MANCHESTER UNITED
The Complete Record

The Most Comprehensive Book of
Facts, Figures and Statistics on
Manchester United Ever Published

Second Edition 2008

Andrew Endlar

First published in paperback in Great Britain in 2007 by Orion Books
This revised and updated edition first published
in paperback in Great Britain in 2008 by
Orion Books
an imprint of the Orion Publishing Group Limited
Orion House, 5 Upper St Martin's Lane,
London WC2H 9EA

An Hachette Livre UK Company

1 3 5 7 9 10 8 6 4 2

A CIP catalogue record for this book is availablefrom the British Library.

ISBN: 978 0 7528 9085 2

Printed and bound in the UK by CPI Mackays, Chatham ME5 8TD

Cover photography

Paul Scholes (most Premiership goals – jointly with Ryan Giggs)
Sir Matt Busby (most seasons as manager)
Alex Stepney (most number of appearances for a goalkeeper)
Ryan Giggs (most overall appearances, most honours won)

All photographs © Manchester United Football Club Limited/Getty Images

The Orion Publishing Group's policy is to use papers that are natural,
renewable and recyclable and made from wood grown in sustainable
forests. The logging and manufacturing processes are expected to
conform to the environmental regulations of the country of origin.

Every effort has been made to fulfil requirements with regard to
reproducing copyright material. The author and publisher will be
glad to rectify any omissions at the earliest possible opportunity.

www.orionbooks.co.uk

MANCHESTER UNITED
The Complete Record

MANCHESTER UNITED
The Complete Record

MANCHESTER UNITED
The Complete Record

Acknowledgements

Daniel Simon Endlar
(Oxford University)
Without whose astonishing spreadsheet work
this publication would not have been possible

Bunny
('Er Indoors)
The other love of my life; who made the sandwiches

Philip Downs MBE
(Secretary, Manchester United Disabled Supporters' Association)
Who proves every single day of his life just what disabled people
can achieve; and is the most inspiring human being whom
I have ever had the privilege to know and work with

Sir Alex Ferguson CBE
For his support and encouragement

Gordon Wise
(Curtis Brown Group)
For his unwavering help and support

Manchester United Football Club
For a lifetime of magical memories,
and in particular, 26th May 1999
(and 21st May 2008)

Andrew Endlar

Introduction and Editorial

Manchester United: The Complete Record is the most complete statistical record of the match and player history of the world's favourite football club ever published. It is the result of eleven years' work and research by the author, who also created and now maintains the club's official statistics website, **www.stretfordend.co.uk**, universally recognised as the definitive resource for Manchester United statistics. **The Complete Record** brings together the vast amount of data available on the website's 14,000 pages and enables the reader to access the information in easy-to-read, accessible, hard copy.

ABBREVIATIONS

The following abbreviations have been used to denote competition names in various sections throughout this volume:–

PREM	FA Premiership	ECWC	European Cup-Winners' Cup
FLD1	Football League Division 1	ICFC	Inter-Cities' Fairs Cup (later UEFA Cup)
FLD2	Football League Division 2	UC	UEFA Cup
FAC	FA Cup	CS	Charity Shield
LC	League Cup	ESC	European Super Cup
EC	European Cup	ICC	Inter-Continental Cup
CL	Champions League	CWC	Club World Championship

TEAM NAMES

In common with Manchester United, many football clubs changed their names in the years following their formation in the late 19th and early 20th centuries. In the same way that Newton Heath became Manchester United; Ardwick, formed in 1887, became Manchester City in 1894, and more elaborately Dial Square, formed in 1886, became Royal Arsenal, then Woolwich Arsenal before becoming simply Arsenal in 1913. For the purposes of continuity, **current** club names have been used throughout this volume.

IS IT A COMPETITIVE MATCH AND INCLUDED IN THE RECORDS?

For the purposes of the match and player records throughout this volume, matches played in the following competitions are classified by the author and Manchester United Football Club as competitive matches:–

FA Premiership, Football Leagues Division 1 and 2, FA Cup, Football League Cup, European Cup/ Champions League, European Cup-Winners' Cup, Inter-Cities' Fairs Cup/UEFA Cup, FA Charity Shield, European Super Cup, Inter-Continental Cup, Club World Championship and Football League Test Matches (the 1890's equivalent of today's play-offs).

Where the term 'OTHER COMPETITIVE MATCHES' is used in this volume, it refers collectively to those matches played in the FA Charity Shield (later referred to as Community Shield), European Super Cup, Inter-Continental Cup, Club World Championship and Football League Test Matches.

Records from the following competitions, although included in this volume for completeness, are **NOT** included in the overall match and player records:–

Football League Division 1 (Season 1939/40) – the competition was abandoned after three matches and the details were expunged from League records.
Football Alliance (1889-1892); War Leagues (1915-1919 and 1939-1946)

MATCHES DECIDED FOLLOWING A DRAWN GAME

The results of all matches which ended in a drawn game and were then decided on penalty kicks or the away goals rule have been classified as drawn matches for the purposes of the match records contained within this volume.

Andrew Endlar

MANCHESTER UNITED
The Complete Record

Chapter 1.1
Season by Season

Newton Heath were not admitted to the Football League until season 1892/93 but competed in the FA Cup on four occasions between 1886 and 1892 as detailed below.

Their very first entry into the FA Cup resulted in a first round elimination at the hands of Fleetwood Rangers and still remains perhaps their most bizarre exit from the competition. The match ended 2-2 after 90 minutes and the referee asked the two clubs to play a period of extra-time in the hope of settling the tie. Newton Heath refused and the tie was consequently awarded to their opponents.

SEASON 1886/87

Match # 1	Saturday 30/10/86	FA Cup 1st Round	at Fleetwood Park	Attendance 2000
Result:	**Fleetwood Rangers 2 Newton Heath 2**			
Teamsheet:	Beckett, Powell, Mitchell, Burke, Davies J, Howells, Earp, Longton, Doughty J, Gotheridge, Davies L			
Scorer(s):	Doughty J 2			

SEASON 1889/90

Match # 2	Saturday 18/01/90	FA Cup 1st Round	at Deepdale	Attendance 7900
Result:	**Preston North End 6 Newton Heath 1**			
Teamsheet:	Hay, Harrison, Powell, Doughty R, Davies J, Owen J, Farman, Craig, Doughty J, Owen G, Wilson			
Scorer(s):	Craig			

SEASON 1890/91

Match # 3	Saturday 04/10/90	FA Cup 1st Qualifying Round	at North Road	Attendance 3000
Result:	**Newton Heath 2 Higher Walton 0**			
Teamsheet:	Slater, Mitchell, Powell, Doughty R, Ramsay, Owen J, Farman, Stewart, Evans, Milarvie, Sharpe			
Scorer(s):	Farman, Evans			

Match # 4	Saturday 25/10/90	FA Cup 2nd Qualifying Round	at Bootle Park	Attendance 500
Result:	**Bootle Reserves 1 Newton Heath 0**			
Teamsheet:	Gyves, Powell, Owen J, Mitchell, Felton, Rattigan, O'Shaughnessy, Dale, Turner, Craig, Donnelly			

SEASON 1891/92

Match # 5	Saturday 03/10/91	FA Cup 1st Qualifying Round	at North Road	Attendance 11000
Result:	**Newton Heath 5 Manchester City 1**			
Teamsheet:	Slater, McFarlane, Clements, Doughty R, Stewart, Owen J, Farman, Edge, Sneddon, Sharpe, Henrys			
Scorer(s):	Farman 2, Doughty R, Edge, Sneddon			

Newton Heath were drawn to play Heywood in the 2nd Qualifying Round. Heywood scratched and the tie was awarded to Newton Heath.

Match # 6	Saturday 14/11/91	FA Cup 3rd Qualifying Round	at Bloomfield Road	Attendance 2000
Result:	**South Shore 0 Newton Heath 2**			
Teamsheet:	Slater, McFarlane, Clements, Owen J, Stewart, Henrys, Farman, Doughty R, Doughty J, Sneddon, Edge			
Scorer(s):	Doughty J, Farman			

Match # 7	Saturday 05/12/91	FA Cup 4th Qualifying Round	at North Road	Attendance 4000
Result:	**Newton Heath 3 Blackpool 4**			
Teamsheet:	Slater, McFarlane, Clements, Doughty R, Stewart, Owen J, Farman, Denman, Sneddon, Henrys, Edge			
Scorer(s):	Edge 2, Farman			

EARLY YEARS SUMMARY

APPEARANCES

PLAYER	LGE	FAC	TOT
Owen J	–	6	6
Doughty R	–	5	5
Farman	–	5	5
Powell	–	4	4
Slater	–	4	4
Stewart	–	4	4
Clements	–	3	3
Doughty J	–	3	3
Edge	–	3	3
Henrys	–	3	3
McFarlane	–	3	3
Mitchell	–	3	3
Sneddon	–	3	3
Craig	–	2	2
Davies J	–	2	2
Sharpe	–	2	2
Beckett	–	1	1
Burke	–	1	1
Dale	–	1	1

APPEARANCES

PLAYER	LGE	FAC	TOT
Davies L	–	1	1
Denman	–	1	1
Donnelly	–	1	1
Earp	–	1	1
Evans	–	1	1
Felton	–	1	1
Gotheridge	–	1	1
Gyves	–	1	1
Harrison	–	1	1
Hay	–	1	1
Howells	–	1	1
Longton	–	1	1
Milarvie	–	1	1
O'Shaughnessy	–	1	1
Owen G	–	1	1
Ramsay	–	1	1
Rattigan	–	1	1
Turner	–	1	1
Wilson	–	1	1

GOALSCORERS

PLAYER	LGE	FAC	TOT
Farman	–	5	5
Doughty J	–	3	3
Edge	–	3	3
Craig	–	1	1
Doughty R	–	1	1
Evans	–	1	1
Sneddon	–	1	1

RESULTS & ATTENDANCES SUMMARY

		P	W	D	L	F	A	TOTAL	AVGE
FA Cup	H	3	2	0	1	10	5	18000	6000
	A	4	1	1	2	5	9	12400	3100
TOTAL		7	3	1	3	15	14	30400	4343

SEASON 1892/93

Match # 8	Saturday 03/09/92	Football League Division 1	at Ewood Park	Attendance 8000
Result:	**Blackburn Rovers 4 Newton Heath 3**			
Teamsheet:	Warner, Clements, Brown, Perrins, Stewart, Erentz, Farman, Coupar, Donaldson, Carson, Mathieson			
Scorer(s):	Coupar, Donaldson, Farman			

Match # 9	Saturday 10/09/92	Football League Division 1	at North Road	Attendance 10000
Result:	**Newton Heath 1 Burnley 1**			
Teamsheet:	Warner, Mitchell, Brown, Perrins, Stewart, Erentz, Farman, Coupar, Donaldson, Carson, Mathieson			
Scorer(s):	Donaldson			

Match # 10	Saturday 17/09/92	Football League Division 1	at Turf Moor	Attendance 7000
Result:	**Burnley 4 Newton Heath 1**			
Teamsheet:	Warner, Mitchell, Brown, Perrins, Stewart, Erentz, Farman, Coupar, Donaldson, Carson, Mathieson			
Scorer(s):	Donaldson			

Match # 11	Saturday 24/09/92	Football League Division 1	at Goodison Park	Attendance 10000
Result:	**Everton 6 Newton Heath 0**			
Teamsheet:	Warner, Mitchell, Brown, Perrins, Stewart, Erentz, Farman, Coupar, Donaldson, Carson, Mathieson			

Match # 12	Saturday 01/10/92	Football League Division 1	at Stoney Lane	Attendance 4000
Result:	**West Bromwich Albion 0 Newton Heath 0**			
Teamsheet:	Warner, Mitchell, Brown, Perrins, Stewart, Erentz, Hood, Coupar, Donaldson, Carson, Mathieson			

Match # 13	Saturday 08/10/92	Football League Division 1	at North Road	Attendance 9000
Result:	**Newton Heath 2 West Bromwich Albion 4**			
Teamsheet:	Warner, Mitchell, Brown, Perrins, Stewart, Erentz, Hood, Coupar, Donaldson, Carson, Mathieson			
Scorer(s):	Donaldson, Hood			

Match # 14	Saturday 15/10/92	Football League Division 1	at North Road	Attendance 4000
Result:	**Newton Heath 10 Wolverhampton Wanderers 1**			
Teamsheet:	Warner, Mitchell, Clements, Perrins, Stewart, Erentz, Farman, Hood, Donaldson, Carson, Hendry			
Scorer(s):	Donaldson 3, Stewart 3, Carson, Farman, Hendry, Hood			

Match # 15	Wednesday 19/10/92	Football League Division 1	at North Road	Attendance 4000
Result:	**Newton Heath 3 Everton 4**			
Teamsheet:	Warner, Mitchell, Clements, Perrins, Stewart, Erentz, Farman, Hood, Donaldson, Carson, Mathieson			
Scorer(s):	Donaldson, Farman, Hood			

Match # 16	Saturday 22/10/92	Football League Division 1	at Olive Grove	Attendance 6000
Result:	**Sheffield Wednesday 1 Newton Heath 0**			
Teamsheet:	Warner, Mitchell, Clements, Perrins, Stewart, Erentz, Farman, Hood, Donaldson, Carson, Hendry			

Match # 17	Saturday 29/10/92	Football League Division 1	at Town Ground	Attendance 6000
Result:	**Nottingham Forest 1 Newton Heath 1**			
Teamsheet:	Warner, Mitchell, Clements, Perrins, Stewart, Erentz, Farman, Hood, Kinloch, Carson, Donaldson			
Scorer(s):	Farman			

Match # 18	Saturday 05/11/92	Football League Division 1	at North Road	Attendance 12000
Result:	**Newton Heath 4 Blackburn Rovers 4**			
Teamsheet:	Warner, Mitchell, Clements, Perrins, Stewart, Erentz, Farman, Hood, Donaldson, Carson, Mathieson			
Scorer(s):	Farman 2, Carson, Hood			

Match # 19	Saturday 12/11/92	Football League Division 1	at North Road	Attendance 8000
Result:	**Newton Heath 1 Notts County 3**			
Teamsheet:	Warner, Mitchell, Clements, Perrins, Stewart, Erentz, Farman, Hood, Donaldson, Carson, Colville			
Scorer(s):	Carson			

Match # 20	Saturday 19/11/92	Football League Division 1	at North Road	Attendance 7000
Result:	**Newton Heath 2 Aston Villa 0**			
Teamsheet:	Warner, Mitchell, Clements, Perrins, Stewart, Erentz, Farman, Hood, Coupar, Fitzsimmons, Colville			
Scorer(s):	Coupar, Fitzsimmons			

Match # 21	Saturday 26/11/92	Football League Division 1	at Thornleyholme Road	Attendance 3000
Result:	**Accrington Stanley 2 Newton Heath 2**			
Teamsheet:	Warner, Mitchell, Clements, Perrins, Henrys, Erentz, Farman, Hood, Coupar, Fitzsimmons, Colville			
Scorer(s):	Colville, Fitzsimmons			

Match # 22	Saturday 03/12/92	Football League Division 1	at Pikes Lane	Attendance 3000
Result:	**Bolton Wanderers 4 Newton Heath 1**			
Teamsheet:	Warner, Mitchell, Clements, Perrins, Stewart, Erentz, Farman, Coupar, Donaldson, Fitzsimmons, Colville			
Scorer(s):	Coupar			

Match # 23	Saturday 10/12/92	Football League Division 1	at North Road	Attendance 4000
Result:	**Newton Heath 1 Bolton Wanderers 0**			
Teamsheet:	Warner, Mitchell, Clements, Perrins, Stewart, Erentz, Farman, Hood, Donaldson, Fitzsimmons, Colville			
Scorer(s):	Donaldson			

Match # 24	Saturday 17/12/92	Football League Division 1	at Molineux	Attendance 5000
Result:	**Wolverhampton Wanderers 2 Newton Heath 0**			
Teamsheet:	Warner, Mitchell, Clements, Perrins, Stewart, Erentz, Farman, Hood, Donaldson, Fitzsimmons, Carson			

Match # 25	Saturday 24/12/92	Football League Division 1	at North Road	Attendance 4000
Result:	**Newton Heath 1 Sheffield Wednesday 5**			
Teamsheet:	Warner, Mitchell, Clements, Perrins, Stewart, Erentz, Farman, Hood, Donaldson, Fitzsimmons, Coupar			
Scorer(s):	Hood			

SEASON 1892/93 (continued)

Match # 26   Monday 26/12/92   Football League Division 1   at Deepdale   Attendance 4000
Result: **Preston North End 2 Newton Heath 1**
Teamsheet: Warner, Mitchell, Clements, Perrins, Stewart, Erentz, Farman, Hood, Donaldson, Fitzsimmons, Coupar
Scorer(s):   Coupar

Match # 27   Saturday 31/12/92   Football League Division 1   at North Road   Attendance 3000
Result: **Newton Heath 7 Derby County 1**
Teamsheet: Warner, Mitchell, Clements, Perrins, Stewart, Erentz, Farman, Hood, Donaldson, Fitzsimmons, Coupar
Scorer(s):   Donaldson 3, Farman 3, Fitzsimmons

Match # 28   Saturday 07/01/93   Football League Division 1   at Victoria Ground   Attendance 1000
Result: **Stoke City 7 Newton Heath 1   (Newton Heath played this match with 10 players)**
Teamsheet: Stewart, Mitchell, Clements, Perrins, Erentz, Farman, Hood, Donaldson, Fitzsimmons, Coupar
Scorer(s):   Coupar

Match # 29   Saturday 14/01/93   Football League Division 1   at North Road   Attendance 8000
Result: **Newton Heath 1 Nottingham Forest 3**
Teamsheet: Davies, Mitchell, Clements, Henrys, Stewart, Erentz, Farman, Hood, Donaldson, Colville, Fitzsimmons
Scorer(s):   Donaldson

Match # 30   Saturday 21/01/93   FA Cup 1st Round   at Ewood Park   Attendance 7000
Result: **Blackburn Rovers 4 Newton Heath 0**
Teamsheet: Davies, Mitchell, Clements, Perrins, Stewart, Erentz, Farman, Hood, Donaldson, Fitzsimmons, Colville

Match # 31   Thursday 26/01/93   Football League Division 1   at Trent Bridge   Attendance 1000
Result: **Notts County 4 Newton Heath 0**
Teamsheet: Davies, Mitchell, Brown, Perrins, Stewart, Erentz, Farman, Hood, Coupar, Colville, Fitzsimmons

Match # 32   Saturday 11/02/93   Football League Division 1   at Racecourse Ground   Attendance 5000
Result: **Derby County 5 Newton Heath 1**
Teamsheet: Warner, Mitchell, Clements, Perrins, Stewart, Henrys, Farman, Hood, Donaldson, Fitzsimmons, Coupar
Scorer(s):   Fitzsimmons

Match # 33   Saturday 04/03/93   Football League Division 1   at North Road   Attendance 15000
Result: **Newton Heath 0 Sunderland 5**
Teamsheet: Warner, Mitchell, Clements, Perrins, Stewart, Erentz, Farman, Hood, Coupar, Fitzsimmons, Colville

Match # 34   Monday 06/03/93   Football League Division 1   at Perry Barr   Attendance 4000
Result: **Aston Villa 2 Newton Heath 0**
Teamsheet: Davies, Mitchell, Clements, Perrins, Stewart, Erentz, Farman, Coupar, Donaldson, Fitzsimmons, Colville

Match # 35   Friday 31/03/93   Football League Division 1   at North Road   Attendance 10000
Result: **Newton Heath 1 Stoke City 0**
Teamsheet: Davies, Mitchell, Clements, Perrins, Stewart, Erentz, Farman, Coupar, Donaldson, Fitzsimmons, Cassidy
Scorer(s):   Farman

Match # 36   Saturday 01/04/93   Football League Division 1   at North Road   Attendance 9000
Result: **Newton Heath 2 Preston North End 1**
Teamsheet: Davies, Mitchell, Clements, Perrins, Stewart, Erentz, Farman, Coupar, Donaldson, Fitzsimmons, Cassidy
Scorer(s):   Donaldson 2

Match # 37   Tuesday 04/04/93   Football League Division 1   at Newcastle Road   Attendance 3500
Result: **Sunderland 6 Newton Heath 0**
Teamsheet: Davies, Mitchell, Clements, Perrins, Stewart, Erentz, Farman, Coupar, Donaldson, Fitzsimmons, Cassidy

Match # 38   Saturday 08/04/93   Football League Division 1   at North Road   Attendance 3000
Result: **Newton Heath 3 Accrington Stanley 3**
Teamsheet: Davies, Mitchell, Clements, Hood, Stewart, Erentz, Farman, Coupar, Donaldson, Fitzsimmons, Cassidy
Scorer(s):   Donaldson, Fitzsimmons, Stewart

By season 1892/93 formal promotion and relegation had not yet been introduced, so the teams at the bottom of the First Division played a 'Test Match' against the teams at the top of the Second Division. Newton Heath finished the season in bottom place in Division One but managed to win their 'Test Match' and keep their top-flight status for the following season.

Match # 39   Saturday 22/04/93   Football League Test Match   at Victoria Ground   Attendance 4000
Result: **Newton Heath 1 Birmingham City 1**
Teamsheet: Davies, Mitchell, Clements, Perrins, Stewart, Erentz, Farman, Coupar, Donaldson, Fitzsimmons, Cassidy
Scorer(s):   Farman

Match # 40   Thursday 27/04/93   Football League Test Match Replay   at Bramall Lane   Attendance 6000
Result: **Newton Heath 5 Birmingham City 2**
Teamsheet: Davies, Mitchell, Clements, Hood, Perrins, Erentz, Farman, Coupar, Donaldson, Fitzsimmons, Cassidy
Scorer(s):   Farman 3, Cassidy, Coupar

SEASON 1892/93 SUMMARY

APPEARANCES

PLAYER	LGE	FAC	TM	TOT
Erentz	29	1	2	32
Mitchell	29	1	2	32
Farman	28	1	2	31
Perrins	28	1	2	31
Stewart	29	1	1	31
Donaldson	26	1	2	29
Clements	24	1	2	27
Coupar	21	–	2	23
Hood	21	1	1	23
Warner	22	–	–	22
Fitzsimmons	18	1	2	21
Carson	13	–	–	13
Colville	9	1	–	10
Davies	7	1	2	10
Mathieson	8	–	–	8
Brown	7	–	–	7
Cassidy	4	–	2	6
Henrys	3	–	–	3
Hendry	2	–	–	2
Kinloch	1	–	–	1

GOALSCORERS

PLAYER	LGE	FAC	TM	TOT
Donaldson	16	–	–	16
Farman	10	–	4	14
Coupar	5	–	1	6
Fitzsimmons	5	–	–	5
Hood	5	–	–	5
Stewart	4	–	–	4
Carson	3	–	–	3
Colville	1	–	–	1
Hendry	1	–	–	1
Cassidy	–	–	1	1

RESULTS & ATTENDANCES SUMMARY

		P	W	D	L	F	A	TOTAL	AVGE
League	H	15	6	3	6	39	35	110000	7333
	A	15	0	3	12	11	50	70500	4700
TOTAL		30	6	6	18	50	85	180500	6017
FA Cup	H	0	0	0	0	0	0	0	n/a
	A	1	0	0	1	0	4	7000	7000
TOTAL		1	0	0	1	0	4	7000	7000
Test	H	0	0	0	0	0	0	0	n/a
Matches	A	0	0	0	0	0	0	0	n/a
	N	2	1	1	0	6	3	10000	5000
TOTAL		2	1	1	0	6	3	10000	5000
Overall	H	15	6	3	6	39	35	110000	7333
	A	16	0	3	13	11	54	77500	4844
	N	2	1	1	0	6	3	10000	5000
TOTAL		33	7	7	19	56	92	197500	5985

FINAL TABLE - LEAGUE DIVISION ONE

		P	W	D	L	F	A	W	D	L	F	A	PTS	GD
				HOME					AWAY					
1	Sunderland	30	13	2	0	58	17	9	2	4	42	19	48	64
2	Preston North End	30	11	2	2	34	10	6	1	8	23	29	37	18
3	Everton	30	9	3	3	44	17	7	1	7	30	34	36	23
4	Aston Villa	30	12	1	2	50	24	4	2	9	23	38	35	11
5	Bolton Wanderers	30	12	1	2	43	21	1	5	9	13	34	32	1
6	Burnley	30	10	2	3	37	15	3	2	10	14	29	30	7
7	Stoke City	30	8	2	5	33	16	4	3	8	25	32	29	10
8	West Bromwich Albion	30	9	2	4	35	17	3	3	9	23	52	29	-11
9	Blackburn Rovers	30	5	8	2	29	24	3	5	7	18	32	29	-9
10	Nottingham Forest	30	7	2	6	30	27	3	6	6	18	25	28	-4
11	Wolverhampton Wanderers	30	11	2	2	32	17	1	2	12	15	51	28	-21
12	Sheffield Wednesday	30	8	2	5	34	28	4	1	10	21	37	27	-10
13	Derby County	30	5	6	4	30	28	4	3	8	22	36	27	-12
14	Notts County	30	8	3	4	34	15	2	1	12	19	46	24	-8
15	Accrington Stanley	30	5	5	5	29	34	1	6	8	28	47	23	-24
16	NEWTON HEATH	30	6	3	6	39	35	0	3	12	11	50	18	-35

SEASON 1893/94

Match # 41 Saturday 02/09/93 Football League Division 1 at North Road Attendance 10000
Result: **Newton Heath 3 Burnley 2**
Teamsheet: Fall, Mitchell, Clements, Perrins, Stewart, Davidson, Farman, McNaught, Fitzsimmons, Peden, Donaldson
Scorer(s): Farman 3

Match # 42 Saturday 09/09/93 Football League Division 1 at Stoney Lane Attendance 4500
Result: **West Bromwich Albion 3 Newton Heath 1**
Teamsheet: Fall, Mitchell, Clements, Perrins, Stewart, Davidson, Farman, McNaught, Fitzsimmons, Peden, Donaldson
Scorer(s): Donaldson

Match # 43 Saturday 16/09/93 Football League Division 1 at Olive Grove Attendance 7000
Result: **Sheffield Wednesday 0 Newton Heath 1**
Teamsheet: Fall, Mitchell, Clements, Erentz, Stewart, Davidson, Farman, Hood, Donaldson, McNaught, Peden
Scorer(s): Farman

Match # 44 Saturday 23/09/93 Football League Division 1 at Bank Street Attendance 10000
Result: **Newton Heath 1 Nottingham Forest 1**
Teamsheet: Fall, Mitchell, Clements, Perrins, Stewart, Davidson, Farman, Erentz, Donaldson, McNaught, Peden
Scorer(s): Donaldson

Match # 45 Saturday 30/09/93 Football League Division 1 at Barley Bank Attendance 4000
Result: **Darwen 1 Newton Heath 0**
Teamsheet: Fall, Mitchell, Clements, Perrins, Stewart, Davidson, Farman, McNaught, Donaldson, Fitzsimmons, Peden

Match # 46 Saturday 07/10/93 Football League Division 1 at Racecourse Ground Attendance 7000
Result: **Derby County 2 Newton Heath 0**
Teamsheet: Fall, Mitchell, Clements, Perrins, Stewart, Davidson, Erentz, McNaught, Donaldson, Fitzsimmons, Peden

Match # 47 Saturday 14/10/93 Football League Division 1 at Bank Street Attendance 8000
Result: **Newton Heath 4 West Bromwich Albion 1**
Teamsheet: Fall, Mitchell, Clements, Perrins, Stewart, Davidson, McNaught, Erentz, Donaldson, Fitzsimmons, Peden
Scorer(s): Peden 2, Donaldson, Erentz

Match # 48 Saturday 21/10/93 Football League Division 1 at Turf Moor Attendance 7000
Result: **Burnley 4 Newton Heath 1**
Teamsheet: Fall, Mitchell, Clements, Perrins, Stewart, Davidson, McNaught, Thompson, Donaldson, Hood, Peden
Scorer(s): Hood

Match # 49 Saturday 28/10/93 Football League Division 1 at Molineux Attendance 4000
Result: **Wolverhampton Wanderers 2 Newton Heath 0**
Teamsheet: Fall, Mitchell, Clements, Perrins, Stewart, Davidson, McNaught, Thompson, Donaldson, Fitzsimmons, Peden

Match # 50 Saturday 04/11/93 Football League Division 1 at Bank Street Attendance 8000
Result: **Newton Heath 0 Darwen 1**
Teamsheet: Fall, Mitchell, Erentz, Hood, Stewart, Davidson, McNaught, Thompson, Peden, Fitzsimmons, Prince

Match # 51 Saturday 11/11/93 Football League Division 1 at Bank Street Attendance 5000
Result: **Newton Heath 1 Wolverhampton Wanderers 0**
Teamsheet: Fall, Mitchell, Erentz, Hood, Stewart, Davidson, Farman, McNaught, Graham, Fitzsimmons, Peden
Scorer(s): Davidson

Match # 52 Saturday 25/11/93 Football League Division 1 at Bramall Lane Attendance 2000
Result: **Sheffield United 3 Newton Heath 1**
Teamsheet: Fall, Mitchell, Clements, Perrins, Stewart, Davidson, McNaught, Campbell, Donaldson, Fitzsimmons, Peden
Scorer(s): Fitzsimmons

Match # 53 Saturday 02/12/93 Football League Division 1 at Bank Street Attendance 6000
Result: **Newton Heath 0 Everton 3**
Teamsheet: Fall, Mitchell, Clements, Perrins, Stewart, Davidson, Rothwell, Campbell, Donaldson, McNaught, Peden

Match # 54 Wednesday 06/12/93 Football League Division 1 at Newcastle Road Attendance 5000
Result: **Sunderland 4 Newton Heath 1**
Teamsheet: Fall, Mitchell, Erentz, Perrins, Stewart, Davidson, Farman, Campbell, Graham, McNaught, Peden
Scorer(s): Campbell

Match # 55 Saturday 09/12/93 Football League Division 1 at Pikes Lane Attendance 5000
Result: **Bolton Wanderers 2 Newton Heath 0**
Teamsheet: Fall, Mitchell, Erentz, Hood, Perrins, Davidson, Farman, Campbell, Donaldson, McNaught, Peden

Match # 56 Saturday 16/12/93 Football League Division 1 at Bank Street Attendance 8000
Result: **Newton Heath 1 Aston Villa 3**
Teamsheet: Fall, Mitchell, Erentz, Perrins, Stewart, Davidson, Farman, Campbell, Donaldson, McNaught, Peden
Scorer(s): Peden

Match # 57 Saturday 23/12/93 Football League Division 1 at Deepdale Attendance 5000
Result: **Preston North End 2 Newton Heath 0**
Teamsheet: Fall, Mitchell, Erentz, Perrins, Stewart, Davidson, Farman, Hood, Donaldson, McNaught, Peden

Match # 58 Saturday 06/01/94 Football League Division 1 at Goodison Park Attendance 8000
Result: **Everton 2 Newton Heath 0**
Teamsheet: Fall, Clements, Erentz, Perrins, Stewart, Davidson, Farman, Hood, Graham, McNaught, Peden

SEASON 1893/94 (continued)

Match # 59   Saturday 13/01/94   Football League Division 1   at Bank Street   Attendance 9000
Result: **Newton Heath 1 Sheffield Wednesday 2**
Teamsheet: Fall, Mitchell, Erentz, Perrins, Stewart, Davidson, Clarkin, Parker, Graham, McNaught, Peden
Scorer(s): Peden

Match # 60   Saturday 27/01/94   FA Cup 1st Round   at Bank Street   Attendance 5000
Result: **Newton Heath 4 Middlesbrough 0**
Teamsheet: Fall, Mitchell, Erentz, Perrins, Stewart, Davidson, Farman, Hood, Donaldson, McNaught, Peden
Scorer(s): Donaldson 2, Farman, Peden

Match # 61   Saturday 03/02/94   Football League Division 1   at Perry Barr   Attendance 5000
Result: **Aston Villa 5 Newton Heath 1**
Teamsheet: Douglas, Mitchell, Erentz, Perrins, Stewart, Davidson, Clarkin, Parker, Donaldson, McNaught, Mathieson
Scorer(s): Mathieson

Match # 62   Saturday 10/02/94   FA Cup 2nd Round   at Bank Street   Attendance 18000
Result: **Newton Heath 0 Blackburn Rovers 0**
Teamsheet: Fall, Mitchell, Erentz, Perrins, Stewart, Davidson, Clarkin, Parker, Donaldson, McNaught, Peden

Match # 63   Saturday 17/02/94   FA Cup 2nd Round Replay   at Ewood Park   Attendance 5000
Result: **Blackburn Rovers 5 Newton Heath 1**
Teamsheet: Fall, Mitchell, Erentz, Perrins, Stewart, Davidson, Clarkin, Hood, Donaldson, McNaught, Peden
Scorer(s): Donaldson

Match # 64   Saturday 03/03/94   Football League Division 1   at Bank Street   Attendance 10000
Result: **Newton Heath 2 Sunderland 4**
Teamsheet: Fall, Mitchell, Erentz, Perrins, Stewart, Davidson, Clarkin, Parker, Donaldson, McNaught, Peden
Scorer(s): McNaught, Peden

Match # 65   Saturday 10/03/94   Football League Division 1   at Bank Street   Attendance 5000
Result: **Newton Heath 0 Sheffield United 2**
Teamsheet: Douglas, Mitchell, Erentz, Hood, Perrins, Davidson, Clarkin, Parker, Donaldson, McNaught, Peden

Match # 66   Monday 12/03/94   Football League Division 1   at Bank Street   Attendance 5000
Result: **Newton Heath 5 Blackburn Rovers 1**
Teamsheet: Fall, Mitchell, Erentz, Perrins, Stewart, McNaught, Clarkin, Farman, Donaldson, Parker, Peden
Scorer(s): Donaldson 3, Clarkin, Farman

Match # 67   Saturday 17/03/94   Football League Division 1   at Bank Street   Attendance 7000
Result: **Newton Heath 2 Derby County 6**
Teamsheet: Fall, Mitchell, Erentz, Perrins, Stewart, McNaught, Clarkin, Farman, Donaldson, Parker, Peden
Scorer(s): Clarkin 2

Match # 68   Friday 23/03/94   Football League Division 1   at Bank Street   Attendance 8000
Result: **Newton Heath 6 Stoke City 2**
Teamsheet: Douglas, Hood, Erentz, Perrins, McNaught, Davidson, Clarkin, Farman, Donaldson, Parker, Peden
Scorer(s): Farman 2, Peden 2, Clarkin, Erentz

Match # 69   Saturday 24/03/94   Football League Division 1   at Bank Street   Attendance 10000
Result: **Newton Heath 2 Bolton Wanderers 2**
Teamsheet: Douglas, Dow, Erentz, Perrins, Stewart, Davidson, Clarkin, Farman, Donaldson, Parker, Peden
Scorer(s): Donaldson, Farman

Match # 70   Monday 26/03/94   Football League Division 1   at Ewood Park   Attendance 5000
Result: **Blackburn Rovers 4 Newton Heath 0**
Teamsheet: Douglas, Dow, Erentz, Perrins, Stone, Davidson, Clarkin, Farman, Parker, Hood, Peden

Match # 71   Saturday 31/03/94   Football League Division 1   at Victoria Ground   Attendance 4000
Result: **Stoke City 3 Newton Heath 1**
Teamsheet: Douglas, Hood, Erentz, Perrins, McNaught, Davidson, Clarkin, Farman, Donaldson, Parker, Peden
Scorer(s): Clarkin

Match # 72   Saturday 07/04/94   Football League Division 1   at Town Ground   Attendance 4000
Result: **Nottingham Forest 2 Newton Heath 0**
Teamsheet: Douglas, Mitchell, Erentz, Perrins, Stewart, Davidson, Clarkin, Farman, Donaldson, Parker, Prince

Match # 73   Saturday 14/04/94   Football League Division 1   at Bank Street   Attendance 4000
Result: **Newton Heath 1 Preston North End 3**
Teamsheet: Fall, Mitchell, Davidson, Perrins, Stewart, Stone, Clarkin, Hood, Donaldson, Mathieson, Peden
Scorer(s): Mathieson

Formal promotion and relegation between the Football League divisions
had still not been introduced, so Newton Heath were again required to
play a 'Test Match' against the team at the top of the Second Division.
This time they were unsuccessful and lost their Division One status.

Match # 74   Saturday 28/04/94   Football League Test Match   at Ewood Park   Attendance 3000
Result: **Newton Heath 0 Liverpool 2**
Teamsheet: Fall, Mitchell, Erentz, Perrins, McNaught, Davidson, Clarkin, Farman, Donaldson, Hood, Peden

SEASON 1893/94 SUMMARY

APPEARANCES

PLAYER	LGE	FAC	TM	TOT
Davidson	28	3	1	32
Peden	28	3	1	32
Perrins	27	3	1	31
McNaught	26	3	1	30
Mitchell	25	3	1	29
Stewart	25	3	–	28
Donaldson	24	3	1	28
Fall	23	3	1	27
Erentz	22	3	1	26
Farman	18	1	1	20
Clarkin	12	2	1	15
Hood	12	2	1	15
Clements	12	–	–	12
Parker	11	1	–	12
Fitzsimmons	9	–	–	9
Douglas	7	–	–	7
Campbell	5	–	–	5
Graham	4	–	–	4
Thompson	3	–	–	3
Dow	2	–	–	2
Mathieson	2	–	–	2
Prince	2	–	–	2
Stone	2	–	–	2
Rothwell	1	–	–	1

GOALSCORERS

PLAYER	LGE	FAC	TM	TOT
Donaldson	7	3	–	10
Farman	8	1	–	9
Peden	7	1	–	8
Clarkin	5	–	–	5
Erentz	2	–	–	2
Mathieson	2	–	–	2
Campbell	1	–	–	1
Davidson	1	–	–	1
Fitzsimmons	1	–	–	1
Hood	1	–	–	1
McNaught	1	–	–	1

RESULTS & ATTENDANCES SUMMARY

		P	W	D	L	F	A	TOTAL	AVGE
League	H	15	5	2	8	29	33	113000	7533
	A	15	1	0	14	7	39	76500	5100
TOTAL		30	6	2	22	36	72	189500	6317
FA Cup	H	2	1	1	0	4	0	23000	11500
	A	1	0	0	1	1	5	5000	5000
TOTAL		3	1	1	1	5	5	28000	9333
Test	H	0	0	0	0	0	0	0	n/a
Matches	A	0	0	0	0	0	0	0	n/a
	N	1	0	0	1	0	2	3000	3000
TOTAL		1	0	0	2	0	2	3000	3000
Overall	H	17	6	3	8	33	33	136000	8000
	A	16	1	0	15	8	44	81500	5094
	N	1	0	0	1	0	2	3000	3000
TOTAL		34	7	3	24	41	79	220500	6485

FINAL TABLE – LEAGUE DIVISION ONE

		P	W	D	L	F	A	W	D	L	F	A	PTS	GD
				HOME						AWAY				
1	Aston Villa	30	12	2	1	49	13	7	4	4	35	29	44	42
2	Sunderland	30	11	3	1	46	14	6	1	8	26	30	38	28
3	Derby County	30	9	2	4	47	32	7	2	6	26	30	36	11
4	Blackburn Rovers	30	13	0	2	48	15	3	2	10	21	38	34	16
5	Burnley	30	13	0	2	43	17	2	4	9	18	34	34	10
6	Everton	30	11	1	3	63	23	4	2	9	27	34	33	33
7	Nottingham Forest	30	10	2	3	38	16	4	2	9	19	32	32	9
8	West Bromwich Albion	30	8	4	3	35	23	6	0	9	31	36	32	7
9	Wolverhampton Wanderers	30	11	1	3	34	24	3	2	10	18	39	31	-11
10	Sheffield United	30	8	3	4	26	22	5	2	8	21	39	31	-14
11	Stoke City	30	13	1	1	45	17	0	2	13	20	62	29	-14
12	Sheffield Wednesday	30	7	3	5	32	21	2	5	8	16	36	26	-9
13	Bolton Wanderers	30	7	3	5	18	14	3	1	11	20	38	24	-14
14	Preston North End	30	7	1	7	25	24	3	2	10	19	32	23	-12
15	Darwen	30	6	4	5	25	28	1	1	13	12	55	19	-46
16	NEWTON HEATH	30	5	2	8	29	33	1	0	14	7	39	14	-36

SEASON 1894/95

Match # 75
Saturday 08/09/94   Football League Division 2   at Derby Turn   Attendance 3000
Result: **Burton Wanderers 1   Newton Heath 0**
Teamsheet: Douglas, McCartney, Erentz, Stewart, McNaught, Davidson, Clarkin, Farman, Dow, Smith, Peters

Match # 76
Saturday 15/09/94   Football League Division 2   at Bank Street   Attendance 6000
Result: **Newton Heath 6   Crewe Alexandra 1**
Teamsheet: Douglas, McCartney, Erentz, Perrins, McNaught, Davidson, Clarkin, Farman, Dow, Smith, Peters
Scorer(s): Dow 2, Smith 2, Clarkin, McCartney

Match # 77
Saturday 22/09/94   Football League Division 2   at Filbert Street   Attendance 6000
Result: **Leicester City 2   Newton Heath 3**
Teamsheet: Douglas, McCartney, Erentz, Perrins, McNaught, Davidson, Clarkin, Donaldson, Dow, Smith, Peters
Scorer(s): Dow 2, Smith

Match # 78
Saturday 06/10/94   Football League Division 2   at Barley Bank   Attendance 6000
Result: **Darwen 1   Newton Heath 1**
Teamsheet: Douglas, McCartney, Erentz, Perrins, McNaught, Davidson, Clarkin, Donaldson, Dow, Smith, Peters
Scorer(s): Donaldson

Match # 79
Saturday 13/10/94   Football League Division 2   at Bank Street   Attendance 4000
Result: **Newton Heath 3   Arsenal 3**
Teamsheet: Douglas, McCartney, Erentz, Perrins, McNaught, Davidson, Clarkin, Donaldson, Dow, Smith, Peters
Scorer(s): Donaldson 2, Clarkin

Match # 80
Saturday 20/10/94   Football League Division 2   at Peel Croft   Attendance 5000
Result: **Burton Swifts 1   Newton Heath 2**
Teamsheet: Douglas, Dow, Erentz, Perrins, McNaught, Davidson, Clarkin, Donaldson, Stewart, Smith, Peters
Scorer(s): Donaldson 2

Match # 81
Saturday 27/10/94   Football League Division 2   at Bank Street   Attendance 3000
Result: **Newton Heath 2   Leicester City 2**
Teamsheet: Douglas, McCartney, Erentz, Perrins, McNaught, Davidson, Clarkin, Donaldson, Stewart, Smith, Peters
Scorer(s): McNaught, Smith

Match # 82
Saturday 03/11/94   Football League Division 2   at Hyde Road   Attendance 14000
Result: **Manchester City 2   Newton Heath 5**
Teamsheet: Douglas, McCartney, Erentz, Perrins, McNaught, Davidson, Clarkin, Donaldson, Dow, Smith, Peters
Scorer(s): Smith 4, Clarkin

Match # 83
Saturday 10/11/94   Football League Division 2   at Bank Street   Attendance 4000
Result: **Newton Heath 3   Rotherham United 2**
Teamsheet: Douglas, McCartney, Erentz, Perrins, McNaught, Davidson, Clarkin, Donaldson, Dow, Smith, Peters
Scorer(s): Davidson, Donaldson, Peters

Match # 84
Saturday 17/11/94   Football League Division 2   at Abbey Park   Attendance 3000
Result: **Grimsby Town 2   Newton Heath 1**
Teamsheet: Douglas, Donaldson, Erentz, Stewart, McNaught, Davidson, Clarkin, Farman, Dow, Smith, Peters
Scorer(s): Clarkin

Match # 85
Saturday 24/11/94   Football League Division 2   at Bank Street   Attendance 5000
Result: **Newton Heath 1   Darwen 1**
Teamsheet: Douglas, McCartney, Erentz, Perrins, McNaught, Davidson, Clarkin, Donaldson, Dow, Smith, Peters
Scorer(s): Donaldson

Match # 86
Saturday 01/12/94   Football League Division 2   at Gresty Road   Attendance 600
Result: **Crewe Alexandra 0   Newton Heath 2**
Teamsheet: Douglas, McCartney, Erentz, Stewart, McNaught, Davidson, Clarkin, Donaldson, Dow, Smith, Peters
Scorer(s): Clarkin, Smith

Match # 87
Saturday 08/12/94   Football League Division 2   at Bank Street   Attendance 4000
Result: **Newton Heath 5   Burton Swifts 1**
Teamsheet: Douglas, McCartney, Erentz, Perrins, Stewart, McNaught, Clarkin, Donaldson, Dow, Smith, Peters
Scorer(s): Peters 2, Smith 2, Dow

Match # 88
Saturday 15/12/94   Football League Division 2   at Trent Bridge   Attendance 3000
Result: **Notts County 1   Newton Heath 1**
Teamsheet: Douglas, McCartney, Erentz, Perrins, Stewart, McNaught, Clarkin, Donaldson, Dow, Smith, Peters
Scorer(s): Donaldson

Match # 89
Saturday 22/12/94   Football League Division 2   at Bank Street   Attendance 2000
Result: **Newton Heath 3   Lincoln City 0**
Teamsheet: Douglas, McCartney, Dow, Perrins, Stewart, Erentz, Clarkin, Donaldson, Millar, Smith, Peters
Scorer(s): Donaldson, Millar, Smith

Match # 90
Monday 24/12/94   Football League Division 2   at Cobridge Stadium   Attendance 1000
Result: **Port Vale 2   Newton Heath 5**
Teamsheet: Douglas, McCartney, Erentz, Perrins, McNaught, Stewart, Clarkin, Donaldson, Millar, Smith, Peters
Scorer(s): Clarkin, Donaldson, McNaught, Millar, Smith

Match # 91
Wednesday 26/12/94   Football League Division 2   at West Bromwich Road   Attendance 1000
Result: **Walsall 1   Newton Heath 2**
Teamsheet: Douglas, Dow, Erentz, Perrins, McNaught, Stewart, Clarkin, Donaldson, Millar, Farman, Peters
Scorer(s): Millar, Stewart

Match # 92
Saturday 29/12/94   Football League Division 2   at John O'Gaunts   Attendance 3000
Result: **Lincoln City 3   Newton Heath 0**
Teamsheet: Douglas, Dow, Erentz, Perrins, McNaught, Stewart, Clarkin, Donaldson, Millar, Smith, Peters

SEASON 1894/95 (continued)

Match # 93	Tuesday 01/01/95	Football League Division 2	at Bank Street	Attendance 5000
Result:	**Newton Heath 3 Port Vale 0**			
Teamsheet:	Douglas, McCartney, Erentz, Donaldson, Stone, McNaught, Clarkin, Rothwell, Millar, Smith, Peters			
Scorer(s):	Millar 2, Rothwell			

Match # 94	Saturday 05/01/95	Football League Division 2	at Bank Street	Attendance 12000
Result:	**Newton Heath 4 Manchester City 1**			
Teamsheet:	Douglas, McCartney, Erentz, Stone, McNaught, Stewart, Clarkin, Donaldson, Dow, Smith, Peters			
Scorer(s):	Clarkin 2, Donaldson, Smith			

Match # 95	Saturday 12/01/95	Football League Division 2	at Millmoor	Attendance 2000
Result:	**Rotherham United 2 Newton Heath 1**			
Teamsheet:	Douglas, McCartney, Erentz, Perrins, McNaught, Stewart, Farman, Donaldson, Dow, Smith, Peters			
Scorer(s):	Erentz			

Match # 96	Saturday 02/02/95	FA Cup 1st Round	at Bank Street	Attendance 7000
Result:	**Newton Heath 2 Stoke City 3**			
Teamsheet:	Douglas, McCartney, Erentz, Perrins, McNaught, Stewart, Clarkin, Donaldson, Millar, Smith, Peters			
Scorer(s):	Peters, Smith			

Match # 97	Saturday 02/03/95	Football League Division 2	at Bank Street	Attendance 6000
Result:	**Newton Heath 1 Burton Wanderers 1**			
Teamsheet:	Douglas, McCartney, Erentz, Perrins, McNaught, Stewart, Clarkin, Donaldson, Dow, Smith, Peters			
Scorer(s):	Peters			

Match # 98	Saturday 23/03/95	Football League Division 2	at Bank Street	Attendance 9000
Result:	**Newton Heath 2 Grimsby Town 0**			
Teamsheet:	Douglas, Dow, Erentz, Perrins, McNaught, Stewart, Clarkin, Donaldson, Cassidy, Smith, Peters			
Scorer(s):	Cassidy 2			

Match # 99	Saturday 30/03/95	Football League Division 2	at Manor Field	Attendance 6000
Result:	**Arsenal 3 Newton Heath 2**			
Teamsheet:	Douglas, Dow, Erentz, Perrins, McNaught, Stewart, Clarkin, Donaldson, Cassidy, Smith, Peters			
Scorer(s):	Clarkin, Donaldson			

Match # 100	Wednesday 03/04/95	Football League Division 2	at Bank Street	Attendance 6000
Result:	**Newton Heath 9 Walsall 0**			
Teamsheet:	Douglas, Dow, Erentz, Perrins, McNaught, Stewart, Clarkin, Donaldson, Cassidy, Smith, Peters			
Scorer(s):	Cassidy 2, Donaldson 2, Peters 2, Smith 2, Clarkin			

Match # 101	Saturday 06/04/95	Football League Division 2	at Bank Street	Attendance 5000
Result:	**Newton Heath 5 Newcastle United 1**			
Teamsheet:	Douglas, Dow, Erentz, Perrins, McNaught, Stewart, Clarkin, Donaldson, Cassidy, Smith, Peters			
Scorer(s):	Cassidy 2, Smith 2, own goal			

Match # 102	Friday 12/04/95	Football League Division 2	at Bank Street	Attendance 15000
Result:	**Newton Heath 2 Bury 2**			
Teamsheet:	Douglas, Dow, Erentz, Perrins, McNaught, Stewart, Clarkin, Donaldson, Cassidy, Smith, Peters			
Scorer(s):	Cassidy, Donaldson			

Match # 103	Saturday 13/04/95	Football League Division 2	at St James' Park	Attendance 4000
Result:	**Newcastle United 3 Newton Heath 0**			
Teamsheet:	Douglas, Donaldson, Dow, Perrins, Stone, Stewart, Clarkin, McFetteridge, Cassidy, Smith, Peters			

Match # 104	Monday 15/04/95	Football League Division 2	at Gigg Lane	Attendance 10000
Result:	**Bury 2 Newton Heath 1**			
Teamsheet:	Douglas, Dow, Cairns, Perrins, Stone, Stewart, Clarkin, Millar, Cassidy, Smith, Peters			
Scorer(s):	Peters			

Match # 105	Saturday 20/04/95	Football League Division 2	at Bank Street	Attendance 12000
Result:	**Newton Heath 3 Notts County 3**			
Teamsheet:	Douglas, Dow, Erentz, Perrins, Longair, Stewart, Clarkin, Donaldson, Cassidy, Smith, Peters			
Scorer(s):	Cassidy, Clarkin, Smith			

As Newton Heath finished in third place in Division Two, they had the
opportunity of being promoted through the 'Test Match' system. This
season's 'Test Match' was against Stoke City, who had finished third
from bottom in Division One. Newton Heath lost the match and so
remained in Division Two for the following season.

Match # 106	Saturday 27/04/95	Football League Test Match	at Cobridge Stadium	Attendance 10000
Result:	**Newton Heath 0 Stoke City 3**			
Teamsheet:	Douglas, Dow, McCartney, Perrins, Stone, Stewart, Clarkin, Donaldson, Cassidy, Smith, Peters			

SEASON 1894/95 SUMMARY

APPEARANCES

PLAYER	LGE	FAC	TM	TOT
Douglas	30	1	1	32
Peters	30	1	1	32
Clarkin	29	1	1	31
Smith	29	1	1	31
Erentz	28	1	–	29
Donaldson	27	1	1	29
Dow	27	–	1	28
McNaught	26	1	–	27
Perrins	25	1	1	27
Stewart	22	1	1	24
McCartney	18	1	1	20
Davidson	12	–	–	12
Cassidy	8	–	1	9
Millar	6	1	–	7
Farman	5	–	–	5
Stone	4	–	1	5
Cairns	1	–	–	1
Longair	1	–	–	1
McFetteridge	1	–	–	1
Rothwell	1	–	–	1

GOALSCORERS

PLAYER	LGE	FAC	TM	TOT
Smith	19	1	–	20
Donaldson	15	–	–	15
Clarkin	11	–	–	11
Cassidy	8	–	–	8
Peters	7	1	–	8
Dow	5	–	–	5
Millar	5	–	–	5
McNaught	2	–	–	2
Davidson	1	–	–	1
Erentz	1	–	–	1
McCartney	1	–	–	1
Rothwell	1	–	–	1
Stewart	1	–	–	1
own goal	1	–	–	1

RESULTS & ATTENDANCES SUMMARY

		P	W	D	L	F	A	TOTAL	AVGE
League	H	15	9	6	0	52	18	98000	6533
	A	15	6	2	7	26	26	67600	4507
TOTAL		30	15	8	7	78	44	165600	5520
FA Cup	H	1	0	0	1	2	3	7000	7000
	A	0	0	0	0	0	0	0	n/a
TOTAL		1	0	0	1	2	3	7000	7000
Test	H	0	0	0	0	0	0	0	n/a
Matches	A	0	0	0	0	0	0	0	n/a
	N	1	0	0	1	0	3	10000	10000
TOTAL		1	0	0	1	0	3	10000	10000
Overall	H	16	9	6	1	54	21	105000	6563
	A	15	6	2	7	26	26	67600	4507
	N	1	0	0	1	0	3	10000	10000
TOTAL		32	15	8	9	80	50	182600	5706

FINAL TABLE - LEAGUE DIVISION TWO

		P	W	D	L	F	A	W	D	L	F	A	PTS	GD
			HOME					AWAY						
1	Bury	30	15	0	0	48	11	8	2	5	30	22	48	45
2	Notts County	30	12	2	1	50	15	5	3	7	25	30	39	30
3	NEWTON HEATH	30	9	6	0	52	18	6	2	7	26	26	38	34
4	Leicester City	30	11	2	2	45	20	4	6	5	27	33	38	19
5	Grimsby Town	30	14	0	1	51	16	4	1	10	28	36	37	27
6	Darwen	30	13	1	1	53	10	3	3	9	21	33	36	31
7	Burton Wanderers	30	10	3	2	49	9	4	4	7	18	30	35	28
8	Arsenal	30	11	3	1	54	20	3	3	9	21	38	34	17
9	Manchester City	30	9	3	3	56	28	5	0	10	26	44	31	10
10	Newcastle United	30	11	1	3	51	28	1	2	12	21	56	27	-12
11	Burton Swifts	30	9	2	4	34	20	2	1	12	18	54	25	-22
12	Rotherham United	30	10	0	5	37	22	1	2	12	18	40	24	-7
13	Lincoln City	30	8	0	7	32	27	2	0	13	20	65	20	-40
14	Walsall	30	8	0	7	35	25	2	0	13	12	67	20	-45
15	Port Vale	30	6	3	5	30	23	1	1	13	9	54	18	-38
16	Crewe Alexandra	30	3	4	8	20	34	0	0	15	6	69	10	-77

SEASON 1895/96

Match # 107   Saturday 07/09/95   Football League Division 2   at Bank Street   Attendance 6000
Result: **Newton Heath 5 Crewe Alexandra 0**
Teamsheet: Douglas, Dow, Erentz, Fitzsimmons, McNaught, Cartwright, Clarkin, Kennedy, Cassidy, Smith, Aitken
Scorer(s):   Cassidy 2, Aitken, Kennedy, Smith

Match # 108   Saturday 14/09/95   Football League Division 2   at The Athletic Ground   Attendance 3000
Result: **Loughborough Town 3 Newton Heath 3**
Teamsheet: Douglas, Dow, Erentz, Fitzsimmons, McNaught, Cartwright, Clarkin, Kennedy, Cassidy, Smith, Peters
Scorer(s):   Cassidy 2, McNaught

Match # 109   Saturday 21/09/95   Football League Division 2   at Bank Street   Attendance 9000
Result: **Newton Heath 5 Burton Swifts 0**
Teamsheet: Douglas, Dow, Erentz, Fitzsimmons, McNaught, Perrins, Clarkin, Kennedy, Donaldson, Smith, Cassidy
Scorer(s):   Cassidy 2, Donaldson 2, Kennedy

Match # 110   Saturday 28/09/95   Football League Division 2   at Gresty Road   Attendance 2000
Result: **Crewe Alexandra 0 Newton Heath 2**
Teamsheet: Douglas, Dow, Erentz, Perrins, McNaught, Fitzsimmons, Clarkin, Kennedy, Cassidy, Smith, Aitken
Scorer(s):   Smith 2

Match # 111   Saturday 05/10/95   Football League Division 2   at Bank Street   Attendance 12000
Result: **Newton Heath 1 Manchester City 1**
Teamsheet: Douglas, Dow, Erentz, Perrins, McNaught, Cartwright, Clarkin, Kennedy, Cassidy, Smith, Peters
Scorer(s):   Clarkin

Match # 112   Saturday 12/10/95   Football League Division 2   at Anfield   Attendance 7000
Result: **Liverpool 7 Newton Heath 1**
Teamsheet: Douglas, Dow, Erentz, Perrins, McNaught, Cartwright, Clarkin, Kennedy, Cassidy, Smith, Peters
Scorer(s):   Cassidy

Match # 113   Saturday 19/10/95   Football League Division 2   at Bank Street   Attendance 8000
Result: **Newton Heath 2 Newcastle United 1**
Teamsheet: Douglas, Dow, Erentz, Perrins, McNaught, Cartwright, Clarkin, Kennedy, Cassidy, Smith, Peters
Scorer(s):   Cassidy, Peters

Match # 114   Saturday 26/10/95   Football League Division 2   at St James' Park   Attendance 8000
Result: **Newcastle United 2 Newton Heath 1**
Teamsheet: Douglas, Dow, McNaught, Fitzsimmons, Perrins, Cartwright, Clarkin, Kennedy, Cassidy, Smith, Peters
Scorer(s):   Kennedy

Match # 115   Saturday 02/11/95   Football League Division 2   at Bank Street   Attendance 10000
Result: **Newton Heath 5 Liverpool 2**
Teamsheet: Douglas, Dow, Erentz, Fitzsimmons, McNaught, Cartwright, Clarkin, Kennedy, Cassidy, Smith, Peters
Scorer(s):   Peters 3, Clarkin, Smith

Match # 116   Saturday 09/11/95   Football League Division 2   at Manor Field   Attendance 9000
Result: **Arsenal 2 Newton Heath 1**
Teamsheet: Douglas, Dow, Erentz, Fitzsimmons, McNaught, Cartwright, Clarkin, Kennedy, Cassidy, Smith, Peters
Scorer(s):   Cassidy

Match # 117   Saturday 16/11/95   Football League Division 2   at Bank Street   Attendance 8000
Result: **Newton Heath 5 Lincoln City 5**
Teamsheet: Douglas, Dow, Collinson, Fitzsimmons, McNaught, Cartwright, Clarkin, Kennedy, Cassidy, Smith, Peters
Scorer(s):   Clarkin 2, Cassidy, Collinson, Peters

Match # 118   Saturday 23/11/95   Football League Division 2   at Trent Bridge   Attendance 3000
Result: **Notts County 0 Newton Heath 2**
Teamsheet: Douglas, Collinson, Erentz, Fitzsimmons, McNaught, Cartwright, Clarkin, Kennedy, Cassidy, Smith, Peters
Scorer(s):   Cassidy, Kennedy

Match # 119   Saturday 30/11/95   Football League Division 2   at Bank Street   Attendance 6000
Result: **Newton Heath 5 Arsenal 1**
Teamsheet: Douglas, Dow, Erentz, Fitzsimmons, McNaught, Cartwright, Clarkin, Kennedy, Cassidy, Smith, Peters
Scorer(s):   Cartwright 2, Clarkin, Kennedy, Peters

Match # 120   Saturday 07/12/95   Football League Division 2   at Hyde Road   Attendance 18000
Result: **Manchester City 2 Newton Heath 1**
Teamsheet: Douglas, Dow, Erentz, Fitzsimmons, McNaught, Cartwright, Clarkin, Kennedy, Cassidy, Smith, Peters
Scorer(s):   Cassidy

Match # 121   Saturday 14/12/95   Football League Division 2   at Bank Street   Attendance 3000
Result: **Newton Heath 3 Notts County 0**
Teamsheet: Douglas, Collinson, Erentz, Fitzsimmons, McNaught, Cartwright, Clarkin, Kennedy, Donaldson, Smith, Cassidy
Scorer(s):   Cassidy, Clarkin, Donaldson

Match # 122   Saturday 21/12/95   Football League Division 2   at Barley Bank   Attendance 3000
Result: **Darwen 3 Newton Heath 0**
Teamsheet: Douglas, Collinson, Erentz, Fitzsimmons, McNaught, Cartwright, Clarkin, Kennedy, Donaldson, Cassidy, Peters

Match # 123   Wednesday 01/01/96   Football League Division 2   at Bank Street   Attendance 8000
Result: **Newton Heath 3 Grimsby Town 2**
Teamsheet: Douglas, Dow, Cartwright, Perrins, McNaught, Fitzsimmons, Clarkin, Kennedy, Donaldson, Smith, Cassidy
Scorer(s):   Cassidy 3

Match # 124   Saturday 04/01/96   Football League Division 2   at Filbert Street   Attendance 7000
Result: **Leicester City 3 Newton Heath 0**
Teamsheet: Douglas, Dow, Collinson, Fitzsimmons, McNaught, Cartwright, Clarkin, Kennedy, Donaldson, Smith, Cassidy

SEASON 1895/96 (continued)

Match # 125 Saturday 11/01/96 Football League Division 2 at Bank Street Attendance 3000
Result: **Newton Heath 3 Rotherham United 0**
Teamsheet: Ridgway, Dow, Collinson, Fitzsimmons, McNaught, Cartwright, Kennedy, Peters, Donaldson, Stephenson, Cassidy
Scorer(s): Donaldson 2, Stephenson

Match # 126 Saturday 01/02/96 FA Cup 1st Round at Bank Street Attendance 6000
Result: **Newton Heath 2 Kettering 1**
Teamsheet: Ridgway, Dow, Collinson, Fitzsimmons, Perrins, Cartwright, Kennedy, Donaldson, Cassidy, Smith, Peters
Scorer(s): Donaldson, Smith

Match # 127 Monday 03/02/96 Football League Division 2 at Bank Street Attendance 1000
Result: **Newton Heath 2 Leicester City 0**
Teamsheet: Ridgway, Collinson, Cartwright, Fitzsimmons, Perrins, Smith, Kennedy, Donaldson, Dow, Vance, Peters
Scorer(s): Kennedy, Smith

Match # 128 Saturday 08/02/96 Football League Division 2 at Peel Croft Attendance 2000
Result: **Burton Swifts 4 Newton Heath 1**
Teamsheet: Ridgway, Collinson, Erentz, Fitzsimmons, McNaught, Cartwright, Kennedy, Donaldson, Dow, Vance, Smith
Scorer(s): Vance

Match # 129 Saturday 15/02/96 FA Cup 2nd Round at Bank Street Attendance 20000
Result: **Newton Heath 1 Derby County 1**
Teamsheet: Ridgway, Collinson, Erentz, Fitzsimmons, McNaught, Cartwright, Clarkin, Donaldson, Kennedy, Smith, Peters
Scorer(s): Kennedy

Match # 130 Wednesday 19/02/96 FA Cup 2nd Round Replay at Baseball Ground Attendance 6000
Result: **Derby County 5 Newton Heath 1**
Teamsheet: Ridgway, Collinson, Erentz, Fitzsimmons, McNaught, Cartwright, Clarkin, Donaldson, Kennedy, Smith, Peters
Scorer(s): Donaldson

Match # 131 Saturday 29/02/96 Football League Division 2 at Bank Street Attendance 1000
Result: **Newton Heath 1 Burton Wanderers 2**
Teamsheet: Perrins, Collinson, Erentz, Fitzsimmons, McNaught, Whitney, Clarkin, Kennedy, Donaldson, Smith, Peters
Scorer(s): McNaught

Match # 132 Saturday 07/03/96 Football League Division 2 at Millmoor Attendance 1500
Result: **Rotherham United 2 Newton Heath 3**
Teamsheet: Cartwright, Collinson, Erentz, Peters, Perrins, Whitney, Clarkin, Kennedy, Donaldson, Vance, Smith
Scorer(s): Donaldson, Kennedy, Smith

Match # 133 Saturday 14/03/96 Football League Division 2 at Abbey Park Attendance 2000
Result: **Grimsby Town 4 Newton Heath 2**
Teamsheet: Whittaker, Collinson, Erentz, Fitzsimmons, McNaught, Cartwright, Clarkin, Kennedy, Donaldson, Vance, Smith
Scorer(s): Kennedy, Smith

Match # 134 Wednesday 18/03/96 Football League Division 2 at Derby Turn Attendance 2000
Result: **Burton Wanderers 5 Newton Heath 1**
Teamsheet: Perrins, Collinson, Erentz, Fitzsimmons, McNaught, Cartwright, Dow, Kennedy, Donaldson, Vance, Smith
Scorer(s): Dow

Match # 135 Monday 23/03/96 Football League Division 2 at Cobridge Stadium Attendance 3000
Result: **Port Vale 3 Newton Heath 0**
Teamsheet: Whittaker, Collinson, Erentz, Fitzsimmons, McNaught, Cartwright, Clarkin, Kennedy, Donaldson, Vance, Smith

Match # 136 Friday 03/04/96 Football League Division 2 at Bank Street Attendance 1000
Result: **Newton Heath 4 Darwen 0**
Teamsheet: Ridgway, Stafford, Erentz, Fitzsimmons, McNaught, Cartwright, Clarkin, Kennedy, Donaldson, Vance, Smith
Scorer(s): Kennedy 3, McNaught

Match # 137 Saturday 04/04/96 Football League Division 2 at Bank Street Attendance 4000
Result: **Newton Heath 2 Loughborough Town 0**
Teamsheet: Ridgway, Stafford, Erentz, Fitzsimmons, McNaught, Cartwright, Clarkin, Kennedy, Donaldson, Vance, Smith
Scorer(s): Donaldson, Smith

Match # 138 Monday 06/04/96 Football League Division 2 at Bank Street Attendance 5000
Result: **Newton Heath 2 Port Vale 1**
Teamsheet: Ridgway, Stafford, Erentz, Fitzsimmons, McNaught, Cartwright, Clarkin, Kennedy, Donaldson, Vance, Smith
Scorer(s): Clarkin, Smith

Match # 139 Saturday 11/04/96 Football League Division 2 at Sincil Bank Attendance 2000
Result: **Lincoln City 2 Newton Heath 0**
Teamsheet: Whittaker, Stafford, Erentz, Fitzsimmons, Perrins, Cartwright, Clarkin, McNaught, Donaldson, Vance, Smith

SEASON 1895/96 SUMMARY

APPEARANCES

PLAYER	LGE	FAC	TOT
Kennedy	29	3	32
Smith	28	3	31
Cartwright	27	3	30
McNaught	28	2	30
Fitzsimmons	26	3	29
Clarkin	26	2	28
Erentz	24	2	26
Cassidy	19	1	20
Donaldson	17	3	20
Dow	19	1	20
Peters	16	3	19
Douglas	18	–	18
Collinson	13	3	16
Perrins	12	1	13
Vance	10	–	10
Ridgway	6	3	9
Stafford	4	–	4
Whittaker	3	–	3
Aitken	2	–	2
Whitney	2	–	2
Stephenson	1	–	1

GOALSCORERS

PLAYER	LGE	FAC	TOT
Cassidy	16	–	16
Kennedy	11	1	12
Smith	9	1	10
Donaldson	7	2	9
Clarkin	7	–	7
Peters	6	–	6
McNaught	3	–	3
Cartwright	2	–	2
Aitken	1	–	1
Collinson	1	–	1
Dow	1	–	1
Stephenson	1	–	1
Vance	1	–	1

RESULTS & ATTENDANCES SUMMARY

		P	W	D	L	F	A	TOTAL	AVGE
League	H	15	12	2	1	48	15	85000	5667
	A	15	3	1	11	18	42	72500	4833
TOTAL		30	15	3	12	66	57	157500	5250
FA Cup	H	2	1	1	0	3	2	26000	13000
	A	1	0	0	1	1	5	6000	6000
TOTAL		3	1	1	1	4	7	32000	10667
Overall	H	17	13	3	1	51	17	111000	6529
	A	16	3	1	12	19	47	78500	4906
TOTAL		33	16	4	13	70	64	189500	5742

FINAL TABLE – LEAGUE DIVISION TWO

		P	HOME W	HOME D	HOME L	HOME F	HOME A	AWAY W	AWAY D	AWAY L	AWAY F	AWAY A	PTS	GD
1	Liverpool	30	14	1	0	65	11	8	1	6	41	21	46	74
2	Manchester City	30	12	3	0	37	9	9	1	5	26	29	46	25
3	Grimsby Town	30	14	1	0	51	9	6	1	8	31	29	42	44
4	Burton Wanderers	30	12	1	2	43	15	7	3	5	26	25	42	29
5	Newcastle United	30	14	0	1	57	14	2	2	11	16	36	34	23
6	NEWTON HEATH	30	12	2	1	48	15	3	1	11	18	42	33	9
7	Arsenal	30	11	1	3	43	11	3	3	9	16	31	32	17
8	Leicester City	30	10	0	5	40	16	4	4	7	17	28	32	13
9	Darwen	30	9	4	2	55	22	3	2	10	17	45	30	5
10	Notts County	30	8	1	6	41	22	4	1	10	16	32	26	3
11	Burton Swifts	30	7	2	6	24	26	3	2	10	15	43	24	-30
12	Loughborough Town	30	7	3	5	32	25	2	2	11	8	42	23	-27
13	Lincoln City	30	7	1	7	36	24	2	3	10	17	51	22	-22
14	Port Vale	30	6	4	5	25	24	1	0	14	18	54	18	-35
15	Rotherham United	30	7	2	6	27	26	0	1	14	7	71	17	-63
16	Crewe Alexandra	30	5	2	8	22	28	0	1	14	8	67	13	-65

SEASON 1896/97

Match # 140
Tuesday 01/09/96   Football League Division 2   at Bank Street   Attendance 4000
Result: **Newton Heath 2 Gainsborough Trinity 0**
Teamsheet: Ridgway, Stafford, Erentz, Draycott, Jenkyns, Cartwright, Bryant, Donaldson, Brown, McNaught, Cassidy
Scorer(s): McNaught 2

Match # 141
Saturday 05/09/96   Football League Division 2   at Peel Croft   Attendance 3000
Result: **Burton Swifts 3 Newton Heath 5**
Teamsheet: Ridgway, Stafford, Erentz, Draycott, Jenkyns, Cartwright, Bryant, Donaldson, Brown, McNaught, Cassidy
Scorer(s): Brown, Bryant, Cassidy, Draycott, McNaught

Match # 142
Monday 07/09/96   Football League Division 2   at Bank Street   Attendance 7000
Result: **Newton Heath 2 Walsall 0**
Teamsheet: Ridgway, Stafford, Erentz, Draycott, Jenkyns, Cartwright, Bryant, Donaldson, Brown, McNaught, Cassidy
Scorer(s): Cassidy, Donaldson

Match # 143
Saturday 12/09/96   Football League Division 2   at Bank Street   Attendance 7000
Result: **Newton Heath 3 Lincoln City 1**
Teamsheet: Ridgway, Stafford, Erentz, Smith, Jenkyns, Cartwright, Bryant, Donaldson, Brown, McNaught, Cassidy
Scorer(s): Cassidy 2, Donaldson

Match # 144
Saturday 19/09/96   Football League Division 2   at Abbey Park   Attendance 3000
Result: **Grimsby Town 2 Newton Heath 0**
Teamsheet: Ridgway, Stafford, Erentz, Draycott, Jenkyns, Smith, Bryant, Donaldson, Brown, McNaught, Cassidy

Match # 145
Monday 21/09/96   Football League Division 2   at Fellows Park   Attendance 7000
Result: **Walsall 2 Newton Heath 3**
Teamsheet: Wetherell, Stafford, Erentz, Draycott, Jenkyns, Smith, Bryant, Donaldson, Brown, McNaught, Cassidy
Scorer(s): Brown, Draycott, McNaught

Match # 146
Saturday 26/09/96   Football League Division 2   at Bank Street   Attendance 7000
Result: **Newton Heath 4 Newcastle United 0**
Teamsheet: Barrett, Stafford, Erentz, Draycott, Jenkyns, Cartwright, Bryant, Donaldson, Smith, McNaught, Cassidy
Scorer(s): Cassidy 3, Donaldson

Match # 147
Saturday 03/10/96   Football League Division 2   at Hyde Road   Attendance 20000
Result: **Manchester City 0 Newton Heath 0**
Teamsheet: Barrett, Stafford, Erentz, Draycott, Jenkyns, Cartwright, Bryant, Donaldson, Cassidy, McNaught, Smith

Match # 148
Saturday 10/10/96   Football League Division 2   at Bank Street   Attendance 7000
Result: **Newton Heath 1 Birmingham City 1**
Teamsheet: Wetherell, Stafford, Erentz, Draycott, Jenkyns, Cartwright, Bryant, Donaldson, Cassidy, McNaught, Smith
Scorer(s): Draycott

Match # 149
Saturday 17/10/96   Football League Division 2   at Raikes Hall Gardens   Attendance 5000
Result: **Blackpool 4 Newton Heath 2**
Teamsheet: Barrett, Stafford, Erentz, Draycott, Jenkyns, Cartwright, Bryant, Donaldson, Brown, McNaught, Smith
Scorer(s): Bryant, Draycott

Match # 150
Wednesday 21/10/96   Football League Division 2   at The Northolme   Attendance 4000
Result: **Gainsborough Trinity 2 Newton Heath 0**
Teamsheet: Barrett, Stafford, Erentz, Draycott, Jenkyns, Cartwright, Bryant, Kennedy, Donaldson, McNaught, Cassidy

Match # 151
Saturday 24/10/96   Football League Division 2   at Bank Street   Attendance 4000
Result: **Newton Heath 3 Burton Wanderers 0**
Teamsheet: Barrett, Stafford, Erentz, Draycott, Jenkyns, Cartwright, Bryant, McNaught, Cassidy, Vance, Smith
Scorer(s): Cassidy 3

Match # 152
Saturday 07/11/96   Football League Division 2   at Bank Street   Attendance 5000
Result: **Newton Heath 4 Grimsby Town 2**
Teamsheet: Barrett, Stafford, Erentz, Draycott, Jenkyns, Cartwright, Bryant, McNaught, Cassidy, Smith, Donaldson
Scorer(s): Cassidy 2, Donaldson, Jenkyns

Match # 153
Saturday 28/11/96   Football League Division 2   at Muntz Street   Attendance 4000
Result: **Birmingham City 1 Newton Heath 0**
Teamsheet: Barrett, Stafford, Erentz, Draycott, Jenkyns, Cartwright, Bryant, McNaught, Cassidy, Gillespie, Donaldson

Match # 154
Saturday 12/12/96   FA Cup 3rd Qualifying Round   at Bank Street   Attendance 6000
Result: **Newton Heath 7 West Manchester 0**
Teamsheet: Barrett, Stafford, Erentz, McNaught, Jenkyns, Draycott, Bryant, Rothwell, Cassidy, Gillespie, Donaldson
Scorer(s): Cassidy 2, Gillespie 2, Rothwell 2, Bryant

Match # 155
Saturday 19/12/96   Football League Division 2   at Trent Bridge   Attendance 5000
Result: **Notts County 3 Newton Heath 0**
Teamsheet: Barrett, Stafford, Erentz, Draycott, Jenkyns, Cartwright, Bryant, McNaught, Cassidy, Gillespie, Donaldson

Match # 156
Friday 25/12/96   Football League Division 2   at Bank Street   Attendance 18000
Result: **Newton Heath 2 Manchester City 1**
Teamsheet: Barrett, Stafford, Erentz, Draycott, Jenkyns, McNaught, Bryant, Smith, Cassidy, Gillespie, Donaldson
Scorer(s): Donaldson, Smith

Match # 157
Saturday 26/12/96   Football League Division 2   at Bank Street   Attendance 9000
Result: **Newton Heath 2 Blackpool 0**
Teamsheet: Barrett, Stafford, Erentz, Draycott, Jenkyns, McNaught, Bryant, Smith, Cassidy, Gillespie, Donaldson
Scorer(s): Cassidy 2

SEASON 1896/97 (continued)

Match # 158 | Monday 28/12/96   Football League Division 2   at Filbert Street   Attendance 8000
Result: **Leicester City 1 Newton Heath 0**
Teamsheet: Barrett, Stafford, Cartwright, Draycott, Jenkyns, McNaught, Bryant, Smith, Cassidy, Gillespie, Donaldson

Match # 159 | Friday 01/01/97   Football League Division 2   at St James' Park   Attendance 17000
Result: **Newcastle United 2 Newton Heath 0**
Teamsheet: Barrett, Stafford, Erentz, Draycott, Jenkyns, Cartwright, Bryant, McNaught, Cassidy, Gillespie, Donaldson

Match # 160 | Saturday 02/01/97   FA Cup 4th Qualifying Round   at Bank Street   Attendance 5000
Result: **Newton Heath 3 Nelson 0**
Teamsheet: Barrett, Stafford, Erentz, Draycott, Jenkyns, McNaught, Bryant, Cassidy, Donaldson, Gillespie, Smith
Scorer(s):   Cassidy, Donaldson, Gillespie

Match # 161 | Saturday 09/01/97   Football League Division 2   at Bank Street   Attendance 3000
Result: **Newton Heath 1 Burton Swifts 1**
Teamsheet: Barrett, Stafford, Erentz, Draycott, Jenkyns, Cartwright, Bryant, McNaught, Cassidy, Gillespie, Donaldson
Scorer(s):   Donaldson

Match # 162 | Saturday 16/01/97   FA Cup 5th Qualifying Round   at Bank Street   Attendance 1500
Result: **Newton Heath 2 Blackpool 2**
Teamsheet: Barrett, Stafford, Erentz, McNaught, Jenkyns, Cartwright, Bryant, Smith, Donaldson, Cassidy, Gillespie
Scorer(s):   Donaldson, Gillespie

Match # 163 | Wednesday 20/01/97   FA Cup 5th Qualifying Round Replay   at Raikes Hall Gardens   Attendance 5000
Result: **Blackpool 1 Newton Heath 2**
Teamsheet: Barrett, Stafford, Erentz, Draycott, Jenkyns, McNaught, Bryant, Donaldson, Boyd, Gillespie, Cassidy
Scorer(s):   Boyd, Cassidy

Match # 164 | Saturday 30/01/97   FA Cup 1st Round   at Bank Street   Attendance 1500
Result: **Newton Heath 5 Kettering 1**
Teamsheet: Barrett, Stafford, Erentz, Draycott, Jenkyns, McNaught, Bryant, Donaldson, Gillespie, Cassidy
Scorer(s):   Cassidy 3, Donaldson 2

Match # 165 | Saturday 06/02/97   Football League Division 2   at Bank Street   Attendance 5000
Result: **Newton Heath 6 Loughborough Town 0**
Teamsheet: Barrett, Stafford, Erentz, Draycott, Jenkyns, McNaught, Smith, Donaldson, Boyd, Gillespie, Cassidy
Scorer(s):   Smith 2, Boyd, Donaldson, Draycott, Jenkyns

Match # 166 | Saturday 13/02/97   FA Cup 2nd Round   at County Cricket Ground   Attendance 8000
Result: **Southampton 1 Newton Heath 1**
Teamsheet: Barrett, Stafford, Erentz, McNaught, Jenkyns, Cartwright, Bryant, Donaldson, Boyd, Gillespie, Cassidy
Scorer(s):   Donaldson

Match # 167 | Wednesday 17/02/97   FA Cup 2nd Round Replay   at Bank Street   Attendance 7000
Result: **Newton Heath 3 Southampton 1**
Teamsheet: Barrett, Stafford, Cartwright, McNaught, Jenkyns, Smith, Bryant, Donaldson, Boyd, Gillespie, Cassidy
Scorer(s):   Bryant 2, Cassidy

Match # 168 | Saturday 20/02/97   Football League Division 2   at Bank Street   Attendance 8000
Result: **Newton Heath 2 Leicester City 1**
Teamsheet: Barrett, Stafford, Cartwright, Draycott, Jenkyns, McNaught, Bryant, Donaldson, Boyd, Gillespie, Cassidy
Scorer(s):   Boyd, Donaldson

Match # 169 | Saturday 27/02/97   FA Cup 3rd Round   at Baseball Ground   Attendance 12000
Result: **Derby County 2 Newton Heath 0**
Teamsheet: Barrett, Stafford, Cartwright, Draycott, Jenkyns, McNaught, Bryant, Donaldson, Boyd, Gillespie, Cassidy

Match # 170 | Tuesday 02/03/97   Football League Division 2   at Bank Street   Attendance 3000
Result: **Newton Heath 3 Darwen 1**
Teamsheet: Barrett, Stafford, Cartwright, Draycott, Morgan, McNaught, Bryant, Donaldson, Boyd, Gillespie, Cassidy
Scorer(s):   Cassidy 2, Boyd

Match # 171 | Saturday 13/03/97   Football League Division 2   at Barley Bank   Attendance 2000
Result: **Darwen 0 Newton Heath 2**
Teamsheet: Barrett, Cartwright, Erentz, Draycott, Jenkyns, McNaught, Bryant, Donaldson, Boyd, Gillespie, Cassidy
Scorer(s):   Cassidy, Gillespie

Match # 172 | Saturday 20/03/97   Football League Division 2   at Derby Turn   Attendance 3000
Result: **Burton Wanderers 1 Newton Heath 2**
Teamsheet: Barrett, Cartwright, Erentz, Draycott, Morgan, McNaught, Bryant, Donaldson, Boyd, Gillespie, Cassidy
Scorer(s):   Gillespie, own goal

Match # 173 | Monday 22/03/97   Football League Division 2   at Bank Street   Attendance 3000
Result: **Newton Heath 1 Arsenal 1**
Teamsheet: Barrett, Cartwright, Erentz, Draycott, Jenkyns, McNaught, Bryant, Donaldson, Boyd, Gillespie, Smith
Scorer(s):   Boyd

Match # 174 | Saturday 27/03/97   Football League Division 2   at Bank Street   Attendance 10000
Result: **Newton Heath 1 Notts County 1**
Teamsheet: Barrett, Cartwright, Erentz, Draycott, Jenkyns, McNaught, Bryant, Donaldson, Boyd, Gillespie, Cassidy
Scorer(s):   Bryant

Match # 175 | Thursday 01/04/97   Football League Division 2   at Sincil Bank   Attendance 1000
Result: **Lincoln City 1 Newton Heath 3**
Teamsheet: Barrett, Cartwright, Erentz, Draycott, Jenkyns, McNaught, Bryant, Donaldson, Boyd, Gillespie, Cassidy
Scorer(s):   Jenkyns 3

SEASON 1896/97 (continued)

Match # 176	Saturday 03/04/97	Football League Division 2	at Manor Field	Attendance 6000
Result:	**Arsenal 0 Newton Heath 2**			
Teamsheet:	Barrett, Cartwright, Erentz, Draycott, Jenkyns, McNaught, Bryant, Donaldson, Boyd, Gillespie, Cassidy			
Scorer(s):	Boyd, Donaldson			

Match # 177	Saturday 10/04/97	Football League Division 2	at The Athletic Ground	Attendance 3000
Result:	**Loughborough Town 2 Newton Heath 0**			
Teamsheet:	Barrett, Stafford, Erentz, Draycott, McNaught, Cartwright, Bryant, Donaldson, Boyd, Gillespie, Cassidy			

Newton Heath were required to play 'Test Matches' against Burnley and
Sunderland. They were unsuccessful and remained in Division Two.

Match # 178	Monday 19/04/97	Football League Test Match	at Turf Moor	Attendance 10000
Result:	**Burnley 2 Newton Heath 0**			
Teamsheet:	Barrett, Cartwright, Erentz, Draycott, Jenkyns, McNaught, Bryant, Doughty, Donaldson, Gillespie, Cassidy			

Match # 179	Wednesday 21/04/97	Football League Test Match	at Bank Street	Attendance 7000
Result:	**Newton Heath 2 Burnley 0**			
Teamsheet:	Barrett, Cartwright, Erentz, Draycott, Jenkyns, McNaught, Bryant, Boyd, Donaldson, Gillespie, Cassidy			
Scorer(s):	Boyd, Jenkyns			

Match # 180	Saturday 24/04/97	Football League Test Match	at Bank Street	Attendance 18000
Result:	**Newton Heath 1 Sunderland 1**			
Teamsheet:	Barrett, Doughty, Erentz, Draycott, Jenkyns, McNaught, Bryant, Boyd, Donaldson, Gillespie, Cassidy			
Scorer(s):	Boyd			

Match # 181	Monday 26/04/97	Football League Test Match	at Newcastle Road	Attendance 6000
Result:	**Sunderland 2 Newton Heath 0**			
Teamsheet:	Barrett, Doughty, Erentz, Draycott, Jenkyns, McNaught, Bryant, Boyd, Donaldson, Gillespie, Cassidy			

SEASON 1896/97 SUMMARY

APPEARANCES

PLAYER	LGE	FAC	TM	TOT
McNaught	30	8	4	42
Bryant	29	8	4	41
Donaldson	29	8	4	41
Cassidy	28	8	4	40
Jenkyns	27	8	4	39
Draycott	29	5	4	38
Erentz	27	6	4	37
Barrett	23	8	4	35
Cartwright	25	5	2	32
Stafford	24	8	–	32
Gillespie	17	8	4	29
Boyd	10	4	3	17
Smith	14	3	–	17
Brown	7	–	–	7
Ridgway	5	–	–	5
Doughty	–	–	3	3
Morgan	2	–	–	2
Wetherell	2	–	–	2
Kennedy	1	–	–	1
Rothwell	–	1	–	1
Vance	1	–	–	1

GOALSCORERS

PLAYER	LGE	FAC	TM	TOT
Cassidy	17	8	–	25
Donaldson	9	5	–	14
Boyd	5	1	2	8
Jenkyns	5	–	1	6
Bryant	3	3	–	6
Gillespie	2	4	–	6
Draycott	5	–	–	5
McNaught	4	–	–	4
Smith	3	–	–	3
Brown	2	–	–	2
Rothwell	–	2	–	2
own goal	1	–	–	1

RESULTS & ATTENDANCES SUMMARY

		P	W	D	L	F	A	TOTAL	AVGE
League	H	15	11	4	0	37	10	100000	6667
	A	15	6	1	8	19	24	91000	6067
	TOTAL	30	17	5	8	56	34	191000	6367
FA Cup	H	5	4	1	0	20	4	21000	4200
	A	3	1	1	1	3	4	25000	8333
	TOTAL	8	5	2	1	23	8	46000	5750
Test Matches	H	2	1	1	0	3	1	25000	12500
	A	2	0	0	2	0	4	16000	8000
	TOTAL	4	1	1	2	3	5	41000	10250
Overall	H	22	16	6	0	60	15	146000	6636
	A	20	7	2	11	22	32	132000	6600
	TOTAL	42	23	8	11	82	47	278000	6619

FINAL TABLE – LEAGUE DIVISION TWO

		P	W	D	L	F	A	W	D	L	F	A	PTS	GD
				HOME					AWAY					
1	Notts County	30	12	1	2	60	18	7	3	5	32	25	42	49
2	NEWTON HEATH	30	11	4	0	37	10	6	1	8	19	24	39	22
3	Grimsby Town	30	12	2	1	44	15	5	2	8	22	30	38	21
4	Birmingham City	30	8	3	4	36	23	8	2	5	33	24	37	22
5	Newcastle United	30	13	1	1	42	13	4	0	11	14	39	35	4
6	Manchester City	30	10	3	2	39	15	2	5	8	19	35	32	8
7	Gainsborough Trinity	30	10	2	3	35	16	2	5	8	15	31	31	3
8	Blackpool	30	11	3	1	39	16	2	2	11	20	40	31	3
9	Leicester City	30	11	2	2	44	19	2	2	11	15	37	30	3
10	Arsenal	30	10	1	4	42	20	3	3	9	26	50	30	-2
11	Darwen	30	13	0	2	54	16	1	0	14	13	45	28	6
12	Walsall	30	8	2	5	37	25	3	2	10	16	44	26	-16
13	Loughborough Town	30	10	0	5	37	14	2	1	12	13	50	25	-14
14	Burton Swifts	30	7	4	4	33	20	2	2	11	13	41	24	-15
15	Burton Wanderers	30	8	1	6	22	22	1	1	13	9	45	20	-36
16	Lincoln City	30	4	2	9	17	27	1	0	14	10	58	12	-58

SEASON 1897/98

Match # 182   Saturday 04/09/97   Football League Division 2   at Bank Street   Attendance 5000
Result: **Newton Heath 5 Lincoln City 0**
Teamsheet: Barrett, Stafford, Erentz F, Morgan, McNaught, Cartwright, Bryant, Dunn, Boyd, Gillespie, Cassidy
Scorer(s):   Boyd 3, Bryant, Cassidy

Match # 183   Saturday 11/09/97   Football League Division 2   at Peel Croft   Attendance 2000
Result: **Burton Swifts 0 Newton Heath 4**
Teamsheet: Barrett, Stafford, Erentz F, Morgan, McNaught, Cartwright, Bryant, Dunn, Boyd, Gillespie, Cassidy
Scorer(s):   Boyd 3, Cassidy

Match # 184   Saturday 18/09/97   Football League Division 2   at Bank Street   Attendance 8000
Result: **Newton Heath 1 Luton Town 2**
Teamsheet: Barrett, Stafford, Erentz F, Morgan, McNaught, Cartwright, Bryant, Dunn, Boyd, Gillespie, Cassidy
Scorer(s):   Cassidy

Match # 185   Saturday 25/09/97   Football League Division 2   at Raikes Hall Gardens   Attendance 2000
Result: **Blackpool 0 Newton Heath 1**
Teamsheet: Barrett, Stafford, Erentz F, McNaught, Jenkyns, Cartwright, Bryant, Donaldson, Boyd, Smith, Cassidy
Scorer(s):   Smith

Match # 186   Saturday 02/10/97   Football League Division 2   at Bank Street   Attendance 6000
Result: **Newton Heath 2 Leicester City 0**
Teamsheet: Barrett, Stafford, Erentz F, McNaught, Jenkyns, Cartwright, Bryant, Donaldson, Boyd, Smith, Cassidy
Scorer(s):   Boyd 2

Match # 187   Saturday 09/10/97   Football League Division 2   at St James' Park   Attendance 12000
Result: **Newcastle United 2 Newton Heath 0**
Teamsheet: Barrett, Stafford, Erentz F, McNaught, Jenkyns, Cartwright, Bryant, Donaldson, Boyd, Smith, Cassidy

Match # 188   Saturday 16/10/97   Football League Division 2   at Bank Street   Attendance 20000
Result: **Newton Heath 1 Manchester City 1**
Teamsheet: Barrett, Stafford, Erentz F, McNaught, Jenkyns, Cartwright, Bryant, Donaldson, Boyd, Gillespie, Cassidy
Scorer(s):   Gillespie

Match # 189   Saturday 23/10/97   Football League Division 2   at Muntz Street   Attendance 6000
Result: **Birmingham City 2 Newton Heath 1**
Teamsheet: Ridgway, Stafford, Erentz F, McNaught, Jenkyns, Cartwright, Bryant, Donaldson, Boyd, Gillespie, Cassidy
Scorer(s):   Bryant

Match # 190   Saturday 30/10/97   Football League Division 2   at Bank Street   Attendance 6000
Result: **Newton Heath 6 Walsall 0**
Teamsheet: Barrett, Stafford, Erentz F, McNaught, Jenkyns, Draycott, Bryant, Donaldson, Boyd, Gillespie, Cassidy
Scorer(s):   Cassidy 2, Donaldson 2, Bryant, Gillespie

Match # 191   Saturday 06/11/97   Football League Division 2   at Sincil Bank   Attendance 2000
Result: **Lincoln City 1 Newton Heath 0**
Teamsheet: Barrett, Stafford, Erentz F, McNaught, Jenkyns, Cartwright, Dunn, Donaldson, Boyd, Gillespie, Cassidy

Match # 192   Saturday 13/11/97   Football League Division 2   at Bank Street   Attendance 7000
Result: **Newton Heath 0 Newcastle United 1**
Teamsheet: Barrett, Cartwright, Erentz F, Draycott, Jenkyns, McNaught, Bryant, Donaldson, Boyd, Gillespie, Cassidy

Match # 193   Saturday 20/11/97   Football League Division 2   at Filbert Street   Attendance 6000
Result: **Leicester City 1 Newton Heath 1**
Teamsheet: Barrett, Stafford, Erentz F, Draycott, McNaught, Cartwright, Bryant, Wedge, Boyd, Cassidy, Dunn
Scorer(s):   Wedge

Match # 194   Saturday 27/11/97   Football League Division 2   at Bank Street   Attendance 5000
Result: **Newton Heath 2 Grimsby Town 1**
Teamsheet: Barrett, Stafford, Erentz F, Draycott, McNaught, Cartwright, Bryant, Wedge, Boyd, Cassidy, Dunn
Scorer(s):   Bryant, Wedge

Match # 195   Saturday 11/12/97   Football League Division 2   at Fellows Park   Attendance 2000
Result: **Walsall 1 Newton Heath 1**
Teamsheet: Barrett, Stafford, Erentz F, Draycott, McNaught, Cartwright, Bryant, Morgan, Boyd, Cassidy, Dunn
Scorer(s):   Boyd

Match # 196   Saturday 25/12/97   Football League Division 2   at Hyde Road   Attendance 16000
Result: **Manchester City 0 Newton Heath 1**
Teamsheet: Barrett, Stafford, Erentz F, Draycott, McNaught, Cartwright, Bryant, Carman, Boyd, Cassidy, Dunn
Scorer(s):   Cassidy

Match # 197   Monday 27/12/97   Football League Division 2   at The Northolme   Attendance 3000
Result: **Gainsborough Trinity 2 Newton Heath 1**
Teamsheet: Barrett, Stafford, Erentz F, Draycott, McNaught, Cartwright, Bryant, Carman, Boyd, Cassidy, Dunn
Scorer(s):   Boyd

Match # 198   Saturday 01/01/98   Football League Division 2   at Bank Street   Attendance 6000
Result: **Newton Heath 4 Burton Swifts 0**
Teamsheet: Barrett, Stafford, Erentz F, Draycott, McNaught, Cartwright, Bryant, Carman, Boyd, Cassidy, Dunn
Scorer(s):   Boyd, Bryant, Carman, McNaught

Match # 199   Saturday 08/01/98   Football League Division 2   at Manor Field   Attendance 8000
Result: **Arsenal 5 Newton Heath 1**
Teamsheet: Barrett, Erentz H, Erentz F, Draycott, McNaught, Cartwright, Bryant, Morgan, Boyd, Cassidy, Gillespie
Scorer(s):   Erentz F

SEASON 1897/98 (continued)

Match # 200
Wednesday 12/01/98   Football League Division 2   at Bank Street   Attendance 7000
Result: **Newton Heath 0 Burnley 0**
Teamsheet: Barrett, Stafford, Erentz F, Draycott, McNaught, Cartwright, Bryant, Collinson, Boyd, Cassidy, Smith

Match # 201
Saturday 15/01/98   Football League Division 2   at Bank Street   Attendance 4000
Result: **Newton Heath 4 Blackpool 0**
Teamsheet: Barrett, Erentz H, Erentz F, Draycott, McNaught, Cartwright, Bryant, Collinson, Boyd, Cassidy, Smith
Scorer(s):   Boyd 2, Cartwright, Cassidy

Match # 202
Saturday 29/01/98   FA Cup 1st Round   at Bank Street   Attendance 6000
Result: **Newton Heath 1 Walsall 0**
Teamsheet: Barrett, Erentz H, Erentz F, Draycott, McNaught, Cartwright, Bryant, Collinson, Boyd, Cassidy, Dunn
Scorer(s):   own goal

Match # 203
Saturday 12/02/98   FA Cup 2nd Round   at Bank Street   Attendance 12000
Result: **Newton Heath 0 Liverpool 0**
Teamsheet: Barrett, Erentz H, Erentz F, Draycott, McNaught, Cartwright, Bryant, Collinson, Boyd, Cassidy, Dunn

Match # 204
Wednesday 16/02/98   FA Cup 2nd Round Replay   at Anfield   Attendance 6000
Result: **Liverpool 2 Newton Heath 1**
Teamsheet: Barrett, Erentz H, Erentz F, Draycott, McNaught, Cartwright, Bryant, Collinson, Boyd, Cassidy, Gillespie
Scorer(s):   Collinson

Match # 205
Saturday 26/02/98   Football League Division 2   at Bank Street   Attendance 6000
Result: **Newton Heath 5 Arsenal 1**
Teamsheet: Barrett, Stafford, Erentz F, Draycott, McNaught, Cartwright, Bryant, Collinson, Boyd, Cassidy, Gillespie
Scorer(s):   Bryant 2, Boyd, Cassidy, Collinson

Match # 206
Monday 07/03/98   Football League Division 2   at Turf Moor   Attendance 3000
Result: **Burnley 6 Newton Heath 3**
Teamsheet: Barrett, Stafford, Erentz F, Draycott, McNaught, Cartwright, Bryant, Collinson, Boyd, Cassidy, Gillespie
Scorer(s):   Bryant 2, Collinson

Match # 207
Saturday 19/03/98   Football League Division 2   at Barley Bank   Attendance 2000
Result: **Darwen 2 Newton Heath 3**
Teamsheet: Ridgway, Stafford, Erentz F, Draycott, McNaught, Cartwright, Bryant, Collinson, Boyd, Cassidy, Gillespie
Scorer(s):   Boyd 2, McNaught

Match # 208
Monday 21/03/98   Football League Division 2   at Dunstable Road   Attendance 2000
Result: **Luton Town 2 Newton Heath 2**
Teamsheet: Ridgway, Stafford, Erentz F, Draycott, McNaught, Cartwright, Bryant, Collinson, Boyd, Cassidy, Gillespie
Scorer(s):   Boyd, Cassidy

Match # 209
Tuesday 29/03/98   Football League Division 2   at Bank Street   Attendance 2000
Result: **Newton Heath 5 Loughborough Town 1**
Teamsheet: Barrett, Erentz H, Cartwright, Morgan, McNaught, Draycott, Bryant, Collinson, Boyd, Cassidy, Gillespie
Scorer(s):   Boyd 3, Cassidy 2

Match # 210
Saturday 02/04/98   Football League Division 2   at Abbey Park   Attendance 2000
Result: **Grimsby Town 1 Newton Heath 3**
Teamsheet: Barrett, Stafford, Erentz H, Draycott, McNaught, Morgan, Bryant, Collinson, Boyd, Cassidy, Gillespie
Scorer(s):   Cassidy 2, Boyd

Match # 211
Friday 08/04/98   Football League Division 2   at Bank Street   Attendance 5000
Result: **Newton Heath 1 Gainsborough Trinity 0**
Teamsheet: Barrett, Erentz H, Erentz F, Draycott, McNaught, Cartwright, Bryant, Collinson, Boyd, Cassidy, Gillespie
Scorer(s):   Cassidy

Match # 212
Saturday 09/04/98   Football League Division 2   at Bank Street   Attendance 4000
Result: **Newton Heath 3 Birmingham City 1**
Teamsheet: Barrett, Stafford, Erentz F, Draycott, McNaught, Cartwright, Bryant, Morgan, Boyd, Cassidy, Gillespie
Scorer(s):   Boyd, Gillespie, Morgan

Match # 213
Saturday 16/04/98   Football League Division 2   at The Athletic Ground   Attendance 1000
Result: **Loughborough Town 0 Newton Heath 0**
Teamsheet: Barrett, Stafford, Erentz F, Draycott, McNaught, Erentz, Bryant, Morgan, Boyd, Cassidy, Gillespie

Match # 214
Saturday 23/04/98   Football League Division 2   at Bank Street   Attendance 4000
Result: **Newton Heath 3 Darwen 2**
Teamsheet: Barrett, Stafford, Erentz F, Draycott, McNaught, Cartwright, Bryant, Collinson, Boyd, Cassidy, Gillespie
Scorer(s):   Collinson 2, Bryant

SEASON 1897/98 SUMMARY

APPEARANCES

PLAYER	LGE	FAC	TOT
Boyd	30	3	33
Cassidy	30	3	33
McNaught	30	3	33
Bryant	29	3	32
Erentz F	28	3	31
Barrett	27	3	30
Cartwright	27	3	30
Stafford	25	–	25
Draycott	21	3	24
Gillespie	19	1	20
Collinson	10	3	13
Dunn	10	2	12
Erentz H	6	3	9
Morgan	9	–	9
Donaldson	8	–	8
Jenkyns	8	–	8
Smith	5	–	5
Carman	3	–	3
Ridgway	3	–	3
Wedge	2	–	2

GOALSCORERS

PLAYER	LGE	FAC	TOT
Boyd	22	–	22
Cassidy	14	–	14
Bryant	10	–	10
Collinson	4	1	5
Gillespie	3	–	3
Donaldson	2	–	2
McNaught	2	–	2
Wedge	2	–	2
Carman	1	–	1
Cartwright	1	–	1
Erentz F	1	–	1
Morgan	1	–	1
Smith	1	–	1
own goal	–	1	1

RESULTS & ATTENDANCES SUMMARY

		P	W	D	L	F	A	TOTAL	AVGE
League	H	15	11	2	2	42	10	95000	6333
	A	15	5	4	6	22	25	69000	4600
TOTAL		30	16	6	8	64	35	164000	5467
FA Cup	H	2	1	1	0	1	0	18000	9000
	A	1	0	0	1	1	2	6000	6000
TOTAL		3	1	1	1	2	2	24000	8000
Overall	H	17	12	3	2	43	10	113000	6647
	A	16	5	4	7	23	27	75000	4688
TOTAL		33	17	7	9	66	37	188000	5697

FINAL TABLE – LEAGUE DIVISION TWO

		P	W	D	L	F	A	W	D	L	F	A	PTS	GD
			HOME					AWAY						
1	Burnley	30	14	1	0	64	13	6	7	2	16	11	48	56
2	Newcastle United	30	14	0	1	43	10	7	3	5	21	22	45	32
3	Manchester City	30	10	4	1	45	15	5	5	5	21	21	39	30
4	NEWTON HEATH	30	11	2	2	42	10	5	4	6	22	25	38	29
5	Arsenal	30	10	4	1	41	14	6	1	8	28	35	37	20
6	Birmingham City	30	11	1	3	37	18	5	3	7	21	32	36	8
7	Leicester City	30	8	5	2	26	11	5	2	8	20	24	33	11
8	Luton Town	30	10	2	3	50	13	3	2	10	18	37	30	18
9	Gainsborough Trinity	30	10	4	1	30	12	2	2	11	20	42	30	-4
10	Walsall	30	9	3	3	42	15	3	2	10	16	43	29	0
11	Blackpool	30	8	4	3	32	15	2	1	12	17	46	25	-12
12	Grimsby Town	30	9	1	5	44	24	1	3	11	8	38	24	-10
13	Burton Swifts	30	7	3	5	25	21	1	2	12	13	48	21	-31
14	Lincoln City	30	6	3	6	27	27	0	2	13	16	55	17	-39
15	Darwen	30	4	1	10	21	32	2	1	12	10	44	14	-45
16	Loughborough Town	30	5	2	8	15	26	1	0	14	9	61	14	-63

SEASON 1898/99

Match # 215 Saturday 03/09/98   Football League Division 2   at The Northolme   Attendance 2000
Result: **Gainsborough Trinity 0 Newton Heath 2**
Teamsheet: Barrett, Stafford, Erentz, Draycott, Morgan, Cartwright, Bryant, Collinson, Jones, Cassidy, Gillespie
Scorer(s):   Bryant, Cassidy

Match # 216 Saturday 10/09/98   Football League Division 2   at Bank Street   Attendance 20000
Result: **Newton Heath 3 Manchester City 0**
Teamsheet: Barrett, Stafford, Erentz, Draycott, Morgan, Cartwright, Bryant, Collinson, Boyd, Cassidy, Gillespie
Scorer(s):   Boyd, Cassidy, Collinson

Match # 217 Saturday 17/09/98   Football League Division 2   at North Road   Attendance 6000
Result: **Glossop 1 Newton Heath 2**
Teamsheet: Barrett, Stafford, Erentz, Draycott, Morgan, Cartwright, Bryant, Collinson, Boyd, Cassidy, Gillespie
Scorer(s):   Bryant, Cassidy

Match # 218 Saturday 24/09/98   Football League Division 2   at Bank Street   Attendance 8000
Result: **Newton Heath 1 Walsall 0**
Teamsheet: Barrett, Stafford, Erentz, Draycott, Morgan, Cartwright, Bryant, Collinson, Boyd, Cassidy, Gillespie
Scorer(s):   Gillespie

Match # 219 Saturday 01/10/98   Football League Division 2   at Peel Croft   Attendance 2000
Result: **Burton Swifts 5 Newton Heath 1**
Teamsheet: Barrett, Stafford, Erentz, Draycott, Morgan, Cartwright, Bryant, Jones, Boyd, Cassidy, Gillespie
Scorer(s):   Boyd

Match # 220 Saturday 08/10/98   Football League Division 2   at Bank Street   Attendance 10000
Result: **Newton Heath 2 Port Vale 1**
Teamsheet: Barrett, Stafford, Erentz, Turner R, Morgan, Cartwright, Bryant, Cairns, Boyd, Cassidy, Gillespie
Scorer(s):   Bryant, Cassidy

Match # 221 Saturday 15/10/98   Football League Division 2   at Muntz Street   Attendance 5000
Result: **Birmingham City 4 Newton Heath 1**
Teamsheet: Barrett, Stafford, Erentz, Draycott, Morgan, Cartwright, Owen, Collinson, Bryant, Cassidy, Gillespie
Scorer(s):   Cassidy

Match # 222 Saturday 22/10/98   Football League Division 2   at Bank Street   Attendance 2000
Result: **Newton Heath 6 Loughborough Town 1**
Teamsheet: Barrett, Stafford, Erentz, Morgan, Turner J, Cartwright, Bryant, Collinson, Brooks, Cassidy, Gillespie
Scorer(s):   Brooks 2, Cassidy 2, Collinson 2

Match # 223 Saturday 05/11/98   Football League Division 2   at Bank Street   Attendance 5000
Result: **Newton Heath 3 Grimsby Town 2**
Teamsheet: Barrett, Stafford, Erentz, Connachan, Turner J, Cartwright, Bryant, Cunningham, Brooks, Cassidy, Gillespie
Scorer(s):   Brooks, Cassidy, Gillespie

Match # 224 Saturday 12/11/98   Football League Division 2   at Bank Street   Attendance 5000
Result: **Newton Heath 0 Barnsley 0**
Teamsheet: Barrett, Stafford, Erentz, Draycott, Collinson, Cartwright, Bryant, Cunningham, Connachan, Cassidy, Gillespie

Match # 225 Saturday 19/11/98   Football League Division 2   at Tower Athletic Ground   Attendance 5000
Result: **New Brighton Tower 0 Newton Heath 3**
Teamsheet: Barrett, Stafford, Erentz, Draycott, Morgan, Cartwright, Bryant, Collinson, Cunningham, Cassidy, Gillespie
Scorer(s):   Collinson 2, Cassidy

Match # 226 Saturday 26/11/98   Football League Division 2   at Bank Street   Attendance 4000
Result: **Newton Heath 1 Lincoln City 0**
Teamsheet: Barrett, Stafford, Erentz, Draycott, Morgan, Cartwright, Bryant, Collinson, Cassidy, Cunningham, Gillespie
Scorer(s):   Bryant

Match # 227 Saturday 03/12/98   Football League Division 2   at Manor Field   Attendance 7000
Result: **Arsenal 5 Newton Heath 1**
Teamsheet: Barrett, Stafford, Erentz, Draycott, Morgan, Cartwright, Bryant, Collinson, Cassidy, Cunningham, Gillespie
Scorer(s):   Collinson

Match # 228 Saturday 10/12/98   Football League Division 2   at Bank Street   Attendance 5000
Result: **Newton Heath 3 Blackpool 1**
Teamsheet: Barrett, Cartwright, Erentz, Draycott, Pepper, Turner J, Connachan, Collinson, Cassidy, Cunningham, Gillespie
Scorer(s):   Cassidy, Collinson, Cunningham

Match # 229 Saturday 17/12/98   Football League Division 2   at Filbert Street   Attendance 8000
Result: **Leicester City 1 Newton Heath 0**
Teamsheet: Barrett, Stafford, Erentz, Draycott, Pepper, Cartwright, Bryant, Connachan, Cassidy, Cunningham, Gillespie

Match # 230 Saturday 24/12/98   Football League Division 2   at Bank Street   Attendance 2000
Result: **Newton Heath 9 Darwen 0**
Teamsheet: Barrett, Stafford, Erentz, Draycott, Pepper, Cartwright, Bryant, Collinson, Boyd, Cassidy, Gillespie
Scorer(s):   Bryant 3, Cassidy 3, Gillespie 2, own goal

Match # 231 Monday 26/12/98   Football League Division 2   at Hyde Road   Attendance 25000
Result: **Manchester City 4 Newton Heath 0**
Teamsheet: Barrett, Stafford, Erentz, Draycott, Pepper, Cartwright, Bryant, Collinson, Cassidy, Brooks, Gillespie

Match # 232 Saturday 31/12/98   Football League Division 2   at Bank Street   Attendance 2000
Result: **Newton Heath 6 Gainsborough Trinity 1**
Teamsheet: Barrett, Stafford, Erentz, Draycott, Pepper, Cartwright, Bryant, Collinson, Cassidy, Boyd, Cunningham
Scorer(s):   Collinson 2, Boyd, Bryant, Cartwright, Draycott

SEASON 1898/99 (continued)

Match # 233 Monday 02/01/99   Football League Division 2   at Bank Street   Attendance 6000
Result: **Newton Heath 2 Burton Swifts 2**
Teamsheet: Barrett, Stafford, Erentz, Draycott, Pepper, Cartwright, Bryant, Collinson, Cassidy, Boyd, Cunningham
Scorer(s): Boyd, Cassidy

Match # 234 Saturday 14/01/99   Football League Division 2   at Bank Street   Attendance 12000
Result: **Newton Heath 3 Glossop 0**
Teamsheet: Barrett, Stafford, Erentz, Draycott, Walker, Cartwright, Bryant, Collinson, Cassidy, Cunningham, Gillespie
Scorer(s): Cunningham, Erentz, Gillespie

Match # 235 Saturday 21/01/99   Football League Division 2   at Fellows Park   Attendance 3000
Result: **Walsall 2 Newton Heath 0**
Teamsheet: Barrett, Stafford, Erentz, Draycott, Walker, Cartwright, Bryant, Collinson, Cassidy, Cunningham, Gillespie

Match # 236 Saturday 28/01/99   FA Cup 1st Round   at Asplins Farm   Attendance 15000
Result: **Tottenham Hotspur 1 Newton Heath 1**
Teamsheet: Barrett, Stafford, Erentz, Draycott, Pepper, Morgan, Bryant, Collinson, Cassidy, Cunningham, Gillespie
Scorer(s): Cassidy

Match # 237 Wednesday 01/02/99   FA Cup 1st Round Replay   at Bank Street   Attendance 6000
Result: **Newton Heath 3 Tottenham Hotspur 5**
Teamsheet: Barrett, Stafford, Erentz, Draycott, Morgan, Cartwright, Bryant, Collinson, Cassidy, Cunningham, Gillespie
Scorer(s): Bryant 3

Match # 238 Saturday 04/02/99   Football League Division 2   at Cobridge Stadium   Attendance 6000
Result: **Port Vale 1 Newton Heath 0**
Teamsheet: Barrett, Stafford, Cartwright, Draycott, Pepper, Morgan, Bryant, Collinson, Boyd, Cassidy, Cunningham

Match # 239 Saturday 18/02/99   Football League Division 2   at The Athletic Ground   Attendance 1500
Result: **Loughborough Town 0 Newton Heath 1**
Teamsheet: Barrett, Stafford, Turner R, Draycott, Gourlay, Morgan, Bryant, Cunningham, Boyd, Cassidy, Roberts
Scorer(s): Bryant

Match # 240 Saturday 25/02/99   Football League Division 2   at Bank Street   Attendance 12000
Result: **Newton Heath 2 Birmingham City 0**
Teamsheet: Barrett, Stafford, Erentz, Draycott, Cartwright, Morgan, Bryant, Cunningham, Boyd, Cassidy, Roberts
Scorer(s): Boyd, Roberts

Match # 241 Saturday 04/03/99   Football League Division 2   at Abbey Park   Attendance 4000
Result: **Grimsby Town 3 Newton Heath 0**
Teamsheet: Barrett, Stafford, Erentz, Draycott, Cartwright, Morgan, Bryant, Collinson, Boyd, Cassidy, Cunningham

Match # 242 Saturday 18/03/99   Football League Division 2   at Bank Street   Attendance 20000
Result: **Newton Heath 1 New Brighton Tower 2**
Teamsheet: Barrett, Stafford, Erentz, Draycott, Cartwright, Morgan, Bryant, Hopkins, Cassidy, Gillespie, Roberts
Scorer(s): Cassidy

Match # 243 Saturday 25/03/99   Football League Division 2   at Sincil Bank   Attendance 3000
Result: **Lincoln City 2 Newton Heath 0**
Teamsheet: Barrett, Stafford, Erentz, Draycott, Cartwright, Morgan, Bryant, Collinson, Lee, Cassidy, Gillespie

Match # 244 Saturday 01/04/99   Football League Division 2   at Bank Street   Attendance 5000
Result: **Newton Heath 2 Arsenal 2**
Teamsheet: Barrett, Stafford, Erentz, Draycott, Griffiths, Morgan, Bryant, Collinson, Cassidy, Cartwright, Gillespie
Scorer(s): Bryant, Cassidy

Match # 245 Monday 03/04/99   Football League Division 2   at Raikes Hall Gardens   Attendance 3000
Result: **Blackpool 0 Newton Heath 1**
Teamsheet: Barrett, Stafford, Erentz, Draycott, Griffiths, Cartwright, Bryant, Morgan, Lee, Gillespie, Cassidy
Scorer(s): Cassidy

Match # 246 Tuesday 04/04/99   Football League Division 2   at Oakwell   Attendance 4000
Result: **Barnsley 0 Newton Heath 2**
Teamsheet: Barrett, Stafford, Erentz, Draycott, Griffiths, Cartwright, Bryant, Morgan, Lee, Gillespie, Cassidy
Scorer(s): Lee 2

Match # 247 Saturday 08/04/99   Football League Division 2   at Dunstable Road   Attendance 1000
Result: **Luton Town 0 Newton Heath 1**
Teamsheet: Barrett, Stafford, Erentz, Draycott, Griffiths, Cartwright, Bryant, Morgan, Lee, Gillespie, Cassidy
Scorer(s): Lee

Match # 248 Wednesday 12/04/99   Football League Division 2   at Bank Street   Attendance 3000
Result: **Newton Heath 5 Luton Town 0**
Teamsheet: Barrett, Stafford, Erentz, Draycott, Griffiths, Cartwright, Radcliffe, Morgan, Lee, Gillespie, Cassidy
Scorer(s): Cartwright, Cassidy, Gillespie, Lee, Morgan

Match # 249 Saturday 15/04/99   Football League Division 2   at Bank Street   Attendance 6000
Result: **Newton Heath 2 Leicester City 2**
Teamsheet: Barrett, Stafford, Erentz, Draycott, Griffiths, Cartwright, Bryant, Morgan, Lee, Gillespie, Cassidy
Scorer(s): Cassidy, Gillespie

Match # 250 Saturday 22/04/99   Football League Division 2   at Barley Bank   Attendance 1000
Result: **Darwen 1 Newton Heath 1**
Teamsheet: Barrett, Stafford, Erentz, Draycott, Griffiths, Cartwright, Bryant, Morgan, Lee, Gillespie, Cassidy
Scorer(s): Morgan

SEASON 1898/99 SUMMARY

APPEARANCES

PLAYER	LGE	FAC	TOT
Barrett	34	2	36
Cassidy	34	2	36
Stafford	33	2	35
Bryant	32	2	34
Cartwright	33	1	34
Erentz	32	2	34
Draycott	31	2	33
Gillespie	28	2	30
Morgan	24	2	26
Collinson	21	2	23
Cunningham	15	2	17
Boyd	12	–	12
Pepper	7	1	8
Griffiths	7	–	7
Lee	7	–	7
Connachan	4	–	4
Brooks	3	–	3
Roberts	3	–	3
Turner J	3	–	3
Jones	2	–	2
Turner R	2	–	2
Walker	2	–	2
Cairns	1	–	1
Gourlay	1	–	1
Hopkins	1	–	1
Owen	1	–	1
Radcliffe	1	–	1

GOALSCORERS

PLAYER	LGE	FAC	TOT
Cassidy	19	1	20
Bryant	10	3	13
Collinson	9	–	9
Gillespie	7	–	7
Boyd	5	–	5
Lee	4	–	4
Brooks	3	–	3
Cartwright	2	–	2
Cunningham	2	–	2
Morgan	2	–	2
Draycott	1	–	1
Erentz	1	–	1
Roberts	1	–	1
own goal	1	–	1

RESULTS & ATTENDANCES SUMMARY

		P	W	D	L	F	A	TOTAL	AVGE
League	H	17	12	4	1	51	14	127000	7471
	A	17	7	1	9	16	29	86500	5088
TOTAL		34	19	5	10	67	43	213500	6279
FA Cup	H	1	0	0	1	3	5	6000	6000
	A	1	0	1	0	1	1	15000	15000
TOTAL		2	0	1	1	4	6	21000	10500
Overall	H	18	12	4	2	54	19	133000	7389
	A	18	7	2	9	17	30	101500	5639
TOTAL		36	19	6	11	71	49	234500	6514

FINAL TABLE – LEAGUE DIVISION TWO

		P	W	D	L	F	A	W	D	L	F	A	PTS	GD
			HOME					AWAY						
1	Manchester City	34	15	1	1	64	10	8	5	4	28	25	52	57
2	Glossop	34	12	1	4	48	13	8	5	4	28	25	46	38
3	Leicester City	34	12	5	0	35	12	6	4	7	29	30	45	22
4	NEWTON HEATH	34	12	4	1	51	14	7	1	9	16	29	43	24
5	New Brighton Tower	34	13	2	2	48	13	5	5	7	23	39	43	19
6	Walsall	34	12	5	0	64	11	3	7	7	15	25	42	43
7	Arsenal	34	14	2	1	55	10	4	3	10	17	31	41	31
8	Birmingham City	34	14	1	2	66	17	3	6	8	19	33	41	35
9	Port Vale	34	12	2	3	35	12	5	3	9	21	22	39	22
10	Grimsby Town	34	10	3	4	39	17	5	2	10	32	43	35	11
11	Barnsley	34	11	4	2	44	18	1	3	13	8	38	31	-4
12	Lincoln City	34	10	5	2	31	16	2	2	13	20	40	31	-5
13	Burton Swifts	34	7	5	5	35	25	3	3	11	16	45	28	-19
14	Gainsborough Trinity	34	8	4	5	40	22	2	1	14	16	50	25	-16
15	Luton Town	34	8	1	8	37	31	2	2	13	14	64	23	-44
16	Blackpool	34	6	3	8	35	30	2	1	14	14	60	20	-41
17	Loughborough Town	34	5	4	8	31	26	1	2	14	7	66	18	-54
18	Darwen	34	2	4	11	16	32	0	1	16	6	109	9	-119

SEASON 1899/1900

Match # 251   Saturday 02/09/99   Football League Division 2   at Bank Street   Attendance 8000
Result: **Newton Heath 2 Gainsborough Trinity 2**
Teamsheet: Barrett, Stafford, Erentz, Morgan, Fitzsimmons, Cartwright, Bryant, Jackson, Lee, Cassidy, Ambler
Scorer(s):   Cassidy, Lee

Match # 252   Saturday 09/09/99   Football League Division 2   at Burnden Park   Attendance 5000
Result: **Bolton Wanderers 2 Newton Heath 1**
Teamsheet: Barrett, Stafford, Erentz, Morgan, Griffiths, Cartwright, Bryant, Jackson, Lee, Cassidy, Ambler
Scorer(s):   Ambler

Match # 253   Saturday 16/09/99   Football League Division 2   at Bank Street   Attendance 6000
Result: **Newton Heath 4 Loughborough Town 0**
Teamsheet: Barrett, Stafford, Erentz, Morgan, Griffiths, Cartwright, Bryant, Jackson, Bain, Cassidy, Lee
Scorer(s):   Bain, Cassidy, Griffiths, own goal

Match # 254   Saturday 23/09/99   Football League Division 2   at Peel Croft   Attendance 2000
Result: **Burton Swifts 0 Newton Heath 0**
Teamsheet: Barrett, Stafford, Erentz, Morgan, Griffiths, Cartwright, Bryant, Jackson, Bain, Cassidy, Roberts

Match # 255   Saturday 30/09/99   Football League Division 2   at Hillsborough   Attendance 8000
Result: **Sheffield Wednesday 2 Newton Heath 1**
Teamsheet: Barrett, Stafford, Erentz, Morgan, Griffiths, Cartwright, Bryant, Jackson, Clark, Cassidy, Roberts
Scorer(s):   Bryant

Match # 256   Saturday 07/10/99   Football League Division 2   at Bank Street   Attendance 5000
Result: **Newton Heath 1 Lincoln City 0**
Teamsheet: Barrett, Stafford, Erentz, Morgan, Griffiths, Cartwright, Roberts, Jackson, Collinson, Cassidy, Gillespie
Scorer(s):   Cassidy

Match # 257   Saturday 14/10/99   Football League Division 2   at Muntz Street   Attendance 10000
Result: **Birmingham City 1 Newton Heath 0**
Teamsheet: Barrett, Stafford, Erentz, Morgan, Griffiths, Cartwright, Sawyer, Jackson, Collinson, Cassidy, Gillespie

Match # 258   Saturday 21/10/99   Football League Division 2   at Bank Street   Attendance 5000
Result: **Newton Heath 2 New Brighton Tower 1**
Teamsheet: Barrett, Stafford, Erentz, Morgan, Griffiths, Fitzsimmons, Bryant, Jackson, Blackmore, Cassidy, Roberts
Scorer(s):   Cassidy 2

Match # 259   Saturday 28/10/99   FA Cup 3rd Qualifying Round   at Bloomfield Road   Attendance 3000
Result: **South Shore 3 Newton Heath 1**
Teamsheet: Barrett, Stafford, Erentz, Morgan, Griffiths, Cartwright, Bryant, Jackson, Blackmore, Cassidy, Roberts
Scorer(s):   Jackson

Match # 260   Saturday 04/11/99   Football League Division 2   at Bank Street   Attendance 5000
Result: **Newton Heath 2 Arsenal 0**
Teamsheet: Barrett, Stafford, Erentz, Morgan, Griffiths, Cartwright, Bryant, Clark, Cassidy, Jackson, Roberts
Scorer(s):   Jackson, Roberts

Match # 261   Saturday 11/11/99   Football League Division 2   at Oakwell   Attendance 3000
Result: **Barnsley 0 Newton Heath 0**
Teamsheet: Barrett, Stafford, Erentz, Morgan, Griffiths, Cartwright, Bryant, Clark, Parkinson, Jackson, Cassidy

Match # 262   Saturday 25/11/99   Football League Division 2   at Dunstable Road   Attendance 3000
Result: **Luton Town 0 Newton Heath 1**
Teamsheet: Barrett, Stafford, Erentz, Morgan, Griffiths, Cartwright, Bryant, Clark, Parkinson, Jackson, Cassidy
Scorer(s):   Jackson

Match # 263   Saturday 02/12/99   Football League Division 2   at Bank Street   Attendance 5000
Result: **Newton Heath 3 Port Vale 0**
Teamsheet: Barrett, Stafford, Erentz, Morgan, Griffiths, Cartwright, Bryant, Clark, Parkinson, Jackson, Cassidy
Scorer(s):   Cassidy 2, Jackson

Match # 264   Saturday 16/12/99   Football League Division 2   at Bank Street   Attendance 4000
Result: **Newton Heath 2 Middlesbrough 1**
Teamsheet: Barrett, Stafford, Erentz, Morgan, Griffiths, Cartwright, Bryant, Heathcote, Parkinson, Jackson, Cassidy
Scorer(s):   Erentz, Parkinson

Match # 265   Saturday 23/12/99   Football League Division 2   at Saltergate   Attendance 2000
Result: **Chesterfield 2 Newton Heath 1**
Teamsheet: Barrett, Stafford, Erentz, Morgan, Griffiths, Cartwright, Bryant, Clark, Parkinson, Cassidy, Roberts
Scorer(s):   Griffiths

Match # 266   Tuesday 26/12/99   Football League Division 2   at Blundell Park   Attendance 2000
Result: **Grimsby Town 0 Newton Heath 7**
Teamsheet: Barrett, Stafford, Erentz, Morgan, Griffiths, Cartwright, Bryant, Clark, Parkinson, Jackson, Cassidy
Scorer(s):   Bryant 2, Cassidy 2, Jackson, Parkinson, own goal

Match # 267   Saturday 30/12/99   Football League Division 2   at The Northolme   Attendance 2000
Result: **Gainsborough Trinity 0 Newton Heath 1**
Teamsheet: Barrett, Stafford, Erentz, Morgan, Griffiths, Cartwright, Bryant, Clark, Parkinson, Jackson, Cassidy
Scorer(s):   Parkinson

Match # 268   Saturday 06/01/00   Football League Division 2   at Bank Street   Attendance 5000
Result: **Newton Heath 1 Bolton Wanderers 2**
Teamsheet: Barrett, Stafford, Erentz, Morgan, Griffiths, Cartwright, Bryant, Clark, Parkinson, Jackson, Cassidy
Scorer(s):   Parkinson

SEASON 1899/1900 (continued)

Match # 269
Saturday 13/01/00 — Football League Division 2 — at The Athletic Ground — Attendance 1000
Result: **Loughborough Town 0 Newton Heath 2**
Teamsheet: Barrett, Stafford, Erentz, Morgan, Griffiths, Cartwright, Sawyer, Gillespie, Parkinson, Jackson, Cassidy
Scorer(s): Jackson, Parkinson

Match # 270
Saturday 20/01/00 — Football League Division 2 — at Bank Street — Attendance 4000
Result: **Newton Heath 4 Burton Swifts 0**
Teamsheet: Barrett, Stafford, Erentz, Morgan, Griffiths, Cartwright, Bryant, Gillespie, Parkinson, Jackson, Cassidy
Scorer(s): Gillespie 3, Parkinson

Match # 271
Saturday 03/02/00 — Football League Division 2 — at Bank Street — Attendance 10000
Result: **Newton Heath 1 Sheffield Wednesday 0**
Teamsheet: Barrett, Stafford, Erentz, Morgan, Griffiths, Cartwright, Bryant, Godsmark, Parkinson, Jackson, Cassidy
Scorer(s): Bryant

Match # 272
Saturday 10/02/00 — Football League Division 2 — at Sincil Bank — Attendance 2000
Result: **Lincoln City 1 Newton Heath 0**
Teamsheet: Barrett, Stafford, Erentz, Morgan, Griffiths, Cartwright, Jackson, Godsmark, Parkinson, Cassidy, Gillespie

Match # 273
Saturday 17/02/00 — Football League Division 2 — at Bank Street — Attendance 10000
Result: **Newton Heath 3 Birmingham City 2**
Teamsheet: Barrett, Collinson, Erentz, Morgan, Griffiths, Cartwright, Bryant, Godsmark, Parkinson, Jackson, Cassidy
Scorer(s): Cassidy, Godsmark, Parkinson

Match # 274
Saturday 24/02/00 — Football League Division 2 — at Tower Athletic Ground — Attendance 8000
Result: **New Brighton Tower 1 Newton Heath 4**
Teamsheet: Barrett, Stafford, Erentz, Morgan, Griffiths, Cartwright, Collinson, Godsmark, Parkinson, Jackson, Smith
Scorer(s): Collinson 2, Godsmark, Smith

Match # 275
Saturday 03/03/00 — Football League Division 2 — at Bank Street — Attendance 4000
Result: **Newton Heath 1 Grimsby Town 0**
Teamsheet: Barrett, Stafford, Erentz, Morgan, Griffiths, Cartwright, Collinson, Godsmark, Parkinson, Jackson, Smith
Scorer(s): Smith

Match # 276
Saturday 10/03/00 — Football League Division 2 — at Manor Field — Attendance 3000
Result: **Arsenal 2 Newton Heath 1**
Teamsheet: Barrett, Stafford, Erentz, Morgan, Griffiths, Cartwright, Bryant, Godsmark, Cassidy, Jackson, Smith
Scorer(s): Cassidy

Match # 277
Saturday 17/03/00 — Football League Division 2 — at Bank Street — Attendance 6000
Result: **Newton Heath 3 Barnsley 0**
Teamsheet: Barrett, Stafford, Erentz, Ambler, Griffiths, Cartwright, Foley, Godsmark, Leigh, Smith, Cassidy
Scorer(s): Cassidy 2, Leigh

Match # 278
Saturday 24/03/00 — Football League Division 2 — at Filbert Street — Attendance 8000
Result: **Leicester City 2 Newton Heath 0**
Teamsheet: Barrett, Collinson, Erentz, Morgan, Griffiths, Foley, Smith, Godsmark, Leigh, Jackson, Cassidy

Match # 279
Saturday 31/03/00 — Football League Division 2 — at Bank Street — Attendance 6000
Result: **Newton Heath 5 Luton Town 0**
Teamsheet: Barrett, Stafford, Erentz, Morgan, Griffiths, Ambler, Smith, Godsmark, Leigh, Jackson, Cassidy
Scorer(s): Cassidy 3, Godsmark 2

Match # 280
Saturday 07/04/00 — Football League Division 2 — at Cobridge Stadium — Attendance 3000
Result: **Port Vale 1 Newton Heath 0**
Teamsheet: Barrett, Stafford, Erentz, Morgan, Griffiths, Ambler, Foley, Smith, Leigh, Jackson, Cassidy

Match # 281
Friday 13/04/00 — Football League Division 2 — at Bank Street — Attendance 10000
Result: **Newton Heath 3 Leicester City 2**
Teamsheet: Barrett, Stafford, Erentz, Ambler, Griffiths, Smith, Foley, Gillespie, Leigh, Jackson, Cassidy
Scorer(s): Gillespie, Griffiths, own goal

Match # 282
Saturday 14/04/00 — Football League Division 2 — at Bank Street — Attendance 4000
Result: **Newton Heath 5 Walsall 0**
Teamsheet: Barrett, Stafford, Erentz, Ambler, Griffiths, Smith, Foley, Gillespie, Leigh, Jackson, Cassidy
Scorer(s): Jackson 2, Erentz, Foley, Gillespie

Match # 283
Tuesday 17/04/00 — Football League Division 2 — at Fellows Park — Attendance 3000
Result: **Walsall 0 Newton Heath 0**
Teamsheet: Barrett, Collinson, Erentz, Morgan, Griffiths, Ambler, Foley, Gillespie, Leigh, Jackson, Smith

Match # 284
Saturday 21/04/00 — Football League Division 2 — at Linthorpe Road — Attendance 8000
Result: **Middlesbrough 2 Newton Heath 0**
Teamsheet: Barrett, Stafford, Erentz, Smith, Griffiths, Ambler, Foley, Gillespie, Leigh, Jackson, Lee

Match # 285
Saturday 28/04/00 — Football League Division 2 — at Bank Street — Attendance 6000
Result: **Newton Heath 2 Chesterfield 1**
Teamsheet: Barrett, Stafford, Erentz, Morgan, Griffiths, Smith, Holt, Gillespie, Leigh, Jackson, Grundy
Scorer(s): Grundy, Holt

SEASON 1899/1900 SUMMARY

APPEARANCES

PLAYER	LGE	FAC	TOT
Barrett	34	1	35
Erentz	34	1	35
Griffiths	33	1	34
Jackson	32	1	33
Stafford	31	1	32
Morgan	30	1	31
Cassidy	29	1	30
Cartwright	25	1	26
Bryant	19	1	20
Parkinson	15	–	15
Smith	12	–	12
Gillespie	10	–	10
Ambler	9	–	9
Clark	9	–	9
Godsmark	9	–	9
Leigh	9	–	9
Collinson	7	–	7
Foley	7	–	7
Roberts	6	1	7
Lee	4	–	4
Bain	2	–	2
Blackmore	1	1	2
Fitzsimmons	2	–	2
Sawyer	2	–	2
Grundy	1	–	1
Heathcote	1	–	1
Holt	1	–	1

GOALSCORERS

PLAYER	LGE	FAC	TOT
Cassidy	16	–	16
Jackson	7	1	8
Parkinson	7	–	7
Gillespie	5	–	5
Bryant	4	–	4
Godsmark	4	–	4
Griffiths	3	–	3
Collinson	2	–	2
Erentz	2	–	2
Smith	2	–	2
Ambler	1	–	1
Bain	1	–	1
Foley	1	–	1
Grundy	1	–	1
Holt	1	–	1
Lee	1	–	1
Leigh	1	–	1
Roberts	1	–	1
own goals	3	–	3

RESULTS & ATTENDANCES SUMMARY

		P	W	D	L	F	A	TOTAL	AVGE
League	H	17	15	1	1	44	11	103000	6059
	A	17	5	3	9	19	16	73000	4294
TOTAL		34	20	4	10	63	27	176000	5176
FA Cup	H	0	0	0	0	0	0	0	n/a
	A	1	0	0	1	1	3	3000	3000
TOTAL		1	0	0	1	1	3	3000	3000
Overall	H	17	15	1	1	44	11	103000	6059
	A	18	5	3	10	20	19	76000	4222
TOTAL		35	20	4	11	64	30	179000	5114

FINAL TABLE – LEAGUE DIVISION TWO

		P	W	D	L	F	A	W	D	L	F	A	PTS	GD
				HOME						AWAY				
1	Sheffield Wednesday	34	17	0	0	61	7	8	4	5	23	15	54	62
2	Bolton Wanderers	34	14	2	1	47	7	8	6	3	32	18	52	54
3	Birmingham City	34	15	1	1	58	12	5	5	7	20	26	46	40
4	NEWTON HEATH	34	15	1	1	44	11	5	3	9	19	16	44	36
5	Leicester City	34	11	5	1	34	8	6	4	7	19	28	43	17
6	Grimsby Town	34	10	3	4	46	24	7	3	7	21	22	40	21
7	Chesterfield	34	10	4	3	35	24	6	2	9	30	36	38	5
8	Arsenal	34	13	1	3	47	12	3	3	11	14	31	36	18
9	Lincoln City	34	11	5	1	31	9	3	3	11	15	34	36	3
10	New Brighton Tower	34	9	4	4	44	22	4	5	8	22	36	35	8
11	Port Vale	34	11	2	4	26	16	3	4	10	13	33	34	–10
12	Walsall	34	10	5	2	35	18	2	3	12	15	37	32	–5
13	Gainsborough Trinity	34	8	4	5	37	24	1	3	13	10	51	25	–28
14	Middlesbrough	34	8	4	5	28	15	0	4	13	11	54	24	–30
15	Burton Swifts	34	8	5	4	31	24	1	1	15	12	60	24	–41
16	Barnsley	34	8	5	4	36	23	0	2	15	10	56	23	–33
17	Luton Town	34	5	3	9	25	25	0	5	12	15	50	18	–35
18	Loughborough Town	34	1	6	10	12	26	0	0	17	6	74	8	–82

SEASON 1900/01

Match # 286   Saturday 01/09/00   Football League Division 2   at North Road   Attendance 8000
Result: **Glossop 1 Newton Heath 0**
Teamsheet: Garvey, Stafford, Erentz, Morgan B, Griffiths, Cartwright, Schofield, Lawson, Leigh, Jackson, Grundy

Match # 287   Saturday 08/09/00   Football League Division 2   at Bank Street   Attendance 5500
Result: **Newton Heath 4 Middlesbrough 0**
Teamsheet: Garvey, Stafford, Erentz, Morgan B, Griffiths, Cartwright, Schofield, Lawson, Leigh, Jackson, Grundy
Scorer(s):   Griffiths, Grundy, Jackson, Leigh

Match # 288   Saturday 15/09/00   Football League Division 2   at Turf Moor   Attendance 4000
Result: **Burnley 1 Newton Heath 0**
Teamsheet: Whitehouse, Stafford, Erentz, Morgan B, Griffiths, Cartwright, Schofield, Lawson, Leigh, Jackson, Grundy

Match # 289   Saturday 22/09/00   Football League Division 2   at Bank Street   Attendance 6000
Result: **Newton Heath 4 Port Vale 0**
Teamsheet: Whitehouse, Stafford, Erentz, Morgan B, Griffiths, Cartwright, Schofield, Smith, Leigh, Jackson, Grundy
Scorer(s):   Grundy, Leigh, Schofield, Smith

Match # 290   Saturday 29/09/00   Football League Division 2   at Filbert Street   Attendance 6000
Result: **Leicester City 1 Newton Heath 0**
Teamsheet: Whitehouse, Stafford, Erentz, Morgan B, Griffiths, Cartwright, Schofield, Smith, Leigh, Jackson, Grundy

Match # 291   Saturday 06/10/00   Football League Division 2   at Bank Street   Attendance 5000
Result: **Newton Heath 1 New Brighton Tower 0**
Teamsheet: Whitehouse, Stafford, Erentz, Morgan B, Griffiths, Cartwright, Schofield, Smith, Leigh, Jackson, Grundy
Scorer(s):   Jackson

Match # 292   Saturday 13/10/00   Football League Division 2   at The Northolme   Attendance 2000
Result: **Gainsborough Trinity 0 Newton Heath 1**
Teamsheet: Whitehouse, Stafford, Erentz, Morgan B, Griffiths, Ambler, Schofield, Smith, Leigh, Jackson, Grundy
Scorer(s):   Leigh

Match # 293   Saturday 20/10/00   Football League Division 2   at Bank Street   Attendance 8000
Result: **Newton Heath 1 Walsall 1**
Teamsheet: Whitehouse, Stafford, Erentz, Morgan B, Griffiths, Cartwright, Schofield, Fisher, Leigh, Jackson, Greenwood
Scorer(s):   Schofield

Match # 294   Saturday 27/10/00   Football League Division 2   at Peel Croft   Attendance 2000
Result: **Burton Swifts 3 Newton Heath 1**
Teamsheet: Whitehouse, Stafford, Erentz, Smith, Griffiths, Jackson, Greenwood, Collinson, Leigh, Fisher, Grundy
Scorer(s):   Leigh

Match # 295   Saturday 10/11/00   Football League Division 2   at Manor Field   Attendance 8000
Result: **Arsenal 2 Newton Heath 1**
Teamsheet: Whitehouse, Stafford, Erentz, Morgan B, Griffiths, Cartwright, Fisher, Jackson, Leigh, Collinson, Schofield
Scorer(s):   Jackson

Match # 296   Saturday 24/11/00   Football League Division 2   at Green Lane   Attendance 5000
Result: **Stockport County 1 Newton Heath 0**
Teamsheet: Whitehouse, Stafford, Erentz, Morgan B, Griffiths, Cartwright, Schofield, Fisher, Leigh, Jackson, Grundy

Match # 297   Saturday 01/12/00   Football League Division 2   at Bank Street   Attendance 5000
Result: **Newton Heath 0 Birmingham City 1**
Teamsheet: Whitehouse, Stafford, Erentz, Morgan B, Griffiths, Cartwright, Schofield, Fisher, Leigh, Jackson, Greenwood

Match # 298   Saturday 08/12/00   Football League Division 2   at Blundell Park   Attendance 4000
Result: **Grimsby Town 2 Newton Heath 0**
Teamsheet: Whitehouse, Stafford, Erentz, Morgan B, Griffiths, Cartwright, Schofield, Fisher, Leigh, Jackson, Grundy

Match # 299   Saturday 15/12/00   Football League Division 2   at Bank Street   Attendance 4000
Result: **Newton Heath 4 Lincoln City 1**
Teamsheet: Garvey, Stafford, Erentz, Morgan B, Griffiths, Cartwright, Schofield, Morgan H, Leigh, Jackson, Fisher
Scorer(s):   Leigh 2, Morgan H, Schofield

Match # 300   Saturday 22/12/00   Football League Division 2   at Saltergate   Attendance 4000
Result: **Chesterfield 2 Newton Heath 1**
Teamsheet: Whitehouse, Stafford, Erentz, Morgan B, Griffiths, Cartwright, Schofield, Morgan H, Leigh, Jackson, Fisher
Scorer(s):   own goal

Match # 301   Wednesday 26/12/00   Football League Division 2   at Bank Street   Attendance 10000
Result: **Newton Heath 4 Blackpool 0**
Teamsheet: Whitehouse, Stafford, Erentz, Morgan B, Griffiths, Cartwright, Schofield, Morgan H, Leigh, Jackson, Booth
Scorer(s):   Griffiths, Leigh, Morgan B, Schofield

Match # 302   Saturday 29/12/00   Football League Division 2   at Bank Street   Attendance 8000
Result: **Newton Heath 3 Glossop 0**
Teamsheet: Whitehouse, Stafford, Erentz, Morgan B, Griffiths, Cartwright, Schofield, Morgan H, Leigh, Jackson, Booth
Scorer(s):   Leigh 2, Morgan H

Match # 303   Tuesday 01/01/01   Football League Division 2   at Linthorpe Road   Attendance 12000
Result: **Middlesbrough 1 Newton Heath 2**
Teamsheet: Whitehouse, Stafford, Erentz, Morgan B, Griffiths, Cartwright, Schofield, Morgan H, Leigh, Jackson, Fisher
Scorer(s):   Schofield 2

SEASON 1900/01 (continued)

Match # 304   Saturday 05/01/01   FA Cup Supplementary Round   at Bank Street   Attendance 5000
Result: **Newton Heath 3 Portsmouth 0**
Teamsheet: Whitehouse, Stafford, Erentz, Morgan B, Griffiths, Cartwright, Schofield, Morgan H, Leigh, Jackson, Fisher
Scorer(s):   Griffiths, Jackson, Stafford

Match # 305   Saturday 12/01/01   Football League Division 2   at Bank Street   Attendance 10000
Result: **Newton Heath 0 Burnley 1**
Teamsheet: Whitehouse, Stafford, Erentz, Morgan B, Griffiths, Cartwright, Schofield, Morgan H, Leigh, Jackson, Fisher

Match # 306   Saturday 19/01/01   Football League Division 2   at Cobridge Stadium   Attendance 1000
Result: **Port Vale 2 Newton Heath 0**
Teamsheet: Whitehouse, Stafford, Erentz, Morgan B, Griffiths, Collinson, Schofield, Morgan H, Leigh, Jackson, Fisher

Match # 307   Saturday 09/02/01   FA Cup 1st Round   at Bank Street   Attendance 8000
Result: **Newton Heath 0 Burnley 0**
Teamsheet: Whitehouse, Stafford, Erentz, Morgan B, Griffiths, Cartwright, Schofield, Morgan H, Leigh, Jackson, Fisher

Match # 308   Wednesday 13/02/01   FA Cup 1st Round Replay   at Turf Moor   Attendance 4000
Result: **Burnley 7 Newton Heath 1**
Teamsheet: Whitehouse, Stafford, Erentz, Morgan B, Collinson, Cartwright, Schofield, Morgan H, Leigh, Heathcote, Fisher
Scorer(s):   Schofield

Match # 309   Saturday 16/02/01   Football League Division 2   at Bank Street   Attendance 7000
Result: **Newton Heath 0 Gainsborough Trinity 0**
Teamsheet: Whitehouse, Stafford, Erentz, Morgan B, Collinson, Cartwright, Schofield, Morgan H, Leigh, Heathcote, Fisher

Match # 310   Tuesday 19/02/01   Football League Division 2   at Tower Athletic Ground   Attendance 2000
Result: **New Brighton Tower 2 Newton Heath 0**
Teamsheet: Whitehouse, Stafford, Erentz, Morgan B, Collinson, Cartwright, Schofield, Morgan H, Leigh, Heathcote, Fisher

Match # 311   Saturday 25/02/01   Football League Division 2   at West Bromwich Road   Attendance 2000
Result: **Walsall 1 Newton Heath 1**
Teamsheet: Garvey, Cartwright, Erentz, Morgan B, Hayes, Whitney, Schofield, Morgan H, Leigh, Whitehouse, Fisher
Scorer(s):   Morgan B

Match # 312   Saturday 02/03/01   Football League Division 2   at Bank Street   Attendance 5000
Result: **Newton Heath 1 Burton Swifts 1**
Teamsheet: Whitehouse, Stafford, Erentz, Morgan B, Griffiths, Cartwright, Schofield, Morgan H, Leigh, Heathcote, Fisher
Scorer(s):   Leigh

Match # 313   Wednesday 13/03/01   Football League Division 2   at Bank Street   Attendance 6000
Result: **Newton Heath 1 Barnsley 0**
Teamsheet: Garvey, Stafford, Erentz, Morgan B, Griffiths, Cartwright, Schofield, Morgan H, Leigh, Jackson, Fisher
Scorer(s):   Leigh

Match # 314   Saturday 16/03/01   Football League Division 2   at Bank Street   Attendance 5000
Result: **Newton Heath 1 Arsenal 0**
Teamsheet: Whitehouse, Stafford, Erentz, Morgan B, Griffiths, Cartwright, Schofield, Morgan H, Leigh, Jackson, Fisher
Scorer(s):   Leigh

Match # 315   Wednesday 20/03/01   Football League Division 2   at Bank Street   Attendance 2000
Result: **Newton Heath 2 Leicester City 3**
Teamsheet: Garvey, Stafford, Collinson, Morgan B, Griffiths, Cartwright, Morgan H, Johnson, Leigh, Jackson, Fisher
Scorer(s):   Fisher, Jackson

Match # 316   Saturday 23/03/01   Football League Division 2   at Bloomfield Road   Attendance 2000
Result: **Blackpool 1 Newton Heath 2**
Teamsheet: Whitehouse, Stafford, Collinson, Morgan B, Griffiths, Cartwright, Schofield, Morgan H, Leigh, Jackson, Fisher
Scorer(s):   Griffiths 2

Match # 317   Saturday 30/03/01   Football League Division 2   at Bank Street   Attendance 4000
Result: **Newton Heath 3 Stockport County 1**
Teamsheet: Whitehouse, Stafford, Collinson, Morgan B, Griffiths, Cartwright, Schofield, Morgan H, Leigh, Jackson, Fisher
Scorer(s):   Leigh, Morgan H, Schofield

Match # 318   Friday 05/04/01   Football League Division 2   at Sincil Bank   Attendance 5000
Result: **Lincoln City 2 Newton Heath 0**
Teamsheet: Whitehouse, Stafford, Erentz, Morgan B, Griffiths, Cartwright, Schofield, Morgan H, Leigh, Jackson, Fisher

Match # 319   Saturday 06/04/01   Football League Division 2   at Muntz Street   Attendance 6000
Result: **Birmingham City 1 Newton Heath 0**
Teamsheet: Whitehouse, Collinson, Erentz, Morgan B, Griffiths, Cartwright, Sawyer, Morgan H, Leigh, Jackson, Fisher

Match # 320   Tuesday 09/04/01   Football League Division 2   at Oakwell   Attendance 3000
Result: **Barnsley 6 Newton Heath 2**
Teamsheet: Whitehouse, Collinson, Erentz, Morgan B, Griffiths, Cartwright, Sawyer, Morgan H, Leigh, Jackson, Fisher
Scorer(s):   Jackson, Morgan B

Match # 321   Saturday 13/04/01   Football League Division 2   at Bank Street   Attendance 3000
Result: **Newton Heath 1 Grimsby Town 0**
Teamsheet: Whitehouse, Collinson, Erentz, Morgan B, Griffiths, Cartwright, Sawyer, Morgan H, Leigh, Jackson, Fisher
Scorer(s):   Morgan H

SEASON 1900/01 (continued)

Match # 322 Saturday 27/04/01   Football League Division 2   at Bank Street   Attendance 1000
Result: **Newton Heath 1 Chesterfield 0**
Teamsheet: Whitehouse, Stafford, Erentz, Morgan B, Griffiths, Cartwright, Schofield, Sawyer, Leigh, Lappin, Fisher
Scorer(s):   Leigh

SEASON 1900/01 SUMMARY

APPEARANCES

PLAYER	LGE	FAC	TOT
Leigh	34	3	37
Morgan B	33	3	36
Cartwright	31	3	34
Erentz	31	3	34
Griffiths	31	2	33
Stafford	30	3	33
Schofield	29	3	32
Whitehouse	29	3	32
Jackson	29	2	31
Fisher	25	3	28
Morgan H	20	3	23
Collinson	11	1	12
Grundy	10	–	10
Garvey	6	–	6
Smith	5	–	5
Heathcote	3	1	4
Sawyer	4	–	4
Greenwood	3	–	3
Lawson	3	–	3
Booth	2	–	2
Ambler	1	–	1
Hayes	1	–	1
Johnson	1	–	1
Lappin	1	–	1
Whitney	1	–	1

GOALSCORERS

PLAYER	LGE	FAC	TOT
Leigh	14	–	14
Schofield	7	1	8
Jackson	5	1	6
Griffiths	4	1	5
Morgan H	4	–	4
Morgan B	3	–	3
Grundy	2	–	2
Fisher	1	–	1
Smith	1	–	1
Stafford	–	1	1
own goal	1	–	1

RESULTS & ATTENDANCES SUMMARY

		P	W	D	L	F	A	TOTAL	AVGE
League	H	17	11	3	3	31	9	94500	5559
	A	17	3	1	13	11	29	76000	4471
	TOTAL	34	14	4	16	42	38	170500	5015
FA Cup	H	2	1	1	0	3	0	13000	6500
	A	1	0	0	1	1	7	4000	4000
	TOTAL	3	1	1	1	4	7	17000	5667
Overall	H	19	12	4	3	34	9	107500	5658
	A	18	3	1	14	12	36	80000	4444
	TOTAL	37	15	5	17	46	45	187500	5068

FINAL TABLE – LEAGUE DIVISION TWO

		P	W	D	L	F	A	W	D	L	F	A	PTS	GD
				HOME						AWAY				
1	Grimsby Town	34	14	3	0	46	11	6	6	5	14	22	49	27
2	Birmingham City	34	14	2	1	41	8	5	8	4	16	16	48	33
3	Burnley	34	15	2	0	39	6	5	2	10	14	23	44	24
4	New Brighton Tower	34	12	5	0	34	8	5	3	9	23	30	42	19
5	Glossop	34	11	2	4	34	9	4	6	7	17	24	38	18
6	Middlesbrough	34	11	4	2	38	13	4	3	10	12	27	37	10
7	Arsenal	34	13	3	1	30	11	2	3	12	9	24	36	4
8	Lincoln City	34	12	3	2	39	11	1	4	12	4	28	33	4
9	Port Vale	34	8	6	3	28	14	3	5	9	17	33	33	-2
10	NEWTON HEATH	34	11	3	3	31	9	3	1	13	11	29	32	4
11	Leicester City	34	9	5	3	30	15	2	5	10	9	22	32	2
12	Blackpool	34	7	6	4	20	11	5	1	11	13	47	31	-25
13	Gainsborough Trinity	34	8	4	5	26	18	2	6	9	19	42	30	-15
14	Chesterfield	34	6	5	6	25	22	3	5	9	21	36	28	-12
15	Barnsley	34	9	3	5	34	23	2	2	13	13	37	27	-13
16	Walsall	34	7	7	3	29	23	0	6	11	11	33	27	-16
17	Stockport County	34	9	2	6	25	21	2	1	14	13	47	25	-30
18	Burton Swifts	34	7	3	7	16	21	1	1	15	18	45	20	-32

SEASON 1901/02

Match # 323	Saturday 07/09/01	Football League Division 2	at Bank Street	Attendance 3000
Result:	**Newton Heath 3 Gainsborough Trinity 0**			
Teamsheet:	Whitehouse, Stafford, Erentz, Morgan, Banks, Cartwright, Schofield, Williams, Preston, Lappin, Fisher			
Scorer(s):	Preston 2, Lappin			

Match # 324	Saturday 14/09/01	Football League Division 2	at Linthorpe Road	Attendance 12000
Result:	**Middlesbrough 5 Newton Heath 0**			
Teamsheet:	Whitehouse, Stafford, Erentz, Morgan, Banks, Cartwright, Smith, Williams, Preston, Lappin, Fisher			

Match # 325	Saturday 21/09/01	Football League Division 2	at Bank Street	Attendance 5000
Result:	**Newton Heath 1 Bristol City 0**			
Teamsheet:	Whitehouse, Stafford, Erentz, Morgan, Griffiths, Banks, Schofield, Williams, Preston, Lappin, Fisher			
Scorer(s):	Griffiths			

Match # 326	Saturday 28/09/01	Football League Division 2	at Bloomfield Road	Attendance 3000
Result:	**Blackpool 2 Newton Heath 4**			
Teamsheet:	Whitehouse, Stafford, Erentz, Morgan, Griffiths, Banks, Schofield, Smith, Preston, Lappin, Fisher			
Scorer(s):	Preston 2, Schofield, own goal			

Match # 327	Saturday 05/10/01	Football League Division 2	at Bank Street	Attendance 5000
Result:	**Newton Heath 3 Stockport County 3**			
Teamsheet:	Whitehouse, Stafford, Cartwright, Morgan, Griffiths, Banks, Schofield, Smith, Preston, Lappin, Fisher			
Scorer(s):	Schofield 2, Preston			

Match # 328	Saturday 12/10/01	Football League Division 2	at Peel Croft	Attendance 3000
Result:	**Burton United 0 Newton Heath 0**			
Teamsheet:	Whitehouse, Stafford, Cartwright, Morgan, Griffiths, Banks, Schofield, Smith, Higgins, Preston, Fisher			

Match # 329	Saturday 19/10/01	Football League Division 2	at North Road	Attendance 7000
Result:	**Glossop 0 Newton Heath 0**			
Teamsheet:	Whitehouse, Morgan, Cartwright, Higgins, Griffiths, Banks, Williams, Smith, Preston, Coupar, Fisher			

Match # 330	Saturday 26/10/01	Football League Division 2	at Bank Street	Attendance 7000
Result:	**Newton Heath 6 Doncaster Rovers 0**			
Teamsheet:	Whitehouse, Morgan, Cartwright, Higgins, Griffiths, Banks, Schofield, Smith, Preston, Coupar, Fisher			
Scorer(s):	Coupar 3, Griffiths, Preston, own goal			

Match # 331	Saturday 09/11/01	Football League Division 2	at Bank Street	Attendance 13000
Result:	**Newton Heath 1 West Bromwich Albion 2**			
Teamsheet:	Whitehouse, Morgan, Cartwright, Higgins, Griffiths, Banks, Schofield, Smith, Preston, Coupar, Fisher			
Scorer(s):	Fisher			

Match # 332	Saturday 16/11/01	Football League Division 2	at Manor Field	Attendance 3000
Result:	**Arsenal 2 Newton Heath 0**			
Teamsheet:	Whitehouse, Morgan, Cartwright, Higgins, Griffiths, Banks, Schofield, Smith, Preston, Lappin, Fisher			

Match # 333	Saturday 23/11/01	Football League Division 2	at Bank Street	Attendance 4000
Result:	**Newton Heath 1 Barnsley 0**			
Teamsheet:	Whitehouse, Stafford, Cartwright, Higgins, Morgan, Banks, Schofield, Smith, Griffiths, Coupar, Fisher			
Scorer(s):	Griffiths			

Match # 334	Saturday 30/11/01	Football League Division 2	at Filbert Street	Attendance 4000
Result:	**Leicester City 3 Newton Heath 2**			
Teamsheet:	Whitehouse, Stafford, Erentz, Higgins, Griffiths, Banks, Schofield, Cartwright, Preston, Lappin, Fisher			
Scorer(s):	Cartwright, Preston			

Match # 335	Saturday 07/12/01	Football League Division 2	at Deepdale	Attendance 2000
Result:	**Preston North End 5 Newton Heath 1**			
Teamsheet:	Whitehouse, Stafford, Erentz, Morgan, Griffiths, Banks, Schofield, Coupar, Smith, Preston, Fisher			
Scorer(s):	Preston			

Match # 336	Saturday 14/12/01	FA Cup Intermediate Round	at Bank Street	Attendance 4000
Result:	**Newton Heath 1 Lincoln City 2**			
Teamsheet:	Whitehouse, Stafford, Erentz, Cartwright, Griffiths, Banks, Schofield, Morgan, Smith, Preston, Fisher			
Scorer(s):	Fisher			

Match # 337	Saturday 21/12/01	Football League Division 2	at Bank Street	Attendance 3000
Result:	**Newton Heath 1 Port Vale 0**			
Teamsheet:	Whitehouse, Cartwright, Erentz, Morgan, Higgins, Banks, Schofield, Heathcote, Richards, Preston, Fisher			
Scorer(s):	Richards			

Match # 338	Thursday 26/12/01	Football League Division 2	at Sincil Bank	Attendance 4000
Result:	**Lincoln City 2 Newton Heath 0**			
Teamsheet:	Saunders, Cartwright, Erentz, Morgan, Griffiths, Banks, Schofield, Heathcote, Richards, Lappin, Fisher			

Match # 339	Wednesday 01/01/02	Football League Division 2	at Bank Street	Attendance 10000
Result:	**Newton Heath 0 Preston North End 2**			
Teamsheet:	Saunders, Stafford, Cartwright, Morgan, Griffiths, Banks, Schofield, Heathcote, Richards, Lappin, Fisher			

Match # 340	Saturday 04/01/02	Football League Division 2	at The Northolme	Attendance 2000
Result:	**Gainsborough Trinity 1 Newton Heath 1**			
Teamsheet:	Saunders, Stafford, Cartwright, Morgan, Griffiths, Banks, Schofield, Preston, Richards, Lappin, Fisher			
Scorer(s):	Lappin			

SEASON 1901/02 (continued)

Match # 341 Saturday 18/01/02 Football League Division 2 at Ashton Gate Attendance 6000
Result: **Bristol City 4 Newton Heath 0**
Teamsheet: Whitehouse, Stafford, Erentz, Morgan, Higgins, Cartwright, Schofield, Smith, Richards, Preston, Lappin

Match # 342 Saturday 25/01/02 Football League Division 2 at Bank Street Attendance 2500
Result: **Newton Heath 0 Blackpool 1**
Teamsheet: Whitehouse, Stafford, Erentz, Morgan, Higgins, Cartwright, Schofield, Smith, Richards, Hayes, Lappin

Match # 343 Saturday 01/02/02 Football League Division 2 at Green Lane Attendance 2000
Result: **Stockport County 1 Newton Heath 0**
Teamsheet: Saunders, Cartwright, Erentz, Morgan, Griffiths, Banks, Schofield, Coupar, Preston, Hayes, Lappin

Match # 344 Tuesday 11/02/02 Football League Division 2 at Bank Street Attendance 1000
Result: **Newton Heath 2 Burnley 0**
Teamsheet: Saunders, Stafford, Erentz, Cartwright, Griffiths, Banks, Morgan, Coupar, Preston, Hayes, Lappin
Scorer(s): Lappin, Preston

Match # 345 Saturday 15/02/02 Football League Division 2 at Bank Street Attendance 5000
Result: **Newton Heath 1 Glossop 0**
Teamsheet: Saunders, Stafford, Erentz, Cartwright, Griffiths, Banks, Morgan, Preston, Richards, Hayes, Lappin
Scorer(s): Erentz

Match # 346 Saturday 22/02/02 Football League Division 2 at Town Moor Avenue Attendance 3000
Result: **Doncaster Rovers 4 Newton Heath 0**
Teamsheet: Saunders, Stafford, Erentz, Morgan, Griffiths, Banks, Smith, Preston, Cartwright, Hayes, Lappin

Match # 347 Saturday 01/03/02 Football League Division 2 at Bank Street Attendance 6000
Result: **Newton Heath 0 Lincoln City 0**
Teamsheet: Saunders, Stafford, Erentz, Morgan, Griffiths, Banks, Schofield, Higson, Preston, Hayes, Cartwright

Match # 348 Saturday 08/03/02 Football League Division 2 at The Hawthorns Attendance 10000
Result: **West Bromwich Albion 4 Newton Heath 0**
Teamsheet: Whitehouse, Stafford, Erentz, Morgan, Griffiths, Banks, Schofield, Higson, Richards, Hayes, Cartwright

Match # 349 Saturday 15/03/02 Football League Division 2 at Bank Street Attendance 4000
Result: **Newton Heath 0 Arsenal 1**
Teamsheet: Whitehouse, Stafford, Erentz, Morgan, Griffiths, Cartwright, Schofield, Higson, Preston, Hayes, Lappin

Match # 350 Monday 17/03/02 Football League Division 2 at Saltergate Attendance 2000
Result: **Chesterfield 3 Newton Heath 0**
Teamsheet: Whitehouse, Morgan, Erentz, Smith, Griffiths, Coupar, Schofield, Preston, Richards, Hayes, Lappin

Match # 351 Saturday 22/03/02 Football League Division 2 at Oakwell Attendance 2500
Result: **Barnsley 3 Newton Heath 2**
Teamsheet: Saunders, Stafford, Erentz, Morgan, Griffiths, Banks, Schofield, Higson, Preston, Hayes, Cartwright
Scorer(s): Cartwright, Higson

Match # 352 Friday 28/03/02 Football League Division 2 at Turf Moor Attendance 3000
Result: **Burnley 1 Newton Heath 0**
Teamsheet: Whitehouse, Stafford, Erentz, Morgan, Griffiths, Banks, Schofield, Smith, Preston, Hayes, Cartwright

Match # 353 Saturday 29/03/02 Football League Division 2 at Bank Street Attendance 2000
Result: **Newton Heath 2 Leicester City 0**
Teamsheet: Saunders, Stafford, Erentz, Morgan, Griffiths, Banks, Schofield, Smith, Preston, Hayes, Cartwright
Scorer(s): Griffiths, Hayes

Match # 354 Monday 07/04/02 Football League Division 2 at Bank Street Attendance 2000
Result: **Newton Heath 1 Middlesbrough 2**
Teamsheet: Whitehouse, Stafford, Erentz, Morgan, Griffiths, Cartwright, Schofield, Higson, Preston, Hayes, O'Brien
Scorer(s): Erentz

Match # 355 Saturday 19/04/02 Football League Division 2 at Cobridge Stadium Attendance 2000
Result: **Port Vale 1 Newton Heath 1**
Teamsheet: Whitehouse, Stafford, Erentz, Morgan, Griffiths, Cartwright, Schofield, Coupar, Preston, Hayes, Lappin
Scorer(s): Schofield

Match # 356 Monday 21/04/02 Football League Division 2 at Bank Street Attendance 500
Result: **Newton Heath 3 Burton United 1**
Teamsheet: Whitehouse, Stafford, Erentz, Morgan, Griffiths, Cartwright, Schofield, Coupar, Preston, Hayes, Lappin
Scorer(s): Cartwright, Griffiths, Preston

Match # 357 Wednesday 23/04/02 Football League Division 2 at Bank Street Attendance 2000
Result: **Newton Heath 2 Chesterfield 0**
Teamsheet: Saunders, Stafford, Erentz, Morgan, Griffiths, Banks, Schofield, Coupar, Preston, Hayes, Lappin
Scorer(s): Coupar, Preston

SEASON 1901/02 SUMMARY

APPEARANCES

PLAYER	LGE	FAC	TOT
Morgan	33	1	34
Cartwright	29	1	30
Griffiths	29	1	30
Preston	29	1	30
Schofield	29	1	30
Banks	27	1	28
Stafford	26	1	27
Erentz	25	1	26
Whitehouse	23	1	24
Lappin	21	–	21
Fisher	17	1	18
Smith	16	1	17
Hayes	16	–	16
Coupar	11	–	11
Saunders	11	–	11
Higgins	10	–	10
Richards	9	–	9
Higson	5	–	5
Williams	4	–	4
Heathcote	3	–	3
O'Brien	1	–	1

GOALSCORERS

PLAYER	LGE	FAC	TOT
Preston	11	–	11
Griffiths	5	–	5
Coupar	4	–	4
Schofield	4	–	4
Cartwright	3	–	3
Lappin	3	–	3
Erentz	2	–	2
Fisher	1	1	2
Hayes	1	–	1
Higson	1	–	1
Richards	1	–	1
own goals	2	–	2

RESULTS & ATTENDANCES SUMMARY

		P	W	D	L	F	A	TOTAL	AVGE
League	H	17	10	2	5	27	12	75000	4412
	A	17	1	4	12	11	41	70500	4147
TOTAL		34	11	6	17	38	53	145500	4279
FA Cup	H	1	0	0	1	1	2	4000	4000
	A	0	0	0	0	0	0	0	n/a
TOTAL		1	0	0	1	1	2	4000	4000
Overall	H	18	10	2	6	28	14	79000	4389
	A	17	1	4	12	11	41	70500	4147
TOTAL		35	11	6	18	39	55	149500	4271

FINAL TABLE - LEAGUE DIVISION TWO

		P	HOME					AWAY					PTS	GD
			W	D	L	F	A	W	D	L	F	A		
1	West Bromwich Albion	34	14	2	1	52	13	11	3	3	30	16	55	53
2	Middlesbrough	34	15	1	1	58	7	8	4	5	32	17	51	66
3	Preston North End	34	12	3	2	50	11	6	3	8	21	21	42	39
4	Arsenal	34	13	2	2	35	9	5	4	8	15	17	42	24
5	Lincoln City	34	11	6	0	26	4	3	7	7	19	31	41	10
6	Bristol City	34	13	1	3	39	12	4	5	8	13	23	40	17
7	Doncaster Rovers	34	12	3	2	39	12	1	5	11	10	46	34	-9
8	Glossop	34	7	6	4	22	15	3	6	8	14	25	32	-4
9	Burnley	34	9	6	2	30	8	1	4	12	11	37	30	-4
10	Burton United	34	8	6	3	32	23	3	2	12	14	31	30	-8
11	Barnsley	34	9	3	5	36	33	3	3	11	15	30	30	-12
12	Port Vale	34	7	7	3	26	17	3	2	12	17	42	29	-16
13	Blackpool	34	9	3	5	27	21	2	4	11	13	35	29	-16
14	Leicester City	34	11	2	4	26	14	1	3	13	12	42	29	-18
15	NEWTON HEATH	34	10	2	5	27	12	1	4	12	11	41	28	-15
16	Chesterfield	34	10	3	4	35	18	1	3	13	12	50	28	-21
17	Stockport County	34	8	3	6	25	20	0	4	13	11	52	23	-36
18	Gainsborough Trinity	34	4	9	4	26	25	0	2	15	4	55	19	-50

Newton Heath officially became Manchester United on 28th April 1902, less than a week after playing their last match of the 1901/02 season.

SEASON 1902/03

Match # 358 Saturday 06/09/02   Football League Division 2   at The Northolme   Attendance 4000
Result: **Gainsborough Trinity 0 Manchester United 1**
Teamsheet: Whitehouse, Stafford, Read, Morgan, Griffiths, Cartwright, Richards, Pegg, Peddie, Williams, Hurst
Scorer(s): Richards

Match # 359 Saturday 13/09/02   Football League Division 2   at Bank Street   Attendance 15000
Result: **Manchester United 1 Burton United 0**
Teamsheet: Whitehouse, Stafford, Read, Morgan, Griffiths, Cartwright, Schofield, Pegg, Peddie, Williams, Hurst
Scorer(s): Hurst

Match # 360 Saturday 20/09/02   Football League Division 2   at Ashton Gate   Attendance 6000
Result: **Bristol City 3 Manchester United 1**
Teamsheet: Whitehouse, Stafford, Read, Morgan, Griffiths, Cartwright, Schofield, Pegg, Peddie, Williams, Hurst
Scorer(s): Hurst

Match # 361 Saturday 27/09/02   Football League Division 2   at Bank Street   Attendance 12000
Result: **Manchester United 1 Glossop 1**
Teamsheet: Whitehouse, Stafford, Read, Morgan, Griffiths, Cartwright, Schofield, Pegg, Peddie, Williams, Hurst
Scorer(s): Hurst

Match # 362 Saturday 04/10/02   Football League Division 2   at Bank Street   Attendance 12000
Result: **Manchester United 2 Chesterfield 1**
Teamsheet: Whitehouse, Bunce, Read, Cartwright, Hayes, Banks, Pegg, Richards, Peddie, Preston, Hurst
Scorer(s): Preston 2

Match # 363 Saturday 11/10/02   Football League Division 2   at Edgeley Park   Attendance 6000
Result: **Stockport County 2 Manchester United 1**
Teamsheet: Whitehouse, Bunce, Read, Cartwright, Hayes, Banks, Pegg, Richards, Peddie, Preston, Hurst
Scorer(s): Pegg

Match # 364 Saturday 25/10/02   Football League Division 2   at Manor Field   Attendance 12000
Result: **Arsenal 0 Manchester United 1**
Teamsheet: Birchenough, Rothwell, Read, Morgan, Griffiths, Banks, Pegg, Richards, Beadsworth, Williams, Hurst
Scorer(s): Beadsworth

Match # 365 Saturday 01/11/02   FA Cup 3rd Qualifying Round   at Bank Street   Attendance 6000
Result: **Manchester United 7 Accrington Stanley 0**
Teamsheet: Whitehouse, Stafford, Read, Morgan, Griffiths, Banks, Pegg, Richards, Peddie, Williams, Hurst
Scorer(s): Williams 3, Morgan, Peddie, Pegg, Richards

Match # 366 Saturday 08/11/02   Football League Division 2   at Sincil Bank   Attendance 3000
Result: **Lincoln City 1 Manchester United 3**
Teamsheet: Birchenough, Rothwell, Read, Morgan, Ball, Banks, Pegg, Beadsworth, Peddie, Williams, Hurst
Scorer(s): Peddie 2, Hurst

Match # 367 Thursday 13/11/02   FA Cup 4th Qualifying Round   at Bank Street   Attendance 5000
Result: **Manchester United 3 Oswaldtwistle Rovers 2**
Teamsheet: Saunders, Rothwell, Read, Morgan, Griffiths, Banks, Schofield, Pegg, Turner, Beadsworth, Williams
Scorer(s): Beadsworth, Pegg, Williams

Match # 368 Saturday 15/11/02   Football League Division 2   at Bank Street   Attendance 25000
Result: **Manchester United 0 Birmingham City 1**
Teamsheet: Birchenough, Stafford, Rothwell, Morgan, Ball, Banks, Pegg, Beadsworth, Peddie, Williams, Hurst

Match # 369 Saturday 22/11/02   Football League Division 2   at Filbert Street   Attendance 5000
Result: **Leicester City 1 Manchester United 1**
Teamsheet: Birchenough, Stafford, Rothwell, Morgan, Downie, Banks, Pegg, Beadsworth, Peddie, Smith, Williams
Scorer(s): Downie

Match # 370 Saturday 29/11/02   FA Cup 5th Qualifying Round   at Bank Street   Attendance 6000
Result: **Manchester United 4 Southport Central 1**
Teamsheet: Birchenough, Rothwell, Read, Downie, Griffiths, Banks, Schofield, Richards, Pegg, Beadsworth, Peddie
Scorer(s): Pegg 3, Banks

Match # 371 Saturday 06/12/02   Football League Division 2   at Turf Moor   Attendance 4000
Result: **Burnley 0 Manchester United 2**
Teamsheet: Birchenough, Read, Rothwell, Downie, Griffiths, Banks, Schofield, Peddie, Pegg, Richards, Hurst
Scorer(s): Pegg, own goal

Match # 372 Saturday 13/12/02   FA Cup Intermediate Round   at Bank Street   Attendance 6000
Result: **Manchester United 1 Burton United 1**
Teamsheet: Birchenough, Rothwell, Read, Downie, Griffiths, Cartwright, Schofield, Richards, Pegg, Peddie, Hurst
Scorer(s): Griffiths

Match # 373 Wednesday 17/12/02   FA Cup Intermediate Round Replay   at Bank Street   Attendance 7000
Result: **Burton United 1 Manchester United 3   (replay venue switched to Bank Street)**
Teamsheet: Birchenough, Rothwell, Read, Downie, Griffiths, Cartwright, Schofield, Beadsworth, Pegg, Peddie, Hurst
Scorer(s): Peddie, Pegg, Schofield

Match # 374 Saturday 20/12/02   Football League Division 2   at Cobridge Stadium   Attendance 1000
Result: **Port Vale 1 Manchester United 1**
Teamsheet: Birchenough, Rothwell, Read, Downie, Griffiths, Cartwright, Schofield, Richards, Pegg, Peddie, Lappin
Scorer(s): Peddie

Match # 375 Thursday 25/12/02   Football League Division 2   at Bank Street   Attendance 40000
Result: **Manchester United 1 Manchester City 1**
Teamsheet: Birchenough, Rothwell, Read, Downie, Griffiths, Cartwright, Schofield, Morrison, Pegg, Peddie, Beadsworth
Scorer(s): Pegg

SEASON 1902/03 (continued)

Match # 376   Friday 26/12/02   Football League Division 2   at Bank Street   Attendance 10000
Result: **Manchester United 2 Blackpool 2**
Teamsheet: Whitehouse, Rothwell, Read, Downie, Griffiths, Cartwright, Morrison, Beadsworth, Pegg, Peddie, Lappin
Scorer(s):   Downie, Morrison

Match # 377   Saturday 27/12/02   Football League Division 2   at Bank Street   Attendance 9000
Result: **Manchester United 2 Barnsley 1**
Teamsheet: Saunders, Stafford, Read, Downie, Griffiths, Morgan, Morrison, Richards, Pegg, Peddie, Lappin
Scorer(s):   Lappin, Peddie

Match # 378   Saturday 03/01/03   Football League Division 2   at Bank Street   Attendance 8000
Result: **Manchester United 3 Gainsborough Trinity 1**
Teamsheet: Birchenough, Rothwell, Read, Morgan, Downie, Ball, Morrison, Preston, Pegg, Peddie, Lappin
Scorer(s):   Downie, Peddie, Pegg

Match # 379   Saturday 10/01/03   Football League Division 2   at Peel Croft   Attendance 3000
Result: **Burton United 3 Manchester United 1**
Teamsheet: Birchenough, Rothwell, Read, Morgan, Beadsworth, Cartwright, Schofield, Morrison, Downie, Peddie, Lappin
Scorer(s):   Peddie

Match # 380   Saturday 17/01/03   Football League Division 2   at Bank Street   Attendance 12000
Result: **Manchester United 1 Bristol City 2**
Teamsheet: Birchenough, Rothwell, Read, Morgan, Downie, Cartwright, Morrison, Richards, Preston, Peddie, Hurst
Scorer(s):   Preston

Match # 381   Saturday 24/01/03   Football League Division 2   at North Road   Attendance 5000
Result: **Glossop 1 Manchester United 3**
Teamsheet: Birchenough, Rothwell, Read, Downie, Griffiths, Banks, Morrison, Peddie, Pegg, Bell, Hurst
Scorer(s):   Downie, Griffiths, Morrison

Match # 382   Saturday 31/01/03   Football League Division 2   at Saltergate   Attendance 6000
Result: **Chesterfield 2 Manchester United 0**
Teamsheet: Birchenough, Stafford, Rothwell, Downie, Griffiths, Banks, Morrison, Pegg, Bell, Peddie, Hurst

Match # 383   Saturday 07/02/03   FA Cup 1st Round   at Bank Street   Attendance 15000
Result: **Manchester United 2 Liverpool 1**
Teamsheet: Birchenough, Stafford, Rothwell, Downie, Griffiths, Cartwright, Street, Pegg, Peddie, Smith, Hurst
Scorer(s):   Peddie 2

Match # 384   Saturday 14/02/03   Football League Division 2   at Bloomfield Road   Attendance 3000
Result: **Blackpool 2 Manchester United 0**
Teamsheet: Birchenough, Stafford, Rothwell, Griffiths, Downie, Banks, Bell, Morrison, Arkesden, Peddie, Hurst

Match # 385   Saturday 21/02/03   FA Cup 2nd Round   at Goodison Park   Attendance 15000
Result: **Everton 3 Manchester United 1**
Teamsheet: Birchenough, Rothwell, Read, Griffiths, Cartwright, Street, Pegg, Peddie, Smith, Hurst
Scorer(s):   Griffiths

Match # 386   Saturday 28/02/03   Football League Division 2   at Town Moor Avenue   Attendance 4000
Result: **Doncaster Rovers 2 Manchester United 2**
Teamsheet: Cartwright, Christie, Read, Downie, Griffiths, Banks, Morrison, Pegg, Peddie, Arkesden, Smith
Scorer(s):   Morrison 2

Match # 387   Saturday 07/03/03   Football League Division 2   at Bank Street   Attendance 4000
Result: **Manchester United 1 Lincoln City 2**
Teamsheet: Birchenough, Stafford, Rothwell, Downie, Griffiths, Cartwright, Morrison, Street, Peddie, Arkesden, Hurst
Scorer(s):   Downie

Match # 388   Monday 09/03/03   Football League Division 2   at Bank Street   Attendance 5000
Result: **Manchester United 3 Arsenal 0**
Teamsheet: Birchenough, Marshall, Read, Ball, Griffiths, Cartwright, Schofield, Morrison, Pegg, Peddie, Arkesden
Scorer(s):   Arkesden, Peddie, Pegg

Match # 389   Saturday 21/03/03   Football League Division 2   at Bank Street   Attendance 8000
Result: **Manchester United 5 Leicester City 1**
Teamsheet: Birchenough, Marshall, Rothwell, Fitchett, Griffiths, Cartwright, Schofield, Morrison, Pegg, Peddie, Smith
Scorer(s):   Fitchett, Griffiths, Morrison, Pegg, Smith

Match # 390   Monday 23/03/03   Football League Division 2   at Bank Street   Attendance 2000
Result: **Manchester United 0 Stockport County 0**
Teamsheet: Birchenough, Marshall, Rothwell, Fitchett, Griffiths, Cartwright, Schofield, Morrison, Pegg, Peddie, Smith

Match # 391   Monday 30/03/03   Football League Division 2   at Bank Street   Attendance 3000
Result: **Manchester United 0 Preston North End 1**
Teamsheet: Birchenough, Marshall, Read, Downie, Griffiths, Cartwright, Schofield, Morrison, Fitchett, Peddie, Hurst

Match # 392   Saturday 04/04/03   Football League Division 2   at Bank Street   Attendance 5000
Result: **Manchester United 4 Burnley 0**
Teamsheet: Birchenough, Rothwell, Read, Downie, Griffiths, Cartwright, Schofield, Morrison, Cleaver, Peddie, Smith
Scorer(s):   Peddie 2, Griffiths, Morrison

Match # 393   Friday 10/04/03   Football League Division 2   at Hyde Road   Attendance 30000
Result: **Manchester City 0 Manchester United 2**
Teamsheet: Birchenough, Rothwell, Read, Downie, Griffiths, Cartwright, Schofield, Morrison, Pegg, Peddie, Arkesden
Scorer(s):   Peddie, Schofield

SEASON 1902/03 (continued)

Match # 394	Saturday 11/04/03	Football League Division 2	at Deepdale	Attendance 7000

Result: **Preston North End 3   Manchester United 1**
Teamsheet: Birchenough, Marshall, Read, Downie, Griffiths, Fitchett, Morrison, Pegg, Arkesden, Peddie, Rothwell
Scorer(s): Pegg

Match # 395	Monday 13/04/03	Football League Division 2	at Bank Street	Attendance 6000

Result: **Manchester United 4   Doncaster Rovers 0**
Teamsheet: Birchenough, Marshall, Read, Downie, Griffiths, Cartwright, Pegg, Morrison, Bell, Arkesden, Smith
Scorer(s): Arkesden, Bell, Griffiths, Morrison

Match # 396	Saturday 18/04/03	Football League Division 2	at Bank Street	Attendance 8000

Result: **Manchester United 2   Port Vale 1**
Teamsheet: Birchenough, Rothwell, Read, Downie, Griffiths, Smith, Morrison, Pegg, Arkesden, Cartwright, Schofield
Scorer(s): Schofield 2

Match # 397	Monday 20/04/03	Football League Division 2	at St Andrews	Attendance 6000

Result: **Birmingham City 2   Manchester United 1**
Teamsheet: Birchenough, Rothwell, Read, Downie, Bell, Banks, Schofield, Peddie, Pegg, Beadsworth, Smith
Scorer(s): Peddie

Match # 398	Saturday 25/04/03	Football League Division 2	at Oakwell	Attendance 2000

Result: **Barnsley 0   Manchester United 0**
Teamsheet: Birchenough, Fitchett, Read, Downie, Griffiths, Banks, Schofield, Pegg, Arkesden, Cartwright, Beadsworth

SEASON 1902/03 SUMMARY

APPEARANCES

PLAYER	LGE	FAC	TOT
Peddie	30	6	36
Pegg	28	7	35
Read	27	6	33
Griffiths	25	7	32
Birchenough	25	5	30
Rothwell	22	6	28
Downie	22	5	27
Cartwright	22	4	26
Hurst	16	5	21
Morrison	20	–	20
Schofield	16	4	20
Banks	13	3	16
Morgan	12	2	14
Beadsworth	9	3	12
Stafford	10	2	12
Richards	8	3	11
Smith	8	2	10

APPEARANCES

PLAYER	LGE	FAC	TOT
Williams	8	2	10
Arkesden	9	–	9
Whitehouse	7	1	8
Marshall	6	–	6
Bell	5	–	5
Fitchett	5	–	5
Lappin	5	–	5
Ball	4	–	4
Preston	4	–	4
Street	1	2	3
Bunce	2	–	2
Hayes	2	–	2
Saunders	1	1	2
Christie	1	–	1
Cleaver	1	–	1
Turner	–	1	1

GOALSCORERS

PLAYER	LGE	FAC	TOT
Peddie	11	4	15
Pegg	7	6	13
Morrison	7	–	7
Griffiths	4	2	6
Downie	5	–	5
Hurst	4	–	4
Schofield	3	1	4
Williams	–	4	4
Preston	3	–	3
Arkesden	2	–	2
Beadsworth	1	1	2
Richards	1	1	2
Bell	1	–	1
Fitchett	1	–	1
Lappin	1	–	1
Smith	1	–	1
Banks	–	1	1
Morgan	–	1	1
own goal	1	–	1

RESULTS & ATTENDANCES SUMMARY

		P	W	D	L	F	A	TOTAL	AVGE
League	H	17	9	4	4	32	15	184000	10824
	A	17	6	4	7	21	23	107000	6294
	TOTAL	34	15	8	11	53	38	291000	8559
FA Cup	H	5	4	1	0	17	5	38000	7600
	A	2	1	0	1	4	4	22000	11000
	TOTAL	7	5	1	1	21	9	60000	8571
Overall	H	22	13	5	4	49	20	222000	10091
	A	19	7	4	8	25	27	129000	6789
	TOTAL	41	20	9	12	74	47	351000	8561

FINAL TABLE – LEAGUE DIVISION TWO

		P	W	D	L	F	A	W	D	L	F	A	PTS	GD
				HOME						AWAY				
1	Manchester City	34	15	1	1	64	15	10	3	4	31	14	54	66
2	Birmingham City	34	17	0	0	57	11	7	3	7	17	25	51	38
3	Arsenal	34	14	2	1	46	9	6	6	5	20	21	48	36
4	Bristol City	34	12	3	2	43	18	5	5	7	16	20	42	21
5	MANCHESTER UNITED	34	9	4	4	32	15	6	4	7	21	23	38	15
6	Chesterfield	34	11	4	2	43	10	3	5	9	24	30	37	27
7	Preston North End	34	10	5	2	39	12	3	5	9	17	28	36	16
8	Barnsley	34	9	4	4	32	13	4	4	9	23	38	34	4
9	Port Vale	34	11	5	1	36	16	2	3	12	21	46	34	-5
10	Lincoln City	34	8	3	6	30	22	4	3	10	16	31	30	-7
11	Glossop	34	9	1	7	26	20	2	6	9	17	38	29	-15
12	Gainsborough Trinity	34	9	4	4	28	14	2	3	12	13	45	29	-18
13	Burton United	34	9	4	4	26	20	2	3	12	13	39	29	-20
14	Blackpool	34	7	5	5	32	24	2	5	10	12	35	28	-15
15	Leicester City	34	5	5	7	20	23	5	3	9	21	42	28	-24
16	Doncaster Rovers	34	8	5	4	27	17	1	2	14	8	55	25	-37
17	Stockport County	34	6	4	7	26	24	1	2	14	13	50	20	-35
18	Burnley	34	6	7	4	25	25	0	1	16	5	52	20	-47

SEASON 1903/04

Match # 399 Saturday 05/09/03   Football League Division 2   at Bank Street   Attendance 40000
Result: **Manchester United 2 Bristol City 2**
Teamsheet: Sutcliffe, Bonthron, Read, Downie, Griffiths, Robertson S, Gaudie, Robertson T, Arkesden, Robertson A, McCartney
Scorer(s):   Griffiths 2

Match # 400 Monday 07/09/03   Football League Division 2   at Turf Moor   Attendance 5000
Result: **Burnley 2 Manchester United 0**
Teamsheet: Sutcliffe, Bonthron, Read, Downie, Griffiths, Cartwright, Gaudie, McCartney, Robertson A, Arkesden, Robertson T

Match # 401 Saturday 12/09/03   Football League Division 2   at Cobridge Stadium   Attendance 3000
Result: **Port Vale 1 Manchester United 0**
Teamsheet: Sutcliffe, Bonthron, Read, Downie, Griffiths, Cartwright, Gaudie, Schofield A, Robertson A, Arkesden, Robertson T

Match # 402 Saturday 19/09/03   Football League Division 2   at North Road   Attendance 3000
Result: **Glossop 0 Manchester United 5**
Teamsheet: Sutcliffe, Bonthron, Read, Downie, Griffiths, Hayes, Schofield A, Gaudie, Arkesden, Bell, Robertson A
Scorer(s):   Griffiths 2, Arkesden, Downie, Robertson A

Match # 403 Saturday 26/09/03   Football League Division 2   at Bank Street   Attendance 30000
Result: **Manchester United 3 Bradford City 1**
Teamsheet: Sutcliffe, Bonthron, Read, Downie, Griffiths, Cartwright, Gaudie, Schofield A, Pegg, Arkesden, Robertson A
Scorer(s):   Pegg 3

Match # 404 Saturday 03/10/03   Football League Division 2   at Manor Field   Attendance 20000
Result: **Arsenal 4 Manchester United 0**
Teamsheet: Sutcliffe, Bonthron, Blackstock, Downie, Griffiths, Cartwright, Hayes, Grassam, Pegg, Arkesden, Morrison

Match # 405 Saturday 10/10/03   Football League Division 2   at Bank Street   Attendance 20000
Result: **Manchester United 4 Barnsley 0**
Teamsheet: Moger, Bonthron, Blackstock, Downie, Griffiths, Cartwright, Schofield A, Grassam, Pegg, Arkesden, Robertson A
Scorer(s):   Pegg 2, Griffiths, Robertson A

Match # 406 Saturday 17/10/03   Football League Division 2   at Sincil Bank   Attendance 5000
Result: **Lincoln City 0 Manchester United 0**
Teamsheet: Sutcliffe, Bonthron, Blackstock, Downie, Griffiths, Cartwright, Schofield A, Grassam, Pegg, Arkesden, Robertson A

Match # 407 Saturday 24/10/03   Football League Division 2   at Bank Street   Attendance 15000
Result: **Manchester United 3 Stockport County 1**
Teamsheet: Sutcliffe, Bonthron, Blackstock, Downie, Griffiths, Robertson S, Schofield A, Grassam, Pegg, Arkesden, Robertson A
Scorer(s):   Arkesden, Grassam, Schofield A

Match # 408 Saturday 07/11/03   Football League Division 2   at Bank Street   Attendance 30000
Result: **Manchester United 0 Bolton Wanderers 0**
Teamsheet: Sutcliffe, Bonthron, Blackstock, Downie, Griffiths, Cartwright, Schofield A, Morrison, Pegg, Arkesden, Robertson A

Match # 409 Saturday 21/11/03   Football League Division 2   at Bank Street   Attendance 15000
Result: **Manchester United 0 Preston North End 2**
Teamsheet: Sutcliffe, Bonthron, Blackstock, Downie, Griffiths, Robertson S, Schofield A, Morrison, Pegg, Arkesden, Robertson A

Match # 410 Saturday 12/12/03   FA Cup Intermediate Round   at Bank Street   Attendance 10000
Result: **Manchester United 1 Birmingham City 1**
Teamsheet: Sutcliffe, Bonthron, Blackstock, Downie, Griffiths, Cartwright, Schofield A, Morrison, Grassam, Pegg, Robertson A
Scorer(s):   Schofield A

Match # 411 Wednesday 16/12/03   FA Cup Intermediate Round Replay   at Muntz Street   Attendance 5000
Result: **Birmingham City 1 Manchester United 1**
Teamsheet: Sutcliffe, Bonthron, Blackstock, Downie, Griffiths, Cartwright, Schofield A, Morrison, Grassam, Arkesden, Robertson A
Scorer(s):   Arkesden

Match # 412 Saturday 19/12/03   Football League Division 2   at Bank Street   Attendance 6000
Result: **Manchester United 4 Gainsborough Trinity 2**
Teamsheet: Sutcliffe, Blackstock, Robertson S, Duckworth, Griffiths, Cartwright, Schofield A, Pegg, Grassam, Arkesden, Robertson A
Scorer(s):   Arkesden, Duckworth, Grassam, Robertson A

Match # 413 Monday 21/12/03   FA Cup Intermediate Round 2nd Replay   at Bramall Lane   Attendance 3000
Result: **Manchester United 1 Birmingham City 1**
Teamsheet: Sutcliffe, Bonthron, Blackstock, Cartwright, Griffiths, Gaudie, Robertson S, Arkesden, Grassam, Morrison, Schofield A
Scorer(s):   Schofield A

Match # 414 Friday 25/12/03   Football League Division 2   at Bank Street   Attendance 15000
Result: **Manchester United 3 Chesterfield 1**
Teamsheet: Sutcliffe, Bonthron, Read, Gaudie, Griffiths, Robertson S, Pegg, McCartney, Grassam, Arkesden, Robertson A
Scorer(s):   Arkesden 2, Robertson A

Match # 415 Saturday 26/12/03   Football League Division 2   at Peel Croft   Attendance 4000
Result: **Burton United 2 Manchester United 2**
Teamsheet: Moger, Bonthron, Hayes, Gaudie, Griffiths, Robertson S, Pegg, McCartney, Grassam, Arkesden, Wilkinson
Scorer(s):   Arkesden 2

Match # 416 Saturday 02/01/04   Football League Division 2   at Ashton Gate   Attendance 8000
Result: **Bristol City 1 Manchester United 1**
Teamsheet: Sutcliffe, Bonthron, Hayes, Bell, McCartney, Griffiths, Arkesden, Robertson A, Grassam, Robertson S, Wilkinson
Scorer(s):   Griffiths

SEASON 1903/04 (continued)

Match # 417   Saturday 09/01/04   Football League Division 2   at Bank Street   Attendance 10000
Result: **Manchester United 2 Port Vale 0**
Teamsheet: Sutcliffe, Bonthron, Read, Bell, Griffiths, Robertson S, McCartney, Grassam, Robertson A, Arkesden, Wilkinson
Scorer(s): Arkesden, Grassam

Match # 418   Monday 11/01/04   FA Cup Intermediate Round 3rd Replay   at Hyde Road   Attendance 9372
Result: **Manchester United 3 Birmingham City 1**
Teamsheet: Sutcliffe, Bonthron, Read, Downie, Griffiths, Cartwright, Schofield A, Morrison, Grassam, Arkesden, Wilkinson
Scorer(s): Arkesden 2, Grassam

Match # 419   Saturday 16/01/04   Football League Division 2   at Bank Street   Attendance 10000
Result: **Manchester United 3 Glossop 1**
Teamsheet: Sutcliffe, Bonthron, Read, Robertson S, Griffiths, Downie, McCartney, Morrison, Grassam, Arkesden, Wilkinson
Scorer(s): Arkesden 2, Downie

Match # 420   Saturday 23/01/04   Football League Division 2   at Valley Parade   Attendance 12000
Result: **Bradford City 3 Manchester United 3**
Teamsheet: Moger, Bonthron, Hayes, Robertson S, Griffiths, Downie, Schofield A, Morrison, Grassam, Arkesden, Wilkinson
Scorer(s): Griffiths 2, Downie

Match # 421   Saturday 30/01/04   Football League Division 2   at Bank Street   Attendance 40000
Result: **Manchester United 1 Arsenal 0**
Teamsheet: Sutcliffe, Bonthron, Hayes, Downie, Griffiths, Robertson S, Schofield A, Morrison, Grassam, Arkesden, Robertson A
Scorer(s): Robertson A

Match # 422   Saturday 06/02/04   FA Cup 1st Round   at Trent Bridge   Attendance 12000
Result: **Notts County 3 Manchester United 3**
Teamsheet: Sutcliffe, Bonthron, Hayes, Downie, Griffiths, Robertson S, Schofield A, Morrison, Grassam, Arkesden, Robertson A
Scorer(s): Arkesden, Downie, Schofield A

Match # 423   Wednesday 10/02/04   FA Cup 1st Round Replay   at Bank Street   Attendance 18000
Result: **Manchester United 2 Notts County 1**
Teamsheet: Sutcliffe, Bonthron, Hayes, Downie, Griffiths, Cartwright, Schofield A, Morrison, Pegg, Arkesden, Robertson A
Scorer(s): Morrison, Pegg

Match # 424   Saturday 13/02/04   Football League Division 2   at Bank Street   Attendance 8000
Result: **Manchester United 2 Lincoln City 0**
Teamsheet: Sutcliffe, Bonthron, Hayes, Downie, Griffiths, Morrison, Schofield A, Pegg, Bell, Arkesden, Robertson A
Scorer(s): Downie, Griffiths

Match # 425   Saturday 20/02/04   FA Cup 2nd Round   at Hillsborough   Attendance 22051
Result: **Sheffield Wednesday 6 Manchester United 0**
Teamsheet: Sutcliffe, Bonthron, Hayes, Downie, Griffiths, Cartwright, Schofield A, Morrison, Pegg, Arkesden, Robertson A

Match # 426   Wednesday 09/03/04   Football League Division 2   at Bloomfield Road   Attendance 3000
Result: **Blackpool 2 Manchester United 1**
Teamsheet: Sutcliffe, Bonthron, Hayes, Downie, Griffiths, Robertson S, Schofield A, Grassam, Kerr, Arkesden, Wilkinson
Scorer(s): Grassam

Match # 427   Saturday 12/03/04   Football League Division 2   at Bank Street   Attendance 14000
Result: **Manchester United 3 Burnley 1**
Teamsheet: Sutcliffe, Bonthron, Hayes, Downie, Griffiths, Robertson S, Schofield A, Morrison, Grassam, Arkesden, Wilkinson
Scorer(s): Grassam 2, Griffiths

Match # 428   Saturday 19/03/04   Football League Division 2   at Deepdale   Attendance 7000
Result: **Preston North End 1 Manchester United 1**
Teamsheet: Sutcliffe, Bonthron, Hayes, Downie, Griffiths, Robertson S, Schofield A, Morrison, Grassam, Arkesden, Wilkinson
Scorer(s): Arkesden

Match # 429   Saturday 26/03/04   Football League Division 2   at Bank Street   Attendance 12000
Result: **Manchester United 2 Grimsby Town 0**
Teamsheet: Sutcliffe, Bonthron, Hayes, Downie, Griffiths, Robertson S, Schofield A, Hall, Kerr, Robertson A, Schofield J
Scorer(s): Robertson A 2

Match # 430   Saturday 28/03/04   Football League Division 2   at Edgeley Park   Attendance 2500
Result: **Stockport County 0 Manchester United 3**
Teamsheet: Moger, Bonthron, Hayes, Downie, Griffiths, Robertson S, Schofield A, Hall, Pegg, Schofield J, Robertson A
Scorer(s): Hall, Pegg, Schofield A

Match # 431   Friday 01/04/04   Football League Division 2   at Saltergate   Attendance 5000
Result: **Chesterfield 0 Manchester United 2**
Teamsheet: Moger, Bonthron, Hayes, Downie, Bell, Cartwright, Schofield A, Hall, Grassam, McCartney, Robertson A
Scorer(s): Bell, Hall

Match # 432   Saturday 02/04/04   Football League Division 2   at Filbert Street   Attendance 4000
Result: **Leicester City 0 Manchester United 1**
Teamsheet: Moger, Bonthron, Hayes, Downie, Bell, Robertson S, Schofield A, Hall, Grassam, McCartney, Robertson A
Scorer(s): McCartney

Match # 433   Tuesday 05/04/04   Football League Division 2   at Oakwell   Attendance 5000
Result: **Barnsley 0 Manchester United 2**
Teamsheet: Moger, Bonthron, Hayes, Downie, Griffiths, Robertson S, Schofield A, McCartney, Grassam, Hall, Robertson A
Scorer(s): Grassam, Schofield A

Match # 434   Saturday 09/04/04   Football League Division 2   at Bank Street   Attendance 10000
Result: **Manchester United 3 Blackpool 1**
Teamsheet: Moger, Bonthron, Hayes, Downie, Griffiths, Robertson S, Schofield A, Hall, Grassam, McCartney, Robertson A
Scorer(s): Grassam 2, Schofield A

SEASON 1903/04 (continued)

Match # 435	Tuesday 12/04/04	Football League Division 2	at Blundell Park	Attendance 8000
Result:	**Grimsby Town 3 Manchester United 1**			
Teamsheet:	Moger, Bonthron, Hayes, Downie, Griffiths, Robertson S, Schofield A, Hall, Grassam, McCartney, Robertson A			
Scorer(s):	Grassam			

Match # 436	Saturday 16/04/04	Football League Division 2	at The Northolme	Attendance 4000
Result:	**Gainsborough Trinity 0 Manchester United 1**			
Teamsheet:	Moger, Bonthron, Hayes, Downie, Griffiths, Robertson S, Schofield A, Hall, Grassam, McCartney, Robertson A			
Scorer(s):	Robertson A			

Match # 437	Saturday 23/04/04	Football League Division 2	at Bank Street	Attendance 8000
Result:	**Manchester United 2 Burton United 0**			
Teamsheet:	Moger, Bonthron, Hayes, Downie, Roberts, Robertson S, Schofield A, Lyons, Grassam, Arkesden, Robertson A			
Scorer(s):	Grassam, Robertson A			

Match # 438	Monday 25/04/04	Football League Division 2	at Burnden Park	Attendance 10000
Result:	**Bolton Wanderers 0 Manchester United 0**			
Teamsheet:	Moger, Bonthron, Hayes, Downie, Roberts, Robertson S, Schofield A, Lyons, Grassam, Robertson A, Arkesden			

Match # 439	Saturday 30/04/04	Football League Division 2	at Bank Street	Attendance 7000
Result:	**Manchester United 5 Leicester City 2**			
Teamsheet:	Moger, Bonthron, Hayes, Downie, Griffiths, Robertson S, Schofield, Pegg, Robertson A, Arkesden, Hartwell			
Scorer(s):	Schofield A 2, Bonthron, Griffiths, Robertson A			

SEASON 1903/04 SUMMARY

APPEARANCES

PLAYER	LGE	FAC	TOT
Bonthron	33	7	40
Griffiths	30	7	37
Downie	29	6	35
Schofield A	26	7	33
Arkesden	26	6	32
Robertson A	27	5	32
Grassam	23	5	28
Sutcliffe	21	7	28
Robertson S	24	2	26
Hayes	21	3	24
Morrison	9	7	16
Pegg	13	3	16
Cartwright	9	6	15
McCartney	13	–	13

APPEARANCES

PLAYER	LGE	FAC	TOT
Moger	13	–	13
Blackstock	7	3	10
Read	8	1	9
Wilkinson	8	1	9
Gaudie	7	1	8
Hall	8	–	8
Robertson T	3	–	3
Kerr	2	–	2
Lyons	2	–	2
Roberts	2	–	2
Schofield J	2	–	2
Duckworth	1	–	1
Hartwell	1	–	1

GOALSCORERS

PLAYER	LGE	FAC	TOT
Arkesden	11	4	15
Grassam	11	1	12
Griffiths	11	–	11
Robertson A	10	–	10
Schofield A	6	3	9
Pegg	6	1	7
Downie	4	1	5
Hall	2	–	2
Bell	1	–	1
Bonthron	1	–	1
Duckworth	1	–	1
McCartney	1	–	1
Morrison	–	1	1

RESULTS & ATTENDANCES SUMMARY

		P	W	D	L	F	A	TOTAL	AVGE
League	H	17	14	2	1	42	14	290000	17059
	A	17	6	6	5	23	19	108500	6382
	TOTAL	34	20	8	6	65	33	398500	11721
FA Cup	H	2	1	1	0	3	2	28000	14000
	A	3	0	2	1	4	10	39051	13017
	N	2	1	1	0	4	2	12372	6186
	TOTAL	7	2	4	1	11	14	79423	11346
Overall	H	19	15	3	1	45	16	318000	16737
	A	20	6	8	6	27	29	147551	7378
	N	2	1	1	0	4	2	12372	6186
	TOTAL	41	22	12	7	76	47	477923	11657

FINAL TABLE – LEAGUE DIVISION TWO

		P	W	D	L	F	A	W	D	L	F	A	PTS	GD
			HOME					AWAY						
1	Preston North End	34	13	4	0	38	10	7	6	4	24	14	50	38
2	Arsenal	34	15	2	0	67	5	6	5	6	24	17	49	69
3	MANCHESTER UNITED	34	14	2	1	42	14	6	6	5	23	19	48	32
4	Bristol City	34	14	2	1	53	12	4	4	9	20	29	42	32
5	Burnley	34	12	2	3	31	20	3	7	7	19	35	39	-5
6	Grimsby Town	34	12	5	0	39	12	2	3	12	11	37	36	1
7	Bolton Wanderers	34	10	3	4	38	11	2	7	8	21	30	34	18
8	Barnsley	34	10	5	2	25	12	1	5	11	13	45	32	-19
9	Gainsborough Trinity	34	10	2	5	34	17	4	1	12	19	43	31	-7
10	Bradford City	34	8	5	4	30	25	4	2	11	15	34	31	-14
11	Chesterfield	34	8	5	4	22	12	3	3	11	15	33	30	-8
12	Lincoln City	34	9	4	4	25	18	2	4	11	16	40	30	-17
13	Port Vale	34	10	3	4	44	20	0	6	11	10	32	29	2
14	Burton United	34	8	6	3	33	16	3	1	13	12	45	29	-16
15	Blackpool	34	8	2	7	25	27	3	3	11	15	40	27	-27
16	Stockport County	34	7	7	3	28	23	1	4	12	12	49	27	-32
17	Glossop	34	7	4	6	42	25	3	2	12	15	39	26	-7
18	Leicester City	34	5	8	4	26	21	1	2	14	16	61	22	-40

SEASON 1904/05

Match # 440	Saturday 03/09/04	Football League Division 2	at Cobridge Stadium	Attendance 4000
Result:	**Port Vale 2 Manchester United 2**		
Teamsheet:	Moger, Bonthron, Hayes, Downie, Roberts, Robertson S, Schofield, Allan, Mackie, Peddie, Arkesden		
Scorer(s):	Allan 2		

Match # 441	Saturday 10/09/04	Football League Division 2	at Bank Street	Attendance 20000
Result:	**Manchester United 4 Bristol City 1**		
Teamsheet:	Moger, Bonthron, Hayes, Downie, Roberts, Robertson S, Schofield, Allan, Mackie, Peddie, Williams		
Scorer(s):	Peddie, Robertson S, Schofield, Williams		

Match # 442	Saturday 17/09/04	Football League Division 2	at Bank Street	Attendance 25000
Result:	**Manchester United 1 Bolton Wanderers 2**		
Teamsheet:	Moger, Bonthron, Hayes, Downie, Roberts, Robertson S, Schofield, Allan, Mackie, Peddie, Williams		
Scorer(s):	Mackie		

Match # 443	Saturday 24/09/04	Football League Division 2	at North Road	Attendance 6000
Result:	**Glossop 1 Manchester United 2**		
Teamsheet:	Moger, Bonthron, Hayes, Downie, Roberts, Bell, Schofield, Allan, Mackie, Peddie, Williams		
Scorer(s):	Allan, Roberts		

Match # 444	Saturday 08/10/04	Football League Division 2	at Valley Parade	Attendance 12000
Result:	**Bradford City 1 Manchester United 1**		
Teamsheet:	Moger, Bonthron, Hayes, Downie, Bell, Robertson S, Schofield, Allan, Peddie, Arkesden, Robertson A		
Scorer(s):	Arkesden		

Match # 445	Saturday 15/10/04	Football League Division 2	at Bank Street	Attendance 15000
Result:	**Manchester United 2 Lincoln City 0**		
Teamsheet:	Moger, Bonthron, Hayes, Downie, Roberts, Bell, Schofield, Allan, Peddie, Arkesden, Williams		
Scorer(s):	Arkesden, Schofield		

Match # 446	Saturday 22/10/04	Football League Division 2	at Filbert Street	Attendance 7000
Result:	**Leicester City 0 Manchester United 3**		
Teamsheet:	Moger, Bonthron, Hayes, Duckworth, Roberts, Bell, Schofield, Allan, Peddie, Arkesden, Williams		
Scorer(s):	Arkesden, Peddie, Schofield		

Match # 447	Saturday 29/10/04	Football League Division 2	at Bank Street	Attendance 15000
Result:	**Manchester United 4 Barnsley 0**		
Teamsheet:	Moger, Bonthron, Hayes, Downie, Bell, Robertson S, Schofield, Allan, Peddie, Arkesden, Williams		
Scorer(s):	Allan, Downie, Peddie, Schofield		

Match # 448	Saturday 05/11/04	Football League Division 2	at The Hawthorns	Attendance 5000
Result:	**West Bromwich Albion 0 Manchester United 2**		
Teamsheet:	Moger, Bonthron, Hayes, Downie, Roberts, Robertson S, Schofield, Allan, Peddie, Arkesden, Williams		
Scorer(s):	Arkesden, Williams		

Match # 449	Saturday 12/11/04	Football League Division 2	at Bank Street	Attendance 15000
Result:	**Manchester United 1 Burnley 0**		
Teamsheet:	Moger, Bonthron, Hayes, Downie, Roberts, Robertson S, Schofield, Allan, Peddie, Arkesden, Williams		
Scorer(s):	Arkesden		

Match # 450	Saturday 19/11/04	Football League Division 2	at Blundell Park	Attendance 4000
Result:	**Grimsby Town 0 Manchester United 1**		
Teamsheet:	Moger, Bonthron, Hayes, Downie, Roberts, Bell, Schofield, Allan, Peddie, Arkesden, Williams		
Scorer(s):	Bell		

Match # 451	Saturday 03/12/04	Football League Division 2	at Town Moor Avenue	Attendance 10000
Result:	**Doncaster Rovers 0 Manchester United 1**		
Teamsheet:	Moger, Bonthron, Hayes, Downie, Roberts, Bell, Schofield, Allan, Peddie, Arkesden, Williams		
Scorer(s):	Peddie		

Match # 452	Saturday 10/12/04	Football League Division 2	at Bank Street	Attendance 12000
Result:	**Manchester United 3 Gainsborough Trinity 1**		
Teamsheet:	Moger, Bonthron, Hayes, Downie, Roberts, Bell, Schofield, Allan, Peddie, Arkesden, Williams		
Scorer(s):	Arkesden 2, Allan		

Match # 453	Saturday 17/12/04	Football League Division 2	at Peel Croft	Attendance 3000
Result:	**Burton United 2 Manchester United 3**		
Teamsheet:	Moger, Bonthron, Hayes, Downie, Roberts, Bell, Schofield, Allan, Peddie, Arkesden, Hartwell		
Scorer(s):	Peddie 3		

Match # 454	Saturday 24/12/04	Football League Division 2	at Bank Street	Attendance 40000
Result:	**Manchester United 3 Liverpool 1**		
Teamsheet:	Moger, Bonthron, Hayes, Downie, Roberts, Bell, Schofield, Allan, Peddie, Arkesden, Williams		
Scorer(s):	Roberts, Arkesden, Williams		

Match # 455	Monday 26/12/04	Football League Division 2	at Bank Street	Attendance 20000
Result:	**Manchester United 3 Chesterfield 0**		
Teamsheet:	Moger, Bonthron, Hayes, Downie, Roberts, Bell, Grassam, Allan, Peddie, Arkesden, Williams		
Scorer(s):	Allan 2, Williams		

Match # 456	Saturday 31/12/04	Football League Division 2	at Bank Street	Attendance 8000
Result:	**Manchester United 6 Port Vale 1**		
Teamsheet:	Moger, Bonthron, Hayes, Downie, Roberts, Bell, Schofield, Allan, Peddie, Arkesden, Williams		
Scorer(s):	Allan 3, Arkesden, Hayes, Roberts		

Match # 457	Monday 02/01/05	Football League Division 2	at Bank Street	Attendance 10000
Result:	**Manchester United 7 Bradford City 0**		
Teamsheet:	Moger, Bonthron, Hayes, Downie, Roberts, Bell, Schofield, Allan, Peddie, Arkesden, Hartwell		
Scorer(s):	Arkesden 2, Roberts 2, Allan, Peddie, own goal		

SEASON 1904/05 (continued)

Match # 458	Tuesday 03/01/05	Football League Division 2	at Burnden Park	Attendance 35000
Result:	**Bolton Wanderers 2 Manchester United 4**		
Teamsheet:	Moger, Bonthron, Hayes, Downie, Roberts, Bell, Schofield, Allan, Peddie, Arkesden, Williams		
Scorer(s):	Allan 2, Peddie, Williams		

Match # 459	Saturday 07/01/05	Football League Division 2	at Ashton Gate	Attendance 12000
Result:	**Bristol City 1 Manchester United 1**		
Teamsheet:	Moger, Bonthron, Blackstock, Downie, Roberts, Bell, Schofield, Grassam, Peddie, Arkesden, Williams		
Scorer(s):	Arkesden		

Match # 460	Saturday 14/01/05	FA Cup Intermediate Round	at Bank Street	Attendance 17000
Result:	**Manchester United 2 Fulham 2**		
Teamsheet:	Moger, Bonthron, Hayes, Downie, Bell, Robertson A, Schofield, Grassam, Mackie, Arkesden, Williams		
Scorer(s):	Arkesden, Mackie		

Match # 461	Wednesday 18/01/05	FA Cup Intermediate Round Replay	at Craven Cottage	Attendance 15000
Result:	**Fulham 0 Manchester United 0**		
Teamsheet:	Moger, Bonthron, Hayes, Downie, Fitchett, Bell, Schofield, Lyons, Grassam, Arkesden, Williams		

Match # 462	Saturday 21/01/05	Football League Division 2	at Bank Street	Attendance 20000
Result:	**Manchester United 4 Glossop 1**		
Teamsheet:	Moger, Bonthron, Hayes, Downie, Fitchett, Bell, Schofield, Grassam, Mackie, Arkesden, Williams		
Scorer(s):	Mackie 2, Arkesden, Grassam		

Match # 463	Monday 23/01/05	FA Cup Intermediate Round 2nd Replay	at Villa Park	Attendance 6000
Result:	**Manchester United 0 Fulham 1**		
Teamsheet:	Moger, Bonthron, Hayes, Downie, Fitchett, Bell, Schofield, Grassam, Mackie, Arkesden, Hartwell		

Match # 464	Saturday 11/02/05	Football League Division 2	at Sincil Bank	Attendance 2000
Result:	**Lincoln City 3 Manchester United 0**		
Teamsheet:	Moger, Bonthron, Hayes, Downie, Roberts, Bell, Schofield, Allan, Peddie, Arkesden, Williams		

Match # 465	Saturday 18/02/05	Football League Division 2	at Bank Street	Attendance 7000
Result:	**Manchester United 4 Leicester City 1**		
Teamsheet:	Moger, Bonthron, Hayes, Downie, Roberts, Bell, Schofield, Allan, Peddie, Arkesden, Williams		
Scorer(s):	Peddie 3, Allan		

Match # 466	Saturday 25/02/05	Football League Division 2	at Oakwell	Attendance 5000
Result:	**Barnsley 0 Manchester United 0**		
Teamsheet:	Moger, Fitchett, Blackstock, Downie, Griffiths, Bell, Beddow, Allan, Peddie, Arkesden, Williams		

Match # 467	Saturday 04/03/05	Football League Division 2	at Bank Street	Attendance 8000
Result:	**Manchester United 2 West Bromwich Albion 0**		
Teamsheet:	Moger, Bonthron, Fitchett, Downie, Roberts, Bell, Beddow, Allan, Peddie, Arkesden, Williams		
Scorer(s):	Peddie, Williams		

Match # 468	Saturday 11/03/05	Football League Division 2	at Turf Moor	Attendance 7000
Result:	**Burnley 2 Manchester United 0**		
Teamsheet:	Moger, Bonthron, Fitchett, Downie, Griffiths, Bell, Beddow, Allan, Peddie, Arkesden, Williams		

Match # 469	Saturday 18/03/05	Football League Division 2	at Bank Street	Attendance 12000
Result:	**Manchester United 2 Grimsby Town 1**		
Teamsheet:	Moger, Bonthron, Fitchett, Downie, Roberts, Bell, Beddow, Allan, Duckworth, Arkesden, Wombwell		
Scorer(s):	Allan, Duckworth		

Match # 470	Saturday 25/03/05	Football League Division 2	at Bloomfield Road	Attendance 6000
Result:	**Blackpool 0 Manchester United 1**		
Teamsheet:	Valentine, Bonthron, Fitchett, Downie, Roberts, Bell, Beddow, Grassam, Duckworth, Peddie, Wombwell		
Scorer(s):	Grassam		

Match # 471	Saturday 01/04/05	Football League Division 2	at Bank Street	Attendance 6000
Result:	**Manchester United 6 Doncaster Rovers 0**		
Teamsheet:	Moger, Bonthron, Fitchett, Downie, Bell, Robertson S, Beddow, Grassam, Duckworth, Peddie, Wombwell		
Scorer(s):	Duckworth 3, Beddow, Peddie, Wombwell		

Match # 472	Saturday 08/04/05	Football League Division 2	at The Northolme	Attendance 6000
Result:	**Gainsborough Trinity 0 Manchester United 0**		
Teamsheet:	Moger, Bonthron, Fitchett, Downie, Roberts, Bell, Beddow, Grassam, Duckworth, Peddie, Wombwell		

Match # 473	Saturday 15/04/05	Football League Division 2	at Bank Street	Attendance 16000
Result:	**Manchester United 5 Burton United 0**		
Teamsheet:	Moger, Bonthron, Fitchett, Downie, Roberts, Bell, Beddow, Duckworth, Peddie, Arkesden, Wombwell		
Scorer(s):	Duckworth 2, Peddie 2, Arkesden		

Match # 474	Friday 21/04/05	Football League Division 2	at Saltergate	Attendance 10000
Result:	**Chesterfield 2 Manchester United 0**		
Teamsheet:	Moger, Bonthron, Fitchett, Downie, Roberts, Bell, Beddow, Allan, Peddie, Arkesden, Wombwell		

Match # 475	Saturday 22/04/05	Football League Division 2	at Anfield	Attendance 28000
Result:	**Liverpool 4 Manchester United 0**		
Teamsheet:	Moger, Bonthron, Fitchett, Downie, Roberts, Bell, Schofield, Duckworth, Peddie, Arkesden, Wombwell		

SEASON 1904/05 (continued)

Match # 476	Monday 24/04/05	Football League Division 2	at Bank Street	Attendance 4000

Result: **Manchester United 3 Blackpool 1**
Teamsheet: Valentine, Holden, Blackstock, Duckworth, Roberts, Bell, Schofield, Allan, Peddie, Arkesden, Wombwell
Scorer(s): Allan, Arkesden, Peddie

SEASON 1904/05 SUMMARY

APPEARANCES

PLAYER	LGE	FAC	TOT
Bonthron	32	3	35
Downie	32	3	35
Moger	32	3	35
Bell	29	3	32
Peddie	32	–	32
Arkesden	28	3	31
Roberts	28	–	28
Allan	27	–	27
Schofield	24	3	27
Hayes	22	3	25
Williams	22	2	24
Fitchett	11	2	13
Beddow	9	–	9
Grassam	6	3	9
Duckworth	8	–	8
Robertson S	8	–	8
Wombwell	8	–	8
Mackie	5	2	7
Blackstock	3	–	3
Hartwell	2	1	3
Griffiths	2	–	2
Robertson A	1	1	2
Valentine	2	–	2
Holden	1	–	1
Lyons	–	1	1

GOALSCORERS

PLAYER	LGE	FAC	TOT
Peddie	17	–	17
Allan	16	–	16
Arkesden	15	1	16
Duckworth	6	–	6
Williams	6	–	6
Roberts	5	–	5
Schofield	4	–	4
Mackie	3	1	4
Grassam	2	–	2
Beddow	1	–	1
Bell	1	–	1
Downie	1	–	1
Hayes	1	–	1
Robertson S	1	–	1
Wombwell	1	–	1
own goal	1	–	1

RESULTS & ATTENDANCES SUMMARY

		P	W	D	L	F	A	TOTAL	AVGE
League	H	17	16	0	1	60	10	253000	14882
	A	17	8	5	4	21	20	162000	9529
TOTAL		34	24	5	5	81	30	415000	12206
FA Cup	H	1	0	1	0	2	2	17000	17000
	A	1	0	1	0	0	0	15000	15000
	N	1	0	0	1	0	1	6000	6000
TOTAL		3	0	2	1	2	3	38000	12667
Overall	H	18	16	1	1	62	12	270000	15000
	A	18	8	6	4	21	20	177000	9833
	N	1	0	0	1	0	1	6000	6000
TOTAL		37	24	7	6	83	33	453000	12243

FINAL TABLE – LEAGUE DIVISION TWO

		P	W	D	L	F	A	W	D	L	F	A	PTS	GD
				HOME						AWAY				
1	Liverpool	34	14	3	0	60	12	13	1	3	33	13	58	68
2	Bolton Wanderers	34	15	0	2	53	16	12	2	3	34	16	56	55
3	MANCHESTER UNITED	34	16	0	1	60	10	8	5	4	21	20	53	51
4	Bristol City	34	12	3	2	40	12	7	1	9	26	33	42	21
5	Chesterfield	34	9	6	2	26	11	5	5	7	18	24	39	9
6	Gainsborough Trinity	34	11	4	2	32	15	3	4	10	29	43	36	3
7	Barnsley	34	11	4	2	29	13	3	1	13	9	43	33	–18
8	Bradford City	34	8	5	4	31	20	4	3	10	14	29	32	–4
9	Lincoln City	34	9	4	4	31	16	3	3	11	11	24	31	2
10	West Bromwich Albion	34	8	2	7	28	20	5	2	10	28	28	30	8
11	Burnley	34	10	1	6	31	21	2	5	10	12	31	30	–9
12	Glossop	34	7	5	5	23	14	3	5	9	14	32	30	–9
13	Grimsby Town	34	9	3	5	22	14	2	5	10	11	32	30	–13
14	Leicester City	34	8	3	6	30	25	3	4	10	10	30	29	–15
15	Blackpool	34	8	5	4	26	15	1	5	11	10	33	28	–12
16	Port Vale	34	7	4	6	28	25	3	3	11	19	47	27	–25
17	Burton United	34	7	2	8	20	29	1	2	14	10	55	20	–54
18	Doncaster Rovers	34	3	2	12	12	32	0	0	17	11	49	8	–58

SEASON 1905/06

Match # 477   Saturday 02/09/05   Football League Division 2   at Bank Street   Attendance 25000
Result: **Manchester United 5 Bristol City 1**
Teamsheet: Moger, Bonthron, Blackstock, Downie, Roberts, Bell, Beddow, Picken, Sagar, Peddie, Arkesden
Scorer(s):   Sagar 3, Beddow, Picken

Match # 478   Monday 04/09/05   Football League Division 2   at Bank Street   Attendance 7000
Result: **Manchester United 2 Blackpool 1**
Teamsheet: Moger, Bonthron, Blackstock, Downie, Roberts, Bell, Beddow, Picken, Sagar, Peddie, Arkesden
Scorer(s):   Peddie 2

Match # 479   Saturday 09/09/05   Football League Division 2   at Blundell Park   Attendance 6000
Result: **Grimsby Town 0 Manchester United 1**
Teamsheet: Moger, Bonthron, Blackstock, Downie, Roberts, Bell, Beddow, Picken, Sagar, Peddie, Wombwell
Scorer(s):   Sagar

Match # 480   Saturday 16/09/05   Football League Division 2   at North Road   Attendance 7000
Result: **Glossop 1 Manchester United 2**
Teamsheet: Montgomery, Bonthron, Blackstock, Downie, Roberts, Bell, Beddow, Picken, Peddie, Arkesden, Wombwell
Scorer(s):   Beddow, Bell

Match # 481   Saturday 23/09/05   Football League Division 2   at Bank Street   Attendance 15000
Result: **Manchester United 3 Stockport County 1**
Teamsheet: Montgomery, Bonthron, Blackstock, Downie, Roberts, Bell, Beddow, Picken, Sagar, Peddie, Wombwell
Scorer(s):   Peddie 2, Sagar

Match # 482   Saturday 30/09/05   Football League Division 2   at Bloomfield Road   Attendance 7000
Result: **Blackpool 0 Manchester United 1**
Teamsheet: Montgomery, Bonthron, Blackstock, Downie, Roberts, Bell, Beddow, Picken, Peddie, Arkesden, Wombwell
Scorer(s):   Roberts

Match # 483   Saturday 07/10/05   Football League Division 2   at Bank Street   Attendance 17000
Result: **Manchester United 0 Bradford City 0**
Teamsheet: Valentine, Bonthron, Blackstock, Downie, Roberts, Bell, Beddow, Picken, Sagar, Peddie, Arkesden

Match # 484   Saturday 14/10/05   Football League Division 2   at The Hawthorns   Attendance 15000
Result: **West Bromwich Albion 1 Manchester United 0**
Teamsheet: Valentine, Bonthron, Blackstock, Downie, Roberts, Bell, Beddow, Lyons, Dyer, Peddie, Wombwell

Match # 485   Saturday 21/10/05   Football League Division 2   at Bank Street   Attendance 12000
Result: **Manchester United 3 Leicester City 2**
Teamsheet: Valentine, Bonthron, Blackstock, Downie, Roberts, Bell, Schofield, Picken, Sagar, Peddie, Wombwell
Scorer(s):   Peddie 2, Sagar

Match # 486   Wednesday 25/10/05   Football League Division 2   at The Northolme   Attendance 4000
Result: **Gainsborough Trinity 2 Manchester United 2**
Teamsheet: Valentine, Bonthron, Blackstock, Downie, Roberts, Bell, Schofield, Picken, Sagar, Peddie, Wombwell
Scorer(s):   Bonthron 2

Match # 487   Saturday 28/10/05   Football League Division 2   at Anlaby Road   Attendance 14000
Result: **Hull City 0 Manchester United 1**
Teamsheet: Valentine, Holden, Blackstock, Downie, Roberts, Bell, Schofield, Picken, Peddie, Arkesden, Wombwell
Scorer(s):   Picken

Match # 488   Saturday 04/11/05   Football League Division 2   at Bank Street   Attendance 15000
Result: **Manchester United 2 Lincoln City 1**
Teamsheet: Valentine, Holden, Blackstock, Downie, Roberts, Bell, Schofield, Donaghy, Sagar, Picken, Wombwell
Scorer(s):   Picken, Roberts

Match # 489   Saturday 11/11/05   Football League Division 2   at Saltergate   Attendance 3000
Result: **Chesterfield 1 Manchester United 0**
Teamsheet: Valentine, Bonthron, Blackstock, Downie, Roberts, Bell, Schofield, Donaghy, Peddie, Picken, Wombwell

Match # 490   Saturday 18/11/05   Football League Division 2   at Bank Street   Attendance 8000
Result: **Manchester United 3 Port Vale 0**
Teamsheet: Moger, Holden, Blackstock, Duckworth, Roberts, Bell, Schofield, Peddie, Beddow, Picken, Williams
Scorer(s):   Beddow, Peddie, own goal

Match # 491   Saturday 25/11/05   Football League Division 2   at Oakwell   Attendance 3000
Result: **Barnsley 0 Manchester United 3**
Teamsheet: Moger, Holden, Blackstock, Duckworth, Roberts, Bell, Schofield, Peddie, Beddow, Picken, Williams
Scorer(s):   Beddow, Picken, own goal

Match # 492   Saturday 02/12/05   Football League Division 2   at Bank Street   Attendance 12000
Result: **Manchester United 4 Leyton Orient 0**
Teamsheet: Moger, Holden, Blackstock, Duckworth, Roberts, Bell, Schofield, Peddie, Beddow, Picken, Williams
Scorer(s):   Peddie 2, Picken 2

Match # 493   Saturday 09/12/05   Football League Division 2   at Turf Moor   Attendance 8000
Result: **Burnley 1 Manchester United 3**
Teamsheet: Moger, Bonthron, Holden, Duckworth, Roberts, Bell, Schofield, Peddie, Beddow, Picken, Williams
Scorer(s):   Beddow, Peddie, Picken

Match # 494   Saturday 23/12/05   Football League Division 2   at Peel Croft   Attendance 5000
Result: **Burton United 0 Manchester United 2**
Teamsheet: Moger, Bonthron, Holden, Downie, Roberts, Bell, Schofield, Peddie, Beddow, Sagar, Williams
Scorer(s):   Schofield 2

SEASON 1905/06 (continued)

Match # 495   Monday 25/12/05   Football League Division 2   at Bank Street   Attendance 35000
Result: **Manchester United 0 Chelsea 0**
Teamsheet: Moger, Bonthron, Holden, Downie, Roberts, Bell, Schofield, Peddie, Beddow, Sagar, Wombwell

Match # 496   Saturday 30/12/05   Football League Division 2   at Ashton Gate   Attendance 18000
Result: **Bristol City 1 Manchester United 1**
Teamsheet: Moger, Bonthron, Holden, Downie, Roberts, Bell, Schofield, Peddie, Beddow, Picken, Williams
Scorer(s):   Roberts

Match # 497   Saturday 06/01/06   Football League Division 2   at Bank Street   Attendance 10000
Result: **Manchester United 5 Grimsby Town 0**
Teamsheet: Moger, Bonthron, Holden, Downie, Roberts, Bell, Schofield, Allan, Beddow, Picken, Williams
Scorer(s):   Beddow 3, Picken 2

Match # 498   Saturday 13/01/06   FA Cup 1st Round   at Bank Street   Attendance 7560
Result: **Manchester United 7 Staple Hill 2**
Teamsheet: Moger, Bonthron, Holden, Downie, Roberts, Bell, Schofield, Allan, Beddow, Picken, Williams
Scorer(s):   Beddow 3, Picken 2, Allan, Williams

Match # 499   Monday 15/01/06   Football League Division 2   at Bank Street   Attendance 6000
Result: **Manchester United 0 Leeds United 3**
Teamsheet: Moger, Holden, Blackstock, Downie, Roberts, Bell, Schofield, Allan, Beddow, Picken, Williams

Match # 500   Saturday 20/01/06   Football League Division 2   at Bank Street   Attendance 7000
Result: **Manchester United 5 Glossop 2**
Teamsheet: Moger, Duckworth, Holden, Downie, Roberts, Robertson, Schofield, Peddie, Beddow, Picken, Williams
Scorer(s):   Picken 2, Beddow, Peddie, Williams

Match # 501   Saturday 27/01/06   Football League Division 2   at Edgeley Park   Attendance 15000
Result: **Stockport County 0 Manchester United 1**
Teamsheet: Moger, Bonthron, Holden, Downie, Roberts, Bell, Schofield, Peddie, Beddow, Picken, Williams
Scorer(s):   Peddie

Match # 502   Saturday 03/02/06   FA Cup 2nd Round   at Bank Street   Attendance 10000
Result: **Manchester United 3 Norwich City 0**
Teamsheet: Moger, Bonthron, Holden, Downie, Roberts, Bell, Schofield, Peddie, Sagar, Picken, Williams
Scorer(s):   Downie, Peddie, Sagar

Match # 503   Saturday 10/02/06   Football League Division 2   at Valley Parade   Attendance 8000
Result: **Bradford City 1 Manchester United 5**
Teamsheet: Moger, Bonthron, Holden, Downie, Roberts, Bell, Schofield, Peddie, Beddow, Picken, Wombwell
Scorer(s):   Beddow 2, Roberts, Schofield, Wombwell

Match # 504   Saturday 17/02/06   Football League Division 2   at Bank Street   Attendance 30000
Result: **Manchester United 0 West Bromwich Albion 0**
Teamsheet: Moger, Bonthron, Holden, Downie, Roberts, Bell, Schofield, Peddie, Beddow, Picken, Wombwell

Match # 505   Saturday 24/02/06   FA Cup 3rd Round   at Bank Street   Attendance 35500
Result: **Manchester United 5 Aston Villa 1**
Teamsheet: Moger, Bonthron, Holden, Downie, Roberts, Bell, Schofield, Peddie, Sagar, Picken, Wombwell
Scorer(s):   Picken 3, Sagar 2

Match # 506   Saturday 03/03/06   Football League Division 2   at Bank Street   Attendance 16000
Result: **Manchester United 5 Hull City 0**
Teamsheet: Moger, Bonthron, Holden, Downie, Roberts, Bell, Schofield, Peddie, Sagar, Picken, Wombwell
Scorer(s):   Picken 2, Peddie, Sagar, Schofield

Match # 507   Saturday 10/03/06   FA Cup 4th Round   at Bank Street   Attendance 26500
Result: **Manchester United 2 Arsenal 3**
Teamsheet: Moger, Bonthron, Holden, Downie, Roberts, Bell, Schofield, Peddie, Sagar, Picken, Wombwell
Scorer(s):   Peddie, Sagar

Match # 508   Saturday 17/03/06   Football League Division 2   at Bank Street   Attendance 16000
Result: **Manchester United 4 Chesterfield 1**
Teamsheet: Moger, Bonthron, Holden, Downie, Roberts, Bell, Schofield, Peddie, Sagar, Picken, Wombwell
Scorer(s):   Picken 3, Sagar

Match # 509   Saturday 24/03/06   Football League Division 2   at Cobridge Stadium   Attendance 3000
Result: **Port Vale 1 Manchester United 0**
Teamsheet: Moger, Bonthron, Holden, Downie, Roberts, Bell, Lyons, Peddie, Sagar, Picken, Wombwell

Match # 510   Thursday 29/03/06   Football League Division 2   at Filbert Street   Attendance 5000
Result: **Leicester City 2 Manchester United 5**
Teamsheet: Moger, Bonthron, Holden, Downie, Roberts, Bell, Schofield, Peddie, Sagar, Picken, Wombwell
Scorer(s):   Peddie 3, Picken, Sagar

Match # 511   Saturday 31/03/06   Football League Division 2   at Bank Street   Attendance 15000
Result: **Manchester United 5 Barnsley 1**
Teamsheet: Moger, Bonthron, Holden, Downie, Roberts, Bell, Schofield, Peddie, Sagar, Picken, Wombwell
Scorer(s):   Sagar 3, Bell, Picken

Match # 512   Saturday 07/04/06   Football League Division 2   at Millfields Road   Attendance 8000
Result: **Leyton Orient 0 Manchester United 1**
Teamsheet: Moger, Bonthron, Holden, Downie, Roberts, Bell, Wombwell, Peddie, Sagar, Picken, Wall
Scorer(s):   Wall

SEASON 1905/06 (continued)

Match # 513   Friday 13/04/06   Football League Division 2   at Stamford Bridge   Attendance 60000
Result: **Chelsea 1   Manchester United 1**
Teamsheet: Moger, Blew, Holden, Downie, Bell, Duckworth, Wombwell, Peddie, Sagar, Picken, Wall
Scorer(s):   Sagar

Match # 514   Saturday 14/04/06   Football League Division 2   at Bank Street   Attendance 12000
Result: **Manchester United 1   Burnley 0**
Teamsheet: Moger, Bonthron, Holden, Downie, Bell, Duckworth, Wombwell, Peddie, Sagar, Picken, Wall
Scorer(s):   Sagar

Match # 515   Monday 16/04/06   Football League Division 2   at Bank Street   Attendance 20000
Result: **Manchester United 2   Gainsborough Trinity 0**
Teamsheet: Valentine, Holden, Blackstock, Downie, Bell, Duckworth, Schofield, Peddie, Allan, Picken, Wombwell
Scorer(s):   Allan 2

Match # 516   Saturday 21/04/06   Football League Division 2   at Elland Road   Attendance 15000
Result: **Leeds United 1   Manchester United 3**
Teamsheet: Moger, Holden, Blackstock, Downie, Roberts, Bell, Wombwell, Peddie, Allan, Sagar, Wall
Scorer(s):   Allan, Peddie, Wombwell

Match # 517   Wednesday 25/04/06   Football League Division 2   at Sincil Bank   Attendance 1500
Result: **Lincoln City 2   Manchester United 3**
Teamsheet: Moger, Holden, Blackstock, Downie, Bell, Duckworth, Donaghy, Allan, Arkesden, Wall
Scorer(s):   Allan 2, Wall

Match # 518   Saturday 28/04/06   Football League Division 2   at Bank Street   Attendance 16000
Result: **Manchester United 6   Burton United 0**
Teamsheet: Moger, Holden, Blackstock, Downie, Roberts, Duckworth, Wombwell, Peddie, Sagar, Picken, Wall
Scorer(s):   Picken 2, Sagar 2, Peddie, Wall

SEASON 1905/06 SUMMARY

APPEARANCES

PLAYER	LGE	FAC	TOT
Bell	36	4	40
Downie	34	4	38
Roberts	34	4	38
Peddie	34	3	37
Picken	33	4	37
Holden	27	4	31
Moger	27	4	31
Bonthron	26	4	30
Schofield	23	4	27
Wombwell	25	2	27
Sagar	20	3	23
Beddow	21	1	22
Blackstock	21	–	21

APPEARANCES

PLAYER	LGE	FAC	TOT
Williams	10	2	12
Duckworth	10	–	10
Valentine	8	–	8
Arkesden	7	–	7
Allan	5	1	6
Wall	6	–	6
Donaghy	3	–	3
Montgomery	3	–	3
Lyons	2	–	2
Blew	1	–	1
Dyer	1	–	1
Robertson	1	–	1

GOALSCORERS

PLAYER	LGE	FAC	TOT
Picken	20	5	25
Peddie	18	2	20
Sagar	16	4	20
Beddow	11	3	14
Allan	5	1	6
Roberts	4	–	4
Schofield	4	–	4
Wall	3	–	3
Bell	2	–	2
Bonthron	2	–	2
Wombwell	2	–	2
Williams	1	1	2
Downie	–	1	1
own goals	2	–	2

RESULTS & ATTENDANCES SUMMARY

		P	W	D	L	F	A	TOTAL	AVGE
League	H	19	15	3	1	55	13	294000	15474
	A	19	13	3	3	35	15	205500	10816
TOTAL		38	28	6	4	90	28	499500	13145
FA Cup	H	4	3	0	1	17	6	79560	19890
	A	0	0	0	0	0	0	0	n/a
TOTAL		4	3	0	1	17	6	79560	19890
Overall	H	23	18	3	2	72	19	373560	16242
	A	19	13	3	3	35	15	205500	10816
TOTAL		42	31	6	5	107	34	579060	13787

FINAL TABLE – LEAGUE DIVISION TWO

		P		HOME						AWAY					PTS	GD
		P	W	D	L	F	A	W	D	L	F	A	PTS	GD
1	Bristol City	38	17	1	1	43	8	13	5	1	40	20	66	55
2	MANCHESTER UNITED	38	15	3	1	55	13	13	3	3	35	15	62	62
3	Chelsea	38	13	4	2	58	16	9	5	5	32	21	53	53
4	West Bromwich Albion	38	13	4	2	53	16	9	4	6	26	20	52	43
5	Hull City	38	10	5	4	38	21	9	1	9	29	33	44	13
6	Leeds United	38	11	5	3	38	19	6	4	9	21	28	43	12
7	Leicester City	38	10	3	6	30	21	5	9	5	23	27	42	5
8	Grimsby Town	38	11	7	1	33	13	4	3	12	13	33	40	0
9	Burnley	38	9	4	6	26	23	6	4	9	16	30	38	-11
10	Stockport County	38	11	6	2	36	16	2	3	14	8	40	35	-12
11	Bradford City	38	7	4	8	21	22	6	4	9	25	38	34	-14
12	Barnsley	38	11	4	4	45	17	1	5	13	15	45	33	-2
13	Lincoln City	38	10	1	8	46	29	2	5	12	23	43	30	-3
14	Blackpool	38	8	3	8	22	21	2	6	11	15	41	29	-25
15	Gainsborough Trinity	38	10	2	7	35	22	2	2	15	9	35	28	-13
16	Glossop	38	9	4	6	36	28	1	4	14	13	43	28	-22
17	Port Vale	38	10	4	5	34	25	2	0	17	15	57	28	-33
18	Chesterfield	38	8	4	7	26	24	2	4	13	14	48	28	-32
19	Burton United	38	9	4	6	26	20	1	2	16	8	47	26	-33
20	Leyton Orient	38	6	4	9	19	22	1	3	15	16	56	21	-43

SEASON 1906/07

Match # 519	Saturday 01/09/06	Football League Division 1	at Ashton Gate	Attendance 5000
Result:	**Bristol City 1 Manchester United 2**			
Teamsheet:	Moger, Bonthron, Holden, Downie, Roberts, Bell, Schofield, Peddie, Sagar, Picken, Wall			
Scorer(s):	Picken, Roberts			

Match # 520	Monday 03/09/06	Football League Division 1	at Baseball Ground	Attendance 5000
Result:	**Derby County 2 Manchester United 2**			
Teamsheet:	Moger, Bonthron, Holden, Downie, Roberts, Bell, Schofield, Peddie, Sagar, Picken, Wall			
Scorer(s):	Schofield 2			

Match # 521	Saturday 08/09/06	Football League Division 1	at Bank Street	Attendance 30000
Result:	**Manchester United 0 Notts County 0**			
Teamsheet:	Moger, Bonthron, Holden, Downie, Roberts, Bell, Schofield, Peddie, Sagar, Picken, Wall			

Match # 522	Saturday 15/09/06	Football League Division 1	at Bramall Lane	Attendance 12000
Result:	**Sheffield United 0 Manchester United 2**			
Teamsheet:	Moger, Bonthron, Holden, Downie, Roberts, Bell, Beddow, Yates, Wombwell, Picken, Wall			
Scorer(s):	Bell, Downie			

Match # 523	Saturday 22/09/06	Football League Division 1	at Bank Street	Attendance 45000
Result:	**Manchester United 1 Bolton Wanderers 2**			
Teamsheet:	Moger, Bonthron, Holden, Downie, Roberts, Bell, Wombwell, Yates, Peddie, Picken, Wall			
Scorer(s):	Peddie			

Match # 524	Saturday 29/09/06	Football League Division 1	at Bank Street	Attendance 25000
Result:	**Manchester United 1 Derby County 1**			
Teamsheet:	Moger, Bonthron, Buckley, Downie, Roberts, Bell, Schofield, Peddie, Allan, Picken, Wall			
Scorer(s):	Bell			

Match # 525	Saturday 06/10/06	Football League Division 1	at Victoria Ground	Attendance 7000
Result:	**Stoke City 1 Manchester United 2**			
Teamsheet:	Moger, Bonthron, Blackstock, Downie, Roberts, Bell, Duckworth, Peddie, Allan, Picken, Wall			
Scorer(s):	Duckworth 2			

Match # 526	Saturday 13/10/06	Football League Division 1	at Bank Street	Attendance 20000
Result:	**Manchester United 1 Blackburn Rovers 1**			
Teamsheet:	Moger, Bonthron, Holden, Downie, Bell, Duckworth, Schofield, Peddie, Allan, Wombwell, Wall			
Scorer(s):	Wall			

Match # 527	Saturday 20/10/06	Football League Division 1	at Roker Park	Attendance 18000
Result:	**Sunderland 4 Manchester United 1**			
Teamsheet:	Moger, Bonthron, Holden, Downie, Roberts, Bell, Duckworth, Peddie, Picken, Wombwell, Wall			
Scorer(s):	Peddie			

Match # 528	Saturday 27/10/06	Football League Division 1	at Bank Street	Attendance 14000
Result:	**Manchester United 2 Birmingham City 1**			
Teamsheet:	Moger, Bonthron, Holden, Downie, Roberts, Bell, Young, Wombwell, Peddie, Picken, Wall			
Scorer(s):	Peddie 2			

Match # 529	Saturday 03/11/06	Football League Division 1	at Goodison Park	Attendance 20000
Result:	**Everton 3 Manchester United 0**			
Teamsheet:	Moger, Bonthron, Holden, Downie, Roberts, Bell, Young, Wombwell, Peddie, Yates, Wall			

Match # 530	Saturday 10/11/06	Football League Division 1	at Bank Street	Attendance 20000
Result:	**Manchester United 1 Arsenal 0**			
Teamsheet:	Moger, Bonthron, Holden, Downie, Duckworth, Bell, Schofield, Wombwell, Peddie, Picken, Wall			
Scorer(s):	Downie			

Match # 531	Saturday 17/11/06	Football League Division 1	at Hillsborough	Attendance 7000
Result:	**Sheffield Wednesday 5 Manchester United 2**			
Teamsheet:	Moger, Bonthron, Holden, Downie, Duckworth, Bell, Berry, Wombwell, Menzies, Peddie, Wall			
Scorer(s):	Menzies, Peddie			

Match # 532	Saturday 24/11/06	Football League Division 1	at Bank Street	Attendance 30000
Result:	**Manchester United 2 Bury 4**			
Teamsheet:	Moger, Bonthron, Blackstock, Downie, Roberts, Bell, Berry, Wombwell, Menzies, Peddie, Wall			
Scorer(s):	Peddie, Wall			

Match # 533	Saturday 01/12/06	Football League Division 1	at Hyde Road	Attendance 40000
Result:	**Manchester City 3 Manchester United 0**			
Teamsheet:	Moger, Bonthron, Duckworth, Downie, Roberts, Bell, Beddow, Wombwell, Menzies, Picken, Wall			

Match # 534	Saturday 08/12/06	Football League Division 1	at Bank Street	Attendance 12000
Result:	**Manchester United 3 Middlesbrough 1**			
Teamsheet:	Moger, Bonthron, Holden, Duckworth, Roberts, Bell, Schofield, Wombwell, Sagar, Picken, Wall			
Scorer(s):	Wall 2, Sagar			

Match # 535	Saturday 15/12/06	Football League Division 1	at Deepdale	Attendance 9000
Result:	**Preston North End 2 Manchester United 0**			
Teamsheet:	Moger, Bonthron, Holden, Duckworth, Roberts, Bell, Schofield, Wombwell, Sagar, Picken, Wall			

Match # 536	Saturday 22/12/06	Football League Division 1	at Bank Street	Attendance 18000
Result:	**Manchester United 1 Newcastle United 3**			
Teamsheet:	Moger, Bonthron, Holden, Duckworth, Roberts, Bell, Schofield, Peddie, Menzies, Picken, Wall			
Scorer(s):	Menzies			

SEASON 1906/07 (continued)

Match # 537 Tuesday 25/12/06   Football League Division 1   at Bank Street   Attendance 20000
Result: **Manchester United 0 Liverpool 0**
Teamsheet: Moger, Holden, Blackstock, Duckworth, Roberts, Bell, Schofield, Berry, Menzies, Picken, Wall

Match # 538 Wednesday 26/12/06   Football League Division 1   at Perry Barr   Attendance 20000
Result: **Aston Villa 2 Manchester United 0**
Teamsheet: Moger, Duckworth, Holden, Downie, Roberts, Wombwell, Berry, Peddie, Menzies, Picken, Wall

Match # 539 Saturday 29/12/06   Football League Division 1   at Bank Street   Attendance 10000
Result: **Manchester United 0 Bristol City 0**
Teamsheet: Moger, Bonthron, Holden, Downie, Roberts, Duckworth, Wombwell, Berry, Menzies, Picken, Wall

Match # 540 Tuesday 01/01/07   Football League Division 1   at Bank Street   Attendance 40000
Result: **Manchester United 1 Aston Villa 0**
Teamsheet: Moger, Bonthron, Burgess, Duckworth, Roberts, Bell, Meredith, Bannister, Menzies, Turnbull, Wall
Scorer(s):   Turnbull

Match # 541 Saturday 05/01/07   Football League Division 1   at Trent Bridge   Attendance 10000
Result: **Notts County 3 Manchester United 0**
Teamsheet: Moger, Bonthron, Burgess, Duckworth, Buckley, Bell, Meredith, Bannister, Menzies, Turnbull, Wall

Match # 542 Saturday 12/01/07   FA Cup 1st Round   at Fratton Park   Attendance 24329
Result: **Portsmouth 2 Manchester United 2**
Teamsheet: Moger, Holden, Blackstock, Duckworth, Roberts, Bell, Meredith, Wombwell, Menzies, Picken, Wall
Scorer(s):   Picken, Wall

Match # 543 Wednesday 16/01/07   FA Cup 1st Round Replay   at Bank Street   Attendance 8000
Result: **Manchester United 1 Portsmouth 2**
Teamsheet: Moger, Bonthron, Holden, Downie, Duckworth, Bell, Meredith, Wombwell, Menzies, Picken, Wall
Scorer(s):   Wall

Match # 544 Saturday 19/01/07   Football League Division 1   at Bank Street   Attendance 15000
Result: **Manchester United 2 Sheffield United 0**
Teamsheet: Moger, Bonthron, Burgess, Duckworth, Holden, Bell, Meredith, Peddie, Beddow, Turnbull, Wall
Scorer(s):   Turnbull, Wall

Match # 545 Saturday 26/01/07   Football League Division 1   at Burnden Park   Attendance 25000
Result: **Bolton Wanderers 0 Manchester United 1**
Teamsheet: Moger, Bonthron, Burgess, Duckworth, Roberts, Bell, Meredith, Picken, Berry, Turnbull, Wall
Scorer(s):   Turnbull

Match # 546 Saturday 02/02/07   Football League Division 1   at St James' Park   Attendance 30000
Result: **Newcastle United 5 Manchester United 0**
Teamsheet: Moger, Holden, Burgess, Duckworth, Roberts, Bell, Meredith, Menzies, Berry, Picken, Wall

Match # 547 Saturday 09/02/07   Football League Division 1   at Bank Street   Attendance 15000
Result: **Manchester United 4 Stoke City 1**
Teamsheet: Moger, Holden, Burgess, Duckworth, Roberts, Bell, Meredith, Picken, Berry, Menzies, Wall
Scorer(s):   Picken 2, Meredith, own goal

Match # 548 Saturday 16/02/07   Football League Division 1   at Ewood Park   Attendance 5000
Result: **Blackburn Rovers 2 Manchester United 4**
Teamsheet: Moger, Holden, Burgess, Duckworth, Roberts, Bell, Meredith, Picken, Sagar, Turnbull, Wall
Scorer(s):   Meredith 2, Sagar, Wall

Match # 549 Saturday 23/02/07   Football League Division 1   at Bank Street   Attendance 16000
Result: **Manchester United 3 Preston North End 0**
Teamsheet: Moger, Holden, Burgess, Duckworth, Roberts, Bell, Berry, Picken, Sagar, Turnbull, Wall
Scorer(s):   Wall 2, Sagar

Match # 550 Saturday 02/03/07   Football League Division 1   at St Andrews   Attendance 20000
Result: **Birmingham City 1 Manchester United 1**
Teamsheet: Moger, Holden, Burgess, Duckworth, Buckley, Bell, Meredith, Picken, Menzies, Turnbull, Wall
Scorer(s):   Menzies

Match # 551 Saturday 16/03/07   Football League Division 1   at Manor Field   Attendance 6000
Result: **Arsenal 4 Manchester United 0**
Teamsheet: Moger, Bonthron, Burgess, Duckworth, Holden, Bell, Meredith, Bannister, Menzies, Turnbull, Wall

Match # 552 Monday 25/03/07   Football League Division 1   at Bank Street   Attendance 12000
Result: **Manchester United 2 Sunderland 0**
Teamsheet: Moger, Holden, Burgess, Duckworth, Roberts, Bell, Meredith, Williams, Menzies, Turnbull, Wall
Scorer(s):   Turnbull, Williams

Match # 553 Saturday 30/03/07   Football League Division 1   at Gigg Lane   Attendance 25000
Result: **Bury 1 Manchester United 2**
Teamsheet: Moger, Holden, Burgess, Duckworth, Roberts, Bell, Meredith, Williams, Menzies, Turnbull, Wall
Scorer(s):   Menzies, Meredith

Match # 554 Monday 01/04/07   Football League Division 1   at Anfield   Attendance 20000
Result: **Liverpool 0 Manchester United 1**
Teamsheet: Moger, Bonthron, Burgess, Duckworth, Roberts, Bell, Meredith, Williams, Menzies, Turnbull, Wall
Scorer(s):   Turnbull

SEASON 1906/07 (continued)

Match # 555	Saturday 06/04/07	Football League Division 1	at Bank Street	Attendance 40000
Result:	**Manchester United 1 Manchester City 1**			
Teamsheet:	Moger, Bonthron, Burgess, Downie, Roberts, Bell, Meredith, Picken, Menzies, Turnbull, Wall			
Scorer(s):	Roberts			

Match # 556	Wednesday 10/04/07	Football League Division 1	at Bank Street	Attendance 10000
Result:	**Manchester United 5 Sheffield Wednesday 0**			
Teamsheet:	Moger, Bonthron, Burgess, Duckworth, Roberts, Downie, Meredith, Picken, Sagar, Turnbull, Wall			
Scorer(s):	Wall 3, Picken, Sagar			

Match # 557	Saturday 13/04/07	Football League Division 1	at Ayresome Park	Attendance 15000
Result:	**Middlesbrough 2 Manchester United 0**			
Teamsheet:	Moger, Bonthron, Burgess, Duckworth, Roberts, Bell, Meredith, Picken, Sagar, Turnbull, Wall			

Match # 558	Monday 22/04/07	Football League Division 1	at Bank Street	Attendance 10000
Result:	**Manchester United 3 Everton 0**			
Teamsheet:	Moger, Holden, Burgess, Duckworth, Roberts, Bell, Meredith, Bannister, Sagar, Turnbull, Wall			
Scorer(s):	Bannister, Meredith, Turnbull			

SEASON 1906/07 SUMMARY

APPEARANCES

PLAYER	LGE	FAC	TOT
Moger	38	2	40
Wall	38	2	40
Bell	35	2	37
Roberts	31	1	32
Duckworth	28	2	30
Bonthron	28	1	29
Holden	27	2	29
Picken	26	2	28
Downie	19	1	20
Menzies	17	2	19
Meredith	16	2	18
Burgess	17	–	17
Peddie	16	–	16
Wombwell	14	2	16
Turnbull	15	–	15
Sagar	10	–	10
Schofield	10	–	10
Berry	9	–	9
Bannister	4	–	4
Blackstock	3	1	4
Allan	3	–	3
Beddow	3	–	3
Buckley	3	–	3
Williams	3	–	3
Yates	3	–	3
Young	2	–	2

GOALSCORERS

PLAYER	LGE	FAC	TOT
Wall	11	2	13
Peddie	6	–	6
Turnbull	6	–	6
Meredith	5	–	5
Picken	4	1	5
Menzies	4	–	4
Sagar	4	–	4
Bell	2	–	2
Downie	2	–	2
Duckworth	2	–	2
Roberts	2	–	2
Schofield	2	–	2
Bannister	1	–	1
Williams	1	–	1
own goal	1	–	1

RESULTS & ATTENDANCES SUMMARY

		P	W	D	L	F	A	TOTAL	AVGE
League	H	19	10	6	3	33	15	402000	21158
	A	19	7	2	10	20	41	299000	15737
TOTAL		38	17	8	13	53	56	701000	18447
FA Cup	H	1	0	0	1	1	2	8000	8000
	A	1	0	1	0	2	2	24329	24329
TOTAL		2	0	1	1	3	4	32329	16165
Overall	H	20	10	6	4	34	17	410000	20500
	A	20	7	3	10	22	43	323329	16166
TOTAL		40	17	9	14	56	60	733329	18333

FINAL TABLE – LEAGUE DIVISION ONE

		P	W	D	L	F	A	W	D	L	F	A	PTS	GD
				HOME						AWAY				
1	Newcastle United	38	18	1	0	51	12	4	6	9	23	34	51	28
2	Bristol City	38	12	3	4	37	18	8	5	6	29	29	48	19
3	Everton	38	16	2	1	50	10	4	3	12	20	36	45	24
4	Sheffield United	38	13	4	2	36	17	4	7	8	21	38	45	2
5	Aston Villa	38	13	4	2	51	19	6	2	11	27	33	44	26
6	Bolton Wanderers	38	10	4	5	35	18	8	4	7	24	29	44	12
7	Arsenal	38	15	1	3	38	15	5	3	11	28	44	44	7
8	MANCHESTER UNITED	38	10	6	3	33	15	7	2	10	20	41	42	-3
9	Birmingham City	38	13	5	1	41	17	2	3	14	11	35	38	0
10	Sunderland	38	10	4	5	42	31	4	5	10	23	35	37	-1
11	Middlesbrough	38	11	2	6	33	21	4	4	11	23	42	36	-7
12	Blackburn Rovers	38	10	3	6	40	25	4	4	11	16	34	35	-3
13	Sheffield Wednesday	38	8	5	6	33	26	4	6	9	16	34	35	-11
14	Preston North End	38	13	4	2	35	19	1	3	15	9	38	35	-13
15	Liverpool	38	9	2	8	45	32	4	5	10	19	33	33	-1
16	Bury	38	9	4	6	30	23	4	2	13	28	45	32	-10
17	Manchester City	38	7	7	5	29	25	3	5	11	24	52	32	-24
18	Notts County	38	6	9	4	31	18	2	6	11	15	32	31	-4
19	Derby County	38	8	6	5	29	19	1	3	15	12	40	27	-18
20	Stoke City	38	7	6	6	27	22	1	4	14	14	42	26	-23

SEASON 1907/08

Match # 559 Monday 02/09/07   Football League Division 1   at Villa Park   Attendance 20000
Result: **Aston Villa 1 Manchester United 4**
Teamsheet: Moger, Holden, Burgess, Duckworth, Roberts, Bell, Meredith, Bannister, Menzies, Turnbull A, Wall
Scorer(s):   Meredith 2, Bannister, Wall

Match # 560 Saturday 07/09/07   Football League Division 1   at Bank Street   Attendance 24000
Result: **Manchester United 4 Liverpool 0**
Teamsheet: Moger, Holden, Burgess, Duckworth, Roberts, Bell, Meredith, Bannister, Menzies, Turnbull A, Wall
Scorer(s):   Turnbull A 3, Wall

Match # 561 Monday 09/09/07   Football League Division 1   at Bank Street   Attendance 20000
Result: **Manchester United 2 Middlesbrough 1**
Teamsheet: Moger, Holden, Burgess, Duckworth, Roberts, Bell, Meredith, Bannister, Menzies, Turnbull A, Wall
Scorer(s):   Turnbull A 2

Match # 562 Saturday 14/09/07   Football League Division 1   at Ayresome Park   Attendance 18000
Result: **Middlesbrough 2 Manchester United 1**
Teamsheet: Moger, Holden, Burgess, Duckworth, Roberts, Thomson, Meredith, Bannister, Menzies, Turnbull A, Wall
Scorer(s):   Bannister

Match # 563 Saturday 21/09/07   Football League Division 1   at Bank Street   Attendance 25000
Result: **Manchester United 2 Sheffield United 1**
Teamsheet: Moger, Holden, Burgess, Duckworth, Roberts, Bell, Meredith, Bannister, Menzies, Turnbull A, Wall
Scorer(s):   Turnbull A 2

Match # 564 Saturday 28/09/07   Football League Division 1   at Stamford Bridge   Attendance 40000
Result: **Chelsea 1 Manchester United 4**
Teamsheet: Moger, Holden, Burgess, Duckworth, Roberts, Bell, Meredith, Bannister, Turnbull J, Turnbull A, Wall
Scorer(s):   Meredith 2, Bannister, Turnbull A

Match # 565 Saturday 05/10/07   Football League Division 1   at Bank Street   Attendance 20000
Result: **Manchester United 4 Nottingham Forest 0**
Teamsheet: Moger, Holden, Burgess, Duckworth, Roberts, Bell, Meredith, Bannister, Turnbull J, Turnbull A, Wall
Scorer(s):   Bannister, Turnbull J, Wall, own goal

Match # 566 Saturday 12/10/07   Football League Division 1   at St James' Park   Attendance 25000
Result: **Newcastle United 1 Manchester United 6**
Teamsheet: Moger, Holden, Stacey, Duckworth, Roberts, Bell, Meredith, Bannister, Turnbull J, Turnbull A, Wall
Scorer(s):   Wall 2, Meredith, Roberts, Turnbull A, Turnbull J

Match # 567 Saturday 19/10/07   Football League Division 1   at Ewood Park   Attendance 30000
Result: **Blackburn Rovers 1 Manchester United 5**
Teamsheet: Moger, Holden, Burgess, Duckworth, Roberts, Bell, Meredith, Bannister, Turnbull J, Turnbull A, Wall
Scorer(s):   Turnbull A 3, Turnbull J 2

Match # 568 Saturday 26/10/07   Football League Division 1   at Bank Street   Attendance 35000
Result: **Manchester United 2 Bolton Wanderers 1**
Teamsheet: Moger, Holden, Burgess, Duckworth, Roberts, Bell, Meredith, Bannister, Turnbull J, Turnbull A, Wall
Scorer(s):   Turnbull A, Turnbull J

Match # 569 Saturday 02/11/07   Football League Division 1   at St Andrews   Attendance 20000
Result: **Birmingham City 3 Manchester United 4**
Teamsheet: Moger, Holden, Burgess, Duckworth, Roberts, Bell, Meredith, Bannister, Turnbull J, Picken, Wall
Scorer(s):   Meredith 2, Turnbull J, Wall

Match # 570 Saturday 09/11/07   Football League Division 1   at Bank Street   Attendance 30000
Result: **Manchester United 4 Everton 3**
Teamsheet: Moger, Holden, Burgess, Duckworth, Roberts, Bell, Meredith, Bannister, Turnbull J, Turnbull A, Wall
Scorer(s):   Wall 2, Meredith, Roberts

Match # 571 Saturday 16/11/07   Football League Division 1   at Roker Park   Attendance 30000
Result: **Sunderland 1 Manchester United 2**
Teamsheet: Moger, Holden, Burgess, Duckworth, Roberts, Bell, Meredith, Bannister, Turnbull J, Turnbull A, Wall
Scorer(s):   Turnbull A 2

Match # 572 Saturday 23/11/07   Football League Division 1   at Bank Street   Attendance 10000
Result: **Manchester United 4 Arsenal 2**
Teamsheet: Moger, Holden, Burgess, Duckworth, Roberts, Bell, Meredith, Bannister, Turnbull J, Turnbull A, Williams
Scorer(s):   Turnbull A 4

Match # 573 Saturday 30/11/07   Football League Division 1   at Hillsborough   Attendance 40000
Result: **Sheffield Wednesday 2 Manchester United 0**
Teamsheet: Moger, Holden, Burgess, Duckworth, Roberts, Bell, Meredith, Bannister, Turnbull J, Turnbull A, Wall

Match # 574 Saturday 07/12/07   Football League Division 1   at Bank Street   Attendance 20000
Result: **Manchester United 2 Bristol City 1**
Teamsheet: Moger, Holden, Stacey, Duckworth, Roberts, Bell, Meredith, Bannister, Turnbull J, Turnbull A, Wall
Scorer(s):   Wall 2

Match # 575 Saturday 14/12/07   Football League Division 1   at Trent Bridge   Attendance 11000
Result: **Notts County 1 Manchester United 1**
Teamsheet: Moger, Holden, Burgess, Duckworth, Roberts, Bell, Meredith, Bannister, Turnbull J, Turnbull A, Wall
Scorer(s):   Meredith

Match # 576 Saturday 21/12/07   Football League Division 1   at Bank Street   Attendance 35000
Result: **Manchester United 3 Manchester City 1**
Teamsheet: Moger, Holden, Burgess, Duckworth, Roberts, Bell, Meredith, Bannister, Turnbull J, Turnbull A, Wall
Scorer(s):   Turnbull A 2, Wall

SEASON 1907/08 (continued)

Match # 577   Wednesday 25/12/07   Football League Division 1   at Bank Street   Attendance 45000
Result: **Manchester United 2   Bury 1**
Teamsheet: Moger, Holden, Stacey, Duckworth, Roberts, Bell, Meredith, Bannister, Turnbull J, Turnbull A, Wall
Scorer(s):   Meredith, Turnbull J

Match # 578   Saturday 28/12/07   Football League Division 1   at Deepdale   Attendance 12000
Result: **Preston North End 0   Manchester United 0**
Teamsheet: Moger, Holden, Stacey, Duckworth, Roberts, Bell, Meredith, Bannister, Turnbull J, Turnbull A, Wall

Match # 579   Wednesday 01/01/08   Football League Division 1   at Gigg Lane   Attendance 29500
Result: **Bury 0   Manchester United 1**
Teamsheet: Moger, Holden, Stacey, Duckworth, Roberts, Bell, Meredith, Bannister, Turnbull J, Turnbull A, Wall
Scorer(s):   Wall

Match # 580   Saturday 11/01/08   FA Cup 1st Round   at Bank Street   Attendance 11747
Result: **Manchester United 3   Blackpool 1**
Teamsheet: Moger, Holden, Stacey, Duckworth, McGillivray, Bell, Meredith, Bannister, Turnbull J, Turnbull A, Wall
Scorer(s):   Wall 2, Bannister

Match # 581   Saturday 18/01/08   Football League Division 1   at Bramall Lane   Attendance 17000
Result: **Sheffield United 2   Manchester United 0**
Teamsheet: Moger, Holden, Burgess, Whiteside, McGillivray, Bell, Meredith, Bannister, Turnbull J, Picken, Wall

Match # 582   Saturday 25/01/08   Football League Division 1   at Bank Street   Attendance 20000
Result: **Manchester United 1   Chelsea 0**
Teamsheet: Moger, Holden, Burgess, Downie, Roberts, Bell, Meredith, Picken, Turnbull J, Menzies, Wall
Scorer(s):   Turnbull J

Match # 583   Saturday 01/02/08   FA Cup 2nd Round   at Bank Street   Attendance 25184
Result: **Manchester United 1   Chelsea 0**
Teamsheet: Moger, Holden, Burgess, Duckworth, Roberts, Bell, Meredith, Bannister, Turnbull J, Turnbull A, Wall
Scorer(s):   Turnbull A

Match # 584   Saturday 08/02/08   Football League Division 1   at Bank Street   Attendance 50000
Result: **Manchester United 1   Newcastle United 1**
Teamsheet: Moger, Holden, Burgess, Duckworth, Downie, Bell, Meredith, Bannister, Turnbull J, Turnbull A, Wall
Scorer(s):   Turnbull J

Match # 585   Saturday 15/02/08   Football League Division 1   at Bank Street   Attendance 15000
Result: **Manchester United 1   Blackburn Rovers 2**
Teamsheet: Moger, Holden, Burgess, Duckworth, Roberts, Bell, Meredith, Bannister, Turnbull J, Turnbull A, Wilson
Scorer(s):   Turnbull A

Match # 586   Saturday 22/02/08   FA Cup 3rd Round   at Villa Park   Attendance 12777
Result: **Aston Villa 0   Manchester United 2**
Teamsheet: Moger, Stacey, Holden, Burgess, Roberts, Bell, Meredith, Bannister, Berry, Turnbull A, Wall
Scorer(s):   Turnbull A, Wall

Match # 587   Saturday 29/02/08   Football League Division 1   at Bank Street   Attendance 12000
Result: **Manchester United 1   Birmingham City 0**
Teamsheet: Moger, Holden, Stacey, Duckworth, Roberts, Bell, Meredith, Bannister, Turnbull J, Turnbull A, Wall
Scorer(s):   Turnbull A

Match # 588   Saturday 07/03/08   FA Cup 4th Round   at Craven Cottage   Attendance 41000
Result: **Fulham 2   Manchester United 1**
Teamsheet: Moger, Stacey, Burgess, Duckworth, Roberts, Bell, Meredith, Bannister, Turnbull J, Turnbull A, Wall
Scorer(s):   Turnbull J

Match # 589   Saturday 14/03/08   Football League Division 1   at Bank Street   Attendance 15000
Result: **Manchester United 3   Sunderland 0**
Teamsheet: Moger, Stacey, Burgess, Duckworth, Roberts, Bell, Meredith, Bannister, Berry, Turnbull A, Wall
Scorer(s):   Bell, Berry, Wall

Match # 590   Saturday 21/03/08   Football League Division 1   at Manor Field   Attendance 20000
Result: **Arsenal 1   Manchester United 0**
Teamsheet: Broomfield, Stacey, Burgess, Duckworth, Roberts, Bell, Meredith, Bannister, Berry, Picken, Wall

Match # 591   Wednesday 25/03/08   Football League Division 1   at Anfield   Attendance 10000
Result: **Liverpool 7   Manchester United 4**
Teamsheet: Moger, Stacey, Dalton, Duckworth, Roberts, Downie, Meredith, Bannister, Turnbull J, Picken, Wall
Scorer(s):   Wall 2, Bannister, Turnbull J

Match # 592   Saturday 28/03/08   Football League Division 1   at Bank Street   Attendance 30000
Result: **Manchester United 4   Sheffield Wednesday 1**
Teamsheet: Broomfield, Stacey, Burgess, Duckworth, Downie, Bell, Meredith, Bannister, Halse, Turnbull A, Wall
Scorer(s):   Wall 2, Halse, Turnbull A

Match # 593   Saturday 04/04/08   Football League Division 1   at Ashton Gate   Attendance 12000
Result: **Bristol City 1   Manchester United 1**
Teamsheet: Broomfield, Stacey, Burgess, Duckworth, Roberts, Bell, Meredith, Bannister, Halse, Turnbull A, Wall
Scorer(s):   Wall

Match # 594   Wednesday 08/04/08   Football League Division 1   at Goodison Park   Attendance 17000
Result: **Everton 1   Manchester United 3**
Teamsheet: Broomfield, Stacey, Burgess, Duckworth, Roberts, Downie, Meredith, Bannister, Halse, Turnbull A, Wall
Scorer(s):   Halse, Turnbull A, Wall

SEASON 1907/08 (continued)

Match # 595 Saturday 11/04/08   Football League Division 1   at Bank Street   Attendance 20000
Result: **Manchester United 0 Notts County 1**
Teamsheet: Broomfield, Stacey, Burgess, Duckworth, Downie, Bell, Berry, Bannister, Turnbull J, Turnbull A, Wall

Match # 596 Friday 17/04/08   Football League Division 1   at City Ground   Attendance 22000
Result: **Nottingham Forest 2 Manchester United 0**
Teamsheet: Broomfield, Stacey, Burgess, Duckworth, Roberts, Bell, Meredith, Halse, Turnbull J, Turnbull A, Wall

Match # 597 Saturday 18/04/08   Football League Division 1   at Hyde Road   Attendance 40000
Result: **Manchester City 0 Manchester United 0**
Teamsheet: Broomfield, Duckworth, Stacey, Downie, Roberts, Bell, Meredith, Bannister, Turnbull J, Turnbull A, Wall

Match # 598 Monday 20/04/08   Football League Division 1   at Bank Street   Attendance 10000
Result: **Manchester United 1 Aston Villa 2**
Teamsheet: Broomfield, Duckworth, Stacey, Downie, Roberts, Bell, Meredith, Bannister, Picken, Turnbull J, Wall
Scorer(s):   Picken

Match # 599 Wednesday 22/04/08   Football League Division 1   at Burnden Park   Attendance 18000
Result: **Bolton Wanderers 2 Manchester United 2**
Teamsheet: Broomfield, Duckworth, Stacey, Downie, Thomson, Bell, Meredith, Bannister, Halse, Picken, Wall
Scorer(s):   Halse, Stacey

Match # 600 Saturday 25/04/08   Football League Division 1   at Bank Street   Attendance 8000
Result: **Manchester United 2 Preston North End 1**
Teamsheet: Moger, Stacey, Hulme, Downie, Thomson, Bell, Meredith, Bannister, Halse, Picken, Wall
Scorer(s):   Halse, own goal

Match # 601 Monday 27/04/08   FA Charity Shield   at Stamford Bridge   Attendance 6000
Result: **Manchester United 1 Queens Park Rangers 1**
Teamsheet: Moger, Stacey, Burgess, Duckworth, Roberts, Bell, Meredith, Bannister, Turnbull J, Turnbull A, Wall
Scorer(s):   Meredith

Match # 602 Wednesday 29/04/08   FA Charity Shield Replay   at Stamford Bridge   Attendance 6000
Result: **Manchester United 4 Queens Park Rangers 0**
Teamsheet: Moger, Stacey, Burgess, Duckworth, Roberts, Bell, Meredith, Bannister, Turnbull J, Picken, Wall
Scorer(s):   Turnbull J 3, Wall

SEASON 1907/08 SUMMARY

APPEARANCES

PLAYER	LGE	FAC	CS	TOT
Meredith	37	4	2	43
Bannister	36	4	2	42
Wall	36	4	2	42
Bell	35	4	2	41
Duckworth	35	3	2	40
Roberts	32	3	2	37
Moger	29	4	2	35
Turnbull A	30	4	1	35
Burgess	27	3	2	32
Turnbull J	26	3	2	31
Holden	26	3	–	29
Stacey	18	3	2	23
Downie	10	–	–	10
Broomfield	9	–	–	9
Picken	8	–	1	9
Halse	6	–	–	6
Menzies	6	–	–	6
Berry	3	1	–	4
Thomson	3	–	–	3
McGillivray	1	1	–	2
Dalton	1	–	–	1
Hulme	1	–	–	1
Whiteside	1	–	–	1
Williams	1	–	–	1
Wilson	1	–	–	1

GOALSCORERS

PLAYER	LGE	FAC	CS	TOT
Turnbull A	25	2	–	27
Wall	19	3	1	23
Turnbull J	10	1	3	14
Meredith	10	–	1	11
Bannister	5	1	–	6
Halse	4	–	–	4
Roberts	2	–	–	2
Bell	1	–	–	1
Berry	1	–	–	1
Picken	1	–	–	1
Stacey	1	–	–	1
own goals	2	–	–	2

RESULTS & ATTENDANCES SUMMARY

		P	W	D	L	F	A	TOTAL	AVGE
League	H	19	15	1	3	43	19	444000	23368
	A	19	8	5	6	38	29	431500	22711
TOTAL		38	23	6	9	81	48	875500	23039
FA Cup	H	2	2	0	0	4	1	36931	18466
	A	2	1	0	1	3	2	53777	26889
TOTAL		4	3	0	1	7	3	90708	22677
Charity	H	0	0	0	0	0	0	0	n/a
Shield	A	0	0	0	0	0	0	0	n/a
	N	2	1	1	0	5	1	12000	6000
TOTAL		2	1	1	0	5	1	12000	6000
Overall	H	21	17	1	3	47	20	480931	22901
	A	21	9	5	7	41	31	485277	23108
	N	2	1	1	0	5	1	12000	6000
TOTAL		44	27	7	10	93	52	978208	22232

FINAL TABLE - LEAGUE DIVISION ONE

		P	HOME					AWAY					PTS	GD
			W	D	L	F	A	W	D	L	F	A		
1	MANCHESTER UNITED	38	15	1	3	43	19	8	5	6	38	29	52	33
2	Aston Villa	38	9	6	4	47	24	8	3	8	30	35	43	18
3	Manchester City	38	12	5	2	36	19	4	6	9	26	35	43	8
4	Newcastle United	38	11	4	4	41	24	4	8	7	24	30	42	11
5	Sheffield Wednesday	38	14	0	5	50	25	5	4	10	23	39	42	9
6	Middlesbrough	38	12	2	5	32	16	5	5	9	22	29	41	9
7	Bury	38	8	7	4	29	22	6	4	9	29	39	39	-3
8	Liverpool	38	11	2	6	43	24	5	4	10	25	37	38	7
9	Nottingham Forest	38	11	6	2	42	21	2	5	12	17	41	37	-3
10	Bristol City	38	8	7	4	29	21	4	5	10	29	40	36	-3
11	Everton	38	11	4	4	34	24	4	2	13	24	40	36	-6
12	Preston North End	38	9	7	3	33	18	3	5	11	14	35	36	-6
13	Chelsea	38	8	3	8	30	35	6	5	8	23	27	36	-9
14	Blackburn Rovers	38	10	7	2	35	23	2	5	12	16	40	36	-12
15	Arsenal	38	9	8	2	32	18	3	4	12	19	45	36	-12
16	Sunderland	38	11	2	6	53	31	5	1	13	25	44	35	3
17	Sheffield United	38	8	6	5	27	22	4	5	10	25	36	35	-6
18	Notts County	38	9	3	7	24	19	4	5	10	15	32	34	-12
19	Bolton Wanderers	38	10	3	6	35	26	4	2	13	17	32	33	-6
20	Birmingham City	38	6	6	7	22	28	3	6	10	18	32	30	-20

SEASON 1908/09

Match # 603 Saturday 05/09/08   Football League Division 1   at Deepdale   Attendance 18000
Result: **Preston North End 0 Manchester United 3**
Teamsheet: Moger, Stacey, Burgess, Duckworth, Roberts, Bell, Meredith, Halse, Turnbull J, Picken, Wall
Scorer(s):   Turnbull J 2, Halse

Match # 604 Monday 07/09/08   Football League Division 1   at Bank Street   Attendance 16000
Result: **Manchester United 2 Bury 1**
Teamsheet: Moger, Stacey, Burgess, Duckworth, Roberts, Bell, Meredith, Halse, Turnbull J, Christie, Wall
Scorer(s):   Turnbull J 2

Match # 605 Saturday 12/09/08   Football League Division 1   at Bank Street   Attendance 25000
Result: **Manchester United 6 Middlesbrough 3**
Teamsheet: Moger, Stacey, Burgess, Duckworth, Roberts, Bell, Meredith, Bannister, Turnbull J, Halse, Wall
Scorer(s):   Turnbull J 4, Halse, Wall

Match # 606 Saturday 19/09/08   Football League Division 1   at Hyde Road   Attendance 40000
Result: **Manchester City 1 Manchester United 2**
Teamsheet: Moger, Duckworth, Stacey, Bannister, Roberts, Downie, Meredith, Hardman, Turnbull J, Halse, Wall
Scorer(s):   Halse, Turnbull J

Match # 607 Saturday 26/09/08   Football League Division 1   at Bank Street   Attendance 25000
Result: **Manchester United 3 Liverpool 2**
Teamsheet: Moger, Duckworth, Stacey, Downie, Roberts, Bell, Meredith, Halse, Turnbull J, Turnbull A, Wall
Scorer(s):   Halse 2, Turnbull J

Match # 608 Saturday 03/10/08   Football League Division 1   at Gigg Lane   Attendance 25000
Result: **Bury 2 Manchester United 2**
Teamsheet: Moger, Hulme, Stacey, Duckworth, Roberts, Downie, Meredith, Halse, Turnbull J, Turnbull A, Wall
Scorer(s):   Halse, Wall

Match # 609 Saturday 10/10/08   Football League Division 1   at Bank Street   Attendance 14000
Result: **Manchester United 2 Sheffield United 1**
Teamsheet: Moger, Hulme, Stacey, Duckworth, Roberts, Bell, Meredith, Bannister, Turnbull J, Turnbull A, Wall
Scorer(s):   Bell 2

Match # 610 Saturday 17/10/08   Football League Division 1   at Villa Park   Attendance 40000
Result: **Aston Villa 3 Manchester United 1**
Teamsheet: Moger, Hulme, Stacey, Duckworth, Roberts, Bell, Meredith, Bannister, Halse, Turnbull A, Wall
Scorer(s):   Halse

Match # 611 Saturday 24/10/08   Football League Division 1   at Bank Street   Attendance 20000
Result: **Manchester United 2 Nottingham Forest 2**
Teamsheet: Wilcox, Linkson, Stacey, Duckworth, Roberts, Downie, Meredith, Halse, Turnbull J, Turnbull A, Wall
Scorer(s):   Turnbull A 2

Match # 612 Saturday 31/10/08   Football League Division 1   at Roker Park   Attendance 30000
Result: **Sunderland 6 Manchester United 1**
Teamsheet: Moger, Stacey, Burgess, Duckworth, Downie, Thomson, Meredith, Halse, Turnbull J, Turnbull A, Wall
Scorer(s):   Turnbull A

Match # 613 Saturday 07/11/08   Football League Division 1   at Bank Street   Attendance 15000
Result: **Manchester United 0 Chelsea 1**
Teamsheet: Moger, Stacey, Hayes, Duckworth, Picken, Bell, Meredith, Bannister, Halse, Turnbull A, Wall

Match # 614 Saturday 14/11/08   Football League Division 1   at Ewood Park   Attendance 25000
Result: **Blackburn Rovers 1 Manchester United 3**
Teamsheet: Moger, Stacey, Hayes, Duckworth, Bell, Downie, Meredith, Halse, Turnbull J, Wall, Hardman
Scorer(s):   Halse, Turnbull J, Wall

Match # 615 Saturday 21/11/08   Football League Division 1   at Bank Street   Attendance 15000
Result: **Manchester United 2 Bradford City 0**
Teamsheet: Moger, Stacey, Hayes, Duckworth, Curry, Downie, Meredith, Halse, Turnbull J, Picken, Wall
Scorer(s):   Picken, Wall

Match # 616 Saturday 28/11/08   Football League Division 1   at Bank Street   Attendance 20000
Result: **Manchester United 3 Sheffield Wednesday 1**
Teamsheet: Moger, Stacey, Hayes, Duckworth, Roberts, Downie, Meredith, Halse, Turnbull J, Picken, Wall
Scorer(s):   Halse, Picken, Turnbull J

Match # 617 Saturday 05/12/08   Football League Division 1   at Goodison Park   Attendance 35000
Result: **Everton 3 Manchester United 2**
Teamsheet: Moger, Stacey, Hayes, Duckworth, Roberts, Bell, Meredith, Bannister, Halse, Wall, Hardman
Scorer(s):   Bannister, Halse

Match # 618 Saturday 12/12/08   Football League Division 1   at Bank Street   Attendance 10000
Result: **Manchester United 4 Leicester City 2**
Teamsheet: Moger, Linkson, Hayes, Duckworth, Curry, Downie, Meredith, Halse, Picken, Wall, Hardman
Scorer(s):   Wall 3, Picken

Match # 619 Saturday 19/12/08   Football League Division 1   at Manor Field   Attendance 10000
Result: **Arsenal 0 Manchester United 1**
Teamsheet: Moger, Linkson, Hayes, Duckworth, Roberts, Downie, Meredith, Bannister, Halse, Picken, Wall
Scorer(s):   Halse

Match # 620 Friday 25/12/08   Football League Division 1   at St James' Park   Attendance 35000
Result: **Newcastle United 2 Manchester United 1**
Teamsheet: Moger, Stacey, Hayes, Duckworth, Roberts, Bell, Meredith, Bannister, Halse, Turnbull A, Wall
Scorer(s):   Wall

SEASON 1908/09 (continued)

Match # 621 Saturday 26/12/08 Football League Division 1 at Bank Street Attendance 40000
Result: **Manchester United 1 Newcastle United 0**
Teamsheet: Moger, Stacey, Hayes, Duckworth, Roberts, Bell, Meredith, Bannister, Halse, Turnbull A, Wall
Scorer(s): Halse

Match # 622 Friday 01/01/09 Football League Division 1 at Bank Street Attendance 15000
Result: **Manchester United 4 Notts County 3**
Teamsheet: Moger, Stacey, Hayes, Duckworth, Roberts, Bell, Meredith, Bannister, Halse, Turnbull A, Wall
Scorer(s): Halse 2, Roberts, Turnbull A

Match # 623 Saturday 02/01/09 Football League Division 1 at Bank Street Attendance 18000
Result: **Manchester United 0 Preston North End 2**
Teamsheet: Moger, Stacey, Hayes, Duckworth, Roberts, Bell, Meredith, Bannister, Picken, Turnbull A, Wall

Match # 624 Saturday 09/01/09 Football League Division 1 at Ayresome Park Attendance 15000
Result: **Middlesbrough 5 Manchester United 0**
Teamsheet: Moger, Stacey, Hayes, Duckworth, Roberts, Bell, Meredith, Bannister, Berry, Turnbull A, Wall

Match # 625 Saturday 16/01/09 FA Cup 1st Round at Bank Street Attendance 8300
Result: **Manchester United 1 Brighton 0**
Teamsheet: Moger, Stacey, Hayes, Duckworth, Roberts, Bell, Meredith, Halse, Turnbull J, Turnbull A, Wall
Scorer(s): Halse

Match # 626 Saturday 23/01/09 Football League Division 1 at Bank Street Attendance 40000
Result: **Manchester United 3 Manchester City 1**
Teamsheet: Moger, Stacey, Hayes, Duckworth, Roberts, Downie, Meredith, Livingstone, Halse, Turnbull A, Wall
Scorer(s): Livingstone 2, Wall

Match # 627 Saturday 30/01/09 Football League Division 1 at Anfield Attendance 30000
Result: **Liverpool 3 Manchester United 1**
Teamsheet: Moger, Stacey, Hayes, Duckworth, Roberts, Downie, Meredith, Livingstone, Halse, Turnbull A, Wall
Scorer(s): Turnbull A

Match # 628 Saturday 06/02/09 FA Cup 2nd Round at Bank Street Attendance 35217
Result: **Manchester United 1 Everton 0**
Teamsheet: Moger, Stacey, Hayes, Duckworth, Roberts, Bell, Halse, Livingstone, Turnbull J, Turnbull A, Wall
Scorer(s): Halse

Match # 629 Saturday 13/02/09 Football League Division 1 at Bramall Lane Attendance 12000
Result: **Sheffield United 0 Manchester United 0**
Teamsheet: Moger, Stacey, Hayes, Downie, Curry, Bell, Halse, Livingstone, Turnbull J, Turnbull A, Wall

Match # 630 Saturday 20/02/09 FA Cup 3rd Round at Bank Street Attendance 38500
Result: **Manchester United 6 Blackburn Rovers 1**
Teamsheet: Moger, Stacey, Hayes, Duckworth, Roberts, Bell, Halse, Livingstone, Turnbull J, Turnbull A, Wall
Scorer(s): Turnbull A 3, Turnbull J 3

Match # 631 Saturday 27/02/09 Football League Division 1 at City Ground Attendance 7000
Result: **Nottingham Forest 2 Manchester United 0**
Teamsheet: Moger, Stacey, Hayes, Downie, Curry, Bell, Payne, Bannister, Turnbull J, Picken, Wall

Match # 632 Wednesday 10/03/09 FA Cup 4th Round at Turf Moor Attendance 16850
Result: **Burnley 2 Manchester United 3**
Teamsheet: Moger, Stacey, Hayes, Duckworth, Roberts, Bell, Meredith, Halse, Turnbull J, Turnbull A, Wall
Scorer(s): Turnbull J 2, Halse

Match # 633 Saturday 13/03/09 Football League Division 1 at Stamford Bridge Attendance 30000
Result: **Chelsea 1 Manchester United 1**
Teamsheet: Moger, Stacey, Hayes, Duckworth, Roberts, Downie, Meredith, Halse, Turnbull J, Turnbull A, Wall
Scorer(s): Wall

Match # 634 Monday 15/03/09 Football League Division 1 at Bank Street Attendance 10000
Result: **Manchester United 2 Sunderland 2**
Teamsheet: Moger, Donnelly, Hayes, Downie, Roberts, Bell, Payne, Livingstone, Turnbull J, Turnbull A, Wall
Scorer(s): Payne, Turnbull J

Match # 635 Saturday 20/03/09 Football League Division 1 at Bank Street Attendance 11000
Result: **Manchester United 0 Blackburn Rovers 3**
Teamsheet: Moger, Holden, Linkson, Duckworth, Curry, Downie, Halse, Livingstone, Turnbull J, Picken, Wall

Match # 636 Saturday 27/03/09 FA Cup Semi-Final at Bramall Lane Attendance 40118
Result: **Manchester United 1 Newcastle United 0**
Teamsheet: Moger, Stacey, Hayes, Duckworth, Roberts, Bell, Meredith, Halse, Turnbull J, Turnbull A, Wall
Scorer(s): Halse

Match # 637 Wednesday 31/03/09 Football League Division 1 at Bank Street Attendance 10000
Result: **Manchester United 0 Aston Villa 2**
Teamsheet: Moger, Holden, Hayes, Duckworth, McGillivray, Downie, Meredith, Bannister, Livingstone, Picken, Ford

Match # 638 Saturday 03/04/09 Football League Division 1 at Hillsborough Attendance 15000
Result: **Sheffield Wednesday 2 Manchester United 0**
Teamsheet: Wilcox, Linkson, Stacey, Curry, Roberts, McGillivray, Meredith, Bannister, Quinn, Livingstone, Ford

SEASON 1908/09 (continued)

Match # 639	Friday 09/04/09	Football League Division 1	at Bank Street	Attendance 18000
Result:	**Manchester United 0 Bristol City 1**			
Teamsheet:	Moger, Hayes, Stacey, Duckworth, Roberts, Downie, Meredith, Bannister, Halse, Livingstone, Wall			

Match # 640	Saturday 10/04/09	Football League Division 1	at Bank Street	Attendance 8000
Result:	**Manchester United 2 Everton 2**			
Teamsheet:	Moger, Stacey, Hayes, Duckworth, Curry, Downie, Meredith, Halse, Turnbull J, Picken, Ford			
Scorer(s):	Turnbull J 2			

Match # 641	Monday 12/04/09	Football League Division 1	at Ashton Gate	Attendance 18000
Result:	**Bristol City 0 Manchester United 0**			
Teamsheet:	Moger, Stacey, Linkson, Duckworth, Roberts, Downie, Meredith, Livingstone, Turnbull J, Picken, Wall			

Match # 642	Tuesday 13/04/09	Football League Division 1	at Trent Bridge	Attendance 7000
Result:	**Notts County 0 Manchester United 1**			
Teamsheet:	Moger, Stacey, Linkson, Duckworth, Roberts, Downie, Meredith, Livingstone, Halse, Picken, Ford			
Scorer(s):	Livingstone			

Match # 643	Saturday 17/04/09	Football League Division 1	at Filbert Street	Attendance 8000
Result:	**Leicester City 3 Manchester United 2**			
Teamsheet:	Moger, Linkson, Hayes, Downie, Curry, Bell, Meredith, Livingstone, Turnbull J, Christie, Wall			
Scorer(s):	Turnbull J, Wall			

Match # 644	Saturday 24/04/09	FA Cup Final	at Crystal Palace	Attendance 71401
Result:	**Manchester United 1 Bristol City 0**			
Teamsheet:	Moger, Stacey, Hayes, Duckworth, Roberts, Bell, Meredith, Halse, Turnbull J, Turnbull A, Wall			
Scorer(s):	Turnbull A			

Match # 645	Tuesday 27/04/09	Football League Division 1	at Bank Street	Attendance 10000
Result:	**Manchester United 1 Arsenal 4**			
Teamsheet:	Moger, Stacey, Linkson, Duckworth, Roberts, Bell, Meredith, Halse, Turnbull J, Turnbull A, Wall			
Scorer(s):	Turnbull J			

Match # 646	Thursday 29/04/09	Football League Division 1	at Valley Parade	Attendance 30000
Result:	**Bradford City 1 Manchester United 0**			
Teamsheet:	Moger, Stacey, Linkson, Duckworth, Roberts, Bell, Meredith, Halse, Turnbull J, Turnbull A, Wall			

SEASON 1908/09 SUMMARY

APPEARANCES

PLAYER	LGE	FAC	TOT
Moger	36	6	42
Wall	34	6	40
Duckworth	33	6	39
Meredith	34	4	38
Stacey	32	6	38
Halse	29	6	35
Roberts	27	6	33
Hayes	22	6	28
Turnbull J	22	6	28
Bell	20	6	26
Turnbull A	19	6	25
Downie	23	–	23
Bannister	16	–	16
Livingstone	11	2	13
Picken	13	–	13
Linkson	10	–	10
Curry	8	–	8
Burgess	4	–	4
Ford	4	–	4
Hardman	4	–	4
Hulme	3	–	3
Christie	2	–	2
Holden	2	–	2
McGillivray	2	–	2
Payne	2	–	2
Wilcox	2	–	2
Berry	1	–	1
Donnelly	1	–	1
Quinn	1	–	1
Thomson	1	–	1

GOALSCORERS

PLAYER	LGE	FAC	TOT
Turnbull J	17	5	22
Halse	14	4	18
Wall	11	–	11
Turnbull A	5	4	9
Livingstone	3	–	3
Picken	3	–	3
Bell	2	–	2
Bannister	1	–	1
Payne	1	–	1
Roberts	1	–	1

RESULTS & ATTENDANCES SUMMARY

		P	W	D	L	F	A	TOTAL	AVGE
League	H	19	10	3	6	37	33	340000	17895
	A	19	5	4	10	21	35	430000	22632
	TOTAL	38	15	7	16	58	68	770000	20263
FA Cup	H	3	3	0	0	8	1	82017	27339
	A	1	1	0	0	3	2	16850	16850
	N	2	2	0	0	2	0	111519	55760
	TOTAL	6	6	0	0	13	3	210386	35064
Overall	H	22	13	3	6	45	34	422017	19183
	A	20	6	4	10	24	37	446850	22343
	N	2	2	0	0	2	0	111519	55760
	TOTAL	44	21	7	16	71	71	980386	22282

FINAL TABLE – LEAGUE DIVISION ONE

		P	W	D	L	F	A	W	D	L	F	A	PTS	GD
				HOME						AWAY				
1	Newcastle United	38	14	1	4	32	20	10	4	5	33	21	53	24
2	Everton	38	11	3	5	51	28	7	7	5	31	29	46	25
3	Sunderland	38	14	0	5	41	23	7	2	10	37	40	44	15
4	Blackburn Rovers	38	6	6	7	29	26	8	7	4	32	24	41	11
5	Sheffield Wednesday	38	15	0	4	48	24	2	6	11	19	37	40	6
6	Arsenal	38	9	3	7	24	18	5	7	7	28	31	38	3
7	Aston Villa	38	8	7	4	31	22	6	3	10	27	34	38	2
8	Bristol City	38	7	7	5	24	25	6	5	8	21	33	38	-13
9	Middlesbrough	38	11	2	6	38	21	3	7	9	21	32	37	6
10	Preston North End	38	8	7	4	29	17	5	4	10	19	27	37	4
11	Chelsea	38	8	7	4	33	22	6	2	11	23	39	37	-5
12	Sheffield United	38	9	5	5	31	25	5	4	10	20	34	37	-8
13	MANCHESTER UNITED	38	10	3	6	37	33	5	4	10	21	35	37	-10
14	Nottingham Forest	38	9	2	8	39	24	5	6	8	27	33	36	9
15	Notts County	38	9	4	6	31	23	5	4	10	20	25	36	3
16	Liverpool	38	9	5	5	36	25	6	1	12	21	40	36	-8
17	Bury	38	9	6	4	35	27	5	2	12	28	50	36	-14
18	Bradford City	38	7	6	6	27	20	5	4	10	20	27	34	0
19	Manchester City	38	12	3	4	50	23	3	1	15	17	46	34	-2
20	Leicester City	38	6	6	7	32	41	2	3	14	22	61	25	-48

SEASON 1909/10

Match # 647   Wednesday 01/09/09   Football League Division 1   at Bank Street   Attendance 12000
Result: **Manchester United 1 Bradford City 0**
Teamsheet: Moger, Stacey, Hayes, Duckworth, Roberts, Bell, Halse, Blott, Bannister, Turnbull A, Wall
Scorer(s):   Wall

Match # 648   Saturday 04/09/09   Football League Division 1   at Bank Street   Attendance 12000
Result: **Manchester United 2 Bury 0**
Teamsheet: Moger, Stacey, Hayes, Duckworth, Roberts, Bell, Halse, Livingstone, Turnbull J, Turnbull A, Wall
Scorer(s):   Turnbull J 2

Match # 649   Monday 06/09/09   Football League Division 1   at Bank Street   Attendance 6000
Result: **Manchester United 2 Notts County 1**
Teamsheet: Moger, Stacey, Hayes, Duckworth, Roberts, Bell, Halse, Livingstone, Turnbull J, Picken, Wall
Scorer(s):   Turnbull J, Wall

Match # 650   Saturday 11/09/09   Football League Division 1   at White Hart Lane   Attendance 40000
Result: **Tottenham Hotspur 2 Manchester United 2**
Teamsheet: Moger, Stacey, Hayes, Duckworth, Roberts, Downie, Blott, Halse, Turnbull J, Turnbull A, Wall
Scorer(s):   Turnbull J, Wall

Match # 651   Saturday 18/09/09   Football League Division 1   at Bank Street   Attendance 13000
Result: **Manchester United 1 Preston North End 1**
Teamsheet: Moger, Stacey, Hayes, Duckworth, Roberts, Downie, Meredith, Halse, Turnbull J, Turnbull A, Wall
Scorer(s):   Roberts

Match # 652   Saturday 25/09/09   Football League Division 1   at Trent Bridge   Attendance 11000
Result: **Notts County 3 Manchester United 2**
Teamsheet: Moger, Stacey, Hayes, Downie, Roberts, Blott, Meredith, Halse, Turnbull J, Turnbull A, Wall
Scorer(s):   Turnbull A 2

Match # 653   Saturday 02/10/09   Football League Division 1   at Bank Street   Attendance 30000
Result: **Manchester United 1 Newcastle United 1**
Teamsheet: Moger, Stacey, Hayes, Duckworth, Roberts, Bell, Meredith, Halse, Turnbull J, Turnbull A, Wall
Scorer(s):   Wall

Match # 654   Saturday 09/10/09   Football League Division 1   at Anfield   Attendance 30000
Result: **Liverpool 3 Manchester United 2**
Teamsheet: Round, Stacey, Hayes, Duckworth, Roberts, Bell, Meredith, Halse, Turnbull J, Turnbull A, Ford
Scorer(s):   Turnbull A 2

Match # 655   Saturday 16/10/09   Football League Division 1   at Bank Street   Attendance 20000
Result: **Manchester United 2 Aston Villa 0**
Teamsheet: Moger, Stacey, Hayes, Duckworth, Roberts, Bell, Meredith, Halse, Turnbull J, Turnbull A, Wall
Scorer(s):   Halse, Turnbull A

Match # 656   Saturday 23/10/09   Football League Division 1   at Bramall Lane   Attendance 30000
Result: **Sheffield United 0 Manchester United 1**
Teamsheet: Moger, Stacey, Hayes, Duckworth, Roberts, Bell, Meredith, Halse, Turnbull J, Turnbull A, Wall
Scorer(s):   Wall

Match # 657   Saturday 30/10/09   Football League Division 1   at Bank Street   Attendance 20000
Result: **Manchester United 1 Arsenal 0**
Teamsheet: Moger, Stacey, Hayes, Duckworth, Roberts, Blott, Meredith, Livingstone, Homer, Turnbull A, Wall
Scorer(s):   Wall

Match # 658   Saturday 06/11/09   Football League Division 1   at Burnden Park   Attendance 20000
Result: **Bolton Wanderers 2 Manchester United 3**
Teamsheet: Moger, Stacey, Hayes, Duckworth, Roberts, Bell, Meredith, Halse, Homer, Turnbull A, Wall
Scorer(s):   Homer 2, Halse

Match # 659   Saturday 13/11/09   Football League Division 1   at Bank Street   Attendance 10000
Result: **Manchester United 2 Chelsea 0**
Teamsheet: Moger, Stacey, Hayes, Duckworth, Roberts, Bell, Meredith, Halse, Homer, Turnbull A, Wall
Scorer(s):   Turnbull A, Wall

Match # 660   Saturday 20/11/09   Football League Division 1   at Ewood Park   Attendance 40000
Result: **Blackburn Rovers 3 Manchester United 2**
Teamsheet: Moger, Holden, Stacey, Duckworth, Roberts, Bell, Meredith, Picken, Homer, Turnbull A, Wall
Scorer(s):   Homer 2

Match # 661   Saturday 27/11/09   Football League Division 1   at Bank Street   Attendance 12000
Result: **Manchester United 2 Nottingham Forest 6**
Teamsheet: Moger, Stacey, Hayes, Duckworth, Roberts, Bell, Meredith, Halse, Homer, Picken, Wall
Scorer(s):   Halse, Wall

Match # 662   Saturday 04/12/09   Football League Division 1   at Roker Park   Attendance 12000
Result: **Sunderland 3 Manchester United 0**
Teamsheet: Moger, Holden, Hayes, Duckworth, Roberts, Bell, Meredith, Livingstone, Homer, Turnbull A, Wall

Match # 663   Saturday 18/12/09   Football League Division 1   at Ayresome Park   Attendance 10000
Result: **Middlesbrough 1 Manchester United 2**
Teamsheet: Moger, Holden, Hayes, Duckworth, Roberts, Bell, Meredith, Homer, Turnbull J, Turnbull A, Wall
Scorer(s):   Homer, Turnbull A

Match # 664   Saturday 25/12/09   Football League Division 1   at Bank Street   Attendance 25000
Result: **Manchester United 0 Sheffield Wednesday 3**
Teamsheet: Moger, Holden, Burgess, Duckworth, Roberts, Bell, Meredith, Homer, Turnbull J, Turnbull A, Wall

SEASON 1909/10 (continued)

Match # 665   Monday 27/12/09   Football League Division 1   at Hillsborough   Attendance 37000
Result: **Sheffield Wednesday 4 Manchester United 1**
Teamsheet: Moger, Stacey, Donnelly, Blott, Whalley, Bell, Meredith, Wall, Homer, Picken, Connor
Scorer(s):   Wall

Match # 666   Saturday 01/01/10   Football League Division 1   at Valley Parade   Attendance 25000
Result: **Bradford City 0 Manchester United 2**
Teamsheet: Moger, Stacey, Hayes, Livingstone, Whalley, Bell, Quinn, Picken, Homer, Turnbull A, Wall
Scorer(s):   Turnbull A, Wall

Match # 667   Saturday 08/01/10   Football League Division 1   at Gigg Lane   Attendance 10000
Result: **Bury 1 Manchester United 1**
Teamsheet: Moger, Stacey, Hayes, Livingstone, Whalley, Bell, Meredith, Picken, Homer, Turnbull A, Connor
Scorer(s):   Homer

Match # 668   Saturday 15/01/10   FA Cup 1st Round   at Turf Moor   Attendance 16628
Result: **Burnley 2 Manchester United 0**
Teamsheet: Moger, Stacey, Hayes, Duckworth, Roberts, Curry, Meredith, Picken, Halse, Turnbull A, Wall

Match # 669   Saturday 22/01/10   Football League Division 1   at Bank Street   Attendance 7000
Result: **Manchester United 5 Tottenham Hotspur 0**
Teamsheet: Moger, Stacey, Hayes, Livingstone, Roberts, Blott, Meredith, Halse, Homer, Hooper, Connor
Scorer(s):   Roberts 2, Connor, Hooper, Meredith

Match # 670   Saturday 05/02/10   Football League Division 1   at Deepdale   Attendance 4000
Result: **Preston North End 1 Manchester United 0**
Teamsheet: Moger, Stacey, Hayes, Livingstone, Roberts, Blott, Meredith, Picken, Halse, Hooper, Wall

Match # 671   Saturday 12/02/10   Football League Division 1   at St James' Park   Attendance 20000
Result: **Newcastle United 3 Manchester United 4**
Teamsheet: Moger, Stacey, Hayes, Livingstone, Roberts, Blott, Meredith, Picken, Halse, Turnbull A, Wall
Scorer(s):   Turnbull A 2, Blott, Roberts

Match # 672   Saturday 19/02/10   Football League Division 1   at Old Trafford   Attendance 45000
Result: **Manchester United 3 Liverpool 4**
Teamsheet: Moger, Stacey, Hayes, Duckworth, Roberts, Blott, Meredith, Halse, Homer, Turnbull A, Wall
Scorer(s):   Homer, Turnbull A, Wall

Match # 673   Saturday 26/02/10   Football League Division 1   at Villa Park   Attendance 20000
Result: **Aston Villa 7 Manchester United 1**
Teamsheet: Round, Stacey, Holden, Duckworth, Roberts, Bell, Meredith, Halse, Homer, Turnbull A, Connor
Scorer(s):   Meredith

Match # 674   Saturday 05/03/10   Football League Division 1   at Old Trafford   Attendance 40000
Result: **Manchester United 1 Sheffield United 0**
Teamsheet: Moger, Stacey, Hayes, Duckworth, Livingstone, Bell, Connor, Halse, Turnbull J, Picken, Wall
Scorer(s):   Picken

Match # 675   Saturday 12/03/10   Football League Division 1   at Manor Field   Attendance 4000
Result: **Arsenal 0 Manchester United 0**
Teamsheet: Moger, Stacey, Hayes, Duckworth, Whalley, Bell, Meredith, Halse, Turnbull J, Picken, Wall

Match # 676   Saturday 19/03/10   Football League Division 1   at Old Trafford   Attendance 20000
Result: **Manchester United 5 Bolton Wanderers 0**
Teamsheet: Moger, Duckworth, Stacey, Livingstone, Roberts, Bell, Meredith, Halse, Turnbull J, Picken, Wall
Scorer(s):   Halse, Meredith, Picken, Turnbull J, Wall

Match # 677   Friday 25/03/10   Football League Division 1   at Old Trafford   Attendance 50000
Result: **Manchester United 2 Bristol City 1**
Teamsheet: Moger, Hayes, Stacey, Whalley, Bell, Meredith, Halse, Turnbull J, Picken, Wall
Scorer(s):   Picken, Turnbull J

Match # 678   Saturday 26/03/10   Football League Division 1   at Stamford Bridge   Attendance 25000
Result: **Chelsea 1 Manchester United 1**
Teamsheet: Moger, Stacey, Hayes, Duckworth, Whalley, Bell, Meredith, Halse, Turnbull J, Turnbull A, Wall
Scorer(s):   Turnbull J

Match # 679   Monday 28/03/10   Football League Division 1   at Ashton Gate   Attendance 18000
Result: **Bristol City 2 Manchester United 1**
Teamsheet: Moger, Duckworth, Hayes, Blott, Whalley, Bell, Meredith, Halse, Turnbull J, Picken, Wall
Scorer(s):   Meredith

Match # 680   Saturday 02/04/10   Football League Division 1   at Old Trafford   Attendance 20000
Result: **Manchester United 2 Blackburn Rovers 0**
Teamsheet: Moger, Stacey, Hayes, Duckworth, Whalley, Livingstone, Meredith, Halse, Turnbull J, Picken, Connor
Scorer(s):   Halse 2

Match # 681   Wednesday 06/04/10   Football League Division 1   at Old Trafford   Attendance 5500
Result: **Manchester United 3 Everton 2**
Teamsheet: Moger, Stacey, Hayes, Duckworth, Whalley, Livingstone, Meredith, Halse, Turnbull J, Picken, Wall
Scorer(s):   Turnbull J 2, Meredith

Match # 682   Saturday 09/04/10   Football League Division 1   at City Ground   Attendance 7000
Result: **Nottingham Forest 2 Manchester United 0**
Teamsheet: Moger, Stacey, Hayes, Livingstone, Roberts, Bell, Meredith, Picken, Halse, Turnbull A, Wall

SEASON 1909/10 (continued)

Match # 683	Saturday 16/04/10	Football League Division 1	at Old Trafford	Attendance 12000
Result:	**Manchester United 2 Sunderland 0**			
Teamsheet:	Moger, Stacey, Donnelly, Livingstone, Roberts, Bell, Meredith, Picken, Homer, Turnbull A, Wall			
Scorer(s):	Turnbull A, Wall			

Match # 684	Saturday 23/04/10	Football League Division 1	at Goodison Park	Attendance 10000
Result:	**Everton 3 Manchester United 3**			
Teamsheet:	Moger, Holden, Donnelly, Duckworth, Roberts, Bell, Connor, Picken, Homer, Turnbull A, Wall			
Scorer(s):	Homer, Turnbull A, Wall			

Match # 685	Saturday 30/04/10	Football League Division 1	at Old Trafford	Attendance 10000
Result:	**Manchester United 4 Middlesbrough 1**			
Teamsheet:	Moger, Holden, Donnelly, Duckworth, Roberts, Livingstone, Meredith, Picken, Homer, Turnbull A, Connor			
Scorer(s):	Picken 4			

SEASON 1909/10 SUMMARY

APPEARANCES

PLAYER	LGE	FAC	TOT
Moger	36	1	37
Stacey	32	1	33
Wall	32	1	33
Meredith	31	1	32
Hayes	30	1	31
Duckworth	29	1	30
Roberts	28	1	29
Halse	27	1	28
Bell	27	–	27
Turnbull A	26	1	27
Picken	19	1	20
Turnbull J	19	–	19
Homer	17	–	17
Livingstone	16	–	16
Blott	10	–	10
Whalley	9	–	9
Connor	8	–	8
Holden	7	–	7
Donnelly	4	–	4
Downie	3	–	3
Hooper	2	–	2
Round	2	–	2
Bannister	1	–	1
Burgess	1	–	1
Curry	–	1	1
Ford	1	–	1
Quinn	1	–	1

GOALSCORERS

PLAYER	LGE	FAC	TOT
Wall	14	–	14
Turnbull A	13	–	13
Turnbull J	9	–	9
Homer	8	–	8
Picken	7	–	7
Halse	6	–	6
Meredith	5	–	5
Roberts	4	–	4
Blott	1	–	1
Connor	1	–	1
Hooper	1	–	1

RESULTS & ATTENDANCES SUMMARY

		P	W	D	L	F	A	TOTAL	AVGE
League	H	19	14	2	3	41	20	369500	19447
	A	19	5	5	9	28	41	373000	19632
TOTAL		38	19	7	12	69	61	742500	19539
FA Cup	H	0	0	0	0	0	0	0	n/a
	A	1	0	0	1	0	2	16628	16628
TOTAL		1	0	0	1	0	2	16628	16628
Overall	H	19	14	2	3	41	20	369500	19447
	A	20	5	5	10	28	43	389628	19481
TOTAL		39	19	7	13	69	63	759128	19465

FINAL TABLE – LEAGUE DIVISION ONE

		P	W	D	L	F	A	W	D	L	F	A	PTS	GD
				HOME					AWAY					
1	Aston Villa	38	17	2	0	62	19	6	5	8	22	23	53	42
2	Liverpool	38	13	3	3	47	23	8	3	8	31	34	48	21
3	Blackburn Rovers	38	13	6	0	47	17	5	3	11	26	38	45	18
4	Newcastle United	38	11	3	5	33	22	8	4	7	37	34	45	14
5	MANCHESTER UNITED	38	14	2	3	41	20	5	5	9	28	41	45	8
6	Sheffield United	38	10	5	4	42	19	6	5	8	20	22	42	21
7	Bradford City	38	12	3	4	38	17	5	5	9	26	30	42	17
8	Sunderland	38	12	3	4	40	18	6	2	11	26	33	41	15
9	Notts County	38	10	5	4	41	26	5	5	9	26	33	40	8
10	Everton	38	8	6	5	30	28	8	2	9	21	28	40	-5
11	Sheffield Wednesday	38	11	4	4	38	28	4	5	10	22	35	39	-3
12	Preston North End	38	14	2	3	36	13	1	3	15	16	45	35	-6
13	Bury	38	8	3	8	35	30	4	6	9	27	36	33	-4
14	Nottingham Forest	38	4	7	8	19	34	7	4	8	35	38	33	-18
15	Tottenham Hotspur	38	10	6	3	35	23	1	4	14	18	46	32	-16
16	Bristol City	38	9	5	5	28	18	3	3	13	17	42	32	-15
17	Middlesbrough	38	8	4	7	34	36	3	5	11	22	37	31	-17
18	Arsenal	38	6	5	8	17	19	5	4	10	20	48	31	-30
19	Chelsea	38	10	4	5	32	24	1	3	15	15	46	29	-23
20	Bolton Wanderers	38	7	2	10	31	34	2	4	13	13	37	24	-27

SEASON 1910/11

Match # 686 Thursday 01/09/10   Football League Division 1   at Manor Field   Attendance 15000
Result: **Arsenal 1 Manchester United 2**
Teamsheet: Moger, Holden, Stacey, Duckworth, Roberts, Bell, Meredith, Halse, West, Turnbull, Wall
Scorer(s):   Halse, West

Match # 687 Saturday 03/09/10   Football League Division 1   at Old Trafford   Attendance 40000
Result: **Manchester United 3 Blackburn Rovers 2**
Teamsheet: Moger, Holden, Stacey, Duckworth, Roberts, Bell, Meredith, Halse, West, Turnbull, Wall
Scorer(s):   Meredith, Turnbull, West

Match # 688 Saturday 10/09/10   Football League Division 1   at City Ground   Attendance 20000
Result: **Nottingham Forest 2 Manchester United 1**
Teamsheet: Moger, Stacey, Hayes, Duckworth, Roberts, Bell, Meredith, Halse, West, Turnbull, Wall
Scorer(s):   Turnbull

Match # 689 Saturday 17/09/10   Football League Division 1   at Old Trafford   Attendance 60000
Result: **Manchester United 2 Manchester City 1**
Teamsheet: Moger, Linkson, Stacey, Duckworth, Roberts, Bell, Meredith, Halse, West, Turnbull, Wall
Scorer(s):   Turnbull, West

Match # 690 Saturday 24/09/10   Football League Division 1   at Goodison Park   Attendance 25000
Result: **Everton 0 Manchester United 1**
Teamsheet: Moger, Holden, Stacey, Duckworth, Roberts, Bell, Meredith, Halse, West, Turnbull, Wall
Scorer(s):   Turnbull

Match # 691 Saturday 01/10/10   Football League Division 1   at Old Trafford   Attendance 20000
Result: **Manchester United 3 Sheffield Wednesday 2**
Teamsheet: Moger, Holden, Stacey, Duckworth, Roberts, Bell, Meredith, Halse, West, Turnbull, Wall
Scorer(s):   Wall 2, West

Match # 692 Saturday 08/10/10   ·   Football League Division 1   at Ashton Gate   Attendance 20000
Result: **Bristol City 0 Manchester United 1**
Teamsheet: Moger, Holden, Stacey, Livingstone, Roberts, Bell, Meredith, Halse, West, Picken, Wall
Scorer(s):   Halse

Match # 693 Saturday 15/10/10   Football League Division 1   at Old Trafford   Attendance 50000
Result: **Manchester United 2 Newcastle United 0**
Teamsheet: Moger, Holden, Stacey, Duckworth, Roberts, Livingstone, Meredith, Halse, West, Turnbull, Wall
Scorer(s):   Halse, Turnbull

Match # 694 Saturday 22/10/10   Football League Division 1   at White Hart Lane   Attendance 30000
Result: **Tottenham Hotspur 2 Manchester United 2**
Teamsheet: Moger, Holden, Stacey, Duckworth, Roberts, Livingstone, Meredith, Halse, West, Turnbull, Connor
Scorer(s):   West 2

Match # 695 Saturday 29/10/10   Football League Division 1   at Old Trafford   Attendance 35000
Result: **Manchester United 1 Middlesbrough 2**
Teamsheet: Moger, Linkson, Stacey, Duckworth, Roberts, Livingstone, Meredith, Halse, West, Turnbull, Connor
Scorer(s):   Turnbull

Match # 696 Saturday 05/11/10   Football League Division 1   at Deepdale   Attendance 13000
Result: **Preston North End 0 Manchester United 2**
Teamsheet: Moger, Linkson, Stacey, Duckworth, Roberts, Curry, Meredith, Halse, West, Turnbull, Connor
Scorer(s):   Turnbull, West

Match # 697 Saturday 12/11/10   Football League Division 1   at Old Trafford   Attendance 13000
Result: **Manchester United 0 Notts County 0**
Teamsheet: Moger, Linkson, Stacey, Duckworth, Roberts, Curry, Meredith, Halse, West, Turnbull, Wall

Match # 698 Saturday 19/11/10   Football League Division 1   at Boundary Park   Attendance 25000
Result: **Oldham Athletic 1 Manchester United 3**
Teamsheet: Moger, Linkson, Stacey, Livingstone, Roberts, Curry, Meredith, Halse, West, Turnbull, Wall
Scorer(s):   Turnbull 2, Wall

Match # 699 Saturday 26/11/10   Football League Division 1   at Anfield   Attendance 8000
Result: **Liverpool 3 Manchester United 2**
Teamsheet: Moger, Linkson, Stacey, Livingstone, Roberts, Curry, Meredith, Halse, Hooper, Turnbull, Wall
Scorer(s):   Roberts, Turnbull

Match # 700 Saturday 03/12/10   Football League Division 1   at Old Trafford   Attendance 7000
Result: **Manchester United 3 Bury 2**
Teamsheet: Moger, Linkson, Stacey, Livingstone, Roberts, Curry, Meredith, Picken, Homer, Turnbull, Wall
Scorer(s):   Homer 2, Turnbull

Match # 701 Saturday 10/12/10   Football League Division 1   at Bramall Lane   Attendance 8000
Result: **Sheffield United 2 Manchester United 0**
Teamsheet: Moger, Holden, Stacey, Livingstone, Roberts, Whalley, Meredith, Picken, Homer, Turnbull, Wall

Match # 702 Saturday 17/12/10   Football League Division 1   at Old Trafford   Attendance 20000
Result: **Manchester United 2 Aston Villa 0**
Teamsheet: Moger, Donnelly, Stacey, Whalley, Roberts, Bell, Meredith, Picken, West, Turnbull, Wall
Scorer(s):   Turnbull, West

Match # 703 Saturday 24/12/10   Football League Division 1   at Roker Park   Attendance 30000
Result: **Sunderland 1 Manchester United 2**
Teamsheet: Moger, Donnelly, Stacey, Whalley, Roberts, Bell, Meredith, Picken, West, Turnbull, Wall
Scorer(s):   Meredith, Turnbull

SEASON 1910/11 (continued)

Match # 704 Monday 26/12/10   Football League Division 1   at Old Trafford   Attendance 40000
Result: **Manchester United 5 Arsenal 0**
Teamsheet: Moger, Donnelly, Stacey, Whalley, Roberts, Bell, Meredith, Picken, West, Turnbull, Wall
Scorer(s): Picken 2, West 2, Meredith

Match # 705 Tuesday 27/12/10   Football League Division 1   at Valley Parade   Attendance 35000
Result: **Bradford City 1 Manchester United 0**
Teamsheet: Moger, Donnelly, Stacey, Whalley, Roberts, Livingstone, Sheldon, Picken, West, Turnbull, Wall

Match # 706 Saturday 31/12/10   Football League Division 1   at Ewood Park   Attendance 20000
Result: **Blackburn Rovers 1 Manchester United 0**
Teamsheet: Moger, Donnelly, Stacey, Whalley, Roberts, Bell, Sheldon, Picken, West, Turnbull, Wall

Match # 707 Monday 02/01/11   Football League Division 1   at Old Trafford   Attendance 40000
Result: **Manchester United 1 Bradford City 0**
Teamsheet: Moger, Donnelly, Stacey, Livingstone, Whalley, Bell, Meredith, Picken, West, Turnbull, Wall
Scorer(s): Meredith

Match # 708 Saturday 07/01/11   Football League Division 1   at Old Trafford   Attendance 10000
Result: **Manchester United 4 Nottingham Forest 2**
Teamsheet: Moger, Donnelly, Stacey, Whalley, Roberts, Bell, Meredith, Picken, Homer, West, Wall
Scorer(s): Homer, Picken, Wall, own goal

Match # 709 Saturday 14/01/11   FA Cup 1st Round   at Bloomfield Road   Attendance 12000
Result: **Blackpool 1 Manchester United 2**
Teamsheet: Moger, Donnelly, Stacey, Duckworth, Roberts, Bell, Meredith, Picken, West, Turnbull, Wall
Scorer(s): Picken, West

Match # 710 Saturday 21/01/11   Football League Division 1   at Hyde Road   Attendance 40000
Result: **Manchester City 1 Manchester United 1**
Teamsheet: Moger, Donnelly, Stacey, Duckworth, Roberts, Bell, Meredith, Halse, West, Turnbull, Wall
Scorer(s): Turnbull

Match # 711 Saturday 28/01/11   Football League Division 1   at Old Trafford   Attendance 45000
Result: **Manchester United 2 Everton 2**
Teamsheet: Moger, Donnelly, Stacey, Duckworth, Roberts, Bell, Sheldon, Halse, West, Turnbull, Wall
Scorer(s): Duckworth, Wall

Match # 712 Saturday 04/02/11   FA Cup 2nd Round   at Old Trafford   Attendance 65101
Result: **Manchester United 2 Aston Villa 1**
Teamsheet: Moger, Donnelly, Stacey, Duckworth, Roberts, Bell, Meredith, Halse, West, Turnbull, Wall
Scorer(s): Halse, Wall

Match # 713 Saturday 11/02/11   Football League Division 1   at Old Trafford   Attendance 14000
Result: **Manchester United 3 Bristol City 1**
Teamsheet: Edmonds, Donnelly, Stacey, Duckworth, Roberts, Bell, Meredith, Homer, West, Picken, Wall
Scorer(s): Homer, Picken, West

Match # 714 Saturday 18/02/11   Football League Division 1   at St James' Park   Attendance 45000
Result: **Newcastle United 0 Manchester United 1**
Teamsheet: Edmonds, Hofton, Donnelly, Duckworth, Roberts, Bell, Meredith, Halse, West, Turnbull, Wall
Scorer(s): Halse

Match # 715 Saturday 25/02/11   FA Cup 3rd Round   at Upton Park   Attendance 26000
Result: **West Ham United 2 Manchester United 1**
Teamsheet: Edmonds, Donnelly, Stacey, Duckworth, Roberts, Bell, Meredith, Halse, West, Turnbull, Wall
Scorer(s): Turnbull

Match # 716 Saturday 04/03/11   Football League Division 1   at Ayresome Park   Attendance 8000
Result: **Middlesbrough 2 Manchester United 2**
Teamsheet: Edmonds, Donnelly, Stacey, Duckworth, Whalley, Bell, Meredith, Homer, West, Turnbull, Wall
Scorer(s): Turnbull, West

Match # 717 Saturday 11/03/11   Football League Division 1   at Old Trafford   Attendance 25000
Result: **Manchester United 5 Preston North End 0**
Teamsheet: Edmonds, Hofton, Stacey, Duckworth, Roberts, Bell, Meredith, Picken, West, Turnbull, Connor
Scorer(s): West 2, Connor, Duckworth, Turnbull

Match # 718 Wednesday 15/03/11   Football League Division 1   at Old Trafford   Attendance 10000
Result: **Manchester United 3 Tottenham Hotspur 2**
Teamsheet: Edmonds, Hofton, Stacey, Duckworth, Roberts, Bell, Meredith, Picken, West, Turnbull, Connor
Scorer(s): Meredith, Turnbull, West

Match # 719 Saturday 18/03/11   Football League Division 1   at Meadow Lane   Attendance 12000
Result: **Notts County 1 Manchester United 0**
Teamsheet: Edmonds, Donnelly, Stacey, Duckworth, Roberts, Bell, Meredith, Picken, West, Turnbull, Connor

Match # 720 Saturday 25/03/11   Football League Division 1   at Old Trafford   Attendance 35000
Result: **Manchester United 0 Oldham Athletic 0**
Teamsheet: Edmonds, Hofton, Stacey, Duckworth, Roberts, Bell, Meredith, Sheldon, West, Turnbull, Wall

Match # 721 Saturday 01/04/11   Football League Division 1   at Old Trafford   Attendance 20000
Result: **Manchester United 2 Liverpool 0**
Teamsheet: Edmonds, Hofton, Stacey, Whalley, Roberts, Bell, Meredith, Halse, West, Turnbull, Sheldon
Scorer(s): West 2

SEASON 1910/11 (continued)

Match # 722	Saturday 08/04/11	Football League Division 1	at Gigg Lane	Attendance 20000
Result:	**Bury 0 Manchester United 3**			
Teamsheet:	Edmonds, Hofton, Stacey, Whalley, Roberts, Bell, Meredith, Halse, Homer, Turnbull, West			
Scorer(s):	Homer 2, Halse			

Match # 723	Saturday 15/04/11	Football League Division 1	at Old Trafford	Attendance 22000
Result:	**Manchester United 1 Sheffield United 1**			
Teamsheet:	Edmonds, Hofton, Stacey, Whalley, Roberts, Bell, Meredith, Halse, Homer, Turnbull, West			
Scorer(s):	West			

Match # 724	Monday 17/04/11	Football League Division 1	at Hillsborough	Attendance 25000
Result:	**Sheffield Wednesday 0 Manchester United 0**			
Teamsheet:	Edmonds, Hofton, Donnelly, Hodge, Bell, Whalley, Meredith, Halse, Hooper, Turnbull, West			

Match # 725	Saturday 22/04/11	Football League Division 1	at Villa Park	Attendance 50000
Result:	**Aston Villa 4 Manchester United 2**			
Teamsheet:	Edmonds, Hofton, Stacey, Duckworth, Whalley, Bell, Meredith, Halse, West, Turnbull, Connor			
Scorer(s):	Halse 2			

Match # 726	Saturday 29/04/11	Football League Division 1	at Old Trafford	Attendance 10000
Result:	**Manchester United 5 Sunderland 1**			
Teamsheet:	Edmonds, Donnelly, Stacey, Duckworth, Whalley, Hodge, Meredith, Halse, West, Turnbull, Blott			
Scorer(s):	Halse 2, Turnbull, West, own goal			

SEASON 1910/11 SUMMARY

APPEARANCES

PLAYER	LGE	FAC	TOT
Stacey	36	3	39
Meredith	35	3	38
Turnbull	35	3	38
West	35	3	38
Roberts	33	3	36
Bell	27	3	30
Wall	26	3	29
Moger	25	2	27
Duckworth	22	3	25
Halse	23	2	25
Donnelly	15	3	18
Picken	14	1	15
Whalley	15	–	15

APPEARANCES

PLAYER	LGE	FAC	TOT
Edmonds	13	1	14
Livingstone	10	–	10
Hofton	9	–	9
Holden	8	–	8
Connor	7	–	7
Homer	7	–	7
Linkson	7	–	7
Curry	5	–	5
Sheldon	5	–	5
Hodge	2	–	2
Hooper	2	–	2
Blott	1	–	1
Hayes	1	–	1

GOALSCORERS

PLAYER	LGE	FAC	TOT
West	19	1	20
Turnbull	18	1	19
Halse	9	1	10
Wall	5	1	6
Homer	6	–	6
Meredith	5	–	5
Picken	4	1	5
Duckworth	2	–	2
Connor	1	–	1
Roberts	1	–	1
own goals	2	–	2

RESULTS & ATTENDANCES SUMMARY

		P	W	D	L	F	A	TOTAL	AVGE
League	H	19	14	4	1	47	18	516000	27158
	A	19	8	4	7	25	22	449000	23632
TOTAL		38	22	8	8	72	40	965000	25395
FA Cup	H	1	1	0	0	2	1	65101	65101
	A	2	1	0	1	3	3	38000	19000
TOTAL		3	2	0	1	5	4	103101	34367
Overall	H	20	15	4	1	49	19	581101	29055
	A	21	9	4	8	28	25	487000	23190
TOTAL		41	24	8	9	77	44	1068101	26051

FINAL TABLE – LEAGUE DIVISION ONE

		P	HOME W	HOME D	HOME L	HOME F	HOME A	AWAY W	AWAY D	AWAY L	AWAY F	AWAY A	PTS	GD
1	MANCHESTER UNITED	38	14	4	1	47	18	8	4	7	25	22	52	32
2	Aston Villa	38	15	3	1	50	18	7	4	8	19	23	51	28
3	Sunderland	38	10	6	3	44	22	5	9	5	23	26	45	19
4	Everton	38	12	3	4	34	17	7	4	8	16	19	45	14
5	Bradford City	38	13	1	5	33	16	7	4	8	18	26	45	9
6	Sheffield Wednesday	38	10	5	4	24	15	7	3	9	23	33	42	-1
7	Oldham Athletic	38	13	4	2	30	12	3	5	11	14	29	41	3
8	Newcastle United	38	8	7	4	37	18	7	3	9	24	25	40	18
9	Sheffield United	38	8	3	8	27	21	7	5	7	22	22	38	6
10	Arsenal	38	9	6	4	24	14	4	6	9	17	35	38	-8
11	Notts County	38	9	6	4	21	16	5	4	10	16	29	38	-8
12	Blackburn Rovers	38	12	2	5	40	14	1	9	9	22	40	37	8
13	Liverpool	38	11	3	5	38	19	4	4	11	15	34	37	0
14	Preston North End	38	8	5	6	25	19	4	6	9	15	30	35	-9
15	Tottenham Hotspur	38	10	5	4	40	23	3	1	15	12	40	32	-11
16	Middlesbrough	38	9	5	5	31	21	2	5	12	18	42	32	-14
17	Manchester City	38	7	5	7	26	26	2	8	9	17	32	31	-15
18	Bury	38	8	9	2	27	18	1	2	16	16	53	29	-28
19	Bristol City	38	8	4	7	23	21	3	1	15	20	45	27	-23
20	Nottingham Forest	38	5	4	10	28	31	4	3	12	27	44	25	-20

SEASON 1911/12

Match # 727 Saturday 02/09/11   Football League Division 1   at Hyde Road   Attendance 35000
Result: **Manchester City 0   Manchester United 0**
Teamsheet: Edmonds, Hofton, Stacey, Duckworth, Roberts, Bell, Meredith, Halse, Homer, Turnbull, Wall

Match # 728 Saturday 09/09/11   Football League Division 1   at Old Trafford   Attendance 20000
Result: **Manchester United 2   Everton 1**
Teamsheet: Edmonds, Hofton, Stacey, Duckworth, Roberts, Bell, Meredith, Halse, Anderson, Turnbull, Wall
Scorer(s):   Halse, Turnbull

Match # 729 Saturday 16/09/11   Football League Division 1   at The Hawthorns   Attendance 35000
Result: **West Bromwich Albion 1   Manchester United 0**
Teamsheet: Edmonds, Hofton, Stacey, Duckworth, Roberts, Bell, Meredith, Hamill, Halse, Turnbull, Wall

Match # 730 Saturday 23/09/11   Football League Division 1   at Old Trafford   Attendance 20000
Result: **Manchester United 2   Sunderland 2**
Teamsheet: Edmonds, Hofton, Stacey, Duckworth, Roberts, Bell, Meredith, Hamill, Halse, Turnbull, Wall
Scorer(s):   Stacey 2

Match # 731 Monday 25/09/11   FA Charity Shield   at Stamford Bridge   Attendance 10000
Result: **Manchester United 8   Swindon Town 4**
Teamsheet: Edmonds, Hofton, Stacey, Duckworth, Roberts, Bell, Meredith, Hamill, Halse, Turnbull, Wall
Scorer(s):   Halse 6, Turnbull, Wall

Match # 732 Saturday 30/09/11   Football League Division 1   at Ewood Park   Attendance 30000
Result: **Blackburn Rovers 2   Manchester United 2**
Teamsheet: Edmonds, Hofton, Stacey, Duckworth, Roberts, Bell, Sheldon, Halse, West, Turnbull, Wall
Scorer(s):   West 2

Match # 733 Saturday 07/10/11   Football League Division 1   at Old Trafford   Attendance 30000
Result: **Manchester United 3   Sheffield Wednesday 1**
Teamsheet: Edmonds, Hofton, Stacey, Duckworth, Roberts, Bell, Meredith, Halse, West, Turnbull, Wall
Scorer(s):   Halse 2, West

Match # 734 Saturday 14/10/11   Football League Division 1   at Gigg Lane   Attendance 18000
Result: **Bury 0   Manchester United 1**
Teamsheet: Edmonds, Hofton, Stacey, Duckworth, Roberts, Bell, Meredith, Halse, West, Turnbull, Wall
Scorer(s):   Turnbull

Match # 735 Saturday 21/10/11   Football League Division 1   at Old Trafford   Attendance 20000
Result: **Manchester United 3   Middlesbrough 4**
Teamsheet: Edmonds, Holden, Stacey, Duckworth, Roberts, Bell, Meredith, Halse, West, Turnbull, Wall
Scorer(s):   Halse, Turnbull, West

Match # 736 Saturday 28/10/11   Football League Division 1   at Meadow Lane   Attendance 15000
Result: **Notts County 0   Manchester United 1**
Teamsheet: Edmonds, Donnelly, Stacey, Whalley, Roberts, Bell, Meredith, Halse, West, Turnbull, Blott
Scorer(s):   Turnbull

Match # 737 Saturday 04/11/11   Football League Division 1   at Old Trafford   Attendance 20000
Result: **Manchester United 1   Tottenham Hotspur 2**
Teamsheet: Edmonds, Donnelly, Stacey, Whalley, Roberts, Bell, Meredith, Halse, West, Turnbull, Wall
Scorer(s):   Halse

Match # 738 Saturday 11/11/11   Football League Division 1   at Old Trafford   Attendance 10000
Result: **Manchester United 0   Preston North End 0**
Teamsheet: Edmonds, Donnelly, Stacey, Duckworth, Roberts, Bell, Meredith, Halse, West, Turnbull, Blott

Match # 739 Saturday 18/11/11   Football League Division 1   at Anfield   Attendance 15000
Result: **Liverpool 3   Manchester United 2**
Teamsheet: Edmonds, Donnelly, Stacey, Duckworth, Roberts, Bell, Meredith, Halse, West, Turnbull, Blott
Scorer(s):   Roberts, West

Match # 740 Saturday 25/11/11   Football League Division 1   at Old Trafford   Attendance 20000
Result: **Manchester United 3   Aston Villa 1**
Teamsheet: Moger, Linkson, Stacey, Duckworth, Roberts, Bell, Meredith, Halse, West, Turnbull, Wall
Scorer(s):   West 2, Roberts

Match # 741 Saturday 02/12/11   Football League Division 1   at St James' Park   Attendance 40000
Result: **Newcastle United 2   Manchester United 3**
Teamsheet: Edmonds, Linkson, Stacey, Duckworth, Roberts, Bell, Meredith, Halse, West, Turnbull, Wall
Scorer(s):   West 2, Halse

Match # 742 Saturday 09/12/11   Football League Division 1   at Old Trafford   Attendance 12000
Result: **Manchester United 1   Sheffield United 0**
Teamsheet: Edmonds, Linkson, Stacey, Duckworth, Roberts, Bell, Meredith, Halse, West, Turnbull, Wall
Scorer(s):   Halse

Match # 743 Saturday 16/12/11   Football League Division 1   at Boundary Park   Attendance 20000
Result: **Oldham Athletic 2   Manchester United 2**
Teamsheet: Edmonds, Linkson, Stacey, Duckworth, Roberts, Bell, Meredith, Halse, West, Turnbull, Wall
Scorer(s):   Turnbull, West

Match # 744 Saturday 23/12/11   Football League Division 1   at Old Trafford   Attendance 20000
Result: **Manchester United 2   Bolton Wanderers 0**
Teamsheet: Edmonds, Linkson, Stacey, Duckworth, Roberts, Bell, Meredith, Halse, West, Turnbull, Wall
Scorer(s):   Halse, Turnbull

SEASON 1911/12 (continued)

Match # 745 Monday 25/12/11 Football League Division 1 at Old Trafford Attendance 50000
Result: **Manchester United 0 Bradford City 1**
Teamsheet: Edmonds, Linkson, Stacey, Duckworth, Roberts, Bell, Meredith, Halse, West, Turnbull, Wall

Match # 746 Tuesday 26/12/11 Football League Division 1 at Valley Parade Attendance 40000
Result: **Bradford City 0 Manchester United 1**
Teamsheet: Edmonds, Linkson, Stacey, Duckworth, Roberts, Whalley, Meredith, Hamill, West, Turnbull, Wall
Scorer(s): West

Match # 747 Saturday 30/12/11 Football League Division 1 at Old Trafford Attendance 50000
Result: **Manchester United 0 Manchester City 0**
Teamsheet: Edmonds, Linkson, Stacey, Duckworth, Roberts, Bell, Meredith, Hamill, West, Turnbull, Wall

Match # 748 Monday 01/01/12 Football League Division 1 at Old Trafford Attendance 20000
Result: **Manchester United 2 Arsenal 0**
Teamsheet: Edmonds, Linkson, Stacey, Duckworth, Roberts, Bell, Meredith, Hamill, West, Turnbull, Wall
Scorer(s): Meredith, West

Match # 749 Saturday 06/01/12 Football League Division 1 at Goodison Park Attendance 12000
Result: **Everton 4 Manchester United 0**
Teamsheet: Edmonds, Holden, Donnelly, Duckworth, Roberts, Bell, Meredith, Hamill, West, Blott, Wall

Match # 750 Saturday 13/01/12 FA Cup 1st Round at Old Trafford Attendance 19579
Result: **Manchester United 3 Huddersfield Town 1**
Teamsheet: Edmonds, Holden, Stacey, Duckworth, Roberts, Bell, Meredith, Halse, West, Turnbull, Wall
Scorer(s): West 2, Halse

Match # 751 Saturday 20/01/12 Football League Division 1 at Old Trafford Attendance 8000
Result: **Manchester United 1 West Bromwich Albion 2**
Teamsheet: Edmonds, Holden, Stacey, Duckworth, Roberts, Bell, Meredith, Halse, McCarthy, Turnbull, Wall
Scorer(s): Wall

Match # 752 Saturday 27/01/12 Football League Division 1 at Roker Park Attendance 12000
Result: **Sunderland 5 Manchester United 0**
Teamsheet: Edmonds, Holden, Stacey, Duckworth, Roberts, Bell, Meredith, Hamill, Whalley, Turnbull, Wall

Match # 753 Saturday 03/02/12 FA Cup 2nd Round at Highfield Road Attendance 17130
Result: **Coventry City 1 Manchester United 5**
Teamsheet: Edmonds, Holden, Stacey, Duckworth, Whalley, Bell, Meredith, Halse, West, Turnbull, Wall
Scorer(s): Halse 2, Turnbull, Wall, West

Match # 754 Saturday 10/02/12 Football League Division 1 at Hillsborough Attendance 25000
Result: **Sheffield Wednesday 3 Manchester United 0**
Teamsheet: Edmonds, Holden, Stacey, Blott, Whalley, Bell, Meredith, Sheldon, West, Turnbull, Wall

Match # 755 Saturday 17/02/12 Football League Division 1 at Old Trafford Attendance 6000
Result: **Manchester United 0 Bury 0**
Teamsheet: Edmonds, Holden, Stacey, Livingstone, Bell, Hodge, Meredith, Halse, West, Turnbull, Wall

Match # 756 Saturday 24/02/12 FA Cup 3rd Round at Elm Park Attendance 24069
Result: **Reading 1 Manchester United 1**
Teamsheet: Edmonds, Linkson, Stacey, Duckworth, Roberts, Bell, Meredith, Halse, West, Turnbull, Wall
Scorer(s): West

Match # 757 Thursday 29/02/12 FA Cup 3rd Round Replay at Old Trafford Attendance 29511
Result: **Manchester United 3 Reading 0**
Teamsheet: Edmonds, Linkson, Stacey, Duckworth, Roberts, Bell, Meredith, Halse, West, Turnbull, Wall
Scorer(s): Turnbull 2, Halse

Match # 758 Saturday 02/03/12 Football League Division 1 at Old Trafford Attendance 10000
Result: **Manchester United 2 Notts County 0**
Teamsheet: Edmonds, Linkson, Stacey, Duckworth, Roberts, Hodge, Sheldon, Halse, West, Turnbull, Wall
Scorer(s): West 2

Match # 759 Saturday 09/03/12 FA Cup 4th Round at Old Trafford Attendance 59300
Result: **Manchester United 1 Blackburn Rovers 1**
Teamsheet: Edmonds, Linkson, Stacey, Duckworth, Roberts, Bell, Meredith, Halse, West, Turnbull, Wall
Scorer(s): own goal

Match # 760 Thursday 14/03/12 FA Cup 4th Round Replay at Ewood Park Attendance 39296
Result: **Blackburn Rovers 4 Manchester United 2**
Teamsheet: Edmonds, Linkson, Stacey, Duckworth, Roberts, Bell, Meredith, Halse, West, Turnbull, Wall
Scorer(s): West 2

Match # 761 Saturday 16/03/12 Football League Division 1 at Deepdale Attendance 7000
Result: **Preston North End 0 Manchester United 0**
Teamsheet: Edmonds, Linkson, Donnelly, Duckworth, Roberts, Hodge, Meredith, Halse, West, Hamill, Wall

Match # 762 Saturday 23/03/12 Football League Division 1 at Old Trafford Attendance 10000
Result: **Manchester United 1 Liverpool 1**
Teamsheet: Royals, Linkson, Donnelly, Duckworth, Roberts, Hodge, Meredith, Hamill, West, Nuttall, Capper
Scorer(s): Nuttall

SEASON 1911/12 (continued)

Match # 763 Saturday 30/03/12   Football League Division 1   at Villa Park   Attendance 15000
Result: **Aston Villa 6 Manchester United 0**
Teamsheet: Royals, Linkson, Donnelly, Duckworth, Knowles, Hodge, Meredith, Halse, West, Turnbull, Blott

Match # 764 Friday 05/04/12   Football League Division 1   at Manor Field   Attendance 14000
Result: **Arsenal 2 Manchester United 1**
Teamsheet: Edmonds, Linkson, Donnelly, Halse, Knowles, Hodge, Meredith, Hamill, West, Turnbull, Wall
Scorer(s): Turnbull

Match # 765 Saturday 06/04/12   Football League Division 1   at Old Trafford   Attendance 14000
Result: **Manchester United 0 Newcastle United 2**
Teamsheet: Moger, Linkson, Donnelly, Hodge, Knowles, Bell, Meredith, Hamill, West, Turnbull, Wall

Match # 766 Tuesday 09/04/12   Football League Division 1   at White Hart Lane   Attendance 20000
Result: **Tottenham Hotspur 1 Manchester United 1**
Teamsheet: Edmonds, Linkson, Donnelly, Hodge, Knowles, Bell, Meredith, Hamill, West, Turnbull, Wall
Scorer(s): Wall

Match # 767 Saturday 13/04/12   Football League Division 1   at Bramall Lane   Attendance 7000
Result: **Sheffield United 6 Manchester United 1**
Teamsheet: Edmonds, Linkson, Donnelly, Hodge, Roberts, Bell, Sheldon, Hamill, West, Nuttall, Wall
Scorer(s): Nuttall

Match # 768 Wednesday 17/04/12   Football League Division 1   at Ayresome Park   Attendance 5000
Result: **Middlesbrough 3 Manchester United 0**
Teamsheet: Moger, Linkson, Donnelly, Hodge, Roberts, Bell, Sheldon, Meredith, West, Nuttall, Wall

Match # 769 Saturday 20/04/12   Football League Division 1   at Old Trafford   Attendance 15000
Result: **Manchester United 3 Oldham Athletic 1**
Teamsheet: Moger, Linkson, Stacey, Knowles, Roberts, Bell, Meredith, Hamill, West, Nuttall, Wall
Scorer(s): West 2, Wall

Match # 770 Saturday 27/04/12   Football League Division 1   at Burnden Park   Attendance 20000
Result: **Bolton Wanderers 1 Manchester United 1**
Teamsheet: Moger, Linkson, Stacey, Knowles, Roberts, Bell, Meredith, Hamill, West, Nuttall, Wall
Scorer(s): Meredith

Match # 771 Monday 29/04/12   Football League Division 1   at Old Trafford   Attendance 20000
Result: **Manchester United 3 Blackburn Rovers 1**
Teamsheet: Moger, Linkson, Stacey, Knowles, Roberts, Bell, Meredith, Hamill, West, Nuttall, Wall
Scorer(s): Hamill, Meredith, West

SEASON 1911/12 SUMMARY

APPEARANCES

PLAYER	LGE	FAC	CS	TOT
Meredith	35	6	1	42
Wall	33	6	1	40
Bell	32	6	1	39
Roberts	32	5	1	38
West	32	6	–	38
Edmonds	30	6	1	37
Turnbull	30	6	1	37
Stacey	29	6	1	36
Duckworth	26	6	1	33
Halse	24	6	1	31
Linkson	21	4	–	25
Hamill	16	–	1	17
Donnelly	13	–	–	13
Hodge	10	–	–	10
Hofton	7	–	1	8
Holden	6	2	–	8
Knowles	7	–	–	7
Blott	6	–	–	6
Moger	6	–	–	6
Nuttall	6	–	–	6
Whalley	5	1	–	6
Sheldon	5	–	–	5
Royals	2	–	–	2
Anderson	1	–	–	1
Capper	1	–	–	1
Homer	1	–	–	1
Livingstone	1	–	–	1
McCarthy	1	–	–	1

GOALSCORERS

PLAYER	LGE	FAC	CS	TOT
West	17	6	–	23
Halse	8	4	6	18
Turnbull	7	3	1	11
Wall	3	1	1	5
Meredith	3	–	–	3
Nuttall	2	–	–	2
Roberts	2	–	–	2
Stacey	2	–	–	2
Hamill	1	–	–	1
own goal	–	1	–	1

RESULTS & ATTENDANCES SUMMARY

		P	W	D	L	F	A	TOTAL	AVGE
League	H	19	9	5	5	29	19	375000	19737
	A	19	4	6	9	16	41	385000	20263
TOTAL		38	13	11	14	45	60	760000	20000
FA Cup	H	3	2	1	0	7	2	108390	36130
	A	3	1	1	1	8	6	80495	26832
TOTAL		6	3	2	1	15	8	188885	31481
Charity	H	0	0	0	0	0	0	0	n/a
Shield	A	0	0	0	0	0	0	0	n/a
	N	1	1	0	0	8	4	10000	10000
TOTAL		1	1	0	0	8	4	10000	10000
Overall	H	22	11	6	5	36	21	483390	21972
	A	22	5	7	10	24	47	465495	21159
	N	1	1	0	0	8	4	10000	10000
TOTAL		45	17	13	15	68	72	958885	21309

FINAL TABLE – LEAGUE DIVISION ONE

		P	W	D	L	F	A	W	D	L	F	A	PTS	GD
				HOME					AWAY					
1	Blackburn Rovers	38	13	6	0	35	10	7	3	9	25	33	49	17
2	Everton	38	13	5	1	29	12	7	1	11	17	30	46	4
3	Newcastle United	38	10	4	5	37	25	8	4	7	27	25	44	14
4	Bolton Wanderers	38	14	2	3	35	15	6	1	12	19	28	43	11
5	Sheffield Wednesday	38	11	3	5	44	17	5	6	8	25	32	41	20
6	Aston Villa	38	12	2	5	48	22	5	5	9	28	41	41	13
7	Middlesbrough	38	11	6	2	35	17	5	2	12	21	28	40	11
8	Sunderland	38	10	6	3	37	14	4	5	10	21	37	39	7
9	West Bromwich Albion	38	10	6	3	23	15	5	3	11	20	32	39	–4
10	Arsenal	38	12	3	4	38	19	3	5	11	17	40	38	–4
11	Bradford City	38	12	3	4	31	15	3	5	11	15	35	38	–4
12	Tottenham Hotspur	38	10	4	5	35	20	4	5	10	18	33	37	0
13	MANCHESTER UNITED	38	9	5	5	29	19	4	6	9	16	41	37	–15
14	Sheffield United	38	10	4	5	47	29	3	6	10	16	27	36	7
15	Manchester City	38	10	5	4	39	20	3	4	12	17	38	35	–2
16	Notts County	38	9	4	6	26	20	5	3	11	20	43	35	–17
17	Liverpool	38	8	4	7	27	23	4	6	9	22	32	34	–6
18	Oldham Athletic	38	10	3	6	32	19	2	7	10	14	35	34	–8
19	Preston North End	38	8	4	7	26	25	5	3	11	14	32	33	–17
20	Bury	38	6	5	8	23	25	0	4	15	9	34	21	–27

SEASON 1912/13

Match # 772 Monday 02/09/12   Football League Division 1   at Manor Field   Attendance 11000
Result: **Arsenal 0 Manchester United 0**
Teamsheet: Beale, Linkson, Stacey, Duckworth, Roberts, Bell, Meredith, Hamill, West, Turnbull, Wall

Match # 773 Saturday 07/09/12   Football League Division 1   at Old Trafford   Attendance 40000
Result: **Manchester United 0 Manchester City 1**
Teamsheet: Beale, Linkson, Stacey, Duckworth, Roberts, Bell, Meredith, Hamill, West, Turnbull, Wall

Match # 774 Saturday 14/09/12   Football League Division 1   at The Hawthorns   Attendance 25000
Result: **West Bromwich Albion 1 Manchester United 2**
Teamsheet: Beale, Holden, Stacey, Whalley, Roberts, Bell, Meredith, Livingstone, West, Turnbull, Wall
Scorer(s): Livingstone, Turnbull

Match # 775 Saturday 21/09/12   Football League Division 1   at Old Trafford   Attendance 40000
Result: **Manchester United 2 Everton 0**
Teamsheet: Beale, Duckworth, Stacey, Whalley, Roberts, Bell, Meredith, Nuttall, West, Turnbull, Wall
Scorer(s): West 2

Match # 776 Saturday 28/09/12   Football League Division 1   at Hillsborough   Attendance 30000
Result: **Sheffield Wednesday 3 Manchester United 3**
Teamsheet: Beale, Linkson, Stacey, Whalley, Bell, Meredith, Nuttall, West, Turnbull, Wall
Scorer(s): West 2, Turnbull

Match # 777 Saturday 05/10/12   Football League Division 1   at Old Trafford   Attendance 45000
Result: **Manchester United 1 Blackburn Rovers 1**
Teamsheet: Beale, Linkson, Duckworth, Whalley, Roberts, Bell, Meredith, Nuttall, West, Turnbull, Wall
Scorer(s): Wall

Match # 778 Saturday 12/10/12   Football League Division 1   at Baseball Ground   Attendance 15000
Result: **Derby County 2 Manchester United 1**
Teamsheet: Beale, Linkson, Donnelly, Duckworth, Roberts, Bell, Meredith, Nuttall, West, Turnbull, Wall
Scorer(s): Turnbull

Match # 779 Saturday 19/10/12   Football League Division 1   at Old Trafford   Attendance 12000
Result: **Manchester United 2 Tottenham Hotspur 0**
Teamsheet: Beale, Linkson, Stacey, Whalley, Roberts, Hodge, Meredith, Nuttall, West, Turnbull, Wall
Scorer(s): Turnbull, West

Match # 780 Saturday 26/10/12   Football League Division 1   at Ayresome Park   Attendance 10000
Result: **Middlesbrough 3 Manchester United 2**
Teamsheet: Mew, Linkson, Stacey, Duckworth, Roberts, Hodge, Meredith, Nuttall, West, Turnbull, Wall
Scorer(s): Nuttall 2

Match # 781 Saturday 02/11/12   Football League Division 1   at Old Trafford   Attendance 12000
Result: **Manchester United 2 Notts County 1**
Teamsheet: Beale, Linkson, Stacey, Duckworth, Roberts, Bell, Meredith, Nuttall, Anderson, Turnbull, Wall
Scorer(s): Anderson, Meredith

Match # 782 Saturday 09/11/12   Football League Division 1   at Roker Park   Attendance 20000
Result: **Sunderland 3 Manchester United 1**
Teamsheet: Beale, Holden, Stacey, Whalley, Roberts, Hodge, Meredith, Anderson, West, Turnbull, Wall
Scorer(s): West

Match # 783 Saturday 16/11/12   Football League Division 1   at Villa Park   Attendance 20000
Result: **Aston Villa 4 Manchester United 2**
Teamsheet: Beale, Linkson, Stacey, Duckworth, Roberts, Bell, Sheldon, Anderson, West, Turnbull, Wall
Scorer(s): Wall, West

Match # 784 Saturday 23/11/12   Football League Division 1   at Old Trafford   Attendance 8000
Result: **Manchester United 3 Liverpool 1**
Teamsheet: Beale, Duckworth, Stacey, Knowles, Roberts, Bell, Meredith, Nuttall, Anderson, West, Wall
Scorer(s): Anderson 2, Wall

Match # 785 Saturday 30/11/12   Football League Division 1   at Burnden Park   Attendance 25000
Result: **Bolton Wanderers 2 Manchester United 1**
Teamsheet: Beale, Duckworth, Stacey, Knowles, Whalley, Bell, Meredith, Nuttall, Anderson, West, Wall
Scorer(s): Wall

Match # 786 Saturday 07/12/12   Football League Division 1   at Old Trafford   Attendance 12000
Result: **Manchester United 4 Sheffield United 0**
Teamsheet: Beale, Linkson, Stacey, Duckworth, Roberts, Bell, Meredith, Turnbull, Anderson, West, Wall
Scorer(s): Anderson, Turnbull, Wall, West

Match # 787 Saturday 14/12/12   Football League Division 1   at St James' Park   Attendance 20000
Result: **Newcastle United 1 Manchester United 3**
Teamsheet: Beale, Linkson, Stacey, Whalley, Duckworth, Bell, Sheldon, Turnbull, Anderson, West, Wall
Scorer(s): West 3

Match # 788 Saturday 21/12/12   Football League Division 1   at Old Trafford   Attendance 30000
Result: **Manchester United 0 Oldham Athletic 0**
Teamsheet: Beale, Linkson, Stacey, Duckworth, Roberts, Bell, Sheldon, Turnbull, Anderson, West, Wall

Match # 789 Wednesday 25/12/12   Football League Division 1   at Stamford Bridge   Attendance 33000
Result: **Chelsea 1 Manchester United 4**
Teamsheet: Beale, Linkson, Stacey, Duckworth, Gipps, Whalley, Sheldon, Turnbull, Anderson, West, Wall
Scorer(s): West 2, Anderson, Whalley

SEASON 1912/13 (continued)

Match # 790	Thursday 26/12/12	Football League Division 1	at Old Trafford	Attendance 20000
Result:	Manchester United 4 Chelsea 2			
Teamsheet:	Beale, Linkson, Stacey, Hamill, Whalley, Gipps, Sheldon, Turnbull, Anderson, West, Wall			
Scorer(s):	Turnbull 2, Anderson, Wall			

Match # 791	Saturday 28/12/12	Football League Division 1	at Hyde Road	Attendance 38000
Result:	Manchester City 0 Manchester United 2			
Teamsheet:	Beale, Hodge, Stacey, Duckworth, Roberts, Whalley, Meredith, Turnbull, Anderson, West, Wall			
Scorer(s):	West 2			

Match # 792	Wednesday 01/01/13	Football League Division 1	at Old Trafford	Attendance 30000
Result:	Manchester United 2 Bradford City 0			
Teamsheet:	Beale, Hodge, Stacey, Duckworth, Roberts, Whalley, Sheldon, Turnbull, Anderson, West, Wall			
Scorer(s):	Anderson 2			

Match # 793	Saturday 04/01/13	Football League Division 1	at Old Trafford	Attendance 25000
Result:	Manchester United 1 West Bromwich Albion 1			
Teamsheet:	Beale, Hodge, Stacey, Duckworth, Roberts, Whalley, Meredith, Turnbull, Anderson, West, Wall			
Scorer(s):	Roberts			

Match # 794	Saturday 11/01/13	FA Cup 1st Round	at Old Trafford	Attendance 11500
Result:	Manchester United 1 Coventry City 1			
Teamsheet:	Beale, Hodge, Stacey, Duckworth, Roberts, Whalley, Meredith, Turnbull, Anderson, West, Wall			
Scorer(s):	Wall			

Match # 795	Thursday 16/01/13	FA Cup 1st Round Replay	at Highfield Road	Attendance 20042
Result:	Coventry City 1 Manchester United 2			
Teamsheet:	Beale, Hodge, Stacey, Duckworth, Roberts, Whalley, Meredith, Turnbull, Anderson, West, Wall			
Scorer(s):	Anderson, Roberts			

Match # 796	Saturday 18/01/13	Football League Division 1	at Goodison Park	Attendance 20000
Result:	Everton 4 Manchester United 1			
Teamsheet:	Beale, Hodge, Stacey, Duckworth, Whalley, Bell, Sheldon, Turnbull, Nuttall, Hamill, Wall			
Scorer(s):	Hamill			

Match # 797	Saturday 25/01/13	Football League Division 1	at Old Trafford	Attendance 45000
Result:	Manchester United 2 Sheffield Wednesday 0			
Teamsheet:	Beale, Hodge, Stacey, Duckworth, Roberts, Whalley, Meredith, Hamill, Anderson, West, Wall			
Scorer(s):	West, Whalley			

Match # 798	Saturday 01/02/13	FA Cup 2nd Round	at Home Park	Attendance 21700
Result:	Plymouth Argyle 0 Manchester United 2			
Teamsheet:	Beale, Hodge, Stacey, Duckworth, Roberts, Whalley, Meredith, Turnbull, Anderson, Hamill, Wall			
Scorer(s):	Anderson, Wall			

Match # 799	Saturday 08/02/13	Football League Division 1	at Ewood Park	Attendance 38000
Result:	Blackburn Rovers 0 Manchester United 0			
Teamsheet:	Beale, Hodge, Stacey, Duckworth, Roberts, Whalley, Meredith, Turnbull, Anderson, West, Wall			

Match # 800	Saturday 15/02/13	Football League Division 1	at Old Trafford	Attendance 30000
Result:	Manchester United 4 Derby County 0			
Teamsheet:	Beale, Hodge, Stacey, Duckworth, Roberts, Whalley, Meredith, Turnbull, Anderson, West, Blott			
Scorer(s):	West 2, Anderson, Turnbull			

Match # 801	Saturday 22/02/13	FA Cup 3rd Round	at Boundary Park	Attendance 26932
Result:	Oldham Athletic 0 Manchester United 0			
Teamsheet:	Beale, Hodge, Stacey, Duckworth, Roberts, Whalley, Meredith, Hamill, Anderson, West, Wall			

Match # 802	Wednesday 26/02/13	FA Cup 3rd Round Replay	at Old Trafford	Attendance 31180
Result:	Manchester United 1 Oldham Athletic 2			
Teamsheet:	Beale, Hodge, Stacey, Duckworth, Roberts, Whalley, Meredith, Turnbull, Anderson, West, Wall			
Scorer(s):	West			

Match # 803	Saturday 01/03/13	Football League Division 1	at Old Trafford	Attendance 15000
Result:	Manchester United 2 Middlesbrough 0			
Teamsheet:	Beale, Hodge, Stacey, Duckworth, Whalley, Bell, Meredith, Turnbull, West, Hamill, Wall			
Scorer(s):	Meredith, Whalley			

Match # 804	Saturday 08/03/13	Football League Division 1	at Meadow Lane	Attendance 10000
Result:	Notts County 1 Manchester United 2			
Teamsheet:	Beale, Hodge, Stacey, Duckworth, Whalley, Bell, Sheldon, Turnbull, Anderson, West, Wall			
Scorer(s):	Anderson, Turnbull			

Match # 805	Saturday 15/03/13	Football League Division 1	at Old Trafford	Attendance 15000
Result:	Manchester United 1 Sunderland 3			
Teamsheet:	Beale, Linkson, Stacey, Livingstone, Whalley, Bell, Sheldon, Turnbull, Anderson, West, Wall			
Scorer(s):	Sheldon			

Match # 806	Friday 21/03/13	Football League Division 1	at Old Trafford	Attendance 20000
Result:	Manchester United 2 Arsenal 0			
Teamsheet:	Beale, Linkson, Stacey, Roberts, Whalley, Hamill, Sheldon, Turnbull, Anderson, West, Wall			
Scorer(s):	Anderson, Whalley			

Match # 807	Saturday 22/03/13	Football League Division 1	at Old Trafford	Attendance 30000
Result:	Manchester United 4 Aston Villa 0			
Teamsheet:	Beale, Linkson, Stacey, Hamill, Whalley, Bell, Sheldon, Turnbull, Anderson, West, Wall			
Scorer(s):	Stacey, Turnbull, Wall, West			

SEASON 1912/13 (continued)

Match # 808	Tuesday 25/03/13	Football League Division 1	at Valley Parade	Attendance 25000
Result:	**Bradford City 1 Manchester United 0**			
Teamsheet:	Beale, Hodge, Stacey, Hamill, Whalley, Bell, Sheldon, Turnbull, Anderson, West, Wall			

Match # 809	Saturday 29/03/13	Football League Division 1	at Anfield	Attendance 12000
Result:	**Liverpool 0 Manchester United 2**			
Teamsheet:	Beale, Hodge, Stacey, Hamill, Whalley, Bell, Sheldon, Turnbull, Hunter, West, Wall			
Scorer(s):	Wall, West			

Match # 810	Monday 31/03/13	Football League Division 1	at White Hart Lane	Attendance 12000
Result:	**Tottenham Hotspur 1 Manchester United 1**			
Teamsheet:	Beale, Hodge, Stacey, Hamill, Whalley, Bell, Sheldon, Turnbull, Anderson, West, Blott			
Scorer(s):	Blott			

Match # 811	Saturday 05/04/13	Football League Division 1	at Old Trafford	Attendance 30000
Result:	**Manchester United 2 Bolton Wanderers 1**			
Teamsheet:	Beale, Hodge, Stacey, Hamill, Whalley, Bell, Sheldon, Turnbull, Anderson, West, Wall			
Scorer(s):	Anderson, Wall			

Match # 812	Saturday 12/04/13	Football League Division 1	at Bramall Lane	Attendance 12000
Result:	**Sheffield United 2 Manchester United 1**			
Teamsheet:	Beale, Hodge, Stacey, Hamill, Roberts, Bell, Sheldon, Turnbull, Anderson, West, Wall			
Scorer(s):	Wall			

Match # 813	Saturday 19/04/13	Football League Division 1	at Old Trafford	Attendance 10000
Result:	**Manchester United 3 Newcastle United 0**			
Teamsheet:	Beale, Hodge, Stacey, Hamill, Roberts, Bell, Meredith, Turnbull, Hunter, West, Wall			
Scorer(s):	Hunter 2, West			

Match # 814	Saturday 26/04/13	Football League Division 1	at Boundary Park	Attendance 3000
Result:	**Oldham Athletic 0 Manchester United 0**			
Teamsheet:	Beale, Hodge, Stacey, Hamill, Roberts, Bell, Meredith, Turnbull, Hunter, West, Wall			

SEASON 1912/13 SUMMARY

APPEARANCES

PLAYER	LGE	FAC	TOT
Beale	37	5	42
Stacey	36	5	41
Wall	36	5	41
West	36	4	40
Turnbull	35	4	39
Whalley	26	5	31
Anderson	24	5	29
Duckworth	24	5	29
Roberts	24	5	29
Meredith	22	5	27
Bell	26	–	26
Hodge	19	5	24

APPEARANCES

PLAYER	LGE	FAC	TOT
Hamill	15	2	17
Linkson	17	–	17
Sheldon	16	–	16
Nuttall	10	–	10
Hunter	3	–	3
Blott	2	–	2
Gipps	2	–	2
Holden	2	–	2
Knowles	2	–	2
Livingstone	2	–	2
Donnelly	1	–	1
Mew	1	–	1

GOALSCORERS

PLAYER	LGE	FAC	TOT
West	21	1	22
Anderson	12	2	14
Wall	10	2	12
Turnbull	10	–	10
Whalley	4	–	4
Hunter	2	–	2
Meredith	2	–	2
Nuttall	2	–	2
Roberts	1	1	2
Blott	1	–	1
Hamill	1	–	1
Livingstone	1	–	1
Sheldon	1	–	1
Stacey	1	–	1

RESULTS & ATTENDANCES SUMMARY

		P	W	D	L	F	A	TOTAL	AVGE
League	H	19	13	3	3	41	14	469000	24684
	A	19	6	5	8	28	29	379000	19947
	TOTAL	38	19	8	11	69	43	848000	22316
FA Cup	H	2	0	1	1	2	3	42680	21340
	A	3	2	1	0	4	1	68674	22891
	TOTAL	5	2	2	1	6	4	111354	22271
Overall	H	21	13	4	4	43	17	511680	24366
	A	22	8	6	8	32	30	447674	20349
	TOTAL	43	21	10	12	75	47	959354	22311

FINAL TABLE – LEAGUE DIVISION ONE

		P		HOME					AWAY					PTS	GD
			W	D	L	F	A	W	D	L	F	A			
1	Sunderland	38	14	2	3	47	17	11	2	6	39	26		54	43
2	Aston Villa	38	13	4	2	57	21	6	8	5	29	31		50	34
3	Sheffield Wednesday	38	12	4	3	44	23	9	3	7	31	32		49	20
4	MANCHESTER UNITED	38	13	3	3	41	14	6	5	8	28	29		46	26
5	Blackburn Rovers	38	10	5	4	54	21	6	8	5	25	22		45	36
6	Manchester City	38	12	3	4	34	15	6	5	8	19	22		44	16
7	Derby County	38	10	2	7	40	29	7	6	6	29	37		42	3
8	Bolton Wanderers	38	10	6	3	36	20	6	4	9	26	43		42	-1
9	Oldham Athletic	38	11	7	1	33	12	3	7	9	17	43		42	-5
10	West Bromwich Albion	38	8	7	4	30	20	5	5	9	27	30		38	7
11	Everton	38	8	2	9	28	31	7	5	7	20	23		37	-6
12	Liverpool	38	12	2	5	40	24	4	3	12	21	47		37	-10
13	Bradford City	38	10	5	4	33	22	2	6	11	17	38		35	-10
14	Newcastle United	38	8	5	6	30	23	5	3	11	17	24		34	0
15	Sheffield United	38	10	5	4	36	24	4	1	14	20	46		34	-14
16	Middlesbrough	38	6	9	4	29	22	5	1	13	26	47		32	-14
17	Tottenham Hotspur	38	9	3	7	28	25	3	3	13	17	47		30	-27
18	Chelsea	38	7	2	10	29	40	4	4	11	22	33		28	-22
19	Notts County	38	6	4	9	19	20	1	5	13	9	36		23	-28
20	Arsenal	38	1	8	10	11	31	2	4	13	15	43		18	-48

SEASON 1913/14

Match # 815 Saturday 06/09/13 Football League Division 1 at Hillsborough Attendance 32000
Result: **Sheffield Wednesday 1 Manchester United 3**
Teamsheet: Beale, Hodge (James), Stacey, Duckworth, Whalley, Hamill, Meredith, Turnbull, Anderson, West, Wall
Scorer(s): Turnbull, West, own goal

Match # 816 Monday 08/09/13 Football League Division 1 at Old Trafford Attendance 25000
Result: **Manchester United 3 Sunderland 1**
Teamsheet: Beale, Hodge (James), Stacey, Duckworth, Whalley, Hamill, Meredith, Turnbull, Anderson, West, Wall
Scorer(s): Anderson, Turnbull, Whalley

Match # 817 Saturday 13/09/13 Football League Division 1 at Old Trafford Attendance 45000
Result: **Manchester United 0 Bolton Wanderers 1**
Teamsheet: Beale, Hodge (James), Stacey, Duckworth, Whalley, Knowles, Meredith, Cashmore, Anderson, West, Wall

Match # 818 Saturday 20/09/13 Football League Division 1 at Stamford Bridge Attendance 40000
Result: **Chelsea 0 Manchester United 2**
Teamsheet: Beale, Hodge (James), Stacey, Duckworth, Whalley, Hamill, Meredith, Turnbull, Anderson, West, Wall
Scorer(s): Anderson, Wall

Match # 819 Saturday 27/09/13 Football League Division 1 at Old Trafford Attendance 55000
Result: **Manchester United 4 Oldham Athletic 1**
Teamsheet: Beale, Hodge (James), Stacey, Duckworth, Whalley, Hamill, Meredith, Turnbull, Anderson, West, Wall
Scorer(s): West 2, Anderson, Wall

Match # 820 Saturday 04/10/13 Football League Division 1 at Old Trafford Attendance 25000
Result: **Manchester United 3 Tottenham Hotspur 1**
Teamsheet: Beale, Hodge (James), Stacey, Duckworth, Whalley, Hamill, Meredith, Hooper, Anderson, West, Wall
Scorer(s): Stacey, Wall, Whalley

Match # 821 Saturday 11/10/13 Football League Division 1 at Turf Moor Attendance 30000
Result: **Burnley 1 Manchester United 2**
Teamsheet: Beale, Chorlton, Stacey, Duckworth, Whalley, Hamill, Meredith, Turnbull, Anderson, West, Wall
Scorer(s): Anderson 2

Match # 822 Saturday 18/10/13 Football League Division 1 at Old Trafford Attendance 30000
Result: **Manchester United 3 Preston North End 0**
Teamsheet: Beale, Hodge (James), Stacey, Duckworth, Whalley, Hamill, Meredith, Turnbull, Anderson, West, Wall
Scorer(s): Anderson 3

Match # 823 Saturday 25/10/13 Football League Division 1 at St James' Park Attendance 35000
Result: **Newcastle United 0 Manchester United 1**
Teamsheet: Beale, Hodge (James), Stacey, Gipps, Whalley, Knowles, Meredith, Turnbull, Anderson, West, Wall
Scorer(s): West

Match # 824 Saturday 01/11/13 Football League Division 1 at Old Trafford Attendance 30000
Result: **Manchester United 3 Liverpool 0**
Teamsheet: Beale, Hodge (James), Stacey, Gipps, Whalley, Hamill, Meredith, Woodcock, Anderson, West, Wall
Scorer(s): Wall 2, West

Match # 825 Saturday 08/11/13 Football League Division 1 at Villa Park Attendance 20000
Result: **Aston Villa 3 Manchester United 1**
Teamsheet: Beale, Hodge (James), Stacey, Gipps, Whalley, Hamill, Meredith, Woodcock, Anderson, West, Wall
Scorer(s): Woodcock

Match # 826 Saturday 15/11/13 Football League Division 1 at Old Trafford Attendance 15000
Result: **Manchester United 0 Middlesbrough 1**
Teamsheet: Beale, Hodge (James), Stacey, Duckworth, Whalley, Hamill, Meredith, Turnbull, Anderson, Hooper, West

Match # 827 Saturday 22/11/13 Football League Division 1 at Bramall Lane Attendance 30000
Result: **Sheffield United 2 Manchester United 0**
Teamsheet: Mew, Hodge (James), Stacey, Gipps, Whalley, Haywood, Meredith, Turnbull, Anderson, West, Wall

Match # 828 Saturday 29/11/13 Football League Division 1 at Old Trafford Attendance 20000
Result: **Manchester United 3 Derby County 3**
Teamsheet: Mew, Hodge (James), Stacey, Gipps, Whalley, Haywood, Meredith, Turnbull, Anderson, Cashmore, Wall
Scorer(s): Turnbull 2, Meredith

Match # 829 Saturday 06/12/13 Football League Division 1 at Hyde Road Attendance 40000
Result: **Manchester City 0 Manchester United 2**
Teamsheet: Beale, Hodge (James), Stacey, Knowles, Whalley, Hamill, Meredith, Turnbull, Anderson, West, Wall
Scorer(s): Anderson 2

Match # 830 Saturday 13/12/13 Football League Division 1 at Old Trafford Attendance 18000
Result: **Manchester United 1 Bradford City 1**
Teamsheet: Beale, Hodge (James), Stacey, Haywood, Knowles, Hamill, Meredith, Turnbull, Anderson, West, Thomson
Scorer(s): Knowles

Match # 831 Saturday 20/12/13 Football League Division 1 at Ewood Park Attendance 35000
Result: **Blackburn Rovers 0 Manchester United 1**
Teamsheet: Beale, Hodge (James), Stacey, Haywood, Knowles, Hamill, Meredith, Turnbull, Anderson, West, Wall
Scorer(s): own goal

Match # 832 Thursday 25/12/13 Football League Division 1 at Old Trafford Attendance 25000
Result: **Manchester United 0 Everton 1**
Teamsheet: Beale, Hodge (James), Stacey, Knowles, Whalley, Hamill, Meredith, Turnbull, Anderson, West, Wall

SEASON 1913/14 (continued)

Match # 833	Friday 26/12/13	Football League Division 1	at Goodison Park	Attendance 40000
Result:	**Everton 5 Manchester United 0**			
Teamsheet:	Beale, Hodge (James), Stacey, Knowles, Whalley, Hamill, Meredith, Potts, West, Turnbull, Wall			

Match # 834	Saturday 27/12/13	Football League Division 1	at Old Trafford	Attendance 10000
Result:	**Manchester United 2 Sheffield Wednesday 1**			
Teamsheet:	Beale, Roberts, Hodge (James), Knowles, Hodge (John), Hamill, Meredith, Potts, Woodcock, Hooper, Wall			
Scorer(s):	Meredith, Wall			

Match # 835	Wednesday 01/01/14	Football League Division 1	at Old Trafford	Attendance 35000
Result:	**Manchester United 1 West Bromwich Albion 0**			
Teamsheet:	Beale, Hodge (James), Stacey, Gipps, Hamill, Haywood, Meredith, Potts, Anderson, Woodcock, Wall			
Scorer(s):	Wall			

Match # 836	Saturday 03/01/14	Football League Division 1	at Burnden Park	Attendance 35000
Result:	**Bolton Wanderers 6 Manchester United 1**			
Teamsheet:	Beale, Roberts, Hodge (James), Gipps, Knowles, Haywood, Meredith, Turnbull, Anderson, West, Wall			
Scorer(s):	West			

Match # 837	Saturday 10/01/14	FA Cup 1st Round	at County Ground	Attendance 18187
Result:	**Swindon Town 1 Manchester United 0**			
Teamsheet:	Beale, Hodge (James), Stacey, Knowles, Livingstone, Whalley, Meredith, Turnbull, Woodcock, West, Wall			

Match # 838	Saturday 17/01/14	Football League Division 1	at Old Trafford	Attendance 20000
Result:	**Manchester United 0 Chelsea 1**			
Teamsheet:	Beale, Hodge (James), Stacey, Knowles, Whalley, Hamill, Meredith, Potts, Woodcock, West, Wall			

Match # 839	Saturday 24/01/14	Football League Division 1	at Boundary Park	Attendance 10000
Result:	**Oldham Athletic 2 Manchester United 2**			
Teamsheet:	Beale, Hodge (James), Stacey, Knowles, Livingstone, Hudson, Meredith, Woodcock, West, Wall, Norton			
Scorer(s):	Wall, Woodcock			

Match # 840	Saturday 07/02/14	Football League Division 1	at White Hart Lane	Attendance 22000
Result:	**Tottenham Hotspur 2 Manchester United 1**			
Teamsheet:	Beale, Hodge (James), Stacey, Hudson, Livingstone, Hamill, Meredith, Travers, West, Turnbull, Wall			
Scorer(s):	Wall			

Match # 841	Saturday 14/02/14	Football League Division 1	at Old Trafford	Attendance 35000
Result:	**Manchester United 0 Burnley 1**			
Teamsheet:	Beale, Hodge (James), Stacey, Haywood, West, Wall, Meredith, Woodcock, Anderson, Travers, Norton			

Match # 842	Saturday 21/02/14	Football League Division 1	at Ayresome Park	Attendance 12000
Result:	**Middlesbrough 3 Manchester United 1**			
Teamsheet:	Beale, Chorlton, Stacey, Haywood, Knowles, Hamill, Meredith, Woodcock, Anderson, West, Wall			
Scorer(s):	Anderson			

Match # 843	Saturday 28/02/14	Football League Division 1	at Old Trafford	Attendance 30000
Result:	**Manchester United 2 Newcastle United 2**			
Teamsheet:	Beale, Chorlton, Stacey, Haywood, Hodge (John), Hamill, Norton, Potts, Anderson, Travers, Wall			
Scorer(s):	Anderson, Potts			

Match # 844	Thursday 05/03/14	Football League Division 1	at Deepdale	Attendance 12000
Result:	**Preston North End 4 Manchester United 2**			
Teamsheet:	Beale, Rowe, Stacey, Haywood, Hodge (John), Hamill, Norton, Potts, Anderson, Travers, Wall			
Scorer(s):	Travers, Wall			

Match # 845	Saturday 14/03/14	Football League Division 1	at Old Trafford	Attendance 30000
Result:	**Manchester United 0 Aston Villa 6**			
Teamsheet:	Beale, Chorlton, Stacey, Livingstone, Hunter, Haywood, Meredith, Woodcock, Anderson, Travers, Wall			

Match # 846	Saturday 04/04/14	Football League Division 1	at Baseball Ground	Attendance 7000
Result:	**Derby County 4 Manchester United 2**			
Teamsheet:	Beale, Hodge (John), Stacey, Haywood, Hunter, Hamill, Meredith, Travers, Anderson, West, Norton			
Scorer(s):	Anderson, Travers			

Match # 847	Friday 10/04/14	Football League Division 1	at Roker Park	Attendance 20000
Result:	**Sunderland 2 Manchester United 0**			
Teamsheet:	Royals, Hodge (James), Hudson, Gipps, Hunter, Haywood, Norton, Travers, Anderson, West, Thomson			

Match # 848	Saturday 11/04/14	Football League Division 1	at Old Trafford	Attendance 36000
Result:	**Manchester United 0 Manchester City 1**			
Teamsheet:	Royals, Hudson, Stacey, Knowles, Hunter, Gipps, Meredith, Travers, Anderson, West, Thomson			

Match # 849	Monday 13/04/14	Football League Division 1	at The Hawthorns	Attendance 20000
Result:	**West Bromwich Albion 2 Manchester United 1**			
Teamsheet:	Royals, Hudson, Stacey, Knowles, Hunter, Gipps, Meredith, Travers, West, Woodcock, Thomson			
Scorer(s):	Travers			

Match # 850	Wednesday 15/04/14	Football League Division 1	at Anfield	Attendance 28000
Result:	**Liverpool 1 Manchester United 2**			
Teamsheet:	Royals, Hudson, Stacey, Knowles, Hunter, Hamill, Meredith, Travers, Anderson, Woodcock, Wall			
Scorer(s):	Travers, Wall			

SEASON 1913/14 (continued)

Match # 851	Saturday 18/04/14	Football League Division 1	at Valley Parade	Attendance 10000
Result:	**Bradford City 1 Manchester United 1**			
Teamsheet:	Royals, Hudson, Stacey, Knowles, Hunter, Hamill, Meredith, Travers, Cashmore, Anderson, Thomson			
Scorer(s):	Thomson			

Match # 852	Wednesday 22/04/14	Football League Division 1	at Old Trafford	Attendance 4500
Result:	**Manchester United 2 Sheffield United 1**			
Teamsheet:	Beale, Hudson, Stacey, Hodge (James), Knowles, Gipps, Meredith, Travers, Anderson, West, Norton			
Scorer(s):	Anderson 2			

Match # 853	Saturday 25/04/14	Football League Division 1	at Old Trafford	Attendance 20000
Result:	**Manchester United 0 Blackburn Rovers 0**			
Teamsheet:	Beale, Hudson, Hodge (James), Haywood, Knowles, Hamill, Norton, Travers, Anderson, West, Thomson			

SEASON 1913/14 SUMMARY

APPEARANCES

PLAYER	LGE	FAC	TOT
Meredith	34	1	35
Stacey	34	1	35
Anderson	32	–	32
Beale	31	1	32
West	30	1	31
Wall	29	1	30
Hodge, James	28	1	29
Hamill	26	–	26
Knowles	18	1	19
Whalley	18	1	19
Turnbull	17	1	18
Haywood	14	–	14
Travers	13	–	13
Woodcock	11	1	12
Gipps	11	–	11
Duckworth	9	–	9
Hudson	9	–	9
Norton	8	–	8
Hunter	7	–	7
Potts	6	–	6
Thomson	6	–	6
Royals	5	–	5
Chorlton	4	–	4
Hodge, John	4	–	4
Livingstone	3	1	4
Cashmore	3	–	3
Hooper	3	–	3
Mew	2	–	2
Roberts	2	–	2
Rowe	1	–	1

GOALSCORERS

PLAYER	LGE	FAC	TOT
Anderson	15	–	15
Wall	11	–	11
West	6	–	6
Travers	4	–	4
Turnbull	4	–	4
Meredith	2	–	2
Whalley	2	–	2
Woodcock	2	–	2
Knowles	1	–	1
Potts	1	–	1
Stacey	1	–	1
Thomson	1	–	1
own goals	2	–	2

RESULTS & ATTENDANCES SUMMARY

		P	W	D	L	F	A	TOTAL	AVGE
League	H	19	8	4	7	27	23	508500	26763
	A	19	7	2	10	25	39	478000	25158
	TOTAL	38	15	6	17	52	62	986500	25961
FA Cup	H	0	0	0	0	0	0	0	n/a
	A	1	0	0	1	0	1	18187	18187
	TOTAL	1	0	0	1	0	1	18187	18187
Overall	H	19	8	4	7	27	23	508500	26763
	A	20	7	2	11	25	40	496187	24809
	TOTAL	39	15	6	18	52	63	1004687	25761

FINAL TABLE – LEAGUE DIVISION ONE

		P	W	D	L	F	A	W	D	L	F	A	PTS	GD
				HOME					AWAY					
1	Blackburn Rovers	38	14	4	1	51	15	6	7	6	27	27	51	36
2	Aston Villa	38	11	3	5	36	21	8	3	8	29	29	44	15
3	Middlesbrough	38	14	2	3	55	20	5	3	11	22	40	43	17
4	Oldham Athletic	38	11	5	3	34	16	6	4	9	21	29	43	10
5	West Bromwich Albion	38	11	7	1	30	16	4	6	9	16	26	43	4
6	Bolton Wanderers	38	13	4	2	41	14	3	6	10	24	38	42	13
7	Sunderland	38	11	3	5	32	17	6	3	10	31	35	40	11
8	Chelsea	38	12	3	4	28	18	4	4	11	18	37	39	–9
9	Bradford City	38	8	6	5	23	17	4	8	7	17	35	38	0
10	Sheffield United	38	11	4	4	36	19	5	1	13	27	41	37	3
11	Newcastle United	38	9	6	4	27	18	4	5	10	12	30	37	–9
12	Burnley	38	10	4	5	43	20	2	8	9	18	33	36	8
13	Manchester City	38	9	3	7	28	23	5	5	9	23	30	36	–2
14	MANCHESTER UNITED	38	8	4	7	27	23	7	2	10	25	39	36	–10
15	Everton	38	8	7	4	32	18	4	4	11	14	37	35	–9
16	Liverpool	38	8	4	7	27	25	6	3	10	19	37	35	–16
17	Tottenham Hotspur	38	9	6	4	30	19	3	4	12	20	43	34	–12
18	Sheffield Wednesday	38	8	4	7	34	34	5	4	10	19	36	34	–17
19	Preston North End	38	9	4	6	39	31	3	2	14	13	38	30	–17
20	Derby County	38	6	5	8	34	32	2	6	11	21	39	27	–16

SEASON 1914/15

Match # 854	Wednesday 02/09/14	Football League Division 1	at Old Trafford	Attendance 13000
Result:	**Manchester United 1 Oldham Athletic 3**			
Teamsheet:	Beale, Hodge (John), Stacey, Hunter, O'Connell, Knowles, Meredith, Anderson, Travers, West, Wall			
Scorer(s):	O'Connell			

Match # 855	Saturday 05/09/14	Football League Division 1	at Old Trafford	Attendance 20000
Result:	**Manchester United 0 Manchester City 0**			
Teamsheet:	Beale, Hodge (John), Stacey, Hunter, O'Connell, Knowles, Meredith, Travers, West, Woodcock, Wall			

Match # 856	Saturday 12/09/14	Football League Division 1	at Burnden Park	Attendance 10000
Result:	**Bolton Wanderers 3 Manchester United 0**			
Teamsheet:	Beale, Hodge (John), Stacey, Hunter, O'Connell, Knowles, Norton, Travers, West, Woodcock, Wall			

Match # 857	Saturday 19/09/14	Football League Division 1	at Old Trafford	Attendance 15000
Result:	**Manchester United 2 Blackburn Rovers 0**			
Teamsheet:	Beale, Hodge (John), Stacey, Gipps, Hunter, Knowles, Meredith, Turnbull, Anderson, West, Wall			
Scorer(s):	West 2			

Match # 858	Saturday 26/09/14	Football League Division 1	at Meadow Lane	Attendance 12000
Result:	**Notts County 4 Manchester United 2**			
Teamsheet:	Beale, Hodge (John), Stacey, Gipps, Hunter, Knowles, Meredith, Turnbull, Anderson, West, Wall			
Scorer(s):	Turnbull, Wall			

Match # 859	Saturday 03/10/14	Football League Division 1	at Old Trafford	Attendance 16000
Result:	**Manchester United 3 Sunderland 0**			
Teamsheet:	Beale, Hodge (John), Stacey, O'Connell, Hunter, Knowles, Meredith, Turnbull, Anderson, West, Norton			
Scorer(s):	Anderson, Stacey, West			

Match # 860	Saturday 10/10/14	Football League Division 1	at Hillsborough	Attendance 19000
Result:	**Sheffield Wednesday 1 Manchester United 0**			
Teamsheet:	Beale, Hodge (John), Stacey, Hunter, O'Connell, Knowles, Meredith, Travers, Anderson, West, Norton			

Match # 861	Saturday 17/10/14	Football League Division 1	at Old Trafford	Attendance 18000
Result:	**Manchester United 0 West Bromwich Albion 0**			
Teamsheet:	Beale, Hodge (John), Stacey, Gipps, O'Connell, Knowles, Woodcock, Potts, Anderson, West, Norton			

Match # 862	Saturday 24/10/14	Football League Division 1	at Goodison Park	Attendance 15000
Result:	**Everton 4 Manchester United 2**			
Teamsheet:	Beale, Hodge (John), Hudson, O'Connell, Whalley, Knowles, Wall, Travers, Anderson, West, Norton			
Scorer(s):	Anderson, Wall			

Match # 863	Saturday 31/10/14	Football League Division 1	at Old Trafford	Attendance 15000
Result:	**Manchester United 2 Chelsea 2**			
Teamsheet:	Beale, Hodge (John), Stacey, Gipps, Hunter, Knowles, Wall, Travers, Anderson, Turnbull, Norton			
Scorer(s):	Anderson, Hunter			

Match # 864	Saturday 07/11/14	Football League Division 1	at Valley Parade	Attendance 12000
Result:	**Bradford City 4 Manchester United 2**			
Teamsheet:	Beale, Hodge (John), Stacey, Gipps, Hunter, Knowles, Wall, Turnbull, Anderson, West, Norton			
Scorer(s):	Hunter, West			

Match # 865	Saturday 14/11/14	Football League Division 1	at Old Trafford	Attendance 12000
Result:	**Manchester United 0 Burnley 2**			
Teamsheet:	Mew, Hodge (John), Stacey, O'Connell, Hunter, Knowles, Meredith, Turnbull, Travers, Woodcock, Wall			

Match # 866	Saturday 21/11/14	Football League Division 1	at White Hart Lane	Attendance 12000
Result:	**Tottenham Hotspur 2 Manchester United 0**			
Teamsheet:	Beale, Stacey, Hudson, O'Connell, Hodge (James), Hunter, Wall, Turnbull, Anderson, West, Norton			

Match # 867	Saturday 28/11/14	Football League Division 1	at Old Trafford	Attendance 5000
Result:	**Manchester United 1 Newcastle United 0**			
Teamsheet:	Beale, Hodge (John), Stacey, O'Connell, Hunter, Knowles, Wall, Turnbull, Anderson, West, Norton			
Scorer(s):	West			

Match # 868	Saturday 05/12/14	Football League Division 1	at Ayresome Park	Attendance 7000
Result:	**Middlesbrough 1 Manchester United 1**			
Teamsheet:	Beale, Hodge (John), Stacey, O'Connell, Hunter, Knowles, Wall, Turnbull, Anderson, West, Norton			
Scorer(s):	Anderson			

Match # 869	Saturday 12/12/14	Football League Division 1	at Old Trafford	Attendance 8000
Result:	**Manchester United 1 Sheffield United 2**			
Teamsheet:	Beale, Hodge (John), Stacey, O'Connell, Hunter, Knowles, Wall, Turnbull, Anderson, West, Norton			
Scorer(s):	Anderson			

Match # 870	Saturday 19/12/14	Football League Division 1	at Villa Park	Attendance 10000
Result:	**Aston Villa 3 Manchester United 3**			
Teamsheet:	Beale, Hodge (John), Stacey, O'Connell, Hunter, Gipps, Meredith, Potts, Anderson, West, Norton			
Scorer(s):	Norton 2, Anderson			

Match # 871	Saturday 26/12/14	Football League Division 1	at Anfield	Attendance 25000
Result:	**Liverpool 1 Manchester United 1**			
Teamsheet:	Beale, Hodge (John), Stacey, Cookson, O'Connell, Gipps, Meredith, Potts, Anderson, West, Norton			
Scorer(s):	Stacey			

SEASON 1914/15 (continued)

Match # 872 Friday 01/01/15   Football League Division 1   at Old Trafford   Attendance 8000
Result: **Manchester United 1 Bradford Park Avenue 2**
Teamsheet: Beale, Hodge (John), Stacey, Gipps, O'Connell, Cookson, Meredith, Potts, Anderson, West, Norton
Scorer(s):   Anderson

Match # 873 Saturday 02/01/15   Football League Division 1   at Hyde Road   Attendance 30000
Result: **Manchester City 1 Manchester United 1**
Teamsheet: Beale, Hodge (John), Stacey, Gipps, O'Connell, Cookson, Meredith, Potts, Anderson, West, Norton
Scorer(s):   West

Match # 874 Saturday 09/01/15   FA Cup 1st Round   at Hillsborough   Attendance 23248
Result: **Sheffield Wednesday 1 Manchester United 0**
Teamsheet: Beale, Hodge (James), Stacey, Hunter, O'Connell, Cookson, Meredith, Fox, Anderson, West, Wall

Match # 875 Saturday 16/01/15   Football League Division 1   at Old Trafford   Attendance 8000
Result: **Manchester United 4 Bolton Wanderers 1**
Teamsheet: Beale, Hodge (John), Stacey, Knowles, O'Connell, Woodcock, Meredith, Potts, Cookson, West, Norton
Scorer(s):   Potts 2, Stacey, Woodcock

Match # 876 Saturday 23/01/15   Football League Division 1   at Ewood Park   Attendance 7000
Result: **Blackburn Rovers 3 Manchester United 3**
Teamsheet: Beale, Hodge (John), Stacey, Knowles, O'Connell, Cookson, Meredith, Potts, Woodcock, West, Norton
Scorer(s):   Woodcock 2, own goal

Match # 877 Saturday 30/01/15   Football League Division 1   at Old Trafford   Attendance 7000
Result: **Manchester United 2 Notts County 2**
Teamsheet: Beale, Hodge (John), Stacey, Knowles, O'Connell, Cookson, Meredith, Potts, Woodcock, West, Norton
Scorer(s):   Potts, Stacey

Match # 878 Saturday 06/02/15   Football League Division 1   at Roker Park   Attendance 5000
Result: **Sunderland 1 Manchester United 0**
Teamsheet: Beale, Spratt, Stacey, Haywood, O'Connell, Cookson, Meredith, Potts, Woodcock, West, Norton

Match # 879 Saturday 13/02/15   Football League Division 1   at Old Trafford   Attendance 7000
Result: **Manchester United 2 Sheffield Wednesday 0**
Teamsheet: Beale, Allman, Spratt, Haywood, O'Connell, Cookson, Meredith, Potts, Woodcock, West, Norton
Scorer(s):   West, Woodcock

Match # 880 Saturday 20/02/15   Football League Division 1   at The Hawthorns   Attendance 10000
Result: **West Bromwich Albion 0 Manchester United 0**
Teamsheet: Beale, Allman, Spratt, Haywood, O'Connell, Cookson, Wall, Potts, Woodcock, Travers, Norton

Match # 881 Saturday 27/02/15   Football League Division 1   at Old Trafford   Attendance 10000
Result: **Manchester United 1 Everton 2**
Teamsheet: Beale, Allman, Spratt, Haywood, O'Connell, Gipps, Meredith, Potts, Woodcock, Prince, Norton
Scorer(s):   Woodcock

Match # 882 Saturday 13/03/15   Football League Division 1   at Old Trafford   Attendance 14000
Result: **Manchester United 1 Bradford City 0**
Teamsheet: Beale, Allman, Spratt, Montgomery, O'Connell, Cookson, Norton, Potts, Woodcock, West, Wall
Scorer(s):   Potts

Match # 883 Saturday 20/03/15   Football League Division 1   at Turf Moor   Attendance 12000
Result: **Burnley 3 Manchester United 0**
Teamsheet: Beale, Allman, Spratt, Montgomery, O'Connell, Cookson, Norton, Potts, Woodcock, West, Wall

Match # 884 Saturday 27/03/15   Football League Division 1   at Old Trafford   Attendance 15000
Result: **Manchester United 1 Tottenham Hotspur 1**
Teamsheet: Beale, Allman, Spratt, Montgomery, Haywood, Meredith, Potts, Woodcock, West, Wall
Scorer(s):   Woodcock

Match # 885 Friday 02/04/15   Football League Division 1   at Old Trafford   Attendance 18000
Result: **Manchester United 2 Liverpool 0**
Teamsheet: Beale, Hodge (John), Spratt, Montgomery, O'Connell, Haywood, Meredith, Potts, Anderson, West, Norton
Scorer(s):   Anderson 2

Match # 886 Saturday 03/04/15   Football League Division 1   at St James' Park   Attendance 12000
Result: **Newcastle United 2 Manchester United 0**
Teamsheet: Beale, Hodge (John), Spratt, Montgomery, O'Connell, Haywood, Meredith, Potts, Anderson, West, Norton

Match # 887 Monday 05/04/15   Football League Division 1   at Park Avenue   Attendance 15000
Result: **Bradford Park Avenue 5 Manchester United 0**
Teamsheet: Beale, Allman, Spratt, Montgomery, O'Connell, Haywood, Meredith, Cookson, Woodcock, West, Norton

Match # 888 Tuesday 06/04/15   Football League Division 1   at Boundary Park   Attendance 2000
Result: **Oldham Athletic 1 Manchester United 0**
Teamsheet: Beale, Allman, Stacey, Montgomery, O'Connell, Knowles, Meredith, Turnbull, Anderson, West, Hodge (James)

Match # 889 Saturday 10/04/15   Football League Division 1   at Old Trafford   Attendance 15000
Result: **Manchester United 2 Middlesbrough 2**
Teamsheet: Beale, Allman, Spratt, Montgomery, O'Connell, Haywood, Meredith, Woodcock, Anderson, Turnbull, Hodge (James)
Scorer(s):   O'Connell, Turnbull

SEASON 1914/15 (continued)

Match # 890	Saturday 17/04/15	Football League Division 1	at Bramall Lane	Attendance 14000
Result:	**Sheffield United 3 Manchester United 1**			
Teamsheet:	Beale, Allman, Spratt, Montgomery, O'Connell, Haywood, Meredith, West, Woodcock, Turnbull, Hodge (James)			
Scorer(s):	West			

Match # 891	Monday 19/04/15	Football League Division 1	at Stamford Bridge	Attendance 13000
Result:	**Chelsea 1 Manchester United 3**			
Teamsheet:	Beale, Allman, Hodge (John), Montgomery, O'Connell, Haywood, Meredith, Woodcock, Anderson, West, Norton			
Scorer(s):	Norton, West, Woodcock			

Match # 892	Monday 26/04/15	Football League Division 1	at Old Trafford	Attendance 8000
Result:	**Manchester United 1 Aston Villa 0**			
Teamsheet:	Beale, Allman, Hodge (John), Montgomery, O'Connell, Haywood, Meredith, Woodcock, Anderson, West, Norton			
Scorer(s):	Anderson			

SEASON 1914/15 SUMMARY

APPEARANCES

PLAYER	LGE	FAC	TOT
Beale	37	1	38
O'Connell	34	1	35
West	33	1	34
Norton	29	–	29
Meredith	26	1	27
Hodge, John	26	–	26
Stacey	24	1	25
Anderson	23	1	24
Knowles	19	–	19
Woodcock	19	–	19
Wall	17	1	18
Potts	17	–	17
Hunter	15	1	16
Cookson	12	1	13
Turnbull	13	–	13
Allman	12	–	12
Haywood	12	–	12
Spratt	12	–	12
Montgomery	11	–	11
Gipps	10	–	10
Travers	8	–	8
Hodge, James	4	1	5
Hudson	2	–	2
Fox	–	1	1
Mew	1	–	1
Prince	1	–	1
Whalley	1	–	1

GOALSCORERS

PLAYER	LGE	FAC	TOT
Anderson	10	–	10
West	9	–	9
Woodcock	7	–	7
Potts	4	–	4
Stacey	4	–	4
Norton	3	–	3
Hunter	2	–	2
O'Connell	2	–	2
Turnbull	2	–	2
Wall	2	–	2
own goal	1	–	1

RESULTS & ATTENDANCES SUMMARY

		P	W	D	L	F	A	TOTAL	AVGE
League	H	19	8	6	5	27	19	232000	12211
	A	19	1	6	12	19	43	242000	12737
	TOTAL	38	9	12	17	46	62	474000	12474
FA Cup	H	0	0	0	0	0	0	0	n/a
	A	1	0	0	1	0	1	23248	23248
	TOTAL	1	0	0	1	0	1	23248	23248
Overall	H	19	8	6	5	27	19	232000	12211
	A	20	1	6	13	19	44	265248	13262
	TOTAL	39	9	12	18	46	63	497248	12750

FINAL TABLE – LEAGUE DIVISION ONE

		P	HOME W	D	L	F	A	AWAY W	D	L	F	A	PTS	GD
1	Everton	38	8	5	6	44	29	11	3	5	32	18	46	29
2	Oldham Athletic	38	11	5	3	46	25	6	6	7	24	31	45	14
3	Blackburn Rovers	38	11	4	4	51	27	7	3	9	32	34	43	22
4	Burnley	38	12	1	6	38	18	6	6	7	23	29	43	14
5	Manchester City	38	9	7	3	29	15	6	6	7	20	24	43	10
6	Sheffield United	38	11	5	3	28	13	4	8	7	21	28	43	8
7	Sheffield Wednesday	38	10	7	2	43	23	5	6	8	18	31	43	7
8	Sunderland	38	11	3	5	46	30	7	2	10	35	42	41	9
9	Bradford Park Avenue	38	11	4	4	40	20	6	3	10	29	45	41	4
10	West Bromwich Albion	38	11	5	3	31	9	4	5	10	18	34	40	6
11	Bradford City	38	11	7	1	40	18	2	7	10	15	31	40	6
12	Middlesbrough	38	10	6	3	42	24	3	6	10	20	50	38	–12
13	Liverpool	38	11	5	3	45	34	3	4	12	20	41	37	–10
14	Aston Villa	38	10	4	5	39	32	3	6	10	23	40	37	–10
15	Newcastle United	38	8	4	7	29	23	3	6	10	17	25	32	–2
16	Notts County	38	8	7	4	28	18	1	6	12	13	39	31	–16
17	Bolton Wanderers	38	8	5	6	35	27	3	3	13	33	57	30	–16
18	MANCHESTER UNITED	38	8	6	5	27	19	1	6	12	19	43	30	–16
19	Chelsea	38	8	6	5	32	25	0	7	12	19	40	29	–14
20	Tottenham Hotspur	38	7	7	5	30	29	1	5	13	27	61	28	–33

SEASON 1919/20

Match # 893 Saturday 30/08/19   Football League Division 1   at Baseball Ground   Attendance 12000
Result: **Derby County 1 Manchester United 1**
Teamsheet: Mew, Moore, Silcock, Montgomery, Hilditch, Whalley, Hodge, Woodcock, Spence, Potts, Hopkin
Scorer(s):   Woodcock

Match # 894 Monday 01/09/19   Football League Division 1   at Old Trafford   Attendance 13000
Result: **Manchester United 0 Sheffield Wednesday 0**
Teamsheet: Mew, Moore, Silcock, Montgomery, Hilditch, Whalley, Hodge, Meehan, Spence, Woodcock, Hopkin

Match # 895 Saturday 06/09/19   Football League Division 1   at Old Trafford   Attendance 15000
Result: **Manchester United 0 Derby County 2**
Teamsheet: Mew, Moore, Silcock, Montgomery, Hilditch, Whalley, Hodge, Woodcock, Spence, Meehan, Hopkin

Match # 896 Monday 08/09/19   Football League Division 1   at Hillsborough   Attendance 10000
Result: **Sheffield Wednesday 1 Manchester United 3**
Teamsheet: Mew, Moore, Silcock, Montgomery, Hilditch, Whalley, Hodge, Woodcock, Spence, Meehan, Hopkin
Scorer(s):   Meehan, Spence, Woodcock

Match # 897 Saturday 13/09/19   Football League Division 1   at Deepdale   Attendance 15000
Result: **Preston North End 2 Manchester United 3**
Teamsheet: Mew, Moore, Silcock, Montgomery, Hilditch, Whalley, Hodge, Woodcock, Spence, Meehan, Hopkin
Scorer(s):   Spence 2, Meehan

Match # 898 Saturday 20/09/19   Football League Division 1   at Old Trafford   Attendance 18000
Result: **Manchester United 5 Preston North End 1**
Teamsheet: Mew, Moore, Silcock, Montgomery, Hilditch, Whalley, Hodge, Woodcock, Spence, Meehan, Hopkin
Scorer(s):   Spence 2, Woodcock 2, Montgomery

Match # 899 Saturday 27/09/19   Football League Division 1   at Ayresome Park   Attendance 20000
Result: **Middlesbrough 1 Manchester United 1**
Teamsheet: Mew, Moore, Silcock, Montgomery, Hilditch, Whalley, Hodge, Woodcock, Spence, Meehan, Hopkin
Scorer(s):   Woodcock

Match # 900 Saturday 04/10/19   Football League Division 1   at Old Trafford   Attendance 28000
Result: **Manchester United 1 Middlesbrough 1**
Teamsheet: Mew, Moore, Silcock, Meehan, Hilditch, Whalley, Hodge, Woodcock, Spence, Toms, Hopkin
Scorer(s):   Woodcock

Match # 901 Saturday 11/10/19   Football League Division 1   at Hyde Road   Attendance 30000
Result: **Manchester City 3 Manchester United 3**
Teamsheet: Mew, Moore, Silcock, Whalley, Grimwood, Meehan, Hodge, Woodcock, Spence, Toms, Hopkin
Scorer(s):   Hodge, Hopkin, Spence

Match # 902 Saturday 18/10/19   Football League Division 1   at Old Trafford   Attendance 40000
Result: **Manchester United 1 Manchester City 0**
Teamsheet: Mew, Moore, Silcock, Meehan, Hilditch, Whalley, Hodge, Hodges, Spence, Woodcock, Hopkin
Scorer(s):   Spence

Match # 903 Saturday 25/10/19   Football League Division 1   at Bramall Lane   Attendance 18000
Result: **Sheffield United 2 Manchester United 2**
Teamsheet: Mew, Moore, Silcock, Meehan, Hilditch, Whalley, Hodge, Hodges, Spence, Woodcock, Hopkin
Scorer(s):   Hopkin, Woodcock

Match # 904 Saturday 01/11/19   Football League Division 1   at Old Trafford   Attendance 24500
Result: **Manchester United 3 Sheffield United 0**
Teamsheet: Mew, Moore, Silcock, Meehan, Hilditch, Whalley, Hodges, Potts, Spence, Woodcock, Hopkin
Scorer(s):   Hodges, Spence, Woodcock

Match # 905 Saturday 08/11/19   Football League Division 1   at Turf Moor   Attendance 15000
Result: **Burnley 2 Manchester United 1**
Teamsheet: Mew, Moore, Silcock, Meehan, Hilditch, Forster, Hodge, Hodges, Spence, Woodcock, Hopkin
Scorer(s):   Hodge

Match # 906 Saturday 15/11/19   Football League Division 1   at Old Trafford   Attendance 25000
Result: **Manchester United 0 Burnley 1**
Teamsheet: Mew, Moore, Silcock, Meehan, Hilditch, Forster, Bissett, Hodges, Spence, Woodcock, Hopkin

Match # 907 Saturday 22/11/19   Football League Division 1   at Boundary Park   Attendance 15000
Result: **Oldham Athletic 0 Manchester United 3**
Teamsheet: Mew, Moore, Silcock, Meehan, Hilditch, Whalley, Bissett, Hodges, Spence, Hodge, Hopkin
Scorer(s):   Hodges, Hopkin, Spence

Match # 908 Saturday 06/12/19   Football League Division 1   at Villa Park   Attendance 40000
Result: **Aston Villa 2 Manchester United 0**
Teamsheet: Mew, Moore, Silcock, Meehan, Hilditch, Whalley, Bissett, Hodge, Spence, Toms, Hopkin

Match # 909 Saturday 13/12/19   Football League Division 1   at Old Trafford   Attendance 30000
Result: **Manchester United 1 Aston Villa 2**
Teamsheet: Mew, Moore, Silcock, Meehan, Hilditch, Montgomery, Hodge, Hodges, Spence, Toms, Hopkin
Scorer(s):   Hilditch

Match # 910 Saturday 20/12/19   Football League Division 1   at Old Trafford   Attendance 20000
Result: **Manchester United 2 Newcastle United 1**
Teamsheet: Mew, Moore, Silcock, Grimwood, Hilditch, Whalley, Hodges, Hodge, Spence, Meehan, Hopkin
Scorer(s):   Hodges, Spence

SEASON 1919/20 (continued)

Match # 911 Friday 26/12/19   Football League Division 1   at Old Trafford   Attendance 45000
Result: **Manchester United 0 Liverpool 0**
Teamsheet: Mew, Moore, Silcock, Grimwood, Hilditch, Whalley, Meredith, Hodges, Spence, Meehan, Hopkin

Match # 912 Saturday 27/12/19   Football League Division 1   at St James' Park   Attendance 45000
Result: **Newcastle United 2 Manchester United 1**
Teamsheet: Mew, Moore, Silcock, Grimwood, Hilditch, Whalley, Bissett, Hodges, Spence, Meehan, Hopkin
Scorer(s):   Hilditch

Match # 913 Thursday 01/01/20   Football League Division 1   at Anfield   Attendance 30000
Result: **Liverpool 0 Manchester United 0**
Teamsheet: Mew, Moore, Silcock, Grimwood, Hilditch, Whalley, Meredith, Hodges, Spence, Woodcock, Hopkin

Match # 914 Saturday 03/01/20   Football League Division 1   at Old Trafford   Attendance 25000
Result: **Manchester United 0 Chelsea 2**
Teamsheet: Mew, Moore, Silcock, Grimwood, Hilditch, Whalley, Meredith, Hodges, Spence, Woodcock, Robinson

Match # 915 Saturday 10/01/20   FA Cup 1st Round   at Old Recreation Ground   Attendance 14549
Result: **Port Vale 0 Manchester United 1**
Teamsheet: Mew, Moore, Silcock, Grimwood, Hilditch, Whalley, Meredith, Meehan, Toms, Woodcock, Hopkin
Scorer(s):   Toms

Match # 916 Saturday 17/01/20   Football League Division 1   at Stamford Bridge   Attendance 40000
Result: **Chelsea 1 Manchester United 0**
Teamsheet: Mew, Moore, Silcock, Grimwood, Hilditch, Whalley, Meredith, Meehan, Spence, Woodcock, Hopkin

Match # 917 Saturday 24/01/20   Football League Division 1   at The Hawthorns   Attendance 20000
Result: **West Bromwich Albion 2 Manchester United 1**
Teamsheet: Mew, Moore, Silcock, Grimwood, Hilditch, Whalley, Meredith, Potts, Woodcock, Toms, Hopkin
Scorer(s):   Woodcock

Match # 918 Saturday 31/01/20   FA Cup 2nd Round   at Old Trafford   Attendance 48600
Result: **Manchester United 1 Aston Villa 2**
Teamsheet: Mew, Moore, Spence, Grimwood, Hilditch, Whalley, Meredith, Potts, Woodcock, Meehan, Hopkin
Scorer(s):   Woodcock

Match # 919 Saturday 07/02/20   Football League Division 1   at Roker Park   Attendance 25000
Result: **Sunderland 3 Manchester United 0**
Teamsheet: Mew, Barlow, Silcock, Grimwood, Hilditch, Meehan, Meredith, Bissett, Spence, Woodcock, Hopkin

Match # 920 Wednesday 11/02/20   Football League Division 1   at Old Trafford   Attendance 15000
Result: **Manchester United 1 Oldham Athletic 1**
Teamsheet: Mew, Barlow, Silcock, Grimwood, Hilditch, Meehan, Meredith, Bissett, Toms, Woodcock, Hopkin
Scorer(s):   Bissett

Match # 921 Saturday 14/02/20   Football League Division 1   at Old Trafford   Attendance 35000
Result: **Manchester United 2 Sunderland 0**
Teamsheet: Mew, Barlow, Silcock, Grimwood, Harris, Hilditch, Bissett, Hodges, Spence, Meehan, Hopkin
Scorer(s):   Harris, Hodges

Match # 922 Saturday 21/02/20   Football League Division 1   at Highbury   Attendance 25000
Result: **Arsenal 0 Manchester United 3**
Teamsheet: Mew, Moore, Silcock, Grimwood, Harris, Hilditch, Bissett, Hodges, Spence, Meehan, Hopkin
Scorer(s):   Spence 2, Hopkin

Match # 923 Wednesday 25/02/20   Football League Division 1   at Old Trafford   Attendance 20000
Result: **Manchester United 1 West Bromwich Albion 2**
Teamsheet: Mew, Moore, Silcock, Grimwood, Harris, Hilditch, Bissett, Hodges, Spence, Meehan, Hopkin
Scorer(s):   Spence

Match # 924 Saturday 28/02/20   Football League Division 1   at Old Trafford   Attendance 20000
Result: **Manchester United 0 Arsenal 1**
Teamsheet: Mew, Moore, Spratt, Grimwood, Harris, Hilditch, Bissett, Hodges, Spence, Meehan, Hopkin

Match # 925 Saturday 06/03/20   Football League Division 1   at Old Trafford   Attendance 25000
Result: **Manchester United 1 Everton 0**
Teamsheet: Mew, Moore, Silcock, Grimwood, Hilditch, Meehan, Meredith, Bissett, Harris, Woodcock, Hopkin
Scorer(s):   Bissett

Match # 926 Saturday 13/03/20   Football League Division 1   at Goodison Park   Attendance 30000
Result: **Everton 0 Manchester United 0**
Teamsheet: Mew, Moore, Silcock, Grimwood, Hilditch, Meehan, Meredith, Bissett, Spence, Woodcock, Hopkin

Match # 927 Saturday 20/03/20   Football League Division 1   at Old Trafford   Attendance 25000
Result: **Manchester United 0 Bradford City 0**
Teamsheet: Mew, Moore, Barlow, Grimwood, Hilditch, Meehan, Meredith, Bissett, Spence, Woodcock, Hopkin

Match # 928 Saturday 27/03/20   Football League Division 1   at Valley Parade   Attendance 18000
Result: **Bradford City 2 Manchester United 1**
Teamsheet: Mew, Moore, Barlow, Grimwood, Harris, Whalley, Meredith, Bissett, Woodcock, Potts, Hopkin
Scorer(s):   Bissett

SEASON 1919/20 (continued)

Match # 929   Friday 02/04/20   Football League Division 1   at Old Trafford   Attendance 30000
Result: **Manchester United 0   Bradford Park Avenue 1**
Teamsheet: Mew, Moore, Silcock, Grimwood, Harris, Meehan, Meredith, Bissett, Spence, Hodges, Prentice

Match # 930   Saturday 03/04/20   Football League Division 1   at Old Trafford   Attendance 39000
Result: **Manchester United 1   Bolton Wanderers 1**
Teamsheet: Mew, Barlow, Silcock, Grimwood, Montgomery, Meehan, Meredith, Woodcock, Toms, Bissett, Hopkin
Scorer(s):   Toms

Match # 931   Tuesday 06/04/20   Football League Division 1   at Park Avenue   Attendance 14000
Result: **Bradford Park Avenue 1   Manchester United 4**
Teamsheet: Mew, Barlow, Silcock, Grimwood, Montgomery, Meehan, Meredith, Woodcock, Toms, Bissett, Hopkin
Scorer(s):   Bissett, Grimwood, Toms, Woodcock

Match # 932   Saturday 10/04/20   Football League Division 1   at Burnden Park   Attendance 25000
Result: **Bolton Wanderers 3   Manchester United 5**
Teamsheet: Mew, Moore, Silcock, Grimwood, Montgomery, Meehan, Meredith, Woodcock, Toms, Bissett, Hopkin
Scorer(s):   Bissett 2, Meredith, Toms, Woodcock

Match # 933   Saturday 17/04/20   Football League Division 1   at Old Trafford   Attendance 40000
Result: **Manchester United 1   Blackburn Rovers 1**
Teamsheet: Mew, Moore, Silcock, Williamson, Montgomery, Meehan, Meredith, Woodcock, Toms, Bissett, Hopkin
Scorer(s):   Hopkin

Match # 934   Saturday 24/04/20   Football League Division 1   at Ewood Park   Attendance 30000
Result: **Blackburn Rovers 5   Manchester United 0**
Teamsheet: Mew, Moore, Silcock, Williamson, Montgomery, Forster, Meredith, Hodges, Toms, Bissett, Hopkin

Match # 935   Monday 26/04/20   Football League Division 1   at Old Trafford   Attendance 30000
Result: **Manchester United 0   Notts County 0**
Teamsheet: Mew, Barlow, Silcock, Forster, Whalley, Meehan, Meredith, Bissett, Toms, Sapsford, Robinson

Match # 936   Saturday 01/05/20   Football League Division 1   at Meadow Lane   Attendance 20000
Result: **Notts County 0   Manchester United 2**
Teamsheet: Mew, Moore, Silcock, Forster, Montgomery, Meehan, Meredith, Bissett, Spence, Sapsford, Hopkin
Scorer(s):   Meredith, Spence

SEASON 1919/20 SUMMARY

APPEARANCES

PLAYER	LGE	FAC	TOT
Mew	42	2	44
Hopkin	39	2	41
Silcock	40	1	41
Meehan	36	2	38
Moore	36	2	38
Hilditch	32	2	34
Spence	32	1	33
Woodcock	28	2	30
Whalley	23	2	25
Grimwood	22	2	24
Bissett	22	–	22
Meredith	19	2	21
Hodges	18	–	18
Hodge	16	–	16
Montgomery	14	–	14
Toms	12	1	13
Barlow	7	–	7
Harris	7	–	7
Forster	5	–	5
Potts	4	1	5
Robinson	2	–	2
Sapsford	2	–	2
Williamson	2	–	2
Prentice	1	–	1
Spratt	1	–	1

GOALSCORERS

PLAYER	LGE	FAC	TOT
Spence	14	–	14
Woodcock	11	1	12
Bissett	6	–	6
Hopkin	5	–	5
Hodges	4	–	4
Toms	3	1	4
Hilditch	2	–	2
Hodge	2	–	2
Meehan	2	–	2
Meredith	2	–	2
Grimwood	1	–	1
Harris	1	–	1
Montgomery	1	–	1

RESULTS & ATTENDANCES SUMMARY

		P	W	D	L	F	A	TOTAL	AVGE
League	H	21	6	8	7	20	17	562500	26786
	A	21	7	6	8	34	33	497000	23667
TOTAL		42	13	14	15	54	50	1059500	25226
FA Cup	H	1	0	0	1	1	2	48600	48600
	A	1	1	0	0	1	0	14549	14549
TOTAL		2	1	0	1	2	2	63149	31575
Overall	H	22	6	8	8	21	19	611100	27777
	A	22	8	6	8	35	33	511549	23252
TOTAL		44	14	14	16	56	52	1122649	25515

FINAL TABLE – LEAGUE DIVISION ONE

		P	W	D	L	F	A	W	D	L	F	A	PTS	GD
			HOME					AWAY						
1	West Bromwich Albion	42	17	1	3	65	21	11	3	7	39	26	60	57
2	Burnley	42	13	5	3	43	27	8	4	9	22	32	51	6
3	Chelsea	42	15	3	3	33	10	7	2	12	23	41	49	5
4	Liverpool	42	12	5	4	35	18	7	5	9	24	26	48	15
5	Sunderland	42	17	2	2	45	16	5	2	14	27	43	48	13
6	Bolton Wanderers	42	11	3	7	35	29	8	6	7	37	36	47	7
7	Manchester City	42	14	5	2	52	27	4	4	13	19	35	45	9
8	Newcastle United	42	11	5	5	31	13	6	4	11	13	26	43	5
9	Aston Villa	42	11	3	7	49	36	7	3	11	26	37	42	2
10	Arsenal	42	11	5	5	32	21	4	7	10	24	37	42	-2
11	Bradford Park Avenue	42	8	6	7	31	26	7	6	8	29	37	42	-3
12	MANCHESTER UNITED	42	6	8	7	20	17	7	6	8	34	33	40	4
13	Middlesbrough	42	10	5	6	35	23	5	5	11	26	42	40	-4
14	Sheffield United	42	14	5	2	43	20	2	3	16	16	49	40	-10
15	Bradford City	42	10	6	5	36	25	4	5	12	18	38	39	-9
16	Everton	42	8	6	7	42	29	4	8	9	27	39	38	1
17	Oldham Athletic	42	12	4	5	33	19	3	4	14	16	33	38	-3
18	Derby County	42	12	5	4	36	18	1	7	13	11	39	38	-10
19	Preston North End	42	9	6	6	35	27	5	4	12	22	46	38	-16
20	Blackburn Rovers	42	11	4	6	48	30	2	7	12	16	47	37	-13
21	Notts County	42	9	8	4	39	25	3	4	14	17	49	36	-18
22	Sheffield Wednesday	42	6	4	11	14	23	1	5	15	14	41	23	-36

SEASON 1920/21

Match # 937 Saturday 28/08/20 Football League Division 1 at Old Trafford Attendance 50000
Result: **Manchester United 2 Bolton Wanderers 3**
Teamsheet: Mew, Moore, Silcock, Meehan, Grimwood, Hilditch, Meredith, Bissett, Goodwin, Sapsford, Hopkin
Scorer(s): Hopkin, Meehan

Match # 9308 Monday 30/08/20 Football League Division 1 at Highbury Attendance 40000
Result: **Arsenal 2 Manchester United 0**
Teamsheet: Mew, Hofton, Silcock, Harris, Hilditch, Meehan, Meredith, Spence, Toms, Sapsford, Hopkin

Match # 939 Saturday 04/09/20 Football League Division 1 at Burnden Park Attendance 35000
Result: **Bolton Wanderers 1 Manchester United 1**
Teamsheet: Mew, Barlow, Silcock, Grimwood, Hilditch, Meehan, Schofield, Myerscough, Spence, Sapsford, Hopkin
Scorer(s): Sapsford

Match # 940 Monday 06/09/20 Football League Division 1 at Old Trafford Attendance 45000
Result: **Manchester United 1 Arsenal 1**
Teamsheet: Mew, Barlow, Silcock, Grimwood, Hilditch, Meehan, Spence, Bissett, Myerscough, Sapsford, Hopkin
Scorer(s): Spence

Match # 941 Saturday 11/09/20 Football League Division 1 at Old Trafford Attendance 40000
Result: **Manchester United 3 Chelsea 1**
Teamsheet: Mew, Barlow, Silcock, Harris, Hilditch, Meehan, Meredith, Hodges, Leonard, Sapsford, Hopkin
Scorer(s): Meehan 2, Leonard

Match # 942 Saturday 18/09/20 Football League Division 1 at Stamford Bridge Attendance 35000
Result: **Chelsea 1 Manchester United 2**
Teamsheet: Mew, Barlow, Silcock, Harris, Hilditch, Meehan, Meredith, Spence, Leonard, Sapsford, Hopkin
Scorer(s): Leonard 2

Match # 943 Saturday 25/09/20 Football League Division 1 at Old Trafford Attendance 50000
Result: **Manchester United 0 Tottenham Hotspur 1**
Teamsheet: Mew, Moore, Barlow, Harris, Hilditch, Meehan, Meredith, Miller, Leonard, Sapsford, Hopkin

Match # 944 Saturday 02/10/20 Football League Division 1 at White Hart Lane Attendance 45000
Result: **Tottenham Hotspur 4 Manchester United 1**
Teamsheet: Mew, Moore, Barlow, Harris, Montgomery, Meehan, Bissett, Miller, Leonard, Spence, Sapsford
Scorer(s): Spence

Match # 945 Saturday 09/10/20 Football League Division 1 at Old Trafford Attendance 50000
Result: **Manchester United 4 Oldham Athletic 1**
Teamsheet: Mew, Barlow, Silcock, Harris, Hilditch, Forster, Meehan, Miller, Spence, Sapsford, Partridge
Scorer(s): Sapsford 2, Meehan, Miller

Match # 946 Saturday 16/10/20 Football League Division 1 at Boundary Park Attendance 20000
Result: **Oldham Athletic 2 Manchester United 2**
Teamsheet: Mew, Barlow, Silcock, Harris, Hilditch, Forster, Meehan, Miller, Spence, Sapsford, Partridge
Scorer(s): Spence, own goal

Match # 947 Saturday 23/10/20 Football League Division 1 at Old Trafford Attendance 42000
Result: **Manchester United 1 Preston North End 0**
Teamsheet: Steward, Barlow, Silcock, Harris, Hilditch, Meehan, Harrison, Hodges, Miller, Sapsford, Partridge
Scorer(s): Miller

Match # 948 Saturday 30/10/20 Football League Division 1 at Deepdale Attendance 25000
Result: **Preston North End 0 Manchester United 0**
Teamsheet: Mew, Barlow, Silcock, Harris, Hilditch, Meehan, Harrison, Miller, Leonard, Sapsford, Hopkin

Match # 949 Saturday 06/11/20 Football League Division 1 at Old Trafford Attendance 30000
Result: **Manchester United 2 Sheffield United 1**
Teamsheet: Mew, Barlow, Silcock, Harris, Hilditch, Forster, Harrison, Miller, Leonard, Partridge, Hopkin
Scorer(s): Leonard 2

Match # 950 Saturday 13/11/20 Football League Division 1 at Bramall Lane Attendance 18000
Result: **Sheffield United 0 Manchester United 0**
Teamsheet: Mew, Moore, Silcock, Harris, Hilditch, Meehan, Harrison, Miller, Leonard, Partridge, Hopkin

Match # 951 Saturday 20/11/20 Football League Division 1 at Old Trafford Attendance 63000
Result: **Manchester United 1 Manchester City 1**
Teamsheet: Mew, Moore, Silcock, Forster, Harris, Meehan, Harrison, Miller, Leonard, Sapsford, Hopkin
Scorer(s): Miller

Match # 952 Saturday 27/11/20 Football League Division 1 at Hyde Road Attendance 35000
Result: **Manchester City 3 Manchester United 0**
Teamsheet: Mew, Moore, Silcock, Harris, Hilditch, Meehan, Harrison, Miller, Leonard, Spence, Hopkin

Match # 953 Saturday 04/12/20 Football League Division 1 at Old Trafford Attendance 25000
Result: **Manchester United 5 Bradford Park Avenue 1**
Teamsheet: Mew, Moore, Silcock, Harris, Grimwood, Forster, Harrison, Myerscough, Miller, Partridge, Hopkin
Scorer(s): Miller 2, Myerscough 2, Partridge

Match # 954 Saturday 11/12/20 Football League Division 1 at Park Avenue Attendance 10000
Result: **Bradford Park Avenue 2 Manchester United 4**
Teamsheet: Mew, Moore, Silcock, Harris, Grimwood, Forster, Harrison, Myerscough, Miller, Partridge, Hopkin
Scorer(s): Myerscough 2, Miller, Partridge

SEASON 1920/21 (continued)

Match # 955	Saturday 18/12/20	Football League Division 1	at Old Trafford	Attendance 40000
Result:	**Manchester United 2 Newcastle United 0**			
Teamsheet:	Mew, Moore, Silcock, Harris, Grimwood, Forster, Harrison, Myerscough, Miller, Partridge, Hopkin			
Scorer(s):	Hopkin, Miller			

Match # 956	Saturday 25/12/20	Football League Division 1	at Villa Park	Attendance 38000
Result:	**Aston Villa 3 Manchester United 4**			
Teamsheet:	Mew, Moore, Silcock, Harris, Grimwood, Forster, Harrison, Myerscough, Miller, Partridge, Hopkin			
Scorer(s):	Grimwood 2, Harrison, Partridge			

Match # 957	Monday 27/12/20	Football League Division 1	at Old Trafford	Attendance 70504
Result:	**Manchester United 1 Aston Villa 3**			
Teamsheet:	Mew, Moore, Silcock, Harris, Grimwood, Forster, Harrison, Myerscough, Miller, Partridge, Hopkin			
Scorer(s):	Harrison			

Match # 958	Saturday 01/01/21	Football League Division 1	at St James' Park	Attendance 40000
Result:	**Newcastle United 6 Manchester United 3**			
Teamsheet:	Mew, Moore, Silcock, Harris, Grimwood, Hilditch, Harrison, Myerscough, Spence, Partridge, Hopkin			
Scorer(s):	Hopkin, Partridge, Silcock			

Match # 959	Saturday 08/01/21	FA Cup 1st Round	at Anfield	Attendance 40000
Result:	**Liverpool 1 Manchester United 1**			
Teamsheet:	Mew, Barlow, Silcock, Harris, Grimwood, Forster, Harrison, Bissett, Miller, Partridge, Hopkin			
Scorer(s):	Miller			

Match # 960	Wednesday 12/01/21	FA Cup 1st Round Replay	at Old Trafford	Attendance 30000
Result:	**Manchester United 1 Liverpool 2**			
Teamsheet:	Mew, Hofton, Silcock, Harris, Grimwood, Albinson, Harrison, Bissett, Miller, Partridge, Hopkin			
Scorer(s):	Partridge			

Match # 961	Saturday 15/01/21	Football League Division 1	at Old Trafford	Attendance 30000
Result:	**Manchester United 1 West Bromwich Albion 4**			
Teamsheet:	Mew, Barlow, Silcock, Harris, Grimwood, Forster, Harrison, Bissett, Miller, Partridge, Hopkin			
Scorer(s):	Partridge			

Match # 962	Saturday 22/01/21	Football League Division 1	at The Hawthorns	Attendance 30000
Result:	**West Bromwich Albion 0 Manchester United 2**			
Teamsheet:	Mew, Silcock, Barlow, Hilditch, Grimwood, Forster, Harrison, Myerscough, Miller, Partridge, Hopkin			
Scorer(s):	Myerscough, Partridge			

Match # 963	Saturday 05/02/21	Football League Division 1	at Old Trafford	Attendance 30000
Result:	**Manchester United 1 Liverpool 1**			
Teamsheet:	Mew, Barlow, Silcock, Hilditch, Grimwood, Forster, Harrison, Myerscough, Miller, Partridge, Hopkin			
Scorer(s):	Grimwood			

Match # 964	Wednesday 09/02/21	Football League Division 1	at Anfield	Attendance 35000
Result:	**Liverpool 2 Manchester United 0**			
Teamsheet:	Mew, Barlow, Silcock, Hilditch, Grimwood, Forster, Meredith, Myerscough, Spence, Partridge, Hopkin			

Match # 965	Saturday 12/02/21	Football League Division 1	at Old Trafford	Attendance 30000
Result:	**Manchester United 1 Everton 2**			
Teamsheet:	Mew, Barlow, Silcock, Hilditch, Grimwood, Forster, Meredith, Myerscough, Miller, Partridge, Hopkin			
Scorer(s):	Meredith			

Match # 966	Sunday 20/02/21	Football League Division 1	at Old Trafford	Attendance 40000
Result:	**Manchester United 3 Sunderland 0**			
Teamsheet:	Mew, Moore, Silcock, Hilditch, Grimwood, Forster, Harrison, Partridge, Goodwin, Sapsford, Robinson			
Scorer(s):	Harrison, Hilditch, Robinson			

Match # 967	Saturday 05/03/21	Football League Division 1	at Roker Park	Attendance 25000
Result:	**Sunderland 2 Manchester United 3**			
Teamsheet:	Mew, Moore, Silcock, Hilditch, Grimwood, Forster, Harrison, Partridge, Goodwin, Sapsford, Robinson			
Scorer(s):	Sapsford 2, Goodwin			

Match # 968	Wednesday 09/03/21	Football League Division 1	at Goodison Park	Attendance 38000
Result:	**Everton 2 Manchester United 0**			
Teamsheet:	Mew, Moore, Barlow, Hilditch, Grimwood, Harris, Harrison, Partridge, Goodwin, Sapsford, Robinson			

Match # 969	Saturday 12/03/21	Football League Division 1	at Old Trafford	Attendance 30000
Result:	**Manchester United 1 Bradford City 1**			
Teamsheet:	Steward, Moore, Barlow, Hilditch, Grimwood, Forster, Harrison, Miller, Goodwin, Sapsford, Robinson			
Scorer(s):	Robinson			

Match # 970	Saturday 19/03/21	Football League Division 1	at Valley Parade	Attendance 25000
Result:	**Bradford City 1 Manchester United 1**			
Teamsheet:	Mew, Moore, Silcock, Hilditch, Montgomery, Forster, Harrison, Myerscough, Sapsford, Partridge, Robinson			
Scorer(s):	Sapsford			

Match # 971	Friday 25/03/21	Football League Division 1	at Turf Moor	Attendance 20000
Result:	**Burnley 1 Manchester United 0**			
Teamsheet:	Mew, Moore, Silcock, Harris, Hilditch, Forster, Harrison, Spence, Miller, Partridge, Hopkin			

Match # 972	Saturday 26/03/21	Football League Division 1	at Leeds Road	Attendance 17000
Result:	**Huddersfield Town 5 Manchester United 2**			
Teamsheet:	Mew, Moore, Silcock, Harris, Hilditch, Forster, Meredith, Spence, Miller, Partridge, Hopkin			
Scorer(s):	Harris, Partridge			

SEASON 1920/21 (continued)

Match # 973 Monday 28/03/21   Football League Division 1   at Old Trafford   Attendance 28000
Result: **Manchester United 0 Burnley 3**
Teamsheet: Mew, Moore, Silcock, Hilditch, Harris, Forster, Harrison, Bissett, Leonard, Sapsford, Partridge

Match # 974 Saturday 02/04/21   Football League Division 1   at Old Trafford   Attendance 30000
Result: **Manchester United 2 Huddersfield Town 0**
Teamsheet: Mew, Moore, Silcock, Hilditch, Grimwood, Forster, Meredith, Bissett, Miller, Partridge, Robinson
Scorer(s): Bissett 2

Match # 975 Saturday 09/04/21   Football League Division 1   at Ayresome Park   Attendance 15000
Result: **Middlesbrough 2 Manchester United 4**
Teamsheet: Mew, Moore, Barlow, Hilditch, Grimwood, Forster, Meredith, Bissett, Spence, Partridge, Hopkin
Scorer(s): Spence 2, Bissett, Grimwood

Match # 976 Saturday 16/04/21   Football League Division 1   at Old Trafford   Attendance 25000
Result: **Manchester United 0 Middlesbrough 1**
Teamsheet: Mew, Moore, Silcock, Hilditch, Grimwood, Forster, Meredith, Bissett, Spence, Partridge, Hopkin

Match # 977 Saturday 23/04/21   Football League Division 1   at Ewood Park   Attendance 18000
Result: **Blackburn Rovers 2 Manchester United 0**
Teamsheet: Mew, Moore, Silcock, Hilditch, Grimwood, Forster, Harrison, Bissett, Miller, Partridge, Hopkin

Match # 978 Saturday 30/04/21   Football League Division 1   at Old Trafford   Attendance 20000
Result: **Manchester United 0 Blackburn Rovers 1**
Teamsheet: Mew, Moore, Silcock, Hilditch, Grimwood, Harris, Meredith, Bissett, Miller, Partridge, Hopkin

Match # 979 Monday 02/05/21   Football League Division 1   at Baseball Ground   Attendance 8000
Result: **Derby County 1 Manchester United 1**
Teamsheet: Mew, Moore, Silcock, Hilditch, Grimwood, Harris, Meredith, Bissett, Hopkin, Sapsford, Robinson
Scorer(s): Bissett

Match # 980 Saturday 07/05/21   Football League Division 1   at Old Trafford   Attendance 10000
Result: **Manchester United 3 Derby County 0**
Teamsheet: Mew, Radford, Silcock, Hilditch, Grimwood, Forster, Meredith, Bissett, Spence, Sapsford, Hopkin
Scorer(s): Spence 2, Sapsford

SEASON 1920/21 SUMMARY

APPEARANCES

PLAYER	LGE	FAC	TOT
Mew	40	2	42
Silcock	37	2	39
Hilditch	34	–	34
Hopkin	31	2	33
Partridge	28	2	30
Harris	26	2	28
Forster	26	1	27
Grimwood	25	2	27
Miller	25	2	27
Moore	26	–	26
Harrison	23	2	25
Sapsford	21	–	21
Barlow	19	1	20
Meehan	15	–	15
Spence	15	–	15
Bissett	12	2	14
Meredith	14	–	14
Myerscough	13	–	13
Leonard	10	–	10
Robinson	7	–	7
Goodwin	5	–	5
Hodges	2	–	2
Hofton	1	1	2
Montgomery	2	–	2
Steward	2	–	2
Albinson	–	1	1
Radford	1	–	1
Schofield	1	–	1
Toms	1	–	1

GOALSCORERS

PLAYER	LGE	FAC	TOT
Miller	7	1	8
Partridge	7	1	8
Sapsford	7	–	7
Spence	7	–	7
Leonard	5	–	5
Myerscough	5	–	5
Bissett	4	–	4
Grimwood	4	–	4
Meehan	4	–	4
Harrison	3	–	3
Hopkin	3	–	3
Robinson	2	–	2
Goodwin	1	–	1
Harris	1	–	1
Hilditch	1	–	1
Meredith	1	–	1
Silcock	1	–	1
own goal	1	–	1

RESULTS & ATTENDANCES SUMMARY

		P	W	D	L	F	A	TOTAL	AVGE
League	H	21	9	4	8	34	26	778504	37072
	A	21	6	6	9	30	42	572000	27238
	TOTAL	42	15	10	17	64	68	1350504	32155
FA Cup	H	1	0	0	1	1	2	30000	30000
	A	1	0	1	0	1	1	40000	40000
	TOTAL	2	0	1	1	2	3	70000	35000
Overall	H	22	9	4	9	35	28	808504	36750
	A	22	6	7	9	31	43	612000	27818
	TOTAL	44	15	11	18	66	71	1420504	32284

FINAL TABLE – LEAGUE DIVISION ONE

		P	W	D	L	F	A	W	D	L	F	A	PTS	GD
				HOME					AWAY					
1	Burnley	42	17	3	1	56	16	6	10	5	23	20	59	43
2	Manchester City	42	19	2	0	50	13	5	4	12	20	37	54	20
3	Bolton Wanderers	42	15	6	0	53	17	4	8	9	24	36	52	24
4	Liverpool	42	11	7	3	41	17	7	8	6	22	18	51	28
5	Newcastle United	42	14	3	4	43	18	6	7	8	23	27	50	21
6	Tottenham Hotspur	42	15	2	4	46	16	4	7	10	24	32	47	22
7	Everton	42	9	8	4	40	26	8	5	8	26	29	47	11
8	Middlesbrough	42	10	6	5	29	21	7	6	8	24	32	46	0
9	Arsenal	42	9	8	4	31	25	6	6	9	28	38	44	-4
10	Aston Villa	42	11	4	6	39	21	7	3	11	24	49	43	-7
11	Blackburn Rovers	42	7	9	5	36	27	6	6	9	21	32	41	-2
12	Sunderland	42	11	4	6	34	19	3	9	9	23	41	41	-3
13	MANCHESTER UNITED	42	9	4	8	34	26	6	6	9	30	42	40	-4
14	West Bromwich Albion	42	8	7	6	31	23	5	7	9	23	35	40	-4
15	Bradford City	42	7	9	5	38	28	5	6	10	23	35	39	-2
16	Preston North End	42	10	4	7	38	25	5	5	11	23	40	39	-4
17	Huddersfield Town	42	11	4	6	26	16	4	5	12	16	33	39	-7
18	Chelsea	42	9	7	5	35	24	4	6	11	13	34	39	-10
19	Oldham Athletic	42	6	9	6	23	26	3	6	12	26	60	33	-37
20	Sheffield United	42	5	11	5	22	19	1	7	13	20	49	30	-26
21	Derby County	42	3	12	6	21	23	2	4	15	11	35	26	-26
22	Bradford Park Avenue	42	6	5	10	29	35	2	3	16	14	41	24	-33

SEASON 1921/22

Match # 981   Saturday 27/08/21   Football League Division 1   at Goodison Park   Attendance 30000
Result: **Everton 5 Manchester United 0**
Teamsheet: Mew, Brett, Silcock, Bennion, Grimwood, Scott, Gibson, Myerscough, Lochhead, Sapsford, Partridge

Match # 982   Monday 29/08/21   Football League Division 1   at Old Trafford   Attendance 20000
Result: **Manchester United 2 West Bromwich Albion 3**
Teamsheet: Mew, Brett, Silcock, Harris, Grimwood, Scott, Harrison, Spence, Goodwin, Partridge, Robinson
Scorer(s):   Partridge, Robinson

Match # 983   Saturday 03/09/21   Football League Division 1   at Old Trafford   Attendance 25000
Result: **Manchester United 2 Everton 1**
Teamsheet: Mew, Brett, Silcock, Harris, Grimwood, Scott, Harrison, Spence, Goodwin, Partridge, Robinson
Scorer(s):   Harrison, Spence

Match # 984   Wednesday 07/09/21   Football League Division 1   at The Hawthorns   Attendance 15000
Result: **West Bromwich Albion 0 Manchester United 0**
Teamsheet: Mew, Brett, Silcock, Harris, Grimwood, Scott, Harrison, Bissett, Spence, Sapsford, Robinson

Match # 985   Saturday 10/09/21   Football League Division 1   at Stamford Bridge   Attendance 35000
Result: **Chelsea 0 Manchester United 0**
Teamsheet: Mew, Brett, Silcock, Harris, Grimwood, Scott, Harrison, Bissett, Spence, Sapsford, Robinson

Match # 986   Saturday 17/09/21   Football League Division 1   at Old Trafford   Attendance 28000
Result: **Manchester United 0 Chelsea 0**
Teamsheet: Mew, Brett, Silcock, Hilditch, Grimwood, Scott, Harrison, Spence, Lochhead, Sapsford, Robinson

Match # 987   Saturday 24/09/21   Football League Division 1   at Deepdale   Attendance 25000
Result: **Preston North End 3 Manchester United 2**
Teamsheet: Mew, Radford, Silcock, Hilditch, Grimwood, Scott, Harrison, Spence, Lochhead, Partridge, Robinson
Scorer(s):   Lochhead, Partridge

Match # 988   Saturday 01/10/21   Football League Division 1   at Old Trafford   Attendance 30000
Result: **Manchester United 1 Preston North End 1**
Teamsheet: Mew, Radford, Brett, Bennion, Hilditch, Scott, Harrison, Spence, Lochhead, Schofield, Partridge
Scorer(s):   Spence

Match # 989   Saturday 08/10/21   Football League Division 1   at White Hart Lane   Attendance 35000
Result: **Tottenham Hotspur 2 Manchester United 2**
Teamsheet: Mew, Radford, Silcock, Bennion, Hilditch, Scott, Bissett, Lochhead, Spence, Sapsford, Partridge
Scorer(s):   Sapsford, Spence

Match # 990   Saturday 15/10/21   Football League Division 1   at Old Trafford   Attendance 30000
Result: **Manchester United 2 Tottenham Hotspur 1**
Teamsheet: Mew, Radford, Silcock, Bennion, Hilditch, Scott, Bissett, Lochhead, Spence, Sapsford, Partridge
Scorer(s):   Sapsford, Spence

Match # 991   Saturday 22/10/21   Football League Division 1   at Hyde Road   Attendance 24000
Result: **Manchester City 4 Manchester United 1**
Teamsheet: Mew, Radford, Brett, Bennion, Hilditch, Scott, Bissett, Lochhead, Spence, Sapsford, Partridge
Scorer(s):   Spence

Match # 992   Saturday 29/10/21   Football League Division 1   at Old Trafford   Attendance 56000
Result: **Manchester United 3 Manchester City 1**
Teamsheet: Mew, Radford, Silcock, Forster, Hilditch, Scott, Harrison, Lochhead, Spence, Sapsford, Partridge
Scorer(s):   Spence 3

Match # 993   Saturday 05/11/21   Football League Division 1   at Old Trafford   Attendance 30000
Result: **Manchester United 3 Middlesbrough 5**
Teamsheet: Mew, Radford, Silcock, Forster, Hilditch, Scott, Harrison, Lochhead, Spence, Sapsford, Partridge
Scorer(s):   Lochhead, Sapsford, Spence

Match # 994   Saturday 12/11/21   Football League Division 1   at Ayresome Park   Attendance 18000
Result: **Middlesbrough 2 Manchester United 0**
Teamsheet: Mew, Radford, Silcock, Forster, Hilditch, Scott, Gibson, Lochhead, Spence, Sapsford, Partridge

Match # 995   Saturday 19/11/21   Football League Division 1   at Villa Park   Attendance 30000
Result: **Aston Villa 3 Manchester United 1**
Teamsheet: Mew, Radford, Barlow, Grimwood, Harris, Scott, Bissett, Lochhead, Spence, Sapsford, Partridge
Scorer(s):   Spence

Match # 996   Saturday 26/11/21   Football League Division 1   at Old Trafford   Attendance 33000
Result: **Manchester United 1 Aston Villa 0**
Teamsheet: Mew, Radford, Silcock, Harris, McBain, Scott, Harrison, Spence, Henderson, Sapsford, Partridge
Scorer(s):   Henderson

Match # 997   Saturday 03/12/21   Football League Division 1   at Valley Parade   Attendance 15000
Result: **Bradford City 2 Manchester United 1**
Teamsheet: Mew, Brett, Silcock, Harris, McBain, Scott, Lochhead, Spence, Henderson, Sapsford, Partridge
Scorer(s):   Spence

Match # 998   Saturday 10/12/21   Football League Division 1   at Old Trafford   Attendance 9000
Result: **Manchester United 1 Bradford City 1**
Teamsheet: Mew, Radford, Scott, Hilditch, McBain, Harris, Gibson, Spence, Henderson, Sapsford, Partridge
Scorer(s):   Henderson

SEASON 1921/22 (continued)

Match # 999   Saturday 17/12/21   Football League Division 1   at Anfield   Attendance 40000
Result: **Liverpool 2 Manchester United 1**
Teamsheet: Mew, Scott, Silcock, Hilditch, McBain, Grimwood, Gibson, Myerscough, Spence, Sapsford, Partridge
Scorer(s):   Sapsford

Match # 1000 Saturday 24/12/21   Football League Division 1   at Old Trafford   Attendance 30000
Result: **Manchester United 0 Liverpool 0**
Teamsheet: Mew, Scott, Silcock, Hilditch, McBain, Grimwood, Gibson, Lochhead, Spence, Partridge, Robinson

Match # 1001 Monday 26/12/21   Football League Division 1   at Old Trafford   Attendance 15000
Result: **Manchester United 0 Burnley 1**
Teamsheet: Mew, Scott, Silcock, Hilditch, McBain, Harris, Gibson, Lochhead, Henderson, Partridge, Robinson

Match # 1002 Tuesday 27/12/21   Football League Division 1   at Turf Moor   Attendance 10000
Result: **Burnley 4 Manchester United 2**
Teamsheet: Mew, Scott, Silcock, Hilditch, McBain, Harris, Gibson, Lochhead, Henderson, Sapsford, Partridge
Scorer(s):   Lochhead, Sapsford

Match # 1003 Saturday 31/12/21   Football League Division 1   at St James' Park   Attendance 20000
Result: **Newcastle United 3 Manchester United 0**
Teamsheet: Mew, Radford, Silcock, Hilditch, Grimwood, Scott, Gibson, Lochhead, Henderson, Spence, Partridge

Match # 1004 Monday 02/01/22   Football League Division 1   at Bramall Lane   Attendance 18000
Result: **Sheffield United 3 Manchester United 0**
Teamsheet: Steward, Howarth, Radford, Hilditch, Harris, Forster, Taylor, Lochhead, Henderson, Spence, Partridge

Match # 1005 Saturday 07/01/22   FA Cup 1st Round   at Old Trafford   Attendance 25726
Result: **Manchester United 1 Cardiff City 4**
Teamsheet: Mew, Radford, Scott, Hilditch, McBain, Harris, Gibson, Lochhead, Spence, Sapsford, Partridge
Scorer(s):   Sapsford

Match # 1006 Saturday 14/01/22   Football League Division 1   at Old Trafford   Attendance 20000
Result: **Manchester United 0 Newcastle United 1**
Teamsheet: Mew, Radford, Silcock, Hilditch, McBain, Grimwood, Gibson, Lochhead, Spence, Sapsford, Partridge

Match # 1007 Saturday 21/01/22   Football League Division 1   at Roker Park   Attendance 10000
Result: **Sunderland 2 Manchester United 1**
Teamsheet: Mew, Radford, Silcock, Hilditch, McBain, Grimwood, Spence, Lochhead, Henderson, Sapsford, Partridge
Scorer(s):   Sapsford

Match # 1008 Saturday 28/01/22   Football League Division 1   at Old Trafford   Attendance 18000
Result: **Manchester United 3 Sunderland 1**
Teamsheet: Mew, Radford, Silcock, Hilditch, McBain, Grimwood, Spence, Lochhead, Henderson, Sapsford, Robinson
Scorer(s):   Lochhead, Sapsford, Spence

Match # 1009 Saturday 11/02/22   Football League Division 1   at Old Trafford   Attendance 30000
Result: **Manchester United 1 Huddersfield Town 1**
Teamsheet: Mew, Radford, Silcock, Hilditch, McBain, Grimwood, Spence, Lochhead, Henderson, Sapsford, Robinson
Scorer(s):   Spence

Match # 1010 Saturday 18/02/22   Football League Division 1   at St Andrews   Attendance 20000
Result: **Birmingham City 0 Manchester United 1**
Teamsheet: Mew, Radford, Silcock, Bennion, McBain, Grimwood, Robinson, Lochhead, Spence, Sapsford, Partridge
Scorer(s):   Spence

Match # 1011 Saturday 25/02/22   Football League Division 1   at Old Trafford   Attendance 35000
Result: **Manchester United 1 Birmingham City 1**
Teamsheet: Mew, Radford, Silcock, Bennion, Haslam, McBain, Harrison, Lochhead, Spence, Sapsford, Partridge
Scorer(s):   Sapsford

Match # 1012 Monday 27/02/22   Football League Division 1   at Leeds Road   Attendance 30000
Result: **Huddersfield Town 1 Manchester United 1**
Teamsheet: Mew, Barlow, Silcock, Bennion, Grimwood, McBain, Harrison, Lochhead, Spence, Sapsford, Partridge
Scorer(s):   Sapsford

Match # 1013 Saturday 11/03/22   Football League Division 1   at Old Trafford   Attendance 30000
Result: **Manchester United 1 Arsenal 0**
Teamsheet: Mew, Radford, Silcock, Bennion, Grimwood, McBain, Harrison, Lochhead, Spence, Sapsford, Partridge
Scorer(s):   Spence

Match # 1014 Saturday 18/03/22   Football League Division 1   at Old Trafford   Attendance 30000
Result: **Manchester United 0 Blackburn Rovers 1**
Teamsheet: Mew, Radford, Silcock, Bennion, Grimwood, McBain, Harrison, Lochhead, Spence, Sapsford, Partridge

Match # 1015 Saturday 25/03/22   Football League Division 1   at Ewood Park   Attendance 15000
Result: **Blackburn Rovers 3 Manchester United 0**
Teamsheet: Mew, Radford, Silcock, Bennion, Grimwood, McBain, Gibson, Hilditch, Spence, Sapsford, Partridge

Match # 1016 Saturday 01/04/22   Football League Division 1   at Old Trafford   Attendance 28000
Result: **Manchester United 0 Bolton Wanderers 1**
Teamsheet: Mew, Barlow, Silcock, Bennion, Hilditch, McBain, Spence, Gibson, Grimwood, Sapsford, Partridge

SEASON 1921/22 (continued)

Match # 1017 Wednesday 05/04/22   Football League Division 1   at Highbury   Attendance 25000
Result: **Arsenal 3 Manchester United 1**
Teamsheet: Mew, Brett, Silcock, Bennion, Hilditch, Grimwood, Harrison, Myerscough, Spence, Lochhead, Partridge
Scorer(s):   Lochhead

Match # 1018 Saturday 08/04/22   Football League Division 1   at Burnden Park   Attendance 28000
Result: **Bolton Wanderers 1 Manchester United 0**
Teamsheet: Mew, Howarth, Silcock, Bennion, Hilditch, Grimwood, Harrison, Myerscough, Spence, Sapsford, Partridge

Match # 1019 Saturday 15/04/22   Football League Division 1   at Old Trafford   Attendance 30000
Result: **Manchester United 0 Oldham Athletic 3**
Teamsheet: Mew, Howarth, Silcock, Bennion, Hilditch, Grimwood, Harrison, McBain, Spence, Sapsford, Partridge

Match # 1020 Monday 17/04/22   Football League Division 1   at Old Trafford   Attendance 28000
Result: **Manchester United 3 Sheffield United 2**
Teamsheet: Mew, Howarth, Silcock, Hilditch, McBain, Grimwood, Harrison, Lochhead, Radford, Partridge, Robinson
Scorer(s):   Harrison, Lochhead, Partridge

Match # 1021 Saturday 22/04/22   Football League Division 1   at Boundary Park   Attendance 30000
Result: **Oldham Athletic 1 Manchester United 1**
Teamsheet: Mew, Radford, Silcock, Hilditch, McBain, Grimwood, Harrison, Myerscough, Lochhead, Partridge, Thomas
Scorer(s):   Lochhead

Match # 1011 Saturday 29/04/22   Football League Division 1   at Old Trafford   Attendance 18000
Result: **Manchester United 1 Cardiff City 1**
Teamsheet: Mew, Radford, Pugh, Hilditch, Harris, Grimwood, Harrison, Myerscough, Lochhead, Partridge, Thomas
Scorer(s):   Partridge

Match # 1023 Saturday 06/05/22   Football League Division 1   at Ninian Park   Attendance 16000
Result: **Cardiff City 3 Manchester United 1**
Teamsheet: Mew, Radford, Silcock, Hilditch, Harris, Grimwood, Harrison, Myerscough, Lochhead, Partridge, Thomas
Scorer(s):   Lochhead

SEASON 1921/22 SUMMARY

APPEARANCES

PLAYER	LGE	FAC	TOT
Mew	41	1	42
Partridge	37	1	38
Silcock	36	1	36
Spence	35	1	36
Lochhead	31	1	32
Hilditch	29	1	30
Sapsford	29	1	30
Grimwood	28	–	28
Radford	26	1	27
Scott	23	1	24
McBain	21	1	22
Harrison	21	–	21
Bennion	15	–	15
Harris	13	1	14
Gibson	11	1	12

APPEARANCES

PLAYER	LGE	FAC	TOT
Robinson	12	–	12
Brett	10	–	10
Henderson	10	–	10
Myerscough	7	–	7
Bissett	6	–	6
Forster	4	–	4
Howarth	4	–	4
Barlow	3	–	3
Thomas	3	–	3
Goodwin	2	–	2
Haslam	1	–	1
Pugh	1	–	1
Schofield	1	–	1
Steward	1	–	1
Taylor	1	–	1

GOALSCORERS

PLAYER	LGE	FAC	TOT
Spence	15	–	15
Sapsford	9	1	10
Lochhead	8	–	8
Partridge	4	–	4
Harrison	2	–	2
Henderson	2	–	2
Robinson	1	–	1

RESULTS & ATTENDANCES SUMMARY

		P	W	D	L	F	A	TOTAL	AVGE
League	H	21	7	7	7	25	26	573000	27286
	A	21	1	5	15	16	47	489000	23286
	TOTAL	42	8	12	22	41	73	1062000	25286
FA Cup	H	1	0	0	1	1	4	25726	25726
	A	0	0	0	0	0	0	0	n/a
	TOTAL	1	0	0	1	1	4	25726	25726
Overall	H	22	7	7	8	26	30	598726	27215
	A	21	1	5	15	16	47	489000	23286
	TOTAL	43	8	12	23	42	77	1087726	25296

FINAL TABLE – LEAGUE DIVISION ONE

		P	HOME W	HOME D	HOME L	HOME F	HOME A	AWAY W	AWAY D	AWAY L	AWAY F	AWAY A	PTS	GD
1	Liverpool	42	15	4	2	43	15	7	9	5	20	21	57	27
2	Tottenham Hotspur	42	15	3	3	43	17	6	6	9	22	22	51	26
3	Burnley	42	16	3	2	49	18	6	2	13	23	36	49	18
4	Cardiff City	42	13	2	6	40	26	6	8	7	21	27	48	8
5	Aston Villa	42	16	3	2	50	19	6	0	15	24	36	47	19
6	Bolton Wanderers	42	12	4	5	40	24	8	3	10	28	35	47	9
7	Newcastle United	42	11	5	5	36	19	7	5	9	23	26	46	14
8	Middlesbrough	42	12	6	3	46	19	4	8	9	33	50	46	10
9	Chelsea	42	9	6	6	17	16	8	6	7	23	27	46	-3
10	Manchester City	42	13	7	1	44	21	5	2	14	21	49	45	-5
11	Sheffield United	42	11	3	7	32	17	4	7	10	27	37	40	5
12	Sunderland	42	13	4	4	46	23	3	4	14	14	39	40	-2
13	West Bromwich Albion	42	8	6	7	26	23	7	4	10	25	40	40	-12
14	Huddersfield Town	42	12	3	6	33	14	3	6	12	20	40	39	-1
15	Blackburn Rovers	42	7	6	8	35	31	6	6	9	19	26	38	-3
16	Preston North End	42	12	7	2	33	20	1	5	15	9	45	38	-23
17	Arsenal	42	10	6	5	27	19	5	1	15	20	37	37	-9
18	Birmingham City	42	9	2	10	25	29	6	5	10	23	31	37	-12
19	Oldham Athletic	42	8	7	6	21	15	5	4	12	17	35	37	-12
20	Everton	42	10	7	4	42	22	2	5	14	15	33	36	2
21	Bradford City	42	8	5	8	28	30	3	5	13	20	42	32	-24
22	MANCHESTER UNITED	42	7	7	7	25	26	1	5	15	16	47	28	-32

SEASON 1922/23

Match # 1024 Saturday 26/08/22   Football League Division 2   at Old Trafford   Attendance 30000
Result: **Manchester United 2   Crystal Palace 1**
Teamsheet: Mew, Radford, Silcock, Hilditch, McBain, Grimwood, Wood, Lochhead, Spence, Partridge, Thomas
Scorer(s):   Spence, Wood

Match # 1025 Monday 28/08/22   Football League Division 2   at Hillsborough   Attendance 12500
Result: **Sheffield Wednesday 1   Manchester United 0**
Teamsheet: Mew, Radford, Silcock, Hilditch, McBain, Grimwood, Wood, Lochhead, Spence, Williams, Thomas

Match # 1026 Saturday 02/09/22   Football League Division 2   at Sydenham Hill   Attendance 8500
Result: **Crystal Palace 2   Manchester United 3**
Teamsheet: Mew, Moore, Silcock, Hilditch, McBain, Grimwood, Wood, Lochhead, Spence, Williams, Thomas
Scorer(s):   Spence 2, Williams

Match # 1027 Monday 04/09/22   Football League Division 2   at Old Trafford   Attendance 22000
Result: **Manchester United 1   Sheffield Wednesday 0**
Teamsheet: Mew, Moore, Silcock, Hilditch, McBain, Grimwood, Wood, Lochhead, Spence, Williams, Thomas
Scorer(s):   Spence

Match # 1028 Saturday 09/09/22   Football League Division 2   at Molineux   Attendance 18000
Result: **Wolverhampton Wanderers 0   Manchester United 1**
Teamsheet: Mew, Moore, Silcock, Hilditch, Barson, McBain, Wood, Lochhead, Spence, Williams, Thomas
Scorer(s):   Williams

Match # 1029 Saturday 16/09/22   Football League Division 2   at Old Trafford   Attendance 28000
Result: **Manchester United 1   Wolverhampton Wanderers 0**
Teamsheet: Mew, Moore, Silcock, Hilditch, Barson, McBain, Wood, Lochhead, Spence, Partridge, Thomas
Scorer(s):   Spence

Match # 1030 Saturday 23/09/22   Football League Division 2   at Highfield Road   Attendance 19000
Result: **Coventry City 2   Manchester United 0**
Teamsheet: Mew, Moore, Silcock, Hilditch, Barson, McBain, Lyner, Sarvis, Spence, Partridge, Thomas

Match # 1031 Saturday 30/09/22   Football League Division 2   at Old Trafford   Attendance 25000
Result: **Manchester United 2   Coventry City 1**
Teamsheet: Mew, Moore, Silcock, Hilditch, Barson, McBain, Lyner, Lochhead, Spence, Henderson, Thomas
Scorer(s):   Henderson, Spence

Match # 1032 Saturday 07/10/22   Football League Division 2   at Old Trafford   Attendance 25000
Result: **Manchester United 1   Port Vale 2**
Teamsheet: Mew, Moore, Silcock, Hilditch, Barson, McBain, Lyner, Lochhead, Spence, Henderson, Thomas
Scorer(s):   Spence

Match # 1033 Saturday 14/10/22   Football League Division 2   at Old Recreation Ground   Attendance 16000
Result: **Port Vale 1   Manchester United 0**
Teamsheet: Mew, Radford, Silcock, Hilditch, Barson, McBain, Wood, Bain, Spence, Partridge, Thomas

Match # 1034 Saturday 21/10/22   Football League Division 2   at Old Trafford   Attendance 18000
Result: **Manchester United 1   Fulham 1**
Teamsheet: Mew, Radford, Pugh, Hilditch, Barson, Grimwood, Wood, Myerscough, Lochhead, Williams, Partridge
Scorer(s):   Myerscough

Match # 1035 Saturday 28/10/22   Football League Division 2   at Craven Cottage   Attendance 20000
Result: **Fulham 0   Manchester United 0**
Teamsheet: Mew, Radford, Silcock, Hilditch, Barson, Grimwood, Wood, Myerscough, Lochhead, McBain, Partridge

Match # 1036 Saturday 04/11/22   Football League Division 2   at Old Trafford   Attendance 16500
Result: **Manchester United 0   Leyton Orient 0**
Teamsheet: Mew, Radford, Silcock, Hilditch, Barson, Grimwood, Wood, Myerscough, Spence, McBain, Partridge

Match # 1037 Saturday 11/11/22   Football League Division 2   at Millfields Road   Attendance 11000
Result: **Leyton Orient 1   Manchester United 1**
Teamsheet: Mew, Radford, Silcock, Hilditch, Barson, Grimwood, Spence, Myerscough, Goldthorpe, McBain, Partridge
Scorer(s):   Goldthorpe

Match # 1038 Saturday 18/11/22   Football League Division 2   at Gigg Lane   Attendance 21000
Result: **Bury 2   Manchester United 2**
Teamsheet: Mew, Radford, Silcock, Hilditch, Barson, Grimwood, Spence, Myerscough, Goldthorpe, McBain, Partridge
Scorer(s):   Goldthorpe 2

Match # 1039 Saturday 25/11/22   Football League Division 2   at Old Trafford   Attendance 28000
Result: **Manchester United 0   Bury 1**
Teamsheet: Mew, Radford, Silcock, Hilditch, Barson, Grimwood, Spence, Myerscough, Goldthorpe, McBain, Partridge

Match # 1040 Saturday 02/12/22   Football League Division 2   at Old Trafford   Attendance 13500
Result: **Manchester United 3   Rotherham United 0**
Teamsheet: Mew, Radford, Silcock, Hilditch, Barson, Grimwood, Wood, Spence, Lochhead, McBain, Partridge
Scorer(s):   Lochhead, McBain, Spence

Match # 1041 Saturday 09/12/22   Football League Division 2   at Millmoor   Attendance 7500
Result: **Rotherham United 1   Manchester United 1**
Teamsheet: Mew, Radford, Moore, Hilditch, Barson, Grimwood, Wood, Spence, Goldthorpe, Lochhead, Partridge
Scorer(s):   Goldthorpe

SEASON 1922/23 (continued)

Match # 1042 Saturday 16/12/22   Football League Division 2   at Old Trafford   Attendance 24000
Result: **Manchester United 1   Stockport County 0**
Teamsheet: Mew, Radford, Silcock, Hilditch, Barson, Grimwood, Cartman, Spence, Goldthorpe, McBain, Partridge
Scorer(s):   McBain

Match # 1043 Saturday 23/12/22   Football League Division 2   at Edgeley Park   Attendance 15500
Result: **Stockport County 1   Manchester United 0**
Teamsheet: Mew, Radford, Silcock, Hilditch, Barson, Grimwood, Cartman, Spence, Goldthorpe, McBain, Partridge

Match # 1044 Monday 25/12/22   Football League Division 2   at Old Trafford   Attendance 17500
Result: **Manchester United 1   West Ham United 2**
Teamsheet: Mew, Radford, Silcock, McBain, Barson, Grimwood, Cartman, Spence, Goldthorpe, Lochhead, Partridge
Scorer(s):   Lochhead

Match # 1045 Tuesday 26/12/22   Football League Division 2   at Upton Park   Attendance 25000
Result: **West Ham United 0   Manchester United 2**
Teamsheet: Mew, Radford, Silcock, Bennion, McBain, Grimwood, Wood, Spence, Goldthorpe, Lochhead, Partridge
Scorer(s):   Lochhead 2

Match # 1046 Saturday 30/12/22   Football League Division 2   at Anlaby Road   Attendance 6750
Result: **Hull City 2   Manchester United 1**
Teamsheet: Mew, Radford, Silcock, Bennion, McBain, Grimwood, Wood, Spence, Goldthorpe, Lochhead, Partridge
Scorer(s):   Lochhead

Match # 1047 Monday 01/01/23   Football League Division 2   at Old Trafford   Attendance 29000
Result: **Manchester United 1   Barnsley 0**
Teamsheet: Mew, Radford, Moore, Hilditch, Barson, Grimwood, Spence, Myerscough, Goldthorpe, Lochhead, Partridge
Scorer(s):   Lochhead

Match # 1048 Saturday 06/01/23   Football League Division 2   at Old Trafford   Attendance 15000
Result: **Manchester United 3   Hull City 2**
Teamsheet: Mew, Radford, Moore, Hilditch, Barson, Grimwood, Wood, Barber, Goldthorpe, Lochhead, Partridge
Scorer(s):   Goldthorpe, Lochhead, own goal

Match # 1049 Saturday 13/01/23   FA Cup 1st Round   at Valley Parade   Attendance 27000
Result: **Bradford City 1   Manchester United 1**
Teamsheet: Mew, Radford, Silcock, Hilditch, Barson, Grimwood, Wood, Lochhead, Spence, Goldthorpe, Partridge
Scorer(s):   Partridge

Match # 1050 Wednesday 17/01/23   FA Cup 1st Round Replay   at Old Trafford   Attendance 27791
Result: **Manchester United 2   Bradford City 0**
Teamsheet: Mew, Radford, Silcock, Hilditch, Barson, Grimwood, Barber, Lochhead, Spence, Goldthorpe, Partridge
Scorer(s):   Barber, Goldthorpe

Match # 1051 Saturday 20/01/23   Football League Division 2   at Old Trafford   Attendance 25000
Result: **Manchester United 0   Leeds United 0**
Teamsheet: Mew, Moore, Silcock, Hilditch, Barson, Grimwood, Lievesley, Barber, Goldthorpe, Lochhead, Partridge

Match # 1052 Saturday 27/01/23   Football League Division 2   at Elland Road   Attendance 24500
Result: **Leeds United 0   Manchester United 1**
Teamsheet: Mew, Radford, Silcock, Hilditch, Barson, Grimwood, Lievesley, Myerscough, Goldthorpe, Lochhead, Partridge
Scorer(s):   Lochhead

Match # 1053 Saturday 03/02/23   FA Cup 2nd Round   at White Hart Lane   Attendance 38333
Result: **Tottenham Hotspur 4   Manchester United 0**
Teamsheet: Mew, Radford, Silcock, Hilditch, Barson, Grimwood, Myerscough, Lochhead, Lievesley, Goldthorpe, Partridge

Match # 1054 Saturday 10/02/23   Football League Division 2   at Meadow Lane   Attendance 10000
Result: **Notts County 1   Manchester United 6**
Teamsheet: Mew, Radford, Silcock, Bennion, Barson, Grimwood, Thomas, Myerscough, Goldthorpe, Lochhead, Partridge
Scorer(s):   Goldthorpe 4, Myerscough 2

Match # 1055 Saturday 17/02/23   Football League Division 2   at Old Trafford   Attendance 27500
Result: **Manchester United 0   Derby County 0**
Teamsheet: Mew, Radford, Silcock, Bennion, Barson, Grimwood, Thomas, Myerscough, Goldthorpe, Lochhead, Partridge

Match # 1056 Wednesday 21/02/23   Football League Division 2   at Old Trafford   Attendance 12100
Result: **Manchester United 1   Notts County 1**
Teamsheet: Mew, Radford, Silcock, Bennion, Barson, Grimwood, Spence, Myerscough, Goldthorpe, Lochhead, Partridge
Scorer(s):   Lochhead

Match # 1057 Saturday 03/03/23   Football League Division 2   at Old Trafford   Attendance 30000
Result: **Manchester United 1   Southampton 2**
Teamsheet: Mew, Radford, Silcock, Hilditch, Barson, Grimwood, Spence, Myerscough, MacDonald, Lochhead, Partridge
Scorer(s):   Lochhead

Match # 1058 Wednesday 14/03/23   Football League Division 2   at Baseball Ground   Attendance 12000
Result: **Derby County 1   Manchester United 1**
Teamsheet: Mew, Radford, Silcock, Bennion, Barson, Grimwood, Spence, Myerscough, MacDonald, Lochhead, Partridge
Scorer(s):   MacDonald

Match # 1059 Saturday 17/03/23   Football League Division 2   at Valley Parade   Attendance 10000
Result: **Bradford City 1   Manchester United 1**
Teamsheet: Mew, Radford, Silcock, Bennion, Barson, Grimwood, Spence, Mann, Goldthorpe, Lochhead, Partridge
Scorer(s):   Goldthorpe

SEASON 1922/23 (continued)

Match # 1060	Wednesday 21/03/23	Football League Division 2	at Old Trafford	Attendance 15000
Result:	**Manchester United 1 Bradford City 1**			
Teamsheet:	Mew, Radford, Moore, Bennion, Barson, Grimwood, Spence, Mann, Goldthorpe, Lochhead, Partridge			
Scorer(s):	Spence			

Match # 1061	Friday 30/03/23	Football League Division 2	at Old Trafford	Attendance 26000
Result:	**Manchester United 3 South Shields 0**			
Teamsheet:	Mew, Radford, Silcock, Hilditch, Barson, Grimwood, Spence, Mann, Goldthorpe, Lochhead, Thomas			
Scorer(s):	Goldthorpe 2, Lochhead			

Match # 1062	Saturday 31/03/23	Football League Division 2	at Bloomfield Road	Attendance 21000
Result:	**Blackpool 1 Manchester United 0**			
Teamsheet:	Mew, Radford, Silcock, Hilditch, Barson, Grimwood, Spence, Mann, Goldthorpe, Lochhead, Thomas			

Match # 1063	Monday 02/04/23	Football League Division 2	at Talbot Road	Attendance 6500
Result:	**South Shields 0 Manchester United 3**			
Teamsheet:	Mew, Radford, Silcock, Bennion, Hilditch, Grimwood, Spence, Mann, Goldthorpe, Lochhead, Thomas			
Scorer(s):	Goldthorpe, Hilditch, Spence			

Match # 1064	Saturday 07/04/23	Football League Division 2	at Old Trafford	Attendance 20000
Result:	**Manchester United 2 Blackpool 1**			
Teamsheet:	Mew, Radford, Silcock, Bennion, Hilditch, Grimwood, Spence, Mann, Goldthorpe, Lochhead, Thomas			
Scorer(s):	Lochhead, Radford			

Match # 1065	Wednesday 11/04/23	Football League Division 2	at The Dell	Attendance 5500
Result:	**Southampton 0 Manchester United 0**			
Teamsheet:	Mew, Radford, Silcock, Bennion, Hilditch, Grimwood, Spence, Mann, Bain, Lochhead, Thomas			

Match # 1066	Saturday 14/04/23	Football League Division 2	at Filbert Street	Attendance 25000
Result:	**Leicester City 0 Manchester United 1**			
Teamsheet:	Steward, Radford, Silcock, Bennion, Hilditch, Grimwood, Spence, Mann, Bain, Lochhead, Partridge			
Scorer(s):	Bain			

Match # 1067	Saturday 21/04/23	Football League Division 2	at Old Trafford	Attendance 30000
Result:	**Manchester United 0 Leicester City 2**			
Teamsheet:	Mew, Radford, Silcock, Bennion, Hilditch, Grimwood, Spence, Mann, Bain, Lochhead, Partridge			

Match # 1068	Saturday 28/04/23	Football League Division 2	at Oakwell	Attendance 8000
Result:	**Barnsley 2 Manchester United 2**			
Teamsheet:	Mew, Radford, Silcock, Bennion, Barson, Grimwood, Mann, Broome, Spence, Lochhead, Thomas			
Scorer(s):	Lochhead, Spence			

SEASON 1922/23 SUMMARY

APPEARANCES

PLAYER	LGE	FAC	TOT
Mew	41	3	44
Silcock	37	3	40
Grimwood	36	3	39
Lochhead	34	3	37
Radford	34	3	37
Spence	35	2	37
Hilditch	32	3	35
Barson	31	3	34
Partridge	30	3	33
Goldthorpe	22	3	25
McBain	21	–	21
Thomas	18	–	18
Wood	15	1	16
Bennion	14	–	14
Myerscough	13	1	14
Moore	12	–	12
Mann	10	–	10
Williams	5	–	5
Bain	4	–	4
Barber	2	1	3
Cartman	3	–	3
Lievesley	2	1	3
Lyner	3	–	3
Henderson	2	–	2
MacDonald	2	–	2
Broome	1	–	1
Pugh	1	–	1
Sarvis	1	–	1
Steward	1	–	1

GOALSCORERS

PLAYER	LGE	FAC	TOT
Goldthorpe	13	1	14
Lochhead	13	–	13
Spence	11	–	11
Myerscough	3	–	3
McBain	2	–	2
Williams	2	–	2
Bain	1	–	1
Henderson	1	–	1
Hilditch	1	–	1
MacDonald	1	–	1
Radford	1	–	1
Wood	1	–	1
Barber	–	1	1
Partridge	–	1	1
own goal	1	–	1

RESULTS & ATTENDANCES SUMMARY

		P	W	D	L	F	A	TOTAL	AVGE
League	H	21	10	6	5	25	17	477100	22719
	A	21	7	8	6	26	19	303250	14440
	TOTAL	42	17	14	11	51	36	780350	18580
FA Cup	H	1	1	0	0	2	0	27791	27791
	A	2	0	1	1	1	5	65333	32667
	TOTAL	3	1	1	1	3	5	93124	31041
Overall	H	22	11	6	5	27	17	504891	22950
	A	23	7	9	7	27	24	368583	16025
	TOTAL	45	18	15	12	54	41	873474	19411

FINAL TABLE – LEAGUE DIVISION TWO

		P	W (HOME)	D	L	F	A	W (AWAY)	D	L	F	A	PTS	GD
1	Notts County	42	16	1	4	29	15	7	6	8	17	19	53	12
2	West Ham United	42	9	8	4	21	11	11	3	7	42	27	51	25
3	Leicester City	42	14	2	5	42	19	7	7	7	23	25	51	21
4	MANCHESTER UNITED	42	10	6	5	25	17	7	8	6	26	19	48	15
5	Blackpool	42	12	4	5	37	14	6	7	8	23	29	47	17
6	Bury	42	14	5	2	41	16	4	6	11	14	30	47	9
7	Leeds United	42	11	8	2	26	10	7	3	11	17	26	47	7
8	Sheffield Wednesday	42	14	3	4	36	16	3	9	9	18	31	46	7
9	Barnsley	42	12	4	5	42	21	5	7	9	20	30	45	11
10	Fulham	42	10	7	4	29	12	6	5	10	14	20	44	11
11	Southampton	42	10	5	6	28	21	4	9	8	12	19	42	0
12	Hull City	42	9	8	4	29	22	5	6	10	14	23	42	-2
13	South Shields	42	11	7	3	26	12	4	3	14	9	32	40	-9
14	Derby County	42	9	5	7	25	16	5	6	10	21	34	39	-4
15	Bradford City	42	8	7	6	27	18	4	6	11	14	27	37	-4
16	Crystal Palace	42	10	7	4	33	16	4	4	14	21	46	37	-8
17	Port Vale	42	8	6	7	23	18	6	3	12	16	33	37	-12
18	Coventry City	42	12	2	7	35	21	3	5	13	11	42	37	-17
19	Leyton Orient	42	9	6	6	26	17	3	6	12	14	33	36	-10
20	Stockport County	42	10	6	5	32	24	4	2	15	11	34	36	-15
21	Rotherham United	42	10	7	4	30	19	3	2	16	14	44	35	-19
22	Wolverhampton Wanderers	42	9	4	8	32	26	0	5	16	10	51	27	-35

SEASON 1923/24

Match # 1069 Saturday 25/08/23 Football League Division 2 at Ashton Gate Attendance 20500
Result: **Bristol City 1 Manchester United 2**
Teamsheet: Mew, Radford, Moore, Bennion, Barson, Hilditch, Ellis, Goldthorpe, MacDonald, Lochhead, McPherson
Scorer(s): Lochhead, MacDonald

Match # 1070 Monday 27/08/23 Football League Division 2 at Old Trafford Attendance 21750
Result: **Manchester United 1 Southampton 0**
Teamsheet: Mew, Radford, Moore, Bennion, Barson, Hilditch, Ellis, Goldthorpe, MacDonald, Lochhead, McPherson
Scorer(s): Goldthorpe

Match # 1071 Saturday 01/09/23 Football League Division 2 at Old Trafford Attendance 21000
Result: **Manchester United 2 Bristol City 1**
Teamsheet: Mew, Radford, Moore, Bennion, Barson, Hilditch, Ellis, Spence, MacDonald, Lochhead, McPherson
Scorer(s): Lochhead, Spence

Match # 1072 Monday 03/09/23 Football League Division 2 at The Dell Attendance 11500
Result: **Southampton 0 Manchester United 0**
Teamsheet: Mew, Radford, Moore, Bennion, Barson, Hilditch, Ellis, Spence, MacDonald, Lochhead, McPherson

Match # 1073 Saturday 08/09/23 Football League Division 2 at Gigg Lane Attendance 19000
Result: **Bury 2 Manchester United 0**
Teamsheet: Mew, Radford, Moore, Bennion, Barson, Hilditch, Ellis, Spence, MacDonald, Lochhead, McPherson

Match # 1074 Saturday 15/09/23 Football League Division 2 at Old Trafford Attendance 43000
Result: **Manchester United 0 Bury 1**
Teamsheet: Steward, Radford, Moore, Hilditch, Barson, Grimwood, Ellis, Mann, Goldthorpe, Lochhead, McPherson

Match # 1075 Saturday 22/09/23 Football League Division 2 at Talbot Road Attendance 9750
Result: **South Shields 1 Manchester United 0**
Teamsheet: Mew, Radford, Moore, Hilditch, Barson, Grimwood, Ellis, Mann, Spence, Lochhead, McPherson

Match # 1076 Saturday 29/09/23 Football League Division 2 at Old Trafford Attendance 22250
Result: **Manchester United 1 South Shields 1**
Teamsheet: Mew, Radford, Moore, Hilditch, Barson, Grimwood, Ellis, Goldthorpe, MacDonald, Lochhead, McPherson
Scorer(s): Lochhead

Match # 1077 Saturday 06/10/23 Football League Division 2 at Boundary Park Attendance 12250
Result: **Oldham Athletic 3 Manchester United 2**
Teamsheet: Mew, Radford, Moore, Bennion, Hilditch, Grimwood, Spence, Lochhead, MacDonald, Kennedy, McPherson
Scorer(s): own goals 2

Match # 1078 Saturday 13/10/23 Football League Division 2 at Old Trafford Attendance 26000
Result: **Manchester United 2 Oldham Athletic 0**
Teamsheet: Steward, Moore, Dennis, Bennion, Haslam, Hilditch, Spence, Mann, Bain, Lochhead, McPherson
Scorer(s): Bain 2

Match # 1079 Saturday 20/10/23 Football League Division 2 at Old Trafford Attendance 31500
Result: **Manchester United 3 Stockport County 0**
Teamsheet: Steward, Moore, Dennis, Bennion, Haslam, Hilditch, Spence, Mann, Bain, Lochhead, McPherson
Scorer(s): Mann 2, Bain

Match # 1080 Saturday 27/10/23 Football League Division 2 at Edgeley Park Attendance 16500
Result: **Stockport County 3 Manchester United 2**
Teamsheet: Steward, Moore, Dennis, Bennion, Haslam, Hilditch, Spence, Barber, Bain, Lochhead, McPherson
Scorer(s): Barber, Lochhead

Match # 1081 Saturday 03/11/23 Football League Division 2 at Filbert Street Attendance 17000
Result: **Leicester City 2 Manchester United 2**
Teamsheet: Steward, Moore, Radford, Bennion, Haslam, Hilditch, Spence, Mann, Bain, Lochhead, McPherson
Scorer(s): Lochhead 2

Match # 1082 Saturday 10/11/23 Football League Division 2 at Old Trafford Attendance 20000
Result: **Manchester United 3 Leicester City 0**
Teamsheet: Steward, Tyler, Moore, Bennion, Grimwood, Hilditch, Spence, Mann, Bain, Lochhead, McPherson
Scorer(s): Lochhead, Mann, Spence

Match # 1083 Saturday 17/11/23 Football League Division 2 at Highfield Road Attendance 13580
Result: **Coventry City 1 Manchester United 1**
Teamsheet: Steward, Radford, Moore, Bennion, Grimwood, Hilditch, Spence, Mann, Bain, Lochhead, McPherson
Scorer(s): own goal

Match # 1084 Saturday 01/12/23 Football League Division 2 at Elland Road Attendance 20000
Result: **Leeds United 0 Manchester United 0**
Teamsheet: Steward, Radford, Moore, Bennion, Barson, Hilditch, Spence, Mann, Bain, Lochhead, McPherson

Match # 1085 Saturday 08/12/23 Football League Division 2 at Old Trafford Attendance 22250
Result: **Manchester United 3 Leeds United 1**
Teamsheet: Steward, Radford, Moore, Bennion, Grimwood, Hilditch, Spence, Mann, Bain, Lochhead, McPherson
Scorer(s): Lochhead 2, Spence

Match # 1086 Saturday 15/12/23 Football League Division 2 at Old Recreation Ground Attendance 7500
Result: **Port Vale 0 Manchester United 1**
Teamsheet: Steward, Radford, Moore, Bennion, Grimwood, Hilditch, Spence, Mann, Bain, Lochhead, Thomas
Scorer(s): Grimwood

SEASON 1923/24 (continued)

Match # 1087   Saturday 22/12/23   Football League Division 2   at Old Trafford   Attendance 11750
Result: **Manchester United 5 Port Vale 0**
Teamsheet: Steward, Radford, Moore, Grimwood, Hilditch, Spence, Mann, Bain, Lochhead, McPherson
Scorer(s):   Bain 3, Lochhead, Spence

Match # 1088   Tuesday 25/12/23   Football League Division 2   at Old Trafford   Attendance 34000
Result: **Manchester United 1 Barnsley 2**
Teamsheet: Steward, Radford, Moore, Hilditch, Grimwood, Bennion, Spence, Mann, Bain, Lochhead, McPherson
Scorer(s):   Grimwood

Match # 1089   Wednesday 26/12/23   Football League Division 2   at Oakwell   Attendance 12000
Result: **Barnsley 1 Manchester United 0**
Teamsheet: Steward, Radford, Moore, Hilditch, Grimwood, Bennion, Spence, Mann, Bain, Lochhead, McPherson

Match # 1090   Saturday 29/12/23   Football League Division 2   at Valley Parade   Attendance 11500
Result: **Bradford City 0 Manchester United 0**
Teamsheet: Steward, Radford, Moore, Bennion, Barson, Hilditch, Spence, Mann, Bain, Lochhead, McPherson

Match # 1091   Wednesday 02/01/24   Football League Division 2   at Old Trafford   Attendance 7000
Result: **Manchester United 1 Coventry City 2**
Teamsheet: Steward, Radford, Moore, Bennion, Barson, Hilditch, Spence, Mann, Bain, Lochhead, McPherson
Scorer(s):   Bain

Match # 1092   Saturday 05/01/24   Football League Division 2   at Old Trafford   Attendance 18000
Result: **Manchester United 3 Bradford City 0**
Teamsheet: Steward, Radford, Moore, Bennion, Barson, Hilditch, Spence, Mann, Bain, Lochhead, McPherson
Scorer(s):   Bain, Lochhead, McPherson

Match # 1093   Saturday 12/01/24   FA Cup 1st Round   at Old Trafford   Attendance 35700
Result: **Manchester United 1 Plymouth Argyle 0**
Teamsheet: Steward, Radford, Moore, Bennion, Barson, Hilditch, Mann, Bain, Spence, Lochhead, McPherson
Scorer(s):   McPherson

Match # 1094   Saturday 19/01/24   Football League Division 2   at Craven Cottage   Attendance 15500
Result: **Fulham 3 Manchester United 1**
Teamsheet: Steward, Radford, Moore, Bennion, Barson, Hilditch, Spence, Smith, Bain, Lochhead, McPherson
Scorer(s):   Lochhead

Match # 1095   Saturday 26/01/24   Football League Division 2   at Old Trafford   Attendance 25000
Result: **Manchester United 0 Fulham 0**
Teamsheet: Steward, Radford, Moore, Bennion, Barson, Hilditch, Spence, Mann, Smith, Lochhead, McPherson

Match # 1096   Saturday 02/02/24   FA Cup 2nd Round   at Old Trafford   Attendance 66673
Result: **Manchester United 0 Huddersfield Town 3**
Teamsheet: Steward, Silcock, Moore, Bennion, Barson, Hilditch, Mann, Henderson, Spence, Lochhead, McPherson

Match # 1097   Wednesday 06/02/24   Football League Division 2   at Bloomfield Road   Attendance 6000
Result: **Blackpool 1 Manchester United 0**
Teamsheet: Steward, Radford, Moore, Bennion, Barson, Hilditch, Spence, Kennedy, Bain, Partridge, Thomas

Match # 1098   Saturday 09/02/24   Football League Division 2   at Old Trafford   Attendance 13000
Result: **Manchester United 0 Blackpool 0**
Teamsheet: Steward, Radford, Moore, Bennion, Barson, Hilditch, Spence, Kennedy, Bain, Lochhead, McPherson

Match # 1099   Saturday 16/02/24   Football League Division 2   at Baseball Ground   Attendance 12000
Result: **Derby County 3 Manchester United 0**
Teamsheet: Steward, Radford, Moore, Bennion, Barson, Grimwood, Ellis, Mann, Spence, Lochhead, McPherson

Match # 1100   Saturday 23/02/24   Football League Division 2   at Old Trafford   Attendance 25000
Result: **Manchester United 0 Derby County 0**
Teamsheet: Steward, Radford, Moore, Bennion, Grimwood, Hilditch, Ellis, Lochhead, Spence, Kennedy, Partridge

Match # 1101   Saturday 01/03/24   Football League Division 2   at Seed Hill   Attendance 2750
Result: **Nelson 0 Manchester United 2**
Teamsheet: Steward, Radford, Moore, Bennion, Grimwood, Hilditch, Ellis, Mann, Spence, Kennedy, McPherson
Scorer(s):   Kennedy, Spence

Match # 1102   Saturday 08/03/24   Football League Division 2   at Old Trafford   Attendance 8500
Result: **Manchester United 0 Nelson 1**
Teamsheet: Steward, Radford, Moore, Bennion, Grimwood, Hilditch, Spence, Mann, Lochhead, Kennedy, McPherson

Match # 1103   Saturday 15/03/24   Football League Division 2   at Old Trafford   Attendance 13000
Result: **Manchester United 1 Hull City 1**
Teamsheet: Mew, Radford, Moore, Bennion, Grimwood, Hilditch, Spence, Smith, Lochhead, Miller, Thomas
Scorer(s):   Lochhead

Match # 1104   Saturday 22/03/24   Football League Division 2   at Anlaby Road   Attendance 6250
Result: **Hull City 1 Manchester United 1**
Teamsheet: Mew, Radford, Moore, Bennion, Grimwood, Hilditch, Spence, Smith, Lochhead, Miller, Thomas
Scorer(s):   Miller

SEASON 1923/24 (continued)

Match # 1105   Saturday 29/03/24   Football League Division 2   at Old Trafford   Attendance 13000
Result: **Manchester United 2   Stoke City 2**
Teamsheet: Mew, Moore, Silcock, Bennion, Grimwood, Hilditch, Spence, Smith, Lochhead, Miller, McPherson
Scorer(s):   Smith 2

Match # 1106   Saturday 05/04/24   Football League Division 2   at Victoria Ground   Attendance 11000
Result: **Stoke City 3   Manchester United 0**
Teamsheet: Mew, Moore, Silcock, Bennion, Grimwood, Hilditch, Spence, Smith, Lochhead, Miller, McPherson

Match # 1107   Saturday 12/04/24   Football League Division 2   at Old Trafford   Attendance 8000
Result: **Manchester United 5   Crystal Palace 1**
Teamsheet: Steward, Moore, Silcock, Mann, Grimwood, Hilditch, Evans, Smith, Spence, Lochhead, Partridge
Scorer(s):   Spence 4, Smith

Match # 1108   Friday 18/04/24   Football League Division 2   at Millfields Road   Attendance 18000
Result: **Leyton Orient 1   Manchester United 0**
Teamsheet: Steward, Moore, Silcock, Mann, Grimwood, Hilditch, Evans, Smith, Spence, Lochhead, Partridge

Match # 1109   Saturday 19/04/24   Football League Division 2   at Sydenham Hill   Attendance 7000
Result: **Crystal Palace 1   Manchester United 1**
Teamsheet: Steward, Moore, Silcock, Mann, Grimwood, Hilditch, Evans, Smith, Spence, Lochhead, Partridge
Scorer(s):   Spence

Match # 1110   Monday 21/04/24   Football League Division 2   at Old Trafford   Attendance 11000
Result: **Manchester United 2   Leyton Orient 2**
Teamsheet: Steward, Moore, Silcock, Bennion, Haslam, Hilditch, Evans, Smith, Spence, Lochhead, McPherson
Scorer(s):   Evans 2

Match # 1111   Saturday 26/04/24   Football League Division 2   at Old Trafford   Attendance 7500
Result: **Manchester United 2   Sheffield Wednesday 0**
Teamsheet: Steward, Moore, Silcock, Mann, Haslam, Hilditch, Evans, Smith, McPherson, Lochhead, Thomas
Scorer(s):   Lochhead, Smith

Match # 1112   Saturday 03/05/24   Football League Division 2   at Hillsborough   Attendance 7250
Result: **Sheffield Wednesday 2   Manchester United 0**
Teamsheet: Steward, Moore, Silcock, Mann, Haslam, Hilditch, Evans, Smith, McPherson, Lochhead, Thomas

SEASON 1923/24 SUMMARY

APPEARANCES

PLAYER	LGE	FAC	TOT
Moore	42	2	44
Hilditch	41	2	43
Lochhead	40	2	42
Spence	36	2	38
Bennion	34	2	36
McPherson	34	2	36
Steward	30	2	32
Radford	30	1	31
Mann	25	2	27
Grimwood	22	–	22
Bain	18	1	19
Barson	17	2	19
Mew	12	–	12
Smith	12	–	12
Ellis	11	–	11
Silcock	8	1	9
Haslam	7	–	7
MacDonald	7	–	7
Evans	6	–	6
Kennedy	6	–	6
Thomas	6	–	6
Partridge	5	–	5
Goldthorpe	4	–	4
Miller	4	–	4
Dennis	3	–	3
Barber	1	–	1
Henderson	–	1	1
Tyler	1	–	1

GOALSCORERS

PLAYER	LGE	FAC	TOT
Lochhead	14	–	14
Spence	10	–	10
Bain	8	–	8
Smith	4	–	4
Mann	3	–	3
Evans	2	–	2
Grimwood	2	–	2
McPherson	1	1	2
Barber	1	–	1
Goldthorpe	1	–	1
Kennedy	1	–	1
MacDonald	1	–	1
Miller	1	–	1
own goals	3	–	3

RESULTS & ATTENDANCES SUMMARY

		P	W	D	L	F	A	TOTAL	AVGE
League	H	21	10	7	4	37	15	402500	19167
	A	21	3	7	11	15	29	256830	12230
	TOTAL	42	13	14	15	52	44	659330	15698
FA Cup	H	2	1	0	1	1	3	102373	51187
	A	0	0	0	0	0	0	0	n/a
	TOTAL	2	1	0	1	1	3	102373	51187
Overall	H	23	11	7	5	38	18	504873	21951
	A	21	3	7	11	15	29	256830	12230
	TOTAL	44	14	14	16	53	47	761703	17311

FINAL TABLE – LEAGUE DIVISION TWO

		P	W	D	L	F	A	W	D	L	F	A	PTS	GD
				HOME					AWAY					
1	Leeds United	42	14	5	2	41	10	7	7	7	20	25	54	26
2	Bury	42	15	5	1	42	7	6	4	11	21	28	51	28
3	Derby County	42	15	4	2	52	15	6	5	10	23	27	51	33
4	Blackpool	42	13	7	1	43	12	5	6	10	29	35	49	25
5	Southampton	42	13	5	3	36	9	4	9	8	16	22	48	21
6	Stoke City	42	9	11	1	27	10	5	7	9	17	32	46	2
7	Oldham Athletic	42	10	10	1	24	12	4	7	10	21	40	45	-7
8	Sheffield Wednesday	42	15	5	1	42	9	1	7	13	12	42	44	3
9	South Shields	42	13	5	3	34	16	4	5	12	15	34	44	-1
10	Leyton Orient	42	11	7	3	27	10	3	8	10	13	26	43	4
11	Barnsley	42	12	7	2	34	16	4	4	13	23	45	43	-4
12	Leicester City	42	13	4	4	43	16	4	4	13	21	38	42	10
13	Stockport County	42	10	7	4	32	21	3	9	9	12	31	42	-8
14	MANCHESTER UNITED	42	10	7	4	37	15	3	7	11	15	29	40	8
15	Crystal Palace	42	11	7	3	37	19	2	6	13	16	46	39	-12
16	Port Vale	42	9	5	7	33	29	4	7	10	17	37	38	-16
17	Hull City	42	8	7	6	32	23	2	10	9	14	28	37	-5
18	Bradford City	42	8	7	6	24	21	3	8	10	11	27	37	-13
19	Coventry City	42	9	6	6	34	23	2	7	12	18	45	35	-16
20	Fulham	42	9	8	4	30	20	1	6	14	15	36	34	-11
21	Nelson	42	8	8	5	32	31	2	5	14	8	43	33	-34
22	Bristol City	42	5	8	8	19	26	2	7	12	13	39	29	-33

SEASON 1924/25

Match # 1113   Saturday 30/08/24   Football League Division 2   at Old Trafford   Attendance 21250
Result: **Manchester United 1 Leicester City 0**
Teamsheet: Steward, Moore, Silcock, Bennion, Barson, Hilditch, Spence, Smith, Goldthorpe, Lochhead, McPherson
Scorer(s):   Goldthorpe

Match # 1114   Monday 01/09/24   Football League Division 2   at Edgeley Park   Attendance 12500
Result: **Stockport County 2 Manchester United 1**
Teamsheet: Steward, Moore, Silcock, Bennion, Barson, Hilditch, Spence, Smith, Henderson, Lochhead, McPherson
Scorer(s):   Lochhead

Match # 1115   Saturday 06/09/24   Football League Division 2   at Victoria Ground   Attendance 15250
Result: **Stoke City 0 Manchester United 0**
Teamsheet: Steward, Moore, Silcock, Mann, Barson, Hilditch, Spence, Smith, Henderson, Lochhead, McPherson

Match # 1116   Monday 08/09/24   Football League Division 2   at Old Trafford   Attendance 9500
Result: **Manchester United 1 Barnsley 0**
Teamsheet: Steward, Moore, Silcock, Mann, Grimwood, Hilditch, Spence, Smith, Henderson, Lochhead, McPherson
Scorer(s):   Henderson

Match # 1117   Saturday 13/09/24   Football League Division 2   at Old Trafford   Attendance 12000
Result: **Manchester United 5 Coventry City 1**
Teamsheet: Steward, Moore, Silcock, Mann, Barson, Grimwood, Spence, Smith, Henderson, Lochhead, McPherson
Scorer(s):   Henderson 2, Lochhead, McPherson, Spence

Match # 1118   Saturday 20/09/24   Football League Division 2   at Boundary Park   Attendance 14500
Result: **Oldham Athletic 0 Manchester United 3**
Teamsheet: Steward, Moore, Silcock, Mann, Barson, Grimwood, Spence, Smith, Henderson, Lochhead, McPherson
Scorer(s):   Henderson 3

Match # 1119   Saturday 27/09/24   Football League Division 2   at Old Trafford   Attendance 29500
Result: **Manchester United 2 Sheffield Wednesday 0**
Teamsheet: Steward, Moore, Silcock, Mann, Barson, Grimwood, Spence, Smith, Henderson, Lochhead, McPherson
Scorer(s):   McPherson, Smith

Match # 1120   Saturday 04/10/24   Football League Division 2   at Millfields Road   Attendance 15000
Result: **Leyton Orient 0 Manchester United 1**
Teamsheet: Steward, Moore, Silcock, Mann, Barson, Grimwood, Spence, Smith, Henderson, Lochhead, McPherson
Scorer(s):   Lochhead

Match # 1121   Saturday 11/10/24   Football League Division 2   at Old Trafford   Attendance 27750
Result: **Manchester United 1 Crystal Palace 0**
Teamsheet: Steward, Moore, Silcock, Mann, Barson, Grimwood, Spence, Smith, Henderson, Lochhead, McPherson
Scorer(s):   Lochhead

Match # 1122   Saturday 18/10/24   Football League Division 2   at The Dell   Attendance 10000
Result: **Southampton 0 Manchester United 2**
Teamsheet: Steward, Moore, Silcock, Mann, Barson, Grimwood, Spence, Smith, Henderson, Lochhead, McPherson
Scorer(s):   Lochhead 2

Match # 1123   Saturday 25/10/24   Football League Division 2   at Molineux   Attendance 17500
Result: **Wolverhampton Wanderers 0 Manchester United 0**
Teamsheet: Steward, Moore, Silcock, Mann, Barson, Grimwood, Spence, Smith, Henderson, Lochhead, McPherson

Match # 1124   Saturday 01/11/24   Football League Division 2   at Old Trafford   Attendance 24000
Result: **Manchester United 2 Fulham 0**
Teamsheet: Steward, Moore, Silcock, Mann, Barson, Grimwood, Spence, Smith, Henderson, Lochhead, McPherson
Scorer(s):   Henderson, Lochhead

Match # 1125   Saturday 08/11/24   Football League Division 2   at Fratton Park   Attendance 19500
Result: **Portsmouth 1 Manchester United 1**
Teamsheet: Steward, Moore, Jones, Mann, Barson, Grimwood, Spence, Smith, Henderson, Lochhead, Thomas
Scorer(s):   Smith

Match # 1126   Saturday 15/11/24   Football League Division 2   at Old Trafford   Attendance 29750
Result: **Manchester United 2 Hull City 0**
Teamsheet: Steward, Moore, Silcock, Mann, Barson, Grimwood, Spence, Smith, Hanson, Lochhead, McPherson
Scorer(s):   Hanson, McPherson

Match # 1127   Saturday 22/11/24   Football League Division 2   at Bloomfield Road   Attendance 9500
Result: **Blackpool 1 Manchester United 1**
Teamsheet: Steward, Moore, Silcock, Mann, Barson, Grimwood, Spence, Smith, Hanson, Lochhead, McPherson
Scorer(s):   Hanson

Match # 1128   Saturday 29/11/24   Football League Division 2   at Old Trafford   Attendance 59500
Result: **Manchester United 1 Derby County 1**
Teamsheet: Steward, Moore, Silcock, Mann, Barson, Grimwood, Spence, Smith, Hanson, Lochhead, McPherson
Scorer(s):   Hanson

Match # 1129   Saturday 06/12/24   Football League Division 2   at Talbot Road   Attendance 6500
Result: **South Shields 1 Manchester United 2**
Teamsheet: Steward, Moore, Silcock, Mann, Barson, Grimwood, Spence, Smith, Henderson, Lochhead, McPherson
Scorer(s):   Henderson, McPherson

Match # 1130   Saturday 13/12/24   Football League Division 2   at Old Trafford   Attendance 18250
Result: **Manchester United 3 Bradford City 0**
Teamsheet: Steward, Jones, Silcock, Mann, Barson, Grimwood, Spence, Smith, Henderson, Lochhead, McPherson
Scorer(s):   Henderson 2, McPherson

SEASON 1924/25 (continued)

Match # 1131 Saturday 20/12/24   Football League Division 2   at Old Recreation Ground   Attendance 11000
Result: **Port Vale 2 Manchester United 1**
Teamsheet: Steward, Jones, Silcock, Mann, Barson, Grimwood, Spence, Smith, Henderson, Lochhead, McPherson
Scorer(s):   Lochhead

Match # 1132 Thursday 25/12/24   Football League Division 2   at Ayresome Park   Attendance 18500
Result: **Middlesbrough 1 Manchester United 1**
Teamsheet: Steward, Moore, Silcock, Mann, Barson, Grimwood, Spence, Smith, Henderson, Kennedy, McPherson
Scorer(s):   Henderson

Match # 1133 Friday 26/12/24   Football League Division 2   at Old Trafford   Attendance 44000
Result: **Manchester United 2 Middlesbrough 0**
Teamsheet: Steward, Moore, Silcock, Mann, Barson, Grimwood, Spence, Smith, Henderson, Kennedy, McPherson
Scorer(s):   Henderson, Smith

Match # 1134 Saturday 27/12/24   Football League Division 2   at Filbert Street   Attendance 18250
Result: **Leicester City 3 Manchester United 0**
Teamsheet: Steward, Moore, Silcock, Mann, Barson, Grimwood, Spence, Smith, Henderson, Kennedy, McPherson

Match # 1135 Thursday 01/01/25   Football League Division 2   at Old Trafford   Attendance 30500
Result: **Manchester United 1 Chelsea 0**
Teamsheet: Steward, Moore, Silcock, Mann, Barson, Grimwood, Spence, Smith, Henderson, Kennedy, McPherson
Scorer(s):   Grimwood

Match # 1136 Saturday 03/01/25   Football League Division 2   at Old Trafford   Attendance 24500
Result: **Manchester United 2 Stoke City 0**
Teamsheet: Steward, Moore, Silcock, Mann, Barson, Grimwood, Spence, Lochhead, Henderson, Kennedy, McPherson
Scorer(s):   Henderson 2

Match # 1137 Saturday 10/01/25   FA Cup 1st Round   at Hillsborough   Attendance 35079
Result: **Sheffield Wednesday 2 Manchester United 0**
Teamsheet: Steward, Moore, Jones, Mann, Grimwood, Hilditch, Spence, Smith, Henderson, Kennedy, McPherson

Match # 1138 Saturday 17/01/25   Football League Division 2   at Highfield Road   Attendance 9000
Result: **Coventry City 1 Manchester United 0**
Teamsheet: Steward, Moore, Silcock, Mann, Haslam, Grimwood, Spence, Taylor, Henderson, Lochhead, McPherson

Match # 1139 Saturday 24/01/25   Football League Division 2   at Old Trafford   Attendance 20000
Result: **Manchester United 0 Oldham Athletic 1**
Teamsheet: Steward, Moore, Silcock, Mann, Barson, Grimwood, Spence, Smith, Henderson, Kennedy, McPherson

Match # 1140 Saturday 07/02/25   Football League Division 2   at Old Trafford   Attendance 18250
Result: **Manchester United 4 Leyton Orient 2**
Teamsheet: Steward, Moore, Silcock, Bennion, Grimwood, Bain, Spence, Lochhead, Pape, Kennedy, McPherson
Scorer(s):   Kennedy 2, McPherson, Pape

Match # 1141 Saturday 14/02/25   Football League Division 2   at Selhurst Park   Attendance 11250
Result: **Crystal Palace 2 Manchester United 1**
Teamsheet: Steward, Moore, Silcock, Bennion, Grimwood, Mann, Spence, Lochhead, Pape, Kennedy, McPherson
Scorer(s):   Lochhead

Match # 1142 Monday 23/02/25   Football League Division 2   at Hillsborough   Attendance 3000
Result: **Sheffield Wednesday 1 Manchester United 1**
Teamsheet: Steward, Moore, Silcock, Bennion, Grimwood, Mann, Spence, Lochhead, Pape, Kennedy, McPherson
Scorer(s):   Pape

Match # 1143 Saturday 28/02/25   Football League Division 2   at Old Trafford   Attendance 21250
Result: **Manchester United 3 Wolverhampton Wanderers 0**
Teamsheet: Steward, Moore, Jones, Bennion, Grimwood, Mann, Spence, Lochhead, Pape, Kennedy, Partridge
Scorer(s):   Spence 2, Kennedy

Match # 1144 Saturday 07/03/25   Football League Division 2   at Craven Cottage   Attendance 16000
Result: **Fulham 1 Manchester United 0**
Teamsheet: Steward, Moore, Jones, Bennion, Grimwood, Mann, Spence, Lochhead, Pape, Kennedy, McPherson

Match # 1145 Saturday 14/03/25   Football League Division 2   at Old Trafford   Attendance 22000
Result: **Manchester United 2 Portsmouth 0**
Teamsheet: Steward, Moore, Jones, Bennion, Grimwood, Mann, Spence, Rennox, Pape, Lochhead, McPherson
Scorer(s):   Lochhead, Spence

Match # 1146 Saturday 21/03/25   Football League Division 2   at Anlaby Road   Attendance 6250
Result: **Hull City 0 Manchester United 1**
Teamsheet: Steward, Moore, Jones, Bennion, Grimwood, Mann, Spence, Rennox, Pape, Lochhead, McPherson
Scorer(s):   Lochhead

Match # 1147 Saturday 28/03/25   Football League Division 2   at Old Trafford   Attendance 26250
Result: **Manchester United 0 Blackpool 0**
Teamsheet: Steward, Moore, Jones, Bennion, Grimwood, Mann, Spence, Rennox, Pape, Lochhead, McPherson

Match # 1148 Saturday 04/04/25   Football League Division 2   at Baseball Ground   Attendance 24000
Result: **Derby County 1 Manchester United 0**
Teamsheet: Steward, Moore, Jones, Mann, Barson, Grimwood, Spence, Rennox, Pape, Lochhead, Thomas

SEASON 1924/25 (continued)

Match # 1149	Friday 10/04/25	Football League Division 2	at Old Trafford	Attendance 43500
Result:	**Manchester United 2 Stockport County 0**			
Teamsheet:	Steward, Moore, Jones, Bennion, Barson, Grimwood, Spence, Smith, Pape, Lochhead, Thomas			
Scorer(s):	Pape 2			

Match # 1150	Saturday 11/04/25	Football League Division 2	at Old Trafford	Attendance 24000
Result:	**Manchester United 1 South Shields 0**			
Teamsheet:	Steward, Moore, Silcock, Bennion, Barson, Grimwood, Spence, Smith, Pape, Lochhead, McPherson			
Scorer(s):	Lochhead			

Match # 1151	Monday 13/04/25	Football League Division 2	at Stamford Bridge	Attendance 16500
Result:	**Chelsea 0 Manchester United 0**			
Teamsheet:	Steward, Moore, Jones, Bennion, Barson, Grimwood, Spence, Smith, Pape, Lochhead, McPherson			

Match # 1152	Saturday 18/04/25	Football League Division 2	at Valley Parade	Attendance 13250
Result:	**Bradford City 0 Manchester United 1**			
Teamsheet:	Steward, Moore, Jones, Bennion, Barson, Grimwood, Spence, Smith, Pape, Lochhead, McPherson			
Scorer(s):	Smith			

Match # 1153	Wednesday 22/04/25	Football League Division 2	at Old Trafford	Attendance 26500
Result:	**Manchester United 1 Southampton 1**			
Teamsheet:	Steward, Moore, Jones, Bennion, Barson, Grimwood, Spence, Smith, Pape, Lochhead, McPherson			
Scorer(s):	Pape			

Match # 1154	Saturday 25/04/25	Football League Division 2	at Old Trafford	Attendance 33500
Result:	**Manchester United 4 Port Vale 0**			
Teamsheet:	Steward, Moore, Jones, Bennion, Barson, Grimwood, Spence, Smith, Pape, Lochhead, McPherson			
Scorer(s):	Lochhead, McPherson, Smith, Spence			

Match # 1155	Saturday 02/05/25	Football League Division 2	at Oakwell	Attendance 11250
Result:	**Barnsley 0 Manchester United 0**			
Teamsheet:	Steward, Moore, Jones, Bennion, Barson, Grimwood, Spence, Smith, Pape, Lochhead, McPherson			

SEASON 1924/25 SUMMARY

APPEARANCES

PLAYER	LGE	FAC	TOT
Spence	42	1	43
Steward	42	1	43
Moore	40	1	41
Grimwood	39	1	40
McPherson	38	1	39
Lochhead	37	–	37
Mann	32	1	33
Barson	32	–	32
Smith	31	1	32
Silcock	29	–	29
Henderson	22	1	23
Bennion	17	–	17

APPEARANCES

PLAYER	LGE	FAC	TOT
Jones	15	1	16
Pape	16	–	16
Kennedy	11	1	12
Hilditch	4	1	5
Rennox	4	–	4
Hanson	3	–	3
Thomas	3	–	3
Bain	1	–	1
Goldthorpe	1	–	1
Haslam	1	–	1
Partridge	1	–	1
Taylor	1	–	1

GOALSCORERS

PLAYER	LGE	FAC	TOT
Henderson	14	–	14
Lochhead	13	–	13
McPherson	7	–	7
Pape	5	–	5
Smith	5	–	5
Spence	5	–	5
Hanson	3	–	3
Kennedy	3	–	3
Goldthorpe	1	–	1
Grimwood	1	–	1

RESULTS & ATTENDANCES SUMMARY

		P	W	D	L	F	A	TOTAL	AVGE
League	H	21	17	3	1	40	6	565750	26940
	A	21	6	8	7	17	17	278500	13262
	TOTAL	42	23	11	8	57	23	844250	20101
FA Cup	H	0	0	0	0	0	0	0	n/a
	A	1	0	0	1	0	2	35079	35079
	TOTAL	1	0	0	1	0	2	35079	35079
Overall	H	21	17	3	1	40	6	565750	26940
	A	22	6	8	8	17	19	313579	14254
	TOTAL	43	23	11	9	57	25	879329	20450

FINAL TABLE – LEAGUE DIVISION TWO

		P	W	D	L	F	A	W	D	L	F	A	PTS	GD
				HOME					AWAY					
1	Leicester City	42	15	4	2	58	9	9	7	5	32	23	59	58
2	MANCHESTER UNITED	42	17	3	1	40	6	6	8	7	17	17	57	34
3	Derby County	42	15	3	3	49	15	7	8	6	22	21	55	35
4	Portsmouth	42	9	13	1	28	14	8	5	8	30	36	48	8
5	Chelsea	42	11	8	2	31	12	5	7	9	20	25	47	14
6	Wolverhampton Wanderers	42	14	1	6	29	19	6	5	10	26	32	46	4
7	Southampton	42	12	8	1	29	10	1	10	10	11	26	44	4
8	Port Vale	42	12	4	5	34	19	5	4	12	14	37	42	-8
9	South Shields	42	9	6	6	33	21	3	11	7	9	17	41	4
10	Hull City	42	12	6	3	40	14	3	5	13	10	35	41	1
11	Leyton Orient	42	8	7	6	22	13	6	5	10	20	29	40	0
12	Fulham	42	11	6	4	26	15	4	4	13	15	41	40	-15
13	Middlesbrough	42	6	10	5	22	21	4	9	8	14	23	39	-8
14	Sheffield Wednesday	42	12	3	6	36	23	3	5	13	14	33	38	-6
15	Barnsley	42	8	8	5	30	23	5	4	12	16	36	38	-13
16	Bradford City	42	11	6	4	26	13	2	6	13	11	37	38	-13
17	Blackpool	42	8	5	8	37	26	6	4	11	28	35	37	4
18	Oldham Athletic	42	9	5	7	24	21	4	6	11	11	30	37	-16
19	Stockport County	42	10	6	5	26	15	3	5	13	11	42	37	-20
20	Stoke City	42	7	8	6	22	17	5	3	13	12	29	35	-12
21	Crystal Palace	42	8	4	9	23	19	4	6	11	15	35	34	-16
22	Coventry City	42	10	6	5	32	26	1	3	17	13	58	31	-39

SEASON 1925/26

Match # 1156	Saturday 29/08/25	Football League Division 1	at Upton Park	Attendance 25630
Result:	**West Ham United 1 Manchester United 0**			
Teamsheet:	Steward, Moore, Silcock, Bennion, Barson, Bain, Spence, Smith, Iddon, Lochhead, McPherson			

Match # 1157	Wednesday 02/09/25	Football League Division 1	at Old Trafford	Attendance 41717
Result:	**Manchester United 3 Aston Villa 0**			
Teamsheet:	Steward, Moore, Silcock, Mann, Barson, Hilditch, Spence, Smith, Pape, Lochhead, McPherson			
Scorer(s):	Barson, Lochhead, Spence			

Match # 1158	Saturday 05/09/25	Football League Division 1	at Old Trafford	Attendance 32288
Result:	**Manchester United 0 Arsenal 1**			
Teamsheet:	Steward, Moore, Silcock, Mann, Barson, Hilditch, Spence, Smith, Pape, Lochhead, McPherson			

Match # 1159	Monday 07/09/25	Football League Division 1	at Villa Park	Attendance 27701
Result:	**Aston Villa 2 Manchester United 2**			
Teamsheet:	Steward, Moore, Silcock, Bennion, Barson, Mann, Spence, Smith, Hanson, Rennox, McPherson			
Scorer(s):	Hanson, Rennox			

Match # 1160	Saturday 12/09/25	Football League Division 1	at Maine Road	Attendance 62994
Result:	**Manchester City 1 Manchester United 1**			
Teamsheet:	Steward, Moore, Silcock, Bennion, Barson, Mann, Spence, Smith, Hanson, Rennox, McPherson			
Scorer(s):	Rennox			

Match # 1161	Wednesday 16/09/25	Football League Division 1	at Old Trafford	Attendance 21275
Result:	**Manchester United 3 Leicester City 2**			
Teamsheet:	Steward, Moore, Silcock, Bennion, Barson, Mann, Spence, Smith, Lochhead, Rennox, McPherson			
Scorer(s):	Rennox 2, Lochhead			

Match # 1162	Saturday 19/09/25	Football League Division 1	at Anfield	Attendance 18824
Result:	**Liverpool 5 Manchester United 0**			
Teamsheet:	Steward, Moore, Silcock, Hilditch, Barson, Mann, Spence, Smith, Lochhead, Rennox, McPherson			

Match # 1163	Saturday 26/09/25	Football League Division 1	at Old Trafford	Attendance 17259
Result:	**Manchester United 6 Burnley 1**			
Teamsheet:	Steward, Moore, Silcock, Hilditch, Barson, Grimwood, Spence, Smith, Hanson, Rennox, Thomas			
Scorer(s):	Rennox 3, Hanson, Hilditch, Smith			

Match # 1164	Saturday 03/10/25	Football League Division 1	at Elland Road	Attendance 26265
Result:	**Leeds United 2 Manchester United 0**			
Teamsheet:	Steward, Moore, Silcock, Hilditch, Barson, Grimwood, Spence, Smith, Hanson, Rennox, Thomas			

Match # 1165	Saturday 10/10/25	Football League Division 1	at Old Trafford	Attendance 39651
Result:	**Manchester United 2 Newcastle United 1**			
Teamsheet:	Steward, Moore, Silcock, Hilditch, Barson, Grimwood, Spence, Smith, Hanson, Rennox, Thomas			
Scorer(s):	Rennox, Thomas			

Match # 1166	Saturday 17/10/25	Football League Division 1	at Old Trafford	Attendance 26496
Result:	**Manchester United 0 Tottenham Hotspur 0**			
Teamsheet:	Steward, Moore, Silcock, Hilditch, Barson, Grimwood, Spence, Smith, Hanson, Rennox, Thomas			

Match # 1167	Saturday 24/10/25	Football League Division 1	at Ninian Park	Attendance 15846
Result:	**Cardiff City 0 Manchester United 2**			
Teamsheet:	Steward, Moore, Silcock, Hilditch, Barson, Grimwood, Spence, Hanson, McPherson, Rennox, Thomas			
Scorer(s):	McPherson 2			

Match # 1168	Saturday 31/10/25	Football League Division 1	at Old Trafford	Attendance 37213
Result:	**Manchester United 1 Huddersfield Town 1**			
Teamsheet:	Steward, Moore, Silcock, Hilditch, Barson, Grimwood, Spence, Hanson, McPherson, Rennox, Thomas			
Scorer(s):	Thomas			

Match # 1169	Saturday 07/11/25	Football League Division 1	at Goodison Park	Attendance 12387
Result:	**Everton 1 Manchester United 3**			
Teamsheet:	Steward, Moore, Silcock, Hilditch, Haslam, Mann, Spence, Smith, McPherson, Rennox, Thomas			
Scorer(s):	McPherson, Rennox, Spence			

Match # 1170	Saturday 14/11/25	Football League Division 1	at Old Trafford	Attendance 23559
Result:	**Manchester United 3 Birmingham City 1**			
Teamsheet:	Steward, Moore, Silcock, Hilditch, Barson, Mann, Spence, Smith, McPherson, Rennox, Thomas			
Scorer(s):	Barson, Spence, Thomas			

Match # 1171	Saturday 21/11/25	Football League Division 1	at Gigg Lane	Attendance 16591
Result:	**Bury 1 Manchester United 3**			
Teamsheet:	Steward, Moore, Silcock, Hilditch, Barson, Mann, Spence, Smith, McPherson, Rennox, Thomas			
Scorer(s):	McPherson 2, Spence			

Match # 1172	Saturday 28/11/25	Football League Division 1	at Old Trafford	Attendance 33660
Result:	**Manchester United 2 Blackburn Rovers 0**			
Teamsheet:	Steward, Moore, Silcock, Hilditch, Barson, Mann, Spence, Smith, McPherson, Rennox, Thomas			
Scorer(s):	McPherson, Thomas			

Match # 1173	Saturday 05/12/25	Football League Division 1	at Roker Park	Attendance 25507
Result:	**Sunderland 2 Manchester United 1**			
Teamsheet:	Steward, Moore, Silcock, Hilditch, Haslam, Mann, Spence, Smith, Hanson, Rennox, Thomas			
Scorer(s):	Rennox			

SEASON 1925/26 (continued)

Match # 1174   Saturday 12/12/25   Football League Division 1   at Old Trafford   Attendance 31132
Result: **Manchester United 1   Sheffield United 2**
Teamsheet: Steward, Moore, Silcock, Hilditch, Barson, Mann, Spence, Smith, McPherson, Rennox, Thomas
Scorer(s):   McPherson

Match # 1175   Saturday 19/12/25   Football League Division 1   at The Hawthorns   Attendance 17651
Result: **West Bromwich Albion 5   Manchester United 1**
Teamsheet: Steward, Moore, Silcock, Bennion, Haslam, Hilditch, Spence, Taylor, McPherson, Rennox, Thomas
Scorer(s):   McPherson

Match # 1176   Friday 25/12/25   Football League Division 1   at Old Trafford   Attendance 38503
Result: **Manchester United 2   Bolton Wanderers 1**
Teamsheet: Steward, Moore, Silcock, Hilditch, Barson, Mann, Spence, Hanson, McPherson, Rennox, Thomas
Scorer(s):   Hanson, Spence

Match # 1177   Monday 28/12/25   Football League Division 1   at Filbert Street   Attendance 28367
Result: **Leicester City 1   Manchester United 3**
Teamsheet: Steward, Moore, Silcock, Mann, Hilditch, Thomas, Spence, Hanson, McPherson, Rennox, Hannaford
Scorer(s):   McPherson 3

Match # 1178   Saturday 02/01/26   Football League Division 1   at Old Trafford   Attendance 29612
Result: **Manchester United 2   West Ham United 1**
Teamsheet: Steward, Moore, Silcock, Hilditch, Grimwood, Mann, Spence, Hanson, McPherson, Rennox, Thomas
Scorer(s):   Rennox 2

Match # 1179   Saturday 09/01/26   FA Cup 3rd Round   at Old Recreation Ground   Attendance 14841
Result: **Port Vale 2   Manchester United 3**
Teamsheet: Steward, Moore, Silcock, Mann, Hilditch, Grimwood, Spence, Smith, McPherson, Rennox, Thomas
Scorer(s):   Spence 2, McPherson

Match # 1180   Saturday 16/01/26   Football League Division 1   at Highbury   Attendance 25252
Result: **Arsenal 3   Manchester United 2**
Teamsheet: Steward, Jones, Silcock, Mann, Hilditch, McCrae, Spence, Hanson, McPherson, Rennox, Thomas
Scorer(s):   McPherson, Spence

Match # 1181   Saturday 23/01/26   Football League Division 1   at Old Trafford   Attendance 48657
Result: **Manchester United 1   Manchester City 6**
Teamsheet: Steward, Jones, Silcock, Bennion, Hilditch, Mann, Spence, Taylor, McPherson, Rennox, Thomas
Scorer(s):   Rennox

Match # 1182   Saturday 30/01/26   FA Cup 4th Round   at White Hart Lane   Attendance 40000
Result: **Tottenham Hotspur 2   Manchester United 2**
Teamsheet: Mew, Moore, Silcock, Hilditch, Haslam, Mann, Spence, Hanson, McPherson, Rennox, Thomas
Scorer(s):   Spence, Thomas

Match # 1183   Wednesday 03/02/26   FA Cup 4th Round Replay   at Old Trafford   Attendance 45000
Result: **Manchester United 2   Tottenham Hotspur 0**
Teamsheet: Mew, Moore, Silcock, Hilditch, Haslam, Mann, Spence, Hanson, McPherson, Rennox, Thomas
Scorer(s):   Rennox, Spence

Match # 1184   Saturday 06/02/26   Football League Division 1   at Turf Moor   Attendance 17141
Result: **Burnley 0   Manchester United 1**
Teamsheet: Mew, Moore, Silcock, McCrae, Haslam, Mann, Hall, Smith, McPherson, Rennox, Hannaford
Scorer(s):   McPherson

Match # 1185   Saturday 13/02/26   Football League Division 1   at Old Trafford   Attendance 29584
Result: **Manchester United 2   Leeds United 1**
Teamsheet: Mew, Moore, Silcock, McCrae, Haslam, Mann, Hall, Hanson, McPherson, Sweeney, Hannaford
Scorer(s):   McPherson, Sweeney

Match # 1186   Saturday 20/02/26   FA Cup 5th Round   at Roker Park   Attendance 50500
Result: **Sunderland 3   Manchester United 3**
Teamsheet: Mew, Moore, Silcock, McCrae, Barson, Mann, Spence, Smith, McPherson, Rennox, Thomas
Scorer(s):   Smith 2, McPherson

Match # 1187   Wednesday 24/02/26   FA Cup 5th Round Replay   at Old Trafford   Attendance 58661
Result: **Manchester United 2   Sunderland 1**
Teamsheet: Mew, Moore, Silcock, McCrae, Barson, Mann, Spence, Smith, McPherson, Rennox, Thomas
Scorer(s):   McPherson, Smith

Match # 1188   Saturday 27/02/26   Football League Division 1   at White Hart Lane   Attendance 25466
Result: **Tottenham Hotspur 0   Manchester United 1**
Teamsheet: Mew, Moore, Jones, McCrae, Haslam, Mann, Hall, Smith, McPherson, Rennox, Thomas
Scorer(s):   Smith

Match # 1189   Saturday 06/03/26   FA Cup 6th Round   at Craven Cottage   Attendance 28699
Result: **Fulham 1   Manchester United 2**
Teamsheet: Mew, Moore, Silcock, McCrae, Barson, Mann, Spence, Smith, McPherson, Rennox, Hannaford
Scorer(s):   McPherson, Smith

Match # 1190   Wednesday 10/03/26   Football League Division 1   at Old Trafford   Attendance 9214
Result: **Manchester United 3   Liverpool 3**
Teamsheet: Mew, Moore, Silcock, Bain, Barson, Mann, Spence, Smith, Hanson, Rennox, Partridge
Scorer(s):   Hanson, Rennox, Spence

Match # 1191   Saturday 13/03/26   Football League Division 1   at Leeds Road   Attendance 27842
Result: **Huddersfield Town 5   Manchester United 0**
Teamsheet: Mew, Moore, Jones, Bennion, Barson, Mann, Spence, Smith, Hanson, Rennox, Partridge

SEASON 1925/26 (continued)

Match # 1192	Wednesday 17/03/26	Football League Division 1	at Burnden Park	Attendance 10794
Result:	**Bolton Wanderers 3 Manchester United 1**			
Teamsheet:	Mew, Moore, Astley, Haslam, Barson, Mann, Spence, Smith, McPherson, Rennox, Thomas			
Scorer(s):	McPherson			

Match # 1193	Saturday 20/03/26	Football League Division 1	at Old Trafford	Attendance 30058
Result:	**Manchester United 0 Everton 0**			
Teamsheet:	Steward, Inglis, Jones, McCrae, Barson, Mann, Spence, Smith, McPherson, Hanson, Thomas			

Match # 1194	Saturday 27/03/26	FA Cup Semi-Final	at Bramall Lane	Attendance 46450
Result:	**Manchester United 0 Manchester City 3**			
Teamsheet:	Steward, Moore, Silcock, McCrae, Barson, Mann, Spence, Smith, McPherson, Rennox, Thomas			

Match # 1195	Friday 02/04/26	Football League Division 1	at Meadow Lane	Attendance 18453
Result:	**Notts County 0 Manchester United 3**			
Teamsheet:	Steward, Moore, Silcock, Mann, Barson, McCrae, Spence, Smith, McPherson, Rennox, Thomas			
Scorer(s):	Rennox 2, McPherson			

Match # 1196	Saturday 03/04/26	Football League Division 1	at Old Trafford	Attendance 41085
Result:	**Manchester United 0 Bury 1**			
Teamsheet:	Steward, Moore, Silcock, Mann, Barson, McCrae, Spence, Hanson, McPherson, Rennox, Thomas			

Match # 1197	Monday 05/04/26	Football League Division 1	at Old Trafford	Attendance 19606
Result:	**Manchester United 0 Notts County 1**			
Teamsheet:	Steward, Moore, Jones, Hanson, McCrae, Mann, Spence, Smith, McPherson, Rennox, Thomas			

Match # 1198	Saturday 10/04/26	Football League Division 1	at Ewood Park	Attendance 15870
Result:	**Blackburn Rovers 7 Manchester United 0**			
Teamsheet:	Steward, Moore, Silcock, Hilditch, Barson, Mann, Spence, Taylor, McPherson, Hanson, Hannaford			

Match # 1199	Wednesday 14/04/26	Football League Division 1	at St James' Park	Attendance 9829
Result:	**Newcastle United 4 Manchester United 1**			
Teamsheet:	Steward, Inglis, Jones, Hilditch, McCrae, Mann, Spence, Smith, Rennox, Hanson, Thomas			
Scorer(s):	Hanson			

Match # 1200	Monday 19/04/26	Football League Division 1	at St Andrews	Attendance 8948
Result:	**Birmingham City 2 Manchester United 1**			
Teamsheet:	Steward, Inglis, Jones, Hilditch, Haslam, Mann, Spence, Smith, Hanson, Rennox, Thomas			
Scorer(s):	Rennox			

Match # 1201	Wednesday 21/04/26	Football League Division 1	at Old Trafford	Attendance 10918
Result:	**Manchester United 5 Sunderland 1**			
Teamsheet:	Steward, Inglis, Jones, Hilditch, Barson, Mann, Spence, Smith, Taylor, Rennox, Thomas			
Scorer(s):	Taylor 3, Smith, Thomas			

Match # 1202	Saturday 24/04/26	Football League Division 1	at Bramall Lane	Attendance 15571
Result:	**Sheffield United 2 Manchester United 0**			
Teamsheet:	Steward, Inglis, Jones, Hilditch, Haslam, Mann, Spence, Smith, Taylor, Rennox, Thomas			

Match # 1203	Wednesday 28/04/26	Football League Division 1	at Old Trafford	Attendance 9116
Result:	**Manchester United 1 Cardiff City 0**			
Teamsheet:	Steward, Inglis, Silcock, Hilditch, Barson, Mann, Spence, Smith, Hanson, Sweeney, Thomas			
Scorer(s):	Inglis			

Match # 1204	Saturday 01/05/26	Football League Division 1	at Old Trafford	Attendance 9974
Result:	**Manchester United 3 West Bromwich Albion 2**			
Teamsheet:	Richardson, Inglis, Silcock, Hilditch, Barson, Mann, Spence, Hanson, Taylor, Sweeney, Partridge			
Scorer(s):	Taylor 3			

SEASON 1925/26 SUMMARY

APPEARANCES

PLAYER	LGE	FAC	TOT
Spence	39	7	46
Mann	34	7	41
Rennox	34	7	41
Moore	33	7	40
Silcock	33	7	40
Steward	35	2	37
McPherson	29	7	36
Smith	30	5	35
Thomas	29	6	35
Barson	28	4	32
Hilditch	28	3	31
Hanson	24	2	26
McCrae	9	4	13
Haslam	9	2	11
Mew	6	5	11
Jones	10	–	10
Grimwood	7	1	8
Bennion	7	–	7
Inglis	7	–	7
Taylor	6	–	6
Hannaford	4	1	5
Lochhead	5	–	5
Hall	3	–	3
Partridge	3	–	3
Sweeney	3	–	3
Bain	2	–	2
Pape	2	–	2
Astley	1	–	1
Iddon	1	–	1
Richardson	1	–	1

GOALSCORERS

PLAYER	LGE	FAC	TOT
McPherson	16	4	20
Rennox	17	1	18
Spence	7	4	11
Smith	3	4	7
Taylor	6	–	6
Thomas	5	1	6
Hanson	5	–	5
Barson	2	–	2
Lochhead	2	–	2
Hilditch	1	–	1
Inglis	1	–	1
Sweeney	1	–	1

RESULTS & ATTENDANCES SUMMARY

		P	W	D	L	F	A	TOTAL	AVGE
League	H	21	12	4	5	40	26	580577	27647
	A	21	7	2	12	26	47	452929	21568
TOTAL		42	19	6	17	66	73	1033506	24607
FA Cup	H	2	2	0	0	4	1	103661	51831
	A	4	2	2	0	10	8	134040	33510
	N	1	0	0	1	0	3	46450	46450
TOTAL		7	4	2	1	14	12	284151	40593
Overall	H	23	14	4	5	44	27	684238	29749
	A	25	9	4	12	36	55	586969	23479
	N	1	0	0	1	0	3	46450	46450
TOTAL		49	23	8	18	80	85	1317657	26891

FINAL TABLE – LEAGUE DIVISION ONE

		P	W	D	L	F	A	W	D	L	F	A	PTS	GD
				HOME						AWAY				
1	Huddersfield Town	42	14	6	1	50	17	9	5	7	42	43	57	32
2	Arsenal	42	16	2	3	57	19	6	6	9	30	44	52	24
3	Sunderland	42	17	2	2	67	30	4	4	13	29	50	48	16
4	Bury	42	12	4	5	55	34	8	3	10	30	43	47	8
5	Sheffield United	42	15	3	3	72	29	4	5	12	30	53	46	20
6	Aston Villa	42	12	7	2	56	25	4	5	12	30	51	44	10
7	Liverpool	42	9	8	4	43	27	5	8	8	27	36	44	7
8	Bolton Wanderers	42	11	6	4	46	31	6	4	11	29	45	44	-1
9	MANCHESTER UNITED	42	12	4	5	40	26	7	2	12	26	47	44	-7
10	Newcastle United	42	13	3	5	59	33	3	7	11	25	42	42	9
11	Everton	42	9	9	3	42	26	3	9	9	30	44	42	2
12	Blackburn Rovers	42	11	6	4	59	33	4	5	12	32	47	41	11
13	West Bromwich Albion	42	13	5	3	59	29	3	3	15	20	49	40	1
14	Birmingham City	42	14	2	5	35	25	2	6	13	31	56	40	-15
15	Tottenham Hotspur	42	11	4	6	45	36	4	5	12	21	43	39	-13
16	Cardiff City	42	8	5	8	30	25	8	2	11	31	51	39	-15
17	Leicester City	42	11	3	7	42	32	3	7	11	28	48	38	-10
18	West Ham United	42	14	2	5	45	27	1	5	15	18	49	37	-13
19	Leeds United	42	11	5	5	38	28	3	3	15	26	48	36	-12
20	Burnley	42	7	7	7	43	35	6	3	12	42	73	36	-23
21	Manchester City	42	8	7	6	48	42	4	4	13	41	58	35	-11
22	Notts County	42	11	4	6	37	26	2	3	16	17	48	33	-20

SEASON 1926/27

Match # 1205 Saturday 28/08/26 Football League Division 1 at Anfield Attendance 34795
Result: **Liverpool 4 Manchester United 2**
Teamsheet: Steward, Inglis, Silcock, Hilditch, Barson, Mann, Spence, Smith, McPherson, Haworth, Thomas
Scorer(s): McPherson 2

Match # 1206 Monday 30/08/26 Football League Division 1 at Bramall Lane Attendance 14844
Result: **Sheffield United 2 Manchester United 2**
Teamsheet: Steward, Inglis, Silcock, Bennion, Haslam, Mann, Spence, Hanson, McPherson, Haworth, Thomas
Scorer(s): McPherson 2

Match # 1207 Saturday 04/09/26 Football League Division 1 at Old Trafford Attendance 26338
Result: **Manchester United 2 Leeds United 2**
Teamsheet: Steward, Inglis, Silcock, Bennion, Barson, Mann, Spence, Hanson, McPherson, Wilson, Partridge
Scorer(s): McPherson 2

Match # 1208 Saturday 11/09/26 Football League Division 1 at St James' Park Attendance 28050
Result: **Newcastle United 4 Manchester United 2**
Teamsheet: Steward, Inglis, Silcock, Bennion, Barson, Mann, Spence, Hanson, McPherson, Rennox, Partridge
Scorer(s): McPherson, Spence

Match # 1209 Wednesday 15/09/26 Football League Division 1 at Old Trafford Attendance 15259
Result: **Manchester United 2 Arsenal 2**
Teamsheet: Steward, Inglis, Jones, Bennion, Barson, Mann, Spence, Hanson, McPherson, Rennox, Partridge
Scorer(s): Hanson, Spence

Match # 1210 Saturday 18/09/26 Football League Division 1 at Old Trafford Attendance 32593
Result: **Manchester United 2 Burnley 1**
Teamsheet: Steward, Inglis, Jones, Bennion, Grimwood, Mann, Chapman, Hanson, Spence, Rennox, McPherson
Scorer(s): Spence 2

Match # 1211 Saturday 25/09/26 Football League Division 1 at Ninian Park Attendance 17267
Result: **Cardiff City 0 Manchester United 2**
Teamsheet: Steward, Jones, Silcock, Bennion, Barson, Wilson, Chapman, Hanson, Spence, Rennox, Hannaford
Scorer(s): Rennox, Spence

Match # 1212 Saturday 02/10/26 Football League Division 1 at Old Trafford Attendance 31234
Result: **Manchester United 2 Aston Villa 1**
Teamsheet: Steward, Jones, Silcock, Bennion, Barson, Wilson, Chapman, Hanson, Spence, Rennox, Hannaford
Scorer(s): Barson, Rennox

Match # 1213 Saturday 09/10/26 Football League Division 1 at Burnden Park Attendance 17869
Result: **Bolton Wanderers 4 Manchester United 0**
Teamsheet: Steward, Jones, Silcock, Bennion, Haslam, Wilson, Chapman, Hanson, McPherson, Rennox, Hannaford

Match # 1214 Saturday 16/10/26 Football League Division 1 at Gigg Lane Attendance 22728
Result: **Bury 0 Manchester United 3**
Teamsheet: Steward, Jones, Silcock, Bennion, Grimwood, Wilson, Chapman, Sweeney, Spence, Rennox, McPherson
Scorer(s): Spence 2, McPherson

Match # 1215 Saturday 23/10/26 Football League Division 1 at Old Trafford Attendance 32010
Result: **Manchester United 0 Birmingham City 1**
Teamsheet: Steward, Jones, Silcock, Bennion, Barson, Wilson, Chapman, Sweeney, Spence, Rennox, McPherson

Match # 1216 Saturday 30/10/26 Football League Division 1 at Upton Park Attendance 19733
Result: **West Ham United 4 Manchester United 0**
Teamsheet: Steward, Moore, Jones, Hilditch, Barson, Mann, Spence, Harris, McPherson, Rennox, Thomas

Match # 1217 Saturday 06/11/26 Football League Division 1 at Old Trafford Attendance 16166
Result: **Manchester United 0 Sheffield Wednesday 0**
Teamsheet: Steward, Moore, Jones, Bennion, Barson, Wilson, Chapman, Smith T, Spence, Rennox, McPherson

Match # 1218 Saturday 13/11/26 Football League Division 1 at Filbert Street Attendance 18521
Result: **Leicester City 2 Manchester United 3**
Teamsheet: Steward, Moore, Jones, Bennion, Grimwood, Wilson, Spence, Smith T, McPherson, Rennox, Thomas
Scorer(s): McPherson 2, Rennox

Match # 1219 Saturday 20/11/26 Football League Division 1 at Old Trafford Attendance 24361
Result: **Manchester United 2 Everton 1**
Teamsheet: Steward, Moore, Jones, Bennion, Grimwood, Wilson, Spence, Smith T, McPherson, Rennox, Thomas
Scorer(s): Rennox 2

Match # 1220 Saturday 27/11/26 Football League Division 1 at Ewood Park Attendance 17280
Result: **Blackburn Rovers 2 Manchester United 1**
Teamsheet: Steward, Moore, Jones, Bennion, Grimwood, Wilson, Spence, Smith T, McPherson, Rennox, Thomas
Scorer(s): Spence

Match # 1221 Saturday 04/12/26 Football League Division 1 at Old Trafford Attendance 33135
Result: **Manchester United 0 Huddersfield Town 0**
Teamsheet: Steward, Moore, Jones, Bennion, Grimwood, Wilson, Spence, Smith T, McPherson, Rennox, Thomas

Match # 1222 Saturday 11/12/26 Football League Division 1 at Roker Park Attendance 15385
Result: **Sunderland 6 Manchester United 0**
Teamsheet: Steward, Moore, Jones, Bennion, Grimwood, Wilson, Spence, Smith T, McPherson, Rennox, Thomas

SEASON 1926/27 (continued)

Match # 1223 Saturday 18/12/26   Football League Division 1   at Old Trafford   Attendance 18585
Result: **Manchester United 2 West Bromwich Albion 0**
Teamsheet: Steward, Moore, Silcock, Bennion, Grimwood, Wilson, Spence, Smith T, McPherson, Sweeney, Thomas
Scorer(s):   Sweeney 2

Match # 1224 Saturday 25/12/26   Football League Division 1   at White Hart Lane   Attendance 37287
Result: **Tottenham Hotspur 1 Manchester United 1**
Teamsheet: Steward, Moore, Silcock, Bennion, Barson, Wilson, Spence, Mann, McPherson, Sweeney, Partridge
Scorer(s):   Spence

Match # 1225 Monday 27/12/26   Football League Division 1   at Old Trafford   Attendance 50665
Result: **Manchester United 2 Tottenham Hotspur 1**
Teamsheet: Steward, Moore, Silcock, Bennion, Barson, Wilson, Spence, Rennox, McPherson, Sweeney, Partridge
Scorer(s):   McPherson 2

Match # 1226 Tuesday 28/12/26   Football League Division 1   at Highbury   Attendance 30111
Result: **Arsenal 1 Manchester United 0**
Teamsheet: Steward, Jones, Silcock, Bennion, Grimwood, Wilson, Spence, Rennox, McPherson, Mann, Partridge

Match # 1227 Saturday 01/01/27   Football League Division 1   at Old Trafford   Attendance 33593
Result: **Manchester United 5 Sheffield United 0**
Teamsheet: Steward, Moore, Silcock, Bennion, Barson, Hilditch, Spence, Rennox, McPherson, Sweeney, Partridge
Scorer(s):   McPherson 2, Barson, Rennox, Sweeney

Match # 1228 Saturday 08/01/27   FA Cup 3rd Round   at Elm Park   Attendance 28918
Result: **Reading 1 Manchester United 1**
Teamsheet: Steward, Moore, Silcock, Bennion, Hilditch, Barson, Spence, Smith T, McPherson, Sweeney, Partridge
Scorer(s):   Bennion

Match # 1229 Wednesday 12/01/27   FA Cup 3rd Round Replay   at Old Trafford   Attendance 29122
Result: **Manchester United 2 Reading 2**
Teamsheet: Steward, Moore, Silcock, Bennion, Hilditch, Barson, Spence, Hanson, McPherson, Sweeney, Partridge
Scorer(s):   Spence, Sweeney

Match # 1230 Saturday 15/01/27   Football League Division 1   at Old Trafford   Attendance 30304
Result: **Manchester United 0 Liverpool 1**
Teamsheet: Steward, Moore, Jones, Bennion, Grimwood, Mann, Spence, Hanson, McPherson, Sweeney, Partridge

Match # 1231 Monday 17/01/27   FA Cup 3rd Round 2nd Replay   at Villa Park   Attendance 16500
Result: **Manchester United 1 Reading 2**
Teamsheet: Steward, Moore, Silcock, Bennion, Hilditch, Barson, Spence, Rennox, McPherson, Sweeney, Partridge
Scorer(s):   McPherson

Match # 1232 Saturday 22/01/27   Football League Division 1   at Elland Road   Attendance 16816
Result: **Leeds United 2 Manchester United 3**
Teamsheet: Steward, Moore, Jones, Bennion, Grimwood, Hilditch, Spence, Rennox, Smith A, Sweeney, McPherson
Scorer(s):   McPherson, Rennox, Spence

Match # 1233 Saturday 05/02/27   Football League Division 1   at Turf Moor   Attendance 22010
Result: **Burnley 1 Manchester United 0**
Teamsheet: Steward, Moore, Jones, Bennion, Barson, Hilditch, Spence, Iddon, Smith A, Sweeney, McPherson

Match # 1234 Wednesday 09/02/27   Football League Division 1   at Old Trafford   Attendance 25402
Result: **Manchester United 3 Newcastle United 1**
Teamsheet: Steward, Moore, Silcock, Mann, Grimwood, Hilditch, Spence, Harris, Hanson, Sweeney, McPherson
Scorer(s):   Hanson, Harris, Spence

Match # 1235 Saturday 12/02/27   Football League Division 1   at Old Trafford   Attendance 26213
Result: **Manchester United 1 Cardiff City 1**
Teamsheet: Steward, Moore, Silcock, Mann, Grimwood, Hilditch, Spence, Harris, Hanson, Sweeney, McPherson
Scorer(s):   Hanson

Match # 1236 Saturday 19/02/27   Football League Division 1   at Villa Park   Attendance 32467
Result: **Aston Villa 2 Manchester United 0**
Teamsheet: Steward, Moore, Silcock, Bennion, Barson, Mann, Spence, Harris, Hanson, Rennox, Thomas

Match # 1237 Saturday 26/02/27   Football League Division 1   at Old Trafford   Attendance 29618
Result: **Manchester United 0 Bolton Wanderers 0**
Teamsheet: Steward, Moore, Silcock, Bennion, Grimwood, Hilditch, Chapman, Smith T, McPherson, Rennox, Hannaford

Match # 1238 Saturday 05/03/27   Football League Division 1   at Old Trafford   Attendance 14709
Result: **Manchester United 1 Bury 2**
Teamsheet: Steward, Moore, Jones, Bennion, Haslam, Hilditch, Chapman, Spence, Smith A, McPherson, Partridge
Scorer(s):   Smith A

Match # 1239 Saturday 12/03/27   Football League Division 1   at St Andrews   Attendance 14392
Result: **Birmingham City 4 Manchester United 0**
Teamsheet: Steward, Moore, Jones, Bennion, Haslam, Hilditch, Chapman, Spence, Smith A, McPherson, Hannaford

Match # 1240 Saturday 19/03/27   Football League Division 1   at Old Trafford   Attendance 18347
Result: **Manchester United 0 West Ham United 3**
Teamsheet: Steward, Moore, Silcock, Bennion, Barson, Wilson, Spence, Hanson, McPherson, Sweeney, Hannaford

SEASON 1926/27 (continued)

Match # 1241   Saturday 26/03/27   Football League Division 1   at Hillsborough   Attendance 11997
Result: **Sheffield Wednesday 2 Manchester United 0**
Teamsheet: Steward, Moore, Silcock, Bennion, Grimwood, Wilson, Spence, Smith T, Hanson, Rennox, Hannaford

Match # 1242   Saturday 02/04/27   Football League Division 1   at Old Trafford   Attendance 17119
Result: **Manchester United 1 Leicester City 0**
Teamsheet: Steward, Moore, Silcock, Bennion, Barson, Hilditch, Chapman, Hanson, Spence, Partridge, McPherson
Scorer(s):   Spence

Match # 1243   Saturday 09/04/27   Football League Division 1   at Goodison Park   Attendance 22564
Result: **Everton 0 Manchester United 0**
Teamsheet: Steward, Moore, Silcock, Bennion, Barson, Hilditch, Chapman, Hanson, Spence, Partridge, Thomas

Match # 1244   Friday 15/04/27   Football League Division 1   at Old Trafford   Attendance 31110
Result: **Manchester United 2 Derby County 2**
Teamsheet: Steward, Moore, Silcock, Bennion, Barson, Hilditch, Chapman, Hanson, Spence, Wilson, McPherson
Scorer(s):   Spence 2

Match # 1245   Saturday 16/04/27   Football League Division 1   at Old Trafford   Attendance 24845
Result: **Manchester United 2 Blackburn Rovers 0**
Teamsheet: Steward, Moore, Silcock, Bennion, Barson, Hilditch, Chapman, Hanson, Spence, Partridge, Thomas
Scorer(s):   Hanson, Spence

Match # 1246   Monday 18/04/27   Football League Division 1   at Baseball Ground   Attendance 17306
Result: **Derby County 2 Manchester United 2**
Teamsheet: Steward, Moore, Silcock, Bennion, Grimwood, Hilditch, Chapman, Hanson, Spence, Partridge, Thomas
Scorer(s):   Spence 2

Match # 1247   Saturday 23/04/27   Football League Division 1   at Leeds Road   Attendance 13870
Result: **Huddersfield Town 0 Manchester United 0**
Teamsheet: Steward, Moore, Silcock, Mann, Barson, Hilditch, Chapman, Sweeney, Spence, Partridge, Thomas

Match # 1248   Saturday 30/04/27   Football League Division 1   at Old Trafford   Attendance 17300
Result: **Manchester United 0 Sunderland 0**
Teamsheet: Steward, Moore, Astley, Bennion, Barson, Wilson, Smith A, Hanson, Spence, Partridge, Thomas

Match # 1249   Thursday 07/05/27   Football League Division 1   at The Hawthorns   Attendance 6668
Result: **West Bromwich Albion 2 Manchester United 2**
Teamsheet: Steward, Moore, Jones, Bennion, Grimwood, Wilson, Chapman, Hanson, Spence, Partridge, Thomas
Scorer(s):   Hanson, Spence

SEASON 1926/27 SUMMARY

APPEARANCES

PLAYER	LGE	FAC	TOT
Steward	42	3	45
Spence	40	3	43
Bennion	37	3	40
McPherson	32	3	35
Moore	30	3	33
Silcock	26	3	29
Barson	21	3	24
Rennox	22	1	23
Hanson	21	1	22
Jones	21	–	21
Wilson	21	–	21
Hilditch	16	3	19
Partridge	16	3	19
Chapman	17	–	17
Grimwood	17	–	17
Sweeney	13	3	16
Thomas	16	–	16
Mann	14	–	14
Smith T	10	1	11
Hannaford	7	–	7
Inglis	6	–	6
Smith A	5	–	5
Harris	4	–	4
Haslam	4	–	4
Haworth	2	–	2
Astley	1	–	1
Iddon	1	–	1

GOALSCORERS

PLAYER	LGE	FAC	TOT
Spence	18	1	19
McPherson	15	1	16
Rennox	7	–	7
Hanson	5	–	5
Sweeney	3	1	4
Barson	2	–	2
Harris	1	–	1
Smith A	1	–	1
Bennion	–	1	1

RESULTS & ATTENDANCES SUMMARY

		P	W	D	L	F	A	TOTAL	AVGE
League	H	21	9	8	4	29	19	548906	26138
	A	21	4	6	11	23	45	431960	20570
TOTAL		42	13	14	15	52	64	980866	23354
FA Cup	H	1	0	1	0	2	2	29122	29122
	A	1	0	1	0	1	1	28918	28918
	N	1	0	0	1	1	2	16500	16500
TOTAL		3	0	2	1	4	5	74540	24847
Overall	H	22	9	9	4	31	21	578028	26274
	A	22	4	7	11	24	46	460878	20949
	N	1	0	0	1	1	2	16500	16500
TOTAL		45	13	16	16	56	69	1055406	23453

FINAL TABLE - LEAGUE DIVISION ONE

		P	W	D	L	F	A	W	D	L	F	A	PTS	GD
				HOME					AWAY					
1	Newcastle United	42	19	1	1	64	20	6	5	10	32	38	56	38
2	Huddersfield Town	42	13	6	2	41	19	4	11	6	35	41	51	16
3	Sunderland	42	15	3	3	70	28	6	4	11	28	42	49	28
4	Bolton Wanderers	42	15	5	1	54	19	4	5	12	30	43	48	22
5	Burnley	42	15	4	2	55	30	4	5	12	36	50	47	11
6	West Ham United	42	9	6	6	50	36	10	2	9	36	34	46	16
7	Leicester City	42	13	4	4	58	33	4	8	9	27	37	46	15
8	Sheffield United	42	12	6	3	46	33	5	4	12	28	53	44	-12
9	Liverpool	42	13	4	4	47	27	5	3	13	22	34	43	8
10	Aston Villa	42	11	4	6	51	34	7	3	11	30	49	43	-2
11	Arsenal	42	12	5	4	47	30	5	4	12	30	56	43	-9
12	Derby County	42	14	4	3	60	28	3	3	15	26	45	41	13
13	Tottenham Hotspur	42	11	4	6	48	33	5	5	11	28	45	41	-2
14	Cardiff City	42	12	3	6	31	17	4	6	11	24	48	41	-10
15	MANCHESTER UNITED	42	9	8	4	29	19	4	6	11	23	45	40	-12
16	Sheffield Wednesday	42	15	3	3	49	29	0	6	15	26	63	39	-17
17	Birmingham City	42	13	3	5	36	17	4	1	16	28	56	38	-9
18	Blackburn Rovers	42	9	5	7	40	40	6	3	12	37	56	38	-19
19	Bury	42	8	5	8	43	38	4	7	10	25	39	36	-9
20	Everton	42	10	6	5	35	30	2	4	15	29	60	34	-26
21	Leeds United	42	9	7	5	43	31	2	1	18	26	57	30	-19
22	West Bromwich Albion	42	10	4	7	47	33	1	4	16	18	53	30	-21

SEASON 1927/28

Match # 1250   Saturday 27/08/27   Football League Division 1   at Old Trafford   Attendance 44957
Result: **Manchester United 3 Middlesbrough 0**
Teamsheet: Steward, Moore, Silcock, Bennion, Barson, Wilson, Chapman, Hanson, Spence, Partridge, McPherson
Scorer(s):   Spence 2, Hanson

Match # 1251   Monday 29/08/27   Football League Division 1   at Hillsborough   Attendance 17944
Result: **Sheffield Wednesday 0 Manchester United 2**
Teamsheet: Steward, Moore, Silcock, Bennion, Hilditch, Wilson, Chapman, Hanson, Spence, Partridge, McPherson
Scorer(s):   Hanson, Partridge

Match # 1252   Saturday 03/09/27   Football League Division 1   at St Andrews   Attendance 25863
Result: **Birmingham City 0 Manchester United 0**
Teamsheet: Steward, Jones, Silcock, Bennion, Barson, Wilson, Chapman, Hanson, Spence, Partridge, McPherson

Match # 1253   Wednesday 07/09/27   Football League Division 1   at Old Trafford   Attendance 18759
Result: **Manchester United 1 Sheffield Wednesday 1**
Teamsheet: Steward, Jones, Silcock, Bennion, Barson, Wilson, Chapman, Hanson, Spence, Partridge, McPherson
Scorer(s):   McPherson

Match # 1254   Saturday 10/09/27   Football League Division 1   at Old Trafford   Attendance 50217
Result: **Manchester United 1 Newcastle United 7**
Teamsheet: Steward, Moore, Silcock, Bennion, Hilditch, Wilson, Chapman, Hanson, Spence, Partridge, Thomas
Scorer(s):   Spence

Match # 1255   Saturday 17/09/27   Football League Division 1   at Leeds Road   Attendance 17307
Result: **Huddersfield Town 4 Manchester United 2**
Teamsheet: Steward, Moore, Silcock, Bennion, Haslam, Hilditch, Chapman, Hanson, Spence, Partridge, Thomas
Scorer(s):   Spence 2

Match # 1256   Monday 19/09/27   Football League Division 1   at Ewood Park   Attendance 18243
Result: **Blackburn Rovers 3 Manchester United 0**
Teamsheet: Steward, Moore, Silcock, Bennion, Haslam, Bain, Chapman, Hanson, Spence, Partridge, Thomas

Match # 1257   Saturday 24/09/27   Football League Division 1   at Old Trafford   Attendance 13952
Result: **Manchester United 3 Tottenham Hotspur 0**
Teamsheet: Richardson, Moore, Silcock, Bennion, Haslam, Mann, Ramsden, Hanson, Spence, Partridge, McPherson
Scorer(s):   Hanson 2, Spence

Match # 1258   Saturday 01/10/27   Football League Division 1   at Filbert Street   Attendance 22385
Result: **Leicester City 1 Manchester United 0**
Teamsheet: Richardson, Moore, Silcock, Bennion, Mann, Wilson, Ramsden, Sweeney, Spence, Partridge, McPherson

Match # 1259   Saturday 08/10/27   Football League Division 1   at Goodison Park   Attendance 40080
Result: **Everton 5 Manchester United 2**
Teamsheet: Richardson, Moore, Silcock, Bennion, Hilditch, Wilson, Williams, Hanson, Spence, Partridge, McPherson
Scorer(s):   Bennion, Spence

Match # 1260   Saturday 15/10/27   Football League Division 1   at Old Trafford   Attendance 31090
Result: **Manchester United 2 Cardiff City 2**
Teamsheet: Richardson, Moore, Silcock, Bennion, Barson, Wilson, Williams, Sweeney, Spence, Johnston, McPherson
Scorer(s):   Spence, Sweeney

Match # 1261   Saturday 22/10/27   Football League Division 1   at Old Trafford   Attendance 18304
Result: **Manchester United 5 Derby County 0**
Teamsheet: Richardson, Jones, Silcock, Bennion, Barson, Wilson, Williams, Sweeney, Spence, Johnston, McPherson
Scorer(s):   Spence 3, Johnston, McPherson

Match # 1262   Saturday 29/10/27   Football League Division 1   at Upton Park   Attendance 21972
Result: **West Ham United 1 Manchester United 2**
Teamsheet: Richardson, Jones, Silcock, Mann, Barson, Wilson, Williams, Hanson, Spence, Johnston, McPherson
Scorer(s):   McPherson, own goal

Match # 1263   Saturday 05/11/27   Football League Division 1   at Old Trafford   Attendance 13119
Result: **Manchester United 2 Portsmouth 0**
Teamsheet: Richardson, Jones, Silcock, Bennion, Barson, Wilson, Williams, Hanson, Spence, Johnston, McPherson
Scorer(s):   McPherson, own goal

Match # 1264   Saturday 12/11/27   Football League Division 1   at Roker Park   Attendance 13319
Result: **Sunderland 4 Manchester United 1**
Teamsheet: Richardson, Jones, Silcock, Bennion, Barson, Wilson, Williams, Hanson, Spence, Johnston, McPherson
Scorer(s):   Spence

Match # 1265   Saturday 19/11/27   Football League Division 1   at Old Trafford   Attendance 25991
Result: **Manchester United 5 Aston Villa 1**
Teamsheet: Richardson, Moore, Jones, Bennion, Barson, Wilson, Williams, Partridge, Spence, Johnston, McPherson
Scorer(s):   Partridge 2, Johnston, McPherson, Spence

Match # 1266   Saturday 26/11/27   Football League Division 1   at Turf Moor   Attendance 18509
Result: **Burnley 4 Manchester United 0**
Teamsheet: Richardson, Moore, Jones, Bennion, Barson, Wilson, Williams, Partridge, Spence, Johnston, McPherson

Match # 1267   Saturday 03/12/27   Football League Division 1   at Old Trafford   Attendance 23581
Result: **Manchester United 0 Bury 1**
Teamsheet: Richardson, Jones, Silcock, Bennion, Hilditch, Wilson, Williams, Partridge, Spence, Johnston, McPherson

SEASON 1927/28 (continued)

Match # 1268   Saturday 10/12/27   Football League Division 1   at Bramall Lane   Attendance 11984
Result: **Sheffield United 2   Manchester United 1**
Teamsheet: Richardson, Moore, Jones, Bennion, Mann, Wilson, Williams, Partridge, Spence, Johnston, Thomas
Scorer(s):   Spence

Match # 1269   Saturday 17/12/27   Football League Division 1   at Old Trafford   Attendance 18120
Result: **Manchester United 4   Arsenal 1**
Teamsheet: Richardson, Moore, Jones, Bennion, Mann, Wilson, Spence, Partridge, Hanson, Johnston, McPherson
Scorer(s):   Hanson, McPherson, Partridge, Spence

Match # 1270   Saturday 24/12/27   Football League Division 1   at Anfield   Attendance 14971
Result: **Liverpool 2   Manchester United 0**
Teamsheet: Richardson, Moore, Jones, Bennion, Mann, Wilson, Spence, Partridge, Hanson, Johnston, McPherson

Match # 1271   Monday 26/12/27   Football League Division 1   at Old Trafford   Attendance 31131
Result: **Manchester United 1   Blackburn Rovers 1**
Teamsheet: Richardson, Moore, Jones, Bennion, Mann, Wilson, Spence, Partridge, Hanson, Johnston, McPherson
Scorer(s):   Spence

Match # 1272   Saturday 31/12/27   Football League Division 1   at Ayresome Park   Attendance 19652
Result: **Middlesbrough 1   Manchester United 2**
Teamsheet: Richardson, Moore, Jones, Bennion, Mann, Wilson, Spence, Taylor, Hanson, Johnston, Partridge
Scorer(s):   Hanson, Johnston

Match # 1273   Saturday 07/01/28   Football League Division 1   at Old Trafford   Attendance 16853
Result: **Manchester United 1   Birmingham City 1**
Teamsheet: Richardson, Moore, Jones, Bennion, Mann, Wilson, Spence, Taylor, Hanson, Johnston, McPherson
Scorer(s):   Hanson

Match # 1274   Saturday 14/01/28   FA Cup 3rd Round   at Old Trafford   Attendance 18538
Result: **Manchester United 7   Brentford 1**
Teamsheet: Richardson, Jones, Silcock, Bennion, Mann, Wilson, Spence, Hanson, McPherson, Johnston, Partridge
Scorer(s):   Hanson 4, Johnston, McPherson, Spence

Match # 1275   Saturday 21/01/28   Football League Division 1   at St James' Park   Attendance 25912
Result: **Newcastle United 4   Manchester United 1**
Teamsheet: Richardson, Jones, Silcock, Bennion, Mann, Wilson, Spence, Partridge, Hanson, Johnston, McPherson
Scorer(s):   Partridge

Match # 1276   Saturday 28/01/28   FA Cup 4th Round   at Gigg Lane   Attendance 25000
Result: **Bury 1   Manchester United 1**
Teamsheet: Richardson, Jones, Silcock, Bennion, Mann, Wilson, Spence, Hanson, McPherson, Johnston, Williams
Scorer(s):   Johnston

Match # 1277   Wednesday 01/02/28   FA Cup 4th Round Replay   at Old Trafford   Attendance 48001
Result: **Manchester United 1   Bury 0**
Teamsheet: Richardson, Jones, Silcock, Bennion, Mann, Wilson, Spence, Hanson, McPherson, Johnston, Williams
Scorer(s):   Spence

Match # 1278   Saturday 04/02/28   Football League Division 1   at White Hart Lane   Attendance 23545
Result: **Tottenham Hotspur 4   Manchester United 1**
Teamsheet: Richardson, Jones, Silcock, McLenahan, Mann, Wilson, Chapman, Hanson, Spence, Johnston, McPherson
Scorer(s):   Johnston

Match # 1279   Saturday 11/02/28   Football League Division 1   at Old Trafford   Attendance 16640
Result: **Manchester United 5   Leicester City 2**
Teamsheet: Richardson, Moore, Jones, Bennion, Mann, Wilson, Spence, Hanson, Nicol, Sweeney, Partridge
Scorer(s):   Nicol 2, Spence 2, Hanson

Match # 1280   Saturday 18/02/28   FA Cup 5th Round   at Old Trafford   Attendance 52568
Result: **Manchester United 1   Birmingham City 0**
Teamsheet: Steward, Jones, Silcock, Bennion, Mann, Wilson, Spence, Hanson, Nicol, Johnston, Partridge
Scorer(s):   Johnston

Match # 1281   Saturday 25/02/28   Football League Division 1   at Ninian Park   Attendance 15579
Result: **Cardiff City 2   Manchester United 0**
Teamsheet: Richardson, Jones, Silcock, Bennion, Mann, Wilson, Spence, Hanson, Nicol, Johnston, Partridge

Match # 1282   Saturday 03/03/28   FA Cup 6th Round   at Ewood Park   Attendance 42312
Result: **Blackburn Rovers 2   Manchester United 0**
Teamsheet: Richardson, Moore, Jones, Bennion, Mann, Wilson, Spence, Hanson, Williams, Johnston, Partridge

Match # 1283   Wednesday 07/03/28   Football League Division 1   at Old Trafford   Attendance 35413
Result: **Manchester United 0   Huddersfield Town 0**
Teamsheet: Richardson, Jones, Silcock, Bennion, Mann, Wilson, Spence, Partridge, Hanson, Johnston, McPherson

Match # 1284   Saturday 10/03/28   Football League Division 1   at Old Trafford   Attendance 21577
Result: **Manchester United 1   West Ham United 1**
Teamsheet: Richardson, Moore, Jones, Bennion, Mann, Wilson, Chapman, Partridge, Hanson, Johnston, McPherson
Scorer(s):   Johnston

Match # 1285   Wednesday 14/03/28   Football League Division 1   at Old Trafford   Attendance 25667
Result: **Manchester United 1   Everton 0**
Teamsheet: Richardson, Moore, Jones, Bennion, Mann, Wilson, Spence, Hanson, Rawlings, Johnston, McPherson
Scorer(s):   Rawlings

SEASON 1927/28 (continued)

Match # 1286   Saturday 17/03/28   Football League Division 1   at Fratton Park   Attendance 25400
Result: **Portsmouth 1 Manchester United 0**
Teamsheet: Richardson, Moore, Jones, Bennion, Barson, Wilson, Spence, Hanson, Rawlings, Johnston, Thomas

Match # 1287   Wednesday 28/03/28   Football League Division 1   at Baseball Ground   Attendance 8323
Result: **Derby County 5 Manchester United 0**
Teamsheet: Richardson, Jones, Silcock, Bennion, Mann, Wilson, Spence, Hanson, Rawlings, Johnston, Thomas

Match # 1288   Saturday 31/03/28   Football League Division 1   at Villa Park   Attendance 24691
Result: **Aston Villa 3 Manchester United 1**
Teamsheet: Richardson, Moore, Jones, Bennion, Mann, McLenahan, Spence, Rawlings, Nicol, Johnston, McPherson
Scorer(s):   Rawlings

Match # 1289   Friday 06/04/28   Football League Division 1   at Burnden Park   Attendance 23795
Result: **Bolton Wanderers 3 Manchester United 2**
Teamsheet: Richardson, Moore, Jones, Bennion, Mann, McLenahan, Spence, Rawlings, Nicol, Johnston, Thomas
Scorer(s):   Spence, Thomas

Match # 1290   Saturday 07/04/28   Football League Division 1   at Old Trafford   Attendance 28311
Result: **Manchester United 4 Burnley 3**
Teamsheet: Richardson, Jones, Silcock, Bennion, Mann, McLenahan, Williams, Ferguson, Rawlings, Johnston, Thomas
Scorer(s):   Rawlings 3, Williams

Match # 1291   Monday 09/04/28   Football League Division 1   at Old Trafford   Attendance 28590
Result: **Manchester United 2 Bolton Wanderers 1**
Teamsheet: Richardson, Jones, Silcock, Hanson, Mann, McLenahan, Williams, Ferguson, Rawlings, Johnston, Thomas
Scorer(s):   Johnston, Rawlings

Match # 1292   Saturday 14/04/28   Football League Division 1   at Gigg Lane   Attendance 17440
Result: **Bury 4 Manchester United 3**
Teamsheet: Richardson, Jones, Silcock, Bennion, Mann, McLenahan, Williams, Ferguson, Rawlings, Johnston, McPherson
Scorer(s):   Johnston, McLenahan, Williams

Match # 1293   Saturday 21/04/28   Football League Division 1   at Old Trafford   Attendance 27137
Result: **Manchester United 2 Sheffield United 3**
Teamsheet: Richardson, Jones, Silcock, Bennion, Mann, McLenahan, Spence, Ferguson, Rawlings, Johnston, Thomas
Scorer(s):   Rawlings, Thomas

Match # 1294   Wednesday 25/04/28   Football League Division 1   at Old Trafford   Attendance 9545
Result: **Manchester United 2 Sunderland 1**
Teamsheet: Steward, Jones, Silcock, McLenahan, Mann, Wilson, Spence, Hanson, Rawlings, Johnston, Thomas
Scorer(s):   Hanson, Johnston

Match # 1295   Saturday 28/04/28   Football League Division 1   at Highbury   Attendance 22452
Result: **Arsenal 0 Manchester United 1**
Teamsheet: Steward, Moore, Jones, McLenahan, Mann, Wilson, Spence, Hanson, Rawlings, Johnston, Thomas
Scorer(s):   Rawlings

Match # 1296   Saturday 05/05/28   Football League Division 1   at Old Trafford   Attendance 30625
Result: **Manchester United 6 Liverpool 1**
Teamsheet: Steward, Moore, Jones, McLenahan, Mann, Wilson, Spence, Hanson, Rawlings, Johnston, Thomas
Scorer(s):   Spence 3, Rawlings 2, Hanson

SEASON 1927/28 SUMMARY

APPEARANCES

PLAYER	LGE	FAC	TOT
Spence	38	5	43
Bennion	36	5	41
Jones	33	5	38
Wilson	33	5	38
Johnston	31	5	36
Richardson	32	4	36
Hanson	30	5	35
Mann	26	5	31
Silcock	26	4	30
McPherson	26	3	29
Moore	25	1	26
Partridge	23	3	26
Williams	13	3	16
Thomas	13	–	13
Rawlings	12	–	12
Barson	11	–	11
Steward	10	1	11
McLenahan	10	–	10
Chapman	9	–	9
Hilditch	5	–	5
Nicol	4	1	5
Ferguson	4	–	4
Sweeney	4	–	4
Haslam	3	–	3
Ramsden	2	–	2
Taylor	2	–	2
Bain	1	–	1

GOALSCORERS

PLAYER	LGE	FAC	TOT
Spence	22	2	24
Hanson	10	4	14
Johnston	8	3	11
Rawlings	10	–	10
McPherson	6	1	7
Partridge	5	–	5
Nicol	2	–	2
Thomas	2	–	2
Williams	2	–	2
Bennion	1	–	1
McLenahan	1	–	1
Sweeney	1	–	1
own goals	2	–	2

RESULTS & ATTENDANCES SUMMARY

		P	W	D	L	F	A	TOTAL	AVGE
League	H	21	12	6	3	51	27	529579	25218
	A	21	4	1	16	21	53	429366	20446
TOTAL		42	16	7	19	72	80	958945	22832
FA Cup	H	3	3	0	0	9	1	119107	39702
	A	2	0	1	1	1	3	67312	33656
TOTAL		5	3	1	1	10	4	186419	37284
Overall	H	24	15	6	3	60	28	648686	27029
	A	23	4	2	17	22	56	496678	21595
TOTAL		47	19	8	20	82	84	1145364	24369

FINAL TABLE – LEAGUE DIVISION ONE

		P	W	D	L	F	A	W	D	L	F	A	PTS	GD
				HOME						AWAY				
1	Everton	42	11	8	2	60	28	9	5	7	42	38	53	36
2	Huddersfield Town	42	15	1	5	57	31	7	6	8	34	37	51	23
3	Leicester City	42	14	5	2	66	25	4	7	10	30	47	48	24
4	Derby County	42	12	4	5	59	30	5	6	10	37	53	44	13
5	Bury	42	13	1	7	53	35	7	3	11	27	45	44	0
6	Cardiff City	42	12	7	2	44	27	5	3	13	26	53	44	-10
7	Bolton Wanderers	42	12	5	4	47	26	4	6	11	34	40	43	15
8	Aston Villa	42	13	3	5	52	30	4	6	11	26	43	43	5
9	Newcastle United	42	9	7	5	49	41	6	6	9	30	40	43	-2
10	Arsenal	42	10	6	5	49	33	3	9	9	33	53	41	-4
11	Birmingham City	42	10	7	4	36	25	3	8	10	34	50	41	-5
12	Blackburn Rovers	42	13	5	3	41	22	3	4	14	25	56	41	-12
13	Sheffield United	42	12	4	5	56	42	3	6	12	23	44	40	-7
14	Sheffield Wednesday	42	9	6	6	45	29	4	7	10	36	49	39	3
15	Sunderland	42	9	5	7	37	29	6	4	11	37	47	39	-2
16	Liverpool	42	10	6	5	54	30	3	7	11	30	51	39	-3
17	West Ham United	42	9	7	5	48	34	5	4	12	33	54	39	-7
18	MANCHESTER UNITED	42	12	6	3	51	27	4	1	16	21	53	39	-8
19	Burnley	42	12	5	4	55	31	4	2	15	27	67	39	-16
20	Portsmouth	42	13	4	4	40	23	3	3	15	26	67	39	-24
21	Tottenham Hotspur	42	12	3	6	47	34	3	5	13	27	52	38	-12
22	Middlesbrough	42	7	9	5	46	35	4	6	11	35	53	37	-7

SEASON 1928/29

Match # 1297 Saturday 25/08/28   Football League Division 1   at Old Trafford   Attendance 20129
Result: **Manchester United 1 Leicester City 1**
Teamsheet: Steward, Dale, Silcock, Bennion, Mann, Wilson, Spence, Hanson, Rawlings, Johnston, Williams
Scorer(s):   Rawlings

Match # 1298 Monday 27/08/28   Football League Division 1   at Villa Park   Attendance 30356
Result: **Aston Villa 0 Manchester United 0**
Teamsheet: Steward, Moore, Silcock, McLenahan, Mann, Wilson, Spence, Hanson, Rawlings, Johnston, Williams

Match # 1299 Saturday 01/09/28   Football League Division 1   at Maine Road   Attendance 61007
Result: **Manchester City 2 Manchester United 2**
Teamsheet: Steward, Moore, Silcock, Bennion, Mann, Wilson, Spence, Hanson, Rawlings, Johnston, Williams
Scorer(s):   Johnston, Wilson

Match # 1300 Saturday 08/09/28   Football League Division 1   at Elland Road   Attendance 28723
Result: **Leeds United 3 Manchester United 2**
Teamsheet: Steward, Moore, Silcock, Bennion, Mann, Wilson, Spence, Hanson, Rawlings, Johnston, Williams
Scorer(s):   Johnston, Spence

Match # 1301 Saturday 15/09/28   Football League Division 1   at Old Trafford   Attendance 24077
Result: **Manchester United 2 Liverpool 2**
Teamsheet: Steward, Moore, Silcock, Bennion, Spencer, Wilson, Spence, Hanson, Rawlings, Johnston, Williams
Scorer(s):   Hanson, Silcock

Match # 1302 Saturday 22/09/28   Football League Division 1   at Upton Park   Attendance 20788
Result: **West Ham United 3 Manchester United 1**
Teamsheet: Steward, Moore, Silcock, Mann, Spencer, Wilson, Hanson, Taylor, Rawlings, Johnston, Williams
Scorer(s):   Rawlings

Match # 1303 Saturday 29/09/28   Football League Division 1   at Old Trafford   Attendance 25243
Result: **Manchester United 5 Newcastle United 0**
Teamsheet: Steward, Moore, Silcock, Bennion, Spencer, Wilson, Spence, Hanson, Rawlings, Johnston, Williams
Scorer(s):   Rawlings 2, Hanson, Johnston, Spence

Match # 1304 Saturday 06/10/28   Football League Division 1   at Turf Moor   Attendance 17493
Result: **Burnley 3 Manchester United 4**
Teamsheet: Steward, Moore, Silcock, Bennion, Spencer, Wilson, Spence, Hanson, Rawlings, Johnston, Williams
Scorer(s):   Hanson 2, Spence 2

Match # 1305 Saturday 13/10/28   Football League Division 1   at Old Trafford   Attendance 26010
Result: **Manchester United 1 Cardiff City 1**
Teamsheet: Steward, Moore, Silcock, Bennion, Spencer, Wilson, Spence, Hanson, Rawlings, Johnston, Williams
Scorer(s):   Johnston

Match # 1306 Saturday 20/10/28   Football League Division 1   at Old Trafford   Attendance 17522
Result: **Manchester United 1 Birmingham City 0**
Teamsheet: Steward, Moore, Silcock, Bennion, Spencer, Wilson, Spence, Hanson, Rawlings, Johnston, Williams
Scorer(s):   Johnston

Match # 1307 Saturday 27/10/28   Football League Division 1   at Leeds Road   Attendance 13648
Result: **Huddersfield Town 1 Manchester United 2**
Teamsheet: Steward, Moore, Silcock, Mann, Spencer, Wilson, Spence, Hanson, Rawlings, Rowley, Thomas
Scorer(s):   Hanson, Spence

Match # 1308 Saturday 03/11/28   Football League Division 1   at Old Trafford   Attendance 31185
Result: **Manchester United 1 Bolton Wanderers 1**
Teamsheet: Steward, Moore, Silcock, Bennion, Spencer, Wilson, Spence, Hanson, Rawlings, Rowley, Williams
Scorer(s):   Hanson

Match # 1309 Saturday 10/11/28   Football League Division 1   at Hillsborough   Attendance 18113
Result: **Sheffield Wednesday 2 Manchester United 1**
Teamsheet: Steward, Moore, Silcock, Bennion, Spencer, Wilson, Spence, Hanson, Rawlings, Rowley, Williams
Scorer(s):   Hanson

Match # 1310 Saturday 17/11/28   Football League Division 1   at Old Trafford   Attendance 26122
Result: **Manchester United 0 Derby County 1**
Teamsheet: Steward, Moore, Silcock, Hilditch, Spencer, Wilson, Spence, Hanson, Rawlings, Rowley, Thomas

Match # 1311 Saturday 24/11/28   Football League Division 1   at Roker Park   Attendance 15932
Result: **Sunderland 5 Manchester United 1**
Teamsheet: Steward, Moore, Silcock, Bennion, Mann, Hilditch, Spence, Hanson, Rawlings, Rowley, Williams
Scorer(s):   Rowley

Match # 1312 Saturday 01/12/28   Football League Division 1   at Old Trafford   Attendance 19589
Result: **Manchester United 1 Blackburn Rovers 4**
Teamsheet: Steward, Moore, Silcock, Bennion, Mann, Hilditch, Ramsden, Hanson, Spence, Rowley, Williams
Scorer(s):   Ramsden

Match # 1313 Saturday 08/12/28   Football League Division 1   at Highbury   Attendance 18923
Result: **Arsenal 3 Manchester United 1**
Teamsheet: Steward, Moore, Dale, Bennion, Spencer, Hilditch, Hanson, Taylor, Rawlings, Rowley, Williams
Scorer(s):   Hanson

Match # 1314 Saturday 15/12/28   Football League Division 1   at Old Trafford   Attendance 17080
Result: **Manchester United 1 Everton 1**
Teamsheet: Richardson, Moore, Dale, Hilditch, Spencer, Wilson, Spence, Hanson, Nicol, Sweeney, Partridge
Scorer(s):   Hanson

SEASON 1928/29 (continued)

Match # 1315 Saturday 22/12/28   Football League Division 1   at Fratton Park   Attendance 12836
Result: **Portsmouth 3 Manchester United 0**
Teamsheet: Richardson, Moore, Dale, Hilditch, Spencer, Wilson, Spence, Hanson, Nicol, Sweeney, Thomas

Match # 1316 Tuesday 25/12/28   Football League Division 1   at Old Trafford   Attendance 22202
Result: **Manchester United 1 Sheffield United 1**
Teamsheet: Richardson, Dale, Silcock, Bennion, Spencer, Wilson, Ramsden, Hanson, Rawlings, Johnston, Partridge
Scorer(s):   Ramsden

Match # 1317 Wednesday 26/12/28   Football League Division 1   at Bramall Lane   Attendance 34696
Result: **Sheffield United 6 Manchester United 1**
Teamsheet: Richardson, Inglis, Dale, Bennion, Spencer, Hilditch, Ramsden, Hanson, Rawlings, Sweeney, Partridge
Scorer(s):   Rawlings

Match # 1318 Saturday 29/12/28   Football League Division 1   at Filbert Street   Attendance 21535
Result: **Leicester City 2 Manchester United 1**
Teamsheet: Richardson, Dale, Silcock, Bennion, Spencer, Hilditch, Ramsden, Sweeney, Hanson, Johnston, Partridge
Scorer(s):   Hanson

Match # 1319 Tuesday 01/01/29   Football League Division 1   at Old Trafford   Attendance 25935
Result: **Manchester United 2 Aston Villa 2**
Teamsheet: Steward, Moore, Silcock, Bennion, Spencer, Hilditch, Spence, Sweeney, Hanson, Rowley, Partridge
Scorer(s):   Hilditch, Rowley

Match # 1320 Saturday 05/01/29   Football League Division 1   at Old Trafford   Attendance 42555
Result: **Manchester United 1 Manchester City 2**
Teamsheet: Steward, Moore, Silcock, Bennion, Spencer, Hilditch, Spence, Hanson, Rawlings, Rowley, Williams
Scorer(s):   Rawlings

Match # 1321 Saturday 12/01/29   FA Cup 3rd Round   at Old Recreation Ground   Attendance 17519
Result: **Port Vale 0 Manchester United 3**
Teamsheet: Steward, Moore, Silcock, Spencer, Mann, Wilson, Spence, Hanson, Williams, Sweeney, Taylor
Scorer(s):   Hanson, Spence, Taylor

Match # 1322 Saturday 19/01/29   Football League Division 1   at Old Trafford   Attendance 21995
Result: **Manchester United 1 Leeds United 2**
Teamsheet: Steward, Moore, Silcock, Mann, Spencer, Wilson, Spence, Taylor, Hanson, Sweeney, Williams
Scorer(s):   Sweeney

Match # 1323 Saturday 26/01/29   FA Cup 4th Round   at Old Trafford   Attendance 40558
Result: **Manchester United 0 Bury 1**
Teamsheet: Steward, Moore, Silcock, Spencer, Mann, Wilson, Spence, Rawlings, Thomas, Sweeney, Thomson

Match # 1324 Saturday 02/02/29   Football League Division 1   at Old Trafford   Attendance 12020
Result: **Manchester United 2 West Ham United 3**
Teamsheet: Steward, Dale, Silcock, Hilditch, Spencer, Wilson, Spence, Hanson, Reid, Rowley, Thomas
Scorer(s):   Reid, Rowley

Match # 1325 Saturday 09/02/29   Football League Division 1   at St James' Park   Attendance 34134
Result: **Newcastle United 5 Manchester United 0**
Teamsheet: Steward, Moore, Silcock, Bennion, Spencer, Mann, Spence, Hanson, Reid, Rowley, Thomas

Match # 1326 Wednesday 13/02/29   Football League Division 1   at Anfield   Attendance 8852
Result: **Liverpool 2 Manchester United 3**
Teamsheet: Steward, Moore, Silcock, Bennion, Spencer, Mann, Spence, Hanson, Reid, Rowley, Thomas
Scorer(s):   Reid 2, Thomas

Match # 1327 Saturday 16/02/29   Football League Division 1   at Old Trafford   Attendance 12516
Result: **Manchester United 1 Burnley 0**
Teamsheet: Steward, Moore, Dale, Bennion, Spencer, Mann, Spence, Hanson, Reid, Rowley, Thomas
Scorer(s):   Rowley

Match # 1328 Saturday 23/02/29   Football League Division 1   at Ninian Park   Attendance 13070
Result: **Cardiff City 2 Manchester United 2**
Teamsheet: Steward, Moore, Dale, Bennion, Spencer, Mann, Spence, Hanson, Reid, Rowley, Thomas
Scorer(s):   Hanson, Reid

Match # 1329 Saturday 02/03/29   Football League Division 1   at St Andrews   Attendance 16738
Result: **Birmingham City 1 Manchester United 1**
Teamsheet: Steward, Moore, Dale, Bennion, Spencer, Mann, Spence, Hanson, Reid, Rowley, Thomas
Scorer(s):   Hanson

Match # 1330 Saturday 09/03/29   Football League Division 1   at Old Trafford   Attendance 28183
Result: **Manchester United 1 Huddersfield Town 0**
Teamsheet: Steward, Moore, Dale, Bennion, Spencer, Mann, Spence, Hanson, Reid, Rowley, Thomas
Scorer(s):   Hanson

Match # 1331 Saturday 16/03/29   Football League Division 1   at Burnden Park   Attendance 17354
Result: **Bolton Wanderers 1 Manchester United 1**
Teamsheet: Steward, Moore, Dale, Bennion, Spencer, Mann, Spence, Hanson, Reid, Rowley, Thomas
Scorer(s):   Hanson

Match # 1332 Saturday 23/03/29   Football League Division 1   at Old Trafford   Attendance 27095
Result: **Manchester United 2 Sheffield Wednesday 1**
Teamsheet: Steward, Moore, Silcock, Bennion, Spencer, Mann, Spence, Hanson, Reid, Rowley, Thomas
Scorer(s):   Reid, Rowley

SEASON 1928/29 (continued)

Match # 1333 Friday 29/03/29   Football League Division 1   at Gigg Lane   Attendance 27167
Result: **Bury 1 Manchester United 3**
Teamsheet: Steward, Moore, Silcock, Bennion, Spencer, Mann, Spence, Hanson, Reid, Rowley, Thomas
Scorer(s): Reid 2, Thomas

Match # 1334 Saturday 30/03/29   Football League Division 1   at Baseball Ground   Attendance 14619
Result: **Derby County 6 Manchester United 1**
Teamsheet: Steward, Moore, Silcock, Bennion, Spencer, Mann, Spence, Hanson, Reid, Boyle, Williams
Scorer(s): Hanson

Match # 1335 Monday 01/04/29   Football League Division 1   at Old Trafford   Attendance 29742
Result: **Manchester United 1 Bury 0**
Teamsheet: Steward, Moore, Dale, Bennion, Spencer, Mann, Spence, Hanson, Reid, Rowley, Thomas
Scorer(s): Thomas

Match # 1336 Saturday 06/04/29   Football League Division 1   at Old Trafford   Attendance 27772
Result: **Manchester United 3 Sunderland 0**
Teamsheet: Steward, Moore, Dale, Bennion, Spencer, Mann, Spence, Hanson, Reid, Rowley, Thomas
Scorer(s): Hanson, Mann, Reid

Match # 1337 Saturday 13/04/29   Football League Division 1   at Ewood Park   Attendance 8193
Result: **Blackburn Rovers 0 Manchester United 3**
Teamsheet: Steward, Moore, Dale, Bennion, Spencer, Mann, Ramsden, Hanson, Reid, Rowley, Thomas
Scorer(s): Reid 2, Ramsden

Match # 1338 Saturday 20/04/29   Football League Division 1   at Old Trafford   Attendance 22858
Result: **Manchester United 4 Arsenal 1**
Teamsheet: Steward, Moore, Dale, Bennion, Spencer, Mann, Spence, Hanson, Reid, Rowley, Thomas
Scorer(s): Reid 2, Hanson, Thomas

Match # 1339 Saturday 27/04/29   Football League Division 1   at Goodison Park   Attendance 19442
Result: **Everton 2 Manchester United 4**
Teamsheet: Steward, Moore, Dale, Bennion, Spencer, Mann, Spence, Hanson, Reid, Rowley, Thomas
Scorer(s): Hanson 2, Reid 2

Match # 1340 Saturday 04/05/29   Football League Division 1   at Old Trafford   Attendance 17728
Result: **Manchester United 0 Portsmouth 0**
Teamsheet: Steward, Moore, Dale, Bennion, Spencer, Mann, Spence, Hanson, Reid, Rowley, Thomas

SEASON 1928/29 SUMMARY

APPEARANCES

PLAYER	LGE	FAC	TOT
Hanson	42	1	43
Moore	37	2	39
Steward	37	2	39
Spence	36	2	38
Spencer	36	2	38
Bennion	34	–	34
Silcock	27	2	29
Mann	25	2	27
Rowley	25	–	25
Wilson	19	2	21
Rawlings	19	1	20
Thomas	19	1	20
Dale	19	–	19
Williams	18	1	19
Reid	17	–	17
Johnston	12	–	12
Hilditch	11	–	11
Sweeney	6	2	8
Partridge	5	–	5
Ramsden	5	–	5
Richardson	5	–	5
Taylor	3	1	4
Nicol	2	–	2
Boyle	1	–	1
Inglis	1	–	1
McLenahan	1	–	1
Thomson	–	1	1

GOALSCORERS

PLAYER	LGE	FAC	TOT
Hanson	19	1	20
Reid	14	–	14
Rawlings	6	–	6
Spence	5	1	6
Johnston	5	–	5
Rowley	5	–	5
Thomas	4	–	4
Ramsden	3	–	3
Hilditch	1	–	1
Mann	1	–	1
Silcock	1	–	1
Sweeney	1	–	1
Wilson	1	–	1
Taylor	–	1	1

RESULTS & ATTENDANCES SUMMARY

		P	W	D	L	F	A	TOTAL	AVGE
League	H	21	8	8	5	32	23	497558	23693
	A	21	6	5	10	34	53	453619	21601
TOTAL		42	14	13	15	66	76	951177	22647
FA Cup	H	1	0	0	1	0	1	40558	40558
	A	1	1	0	0	3	0	17519	17519
TOTAL		2	1	0	1	3	1	58077	29039
Overall	H	22	8	8	6	32	24	538116	24460
	A	22	7	5	10	37	53	471138	21415
TOTAL		44	15	13	16	69	77	1009254	22938

FINAL TABLE – LEAGUE DIVISION ONE

		P	W	D	L	F	A	W	D	L	F	A	PTS	GD
					HOME					AWAY				
1	Sheffield Wednesday	42	18	3	0	55	16	3	7	11	31	46	52	24
2	Leicester City	42	16	5	0	67	22	5	4	12	29	45	51	29
3	Aston Villa	42	16	2	3	62	30	7	2	12	36	51	50	17
4	Sunderland	42	16	2	3	67	30	4	5	12	26	45	47	18
5	Liverpool	42	11	4	6	53	28	6	8	7	37	36	46	26
6	Derby County	42	12	5	4	56	24	6	5	10	30	47	46	15
7	Blackburn Rovers	42	11	6	4	42	26	6	5	10	30	37	45	9
8	Manchester City	42	12	3	6	63	40	6	6	9	32	46	45	9
9	Arsenal	42	11	6	4	43	25	5	7	9	34	47	45	5
10	Newcastle United	42	15	2	4	48	29	4	4	13	22	43	44	-2
11	Sheffield United	42	12	5	4	57	30	3	6	12	29	55	41	1
12	MANCHESTER UNITED	42	8	8	5	32	23	6	5	10	34	53	41	-10
13	Leeds United	42	11	5	5	42	28	5	4	12	29	56	41	-13
14	Bolton Wanderers	42	10	6	5	44	25	4	6	11	29	55	40	-7
15	Birmingham City	42	8	7	6	37	32	7	3	11	31	45	40	-9
16	Huddersfield Town	42	9	6	6	45	23	5	5	11	25	38	39	9
17	West Ham United	42	11	6	4	55	31	4	3	14	31	65	39	-10
18	Everton	42	11	2	8	38	31	6	2	13	25	44	38	-12
19	Burnley	42	12	5	4	55	32	3	3	15	26	71	38	-22
20	Portsmouth	42	13	2	6	43	26	2	4	15	13	54	36	-24
21	Bury	42	9	5	7	38	35	3	2	16	24	64	31	-37
22	Cardiff City	42	7	7	7	34	26	1	6	14	9	33	29	-16

SEASON 1929/30

Match # 1341 Saturday 31/08/29 Football League Division 1 at St James' Park Attendance 43489
Result: **Newcastle United 4 Manchester United 1**
Teamsheet: Steward, Moore, Dale, Bennion, Spencer, Mann, Spence, Hanson, Reid, Rowley, Thomas
Scorer(s): Spence

Match # 1342 Monday 02/09/29 Football League Division 1 at Filbert Street Attendance 20490
Result: **Leicester City 4 Manchester United 1**
Teamsheet: Steward, Moore, Dale, Bennion, Spencer, Mann, Spence, Hanson, Reid, Rowley, Thomas
Scorer(s): Rowley

Match # 1343 Saturday 07/09/29 Football League Division 1 at Old Trafford Attendance 22362
Result: **Manchester United 1 Blackburn Rovers 0**
Teamsheet: Steward, Moore, Silcock, Bennion, Spencer, Mann, Spence, Hanson, Reid, Rowley, Thomas
Scorer(s): Mann

Match # 1344 Wednesday 11/09/29 Football League Division 1 at Old Trafford Attendance 16445
Result: **Manchester United 2 Leicester City 1**
Teamsheet: Steward, Moore, Silcock, Bennion, Spencer, Mann, Spence, Hanson, Ball, Rowley, Thomas
Scorer(s): Ball, Spence

Match # 1345 Saturday 14/09/29 Football League Division 1 at Ayresome Park Attendance 26428
Result: **Middlesbrough 2 Manchester United 3**
Teamsheet: Steward, Moore, Dale, Bennion, Spencer, Mann, Spence, Hanson, Rawlings, Rowley, Thomas
Scorer(s): Rawlings 3

Match # 1346 Saturday 21/09/29 Football League Division 1 at Old Trafford Attendance 20788
Result: **Manchester United 1 Liverpool 2**
Teamsheet: Steward, Moore, Dale, Bennion, Spencer, Mann, Spence, Hanson, Rawlings, Rowley, Thomas
Scorer(s): Spence

Match # 1347 Saturday 28/09/29 Football League Division 1 at Upton Park Attendance 20695
Result: **West Ham United 2 Manchester United 1**
Teamsheet: Steward, Moore, Dale, Bennion, Mann, Wilson, Spence, Hanson, Rawlings, Rowley, Thomas
Scorer(s): Hanson

Match # 1348 Saturday 05/10/29 Football League Division 1 at Old Trafford Attendance 57201
Result: **Manchester United 1 Manchester City 3**
Teamsheet: Steward, Moore, Silcock, Bennion, Spencer, Mann, Spence, Hanson, Reid, Rowley, Thomas
Scorer(s): Thomas

Match # 1349 Monday 07/10/29 Football League Division 1 at Bramall Lane Attendance 7987
Result: **Sheffield United 3 Manchester United 1**
Teamsheet: Steward, Moore, Silcock, Bennion, Spencer, Mann, Spence, Boyle, Rawlings, Sweeney, Thomas
Scorer(s): Boyle

Match # 1350 Saturday 12/10/29 Football League Division 1 at Old Trafford Attendance 21494
Result: **Manchester United 2 Grimsby Town 5**
Teamsheet: Steward, Moore, Dale, Hilditch, Taylor, McLenahan, Spence, Boyle, Ball, Rowley, Thomas
Scorer(s): Ball, Rowley

Match # 1351 Saturday 19/10/29 Football League Division 1 at Fratton Park Attendance 18070
Result: **Portsmouth 3 Manchester United 0**
Teamsheet: Steward, Moore, Dale, Bennion, Taylor, Mann, Spence, Boyle, Reid, Rowley, Thomas

Match # 1352 Saturday 26/10/29 Football League Division 1 at Old Trafford Attendance 12662
Result: **Manchester United 1 Arsenal 0**
Teamsheet: Steward, Moore, Dale, Taylor, Spencer, Mann, Spence, Hanson, Ball, Rowley, Thomas
Scorer(s): Ball

Match # 1353 Saturday 02/11/29 Football League Division 1 at Villa Park Attendance 24292
Result: **Aston Villa 1 Manchester United 0**
Teamsheet: Steward, Moore, Dale, Taylor, Spencer, Mann, Spence, Hanson, Ball, Rowley, Thomas

Match # 1354 Saturday 09/11/29 Football League Division 1 at Old Trafford Attendance 15174
Result: **Manchester United 3 Derby County 2**
Teamsheet: Steward, Moore, Dale, Bennion, Taylor, Mann, Spence, Hanson, Ball, Rowley, Thomas
Scorer(s): Ball, Hanson, Rowley

Match # 1355 Saturday 16/11/29 Football League Division 1 at Hillsborough Attendance 14264
Result: **Sheffield Wednesday 7 Manchester United 2**
Teamsheet: Steward, Moore, Dale, Bennion, Taylor, Mann, Spence, Hanson, Ball, Rowley, Thomas
Scorer(s): Ball, Hanson

Match # 1356 Saturday 23/11/29 Football League Division 1 at Old Trafford Attendance 9060
Result: **Manchester United 1 Burnley 0**
Teamsheet: Steward, Moore, Dale, Bennion, Wilson, Spence, Hanson, Ball, Rowley, Thomas
Scorer(s): Rowley

Match # 1357 Saturday 30/11/29 Football League Division 1 at Roker Park Attendance 11508
Result: **Sunderland 2 Manchester United 4**
Teamsheet: Steward, Moore, Dale, Hilditch, Taylor, Wilson, Spence, Hanson, Ball, Rowley, Thomas
Scorer(s): Spence 2, Ball, Hanson

Match # 1358 Saturday 07/12/29 Football League Division 1 at Old Trafford Attendance 5656
Result: **Manchester United 1 Bolton Wanderers 1**
Teamsheet: Steward, Moore, Dale, Hilditch, Taylor, Wilson, Spence, Hanson, Ball, Rowley, Thomas
Scorer(s): Ball

SEASON 1929/30 (continued)

Match # 1359 Saturday 14/12/29   Football League Division 1   at Goodison Park   Attendance 18182
Result: **Everton 0   Manchester United 0**
Teamsheet: Steward, Moore, Dale, Hilditch, Taylor, Wilson, Spence, Hanson, Ball, Rowley, Thomas

Match # 1360 Saturday 21/12/29   Football League Division 1   at Old Trafford   Attendance 15054
Result: **Manchester United 3   Leeds United 1**
Teamsheet: Steward, Moore, Jones, Hilditch, Taylor, Wilson, Spence, Hanson, Ball, Rowley, McLachlan
Scorer(s):   Ball 2, Hanson

Match # 1361 Wednesday 25/12/29   Football League Division 1   at Old Trafford   Attendance 18626
Result: **Manchester United 0   Birmingham City 0**
Teamsheet: Steward, Moore, Jones, Hilditch, Taylor, Wilson, Spence, Hanson, Ball, Rowley, McLachlan

Match # 1362 Thursday 26/12/29   Football League Division 1   at St Andrews   Attendance 35682
Result: **Birmingham City 0   Manchester United 1**
Teamsheet: Steward, Moore, Jones, Hilditch, Taylor, Wilson, Spence, Boyle, Ball, Rowley, McLachlan
Scorer(s):   Rowley

Match # 1363 Saturday 28/12/29   Football League Division 1   at Old Trafford   Attendance 14862
Result: **Manchester United 5   Newcastle United 0**
Teamsheet: Chesters, Moore, Jones, Hilditch, Taylor, Wilson, Spence, Boyle, Ball, Rowley, McLachlan
Scorer(s):   Boyle 2, McLachlan, Rowley, Spence

Match # 1364 Saturday 04/01/30   Football League Division 1   at Ewood Park   Attendance 23923
Result: **Blackburn Rovers 5   Manchester United 4**
Teamsheet: Steward, Moore, Jones, Hilditch, Taylor, Wilson, Spence, Boyle, Ball, Rowley, McLachlan
Scorer(s):   Boyle 2, Ball, Rowley

Match # 1365 Saturday 11/01/30   FA Cup 3rd Round   at Old Trafford   Attendance 33226
Result: **Manchester United 0   Swindon Town 2**
Teamsheet: Steward, Moore, Jones, Taylor, Hilditch, Wilson, Spence, Ball, McLachlan, Rowley, Boyle

Match # 1366 Saturday 18/01/30   Football League Division 1   at Old Trafford   Attendance 21028
Result: **Manchester United 0   Middlesbrough 3**
Teamsheet: Steward, Moore, Jones, Hilditch, Taylor, Wilson, Spence, Boyle, Ball, Rowley, McLachlan

Match # 1367 Saturday 25/01/30   Football League Division 1   at Anfield   Attendance 28592
Result: **Liverpool 1   Manchester United 0**
Teamsheet: Steward, Dale, Silcock, Bennion, Hilditch, Wilson, Spence, Boyle, Reid, Rowley, McLachlan

Match # 1368 Saturday 01/02/30   Football League Division 1   at Old Trafford   Attendance 15424
Result: **Manchester United 4   West Ham United 2**
Teamsheet: Steward, Dale, Silcock, Bennion, Hilditch, Wilson, Spence, Boyle, Reid, Rowley, McLachlan
Scorer(s):   Spence 4

Match # 1369 Saturday 08/02/30   Football League Division 1   at Maine Road   Attendance 64472
Result: **Manchester City 0   Manchester United 1**
Teamsheet: Steward, Jones, Silcock, Bennion, Hilditch, Wilson, Spence, Boyle, Reid, Rowley, McLachlan
Scorer(s):   Reid

Match # 1370 Saturday 15/02/30   Football League Division 1   at Blundell Park   Attendance 9337
Result: **Grimsby Town 2   Manchester United 2**
Teamsheet: Steward, Moore, Silcock, Bennion, Hilditch, Wilson, Spence, Boyle, Reid, Rowley, McLachlan
Scorer(s):   Reid, Rowley

Match # 1371 Saturday 22/02/30   Football League Division 1   at Old Trafford   Attendance 17317
Result: **Manchester United 3   Portsmouth 0**
Teamsheet: Steward, Moore, Silcock, Bennion, Hilditch, Wilson, Spence, Boyle, Reid, Rowley, McLachlan
Scorer(s):   Reid 2, Boyle

Match # 1372 Saturday 01/03/30   Football League Division 1   at Burnden Park   Attendance 17714
Result: **Bolton Wanderers 4   Manchester United 1**
Teamsheet: Steward, Moore, Silcock, Bennion, Hilditch, Wilson, Spence, Boyle, Reid, Rowley, McLachlan
Scorer(s):   Reid

Match # 1373 Saturday 08/03/30   Football League Division 1   at Old Trafford   Attendance 25407
Result: **Manchester United 2   Aston Villa 3**
Teamsheet: Steward, Dale, Silcock, Bennion, Hilditch, Wilson, Spence, Warburton, Reid, Rowley, McLachlan
Scorer(s):   McLachlan, Warburton

Match # 1374 Wednesday 12/03/30   Football League Division 1   at Highbury   Attendance 18082
Result: **Arsenal 4   Manchester United 2**
Teamsheet: Steward, Dale, Silcock, Bennion, Hilditch, Wilson, Spence, Warburton, Ball, McLachlan, Thomas
Scorer(s):   Ball, Wilson

Match # 1375 Saturday 15/03/30   Football League Division 1   at Baseball Ground   Attendance 9102
Result: **Derby County 1   Manchester United 1**
Teamsheet: Chesters, Jones, Silcock, McLenahan, Hilditch, Wilson, Spence, Boyle, Ball, Rowley, McLachlan
Scorer(s):   Rowley

Match # 1376 Saturday 29/03/30   Football League Division 1   at Turf Moor   Attendance 11659
Result: **Burnley 4   Manchester United 0**
Teamsheet: Chesters, Jones, Silcock, McLenahan, Hilditch, Wilson, Spence, Boyle, Ball, Rowley, McLachlan

SEASON 1929/30 (continued)

Match # 1377 Saturday 05/04/30   Football League Division 1   at Old Trafford   Attendance 13230
Result: **Manchester United 2 Sunderland 1**
Teamsheet: Steward, Jones, Silcock, Bennion, Hilditch, Wilson, Spence, McLenahan, Ball, Rowley, McLachlan
Scorer(s): McLenahan 2

Match # 1378 Monday 14/04/30   Football League Division 1   at Old Trafford   Attendance 12806
Result: **Manchester United 2 Sheffield Wednesday 2**
Teamsheet: Steward, Jones, Silcock, Bennion, Hilditch, Wilson, Spence, McLenahan, Reid, Rowley, McLachlan
Scorer(s): McLenahan, Rowley

Match # 1379 Friday 18/04/30   Football League Division 1   at Old Trafford   Attendance 26496
Result: **Manchester United 1 Huddersfield Town 0**
Teamsheet: Steward, Jones, Silcock, Bennion, Hilditch, Wilson, Spence, McLenahan, McLachlan, Rowley, Thomas
Scorer(s): McLenahan

Match # 1380 Saturday 19/04/30   Football League Division 1   at Old Trafford   Attendance 13320
Result: **Manchester United 3 Everton 3**
Teamsheet: Steward, Jones, Silcock, Bennion, Hilditch, Wilson, Spence, McLenahan, Thomson, Rowley, McLachlan
Scorer(s): McLenahan, Rowley, Spence

Match # 1381 Tuesday 22/04/30   Football League Division 1   at Leeds Road   Attendance 20716
Result: **Huddersfield Town 2 Manchester United 2**
Teamsheet: Steward, Jones, Silcock, Bennion, Hilditch, Wilson, Spence, McLenahan, Ball, Rowley, McLachlan
Scorer(s): Hilditch, McLenahan

Match # 1382 Saturday 26/04/30   Football League Division 1   at Elland Road   Attendance 10596
Result: **Leeds United 3 Manchester United 1**
Teamsheet: Steward, Jones, Silcock, Bennion, Hilditch, Wilson, Spence, McLenahan, Ball, Rowley, McLachlan
Scorer(s): Spence

Match # 1383 Saturday 03/05/30   Football League Division 1   at Old Trafford   Attendance 15268
Result: **Manchester United 1 Sheffield United 5**
Teamsheet: Steward, Jones, Silcock, Bennion, Hilditch, Wilson, Spence, McLenahan, Ball, Rowley, McLachlan
Scorer(s): Rowley

SEASON 1929/30 SUMMARY

APPEARANCES

PLAYER	LGE	FAC	TOT
Spence	42	1	43
Rowley	40	1	41
Steward	39	1	40
Moore	28	1	29
Wilson	28	1	29
Bennion	28	–	28
Hilditch	27	1	28
Ball	23	1	24
McLachlan	23	1	24
Silcock	21	–	21
Thomas	21	–	21
Dale	19	–	19
Hanson	18	–	18

APPEARANCES

PLAYER	LGE	FAC	TOT
Jones	16	1	17
Taylor	16	1	17
Boyle	15	1	16
Mann	14	–	14
Reid	13	–	13
McLenahan	10	–	10
Spencer	10	–	10
Rawlings	4	–	4
Chesters	3	–	3
Warburton	2	–	2
Sweeney	1	–	1
Thomson	1	–	1

GOALSCORERS

PLAYER	LGE	FAC	TOT
Rowley	12	–	12
Spence	12	–	12
Ball	11	–	11
Boyle	6	–	6
McLenahan	6	–	6
Hanson	5	–	5
Reid	5	–	5
Rawlings	3	–	3
McLachlan	2	–	2
Hilditch	1	–	1
Mann	1	–	1
Thomas	1	–	1
Warburton	1	–	1
Wilson	1	–	1

RESULTS & ATTENDANCES SUMMARY

		P	W	D	L	F	A	TOTAL	AVGE
League	H	21	11	4	6	39	34	389680	18556
	A	21	4	4	13	28	54	455280	21680
	TOTAL	42	15	8	19	67	88	844960	20118
FA Cup	H	1	0	0	1	0	2	33226	33226
	A	0	0	0	0	0	0	0	n/a
	TOTAL	1	0	0	1	0	2	33226	33226
Overall	H	22	11	4	7	39	36	422906	19223
	A	21	4	4	13	28	54	455280	21680
	TOTAL	43	15	8	20	67	90	878186	20423

FINAL TABLE - LEAGUE DIVISION ONE

		P	HOME W	HOME D	HOME L	HOME F	HOME A	AWAY W	AWAY D	AWAY L	AWAY F	AWAY A	PTS	GD
1	Sheffield Wednesday	42	15	4	2	56	20	11	4	6	49	37	60	48
2	Derby County	42	16	4	1	61	32	5	4	12	29	50	50	8
3	Manchester City	42	12	5	4	51	33	7	4	10	40	48	47	10
4	Aston Villa	42	13	1	7	54	33	8	4	9	38	50	47	9
5	Leeds United	42	15	2	4	52	22	5	4	12	27	41	46	16
6	Blackburn Rovers	42	15	2	4	65	36	4	5	12	34	57	45	6
7	West Ham United	42	14	2	5	51	26	5	3	13	35	53	43	7
8	Leicester City	42	12	5	4	57	42	5	4	12	29	48	43	-4
9	Sunderland	42	13	3	5	50	35	5	4	12	26	45	43	-4
10	Huddersfield Town	42	9	7	5	32	21	8	2	11	31	48	43	-6
11	Birmingham City	42	13	3	5	40	21	3	6	12	27	41	41	5
12	Liverpool	42	11	5	5	33	29	5	4	12	30	50	41	-16
13	Portsmouth	42	10	6	5	43	25	5	4	12	23	37	40	4
14	Arsenal	42	10	2	9	49	26	4	9	8	29	40	39	12
15	Bolton Wanderers	42	11	5	5	46	24	4	4	13	28	50	39	0
16	Middlesbrough	42	11	3	7	48	31	5	3	13	34	53	38	-2
17	MANCHESTER UNITED	42	11	4	6	39	34	4	4	13	28	54	38	-21
18	Grimsby Town	42	8	6	7	39	39	7	1	13	34	50	37	-16
19	Newcastle United	42	13	4	4	52	32	2	3	16	19	60	37	-21
20	Sheffield United	42	12	2	7	59	35	3	4	14	32	57	36	-5
21	Burnley	42	11	5	5	53	34	3	3	15	26	63	36	-18
22	Everton	42	6	7	8	48	46	6	4	11	32	46	35	-12

SEASON 1930/31

Match # 1384 Saturday 30/08/30 Football League Division 1 at Old Trafford Attendance 18004
Result: **Manchester United 3 Aston Villa 4**
Teamsheet: Steward, Jones, Silcock, Bennion, McLenahan, Wilson, Spence, Warburton, Reid, Rowley, McLachlan
Scorer(s): Reid, Rowley, Warburton

Match # 1385 Wednesday 03/09/30 Football League Division 1 at Ayresome Park Attendance 15712
Result: **Middlesbrough 3 Manchester United 1**
Teamsheet: Chesters, Dale, Silcock, Bennion, McLenahan, Wilson, Ramsden, Warburton, Reid, Rowley, McLachlan
Scorer(s): Rowley

Match # 1386 Saturday 06/09/30 Football League Division 1 at Stamford Bridge Attendance 68648
Result: **Chelsea 6 Manchester United 2**
Teamsheet: Chesters, Dale, Silcock, Bennion, McLenahan, Hilditch, Spence, Warburton, Reid, Rowley, McLachlan
Scorer(s): Reid, Spence

Match # 1387 Wednesday 10/09/30 Football League Division 1 at Old Trafford Attendance 11836
Result: **Manchester United 0 Huddersfield Town 6**
Teamsheet: Chesters, Dale, Silcock, Bennion, Hilditch, McLenahan, Spence, Warburton, Reid, Rowley, McLachlan

Match # 1388 Saturday 13/09/30 Football League Division 1 at Old Trafford Attendance 10907
Result: **Manchester United 4 Newcastle United 7**
Teamsheet: Chesters, Dale, Silcock, Williams, Hilditch, McLenahan, Spence, Warburton, Reid, Rowley, McLachlan
Scorer(s): Reid 3, Rowley

Match # 1389 Monday 15/09/30 Football League Division 1 at Leeds Road Attendance 14028
Result: **Huddersfield Town 3 Manchester United 0**
Teamsheet: Steward, Mellor, Silcock, Williams, Dale, McLenahan, Spence, Warburton, Reid, Rowley, McLachlan

Match # 1390 Saturday 20/09/30 Football League Division 1 at Hillsborough Attendance 18705
Result: **Sheffield Wednesday 3 Manchester United 0**
Teamsheet: Steward, Mellor, Silcock, Williams, Dale, McLenahan, Spence, Warburton, Bullock, Rowley, McLachlan

Match # 1391 Saturday 27/09/30 Football League Division 1 at Old Trafford Attendance 14695
Result: **Manchester United 0 Grimsby Town 2**
Teamsheet: Steward, Jones, Silcock, Bennion, Dale, McLenahan, Spence, Reid, Bullock, Rowley, McLachlan

Match # 1392 Saturday 04/10/30 Football League Division 1 at Maine Road Attendance 41757
Result: **Manchester City 4 Manchester United 1**
Teamsheet: Steward, Jones, Silcock, Hilditch, McLenahan, Wilson, Spence, Warburton, Reid, Rowley, McLachlan
Scorer(s): Spence

Match # 1393 Saturday 11/10/30 Football League Division 1 at Upton Park Attendance 20003
Result: **West Ham United 5 Manchester United 1**
Teamsheet: Steward, Mellor, Dale, Bennion, Parker, Wilson, Spence, Gallimore, Reid, Rowley, McLachlan
Scorer(s): Reid

Match # 1394 Saturday 18/10/30 Football League Division 1 at Old Trafford Attendance 23406
Result: **Manchester United 1 Arsenal 2**
Teamsheet: Steward, Mellor, Silcock, Bennion, Parker, Wilson, Spence, Gallimore, Reid, Rowley, McLachlan
Scorer(s): McLachlan

Match # 1395 Saturday 25/10/30 Football League Division 1 at Fratton Park Attendance 19262
Result: **Portsmouth 4 Manchester United 1**
Teamsheet: Steward, Mellor, Silcock, Bennion, Parker, Wilson, Spence, Gallimore, Reid, Rowley, McLachlan
Scorer(s): Rowley

Match # 1396 Saturday 01/11/30 Football League Division 1 at Old Trafford Attendance 11479
Result: **Manchester United 2 Birmingham City 0**
Teamsheet: Steward, Mellor, Silcock, Bennion, Parker, Wilson, Spence, Gallimore, Bullock, Rowley, McLachlan
Scorer(s): Gallimore, Rowley

Match # 1397 Saturday 08/11/30 Football League Division 1 at Filbert Street Attendance 17466
Result: **Leicester City 5 Manchester United 4**
Teamsheet: Steward, Mellor, Silcock, Bennion, Parker, Wilson, Spence, Gallimore, Bullock, Rowley, McLachlan
Scorer(s): Bullock 3, McLachlan

Match # 1398 Saturday 15/11/30 Football League Division 1 at Old Trafford Attendance 14765
Result: **Manchester United 0 Blackpool 0**
Teamsheet: Steward, Mellor, Dale, Bennion, Parker, Wilson, Spence, Gallimore, Bullock, Rowley, McLachlan

Match # 1399 Saturday 22/11/30 Football League Division 1 at Bramall Lane Attendance 12698
Result: **Sheffield United 3 Manchester United 1**
Teamsheet: Steward, Mellor, Dale, Bennion, Parker, Wilson, Spence, Gallimore, Bullock, Rowley, McLachlan
Scorer(s): Gallimore

Match # 1400 Saturday 29/11/30 Football League Division 1 at Old Trafford Attendance 10971
Result: **Manchester United 1 Sunderland 1**
Teamsheet: Steward, Mellor, Silcock, Bennion, Parker, Wilson, Ramsden, Gallimore, Bullock, Rowley, McLachlan
Scorer(s): Gallimore

Match # 1401 Saturday 06/12/30 Football League Division 1 at Ewood Park Attendance 10802
Result: **Blackburn Rovers 4 Manchester United 1**
Teamsheet: Steward, Mellor, Silcock, Bennion, Parker, McLenahan, Ramsden, Gallimore, Bullock, Rowley, McLachlan
Scorer(s): Rowley

SEASON 1930/31 (continued)

Match # 1402 Saturday 13/12/30   Football League Division 1   at Old Trafford   Attendance 9701
Result: **Manchester United 2 Derby County 1**
Teamsheet: Steward, Mellor, Silcock, Bennion, McLenahan, Wilson, Spence, Gallimore, Reid, Rowley, McLachlan
Scorer(s):   Reid, Spence

Match # 1403 Saturday 20/12/30   Football League Division 1   at Elland Road   Attendance 11282
Result: **Leeds United 5 Manchester United 0**
Teamsheet: Steward, Mellor, Silcock, Bennion, McLenahan, Wilson, Spence, Gallimore, Reid, Rowley, McLachlan

Match # 1404 Thursday 25/12/30   Football League Division 1   at Burnden Park   Attendance 22662
Result: **Bolton Wanderers 3 Manchester United 1**
Teamsheet: Steward, Mellor, Silcock, Bennion, McLenahan, Lydon, Spence, Gallimore, Reid, Wilson, McLachlan
Scorer(s):   Reid

Match # 1405 Friday 26/12/30   Football League Division 1   at Old Trafford   Attendance 12741
Result: **Manchester United 1 Bolton Wanderers 1**
Teamsheet: Steward, Mellor, Silcock, Bennion, Hilditch, Wilson, Ramsden, Gallimore, Reid, Rowley, McLachlan
Scorer(s):   Reid

Match # 1406 Saturday 27/12/30   Football League Division 1   at Villa Park   Attendance 32505
Result: **Aston Villa 7 Manchester United 0**
Teamsheet: Steward, Mellor, Dale, Bennion, Hilditch, Wilson, Ramsden, Gallimore, Reid, Rowley, McLachlan

Match # 1407 Thursday 01/01/31   Football League Division 1   at Old Trafford   Attendance 9875
Result: **Manchester United 0 Leeds United 0**
Teamsheet: Steward, Mellor, Dale, Bennion, Hilditch, Wilson, Ramsden, Gallimore, Reid, Rowley, McLachlan

Match # 1408 Saturday 03/01/31   Football League Division 1   at Old Trafford   Attendance 8966
Result: **Manchester United 1 Chelsea 0**
Teamsheet: Steward, Mellor, Dale, Bennion, Hilditch, Wilson, Ramsden, Warburton, Reid, Gallimore, McLachlan
Scorer(s):   Warburton

Match # 1409 Saturday 10/01/31   FA Cup 3rd Round   at Victoria Ground   Attendance 23415
Result: **Stoke City 3 Manchester United 3**
Teamsheet: Steward, Mellor, Dale, Bennion, Hilditch, Wilson, Ramsden, Warburton, Reid, Gallimore, McLachlan
Scorer(s):   Reid 3

Match # 1410 Wednesday 14/01/31   FA Cup 3rd Round Replay   at Old Trafford   Attendance 22013
Result: **Manchester United 0 Stoke City 0**
Teamsheet: Steward, Mellor, Dale, Bennion, Hilditch, Wilson, Ramsden, Warburton, Reid, Gallimore, McLachlan

Match # 1411 Saturday 17/01/31   Football League Division 1   at St James' Park   Attendance 24835
Result: **Newcastle United 4 Manchester United 3**
Teamsheet: Steward, Mellor, Silcock, Bennion, Hilditch, McLachlan, Spence, Warburton, Reid, Gallimore, Hopkinson
Scorer(s):   Warburton 2, Reid

Match # 1412 Monday 19/01/31   FA Cup 3rd Round 2nd Replay   at Anfield   Attendance 11788
Result: **Manchester United 4 Stoke City 2**
Teamsheet: Steward, Mellor, Dale, Bennion, Hilditch, McLachlan, Spence, Warburton, Thomson, Gallimore, Hopkinson
Scorer(s):   Hopkinson 2, Gallimore, Spence

Match # 1413 Saturday 24/01/31   FA Cup 4th Round   at Blundell Park   Attendance 15000
Result: **Grimsby Town 1 Manchester United 0**
Teamsheet: Steward, Mellor, Dale, Bennion, Hilditch, McLachlan, Spence, Warburton, Reid, Gallimore, Hopkinson

Match # 1414 Wednesday 28/01/31   Football League Division 1   at Old Trafford   Attendance 6077
Result: **Manchester United 4 Sheffield Wednesday 1**
Teamsheet: Steward, Mellor, Dale, Bennion, Hilditch, McLachlan, Spence, Warburton, Reid, Rowley, Hopkinson
Scorer(s):   Hopkinson, Reid, Spence, Warburton

Match # 1415 Saturday 31/01/31   Football League Division 1   at Blundell Park   Attendance 9305
Result: **Grimsby Town 2 Manchester United 1**
Teamsheet: Steward, Mellor, Dale, Bennion, Hilditch, McLachlan, Spence, Warburton, Reid, Rowley, Hopkinson
Scorer(s):   Reid

Match # 1416 Saturday 07/02/31   Football League Division 1   at Old Trafford   Attendance 39876
Result: **Manchester United 1 Manchester City 3**
Teamsheet: Steward, Mellor, Dale, Bennion, Hilditch, McLachlan, Spence, Warburton, Reid, Gallimore, Hopkinson
Scorer(s):   Spence

Match # 1417 Saturday 14/02/31   Football League Division 1   at Old Trafford   Attendance 9745
Result: **Manchester United 1 West Ham United 0**
Teamsheet: Steward, Mellor, Dale, Bennion, Hilditch, McLachlan, Spence, Thomson, Reid, Gallimore, Hopkinson
Scorer(s):   Gallimore

Match # 1418 Saturday 21/02/31   Football League Division 1   at Highbury   Attendance 41510
Result: **Arsenal 4 Manchester United 1**
Teamsheet: Steward, Mellor, Dale, Bennion, Hilditch, McLachlan, Spence, Thomson, Bullock, Gallimore, Hopkinson
Scorer(s):   Thomson

Match # 1419 Saturday 07/03/31   Football League Division 1   at St Andrews   Attendance 17678
Result: **Birmingham City 0 Manchester United 0**
Teamsheet: Steward, Mellor, Dale, Bennion, Hilditch, McLachlan, Spence, Warburton, Bullock, Gallimore, Hopkinson

SEASON 1930/31 (continued)

Match # 1420 Monday 16/03/31   Football League Division 1   at Old Trafford   Attendance 4808
Result: **Manchester United 0 Portsmouth 1**
Teamsheet: Steward, Mellor, Dale, Bennion, Hilditch, McLachlan, Spence, Warburton, Reid, Gallimore, Hopkinson

Match # 1421 Saturday 21/03/31   Football League Division 1   at Bloomfield Road   Attendance 13162
Result: **Blackpool 5 Manchester United 1**
Teamsheet: Steward, Mellor, Jones, Bennion, Hilditch, McLachlan, Spence, Warburton, Reid, Gallimore, Hopkinson
Scorer(s):   Hopkinson

Match # 1422 Wednesday 25/03/31   Football League Division 1   at Old Trafford   Attendance 3679
Result: **Manchester United 0 Leicester City 0**
Teamsheet: Steward, Mellor, Dale, McLenahan, Hilditch, McLachlan, Spence, Warburton, Gallimore, Rowley, Hopkinson

Match # 1423 Saturday 28/03/31   Football League Division 1   at Old Trafford   Attendance 5420
Result: **Manchester United 1 Sheffield United 2**
Teamsheet: Steward, Mellor, Dale, McLenahan, Hilditch, McLachlan, Spence, Warburton, Wilson, Gallimore, Hopkinson
Scorer(s):   Hopkinson

Match # 1424 Friday 03/04/31   Football League Division 1   at Anfield   Attendance 27782
Result: **Liverpool 1 Manchester United 1**
Teamsheet: Steward, Mellor, Silcock, Bennion, Hilditch, McLachlan, Spence, McLenahan, Wilson, Rowley, Hopkinson
Scorer(s):   Wilson

Match # 1425 Saturday 04/04/31   Football League Division 1   at Roker Park   Attendance 13590
Result: **Sunderland 1 Manchester United 2**
Teamsheet: Steward, Mellor, Silcock, Bennion, Hilditch, McLachlan, Spence, McLenahan, Reid, Gallimore, Hopkinson
Scorer(s):   Hopkinson, Reid

Match # 1426 Monday 06/04/31   Football League Division 1   at Old Trafford   Attendance 8058
Result: **Manchester United 4 Liverpool 1**
Teamsheet: Steward, Mellor, Silcock, Bennion, Hilditch, McLachlan, Spence, McLenahan, Reid, Rowley, Hopkinson
Scorer(s):   Reid 2, McLenahan, Rowley

Match # 1427 Saturday 11/04/31   Football League Division 1   at Old Trafford   Attendance 6414
Result: **Manchester United 0 Blackburn Rovers 1**
Teamsheet: Steward, Mellor, Silcock, Bennion, Hilditch, McLachlan, Spence, McLenahan, Reid, Rowley, Hopkinson

Match # 1428 Saturday 18/04/31   Football League Division 1   at Baseball Ground   Attendance 6610
Result: **Derby County 6 Manchester United 1**
Teamsheet: Steward, Mellor, Silcock, Bennion, Hilditch, McLachlan, Spence, McLenahan, Reid, Gallimore, Hopkinson
Scorer(s):   Spence

Match # 1429 Saturday 02/05/31   Football League Division 1   at Old Trafford   Attendance 3969
Result: **Manchester United 4 Middlesbrough 4**
Teamsheet: Steward, Mellor, Jones, Bennion, Hilditch, McLachlan, Spence, McLenahan, Reid, Gallimore, Hopkinson
Scorer(s):   Reid 2, Bennion, Gallimore

SEASON 1930/31 SUMMARY

APPEARANCES

PLAYER	LGE	FAC	TOT
McLachlan	42	4	46
Steward	38	4	42
Bennion	36	4	40
Mellor	35	4	39
Spence	35	2	37
Reid	30	3	33
Gallimore	28	4	32
Hilditch	25	4	29
Rowley	29	–	29
Dale	22	4	26
Silcock	25	–	25
Warburton	18	4	22
Wilson	20	2	22
McLenahan	21	–	21
Hopkinson	17	2	19
Bullock	10	–	10
Parker	9	–	9
Ramsden	7	2	9
Jones	5	–	5
Chesters	4	–	4
Thomson	2	1	3
Williams	3	–	3
Lydon	1	–	1

GOALSCORERS

PLAYER	LGE	FAC	TOT
Reid	17	3	20
Rowley	7	–	7
Spence	6	1	7
Gallimore	5	1	6
Hopkinson	4	2	6
Warburton	5	–	5
Bullock	3	–	3
McLachlan	2	–	2
Bennion	1	–	1
McLenahan	1	–	1
Thomson	1	–	1
Wilson	1	–	1

RESULTS & ATTENDANCES SUMMARY

		P	W	D	L	F	A	TOTAL	AVGE
League	H	21	6	6	9	30	37	245392	11685
	A	21	1	2	18	23	78	460002	21905
TOTAL		42	7	8	27	53	115	705394	16795
FA Cup	H	1	0	1	0	0	0	22013	22013
	A	2	0	1	1	3	4	38415	19208
	N	1	1	0	0	4	2	11788	11788
TOTAL		4	1	2	1	7	6	72216	18054
Overall	H	22	6	7	9	30	37	267405	12155
	A	23	1	3	19	26	82	498417	21670
	N	1	1	0	0	4	2	11788	11788
TOTAL		46	8	10	28	60	121	777610	16905

FINAL TABLE – LEAGUE DIVISION ONE

		P	HOME W	HOME D	HOME L	HOME F	HOME A	AWAY W	AWAY D	AWAY L	AWAY F	AWAY A	PTS	GD
1	Arsenal	42	14	5	2	67	27	14	5	2	60	32	66	68
2	Aston Villa	42	17	3	1	86	34	8	6	7	42	44	59	50
3	Sheffield Wednesday	42	14	3	4	65	32	8	5	8	37	43	52	27
4	Portsmouth	42	11	7	3	46	26	7	6	8	38	41	49	17
5	Huddersfield Town	42	10	8	3	45	27	8	4	9	36	38	48	16
6	Derby County	42	12	6	3	56	31	6	4	11	38	48	46	15
7	Middlesbrough	42	13	5	3	57	28	6	3	12	41	62	46	8
8	Manchester City	42	13	2	6	41	29	5	8	8	34	41	46	5
9	Liverpool	42	11	6	4	48	28	4	6	11	38	57	42	1
10	Blackburn Rovers	42	14	3	4	54	28	3	5	13	29	56	42	–1
11	Sunderland	42	12	4	5	61	38	4	5	12	28	47	41	4
12	Chelsea	42	13	4	4	42	19	2	6	13	22	48	40	–3
13	Grimsby Town	42	13	2	6	55	31	4	3	14	27	56	39	–5
14	Bolton Wanderers	42	12	6	3	45	26	3	3	15	23	55	39	–13
15	Sheffield United	42	10	7	4	49	31	4	3	14	29	53	38	–6
16	Leicester City	42	12	4	5	50	38	4	2	15	30	57	38	–15
17	Newcastle United	42	9	2	10	41	45	6	4	11	37	42	36	–9
18	West Ham United	42	11	3	7	56	44	3	5	13	23	50	36	–15
19	Birmingham City	42	11	3	7	37	28	2	7	12	18	42	36	–15
20	Blackpool	42	8	7	6	41	44	3	3	15	30	81	32	–54
21	Leeds United	42	10	3	8	49	31	2	4	15	19	50	31	–13
22	MANCHESTER UNITED	42	6	6	9	30	37	1	2	18	23	78	22	–62

SEASON 1931/32

Match # 1430   Saturday 29/08/31   Football League Division 2   at Park Avenue   Attendance 16239
Result: **Bradford Park Avenue 3 Manchester United 1**
Teamsheet: Steward, Mellor, Silcock, Bennion, Parker, McLachlan, Ferguson, Warburton, Reid, Johnston, Mann
Scorer(s):   Reid

Match # 1431   Wednesday 02/09/31   Football League Division 2   at Old Trafford   Attendance 3507
Result: **Manchester United 2 Southampton 3**
Teamsheet: Steward, Mellor, Silcock, Bennion, Parker, McLenahan, Ferguson, Warburton, Reid, Johnston, McLachlan
Scorer(s):   Ferguson, Johnston

Match # 1432   Saturday 05/09/31   Football League Division 2   at Old Trafford   Attendance 6763
Result: **Manchester United 2 Swansea City 1**
Teamsheet: Steward, Mellor, Silcock, McLenahan, Parker, McLachlan, Ferguson, Spence, Reid, Johnston, Hopkinson
Scorer(s):   Hopkinson, Reid

Match # 1433   Monday 07/09/31   Football League Division 2   at Victoria Ground   Attendance 10518
Result: **Stoke City 3 Manchester United 0**
Teamsheet: Steward, Mellor, Silcock, McLenahan, Parker, McLachlan, Spence, Johnston, Reid, Rowley, Hopkinson

Match # 1434   Saturday 12/09/31   Football League Division 2   at Old Trafford   Attendance 9557
Result: **Manchester United 1 Tottenham Hotspur 1**
Teamsheet: Steward, Mellor, Silcock, Bennion, Hilditch, Wilson, Ferguson, Gallimore, Spence, Johnston, Hopkinson
Scorer(s):   Johnston

Match # 1435   Wednesday 16/09/31   Football League Division 2   at Old Trafford   Attendance 5025
Result: **Manchester United 1 Stoke City 1**
Teamsheet: Steward, Mellor, Silcock, Bennion, Hilditch, Wilson, Ferguson, Gallimore, Spence, Johnston, Mann
Scorer(s):   Spence

Match # 1436   Saturday 19/09/31   Football League Division 2   at City Ground   Attendance 10166
Result: **Nottingham Forest 2 Manchester United 1**
Teamsheet: Steward, Jones, Silcock, Bennion, Parker, Wilson, Ferguson, Gallimore, Reid, Johnston, Hopkinson
Scorer(s):   Gallimore

Match # 1437   Saturday 26/09/31   Football League Division 2   at Old Trafford   Attendance 10834
Result: **Manchester United 3 Chesterfield 1**
Teamsheet: Steward, Jones, Silcock, Bennion, Hilditch, Wilson, Ferguson, Warburton, Dean, Johnston, Robinson
Scorer(s):   Warburton 2, Johnston

Match # 1438   Saturday 03/10/31   Football League Division 2   at Turf Moor   Attendance 9719
Result: **Burnley 2 Manchester United 0**
Teamsheet: Steward, Jones, Silcock, Bennion, Hilditch, Wilson, Ferguson, Warburton, Dean, Johnston, Robinson

Match # 1439   Saturday 10/10/31   Football League Division 2   at Old Trafford   Attendance 8496
Result: **Manchester United 3 Preston North End 2**
Teamsheet: Steward, Mellor, Silcock, Bennion, Hilditch, McLenahan, Mann, Gallimore, Spence, Johnston, Robinson
Scorer(s):   Gallimore, Johnston, Spence

Match # 1440   Saturday 17/10/31   Football League Division 2   at Oakwell   Attendance 4052
Result: **Barnsley 0 Manchester United 0**
Teamsheet: Steward, Mellor, Silcock, Bennion, Hilditch, McLenahan, Mann, Gallimore, Spence, Johnston, Robinson

Match # 1441   Saturday 24/10/31   Football League Division 2   at Old Trafford   Attendance 6694
Result: **Manchester United 3 Notts County 3**
Teamsheet: Steward, Mellor, Silcock, Bennion, Hilditch, Wilson, Mann, Gallimore, Spence, Johnston, Robinson
Scorer(s):   Gallimore, Mann, Spence

Match # 1442   Saturday 31/10/31   Football League Division 2   at Home Park   Attendance 22555
Result: **Plymouth Argyle 3 Manchester United 1**
Teamsheet: Steward, Mellor, Silcock, Bennion, Wilson, McLachlan, Mann, Gallimore, Spence, Johnston, Robinson
Scorer(s):   Johnston

Match # 1443   Saturday 07/11/31   Football League Division 2   at Old Trafford   Attendance 9512
Result: **Manchester United 2 Leeds United 5**
Teamsheet: Steward, Mellor, Silcock, Bennion, Hilditch, McLachlan, Mann, Gallimore, Spence, Johnston, Robinson
Scorer(s):   Spence 2

Match # 1444   Saturday 14/11/31   Football League Division 2   at Boundary Park   Attendance 10922
Result: **Oldham Athletic 1 Manchester United 5**
Teamsheet: Steward, Mellor, Dale, Bennion, Parker, McLachlan, Mann, Gallimore, Spence, Johnston, Robinson
Scorer(s):   Johnston 2, Spence 2, Mann

Match # 1445   Saturday 21/11/31   Football League Division 2   at Old Trafford   Attendance 11745
Result: **Manchester United 1 Bury 2**
Teamsheet: Steward, Mellor, Dale, Bennion, Hilditch, McLenahan, Mann, Gallimore, Spence, Johnston, Robinson
Scorer(s):   Spence

Match # 1446   Saturday 28/11/31   Football League Division 2   at Old Recreation Ground   Attendance 6955
Result: **Port Vale 1 Manchester United 2**
Teamsheet: Steward, Mellor, Dale, Bennion, Hilditch, McLenahan, Mann, Johnston, Spence, Robinson, Gallimore
Scorer(s):   Spence 2

Match # 1447   Saturday 05/12/31   Football League Division 2   at Old Trafford   Attendance 6396
Result: **Manchester United 2 Millwall 0**
Teamsheet: Steward, Mellor, Dale, Lydon, Hilditch, Manley, Mann, Johnston, Spence, Reid, Gallimore
Scorer(s):   Gallimore, Spence

SEASON 1931/32 (continued)

Match # 1448 Saturday 12/12/31   Football League Division 2   at Valley Parade   Attendance 13215
Result: **Bradford City 4 Manchester United 3**
Teamsheet: Steward, Mellor, Silcock, Lydon, Hilditch, Manley, Mann, Johnston, Spence, Reid, Gallimore
Scorer(s):   Spence 2, Johnston

Match # 1449 Saturday 19/12/31   Football League Division 2   at Old Trafford   Attendance 4697
Result: **Manchester United 0 Bristol City 1**
Teamsheet: Chesters, Mellor, Silcock, Bennion, Hilditch, Manley, Mann, Johnston, Spence, Reid, Gallimore

Match # 1450 Friday 25/12/31   Football League Division 2   at Old Trafford   Attendance 33123
Result: **Manchester United 3 Wolverhampton Wanderers 2**
Teamsheet: Chesters, Mellor, Silcock, Bennion, Hilditch, McLachlan, Hopkinson, Ridding, Spence, Reid, Gallimore
Scorer(s):   Hopkinson, Reid, Spence

Match # 1451 Saturday 26/12/31   Football League Division 2   at Molineux   Attendance 37207
Result: **Wolverhampton Wanderers 7 Manchester United 0**
Teamsheet: Steward, Mellor, Silcock, Bennion, Hilditch, McLachlan, Hopkinson, Ridding, Spence, Johnston, Gallimore

Match # 1452 Saturday 02/01/32   Football League Division 2   at Old Trafford   Attendance 6056
Result: **Manchester United 0 Bradford Park Avenue 2**
Teamsheet: Steward, Mellor, Silcock, Bennion, Hilditch, McLachlan, Hopkinson, Ridding, Spence, Reid, Gallimore

Match # 1453 Saturday 09/01/32   FA Cup 3rd Round   at Home Park   Attendance 28000
Result: **Plymouth Argyle 4 Manchester United 1**
Teamsheet: Steward, Mellor, Silcock, Bennion, McLenahan, Hilditch, Spence, Johnston, Ridding, Reid, McLachlan
Scorer(s):   Reid

Match # 1454 Saturday 16/01/32   Football League Division 2   at Vetch Field   Attendance 5888
Result: **Swansea City 3 Manchester United 1**
Teamsheet: Steward, Mellor, Silcock, Bennion, Parker, McLachlan, Spence, Warburton, Reid, Johnston, Whittle
Scorer(s):   Warburton

Match # 1455 Saturday 23/01/32   Football League Division 2   at White Hart Lane   Attendance 19139
Result: **Tottenham Hotspur 4 Manchester United 1**
Teamsheet: Steward, Mellor, Silcock, Bennion, Parker, McLachlan, Spence, Ridding, Reid, Gallimore, Hopkinson
Scorer(s):   Reid

Match # 1456 Saturday 30/01/32   Football League Division 2   at Old Trafford   Attendance 11152
Result: **Manchester United 3 Nottingham Forest 2**
Teamsheet: Steward, Mellor, Silcock, Bennion, Hilditch, McLachlan, Spence, Warburton, Reid, Gallimore, Hopkinson
Scorer(s):   Reid 3

Match # 1457 Saturday 06/02/32   Football League Division 2   at Saltergate   Attendance 9457
Result: **Chesterfield 1 Manchester United 3**
Teamsheet: Steward, Mellor, Jones, Bennion, Vincent, McLachlan, Spence, Ridding, Reid, Gallimore, Hopkinson
Scorer(s):   Reid 2, Spence

Match # 1458 Wednesday 17/02/32   Football League Division 2   at Old Trafford   Attendance 11036
Result: **Manchester United 5 Burnley 1**
Teamsheet: Steward, Jones, Silcock, Bennion, Vincent, McLachlan, Spence, Gallimore, Ridding, Johnston, Hopkinson
Scorer(s):   Johnston 2, Ridding 2, Gallimore

Match # 1459 Saturday 20/02/32   Football League Division 2   at Deepdale   Attendance 13353
Result: **Preston North End 0 Manchester United 0**
Teamsheet: Steward, Jones, Silcock, McLenahan, Vincent, McLachlan, Spence, Warburton, Ridding, Gallimore, Hopkinson

Match # 1460 Saturday 27/02/32   Football League Division 2   at Old Trafford   Attendance 18223
Result: **Manchester United 3 Barnsley 0**
Teamsheet: Steward, Jones, Silcock, McLenahan, Vincent, McLachlan, Spence, Gallimore, Reid, Johnston, Hopkinson
Scorer(s):   Hopkinson 2, Gallimore

Match # 1461 Saturday 05/03/32   Football League Division 2   at Meadow Lane   Attendance 10817
Result: **Notts County 1 Manchester United 2**
Teamsheet: Steward, Mellor, Jones, McLenahan, Vincent, McLachlan, Spence, Gallimore, Reid, Johnston, Hopkinson
Scorer(s):   Hopkinson, Reid

Match # 1462 Saturday 12/03/32   Football League Division 2   at Old Trafford   Attendance 24827
Result: **Manchester United 2 Plymouth Argyle 1**
Teamsheet: Steward, Mellor, Jones, Wilson, Vincent, McLachlan, Spence, Ridding, Reid, Johnston, Hopkinson
Scorer(s):   Spence 2

Match # 1463 Saturday 19/03/32   Football League Division 2   at Elland Road   Attendance 13644
Result: **Leeds United 1 Manchester United 4**
Teamsheet: Steward, Jones, Silcock, Wilson, Vincent, McLachlan, Spence, Ridding, Reid, Johnston, Hopkinson
Scorer(s):   Reid 2, Johnston, Ridding

Match # 1464 Friday 25/03/32   Football League Division 2   at Old Trafford   Attendance 37012
Result: **Manchester United 0 Charlton Athletic 2**
Teamsheet: Steward, Jones, Silcock, Lievesley, Vincent, McLachlan, Spence, Ridding, Reid, Gallimore, Page

Match # 1465 Saturday 26/03/32   Football League Division 2   at Old Trafford   Attendance 17886
Result: **Manchester United 5 Oldham Athletic 1**
Teamsheet: Moody, Jones, Silcock, Lievesley, Vincent, McLachlan, Spence, Ridding, Reid, Page, Fitton
Scorer(s):   Reid 3, Fitton, Spence

SEASON 1931/32 (continued)

Match # 1466	Monday 28/03/32	Football League Division 2	at The Valley	Attendance 16256
Result:	**Charlton Athletic 1 Manchester United 0**			
Teamsheet:	Moody, Mellor, Silcock, Bennion, Vincent, McLachlan, Spence, Ridding, Reid, Page, Fitton			

Match # 1467	Saturday 02/04/32	Football League Division 2	at Gigg Lane	Attendance 12592
Result:	**Bury 0 Manchester United 0**			
Teamsheet:	Moody, Mellor, Silcock, Bennion, Vincent, McLachlan, Spence, Ridding, Reid, Page, Fitton			

Match # 1468	Saturday 09/04/32	Football League Division 2	at Old Trafford	Attendance 10916
Result:	**Manchester United 2 Port Vale 0**			
Teamsheet:	Moody, Mellor, Silcock, Bennion, Vincent, McLachlan, Spence, Page, Reid, Johnston, Fitton			
Scorer(s):	Reid, Spence			

Match # 1469	Saturday 16/04/32	Football League Division 2	at The Den	Attendance 9087
Result:	**Millwall 1 Manchester United 1**			
Teamsheet:	Moody, Mellor, Silcock, Hopkinson, Vincent, McLachlan, Spence, Ridding, Reid, Page, Fitton			
Scorer(s):	Reid			

Match # 1470	Saturday 23/04/32	Football League Division 2	at Old Trafford	Attendance 17765
Result:	**Manchester United 1 Bradford City 0**			
Teamsheet:	Moody, Mellor, Silcock, Hopkinson, Vincent, McLachlan, Spence, McDonald, Black, Page, Fitton			
Scorer(s):	Fitton			

Match # 1471	Saturday 30/04/32	Football League Division 2	at Ashton Gate	Attendance 5874
Result:	**Bristol City 2 Manchester United 1**			
Teamsheet:	Moody, Mellor, Silcock, Bennion, Vincent, McLachlan, Spence, Page, Black, Reid, Fitton			
Scorer(s):	Black			

Match # 1472	Saturday 07/05/32	Football League Division 2	at The Dell	Attendance 6128
Result:	**Southampton 1 Manchester United 1**			
Teamsheet:	Moody, Mellor, Silcock, Hopkinson, Vincent, McLachlan, Spence, McDonald, Black, Page, Fitton			
Scorer(s):	Black			

SEASON 1931/32 SUMMARY

APPEARANCES

PLAYER	LGE	FAC	TOT
Spence	37	1	38
Silcock	35	1	36
Mellor	33	1	34
Steward	32	1	33
Bennion	28	1	29
Johnston	28	1	29
McLachlan	28	1	29
Reid	25	1	26
Gallimore	25	–	25
Hopkinson	19	–	19
Hilditch	17	1	18
Vincent	16	–	16
Ridding	14	1	15
Mann	13	–	13
Jones	12	–	12
McLenahan	11	1	12
Robinson	10	–	10

APPEARANCES

PLAYER	LGE	FAC	TOT
Page	9	–	9
Wilson	9	–	9
Ferguson	8	–	8
Fitton	8	–	8
Moody	8	–	8
Parker	8	–	8
Warburton	7	–	7
Dale	4	–	4
Black	3	–	3
Manley	3	–	3
Chesters	2	–	2
Dean	2	–	2
Lievesley	2	–	2
Lydon	2	–	2
McDonald	2	–	2
Rowley	1	–	1
Whittle	1	–	1

GOALSCORERS

PLAYER	LGE	FAC	TOT
Spence	19	–	19
Reid	17	1	18
Johnston	11	–	11
Gallimore	6	–	6
Hopkinson	5	–	5
Ridding	3	–	3
Warburton	3	–	3
Black	2	–	2
Fitton	2	–	2
Mann	2	–	2
Ferguson	1	–	1

RESULTS & ATTENDANCES SUMMARY

		P	W	D	L	F	A	TOTAL	AVGE
League	H	21	12	3	6	44	31	271222	12915
	A	21	5	5	11	27	41	263783	12561
	TOTAL	42	17	8	17	71	72	535005	12738
FA Cup	H	0	0	0	0	0	0	0	n/a
	A	1	0	0	1	1	4	28000	28000
	TOTAL	1	0	0	1	1	4	28000	28000
Overall	H	21	12	3	6	44	31	271222	12915
	A	22	5	5	12	28	45	291783	13263
	N	0	0	0	0	0	0	0	n/a
	TOTAL	43	17	8	18	72	76	563005	13093

FINAL TABLE – LEAGUE DIVISION TWO

		P	W	D	L	F	A	W	D	L	F	A	PTS	GD
				HOME						AWAY				
1	Wolverhampton Wanderers	42	17	3	1	71	11	7	5	9	44	38	56	66
2	Leeds United	42	12	5	4	36	22	10	5	6	42	32	54	24
3	Stoke City	42	14	6	1	47	19	5	8	8	22	29	52	21
4	Plymouth Argyle	42	14	4	3	69	29	6	5	10	31	37	49	34
5	Bury	42	13	4	4	44	21	8	3	10	26	37	49	12
6	Bradford Park Avenue	42	17	2	2	44	18	4	5	12	28	45	49	9
7	Bradford City	42	10	7	4	53	26	6	6	9	27	35	45	19
8	Tottenham Hotspur	42	11	6	4	58	37	5	5	11	29	41	43	9
9	Millwall	42	13	3	5	43	21	4	6	11	18	40	43	0
10	Charlton Athletic	42	11	5	5	38	28	6	4	11	23	38	43	-5
11	Nottingham Forest	42	13	4	4	49	27	3	6	12	28	45	42	5
12	MANCHESTER UNITED	42	12	3	6	44	31	5	5	11	27	41	42	-1
13	Preston North End	42	11	6	4	37	25	5	4	12	38	52	42	-2
14	Southampton	42	10	5	6	39	30	7	2	12	27	47	41	-11
15	Swansea City	42	12	4	5	45	22	4	3	14	28	53	39	-2
16	Notts County	42	10	4	7	43	30	3	8	10	32	45	38	0
17	Chesterfield	42	11	3	7	43	33	2	8	11	21	53	37	-22
18	Oldham Athletic	42	10	4	7	41	34	3	6	12	21	50	36	-22
19	Burnley	42	7	8	6	36	36	6	1	14	23	51	35	-28
20	Port Vale	42	8	4	9	30	33	5	3	13	28	56	33	-31
21	Barnsley	42	8	7	6	35	30	4	2	15	20	61	33	-36
22	Bristol City	42	4	7	10	22	37	2	4	15	17	41	23	-39

SEASON 1932/33

Match # 1473	Saturday 27/08/32	Football League Division 2	at Old Trafford	Attendance 24996
Result:	**Manchester United 0 Stoke City 2**			
Teamsheet:	Moody, Mellor, Silcock, McLenahan, Vincent, McLachlan, Spence, Ridding, Black, McDonald, Page			

Match # 1474	Monday 29/08/32	Football League Division 2	at The Valley	Attendance 12946
Result:	**Charlton Athletic 0 Manchester United 1**			
Teamsheet:	Moody, Mellor, Silcock, McLenahan, Vincent, McLachlan, Spence, Warburton, Reid, McDonald, Fitton			
Scorer(s):	Spence			

Match # 1475	Saturday 03/09/32	Football League Division 2	at The Dell	Attendance 7978
Result:	**Southampton 4 Manchester United 2**			
Teamsheet:	Moody, Mellor, Silcock, McLenahan, Vincent, McLachlan, Spence, Warburton, Reid, McDonald, Hopkinson			
Scorer(s):	Reid, own goal			

Match # 1476	Wednesday 07/09/32	Football League Division 2	at Old Trafford	Attendance 9480
Result:	**Manchester United 1 Charlton Athletic 1**			
Teamsheet:	Moody, Mellor, Silcock, McLenahan, Vincent, McLachlan, Spence, McDonald, Reid, Page, Hopkinson			
Scorer(s):	McLenahan			

Match # 1477	Saturday 10/09/32	Football League Division 2	at White Hart Lane	Attendance 23333
Result:	**Tottenham Hotspur 6 Manchester United 1**			
Teamsheet:	Moody, Mellor, Silcock, Hopkinson, McLenahan, McLachlan, Spence, McDonald, Ridding, Gallimore, Fitton			
Scorer(s):	Ridding			

Match # 1478	Saturday 17/09/32	Football League Division 2	at Old Trafford	Attendance 17662
Result:	**Manchester United 1 Grimsby Town 1**			
Teamsheet:	Moody, Mellor, Silcock, Manley, McLenahan, McLachlan, Brown, McDonald, Spence, Page, Fitton			
Scorer(s):	Brown			

Match # 1479	Saturday 24/09/32	Football League Division 2	at Boundary Park	Attendance 14403
Result:	**Oldham Athletic 1 Manchester United 1**			
Teamsheet:	Moody, Mellor, Silcock, Manley, Vincent, McLachlan, Brown, McLenahan, Spence, Gallimore, Hopkinson			
Scorer(s):	Spence			

Match # 1480	Saturday 01/10/32	Football League Division 2	at Old Trafford	Attendance 20800
Result:	**Manchester United 0 Preston North End 0**			
Teamsheet:	Moody, Mellor, Silcock, Vincent, Frame, McLenahan, Spence, Chalmers, Reid, Gallimore, Brown			

Match # 1481	Saturday 08/10/32	Football League Division 2	at Turf Moor	Attendance 5314
Result:	**Burnley 2 Manchester United 3**			
Teamsheet:	Moody, Mellor, Silcock, Vincent, Frame, McLenahan, Spence, Chalmers, Reid, Gallimore, Brown			
Scorer(s):	Brown, Gallimore, Spence			

Match # 1482	Saturday 15/10/32	Football League Division 2	at Old Trafford	Attendance 18918
Result:	**Manchester United 2 Bradford Park Avenue 1**			
Teamsheet:	Moody, Mellor, Silcock, Vincent, Frame, McLenahan, Spence, Chalmers, Reid, Gallimore, Brown			
Scorer(s):	Reid 2			

Match # 1483	Saturday 22/10/32	Football League Division 2	at Old Trafford	Attendance 15860
Result:	**Manchester United 7 Millwall 1**			
Teamsheet:	Moody, Mellor, Silcock, Vincent, Frame, McLenahan, Spence, Chalmers, Reid, Gallimore, Brown			
Scorer(s):	Reid 3, Brown 2, Gallimore, Spence			

Match # 1484	Saturday 29/10/32	Football League Division 2	at Old Recreation Ground	Attendance 7138
Result:	**Port Vale 3 Manchester United 3**			
Teamsheet:	Moody, Mellor, Manley, Vincent, Frame, McLenahan, Spence, Chalmers, Ridding, Gallimore, Brown			
Scorer(s):	Ridding 2, Brown			

Match # 1485	Saturday 05/11/32	Football League Division 2	at Old Trafford	Attendance 24178
Result:	**Manchester United 2 Notts County 0**			
Teamsheet:	Moody, Mellor, Manley, Vincent, Frame, McLenahan, Spence, Chalmers, Ridding, Gallimore, Brown			
Scorer(s):	Gallimore, Ridding			

Match # 1486	Saturday 12/11/32	Football League Division 2	at Gigg Lane	Attendance 21663
Result:	**Bury 2 Manchester United 2**			
Teamsheet:	Moody, Mellor, Silcock, Vincent, Frame, McLenahan, Brown, Warburton, Ridding, McDonald, Fitton			
Scorer(s):	Brown, Ridding			

Match # 1487	Saturday 19/11/32	Football League Division 2	at Old Trafford	Attendance 28803
Result:	**Manchester United 4 Fulham 3**			
Teamsheet:	Moody, Mellor, Jones, Vincent, Frame, McLenahan, Brown, Chalmers, Ridding, Gallimore, Stewart			
Scorer(s):	Gallimore 2, Brown, Ridding			

Match # 1488	Saturday 26/11/32	Football League Division 2	at Saltergate	Attendance 10277
Result:	**Chesterfield 1 Manchester United 1**			
Teamsheet:	Moody, Mellor, Jones, Vincent, Frame, McLenahan, Brown, Chalmers, Ridding, Gallimore, Stewart			
Scorer(s):	Ridding			

Match # 1489	Saturday 03/12/32	Football League Division 2	at Old Trafford	Attendance 28513
Result:	**Manchester United 0 Bradford City 1**			
Teamsheet:	Moody, Mellor, Jones, Vincent, Frame, McLenahan, Brown, Chalmers, Ridding, McDonald, Stewart			

Match # 1490	Saturday 10/12/32	Football League Division 2	at Upton Park	Attendance 13435
Result:	**West Ham United 3 Manchester United 1**			
Teamsheet:	Moody, Mellor, Silcock, Vincent, Frame, McLenahan, Brown, Chalmers, Ridding, Gallimore, Stewart			
Scorer(s):	Ridding			

SEASON 1932/33 (continued)

Match # 1491 Saturday 17/12/32   Football League Division 2   at Old Trafford   Attendance 18021
Result: **Manchester United 4 Lincoln City 1**
Teamsheet: Moody, Mellor, Silcock, Vincent, Frame, McLenahan, Brown, Ridding, Reid, Chalmers, Stewart
Scorer(s):   Reid 3, own goal

Match # 1492 Saturday 24/12/32   Football League Division 2   at Vetch Field   Attendance 10727
Result: **Swansea City 2 Manchester United 1**
Teamsheet: Moody, Mellor, Silcock, Vincent, Frame, McLenahan, Brown, Ridding, Reid, Chalmers, Stewart
Scorer(s):   Brown

Match # 1493 Monday 26/12/32   Football League Division 2   at Home Park   Attendance 33776
Result: **Plymouth Argyle 2 Manchester United 3**
Teamsheet: Moody, Jones, Silcock, Vincent, Frame, Manley, Spence, Ridding, Reid, Chalmers, Stewart
Scorer(s):   Spence 2, Reid

Match # 1494 Saturday 31/12/32   Football League Division 2   at Victoria Ground   Attendance 14115
Result: **Stoke City 0 Manchester United 0**
Teamsheet: Moody, Mellor, Silcock, Vincent, Frame, Manley, Spence, Ridding, Reid, Chalmers, Stewart

Match # 1495 Monday 02/01/33   Football League Division 2   at Old Trafford   Attendance 30257
Result: **Manchester United 4 Plymouth Argyle 0**
Teamsheet: Moody, Jones, Silcock, Vincent, Frame, McLenahan, Spence, McDonald, Ridding, Chalmers, McLachlan
Scorer(s):   Ridding 2, Chalmers, Spence

Match # 1496 Saturday 07/01/33   Football League Division 2   at Old Trafford   Attendance 21364
Result: **Manchester United 1 Southampton 2**
Teamsheet: Moody, Mellor, Silcock, Manley, Vincent, McLenahan, Spence, McDonald, Ridding, Chalmers, Stewart
Scorer(s):   McDonald

Match # 1497 Saturday 14/01/33   FA Cup 3rd Round   at Old Trafford   Attendance 36991
Result: **Manchester United 1 Middlesbrough 4**
Teamsheet: Moody, Mellor, Silcock, Vincent, Frame, McLenahan, Spence, Chalmers, Ridding, Reid, Stewart
Scorer(s):   Spence

Match # 1498 Saturday 21/01/33   Football League Division 2   at Old Trafford   Attendance 20661
Result: **Manchester United 2 Tottenham Hotspur 1**
Teamsheet: Moody, Mellor, Silcock, Vincent, Frame, Manley, Brown, Chalmers, Ridding, McDonald, Stewart
Scorer(s):   Frame, McDonald

Match # 1499 Tuesday 31/01/33   Football League Division 2   at Blundell Park   Attendance 4020
Result: **Grimsby Town 1 Manchester United 1**
Teamsheet: Moody, Mellor, Jones, Vincent, Frame, Manley, Brown, Chalmers, Ridding, McDonald, Stewart
Scorer(s):   Stewart

Match # 1500 Saturday 04/02/33   Football League Division 2   at Old Trafford   Attendance 15275
Result: **Manchester United 2 Oldham Athletic 0**
Teamsheet: Moody, Mellor, Jones, Vincent, Frame, Manley, Spence, Chalmers, Ridding, McDonald, Stewart
Scorer(s):   Ridding, Stewart

Match # 1501 Saturday 11/02/33   Football League Division 2   at Deepdale   Attendance 15662
Result: **Preston North End 3 Manchester United 3**
Teamsheet: Moody, Mellor, Jones, Vincent, Frame, Manley, Hopkinson, Hine, Dewar, McDonald, Stewart
Scorer(s):   Dewar, Hopkinson, Stewart

Match # 1502 Wednesday 22/02/33   Football League Division 2   at Old Trafford   Attendance 18533
Result: **Manchester United 2 Burnley 1**
Teamsheet: Moody, Mellor, Silcock, Vincent, Frame, Manley, Warburton, Hine, Dewar, McDonald, Stewart
Scorer(s):   McDonald, Warburton

Match # 1503 Saturday 04/03/33   Football League Division 2   at The Den   Attendance 22587
Result: **Millwall 2 Manchester United 0**
Teamsheet: Moody, Mellor, Jones, Vincent, Frame, McLachlan, Warburton, Hine, Dewar, McDonald, Stewart

Match # 1504 Saturday 11/03/33   Football League Division 2   at Old Trafford   Attendance 24690
Result: **Manchester United 1 Port Vale 1**
Teamsheet: Moody, Mellor, Jones, Vincent, Frame, Manley, Warburton, Ridding, Dewar, Hine, Stewart
Scorer(s):   Hine

Match # 1505 Saturday 18/03/33   Football League Division 2   at Meadow Lane   Attendance 13018
Result: **Notts County 1 Manchester United 0**
Teamsheet: Moody, Mellor, Silcock, Vincent, Frame, McLenahan, Mitchell, Ridding, Dewar, Hine, Stewart

Match # 1506 Saturday 25/03/33   Football League Division 2   at Old Trafford   Attendance 27687
Result: **Manchester United 1 Bury 3**
Teamsheet: Moody, Mellor, Silcock, McLenahan, Vincent, McLachlan, Ridding, Hine, Dewar, McDonald, Stewart
Scorer(s):   McLenahan

Match # 1507 Saturday 01/04/33   Football League Division 2   at Craven Cottage   Attendance 21477
Result: **Fulham 3 Manchester United 1**
Teamsheet: Moody, Mellor, Silcock, Vincent, Frame, McLachlan, Spence, Ridding, Dewar, Hine, Stewart
Scorer(s):   Dewar

Match # 1508 Wednesday 05/04/33   Football League Division 2   at Park Avenue   Attendance 6314
Result: **Bradford Park Avenue 1 Manchester United 1**
Teamsheet: Moody, Mellor, Topping, Vincent, Frame, McLachlan, Brown, Ridding, Dewar, Hine, Stewart
Scorer(s):   Vincent

SEASON 1932/33 (continued)

Match # 1509 Saturday 08/04/33   Football League Division 2   at Old Trafford   Attendance 16031
Result: **Manchester United 2 Chesterfield 1**
Teamsheet: Moody, Mellor, Topping, Vincent, Frame, McLachlan, Brown, Chalmers, Dewar, Gallimore, Stewart
Scorer(s): Dewar, Frame

Match # 1510 Friday 14/04/33   Football League Division 2   at City Ground   Attendance 12963
Result: **Nottingham Forest 3 Manchester United 2**
Teamsheet: Moody, Mellor, Topping, Vincent, Frame, Manley, Brown, Chalmers, Dewar, Hine, McLachlan
Scorer(s): Brown, Dewar

Match # 1511 Saturday 15/04/33   Football League Division 2   at Valley Parade   Attendance 11195
Result: **Bradford City 1 Manchester United 2**
Teamsheet: Moody, Mellor, Silcock, Vincent, Frame, Manley, Brown, Hine, Dewar, McDonald, McLachlan
Scorer(s): Brown, Hine

Match # 1512 Monday 17/04/33   Football League Division 2   at Old Trafford   Attendance 16849
Result: **Manchester United 2 Nottingham Forest 1**
Teamsheet: Moody, Mellor, Silcock, Vincent, Frame, Manley, Brown, Hine, Dewar, McDonald, McLachlan
Scorer(s): Hine, McDonald

Match # 1513 Saturday 22/04/33   Football League Division 2   at Old Trafford   Attendance 14958
Result: **Manchester United 1 West Ham United 2**
Teamsheet: Moody, Mellor, Topping, Vincent, Frame, Manley, Brown, Hine, Dewar, McDonald, McLachlan
Scorer(s): Dewar

Match # 1514 Saturday 29/04/33   Football League Division 2   at Sincil Bank   Attendance 8507
Result: **Lincoln City 3 Manchester United 2**
Teamsheet: Moody, Mellor, Silcock, Vincent, Frame, Manley, Brown, Hine, Dewar, McDonald, Hopkinson
Scorer(s): Hine, Dewar

Match # 1515 Saturday 06/05/33   Football League Division 2   at Old Trafford   Attendance 65988
Result: **Manchester United 1 Swansea City 1**
Teamsheet: Moody, Mellor, Topping, Vincent, Frame, Manley, Heywood, Hine, Dewar, Chalmers, Brown
Scorer(s): Hine

SEASON 1932/33 SUMMARY

APPEARANCES

PLAYER	LGE	FAC	TOT
Moody	42	1	43
Mellor	40	1	41
Vincent	40	1	41
Frame	33	1	34
Silcock	27	1	28
Brown	25	–	25
McLenahan	24	1	25
Ridding	23	1	24
Chalmers	22	1	23
Stewart	21	1	22
McDonald	21	–	21
Spence	19	1	20
Manley	19	–	19
McLachlan	17	–	17

APPEARANCES

PLAYER	LGE	FAC	TOT
Dewar	15	–	15
Hine	14	–	14
Gallimore	12	–	12
Reid	11	1	12
Jones	10	–	10
Hopkinson	6	–	6
Warburton	6	–	6
Topping	5	–	5
Fitton	4	–	4
Page	3	–	3
Black	1	–	1
Heywood	1	–	1
Mitchell	1	–	1

GOALSCORERS

PLAYER	LGE	FAC	TOT
Ridding	11	–	11
Brown	10	–	10
Reid	10	–	10
Spence	7	1	8
Dewar	6	–	6
Gallimore	5	–	5
Hine	5	–	5
McDonald	4	–	4
Stewart	3	–	3
Frame	2	–	2
McLenahan	2	–	2
Chalmers	1	–	1
Hopkinson	1	–	1
Vincent	1	–	1
Warburton	1	–	1
own goals	2	–	2

RESULTS & ATTENDANCES SUMMARY

		P	W	D	L	F	A	TOTAL	AVGE
League	H	21	11	5	5	40	24	479524	22834
	A	21	4	8	9	31	44	290848	13850
TOTAL		42	15	13	14	71	68	770372	18342
FA Cup	H	1	0	0	1	1	4	36991	36991
	A	0	0	0	0	0	0	0	n/a
TOTAL		1	0	0	1	1	4	36991	36991
Overall	H	22	11	5	6	41	28	516515	23478
	A	21	4	8	9	31	44	290848	13850
TOTAL		43	15	13	15	72	72	807363	18776

FINAL TABLE - LEAGUE DIVISION TWO

		P	W	D	L	F	A	W	D	L	F	A	PTS	GD
				HOME					AWAY					
1	Stoke City	42	13	3	5	40	15	12	3	6	38	24	56	39
2	Tottenham Hotspur	42	14	7	0	58	19	6	8	7	38	32	55	45
3	Fulham	42	12	5	4	46	31	8	5	8	32	34	50	13
4	Bury	42	13	7	1	55	23	7	2	12	29	36	49	25
5	Nottingham Forest	42	9	8	4	37	28	8	7	6	30	31	49	8
6	MANCHESTER UNITED	42	11	5	5	40	24	4	8	9	31	44	43	3
7	Millwall	42	11	7	3	40	20	5	4	12	19	37	43	2
8	Bradford Park Avenue	42	13	4	4	51	27	4	4	13	26	44	42	6
9	Preston North End	42	12	2	7	53	36	4	8	9	21	34	42	4
10	Swansea City	42	17	0	4	36	12	2	4	15	14	42	42	-4
11	Bradford City	42	10	6	5	43	24	4	7	10	22	37	41	4
12	Southampton	42	15	3	3	48	22	3	2	16	18	44	41	0
13	Grimsby Town	42	8	10	3	49	34	6	3	12	30	50	41	-5
14	Plymouth Argyle	42	13	4	4	45	22	3	5	13	18	45	41	-4
15	Notts County	42	10	4	7	41	31	5	6	10	26	47	40	-11
16	Oldham Athletic	42	10	4	7	38	31	5	4	12	29	49	38	-13
17	Port Vale	42	12	3	6	49	27	2	7	12	17	52	38	-13
18	Lincoln City	42	11	6	4	46	28	1	7	13	26	59	37	-15
19	Burnley	42	8	9	4	35	20	3	5	13	32	59	36	-12
20	West Ham United	42	12	6	3	56	31	1	3	17	19	62	35	-18
21	Chesterfield	42	10	5	6	36	25	2	5	14	25	59	34	-23
22	Charlton Athletic	42	9	3	9	35	35	3	4	14	25	56	31	-31

SEASON 1933/34

Match # 1516 Saturday 26/08/33   Football League Division 2   at Home Park   Attendance 25700
Result: **Plymouth Argyle 4 Manchester United 0**
Teamsheet: Hillam, Mellor, Jones, McLenahan, Vose, Manley, McGillivray, Hine, Dewar, Green, Stewart

Match # 1517 Wednesday 30/08/33   Football League Division 2   at Old Trafford   Attendance 16934
Result: **Manchester United 0 Nottingham Forest 1**
Teamsheet: Hillam, Mellor, Jones, McLenahan, Vose, Manley, McGillivray, Hine, Dewar, Green, Stewart

Match # 1518 Saturday 02/09/33   Football League Division 2   at Old Trafford   Attendance 16987
Result: **Manchester United 1 Lincoln City 1**
Teamsheet: Hillam, Mellor, Jones, Vincent, Frame, McLenahan, McGillivray, Hine, Dewar, Green, Stewart
Scorer(s):   Green

Match # 1519 Thursday 07/09/33   Football League Division 2   at City Ground   Attendance 10650
Result: **Nottingham Forest 1 Manchester United 1**
Teamsheet: Hillam, Mellor, Jones, Vose, Frame, McLenahan, McGillivray, Hine, Dewar, Chalmers, Stewart
Scorer(s):   Stewart

Match # 1520 Saturday 09/09/33   Football League Division 2   at Old Trafford   Attendance 21779
Result: **Manchester United 1 Bolton Wanderers 5**
Teamsheet: Hillam, Mellor, Jones, Vincent, Frame, McLenahan, McGillivray, Hine, Dewar, Chalmers, Stewart
Scorer(s):   Stewart

Match # 1521 Saturday 16/09/33   Football League Division 2   at Griffin Park   Attendance 17180
Result: **Brentford 3 Manchester United 4**
Teamsheet: Hillam, Jones, Silcock, Frame, McMillen, Manley, Brown, Warburton, Dewar, Hine, Stewart
Scorer(s):   Brown 2, Frame, Hine

Match # 1522 Saturday 23/09/33   Football League Division 2   at Old Trafford   Attendance 18411
Result: **Manchester United 5 Burnley 2**
Teamsheet: Hillam, Jones, Silcock, Vose, McMillen, Manley, Brown, Frame, Dewar, Hine, Stewart
Scorer(s):   Dewar 4, Brown

Match # 1523 Saturday 30/09/33   Football League Division 2   at Boundary Park   Attendance 22736
Result: **Oldham Athletic 2 Manchester United 0**
Teamsheet: Hall, Jones, Silcock, Vose, McMillen, Manley, Brown, Frame, Dewar, Hine, Stewart

Match # 1524 Saturday 07/10/33   Football League Division 2   at Old Trafford   Attendance 22303
Result: **Manchester United 1 Preston North End 0**
Teamsheet: Hall, Jones, Silcock, Vose, McMillen, Manley, Brown, Chalmers, Dewar, Hine, Hopkinson
Scorer(s):   Hine

Match # 1525 Saturday 14/10/33   Football League Division 2   at Park Avenue   Attendance 11033
Result: **Bradford Park Avenue 6 Manchester United 1**
Teamsheet: Hall, Jones, McLenahan, Vose, Vincent, Manley, Brown, Ridding, Dewar, Hine, Hopkinson
Scorer(s):   Hine

Match # 1526 Saturday 21/10/33   Football League Division 2   at Gigg Lane   Attendance 15008
Result: **Bury 2 Manchester United 1**
Teamsheet: Hall, Jones, Silcock, McLenahan, McMillen, Manley, Warburton, Dewar, Byrne, Hine, Stewart
Scorer(s):   Byrne

Match # 1527 Saturday 28/10/33   Football League Division 2   at Old Trafford   Attendance 16269
Result: **Manchester United 4 Hull City 1**
Teamsheet: Hall, Jones, Silcock, McLenahan, McMillen, Manley, Heywood, Hine, Dewar, Green, Stewart
Scorer(s):   Heywood 2, Green, Hine

Match # 1528 Saturday 04/11/33   Football League Division 2   at Craven Cottage   Attendance 17049
Result: **Fulham 0 Manchester United 2**
Teamsheet: Hall, Jones, Silcock, McLenahan, McMillen, Manley, Heywood, Hine, Dewar, Green, Stewart
Scorer(s):   Stewart, own goal

Match # 1529 Saturday 11/11/33   Football League Division 2   at Old Trafford   Attendance 18149
Result: **Manchester United 1 Southampton 0**
Teamsheet: Hall, Jones, Silcock, McLenahan, McMillen, Manley, Heywood, Hine, Dewar, Green, Stewart
Scorer(s):   Manley

Match # 1530 Saturday 18/11/33   Football League Division 2   at Bloomfield Road   Attendance 14384
Result: **Blackpool 3 Manchester United 1**
Teamsheet: Hall, Jones, Silcock, McLenahan, McMillen, Manley, Brown, Hine, Dewar, Green, Stewart
Scorer(s):   Brown

Match # 1531 Saturday 25/11/33   Football League Division 2   at Old Trafford   Attendance 20902
Result: **Manchester United 2 Bradford City 1**
Teamsheet: Hall, Jones, Silcock, Vincent, Vose, Manley, Brown, Ridding, Dewar, Hine, Black
Scorer(s):   Dewar, own goal

Match # 1532 Saturday 02/12/33   Football League Division 2   at Old Recreation Ground   Attendance 10316
Result: **Port Vale 2 Manchester United 3**
Teamsheet: Hall, Jones, Topping, Vincent, Vose, Manley, Brown, Ridding, Dewar, Hine, Black
Scorer(s):   Black, Brown, Dewar

Match # 1533 Saturday 09/12/33   Football League Division 2   at Old Trafford   Attendance 15564
Result: **Manchester United 1 Notts County 2**
Teamsheet: Hall, Jones, Silcock, Vincent, Vose, McLenahan, Brown, Ridding, Dewar, Hine, Black
Scorer(s):   Dewar

SEASON 1933/34 (continued)

Match # 1534 Saturday 16/12/33   Football League Division 2   at Vetch Field   Attendance 6591
Result: **Swansea City 2 Manchester United 1**
Teamsheet: Hall, Jones, Silcock, McLenahan, Vose, Manley, Brown, Chalmers, Dewar, Hine, Black
Scorer(s): Hine

Match # 1535 Saturday 23/12/33   Football League Division 2   at Old Trafford   Attendance 12043
Result: **Manchester United 1 Millwall 1**
Teamsheet: Hall, Jones, Frame, McLenahan, McMillen, Manley, Brown, Chalmers, Dewar, Hine, Hopkinson
Scorer(s): Dewar

Match # 1536 Monday 25/12/33   Football League Division 2   at Old Trafford   Attendance 29443
Result: **Manchester United 1 Grimsby Town 3**
Teamsheet: Hall, Jones, Frame, Vose, McMillen, Manley, Byrne, Hine, Dewar, Chalmers, Stewart
Scorer(s): Vose

Match # 1537 Tuesday 26/12/33   Football League Division 2   at Blundell Park   Attendance 15801
Result: **Grimsby Town 7 Manchester United 3**
Teamsheet: Hall, Frame, Topping, Vose, McMillen, Manley, McGillivray, McDonald, Byrne, Chalmers, Stewart
Scorer(s): Byrne 2, Frame

Match # 1538 Saturday 30/12/33   Football League Division 2   at Old Trafford   Attendance 12206
Result: **Manchester United 0 Plymouth Argyle 3**
Teamsheet: Hall, Frame, Jones, Vose, McMillen, Manley, Byrne, Hine, Ball, Chalmers, Stewart

Match # 1539 Saturday 06/01/34   Football League Division 2   at Sincil Bank   Attendance 6075
Result: **Lincoln City 5 Manchester United 1**
Teamsheet: Hall, Nevin, Topping, Frame, McMillen, Manley, Brown, McGillivray, Ball, McLenahan, Stewart
Scorer(s): Brown

Match # 1540 Saturday 13/01/34   FA Cup 3rd Round   at Old Trafford   Attendance 23283
Result: **Manchester United 1 Portsmouth 1**
Teamsheet: Hall, Jones, Silcock, Vose, McMillen, Manley, Hine, McGillivray, Ball, McLenahan, Stewart
Scorer(s): McLenahan

Match # 1541 Wednesday 17/01/34   FA Cup 3rd Round Replay   at Fratton Park   Attendance 18748
Result: **Portsmouth 4 Manchester United 1**
Teamsheet: Hall, Jones, Nevin, Vose, McMillen, Manley, Brown, Hine, Ball, McLenahan, Stewart
Scorer(s): Ball

Match # 1542 Saturday 20/01/34   Football League Division 2   at Burnden Park   Attendance 11887
Result: **Bolton Wanderers 3 Manchester United 1**
Teamsheet: Hall, Nevin, Silcock, Frame, McMillen, Manley, McGillivray, Hine, Ball, McDonald, Stewart
Scorer(s): Ball

Match # 1543 Saturday 27/01/34   Football League Division 2   at Old Trafford   Attendance 16891
Result: **Manchester United 1 Brentford 3**
Teamsheet: Hall, Jones, Silcock, McLenahan, McMillen, Manley, Cape, Hine, Ball, McDonald, Stewart
Scorer(s): Ball

Match # 1544 Saturday 03/02/34   Football League Division 2   at Turf Moor   Attendance 9906
Result: **Burnley 1 Manchester United 4**
Teamsheet: Hall, Jones, Nevin, Manns, Newton, Manley, Cape, McLenahan, Ball, Green, Stewart
Scorer(s): Cape 2, Green, Stewart

Match # 1545 Saturday 10/02/34   Football League Division 2   at Old Trafford   Attendance 24480
Result: **Manchester United 2 Oldham Athletic 3**
Teamsheet: Hall, Jones, Nevin, Manns, Newton, Manley, Cape, McLenahan, Ball, Green, Stewart
Scorer(s): Cape, Green

Match # 1546 Wednesday 21/02/34   Football League Division 2   at Deepdale   Attendance 9173
Result: **Preston North End 3 Manchester United 2**
Teamsheet: Hall, Jones, Topping, McLenahan, Frame, Manley, Cape, Chalmers, Ball, Gallimore, Stewart
Scorer(s): Gallimore 2

Match # 1547 Saturday 24/02/34   Football League Division 2   at Old Trafford   Attendance 13389
Result: **Manchester United 0 Bradford Park Avenue 4**
Teamsheet: Hall, Jones, Topping, McLenahan, Frame, Manley, Cape, Hine, Ball, Gallimore, Stewart

Match # 1548 Saturday 03/03/34   Football League Division 2   at Old Trafford   Attendance 11176
Result: **Manchester United 2 Bury 1**
Teamsheet: Behan, Jones, Silcock, McLenahan, Vose, Hopkinson, Cape, Ainsworth, Ball, Gallimore, Stewart
Scorer(s): Ball, Gallimore

Match # 1549 Saturday 10/03/34   Football League Division 2   at Anlaby Road   Attendance 5771
Result: **Hull City 4 Manchester United 1**
Teamsheet: Hillam, Jones, Silcock, McMillen, Vose, Hopkinson, Cape, McDonald, Ball, Gallimore, Stewart
Scorer(s): Ball

Match # 1550 Saturday 17/03/34   Football League Division 2   at Old Trafford   Attendance 17565
Result: **Manchester United 1 Fulham 0**
Teamsheet: Hacking, Griffiths, Jones, Robertson, Frame, McKay, Cape, Ainsworth, Ball, Gallimore, Hopkinson
Scorer(s): Ball

Match # 1551 Saturday 24/03/34   Football League Division 2   at The Dell   Attendance 4840
Result: **Southampton 1 Manchester United 0**
Teamsheet: Hacking, Griffiths, Jones, Robertson, Frame, McKay, Cape, Ridding, Ball, Gallimore, Manley

SEASON 1933/34 (continued)

Match # 1552 Friday 30/03/34   Football League Division 2   at Old Trafford   Attendance 29114
Result: **Manchester United 0   West Ham United 1**
Teamsheet: Hacking, Griffiths, Jones, Robertson, Frame, McKay, Cape, McMillen, Ball, Hine, Gallimore

Match # 1553 Saturday 31/03/34   Football League Division 2   at Old Trafford   Attendance 20038
Result: **Manchester United 2   Blackpool 0**
Teamsheet: Hacking, Griffiths, Jones, Robertson, Frame, McKay, Cape, Chalmers, Ball, Hine, Manley
Scorer(s):   Cape, Hine

Match # 1554 Monday 02/04/34   Football League Division 2   at Upton Park   Attendance 20085
Result: **West Ham United 2   Manchester United 1**
Teamsheet: Hacking, Griffiths, Jones, Robertson, McMillen, McKay, Cape, Chalmers, Ball, Hine, Manley
Scorer(s):   Cape

Match # 1555 Saturday 07/04/34   Football League Division 2   at Valley Parade   Attendance 9258
Result: **Bradford City 1   Manchester United 1**
Teamsheet: Hacking, Griffiths, Jones, Robertson, McMillen, McKay, Cape, Chalmers, Ball, Hine, Brown
Scorer(s):   Cape

Match # 1556 Saturday 14/04/34   Football League Division 2   at Old Trafford   Attendance 14777
Result: **Manchester United 2   Port Vale 0**
Teamsheet: Hacking, Griffiths, Jones, Robertson, Vincent, McKay, Cape, McMillen, Brown, Hine, Hopkinson
Scorer(s):   Brown, McMillen

Match # 1557 Saturday 21/04/34   Football League Division 2   at Meadow Lane   Attendance 9645
Result: **Notts County 0   Manchester United 0**
Teamsheet: Hacking, Griffiths, Jones, Robertson, Vincent, McKay, Cape, McMillen, Brown, Hine, Hopkinson

Match # 1558 Saturday 28/04/34   Football League Division 2   at Old Trafford   Attendance 16678
Result: **Manchester United 1   Swansea City 1**
Teamsheet: Hacking, Griffiths, Jones, Robertson, McMillen, Hopkinson, Cape, McKay, Ball, Hine, Topping
Scorer(s):   Topping

Match # 1559 Saturday 05/05/34   Football League Division 2   at The Den   Attendance 24003
Result: **Millwall 0   Manchester United 2**
Teamsheet: Hacking, Griffiths, Jones, Robertson, Vose, McKay, Cape, McLenahan, Ball, Hine, Manley
Scorer(s):   Cape, Manley

SEASON 1933/34 SUMMARY

APPEARANCES

PLAYER	LGE	FAC	TOT
Jones	39	2	41
Hine	33	2	35
Manley	30	2	32
Stewart	25	2	27
Hall	23	2	25
McMillen	23	2	25
McLenahan	22	2	24
Dewar	21	–	21
Ball	18	2	20
Vose	17	2	19
Frame	18	–	18
Cape	17	–	17
Silcock	16	1	17
Brown	15	1	16
Chalmers	12	–	12
Griffiths	10	–	10
Hacking	10	–	10
McKay	10	–	10
Robertson	10	–	10
Green	9	–	9
Hopkinson	9	–	9
McGillivray	8	1	9
Hillam	8	–	8
Vincent	8	–	8
Gallimore	7	–	7
Topping	6	–	6
Mellor	5	–	5
Nevin	4	1	5
Ridding	5	–	5
Black	4	–	4
Byrne	4	–	4
McDonald	4	–	4
Heywood	3	–	3
Ainsworth	2	–	2
Manns	2	–	2
Newton	2	–	2
Warburton	2	–	2
Behan	1	–	1

GOALSCORERS

PLAYER	LGE	FAC	TOT
Dewar	8	–	8
Brown	7	–	7
Cape	7	–	7
Hine	6	–	6
Ball	5	1	6
Green	4	–	4
Stewart	4	–	4
Byrne	3	–	3
Gallimore	3	–	3
Frame	2	–	2
Heywood	2	–	2
Manley	2	–	2
Black	1	–	1
McMillen	1	–	1
Topping	1	–	1
Vose	1	–	1
McLenahan	–	1	1
own goals	2	–	2

RESULTS & ATTENDANCES SUMMARY

		P	W	D	L	F	A	TOTAL	AVGE
League	H	21	9	3	9	29	33	385098	18338
	A	21	5	3	13	30	52	277091	13195
	TOTAL	42	14	6	22	59	85	662189	15766
FA Cup	H	1	0	1	0	1	1	23283	23283
	A	1	0	0	1	1	4	18748	18748
	TOTAL	2	0	1	1	2	5	42031	21016
Overall	H	22	9	4	9	30	34	408381	18563
	A	22	5	3	14	31	56	295839	13447
	TOTAL	44	14	7	23	61	90	704220	16005

FINAL TABLE – LEAGUE DIVISION TWO

		P	W	D	L	F	A	W	D	L	F	A	PTS	GD
				HOME					AWAY					
1	Grimsby Town	42	15	3	3	62	28	12	2	7	41	31	59	44
2	Preston North End	42	15	3	3	47	20	8	3	10	24	32	52	19
3	Bolton Wanderers	42	14	2	5	45	22	7	7	7	34	33	51	24
4	Brentford	42	15	2	4	52	24	7	5	9	33	36	51	25
5	Bradford Park Avenue	42	16	2	3	63	27	7	1	13	23	40	49	19
6	Bradford City	42	14	4	3	46	25	6	2	13	27	42	46	6
7	West Ham United	42	13	3	5	51	28	4	8	9	27	42	45	8
8	Port Vale	42	14	4	3	39	14	5	3	13	21	41	45	5
9	Oldham Athletic	42	12	5	4	48	28	5	5	11	24	32	44	12
10	Plymouth Argyle	42	12	7	2	43	20	3	6	12	26	50	43	–1
11	Blackpool	42	10	8	3	39	27	5	5	11	23	37	43	–2
12	Bury	42	12	4	5	43	31	5	5	11	27	42	43	–3
13	Burnley	42	14	2	5	40	29	4	4	13	20	43	42	–12
14	Southampton	42	15	2	4	40	21	0	6	15	14	37	38	–4
15	Hull City	42	11	4	6	33	20	2	8	11	19	48	38	–16
16	Fulham	42	13	3	5	29	17	2	4	15	19	50	37	–19
17	Nottingham Forest	42	11	4	6	50	27	2	5	14	23	47	35	–1
18	Notts County	42	9	7	5	32	22	3	4	14	21	40	35	–9
19	Swansea City	42	10	9	2	36	19	0	6	15	15	41	35	–9
20	MANCHESTER UNITED	42	9	3	9	29	33	5	3	13	30	52	34	–26
21	Millwall	42	8	8	5	21	17	3	3	15	18	51	33	–29
22	Lincoln City	42	7	7	7	31	23	2	1	18	13	52	26	–31

SEASON 1934/35

Match # 1560   Saturday 25/08/34   Football League Division 2   at Old Trafford   Attendance 27573
Result: **Manchester United 2 Bradford City 0**
Teamsheet: Hacking, Griffiths, Jones (Tom), Robertson, Vose, McKay, Cape, Mutch, Ball, Jones (Tommy), Manley
Scorer(s):   Manley 2

Match # 1561   Saturday 01/09/34   Football League Division 2   at Bramall Lane   Attendance 18468
Result: **Sheffield United 3 Manchester United 2**
Teamsheet: Hacking, Griffiths, Jones (Tom), Robertson, Vose, McKay, Cape, Mutch, Ball, Jones (Tommy), Manley
Scorer(s):   Ball, Manley

Match # 1562   Monday 03/09/34   Football League Division 2   at Burnden Park   Attendance 16238
Result: **Bolton Wanderers 3 Manchester United 1**
Teamsheet: Hacking, Griffiths, Jones (Tom), Robertson, Vose, McKay, Cape, Mutch, Ball, Jones (Tommy), Manley
Scorer(s):   own goal

Match # 1563   Saturday 08/09/34   Football League Division 2   at Old Trafford   Attendance 22315
Result: **Manchester United 4 Barnsley 1**
Teamsheet: Hacking, Griffiths, Jones (Tom), McLenahan, Vose, McKay, Cape, Mutch, Ball, Jones (Tommy), Manley
Scorer(s):   Mutch 3, Manley

Match # 1564   Wednesday 12/09/34   Football League Division 2   at Old Trafford   Attendance 24760
Result: **Manchester United 0 Bolton Wanderers 3**
Teamsheet: Hacking, Griffiths, Jones (Tom), McLenahan, Vose, McKay, Cape, Mutch, Ball, Jones (Tommy), Manley

Match # 1565   Saturday 15/09/34   Football League Division 2   at Old Recreation Ground   Attendance 9307
Result: **Port Vale 3 Manchester United 2**
Teamsheet: Hacking, Jones (Tom), Topping, McLenahan, Vose, McKay, Cape, Mutch, Ball, Hine, Jones (Tommy)
Scorer(s):   Jones (Tommy), Mutch

Match # 1566   Saturday 22/09/34   Football League Division 2   at Old Trafford   Attendance 13052
Result: **Manchester United 5 Norwich City 0**
Teamsheet: Langford, Mellor, Jones (Tom), Robertson, Vose, McKay, Jones (Tommy), Mutch, Cape, McLenahan, Owen
Scorer(s):   Cape, Jones (Tommy), McLenahan, Mutch, Owen

Match # 1567   Saturday 29/09/34   Football League Division 2   at Old Trafford   Attendance 14865
Result: **Manchester United 3 Swansea City 1**
Teamsheet: Langford, Griffiths, Jones (Tom), Robertson, Vose, Manley, Jones (Tommy), Mutch, Cape, McKay, Owen
Scorer(s):   Cape 2, Mutch

Match # 1568   Saturday 06/10/34   Football League Division 2   at Turf Moor   Attendance 16757
Result: **Burnley 1 Manchester United 2**
Teamsheet: Hacking, Griffiths, Jones (Tom), Robertson, Vose, Manley, Jones (Tommy), Mutch, Cape, McKay, Owen
Scorer(s):   Capey, Manley

Match # 1569   Saturday 13/10/34   Football League Division 2   at Old Trafford   Attendance 29143
Result: **Manchester United 4 Oldham Athletic 0**
Teamsheet: Hacking, Griffiths, Jones (Tom), Robertson, Vose, Manley, Jones (Tommy), Mutch, Hine, McKay, Owen
Scorer(s):   Manley 2, McKay, Mutch

Match # 1570   Saturday 20/10/34   Football League Division 2   at St James' Park   Attendance 24752
Result: **Newcastle United 0 Manchester United 1**
Teamsheet: Hacking, Griffiths, Jones (Tom), Robertson, Vose, Manley, Jones (Tommy), Mutch, Bamford, McKay, Owen
Scorer(s):   Bamford

Match # 1571   Saturday 27/10/34   Football League Division 2   at Old Trafford   Attendance 31950
Result: **Manchester United 3 West Ham United 1**
Teamsheet: Hacking, Griffiths, Jones (Tom), Robertson, Vose, Manley, Jones (Tommy), Mutch, Bamford, McKay, Owen
Scorer(s):   Mutch 2, McKay

Match # 1572   Saturday 03/11/34   Football League Division 2   at Bloomfield Road   Attendance 15663
Result: **Blackpool 1 Manchester United 2**
Teamsheet: Hacking, Griffiths, Jones (Tom), Robertson, Vose, Manley, Bryant, Mutch, Bamford, McKay, Jones (Tommy)
Scorer(s):   Bryant, McKay

Match # 1573   Saturday 10/11/34   Football League Division 2   at Old Trafford   Attendance 41415
Result: **Manchester United 1 Bury 0**
Teamsheet: Hacking, Griffiths, Jones (Tom), Robertson, Vose, Manley, Bryant, Mutch, Bamford, McKay, Jones (Tommy)
Scorer(s):   Mutch

Match # 1574   Saturday 17/11/34   Football League Division 2   at Anlaby Road   Attendance 6494
Result: **Hull City 3 Manchester United 2**
Teamsheet: Hacking, Griffiths, Jones (Tom), Robertson, Vose, Manley, Bryant, Mutch, Bamford, McKay, Owen
Scorer(s):   Bamford 2

Match # 1575   Saturday 24/11/34   Football League Division 2   at Old Trafford   Attendance 27192
Result: **Manchester United 3 Nottingham Forest 2**
Teamsheet: Hacking, Griffiths, Jones (Tom), Robertson, Vose, Manley, Bryant, Mutch, Bamford, Hine, McLenahan
Scorer(s):   Mutch 2, Hine

Match # 1576   Saturday 01/12/34   Football League Division 2   at Griffin Park   Attendance 21744
Result: **Brentford 3 Manchester United 1**
Teamsheet: Hacking, Griffiths, Jones (Tom), Robertson, Vose, Manley, Bryant, McKay, Bamford, Hine, McLenahan
Scorer(s):   Bamford

Match # 1577   Saturday 08/12/34   Football League Division 2   at Old Trafford   Attendance 25706
Result: **Manchester United 1 Fulham 0**
Teamsheet: Hacking, Griffiths, Jones (Tom), McLenahan, Vose, McKay, Bryant, Mutch, Bamford, Rowley, Manley
Scorer(s):   Mutch

SEASON 1934/35 (continued)

Match # 1578   Saturday 15/12/34   Football League Division 2   at Park Avenue   Attendance 8405
Result: **Bradford Park Avenue 1   Manchester United 2**
Teamsheet: Hacking, Griffiths, Jones (Tom), Robertson, Vose, McKay, Bryant, Mutch, Bamford, Rowley, Manley
Scorer(s):   Manley, Mutch

Match # 1579   Saturday 22/12/34   Football League Division 2   at Old Trafford   Attendance 24896
Result: **Manchester United 3   Plymouth Argyle 1**
Teamsheet: Hacking, Griffiths, Jones (Tom), Robertson, Vose, McKay, Bryant, Mutch, Bamford, Rowley, Manley
Scorer(s):   Bamford, Bryant, Rowley

Match # 1580   Tuesday 25/12/34   Football League Division 2   at Old Trafford   Attendance 32965
Result: **Manchester United 2   Notts County 1**
Teamsheet: Hacking, Griffiths, Jones (Tom), Robertson, Vose, McKay, Bryant, Mutch, Bamford, Rowley, Owen
Scorer(s):   Mutch, Rowley

Match # 1581   Wednesday 26/12/34   Football League Division 2   at Meadow Lane   Attendance 24599
Result: **Notts County 1   Manchester United 0**
Teamsheet: Hacking, Griffiths, Jones (Tom), Robertson, McMillen, McKay, Bryant, Mutch, Bamford, Rowley, Owen

Match # 1582   Saturday 29/12/34   Football League Division 2   at Valley Parade   Attendance 11908
Result: **Bradford City 2   Manchester United 0**
Teamsheet: Langford, Griffiths, Jones (Tom), Robertson, Vose, McKay, Bryant, Mutch, Cape, Rowley, Owen

Match # 1583   Tuesday 01/01/35   Football League Division 2   at Old Trafford   Attendance 15174
Result: **Manchester United 3   Southampton 0**
Teamsheet: Hall, Griffiths, Jones (Tom), Robertson, Vose, McKay, Bryant, Mutch, Cape, Rowley, Manley
Scorer(s):   Cape 2, Rowley

Match # 1584   Saturday 05/01/35   Football League Division 2   at Old Trafford   Attendance 28300
Result: **Manchester United 3   Sheffield United 3**
Teamsheet: Hall, Griffiths, Jones (Tom), Robertson, Vose, McKay, Bryant, Mutch, Cape, Rowley, Manley
Scorer(s):   Bryant, Mutch, Rowley

Match # 1585   Saturday 12/01/35   FA Cup 3rd Round   at Eastville   Attendance 20400
Result: **Bristol Rovers 1   Manchester United 3**
Teamsheet: Hall, Griffiths, Jones (Tom), Robertson, Vose, McKay, Bryant, Mutch, Bamford, Rowley, Manley
Scorer(s):   Bamford 2, Mutch

Match # 1586   Saturday 19/01/35   Football League Division 2   at Oakwell   Attendance 10177
Result: **Barnsley 0   Manchester United 2**
Teamsheet: Hacking, Griffiths, Porter, Robertson, Vose, McKay, Bryant, Mutch, Bamford, Rowley, Jones (Tommy)
Scorer(s):   Bryant, Jones (Tommy)

Match # 1587   Saturday 26/01/35   FA Cup 4th Round   at City Ground   Attendance 32862
Result: **Nottingham Forest 0   Manchester United 0**
Teamsheet: Hacking, Griffiths, Porter, Robertson, Vose, McKay, Cape, Mutch, Bamford, Rowley, Jones (Tommy)

Match # 1588   Wednesday 30/01/35   FA Cup 4th Round Replay   at Old Trafford   Attendance 33851
Result: **Manchester United 0   Nottingham Forest 3**
Teamsheet: Hacking, Griffiths, Jones (Tom), Robertson, Vose, McKay, Bryant, Mutch, Bamford, Rowley, Jones (Tommy)

Match # 1589   Saturday 02/02/35   Football League Division 2   at The Nest   Attendance 14260
Result: **Norwich City 3   Manchester United 2**
Teamsheet: Hacking, Griffiths, Jones (Tom), Robertson, Vose, McKay, Jones (Tommy), Mutch, Cape, Rowley, Manley
Scorer(s):   Manley, Rowley

Match # 1590   Wednesday 06/02/35   Football League Division 2   at Old Trafford   Attendance 7372
Result: **Manchester United 2   Port Vale 1**
Teamsheet: Hall, Griffiths, Jones (Tom), McKay, Robertson, Manley, Bryant, Mutch, Cape, Rowley, Jones (Tommy)
Scorer(s):   Jones (Tommy), Rowley

Match # 1591   Saturday 09/02/35   Football League Division 2   at Vetch Field   Attendance 8876
Result: **Swansea City 1   Manchester United 0**
Teamsheet: Hall, Griffiths, Porter, Robertson, McLenahan, McKay, Bryant, Mutch, Boyd, Rowley, Jones (Tommy)

Match # 1592   Saturday 23/02/35   Football League Division 2   at Boundary Park   Attendance 14432
Result: **Oldham Athletic 3   Manchester United 1**
Teamsheet: Hall, Griffiths, Porter, McKay, Vose, Manley, Bryant, Mutch, Boyd, Rowley, Jones (Tommy)
Scorer(s):   Mutch

Match # 1593   Saturday 02/03/35   Football League Division 2   at Old Trafford   Attendance 20728
Result: **Manchester United 0   Newcastle United 1**
Teamsheet: Langford, Griffiths, Porter, Robertson, Vose, McKay, Cape, Mutch, Boyd, Rowley, Manley

Match # 1594   Saturday 09/03/35   Football League Division 2   at Upton Park   Attendance 19718
Result: **West Ham United 0   Manchester United 0**
Teamsheet: Langford, Griffiths, Porter, Robertson, Vose, McKay, Cape, Mutch, Boyd, Rowley, Manley

Match # 1595   Saturday 16/03/35   Football League Division 2   at Old Trafford   Attendance 25704
Result: **Manchester United 3   Blackpool 2**
Teamsheet: Langford, Griffiths, Porter, Robertson, Vose, Manley, Bryant, Mutch, Bamford, Rowley, McMillen
Scorer(s):   Bamford, Mutch, Rowley

SEASON 1934/35 (continued)

Match # 1596   Saturday 23/03/35   Football League Division 2   at Gigg Lane   Attendance 7229
Result: **Bury 0 Manchester United 1**
Teamsheet: Langford, Griffiths, Porter, Robertson, Vose, Manley, Cape, Mutch, Bamford, Rowley, McMillen
Scorer(s):   Cape

Match # 1597   Wednesday 27/03/35   Football League Division 2   at Old Trafford   Attendance 10247
Result: **Manchester United 3 Burnley 4**
Teamsheet: Langford, Griffiths, Porter, McKay, Vose, Manley, Cape, Mutch, Boyd, Rowley, McMillen
Scorer(s):   Boyd, Cape, McMillen

Match # 1598   Saturday 30/03/35   Football League Division 2   at Old Trafford   Attendance 15358
Result: **Manchester United 3 Hull City 0**
Teamsheet: Langford, Griffiths, Porter, Robertson, Vose, Owen, Cape, Mutch, Boyd, McKay, Rowley
Scorer(s):   Boyd 3

Match # 1599   Saturday 06/04/35   Football League Division 2   at City Ground   Attendance 8618
Result: **Nottingham Forest 2 Manchester United 2**
Teamsheet: Langford, Griffiths, Porter, Robertson, Vose, Owen, Bryant, Mutch, Cape, McKay, Rowley
Scorer(s):   Bryant 2

Match # 1600   Saturday 13/04/35   Football League Division 2   at Old Trafford   Attendance 32969
Result: **Manchester United 0 Brentford 0**
Teamsheet: Langford, Griffiths, Porter, Robertson, Vose, McKay, Bryant, Mutch, Cape, Rowley, Owen

Match # 1601   Saturday 20/04/35   Football League Division 2   at Craven Cottage   Attendance 11059
Result: **Fulham 3 Manchester United 1**
Teamsheet: Langford, Griffiths, Porter, Robertson, Vose, McLenahan, Bryant, Mutch, Bamford, McKay, Jones (Tommy)
Scorer(s):   Bamford

Match # 1602   Monday 22/04/35   Football League Division 2   at The Dell   Attendance 12458
Result: **Southampton 1 Manchester United 0**
Teamsheet: Hall, Griffiths, Porter, Robertson, Vose, McLenahan, Bryant, Mutch, Bamford, McKay, Rowley

Match # 1603   Saturday 27/04/35   Football League Division 2   at Old Trafford   Attendance 8606
Result: **Manchester United 2 Bradford Park Avenue 0**
Teamsheet: Hall, Griffiths, Porter, Robertson, Vose, Manley, Bryant, McKay, Bamford, Rowley, Owen
Scorer(s):   Bamford, Robertson

Match # 1604   Saturday 04/05/35   Football League Division 2   at Home Park   Attendance 10767
Result: **Plymouth Argyle 0 Manchester United 2**
Teamsheet: Hall, Griffiths, Porter, Robertson, Vose, Manley, Bryant, Mutch, Bamford, Rowley, Owen
Scorer(s):   Bamford, Rowley

SEASON 1934/35 SUMMARY

APPEARANCES

PLAYER	LGE	FAC	TOT
Griffiths	40	3	43
Mutch	40	3	43
Vose	39	3	42
McKay	38	3	41
Robertson	36	3	39
Manley	30	1	31
Jones,Tom	27	2	29
Rowley	24	3	27
Bryant	24	2	26
Hacking	22	2	24
Bamford	19	3	22
Cape	21	1	22
Jones,Tommy	20	2	22
Porter	15	1	16
Owen	15	–	15
Langford	12	–	12
McLenahan	10	–	10
Hall	8	1	9
Ball	6	–	6
Boyd	6	–	6
Hine	4	–	4
McMillen	4	–	4
Mellor	1	–	1
Topping	1	–	1

GOALSCORERS

PLAYER	LGE	FAC	TOT
Mutch	18	1	19
Bamford	9	2	11
Manley	9	–	9
Cape	8	–	8
Rowley	8	–	8
Bryant	6	–	6
Boyd	4	–	4
Jones,Tommy	4	–	4
McKay	3	–	3
Ball	1	–	1
Hine	1	–	1
McLenahan	1	–	1
McMillen	1	–	1
Owen	1	–	1
Robertson	1	–	1
own goal	1	–	1

RESULTS & ATTENDANCES SUMMARY

		P	W	D	L	F	A	TOTAL	AVGE
League	H	21	16	2	3	50	21	480290	22871
	A	21	7	2	12	26	34	291929	13901
TOTAL		42	23	4	15	76	55	772219	18386
FA Cup	H	1	0	0	1	0	3	33851	33851
	A	2	1	1	0	3	1	53262	26631
TOTAL		3	1	1	1	3	4	87113	29038
Overall	H	22	16	2	4	50	24	514141	23370
	A	23	8	3	12	29	35	345191	15008
TOTAL		45	24	5	16	79	59	859332	19096

FINAL TABLE – LEAGUE DIVISION TWO

		P	W	D	L	F	A	W	D	L	F	A	PTS	GD
			HOME					AWAY						
1	Brentford	42	19	2	0	59	14	7	7	7	34	34	61	45
2	Bolton Wanderers	42	17	1	3	63	15	9	3	9	33	33	56	48
3	West Ham United	42	18	1	2	46	17	8	3	10	34	46	56	17
4	Blackpool	42	16	4	1	46	18	5	7	9	33	39	53	22
5	MANCHESTER UNITED	42	16	2	3	50	21	7	2	12	26	34	50	21
6	Newcastle United	42	14	2	5	55	25	8	2	11	34	43	48	21
7	Fulham	42	15	3	3	62	26	2	9	10	14	30	46	20
8	Plymouth Argyle	42	13	3	5	48	26	6	5	10	27	38	46	11
9	Nottingham Forest	42	12	5	4	46	23	5	3	13	30	47	42	6
10	Bury	42	14	1	6	38	26	5	3	13	24	47	42	-11
11	Sheffield United	42	11	4	6	51	30	5	5	11	28	40	41	9
12	Burnley	42	11	2	8	43	32	5	7	9	20	41	41	-10
13	Hull City	42	9	6	6	32	22	7	2	12	31	52	40	-11
14	Norwich City	42	11	6	4	51	23	3	5	13	20	38	39	10
15	Bradford Park Avenue	42	7	8	6	32	28	4	8	9	23	35	38	-8
16	Barnsley	42	8	10	3	32	22	5	2	14	28	61	38	-23
17	Swansea City	42	13	5	3	41	22	1	3	17	15	45	36	-11
18	Port Vale	42	10	7	4	42	28	1	5	15	13	46	34	-19
19	Southampton	42	9	8	4	28	19	2	4	15	18	56	34	-29
20	Bradford City	42	10	7	4	34	20	2	1	18	16	48	32	-18
21	Oldham Athletic	42	10	3	8	44	40	0	3	18	12	55	26	-39
22	Notts County	42	8	3	10	29	33	1	4	16	17	64	25	-51

SEASON 1935/36

Match # 1605 Saturday 31/08/35   Football League Division 2   at Home Park   Attendance 22366
Result: **Plymouth Argyle 3 Manchester United 1**
Teamsheet: Breedon, Griffiths, Porter, Brown, Vose, McKay, Bryant, Mutch, Bamford, Rowley, Chester
Scorer(s):   Bamford

Match # 1606 Wednesday 04/09/35   Football League Division 2   at Old Trafford   Attendance 21211
Result: **Manchester United 3 Charlton Athletic 0**
Teamsheet: Hall, Griffiths, Porter, Brown, Vose, McKay, Cape, Mutch, Bamford, Ferrier, Chester
Scorer(s):   Bamford, Cape, Chester

Match # 1607 Saturday 07/09/35   Football League Division 2   at Old Trafford   Attendance 30754
Result: **Manchester United 3 Bradford City 1**
Teamsheet: Hall, Griffiths, Porter, Brown, Vose, McKay, Cape, Mutch, Bamford, Ferrier, Chester
Scorer(s):   Bamford 2, Mutch

Match # 1608 Monday 09/09/35   Football League Division 2   at The Valley   Attendance 13178
Result: **Charlton Athletic 0 Manchester United 0**
Teamsheet: Hall, Griffiths, Porter, Brown, Vose, McKay, Cape, Mutch, Bamford, Ferrier, Chester

Match # 1609 Saturday 14/09/35   Football League Division 2   at St James' Park   Attendance 28520
Result: **Newcastle United 0 Manchester United 2**
Teamsheet: Hall, Griffiths, Porter, Brown, Vose, Manley, Cape, Mutch, Bamford, Rowley, Chester
Scorer(s):   Bamford, Rowley

Match # 1610 Wednesday 18/09/35   Football League Division 2   at Old Trafford   Attendance 15739
Result: **Manchester United 2 Hull City 0**
Teamsheet: Hall, Griffiths, Porter, Brown, Vose, Manley, Bryant, Mutch, Bamford, Rowley, Chester
Scorer(s):   Bamford 2

Match # 1611 Saturday 21/09/35   Football League Division 2   at Old Trafford   Attendance 34718
Result: **Manchester United 0 Tottenham Hotspur 0**
Teamsheet: Breedon, Redwood, Porter, Brown, Vose, McKay, Bryant, Mutch, Bamford, Manley, Chester

Match # 1612 Saturday 28/09/35   Football League Division 2   at The Dell   Attendance 17678
Result: **Southampton 2 Manchester United 1**
Teamsheet: Hall, Griffiths, Porter, Brown, Vose, McKay, Robbie, Mutch, Bamford, Rowley, Chester
Scorer(s):   Rowley

Match # 1613 Saturday 05/10/35   Football League Division 2   at Old Recreation Ground   Attendance 9703
Result: **Port Vale 0 Manchester United 3**
Teamsheet: Hall, Griffiths, Porter, Brown, Vose, McKay, Cape, Mutch, Bamford, Rowley, Chester
Scorer(s):   Mutch 2, Bamford

Match # 1614 Saturday 12/10/35   Football League Division 2   at Old Trafford   Attendance 22723
Result: **Manchester United 1 Fulham 0**
Teamsheet: Hall, Griffiths, Porter, Brown, Vose, McKay, Cape, Mutch, Bamford, Rowley, Chester
Scorer(s):   Rowley

Match # 1615 Saturday 19/10/35   Football League Division 2   at Old Trafford   Attendance 18636
Result: **Manchester United 3 Sheffield United 1**
Teamsheet: Hall, Griffiths, Porter, Brown, Vose, McKay, Cape, Mutch, Bamford, Rowley, Chester
Scorer(s):   Cape, Mutch, Rowley

Match # 1616 Saturday 26/10/35   Football League Division 2   at Park Avenue   Attendance 12216
Result: **Bradford Park Avenue 1 Manchester United 0**
Teamsheet: Hall, Griffiths, Porter, Brown, Vose, McKay, Cape, Mutch, Bamford, Rowley, Chester

Match # 1617 Saturday 02/11/35   Football League Division 2   at Old Trafford   Attendance 39074
Result: **Manchester United 0 Leicester City 1**
Teamsheet: Hall, Griffiths, Porter, Brown, Vose, McKay, Cape, Mutch, Bamford, Rowley, Owen

Match # 1618 Saturday 09/11/35   Football League Division 2   at Vetch Field   Attendance 9731
Result: **Swansea City 2 Manchester United 1**
Teamsheet: Hall, Griffiths, Porter, Brown, Vose, Manley, Wassall, Mutch, Bamford, Rowley, Owen
Scorer(s):   Bamford

Match # 1619 Saturday 16/11/35   Football League Division 2   at Old Trafford   Attendance 24440
Result: **Manchester United 2 West Ham United 3**
Teamsheet: Hall, Griffiths, Porter, Brown, Vose, McKay, Wassall, Mutch, Morton, Rowley, Chester
Scorer(s):   Rowley 2

Match # 1620 Saturday 23/11/35   Football League Division 2   at Carrow Road   Attendance 17266
Result: **Norwich City 3 Manchester United 5**
Teamsheet: Langford, Griffiths, Porter, Brown, Vose, McKay, Cape, Mutch, Bamford, Rowley, Manley
Scorer(s):   Rowley 3, Manley 2

Match # 1621 Saturday 30/11/35   Football League Division 2   at Old Trafford   Attendance 23569
Result: **Manchester United 0 Doncaster Rovers 0**
Teamsheet: Langford, Griffiths, Porter, Whalley, Vose, McKay, Cape, Mutch, Bamford, Rowley, Manley

Match # 1622 Saturday 07/12/35   Football League Division 2   at Bloomfield Road   Attendance 13218
Result: **Blackpool 4 Manchester United 1**
Teamsheet: Langford, Griffiths, Porter, Robertson, Vose, McKay, Cape, Mutch, Bamford, Rowley, Manley
Scorer(s):   Mutch

SEASON 1935/36 (continued)

Match # 1623 Saturday 14/12/35   Football League Division 2   at Old Trafford   Attendance 15284
Result: **Manchester United 5 Nottingham Forest 0**
Teamsheet: Hall, Griffiths, Porter, Brown, Vose, McKay, Cape, Mutch, Bamford, Rowley, Manley
Scorer(s): Bamford 2, Manley, Mutch, Rowley

Match # 1624 Thursday 26/12/35   Football League Division 2   at Old Trafford   Attendance 20993
Result: **Manchester United 1 Barnsley 1**
Teamsheet: Hall, Griffiths, Porter, Brown, Vose, McKay, Cape, Mutch, Bamford, Rowley, Manley
Scorer(s): Mutch

Match # 1625 Saturday 28/12/35   Football League Division 2   at Old Trafford   Attendance 20894
Result: **Manchester United 3 Plymouth Argyle 2**
Teamsheet: Hall, Griffiths, Porter, Brown, Vose, McKay, Cape, Gardner, Mutch, Rowley, Manley
Scorer(s): Mutch 2, Manley

Match # 1626 Wednesday 01/01/36   Football League Division 2   at Oakwell   Attendance 20957
Result: **Barnsley 0 Manchester United 3**
Teamsheet: Hall, Griffiths, Porter, Brown, Vose, McKay, Cape, Gardner, Mutch, Ferrier, Manley
Scorer(s): Gardner, Manley, Mutch

Match # 1627 Saturday 04/01/36   Football League Division 2   at Valley Parade   Attendance 11286
Result: **Bradford City 1 Manchester United 0**
Teamsheet: Hall, Griffiths, Porter, Brown, Vose, McKay, Cape, Gardner, Mutch, Rowley, Manley

Match # 1628 Saturday 11/01/36   FA Cup 3rd Round   at Elm Park   Attendance 25844
Result: **Reading 1 Manchester United 3**
Teamsheet: Hall, Griffiths, Porter, Brown, Vose, McKay, Bamford, Gardner, Mutch, Rowley, Manley
Scorer(s): Mutch 2, Manley

Match # 1629 Saturday 18/01/36   Football League Division 2   at Old Trafford   Attendance 22968
Result: **Manchester United 3 Newcastle United 1**
Teamsheet: Hall, Griffiths, Porter, Brown, Vose, McKay, Bamford, Gardner, Mutch, Rowley, Manley
Scorer(s): Mutch 2, Rowley

Match # 1630 Saturday 25/01/36   FA Cup 4th Round   at Victoria Ground   Attendance 32286
Result: **Stoke City 0 Manchester United 0**
Teamsheet: Hall, Griffiths, Porter, Brown, Vose, McKay, Bamford, Gardner, Mutch, Rowley, Manley

Match # 1631 Wednesday 29/01/36   FA Cup 4th Round Replay   at Old Trafford   Attendance 34440
Result: **Manchester United 0 Stoke City 2**
Teamsheet: Hall, Griffiths, Porter, Brown, Vose, McKay, Bryant, Rowley, Mutch, Ferrier, Manley

Match # 1632 Saturday 01/02/36   Football League Division 2   at Old Trafford   Attendance 23205
Result: **Manchester United 4 Southampton 0**
Teamsheet: Hall, Griffiths, Porter, Brown, Vose, McKay, Bryant, Gardner, Mutch, Rowley, Manley
Scorer(s): Mutch 2, Bryant, own goal

Match # 1633 Wednesday 05/02/36   Football League Division 2   at White Hart Lane   Attendance 20085
Result: **Tottenham Hotspur 0 Manchester United 0**
Teamsheet: Hall, Griffiths, Porter, Brown, Vose, McKay, Bryant, Ferrier, Mutch, Rowley, Manley

Match # 1634 Saturday 08/02/36   Football League Division 2   at Old Trafford   Attendance 22265
Result: **Manchester United 7 Port Vale 2**
Teamsheet: Hall, Griffiths, Porter, Brown, Vose, McKay, Bryant, Gardner, Mutch, Rowley, Manley
Scorer(s): Manley 4, Rowley 2, Mutch

Match # 1635 Saturday 22/02/36   Football League Division 2   at Bramall Lane   Attendance 25852
Result: **Sheffield United 1 Manchester United 1**
Teamsheet: Hall, Griffiths, Porter, Brown, Vose, McKay, Bryant, Gardner, Mutch, Rowley, Manley
Scorer(s): Manley

Match # 1636 Saturday 29/02/36   Football League Division 2   at Old Trafford   Attendance 18423
Result: **Manchester United 3 Blackpool 2**
Teamsheet: Hall, Griffiths, Porter, Brown, Vose, McKay, Bryant, Gardner, Mutch, Rowley, Manley
Scorer(s): Bryant, Manley, Mutch

Match # 1637 Saturday 07/03/36   Football League Division 2   at Upton Park   Attendance 29684
Result: **West Ham United 1 Manchester United 2**
Teamsheet: Hall, Griffiths, Porter, Brown, Vose, McKay, Bryant, Gardner, Mutch, Rowley, Manley
Scorer(s): Bryant, Mutch

Match # 1638 Saturday 14/03/36   Football League Division 2   at Old Trafford   Attendance 27580
Result: **Manchester United 3 Swansea City 0**
Teamsheet: Hall, Griffiths, Porter, Brown, Vose, McKay, Bryant, Gardner, Mutch, Rowley, Manley
Scorer(s): Manley, Mutch, Rowley

Match # 1639 Saturday 21/03/36   Football League Division 2   at Filbert Street   Attendance 18200
Result: **Leicester City 1 Manchester United 1**
Teamsheet: Hall, Griffiths, Porter, Brown, Vose, McKay, Bryant, Gardner, Mutch, Rowley, Manley
Scorer(s): Bryant

Match # 1640 Saturday 28/03/36   Football League Division 2   at Old Trafford   Attendance 31596
Result: **Manchester United 2 Norwich City 1**
Teamsheet: Hall, Griffiths, Porter, Brown, Vose, McKay, Bryant, Ferrier, Mutch, Rowley, Manley
Scorer(s): Rowley 2

SEASON 1935/36 (continued)

Match # 1641   Wednesday 01/04/36   Football League Division 2   at Craven Cottage   Attendance 11137
Result: **Fulham 2 Manchester United 2**
Teamsheet: Hall, Griffiths, Porter, Brown, Vose, McKay, Bryant, Ferrier, Mutch, Rowley, Manley
Scorer(s):   Bryant, Griffiths

Match # 1642   Saturday 04/04/36   Football League Division 2   at Belle Vue Stadium   Attendance 13474
Result: **Doncaster Rovers 0 Manchester United 0**
Teamsheet: Hall, Griffiths, Porter, Brown, Vose, McKay, Bryant, Gardner, Mutch, Rowley, Manley

Match # 1643   Friday 10/04/36   Football League Division 2   at Turf Moor   Attendance 27245
Result: **Burnley 2 Manchester United 2**
Teamsheet: Hall, Griffiths, Porter, Brown, Vose, McKay, Bryant, Mutch, Bamford, Rowley, Manley
Scorer(s):   Bamford 2

Match # 1644   Saturday 11/04/36   Football League Division 2   at Old Trafford   Attendance 33517
Result: **Manchester United 4 Bradford Park Avenue 0**
Teamsheet: Breedon, Griffiths, Porter, Brown, Vose, Manley, Bryant, Mutch, Bamford, Rowley, Lang
Scorer(s):   Mutch 2, Bamford, Bryant

Match # 1645   Monday 13/04/36   Football League Division 2   at Old Trafford   Attendance 39855
Result: **Manchester United 4 Burnley 0**
Teamsheet: Hall, Griffiths, Porter, Whalley, Brown, Manley, Bryant, Mutch, Bamford, Rowley, Lang
Scorer(s):   Bryant 2, Rowley 2

Match # 1646   Saturday 18/04/36   Football League Division 2   at City Ground   Attendance 12156
Result: **Nottingham Forest 1 Manchester United 1**
Teamsheet: Hall, Griffiths, Porter, Brown, Vose, Manley, Bryant, Mutch, Bamford, Rowley, Lang
Scorer(s):   Bamford

Match # 1647   Saturday 25/04/36   Football League Division 2   at Old Trafford   Attendance 35027
Result: **Manchester United 2 Bury 1**
Teamsheet: Hall, Griffiths, Porter, Brown, Vose, Manley, Bryant, Mutch, Bamford, Rowley, Lang
Scorer(s):   Lang, Rowley

Match # 1648   Wednesday 29/04/36   Football League Division 2   at Gigg Lane   Attendance 31562
Result: **Bury 2 Manchester United 3**
Teamsheet: Hall, Griffiths, Porter, Brown, Vose, McKay, Bryant, Mutch, Bamford, Rowley, Manley
Scorer(s):   Manley 2, Mutch

Match # 1649   Saturday 02/05/36   Football League Division 2   at Anlaby Road   Attendance 4540
Result: **Hull City 1 Manchester United 1**
Teamsheet: Hall, Griffiths, Porter, Brown, Vose, McKay, Bryant, Mutch, Bamford, Rowley, Manley
Scorer(s):   Bamford

SEASON 1935/36 SUMMARY

APPEARANCES

PLAYER	LGE	FAC	TOT
Mutch	42	3	45
Porter	42	3	45
Griffiths	41	3	44
Vose	41	3	44
Brown	40	3	43
Rowley	37	3	40
Hall	36	3	39
McKay	35	3	38
Manley	31	3	34
Bamford	27	2	29
Bryant	21	1	22
Cape	17	–	17
Gardner	12	2	14
Chester	13	–	13
Ferrier	7	1	8
Lang	4	–	4
Breedon	3	–	3
Langford	3	–	3
Owen	2	–	2
Wassall	2	–	2
Whalley	2	–	2
Morton	1	–	1
Redwood	1	–	1
Robbie	1	–	1
Robertson	1	–	1

GOALSCORERS

PLAYER	LGE	FAC	TOT
Mutch	21	2	23
Rowley	19	–	19
Bamford	16	–	16
Manley	14	1	15
Bryant	8	–	8
Cape	2	–	2
Chester	1	–	1
Gardner	1	–	1
Griffiths	1	–	1
Lang	1	–	1
own goal	1	–	1

RESULTS & ATTENDANCES SUMMARY

		P	W	D	L	F	A	TOTAL	AVGE
League	H	21	16	3	2	55	16	542471	25832
	A	21	6	9	6	30	27	370054	17622
	TOTAL	42	22	12	8	85	43	912525	21727
FA Cup	H	1	0	0	1	0	2	34440	34440
	A	2	1	1	0	3	1	58130	29065
	TOTAL	3	1	1	1	3	3	92570	30857
Overall	H	22	16	3	3	55	18	576911	26223
	A	23	7	10	6	33	28	428184	18617
	TOTAL	45	23	13	9	88	46	1005095	22335

FINAL TABLE - LEAGUE DIVISION TWO

		P	HOME W	HOME D	HOME L	HOME F	HOME A	AWAY W	AWAY D	AWAY L	AWAY F	AWAY A	PTS	GD
1	MANCHESTER UNITED	42	16	3	2	55	16	6	9	6	30	27	56	42
2	Charlton Athletic	42	15	6	0	53	17	7	5	9	32	41	55	27
3	Sheffield United	42	15	4	2	51	15	5	8	8	28	35	52	29
4	West Ham United	42	13	5	3	51	23	9	3	9	39	45	52	22
5	Tottenham Hotspur	42	12	6	3	60	25	6	7	8	31	30	49	36
6	Leicester City	42	14	5	2	53	19	5	5	11	26	38	48	22
7	Plymouth Argyle	42	15	2	4	50	20	5	6	10	21	37	48	14
8	Newcastle United	42	13	5	3	56	27	7	1	13	32	52	46	9
9	Fulham	42	11	6	4	58	24	4	8	9	18	28	44	24
10	Blackpool	42	14	3	4	64	34	4	4	13	29	38	43	21
11	Norwich City	42	14	2	5	47	24	3	7	11	25	41	43	7
12	Bradford City	42	12	7	2	32	18	3	6	12	23	47	43	-10
13	Swansea City	42	11	3	7	42	26	4	6	11	25	50	39	-9
14	Bury	42	10	6	5	41	27	3	6	12	25	57	38	-18
15	Burnley	42	9	8	4	35	21	3	5	13	15	38	37	-9
16	Bradford Park Avenue	42	13	6	2	43	26	1	3	17	19	58	37	-22
17	Southampton	42	11	3	7	32	24	3	6	12	15	41	37	-18
18	Doncaster Rovers	42	10	7	4	28	17	4	2	15	23	54	37	-20
19	Nottingham Forest	42	8	8	5	43	22	4	3	14	26	54	35	-7
20	Blackburn	42	9	4	8	40	32	3	5	13	14	48	33	-26
21	Port Vale	42	10	5	6	34	30	2	3	16	22	76	32	-50
22	Hull City	42	4	7	10	33	45	1	3	17	14	66	20	-64

SEASON 1936/37

Match # 1650	Saturday 29/08/36	Football League Division 1	at Old Trafford	Attendance 42731
Result:	**Manchester United 1 Wolverhampton Wanderers 1**
Teamsheet:	John, Redwood, Porter, Brown, Vose, McKay, Bryant, Mutch, Bamford, Rowley, Manley
Scorer(s):	Bamford

Match # 1651	Wednesday 02/09/36	Football League Division 1	at Leeds Road	Attendance 12612
Result:	**Huddersfield Town 3 Manchester United 1**
Teamsheet:	John, Redwood, McLenahan, Brown, Vose, McKay, Bryant, McClelland, Bamford, Rowley, Manley
Scorer(s):	Manley

Match # 1652	Saturday 05/09/36	Football League Division 1	at Baseball Ground	Attendance 21194
Result:	**Derby County 5 Manchester United 4**
Teamsheet:	John, Redwood, McLenahan, Brown, Vose, McKay, Bryant, Wassall, Bamford, Ferrier, Manley
Scorer(s):	Bamford 3, Wassall

Match # 1653	Wednesday 09/09/36	Football League Division 1	at Old Trafford	Attendance 26839
Result:	**Manchester United 3 Huddersfield Town 1**
Teamsheet:	John, Redwood, Mellor, Brown, Vose, McKay, Bryant, Wassall, Bamford, Mutch, Manley
Scorer(s):	Bamford, Bryant, Mutch

Match # 1654	Saturday 12/09/36	Football League Division 1	at Old Trafford	Attendance 68796
Result:	**Manchester United 3 Manchester City 2**
Teamsheet:	John, Redwood, Roughton, Brown, Vose, McKay, Bryant, Wassall, Bamford, Mutch, Manley
Scorer(s):	Bamford, Bryant, Manley

Match # 1655	Saturday 19/09/36	Football League Division 1	at Old Trafford	Attendance 40933
Result:	**Manchester United 1 Sheffield Wednesday 1**
Teamsheet:	John, Redwood, Roughton, Brown, Vose, McKay, Bryant, Wassall, Bamford, Mutch, Manley
Scorer(s):	Bamford

Match # 1656	Saturday 26/09/36	Football League Division 1	at Deepdale	Attendance 24149
Result:	**Preston North End 3 Manchester United 1**
Teamsheet:	John, Redwood, Roughton, Brown, Vose, McKay, Bryant, Wassall, Bamford, Ferrier, Manley
Scorer(s):	Bamford

Match # 1657	Saturday 03/10/36	Football League Division 1	at Old Trafford	Attendance 55884
Result:	**Manchester United 2 Arsenal 0**
Teamsheet:	John, Redwood, Roughton, Brown, Vose, McKay, Bryant, Mutch, Bamford, Rowley, Manley
Scorer(s):	Bryant, Rowley

Match # 1658	Saturday 10/10/36	Football League Division 1	at Griffin Park	Attendance 28019
Result:	**Brentford 4 Manchester United 0**
Teamsheet:	John, Redwood, Roughton, Brown, Vose, McKay, Bryant, Mutch, Bamford, Rowley, Manley

Match # 1659	Saturday 17/10/36	Football League Division 1	at Fratton Park	Attendance 19845
Result:	**Portsmouth 2 Manchester United 1**
Teamsheet:	John, Griffiths, Roughton, Brown, Vose, McKay, Bryant, Wassall, Bamford, Rowley, Manley
Scorer(s):	Manley

Match # 1660	Saturday 24/10/36	Football League Division 1	at Old Trafford	Attendance 29859
Result:	**Manchester United 0 Chelsea 0**
Teamsheet:	John, Griffiths, Roughton, Brown, Vose, Whalley, Bryant, Mutch, Bamford, Rowley, Manley

Match # 1661	Saturday 31/10/36	Football League Division 1	at Victoria Ground	Attendance 22464
Result:	**Stoke City 3 Manchester United 0**
Teamsheet:	John, Griffiths, Roughton, Brown, Vose, Whalley, Bryant, Mutch, Bamford, Rowley, Manley

Match # 1662	Saturday 07/11/36	Football League Division 1	at Old Trafford	Attendance 26084
Result:	**Manchester United 0 Charlton Athletic 0**
Teamsheet:	John, Griffiths, Roughton, Brown, Vose, McKay, Bryant, Mutch, Bamford, Ferrier, Manley

Match # 1663	Saturday 14/11/36	Football League Division 1	at Blundell Park	Attendance 9844
Result:	**Grimsby Town 6 Manchester United 2**
Teamsheet:	John, Griffiths, Mellor, Brown, Vose, McKay, Bryant, Mutch, Bamford, Ferrier, Manley
Scorer(s):	Bryant, Mutch

Match # 1664	Saturday 21/11/36	Football League Division 1	at Old Trafford	Attendance 26419
Result:	**Manchester United 2 Liverpool 5**
Teamsheet:	John, Griffiths, Roughton, Brown, McLenahan, McKay, Bryant, Mutch, Thompson, Ferrier, Manley
Scorer(s):	Manley, Thompson

Match # 1665	Saturday 28/11/36	Football League Division 1	at Elland Road	Attendance 17610
Result:	**Leeds United 2 Manchester United 1**
Teamsheet:	Breen, Roughton, Porter, Winterbottom, Brown, McKay, Bryant, Mutch, Bamford, Thompson, Manley
Scorer(s):	Bryant

Match # 1666	Saturday 05/12/36	Football League Division 1	at Old Trafford	Attendance 16544
Result:	**Manchester United 1 Birmingham City 2**
Teamsheet:	Breen, Redwood, Roughton, Winterbottom, Vose, McKay, Bryant, Mutch, Bamford, Rowley, Manley
Scorer(s):	Mutch

Match # 1667	Saturday 12/12/36	Football League Division 1	at Ayresome Park	Attendance 11970
Result:	**Middlesbrough 3 Manchester United 2**
Teamsheet:	Breen, Redwood, Roughton, Winterbottom, Brown, Manley, Bryant, Wassall, Mutch, Rowley, Halton
Scorer(s):	Halton, Manley

SEASON 1936/37 (continued)

Match # 1668 Saturday 19/12/36   Football League Division 1   at Old Trafford   Attendance 21051
Result: **Manchester United 2 West Bromwich Albion 2**
Teamsheet: Breen, Redwood, Roughton, Winterbottom, Brown, Manley, Bryant, Mutch, Bamford, McKay, Halton
Scorer(s):   McKay, Mutch

Match # 1669 Friday 25/12/36   Football League Division 1   at Old Trafford   Attendance 47658
Result: **Manchester United 1 Bolton Wanderers 0**
Teamsheet: Breen, Redwood, Roughton, Brown, Winterbottom, Manley, Bryant, Mutch, Bamford, McKay, Halton
Scorer(s):   Bamford

Match # 1670 Saturday 26/12/36   Football League Division 1   at Molineux   Attendance 41525
Result: **Wolverhampton Wanderers 3 Manchester United 1**
Teamsheet: Breen, Redwood, Roughton, Brown, Winterbottom, Manley, Bryant, Mutch, Bamford, McKay, Halton
Scorer(s):   McKay

Match # 1671 Tuesday 28/12/36   Football League Division 1   at Burnden Park   Attendance 11801
Result: **Bolton Wanderers 0 Manchester United 4**
Teamsheet: Breen, Redwood, Roughton, Brown, Winterbottom, Whalley, Bryant, Mutch, Bamford, McKay, Lang
Scorer(s):   Bryant 2, McKay 2

Match # 1672 Friday 01/01/37   Football League Division 1   at Old Trafford   Attendance 46257
Result: **Manchester United 2 Sunderland 1**
Teamsheet: Breen, Redwood, Roughton, Brown, Winterbottom, Whalley, Bryant, Mutch, Bamford, McKay, Lang
Scorer(s):   Bryant, Mutch

Match # 1673 Saturday 02/01/37   Football League Division 1   at Old Trafford   Attendance 31883
Result: **Manchester United 2 Derby County 2**
Teamsheet: Breedon, Redwood, Roughton, Brown, Winterbottom, Whalley, Cape, Mutch, Rowley, McKay, Lang
Scorer(s):   Rowley 2

Match # 1674 Saturday 09/01/37   Football League Division 1   at Maine Road   Attendance 64862
Result: **Manchester City 1 Manchester United 0**
Teamsheet: Breen, Redwood, Roughton, Brown, Winterbottom, Whalley, Mutch, Vose, Rowley, McKay, Lang

Match # 1675 Saturday 16/01/37   FA Cup 3rd Round   at Old Trafford   Attendance 36668
Result: **Manchester United 1 Reading 0**
Teamsheet: Breen, Vose, Roughton, Brown, Winterbottom, Whalley, Bryant, Mutch, Bamford, McKay, Lang
Scorer(s):   Bamford

Match # 1676 Saturday 23/01/37   Football League Division 1   at Hillsborough   Attendance 8658
Result: **Sheffield Wednesday 1 Manchester United 0**
Teamsheet: Breen, Redwood, Roughton, Brown, Winterbottom, Whalley, Bryant, Mutch, Bamford, Baird, Wrigglesworth

Match # 1675 Saturday 30/01/37   FA Cup 4th Round   at Highbury   Attendance 45637
Result: **Arsenal 5 Manchester United 0**
Teamsheet: Breen, Redwood, Roughton, Brown, Winterbottom, Whalley, Bryant, Mutch, Bamford, McKay, Wrigglesworth

Match # 1678 Wednesday 03/02/37   Football League Division 1   at Old Trafford   Attendance 13225
Result: **Manchester United 1 Preston North End 1**
Teamsheet: Breen, Redwood, Roughton, Brown, Winterbottom, Whalley, Bryant, Baird, Rowley, McKay, Wrigglesworth
Scorer(s):   Wrigglesworth

Match # 1679 Saturday 06/02/37   Football League Division 1   at Highbury   Attendance 37236
Result: **Arsenal 1 Manchester United 1**
Teamsheet: Breen, Griffiths, Winterbottom, Whalley, Vose, Manley, Bryant, Baird, Rowley, McKay, Lang
Scorer(s):   Rowley

Match # 1680 Saturday 13/02/37   Football League Division 1   at Old Trafford   Attendance 31942
Result: **Manchester United 1 Brentford 3**
Teamsheet: Breen, Griffiths, Winterbottom, Whalley, Vose, Manley, Bryant, Baird, Rowley, McKay, Lang
Scorer(s):   Baird

Match # 1681 Saturday 20/02/37   Football League Division 1   at Old Trafford   Attendance 19416
Result: **Manchester United 0 Portsmouth 1**
Teamsheet: Breen, Griffiths, Roughton, Winterbottom, Vose, Whalley, Bryant, Mutch, Rowley, Baird, Manley

Match # 1682 Saturday 27/02/37   Football League Division 1   at Stamford Bridge   Attendance 16382
Result: **Chelsea 4 Manchester United 2**
Teamsheet: Breen, Griffiths, Roughton, Winterbottom, Vose, Whalley, Bryant, Gladwin, Bamford, Baird, Wrigglesworth
Scorer(s):   Bamford, Gladwin

Match # 1683 Saturday 06/03/37   Football League Division 1   at Old Trafford   Attendance 24660
Result: **Manchester United 2 Stoke City 1**
Teamsheet: Breen, Griffiths, Roughton, Whalley, Winterbottom, McKay, Bryant, McClelland, Bamford, Baird, Wrigglesworth
Scorer(s):   Baird, McClelland

Match # 1684 Saturday 13/03/37   Football League Division 1   at The Valley   Attendance 25943
Result: **Charlton Athletic 3 Manchester United 0**
Teamsheet: Breen, Griffiths, Roughton, Whalley, Winterbottom, McKay, Bryant, Mutch, Bamford, Baird, Wrigglesworth

Match # 1685 Saturday 20/03/37   Football League Division 1   at Old Trafford   Attendance 26636
Result: **Manchester United 1 Grimsby Town 1**
Teamsheet: Breen, Griffiths, Roughton, Brown, Winterbottom, Whalley, Cape, Gladwin, Rowley, Baird, Bryant
Scorer(s):   Cape

SEASON 1936/37 (continued)

Match # 1686   Friday 26/03/37   Football League Division 1   at Old Trafford   Attendance 30071
Result: **Manchester United 2 Everton 1**
Teamsheet: Breen, Griffiths, Roughton, Brown, Winterbottom, Whalley, Cape, Gladwin, Mutch, Baird, Manley
Scorer(s):   Baird, Mutch

Match # 1687   Saturday 27/03/37   Football League Division 1   at Anfield   Attendance 25319
Result: **Liverpool 2 Manchester United 0**
Teamsheet: Breen, Griffiths, Roughton, Brown, Winterbottom, Whalley, Cape, Gladwin, Mutch, Baird, Manley

Match # 1688   Monday 29/03/37   Football League Division 1   at Goodison Park   Attendance 28395
Result: **Everton 2 Manchester United 3**
Teamsheet: Breen, Griffiths, Roughton, Brown, Vose, Manley, Bryant, Baird, Mutch, Ferrier, Lang
Scorer(s):   Bryant, Ferrier, Mutch

Match # 1689   Saturday 03/04/37   Football League Division 1   at Old Trafford   Attendance 34429
Result: **Manchester United 0 Leeds United 0**
Teamsheet: Breen, Griffiths, Roughton, Brown, Vose, Manley, Bryant, Baird, Mutch, Rowley, Lang

Match # 1690   Saturday 10/04/37   Football League Division 1   at St Andrews   Attendance 19130
Result: **Birmingham City 2 Manchester United 2**
Teamsheet: Breen, Griffiths, Jones, Gladwin, Vose, Whalley, Wrigglesworth, Gardner, Bamford, McClelland, Manley
Scorer(s):   Bamford 2

Match # 1691   Saturday 17/04/37   Football League Division 1   at Old Trafford   Attendance 17656
Result: **Manchester United 2 Middlesbrough 1**
Teamsheet: Breen, Griffiths, Redwood, Gladwin, Vose, Whalley, Bryant, Gardner, Bamford, McClelland, Wrigglesworth
Scorer(s):   Bamford, Bryant

Match # 1692   Wednesday 21/04/37   Football League Division 1   at Roker Park   Attendance 12876
Result: **Sunderland 1 Manchester United 1**
Teamsheet: Breen, Griffiths, Roughton, Gladwin, Vose, McKay, Bryant, Gardner, Bamford, McClelland, Manley
Scorer(s):   Bamford

Match # 1693   Saturday 24/04/37   Football League Division 1   at The Hawthorns   Attendance 16234
Result: **West Bromwich Albion 1 Manchester United 0**
Teamsheet: Breen, Griffiths, Roughton, Gladwin, Vose, McKay, Bryant, Gardner, Bamford, Baird, Manley

SEASON 1936/37 SUMMARY

APPEARANCES

PLAYER	LGE	FAC	TOT
Bryant	37	2	39
Roughton	33	2	35
Brown	31	2	33
Bamford	29	2	31
Manley	31	–	31
McKay	29	2	31
Mutch	28	2	30
Breen	26	2	28
Vose	26	1	27
Winterbottom	21	2	23
Redwood	21	1	22
Griffiths	21	–	21
Whalley	19	2	21
Rowley	17	–	17
John	15	–	15
Baird	14	–	14
Lang	8	1	9
Gladwin	8	–	8
Wrigglesworth	7	1	8
Wassall	7	–	7
Ferrier	6	–	6
McClelland	5	–	5
Cape	4	–	4
Gardner	4	–	4
Halton	4	–	4
McLenahan	3	–	3
Mellor	2	–	2
Porter	2	–	2
Thompson	2	–	2
Breedon	1	–	1
Jones	1	–	1

GOALSCORERS

PLAYER	LGE	FAC	TOT
Bamford	14	1	15
Bryant	10	–	10
Mutch	7	–	7
Manley	5	–	5
McKay	4	–	4
Rowley	4	–	4
Baird	3	–	3
Cape	1	–	1
Ferrier	1	–	1
Gladwin	1	–	1
Halton	1	–	1
McClelland	1	–	1
Thompson	1	–	1
Wassall	1	–	1
Wrigglesworth	1	–	1

RESULTS & ATTENDANCES SUMMARY

		P	W	D	L	F	A	TOTAL	AVGE
League	H	21	8	9	4	29	26	678973	32332
	A	21	2	3	16	26	52	476068	22670
TOTAL		42	10	12	20	55	78	1155041	27501
FA Cup	H	1	1	0	0	1	0	36668	36668
	A	1	0	0	1	0	5	45637	45637
TOTAL		2	1	0	1	1	5	82305	41153
Overall	H	22	9	9	4	30	26	715641	32529
	A	22	2	3	17	26	57	521705	23714
TOTAL		44	11	12	21	56	83	1237346	28122

FINAL TABLE – LEAGUE DIVISION ONE

		P	W	D	L	F	A	W	D	L	F	A	PTS	GD
			HOME					AWAY						
1	Manchester City	42	15	5	1	56	22	7	8	6	51	39	57	46
2	Charlton Athletic	42	15	5	1	37	13	6	7	8	21	36	54	9
3	Arsenal	42	10	10	1	43	20	8	6	7	37	29	52	31
4	Derby County	42	13	3	5	58	39	8	4	9	38	51	49	6
5	Wolverhampton Wanderers	42	16	2	3	63	24	5	3	13	21	43	47	17
6	Brentford	42	14	5	2	58	32	4	5	12	24	46	46	4
7	Middlesbrough	42	14	6	1	49	22	5	2	14	25	49	46	3
8	Sunderland	42	17	2	2	59	24	2	4	15	30	63	44	2
9	Portsmouth	42	13	3	5	41	29	4	7	10	21	37	44	-4
10	Stoke City	42	12	6	3	52	27	3	6	12	20	30	42	15
11	Birmingham City	42	9	7	5	36	24	4	8	9	28	36	41	4
12	Grimsby Town	42	13	3	5	60	32	4	4	13	26	49	41	5
13	Chelsea	42	11	6	4	36	21	3	7	11	16	34	41	-3
14	Preston North End	42	10	6	5	35	28	4	7	10	21	39	41	-11
15	Huddersfield Town	42	12	5	4	39	21	0	10	11	23	43	39	-2
16	West Bromwich Albion	42	13	3	5	45	32	3	3	15	32	66	38	-21
17	Everton	42	12	7	2	56	23	2	2	17	25	55	37	3
18	Liverpool	42	9	8	4	38	26	3	3	15	24	58	35	-22
19	Leeds United	42	14	3	4	44	20	1	1	19	16	60	34	-20
20	Bolton Wanderers	42	6	6	9	22	33	4	8	9	21	33	34	-23
21	MANCHESTER UNITED	42	8	9	4	29	26	2	3	16	26	52	32	-23
22	Sheffield Wednesday	42	8	5	8	32	29	1	7	13	21	40	30	-16

SEASON 1937/38

Match # 1694	Saturday 28/08/37	Football League Division 2	at Old Trafford	Attendance 29446

Match # 1694 — Saturday 28/08/37 — Football League Division 2 — at Old Trafford — Attendance 29446
Result: **Manchester United 3 Newcastle United 0**
Teamsheet: Breen, Griffiths, Roughton, Gladwin, Vose, McKay, Bryant, Murray, Bamford, Baird, Manley
Scorer(s): Manley 2, Bryant

Match # 1695 — Monday 30/08/37 — Football League Division 2 — at Highfield Road — Attendance 30575
Result: **Coventry City 1 Manchester United 0**
Teamsheet: Breen, Griffiths, Roughton, Gladwin, Vose, McKay, Bryant, Murray, Bamford, Baird, Manley

Match # 1696 — Saturday 04/09/37 — Football League Division 2 — at Kenilworth Road — Attendance 20610
Result: **Luton Town 1 Manchester United 0**
Teamsheet: Breen, Griffiths, Roughton, Gladwin, Vose, McKay, Bryant, Murray, Mutch, Baird, Manley

Match # 1697 — Wednesday 08/09/37 — Football League Division 2 — at Old Trafford — Attendance 17455
Result: **Manchester United 2 Coventry City 2**
Teamsheet: Breen, Griffiths, Roughton, Gladwin, Vose, McKay, Bryant, Wassall, Bamford, Baird, Manley
Scorer(s): Bamford, Bryant

Match # 1698 — Saturday 11/09/37 — Football League Division 2 — at Old Trafford — Attendance 22934
Result: **Manchester United 4 Barnsley 1**
Teamsheet: Breen, Griffiths, Roughton, Brown, Winterbottom, McKay, Bryant, Wassall, Bamford, Ferrier, Manley
Scorer(s): Bamford 3, Manley

Match # 1699 — Monday 13/09/37 — Football League Division 2 — at Gigg Lane — Attendance 9954
Result: **Bury 1 Manchester United 2**
Teamsheet: Breen, Griffiths, Roughton, Brown, Winterbottom, McKay, Bryant, Wassall, Bamford, Ferrier, Manley
Scorer(s): Ferrier 2

Match # 1700 — Saturday 18/09/37 — Football League Division 2 — at Edgeley Park — Attendance 24386
Result: **Stockport County 1 Manchester United 0**
Teamsheet: Breen, Griffiths, Roughton, Brown, Winterbottom, McKay, Bryant, Mutch, Bamford, Ferrier, Manley

Match # 1701 — Saturday 25/09/37 — Football League Division 2 — at Old Trafford — Attendance 22729
Result: **Manchester United 1 Southampton 2**
Teamsheet: Breen, Griffiths, Roughton, Brown, Winterbottom, McKay, Bryant, Gladwin, Thompson, Carey, Manley
Scorer(s): Manley

Match # 1702 — Saturday 02/10/37 — Football League Division 2 — at Old Trafford — Attendance 20105
Result: **Manchester United 0 Sheffield United 1**
Teamsheet: Breen, Griffiths, Roughton, Brown, Vose, McKay, Bryant, Carey, Bamford, Baird, Manley

Match # 1703 — Saturday 09/10/37 — Football League Division 2 — at White Hart Lane — Attendance 31189
Result: **Tottenham Hotspur 0 Manchester United 1**
Teamsheet: Breen, Griffiths, Roughton, Brown, Vose, McKay, Bryant, Wassall, Ferrier, Baird, Manley
Scorer(s): Manley

Match # 1704 — Saturday 16/10/37 — Football League Division 2 — at Ewood Park — Attendance 19580
Result: **Blackburn Rovers 1 Manchester United 1**
Teamsheet: Breen, Griffiths, Roughton, Brown, Vose, McKay, Bryant, Wassall, Bamford, Baird, Wrigglesworth
Scorer(s): Bamford

Match # 1705 — Saturday 23/10/37 — Football League Division 2 — at Old Trafford — Attendance 16379
Result: **Manchester United 1 Sheffield Wednesday 0**
Teamsheet: Breedon, Griffiths, Roughton, Brown, Vose, McKay, Bryant, Murray, Bamford, Ferrier, Rowley
Scorer(s): Ferrier

Match # 1706 — Saturday 30/10/37 — Football League Division 2 — at Craven Cottage — Attendance 17350
Result: **Fulham 1 Manchester United 0**
Teamsheet: Breen, Griffiths, Roughton, Brown, Vose, McKay, Wrigglesworth, Wassall, Bamford, Whalley, Manley

Match # 1707 — Saturday 06/11/37 — Football League Division 2 — at Old Trafford — Attendance 18359
Result: **Manchester United 0 Plymouth Argyle 0**
Teamsheet: Breen, Redwood, Roughton, Brown, Vose, Whalley, Wrigglesworth, Wassall, Bamford, McKay, Manley

Match # 1708 — Saturday 13/11/37 — Football League Division 2 — at Saltergate — Attendance 17407
Result: **Chesterfield 1 Manchester United 7**
Teamsheet: Breedon, Redwood, Roughton, Brown, Vose, Whalley, Bryant, Baird, Bamford, Pearson, Manley
Scorer(s): Bamford 4, Baird, Bryant, Manley

Match # 1709 — Saturday 20/11/37 — Football League Division 2 — at Old Trafford — Attendance 33193
Result: **Manchester United 3 Aston Villa 1**
Teamsheet: Breedon, Redwood, Roughton, Brown, Vose, McKay, Bryant, Baird, Bamford, Pearson, Manley
Scorer(s): Bamford, Manley, Pearson

Match # 1710 — Saturday 27/11/37 — Football League Division 2 — at Carrow Road — Attendance 17397
Result: **Norwich City 2 Manchester United 3**
Teamsheet: Breedon, Redwood, Roughton, Brown, Vose, McKay, Bryant, Baird, Bamford, Pearson, Manley
Scorer(s): Baird, Bryant, Pearson

Match # 1711 — Saturday 04/12/37 — Football League Division 2 — at Old Trafford — Attendance 17782
Result: **Manchester United 5 Swansea City 1**
Teamsheet: Breedon, Redwood, Roughton, Whalley, Vose, McKay, Bryant, Baird, Bamford, Pearson, Rowley
Scorer(s): Rowley 4, Bryant

SEASON 1937/38 (continued)

Match # 1712 Saturday 11/12/37   Football League Division 2   at Park Avenue   Attendance 12004
Result: **Bradford Park Avenue 4 Manchester United 0**
Teamsheet: Breedon, Redwood, Roughton, Whalley, Jones, McKay, Bryant, Baird, Bamford, Pearson, Rowley

Match # 1713 Monday 27/12/37   Football League Division 2   at Old Trafford   Attendance 30778
Result: **Manchester United 4 Nottingham Forest 3**
Teamsheet: Breedon, Redwood, Roughton, Whalley, Vose, McKay, Wrigglesworth, Baird, Bamford, Pearson, Rowley
Scorer(s):   Baird 2, McKay, Wrigglesworth

Match # 1714 Tuesday 28/12/37   Football League Division 2   at City Ground   Attendance 19283
Result: **Nottingham Forest 2 Manchester United 3**
Teamsheet: Breedon, Redwood, Roughton, Griffiths, Vose, McKay, Bryant, Baird, Bamford, Carey, Rowley
Scorer(s):   Bamford, Bryant, Carey

Match # 1715 Saturday 01/01/38   Football League Division 2   at St James' Park   Attendance 40088
Result: **Newcastle United 2 Manchester United 2**
Teamsheet: Breedon, Redwood, Roughton, Savage, Griffiths, McKay, Bryant, Baird, Bamford, Carey, Rowley
Scorer(s):   Bamford, Rowley

Match # 1716 Saturday 08/01/38   FA Cup 3rd Round   at Old Trafford   Attendance 49004
Result: **Manchester United 3 Yeovil Town 0**
Teamsheet: Breen, Redwood, Roughton, Brown, Vose, McKay, Bryant, Baird, Bamford, Pearson, Rowley
Scorer(s):   Baird, Bamford, Pearson

Match # 1717 Saturday 15/01/38   Football League Division 2   at Old Trafford   Attendance 16845
Result: **Manchester United 4 Luton Town 2**
Teamsheet: Breen, Redwood, Roughton, Savage, Vose, McKay, Bryant, Baird, Bamford, Carey, Rowley
Scorer(s):   Bamford, Bryant, Carey, McKay

Match # 1718 Saturday 22/01/38   FA Cup 4th Round   at Oakwell   Attendance 35549
Result: **Barnsley 2 Manchester United 2**
Teamsheet: Breen, Redwood, Roughton, Brown, Vose, McKay, Bryant, Baird, Bamford, Carey, Rowley
Scorer(s):   Baird, Carey

Match # 1719 Wednesday 26/01/38   FA Cup 4th Round Replay   at Old Trafford   Attendance 33601
Result: **Manchester United 1 Barnsley 0**
Teamsheet: Breen, Redwood, Roughton, Savage, Vose, McKay, Bryant, Baird, Bamford, Carey, Rowley
Scorer(s):   Baird

Match # 1720 Saturday 29/01/38   Football League Division 2   at Old Trafford   Attendance 31852
Result: **Manchester United 3 Stockport County 1**
Teamsheet: Breen, Griffiths, Redwood, Savage, Vose, McKay, Bryant, Baird, Bamford, Carey, Rowley
Scorer(s):   Bamford, Bryant, McKay

Match # 1721 Wednesday 02/02/38   Football League Division 2   at Oakwell   Attendance 7859
Result: **Barnsley 2 Manchester United 2**
Teamsheet: Breen, Griffiths, Redwood, Savage, Vose, Porter, Bryant, Baird, Smith, Carey, Rowley
Scorer(s):   Rowley, Smith

Match # 1722 Saturday 05/02/38   Football League Division 2   at The Dell   Attendance 20354
Result: **Southampton 3 Manchester United 3**
Teamsheet: Breen, Griffiths, Redwood, Brown, Vose, Porter, Bryant, Baird, Smith, Carey, Rowley
Scorer(s):   Redwood 2, Baird

Match # 1723 Saturday 12/02/38   FA Cup 5th Round   at Griffin Park   Attendance 24147
Result: **Brentford 2 Manchester United 0**
Teamsheet: Breen, Redwood, Roughton, Brown, Vose, Manley, Bryant, Baird, Bamford, Carey, Rowley

Match # 1724 Thursday 17/02/38   Football League Division 2   at Bramall Lane   Attendance 17754
Result: **Sheffield United 1 Manchester United 2**
Teamsheet: Breen, Redwood, Roughton, Brown, Vose, Manley, Bryant, Baird, Smith, Carey, Rowley
Scorer(s):   Bryant, Smith

Match # 1725 Saturday 19/02/38   Football League Division 2   at Old Trafford   Attendance 34631
Result: **Manchester United 0 Tottenham Hotspur 0**
Teamsheet: Breen, Redwood, Roughton, Brown, Vose, McKay, Bryant, Baird, Smith, Carey, Manley

Match # 1726 Wednesday 23/02/38   Football League Division 2   at Old Trafford   Attendance 14572
Result: **Manchester United 4 West Ham United 0**
Teamsheet: Breen, Redwood, Roughton, Brown, Manley, McKay, Bryant, Wassall, Smith, Baird, Rowley
Scorer(s):   Baird 2, Smith, Wassall

Match # 1727 Saturday 26/02/38   Football League Division 2   at Old Trafford   Attendance 30892
Result: **Manchester United 2 Blackburn Rovers 1**
Teamsheet: Breen, Redwood, Roughton, Brown, Manley, McKay, Bryant, Wassall, Smith, Baird, Rowley
Scorer(s):   Baird, Bryant

Match # 1728 Saturday 05/03/38   Football League Division 2   at Hillsborough   Attendance 37156
Result: **Sheffield Wednesday 1 Manchester United 3**
Teamsheet: Breen, Redwood, Roughton, Brown, Vose, McKay, Bryant, Baird, Smith, Carey, Rowley
Scorer(s):   Baird, Brown, Rowley

Match # 1729 Saturday 12/03/38   Football League Division 2   at Old Trafford   Attendance 30636
Result: **Manchester United 1 Fulham 0**
Teamsheet: Breen, Redwood, Roughton, Brown, Vose, McKay, Bryant, Baird, Smith, Carey, Rowley
Scorer(s):   Baird

SEASON 1937/38 (continued)

Match # 1730 Saturday 19/03/38   Football League Division 2   at Home Park   Attendance 20311
Result: **Plymouth Argyle 1 Manchester United 1**
Teamsheet: Breen, Redwood, Roughton, Brown, Vose, McKay, Bryant, Baird, Bamford, Carey, Rowley
Scorer(s):   Rowley

Match # 1731 Saturday 26/03/38   Football League Division 2   at Old Trafford   Attendance 27311
Result: **Manchester United 4 Chesterfield 1**
Teamsheet: Breen, Redwood, Roughton, Brown, Vose, McKay, Bryant, Baird, Smith, Carey, Rowley
Scorer(s):   Smith 2, Bryant, Carey

Match # 1732 Saturday 02/04/38   Football League Division 2   at Villa Park   Attendance 54654
Result: **Aston Villa 3 Manchester United 0**
Teamsheet: Breen, Redwood, Roughton, Brown, Vose, McKay, Bryant, Baird, Smith, Carey, Rowley

Match # 1733 Saturday 09/04/38   Football League Division 2   at Old Trafford   Attendance 25879
Result: **Manchester United 0 Norwich City 0**
Teamsheet: Breen, Redwood, Roughton, Brown, Vose, McKay, Bryant, Baird, Smith, Carey, Rowley

Match # 1734 Friday 15/04/38   Football League Division 2   at Turf Moor   Attendance 28459
Result: **Burnley 1 Manchester United 0**
Teamsheet: Breen, Redwood, Roughton, Brown, Vose, McKay, Bryant, Baird, Smith, Pearson, Rowley

Match # 1735 Saturday 16/04/38   Football League Division 2   at Vetch Field   Attendance 13811
Result: **Swansea City 2 Manchester United 2**
Teamsheet: Breen, Redwood, Roughton, Gladwin, Vose, Manley, Bryant, Baird, Bamford, Smith, Rowley
Scorer(s):   Rowley, Smith

Match # 1736 Monday 18/04/38   Football League Division 2   at Old Trafford   Attendance 35808
Result: **Manchester United 4 Burnley 0**
Teamsheet: Breen, Redwood, Roughton, Brown, Vose, McKay, Bryant, Baird, Smith, Pearson, Rowley
Scorer(s):   McKay 2, Baird, Bryant

Match # 1737 Saturday 23/04/38   Football League Division 2   at Old Trafford   Attendance 28919
Result: **Manchester United 3 Bradford Park Avenue 1**
Teamsheet: Breen, Redwood, Roughton, Brown, Vose, McKay, Bryant, Baird, Smith, Pearson, Rowley
Scorer(s):   Baird, McKay, Smith

Match # 1738 Saturday 30/04/38   Football League Division 2   at Upton Park   Attendance 14816
Result: **West Ham United 1 Manchester United 0**
Teamsheet: Breen, Redwood, Roughton, Gladwin, Vose, McKay, Bryant, Baird, Smith, Pearson, Rowley

Match # 1739 Saturday 07/05/38   Football League Division 2   at Old Trafford   Attendance 53604
Result: **Manchester United 2 Bury 0**
Teamsheet: Breen, Redwood, Roughton, Brown, Manley, McKay, Bryant, Baird, Smith, Pearson, Rowley
Scorer(s):   McKay, Smith

SEASON 1937/38 SUMMARY

APPEARANCES

PLAYER	LGE	FAC	TOT
Bryant	39	4	43
Roughton	39	4	43
McKay	37	3	40
Baird	35	4	39
Breen	33	4	37
Vose	33	4	37
Redwood	29	4	33
Brown	28	3	31
Rowley	25	4	29
Bamford	23	4	27
Manley	21	1	22
Carey	16	3	19
Griffiths	18	–	18
Smith	17	–	17
Pearson	11	1	12
Breedon	9	–	9
Wassall	9	–	9
Gladwin	7	–	7
Whalley	6	–	6
Ferrier	5	–	5
Savage	4	1	5
Murray	4	–	4
Winterbottom	4	–	4
Wrigglesworth	4	–	4
Mutch	2	–	2
Porter	2	–	2
Jones	1	–	1
Thompson	1	–	1

GOALSCORERS

PLAYER	LGE	FAC	TOT
Bamford	14	1	15
Baird	12	3	15
Bryant	12	–	12
Rowley	9	–	9
Smith	8	–	8
Manley	7	–	7
McKay	7	–	7
Carey	3	1	4
Ferrier	3	–	3
Pearson	2	1	3
Redwood	2	–	2
Brown	1	–	1
Wassall	1	–	1
Wrigglesworth	1	–	1

RESULTS & ATTENDANCES SUMMARY

		P	W	D	L	F	A	TOTAL	AVGE
League	H	21	15	3	3	50	18	560109	26672
	A	21	7	6	8	32	32	474997	22619
	TOTAL	42	22	9	11	82	50	1035106	24645
FA Cup	H	2	2	0	0	4	0	82605	41303
	A	2	0	1	1	2	4	59696	29848
	TOTAL	4	2	1	1	6	4	142301	35575
Overall	H	23	17	3	3	54	18	642714	27944
	A	23	7	7	9	34	36	534693	23248
	TOTAL	46	24	10	12	88	54	1177407	25596

FINAL TABLE – LEAGUE DIVISION TWO

		P	HOME W	HOME D	HOME L	HOME F	HOME A	AWAY W	AWAY D	AWAY L	AWAY F	AWAY A	PTS	GD
1	Aston Villa	42	17	2	2	50	12	8	5	8	23	23	57	38
2	MANCHESTER UNITED	42	15	3	3	50	18	7	6	8	32	32	53	32
3	Sheffield United	42	15	4	2	46	19	7	5	9	27	37	53	17
4	Coventry City	42	12	5	4	31	15	8	7	6	35	30	52	21
5	Tottenham Hotspur	42	14	3	4	46	16	5	3	13	30	38	44	22
6	Burnley	42	15	4	2	35	11	2	6	13	19	43	44	0
7	Bradford Park Avenue	42	13	4	4	51	22	4	5	12	18	34	43	13
8	Fulham	42	10	7	4	44	23	6	4	11	17	34	43	4
9	West Ham United	42	13	5	3	34	16	1	9	11	19	36	42	1
10	Bury	42	12	3	6	43	26	6	2	13	20	34	41	3
11	Chesterfield	42	12	2	7	39	24	4	7	10	24	39	41	0
12	Luton Town	42	10	6	5	53	36	5	4	12	36	50	40	3
13	Plymouth Argyle	42	10	7	4	40	30	4	5	12	17	35	40	-8
14	Norwich City	42	11	5	5	35	28	3	6	12	21	47	39	-19
15	Southampton	42	12	6	3	42	26	3	3	15	13	51	39	-22
16	Blackburn Rovers	42	13	6	2	51	30	1	4	16	20	50	38	-9
17	Sheffield Wednesday	42	10	5	6	27	21	4	5	12	22	35	38	-7
18	Swansea City	42	12	6	3	31	21	1	6	14	14	52	38	-28
19	Newcastle United	42	12	4	5	38	18	2	4	15	13	40	36	-7
20	Nottingham Forest	42	12	3	6	29	21	2	5	14	18	39	36	-13
21	Barnsley	42	7	11	3	30	20	4	3	14	20	44	36	-14
22	Stockport County	42	8	6	7	24	24	3	3	15	19	46	31	-27

SEASON 1938/39

Match # 1740 Saturday 27/08/38   Football League Division 1   at Ayresome Park   Attendance 25539
Result: **Middlesbrough 3 Manchester United 1**
Teamsheet: Breen, Redwood, Roughton, Gladwin, Vose, McKay, Bryant, Wassall, Smith, Craven, Rowley
Scorer(s):   Smith

Match # 1741 Wednesday 31/08/38   Football League Division 1   at Old Trafford   Attendance 37950
Result: **Manchester United 2 Bolton Wanderers 2**
Teamsheet: Breedon, Redwood, Roughton, Gladwin, Vose, McKay, Bryant, Craven, Smith, Pearson, Rowley
Scorer(s):   Craven, own goal

Match # 1742 Saturday 03/09/38   Football League Division 1   at Old Trafford   Attendance 22228
Result: **Manchester United 4 Birmingham City 1**
Teamsheet: Breedon, Griffiths, Redwood, Gladwin, Vose, Manley, Bryant, Craven, Smith, Pearson, Rowley
Scorer(s):   Smith 2, Bryant, Craven

Match # 1743 Wednesday 07/09/38   Football League Division 1   at Anfield   Attendance 25070
Result: **Liverpool 1 Manchester United 0**
Teamsheet: Breedon, Griffiths, Redwood, Gladwin, Vose, Manley, Bryant, Craven, Smith, Pearson, Rowley

Match # 1744 Saturday 10/09/38   Football League Division 1   at Blundell Park   Attendance 14077
Result: **Grimsby Town 1 Manchester United 0**
Teamsheet: Breedon, Griffiths, Redwood, Gladwin, Vose, Manley, Bryant, Craven, Smith, Carey, Rowley

Match # 1745 Saturday 17/09/38   Football League Division 1   at Victoria Ground   Attendance 21526
Result: **Stoke City 1 Manchester United 1**
Teamsheet: Breedon, Redwood, Roughton, Gladwin, Vose, Manley, Bryant, Craven, Smith, Carey, Rowley
Scorer(s):   Smith

Match # 1746 Saturday 24/09/38   Football League Division 1   at Old Trafford   Attendance 34557
Result: **Manchester United 5 Chelsea 1**
Teamsheet: Breedon, Redwood, Griffiths, Gladwin, Vose, Manley, Bryant, Craven, Smith, Carey, Rowley
Scorer(s):   Carey, Manley, Redwood, Rowley, Smith

Match # 1747 Saturday 01/10/38   Football League Division 1   at Deepdale   Attendance 25964
Result: **Preston North End 1 Manchester United 1**
Teamsheet: Breedon, Redwood, Griffiths, Gladwin, Vose, Manley, Bryant, Craven, Smith, Carey, Rowley
Scorer(s):   Bryant

Match # 1748 Saturday 08/10/38   Football League Division 1   at Old Trafford   Attendance 35730
Result: **Manchester United 0 Charlton Athletic 2**
Teamsheet: Breedon, Redwood, Griffiths, Gladwin, Vose, Manley, Bryant, Craven, Smith, Carey, Rowley

Match # 1749 Saturday 15/10/38   Football League Division 1   at Old Trafford   Attendance 39723
Result: **Manchester United 0 Blackpool 0**
Teamsheet: Breedon, Redwood, Griffiths, Gladwin, Vose, Manley, Wrigglesworth, Wassall, Smith, Carey, Rowley

Match # 1750 Saturday 22/10/38   Football League Division 1   at Baseball Ground   Attendance 26612
Result: **Derby County 5 Manchester United 1**
Teamsheet: Breedon, Griffiths, Roughton, Gladwin, Vose, Manley, Wrigglesworth, Wassall, Smith, Carey, Rowley
Scorer(s):   Smith

Match # 1751 Saturday 29/10/38   Football League Division 1   at Old Trafford   Attendance 33565
Result: **Manchester United 0 Sunderland 1**
Teamsheet: Breedon, Redwood, Roughton, Brown, Manley, McKay, Bryant, Carey, Smith, Pearson, Wrigglesworth

Match # 1752 Saturday 05/11/38   Football League Division 1   at Villa Park   Attendance 38357
Result: **Aston Villa 0 Manchester United 2**
Teamsheet: Breen, Redwood, Griffiths, Warner, Vose, McKay, Rowley, Carey, Smith, Pearson, Wrigglesworth
Scorer(s):   Rowley, Wrigglesworth

Match # 1753 Saturday 12/11/38   Football League Division 1   at Old Trafford   Attendance 32821
Result: **Manchester United 1 Wolverhampton Wanderers 3**
Teamsheet: Breedon, Redwood, Griffiths, Warner, Vose, McKay, Rowley, Carey, Smith, Pearson, Wrigglesworth
Scorer(s):   Rowley

Match # 1754 Saturday 19/11/38   Football League Division 1   at Goodison Park   Attendance 31809
Result: **Everton 3 Manchester United 0**
Teamsheet: Breedon, Redwood, Roughton, Warner, Manley, Whalley, Rowley, Gladwin, Smith, Carey, Wrigglesworth

Match # 1755 Saturday 26/11/38   Football League Division 1   at Old Trafford   Attendance 23164
Result: **Manchester United 1 Huddersfield Town 1**
Teamsheet: Breedon, Redwood, Griffiths, Warner, Vose, Manley, Bryant, Wassall, Hanlon, Craven, Rowley
Scorer(s):   Hanlon

Match # 1756 Saturday 03/12/38   Football League Division 1   at Fratton Park   Attendance 18692
Result: **Portsmouth 0 Manchester United 0**
Teamsheet: Breedon, Redwood, Griffiths, Warner, Vose, Manley, Wrigglesworth, Wassall, Hanlon, Craven, Rowley

Match # 1757 Saturday 10/12/38   Football League Division 1   at Old Trafford   Attendance 42008
Result: **Manchester United 1 Arsenal 0**
Teamsheet: Breedon, Redwood, Griffiths, Warner, Vose, Manley, Bryant, Wassall, Hanlon, Carey, Rowley
Scorer(s):   Bryant

SEASON 1938/39 (continued)

Match # 1758   Saturday 17/12/38   Football League Division 1   at Griffin Park   Attendance 14919
Result: **Brentford 2 Manchester United 5**
Teamsheet: Breedon, Redwood, Griffiths, Warner, Vose, Manley, Bryant, Wassall, Hanlon, Carey, Rowley
Scorer(s):   Hanlon 2, Bryant, Manley, Rowley

Match # 1759   Saturday 24/12/38   Football League Division 1   at Old Trafford   Attendance 33235
Result: **Manchester United 1 Middlesbrough 1**
Teamsheet: Breedon, Redwood, Griffiths, Warner, Vose, McKay, Bryant, Wassall, Hanlon, Carey, Rowley
Scorer(s):   Wassall

Match # 1760   Monday 26/12/38   Football League Division 1   at Old Trafford   Attendance 26332
Result: **Manchester United 3 Leicester City 0**
Teamsheet: Tapken, Redwood, Griffiths, Warner, Vose, Brown, Wrigglesworth, Wassall, Hanlon, Carey, Rowley
Scorer(s):   Wrigglesworth 2, Carey

Match # 1761   Tuesday 27/12/38   Football League Division 1   at Filbert Street   Attendance 21434
Result: **Leicester City 1 Manchester United 1**
Teamsheet: Tapken, Redwood, Griffiths, Warner, Vose, Brown, Wrigglesworth, Wassall, Hanlon, Carey, Rowley
Scorer(s):   Hanlon

Match # 1762   Saturday 31/12/38   Football League Division 1   at St Andrews   Attendance 20787
Result: **Birmingham City 3 Manchester United 3**
Teamsheet: Tapken, Redwood, Griffiths, Warner, Vose, McKay, Wassall, Carey, Hanlon, Pearson, Wrigglesworth
Scorer(s):   Hanlon, McKay, Pearson

Match # 1763   Saturday 07/01/39   FA Cup 3rd Round   at The Hawthorns   Attendance 23900
Result: **West Bromwich Albion 0 Manchester United 0**
Teamsheet: Tapken, Redwood, Griffiths, Warner, Vose, McKay, Wrigglesworth, Wassall, Hanlon, Carey, Rowley

Match # 1764   Wednesday 11/01/39   FA Cup 3rd Round Replay   at Old Trafford   Attendance 17641
Result: **Manchester United 1 West Bromwich Albion 5**
Teamsheet: Tapken, Redwood, Griffiths, Warner, Gladwin, McKay, Wrigglesworth, Wassall, Hanlon, Carey, Smith
Scorer(s):   Redwood

Match # 1765   Saturday 14/01/39   Football League Division 1   at Old Trafford   Attendance 25654
Result: **Manchester United 3 Grimsby Town 1**
Teamsheet: Tapken, Redwood, Griffiths, Warner, Vose, McKay, Bryant, Wassall, Hanlon, Carey, Rowley
Scorer(s):   Rowley 2, Wassall

Match # 1766   Saturday 21/01/39   Football League Division 1   at Old Trafford   Attendance 37384
Result: **Manchester United 0 Stoke City 1**
Teamsheet: Tapken, Redwood, Griffiths, Warner, Vose, McKay, Bryant, Wassall, Hanlon, Carey, Rowley

Match # 17679 Saturday 28/01/39   Football League Division 1   at Stamford Bridge   Attendance 31265
Result: **Chelsea 0 Manchester United 1**
Teamsheet: Tapken, Redwood, Griffiths, Warner, Vose, McKay, Bryant, Wassall, Hanlon, Bradbury, Rowley
Scorer(s):   Bradbury

Match # 1768   Saturday 04/02/39   Football League Division 1   at Old Trafford   Attendance 41061
Result: **Manchester United 1 Preston North End 1**
Teamsheet: Tapken, Redwood, Griffiths, Warner, Vose, McKay, Bryant, Wassall, Hanlon, Carey, Rowley
Scorer(s):   Rowley

Match # 1769   Saturday 11/02/39   Football League Division 1   at The Valley   Attendance 23721
Result: **Charlton Athletic 7 Manchester United 1**
Teamsheet: Tapken, Redwood, Griffiths, Warner, Vose, McKay, Bryant, Wassall, Hanlon, Bradbury, Rowley
Scorer(s):   Hanlon

Match # 1770   Saturday 18/02/39   Football League Division 1   at Bloomfield Road   Attendance 15253
Result: **Blackpool 3 Manchester United 5**
Teamsheet: Tapken, Redwood, Griffiths, Warner, Vose, McKay, Bryant, Wassall, Hanlon, Carey, Rowley
Scorer(s):   Hanlon 3, Bryant, Carey

Match # 1771   Saturday 25/02/39   Football League Division 1   at Old Trafford   Attendance 37166
Result: **Manchester United 1 Derby County 1**
Teamsheet: Tapken, Redwood, Griffiths, Warner, Vose, McKay, Bryant, Wassall, Hanlon, Carey, Rowley
Scorer(s):   Carey

Match # 1772   Saturday 04/03/39   Football League Division 1   at Roker Park   Attendance 11078
Result: **Sunderland 5 Manchester United 2**
Teamsheet: Tapken, Redwood, Griffiths, Warner, Vose, McKay, Rowley, Wassall, Hanlon, Carey, Manley
Scorer(s):   Manley, Rowley

Match # 1773   Saturday 11/03/39   Football League Division 1   at Old Trafford   Attendance 28292
Result: **Manchester United 1 Aston Villa 1**
Teamsheet: Breen, Redwood, Griffiths, Warner, Vose, Manley, Smith, Wassall, Hanlon, Carey, Rowley
Scorer(s):   Wassall

Match # 1774   Saturday 18/03/39   Football League Division 1   at Molineux   Attendance 31498
Result: **Wolverhampton Wanderers 3 Manchester United 0**
Teamsheet: Breen, Redwood, Griffiths, Warner, Vose, Manley, Bryant, Wassall, Hanlon, Carey, Rowley

Match # 1775   Wednesday 29/03/39   Football League Division 1   at Old Trafford   Attendance 18438
Result: **Manchester United 0 Everton 2**
Teamsheet: Breen, Redwood, Griffiths, Warner, Vose, Manley, Dougan, Wassall, Hanlon, Pearson, Rowley

SEASON 1938/39 (continued)

Match # 1776	Saturday 01/04/39	Football League Division 1	at Leeds Road	Attendance 14007
Result:	**Huddersfield Town 1 Manchester United 1**			
Teamsheet:	Breen, Griffiths, Roughton, Warner, Vose, Manley, Dougan, Smith, Hanlon, Pearson, Rowley			
Scorer(s):	Rowley			

Match # 1777	Friday 07/04/39	Football League Division 1	at Old Trafford	Attendance 35564
Result:	**Manchester United 0 Leeds United 0**			
Teamsheet:	Tapken, Griffiths, Roughton, Warner, Vose, Manley, Dougan, Smith, Hanlon, Carey, Rowley			

Match # 1778	Saturday 08/04/39	Football League Division 1	at Old Trafford	Attendance 25457
Result:	**Manchester United 1 Portsmouth 1**			
Teamsheet:	Tapken, Griffiths, Roughton, Warner, Vose, Manley, Dougan, Wassall, Hanlon, Carey, Rowley			
Scorer(s):	Rowley			

Match # 1779	Monday 10/04/39	Football League Division 1	at Elland Road	Attendance 13771
Result:	**Leeds United 3 Manchester United 1**			
Teamsheet:	Tapken, Griffiths, Roughton, Whalley, Manley, McKay, Bryant, Smith, Hanlon, Carey, Rowley			
Scorer(s):	Carey			

Match # 1780	Saturday 15/04/39	Football League Division 1	at Highbury	Attendance 25741
Result:	**Arsenal 2 Manchester United 1**			
Teamsheet:	Breedon, Griffiths, Roughton, Warner, Vose, McKay, Bryant, Wassall, Hanlon, Carey, Rowley			
Scorer(s):	Hanlon			

Match # 1781	Saturday 22/04/39	Football League Division 1	at Old Trafford	Attendance 15353
Result:	**Manchester United 3 Brentford 0**			
Teamsheet:	Breedon, Griffiths, Roughton, Warner, Vose, McKay, Bryant, Wassall, Hanlon, Carey, Wrigglesworth			
Scorer(s):	Bryant, Carey, Wassall			

Match # 1782	Saturday 29/04/39	Football League Division 1	at Burnden Park	Attendance 10314
Result:	**Bolton Wanderers 0 Manchester United 0**			
Teamsheet:	Breedon, Redwood, Roughton, Warner, Vose, McKay, Bryant, Wassall, Hanlon, Carey, Wrigglesworth			

Match # 1783	Saturday 06/05/39	Football League Division 1	at Old Trafford	Attendance 12073
Result:	**Manchester United 2 Liverpool 0**			
Teamsheet:	Breedon, Redwood, Roughton, Warner, Vose, McKay, Bryant, Wassall, Hanlon, Carey, Rowley			
Scorer(s):	Hanlon 2			

SEASON 1939/40

	Saturday 26/08/39	Football League Division 1	at Old Trafford	Attendance 22537
Result:	**Manchester United 4 Grimsby Town 0**			
Teamsheet:	Breedon, Redwood, Griffiths, Warner, Vose, McKay, Bryant, Carey, Smith, Pearson, Wrigglesworth			
Scorer(s):	Bryant, Carey, Pearson, Wrigglesworth			

	Wednesday 30/08/39	Football League Division 1	at Stamford Bridge	Attendance 15157
Result:	**Chelsea 1 Manchester United 1**			
Teamsheet:	Breedon, Redwood, Griffiths, Warner, Vose, McKay, Bryant, Carey, Hanlon, Pearson, Wrigglesworth			
Scorer(s):	Bryant			

	Saturday 26/08/39	Football League Division 1	at The Valley	Attendance 8608
Result:	**Charlton Athletic 2 Manchester United 0**			
Teamsheet:	Breedon, Redwood, Griffiths, Warner, Chilton, Whalley, Bryant, Wassall, Asquith, Pearson, Wrigglesworth			

Football was suspended in September 1939 following the outbreak of the Second World War. Three matches had already been played but the details were expunged from League records following the suspension of the competition. The above details appear for informative purposes only and the appearance and goalscoring records are not included in the overall match statistics and player records which appear in this volume. Football re-commenced in 1946 with only the FA Cup competition.

SEASON 1945/46

Match # 1784	Saturday 05/01/46	FA Cup 3rd Round 1st Leg	at Peel Park	Attendance 9968
Result:	**Accrington Stanley 2 Manchester United 2**			
Teamsheet:	Crompton, Whalley, Roach, Warner, Chilton, Cockburn, Hanlon, Carey, Smith, Rowley, Wrigglesworth			
Scorer(s):	Smith, Wrigglesworth			

Match # 1785	Wednesday 09/01/46	FA Cup 3rd Round 2nd Leg	at Maine Road	Attendance 15339
Result:	**Manchester United 5 Accrington Stanley 1**			
Teamsheet:	Crompton, Whalley, Roach, Warner, Carey, Cockburn, Hanlon, Rowley, Smith, Bainbridge, Wrigglesworth			
Scorer(s):	Rowley 2, Bainbridge, Wrigglesworth, own goal			

Match # 1786	Saturday 26/01/46	FA Cup 4th Round 1st Leg	at Maine Road	Attendance 36237
Result:	**Manchester United 1 Preston North End 0**			
Teamsheet:	Crompton, Whalley, Walton, Warner, Chilton, Cockburn, Hanlon, Smith, Rowley, Carey, Wrigglesworth			
Scorer(s):	Hanlon			

Match # 1787	Wednesday 30/01/46	FA Cup 4th Round 2nd Leg	at Deepdale	Attendance 21000
Result:	**Preston North End 3 Manchester United 1**			
Teamsheet:	Crompton, Whalley, Walton, Warner, Chilton, Cockburn, Hanlon, Smith, Rowley, Carey, Wrigglesworth			
Scorer(s):	Hanlon			

SEASON 1938/39 SUMMARY

APPEARANCES

PLAYER	LGE	FAC	TOT
Vose	39	1	40
Rowley	38	1	39
Griffiths	35	2	37
Redwood	35	2	37
Carey	32	2	34
Warner	29	2	31
Hanlon	27	2	29
Wassall	27	2	29
Bryant	27	–	27
Manley	23	–	23
Breedon	22	–	22
McKay	20	2	22
Smith	19	1	20
Tapken	14	2	16
Roughton	14	–	14
Wrigglesworth	12	2	14
Gladwin	12	1	13
Craven	11	–	11
Pearson	9	–	9
Breen	6	–	6
Dougan	4	–	4
Brown	3	–	3
Bradbury	2	–	2
Whalley	2	–	2

GOALSCORERS

PLAYER	LGE	FAC	TOT
Hanlon	12	–	12
Rowley	10	–	10
Bryant	6	–	6
Carey	6	–	6
Smith	6	–	6
Wassall	4	–	4
Manley	3	–	3
Wrigglesworth	3	–	3
Craven	2	–	2
Redwood	1	1	2
Bradbury	1	–	1
McKay	1	–	1
Pearson	1	–	1
own goal	1	–	1

RESULTS & ATTENDANCES SUMMARY

		P	W	D	L	F	A	TOTAL	AVGE
League	H	21	7	9	5	30	20	637755	30369
	A	21	4	7	10	27	45	461434	21973
	TOTAL	42	11	16	15	57	65	1099189	26171
FA Cup	H	1	0	0	1	1	5	17641	17641
	A	1	0	1	0	0	0	23900	23900
	TOTAL	2	0	1	1	1	5	41541	20771
Overall	H	22	7	9	6	31	25	655396	29791
	A	22	4	8	10	27	45	485334	22061
	TOTAL	44	11	17	16	58	70	1140730	25926

FINAL TABLE – LEAGUE DIVISION ONE

		P	W	D	L	F	A	W	D	L	F	A	PTS	GD
				HOME						AWAY				
1	Everton	42	17	3	1	60	18	10	2	9	28	34	59	36
2	Wolverhampton Wanderers	42	14	6	1	55	12	8	5	8	33	27	55	49
3	Charlton Athletic	42	16	3	2	49	24	6	3	12	26	35	50	16
4	Middlesbrough	42	13	6	2	64	27	7	3	11	29	47	49	19
5	Arsenal	42	14	3	4	34	14	5	6	10	21	27	47	14
6	Derby County	42	12	3	6	39	22	7	5	9	27	33	46	11
7	Stoke City	42	13	6	2	50	25	4	6	11	21	43	46	3
8	Bolton Wanderers	42	10	6	5	39	25	5	9	7	28	33	45	9
9	Preston North End	42	13	7	1	44	19	3	5	13	19	40	44	4
10	Grimsby Town	42	11	6	4	38	26	5	5	11	23	43	43	-8
11	Liverpool	42	12	6	3	40	24	2	8	11	22	39	42	-1
12	Aston Villa	42	11	3	7	44	25	5	6	10	27	35	41	11
13	Leeds United	42	11	5	5	40	27	5	4	12	19	40	41	-8
14	MANCHESTER UNITED	42	7	9	5	30	20	4	7	10	27	45	38	-8
15	Blackpool	42	9	8	4	37	26	3	6	12	19	42	38	-12
16	Sunderland	42	7	7	7	30	29	6	5	10	24	38	38	-13
17	Portsmouth	42	10	7	4	25	15	2	6	13	22	55	37	-23
18	Brentford	42	11	2	8	30	27	3	6	12	23	47	36	-21
19	Huddersfield Town	42	11	4	6	38	18	1	7	13	20	46	35	-6
20	Chelsea	42	10	5	6	43	29	2	4	15	21	51	33	-16
21	Birmingham City	42	10	5	6	40	27	2	3	16	22	57	32	-22
22	Leicester City	42	7	6	8	35	35	2	5	14	13	47	29	-34

SEASON 1945/46 SUMMARY

APPEARANCES

PLAYER	LGE	FAC	TOT
Carey	–	4	4
Cockburn	–	4	4
Crompton	–	4	4
Hanlon	–	4	4
Rowley	–	4	4
Smith	–	4	4
Warner	–	4	4
Whalley	–	4	4
Wrigglesworth	–	4	4
Chilton	–	3	3
Roach	–	2	2
Walton	–	2	2
Bainbridge	–	1	1

GOALSCORERS

PLAYER	LGE	FAC	TOT
Hanlon	–	2	2
Rowley	–	2	2
Wrigglesworth	–	2	2
Bainbridge	–	1	1
Smith	–	1	1
own goal	–	1	1

RESULTS & ATTENDANCES SUMMARY

		P	W	D	L	F	A	TOTAL	AVGE
FA Cup	H	2	2	0	0	6	1	51576	25788
	A	2	0	1	1	3	5	30968	15484
	TOTAL	4	2	1	1	9	6	82544	20636

SEASON 1946/47

Match # 1788	Saturday 31/08/46 Football League Division 1	at Maine Road	Attendance 41025
Result:	**Manchester United 2 Grimsby Town 1**		
Teamsheet:	Crompton, Carey, McGlen, Warner, Chilton, Cockburn, Delaney, Pearson, Hanlon, Rowley, Mitten		
Scorer(s):	Mitten, Rowley		

Match # 1789	Wednesday 04/09/46 Football League Division 1	at Stamford Bridge	Attendance 27750
Result:	**Chelsea 0 Manchester United 3**		
Teamsheet:	Crompton, Carey, McGlen, Warner, Chilton, Cockburn, Delaney, Pearson, Hanlon, Rowley, Mitten		
Scorer(s):	Mitten, Pearson, Rowley		

Match # 1790	Saturday 07/09/46 Football League Division 1	at The Valley	Attendance 44088
Result:	**Charlton Athletic 1 Manchester United 3**		
Teamsheet:	Crompton, Carey, McGlen, Warner, Chilton, Cockburn, Delaney, Pearson, Hanlon, Rowley, Mitten		
Scorer(s):	Hanlon, Rowley, own goal		

Match # 1791	Wednesday 11/09/46 Football League Division 1	at Maine Road	Attendance 41657
Result:	**Manchester United 5 Liverpool 0**		
Teamsheet:	Crompton, Carey, McGlen, Warner, Chilton, Cockburn, Delaney, Pearson, Hanlon, Rowley, Mitten		
Scorer(s):	Pearson 3, Mitten, Rowley		

Match # 1792	Saturday 14/09/46 Football League Division 1	at Maine Road	Attendance 65112
Result:	**Manchester United 1 Middlesbrough 0**		
Teamsheet:	Crompton, Carey, McGlen, Warner, Chilton, Cockburn, Delaney, Pearson, Hanlon, Rowley, Mitten		
Scorer(s):	Rowley		

Match # 1793	Wednesday 18/09/46 Football League Division 1	at Maine Road	Attendance 30275
Result:	**Manchester United 1 Chelsea 1**		
Teamsheet:	Crompton, Carey, Chilton, Warner, Whalley, Cockburn, Delaney, Aston, Hanlon, Pearson, Mitten		
Scorer(s):	Chilton		

Match # 1794	Saturday 21/09/46 Football League Division 1	at Victoria Ground	Attendance 41699
Result:	**Stoke City 3 Manchester United 2**		
Teamsheet:	Crompton, Carey, McGlen, Warner, Chilton, Cockburn, Delaney, Pearson, Hanlon, Rowley, Mitten		
Scorer(s):	Delaney, Hanlon		

Match # 1795	Saturday 28/09/46 Football League Division 1	at Maine Road	Attendance 62718
Result:	**Manchester United 5 Arsenal 2**		
Teamsheet:	Crompton, Walton, McGlen, Warner, Chilton, Aston, Delaney, Pearson, Hanlon, Rowley, Wrigglesworth		
Scorer(s):	Hanlon 2, Rowley 2, Wrigglesworth		

Match # 1796	Saturday 05/10/46 Football League Division 1	at Maine Road	Attendance 55395
Result:	**Manchester United 1 Preston North End 1**		
Teamsheet:	Crompton, Carey, McGlen, Warner, Chilton, Cockburn, Delaney, Pearson, Hanlon, Rowley, Wrigglesworth		
Scorer(s):	Wrigglesworth		

Match # 17979	Saturday 12/10/46 Football League Division 1	at Bramall Lane	Attendance 35543
Result:	**Sheffield United 2 Manchester United 2**		
Teamsheet:	Crompton, Walton, McGlen, Warner, Chilton, Carey, Delaney, Pearson, Hanlon, Rowley, Wrigglesworth		
Scorer(s):	Rowley 2		

Match # 1798	Saturday 19/10/46 Football League Division 1	at Bloomfield Road	Attendance 26307
Result:	**Blackpool 3 Manchester United 1**		
Teamsheet:	Crompton, Walton, McGlen, Carey, Chilton, Cockburn, Delaney, Pearson, Hanlon, Rowley, Wrigglesworth		
Scorer(s):	Delaney		

Match # 1799	Saturday 26/10/46 Football League Division 1	at Maine Road	Attendance 48385
Result:	**Manchester United 0 Sunderland 3**		
Teamsheet:	Crompton, Walton, McGlen, Warner, Chilton, Cockburn, Delaney, Morris, Burke, Pearson, Rowley		

Match # 1800	Saturday 02/11/46 Football League Division 1	at Villa Park	Attendance 53668
Result:	**Aston Villa 0 Manchester United 0**		
Teamsheet:	Collinson, Walton, McGlen, Warner, Chilton, Cockburn, Delaney, Morris, Rowley, Pearson, Mitten		

Match # 1801	Saturday 09/11/46 Football League Division 1	at Maine Road	Attendance 57340
Result:	**Manchester United 4 Derby County 1**		
Teamsheet:	Collinson, Walton, McGlen, Warner, Chilton, Cockburn, Delaney, Morris, Rowley, Pearson, Mitten		
Scorer(s):	Pearson 2, Mitten, Rowley		

Match # 1802	Saturday 16/11/46 Football League Division 1	at Goodison Park	Attendance 45832
Result:	**Everton 2 Manchester United 2**		
Teamsheet:	Collinson, Walton, McGlen, Warner, Chilton, Cockburn, Delaney, Morris, Rowley, Pearson, Mitten		
Scorer(s):	Pearson, Rowley		

Match # 1803	Saturday 23/11/46 Football League Division 1	at Maine Road	Attendance 39216
Result:	**Manchester United 5 Huddersfield Town 2**		
Teamsheet:	Collinson, Walton, McGlen, Carey, Chilton, Cockburn, Delaney, Morris, Rowley, Pearson, Mitten		
Scorer(s):	Mitten 2, Morris 2, Rowley		

Match # 1804	Saturday 30/11/46 Football League Division 1	at Molineux	Attendance 46704
Result:	**Wolverhampton Wanderers 3 Manchester United 2**		
Teamsheet:	Collinson, Worrall, McGlen, Carey, Chilton, Cockburn, Delaney, Morris, Hanlon, Pearson, Mitten		
Scorer(s):	Delaney, Hanlon		

Match # 1805	Saturday 07/12/46 Football League Division 1	at Maine Road	Attendance 31962
Result:	**Manchester United 4 Brentford 1**		
Teamsheet:	Collinson, Carey, McGlen, Warner, Chilton, Cockburn, Hanlon, Morris, Rowley, Pearson, Mitten		
Scorer(s):	Rowley 3, Mitten		

SEASON 1946/47 (continued)

Match # 1806 Saturday 14/12/46 Football League Division 1 at Ewood Park Attendance 21455
Result: **Blackburn Rovers 2 Manchester United 1**
Teamsheet: Collinson, Carey, McGlen, Warner, Chilton, Cockburn, Hanlon, Morris, Rowley, Pearson, Mitten
Scorer(s): Morris

Match # 1807 Wednesday 25/12/46 Football League Division 1 at Burnden Park Attendance 28505
Result: **Bolton Wanderers 2 Manchester United 2**
Teamsheet: Crompton, Carey, McGlen, Warner, Chilton, Cockburn, Delaney, Morris, Rowley, Pearson, Mitten
Scorer(s): Rowley 2

Match # 1808 Thursday 26/12/46 Football League Division 1 at Maine Road Attendance 57186
Result: **Manchester United 1 Bolton Wanderers 0**
Teamsheet: Crompton, Carey, McGlen, Warner, Chilton, Cockburn, Delaney, Morris, Rowley, Pearson, Mitten
Scorer(s): Pearson

Match # 1809 Saturday 28/12/46 Football League Division 1 at Blundell Park Attendance 17183
Result: **Grimsby Town 0 Manchester United 0**
Teamsheet: Crompton, Whalley, Aston, Warner, Chilton, Cockburn, Delaney, Morris, Rowley, Pearson, Mitten

Match # 1810 Saturday 04/01/47 Football League Division 1 at Maine Road Attendance 43406
Result: **Manchester United 4 Charlton Athletic 1**
Teamsheet: Crompton, Aston, McGlen, Warner, Chilton, Cockburn, Delaney, Morris, Burke, Pearson, Buckle
Scorer(s): Burke 2, Buckle, Pearson

Match # 1811 Saturday 11/01/47 FA Cup 3rd Round at Park Avenue Attendance 26990
Result: **Bradford Park Avenue 0 Manchester United 3**
Teamsheet: Crompton, Aston, McGlen, Warner, Chilton, Carey, Delaney, Morris, Rowley, Pearson, Buckle
Scorer(s): Rowley 2, Buckle

Match # 1812 Saturday 18/01/47 Football League Division 1 at Ayresome Park Attendance 37435
Result: **Middlesbrough 2 Manchester United 4**
Teamsheet: Crompton, Aston, McGlen, Warner, Chilton, Carey, Delaney, Morris, Rowley, Pearson, Buckle
Scorer(s): Pearson 2, Buckle, Morris

Match # 1813 Saturday 25/01/47 FA Cup 4th Round at Maine Road Attendance 34059
Result: **Manchester United 0 Nottingham Forest 2**
Teamsheet: Fielding, Aston, McGlen, Warner, Chilton, Carey, Delaney, Morris, Rowley, Pearson, Buckle

Match # 1814 Saturday 01/02/47 Football League Division 1 at Highbury Attendance 29415
Result: **Arsenal 6 Manchester United 2**
Teamsheet: Fielding, Aston, McGlen, Warner, Chilton, Cockburn, Delaney, Morris, Hanlon, Pearson, Buckle
Scorer(s): Morris, Pearson

Match # 1815 Wednesday 05/02/47 Football League Division 1 at Maine Road Attendance 8456
Result: **Manchester United 1 Stoke City 1**
Teamsheet: Fielding, Aston, Walton, Warner, Chilton, Cockburn, Delaney, Morris, Hanlon, Pearson, Buckle
Scorer(s): Buckle

Match # 1816 Saturday 22/02/47 Football League Division 1 at Maine Road Attendance 29993
Result: **Manchester United 3 Blackpool 0**
Teamsheet: Fielding, Aston, Walton, Warner, Chilton, Carey, Delaney, Morris, Hanlon, Pearson, Rowley
Scorer(s): Rowley 2, Hanlon

Match # 1817 Saturday 01/03/47 Football League Division 1 at Roker Park Attendance 25038
Result: **Sunderland 1 Manchester United 1**
Teamsheet: Fielding, Aston, Walton, Warner, Chilton, Cockburn, Delaney, Morris, Hanlon, Pearson, Rowley
Scorer(s): Delaney

Match # 1818 Saturday 08/03/47 Football League Division 1 at Maine Road Attendance 36965
Result: **Manchester United 2 Aston Villa 1**
Teamsheet: Fielding, Aston, Walton, Warner, Chilton, Carey, Delaney, Morris, Burke, Pearson, Rowley
Scorer(s): Burke, Pearson

Match # 1819 Saturday 15/03/47 Football League Division 1 at Baseball Ground Attendance 19579
Result: **Derby County 4 Manchester United 3**
Teamsheet: Fielding, Walton, McGlen, Warner, Chilton, Carey, Delaney, Morris, Burke, Pearson, Rowley
Scorer(s): Burke 2, Pearson

Match # 1820 Saturday 22/03/47 Football League Division 1 at Maine Road Attendance 43441
Result: **Manchester United 3 Everton 0**
Teamsheet: Crompton, Carey, McGlen, Warner, Chilton, Cockburn, Delaney, Morris, Burke, Pearson, Rowley
Scorer(s): Burke, Delaney, Warner

Match # 1821 Saturday 29/03/47 Football League Division 1 at Leeds Road Attendance 18509
Result: **Huddersfield Town 2 Manchester United 2**
Teamsheet: Crompton, Carey, Aston, Cockburn, Chilton, McGlen, Delaney, Hanlon, Burke, Pearson, Rowley
Scorer(s): Delaney, Pearson

Match # 1822 Saturday 05/04/47 Football League Division 1 at Maine Road Attendance 66967
Result: **Manchester United 3 Wolverhampton Wanderers 1**
Teamsheet: Crompton, Carey, Aston, Cockburn, Chilton, McGlen, Delaney, Hanlon, Burke, Pearson, Rowley
Scorer(s): Rowley 2, Hanlon

Match # 1823 Monday 07/04/47 Football League Division 1 at Maine Road Attendance 41772
Result: **Manchester United 3 Leeds United 1**
Teamsheet: Crompton, Carey, Aston, Cockburn, Chilton, McGlen, Delaney, Hanlon, Burke, Pearson, Rowley
Scorer(s): Burke 2, Delaney

SEASON 1946/47 (continued)

Match # 1824	Tuesday 08/04/47	Football League Division 1	at Elland Road	Attendance 15528
Result:	**Leeds United 0 Manchester United 2**			
Teamsheet:	Crompton, Carey, Aston, Cockburn, Chilton, McGlen, Delaney, Hanlon, Burke, Pearson, Rowley			
Scorer(s):	Burke, McGlen			

Match # 1825	Saturday 12/04/47	Football League Division 1	at Griffin Park	Attendance 21714
Result:	**Brentford 0 Manchester United 0**			
Teamsheet:	Crompton, Carey, Aston, Warner, Chilton, Cockburn, Rowley, Hanlon, Burke, Pearson, Mitten			

Match # 1826	Saturday 19/04/47	Football League Division 1	at Maine Road	Attendance 46196
Result:	**Manchester United 4 Blackburn Rovers 0**			
Teamsheet:	Crompton, Carey, Aston, Warner, Whalley, Cockburn, Delaney, Morris, Hanlon, Pearson, Rowley			
Scorer(s):	Pearson 2, Rowley, own goal			

Match # 1827	Saturday 26/04/47	Football League Division 1	at Fratton Park	Attendance 30623
Result:	**Portsmouth 0 Manchester United 1**			
Teamsheet:	Crompton, Carey, Aston, Cockburn, Chilton, McGlen, Delaney, Hanlon, Burke, Pearson, Rowley			
Scorer(s):	Delaney			

Match # 1828	Saturday 03/05/47	Football League Division 1	at Anfield	Attendance 48800
Result:	**Liverpool 1 Manchester United 0**			
Teamsheet:	Crompton, Carey, Aston, Warner, Chilton, McGlen, Delaney, Hanlon, Burke, Pearson, Rowley			

Match # 1829	Saturday 10/05/47	Football League Division 1	at Deepdale	Attendance 23278
Result:	**Preston North End 1 Manchester United 1**			
Teamsheet:	Crompton, Walton, Aston, Warner, Chilton, McGlen, Delaney, Morris, Burke, Pearson, Rowley			
Scorer(s):	Pearson			

Match # 1830	Saturday 17/05/47	Football League Division 1	at Maine Road	Attendance 37614
Result:	**Manchester United 3 Portsmouth 0**			
Teamsheet:	Crompton, Walton, Aston, Warner, Chilton, Carey, Buckle, Morris, Rowley, Pearson, Mitten			
Scorer(s):	Mitten, Morris, Rowley			

Match # 1831	Monday 26/05/47	Football League Division 1	at Maine Road	Attendance 34059
Result:	**Manchester United 6 Sheffield United 2**			
Teamsheet:	Crompton, Carey, Aston, Warner, Chilton, McGlen, Hanlon, Morris, Rowley, Pearson, Mitten			
Scorer(s):	Rowley 3, Morris 2, Pearson			

SEASON 1946/47 SUMMARY

APPEARANCES

PLAYER	LGE	FAC	TOT
Pearson	42	2	44
Chilton	41	2	43
Delaney	37	2	39
Rowley	37	2	39
Warner	34	2	36
McGlen	33	2	35
Carey	31	2	33
Cockburn	32	–	32
Crompton	29	1	30
Hanlon	27	–	27
Morris	24	2	26
Aston	21	2	23
Mitten	20	–	20
Walton	15	–	15
Burke	13	–	13
Buckle	5	2	7
Collinson	7	–	7
Fielding	6	1	7
Wrigglesworth	4	–	4
Whalley	3	–	3
Worrall	1	–	1

GOALSCORERS

PLAYER	LGE	FAC	TOT
Rowley	26	2	28
Pearson	19	–	19
Burke	9	–	9
Delaney	8	–	8
Mitten	8	–	8
Morris	8	–	8
Hanlon	7	–	7
Buckle	3	1	4
Wrigglesworth	2	–	2
Chilton	1	–	1
McGlen	1	–	1
Warner	1	–	1
own goals	2	–	2

RESULTS & ATTENDANCES SUMMARY

		P	W	D	L	F	A	TOTAL	AVGE
League	H	21	17	3	1	61	19	919140	43769
	A	21	5	9	7	34	35	658653	31364
	TOTAL	42	22	12	8	95	54	1577793	37567
FA Cup	H	1	0	0	1	0	2	34059	34059
	A	1	1	0	0	3	0	26990	26990
	TOTAL	2	1	0	1	3	2	61049	30525
Overall	H	22	17	3	2	61	21	953199	43327
	A	22	6	9	7	37	35	685643	31166
	TOTAL	44	23	12	9	98	56	1638842	37246

FINAL TABLE – LEAGUE DIVISION ONE

		P	HOME					AWAY					PTS	GD
			W	D	L	F	A	W	D	L	F	A		
1	Liverpool	42	13	3	5	42	24	12	4	5	42	28	57	32
2	MANCHESTER UNITED	42	17	3	1	61	19	5	9	7	34	35	56	41
3	Wolverhampton Wanderers	42	15	1	5	66	31	10	5	6	32	25	56	42
4	Stoke City	42	14	5	2	52	21	10	2	9	38	32	55	37
5	Blackpool	42	14	1	6	38	32	8	5	8	33	38	50	1
6	Sheffield United	42	12	4	5	51	32	9	3	9	38	43	49	14
7	Preston North End	42	10	7	4	45	27	8	4	9	31	47	47	2
8	Aston Villa	42	9	6	6	39	24	9	3	9	28	29	45	14
9	Sunderland	42	11	3	7	33	27	7	5	9	32	39	44	-1
10	Everton	42	13	5	3	40	24	4	4	13	22	43	43	-5
11	Middlesbrough	42	11	3	7	46	32	6	5	10	27	36	42	5
12	Portsmouth	42	11	3	7	42	27	5	6	10	24	33	41	6
13	Arsenal	42	9	5	7	43	33	7	4	10	29	37	41	2
14	Derby County	42	13	2	6	44	28	5	3	13	29	51	41	-6
15	Chelsea	42	9	3	9	33	39	7	4	10	36	45	39	-15
16	Grimsby Town	42	9	6	6	37	35	4	6	11	24	47	38	-21
17	Blackburn Rovers	42	6	5	10	23	27	8	3	10	22	26	36	-8
18	Bolton Wanderers	42	8	5	8	30	28	5	3	13	27	41	34	-12
19	Charlton Athletic	42	6	6	9	34	32	5	6	10	23	39	34	-14
20	Huddersfield Town	42	11	4	6	34	24	2	3	16	19	55	33	-26
21	Brentford	42	5	5	11	19	35	4	2	15	26	53	25	-43
22	Leeds United	42	6	5	10	30	30	0	1	20	15	60	18	-45

SEASON 1947/48

Match # 1832 Saturday 23/08/47   Football League Division 1   at Ayresome Park   Attendance 39554
Result: **Middlesbrough 2 Manchester United 2**
Teamsheet: Crompton, Carey, Aston, Warner, Chilton, McGlen, Delaney, Morris, Rowley, Pearson, Mitten
Scorer(s):   Rowley 2

Match # 1833 Wednesday 27/08/47   Football League Division 1   at Maine Road   Attendance 52385
Result: **Manchester United 2 Liverpool 0**
Teamsheet: Crompton, Carey, Aston, Warner, Chilton, McGlen, Delaney, Morris, Rowley, Pearson, Mitten
Scorer(s):   Morris, Pearson

Match # 1834 Saturday 30/08/47   Football League Division 1   at Maine Road   Attendance 52659
Result: **Manchester United 6 Charlton Athletic 2**
Teamsheet: Crompton, Carey, Aston, Warner, Chilton, McGlen, Delaney, Morris, Rowley, Pearson, Mitten
Scorer(s):   Rowley 4, Morris, Pearson

Match # 1835 Wednesday 03/09/47   Football League Division 1   at Anfield   Attendance 48081
Result: **Liverpool 2 Manchester United 2**
Teamsheet: Crompton, Carey, Aston, Warner, Chilton, McGlen, Delaney, Morris, Rowley, Pearson, Mitten
Scorer(s):   Mitten, Pearson

Match # 1836 Saturday 06/09/47   Football League Division 1   at Highbury   Attendance 64905
Result: **Arsenal 2 Manchester United 1**
Teamsheet: Crompton, Carey, Aston, Warner, Chilton, McGlen, Delaney, Morris, Rowley, Pearson, Mitten
Scorer(s):   Morris

Match # 1837 Monday 08/09/47   Football League Division 1   at Turf Moor   Attendance 37517
Result: **Burnley 0 Manchester United 0**
Teamsheet: Crompton, Carey, Aston, Warner, Chilton, McGlen, Delaney, Morris, Rowley, Pearson, Mitten

Match # 1838 Saturday 13/09/47   Football League Division 1   at Maine Road   Attendance 49808
Result: **Manchester United 0 Sheffield United 1**
Teamsheet: Crompton, Carey, Aston, Warner, Chilton, McGlen, Delaney, Morris, Burke, Pearson, Rowley

Match # 1839 Saturday 20/09/47   Football League Division 1   at Maine Road   Attendance 71364
Result: **Manchester City 0 Manchester United 0**
Teamsheet: Crompton, Carey, Aston, Warner, Chilton, McGlen, Delaney, Morris, Rowley, Pearson, Mitten

Match # 1840 Saturday 27/09/47   Football League Division 1   at Deepdale   Attendance 34372
Result: **Preston North End 2 Manchester United 1**
Teamsheet: Crompton, Aston, McGlen, Warner, Chilton, Cockburn, Dale, Morris, Hanlon, Pearson, Rowley
Scorer(s):   Morris

Match # 1841 Saturday 04/10/47   Football League Division 1   at Maine Road   Attendance 45745
Result: **Manchester United 1 Stoke City 1**
Teamsheet: Crompton, Aston, McGlen, Warner, Chilton, Cockburn, Dale, Morris, Hanlon, Pearson, Rowley
Scorer(s):   Hanlon

Match # 1842 Saturday 11/10/47   Football League Division 1   at Maine Road   Attendance 40035
Result: **Manchester United 3 Grimsby Town 4**
Teamsheet: Crompton, Aston, McGlen, Warner, Chilton, Pearson, Delaney, Morris, Hanlon, Rowley, Mitten
Scorer(s):   Mitten, Morris, Rowley

Match # 1843 Saturday 18/10/47   Football League Division 1   at Roker Park   Attendance 37148
Result: **Sunderland 1 Manchester United 0**
Teamsheet: Crompton, Walton, Aston, Carey, Chilton, McGlen, Delaney, Pearson, Hanlon, Rowley, Mitten

Match # 1844 Saturday 25/10/47   Football League Division 1   at Maine Road   Attendance 47078
Result: **Manchester United 2 Aston Villa 0**
Teamsheet: Crompton, Aston, Worrall, Carey, Chilton, Cockburn, Delaney, Morris, Rowley, Pearson, Mitten
Scorer(s):   Delaney, Rowley

Match # 1845 Saturday 01/11/47   Football League Division 1   at Molineux   Attendance 44309
Result: **Wolverhampton Wanderers 2 Manchester United 6**
Teamsheet: Crompton, Aston, Worrall, Carey, Chilton, Cockburn, Morris, Rowley, Pearson, Mitten
Scorer(s):   Morris 2, Pearson 2, Delaney, Mitten

Match # 1846 Saturday 08/11/47   Football League Division 1   at Maine Road   Attendance 59772
Result: **Manchester United 4 Huddersfield Town 4**
Teamsheet: Crompton, Aston, Worrall, Carey, Chilton, Cockburn, Delaney, Morris, Rowley, Pearson, Mitten
Scorer(s):   Rowley 4

Match # 1847 Saturday 15/11/47   Football League Division 1   at Baseball Ground   Attendance 32990
Result: **Derby County 1 Manchester United 1**
Teamsheet: Pegg, Aston, Worrall, Carey, Chilton, Cockburn, Delaney, Morris, Rowley, Pearson, Mitten
Scorer(s):   Carey

Match # 1848 Saturday 22/11/47   Football League Division 1   at Maine Road   Attendance 35509
Result: **Manchester United 2 Everton 2**
Teamsheet: Pegg, Aston, Worrall, Carey, Chilton, Cockburn, Delaney, Morris, Rowley, Pearson, Mitten
Scorer(s):   Cockburn, Morris

Match # 1849 Saturday 29/11/47   Football League Division 1   at Stamford Bridge   Attendance 43617
Result: **Chelsea 0 Manchester United 4**
Teamsheet: Crompton, Aston, Walton, Carey, Chilton, Cockburn, Delaney, Morris, Rowley, Pearson, Mitten
Scorer(s):   Morris 3, Rowley

SEASON 1947/48 (continued)

Match # 1850 Saturday 06/12/47   Football League Division 1   at Maine Road   Attendance 63683
Result: **Manchester United 1 Blackpool 1**
Teamsheet: Crompton, Walton, Aston, Carey, Chilton, Cockburn, Delaney, Morris, Rowley, Pearson, Mitten
Scorer(s):   Pearson

Match # 1851 Saturday 13/12/47   Football League Division 1   at Ewood Park   Attendance 22784
Result: **Blackburn Rovers 1 Manchester United 1**
Teamsheet: Crompton, Walton, Aston, Carey, Chilton, Cockburn, Delaney, Morris, Rowley, Pearson, Mitten
Scorer(s):   Morris

Match # 1852 Saturday 20/12/47   Football League Division 1   at Maine Road   Attendance 46666
Result: **Manchester United 2 Middlesbrough 1**
Teamsheet: Crompton, Walton, Aston, Anderson, Chilton, Cockburn, Delaney, Morris, Rowley, Pearson, Mitten
Scorer(s):   Pearson 2

Match # 1853 Thursday 25/12/47   Football League Division 1   at Maine Road   Attendance 42776
Result: **Manchester United 3 Portsmouth 2**
Teamsheet: Crompton, Walton, Aston, Carey, Chilton, Cockburn, Delaney, Morris, Rowley, Pearson, Mitten
Scorer(s):   Morris 2, Rowley

Match # 1854 Saturday 27/12/47   Football League Division 1   at Fratton Park   Attendance 27674
Result: **Portsmouth 1 Manchester United 3**
Teamsheet: Crompton, Carey, Aston, Anderson, Chilton, Cockburn, Delaney, Morris, Rowley, Pearson, Mitten
Scorer(s):   Morris 2, Delaney

Match # 1855 Monday 01/01/48   Football League Division 1   at Maine Road   Attendance 59838
Result: **Manchester United 5 Burnley 0**
Teamsheet: Crompton, Carey, Aston, Anderson, Chilton, Cockburn, Delaney, Morris, Rowley, Pearson, Mitten
Scorer(s):   Rowley 3, Mitten 2

Match # 1856 Saturday 03/01/48   Football League Division 1   at The Valley   Attendance 40484
Result: **Charlton Athletic 1 Manchester United 2**
Teamsheet: Crompton, Carey, Aston, Warner, Chilton, Lynn, Delaney, Morris, Rowley, Pearson, Mitten
Scorer(s):   Morris, Pearson

Match # 1857 Saturday 10/01/48   FA Cup 3rd Round   at Villa Park   Attendance 58683
Result: **Aston Villa 4 Manchester United 6**
Teamsheet: Crompton, Carey, Aston, Anderson, Chilton, Cockburn, Delaney, Morris, Rowley, Pearson, Mitten
Scorer(s):   Morris 2, Pearson 2, Delaney, Rowley

Match # 1858 Saturday 17/01/48   Football League Division 1   at Maine Road   Attendance 81962
Result: **Manchester United 1 Arsenal 1**
Teamsheet: Crompton, Carey, Aston, Anderson, Chilton, Cockburn, Delaney, Morris, Rowley, Pearson, Mitten
Scorer(s):   Rowley

Match # 1859 Saturday 24/01/48   FA Cup 4th Round   at Goodison Park   Attendance 74000
Result: **Manchester United 3 Liverpool 0**
Teamsheet: Crompton, Carey, Aston, Anderson, Chilton, Cockburn, Delaney, Morris, Rowley, Pearson, Mitten
Scorer(s):   Mitten, Morris, Rowley

Match # 1860 Saturday 31/01/48   Football League Division 1   at Bramall Lane   Attendance 45189
Result: **Sheffield United 2 Manchester United 1**
Teamsheet: Brown, Carey, Aston, Anderson, Chilton, Cockburn, Delaney, Morris, Rowley, Pearson, Mitten
Scorer(s):   Rowley

Match # 1861 Saturday 07/02/48   FA Cup 5th Round   at Leeds Road   Attendance 33312
Result: **Manchester United 2 Charlton Athletic 0**
Teamsheet: Crompton, Carey, Aston, Warner, Chilton, Cockburn, Delaney, Morris, Rowley, Pearson, Mitten
Scorer(s):   Mitten, Warner

Match # 1862 Saturday 14/02/48   Football League Division 1   at Maine Road   Attendance 61765
Result: **Manchester United 1 Preston North End 1**
Teamsheet: Crompton, Carey, Aston, Warner, Chilton, Cockburn, Delaney, Morris, Rowley, Pearson, Mitten
Scorer(s):   Delaney

Match # 1863 Saturday 21/02/48   Football League Division 1   at Victoria Ground   Attendance 36794
Result: **Stoke City 0 Manchester United 2**
Teamsheet: Crompton, Carey, Aston, Anderson, Chilton, Cockburn, Delaney, Morris, Rowley, Pearson, Buckle
Scorer(s):   Buckle, Pearson

Match # 1864 Saturday 28/02/48   FA Cup 6th Round   at Maine Road   Attendance 74213
Result: **Manchester United 4 Preston North End 2**
Teamsheet: Crompton, Carey, Aston, Anderson, Chilton, Cockburn, Delaney, Morris, Rowley, Pearson, Mitten
Scorer(s):   Pearson 2, Mitten, Rowley

Match # 1865 Saturday 06/03/48   Football League Division 1   at Maine Road   Attendance 55160
Result: **Manchester United 3 Sunderland 1**
Teamsheet: Crompton, Carey, Aston, Anderson, Chilton, Cockburn, Delaney, Morris, Rowley, Pearson, Mitten
Scorer(s):   Delaney, Mitten, Rowley

Match # 1866 Saturday 13/03/48   FA Cup Semi-Final   at Hillsborough   Attendance 60000
Result: **Manchester United 3 Derby County 1**
Teamsheet: Crompton, Carey, Aston, Anderson, Chilton, Cockburn, Delaney, Morris, Rowley, Pearson, Mitten
Scorer(s):   Pearson 3

Match # 1867 Wednesday 17/03/48   Football League Division 1   at Blundell Park   Attendance 12284
Result: **Grimsby Town 1 Manchester United 1**
Teamsheet: Crompton, Carey, Aston, Anderson, Chilton, Cockburn, Delaney, Hanlon, Rowley, Pearson, Mitten
Scorer(s):   Rowley

SEASON 1947/48 (continued)

Match # 1868 Saturday 20/03/48   Football League Division 1   at Maine Road   Attendance 50667
Result: **Manchester United 3 Wolverhampton Wanderers 2**
Teamsheet: Crompton, Carey, Aston, Warner, Chilton, Anderson, Delaney, Morris, Rowley, Pearson, Mitten
Scorer(s):   Delaney, Mitten, Morris

Match # 1869 Monday 22/03/48   Football League Division 1   at Villa Park   Attendance 52368
Result: **Aston Villa 0 Manchester United 1**
Teamsheet: Crompton, Carey, Aston, Anderson, Chilton, Lynn, Delaney, Morris, Rowley, Pearson, Mitten
Scorer(s):   Pearson

Match # 1870 Friday 26/03/48   Football League Division 1   at Maine Road   Attendance 71623
Result: **Manchester United 0 Bolton Wanderers 2**
Teamsheet: Crompton, Carey, Aston, Anderson, Chilton, Lynn, Delaney, Morris, Rowley, Pearson, Mitten

Match # 1871 Saturday 27/03/48   Football League Division 1   at Leeds Road   Attendance 38266
Result: **Huddersfield Town 0 Manchester United 2**
Teamsheet: Brown, Carey, Aston, Warner, McGlen, Cockburn, Delaney, Morris, Burke, Pearson, Mitten
Scorer(s):   Burke, Pearson

Match # 1872 Monday 29/03/48   Football League Division 1   at Burnden Park   Attendance 44225
Result: **Bolton Wanderers 0 Manchester United 1**
Teamsheet: Brown, Carey, Aston, Anderson, Chilton, Cockburn, Hanlon, Morris, Burke, Pearson, Mitten
Scorer(s):   Anderson

Match # 1873 Saturday 03/04/48   Football League Division 1   at Maine Road   Attendance 49609
Result: **Manchester United 1 Derby County 0**
Teamsheet: Crompton, Carey, Aston, Anderson, Chilton, Cockburn, Delaney, Morris, Rowley, Pearson, Mitten
Scorer(s):   Pearson

Match # 1874 Wednesday 07/04/48   Football League Division 1   at Maine Road   Attendance 71690
Result: **Manchester United 1 Manchester City 1**
Teamsheet: Crompton, Carey, Aston, Anderson, Chilton, Lowrie, Hanlon, Morris, Burke, Rowley, Mitten
Scorer(s):   Rowley

Match # 1875 Saturday 10/04/48   Football League Division 1   at Goodison Park   Attendance 44198
Result: **Everton 2 Manchester United 0**
Teamsheet: Crompton, Ball, Aston, Anderson, Chilton, Lowrie, Buckle, Morris, Burke, Cassidy, Mitten

Match # 1876 Saturday 17/04/48   Football League Division 1   at Maine Road   Attendance 43225
Result: **Manchester United 5 Chelsea 0**
Teamsheet: Crompton, Carey, Aston, Anderson, Chilton, Cockburn, Delaney, Morris, Rowley, Pearson, Mitten
Scorer(s):   Pearson 2, Delaney, Mitten, Rowley

Match # 1877 Saturday 24/04/48   FA Cup Final   at Wembley   Attendance 99000
Result: **Manchester United 4 Blackpool 2**
Teamsheet: Crompton, Carey, Aston, Anderson, Chilton, Cockburn, Delaney, Morris, Rowley, Pearson, Mitten
Scorer(s):   Rowley 2, Anderson, Pearson

Match # 1878 Wednesday 28/04/48   Football League Division 1   at Bloomfield Road   Attendance 32236
Result: **Blackpool 1 Manchester United 0**
Teamsheet: Crompton, Carey, Aston, Anderson, Chilton, Cockburn, Buckle, Hanlon, Rowley, Pearson, Mitten

Match # 1879 Saturday 01/05/48   Football League Division 1   at Maine Road   Attendance 44439
Result: **Manchester United 4 Blackburn Rovers 1**
Teamsheet: Crompton, Carey, Aston, Anderson, Chilton, Cockburn, Delaney, Burke, Rowley, Pearson, Mitten
Scorer(s):   Paerson 3, Delaney

SEASON 1947/48 SUMMARY

APPEARANCES

PLAYER	LGE	FAC	TOT
Aston	42	6	48
Chilton	41	6	47
Pearson	40	6	46
Rowley	39	6	45
Mitten	38	6	44
Morris	38	6	44
Carey	37	6	43
Crompton	37	6	43
Delaney	36	6	42
Cockburn	26	6	32
Anderson	18	5	23
Warner	15	1	16
McGlen	13	–	13
Hanlon	8	–	8
Burke	6	–	6
Walton	6	–	6
Worrall	5	–	5
Brown	3	–	3
Buckle	3	–	3
Lynn	3	–	3
Dale	2	–	2
Lowrie	2	–	2
Pegg	2	–	2
Ball	1	–	1
Cassidy	1	–	1

GOALSCORERS

PLAYER	LGE	FAC	TOT
Rowley	23	5	28
Pearson	18	8	26
Morris	18	3	21
Mitten	8	3	11
Delaney	8	1	9
Anderson	1	1	2
Buckle	1	–	1
Burke	1	–	1
Carey	1	–	1
Cockburn	1	–	1
Hanlon	1	–	1
Warner	–	1	1

RESULTS & ATTENDANCES SUMMARY

		P	W	D	L	F	A	TOTAL	AVGE
League	H	21	11	7	3	50	27	1126094	53624
	A	21	8	7	6	31	21	850359	40493
	TOTAL	42	19	14	9	81	48	1976453	47058
FA Cup	H	3	3	0	0	9	2	181525	60508
	A	1	1	0	0	6	4	58683	58683
	N	2	2	0	0	7	3	159000	79500
	TOTAL	6	6	0	0	22	9	399208	66535
Overall	H	24	14	7	3	59	29	1307619	54484
	A	22	9	7	6	37	25	909042	41320
	N	2	2	0	0	7	3	159000	79500
	TOTAL	48	25	14	9	103	57	2375661	49493

FINAL TABLE – LEAGUE DIVISION ONE

		P	HOME W	HOME D	HOME L	HOME F	HOME A	AWAY W	AWAY D	AWAY L	AWAY F	AWAY A	PTS	GD
1	Arsenal	42	15	3	3	56	15	8	10	3	25	17	59	49
2	MANCHESTER UNITED	42	11	7	3	50	27	8	7	6	31	21	52	33
3	Burnley	42	12	5	4	31	12	8	7	6	25	31	52	13
4	Derby County	42	11	6	4	38	24	8	6	7	39	33	50	20
5	Wolverhampton Wanderers	42	12	4	5	45	29	7	5	9	38	41	47	13
6	Aston Villa	42	13	5	3	42	22	6	4	11	23	35	47	8
7	Preston North End	42	13	4	4	43	35	7	3	11	24	33	47	–1
8	Portsmouth	42	13	5	3	44	17	6	2	13	24	33	45	18
9	Blackpool	42	13	4	4	37	14	4	6	11	20	27	44	16
10	Manchester City	42	13	3	5	37	22	2	9	10	15	25	42	5
11	Liverpool	42	9	8	4	39	23	7	2	12	26	38	42	4
12	Sheffield United	42	13	4	4	44	24	3	6	12	21	46	42	–5
13	Charlton Athletic	42	8	4	9	33	29	9	2	10	24	37	40	–9
14	Everton	42	10	2	9	30	26	7	4	10	22	40	40	–14
15	Stoke City	42	9	5	7	29	23	5	5	11	12	32	38	–14
16	Middlesbrough	42	8	7	6	37	27	6	2	13	34	46	37	–2
17	Bolton Wanderers	42	11	2	8	29	25	5	3	13	17	33	37	–12
18	Chelsea	42	11	6	4	38	27	3	3	15	15	44	37	–18
19	Huddersfield Town	42	7	6	8	25	24	5	6	10	26	36	36	–9
20	Sunderland	42	11	4	6	33	18	2	6	13	23	49	36	–11
21	Blackburn Rovers	42	8	5	8	35	30	3	5	13	19	42	32	–18
22	Grimsby Town	42	5	5	11	20	35	3	1	17	25	76	22	–66

SEASON 1948/49

Match # 1880	Saturday 21/08/48	Football League Division 1	at Maine Road	Attendance 52620
Result:	**Manchester United 1 Derby County 2**			
Teamsheet:	Crompton, Carey, Aston, Anderson, Chilton, Cockburn, Delaney, Morris, Rowley, Pearson, Mitten			
Scorer(s):	Pearson			

Match # 1881	Monday 23/08/48	Football League Division 1	at Bloomfield Road	Attendance 36880
Result:	**Blackpool 0 Manchester United 3**			
Teamsheet:	Crompton, Ball, Carey, Anderson, Chilton, McGlen, Delaney, Morris, Rowley, Pearson, Mitten			
Scorer(s):	Rowley 2, Mitten			

Match # 1882	Saturday 28/08/48	Football League Division 1	at Highbury	Attendance 64150
Result:	**Arsenal 0 Manchester United 1**			
Teamsheet:	Crompton, Carey, Aston, Anderson, Chilton, Cockburn, Delaney, Morris, Rowley, Pearson, Mitten			
Scorer(s):	Mitten			

Match # 1883	Wednesday 01/09/48	Football League Division 1	at Maine Road	Attendance 51187
Result:	**Manchester United 3 Blackpool 4**			
Teamsheet:	Brown, Carey, Aston, Anderson, Chilton, Cockburn, Delaney, Morris, Rowley, Pearson, Mitten			
Scorer(s):	Delaney, Mitten, Morris			

Match # 1884	Saturday 04/09/48	Football League Division 1	at Maine Road	Attendance 57714
Result:	**Manchester United 4 Huddersfield Town 1**			
Teamsheet:	Crompton, Carey, Aston, Anderson, Chilton, McGlen, Delaney, Morris, Rowley, Pearson, Mitten			
Scorer(s):	Pearson 2, Delaney, Mitten			

Match # 1884	Wednesday 08/09/48	Football League Division 1	at Molineux	Attendance 42617
Result:	**Wolverhampton Wanderers 3 Manchester United 2**			
Teamsheet:	Crompton, Carey, Aston, Anderson, Chilton, McGlen, Delaney, Morris, Rowley, Pearson, Mitten			
Scorer(s):	Morris, Rowley			

Match # 1886	Saturday 11/09/48	Football League Division 1	at Maine Road	Attendance 64502
Result:	**Manchester City 0 Manchester United 0**			
Teamsheet:	Crompton, Carey, Aston, Cockburn, Chilton, McGlen, Delaney, Morris, Rowley, Pearson, Mitten			

Match # 1887	Wednesday 15/09/48	Football League Division 1	at Maine Road	Attendance 33871
Result:	**Manchester United 2 Wolverhampton Wanderers 0**			
Teamsheet:	Crompton, Carey, Aston, Anderson, Chilton, Cockburn, Buckle, Morris, Rowley, Pearson, Mitten			
Scorer(s):	Buckle, Pearson			

Match # 1888	Saturday 18/09/48	Football League Division 1	at Bramall Lane	Attendance 36880
Result:	**Sheffield United 2 Manchester United 2**			
Teamsheet:	Crompton, Carey, Aston, Cockburn, Chilton, McGlen, Buckle, Morris, Rowley, Pearson, Mitten			
Scorer(s):	Buckle, Pearson			

Match # 1889	Saturday 25/09/48	Football League Division 1	at Maine Road	Attendance 53820
Result:	**Manchester United 3 Aston Villa 1**			
Teamsheet:	Crompton, Carey, Aston, Cockburn, Chilton, McGlen, Delaney, Hanlon, Rowley, Pearson, Mitten			
Scorer(s):	Mitten 2, Pearson			

Match # 1890	Saturday 02/10/48	Football League Division 1	at Roker Park	Attendance 54419
Result:	**Sunderland 2 Manchester United 1**			
Teamsheet:	Crompton, Carey, Aston, Cockburn, Chilton, McGlen, Delaney, Buckle, Rowley, Pearson, Mitten			
Scorer(s):	Rowley			

Match # 1891	Wednesday 06/10/48	FA Charity Shield	at Highbury	Attendance 31000
Result:	**Arsenal 4 Manchester United 3**			
Teamsheet:	Crompton, Carey, Aston, Anderson, Chilton, Warner, Delaney, Morris, Burke, Rowley, Mitten			
Scorer(s):	Burke, Rowley, own goal			

Match # 1892	Saturday 09/10/48	Football League Division 1	at Maine Road	Attendance 46964
Result:	**Manchester United 1 Charlton Athletic 1**			
Teamsheet:	Crompton, Ball, Aston, Anderson, Chilton, Warner, Delaney, Morris, Burke, Rowley, Mitten			
Scorer(s):	Burke			

Match # 1893	Saturday 16/10/48	Football League Division 1	at Victoria Ground	Attendance 45830
Result:	**Stoke City 2 Manchester United 1**			
Teamsheet:	Crompton, Carey, Aston, Anderson, Chilton, Cockburn, Delaney, Morris, Rowley, Pearson, Mitten			
Scorer(s):	Morris			

Match # 1894	Saturday 23/10/48	Football League Division 1	at Maine Road	Attendance 47093
Result:	**Manchester United 1 Burnley 1**			
Teamsheet:	Crompton, Carey, Aston, Anderson, Chilton, Cockburn, Delaney, Morris, Rowley, Pearson, Mitten			
Scorer(s):	Mitten			

Match # 1895	Saturday 30/10/48	Football League Division 1	at Deepdale	Attendance 37372
Result:	**Preston North End 1 Manchester United 6**			
Teamsheet:	Crompton, Carey, Aston, Warner, Chilton, Cockburn, Delaney, Morris, Rowley, Pearson, Mitten			
Scorer(s):	Mitten 2, Pearson 2, Morris, Rowley			

Match # 1896	Saturday 06/11/48	Football League Division 1	at Maine Road	Attendance 42789
Result:	**Manchester United 2 Everton 0**			
Teamsheet:	Crompton, Carey, Aston, Warner, Chilton, Cockburn, Delaney, Morris, Rowley, Pearson, Mitten			
Scorer(s):	Delaney, Morris			

Match # 1897	Saturday 13/11/48	Football League Division 1	at Stamford Bridge	Attendance 62542
Result:	**Chelsea 1 Manchester United 1**			
Teamsheet:	Crompton, Carey, Aston, Anderson, Chilton, Cockburn, Delaney, Morris, Rowley, Pearson, Mitten			
Scorer(s):	Rowley			

SEASON 1948/49 (continued)

Match # 1898 Saturday 20/11/48 Football League Division 1 at Maine Road Attendance 45482
Result: **Manchester United 3 Birmingham City 0**
Teamsheet: Crompton, Carey, Aston, Cockburn, McGlen, Chilton, Delaney, Morris, Rowley, Pearson, Mitten
Scorer(s): Morris, Pearson, Rowley

Match # 1899 Saturday 27/11/48 Football League Division 1 at Ayresome Park Attendance 31331
Result: **Middlesbrough 1 Manchester United 4**
Teamsheet: Crompton, Carey, Aston, Cockburn, McGlen, Chilton, Delaney, Morris, Rowley, Pearson, Mitten
Scorer(s): Rowley 3, Delaney

Match # 1900 Saturday 04/12/48 Football League Division 1 at Maine Road Attendance 70787
Result: **Manchester United 1 Newcastle United 1**
Teamsheet: Crompton, Carey, Aston, Cockburn, McGlen, Chilton, Delaney, Morris, Rowley, Pearson, Mitten
Scorer(s): Mitten

Match # 1901 Saturday 11/12/48 Football League Division 1 at Fratton Park Attendance 29966
Result: **Portsmouth 2 Manchester United 2**
Teamsheet: Crompton, Carey, Aston, Cockburn, McGlen, Chilton, Delaney, Morris, Rowley, Pearson, Mitten
Scorer(s): McGlen, Mitten

Match # 1902 Saturday 18/12/48 Football League Division 1 at Baseball Ground Attendance 31498
Result: **Derby County 1 Manchester United 3**
Teamsheet: Crompton, Carey, Aston, Cockburn, McGlen, Chilton, Delaney, Pearson, Burke, Rowley, Mitten
Scorer(s): Burke 2, Pearson

Match # 1903 Saturday 25/12/48 Football League Division 1 at Maine Road Attendance 47788
Result: **Manchester United 0 Liverpool 0**
Teamsheet: Crompton, Carey, Aston, Cockburn, McGlen, Chilton, Delaney, Pearson, Burke, Rowley, Mitten

Match # 1904 Sunday 26/12/48 Football League Division 1 at Anfield Attendance 53325
Result: **Liverpool 0 Manchester United 2**
Teamsheet: Crompton, Carey, Aston, Cockburn, McGlen, Chilton, Buckle, Pearson, Burke, Rowley, Mitten
Scorer(s): Burke, Pearson

Match # 1905 Saturday 01/01/49 Football League Division 1 at Maine Road Attendance 58688
Result: **Manchester United 2 Arsenal 0**
Teamsheet: Crompton, Carey, Aston, Cockburn, Chilton, McGlen, Delaney, Morris, Burke, Pearson, Mitten
Scorer(s): Burke, Mitten

Match # 1906 Saturday 08/01/49 FA Cup 3rd Round at Maine Road Attendance 55012
Result: **Manchester United 6 Bournemouth 0**
Teamsheet: Crompton, Carey, Aston, Cockburn, Chilton, McGlen, Delaney, Pearson, Burke, Rowley, Mitten
Scorer(s): Burke 2, Rowley 2, Mitten, Pearson

Match # 1907 Saturday 22/01/49 Football League Division 1 at Maine Road Attendance 66485
Result: **Manchester United 0 Manchester City 0**
Teamsheet: Crompton, Carey, Aston, Cockburn, Chilton, McGlen, Delaney, Morris, Rowley, Pearson, Mitten

Match # 1908 Saturday 29/01/49 FA Cup 4th Round at Maine Road Attendance 82771
Result: **Manchester United 1 Bradford Park Avenue 1**
Teamsheet: Crompton, Carey, Aston, Cockburn, Chilton, McGlen, Delaney, Morris, Rowley, Pearson, Mitten
Scorer(s): Mitten

Match # 1909 Saturday 05/02/49 FA Cup 4th Round Replay at Park Avenue Attendance 30000
Result: **Bradford Park Avenue 1 Manchester United 1**
Teamsheet: Crompton, Carey, Aston, Cockburn, Chilton, McGlen, Buckle, Pearson, Burke, Rowley, Mitten
Scorer(s): Mitten

Match # 1910 Monday 07/02/49 FA Cup 4th Round 2nd Replay at Maine Road Attendance 70434
Result: **Manchester United 5 Bradford Park Avenue 0**
Teamsheet: Crompton, Carey, Aston, Cockburn, Chilton, McGlen, Buckle, Pearson, Burke, Rowley, Mitten
Scorer(s): Burke 2, Rowley 2, Pearson

Match # 1911 Saturday 12/02/49 FA Cup 5th Round at Maine Road Attendance 81565
Result: **Manchester United 8 Yeovil Town 0**
Teamsheet: Crompton, Carey, Aston, Cockburn, Chilton, McGlen, Delaney, Pearson, Burke, Rowley, Mitten
Scorer(s): Rowley 5, Burke 2, Mitten

Match # 1912 Saturday 19/02/49 Football League Division 1 at Villa Park Attendance 68354
Result: **Aston Villa 2 Manchester United 1**
Teamsheet: Crompton, Carey, Aston, Cockburn, Chilton, McGlen, Delaney, Pearson, Burke, Rowley, Mitten
Scorer(s): Rowley

Match # 1913 Saturday 26/02/49 FA Cup 6th Round at Boothferry Park Attendance 55000
Result: **Hull City 0 Manchester United 1**
Teamsheet: Crompton, Ball, Aston, Cockburn, Chilton, McGlen, Delaney, Pearson, Burke, Rowley, Mitten
Scorer(s): Pearson

Match # 1914 Saturday 05/03/49 Football League Division 1 at The Valley Attendance 55291
Result: **Charlton Athletic 2 Manchester United 3**
Teamsheet: Crompton, Carey, Aston, Cockburn, Chilton, McGlen, Delaney, Downie, Rowley, Pearson, Mitten
Scorer(s): Pearson 2, Downie

Match # 1915 Saturday 12/03/49 Football League Division 1 at Maine Road Attendance 55949
Result: **Manchester United 3 Stoke City 0**
Teamsheet: Crompton, Carey, Aston, Cockburn, Chilton, McGlen, Delaney, Downie, Rowley, Pearson, Mitten
Scorer(s): Downie, Mitten, Rowley

SEASON 1948/49 (continued)

Match # 1916 Saturday 19/03/49 Football League Division 1 at St Andrews Attendance 46819
Result: **Birmingham City 1 Manchester United 0**
Teamsheet: Crompton, Carey, Aston, Cockburn, Chilton, McGlen, Delaney, Anderson, Rowley, Pearson, Mitten

Match # 1917 Saturday 26/03/49 FA Cup Semi-Final at Hillsborough Attendance 62250
Result: **Manchester United 1 Wolverhampton Wanderers 1**
Teamsheet: Crompton, Carey, Aston, Cockburn, Chilton, McGlen, Delaney, Anderson, Rowley, Pearson, Mitten
Scorer(s): Mitten

Match # 1918 Saturday 02/04/49 FA Cup Semi-Final Replay at Goodison Park Attendance 73000
Result: **Manchester United 0 Wolverhampton Wanderers 1**
Teamsheet: Crompton, Carey, Aston, Cockburn, Chilton, McGlen, Delaney, Pearson, Burke, Rowley, Mitten

Match # 1919 Wednesday 06/04/49 Football League Division 1 at Leeds Road Attendance 17256
Result: **Huddersfield Town 2 Manchester United 1**
Teamsheet: Crompton, Carey, Ball, Anderson, Chilton, McGlen, Delaney, Downie, Burke, Rowley, Mitten
Scorer(s): Rowley

Match # 1920 Saturday 09/04/49 Football League Division 1 at Maine Road Attendance 27304
Result: **Manchester United 1 Chelsea 1**
Teamsheet: Crompton, Carey, Ball, Anderson, Chilton, McGlen, Buckle, Downie, Burke, Rowley, Mitten
Scorer(s): Mitten

Match # 1921 Friday 15/04/49 Football League Division 1 at Burnden Park Attendance 44999
Result: **Bolton Wanderers 0 Manchester United 1**
Teamsheet: Crompton, Ball, Aston, Lowrie, Chilton, Cockburn, Carey, Downie, Rowley, Pearson, Mitten
Scorer(s): Carey

Match # 1922 Saturday 16/04/49 Football League Division 1 at Turf Moor Attendance 37722
Result: **Burnley 0 Manchester United 2**
Teamsheet: Crompton, Ball, Aston, Lowrie, Chilton, Cockburn, Carey, Downie, Rowley, Pearson, Mitten
Scorer(s): Rowley 2

Match # 1923 Monday 18/04/49 Football League Division 1 at Maine Road Attendance 47653
Result: **Manchester United 3 Bolton Wanderers 0**
Teamsheet: Crompton, Ball, Aston, Lowrie, Chilton, Cockburn, Delaney, Carey, Rowley, Pearson, Mitten
Scorer(s): Rowley 2, Mitten

Match # 1924 Thursday 21/04/49 Football League Division 1 at Maine Road Attendance 30640
Result: **Manchester United 1 Sunderland 2**
Teamsheet: Crompton, Ball, Aston, Lowrie, Chilton, Cockburn, Delaney, Carey, Rowley, Pearson, Mitten
Scorer(s): Mitten

Match # 1925 Saturday 23/04/49 Football League Division 1 at Maine Road Attendance 43214
Result: **Manchester United 2 Preston North End 2**
Teamsheet: Crompton, Carey, Aston, Lowrie, Chilton, Cockburn, Delaney, Downie, Rowley, Pearson, Mitten
Scorer(s): Downie 2

Match # 1926 Wednesday 27/04/49 Football League Division 1 at Goodison Park Attendance 39106
Result: **Everton 2 Manchester United 0**
Teamsheet: Crompton, Carey, Aston, Lowrie, Chilton, Cockburn, Delaney, Downie, Cassidy, Pearson, Mitten

Match # 1927 Saturday 30/04/49 Football League Division 1 at St James' Park Attendance 38266
Result: **Newcastle United 0 Manchester United 1**
Teamsheet: Crompton, Carey, Aston, Lowrie, Chilton, Cockburn, Delaney, Downie, Burke, Pearson, Mitten
Scorer(s): Burke

Match # 1928 Monday 02/05/49 Football League Division 1 at Maine Road Attendance 20158
Result: **Manchester United 1 Middlesbrough 0**
Teamsheet: Crompton, Carey, Aston, Lowrie, Chilton, Cockburn, Delaney, Downie, Rowley, Pearson, Mitten
Scorer(s): Rowley

Match # 1929 Wednesday 04/05/49 Football League Division 1 at Maine Road Attendance 20880
Result: **Manchester United 3 Sheffield United 2**
Teamsheet: Crompton, Carey, Aston, Cockburn, Chilton, McGlen, Delaney, Downie, Rowley, Pearson, Mitten
Scorer(s): Downie, Mitten, Pearson

Match # 1930 Saturday 07/05/49 Football League Division 1 at Maine Road Attendance 49808
Result: **Manchester United 3 Portsmouth 2**
Teamsheet: Crompton, Carey, Aston, Anderson, Chilton, Cockburn, Delaney, Downie, Rowley, Pearson, Mitten
Scorer(s): Rowley 2, Mitten

SEASON 1948/49 SUMMARY

APPEARANCES

PLAYER	LGE	FAC	CS	TOT
Chilton	42	8	1	51
Mitten	42	8	1	51
Crompton	41	8	1	50
Carey	41	7	1	49
Aston	39	8	1	48
Rowley	39	8	1	48
Pearson	39	8	–	47
Cockburn	36	8	–	44
Delaney	36	6	1	43
McGlen	23	8	–	31
Morris	21	1	1	23
Anderson	15	1	1	17
Burke	9	6	1	16
Downie	12	–	–	12
Ball	8	1	–	9
Lowrie	8	–	–	8
Buckle	5	2	–	7
Warner	3	–	1	4
Brown	1	–	–	1
Cassidy	1	–	–	1
Hanlon	1	–	–	1

GOALSCORERS

PLAYER	LGE	FAC	CS	TOT
Rowley	20	9	1	30
Mitten	18	5	–	23
Pearson	14	3	–	17
Burke	6	6	1	13
Morris	6	–	–	6
Downie	5	–	–	5
Delaney	4	–	–	4
Buckle	2	–	–	2
Carey	1	–	–	1
McGlen	1	–	–	1
own goal	–	–	1	1

RESULTS & ATTENDANCES SUMMARY

		P	W	D	L	F	A	TOTAL	AVGE
League	H	21	11	7	3	40	20	970894	46233
	A	21	10	4	7	37	24	939125	44720
	TOTAL	42	21	11	10	77	44	1910019	45477
FA Cup	H	4	3	1	0	20	1	289782	72446
	A	2	1	1	0	2	1	85000	42500
	N	2	0	1	1	1	2	135250	67625
	TOTAL	8	4	3	1	23	4	510032	63754
Charity Shield	H	0	0	0	0	0	0	0	n/a
	A	1	0	0	1	3	4	31000	31000
	TOTAL	1	0	0	1	3	4	31000	31000
Overall	H	25	14	8	3	60	21	1260676	50427
	A	24	11	5	8	42	29	1055125	43964
	N	2	0	1	1	1	2	135250	67625
	TOTAL	51	25	14	12	103	52	2451051	48060

FINAL TABLE – LEAGUE DIVISION ONE

		P	W	D	L	F	A	W	D	L	F	A	PTS	GD
			HOME					AWAY						
1	Portsmouth	42	18	3	0	52	12	7	5	9	32	30	58	42
2	MANCHESTER UNITED	42	11	7	3	40	20	10	4	7	37	24	53	33
3	Derby County	42	17	2	2	48	22	5	7	9	26	33	53	19
4	Newcastle United	42	12	5	4	35	29	8	7	6	35	27	52	14
5	Arsenal	42	13	5	3	51	18	5	8	8	23	26	49	30
6	Wolverhampton Wanderers	42	13	5	3	48	19	4	7	10	31	47	46	13
7	Manchester City	42	10	8	3	28	21	5	7	9	19	30	45	-4
8	Sunderland	42	8	10	3	27	19	5	7	9	22	39	43	-9
9	Charlton Athletic	42	10	5	6	38	31	5	7	9	25	36	42	-4
10	Aston Villa	42	10	6	5	40	36	6	4	11	20	40	42	-16
11	Stoke City	42	14	3	4	43	24	2	6	13	23	44	41	-2
12	Liverpool	42	5	10	6	25	18	8	4	9	28	25	40	10
13	Chelsea	42	10	6	5	43	27	2	8	11	26	41	38	1
14	Bolton Wanderers	42	10	4	7	43	32	4	6	11	16	36	38	-9
15	Burnley	42	10	6	5	27	19	2	8	11	16	31	38	-7
16	Blackpool	42	8	8	5	24	25	3	8	10	30	42	38	-13
17	Birmingham City	42	9	7	5	19	10	2	8	11	17	28	37	-2
18	Everton	42	12	5	4	33	25	1	6	14	8	38	37	-22
19	Middlesbrough	42	10	6	5	37	23	1	6	14	9	34	34	-11
20	Huddersfield Town	42	6	7	8	19	24	6	3	12	21	45	34	-29
21	Preston North End	42	8	6	7	36	36	3	5	13	26	39	33	-13
22	Sheffield United	42	8	9	4	32	25	3	2	16	25	53	33	-21

SEASON 1949/50

Match # 1931 Saturday 20/08/49 Football League Division 1 at Baseball Ground Attendance 35687
Result: **Derby County 0 Manchester United 1**
Teamsheet: Crompton, Carey, Aston, Warner, Lynn, Cockburn, Delaney, Downie, Rowley, Pearson, Mitten
Scorer(s): Rowley

Match # 1932 Wednesday 24/08/49 Football League Division 1 at Old Trafford Attendance 41748
Result: **Manchester United 3 Bolton Wanderers 0**
Teamsheet: Crompton, Carey, Aston, Warner, Lynn, Cockburn, Delaney, Downie, Rowley, Pearson, Mitten
Scorer(s): Mitten, Rowley, own goal

Match # 1933 Saturday 27/08/49 Football League Division 1 at Old Trafford Attendance 44655
Result: **Manchester United 1 West Bromwich Albion 1**
Teamsheet: Crompton, Carey, Aston, Warner, Lynn, Cockburn, Delaney, Pearson, Rowley, Birch, Mitten
Scorer(s): Pearson

Match # 1934 Wednesday 31/08/49 Football League Division 1 at Burnden Park Attendance 36277
Result: **Bolton Wanderers 1 Manchester United 2**
Teamsheet: Crompton, Carey, Aston, Warner, Lynn, Cockburn, Delaney, Pearson, Rowley, Buckle, Mitten
Scorer(s): Mitten, Pearson

Match # 1935 Saturday 03/09/49 Football League Division 1 at Old Trafford Attendance 47760
Result: **Manchester United 2 Manchester City 1**
Teamsheet: Crompton, Carey, Aston, Warner, Lynn, Cockburn, Delaney, Pearson, Rowley, Buckle, Mitten
Scorer(s): Pearson 2

Match # 1936 Wednesday 07/09/49 Football League Division 1 at Anfield Attendance 51587
Result: **Liverpool 1 Manchester United 1**
Teamsheet: Crompton, Carey, Aston, Lowrie, Lynn, Chilton, Delaney, Pearson, Rowley, Buckle, Mitten
Scorer(s): Mitten

Match # 1937 Saturday 10/09/49 Football League Division 1 at Stamford Bridge Attendance 61357
Result: **Chelsea 1 Manchester United 1**
Teamsheet: Crompton, Carey, Aston, Lowrie, Lynn, Chilton, Delaney, Pearson, Rowley, Buckle, Mitten
Scorer(s): Rowley

Match # 1938 Saturday 17/09/49 Football League Division 1 at Old Trafford Attendance 43522
Result: **Manchester United 2 Stoke City 2**
Teamsheet: Crompton, Carey, Aston, Chilton, Lynn, Cockburn, Delaney, Pearson, Rowley, Buckle, Mitten
Scorer(s): Rowley 2

Match # 1939 Saturday 24/09/49 Football League Division 1 at Turf Moor Attendance 41072
Result: **Burnley 1 Manchester United 0**
Teamsheet: Crompton, Carey, Aston, Chilton, Lynn, Cockburn, Delaney, Pearson, Rowley, Buckle, Mitten

Match # 1940 Saturday 01/10/49 Football League Division 1 at Old Trafford Attendance 49260
Result: **Manchester United 1 Sunderland 3**
Teamsheet: Crompton, Carey, Aston, Lowrie, Chilton, Cockburn, Delaney, Pearson, Rowley, Buckle, Mitten
Scorer(s): Pearson

Match # 1941 Saturday 08/10/49 Football League Division 1 at Old Trafford Attendance 43809
Result: **Manchester United 3 Charlton Athletic 2**
Teamsheet: Crompton, Ball, Aston, Warner, Chilton, McGlen, Delaney, Bogan, Rowley, Pearson, Mitten
Scorer(s): Mitten 2, Rowley

Match # 1942 Saturday 15/10/49 Football League Division 1 at Villa Park Attendance 47483
Result: **Aston Villa 0 Manchester United 4**
Teamsheet: Crompton, Ball, Carey, Warner, Lynn, Cockburn, Delaney, Bogan, Rowley, Pearson, Mitten
Scorer(s): Mitten 2, Bogan, Rowley

Match # 1943 Saturday 22/10/49 Football League Division 1 at Old Trafford Attendance 51427
Result: **Manchester United 3 Wolverhampton Wanderers 0**
Teamsheet: Crompton, Carey, Aston, Warner, Chilton, Cockburn, Delaney, Bogan, Rowley, Pearson, Mitten
Scorer(s): Pearson 2, Bogan

Match # 1944 Saturday 29/10/49 Football League Division 1 at Fratton Park Attendance 41098
Result: **Portsmouth 0 Manchester United 0**
Teamsheet: Crompton, Carey, Aston, Warner, Chilton, Cockburn, Delaney, Bogan, Rowley, Pearson, Mitten

Match # 1945 Saturday 05/11/49 Football League Division 1 at Old Trafford Attendance 40295
Result: **Manchester United 6 Huddersfield Town 0**
Teamsheet: Feehan, Carey, Aston, Cockburn, Chilton, McGlen, Delaney, Bogan, Rowley, Pearson, Mitten
Scorer(s): Pearson 2, Rowley 2, Delaney, Mitten

Match # 1946 Saturday 12/11/49 Football League Division 1 at Goodison Park Attendance 46672
Result: **Everton 0 Manchester United 0**
Teamsheet: Crompton, Carey, Aston, Warner, Chilton, Cockburn, Delaney, Bogan, Rowley, Pearson, Mitten

Match # 1947 Saturday 19/11/49 Football League Division 1 at Old Trafford Attendance 42626
Result: **Manchester United 2 Middlesbrough 0**
Teamsheet: Crompton, Carey, Aston, Cockburn, Chilton, McGlen, Delaney, Bogan, Rowley, Pearson, Mitten
Scorer(s): Pearson, Rowley

Match # 1948 Saturday 26/11/49 Football League Division 1 at Bloomfield Road Attendance 27742
Result: **Blackpool 3 Manchester United 3**
Teamsheet: Feehan, Carey, Aston, Cockburn, Chilton, McGlen, Delaney, Rowley, Bogan, Pearson, Mitten
Scorer(s): Pearson 2, Bogan

SEASON 1949/50 (continued)

Match # 1949 Saturday 03/12/49   Football League Division 1   at Old Trafford   Attendance 30343
Result: **Manchester United 1 Newcastle United 1**
Teamsheet: Wood, Carey, Aston, Cockburn, Chilton, McGlen, Delaney, Downie, Bogan, Pearson, Mitten
Scorer(s): Mitten

Match # 1950 Saturday 10/12/49   Football League Division 1   at Craven Cottage   Attendance 35362
Result: **Fulham 1 Manchester United 0**
Teamsheet: Feehan, Carey, Aston, Cockburn, Chilton, McGlen, Delaney, Bogan, Rowley, Pearson, Mitten

Match # 1951 Saturday 17/12/49   Football League Division 1   at Old Trafford   Attendance 33753
Result: **Manchester United 0 Derby County 1**
Teamsheet: Feehan, Carey, Aston, Cockburn, Chilton, McGlen, Delaney, Bogan, Rowley, Pearson, Mitten

Match # 1952 Saturday 24/12/49   Football League Division 1   at The Hawthorns   Attendance 46973
Result: **West Bromwich Albion 1 Manchester United 2**
Teamsheet: Feehan, Carey, Aston, Cockburn, Chilton, McGlen, Delaney, Bogan, Rowley, Pearson, Mitten
Scorer(s): Bogan, Rowley

Match # 1953 Monday 26/12/49   Football League Division 1   at Old Trafford   Attendance 53928
Result: **Manchester United 2 Arsenal 0**
Teamsheet: Feehan, Carey, Aston, Warner, Chilton, McGlen, Delaney, Bogan, Rowley, Pearson, Mitten
Scorer(s): Pearson 2

Match # 1954 Tuesday 27/12/49   Football League Division 1   at Highbury   Attendance 65133
Result: **Arsenal 0 Manchester United 0**
Teamsheet: Feehan, Carey, Aston, Warner, Chilton, McGlen, Delaney, Bogan, Rowley, Pearson, Mitten

Match # 1955 Saturday 31/12/49   Football League Division 1   at Maine Road   Attendance 63704
Result: **Manchester City 1 Manchester United 2**
Teamsheet: Feehan, Carey, Aston, Warner, Chilton, McGlen, Delaney, Bogan, Rowley, Pearson, Mitten
Scorer(s): Delaney, Pearson

Match # 1956 Saturday 07/01/50   FA Cup 3rd Round   at Old Trafford   Attendance 38284
Result: **Manchester United 4 Weymouth Town 0**
Teamsheet: Feehan, Carey, Aston, Cockburn, Chilton, McGlen, Delaney, Bogan, Rowley, Pearson, Mitten
Scorer(s): Rowley 2, Delaney, Pearson

Match # 1957 Saturday 14/01/50   Football League Division 1   at Old Trafford   Attendance 46954
Result: **Manchester United 1 Chelsea 0**
Teamsheet: Lancaster, Carey, Aston, Cockburn, Chilton, McGlen, Delaney, Downie, Rowley, Pearson, Mitten
Scorer(s): Mitten

Match # 1958 Saturday 21/01/50   Football League Division 1   at Victoria Ground   Attendance 38877
Result: **Stoke City 3 Manchester United 1**
Teamsheet: Feehan, Carey, Aston, Cockburn, Chilton, McGlen, Delaney, Bogan, Rowley, Pearson, Mitten
Scorer(s): Mitten

Match # 1959 Saturday 28/01/50   FA Cup 4th Round   at Vicarage Road   Attendance 32800
Result: **Watford 0 Manchester United 1**
Teamsheet: Lancaster, Carey, Aston, Warner, Chilton, Cockburn, Delaney, Bogan, Rowley, Pearson, Mitten
Scorer(s): Rowley

Match # 1960 Saturday 04/02/50   Football League Division 1   at Old Trafford   Attendance 46702
Result: **Manchester United 3 Burnley 2**
Teamsheet: Lancaster, Carey, Aston, Warner, Chilton, Cockburn, Delaney, Bogan, Rowley, Pearson, Mitten
Scorer(s): Rowley 2, Mitten

Match # 1961 Saturday 11/02/50   FA Cup 5th Round   at Old Trafford   Attendance 53688
Result: **Manchester United 3 Portsmouth 3**
Teamsheet: Lancaster, Carey, Aston, Warner, Chilton, Cockburn, Delaney, Bogan, Rowley, Pearson, Mitten
Scorer(s): Mitten 2, Pearson

Match # 1962 Wednesday 15/02/50   FA Cup 5th Round Replay   at Fratton Park   Attendance 49962
Result: **Portsmouth 1 Manchester United 3**
Teamsheet: Feehan, Carey, Aston, Warner, Chilton, Cockburn, Delaney, Bogan, Rowley, Downie, Mitten
Scorer(s): Delaney, Downie, Mitten

Match # 1963 Saturday 18/02/50   Football League Division 1   at Roker Park   Attendance 63251
Result: **Sunderland 2 Manchester United 2**
Teamsheet: Feehan, Carey, Aston, Warner, Chilton, Cockburn, Delaney, Clempson, Rowley, Downie, Mitten
Scorer(s): Chilton, Rowley

Match # 1964 Saturday 25/02/50   Football League Division 1   at The Valley   Attendance 44920
Result: **Charlton Athletic 1 Manchester United 2**
Teamsheet: Crompton, Ball, Aston, Carey, Chilton, Cockburn, Delaney, Downie, Rowley, Pearson, Mitten
Scorer(s): Carey, Rowley

Match # 1965 Saturday 04/03/50   FA Cup 6th Round   at Stamford Bridge   Attendance 70362
Result: **Chelsea 2 Manchester United 0**
Teamsheet: Crompton, Carey, Aston, Warner, Chilton, Cockburn, Delaney, Downie, Rowley, Pearson, Mitten

Match # 1966 Wednesday 08/03/50   Football League Division 1   at Old Trafford   Attendance 22149
Result: **Manchester United 7 Aston Villa 0**
Teamsheet: Crompton, Ball, Aston, Warner, Carey, Cockburn, Delaney, Downie, Rowley, Pearson, Mitten
Scorer(s): Mitten 4, Downie 2, Rowley

SEASON 1949/50 (continued)

Match # 1967	Saturday 11/03/50 Football League Division 1	at Ayresome Park	Attendance 46702
Result:	**Middlesbrough 2 Manchester United 3**		
Teamsheet:	Crompton, Ball, Aston, Warner, Chilton, Carey, Delaney, Downie, Rowley, Pearson, Mitten		
Scorer(s):	Downie 2, Rowley		

Match # 1968	Wednesday 15/03/50 Football League Division 1	at Old Trafford	Attendance 43456
Result:	**Manchester United 0 Liverpool 0**		
Teamsheet:	Crompton, Carey, Aston, Warner, Chilton, Cockburn, Delaney, Downie, Rowley, Pearson, Mitten		

Match # 1969	Saturday 18/03/50 Football League Division 1	at Old Trafford	Attendance 53688
Result:	**Manchester United 1 Blackpool 2**		
Teamsheet:	Crompton, Carey, Aston, Warner, Chilton, Cockburn, Bogan, Downie, Delaney, Pearson, Mitten		
Scorer(s):	Delaney		

Match # 1970	Saturday 25/03/50 Football League Division 1	at Leeds Road	Attendance 34348
Result:	**Huddersfield Town 3 Manchester United 1**		
Teamsheet:	Crompton, Ball, Aston, Warner, Chilton, Cockburn, Delaney, Downie, Carey, Pearson, Mitten		
Scorer(s):	Downie		

Match # 1971	Saturday 01/04/50 Football League Division 1	at Old Trafford	Attendance 35381
Result:	**Manchester United 1 Everton 1**		
Teamsheet:	Feehan, Ball, Aston, Carey, Chilton, Cockburn, Delaney, Downie, Rowley, Pearson, Mitten		
Scorer(s):	Delaney		

Match # 1972	Friday 07/04/50 Football League Division 1	at Old Trafford	Attendance 47170
Result:	**Manchester United 0 Birmingham City 2**		
Teamsheet:	Feehan, Ball, Aston, Carey, Chilton, Cockburn, Delaney, Pearson, Rowley, Downie, Mitten		

Match # 1973	Saturday 08/04/50 Football League Division 1	at Molineux	Attendance 54296
Result:	**Wolverhampton Wanderers 1 Manchester United 1**		
Teamsheet:	Crompton, Ball, Aston, Carey, Chilton, Cockburn, Delaney, Pearson, Rowley, Downie, Mitten		
Scorer(s):	Rowley		

Match # 1974	Monday 10/04/50 Football League Division 1	at St Andrews	Attendance 35863
Result:	**Birmingham City 0 Manchester United 0**		
Teamsheet:	Crompton, Ball, Aston, Carey, Chilton, Cockburn, Delaney, Pearson, Rowley, Downie, Mitten		

Match # 1975	Saturday 15/04/50 Football League Division 1	at Old Trafford	Attendance 44908
Result:	**Manchester United 0 Portsmouth 2**		
Teamsheet:	Crompton, McNulty, Ball, Whitefoot, Chilton, Cockburn, Delaney, Pearson, Rowley, Downie, Mitten		

Match # 1976	Saturday 22/04/50 Football League Division 1	at St James' Park	Attendance 52203
Result:	**Newcastle United 2 Manchester United 1**		
Teamsheet:	Crompton, Ball, Aston, Warner, Chilton, Cockburn, Delaney, Pearson, Rowley, Downie, Mitten		
Scorer(s):	Downie		

Match # 1977	Saturday 29/04/50 Football League Division 1	at Old Trafford	Attendance 11968
Result:	**Manchester United 3 Fulham 0**		
Teamsheet:	Crompton, McNulty, Ball, Aston, Chilton, Cockburn, Delaney, Pearson, Rowley, Downie, Mitten		
Scorer(s):	Rowley 2, Cockburn		

SEASON 1949/50 SUMMARY

APPEARANCES

PLAYER	LGE	FAC	TOT
Delaney	42	5	47
Mitten	42	5	47
Aston	40	5	45
Pearson	41	4	45
Rowley	39	5	44
Carey	38	5	43
Chilton	35	5	40
Cockburn	35	5	40
Crompton	27	1	28
Warner	21	4	25
Bogan	18	4	22
Downie	18	2	20
Feehan	12	2	14
McGlen	13	1	14
Ball	13	–	13
Lynn	10	–	10
Buckle	7	–	7
Lancaster	2	2	4
Lowrie	3	–	3
McNulty	2	–	2
Birch	1	–	1
Clempson	1	–	1
Whitefoot	1	–	1
Wood	1	–	1

GOALSCORERS

PLAYER	LGE	FAC	TOT
Rowley	20	3	23
Mitten	16	3	19
Pearson	15	2	17
Downie	6	1	7
Delaney	4	2	6
Bogan	4	–	4
Carey	1	–	1
Chilton	1	–	1
Cockburn	1	–	1
own goal	1	–	1

RESULTS & ATTENDANCES SUMMARY

		P	W	D	L	F	A	TOTAL	AVGE
League	H	21	11	5	5	42	20	875502	41691
	A	21	7	9	5	27	24	970607	46219
	TOTAL	42	18	14	10	69	44	1846109	43955
FA Cup	H	2	1	1	0	7	3	91972	45986
	A	3	2	0	1	4	3	153124	51041
	TOTAL	5	3	1	1	11	6	245096	49019
Overall	H	23	12	6	5	49	23	967474	42064
	A	24	9	9	6	31	27	1123731	46822
	TOTAL	47	21	15	11	80	50	2091205	44494

FINAL TABLE - LEAGUE DIVISION ONE

		P	HOME W	HOME D	HOME L	HOME F	HOME A	AWAY W	AWAY D	AWAY L	AWAY F	AWAY A	PTS	GD
1	Portsmouth	42	12	7	2	44	15	10	2	9	30	23	53	36
2	Wolverhampton Wanderers	42	11	8	2	47	21	9	5	7	29	28	53	27
3	Sunderland	42	14	6	1	50	23	7	4	10	33	39	52	21
4	MANCHESTER UNITED	42	11	5	5	42	20	7	9	5	27	24	50	25
5	Newcastle United	42	14	4	3	49	23	5	8	8	28	32	50	22
6	Arsenal	42	12	4	5	48	24	7	7	7	31	31	49	24
7	Blackpool	42	10	8	3	29	14	7	7	7	17	21	49	11
8	Liverpool	42	10	7	4	37	23	7	7	7	27	31	48	10
9	Middlesbrough	42	14	2	5	37	18	6	5	10	22	30	47	11
10	Burnley	42	9	7	5	23	17	7	6	8	17	23	45	0
11	Derby County	42	11	5	5	46	26	6	5	10	23	35	44	8
12	Aston Villa	42	10	7	4	31	19	5	5	11	30	42	42	0
13	Chelsea	42	7	7	7	31	30	5	9	7	27	35	40	-7
14	West Bromwich Albion	42	9	7	5	28	16	5	5	11	19	37	40	-6
15	Huddersfield Town	42	11	4	6	34	22	3	5	13	18	51	37	-21
16	Bolton Wanderers	42	10	5	6	34	22	0	9	12	11	37	34	-14
17	Fulham	42	8	6	7	24	19	2	8	11	17	35	34	-13
18	Everton	42	6	8	7	24	20	4	6	11	18	46	34	-24
19	Stoke City	42	10	4	7	27	28	1	8	12	18	47	34	-30
20	Charlton Athletic	42	7	5	9	33	35	6	1	14	20	30	32	-12
21	Manchester City	42	7	8	6	27	24	1	5	15	9	44	29	-32
22	Birmingham City	42	6	8	7	19	24	1	6	14	12	43	28	-36

SEASON 1950/51

Match # 1978 Saturday 19/08/50 Football League Division 1 at Old Trafford Attendance 44042
Result: **Manchester United 1 Fulham 0**
Teamsheet: Allen, Carey, Aston, McIlvenny, Chilton, Cockburn, Delaney, Downie, Rowley, Pearson, McGlen
Scorer(s): Pearson

Match # 1979 Wednesday 23/08/50 Football League Division 1 at Anfield Attendance 30211
Result: **Liverpool 2 Manchester United 1**
Teamsheet: Allen, Carey, Aston, McIlvenny, Chilton, Cockburn, Delaney, Downie, Rowley, Pearson, McGlen
Scorer(s): Rowley

Match # 1980 Saturday 26/08/50 Football League Division 1 at Burnden Park Attendance 40431
Result: **Bolton Wanderers 1 Manchester United 0**
Teamsheet: Allen, Carey, Aston, Gibson, Chilton, Cockburn, Delaney, Downie, Rowley, Pearson, McGlen

Match # 1981 Wednesday 30/08/50 Football League Division 1 at Old Trafford Attendance 34835
Result: **Manchester United 1 Liverpool 0**
Teamsheet: Allen, Carey, Aston, Gibson, Chilton, Cockburn, Bogan, Downie, Rowley, Pearson, McGlen
Scorer(s): Downie

Match # 1982 Saturday 02/09/50 Football League Division 1 at Old Trafford Attendance 53260
Result: **Manchester United 1 Blackpool 0**
Teamsheet: Allen, Carey, Aston, Gibson, Chilton, Cockburn, Bogan, Downie, Rowley, Pearson, McGlen
Scorer(s): Bogan

Match # 1983 Monday 04/09/50 Football League Division 1 at Villa Park Attendance 42724
Result: **Aston Villa 1 Manchester United 3**
Teamsheet: Allen, Carey, Aston, Gibson, Chilton, Cockburn, Bogan, Downie, Rowley, Pearson, McGlen
Scorer(s): Rowley 2, Pearson

Match # 1984 Saturday 09/09/50 Football League Division 1 at White Hart Lane Attendance 60621
Result: **Tottenham Hotspur 1 Manchester United 0**
Teamsheet: Allen, Carey, Aston, Gibson, Chilton, Cockburn, Bogan, Downie, Rowley, Pearson, McGlen

Match # 1985 Wednesday 13/09/50 Football League Division 1 at Old Trafford Attendance 33021
Result: **Manchester United 0 Aston Villa 0**
Teamsheet: Allen, Carey, Aston, Gibson, Chilton, Cockburn, Delaney, Bogan, Rowley, Cassidy, McShane

Match # 1986 Saturday 16/09/50 Football League Division 1 at Old Trafford Attendance 36619
Result: **Manchester United 3 Charlton Athletic 0**
Teamsheet: Allen, Carey, Aston, Gibson, Chilton, Cockburn, Delaney, Downie, Rowley, Pearson, McShane
Scorer(s): Delaney, Pearson, Rowley

Match # 1987 Saturday 23/09/50 Football League Division 1 at Ayresome Park Attendance 48051
Result: **Middlesbrough 1 Manchester United 2**
Teamsheet: Allen, Carey, Aston, Gibson, Chilton, Cockburn, Delaney, Downie, Rowley, Pearson, McShane
Scorer(s): Pearson 2

Match # 1988 Saturday 30/09/50 Football League Division 1 at Molineux Attendance 45898
Result: **Wolverhampton Wanderers 0 Manchester United 0**
Teamsheet: Allen, Carey, Aston, Gibson, Chilton, Cockburn, Delaney, Downie, Rowley, Pearson, McShane

Match # 1989 Saturday 07/10/50 Football League Division 1 at Old Trafford Attendance 40651
Result: **Manchester United 3 Sheffield Wednesday 1**
Teamsheet: Allen, Carey, Redman, Gibson, Jones, McGlen, Delaney, Downie, Rowley, Pearson, McShane
Scorer(s): Downie, McShane, Rowley

Match # 1990 Saturday 14/10/50 Football League Division 1 at Highbury Attendance 66150
Result: **Arsenal 3 Manchester United 0**
Teamsheet: Allen, Carey, Aston, Gibson, Chilton, Cockburn, Delaney, Downie, Rowley, Pearson, McShane

Match # 1991 Saturday 21/10/50 Football League Division 1 at Old Trafford Attendance 41842
Result: **Manchester United 0 Portsmouth 0**
Teamsheet: Allen, Carey, Aston, Gibson, Chilton, McGlen, Delaney, Downie, Rowley, Pearson, McShane

Match # 1992 Saturday 28/10/50 Football League Division 1 at Goodison Park Attendance 51142
Result: **Everton 1 Manchester United 4**
Teamsheet: Crompton, Carey, Aston, Gibson, Jones, Cockburn, Delaney, Bogan, Rowley, Pearson, McShane
Scorer(s): Rowley 2, Aston, Pearson

Match # 1993 Saturday 04/11/50 Football League Division 1 at Old Trafford Attendance 39454
Result: **Manchester United 1 Burnley 1**
Teamsheet: Allen, Carey, Aston, Gibson, Chilton, Cockburn, Delaney, Bogan, Rowley, Pearson, McShane
Scorer(s): McShane

Match # 1994 Saturday 11/11/50 Football League Division 1 at Stamford Bridge Attendance 51882
Result: **Chelsea 1 Manchester United 0**
Teamsheet: Allen, Carey, Aston, Gibson, Chilton, Cockburn, Delaney, Pearson, Rowley, Downie, McShane

Match # 1995 Saturday 18/11/50 Football League Division 1 at Old Trafford Attendance 30031
Result: **Manchester United 0 Stoke City 0**
Teamsheet: Allen, Carey, Aston, Gibson, Chilton, Cockburn, Bogan, Pearson, Rowley, Birch, McShane

SEASON 1950/51 (continued)

Match # 1996   Saturday 25/11/50   Football League Division 1   at The Hawthorns   Attendance 28146
Result: **West Bromwich Albion 0 Manchester United 1**
Teamsheet: Allen, McNulty, Aston, Gibson, Chilton, Cockburn, Bogan, Pearson, Rowley, Birch, McShane
Scorer(s):   Birch

Match # 1997   Saturday 02/12/50   Football League Division 1   at Old Trafford   Attendance 34502
Result: **Manchester United 1 Newcastle United 2**
Teamsheet: Allen, Carey, Aston, Gibson, Chilton, Cockburn, Birkett, Pearson, Rowley, Birch, McShane
Scorer(s):   Birch

Match # 1998   Saturday 09/12/50   Football League Division 1   at Leeds Road   Attendance 26713
Result: **Huddersfield Town 2 Manchester United 3**
Teamsheet: Allen, McNulty, McGlen, Gibson, Chilton, Cockburn, Birkett, Pearson, Aston, Birch, McShane
Scorer(s):   Aston 2, Birkett

Match # 1999   Saturday 16/12/50   Football League Division 1   at Craven Cottage   Attendance 19649
Result: **Fulham 2 Manchester United 2**
Teamsheet: Allen, McNulty, McGlen, Gibson, Chilton, Cockburn, Birkett, Pearson, Aston, Downie, McShane
Scorer(s):   Pearson 2

Match # 2000   Saturday 23/12/50   Football League Division 1   at Old Trafford   Attendance 35382
Result: **Manchester United 2 Bolton Wanderers 3**
Teamsheet: Allen, Carey, McGlen, Gibson, Chilton, Cockburn, Birkett, Pearson, Aston, Downie, McShane
Scorer(s):   Aston, Pearson

Match # 2001   Monday 25/12/50   Football League Division 1   at Roker Park   Attendance 41215
Result: **Sunderland 2 Manchester United 1**
Teamsheet: Allen, Carey, McGlen, Gibson, Chilton, Cockburn, Birkett, Pearson, Aston, Birch, Rowley
Scorer(s):   Aston

Match # 2002   Tuesday 26/12/50   Football League Division 1   at Old Trafford   Attendance 35176
Result: **Manchester United 3 Sunderland 5**
Teamsheet: Allen, Carey, McGlen, Gibson, Chilton, Cockburn, McShane, Pearson, Aston, Bogan, Rowley
Scorer(s):   Bogan 2, Aston

Match # 2003   Saturday 06/01/51   FA Cup 3rd Round   at Old Trafford   Attendance 37161
Result: **Manchester United 4 Oldham Athletic 1**
Teamsheet: Allen, Carey, McGlen, Lowrie, Chilton, Cockburn, Birkett, Pearson, Aston, Birch, McShane
Scorer(s):   Aston, Birch, Pearson, own goal

Match # 2004   Saturday 13/01/51   Football League Division 1   at Old Trafford   Attendance 43283
Result: **Manchester United 2 Tottenham Hotspur 1**
Teamsheet: Allen, Carey, Redman, Gibson, Chilton, Cockburn, Birkett, Birch, Aston, Pearson, Rowley
Scorer(s):   Birch, Rowley

Match # 2005   Saturday 20/01/51   Football League Division 1   at The Valley   Attendance 31978
Result: **Charlton Athletic 1 Manchester United 2**
Teamsheet: Crompton, Carey, Redman, Gibson, Chilton, Cockburn, Birkett, Birch, Aston, Pearson, Rowley
Scorer(s):   Aston, Birkett

Match # 2006   Saturday 27/01/51   FA Cup 4th Round   at Old Trafford   Attendance 55434
Result: **Manchester United 4 Leeds United 0**
Teamsheet: Allen, Carey, Redman, Gibson, Chilton, Cockburn, Birkett, Pearson, Aston, Birch, Rowley
Scorer(s):   Pearson 3, Rowley

Match # 2007   Saturday 03/02/51   Football League Division 1   at Old Trafford   Attendance 44633
Result: **Manchester United 1 Middlesbrough 0**
Teamsheet: Allen, Carey, Redman, Gibson, Chilton, Cockburn, Birkett, Bogan, Aston, Pearson, Rowley
Scorer(s):   Pearson

Match # 2008   Saturday 10/02/51   FA Cup 5th Round   at Old Trafford   Attendance 55058
Result: **Manchester United 1 Arsenal 0**
Teamsheet: Allen, Carey, Redman, Gibson, Chilton, Cockburn, Birkett, Pearson, Aston, Birch, Rowley
Scorer(s):   Pearson

Match # 2009   Saturday 17/02/51   Football League Division 1   at Old Trafford   Attendance 42022
Result: **Manchester United 2 Wolverhampton Wanderers 1**
Teamsheet: Allen, McNulty, Carey, Gibson, Chilton, Cockburn, Birkett, Pearson, Aston, Birch, Rowley
Scorer(s):   Birch, Rowley

Match # 2010   Saturday 24/02/51   FA Cup 6th Round   at St Andrews   Attendance 50000
Result: **Birmingham City 1 Manchester United 0**
Teamsheet: Allen, McNulty, Carey, Gibson, Chilton, Cockburn, Birkett, Pearson, Aston, Birch, Rowley

Match # 2011   Monday 26/02/51   Football League Division 1   at Hillsborough   Attendance 25693
Result: **Sheffield Wednesday 0 Manchester United 4**
Teamsheet: Allen, Carey, McGlen, Gibson, Jones, Cockburn, McShane, Pearson, Aston, Downie, Rowley
Scorer(s):   Downie, McShane, Pearson, Rowley

Match # 2012   Saturday 03/03/51   Football League Division 1   at Old Trafford   Attendance 46202
Result: **Manchester United 3 Arsenal 1**
Teamsheet: Allen, Carey, Redman, Whitefoot, Jones, Cockburn, McShane, Pearson, Aston, Downie, Rowley
Scorer(s):   Aston 2, Downie

Match # 2013   Saturday 10/03/51   Football League Division 1   at Fratton Park   Attendance 33148
Result: **Portsmouth 0 Manchester United 0**
Teamsheet: Allen, Carey, Redman, Whitefoot, Chilton, McGlen, McShane, Pearson, Aston, Downie, Rowley

SEASON 1950/51 (continued)

Match # 2014	Saturday 17/03/51 Football League Division 1	at Old Trafford	Attendance 29317
Result:	**Manchester United 3 Everton 0**		
Teamsheet:	Allen, Carey, Redman, Gibson, Chilton, McGlen, McShane, Pearson, Aston, Downie, Rowley		
Scorer(s):	Aston, Downie, Pearson		

Match # 2015	Friday 23/03/51 Football League Division 1	at Old Trafford	Attendance 42009
Result:	**Manchester United 2 Derby County 0**		
Teamsheet:	Allen, Carey, Redman, Gibson, Chilton, McGlen, McShane, Clempson, Aston, Downie, Rowley		
Scorer(s):	Aston, Downie		

Match # 2016	Saturday 24/03/51 Football League Division 1	at Turf Moor	Attendance 36656
Result:	**Burnley 1 Manchester United 2**		
Teamsheet:	Allen, Carey, Redman, Gibson, Chilton, McGlen, McShane, Clempson, Aston, Downie, Rowley		
Scorer(s):	Aston, McShane		

Match # 2017	Monday 26/03/51 Football League Division 1	at Baseball Ground	Attendance 25860
Result:	**Derby County 2 Manchester United 4**		
Teamsheet:	Allen, Carey, Redman, Cockburn, Chilton, McGlen, McShane, Pearson, Aston, Downie, Rowley		
Scorer(s):	Aston, Downie, Pearson, Rowley		

Match # 2018	Saturday 31/03/51 Football League Division 1	at Old Trafford	Attendance 25779
Result:	**Manchester United 4 Chelsea 1**		
Teamsheet:	Allen, Carey, Redman, Cockburn, Chilton, McGlen, McShane, Pearson, Aston, Downie, Rowley		
Scorer(s):	Pearson 3, McShane		

Match # 2019	Saturday 07/04/51 Football League Division 1	at Victoria Ground	Attendance 25690
Result:	**Stoke City 2 Manchester United 0**		
Teamsheet:	Allen, Carey, Redman, Cockburn, Chilton, McGlen, McShane, Pearson, Aston, Downie, Rowley		

Match # 2020	Saturday 14/04/51 Football League Division 1	at Old Trafford	Attendance 24764
Result:	**Manchester United 3 West Bromwich Albion 0**		
Teamsheet:	Allen, Carey, Redman, Gibson, Chilton, McGlen, McShane, Pearson, Aston, Downie, Rowley		
Scorer(s):	Downie, Pearson, Rowley		

Match # 2021	Saturday 21/04/51 Football League Division 1	at St James' Park	Attendance 45209
Result:	**Newcastle United 0 Manchester United 2**		
Teamsheet:	Allen, Carey, Redman, Cockburn, Chilton, McGlen, McShane, Pearson, Aston, Downie, Rowley		
Scorer(s):	Pearson, Rowley		

Match # 2022	Saturday 28/04/51 Football League Division 1	at Old Trafford	Attendance 25560
Result:	**Manchester United 6 Huddersfield Town 0**		
Teamsheet:	Allen, Carey, Redman, Cockburn, Chilton, McGlen, McShane, Pearson, Aston, Downie, Rowley		
Scorer(s):	Aston 2, McShane 2, Downie, Rowley		

Match # 2023	Saturday 05/05/51 Football League Division 1	at Bloomfield Road	Attendance 22864
Result:	**Blackpool 1 Manchester United 1**		
Teamsheet:	Allen, Carey, Redman, Cockburn, Chilton, McGlen, McShane, Pearson, Aston, Downie, Rowley		
Scorer(s):	Downie		

SEASON 1950/51 SUMMARY

APPEARANCES

PLAYER	LGE	FAC	TOT
Aston	41	4	45
Allen	40	4	44
Carey	39	4	43
Pearson	39	4	43
Chilton	38	4	42
Rowley	39	3	42
Cockburn	35	4	39
Gibson	32	3	35
McShane	30	1	31
Downie	29	–	29
McGlen	26	1	27
Redman	16	2	18
Birkett	9	4	13
Delaney	13	–	13
Birch	8	4	12
Bogan	11	–	11
McNulty	4	1	5
Jones	4	–	4
Clempson	2	–	2
Crompton	2	–	2
McIlvenny	2	–	2
Whitefoot	2	–	2
Cassidy	1	–	1
Lowrie	–	1	1

GOALSCORERS

PLAYER	LGE	FAC	TOT
Pearson	18	5	23
Aston	15	1	16
Rowley	14	1	15
Downie	10	–	10
McShane	7	–	7
Birch	4	1	5
Bogan	3	–	3
Birkett	2	–	2
Delaney	1	–	1
own goal	–	1	1

RESULTS & ATTENDANCES SUMMARY

		P	W	D	L	F	A	TOTAL	AVGE
League	H	21	14	4	3	42	16	782384	37256
	A	21	10	4	7	32	24	799931	38092
	TOTAL	42	24	8	10	74	40	1582315	37674
FA Cup	H	3	3	0	0	9	1	147653	49218
	A	1	0	0	1	0	1	50000	50000
	TOTAL	4	3	0	1	9	2	197653	49413
Overall	H	24	17	4	3	51	17	930037	38752
	A	22	10	4	8	32	25	849931	38633
	TOTAL	46	27	8	11	83	42	1779968	38695

FINAL TABLE – LEAGUE DIVISION ONE

		P	HOME W	HOME D	HOME L	HOME F	HOME A	AWAY W	AWAY D	AWAY L	AWAY F	AWAY A	PTS	GD
1	Tottenham Hotspur	42	17	2	2	54	21	8	8	5	28	23	60	38
2	MANCHESTER UNITED	42	14	4	3	42	16	10	4	7	32	24	56	34
3	Blackpool	42	12	6	3	43	19	8	4	9	36	34	50	26
4	Newcastle United	42	10	6	5	36	22	8	7	6	26	31	49	9
5	Arsenal	42	11	5	5	47	28	8	4	9	26	28	47	17
6	Middlesbrough	42	12	7	2	51	25	6	4	11	25	40	47	11
7	Portsmouth	42	8	10	3	39	30	8	5	8	32	38	47	3
8	Bolton Wanderers	42	11	2	8	31	20	8	5	8	33	41	45	3
9	Liverpool	42	11	5	5	28	25	5	6	10	25	34	43	–6
10	Burnley	42	9	7	5	27	16	5	7	9	21	27	42	5
11	Derby County	42	10	5	6	53	33	6	3	12	28	42	40	6
12	Sunderland	42	8	9	4	30	21	4	7	10	33	52	40	–10
13	Stoke City	42	10	5	6	28	19	3	9	9	22	40	40	–9
14	Wolverhampton Wanderers	42	9	3	9	44	30	6	5	10	30	31	38	13
15	Aston Villa	42	9	6	6	39	29	3	7	11	27	39	37	–2
16	West Bromwich Albion	42	7	4	10	30	27	6	7	8	23	34	37	–8
17	Charlton Athletic	42	9	4	8	35	31	5	5	11	28	49	37	–17
18	Fulham	42	8	5	8	35	37	5	6	10	17	31	37	–16
19	Huddersfield Town	42	8	4	9	40	40	7	2	12	24	52	36	–28
20	Chelsea	42	9	4	8	31	25	3	4	14	22	40	32	–12
21	Sheffield Wednesday	42	9	6	6	43	32	3	2	16	21	51	32	–19
22	Everton	42	7	5	9	26	35	5	3	13	22	51	32	–38

SEASON 1951/52

Match # 2024	Saturday 18/08/51 Football League Division 1	at The Hawthorns	Attendance 27486
Result:	**West Bromwich Albion 3 Manchester United 3**		
Teamsheet:	Allen, Carey, Redman, Cockburn, Chilton, McGlen, McShane, Pearson, Rowley, Downie, Bond		
Scorer(s):	Rowley 3		

Match # 2025	Wednesday 22/08/51 Football League Division 1	at Old Trafford	Attendance 37339
Result:	**Manchester United 4 Middlesbrough 2**		
Teamsheet:	Allen, Carey, Redman, Gibson, Chilton, Cockburn, McShane, Pearson, Rowley, Downie, Bond		
Scorer(s):	Rowley 3, Pearson		

Match # 2026	Saturday 25/08/51 Football League Division 1	at Old Trafford	Attendance 51850
Result:	**Manchester United 2 Newcastle United 1**		
Teamsheet:	Allen, Carey, Redman, Gibson, Chilton, Cockburn, McShane, Pearson, Rowley, Downie, Bond		
Scorer(s):	Downie, Rowley		

Match # 2027	Wednesday 29/08/51 Football League Division 1	at Ayresome Park	Attendance 44212
Result:	**Middlesbrough 1 Manchester United 4**		
Teamsheet:	Allen, Carey, Redman, Gibson, Chilton, Cockburn, McShane, Pearson, Rowley, Downie, Bond		
Scorer(s):	Pearson 2, Rowley 2		

Match # 2028	Saturday 01/09/51 Football League Division 1	at Burnden Park	Attendance 52239
Result:	**Bolton Wanderers 1 Manchester United 0**		
Teamsheet:	Allen, Carey, Redman, Gibson, Chilton, Cockburn, Berry, Pearson, Rowley, Downie, Bond		

Match # 2029	Wednesday 05/09/51 Football League Division 1	at Old Trafford	Attendance 26773
Result:	**Manchester United 3 Charlton Athletic 2**		
Teamsheet:	Allen, Carey, Redman, Gibson, Chilton, Cockburn, Berry, Pearson, Rowley, Downie, Bond		
Scorer(s):	Rowley 2, Downie		

Match # 2030	Saturday 08/09/51 Football League Division 1	at Old Trafford	Attendance 48660
Result:	**Manchester United 4 Stoke City 0**		
Teamsheet:	Allen, Carey, Redman, Gibson, Chilton, Cockburn, Berry, Pearson, Rowley, Downie, McShane		
Scorer(s):	Rowley 3, Pearson		

Match # 2031	Wednesday 12/09/51 Football League Division 1	at The Valley	Attendance 28806
Result:	**Charlton Athletic 2 Manchester United 2**		
Teamsheet:	Allen, Carey, Redman, Gibson, Chilton, Cockburn, Berry, Pearson, Rowley, Downie, McShane		
Scorer(s):	Downie 2		

Match # 2032	Saturday 15/09/51 Football League Division 1	at Maine Road	Attendance 52571
Result:	**Manchester City 1 Manchester United 2**		
Teamsheet:	Allen, Carey, Redman, Gibson, Chilton, Cockburn, Berry, Pearson, Cassidy, Downie, McShane		
Scorer(s):	Berry, McShane		

Match # 2033	Saturday 22/09/51 Football League Division 1	at White Hart Lane	Attendance 70882
Result:	**Tottenham Hotspur 2 Manchester United 0**		
Teamsheet:	Allen, Carey, Redman, Gibson, Chilton, Cockburn, Berry, Pearson, Rowley, Downie, McShane		

Match # 2034	Saturday 29/09/51 Football League Division 1	at Old Trafford	Attendance 53454
Result:	**Manchester United 1 Preston North End 2**		
Teamsheet:	Allen, Carey, Redman, Gibson, Chilton, Cockburn, Berry, Walton, Aston, Pearson, Rowley		
Scorer(s):	Aston		

Match # 2035	Saturday 06/10/51 Football League Division 1	at Old Trafford	Attendance 39767
Result:	**Manchester United 2 Derby County 1**		
Teamsheet:	Allen, Carey, Redman, Gibson, Chilton, Cockburn, Berry, Walton, Rowley, Pearson, McShane		
Scorer(s):	Berry, Pearson		

Match # 2036	Saturday 13/10/51 Football League Division 1	at Villa Park	Attendance 47795
Result:	**Aston Villa 2 Manchester United 5**		
Teamsheet:	Allen, McNulty, Redman, Gibson, Chilton, Berry, Pearson, Rowley, Downie, Bond		
Scorer(s):	Pearson 2, Rowley 2, Bond		

Match # 2037	Saturday 20/10/51 Football League Division 1	at Old Trafford	Attendance 40915
Result:	**Manchester United 0 Sunderland 1**		
Teamsheet:	Allen, Carey, Redman, Gibson, Chilton, McGlen, Berry, Downie, Rowley, Pearson, McShane		

Match # 2038	Saturday 27/10/51 Football League Division 1	at Molineux	Attendance 46167
Result:	**Wolverhampton Wanderers 0 Manchester United 2**		
Teamsheet:	Allen, Carey, Redman, Gibson, Chilton, Cockburn, McShane, Pearson, Rowley, Birch, Bond		
Scorer(s):	Pearson, Rowley		

Match # 2039	Saturday 03/11/51 Football League Division 1	at Old Trafford	Attendance 25616
Result:	**Manchester United 1 Huddersfield Town 1**		
Teamsheet:	Allen, Carey, Redman, Gibson, Chilton, Cockburn, McShane, Pearson, Rowley, Birch, Bond		
Scorer(s):	Pearson		

Match # 2040	Saturday 10/11/51 Football League Division 1	at Stamford Bridge	Attendance 48960
Result:	**Chelsea 4 Manchester United 2**		
Teamsheet:	Allen, Carey, Redman, Gibson, Chilton, Berry, Pearson, Aston, Downie, Rowley		
Scorer(s):	Pearson, Rowley		

Match # 2041	Saturday 17/11/51 Football League Division 1	at Old Trafford	Attendance 35914
Result:	**Manchester United 1 Portsmouth 3**		
Teamsheet:	Allen, Carey, Redman, Gibson, Chilton, Cockburn, Berry, Pearson, Aston, Downie, Rowley		
Scorer(s):	Downie		

SEASON 1951/52 (continued)

Match # 2042 Saturday 24/11/51   Football League Division 1   at Anfield   Attendance 42378
Result: **Liverpool 0 Manchester United 0**
Teamsheet: Crompton, Carey, Byrne, Blanchflower, Chilton, Cockburn, Berry, Pearson, Rowley, Downie, Bond

Match # 2043 Saturday 01/12/51   Football League Division 1   at Old Trafford   Attendance 34154
Result: **Manchester United 3 Blackpool 1**
Teamsheet: Crompton, McNulty, Byrne, Carey, Chilton, Cockburn, Berry, Pearson, Rowley, Downie, Bond
Scorer(s): Downie 2, Rowley

Match # 2044 Saturday 08/12/51   Football League Division 1   at Highbury   Attendance 55451
Result: **Arsenal 1 Manchester United 3**
Teamsheet: Crompton, McNulty, Byrne, Carey, Chilton, Cockburn, Berry, Pearson, Rowley, Downie, Bond
Scorer(s): Pearson, Rowley, own goal

Match # 2045 Saturday 15/12/51   Football League Division 1   at Old Trafford   Attendance 27584
Result: **Manchester United 5 West Bromwich Albion 1**
Teamsheet: Allen, McNulty, Byrne, Carey, Chilton, Cockburn, Berry, Pearson, Rowley, Downie, Bond
Scorer(s): Downie 2, Pearson 2, Berry

Match # 2046 Saturday 22/12/51   Football League Division 1   at St James' Park   Attendance 45414
Result: **Newcastle United 2 Manchester United 2**
Teamsheet: Allen, McNulty, Byrne, Carey, Chilton, Cockburn, Berry, Pearson, Rowley, Downie, Bond
Scorer(s): Bond, Cockburn

Match # 2047 Tuesday 25/12/51   Football League Division 1   at Old Trafford   Attendance 33802
Result: **Manchester United 3 Fulham 2**
Teamsheet: Allen, McNulty, Byrne, Chilton, Jones, Cockburn, Berry, Pearson, Rowley, Downie, Bond
Scorer(s): Berry, Bond, Rowley

Match # 2048 Wednesday 26/12/51   Football League Division 1   at Craven Cottage   Attendance 32671
Result: **Fulham 3 Manchester United 3**
Teamsheet: Allen, McNulty, Byrne, Chilton, Jones, Cockburn, Berry, Pearson, Rowley, Downie, Bond
Scorer(s): Bond, Pearson, Rowley

Match # 2049 Saturday 29/12/51   Football League Division 1   at Old Trafford   Attendance 53205
Result: **Manchester United 1 Bolton Wanderers 0**
Teamsheet: Allen, McNulty, Byrne, Chilton, Jones, Cockburn, Berry, Pearson, Rowley, Downie, Bond
Scorer(s): Pearson

Match # 2050 Saturday 05/01/52   Football League Division 1   at Victoria Ground   Attendance 36389
Result: **Stoke City 0 Manchester United 0**
Teamsheet: Allen, McNulty, Byrne, Carey, Chilton, Cockburn, Berry, Pearson, Rowley, Downie, Bond

Match # 2051 Saturday 12/01/52   FA Cup 3rd Round   at Old Trafford   Attendance 43517
Result: **Manchester United 0 Hull City 2**
Teamsheet: Allen, McNulty, Byrne, Carey, Chilton, Cockburn, Berry, Pearson, Rowley, Downie, Bond

Match # 2052 Saturday 19/01/52   Football League Division 1   at Old Trafford   Attendance 54245
Result: **Manchester United 1 Manchester City 1**
Teamsheet: Allen, McNulty, Byrne, Carey, Chilton, Cockburn, Berry, Pearson, Aston, Downie, Rowley
Scorer(s): Carey

Match # 2053 Saturday 26/01/52   Football League Division 1   at Old Trafford   Attendance 40845
Result: **Manchester United 2 Tottenham Hotspur 0**
Teamsheet: Allen, McNulty, Byrne, Carey, Chilton, Cockburn, Berry, Clempson, Aston, Pearson, Rowley
Scorer(s): Pearson, own goal

Match # 2054 Saturday 09/02/52   Football League Division 1   at Deepdale   Attendance 38792
Result: **Preston North End 1 Manchester United 2**
Teamsheet: Allen, McNulty, Byrne, Carey, Chilton, Cockburn, Berry, Clempson, Aston, Pearson, Rowley
Scorer(s): Aston, Berry

Match # 2055 Saturday 16/02/52   Football League Division 1   at Baseball Ground   Attendance 27693
Result: **Derby County 0 Manchester United 3**
Teamsheet: Crompton, McNulty, Byrne, Carey, Chilton, Cockburn, Berry, Clempson, Aston, Pearson, Rowley
Scorer(s): Aston, Pearson, Rowley

Match # 2056 Saturday 01/03/52   Football League Division 1   at Old Trafford   Attendance 38910
Result: **Manchester United 1 Aston Villa 1**
Teamsheet: Crompton, McNulty, Byrne, Carey, Chilton, Cockburn, Berry, Clempson, Aston, Pearson, Rowley
Scorer(s): Berry

Match # 2057 Saturday 08/03/52   Football League Division 1   at Roker Park   Attendance 48078
Result: **Sunderland 1 Manchester United 2**
Teamsheet: Crompton, McNulty, Byrne, Carey, Chilton, Cockburn, Berry, Clempson, Aston, Pearson, Rowley
Scorer(s): Cockburn, Rowley

Match # 2058 Saturday 15/03/52   Football League Division 1   at Old Trafford   Attendance 45109
Result: **Manchester United 2 Wolverhampton Wanderers 0**
Teamsheet: Crompton, McNulty, Byrne, Carey, Chilton, Cockburn, Berry, Clempson, Aston, Pearson, Rowley
Scorer(s): Aston, Clempson

Match # 2059 Saturday 22/03/52   Football League Division 1   at Leeds Road   Attendance 30316
Result: **Huddersfield Town 3 Manchester United 2**
Teamsheet: Crompton, McNulty, Byrne, Carey, Chilton, Cockburn, Berry, Clempson, Aston, Pearson, Rowley
Scorer(s): Clempson, Pearson

SEASON 1951/52 (continued)

Match # 2060 Saturday 05/04/52   Football League Division 1   at Fratton Park   Attendance 25522
Result: **Portsmouth 1 Manchester United 0**
Teamsheet: Crompton, McNulty, Byrne, Carey, Chilton, Whitefoot, Berry, Clempson, Aston, Downie, Bond

Match # 2061 Friday 11/04/52   Football League Division 1   at Turf Moor   Attendance 38907
Result: **Burnley 1 Manchester United 1**
Teamsheet: Allen, McNulty, Aston, Carey, Chilton, Cockburn, Berry, Downie, Rowley, Pearson, Byrne
Scorer(s):   Byrne

Match # 2062 Saturday 12/04/52   Football League Division 1   at Old Trafford   Attendance 42970
Result: **Manchester United 4 Liverpool 0**
Teamsheet: Allen, McNulty, Aston, Carey, Chilton, Whitefoot, Berry, Downie, Rowley, Pearson, Byrne
Scorer(s):   Byrne 2, Downie, Rowley

Match # 2063 Monday 14/04/52   Football League Division 1   at Old Trafford   Attendance 44508
Result: **Manchester United 6 Burnley 1**
Teamsheet: Allen, McNulty, Aston, Carey, Chilton, Whitefoot, Berry, Downie, Rowley, Pearson, Byrne
Scorer(s):   Byrne 2, Carey, Downie, Pearson, Rowley

Match # 2064 Saturday 19/04/52   Football League Division 1   at Bloomfield Road   Attendance 29118
Result: **Blackpool 2 Manchester United 2**
Teamsheet: Allen, McNulty, Aston, Carey, Chilton, Cockburn, Berry, Downie, Rowley, Pearson, Byrne
Scorer(s):   Byrne, Rowley

Match # 2065 Monday 21/04/52   Football League Division 1   at Old Trafford   Attendance 37436
Result: **Manchester United 3 Chelsea 0**
Teamsheet: Allen, McNulty, Aston, Carey, Chilton, Cockburn, Berry, Downie, Rowley, Pearson, Byrne
Scorer(s):   Carey, Pearson, own goal

Match # 2066 Saturday 26/04/52   Football League Division 1   at Old Trafford   Attendance 53651
Result: **Manchester United 6 Arsenal 1**
Teamsheet: Allen, McNulty, Aston, Carey, Chilton, Cockburn, Berry, Downie, Rowley, Pearson, Byrne
Scorer(s):   Rowley 3, Pearson 2, Byrne

SEASON 1951/52 SUMMARY

APPEARANCES

PLAYER	LGE	FAC	TOT
Chilton	42	1	43
Pearson	41	1	42
Rowley	40	1	41
Carey	38	1	39
Cockburn	38	1	39
Berry	36	1	37
Allen	33	1	34
Downie	31	1	32
Byrne	24	1	25
McNulty	24	1	25
Bond	19	1	20
Aston	18	–	18

APPEARANCES

PLAYER	LGE	FAC	TOT
Redman	18	–	18
Gibson	17	–	17
McShane	12	–	12
Crompton	9	–	9
Clempson	8	–	8
Jones	3	–	3
Birch	2	–	2
McGlen	2	–	2
Walton	2	–	2
Blanchflower	1	–	1
Cassidy	1	–	1

GOALSCORERS

PLAYER	LGE	FAC	TOT
Rowley	30	–	30
Pearson	22	–	22
Downie	11	–	11
Byrne	7	–	7
Berry	6	–	6
Aston	4	–	4
Bond	4	–	4
Carey	3	–	3
Clempson	2	–	2
Cockburn	2	–	2
McShane	1	–	1
own goals	3	–	3

RESULTS & ATTENDANCES SUMMARY

		P	W	D	L	F	A	TOTAL	AVGE
League	H	21	15	3	3	55	21	866707	41272
	A	21	8	8	5	40	31	869847	41421
	TOTAL	42	23	11	8	95	52	1736554	41347
FA Cup	H	1	0	0	1	0	2	43517	43517
	A	0	0	0	0	0	0	0	n/a
	TOTAL	1	0	0	1	0	2	43517	43517
Overall	H	22	15	3	4	55	23	910224	41374
	A	21	8	8	5	40	31	869847	41421
	TOTAL	43	23	11	9	95	54	1780071	41397

FINAL TABLE – LEAGUE DIVISION ONE

		P	HOME					AWAY					PTS	GD
		P	W	D	L	F	A	W	D	L	F	A	PTS	GD
1	MANCHESTER UNITED	42	15	3	3	55	21	8	8	5	40	31	57	43
2	Tottenham Hotspur	42	16	1	4	45	20	6	8	7	31	33	53	25
3	Arsenal	42	13	7	1	54	30	8	4	9	26	31	53	19
4	Portsmouth	42	13	3	5	42	25	7	5	9	26	33	48	10
5	Bolton Wanderers	42	11	7	3	35	26	8	3	10	30	35	48	4
6	Aston Villa	42	13	3	5	49	28	6	6	9	30	42	47	9
7	Preston North End	42	10	5	6	39	22	7	7	7	35	32	46	20
8	Newcastle United	42	12	4	5	62	28	6	5	10	36	45	45	25
9	Blackpool	42	12	5	4	40	27	6	4	11	24	37	45	0
10	Charlton Athletic	42	12	5	4	41	24	5	5	11	27	39	44	5
11	Liverpool	42	6	11	4	31	25	6	8	7	26	36	43	-4
12	Sunderland	42	8	6	7	41	28	7	6	8	29	33	42	9
13	West Bromwich Albion	42	8	9	4	38	29	6	4	11	36	48	41	-3
14	Burnley	42	9	6	6	32	19	6	4	11	24	44	40	-7
15	Manchester City	42	7	5	9	29	28	6	8	7	29	33	39	-3
16	Wolverhampton Wanderers	42	8	6	7	40	33	4	8	9	33	40	38	0
17	Derby County	42	10	4	7	43	37	5	3	13	20	43	37	-17
18	Middlesbrough	42	12	4	5	37	25	3	2	16	27	63	36	-24
19	Chelsea	42	10	3	8	31	29	4	5	12	21	43	36	-20
20	Stoke City	42	8	6	7	34	32	4	1	16	15	56	31	-39
21	Huddersfield Town	42	9	3	9	32	35	1	5	15	17	47	28	-33
22	Fulham	42	5	7	9	38	31	3	4	14	20	46	27	-19

SEASON 1952/53

Match # 2067 Saturday 23/08/52   Football League Division 1   at Old Trafford   Attendance 43629
Result: **Manchester United 2 Chelsea 0**
Teamsheet: Wood, McNulty, Aston, Carey, Chilton, Gibson, Berry, Downie, Rowley, Pearson, Byrne
Scorer(s): Berry, Downie

Match # 2068 Wednesday 27/08/52   Football League Division 1   at Highbury   Attendance 58831
Result: **Arsenal 2 Manchester United 1**
Teamsheet: Crompton, McNulty, Aston, Carey, Chilton, Cockburn, Berry, Downie, Rowley, Pearson, Byrne
Scorer(s): Rowley

Match # 2069 Saturday 30/08/52   Football League Division 1   at Maine Road   Attendance 56140
Result: **Manchester City 2 Manchester United 1**
Teamsheet: Crompton, McNulty, Aston, Carey, Chilton, Cockburn, Berry, Downie, Rowley, Pearson, Byrne
Scorer(s): Downie

Match # 2070 Wednesday 03/09/52   Football League Division 1   at Old Trafford   Attendance 39193
Result: **Manchester United 0 Arsenal 0**
Teamsheet: Crompton, Carey, Byrne, Gibson, Chilton, Cockburn, Berry, Clempson, Aston, Pearson, Bond

Match # 2071 Saturday 06/09/52   Football League Division 1   at Fratton Park   Attendance 37278
Result: **Portsmouth 2 Manchester United 0**
Teamsheet: Crompton, McNulty, Byrne, Gibson, Chilton, Cockburn, Berry, Clempson, Aston, Pearson, Rowley

Match # 2072 Wednesday 10/09/52   Football League Division 1   at Baseball Ground   Attendance 20226
Result: **Derby County 2 Manchester United 3**
Teamsheet: Crompton, McNulty, Aston, Carey, Chilton, Gibson, Berry, Downie, Rowley, Pearson, Byrne
Scorer(s): Pearson 3

Match # 2073 Saturday 13/09/52   Football League Division 1   at Old Trafford   Attendance 40531
Result: **Manchester United 1 Bolton Wanderers 0**
Teamsheet: Allen, McNulty, Aston, Carey, Chilton, Gibson, Berry, Downie, Rowley, Pearson, Byrne
Scorer(s): Berry

Match # 2074 Saturday 20/09/52   Football League Division 1   at Villa Park   Attendance 43490
Result: **Aston Villa 3 Manchester United 3**
Teamsheet: Wood, McNulty, Aston, Carey, Chilton, Gibson, Berry, Downie, Rowley, Pearson, Byrne
Scorer(s): Rowley 2, Downie

Match # 2075 Wednesday 24/09/52   FA Charity Shield   at Old Trafford   Attendance 11381
Result: **Manchester United 4 Newcastle United 2**
Teamsheet: Wood, McNulty, Aston, Carey, Chilton, Gibson, Berry, Downie, Rowley, Pearson, Byrne
Scorer(s): Rowley 2, Byrne, Downie

Match # 2076 Saturday 27/09/52   Football League Division 1   at Old Trafford   Attendance 28967
Result: **Manchester United 0 Sunderland 1**
Teamsheet: Wood, McNulty, Aston, Jones, Chilton, Gibson, Berry, Downie, Clempson, Pearson, Byrne

Match # 2077 Saturday 04/10/52   Football League Division 1   at Molineux   Attendance 40132
Result: **Wolverhampton Wanderers 6 Manchester United 2**
Teamsheet: Allen, McNulty, Aston, Carey, Chilton, Gibson, Berry, Downie, Rowley, Pearson, Scott
Scorer(s): Rowley 2

Match # 2078 Saturday 11/10/52   Football League Division 1   at Old Trafford   Attendance 28968
Result: **Manchester United 0 Stoke City 2**
Teamsheet: Wood, McNulty, Aston, Carey, Chilton, Gibson, Berry, Clempson, Rowley, Downie, Scott

Match # 2079 Saturday 18/10/52   Football League Division 1   at Deepdale   Attendance 33502
Result: **Preston North End 0 Manchester United 5**
Teamsheet: Crompton, Carey, Byrne, Whitefoot, Chilton, Gibson, Berry, Downie, Aston, Pearson, Rowley
Scorer(s): Aston 2, Pearson 2, Rowley

Match # 2080 Saturday 25/10/52   Football League Division 1   at Old Trafford   Attendance 36913
Result: **Manchester United 1 Burnley 3**
Teamsheet: Crompton, Carey, Byrne, Whitefoot, Chilton, Gibson, Berry, Downie, Aston, Pearson, Rowley
Scorer(s): Aston

Match # 2081 Saturday 01/11/52   Football League Division 1   at White Hart Lane   Attendance 44300
Result: **Tottenham Hotspur 1 Manchester United 2**
Teamsheet: Crompton, McNulty, Byrne, Whitefoot, Chilton, Gibson, Berry, Downie, Aston, Pearson, McShane
Scorer(s): Berry 2

Match # 2082 Saturday 08/11/52   Football League Division 1   at Old Trafford   Attendance 48571
Result: **Manchester United 1 Sheffield Wednesday 1**
Teamsheet: Crompton, McNulty, Byrne, Whitefoot, Chilton, Gibson, Berry, Downie, Aston, Pearson, McShane
Scorer(s): Pearson

Match # 2083 Saturday 15/11/52   Football League Division 1   at Ninian Park   Attendance 40096
Result: **Cardiff City 1 Manchester United 2**
Teamsheet: Crompton, McNulty, Byrne, Cockburn, Chilton, Gibson, Berry, Downie, Aston, Pearson, McShane
Scorer(s): Aston, Pearson

Match # 2084 Saturday 22/11/52   Football League Division 1   at Old Trafford   Attendance 33528
Result: **Manchester United 2 Newcastle United 2**
Teamsheet: Crompton, McNulty, Byrne, Cockburn, Chilton, Gibson, Berry, Downie, Aston, Pearson, McShane
Scorer(s): Aston, Pearson

SEASON 1952/53 (continued)

Match # 2085 Saturday 29/11/52   Football League Division 1   at The Hawthorns   Attendance 23499
Result: **West Bromwich Albion 3 Manchester United 1**
Teamsheet: Crompton, McNulty, Byrne, Cockburn, Chilton, Gibson, Berry, Downie, Lewis, Pearson, McShane
Scorer(s):   Lewis

Match # 2086 Saturday 06/12/52   Football League Division 1   at Old Trafford   Attendance 27617
Result: **Manchester United 3 Middlesbrough 2**
Teamsheet: Crompton, McNulty, Byrne, Carey, Chilton, Cockburn, Berry, Doherty, Aston, Pearson, Pegg
Scorer(s):   Pearson 2, Aston

Match # 2087 Saturday 13/12/52   Football League Division 1   at Anfield   Attendance 34450
Result: **Liverpool 1 Manchester United 2**
Teamsheet: Crompton, Foulkes, Byrne, Carey, Chilton, Cockburn, Berry, Doherty, Aston, Pearson, Pegg
Scorer(s):   Aston, Pearson

Match # 2088 Saturday 20/12/52   Football League Division 1   at Stamford Bridge   Attendance 23261
Result: **Chelsea 2 Manchester United 3**
Teamsheet: Crompton, Foulkes, Byrne, Carey, Chilton, Cockburn, Berry, Doherty, Aston, Pearson, Pegg
Scorer(s):   Doherty 2, Aston

Match # 2089 Thursday 25/12/52   Football League Division 1   at Bloomfield Road   Attendance 27778
Result: **Blackpool 0 Manchester United 0**
Teamsheet: Wood, McNulty, Byrne, Carey, Chilton, Cockburn, Berry, Doherty, Aston, Pearson, Pegg

Match # 2090 Friday 26/12/52   Football League Division 1   at Old Trafford   Attendance 48077
Result: **Manchester United 2 Blackpool 1**
Teamsheet: Wood, McNulty, Byrne, Carey, Chilton, Cockburn, Berry, Lewis, Aston, Pearson, Pegg
Scorer(s):   Carey, Lewis

Match # 2091 Thursday 01/01/53   Football League Division 1   at Old Trafford   Attendance 34813
Result: **Manchester United 1 Derby County 0**
Teamsheet: Wood, Redman, Byrne, Carey, Chilton, Cockburn, Berry, Aston, Lewis, Pearson, Pegg
Scorer(s):   Lewis

Match # 2092 Saturday 03/01/53   Football League Division 1   at Old Trafford   Attendance 47883
Result: **Manchester United 1 Manchester City 1**
Teamsheet: Wood, Aston, Byrne, Carey, Chilton, Whitefoot, Berry, Doherty, Lewis, Pearson, Pegg
Scorer(s):   Pearson

Match # 2093 Saturday 10/01/53   FA Cup 3rd Round   at The Den   Attendance 35652
Result: **Millwall 0 Manchester United 1**
Teamsheet: Wood, Aston, Byrne, Carey, Chilton, Cockburn, Berry, Downie, Lewis, Pearson, Rowley
Scorer(s):   Pearson

Match # 2094 Saturday 17/01/53   Football League Division 1   at Old Trafford   Attendance 32341
Result: **Manchester United 1 Portsmouth 0**
Teamsheet: Wood, Aston, Byrne, Carey, Chilton, Cockburn, Berry, Downie, Lewis, Pearson, Pegg
Scorer(s):   Lewis

Match # 2095 Saturday 24/01/53   Football League Division 1   at Burnden Park   Attendance 43638
Result: **Bolton Wanderers 2 Manchester United 1**
Teamsheet: Wood, Aston, Byrne, Carey, Chilton, Cockburn, Berry, Downie, Lewis, Pearson, Pegg
Scorer(s):   Lewis

Match # 2096 Saturday 31/01/53   FA Cup 4th Round   at Old Trafford   Attendance 34748
Result: **Manchester United 1 Walthamstow Avenue 1**
Teamsheet: Wood, Aston, Byrne, Carey, Chilton, Cockburn, Berry, Downie, Lewis, Pearson, Rowley
Scorer(s):   Lewis

Match # 2097 Thursday 05/02/53   FA Cup 4th Round Replay   at Highbury   Attendance 49119
Result: **Walthamstow Avenue 2 Manchester United 5**
Teamsheet: Wood, Aston, Byrne, Carey, Chilton, Cockburn, Berry, Lewis, Rowley, Pearson, Pegg
Scorer(s):   Rowley 2, Byrne, Lewis, Pearson

Match # 2098 Saturday 07/02/53   Football League Division 1   at Old Trafford   Attendance 34339
Result: **Manchester United 3 Aston Villa 1**
Teamsheet: Wood, Aston, Byrne, Carey, Chilton, Cockburn, Berry, Lewis, Rowley, Pearson, Pegg
Scorer(s):   Rowley 2, Lewis

Match # 2099 Saturday 14/02/53   FA Cup 5th Round   at Goodison Park   Attendance 77920
Result: **Everton 2 Manchester United 1**
Teamsheet: Wood, Aston, Byrne, Carey, Chilton, Cockburn, Berry, Lewis, Rowley, Pearson, Pegg
Scorer(s):   Rowley

Match # 2100 Wednesday 18/02/53   Football League Division 1   at Roker Park   Attendance 24263
Result: **Sunderland 2 Manchester United 2**
Teamsheet: Carey, Aston, Byrne, Gibson, Chilton, Cockburn, Berry, Lewis, Rowley, Pearson, Pegg
Scorer(s):   Lewis, Pegg

Match # 2101 Saturday 21/02/53   Football League Division 1   at Old Trafford   Attendance 38269
Result: **Manchester United 0 Wolverhampton Wanderers 3**
Teamsheet: Wood, Aston, Byrne, Carey, Chilton, Cockburn, Berry, Lewis, Rowley, Pearson, Pegg

Match # 2102 Saturday 28/02/53   Football League Division 1   at Victoria Ground   Attendance 30219
Result: **Stoke City 3 Manchester United 1**
Teamsheet: Crompton, McNulty, Byrne, Chilton, Jones, Gibson, Berry, Aston, Rowley, Downie, Pegg
Scorer(s):   Berry

SEASON 1952/53 (continued)

Match # 2103 Saturday 07/03/53   Football League Division 1   at Old Trafford   Attendance 52590
Result: **Manchester United 5   Preston North End 2**
Teamsheet: Crompton, Aston, Byrne, Carey, Chilton, Cockburn, Berry, Rowley, Taylor, Pearson, Pegg
Scorer(s):   Pegg 2, Taylor 2, Rowley

Match # 2104 Saturday 14/03/53   Football League Division 1   at Turf Moor   Attendance 45682
Result: **Burnley 2   Manchester United 1**
Teamsheet: Crompton, Aston, Byrne, Carey, Chilton, Cockburn, Berry, Rowley, Taylor, Pearson, Pegg
Scorer(s):   Byrne

Match # 2105 Wednesday 25/03/53   Football League Division 1   at Old Trafford   Attendance 18384
Result: **Manchester United 3   Tottenham Hotspur 2**
Teamsheet: Crompton, Aston, Byrne, Gibson, Chilton, Cockburn, Berry, Rowley, Taylor, Pearson, Pegg
Scorer(s):   Pearson 2, Pegg

Match # 2106 Saturday 28/03/53   Football League Division 1   at Hillsborough   Attendance 36509
Result: **Sheffield Wednesday 0   Manchester United 0**
Teamsheet: Crompton, Aston, Byrne, Carey, Chilton, Cockburn, Berry, Rowley, Taylor, Pearson, Pegg

Match # 2107 Friday 03/04/53   Football League Division 1   at The Valley   Attendance 41814
Result: **Charlton Athletic 2   Manchester United 2**
Teamsheet: Crompton, Aston, Byrne, Carey, Chilton, Blanchflower, Berry, Rowley, Taylor, Pearson, Pegg
Scorer(s):   Berry, Taylor

Match # 2108 Saturday 04/04/53   Football League Division 1   at Old Trafford   Attendance 37163
Result: **Manchester United 1   Cardiff City 4**
Teamsheet: Crompton, Aston, Byrne, Gibson, Chilton, Edwards, Berry, Rowley, Taylor, Pearson, Pegg
Scorer(s):   Byrne

Match # 2109 Monday 06/04/53   Football League Division 1   at Old Trafford   Attendance 30105
Result: **Manchester United 3   Charlton Athletic 2**
Teamsheet: Crompton, McNulty, Byrne, Carey, Chilton, Whitefoot, Berry, Lewis, Taylor, Pearson, Rowley
Scorer(s):   Taylor 2, Rowley

Match # 2110 Saturday 11/04/53   Football League Division 1   at St James' Park   Attendance 38970
Result: **Newcastle United 1   Manchester United 2**
Teamsheet: Olive, McNulty, Byrne, Carey, Chilton, Whitefoot, Viollet, Pearson, Aston, Taylor, Rowley
Scorer(s):   Taylor 2

Match # 2111 Saturday 18/04/53   Football League Division 1   at Old Trafford   Attendance 31380
Result: **Manchester United 2   West Bromwich Albion 2**
Teamsheet: Olive, McNulty, Byrne, Carey, Chilton, Whitefoot, Viollet, Pearson, Aston, Taylor, Rowley
Scorer(s):   Pearson, Viollet

Match # 2112 Monday 20/04/53   Football League Division 1   at Old Trafford   Attendance 20869
Result: **Manchester United 3   Liverpool 1**
Teamsheet: Crompton, Aston, Byrne, Carey, Chilton, Whitefoot, Berry, Downie, Taylor, Pearson, Rowley
Scorer(s):   Berry, Pearson, Rowley

Match # 2113 Saturday 25/04/53   Football League Division 1   at Ayresome Park   Attendance 34344
Result: **Middlesbrough 5   Manchester United 0**
Teamsheet: Crompton, McNulty, Byrne, Carey, Chilton, Whitefoot, Berry, Viollet, Aston, Taylor, Rowley

SEASON 1952/53 SUMMARY

APPEARANCES

PLAYER	LGE	FAC	CS	TOT
Chilton	42	4	1	47
Aston	40	4	1	45
Berry	40	4	1	45
Byrne	40	4	1	45
Pearson	39	4	1	44
Carey	32	4	1	37
Rowley	26	4	1	31
Cockburn	22	4	–	26
Crompton	25	–	–	25
McNulty	23	–	1	24
Downie	20	2	1	23
Gibson	20	–	1	21
Pegg	19	2	–	21
Wood	12	4	1	17
Lewis	10	4	–	14
Taylor	11	–	–	11
Whitefoot	10	–	–	10
Doherty	5	–	–	5
McShane	5	–	–	5
Clempson	4	–	–	4
Viollet	3	–	–	3
Allen	2	–	–	2
Foulkes	2	–	–	2
Jones	2	–	–	2
Olive	2	–	–	2
Scott	2	–	–	2
Blanchflower	1	–	–	1
Bond	1	–	–	1
Edwards	1	–	–	1
Redman	1	–	–	1

GOALSCORERS

PLAYER	LGE	FAC	CS	TOT
Pearson	16	2	–	18
Rowley	11	3	2	16
Lewis	7	2	–	9
Aston	8	–	–	8
Berry	7	–	–	7
Taylor	7	–	–	7
Pegg	4	–	–	4
Downie	3	–	1	4
Byrne	2	1	1	4
Doherty	2	–	–	2
Carey	1	–	–	1
Viollet	1	–	–	1

RESULTS & ATTENDANCES SUMMARY

		P	W	D	L	F	A	TOTAL	AVGE
League	H	21	11	5	5	35	30	754130	35911
	A	21	7	5	9	34	42	778422	37068
	TOTAL	42	18	10	14	69	72	1532552	36489
FA Cup	H	1	0	1	0	1	1	34748	34748
	A	3	2	0	1	7	4	162691	54230
	TOTAL	4	2	1	1	8	5	197439	49360
Charity	H	1	1	0	0	4	2	11381	11381
Shield	A	0	0	0	0	0	0	0	n/a
	TOTAL	1	1	0	0	4	2	11381	11381
Overall	H	23	12	6	5	40	33	800259	34794
	A	24	9	5	10	41	46	941113	39213
	TOTAL	47	21	11	15	81	79	1741372	37050

FINAL TABLE – LEAGUE DIVISION ONE

		P	W	D	L	F	A	W	D	L	F	A	PTS	GD
				HOME						AWAY				
1	Arsenal	42	15	3	3	60	30	6	9	6	37	34	54	33
2	Preston North End	42	15	3	3	46	25	6	9	6	39	35	54	25
3	Wolverhampton Wanderers	42	13	5	3	54	27	6	8	7	32	36	51	23
4	West Bromwich Albion	42	13	3	5	35	19	8	5	8	31	41	50	6
5	Charlton Athletic	42	12	8	1	47	22	7	3	11	30	41	49	14
6	Burnley	42	11	6	4	36	20	7	6	8	31	32	48	15
7	Blackpool	42	13	5	3	45	22	6	4	11	26	48	47	1
8	MANCHESTER UNITED	42	11	5	5	35	30	7	5	9	34	42	46	-3
9	Sunderland	42	11	9	1	42	27	4	4	13	26	55	43	-14
10	Tottenham Hotspur	42	11	6	4	55	37	4	5	12	23	32	41	9
11	Aston Villa	42	9	7	5	36	23	5	6	10	27	38	41	2
12	Cardiff City	42	7	8	6	32	17	7	4	10	22	29	40	8
13	Middlesbrough	42	12	5	4	46	27	2	6	13	24	50	39	-7
14	Bolton Wanderers	42	9	4	8	39	35	6	5	10	22	34	39	-8
15	Portsmouth	42	10	6	5	44	34	4	4	13	30	49	38	-9
16	Newcastle United	42	9	5	7	34	33	5	4	12	25	37	37	-11
17	Liverpool	42	10	6	5	36	28	4	2	15	25	54	36	-21
18	Sheffield Wednesday	42	8	6	7	35	32	4	5	12	27	40	35	-10
19	Chelsea	42	10	4	7	35	24	2	7	12	21	42	35	-10
20	Manchester City	42	12	2	7	45	28	2	5	14	27	59	35	-15
21	Stoke City	42	10	4	7	35	26	2	6	13	18	40	34	-13
22	Derby County	42	9	6	6	41	29	2	4	15	18	45	32	-15

SEASON 1953/54

Match # 2114   Wednesday 19/08/53   Football League Division 1   at Old Trafford   Attendance 28936
Result: **Manchester United 1 Chelsea 1**
Teamsheet: Crompton, Aston, Byrne, Gibson, Chilton, Cockburn, Berry, Rowley, Taylor, Pearson, Pegg
Scorer(s):   Pearson

Match # 2115   Saturday 22/08/53   Football League Division 1   at Anfield   Attendance 48422
Result: **Liverpool 4 Manchester United 4**
Teamsheet: Crompton, Aston, Byrne, Gibson, Chilton, Cockburn, Berry, Rowley, Taylor, Lewis, Pegg
Scorer(s):   Byrne, Lewis, Rowley, Taylor

Match # 2116   Wednesday 26/08/53   Football League Division 1   at Old Trafford   Attendance 31806
Result: **Manchester United 1 West Bromwich Albion 3**
Teamsheet: Crompton, Aston, Byrne, Gibson, Chilton, Cockburn, Berry, Rowley, Taylor, Lewis, Pegg
Scorer(s):   Taylor

Match # 2117   Saturday 29/08/53   Football League Division 1   at Old Trafford   Attendance 27837
Result: **Manchester United 1 Newcastle United 1**
Teamsheet: Wood, McNulty, Aston, Whitefoot, Chilton, Cockburn, Berry, Byrne, Taylor, Lewis, Rowley
Scorer(s):   Chilton

Match # 2118   Wednesday 02/09/53   Football League Division 1   at The Hawthorns   Attendance 28892
Result: **West Bromwich Albion 2 Manchester United 0**
Teamsheet: Wood, Aston, Byrne, Whitefoot, Chilton, Cockburn, Berry, Lewis, Taylor, Viollet, Rowley

Match # 2119   Saturday 05/09/53   Football League Division 1   at Maine Road   Attendance 53097
Result: **Manchester City 2 Manchester United 0**
Teamsheet: Wood, Aston, Byrne, Whitefoot, Chilton, Cockburn, Berry, Viollet, Taylor, Pearson, Rowley

Match # 2120   Wednesday 09/09/53   Football League Division 1   at Old Trafford   Attendance 18161
Result: **Manchester United 2 Middlesbrough 2**
Teamsheet: Wood, McNulty, Byrne, Whitefoot, Chilton, Cockburn, Berry, Lewis, Rowley, Pearson, McShane
Scorer(s):   Rowley 2

Match # 2121   Saturday 12/09/53   Football League Division 1   at Burnden Park   Attendance 43544
Result: **Bolton Wanderers 0 Manchester United 0**
Teamsheet: Wood, McNulty, Byrne, Whitefoot, Chilton, Cockburn, Berry, Taylor, Rowley, Pearson, McShane

Match # 2122   Wednesday 16/09/53   Football League Division 1   at Ayresome Park   Attendance 23607
Result: **Middlesbrough 1 Manchester United 4**
Teamsheet: Wood, McNulty, Byrne, Whitefoot, Chilton, Cockburn, Berry, Taylor, Rowley, Pearson, McShane
Scorer(s):   Taylor 2, Byrne, Rowley

Match # 2123   Saturday 19/09/53   Football League Division 1   at Old Trafford   Attendance 41171
Result: **Manchester United 1 Preston North End 0**
Teamsheet: Wood, Foulkes, Byrne, Whitefoot, Chilton, Cockburn, Berry, Taylor, Rowley, Pearson, McShane
Scorer(s):   Byrne

Match # 2124   Saturday 26/09/53   Football League Division 1   at White Hart Lane   Attendance 52837
Result: **Tottenham Hotspur 1 Manchester United 1**
Teamsheet: Wood, Foulkes, Byrne, Whitefoot, Chilton, Cockburn, Berry, Taylor, Rowley, Pearson, McShane
Scorer(s):   Rowley

Match # 2125   Saturday 03/10/53   Football League Division 1   at Old Trafford   Attendance 37696
Result: **Manchester United 1 Burnley 2**
Teamsheet: Wood, Foulkes, Byrne, Whitefoot, Chilton, Cockburn, Berry, Taylor, Rowley, Pearson, McShane
Scorer(s):   Pearson

Match # 2126   Saturday 10/10/53   Football League Division 1   at Old Trafford   Attendance 34617
Result: **Manchester United 1 Sunderland 0**
Teamsheet: Wood, Aston, Byrne, Whitefoot, Chilton, Cockburn, Berry, Taylor, Rowley, Pearson, McShane
Scorer(s):   Rowley

Match # 2127   Saturday 17/10/53   Football League Division 1   at Molineux   Attendance 40084
Result: **Wolverhampton Wanderers 3 Manchester United 1**
Teamsheet: Wood, Foulkes, Byrne, Whitefoot, Chilton, Cockburn, Berry, Pearson, Taylor, Rowley, McShane
Scorer(s):   Taylor

Match # 2128   Saturday 24/10/53   Football League Division 1   at Old Trafford   Attendance 30266
Result: **Manchester United 1 Aston Villa 0**
Teamsheet: Wood, Foulkes, Byrne, Whitefoot, Chilton, Cockburn, Berry, Pearson, Taylor, Rowley, McShane
Scorer(s):   Berry

Match # 2129   Saturday 31/10/53   Football League Division 1   at Leeds Road   Attendance 34175
Result: **Huddersfield Town 0 Manchester United 0**
Teamsheet: Wood, Foulkes, Byrne, Whitefoot, Chilton, Edwards, Berry, Blanchflower, Taylor, Viollet, Rowley

Match # 2130   Saturday 07/11/53   Football League Division 1   at Old Trafford   Attendance 28141
Result: **Manchester United 2 Arsenal 2**
Teamsheet: Wood, Foulkes, Byrne, Whitefoot, Chilton, Edwards, Berry, Blanchflower, Taylor, Viollet, Rowley
Scorer(s):   Blanchflower, Rowley

Match # 2131   Saturday 14/11/53   Football League Division 1   at Ninian Park   Attendance 26844
Result: **Cardiff City 1 Manchester United 6**
Teamsheet: Wood, Foulkes, Byrne, Whitefoot, Chilton, Edwards, Berry, Blanchflower, Taylor, Viollet, Rowley
Scorer(s):   Viollet 2, Berry, Blanchflower, Rowley, Taylor

SEASON 1953/54 (continued)

Match # 2132	Saturday 21/11/53	Football League Division 1	at Old Trafford	Attendance 49853
Result:	**Manchester United 4 Blackpool 1**			
Teamsheet:	Wood, Foulkes, Byrne, Whitefoot, Chilton, Edwards, Berry, Blanchflower, Taylor, Viollet, Rowley			
Scorer(s):	Taylor 3, Viollet			

Match # 2133	Saturday 28/11/53	Football League Division 1	at Fratton Park	Attendance 29233
Result:	**Portsmouth 1 Manchester United 1**			
Teamsheet:	Wood, Foulkes, Byrne, Whitefoot, Chilton, Edwards, Webster, Blanchflower, Taylor, Viollet, Rowley			
Scorer(s):	Taylor			

Match # 2134	Saturday 05/12/53	Football League Division 1	at Old Trafford	Attendance 31693
Result:	**Manchester United 2 Sheffield United 2**			
Teamsheet:	Wood, Foulkes, Byrne, Whitefoot, Chilton, Edwards, Berry, Blanchflower, Taylor, Viollet, Rowley			
Scorer(s):	Blanchflower 2			

Match # 2135	Saturday 12/12/53	Football League Division 1	at Stamford Bridge	Attendance 37153
Result:	**Chelsea 3 Manchester United 1**			
Teamsheet:	Wood, Foulkes, Byrne, Whitefoot, Chilton, Edwards, Berry, Blanchflower, Taylor, Viollet, Rowley			
Scorer(s):	Berry			

Match # 2136	Saturday 19/12/53	Football League Division 1	at Old Trafford	Attendance 26074
Result:	**Manchester United 5 Liverpool 1**			
Teamsheet:	Wood, Foulkes, Byrne, Whitefoot, Chilton, Edwards, Berry, Blanchflower, Taylor, Viollet, Rowley			
Scorer(s):	Blanchflower 2, Taylor 2, Viollet			

Match # 2137	Friday 25/12/53	Football League Division 1	at Old Trafford	Attendance 27123
Result:	**Manchester United 5 Sheffield Wednesday 2**			
Teamsheet:	Wood, Foulkes, Byrne, Whitefoot, Chilton, Edwards, Berry, Blanchflower, Taylor, Viollet, Rowley			
Scorer(s):	Taylor 3, Blanchflower, Viollet			

Match # 2138	Saturday 26/12/53	Football League Division 1	at Hillsborough	Attendance 44196
Result:	**Sheffield Wednesday 0 Manchester United 1**			
Teamsheet:	Wood, Foulkes, Byrne, Whitefoot, Chilton, Edwards, Berry, Blanchflower, Taylor, Viollet, Rowley			
Scorer(s):	Viollet			

Match # 2139	Saturday 02/01/54	Football League Division 1	at St James' Park	Attendance 55780
Result:	**Newcastle United 1 Manchester United 2**			
Teamsheet:	Wood, Foulkes, Byrne, Whitefoot, Chilton, Edwards, Berry, Blanchflower, Taylor, Viollet, Rowley			
Scorer(s):	Blanchflower, Foulkes			

Match # 2140	Saturday 09/01/54	FA Cup 3rd Round	at Turf Moor	Attendance 54000
Result:	**Burnley 5 Manchester United 3**			
Teamsheet:	Wood, Foulkes, Byrne, Whitefoot, Chilton, Edwards, Berry, Blanchflower, Taylor, Viollet, Rowley			
Scorer(s):	Blanchflower, Taylor, Viollet			

Match # 2141	Saturday 16/01/54	Football League Division 1	at Old Trafford	Attendance 46379
Result:	**Manchester United 1 Manchester City 1**			
Teamsheet:	Wood, Foulkes, Byrne, Whitefoot, Chilton, Edwards, Berry, Blanchflower, Taylor, Viollet, Pegg			
Scorer(s):	Berry			

Match # 2142	Saturday 23/01/54	Football League Division 1	at Old Trafford	Attendance 46663
Result:	**Manchester United 1 Bolton Wanderers 5**			
Teamsheet:	Wood, Foulkes, Byrne, Whitefoot, Chilton, Edwards, Berry, Blanchflower, Taylor, Viollet, Pegg			
Scorer(s):	Taylor			

Match # 2143	Saturday 06/02/54	Football League Division 1	at Deepdale	Attendance 30064
Result:	**Preston North End 1 Manchester United 3**			
Teamsheet:	Crompton, Foulkes, Byrne, Whitefoot, Chilton, Edwards, Berry, Blanchflower, Taylor, Viollet, Rowley			
Scorer(s):	Blanchflower, Rowley, Taylor			

Match # 2144	Saturday 13/02/54	Football League Division 1	at Old Trafford	Attendance 35485
Result:	**Manchester United 2 Tottenham Hotspur 0**			
Teamsheet:	Crompton, Foulkes, Byrne, Whitefoot, Chilton, Edwards, McFarlane, Blanchflower, Taylor, Viollet, Rowley			
Scorer(s):	Rowley, Taylor			

Match # 2145	Saturday 20/02/54	Football League Division 1	at Turf Moor	Attendance 29576
Result:	**Burnley 2 Manchester United 0**			
Teamsheet:	Crompton, Foulkes, Byrne, Whitefoot, Chilton, Edwards, Berry, Blanchflower, Taylor, Viollet, Pegg			

Match # 2146	Saturday 27/02/54	Football League Division 1	at Roker Park	Attendance 58440
Result:	**Sunderland 0 Manchester United 2**			
Teamsheet:	Wood, Foulkes, Byrne, Whitefoot, Chilton, Edwards, Berry, Blanchflower, Taylor, Viollet, Rowley			
Scorer(s):	Blanchflower, Taylor			

Match # 2147	Saturday 06/03/54	Football League Division 1	at Old Trafford	Attendance 38939
Result:	**Manchester United 1 Wolverhampton Wanderers 0**			
Teamsheet:	Wood, Foulkes, Redman, Whitefoot, Chilton, Edwards, Berry, Blanchflower, Taylor, Viollet, Rowley			
Scorer(s):	Berry			

Match # 2148	Saturday 13/03/54	Football League Division 1	at Villa Park	Attendance 26023
Result:	**Aston Villa 2 Manchester United 2**			
Teamsheet:	Crompton, Foulkes, Byrne, Whitefoot, Chilton, Cockburn, Berry, Blanchflower, Taylor, Viollet, Rowley			
Scorer(s):	Taylor 2			

Match # 2149	Saturday 20/03/54	Football League Division 1	at Old Trafford	Attendance 40181
Result:	**Manchester United 3 Huddersfield Town 1**			
Teamsheet:	Crompton, Foulkes, Byrne, Whitefoot, Chilton, Edwards, Berry, Blanchflower, Taylor, Viollet, Rowley			
Scorer(s):	Blanchflower, Rowley, Viollet			

SEASON 1953/54 (continued)

Match # 2150	Saturday 27/03/54 · Football League Division 1	at Highbury	Attendance 42753
Result:	**Arsenal 3 Manchester United 1**		
Teamsheet:	Crompton, Foulkes, Byrne, Gibson, Chilton, Edwards, Berry, Blanchflower, Taylor, Viollet, Rowley		
Scorer(s):	Taylor		

Match # 2151	Saturday 03/04/54 Football League Division 1	at Old Trafford	Attendance 22832
Result:	**Manchester United 2 Cardiff City 3**		
Teamsheet:	Crompton, Foulkes, Byrne, Whitefoot, Chilton, Edwards, Berry, Blanchflower, Lewis, Viollet, Rowley		
Scorer(s):	Rowley, Viollet		

Match # 2152	Saturday 10/04/54 Football League Division 1	at Bloomfield Road	Attendance 25996
Result:	**Blackpool 2 Manchester United 0**		
Teamsheet:	Crompton, Foulkes, Byrne, Whitefoot, Chilton, Edwards, Berry, Blanchflower, Aston, Viollet, Rowley		

Match # 2153	Friday 16/04/54 Football League Division 1	at Old Trafford	Attendance 31876
Result:	**Manchester United 2 Charlton Athletic 0**		
Teamsheet:	Crompton, Foulkes, Byrne, Whitefoot, Chilton, Edwards, Gibson, Blanchflower, Aston, Viollet, Pegg		
Scorer(s):	Aston, Viollet		

Match # 2154	Saturday 17/04/54 Football League Division 1	at Old Trafford	Attendance 29663
Result:	**Manchester United 2 Portsmouth 0**		
Teamsheet:	Crompton, Foulkes, Byrne, Whitefoot, Chilton, Edwards, Gibson, Blanchflower, Aston, Viollet, Pegg		
Scorer(s):	Blanchflower, Viollet		

Match # 2155	Monday 19/04/54 Football League Division 1	at The Valley	Attendance 19111
Result:	**Charlton Athletic 1 Manchester United 0**		
Teamsheet:	Crompton, Foulkes, Byrne, Whitefoot, Chilton, Cockburn, Gibson, Blanchflower, Aston, Viollet, Pegg		

Match # 2156	Saturday 24/04/54 Football League Division 1	at Bramall Lane	Attendance 29189
Result:	**Sheffield United 1 Manchester United 3**		
Teamsheet:	Crompton, Foulkes, Byrne, Whitefoot, Chilton, Cockburn, Berry, Blanchflower, Aston, Viollet, Rowley		
Scorer(s):	Aston, Blanchflower, Viollet		

SEASON 1953/54 SUMMARY

APPEARANCES

PLAYER	LGE	FAC	TOT
Chilton	42	1	43
Byrne	41	1	42
Whitefoot	38	1	39
Berry	37	1	38
Rowley	36	1	37
Taylor	35	1	36
Foulkes	32	1	33
Viollet	29	1	30
Blanchflower	27	1	28
Wood	27	1	28
Edwards	24	1	25
Cockburn	18	–	18

APPEARANCES

PLAYER	LGE	FAC	TOT
Crompton	15	–	15
Aston	12	–	12
Pearson	11	–	11
McShane	9	–	9
Pegg	9	–	9
Gibson	7	–	7
Lewis	6	–	6
McNulty	4	–	4
McFarlane	1	–	1
Redman	1	–	1
Webster	1	–	1

GOALSCORERS

PLAYER	LGE	FAC	TOT
Taylor	22	1	23
Blanchflower	13	1	14
Rowley	12	–	12
Viollet	11	1	12
Berry	5	–	5
Byrne	3	–	3
Aston	2	–	2
Pearson	2	–	2
Chilton	1	–	1
Foulkes	1	–	1
Lewis	1	–	1

RESULTS & ATTENDANCES SUMMARY

		P	W	D	L	F	A	TOTAL	AVGE
League	H	21	11	6	4	41	27	705392	33590
	A	21	7	6	8	32	31	779016	37096
	TOTAL	42	18	12	12	73	58	1484408	35343
FA Cup	H	0	0	0	0	0	0	0	n/a
	A	1	0	0	1	3	5	54000	54000
	TOTAL	1	0	0	1	3	5	54000	54000
Overall	H	21	11	6	4	41	27	705392	33590
	A	22	7	6	9	35	36	833016	37864
	TOTAL	43	18	12	13	76	63	1538408	35777

FINAL TABLE – LEAGUE DIVISION ONE

		P	W	D	L	F	A	W	D	L	F	A	PTS	GD
				HOME					AWAY					
1	Wolverhampton Wanderers	42	16	1	4	61	25	9	6	6	35	31	57	40
2	West Bromwich Albion	42	13	5	3	51	24	9	4	8	35	39	53	23
3	Huddersfield Town	42	13	6	2	45	24	7	5	9	33	37	51	17
4	MANCHESTER UNITED	42	11	6	4	41	27	7	6	8	32	31	48	15
5	Bolton Wanderers	42	14	6	1	45	20	4	6	11	30	40	48	15
6	Blackpool	42	13	6	2	43	19	6	4	11	37	50	48	11
7	Burnley	42	16	2	3	51	23	5	2	14	27	44	46	11
8	Chelsea	42	12	3	6	45	26	4	9	8	29	42	44	6
9	Charlton Athletic	42	14	4	3	51	26	5	2	14	24	51	44	-2
10	Cardiff City	42	12	4	5	32	27	6	4	11	19	44	44	-20
11	Preston North End	42	12	2	7	43	24	7	3	11	44	34	43	29
12	Arsenal	42	8	8	5	42	37	7	5	9	33	36	43	2
13	Aston Villa	42	12	5	4	50	28	4	4	13	20	40	41	2
14	Portsmouth	42	13	5	3	53	31	1	6	14	28	58	39	-8
15	Newcastle United	42	9	2	10	43	40	5	8	8	29	37	38	-5
16	Tottenham Hotspur	42	11	3	7	38	33	5	2	14	27	43	37	-11
17	Manchester City	42	10	4	7	35	31	4	5	12	27	46	37	-15
18	Sunderland	42	11	4	6	50	37	3	4	14	31	52	36	-8
19	Sheffield Wednesday	42	12	4	5	43	30	3	2	16	27	61	36	-21
20	Sheffield United	42	9	5	7	43	38	2	6	13	26	52	33	-21
21	Middlesbrough	42	6	6	9	29	35	4	4	13	31	56	30	-31
22	Liverpool	42	7	8	6	49	38	2	2	17	19	59	28	-29

SEASON 1954/55

Match # 2157	Saturday 21/08/54	Football League Division 1	at Old Trafford	Attendance 38203
Result:	Manchester United 1 Portsmouth 3			
Teamsheet:	Wood, Foulkes, Byrne, Whitefoot, Chilton, Edwards, Berry, Blanchflower, Webster, Viollet, Rowley			
Scorer(s):	Rowley			

Match # 2158	Monday 23/08/54	Football League Division 1	at Hillsborough	Attendance 38118
Result:	Sheffield Wednesday 2 Manchester United 4			
Teamsheet:	Wood, Foulkes, Byrne, Whitefoot, Chilton, Edwards, Berry, Blanchflower, Webster, Viollet, Rowley			
Scorer(s):	Blanchflower 2, Viollet 2			

Match # 2159	Saturday 28/08/54	Football League Division 1	at Bloomfield Road	Attendance 31855
Result:	Blackpool 2 Manchester United 4			
Teamsheet:	Wood, Foulkes, Byrne, Whitefoot, Chilton, Edwards, Berry, Blanchflower, Webster, Viollet, Rowley			
Scorer(s):	Webster 2, Blanchflower, Viollet			

Match # 2160	Wednesday 01/09/54	Football League Division 1	at Old Trafford	Attendance 31371
Result:	Manchester United 2 Sheffield Wednesday 0			
Teamsheet:	Wood, Foulkes, Byrne, Whitefoot, Chilton, Edwards, Berry, Blanchflower, Webster, Viollet, Rowley			
Scorer(s):	Viollet 2			

Match # 2161	Saturday 04/09/54	Football League Division 1	at Old Trafford	Attendance 38105
Result:	Manchester United 3 Charlton Athletic 1			
Teamsheet:	Wood, Foulkes, Byrne, Whitefoot, Chilton, Edwards, Berry, Blanchflower, Taylor, Viollet, Rowley			
Scorer(s):	Rowley 2, Taylor			

Match # 2162	Wednesday 08/09/54	Football League Division 1	at White Hart Lane	Attendance 35162
Result:	Tottenham Hotspur 0 Manchester United 2			
Teamsheet:	Wood, Foulkes, Byrne, Whitefoot, Chilton, Edwards, Berry, Blanchflower, Webster, Viollet, Rowley			
Scorer(s):	Berry, Webster			

Match # 2163	Saturday 11/09/54	Football League Division 1	at Burnden Park	Attendance 44661
Result:	Bolton Wanderers 1 Manchester United 1			
Teamsheet:	Wood, Foulkes, Byrne, Whitefoot, Chilton, Edwards, Berry, Blanchflower, Webster, Viollet, Rowley			
Scorer(s):	Webster			

Match # 2164	Wednesday 15/09/54	Football League Division 1	at Old Trafford	Attendance 29212
Result:	Manchester United 2 Tottenham Hotspur 1			
Teamsheet:	Wood, Foulkes, Byrne, Whitefoot, Chilton, Edwards, Berry, Blanchflower, Taylor, Viollet, Rowley			
Scorer(s):	Rowley, Viollet			

Match # 2165	Saturday 18/09/54	Football League Division 1	at Old Trafford	Attendance 45648
Result:	Manchester United 1 Huddersfield Town 1			
Teamsheet:	Wood, Foulkes, Byrne, Whitefoot, Chilton, Edwards, Berry, Blanchflower, Taylor, Viollet, Rowley			
Scorer(s):	Viollet			

Match # 2166	Saturday 25/09/54	Football League Division 1	at Maine Road	Attendance 54105
Result:	Manchester City 3 Manchester United 2			
Teamsheet:	Wood, Foulkes, Byrne, Gibson, Chilton, Edwards, Berry, Blanchflower, Taylor, Viollet, Rowley			
Scorer(s):	Blanchflower, Taylor			

Match # 2167	Saturday 02/10/54	Football League Division 1	at Molineux	Attendance 39617
Result:	Wolverhampton Wanderers 4 Manchester United 2			
Teamsheet:	Crompton, Greaves, Kennedy, Gibson, Chilton, Cockburn, Berry, Edwards, Taylor, Viollet, Rowley			
Scorer(s):	Rowley, Viollet			

Match # 2168	Saturday 09/10/54	Football League Division 1	at Old Trafford	Attendance 39378
Result:	Manchester United 5 Cardiff City 2			
Teamsheet:	Wood, Foulkes, Byrne, Gibson, Chilton, Edwards, Berry, Blanchflower, Taylor, Viollet, Rowley			
Scorer(s):	Taylor 4, Viollet			

Match # 2169	Saturday 16/10/54	Football League Division 1	at Stamford Bridge	Attendance 55966
Result:	Chelsea 5 Manchester United 6			
Teamsheet:	Wood, Foulkes, Byrne, Gibson, Chilton, Edwards, Berry, Blanchflower, Taylor, Viollet, Rowley			
Scorer(s):	Viollet 3, Taylor 2, Blanchflower			

Match # 2170	Saturday 23/10/54	Football League Division 1	at Old Trafford	Attendance 29217
Result:	Manchester United 2 Newcastle United 2			
Teamsheet:	Wood, Foulkes, Byrne, Gibson, Chilton, Edwards, Berry, Blanchflower, Taylor, Viollet, Rowley			
Scorer(s):	Taylor, own goal			

Match # 2171	Saturday 30/10/54	Football League Division 1	at Goodison Park	Attendance 63021
Result:	Everton 4 Manchester United 2			
Teamsheet:	Wood, Foulkes, Byrne, Gibson, Chilton, Edwards, Berry, Blanchflower, Taylor, Viollet, Rowley			
Scorer(s):	Rowley, Taylor			

Match # 2172	Saturday 06/11/54	Football League Division 1	at Old Trafford	Attendance 30063
Result:	Manchester United 2 Preston North End 1			
Teamsheet:	Wood, Foulkes, Byrne, Gibson, Chilton, Edwards, Berry, Blanchflower, Taylor, Viollet, Rowley			
Scorer(s):	Viollet 2			

Match # 2173	Saturday 13/11/54	Football League Division 1	at Bramall Lane	Attendance 26257
Result:	Sheffield United 3 Manchester United 0			
Teamsheet:	Wood, Foulkes, Byrne, Gibson, Chilton, Edwards, Berry, Blanchflower, Taylor, Viollet, Rowley			

Match # 2174	Saturday 20/11/54	Football League Division 1	at Old Trafford	Attendance 33373
Result:	Manchester United 2 Arsenal 1			
Teamsheet:	Wood, Foulkes, Byrne, Gibson, Chilton, Goodwin, Berry, Blanchflower, Taylor, Viollet, Scanlon			
Scorer(s):	Blanchflower, Taylor			

SEASON 1954/55 (continued)

Match # 2175 Saturday 27/11/54   Football League Division 1   at The Hawthorns   Attendance 33931
Result: **West Bromwich Albion 2 Manchester United 0**
Teamsheet: Wood, Foulkes, Byrne, Gibson, Chilton, Edwards, Berry, Blanchflower, Taylor, Viollet, Scanlon

Match # 2176 Saturday 04/12/54   Football League Division 1   at Old Trafford   Attendance 19369
Result: **Manchester United 3 Leicester City 1**
Teamsheet: Wood, Foulkes, Byrne, Gibson, Chilton, Whitefoot, Berry, Blanchflower, Webster, Viollet, Rowley
Scorer(s):   Rowley, Viollet, Webster

Match # 2177 Saturday 11/12/54   Football League Division 1   at Turf Moor   Attendance 24977
Result: **Burnley 2 Manchester United 4**
Teamsheet: Wood, Foulkes, Bent, Gibson, Chilton, Whitefoot, Berry, Blanchflower, Webster, Viollet, Rowley
Scorer(s):   Webster 3, Viollet

Match # 2178 Saturday 18/12/54   Football League Division 1   at Fratton Park   Attendance 26019
Result: **Portsmouth 0 Manchester United 0**
Teamsheet: Wood, Foulkes, Byrne, Gibson, Chilton, Edwards, Berry, Blanchflower, Webster, Viollet, Rowley

Match # 2179 Monday 27/12/54   Football League Division 1   at Old Trafford   Attendance 49136
Result: **Manchester United 0 Aston Villa 1**
Teamsheet: Wood, Foulkes, Byrne, Gibson, Chilton, Edwards, Berry, Blanchflower, Webster, Viollet, Rowley

Match # 2180 Tuesday 28/12/54   Football League Division 1   at Villa Park   Attendance 48718
Result: **Aston Villa 2 Manchester United 1**
Teamsheet: Wood, Foulkes, Byrne, Gibson, Chilton, Edwards, Berry, Webster, Taylor, Viollet, Pegg
Scorer(s):   Taylor

Match # 2181 Saturday 01/01/55   Football League Division 1   at Old Trafford   Attendance 51918
Result: **Manchester United 4 Blackpool 1**
Teamsheet: Wood, Foulkes, Byrne, Gibson, Chilton, Edwards, Berry, Blanchflower, Taylor, Viollet, Pegg
Scorer(s):   Blanchflower 2, Edwards, Viollet

Match # 2182 Saturday 08/01/55   FA Cup 3rd Round   at Elm Park   Attendance 26000
Result: **Reading 1 Manchester United 1**
Teamsheet: Wood, Foulkes, Byrne, Gibson, Chilton, Edwards, Berry, Blanchflower, Webster, Viollet, Rowley
Scorer(s):   Webster

Match # 2183 Wednesday 12/01/55   FA Cup 3rd Round Replay   at Old Trafford   Attendance 24578
Result: **Manchester United 4 Reading 1**
Teamsheet: Wood, Foulkes, Byrne, Gibson, Chilton, Edwards, Berry, Blanchflower, Webster, Viollet, Rowley
Scorer(s):   Webster 2, Rowley, Viollet

Match # 2184 Saturday 22/01/55   Football League Division 1   at Old Trafford   Attendance 39873
Result: **Manchester United 1 Bolton Wanderers 1**
Teamsheet: Wood, Foulkes, Byrne, Gibson, Chilton, Edwards, Berry, Blanchflower, Taylor, Viollet, Rowley
Scorer(s):   Taylor

Match # 2185 Saturday 05/02/55   Football League Division 1   at Leeds Road   Attendance 31408
Result: **Huddersfield Town 1 Manchester United 3**
Teamsheet: Wood, Foulkes, Byrne, Gibson, Chilton, Whitefoot, Berry, Blanchflower, Webster, Edwards, Pegg
Scorer(s):   Berry, Edwards, Pegg

Match # 2186 Saturday 12/02/55   Football League Division 1   at Old Trafford   Attendance 47914
Result: **Manchester United 0 Manchester City 5**
Teamsheet: Wood, Foulkes, Byrne, Gibson, Chilton, Whitefoot, Berry, Blanchflower, Webster, Edwards, Pegg

Match # 2187 Saturday 19/02/55   FA Cup 4th Round   at Maine Road   Attendance 75000
Result: **Manchester City 2 Manchester United 0**
Teamsheet: Wood, Foulkes, Byrne, Gibson, Chilton, Edwards, Berry, Blanchflower, Taylor, Viollet, Rowley

Match # 2188 Wednesday 23/02/55   Football League Division 1   at Old Trafford   Attendance 15679
Result: **Manchester United 2 Wolverhampton Wanderers 4**
Teamsheet: Wood, Foulkes, Byrne, Gibson, Chilton, Whitefoot, Webster, Viollet, Taylor, Edwards, Pegg
Scorer(s):   Edwards, Taylor

Match # 2189 Saturday 26/02/55   Football League Division 1   at Ninian Park   Attendance 16329
Result: **Cardiff City 3 Manchester United 0**
Teamsheet: Wood, Foulkes, Byrne, Gibson, Jones, Whitefoot, Webster, Viollet, Taylor, Edwards, Pegg

Match # 2190 Saturday 05/03/55   Football League Division 1   at Old Trafford   Attendance 31729
Result: **Manchester United 1 Burnley 0**
Teamsheet: Wood, Foulkes, Byrne, Gibson, Jones, Whitefoot, Berry, Taylor, Webster, Edwards, Scanlon
Scorer(s):   Edwards

Match # 2191 Saturday 19/03/55   Football League Division 1   at Old Trafford   Attendance 32295
Result: **Manchester United 1 Everton 2**
Teamsheet: Wood, Foulkes, Byrne, Gibson, Jones, Whitefoot, Berry, Taylor, Webster, Edwards, Scanlon
Scorer(s):   Scanlon

Match # 2192 Saturday 26/03/55   Football League Division 1   at Deepdale   Attendance 13327
Result: **Preston North End 0 Manchester United 2**
Teamsheet: Wood, Foulkes, Byrne, Gibson, Jones, Whitefoot, Berry, Whelan, Taylor, Edwards, Scanlon
Scorer(s):   Byrne, Scanlon

SEASON 1954/55 (continued)

Match # 2193 Saturday 02/04/55   Football League Division 1   at Old Trafford   Attendance 21158
Result: **Manchester United 5 Sheffield United 0**
Teamsheet: Wood, Foulkes, Bent, Gibson, Jones, Whitefoot, Berry, Whelan, Taylor, Viollet, Scanlon
Scorer(s):   Taylor 2, Berry, Viollet, Whelan

Match # 2194 Friday 08/04/55   Football League Division 1   at Roker Park   Attendance 43882
Result: **Sunderland 4 Manchester United 3**
Teamsheet: Wood, Foulkes, Byrne, Gibson, Jones, Whitefoot, Berry, Whelan, Taylor, Edwards, Scanlon
Scorer(s):   Edwards 2, Scanlon

Match # 2195 Saturday 09/04/55   Football League Division 1   at Filbert Street   Attendance 34362
Result: **Leicester City 1 Manchester United 0**
Teamsheet: Crompton, Foulkes, Byrne, Gibson, Jones, Whitefoot, Berry, Whelan, Taylor, Edwards, Scanlon

Match # 2196 Monday 11/04/55   Football League Division 1   at Old Trafford   Attendance 36013
Result: **Manchester United 2 Sunderland 2**
Teamsheet: Crompton, Foulkes, Byrne, Gibson, Jones, Whitefoot, Berry, Whelan, Taylor, Edwards, Scanlon
Scorer(s):   Byrne, Taylor

Match # 2197 Saturday 16/04/55   Football League Division 1   at Old Trafford   Attendance 24765
Result: **Manchester United 3 West Bromwich Albion 0**
Teamsheet: Crompton, Foulkes, Byrne, Goodwin, Jones, Whitefoot, Berry, Whelan, Taylor, Viollet, Scanlon
Scorer(s):   Taylor 2, Viollet

Match # 2198 Monday 18/04/55   Football League Division 1   at St James' Park   Attendance 35540
Result: **Newcastle United 2 Manchester United 0**
Teamsheet: Crompton, Foulkes, Byrne, Gibson, Jones, Whitefoot, Berry, Whelan, Taylor, Viollet, Scanlon

Match # 2199 Saturday 23/04/55   Football League Division 1   at Highbury   Attendance 42754
Result: **Arsenal 2 Manchester United 3**
Teamsheet: Wood, Foulkes, Byrne, Gibson, Jones, Goodwin, Berry, Blanchflower, Taylor, Viollet, Scanlon
Scorer(s):   Blanchflower 2, own goal

Match # 2200 Tuesday 26/04/55   Football League Division 1   at The Valley   Attendance 18149
Result: **Charlton Athletic 1 Manchester United 1**
Teamsheet: Wood, Foulkes, Byrne, Gibson, Jones, Goodwin, Berry, Blanchflower, Taylor, Viollet, Scanlon
Scorer(s):   Viollet

Match # 2201 Saturday 30/04/55   Football League Division 1   at Old Trafford   Attendance 34933
Result: **Manchester United 2 Chelsea 1**
Teamsheet: Wood, Foulkes, Byrne, Gibson, Jones, Goodwin, Berry, Blanchflower, Taylor, Viollet, Scanlon
Scorer(s):   Scanlon, Taylor

SEASON 1954/55 SUMMARY

APPEARANCES

PLAYER	LGE	FAC	TOT
Foulkes	41	3	44
Berry	40	3	43
Byrne	39	3	42
Wood	37	3	40
Viollet	34	3	37
Edwards	33	3	36
Gibson	32	3	35
Blanchflower	29	3	32
Chilton	29	3	32
Taylor	30	1	31
Rowley	22	3	25
Whitefoot	24	–	24
Webster	17	2	19
Scanlon	14	–	14
Jones	13	–	13
Whelan	7	–	7
Pegg	6	–	6
Crompton	5	–	5
Goodwin	5	–	5
Bent	2	–	2
Cockburn	1	–	1
Greaves	1	–	1
Kennedy	1	–	1

GOALSCORERS

PLAYER	LGE	FAC	TOT
Viollet	20	1	21
Taylor	20	–	20
Webster	8	3	11
Blanchflower	10	–	10
Rowley	7	1	8
Edwards	6	–	6
Scanlon	4	–	4
Berry	3	–	3
Byrne	2	–	2
Pegg	1	–	1
Whelan	1	–	1
own goals	2	–	2

RESULTS & ATTENDANCES SUMMARY

		P	W	D	L	F	A	TOTAL	AVGE
League	H	21	12	4	5	44	30	719352	34255
	A	21	8	3	10	40	44	758158	36103
	TOTAL	42	20	7	15	84	74	1477510	35179
FA Cup	H	1	1	0	0	4	1	24578	24578
	A	2	0	1	1	1	3	101000	50500
	TOTAL	3	1	1	1	5	4	125578	41859
Overall	H	22	13	4	5	48	31	743930	33815
	A	23	8	4	11	41	47	859158	37355
	TOTAL	45	21	8	16	89	78	1603088	35624

FINAL TABLE - LEAGUE DIVISION ONE

		P	W	D	L	F	A	W	D	L	F	A	PTS	GD
				HOME						AWAY				
1	Chelsea	42	11	5	5	43	29	9	7	5	38	28	52	24
2	Wolverhampton Wanderers	42	13	5	3	58	30	6	5	10	31	40	48	19
3	Portsmouth	42	13	5	3	44	21	5	7	9	30	41	48	12
4	Sunderland	42	8	11	2	39	27	7	7	7	25	27	48	10
5	MANCHESTER UNITED	42	12	4	5	44	30	8	3	10	40	44	47	10
6	Aston Villa	42	11	3	7	38	31	9	4	8	34	42	47	-1
7	Manchester City	42	11	5	5	45	36	7	5	9	31	33	46	7
8	Newcastle United	42	12	5	4	53	27	5	4	12	36	50	43	12
9	Arsenal	42	12	3	6	44	25	5	6	10	25	38	43	6
10	Burnley	42	11	3	7	29	19	6	6	9	22	29	43	3
11	Everton	42	9	6	6	32	24	7	4	10	30	44	42	-6
12	Huddersfield Town	42	10	4	7	28	23	4	9	8	35	45	41	-5
13	Sheffield United	42	10	3	8	41	34	7	4	10	29	52	41	-16
14	Preston North End	42	8	5	8	47	33	8	3	10	36	31	40	19
15	Charlton Athletic	42	8	6	7	43	34	7	4	10	33	41	40	1
16	Tottenham Hotspur	42	9	4	8	42	35	7	4	10	30	38	40	-1
17	West Bromwich Albion	42	11	5	5	44	33	5	3	13	32	63	40	-20
18	Bolton Wanderers	42	11	6	4	45	29	2	7	12	17	40	39	-7
19	Blackpool	42	8	6	7	33	26	6	4	11	27	38	38	-4
20	Cardiff City	42	9	4	8	41	38	4	7	10	21	38	37	-14
21	Leicester City	42	9	6	6	43	32	3	5	13	31	54	35	-12
22	Sheffield Wednesday	42	7	7	7	42	38	1	3	17	21	62	26	-37

SEASON 1955/56

Match # 2202	Saturday 20/08/55 Football League Division 1	at St Andrews	Attendance 37994
Result:	**Birmingham City 2 Manchester United 2**		
Teamsheet:	Wood, Foulkes, Byrne, Whitefoot, Jones, Edwards, Webster, Blanchflower, Taylor, Viollet, Scanlon		
Scorer(s):	Viollet 2		

Match # 2203	Wednesday 24/08/55 Football League Division 1	at Old Trafford	Attendance 25406
Result:	**Manchester United 2 Tottenham Hotspur 2**		
Teamsheet:	Wood, Foulkes, Byrne, Whitefoot, Jones, Edwards, Berry, Blanchflower, Webster, Viollet, Scanlon		
Scorer(s):	Berry, Webster		

Match # 2204	Saturday 27/08/55 Football League Division 1	at Old Trafford	Attendance 31996
Result:	**Manchester United 3 West Bromwich Albion 1**		
Teamsheet:	Wood, Foulkes, Byrne, Whitefoot, Jones, Edwards, Webster, Blanchflower, Lewis, Viollet, Scanlon		
Scorer(s):	Lewis, Scanlon, Viollet		

Match # 2205	Wednesday 31/08/55 Football League Division 1	at White Hart Lane	Attendance 27453
Result:	**Tottenham Hotspur 1 Manchester United 2**		
Teamsheet:	Wood, Foulkes, Byrne, Whitefoot, Jones, Edwards, Webster, Blanchflower, Lewis, Viollet, Scanlon		
Scorer(s):	Edwards 2		

Match # 2206	Saturday 03/09/55 Football League Division 1	at Maine Road	Attendance 59162
Result:	**Manchester City 1 Manchester United 0**		
Teamsheet:	Wood, Foulkes, Byrne, Whitefoot, Jones, Goodwin, Webster, Blanchflower, Lewis, Edwards, Scanlon		

Match # 2207	Wednesday 07/09/55 Football League Division 1	at Old Trafford	Attendance 27843
Result:	**Manchester United 2 Everton 1**		
Teamsheet:	Wood, Foulkes, Byrne, Whitefoot, Jones, Goodwin, Webster, Blanchflower, Lewis, Edwards, Scanlon		
Scorer(s):	Blanchflower, Edwards		

Match # 2208	Saturday 10/09/55 Football League Division 1	at Bramall Lane	Attendance 28241
Result:	**Sheffield United 1 Manchester United 0**		
Teamsheet:	Wood, Foulkes, Byrne, Whitefoot, Jones, Goodwin, Berry, Whelan, Webster, Blanchflower, Pegg		

Match # 2209	Wednesday 14/09/55 Football League Division 1	at Goodison Park	Attendance 34897
Result:	**Everton 4 Manchester United 2**		
Teamsheet:	Wood, Foulkes, Byrne, Whitehurst, Jones, Goodwin, Webster, Whelan, Blanchflower, Doherty, Berry		
Scorer(s):	Blanchflower, Webster		

Match # 2210	Saturday 17/09/55 Football League Division 1	at Old Trafford	Attendance 33078
Result:	**Manchester United 3 Preston North End 2**		
Teamsheet:	Wood, Foulkes, Byrne, Whitefoot, Jones, Goodwin, Webster, Blanchflower, Taylor, Viollet, Pegg		
Scorer(s):	Pegg, Taylor, Viollet		

Match # 2211	Saturday 24/09/55 Football League Division 1	at Turf Moor	Attendance 26873
Result:	**Burnley 0 Manchester United 0**		
Teamsheet:	Wood, Foulkes, Byrne, Whitefoot, Jones, Goodwin, Webster, Blanchflower, Taylor, Viollet, Pegg		

Match # 2212	Saturday 01/10/55 Football League Division 1	at Old Trafford	Attendance 34409
Result:	**Manchester United 3 Luton Town 1**		
Teamsheet:	Wood, Foulkes, Bent, Whitefoot, Jones, Goodwin, Berry, Blanchflower, Taylor, Webster, Pegg		
Scorer(s):	Taylor 2, Webster		

Match # 2213	Saturday 08/10/55 Football League Division 1	at Old Trafford	Attendance 48638
Result:	**Manchester United 4 Wolverhampton Wanderers 3**		
Teamsheet:	Wood, Byrne, Bent, Whitefoot, Jones, McGuinness, Berry, Doherty, Taylor, Webster, Pegg		
Scorer(s):	Taylor 2, Doherty, Pegg		

Match # 2214	Saturday 15/10/55 Football League Division 1	at Villa Park	Attendance 29478
Result:	**Aston Villa 4 Manchester United 4**		
Teamsheet:	Wood, Foulkes, Byrne, Whitefoot, Jones, McGuinness, Berry, Blanchflower, Taylor, Webster, Pegg		
Scorer(s):	Pegg 2, Blanchflower, Webster		

Match # 2215	Saturday 22/10/55 Football League Division 1	at Old Trafford	Attendance 34150
Result:	**Manchester United 3 Huddersfield Town 0**		
Teamsheet:	Crompton, Foulkes, Bent, Whitefoot, Jones, Edwards, Berry, Blanchflower, Taylor, Viollet, Pegg		
Scorer(s):	Berry, Pegg, Taylor		

Match # 2216	Saturday 29/10/55 Football League Division 1	at Ninian Park	Attendance 27795
Result:	**Cardiff City 0 Manchester United 1**		
Teamsheet:	Wood, Foulkes, Byrne, Whitefoot, Jones, Edwards, Berry, Blanchflower, Taylor, Viollet, Pegg		
Scorer(s):	Taylor		

Match # 2217	Saturday 05/11/55 Football League Division 1	at Old Trafford	Attendance 41586
Result:	**Manchester United 1 Arsenal 1**		
Teamsheet:	Wood, Foulkes, Byrne, Whitefoot, Jones, Edwards, Berry, Blanchflower, Taylor, Viollet, Pegg		
Scorer(s):	Taylor		

Match # 2218	Saturday 12/11/55 Football League Division 1	at Burnden Park	Attendance 38109
Result:	**Bolton Wanderers 3 Manchester United 1**		
Teamsheet:	Wood, Foulkes, Byrne, Colman, Jones, Edwards, Berry, Blanchflower, Taylor, Webster, Pegg		
Scorer(s):	Taylor		

Match # 2219	Saturday 19/11/55 Football League Division 1	at Old Trafford	Attendance 22192
Result:	**Manchester United 3 Chelsea 0**		
Teamsheet:	Wood, Foulkes, Byrne, Colman, Jones, Edwards, Berry, Doherty, Taylor, Viollet, Pegg		
Scorer(s):	Taylor 2, Byrne		

SEASON 1955/56 (continued)

Match # 2220 Saturday 26/11/55   Football League Division 1   at Bloomfield Road   Attendance 26240
Result: **Blackpool 0 Manchester United 0**
Teamsheet: Wood, Greaves, Byrne, Colman, Jones, Edwards, Berry, Doherty, Taylor, Viollet, Pegg

Match # 2221 Saturday 03/12/55   Football League Division 1   at Old Trafford   Attendance 39901
Result: **Manchester United 2 Sunderland 1**
Teamsheet: Wood, Foulkes, Byrne, Colman, Jones, Edwards, Berry, Doherty, Taylor, Viollet, Pegg
Scorer(s):   Doherty, Viollet

Match # 2222 Saturday 10/12/55   Football League Division 1   at Fratton Park   Attendance 24594
Result: **Portsmouth 3 Manchester United 2**
Teamsheet: Wood, Foulkes, Byrne, Colman, Jones, Edwards, Berry, Doherty, Taylor, Viollet, Pegg
Scorer(s):   Pegg, Taylor

Match # 2223 Saturday 17/12/55   Football League Division 1   at Old Trafford   Attendance 27704
Result: **Manchester United 2 Birmingham City 1**
Teamsheet: Wood, Foulkes, Byrne, Colman, Jones, Edwards, Berry, Doherty, Taylor, Viollet, Pegg
Scorer(s):   Jones, Viollet

Match # 2224 Saturday 24/12/55   Football League Division 1   at The Hawthorns   Attendance 25168
Result: **West Bromwich Albion 1 Manchester United 4**
Teamsheet: Wood, Foulkes, Byrne, Colman, Jones, Edwards, Berry, Doherty, Taylor, Viollet, Pegg
Scorer(s):   Viollet 3, Taylor

Match # 2225 Monday 26/12/55   Football League Division 1   at Old Trafford   Attendance 44611
Result: **Manchester United 5 Charlton Athletic 1**
Teamsheet: Wood, Foulkes, Byrne, Colman, Jones, Edwards, Berry, Doherty, Taylor, Viollet, Pegg
Scorer(s):   Viollet 2, Byrne, Doherty, Taylor

Match # 2226 Tuesday 27/12/55   Football League Division 1   at The Valley   Attendance 42040
Result: **Charlton Athletic 3 Manchester United 0**
Teamsheet: Wood, Foulkes, Byrne, Colman, Jones, Edwards, Berry, Doherty, Taylor, Viollet, Pegg

Match # 2227 Saturday 31/12/55   Football League Division 1   at Old Trafford   Attendance 60956
Result: **Manchester United 2 Manchester City 1**
Teamsheet: Wood, Foulkes, Byrne, Colman, Jones, Edwards, Berry, Doherty, Taylor, Viollet, Pegg
Scorer(s):   Taylor, Viollet

Match # 2228 Saturday 07/01/56   FA Cup 3rd Round   at Eastville   Attendance 35872
Result: **Bristol Rovers 4 Manchester United 0**
Teamsheet: Wood, Foulkes, Byrne, Colman, Jones, Whitefoot, Berry, Doherty, Taylor, Viollet, Pegg

Match # 2229 Saturday 14/01/56   Football League Division 1   at Old Trafford   Attendance 30162
Result: **Manchester United 3 Sheffield United 1**
Teamsheet: Wood, Foulkes, Byrne, Colman, Jones, Edwards, Berry, Whelan, Taylor, Viollet, Pegg
Scorer(s):   Berry, Pegg, Taylor

Match # 2230 Saturday 21/01/56   Football League Division 1   at Deepdale   Attendance 28047
Result: **Preston North End 3 Manchester United 1**
Teamsheet: Wood, Foulkes, Byrne, Colman, Jones, Edwards, Scott, Whelan, Webster, Viollet, Pegg
Scorer(s):   Whelan

Match # 2231 Saturday 04/02/56   Football League Division 1   at Old Trafford   Attendance 27342
Result: **Manchester United 2 Burnley 0**
Teamsheet: Wood, Greaves, Byrne, Colman, Jones, Edwards, Berry, Whelan, Taylor, Viollet, Pegg
Scorer(s):   Taylor, Viollet

Match # 2232 Saturday 11/02/56   Football League Division 1   at Kenilworth Road   Attendance 16354
Result: **Luton Town 0 Manchester United 2**
Teamsheet: Wood, Greaves, Byrne, Goodwin, Jones, Blanchflower, Berry, Whelan, Taylor, Viollet, Pegg
Scorer(s):   Viollet, Whelan

Match # 2233 Saturday 18/02/56   Football League Division 1   at Molineux   Attendance 40014
Result: **Wolverhampton Wanderers 0 Manchester United 2**
Teamsheet: Wood, Greaves, Byrne, Colman, Jones, Edwards, Berry, Whelan, Taylor, Viollet, Pegg
Scorer(s):   Taylor 2

Match # 2234 Saturday 25/02/56   Football League Division 1   at Old Trafford   Attendance 36277
Result: **Manchester United 1 Aston Villa 0**
Teamsheet: Wood, Greaves, Byrne, Colman, Jones, Edwards, Berry, Whelan, Taylor, Viollet, Pegg
Scorer(s):   Whelan

Match # 2235 Saturday 03/03/56   Football League Division 1   at Stamford Bridge   Attendance 32050
Result: **Chelsea 2 Manchester United 4**
Teamsheet: Wood, Greaves, Byrne, Colman, Jones, Edwards, Berry, Whelan, Taylor, Viollet, Pegg
Scorer(s):   Viollet 2, Pegg, Taylor

Match # 2236 Saturday 10/03/56   Football League Division 1   at Old Trafford   Attendance 44693
Result: **Manchester United 1 Cardiff City 1**
Teamsheet: Wood, Greaves, Byrne, Colman, Jones, Edwards, Berry, Whelan, Taylor, Viollet, Pegg
Scorer(s):   Byrne

Match # 2237 Saturday 17/03/56   Football League Division 1   at Highbury   Attendance 50758
Result: **Arsenal 1 Manchester United 1**
Teamsheet: Wood, Greaves, Byrne, Colman, Jones, Edwards, Berry, Whelan, Taylor, Viollet, Pegg
Scorer(s):   Viollet

SEASON 1955/56 (continued)

Match # 2238 Saturday 24/03/56   Football League Division 1   at Old Trafford   Attendance 46114
Result: **Manchester United 1 Bolton Wanderers 0**
Teamsheet: Wood, Greaves, Byrne, Colman, Jones, Edwards, Berry, Whelan, Taylor, Viollet, Pegg
Scorer(s): Taylor

Match # 2239 Friday 30/03/56   Football League Division 1   at Old Trafford   Attendance 58994
Result: **Manchester United 5 Newcastle United 2**
Teamsheet: Wood, Greaves, Byrne, Colman, Jones, Edwards, Berry, Doherty, Taylor, Viollet, Pegg
Scorer(s): Viollet 2, Doherty, Pegg, Taylor

Match # 2240 Saturday 31/03/56   Football League Division 1   at Leeds Road   Attendance 37780
Result: **Huddersfield Town 0 Manchester United 2**
Teamsheet: Wood, Greaves, Byrne, Colman, Jones, Edwards, Berry, Doherty, Taylor, Viollet, Pegg
Scorer(s): Taylor 2

Match # 2241 Monday 02/04/56   Football League Division 1   at St James' Park   Attendance 37395
Result: **Newcastle United 0 Manchester United 0**
Teamsheet: Wood, Greaves, Byrne, Colman, Jones, Edwards, Berry, Doherty, Taylor, Viollet, Pegg

Match # 2242 Saturday 07/04/56   Football League Division 1   at Old Trafford   Attendance 62277
Result: **Manchester United 2 Blackpool 1**
Teamsheet: Wood, Greaves, Byrne, Colman, Jones, Edwards, Berry, Doherty, Taylor, Viollet, Pegg
Scorer(s): Berry, Taylor

Match # 2243 Saturday 14/04/56   Football League Division 1   at Roker Park   Attendance 19865
Result: **Sunderland 2 Manchester United 2**
Teamsheet: Wood, Greaves, Bent, Colman, Jones, McGuinness, Berry, Whelan, Blanchflower, Viollet, Pegg
Scorer(s): McGuinness, Whelan

Match # 2244 Saturday 21/04/56   Football League Division 1   at Old Trafford   Attendance 38417
Result: **Manchester United 1 Portsmouth 0**
Teamsheet: Wood, Greaves, Byrne, Colman, Jones, Edwards, Berry, Doherty, Taylor, Viollet, Pegg
Scorer(s): Viollet

SEASON 1955/56 SUMMARY

APPEARANCES

PLAYER	LGE	FAC	TOT
Jones	42	1	43
Wood	41	1	42
Byrne	39	1	40
Pegg	35	1	35
Berry	34	1	35
Viollet	34	1	35
Taylor	33	1	34
Edwards	33	–	33
Foulkes	26	1	27
Colman	25	1	26
Blanchflower	18	–	18
Doherty	16	1	17

APPEARANCES

PLAYER	LGE	FAC	TOT
Whitefoot	15	1	16
Greaves	15	–	15
Webster	15	–	15
Whelan	13	–	13
Goodwin	8	–	8
Scanlon	6	–	6
Bent	4	–	4
Lewis	4	–	4
McGuinness	3	–	3
Crompton	1	–	1
Scott	1	–	1
Whitehurst	1	–	1

GOALSCORERS

PLAYER	LGE	FAC	TOT
Taylor	25	–	25
Viollet	20	–	20
Pegg	9	–	9
Berry	4	–	4
Doherty	4	–	4
Webster	4	–	4
Whelan	4	–	4
Blanchflower	3	–	3
Byrne	3	–	3
Edwards	3	–	3
Jones	1	–	1
Lewis	1	–	1
McGuinness	1	–	1
Scanlon	1	–	1

RESULTS & ATTENDANCES SUMMARY

		P	W	D	L	F	A	TOTAL	AVGE
League	H	21	18	3	0	51	20	816746	38893
	A	21	7	7	7	32	31	690307	32872
	TOTAL	42	25	10	7	83	51	1507053	35882
FA Cup	H	0	0	0	0	0	0	0	n/a
	A	1	0	0	1	0	4	35872	35872
	TOTAL	1	0	0	1	0	4	35872	35872
Overall	H	21	18	3	0	51	20	816746	38893
	A	22	7	7	8	32	35	726179	33008
	TOTAL	43	25	10	8	83	55	1542925	35882

FINAL TABLE - LEAGUE DIVISION ONE

		P	W	D	L	F	A	W	D	L	F	A	PTS	GD
				HOME					AWAY					
1	MANCHESTER UNITED	42	18	3	0	51	20	7	7	7	32	31	60	32
2	Blackpool	42	13	4	4	56	27	7	5	9	30	35	49	24
3	Wolverhampton Wanderers	42	15	2	4	51	27	5	7	9	38	38	49	24
4	Manchester City	42	11	5	5	40	27	7	5	9	42	42	46	13
5	Arsenal	42	13	4	4	38	22	5	6	10	22	39	46	-1
6	Birmingham City	42	12	4	5	51	26	6	5	10	24	31	45	18
7	Burnley	42	11	3	7	37	20	7	5	9	27	34	44	10
8	Bolton Wanderers	42	13	3	5	50	24	5	4	12	21	34	43	13
9	Sunderland	42	10	8	3	44	36	7	1	13	36	59	43	-15
10	Luton Town	42	12	4	5	44	27	5	4	12	22	37	42	2
11	Newcastle United	42	12	4	5	49	24	5	3	13	36	46	41	15
12	Portsmouth	42	9	8	4	46	38	7	1	13	32	47	41	-7
13	West Bromwich Albion	42	13	3	5	37	25	5	2	14	21	45	41	-12
14	Charlton Athletic	42	13	2	6	47	26	4	4	13	28	55	40	-6
15	Everton	42	11	5	5	37	29	4	5	12	18	40	40	-14
16	Chelsea	42	10	4	7	32	26	4	7	10	32	51	39	-13
17	Cardiff City	42	11	4	6	36	32	4	5	12	19	37	39	-14
18	Tottenham Hotspur	42	9	4	8	37	33	6	3	12	24	38	37	-10
19	Preston North End	42	6	5	10	32	36	8	3	10	41	36	36	1
20	Aston Villa	42	9	6	6	32	29	2	7	12	20	40	35	-17
21	Huddersfield Town	42	9	4	8	32	30	5	3	13	22	53	35	-29
22	Sheffield United	42	8	6	7	31	35	4	3	14	32	42	33	-14

SEASON 1956/57

Match # 2245   Saturday 18/08/56   Football League Division 1   at Old Trafford   Attendance 32752
Result: **Manchester United 2 Birmingham City 2**
Teamsheet: Wood, Foulkes, Byrne, Colman, Jones, Edwards, Berry, Whelan, Taylor, Viollet, Pegg
Scorer(s):   Viollet 2

Match # 2246   Monday 20/08/56   Football League Division 1   at Deepdale   Attendance 32569
Result: **Preston North End 1 Manchester United 3**
Teamsheet: Wood, Foulkes, Byrne, Colman, Jones, Edwards, Berry, Whelan, Taylor, Viollet, Pegg
Scorer(s):   Taylor 2, Whelan

Match # 2247   Saturday 25/08/56   Football League Division 1   at The Hawthorns   Attendance 26387
Result: **West Bromwich Albion 2 Manchester United 3**
Teamsheet: Wood, Foulkes, Byrne, Colman, Jones, Edwards, Berry, Whelan, Taylor, Viollet, Pegg
Scorer(s):   Taylor, Viollet, Whelan

Match # 2248   Wednesday 29/08/56   Football League Division 1   at Old Trafford   Attendance 32515
Result: **Manchester United 3 Preston North End 2**
Teamsheet: Wood, Foulkes, Byrne, Colman, Jones, Edwards, Berry, Whelan, Taylor, Viollet, Pegg
Scorer(s):   Viollet 3

Match # 2249   Saturday 01/09/56   Football League Division 1   at Old Trafford   Attendance 40369
Result: **Manchester United 3 Portsmouth 0**
Teamsheet: Wood, Foulkes, Byrne, Colman, Jones, Edwards, Berry, Whelan, Taylor, Viollet, Pegg
Scorer(s):   Berry, Pegg, Viollet

Match # 2250   Wednesday 05/09/56   Football League Division 1   at Stamford Bridge   Attendance 29082
Result: **Chelsea 1 Manchester United 2**
Teamsheet: Wood, Foulkes, Byrne, Colman, Jones, Edwards, Berry, Whelan, Taylor, Viollet, Pegg
Scorer(s):   Taylor, Whelan

Match # 2251   Saturday 08/09/56   Football League Division 1   at St James' Park   Attendance 50130
Result: **Newcastle United 1 Manchester United 1**
Teamsheet: Wood, Foulkes, Byrne, Colman, Jones, Edwards, Berry, Whelan, Taylor, Viollet, Pegg
Scorer(s):   Whelan

Match # 2252   Wednesday 12/09/56   European Cup Preliminary Round 1st Leg   at Park Astrid   Attendance 35000
Result: **Anderlecht 0 Manchester United 2**
Teamsheet: Wood, Foulkes, Byrne, Colman, Jones, Blanchflower, Berry, Whelan, Taylor, Viollet, Pegg
Scorer(s):   Taylor, Viollet

Match # 2253   Saturday 15/09/56   Football League Division 1   at Old Trafford   Attendance 48078
Result: **Manchester United 4 Sheffield Wednesday 1**
Teamsheet: Wood, Foulkes, Byrne, Colman, Jones, Edwards, Berry, Whelan, Taylor, Viollet, Pegg
Scorer(s):   Berry, Taylor, Viollet, Whelan

Match # 2254   Saturday 22/09/56   Football League Division 1   at Old Trafford   Attendance 53525
Result: **Manchester United 2 Manchester City 0**
Teamsheet: Wood, Foulkes, Byrne, Colman, Jones, Edwards, Berry, Whelan, Taylor, Viollet, Pegg
Scorer(s):   Viollet, Whelan

Match # 2255   Wednesday 26/09/56   European Cup Preliminary Round 2nd Leg   at Maine Road   Attendance 40000
Result: **Manchester United 10 Anderlecht 0**
Teamsheet: Wood, Foulkes, Byrne, Colman, Jones, Edwards, Berry, Whelan, Taylor, Viollet, Pegg
Scorer(s):   Viollet 4, Taylor 3, Whelan 2, Berry

Match # 2256   Saturday 29/09/56   Football League Division 1   at Highbury   Attendance 62479
Result: **Arsenal 1 Manchester United 2**
Teamsheet: Wood, Foulkes, Byrne, Colman, Cope, Edwards, Berry, Whelan, Taylor, Viollet, Pegg
Scorer(s):   Berry, Whelan

Match # 2257   Saturday 06/10/56   Football League Division 1   at Old Trafford   Attendance 41439
Result: **Manchester United 4 Charlton Athletic 2**
Teamsheet: Wood, Foulkes, Bent, Colman, Jones, McGuinness, Berry, Whelan, Charlton, Viollet, Pegg
Scorer(s):   Charlton 2, Berry, Whelan

Match # 2258   Saturday 13/10/56   Football League Division 1   at Roker Park   Attendance 49487
Result: **Sunderland 1 Manchester United 3**
Teamsheet: Wood, Foulkes, Byrne, Colman, Jones, Edwards, Berry, Whelan, Taylor, Viollet, Pegg
Scorer(s):   Viollet, Whelan, own goal

Match # 2259   Wednesday 17/10/56   European Cup 1st Round 1st Leg   at Maine Road   Attendance 75598
Result: **Manchester United 3 Borussia Dortmund 2**
Teamsheet: Wood, Foulkes, Byrne, Colman, Jones, Edwards, Berry, Whelan, Taylor, Viollet, Pegg
Scorer(s):   Viollet 2, Pegg

Match # 2260   Saturday 20/10/56   Football League Division 1   at Old Trafford   Attendance 43151
Result: **Manchester United 2 Everton 5**
Teamsheet: Wood, Foulkes, Byrne, Colman, Jones, Edwards, Berry, Whelan, Taylor, Charlton, Pegg
Scorer(s):   Charlton, Whelan

Match # 2261   Wednesday 24/10/56   FA Charity Shield   at Maine Road   Attendance 30495
Result: **Manchester City 0 Manchester United 1**
Teamsheet: Wood, Foulkes, Byrne, Colman, Jones, Edwards, Berry, Whelan, Taylor, Viollet, Pegg
Scorer(s):   Viollet

Match # 2262   Saturday 27/10/56   Football League Division 1   at Bloomfield Road   Attendance 32632
Result: **Blackpool 2 Manchester United 2**
Teamsheet: Hawksworth, Foulkes, Byrne, Colman, Jones, Edwards, Berry, Whelan, Taylor, Viollet, Pegg
Scorer(s):   Taylor 2

SEASON 1956/57 (continued)

Match # 2263   Saturday 03/11/56   Football League Division 1   at Old Trafford   Attendance 59835
Result: **Manchester United 3 Wolverhampton Wanderers 0**
Teamsheet: Wood, Foulkes, Byrne, Colman, Jones, Edwards, Berry, Whelan, Taylor, Charlton, Pegg
Scorer(s):   Pegg, Taylor, Whelan

Match # 2264   Saturday 10/11/56   Football League Division 1   at Burnden Park   Attendance 39922
Result: **Bolton Wanderers 2 Manchester United 0**
Teamsheet: Wood, Foulkes, Byrne, Colman, Jones, Edwards, Berry, Whelan, Taylor, Charlton, Pegg

Match # 2265   Saturday 17/11/56   Football League Division 1   at Old Trafford   Attendance 51131
Result: **Manchester United 3 Leeds United 2**
Teamsheet: Wood, Foulkes, Byrne, Colman, Jones, McGuinness, Berry, Whelan, Taylor, Charlton, Pegg
Scorer(s):   Whelan 2, Charlton

Match # 2266   Wednesday 21/11/56   European Cup 1st Round 2nd Leg   at Rote Erde Stadion   Attendance 44570
Result: **Borussia Dortmund 0 Manchester United 0**
Teamsheet: Wood, Foulkes, Byrne, Colman, Jones, McGuinness, Berry, Whelan, Taylor, Edwards, Pegg

Match # 2267   Saturday 24/11/56   Football League Division 1   at White Hart Lane   Attendance 57724
Result: **Tottenham Hotspur 2 Manchester United 2**
Teamsheet: Wood, Foulkes, Byrne, Colman, Blanchflower, McGuinness, Berry, Whelan, Taylor, Edwards, Pegg
Scorer(s):   Berry, Colman

Match # 2268   Saturday 01/12/56   Football League Division 1   at Old Trafford   Attendance 34736
Result: **Manchester United 3 Luton Town 1**
Teamsheet: Wood, Foulkes, Byrne, Colman, Jones, McGuinness, Berry, Whelan, Taylor, Edwards, Pegg
Scorer(s):   Edwards, Pegg, Taylor

Match # 2269   Saturday 08/12/56   Football League Division 1   at Villa Park   Attendance 42530
Result: **Aston Villa 1 Manchester United 3**
Teamsheet: Wood, Foulkes, Bent, Colman, Jones, Edwards, Berry, Whelan, Taylor, Viollet, Pegg
Scorer(s):   Taylor 2, Viollet

Match # 2270   Saturday 15/12/56   Football League Division 1   at St Andrews   Attendance 36146
Result: **Birmingham City 3 Manchester United 1**
Teamsheet: Wood, Foulkes, Bent, Colman, Jones, Edwards, Berry, Whelan, Taylor, Viollet, Pegg
Scorer(s):   Whelan

Match # 2271   Wednesday 26/12/56   Football League Division 1   at Old Trafford   Attendance 28607
Result: **Manchester United 3 Cardiff City 1**
Teamsheet: Wood, Foulkes, Byrne, Colman, Jones, Edwards, Berry, Whelan, Taylor, Viollet, Pegg
Scorer(s):   Taylor, Viollet, Whelan

Match # 2272   Saturday 29/12/56   Football League Division 1   at Fratton Park   Attendance 32147
Result: **Portsmouth 1 Manchester United 3**
Teamsheet: Wood, Foulkes, Byrne, Colman, Jones, McGuinness, Berry, Whelan, Edwards, Viollet, Pegg
Scorer(s):   Edwards, Pegg, Viollet

Match # 2273   Tuesday 01/01/57   Football League Division 1   at Old Trafford   Attendance 42116
Result: **Manchester United 3 Chelsea 0**
Teamsheet: Wood, Foulkes, Byrne, Colman, Jones, Edwards, Berry, Whelan, Taylor, Viollet, Pegg
Scorer(s):   Taylor 2, Whelan

Match # 2274   Saturday 05/01/57   FA Cup 3rd Round   at Victoria Ground   Attendance 17264
Result: **Hartlepool United 3 Manchester United 4**
Teamsheet: Wood, Foulkes, Byrne, Colman, Jones, Edwards, Berry, Whelan, Taylor, Viollet, Pegg
Scorer(s):   Whelan 2, Berry, Taylor

Match # 2275   Saturday 12/01/57   Football League Division 1   at Old Trafford   Attendance 44911
Result: **Manchester United 6 Newcastle United 1**
Teamsheet: Wood, Foulkes, Byrne, Colman, Jones, Edwards, Berry, Whelan, Taylor, Viollet, Pegg
Scorer(s):   Pegg 2, Viollet 2, Whelan 2

Match # 2276   Wednesday 16/01/57   European Cup Quarter-Final 1st Leg   at Estadio San Mames   Attendance 60000
Result: **Athletic Bilbao 5 Manchester United 3**
Teamsheet: Wood, Foulkes, Byrne, Colman, Jones, Edwards, Berry, Whelan, Taylor, Viollet, Pegg
Scorer(s):   Taylor, Viollet, Whelan

Match # 2277   Saturday 19/01/57   Football League Division 1   at Hillsborough   Attendance 51068
Result: **Sheffield Wednesday 2 Manchester United 1**
Teamsheet: Wood, Foulkes, Byrne, Colman, Jones, Edwards, Berry, Whelan, Taylor, Viollet, Pegg
Scorer(s):   Taylor

Match # 2278   Wednesday 26/01/57   FA Cup 4th Round   at Racecourse Ground   Attendance 34445
Result: **Wrexham 0 Manchester United 5**
Teamsheet: Wood, Foulkes, Byrne, Colman, Jones, Edwards, Berry, Whelan, Taylor, Viollet, Pegg
Scorer(s):   Taylor 2, Whelan 2, Byrne

Match # 2279   Saturday 02/02/57   Football League Division 1   at Maine Road   Attendance 63872
Result: **Manchester City 2 Manchester United 4**
Teamsheet: Wood, Foulkes, Byrne, Colman, Jones, Edwards, Berry, Whelan, Taylor, Viollet, Pegg
Scorer(s):   Edwards, Taylor, Viollet, Whelan

Match # 2280   Wednesday 06/02/57   European Cup Quarter-Final 2nd Leg   at Maine Road   Attendance 70000
Result: **Manchester United 3 Athletic Bilbao 0**
Teamsheet: Wood, Foulkes, Byrne, Colman, Jones, Edwards, Berry, Whelan, Taylor, Viollet, Pegg
Scorer(s):   Berry, Taylor, Viollet

SEASON 1956/57 (continued)

Match # 2281 Saturday 09/02/57   Football League Division 1   at Old Trafford   Attendance 60384
Result: **Manchester United 6 Arsenal 2**
Teamsheet: Wood, Foulkes, Byrne, Colman, Jones, Edwards, Berry, Whelan, Taylor, Viollet, Pegg
Scorer(s): Berry 2, Whelan 2, Edwards, Taylor

Match # 2282 Saturday 16/02/57   FA Cup 5th Round   at Old Trafford   Attendance 61803
Result: **Manchester United 1 Everton 0**
Teamsheet: Wood, Foulkes, Byrne, Colman, Jones, Edwards, Webster, Whelan, Taylor, Viollet, Pegg
Scorer(s): Edwards

Match # 2283 Monday 18/02/57   Football League Division 1   at The Valley   Attendance 16308
Result: **Charlton Athletic 1 Manchester United 5**
Teamsheet: Wood, Byrne, Bent, Colman, Jones, McGuinness, Berry, Whelan, Taylor, Charlton, Pegg
Scorer(s): Charlton 3, Taylor 2

Match # 2284 Saturday 23/02/57   Football League Division 1   at Old Trafford   Attendance 42602
Result: **Manchester United 0 Blackpool 2**
Teamsheet: Wood, Foulkes, Byrne, Colman, Jones, Edwards, Berry, Whelan, Taylor, Charlton, Pegg

Match # 2285 Saturday 02/03/57   FA Cup 6th Round   at Dean Court   Attendance 28799
Result: **Bournemouth 1 Manchester United 2**
Teamsheet: Wood, Foulkes, Byrne, Colman, Jones, McGuinness, Berry, Whelan, Edwards, Viollet, Pegg
Scorer(s): Berry 2

Match # 2286 Wednesday 06/03/57   Football League Division 1   at Goodison Park   Attendance 34029
Result: **Everton 1 Manchester United 2**
Teamsheet: Wood, Byrne, Bent, Goodwin, Blanchflower, McGuinness, Berry, Whelan, Webster, Doherty, Pegg
Scorer(s): Webster 2

Match # 2287 Saturday 09/03/57   Football League Division 1   at Old Trafford   Attendance 55484
Result: **Manchester United 1 Aston Villa 1**
Teamsheet: Wood, Foulkes, Byrne, Goodwin, Blanchflower, McGuinness, Berry, Whelan, Edwards, Charlton, Pegg
Scorer(s): Charlton

Match # 2288 Saturday 16/03/57   Football League Division 1   at Molineux   Attendance 53228
Result: **Wolverhampton Wanderers 1 Manchester United 1**
Teamsheet: Clayton, Foulkes, Byrne, Colman, Blanchflower, Edwards, Berry, Whelan, Webster, Charlton, Pegg
Scorer(s): Charlton

Match # 2289 Saturday 23/03/57   FA Cup Semi-Final   at Hillsborough   Attendance 65107
Result: **Manchester United 2 Birmingham City 0**
Teamsheet: Wood, Foulkes, Byrne, Colman, Blanchflower, Edwards, Berry, Whelan, Charlton, Viollet, Pegg
Scorer(s): Berry, Charlton

Match # 2290 Monday 25/03/57   Football League Division 1   at Old Trafford   Attendance 60862
Result: **Manchester United 0 Bolton Wanderers 2**
Teamsheet: Wood, Foulkes, Byrne, Colman, Blanchflower, McGuinness, Berry, Whelan, Edwards, Charlton, Pegg

Match # 2291 Saturday 30/03/57   Football League Division 1   at Elland Road   Attendance 47216
Result: **Leeds United 1 Manchester United 2**
Teamsheet: Wood, Foulkes, Byrne, Colman, Blanchflower, Edwards, Berry, Whelan, Webster, Charlton, Pegg
Scorer(s): Berry, Charlton

Match # 2292 Saturday 06/04/57   Football League Division 1   at Old Trafford   Attendance 60349
Result: **Manchester United 0 Tottenham Hotspur 0**
Teamsheet: Wood, Foulkes, Bent, Colman, Blanchflower, McGuinness, Berry, Whelan, Taylor, Viollet, Scanlon

Match # 2293 Thursday 11/04/57   European Cup Semi-Final 1st Leg   at Bernabeu Stadium   Attendance 135000
Result: **Real Madrid 3 Manchester United 1**
Teamsheet: Wood, Foulkes, Byrne, Colman, Blanchflower, Edwards, Berry, Whelan, Taylor, Viollet, Pegg
Scorer(s): Taylor

Match # 2294 Saturday 13/04/57   Football League Division 1   at Kenilworth Road   Attendance 21227
Result: **Luton Town 0 Manchester United 2**
Teamsheet: Wood, Foulkes, Byrne, Goodwin, Blanchflower, Edwards, Berry, Viollet, Taylor, Charlton, Scanlon
Scorer(s): Taylor 2

Match # 2295 Friday 19/04/57   Football League Division 1   at Turf Moor   Attendance 41321
Result: **Burnley 1 Manchester United 3**
Teamsheet: Wood, Foulkes, Byrne, Goodwin, Blanchflower, Edwards, Berry, Whelan, Taylor, Charlton, Pegg
Scorer(s): Whelan 3

Match # 2296 Saturday 20/04/57   Football League Division 1   at Old Trafford   Attendance 58725
Result: **Manchester United 4 Sunderland 0**
Teamsheet: Wood, Foulkes, Byrne, Colman, Blanchflower, Edwards, Berry, Whelan, Taylor, Charlton, Pegg
Scorer(s): Whelan 2, Edwards, Taylor

Match # 2297 Monday 22/04/57   Football League Division 1   at Old Trafford   Attendance 41321
Result: **Manchester United 2 Burnley 0**
Teamsheet: Wood, Foulkes, Greaves, Goodwin, Cope, McGuinness, Webster, Doherty, Dawson, Viollet, Scanlon
Scorer(s): Dawson, Webster

Match # 2298 Thursday 25/04/57   European Cup Semi-Final 2nd Leg   at Old Trafford   Attendance 65000
Result: **Manchester United 2 Real Madrid 2**
Teamsheet: Wood, Foulkes, Byrne, Colman, Blanchflower, Edwards, Berry, Whelan, Taylor, Charlton, Pegg
Scorer(s): Charlton, Taylor

SEASON 1956/57 (continued)

Match # 2299	Saturday 27/04/57	Football League Division 1	at Ninian Park	Attendance 17708
Result:	**Cardiff City 2 Manchester United 3**		
Teamsheet:	Wood, Foulkes, Greaves, Colman, Blanchflower, McGuinness, Webster, Whelan, Dawson, Viollet, Scanlon		
Scorer(s):	Scanlon 2, Dawson		

Match # 2300	Monday 29/04/57	Football League Division 1	at Old Trafford	Attendance 20357
Result:	**Manchester United 1 West Bromwich Albion 1**		
Teamsheet:	Clayton, Greaves, Byrne, Goodwin, Jones, McGuinness, Berry, Doherty, Dawson, Viollet, Scanlon		
Scorer(s):	Dawson		

Match # 2301	Saturday 04/05/57	FA Cup Final	at Wembley	Attendance 100000
Result:	**Manchester United 1 Aston Villa 2**		
Teamsheet:	Wood, Foulkes, Byrne, Colman, Blanchflower, Edwards, Berry, Whelan, Taylor, Charlton, Pegg		
Scorer(s):	Taylor		

SEASON 1956/57 SUMMARY

APPEARANCES

PLAYER	LGE	FAC	EC	CS	TOT
Berry	40	5	8	1	54
Foulkes	39	6	8	1	54
Whelan	39	6	8	1	54
Wood	39	6	8	1	54
Pegg	37	6	8	1	52
Byrne	36	6	8	1	51
Colman	36	6	8	1	51
Edwards	34	6	7	1	48
Taylor	32	4	8	1	45
Jones	29	4	6	1	40
Viollet	27	5	6	1	39
Charlton	14	2	1	–	17
Blanchflower	11	2	3	–	16
McGuinness	13	1	1	–	15
Bent	6	–	–	–	6
Goodwin	6	–	–	–	6
Webster	5	1	–	–	6
Scanlon	5	–	–	–	5
Dawson	3	–	–	–	3
Doherty	3	–	–	–	3
Greaves	3	–	–	–	3
Clayton	2	–	–	–	2
Cope	2	–	–	–	2
Hawksworth	1	–	–	–	1

GOALSCORERS

PLAYER	LGE	FAC	EC	CS	TOT
Taylor	22	4	8	–	34
Whelan	26	4	3	–	33
Viollet	16	–	9	1	26
Berry	8	4	2	–	14
Charlton	10	1	1	–	12
Pegg	6	–	1	–	7
Edwards	5	1	–	–	6
Dawson	3	–	–	–	3
Webster	3	–	–	–	3
Scanlon	2	–	–	–	2
Colman	1	–	–	–	1
Byrne	–	1	–	–	1
own goal	1	–	–	–	1

RESULTS & ATTENDANCES SUMMARY

		P	W	D	L	F	A	TOTAL	AVGE
League	H	21	14	4	3	55	25	953249	45393
	A	21	14	4	3	48	29	837212	39867
TOTAL		42	28	8	6	103	54	1790461	42630
FA Cup	H	1	1	0	0	1	0	61803	61803
	A	3	3	0	0	11	4	80508	26836
	N	2	1	0	1	3	2	165107	82554
TOTAL		6	5	0	1	15	6	307418	51236
European	H	4	3	1	0	18	4	250598	62650
Cup	A	4	1	1	2	6	8	274570	68643
TOTAL		8	4	2	2	24	12	525168	65646
Charity	H	0	0	0	0	0	0	0	n/a
Shield	A	1	1	0	0	1	0	30495	30495
TOTAL		1	1	0	0	1	0	30495	30495
Overall	H	26	18	5	3	74	29	1265650	48679
	A	29	19	5	5	66	41	1222785	42165
	N	2	1	0	1	3	2	165107	82554
TOTAL		57	38	10	9	143	72	2653542	46553

FINAL TABLE – LEAGUE DIVISION ONE

		P		HOME					AWAY				PTS	GD
			W	D	L	F	A	W	D	L	F	A		
1	MANCHESTER UNITED	42	14	4	3	55	25	14	4	3	48	29	64	49
2	Tottenham Hotspur	42	15	4	2	70	24	7	8	6	34	32	56	48
3	Preston North End	42	15	4	2	50	19	8	6	7	34	37	56	28
4	Blackpool	42	14	3	4	55	26	8	6	7	38	39	53	28
5	Arsenal	42	12	5	4	45	21	9	3	9	40	48	50	16
6	Wolverhampton Wanderers	42	17	2	2	70	29	3	6	12	24	41	48	24
7	Burnley	42	14	5	2	41	21	4	5	12	15	29	46	6
8	Leeds United	42	10	8	3	42	18	5	6	10	30	45	44	9
9	Bolton Wanderers	42	13	6	2	42	23	3	6	12	23	42	44	0
10	Aston Villa	42	10	8	3	45	25	4	7	10	20	30	43	10
11	West Bromwich Albion	42	8	8	5	31	25	6	6	9	28	36	42	-2
12	Birmingham City	42	12	5	4	52	25	3	4	14	17	44	39	0
13	Chelsea	42	7	8	6	43	36	6	5	10	30	37	39	0
14	Sheffield Wednesday	42	14	3	4	55	29	2	3	16	27	59	38	-6
15	Everton	42	10	5	6	34	28	4	5	12	27	51	38	-18
16	Luton Town	42	10	4	7	32	26	4	5	12	26	50	37	-18
17	Newcastle United	42	10	5	6	43	31	4	3	14	24	56	36	-20
18	Manchester City	42	10	2	9	48	42	3	7	11	30	46	35	-10
19	Portsmouth	42	8	6	7	37	35	2	7	12	25	57	33	-30
20	Sunderland	42	9	5	7	40	30	3	3	15	27	58	32	-21
21	Cardiff City	42	7	6	8	35	34	3	3	15	18	54	29	-35
22	Charlton Athletic	42	7	3	11	31	44	2	1	18	31	76	22	-58

SEASON 1957/58

Match # 2302   Saturday 24/08/57   Football League Division 1   at Filbert Street   Attendance 40214
Result: **Leicester City 0 Manchester United 3**
Teamsheet: Wood, Foulkes, Byrne, Colman, Blanchflower, Edwards, Berry, Whelan, Taylor T, Viollet, Pegg
Scorer(s):   Whelan 3

Match # 2303   Wednesday 28/08/57   Football League Division 1   at Old Trafford   Attendance 59103
Result: **Manchester United 3 Everton 0**
Teamsheet: Wood, Foulkes, Byrne, Colman, Blanchflower, Edwards, Berry, Whelan, Taylor T, Viollet, Pegg
Scorer(s):   Taylor T, Viollet, own goal

Match # 2304   Saturday 31/08/57   Football League Division 1   at Old Trafford   Attendance 63347
Result: **Manchester United 4 Manchester City 1**
Teamsheet: Wood, Foulkes, Byrne, Colman, Blanchflower, Edwards, Berry, Whelan, Taylor T, Viollet, Pegg
Scorer(s):   Berry, Edwards, Taylor T, Viollet

Match # 2305   Wednesday 04/09/57   Football League Division 1   at Goodison Park   Attendance 72077
Result: **Everton 3 Manchester United 3**
Teamsheet: Wood, Foulkes, Byrne, Colman, Blanchflower, Edwards, Berry, Whelan, Taylor T, Viollet, Pegg
Scorer(s):   Berry, Viollet, Whelan

Match # 2306   Saturday 07/09/57   Football League Division 1   at Old Trafford   Attendance 50842
Result: **Manchester United 5 Leeds United 0**
Teamsheet: Wood, Foulkes, Byrne, Colman, Blanchflower, Edwards, Berry, Whelan, Taylor T, Viollet, Pegg
Scorer(s):   Berry 2, Taylor T 2, Viollet

Match # 2307   Monday 09/09/57   Football League Division 1   at Bloomfield Road   Attendance 34181
Result: **Blackpool 1 Manchester United 4**
Teamsheet: Wood, Foulkes, Byrne, Colman, Blanchflower, Edwards, Berry, Whelan, Taylor T, Viollet, Pegg
Scorer(s):   Viollet 2, Whelan 2

Match # 2308   Saturday 14/09/57   Football League Division 1   at Burnden Park   Attendance 48003
Result: **Bolton Wanderers 4 Manchester United 0**
Teamsheet: Wood, Foulkes, Byrne, Colman, Blanchflower, Edwards, Berry, Whelan, Taylor T, Viollet, Pegg

Match # 2309   Wednesday 18/09/57   Football League Division 1   at Old Trafford   Attendance 40763
Result: **Manchester United 1 Blackpool 2**
Teamsheet: Wood, Foulkes, Byrne, Colman, Blanchflower, Edwards, Berry, Whelan, Taylor T, Viollet, Pegg
Scorer(s):   Edwards

Match # 2310   Saturday 21/09/57   Football League Division 1   at Old Trafford   Attendance 47142
Result: **Manchester United 4 Arsenal 2**
Teamsheet: Wood, Foulkes, Byrne, Colman, Blanchflower, Edwards, Berry, Whelan, Taylor T, Viollet, Pegg
Scorer(s):   Whelan 2, Pegg, Taylor T

Match # 2311   Wednesday 25/09/57   European Cup Preliminary Round 1st Leg   at Dalymount Park   Attendance 45000
Result: **Shamrock Rovers 0 Manchester United 6**
Teamsheet: Wood, Foulkes, Byrne, Goodwin, Blanchflower, Edwards, Berry, Whelan, Taylor T, Viollet, Pegg
Scorer(s):   Taylor T 2, Whelan 2, Berry, Pegg

Match # 2312   Saturday 28/09/57   Football League Division 1   at Molineux   Attendance 48825
Result: **Wolverhampton Wanderers 3 Manchester United 1**
Teamsheet: Wood, Foulkes, McGuinness, Goodwin, Blanchflower, Edwards, Berry, Doherty, Taylor T, Charlton, Pegg
Scorer(s):   Doherty

Match # 2313   Wednesday 02/10/57   European Cup Preliminary Round 2nd Leg   at Old Trafford   Attendance 33754
Result: **Manchester United 3 Shamrock Rovers 2**
Teamsheet: Wood, Foulkes, Byrne, Colman, Jones M, McGuinness, Berry, Webster, Taylor T, Viollet, Pegg
Scorer(s):   Viollet 2, Pegg

Match # 2314   Saturday 05/10/57   Football League Division 1   at Old Trafford   Attendance 43102
Result: **Manchester United 4 Aston Villa 1**
Teamsheet: Wood, Foulkes, Byrne, Colman, Jones M, McGuinness, Berry, Whelan, Taylor T, Charlton, Pegg
Scorer(s):   Taylor T 2, Pegg, own goal

Match # 2315   Saturday 12/10/57   Football League Division 1   at City Ground   Attendance 47654
Result: **Nottingham Forest 1 Manchester United 2**
Teamsheet: Wood, Foulkes, Byrne, Colman, Blanchflower, Edwards, Berry, Whelan, Taylor T, Viollet, Pegg
Scorer(s):   Viollet, Whelan

Match # 2316   Saturday 19/10/57   Football League Division 1   at Old Trafford   Attendance 38253
Result: **Manchester United 0 Portsmouth 3**
Teamsheet: Wood, Foulkes, Jones P, Colman, Blanchflower, McGuinness, Berry, Whelan, Dawson, Viollet, Pegg

Match # 2317   Tuesday 22/10/57   FA Charity Shield   at Old Trafford   Attendance 27293
Result: **Manchester United 4 Aston Villa 0**
Teamsheet: Wood, Foulkes, Byrne, Goodwin, Blanchflower, Edwards, Berry, Whelan, Taylor T, Viollet, Pegg
Scorer(s):   Taylor T 3, Berry

Match # 2318   Saturday 26/10/57   Football League Division 1   at The Hawthorns   Attendance 52160
Result: **West Bromwich Albion 4 Manchester United 3**
Teamsheet: Wood, Foulkes, Byrne, Goodwin, Blanchflower, Edwards, Berry, Whelan, Taylor T, Charlton, Pegg
Scorer(s):   Taylor T 2, Whelan

Match # 2319   Saturday 02/11/57   Football League Division 1   at Old Trafford   Attendance 49449
Result: **Manchester United 1 Burnley 0**
Teamsheet: Wood, Foulkes, Byrne, Goodwin, Blanchflower, Edwards, Berry, Whelan, Taylor T, Webster, Pegg
Scorer(s):   Taylor T

SEASON 1957/58 (continued)

Match # 2320   Saturday 09/11/57   Football League Division 1   at Deepdale   Attendance 39063
Result: **Preston North End 1   Manchester United 1**
Teamsheet: Wood, Foulkes, Byrne, Goodwin, Blanchflower, Edwards, Berry, Whelan, Taylor T, Webster, Pegg
Scorer(s):   Whelan

Match # 2321   Saturday 16/11/57   Football League Division 1   at Old Trafford   Attendance 40366
Result: **Manchester United 2   Sheffield Wednesday 1**
Teamsheet: Wood, Foulkes, Byrne, Colman, Blanchflower, Edwards, Berry, Whelan, Taylor T, Webster, Pegg
Scorer(s):   Webster 2

Match # 2322   Wednesday 20/11/57   European Cup 1st Round 1st Leg   at Old Trafford   Attendance 60000
Result: **Manchester United 3   Dukla Prague 0**
Teamsheet: Wood, Foulkes, Byrne, Colman, Blanchflower, Edwards, Berry, Whelan, Taylor T, Webster, Pegg
Scorer(s):   Pegg, Taylor T, Webster

Match # 2323   Saturday 23/11/57   Football League Division 1   at St James' Park   Attendance 53890
Result: **Newcastle United 1   Manchester United 2**
Teamsheet: Wood, Foulkes, Byrne, Colman, Blanchflower, Edwards, Scanlon, Whelan, Taylor T, Webster, Pegg
Scorer(s):   Edwards, Taylor T

Match # 2324   Saturday 30/11/57   Football League Division 1   at Old Trafford   Attendance 43077
Result: **Manchester United 3   Tottenham Hotspur 4**
Teamsheet: Gaskell, Foulkes, Byrne, Colman, Blanchflower, Edwards, Scanlon, Whelan, Webster, Charlton, Pegg
Scorer(s):   Pegg 2, Whelan

Match # 2325   Wednesday 04/12/57   European Cup 1st Round 2nd Leg   at Stadium Strahov   Attendance 35000
Result: **Dukla Prague 1   Manchester United 0**
Teamsheet: Wood, Foulkes, Byrne, Colman, Jones M, Edwards, Scanlon, Whelan, Taylor T, Webster, Pegg

Match # 2326   Saturday 07/12/57   Football League Division 1   at St Andrews   Attendance 35791
Result: **Birmingham City 3   Manchester United 3**
Teamsheet: Wood, Foulkes, Byrne, Colman, Jones M, Edwards, Berry, Whelan, Taylor T, Viollet, Pegg
Scorer(s):   Viollet 2, Taylor T

Match # 2327   Saturday 14/12/57   Football League Division 1   at Old Trafford   Attendance 36853
Result: **Manchester United 0   Chelsea 1**
Teamsheet: Wood, Foulkes, Byrne, Colman, Jones M, Edwards, Berry, Whelan, Taylor T, Viollet, Pegg

Match # 2328   Saturday 21/12/57   Football League Division 1   at Old Trafford   Attendance 41631
Result: **Manchester United 4   Leicester City 0**
Teamsheet: Gregg, Foulkes, Byrne, Colman, Jones M, Edwards, Morgans, Charlton, Taylor T, Viollet, Scanlon
Scorer(s):   Viollet 2, Charlton, Scanlon

Match # 2329   Wednesday 25/12/57   Football League Division 1   at Old Trafford   Attendance 39444
Result: **Manchester United 3   Luton Town 0**
Teamsheet: Gregg, Foulkes, Byrne, Colman, Jones M, Edwards, Morgans, Charlton, Taylor T, Viollet, Scanlon
Scorer(s):   Charlton, Edwards, Taylor T

Match # 2330   Thursday 26/12/57   Football League Division 1   at Kenilworth Road   Attendance 26458
Result: **Luton Town 2   Manchester United 2**
Teamsheet: Gregg, Foulkes, Byrne, Colman, Jones M, Edwards, Berry, Charlton, Taylor T, Viollet, Scanlon
Scorer(s):   Scanlon, Taylor T

Match # 2331   Saturday 28/12/57   Football League Division 1   at Maine Road   Attendance 70483
Result: **Manchester City 2   Manchester United 2**
Teamsheet: Gregg, Foulkes, Byrne, Colman, Jones M, Edwards, Morgans, Charlton, Webster, Viollet, Scanlon
Scorer(s):   Charlton, Viollet

Match # 2332   Saturday 04/01/58   FA Cup 3rd Round   at Borough Park   Attendance 21000
Result: **Workington 1   Manchester United 3**
Teamsheet: Gregg, Foulkes, Byrne, Colman, Jones M, Edwards, Morgans, Charlton, Taylor T, Viollet, Scanlon
Scorer(s):   Viollet 3

Match # 2333   Saturday 11/01/58   Football League Division 1   at Elland Road   Attendance 39401
Result: **Leeds United 1   Manchester United 1**
Teamsheet: Gregg, Foulkes, Byrne, Colman, Jones M, Edwards, Morgans, Charlton, Taylor T, Viollet, Scanlon
Scorer(s):   Viollet

Match # 2334   Tuesday 14/01/58   European Cup Quarter-Final 1st Leg   at Old Trafford   Attendance 60000
Result: **Manchester United 2   Red Star Belgrade 1**
Teamsheet: Gregg, Foulkes, Byrne, Colman, Jones M, Edwards, Morgans, Charlton, Taylor T, Viollet, Scanlon
Scorer(s):   Charlton, Colman

Match # 2335   Saturday 18/01/58   Football League Division 1   at Old Trafford   Attendance 41141
Result: **Manchester United 7   Bolton Wanderers 2**
Teamsheet: Gregg, Foulkes, Byrne, Colman, Jones M, Edwards, Morgans, Charlton, Taylor T, Viollet, Scanlon
Scorer(s):   Charlton 3, Viollet 2, Edwards, Scanlon

Match # 2336   Saturday 25/01/58   FA Cup 4th Round   at Old Trafford   Attendance 53550
Result: **Manchester United 2   Ipswich Town 0**
Teamsheet: Gregg, Foulkes, Byrne, Colman, Jones M, Edwards, Morgans, Charlton, Taylor T, Viollet, Scanlon
Scorer(s):   Charlton 2

Match # 2337   Saturday 01/02/58   Football League Division 1   at Highbury   Attendance 63578
Result: **Arsenal 4   Manchester United 5**
Teamsheet: Gregg, Foulkes, Byrne, Colman, Jones M, Edwards, Morgans, Charlton, Taylor T, Viollet, Scanlon
Scorer(s):   Taylor T 2, Charlton, Edwards, Viollet

SEASON 1957/58 (continued)

Match # 2338 Wednesday 05/02/58   European Cup Quarter-Final 2nd Leg   at Stadion JNA   Attendance 55000
Result: **Red Star Belgrade 3 Manchester United 3**
Teamsheet: Gregg, Foulkes, Byrne, Colman, Jones M, Edwards, Morgans, Charlton, Taylor T, Viollet, Scanlon
Scorer(s):   Charlton 2, Viollet

Match # 2339 Wednesday 19/02/58   FA Cup 5th Round   at Old Trafford   Attendance 59848
Result: **Manchester United 3 Sheffield Wednesday 0**
Teamsheet: Gregg, Foulkes, Greaves, Goodwin, Cope, Crowther, Webster, Taylor E, Dawson, Pearson, Brennan
Scorer(s):   Brennan 2, Dawson

Match # 2340 Saturday 22/02/58   Football League Division 1   at Old Trafford   Attendance 66124
Result: **Manchester United 1 Nottingham Forest 1**
Teamsheet: Gregg, Foulkes, Greaves, Goodwin, Cope, Crowther, Webster, Taylor E, Dawson, Pearson, Brennan
Scorer(s):   Dawson

Match # 2341 Saturday 01/03/58   FA Cup 6th Round   at The Hawthorns   Attendance 58250
Result: **West Bromwich Albion 2 Manchester United 2**
Teamsheet: Gregg, Foulkes, Greaves, Goodwin, Cope, Crowther, Webster, Taylor E, Dawson, Pearson, Charlton
Scorer(s):   Dawson, Taylor E

Match # 2342 Wednesday 05/03/58   FA Cup 6th Round Replay   at Old Trafford   Attendance 60000
Result: **Manchester United 1 West Bromwich Albion 0**
Teamsheet: Gregg, Foulkes, Greaves, Goodwin, Cope, Harrop, Webster, Taylor E, Dawson, Pearson, Charlton
Scorer(s):   Webster

Match # 2343 Saturday 08/03/58   Football League Division 1   at Old Trafford   Attendance 63278
Result: **Manchester United 0 West Bromwich Albion 4**
Teamsheet: Gregg, Foulkes, Greaves, Goodwin, Cope, Harrop, Webster, Taylor E, Dawson, Pearson, Charlton

Match # 2344 Saturday 15/03/58   Football League Division 1   at Turf Moor   Attendance 37247
Result: **Burnley 3 Manchester United 0**
Teamsheet: Gregg, Foulkes, Greaves, Goodwin, Cope, Crowther, Webster, Harrop, Dawson, Pearson, Charlton

Match # 2345 Saturday 22/03/58   FA Cup Semi-Final   at Villa Park   Attendance 69745
Result: **Manchester United 2 Fulham 2**
Teamsheet: Gregg, Foulkes, Greaves, Goodwin, Cope, Crowther, Webster, Taylor E, Dawson, Charlton, Pearson
Scorer(s):   Charlton 2

Match # 2346 Wednesday 26/03/58   FA Cup Semi-Final Replay   at Highbury   Attendance 38000
Result: **Manchester United 5 Fulham 3**
Teamsheet: Gregg, Foulkes, Greaves, Goodwin, Cope, Crowther, Webster, Taylor E, Dawson, Charlton, Brennan
Scorer(s):   Dawson 3, Brennan, Charlton

Match # 2347 Saturday 29/03/58   Football League Division 1   at Hillsborough   Attendance 35608
Result: **Sheffield Wednesday 1 Manchester United 0**
Teamsheet: Gregg, Foulkes, Cope, Goodwin, Harrop, Crowther, Webster, Taylor E, Dawson, Charlton, Brennan

Match # 2348 Monday 31/03/58   Football League Division 1   at Villa Park   Attendance 16631
Result: **Aston Villa 3 Manchester United 2**
Teamsheet: Gregg, Foulkes, Cope, Goodwin, Harrop, Crowther, Webster, Pearson, Dawson, Charlton, Brennan
Scorer(s):   Dawson, Webster

Match # 2349 Friday 04/04/58   Football League Division 1   at Old Trafford   Attendance 47421
Result: **Manchester United 2 Sunderland 2**
Teamsheet: Gregg, Foulkes, Greaves, Goodwin, Cope, Crowther, Webster, Taylor E, Dawson, Charlton, Brennan
Scorer(s):   Charlton, Dawson

Match # 2350 Saturday 05/04/58   Football League Division 1   at Old Trafford   Attendance 47816
Result: **Manchester United 0 Preston North End 0**
Teamsheet: Gregg, Foulkes, Greaves, Goodwin, Cope, Crowther, Morgans, Taylor E, Webster, Charlton, Heron

Match # 2351 Monday 07/04/58   Football League Division 1   at Roker Park   Attendance 51302
Result: **Sunderland 1 Manchester United 2**
Teamsheet: Gregg, Foulkes, Greaves, Goodwin, Harrop, McGuinness, Morgans, Taylor E, Webster, Charlton, Pearson
Scorer(s):   Webster 2

Match # 2352 Saturday 12/04/58   Football League Division 1   at White Hart Lane   Attendance 59836
Result: **Tottenham Hotspur 1 Manchester United 0**
Teamsheet: Gregg, Foulkes, Greaves, Goodwin, Cope, Crowther, Morgans, Taylor E, Webster, Charlton, Pearson

Match # 2353 Wednesday 16/04/58   Football League Division 1   at Fratton Park   Attendance 39975
Result: **Portsmouth 3 Manchester United 3**
Teamsheet: Gaskell, Foulkes, Greaves, Crowther, Cope, McGuinness, Dawson, Taylor E, Webster, Pearson, Morgans
Scorer(s):   Dawson, Taylor, Webster

Match # 2354 Saturday 19/04/58   Football League Division 1   at Old Trafford   Attendance 38991
Result: **Manchester United 0 Birmingham City 2**
Teamsheet: Gregg, Foulkes, Greaves, Goodwin, Cope, Crowther, Dawson, Taylor E, Webster, Pearson, Morgans

Match # 2355 Monday 21/04/58   Football League Division 1   at Old Trafford   Attendance 33267
Result: **Manchester United 0 Wolverhampton Wanderers 4**
Teamsheet: Gaskell, Foulkes, Greaves, Goodwin, Cope, McGuinness, Dawson, Brennan, Webster, Viollet, Morgans

SEASON 1957/58 (continued)

Match # 2356   Wednesday 23/04/58   Football League Division 1   at Old Trafford   Attendance 28393
Result: **Manchester United 1 Newcastle United 1**
Teamsheet: Gregg, Foulkes, Greaves, Crowther, Cope, McGuinness, Dawson, Taylor E, Webster, Charlton, Morgans
Scorer(s):   Dawson

Match # 2357   Saturday 26/04/58   Football League Division 1   at Stamford Bridge   Attendance 45011
Result: **Chelsea 2 Manchester United 1**
Teamsheet: Gregg, Foulkes, Greaves, Goodwin, Cope, Crowther, Dawson, Taylor E, Charlton, Viollet, Webster
Scorer(s):   Taylor E

Match # 2358   Saturday 03/05/58   FA Cup Final   at Wembley   Attendance 100000
Result: **Manchester United 0 Bolton Wanderers 2**
Teamsheet: Gregg, Foulkes, Greaves, Goodwin, Cope, Crowther, Dawson, Taylor E, Charlton, Viollet, Webster

Match # 2359   Thursday 08/05/58   European Cup Semi-Final 1st Leg   at Old Trafford   Attendance 44880
Result: **Manchester United 2 AC Milan 1**
Teamsheet: Gregg, Foulkes, Greaves, Goodwin, Cope, Crowther, Morgans, Taylor E, Webster, Viollet, Pearson
Scorer(s):   Taylor E, Viollet

Match # 2360   Wednesday 14/05/58   European Cup Semi-Final 2nd Leg   at Stadio San Siro   Attendance 80000
Result: **AC Milan 4 Manchester United 0**
Teamsheet: Gregg, Foulkes, Greaves, Goodwin, Cope, Crowther, Morgans, Taylor E, Webster, Viollet, Pearson

SEASON 1957/58 SUMMARY

APPEARANCES

PLAYER	LGE	FAC	EC	CS	TOT
Foulkes	42	8	8	1	59
Byrne	26	2	6	1	35
Edwards	26	2	5	1	34
Taylor T	25	2	6	1	34
Viollet	22	3	6	1	32
Colman	24	2	5	–	31
Gregg	19	8	4	–	31
Webster	20	6	5	–	31
Charlton	21	7	2	–	30
Goodwin	16	6	3	1	26
Pegg	21	–	4	1	26
Wood	20	–	4	1	25
Berry	20	–	3	1	24
Whelan	20	–	3	1	24
Blanchflower	18	–	2	1	21
Cope	13	6	2	–	21
Greaves	12	6	2	–	20
Morgans	13	2	4	–	19
Taylor E	11	6	2	–	19
Crowther	11	5	2	–	18
Dawson	12	6	–	–	18
Jones M	10	2	4	–	16
Pearson	8	4	2	–	14
Scanlon	9	2	3	–	14
McGuinness	7	–	1	–	8
Brennan	5	2	–	–	7
Harrop	5	1	–	–	6
Gaskell	3	–	–	–	3
Doherty	1	–	–	–	1
Heron	1	–	–	–	1
Jones P	1	–	–	–	1

GOALSCORERS

PLAYER	LGE	FAC	EC	CS	TOT
Viollet	16	3	4	–	23
Taylor T	16	–	3	3	22
Charlton	8	5	3	–	16
Whelan	12	–	2	–	14
Dawson	5	5	–	–	10
Webster	6	1	1	–	8
Pegg	4	–	3	–	7
Edwards	6	–	–	–	6
Berry	4	–	1	1	6
Taylor E	2	1	1	–	4
Scanlon	3	–	–	–	3
Brennan	–	3	–	–	3
Doherty	1	–	–	–	1
Colman	–	–	1	–	1
own goals	2	–	–	–	2

RESULTS & ATTENDANCES SUMMARY

		P	W	D	L	F	A	TOTAL	AVGE
League	H	21	10	4	7	45	31	959803	45705
	A	21	6	7	8	40	44	957388	45590
	TOTAL	42	16	11	15	85	75	1917191	45647
FA Cup	H	3	3	0	0	6	0	173398	57799
	A	2	1	1	0	5	3	79250	39625
	N	3	1	1	1	7	7	207745	69248
	TOTAL	8	5	2	1	18	10	460393	57549
European Cup	H	4	4	0	0	10	4	198634	49659
	A	4	1	1	2	9	8	215000	53750
	TOTAL	8	5	1	2	19	12	413634	51704
Charity Shield	H	1	1	0	0	4	0	27293	27293
	A	0	0	0	0	0	0	0	n/a
	TOTAL	1	1	0	0	4	0	27293	27293
Overall	H	29	18	4	7	65	35	1359128	46866
	A	27	8	9	10	54	55	1251638	46357
	N	3	1	1	1	7	7	207745	69248
	TOTAL	59	27	14	18	126	97	2818511	47771

FINAL TABLE – LEAGUE DIVISION ONE

		P	W	D	L	F	A	W	D	L	F	A	PTS	GD
			HOME						AWAY					
1	Wolverhampton Wanderers	42	17	3	1	60	21	11	5	5	43	26	64	56
2	Preston North End	42	18	2	1	63	14	8	5	8	37	37	59	49
3	Tottenham Hotspur	42	13	4	4	58	33	8	5	8	35	44	51	16
4	West Bromwich Albion	42	14	4	3	59	29	4	10	7	33	41	50	22
5	Manchester City	42	14	4	3	58	33	8	1	12	46	67	49	4
6	Burnley	42	16	2	3	52	21	5	3	13	28	53	47	6
7	Blackpool	42	11	2	8	47	35	8	4	9	33	32	44	13
8	Luton Town	42	13	3	5	45	22	6	3	12	24	41	44	6
9	MANCHESTER UNITED	42	10	4	7	45	31	6	7	8	40	44	43	10
10	Nottingham Forest	42	10	4	7	41	27	6	6	9	28	36	42	6
11	Chelsea	42	10	5	6	47	34	5	7	9	36	45	42	4
12	Arsenal	42	10	4	7	48	39	6	3	12	25	46	39	–12
13	Birmingham City	42	8	6	7	43	37	6	5	10	33	52	39	–13
14	Aston Villa	42	12	4	5	46	26	4	3	14	27	60	39	–13
15	Bolton Wanderers	42	9	5	7	38	35	5	5	11	27	52	38	–22
16	Everton	42	5	9	7	34	35	8	2	11	31	40	37	–10
17	Leeds United	42	10	6	5	33	23	4	3	14	18	40	37	–12
18	Leicester City	42	11	4	6	59	41	3	1	17	32	71	33	–21
19	Newcastle United	42	6	4	11	38	42	6	4	11	35	39	32	–8
20	Portsmouth	42	10	6	5	45	34	2	2	17	28	54	32	–15
21	Sunderland	42	7	7	7	32	33	3	5	13	22	64	32	–43
22	Sheffield Wednesday	42	12	2	7	45	40	0	5	16	24	52	31	–23

SEASON 1958/59

Match # 2361	Saturday 23/08/58	Football League Division 1	at Old Trafford	Attendance 52382
Result:	**Manchester United 5 Chelsea 2**		
Teamsheet:	Gregg, Foulkes, Greaves, Goodwin, Cope, McGuinness, Dawson, Taylor, Viollet, Charlton, Scanlon		
Scorer(s):	Charlton 3, Dawson 2		

Match # 2362	Wednesday 27/08/58	Football League Division 1	at City Ground	Attendance 44971
Result:	**Nottingham Forest 0 Manchester United 3**		
Teamsheet:	Gregg, Foulkes, Greaves, Goodwin, Cope, McGuinness, Dawson, Taylor, Viollet, Charlton, Scanlon		
Scorer(s):	Charlton 2, Scanlon		

Match # 2363	Saturday 30/08/58	Football League Division 1	at Bloomfield Road	Attendance 26719
Result:	**Blackpool 2 Manchester United 1**		
Teamsheet:	Gregg, Foulkes, Greaves, Goodwin, Cope, McGuinness, Dawson, Taylor, Viollet, Charlton, Scanlon		
Scorer(s):	Viollet		

Match # 2364	Wednesday 03/09/58	Football League Division 1	at Old Trafford	Attendance 51880
Result:	**Manchester United 1 Nottingham Forest 1**		
Teamsheet:	Gregg, Foulkes, Greaves, Goodwin, Cope, McGuinness, Dawson, Taylor, Viollet, Charlton, Scanlon		
Scorer(s):	Charlton		

Match # 2365	Saturday 06/09/58	Football League Division 1	at Old Trafford	Attendance 65187
Result:	**Manchester United 6 Blackburn Rovers 1**		
Teamsheet:	Gregg, Foulkes, Greaves, Goodwin, Cope, McGuinness, Webster, Taylor, Viollet, Charlton, Scanlon		
Scorer(s):	Charlton 2, Viollet 2, Scanlon, Webster		

Match # 2366	Monday 08/09/58	Football League Division 1	at Upton Park	Attendance 35672
Result:	**West Ham United 3 Manchester United 2**		
Teamsheet:	Gregg, Foulkes, Greaves, Goodwin, Cope, McGuinness, Webster, Taylor, Viollet, Charlton, Scanlon		
Scorer(s):	McGuinness, Webster		

Match # 2367	Saturday 13/09/58	Football League Division 1	at St James' Park	Attendance 60670
Result:	**Newcastle United 1 Manchester United 1**		
Teamsheet:	Gregg, Foulkes, Greaves, Goodwin, Cope, Crowther, Webster, Taylor, Viollet, Charlton, Scanlon		
Scorer(s):	Charlton		

Match # 2368	Wednesday 17/09/58	Football League Division 1	at Old Trafford	Attendance 53276
Result:	**Manchester United 4 West Ham United 1**		
Teamsheet:	Gregg, Foulkes, Greaves, Goodwin, Cope, McGuinness, Webster, Taylor, Dawson, Charlton, Scanlon		
Scorer(s):	Scanlon 3, Webster		

Match # 2369	Saturday 20/09/58	Football League Division 1	at Old Trafford	Attendance 62277
Result:	**Manchester United 2 Tottenham Hotspur 2**		
Teamsheet:	Gregg, Foulkes, Greaves, Goodwin, Cope, McGuinness, Webster, Quixall, Dawson, Charlton, Scanlon		
Scorer(s):	Webster 2		

Match # 2370	Saturday 27/09/58	Football League Division 1	at Maine Road	Attendance 62912
Result:	**Manchester City 1 Manchester United 1**		
Teamsheet:	Gregg, Foulkes, Greaves, Goodwin, Cope, McGuinness, Viollet, Quixall, Webster, Charlton, Scanlon		
Scorer(s):	Charlton		

Match # 2371	Saturday 04/10/58	Football League Division 1	at Molineux	Attendance 36840
Result:	**Wolverhampton Wanderers 4 Manchester United 0**		
Teamsheet:	Wood, Foulkes, Greaves, Goodwin, Harrop, Crowther, Viollet, Quixall, Webster, Pearson, Scanlon		

Match # 2372	Wednesday 08/10/58	Football League Division 1	at Old Trafford	Attendance 46163
Result:	**Manchester United 0 Preston North End 2**		
Teamsheet:	Gregg, Foulkes, Greaves, Goodwin, Cope, McGuinness, Viollet, Taylor, Dawson, Charlton, Scanlon		

Match # 2373	Saturday 11/10/58	Football League Division 1	at Old Trafford	Attendance 56148
Result:	**Manchester United 1 Arsenal 1**		
Teamsheet:	Gregg, Foulkes, Greaves, Goodwin, Cope, McGuinness, Viollet, Quixall, Charlton, Taylor, Scanlon		
Scorer(s):	Viollet		

Match # 2374	Saturday 18/10/58	Football League Division 1	at Goodison Park	Attendance 64079
Result:	**Everton 3 Manchester United 2**		
Teamsheet:	Gregg, Foulkes, Greaves, Goodwin, Cope, McGuinness, Viollet, Quixall, Charlton, Taylor, Scanlon		
Scorer(s):	Cope 2		

Match # 2375	Saturday 25/10/58	Football League Division 1	at Old Trafford	Attendance 51721
Result:	**Manchester United 1 West Bromwich Albion 2**		
Teamsheet:	Gregg, Foulkes, Greaves, Goodwin, Harrop, McGuinness, Viollet, Quixall, Dawson, Charlton, Scanlon		
Scorer(s):	Goodwin		

Match # 2376	Saturday 01/11/58	Football League Division 1	at Elland Road	Attendance 48574
Result:	**Leeds United 1 Manchester United 2**		
Teamsheet:	Gregg, Foulkes, Greaves, Goodwin, Harrop, McGuinness, Morgans, Quixall, Dawson, Charlton, Scanlon		
Scorer(s):	Goodwin, Scanlon		

Match # 2377	Saturday 08/11/58	Football League Division 1	at Old Trafford	Attendance 48509
Result:	**Manchester United 1 Burnley 3**		
Teamsheet:	Gregg, Foulkes, Greaves, Goodwin, Harrop, McGuinness, Morgans, Quixall, Dawson, Charlton, Scanlon		
Scorer(s):	Quixall		

Match # 2378	Saturday 15/11/58	Football League Division 1	at Burnden Park	Attendance 33358
Result:	**Bolton Wanderers 6 Manchester United 3**		
Teamsheet:	Gregg, Foulkes, Greaves, Goodwin, Cope, McGuinness, Bradley, Quixall, Dawson, Charlton, Scanlon		
Scorer(s):	Dawson 2, Charlton		

SEASON 1958/59 (continued)

Match # 2379 Saturday 22/11/58   Football League Division 1   at Old Trafford   Attendance 42428
Result: **Manchester United 2 Luton Town 1**
Teamsheet: Gregg, Foulkes, Carolan, Goodwin, Cope, McGuinness, Bradley, Quixall, Viollet, Charlton, Scanlon
Scorer(s): Charlton, Viollet

Match # 2380 Saturday 29/11/58   Football League Division 1   at St Andrews   Attendance 28658
Result: **Birmingham City 0 Manchester United 4**
Teamsheet: Gregg, Foulkes, Carolan, Goodwin, Cope, McGuinness, Bradley, Quixall, Viollet, Charlton, Scanlon
Scorer(s): Charlton 2, Bradley, Scanlon

Match # 2381 Saturday 06/12/58   Football League Division 1   at Old Trafford   Attendance 38482
Result: **Manchester United 4 Leicester City 1**
Teamsheet: Gregg, Foulkes, Carolan, Goodwin, Cope, McGuinness, Bradley, Quixall, Viollet, Charlton, Scanlon
Scorer(s): Bradley, Charlton, Scanlon, Viollet

Match # 2382 Saturday 13/12/58   Football League Division 1   at Deepdale   Attendance 26290
Result: **Preston North End 3 Manchester United 4**
Teamsheet: Gregg, Foulkes, Carolan, Goodwin, Cope, McGuinness, Bradley, Quixall, Viollet, Charlton, Scanlon
Scorer(s): Bradley, Charlton, Scanlon, Viollet

Match # 2383 Saturday 20/12/58   Football League Division 1   at Stamford Bridge   Attendance 48550
Result: **Chelsea 2 Manchester United 3**
Teamsheet: Gregg, Foulkes, Carolan, Goodwin, Cope, McGuinness, Bradley, Quixall, Viollet, Charlton, Scanlon
Scorer(s): Charlton, Goodwin, own goal

Match # 2384 Friday 26/12/58   Football League Division 1   at Old Trafford   Attendance 63098
Result: **Manchester United 2 Aston Villa 1**
Teamsheet: Gregg, Foulkes, Carolan, Goodwin, Cope, McGuinness, Bradley, Quixall, Viollet, Pearson, Scanlon
Scorer(s): Quixall, Viollet

Match # 2385 Saturday 27/12/58   Football League Division 1   at Villa Park   Attendance 56450
Result: **Aston Villa 0 Manchester United 2**
Teamsheet: Gregg, Foulkes, Greaves, Goodwin, Cope, McGuinness, Hunter, Quixall, Viollet, Pearson, Scanlon
Scorer(s): Pearson, Viollet

Match # 2386 Saturday 03/01/59   Football League Division 1   at Old Trafford   Attendance 61961
Result: **Manchester United 3 Blackpool 1**
Teamsheet: Gregg, Foulkes, Carolan, Goodwin, Cope, McGuinness, Bradley, Quixall, Viollet, Charlton, Scanlon
Scorer(s): Charlton 2, Viollet

Match # 2387 Saturday 10/01/59   FA Cup 3rd Round   at Carrow Road   Attendance 38000
Result: **Norwich City 3 Manchester United 0**
Teamsheet: Gregg, Foulkes, Carolan, Goodwin, Cope, McGuinness, Bradley, Quixall, Viollet, Charlton, Scanlon

Match # 2388 Saturday 31/01/59   Football League Division 1   at Old Trafford   Attendance 49008
Result: **Manchester United 4 Newcastle United 4**
Teamsheet: Gregg, Foulkes, Carolan, Harrop, Goodwin, McGuinness, Bradley, Quixall, Viollet, Charlton, Scanlon
Scorer(s): Charlton, Quixall, Scanlon, Viollet

Match # 2389 Saturday 07/02/59   Football League Division 1   at White Hart Lane   Attendance 48401
Result: **Tottenham Hotspur 1 Manchester United 3**
Teamsheet: Gregg, Greaves, Carolan, Goodwin, Cope, McGuinness, Bradley, Quixall, Viollet, Charlton, Scanlon
Scorer(s): Charlton 2, Scanlon

Match # 2390 Monday 16/02/59   Football League Division 1   at Old Trafford   Attendance 59846
Result: **Manchester United 4 Manchester City 1**
Teamsheet: Gregg, Greaves, Carolan, Goodwin, Cope, McGuinness, Bradley, Quixall, Viollet, Charlton, Scanlon
Scorer(s): Bradley 2, Goodwin, Scanlon

Match # 2391 Saturday 21/02/59   Football League Division 1   at Old Trafford   Attendance 62794
Result: **Manchester United 2 Wolverhampton Wanderers 1**
Teamsheet: Gregg, Greaves, Carolan, Goodwin, Cope, McGuinness, Bradley, Quixall, Viollet, Charlton, Scanlon
Scorer(s): Charlton, Viollet

Match # 2392 Saturday 28/02/59   Football League Division 1   at Highbury   Attendance 67162
Result: **Arsenal 3 Manchester United 2**
Teamsheet: Gregg, Greaves, Carolan, Goodwin, Cope, McGuinness, Bradley, Quixall, Viollet, Charlton, Scanlon
Scorer(s): Bradley, Viollet

Match # 2393 Monday 02/03/59   Football League Division 1   at Ewood Park   Attendance 40401
Result: **Blackburn Rovers 1 Manchester United 3**
Teamsheet: Gregg, Greaves, Carolan, Goodwin, Cope, McGuinness, Bradley, Quixall, Viollet, Charlton, Scanlon
Scorer(s): Bradley 2, Scanlon

Match # 2394 Saturday 07/03/59   Football League Division 1   at Old Trafford   Attendance 51254
Result: **Manchester United 2 Everton 1**
Teamsheet: Gregg, Greaves, Carolan, Goodwin, Cope, McGuinness, Bradley, Quixall, Viollet, Charlton, Scanlon
Scorer(s): Goodwin, Scanlon

Match # 2395 Saturday 14/03/59   Football League Division 1   at The Hawthorns   Attendance 35463
Result: **West Bromwich Albion 1 Manchester United 3**
Teamsheet: Gregg, Greaves, Carolan, Goodwin, Cope, McGuinness, Bradley, Quixall, Viollet, Charlton, Scanlon
Scorer(s): Bradley, Scanlon, Viollet

Match # 2396 Saturday 21/03/59   Football League Division 1   at Old Trafford   Attendance 45473
Result: **Manchester United 4 Leeds United 0**
Teamsheet: Gregg, Greaves, Carolan, Goodwin, Cope, McGuinness, Bradley, Quixall, Viollet, Charlton, Scanlon
Scorer(s): Viollet 3, Charlton

SEASON 1958/59 (continued)

Match # 2397	Friday 27/03/59	Football League Division 1	at Old Trafford	Attendance 52004
Result:	**Manchester United 6 Portsmouth 1**			
Teamsheet:	Gregg, Greaves, Carolan, Goodwin, Cope, McGuinness, Bradley, Quixall, Viollet, Charlton, Scanlon			
Scorer(s):	Charlton 2, Viollet 2, Bradley, own goal			

Match # 2398	Saturday 28/03/59	Football League Division 1	at Turf Moor	Attendance 44577
Result:	**Burnley 4 Manchester United 2**			
Teamsheet:	Gregg, Greaves, Carolan, Goodwin, Cope, McGuinness, Bradley, Quixall, Viollet, Charlton, Scanlon			
Scorer(s):	Goodwin, Viollet			

Match # 2399	Monday 30/03/59	Football League Division 1	at Fratton Park	Attendance 29359
Result:	**Portsmouth 1 Manchester United 3**			
Teamsheet:	Gregg, Greaves, Carolan, Goodwin, Foulkes, McGuinness, Bradley, Quixall, Viollet, Charlton, Scanlon			
Scorer(s):	Charlton 2, Bradley			

Match # 2400	Saturday 04/04/59	Football League Division 1	at Old Trafford	Attendance 61528
Result:	**Manchester United 3 Bolton Wanderers 0**			
Teamsheet:	Gregg, Greaves, Carolan, Goodwin, Foulkes, McGuinness, Bradley, Quixall, Viollet, Charlton, Scanlon			
Scorer(s):	Charlton, Scanlon, Viollet			

Match # 2401	Saturday 11/04/59	Football League Division 1	at Kenilworth Road	Attendance 27025
Result:	**Luton Town 0 Manchester United 0**			
Teamsheet:	Gregg, Greaves, Carolan, Goodwin, Foulkes, McGuinness, Bradley, Quixall, Viollet, Pearson, Scanlon			

Match # 2402	Saturday 18/04/59	Football League Division 1	at Old Trafford	Attendance 43006
Result:	**Manchester United 1 Birmingham City 0**			
Teamsheet:	Gregg, Greaves, Carolan, Goodwin, Foulkes, McGuinness, Bradley, Quixall, Viollet, Charlton, Scanlon			
Scorer(s):	Quixall			

Match # 2403	Saturday 25/04/59	Football League Division 1	at Filbert Street	Attendance 38466
Result:	**Leicester City 2 Manchester United 1**			
Teamsheet:	Gregg, Greaves, Carolan, Goodwin, Foulkes, Brennan, Bradley, Quixall, Viollet, Charlton, Scanlon			
Scorer(s):	Bradley			

SEASON 1958/59 SUMMARY

APPEARANCES

PLAYER	LGE	FAC	TOT
Goodwin	42	1	43
Scanlon	42	1	43
Gregg	41	1	42
McGuinness	39	1	40
Charlton	38	1	39
Viollet	37	1	38
Greaves	34	–	34
Quixall	33	1	34
Cope	32	1	33
Foulkes	32	1	33
Bradley	24	1	25

APPEARANCES

PLAYER	LGE	FAC	TOT
Carolan	23	1	24
Dawson	11	–	11
Taylor	11	–	11
Webster	7	–	7
Harrop	5	–	5
Pearson	4	–	4
Crowther	2	–	2
Morgans	2	–	2
Brennan	1	–	1
Hunter	1	–	1
Wood	1	–	1

GOALSCORERS

PLAYER	LGE	FAC	TOT
Charlton	29	–	29
Viollet	21	–	21
Scanlon	16	–	16
Bradley	12	–	12
Goodwin	6	–	6
Webster	5	–	5
Dawson	4	–	4
Quixall	4	–	4
Cope	2	–	2
McGuinness	1	–	1
Pearson	1	–	1
own goals	2	–	2

RESULTS & ATTENDANCES SUMMARY

		P	W	D	L	F	A	TOTAL	AVGE
League	H	21	14	4	3	58	27	1118425	53258
	A	21	10	3	8	45	39	904597	43076
	TOTAL	42	24	7	11	103	66	2023022	48167
FA Cup	H	0	0	0	0	0	0	0	n/a
	A	1	0	0	1	0	3	38000	38000
	TOTAL	1	0	0	1	0	3	38000	38000
Overall	H	21	14	4	3	58	27	1118425	53258
	A	22	10	3	9	45	42	942597	42845
	TOTAL	43	24	7	12	103	69	2061022	47931

FINAL TABLE – LEAGUE DIVISION ONE

		P	HOME W	HOME D	HOME L	HOME F	HOME A	AWAY W	AWAY D	AWAY L	AWAY F	AWAY A	PTS	GD
1	Wolverhampton Wanderers	42	15	3	3	68	19	13	2	6	42	30	61	61
2	MANCHESTER UNITED	42	14	4	3	58	27	10	3	8	45	39	55	37
3	Arsenal	42	14	3	4	53	29	7	5	9	35	39	50	20
4	Bolton Wanderers	42	14	3	4	56	30	6	7	8	23	36	50	13
5	West Bromwich Albion	42	8	7	6	41	33	10	6	5	47	35	49	20
6	West Ham United	42	15	3	3	59	29	6	3	12	26	41	48	15
7	Burnley	42	11	4	6	41	29	8	6	7	40	41	48	11
8	Blackpool	42	12	7	2	39	13	6	4	11	27	36	47	17
9	Birmingham City	42	14	1	6	54	35	6	5	10	30	33	46	16
10	Blackburn Rovers	42	12	3	6	48	28	5	7	9	28	42	44	6
11	Newcastle United	42	11	3	7	40	29	6	4	11	40	51	41	0
12	Preston North End	42	9	3	9	40	39	8	4	9	30	38	41	–7
13	Nottingham Forest	42	9	4	8	37	32	8	2	11	34	42	40	–3
14	Chelsea	42	13	2	6	52	37	5	2	14	25	61	40	–21
15	Leeds United	42	8	7	6	28	27	7	2	12	29	47	39	–17
16	Everton	42	11	3	7	39	38	6	1	14	32	49	38	–16
17	Luton Town	42	11	6	4	50	26	1	7	13	18	45	37	–3
18	Tottenham Hotspur	42	10	3	8	56	42	3	7	11	29	53	36	–10
19	Leicester City	42	7	6	8	34	36	4	4	13	33	62	32	–31
20	Manchester City	42	8	7	6	40	32	3	2	16	24	63	31	–31
21	Aston Villa	42	8	5	8	31	33	3	3	15	27	54	30	–29
22	Portsmouth	42	5	4	12	38	47	1	5	15	26	65	21	–48

SEASON 1959/60

Match # 2404   Saturday 22/08/59   Football League Division 1   at The Hawthorns   Attendance 40076
Result: **West Bromwich Albion 3 Manchester United 2**
Teamsheet: Gregg, Greaves, Carolan, Goodwin, Foulkes, McGuinness, Bradley, Quixall, Viollet, Charlton, Scanlon
Scorer(s):   Viollet 2

Match # 2405   Wednesday 26/08/59   Football League Division 1   at Old Trafford   Attendance 57674
Result: **Manchester United 0 Chelsea 1**
Teamsheet: Gregg, Greaves, Carolan, Goodwin, Foulkes, McGuinness, Bradley, Quixall, Dawson, Viollet, Charlton

Match # 2406   Saturday 29/08/59   Football League Division 1   at Old Trafford   Attendance 53257
Result: **Manchester United 3 Newcastle United 2**
Teamsheet: Gregg, Cope, Carolan, Brennan, Foulkes, McGuinness, Bradley, Quixall, Viollet, Charlton, Scanlon
Scorer(s):   Viollet 2, Charlton

Match # 2407   Wednesday 02/09/59   Football League Division 1   at Stamford Bridge   Attendance 66579
Result: **Chelsea 3 Manchester United 6**
Teamsheet: Gregg, Cope, Carolan, Brennan, Foulkes, McGuinness, Bradley, Quixall, Viollet, Charlton, Scanlon
Scorer(s):   Bradley 2, Viollet 2, Charlton, Quixall

Match # 2408   Saturday 05/09/59   Football League Division 1   at St Andrews   Attendance 38220
Result: **Birmingham City 1 Manchester United 1**
Teamsheet: Gregg, Cope, Carolan, Brennan, Foulkes, McGuinness, Bradley, Quixall, Viollet, Charlton, Scanlon
Scorer(s):   Quixall

Match # 2409   Wednesday 09/09/59   Football League Division 1   at Old Trafford   Attendance 48407
Result: **Manchester United 6 Leeds United 0**
Teamsheet: Gregg, Cope, Carolan, Brennan, Foulkes, McGuinness, Bradley, Quixall, Viollet, Charlton, Scanlon
Scorer(s):   Bradley 2, Charlton 2, Scanlon, Viollet

Match # 2410   Saturday 12/09/59   Football League Division 1   at Old Trafford   Attendance 55402
Result: **Manchester United 1 Tottenham Hotspur 5**
Teamsheet: Gregg, Cope, Carolan, Goodwin, Foulkes, McGuinness, Bradley, Giles, Viollet, Charlton, Scanlon
Scorer(s):   Viollet

Match # 2411   Wednesday 16/09/59   Football League Division 1   at Elland Road   Attendance 34048
Result: **Leeds United 2 Manchester United 2**
Teamsheet: Gregg, Foulkes, Carolan, Brennan, Cope, McGuinness, Bradley, Quixall, Viollet, Charlton, Scanlon
Scorer(s):   Charlton, own goal

Match # 2412   Saturday 19/09/59   Football League Division 1   at Maine Road   Attendance 58300
Result: **Manchester City 3 Manchester United 0**
Teamsheet: Gregg, Foulkes, Carolan, Brennan, Cope, McGuinness, Bradley, Quixall, Viollet, Charlton, Scanlon

Match # 2413   Saturday 26/09/59   Football League Division 1   at Deepdale   Attendance 35016
Result: **Preston North End 4 Manchester United 0**
Teamsheet: Gregg, Foulkes, Carolan, Viollet, Cope, McGuinness, Bradley, Quixall, Dawson, Charlton, Scanlon

Match # 2414   Saturday 03/10/59   Football League Division 1   at Old Trafford   Attendance 41637
Result: **Manchester United 4 Leicester City 1**
Teamsheet: Gaskell, Foulkes, Carolan, Goodwin, Cope, McGuinness, Bradley, Quixall, Viollet, Charlton, Scanlon
Scorer(s):   Viollet 2, Charlton, Quixall

Match # 2415   Saturday 10/10/59   Football League Division 1   at Old Trafford   Attendance 51626
Result: **Manchester United 4 Arsenal 2**
Teamsheet: Gregg, Foulkes, Carolan, Goodwin, Cope, McGuinness, Bradley, Quixall, Viollet, Charlton, Scanlon
Scorer(s):   Charlton, Quixall, Viollet, own goal

Match # 2416   Saturday 17/10/59   Football League Division 1   at Molineux   Attendance 45451
Result: **Wolverhampton Wanderers 3 Manchester United 2**
Teamsheet: Gregg, Foulkes, Carolan, Goodwin, Cope, McGuinness, Bradley, Giles, Viollet, Pearson, Scanlon
Scorer(s):   Viollet, own goal

Match # 2417   Saturday 24/10/59   Football League Division 1   at Old Trafford   Attendance 39259
Result: **Manchester United 3 Sheffield Wednesday 1**
Teamsheet: Gregg, Foulkes, Carolan, Goodwin, Cope, McGuinness, Bradley, Quixall, Viollet, Charlton, Scanlon
Scorer(s):   Viollet 2, Bradley

Match # 2418   Saturday 31/10/59   Football League Division 1   at Ewood Park   Attendance 39621
Result: **Blackburn Rovers 1 Manchester United 1**
Teamsheet: Gregg, Foulkes, Carolan, Goodwin, Cope, McGuinness, Bradley, Quixall, Viollet, Charlton, Scanlon
Scorer(s):   Quixall

Match # 2419   Saturday 07/11/59   Football League Division 1   at Old Trafford   Attendance 44063
Result: **Manchester United 3 Fulham 3**
Teamsheet: Gregg, Foulkes, Carolan, Goodwin, Cope, McGuinness, Bradley, Quixall, Viollet, Charlton, Scanlon
Scorer(s):   Charlton, Scanlon, Viollet

Match # 2420   Saturday 14/11/59   Football League Division 1   at Burnden Park   Attendance 37892
Result: **Bolton Wanderers 1 Manchester United 1**
Teamsheet: Gregg, Foulkes, Carolan, Goodwin, Cope, McGuinness, Bradley, Quixall, Viollet, Charlton, Dawson
Scorer(s):   Dawson

Match # 2421   Saturday 21/11/59   Football League Division 1   at Old Trafford   Attendance 40572
Result: **Manchester United 4 Luton Town 1**
Teamsheet: Gregg, Foulkes, Carolan, Goodwin, Cope, McGuinness, Bradley, Quixall, Viollet, Charlton, Scanlon
Scorer(s):   Viollet 2, Goodwin, Quixall

SEASON 1959/60 (continued)

Match # 2422 | Saturday 28/11/59 | Football League Division 1 | at Goodison Park | Attendance 46095
Result: **Everton 2 Manchester United 1**
Teamsheet: Gregg, Foulkes, Carolan, Goodwin, Cope, McGuinness, Bradley, Quixall, Viollet, Charlton, Scanlon
Scorer(s): Viollet

Match # 2423 | Saturday 05/12/59 | Football League Division 1 | at Old Trafford | Attendance 45558
Result: **Manchester United 3 Blackpool 1**
Teamsheet: Gaskell, Foulkes, Carolan, Goodwin, Cope, Brennan, Dawson, Quixall, Viollet, Pearson, Scanlon
Scorer(s): Viollet 2, Pearson

Match # 2424 | Saturday 12/12/59 | Football League Division 1 | at City Ground | Attendance 31666
Result: **Nottingham Forest 1 Manchester United 5**
Teamsheet: Gaskell, Foulkes, Carolan, Goodwin, Cope, Brennan, Dawson, Quixall, Viollet, Pearson, Scanlon
Scorer(s): Viollet 3, Dawson, Scanlon

Match # 2425 | Saturday 19/12/59 | Football League Division 1 | at Old Trafford | Attendance 33677
Result: **Manchester United 2 West Bromwich Albion 3**
Teamsheet: Gaskell, Foulkes, Carolan, Goodwin, Cope, Brennan, Dawson, Quixall, Viollet, Pearson, Scanlon
Scorer(s): Dawson, Quixall

Match # 2426 | Saturday 26/12/59 | Football League Division 1 | at Old Trafford | Attendance 62376
Result: **Manchester United 1 Burnley 2**
Teamsheet: Gaskell, Foulkes, Carolan, Goodwin, Cope, Brennan, Dawson, Quixall, Viollet, Charlton, Scanlon
Scorer(s): Quixall

Match # 2427 | Monday 28/12/59 | Football League Division 1 | at Turf Moor | Attendance 47253
Result: **Burnley 1 Manchester United 4**
Teamsheet: Gaskell, Foulkes, Carolan, Goodwin, Cope, Brennan, Dawson, Quixall, Viollet, Charlton, Scanlon
Scorer(s): Scanlon 2, Viollet 2

Match # 2428 | Saturday 02/01/60 | Football League Division 1 | at St James' Park | Attendance 57200
Result: **Newcastle United 7 Manchester United 3**
Teamsheet: Gaskell, Foulkes, Carolan, Goodwin, Cope, Brennan, Dawson, Quixall, Viollet, Charlton, Scanlon
Scorer(s): Quixall 2, Dawson

Match # 2429 | Saturday 09/01/60 | FA Cup 3rd Round | at Baseball Ground | Attendance 33297
Result: **Derby County 2 Manchester United 4**
Teamsheet: Gregg, Foulkes, Carolan, Goodwin, Cope, Brennan, Dawson, Quixall, Viollet, Charlton, Scanlon
Scorer(s): Charlton, Goodwin, Scanlon, own goal

Match # 2430 | Saturday 16/01/60 | Football League Division 1 | at Old Trafford | Attendance 47361
Result: **Manchester United 2 Birmingham City 1**
Teamsheet: Gregg, Foulkes, Carolan, Setters, Cope, Brennan, Bradley, Quixall, Viollet, Charlton, Scanlon
Scorer(s): Quixall, Viollet

Match # 2431 | Saturday 23/01/60 | Football League Division 1 | at White Hart Lane | Attendance 62602
Result: **Tottenham Hotspur 2 Manchester United 1**
Teamsheet: Gregg, Foulkes, Carolan, Setters, Cope, Brennan, Bradley, Quixall, Viollet, Charlton, Scanlon
Scorer(s): Bradley

Match # 2432 | Saturday 30/01/60 | FA Cup 4th Round | at Anfield | Attendance 56736
Result: **Liverpool 1 Manchester United 3**
Teamsheet: Gregg, Foulkes, Carolan, Setters, Cope, Brennan, Bradley, Quixall, Viollet, Charlton, Scanlon
Scorer(s): Charlton 2, Bradley

Match # 2433 | Saturday 06/02/60 | Football League Division 1 | at Old Trafford | Attendance 59450
Result: **Manchester United 0 Manchester City 0**
Teamsheet: Gregg, Foulkes, Carolan, Setters, Cope, Brennan, Bradley, Quixall, Viollet, Charlton, Scanlon

Match # 2434 | Saturday 13/02/60 | Football League Division 1 | at Old Trafford | Attendance 44014
Result: **Manchester United 1 Preston North End 1**
Teamsheet: Gregg, Foulkes, Carolan, Setters, Cope, Brennan, Bradley, Quixall, Viollet, Charlton, Scanlon
Scorer(s): Viollet

Match # 2435 | Saturday 20/02/60 | FA Cup 5th Round | at Old Trafford | Attendance 66350
Result: **Manchester United 0 Sheffield Wednesday 1**
Teamsheet: Gregg, Foulkes, Carolan, Setters, Cope, Brennan, Bradley, Quixall, Viollet, Charlton, Scanlon

Match # 2436 | Wednesday 24/02/60 | Football League Division 1 | at Filbert Street | Attendance 33191
Result: **Leicester City 3 Manchester United 1**
Teamsheet: Gregg, Foulkes, Carolan, Setters, Cope, Brennan, Viollet, Quixall, Dawson, Charlton, Scanlon
Scorer(s): Scanlon

Match # 2437 | Saturday 27/02/60 | Football League Division 1 | at Bloomfield Road | Attendance 23996
Result: **Blackpool 0 Manchester United 6**
Teamsheet: Gregg, Foulkes, Carolan, Setters, Cope, Brennan, Viollet, Quixall, Dawson, Charlton, Scanlon
Scorer(s): Charlton 3, Viollet 2, Scanlon

Match # 2438 | Saturday 05/03/60 | Football League Division 1 | at Old Trafford | Attendance 60560
Result: **Manchester United 0 Wolverhampton Wanderers 2**
Teamsheet: Gregg, Foulkes, Carolan, Setters, Cope, Brennan, Viollet, Quixall, Dawson, Charlton, Scanlon

Match # 2439 | Saturday 19/03/60 | Football League Division 1 | at Old Trafford | Attendance 35269
Result: **Manchester United 3 Nottingham Forest 1**
Teamsheet: Gregg, Foulkes, Carolan, Setters, Cope, Brennan, Giles, Viollet, Dawson, Pearson, Charlton
Scorer(s): Charlton 2, Dawson

SEASON 1959/60 (continued)

Match # 2440 Saturday 26/03/60 Football League Division 1 at Craven Cottage Attendance 38250
Result: **Fulham 0 Manchester United 5**
Teamsheet: Gregg, Foulkes, Carolan, Setters, Cope, Brennan, Giles, Viollet, Dawson, Pearson, Charlton
Scorer(s): Viollet 2, Dawson, Giles, Pearson

Match # 2441 Wednesday 30/03/60 Football League Division 1 at Hillsborough Attendance 26821
Result: **Sheffield Wednesday 4 Manchester United 2**
Teamsheet: Gaskell, Foulkes, Heron, Setters, Cope, Brennan, Bradley, Viollet, Dawson, Pearson, Charlton
Scorer(s): Charlton, Viollet

Match # 2442 Saturday 02/04/60 Football League Division 1 at Old Trafford Attendance 45298
Result: **Manchester United 2 Bolton Wanderers 0**
Teamsheet: Gaskell, Foulkes, Carolan, Setters, Cope, Brennan, Bradley, Giles, Dawson, Pearson, Charlton
Scorer(s): Charlton 2

Match # 2443 Saturday 09/04/60 Football League Division 1 at Kenilworth Road Attendance 21242
Result: **Luton Town 2 Manchester United 3**
Teamsheet: Gregg, Foulkes, Carolan, Setters, Cope, Brennan, Bradley, Giles, Dawson, Lawton, Scanlon
Scorer(s): Dawson 2, Bradley

Match # 2444 Friday 15/04/60 Football League Division 1 at Upton Park Attendance 34969
Result: **West Ham United 2 Manchester United 1**
Teamsheet: Gregg, Foulkes, Carolan, Setters, Cope, Brennan, Bradley, Giles, Dawson, Lawton, Charlton
Scorer(s): Dawson

Match # 2445 Saturday 16/04/60 Football League Division 1 at Old Trafford Attendance 45945
Result: **Manchester United 1 Blackburn Rovers 0**
Teamsheet: Gregg, Foulkes, Carolan, Setters, Cope, Brennan, Bradley, Giles, Dawson, Lawton, Charlton
Scorer(s): Dawson

Match # 2446 Monday 18/04/60 Football League Division 1 at Old Trafford Attendance 34676
Result: **Manchester United 5 West Ham United 3**
Teamsheet: Gregg, Foulkes, Carolan, Setters, Cope, Brennan, Giles, Quixall, Dawson, Viollet, Charlton
Scorer(s): Charlton 2, Dawson 2, Quixall

Match # 2447 Saturday 23/04/60 Football League Division 1 at Highbury Attendance 41057
Result: **Arsenal 5 Manchester United 2**
Teamsheet: Gregg, Foulkes, Carolan, Setters, Cope, Brennan, Giles, Quixall, Dawson, Pearson, Charlton
Scorer(s): Giles, Pearson

Match # 2448 Saturday 30/04/60 Football League Division 1 at Old Trafford Attendance 43823
Result: **Manchester United 5 Everton 0**
Teamsheet: Gregg, Foulkes, Carolan, Setters, Cope, Brennan, Bradley, Quixall, Dawson, Pearson, Charlton
Scorer(s): Dawson 3, Bradley, Quixall

SEASON 1959/60 SUMMARY

APPEARANCES

PLAYER	LGE	FAC	TOT
Foulkes	42	3	45
Carolan	41	3	44
Cope	40	3	43
Charlton	37	3	40
Viollet	36	3	39
Gregg	33	3	36
Quixall	33	3	36
Scanlon	31	3	34
Brennan	29	3	32
Bradley	29	2	31
Dawson	22	1	23
Goodwin	18	1	19
McGuinness	19	–	19
Setters	17	2	19
Giles	10	–	10
Pearson	10	–	10
Gaskell	9	–	9
Lawton	3	–	3
Greaves	2	–	2
Heron	1	–	1

GOALSCORERS

PLAYER	LGE	FAC	TOT
Viollet	32	–	32
Charlton	18	3	21
Dawson	15	–	15
Quixall	13	–	13
Bradley	8	1	9
Scanlon	7	1	8
Pearson	3	–	3
Giles	2	–	2
Goodwin	1	1	2
own goals	3	1	4

RESULTS & ATTENDANCES SUMMARY

		P	W	D	L	F	A	TOTAL	AVGE
League	H	21	13	3	5	53	30	989904	47138
	A	21	6	4	11	49	50	859545	40931
TOTAL		42	19	7	16	102	80	1849449	44035
FA Cup	H	1	0	0	1	0	1	66350	66350
	A	2	2	0	0	7	3	90033	45017
TOTAL		3	2	0	1	7	4	156383	52128
Overall	H	22	13	3	6	53	31	1056254	48012
	A	23	8	4	11	56	53	949578	41286
TOTAL		45	21	7	17	109	84	2005832	44574

FINAL TABLE – LEAGUE DIVISION ONE

		P	W	D	L	F	A	W	D	L	F	A	PTS	GD
				HOME					AWAY					
1	Burnley	42	15	2	4	52	28	9	5	7	33	33	55	24
2	Wolverhampton Wanderers	42	15	3	3	63	28	9	3	9	43	39	54	39
3	Tottenham Hotspur	42	10	6	5	43	24	11	5	5	43	26	53	36
4	West Bromwich Albion	42	12	4	5	48	25	7	7	7	35	32	49	26
5	Sheffield Wednesday	42	12	7	2	48	20	7	4	10	32	39	49	21
6	Bolton Wanderers	42	12	5	4	37	27	8	3	10	22	24	48	8
7	MANCHESTER UNITED	42	13	3	5	53	30	6	4	11	49	50	45	22
8	Newcastle United	42	10	5	6	42	32	8	3	10	40	46	44	4
9	Preston North End	42	10	6	5	43	34	6	6	9	36	42	44	3
10	Fulham	42	12	4	5	42	28	5	6	10	31	52	44	-7
11	Blackpool	42	9	6	6	32	32	6	4	11	27	39	40	-12
12	Leicester City	42	8	6	7	38	32	5	7	9	28	43	39	-9
13	Arsenal	42	9	5	7	39	38	6	4	11	29	42	39	-12
14	West Ham United	42	12	3	6	47	33	4	3	14	28	58	38	-16
15	Everton	42	13	3	5	50	20	0	8	13	23	58	37	-5
16	Manchester City	42	11	2	8	47	34	6	1	14	31	50	37	-6
17	Blackburn Rovers	42	12	3	6	38	29	4	2	15	22	41	37	-10
18	Chelsea	42	7	5	9	44	50	7	4	10	32	41	37	-15
19	Birmingham City	42	9	5	7	37	36	4	5	12	26	44	36	-17
20	Nottingham Forest	42	8	6	7	30	28	5	3	13	20	46	35	-24
21	Leeds United	42	7	5	9	37	46	5	5	11	28	46	34	-27
22	Luton Town	42	6	5	10	25	29	3	7	11	25	44	30	-23

SEASON 1960/61

Match # 2449
Saturday 20/08/60   Football League Division 1   at Old Trafford   Attendance 47778
Result: **Manchester United 1 Blackburn Rovers 3**
Teamsheet: Gregg, Cope, Carolan, Setters, Haydock, Brennan, Giles, Quixall, Viollet, Charlton, Scanlon
Scorer(s): Charlton

Match # 2450
Wednesday 24/08/60   Football League Division 1   at Goodison Park   Attendance 51602
Result: **Everton 4 Manchester United 0**
Teamsheet: Gregg, Brennan, Carolan, Setters, Haydock, Nicholson, Giles, Quixall, Viollet, Charlton, Scanlon

Match # 2451
Wednesday 31/08/60   Football League Division 1   at Old Trafford   Attendance 51818
Result: **Manchester United 4 Everton 0**
Teamsheet: Gregg, Foulkes, Brennan, Setters, Haydock, Nicholson, Quixall, Giles, Dawson, Viollet, Charlton
Scorer(s): Dawson 2, Charlton, Nicholson

Match # 2452
Saturday 03/09/60   Football League Division 1   at White Hart Lane   Attendance 55445
Result: **Tottenham Hotspur 4 Manchester United 1**
Teamsheet: Gregg, Foulkes, Brennan, Setters, Haydock, Nicholson, Quixall, Giles, Dawson, Viollet, Charlton
Scorer(s): Viollet

Match # 2453
Monday 05/09/60   Football League Division 1   at Upton Park   Attendance 30506
Result: **West Ham United 2 Manchester United 1**
Teamsheet: Gregg, Foulkes, Brennan, Setters, Cope, Nicholson, Quixall, Giles, Dawson, Viollet, Charlton
Scorer(s): Quixall

Match # 2454
Saturday 10/09/60   Football League Division 1   at Old Trafford   Attendance 35493
Result: **Manchester United 1 Leicester City 1**
Teamsheet: Gregg, Foulkes, Brennan, Setters, Cope, Nicholson, Quixall, Giles, Dawson, Viollet, Charlton
Scorer(s): Giles

Match # 2455
Wednesday 14/09/60   Football League Division 1   at Old Trafford   Attendance 33695
Result: **Manchester United 6 West Ham United 1**
Teamsheet: Gregg, Foulkes, Brennan, Setters, Cope, Nicholson, Quixall, Giles, Viollet, Charlton, Scanlon
Scorer(s): Charlton 2, Viollet 2, Quixall, Scanlon

Match # 2456
Saturday 17/09/60   Football League Division 1   at Villa Park   Attendance 43593
Result: **Aston Villa 3 Manchester United 1**
Teamsheet: Gregg, Foulkes, Brennan, Setters, Cope, Nicholson, Giles, Quixall, Viollet, Charlton, Scanlon
Scorer(s): Viollet

Match # 2457
Saturday 24/09/60   Football League Division 1   at Old Trafford   Attendance 44458
Result: **Manchester United 1 Wolverhampton Wanderers 3**
Teamsheet: Gregg, Foulkes, Brennan, Setters, Cope, Nicholson, Giles, Quixall, Viollet, Charlton, Scanlon
Scorer(s): Charlton

Match # 2458
Saturday 01/10/60   Football League Division 1   at Burnden Park   Attendance 39197
Result: **Bolton Wanderers 1 Manchester United 1**
Teamsheet: Gregg, Setters, Brennan, Stiles, Foulkes, Nicholson, Moir, Giles, Dawson, Charlton, Scanlon
Scorer(s): Giles

Match # 2459
Saturday 15/10/60   Football League Division 1   at Turf Moor   Attendance 32011
Result: **Burnley 5 Manchester United 3**
Teamsheet: Gregg, Setters, Dunne, Stiles, Foulkes, Nicholson, Quixall, Giles, Viollet, Pearson, Charlton
Scorer(s): Viollet 3

Match # 2460
Wednesday 19/10/60   League Cup 1st Round   at St James' Park   Attendance 14494
Result: **Exeter City 1 Manchester United 1**
Teamsheet: Gregg, Setters, Brennan, Stiles, Foulkes, Nicholson, Dawson, Lawton, Viollet, Pearson, Scanlon
Scorer(s): Dawson

Match # 2461
Saturday 22/10/60   Football League Division 1   at Old Trafford   Attendance 37516
Result: **Manchester United 3 Newcastle United 2**
Teamsheet: Gregg, Setters, Brennan, Stiles, Foulkes, Nicholson, Dawson, Giles, Viollet, Charlton, Scanlon
Scorer(s): Dawson, Setters, Stiles

Match # 2462
Monday 24/10/60   Football League Division 1   at Old Trafford   Attendance 23628
Result: **Manchester United 2 Nottingham Forest 1**
Teamsheet: Gregg, Dunne, Brennan, Stiles, Foulkes, Nicholson, Dawson, Giles, Viollet, Pearson, Scanlon
Scorer(s): Viollet 2

Match # 2463
Wednesday 26/10/60   League Cup 1st Round Replay   at Old Trafford   Attendance 15662
Result: **Manchester United 4 Exeter City 1**
Teamsheet: Gaskell, Dunne, Carolan, Stiles, Cope, Nicholson, Dawson, Giles, Quixall, Pearson, Scanlon
Scorer(s): Quixall 2, Giles, Pearson

Match # 2464
Saturday 29/10/60   Football League Division 1   at Highbury   Attendance 45715
Result: **Arsenal 2 Manchester United 1**
Teamsheet: Gregg, Brennan, Heron, Stiles, Foulkes, Nicholson, Dawson, Giles, Viollet, Quixall, Charlton
Scorer(s): Quixall

Match # 2465
Wednesday 02/11/60   League Cup 2nd Round   at Valley Parade   Attendance 4670
Result: **Bradford City 2 Manchester United 1**
Teamsheet: Gregg, Setters, Brennan, Bratt, Foulkes, Nicholson, Dawson, Giles, Viollet, Pearson, Scanlon
Scorer(s): Viollet

Match # 2466
Saturday 05/11/60   Football League Division 1   at Old Trafford   Attendance 36855
Result: **Manchester United 0 Sheffield Wednesday 0**
Teamsheet: Gregg, Setters, Brennan, Stiles, Foulkes, Nicholson, Dawson, Giles, Viollet, Quixall, Charlton

SEASON 1960/61 (continued)

Match # 2467	Saturday 12/11/60	Football League Division 1	at St Andrews	Attendance 31549
Result:	**Birmingham City 3 Manchester United 1**			
Teamsheet:	Gregg, Setters, Brennan, Stiles, Foulkes, Nicholson, Dawson, Giles, Viollet, Pearson, Charlton			
Scorer(s):	Charlton			

Match # 2468	Saturday 19/11/60	Football League Division 1	at Old Trafford	Attendance 32756
Result:	**Manchester United 3 West Bromwich Albion 0**			
Teamsheet:	Gregg, Setters, Brennan, Stiles, Foulkes, Nicholson, Bradley, Quixall, Dawson, Viollet, Charlton			
Scorer(s):	Dawson, Quixall, Viollet			

Match # 2469	Saturday 26/11/60	Football League Division 1	at Ninian Park	Attendance 21122
Result:	**Cardiff City 3 Manchester United 0**			
Teamsheet:	Gregg, Brennan, Cantwell, Setters, Foulkes, Nicholson, Bradley, Quixall, Dawson, Viollet, Charlton			

Match # 2470	Saturday 03/12/60	Football League Division 1	at Old Trafford	Attendance 24904
Result:	**Manchester United 1 Preston North End 0**			
Teamsheet:	Gregg, Brennan, Cantwell, Setters, Foulkes, Nicholson, Bradley, Quixall, Dawson, Pearson, Charlton			
Scorer(s):	Dawson			

Match # 2471	Saturday 10/12/60	Football League Division 1	at Craven Cottage	Attendance 23625
Result:	**Fulham 4 Manchester United 4**			
Teamsheet:	Gregg, Brennan, Cantwell, Setters, Foulkes, Nicholson, Bradley, Quixall, Dawson, Pearson, Charlton			
Scorer(s):	Quixall 2, Charlton, Dawson			

Match # 2472	Saturday 17/12/60	Football League Division 1	at Ewood Park	Attendance 17285
Result:	**Blackburn Rovers 1 Manchester United 2**			
Teamsheet:	Gregg, Brennan, Cantwell, Setters, Foulkes, Nicholson, Quixall, Stiles, Dawson, Pearson, Charlton			
Scorer(s):	Pearson 2			

Match # 2473	Saturday 24/12/60	Football League Division 1	at Stamford Bridge	Attendance 37601
Result:	**Chelsea 1 Manchester United 2**			
Teamsheet:	Gregg, Brennan, Cantwell, Setters, Foulkes, Nicholson, Quixall, Stiles, Dawson, Pearson, Charlton			
Scorer(s):	Charlton, Dawson			

Match # 2474	Monday 26/12/60	Football League Division 1	at Old Trafford	Attendance 50164
Result:	**Manchester United 6 Chelsea 0**			
Teamsheet:	Gregg, Brennan, Cantwell, Setters, Foulkes, Nicholson, Quixall, Stiles, Dawson, Pearson, Charlton			
Scorer(s):	Dawson 3, Nicholson 2, Charlton			

Match # 2475	Saturday 31/12/60	Football League Division 1	at Old Trafford	Attendance 61213
Result:	**Manchester United 5 Manchester City 1**			
Teamsheet:	Gregg, Brennan, Cantwell, Setters, Foulkes, Nicholson, Quixall, Stiles, Dawson, Pearson, Charlton			
Scorer(s):	Dawson 3, Charlton 2			

Match # 2476	Saturday 07/01/61	FA Cup 3rd Round	at Old Trafford	Attendance 49184
Result:	**Manchester United 3 Middlesbrough 0**			
Teamsheet:	Gregg, Brennan, Cantwell, Setters, Foulkes, Nicholson, Quixall, Stiles, Dawson, Pearson, Charlton			
Scorer(s):	Dawson 2, Cantwell			

Match # 2477	Saturday 14/01/61	Football League Division 1	at Old Trafford	Attendance 65295
Result:	**Manchester United 2 Tottenham Hotspur 0**			
Teamsheet:	Gregg, Brennan, Cantwell, Setters, Foulkes, Nicholson, Quixall, Stiles, Dawson, Pearson, Charlton			
Scorer(s):	Pearson, Stiles			

Match # 2478	Saturday 21/01/61	Football League Division 1	at Filbert Street	Attendance 31308
Result:	**Leicester City 6 Manchester United 0**			
Teamsheet:	Briggs, Brennan, Cantwell, Setters, Foulkes, Nicholson, Quixall, Stiles, Dawson, Pearson, Charlton			

Match # 2479	Saturday 28/01/61	FA Cup 4th Round	at Hillsborough	Attendance 58000
Result:	**Sheffield Wednesday 1 Manchester United 1**			
Teamsheet:	Briggs, Brennan, Cantwell, Setters, Foulkes, Nicholson, Viollet, Stiles, Dawson, Pearson, Charlton			
Scorer(s):	Cantwell			

Match # 2480	Wednesday 01/02/61	FA Cup 4th Round Replay	at Old Trafford	Attendance 65243
Result:	**Manchester United 2 Sheffield Wednesday 7**			
Teamsheet:	Briggs, Brennan, Cantwell, Setters, Foulkes, Nicholson, Quixall, Stiles, Dawson, Pearson, Charlton			
Scorer(s):	Dawson, Pearson			

Match # 2481	Saturday 04/02/61	Football League Division 1	at Old Trafford	Attendance 33525
Result:	**Manchester United 1 Aston Villa 1**			
Teamsheet:	Pinner, Brennan, Cantwell, Setters, Foulkes, Nicholson, Quixall, Stiles, Dawson, Pearson, Charlton			
Scorer(s):	Charlton			

Match # 2482	Saturday 11/02/61	Football League Division 1	at Molineux	Attendance 38526
Result:	**Wolverhampton Wanderers 2 Manchester United 1**			
Teamsheet:	Pinner, Brennan, Cantwell, Setters, Foulkes, Nicholson, Quixall, Stiles, Dawson, Pearson, Charlton			
Scorer(s):	Nicholson			

Match # 2483	Saturday 18/02/61	Football League Division 1	at Old Trafford	Attendance 37558
Result:	**Manchester United 3 Bolton Wanderers 1**			
Teamsheet:	Pinner, Brennan, Cantwell, Stiles, Foulkes, Setters, Morgans, Quixall, Dawson, Pearson, Charlton			
Scorer(s):	Dawson 2, Quixall			

Match # 2484	Saturday 25/02/61	Football League Division 1	at City Ground	Attendance 26850
Result:	**Nottingham Forest 3 Manchester United 2**			
Teamsheet:	Gregg, Brennan, Cantwell, Setters, Foulkes, Nicholson, Morgans, Quixall, Dawson, Pearson, Charlton			
Scorer(s):	Charlton, Quixall			

SEASON 1960/61 (continued)

Match # 2485 Saturday 04/03/61 Football League Division 1 at Maine Road Attendance 50479
Result: **Manchester City 1 Manchester United 3**
Teamsheet: Gregg, Brennan, Cantwell, Setters, Foulkes, Stiles, Moir, Quixall, Dawson, Pearson, Charlton
Scorer(s): Charlton, Dawson, Pearson

Match # 2486 Saturday 11/03/61 Football League Division 1 at St James' Park Attendance 28870
Result: **Newcastle United 1 Manchester United 1**
Teamsheet: Pinner, Brennan, Cantwell, Setters, Foulkes, Stiles, Moir, Quixall, Lawton, Pearson, Charlton
Scorer(s): Charlton

Match # 2487 Saturday 18/03/61 Football League Division 1 at Old Trafford Attendance 29732
Result: **Manchester United 1 Arsenal 1**
Teamsheet: Gaskell, Brennan, Cantwell, Setters, Foulkes, Stiles, Moir, Quixall, Dawson, Pearson, Charlton
Scorer(s): Moir

Match # 2488 Saturday 25/03/61 Football League Division 1 at Hillsborough Attendance 35901
Result: **Sheffield Wednesday 5 Manchester United 1**
Teamsheet: Gaskell, Brennan, Cantwell, Setters, Foulkes, Stiles, Moir, Quixall, Dawson, Pearson, Charlton
Scorer(s): Charlton

Match # 2489 Friday 31/03/61 Football League Division 1 at Bloomfield Road Attendance 30835
Result: **Blackpool 2 Manchester United 0**
Teamsheet: Gaskell, Brennan, Cantwell, Setters, Foulkes, Stiles, Moir, Quixall, Dawson, Pearson, Charlton

Match # 2490 Saturday 01/04/61 Football League Division 1 at Old Trafford Attendance 24654
Result: **Manchester United 3 Fulham 1**
Teamsheet: Gaskell, Brennan, Cantwell, Setters, Foulkes, Nicholson, Giles, Quixall, Viollet, Pearson, Charlton
Scorer(s): Charlton, Quixall, Viollet

Match # 2491 Monday 03/04/61 Football League Division 1 at Old Trafford Attendance 39169
Result: **Manchester United 2 Blackpool 0**
Teamsheet: Gaskell, Brennan, Cantwell, Setters, Foulkes, Nicholson, Giles, Quixall, Viollet, Pearson, Charlton
Scorer(s): Nicholson, own goal

Match # 2492 Saturday 08/04/61 Football League Division 1 at The Hawthorns Attendance 27750
Result: **West Bromwich Albion 1 Manchester United 1**
Teamsheet: Gaskell, Brennan, Cantwell, Setters, Foulkes, Nicholson, Giles, Quixall, Viollet, Pearson, Charlton
Scorer(s): Pearson

Match # 2493 Wednesday 12/04/61 Football League Division 1 at Old Trafford Attendance 25019
Result: **Manchester United 6 Burnley 0**
Teamsheet: Gaskell, Brennan, Cantwell, Setters, Foulkes, Stiles, Giles, Quixall, Viollet, Pearson, Moir
Scorer(s): Quixall 3, Viollet 3

Match # 2494 Saturday 15/04/61 Football League Division 1 at Old Trafford Attendance 28376
Result: **Manchester United 4 Birmingham City 1**
Teamsheet: Gaskell, Brennan, Cantwell, Setters, Foulkes, Stiles, Giles, Quixall, Viollet, Pearson, Moir
Scorer(s): Pearson 2, Quixall, Viollet

Match # 2495 Saturday 22/04/61 Football League Division 1 at Deepdale Attendance 21252
Result: **Preston North End 2 Manchester United 4**
Teamsheet: Gaskell, Dunne, Brennan, Setters, Foulkes, Stiles, Giles, Quixall, Viollet, Pearson, Charlton
Scorer(s): Charlton 2, Setters 2

Match # 2496 Saturday 29/04/61 Football League Division 1 at Old Trafford Attendance 30320
Result: **Manchester United 3 Cardiff City 3**
Teamsheet: Gaskell, Brennan, Cantwell, Setters, Foulkes, Stiles, Giles, Quixall, Viollet, Pearson, Charlton
Scorer(s): Charlton 2, Setters

SEASON 1960/61 SUMMARY

APPEARANCES

PLAYER	LGE	FAC	LC	TOT
Brennan	41	3	2	46
Foulkes	40	3	2	45
Setters	40	3	2	45
Charlton	39	3	–	42
Quixall	38	2	1	41
Nicholson	31	3	3	37
Dawson	28	3	3	34
Pearson	27	3	3	33
Stiles	26	3	2	31
Gregg	27	1	2	30
Cantwell	24	3	–	27
Viollet	24	1	2	27
Giles	23	–	2	25
Gaskell	10	–	1	11
Scanlon	8	–	3	11
Moir	8	–	–	8
Cope	6	–	1	7
Bradley	4	–	–	4
Dunne	3	–	1	4
Haydock	4	–	–	4
Pinner	4	–	–	4
Briggs	1	2	–	3
Carolan	2	–	1	3
Lawton	1	–	1	2
Morgans	2	–	–	2
Bratt	–	–	1	1
Heron	1	–	–	1

GOALSCORERS

PLAYER	LGE	FAC	LC	TOT
Charlton	21	–	–	21
Dawson	16	3	1	20
Viollet	15	–	1	16
Quixall	13	–	2	15
Pearson	7	1	1	9
Nicholson	5	–	–	5
Setters	4	–	–	4
Giles	2	–	1	3
Stiles	2	–	–	2
Cantwell	–	2	–	2
Moir	1	–	–	1
Scanlon	1	–	–	1
own goal	1	–	–	1

RESULTS & ATTENDANCES SUMMARY

		P	W	D	L	F	A	TOTAL	AVGE
League	H	21	14	5	2	58	20	793926	37806
	A	21	4	4	13	30	56	721022	34334
	TOTAL	42	18	9	15	88	76	1514948	36070
FA Cup	H	2	1	0	1	5	7	114427	57214
	A	1	0	1	0	1	1	58000	58000
	TOTAL	3	1	1	1	6	8	172427	57476
League Cup	H	1	1	0	0	4	1	15662	15662
	A	2	0	1	1	2	3	19164	9582
	TOTAL	3	1	1	1	6	4	34826	11609
Overall	H	24	16	5	3	67	28	924015	38501
	A	24	4	6	14	33	60	798186	33258
	TOTAL	48	20	11	17	100	88	1722201	35879

FINAL TABLE – LEAGUE DIVISION ONE

		P	HOME W	HOME D	HOME L	HOME F	HOME A	AWAY W	AWAY D	AWAY L	AWAY F	AWAY A	PTS	GD
1	Tottenham Hotspur	42	15	3	3	65	28	16	1	4	50	27	66	60
2	Sheffield Wednesday	42	15	4	2	45	17	8	8	5	33	30	58	31
3	Wolverhampton Wanderers	42	17	2	2	61	32	8	5	8	42	43	57	28
4	Burnley	42	11	4	6	58	40	11	3	7	44	37	51	25
5	Everton	42	13	4	4	47	23	9	2	10	40	46	50	18
6	Leicester City	42	12	4	5	54	31	6	5	10	33	39	45	17
7	MANCHESTER UNITED	42	14	5	2	58	20	4	4	13	30	56	45	12
8	Blackburn Rovers	42	12	3	6	48	34	3	10	8	29	42	43	1
9	Aston Villa	42	13	3	5	48	28	4	6	11	30	49	43	1
10	West Bromwich Albion	42	10	3	8	43	32	8	2	11	24	39	41	-4
11	Arsenal	42	12	3	6	44	35	3	8	10	33	50	41	-8
12	Chelsea	42	10	5	6	61	48	5	2	14	37	52	37	-2
13	Manchester City	42	10	5	6	41	30	3	6	12	38	60	37	-11
14	Nottingham Forest	42	8	7	6	34	33	6	2	13	28	45	37	-16
15	Cardiff City	42	11	5	5	34	26	2	6	13	26	59	37	-25
16	West Ham United	42	12	4	5	53	31	1	6	14	24	57	36	-11
17	Fulham	42	8	8	5	39	39	6	0	15	33	56	36	-23
18	Bolton Wanderers	42	9	5	7	38	29	3	6	12	20	44	35	-15
19	Birmingham City	42	10	4	7	35	31	4	2	15	27	53	34	-22
20	Blackpool	42	9	3	9	44	34	3	6	12	24	39	33	-5
21	Newcastle United	42	7	7	7	51	49	4	3	14	35	60	32	-23
22	Preston North End	42	7	6	8	28	25	3	4	14	15	46	30	-28

SEASON 1961/62

Match # 2497 Saturday 19/08/61 Football League Division 1 at Upton Park Attendance 32628
Result: **West Ham United 1 Manchester United 1**
Teamsheet: Gregg, Brennan, Cantwell, Stiles, Foulkes, Setters, Quixall, Viollet, Herd, Pearson, Charlton
Scorer(s): Stiles

Match # 2498 Wednesday 23/08/61 Football League Division 1 at Old Trafford Attendance 45847
Result: **Manchester United 3 Chelsea 2**
Teamsheet: Gregg, Brennan, Cantwell, Stiles, Foulkes, Setters, Quixall, Viollet, Herd, Pearson, Charlton
Scorer(s): Herd, Pearson, Viollet

Match # 2499 Saturday 26/08/61 Football League Division 1 at Old Trafford Attendance 45302
Result: **Manchester United 6 Blackburn Rovers 1**
Teamsheet: Gregg, Brennan, Cantwell, Stiles, Foulkes, Setters, Quixall, Viollet, Herd, Pearson, Charlton
Scorer(s): Herd 2, Quixall 2, Charlton, Setters

Match # 2500 Wednesday 30/08/61 Football League Division 1 at Stamford Bridge Attendance 42248
Result: **Chelsea 2 Manchester United 0**
Teamsheet: Gregg, Brennan, Cantwell, Stiles, Foulkes, Setters, Quixall, Viollet, Herd, Pearson, Charlton

Match # 2501 Saturday 02/09/61 Football League Division 1 at Bloomfield Road Attendance 28156
Result: **Blackpool 2 Manchester United 3**
Teamsheet: Gregg, Brennan, Cantwell, Stiles, Foulkes, Setters, Bradley, Viollet, Herd, Pearson, Charlton
Scorer(s): Viollet 2, Charlton

Match # 2502 Saturday 09/09/61 Football League Division 1 at Old Trafford Attendance 57135
Result: **Manchester United 1 Tottenham Hotspur 0**
Teamsheet: Gregg, Brennan, Cantwell, Stiles, Foulkes, Setters, Quixall, Viollet, Herd, Pearson, Charlton
Scorer(s): Quixall

Match # 2503 Saturday 16/09/61 Football League Division 1 at Ninian Park Attendance 29251
Result: **Cardiff City 1 Manchester United 2**
Teamsheet: Gregg, Brennan, Cantwell, Stiles, Foulkes, Setters, Quixall, Viollet, Dawson, Pearson, Charlton
Scorer(s): Dawson, Quixall

Match # 2504 Monday 18/09/61 Football League Division 1 at Villa Park Attendance 38837
Result: **Aston Villa 1 Manchester United 1**
Teamsheet: Gaskell, Brennan, Dunne, Stiles, Foulkes, Setters, Quixall, Viollet, Herd, Pearson, Charlton
Scorer(s): Stiles

Match # 2505 Saturday 23/09/61 Football League Division 1 at Old Trafford Attendance 56345
Result: **Manchester United 3 Manchester City 2**
Teamsheet: Gregg, Brennan, Dunne, Stiles, Foulkes, Setters, Quixall, Viollet, Herd, Pearson, Charlton
Scorer(s): Stiles, Viollet, own goal

Match # 2506 Saturday 30/09/61 Football League Division 1 at Old Trafford Attendance 39457
Result: **Manchester United 0 Wolverhampton Wanderers 2**
Teamsheet: Gregg, Brennan, Cantwell, Stiles, Foulkes, Lawton, Quixall, Giles, Dawson, Pearson, Charlton

Match # 2507 Saturday 07/10/61 Football League Division 1 at The Hawthorns Attendance 25645
Result: **West Bromwich Albion 1 Manchester United 1**
Teamsheet: Gaskell, Brennan, Cantwell, Stiles, Foulkes, Lawton, Moir, Quixall, Dawson, Giles, Charlton
Scorer(s): Dawson

Match # 2508 Saturday 14/10/61 Football League Division 1 at Old Trafford Attendance 30674
Result: **Manchester United 0 Birmingham City 2**
Teamsheet: Gregg, Brennan, Cantwell, Stiles, Haydock, Lawton, Bradley, Giles, Dawson, Herd, Moir

Match # 2509 Saturday 21/10/61 Football League Division 1 at Highbury Attendance 54245
Result: **Arsenal 5 Manchester United 1**
Teamsheet: Gregg, Brennan, Cantwell, Nicholson, Foulkes, Lawton, Moir, Giles, Herd, Viollet, Charlton
Scorer(s): Viollet

Match # 2510 Saturday 28/10/61 Football League Division 1 at Old Trafford Attendance 31442
Result: **Manchester United 0 Bolton Wanderers 3**
Teamsheet: Gregg, Brennan, Dunne, Nicholson, Foulkes, Setters, Moir, Quixall, Herd, Viollet, Charlton

Match # 2511 Saturday 04/11/61 Football League Division 1 at Hillsborough Attendance 35998
Result: **Sheffield Wednesday 3 Manchester United 1**
Teamsheet: Gregg, Brennan, Cantwell, Stiles, Foulkes, Setters, Bradley, Giles, Viollet, Charlton, McMillan
Scorer(s): Viollet

Match # 2512 Saturday 11/11/61 Football League Division 1 at Old Trafford Attendance 21567
Result: **Manchester United 2 Leicester City 2**
Teamsheet: Gaskell, Brennan, Cantwell, Stiles, Foulkes, Setters, Bradley, Giles, Viollet, Charlton, McMillan
Scorer(s): Giles, Viollet

Match # 2513 Saturday 18/11/61 Football League Division 1 at Portman Road Attendance 25755
Result: **Ipswich Town 4 Manchester United 1**
Teamsheet: Gaskell, Brennan, Dunne, Stiles, Foulkes, Setters, Bradley, Giles, Herd, Charlton, McMillan
Scorer(s): McMillan

Match # 2514 Saturday 25/11/61 Football League Division 1 at Old Trafford Attendance 41029
Result: **Manchester United 1 Burnley 4**
Teamsheet: Gaskell, Brennan, Dunne, Stiles, Foulkes, Setters, Bradley, Giles, Herd, Quixall, Charlton
Scorer(s): Herd

SEASON 1961/62 (continued)

Match # 2515 Saturday 02/12/61   Football League Division 1   at Goodison Park   Attendance 48099
Result: **Everton 5   Manchester United 1**
Teamsheet: Gaskell, Brennan, Dunne, Nicholson, Foulkes, Setters, Chisnall, Giles, Herd, Lawton, Charlton
Scorer(s): Herd

Match # 2516 Saturday 09/12/61   Football League Division 1   at Old Trafford   Attendance 22193
Result: **Manchester United 3   Fulham 0**
Teamsheet: Gaskell, Brennan, Dunne, Nicholson, Foulkes, Setters, Chisnall, Giles, Herd, Lawton, Charlton
Scorer(s): Herd 2, Lawton

Match # 2517 Saturday 16/12/61   Football League Division 1   at Old Trafford   Attendance 29472
Result: **Manchester United 1   West Ham United 2**
Teamsheet: Gaskell, Brennan, Dunne, Nicholson, Foulkes, Setters, Chisnall, Giles, Herd, Lawton, Charlton
Scorer(s): Herd

Match # 2518 Tuesday 26/12/61   Football League Division 1   at Old Trafford   Attendance 30822
Result: **Manchester United 6   Nottingham Forest 3**
Teamsheet: Gaskell, Brennan, Dunne, Nicholson, Foulkes, Setters, Chisnall, Giles, Herd, Lawton, Charlton
Scorer(s): Lawton 3, Brennan, Charlton, Herd

Match # 2519 Saturday 06/01/62   FA Cup 3rd Round   at Old Trafford   Attendance 42202
Result: **Manchester United 2   Bolton Wanderers 1**
Teamsheet: Gaskell, Brennan, Dunne, Nicholson, Foulkes, Setters, Chisnall, Giles, Herd, Lawton, Bradley
Scorer(s): Herd, Nicholson

Match # 2520 Saturday 13/01/62   Football League Division 1   at Old Trafford   Attendance 26999
Result: **Manchester United 0   Blackpool 1**
Teamsheet: Gaskell, Brennan, Dunne, Nicholson, Foulkes, Setters, Chisnall, Giles, Herd, Lawton, Charlton

Match # 2521 Monday 15/01/62   Football League Division 1   at Old Trafford   Attendance 20807
Result: **Manchester United 2   Aston Villa 0**
Teamsheet: Gaskell, Brennan, Dunne, Nicholson, Foulkes, Setters, Chisnall, Giles, Quixall, Lawton, Charlton
Scorer(s): Charlton, Quixall

Match # 2522 Saturday 20/01/62   Football League Division 1   at White Hart Lane   Attendance 55225
Result: **Tottenham Hotspur 2   Manchester United 2**
Teamsheet: Gaskell, Brennan, Dunne, Nicholson, Foulkes, Setters, Stiles, Lawton, Giles, Charlton
Scorer(s): Charlton, Stiles

Match # 2523 Wednesday 31/01/62   FA Cup 4th Round   at Old Trafford   Attendance 54082
Result: **Manchester United 1   Arsenal 0**
Teamsheet: Gaskell, Brennan, Dunne, Nicholson, Foulkes, Setters, Chisnall, Stiles, Lawton, Giles, Charlton
Scorer(s): Setters

Match # 2524 Saturday 03/02/62   Football League Division 1   at Old Trafford   Attendance 29200
Result: **Manchester United 3   Cardiff City 0**
Teamsheet: Gaskell, Brennan, Dunne, Nicholson, Foulkes, Setters, Chisnall, Stiles, Lawton, Giles, Charlton
Scorer(s): Giles, Lawton, Stiles

Match # 2525 Saturday 10/02/62   Football League Division 1   at Maine Road   Attendance 49959
Result: **Manchester City 0   Manchester United 2**
Teamsheet: Gaskell, Brennan, Dunne, Stiles, Setters, Nicholson, Chisnall, Giles, Herd, Lawton, Charlton
Scorer(s): Chisnall, Herd

Match # 2526 Saturday 17/02/62   FA Cup 5th Round   at Old Trafford   Attendance 59553
Result: **Manchester United 0   Sheffield Wednesday 0**
Teamsheet: Gaskell, Brennan, Dunne, Setters, Foulkes, Nicholson, Chisnall, Giles, Herd, Lawton, Charlton

Match # 2527 Wednesday 21/02/62   FA Cup 5th Round Replay   at Hillsborough   Attendance 62969
Result: **Sheffield Wednesday 0   Manchester United 2**
Teamsheet: Gaskell, Brennan, Dunne, Stiles, Foulkes, Setters, Quixall, Giles, Herd, Lawton, Charlton
Scorer(s): Charlton, Giles

Match # 2528 Saturday 24/02/62   Football League Division 1   at Old Trafford   Attendance 32456
Result: **Manchester United 4   West Bromwich Albion 1**
Teamsheet: Briggs, Brennan, Dunne, Stiles, Foulkes, Setters, Quixall, Giles, Herd, Lawton, Charlton
Scorer(s): Charlton 2, Quixall, Setters

Match # 2529 Wednesday 28/02/62   Football League Division 1   at Molineux   Attendance 27565
Result: **Wolverhampton Wanderers 2   Manchester United 2**
Teamsheet: Briggs, Brennan, Dunne, Setters, Foulkes, Nicholson, Quixall, Stiles, Herd, Lawton, Charlton
Scorer(s): Herd, Lawton

Match # 2530 Saturday 03/03/62   Football League Division 1   at St Andrews   Attendance 25817
Result: **Birmingham City 1   Manchester United 0**
Teamsheet: Briggs, Brennan, Dunne, Stiles, Foulkes, Setters, Quixall, Giles, Herd, Lawton, Charlton
Scorer(s): Herd

Match # 2531 Saturday 10/03/62   FA Cup 6th Round   at Deepdale   Attendance 37521
Result: **Preston North End 0   Manchester United 0**
Teamsheet: Gaskell, Brennan, Dunne, Nicholson, Foulkes, Setters, Chisnall, Giles, Cantwell, Lawton, Charlton

Match # 2532 Wednesday 14/03/62   FA Cup 6th Round Replay   at Old Trafford   Attendance 63468
Result: **Manchester United 2   Preston North End 1**
Teamsheet: Gaskell, Brennan, Dunne, Stiles, Foulkes, Setters, Quixall, Giles, Herd, Lawton, Charlton
Scorer(s): Charlton, Herd

SEASON 1961/62 (continued)

Match # 2533 Saturday 17/03/62	Football League Division 1	at Burnden Park	Attendance 34366
Result:	**Bolton Wanderers 1 Manchester United 0**
Teamsheet:	Briggs, Brennan, Dunne, Nicholson, Foulkes, Setters, Quixall, Giles, Lawton, Stiles, Charlton

Match # 2534 Tuesday 20/03/62	Football League Division 1	at City Ground	Attendance 27833
Result:	**Nottingham Forest 1 Manchester United 0**
Teamsheet:	Briggs, Brennan, Dunne, Nicholson, Foulkes, Setters, Quixall, Giles, Lawton, Stiles, Moir

Match # 2535 Saturday 24/03/62	Football League Division 1	at Old Trafford	Attendance 31322
Result:	**Manchester United 1 Sheffield Wednesday 1**
Teamsheet:	Gaskell, Brennan, Dunne, Stiles, Foulkes, Setters, Moir, Giles, Quixall, Lawton, Charlton
Scorer(s):	Charlton

Match # 2536 Saturday 31/03/62	FA Cup Semi-Final	at Hillsborough	Attendance 65000
Result:	**Manchester United 1 Tottenham Hotspur 3**
Teamsheet:	Gaskell, Dunne, Cantwell, Stiles, Foulkes, Setters, Quixall, Giles, Herd, Lawton, Charlton
Scorer(s):	Herd

Match # 2537 Wednesday 04/04/62	Football League Division 1	at Filbert Street	Attendance 15318
Result:	**Leicester City 4 Manchester United 3**
Teamsheet:	Gaskell, Setters, Dunne, Stiles, Foulkes, Nicholson, Moir, Quixall, Herd, Lawton, McMillan
Scorer(s):	McMillan 2, Quixall

Match # 2538 Saturday 07/04/62	Football League Division 1	at Old Trafford	Attendance 24976
Result:	**Manchester United 5 Ipswich Town 0**
Teamsheet:	Briggs, Brennan, Dunne, Stiles, Foulkes, Setters, Moir, Giles, Quixall, McMillan, Charlton
Scorer(s):	Quixall 3, Setters, Stiles

Match # 2539 Tuesday 10/04/62	Football League Division 1	at Ewood Park	Attendance 14623
Result:	**Blackburn Rovers 3 Manchester United 0**
Teamsheet:	Gaskell, Brennan, Dunne, Stiles, Foulkes, Setters, Moir, Giles, Cantwell, Pearson, McMillan

Match # 2540 Saturday 14/04/62	Football League Division 1	at Turf Moor	Attendance 36240
Result:	**Burnley 1 Manchester United 3**
Teamsheet:	Briggs, Brennan, Dunne, Stiles, Foulkes, Setters, Giles, Pearson, Cantwell, Herd, McMillan
Scorer(s):	Brennan, Cantwell, Herd

Match # 2541 Monday 16/04/62	Football League Division 1	at Old Trafford	Attendance 24258
Result:	**Manchester United 2 Arsenal 3**
Teamsheet:	Briggs, Brennan, Cantwell, Stiles, Foulkes, Setters, Giles, Pearson, Herd, McMillan, Charlton
Scorer(s):	Cantwell, McMillan

Match # 2542 Saturday 21/04/62	Football League Division 1	at Old Trafford	Attendance 31926
Result:	**Manchester United 1 Everton 1**
Teamsheet:	Gaskell, Brennan, Dunne, Stiles, Foulkes, Setters, Giles, Pearson, Cantwell, Herd, Charlton
Scorer(s):	Herd

Match # 2543 Monday 23/04/62	Football League Division 1	at Old Trafford	Attendance 30073
Result:	**Manchester United 0 Sheffield United 1**
Teamsheet:	Gaskell, Brennan, Dunne, Stiles, Foulkes, Setters, Giles, Pearson, Herd, McMillan, Charlton

Match # 2544 Tuesday 24/04/62	Football League Division 1	at Bramall Lane	Attendance 25324
Result:	**Sheffield United 2 Manchester United 3**
Teamsheet:	Gaskell, Brennan, Dunne, Nicholson, Foulkes, Setters, Giles, Pearson, McMillan, Stiles, Charlton
Scorer(s):	McMillan 2, Stiles

Match # 2545 Saturday 28/04/62	Football League Division 1	at Craven Cottage	Attendance 40113
Result:	**Fulham 2 Manchester United 0**
Teamsheet:	Gaskell, Brennan, Dunne, Setters, Foulkes, Nicholson, Giles, Pearson, McMillan, Stiles, Charlton

SEASON 1961/62 SUMMARY

APPEARANCES

PLAYER	LGE	FAC	TOT
Brennan	41	6	47
Foulkes	40	7	47
Setters	38	7	45
Charlton	37	6	43
Stiles	34	4	38
Giles	30	7	37
Dunne	28	7	35
Herd	27	5	32
Gaskell	21	7	28
Lawton	20	7	27
Quixall	21	3	24
Nicholson	17	4	21
Cantwell	17	2	19
Pearson	17	–	17
Chisnall	9	4	13
Gregg	13	–	13
Viollet	13	–	13
McMillan	11	–	11
Moir	9	–	9
Briggs	8	–	8
Bradley	6	1	7
Dawson	4	–	4
Haydock	1	–	1

GOALSCORERS

PLAYER	LGE	FAC	TOT
Herd	14	3	17
Quixall	10	–	10
Charlton	8	2	10
Stiles	7	–	7
Viollet	7	–	7
Lawton	6	–	6
McMillan	6	–	6
Setters	3	1	4
Giles	2	1	3
Brennan	2	–	2
Cantwell	2	–	2
Dawson	2	–	2
Chisnall	1	–	1
Pearson	1	–	1
Nicholson	–	1	1
own goal	1	–	1

RESULTS & ATTENDANCES SUMMARY

		P	W	D	L	F	A	TOTAL	AVGE
League	H	21	10	3	8	44	31	703302	33491
	A	21	5	6	10	28	44	713245	33964
TOTAL		42	15	9	18	72	75	1416547	33727
FA Cup	H	4	3	1	0	5	2	219305	54826
	A	2	1	1	0	2	0	100490	50245
	N	1	0	0	1	1	3	65000	65000
TOTAL		7	4	2	1	8	5	384795	54971
Overall	H	25	13	4	8	49	33	922607	36904
	A	23	6	7	10	30	44	813735	35380
	N	1	0	0	1	1	3	65000	65000
TOTAL		49	19	11	19	80	80	1801342	36762

FINAL TABLE – LEAGUE DIVISION ONE

		P	W	D	L	F	A	W	D	L	F	A	PTS	GD
				HOME						AWAY				
1	Ipswich Town	42	17	2	2	58	28	7	6	8	35	39	56	26
2	Burnley	42	14	4	3	57	26	7	7	7	44	41	53	34
3	Tottenham Hotspur	42	14	4	3	59	34	7	6	8	29	35	52	19
4	Everton	42	17	2	2	64	21	3	9	9	24	33	51	34
5	Sheffield United	42	13	5	3	37	23	6	4	11	24	46	47	–8
6	Sheffield Wednesday	42	14	4	3	47	23	6	2	13	25	35	46	14
7	Aston Villa	42	13	5	3	45	20	5	3	13	20	36	44	9
8	West Ham United	42	11	6	4	49	37	6	4	11	27	45	44	–6
9	West Bromwich Albion	42	10	7	4	50	23	5	6	10	33	44	43	16
10	Arsenal	42	9	6	6	39	31	7	5	9	32	41	43	–1
11	Bolton Wanderers	42	11	7	3	35	22	5	3	13	27	44	42	–4
12	Manchester City	42	11	3	7	46	38	6	4	11	32	43	41	–3
13	Blackpool	42	10	4	7	41	30	5	7	9	29	45	41	–5
14	Leicester City	42	12	2	7	38	27	5	4	12	34	44	40	1
15	MANCHESTER UNITED	42	10	3	8	44	31	5	6	10	28	44	39	–3
16	Blackburn Rovers	42	10	6	5	33	22	4	5	12	17	36	39	–8
17	Birmingham City	42	9	6	6	37	35	5	4	12	28	46	38	–16
18	Wolverhampton Wanderers	42	8	7	6	38	34	5	3	13	35	52	36	–13
19	Nottingham Forest	42	12	4	5	39	23	1	6	14	24	56	36	–16
20	Fulham	42	8	3	10	38	34	5	4	12	28	40	33	–8
21	Cardiff City	42	6	9	6	30	33	3	5	13	20	48	32	–31
22	Chelsea	42	7	7	7	34	29	2	3	16	29	65	28	–31

SEASON 1962/63

Match # 2546   Saturday 18/08/62   Football League Division 1   at Old Trafford   Attendance 51685
Result: **Manchester United 2   West Bromwich Albion 2**
Teamsheet: Gaskell, Brennan, Dunne, Stiles, Foulkes, Setters, Giles, Quixall, Herd, Law, Moir
Scorer(s):   Herd, Law

Match # 2547   Wednesday 22/08/62   Football League Division 1   at Goodison Park   Attendance 69501
Result: **Everton 3   Manchester United 1**
Teamsheet: Gaskell, Brennan, Dunne, Stiles, Foulkes, Setters, Giles, Pearson, Herd, Law, Moir
Scorer(s):   Moir

Match # 2548   Saturday 25/08/62   Football League Division 1   at Highbury   Attendance 62308
Result: **Arsenal 1   Manchester United 3**
Teamsheet: Gaskell, Brennan, Dunne, Nicholson, Foulkes, Lawton, Giles, Chisnall, Herd, Law, Moir
Scorer(s):   Herd 2, Chisnall

Match # 2549   Wednesday 29/08/62   Football League Division 1   at Old Trafford   Attendance 63437
Result: **Manchester United 0   Everton 1**
Teamsheet: Gaskell, Brennan, Dunne, Nicholson, Foulkes, Lawton, Giles, Chisnall, Herd, Law, Moir

Match # 2550   Saturday 01/09/62   Football League Division 1   at Old Trafford   Attendance 39847
Result: **Manchester United 2   Birmingham City 0**
Teamsheet: Gaskell, Brennan, Dunne, Nicholson, Foulkes, Lawton, Giles, Chisnall, Herd, Law, Moir
Scorer(s):   Giles, Herd

Match # 2551   Wednesday 05/09/62   Football League Division 1   at Burnden Park   Attendance 44859
Result: **Bolton Wanderers 3   Manchester United 0**
Teamsheet: Gaskell, Brennan, Dunne, Nicholson, Foulkes, Lawton, Giles, Quixall, Herd, Law, Moir

Match # 2552   Saturday 08/09/62   Football League Division 1   at Brisbane Road   Attendance 24901
Result: **Leyton Orient 1   Manchester United 0**
Teamsheet: Gaskell, Brennan, Dunne, Nicholson, Foulkes, Lawton, Moir, Setters, Herd, Law, McMillan

Match # 2553   Wednesday 12/09/62   Football League Division 1   at Old Trafford   Attendance 37721
Result: **Manchester United 3   Bolton Wanderers 0**
Teamsheet: Gaskell, Brennan, Dunne, Stiles, Foulkes, Setters, Giles, Lawton, Herd, Law, Cantwell
Scorer(s):   Herd 2, Cantwell

Match # 2554   Saturday 15/09/62   Football League Division 1   at Old Trafford   Attendance 49193
Result: **Manchester United 2   Manchester City 3**
Teamsheet: Gaskell, Brennan, Dunne, Stiles, Foulkes, Nicholson, Giles, Lawton, Herd, Law, Cantwell
Scorer(s):   Law 2

Match # 2555   Saturday 22/09/62   Football League Division 1   at Old Trafford   Attendance 45954
Result: **Manchester United 2   Burnley 5**
Teamsheet: Gaskell, Brennan, Dunne, Stiles, Foulkes, Lawton, Giles, Law, Herd, Pearson, Moir
Scorer(s):   Law, Stiles

Match # 2556   Saturday 29/09/62   Football League Division 1   at Hillsborough   Attendance 40520
Result: **Sheffield Wednesday 1   Manchester United 0**
Teamsheet: Gregg, Brennan, Dunne, Stiles, Foulkes, Lawton, Giles, Law, Quixall, Chisnall, McMillan

Match # 2557   Saturday 06/10/62   Football League Division 1   at Bloomfield Road   Attendance 33242
Result: **Blackpool 2   Manchester United 2**
Teamsheet: Gregg, Brennan, Dunne, Stiles, Foulkes, Nicholson, Giles, Law, Herd, Lawton, McMillan
Scorer(s):   Herd 2

Match # 2558   Saturday 13/10/62   Football League Division 1   at Old Trafford   Attendance 42252
Result: **Manchester United 0   Blackburn Rovers 3**
Teamsheet: Gregg, Brennan, Dunne, Stiles, Foulkes, Nicholson, Giles, Law, Herd, Charlton, McMillan

Match # 2559   Wednesday 24/10/62   Football League Division 1   at White Hart Lane   Attendance 51314
Result: **Tottenham Hotspur 6   Manchester United 2**
Teamsheet: Gregg, Brennan, Cantwell, Stiles, Foulkes, Setters, Giles, Quixall, Herd, Law, Charlton
Scorer(s):   Herd, Quixall

Match # 2560   Saturday 27/10/62   Football League Division 1   at Old Trafford   Attendance 29204
Result: **Manchester United 3   West Ham United 1**
Teamsheet: Gregg, Brennan, Cantwell, Stiles, Foulkes, Setters, Giles, Quixall, Herd, Law, Charlton
Scorer(s):   Quixall 2, Law

Match # 2561   Saturday 03/11/62   Football League Division 1   at Portman Road   Attendance 18483
Result: **Ipswich Town 3   Manchester United 5**
Teamsheet: Gregg, Brennan, Cantwell, Stiles, Foulkes, Setters, Giles, Quixall, Herd, Law, Charlton
Scorer(s):   Law 4, Herd

Match # 2562   Saturday 10/11/62   Football League Division 1   at Old Trafford   Attendance 43810
Result: **Manchester United 3   Liverpool 3**
Teamsheet: Gregg, Brennan, Cantwell, Stiles, Foulkes, Setters, Giles, Quixall, Herd, Law, Charlton
Scorer(s):   Giles, Herd, Quixall

Match # 2563   Saturday 17/11/62   Football League Division 1   at Molineux   Attendance 27305
Result: **Wolverhampton Wanderers 2   Manchester United 3**
Teamsheet: Gregg, Brennan, Cantwell, Stiles, Foulkes, Setters, Giles, Quixall, Herd, Law, Charlton
Scorer(s):   Law 2, Herd

SEASON 1962/63 (continued)

Match # 2564 Saturday 24/11/62   Football League Division 1   at Old Trafford   Attendance 36852
Result: **Manchester United 2 Aston Villa 2**
Teamsheet: Gregg, Brennan, Cantwell, Stiles, Foulkes, Setters, Giles, Quixall, Herd, Law, Charlton
Scorer(s):   Quixall 2

Match # 2565 Saturday 01/12/62   Football League Division 1   at Bramall Lane   Attendance 25173
Result: **Sheffield United 1 Manchester United 1**
Teamsheet: Gregg, Brennan, Cantwell, Stiles, Foulkes, Setters, Giles, Quixall, Herd, Lawton, Charlton
Scorer(s):   Charlton

Match # 2566 Saturday 08/12/62   Football League Division 1   at Old Trafford   Attendance 27496
Result: **Manchester United 5 Nottingham Forest 1**
Teamsheet: Gregg, Brennan, Cantwell, Nicholson, Foulkes, Lawton, Giles, Quixall, Herd, Law, Charlton
Scorer(s):   Herd 2, Charlton, Giles, Law

Match # 2567 Saturday 15/12/62   Football League Division 1   at The Hawthorns   Attendance 18113
Result: **West Bromwich Albion 3 Manchester United 0**
Teamsheet: Gregg, Brennan, Cantwell, Stiles, Foulkes, Nicholson, Giles, Quixall, Herd, Law, Moir

Match # 2568 Wednesday 26/12/62   Football League Division 1   at Craven Cottage   Attendance 23928
Result: **Fulham 0 Manchester United 1**
Teamsheet: Gregg, Brennan, Cantwell, Stiles, Foulkes, Setters, Giles, Quixall, Herd, Law, Charlton
Scorer(s):   Charlton

Match # 2569 Saturday 23/02/63   Football League Division 1   at Old Trafford   Attendance 43121
Result: **Manchester United 1 Blackpool 1**
Teamsheet: Gregg, Brennan, Cantwell, Crerand, Foulkes, Setters, Giles, Quixall, Herd, Chisnall, Charlton
Scorer(s):   Herd

Match # 2570 Saturday 02/03/63   Football League Division 1   at Ewood Park   Attendance 27924
Result: **Blackburn Rovers 2 Manchester United 2**
Teamsheet: Gregg, Brennan, Cantwell, Crerand, Foulkes, Setters, Giles, Quixall, Herd, Law, Charlton
Scorer(s):   Charlton, Law

Match # 2571 Monday 04/03/63   FA Cup 3rd Round   at Old Trafford   Attendance 47703
Result: **Manchester United 5 Huddersfield Town 0**
Teamsheet: Gregg, Brennan, Cantwell, Stiles, Foulkes, Setters, Giles, Quixall, Herd, Law, Charlton
Scorer(s):   Law 3, Giles, Quixall

Match # 2572 Saturday 09/03/63   Football League Division 1   at Old Trafford   Attendance 53416
Result: **Manchester United 0 Tottenham Hotspur 2**
Teamsheet: Gregg, Brennan, Cantwell, Crerand, Foulkes, Stiles, Giles, Quixall, Herd, Law, Charlton

Match # 2573 Monday 11/03/63   FA Cup 4th Round   at Old Trafford   Attendance 52265
Result: **Manchester United 1 Aston Villa 0**
Teamsheet: Gregg, Brennan, Cantwell, Stiles, Foulkes, Setters, Giles, Quixall, Herd, Law, Charlton
Scorer(s):   Quixall

Match # 2574 Saturday 16/03/63   FA Cup 5th Round   at Old Trafford   Attendance 48298
Result: **Manchester United 2 Chelsea 1**
Teamsheet: Gregg, Brennan, Cantwell, Stiles, Foulkes, Setters, Giles, Quixall, Herd, Law, Charlton
Scorer(s):   Law, Quixall

Match # 2575 Monday 18/03/63   Football League Division 1   at Upton Park   Attendance 28950
Result: **West Ham United 3 Manchester United 1**
Teamsheet: Gregg, Brennan, Cantwell, Crerand, Foulkes, Setters, Giles, Stiles, Herd, Law, Charlton
Scorer(s):   Herd

Match # 2576 Saturday 23/03/63   Football League Division 1   at Old Trafford   Attendance 32792
Result: **Manchester United 0 Ipswich Town 1**
Teamsheet: Gregg, Brennan, Cantwell, Crerand, Foulkes, Setters, Giles, Quixall, Herd, Law, Charlton

Match # 2577 Saturday 30/03/63   FA Cup 6th Round   at Highfield Road   Attendance 44000
Result: **Coventry City 1 Manchester United 3**
Teamsheet: Gregg, Brennan, Dunne, Crerand, Foulkes, Setters, Giles, Quixall, Herd, Law, Charlton
Scorer(s):   Charlton 2, Quixall

Match # 2578 Monday 01/04/63   Football League Division 1   at Old Trafford   Attendance 28124
Result: **Manchester United 0 Fulham 2**
Teamsheet: Gregg, Brennan, Dunne, Crerand, Foulkes, Setters, Giles, Chisnall, Quixall, Law, Charlton

Match # 2579 Tuesday 09/04/63   Football League Division 1   at Villa Park   Attendance 26867
Result: **Aston Villa 1 Manchester United 2**
Teamsheet: Gregg, Brennan, Cantwell, Crerand, Foulkes, Setters, Giles, Stiles, Herd, Quixall, Charlton
Scorer(s):   Charlton, Stiles

Match # 2580 Saturday 13/04/63   Football League Division 1   at Anfield   Attendance 51529
Result: **Liverpool 1 Manchester United 0**
Teamsheet: Gregg, Brennan, Dunne, Crerand, Foulkes, Setters, Giles, Stiles, Quixall, Law, Charlton

Match # 2581 Monday 15/04/63   Football League Division 1   at Old Trafford   Attendance 50005
Result: **Manchester United 2 Leicester City 2**
Teamsheet: Gregg, Brennan, Dunne, Crerand, Foulkes, Setters, Quixall, Stiles, Herd, Law, Charlton
Scorer(s):   Charlton, Herd

SEASON 1962/63 (continued)

Match # 2582   Tuesday 16/04/63   Football League Division 1   at Filbert Street   Attendance 37002
Result: **Leicester City 4 Manchester United 3**
Teamsheet: Gregg, Brennan, Dunne, Crerand, Foulkes, Setters, Quixall, Stiles, Herd, Law, Charlton
Scorer(s):   Law 3

Match # 2583   Saturday 20/04/63   Football League Division 1   at Old Trafford   Attendance 31179
Result: **Manchester United 1 Sheffield United 1**
Teamsheet: Gregg, Brennan, Dunne, Crerand, Foulkes, Setters, Quixall, Stiles, Herd, Law, Charlton
Scorer(s):   Law

Match # 2584   Monday 22/04/63   Football League Division 1   at Old Trafford   Attendance 36147
Result: **Manchester United 2 Wolverhampton Wanderers 1**
Teamsheet: Gaskell, Brennan, Dunne, Crerand, Foulkes, Setters, Quixall, Stiles, Herd, Law, Charlton
Scorer(s):   Herd, Law

Match # 2585   Saturday 27/04/63   FA Cup Semi-Final   at Villa Park   Attendance 65000
Result: **Manchester United 1 Southampton 0**
Teamsheet: Gaskell, Dunne, Cantwell, Crerand, Foulkes, Setters, Giles, Stiles, Herd, Law, Charlton
Scorer(s):   Law

Match # 2586   Wednesday 01/05/63   Football League Division 1   at Old Trafford   Attendance 31878
Result: **Manchester United 1 Sheffield Wednesday 3**
Teamsheet: Gaskell, Brennan, Cantwell, Crerand, Foulkes, Setters, Quixall, Stiles, Herd, Law, Charlton
Scorer(s):   Setters

Match # 2587   Saturday 04/05/63   Football League Division 1   at Turf Moor   Attendance 30266
Result: **Burnley 0 Manchester United 1**
Teamsheet: Gaskell, Dunne, Cantwell, Crerand, Foulkes, Setters, Giles, Stiles, Quixall, Law, Charlton
Scorer(s):   Law

Match # 2588   Monday 06/05/63   Football League Division 1   at Old Trafford   Attendance 35999
Result: **Manchester United 2 Arsenal 3**
Teamsheet: Gaskell, Dunne, Cantwell, Crerand, Foulkes, Setters, Giles, Stiles, Quixall, Law, Charlton
Scorer(s):   Law 2

Match # 2589   Friday 10/05/63   Football League Division 1   at St Andrews   Attendance 21814
Result: **Birmingham City 2 Manchester United 1**
Teamsheet: Gaskell, Dunne, Cantwell, Crerand, Foulkes, Stiles, Quixall, Giles, Herd, Law, Charlton
Scorer(s):   Law

Match # 2590   Wednesday 15/05/63   Football League Division 1   at Maine Road   Attendance 52424
Result: **Manchester City 1 Manchester United 1**
Teamsheet: Gaskell, Dunne, Cantwell, Crerand, Foulkes, Stiles, Quixall, Giles, Herd, Law, Charlton
Scorer(s):   Quixall

Match # 2591   Saturday 18/05/63   Football League Division 1   at Old Trafford   Attendance 32759
Result: **Manchester United 3 Leyton Orient 1**
Teamsheet: Gaskell, Dunne, Cantwell, Crerand, Foulkes, Setters, Quixall, Giles, Herd, Law, Charlton
Scorer(s):   Charlton, Law, own goal

Match # 2592   Monday 20/05/63   Football League Division 1   at City Ground   Attendance 16130
Result: **Nottingham Forest 3 Manchester United 2**
Teamsheet: Gaskell, Dunne, Cantwell, Crerand, Haydock, Brennan, Quixall, Stiles, Herd, Giles, Walker
Scorer(s):   Giles, Herd

Match # 2593   Saturday 25/05/63   FA Cup Final   at Wembley   Attendance 100000
Result: **Manchester United 3 Leicester City 1**
Teamsheet: Gaskell, Dunne, Cantwell, Crerand, Foulkes, Setters, Giles, Quixall, Herd, Law, Charlton
Scorer(s):   Herd 2, Law

SEASON 1962/63 SUMMARY

APPEARANCES

PLAYER	LGE	FAC	TOT
Foulkes	41	6	47
Law	38	6	44
Herd	37	6	43
Giles	36	6	42
Brennan	37	4	41
Quixall	31	5	36
Stiles	31	4	35
Charlton	28	6	34
Setters	27	6	33
Cantwell	25	5	30
Dunne	25	3	28
Gregg	24	4	28
Crerand	19	3	22
Gaskell	18	2	20
Lawton	12	–	12
Nicholson	10	–	10
Moir	9	–	9
Chisnall	6	–	6
McMillan	4	–	4
Pearson	2	–	2
Haydock	1	–	1
Walker	1	–	1

GOALSCORERS

PLAYER	LGE	FAC	TOT
Law	23	6	29
Herd	19	2	21
Quixall	7	4	11
Charlton	7	2	9
Giles	4	1	5
Stiles	2	–	2
Cantwell	1	–	1
Chisnall	1	–	1
Moir	1	–	1
Setters	1	–	1
own goal	1	–	1

RESULTS & ATTENDANCES SUMMARY

		P	W	D	L	F	A	TOTAL	AVGE
League	H	21	6	6	9	36	38	842871	40137
	A	21	6	4	11	31	43	732553	34883
	TOTAL	42	12	10	20	67	81	1575424	37510
FA Cup	H	3	3	0	0	8	1	148266	49422
	A	1	1	0	0	3	1	44000	44000
	N	2	2	0	0	4	1	165000	82500
	TOTAL	6	6	0	0	15	3	357266	59544
Overall	H	24	9	6	9	44	39	991137	41297
	A	22	7	4	11	34	44	776553	35298
	N	2	2	0	0	4	1	165000	82500
	TOTAL	48	18	10	20	82	84	1932690	40264

FINAL TABLE – LEAGUE DIVISION ONE

		P	W	D	L	F	A	W	D	L	F	A	PTS	GD
				HOME						AWAY				
1	Everton	42	14	7	0	48	17	11	4	6	36	25	61	42
2	Tottenham Hotspur	42	14	6	1	72	28	9	3	9	39	34	55	49
3	Burnley	42	14	4	3	41	17	8	6	7	37	40	54	21
4	Leicester City	42	14	6	1	53	23	6	6	9	26	30	52	26
5	Wolverhampton Wanderers	42	11	6	4	51	25	9	4	8	42	40	50	28
6	Sheffield Wednesday	42	10	5	6	38	26	9	5	7	39	37	48	14
7	Arsenal	42	11	4	6	44	33	7	6	8	42	44	46	9
8	Liverpool	42	13	3	5	45	22	4	7	10	26	37	44	12
9	Nottingham Forest	42	12	4	5	39	28	5	6	10	28	41	44	-2
10	Sheffield United	42	11	7	3	33	20	5	5	11	25	40	44	-2
11	Blackburn Rovers	42	11	4	6	55	34	4	8	9	24	37	42	8
12	West Ham United	42	8	6	7	39	34	6	6	9	34	35	40	4
13	Blackpool	42	8	7	6	34	27	5	7	9	24	37	40	-6
14	West Bromwich Albion	42	11	1	9	40	37	5	6	10	31	42	39	-8
15	Aston Villa	42	12	2	7	38	23	3	6	12	24	45	38	-6
16	Fulham	42	8	6	7	28	30	6	4	11	22	41	38	-21
17	Ipswich Town	42	5	8	8	34	39	7	3	11	25	39	35	-19
18	Bolton Wanderers	42	13	3	5	35	18	2	2	17	20	57	35	-20
19	MANCHESTER UNITED	42	6	6	9	36	38	6	4	11	31	43	34	-14
20	Birmingham City	42	6	8	7	40	40	4	5	12	23	50	33	-27
21	Manchester City	42	7	5	9	30	45	3	6	12	28	57	31	-44
22	Leyton Orient	42	4	5	12	22	37	2	4	15	15	44	21	-44

SEASON 1963/64

Match # 2594 Saturday 17/08/63   FA Charity Shield   at Goodison Park   Attendance 54840
Result: **Everton 4 Manchester United 0**
Teamsheet: Gaskell, Dunne, Cantwell, Crerand, Foulkes, Setters, Giles, Quixall, Herd, Law, Charlton

Match # 2595 Saturday 24/08/63   Football League Division 1   at Hillsborough   Attendance 32177
Result: **Sheffield Wednesday 3 Manchester United 3**
Teamsheet: Gregg, Dunne, Cantwell, Crerand, Foulkes, Setters, Moir, Chisnall, Sadler, Law, Charlton
Scorer(s):   Charlton 2, Moir

Match # 2596 Wednesday 28/08/63   Football League Division 1   at Old Trafford   Attendance 39921
Result: **Manchester United 2 Ipswich Town 0**
Teamsheet: Gregg, Dunne, Cantwell, Crerand, Foulkes, Setters, Moir, Chisnall, Sadler, Law, Charlton
Scorer(s):   Law 2

Match # 2597 Saturday 31/08/63   Football League Division 1   at Old Trafford   Attendance 62965
Result: **Manchester United 5 Everton 1**
Teamsheet: Gregg, Dunne, Cantwell, Crerand, Foulkes, Stiles, Moir, Chisnall, Sadler, Law, Charlton
Scorer(s):   Chisnall 2, Law 2, Sadler

Match # 2598 Tuesday 03/09/63   Football League Division 1   at Portman Road   Attendance 28113
Result: **Ipswich Town 2 Manchester United 7**
Teamsheet: Gregg, Dunne, Cantwell, Crerand, Foulkes, Setters, Moir, Chisnall, Sadler, Law, Charlton
Scorer(s):   Law 3, Chisnall, Moir, Sadler, Setters

Match # 2599 Saturday 07/09/63   Football League Division 1   at St Andrews   Attendance 36874
Result: **Birmingham City 1 Manchester United 1**
Teamsheet: Gregg, Dunne, Cantwell, Crerand, Foulkes, Setters, Moir, Chisnall, Sadler, Law, Charlton
Scorer(s):   Chisnall

Match # 2600 Wednesday 11/09/63   Football League Division 1   at Old Trafford   Attendance 47400
Result: **Manchester United 3 Blackpool 0**
Teamsheet: Gregg, Dunne, Cantwell, Crerand, Foulkes, Setters, Moir, Chisnall, Sadler, Law, Charlton
Scorer(s):   Charlton 2, Law

Match # 2601 Saturday 14/09/63   Football League Division 1   at Old Trafford   Attendance 50453
Result: **Manchester United 1 West Bromwich Albion 0**
Teamsheet: Gregg, Dunne, Cantwell, Crerand, Foulkes, Setters, Best, Stiles, Sadler, Chisnall, Charlton
Scorer(s):   Sadler

Match # 2602 Monday 16/09/63   Football League Division 1   at Bloomfield Road   Attendance 29806
Result: **Blackpool 1 Manchester United 0**
Teamsheet: Gregg, Dunne, Cantwell, Crerand, Foulkes, Setters, Moir, Stiles, Sadler, Chisnall, Charlton

Match # 2603 Saturday 21/09/63   Football League Division 1   at Highbury   Attendance 56776
Result: **Arsenal 2 Manchester United 1**
Teamsheet: Gregg, Dunne, Cantwell, Crerand, Foulkes, Setters, Herd, Chisnall, Sadler, Law, Charlton
Scorer(s):   Herd

Match # 2604 Wednesday 25/09/63   European CWC 1st Round 1st Leg   at Feyenoord Stadion   Attendance 20000
Result: **Willem II 1 Manchester United 1**
Teamsheet: Gregg, Dunne, Cantwell, Crerand, Foulkes, Setters, Herd, Chisnall, Sadler, Law, Charlton
Scorer(s):   Herd

Match # 2605 Saturday 28/09/63   Football League Division 1   at Old Trafford   Attendance 41374
Result: **Manchester United 3 Leicester City 1**
Teamsheet: Gregg, Dunne, Cantwell, Crerand, Foulkes, Setters, Moir, Chisnall, Sadler, Herd, Charlton
Scorer(s):   Herd 2, Setters

Match # 2606 Wednesday 02/10/63   Football League Division 1   at Stamford Bridge   Attendance 45351
Result: **Chelsea 1 Manchester United 1**
Teamsheet: Gregg, Dunne, Cantwell, Crerand, Foulkes, Setters, Moir, Chisnall, Sadler, Herd, Charlton
Scorer(s):   Setters

Match # 2607 Saturday 05/10/63   Football League Division 1   at Burnden Park   Attendance 35872
Result: **Bolton Wanderers 0 Manchester United 1**
Teamsheet: Gregg, Dunne, Cantwell, Crerand, Foulkes, Setters, Herd, Chisnall, Sadler, Stiles, Charlton
Scorer(s):   Herd

Match # 2608 Tuesday 15/10/63   European CWC 1st Round 2nd Leg   at Old Trafford   Attendance 46272
Result: **Manchester United 6 Willem II 1**
Teamsheet: Gregg, Dunne, Cantwell, Crerand, Foulkes, Setters, Quixall, Chisnall, Herd, Law, Charlton
Scorer(s):   Law 3, Charlton, Chisnall, Setters

Match # 2609 Saturday 19/10/63   Football League Division 1   at City Ground   Attendance 41426
Result: **Nottingham Forest 1 Manchester United 2**
Teamsheet: Gregg, Dunne, Cantwell, Crerand, Foulkes, Setters, Quixall, Chisnall, Herd, Law, Charlton
Scorer(s):   Chisnall, Quixall

Match # 2610 Saturday 26/10/63   Football League Division 1   at Old Trafford   Attendance 45120
Result: **Manchester United 0 West Ham United 1**
Teamsheet: Gregg, Dunne, Cantwell, Crerand, Foulkes, Stiles, Moir, Chisnall, Herd, Law, Charlton

Match # 2611 Monday 28/10/63   Football League Division 1   at Old Trafford   Attendance 41169
Result: **Manchester United 2 Blackburn Rovers 2**
Teamsheet: Gregg, Dunne, Cantwell, Crerand, Foulkes, Setters, Moir, Chisnall, Quixall, Law, Charlton
Scorer(s):   Quixall 2

SEASON 1963/64 (continued)

Match # 2612 Saturday 02/11/63   Football League Division 1   at Molineux   Attendance 34159
Result: **Wolverhampton Wanderers 2   Manchester United 0**
Teamsheet: Gregg, Dunne, Cantwell, Crerand, Foulkes, Setters, Moir, Chisnall, Quixall, Law, Charlton

Match # 2613 Saturday 09/11/63   Football League Division 1   at Old Trafford   Attendance 57413
Result: **Manchester United 4   Tottenham Hotspur 1**
Teamsheet: Gregg, Dunne, Cantwell, Crerand, Foulkes, Setters, Quixall, Moore, Herd, Law, Charlton
Scorer(s): Law 3, Herd

Match # 2614 Saturday 16/11/63   Football League Division 1   at Villa Park   Attendance 36276
Result: **Aston Villa 4   Manchester United 0**
Teamsheet: Gregg, Dunne, Cantwell, Crerand, Foulkes, Setters, Quixall, Moore, Herd, Law, Charlton

Match # 2615 Saturday 23/11/63   Football League Division 1   at Old Trafford   Attendance 54654
Result: **Manchester United 0   Liverpool 1**
Teamsheet: Gregg, Dunne, Cantwell, Crerand, Foulkes, Setters, Quixall, Moore, Herd, Law, Charlton

Match # 2616 Saturday 30/11/63   Football League Division 1   at Bramall Lane   Attendance 30615
Result: **Sheffield United 1   Manchester United 2**
Teamsheet: Gaskell, Dunne, Cantwell, Crerand, Foulkes, Setters, Quixall, Moore, Herd, Law, Charlton
Scorer(s): Law 2

Match # 2617 Tuesday 03/12/63   European CWC 2nd Round 1st Leg   at White Hart Lane   Attendance 57447
Result: **Tottenham Hotspur 2   Manchester United 0**
Teamsheet: Gaskell, Dunne, Cantwell, Crerand, Foulkes, Setters, Quixall, Stiles, Herd, Law, Charlton

Match # 2618 Saturday 07/12/63   Football League Division 1   at Old Trafford   Attendance 52232
Result: **Manchester United 5   Stoke City 2**
Teamsheet: Gaskell, Dunne, Cantwell, Crerand, Foulkes, Setters, Quixall, Moore, Herd, Law, Charlton
Scorer(s): Law 4, Herd

Match # 2619 Tuesday 10/12/63   European CWC 2nd Round 2nd Leg   at Old Trafford   Attendance 50000
Result: **Manchester United 4   Tottenham Hotspur 1**
Teamsheet: Gaskell, Dunne, Cantwell, Crerand, Foulkes, Setters, Quixall, Chisnall, Sadler, Herd, Charlton
Scorer(s): Charlton 2, Herd 2

Match # 2620 Saturday 14/12/63   Football League Division 1   at Old Trafford   Attendance 35139
Result: **Manchester United 3   Sheffield Wednesday 1**
Teamsheet: Gaskell, Brennan, Dunne, Crerand, Foulkes, Setters, Chisnall, Moore, Sadler, Herd, Charlton
Scorer(s): Herd 3

Match # 2621 Saturday 21/12/63   Football League Division 1   at Goodison Park   Attendance 48027
Result: **Everton 4   Manchester United 0**
Teamsheet: Gaskell, Dunne, Cantwell, Crerand, Foulkes, Setters, Moir, Moore, Sadler, Herd, Charlton

Match # 2622 Thursday 26/12/63   Football League Division 1   at Turf Moor   Attendance 35764
Result: **Burnley 6   Manchester United 1**
Teamsheet: Gaskell, Dunne, Cantwell, Crerand, Foulkes, Setters, Quixall, Moore, Charlton, Herd, Brennan
Scorer(s): Herd

Match # 2623 Saturday 28/12/63   Football League Division 1   at Old Trafford   Attendance 47834
Result: **Manchester United 5   Burnley 1**
Teamsheet: Gaskell, Dunne, Cantwell, Crerand, Foulkes, Setters, Anderson, Moore, Charlton, Herd, Best
Scorer(s): Herd 2, Moore 2, Best

Match # 2624 Saturday 04/01/64   FA Cup 3rd Round   at The Dell   Attendance 29164
Result: **Southampton 2   Manchester United 3**
Teamsheet: Gaskell, Dunne, Cantwell, Crerand, Foulkes, Setters, Anderson, Moore, Charlton, Herd, Best
Scorer(s): Crerand, Herd, Moore

Match # 2625 Saturday 11/01/64   Football League Division 1   at Old Trafford   Attendance 44695
Result: **Manchester United 1   Birmingham City 2**
Teamsheet: Gaskell, Dunne, Cantwell, Crerand, Foulkes, Setters, Herd, Moore, Sadler, Law, Best
Scorer(s): Sadler

Match # 2626 Saturday 18/01/64   Football League Division 1   at The Hawthorns   Attendance 25624
Result: **West Bromwich Albion 1   Manchester United 4**
Teamsheet: Gaskell, Dunne, Cantwell, Crerand, Foulkes, Setters, Herd, Moore, Charlton, Law, Best
Scorer(s): Law 2, Best, Charlton

Match # 2627 Saturday 25/01/64   FA Cup 4th Round   at Old Trafford   Attendance 55772
Result: **Manchester United 4   Bristol Rovers 1**
Teamsheet: Gaskell, Dunne, Cantwell, Crerand, Foulkes, Setters, Herd, Chisnall, Charlton, Law, Best
Scorer(s): Law 3, Herd

Match # 2628 Saturday 01/02/64   Football League Division 1   at Old Trafford   Attendance 48340
Result: **Manchester United 3   Arsenal 1**
Teamsheet: Gaskell, Brennan, Dunne, Stiles, Foulkes, Setters, Herd, Moore, Charlton, Law, Best
Scorer(s): Herd, Law, Setters

Match # 2629 Saturday 08/02/64   Football League Division 1   at Filbert Street   Attendance 35538
Result: **Leicester City 3   Manchester United 2**
Teamsheet: Gaskell, Brennan, Dunne, Crerand, Foulkes, Setters, Herd, Moore, Charlton, Law, Best
Scorer(s): Herd, Law

SEASON 1963/64 (continued)

Match # 2630 Saturday 15/02/64   FA Cup 5th Round   at Oakwell   Attendance 38076
Result: **Barnsley 0 Manchester United 4**
Teamsheet: Gaskell, Brennan, Dunne, Crerand, Foulkes, Setters, Herd, Stiles, Charlton, Law, Best
Scorer(s): Law 2, Best, Herd

Match # 2631 Wednesday 19/02/64   Football League Division 1   at Old Trafford   Attendance 33926
Result: **Manchester United 5 Bolton Wanderers 0**
Teamsheet: Gaskell, Brennan, Dunne, Crerand, Foulkes, Setters, Herd, Stiles, Charlton, Law, Best
Scorer(s): Best 2, Herd 2, Charlton

Match # 2632 Saturday 22/02/64   Football League Division 1   at Ewood Park   Attendance 36726
Result: **Blackburn Rovers 1 Manchester United 3**
Teamsheet: Gaskell, Brennan, Dunne, Crerand, Foulkes, Setters, Herd, Chisnall, Charlton, Law, Best
Scorer(s): Law 2, Chisnall

Match # 2633 Wednesday 26/02/64   European CWC Quarter-Final 1st Leg   at Old Trafford   Attendance 60000
Result: **Manchester United 4 Sporting Lisbon 1**
Teamsheet: Gaskell, Brennan, Dunne, Crerand, Foulkes, Setters, Herd, Stiles, Charlton, Law, Best
Scorer(s): Law 3, Charlton

Match # 2634 Saturday 29/02/64   FA Cup 6th Round   at Old Trafford   Attendance 63700
Result: **Manchester United 3 Sunderland 3**
Teamsheet: Gaskell, Brennan, Dunne, Crerand, Foulkes, Setters, Herd, Stiles, Charlton, Law, Best
Scorer(s): Best, Charlton, own goal

Match # 2635 Wednesday 04/03/64   FA Cup 6th Round Replay   at Roker Park   Attendance 68000
Result: **Sunderland 2 Manchester United 2**
Teamsheet: Gaskell, Brennan, Dunne, Crerand, Foulkes, Setters, Herd, Chisnall, Charlton, Law, Best
Scorer(s): Charlton, Law

Match # 2636 Saturday 07/03/64   Football League Division 1   at Upton Park   Attendance 27027
Result: **West Ham United 0 Manchester United 2**
Teamsheet: Gaskell, Brennan, Dunne, Crerand, Tranter, Stiles, Anderson, Chisnall, Sadler, Herd, Moir
Scorer(s): Herd, Sadler

Match # 2637 Monday 09/03/64   FA Cup 6th Round 2nd Replay   at Leeds Road   Attendance 54952
Result: **Manchester United 5 Sunderland 1**
Teamsheet: Gaskell, Brennan, Dunne, Crerand, Foulkes, Setters, Herd, Chisnall, Charlton, Law, Best
Scorer(s): Law 3, Chisnall, Herd

Match # 2638 Saturday 14/03/64   FA Cup Semi-Final   at Hillsborough   Attendance 65000
Result: **Manchester United 1 West Ham United 3**
Teamsheet: Gaskell, Brennan, Dunne, Crerand, Foulkes, Setters, Herd, Chisnall, Charlton, Law, Best
Scorer(s): Law

Match # 2639 Wednesday 18/03/64   European CWC Quarter-Final 2nd Leg   at de Jose Alvalade   Attendance 40000
Result: **Sporting Lisbon 5 Manchester United 0**
Teamsheet: Gaskell, Brennan, Dunne, Crerand, Foulkes, Setters, Herd, Chisnall, Charlton, Law, Best

Match # 2640 Saturday 21/03/64   Football League Division 1   at White Hart Lane   Attendance 56392
Result: **Tottenham Hotspur 2 Manchester United 3**
Teamsheet: Gaskell, Brennan, Dunne, Crerand, Foulkes, Stiles, Best, Moore, Sadler, Law, Charlton
Scorer(s): Charlton, Law, Moore

Match # 2641 Monday 23/03/64   Football League Division 1   at Old Trafford   Attendance 42931
Result: **Manchester United 1 Chelsea 1**
Teamsheet: Gaskell, Brennan, Dunne, Crerand, Foulkes, Stiles, Best, Moore, Sadler, Law, Charlton
Scorer(s): Law

Match # 2642 Friday 27/03/64   Football League Division 1   at Craven Cottage   Attendance 41769
Result: **Fulham 2 Manchester United 2**
Teamsheet: Gaskell, Brennan, Dunne, Crerand, Foulkes, Stiles, Best, Moore, Herd, Law, Charlton
Scorer(s): Herd, Law

Match # 2643 Saturday 28/03/64   Football League Division 1   at Old Trafford   Attendance 44470
Result: **Manchester United 2 Wolverhampton Wanderers 2**
Teamsheet: Gregg, Brennan, Cantwell, Crerand, Foulkes, Stiles, Best, Chisnall, Herd, Setters, Charlton
Scorer(s): Charlton, Herd

Match # 2644 Monday 30/03/64   Football League Division 1   at Old Trafford   Attendance 42279
Result: **Manchester United 3 Fulham 0**
Teamsheet: Gregg, Brennan, Dunne, Crerand, Foulkes, Stiles, Moir, Moore, Herd, Law, Charlton
Scorer(s): Crerand, Foulkes, Herd

Match # 2645 Saturday 04/04/64   Football League Division 1   at Anfield   Attendance 52559
Result: **Liverpool 3 Manchester United 0**
Teamsheet: Gregg, Brennan, Dunne, Crerand, Foulkes, Setters, Best, Stiles, Herd, Law, Charlton

Match # 2646 Monday 06/04/64   Football League Division 1   at Old Trafford   Attendance 25848
Result: **Manchester United 1 Aston Villa 0**
Teamsheet: Gregg, Brennan, Dunne, Crerand, Foulkes, Stiles, Best, Charlton, Herd, Law, Moir
Scorer(s): Law

Match # 2647 Monday 13/04/64   Football League Division 1   at Old Trafford   Attendance 27587
Result: **Manchester United 2 Sheffield United 1**
Teamsheet: Gregg, Brennan, Cantwell, Crerand, Foulkes, Stiles, Best, Charlton, Herd, Law, Moir
Scorer(s): Law, Moir

SEASON 1963/64 (continued)

Match # 2648   Saturday 18/04/64   Football League Division 1   at Victoria Ground   Attendance 45670
Result: **Stoke City 3   Manchester United 1**
Teamsheet: Gregg, Brennan, Dunne, Crerand, Foulkes, Stiles, Best, Charlton, Sadler, Herd, Moir
Scorer(s):   Charlton

Match # 2649   Saturday 25/04/64   Football League Division 1   at Old Trafford   Attendance 31671
Result: **Manchester United 3   Nottingham Forest 1**
Teamsheet: Gaskell, Brennan, Dunne, Crerand, Foulkes, Setters, Best, Moore, Herd, Law, Charlton
Scorer(s):   Law 2, Moore

SEASON 1963/64 SUMMARY

APPEARANCES

PLAYER	LGE	FAC	ECWC	CS	TOT
Crerand	41	7	6	1	55
Foulkes	41	7	6	1	55
Charlton	40	7	6	1	54
Dunne A	40	7	6	1	54
Setters	32	7	6	1	46
Herd	30	7	6	1	44
Law	30	6	5	1	42
Cantwell	28	2	4	1	35
Gaskell	17	7	4	1	29
Chisnall	20	4	4	–	28
Gregg	25	–	2	–	27
Best	17	7	2	–	26
Brennan	17	5	2	–	24
Sadler	19	–	2	–	21
Stiles	17	2	2	–	21
Moore	18	1	–	–	19
Moir	18	–	–	–	18
Quixall	9	–	3	1	13
Anderson	2	1	–	–	3
Giles	–	–	–	1	1
Tranter	1	–	–	–	1

GOALSCORERS

PLAYER	LGE	FAC	ECWC	CS	TOT
Law	30	10	6	–	46
Herd	20	4	3	–	27
Charlton	9	2	4	–	15
Chisnall	6	1	1	–	8
Best	4	2	–	–	6
Sadler	5	–	–	–	5
Moore	4	1	–	–	5
Setters	4	–	1	–	5
Moir	3	–	–	–	3
Quixall	3	–	–	–	3
Crerand	1	1	–	–	2
Foulkes	1	–	–	–	1
own goal	–	1	–	–	1

RESULTS & ATTENDANCES SUMMARY

		P	W	D	L	F	A	TOTAL	AVGE
League	H	21	15	3	3	54	19	917421	43687
	A	21	8	4	9	36	43	812541	38692
	TOTAL	42	23	7	12	90	62	1729962	41190
FA Cup	H	2	1	1	0	7	4	119472	59736
	A	3	2	1	0	9	4	135240	45080
	N	2	1	0	1	6	4	119952	59976
	TOTAL	7	4	2	1	22	12	374664	53523
European	H	3	3	0	0	14	3	156272	52091
CWC	A	3	0	1	2	1	8	117447	39149
	TOTAL	6	3	1	2	15	11	273719	45620
Charity	H	0	0	0	0	0	0	0	n/a
Shield	A	1	0	0	1	0	4	54840	54840
	TOTAL	1	0	0	1	0	4	54840	54840
Overall	H	26	19	4	3	75	26	1193165	45891
	A	28	10	6	12	46	59	1120068	40002
	N	2	1	0	1	6	4	119952	59976
	TOTAL	56	30	10	16	127	89	2433185	43450

FINAL TABLE – LEAGUE DIVISION ONE

		P	W	D	L	F	A	W	D	L	F	A	PTS	GD
				HOME						AWAY				
1	Liverpool	42	16	0	5	60	18	10	5	6	32	27	57	47
2	MANCHESTER UNITED	42	15	3	3	54	19	8	4	9	36	43	53	28
3	Everton	42	14	4	3	53	26	7	6	8	31	38	52	20
4	Tottenham Hotspur	42	13	3	5	54	31	9	4	8	43	50	51	16
5	Chelsea	42	12	3	6	36	24	8	7	6	36	32	50	16
6	Sheffield Wednesday	42	15	3	3	50	24	4	8	9	34	43	49	17
7	Blackburn Rovers	42	10	4	7	44	28	8	6	7	45	37	46	24
8	Arsenal	42	10	7	4	56	37	7	4	10	34	45	45	8
9	Burnley	42	14	3	4	46	23	3	7	11	25	41	44	7
10	West Bromwich Albion	42	9	6	6	43	35	7	5	9	27	26	43	9
11	Leicester City	42	9	4	8	33	27	7	7	7	28	31	43	3
12	Sheffield United	42	10	6	5	35	22	6	5	10	26	42	43	-3
13	Nottingham Forest	42	9	5	7	34	24	7	4	10	30	44	41	-4
14	West Ham United	42	8	7	6	45	38	6	5	10	24	36	40	-5
15	Fulham	42	11	8	2	45	23	2	5	14	13	42	39	-7
16	Wolverhampton Wanderers	42	6	9	6	36	34	6	6	9	34	46	39	-10
17	Stoke City	42	9	6	6	49	33	5	4	12	28	45	38	-1
18	Blackpool	42	8	6	7	26	29	5	3	13	26	44	35	-21
19	Aston Villa	42	8	6	7	35	29	3	6	12	27	42	34	-9
20	Birmingham City	42	7	7	7	33	32	4	0	17	21	60	29	-38
21	Bolton Wanderers	42	6	5	10	30	35	4	3	17	18	45	28	-32
22	Ipswich Town	42	9	3	9	38	45	0	4	14	18	76	25	-65

SEASON 1964/65

Match # 2650 Saturday 22/08/64 Football League Division 1 at Old Trafford Attendance 52007
Result: **Manchester United 2 West Bromwich Albion 2**
Teamsheet: Gaskell, Brennan, Dunne A, Setters, Foulkes, Stiles, Connelly, Charlton, Herd, Law, Best
Scorer(s): Charlton, Law

Match # 2651 Monday 24/08/64 Football League Division 1 at Upton Park Attendance 37070
Result: **West Ham United 3 Manchester United 1**
Teamsheet: Gaskell, Brennan, Dunne A, Setters, Foulkes, Stiles, Connelly, Charlton, Herd, Law, Best
Scorer(s): Law

Match # 2652 Saturday 29/08/64 Football League Division 1 at Filbert Street Attendance 32373
Result: **Leicester City 2 Manchester United 2**
Teamsheet: Gaskell, Brennan, Dunne A, Crerand, Foulkes, Stiles, Connelly, Charlton, Sadler, Law, Best
Scorer(s): Law, Sadler

Match # 2653 Wednesday 02/09/64 Football League Division 1 at Old Trafford Attendance 45123
Result: **Manchester United 3 West Ham United 1**
Teamsheet: Gaskell, Brennan, Dunne A, Crerand, Foulkes, Stiles, Connelly, Charlton, Sadler, Law, Best
Scorer(s): Best, Connelly, Law

Match # 2654 Saturday 05/09/64 Football League Division 1 at Craven Cottage Attendance 36291
Result: **Fulham 2 Manchester United 1**
Teamsheet: Gaskell, Brennan, Dunne A, Crerand, Foulkes, Stiles, Connelly, Charlton, Sadler, Law, Best
Scorer(s): Connelly

Match # 2655 Tuesday 08/09/64 Football League Division 1 at Goodison Park Attendance 63024
Result: **Everton 3 Manchester United 3**
Teamsheet: Dunne P, Brennan, Dunne A, Crerand, Foulkes, Stiles, Connelly, Charlton, Herd, Law, Best
Scorer(s): Connelly, Herd, Law

Match # 2656 Saturday 12/09/64 Football League Division 1 at Old Trafford Attendance 45012
Result: **Manchester United 3 Nottingham Forest 0**
Teamsheet: Dunne P, Brennan, Dunne A, Crerand, Foulkes, Setters, Connelly, Charlton, Herd, Stiles, Best
Scorer(s): Herd 2, Connelly

Match # 2657 Wednesday 16/09/64 Football League Division 1 at Old Trafford Attendance 49968
Result: **Manchester United 2 Everton 1**
Teamsheet: Dunne P, Brennan, Dunne A, Crerand, Foulkes, Stiles, Connelly, Charlton, Herd, Law, Best
Scorer(s): Best, Law

Match # 2658 Saturday 19/09/64 Football League Division 1 at Victoria Ground Attendance 40031
Result: **Stoke City 1 Manchester United 2**
Teamsheet: Dunne P, Brennan, Dunne A, Crerand, Foulkes, Setters, Connelly, Charlton, Herd, Stiles, Best
Scorer(s): Connelly, Herd

Match # 2659 Wednesday 23/09/64 Inter-Cities' Fairs Cup 1st Round 1st Leg at Roasunda Stadion Attendance 6537
Result: **Djurgardens 1 Manchester United 1**
Teamsheet: Dunne P, Brennan, Dunne A, Crerand, Foulkes, Stiles, Connelly, Charlton, Herd, Setters, Best
Scorer(s): Herd

Match # 2660 Saturday 26/09/64 Football League Division 1 at Old Trafford Attendance 53058
Result: **Manchester United 4 Tottenham Hotspur 1**
Teamsheet: Dunne P, Brennan, Dunne A, Crerand, Foulkes, Stiles, Connelly, Charlton, Herd, Law, Best
Scorer(s): Crerand 2, Law 2

Match # 2661 Wednesday 30/09/64 Football League Division 1 at Stamford Bridge Attendance 60769
Result: **Chelsea 0 Manchester United 2**
Teamsheet: Dunne P, Brennan, Dunne A, Crerand, Foulkes, Stiles, Connelly, Charlton, Herd, Law, Best
Scorer(s): Best, Law

Match # 2662 Saturday 03/10/64 Football League Division 1 at Turf Moor Attendance 30761
Result: **Burnley 0 Manchester United 0**
Teamsheet: Dunne P, Brennan, Dunne A, Crerand, Foulkes, Stiles, Connelly, Charlton, Herd, Law, Best

Match # 2663 Saturday 10/10/64 Football League Division 1 at Old Trafford Attendance 48577
Result: **Manchester United 1 Sunderland 0**
Teamsheet: Dunne P, Brennan, Dunne A, Crerand, Foulkes, Stiles, Connelly, Charlton, Herd, Law, Best
Scorer(s): Herd

Match # 2664 Saturday 17/10/64 Football League Division 1 at Molineux Attendance 26763
Result: **Wolverhampton Wanderers 2 Manchester United 4**
Teamsheet: Dunne P, Brennan, Dunne A, Crerand, Foulkes, Stiles, Connelly, Charlton, Herd, Law, Best
Scorer(s): Law 2, Herd, own goal

Match # 2665 Saturday 24/10/64 Football League Division 1 at Old Trafford Attendance 35807
Result: **Manchester United 7 Aston Villa 0**
Teamsheet: Dunne P, Brennan, Dunne A, Crerand, Foulkes, Setters, Connelly, Stiles, Herd, Law, Best
Scorer(s): Law 4, Herd 2, Connelly

Match # 2666 Tuesday 27/10/64 Inter-Cities' Fairs Cup 1st Round 2nd Leg at Old Trafford Attendance 38437
Result: **Manchester United 6 Djurgardens 1**
Teamsheet: Dunne P, Brennan, Dunne A, Crerand, Foulkes, Stiles, Connelly, Charlton, Herd, Law, Best
Scorer(s): Law 3, Charlton 2, Best

Match # 2667 Saturday 31/10/64 Football League Division 1 at Anfield Attendance 52402
Result: **Liverpool 0 Manchester United 2**
Teamsheet: Dunne P, Brennan, Dunne A, Crerand, Foulkes, Stiles, Connelly, Charlton, Herd, Law, Best
Scorer(s): Crerand, Herd

SEASON 1964/65 (continued)

Match # 2668 Saturday 07/11/64 Football League Division 1 at Old Trafford Attendance 50178
Result: **Manchester United 1 Sheffield Wednesday 0**
Teamsheet: Dunne P, Brennan, Dunne A, Crerand, Foulkes, Stiles, Connelly, Charlton, Herd, Law, Best
Scorer(s): Herd

Match # 2669 Wednesday 11/11/64 Inter-Cities' Fairs Cup 2nd Round 1st Leg at Rote Erde Stadion Attendance 25000
Result: **Borussia Dortmund 1 Manchester United 6**
Teamsheet: Dunne P, Brennan, Dunne A, Crerand, Foulkes, Stiles, Connelly, Charlton, Herd, Law, Best
Scorer(s): Charlton 3, Best, Herd, Law

Match # 2670 Saturday 14/11/64 Football League Division 1 at Bloomfield Road Attendance 31129
Result: **Blackpool 1 Manchester United 2**
Teamsheet: Dunne P, Brennan, Dunne A, Crerand, Foulkes, Stiles, Connelly, Charlton, Herd, Law, Moir
Scorer(s): Connelly, Herd

Match # 2671 Saturday 21/11/64 Football League Division 1 at Old Trafford Attendance 49633
Result: **Manchester United 3 Blackburn Rovers 0**
Teamsheet: Dunne P, Brennan, Dunne A, Crerand, Foulkes, Stiles, Connelly, Charlton, Herd, Law, Best
Scorer(s): Best, Connelly, Herd

Match # 2672 Saturday 28/11/64 Football League Division 1 at Highbury Attendance 59627
Result: **Arsenal 2 Manchester United 3**
Teamsheet: Dunne P, Brennan, Dunne A, Crerand, Foulkes, Stiles, Connelly, Charlton, Herd, Law, Best
Scorer(s): Law 2, Connelly

Match # 2673 Wednesday 02/12/64 Inter-Cities' Fairs Cup 2nd Round 2nd Leg at Old Trafford Attendance 31896
Result: **Manchester United 4 Borussia Dortmund 0**
Teamsheet: Dunne P, Brennan, Dunne A, Crerand, Foulkes, Stiles, Connelly, Charlton, Herd, Law, Best
Scorer(s): Charlton 2, Connelly, Law

Match # 2674 Saturday 05/12/64 Football League Division 1 at Old Trafford Attendance 53374
Result: **Manchester United 0 Leeds United 1**
Teamsheet: Dunne P, Brennan, Dunne A, Crerand, Foulkes, Stiles, Connelly, Charlton, Herd, Law, Best

Match # 2675 Saturday 12/12/64 Football League Division 1 at The Hawthorns Attendance 28126
Result: **West Bromwich Albion 1 Manchester United 1**
Teamsheet: Dunne P, Brennan, Dunne A, Crerand, Foulkes, Stiles, Connelly, Charlton, Herd, Law, Best
Scorer(s): Law

Match # 2676 Wednesday 16/12/64 Football League Division 1 at Old Trafford Attendance 25721
Result: **Manchester United 1 Birmingham City 1**
Teamsheet: Dunne P, Brennan, Dunne A, Crerand, Foulkes, Stiles, Connelly, Charlton, Sadler, Herd, Best
Scorer(s): Charlton

Match # 2677 Saturday 26/12/64 Football League Division 1 at Bramall Lane Attendance 37295
Result: **Sheffield United 0 Manchester United 1**
Teamsheet: Dunne P, Brennan, Dunne A, Crerand, Foulkes, Stiles, Connelly, Charlton, Sadler, Herd, Best
Scorer(s): Best

Match # 2678 Monday 28/12/64 Football League Division 1 at Old Trafford Attendance 42219
Result: **Manchester United 1 Sheffield United 1**
Teamsheet: Dunne P, Brennan, Dunne A, Crerand, Foulkes, Stiles, Connelly, Charlton, Sadler, Herd, Best
Scorer(s): Herd

Match # 2679 Saturday 09/01/65 FA Cup 3rd Round at Old Trafford Attendance 40000
Result: **Manchester United 2 Chester City 1**
Teamsheet: Dunne P, Brennan, Dunne A, Crerand, Foulkes, Stiles, Connelly, Charlton, Herd, Kinsey, Best
Scorer(s): Best, Kinsey

Match # 2680 Saturday 16/01/65 Football League Division 1 at City Ground Attendance 43009
Result: **Nottingham Forest 2 Manchester United 2**
Teamsheet: Dunne P, Brennan, Dunne A, Crerand, Foulkes, Stiles, Connelly, Charlton, Herd, Law, Best
Scorer(s): Law 2

Match # 2681 Wednesday 20/01/65 Inter-Cities' Fairs Cup 3rd Round 1st Leg at Old Trafford Attendance 50000
Result: **Manchester United 1 Everton 1**
Teamsheet: Dunne P, Brennan, Dunne A, Crerand, Foulkes, Stiles, Connelly, Charlton, Herd, Law, Best
Scorer(s): Connelly

Match # 2682 Saturday 23/01/65 Football League Division 1 at Old Trafford Attendance 50392
Result: **Manchester United 1 Stoke City 1**
Teamsheet: Dunne P, Brennan, Dunne A, Crerand, Foulkes, Stiles, Connelly, Charlton, Herd, Law, Best
Scorer(s): Law

Match # 2683 Saturday 30/01/65 FA Cup 4th Round at Victoria Ground Attendance 53009
Result: **Stoke City 0 Manchester United 0**
Teamsheet: Dunne P, Brennan, Dunne A, Crerand, Foulkes, Stiles, Connelly, Charlton, Herd, Law, Best

Match # 2684 Wednesday 03/02/65 FA Cup 4th Round Replay at Old Trafford Attendance 50814
Result: **Manchester United 1 Stoke City 0**
Teamsheet: Dunne P, Brennan, Dunne A, Crerand, Foulkes, Stiles, Connelly, Charlton, Herd, Law, Best
Scorer(s): Herd

Match # 2685 Saturday 06/02/65 Football League Division 1 at White Hart Lane Attendance 58639
Result: **Tottenham Hotspur 1 Manchester United 0**
Teamsheet: Dunne P, Brennan, Dunne A, Crerand, Foulkes, Stiles, Connelly, Charlton, Herd, Law, Best

SEASON 1964/65 (continued)

Match # 2686 Tuesday 09/02/65   Inter-Cities' Fairs Cup 3rd Round 2nd Leg   at Goodison Park   Attendance 54397
Result: **Everton 1 Manchester United 2**
Teamsheet: Dunne P, Brennan, Dunne A, Crerand, Foulkes, Stiles, Connelly, Charlton, Herd, Law, Best
Scorer(s):   Connelly, Herd

Match # 2687 Saturday 13/02/65   Football League Division 1   at Old Trafford   Attendance 38865
Result: **Manchester United 3 Burnley 2**
Teamsheet: Dunne P, Brennan, Dunne A, Crerand, Foulkes, Stiles, Connelly, Charlton, Herd, Law, Best
Scorer(s):   Best, Charlton, Herd

Match # 2688 Saturday 20/02/65   FA Cup 5th Round   at Old Trafford   Attendance 54000
Result: **Manchester United 2 Burnley 1**
Teamsheet: Dunne P, Brennan, Dunne A, Crerand, Foulkes, Stiles, Connelly, Charlton, Herd, Law, Best
Scorer(s):   Crerand, Law

Match # 2689 Wednesday 24/02/65   Football League Division 1   at Roker Park   Attendance 51336
Result: **Sunderland 1 Manchester United 0**
Teamsheet: Dunne P, Brennan, Dunne A, Crerand, Foulkes, Fitzpatrick, Connelly, Charlton, Herd, Law, Best

Match # 2690 Saturday 27/02/65   Football League Division 1   at Old Trafford   Attendance 37018
Result: **Manchester United 3 Wolverhampton Wanderers 0**
Teamsheet: Dunne P, Brennan, Dunne A, Crerand, Foulkes, Stiles, Connelly, Charlton, Herd, Law, Best
Scorer(s):   Charlton 2, Connelly

Match # 2691 Wednesday 10/03/65   FA Cup 6th Round   at Molineux   Attendance 53581
Result: **Wolverhampton Wanderers 3 Manchester United 5**
Teamsheet: Dunne P, Brennan, Dunne A, Crerand, Foulkes, Stiles, Connelly, Charlton, Herd, Law, Best
Scorer(s):   Law 2, Best, Crerand, Herd

Match # 2692 Saturday 13/03/65   Football League Division 1   at Old Trafford   Attendance 56261
Result: **Manchester United 4 Chelsea 0**
Teamsheet: Dunne P, Brennan, Dunne A, Crerand, Foulkes, Stiles, Connelly, Charlton, Herd, Law, Best
Scorer(s):   Herd 2, Best, Law

Match # 2693 Monday 15/03/65   Football League Division 1   at Old Trafford   Attendance 45402
Result: **Manchester United 4 Fulham 1**
Teamsheet: Dunne P, Brennan, Dunne A, Crerand, Foulkes, Stiles, Connelly, Charlton, Herd, Law, Best
Scorer(s):   Connelly 2, Herd 2

Match # 2694 Saturday 20/03/65   Football League Division 1   at Hillsborough   Attendance 33549
Result: **Sheffield Wednesday 1 Manchester United 0**
Teamsheet: Dunne P, Brennan, Dunne A, Crerand, Foulkes, Stiles, Connelly, Charlton, Herd, Law, Best

Match # 2695 Monday 22/03/65   Football League Division 1   at Old Trafford   Attendance 42318
Result: **Manchester United 2 Blackpool 0**
Teamsheet: Dunne P, Brennan, Dunne A, Crerand, Foulkes, Stiles, Connelly, Charlton, Herd, Law, Best
Scorer(s):   Law 2

Match # 2696 Saturday 27/03/65   FA Cup Semi-Final   at Hillsborough   Attendance 65000
Result: **Manchester United 0 Leeds United 0**
Teamsheet: Dunne P, Brennan, Dunne A, Crerand, Foulkes, Stiles, Connelly, Charlton, Herd, Law, Best

Match # 2697 Wednesday 31/03/65   FA Cup Semi-Final Replay   at City Ground   Attendance 46300
Result: **Manchester United 0 Leeds United 1**
Teamsheet: Dunne P, Brennan, Dunne A, Crerand, Foulkes, Stiles, Connelly, Charlton, Herd, Law, Best

Match # 2698 Saturday 03/04/65   Football League Division 1   at Ewood Park   Attendance 29363
Result: **Blackburn Rovers 0 Manchester United 5**
Teamsheet: Dunne P, Brennan, Dunne A, Crerand, Foulkes, Stiles, Connelly, Charlton, Herd, Law, Best
Scorer(s):   Charlton 3, Connelly, Herd

Match # 2699 Monday 12/04/65   Football League Division 1   at Old Trafford   Attendance 34114
Result: **Manchester United 1 Leicester City 0**
Teamsheet: Dunne P, Brennan, Dunne A, Crerand, Foulkes, Stiles, Connelly, Charlton, Herd, Best, Aston
Scorer(s):   Herd

Match # 2700 Saturday 17/04/65   Football League Division 1   at Elland Road   Attendance 52368
Result: **Leeds United 0 Manchester United 1**
Teamsheet: Dunne P, Brennan, Dunne A, Crerand, Foulkes, Stiles, Connelly, Charlton, Herd, Law, Best
Scorer(s):   Connelly

Match # 2701 Monday 19/04/65   Football League Division 1   at St Andrews   Attendance 28907
Result: **Birmingham City 2 Manchester United 4**
Teamsheet: Dunne P, Brennan, Dunne A, Crerand, Foulkes, Stiles, Connelly, Charlton, Cantwell, Law, Best
Scorer(s):   Best 2, Cantwell, Charlton

Match # 2702 Saturday 24/04/65   Football League Division 1   at Old Trafford   Attendance 55772
Result: **Manchester United 3 Liverpool 0**
Teamsheet: Dunne P, Brennan, Dunne A, Crerand, Foulkes, Stiles, Connelly, Charlton, Cantwell, Law, Best
Scorer(s):   Law 2, Connelly

Match # 2703 Monday 26/04/65   Football League Division 1   at Old Trafford   Attendance 51625
Result: **Manchester United 3 Arsenal 1**
Teamsheet: Dunne P, Brennan, Dunne A, Crerand, Foulkes, Stiles, Connelly, Charlton, Herd, Law, Best
Scorer(s):   Law 2, Best

SEASON 1964/65 (continued)

Match # 2704 Wednesday 28/04/65   Football League Division 1   at Villa Park   Attendance 36081
Result: **Aston Villa 2 Manchester United 1**
Teamsheet: Dunne P, Brennan, Dunne A, Fitzpatrick, Foulkes, Stiles, Connelly, Charlton, Herd, Law, Best
Scorer(s):   Charlton

Match # 2705 Wednesday 12/05/65   Inter-Cities' Fairs Cup Quarter-Final 1st Leg   at Stade de la Meinau   Attendance 30000
Result: **Strasbourg 0 Manchester United 5**
Teamsheet: Dunne P, Brennan, Dunne A, Crerand, Foulkes, Stiles, Connelly, Charlton, Herd, Law, Best
Scorer(s):   Law 2, Charlton, Connelly, Herd

Match # 2706 Wednesday 19/05/65   Inter-Cities' Fairs Cup Quarter-Final 2nd Leg at Old Trafford   Attendance 34188
Result: **Manchester United 0 Strasbourg 0**
Teamsheet: Dunne P, Brennan, Dunne A, Crerand, Foulkes, Stiles, Connelly, Charlton, Herd, Law, Best

Match # 2707 Monday 31/05/65   Inter-Cities' Fairs Cup Semi-Final 1st Leg   at Old Trafford   Attendance 39902
Result: **Manchester United 3 Ferencvaros 2**
Teamsheet: Dunne P, Brennan, Dunne A, Crerand, Foulkes, Stiles, Connelly, Charlton, Herd, Law, Best
Scorer(s):   Herd 2, Law

Match # 2708 Sunday 06/06/65   Inter-Cities' Fairs Cup Semi-Final 2nd Leg   at Nep Stadion   Attendance 50000
Result: **Ferencvaros 1 Manchester United 0**
Teamsheet: Dunne P, Brennan, Dunne A, Crerand, Foulkes, Stiles, Connelly, Charlton, Herd, Law, Best

Match # 2709 Wednesday 16/06/65   Inter-Cities' Fairs Cup Semi-Final Replay   at Nep Stadion   Attendance 60000
Result: **Ferencvaros 2 Manchester United 1**
Teamsheet: Dunne P, Brennan, Dunne A, Crerand, Foulkes, Stiles, Connelly, Charlton, Herd, Law, Best
Scorer(s):   Connelly

SEASON 1964/65 SUMMARY

APPEARANCES

PLAYER	LGE	FAC	ICFC	TOT
Brennan	42	7	11	60
Connelly	42	7	11	60
Dunne A	42	7	11	60
Foulkes	42	7	11	60
Best	41	7	11	59
Charlton	41	7	11	59
Stiles	41	7	11	59
Crerand	39	7	11	57
Dunne P	37	7	11	55
Herd	37	7	11	55
Law	36	6	10	52
Sadler	6	–	–	6
Setters	5	–	1	6
Gaskell	5	–	–	5
Cantwell	2	–	–	2
Fitzpatrick	2	–	–	2
Aston	1	–	–	1
Kinsey	–	1	–	1
Moir	1	–	–	1

GOALSCORERS

PLAYER	LGE	FAC	ICFC	TOT
Law	28	3	8	39
Herd	20	2	6	28
Connelly	15	–	5	20
Charlton	10	–	8	18
Best	10	2	2	14
Crerand	3	2	–	5
Cantwell	1	–	–	1
Sadler	1	–	–	1
Kinsey	–	1	–	1
own goal	1	–	–	1

RESULTS & ATTENDANCES SUMMARY

		P	W	D	L	F	A	TOTAL	AVGE
League	H	21	16	4	1	52	13	962444	45831
	A	21	10	5	6	37	26	868913	41377
	TOTAL	42	26	9	7	89	39	1831357	43604
FA Cup	H	3	3	0	0	5	2	144814	48271
	A	2	1	1	0	5	3	106590	53295
	N	2	0	1	1	0	1	111300	55650
	TOTAL	7	4	2	1	10	6	362704	51815
ICFC	H	5	3	2	0	14	4	194423	38885
	A	6	3	1	2	15	6	225934	37656
	TOTAL	11	6	3	2	29	10	420357	38214
Overall	H	29	22	6	1	71	19	1301681	44886
	A	29	14	7	8	57	35	1201437	41429
	N	2	0	1	1	0	1	111300	55650
	TOTAL	60	36	14	10	128	55	2614418	43574

FINAL TABLE – LEAGUE DIVISION ONE

		P	W	D	L	F	A	W	D	L	F	A	PTS	GD
				HOME						AWAY				
1	MANCHESTER UNITED	42	16	4	1	52	13	10	5	6	37	26	61	50
2	Leeds United	42	16	3	2	53	23	10	6	5	30	29	61	31
3	Chelsea	42	15	2	4	48	19	9	6	6	41	35	56	35
4	Everton	42	9	10	2	37	22	8	5	8	32	38	49	9
5	Nottingham Forest	42	10	7	4	45	33	7	6	8	26	34	47	4
6	Tottenham Hotspur	42	18	3	0	65	20	1	4	16	22	51	45	16
7	Liverpool	42	12	5	4	42	33	5	5	11	25	40	44	-6
8	Sheffield Wednesday	42	13	5	3	37	15	3	6	12	20	40	43	2
9	West Ham United	42	14	2	5	48	25	5	2	14	34	46	42	11
10	Blackburn Rovers	42	12	2	7	46	33	4	8	9	37	46	42	4
11	Stoke City	42	11	4	6	40	27	5	6	10	27	39	42	1
12	Burnley	42	9	9	3	39	26	7	1	13	31	44	42	0
13	Arsenal	42	11	5	5	42	31	6	2	13	27	44	41	-6
14	West Bromwich Albion	42	10	4	7	45	25	3	8	10	25	40	39	5
15	Sunderland	42	12	6	3	45	26	2	3	16	19	48	37	-10
16	Aston Villa	42	14	1	6	36	24	2	4	15	21	58	37	-25
17	Blackpool	42	9	7	5	41	28	3	4	14	26	50	35	-11
18	Leicester City	42	9	6	6	43	36	2	7	12	26	49	35	-16
19	Sheffield United	42	7	5	9	30	29	5	6	10	20	35	35	-14
20	Fulham	42	10	5	6	44	32	1	7	13	16	46	34	-18
21	Wolverhampton Wanderers	42	8	2	11	33	36	5	2	14	26	53	30	-30
22	Birmingham City	42	6	8	7	36	40	2	3	16	28	56	27	-32

SEASON 1965/66

Match # 2710 Saturday 14/08/65   FA Charity Shield   at Old Trafford   Attendance 48502
Result: **Manchester United 2 Liverpool 2   (TROPHY SHARED)**
Teamsheet: Dunne P, Brennan, Dunne A, Crerand, Cantwell, Stiles, Best, Charlton, Herd, Law, Aston
Scorer(s):   Best, Herd

Match # 2711 Saturday 21/08/65   Football League Division 1   at Old Trafford   Attendance 37524
Result: **Manchester United 1 Sheffield Wednesday 0**
Teamsheet: Dunne P, Brennan, Dunne A, Crerand, Foulkes, Stiles, Anderson, Charlton, Herd, Best, Aston
Scorer(s):   Herd

Match # 2712 Tuesday 24/08/65   Football League Division 1   at City Ground   Attendance 33744
Result: **Nottingham Forest 4 Manchester United 2**
Teamsheet: Dunne P, Brennan, Dunne A, Crerand, Foulkes, Stiles, Connelly, Charlton, Herd, Best, Aston
Scorer(s):   Aston, Best

Match # 2713 Saturday 28/08/65   Football League Division 1   at County Ground   Attendance 21140
Result: **Northampton Town 1 Manchester United 1**
Teamsheet: Gaskell, Dunne A, Cantwell, Crerand, Foulkes, Stiles, Connelly, Charlton, Herd, Law, Best
Scorer(s):   Connelly

Match # 2714 Wednesday 01/09/65   Football League Division 1   at Old Trafford   Attendance 38777
Result: **Manchester United 0 Nottingham Forest 0**
Teamsheet: Gaskell, Brennan, Dunne A, Crerand, Foulkes, Stiles, Connelly, Charlton, Herd, Law, Best

Match # 2715 Saturday 04/09/65   Football League Division 1   at Old Trafford   Attendance 37603
Result: **Manchester United 1 Stoke City 1**
Teamsheet: Gaskell, Brennan, Dunne A, Crerand, Foulkes, Stiles, Connelly, Charlton, Herd, Law, Best
Scorer(s):   Herd

Match # 2716 Wednesday 08/09/65   Football League Division 1   at St James' Park   Attendance 57380
Result: **Newcastle United 1 Manchester United 2**
Teamsheet: Gaskell, Brennan, Dunne A, Crerand, Foulkes, Stiles, Connelly, Charlton, Herd, Law, Best
Scorer(s):   Herd, Law

Match # 2717 Saturday 11/09/65   Football League Division 1   at Turf Moor   Attendance 30235
Result: **Burnley 3 Manchester United 0**
Teamsheet: Gaskell, Brennan, Dunne A, Crerand, Foulkes, Stiles, Connelly, Charlton, Herd, Law, Best

Match # 2718 Wednesday 15/09/65   Football League Division 1   at Old Trafford   Attendance 30401
Result: **Manchester United 1 Newcastle United 1**
Teamsheet: Gaskell, Brennan, Dunne A, Crerand, Foulkes, Stiles, Connelly, Charlton, Herd, Law, Best
Scorer(s):   Stiles

Match # 2719 Saturday 18/09/65   Football League Division 1   at Old Trafford   Attendance 37917
Result: **Manchester United 4 Chelsea 1**
Teamsheet: Gaskell, Brennan, Dunne A, Crerand, Foulkes, Stiles, Connelly, Charlton, Herd, Law, Aston
Scorer(s):   Law 3, Charlton

Match # 2720 Wednesday 22/09/65   European Cup Preliminary Round 1st Leg   at Olympiastadion   Attendance 25000
Result: **HJK Helsinki 2 Manchester United 3**
Teamsheet: Gaskell, Brennan, Dunne A, Fitzpatrick, Foulkes, Stiles, Connelly, Charlton, Herd, Law, Aston
Scorer(s):   Connelly, Herd, Law

Match # 2721 Saturday 25/09/65   Football League Division 1   at Highbury   Attendance 56757
Result: **Arsenal 4 Manchester United 2**
Teamsheet: Dunne P, Brennan, Dunne A, Crerand, Foulkes, Stiles, Connelly, Charlton, Herd, Law, Aston
Scorer(s):   Aston, Charlton

Match # 2722 Wednesday 06/10/65   European Cup Preliminary Round 2nd Leg   at Old Trafford   Attendance 30388
Result: **Manchester United 6 HJK Helsinki 0**
Teamsheet: Dunne P, Brennan, Dunne A, Crerand, Foulkes, Stiles, Connelly, Best, Charlton, Law, Aston
Scorer(s):   Connelly 3, Best 2, Charlton

Match # 2723 Saturday 09/10/65   Football League Division 1   at Old Trafford   Attendance 58161
Result: **Manchester United 2 Liverpool 0**
Teamsheet: Dunne P, Brennan, Dunne A, Crerand, Foulkes, Stiles, Connelly, Best, Charlton, Law, Aston
Scorer(s):   Best, Law

Match # 2724 Saturday 16/10/65   Football League Division 1   at White Hart Lane   Attendance 58051
Result: **Tottenham Hotspur 5 Manchester United 1**
Teamsheet: Dunne P, Brennan, Dunne A, Crerand, Foulkes, Stiles, Connelly, Best, Charlton, Law, Aston
Substitute(s):   Fitzpatrick   Scorer(s):   Charlton

Match # 2725 Saturday 23/10/65   Football League Division 1   at Old Trafford   Attendance 32716
Result: **Manchester United 4 Fulham 1**
Teamsheet: Dunne P, Brennan, Dunne A, Crerand, Foulkes, Stiles, Connelly, Best, Charlton, Herd, Aston
Scorer(s):   Herd 3, Charlton

Match # 2726 Saturday 30/10/65   Football League Division 1   at Bloomfield Road   Attendance 24703
Result: **Blackpool 1 Manchester United 2**
Teamsheet: Gregg, Brennan, Dunne A, Crerand, Foulkes, Stiles, Connelly, Best, Charlton, Herd, Aston
Scorer(s):   Herd 2

Match # 2727 Saturday 06/11/65   Football League Division 1   at Old Trafford   Attendance 38823
Result: **Manchester United 2 Blackburn Rovers 2**
Teamsheet: Gregg, Brennan, Dunne A, Crerand, Foulkes, Stiles, Best, Law, Charlton, Herd, Aston
Substitute(s):   Connelly   Scorer(s):   Charlton, Law

SEASON 1965/66 (continued)

Match # 2728   Saturday 13/11/65   Football League Division 1   at Filbert Street   Attendance 34551
Result: **Leicester City 0 Manchester United 5**
Teamsheet: Gregg, Dunne A, Cantwell, Crerand, Foulkes, Stiles, Best, Law, Charlton, Herd, Connelly
Scorer(s):   Herd 2, Best, Charlton, Connelly

Match # 2729   Wednesday 17/11/65   European Cup 1st Round 1st Leg   at Walter Ulbricht Stadium   Attendance 40000
Result: **ASK Vorwaerts 0 Manchester United 2**
Teamsheet: Gregg, Dunne A, Cantwell, Crerand, Foulkes, Stiles, Best, Law, Charlton, Herd, Connelly
Scorer(s):   Connelly, Law

Match # 2730   Saturday 20/11/65   Football League Division 1   at Old Trafford   Attendance 37922
Result: **Manchester United 3 Sheffield United 1**
Teamsheet: Gregg, Dunne A, Cantwell, Crerand, Sadler, Stiles, Best, Law, Charlton, Herd, Connelly
Scorer(s):   Best 2, Law

Match # 2731   Wednesday 01/12/65   European Cup 1st Round 2nd Leg   at Old Trafford   Attendance 30082
Result: **Manchester United 3 ASK Vorwaerts 1**
Teamsheet: Dunne P, Dunne A, Cantwell, Crerand, Foulkes, Stiles, Best, Law, Charlton, Herd, Connelly
Scorer(s):   Herd 3

Match # 2732   Saturday 04/12/65   Football League Division 1   at Old Trafford   Attendance 32924
Result: **Manchester United 0 West Ham United 0**
Teamsheet: Dunne P, Dunne A, Cantwell, Crerand, Foulkes, Stiles, Best, Law, Charlton, Herd, Connelly

Match # 2733   Saturday 11/12/65   Football League Division 1   at Roker Park   Attendance 37417
Result: **Sunderland 2 Manchester United 3**
Teamsheet: Dunne P, Dunne A, Cantwell, Crerand, Foulkes, Stiles, Best, Law, Charlton, Herd, Connelly
Scorer(s):   Best 2, Herd

Match # 2734   Wednesday 15/12/65   Football League Division 1   at Old Trafford   Attendance 32624
Result: **Manchester United 3 Everton 0**
Teamsheet: Gregg, Dunne A, Cantwell, Crerand, Foulkes, Stiles, Best, Law, Charlton, Herd, Connelly
Scorer(s):   Best, Charlton, Herd

Match # 2735   Saturday 18/12/65   Football League Division 1   at Old Trafford   Attendance 39270
Result: **Manchester United 5 Tottenham Hotspur 1**
Teamsheet: Gregg, Dunne A, Cantwell, Crerand, Foulkes, Stiles, Best, Law, Charlton, Herd, Connelly
Scorer(s):   Law 2, Charlton, Herd, own goal

Match # 2736   Monday 27/12/65   Football League Division 1   at Old Trafford   Attendance 54102
Result: **Manchester United 1 West Bromwich Albion 1**
Teamsheet: Gregg, Dunne A, Cantwell, Crerand, Foulkes, Stiles, Best, Law, Charlton, Herd, Connelly
Scorer(s):   Law

Match # 2737   Saturday 01/01/66   Football League Division 1   at Anfield   Attendance 53790
Result: **Liverpool 2 Manchester United 1**
Teamsheet: Gregg, Dunne A, Cantwell, Crerand, Foulkes, Stiles, Best, Law, Charlton, Herd, Connelly
Scorer(s):   Law

Match # 2738   Saturday 08/01/66   Football League Division 1   at Old Trafford   Attendance 39162
Result: **Manchester United 1 Sunderland 1**
Teamsheet: Gregg, Dunne A, Cantwell, Crerand, Foulkes, Stiles, Best, Law, Charlton, Herd, Aston
Scorer(s):   Best

Match # 2739   Wednesday 12/01/66   Football League Division 1   at Elland Road   Attendance 49672
Result: **Leeds United 1 Manchester United 1**
Teamsheet: Gregg, Dunne A, Cantwell, Crerand, Foulkes, Stiles, Best, Law, Charlton, Herd, Aston
Scorer(s):   Herd

Match # 2740   Saturday 15/01/66   Football League Division 1   at Craven Cottage   Attendance 33018
Result: **Fulham 0 Manchester United 1**
Teamsheet: Gregg, Dunne A, Cantwell, Crerand, Foulkes, Stiles, Best, Law, Charlton, Herd, Aston
Scorer(s):   Charlton

Match # 2741   Saturday 22/01/66   FA Cup 3rd Round   at Baseball Ground   Attendance 33827
Result: **Derby County 2 Manchester United 5**
Teamsheet: Gregg, Dunne A, Cantwell, Crerand, Foulkes, Stiles, Best, Law, Charlton, Herd, Aston
Scorer(s):   Best 2, Law 2, Herd

Match # 2742   Saturday 29/01/66   Football League Division 1   at Hillsborough   Attendance 39281
Result: **Sheffield Wednesday 0 Manchester United 0**
Teamsheet: Gregg, Dunne A, Cantwell, Crerand, Foulkes, Stiles, Best, Law, Charlton, Herd, Aston

Match # 2743   Wednesday 02/02/66   European Cup Quarter-Final 1st Leg   at Old Trafford   Attendance 64035
Result: **Manchester United 3 Benfica 2**
Teamsheet: Gregg, Dunne A, Cantwell, Crerand, Foulkes, Stiles, Best, Law, Charlton, Herd, Connelly
Scorer(s):   Foulkes, Herd, Law

Match # 2744   Saturday 05/02/66   Football League Division 1   at Old Trafford   Attendance 34986
Result: **Manchester United 6 Northampton Town 2**
Teamsheet: Gregg, Dunne A, Cantwell, Crerand, Foulkes, Stiles, Best, Law, Charlton, Herd, Connelly
Scorer(s):   Charlton 3, Law 2, Connelly

Match # 2745   Saturday 12/02/66   FA Cup 4th Round   at Old Trafford   Attendance 54263
Result: **Manchester United 0 Rotherham United 0**
Teamsheet: Gregg, Dunne A, Cantwell, Crerand, Foulkes, Stiles, Best, Law, Charlton, Herd, Connelly

SEASON 1965/66 (continued)

Match # 2746	Tuesday 15/02/66	FA Cup 4th Round Replay	at Millmoor	Attendance 23500

Result: **Rotherham United 0 Manchester United 1**
Teamsheet: Gregg, Brennan, Dunne A, Crerand, Foulkes, Stiles, Best, Law, Charlton, Herd, Connelly
Scorer(s): Connelly

Match # 2747 Saturday 19/02/66 Football League Division 1 at Victoria Ground Attendance 36667
Result: **Stoke City 2 Manchester United 2**
Teamsheet: Gregg, Brennan, Dunne A, Crerand, Foulkes, Stiles, Connelly, Best, Charlton, Herd, Aston
Scorer(s): Connelly, Herd

Match # 2748 Saturday 26/02/66 Football League Division 1 at Old Trafford Attendance 49892
Result: **Manchester United 4 Burnley 2**
Teamsheet: Gregg, Brennan, Dunne A, Crerand, Foulkes, Stiles, Best, Law, Charlton, Herd, Connelly
Scorer(s): Herd 3, Charlton

Match # 2749 Saturday 05/03/66 FA Cup 5th Round at Molineux Attendance 53500
Result: **Wolverhampton Wanderers 2 Manchester United 4**
Teamsheet: Gregg, Brennan, Dunne A, Crerand, Foulkes, Stiles, Best, Law, Charlton, Herd, Connelly
Scorer(s): Law 2, Best, Herd

Match # 2750 Wednesday 09/03/66 European Cup Quarter-Final 2nd Leg at Estadio da Luz Attendance 75000
Result: **Benfica 1 Manchester United 5**
Teamsheet: Gregg, Brennan, Dunne A, Crerand, Foulkes, Stiles, Best, Law, Charlton, Herd, Connelly
Scorer(s): Best 2, Charlton, Connelly, Crerand

Match # 2751 Saturday 12/03/66 Football League Division 1 at Stamford Bridge Attendance 60269
Result: **Chelsea 2 Manchester United 0**
Teamsheet: Gregg, Brennan, Dunne A, Crerand, Foulkes, Stiles, Best, Law, Charlton, Herd, Connelly

Match # 2752 Saturday 19/03/66 Football League Division 1 at Old Trafford Attendance 47246
Result: **Manchester United 2 Arsenal 1**
Teamsheet: Gregg, Brennan, Dunne A, Crerand, Foulkes, Stiles, Best, Law, Charlton, Herd, Connelly
Scorer(s): Law, Stiles

Match # 2753 Saturday 26/03/66 FA Cup 6th Round at Deepdale Attendance 37876
Result: **Preston North End 1 Manchester United 1**
Teamsheet: Gregg, Brennan, Dunne A, Crerand, Foulkes, Stiles, Best, Law, Charlton, Herd, Connelly
Scorer(s): Herd

Match # 2754 Wednesday 30/03/66 FA Cup 6th Round Replay at Old Trafford Attendance 60433
Result: **Manchester United 3 Preston North End 1**
Teamsheet: Gregg, Brennan, Dunne A, Crerand, Foulkes, Stiles, Connelly, Law, Charlton, Herd, Aston
Scorer(s): Law 2, Connelly

Match # 2755 Wednesday 06/04/66 Football League Division 1 at Villa Park Attendance 28211
Result: **Aston Villa 1 Manchester United 1**
Teamsheet: Gaskell, Brennan, Dunne A, Crerand, Foulkes, Fitzpatrick, Connelly, Law, Anderson, Cantwell, Aston
Scorer(s): Cantwell

Match # 2756 Saturday 09/04/66 Football League Division 1 at Old Trafford Attendance 42593
Result: **Manchester United 1 Leicester City 2**
Teamsheet: Gregg, Brennan, Noble, Crerand, Sadler, Stiles, Best, Anderson, Charlton, Herd, Connelly
Scorer(s): Connelly

Match # 2757 Wednesday 13/04/66 European Cup Semi-Final 1st Leg at Stadion JNA Attendance 60000
Result: **Partizan Belgrade 2 Manchester United 0**
Teamsheet: Gregg, Brennan, Dunne A, Crerand, Foulkes, Stiles, Best, Law, Charlton, Herd, Connelly

Match # 2758 Saturday 16/04/66 Football League Division 1 at Bramall Lane Attendance 22330
Result: **Sheffield United 3 Manchester United 1**
Teamsheet: Gregg, Brennan, Cantwell, Fitzpatrick, Foulkes, Stiles, Connelly, Anderson, Sadler, Herd, Aston
Scorer(s): Sadler

Match # 2759 Wednesday 20/04/66 European Cup Semi-Final 2nd Leg at Old Trafford Attendance 62500
Result: **Manchester United 1 Partizan Belgrade 0**
Teamsheet: Gregg, Brennan, Dunne A, Crerand, Foulkes, Stiles, Anderson, Law, Charlton, Herd, Connelly
Scorer(s): Stiles

Match # 2760 Saturday 23/04/66 FA Cup Semi-Final at Burnden Park Attendance 60000
Result: **Manchester United 0 Everton 1**
Teamsheet: Gregg, Brennan, Dunne A, Crerand, Foulkes, Stiles, Anderson, Law, Charlton, Herd, Connelly

Match # 2761 Monday 25/04/66 Football League Division 1 at Goodison Park Attendance 50843
Result: **Everton 0 Manchester United 0**
Teamsheet: Gregg, Brennan, Dunne A, Crerand, Cantwell, Stiles, Anderson, Law, Sadler, Charlton, Aston

Match # 2762 Wednesday 27/04/66 Football League Division 1 at Old Trafford Attendance 26953
Result: **Manchester United 2 Blackpool 1**
Teamsheet: Gregg, Brennan, Dunne A, Crerand, Cantwell, Stiles, Connelly, Law, Sadler, Charlton, Aston
Scorer(s): Charlton, Law

Match # 2763 Saturday 30/04/66 Football League Division 1 at Upton Park Attendance 36416
Result: **West Ham United 3 Manchester United 2**
Teamsheet: Gregg, Brennan, Dunne A, Crerand, Cantwell, Stiles, Connelly, Law, Sadler, Charlton, Aston
Substitute(s): Herd   Scorer(s): Aston, Cantwell

SEASON 1965/66 (continued)

Match # 2764	Wednesday 04/05/66 Football League Division 1 at The Hawthorns Attendance 22609
Result:	**West Bromwich Albion 3 Manchester United 3**
Teamsheet:	Gregg, Brennan, Dunne A, Crerand, Cantwell, Fitzpatrick, Ryan, Law, Sadler, Herd, Aston
Substitute(s):	Anderson Scorer(s): Aston, Dunne A, Herd

Match # 2765	Saturday 07/05/66 Football League Division 1 at Ewood Park Attendance 14513
Result:	**Blackburn Rovers 1 Manchester United 4**
Teamsheet:	Gregg, Brennan, Dunne A, Crerand, Cantwell, Stiles, Ryan, Charlton, Sadler, Herd, Aston
Scorer(s):	Herd 2, Charlton, Sadler

Match # 2766	Monday 09/05/66 Football League Division 1 at Old Trafford Attendance 23039
Result:	**Manchester United 6 Aston Villa 1**
Teamsheet:	Gregg, Brennan, Dunne A, Crerand, Cantwell, Stiles, Ryan, Herd, Sadler, Charlton, Aston
Scorer(s):	Herd 2, Sadler 2, Charlton, Ryan

Match # 2767	Thursday 19/05/66 Football League Division 1 at Old Trafford Attendance 35008
Result:	**Manchester United 1 Leeds United 1**
Teamsheet:	Gregg, Brennan, Noble, Crerand, Cantwell, Dunne A, Ryan, Herd, Sadler, Law, Aston
Scorer(s):	Herd

SEASON 1965/66 SUMMARY

APPEARANCES

PLAYER	LGE	FAC	EC	CS	TOTAL
Crerand	41	7	7	1	56
Dunne A	40	7	8	1	56
Stiles	39	7	8	1	55
Charlton	38	7	8	1	54
Herd	36 (1)	7	7	1	51 (1)
Law	33	7	8	1	49
Foulkes	33	7	8	–	48
Connelly	31 (1)	6	8	–	45 (1)
Best	31	5	6	1	43
Brennan	28	5	5	1	39
Gregg	26	7	5	–	38
Cantwell	23	2	3	1	29
Aston	23	2	2	1	28
Dunne P	8	–	2	1	11
Sadler	10	–	–	–	10
Gaskell	8	–	1	–	9
Anderson	5 (1)	1	1	–	7 (1)
Fitzpatrick	3 (1)	–	1	–	4 (1)
Ryan	4	–	–	–	4
Noble	2	–	–	–	2

GOALSCORERS

PLAYER	LGE	FAC	EC	CS	TOT
Herd	24	3	5	1	33
Law	15	6	3	–	24
Charlton	16	–	2	–	18
Best	9	3	4	1	17
Connelly	5	2	6	–	13
Aston	4	–	–	–	4
Sadler	4	–	–	–	4
Stiles	2	–	1	–	3
Cantwell	2	–	–	–	2
Dunne A	1	–	–	–	1
Ryan	1	–	–	–	1
Crerand	–	–	1	–	1
Foulkes	–	–	1	–	1
own goal	1	–	–	–	1

RESULTS & ATTENDANCES SUMMARY

		P	W	D	L	F	A	TOTAL	AVGE
League	H	21	12	8	1	50	20	807643	38459
	A	21	6	7	8	34	39	801597	38171
TOTAL		42	18	15	9	84	59	1609240	38315
FA Cup	H	2	1	1	0	3	1	114696	57348
	A	4	3	1	0	11	5	148703	37176
	N	1	0	0	1	0	1	60000	60000
TOTAL		7	4	2	1	14	7	323399	46200
European	H	4	4	0	0	13	3	187005	46751
Cup	A	4	3	0	1	10	5	200000	50000
TOTAL		8	7	0	1	23	8	387005	48376
Charity	H	1	0	1	0	2	2	48502	48502
Shield	A	0	0	0	0	0	0	0	n/a
TOTAL		1	0	1	0	2	2	48502	48502
Overall	H	28	17	10	1	68	26	1157846	41352
	A	29	12	8	9	55	49	1150300	39666
	N	1	0	0	1	0	1	60000	60000
TOTAL		58	29	18	11	123	76	2368146	40830

FINAL TABLE – LEAGUE DIVISION ONE

		P	HOME W	HOME D	HOME L	HOME F	HOME A	AWAY W	AWAY D	AWAY L	AWAY F	AWAY A	PTS	GD
1	Liverpool	42	17	2	2	52	15	9	7	5	27	19	61	45
2	Leeds United	42	14	4	3	49	15	9	5	7	30	23	55	41
3	Burnley	42	15	3	3	45	20	9	4	8	34	27	55	32
4	MANCHESTER UNITED	42	12	8	1	50	20	6	7	8	34	39	51	25
5	Chelsea	42	11	4	6	30	21	11	3	7	35	32	51	12
6	West Bromwich Albion	42	11	6	4	58	34	8	6	7	33	35	50	22
7	Leicester City	42	12	4	5	40	28	9	3	9	40	37	49	15
8	Tottenham Hotspur	42	11	6	4	55	37	5	6	10	20	29	44	9
9	Sheffield United	42	11	6	4	37	25	5	5	11	19	34	43	-3
10	Stoke City	42	12	6	3	42	22	3	6	12	23	42	42	1
11	Everton	42	12	6	3	39	19	3	5	13	17	43	41	-6
12	West Ham United	42	12	5	4	46	33	3	4	14	24	50	39	-13
13	Blackpool	42	9	5	7	36	29	5	4	12	19	36	37	-10
14	Arsenal	42	8	8	5	36	31	4	5	12	26	44	37	-13
15	Newcastle United	42	10	5	6	26	20	4	4	13	24	43	37	-13
16	Aston Villa	42	10	3	8	39	34	5	3	13	30	46	36	-11
17	Sheffield Wednesday	42	11	6	4	35	18	3	2	16	21	48	36	-10
18	Nottingham Forest	42	11	3	7	31	26	3	5	13	25	46	36	-16
19	Sunderland	42	13	2	6	36	28	1	6	14	15	44	36	-21
20	Fulham	42	9	4	8	34	37	5	3	13	33	48	35	-18
21	Northampton Town	42	8	6	7	31	32	2	7	12	24	60	33	-37
22	Blackburn Rovers	42	6	1	14	30	36	2	3	16	27	52	20	-31

SEASON 1966/67

Match # 2768 Saturday 20/08/66 Football League Division 1 at Old Trafford Attendance 41343
Result: **Manchester United 5 West Bromwich Albion 3**
Teamsheet: Gaskell, Brennan, Dunne A, Fitzpatrick, Foulkes, Stiles, Best, Law, Charlton, Herd, Connelly
Scorer(s): Law 2, Best, Herd, Stiles

Match # 2769 Tuesday 23/08/66 Football League Division 1 at Goodison Park Attendance 60657
Result: **Everton 1 Manchester United 2**
Teamsheet: Gaskell, Brennan, Dunne A, Fitzpatrick, Foulkes, Stiles, Best, Law, Charlton, Herd, Connelly
Scorer(s): Law 2

Match # 2770 Saturday 27/08/66 Football League Division 1 at Elland Road Attendance 45092
Result: **Leeds United 3 Manchester United 1**
Teamsheet: Gaskell, Brennan, Dunne A, Fitzpatrick, Foulkes, Stiles, Best, Law, Charlton, Herd, Connelly
Scorer(s): Best

Match # 2771 Wednesday 31/08/66 Football League Division 1 at Old Trafford Attendance 61114
Result: **Manchester United 3 Everton 0**
Teamsheet: Gaskell, Brennan, Dunne A, Crerand, Foulkes, Stiles, Connelly, Law, Charlton, Herd, Best
Scorer(s): Connelly, Foulkes, Law

Match # 2772 Saturday 03/09/66 Football League Division 1 at Old Trafford Attendance 44448
Result: **Manchester United 3 Newcastle United 2**
Teamsheet: Gregg, Brennan, Dunne A, Crerand, Foulkes, Stiles, Connelly, Law, Charlton, Herd, Best
Scorer(s): Connelly, Herd, Law

Match # 2773 Wednesday 07/09/66 Football League Division 1 at Victoria Ground Attendance 44337
Result: **Stoke City 3 Manchester United 0**
Teamsheet: Gregg, Brennan, Dunne A, Crerand, Foulkes, Stiles, Connelly, Law, Charlton, Herd, Best

Match # 2774 Saturday 10/09/66 Football League Division 1 at White Hart Lane Attendance 56295
Result: **Tottenham Hotspur 2 Manchester United 1**
Teamsheet: Gaskell, Brennan, Dunne A, Crerand, Foulkes, Stiles, Best, Law, Sadler, Herd, Charlton
Substitute(s): Aston Scorer(s): Law

Match # 2775 Wednesday 14/09/66 League Cup 2nd Round at Bloomfield Road Attendance 15570
Result: **Blackpool 5 Manchester United 1**
Teamsheet: Dunne P, Brennan, Dunne A, Crerand, Foulkes, Stiles, Connelly, Best, Sadler, Herd, Aston
Scorer(s): Herd

Match # 2776 Saturday 17/09/66 Football League Division 1 at Old Trafford Attendance 62085
Result: **Manchester United 1 Manchester City 0**
Teamsheet: Stepney, Brennan, Dunne A, Crerand, Foulkes, Stiles, Best, Law, Sadler, Charlton, Aston
Scorer(s): Law

Match # 2777 Saturday 24/09/66 Football League Division 1 at Old Trafford Attendance 52697
Result: **Manchester United 4 Burnley 1**
Teamsheet: Stepney, Brennan, Dunne A, Crerand, Foulkes, Stiles, Herd, Law, Sadler, Charlton, Best
Substitute(s): Aston Scorer(s): Crerand, Herd, Law, Sadler

Match # 2778 Saturday 01/10/66 Football League Division 1 at City Ground Attendance 41854
Result: **Nottingham Forest 4 Manchester United 1**
Teamsheet: Stepney, Brennan, Dunne A, Crerand, Foulkes, Stiles, Best, Charlton, Sadler, Herd, Aston
Scorer(s): Charlton

Match # 2779 Saturday 08/10/66 Football League Division 1 at Bloomfield Road Attendance 33555
Result: **Blackpool 1 Manchester United 2**
Teamsheet: Stepney, Dunne A, Noble, Crerand, Cantwell, Stiles, Herd, Law, Sadler, Charlton, Best
Scorer(s): Law 2

Match # 2780 Saturday 15/10/66 Football League Division 1 at Old Trafford Attendance 56789
Result: **Manchester United 1 Chelsea 1**
Teamsheet: Stepney, Dunne A, Noble, Crerand, Cantwell, Stiles, Herd, Law, Sadler, Charlton, Best
Scorer(s): Law

Match # 2781 Saturday 29/10/66 Football League Division 1 at Old Trafford Attendance 45387
Result: **Manchester United 1 Arsenal 0**
Teamsheet: Stepney, Dunne A, Noble, Crerand, Cantwell, Stiles, Herd, Law, Sadler, Charlton, Best
Scorer(s): Sadler

Match # 2782 Saturday 05/11/66 Football League Division 1 at Stamford Bridge Attendance 55958
Result: **Chelsea 1 Manchester United 3**
Teamsheet: Stepney, Brennan, Noble, Crerand, Foulkes, Stiles, Herd, Aston, Sadler, Charlton, Best
Scorer(s): Aston 2, Best

Match # 2783 Saturday 12/11/66 Football League Division 1 at Old Trafford Attendance 46942
Result: **Manchester United 2 Sheffield Wednesday 0**
Teamsheet: Stepney, Dunne A, Noble, Crerand, Foulkes, Stiles, Herd, Law, Sadler, Charlton, Best
Substitute(s): Aston Scorer(s): Charlton, Herd

Match # 2784 Saturday 19/11/66 Football League Division 1 at The Dell Attendance 29458
Result: **Southampton 1 Manchester United 2**
Teamsheet: Stepney, Dunne A, Noble, Crerand, Cantwell, Stiles, Herd, Law, Sadler, Charlton, Best
Substitute(s): Aston Scorer(s): Charlton 2

Match # 2785 Saturday 26/11/66 Football League Division 1 at Old Trafford Attendance 44687
Result: **Manchester United 5 Sunderland 0**
Teamsheet: Stepney, Dunne A, Noble, Crerand, Sadler, Stiles, Best, Law, Charlton, Herd, Aston
Scorer(s): Herd 4, Law

SEASON 1966/67 (continued)

Match # 2786 Wednesday 30/11/66   Football League Division 1   at Filbert Street   Attendance 39014
Result: **Leicester City 1 Manchester United 2**
Teamsheet: Stepney, Dunne A, Noble, Crerand, Sadler, Stiles, Best, Law, Charlton, Herd, Aston
Scorer(s): Best, Law

Match # 2787 Saturday 03/12/66   Football League Division 1   at Villa Park   Attendance 39937
Result: **Aston Villa 2 Manchester United 1**
Teamsheet: Stepney, Dunne A, Noble, Crerand, Sadler, Stiles, Best, Law, Charlton, Herd, Aston
Scorer(s): Herd

Match # 2788 Saturday 10/12/66   Football League Division 1   at Old Trafford   Attendance 61768
Result: **Manchester United 2 Liverpool 2**
Teamsheet: Stepney, Brennan, Noble, Crerand, Sadler, Dunne A, Best, Ryan, Charlton, Herd, Aston
Substitute(s): Anderson   Scorer(s): Best 2

Match # 2789 Saturday 17/12/66   Football League Division 1   at The Hawthorns   Attendance 32080
Result: **West Bromwich Albion 3 Manchester United 4**
Teamsheet: Stepney, Brennan, Noble, Crerand, Sadler, Stiles, Best, Law, Charlton, Herd, Aston
Scorer(s): Herd 3, Law

Match # 2790 Monday 26/12/66   Football League Division 1   at Bramall Lane   Attendance 42752
Result: **Sheffield United 2 Manchester United 1**
Teamsheet: Stepney, Dunne A, Noble, Crerand, Foulkes, Sadler, Best, Law, Charlton, Herd, Aston
Scorer(s): Herd

Match # 2791 Tuesday 27/12/66   Football League Division 1   at Old Trafford   Attendance 59392
Result: **Manchester United 2 Sheffield United 0**
Teamsheet: Stepney, Dunne A, Noble, Crerand, Foulkes, Sadler, Best, Law, Charlton, Herd, Aston
Scorer(s): Crerand, Herd

Match # 2792 Saturday 31/12/66   Football League Division 1   at Old Trafford   Attendance 53486
Result: **Manchester United 0 Leeds United 0**
Teamsheet: Stepney, Dunne A, Noble, Crerand, Foulkes, Sadler, Best, Law, Charlton, Herd, Aston

Match # 2793 Saturday 14/01/67   Football League Division 1   at Old Trafford   Attendance 57366
Result: **Manchester United 1 Tottenham Hotspur 0**
Teamsheet: Stepney, Dunne A, Noble, Crerand, Foulkes, Sadler, Best, Ryan, Charlton, Herd, Aston
Scorer(s): Herd

Match # 2794 Saturday 21/01/67   Football League Division 1   at Maine Road   Attendance 62983
Result: **Manchester City 1 Manchester United 1**
Teamsheet: Stepney, Dunne A, Noble, Crerand, Foulkes, Stiles, Ryan, Charlton, Sadler, Herd, Best
Scorer(s): Foulkes

Match # 2795 Saturday 28/01/67   FA Cup 3rd Round   at Old Trafford   Attendance 63500
Result: **Manchester United 2 Stoke City 0**
Teamsheet: Stepney, Dunne A, Noble, Crerand, Foulkes, Stiles, Best, Law, Sadler, Herd, Charlton
Scorer(s): Herd, Law

Match # 2796 Saturday 04/02/67   Football League Division 1   at Turf Moor   Attendance 40165
Result: **Burnley 1 Manchester United 1**
Teamsheet: Stepney, Dunne A, Noble, Crerand, Foulkes, Stiles, Best, Law, Sadler, Herd, Charlton
Scorer(s): Sadler

Match # 2797 Saturday 11/02/67   Football League Division 1   at Old Trafford   Attendance 62727
Result: **Manchester United 1 Nottingham Forest 0**
Teamsheet: Stepney, Dunne A, Noble, Crerand, Foulkes, Stiles, Best, Law, Sadler, Herd, Charlton
Substitute(s): Ryan   Scorer(s): Law

Match # 2798 Saturday 18/02/67   FA Cup 4th Round   at Old Trafford   Attendance 63409
Result: **Manchester United 1 Norwich City 2**
Teamsheet: Stepney, Dunne A, Noble, Crerand, Sadler, Stiles, Ryan, Law, Charlton, Herd, Best
Scorer(s): Law

Match # 2799 Saturday 25/02/67   Football League Division 1   at Old Trafford   Attendance 47158
Result: **Manchester United 4 Blackpool 0**
Teamsheet: Stepney, Dunne A, Noble, Crerand, Foulkes, Stiles, Best, Law, Sadler, Charlton, Aston
Scorer(s): Charlton 2, Law, own goal

Match # 2800 Friday 03/03/67   Football League Division 1   at Highbury   Attendance 63363
Result: **Arsenal 1 Manchester United 1**
Teamsheet: Stepney, Dunne A, Noble, Crerand, Foulkes, Stiles, Best, Law, Sadler, Charlton, Aston
Scorer(s): Aston

Match # 2801 Saturday 11/03/67   Football League Division 1   at St James' Park   Attendance 37430
Result: **Newcastle United 0 Manchester United 0**
Teamsheet: Stepney, Dunne A, Noble, Crerand, Foulkes, Stiles, Best, Law, Sadler, Charlton, Aston

Match # 2802 Saturday 18/03/67   Football League Division 1   at Old Trafford   Attendance 50281
Result: **Manchester United 5 Leicester City 2**
Teamsheet: Stepney, Dunne A, Noble, Crerand, Foulkes, Stiles, Best, Law, Charlton, Herd, Aston
Substitute(s): Sadler   Scorer(s): Aston, Charlton, Herd, Law, Sadler

Match # 2803 Saturday 25/03/67   Football League Division 1   at Anfield   Attendance 53813
Result: **Liverpool 0 Manchester United 0**
Teamsheet: Stepney, Dunne A, Noble, Crerand, Foulkes, Stiles, Best, Law, Sadler, Charlton, Aston

SEASON 1966/67 (continued)

Match # 2804   Monday 27/03/67   Football League Division 1   at Craven Cottage   Attendance 47290
Result: **Fulham 2 Manchester United 2**
Teamsheet: Stepney, Dunne A, Noble, Crerand, Foulkes, Stiles, Best, Law, Sadler, Charlton, Aston
Scorer(s):   Best, Stiles

Match # 2805   Tuesday 28/03/67   Football League Division 1   at Old Trafford   Attendance 51673
Result: **Manchester United 2 Fulham 1**
Teamsheet: Stepney, Dunne A, Noble, Crerand, Foulkes, Stiles, Best, Law, Sadler, Charlton, Aston
Scorer(s):   Foulkes, Stiles

Match # 2806   Saturday 01/04/67   Football League Division 1   at Old Trafford   Attendance 61308
Result: **Manchester United 3 West Ham United 0**
Teamsheet: Stepney, Dunne A, Noble, Crerand, Foulkes, Stiles, Best, Law, Sadler, Charlton, Aston
Scorer(s):   Best, Charlton, Law

Match # 2807   Monday 10/04/67   Football League Division 1   at Hillsborough   Attendance 51101
Result: **Sheffield Wednesday 2 Manchester United 2**
Teamsheet: Stepney, Dunne A, Noble, Crerand, Foulkes, Stiles, Best, Law, Sadler, Charlton, Aston
Scorer(s):   Charlton 2

Match # 2808   Tuesday 18/04/67   Football League Division 1   at Old Trafford   Attendance 54291
Result: **Manchester United 3 Southampton 0**
Teamsheet: Stepney, Dunne A, Noble, Crerand, Foulkes, Stiles, Best, Law, Sadler, Charlton, Aston
Scorer(s):   Charlton, Law, Sadler

Match # 2809   Saturday 22/04/67   Football League Division 1   at Roker Park   Attendance 43570
Result: **Sunderland 0 Manchester United 0**
Teamsheet: Stepney, Dunne A, Noble, Crerand, Foulkes, Stiles, Best, Law, Sadler, Charlton, Aston

Match # 2810   Saturday 29/04/67   Football League Division 1   at Old Trafford   Attendance 55782
Result: **Manchester United 3 Aston Villa 1**
Teamsheet: Stepney, Brennan, Dunne A, Crerand, Foulkes, Stiles, Best, Law, Sadler, Charlton, Aston
Scorer(s):   Aston, Best, Law

Match # 2811   Saturday 06/05/67   Football League Division 1   at Upton Park   Attendance 38424
Result: **West Ham United 1 Manchester United 6**
Teamsheet: Stepney, Brennan, Dunne A, Crerand, Foulkes, Stiles, Best, Law, Sadler, Charlton, Aston
Scorer(s):   Law 2, Best, Charlton, Crerand, Foulkes

Match # 2812   Saturday 13/05/67   Football League Division 1   at Old Trafford   Attendance 61071
Result: **Manchester United 0 Stoke City 0**
Teamsheet: Stepney, Brennan, Dunne A, Crerand, Foulkes, Stiles, Best, Ryan, Sadler, Charlton, Aston

SEASON 1966/67 SUMMARY

APPEARANCES

PLAYER	LGE	FAC	LC	TOTAL
Best	42	2	1	45
Charlton	42	2	–	44
Dunne A	40	2	1	43
Crerand	39	2	1	42
Stiles	37	2	1	40
Sadler	35 (1)	2	1	38 (1)
Law	36	2	–	38
Stepney	35	2	–	37
Foulkes	33	1	1	35
Herd	28	2	1	31
Noble	29	2	–	31
Aston	26 (4)	–	1	27 (4)
Brennan	16	–	1	17
Connelly	6	–	1	7
Ryan	4 (1)	1	–	5 (1)
Gaskell	5	–	–	5
Cantwell	4	–	–	4
Fitzpatrick	3	–	–	3
Gregg	2	–	–	2
Dunne P	–	–	1	1
Anderson	– (1)	–	–	– (1)

GOALSCORERS

PLAYER	LGE	FAC	LC	TOT
Law	23	2	–	25
Herd	16	1	1	18
Charlton	12	–	–	12
Best	10	–	–	10
Aston	5	–	–	5
Sadler	5	–	–	5
Foulkes	4	–	–	4
Crerand	3	–	–	3
Stiles	3	–	–	3
Connelly	2	–	–	2
own goal	1	–	–	1

RESULTS & ATTENDANCES SUMMARY

		P	W	D	L	F	A	TOTAL	AVGE
League	H	21	17	4	0	51	13	1131795	53895
	A	21	7	8	6	33	32	959128	45673
	TOTAL	42	24	12	6	84	45	2090923	49784
FA Cup	H	2	1	0	1	3	2	126909	63455
	A	0	0	0	0	0	0	0	n/a
	TOTAL	2	1	0	1	3	2	126909	63455
League Cup	H	0	0	0	0	0	0	0	n/a
	A	1	0	0	1	1	5	15570	15570
	TOTAL	1	0	0	1	1	5	15570	15570
Overall	H	23	18	4	1	54	15	1258704	54726
	A	22	7	8	7	34	37	974698	44304
	TOTAL	45	25	12	8	88	52	2233402	49631

FINAL TABLE – LEAGUE DIVISION ONE

		P	HOME W	HOME D	HOME L	HOME F	HOME A	AWAY W	AWAY D	AWAY L	AWAY F	AWAY A	PTS	GD
1	MANCHESTER UNITED	42	17	4	0	51	13	7	8	6	33	32	60	39
2	Nottingham Forest	42	16	4	1	41	13	7	6	8	23	28	56	23
3	Tottenham Hotspur	42	15	3	3	44	21	9	5	7	27	27	56	23
4	Leeds United	42	15	4	2	41	17	7	7	7	21	25	55	20
5	Liverpool	42	12	7	2	36	17	7	6	8	28	30	51	17
6	Everton	42	11	4	6	39	22	8	6	7	26	24	48	19
7	Arsenal	42	11	6	4	32	20	5	8	8	26	27	46	11
8	Leicester City	42	12	4	5	47	28	6	4	11	31	43	44	7
9	Chelsea	42	7	9	5	33	29	8	5	8	34	33	44	5
10	Sheffield United	42	11	5	5	34	22	5	5	11	18	37	42	-7
11	Sheffield Wednesday	42	9	7	5	39	19	5	6	10	17	28	41	9
12	Stoke City	42	11	5	5	40	21	6	2	13	23	37	41	5
13	West Bromwich Albion	42	11	1	9	40	28	5	6	10	37	45	39	4
14	Burnley	42	11	4	6	43	28	4	5	12	23	48	39	-10
15	Manchester City	42	8	9	4	27	25	4	6	11	16	27	39	-9
16	West Ham United	42	8	6	7	40	31	6	2	13	40	53	36	-4
17	Sunderland	42	12	3	6	39	26	2	5	14	19	46	36	-14
18	Fulham	42	8	7	6	49	34	3	5	13	22	49	34	-12
19	Southampton	42	10	3	8	49	41	4	3	14	25	51	34	-18
20	Newcastle United	42	9	5	7	24	27	3	4	14	15	54	33	-42
21	Aston Villa	42	7	5	9	30	33	4	2	15	24	52	29	-31
22	Blackpool	42	1	5	15	18	36	5	4	12	23	40	21	-35

SEASON 1967/68

Match # 2813 Saturday 12/08/67   FA Charity Shield   at Old Trafford   Attendance 54106
Result: **Manchester United 3 Tottenham Hotspur 3   (TROPHY SHARED)**
Teamsheet: Stepney, Brennan, Dunne, Crerand, Foulkes, Stiles, Best, Kidd, Charlton, Law, Aston
Scorer(s): Charlton 2, Law

Match # 2814 Saturday 19/08/67   Football League Division 1   at Goodison Park   Attendance 61452
Result: **Everton 3 Manchester United 1**
Teamsheet: Stepney, Brennan, Dunne, Crerand, Foulkes, Stiles, Best, Law, Charlton, Kidd, Aston
Substitute(s): Sadler   Scorer(s):   Charlton

Match # 2815 Wednesday 23/08/67   Football League Division 1   at Old Trafford   Attendance 53016
Result: **Manchester United 1 Leeds United 0**
Teamsheet: Stepney, Brennan, Dunne, Crerand, Foulkes, Stiles, Ryan, Law, Charlton, Kidd, Aston
Scorer(s): Charlton

Match # 2816 Saturday 26/08/67   Football League Division 1   at Old Trafford   Attendance 51256
Result: **Manchester United 1 Leicester City 1**
Teamsheet: Stepney, Brennan, Dunne, Sadler, Foulkes, Stiles, Best, Law, Charlton, Kidd, Aston
Scorer(s): Foulkes

Match # 2817 Saturday 02/09/67   Football League Division 1   at Upton Park   Attendance 36562
Result: **West Ham United 1 Manchester United 3**
Teamsheet: Stepney, Dunne, Burns, Crerand, Foulkes, Stiles, Ryan, Sadler, Charlton, Kidd, Best
Scorer(s): Kidd, Ryan, Sadler

Match # 2818 Wednesday 06/09/67   Football League Division 1   at Roker Park   Attendance 51527
Result: **Sunderland 1 Manchester United 1**
Teamsheet: Stepney, Dunne, Burns, Crerand, Foulkes, Stiles, Ryan, Sadler, Charlton, Kidd, Best
Substitute(s): Fitzpatrick   Scorer(s):   Kidd

Match # 2819 Saturday 09/09/67   Football League Division 1   at Old Trafford   Attendance 55809
Result: **Manchester United 2 Burnley 2**
Teamsheet: Stepney, Dunne, Burns, Crerand, Foulkes, Fitzpatrick, Ryan, Sadler, Charlton, Kidd, Best
Substitute(s): Kopel   Scorer(s):   Burns, Crerand

Match # 2820 Saturday 16/09/67   Football League Division 1   at Hillsborough   Attendance 47274
Result: **Sheffield Wednesday 1 Manchester United 1**
Teamsheet: Stepney, Dunne, Burns, Crerand, Foulkes, Stiles, Best, Sadler, Charlton, Law, Kidd
Scorer(s): Best

Match # 2821 Wednesday 20/09/67   European Cup 1st Round 1st Leg   at Old Trafford   Attendance 43912
Result: **Manchester United 4 Hibernians Malta 0**
Teamsheet: Stepney, Dunne, Burns, Crerand, Foulkes, Stiles, Best, Sadler, Charlton, Law, Kidd
Scorer(s): Law 2, Sadler 2

Match # 2822 Saturday 23/09/67   Football League Division 1   at Old Trafford   Attendance 58779
Result: **Manchester United 3 Tottenham Hotspur 1**
Teamsheet: Stepney, Dunne, Burns, Crerand, Foulkes, Stiles, Best, Sadler, Charlton, Law, Kidd
Scorer(s): Best 2, Law

Match # 2823 Wednesday 27/09/67   European Cup 1st Round 2nd Leg   at Empire Stadium   Attendance 25000
Result: **Hibernians Malta 0 Manchester United 0**
Teamsheet: Stepney, Dunne, Burns, Crerand, Foulkes, Stiles, Best, Sadler, Charlton, Law, Kidd

Match # 2824 Saturday 30/09/67   Football League Division 1   at Maine Road   Attendance 62942
Result: **Manchester City 1 Manchester United 2**
Teamsheet: Stepney, Dunne, Burns, Crerand, Foulkes, Stiles, Best, Sadler, Charlton, Law, Kidd
Substitute(s): Aston   Scorer(s):   Charlton 2

Match # 2825 Saturday 07/10/67   Football League Division 1   at Old Trafford   Attendance 60197
Result: **Manchester United 1 Arsenal 0**
Teamsheet: Stepney, Dunne, Burns, Crerand, Sadler, Stiles, Best, Kidd, Charlton, Law, Aston
Scorer(s): Aston

Match # 2826 Saturday 14/10/67   Football League Division 1   at Bramall Lane   Attendance 29170
Result: **Sheffield United 0 Manchester United 3**
Teamsheet: Stepney, Dunne, Burns, Crerand, Sadler, Stiles, Best, Kidd, Charlton, Law, Aston
Substitute(s): Fitzpatrick   Scorer(s):   Aston, Kidd, Law

Match # 2827 Wednesday 25/10/67   Football League Division 1   at Old Trafford   Attendance 54253
Result: **Manchester United 4 Coventry City 0**
Teamsheet: Stepney, Dunne, Burns, Crerand, Sadler, Fitzpatrick, Best, Kidd, Charlton, Law, Aston
Scorer(s): Aston 2, Best, Charlton

Match # 2828 Saturday 28/10/67   Football League Division 1   at City Ground   Attendance 49946
Result: **Nottingham Forest 3 Manchester United 1**
Teamsheet: Stepney, Kopel, Burns, Crerand, Sadler, Fitzpatrick, Best, Kidd, Charlton, Law, Aston
Scorer(s): Best

Match # 2829 Saturday 04/11/67   Football League Division 1   at Old Trafford   Attendance 51041
Result: **Manchester United 1 Stoke City 0**
Teamsheet: Stepney, Dunne, Burns, Crerand, Foulkes, Sadler, Ryan, Kidd, Charlton, Best, Aston
Scorer(s): Charlton

Match # 2830 Wednesday 08/11/67   Football League Division 1   at Elland Road   Attendance 43999
Result: **Leeds United 1 Manchester United 0**
Teamsheet: Stepney, Dunne, Burns, Crerand, Foulkes, Sadler, Ryan, Kidd, Charlton, Best, Aston
Substitute(s): Fitzpatrick

SEASON 1967/68 (continued)

Match # 2831   Saturday 11/11/67   Football League Division 1   at Anfield   Attendance 54515
Result: **Liverpool 1 Manchester United 2**
Teamsheet: Stepney, Dunne, Burns, Crerand, Foulkes, Sadler, Fitzpatrick, Kidd, Charlton, Best, Aston
Scorer(s):   Best 2

Match # 2832   Wednesday 15/11/67   European Cup 2nd Round 1st Leg   at Stadion Kosevo   Attendance 45000
Result: **Sarajevo 0 Manchester United 0**
Teamsheet: Stepney, Dunne, Burns, Crerand, Foulkes, Sadler, Fitzpatrick, Kidd, Charlton, Best, Aston

Match # 2833   Saturday 18/11/67   Football League Division 1   at Old Trafford   Attendance 48732
Result: **Manchester United 3 Southampton 2**
Teamsheet: Stepney, Dunne, Burns, Crerand, Foulkes, Sadler, Fitzpatrick, Kidd, Charlton, Best, Aston
Scorer(s):   Aston, Charlton, Kidd

Match # 2834   Saturday 25/11/67   Football League Division 1   at Stamford Bridge   Attendance 54712
Result: **Chelsea 1 Manchester United 1**
Teamsheet: Stepney, Brennan, Dunne, Crerand, Foulkes, Sadler, Burns, Kidd, Charlton, Best, Aston
Scorer(s):   Kidd

Match # 2835   Wednesday 29/11/67   European Cup 2nd Round 2nd Leg   at Old Trafford   Attendance 62801
Result: **Manchester United 2 Sarajevo 1**
Teamsheet: Stepney, Brennan, Dunne, Crerand, Foulkes, Sadler, Burns, Kidd, Charlton, Best, Aston
Scorer(s):   Aston, Best

Match # 2836   Saturday 02/12/67   Football League Division 1   at Old Trafford   Attendance 52568
Result: **Manchester United 2 West Bromwich Albion 1**
Teamsheet: Stepney, Brennan, Dunne, Crerand, Foulkes, Sadler, Burns, Kidd, Charlton, Best, Aston
Scorer(s):   Best 2

Match # 2837   Saturday 09/12/67   Football League Division 1   at St James' Park   Attendance 48639
Result: **Newcastle United 2 Manchester United 2**
Teamsheet: Stepney, Brennan, Dunne, Crerand, Foulkes, Sadler, Burns, Kidd, Charlton, Best, Aston
Scorer(s):   Dunne, Kidd

Match # 2838   Saturday 16/12/67   Football League Division 1   at Old Trafford   Attendance 60736
Result: **Manchester United 3 Everton 1**
Teamsheet: Stepney, Dunne, Burns, Crerand, Foulkes, Sadler, Best, Kidd, Charlton, Law, Aston
Scorer(s):   Aston, Law, Sadler

Match # 2839   Saturday 23/12/67   Football League Division 1   at Filbert Street   Attendance 40104
Result: **Leicester City 2 Manchester United 2**
Teamsheet: Stepney, Dunne, Burns, Crerand, Foulkes, Sadler, Best, Kidd, Charlton, Law, Aston
Scorer(s):   Charlton, Law

Match # 2840   Tuesday 26/12/67   Football League Division 1   at Old Trafford   Attendance 63450
Result: **Manchester United 4 Wolverhampton Wanderers 0**
Teamsheet: Stepney, Dunne, Burns, Crerand, Foulkes, Sadler, Best, Kidd, Charlton, Law, Aston
Scorer(s):   Best 2, Charlton, Kidd

Match # 2841   Saturday 30/12/67   Football League Division 1   at Molineux   Attendance 53940
Result: **Wolverhampton Wanderers 2 Manchester United 3**
Teamsheet: Stepney, Dunne, Burns, Crerand, Foulkes, Sadler, Best, Kidd, Charlton, Law, Aston
Scorer(s):   Aston, Charlton, Kidd

Match # 2842   Saturday 06/01/68   Football League Division 1   at Old Trafford   Attendance 54498
Result: **Manchester United 3 West Ham United 1**
Teamsheet: Stepney, Dunne, Burns, Crerand, Sadler, Fitzpatrick, Best, Kidd, Charlton, Law, Aston
Scorer(s):   Aston, Best, Charlton

Match # 2843   Saturday 20/01/68   Football League Division 1   at Old Trafford   Attendance 55254
Result: **Manchester United 4 Sheffield Wednesday 2**
Teamsheet: Stepney, Dunne, Burns, Crerand, Sadler, Fitzpatrick, Best, Kidd, Charlton, Law, Aston
Scorer(s):   Best 2, Charlton, Kidd

Match # 2844   Saturday 27/01/68   FA Cup 3rd Round   at Old Trafford   Attendance 63500
Result: **Manchester United 2 Tottenham Hotspur 2**
Teamsheet: Stepney, Dunne, Burns, Crerand, Sadler, Fitzpatrick, Best, Kidd, Charlton, Law, Aston
Scorer(s):   Best, Charlton

Match # 2845   Wednesday 31/01/68   FA Cup 3rd Round Replay   at White Hart Lane   Attendance 57200
Result: **Tottenham Hotspur 1 Manchester United 0**
Teamsheet: Stepney, Dunne, Burns, Crerand, Sadler, Fitzpatrick, Best, Kidd, Charlton, Herd, Aston

Match # 2846   Saturday 03/02/68   Football League Division 1   at White Hart Lane   Attendance 57790
Result: **Tottenham Hotspur 1 Manchester United 2**
Teamsheet: Stepney, Dunne, Burns, Crerand, Sadler, Fitzpatrick, Best, Kidd, Charlton, Herd, Aston
Scorer(s):   Best, Charlton

Match # 2847   Saturday 17/02/68   Football League Division 1   at Turf Moor   Attendance 31965
Result: **Burnley 2 Manchester United 1**
Teamsheet: Stepney, Dunne, Burns, Crerand, Sadler, Stiles, Best, Kidd, Charlton, Law, Aston
Scorer(s):   Best

Match # 2848   Saturday 24/02/68   Football League Division 1   at Highbury   Attendance 46417
Result: **Arsenal 0 Manchester United 2**
Teamsheet: Stepney, Dunne, Burns, Crerand, Sadler, Stiles, Best, Kidd, Fitzpatrick, Law, Aston
Scorer(s):   Best, own goal

SEASON 1967/68 (continued)

Match # 2849
Result:
Teamsheet:
Scorer(s):

Wednesday 28/02/68   European Cup Quarter-Final 1st Leg   at Old Trafford   Attendance 63456
Manchester United 2 Gornik Zabrze 0
Stepney, Dunne, Burns, Crerand, Sadler, Stiles, Best, Kidd, Charlton, Ryan, Aston
Kidd, own goal

Match # 2850
Result:
Teamsheet:
Scorer(s):

Saturday 02/03/68   Football League Division 1   at Old Trafford   Attendance 62978
Manchester United 1 Chelsea 3
Stepney, Dunne, Burns, Crerand, Sadler, Stiles, Best, Kidd, Charlton, Ryan, Aston
Kidd

Match # 2851
Result:
Teamsheet:

Wednesday 13/03/68   European Cup Quarter-Final 2nd Leg   at Stadion Slaski   Attendance 105000
Gornik Zabrze 1 Manchester United 0
Stepney, Dunne, Burns, Crerand, Sadler, Stiles, Fitzpatrick, Charlton, Herd, Kidd, Best

Match # 2852
Result:
Teamsheet:
Substitute(s):

Saturday 16/03/68   Football League Division 1   at Highfield Road   Attendance 47110
Coventry City 2 Manchester United 0
Stepney, Brennan, Burns, Crerand, Sadler, Stiles, Best, Kidd, Charlton, Fitzpatrick, Herd
Aston

Match # 2853
Result:
Teamsheet:
Scorer(s):

Saturday 23/03/68   Football League Division 1   at Old Trafford   Attendance 61978
Manchester United 3 Nottingham Forest 0
Stepney, Brennan, Burns, Crerand, Sadler, Stiles, Fitzpatrick, Herd, Charlton, Best, Aston
Brennan, Burns, Herd

Match # 2854
Result:
Teamsheet:
Substitute(s):

Wednesday 27/03/68   Football League Division 1   at Old Trafford   Attendance 63004
Manchester United 1 Manchester City 3
Stepney, Brennan, Burns, Crerand, Sadler, Stiles, Fitzpatrick, Law, Charlton, Best, Herd
Aston   Scorer(s):   Best

Match # 2855
Result:
Teamsheet:
Substitute(s):

Saturday 30/03/68   Football League Division 1   at Victoria Ground   Attendance 30141
Stoke City 2 Manchester United 4
Stepney, Brennan, Burns, Crerand, Sadler, Fitzpatrick, Best, Gowling, Charlton, Herd, Aston
Ryan   Scorer(s):   Aston, Best, Gowling, Ryan

Match # 2856
Result:
Teamsheet:
Scorer(s):

Saturday 06/04/68   Football League Division 1   at Old Trafford   Attendance 63059
Manchester United 1 Liverpool 2
Stepney, Dunne, Burns, Crerand, Sadler, Fitzpatrick, Best, Gowling, Charlton, Herd, Aston
Best

Match # 2857
Result:
Teamsheet:
Scorer(s):

Friday 12/04/68   Football League Division 1   at Craven Cottage   Attendance 40152
Fulham 0 Manchester United 4
Stepney, Dunne, Burns, Crerand, Sadler, Stiles, Best, Kidd, Charlton, Law, Aston
Best 2, Kidd, Law

Match # 2858
Result:
Teamsheet:
Scorer(s):

Saturday 13/04/68   Football League Division 1   at The Dell   Attendance 30079
Southampton 2 Manchester United 2
Stepney, Dunne, Burns, Crerand, Foulkes, Sadler, Best, Kidd, Charlton, Gowling, Aston
Best, Charlton

Match # 2859
Result:
Teamsheet:
Scorer(s):

Monday 15/04/68   Football League Division 1   at Old Trafford   Attendance 60465
Manchester United 3 Fulham 0
Rimmer, Dunne, Burns, Crerand, Foulkes, Sadler, Best, Kidd, Charlton, Law, Aston
Aston, Best, Charlton

Match # 2860
Result:
Teamsheet:
Scorer(s):

Saturday 20/04/68   Football League Division 1   at Old Trafford   Attendance 55033
Manchester United 1 Sheffield United 0
Stepney, Brennan, Dunne, Crerand, Sadler, Stiles, Best, Kidd, Charlton, Law, Aston
Law

Match # 2861
Result:
Teamsheet:
Scorer(s):

Wednesday 24/04/68   European Cup Semi-Final 1st Leg   at Old Trafford   Attendance 63500
Manchester United 1 Real Madrid 0
Stepney, Dunne, Burns, Crerand, Sadler, Stiles, Best, Kidd, Charlton, Law, Aston
Best

Match # 2862
Result:
Teamsheet:
Scorer(s):

Saturday 27/04/68   Football League Division 1   at The Hawthorns   Attendance 43412
West Bromwich Albion 6 Manchester United 3
Stepney, Dunne, Burns, Crerand, Sadler, Stiles, Best, Kidd, Charlton, Law, Aston
Kidd 2, Law

Match # 2863
Result:
Teamsheet:
Scorer(s):

Saturday 04/05/68   Football League Division 1   at Old Trafford   Attendance 59976
Manchester United 6 Newcastle United 0
Stepney, Brennan, Dunne, Crerand, Foulkes, Sadler, Best, Kidd, Charlton, Gowling, Aston
Best 3, Kidd 2, Sadler

Match # 2864
Result:
Teamsheet:
Substitute(s):

Saturday 11/05/68   Football League Division 1   at Old Trafford   Attendance 62963
Manchester United 1 Sunderland 2
Stepney, Brennan, Dunne, Crerand, Foulkes, Stiles, Best, Kidd, Charlton, Sadler, Aston
Gowling   Scorer(s):   Best

Match # 2865
Result:
Teamsheet:
Scorer(s):

Wednesday 15/05/68   European Cup Semi-Final 2nd Leg   at Bernabeu Stadium   Attendance 125000
Real Madrid 3 Manchester United 3
Stepney, Brennan, Dunne, Crerand, Foulkes, Stiles, Best, Kidd, Charlton, Sadler, Aston
Foulkes, Sadler, own goal

Match # 2866
Result:
Teamsheet:
Scorer(s):

Wednesday 29/05/68   European Cup Final   at Wembley   Attendance 100000
Manchester United 4 Benfica 1
Stepney, Brennan, Dunne, Crerand, Foulkes, Stiles, Best, Kidd, Charlton, Sadler, Aston
Charlton 2, Best, Kidd

SEASON 1967/68 SUMMARY

APPEARANCES

PLAYER	LGE	FAC	EC	CS	TOTAL
Best	41	2	9	1	53
Charlton	41	2	9	1	53
Crerand	41	2	9	1	53
Stepney	41	2	9	1	53
Sadler	40 (1)	2	9	–	51 (1)
Kidd	38	2	9	1	50
Dunne	37	2	9	1	49
Burns	36	2	7	–	45
Aston	34 (3)	2	6	1	43 (3)
Foulkes	24	–	6	1	31
Law	23	1	3	1	28
Stiles	20	–	7	1	28
Fitzpatrick	14 (3)	2	2	–	18 (3)
Brennan	13	–	3	1	17
Ryan	7 (1)	–	1	–	8 (1)
Herd	6	1	1	–	8
Gowling	4 (1)	–	–	–	4 (1)
Kopel	1 (1)	–	–	–	1 (1)
Rimmer	1	–	–	–	1

GOALSCORERS

PLAYER	LGE	FAC	EC	CS	TOT
Best	28	1	3	–	32
Charlton	15	1	2	2	20
Kidd	15	–	2	–	17
Aston	10	–	1	–	11
Law	7	–	2	1	10
Sadler	3	–	3	–	6
Burns	2	–	–	–	2
Ryan	2	–	–	–	2
Foulkes	1	–	1	–	2
Brennan	1	–	–	–	1
Crerand	1	–	–	–	1
Dunne	1	–	–	–	1
Gowling	1	–	–	–	1
Herd	1	–	–	–	1
own goals	1	–	2	–	3

RESULTS & ATTENDANCES SUMMARY

		P	W	D	L	F	A	TOTAL	AVGE
League	H	21	15	2	4	49	21	1209045	57574
	A	21	9	6	6	40	34	961848	45802
	TOTAL	42	24	8	10	89	55	2170893	51688
FA Cup	H	1	0	1	0	2	2	63500	63500
	A	1	0	0	1	0	1	57200	57200
	TOTAL	2	0	1	1	2	3	120700	60350
European	H	4	4	0	0	9	1	233669	58417
Cup	A	4	0	3	1	3	4	300000	75000
	N	1	1	0	0	4	1	100000	100000
	TOTAL	9	5	3	1	16	6	633669	70408
Charity	H	1	0	1	0	3	3	54106	54106
Shield	A	0	0	0	0	0	0	0	n/a
	TOTAL	1	0	1	0	3	3	54106	54106
Overall	H	27	19	4	4	63	27	1560320	57790
	A	26	9	9	8	43	39	1319048	50733
	N	1	1	0	0	4	1	100000	100000
	TOTAL	54	29	13	12	110	67	2979368	55173

FINAL TABLE – LEAGUE DIVISION ONE

		P	HOME W	D	L	F	A	AWAY W	D	L	F	A	PTS	GD
1	Manchester City	42	17	2	2	52	16	9	4	8	34	27	58	43
2	MANCHESTER UNITED	42	15	2	4	49	21	9	6	6	40	34	56	34
3	Liverpool	42	17	2	2	51	17	5	9	7	20	23	55	31
4	Leeds United	42	17	3	1	49	14	5	6	10	22	27	53	30
5	Everton	42	18	1	2	43	13	5	5	11	24	27	52	27
6	Chelsea	42	11	7	3	34	25	7	5	9	28	43	48	-6
7	Tottenham Hotspur	42	11	7	3	44	20	8	2	11	26	39	47	11
8	West Bromwich Albion	42	12	4	5	45	25	5	8	8	30	37	46	13
9	Arsenal	42	12	6	3	37	23	5	4	12	23	33	44	4
10	Newcastle United	42	12	7	2	38	20	1	8	12	16	47	41	-13
11	Nottingham Forest	42	11	6	4	34	22	3	5	13	18	42	39	-12
12	West Ham United	42	8	5	8	43	30	6	5	10	30	39	38	4
13	Leicester City	42	7	7	7	37	34	6	5	10	27	35	38	-5
14	Burnley	42	12	7	2	38	16	2	3	16	26	55	38	-7
15	Sunderland	42	8	7	6	28	28	5	4	12	23	33	37	-10
16	Southampton	42	9	8	4	37	31	4	3	14	29	52	37	-17
17	Wolverhampton Wanderers	42	10	4	7	45	36	4	4	13	21	39	36	-9
18	Stoke City	42	10	3	8	30	29	4	4	13	20	44	35	-23
19	Sheffield Wednesday	42	6	10	5	32	24	5	2	14	19	39	34	-12
20	Coventry City	42	8	5	8	32	32	1	10	10	19	39	33	-20
21	Sheffield United	42	7	4	10	25	31	4	6	11	24	39	32	-21
22	Fulham	42	6	4	11	27	41	4	3	14	29	57	27	-42

SEASON 1968/69

Match # 2867 Saturday 10/08/68 Football League Division 1 at Old Trafford Attendance 61311
Result: **Manchester United 2 Everton 1**
Teamsheet: Stepney, Brennan, Dunne, Crerand, Foulkes, Stiles, Best, Kidd, Charlton, Law, Aston
Scorer(s): Best, Charlton

Match # 2868 Wednesday 14/08/68 Football League Division 1 at The Hawthorns Attendance 38299
Result: **West Bromwich Albion 3 Manchester United 1**
Teamsheet: Stepney, Brennan, Dunne, Crerand, Foulkes, Stiles, Best, Kidd, Charlton, Law, Aston
Substitute(s): Sadler Scorer(s): Charlton

Match # 2869 Saturday 17/08/68 Football League Division 1 at Maine Road Attendance 63052
Result: **Manchester City 0 Manchester United 0**
Teamsheet: Stepney, Kopel, Dunne, Fitzpatrick, Sadler, Stiles, Best, Gowling, Charlton, Kidd, Aston
Substitute(s): Burns

Match # 2870 Wednesday 21/08/68 Football League Division 1 at Old Trafford Attendance 51201
Result: **Manchester United 1 Coventry City 0**
Teamsheet: Stepney, Kopel, Dunne, Fitzpatrick, Sadler, Stiles, Ryan, Kidd, Charlton, Burns, Best
Scorer(s): Ryan

Match # 2871 Saturday 24/08/68 Football League Division 1 at Old Trafford Attendance 55114
Result: **Manchester United 0 Chelsea 4**
Teamsheet: Stepney, Kopel, Dunne, Crerand, Sadler, Stiles, Ryan, Kidd, Charlton, Burns, Best

Match # 2872 Wednesday 28/08/68 Football League Division 1 at Old Trafford Attendance 62689
Result: **Manchester United 3 Tottenham Hotspur 1**
Teamsheet: Stepney, Brennan, Dunne, Fitzpatrick, Sadler, Stiles, Morgan, Kidd, Charlton, Law, Best
Scorer(s): Fitzpatrick 2, own goal

Match # 2873 Saturday 31/08/68 Football League Division 1 at Hillsborough Attendance 50490
Result: **Sheffield Wednesday 5 Manchester United 4**
Teamsheet: Stepney, Brennan, Dunne, Fitzpatrick, Sadler, Stiles, Morgan, Kidd, Charlton, Law, Best
Substitute(s): Burns Scorer(s): Law 2, Best, Charlton

Match # 2874 Saturday 07/09/68 Football League Division 1 at Old Trafford Attendance 63274
Result: **Manchester United 1 West Ham United 1**
Teamsheet: Stepney, Dunne, Burns, Fitzpatrick, Foulkes, Stiles, Morgan, Sadler, Charlton, Law, Best
Scorer(s): Law

Match # 2875 Saturday 14/09/68 Football League Division 1 at Turf Moor Attendance 32935
Result: **Burnley 1 Manchester United 0**
Teamsheet: Stepney, Dunne, Burns, Fitzpatrick, Foulkes, Stiles, Morgan, Sadler, Charlton, Law, Best

Match # 2876 Wednesday 18/09/68 European Cup 1st Round 1st Leg at Lansdowne Road Attendance 48000
Result: **Waterford 1 Manchester United 3**
Teamsheet: Stepney, Dunne, Burns, Crerand, Foulkes, Stiles, Best, Law, Charlton, Sadler, Kidd
Substitute(s): Rimmer Scorer(s): Law 3

Match # 2877 Saturday 21/09/68 Football League Division 1 at Old Trafford Attendance 47262
Result: **Manchester United 3 Newcastle United 1**
Teamsheet: Stepney, Dunne, Burns, Crerand, Sadler, Stiles, Morgan, Fitzpatrick, Charlton, Law, Best
Substitute(s): Kidd Scorer(s): Best 2, Law

Match # 2878 Wednesday 25/09/68 Inter-Continental Cup Final 1st Leg at Boca Juniors Stadium Attendance 55000
Result: **Estudiantes de la Plata 1 Manchester United 0**
Teamsheet: Stepney, Dunne, Burns, Crerand, Foulkes, Stiles, Morgan, Sadler, Charlton, Law, Best

Match # 2879 Wednesday 02/10/68 European Cup 1st Round 2nd Leg at Old Trafford Attendance 41750
Result: **Manchester United 7 Waterford 1**
Teamsheet: Stepney, Dunne, Burns, Crerand, Foulkes, Stiles, Best, Law, Charlton, Sadler, Kidd
Scorer(s): Law 4, Burns, Charlton, Stiles

Match # 2880 Saturday 05/10/68 Football League Division 1 at Old Trafford Attendance 61843
Result: **Manchester United 0 Arsenal 0**
Teamsheet: Stepney, Dunne, Burns, Crerand, Foulkes, Stiles, Morgan, Fitzpatrick, Charlton, Law, Best

Match # 2881 Wednesday 09/10/68 Football League Division 1 at White Hart Lane Attendance 56205
Result: **Tottenham Hotspur 2 Manchester United 2**
Teamsheet: Stepney, Dunne, Burns, Crerand, Foulkes, Stiles, Morgan, Fitzpatrick, Charlton, Law, Best
Substitute(s): Sartori Scorer(s): Crerand, Law

Match # 2882 Saturday 12/10/68 Football League Division 1 at Anfield Attendance 53392
Result: **Liverpool 2 Manchester United 0**
Teamsheet: Stepney, Brennan, Kopel, Crerand, James, Stiles, Ryan, Fitzpatrick, Charlton, Gowling, Sartori

Match # 2883 Wednesday 16/10/68 Inter-Continental Cup Final 2nd Leg at Old Trafford Attendance 63500
Result: **Manchester United 1 Estudiantes de la Plata 1**
Teamsheet: Stepney, Brennan, Dunne, Crerand, Foulkes, Sadler, Morgan, Kidd, Charlton, Law, Best
Scorer(s): Morgan

Match # 2884 Saturday 19/10/68 Football League Division 1 at Old Trafford Attendance 46526
Result: **Manchester United 1 Southampton 2**
Teamsheet: Stepney, Kopel, Dunne, Crerand, Foulkes, Stiles, Morgan, Sadler, Charlton, Sartori, Best
Substitute(s): Fitzpatrick Scorer(s): Best

SEASON 1968/69 (continued)

Match # 2885 Saturday 26/10/68   Football League Division 1   at Loftus Road   Attendance 31138
Result: **Queens Park Rangers 2 Manchester United 3**
Teamsheet: Stepney, Brennan, Dunne, Crerand, Sadler, Stiles, Morgan, Kidd, Charlton, Law, Best
Scorer(s):   Best 2, Law

Match # 2886 Saturday 02/11/68   Football League Division 1   at Old Trafford   Attendance 53839
Result: **Manchester United 0 Leeds United 0**
Teamsheet: Stepney, Brennan, Dunne, Crerand, Sadler, Stiles, Morgan, Kidd, Charlton, Law, Best

Match # 2887 Saturday 09/11/68   Football League Division 1   at Roker Park   Attendance 33151
Result: **Sunderland 1 Manchester United 1**
Teamsheet: Stepney, Brennan, Dunne, Crerand, Sadler, Stiles, Morgan, Kidd, Charlton, Sartori, Best
Scorer(s):   own goal

Match # 2888 Wednesday 13/11/68   European Cup 2nd Round 1st Leg   at Old Trafford   Attendance 51000
Result: **Manchester United 3 Anderlecht 0**
Teamsheet: Stepney, Brennan, Dunne, Crerand, Sadler, Stiles, Ryan, Kidd, Charlton, Law, Sartori
Scorer(s):   Law 2, Kidd

Match # 2889 Saturday 16/11/68   Football League Division 1   at Old Trafford   Attendance 45796
Result: **Manchester United 0 Ipswich Town 0**
Teamsheet: Stepney, Brennan, Dunne, Crerand, James, Stiles, Morgan, Kidd, Charlton, Law, Best
Substitute(s): Kopel

Match # 2890 Saturday 23/11/68   Football League Division 1   at Victoria Ground   Attendance 30562
Result: **Stoke City 0 Manchester United 0**
Teamsheet: Stepney, Kopel, Dunne, Crerand, James, Stiles, Morgan, Best, Charlton, Fitzpatrick, Sartori

Match # 2891 Wednesday 27/11/68   European Cup 2nd Round 2nd Leg   at Park Astrid   Attendance 40000
Result: **Anderlecht 3 Manchester United 1**
Teamsheet: Stepney, Kopel, Dunne, Crerand, Foulkes, Stiles, Fitzpatrick, Law, Charlton, Sadler, Sartori
Scorer(s):   Sartori

Match # 2892 Saturday 30/11/68   Football League Division 1   at Old Trafford   Attendance 50165
Result: **Manchester United 2 Wolverhampton Wanderers 0**
Teamsheet: Stepney, Kopel, Dunne, Crerand, Sadler, Stiles, Morgan, Sartori, Charlton, Law, Best
Substitute(s): Fitzpatrick   Scorer(s):   Best, Law

Match # 2893 Saturday 07/12/68   Football League Division 1   at Filbert Street   Attendance 36303
Result: **Leicester City 2 Manchester United 1**
Teamsheet: Stepney, Dunne, Burns, Crerand, Sadler, Stiles, Morgan, Sartori, Charlton, Law, Best
Scorer(s):   Law

Match # 2894 Saturday 14/12/68   Football League Division 1   at Old Trafford   Attendance 55354
Result: **Manchester United 1 Liverpool 0**
Teamsheet: Stepney, Dunne, Burns, Crerand, James, Stiles, Best, Sadler, Charlton, Law, Sartori
Scorer(s):   Law

Match # 2895 Saturday 21/12/68   Football League Division 1   at The Dell   Attendance 26194
Result: **Southampton 2 Manchester United 0**
Teamsheet: Stepney, Dunne, Burns, Crerand, James, Stiles, Best, Sadler, Charlton, Law, Sartori

Match # 2896 Thursday 26/12/68   Football League Division 1   at Highbury   Attendance 62300
Result: **Arsenal 3 Manchester United 0**
Teamsheet: Stepney, Dunne, Burns, Crerand, James, Stiles, Best, Sadler, Charlton, Law, Kidd
Substitute(s): Sartori

Match # 2897 Saturday 04/01/69   FA Cup 3rd Round   at St James' Park   Attendance 18500
Result: **Exeter City 1 Manchester United 3**
Teamsheet: Stepney, Dunne, Burns, Fitzpatrick, James, Stiles, Best, Kidd, Charlton, Law, Sartori
Substitute(s): Sadler   Scorer(s):   Fitzpatrick, Kidd, own goal

Match # 2898 Saturday 11/01/69   Football League Division 1   at Elland Road   Attendance 48145
Result: **Leeds United 2 Manchester United 1**
Teamsheet: Stepney, Dunne, Burns, Crerand, James, Stiles, Best, Fitzpatrick, Charlton, Law, Sartori
Scorer(s):   Charlton

Match # 2899 Saturday 18/01/69   Football League Division 1   at Old Trafford   Attendance 45670
Result: **Manchester United 4 Sunderland 1**
Teamsheet: Rimmer, Dunne, Burns, Fitzpatrick, James, Stiles, Morgan, Sartori, Charlton, Law, Best
Scorer(s):   Law 3, Best

Match # 2900 Saturday 25/01/69   FA Cup 4th Round   at Old Trafford   Attendance 63498
Result: **Manchester United 1 Watford 1**
Teamsheet: Rimmer, Kopel, Dunne, Fitzpatrick, James, Stiles, Morgan, Best, Charlton, Law, Sartori
Scorer(s):   Law

Match # 2901 Saturday 01/02/69   Football League Division 1   at Portman Road   Attendance 30837
Result: **Ipswich Town 1 Manchester United 0**
Teamsheet: Stepney, Fitzpatrick, Dunne, Crerand, James, Stiles, Morgan, Kidd, Charlton, Law, Best

Match # 2902 Monday 03/02/69   FA Cup 4th Round Replay   at Vicarage Road   Attendance 34000
Result: **Watford 0 Manchester United 2**
Teamsheet: Stepney, Fitzpatrick, Dunne, Crerand, James, Stiles, Morgan, Kidd, Charlton, Law, Best
Scorer(s):   Law 2

SEASON 1968/69 (continued)

Match # 2903 Saturday 08/02/69   FA Cup 5th Round   at St Andrews   Attendance 52500
Result: **Birmingham City 2 Manchester United 2**
Teamsheet: Stepney, Fitzpatrick, Dunne, Crerand, James, Stiles, Morgan, Kidd, Charlton, Law, Best
Scorer(s):   Best, Law

Match # 2904 Saturday 15/02/69   Football League Division 1   at Molineux   Attendance 44023
Result: **Wolverhampton Wanderers 2 Manchester United 2**
Teamsheet: Stepney, Fitzpatrick, Dunne, Crerand, James, Sadler, Morgan, Kidd, Charlton, Sartori, Best
Substitute(s):   Foulkes   Scorer(s):   Best, Charlton

Match # 2905 Monday 24/02/69   FA Cup 5th Round Replay   at Old Trafford   Attendance 61932
Result: **Manchester United 6 Birmingham City 2**
Teamsheet: Stepney, Fitzpatrick, Dunne, Crerand, James, Stiles, Morgan, Kidd, Charlton, Law, Best
Scorer(s):   Law 3, Crerand, Kidd, Morgan

Match # 2906 Wednesday 26/02/69   European Cup Quarter-Final 1st Leg   at Old Trafford   Attendance 61932
Result: **Manchester United 3 Rapid Vienna 0**
Teamsheet: Stepney, Fitzpatrick, Dunne, Crerand, James, Stiles, Morgan, Kidd, Charlton, Law, Best
Scorer(s):   Best 2, Morgan

Match # 2907 Saturday 01/03/69   FA Cup 6th Round   at Old Trafford   Attendance 63464
Result: **Manchester United 0 Everton 1**
Teamsheet: Stepney, Fitzpatrick, Dunne, Crerand, James, Stiles, Morgan, Kidd, Charlton, Law, Best

Match # 2908 Wednesday 05/03/69   European Cup Quarter-Final 2nd Leg   at Wiener Stadion   Attendance 52000
Result: **Rapid Vienna 0 Manchester United 0**
Teamsheet: Stepney, Fitzpatrick, Dunne, Crerand, James, Stiles, Morgan, Kidd, Charlton, Sadler, Best

Match # 2909 Saturday 08/03/69   Football League Division 1   at Old Trafford   Attendance 63264
Result: **Manchester United 0 Manchester City 1**
Teamsheet: Stepney, Brennan, Fitzpatrick, Crerand, Foulkes, Stiles, Morgan, Kidd, Charlton, Sadler, Best

Match # 2910 Monday 10/03/69   Football League Division 1   at Goodison Park   Attendance 57514
Result: **Everton 0 Manchester United 0**
Teamsheet: Stepney, Brennan, Dunne, Crerand, James, Stiles, Best, Kidd, Fitzpatrick, Sadler, Aston
Substitute(s):   Foulkes

Match # 2911 Saturday 15/03/69   Football League Division 1   at Stamford Bridge   Attendance 60436
Result: **Chelsea 3 Manchester United 2**
Teamsheet: Stepney, Fitzpatrick, Dunne, Crerand, James, Stiles, Morgan, Kidd, Sadler, Law, Best
Scorer(s):   James, Law

Match # 2912 Wednesday 19/03/69   Football League Division 1   at Old Trafford   Attendance 36638
Result: **Manchester United 8 Queens Park Rangers 1**
Teamsheet: Stepney, Fitzpatrick, Dunne, Crerand, James, Stiles, Morgan, Kidd, Aston, Law, Best
Scorer(s):   Morgan 3, Best 2, Aston, Kidd, Stiles

Match # 2913 Saturday 22/03/69   Football League Division 1   at Old Trafford   Attendance 45527
Result: **Manchester United 1 Sheffield Wednesday 0**
Teamsheet: Stepney, Fitzpatrick, Dunne, Crerand, James, Stiles, Morgan, Kidd, Best, Law, Aston
Scorer(s):   Best

Match # 2914 Monday 24/03/69   Football League Division 1   at Old Trafford   Attendance 39931
Result: **Manchester United 1 Stoke City 1**
Teamsheet: Stepney, Fitzpatrick, Dunne, Crerand, James, Stiles, Morgan, Kidd, Aston, Law, Best
Substitute(s):   Sadler   Scorer(s):   Aston

Match # 2915 Saturday 29/03/69   Football League Division 1   at Upton Park   Attendance 41546
Result: **West Ham United 0 Manchester United 0**
Teamsheet: Stepney, Fitzpatrick, Dunne, Crerand, James, Stiles, Ryan, Kidd, Aston, Law, Best
Substitute(s):   Sadler

Match # 2916 Monday 31/03/69   Football League Division 1   at City Ground   Attendance 41892
Result: **Nottingham Forest 0 Manchester United 1**
Teamsheet: Stepney, Fitzpatrick, Stiles, Crerand, James, Sadler, Ryan, Kidd, Aston, Law, Best
Scorer(s):   Best

Match # 2917 Wednesday 02/04/69   Football League Division 1   at Old Trafford   Attendance 38846
Result: **Manchester United 2 West Bromwich Albion 1**
Teamsheet: Stepney, Fitzpatrick, Stiles, Crerand, James, Sadler, Morgan, Ryan, Aston, Kidd, Best
Substitute(s):   Foulkes   Scorer(s):   Best 2

Match # 2918 Saturday 05/04/69   Football League Division 1   at Old Trafford   Attendance 51952
Result: **Manchester United 3 Nottingham Forest 1**
Teamsheet: Stepney, Fitzpatrick, Stiles, Crerand, James, Sadler, Morgan, Kidd, Aston, Law, Best
Scorer(s):   Morgan 2, Best

Match # 2919 Tuesday 08/04/69   Football League Division 1   at Highfield Road   Attendance 45402
Result: **Coventry City 2 Manchester United 1**
Teamsheet: Stepney, Fitzpatrick, Stiles, Crerand, James, Sadler, Morgan, Kidd, Aston, Charlton, Best
Scorer(s):   Fitzpatrick

Match # 2920 Saturday 12/04/69   Football League Division 1   at St James' Park   Attendance 46379
Result: **Newcastle United 2 Manchester United 0**
Teamsheet: Rimmer, Fitzpatrick, Stiles, Crerand, James, Sadler, Morgan, Kidd, Charlton, Law, Best

SEASON 1968/69 (continued)

Match # 2921	Saturday 19/04/69	Football League Division 1	at Old Trafford	Attendance 52626
Result: **Manchester United 2 Burnley 0**
Teamsheet: Rimmer, Brennan, Fitzpatrick, Crerand, Foulkes, Stiles, Morgan, Kidd, Aston, Law, Best
Scorer(s): Best, own goal

Match # 2922	Wednesday 23/04/69	European Cup Semi-Final 1st Leg	at Stadio San Siro	Attendance 80000
Result: **AC Milan 2 Manchester United 0**
Teamsheet: Rimmer, Brennan, Fitzpatrick, Crerand, Foulkes, Stiles, Morgan, Kidd, Charlton, Law, Best
Substitute(s): Burns

Match # 2923	Thursday 15/05/69	European Cup Semi-Final 2nd Leg	at Old Trafford	Attendance 63103
Result: **Manchester United 1 AC Milan 0**
Teamsheet: Rimmer, Brennan, Burns, Crerand, Foulkes, Stiles, Morgan, Kidd, Charlton, Law, Best
Scorer(s): Charlton

Match # 2924	Saturday 17/05/69	Football League Division 1	at Old Trafford	Attendance 45860
Result: **Manchester United 3 Leicester City 2**
Teamsheet: Rimmer, Brennan, Burns, Crerand, Foulkes, Stiles, Morgan, Kidd, Charlton, Law, Best
Scorer(s): Best, Law, Morgan

SEASON 1968/69 SUMMARY

APPEARANCES

PLAYER	LGE	FAC	EC	ICC	TOTAL
Stiles	41	6	8	1	56
Best	41	6	6	2	55
Stepney	38	5	6	2	51
Crerand	35	4	8	2	49
Charlton	32	6	8	2	48
Dunne	33	6	6	2	47
Law	30	6	7	2	45
Kidd	28 (1)	5	7	1	41 (1)
Morgan	29	5	4	2	40
Fitzpatrick	28 (2)	6	4	–	38 (2)
Sadler	26 (3)	– (1)	5	2	33 (4)
James	21	6	2	–	29
Burns	14 (2)	1	3 (1)	1	19 (3)
Foulkes	10 (3)	–	5	2	17 (3)
Brennan	13	–	3	1	17
Sartori	11 (2)	2	2	–	15 (2)
Aston	13	–	–	–	13
Kopel	7 (1)	1	1	–	9 (1)
Rimmer	4	1	2 (1)	–	7 (1)
Ryan	6	–	1	–	7
Gowling	2	–	–	–	2

GOALSCORERS

PLAYER	LGE	FAC	EC	ICC	TOT
Law	14	7	9	–	30
Best	19	1	2	–	22
Morgan	6	1	1	1	9
Charlton	5	–	2	–	7
Fitzpatrick	3	1	–	–	4
Kidd	1	2	1	–	4
Aston	2	–	–	–	2
Crerand	1	1	–	–	2
Stiles	1	–	1	–	2
James	1	–	–	–	1
Ryan	1	–	–	–	1
Burns	–	–	1	–	1
Sartori	–	–	1	–	1
own goals	3	1	–	–	4

RESULTS & ATTENDANCES SUMMARY

		P	W	D	L	F	A	TOTAL	AVGE
League	H	21	13	5	3	38	18	1074688	51176
	A	21	2	7	12	19	35	930195	44295
	TOTAL	42	15	12	15	57	53	2004883	47735
FA Cup	H	3	1	1	1	7	4	188894	62965
	A	3	2	1	0	7	3	105000	35000
	TOTAL	6	3	2	1	14	7	293894	48982
European	H	4	4	0	0	14	1	217785	54446
Cup	A	4	1	1	2	4	6	220000	55000
	TOTAL	8	5	1	2	18	7	437785	54723
ICC	H	1	0	1	0	1	1	63500	63500
	A	1	0	0	1	0	1	55000	55000
	TOTAL	2	0	1	1	1	2	118500	59250
Overall	H	29	18	7	4	60	24	1544867	53271
	A	29	5	9	15	30	45	1310195	45179
	TOTAL	58	23	16	19	90	69	2855062	49225

FINAL TABLE – LEAGUE DIVISION ONE

		P	HOME					AWAY					PTS	GD
			W	D	L	F	A	W	D	L	F	A		
1	Leeds United	42	18	3	0	41	9	9	10	2	25	17	67	40
2	Liverpool	42	16	4	1	36	10	9	7	5	27	14	61	39
3	Everton	42	14	5	2	43	10	7	10	4	34	26	57	41
4	Arsenal	42	12	6	3	31	12	10	6	5	25	15	56	29
5	Chelsea	42	11	7	3	40	24	9	3	9	33	29	50	20
6	Tottenham Hotspur	42	10	8	3	39	22	4	9	8	22	29	45	10
7	Southampton	42	10	5	3	41	21	3	8	10	16	27	45	9
8	West Ham United	42	10	8	3	47	22	3	10	8	19	28	44	16
9	Newcastle United	42	12	7	2	40	20	3	7	11	21	35	44	6
10	West Bromwich Albion	42	11	7	3	43	26	5	4	12	21	41	43	–3
11	**MANCHESTER UNITED**	42	13	5	3	38	18	2	7	12	19	35	42	4
12	Ipswich Town	42	10	4	7	32	26	5	7	9	27	34	41	–1
13	Manchester City	42	13	6	2	49	20	2	4	15	15	35	40	9
14	Burnley	42	11	6	4	36	25	4	3	14	19	57	39	–27
15	Sheffield Wednesday	42	7	9	5	27	26	3	7	11	14	28	36	–13
16	Wolverhampton Wanderers	42	7	10	4	26	22	3	5	13	15	36	35	–17
17	Sunderland	42	10	6	5	28	18	1	6	14	15	49	34	–24
18	Nottingham Forest	42	6	6	9	17	22	4	7	10	28	35	33	–12
19	Stoke City	42	9	7	5	24	24	0	8	13	16	39	33	–23
20	Coventry City	42	8	6	7	32	22	2	5	14	14	42	31	–18
21	Leicester City	42	8	8	5	27	24	1	4	16	12	44	30	–29
22	Queens Park Rangers	42	4	7	10	20	33	0	3	18	19	62	18	–56

SEASON 1969/70

Match # 2925 Saturday 09/08/69   Football League Division 1   at Selhurst Park   Attendance 48610
Result: **Crystal Palace 2   Manchester United 2**
Teamsheet: Rimmer, Dunne, Burns, Crerand, Foulkes, Sadler, Morgan, Kidd, Charlton, Law, Best
Substitute(s):   Givens   Scorer(s):   Charlton, Morgan

Match # 2926 Wednesday 13/08/69   Football League Division 1   at Old Trafford   Attendance 57752
Result: **Manchester United 0   Everton 2**
Teamsheet: Rimmer, Brennan, Burns, Crerand, Foulkes, Sadler, Morgan, Kidd, Charlton, Law, Best
Substitute(s):   Givens

Match # 2927 Saturday 16/08/69   Football League Division 1   at Old Trafford   Attendance 46328
Result: **Manchester United 1   Southampton 4**
Teamsheet: Rimmer, Brennan, Burns, Crerand, Foulkes, Sadler, Morgan, Kidd, Charlton, Law, Best
Scorer(s):   Morgan

Match # 2928 Tuesday 19/08/69   Football League Division 1   at Goodison Park   Attendance 53185
Result: **Everton 3   Manchester United 0**
Teamsheet: Stepney, Fitzpatrick, Burns, Crerand, Edwards, Sadler, Morgan, Kidd, Givens, Best, Aston

Match # 2929 Saturday 23/08/69   Football League Division 1   at Molineux   Attendance 50783
Result: **Wolverhampton Wanderers 0   Manchester United 0**
Teamsheet: Stepney, Fitzpatrick, Burns, Crerand, Ure, Sadler, Morgan, Kidd, Charlton, Law, Best
Substitute(s):   Givens

Match # 2930 Wednesday 27/08/69   Football League Division 1   at Old Trafford   Attendance 52774
Result: **Manchester United 0   Newcastle United 0**
Teamsheet: Stepney, Fitzpatrick, Dunne, Crerand, Ure, Sadler, Morgan, Kidd, Charlton, Givens, Best

Match # 2931 Saturday 30/08/69   Football League Division 1   at Old Trafford   Attendance 50570
Result: **Manchester United 3   Sunderland 1**
Teamsheet: Stepney, Fitzpatrick, Dunne, Crerand, Ure, Sadler, Morgan, Kidd, Charlton, Givens, Best
Scorer(s):   Best, Kidd, Givens

Match # 2932 Wednesday 03/09/69   League Cup 2nd Round   at Old Trafford   Attendance 38938
Result: **Manchester United 1   Middlesbrough 0**
Teamsheet: Stepney, Fitzpatrick, Dunne, Crerand, James, Sadler, Morgan, Kidd, Charlton, Givens, Best
Substitute(s):   Gowling   Scorer(s):   Sadler

Match # 2933 Saturday 06/09/69   Football League Division 1   at Elland Road   Attendance 44271
Result: **Leeds United 2   Manchester United 2**
Teamsheet: Stepney, Fitzpatrick, Dunne, Burns, Ure, Sadler, Morgan, Givens, Charlton, Gowling, Best
Scorer(s):   Best 2

Match # 2934 Saturday 13/09/69   Football League Division 1   at Old Trafford   Attendance 56509
Result: **Manchester United 1   Liverpool 0**
Teamsheet: Stepney, Fitzpatrick, Dunne, Burns, Ure, Sadler, Morgan, Kidd, Charlton, Gowling, Best
Scorer(s):   Morgan

Match # 2935 Wednesday 17/09/69   Football League Division 1   at Hillsborough   Attendance 39298
Result: **Sheffield Wednesday 1   Manchester United 3**
Teamsheet: Stepney, Fitzpatrick, Dunne, Burns, Ure, Sadler, Morgan, Kidd, Charlton, Gowling, Best
Substitute(s):   Aston   Scorer(s):   Best 2, Kidd

Match # 2936 Saturday 20/09/69   Football League Division 1   at Highbury   Attendance 59498
Result: **Arsenal 2   Manchester United 2**
Teamsheet: Stepney, Fitzpatrick, Dunne, Burns, Ure, Sadler, Morgan, Kidd, Charlton, Aston, Best
Scorer(s):   Best, Sadler

Match # 2937 Tuesday 23/09/69   League Cup 3rd Round   at Old Trafford   Attendance 48347
Result: **Manchester United 2   Wrexham 0**
Teamsheet: Stepney, Fitzpatrick, Dunne, Burns, Ure, Sadler, Morgan, Kidd, Charlton, Aston, Best
Scorer(s):   Best, Kidd

Match # 2938 Saturday 27/09/69   Football League Division 1   at Old Trafford   Attendance 58579
Result: **Manchester United 5   West Ham United 2**
Teamsheet: Stepney, Fitzpatrick, Dunne, Burns, Ure, Sadler, Morgan, Kidd, Charlton, Aston, Best
Scorer(s):   Best 2, Burns, Charlton, Kidd

Match # 2939 Saturday 04/10/69   Football League Division 1   at Baseball Ground   Attendance 40724
Result: **Derby County 2   Manchester United 0**
Teamsheet: Stepney, Fitzpatrick, Dunne, Burns, Ure, Sadler, Morgan, Kidd, Charlton, Aston, Best
Substitute(s):   Sartori

Match # 2940 Wednesday 08/10/69   Football League Division 1   at The Dell   Attendance 31044
Result: **Southampton 0   Manchester United 3**
Teamsheet: Stepney, Fitzpatrick, Dunne, Burns, Ure, Sadler, Morgan, Kidd, Charlton, Aston, Best
Scorer(s):   Best, Burns, Kidd

Match # 2941 Saturday 11/10/69   Football League Division 1   at Old Trafford   Attendance 52281
Result: **Manchester United 2   Ipswich Town 1**
Teamsheet: Stepney, Fitzpatrick, Dunne, Burns, Ure, Sadler, Morgan, Kidd, Charlton, Aston, Best
Substitute(s):   Brennan   Scorer(s):   Best, Kidd

Match # 2942 Tuesday 14/10/69   League Cup 4th Round   at Turf Moor   Attendance 27959
Result: **Burnley 0   Manchester United 0**
Teamsheet: Stepney, Fitzpatrick, Dunne, Burns, Ure, Sadler, Morgan, Kidd, Charlton, Aston, Best

SEASON 1969/70 (continued)

Match # 2943	Saturday 18/10/69	Football League Division 1	at Old Trafford	Attendance 53702
Result:	**Manchester United 1 Nottingham Forest 1**			
Teamsheet:	Stepney, Fitzpatrick, Dunne, Burns, Ure, Sadler, Morgan, Kidd, Charlton, Aston, Best			
Scorer(s):	Best			

Match # 2944	Monday 20/10/69	League Cup 4th Round Replay	at Old Trafford	Attendance 50275
Result:	**Manchester United 1 Burnley 0**			
Teamsheet:	Stepney, Fitzpatrick, Dunne, Burns, Ure, Sadler, Morgan, Kidd, Charlton, Aston, Best			
Substitute(s):	Sartori	Scorer(s): Best		

Match # 2945	Saturday 25/10/69	Football League Division 1	at The Hawthorns	Attendance 45120
Result:	**West Bromwich Albion 2 Manchester United 1**			
Teamsheet:	Stepney, Brennan, Dunne, Burns, Ure, Sadler, Sartori, Kidd, Charlton, Aston, Best			
Substitute(s):	Givens	Scorer(s): Kidd		

Match # 2946	Saturday 01/11/69	Football League Division 1	at Old Trafford	Attendance 53406
Result:	**Manchester United 1 Stoke City 1**			
Teamsheet:	Stepney, Brennan, Dunne, Burns, Ure, Sadler, Law, Kidd, Charlton, Aston, Best			
Scorer(s):	Charlton			

Match # 2947	Saturday 08/11/69	Football League Division 1	at Highfield Road	Attendance 43446
Result:	**Coventry City 1 Manchester United 2**			
Teamsheet:	Stepney, Brennan, Dunne, Burns, Ure, Sadler, Sartori, Best, Charlton, Law, Aston			
Scorer(s):	Aston, Law			

Match # 2948	Wednesday 12/11/69	League Cup 5th Round	at Baseball Ground	Attendance 38895
Result:	**Derby County 0 Manchester United 0**			
Teamsheet:	Stepney, Brennan, Dunne, Burns, Ure, Sadler, Sartori, Best, Charlton, Law, Aston			

Match # 2949	Saturday 15/11/69	Football League Division 1	at Maine Road	Attendance 63013
Result:	**Manchester City 4 Manchester United 0**			
Teamsheet:	Stepney, Brennan, Dunne, Burns, Ure, Sadler, Sartori, Best, Charlton, Law, Aston			
Substitute(s):	Kidd			

Match # 2950	Wednesday 19/11/69	League Cup 5th Round Replay	at Old Trafford	Attendance 57393
Result:	**Manchester United 1 Derby County 0**			
Teamsheet:	Stepney, Fitzpatrick, Dunne, Burns, Ure, Sadler, Best, Kidd, Charlton, Law, Aston			
Substitute(s):	Sartori	Scorer(s): Kidd		

Match # 2951	Saturday 22/11/69	Football League Division 1	at Old Trafford	Attendance 50003
Result:	**Manchester United 3 Tottenham Hotspur 1**			
Teamsheet:	Stepney, Fitzpatrick, Dunne, Burns, Ure, Sadler, Sartori, Kidd, Charlton, Best, Aston			
Substitute(s):	Edwards	Scorer(s): Charlton 2, Burns		

Match # 2952	Saturday 29/11/69	Football League Division 1	at Turf Moor	Attendance 23770
Result:	**Burnley 1 Manchester United 1**			
Teamsheet:	Stepney, Edwards, Dunne, Burns, Ure, Sadler, Best, Kidd, Charlton, Stiles, Aston			
Scorer(s):	Best			

Match # 2953	Wednesday 03/12/69	League Cup Semi-Final 1st Leg	at Maine Road	Attendance 55799
Result:	**Manchester City 2 Manchester United 1**			
Teamsheet:	Stepney, Edwards, Dunne, Burns, Ure, Sadler, Best, Kidd, Charlton, Stiles, Aston			
Scorer(s):	Charlton			

Match # 2954	Saturday 06/12/69	Football League Division 1	at Old Trafford	Attendance 49344
Result:	**Manchester United 0 Chelsea 2**			
Teamsheet:	Stepney, Edwards, Dunne, Burns, Ure, Sadler, Best, Kidd, Charlton, Stiles, Aston			
Substitute(s):	Ryan			

Match # 2955	Saturday 13/12/69	Football League Division 1	at Anfield	Attendance 47682
Result:	**Liverpool 1 Manchester United 4**			
Teamsheet:	Stepney, Brennan, Dunne, Burns, Ure, Sadler, Morgan, Best, Charlton, Crerand, Aston			
Substitute(s):	Sartori	Scorer(s): Charlton, Morgan, Ure, own goal		

Match # 2956	Wednesday 17/12/69	League Cup Semi-Final 2nd Leg	at Old Trafford	Attendance 63418
Result:	**Manchester United 2 Manchester City 2**			
Teamsheet:	Stepney, Edwards, Dunne, Stiles, Ure, Sadler, Morgan, Crerand, Charlton, Law, Best			
Scorer(s):	Edwards, Law			

Match # 2957	Friday 26/12/69	Football League Division 1	at Old Trafford	Attendance 50806
Result:	**Manchester United 0 Wolverhampton Wanderers 0**			
Teamsheet:	Stepney, Edwards, Dunne, Burns, Ure, Sadler, Morgan, Crerand, Charlton, Kidd, Best			

Match # 2958	Saturday 27/12/69	Football League Division 1	at Roker Park	Attendance 36504
Result:	**Sunderland 1 Manchester United 1**			
Teamsheet:	Stepney, Edwards, Brennan, Burns, Ure, Sadler, Morgan, Crerand, Charlton, Kidd, Best			
Scorer(s):	Kidd			

Match # 2959	Saturday 03/01/70	FA Cup 3rd Round	at Portman Road	Attendance 29552
Result:	**Ipswich Town 0 Manchester United 1**			
Teamsheet:	Stepney, Edwards, Brennan, Burns, Ure, Sadler, Morgan, Crerand, Charlton, Kidd, Best			
Substitute(s):	Aston	Scorer(s): own goal		

Match # 2960	Saturday 10/01/70	Football League Division 1	at Old Trafford	Attendance 41055
Result:	**Manchester United 2 Arsenal 1**			
Teamsheet:	Stepney, Edwards, Dunne, Burns, Ure, Sadler, Morgan, Crerand, Charlton, Kidd, Aston			
Substitute(s):	Sartori	Scorer(s): Morgan, Sartori		

SEASON 1969/70 (continued)

Match # 2961 Saturday 17/01/70   Football League Division 1   at Upton Park   Attendance 41643
Result: **West Ham United 0 Manchester United 0**
Teamsheet: Rimmer, Edwards, Burns, Crerand, Ure, Sadler, Morgan, Sartori, Charlton, Kidd, Aston

Match # 2962 Saturday 24/01/70   FA Cup 4th Round   at Old Trafford   Attendance 63417
Result: **Manchester United 3 Manchester City 0**
Teamsheet: Stepney, Edwards, Burns, Crerand, Ure, Sadler, Morgan, Sartori, Charlton, Kidd, Aston
Scorer(s):   Kidd 2, Morgan

Match # 2963 Monday 26/01/70   Football League Division 1   at Old Trafford   Attendance 59879
Result: **Manchester United 2 Leeds United 2**
Teamsheet: Stepney, Edwards, Burns, Crerand, Ure, Sadler, Morgan, Sartori, Charlton, Kidd, Aston
Scorer(s):   Kidd, Sadler

Match # 2964 Saturday 31/01/70   Football League Division 1   at Old Trafford   Attendance 59315
Result: **Manchester United 1 Derby County 0**
Teamsheet: Stepney, Edwards, Burns, Crerand, Ure, Sadler, Morgan, Sartori, Charlton, Kidd, Aston
Scorer(s):   Charlton

Match # 2965 Saturday 07/02/70   FA Cup 5th Round   at County Ground   Attendance 21771
Result: **Northampton Town 2 Manchester United 8**
Teamsheet: Stepney, Edwards, Dunne, Crerand, Ure, Sadler, Morgan, Sartori, Charlton, Kidd, Best
Substitute(s): Burns   Scorer(s):   Best 6, Kidd 2

Match # 2966 Tuesday 10/02/70   Football League Division 1   at Portman Road   Attendance 29755
Result: **Ipswich Town 0 Manchester United 1**
Teamsheet: Stepney, Edwards, Dunne, Crerand, Ure, Sadler, Morgan, Sartori, Charlton, Kidd, Best
Scorer(s):   Kidd

Match # 2967 Saturday 14/02/70   Football League Division 1   at Old Trafford   Attendance 54711
Result: **Manchester United 1 Crystal Palace 1**
Teamsheet: Stepney, Edwards, Dunne, Crerand, Ure, Sadler, Morgan, Sartori, Charlton, Kidd, Best
Scorer(s):   Kidd

Match # 2968 Saturday 21/02/70   FA Cup 6th Round   at Ayresome Park   Attendance 40000
Result: **Middlesbrough 1 Manchester United 1**
Teamsheet: Stepney, Edwards, Dunne, Crerand, Ure, Sadler, Morgan, Sartori, Charlton, Kidd, Best
Scorer(s):   Sartori

Match # 2969 Wednesday 25/02/70   FA Cup 6th Round Replay   at Old Trafford   Attendance 63418
Result: **Manchester United 2 Middlesbrough 1**
Teamsheet: Stepney, Dunne, Burns, Crerand, Ure, Sadler, Morgan, Sartori, Charlton, Kidd, Best
Scorer(s):   Charlton, Morgan

Match # 2970 Saturday 28/02/70   Football League Division 1   at Victoria Ground   Attendance 38917
Result: **Stoke City 2 Manchester United 2**
Teamsheet: Stepney, Edwards, Dunne, Crerand, Ure, Sadler, Morgan, Sartori, Charlton, Kidd, Best
Substitute(s): Burns   Scorer(s):   Morgan, Sartori

Match # 2971 Saturday 14/03/70   FA Cup Semi-Final   at Hillsborough   Attendance 55000
Result: **Leeds United 0 Manchester United 0**
Teamsheet: Stepney, Edwards, Dunne, Crerand, Ure, Sadler, Morgan, Sartori, Charlton, Kidd, Best

Match # 2972 Tuesday 17/03/70   Football League Division 1   at Old Trafford   Attendance 38377
Result: **Manchester United 3 Burnley 3**
Teamsheet: Rimmer, Edwards, Dunne, Crerand, Ure, Sadler, Morgan, Sartori, Charlton, Law, Best
Scorer(s):   Best, Crerand, Law

Match # 2973 Saturday 21/03/70   Football League Division 1   at Stamford Bridge   Attendance 61479
Result: **Chelsea 2 Manchester United 1**
Teamsheet: Stepney, Edwards, Burns, Crerand, Ure, Stiles, Morgan, Sartori, Charlton, Law, Best
Scorer(s):   Morgan

Match # 2974 Monday 23/03/70   FA Cup Semi-Final Replay   at Villa Park   Attendance 62500
Result: **Leeds United 0 Manchester United 0**
Teamsheet: Stepney, Edwards, Dunne, Crerand, Sadler, Stiles, Morgan, Sartori, Charlton, Kidd, Best
Substitute(s): Law

Match # 2975 Thursday 26/03/70   FA Cup Semi-Final 2nd Replay   at Burnden Park   Attendance 56000
Result: **Leeds United 1 Manchester United 0**
Teamsheet: Stepney, Edwards, Dunne, Crerand, Sadler, Stiles, Morgan, Sartori, Charlton, Kidd, Best
Substitute(s): Law

Match # 2976 Saturday 28/03/70   Football League Division 1   at Old Trafford   Attendance 59777
Result: **Manchester United 1 Manchester City 2**
Teamsheet: Stepney, Edwards, Dunne, Crerand, Sadler, Burns, Morgan, Sartori, Charlton, Kidd, Best
Substitute(s): Law   Scorer(s):   Kidd

Match # 2977 Monday 30/03/70   Football League Division 1   at Old Trafford   Attendance 38647
Result: **Manchester United 1 Coventry City 1**
Teamsheet: Stepney, Edwards, Dunne, Fitzpatrick, Ure, Sadler, Morgan, Best, Law, Kidd, Aston
Substitute(s): Burns   Scorer(s):   Kidd

Match # 2978 Tuesday 31/03/70   Football League Division 1   at City Ground   Attendance 39228
Result: **Nottingham Forest 1 Manchester United 2**
Teamsheet: Stepney, Stiles, Dunne, Crerand, James, Sadler, Morgan, Fitzpatrick, Charlton, Gowling, Best
Scorer(s):   Charlton, Gowling

SEASON 1969/70 (continued)

Match # 2979   Saturday 04/04/70   Football League Division 1   at St James' Park   Attendance 43094
Result: **Newcastle United 5   Manchester United 1**
Teamsheet: Stepney, Fitzpatrick, Dunne, Crerand, James, Sadler, Morgan, Gowling, Charlton, Stiles, Aston
Substitute(s):   Sartori   Scorer(s):   Charlton

Match # 2980   Wednesday 08/04/70   Football League Division 1   at Old Trafford   Attendance 26582
Result: **Manchester United 7   West Bromwich Albion 0**
Teamsheet: Stepney, Stiles, Dunne, Crerand, Ure, Sadler, Morgan, Fitzpatrick, Charlton, Gowling, Best
Scorer(s):   Charlton 2, Fitzpatrick 2, Gowling 2, Best

Match # 2981   Friday 10/04/70   FA Cup 3rd Place Play-Off   at Highbury   Attendance 15105
Result: **Manchester United 2   Watford 0**
Teamsheet: Stepney, Stiles, Dunne, Crerand, Ure, Sadler, Morgan, Fitzpatrick, Charlton, Kidd, Best
Scorer(s):   Kidd 2

Match # 2982   Monday 13/04/70   Football League Division 1   at White Hart Lane   Attendance 41808
Result: **Tottenham Hotspur 2   Manchester United 1**
Teamsheet: Stepney, Edwards, Dunne, Crerand, Ure, Stiles, Morgan, Fitzpatrick, Charlton, Kidd, Best
Substitute(s):   Gowling   Scorer(s):   Fitzpatrick

Match # 2983   Wednesday 15/04/70   Football League Division 1   at Old Trafford   Attendance 36649
Result: **Manchester United 2   Sheffield Wednesday 2**
Teamsheet: Stepney, Edwards, Dunne, Crerand, Sadler, Stiles, Morgan, Fitzpatrick, Charlton, Kidd, Best
Scorer(s):   Best, Charlton

SEASON 1969/70 SUMMARY

APPEARANCES

PLAYER	LGE	FAC	LC	TOTAL
Charlton	40	9	8	57
Sadler	40	9	8	57
Stepney	37	9	8	54
Best	37	8	8	53
Morgan	35	9	5	49
Kidd	33 (1)	9	6	48 (1)
Dunne	33	7	8	48
Ure	34	7	7	48
Burns	30 (2)	3 (1)	6	39 (3)
Crerand	25	9	2	36
Aston	21 (1)	1 (1)	6	28 (2)
Edwards	18 (1)	7	2	27 (1)
Fitzpatrick	20	1	5	26
Sartori	13 (4)	7	1 (2)	21 (6)
Law	10 (1)	– (2)	3	13 (3)
Stiles	8	3	2	13
Brennan	8 (1)	1	1	10 (1)
Gowling	6 (1)	–	– (1)	6 (2)
Givens	4 (4)	–	1	5 (4)
Rimmer	5	–	–	5
Foulkes	3	–	–	3
James	2	–	1	3
Ryan	– (1)	–	–	– (1)

GOALSCORERS

PLAYER	LGE	FAC	LC	TOT
Best	15	6	2	23
Kidd	12	6	2	20
Charlton	12	1	1	14
Morgan	7	2	–	9
Burns	3	–	–	3
Fitzpatrick	3	–	–	3
Gowling	3	–	–	3
Law	2	–	1	3
Sadler	2	–	1	3
Sartori	2	1	–	3
Aston	1	–	–	1
Crerand	1	–	–	1
Givens	1	–	–	1
Ure	1	–	–	1
Edwards	–	–	1	1
own goals	1	1	–	2

RESULTS & ATTENDANCES SUMMARY

		P	W	D	L	F	A	TOTAL	AVGE
League	H	21	8	9	4	37	27	1047046	49859
	A	21	6	8	7	29	34	922872	43946
TOTAL		42	14	17	11	66	61	1969918	46903
FA Cup	H	2	2	0	0	5	1	126835	63418
	A	3	2	1	0	10	3	91323	30441
	N	4	1	2	1	2	1	188605	47151
TOTAL		9	5	3	1	17	5	406763	45196
League	H	5	4	1	0	7	2	258371	51674
Cup	A	3	0	2	1	1	2	122653	40884
TOTAL		8	4	3	1	8	4	381024	47628
Overall	H	28	14	10	4	49	30	1432252	51152
	A	27	8	11	8	40	39	1136848	42105
	N	4	1	2	1	2	1	188605	47151
TOTAL		59	23	23	13	91	70	2757705	46741

FINAL TABLE – LEAGUE DIVISION ONE

		P	W	D	L	F	A	W	D	L	F	A	PTS	GD
				— HOME —					— AWAY —					
1	Everton	42	17	3	1	46	19	12	5	4	26	15	66	38
2	Leeds United	42	15	4	2	50	19	6	11	4	34	30	57	35
3	Chelsea	42	13	7	1	36	18	8	6	7	34	32	55	20
4	Derby County	42	15	3	3	45	14	7	6	8	19	23	53	27
5	Liverpool	42	10	7	4	34	20	10	4	7	31	22	51	23
6	Coventry City	42	9	6	6	35	28	10	5	6	23	20	49	10
7	Newcastle United	42	14	2	5	42	16	3	11	7	15	19	47	22
8	MANCHESTER UNITED	42	8	9	4	37	27	6	8	7	29	34	45	5
9	Stoke City	42	10	7	4	31	23	5	8	8	25	29	45	4
10	Manchester City	42	8	6	7	25	22	8	5	8	30	26	43	7
11	Tottenham Hotspur	42	11	2	8	27	21	6	7	8	27	34	43	-1
12	Arsenal	42	7	10	4	29	23	5	8	8	22	26	42	2
13	Wolverhampton Wanderers	42	8	8	5	30	23	4	8	9	25	34	40	-2
14	Burnley	42	7	7	7	33	29	5	8	8	23	32	39	-5
15	Nottingham Forest	42	8	9	4	28	28	2	9	10	22	43	38	-21
16	West Bromwich Albion	42	10	6	5	39	25	4	3	14	19	41	37	-8
17	West Ham United	42	8	8	5	28	21	4	4	13	23	39	36	-9
18	Ipswich Town	42	9	5	7	23	20	1	6	14	17	43	31	-23
19	Southampton	42	3	12	6	24	27	3	5	13	22	40	29	-21
20	Crystal Palace	42	5	6	10	20	36	1	9	11	14	32	27	-34
21	Sunderland	42	4	11	6	17	24	2	3	16	13	44	26	-38
22	Sheffield United	42	6	5	10	23	27	2	4	15	17	44	25	-31

SEASON 1970/71

Match # 2984 Saturday 15/08/70 Football League Division 1 at Old Trafford Attendance 59365
Result: **Manchester United 0 Leeds United 1**
Teamsheet: Stepney, Edwards, Dunne, Crerand, Ure, Sadler, Fitzpatrick, Stiles, Charlton, Kidd, Best
Substitute(s): Gowling

Match # 2985 Wednesday 19/08/70 Football League Division 1 at Old Trafford Attendance 50979
Result: **Manchester United 0 Chelsea 0**
Teamsheet: Stepney, Edwards, Dunne, Crerand, Ure, Sadler, Morgan, Fitzpatrick, Charlton, Stiles, Best

Match # 2986 Saturday 22/08/70 Football League Division 1 at Highbury Attendance 54117
Result: **Arsenal 4 Manchester United 0**
Teamsheet: Stepney, Stiles, Dunne, Crerand, Ure, Sadler, Morgan, Fitzpatrick, Charlton, Law, Best
Substitute(s): Edwards

Match # 2987 Tuesday 25/08/70 Football League Division 1 at Turf Moor Attendance 29385
Result: **Burnley 0 Manchester United 2**
Teamsheet: Rimmer, Edwards, Dunne, Fitzpatrick, Ure, Sadler, Morgan, Law, Charlton, Stiles, Best
Substitute(s): Gowling Scorer(s): Law 2

Match # 2988 Saturday 29/08/70 Football League Division 1 at Old Trafford Attendance 50643
Result: **Manchester United 1 West Ham United 1**
Teamsheet: Rimmer, Edwards, Dunne, Fitzpatrick, Ure, Sadler, Morgan, Law, Charlton, Stiles, Best
Substitute(s): Young Scorer(s): Fitzpatrick

Match # 2989 Wednesday 02/09/70 Football League Division 1 at Old Trafford Attendance 51346
Result: **Manchester United 2 Everton 0**
Teamsheet: Rimmer, Edwards, Dunne, Fitzpatrick, Ure, Sadler, Stiles, Law, Charlton, Kidd, Best
Scorer(s): Best, Charlton

Match # 2990 Saturday 05/09/70 Football League Division 1 at Anfield Attendance 52542
Result: **Liverpool 1 Manchester United 1**
Teamsheet: Rimmer, Edwards, Dunne, Fitzpatrick, Ure, Sadler, Stiles, Law, Charlton, Kidd, Best
Scorer(s): Kidd

Match # 2991 Wednesday 09/09/70 League Cup 2nd Round at Recreation Ground Attendance 18509
Result: **Aldershot 1 Manchester United 3**
Teamsheet: Rimmer, Edwards, Dunne, Fitzpatrick, Ure, Sadler, Stiles, Law, Charlton, Kidd, Best
Substitute(s): James Scorer(s): Best, Kidd, Law

Match # 2992 Saturday 12/09/70 Football League Division 1 at Old Trafford Attendance 48939
Result: **Manchester United 2 Coventry City 0**
Teamsheet: Rimmer, Edwards, Dunne, Fitzpatrick, Ure, Sadler, Stiles, Law, Charlton, Kidd, Best
Scorer(s): Best, Charlton

Match # 2993 Saturday 19/09/70 Football League Division 1 at Portman Road Attendance 27776
Result: **Ipswich Town 4 Manchester United 0**
Teamsheet: Rimmer, Edwards, Dunne, Fitzpatrick, Ure, Sadler, Stiles, Law, Charlton, Gowling, Best

Match # 2994 Saturday 26/09/70 Football League Division 1 at Old Trafford Attendance 46647
Result: **Manchester United 1 Blackpool 1**
Teamsheet: Rimmer, Watson, Burns, Fitzpatrick, James, Sadler, Morgan, Gowling, Charlton, Kidd, Best
Scorer(s): Best

Match # 2995 Saturday 03/10/70 Football League Division 1 at Molineux Attendance 38629
Result: **Wolverhampton Wanderers 3 Manchester United 2**
Teamsheet: Rimmer, Watson, Burns, Fitzpatrick, James, Sadler, Morgan, Gowling, Charlton, Kidd, Best
Substitute(s): Sartori Scorer(s): Gowling, Kidd

Match # 2996 Wednesday 07/10/70 League Cup 3rd Round at Old Trafford Attendance 32068
Result: **Manchester United 1 Portsmouth 0**
Teamsheet: Rimmer, Donald, Burns, Fitzpatrick, Ure, Sadler, Morgan, Gowling, Charlton, Kidd, Best
Substitute(s): Aston Scorer(s): Charlton

Match # 2997 Saturday 10/10/70 Football League Division 1 at Old Trafford Attendance 42979
Result: **Manchester United 0 Crystal Palace 1**
Teamsheet: Rimmer, Edwards, Dunne, Fitzpatrick, Ure, Stiles, Morgan, Best, Charlton, Kidd, Aston

Match # 2998 Saturday 17/10/70 Football League Division 1 at Elland Road Attendance 50190
Result: **Leeds United 2 Manchester United 2**
Teamsheet: Rimmer, Edwards, Dunne, Fitzpatrick, Ure, Stiles, Burns, Best, Charlton, Kidd, Aston
Substitute(s): Sartori Scorer(s): Charlton, Fitzpatrick

Match # 2999 Saturday 24/10/70 Football League Division 1 at Old Trafford Attendance 43278
Result: **Manchester United 2 West Bromwich Albion 1**
Teamsheet: Rimmer, Edwards, Dunne, Fitzpatrick, Ure, Burns, Law, Best, Charlton, Kidd, Aston
Scorer(s): Kidd, Law

Match # 3000 Wednesday 28/10/70 League Cup 4th Round at Old Trafford Attendance 47565
Result: **Manchester United 2 Chelsea 1**
Teamsheet: Rimmer, Edwards, Dunne, Fitzpatrick, James, Sadler, Aston, Best, Charlton, Kidd, Law
Substitute(s): Burns Scorer(s): Best, Charlton

Match # 3001 Saturday 31/10/70 Football League Division 1 at St James' Park Attendance 45140
Result: **Newcastle United 1 Manchester United 0**
Teamsheet: Rimmer, Edwards, Dunne, Fitzpatrick, James, Sadler, Burns, Best, Charlton, Kidd, Aston

SEASON 1970/71 (continued)

Match # 3002 Saturday 07/11/70   Football League Division 1   at Old Trafford   Attendance 47451
Result: **Manchester United 2 Stoke City 2**
Teamsheet: Rimmer, Edwards, Burns, Fitzpatrick, James, Sadler, Law, Best, Charlton, Kidd, Aston
Scorer(s):   Law, Sadler

Match # 3003 Saturday 14/11/70   Football League Division 1   at City Ground   Attendance 36364
Result: **Nottingham Forest 1 Manchester United 2**
Teamsheet: Rimmer, Watson, Dunne, Fitzpatrick, James, Sadler, Law, Best, Charlton, Gowling, Sartori
Scorer(s):   Gowling, Sartori

Match # 3004 Wednesday 18/11/70   League Cup 5th Round   at Old Trafford   Attendance 48961
Result: **Manchester United 4 Crystal Palace 2**
Teamsheet: Rimmer, Watson, Dunne, Fitzpatrick, James, Sadler, Law, Best, Charlton, Kidd, Aston
Scorer(s):   Kidd 2, Charlton, Fitzpatrick

Match # 3005 Saturday 21/11/70   Football League Division 1   at The Dell   Attendance 30202
Result: **Southampton 1 Manchester United 0**
Teamsheet: Rimmer, Watson, Dunne, Fitzpatrick, James, Sadler, Law, Best, Charlton, Kidd, Aston
Substitute(s): Sartori

Match # 3006 Saturday 28/11/70   Football League Division 1   at Old Trafford   Attendance 45306
Result: **Manchester United 1 Huddersfield Town 1**
Teamsheet: Rimmer, Watson, Dunne, Fitzpatrick, James, Sadler, Law, Best, Charlton, Kidd, Aston
Scorer(s):   Best

Match # 3007 Saturday 05/12/70   Football League Division 1   at White Hart Lane   Attendance 55693
Result: **Tottenham Hotspur 2 Manchester United 2**
Teamsheet: Rimmer, Watson, Dunne, Fitzpatrick, James, Sadler, Law, Best, Charlton, Kidd, Aston
Scorer(s):   Best, Law

Match # 3008 Saturday 12/12/70   Football League Division 1   at Old Trafford   Attendance 52636
Result: **Manchester United 1 Manchester City 4**
Teamsheet: Rimmer, Watson, Dunne, Fitzpatrick, James, Stiles, Law, Best, Charlton, Kidd, Aston
Substitute(s): Sartori   Scorer(s):   Kidd

Match # 3009 Wednesday 16/12/70   League Cup Semi-Final 1st Leg   at Old Trafford   Attendance 48889
Result: **Manchester United 1 Aston Villa 1**
Teamsheet: Rimmer, Watson, Dunne, Fitzpatrick, James, Stiles, Sartori, Best, Charlton, Kidd, Aston
Scorer(s):   Kidd

Match # 3010 Saturday 19/12/70   Football League Division 1   at Old Trafford   Attendance 33182
Result: **Manchester United 1 Arsenal 3**
Teamsheet: Rimmer, Watson, Dunne, Crerand, James, Fitzpatrick, Morgan, Best, Charlton, Kidd, Sartori
Scorer(s):   Sartori

Match # 3011 Wednesday 23/12/70   League Cup Semi-Final 2nd Leg   at Villa Park   Attendance 58667
Result: **Aston Villa 2 Manchester United 1**
Teamsheet: Rimmer, Fitzpatrick, Dunne, Crerand, Ure, Sadler, Morgan, Best, Charlton, Kidd, Law
Scorer(s):   Kidd

Match # 3012 Saturday 26/12/70   Football League Division 1   at Baseball Ground   Attendance 34068
Result: **Derby County 4 Manchester United 4**
Teamsheet: Rimmer, Fitzpatrick, Dunne, Crerand, Ure, Sadler, Morgan, Best, Charlton, Kidd, Law
Scorer(s):   Law 2, Best, Kidd

Match # 3013 Saturday 02/01/71   FA Cup 3rd Round   at Old Trafford   Attendance 47824
Result: **Manchester United 0 Middlesbrough 0**
Teamsheet: Rimmer, Fitzpatrick, Dunne, Crerand, Ure, Sadler, Morgan, Best, Charlton, Kidd, Law

Match # 3014 Tuesday 05/01/71   FA Cup 3rd Round Replay   at Ayresome Park   Attendance 41000
Result: **Middlesbrough 2 Manchester United 1**
Teamsheet: Rimmer, Fitzpatrick, Dunne, Crerand, Edwards, Sadler, Morgan, Best, Charlton, Kidd, Law
Substitute(s): Gowling   Scorer(s):   Best

Match # 3015 Saturday 09/01/71   Football League Division 1   at Stamford Bridge   Attendance 53482
Result: **Chelsea 1 Manchester United 2**
Teamsheet: Stepney, Fitzpatrick, Dunne, Crerand, Edwards, Stiles, Morgan, Law, Charlton, Gowling, Aston
Scorer(s):   Gowling, Morgan

Match # 3016 Saturday 16/01/71   Football League Division 1   at Old Trafford   Attendance 40135
Result: **Manchester United 1 Burnley 1**
Teamsheet: Stepney, Fitzpatrick, Dunne, Crerand, Edwards, Stiles, Morgan, Law, Charlton, Gowling, Aston
Scorer(s):   Aston

Match # 3017 Saturday 30/01/71   Football League Division 1   at Leeds Road   Attendance 41464
Result: **Huddersfield Town 1 Manchester United 2**
Teamsheet: Stepney, Fitzpatrick, Burns, Crerand, Edwards, Sadler, Morgan, Law, Charlton, Gowling, Best
Substitute(s): Aston   Scorer(s):   Aston, Law

Match # 3018 Saturday 06/02/71   Football League Division 1   at Old Trafford   Attendance 48965
Result: **Manchester United 2 Tottenham Hotspur 1**
Teamsheet: Stepney, Fitzpatrick, Burns, Crerand, Edwards, Sadler, Morgan, Kidd, Charlton, Gowling, Best
Scorer(s):   Best, Morgan

Match # 3019 Saturday 20/02/71   Football League Division 1   at Old Trafford   Attendance 36060
Result: **Manchester United 5 Southampton 1**
Teamsheet: Stepney, Fitzpatrick, Burns, Crerand, Edwards, Sadler, Morgan, Best, Charlton, Gowling, Aston
Scorer(s):   Gowling 4, Morgan

SEASON 1970/71 (continued)

Match # 3020	Tuesday 23/02/71	Football League Division 1	at Goodison Park	Attendance 52544
Result:	**Everton 1 Manchester United 0**			
Teamsheet:	Stepney, Fitzpatrick, Dunne, Crerand, Edwards, Sadler, Morgan, Best, Charlton, Gowling, Aston			
Substitute(s):	Burns			

Match # 3021	Saturday 27/02/71	Football League Division 1	at Old Trafford	Attendance 41902
Result:	**Manchester United 1 Newcastle United 0**			
Teamsheet:	Stepney, Fitzpatrick, Dunne, Crerand, Edwards, Sadler, Morgan, Best, Charlton, Kidd, Aston			
Scorer(s):	Kidd			

Match # 3022	Saturday 06/03/71	Football League Division 1	at The Hawthorns	Attendance 41112
Result:	**West Bromwich Albion 4 Manchester United 3**			
Teamsheet:	Stepney, Fitzpatrick, Dunne, Crerand, Edwards, Sadler, Morgan, Best, Charlton, Kidd, Aston			
Scorer(s):	Aston, Best, Kidd			

Match # 3023	Saturday 13/03/71	Football League Division 1	at Old Trafford	Attendance 40473
Result:	**Manchester United 2 Nottingham Forest 0**			
Teamsheet:	Stepney, Fitzpatrick, Dunne, Crerand, Edwards, Sadler, Morgan, Best, Charlton, Law, Aston			
Substitute(s):	Burns	Scorer(s): Best, Law		

Match # 3024	Saturday 20/03/71	Football League Division 1	at Victoria Ground	Attendance 40005
Result:	**Stoke City 1 Manchester United 2**			
Teamsheet:	Stepney, Fitzpatrick, Dunne, Crerand, Edwards, Sadler, Morgan, Best, Charlton, Law, Aston			
Scorer(s):	Best 2			

Match # 3025	Saturday 03/04/71	Football League Division 1	at Upton Park	Attendance 38507
Result:	**West Ham United 2 Manchester United 1**			
Teamsheet:	Stepney, Fitzpatrick, Dunne, Crerand, Edwards, Sadler, Morgan, Best, Charlton, Law, Aston			
Substitute(s):	Burns	Scorer(s): Best		

Match # 3026	Saturday 10/04/71	Football League Division 1	at Old Trafford	Attendance 45691
Result:	**Manchester United 1 Derby County 2**			
Teamsheet:	Stepney, Dunne, Burns, Crerand, Edwards, Stiles, Morgan, Best, Charlton, Law, Aston			
Substitute(s):	Gowling	Scorer(s): Law		

Match # 3027	Monday 12/04/71	Football League Division 1	at Old Trafford	Attendance 41886
Result:	**Manchester United 1 Wolverhampton Wanderers 0**			
Teamsheet:	Stepney, Dunne, Burns, Crerand, Edwards, Stiles, Best, Gowling, Charlton, Law, Morgan			
Substitute(s):	Kidd	Scorer(s): Gowling		

Match # 3028	Tuesday 13/04/71	Football League Division 1	at Highfield Road	Attendance 33818
Result:	**Coventry City 2 Manchester United 1**			
Teamsheet:	Stepney, Dunne, Burns, Crerand, Edwards, Stiles, Best, Gowling, Charlton, Kidd, Morgan			
Scorer(s):	Best			

Match # 3029	Saturday 17/04/71	Football League Division 1	at Selhurst Park	Attendance 39145
Result:	**Crystal Palace 3 Manchester United 5**			
Teamsheet:	Stepney, Fitzpatrick, Dunne, Crerand, Edwards, Sadler, Best, Gowling, Charlton, Law, Morgan			
Substitute(s):	Burns	Scorer(s): Law 3, Best 2		

Match # 3030	Monday 19/04/71	Football League Division 1	at Old Trafford	Attendance 44004
Result:	**Manchester United 0 Liverpool 2**			
Teamsheet:	Stepney, Dunne, Burns, Crerand, Edwards, Sadler, Best, Gowling, Charlton, Law, Morgan			

Match # 3031	Saturday 24/04/71	Football League Division 1	at Old Trafford	Attendance 33566
Result:	**Manchester United 3 Ipswich Town 2**			
Teamsheet:	Stepney, Dunne, Burns, Crerand, James, Sadler, Law, Gowling, Charlton, Kidd, Best			
Substitute(s):	Sartori	Scorer(s): Best, Charlton, Kidd		

Match # 3032	Saturday 01/05/71	Football League Division 1	at Bloomfield Road	Attendance 29857
Result:	**Blackpool 1 Manchester United 1**			
Teamsheet:	Stepney, Dunne, Burns, Crerand, James, Sadler, Law, Gowling, Charlton, Kidd, Best			
Scorer(s):	Law			

Match # 3033	Wednesday 05/05/71	Football League Division 1	at Maine Road	Attendance 43626
Result:	**Manchester City 3 Manchester United 4**			
Teamsheet:	Stepney, O'Neil, Burns, Crerand, James, Sadler, Law, Gowling, Charlton, Kidd, Best			
Scorer(s):	Best 2, Charlton, Law			

SEASON 1970/71 SUMMARY

APPEARANCES

PLAYER	LGE	FAC	LC	TOTAL
Charlton	42	2	6	50
Best	40	2	6	48
Fitzpatrick	35	2	6	43
Dunne	35	2	5	42
Sadler	32	2	5	39
Law	28	2	4	34
Edwards	29 (1)	1	2	32 (1)
Kidd	24 (1)	2	6	32 (1)
Morgan	25	2	2	29
Rimmer	20	2	6	28
Crerand	24	2	1	27
Aston	19 (1)	–	3 (1)	22 (2)
Stepney	22	–	–	22
Stiles	17	–	2	19
Gowling	17 (3)	– (1)	1	18 (4)
Burns	16 (4)	–	1 (1)	17 (5)
Ure	13	1	3	17
James	13	–	3 (1)	16 (1)
Watson	8	–	2	10
Sartori	2 (5)	–	1	3 (5)
Donald	–	–	1	1
O'Neil	1	–	–	1
Young	– (1)	–	–	– (1)

GOALSCORERS

PLAYER	LGE	FAC	LC	TOT
Best	18	1	2	21
Law	15	–	1	16
Kidd	8	–	5	13
Gowling	8	–	–	8
Charlton	5	–	3	8
Aston	3	–	–	3
Morgan	3	–	–	3
Fitzpatrick	2	–	1	3
Sartori	2	–	–	2
Sadler	1	–	–	1

RESULTS & ATTENDANCES SUMMARY

		P	W	D	L	F	A	TOTAL	AVGE
League	H	21	9	6	6	29	24	945433	45021
	A	21	7	5	9	36	42	867666	41317
TOTAL		42	16	11	15	65	66	1813099	43169
FA Cup	H	1	0	1	0	0	0	47824	47824
	A	1	0	0	1	1	2	41000	41000
TOTAL		2	0	1	1	1	2	88824	44412
League	H	4	3	1	0	8	4	177483	44371
Cup	A	2	1	0	1	4	3	77176	38588
TOTAL		6	4	1	1	12	7	254659	42443
Overall	H	26	12	8	6	37	28	1170740	45028
	A	24	8	5	11	41	47	985842	41077
TOTAL		50	20	13	17	78	75	2156582	43132

FINAL TABLE – LEAGUE DIVISION ONE

		P	W	D	L	F	A	W	D	L	F	A	PTS	GD
				HOME						AWAY				
1	Arsenal	42	18	3	0	41	6	11	4	6	30	23	65	42
2	Leeds United	42	16	2	3	40	12	11	8	2	32	18	64	42
3	Tottenham Hotspur	42	11	5	5	33	19	8	9	4	21	14	52	21
4	Wolverhampton Wanderers	42	13	3	5	33	22	9	5	7	31	32	52	10
5	Liverpool	42	11	10	0	30	10	6	7	8	12	14	51	18
6	Chelsea	42	12	6	3	34	21	6	9	6	18	21	51	10
7	Southampton	42	12	5	4	35	15	5	7	9	21	29	46	12
8	MANCHESTER UNITED	42	9	6	6	29	24	7	5	9	36	42	43	-1
9	Derby County	42	9	5	7	32	26	7	5	9	24	28	42	2
10	Coventry City	42	12	4	5	24	12	4	6	11	13	26	42	-1
11	Manchester City	42	7	9	5	30	22	5	8	8	17	20	41	5
12	Newcastle United	42	9	9	3	27	16	5	4	12	17	30	41	-2
13	Stoke City	42	10	7	4	28	11	2	6	13	16	37	37	-4
14	Everton	42	10	7	4	32	16	2	6	13	22	44	37	-6
15	Huddersfield Town	42	7	8	6	19	16	4	6	11	21	33	36	-9
16	Nottingham Forest	42	9	4	8	29	26	5	4	12	13	35	36	-19
17	West Bromwich Albion	42	9	8	4	34	25	1	7	13	24	50	35	-17
18	Crystal Palace	42	9	5	7	24	24	3	6	12	15	33	35	-18
19	Ipswich Town	42	9	4	8	28	22	3	6	12	14	26	34	-6
20	West Ham United	42	6	8	7	28	30	4	6	11	19	30	34	-13
21	Burnley	42	4	8	9	20	31	3	5	13	9	32	27	-34
22	Blackpool	42	3	9	9	22	31	1	6	14	12	35	23	-32

SEASON 1971/72

Match # 3034 Saturday 14/08/71 Football League Division 1 at Baseball Ground Attendance 35886
Result: **Derby County 2 Manchester United 2**
Teamsheet: Stepney, O'Neil, Dunne, Gowling, James, Sadler, Morgan, Kidd, Charlton, Law, Best
Scorer(s): Gowling, Law

Match # 3035 Wednesday 18/08/71 Football League Division 1 at Stamford Bridge Attendance 54763
Result: **Chelsea 2 Manchester United 3**
Teamsheet: Stepney, Fitzpatrick, Dunne, Gowling, James, Sadler, Morgan, Kidd, Charlton, Law, Best
Scorer(s): Charlton, Kidd, Morgan

Match # 3036 Friday 20/08/71 Football League Division 1 at Anfield Attendance 27649
Result: **Manchester United 3 Arsenal 1**
Teamsheet: Stepney, O'Neil, Dunne, Gowling, James, Sadler, Morgan, Kidd, Charlton, Law, Best
Substitute(s): Aston Scorer(s): Charlton, Gowling, Kidd

Match # 3037 Monday 23/08/71 Football League Division 1 at Victoria Ground Attendance 23146
Result: **Manchester United 3 West Bromwich Albion 1**
Teamsheet: Stepney, O'Neil, Dunne, Gowling, James, Sadler, Morgan, Kidd, Charlton, Best, Aston
Substitute(s): Burns Scorer(s): Best 2, Gowling

Match # 3038 Saturday 28/08/71 Football League Division 1 at Molineux Attendance 46471
Result: **Wolverhampton Wanderers 1 Manchester United 1**
Teamsheet: Stepney, O'Neil, Dunne, Gowling, James, Sadler, Morgan, Kidd, Charlton, Law, Best
Scorer(s): Best

Match # 3039 Tuesday 31/08/71 Football League Division 1 at Goodison Park Attendance 52151
Result: **Everton 1 Manchester United 0**
Teamsheet: Stepney, O'Neil, Dunne, Gowling, James, Sadler, Morgan, Kidd, Charlton, Law, Best

Match # 3040 Saturday 04/09/71 Football League Division 1 at Old Trafford Attendance 45656
Result: **Manchester United 1 Ipswich Town 0**
Teamsheet: Stepney, O'Neil, Dunne, Gowling, James, Sadler, Morgan, Kidd, Charlton, Law, Best
Substitute(s): Aston Scorer(s): Best

Match # 3041 Tuesday 07/09/71 League Cup 2nd Round at Portman Road Attendance 28143
Result: **Ipswich Town 1 Manchester United 3**
Teamsheet: Stepney, O'Neil, Dunne, Gowling, James, Sadler, Morgan, Kidd, Charlton, Best, Aston
Scorer(s): Best 2, Morgan

Match # 3042 Saturday 11/09/71 Football League Division 1 at Selhurst Park Attendance 44020
Result: **Crystal Palace 1 Manchester United 3**
Teamsheet: Stepney, O'Neil, Dunne, Gowling, James, Sadler, Morgan, Kidd, Charlton, Law, Best
Substitute(s): Aston Scorer(s): Law 2, Kidd

Match # 3043 Saturday 18/09/71 Football League Division 1 at Old Trafford Attendance 55339
Result: **Manchester United 4 West Ham United 2**
Teamsheet: Stepney, O'Neil, Dunne, Gowling, James, Sadler, Morgan, Kidd, Charlton, Law, Best
Scorer(s): Best 3, Charlton

Match # 3044 Saturday 25/09/71 Football League Division 1 at Anfield Attendance 55634
Result: **Liverpool 2 Manchester United 2**
Teamsheet: Stepney, O'Neil, Burns, Gowling, James, Sadler, Morgan, Kidd, Charlton, Law, Best
Scorer(s): Charlton, Law

Match # 3045 Saturday 02/10/71 Football League Division 1 at Old Trafford Attendance 51735
Result: **Manchester United 2 Sheffield United 0**
Teamsheet: Stepney, O'Neil, Dunne, Gowling, James, Sadler, Morgan, Kidd, Charlton, Best, Aston
Substitute(s): Burns Scorer(s): Best, Gowling

Match # 3046 Wednesday 06/10/71 League Cup 3rd Round at Old Trafford Attendance 44600
Result: **Manchester United 1 Burnley 1**
Teamsheet: Stepney, O'Neil, Dunne, Gowling, James, Sadler, Morgan, Kidd, Charlton, Best, Aston
Scorer(s): Charlton

Match # 3047 Saturday 09/10/71 Football League Division 1 at Leeds Road Attendance 33458
Result: **Huddersfield Town 0 Manchester United 3**
Teamsheet: Stepney, O'Neil, Dunne, Gowling, James, Sadler, Morgan, Kidd, Charlton, Law, Best
Scorer(s): Best, Charlton, Law

Match # 3048 Saturday 16/10/71 Football League Division 1 at Old Trafford Attendance 53247
Result: **Manchester United 1 Derby County 0**
Teamsheet: Stepney, O'Neil, Dunne, Gowling, James, Sadler, Morgan, Kidd, Charlton, Law, Best
Scorer(s): Best

Match # 3049 Monday 18/10/71 League Cup 3rd Round Replay at Turf Moor Attendance 27511
Result: **Burnley 0 Manchester United 1**
Teamsheet: Stepney, O'Neil, Dunne, Gowling, James, Sadler, Morgan, Kidd, Charlton, Law, Best
Scorer(s): Charlton

Match # 3050 Saturday 23/10/71 Football League Division 1 at St James' Park Attendance 52411
Result: **Newcastle United 0 Manchester United 1**
Teamsheet: Stepney, O'Neil, Dunne, Gowling, James, Sadler, Morgan, Kidd, Charlton, Law, Best
Substitute(s): Aston Scorer(s): Best

Match # 3051 Wednesday 27/10/71 League Cup 4th Round at Old Trafford Attendance 47062
Result: **Manchester United 1 Stoke City 1**
Teamsheet: Stepney, O'Neil, Burns, Gowling, James, Sadler, Morgan, Kidd, Charlton, Law, Best
Substitute(s): Aston Scorer(s): Gowling

SEASON 1971/72 (continued)

Match # 3052   Saturday 30/10/71   Football League Division 1   at Old Trafford   Attendance 53960
Result: **Manchester United 0   Leeds United 1**
Teamsheet: Stepney, O'Neil, Dunne, Gowling, James, Sadler, Morgan, Kidd, Charlton, Law, Best
Substitute(s):   Sartori

Match # 3053   Saturday 06/11/71   Football League Division 1   at Maine Road   Attendance 63326
Result: **Manchester City 3   Manchester United 3**
Teamsheet: Stepney, O'Neil, Dunne, Gowling, James, Sadler, Morgan, Kidd, Charlton, McIlroy, Best
Substitute(s):   Aston   Scorer(s):   Gowling, Kidd, McIlroy

Match # 3054   Monday 08/11/71   League Cup 4th Round Replay   at Victoria Ground   Attendance 40805
Result: **Stoke City 0   Manchester United 0**
Teamsheet: Stepney, O'Neil, Burns, Gowling, James, Sadler, Morgan, Kidd, Charlton, McIlroy, Best
Substitute(s):   Aston

Match # 3055   Saturday 13/11/71   Football League Division 1   at Old Trafford   Attendance 54058
Result: **Manchester United 3   Tottenham Hotspur 1**
Teamsheet: Stepney, O'Neil, Burns, Gowling, James, Sadler, Morgan, McIlroy, Charlton, Law, Best
Scorer(s):   Law 2, McIlroy

Match # 3056   Monday 15/11/71   League Cup 4th Round 2nd Replay   at Victoria Ground   Attendance 42249
Result: **Stoke City 2   Manchester United 1**
Teamsheet: Stepney, O'Neil, Burns, Gowling, James, Sadler, Morgan, McIlroy, Charlton, Sartori, Best
Scorer(s):   Best

Match # 3057   Saturday 20/11/71   Football League Division 1   at Old Trafford   Attendance 48757
Result: **Manchester United 3   Leicester City 2**
Teamsheet: Stepney, O'Neil, Burns, Gowling, James, Edwards, Morgan, Kidd, Charlton, Law, Best
Substitute(s):   McIlroy   Scorer(s):   Law 2, Kidd

Match # 3058   Saturday 27/11/71   Football League Division 1   at The Dell   Attendance 30323
Result: **Southampton 2   Manchester United 5**
Teamsheet: Stepney, O'Neil, Burns, Gowling, James, Sadler, Morgan, Kidd, Charlton, Law, Best
Substitute(s):   Aston   Scorer(s):   Best 3, Kidd, McIlroy

Match # 3059   Saturday 04/12/71   Football League Division 1   at Old Trafford   Attendance 45411
Result: **Manchester United 3   Nottingham Forest 2**
Teamsheet: Stepney, O'Neil, Burns, Gowling, James, Sadler, Morgan, Kidd, Charlton, Law, Best
Scorer(s):   Kidd 2, Law

Match # 3060   Saturday 11/12/71   Football League Division 1   at Victoria Ground   Attendance 33857
Result: **Stoke City 1   Manchester United 1**
Teamsheet: Stepney, O'Neil, Burns, Gowling, James, Sadler, Morgan, Kidd, Charlton, Law, Best
Substitute(s):   McIlroy   Scorer(s):   Law

Match # 3061   Saturday 18/12/71   Football League Division 1   at Portman Road   Attendance 29229
Result: **Ipswich Town 0   Manchester United 0**
Teamsheet: Stepney, Dunne, Burns, Gowling, James, Sadler, Morgan, Kidd, Charlton, Law, Best

Match # 3062   Monday 27/12/71   Football League Division 1   at Old Trafford   Attendance 52117
Result: **Manchester United 2   Coventry City 2**
Teamsheet: Stepney, Dunne, Burns, Gowling, James, Sadler, Morgan, Kidd, Charlton, Law, Best
Substitute(s):   McIlroy   Scorer(s):   James, Law

Match # 3063   Saturday 01/01/72   Football League Division 1   at Upton Park   Attendance 41892
Result: **West Ham United 3   Manchester United 0**
Teamsheet: Stepney, Dunne, Burns, Gowling, Edwards, Sadler, Morgan, Kidd, Charlton, Law, Best

Match # 3064   Saturday 08/01/72   Football League Division 1   at Old Trafford   Attendance 46781
Result: **Manchester United 1   Wolverhampton Wanderers 3**
Teamsheet: Stepney, Dunne, Burns, Gowling, Edwards, Sadler, Morgan, Kidd, Charlton, Law, McIlroy
Substitute(s):   Sartori   Scorer(s):   McIlroy

Match # 3065   Saturday 15/01/72   FA Cup 3rd Round   at The Dell   Attendance 30190
Result: **Southampton 1   Manchester United 1**
Teamsheet: Stepney, O'Neil, Burns, Gowling, Edwards, Sadler, Morgan, Kidd, Charlton, Law, Best
Substitute(s):   McIlroy   Scorer(s):   Charlton

Match # 3066   Wednesday 19/01/72   FA Cup 3rd Round Replay   at Old Trafford   Attendance 50960
Result: **Manchester United 4   Southampton 1**
Teamsheet: Stepney, O'Neil, Burns, Gowling, Edwards, Sadler, Morgan, McIlroy, Charlton, Law, Best
Substitute(s):   Aston   Scorer(s):   Best 2, Aston, Sadler

Match # 3067   Saturday 22/01/72   Football League Division 1   at Old Trafford   Attendance 55927
Result: **Manchester United 0   Chelsea 1**
Teamsheet: Stepney, O'Neil, Burns, Gowling, Edwards, Sadler, Morgan, McIlroy, Charlton, Law, Best
Substitute(s):   Aston

Match # 3068   Saturday 29/01/72   Football League Division 1   at The Hawthorns   Attendance 47012
Result: **West Bromwich Albion 2   Manchester United 1**
Teamsheet: Stepney, O'Neil, Dunne, Burns, James, Sadler, Morgan, Kidd, Charlton, Law, Best
Scorer(s):   Kidd

Match # 3069   Saturday 05/02/72   FA Cup 4th Round   at Deepdale   Attendance 27025
Result: **Preston North End 0   Manchester United 2**
Teamsheet: Stepney, O'Neil, Burns, Gowling, James, Sadler, Morgan, Kidd, Charlton, Law, Best
Scorer(s):   Gowling 2

SEASON 1971/72 (continued)

Match # 3070   Saturday 12/02/72   Football League Division 1   at Old Trafford   Attendance 44983
Result: **Manchester United 0 Newcastle United 2**
Teamsheet: Stepney, O'Neil, Burns, Gowling, James, Sadler, Morgan, Kidd, Charlton, Law, Best

Match # 3071   Saturday 19/02/72   Football League Division 1   at Elland Road   Attendance 45399
Result: **Leeds United 5 Manchester United 1**
Teamsheet: Stepney, O'Neil, Dunne, Burns, James, Sadler, Morgan, Kidd, Charlton, Gowling, Best
Substitute(s):   McIlroy   Scorer(s):   Burns

Match # 3072   Saturday 26/02/72   FA Cup 5th Round   at Old Trafford   Attendance 53850
Result: **Manchester United 0 Middlesbrough 0**
Teamsheet: Stepney, O'Neil, Dunne, Burns, James, Sadler, Morgan, Gowling, Charlton, Law, Best

Match # 3073   Tuesday 29/02/72   FA Cup 5th Round Replay   at Ayresome Park   Attendance 39683
Result: **Middlesbrough 0 Manchester United 3**
Teamsheet: Stepney, O'Neil, Dunne, Burns, James, Sadler, Morgan, Gowling, Charlton, Law, Best
Scorer(s):   Best, Charlton, Morgan

Match # 3074   Saturday 04/03/72   Football League Division 1   at White Hart Lane   Attendance 54814
Result: **Tottenham Hotspur 2 Manchester United 0**
Teamsheet: Stepney, O'Neil, Dunne, Buchan, James, Sadler, Morgan, Gowling, Charlton, Law, Best

Match # 3075   Wednesday 08/03/72   Football League Division 1   at Old Trafford   Attendance 38415
Result: **Manchester United 0 Everton 0**
Teamsheet: Stepney, O'Neil, Dunne, Buchan, James, Sadler, Burns, Gowling, Kidd, Law, Best
Substitute(s):   McIlroy

Match # 3076   Saturday 11/03/72   Football League Division 1   at Old Trafford   Attendance 53581
Result: **Manchester United 2 Huddersfield Town 0**
Teamsheet: Stepney, O'Neil, Dunne, Buchan, James, Sadler, Morgan, Kidd, Charlton, Best, Storey-Moore
Scorer(s):   Best, Storey-Moore

Match # 3077   Saturday 18/03/72   FA Cup 6th Round   at Old Trafford   Attendance 54226
Result: **Manchester United 1 Stoke City 1**
Teamsheet: Stepney, O'Neil, Dunne, Buchan, James, Sadler, Morgan, Kidd, Charlton, Law, Best
Substitute(s):   Gowling   Scorer(s):   Best

Match # 3078   Wednesday 22/03/72   FA Cup 6th Round Replay   at Victoria Ground   Attendance 49192
Result: **Stoke City 2 Manchester United 1**
Teamsheet: Stepney, O'Neil, Dunne, Gowling, James, Buchan, Morgan, Kidd, Charlton, Law, Best
Substitute(s):   McIlroy   Scorer(s):   Best

Match # 3079   Saturday 25/03/72   Football League Division 1   at Old Trafford   Attendance 41550
Result: **Manchester United 4 Crystal Palace 0**
Teamsheet: Stepney, O'Neil, Dunne, Buchan, James, Gowling, Best, Kidd, Charlton, Law, Storey-Moore
Substitute(s):   McIlroy   Scorer(s):   Charlton, Gowling, Law, Storey-Moore

Match # 3080   Saturday 01/04/72   Football League Division 1   at Highfield Road   Attendance 37901
Result: **Coventry City 2 Manchester United 3**
Teamsheet: Stepney, O'Neil, Dunne, Buchan, James, Gowling, Morgan, Best, Charlton, Law, Storey-Moore
Scorer(s):   Best, Charlton, Storey-Moore

Match # 3081   Monday 03/04/72   Football League Division 1   at Old Trafford   Attendance 53826
Result: **Manchester United 0 Liverpool 3**
Teamsheet: Stepney, O'Neil, Dunne, Buchan, James, Gowling, Morgan, Best, Charlton, Law, Storey-Moore
Substitute(s):   Young

Match # 3082   Tuesday 04/04/72   Football League Division 1   at Bramall Lane   Attendance 45045
Result: **Sheffield United 1 Manchester United 1**
Teamsheet: Connaughton, O'Neil, Dunne, Buchan, James, Sadler, Best, McIlroy, Charlton, Young, Storey-Moore
Scorer(s):   Sadler

Match # 3083   Saturday 08/04/72   Football League Division 1   at Filbert Street   Attendance 35970
Result: **Leicester City 2 Manchester United 0**
Teamsheet: Connaughton, O'Neil, Dunne, Buchan, Sadler, Morgan, Best, McIlroy, Charlton, Young, Storey-Moore
Substitute(s):   Gowling

Match # 3084   Wednesday 12/04/72   Football League Division 1   at Old Trafford   Attendance 56362
Result: **Manchester United 1 Manchester City 3**
Teamsheet: Connaughton, O'Neil, Dunne, Buchan, James, Sadler, Best, Gowling, Charlton, Kidd, Storey-Moore
Substitute(s):   Law   Scorer(s):   Buchan

Match # 3085   Saturday 15/04/72   Football League Division 1   at Old Trafford   Attendance 38437
Result: **Manchester United 3 Southampton 2**
Teamsheet: Stepney, O'Neil, Dunne, Buchan, James, Sadler, Best, Young, Kidd, Law, Storey-Moore
Substitute(s):   McIlroy   Scorer(s):   Best, Kidd, Storey-Moore

Match # 3086   Saturday 22/04/72   Football League Division 1   at City Ground   Attendance 35063
Result: **Nottingham Forest 0 Manchester United 0**
Teamsheet: Stepney, O'Neil, Dunne, Buchan, James, Sadler, Morgan, Kidd, Charlton, Law, Storey-Moore
Substitute(s):   Young

Match # 3087   Tuesday 25/04/72   Football League Division 1   at Highbury   Attendance 49125
Result: **Arsenal 3 Manchester United 0**
Teamsheet: Stepney, O'Neil, Dunne, Buchan, Sadler, Gowling, Best, Young, Charlton, Kidd, Storey-Moore
Substitute(s):   McIlroy

SEASON 1971/72 (continued)

Match # 3088	Saturday 29/04/72 Football League Division 1 at Old Trafford Attendance 34959
Result:	**Manchester United 3 Stoke City 0**
Teamsheet:	Stepney, O'Neil, Dunne, Buchan, James, Young, Best, McIlroy, Charlton, Law, Storey-Moore
Substitute(s):	Gowling Scorer(s): Best, Charlton, Storey-Moore

SEASON 1971/72 SUMMARY

APPEARANCES

PLAYER	LGE	FAC	LC	TOTAL
Best	40	7	6	53
Charlton	40	7	6	53
Stepney	39	7	6	52
O'Neil	37	7	6	50
Sadler	37	6	6	49
James	37	5	6	48
Morgan	35	7	6	48
Gowling	35 (2)	6 (1)	6	47 (3)
Kidd	34	4	5	43
Law	32 (1)	7	2	41 (1)
Dunne	34	4	3	41
Burns	15 (2)	5	3	23 (2)
Buchan	13	2	–	15
McIlroy	8 (8)	1 (2)	2	11(10)
Storey-Moore	11	–	–	11
Edwards	4	2	–	6
Young	5 (2)	–	–	5 (2)
Aston	2 (7)	– (1)	2 (2)	4(10)
Connaughton	3	–	–	3
Sartori	– (2)	–	1	1 (2)
Fitzpatrick	1	–	–	1

GOALSCORERS

PLAYER	LGE	FAC	LC	TOT
Best	18	5	3	26
Law	13	–	–	13
Charlton	8	2	2	12
Kidd	10	–	–	10
Gowling	6	2	1	9
Storey-Moore	5	–	–	5
McIlroy	4	–	–	4
Morgan	1	1	1	3
Sadler	1	1	–	2
Buchan	1	–	–	1
Burns	1	–	–	1
James	1	–	–	1
Aston	–	1	–	1

RESULTS & ATTENDANCES SUMMARY

		P	W	D	L	F	A	TOTAL	AVGE
League	H	21	13	2	6	39	26	975896	46471
	A	21	6	8	7	30	35	923750	43988
	TOTAL	42	19	10	13	69	61	1899646	45230
FA Cup	H	3	1	2	0	5	2	159036	53012
	A	4	2	1	1	7	3	146090	36523
	TOTAL	7	3	3	1	12	5	305126	43589
League	H	2	0	2	0	2	2	91662	45831
Cup	A	4	2	1	1	5	3	138708	34677
	TOTAL	6	2	3	1	7	5	230370	38395
Overall	H	26	14	6	6	46	30	1226594	47177
	A	29	10	10	9	42	41	1208548	41674
	TOTAL	55	24	16	15	88	71	2435142	44275

FINAL TABLE – LEAGUE DIVISION ONE

		P	HOME					AWAY					PTS	GD
			W	D	L	F	A	W	D	L	F	A		
1	Derby County	42	16	4	1	43	10	8	6	7	26	23	58	36
2	Leeds United	42	17	4	0	54	10	7	5	9	19	21	57	42
3	Liverpool	42	17	3	1	48	16	7	6	8	16	14	57	34
4	Manchester City	42	16	3	2	48	15	7	8	6	29	30	57	32
5	Arsenal	42	15	2	4	36	13	7	6	8	22	27	52	18
6	Tottenham Hotspur	42	16	3	2	45	13	3	10	8	18	29	51	21
7	Chelsea	42	12	7	2	41	20	6	5	10	17	29	48	9
8	MANCHESTER UNITED	42	13	2	6	39	26	6	8	7	30	35	48	8
9	Wolverhampton Wanderers	42	10	7	4	35	23	8	4	9	30	34	47	8
10	Sheffield United	42	10	8	3	39	26	7	4	10	22	34	46	1
11	Newcastle United	42	10	6	5	30	18	5	5	11	19	34	41	-3
12	Leicester City	42	9	6	6	18	11	4	7	10	23	35	39	-5
13	Ipswich Town	42	7	8	6	19	19	4	8	9	20	34	38	-14
14	West Ham United	42	10	6	5	31	19	2	6	13	16	32	36	-4
15	Everton	42	8	9	4	28	17	1	9	11	9	31	36	-11
16	West Bromwich Albion	42	6	7	8	22	23	6	4	11	20	31	35	-12
17	Stoke City	42	6	10	5	26	25	4	5	12	13	31	35	-17
18	Coventry City	42	7	10	4	27	23	2	5	14	17	44	33	-23
19	Southampton	42	8	5	8	31	28	4	2	15	21	52	31	-28
20	Crystal Palace	42	4	8	9	26	31	4	5	12	13	34	29	-26
21	Nottingham Forest	42	6	4	11	25	29	2	5	14	22	52	25	-34
22	Huddersfield Town	42	4	7	10	12	22	2	6	13	15	37	25	-32

SEASON 1972/73

Match # 3089 Saturday 12/08/72 Football League Division 1 at Old Trafford Attendance 51459
Result: **Manchester United 1 Ipswich Town 2**
Teamsheet: Stepney, O'Neil, Dunne, Morgan, James, Buchan, Best, Kidd, Charlton, Law, Storey-Moore
Substitute(s): McIlroy Scorer(s): Law

Match # 3090 Tuesday 15/08/72 Football League Division 1 at Anfield Attendance 54789
Result: **Liverpool 2 Manchester United 0**
Teamsheet: Stepney, O'Neil, Dunne, Young, James, Buchan, Morgan, Kidd, Charlton, Best, Storey-Moore
Substitute(s): McIlroy

Match # 3091 Saturday 19/08/72 Football League Division 1 at Goodison Park Attendance 52348
Result: **Everton 2 Manchester United 0**
Teamsheet: Stepney, O'Neil, Dunne, Buchan, James, Sadler, Morgan, Fitzpatrick, Kidd, Best, Storey-Moore
Substitute(s): McIlroy

Match # 3092 Wednesday 23/08/72 Football League Division 1 at Old Trafford Attendance 40067
Result: **Manchester United 1 Leicester City 1**
Teamsheet: Stepney, O'Neil, Dunne, Buchan, James, Sadler, Morgan, Fitzpatrick, McIlroy, Best, Storey-Moore
Substitute(s): Kidd Scorer(s): Best

Match # 3093 Saturday 26/08/72 Football League Division 1 at Old Trafford Attendance 48108
Result: **Manchester United 0 Arsenal 0**
Teamsheet: Stepney, O'Neil, Dunne, Buchan, James, Sadler, Morgan, Young, McIlroy, Best, Storey-Moore

Match # 3094 Wednesday 30/08/72 Football League Division 1 at Old Trafford Attendance 44482
Result: **Manchester United 0 Chelsea 0**
Teamsheet: Stepney, O'Neil, Dunne, Buchan, James, Sadler, Morgan, Fitzpatrick, Law, Best, Storey-Moore
Substitute(s): Charlton

Match # 3095 Saturday 02/09/72 Football League Division 1 at Upton Park Attendance 31939
Result: **West Ham United 2 Manchester United 2**
Teamsheet: Stepney, O'Neil, Dunne, Buchan, James, Sadler, Morgan, Law, Charlton, Best, Storey-Moore
Substitute(s): McIlroy Scorer(s): Best, Storey-Moore

Match # 3096 Wednesday 06/09/72 League Cup 2nd Round at Manor Ground Attendance 16560
Result: **Oxford United 2 Manchester United 2**
Teamsheet: Stepney, O'Neil, Dunne, Buchan, James, Sadler, Morgan, Law, Charlton, Best, Storey-Moore
Substitute(s): McIlroy Scorer(s): Charlton, Law

Match # 3097 Saturday 09/09/72 Football League Division 1 at Old Trafford Attendance 37073
Result: **Manchester United 0 Coventry City 1**
Teamsheet: Stepney, O'Neil, Buchan, Fitzpatrick, James, Sadler, McIlroy, Law, Charlton, Best, Storey-Moore
Substitute(s): Young

Match # 3098 Tuesday 12/09/72 League Cup 2nd Round Replay at Old Trafford Attendance 21486
Result: **Manchester United 3 Oxford United 1**
Teamsheet: Stepney, Fitzpatrick, Buchan, Young, James, Sadler, Morgan, Law, Charlton, Best, Storey-Moore
Substitute(s): McIlroy Scorer(s): Best 2, Storey-Moore

Match # 3099 Saturday 16/09/72 Football League Division 1 at Molineux Attendance 34049
Result: **Wolverhampton Wanderers 2 Manchester United 0**
Teamsheet: Stepney, Buchan, Dunne, Fitzpatrick, James, Sadler, Young, McIlroy, Charlton, Best, Storey-Moore
Substitute(s): Kidd

Match # 3100 Saturday 23/09/72 Football League Division 1 at Old Trafford Attendance 48255
Result: **Manchester United 3 Derby County 0**
Teamsheet: Stepney, Donald, Dunne, Young, James, Buchan, Morgan, Davies, Charlton, Best, Storey-Moore
Scorer(s): Davies, Morgan, Storey-Moore

Match # 3101 Saturday 30/09/72 Football League Division 1 at Bramall Lane Attendance 37347
Result: **Sheffield United 1 Manchester United 0**
Teamsheet: Stepney, Donald, Dunne, Young, James, Buchan, Morgan, Davies, Charlton, Best, Storey-Moore
Substitute(s): McIlroy

Match # 3102 Tuesday 03/10/72 League Cup 3rd Round at Eastville Attendance 33957
Result: **Bristol Rovers 1 Manchester United 1**
Teamsheet: Stepney, Donald, Dunne, Young, James, Buchan, Morgan, Kidd, Charlton, Best, Storey-Moore
Scorer(s): Morgan

Match # 3103 Saturday 07/10/72 Football League Division 1 at The Hawthorns Attendance 32909
Result: **West Bromwich Albion 2 Manchester United 2**
Teamsheet: Stepney, Donald, Dunne, Young, James, Buchan, Morgan, MacDougall, Davies, Best, Storey-Moore
Scorer(s): Best, Storey-Moore

Match # 3104 Wednesday 11/10/72 League Cup 3rd Round Replay at Old Trafford Attendance 29349
Result: **Manchester United 1 Bristol Rovers 2**
Teamsheet: Stepney, Watson, Dunne, Young, James, Buchan, Morgan, Kidd, Charlton, Best, Storey-Moore
Substitute(s): McIlroy Scorer(s): McIlroy

Match # 3105 Saturday 14/10/72 Football League Division 1 at Old Trafford Attendance 52104
Result: **Manchester United 1 Birmingham City 0**
Teamsheet: Stepney, Watson, Dunne, Young, Sadler, Buchan, Morgan, MacDougall, Davies, Best, Storey-Moore
Scorer(s): MacDougall

Match # 3106 Saturday 21/10/72 Football League Division 1 at St James' Park Attendance 38170
Result: **Newcastle United 2 Manchester United 1**
Teamsheet: Stepney, Watson, Dunne, Young, Sadler, Buchan, Morgan, MacDougall, Davies, Best, Storey-Moore
Substitute(s): Charlton Scorer(s): Charlton

SEASON 1972/73 (continued)

Match # 3107 Saturday 28/10/72   Football League Division 1   at Old Trafford   Attendance 52497
Result: **Manchester United 1 Tottenham Hotspur 4**
Teamsheet: Stepney, Watson, Dunne, Law, Sadler, Buchan, Morgan, MacDougall, Davies, Best, Charlton
Scorer(s):   Charlton

Match # 3108 Saturday 04/11/72   Football League Division 1   at Filbert Street   Attendance 32575
Result: **Leicester City 2 Manchester United 2**
Teamsheet: Stepney, Donald, Dunne, Morgan, Sadler, Buchan, Best, MacDougall, Davies, Charlton, Storey-Moore
Scorer(s):   Best, Davies

Match # 3109 Saturday 11/11/72   Football League Division 1   at Old Trafford   Attendance 53944
Result: **Manchester United 2 Liverpool 0**
Teamsheet: Stepney, O'Neil, Dunne, Morgan, Sadler, Buchan, Best, MacDougall, Charlton, Davies, Storey-Moore
Substitute(s): McIlroy   Scorer(s):   Davies, MacDougall

Match # 3110 Saturday 18/11/72   Football League Division 1   at Maine Road   Attendance 52050
Result: **Manchester City 3 Manchester United 0**
Teamsheet: Stepney, O'Neil, Dunne, Morgan, Sadler, Buchan, Best, MacDougall, Charlton, Davies, Storey-Moore
Substitute(s): Kidd

Match # 3111 Saturday 25/11/72   Football League Division 1   at Old Trafford   Attendance 36073
Result: **Manchester United 2 Southampton 1**
Teamsheet: Stepney, O'Neil, Dunne, Morgan, Edwards, Buchan, Best, MacDougall, Charlton, Davies, Storey-Moore
Scorer(s):   Davies, MacDougall

Match # 3112 Saturday 02/12/72   Football League Division 1   at Carrow Road   Attendance 35910
Result: **Norwich City 0 Manchester United 2**
Teamsheet: Stepney, O'Neil, Dunne, Morgan, Sadler, Buchan, Young, MacDougall, Charlton, Davies, Storey-Moore
Scorer(s):   MacDougall, Storey-Moore

Match # 3113 Saturday 09/12/72   Football League Division 1   at Old Trafford   Attendance 41347
Result: **Manchester United 0 Stoke City 2**
Teamsheet: Stepney, O'Neil, Dunne, Young, Sadler, Buchan, Morgan, MacDougall, Charlton, Davies, Storey-Moore
Substitute(s): Law

Match # 3114 Saturday 16/12/72   Football League Division 1   at Selhurst Park   Attendance 39484
Result: **Crystal Palace 5 Manchester United 0**
Teamsheet: Stepney, O'Neil, Dunne, Young, Sadler, Buchan, Morgan, MacDougall, Kidd, Davies, Storey-Moore
Substitute(s): Law

Match # 3115 Saturday 23/12/72   Football League Division 1   at Old Trafford   Attendance 46382
Result: **Manchester United 1 Leeds United 1**
Teamsheet: Stepney, O'Neil, Dunne, Law, Sadler, Buchan, Morgan, MacDougall, Charlton, Davies, Storey-Moore
Substitute(s): Kidd   Scorer(s):   MacDougall

Match # 3116 Tuesday 26/12/72   Football League Division 1   at Baseball Ground   Attendance 35098
Result: **Derby County 3 Manchester United 1**
Teamsheet: Stepney, O'Neil, Dunne, Kidd, Sadler, Buchan, Morgan, MacDougall, Charlton, Davies, Storey-Moore
Substitute(s): Young   Scorer(s):   Storey-Moore

Match # 3117 Saturday 06/01/73   Football League Division 1   at Highbury   Attendance 51194
Result: **Arsenal 3 Manchester United 1**
Teamsheet: Stepney, Young, Forsyth, Graham, Sadler, Buchan, Morgan, Kidd, Charlton, Law, Storey-Moore
Scorer(s):   Kidd

Match # 3118 Saturday 13/01/73   FA Cup 3rd Round   at Molineux   Attendance 40005
Result: **Wolverhampton Wanderers 1 Manchester United 0**
Teamsheet: Stepney, Young, Forsyth, Law, Sadler, Buchan, Morgan, Kidd, Charlton, Davies, Graham
Substitute(s): Dunne

Match # 3119 Saturday 20/01/73   Football League Division 1   at Old Trafford   Attendance 50878
Result: **Manchester United 2 West Ham United 2**
Teamsheet: Stepney, Young, Forsyth, Law, Holton, Buchan, Morgan, MacDougall, Charlton, Macari, Graham
Substitute(s): Davies   Scorer(s):   Charlton, Macari

Match # 3120 Wednesday 24/01/73   Football League Division 1   at Old Trafford   Attendance 58970
Result: **Manchester United 0 Everton 0**
Teamsheet: Stepney, Young, Forsyth, Martin, Holton, Buchan, Morgan, MacDougall, Charlton, Macari, Graham
Substitute(s): Kidd

Match # 3121 Saturday 27/01/73   Football League Division 1   at Highfield Road   Attendance 42767
Result: **Coventry City 1 Manchester United 1**
Teamsheet: Stepney, Young, Forsyth, Graham, Holton, Buchan, Morgan, MacDougall, Charlton, Macari, Martin
Scorer(s):   Holton

Match # 3122 Saturday 10/02/73   Football League Division 1   at Old Trafford   Attendance 52089
Result: **Manchester United 2 Wolverhampton Wanderers 1**
Teamsheet: Stepney, Young, Forsyth, Graham, Holton, Buchan, Morgan, MacDougall, Charlton, Macari, Martin
Scorer(s):   Charlton 2

Match # 3123 Saturday 17/02/73   Football League Division 1   at Portman Road   Attendance 31918
Result: **Ipswich Town 4 Manchester United 1**
Teamsheet: Stepney, Forsyth, Dunne, Graham, Holton, Buchan, Martin, MacDougall, Charlton, Macari, Kidd
Scorer(s):   Macari

Match # 3124 Saturday 03/03/73   Football League Division 1   at Old Trafford   Attendance 46735
Result: **Manchester United 2 West Bromwich Albion 1**
Teamsheet: Stepney, Young, Forsyth, Graham, James, Buchan, Morgan, Kidd, Charlton, Macari, Storey-Moore
Substitute(s): Martin   Scorer(s):   Kidd, Macari

SEASON 1972/73 (continued)

Match # 3125 Saturday 10/03/73   Football League Division 1   at St Andrews   Attendance 51278
Result: **Birmingham City 3 Manchester United 1**
Teamsheet: Rimmer, Young, Forsyth, Graham, James, Buchan, Morgan, Kidd, Charlton, Macari, Storey-Moore
Substitute(s): Martin   Scorer(s):   Macari

Match # 3126 Saturday 17/03/73   Football League Division 1   at Old Trafford   Attendance 48426
Result: **Manchester United 2 Newcastle United 1**
Teamsheet: Rimmer, Young, James, Graham, Holton, Buchan, Morgan, Kidd, Charlton, Macari, Martin
Scorer(s):   Holton, Martin

Match # 3127 Saturday 24/03/73   Football League Division 1   at White Hart Lane   Attendance 49751
Result: **Tottenham Hotspur 1 Manchester United 1**
Teamsheet: Rimmer, Young, James, Graham, Holton, Buchan, Morgan, Kidd, Charlton, Macari, Martin
Scorer(s):   Graham

Match # 3128 Saturday 31/03/73   Football League Division 1   at The Dell   Attendance 23161
Result: **Southampton 0 Manchester United 2**
Teamsheet: Rimmer, Young, James, Graham, Holton, Buchan, Morgan, Kidd, Charlton, Macari, Martin
Substitute(s): Anderson   Scorer(s):   Charlton, Holton

Match # 3129 Saturday 07/04/73   Football League Division 1   at Old Trafford   Attendance 48593
Result: **Manchester United 1 Norwich City 0**
Teamsheet: Stepney, Young, James, Graham, Holton, Buchan, Morgan, Kidd, Charlton, Law, Martin
Substitute(s): Anderson   Scorer(s):   Martin

Match # 3130 Wednesday 11/04/73   Football League Division 1   at Old Trafford   Attendance 46891
Result: **Manchester United 2 Crystal Palace 0**
Teamsheet: Stepney, Young, James, Graham, Holton, Buchan, Morgan, Kidd, Charlton, Macari, Martin
Substitute(s): Anderson   Scorer(s):   Kidd, Morgan

Match # 3131 Saturday 14/04/73   Football League Division 1   at Victoria Ground   Attendance 37051
Result: **Stoke City 2 Manchester United 2**
Teamsheet: Stepney, Young, James, Graham, Holton, Buchan, Morgan, Anderson, Charlton, Macari, Martin
Substitute(s): Fletcher   Scorer(s):   Macari, Morgan

Match # 3132 Wednesday 18/04/73   Football League Division 1   at Elland Road   Attendance 45450
Result: **Leeds United 0 Manchester United 1**
Teamsheet: Stepney, Young, James, Graham, Holton, Buchan, Morgan, Anderson, Charlton, Macari, Martin
Substitute(s): Fletcher   Scorer(s):   Anderson

Match # 3133 Saturday 21/04/73   Football League Division 1   at Old Trafford   Attendance 61676
Result: **Manchester United 0 Manchester City 0**
Teamsheet: Stepney, Young, James, Graham, Holton, Buchan, Morgan, Kidd, Charlton, Macari, Martin
Substitute(s): Anderson

Match # 3134 Monday 23/04/73   Football League Division 1   at Old Trafford   Attendance 57280
Result: **Manchester United 1 Sheffield United 2**
Teamsheet: Stepney, Young, Sidebottom, Graham, Holton, Buchan, Morgan, Kidd, Charlton, Macari, Martin
Scorer(s):   Kidd

Match # 3135 Saturday 28/04/73   Football League Division 1   at Stamford Bridge   Attendance 44184
Result: **Chelsea 1 Manchester United 0**
Teamsheet: Stepney, Young, Sidebottom, Graham, Holton, Buchan, Morgan, Kidd, Charlton, Macari, Martin
Substitute(s): Anderson

SEASON 1972/73 SUMMARY

APPEARANCES

PLAYER	LGE	FAC	LC	TOTAL
Buchan	42	1	4	47
Morgan	39	1	4	44
Stepney	38	1	4	43
Charlton	34 (2)	1	4	39 (2)
Young	28 (2)	1	3	32 (2)
Storey-Moore	26	–	4	30
Dunne	24	– (1)	3	27 (1)
James	22	–	4	26
Best	19	–	4	23
Sadler	19	1	2	22
Kidd	17 (5)	1	2	20 (5)
Graham	18	1	–	19
MacDougall	18	–	–	18
O'Neil	16	–	1	17
Davies	15 (1)	1	–	16 (1)
Macari	16	–	–	16
Holton	15	–	–	15
Martin	14 (2)	–	–	14 (2)
Law	9 (2)	1	2	12 (2)
Forsyth	8	1	–	9
Fitzpatrick	5	–	1	6
Donald	4	–	1	5
McIlroy	4 (6)	–	– (3)	4 (9)
Rimmer	4	–	–	4
Watson	3	–	1	4
Anderson	2 (5)	–	–	2 (5)
Sidebottom	2	–	–	2
Edwards	1	–	–	1
Fletcher	– (2)	–	–	– (2)

GOALSCORERS

PLAYER	LGE	FAC	LC	TOT
Charlton	6	–	1	7
Storey-Moore	5	–	1	6
Best	4	–	2	6
Macari	5	–	–	5
MacDougall	5	–	–	5
Davies	4	–	–	4
Kidd	4	–	–	4
Morgan	3	–	1	4
Holton	3	–	–	3
Martin	2	–	–	2
Law	1	–	1	2
Anderson	1	–	–	1
Graham	1	–	–	1
McIlroy	–	–	1	1

RESULTS & ATTENDANCES SUMMARY

		P	W	D	L	F	A	TOTAL	AVGE
League	H	21	9	7	5	24	19	1023329	48730
	A	21	3	6	12	20	41	853422	40639
	TOTAL	42	12	13	17	44	60	1876511	44685
FA Cup	H	0	0	0	0	0	0	0	n/a
	A	1	0	0	1	0	1	40005	40005
	TOTAL	1	0	0	1	0	1	40005	40005
League	H	2	1	0	1	4	3	50835	25418
Cup	A	2	0	2	0	3	3	50517	25259
	TOTAL	4	1	2	1	7	6	101352	25338
Overall	H	23	10	7	6	28	22	1074164	46703
	A	24	3	8	13	23	45	943944	39331
	TOTAL	47	13	15	19	51	67	2018108	42938

FINAL TABLE – LEAGUE DIVISION ONE

		P	HOME W	HOME D	HOME L	HOME F	HOME A	AWAY W	AWAY D	AWAY L	AWAY F	AWAY A	PTS	GD
1	Liverpool	42	17	3	1	45	19	8	7	6	27	23	60	30
2	Arsenal	42	14	5	2	31	14	9	6	6	26	29	57	14
3	Leeds United	42	15	4	2	45	13	6	7	8	26	32	53	26
4	Ipswich Town	42	10	7	4	34	20	7	7	7	21	25	48	10
5	Wolverhampton Wanderers	42	13	3	5	43	23	5	8	8	23	31	47	12
6	West Ham United	42	12	5	4	45	25	5	7	9	22	28	46	14
7	Derby County	42	15	3	3	43	18	4	5	12	13	36	46	2
8	Tottenham Hotspur	42	10	5	6	33	23	6	8	7	25	25	45	10
9	Newcastle United	42	12	6	3	35	19	4	7	10	25	32	45	9
10	Birmingham City	42	11	7	3	39	22	4	5	12	14	32	42	–1
11	Manchester City	42	12	4	5	36	20	3	7	11	21	40	41	–3
12	Chelsea	42	9	6	6	30	22	4	8	9	19	29	40	–2
13	Southampton	42	8	11	2	26	17	3	7	11	21	35	40	–5
14	Sheffield United	42	11	4	6	28	18	4	6	11	23	41	40	–8
15	Stoke City	42	11	8	2	38	17	3	2	16	23	39	38	5
16	Leicester City	42	7	9	5	23	18	3	8	10	17	28	37	–6
17	Everton	42	9	5	7	27	21	4	6	11	14	28	37	–8
18	MANCHESTER UNITED	42	9	7	5	24	19	3	6	12	20	41	37	–16
19	Coventry City	42	9	5	7	27	24	4	4	13	13	31	35	–15
20	Norwich City	42	7	9	5	22	19	4	1	16	14	44	32	–27
21	Crystal Palace	42	7	7	7	25	21	2	5	14	16	37	30	–17
22	West Bromwich Albion	42	8	7	6	25	24	1	3	17	13	38	28	–24

SEASON 1973/74

Match # 3136	Saturday 25/08/73	Football League Division 1	at Highbury	Attendance 51501

Match # 3136 Saturday 25/08/73 Football League Division 1 at Highbury Attendance 51501
Result: **Arsenal 3 Manchester United 0**
Teamsheet: Stepney, Young, Buchan M, Daly, Holton, James, Morgan, Anderson, Macari, Graham, Martin
Substitute(s): McIlroy

Match # 3137 Wednesday 29/08/73 Football League Division 1 at Old Trafford Attendance 43614
Result: **Manchester United 1 Stoke City 0**
Teamsheet: Stepney, Young, Buchan M, Martin, Holton, James, Morgan, Anderson, Macari, Graham, McIlroy
Substitute(s): Fletcher Scorer(s): James

Match # 3138 Saturday 01/09/73 Football League Division 1 at Old Trafford Attendance 44156
Result: **Manchester United 2 Queens Park Rangers 1**
Teamsheet: Stepney, Young, Buchan M, Martin, Holton, Sidebottom, Morgan, Anderson, Macari, Graham, McIlroy
Substitute(s): Fletcher Scorer(s): Holton, McIlroy

Match # 3139 Wednesday 05/09/73 Football League Division 1 at Filbert Street Attendance 29152
Result: **Leicester City 1 Manchester United 0**
Teamsheet: Stepney, Young, Buchan M, Daly, Holton, Sadler, Morgan, Anderson, Kidd, Graham, McIlroy
Substitute(s): Martin

Match # 3140 Saturday 08/09/73 Football League Division 1 at Portman Road Attendance 22023
Result: **Ipswich Town 2 Manchester United 1**
Teamsheet: Stepney, Young, Buchan M, Daly, Sadler, Greenhoff, Morgan, Anderson, Kidd, Graham, McIlroy
Substitute(s): Macari Scorer(s): Anderson

Match # 3141 Wednesday 12/09/73 Football League Division 1 at Old Trafford Attendance 40793
Result: **Manchester United 1 Leicester City 2**
Teamsheet: Stepney, Buchan M, Young, Martin, Holton, James, Morgan, Anderson, Macari, Graham, Storey-Moore
Scorer(s): Stepney

Match # 3142 Saturday 15/09/73 Football League Division 1 at Old Trafford Attendance 44757
Result: **Manchester United 3 West Ham United 1**
Teamsheet: Stepney, Buchan M, Young, Martin, Holton, James, Morgan, Kidd, Anderson, Graham, Storey-Moore
Substitute(s): Buchan G Scorer(s): Kidd 2, Storey-Moore

Match # 3143 Saturday 22/09/73 Football League Division 1 at Elland Road Attendance 47058
Result: **Leeds United 0 Manchester United 0**
Teamsheet: Stepney, Buchan M, Young, Greenhoff, Holton, James, Morgan, Anderson, Macari, Kidd, Graham
Substitute(s): Buchan G

Match # 3144 Saturday 29/09/73 Football League Division 1 at Old Trafford Attendance 53862
Result: **Manchester United 0 Liverpool 0**
Teamsheet: Stepney, Buchan M, Young, Greenhoff, Holton, James, Morgan, Anderson, Macari, Kidd, Graham
Substitute(s): Buchan G

Match # 3145 Saturday 06/10/73 Football League Division 1 at Molineux Attendance 32962
Result: **Wolverhampton Wanderers 2 Manchester United 1**
Teamsheet: Stepney, Buchan M, Young, Greenhoff, Holton, James, Morgan, Anderson, Macari, Kidd, Graham
Substitute(s): McIlroy Scorer(s): McIlroy

Match # 3146 Monday 08/10/73 League Cup 2nd Round at Old Trafford Attendance 23906
Result: **Manchester United 0 Middlesbrough 1**
Teamsheet: Stepney, Buchan M, Young, Greenhoff, Holton, James, Morgan, Daly, Macari, Kidd, Graham
Substitute(s): Buchan G

Match # 3147 Saturday 13/10/73 Football League Division 1 at Old Trafford Attendance 43724
Result: **Manchester United 0 Derby County 1**
Teamsheet: Stepney, Buchan M, Forsyth, Greenhoff, Holton, James, Morgan, Young, Kidd, Anderson, Graham

Match # 3148 Saturday 20/10/73 Football League Division 1 at Old Trafford Attendance 48937
Result: **Manchester United 1 Birmingham City 0**
Teamsheet: Stepney, Buchan M, Young, Greenhoff, Holton, James, Morgan, Kidd, Macari, Graham, Best
Substitute(s): Martin Scorer(s): Stepney

Match # 3149 Saturday 27/10/73 Football League Division 1 at Turf Moor Attendance 31976
Result: **Burnley 0 Manchester United 0**
Teamsheet: Stepney, Buchan M, Young, Greenhoff, James, Griffiths, Morgan, Kidd, Macari, Graham, Best
Substitute(s): Sadler

Match # 3150 Saturday 03/11/73 Football League Division 1 at Old Trafford Attendance 48036
Result: **Manchester United 2 Chelsea 2**
Teamsheet: Stepney, Buchan M, Young, Greenhoff, James, Griffiths, Morgan, Macari, Kidd, Graham, Best
Scorer(s): Greenhoff, Young

Match # 3151 Saturday 10/11/73 Football League Division 1 at White Hart Lane Attendance 42756
Result: **Tottenham Hotspur 2 Manchester United 1**
Teamsheet: Stepney, Buchan M, Young, Greenhoff, Holton, James, Morgan, Macari, Kidd, Graham, Best
Scorer(s): Best

Match # 3152 Saturday 17/11/73 Football League Division 1 at St James' Park Attendance 41768
Result: **Newcastle United 3 Manchester United 2**
Teamsheet: Stepney, Buchan M, Young, Greenhoff, Holton, James, Morgan, Macari, Kidd, Graham, Best
Scorer(s): Graham, Macari

Match # 3153 Saturday 24/11/73 Football League Division 1 at Old Trafford Attendance 36338
Result: **Manchester United 0 Norwich City 0**
Teamsheet: Stepney, Buchan M, Young, Greenhoff, Holton, James, Morgan, Macari, Kidd, Graham, Best
Substitute(s): Fletcher

SEASON 1973/74 (continued)

Match # 3154	Saturday 08/12/73	Football League Division 1	at Old Trafford	Attendance 31648
Result:	**Manchester United 0 Southampton 0**			
Teamsheet:	Stepney, Buchan M, Forsyth, Greenhoff, James, Griffiths, Morgan, Young, Kidd, McIlroy, Best			
Substitute(s):	Anderson			

Match # 3155	Saturday 15/12/73	Football League Division 1	at Old Trafford	Attendance 28589
Result:	**Manchester United 2 Coventry City 3**			
Teamsheet:	Stepney, Buchan M, Forsyth, Greenhoff, James, Griffiths, Morgan, Macari, McIlroy, Young, Best			
Substitute(s):	Martin	Scorer(s): Best, Morgan		

Match # 3156	Saturday 22/12/73	Football League Division 1	at Anfield	Attendance 40420
Result:	**Liverpool 2 Manchester United 0**			
Teamsheet:	Stepney, Buchan M, Young, Greenhoff, Sidebottom, Griffiths, Morgan, Macari, Kidd, Graham, Best			
Substitute(s):	McIlroy			

Match # 3157	Wednesday 26/12/73	Football League Division 1	at Old Trafford	Attendance 38653
Result:	**Manchester United 1 Sheffield United 2**			
Teamsheet:	Stepney, Young, Griffiths, Greenhoff, Holton, Buchan M, Morgan, Macari, McIlroy, Graham, Best			
Scorer(s):	Macari			

Match # 3158	Saturday 29/12/73	Football League Division 1	at Old Trafford	Attendance 36365
Result:	**Manchester United 2 Ipswich Town 0**			
Teamsheet:	Stepney, Young, Griffiths, Greenhoff, Holton, Buchan M, Morgan, Macari, McIlroy, Graham, Best			
Scorer(s):	Macari, McIlroy			

Match # 3159	Tuesday 01/01/74	Football League Division 1	at Loftus Road	Attendance 32339
Result:	**Queens Park Rangers 3 Manchester United 0**			
Teamsheet:	Stepney, Young, Houston, Greenhoff, Holton, Buchan M, Morgan, Macari, McIlroy, Graham, Best			

Match # 3160	Saturday 05/01/74	FA Cup 3rd Round	at Old Trafford	Attendance 31810
Result:	**Manchester United 1 Plymouth Argyle 0**			
Teamsheet:	Stepney, Young, Forsyth, Greenhoff, Holton, Buchan M, Morgan, Macari, Kidd, Graham, Martin			
Substitute(s):	McIlroy	Scorer(s): Macari		

Match # 3161	Saturday 12/01/74	Football League Division 1	at Upton Park	Attendance 34147
Result:	**West Ham United 2 Manchester United 1**			
Teamsheet:	Stepney, Forsyth, Houston, Greenhoff, Holton, Buchan M, Morgan, Macari, Kidd, Young, Graham			
Substitute(s):	McIlroy	Scorer(s): McIlroy		

Match # 3162	Saturday 19/01/74	Football League Division 1	at Old Trafford	Attendance 38589
Result:	**Manchester United 1 Arsenal 1**			
Teamsheet:	Stepney, Buchan M, Houston, Greenhoff, Holton, James, Morgan, Macari, McIlroy, Young, Martin			
Scorer(s):	James			

Match # 3163	Saturday 26/01/74	FA Cup 4th Round	at Old Trafford	Attendance 37177
Result:	**Manchester United 0 Ipswich Town 1**			
Teamsheet:	Stepney, Buchan M, Forsyth, Greenhoff, Holton, James, Morgan, Macari, McIlroy, Young, Martin			
Substitute(s):	Kidd			

Match # 3164	Saturday 02/02/74	Football League Division 1	at Highfield Road	Attendance 25313
Result:	**Coventry City 1 Manchester United 0**			
Teamsheet:	Stepney, Buchan M, Houston, Greenhoff, Holton, James, Morgan, Macari, McIlroy, Kidd, Young			
Substitute(s):	Forsyth			

Match # 3165	Saturday 09/02/74	Football League Division 1	at Old Trafford	Attendance 60025
Result:	**Manchester United 0 Leeds United 2**			
Teamsheet:	Stepney, Buchan M, Houston, Greenhoff, Holton, James, Morgan, Macari, Kidd, Young, Forsyth			
Substitute(s):	McIlroy			

Match # 3166	Saturday 16/02/74	Football League Division 1	at Baseball Ground	Attendance 29987
Result:	**Derby County 2 Manchester United 2**			
Teamsheet:	Stepney, Forsyth, Houston, Greenhoff, Holton, Buchan M, Morgan, Fletcher, Kidd, Macari, McIlroy			
Substitute(s):	Daly	Scorer(s): Greenhoff, Houston		

Match # 3167	Saturday 23/02/74	Football League Division 1	at Old Trafford	Attendance 39260
Result:	**Manchester United 0 Wolverhampton Wanderers 0**			
Teamsheet:	Stepney, Forsyth, Houston, Greenhoff, Holton, Buchan M, Morgan, Fletcher, Kidd, Macari, McIlroy			
Substitute(s):	Daly			

Match # 3168	Saturday 02/03/74	Football League Division 1	at Bramall Lane	Attendance 29203
Result:	**Sheffield United 0 Manchester United 1**			
Teamsheet:	Stepney, Forsyth, Houston, Greenhoff, Holton, Buchan M, Morgan, Macari, McIlroy, Daly, Martin			
Scorer(s):	Macari			

Match # 3169	Wednesday 13/03/74	Football League Division 1	at Maine Road	Attendance 51331
Result:	**Manchester City 0 Manchester United 0**			
Teamsheet:	Stepney, Forsyth, Houston, Martin, Holton, Buchan M, Morgan, Macari, Greenhoff, Daly, Bielby			
Substitute(s):	Graham			

Match # 3170	Saturday 16/03/74	Football League Division 1	at St Andrews	Attendance 37768
Result:	**Birmingham City 1 Manchester United 0**			
Teamsheet:	Stepney, Forsyth, Houston, Martin, Holton, Buchan M, McCalliog, Macari, Greenhoff, Graham, Bielby			

Match # 3171	Saturday 23/03/74	Football League Division 1	at Old Trafford	Attendance 36278
Result:	**Manchester United 0 Tottenham Hotspur 1**			
Teamsheet:	Stepney, Forsyth, Houston, Greenhoff, James, Buchan M, Morgan, McIlroy, Kidd, McCalliog, Daly			
Substitute(s):	Bielby			

SEASON 1973/74 (continued)

Match # 3172 Saturday 30/03/74   Football League Division 1   at Stamford Bridge   Attendance 29602
Result: **Chelsea 1 Manchester United 3**
Teamsheet: Stepney, Forsyth, Houston, Daly, James, Buchan M, Morgan, McIlroy, Greenhoff, McCalliog, Martin
Substitute(s): Bielby   Scorer(s):   Daly, McIlroy, Morgan

Match # 3173 Wednesday 03/04/74   Football League Division 1   at Old Trafford   Attendance 33336
Result: **Manchester United 3 Burnley 3**
Teamsheet: Stepney, Forsyth, Houston, Daly, Holton, Buchan M, Morgan, McIlroy, Greenhoff, McCalliog, Martin
Scorer(s):   Forsyth, Holton, McIlroy

Match # 3174 Saturday 06/04/74   Football League Division 1   at Carrow Road   Attendance 28223
Result: **Norwich City 0 Manchester United 2**
Teamsheet: Stepney, Forsyth, Houston, Greenhoff, Holton, Buchan M, Morgan, Macari, McIlroy, McCalliog, Daly
Scorer(s):   Greenhoff, Macari

Match # 3175 Saturday 13/04/74   Football League Division 1   at Old Trafford   Attendance 44751
Result: **Manchester United 1 Newcastle United 0**
Teamsheet: Stepney, Forsyth, Houston, Greenhoff, Holton, Buchan M, Morgan, Daly, McCalliog, Macari, McIlroy
Scorer(s):   McCalliog

Match # 3176 Monday 15/04/74   Football League Division 1   at Old Trafford   Attendance 48424
Result: **Manchester United 3 Everton 0**
Teamsheet: Stepney, Young, Houston, Greenhoff, Holton, Buchan M, Morgan, Macari, McIlroy, McCalliog, Daly
Substitute(s): Martin   Scorer(s):   McCalliog 2, Houston

Match # 3177 Saturday 20/04/74   Football League Division 1   at The Dell   Attendance 30789
Result: **Southampton 1 Manchester United 1**
Teamsheet: Stepney, Young, Houston, Greenhoff, Holton, Buchan M, Morgan, Macari, McIlroy, McCalliog, Daly
Scorer(s):   McCalliog

Match # 3178 Tuesday 23/04/74   Football League Division 1   at Goodison Park   Attendance 46093
Result: **Everton 1 Manchester United 0**
Teamsheet: Stepney, Forsyth, Houston, Greenhoff, Holton, Buchan M, Morgan, Macari, McIlroy, McCalliog, Daly

Match # 3179 Saturday 27/04/74   Football League Division 1   at Old Trafford   Attendance 56996
Result: **Manchester United 0 Manchester City 1**
Teamsheet: Stepney, Forsyth, Houston, Greenhoff, Holton, Buchan M, Morgan, Macari, McIlroy, McCalliog, Daly

Match # 3180 Monday 29/04/74   Football League Division 1   at Victoria Ground   Attendance 27392
Result: **Stoke City 1 Manchester United 0**
Teamsheet: Stepney, Forsyth, Houston, Greenhoff, Holton, Buchan M, Morgan, Macari, McIlroy, McCalliog, Martin

SEASON 1973/74 SUMMARY

APPEARANCES

PLAYER	LGE	FAC	LC	TOTAL
Buchan M	42	2	1	45
Stepney	42	2	1	45
Morgan	41	2	1	44
Greenhoff	36	2	1	39
Macari	34 (1)	2	1	37 (1)
Holton	34	2	1	37
Young	29	2	1	32
McIlroy	24 (5)	1 (1)	–	25 (6)
Graham	23 (1)	1	1	25 (1)
Kidd	21	1 (1)	1	23 (1)
James	21	1	1	23
Forsyth	18 (1)	2	–	20 (1)
Houston	20	–	–	20
Daly	14 (2)	–	1	15 (2)
Martin	12 (4)	2	–	14 (4)
Best	12	–	–	12
Anderson	11 (1)	–	–	11 (1)
McCalliog	11	–	–	11
Griffiths	7	–	–	7
Fletcher	2 (3)	–	–	2 (3)
Bielby	2 (2)	–	–	2 (2)
Sadler	2 (1)	–	–	2 (1)
Sidebottom	2	–	–	2
Storey-Moore	2	–	–	2
Buchan G	– (3)	–	– (1)	– (4)

GOALSCORERS

PLAYER	LGE	FAC	LC	TOT
McIlroy	6	–	–	6
Macari	5	1	–	6
McCalliog	4	–	–	4
Greenhoff	3	–	–	3
Best	2	–	–	2
Holton	2	–	–	2
Houston	2	–	–	2
James	2	–	–	2
Kidd	2	–	–	2
Morgan	2	–	–	2
Stepney	2	–	–	2
Anderson	1	–	–	1
Daly	1	–	–	1
Forsyth	1	–	–	1
Graham	1	–	–	1
Storey-Moore	1	–	–	1
Young	1	–	–	1

RESULTS & ATTENDANCES SUMMARY

		P	W	D	L	F	A	TOTAL	AVGE
League	H	21	7	7	7	23	20	897131	42721
	A	21	3	5	13	15	28	741803	35324
	TOTAL	42	10	12	20	38	48	1638934	39022
FA Cup	H	2	1	0	1	1	1	68987	34494
	A	0	0	0	0	0	0	0	n/a
	TOTAL	2	1	0	1	1	1	68987	34494
League Cup	H	1	0	0	1	0	1	23906	23906
	A	0	0	0	0	0	0	0	n/a
	TOTAL	1	0	0	1	0	1	23906	23906
Overall	H	24	8	7	9	24	22	990024	41251
	A	21	3	5	13	15	28	741803	35324
	TOTAL	45	11	12	22	39	50	1731827	38485

FINAL TABLE – LEAGUE DIVISION ONE

		P	W	D	L	F	A	W	D	L	F	A	PTS	GD
			HOME					AWAY						
1	Leeds United	42	12	8	1	38	18	12	6	3	28	13	62	35
2	Liverpool	42	18	2	1	34	11	4	11	6	18	20	57	21
3	Derby County	42	13	7	1	40	16	4	7	10	12	26	48	10
4	Ipswich Town	42	10	7	4	38	21	8	4	9	29	37	47	9
5	Stoke City	42	13	6	2	39	15	2	10	9	15	27	46	12
6	Burnley	42	10	9	2	29	16	6	5	10	27	37	46	3
7	Everton	42	12	7	2	29	14	4	5	12	21	34	44	2
8	Queens Park Rangers	42	8	10	3	30	17	5	7	9	26	35	43	4
9	Leicester City	42	10	7	4	35	17	3	9	9	16	24	42	10
10	Arsenal	42	9	7	5	23	16	5	7	9	26	35	42	-2
11	Tottenham Hotspur	42	9	4	8	26	27	5	10	6	19	23	42	-5
12	Wolverhampton Wanderers	42	11	6	4	30	18	2	9	10	19	31	41	0
13	Sheffield United	42	7	7	7	25	22	7	5	9	19	27	40	-5
14	Manchester City	42	10	7	4	25	17	4	5	12	14	29	40	-7
15	Newcastle United	42	9	6	6	28	21	4	6	11	21	27	38	1
16	Coventry City	42	10	5	6	25	18	4	5	12	18	36	38	-11
17	Chelsea	42	9	4	8	36	29	3	9	9	20	31	37	-4
18	West Ham United	42	7	7	7	36	32	4	8	9	19	28	37	-5
19	Birmingham City	42	10	7	4	30	21	2	6	13	22	43	37	-12
20	Southampton	42	8	10	3	30	20	3	4	14	17	48	36	-21
21	MANCHESTER UNITED	42	7	7	7	23	20	3	5	13	15	28	32	-10
22	Norwich City	42	6	9	6	25	27	1	6	14	12	35	29	-25

SEASON 1974/75

Match # 3181   Saturday 17/08/74   Football League Division 2   at Brisbane Road   Attendance 17772
Result: **Leyton Orient 0   Manchester United 2**
Teamsheet: Stepney, Forsyth, Houston, Greenhoff, Holton, Buchan, Morgan, Macari, Pearson, McCalliog, Daly
Substitute(s):   McIlroy   Scorer(s):   Houston, Morgan

Match # 3182   Saturday 24/08/74   Football League Division 2   at Old Trafford   Attendance 44756
Result: **Manchester United 4   Millwall 0**
Teamsheet: Stepney, Forsyth, Houston, Greenhoff, Holton, Buchan, Morgan, McIlroy, Pearson, Martin, Daly
Scorer(s):   Daly 3, Pearson

Match # 3183   Wednesday 28/08/74   Football League Division 2   at Old Trafford   Attendance 42547
Result: **Manchester United 2   Portsmouth 1**
Teamsheet: Stepney, Forsyth, Houston, Greenhoff, Holton, Buchan, Morgan, McIlroy, Pearson, Martin, Daly
Scorer(s):   Daly, McIlroy

Match # 3184   Saturday 31/08/74   Football League Division 2   at Ninian Park   Attendance 22344
Result: **Cardiff City 0   Manchester United 1**
Teamsheet: Stepney, Forsyth, Houston, Greenhoff, Holton, Buchan, Morgan, McIlroy, Pearson, Martin, Daly
Substitute(s):   Young   Scorer(s):   Daly

Match # 3185   Saturday 07/09/74   Football League Division 2   at Old Trafford   Attendance 40671
Result: **Manchester United 2   Nottingham Forest 2**
Teamsheet: Stepney, Forsyth, Houston, Greenhoff, Holton, Buchan, Morgan, McIlroy, Martin, McCalliog, Daly
Substitute(s):   Macari   Scorer(s):   Greenhoff, McIlroy

Match # 3186   Wednesday 11/09/74   League Cup 2nd Round   at Old Trafford   Attendance 21616
Result: **Manchester United 5   Charlton Athletic 1**
Teamsheet: Stepney, Forsyth, Houston, Martin, Holton, Buchan, Morgan, McIlroy, Macari, McCalliog, Daly
Substitute(s):   Young   Scorer(s):   Macari 2, Houston, McIlroy, own goal

Match # 3187   Saturday 14/09/74   Football League Division 2   at The Hawthorns   Attendance 23721
Result: **West Bromwich Albion 1   Manchester United 1**
Teamsheet: Stepney, Forsyth, Houston, Martin, Holton, Buchan, Morgan, McIlroy, Pearson, McCalliog, Daly
Substitute(s):   Greenhoff   Scorer(s):   Pearson

Match # 3188   Monday 16/09/74   Football League Division 2   at The Den   Attendance 16988
Result: **Millwall 0   Manchester United 1**
Teamsheet: Stepney, Forsyth, Houston, Greenhoff, Sidebottom, Buchan, Morgan, McIlroy, Macari, McCalliog, Daly
Substitute(s):   Young   Scorer(s):   Daly

Match # 3189   Saturday 21/09/74   Football League Division 2   at Old Trafford   Attendance 42948
Result: **Manchester United 2   Bristol Rovers 0**
Teamsheet: Stepney, Forsyth, Houston, Greenhoff, Holton, Buchan, Morgan, McIlroy, Macari, McCalliog, Daly
Substitute(s):   Young   Scorer(s):   Greenhoff, own goal

Match # 3190   Wednesday 25/09/74   Football League Division 2   at Old Trafford   Attendance 47084
Result: **Manchester United 3   Bolton Wanderers 0**
Teamsheet: Stepney, Forsyth, Houston, Greenhoff, Sidebottom, Buchan, Morgan, McIlroy, Macari, McCalliog, Daly
Scorer(s):   Houston, Macari, own goal

Match # 3191   Saturday 28/09/74   Football League Division 2   at Carrow Road   Attendance 24586
Result: **Norwich City 2   Manchester United 0**
Teamsheet: Stepney, Forsyth, Houston, Greenhoff, Sidebottom, Buchan, Morgan, McIlroy, Macari, McCalliog, Daly
Substitute(s):   Young

Match # 3192   Saturday 05/10/74   Football League Division 2   at Craven Cottage   Attendance 26513
Result: **Fulham 1   Manchester United 2**
Teamsheet: Stepney, Forsyth, Houston, Greenhoff, Holton, Buchan, Morgan, McIlroy, Pearson, McCalliog, Daly
Substitute(s):   Macari   Scorer(s):   Pearson 2

Match # 3193   Wednesday 09/10/74   League Cup 3rd Round   at Old Trafford   Attendance 55169
Result: **Manchester United 1   Manchester City 0**
Teamsheet: Stepney, Forsyth, Albiston, Greenhoff, Holton, Buchan, Morgan, McIlroy, Pearson, McCalliog, Daly
Substitute(s):   Macari   Scorer(s):   Daly

Match # 3194   Saturday 12/10/74   Football League Division 2   at Old Trafford   Attendance 46565
Result: **Manchester United 1   Notts County 0**
Teamsheet: Stepney, Forsyth, Houston, Greenhoff, Holton, Buchan, Morgan, McIlroy, Macari, McCalliog, Daly
Substitute(s):   Young   Scorer(s):   McIlroy

Match # 3195   Tuesday 15/10/74   Football League Division 2   at Fratton Park   Attendance 25608
Result: **Portsmouth 0   Manchester United 0**
Teamsheet: Stepney, Forsyth, Albiston, Greenhoff, Holton, Buchan, Morgan, McIlroy, Macari, McCalliog, Daly
Substitute(s):   McCreery

Match # 3196   Saturday 19/10/74   Football League Division 2   at Bloomfield Road   Attendance 25370
Result: **Blackpool 0   Manchester United 3**
Teamsheet: Stepney, Forsyth, Houston, Greenhoff, Holton, Buchan, Morgan, McIlroy, Macari, McCalliog, Daly
Substitute(s):   McCreery   Scorer(s):   Forsyth, Macari, McCalliog

Match # 3197   Saturday 26/10/74   Football League Division 2   at Old Trafford   Attendance 48724
Result: **Manchester United 1   Southampton 0**
Teamsheet: Stepney, Forsyth, Houston, Greenhoff, Holton, Buchan, Morgan, McIlroy, Macari, McCalliog, Daly
Substitute(s):   Pearson   Scorer(s):   Pearson

Match # 3198   Saturday 02/11/74   Football League Division 2   at Old Trafford   Attendance 41909
Result: **Manchester United 4   Oxford United 0**
Teamsheet: Stepney, Forsyth, Houston, Greenhoff, Sidebottom, Buchan, Macari, McIlroy, Pearson, McCalliog, Daly
Substitute(s):   Morgan   Scorer(s):   Pearson 3, Macari

SEASON 1974/75 (continued)

Match # 3199   Saturday 09/11/74   Football League Division 2   at Ashton Gate   Attendance 28104
Result: **Bristol City 1   Manchester United 0**
Teamsheet: Stepney, Forsyth, Houston, Greenhoff, Sidebottom, Buchan, Macari, McIlroy, Pearson, McCalliog, Daly
Substitute(s):   Graham

Match # 3200   Wednesday 13/11/74   League Cup 4th Round   at Old Trafford   Attendance 46275
Result: **Manchester United 3   Burnley 2**
Teamsheet: Stepney, Forsyth, Houston, Greenhoff, Sidebottom, Buchan, Macari, McIlroy, Pearson, McCalliog, Daly
Substitute(s):   Morgan   Scorer(s):   Macari 2, Morgan

Match # 3201   Saturday 16/11/74   Football League Division 2   at Old Trafford   Attendance 55615
Result: **Manchester United 2   Aston Villa 1**
Teamsheet: Stepney, Forsyth, Houston, Macari, Sidebottom, Buchan, Morgan, McIlroy, Pearson, McCalliog, Daly
Substitute(s):   Greenhoff   Scorer(s):   Daly 2

Match # 3020   Saturday 23/11/74   Football League Division 2   at Boothferry Park   Attendance 23287
Result: **Hull City 2   Manchester United 0**
Teamsheet: Stepney, Forsyth, Houston, Macari, Sidebottom, Buchan, Morgan, McIlroy, Greenhoff, McCalliog, Daly

Match # 3203   Saturday 30/11/74   Football League Division 2   at Old Trafford   Attendance 60585
Result: **Manchester United 3   Sunderland 2**
Teamsheet: Stepney, Forsyth, Houston, Greenhoff, Holton, Buchan, Morgan, McIlroy, Pearson, Macari, Daly
Substitute(s):   Davies   Scorer(s):   McIlroy, Morgan, Pearson

Match # 3204   Wednesday 04/12/74   League Cup 5th Round   at Ayresome Park   Attendance 36005
Result: **Middlesbrough 0   Manchester United 0**
Teamsheet: Stepney, Forsyth, Houston, Greenhoff, Holton, Buchan, Morgan, McIlroy, Pearson, Macari, Daly
Substitute(s):   Young

Match # 3205   Saturday 07/12/74   Football League Division 2   at Hillsborough   Attendance 35230
Result: **Sheffield Wednesday 4   Manchester United 4**
Teamsheet: Stepney, Forsyth, Houston, Greenhoff, Holton, Buchan, Morgan, McIlroy, Pearson, Macari, McCalliog
Substitute(s):   Davies   Scorer(s):   Macari 2, Houston, Pearson

Match # 3206   Saturday 14/12/74   Football League Division 2   at Old Trafford   Attendance 41200
Result: **Manchester United 0   Leyton Orient 0**
Teamsheet: Stepney, Forsyth, Houston, Greenhoff, Sidebottom, Buchan, Morgan, McIlroy, Pearson, Macari, Daly
Substitute(s):   Davies

Match # 3207   Wednesday 18/12/74   League Cup 5th Round Replay   at Old Trafford   Attendance 49501
Result: **Manchester United 3   Middlesbrough 0**
Teamsheet: Stepney, Young, Houston, Greenhoff, Sidebottom, Buchan, Morgan, McIlroy, Pearson, Macari, Daly
Substitute(s):   McCalliog   Scorer(s):   Macari, McIlroy, Pearson

Match # 3208   Saturday 21/12/74   Football League Division 2   at Bootham Crescent   Attendance 15567
Result: **York City 0   Manchester United 1**
Teamsheet: Stepney, Young, Houston, Greenhoff, Sidebottom, Buchan, Morgan, McIlroy, Pearson, Macari, Daly
Substitute(s):   Davies   Scorer(s):   Pearson

Match # 3209   Thursday 26/12/74   Football League Division 2   at Old Trafford   Attendance 51104
Result: **Manchester United 2   West Bromwich Albion 1**
Teamsheet: Stepney, Young, Houston, Greenhoff, Sidebottom, Buchan, Morgan, McIlroy, Pearson, Macari, Daly
Scorer(s):   Daly, McIlroy

Match # 3210   Saturday 28/12/74   Football League Division 2   at Boundary Park   Attendance 26384
Result: **Oldham Athletic 1   Manchester United 0**
Teamsheet: Stepney, Young, Albiston, Greenhoff, Sidebottom, Buchan, Morgan, McIlroy, Pearson, Macari, Daly
Substitute(s):   Davies

Match # 3211   Saturday 04/01/75   FA Cup 3rd Round   at Old Trafford   Attendance 43353
Result: **Manchester United 0   Walsall 0**
Teamsheet: Stepney, Young, Houston, Greenhoff, Sidebottom, Buchan, Morgan, McIlroy, Pearson, Macari, Daly
Substitute(s):   Davies

Match # 3212   Tuesday 07/01/75   FA Cup 3rd Round Replay   at Fellows Park   Attendance 18105
Result: **Walsall 3   Manchester United 2**
Teamsheet: Stepney, Young, Houston, Greenhoff, Sidebottom, Buchan, McCalliog, McIlroy, Pearson, Macari, Daly
Substitute(s):   Davies   Scorer(s):   Daly, McIlroy

Match # 3213   Saturday 11/01/75   Football League Division 2   at Old Trafford   Attendance 45662
Result: **Manchester United 2   Sheffield Wednesday 0**
Teamsheet: Stepney, Forsyth, Houston, Greenhoff, James, Buchan, Morgan, McIlroy, Pearson, Macari, McCalliog
Substitute(s):   Daly   Scorer(s):   McCalliog 2

Match # 3214   Wednesday 15/01/75   League Cup Semi-Final 1st Leg   at Old Trafford   Attendance 58010
Result: **Manchester United 2   Norwich City 2**
Teamsheet: Stepney, Forsyth, Houston, Greenhoff, James, Buchan, Morgan, McIlroy, Daly, Macari, McCalliog
Substitute(s):   Young   Scorer(s):   Macari 2

Match # 3215   Saturday 18/01/75   Football League Division 2   at Roker Park   Attendance 45976
Result: **Sunderland 0   Manchester United 0**
Teamsheet: Stepney, Forsyth, Houston, Greenhoff, James, Buchan, Morgan, McIlroy, Baldwin, Macari, McCalliog

Match # 3216   Wednesday 22/01/75   League Cup Semi-Final 2nd Leg   at Carrow Road   Attendance 31621
Result: **Norwich City 1   Manchester United 0**
Teamsheet: Stepney, Forsyth, Houston, Greenhoff, James, Buchan, Morgan, McIlroy, Daly, Macari, McCalliog
Substitute(s):   Young

SEASON 1974/75 (continued)

Match # 3217 Saturday 01/02/75   Football League Division 2   at Old Trafford   Attendance 47118
Result: **Manchester United 0   Bristol City 1**
Teamsheet: Stepney, Forsyth, Houston, Daly, James, Buchan, Morgan, McIlroy, Baldwin, Macari, McCalliog
Substitute(s): Young

Match # 3218 Saturday 08/02/75   Football League Division 2   at Manor Ground   Attendance 15959
Result: **Oxford United 1   Manchester United 0**
Teamsheet: Roche, Forsyth, Houston, Greenhoff, James, Buchan, Morgan, McIlroy, Pearson, Macari, Young
Substitute(s): Davies

Match # 3219 Saturday 15/02/75   Football League Division 2   at Old Trafford   Attendance 44712
Result: **Manchester United 2   Hull City 0**
Teamsheet: Roche, Forsyth, Houston, Greenhoff, James, Buchan, Young, McIlroy, Pearson, Macari, Martin
Substitute(s): Davies   Scorer(s):   Houston, Pearson

Match # 3220 Saturday 22/02/75   Football League Division 2   at Villa Park   Attendance 39156
Result: **Aston Villa 2   Manchester United 0**
Teamsheet: Stepney, Forsyth, Houston, Greenhoff, Sidebottom, Buchan, Young, McIlroy, Pearson, Macari, Martin
Substitute(s): Davies

Match # 3221 Saturday 01/03/75   Football League Division 2   at Old Trafford   Attendance 43601
Result: **Manchester United 4   Cardiff City 0**
Teamsheet: Stepney, Forsyth, Houston, Greenhoff, James, Buchan, Morgan, McIlroy, Pearson, Macari, Daly
Substitute(s): Coppell   Scorer(s):   Houston, Macari, McIlroy, Pearson

Match # 3222 Saturday 08/03/75   Football League Division 2   at Burnden Park   Attendance 38152
Result: **Bolton Wanderers 0   Manchester United 1**
Teamsheet: Stepney, Forsyth, Houston, Greenhoff, James, Buchan, Coppell, McIlroy, Pearson, Macari, Daly
Substitute(s): Young   Scorer(s):   Pearson

Match # 3223 Saturday 15/03/75   Football League Division 2   at Old Trafford   Attendance 56202
Result: **Manchester United 1   Norwich City 1**
Teamsheet: Stepney, Forsyth, Houston, Greenhoff, James, Buchan, Coppell, McIlroy, Pearson, Macari, Daly
Substitute(s): Young   Scorer(s):   Pearson

Match # 3224 Saturday 22/03/75   Football League Division 2   at City Ground   Attendance 21893
Result: **Nottingham Forest 0   Manchester United 1**
Teamsheet: Stepney, Forsyth, Houston, Greenhoff, James, Buchan, Coppell, McIlroy, Pearson, Macari, Daly
Scorer(s): Daly

Match # 3225 Friday 28/03/75   Football League Division 2   at Eastville   Attendance 19337
Result: **Bristol Rovers 1   Manchester United 1**
Teamsheet: Stepney, Forsyth, Houston, Greenhoff, James, Buchan, Coppell, McIlroy, Pearson, Macari, Daly
Substitute(s): Morgan   Scorer(s):   Macari

Match # 3226 Saturday 29/03/75   Football League Division 2   at Old Trafford   Attendance 46802
Result: **Manchester United 2   York City 1**
Teamsheet: Stepney, Forsyth, Houston, Morgan, Greenhoff, Buchan, Coppell, McIlroy, Pearson, Macari, Daly
Scorer(s): Macari, Morgan

Match # 3227 Monday 31/03/75   Football League Division 2   at Old Trafford   Attendance 56618
Result: **Manchester United 3   Oldham Athletic 2**
Teamsheet: Stepney, Forsyth, Houston, Morgan, Greenhoff, Buchan, Coppell, McIlroy, Pearson, Macari, Daly
Substitute(s): Martin   Scorer(s):   Coppell, Macari, McIlroy

Match # 3228 Saturday 05/04/75   Football League Division 2   at The Dell   Attendance 21866
Result: **Southampton 0   Manchester United 1**
Teamsheet: Stepney, Forsyth, Houston, Young, Greenhoff, Buchan, Morgan, McIlroy, Pearson, Macari, Daly
Substitute(s): Nicholl   Scorer(s):   Macari

Match # 3229 Saturday 12/04/75   Football League Division 2   at Old Trafford   Attendance 52971
Result: **Manchester United 1   Fulham 0**
Teamsheet: Stepney, Forsyth, Houston, Greenhoff, James, Morgan, Coppell, McIlroy, Pearson, Macari, Daly
Scorer(s): Daly

Match # 3230 Saturday 19/04/75   Football League Division 2   at Meadow Lane   Attendance 17320
Result: **Notts County 2   Manchester United 2**
Teamsheet: Stepney, Forsyth, Houston, Greenhoff, James, Buchan, Coppell, McIlroy, Pearson, Macari, Daly
Scorer(s): Greenhoff, Houston

Match # 3231 Saturday 26/04/75   Football League Division 2   at Old Trafford   Attendance 58769
Result: **Manchester United 4   Blackpool 0**
Teamsheet: Stepney, Forsyth, Houston, Greenhoff, James, Buchan, Coppell, McIlroy, Pearson, Macari, Daly
Scorer(s): Pearson 2, Greenhoff, Macari

SEASON 1974/75 SUMMARY

APPEARANCES

PLAYER	LGE	FAC	LC	TOTAL
McIlroy	41 (1)	2	7	50 (1)
Buchan	41	2	7	50
Stepney	40	2	7	49
Houston	40	2	6	48
Greenhoff	39 (2)	2	6	47 (2)
Daly	36 (1)	2	7	45 (1)
Forsyth	39	–	6	45
Macari	36 (2)	2	6 (1)	44 (3)
Morgan	32 (2)	1	6 (1)	39 (3)
Pearson	30 (1)	2	4	36 (1)
McCalliog	20	1	5 (1)	26 (1)
Holton	14	–	3	17
Sidebottom	12	2	2	16
James	13	–	2	15
Young	7 (8)	2	1 (4)	10 (12)
Coppell	9 (1)	–	–	9 (1)
Martin	7 (1)	–	1	8 (1)
Albiston	2	–	1	3
Baldwin	2	–	–	2
Roche	2	–	–	2
Davies	– (8)	– (2)	–	– (10)
McCreery	– (2)	–	–	– (2)
Graham	– (1)	–	–	– (1)
Nicholl	– (1)	–	–	– (1)

GOALSCORERS

PLAYER	LGE	FAC	LC	TOT
Pearson	17	–	1	18
Macari	11	–	7	18
Daly	11	1	1	13
McIlroy	7	1	2	10
Houston	6	–	1	7
Greenhoff	4	–	–	4
Morgan	3	–	1	4
McCalliog	3	–	–	3
Coppell	1	–	–	1
Forsyth	1	–	–	1
own goals	2	–	1	3

RESULTS & ATTENDANCES SUMMARY

		P	W	D	L	F	A	TOTAL	AVGE
League	H	21	17	3	1	45	12	1016163	48389
	A	21	9	6	6	21	18	531133	25292
	TOTAL	42	26	9	7	66	30	1547296	36840
FA Cup	H	1	0	1	0	0	0	43353	43353
	A	1	0	0	1	2	3	18105	18105
	TOTAL	2	0	1	1	2	3	61458	30729
League	H	5	4	1	0	14	5	230571	46114
Cup	A	2	0	1	1	0	1	67626	33813
	TOTAL	7	4	2	1	14	6	298197	42600
Overall	H	27	21	5	1	59	17	1290087	47781
	A	24	9	7	8	23	22	616864	25703
	TOTAL	51	30	12	9	82	39	1906951	37391

FINAL TABLE – LEAGUE DIVISION TWO

		P	W	D	L	F	A	W	D	L	F	A	PTS	GD
				HOME						AWAY				
1	MANCHESTER UNITED	42	17	3	1	45	12	9	6	6	21	18	61	36
2	Aston Villa	42	16	4	1	47	6	9	4	8	32	26	58	47
3	Norwich City	42	14	3	4	34	17	6	10	5	24	20	53	21
4	Sunderland	42	14	6	1	41	8	5	7	9	24	27	51	30
5	Bristol City	42	14	5	2	31	10	7	3	11	16	23	50	14
6	West Bromwich Albion	42	13	4	4	33	15	5	5	11	21	27	45	12
7	Blackpool	42	12	6	3	31	17	2	11	8	7	16	45	5
8	Hull City	42	12	8	1	25	10	3	6	12	15	43	44	-13
9	Fulham	42	9	8	4	29	17	4	8	9	15	22	42	5
10	Bolton Wanderers	42	9	7	5	27	16	6	5	10	18	25	42	4
11	Oxford United	42	14	3	4	30	19	1	9	11	11	32	42	-10
12	Leyton Orient	42	8	9	4	17	16	3	11	7	11	23	42	-11
13	Southampton	42	10	6	5	29	20	5	5	11	24	34	41	-1
14	Notts County	42	7	11	3	34	26	5	5	11	15	33	40	-10
15	York City	42	9	7	5	28	18	5	3	13	23	37	38	-4
16	Nottingham Forest	42	7	7	7	24	23	5	7	9	19	32	38	-12
17	Portsmouth	42	9	7	5	28	20	3	6	12	16	34	37	-10
18	Oldham Athletic	42	10	7	4	28	16	0	8	13	12	32	35	-8
19	Bristol Rovers	42	10	4	7	25	23	2	7	12	17	41	35	-22
20	Millwall	42	8	9	4	31	19	2	3	16	13	37	32	-12
21	Cardiff City	42	7	8	6	24	21	2	6	13	12	41	32	-26
22	Sheffield Wednesday	42	3	7	11	17	29	2	4	15	12	35	21	-35

SEASON 1975/76

Match # 3232 Saturday 16/08/75   Football League Division 1   at Molineux   Attendance 32348
Result: **Wolverhampton Wanderers 0 Manchester United 2**
Teamsheet: Stepney, Forsyth, Houston, Jackson, Greenhoff, Buchan, Coppell, McIlroy, Pearson, Macari, Daly
Substitute(s): Nicholl   Scorer(s):   Macari 2

Match # 3233 Tuesday 19/08/75   Football League Division 1   at St Andrews   Attendance 33177
Result: **Birmingham City 0 Manchester United 2**
Teamsheet: Stepney, Forsyth, Houston, Jackson, Greenhoff, Buchan, Coppell, McIlroy, McCreery, Macari, Daly
Substitute(s): Nicholl   Scorer(s):   McIlroy 2

Match # 3234 Saturday 23/08/75   Football League Division 1   at Old Trafford   Attendance 55949
Result: **Manchester United 5 Sheffield United 1**
Teamsheet: Stepney, Forsyth, Houston, Jackson, Greenhoff, Buchan, Coppell, McIlroy, Pearson, Macari, Daly
Substitute(s): Nicholl   Scorer(s):   Pearson 2, Daly, McIlroy, own goal

Match # 3235 Wednesday 27/08/75   Football League Division 1   at Old Trafford   Attendance 52169
Result: **Manchester United 1 Coventry City 1**
Teamsheet: Stepney, Forsyth, Houston, Jackson, Greenhoff, Buchan, Coppell, McIlroy, Pearson, Macari, Daly
Scorer(s): Pearson

Match # 3236 Saturday 30/08/75   Football League Division 1   at Victoria Ground   Attendance 33092
Result: **Stoke City 0 Manchester United 1**
Teamsheet: Stepney, Forsyth, Houston, Jackson, Greenhoff, Buchan, Coppell, McIlroy, Pearson, Macari, Daly
Scorer(s): own goal

Match # 3237 Saturday 06/09/75   Football League Division 1   at Old Trafford   Attendance 51641
Result: **Manchester United 3 Tottenham Hotspur 2**
Teamsheet: Stepney, Nicholl, Houston, Jackson, Greenhoff, Buchan, Coppell, McIlroy, Pearson, Macari, Daly
Scorer(s): Daly 2, own goal

Match # 3238 Wednesday 10/09/75   League Cup 2nd Round   at Old Trafford   Attendance 25286
Result: **Manchester United 2 Brentford 1**
Teamsheet: Stepney, Nicholl, Houston, Jackson, Greenhoff, Buchan, Coppell, McIlroy, Pearson, Macari, Daly
Substitute(s): Grimshaw   Scorer(s):   Macari, McIlroy

Match # 3239 Saturday 13/09/75   Football League Division 1   at Loftus Road   Attendance 29237
Result: **Queens Park Rangers 1 Manchester United 0**
Teamsheet: Stepney, Nicholl, Albiston, Jackson, Houston, Buchan, Coppell, McIlroy, Pearson, Macari, Daly
Substitute(s): Young

Match # 3240 Saturday 20/09/75   Football League Division 1   at Old Trafford   Attendance 50513
Result: **Manchester United 1 Ipswich Town 0**
Teamsheet: Stepney, Nicholl, Houston, McCreery, Greenhoff, Buchan, Coppell, McIlroy, Pearson, Macari, Daly
Scorer(s): Houston

Match # 3241 Wednesday 24/09/75   Football League Division 1   at Baseball Ground   Attendance 33187
Result: **Derby County 2 Manchester United 1**
Teamsheet: Stepney, Nicholl, Houston, McCreery, Greenhoff, Buchan, Coppell, McIlroy, Pearson, Macari, Daly
Scorer(s): Daly

Match # 3242 Saturday 27/09/75   Football League Division 1   at Maine Road   Attendance 46931
Result: **Manchester City 2 Manchester United 2**
Teamsheet: Stepney, Nicholl, Houston, McCreery, Greenhoff, Buchan, Coppell, McIlroy, Pearson, Macari, Daly
Scorer(s): Macari, McCreery

Match # 3243 Saturday 04/10/75   Football League Division 1   at Old Trafford   Attendance 47878
Result: **Manchester United 0 Leicester City 0**
Teamsheet: Stepney, Nicholl, Houston, Jackson, Greenhoff, Buchan, Coppell, McIlroy, Pearson, Macari, Daly
Substitute(s): McCreery

Match # 3244 Wednesday 08/10/75   League Cup 3rd Round   at Villa Park   Attendance 41447
Result: **Aston Villa 1 Manchester United 2**
Teamsheet: Stepney, Nicholl, Houston, Jackson, Greenhoff, Buchan, Coppell, McIlroy, Pearson, Macari, Daly
Scorer(s): Coppell, Macari

Match # 3245 Saturday 11/10/75   Football League Division 1   at Elland Road   Attendance 40264
Result: **Leeds United 1 Manchester United 2**
Teamsheet: Stepney, Nicholl, Houston, Jackson, Greenhoff, Buchan, Coppell, McIlroy, Pearson, Macari, Daly
Substitute(s): Grimshaw   Scorer(s):   McIlroy 2

Match # 3246 Saturday 18/10/75   Football League Division 1   at Old Trafford   Attendance 53885
Result: **Manchester United 3 Arsenal 1**
Teamsheet: Stepney, Nicholl, Houston, Jackson, Greenhoff, Buchan, Coppell, McIlroy, Pearson, Macari, Daly
Scorer(s): Coppell 2, Pearson

Match # 3247 Saturday 25/10/75   Football League Division 1   at Upton Park   Attendance 38528
Result: **West Ham United 2 Manchester United 1**
Teamsheet: Stepney, Nicholl, Houston, Jackson, Greenhoff, Buchan, Coppell, McIlroy, Pearson, Macari, Daly
Substitute(s): McCreery   Scorer(s):   Macari

Match # 3248 Saturday 01/11/75   Football League Division 1   at Old Trafford   Attendance 50587
Result: **Manchester United 1 Norwich City 0**
Teamsheet: Roche, Nicholl, Houston, Jackson, Greenhoff, Buchan, Coppell, McIlroy, Pearson, Macari, Daly
Scorer(s): Pearson

Match # 3249 Saturday 08/11/75   Football League Division 1   at Anfield   Attendance 49136
Result: **Liverpool 3 Manchester United 1**
Teamsheet: Roche, Nicholl, Houston, Jackson, Greenhoff, Buchan, Coppell, McIlroy, Pearson, Macari, Daly
Substitute(s): McCreery   Scorer(s):   Coppell

SEASON 1975/76 (continued)

Match # 3250   Wednesday 12/11/75   League Cup 4th Round   at Maine Road   Attendance 50182
Result: **Manchester City 4   Manchester United 0**
Teamsheet: Roche, Nicholl, Houston, Jackson, Greenhoff, Buchan, Coppell, McIlroy, Pearson, Macari, Daly
Substitute(s):   McCreery

Match # 3251   Saturday 15/11/75   Football League Division 1   at Old Trafford   Attendance 51682
Result: **Manchester United 2   Aston Villa 0**
Teamsheet: Roche, Nicholl, Houston, Daly, Greenhoff, Buchan, Coppell, McIlroy, Pearson, Macari, Hill
Substitute(s):   McCreery   Scorer(s):   Coppell, McIlroy

Match # 3252   Saturday 22/11/75   Football League Division 1   at Highbury   Attendance 40102
Result: **Arsenal 3   Manchester United 1**
Teamsheet: Roche, Nicholl, Houston, Daly, Greenhoff, Buchan, Coppell, McIlroy, Pearson, Macari, Hill
Substitute(s):   McCreery   Scorer(s):   Pearson

Match # 3253   Saturday 29/11/75   Football League Division 1   at Old Trafford   Attendance 52624
Result: **Manchester United 1   Newcastle United 0**
Teamsheet: Stepney, Nicholl, Houston, Daly, Greenhoff, Buchan, Coppell, McIlroy, Pearson, Macari, Hill
Substitute(s):   McCreery   Scorer(s):   Daly

Match # 32546   Saturday 06/12/75   Football League Division 1   at Ayresome Park   Attendance 32454
Result: **Middlesbrough 0   Manchester United 0**
Teamsheet: Stepney, Forsyth, Houston, Daly, Greenhoff, Buchan, Coppell, McIlroy, Pearson, Macari, Hill
Substitute(s):   Nicholl

Match # 3255   Saturday 13/12/75   Football League Division 1   at Bramall Lane   Attendance 31741
Result: **Sheffield United 1   Manchester United 4**
Teamsheet: Stepney, Forsyth, Houston, Daly, Greenhoff, Buchan, Coppell, McIlroy, Pearson, Macari, Hill
Substitute(s):   McCreery   Scorer(s):   Pearson 2, Hill, Macari

Match # 3256   Saturday 20/12/75   Football League Division 1   at Old Trafford   Attendance 44269
Result: **Manchester United 1   Wolverhampton Wanderers 0**
Teamsheet: Stepney, Forsyth, Houston, Daly, Greenhoff, Buchan, Coppell, McIlroy, Pearson, Macari, Hill
Substitute(s):   Kelly   Scorer(s):   Hill

Match # 3257   Tuesday 23/12/75   Football League Division 1   at Goodison Park   Attendance 41732
Result: **Everton 1   Manchester United 1**
Teamsheet: Stepney, Forsyth, Houston, Daly, Greenhoff, Buchan, Coppell, McIlroy, Pearson, Macari, Hill
Scorer(s):   Macari

Match # 3258   Saturday 27/12/75   Football League Division 1   at Old Trafford   Attendance 59726
Result: **Manchester United 2   Burnley 1**
Teamsheet: Stepney, Forsyth, Houston, Daly, Greenhoff, Buchan, Coppell, McIlroy, Pearson, Macari, Hill
Substitute(s):   McCreery   Scorer(s):   Macari, McIlroy

Match # 3259   Saturday 03/01/76   FA Cup 3rd Round   at Old Trafford   Attendance 41082
Result: **Manchester United 2   Oxford United 1**
Teamsheet: Stepney, Forsyth, Houston, Daly, Greenhoff, Buchan, Coppell, McIlroy, Pearson, Macari, Hill
Substitute(s):   Nicholl   Scorer(s):   Daly 2

Match # 3260   Saturday 10/01/76   Football League Division 1   at Old Trafford   Attendance 58302
Result: **Manchester United 2   Queens Park Rangers 1**
Teamsheet: Stepney, Forsyth, Houston, Daly, Greenhoff, Buchan, Coppell, McIlroy, Pearson, Macari, Hill
Scorer(s):   Hill, McIlroy

Match # 3261   Saturday 17/01/76   Football League Division 1   at White Hart Lane   Attendance 49189
Result: **Tottenham Hotspur 1   Manchester United 1**
Teamsheet: Stepney, Forsyth, Houston, Daly, Greenhoff, Buchan, Coppell, McIlroy, Pearson, Macari, Hill
Substitute(s):   McCreery   Scorer(s):   Hill

Match # 3262   Saturday 24/01/76   FA Cup 4th Round   at Old Trafford   Attendance 56352
Result: **Manchester United 3   Peterborough United 1**
Teamsheet: Stepney, Forsyth, Houston, Daly, Greenhoff, Buchan, Coppell, McIlroy, Pearson, Macari, Hill
Scorer(s):   Forsyth, Hill, McIlroy

Match # 3263   Saturday 31/01/76   Football League Division 1   at Old Trafford   Attendance 50724
Result: **Manchester United 3   Birmingham City 1**
Teamsheet: Stepney, Forsyth, Houston, Daly, Greenhoff, Buchan, Coppell, McIlroy, Pearson, Macari, Hill
Substitute(s):   McCreery   Scorer(s):   Forsyth, Macari, McIlroy

Match # 3264   Saturday 07/02/76   Football League Division 1   at Highfield Road   Attendance 33922
Result: **Coventry City 1   Manchester United 1**
Teamsheet: Stepney, Forsyth, Houston, Daly, Greenhoff, Buchan, Coppell, McIlroy, Pearson, Macari, Hill
Substitute(s):   McCreery   Scorer(s):   Macari

Match # 3265   Saturday 14/02/76   FA Cup 5th Round   at Filbert Street   Attendance 34000
Result: **Leicester City 1   Manchester United 2**
Teamsheet: Stepney, Forsyth, Houston, Daly, Greenhoff, Buchan, Coppell, McIlroy, Pearson, Macari, Hill
Substitute(s):   McCreery   Scorer(s):   Daly, Macari

Match # 3266   Wednesday 18/02/76   Football League Division 1   at Old Trafford   Attendance 59709
Result: **Manchester United 0   Liverpool 0**
Teamsheet: Stepney, Forsyth, Houston, Daly, Greenhoff, Buchan, Coppell, McIlroy, Pearson, Macari, Hill
Substitute(s):   McCreery

Match # 3267   Saturday 21/02/76   Football League Division 1   at Villa Park   Attendance 50094
Result: **Aston Villa 2   Manchester United 1**
Teamsheet: Stepney, Forsyth, Houston, Daly, Greenhoff, Buchan, Coppell, McIlroy, Pearson, Macari, Hill
Substitute(s):   Coyne   Scorer(s):   Macari

SEASON 1975/76 (continued)

Match # 3268 Wednesday 25/02/76 Football League Division 1 at Old Trafford Attendance 59632
Result: **Manchester United 1 Derby County 1**
Teamsheet: Stepney, Forsyth, Houston, Daly, Greenhoff, Buchan, Coppell, McIlroy, Pearson, Macari, Hill
Substitute(s): McCreery Scorer(s): Pearson

Match # 3269 Saturday 28/02/76 Football League Division 1 at Old Trafford Attendance 57220
Result: **Manchester United 4 West Ham United 0**
Teamsheet: Stepney, Forsyth, Houston, Daly, Greenhoff, Buchan, Coppell, McIlroy, Pearson, Macari, Hill
Substitute(s): McCreery Scorer(s): Forsyth, Macari, McCreery, Pearson

Match # 3270 Saturday 06/03/76 FA Cup 6th Round at Old Trafford Attendance 59433
Result: **Manchester United 1 Wolverhampton Wanderers 1**
Teamsheet: Stepney, Forsyth, Houston, Daly, Greenhoff, Buchan, Coppell, McIlroy, Pearson, Macari, Hill
Scorer(s): Daly

Match # 3271 Tuesday 09/03/76 FA Cup 6th Round Replay at Molineux Attendance 44373
Result: **Wolverhampton Wanderers 2 Manchester United 3**
Teamsheet: Stepney, Forsyth, Houston, Daly, Greenhoff, Buchan, Coppell, McIlroy, Pearson, Macari, Hill
Substitute(s): Nicholl Scorer(s): Greenhoff, McIlroy, Pearson

Match # 3272 Saturday 13/03/76 Football League Division 1 at Old Trafford Attendance 59429
Result: **Manchester United 3 Leeds United 2**
Teamsheet: Stepney, Forsyth, Houston, Daly, Greenhoff, Buchan, Coppell, McIlroy, Pearson, McCreery, Hill
Scorer(s): Daly, Houston, Pearson

Match # 3273 Tuesday 16/03/76 Football League Division 1 at Carrow Road Attendance 27787
Result: **Norwich City 1 Manchester United 1**
Teamsheet: Stepney, Forsyth, Houston, Daly, Greenhoff, Buchan, Coppell, McIlroy, Pearson, McCreery, Hill
Scorer(s): Hill

Match # 3274 Saturday 20/03/76 Football League Division 1 at St James' Park Attendance 45048
Result: **Newcastle United 3 Manchester United 4**
Teamsheet: Stepney, Forsyth, Houston, Daly, Greenhoff, Buchan, Coppell, McIlroy, Pearson, McCreery, Hill
Scorer(s): Pearson 2, own goals 2

Match # 3275 Saturday 27/03/76 Football League Division 1 at Old Trafford Attendance 58527
Result: **Manchester United 3 Middlesbrough 0**
Teamsheet: Stepney, Forsyth, Houston, Daly, Greenhoff, Buchan, Coppell, McIlroy, Pearson, McCreery, Hill
Scorer(s): Daly, Hill, McCreery

Match # 3276 Saturday 03/04/76 FA Cup Semi-Final at Hillsborough Attendance 55000
Result: **Manchester United 2 Derby County 0**
Teamsheet: Stepney, Forsyth, Houston, Daly, Greenhoff, Buchan, Coppell, McIlroy, Pearson, McCreery, Hill
Scorer(s): Hill 2

Match # 3277 Saturday 10/04/76 Football League Division 1 at Portman Road Attendance 34886
Result: **Ipswich Town 3 Manchester United 0**
Teamsheet: Stepney, Forsyth, Houston, Daly, Greenhoff, Buchan, Coppell, McIlroy, Pearson, McCreery, Hill

Match # 3278 Saturday 17/04/76 Football League Division 1 at Old Trafford Attendance 61879
Result: **Manchester United 2 Everton 1**
Teamsheet: Stepney, Forsyth, Houston, Daly, Greenhoff, Buchan, Coppell, McIlroy, Pearson, Macari, Hill
Substitute(s): McCreery Scorer(s): McCreery, own goal

Match # 3279 Monday 19/04/76 Football League Division 1 at Turf Moor Attendance 27418
Result: **Burnley 0 Manchester United 1**
Teamsheet: Stepney, Forsyth, Houston, Daly, Greenhoff, Buchan, McCreery, McIlroy, Pearson, Macari, Hill
Substitute(s): Jackson Scorer(s): Macari

Match # 3280 Wednesday 21/04/76 Football League Division 1 at Old Trafford Attendance 53879
Result: **Manchester United 0 Stoke City 1**
Teamsheet: Stepney, Forsyth, Houston, Daly, Greenhoff, Buchan, Jackson, McIlroy, McCreery, Macari, Hill
Substitute(s): Nicholl

Match # 3281 Saturday 24/04/76 Football League Division 1 at Filbert Street Attendance 31053
Result: **Leicester City 2 Manchester United 1**
Teamsheet: Stepney, Forsyth, Houston, Nicholl, Greenhoff, Buchan, Jackson, McCreery, Coyne, Macari, Hill
Substitute(s): Albiston Scorer(s): Coyne

Match # 3282 Saturday 01/05/76 FA Cup Final at Wembley Attendance 100000
Result: **Manchester United 0 Southampton 1**
Teamsheet: Stepney, Forsyth, Houston, Daly, Greenhoff, Buchan, Coppell, McIlroy, Pearson, Macari, Hill
Substitute(s): McCreery

Match # 3283 Tuesday 04/05/76 Football League Division 1 at Old Trafford Attendance 59517
Result: **Manchester United 2 Manchester City 0**
Teamsheet: Stepney, Forsyth, Houston, Daly, Albiston, Buchan, Coppell, McIlroy, Pearson, Jackson, Hill
Substitute(s): McCreery Scorer(s): Hill, McIlroy

SEASON 1975/76 SUMMARY

APPEARANCES

PLAYER	LGE	FAC	LC	TOTAL
Buchan	42	7	3	52
Houston	42	7	3	52
Daly	41	7	3	51
McIlroy	41	7	3	51
Greenhoff	40	7	3	50
Coppell	39	7	3	49
Pearson	39	7	3	49
Stepney	38	7	2	47
Macari	36	6	3	45
Forsyth	28	7	–	35
Hill	26	7	–	33
Jackson	16 (1)	–	3	19 (1)
Nicholl	15 (5)	– (2)	3	18 (7)
McCreery	12 (16)	1 (2)	– (1)	13 (19)
Roche	4	–	1	5
Albiston	2 (1)	–	–	2 (1)
Coyne	1 (1)	–	–	1 (1)
Grimshaw	– (1)	–	– (1)	– (2)
Kelly	– (1)	–	–	– (1)
Young	– (1)	–	–	– (1)

GOALSCORERS

PLAYER	LGE	FAC	LC	TOT
Macari	12	1	2	15
Pearson	13	1	–	14
McIlroy	10	2	1	13
Daly	7	4	–	11
Hill	7	3	–	10
Coppell	4	–	1	5
McCreery	4	–	–	4
Forsyth	2	1	–	3
Houston	2	–	–	2
Coyne	1	–	–	1
Greenhoff	–	1	–	1
own goals	6	–	–	6

RESULTS & ATTENDANCES SUMMARY

		P	W	D	L	F	A	TOTAL	AVGE
League	H	21	16	4	1	40	13	1149741	54750
	A	21	7	6	8	28	29	781326	37206
	TOTAL	42	23	10	9	68	42	1931067	45978
FA Cup	H	3	2	1	0	6	3	156867	52289
	A	2	2	0	0	5	3	78373	39187
	N	2	1	0	1	2	1	155000	77500
	TOTAL	7	5	1	1	13	7	390240	55749
League	H	1	1	0	0	2	1	25286	25286
Cup	A	2	1	0	1	2	5	91629	45815
	TOTAL	3	2	0	1	4	6	116915	38972
Overall	H	25	19	5	1	48	17	1331894	53276
	A	25	10	6	9	35	37	951328	38053
	N	2	1	0	1	2	1	155000	77500
	TOTAL	52	30	11	11	85	55	2438222	46889

FINAL TABLE - LEAGUE DIVISION ONE

		P	HOME					AWAY					PTS	GD
			W	D	L	F	A	W	D	L	F	A		
1	Liverpool	42	14	5	2	41	21	9	9	3	25	10	60	35
2	Queens Park Rangers	42	17	4	0	42	13	7	7	7	25	20	59	34
3	MANCHESTER UNITED	42	16	4	1	40	13	7	6	8	28	29	56	26
4	Derby County	42	15	3	3	45	30	6	8	7	30	28	53	17
5	Leeds United	42	13	3	5	37	19	8	6	7	28	27	51	19
6	Ipswich Town	42	11	6	4	36	23	5	8	8	18	25	46	6
7	Leicester City	42	9	9	3	29	24	4	10	7	19	27	45	-3
8	Manchester City	42	14	5	2	46	18	2	6	13	18	28	43	18
9	Tottenham Hotspur	42	6	10	5	33	32	8	5	8	30	31	43	0
10	Norwich City	42	10	5	6	33	26	6	5	10	25	32	42	0
11	Everton	42	10	7	4	37	24	5	5	11	23	42	42	-6
12	Stoke City	42	8	5	8	25	24	7	6	8	23	26	41	-2
13	Middlesbrough	42	9	7	5	23	11	6	3	12	23	34	40	1
14	Coventry City	42	6	9	6	22	22	7	5	9	25	35	40	-10
15	Newcastle United	42	11	4	6	51	26	4	5	12	20	36	39	9
16	Aston Villa	42	11	8	2	32	17	0	9	12	19	42	39	-8
17	Arsenal	42	11	4	6	33	19	2	6	13	14	34	36	-6
18	West Ham United	42	10	5	6	26	23	3	5	13	22	48	36	-23
19	Birmingham City	42	11	5	5	36	26	2	2	17	21	49	33	-18
20	Wolverhampton Wanderers	42	7	6	8	27	25	3	4	14	24	43	30	-17
21	Burnley	42	6	6	9	23	26	3	4	14	20	40	28	-23
22	Sheffield United	42	4	7	10	19	32	2	3	16	14	50	22	-49

SEASON 1976/77

Match # 3284 Saturday 21/08/76   Football League Division 1   at Old Trafford   Attendance 58898
Result: **Manchester United 2 Birmingham City 2**
Teamsheet: Stepney, Nicholl, Houston, Daly, Greenhoff B, Buchan, Coppell, McIlroy, Pearson, Macari, Hill
Substitute(s): Foggon   Scorer(s):   Coppell, Pearson

Match # 3285 Tuesday 24/08/76   Football League Division 1   at Highfield Road   Attendance 26775
Result: **Coventry City 0 Manchester United 2**
Teamsheet: Stepney, Nicholl, Houston, Daly, Greenhoff B, Buchan, Coppell, McIlroy, Pearson, Macari, Hill
Scorer(s): Hill, Macari

Match # 3286 Saturday 28/08/76   Football League Division 1   at Baseball Ground   Attendance 30054
Result: **Derby County 0 Manchester United 0**
Teamsheet: Stepney, Nicholl, Houston, Daly, Greenhoff B, Buchan, Coppell, McIlroy, Pearson, Macari, Hill

Match # 3287 Wednesday 01/09/76   League Cup 2nd Round   at Old Trafford   Attendance 37586
Result: **Manchester United 5 Tranmere Rovers 0**
Teamsheet: Stepney, Nicholl, Houston, Daly, Greenhoff B, Buchan, Coppell, McIlroy, Pearson, Macari, Hill
Substitute(s): McCreery   Scorer(s):   Daly 2, Hill, Macari, Pearson

Match # 3288 Saturday 04/09/76   Football League Division 1   at Old Trafford   Attendance 60723
Result: **Manchester United 2 Tottenham Hotspur 3**
Teamsheet: Stepney, Nicholl, Houston, Daly, Greenhoff B, Buchan, Coppell, McIlroy, Pearson, Macari, Hill
Substitute(s): McCreery   Scorer(s):   Coppell, Pearson

Match # 3289 Saturday 11/09/76   Football League Division 1   at St James' Park   Attendance 39037
Result: **Newcastle United 2 Manchester United 2**
Teamsheet: Stepney, Nicholl, Houston, Daly, Greenhoff B, Buchan, Coppell, McIlroy, Pearson, Macari, Hill
Substitute(s): Foggon   Scorer(s):   Greenhoff B, Pearson

Match # 3290 Wednesday 15/09/76   UEFA Cup 1st Round 1st Leg   at Olympisch Stadion   Attendance 30000
Result: **Ajax 1 Manchester United 0**
Teamsheet: Stepney, Nicholl, Houston, Daly, Greenhoff B, Buchan, Coppell, McIlroy, Pearson, Macari, Hill
Substitute(s): McCreery

Match # 3291 Saturday 18/09/76   Football League Division 1   at Old Trafford   Attendance 56712
Result: **Manchester United 2 Middlesbrough 0**
Teamsheet: Stepney, Nicholl, Houston, Daly, Greenhoff B, Buchan, Coppell, McIlroy, Pearson, Macari, Hill
Substitute(s): Foggon   Scorer(s):   Pearson, own goal

Match # 3292 Wednesday 22/09/76   League Cup 3rd Round   at Old Trafford   Attendance 46170
Result: **Manchester United 2 Sunderland 2**
Teamsheet: Stepney, Nicholl, Houston, Daly, Greenhoff B, Buchan, McCreery, McIlroy, Pearson, Macari, Hill
Scorer(s): Pearson, own goal

Match # 3293 Saturday 25/09/76   Football League Division 1   at Maine Road   Attendance 48861
Result: **Manchester City 1 Manchester United 3**
Teamsheet: Stepney, Nicholl, Houston, Daly, Greenhoff B, Buchan, Coppell, McIlroy, Pearson, Macari, Hill
Substitute(s): McCreery   Scorer(s):   Daly, Coppell, McCreery

Match # 3294 Wednesday 29/09/76   UEFA Cup 1st Round 2nd Leg   at Old Trafford   Attendance 58918
Result: **Manchester United 2 Ajax 0**
Teamsheet: Stepney, Nicholl, Houston, Daly, Greenhoff B, Buchan, Coppell, McIlroy, McCreery, Macari, Hill
Substitute(s): Albiston, Paterson   Scorer(s):   Macari, McIlroy

Match # 3295 Saturday 02/10/76   Football League Division 1   at Elland Road   Attendance 44512
Result: **Leeds United 0 Manchester United 2**
Teamsheet: Stepney, Nicholl, Houston, Daly, Greenhoff B, Buchan, Coppell, McIlroy, Pearson, Macari, Hill
Substitute(s): McCreery   Scorer(s):   Coppell, Daly

Match # 3296 Monday 04/10/76   League Cup 3rd Round Replay   at Roker Park   Attendance 46170
Result: **Sunderland 2 Manchester United 2**
Teamsheet: Stepney, Nicholl, Houston, Daly, Waldron, Buchan, Coppell, McIlroy, McCreery, Greenhoff B, Hill
Substitute(s): Albiston   Scorer(s):   Daly, Greenhoff B

Match # 3297 Wednesday 06/10/76   League Cup 3rd Round 2nd Replay   at Old Trafford   Attendance 47689
Result: **Manchester United 1 Sunderland 0**
Teamsheet: Stepney, Nicholl, Houston, Daly, Greenhoff B, Buchan, Coppell, McIlroy, McCreery, Macari, Hill
Substitute(s): Albiston   Scorer(s):   Greenhoff B

Match # 3298 Saturday 16/10/76   Football League Division 1   at The Hawthorns   Attendance 36615
Result: **West Bromwich Albion 4 Manchester United 0**
Teamsheet: Stepney, Nicholl, Houston, Daly, Greenhoff B, Waldron, Coppell, McIlroy, Pearson, Macari, Hill
Substitute(s): McCreery

Match # 3299 Wednesday 20/10/76   UEFA Cup 2nd Round 1st Leg   at Old Trafford   Attendance 59000
Result: **Manchester United 1 Juventus 0**
Teamsheet: Stepney, Nicholl, Albiston, Daly, Greenhoff B, Houston, Coppell, McIlroy, Pearson, Macari, Hill
Substitute(s): McCreery   Scorer(s):   Hill

Match # 3300 Saturday 23/10/76   Football League Division 1   at Old Trafford   Attendance 54356
Result: **Manchester United 2 Norwich City 2**
Teamsheet: Stepney, Nicholl, Houston, Daly, Greenhoff B, Waldron, Coppell, McIlroy, Pearson, Macari, Hill
Substitute(s): McGrath   Scorer(s):   Daly, Hill

Match # 3301 Wednesday 27/10/76   League Cup 4th Round   at Old Trafford   Attendance 52002
Result: **Manchester United 7 Newcastle United 2**
Teamsheet: Stepney, Nicholl, Albiston, Daly, Greenhoff B, Houston, Coppell, McIlroy, Pearson, Macari, Hill
Substitute(s): McGrath   Scorer(s):   Hill 3, Coppell, Houston, Nicholl, Pearson

SEASON 1976/77 (continued)

Match # 3302   Saturday 30/10/76   Football League Division 1   at Old Trafford   Attendance 57416
Result: **Manchester United 0 Ipswich Town 1**
Teamsheet: Stepney, Nicholl, Albiston, Daly, Greenhoff B, Houston, Coppell, McIlroy, Pearson, Macari, Hill
Substitute(s): McCreery

Match # 3303   Wednesday 03/11/76   UEFA Cup 2nd Round 2nd Leg   at Stadio Comunale   Attendance 66632
Result: **Juventus 3 Manchester United 0**
Teamsheet: Stepney, Nicholl, Albiston, Daly, Greenhoff B, Houston, Coppell, McIlroy, Pearson, Macari, Hill
Substitute(s): McCreery, Paterson

Match # 3304   Saturday 06/11/76   Football League Division 1   at Villa Park   Attendance 44789
Result: **Aston Villa 3 Manchester United 2**
Teamsheet: Stepney, Nicholl, Albiston, Daly, Greenhoff B, Houston, McGrath, McIlroy, Pearson, Coppell, Hill
Scorer(s):   Hill, Pearson

Match # 3305   Wednesday 10/11/76   Football League Division 1   at Old Trafford   Attendance 42685
Result: **Manchester United 3 Sunderland 3**
Teamsheet: Roche, Albiston, Houston, Daly, Paterson, Waldron, Coppell, Greenhoff B, Pearson, Macari, Hill
Substitute(s): Clark   Scorer(s):   Greenhoff B, Hill, Pearson

Match # 3306   Saturday 20/11/76   Football League Division 1   at Filbert Street   Attendance 26421
Result: **Leicester City 1 Manchester United 1**
Teamsheet: Stepney, Nicholl, Albiston, Daly, Greenhoff B, Paterson, Coppell, McIlroy, Pearson, Greenhoff J, Hill
Scorer(s):   Daly

Match # 3307   Saturday 27/11/76   Football League Division 1   at Old Trafford   Attendance 55366
Result: **Manchester United 0 West Ham United 2**
Teamsheet: Stepney, Forsyth, Albiston, Daly, Greenhoff B, Houston, Coppell, McIlroy, Pearson, Greenhoff J, Hill

Match # 3308   Wednesday 01/12/76   League Cup 5th Round   at Old Trafford   Attendance 57738
Result: **Manchester United 0 Everton 3**
Teamsheet: Stepney, Forsyth, Albiston, Daly, Paterson, Greenhoff B, Coppell, McIlroy, Pearson, Jackson, Hill
Substitute(s): McCreery

Match # 3309   Saturday 18/12/76   Football League Division 1   at Highbury   Attendance 39572
Result: **Arsenal 3 Manchester United 1**
Teamsheet: Stepney, Forsyth, Houston, McIlroy, Greenhoff B, Buchan, McCreery, Greenhoff J, Pearson, Macari, Hill
Substitute(s): McGrath   Scorer(s):   McIlroy

Match # 3310   Monday 27/12/76   Football League Division 1   at Old Trafford   Attendance 56786
Result: **Manchester United 4 Everton 0**
Teamsheet: Stepney, Nicholl, Houston, McIlroy, Greenhoff B, Buchan, Coppell, Greenhoff J, Pearson, Macari, Hill
Substitute(s): McCreery   Scorer(s):   Greenhoff J, Hill, Macari, Pearson

Match # 3311   Saturday 01/01/77   Football League Division 1   at Old Trafford   Attendance 55446
Result: **Manchester United 2 Aston Villa 0**
Teamsheet: Stepney, Nicholl, Houston, McIlroy, Greenhoff B, Buchan, Coppell, Greenhoff J, Pearson, Macari, Hill
Substitute(s): McCreery   Scorer(s):   Pearson 2

Match # 3312   Monday 03/01/77   Football League Division 1   at Portman Road   Attendance 30105
Result: **Ipswich Town 2 Manchester United 1**
Teamsheet: Stepney, Nicholl, Albiston, McIlroy, Greenhoff B, Buchan, McCreery, Greenhoff J, Pearson, Macari, Hill
Substitute(s): McGrath   Scorer(s):   Pearson

Match # 3313   Saturday 08/01/77   FA Cup 3rd Round   at Old Trafford   Attendance 48870
Result: **Manchester United 1 Walsall 0**
Teamsheet: Stepney, Nicholl, Houston, McIlroy, Greenhoff B, Buchan, Coppell, Greenhoff J, Pearson, Macari, Hill
Substitute(s): Daly   Scorer(s):   Hill

Match # 3314   Saturday 15/01/77   Football League Division 1   at Old Trafford   Attendance 46567
Result: **Manchester United 2 Coventry City 0**
Teamsheet: Stepney, Nicholl, Houston, McIlroy, Greenhoff B, Buchan, Coppell, Greenhoff J, Pearson, Macari, Hill
Substitute(s): McCreery   Scorer(s):   Macari 2

Match # 3315   Wednesday 19/01/77   Football League Division 1   at Old Trafford   Attendance 43051
Result: **Manchester United 2 Bristol City 1**
Teamsheet: Stepney, Nicholl, Houston, McIlroy, Greenhoff B, Buchan, Coppell, Greenhoff J, Pearson, Macari, Hill
Scorer(s):   Greenhoff B, Pearson

Match # 3316   Saturday 22/01/77   Football League Division 1   at St Andrews   Attendance 35316
Result: **Birmingham City 2 Manchester United 3**
Teamsheet: Stepney, Nicholl, Houston, McIlroy, Greenhoff B, Buchan, Coppell, Greenhoff J, Pearson, Macari, Hill
Substitute(s): Daly   Scorer(s):   Greenhoff J, Houston, Pearson

Match # 3317   Saturday 29/01/77   FA Cup 4th Round   at Old Trafford   Attendance 57422
Result: **Manchester United 1 Queens Park Rangers 0**
Teamsheet: Stepney, Nicholl, McIlroy, Greenhoff B, Buchan, Coppell, Greenhoff J, Pearson, Macari, Hill
Scorer(s):   Macari

Match # 3318   Saturday 05/02/77   Football League Division 1   at Old Trafford   Attendance 54044
Result: **Manchester United 3 Derby County 1**
Teamsheet: Stepney, Nicholl, Houston, McIlroy, Greenhoff B, Buchan, Coppell, Greenhoff J, Pearson, Macari, Daly
Scorer(s):   Houston, Macari, own goal

Match # 3319   Saturday 12/02/77   Football League Division 1   at White Hart Lane   Attendance 46946
Result: **Tottenham Hotspur 1 Manchester United 3**
Teamsheet: Stepney, Nicholl, Houston, McIlroy, Greenhoff B, Buchan, Coppell, Greenhoff J, Pearson, Macari, Hill
Scorer(s):   Hill, Macari, McIlroy

SEASON 1976/77 (continued)

Match # 3320 Wednesday 16/02/77 Football League Division 1 at Old Trafford Attendance 57487
Result: **Manchester United 0 Liverpool 0**
Teamsheet: Stepney, Nicholl, Houston, McIlroy, Greenhoff B, Buchan, Coppell, Greenhoff J, Pearson, Macari, Hill

Match # 3321 Saturday 19/02/77 Football League Division 1 at Old Trafford Attendance 51828
Result: **Manchester United 3 Newcastle United 1**
Teamsheet: Stepney, Nicholl, Houston, McIlroy, Greenhoff B, Buchan, Coppell, Greenhoff J, Pearson, Macari, Hill
Substitute(s): Albiston Scorer(s): Greenhoff J 3

Match # 3322 Saturday 26/02/77 FA Cup 5th Round at The Dell Attendance 29137
Result: **Southampton 2 Manchester United 2**
Teamsheet: Stepney, Nicholl, Houston, McIlroy, Greenhoff B, Buchan, Coppell, Greenhoff J, Pearson, Macari, Hill
Substitute(s): McCreery Scorer(s): Hill, Macari

Match # 3323 Saturday 05/03/77 Football League Division 1 at Old Trafford Attendance 58595
Result: **Manchester United 3 Manchester City 1**
Teamsheet: Stepney, Nicholl, Houston, McIlroy, Greenhoff B, Buchan, Coppell, Greenhoff J, Pearson, Macari, Hill
Substitute(s): McCreery Scorer(s): Coppell, Hill, Pearson

Match # 3324 Tuesday 08/03/77 FA Cup 5th Round Replay at Old Trafford Attendance 58103
Result: **Manchester United 2 Southampton 1**
Teamsheet: Stepney, Nicholl, Houston, McIlroy, Greenhoff B, Buchan, Coppell, Greenhoff J, Pearson, Macari, Hill
Scorer(s): Greenhoff J 2

Match # 3325 Saturday 12/03/77 Football League Division 1 at Old Trafford Attendance 60612
Result: **Manchester United 1 Leeds United 0**
Teamsheet: Stepney, Nicholl, Houston, McIlroy, Greenhoff B, Buchan, Coppell, Greenhoff J, Pearson, Macari, Hill
Substitute(s): McCreery Scorer(s): own goal

Match # 3326 Saturday 19/03/77 FA Cup 6th Round at Old Trafford Attendance 57089
Result: **Manchester United 2 Aston Villa 1**
Teamsheet: Stepney, Nicholl, Houston, McIlroy, Greenhoff B, Buchan, Coppell, Greenhoff J, Pearson, Macari, Hill
Substitute(s): McCreery Scorer(s): Houston, Macari

Match # 3327 Wednesday 23/03/77 Football League Division 1 at Old Trafford Attendance 51053
Result: **Manchester United 2 West Bromwich Albion 2**
Teamsheet: Stepney, Nicholl, Albiston, McIlroy, Houston, Buchan, Coppell, Greenhoff J, Pearson, Macari, Hill
Substitute(s): McCreery Scorer(s): Coppell, Hill

Match # 3328 Saturday 02/04/77 Football League Division 1 at Carrow Road Attendance 24161
Result: **Norwich City 2 Manchester United 1**
Teamsheet: Stepney, Nicholl, Houston, McIlroy, Greenhoff B, Buchan, Coppell, Greenhoff J, McCreery, Macari, Hill
Substitute(s): McGrath Scorer(s): own goal

Match # 3329 Tuesday 05/04/77 Football League Division 1 at Goodison Park Attendance 38216
Result: **Everton 1 Manchester United 2**
Teamsheet: Stepney, Nicholl, Houston, McIlroy, Greenhoff B, Buchan, Coppell, Greenhoff J, Pearson, McCreery, Hill
Substitute(s): Albiston Scorer(s): Hill 2

Match # 3330 Saturday 09/04/77 Football League Division 1 at Old Trafford Attendance 53102
Result: **Manchester United 3 Stoke City 0**
Teamsheet: Stepney, Nicholl, Houston, McIlroy, Greenhoff B, Buchan, Coppell, Greenhoff J, Pearson, Macari, Hill
Substitute(s): McCreery Scorer(s): Houston, Macari, Pearson

Match # 3331 Monday 11/04/77 Football League Division 1 at Roker Park Attendance 38785
Result: **Sunderland 2 Manchester United 1**
Teamsheet: Stepney, Nicholl, Houston, McIlroy, Greenhoff B, Buchan, Coppell, McCreery, Pearson, Macari, Hill
Substitute(s): Albiston Scorer(s): Hill

Match # 3332 Saturday 16/04/77 Football League Division 1 at Old Trafford Attendance 49161
Result: **Manchester United 1 Leicester City 1**
Teamsheet: Stepney, Nicholl, Albiston, McIlroy, Greenhoff B, Buchan, Coppell, Greenhoff J, Pearson, Macari, McCreery
Substitute(s): Hill Scorer(s): Greenhoff J

Match # 3333 Tuesday 19/04/77 Football League Division 1 at Loftus Road Attendance 28848
Result: **Queens Park Rangers 4 Manchester United 0**
Teamsheet: Stepney, Nicholl, Albiston, McIlroy, Greenhoff B, Houston, Coppell, Greenhoff J, Pearson, Macari, McCreery
Substitute(s): Forsyth

Match # 3334 Saturday 23/04/77 FA Cup Semi-Final at Hillsborough Attendance 55000
Result: **Manchester United 2 Leeds United 1**
Teamsheet: Stepney, Nicholl, Houston, McIlroy, Greenhoff B, Buchan, Coppell, Greenhoff J, Pearson, Macari, Hill
Scorer(s): Coppell, Greenhoff J

Match # 3335 Tuesday 26/04/77 Football League Division 1 at Ayresome Park Attendance 21744
Result: **Middlesbrough 3 Manchester United 0**
Teamsheet: Stepney, Nicholl, Houston, McIlroy, Greenhoff B, Buchan, Coppell, Greenhoff J, Pearson, Macari, Hill

Match # 3336 Saturday 30/04/77 Football League Division 1 at Old Trafford Attendance 50788
Result: **Manchester United 1 Queens Park Rangers 0**
Teamsheet: Stepney, Nicholl, Houston, McIlroy, Greenhoff B, Buchan, Coppell, Greenhoff J, Pearson, Macari, Hill
Substitute(s): McCreery Scorer(s): Macari

Match # 3337 Tuesday 03/05/77 Football League Division 1 at Anfield Attendance 53046
Result: **Liverpool 1 Manchester United 0**
Teamsheet: Stepney, Nicholl, Houston, McIlroy, Forsyth, Albiston, Coppell, Greenhoff J, Pearson, Macari, Hill
Substitute(s): McCreery

SEASON 1976/77 (continued)

Match # 3338 Saturday 07/05/77   Football League Division 1   at Ashton Gate   Attendance 28864
Result: **Bristol City 1 Manchester United 1**
Teamsheet: Stepney, Nicholl, Houston, Jackson, Greenhoff B, Buchan, Coppell, Greenhoff J, McCreery, Macari, Albiston
Substitute(s): McIlroy   Scorer(s):   Greenhoff J

Match # 3339 Wednesday 11/05/77   Football League Division 1   at Victoria Ground   Attendance 24204
Result: **Stoke City 3 Manchester United 3**
Teamsheet: Stepney, Nicholl, Albiston, Jackson, Greenhoff B, Buchan, Coppell, McCreery, McGrath, Macari, Hill
Scorer(s):   Hill 2, McCreery

Match # 3340 Saturday 14/05/77   Football League Division 1   at Old Trafford   Attendance 53232
Result: **Manchester United 3 Arsenal 2**
Teamsheet: Stepney, Nicholl, Albiston, McIlroy, Greenhoff B, Buchan, Coppell, Greenhoff J, Pearson, Macari, Hill
Substitute(s): McCreery   Scorer(s):   Greenhoff J, Hill, Macari

Match # 3341 Monday 16/05/77   Football League Division 1   at Upton Park   Attendance 29904
Result: **West Ham United 4 Manchester United 2**
Teamsheet: Roche, Nicholl, Albiston, McIlroy, Greenhoff B, Buchan, Coppell, Greenhoff J, Pearson, Macari, Hill
Substitute(s): McCreery   Scorer(s):   Hill, Pearson

Match # 3342 Saturday 21/05/77   FA Cup Final   at Wembley   Attendance 100000
Result: **Manchester United 2 Liverpool 1**
Teamsheet: Stepney, Nicholl, Albiston, McIlroy, Greenhoff B, Buchan, Coppell, Greenhoff J, Pearson, Macari, Hill
Substitute(s): McCreery   Scorer(s):   Greenhoff J, Pearson

SEASON 1976/77 SUMMARY

APPEARANCES

PLAYER	LGE	FAC	LC	UC	TOTAL
Greenhoff B	40	7	6	4	57
Stepney	40	7	6	4	57
McIlroy	39 (1)	7	6	4	56 (1)
Coppell	40	7	5	4	56
Hill	38 (1)	7	6	4	55 (1)
Nicholl	39	7	5	4	55
Macari	38	7	4	4	53
Pearson	39	7	4	3	53
Houston	36	6	5	4	51
Buchan	33	7	4	2	46
Greenhoff J	27	7	–	–	34
Daly	16 (1)	– (1)	6	4	26 (2)
Albiston	14 (3)	1	2 (2)	2 (1)	19 (6)
McCreery	9 (16)	– (3)	3 (2)	1 (3)	13 (24)
Forsyth	3 (1)	–	1	–	4 (1)
Waldron	3	–	1	–	4
Paterson	2	–	1	– (2)	3 (2)
Jackson	2	–	1	–	3
McGrath	2 (4)	–	– (1)	–	2 (5)
Roche	2	–	–	–	2
Foggon	– (3)	–	–	–	– (3)
Clark	– (1)	–	–	–	– (1)

GOALSCORERS

PLAYER	LGE	FAC	LC	UC	TOT
Hill	15	2	4	1	22
Pearson	15	1	3	–	19
Macari	9	3	1	1	14
Greenhoff J	8	4	–	–	12
Coppell	6	1	1	–	8
Daly	4	–	3	–	7
Greenhoff B	3	–	2	–	5
Houston	3	1	1	–	5
McIlroy	2	–	–	1	3
McCreery	2	–	–	–	2
Nicholl	–	–	1	–	1
own goals	4	–	1	–	5

RESULTS & ATTENDANCES SUMMARY

		P	W	D	L	F	A	TOTAL	AVGE
League	H	21	12	6	3	41	22	1127908	53710
	A	21	6	5	10	30	40	736775	35085
	TOTAL	42	18	11	13	71	62	1864683	44397
FA Cup	H	4	4	0	0	6	2	221484	55371
	A	1	0	1	0	2	2	29137	29137
	N	2	2	0	0	4	2	155000	77500
	TOTAL	7	6	1	0	12	6	405621	57946
League Cup	H	5	3	1	1	15	7	241185	48237
	A	1	0	1	0	2	2	46170	46170
	TOTAL	6	3	2	1	17	9	287355	47893
UEFA Cup	H	2	2	0	0	3	0	117918	58959
	A	2	0	0	2	0	4	96632	48316
	TOTAL	4	2	0	2	3	4	214550	53638
Overall	H	32	21	7	4	65	31	1708495	53390
	A	25	6	7	12	34	48	908714	36349
	N	2	2	0	0	4	2	155000	77500
	TOTAL	59	29	14	16	103	81	2772209	46987

FINAL TABLE – LEAGUE DIVISION ONE

		P	W	D	L	F	A	W	D	L	F	A	PTS	GD
				HOME					AWAY					
1	Liverpool	42	18	3	0	47	11	5	8	8	15	22	57	29
2	Manchester City	42	15	5	1	38	13	6	9	6	22	21	56	26
3	Ipswich Town	42	15	4	2	41	11	7	4	10	25	28	52	27
4	Aston Villa	42	17	3	1	55	17	5	4	12	21	33	51	26
5	Newcastle United	42	14	6	1	40	15	4	7	10	24	34	49	15
6	MANCHESTER UNITED	42	12	6	3	41	22	6	5	10	30	40	47	9
7	West Bromwich Albion	42	10	6	5	38	22	6	7	8	24	34	45	6
8	Arsenal	42	11	6	4	37	20	5	5	11	27	39	43	5
9	Everton	42	9	7	5	35	24	5	7	9	27	40	42	-2
10	Leeds United	42	8	8	5	28	26	7	4	10	20	25	42	-3
11	Leicester City	42	8	9	4	30	28	4	9	8	17	32	42	-13
12	Middlesbrough	42	11	6	4	25	14	3	7	11	15	31	41	-5
13	Birmingham City	42	10	6	5	38	25	3	6	12	25	36	38	2
14	Queens Park Rangers	42	10	7	4	31	21	3	5	13	16	31	38	-5
15	Derby County	42	9	9	3	36	18	0	10	11	14	37	37	-5
16	Norwich City	42	12	4	5	30	23	2	5	14	17	41	37	-17
17	West Ham United	42	9	6	6	28	23	2	8	11	18	42	36	-19
18	Bristol City	42	8	7	6	25	19	3	6	12	13	29	35	-10
19	Coventry City	42	7	9	5	34	26	3	6	12	14	33	35	-11
20	Sunderland	42	9	5	7	29	16	2	7	12	17	38	34	-8
21	Stoke City	42	9	8	4	21	16	1	6	14	7	35	34	-23
22	Tottenham Hotspur	42	9	7	5	26	20	3	2	16	22	52	33	-24

SEASON 1977/78

Match # 3343 Saturday 13/08/77   FA Charity Shield   at Wembley   Attendance 82000
Result: **Manchester United 0 Liverpool 0 (TROPHY SHARED)**
Teamsheet: Stepney, Nicholl, Albiston, McIlroy, Greenhoff B, Buchan, Coppell, Greenhoff J, Pearson, Macari, Hill
Substitute(s): McCreery

Match # 3344 Saturday 20/08/77   Football League Division 1   at St Andrews   Attendance 28005
Result: **Birmingham City 1 Manchester United 4**
Teamsheet: Stepney, Nicholl, Albiston, McIlroy, Greenhoff B, Buchan, Coppell, McCreery, Pearson, Macari, Hill
Substitute(s): Grimes   Scorer(s): Macari 3, Hill

Match # 3345 Wednesday 24/08/77   Football League Division 1   at Old Trafford   Attendance 55726
Result: **Manchester United 2 Coventry City 1**
Teamsheet: Stepney, Nicholl, Albiston, McIlroy, Greenhoff B, Buchan, Coppell, McCreery, Pearson, Macari, Hill
Scorer(s): Hill, McCreery

Match # 3346 Saturday 27/08/77   Football League Division 1   at Old Trafford   Attendance 57904
Result: **Manchester United 0 Ipswich Town 0**
Teamsheet: Stepney, Nicholl, Albiston, McIlroy, Greenhoff B, Buchan, McGrath, McCreery, Coppell, Macari, Hill
Substitute(s): Grimes

Match # 3347 Tuesday 30/08/77   League Cup 2nd Round   at Highbury   Attendance 36171
Result: **Arsenal 3 Manchester United 2**
Teamsheet: Stepney, Nicholl, Albiston, Grimes, Greenhoff B, Buchan, Coppell, McCreery, Pearson, Macari, Hill
Substitute(s): McGrath   Scorer(s): McCreery, Pearson

Match # 3348 Saturday 03/09/77   Football League Division 1   at Baseball Ground   Attendance 21279
Result: **Derby County 0 Manchester United 1**
Teamsheet: Stepney, Forsyth, Albiston, McIlroy, Nicholl, Buchan, Coppell, McCreery, Pearson, Macari, Hill
Scorer(s): Macari

Match # 3349 Saturday 10/09/77   Football League Division 1   at Maine Road   Attendance 50856
Result: **Manchester City 3 Manchester United 1**
Teamsheet: Stepney, Forsyth, Albiston, McIlroy, Nicholl, Buchan, Coppell, McCreery, Pearson, Macari, Hill
Substitute(s): McGrath   Scorer(s): Nicholl

Match # 3350 Wednesday 14/09/77   European CWC 1st Round 1st Leg   at Stade Geoffrey Guichard   Attendance 33678
Result: **St Etienne 1 Manchester United 1**
Teamsheet: Stepney, Nicholl, Albiston, McIlroy, Greenhoff B, Buchan, McGrath, McCreery, Pearson, Coppell, Hill
Substitute(s): Grimes, Houston   Scorer(s): Hill

Match # 3351 Saturday 17/09/77   Football League Division 1   at Old Trafford   Attendance 54951
Result: **Manchester United 0 Chelsea 1**
Teamsheet: Stepney, Nicholl, Albiston, McIlroy, Greenhoff B, Buchan, Coppell, McCreery, Pearson, Macari, Hill
Substitute(s): McGrath

Match # 3352 Saturday 24/09/77   Football League Division 1   at Elland Road   Attendance 33517
Result: **Leeds United 1 Manchester United 1**
Teamsheet: Stepney, Nicholl, Albiston, McIlroy, Greenhoff B, Houston, McGrath, Coppell, Pearson, Macari, Hill
Scorer(s): Hill

Match # 3353 Saturday 01/10/77   Football League Division 1   at Old Trafford   Attendance 55089
Result: **Manchester United 2 Liverpool 0**
Teamsheet: Stepney, Nicholl, Albiston, McIlroy, Greenhoff B, Buchan, McGrath, Coppell, Greenhoff J, Macari, Hill
Scorer(s): Macari, McIlroy

Match # 3354 Wednesday 05/10/77   European CWC 1st Round 2nd Leg   at Home Park   Attendance 31634
Result: **Manchester United 2 St Etienne 0**
Teamsheet: Stepney, Nicholl, Albiston, McIlroy, Greenhoff B, Buchan, Coppell, Greenhoff J, Pearson, Macari, Hill
Substitute(s): McGrath   Scorer(s): Coppell, Pearson

Match # 3355 Saturday 08/10/77   Football League Division 1   at Ayresome Park   Attendance 26882
Result: **Middlesbrough 2 Manchester United 1**
Teamsheet: Stepney, Nicholl, Albiston, McCreery, Greenhoff B, Buchan, McGrath, Greenhoff J, Coppell, Macari, Hill
Scorer(s): Coppell

Match # 3356 Saturday 15/10/77   Football League Division 1   at Old Trafford   Attendance 55056
Result: **Manchester United 3 Newcastle United 2**
Teamsheet: Stepney, Nicholl, Albiston, McIlroy, Houston, Buchan, McGrath, Greenhoff J, Coppell, Macari, Hill
Scorer(s): Coppell, Greenhoff J, Macari

Match # 3357 Wednesday 19/10/77   European CWC 2nd Round 1st Leg   at Estadio das Antas   Attendance 70000
Result: **Porto 4 Manchester United 0**
Teamsheet: Stepney, Nicholl, Albiston, McIlroy, Houston, Buchan, McGrath, McCreery, Coppell, Macari, Hill
Substitute(s): Forsyth, Grimes

Match # 3358 Saturday 22/10/77   Football League Division 1   at The Hawthorns   Attendance 27526
Result: **West Bromwich Albion 4 Manchester United 0**
Teamsheet: Stepney, Forsyth, Rogers, McIlroy, Nicholl, Buchan, Coppell, McCreery, Pearson, Macari, Hill
Substitute(s): McGrath

Match # 3359 Saturday 29/10/77   Football League Division 1   at Villa Park   Attendance 39144
Result: **Aston Villa 2 Manchester United 1**
Teamsheet: Stepney, Nicholl, Albiston, McIlroy, Houston, Buchan, McGrath, Coppell, Pearson, McCreery, Hill
Substitute(s): Grimes   Scorer(s): Nicholl

Match # 3360 Wednesday 02/11/77   European CWC 2nd Round 2nd Leg   at Old Trafford   Attendance 51831
Result: **Manchester United 5 Porto 2**
Teamsheet: Stepney, Nicholl, Albiston, McIlroy, Houston, Buchan, McGrath, Coppell, Pearson, McCreery, Hill
Scorer(s): Coppell 2, Nicholl, own goals 2

SEASON 1977/78 (continued)

Match # 3361 Saturday 05/11/77   Football League Division 1   at Old Trafford   Attendance 53055
Result: **Manchester United 1 Arsenal 2**
Teamsheet: Stepney, Nicholl, Albiston, McIlroy, Houston, Buchan, McGrath, Coppell, Pearson, McCreery, Hill
Substitute(s): Grimes   Scorer(s):   Hill

Match # 3362 Saturday 12/11/77   Football League Division 1   at City Ground   Attendance 30183
Result: **Nottingham Forest 2 Manchester United 1**
Teamsheet: Roche, Nicholl, Houston, McIlroy, Greenhoff B, Buchan, McGrath, Coppell, Pearson, McCreery, Hill
Scorer(s):   Pearson

Match # 3363 Saturday 19/11/77   Football League Division 1   at Old Trafford   Attendance 48729
Result: **Manchester United 1 Norwich City 0**
Teamsheet: Roche, Nicholl, Houston, McIlroy, Greenhoff B, Buchan, Coppell, Greenhoff J, Pearson, Macari, Hill
Substitute(s): McCreery   Scorer(s):   Pearson

Match # 3364 Saturday 26/11/77   Football League Division 1   at Loftus Road   Attendance 25367
Result: **Queens Park Rangers 2 Manchester United 2**
Teamsheet: Roche, Nicholl, Houston, Grimes, Greenhoff B, Buchan, Coppell, Greenhoff J, Pearson, Macari, Hill
Substitute(s): McGrath   Scorer(s):   Hill 2

Match # 3365 Saturday 03/12/77   Football League Division 1   at Old Trafford   Attendance 48874
Result: **Manchester United 3 Wolverhampton Wanderers 1**
Teamsheet: Roche, Nicholl, Albiston, McIlroy, Greenhoff B, Houston, Coppell, Greenhoff J, Pearson, Grimes, Hill
Substitute(s): McGrath   Scorer(s):   Greenhoff J, McIlroy, Pearson

Match # 3366 Saturday 10/12/77   Football League Division 1   at Upton Park   Attendance 20242
Result: **West Ham United 2 Manchester United 1**
Teamsheet: Roche, Nicholl, Albiston, Coppell, Greenhoff B, Houston, McGrath, Greenhoff J, Pearson, Grimes, Hill
Scorer(s):   McGrath

Match # 3367 Saturday 17/12/77   Football League Division 1   at Old Trafford   Attendance 54374
Result: **Manchester United 0 Nottingham Forest 4**
Teamsheet: Roche, Nicholl, Houston, McIlroy, Greenhoff B, Buchan, Coppell, Greenhoff J, Pearson, Macari, Hill
Substitute(s): Grimes

Match # 3368 Monday 26/12/77   Football League Division 1   at Goodison Park   Attendance 48335
Result: **Everton 2 Manchester United 6**
Teamsheet: Roche, Nicholl, Houston, McIlroy, Greenhoff B, Buchan, Coppell, Greenhoff J, Ritchie, Macari, Hill
Substitute(s): Grimes   Scorer(s):   Macari 2, Coppell, Greenhoff J, Hill, McIlroy

Match # 3369 Tuesday 27/12/77   Football League Division 1   at Old Trafford   Attendance 57396
Result: **Manchester United 3 Leicester City 1**
Teamsheet: Roche, Nicholl, Albiston, McIlroy, Houston, Buchan, Coppell, Greenhoff J, Ritchie, Macari, Hill
Scorer(s):   Coppell, Greenhoff J, Hill

Match # 3370 Saturday 31/12/77   Football League Division 1   at Highfield Road   Attendance 24706
Result: **Coventry City 3 Manchester United 0**
Teamsheet: Roche, Nicholl, Houston, McIlroy, Greenhoff B, Buchan, Coppell, Greenhoff J, Ritchie, Macari, Hill
Substitute(s): McGrath

Match # 3371 Monday 02/01/78   Football League Division 1   at Old Trafford   Attendance 53501
Result: **Manchester United 1 Birmingham City 2**
Teamsheet: Roche, Nicholl, Albiston, McIlroy, Greenhoff B, Buchan, Coppell, Greenhoff J, Ritchie, Macari, Hill
Scorer(s):   Greenhoff J

Match # 3372 Saturday 07/01/78   FA Cup 3rd Round   at Brunton Park   Attendance 21710
Result: **Carlisle United 1 Manchester United 1**
Teamsheet: Roche, Nicholl, Albiston, McIlroy, Greenhoff B, Buchan, Coppell, Greenhoff J, Pearson, Macari, Grimes
Substitute(s): McCreery   Scorer(s):   Macari

Match # 3373 Wednesday 11/01/78   FA Cup 3rd Round Replay   at Old Trafford   Attendance 54156
Result: **Manchester United 4 Carlisle United 2**
Teamsheet: Roche, Nicholl, Albiston, McIlroy, Houston, Buchan, Coppell, Greenhoff J, Pearson, Macari, Hill
Scorer(s):   Macari 2, Pearson 2

Match # 3374 Saturday 14/01/78   Football League Division 1   at Portman Road   Attendance 23321
Result: **Ipswich Town 1 Manchester United 2**
Teamsheet: Roche, Nicholl, Albiston, McIlroy, Houston, Buchan, Coppell, Greenhoff J, Pearson, Macari, Hill
Scorer(s):   McIlroy, Pearson

Match # 3375 Saturday 21/01/78   Football League Division 1   at Old Trafford   Attendance 57115
Result: **Manchester United 4 Derby County 0**
Teamsheet: Roche, Nicholl, Albiston, McIlroy, Houston, Buchan, Coppell, Greenhoff J, Pearson, Macari, Hill
Scorer(s):   Hill 2, Buchan, Pearson

Match # 3376 Saturday 28/01/78   FA Cup 4th Round   at Old Trafford   Attendance 57056
Result: **Manchester United 1 West Bromwich Albion 1**
Teamsheet: Roche, Nicholl, Albiston, McIlroy, Houston, Buchan, Coppell, Jordan, Pearson, Macari, Hill
Scorer(s):   Coppell

Match # 3377 Wednesday 01/02/78   FA Cup 4th Round Replay   at The Hawthorns   Attendance 37086
Result: **West Bromwich Albion 3 Manchester United 2**
Teamsheet: Roche, Nicholl, Albiston, McIlroy, Houston, Buchan, Coppell, Jordan, Pearson, Macari, Hill
Substitute(s): Greenhoff J   Scorer(s):   Hill, Pearson

Match # 3378 Wednesday 08/02/78   Football League Division 1   at Old Trafford   Attendance 43457
Result: **Manchester United 1 Bristol City 1**
Teamsheet: Roche, Nicholl, Albiston, McIlroy, Houston, Buchan, Coppell, Jordan, Pearson, Macari, Hill
Substitute(s): Greenhoff J   Scorer(s):   Hill

SEASON 1977/78 (continued)

Match # 3379   Saturday 11/02/78   Football League Division 1   at Stamford Bridge   Attendance 32849
Result: **Chelsea 2 Manchester United 2**
Teamsheet: Roche, Nicholl, Albiston, McIlroy, Houston, Greenhoff B, Coppell, Jordan, Pearson, Macari, Hill
Scorer(s):   Hill, McIlroy

Match # 3380   Saturday 25/02/78   Football League Division 1   at Anfield   Attendance 49095
Result: **Liverpool 3 Manchester United 1**
Teamsheet: Roche, Nicholl, Albiston, McIlroy, McQueen, Houston, Coppell, Jordan, Pearson, Macari, Hill
Scorer(s):   McIlroy

Match # 3381   Wednesday 01/03/78   Football League Division 1   at Old Trafford   Attendance 49101
Result: **Manchester United 0 Leeds United 1**
Teamsheet: Roche, Nicholl, Albiston, McIlroy, Greenhoff B, Houston, Coppell, Greenhoff J, Jordan, Macari, Hill
Substitute(s):   McGrath

Match # 3382   Saturday 04/03/78   Football League Division 1   at Old Trafford   Attendance 46322
Result: **Manchester United 0 Middlesbrough 0**
Teamsheet: Roche, Nicholl, Houston, McIlroy, McQueen, Greenhoff B, Coppell, Greenhoff J, Jordan, Macari, Hill

Match # 3383   Saturday 11/03/78   Football League Division 1   at St James' Park   Attendance 25825
Result: **Newcastle United 2 Manchester United 2**
Teamsheet: Roche, Nicholl, Houston, McIlroy, McQueen, Greenhoff B, Coppell, Greenhoff J, Jordan, Macari, Hill
Scorer(s):   Jordan, Hill

Match # 3384   Wednesday 15/03/78   Football League Division 1   at Old Trafford   Attendance 58398
Result: **Manchester United 2 Manchester City 2**
Teamsheet: Stepney, Nicholl, Houston, McIlroy, McQueen, Greenhoff B, Coppell, Greenhoff J, Jordan, Macari, Hill
Substitute(s):   Albiston   Scorer(s):   Hill 2

Match # 3385   Saturday 18/03/78   Football League Division 1   at Old Trafford   Attendance 46329
Result: **Manchester United 1 West Bromwich Albion 1**
Teamsheet: Stepney, Nicholl, Houston, McIlroy, McQueen, Greenhoff B, Coppell, Greenhoff J, Pearson, Macari, Hill
Substitute(s):   McGrath   Scorer(s):   McQueen

Match # 3386   Saturday 25/03/78   Football League Division 1   at Filbert Street   Attendance 20299
Result: **Leicester City 2 Manchester United 3**
Teamsheet: Stepney, Nicholl, Albiston, McIlroy, McQueen, Greenhoff B, Coppell, Greenhoff J, Pearson, Macari, Hill
Scorer(s):   Greenhoff J, Hill, Pearson

Match # 3387   Monday 27/03/78   Football League Division 1   at Old Trafford   Attendance 55277
Result: **Manchester United 1 Everton 2**
Teamsheet: Stepney, Nicholl, Houston, McIlroy, McQueen, Greenhoff B, Coppell, Greenhoff J, Pearson, Macari, Hill
Scorer(s):   Hill

Match # 3388   Wednesday 29/03/78   Football League Division 1   at Old Trafford   Attendance 41625
Result: **Manchester United 1 Aston Villa 1**
Teamsheet: Stepney, Greenhoff B, Houston, McIlroy, McQueen, Buchan, Coppell, Greenhoff J, Pearson, Macari, Jordan
Substitute(s):   McCreery   Scorer(s):   McIlroy

Match # 3389   Saturday 01/04/78   Football League Division 1   at Highbury   Attendance 40829
Result: **Arsenal 3 Manchester United 1**
Teamsheet: Stepney, Greenhoff B, Houston, McIlroy, McQueen, Buchan, Coppell, Jordan, Pearson, Macari, Hill
Substitute(s):   McCreery   Scorer(s):   Jordan

Match # 3390   Saturday 08/04/78   Football League Division 1   at Old Trafford   Attendance 42677
Result: **Manchester United 3 Queens Park Rangers 1**
Teamsheet: Stepney, Greenhoff B, Houston, McIlroy, McQueen, Buchan, Coppell, Jordan, Pearson, Grimes, McCreery
Scorer(s):   Pearson 2, Grimes

Match # 3391   Saturday 15/04/78   Football League Division 1   at Carrow Road   Attendance 19778
Result: **Norwich City 1 Manchester United 3**
Teamsheet: Stepney, Albiston, Houston, McIlroy, McQueen, Buchan, Coppell, Jordan, Pearson, Greenhoff B, McCreery
Substitute(s):   McGrath   Scorer(s):   Coppell, Jordan, McIlroy

Match # 3392   Saturday 22/04/78   Football League Division 1   at Old Trafford   Attendance 54089
Result: **Manchester United 3 West Ham United 0**
Teamsheet: Stepney, Albiston, Houston, McIlroy, McQueen, Buchan, Coppell, Jordan, Pearson, Grimes, Greenhoff B
Scorer(s):   Grimes, McIlroy, Pearson

Match # 3393   Tuesday 25/04/78   Football League Division 1   at Ashton Gate   Attendance 26035
Result: **Bristol City 0 Manchester United 1**
Teamsheet: Roche, Albiston, Houston, McIlroy, McQueen, Nicholl, Coppell, Jordan, Pearson, Grimes, Greenhoff B
Substitute(s):   McCreery   Scorer(s):   Pearson

Match # 3394   Saturday 29/04/78   Football League Division 1   at Molineux   Attendance 24774
Result: **Wolverhampton Wanderers 2 Manchester United 1**
Teamsheet: Stepney, Albiston, Houston, McIlroy, McQueen, Nicholl, Coppell, Jordan, Pearson, Greenhoff B, Grimes
Scorer(s):   Greenhoff B

SEASON 1977/78 SUMMARY

APPEARANCES

PLAYER	LGE	FAC	LC	ECWC	CS	TOTAL
Coppell	42	4	1	4	1	52
McIlroy	39	4	–	4	1	48
Nicholl	37	4	1	4	1	47
Hill	36	3	1	4	1	45
Macari	32	4	1	2	1	40
Pearson	30	4	1	3	1	39
Buchan	28	4	1	4	1	38
Albiston	27 (1)	4	1	4	1	37 (1)
Houston	31	3	–	2 (1)	–	36 (1)
Greenhoff B	31	1	1	2	1	36
Stepney	23	–	1	4	1	29
Greenhoff J	22 (1)	2 (1)	–	1	1	26 (2)
Roche	19	4	–	–	–	23
McCreery	13 (4)	– (1)	1	3	– (1)	17 (6)
Jordan	14	2	–	–	–	16
McQueen	14	–	–	–	–	14
McGrath	9 (9)	–	– (1)	3 (1)	–	12 (11)
Grimes	7 (6)	1	1	– (2)	–	9 (8)
Ritchie	4	–	–	–	–	4
Forsyth	3	–	–	– (1)	–	3 (1)
Rogers	1	–	–	–	–	1

GOALSCORERS

PLAYER	LGE	FAC	LC	ECWC	CS	TOTAL
Hill	17	1	–	1	–	19
Pearson	10	3	1	1	–	15
Macari	8	3	–	–	–	11
McIlroy	9	–	–	–	–	9
Coppell	5	1	–	3	–	9
Greenhoff J	6	–	–	–	–	6
Jordan	3	–	–	–	–	3
Nicholl	2	–	–	1	–	3
Grimes	2	–	–	–	–	2
McCreery	1	–	1	–	–	2
Buchan	1	–	–	–	–	1
Greenhoff B	1	–	–	–	–	1
McGrath	1	–	–	–	–	1
McQueen	1	–	–	–	–	1
own goals	–	–	–	2	–	2

RESULTS & ATTENDANCES SUMMARY

		P	W	D	L	F	A	TOTAL	AVGE
League	H	21	9	6	6	32	23	1089045	51859
	A	21	7	4	10	35	40	638847	30421
	TOTAL	42	16	10	16	67	63	1727892	41140
FA Cup	H	2	1	1	0	5	3	111212	55606
	A	2	0	1	1	3	4	58796	29398
	TOTAL	4	1	2	1	8	7	170008	42502
League	H	0	0	0	0	0	0	0	n/a
Cup	A	1	0	0	1	2	3	36171	36171
	TOTAL	1	0	0	1	2	3	36171	36171
European	H	2	2	0	0	7	2	83465	41733
CWC	A	2	0	1	1	1	5	103678	51839
	TOTAL	4	2	1	1	8	7	187143	46786
Charity	H	0	0	0	0	0	0	0	n/a
Shield	A	0	0	0	0	0	0	0	n/a
	N	1	0	1	0	0	0	82000	82000
	TOTAL	1	0	1	0	0	0	82000	82000
Overall	H	25	12	7	6	44	28	1283722	51349
	A	26	7	6	13	41	52	837492	32211
	N	1	0	1	0	0	0	82000	82000
	TOTAL	52	19	14	19	85	80	2203214	42370

FINAL TABLE - LEAGUE DIVISION ONE

		P	W	D	L	F	A	W	D	L	F	A	PTS	GD
			HOME					AWAY						
1	Nottingham Forest	42	15	6	0	37	8	10	8	3	32	16	64	45
2	Liverpool	42	15	4	2	37	11	9	5	7	28	23	57	31
3	Everton	42	14	4	3	47	22	8	7	6	29	23	55	31
4	Manchester City	42	14	5	2	38	12	7	5	9	22	25	52	23
5	Arsenal	42	14	4	3	46	21	6	8	7	28	30	52	23
6	West Bromwich Albion	42	13	5	3	35	18	5	9	7	27	35	50	9
7	Coventry City	42	13	5	3	48	23	5	7	9	27	39	48	13
8	Aston Villa	42	11	4	6	33	18	7	6	8	24	24	46	15
9	Leeds United	42	12	4	5	39	21	6	6	9	24	32	46	10
10	MANCHESTER UNITED	42	9	6	6	32	23	7	4	10	35	40	42	4
11	Birmingham City	42	8	5	8	32	30	8	4	9	23	30	41	-5
12	Derby County	42	10	7	4	37	24	4	6	11	17	35	41	-5
13	Norwich City	42	10	8	3	28	20	1	10	10	24	46	40	-14
14	Middlesbrough	42	8	8	5	25	19	4	7	10	17	35	39	-12
15	Wolverhampton Wanderers	42	7	8	6	30	27	5	4	12	21	37	36	-13
16	Chelsea	42	7	11	3	28	20	4	3	14	18	49	36	-23
17	Bristol City	42	9	6	6	37	26	2	7	12	12	27	35	-4
18	Ipswich Town	42	10	5	6	32	24	1	8	12	15	37	35	-14
19	Queens Park Rangers	42	8	8	5	27	26	1	7	13	20	38	33	-17
20	West Ham United	42	8	6	7	31	28	4	2	15	21	41	32	-17
21	Newcastle United	42	4	6	11	26	37	2	4	15	16	41	22	-36
22	Leicester City	42	4	7	10	16	32	1	5	15	10	38	22	-44

SEASON 1978/79

Match # 3395   Saturday 19/08/78   Football League Division 1   at Old Trafford   Attendance 56139
Result: **Manchester United 1 Birmingham City 0**
Teamsheet: Roche, Greenhoff B, Albiston, McIlroy, McQueen, Buchan, Coppell, Greenhoff J, Jordan, Macari, McCreery
Scorer(s):   Jordan

Match # 3396   Wednesday 23/08/78   Football League Division 1   at Elland Road   Attendance 36845
Result: **Leeds United 2 Manchester United 3**
Teamsheet: Roche, Greenhoff B, Albiston, McIlroy, McQueen, Buchan, Coppell, Greenhoff J, Jordan, Macari, McCreery
Scorer(s):   Macari, McIlroy, McQueen

Match # 3397   Saturday 26/08/78   Football League Division 1   at Portman Road   Attendance 21802
Result: **Ipswich Town 3 Manchester United 0**
Teamsheet: Roche, Greenhoff B, Albiston, McIlroy, McQueen, Buchan, Coppell, Greenhoff J, Jordan, Macari, McCreery
Substitute(s):   McGrath

Match # 3398   Wednesday 30/08/78   League Cup 2nd Round   at Old Trafford   Attendance 41761
Result: **Stockport County 2 Manchester United 3**   **(United drawn away - tie switched to Old Trafford)**
Teamsheet: Roche, Greenhoff B, Albiston, McIlroy, McQueen, Buchan, Coppell, Greenhoff J, Jordan, Macari, Grimes
Scorer(s):   Greenhoff J, Jordan, McIlroy

Match # 3399   Saturday 02/09/78   Football League Division 1   at Old Trafford   Attendance 53982
Result: **Manchester United 1 Everton 1**
Teamsheet: Roche, Nicholl, Albiston, McIlroy, Greenhoff B, Buchan, Coppell, Greenhoff J, Jordan, Macari, McCreery
Substitute(s):   Grimes   Scorer(s):   Buchan

Match # 3400   Saturday 09/09/78   Football League Division 1   at Loftus Road   Attendance 23477
Result: **Queens Park Rangers 1 Manchester United 1**
Teamsheet: Roche, Greenhoff B, Albiston, McIlroy, McQueen, Buchan, Coppell, Greenhoff J, Jordan, Macari, McCreery
Scorer(s):   Greenhoff J

Match # 3401   Saturday 16/09/78   Football League Division 1   at Old Trafford   Attendance 53039
Result: **Manchester United 1 Nottingham Forest 1**
Teamsheet: Roche, Greenhoff B, Albiston, McIlroy, McQueen, Buchan, Coppell, Greenhoff J, Jordan, Macari, McCreery
Substitute(s):   Grimes   Scorer(s):   Greenhoff J

Match # 3402   Saturday 23/09/78   Football League Division 1   at Highbury   Attendance 45393
Result: **Arsenal 1 Manchester United 1**
Teamsheet: Roche, Albiston, Houston, Greenhoff B, McQueen, Buchan, Coppell, Greenhoff J, Jordan, Macari, McIlroy
Scorer(s):   Coppell

Match # 3403   Saturday 30/09/78   Football League Division 1   at Old Trafford   Attendance 55301
Result: **Manchester United 1 Manchester City 0**
Teamsheet: Roche, Albiston, Houston, Greenhoff B, McQueen, Buchan, Coppell, Greenhoff J, Jordan, Macari, McIlroy
Scorer(s):   Jordan

Match # 3404   Wednesday 04/10/78   League Cup 3rd Round   at Old Trafford   Attendance 40534
Result: **Manchester United 1 Watford 2**
Teamsheet: Roche, Albiston, Houston, Greenhoff B, McQueen, Buchan, Coppell, Greenhoff J, Jordan, McIlroy, Grimes
Substitute(s):   McCreery   Scorer(s):   Jordan

Match # 3405   Saturday 07/10/78   Football League Division 1   at Old Trafford   Attendance 45402
Result: **Manchester United 3 Middlesbrough 2**
Teamsheet: Roche, Albiston, Houston, McIlroy, McQueen, Buchan, Coppell, Greenhoff J, Jordan, Macari, McCreery
Substitute(s):   Grimes   Scorer(s):   Macari 2, Jordan

Match # 3406   Saturday 14/10/78   Football League Division 1   at Villa Park   Attendance 36204
Result: **Aston Villa 2 Manchester United 2**
Teamsheet: Roche, Albiston, Houston, McIlroy, McQueen, Buchan, Coppell, Greenhoff J, Jordan, Macari, Grimes
Scorer(s):   Macari, McIlroy

Match # 3407   Saturday 21/10/78   Football League Division 1   at Old Trafford   Attendance 47211
Result: **Manchester United 1 Bristol City 3**
Teamsheet: Roche, Albiston, Houston, McIlroy, McQueen, Buchan, Coppell, Greenhoff J, Jordan, Macari, Grimes
Substitute(s):   Greenhoff B   Scorer(s):   Greenhoff J

Match # 3408   Saturday 28/10/78   Football League Division 1   at Molineux   Attendance 23141
Result: **Wolverhampton Wanderers 2 Manchester United 4**
Teamsheet: Roche, Nicholl, Houston, Greenhoff B, McQueen, Buchan, Coppell, Greenhoff J, Jordan, Macari, McIlroy
Substitute(s):   Grimes   Scorer(s):   Greenhoff J 2, Greenhoff B, Jordan

Match # 3409   Saturday 04/11/78   Football League Division 1   at Old Trafford   Attendance 46259
Result: **Manchester United 1 Southampton 1**
Teamsheet: Roche, Nicholl, Houston, McIlroy, Greenhoff B, Buchan, Coppell, Greenhoff J, Jordan, Macari, Grimes
Scorer(s):   Greenhoff J

Match # 3410   Saturday 11/11/78   Football League Division 1   at St Andrews   Attendance 23550
Result: **Birmingham City 5 Manchester United 1**
Teamsheet: Roche, Nicholl, Houston, McCreery, Greenhoff B, Buchan, Coppell, Greenhoff J, Jordan, Macari, McIlroy
Substitute(s):   Albiston   Scorer(s):   Jordan

Match # 3411   Saturday 18/11/78   Football League Division 1   at Old Trafford   Attendance 42109
Result: **Manchester United 2 Ipswich Town 0**
Teamsheet: Bailey, Albiston, Houston, Greenhoff B, McQueen, Buchan, Coppell, Greenhoff J, Jordan, Sloan, McIlroy
Substitute(s):   McGrath   Scorer(s):   Coppell, Greenhoff J

Match # 3412   Tuesday 21/11/78   Football League Division 1   at Goodison Park   Attendance 42126
Result: **Everton 3 Manchester United 0**
Teamsheet: Bailey, Albiston, Houston, Greenhoff B, McQueen, Buchan, Coppell, Greenhoff J, Jordan, Sloan, McIlroy
Substitute(s):   Macari

SEASON 1978/79 (continued)

Match # 3413 | Saturday 25/11/78 | Football League Division 1 | at Stamford Bridge | Attendance 28162
Result: **Chelsea 0 Manchester United 1**
Teamsheet: Bailey, Greenhoff B, Houston, McIlroy, McQueen, Buchan, Coppell, Greenhoff J, Jordan, Macari, Thomas
Scorer(s): Greenhoff J

Match # 3414 | Saturday 09/12/78 | Football League Division 1 | at Baseball Ground | Attendance 23180
Result: **Derby County 1 Manchester United 3**
Teamsheet: Bailey, Greenhoff B, Houston, McIlroy, McQueen, Buchan, Coppell, Greenhoff J, Ritchie, Macari, Thomas
Scorer(s): Ritchie 2, Greenhoff J

Match # 3415 | Saturday 16/12/78 | Football League Division 1 | at Old Trafford | Attendance 52026
Result: **Manchester United 2 Tottenham Hotspur 0**
Teamsheet: Bailey, Greenhoff B, Houston, McIlroy, McQueen, Buchan, Coppell, Greenhoff J, Ritchie, Macari, Thomas
Substitute(s): Paterson Scorer(s): McIlroy, Ritchie

Match # 3416 | Friday 22/12/78 | Football League Division 1 | at Burnden Park | Attendance 32390
Result: **Bolton Wanderers 3 Manchester United 0**
Teamsheet: Bailey, Greenhoff B, Connell, McIlroy, McQueen, Buchan, Coppell, Greenhoff J, Ritchie, Macari, Thomas
Substitute(s): Nicholl

Match # 3417 | Tuesday 26/12/78 | Football League Division 1 | at Old Trafford | Attendance 54910
Result: **Manchester United 0 Liverpool 3**
Teamsheet: Bailey, Greenhoff B, Connell, McIlroy, McQueen, Buchan, Coppell, Greenhoff J, Ritchie, Macari, Thomas

Match # 3418 | Saturday 30/12/78 | Football League Division 1 | at Old Trafford | Attendance 45091
Result: **Manchester United 3 West Bromwich Albion 5**
Teamsheet: Bailey, Greenhoff B, Houston, McIlroy, McQueen, Buchan, Coppell, Greenhoff J, Ritchie, McCreery, Thomas
Substitute(s): Sloan Scorer(s): Greenhoff B, McIlroy, McQueen

Match # 3419 | Monday 15/01/79 | FA Cup 3rd Round | at Old Trafford | Attendance 38743
Result: **Manchester United 3 Chelsea 0**
Teamsheet: Bailey, Greenhoff B, Houston, McIlroy, McQueen, Buchan, Coppell, Greenhoff J, Pearson, Nicholl, Grimes
Scorer(s): Coppell, Greenhoff J, Grimes

Match # 3420 | Wednesday 31/01/79 | FA Cup 4th Round | at Craven Cottage | Attendance 25229
Result: **Fulham 1 Manchester United 1**
Teamsheet: Bailey, Greenhoff B, Houston, McIlroy, McQueen, Buchan, Coppell, Greenhoff J, Pearson, Macari, Thomas
Substitute(s): Nicholl Scorer(s): Greenhoff J

Match # 3421 | Saturday 03/02/79 | Football League Division 1 | at Old Trafford | Attendance 45460
Result: **Manchester United 0 Arsenal 2**
Teamsheet: Bailey, Greenhoff B, Houston, Nicholl, McQueen, Buchan, Coppell, Greenhoff J, Macari, McIlroy, Thomas
Substitute(s): Ritchie

Match # 3422 | Saturday 10/02/79 | Football League Division 1 | at Maine Road | Attendance 46151
Result: **Manchester City 0 Manchester United 3**
Teamsheet: Bailey, Greenhoff B, Albiston, McIlroy, McQueen, Buchan, Coppell, Greenhoff J, Ritchie, Macari, Thomas
Scorer(s): Coppell 2, Ritchie

Match # 3423 | Monday 12/02/79 | FA Cup 4th Round Replay | at Old Trafford | Attendance 41200
Result: **Manchester United 1 Fulham 0**
Teamsheet: Bailey, Greenhoff B, Albiston, McIlroy, McQueen, Buchan, Coppell, Greenhoff J, Ritchie, Macari, Thomas
Scorer(s): Greenhoff J

Match # 3424 | Tuesday 20/02/79 | FA Cup 5th Round | at Layer Road | Attendance 13171
Result: **Colchester United 0 Manchester United 1**
Teamsheet: Bailey, Greenhoff B, Albiston, McIlroy, McQueen, Buchan, Coppell, Greenhoff J, Ritchie, Macari, Thomas
Substitute(s): Nicholl Scorer(s): Greenhoff J

Match # 3425 | Saturday 24/02/79 | Football League Division 1 | at Old Trafford | Attendance 44437
Result: **Manchester United 1 Aston Villa 1**
Teamsheet: Bailey, Greenhoff B, Albiston, McIlroy, McQueen, Buchan, Coppell, Greenhoff J, Ritchie, Macari, Thomas
Substitute(s): Nicholl Scorer(s): Greenhoff J

Match # 3426 | Wednesday 28/02/79 | Football League Division 1 | at Old Trafford | Attendance 36085
Result: **Manchester United 2 Queens Park Rangers 0**
Teamsheet: Bailey, Greenhoff B, Albiston, McIlroy, McQueen, Buchan, Coppell, Greenhoff J, Ritchie, Nicholl, Thomas
Scorer(s): Coppell, Greenhoff J

Match # 3427 | Saturday 03/03/79 | Football League Division 1 | at Ashton Gate | Attendance 24583
Result: **Bristol City 1 Manchester United 2**
Teamsheet: Bailey, Nicholl, Albiston, McIlroy, McQueen, Buchan, Coppell, Greenhoff J, Ritchie, Grimes, Thomas
Scorer(s): McQueen, Ritchie

Match # 3428 | Saturday 10/03/79 | FA Cup 6th Round | at White Hart Lane | Attendance 51800
Result: **Tottenham Hotspur 1 Manchester United 1**
Teamsheet: Bailey, Nicholl, Albiston, McIlroy, McQueen, Buchan, Coppell, Greenhoff J, Ritchie, Grimes, Thomas
Substitute(s): Jordan Scorer(s): Thomas

Match # 3429 | Wednesday 14/03/79 | FA Cup 6th Round Replay | at Old Trafford | Attendance 55584
Result: **Manchester United 2 Tottenham Hotspur 0**
Teamsheet: Bailey, Nicholl, Albiston, McIlroy, McQueen, Buchan, Coppell, Greenhoff J, Jordan, Grimes, Thomas
Scorer(s): McIlroy, Jordan

Match # 3430 | Tuesday 20/03/79 | Football League Division 1 | at Highfield Road | Attendance 25382
Result: **Coventry City 4 Manchester United 3**
Teamsheet: Bailey, Nicholl, Albiston, McIlroy, McQueen, Buchan, Coppell, Greenhoff J, Jordan, Greenhoff B, Thomas
Scorer(s): Coppell 2, McIlroy

SEASON 1978/79 (continued)

Match # 3431	Saturday 24/03/79	Football League Division 1	at Old Trafford	Attendance 51191

Result: **Manchester United 4 Leeds United 1**
Teamsheet: Bailey, Nicholl, Albiston, McIlroy, McQueen, Buchan, Coppell, Greenhoff J, Ritchie, Greenhoff B, Thomas
Substitute(s): Paterson   Scorer(s):   Ritchie 3, Thomas

Match # 3432	Tuesday 27/03/79	Football League Division 1	at Ayresome Park	Attendance 20138

Result: **Middlesbrough 2 Manchester United 2**
Teamsheet: Bailey, Nicholl, Albiston, McIlroy, McQueen, Buchan, Coppell, Greenhoff J, Jordan, Greenhoff B, Thomas
Scorer(s): Coppell, McQueen

Match # 3433	Saturday 31/03/79	FA Cup Semi-Final	at Maine Road	Attendance 52524

Result: **Manchester United 2 Liverpool 2**
Teamsheet: Bailey, Nicholl, Albiston, McIlroy, McQueen, Buchan, Coppell, Greenhoff J, Jordan, Greenhoff B, Thomas
Scorer(s): Greenhoff B, Jordan

Match # 3434	Wednesday 04/04/79	FA Cup Semi-Final Replay	at Goodison Park	Attendance 53069

Result: **Manchester United 1 Liverpool 0**
Teamsheet: Bailey, Nicholl, Albiston, McIlroy, McQueen, Buchan, Coppell, Greenhoff J, Jordan, Macari, Thomas
Substitute(s): Ritchie   Scorer(s):   Greenhoff J

Match # 3435	Saturday 07/04/79	Football League Division 1	at Carrow Road	Attendance 19382

Result: **Norwich City 2 Manchester United 2**
Teamsheet: Bailey, Albiston, Houston, McIlroy, McQueen, Buchan, Coppell, Greenhoff J, Jordan, Macari, Thomas
Scorer(s): Macari, McQueen

Match # 3436	Wednesday 11/04/79	Football League Division 1	at Old Trafford	Attendance 49617

Result: **Manchester United 1 Bolton Wanderers 2**
Teamsheet: Bailey, Nicholl, Albiston, McIlroy, McQueen, Buchan, Coppell, Ritchie, Jordan, Macari, Thomas
Scorer(s): Buchan

Match # 3437	Saturday 14/04/79	Football League Division 1	at Anfield	Attendance 46608

Result: **Liverpool 2 Manchester United 0**
Teamsheet: Bailey, Nicholl, Albiston, McIlroy, Greenhoff B, Buchan, Coppell, Ritchie, Jordan, Macari, Thomas
Substitute(s): Houston

Match # 3438	Monday 16/04/79	Football League Division 1	at Old Trafford	Attendance 46035

Result: **Manchester United 0 Coventry City 0**
Teamsheet: Bailey, Nicholl, Albiston, McIlroy, McQueen, Buchan, Coppell, Ritchie, Jordan, Greenhoff B, Thomas
Substitute(s): McCreery

Match # 3439	Wednesday 18/04/79	Football League Division 1	at City Ground	Attendance 33074

Result: **Nottingham Forest 1 Manchester United 1**
Teamsheet: Bailey, Nicholl, Albiston, McIlroy, McQueen, Buchan, Coppell, McCreery, Jordan, Greenhoff B, Thomas
Substitute(s): Grimes   Scorer(s):   Jordan

Match # 3440	Saturday 21/04/79	Football League Division 1	at White Hart Lane	Attendance 36665

Result: **Tottenham Hotspur 1 Manchester United 1**
Teamsheet: Bailey, Nicholl, Albiston, McIlroy, McQueen, Greenhoff B, Coppell, McCreery, Jordan, Macari, Thomas
Substitute(s): Grimes   Scorer(s):   McQueen

Match # 3441	Wednesday 25/04/79	Football League Division 1	at Old Trafford	Attendance 33678

Result: **Manchester United 1 Norwich City 0**
Teamsheet: Bailey, Nicholl, Albiston, McIlroy, McQueen, Buchan, Coppell, McCreery, Jordan, Macari, Thomas
Substitute(s): Grimes   Scorer(s):   Macari

Match # 3442	Saturday 28/04/79	Football League Division 1	at Old Trafford	Attendance 42546

Result: **Manchester United 0 Derby County 0**
Teamsheet: Bailey, McCreery, Albiston, McIlroy, Nicholl, Houston, Coppell, Ritchie, Jordan, Macari, Thomas
Substitute(s): Grimes

Match # 3443	Monday 30/04/79	Football League Division 1	at The Dell	Attendance 21616

Result: **Southampton 1 Manchester United 1**
Teamsheet: Bailey, Albiston, Houston, Sloan, McQueen, Moran, Coppell, Paterson, Ritchie, Macari, Grimes
Scorer(s): Ritchie

Match # 3444	Saturday 05/05/79	Football League Division 1	at The Hawthorns	Attendance 27960

Result: **West Bromwich Albion 1 Manchester United 0**
Teamsheet: Bailey, Albiston, Houston, McIlroy, McQueen, Greenhoff B, Coppell, Greenhoff J, Jordan, Macari, Thomas
Substitute(s): Grimes

Match # 3445	Monday 07/05/79	Football League Division 1	at Old Trafford	Attendance 39402

Result: **Manchester United 3 Wolverhampton Wanderers 2**
Teamsheet: Bailey, Nicholl, Albiston, Greenhoff B, Houston, Buchan, Coppell, Ritchie, Jordan, Macari, Thomas
Substitute(s): Grimes   Scorer(s):   Coppell 2, Ritchie

Match # 3446	Saturday 12/05/79	FA Cup Final	at Wembley	Attendance 100000

Result: **Manchester United 2 Arsenal 3**
Teamsheet: Bailey, Nicholl, Albiston, McIlroy, McQueen, Buchan, Coppell, Greenhoff J, Jordan, Macari, Thomas
Scorer(s): McIlroy, McQueen

Match # 3447	Wednesday 16/05/79	Football League Division 1	at Old Trafford	Attendance 38109

Result: **Manchester United 1 Chelsea 1**
Teamsheet: Bailey, Albiston, Houston, McIlroy, McQueen, Nicholl, Coppell, Greenhoff J, Jordan, McCreery, Thomas
Substitute(s): Grimes   Scorer(s):   Coppell

SEASON 1978/79 SUMMARY

APPEARANCES

PLAYER	LGE	FAC	LC	TOTAL
Coppell	42	9	2	53
McIlroy	40	9	2	51
Buchan	37	9	2	48
McQueen	36	9	2	47
Greenhoff J	33	9	2	44
Albiston	32 (1)	7	2	41 (1)
Greenhoff B	32 (1)	5	2	39 (1)
Macari	31 (1)	5	1	37 (1)
Bailey	28	9	–	37
Jordan	30	4 (1)	2	36 (1)
Thomas	25	8		33
Nicholl	19 (2)	6 (2)	–	25 (4)
Houston	21 (1)	2	1	24 (1)
Ritchie	16 (1)	3 (1)	–	19 (2)
Roche	14	–	2	16
McCreery	14 (1)	–	– (1)	14 (2)
Grimes	5 (11)	3	2	10 (11)
Sloan	3 (1)	–	–	3 (1)
Connell	2	–	–	2
Pearson	–	2	–	2
Paterson	1 (2)	–	–	1 (2)
Moran	1	–	–	1
McGrath	– (2)	–	–	– (2)

GOALSCORERS

PLAYER	LGE	FAC	LC	TOT
Greenhoff J	11	5	1	17
Coppell	11	1	–	12
Ritchie	10	–	–	10
Jordan	6	2	2	10
McIlroy	5	2	1	8
McQueen	6	1	–	7
Macari	6	–	–	6
Greenhoff B	2	1	–	3
Buchan	2	–	–	2
Thomas	1	1	–	2
Grimes	–	1	–	1

RESULTS & ATTENDANCES SUMMARY

		P	W	D	L	F	A	TOTAL	AVGE
League	H	21	9	7	5	29	25	978029	46573
	A	21	6	8	7	31	38	637829	30373
	TOTAL	42	15	15	12	60	63	1615858	38473
FA Cup	H	3	3	0	0	6	0	135527	45176
	A	3	1	2	0	3	2	90200	30067
	N	3	1	1	1	5	5	205593	68531
	TOTAL	9	5	3	1	14	7	431320	47924
League Cup	H	1	0	0	1	1	2	40534	40534
	A	1	1	0	0	3	2	41761	41761
	TOTAL	2	1	0	1	4	4	82295	41148
Overall	H	25	12	7	6	36	27	1154090	46164
	A	25	8	10	7	37	42	769790	30792
	N	3	1	1	1	5	5	205593	68531
	TOTAL	53	21	18	14	78	74	2129473	40179

FINAL TABLE – LEAGUE DIVISION ONE

		P	W	D	L	F	A	W	D	L	F	A	PTS	GD
				HOME						AWAY				
1	Liverpool	42	19	2	0	51	4	11	6	4	34	12	68	69
2	Nottingham Forest	42	11	10	0	34	10	10	8	3	27	16	60	35
3	West Bromwich Albion	42	13	5	3	38	15	11	6	4	34	20	59	37
4	Everton	42	12	7	2	32	17	5	10	6	20	23	51	12
5	Leeds United	42	11	4	6	41	25	7	10	4	29	27	50	18
6	Ipswich Town	42	11	4	6	34	21	9	5	7	29	28	49	14
7	Arsenal	42	11	8	2	37	18	6	6	9	24	30	48	13
8	Aston Villa	42	8	9	4	37	26	7	7	7	22	23	46	10
9	MANCHESTER UNITED	42	9	7	5	29	25	6	8	7	31	38	45	-3
10	Coventry City	42	11	7	3	41	29	3	9	9	17	39	44	-10
11	Tottenham Hotspur	42	7	8	6	19	25	6	7	8	29	36	41	-13
12	Middlesbrough	42	10	5	6	33	21	5	5	11	24	29	40	7
13	Bristol City	42	11	6	4	34	19	4	4	13	13	32	40	-4
14	Southampton	42	9	10	2	35	20	3	6	12	12	33	40	-6
15	Manchester City	42	9	5	7	34	28	4	8	9	24	28	39	2
16	Norwich City	42	7	10	4	29	19	0	13	8	22	38	37	-6
17	Bolton Wanderers	42	10	5	6	36	28	2	6	13	18	47	35	-21
18	Wolverhampton Wanderers	42	10	4	7	26	26	3	4	14	18	42	34	-24
19	Derby County	42	8	5	8	25	25	2	6	13	19	46	31	-27
20	Queens Park Rangers	42	4	9	8	24	33	2	4	15	21	40	25	-28
21	Birmingham City	42	5	9	7	24	25	1	1	19	13	39	22	-27
22	Chelsea	42	3	5	13	23	42	2	5	14	21	50	20	-48

SEASON 1979/80

Match # 3448   Saturday 18/08/79   Football League Division 1   at The Dell   Attendance 21768
Result: **Southampton 1   Manchester United 1**
Teamsheet: Bailey, Nicholl, Albiston, McIlroy, McQueen, Buchan, Coppell, Wilkins, Jordan, Macari, Thomas
Scorer(s):   McQueen

Match # 3449   Wednesday 22/08/79   Football League Division 1   at Old Trafford   Attendance 53377
Result: **Manchester United 2   West Bromwich Albion 0**
Teamsheet: Bailey, Nicholl, Albiston, McIlroy, McQueen, Buchan, Coppell, Wilkins, Jordan, Macari, Thomas
Substitute(s):   Ritchie   Scorer(s):   Coppell, McQueen

Match # 3450   Saturday 25/08/79   Football League Division 1   at Highbury   Attendance 44380
Result: **Arsenal 0   Manchester United 0**
Teamsheet: Bailey, Nicholl, Albiston, McIlroy, McQueen, Buchan, Coppell, Wilkins, Jordan, Macari, Thomas
Substitute(s):   Paterson

Match # 3451   Wednesday 29/08/79   League Cup 2nd Round 1st Leg   at White Hart Lane   Attendance 29163
Result: **Tottenham Hotspur 2   Manchester United 1**
Teamsheet: Bailey, Nicholl, Albiston, Paterson, McQueen, Buchan, Ritchie, Wilkins, Jordan, Macari, Thomas
Scorer(s):   Thomas

Match # 3452   Saturday 01/09/79   Football League Division 1   at Old Trafford   Attendance 51015
Result: **Manchester United 2   Middlesbrough 1**
Teamsheet: Bailey, Nicholl, Albiston, McIlroy, McQueen, Buchan, Coppell, Wilkins, Jordan, Macari, Thomas
Scorer(s):   Macari 2

Match # 3453   Wednesday 05/09/79   League Cup 2nd Round 2nd Leg   at Old Trafford   Attendance 48292
Result: **Manchester United 3   Tottenham Hotspur 1**
Teamsheet: Bailey, Nicholl, Albiston, McIlroy, Houston, Buchan, Coppell, Wilkins, Jordan, Macari, Thomas
Substitute(s):   Ritchie   Scorer(s):   Coppell, Thomas, own goal

Match # 3454   Saturday 08/09/79   Football League Division 1   at Villa Park   Attendance 34859
Result: **Aston Villa 0   Manchester United 3**
Teamsheet: Bailey, Nicholl, Albiston, McIlroy, McQueen, Buchan, Coppell, Wilkins, Jordan, Macari, Thomas
Substitute(s):   Grimes   Scorer(s):   Coppell, Grimes, Thomas

Match # 3455   Saturday 15/09/79   Football League Division 1   at Old Trafford   Attendance 54308
Result: **Manchester United 1   Derby County 0**
Teamsheet: Bailey, Nicholl, Albiston, McIlroy, McQueen, Buchan, Coppell, Wilkins, Ritchie, Macari, Grimes
Scorer(s):   Grimes

Match # 3456   Saturday 22/09/79   Football League Division 1   at Molineux   Attendance 35503
Result: **Wolverhampton Wanderers 3   Manchester United 1**
Teamsheet: Bailey, Nicholl, Albiston, McIlroy, McQueen, Buchan, Grimes, Wilkins, Coppell, Macari, Thomas
Scorer(s):   Macari

Match # 3457   Wednesday 26/09/79   League Cup 3rd Round   at Carrow Road   Attendance 18312
Result: **Norwich City 4   Manchester United 1**
Teamsheet: Bailey, Nicholl, Albiston, McIlroy, McQueen, Buchan, Grimes, Wilkins, Coppell, Macari, Thomas
Substitute(s):   Ritchie   Scorer(s):   McIlroy

Match # 3458   Saturday 29/09/79   Football League Division 1   at Old Trafford   Attendance 52596
Result: **Manchester United 4   Stoke City 0**
Teamsheet: Bailey, Nicholl, Albiston, McIlroy, McQueen, Buchan, Grimes, Wilkins, Coppell, Macari, Thomas
Substitute(s):   Sloan   Scorer(s):   McQueen 2, McIlroy, Wilkins

Match # 3459   Saturday 06/10/79   Football League Division 1   at Old Trafford   Attendance 52641
Result: **Manchester United 2   Brighton 0**
Teamsheet: Bailey, Nicholl, Albiston, McIlroy, McQueen, Buchan, Grimes, Wilkins, Coppell, Macari, Thomas
Scorer(s):   Coppell, Macari

Match # 3460   Wednesday 10/10/79   Football League Division 1   at The Hawthorns   Attendance 27713
Result: **West Bromwich Albion 2   Manchester United 0**
Teamsheet: Bailey, Nicholl, Albiston, McIlroy, McQueen, Buchan, Grimes, Wilkins, Coppell, Macari, Thomas

Match # 3461   Saturday 13/10/79   Football League Division 1   at Ashton Gate   Attendance 28305
Result: **Bristol City 1   Manchester United 1**
Teamsheet: Bailey, Nicholl, Albiston, McIlroy, McQueen, Buchan, Grimes, Wilkins, Coppell, Macari, Thomas
Scorer(s):   Macari

Match # 3462   Saturday 20/10/79   Football League Division 1   at Old Trafford   Attendance 50826
Result: **Manchester United 1   Ipswich Town 0**
Teamsheet: Bailey, Nicholl, Albiston, McIlroy, McQueen, Buchan, Grimes, Wilkins, Coppell, Macari, Thomas
Scorer(s):   Grimes

Match # 3463   Saturday 27/10/79   Football League Division 1   at Goodison Park   Attendance 37708
Result: **Everton 0   Manchester United 0**
Teamsheet: Bailey, Nicholl, Albiston, McIlroy, McQueen, Buchan, Grimes, Wilkins, Coppell, Macari, Thomas
Substitute(s):   Sloan

Match # 3464   Saturday 03/11/79   Football League Division 1   at Old Trafford   Attendance 50215
Result: **Manchester United 1   Southampton 0**
Teamsheet: Bailey, Nicholl, Houston, McIlroy, Moran, Buchan, Grimes, Wilkins, Coppell, Macari, Thomas
Scorer(s):   Macari

Match # 3465   Saturday 10/11/79   Football League Division 1   at Maine Road   Attendance 50067
Result: **Manchester City 2   Manchester United 0**
Teamsheet: Bailey, Nicholl, Houston, McIlroy, Moran, Buchan, Grimes, Wilkins, Coppell, Macari, Thomas

SEASON 1979/80 (continued)

Match # 3466	Saturday 17/11/79	Football League Division 1	at Old Trafford	Attendance 52800
Result:	**Manchester United 1 Crystal Palace 1**			
Teamsheet:	Bailey, Nicholl, Houston, McIlroy, Moran, Buchan, Coppell, Wilkins, Jordan, Macari, Thomas			
Substitute(s):	Grimes	Scorer(s): Jordan		

Match # 3467	Saturday 24/11/79	Football League Division 1	at Old Trafford	Attendance 46540
Result:	**Manchester United 5 Norwich City 0**			
Teamsheet:	Bailey, Nicholl, Grimes, McIlroy, Moran, Buchan, Coppell, Wilkins, Jordan, Macari, Thomas			
Scorer(s):	Jordan 2, Coppell, Macari, Moran			

Match # 3468	Saturday 01/12/79	Football League Division 1	at White Hart Lane	Attendance 51389
Result:	**Tottenham Hotspur 1 Manchester United 2**			
Teamsheet:	Bailey, Nicholl, Grimes, McIlroy, Moran, Buchan, Coppell, Wilkins, Jordan, Macari, Thomas			
Scorer(s):	Coppell, Macari			

Match # 3469	Saturday 08/12/79	Football League Division 1	at Old Trafford	Attendance 58348
Result:	**Manchester United 1 Leeds United 1**			
Teamsheet:	Bailey, Nicholl, Grimes, McIlroy, Moran, Buchan, Coppell, Wilkins, Jordan, Macari, Thomas			
Scorer(s):	Thomas			

Match # 3470	Saturday 15/12/79	Football League Division 1	at Highfield Road	Attendance 25541
Result:	**Coventry City 1 Manchester United 2**			
Teamsheet:	Bailey, Nicholl, Houston, McIlroy, McQueen, Buchan, Coppell, Wilkins, Jordan, Macari, Thomas			
Scorer(s):	Macari, McQueen			

Match # 3471	Saturday 22/12/79	Football League Division 1	at Old Trafford	Attendance 54607
Result:	**Manchester United 3 Nottingham Forest 0**			
Teamsheet:	Bailey, Nicholl, Houston, McIlroy, McQueen, Buchan, Coppell, Wilkins, Jordan, Macari, Thomas			
Scorer(s):	Jordan 2, McQueen			

Match # 3472	Wednesday 26/12/79	Football League Division 1	at Anfield	Attendance 51073
Result:	**Liverpool 2 Manchester United 0**			
Teamsheet:	Bailey, Nicholl, Houston, McIlroy, McQueen, Buchan, Coppell, Wilkins, Jordan, Macari, Thomas			
Substitute(s):	Grimes			

Match # 3473	Saturday 29/12/79	Football League Division 1	at Old Trafford	Attendance 54295
Result:	**Manchester United 3 Arsenal 0**			
Teamsheet:	Bailey, Nicholl, Houston, McIlroy, McQueen, Buchan, Coppell, Wilkins, Jordan, Macari, Thomas			
Scorer(s):	Jordan, McIlroy, McQueen			

Match # 3474	Saturday 05/01/80	FA Cup 3rd Round	at White Hart Lane	Attendance 45207
Result:	**Tottenham Hotspur 1 Manchester United 1**			
Teamsheet:	Bailey, Nicholl, Houston, McIlroy, McQueen, Buchan, Coppell, Wilkins, Jordan, Macari, Thomas			
Scorer(s):	McIlroy			

Match # 3475	Wednesday 09/01/80	FA Cup 3rd Round Replay	at Old Trafford	Attendance 53762
Result:	**Manchester United 0 Tottenham Hotspur 1**			
Teamsheet:	Bailey, Nicholl, Houston, McIlroy, McQueen, Buchan, Coppell, Wilkins, Jordan, Macari, Thomas			

Match # 3476	Saturday 12/01/80	Football League Division 1	at Ayresome Park	Attendance 30587
Result:	**Middlesbrough 1 Manchester United 1**			
Teamsheet:	Bailey, Nicholl, Houston, McIlroy, McQueen, Buchan, Coppell, Wilkins, Jordan, Macari, Thomas			
Substitute(s):	McGrath	Scorer(s): Thomas		

Match # 3477	Saturday 02/02/80	Football League Division 1	at Baseball Ground	Attendance 27783
Result:	**Derby County 1 Manchester United 3**			
Teamsheet:	Bailey, Nicholl, Houston, McIlroy, McQueen, Buchan, Coppell, Jovanovic, Jordan, Macari, Thomas			
Substitute(s):	Grimes	Scorer(s): McIlroy, Thomas, own goal		

Match # 3478	Saturday 09/02/80	Football League Division 1	at Old Trafford	Attendance 51568
Result:	**Manchester United 0 Wolverhampton Wanderers 1**			
Teamsheet:	Bailey, Nicholl, Houston, McIlroy, McQueen, Buchan, Coppell, Wilkins, Jordan, Macari, Thomas			
Substitute(s):	Grimes			

Match # 3479	Saturday 16/02/80	Football League Division 1	at Victoria Ground	Attendance 28389
Result:	**Stoke City 1 Manchester United 1**			
Teamsheet:	Bailey, Nicholl, Houston, McIlroy, McQueen, Buchan, Coppell, Wilkins, Jordan, Macari, Grimes			
Substitute(s):	Ritchie	Scorer(s): Coppell		

Match # 3480	Saturday 23/02/80	Football League Division 1	at Old Trafford	Attendance 43329
Result:	**Manchester United 4 Bristol City 0**			
Teamsheet:	Bailey, Nicholl, Houston, McIlroy, McQueen, Buchan, Coppell, Wilkins, Jordan, Macari, Grimes			
Substitute(s):	Ritchie	Scorer(s): Jordan 2, McIlroy, own goal		

Match # 3481	Wednesday 27/02/80	Football League Division 1	at Old Trafford	Attendance 47546
Result:	**Manchester United 2 Bolton Wanderers 0**			
Teamsheet:	Bailey, Nicholl, Houston, McIlroy, McQueen, Buchan, Coppell, Wilkins, Jordan, Macari, Grimes			
Substitute(s):	Sloan	Scorer(s): Coppell, McQueen		

Match # 3482	Saturday 01/03/80	Football League Division 1	at Portman Road	Attendance 30229
Result:	**Ipswich Town 6 Manchester United 0**			
Teamsheet:	Bailey, Nicholl, Houston, McIlroy, McQueen, Buchan, Coppell, Sloan, Jordan, Macari, Grimes			
Substitute(s):	Jovanovic			

Match # 3483	Wednesday 12/03/80	Football League Division 1	at Old Trafford	Attendance 45515
Result:	**Manchester United 0 Everton 0**			
Teamsheet:	Bailey, Nicholl, Albiston, McIlroy, McQueen, Buchan, Coppell, Wilkins, Jordan, Macari, Grimes			
Substitute(s):	Greenhoff			

SEASON 1979/80 (continued)

Match # 3484   Saturday 15/03/80   Football League Division 1   at Goldstone Ground   Attendance 29621
Result: **Brighton 0 Manchester United 0**
Teamsheet: Bailey, Nicholl, Albiston, McIlroy, McQueen, Buchan, Coppell, Wilkins, Jordan, Macari, Grimes

Match # 3485   Saturday 22/03/80   Football League Division 1   at Old Trafford   Attendance 56387
Result: **Manchester United 1 Manchester City 0**
Teamsheet: Bailey, Nicholl, Albiston, McIlroy, McQueen, Buchan, Coppell, Wilkins, Jordan, Macari, Thomas
Substitute(s):   Grimes   Scorer(s):   Thomas

Match # 3486   Saturday 29/03/80   Football League Division 1   at Selhurst Park   Attendance 33056
Result: **Crystal Palace 0 Manchester United 2**
Teamsheet: Bailey, Nicholl, Albiston, McIlroy, McQueen, Buchan, Coppell, Wilkins, Jordan, Macari, Thomas
Scorer(s):   Jordan, Thomas

Match # 3487   Wednesday 02/04/80   Football League Division 1   at City Ground   Attendance 31417
Result: **Nottingham Forest 2 Manchester United 0**
Teamsheet: Bailey, Nicholl, Albiston, McIlroy, McQueen, Buchan, Coppell, Wilkins, Jordan, Macari, Thomas

Match # 3488   Saturday 05/04/80   Football League Division 1   at Old Trafford   Attendance 57342
Result: **Manchester United 2 Liverpool 1**
Teamsheet: Bailey, Nicholl, Albiston, Greenhoff, McQueen, Buchan, Coppell, Wilkins, Jordan, Macari, Thomas
Scorer(s):   Greenhoff J, Thomas

Match # 3489   Monday 07/04/80   Football League Division 1   at Burnden Park   Attendance 31902
Result: **Bolton Wanderers 1 Manchester United 3**
Teamsheet: Bailey, Nicholl, Albiston, McIlroy, McQueen, Buchan, Coppell, Wilkins, Jordan, Grimes, Thomas
Substitute(s):   Ritchie   Scorer(s):   Coppell, McQueen, Thomas

Match # 3490   Saturday 12/04/80   Football League Division 1   at Old Trafford   Attendance 53151
Result: **Manchester United 4 Tottenham Hotspur 1**
Teamsheet: Bailey, Nicholl, Albiston, McIlroy, McQueen, Buchan, Coppell, Wilkins, Jordan, Ritchie, Thomas
Scorer(s):   Ritchie 3, Wilkins

Match # 3491   Saturday 19/04/80   Football League Division 1   at Carrow Road   Attendance 23274
Result: **Norwich City 0 Manchester United 2**
Teamsheet: Bailey, Nicholl, Albiston, McIlroy, Moran, Buchan, Coppell, Wilkins, Jordan, Ritchie, Thomas
Scorer(s):   Jordan 2

Match # 3492   Wednesday 23/04/80   Football League Division 1   at Old Trafford   Attendance 45201
Result: **Manchester United 2 Aston Villa 1**
Teamsheet: Bailey, Nicholl, Albiston, McIlroy, Moran, Buchan, Coppell, Greenhoff, Jordan, Macari, Thomas
Scorer(s):   Jordan 2

Match # 3493   Saturday 26/04/80   Football League Division 1   at Old Trafford   Attendance 52154
Result: **Manchester United 2 Coventry City 1**
Teamsheet: Bailey, Nicholl, Albiston, McIlroy, Moran, Buchan, Coppell, Greenhoff, Jordan, Macari, Thomas
Substitute(s):   Sloan   Scorer(s):   McIlroy 2

Match # 3494   Saturday 03/05/80   Football League Division 1   at Elland Road   Attendance 39625
Result: **Leeds United 2 Manchester United 0**
Teamsheet: Bailey, Nicholl, Albiston, McIlroy, McQueen, Buchan, Coppell, Greenhoff, Jordan, Macari, Thomas
Substitute(s):   Ritchie

SEASON 1979/80 SUMMARY

APPEARANCES

PLAYER	LGE	FAC	LC	TOTAL
Bailey	42	2	3	47
Buchan	42	2	3	47
Nicholl	42	2	3	47
Coppell	42	2	2	46
McIlroy	42	2	2	45
Macari	39	2	3	44
Wilkins	37	2	3	42
Thomas	35	2	3	40
McQueen	33	2	2	37
Jordan	32	2	2	36
Albiston	25	–	3	28
Grimes	20 (6)	–	1	21 (6)
Houston	14	2	1	17
Moran	9	–	–	9
Ritchie	3 (5)	–	1 (2)	4 (7)
Greenhoff	4 (1)	–	–	4 (1)
Sloan	1 (4)	–	–	1 (4)
Jovanovic	1 (1)	–	–	1 (1)
Paterson	– (1)	–	1	1 (1)
McGrath	– (1)	–	–	– (1)

GOALSCORERS

PLAYER	LGE	FAC	LC	TOT
Jordan	13	–	–	13
Thomas	8	–	2	10
Macari	9	–	–	9
McQueen	9	–	–	9
Coppell	8	–	1	9
McIlroy	6	1	1	8
Grimes	3	–	–	3
Ritchie	3	–	–	3
Wilkins	2	–	–	2
Greenhoff	1	–	–	1
Moran	1	–	–	1
own goals	2	–	1	3

RESULTS & ATTENDANCES SUMMARY

		P	W	D	L	F	A	TOTAL	AVGE
League	H	21	17	3	1	43	8	1083761	51608
	A	21	7	7	7	22	27	714189	34009
	TOTAL	42	24	10	8	65	35	1797950	42808
FA Cup	H	1	0	0	1	0	1	53762	53762
	A	1	0	1	0	1	1	45207	45207
	TOTAL	2	0	1	1	1	2	98969	49485
League Cup	H	1	1	0	0	3	1	48292	48292
	A	2	0	0	2	2	6	47475	23738
	TOTAL	3	1	0	2	5	7	95767	31922
Overall	H	23	18	3	2	46	10	1185815	51557
	A	24	7	8	9	25	34	806871	33620
	TOTAL	47	25	11	11	71	44	1992686	42398

FINAL TABLE – LEAGUE DIVISION ONE

		P	W	D	L	F	A	W	D	L	F	A	PTS	GD
			HOME						AWAY					
1	Liverpool	42	15	6	0	46	8	10	4	7	35	22	60	51
2	MANCHESTER UNITED	42	17	3	1	43	8	7	7	7	22	27	58	30
3	Ipswich Town	42	14	4	3	43	13	8	5	8	25	26	53	29
4	Arsenal	42	8	10	3	24	12	10	6	5	28	24	52	16
5	Nottingham Forest	42	16	4	1	44	11	4	4	13	19	32	48	20
6	Wolverhampton Wanderers	42	9	6	6	29	20	10	3	8	29	27	47	11
7	Aston Villa	42	11	5	5	29	22	5	9	7	22	28	46	1
8	Southampton	42	14	2	5	53	24	4	7	10	12	29	45	12
9	Middlesbrough	42	11	7	3	31	14	5	5	11	19	30	44	6
10	West Bromwich Albion	42	9	8	4	37	23	2	11	8	17	27	41	4
11	Leeds United	42	10	7	4	30	17	3	7	11	16	33	40	-4
12	Norwich City	42	10	8	3	38	30	3	6	12	20	36	40	-8
13	Crystal Palace	42	9	9	3	26	13	3	7	11	15	37	40	-9
14	Tottenham Hotspur	42	11	5	5	30	22	4	5	12	22	40	40	-10
15	Coventry City	42	12	2	7	34	24	4	5	12	22	42	39	-10
16	Brighton & Hove Albion	42	8	8	5	25	20	3	7	11	22	37	37	-10
17	Manchester City	42	8	8	5	28	25	4	5	12	15	41	37	-23
18	Stoke City	42	9	4	8	27	26	4	6	11	17	32	36	-14
19	Everton	42	7	7	7	28	25	2	10	9	15	26	35	-8
20	Bristol City	42	6	6	9	22	30	3	7	11	15	36	31	-29
21	Derby County	42	9	4	8	36	29	2	4	15	11	38	30	-20
22	Bolton Wanderers	42	5	11	5	19	21	0	4	17	19	52	25	-35

SEASON 1980/81

Match # 3495 Saturday 16/08/80   Football League Division 1   at Old Trafford   Attendance 54394
Result: **Manchester United 3   Middlesbrough 0**
Teamsheet: Bailey, Nicholl, Albiston, McIlroy, Moran, Buchan, Coppell, Greenhoff, Jordan, Macari, Thomas
Substitute(s):   Grimes   Scorer(s):   Grimes, Macari, Thomas

Match # 3496 Tuesday 19/08/80   Football League Division 1   at Molineux   Attendance 31955
Result: **Wolverhampton Wanderers 1   Manchester United 0**
Teamsheet: Roche, Nicholl, Albiston, McIlroy, Moran, Buchan, Grimes, Greenhoff, Coppell, Macari, Thomas
Substitute(s):   Ritchie

Match # 3497 Saturday 23/08/80   Football League Division 1   at St Andrews   Attendance 28661
Result: **Birmingham City 0   Manchester United 0**
Teamsheet: Roche, Nicholl, Albiston, McIlroy, Moran, Buchan, McGrath, Coppell, Ritchie, Macari, Thomas
Substitute(s):   Duxbury

Match # 3498 Wednesday 27/08/80   League Cup 2nd Round 1st Leg   at Old Trafford   Attendance 31656
Result: **Manchester United 0   Coventry City 1**
Teamsheet: Bailey, Nicholl, Albiston, McIlroy, Jovanovic, Buchan, Coppell, Greenhoff, Ritchie, Macari, Thomas
Substitute(s):   Sloan

Match # 3499 Saturday 30/08/80   Football League Division 1   at Old Trafford   Attendance 51498
Result: **Manchester United 1   Sunderland 1**
Teamsheet: Bailey, Nicholl, Albiston, McIlroy, Jovanovic, Buchan, Coppell, Greenhoff, Ritchie, Macari, Thomas
Scorer(s):   Jovanovic

Match # 3500 Tuesday 02/09/80   League Cup 2nd Round 2nd Leg   at Highfield Road   Attendance 18946
Result: **Coventry City 1   Manchester United 0**
Teamsheet: Bailey, Nicholl, Albiston, McIlroy, Jovanovic, Buchan, Coppell, Greenhoff, Ritchie, Macari, Thomas

Match # 3501 Saturday 06/09/80   Football League Division 1   at White Hart Lane   Attendance 40995
Result: **Tottenham Hotspur 0   Manchester United 0**
Teamsheet: Bailey, Nicholl, Albiston, McIlroy, Jovanovic, Buchan, Coppell, Greenhoff, Ritchie, Macari, Thomas
Substitute(s):   Duxbury

Match # 3502 Saturday 13/09/80   Football League Division 1   at Old Trafford   Attendance 43229
Result: **Manchester United 5   Leicester City 0**
Teamsheet: Bailey, Nicholl, Albiston, McIlroy, Jovanovic, Buchan, Grimes, Greenhoff, Coppell, Macari, Thomas
Substitute(s):   McGarvey   Scorer(s):   Jovanovic 2, Coppell, Grimes, Macari

Match # 3503 Wednesday 17/09/80   UEFA Cup 1st Round 1st Leg   at Old Trafford   Attendance 38037
Result: **Manchester United 1   Widzew Lodz 1**
Teamsheet: Bailey, Nicholl, Albiston, McIlroy, Jovanovic, Buchan, Grimes, Greenhoff, Coppell, Macari, Thomas
Substitute(s):   Duxbury   Scorer(s):   McIlroy

Match # 3504 Saturday 20/09/80   Football League Division 1   at Elland Road   Attendance 32539
Result: **Leeds United 0   Manchester United 0**
Teamsheet: Bailey, Nicholl, Albiston, McIlroy, Jovanovic, Buchan, Grimes, Greenhoff, Coppell, Macari, Thomas
Substitute(s):   Duxbury

Match # 3505 Saturday 27/09/80   Football League Division 1   at Old Trafford   Attendance 55918
Result: **Manchester United 2   Manchester City 2**
Teamsheet: Bailey, Nicholl, Albiston, McIlroy, McQueen, Buchan, Grimes, Greenhoff, Coppell, Duxbury, Thomas
Substitute(s):   Sloan   Scorer(s):   Albiston, Coppell

Match # 3506 Wednesday 01/10/80   UEFA Cup 1st Round 2nd Leg   at Stadio TKS   Attendance 40000
Result: **Widzew Lodz 0   Manchester United 0   (United lost the tie on away goals rule)**
Teamsheet: Bailey, Nicholl, Albiston, McIlroy, Jovanovic, Buchan, Grimes, Coppell, Jordan, Duxbury, Thomas
Substitute(s):   Moran

Match # 3507 Saturday 04/10/80   Football League Division 1   at City Ground   Attendance 29801
Result: **Nottingham Forest 1   Manchester United 2**
Teamsheet: Bailey, Nicholl, Albiston, McIlroy, Jovanovic, Moran, Duxbury, Coppell, Jordan, Macari, Thomas
Scorer(s):   Coppell, Macari

Match # 3508 Wednesday 08/10/80   Football League Division 1   at Old Trafford   Attendance 38831
Result: **Manchester United 3   Aston Villa 3**
Teamsheet: Bailey, Nicholl, Albiston, McIlroy, Jovanovic, Moran, Duxbury, Coppell, Jordan, Macari, Thomas
Substitute(s):   Greenhoff   Scorer(s):   McIlroy 2, Coppell

Match # 3509 Saturday 11/10/80   Football League Division 1   at Old Trafford   Attendance 49036
Result: **Manchester United 0   Arsenal 0**
Teamsheet: Bailey, Nicholl, Albiston, McIlroy, Jovanovic, Moran, Grimes, Coppell, Jordan, Duxbury, Thomas

Match # 3510 Saturday 18/10/80   Football League Division 1   at Portman Road   Attendance 28572
Result: **Ipswich Town 1   Manchester United 1**
Teamsheet: Bailey, Nicholl, Albiston, McIlroy, Jovanovic, Moran, Coppell, Duxbury, Jordan, Macari, Thomas
Scorer(s):   McIlroy

Match # 3511 Wednesday 22/10/80   Football League Division 1   at Victoria Ground   Attendance 24534
Result: **Stoke City 1   Manchester United 2**
Teamsheet: Bailey, Nicholl, Albiston, McIlroy, Jovanovic, Moran, Coppell, Birtles, Jordan, Macari, Thomas
Substitute(s):   Duxbury   Scorer(s):   Jordan, Macari

Match # 3512 Saturday 25/10/80   Football League Division 1   at Old Trafford   Attendance 54260
Result: **Manchester United 2   Everton 0**
Teamsheet: Bailey, Nicholl, Albiston, McIlroy, Moran, Duxbury, Coppell, Birtles, Jordan, Macari, Thomas
Scorer(s):   Coppell, Jordan

SEASON 1980/81 (continued)

Match # 3513 Saturday 01/11/80   Football League Division 1   at Selhurst Park   Attendance 31449
Result: **Crystal Palace 1 Manchester United 0**
Teamsheet: Bailey, Nicholl, Albiston, McIlroy, Jovanovic, Moran, Coppell, Birtles, Jordan, Macari, Thomas

Match # 3514 Saturday 08/11/80   Football League Division 1   at Old Trafford   Attendance 42794
Result: **Manchester United 0 Coventry City 0**
Teamsheet: Bailey, Nicholl, Albiston, McIlroy, Jovanovic, Moran, Coppell, Birtles, Jordan, Macari, Thomas
Substitute(s): Sloan

Match # 3515 Wednesday 12/11/80   Football League Division 1   at Old Trafford   Attendance 37959
Result: **Manchester United 0 Wolverhampton Wanderers 0**
Teamsheet: Bailey, Nicholl, Albiston, McIlroy, Moran, Duxbury, Coppell, Birtles, Jordan, Macari, Thomas

Match # 3516 Saturday 15/11/80   Football League Division 1   at Ayresome Park   Attendance 20606
Result: **Middlesbrough 1 Manchester United 1**
Teamsheet: Bailey, Nicholl, Albiston, McIlroy, Moran, Duxbury, Coppell, Birtles, Jordan, Macari, Thomas
Scorer(s): Jordan

Match # 3517 Saturday 22/11/80   Football League Division 1   at Goldstone Ground   Attendance 23923
Result: **Brighton 1 Manchester United 4**
Teamsheet: Bailey, Nicholl, Albiston, McIlroy, Jovanovic, Moran, Coppell, Birtles, Jordan, Duxbury, Thomas
Substitute(s): Grimes   Scorer(s):   Jordan 2, Duxbury, McIlroy

Match # 3518 Saturday 29/11/80   Football League Division 1   at Old Trafford   Attendance 46840
Result: **Manchester United 1 Southampton 1**
Teamsheet: Bailey, Jovanovic, Albiston, McIlroy, Moran, Duxbury, Coppell, Birtles, Jordan, Macari, Grimes
Substitute(s): Whelan   Scorer(s):   Jordan

Match # 3519 Saturday 06/12/80   Football League Division 1   at Carrow Road   Attendance 18780
Result: **Norwich City 2 Manchester United 2**
Teamsheet: Bailey, Nicholl, Albiston, McIlroy, Jovanovic, Buchan, Coppell, Greenhoff, Jordan, Macari, Duxbury
Scorer(s): Coppell, own goal

Match # 3520 Saturday 13/12/80   Football League Division 1   at Old Trafford   Attendance 39568
Result: **Manchester United 2 Stoke City 2**
Teamsheet: Bailey, Nicholl, Albiston, McIlroy, Moran, Coppell, Duxbury, Jordan, Macari, Thomas
Scorer(s): Jordan, Macari

Match # 3521 Saturday 20/12/80   Football League Division 1   at Highbury   Attendance 33730
Result: **Arsenal 2 Manchester United 1**
Teamsheet: Bailey, Nicholl, Albiston, McIlroy, Moran, Coppell, Duxbury, Jordan, Macari, Thomas
Scorer(s): Macari

Match # 3522 Friday 26/12/80   Football League Division 1   at Old Trafford   Attendance 57049
Result: **Manchester United 0 Liverpool 0**
Teamsheet: Bailey, Nicholl, Albiston, McIlroy, Moran, Coppell, Duxbury, Jordan, Macari, Thomas

Match # 3523 Saturday 27/12/80   Football League Division 1   at The Hawthorns   Attendance 30326
Result: **West Bromwich Albion 3 Manchester United 1**
Teamsheet: Bailey, Nicholl, Albiston, McIlroy, Jovanovic, Moran, Coppell, Duxbury, Jordan, Macari, Thomas
Scorer(s): Jovanovic

Match # 3524 Saturday 03/01/81   FA Cup 3rd Round   at Old Trafford   Attendance 42199
Result: **Manchester United 2 Brighton 2**
Teamsheet: Bailey, Nicholl, Albiston, McIlroy, Jovanovic, Moran, Coppell, Birtles, Jordan, Macari, Thomas
Substitute(s): Duxbury   Scorer(s):   Duxbury, Thomas

Match # 3525 Wednesday 07/01/81   FA Cup 3rd Round Replay   at Goldstone Ground   Attendance 26915
Result: **Brighton 0 Manchester United 2**
Teamsheet: Bailey, Nicholl, Albiston, Wilkins, McQueen, Buchan, Coppell, Birtles, Jordan, Macari, Thomas
Substitute(s): Duxbury   Scorer(s):   Birtles, Nicholl

Match # 3526 Saturday 10/01/81   Football League Division 1   at Old Trafford   Attendance 42208
Result: **Manchester United 2 Brighton 1**
Teamsheet: Bailey, Nicholl, Albiston, Wilkins, McQueen, Buchan, Coppell, Birtles, Jordan, Macari, Thomas
Substitute(s): Duxbury   Scorer(s):   Macari, McQueen

Match # 3527 Saturday 24/01/81   FA Cup 4th Round   at City Ground   Attendance 34110
Result: **Nottingham Forest 1 Manchester United 0**
Teamsheet: Bailey, Nicholl, Albiston, Wilkins, McQueen, Buchan, Coppell, Birtles, Jordan, Macari, Thomas

Match # 3528 Wednesday 28/01/81   Football League Division 1   at Roker Park   Attendance 31910
Result: **Sunderland 2 Manchester United 0**
Teamsheet: Bailey, Nicholl, Albiston, Duxbury, McQueen, Buchan, Coppell, Birtles, Jordan, Macari, Thomas

Match # 3529 Saturday 31/01/81   Football League Division 1   at Old Trafford   Attendance 39081
Result: **Manchester United 2 Birmingham City 0**
Teamsheet: Bailey, Nicholl, Albiston, Duxbury, McQueen, Buchan, Coppell, Birtles, Jordan, Macari, Thomas
Substitute(s): McIlroy   Scorer(s):   Jordan, Macari

Match # 3530 Saturday 07/02/81   Football League Division 1   at Filbert Street   Attendance 26085
Result: **Leicester City 1 Manchester United 0**
Teamsheet: Bailey, Nicholl, Albiston, Duxbury, Jovanovic, Buchan, Coppell, Birtles, Jordan, Macari, Thomas
Substitute(s): Wilkins

SEASON 1980/81 (continued)

Match # 3531	Tuesday 17/02/81	Football League Division 1	at Old Trafford	Attendance 40642
Result:	**Manchester United 0 Tottenham Hotspur 0**			
Teamsheet:	Bailey, Nicholl, Albiston, Duxbury, Moran, Buchan, Coppell, Wilkins, Birtles, Macari, McIlroy			

Match # 3532	Saturday 21/02/81	Football League Division 1	at Maine Road	Attendance 50114
Result:	**Manchester City 1 Manchester United 0**			
Teamsheet:	Bailey, Nicholl, Albiston, Duxbury, Moran, Buchan, Coppell, Wilkins, Birtles, Macari, McIlroy			
Substitute(s):	McGarvey			

Match # 3533	Saturday 28/02/81	Football League Division 1	at Old Trafford	Attendance 45733
Result:	**Manchester United 0 Leeds United 1**			
Teamsheet:	Bailey, Nicholl, Albiston, Wilkins, Moran, Buchan, Coppell, Birtles, Jordan, Macari, McIlroy			

Match # 3534	Saturday 07/03/81	Football League Division 1	at The Dell	Attendance 22698
Result:	**Southampton 1 Manchester United 0**			
Teamsheet:	Bailey, Nicholl, Albiston, Wilkins, Moran, Buchan, Coppell, Birtles, Jordan, Macari, McIlroy			

Match # 3535	Saturday 14/03/81	Football League Division 1	at Villa Park	Attendance 42182
Result:	**Aston Villa 3 Manchester United 3**			
Teamsheet:	Bailey, Nicholl, Albiston, Wilkins, Moran, Buchan, Coppell, Birtles, Jordan, Macari, McIlroy			
Scorer(s):	Jordan 2, McIlroy			

Match # 3536	Wednesday 18/03/81	Football League Division 1	at Old Trafford	Attendance 38205
Result:	**Manchester United 1 Nottingham Forest 1**			
Teamsheet:	Bailey, Nicholl, Albiston, Wilkins, Moran, Buchan, Coppell, Birtles, Jordan, Macari, McIlroy			
Substitute(s):	Duxbury	Scorer(s): own goal		

Match # 3537	Saturday 21/03/81	Football League Division 1	at Old Trafford	Attendance 46685
Result:	**Manchester United 2 Ipswich Town 1**			
Teamsheet:	Bailey, Nicholl, Albiston, Moran, McQueen, Buchan, Coppell, Birtles, Jordan, Duxbury, Thomas			
Scorer(s):	Nicholl, Thomas			

Match # 3538	Saturday 28/03/81	Football League Division 1	at Goodison Park	Attendance 25856
Result:	**Everton 0 Manchester United 1**			
Teamsheet:	Bailey, Nicholl, Albiston, Moran, McQueen, Buchan, Coppell, Birtles, Jordan, Duxbury, Thomas			
Substitute(s):	Macari	Scorer(s): Jordan		

Match # 3539	Saturday 04/04/81	Football League Division 1	at Old Trafford	Attendance 37954
Result:	**Manchester United 1 Crystal Palace 0**			
Teamsheet:	Bailey, Duxbury, Albiston, Moran, McQueen, Buchan, Coppell, Birtles, Jordan, Macari, Thomas			
Substitute(s):	Wilkins	Scorer(s): Duxbury		

Match # 3540	Saturday 11/04/81	Football League Division 1	at Highfield Road	Attendance 20201
Result:	**Coventry City 0 Manchester United 2**			
Teamsheet:	Bailey, Duxbury, Albiston, Moran, McQueen, Buchan, Coppell, Birtles, Jordan, Macari, Wilkins			
Scorer(s):	Jordan 2			

Match # 3541	Tuesday 14/04/81	Football League Division 1	at Anfield	Attendance 31276
Result:	**Liverpool 0 Manchester United 1**			
Teamsheet:	Bailey, Duxbury, Albiston, Moran, McQueen, Buchan, Coppell, Birtles, Jordan, Macari, Wilkins			
Scorer(s):	McQueen			

Match # 3542	Saturday 18/04/81	Football League Division 1	at Old Trafford	Attendance 44442
Result:	**Manchester United 2 West Bromwich Albion 1**			
Teamsheet:	Bailey, Duxbury, Albiston, Moran, McQueen, Buchan, Coppell, Birtles, Jordan, Macari, Wilkins			
Scorer(s):	Jordan, Macari			

Match # 3543	Saturday 25/04/81	Football League Division 1	at Old Trafford	Attendance 40165
Result:	**Manchester United 1 Norwich City 0**			
Teamsheet:	Bailey, Duxbury, Albiston, Moran, McQueen, Buchan, Coppell, Birtles, Jordan, Macari, Wilkins			
Scorer(s):	Jordan			

SEASON 1980/81 SUMMARY

APPEARANCES

PLAYER	LGE	FAC	LC	UC	TOTAL
Albiston	42	3	2	2	49
Coppell	42	3	2	2	49
Bailey	40	3	2	2	47
Macari	37 (1)	3	2	1	43 (1)
Nicholl	36	3	2	2	43
Jordan	33	3	–	1	37
Thomas	30	3	2	2	37
McIlroy	31 (1)	1	2	2	36 (1)
Moran	32	1	–	– (1)	33 (1)
Buchan	26	2	2	2	32
Duxbury	27 (6)	– (2)	–	1 (1)	28 (9)
Birtles	25	3	–	–	28
Jovanovic	19	1	2	2	24
Wilkins	11 (2)	2	–	–	13 (2)
McQueen	11	2	–	–	13
Greenhoff	8 (1)	–	2	1	11 (1)
Grimes	6 (2)	–	–	2	8 (2)
Ritchie	3 (1)	–	2	–	5 (1)
Roche	2	–	–	–	2
McGrath	1	–	–	–	1
Sloan	– (2)	–	– (1)	–	– (3)
McGarvey	– (2)	–	–	–	– (2)
Whelan	– (1)	–	–	–	– (1)

GOALSCORERS

PLAYER	LGE	FAC	LC	UC	TOT
Jordan	15	–	–	–	15
Macari	9	–	–	–	9
Coppell	6	–	–	–	6
McIlroy	5	–	–	1	6
Jovanovic	4	–	–	–	4
Duxbury	2	1	–	–	3
Thomas	2	1	–	–	3
Grimes	2	–	–	–	2
McQueen	2	–	–	–	2
Nicholl	1	1	–	–	2
Albiston	1	–	–	–	1
Birtles	–	1	–	–	1
own goals	2	–	–	–	2

RESULTS & ATTENDANCES SUMMARY

		P	W	D	L	F	A	TOTAL	AVGE
League	H	21	9	11	1	30	14	946491	45071
	A	21	6	7	8	21	22	626193	29819
	TOTAL	42	15	18	9	51	36	1572684	37445
FA Cup	H	1	0	1	0	2	2	42199	42199
	A	2	1	0	1	2	1	61025	30513
	TOTAL	3	1	1	1	4	3	103224	34408
League Cup	H	1	0	0	1	0	1	31656	31656
	A	1	0	0	1	0	1	18946	18946
	TOTAL	2	0	0	2	0	2	50602	25301
UEFA Cup	H	1	0	1	0	1	1	38037	38037
	A	1	0	1	0	0	0	40000	40000
	TOTAL	2	0	2	0	1	1	78037	39019
Overall	H	24	9	13	2	33	18	1058383	44099
	A	25	7	8	10	23	24	746164	29847
	TOTAL	49	16	21	12	56	42	1804547	36827

FINAL TABLE – LEAGUE DIVISION ONE

		P		HOME					AWAY				PTS	GD
			W	D	L	F	A	W	D	L	F	A		
1	Aston Villa	42	16	3	2	40	13	10	5	6	32	27	60	32
2	Ipswich Town	42	15	4	2	45	14	8	6	7	32	29	56	34
3	Arsenal	42	13	8	0	36	17	6	7	8	25	28	53	16
4	West Bromwich Albion	42	15	4	2	40	15	5	8	8	20	27	52	18
5	Liverpool	42	13	5	3	38	15	4	12	5	24	27	51	20
6	Southampton	42	15	4	2	47	22	5	6	10	29	34	50	20
7	Nottingham Forest	42	15	3	3	44	20	4	9	8	18	24	50	18
8	MANCHESTER UNITED	42	9	11	1	30	14	6	7	8	21	22	48	15
9	Leeds United	42	10	5	6	19	19	7	5	9	20	28	44	–8
10	Tottenham Hotspur	42	9	9	3	44	31	5	6	10	26	37	43	2
11	Stoke City	42	8	9	4	31	23	4	9	8	20	37	42	–9
12	Manchester City	42	10	7	4	35	25	4	4	13	21	34	39	–3
13	Birmingham City	42	11	5	5	32	23	2	7	12	18	38	38	–11
14	Middlesbrough	42	14	4	3	38	16	2	1	18	15	45	37	–8
15	Everton	42	8	6	7	32	25	5	4	12	23	33	36	–3
16	Coventry City	42	9	6	6	31	30	4	4	13	17	38	36	–20
17	Sunderland	42	10	4	7	32	19	4	3	14	20	34	35	–1
18	Wolverhampton Wanderers	42	11	2	8	26	20	2	7	12	17	35	35	–12
19	Brighton & Hove Albion	42	10	3	8	30	26	4	4	13	24	41	35	–13
20	Norwich City	42	9	7	5	34	25	4	0	17	15	48	33	–24
21	Leicester City	42	7	5	9	20	23	6	1	14	20	44	32	–27
22	Crystal Palace	42	6	4	11	32	37	0	3	18	15	46	19	–36

SEASON 1981/82

Match # 3544 Saturday 29/08/81   Football League Division 1   at Highfield Road   Attendance 19329
Result: **Coventry City 2 Manchester United 1**
Teamsheet: Bailey, Gidman, Albiston, Wilkins, McQueen, Buchan, Coppell, Birtles, Stapleton, Macari, McIlroy
Scorer(s): Macari

Match # 3545 Monday 31/08/81   Football League Division 1   at Old Trafford   Attendance 51496
Result: **Manchester United 0 Nottingham Forest 0**
Teamsheet: Bailey, Gidman, Albiston, Wilkins, McQueen, Buchan, Coppell, Birtles, Stapleton, Macari, McIlroy

Match # 3546 Saturday 05/09/81   Football League Division 1   at Old Trafford   Attendance 45555
Result: **Manchester United 1 Ipswich Town 2**
Teamsheet: Bailey, Gidman, Albiston, Wilkins, McQueen, Buchan, Coppell, Birtles, Stapleton, Macari, McIlroy
Substitute(s): Duxbury   Scorer(s): Stapleton

Match # 3547 Saturday 12/09/81   Football League Division 1   at Villa Park   Attendance 37661
Result: **Aston Villa 1 Manchester United 1**
Teamsheet: Bailey, Gidman, Albiston, Wilkins, McQueen, Buchan, Coppell, Birtles, Stapleton, Macari, McIlroy
Scorer(s): Stapleton

Match # 3548 Saturday 19/09/81   Football League Division 1   at Old Trafford   Attendance 47309
Result: **Manchester United 1 Swansea City 0**
Teamsheet: Bailey, Gidman, Albiston, Wilkins, McQueen, Buchan, Coppell, Birtles, Stapleton, Macari, McIlroy
Substitute(s): Moses   Scorer(s): Birtles

Match # 3549 Tuesday 22/09/81   Football League Division 1   at Ayresome Park   Attendance 19895
Result: **Middlesbrough 0 Manchester United 2**
Teamsheet: Bailey, Gidman, Albiston, Wilkins, McQueen, Buchan, Coppell, Birtles, Stapleton, Macari, Moses
Substitute(s): Duxbury   Scorer(s): Birtles, Stapleton

Match # 3550 Saturday 26/09/81   Football League Division 1   at Highbury   Attendance 39795
Result: **Arsenal 0 Manchester United 0**
Teamsheet: Bailey, Gidman, Albiston, Wilkins, McQueen, Buchan, Coppell, Birtles, Stapleton, Macari, Moses

Match # 3551 Wednesday 30/09/81   Football League Division 1   at Old Trafford   Attendance 47019
Result: **Manchester United 1 Leeds United 0**
Teamsheet: Bailey, Gidman, Albiston, Wilkins, McQueen, Buchan, Coppell, Birtles, Stapleton, McIlroy, Moses
Substitute(s): Duxbury   Scorer(s): Stapleton

Match # 3552 Saturday 03/10/81   Football League Division 1   at Old Trafford   Attendance 46837
Result: **Manchester United 5 Wolverhampton Wanderers 0**
Teamsheet: Bailey, Gidman, Albiston, Moran, Buchan, Coppell, Birtles, Stapleton, McIlroy, Moses
Scorer(s): McIlroy 3, Birtles, Stapleton

Match # 3553 Wednesday 07/10/81   League Cup 2nd Round 1st Leg   at White Hart Lane   Attendance 39333
Result: **Tottenham Hotspur 1 Manchester United 0**
Teamsheet: Bailey, Gidman, Albiston, Wilkins, Moran, Buchan, Coppell, Birtles, Stapleton, McIlroy, Robson
Substitute(s): Duxbury

Match # 3554 Saturday 10/10/81   Football League Division 1   at Maine Road   Attendance 52037
Result: **Manchester City 0 Manchester United 0**
Teamsheet: Bailey, Gidman, Albiston, Wilkins, Moran, Buchan, Robson, Birtles, Stapleton, McIlroy, Moses
Substitute(s): Coppell

Match # 3555 Saturday 17/10/81   Football League Division 1   at Old Trafford   Attendance 48800
Result: **Manchester United 1 Birmingham City 1**
Teamsheet: Bailey, Gidman, Albiston, Wilkins, Moran, Buchan, Robson, Birtles, Stapleton, Moses, Coppell
Scorer(s): Coppell

Match # 3556 Wednesday 21/10/81   Football League Division 1   at Old Trafford   Attendance 38342
Result: **Manchester United 1 Middlesbrough 0**
Teamsheet: Bailey, Gidman, Albiston, Wilkins, Duxbury, Buchan, Robson, Birtles, Stapleton, Moses, Coppell
Scorer(s): Moses

Match # 3557 Saturday 24/10/81   Football League Division 1   at Anfield   Attendance 41438
Result: **Liverpool 1 Manchester United 2**
Teamsheet: Bailey, Gidman, Albiston, Wilkins, Moran, Buchan, Robson, Birtles, Stapleton, Moses, Coppell
Scorer(s): Albiston, Moran

Match # 3558 Wednesday 28/10/81   League Cup 2nd Round 2nd Leg   at Old Trafford   Attendance 55890
Result: **Manchester United 0 Tottenham Hotspur 1**
Teamsheet: Bailey, Gidman, Albiston, Wilkins, Moran, Buchan, Robson, Birtles, Stapleton, Moses, Coppell

Match # 3559 Saturday 31/10/81   Football League Division 1   at Old Trafford   Attendance 45928
Result: **Manchester United 2 Notts County 1**
Teamsheet: Bailey, Gidman, Albiston, Wilkins, Duxbury, Buchan, Robson, Birtles, Stapleton, Moses, Coppell
Substitute(s): Macari   Scorer(s): Birtles, Moses

Match # 3560 Saturday 07/11/81   Football League Division 1   at Roker Park   Attendance 27070
Result: **Sunderland 1 Manchester United 5**
Teamsheet: Bailey, Gidman, Albiston, Wilkins, Moran, Buchan, Robson, Birtles, Stapleton, Moses, Coppell
Substitute(s): Duxbury   Scorer(s): Stapleton 2, Birtles, Moran, Robson

Match # 3561 Saturday 21/11/81   Football League Division 1   at White Hart Lane   Attendance 35534
Result: **Tottenham Hotspur 3 Manchester United 1**
Teamsheet: Roche, Duxbury, Albiston, Wilkins, Moran, Buchan, Robson, Birtles, Stapleton, Moses, McIlroy
Substitute(s): Nicholl   Scorer(s): Birtles

SEASON 1981/82 (continued)

Match # 3562   Saturday 28/11/81   Football League Division 1   at Old Trafford   Attendance 41911
Result: **Manchester United 2 Brighton 0**
Teamsheet: Roche, Gidman, Albiston, Wilkins, Moran, McQueen, Robson, Birtles, Stapleton, Moses, McIlroy
Scorer(s):   Birtles, Stapleton

Match # 3563   Saturday 05/12/81   Football League Division 1   at The Dell   Attendance 24404
Result: **Southampton 3 Manchester United 2**
Teamsheet: Roche, Gidman, Albiston, Wilkins, Moran, McQueen, Robson, Birtles, Stapleton, Moses, McIlroy
Scorer(s):   Robson, Stapleton

Match # 3564   Saturday 02/01/82   FA Cup 3rd Round   at Vicarage Road   Attendance 26104
Result: **Watford 1 Manchester United 0**
Teamsheet: Bailey, Gidman, Albiston, Wilkins, Moran, Buchan, Robson, Birtles, Stapleton, Moses, McIlroy
Substitute(s):   Macari

Match # 3565   Wednesday 06/01/82   Football League Division 1   at Old Trafford   Attendance 40451
Result: **Manchester United 1 Everton 1**
Teamsheet: Bailey, Gidman, Albiston, Wilkins, Moran, Buchan, Robson, McGarvey, Stapleton, McIlroy, Coppell
Scorer(s):   Stapleton

Match # 3566   Saturday 23/01/82   Football League Division 1   at Victoria Ground   Attendance 19793
Result: **Stoke City 0 Manchester United 3**
Teamsheet: Bailey, Duxbury, Albiston, Wilkins, Moran, McQueen, Robson, Birtles, Stapleton, Macari, Coppell
Scorer(s):   Birtles, Coppell, Stapleton

Match # 3567   Wednesday 27/01/82   Football League Division 1   at Old Trafford   Attendance 41291
Result: **Manchester United 1 West Ham United 0**
Teamsheet: Bailey, Duxbury, Albiston, Wilkins, Moran, McQueen, Robson, Birtles, Stapleton, Macari, Coppell
Scorer(s):   Macari

Match # 3568   Saturday 30/01/82   Football League Division 1   at Vetch Field   Attendance 24115
Result: **Swansea City 2 Manchester United 0**
Teamsheet: Bailey, Duxbury, Albiston, Wilkins, Moran, McQueen, Robson, Birtles, Stapleton, Macari, Coppell
Substitute(s):   Gidman

Match # 3569   Saturday 06/02/82   Football League Division 1   at Old Trafford   Attendance 43184
Result: **Manchester United 4 Aston Villa 1**
Teamsheet: Bailey, Gidman, Albiston, Wilkins, Moran, Buchan, Robson, Birtles, Stapleton, Duxbury, Coppell
Substitute(s):   McGarvey   Scorer(s):   Moran 2, Coppell, Robson

Match # 3570   Saturday 13/02/82   Football League Division 1   at Molineux   Attendance 22481
Result: **Wolverhampton Wanderers 0 Manchester United 1**
Teamsheet: Bailey, Gidman, Albiston, Wilkins, Moran, Buchan, Robson, Birtles, Stapleton, Duxbury, Coppell
Scorer(s):   Birtles

Match # 3571   Saturday 20/02/82   Football League Division 1   at Old Trafford   Attendance 43833
Result: **Manchester United 0 Arsenal 0**
Teamsheet: Bailey, Gidman, Albiston, Wilkins, Moran, Buchan, Robson, Birtles, Stapleton, Duxbury, Coppell

Match # 3572   Saturday 27/02/82   Football League Division 1   at Old Trafford   Attendance 57830
Result: **Manchester United 1 Manchester City 1**
Teamsheet: Bailey, Gidman, Albiston, Wilkins, Moran, Buchan, Robson, Birtles, Stapleton, Duxbury, Coppell
Scorer(s):   Moran

Match # 3573   Saturday 06/03/82   Football League Division 1   at St Andrews   Attendance 19637
Result: **Birmingham City 0 Manchester United 1**
Teamsheet: Bailey, Gidman, Albiston, Wilkins, Moran, Buchan, Robson, Birtles, Stapleton, Duxbury, Coppell
Substitute(s):   McGarvey   Scorer(s):   Birtles

Match # 3574   Wednesday 17/03/82   Football League Division 1   at Old Trafford   Attendance 34499
Result: **Manchester United 0 Coventry City 1**
Teamsheet: Bailey, Gidman, Albiston, Wilkins, Moran, Buchan, Robson, Birtles, Stapleton, Moses, Coppell
Substitute(s):   Duxbury

Match # 3575   Saturday 20/03/82   Football League Division 1   at Meadow Lane   Attendance 17048
Result: **Notts County 1 Manchester United 3**
Teamsheet: Bailey, Gidman, Albiston, Wilkins, Moran, Buchan, Robson, Birtles, Stapleton, Moses, Coppell
Substitute(s):   McGarvey   Scorer(s):   Coppell 2, Stapleton

Match # 3576   Saturday 27/03/82   Football League Division 1   at Old Trafford   Attendance 40776
Result: **Manchester United 0 Sunderland 0**
Teamsheet: Bailey, Gidman, Albiston, Wilkins, McQueen, Buchan, Robson, Birtles, Stapleton, Moses, Coppell
Substitute(s):   McGarvey

Match # 3577   Saturday 03/04/82   Football League Division 1   at Elland Road   Attendance 30953
Result: **Leeds United 0 Manchester United 0**
Teamsheet: Bailey, Duxbury, Albiston, Wilkins, Moran, Buchan, Robson, McGarvey, Stapleton, Moses, Coppell

Match # 3578   Wednesday 07/04/82   Football League Division 1   at Old Trafford   Attendance 48371
Result: **Manchester United 0 Liverpool 1**
Teamsheet: Bailey, Duxbury, Albiston, Wilkins, Moran, Buchan, Robson, McGarvey, Stapleton, Moses, Coppell
Substitute(s):   Grimes

Match # 3579   Saturday 10/04/82   Football League Division 1   at Goodison Park   Attendance 29306
Result: **Everton 3 Manchester United 3**
Teamsheet: Bailey, Gidman, Albiston, Wilkins, Moran, Duxbury, Robson, McGarvey, Stapleton, Moses, Coppell
Substitute(s):   Grimes   Scorer(s):   Coppell 2, Grimes

SEASON 1981/82 (continued)

Match # 3580	Monday 12/04/82	Football League Division 1	at Old Trafford	Attendance 38717
Result:	**Manchester United 1 West Bromwich Albion 0**			
Teamsheet:	Bailey, Gidman, Albiston, Wilkins, Moran, McQueen, Robson, McGarvey, Stapleton, Grimes, Coppell			
Scorer(s):	Moran			

Match # 3581	Saturday 17/04/82	Football League Division 1	at Old Trafford	Attendance 50724
Result:	**Manchester United 2 Tottenham Hotspur 0**			
Teamsheet:	Bailey, Gidman, Albiston, Wilkins, Moran, McQueen, Robson, McGarvey, Stapleton, Grimes, Coppell			
Scorer(s):	Coppell, McGarvey			

Match # 3582	Tuesday 20/04/82	Football League Division 1	at Portman Road	Attendance 25744
Result:	**Ipswich Town 2 Manchester United 1**			
Teamsheet:	Bailey, Gidman, Albiston, Wilkins, Moran, McQueen, Robson, McGarvey, Stapleton, Grimes, Duxbury			
Substitute(s):	Birtles	Scorer(s): Gidman		

Match # 3583	Saturday 24/04/82	Football League Division 1	at Goldstone Ground	Attendance 20750
Result:	**Brighton 0 Manchester United 1**			
Teamsheet:	Bailey, Gidman, Albiston, Wilkins, Moran, McQueen, Robson, McGarvey, Stapleton, Grimes, Duxbury			
Substitute(s):	Whiteside	Scorer(s): Wilkins		

Match # 3584	Saturday 01/05/82	Football League Division 1	at Old Trafford	Attendance 40038
Result:	**Manchester United 1 Southampton 0**			
Teamsheet:	Bailey, Gidman, Albiston, Wilkins, Duxbury, McQueen, Robson, McGarvey, Stapleton, Grimes, Davies			
Scorer(s):	McGarvey			

Match # 3585	Wednesday 05/05/82	Football League Division 1	at City Ground	Attendance 18449
Result:	**Nottingham Forest 0 Manchester United 1**			
Teamsheet:	Bailey, Gidman, Albiston, Wilkins, Moran, Duxbury, Robson, McGarvey, Stapleton, Grimes, Coppell			
Scorer(s):	Stapleton			

Match # 3586	Saturday 08/05/82	Football League Division 1	at Upton Park	Attendance 26337
Result:	**West Ham United 1 Manchester United 1**			
Teamsheet:	Bailey, Gidman, Albiston, Wilkins, Moran, Duxbury, Moses, Birtles, Stapleton, Grimes, Coppell			
Substitute(s):	McGarvey	Scorer(s): Moran		

Match # 3587	Wednesday 12/05/82	Football League Division 1	at The Hawthorns	Attendance 19707
Result:	**West Bromwich Albion 0 Manchester United 3**			
Teamsheet:	Bailey, Gidman, Albiston, Wilkins, Moran, McQueen, Robson, Birtles, Stapleton, Grimes, Coppell			
Scorer(s):	Birtles, Coppell, Robson			

Match # 3588	Saturday 15/05/82	Football League Division 1	at Old Trafford	Attendance 43072
Result:	**Manchester United 2 Stoke City 0**			
Teamsheet:	Bailey, Gidman, Albiston, Wilkins, Moran, McQueen, Robson, Birtles, Whiteside, Grimes, Coppell			
Substitute(s):	McGarvey	Scorer(s): Robson, Whiteside		

SEASON 1981/82 SUMMARY

APPEARANCES

PLAYER	LGE	FAC	LC	TOTAL
Albiston	42	1	2	45
Wilkins	42	1	2	45
Stapleton	41	1	2	44
Bailey	39	1	2	42
Gidman	36 (1)	1	2	39 (1)
Coppell	35 (1)	–	2	37 (1)
Birtles	32 (1)	1	2	35 (1)
Robson	32	1	2	35
Moran	30	1	2	33
Buchan	27	1	2	30
Moses	20 (1)	1	1	22 (1)
McQueen	21	–	–	21
Duxbury	19 (5)	–	– (1)	19 (6)
McIlroy	12	1	1	14
McGarvey	10 (6)	–	–	10 (6)
Macari	10 (1)	– (1)	–	10 (2)
Grimes	9 (2)	–	–	9 (2)
Roche	3	–	–	3
Whiteside	1 (1)	–	–	1 (1)
Davies	1	–	–	1
Nicholl	– (1)	–	–	– (1)

GOALSCORERS

PLAYER	LGE	FAC	LC	TOT
Stapleton	13	–	–	13
Birtles	11	–	–	11
Coppell	9	–	–	9
Moran	7	–	–	7
Robson	5	–	–	5
McIlroy	3	–	–	3
Macari	2	–	–	2
McGarvey	2	–	–	2
Moses	2	–	–	2
Albiston	1	–	–	1
Gidman	1	–	–	1
Grimes	1	–	–	1
Whiteside	1	–	–	1
Wilkins	1	–	–	1

RESULTS & ATTENDANCES SUMMARY

		P	W	D	L	F	A	TOTAL	AVGE
League	H	21	12	6	3	27	9	935983	44571
	A	21	10	6	5	32	20	571483	27213
	TOTAL	42	22	12	8	59	29	1507466	35892
FA Cup	H	0	0	0	0	0	0	0	n/a
	A	1	0	0	1	0	1	26104	26104
	TOTAL	1	0	0	1	0	1	26104	26104
League	H	1	0	0	1	0	1	55890	55890
Cup	A	1	0	0	1	0	1	39333	39333
	TOTAL	2	0	0	2	0	2	95223	47612
Overall	H	22	12	6	4	27	10	991873	45085
	A	23	10	6	7	32	22	636920	27692
	TOTAL	45	22	12	11	59	32	1628793	36195

FINAL TABLE - LEAGUE DIVISION ONE

		P	W	D	L	F	A	W	D	L	F	A	PTS	GD
				HOME					AWAY					
1	Liverpool	42	14	3	4	39	14	12	6	3	41	18	87	48
2	Ipswich Town	42	17	1	3	47	25	9	4	8	28	28	83	22
3	MANCHESTER UNITED	42	12	6	3	27	9	10	6	5	32	20	78	30
4	Tottenham Hotspur	42	12	4	5	41	26	8	7	6	26	22	71	19
5	Arsenal	42	13	5	3	27	15	7	6	8	21	22	71	11
6	Swansea City	42	13	3	5	34	16	8	3	10	24	35	69	7
7	Southampton	42	15	2	4	49	30	4	7	10	23	37	66	5
8	Everton	42	11	7	3	33	21	6	6	9	23	29	64	6
9	West Ham United	42	9	10	2	42	29	5	6	10	24	28	58	9
10	Manchester City	42	9	7	5	32	23	6	6	9	17	27	58	-1
11	Aston Villa	42	9	6	6	28	24	6	6	9	27	29	57	2
12	Nottingham Forest	42	7	7	7	19	20	8	5	8	23	28	57	-6
13	Brighton & Hove Albion	42	8	7	6	30	24	5	6	10	13	28	52	-9
14	Coventry City	42	9	4	8	31	24	4	7	10	25	38	50	-6
15	Notts County	42	8	5	8	32	33	5	3	13	29	36	47	-8
16	Birmingham City	42	8	6	7	29	25	2	8	11	24	36	44	-8
17	West Bromwich Albion	42	6	6	9	24	25	5	5	11	22	32	44	-11
18	Stoke City	42	9	2	10	27	28	3	6	12	17	35	44	-19
19	Sunderland	42	6	5	10	19	26	5	6	10	19	32	44	-20
20	Leeds United	42	6	11	4	23	20	4	1	16	16	41	42	-22
21	Wolverhampton Wanderers	42	8	5	8	19	20	2	5	14	13	43	40	-31
22	Middlesbrough	42	5	9	7	20	24	3	6	12	14	28	39	-18

SEASON 1982/83

Match # 3589	Saturday 28/08/82	Football League Division 1	at Old Trafford	Attendance 48673
Result:	**Manchester United 3 Birmingham City 0**		
Teamsheet:	Bailey, Duxbury, Albiston, Wilkins, Moran, McQueen, Robson, Muhren, Stapleton, Whiteside, Coppell		
Scorer(s):	Coppell, Moran, Stapleton		

Match # 3590	Wednesday 01/09/82	Football League Division 1	at City Ground	Attendance 23956
Result:	**Nottingham Forest 0 Manchester United 3**		
Teamsheet:	Bailey, Duxbury, Albiston, Wilkins, Moran, McQueen, Robson, Muhren, Stapleton, Whiteside, Coppell		
Scorer(s):	Robson, Whiteside, Wilkins		

Match # 3591	Saturday 04/09/82	Football League Division 1	at The Hawthorns	Attendance 24928
Result:	**West Bromwich Albion 3 Manchester United 1**		
Teamsheet:	Bailey, Duxbury, Albiston, Wilkins, Moran, McQueen, Robson, Muhren, Stapleton, Whiteside, Coppell		
Scorer(s):	Robson		

Match # 3592	Wednesday 08/09/82	Football League Division 1	at Old Trafford	Attendance 43186
Result:	**Manchester United 2 Everton 1**		
Teamsheet:	Bailey, Duxbury, Albiston, Wilkins, Moran, McQueen, Robson, Muhren, Stapleton, Whiteside, Coppell		
Scorer(s):	Robson, Whiteside		

Match # 3593	Saturday 11/09/82	Football League Division 1	at Old Trafford	Attendance 43140
Result:	**Manchester United 3 Ipswich Town 1**		
Teamsheet:	Bailey, Duxbury, Albiston, Wilkins, Moran, McQueen, Robson, Muhren, Stapleton, Whiteside, Coppell		
Scorer(s):	Whiteside 2, Coppell		

Match # 3594	Wednesday 15/09/82	UEFA Cup 1st Round 1st Leg	at Old Trafford	Attendance 46588
Result:	**Manchester United 0 Valencia 0**		
Teamsheet:	Bailey, Duxbury, Albiston, Wilkins, Buchan, McQueen, Robson, Grimes, Stapleton, Whiteside, Coppell		

Match # 3595	Saturday 18/09/82	Football League Division 1	at The Dell	Attendance 21700
Result:	**Southampton 0 Manchester United 1**		
Teamsheet:	Bailey, Duxbury, Albiston, Wilkins, Buchan, McQueen, Robson, Grimes, Stapleton, Whiteside, Coppell		
Substitute(s):	Macari Scorer(s): Macari		

Match # 3596	Saturday 25/09/82	Football League Division 1	at Old Trafford	Attendance 43198
Result:	**Manchester United 0 Arsenal 0**		
Teamsheet:	Bailey, Duxbury, Albiston, Wilkins, Moran, McQueen, Robson, Grimes, Stapleton, Whiteside, Macari		

Match # 3597	Wednesday 29/09/82	UEFA Cup 1st Round 2nd Leg	at Luis Casanova	Attendance 35000
Result:	**Valencia 2 Manchester United 1**		
Teamsheet:	Bailey, Duxbury, Albiston, Wilkins, Moran, Buchan, Robson, Grimes, Stapleton, Whiteside, Moses		
Substitute(s):	Coppell, Macari Scorer(s): Robson		

Match # 3598	Saturday 02/10/82	Football League Division 1	at Kenilworth Road	Attendance 17009
Result:	**Luton Town 1 Manchester United 1**		
Teamsheet:	Bailey, Duxbury, Albiston, Wilkins, Moran, McQueen, Robson, Grimes, Stapleton, Whiteside, Moses		
Scorer(s):	Grimes		

Match # 3599	Wednesday 06/10/82	League Cup 2nd Round 1st Leg	at Old Trafford	Attendance 22091
Result:	**Manchester United 2 Bournemouth 0**		
Teamsheet:	Bailey, Duxbury, Albiston, Wilkins, Moran, McQueen, Robson, Grimes, Stapleton, Beardsley, Moses		
Substitute(s):	Whiteside Scorer(s): Stapleton, own goal		

Match # 3600	Saturday 09/10/82	Football League Division 1	at Old Trafford	Attendance 43132
Result:	**Manchester United 1 Stoke City 0**		
Teamsheet:	Bailey, Duxbury, Albiston, Wilkins, Moran, McQueen, Robson, Grimes, Stapleton, Whiteside, Moses		
Scorer(s):	Robson		

Match # 3601	Saturday 16/10/82	Football League Division 1	at Anfield	Attendance 40853
Result:	**Liverpool 0 Manchester United 0**		
Teamsheet:	Bailey, Duxbury, Albiston, Wilkins, Moran, McQueen, Robson, Grimes, Stapleton, Whiteside, Coppell		

Match # 3602	Saturday 23/10/82	Football League Division 1	at Old Trafford	Attendance 57334
Result:	**Manchester United 2 Manchester City 2**		
Teamsheet:	Bailey, Duxbury, Albiston, Wilkins, Moran, McQueen, Robson, Muhren, Stapleton, Whiteside, Coppell		
Substitute(s):	Macari Scorer(s): Stapleton 2		

Match # 3603	Tuesday 26/10/82	League Cup 2nd Round 2nd Leg	at Dean Court	Attendance 13226
Result:	**Bournemouth 2 Manchester United 2**		
Teamsheet:	Bailey, Duxbury, Albiston, Wilkins, Grimes, Buchan, Robson, Muhren, Stapleton, Whiteside, Coppell		
Substitute(s):	Macari Scorer(s): Coppell, Muhren		

Match # 3604	Saturday 30/10/82	Football League Division 1	at Upton Park	Attendance 31684
Result:	**West Ham United 3 Manchester United 1**		
Teamsheet:	Bailey, Duxbury, Albiston, Grimes, Moran, Buchan, Robson, Muhren, Stapleton, Whiteside, Coppell		
Scorer(s):	Moran		

Match # 3605	Saturday 06/11/82	Football League Division 1	at Goldstone Ground	Attendance 18379
Result:	**Brighton 1 Manchester United 0**		
Teamsheet:	Bailey, Duxbury, Albiston, Moses, Moran, McQueen, Robson, Muhren, Stapleton, Whiteside, Coppell		
Substitute(s):	Macari		

Match # 3606	Wednesday 10/11/82	League Cup 3rd Round	at Valley Parade	Attendance 15568
Result:	**Bradford City 0 Manchester United 0**		
Teamsheet:	Bailey, Duxbury, Albiston, Moses, McGrath, McQueen, Robson, Muhren, Stapleton, Whiteside, Coppell		

SEASON 1982/83 (continued)

Match # 3607   Saturday 13/11/82   Football League Division 1   at Old Trafford   Attendance 47869
Result: **Manchester United 1 Tottenham Hotspur 0**
Teamsheet: Bailey, Duxbury, Albiston, Moses, McGrath, McQueen, Robson, Muhren, Stapleton, Whiteside, Coppell
Scorer(s):   Muhren

Match # 3608   Saturday 20/11/82   Football League Division 1   at Villa Park   Attendance 35487
Result: **Aston Villa 2 Manchester United 1**
Teamsheet: Bailey, Duxbury, Albiston, Moses, Moran, McQueen, Robson, Muhren, Stapleton, Whiteside, Coppell
Substitute(s): McGarvey   Scorer(s):   Stapleton

Match # 3609   Wednesday 24/11/82   League Cup 3rd Round Replay   at Old Trafford   Attendance 24507
Result: **Manchester United 4 Bradford City 1**
Teamsheet: Bailey, Duxbury, Albiston, Moses, Moran, McQueen, Robson, Muhren, Stapleton, Macari, Coppell
Substitute(s): Whiteside   Scorer(s):   Albiston, Coppell, Moran, Moses

Match # 3610   Saturday 27/11/82   Football League Division 1   at Old Trafford   Attendance 34579
Result: **Manchester United 3 Norwich City 0**
Teamsheet: Bailey, Duxbury, Albiston, Moses, Moran, McQueen, Robson, Muhren, Stapleton, Whiteside, Coppell
Scorer(s):   Robson 2, Muhren

Match # 3611   Wednesday 01/12/82   League Cup 4th Round   at Old Trafford   Attendance 28378
Result: **Manchester United 2 Southampton 0**
Teamsheet: Bailey, Duxbury, Albiston, Moses, Moran, McQueen, Robson, Muhren, Stapleton, Whiteside, Coppell
Scorer(s):   McQueen, Whiteside

Match # 3612   Saturday 04/12/82   Football League Division 1   at Vicarage Road   Attendance 25669
Result: **Watford 0 Manchester United 1**
Teamsheet: Bailey, Duxbury, Albiston, Moses, Buchan, McQueen, Robson, Muhren, Stapleton, Whiteside, Coppell
Scorer(s):   Whiteside

Match # 3613   Saturday 11/12/82   Football League Division 1   at Old Trafford   Attendance 33618
Result: **Manchester United 4 Notts County 0**
Teamsheet: Bailey, Duxbury, Albiston, Moses, Moran, McQueen, Robson, Muhren, Stapleton, Whiteside, Coppell
Substitute(s): Grimes   Scorer(s):   Duxbury, Robson, Stapleton, Whiteside

Match # 3614   Saturday 18/12/82   Football League Division 1   at Vetch Field   Attendance 15748
Result: **Swansea City 0 Manchester United 0**
Teamsheet: Bailey, Duxbury, Albiston, Moses, Moran, McQueen, Robson, Muhren, Stapleton, Whiteside, Coppell

Match # 3615   Monday 27/12/82   Football League Division 1   at Old Trafford   Attendance 47783
Result: **Manchester United 0 Sunderland 0**
Teamsheet: Bailey, Duxbury, Albiston, Moses, Moran, McQueen, Robson, Muhren, Stapleton, Whiteside, Coppell

Match # 3616   Tuesday 28/12/82   Football League Division 1   at Highfield Road   Attendance 18945
Result: **Coventry City 3 Manchester United 0**
Teamsheet: Bailey, Duxbury, Albiston, Moses, Moran, McQueen, Robson, Wilkins, Stapleton, McGarvey, Grimes

Match # 3617   Saturday 01/01/83   Football League Division 1   at Old Trafford   Attendance 41545
Result: **Manchester United 3 Aston Villa 1**
Teamsheet: Bailey, Duxbury, Albiston, Moses, Moran, McQueen, Robson, Muhren, Stapleton, Whiteside, Coppell
Scorer(s):   Stapleton 2, Coppell

Match # 3618   Monday 03/01/83   Football League Division 1   at Old Trafford   Attendance 39123
Result: **Manchester United 0 West Bromwich Albion 0**
Teamsheet: Bailey, Duxbury, Albiston, Moses, Moran, McQueen, Robson, Muhren, Stapleton, Whiteside, Coppell

Match # 3619   Saturday 08/01/83   FA Cup 3rd Round   at Old Trafford   Attendance 44143
Result: **Manchester United 2 West Ham United 0**
Teamsheet: Bailey, Duxbury, Albiston, Moses, Moran, McQueen, Robson, Muhren, Stapleton, Whiteside, Coppell
Scorer(s):   Coppell, Stapleton

Match # 3620   Saturday 15/01/83   Football League Division 1   at St Andrews   Attendance 19333
Result: **Birmingham City 1 Manchester United 2**
Teamsheet: Bailey, Duxbury, Albiston, Moses, Moran, McQueen, Robson, Muhren, Stapleton, Whiteside, Coppell
Scorer(s):   Robson, Whiteside

Match # 3621   Wednesday 19/01/83   League Cup 5th Round   at Old Trafford   Attendance 44413
Result: **Manchester United 4 Nottingham Forest 0**
Teamsheet: Bailey, Duxbury, Albiston, Moses, Moran, McQueen, Robson, Muhren, Stapleton, Whiteside, Coppell
Scorer(s):   McQueen 2, Coppell, Robson

Match # 3622   Saturday 22/01/83   Football League Division 1   at Old Trafford   Attendance 38615
Result: **Manchester United 2 Nottingham Forest 0**
Teamsheet: Bailey, Duxbury, Albiston, Moses, Moran, McQueen, Robson, Muhren, Stapleton, Whiteside, Coppell
Scorer(s):   Coppell, Muhren

Match # 3623   Saturday 29/01/83   FA Cup 4th Round   at Kenilworth Road   Attendance 20516
Result: **Luton Town 0 Manchester United 2**
Teamsheet: Bailey, Duxbury, Albiston, Moses, Moran, McQueen, Robson, Muhren, Stapleton, Whiteside, Coppell
Scorer(s):   Moran, Moses

Match # 3624   Saturday 05/02/83   Football League Division 1   at Portman Road   Attendance 23804
Result: **Ipswich Town 1 Manchester United 1**
Teamsheet: Bailey, Duxbury, Albiston, Moses, Moran, McQueen, Robson, Muhren, Stapleton, Whiteside, Coppell
Scorer(s):   Stapleton

SEASON 1982/83 (continued)

Match # 3625   Tuesday 15/02/83   League Cup Semi-Final 1st Leg   at Highbury   Attendance 43136
Result: **Arsenal 2 Manchester United 4**
Teamsheet: Bailey, Duxbury, Albiston, Moses, Moran, McQueen, Robson, Muhren, Stapleton, Whiteside, Coppell
Scorer(s):   Coppell 2, Stapleton, Whiteside

Match # 3626   Saturday 19/02/83   FA Cup 5th Round   at Baseball Ground   Attendance 33022
Result: **Derby County 0 Manchester United 1**
Teamsheet: Bailey, Duxbury, Albiston, Moses, Moran, McQueen, Robson, Muhren, Stapleton, Whiteside, Coppell
Scorer(s):   Whiteside

Match # 3627   Wednesday 23/02/83   League Cup Semi-Final 2nd Leg   at Old Trafford   Attendance 56635
Result: **Manchester United 2 Arsenal 1**
Teamsheet: Bailey, Duxbury, Albiston, Moses, Moran, McQueen, Robson, Muhren, Stapleton, Whiteside, Coppell
Substitute(s):   Wilkins   Scorer(s):   Coppell, Moran

Match # 3628   Saturday 26/02/83   Football League Division 1   at Old Trafford   Attendance 57397
Result: **Manchester United 1 Liverpool 1**
Teamsheet: Bailey, Duxbury, Albiston, Moses, Moran, McQueen, Wilkins, Muhren, Stapleton, Whiteside, Coppell
Substitute(s):   Macari   Scorer(s):   Muhren

Match # 3629   Wednesday 02/03/83   Football League Division 1   at Victoria Ground   Attendance 21266
Result: **Stoke City 1 Manchester United 0**
Teamsheet: Bailey, Duxbury, Albiston, Moses, McGrath, McQueen, Wilkins, Muhren, Stapleton, Whiteside, Coppell

Match # 3630   Saturday 05/03/83   Football League Division 1   at Maine Road   Attendance 45400
Result: **Manchester City 1 Manchester United 2**
Teamsheet: Bailey, Duxbury, Albiston, Moses, McGrath, McQueen, Wilkins, Muhren, Stapleton, Whiteside, Coppell
Scorer(s):   Stapleton 2

Match # 3631   Saturday 12/03/83   FA Cup 6th Round   at Old Trafford   Attendance 58198
Result: **Manchester United 1 Everton 0**
Teamsheet: Bailey, Duxbury, Albiston, Moses, Moran, McQueen, Wilkins, Muhren, Stapleton, Whiteside, Coppell
Substitute(s):   Macari   Scorer(s):   Stapleton

Match # 3632   Saturday 19/03/83   Football League Division 1   at Old Trafford   Attendance 36264
Result: **Manchester United 1 Brighton 1**
Teamsheet: Bailey, Gidman, Albiston, Grimes, McGrath, Duxbury, Wilkins, Muhren, Stapleton, Whiteside, Coppell
Substitute(s):   Macari   Scorer(s):   Albiston

Match # 3633   Tuesday 22/03/83   Football League Division 1   at Old Trafford   Attendance 30227
Result: **Manchester United 2 West Ham United 1**
Teamsheet: Bailey, Gidman, Albiston, Moses, McGrath, Duxbury, Wilkins, Muhren, Stapleton, McGarvey, Coppell
Substitute(s):   Macari   Scorer(s):   McGarvey, Stapleton

Match # 3634   Saturday 26/03/83   League Cup Final   at Wembley   Attendance 100000
Result: **Manchester United 1 Liverpool 2**
Teamsheet: Bailey, Duxbury, Albiston, Moses, Moran, McQueen, Wilkins, Muhren, Stapleton, Whiteside, Coppell
Substitute(s):   Macari   Scorer(s):   Whiteside

Match # 3635   Saturday 02/04/83   Football League Division 1   at Old Trafford   Attendance 36814
Result: **Manchester United 3 Coventry City 0**
Teamsheet: Wealands, Duxbury, Albiston, Moses, McGrath, McQueen, Wilkins, Muhren, Stapleton, Whiteside, Coppell
Substitute(s):   Macari   Scorer(s):   Macari, Stapleton, own goal

Match # 3636   Monday 04/04/83   Football League Division 1   at Roker Park   Attendance 31486
Result: **Sunderland 0 Manchester United 0**
Teamsheet: Wealands, Duxbury, Albiston, Moses, McGrath, McQueen, Wilkins, Muhren, Stapleton, Macari, Coppell
Substitute(s):   McGarvey

Match # 3637   Saturday 09/04/83   Football League Division 1   at Old Trafford   Attendance 37120
Result: **Manchester United 1 Southampton 1**
Teamsheet: Bailey, Duxbury, Albiston, Moses, McGrath, McQueen, Robson, Muhren, Stapleton, Whiteside, Wilkins
Scorer(s):   Robson

Match # 3638   Saturday 16/04/83   FA Cup Semi-Final   at Villa Park   Attendance 46535
Result: **Manchester United 2 Arsenal 1**
Teamsheet: Bailey, Duxbury, Albiston, Moses, Moran, McQueen, Robson, Wilkins, Stapleton, Whiteside, Grimes
Substitute(s):   McGrath   Scorer(s):   Robson, Whiteside

Match # 3639   Tuesday 19/04/83   Football League Division 1   at Goodison Park   Attendance 21715
Result: **Everton 2 Manchester United 0**
Teamsheet: Wealands, Duxbury, Albiston, Moses, McGrath, McQueen, Robson, Wilkins, Stapleton, Whiteside, Grimes
Substitute(s):   Cunningham

Match # 3640   Saturday 23/04/83   Football League Division 1   at Old Trafford   Attendance 43048
Result: **Manchester United 2 Watford 0**
Teamsheet: Wealands, Duxbury, Albiston, Moses, McGrath, McQueen, Robson, Wilkins, Stapleton, Whiteside, Grimes
Substitute(s):   Cunningham   Scorer(s):   Cunningham, Grimes

Match # 3641   Saturday 30/04/83   Football League Division 1   at Carrow Road   Attendance 22233
Result: **Norwich City 1 Manchester United 1**
Teamsheet: Bailey, Duxbury, Grimes, Moses, Moran, McQueen, Robson, Wilkins, Stapleton, Whiteside, Cunningham
Scorer(s):   Whiteside

Match # 3642   Monday 02/05/83   Football League Division 1   at Highbury   Attendance 23602
Result: **Arsenal 3 Manchester United 0**
Teamsheet: Bailey, Duxbury, Grimes, Moses, Moran, McQueen, McGrath, Wilkins, McGarvey, Whiteside, Cunningham

SEASON 1982/83 (continued)

Match # 3643	Saturday 07/05/83	Football League Division 1	at Old Trafford	Attendance 35724

Result: **Manchester United 2 Swansea City 1**
Teamsheet: Bailey, Duxbury, Grimes, Wilkins, Moran, McQueen, Robson, Muhren, Stapleton, Whiteside, Cunningham
Substitute(s): Davies   Scorer(s):   Robson, Stapleton

Match # 3644	Monday 09/05/83	Football League Division 1	at Old Trafford	Attendance 34213

Result: **Manchester United 3 Luton Town 0**
Teamsheet: Bailey, Duxbury, Grimes, McGrath, Moran, McQueen, Robson, Muhren, Stapleton, Whiteside, Davies
Substitute(s): McGarvey   Scorer(s):   McGrath 2, Stapleton

Match # 3645	Wednesday 11/05/83	Football League Division 1	at White Hart Lane	Attendance 32803

Result: **Tottenham Hotspur 2 Manchester United 0**
Teamsheet: Bailey, Duxbury, Albiston, Moses, Moran, McGrath, Robson, Muhren, Stapleton, Whiteside, Grimes
Substitute(s): McGarvey

Match # 3646	Saturday 14/05/83	Football League Division 1	at Meadow Lane	Attendance 14395

Result: **Notts County 3 Manchester United 2**
Teamsheet: Wealands, Gidman, Albiston, Moses, McGrath, Duxbury, Wilkins, Muhren, Stapleton, Whiteside, Davies
Scorer(s): McGrath, Muhren

Match # 3647	Saturday 21/05/83	FA Cup Final	at Wembley	Attendance 100000

Result: **Manchester United 2 Brighton 2**
Teamsheet: Bailey, Duxbury, Albiston, Wilkins, Moran, McQueen, Robson, Muhren, Stapleton, Whiteside, Davies
Scorer(s): Stapleton, Wilkins

Match # 3648	Thursday 26/05/83	FA Cup Final Replay	at Wembley	Attendance 92000

Result: **Manchester United 4 Brighton 0**
Teamsheet: Bailey, Duxbury, Albiston, Wilkins, Moran, McQueen, Robson, Muhren, Stapleton, Whiteside, Davies
Scorer(s): Robson 2, Muhren, Whiteside

SEASON 1982/83 SUMMARY

APPEARANCES

PLAYER	LGE	FAC	LC	UC	TOTAL
Duxbury	42	7	9	2	60
Stapleton	41	7	9	2	59
Albiston	38	7	9	2	56
Whiteside	39	7	7 (2)	2	55 (2)
Bailey	37	7	9	2	55
McQueen	37	7	8	1	53
Robson	33	6	8	2	49
Muhren	32	6	8	–	46
Moran	29	7	7	1	44
Moses	29	5	8	1	43
Coppell	29	4	8	1 (1)	42 (1)
Wilkins	26	4	3 (1)	2	35 (1)
Grimes	15 (1)	1	2	2	20 (1)
McGrath	14	– (1)	1	–	15 (1)
Buchan	3	–	1	2	6
Wealands	5	–	–	–	5
Davies	2 (1)	2	–	–	4 (1)
Macari	2 (7)	– (1)	1 (2)	– (1)	3 (11)
McGarvey	3 (4)	–	–	–	3 (4)
Cunningham	3 (2)	–	–	–	3 (2)
Gidman	3	–	–	–	3
Beardsley	–	–	1	–	1

GOALSCORERS

PLAYER	LGE	FAC	LC	UC	TOT
Stapleton	14	3	2	–	19
Robson	10	3	1	1	15
Whiteside	8	3	3	–	14
Coppell	4	1	6	–	11
Muhren	5	1	1	–	7
Moran	2	1	2	–	5
McGrath	3	–	–	–	3
McQueen	–	–	3	–	3
Grimes	2	–	–	–	2
Macari	2	–	–	–	2
Albiston	1	–	1	–	2
Moses	–	1	1	–	2
Wilkins	1	1	–	–	2
Cunningham	1	–	–	–	1
Duxbury	1	–	–	–	1
McGarvey	1	–	–	–	1
own goals	1	–	1	–	2

RESULTS & ATTENDANCES SUMMARY

		P	W	D	L	F	A	TOTAL	AVGE
League	H	21	14	7	0	39	10	872602	41552
	A	21	5	6	10	17	28	530395	25257
	TOTAL	42	19	13	10	56	38	1402997	33405
FA Cup	H	2	2	0	0	3	0	102341	51171
	A	2	2	0	0	3	0	53538	26769
	N	3	2	1	0	8	3	238535	79512
	TOTAL	7	6	1	0	14	3	394414	56345
League Cup	H	5	5	0	0	14	2	176024	35205
	A	3	1	2	0	6	4	71930	23977
	N	1	0	0	1	1	2	100000	100000
	TOTAL	9	6	2	1	21	8	347954	38662
UEFA Cup	H	1	0	1	0	0	0	46588	46588
	A	1	0	0	1	1	2	35000	35000
	TOTAL	2	0	1	1	1	2	81588	40794
Overall	H	29	21	8	0	56	12	1197555	41295
	A	27	8	8	11	27	34	690863	25588
	N	4	2	1	1	9	5	338535	84634
	TOTAL	60	31	17	12	92	51	2226953	37116

FINAL TABLE – LEAGUE DIVISION ONE

		P	HOME					AWAY					PTS	GD
			W	D	L	F	A	W	D	L	F	A		
1	Liverpool	42	16	4	1	55	16	8	6	7	32	21	82	50
2	Watford	42	16	2	3	49	20	6	3	12	25	37	71	17
3	MANCHESTER UNITED	42	14	7	0	39	10	5	6	10	17	28	70	18
4	Tottenham Hotspur	42	15	4	2	50	15	5	5	11	15	35	69	15
5	Nottingham Forest	42	12	5	4	34	18	8	4	9	28	32	69	12
6	Aston Villa	42	17	2	2	47	15	4	3	14	15	35	68	12
7	Everton	42	13	6	2	43	19	5	4	12	23	29	64	18
8	West Ham United	42	13	3	5	41	23	7	1	13	27	39	64	6
9	Ipswich Town	42	11	3	7	39	23	4	10	7	25	27	58	14
10	Arsenal	42	11	6	4	36	19	5	4	12	22	37	58	2
11	West Bromwich Albion	42	11	5	5	35	20	4	7	10	16	29	57	2
12	Southampton	42	11	5	5	36	22	4	7	10	18	36	57	–4
13	Stoke City	42	13	4	4	34	21	3	5	13	19	43	57	–11
14	Norwich City	42	10	6	5	30	18	4	6	11	22	40	54	–6
15	Notts County	42	12	4	5	37	25	3	3	15	18	46	52	–16
16	Sunderland	42	7	10	4	30	22	5	4	12	18	39	50	–13
17	Birmingham City	42	9	7	5	29	24	3	7	11	11	31	50	–15
18	Luton Town	42	7	7	7	34	33	5	6	10	31	51	49	–19
19	Coventry City	42	10	5	6	29	17	3	4	14	19	42	48	–11
20	Manchester City	42	9	5	7	26	23	4	3	14	21	47	47	–23
21	Swansea City	42	10	4	7	32	29	0	7	14	19	40	41	–18
22	Brighton & Hove Albion	42	8	7	6	25	22	1	6	14	13	46	40	–30

SEASON 1983/84

Match # 3649   Saturday 20/08/83   FA Charity Shield   at Wembley   Attendance 92000
Result: **Manchester United 2 Liverpool 0**
Teamsheet: Bailey, Duxbury, Albiston, Wilkins, Moran, McQueen, Robson, Muhren, Stapleton, Whiteside, Graham
Substitute(s):   Gidman   Scorer(s): Robson 2

Match # 3650   Saturday 27/08/83   Football League Division 1   at Old Trafford   Attendance 48742
Result: **Manchester United 3 Queens Park Rangers 1**
Teamsheet: Bailey, Duxbury, Albiston, Wilkins, Moran, McQueen, Robson, Muhren, Stapleton, Whiteside, Graham
Substitute(s):   Macari   Scorer(s): Muhren 2, Stapleton

Match # 3651   Monday 29/08/83   Football League Division 1   at Old Trafford   Attendance 43005
Result: **Manchester United 1 Nottingham Forest 2**
Teamsheet: Bailey, Duxbury, Albiston, Wilkins, Moran, McQueen, Robson, Muhren, Stapleton, Whiteside, Graham
Substitute(s):   Macari   Scorer(s): Moran

Match # 3652   Saturday 03/09/83   Football League Division 1   at Victoria Ground   Attendance 23704
Result: **Stoke City 0 Manchester United 1**
Teamsheet: Bailey, Gidman, Albiston, Wilkins, Moran, McQueen, Robson, Muhren, Stapleton, Whiteside, Graham
Scorer(s):   Muhren

Match # 3653   Tuesday 06/09/83   Football League Division 1   at Highbury   Attendance 42703
Result: **Arsenal 2 Manchester United 3**
Teamsheet: Bailey, Gidman, Albiston, Wilkins, Moran, McQueen, Robson, Muhren, Stapleton, Whiteside, Graham
Substitute(s):   Moses   Scorer(s): Moran, Robson, Stapleton

Match # 3654   Saturday 10/09/83   Football League Division 1   at Old Trafford   Attendance 41013
Result: **Manchester United 2 Luton Town 0**
Teamsheet: Bailey, Gidman, Albiston, Wilkins, Moran, McQueen, Robson, Muhren, Stapleton, Whiteside, Graham
Substitute(s):   Moses   Scorer(s): Albiston, Muhren

Match # 3655   Wednesday 14/09/83   European CWC 1st Round 1st Leg   at Old Trafford   Attendance 39745
Result: **Manchester United 1 Dukla Prague 1**
Teamsheet: Bailey, Duxbury, Albiston, Wilkins, Moran, McQueen, Robson, Muhren, Stapleton, Macari, Graham
Substitute(s):   Gidman, Moses   Scorer(s): Wilkins

Match # 3656   Saturday 17/09/83   Football League Division 1   at The Dell   Attendance 20674
Result: **Southampton 3 Manchester United 0**
Teamsheet: Bailey, Duxbury, Albiston, Wilkins, Moran, McQueen, Moses, Muhren, Stapleton, Whiteside, Graham

Match # 3657   Saturday 24/09/83   Football League Division 1   at Old Trafford   Attendance 56121
Result: **Manchester United 1 Liverpool 0**
Teamsheet: Bailey, Duxbury, Albiston, Wilkins, Moran, McQueen, Robson, Muhren, Stapleton, Whiteside, Graham
Scorer(s):   Stapleton

Match # 3658   Tuesday 27/09/83   European CWC 1st Round 2nd Leg   at Stadion Juliska   Attendance 28850
Result: **Dukla Prague 2 Manchester United 2   (United won the tie on away goals rule)**
Teamsheet: Bailey, Duxbury, Albiston, Wilkins, Moran, McQueen, Robson, Muhren, Stapleton, Whiteside, Graham
Scorer(s):   Robson, Stapleton

Match # 3659   Saturday 01/10/83   Football League Division 1   at Carrow Road   Attendance 19290
Result: **Norwich City 3 Manchester United 3**
Teamsheet: Bailey, Duxbury, Albiston, Wilkins, Moran, McGrath, Robson, Muhren, Stapleton, Whiteside, Graham
Substitute(s):   Moses   Scorer(s): Whiteside 2, Stapleton

Match # 3660   Monday 03/10/83   League Cup 2nd Round 1st Leg   at Vale Park   Attendance 19885
Result: **Port Vale 0 Manchester United 1**
Teamsheet: Bailey, Duxbury, Albiston, Wilkins, Moran, McGrath, Robson, Muhren, Stapleton, Whiteside, Graham
Substitute(s):   Moses   Scorer(s): Stapleton

Match # 3661   Saturday 15/10/83   Football League Division 1   at Old Trafford   Attendance 42221
Result: **Manchester United 3 West Bromwich Albion 0**
Teamsheet: Bailey, Duxbury, Albiston, Wilkins, Moran, McQueen, Robson, Muhren, Stapleton, Whiteside, Graham
Scorer(s):   Albiston, Graham, Whiteside

Match # 3662   Wednesday 19/10/83   European CWC 2nd Round 1st Leg   at Stad Yuri Gargarin   Attendance 40000
Result: **Spartak Varna 1 Manchester United 2**
Teamsheet: Bailey, Duxbury, Albiston, Wilkins, Moran, McQueen, Robson, Muhren, Stapleton, Whiteside, Graham
Scorer(s):   Graham, Robson

Match # 3663   Saturday 22/10/83   Football League Division 1   at Roker Park   Attendance 26826
Result: **Sunderland 0 Manchester United 1**
Teamsheet: Bailey, Duxbury, Albiston, Wilkins, Moran, McQueen, Robson, Moses, Stapleton, Whiteside, Graham
Substitute(s):   Macari   Scorer(s): Wilkins

Match # 3664   Wednesday 26/10/83   League Cup 2nd Round 2nd Leg   at Old Trafford   Attendance 23589
Result: **Manchester United 2 Port Vale 0**
Teamsheet: Bailey, Gidman, Albiston, Wilkins, Duxbury, McQueen, Robson, Moses, Stapleton, Whiteside, Graham
Substitute(s):   Hughes   Scorer(s): Whiteside, Wilkins

Match # 3665   Saturday 29/10/83   Football League Division 1   at Old Trafford   Attendance 41880
Result: **Manchester United 3 Wolverhampton Wanderers 0**
Teamsheet: Bailey, Gidman, Albiston, Wilkins, Duxbury, McQueen, Robson, Muhren, Stapleton, Whiteside, Graham
Substitute(s):   Moses   Scorer(s): Stapleton 2, Robson

Match # 3666   Wednesday 02/11/83   European CWC 2nd Round 2nd Leg   at Old Trafford   Attendance 39079
Result: **Manchester United 2 Spartak Varna 0**
Teamsheet: Bailey, Duxbury, Albiston, Moses, Moran, McQueen, Robson, Macari, Stapleton, Whiteside, Graham
Substitute(s):   Dempsey, Hughes   Scorer(s): Stapleton 2

SEASON 1983/84 (continued)

Match # 3667   Saturday 05/11/83   Football League Division 1   at Old Trafford   Attendance 45077
Result: **Manchester United 1 Aston Villa 2**
Teamsheet: Bailey, Duxbury, Albiston, Wilkins, Moran, McQueen, Robson, Moses, Stapleton, Whiteside, Graham
Substitute(s):   Macari   Scorer(s): Robson

Match # 3668   Tuesday 08/11/83   League Cup 3rd Round   at Layer Road   Attendance 13031
Result: **Colchester United 0 Manchester United 2**
Teamsheet: Bailey, Duxbury, Albiston, Wilkins, Moran, McQueen, Robson, Moses, Stapleton, Whiteside, Graham
Substitute(s):   Macari   Scorer(s): McQueen, Moses

Match # 3669   Saturday 12/11/83   Football League Division 1   at Filbert Street   Attendance 24409
Result: **Leicester City 1 Manchester United 1**
Teamsheet: Bailey, Duxbury, Albiston, Wilkins, Moran, McQueen, Robson, Moses, Stapleton, Whiteside, Graham
Scorer(s):   Robson

Match # 3670   Saturday 19/11/83   Football League Division 1   at Old Trafford   Attendance 43111
Result: **Manchester United 4 Watford 1**
Teamsheet: Bailey, Moses, Albiston, Wilkins, Duxbury, McQueen, Robson, Muhren, Stapleton, Crooks, Graham
Scorer(s):   Stapleton 3, Robson

Match # 3671   Sunday 27/11/83   Football League Division 1   at Upton Park   Attendance 23355
Result: **West Ham United 1 Manchester United 1**
Teamsheet: Bailey, Moses, Albiston, Wilkins, Duxbury, McQueen, Robson, Muhren, Stapleton, Crooks, Graham
Substitute(s):   Whiteside   Scorer(s): Wilkins

Match # 3672   Wednesday 30/11/83   League Cup 4th Round   at Manor Ground   Attendance 13739
Result: **Oxford United 1 Manchester United 1**
Teamsheet: Bailey, Duxbury, Albiston, Wilkins, Moran, McQueen, Robson, Moses, Stapleton, Whiteside, Hughes
Scorer(s):   Hughes

Match # 3673   Saturday 03/12/83   Football League Division 1   at Old Trafford   Attendance 43664
Result: **Manchester United 0 Everton 1**
Teamsheet: Bailey, Duxbury, Albiston, Wilkins, Moran, McQueen, Robson, Moses, Stapleton, Crooks, Whiteside

Match # 3674   Wednesday 07/12/83   League Cup 4th Round Replay   at Old Trafford   Attendance 27459
Result: **Manchester United 1 Oxford United 1**
Teamsheet: Bailey, Duxbury, Albiston, Wilkins, Moran, McQueen, Robson, Moses, Stapleton, Whiteside, Graham
Scorer(s):   Stapleton

Match # 3675   Saturday 10/12/83   Football League Division 1   at Portman Road   Attendance 19779
Result: **Ipswich Town 0 Manchester United 2**
Teamsheet: Bailey, Duxbury, Albiston, Wilkins, Moran, McQueen, Robson, Moses, Stapleton, Crooks, Graham
Scorer(s):   Crooks, Graham

Match # 3676   Friday 16/12/83   Football League Division 1   at Old Trafford   Attendance 33616
Result: **Manchester United 4 Tottenham Hotspur 2**
Teamsheet: Bailey, Moses, Albiston, Wilkins, Moran, Duxbury, Robson, Muhren, Stapleton, Whiteside, Graham
Substitute(s):   Macari   Scorer(s): Graham 2, Moran 2

Match # 3677   Monday 19/12/83   League Cup 4th Round 2nd Replay   at Manor Ground   Attendance 13912
Result: **Oxford United 2 Manchester United 1**
Teamsheet: Wealands, Moses, Albiston, Wilkins, Moran, Duxbury, Robson, Muhren, Stapleton, Whiteside, Graham
Substitute(s):   Macari   Scorer(s): Graham

Match # 3678   Monday 26/12/83   Football League Division 1   at Highfield Road   Attendance 21553
Result: **Coventry City 1 Manchester United 1**
Teamsheet: Bailey, Duxbury, Albiston, Wilkins, Moran, McQueen, Moses, Muhren, Stapleton, Crooks, Graham
Scorer(s):   Muhren

Match # 3679   Tuesday 27/12/83   Football League Division 1   at Old Trafford   Attendance 41544
Result: **Manchester United 3 Notts County 3**
Teamsheet: Wealands, Duxbury, Albiston, Wilkins, Moran, McQueen, Moses, Muhren, Stapleton, Crooks, Graham
Substitute(s):   Whiteside   Scorer(s): Crooks, McQueen, Moran

Match # 3680   Saturday 31/12/83   Football League Division 1   at Old Trafford   Attendance 40164
Result: **Manchester United 1 Stoke City 0**
Teamsheet: Wealands, Duxbury, Albiston, Wilkins, Moran, McQueen, Moses, Muhren, Stapleton, Whiteside, Graham
Scorer(s):   Graham

Match # 3681   Monday 02/01/84   Football League Division 1   at Anfield   Attendance 44622
Result: **Liverpool 1 Manchester United 1**
Teamsheet: Bailey, Duxbury, Albiston, Wilkins, Moran, McQueen, Moses, Muhren, Stapleton, Whiteside, Graham
Substitute(s):   Crooks   Scorer(s): Whiteside

Match # 3682   Saturday 07/01/84   FA Cup 3rd Round   at Dean Court   Attendance 14782
Result: **Bournemouth 2 Manchester United 0**
Teamsheet: Bailey, Moses, Albiston, Wilkins, Hogg, Duxbury, Robson, Muhren, Stapleton, Whiteside, Graham
Substitute(s):   Macari

Match # 3683   Friday 13/01/84   Football League Division 1   at Loftus Road   Attendance 16308
Result: **Queens Park Rangers 1 Manchester United 1**
Teamsheet: Bailey, Duxbury, Moses, Wilkins, Moran, Hogg, Robson, Muhren, Stapleton, Whiteside, Graham
Scorer(s):   Robson

Match # 3684   Saturday 21/01/84   Football League Division 1   at Old Trafford   Attendance 40371
Result: **Manchester United 3 Southampton 2**
Teamsheet: Bailey, Duxbury, Moses, Wilkins, Moran, Hogg, Robson, Muhren, Stapleton, Whiteside, Graham
Substitute(s):   Hughes   Scorer(s): Muhren, Robson, Stapleton

SEASON 1983/84 (continued)

Match # 3685 Saturday 04/02/84 Football League Division 1 at Old Trafford Attendance 36851
Result: **Manchester United 0 Norwich City 0**
Teamsheet: Bailey, Moses, Albiston, Wilkins, Moran, Duxbury, Robson, Muhren, Stapleton, Whiteside, Graham

Match # 3686 Tuesday 07/02/84 Football League Division 1 at St Andrews Attendance 19957
Result: **Birmingham City 2 Manchester United 2**
Teamsheet: Bailey, Duxbury, Albiston, Wilkins, Moran, Hogg, Robson, Moses, Stapleton, Whiteside, Graham
Scorer(s): Hogg, Whiteside

Match # 3687 Sunday 12/02/84 Football League Division 1 at Kenilworth Road Attendance 11265
Result: **Luton Town 0 Manchester United 5**
Teamsheet: Bailey, Duxbury, Albiston, Wilkins, Moran, Hogg, Robson, Muhren, Stapleton, Whiteside, Moses
Substitute(s): Graham Scorer(s): Robson 2, Whiteside 2, Stapleton

Match # 3688 Saturday 18/02/84 Football League Division 1 at Molineux Attendance 20676
Result: **Wolverhampton Wanderers 1 Manchester United 1**
Teamsheet: Bailey, Duxbury, Albiston, Wilkins, Moran, Hogg, Robson, Muhren, Stapleton, Whiteside, Moses
Substitute(s): Graham Scorer(s): Whiteside

Match # 3689 Saturday 25/02/84 Football League Division 1 at Old Trafford Attendance 40615
Result: **Manchester United 2 Sunderland 1**
Teamsheet: Bailey, Duxbury, Albiston, Wilkins, Moran, Hogg, Robson, Muhren, Stapleton, Whiteside, Moses
Substitute(s): Graham Scorer(s): Moran 2

Match # 3690 Saturday 03/03/84 Football League Division 1 at Villa Park Attendance 32874
Result: **Aston Villa 0 Manchester United 3**
Teamsheet: Bailey, Duxbury, Albiston, Wilkins, McGrath, Hogg, Robson, Muhren, Stapleton, Whiteside, Moses
Substitute(s): Graham Scorer(s): Moses, Robson, Whiteside

Match # 3691 Wednesday 07/03/84 European CWC 3rd Round 1st Leg at Estadio Camp Nou Attendance 70000
Result: **Barcelona 2 Manchester United 0**
Teamsheet: Bailey, Duxbury, Albiston, Wilkins, Moran, Hogg, Robson, Muhren, Stapleton, Hughes, Moses
Substitute(s): Graham

Match # 3692 Saturday 10/03/84 Football League Division 1 at Old Trafford Attendance 39473
Result: **Manchester United 2 Leicester City 0**
Teamsheet: Bailey, Duxbury, Albiston, Wilkins, Moran, Hogg, Robson, Muhren, Stapleton, Hughes, Moses
Scorer(s): Hughes, Moses

Match # 3693 Saturday 17/03/84 Football League Division 1 at Old Trafford Attendance 48942
Result: **Manchester United 4 Arsenal 0**
Teamsheet: Bailey, Duxbury, Albiston, Wilkins, Moran, Hogg, Robson, Muhren, Stapleton, Whiteside, Moses
Substitute(s): Hughes Scorer(s): Muhren 2, Robson, Stapleton

Match # 3694 Wednesday 21/03/84 European CWC 3rd Round 2nd Leg at Old Trafford Attendance 58547
Result: **Manchester United 3 Barcelona 0**
Teamsheet: Bailey, Duxbury, Albiston, Wilkins, Moran, Hogg, Robson, Muhren, Stapleton, Whiteside, Moses
Substitute(s): Hughes Scorer(s): Robson 2, Stapleton

Match # 3695 Saturday 31/03/84 Football League Division 1 at The Hawthorns Attendance 28104
Result: **West Bromwich Albion 2 Manchester United 0**
Teamsheet: Bailey, Duxbury, Albiston, Wilkins, Moran, Hogg, Robson, Graham, Stapleton, Whiteside, Moses

Match # 3696 Saturday 07/04/84 Football League Division 1 at Old Trafford Attendance 39896
Result: **Manchester United 1 Birmingham City 0**
Teamsheet: Bailey, Duxbury, Albiston, Wilkins, Moran, Hogg, Robson, Graham, Stapleton, Whiteside, Moses
Substitute(s): Hughes Scorer(s): Robson

Match # 3697 Wednesday 11/04/84 European CWC Semi-Final 1st Leg at Old Trafford Attendance 58171
Result: **Manchester United 1 Juventus 1**
Teamsheet: Bailey, Duxbury, Albiston, McGrath, Moran, Hogg, Graham, Moses, Stapleton, Whiteside, Gidman
Substitute(s): Davies Scorer(s): Davies

Match # 3698 Saturday 14/04/84 Football League Division 1 at Meadow Lane Attendance 13911
Result: **Notts County 1 Manchester United 0**
Teamsheet: Bailey, Duxbury, Albiston, Wilkins, Moran, Hogg, McGrath, Moses, Stapleton, Whiteside, Davies
Substitute(s): Hughes

Match # 3699 Tuesday 17/04/84 Football League Division 1 at Vicarage Road Attendance 20764
Result: **Watford 0 Manchester United 0**
Teamsheet: Bailey, Duxbury, Albiston, Wilkins, Moran, Hogg, Davies, McGrath, Stapleton, Whiteside, Graham

Match # 3700 Saturday 21/04/84 Football League Division 1 at Old Trafford Attendance 38524
Result: **Manchester United 4 Coventry City 1**
Teamsheet: Bailey, Duxbury, Albiston, Wilkins, Moran, Hogg, McGrath, Moses, Stapleton, Hughes, Graham
Substitute(s): Whiteside Scorer(s): Hughes 2, McGrath, Wilkins

Match # 3701 Wednesday 25/04/84 European CWC Semi-Final 2nd Leg at Stadio Comunale Attendance 64655
Result: **Juventus 2 Manchester United 1**
Teamsheet: Bailey, Duxbury, Albiston, Wilkins, Moran, Hogg, McGrath, Moses, Stapleton, Hughes, Graham
Substitute(s): Whiteside Scorer(s): Whiteside

Match # 3702 Saturday 28/04/84 Football League Division 1 at Old Trafford Attendance 44124
Result: **Manchester United 0 West Ham United 0**
Teamsheet: Bailey, Duxbury, Albiston, Wilkins, Moran, Hogg, McGrath, Moses, Stapleton, Hughes, Graham
Substitute(s): Whiteside

SEASON 1983/84 (continued)

Match # 3703   Saturday 05/05/84   Football League Division 1   at Goodison Park   Attendance 28802
Result: **Everton 1 Manchester United 1**
Teamsheet: Bailey, Duxbury, Albiston, Wilkins, Moran, Hogg, Robson, Moses, Stapleton, Hughes, Davies
Substitute(s):   Whiteside   Scorer(s):   Stapleton

Match # 3704   Monday 07/05/84   Football League Division 1   at Old Trafford   Attendance 44257
Result: **Manchester United 1 Ipswich Town 2**
Teamsheet: Bailey, Duxbury, Albiston, Wilkins, Moran, McGrath, Robson, Moses, Stapleton, Hughes, Graham
Substitute(s):   Whiteside   Scorer(s):   Hughes

Match # 3705   Saturday 12/05/84   Football League Division 1   at White Hart Lane   Attendance 39790
Result: **Tottenham Hotspur 1 Manchester United 1**
Teamsheet: Bailey, Duxbury, Albiston, Wilkins, Moran, McGrath, Robson, Moses, Stapleton, Hughes, Graham
Substitute(s):   Whiteside   Scorer(s):   Whiteside

Match # 3706   Wednesday 16/05/84   Football League Division 1   at City Ground   Attendance 23651
Result: **Nottingham Forest 2 Manchester United 0**
Teamsheet: Bailey, Duxbury, Albiston, Wilkins, Moran, McGrath, Robson, Blackmore, Stapleton, Hughes, Graham

SEASON 1983/84 SUMMARY

APPEARANCES

PLAYER	LGE	FAC	LC	ECWC	CS	TOTAL
Stapleton	42	1	6	8	1	58
Albiston	40	1	6	8	1	56
Wilkins	42	1	6	6	1	56
Bailey	40	1	5	8	1	55
Duxbury	39	1	6	8	1	55
Moran	38	–	5	8	1	52
Robson	33	1	6	6	1	47
Graham	33 (4)	1	5	6 (1)	1	46 (5)
Whiteside	30 (7)	1	6	5 (1)	1	43 (8)
Moses	31 (4)	1	5 (1)	5 (1)	–	42 (6)
Muhren	26	1	2	5	1	35
McQueen	20	–	4	4	1	29
Hogg	16	1	–	4	–	21
McGrath	9	–	1	2	–	12
Hughes	7 (4)	–	1 (1)	2 (2)	–	10 (7)
Gidman	4	–	1	1 (1)	– (1)	6 (2)
Crooks	6 (1)	–	–	–	–	6 (1)
Davies	3	–	–	– (1)	–	3 (1)
Wealands	2	–	1	–	–	3
Macari	– (5)	– (1)	– (2)	2	–	2 (8)
Blackmore	1	–	–	–	–	1
Dempsey	–	–	–	– (1)	–	– (1)

GOALSCORERS

PLAYER	LGE	FAC	LC	ECWC	CS	TOTAL
Stapleton	13	–	2	4	–	19
Robson	12	–	–	4	2	18
Whiteside	10	–	1	1	–	12
Muhren	8	–	–	–	–	8
Moran	7	–	–	–	–	7
Graham	5	–	1	1	–	7
Hughes	4	–	1	–	–	5
Wilkins	3	–	1	1	–	5
Moses	2	–	1	–	–	3
Albiston	2	–	–	–	–	2
Crooks	2	–	–	–	–	2
McQueen	1	–	1	–	–	2
Hogg	1	–	–	–	–	1
McGrath	1	–	–	–	–	1
Davies	–	–	–	1	–	1

RESULTS & ATTENDANCES SUMMARY

		P	W	D	L	F	A	TOTAL	AVGE
League	H	21	14	3	4	43	18	893211	42534
	A	21	6	11	4	28	23	523017	24906
TOTAL		42	20	14	8	71	41	1416228	33720
FA Cup	H	0	0	0	0	0	0	0	n/a
	A	1	0	0	1	0	2	14782	14782
TOTAL		1	0	0	1	0	2	14782	14782
League	H	2	1	1	0	3	1	51048	25524
Cup	A	4	2	1	1	5	3	60567	15142
TOTAL		6	3	2	1	8	4	111615	18603
European	H	4	2	2	0	7	2	195542	48886
CWC	A	4	1	1	2	5	7	203505	50876
TOTAL		8	3	3	2	12	9	399047	49881
Charity	H	0	0	0	0	0	0	0	n/a
Shield	A	0	0	0	0	0	0	0	n/a
	N	1	1	0	0	2	0	92000	92000
TOTAL		1	1	0	0	2	0	92000	92000
Overall	H	27	17	6	4	53	21	1139801	42215
	A	30	9	13	8	38	35	801871	26729
	N	1	1	0	0	2	0	92000	92000
TOTAL		58	27	19	12	93	56	2033672	35063

FINAL TABLE – LEAGUE DIVISION ONE

		P	W	D	L	F	A	W	D	L	F	A	PTS	GD
				HOME					AWAY					
1	Liverpool	42	14	5	2	50	12	8	9	4	23	20	80	41
2	Southampton	42	15	4	2	44	17	7	7	7	22	21	77	28
3	Nottingham Forest	42	14	4	3	47	17	8	4	9	29	28	74	31
4	MANCHESTER UNITED	42	14	3	4	43	18	6	11	4	28	23	74	30
5	Queens Park Rangers	42	14	4	3	37	12	8	3	10	30	25	73	30
6	Arsenal	42	10	5	6	41	29	8	4	9	33	31	63	14
7	Everton	42	9	9	3	21	12	7	5	9	23	30	62	2
8	Tottenham Hotspur	42	11	4	6	31	24	6	6	9	33	41	61	-1
9	West Ham United	42	10	4	7	39	24	7	5	9	21	31	60	5
10	Aston Villa	42	14	3	4	34	22	3	6	12	25	39	60	-2
11	Watford	42	9	7	5	36	31	7	2	12	32	46	57	-9
12	Ipswich Town	42	11	4	6	34	23	4	4	13	21	34	53	-2
13	Sunderland	42	8	9	4	26	18	5	4	12	16	35	52	-11
14	Norwich City	42	9	8	4	34	20	3	7	11	14	29	51	-1
15	Leicester City	42	11	5	5	40	30	2	7	12	25	38	51	-3
16	Luton Town	42	7	5	9	30	33	7	4	10	23	33	51	-13
17	West Bromwich Albion	42	10	4	7	30	25	4	5	12	18	37	51	-14
18	Stoke City	42	11	4	6	30	23	2	7	12	14	40	50	-19
19	Coventry City	42	8	5	8	33	33	5	6	10	24	44	50	-20
20	Birmingham City	42	7	7	7	19	18	5	5	11	20	32	48	-11
21	Notts County	42	6	7	8	31	36	4	4	13	19	36	41	-22
22	Wolverhampton Wanderers	42	4	8	9	15	28	2	3	16	12	52	29	-53

SEASON 1984/85

Match # 3707 Saturday 25/08/84   Football League Division 1   at Old Trafford   Attendance 53668
Result: **Manchester United 1 Watford 1**
Teamsheet: Bailey, Duxbury, Albiston, Moses, Moran, Hogg, Robson, Strachan, Hughes, Brazil, Olsen
Substitute(s): Whiteside   Scorer(s):   Strachan

Match # 3708 Tuesday 28/08/84   Football League Division 1   at The Dell   Attendance 22183
Result: **Southampton 0 Manchester United 0**
Teamsheet: Bailey, Duxbury, Albiston, Moses, Moran, Hogg, Robson, Strachan, Hughes, Brazil, Olsen

Match # 3709 Saturday 01/09/84   Football League Division 1   at Portman Road   Attendance 20876
Result: **Ipswich Town 1 Manchester United 1**
Teamsheet: Bailey, Duxbury, Albiston, Moses, Moran, Hogg, Robson, Strachan, Hughes, Brazil, Olsen
Substitute(s): Whiteside   Scorer(s):   Hughes

Match # 3710 Wednesday 05/09/84   Football League Division 1   at Old Trafford   Attendance 48398
Result: **Manchester United 1 Chelsea 1**
Teamsheet: Bailey, Duxbury, Albiston, Moses, Moran, Hogg, Robson, Strachan, Hughes, Whiteside, Olsen
Scorer(s):   Olsen

Match # 3711 Saturday 08/09/84   Football League Division 1   at Old Trafford   Attendance 54915
Result: **Manchester United 5 Newcastle United 0**
Teamsheet: Bailey, Duxbury, Albiston, Moses, Moran, Hogg, Robson, Strachan, Hughes, Whiteside, Olsen
Scorer(s):   Strachan 2, Hughes, Moses, Olsen

Match # 3712 Saturday 15/09/84   Football League Division 1   at Highfield Road   Attendance 18312
Result: **Coventry City 0 Manchester United 3**
Teamsheet: Bailey, Duxbury, Albiston, Moses, Moran, Hogg, Robson, Strachan, Hughes, Whiteside, Olsen
Scorer(s):   Whiteside 2, Robson

Match # 3713 Wednesday 19/09/84   UEFA Cup 1st Round 1st Leg   at Old Trafford   Attendance 33119
Result: **Manchester United 3 Raba Vasas 0**
Teamsheet: Bailey, Duxbury, Albiston, Moses, Moran, Hogg, Robson, Muhren, Hughes, Whiteside, Olsen
Scorer(s):   Hughes, Muhren, Robson

Match # 3714 Saturday 22/09/84   Football League Division 1   at Old Trafford   Attendance 56638
Result: **Manchester United 1 Liverpool 1**
Teamsheet: Bailey, Duxbury, Albiston, Moses, Moran, Hogg, Robson, Strachan, Hughes, Whiteside, Olsen
Substitute(s): Muhren   Scorer(s):   Strachan

Match # 3715 Wednesday 26/09/84   League Cup 2nd Round 1st Leg   at Old Trafford   Attendance 28383
Result: **Manchester United 4 Burnley 0**
Teamsheet: Bailey, Duxbury, Albiston, Moses, Garton, Hogg, Robson, Graham, Hughes, Whiteside, Muhren
Substitute(s): Brazil   Scorer(s):   Hughes 3, Robson

Match # 3716 Saturday 29/09/84   Football League Division 1   at The Hawthorns   Attendance 26292
Result: **West Bromwich Albion 1 Manchester United 2**
Teamsheet: Bailey, Duxbury, Albiston, Moses, Moran, Hogg, Robson, Strachan, Hughes, Brazil, Olsen
Scorer(s):   Robson, Strachan

Match # 3717 Wednesday 03/10/84   UEFA Cup 1st Round 2nd Leg   at Raba ETO Stadium   Attendance 26000
Result: **Raba Vasas 2 Manchester United 2**
Teamsheet: Bailey, Duxbury, Albiston, Moses, Moran, Hogg, Robson, Muhren, Hughes, Brazil, Olsen
Substitute(s): Gidman   Scorer(s):   Brazil, Muhren

Match # 3718 Saturday 06/10/84   Football League Division 1   at Villa Park   Attendance 37131
Result: **Aston Villa 3 Manchester United 0**
Teamsheet: Bailey, Duxbury, Albiston, Moses, Moran, Hogg, Strachan, Muhren, Hughes, Brazil, Olsen

Match # 3719 Tuesday 09/10/84   League Cup 2nd Round 2nd Leg   at Turf Moor   Attendance 12690
Result: **Burnley 0 Manchester United 3**
Teamsheet: Bailey, Duxbury, Albiston, Moses, Moran, Hogg, Strachan, Blackmore, Stapleton, Brazil, Olsen
Scorer(s):   Brazil 2, Olsen

Match # 3720 Saturday 13/10/84   Football League Division 1   at Old Trafford   Attendance 47559
Result: **Manchester United 5 West Ham United 1**
Teamsheet: Bailey, Duxbury, Albiston, Moses, McQueen, Hogg, Robson, Strachan, Hughes, Brazil, Olsen
Scorer(s):   Brazil, Hughes, McQueen, Moses, Strachan

Match # 3721 Saturday 20/10/84   Football League Division 1   at Old Trafford   Attendance 54516
Result: **Manchester United 1 Tottenham Hotspur 0**
Teamsheet: Bailey, Gidman, Albiston, Moses, Moran, Hogg, Robson, Strachan, Hughes, Brazil, Olsen
Scorer(s):   Hughes

Match # 3722 Wednesday 24/10/84   UEFA Cup 2nd Round 1st Leg   at Philipstadion   Attendance 27500
Result: **PSV Eindhoven 0 Manchester United 0**
Teamsheet: Bailey, Gidman, Albiston, Moses, Moran, Hogg, Robson, Strachan, Hughes, Brazil, Olsen

Match # 3723 Saturday 27/10/84   Football League Division 1   at Goodison Park   Attendance 40742
Result: **Everton 5 Manchester United 0**
Teamsheet: Bailey, Moran, Albiston, Moses, McQueen, Hogg, Robson, Strachan, Hughes, Brazil, Olsen
Substitute(s): Stapleton

Match # 3724 Tuesday 30/10/84   League Cup 3rd Round   at Old Trafford   Attendance 50918
Result: **Manchester United 1 Everton 2**
Teamsheet: Bailey, Gidman, Albiston, Moses, Moran, Hogg, Robson, Strachan, Hughes, Brazil, Olsen
Substitute(s): Stapleton   Scorer(s):   Brazil

SEASON 1984/85 (continued)

Match # 3725   Friday 02/11/84   Football League Division 1   at Old Trafford   Attendance 32279
Result: **Manchester United 4 Arsenal 2**
Teamsheet: Bailey, Gidman, Albiston, Moses, Moran, Hogg, Robson, Strachan, Hughes, Stapleton, Olsen
Scorer(s):   Strachan 2, Hughes, Robson

Match # 3726   Wednesday 07/11/84   UEFA Cup 2nd Round 2nd Leg   at Old Trafford   Attendance 39281
Result: **Manchester United 1 PSV Eindhoven 0**
Teamsheet: Bailey, Gidman, Albiston, Moses, Moran, Hogg, Robson, Strachan, Hughes, Stapleton, Olsen
Substitute(s):   Garton, Whiteside   Scorer(s):   Strachan

Match # 3727   Saturday 10/11/84   Football League Division 1   at Filbert Street   Attendance 23840
Result: **Leicester City 2 Manchester United 3**
Teamsheet: Bailey, Gidman, Albiston, Moses, Garton, Hogg, Robson, Strachan, Hughes, Brazil, Olsen
Substitute(s):   Whiteside   Scorer(s):   Brazil, Hughes, Strachan

Match # 3728   Saturday 17/11/84   Football League Division 1   at Old Trafford   Attendance 41630
Result: **Manchester United 2 Luton Town 0**
Teamsheet: Bailey, Gidman, Albiston, Moses, McQueen, Duxbury, Robson, Strachan, Hughes, Whiteside, Olsen
Substitute(s):   Stapleton   Scorer(s):   Whiteside 2

Match # 3729   Saturday 24/11/84   Football League Division 1   at Roker Park   Attendance 25405
Result: **Sunderland 3 Manchester United 2**
Teamsheet: Bailey, Gidman, Duxbury, Moses, McQueen, Garton, Robson, Strachan, Hughes, Whiteside, Olsen
Substitute(s):   Muhren   Scorer(s):   Hughes, Robson

Match # 3730   Wednesday 28/11/84   UEFA Cup 3rd Round 1st Leg   at Old Trafford   Attendance 48278
Result: **Manchester United 2 Dundee United 2**
Teamsheet: Bailey, Gidman, Albiston, Moses, McQueen, Duxbury, Robson, Strachan, Hughes, Whiteside, Olsen
Substitute(s):   Stapleton   Scorer(s):   Robson, Strachan

Match # 3731   Saturday 01/12/84   Football League Division 1   at Old Trafford   Attendance 36635
Result: **Manchester United 2 Norwich City 0**
Teamsheet: Bailey, Gidman, Duxbury, Moses, McQueen, McGrath, Robson, Strachan, Hughes, Whiteside, Olsen
Scorer(s):   Hughes, Robson

Match # 3732   Saturday 08/12/84   Football League Division 1   at City Ground   Attendance 25902
Result: **Nottingham Forest 3 Manchester United 2**
Teamsheet: Bailey, Duxbury, Blackmore, Moses, McQueen, McGrath, Robson, Strachan, Stapleton, Brazil, Muhren
Scorer(s):   Strachan 2

Match # 3733   Wednesday 12/12/84   UEFA Cup 3rd Round 2nd Leg   at Tannadice Park   Attendance 21821
Result: **Dundee United 2 Manchester United 3**
Teamsheet: Bailey, Gidman, Albiston, Moses, McQueen, Duxbury, Robson, Strachan, Stapleton, Hughes, Muhren
Scorer(s):   Hughes, Muhren, own goal

Match # 3734   Saturday 15/12/84   Football League Division 1   at Old Trafford   Attendance 36134
Result: **Manchester United 3 Queens Park Rangers 0**
Teamsheet: Bailey, Gidman, Albiston, Moses, McQueen, Duxbury, Robson, Strachan, Stapleton, Brazil, Olsen
Scorer(s):   Brazil, Duxbury, Gidman

Match # 3735   Saturday 22/12/84   Football League Division 1   at Old Trafford   Attendance 35168
Result: **Manchester United 3 Ipswich Town 0**
Teamsheet: Bailey, Gidman, Albiston, Moses, McQueen, Duxbury, Robson, Strachan, Hughes, Stapleton, Olsen
Scorer(s):   Gidman, Robson, Strachan

Match # 3736   Wednesday 26/12/84   Football League Division 1   at Victoria Ground   Attendance 20985
Result: **Stoke City 2 Manchester United 1**
Teamsheet: Bailey, Gidman, Albiston, Moses, McQueen, Duxbury, Robson, Strachan, Hughes, Stapleton, Muhren
Substitute(s):   Brazil   Scorer(s):   Stapleton

Match # 3737   Saturday 29/12/84   Football League Division 1   at Stamford Bridge   Attendance 42197
Result: **Chelsea 1 Manchester United 3**
Teamsheet: Bailey, Duxbury, Albiston, Moses, McQueen, McGrath, Robson, Strachan, Stapleton, Hughes, Muhren
Scorer(s):   Hughes, Moses, Stapleton

Match # 3738   Tuesday 01/01/85   Football League Division 1   at Old Trafford   Attendance 47625
Result: **Manchester United 1 Sheffield Wednesday 2**
Teamsheet: Bailey, Duxbury, Albiston, Moses, McQueen, McGrath, Robson, Strachan, Hughes, Brazil, Muhren
Scorer(s):   Hughes

Match # 3739   Saturday 05/01/85   FA Cup 3rd Round   at Old Trafford   Attendance 32080
Result: **Manchester United 3 Bournemouth 0**
Teamsheet: Bailey, Duxbury, Albiston, Moses, McQueen, McGrath, Robson, Strachan, Stapleton, Hughes, Muhren
Scorer(s):   McQueen, Stapleton, Strachan

Match # 3740   Saturday 12/01/85   Football League Division 1   at Old Trafford   Attendance 35992
Result: **Manchester United 0 Coventry City 1**
Teamsheet: Pears, Duxbury, Albiston, Moses, McQueen, McGrath, Robson, Strachan, Stapleton, Hughes, Muhren
Substitute(s):   Brazil

Match # 3741   Saturday 26/01/85   FA Cup 4th Round   at Old Trafford   Attendance 38039
Result: **Manchester United 2 Coventry City 1**
Teamsheet: Pears, Gidman, Albiston, Moses, Moran, Hogg, McGrath, Strachan, Whiteside, Hughes, Olsen
Substitute(s):   Brazil   Scorer(s):   Hughes, McGrath

Match # 3742   Saturday 02/02/85   Football League Division 1   at Old Trafford   Attendance 36681
Result: **Manchester United 2 West Bromwich Albion 0**
Teamsheet: Pears, Gidman, Albiston, Moses, Moran, Hogg, McGrath, Strachan, Hughes, Whiteside, Olsen
Scorer(s):   Strachan 2

SEASON 1984/85 (continued)

Match # 3743 Saturday 09/02/85 Football League Division 1 at St James' Park Attendance 32555
Result: **Newcastle United 1 Manchester United 1**
Teamsheet: Pears, Gidman, Albiston, Moses, Moran, Hogg, McGrath, Strachan, Hughes, Whiteside, Olsen
Substitute(s): Stapleton Scorer(s): Moran

Match # 3744 Friday 15/02/85 FA Cup 5th Round at Ewood Park Attendance 22692
Result: **Blackburn Rovers 0 Manchester United 2**
Teamsheet: Bailey, Gidman, Albiston, Moses, Moran, Hogg, McGrath, Strachan, Hughes, Whiteside, Olsen
Scorer(s): McGrath, Strachan

Match # 3745 Saturday 23/02/85 Football League Division 1 at Highbury Attendance 48612
Result: **Arsenal 0 Manchester United 1**
Teamsheet: Bailey, Gidman, Albiston, Duxbury, Moran, Hogg, McGrath, Strachan, Hughes, Stapleton, Olsen
Substitute(s): Whiteside Scorer(s): Whiteside

Match # 3746 Saturday 02/03/85 Football League Division 1 at Old Trafford Attendance 51150
Result: **Manchester United 1 Everton 1**
Teamsheet: Bailey, Gidman, Albiston, Duxbury, McGrath, Hogg, Strachan, Brazil, Hughes, Whiteside, Olsen
Scorer(s): Olsen

Match # 3747 Wednesday 06/03/85 UEFA Cup Quarter-Final 1st Leg at Old Trafford Attendance 35432
Result: **Manchester United 1 Videoton 0**
Teamsheet: Bailey, Gidman, Albiston, Duxbury, McGrath, Hogg, Strachan, Whiteside, Hughes, Stapleton, Olsen
Scorer(s): Stapleton

Match # 3748 Saturday 09/03/85 FA Cup 6th Round at Old Trafford Attendance 46769
Result: **Manchester United 4 West Ham United 2**
Teamsheet: Bailey, Gidman, Albiston, Duxbury, McGrath, Hogg, Strachan, Whiteside, Hughes, Stapleton, Olsen
Scorer(s): Whiteside 3, Hughes

Match # 3749 Tuesday 12/03/85 Football League Division 1 at White Hart Lane Attendance 42908
Result: **Tottenham Hotspur 1 Manchester United 2**
Teamsheet: Bailey, Gidman, Albiston, Duxbury, McGrath, Hogg, Strachan, Whiteside, Hughes, Stapleton, Olsen
Scorer(s): Hughes, Whiteside

Match # 3750 Friday 15/03/85 Football League Division 1 at Upton Park Attendance 16674
Result: **West Ham United 2 Manchester United 2**
Teamsheet: Bailey, Gidman, Albiston, Duxbury, McGrath, Hogg, Strachan, Whiteside, Hughes, Stapleton, Olsen
Substitute(s): Robson Scorer(s): Robson, Stapleton

Match # 3751 Wednesday 20/03/85 UEFA Cup Quarter-Final 2nd Leg at Sostoi Stadion Attendance 25000
Result: **Videoton 1 Manchester United 0 (United lost the tie 4-5 on penalty kicks)**
Teamsheet: Bailey, Gidman, Albiston, Duxbury, McGrath, Hogg, Robson, Strachan, Hughes, Stapleton, Whiteside
Substitute(s): Olsen

Match # 3752 Saturday 23/03/85 Football League Division 1 at Old Trafford Attendance 40941
Result: **Manchester United 4 Aston Villa 0**
Teamsheet: Bailey, Gidman, Albiston, Whiteside, McGrath, Hogg, Robson, Strachan, Hughes, Stapleton, Olsen
Scorer(s): Hughes 3, Whiteside

Match # 3753 Sunday 31/03/85 Football League Division 1 at Anfield Attendance 34886
Result: **Liverpool 0 Manchester United 1**
Teamsheet: Bailey, Gidman, Albiston, Whiteside, McGrath, Hogg, Robson, Strachan, Hughes, Stapleton, Olsen
Scorer(s): Stapleton

Match # 3754 Wednesday 03/04/85 Football League Division 1 at Old Trafford Attendance 35950
Result: **Manchester United 2 Leicester City 1**
Teamsheet: Bailey, Gidman, Albiston, Whiteside, McGrath, Hogg, Robson, Strachan, Hughes, Stapleton, Olsen
Scorer(s): Robson, Stapleton

Match # 3755 Saturday 06/04/85 Football League Division 1 at Old Trafford Attendance 42940
Result: **Manchester United 5 Stoke City 0**
Teamsheet: Bailey, Gidman, Albiston, Whiteside, McGrath, Hogg, Robson, Strachan, Hughes, Stapleton, Olsen
Substitute(s): Duxbury Scorer(s): Hughes 2, Olsen 2, Whiteside

Match # 3756 Tuesday 09/04/85 Football League Division 1 at Hillsborough Attendance 39380
Result: **Sheffield Wednesday 1 Manchester United 0**
Teamsheet: Pears, Gidman, Albiston, Duxbury, McGrath, Hogg, Robson, Strachan, Hughes, Stapleton, Olsen
Substitute(s): Brazil

Match # 3757 Saturday 13/04/85 FA Cup Semi-Final at Goodison Park Attendance 51690
Result: **Manchester United 2 Liverpool 2**
Teamsheet: Bailey, Gidman, Albiston, Whiteside, McGrath, Hogg, Robson, Strachan, Hughes, Stapleton, Olsen
Scorer(s): Robson, Stapleton

Match # 3758 Wednesday 17/04/85 FA Cup Semi-Final Replay at Maine Road Attendance 45775
Result: **Manchester United 2 Liverpool 1**
Teamsheet: Bailey, Gidman, Albiston, Whiteside, McGrath, Hogg, Robson, Strachan, Hughes, Stapleton, Olsen
Scorer(s): Hughes, Robson

Match # 3759 Sunday 21/04/85 Football League Division 1 at Kenilworth Road Attendance 10320
Result: **Luton Town 2 Manchester United 1**
Teamsheet: Bailey, Gidman, Albiston, Whiteside, McGrath, Hogg, Robson, Muhren, Hughes, Stapleton, Olsen
Scorer(s): Whiteside

Match # 3760 Wednesday 24/04/85 Football League Division 1 at Old Trafford Attendance 31291
Result: **Manchester United 0 Southampton 0**
Teamsheet: Bailey, Gidman, Albiston, Whiteside, McGrath, Hogg, Robson, Strachan, Hughes, Stapleton, Olsen
Substitute(s): Duxbury

SEASON 1984/85 (continued)

Match # 3761 Saturday 27/04/85 Football League Division 1 at Old Trafford	Attendance 38979
Result: **Manchester United 2 Sunderland 2**	
Teamsheet: Bailey, Gidman, Albiston, Whiteside, McGrath, Moran, Robson, Strachan, Hughes, Brazil, Olsen	
Substitute(s): Duxbury Scorer(s): Moran, Robson	

Match # 3762 Saturday 04/05/85 Football League Division 1 at Carrow Road	Attendance 15502
Result: **Norwich City 0 Manchester United 1**	
Teamsheet: Bailey, Gidman, Albiston, Whiteside, McGrath, Moran, Robson, Strachan, Hughes, Stapleton, Olsen	
Scorer(s): Moran	

Match # 3763 Monday 06/05/85 Football League Division 1 at Old Trafford	Attendance 41775
Result: **Manchester United 2 Nottingham Forest 0**	
Teamsheet: Bailey, Gidman, Albiston, Whiteside, McGrath, Moran, Robson, Strachan, Stapleton, Brazil, Olsen	
Substitute(s): Muhren Scorer(s): Gidman, Stapleton	

Match # 3764 Saturday 11/05/85 Football League Division 1 at Loftus Road	Attendance 20483
Result: **Queens Park Rangers 1 Manchester United 3**	
Teamsheet: Bailey, Gidman, Albiston, Whiteside, McGrath, Hogg, Duxbury, Strachan, Stapleton, Brazil, Olsen	
Substitute(s): Muhren Scorer(s): Brazil 2, Strachan	

Match # 3765 Monday 13/05/85 Football League Division 1 at Vicarage Road	Attendance 20500
Result: **Watford 5 Manchester United 1**	
Teamsheet: Bailey, Gidman, Albiston, Whiteside, McGrath, Moran, Duxbury, Strachan, Hughes, Stapleton, Brazil	
Substitute(s): Muhren Scorer(s): Moran	

Match # 3766 Saturday 18/05/85 FA Cup Final at Wembley	Attendance 100000
Result: **Manchester United 1 Everton 0**	
Teamsheet: Bailey, Gidman, Albiston, Whiteside, McGrath, Moran, Robson, Strachan, Hughes, Stapleton, Olsen	
Substitute(s): Duxbury Scorer(s): Whiteside	

SEASON 1984/85 SUMMARY

APPEARANCES

PLAYER	LGE	FAC	LC	UC	TOTAL
Albiston	39	7	3	8	57
Strachan	41	7	2	6	56
Bailey	38	6	3	8	55
Hughes	38	7	2	8	55
Olsen	36	6	2	6 (1)	50 (1)
Robson	32 (1)	4	2	7	45 (1)
Hogg	29	5	3	6	43
Gidman	27	6	1	6 (1)	40 (1)
Moses	26	3	3	6	38
Duxbury	27 (3)	2 (1)	2	6	37 (4)
Whiteside	23 (4)	6	1	4 (1)	34 (5)
McGrath	23	7	–	2	32
Stapleton	21 (3)	5	1 (1)	4 (1)	31 (5)
Moran	19	3	2	4	28
Brazil	17 (3)	– (1)	2 (1)	2	21 (5)
McQueen	12	1	–	2	15
Muhren	7 (5)	1	1	3	12 (5)
Pears	4	1	–	–	5
Garton	2	–	1	– (1)	3 (1)
Blackmore	1	–	1	–	2
Graham	–	–	1	–	1

GOALSCORERS

PLAYER	LGE	FAC	LC	UC	TOT
Hughes	16	3	3	2	24
Strachan	15	2	–	2	19
Robson	9	2	1	2	14
Whiteside	9	4	–	–	13
Stapleton	6	2	–	1	9
Brazil	5	–	3	1	9
Olsen	5	–	1	–	6
Moran	4	–	–	–	4
Gidman	3	–	–	–	3
Moses	3	–	–	–	3
Muhren	–	–	3	–	3
McQueen	1	1	–	–	2
McGrath	–	2	–	–	2
Duxbury	1	–	–	–	1
own goal	–	–	–	1	1

RESULTS & ATTENDANCES SUMMARY

		P	W	D	L	F	A	TOTAL	AVGE
League	H	21	13	6	2	47	13	900864	42898
	A	21	9	4	8	30	34	585685	27890
	TOTAL	42	22	10	10	77	47	1486549	35394
FA Cup	H	3	3	0	0	9	3	116888	38963
	A	1	1	0	0	2	0	22692	22692
	N	3	2	1	0	5	3	197465	65822
	TOTAL	7	6	1	0	16	6	337045	48149
League Cup	H	2	1	0	1	5	2	79301	39651
	A	1	1	0	0	3	0	12690	12690
	TOTAL	3	2	0	1	8	2	91991	30664
UEFA Cup	H	4	3	1	0	7	2	156110	39028
	A	4	1	2	1	5	5	100321	25080
	TOTAL	8	4	3	1	12	7	256431	32054
Overall	H	30	20	7	3	68	20	1253163	41772
	A	27	12	6	9	40	39	721388	26718
	N	3	2	1	0	5	3	197465	65822
	TOTAL	60	34	14	12	113	62	2172016	36200

FINAL TABLE - LEAGUE DIVISION ONE

		P	W	D	L	F	A	W	D	L	F	A	PTS	GD
			HOME					AWAY						
1	Everton	42	16	3	2	58	17	12	3	6	30	26	90	45
2	Liverpool	42	12	4	5	36	19	10	7	4	32	16	77	33
3	Tottenham Hotspur	42	11	3	7	46	31	12	5	4	32	20	77	27
4	MANCHESTER UNITED	42	13	6	2	47	13	9	4	8	30	34	76	30
5	Southampton	42	13	4	4	29	18	6	7	8	27	29	68	9
6	Chelsea	42	13	3	5	38	20	5	9	7	25	28	66	15
7	Arsenal	42	14	5	2	37	14	5	4	12	24	35	66	12
8	Sheffield Wednesday	42	12	7	2	39	21	5	7	9	19	24	65	13
9	Nottingham Forest	42	13	4	4	35	18	6	3	12	21	30	64	8
10	Aston Villa	42	10	7	4	34	20	5	4	12	26	40	56	0
11	Watford	42	10	5	6	48	30	4	8	9	33	41	55	10
12	West Bromwich Albion	42	11	4	6	36	23	5	3	13	22	39	55	–4
13	Luton Town	42	12	5	4	40	22	3	4	14	17	39	54	–4
14	Newcastle United	42	11	4	6	33	26	2	9	10	22	44	52	–15
15	Leicester City	42	10	4	7	39	25	5	2	14	26	48	51	–8
16	West Ham United	42	7	8	6	27	23	6	4	11	24	45	51	–17
17	Ipswich Town	42	8	7	6	27	20	5	4	12	19	37	50	–11
18	Coventry City	42	11	3	7	29	22	4	2	15	18	42	50	–17
19	Queens Park Rangers	42	11	6	4	41	30	2	5	14	12	42	50	–19
20	Norwich City	42	9	6	6	28	24	4	4	13	18	40	49	–18
21	Sunderland	42	7	6	8	20	26	3	4	14	20	36	40	–22
22	Stoke City	42	3	3	15	18	41	0	5	16	6	50	17	–67

SEASON 1985/86

Match # 3767	Saturday 10/08/85	FA Charity Shield	at Wembley	Attendance 82000

Result: **Manchester United 0 Everton 2**
Teamsheet: Bailey, Gidman, Albiston, Whiteside, McGrath, Hogg, Robson, Duxbury, Hughes, Stapleton, Olsen
Substitute(s): Moses

Match # 3768 Saturday 17/08/85 Football League Division 1 at Old Trafford Attendance 49743
Result: **Manchester United 4 Aston Villa 0**
Teamsheet: Bailey, Gidman, Albiston, Whiteside, McGrath, Hogg, Robson, Moses, Hughes, Stapleton, Olsen
Substitute(s): Duxbury   Scorer(s): Hughes 2, Olsen, Whiteside

Match # 3769 Tuesday 20/08/85 Football League Division 1 at Portman Road Attendance 18777
Result: **Ipswich Town 0 Manchester United 1**
Teamsheet: Bailey, Gidman, Albiston, Whiteside, McGrath, Hogg, Robson, Strachan, Hughes, Stapleton, Olsen
Substitute(s): Duxbury   Scorer(s): Robson

Match # 3770 Saturday 24/08/85 Football League Division 1 at Highbury Attendance 37145
Result: **Arsenal 1 Manchester United 2**
Teamsheet: Bailey, Duxbury, Albiston, Whiteside, McGrath, Hogg, Robson, Strachan, Hughes, Stapleton, Olsen
Scorer(s): Hughes, McGrath

Match # 3771 Monday 26/08/85 Football League Division 1 at Old Trafford Attendance 50773
Result: **Manchester United 2 West Ham United 0**
Teamsheet: Bailey, Duxbury, Albiston, Whiteside, McGrath, Hogg, Robson, Strachan, Hughes, Stapleton, Olsen
Scorer(s): Hughes, Strachan

Match # 3772 Saturday 31/08/85 Football League Division 1 at City Ground Attendance 26274
Result: **Nottingham Forest 1 Manchester United 3**
Teamsheet: Bailey, Duxbury, Albiston, Whiteside, McGrath, Hogg, Robson, Strachan, Hughes, Stapleton, Barnes
Substitute(s): Brazil   Scorer(s): Barnes, Hughes, Stapleton

Match # 3773 Wednesday 04/09/85 Football League Division 1 at Old Trafford Attendance 51102
Result: **Manchester United 3 Newcastle United 0**
Teamsheet: Bailey, Duxbury, Albiston, Whiteside, McGrath, Hogg, Robson, Strachan, Hughes, Stapleton, Barnes
Substitute(s): Brazil   Scorer(s): Stapleton 2, Hughes

Match # 3774 Saturday 07/09/85 Football League Division 1 at Old Trafford Attendance 51820
Result: **Manchester United 3 Oxford United 0**
Teamsheet: Bailey, Duxbury, Albiston, Whiteside, McGrath, Hogg, Robson, Strachan, Hughes, Stapleton, Barnes
Substitute(s): Brazil   Scorer(s): Barnes, Robson, Whiteside

Match # 3775 Saturday 14/09/85 Football League Division 1 at Maine Road Attendance 48773
Result: **Manchester City 0 Manchester United 3**
Teamsheet: Bailey, Duxbury, Albiston, Whiteside, McGrath, Hogg, Robson, Strachan, Hughes, Stapleton, Barnes
Substitute(s): Brazil   Scorer(s): Albiston, Duxbury, Robson

Match # 3776 Saturday 21/09/85 Football League Division 1 at The Hawthorns Attendance 25068
Result: **West Bromwich Albion 1 Manchester United 5**
Teamsheet: Bailey, Duxbury, Albiston, Whiteside, McGrath, Hogg, Robson, Strachan, Brazil, Stapleton, Blackmore
Substitute(s): Moran   Scorer(s): Brazil 2, Blackmore, Stapleton, Strachan

Match # 3777 Tuesday 24/09/85 League Cup 2nd Round 1st Leg at Selhurst Park Attendance 21507
Result: **Crystal Palace 0 Manchester United 1**
Teamsheet: Bailey, Duxbury, Albiston, Whiteside, McGrath, Moran, Robson, Blackmore, Brazil, Stapleton, Barnes
Scorer(s): Barnes

Match # 3778 Saturday 28/09/85 Football League Division 1 at Old Trafford Attendance 52449
Result: **Manchester United 1 Southampton 0**
Teamsheet: Bailey, Duxbury, Albiston, Whiteside, McGrath, Moran, Robson, Moses, Hughes, Stapleton, Barnes
Substitute(s): Brazil   Scorer(s): Hughes

Match # 3779 Saturday 05/10/85 Football League Division 1 at Kenilworth Road Attendance 17454
Result: **Luton Town 1 Manchester United 1**
Teamsheet: Bailey, Duxbury, Albiston, Whiteside, McGrath, Moran, Robson, Moses, Hughes, Stapleton, Barnes
Scorer(s): Hughes

Match # 3780 Wednesday 09/10/85 League Cup 2nd Round 2nd Leg at Old Trafford Attendance 26118
Result: **Manchester United 1 Crystal Palace 0**
Teamsheet: Bailey, Duxbury, Albiston, Whiteside, McGrath, Moran, Robson, Olsen, Hughes, Stapleton, Barnes
Substitute(s): Brazil   Scorer(s): Whiteside

Match # 3781 Saturday 12/10/85 Football League Division 1 at Old Trafford Attendance 48845
Result: **Manchester United 2 Queens Park Rangers 0**
Teamsheet: Bailey, Duxbury, Albiston, Whiteside, McGrath, Moran, Robson, Olsen, Hughes, Stapleton, Barnes
Scorer(s): Hughes, Olsen

Match # 3782 Saturday 19/10/85 Football League Division 1 at Old Trafford Attendance 54492
Result: **Manchester United 1 Liverpool 1**
Teamsheet: Bailey, Duxbury, Albiston, Whiteside, Moran, Hogg, McGrath, Moses, Hughes, Stapleton, Olsen
Substitute(s): Barnes   Scorer(s): McGrath

Match # 3783 Saturday 26/10/85 Football League Division 1 at Stamford Bridge Attendance 42485
Result: **Chelsea 1 Manchester United 2**
Teamsheet: Bailey, Duxbury, Albiston, Whiteside, Moran, Hogg, McGrath, Olsen, Hughes, Stapleton, Barnes
Scorer(s): Hughes, Olsen

Match # 3784 Tuesday 29/10/85 League Cup 3rd Round at Old Trafford Attendance 32056
Result: **Manchester United 1 West Ham United 0**
Teamsheet: Bailey, Duxbury, Albiston, Whiteside, Moran, Hogg, McGrath, Olsen, Hughes, Stapleton, Barnes
Substitute(s): Brazil   Scorer(s): Whiteside

SEASON 1985/86 (continued)

Match # 3785 Saturday 02/11/85   Football League Division 1   at Old Trafford   Attendance 46748
Result: **Manchester United 2 Coventry City 0**
Teamsheet: Bailey, Garton, Albiston, Whiteside, Moran, Hogg, McGrath, Olsen, Hughes, Stapleton, Barnes
Scorer(s):   Olsen 2

Match # 3786 Saturday 09/11/85   Football League Division 1   at Hillsborough   Attendance 48105
Result: **Sheffield Wednesday 1 Manchester United 0**
Teamsheet: Bailey, Gidman, Albiston, Whiteside, McGrath, Moran, Robson, Olsen, Hughes, Stapleton, Barnes
Substitute(s): Strachan

Match # 3787 Saturday 16/11/85   Football League Division 1   at Old Trafford   Attendance 54575
Result: **Manchester United 0 Tottenham Hotspur 0**
Teamsheet: Bailey, Gidman, Albiston, Whiteside, McGrath, Moran, Strachan, Olsen, Hughes, Stapleton, Barnes

Match # 3788 Saturday 23/11/85   Football League Division 1   at Filbert Street   Attendance 22008
Result: **Leicester City 3 Manchester United 0**
Teamsheet: Bailey, Gidman, Albiston, Whiteside, Moran, Hogg, McGrath, Strachan, Hughes, Stapleton, Olsen
Substitute(s): Brazil

Match # 3789 Tuesday 26/11/85   League Cup 4th Round   at Anfield   Attendance 41291
Result: **Liverpool 2 Manchester United 1**
Teamsheet: Bailey, Gidman, Blackmore, Whiteside, Moran, Hogg, McGrath, Strachan, Stapleton, Brazil, Olsen
Scorer(s):   McGrath

Match # 3790 Saturday 30/11/85   Football League Division 1   at Old Trafford   Attendance 42181
Result: **Manchester United 1 Watford 1**
Teamsheet: Bailey, Gidman, Gibson C, Whiteside, Moran, Hogg, McGrath, Strachan, Hughes, Stapleton, Olsen
Substitute(s): Brazil   Scorer(s):   Brazil

Match # 3791 Saturday 07/12/85   Football League Division 1   at Old Trafford   Attendance 37981
Result: **Manchester United 1 Ipswich Town 0**
Teamsheet: Bailey, Gidman, Gibson C, Whiteside, McGrath, Hogg, Dempsey, Strachan, Hughes, Stapleton, Olsen
Substitute(s): Brazil   Scorer(s):   Stapleton

Match # 3792 Saturday 14/12/85   Football League Division 1   at Villa Park   Attendance 27626
Result: **Aston Villa 1 Manchester United 3**
Teamsheet: Turner, Gidman, Gibson C, Whiteside, McGrath, Garton, Blackmore, Strachan, Hughes, Stapleton, Olsen
Substitute(s): Brazil   Scorer(s):   Blackmore, Hughes, Strachan

Match # 3793 Saturday 21/12/85   Football League Division 1   at Old Trafford   Attendance 44386
Result: **Manchester United 0 Arsenal 1**
Teamsheet: Bailey, Gidman, Gibson C, Whiteside, McGrath, Garton, Blackmore, Strachan, Hughes, Stapleton, Olsen

Match # 3794 Thursday 26/12/85   Football League Division 1   at Goodison Park   Attendance 42551
Result: **Everton 3 Manchester United 1**
Teamsheet: Bailey, Gidman, Gibson C, Whiteside, McGrath, Hogg, Blackmore, Strachan, Hughes, Stapleton, Olsen
Substitute(s): Wood   Scorer(s):   Stapleton

Match # 3795 Wednesday 01/01/86   Football League Division 1   at Old Trafford   Attendance 43095
Result: **Manchester United 1 Birmingham City 0**
Teamsheet: Turner, Gidman, Albiston, Whiteside, McGrath, Garton, Blackmore, Strachan, Hughes, Stapleton, Gibson C
Substitute(s): Brazil   Scorer(s):   Gibson C

Match # 3796 Thursday 09/01/86   FA Cup 3rd Round   at Old Trafford   Attendance 40223
Result: **Manchester United 2 Rochdale 0**
Teamsheet: Turner, Duxbury, Albiston, Whiteside, Higgins, Garton, Blackmore, Strachan, Hughes, Stapleton, Gibson C
Substitute(s): Olsen   Scorer(s):   Hughes, Stapleton

Match # 3797 Saturday 11/01/86   Football League Division 1   at Manor Ground   Attendance 13280
Result: **Oxford United 1 Manchester United 3**
Teamsheet: Bailey, Gidman, Albiston, Whiteside, Moran, Garton, Blackmore, Strachan, Hughes, Stapleton, Gibson C
Scorer(s):   Gibson C, Hughes, Whiteside

Match # 3798 Saturday 18/01/86   Football League Division 1   at Old Trafford   Attendance 46717
Result: **Manchester United 2 Nottingham Forest 3**
Teamsheet: Bailey, Gidman, Albiston, Whiteside, Moran, Garton, Olsen, Strachan, Hughes, Stapleton, Gibson C
Scorer(s):   Olsen 2

Match # 3799 Saturday 25/01/86   FA Cup 4th Round   at Roker Park   Attendance 35484
Result: **Sunderland 0 Manchester United 0**
Teamsheet: Bailey, Gidman, Albiston, Whiteside, McGrath, Moran, Robson, Strachan, Stapleton, Blackmore, Olsen

Match # 3800 Wednesday 29/01/86   FA Cup 4th Round Replay   at Old Trafford   Attendance 43402
Result: **Manchester United 3 Sunderland 0**
Teamsheet: Bailey, Gidman, Albiston, Whiteside, McGrath, Moran, Robson, Strachan, Stapleton, Olsen, Gibson C
Substitute(s): Blackmore   Scorer(s):   Olsen 2, Whiteside

Match # 3801 Sunday 02/02/86   Football League Division 1   at Upton Park   Attendance 22642
Result: **West Ham United 2 Manchester United 1**
Teamsheet: Bailey, Gidman, Albiston, Whiteside, McGrath, Moran, Robson, Olsen, Hughes, Stapleton, Gibson C
Substitute(s): Gibson T   Scorer(s):   Robson

Match # 3802 Sunday 09/02/86   Football League Division 1   at Anfield   Attendance 35064
Result: **Liverpool 1 Manchester United 1**
Teamsheet: Turner, Gidman, Albiston, Whiteside, McGrath, Moran, Sivebaek, Gibson T, Hughes, Gibson C, Olsen
Substitute(s): Stapleton   Scorer(s):   Gibson C

SEASON 1985/86 (continued)

Match # 3803 Saturday 22/02/86   Football League Division 1   at Old Trafford   Attendance 45193
Result: **Manchester United 3 West Bromwich Albion 0**
Teamsheet: Turner, Gidman, Albiston, Blackmore, McGrath, Moran, Strachan, Gibson C, Hughes, Stapleton, Olsen
Substitute(s): Gibson T   Scorer(s):   Olsen 3

Match # 3804 Saturday 01/03/86   Football League Division 1   at The Dell   Attendance 19012
Result: **Southampton 1 Manchester United 0**
Teamsheet: Turner, Duxbury, Albiston, Gibson C, McGrath, Moran, Robson, Strachan, Hughes, Stapleton, Olsen
Substitute(s): Gibson T

Match # 3805 Wednesday 05/03/86   FA Cup 5th Round   at Upton Park   Attendance 26441
Result: **West Ham United 1 Manchester United 1**
Teamsheet: Turner, Duxbury, Albiston, Whiteside, McGrath, Moran, Robson, Strachan, Hughes, Stapleton, Gibson C
Substitute(s): Olsen   Scorer(s):   Stapleton

Match # 3806 Sunday 09/03/86   FA Cup 5th Round Replay   at Old Trafford   Attendance 30441
Result: **Manchester United 0 West Ham United 2**
Teamsheet: Turner, Duxbury, Albiston, Whiteside, McGrath, Higgins, Olsen, Strachan, Hughes, Stapleton, Gibson C
Substitute(s): Blackmore

Match # 3807 Saturday 15/03/86   Football League Division 1   at Loftus Road   Attendance 23407
Result: **Queens Park Rangers 1 Manchester United 0**
Teamsheet: Turner, Duxbury, Albiston, Blackmore, McGrath, Moran, Olsen, Strachan, Davenport, Stapleton, Gibson C
Substitute(s): Gibson T

Match # 3808 Wednesday 19/03/86   Football League Division 1   at Old Trafford   Attendance 33668
Result: **Manchester United 2 Luton Town 0**
Teamsheet: Turner, Duxbury, Albiston, Whiteside, McGrath, Moran, Gibson C, Strachan, Hughes, Davenport, Olsen
Substitute(s): Stapleton   Scorer(s):   Hughes, McGrath

Match # 3809 Saturday 22/03/86   Football League Division 1   at Old Trafford   Attendance 51274
Result: **Manchester United 2 Manchester City 2**
Teamsheet: Turner, Duxbury, Albiston, Whiteside, McGrath, Higgins, Gibson C, Strachan, Hughes, Davenport, Barnes
Substitute(s): Stapleton   Scorer(s):   Gibson C, Strachan

Match # 3810 Saturday 29/03/86   Football League Division 1   at St Andrews   Attendance 22551
Result: **Birmingham City 1 Manchester United 1**
Teamsheet: Turner, Gidman, Albiston, Whiteside, McGrath, Higgins, Robson, Strachan, Hughes, Davenport, Gibson C
Substitute(s): Stapleton   Scorer(s):   Robson

Match # 3811 Monday 31/03/86   Football League Division 1   at Old Trafford   Attendance 51189
Result: **Manchester United 0 Everton 0**
Teamsheet: Turner, Gidman, Albiston, Whiteside, McGrath, Higgins, Robson, Strachan, Hughes, Davenport, Gibson C
Substitute(s): Stapleton

Match # 3812 Saturday 05/04/86   Football League Division 1   at Highfield Road   Attendance 17160
Result: **Coventry City 1 Manchester United 3**
Teamsheet: Turner, Gidman, Albiston, Whiteside, McGrath, Higgins, Robson, Strachan, Hughes, Davenport, Gibson C
Substitute(s): Stapleton   Scorer(s):   Gibson C, Robson, Strachan

Match # 3813 Wednesday 09/04/86   Football League Division 1   at Old Trafford   Attendance 45355
Result: **Manchester United 1 Chelsea 2**
Teamsheet: Turner, Gidman, Albiston, Duxbury, McGrath, Higgins, Robson, Strachan, Hughes, Davenport, Olsen
Substitute(s): Stapleton   Scorer(s):   Olsen

Match # 3814 Sunday 13/04/86   Football League Division 1   at Old Trafford   Attendance 32331
Result: **Manchester United 0 Sheffield Wednesday 2**
Teamsheet: Turner, Gidman, Albiston, Duxbury, McGrath, Higgins, Robson, Sivebaek, Hughes, Davenport, Olsen
Substitute(s): Gibson T

Match # 3815 Wednesday 16/04/86   Football League Division 1   at St James' Park   Attendance 31840
Result: **Newcastle United 2 Manchester United 4**
Teamsheet: Turner, Gidman, Albiston, Whiteside, McGrath, Garton, Robson, Gibson T, Hughes, Stapleton, Blackmore
Substitute(s): Sivebaek   Scorer(s):   Hughes 2, Robson, Whiteside

Match # 3816 Saturday 19/04/86   Football League Division 1   at White Hart Lane   Attendance 32357
Result: **Tottenham Hotspur 0 Manchester United 0**
Teamsheet: Turner, Gidman, Albiston, Whiteside, McGrath, Garton, Duxbury, Davenport, Hughes, Stapleton, Blackmore
Substitute(s): Olsen

Match # 3817 Saturday 26/04/86   Football League Division 1   at Old Trafford   Attendance 38840
Result: **Manchester United 4 Leicester City 0**
Teamsheet: Turner, Gidman, Albiston, Whiteside, McGrath, Garton, Duxbury, Davenport, Hughes, Stapleton, Blackmore
Substitute(s): Olsen   Scorer(s):   Blackmore, Davenport, Hughes, Stapleton

Match # 3818 Saturday 03/05/86   Football League Division 1   at Vicarage Road   Attendance 18414
Result: **Watford 1 Manchester United 1**
Teamsheet: Turner, Garton, Albiston, Whiteside, McGrath, Hogg, Duxbury, Davenport, Hughes, Stapleton, Blackmore
Substitute(s): Olsen   Scorer(s):   Hughes

SEASON 1985/86 SUMMARY

APPEARANCES

PLAYER	LGE	FAC	LC	CS	TOTAL
McGrath	40	4	4	1	49
Whiteside	37	5	4	1	47
Albiston	37	5	3	1	46
Hughes	40	3	2	1	46
Stapleton	34 (7)	5	4	1	44 (7)
Strachan	27 (1)	5	1	–	33 (1)
Olsen	25 (3)	3 (2)	3	1	32 (5)
Bailey	25	2	4	1	32
Duxbury	21 (2)	3	3	1	28 (2)
Gidman	24	2	1	1	28
Robson	21	3	2	1	27
Moran	18 (1)	3	4	–	25 (1)
Gibson C	18	4	–	–	22
Hogg	17	–	2	1	20
Turner	17	3	–	–	20
Blackmore	12	2 (2)	2	–	16 (2)
Barnes	12 (1)	–	3	–	15 (1)
Davenport	11	–	–	–	11
Garton	10	1	–	–	11
Higgins	6	2	–	–	8
Moses	4	–	–	– (1)	4 (1)
Brazil	1 (10)	–	2 (2)	–	3 (12)
Gibson T	2 (5)	–	–	–	2 (5)
Sivebaek	2 (1)	–	–	–	2 (1)
Dempsey	1	–	–	–	1
Wood	– (1)	–	–	–	– (1)

GOALSCORERS

PLAYER	LGE	FAC	LC	CS	TOT
Hughes	17	1	–	–	18
Olsen	11	2	–	–	13
Stapleton	7	2	–	–	9
Robson	7	–	–	–	7
Whiteside	4	1	2	–	7
Gibson C	5	–	–	–	5
Strachan	5	–	–	–	5
McGrath	3	–	1	–	4
Blackmore	3	–	–	–	3
Brazil	3	–	–	–	3
Barnes	2	–	1	–	3
Albiston	1	–	–	–	1
Davenport	1	–	–	–	1
Duxbury	1	–	–	–	1

RESULTS & ATTENDANCES SUMMARY

		P	W	D	L	F	A	TOTAL	AVGE
League	H	21	12	5	4	35	12	972757	46322
	A	21	10	5	6	35	24	591993	28190
	TOTAL	42	22	10	10	70	36	1564750	37256
FA Cup	H	3	2	0	1	5	2	114066	38022
	A	2	0	2	0	1	1	61925	30963
	TOTAL	5	2	2	1	6	3	175991	35198
League	H	2	2	0	0	2	0	58174	29087
Cup	A	2	1	0	1	2	2	62798	31399
	TOTAL	4	3	0	1	4	2	120972	30243
Charity	H	0	0	0	0	0	0	0	n/a
Shield	A	0	0	0	0	0	0	0	n/a
	N	1	0	0	1	0	2	82000	82000
	TOTAL	1	0	0	1	0	2	82000	82000
Overall	H	26	16	5	5	42	14	1144997	44038
	A	25	11	7	7	38	27	716716	28669
	N	1	0	0	1	0	2	82000	82000
	TOTAL	52	27	12	13	80	43	1943713	37379

FINAL TABLE – LEAGUE DIVISION ONE

		P	W	D	L	F	A	W	D	L	F	A	PTS	GD
				HOME						AWAY				
1	Liverpool	42	16	4	1	58	14	10	6	5	31	23	88	52
2	Everton	42	16	3	2	54	18	10	5	6	33	23	86	46
3	West Ham United	42	17	2	2	48	16	9	4	8	26	24	84	34
4	MANCHESTER UNITED	42	12	5	4	35	12	10	5	6	35	24	76	34
5	Sheffield Wednesday	42	13	6	2	36	23	8	4	9	27	31	73	9
6	Chelsea	42	12	4	5	32	27	8	7	6	25	29	71	1
7	Arsenal	42	13	5	3	29	15	7	4	10	20	32	69	2
8	Nottingham Forest	42	11	5	5	38	25	8	6	7	31	28	68	16
9	Luton Town	42	12	6	3	37	15	6	6	9	24	29	66	17
10	Tottenham Hotspur	42	12	2	7	47	25	7	6	8	27	27	65	22
11	Newcastle United	42	12	5	4	46	31	5	7	9	21	41	63	-5
12	Watford	42	11	6	4	40	22	5	5	11	29	40	59	7
13	Queens Park Rangers	42	12	3	6	33	20	3	4	14	20	44	52	-11
14	Southampton	42	10	6	5	32	18	2	4	15	19	44	46	-11
15	Manchester City	42	7	7	7	25	26	4	5	12	18	31	45	-14
16	Aston Villa	42	7	6	8	27	28	3	8	10	24	39	44	-16
17	Coventry City	42	6	5	10	31	35	5	5	11	17	36	43	-23
18	Oxford United	42	7	7	7	34	27	3	5	13	28	53	42	-18
19	Leicester City	42	7	8	6	35	35	3	4	14	19	41	42	-22
20	Ipswich Town	42	8	5	8	20	24	3	3	15	12	31	41	-23
21	Birmingham City	42	5	2	14	13	25	3	3	15	17	48	29	-43
22	West Bromwich Albion	42	3	8	10	21	36	1	4	16	14	53	24	-54

SEASON 1986/87

Match # 3819 Saturday 23/08/86   Football League Division 1   at Highbury   Attendance 41382
Result: **Arsenal 1 Manchester United 0**
Teamsheet: Turner, Duxbury, Albiston, Whiteside, McGrath, Moran, Strachan, Blackmore, Stapleton, Davenport, Gibson C
Substitute(s):   Olsen

Match # 3820 Monday 25/08/86   Football League Division 1   at Old Trafford   Attendance 43306
Result: **Manchester United 2 West Ham United 3**
Teamsheet: Turner, Duxbury, Albiston, Whiteside, McGrath, Moran, Strachan, Blackmore, Stapleton, Davenport, Gibson C
Substitute(s):   Olsen   Scorer(s):   Davenport, Stapleton

Match # 3821 Saturday 30/08/86   Football League Division 1   at Old Trafford   Attendance 37544
Result: **Manchester United 0 Charlton Athletic 1**
Teamsheet: Turner, Duxbury, Albiston, Whiteside, McGrath, Moran, Strachan, Blackmore, Stapleton, Davenport, Olsen
Substitute(s):   Gibson T

Match # 3822 Saturday 06/09/86   Football League Division 1   at Filbert Street   Attendance 16785
Result: **Leicester City 1 Manchester United 1**
Teamsheet: Turner, Sivebaek, Albiston, Whiteside, McGrath, Hogg, Strachan, Duxbury, Stapleton, Gibson T, Olsen
Substitute(s):   Davenport   Scorer(s):   Whiteside

Match # 3823 Saturday 13/09/86   Football League Division 1   at Old Trafford   Attendance 40135
Result: **Manchester United 5 Southampton 1**
Teamsheet: Turner, Sivebaek, Albiston, Whiteside, McGrath, Moran, Robson, Strachan, Stapleton, Davenport, Olsen
Substitute(s):   Gibson T   Scorer(s):   Stapleton 2, Davenport, Olsen, Whiteside

Match # 3824 Tuesday 16/09/86   Football League Division 1   at Vicarage Road   Attendance 21650
Result: **Watford 1 Manchester United 0**
Teamsheet: Turner, Sivebaek, Albiston, Moses, McGrath, Moran, Robson, Blackmore, Stapleton, Davenport, Olsen

Match # 3825 Sunday 21/09/86   Football League Division 1   at Goodison Park   Attendance 25843
Result: **Everton 3 Manchester United 1**
Teamsheet: Turner, Sivebaek, Albiston, Whiteside, McGrath, Moran, Robson, Strachan, Stapleton, Davenport, Moses
Substitute(s):   Olsen   Scorer(s):   Robson

Match # 3826 Wednesday 24/09/86   League Cup 2nd Round 1st Leg   at Old Trafford   Attendance 18906
Result: **Manchester United 2 Port Vale 0**
Teamsheet: Turner, Duxbury, Albiston, Whiteside, McGrath, Moran, Robson, Strachan, Stapleton, Davenport, Moses
Scorer(s):   Stapleton, Whiteside

Match # 3827 Sunday 28/09/86   Football League Division 1   at Old Trafford   Attendance 33340
Result: **Manchester United 0 Chelsea 1**
Teamsheet: Turner, Sivebaek, Albiston, Whiteside, McGrath, Moran, Robson, Strachan, Stapleton, Davenport, Moses
Substitute(s):   Olsen

Match # 3828 Saturday 04/10/86   Football League Division 1   at City Ground   Attendance 34828
Result: **Nottingham Forest 1 Manchester United 1**
Teamsheet: Turner, Sivebaek, Albiston, Whiteside, McGrath, Moran, Robson, Strachan, Stapleton, Davenport, Olsen
Scorer(s):   Robson

Match # 3829 Tuesday 07/10/86   League Cup 2nd Round 2nd Leg   at Vale Park   Attendance 10486
Result: **Port Vale 2 Manchester United 5**
Teamsheet: Turner, Sivebaek, Albiston, Moses, McGrath, Moran, Robson, Strachan, Stapleton, Davenport, Barnes
Substitute(s):   Gibson T, Whiteside   Scorer(s):   Moses 2, Barnes, Davenport, Stapleton

Match # 3830 Saturday 11/10/86   Football League Division 1   at Old Trafford   Attendance 45890
Result: **Manchester United 3 Sheffield Wednesday 1**
Teamsheet: Turner, Sivebaek, Albiston, Whiteside, McGrath, Hogg, Robson, Strachan, Stapleton, Davenport, Barnes
Scorer(s):   Davenport 2, Whiteside

Match # 3831 Saturday 18/10/86   Football League Division 1   at Old Trafford   Attendance 39927
Result: **Manchester United 1 Luton Town 0**
Teamsheet: Turner, Sivebaek, Albiston, Whiteside, McGrath, Hogg, Robson, Strachan, Stapleton, Davenport, Barnes
Substitute(s):   Gibson T   Scorer(s):   Stapleton

Match # 3832 Saturday 25/10/86   Football League Division 1   at Maine Road   Attendance 32440
Result: **Manchester City 1 Manchester United 1**
Teamsheet: Turner, Sivebaek, Albiston, Whiteside, McGrath, Hogg, Robson, Moses, Stapleton, Davenport, Barnes
Scorer(s):   Stapleton

Match # 3833 Wednesday 29/10/86   League Cup 3rd Round   at Old Trafford   Attendance 23639
Result: **Manchester United 0 Southampton 0**
Teamsheet: Turner, Duxbury, Albiston, Whiteside, McGrath, Hogg, Robson, Moses, Stapleton, Davenport, Barnes
Substitute(s):   Gibson T, Olsen

Match # 3834 Saturday 01/11/86   Football League Division 1   at Old Trafford   Attendance 36946
Result: **Manchester United 1 Coventry City 1**
Teamsheet: Turner, Sivebaek, Albiston, Whiteside, McGrath, Hogg, Robson, Strachan, Stapleton, Davenport, Olsen
Substitute(s):   Moses   Scorer(s):   Davenport

Match # 3835 Tuesday 04/11/86   League Cup 3rd Round Replay   at The Dell   Attendance 17915
Result: **Southampton 4 Manchester United 1**
Teamsheet: Turner, Duxbury, Albiston, Whiteside, McGrath, Hogg, Moses, Olsen, Stapleton, Davenport, Gibson C
Substitute(s):   Moran, Wood   Scorer(s):   Davenport

Match # 3836 Saturday 08/11/86   Football League Division 1   at Manor Ground   Attendance 13545
Result: **Oxford United 2 Manchester United 0**
Teamsheet: Turner, Duxbury, Albiston, Moran, McGrath, Hogg, Blackmore, Moses, Stapleton, Davenport, Barnes
Substitute(s):   Olsen

SEASON 1986/87 (continued)

Match # 3837 Saturday 15/11/86   Football League Division 1   at Carrow Road   Attendance 22684
Result: **Norwich City 0 Manchester United 0**
Teamsheet: Turner, Sivebaek, Duxbury, Moses, McGrath, Hogg, Olsen, Blackmore, Stapleton, Davenport, Barnes
Substitute(s):   Moran

Match # 3838 Saturday 22/11/86   Football League Division 1   at Old Trafford   Attendance 42235
Result: **Manchester United 1 Queens Park Rangers 0**
Teamsheet: Turner, Sivebaek, Duxbury, Moses, McGrath, Hogg, Olsen, Blackmore, Stapleton, Davenport, Barnes
Substitute(s):   Strachan   Scorer(s):   Sivebaek

Match # 3839 Saturday 29/11/86   Football League Division 1   at Plough Lane   Attendance 12112
Result: **Wimbledon 1 Manchester United 0**
Teamsheet: Turner, Sivebaek, Duxbury, Moses, McGrath, Moran, Olsen, Blackmore, Stapleton, Davenport, Barnes
Substitute(s):   Robson

Match # 3840 Sunday 07/12/86   Football League Division 1   at Old Trafford   Attendance 35957
Result: **Manchester United 3 Tottenham Hotspur 3**
Teamsheet: Turner, Sivebaek, Duxbury, Moses, McGrath, Moran, Robson, Strachan, Whiteside, Davenport, Olsen
Substitute(s):   Stapleton   Scorer(s):   Davenport 2, Whiteside

Match # 3841 Saturday 13/12/86   Football League Division 1   at Villa Park   Attendance 29205
Result: **Aston Villa 3 Manchester United 3**
Teamsheet: Walsh, Sivebaek, Duxbury, Moses, Moran, Hogg, Robson, Strachan, Whiteside, Davenport, Olsen
Substitute(s):   Stapleton   Scorer(s):   Davenport 2, Whiteside

Match # 3842 Saturday 20/12/86   Football League Division 1   at Old Trafford   Attendance 34150
Result: **Manchester United 2 Leicester City 0**
Teamsheet: Walsh, Sivebaek, Gibson C, O'Brien, Moran, Hogg, Robson, Strachan, Whiteside, Davenport, Olsen
Substitute(s):   Stapleton   Scorer(s):   Gibson C, Stapleton

Match # 3843 Friday 26/12/86   Football League Division 1   at Anfield   Attendance 40663
Result: **Liverpool 0 Manchester United 1**
Teamsheet: Walsh, Sivebaek, Gibson C, Whiteside, Moran, Duxbury, Robson, Strachan, Stapleton, Davenport, Olsen
Scorer(s):   Whiteside

Match # 3844 Saturday 27/12/86   Football League Division 1   at Old Trafford   Attendance 44610
Result: **Manchester United 0 Norwich City 1**
Teamsheet: Walsh, Sivebaek, Gibson C, Whiteside, Garton, Duxbury, Robson, Strachan, Stapleton, Davenport, Olsen
Substitute(s):   O'Brien

Match # 3845 Thursday 01/01/87   Football League Division 1   at Old Trafford   Attendance 43334
Result: **Manchester United 4 Newcastle United 1**
Teamsheet: Turner, Sivebaek, Gibson C, O'Brien, Garton, Moran, Duxbury, Strachan, Whiteside, Davenport, Olsen
Substitute(s):   Stapleton   Scorer(s):   Olsen, Stapleton, Whiteside, own goal

Match # 3846 Saturday 03/01/87   Football League Division 1   at The Dell   Attendance 20409
Result: **Southampton 1 Manchester United 1**
Teamsheet: Turner, Duxbury, Gibson C, O'Brien, Garton, Moran, Gill, Strachan, Stapleton, Gibson T, Olsen
Substitute(s):   Davenport   Scorer(s):   Olsen

Match # 3847 Saturday 10/01/87   FA Cup 3rd Round   at Old Trafford   Attendance 54294
Result: **Manchester United 1 Manchester City 0**
Teamsheet: Turner, Sivebaek, Gibson C, Whiteside, Garton, Moran, Duxbury, Strachan, Stapleton, Davenport, Olsen
Substitute(s):   Gibson T   Scorer(s):   Whiteside

Match # 3848 Saturday 24/01/87   Football League Division 1   at Old Trafford   Attendance 51367
Result: **Manchester United 2 Arsenal 0**
Teamsheet: Turner, Sivebaek, Duxbury, Whiteside, Garton, Moran, Blackmore, Strachan, Stapleton, Gibson T, Olsen
Substitute(s):   McGrath   Scorer(s):   Gibson T, Strachan

Match # 3849 Saturday 31/01/87   FA Cup 4th Round   at Old Trafford   Attendance 49082
Result: **Manchester United 0 Coventry City 1**
Teamsheet: Turner, Sivebaek, Duxbury, Whiteside, Garton, Moran, Blackmore, Strachan, Stapleton, Gibson T, Olsen
Substitute(s):   Davenport, McGrath

Match # 3850 Saturday 07/02/87   Football League Division 1   at Selhurst Park   Attendance 15482
Result: **Charlton Athletic 0 Manchester United 0**
Teamsheet: Turner, Sivebaek, Gibson C, Duxbury, Garton, Moran, Robson, Strachan, Stapleton, Gibson T, Olsen
Substitute(s):   Davenport

Match # 3851 Saturday 14/02/87   Football League Division 1   at Old Trafford   Attendance 35763
Result: **Manchester United 3 Watford 1**
Teamsheet: Turner, Garton, Gibson C, Duxbury, McGrath, Moran, Robson, Strachan, Davenport, Gibson T, Olsen
Substitute(s):   Stapleton   Scorer(s):   Davenport, McGrath, Strachan

Match # 3852 Saturday 21/02/87   Football League Division 1   at Stamford Bridge   Attendance 26516
Result: **Chelsea 1 Manchester United 1**
Teamsheet: Bailey, Duxbury, Gibson C, Whiteside, McGrath, Moran, Robson, Strachan, Davenport, Gibson T, Olsen
Substitute(s):   Stapleton   Scorer(s):   Davenport

Match # 3853 Saturday 28/02/87   Football League Division 1   at Old Trafford   Attendance 47421
Result: **Manchester United 0 Everton 0**
Teamsheet: Bailey, Duxbury, Gibson C, Whiteside, McGrath, Moran, Robson, Hogg, Davenport, Gibson T, Strachan
Substitute(s):   O'Brien

Match # 3854 Saturday 07/03/87   Football League Division 1   at Old Trafford   Attendance 48619
Result: **Manchester United 2 Manchester City 0**
Teamsheet: Bailey, Sivebaek, Gibson C, Duxbury, McGrath, Moran, Robson, Strachan, Whiteside, Gibson T, O'Brien
Substitute(s):   Davenport   Scorer(s):   Robson, own goal

SEASON 1986/87 (continued)

Match # 3855 Saturday 14/03/87   Football League Division 1   at Kenilworth Road   Attendance 12509
Result: **Luton Town 2 Manchester United 1**
Teamsheet: Bailey, Sivebaek, Gibson C, Duxbury, McGrath, Moran, Robson, Strachan, Whiteside, Gibson T, O'Brien
Substitute(s): Davenport   Scorer(s):   Robson

Match # 3856 Saturday 21/03/87   Football League Division 1   at Hillsborough   Attendance 29888
Result: **Sheffield Wednesday 1 Manchester United 0**
Teamsheet: Bailey, Garton, Duxbury, O'Brien, McGrath, Moran, Robson, Strachan, Whiteside, Davenport, Gibson C
Substitute(s): Gibson T

Match # 3857 Saturday 28/03/87   Football League Division 1   at Old Trafford   Attendance 39182
Result: **Manchester United 2 Nottingham Forest 0**
Teamsheet: Walsh, Sivebaek, Gibson C, O'Brien, McGrath, Duxbury, Robson, Moses, Stapleton, Whiteside, Wood
Substitute(s): Albiston   Scorer(s):   McGrath, Robson

Match # 3858 Saturday 04/04/87   Football League Division 1   at Old Trafford   Attendance 32443
Result: **Manchester United 3 Oxford United 2**
Teamsheet: Walsh, Sivebaek, Gibson C, O'Brien, McGrath, Duxbury, Robson, Moses, Stapleton, Wood, Davenport
Substitute(s): Albiston   Scorer(s):   Davenport 2, Robson

Match # 3859 Tuesday 14/04/87   Football League Division 1   at Upton Park   Attendance 23486
Result: **West Ham United 0 Manchester United 0**
Teamsheet: Walsh, Duxbury, Gibson C, Moses, McGrath, Moran, Robson, Strachan, Stapleton, Gibson T, Davenport
Substitute(s): Albiston

Match # 3860 Saturday 18/04/87   Football League Division 1   at St James' Park   Attendance 32706
Result: **Newcastle United 2 Manchester United 1**
Teamsheet: Walsh, Duxbury, Gibson C, Moses, McGrath, Moran, O'Brien, Strachan, Gibson T, Whiteside, Davenport
Substitute(s): Stapleton   Scorer(s):   Strachan

Match # 3861 Monday 20/04/87   Football League Division 1   at Old Trafford   Attendance 54103
Result: **Manchester United 1 Liverpool 0**
Teamsheet: Walsh, Sivebaek, Albiston, Moses, McGrath, Moran, Duxbury, Strachan, Whiteside, Davenport, Gibson C
Substitute(s): Stapleton   Scorer(s):   Davenport

Match # 3862 Saturday 25/04/87   Football League Division 1   at Loftus Road   Attendance 17414
Result: **Queens Park Rangers 1 Manchester United 1**
Teamsheet: Walsh, Duxbury, Albiston, Moses, McGrath, Moran, Robson, Strachan, Whiteside, Davenport, Gibson C
Substitute(s): Sivebaek   Scorer(s):   Strachan

Match # 3863 Saturday 02/05/87   Football League Division 1   at Old Trafford   Attendance 31686
Result: **Manchester United 0 Wimbledon 1**
Teamsheet: Walsh, Duxbury, Albiston, Moses, McGrath, Moran, Robson, Strachan, Davenport, Olsen, Gibson C
Substitute(s): Stapleton

Match # 3864 Monday 04/05/87   Football League Division 1   at White Hart Lane   Attendance 36692
Result: **Tottenham Hotspur 4 Manchester United 0**
Teamsheet: Walsh, Sivebaek, Gibson C, Duxbury, McGrath, Moran, Robson, Strachan, Gibson T, Whiteside, Olsen
Substitute(s): Blackmore

Match # 3865 Wednesday 06/05/87   Football League Division 1   at Highfield Road   Attendance 23407
Result: **Coventry City 1 Manchester United 1**
Teamsheet: Walsh, Garton, Albiston, Duxbury, McGrath, Moran, Robson, Strachan, Whiteside, Davenport, Gibson C
Substitute(s): Blackmore   Scorer(s):   Whiteside

Match # 3866 Saturday 09/05/87   Football League Division 1   at Old Trafford   Attendance 35179
Result: **Manchester United 3 Aston Villa 1**
Teamsheet: Walsh, Garton, Albiston, Duxbury, McGrath, Moran, Robson, Blackmore, Whiteside, Davenport, Gibson C
Substitute(s): Olsen   Scorer(s):   Blackmore, Duxbury, Robson

SEASON 1986/87 SUMMARY

APPEARANCES

PLAYER	LGE	FAC	LC	TOTAL
Davenport	34 (5)	1 (1)	4	39 (6)
McGrath	34 (1)	– (1)	4	38 (2)
Strachan	33 (1)	2	2	37 (1)
Duxbury	32	2	3	37
Moran	32 (1)	2	2 (1)	36 (2)
Whiteside	31	2	3 (1)	36 (1)
Robson	29 (1)	–	3	32 (1)
Stapleton	25 (9)	2	4	31 (9)
Sivebaek	27 (1)	2	1	30 (1)
Turner	23	2	4	29
Gibson C	24	1	1	26
Olsen	22 (6)	2	1 (1)	25 (7)
Albiston	19 (3)	–	4	23 (3)
Moses	17 (1)	–	4	21 (1)
Walsh	14	–	–	14
Gibson T	12 (4)	1 (1)	– (2)	13 (7)
Hogg	11	–	2	13
Blackmore	10 (2)	1	–	11 (2)
Garton	9	2	–	11
O'Brien	9 (2)	–	–	9 (2)
Barnes	7	–	2	9
Bailey	5	–	–	5
Wood	2	–	– (1)	2 (1)
Gill	1	–	–	1

GOALSCORERS

PLAYER	LGE	FAC	LC	TOT
Davenport	14	–	2	16
Whiteside	8	1	1	10
Stapleton	7	–	2	9
Robson	7	–	–	7
Strachan	4	–	–	4
Olsen	3	–	–	3
McGrath	2	–	–	2
Moses	–	–	2	2
Blackmore	1	–	–	1
Duxbury	1	–	–	1
Gibson C	1	–	–	1
Gibson T	1	–	–	1
Sivebaek	1	–	–	1
Barnes	–	–	1	1
own goals	2	–	–	2

RESULTS & ATTENDANCES SUMMARY

		P	W	D	L	F	A	TOTAL	AVGE
League	H	21	13	3	5	38	18	853137	40626
	A	21	1	11	9	14	27	529646	25221
TOTAL		42	14	14	14	52	45	1382783	32923
FA Cup	H	2	1	0	1	1	1	103376	51688
	A	0	0	0	0	0	0	0	n/a
TOTAL		2	1	0	1	1	1	103376	51688
League Cup	H	2	1	1	0	2	0	42545	21273
	A	2	1	0	1	6	6	28401	14201
TOTAL		4	2	1	1	8	6	70946	17737
Overall	H	25	15	4	6	41	19	999058	39962
	A	23	2	11	10	20	33	558047	24263
TOTAL		48	17	15	16	61	52	1557105	32440

FINAL TABLE – LEAGUE DIVISION ONE

		P	W	D	L	F	A	W	D	L	F	A	PTS	GD
			HOME					AWAY						
1	Everton	42	16	4	1	49	11	10	4	7	27	20	86	45
2	Liverpool	42	15	3	3	43	16	8	5	8	29	26	77	30
3	Tottenham Hotspur	42	14	3	4	40	14	7	5	9	28	29	71	25
4	Arsenal	42	12	5	4	31	12	8	5	8	27	23	70	23
5	Norwich City	42	9	10	2	27	20	8	7	6	26	31	68	2
6	Wimbledon	42	11	5	5	32	22	8	4	9	25	28	66	7
7	Luton Town	42	14	5	2	29	13	4	7	10	18	32	66	2
8	Nottingham Forest	42	12	8	1	36	14	6	3	12	28	37	65	13
9	Watford	42	12	5	4	38	20	6	4	11	29	34	63	13
10	Coventry City	42	14	4	3	35	17	3	8	10	15	28	63	5
11	MANCHESTER UNITED	42	13	3	5	38	18	1	11	9	14	27	56	7
12	Southampton	42	11	5	5	44	24	3	5	13	25	44	52	1
13	Sheffield Wednesday	42	9	7	5	39	24	4	6	11	19	35	52	–1
14	Chelsea	42	8	6	7	30	30	5	7	9	23	34	52	–11
15	West Ham United	42	10	4	7	33	28	4	6	11	19	39	52	–15
16	Queens Park Rangers	42	9	7	5	31	27	4	4	13	17	37	50	–16
17	Newcastle United	42	10	4	7	33	29	2	7	12	14	36	47	–18
18	Oxford United	42	8	8	5	30	25	3	5	13	14	44	46	–25
19	Charlton Athletic	42	7	7	7	26	22	4	4	13	19	33	44	–10
20	Leicester City	42	9	7	5	39	24	2	2	17	15	52	42	–22
21	Manchester City	42	8	6	7	28	24	0	9	12	8	33	39	–21
22	Aston Villa	42	7	7	7	25	25	1	5	15	20	54	36	–34

SEASON 1987/88

Match # 3867	Saturday 15/08/87	Football League Division 1	at The Dell	Attendance 21214
Result:	**Southampton 2 Manchester United 2**			
Teamsheet:	Walsh, Anderson, Duxbury, Moses, McGrath, Moran, Robson, Strachan, McClair, Whiteside, Olsen			
Substitute(s):	Albiston, Davenport	Scorer(s): Whiteside 2		

Match # 3868	Wednesday 19/08/87	Football League Division 1	at Old Trafford	Attendance 43893
Result:	**Manchester United 0 Arsenal 0**			
Teamsheet:	Walsh, Anderson, Duxbury, Moses, McGrath, Moran, Robson, Strachan, McClair, Whiteside, Olsen			

Match # 3869	Saturday 22/08/87	Football League Division 1	at Old Trafford	Attendance 38769
Result:	**Manchester United 2 Watford 0**			
Teamsheet:	Walsh, Anderson, Duxbury, Moses, McGrath, Moran, Robson, Strachan, McClair, Whiteside, Olsen			
Substitute(s):	Albiston, Davenport	Scorer(s): McClair, McGrath		

Match # 3870	Saturday 29/08/87	Football League Division 1	at Selhurst Park	Attendance 14046
Result:	**Charlton Athletic 1 Manchester United 3**			
Teamsheet:	Walsh, Anderson, Duxbury, Moses, McGrath, Moran, Robson, Strachan, McClair, Whiteside, Olsen			
Substitute(s):	Davenport, Gibson	Scorer(s): McClair, McGrath, Robson		

Match # 3871	Monday 31/08/87	Football League Division 1	at Old Trafford	Attendance 46616
Result:	**Manchester United 3 Chelsea 1**			
Teamsheet:	Walsh, Anderson, Albiston, Moses, McGrath, Moran, Duxbury, Strachan, McClair, Whiteside, Olsen			
Substitute(s):	Gibson	Scorer(s): McClair, Strachan, Whiteside		

Match # 3872	Saturday 05/09/87	Football League Division 1	at Highfield Road	Attendance 27125
Result:	**Coventry City 0 Manchester United 0**			
Teamsheet:	Walsh, Anderson, Albiston, Moses, McGrath, Moran, Duxbury, Strachan, McClair, Whiteside, Olsen			
Substitute(s):	Davenport, Gibson			

Match # 3873	Saturday 12/09/87	Football League Division 1	at Old Trafford	Attendance 45619
Result:	**Manchester United 2 Newcastle United 2**			
Teamsheet:	Walsh, Anderson, Duxbury, Moses, McGrath, Moran, Robson, Strachan, McClair, Whiteside, Olsen			
Substitute(s):	Davenport	Scorer(s): McClair, Olsen		

Match # 3874	Saturday 19/09/87	Football League Division 1	at Goodison Park	Attendance 38439
Result:	**Everton 2 Manchester United 1**			
Teamsheet:	Walsh, Anderson, Duxbury, Moses, McGrath, Hogg, Robson, Strachan, McClair, Whiteside, Olsen			
Substitute(s):	Davenport, Garton	Scorer(s): Whiteside		

Match # 3875	Wednesday 23/09/87	League Cup 2nd Round 1st Leg	at Old Trafford	Attendance 25041
Result:	**Manchester United 5 Hull City 0**			
Teamsheet:	Walsh, Anderson, Gibson, Moses, McGrath, Duxbury, Robson, Strachan, McClair, Whiteside, Davenport			
Substitute(s):	Garton	Scorer(s): Davenport, McClair, McGrath, Strachan, Whiteside		

Match # 3876	Saturday 26/09/87	Football League Division 1	at Old Trafford	Attendance 48087
Result:	**Manchester United 1 Tottenham Hotspur 0**			
Teamsheet:	Walsh, Anderson, Gibson, Garton, McGrath, Duxbury, Robson, Strachan, McClair, Whiteside, Olsen			
Substitute(s):	Blackmore, Davenport	Scorer(s): McClair		

Match # 3877	Saturday 03/10/87	Football League Division 1	at Kenilworth Road	Attendance 9137
Result:	**Luton Town 1 Manchester United 1**			
Teamsheet:	Walsh, Blackmore, Gibson, Garton, McGrath, Duxbury, Robson, Strachan, McClair, Whiteside, Olsen			
Substitute(s):	O'Brien	Scorer(s): McClair		

Match # 3878	Wednesday 07/10/87	League Cup 2nd Round 2nd Leg	at Boothferry Park	Attendance 13586
Result:	**Hull City 0 Manchester United 1**			
Teamsheet:	Turner, Blackmore, Gibson, Garton, McGrath, Duxbury, Robson, Strachan, McClair, Whiteside, Olsen			
Substitute(s):	Graham, O'Brien	Scorer(s): McClair		

Match # 3879	Saturday 10/10/87	Football League Division 1	at Hillsborough	Attendance 32779
Result:	**Sheffield Wednesday 2 Manchester United 4**			
Teamsheet:	Walsh, Garton, Gibson, Duxbury, McGrath, Moran, Robson, Strachan, McClair, Whiteside, Olsen			
Substitute(s):	Blackmore, Davenport	Scorer(s): McClair 2, Blackmore, Robson		

Match # 3880	Saturday 17/10/87	Football League Division 1	at Old Trafford	Attendance 39821
Result:	**Manchester United 2 Norwich City 1**			
Teamsheet:	Walsh, Garton, Gibson, Duxbury, McGrath, Davenport, Robson, Blackmore, McClair, Whiteside, Olsen			
Substitute(s):	Moran, O'Brien	Scorer(s): Davenport, Robson		

Match # 3881	Saturday 24/10/87	Football League Division 1	at Upton Park	Attendance 19863
Result:	**West Ham United 1 Manchester United 1**			
Teamsheet:	Walsh, Anderson, Gibson, Duxbury, McGrath, Moran, Robson, Strachan, McClair, Davenport, Olsen			
Substitute(s):	Blackmore	Scorer(s): Gibson		

Match # 3882	Wednesday 28/10/87	League Cup 3rd Round	at Old Trafford	Attendance 27283
Result:	**Manchester United 2 Crystal Palace 1**			
Teamsheet:	Turner, Anderson, Gibson, Duxbury, Garton, Moran, Robson, Strachan, McClair, Whiteside, Davenport			
Substitute(s):	Blackmore, Olsen	Scorer(s): McClair 2		

Match # 3883	Saturday 31/10/87	Football League Division 1	at Old Trafford	Attendance 44669
Result:	**Manchester United 2 Nottingham Forest 2**			
Teamsheet:	Walsh, Anderson, Gibson, Duxbury, Garton, Moran, Robson, Davenport, McClair, Whiteside, Olsen			
Substitute(s):	Strachan	Scorer(s): Robson, Whiteside		

Match # 3884	Sunday 15/11/87	Football League Division 1	at Old Trafford	Attendance 47106
Result:	**Manchester United 1 Liverpool 1**			
Teamsheet:	Walsh, Anderson, Gibson, Duxbury, Blackmore, Moran, Robson, Strachan, McClair, Whiteside, Olsen			
Substitute(s):	Davenport	Scorer(s): Whiteside		

SEASON 1987/88 (continued)

Match # 3885	Wednesday 18/11/87 League Cup 4th Round	at Old Trafford	Attendance 33519
Result:	**Bury 1 Manchester United 2** **(United drawn away - tie switched to Old Trafford)**		
Teamsheet:	Walsh, Anderson, Gibson, Duxbury, Blackmore, Davenport, Robson, Strachan, McClair, Whiteside, Olsen		
Substitute(s):	Moses, O'Brien Scorer(s): McClair, Whiteside		

Match # 3886	Saturday 21/11/87 Football League Division 1	at Plough Lane	Attendance 11532
Result:	**Wimbledon 2 Manchester United 1**		
Teamsheet:	Walsh, Anderson, Duxbury, Moses, Blackmore, Moran, Robson, Graham, McClair, Whiteside, Olsen		
Substitute(s):	Albiston, O'Brien Scorer(s): Blackmore		

Match # 3887	Saturday 05/12/87 Football League Division 1	at Loftus Road	Attendance 20632
Result:	**Queens Park Rangers 0 Manchester United 2**		
Teamsheet:	Turner, Duxbury, Albiston, Moses, Moran, O'Brien, Robson, Strachan, McClair, Davenport, Olsen		
Scorer(s):	Davenport, Robson		

Match # 3888	Saturday 12/12/87 Football League Division 1	at Old Trafford	Attendance 34709
Result:	**Manchester United 3 Oxford United 1**		
Teamsheet:	Turner, Duxbury, Gibson, Moses, Moran, Davenport, Robson, Strachan, McClair, Whiteside, Olsen		
Substitute(s):	Albiston Scorer(s): Strachan 2, Olsen		

Match # 3889	Saturday 19/12/87 Football League Division 1	at Fratton Park	Attendance 22207
Result:	**Portsmouth 1 Manchester United 2**		
Teamsheet:	Turner, Duxbury, Gibson, Bruce, Moran, Moses, Robson, Strachan, McClair, Whiteside, Olsen		
Substitute(s):	Davenport Scorer(s): McClair, Robson		

Match # 3890	Saturday 26/12/87 Football League Division 1	at St James' Park	Attendance 26461
Result:	**Newcastle United 1 Manchester United 0**		
Teamsheet:	Turner, Duxbury, Gibson, Bruce, Moran, Moses, Robson, Strachan, McClair, Whiteside, Davenport		
Substitute(s):	Anderson, Olsen		

Match # 3891	Monday 28/12/87 Football League Division 1	at Old Trafford	Attendance 47024
Result:	**Manchester United 2 Everton 1**		
Teamsheet:	Turner, Anderson, Gibson, Bruce, Moran, Duxbury, Robson, Strachan, McClair, Whiteside, Olsen		
Substitute(s):	Davenport, Moses Scorer(s): McClair 2		

Match # 3892	Friday 01/01/88 Football League Division 1	at Old Trafford	Attendance 37257
Result:	**Manchester United 0 Charlton Athletic 0**		
Teamsheet:	Turner, Anderson, Gibson, Bruce, Duxbury, Moses, Robson, Strachan, McClair, Davenport, Olsen		
Substitute(s):	Blackmore, O'Brien		

Match # 3893	Saturday 02/01/88 Football League Division 1	at Vicarage Road	Attendance 18038
Result:	**Watford 0 Manchester United 1**		
Teamsheet:	Turner, Anderson, Albiston, Bruce, Moran, Duxbury, Robson, Strachan, McClair, Whiteside, Gibson		
Substitute(s):	Davenport, O'Brien Scorer(s): McClair		

Match # 3894	Sunday 10/01/88 FA Cup 3rd Round	at Portman Road	Attendance 23012
Result:	**Ipswich Town 1 Manchester United 2**		
Teamsheet:	Turner, Anderson, Duxbury, Bruce, Moran, Moses, Robson, Strachan, McClair, Whiteside, Gibson		
Substitute(s):	Davenport, Olsen Scorer(s): Anderson, own goal		

Match # 3895	Saturday 16/01/88 Football League Division 1	at Old Trafford	Attendance 35716
Result:	**Manchester United 0 Southampton 2**		
Teamsheet:	Turner, Anderson, Gibson, Bruce, Moran, Moses, Robson, Duxbury, McClair, Davenport, Olsen		
Substitute(s):	O'Brien, Strachan		

Match # 3896	Wednesday 20/01/88 League Cup 5th Round	at Manor Ground	Attendance 12658
Result:	**Oxford United 2 Manchester United 0**		
Teamsheet:	Turner, Anderson, Gibson, Blackmore, Moran, Duxbury, Robson, Strachan, McClair, Whiteside, Olsen		
Substitute(s):	Davenport, Hogg		

Match # 3897	Sunday 24/01/88 Football League Division 1	at Highbury	Attendance 29392
Result:	**Arsenal 1 Manchester United 2**		
Teamsheet:	Turner, Anderson, Duxbury, Bruce, Blackmore, Hogg, Robson, Strachan, McClair, Whiteside, Olsen		
Substitute(s):	O'Brien Scorer(s): McClair, Strachan		

Match # 3898	Saturday 30/01/88 FA Cup 4th Round	at Old Trafford	Attendance 50716
Result:	**Manchester United 2 Chelsea 0**		
Teamsheet:	Turner, Anderson, Duxbury, Bruce, Blackmore, Hogg, Robson, Strachan, McClair, Whiteside, Olsen		
Substitute(s):	O'Brien Scorer(s): McClair, Whiteside		

Match # 3899	Saturday 06/02/88 Football League Division 1	at Old Trafford	Attendance 37144
Result:	**Manchester United 1 Coventry City 0**		
Teamsheet:	Turner, Anderson, Duxbury, Bruce, O'Brien, Hogg, Robson, Strachan, McClair, Whiteside, Olsen		
Substitute(s):	Albiston Scorer(s): O'Brien		

Match # 3900	Wednesday 10/02/88 Football League Division 1	at Baseball Ground	Attendance 20016
Result:	**Derby County 1 Manchester United 2**		
Teamsheet:	Turner, Anderson, Duxbury, Bruce, O'Brien, Hogg, Robson, Strachan, McClair, Whiteside, Olsen		
Substitute(s):	Albiston, Davenport Scorer(s): Strachan, Whiteside		

Match # 3901	Saturday 13/02/88 Football League Division 1	at Stamford Bridge	Attendance 25014
Result:	**Chelsea 1 Manchester United 2**		
Teamsheet:	Turner, Anderson, Albiston, Bruce, O'Brien, Hogg, Robson, Davenport, McClair, Whiteside, Gibson		
Substitute(s):	Blackmore Scorer(s): Bruce, O'Brien		

Match # 3902	Saturday 20/02/88 FA Cup 5th Round	at Highbury	Attendance 54161
Result:	**Arsenal 2 Manchester United 1**		
Teamsheet:	Turner, Anderson, Gibson, Bruce, Duxbury, Hogg, Davenport, Strachan, McClair, Whiteside, Olsen		
Substitute(s):	Blackmore, O'Brien Scorer(s): McClair		

SEASON 1987/88 (continued)

Match # 3903 Tuesday 23/02/88   Football League Division 1   at White Hart Lane   Attendance 25731
Result: **Tottenham Hotspur 1 Manchester United 1**
Teamsheet: Turner, Anderson, Duxbury, Bruce, O'Brien, Hogg, Davenport, Blackmore, McClair, Whiteside, Gibson
Substitute(s): Olsen, Strachan   Scorer(s):   McClair

Match # 3904 Saturday 05/03/88   Football League Division 1   at Carrow Road   Attendance 19129
Result: **Norwich City 1 Manchester United 0**
Teamsheet: Turner, Blackmore, Duxbury, Bruce, O'Brien, Moran, Robson, Strachan, McClair, Davenport, Gibson
Substitute(s): Olsen

Match # 3905 Saturday 12/03/88   Football League Division 1   at Old Trafford   Attendance 33318
Result: **Manchester United 4 Sheffield Wednesday 1**
Teamsheet: Turner, Blackmore, Gibson, Bruce, Duxbury, Hogg, Robson, Strachan, McClair, Davenport, Olsen
Substitute(s): O'Brien   Scorer(s):   McClair 2, Blackmore, Davenport

Match # 3906 Saturday 19/03/88   Football League Division 1   at City Ground   Attendance 27598
Result: **Nottingham Forest 0 Manchester United 0**
Teamsheet: Turner, Anderson, Blackmore, Bruce, Duxbury, Hogg, Whiteside, Olsen, McClair, Davenport, Gibson
Substitute(s): McGrath, O'Brien

Match # 3907 Saturday 26/03/88   Football League Division 1   at Old Trafford   Attendance 37269
Result: **Manchester United 3 West Ham United 1**
Teamsheet: Turner, Anderson, Blackmore, Bruce, McGrath, Duxbury, Robson, Strachan, McClair, Davenport, Gibson
Substitute(s): Olsen   Scorer(s):   Anderson, Robson, Strachan

Match # 3908 Saturday 02/04/88   Football League Division 1   at Old Trafford   Attendance 40146
Result: **Manchester United 4 Derby County 1**
Teamsheet: Turner, Anderson, Blackmore, Duxbury, McGrath, Hogg, Robson, Strachan, McClair, Davenport, Gibson
Substitute(s): O'Brien, Olsen   Scorer(s):   McClair 3, Gibson

Match # 3909 Monday 04/04/88   Football League Division 1   at Anfield   Attendance 43497
Result: **Liverpool 3 Manchester United 3**
Teamsheet: Turner, Anderson, Blackmore, Bruce, McGrath, Duxbury, Robson, Strachan, McClair, Davenport, Gibson
Substitute(s): Olsen, Whiteside   Scorer(s):   Robson 2, Strachan

Match # 3910 Tuesday 12/04/88   Football League Division 1   at Old Trafford   Attendance 28830
Result: **Manchester United 3 Luton Town 0**
Teamsheet: Turner, Anderson, Blackmore, Bruce, McGrath, Duxbury, Robson, Strachan, McClair, Davenport, Gibson
Substitute(s): Olsen   Scorer(s):   Davenport, McClair, Robson

Match # 3911 Saturday 30/04/88   Football League Division 1   at Old Trafford   Attendance 35733
Result: **Manchester United 2 Queens Park Rangers 1**
Teamsheet: Turner, Anderson, Blackmore, Bruce, McGrath, Duxbury, Robson, Strachan, McClair, Davenport, Olsen
Substitute(s): O'Brien   Scorer(s):   Bruce, own goal

Match # 3912 Monday 02/05/88   Football League Division 1   at Manor Ground   Attendance 8966
Result: **Oxford United 0 Manchester United 2**
Teamsheet: Turner, Anderson, Gibson, Bruce, McGrath, Duxbury, Robson, Strachan, McClair, Davenport, Olsen
Substitute(s): Blackmore   Scorer(s):   Anderson, Strachan

Match # 3913 Saturday 07/05/88   Football League Division 1   at Old Trafford   Attendance 35105
Result: **Manchester United 4 Portsmouth 1**
Teamsheet: Turner, Anderson, Gibson, Bruce, McGrath, Duxbury, Robson, Strachan, McClair, Davenport, Olsen
Substitute(s): Blackmore, Hogg   Scorer(s):   McClair 2, Davenport, Robson

Match # 3914 Monday 09/05/88   Football League Division 1   at Old Trafford   Attendance 28040
Result: **Manchester United 2 Wimbledon 1**
Teamsheet: Turner, Duxbury, Blackmore, Bruce, McGrath, Moses, Robson, Strachan, McClair, Davenport, Gibson
Substitute(s): Martin   Scorer(s):   McClair 2

SEASON 1987/88 SUMMARY

APPEARANCES

PLAYER	LGE	FAC	LC	TOTAL
McClair	40	3	5	48
Duxbury	39	3	5	47
Robson	36	2	5	43
Strachan	33 (3)	3	5	41 (3)
Anderson	30 (1)	3	4	37 (1)
Olsen	30 (7)	2 (1)	3 (1)	35 (9)
Whiteside	26 (1)	3	5	34 (1)
Gibson	26 (3)	2	5	33 (3)
Turner	24	3	3	30
Davenport	21 (13)	1 (1)	3 (1)	25 (15)
Bruce	21	3	–	24
McGrath	21 (1)	–	2	23 (1)
Moran	20 (1)	1	2	23 (1)
Blackmore	15 (7)	1 (1)	3 (1)	19 (9)
Moses	16 (1)	1	1 (1)	18 (2)
Walsh	16	–	2	18
Hogg	9 (1)	2	– (1)	11 (2)
Garton	5 (1)	–	2 (1)	7 (2)
O'Brien	6 (11)	– (2)	– (2)	6 (15)
Albiston	5 (6)	–	–	5 (6)
Graham	1	–	– (1)	1 (1)
Martin	– (1)	–	–	– (1)

GOALSCORERS

PLAYER	LGE	FAC	LC	TOT
McClair	24	2	5	31
Robson	11	–	–	11
Whiteside	7	1	2	10
Strachan	8	–	1	9
Davenport	5	–	1	6
Blackmore	3	–	–	3
Anderson	2	1	–	3
McGrath	2	–	1	3
Bruce	2	–	–	2
Gibson	2	–	–	2
O'Brien	2	–	–	2
Olsen	2	–	–	2
own goals	1	1	–	2

RESULTS & ATTENDANCES SUMMARY

		P	W	D	L	F	A	TOTAL	AVGE
League	H	20	14	5	1	41	17	784871	39244
	A	20	9	7	4	30	21	460816	23041
TOTAL		40	23	12	5	71	38	1245687	31142
FA Cup	H	1	1	0	0	2	0	50716	50716
	A	2	1	0	1	3	3	77173	38587
TOTAL		3	2	0	1	5	3	127889	42630
League Cup	H	2	2	0	0	7	1	52324	26162
	A	3	2	0	1	3	3	59763	19921
TOTAL		5	4	0	1	10	4	112087	22417
Overall	H	23	17	5	1	50	18	887911	38605
	A	25	12	7	6	36	27	597752	23910
TOTAL		48	29	12	7	86	45	1485663	30951

FINAL TABLE - LEAGUE DIVISION ONE

		P	HOME W	HOME D	HOME L	HOME F	HOME A	AWAY W	AWAY D	AWAY L	AWAY F	AWAY A	PTS	GD
1	Liverpool	40	15	5	0	49	9	11	7	2	38	15	90	63
2	MANCHESTER UNITED	40	14	5	1	41	17	9	7	4	30	21	81	33
3	Nottingham Forest	40	11	7	2	40	17	9	6	5	27	22	73	28
4	Everton	40	14	4	2	34	11	5	9	6	19	16	70	26
5	Queens Park Rangers	40	12	4	4	30	14	7	6	7	18	24	67	10
6	Arsenal	40	11	4	5	35	16	7	8	5	23	23	66	19
7	Wimbledon	40	8	9	3	32	20	6	6	8	26	27	57	11
8	Newcastle United	40	9	6	5	32	23	5	8	7	23	30	56	2
9	Luton Town	40	11	6	3	40	21	3	5	12	17	37	53	–1
10	Coventry City	40	6	8	6	23	25	7	6	7	23	28	53	–7
11	Sheffield Wednesday	40	10	2	8	27	30	5	6	9	25	36	53	–14
12	Southampton	40	6	8	6	27	26	6	6	8	22	27	50	–4
13	Tottenham Hotspur	40	9	5	6	26	23	3	6	11	12	25	47	–10
14	Norwich City	40	7	5	8	26	26	5	4	11	14	26	45	–12
15	Derby County	40	6	7	7	18	17	4	6	10	17	28	43	–10
16	West Ham United	40	6	9	5	23	21	3	6	11	17	31	42	–12
17	Charlton Athletic	40	7	7	6	23	21	2	8	10	15	31	42	–14
18	Chelsea	40	7	11	2	24	17	2	4	14	26	51	42	–18
19	Portsmouth	40	4	8	8	21	27	3	6	11	15	39	35	–30
20	Watford	40	4	5	11	15	24	3	6	11	12	27	32	–24
21	Oxford United	40	5	7	8	24	34	1	6	13	20	46	31	–36

SEASON 1988/89

Match # 3915 Saturday 27/08/88 Football League Division 1 at Old Trafford Attendance 46377
Result: **Manchester United 0 Queens Park Rangers 0**
Teamsheet: Leighton, Blackmore, Martin, Bruce, McGrath, McClair, Robson, Strachan, Davenport, Hughes, Olsen
Substitute(s): O'Brien

Match # 3916 Saturday 03/09/88 Football League Division 1 at Anfield Attendance 42026
Result: **Liverpool 1 Manchester United 0**
Teamsheet: Leighton, Anderson, Blackmore, Bruce, McGrath, Duxbury, Robson, Strachan, McClair, Hughes, Olsen
Substitute(s): Davenport, Garton

Match # 3917 Saturday 10/09/88 Football League Division 1 at Old Trafford Attendance 40422
Result: **Manchester United 1 Middlesbrough 0**
Teamsheet: Leighton, Garton, Blackmore, Bruce, McGrath, Duxbury, Robson, Davenport, McClair, Hughes, Olsen
Scorer(s): Robson

Match # 3918 Saturday 17/09/88 Football League Division 1 at Kenilworth Road Attendance 11010
Result: **Luton Town 0 Manchester United 2**
Teamsheet: Leighton, Garton, Blackmore, Bruce, McGrath, Duxbury, Robson, Davenport, McClair, Hughes, Olsen
Scorer(s): Davenport, Robson

Match # 3919 Saturday 24/09/88 Football League Division 1 at Old Trafford Attendance 39941
Result: **Manchester United 2 West Ham United 0**
Teamsheet: Leighton, Blackmore, Sharpe, Bruce, Garton, Duxbury, Robson, Strachan, McClair, Hughes, Davenport
Substitute(s): Beardsmore, Olsen Scorer(s): Davenport, Hughes

Match # 3920 Wednesday 28/09/88 League Cup 2nd Round 1st Leg at Millmoor Attendance 12588
Result: **Rotherham United 0 Manchester United 1**
Teamsheet: Leighton, Blackmore, Sharpe, Bruce, McGrath, Duxbury, Robson, Strachan, McClair, Hughes, Davenport
Substitute(s): Beardsmore, Olsen Scorer(s): Davenport

Match # 3921 Saturday 01/10/88 Football League Division 1 at White Hart Lane Attendance 29318
Result: **Tottenham Hotspur 2 Manchester United 2**
Teamsheet: Leighton, Garton, Sharpe, Bruce, McGrath, Duxbury, Robson, Strachan, McClair, Hughes, Davenport
Substitute(s): Anderson, Olsen Scorer(s): Hughes, McClair

Match # 3922 Wednesday 12/10/88 League Cup 2nd Round 2nd Leg at Old Trafford Attendance 20597
Result: **Manchester United 5 Rotherham United 0**
Teamsheet: Leighton, Beardsmore, Blackmore, Bruce, Garton, Duxbury, Robson, Strachan, McClair, Hughes, Sharpe
Substitute(s): Davenport, Robins Scorer(s): McClair 3, Bruce, Robson

Match # 3923 Saturday 22/10/88 Football League Division 1 at Plough Lane Attendance 12143
Result: **Wimbledon 1 Manchester United 1**
Teamsheet: Leighton, Blackmore, Sharpe, Bruce, Garton, Duxbury, Robson, Strachan, McClair, Hughes, Davenport
Substitute(s): Beardsmore, Robins Scorer(s): Hughes

Match # 3924 Wednesday 26/10/88 Football League Division 1 at Old Trafford Attendance 36998
Result: **Manchester United 1 Norwich City 2**
Teamsheet: Leighton, Blackmore, Sharpe, Bruce, Garton, Duxbury, Robson, Strachan, McClair, Hughes, Davenport
Substitute(s): Olsen Scorer(s): Hughes

Match # 3925 Sunday 30/10/88 Football League Division 1 at Goodison Park Attendance 27005
Result: **Everton 1 Manchester United 1**
Teamsheet: Leighton, Garton, Blackmore, Bruce, Duxbury, Donaghy, Robson, Strachan, McClair, Hughes, Olsen
Substitute(s): Gibson, O'Brien Scorer(s): Hughes

Match # 3926 Wednesday 02/11/88 League Cup 3rd Round at Plough Lane Attendance 10864
Result: **Wimbledon 2 Manchester United 1**
Teamsheet: Leighton, Blackmore, Gibson, Bruce, Garton, Duxbury, Robson, O'Brien, McClair, Hughes, Olsen
Substitute(s): Anderson, Strachan Scorer(s): Robson

Match # 3927 Saturday 05/11/88 Football League Division 1 at Old Trafford Attendance 44804
Result: **Manchester United 1 Aston Villa 1**
Teamsheet: Leighton, Blackmore, Gibson, Bruce, O'Brien, Donaghy, Robson, Strachan, McClair, Hughes, Olsen
Substitute(s): Duxbury Scorer(s): Bruce

Match # 3928 Saturday 12/11/88 Football League Division 1 at Baseball Ground Attendance 24080
Result: **Derby County 2 Manchester United 2**
Teamsheet: Leighton, Garton, Blackmore, Bruce, Duxbury, Donaghy, Robson, Strachan, McClair, Hughes, Sharpe
Substitute(s): Olsen Scorer(s): Hughes, McClair

Match # 3929 Saturday 19/11/88 Football League Division 1 at Old Trafford Attendance 37277
Result: **Manchester United 2 Southampton 2**
Teamsheet: Leighton, Garton, Sharpe, Bruce, Blackmore, Donaghy, Robson, Strachan, McClair, Hughes, Milne
Substitute(s): Gill Scorer(s): Hughes, Robson

Match # 3930 Wednesday 23/11/88 Football League Division 1 at Old Trafford Attendance 30849
Result: **Manchester United 1 Sheffield Wednesday 1**
Teamsheet: Leighton, Garton, Sharpe, Bruce, Blackmore, Donaghy, Robson, Strachan, McClair, Hughes, Milne
Substitute(s): Gill, Wilson Scorer(s): Hughes

Match # 3931 Sunday 27/11/88 Football League Division 1 at St James' Park Attendance 20350
Result: **Newcastle United 0 Manchester United 0**
Teamsheet: Leighton, Garton, Blackmore, Bruce, Gill, Donaghy, Robson, Milne, McClair, Hughes, Sharpe
Substitute(s): Martin, Robins

Match # 3932 Saturday 03/12/88 Football League Division 1 at Old Trafford Attendance 31173
Result: **Manchester United 3 Charlton Athletic 0**
Teamsheet: Leighton, Garton, Martin, Bruce, Blackmore, Donaghy, Robson, Strachan, McClair, Hughes, Milne
Scorer(s): Hughes, McClair, Milne

SEASON 1988/89 (continued)

Match # 3933 Saturday 10/12/88   Football League Division 1   at Highfield Road   Attendance 19936
Result: **Coventry City 1 Manchester United 0**
Teamsheet: Leighton, Garton, Martin, Bruce, Blackmore, Donaghy, Robson, Strachan, McClair, Hughes, Sharpe
Substitute(s): Gill, Milne

Match # 3934 Saturday 17/12/88   Football League Division 1   at Highbury   Attendance 37422
Result: **Arsenal 2 Manchester United 1**
Teamsheet: Leighton, Martin, Sharpe, Bruce, Blackmore, Donaghy, Robson, Strachan, McClair, Hughes, Milne
Substitute(s): Beardsmore, Gill   Scorer(s):   Hughes

Match # 3935 Monday 26/12/88   Football League Division 1   at Old Trafford   Attendance 39582
Result: **Manchester United 2 Nottingham Forest 0**
Teamsheet: Leighton, Martin, Sharpe, Bruce, Beardsmore, Donaghy, Robson, Strachan, McClair, Hughes, Milne
Scorer(s):   Hughes, Milne

Match # 3936 Sunday 01/01/89   Football League Division 1   at Old Trafford   Attendance 44745
Result: **Manchester United 3 Liverpool 1**
Teamsheet: Leighton, Martin, Sharpe, Bruce, Beardsmore, Donaghy, Robson, Strachan, McClair, Hughes, Milne
Substitute(s): McGrath, Robins   Scorer(s):   Beardsmore, Hughes, McClair

Match # 3937 Monday 02/01/89   Football League Division 1   at Ayresome Park   Attendance 24411
Result: **Middlesbrough 1 Manchester United 0**
Teamsheet: Leighton, Gill, Sharpe, Bruce, McGrath, Donaghy, Robson, Beardsmore, McClair, Hughes, Milne
Substitute(s): Robins, Wilson

Match # 3938 Saturday 07/01/89   FA Cup 3rd Round   at Old Trafford   Attendance 36222
Result: **Manchester United 0 Queens Park Rangers 0**
Teamsheet: Leighton, Gill, Martin, Bruce, Beardsmore, Donaghy, Robson, Robins, McClair, Hughes, Milne
Substitute(s): Wilson

Match # 3939 Wednesday 11/01/89   FA Cup 3rd Round Replay   at Loftus Road   Attendance 22236
Result: **Queens Park Rangers 2 Manchester United 2**
Teamsheet: Leighton, Martin, Sharpe, Bruce, Beardsmore, Donaghy, Gill, Blackmore, McClair, Hughes, Milne
Substitute(s): Graham, Wilson   Scorer(s):   Gill, Graham

Match # 3940 Saturday 14/01/89   Football League Division 1   at Old Trafford   Attendance 40931
Result: **Manchester United 3 Millwall 0**
Teamsheet: Leighton, Martin, Sharpe, Bruce, Beardsmore, Donaghy, Gill, Blackmore, McClair, Hughes, Milne
Substitute(s): Maiorana, Wilson   Scorer(s):   Blackmore, Gill, Hughes

Match # 3941 Saturday 21/01/89   Football League Division 1   at Upton Park   Attendance 29822
Result: **West Ham United 1 Manchester United 3**
Teamsheet: Leighton, Gill, Martin, Bruce, Blackmore, Donaghy, Robson, Strachan, McClair, Hughes, Milne
Substitute(s): Sharpe   Scorer(s):   Martin, McClair, Strachan

Match # 3942 Monday 23/01/89   FA Cup 3rd Round 2nd Replay   at Old Trafford   Attendance 46257
Result: **Manchester United 3 Queens Park Rangers 0**
Teamsheet: Leighton, Martin, Sharpe, Bruce, Blackmore, Donaghy, Robson, Strachan, McClair, Hughes, Milne
Substitute(s): Beardsmore, McGrath   Scorer(s):   McClair 2, Robson

Match # 3943 Saturday 28/01/89   FA Cup 4th Round   at Old Trafford   Attendance 47745
Result: **Manchester United 4 Oxford United 0**
Teamsheet: Leighton, Blackmore, Sharpe, Bruce, McGrath, Donaghy, Robson, Strachan, McClair, Hughes, Milne
Substitute(s): Beardsmore, Gill   Scorer(s):   Bruce, Hughes, Robson, own goal

Match # 3944 Sunday 05/02/89   Football League Division 1   at Old Trafford   Attendance 41423
Result: **Manchester United 1 Tottenham Hotspur 0**
Teamsheet: Leighton, Martin, Sharpe, Bruce, Blackmore, Donaghy, Robson, Strachan, McClair, Hughes, Milne
Substitute(s): Beardsmore, McGrath   Scorer(s):   McClair

Match # 3945 Saturday 11/02/89   Football League Division 1   at Hillsborough   Attendance 34820
Result: **Sheffield Wednesday 0 Manchester United 2**
Teamsheet: Leighton, Blackmore, Martin, Bruce, McGrath, Donaghy, Robson, Strachan, McClair, Hughes, Milne
Substitute(s): Beardsmore   Scorer(s):   McClair 2

Match # 3946 Saturday 18/02/89   FA Cup 5th Round   at Dean Court   Attendance 12708
Result: **Bournemouth 1 Manchester United 1**
Teamsheet: Leighton, Blackmore, Martin, Bruce, McGrath, Donaghy, Robson, Strachan, McClair, Hughes, Milne
Substitute(s): Sharpe   Scorer(s):   Hughes

Match # 3947 Wednesday 22/02/89   FA Cup 5th Round Replay   at Old Trafford   Attendance 52422
Result: **Manchester United 1 Bournemouth 0**
Teamsheet: Leighton, Blackmore, Sharpe, Bruce, McGrath, Donaghy, Robson, Strachan, McClair, Hughes, Milne
Substitute(s): Gill   Scorer(s):   McClair

Match # 3948 Saturday 25/02/89   Football League Division 1   at Carrow Road   Attendance 23155
Result: **Norwich City 2 Manchester United 1**
Teamsheet: Leighton, Blackmore, Sharpe, Bruce, McGrath, Donaghy, Robson, Strachan, McClair, Hughes, Milne
Substitute(s): Beardsmore, Martin   Scorer(s):   McGrath

Match # 3949 Sunday 12/03/89   Football League Division 1   at Villa Park   Attendance 28332
Result: **Aston Villa 0 Manchester United 0**
Teamsheet: Leighton, Beardsmore, Martin, Bruce, McGrath, Donaghy, Robson, Strachan, McClair, Hughes, Sharpe
Substitute(s): Blackmore, Milne

Match # 3950 Saturday 18/03/89   FA Cup 6th Round   at Old Trafford   Attendance 55040
Result: **Manchester United 0 Nottingham Forest 1**
Teamsheet: Leighton, Beardsmore, Sharpe, Bruce, McGrath, Donaghy, Robson, Strachan, McClair, Hughes, Milne
Substitute(s): Blackmore, Martin

SEASON 1988/89 (continued)

Match # 3951 Saturday 25/03/89   Football League Division 1   at Old Trafford   Attendance 36335
Result: **Manchester United 2 Luton Town 0**
Teamsheet: Leighton, Martin, Blackmore, Bruce, McGrath, Donaghy, Robson, Beardsmore, McClair, Hughes, Milne
Substitute(s):   Maiorana   Scorer(s):   Blackmore, Milne

Match # 3952 Monday 27/03/89   Football League Division 1   at City Ground   Attendance 30092
Result: **Nottingham Forest 2 Manchester United 0**
Teamsheet: Leighton, Anderson, Blackmore, Bruce, McGrath, Donaghy, Robson, Beardsmore, McClair, Hughes, Milne
Substitute(s):   Gill, Martin

Match # 3953 Sunday 02/04/89   Football League Division 1   at Old Trafford   Attendance 37977
Result: **Manchester United 1 Arsenal 1**
Teamsheet: Leighton, Anderson, Donaghy, Bruce, McGrath, Whiteside, Robson, Beardsmore, McClair, Hughes, Maiorana
Substitute(s):   Blackmore, Martin   Scorer(s):   own goal

Match # 3954 Saturday 08/04/89   Football League Division 1   at The Den   Attendance 17523
Result: **Millwall 0 Manchester United 0**
Teamsheet: Leighton, Anderson, Donaghy, Bruce, McGrath, Whiteside, Robson, Beardsmore, McClair, Hughes, Martin
Substitute(s):   Maiorana

Match # 3955 Saturday 15/04/89   Football League Division 1   at Old Trafford   Attendance 34145
Result: **Manchester United 0 Derby County 2**
Teamsheet: Leighton, Anderson, Martin, Bruce, McGrath, Donaghy, Robins, Beardsmore, McClair, Hughes, Maiorana
Substitute(s):   Duxbury, Wilson

Match # 3956 Saturday 22/04/89   Football League Division 1   at Selhurst Park   Attendance 12055
Result: **Charlton Athletic 1 Manchester United 0**
Teamsheet: Leighton, Duxbury, Donaghy, Bruce, McGrath, Whiteside, Robson, Beardsmore, McClair, Hughes, Milne
Substitute(s):   Robins

Match # 3957 Saturday 29/04/89   Football League Division 1   at Old Trafford   Attendance 29799
Result: **Manchester United 0 Coventry City 1**
Teamsheet: Leighton, Duxbury, Donaghy, Bruce, McGrath, Whiteside, Robson, Beardsmore, McClair, Hughes, Martin
Substitute(s):   Robins

Match # 3958 Tuesday 02/05/89   Football League Division 1   at Old Trafford   Attendance 23368
Result: **Manchester United 1 Wimbledon 0**
Teamsheet: Leighton, Duxbury, Donaghy, Bruce, McGrath, Whiteside, Robson, Beardsmore, McClair, Hughes, Martin
Substitute(s):   Maiorana   Scorer(s):   McClair

Match # 3959 Saturday 06/05/89   Football League Division 1   at The Dell   Attendance 17021
Result: **Southampton 2 Manchester United 1**
Teamsheet: Leighton, Duxbury, Donaghy, Bruce, McGrath, Whiteside, Robson, Beardsmore, McClair, Hughes, Martin
Substitute(s):   Milne, Sharpe   Scorer(s):   Beardsmore

Match # 3960 Monday 08/05/89   Football League Division 1   at Loftus Road   Attendance 10017
Result: **Queens Park Rangers 3 Manchester United 2**
Teamsheet: Leighton, Duxbury, Sharpe, Bruce, Blackmore, Donaghy, Milne, Beardsmore, McClair, Hughes, Martin
Substitute(s):   Robins   Scorer(s):   Blackmore, Bruce

Match # 3961 Wednesday 10/05/89   Football League Division 1   at Old Trafford   Attendance 26722
Result: **Manchester United 1 Everton 2**
Teamsheet: Leighton, Duxbury, Sharpe, Bruce, Blackmore, Donaghy, Milne, Beardsmore, McClair, Hughes, Martin
Substitute(s):   Brazil, Robins   Scorer(s):   Hughes

Match # 3962 Saturday 13/05/89   Football League Division 1   at Old Trafford   Attendance 30379
Result: **Manchester United 2 Newcastle United 0**
Teamsheet: Leighton, Duxbury, Martin, Bruce, Blackmore, Donaghy, Robson, Beardsmore, McClair, Hughes, Milne
Substitute(s):   Robins, Sharpe   Scorer(s):   McClair, Robson

SEASON 1988/89 SUMMARY

APPEARANCES

PLAYER	LGE	FAC	LC	TOTAL
Bruce	38	7	3	48
Hughes	38	7	3	48
Leighton	38	7	3	48
McClair	38	7	3	48
Robson	34	6	3	43
Donaghy	30	7	–	37
Blackmore	26 (2)	5 (1)	3	34 (3)
Strachan	21	5	2 (1)	28 (1)
Sharpe	19 (3)	5 (1)	2	26 (4)
Milne	19 (3)	7	–	26 (3)
Martin	20 (4)	4 (1)	–	24 (5)
McGrath	18 (2)	4 (1)	1	23 (3)
Beardsmore	17 (6)	3 (2)	1 (1)	21 (9)
Duxbury	16 (2)	–	3	19 (2)
Garton	13 (1)	–	2	15 (1)
Davenport	7 (1)	–	1 (1)	8 (2)
Olsen	6 (4)	–	1 (1)	7 (5)
Gill	4 (5)	2 (2)	–	6 (7)
Whiteside	6	–	–	6
Anderson	5 (1)	–	– (1)	5 (2)
Robins	1 (9)	1	– (1)	2 (10)
Maiorana	2 (4)	–	–	2 (4)
O'Brien	1 (2)	–	1	2 (2)
Gibson	1 (1)	–	1	2 (1)
Wilson	– (4)	– (2)	–	– (6)
Brazil	– (1)	–	–	– (1)
Graham	–	– (1)	–	– (1)

GOALSCORERS

PLAYER	LGE	FAC	LC	TOT
Hughes	14	2	–	16
McClair	10	3	3	16
Robson	4	2	2	8
Bruce	2	1	1	4
Blackmore	3	–	–	3
Milne	3	–	–	3
Davenport	2	–	1	3
Beardsmore	2	–	–	2
Gill	1	1	–	2
Martin	1	–	–	1
McGrath	1	–	–	1
Strachan	1	–	–	1
Graham	–	1	–	1
own goals	1	1	–	2

RESULTS & ATTENDANCES SUMMARY

		P	W	D	L	F	A	TOTAL	AVGE
League	H	19	10	5	4	27	13	693247	36487
	A	19	3	7	9	18	22	450538	23713
	TOTAL	38	13	12	13	45	35	1143785	30100
FA Cup	H	5	3	1	1	8	1	237686	47537
	A	2	0	2	0	3	3	34944	17472
	TOTAL	7	3	3	1	11	4	272630	38947
League Cup	H	1	1	0	0	5	0	20597	20597
	A	2	1	0	1	2	2	23452	11726
	TOTAL	3	2	0	1	7	2	44049	14683
Overall	H	25	14	6	5	40	14	951530	38061
	A	23	4	9	10	23	27	508934	22128
	TOTAL	48	18	15	15	63	41	1460464	30426

FINAL TABLE – LEAGUE DIVISION ONE

		P	W	D	L	F	A	W	D	L	F	A	PTS	GD
				HOME						AWAY				
1	Arsenal	38	10	6	3	35	19	12	4	3	38	17	76	37
2	Liverpool	38	11	5	3	33	11	11	5	3	32	17	76	37
3	Nottingham Forest	38	8	7	4	31	16	9	6	4	33	27	64	21
4	Norwich City	38	8	7	4	23	20	9	4	6	25	25	62	3
5	Derby County	38	9	3	7	23	18	8	4	7	17	20	58	2
6	Tottenham Hotspur	38	8	6	5	31	24	7	6	6	29	22	57	14
7	Coventry City	38	9	4	6	28	23	5	9	5	19	19	55	5
8	Everton	38	10	7	2	33	18	4	5	10	17	27	54	5
9	Queens Park Rangers	38	9	5	5	23	16	5	6	8	20	21	53	6
10	Millwall	38	10	3	6	27	21	4	8	7	20	31	53	-5
11	MANCHESTER UNITED	38	10	5	4	27	13	3	7	9	18	22	51	10
12	Wimbledon	38	10	3	6	30	19	4	6	9	20	27	51	4
13	Southampton	38	6	7	6	25	26	4	8	7	27	40	45	-14
14	Charlton Athletic	38	6	7	6	25	24	4	5	10	19	34	42	-14
15	Sheffield Wednesday	38	6	6	7	21	25	4	6	9	13	26	42	-17
16	Luton Town	38	8	6	5	32	21	2	5	12	10	31	41	-10
17	Aston Villa	38	7	6	6	25	22	2	7	10	20	34	40	-11
18	Middlesbrough	38	6	7	6	28	30	3	5	11	16	31	39	-17
19	West Ham United	38	3	6	10	19	30	7	2	10	18	32	38	-25
20	Newcastle United	38	3	6	10	19	28	4	4	11	13	35	31	-31

SEASON 1989/90

Match # 3963   Saturday 19/08/89   Football League Division 1   at Old Trafford   Attendance 47245
Result: **Manchester United 4 Arsenal 1**
Teamsheet: Leighton, Duxbury, Blackmore, Bruce, Phelan, Donaghy, Robson, Webb, McClair, Hughes, Sharpe
Substitute(s):   Martin   Scorer(s):   Bruce, Hughes, McClair, Webb

Match # 3964   Tuesday 22/08/89   Football League Division 1   at Selhurst Park   Attendance 22423
Result: **Crystal Palace 1 Manchester United 1**
Teamsheet: Leighton, Duxbury, Blackmore, Bruce, Phelan, Donaghy, Robson, Webb, McClair, Hughes, Sharpe
Scorer(s):   Robson

Match # 3965   Saturday 26/08/89   Football League Division 1   at Baseball Ground   Attendance 22175
Result: **Derby County 2 Manchester United 0**
Teamsheet: Leighton, Duxbury, Martin, Bruce, Phelan, Blackmore, Robson, Webb, McClair, Hughes, Sharpe
Substitute(s):   Graham

Match # 3966   Wednesday 30/08/89   Football League Division 1   at Old Trafford   Attendance 41610
Result: **Manchester United 0 Norwich City 2**
Teamsheet: Leighton, Duxbury, Blackmore, Bruce, Phelan, Pallister, Robson, Webb, McClair, Hughes, Sharpe
Substitute(s):   Martin, Robins

Match # 3967   Saturday 09/09/89   Football League Division 1   at Goodison Park   Attendance 37916
Result: **Everton 3 Manchester United 2**
Teamsheet: Leighton, Duxbury, Martin, Bruce, Phelan, Pallister, Donaghy, Blackmore, McClair, Hughes, Sharpe
Substitute(s):   Anderson, Beardsmore   Scorer(s):   Beardsmore, McClair

Match # 3968   Saturday 16/09/89   Football League Division 1   at Old Trafford   Attendance 42746
Result: **Manchester United 5 Millwall 1**
Teamsheet: Leighton, Anderson, Donaghy, Bruce, Phelan, Pallister, Robson, Ince, McClair, Hughes, Sharpe
Substitute(s):   Beardsmore, Duxbury   Scorer(s):   Hughes 3, Robson, Sharpe

Match # 3969   Wednesday 20/09/89   League Cup 2nd Round 1st Leg   at Fratton Park   Attendance 18072
Result: **Portsmouth 2 Manchester United 3**
Teamsheet: Leighton, Anderson, Donaghy, Beardsmore, Phelan, Pallister, Robson, Ince, McClair, Hughes, Wallace
Substitute(s):   Duxbury, Sharpe   Scorer(s):   Ince 2, Wallace

Match # 3970   Saturday 23/09/89   Football League Division 1   at Maine Road   Attendance 43246
Result: **Manchester City 5 Manchester United 1**
Teamsheet: Leighton, Anderson, Donaghy, Duxbury, Phelan, Pallister, Beardsmore, Ince, McClair, Hughes, Wallace
Substitute(s):   Sharpe   Scorer(s):   Hughes

Match # 3971   Tuesday 03/10/89   League Cup 2nd Round 2nd Leg   at Old Trafford   Attendance 26698
Result: **Manchester United 0 Portsmouth 0**
Teamsheet: Leighton, Duxbury, Donaghy, Bruce, Phelan, Pallister, Robson, Ince, McClair, Hughes, Wallace

Match # 3972   Saturday 14/10/89   Football League Division 1   at Old Trafford   Attendance 41492
Result: **Manchester United 0 Sheffield Wednesday 0**
Teamsheet: Leighton, Duxbury, Donaghy, Bruce, Phelan, Pallister, Robson, Ince, McClair, Hughes, Wallace
Substitute(s):   Martin, Sharpe

Match # 3973   Saturday 21/10/89   Football League Division 1   at Highfield Road   Attendance 19625
Result: **Coventry City 1 Manchester United 4**
Teamsheet: Leighton, Donaghy, Martin, Bruce, Phelan, Pallister, Robson, Ince, McClair, Hughes, Sharpe
Substitute(s):   Duxbury, Maiorana   Scorer(s):   Hughes 2, Bruce, Phelan

Match # 3974   Wednesday 25/10/89   League Cup 3rd Round   at Old Trafford   Attendance 45759
Result: **Manchester United 0 Tottenham Hotspur 3**
Teamsheet: Leighton, Donaghy, Martin, Bruce, Phelan, Pallister, Robson, Ince, McClair, Hughes, Sharpe
Substitute(s):   Maiorana

Match # 3975   Saturday 28/10/89   Football League Division 1   at Old Trafford   Attendance 37122
Result: **Manchester United 2 Southampton 1**
Teamsheet: Leighton, Donaghy, Martin, Bruce, Phelan, Pallister, Robson, Ince, McClair, Hughes, Sharpe
Substitute(s):   Blackmore   Scorer(s):   McClair 2

Match # 3976   Saturday 04/11/89   Football League Division 1   at Selhurst Park   Attendance 16065
Result: **Charlton Athletic 2 Manchester United 0**
Teamsheet: Leighton, Donaghy, Martin, Bruce, Phelan, Pallister, Robson, Ince, McClair, Hughes, Sharpe
Substitute(s):   Blackmore, Wallace

Match # 3977   Sunday 12/11/89   Football League Division 1   at Old Trafford   Attendance 34182
Result: **Manchester United 1 Nottingham Forest 0**
Teamsheet: Leighton, Blackmore, Martin, Bruce, Phelan, Pallister, Robson, Ince, McClair, Hughes, Wallace
Substitute(s):   Sharpe   Scorer(s):   Pallister

Match # 3978   Saturday 18/11/89   Football League Division 1   at Kenilworth Road   Attendance 11141
Result: **Luton Town 1 Manchester United 3**
Teamsheet: Leighton, Blackmore, Martin, Bruce, Phelan, Pallister, Robson, Ince, McClair, Hughes, Wallace
Scorer(s):   Blackmore, Hughes, Wallace

Match # 3979   Saturday 25/11/89   Football League Division 1   at Old Trafford   Attendance 46975
Result: **Manchester United 0 Chelsea 0**
Teamsheet: Leighton, Blackmore, Martin, Bruce, Phelan, Pallister, Robson, Ince, McClair, Hughes, Wallace
Substitute(s):   Beardsmore, Duxbury

Match # 3980   Sunday 03/12/89   Football League Division 1   at Highbury   Attendance 34484
Result: **Arsenal 1 Manchester United 0**
Teamsheet: Leighton, Blackmore, Martin, Bruce, Phelan, Pallister, Robson, Ince, McClair, Hughes, Wallace
Substitute(s):   Beardsmore

SEASON 1989/90 (continued)

Match # 3981   Saturday 09/12/89   Football League Division 1   at Old Trafford   Attendance 33514
Result: **Manchester United 1   Crystal Palace 2**
Teamsheet: Leighton, Beardsmore, Martin, Bruce, Phelan, Pallister, Robson, Ince, McClair, Sharpe, Wallace
Substitute(s):   Blackmore, Hughes   Scorer(s):   Beardsmore

Match # 3982   Saturday 16/12/89   Football League Division 1   at Old Trafford   Attendance 36230
Result: **Manchester United 0   Tottenham Hotspur 1**
Teamsheet: Leighton, Beardsmore, Sharpe, Bruce, Phelan, Pallister, Robson, Ince, McClair, Hughes, Wallace
Substitute(s):   Anderson, Blackmore

Match # 3983   Saturday 23/12/89   Football League Division 1   at Anfield   Attendance 37426
Result: **Liverpool 0   Manchester United 0**
Teamsheet: Leighton, Blackmore, Martin, Bruce, Phelan, Pallister, Robson, Ince, McClair, Hughes, Wallace
Substitute(s):   Sharpe

Match # 3984   Tuesday 26/12/89   Football League Division 1   at Villa Park   Attendance 41247
Result: **Aston Villa 3   Manchester United 0**
Teamsheet: Leighton, Anderson, Martin, Bruce, Phelan, Pallister, Blackmore, Ince, McClair, Hughes, Sharpe
Substitute(s):   Duxbury, Robins

Match # 3985   Saturday 30/12/89   Football League Division 1   at Plough Lane   Attendance 9622
Result: **Wimbledon 2   Manchester United 2**
Teamsheet: Leighton, Anderson, Martin, Bruce, Phelan, Pallister, Blackmore, Ince, McClair, Hughes, Robins
Substitute(s):   Sharpe   Scorer(s):   Hughes, Robins

Match # 3986   Monday 01/01/90   Football League Division 1   at Old Trafford   Attendance 34824
Result: **Manchester United 0   Queens Park Rangers 0**
Teamsheet: Leighton, Anderson, Martin, Bruce, Phelan, Pallister, Sharpe, Blackmore, McClair, Hughes, Robins
Substitute(s):   Beardsmore, Duxbury

Match # 3987   Sunday 07/01/90   FA Cup 3rd Round   at City Ground   Attendance 23072
Result: **Nottingham Forest 0   Manchester United 1**
Teamsheet: Leighton, Anderson, Martin, Bruce, Phelan, Pallister, Beardsmore, Blackmore, McClair, Hughes, Robins
Substitute(s):   Duxbury   Scorer(s):   Robins

Match # 3988   Saturday 13/01/90   Football League Division 1   at Old Trafford   Attendance 38985
Result: **Manchester United 1   Derby County 2**
Teamsheet: Leighton, Anderson, Martin, Bruce, Phelan, Pallister, Beardsmore, Blackmore, McClair, Hughes, Robins
Substitute(s):   Duxbury, Milne   Scorer(s):   Pallister

Match # 3989   Sunday 21/01/90   Football League Division 1   at Carrow Road   Attendance 17370
Result: **Norwich City 2   Manchester United 0**
Teamsheet: Leighton, Anderson, Martin, Bruce, Phelan, Pallister, Robins, Ince, McClair, Hughes, Wallace
Substitute(s):   Beardsmore, Blackmore

Match # 3990   Sunday 28/01/90   FA Cup 4th Round   at Edgar Street   Attendance 13777
Result: **Hereford United 0   Manchester United 1**
Teamsheet: Leighton, Anderson, Martin, Donaghy, Duxbury, Pallister, Blackmore, Ince, McClair, Hughes, Wallace
Substitute(s):   Beardsmore   Scorer(s):   Blackmore

Match # 3991   Saturday 03/02/90   Football League Division 1   at Old Trafford   Attendance 40274
Result: **Manchester United 1   Manchester City 1**
Teamsheet: Leighton, Anderson, Martin, Donaghy, Phelan, Pallister, Blackmore, Duxbury, McClair, Hughes, Wallace
Substitute(s):   Beardsmore, Robins   Scorer(s):   Blackmore

Match # 3992   Saturday 10/02/90   Football League Division 1   at The Den   Attendance 15491
Result: **Millwall 1   Manchester United 2**
Teamsheet: Leighton, Anderson, Martin, Beardsmore, Phelan, Pallister, Blackmore, Duxbury, McClair, Hughes, Wallace
Substitute(s):   Brazil, Robins   Scorer(s):   Hughes, Wallace

Match # 3993   Sunday 18/02/90   FA Cup 5th Round   at St James' Park   Attendance 31748
Result: **Newcastle United 2   Manchester United 3**
Teamsheet: Leighton, Anderson, Martin, Bruce, Phelan, Pallister, Robins, Duxbury, McClair, Hughes, Wallace
Substitute(s):   Beardsmore, Ince   Scorer(s):   McClair, Robins, Wallace

Match # 3994   Saturday 24/02/90   Football League Division 1   at Stamford Bridge   Attendance 29979
Result: **Chelsea 1   Manchester United 0**
Teamsheet: Leighton, Anderson, Martin, Bruce, Phelan, Pallister, Duxbury, Ince, McClair, Hughes, Wallace
Substitute(s):   Beardsmore, Donaghy

Match # 3995   Saturday 03/03/90   Football League Division 1   at Old Trafford   Attendance 35327
Result: **Manchester United 4   Luton Town 1**
Teamsheet: Leighton, Anderson, Martin, Bruce, Phelan, Pallister, Robins, Ince, McClair, Hughes, Wallace
Substitute(s):   Beardsmore   Scorer(s):   Hughes, McClair, Robins, Wallace

Match # 3996   Sunday 11/03/90   FA Cup 6th Round   at Bramall Lane   Attendance 34344
Result: **Sheffield United 0   Manchester United 1**
Teamsheet: Leighton, Anderson, Martin, Bruce, Phelan, Pallister, Robins, Ince, McClair, Hughes, Wallace
Substitute(s):   Duxbury   Scorer(s):   McClair

Match # 3997   Wednesday 14/03/90   Football League Division 1   at Old Trafford   Attendance 37398
Result: **Manchester United 0   Everton 0**
Teamsheet: Leighton, Duxbury, Martin, Bruce, Phelan, Pallister, Robins, Ince, McClair, Hughes, Wallace
Substitute(s):   Beardsmore, Blackmore

Match # 3998   Sunday 18/03/90   Football League Division 1   at Old Trafford   Attendance 46629
Result: **Manchester United 1   Liverpool 2**
Teamsheet: Leighton, Anderson, Martin, Bruce, Phelan, Pallister, Blackmore, Ince, McClair, Hughes, Wallace
Substitute(s):   Beardsmore, Duxbury   Scorer(s):   own goal

SEASON 1989/90 (continued)

Match # 3999 Wednesday 21/03/90   Football League Division 1   at Hillsborough   Attendance 33260
Result: **Sheffield Wednesday 1 Manchester United 0**
Teamsheet: Leighton, Donaghy, Martin, Bruce, Phelan, Pallister, Beardsmore, Gibson, McClair, Hughes, Blackmore
Substitute(s): Ince, Wallace

Match # 4000 Saturday 24/03/90   Football League Division 1   at The Dell   Attendance 20510
Result: **Southampton 0 Manchester United 2**
Teamsheet: Leighton, Donaghy, Martin, Bruce, Phelan, Pallister, Gibson, Ince, McClair, Hughes, Wallace
Substitute(s): Robins, Webb   Scorer(s):   Gibson, Robins

Match # 4001 Saturday 31/03/90   Football League Division 1   at Old Trafford   Attendance 39172
Result: **Manchester United 3 Coventry City 0**
Teamsheet: Leighton, Donaghy, Gibson, Bruce, Phelan, Pallister, Webb, Ince, McClair, Hughes, Wallace
Substitute(s): Martin, Robins   Scorer(s):   Hughes 2, Robins

Match # 4002 Sunday 08/04/90   FA Cup Semi-Final   at Maine Road   Attendance 44026
Result: **Manchester United 3 Oldham Athletic 3**
Teamsheet: Leighton, Martin, Gibson, Bruce, Phelan, Pallister, Robson, Ince, McClair, Hughes, Webb
Substitute(s): Robins, Wallace   Scorer(s):   Robson, Wallace, Webb

Match # 4003 Wednesday 11/04/90   FA Cup Semi-Final Replay   at Maine Road   Attendance 35005
Result: **Manchester United 2 Oldham Athletic 1**
Teamsheet: Leighton, Ince, Martin, Bruce, Phelan, Pallister, Robson, Webb, McClair, Hughes, Wallace
Substitute(s): Gibson, Robins   Scorer(s):   McClair, Robins

Match # 4004 Saturday 14/04/90   Football League Division 1   at Loftus Road   Attendance 18997
Result: **Queens Park Rangers 1 Manchester United 2**
Teamsheet: Sealey, Ince, Martin, Bruce, Phelan, Pallister, Robson, Webb, McClair, Hughes, Wallace
Substitute(s): Gibson, Robins   Scorer(s):   Robins, Webb

Match # 4005 Tuesday 17/04/90   Football League Division 1   at Old Trafford   Attendance 44080
Result: **Manchester United 2 Aston Villa 0**
Teamsheet: Sealey, Anderson, Gibson, Robins, Phelan, Pallister, Robson, Webb, McClair, Hughes, Wallace
Substitute(s): Beardsmore, Blackmore   Scorer(s):   Robins 2

Match # 4006 Saturday 21/04/90   Football League Division 1   at White Hart Lane   Attendance 33317
Result: **Tottenham Hotspur 2 Manchester United 1**
Teamsheet: Leighton, Robins, Martin, Bruce, Phelan, Pallister, Robson, Webb, McClair, Hughes, Wallace
Substitute(s): Beardsmore, Blackmore   Scorer(s):   Bruce

Match # 4007 Monday 30/04/90   Football League Division 1   at Old Trafford   Attendance 29281
Result: **Manchester United 0 Wimbledon 0**
Teamsheet: Bosnich, Anderson, Martin, Bruce, Phelan, Pallister, Robson, Ince, Robins, Hughes, Gibson
Substitute(s): Blackmore, Wallace

Match # 4008 Wednesday 02/05/90   Football League Division 1   at City Ground   Attendance 21186
Result: **Nottingham Forest 4 Manchester United 0**
Teamsheet: Leighton, Duxbury, Blackmore, Bruce, Phelan, Pallister, Beardsmore, Webb, McClair, Robins, Wallace

Match # 4009 Saturday 05/05/90   Football League Division 1   at Old Trafford   Attendance 35389
Result: **Manchester United 1 Charlton Athletic 0**
Teamsheet: Leighton, Ince, Martin, Bruce, Phelan, Pallister, Beardsmore, Webb, McClair, Hughes, Wallace
Scorer(s):   Pallister

Match # 4010 Saturday 12/05/90   FA Cup Final   at Wembley   Attendance 80000
Result: **Manchester United 3 Crystal Palace 3**
Teamsheet: Leighton, Ince, Martin, Bruce, Phelan, Pallister, Robson, Webb, McClair, Hughes, Wallace
Substitute(s): Blackmore, Robins   Scorer(s):   Hughes 2, Robson

Match # 4011 Thursday 17/05/90   FA Cup Final Replay   at Wembley   Attendance 80000
Result: **Manchester United 1 Crystal Palace 0**
Teamsheet: Sealey, Ince, Martin, Bruce, Phelan, Pallister, Robson, Webb, McClair, Hughes, Wallace
Scorer(s):   Martin

SEASON 1989/90 SUMMARY

APPEARANCES

PLAYER	LGE	FAC	LC	TOTAL
McClair	37	8	3	48
Phelan	38	7	3	48
Hughes	36 (1)	8	3	47 (1)
Pallister	35	8	3	46
Leighton	35	7	3	45
Bruce	34	7	2	43
Martin	28 (4)	8	1	37 (4)
Ince	25 (1)	6 (1)	3	34 (2)
Wallace	23 (3)	6 (1)	2	31 (4)
Robson	20	4	3	27
Blackmore	19 (9)	2 (1)	–	21 (10)
Anderson	14 (2)	4	1	19 (2)
Donaghy	13 (1)	1	3	17 (1)
Duxbury	12 (7)	2 (2)	1 (1)	15 (10)
Sharpe	13 (5)	–	1 (1)	14 (6)
Webb	10 (1)	4	–	14 (1)
Robins	10 (7)	3 (3)	–	13 (10)
Beardsmore	8 (13)	1 (2)	1	10 (15)
Gibson	5 (1)	1 (1)	–	6 (2)
Sealey	2	1	–	3
Bosnich	1	–	–	1
Maiorana	– (1)	–	– (1)	– (2)
Brazil	– (1)	–	–	– (1)
Graham	– (1)	–	–	– (1)
Milne	– (1)	–	–	– (1)

GOALSCORERS

PLAYER	LGE	FAC	LC	TOT
Hughes	13	2	–	15
Robins	7	3	–	10
McClair	5	3	–	8
Wallace	3	2	1	6
Robson	2	2	–	4
Bruce	3	–	–	3
Pallister	3	–	–	3
Blackmore	2	1	–	3
Webb	2	1	–	3
Beardsmore	2	–	–	2
Ince	–	–	2	2
Gibson	1	–	–	1
Phelan	1	–	–	1
Sharpe	1	–	–	1
Martin	–	1	–	1
own goal	1	–	–	1

RESULTS & ATTENDANCES SUMMARY

		P	W	D	L	F	A	TOTAL	AVGE
League	H	19	8	6	5	26	14	742475	39078
	A	19	5	3	11	20	33	485480	25552
TOTAL		38	13	9	16	46	47	1227955	32315
FA Cup	H	0	0	0	0	0	0	0	n/a
	A	4	4	0	0	6	2	102941	25735
	N	4	2	2	0	9	7	239031	59758
TOTAL		8	6	2	0	15	9	341972	42747
League Cup	H	2	0	1	1	0	3	72457	36229
	A	1	1	0	0	3	2	18072	18072
TOTAL		3	1	1	1	3	5	90529	30176
Overall	H	21	8	7	6	26	17	814932	38806
	A	24	10	3	11	29	37	606493	25271
	N	4	2	2	0	9	7	239031	59758
TOTAL		49	20	12	17	64	61	1660456	33887

FINAL TABLE – LEAGUE DIVISION ONE

		P	HOME W	D	L	F	A	AWAY W	D	L	F	A	PTS	GD
1	Liverpool	38	13	5	1	38	15	10	5	4	40	22	79	41
2	Aston Villa	38	13	3	3	36	20	8	4	7	21	18	70	19
3	Tottenham Hotspur	38	12	1	6	35	24	7	5	7	24	23	63	12
4	Arsenal	38	14	3	2	38	11	4	5	10	16	27	62	16
5	Chelsea	38	8	7	4	31	24	8	5	6	27	26	60	8
6	Everton	38	14	3	2	40	16	3	5	11	17	30	59	11
7	Southampton	38	10	5	4	40	27	5	5	9	31	36	55	8
8	Wimbledon	38	5	8	6	22	23	8	8	3	25	17	55	7
9	Nottingham Forest	38	9	4	6	31	21	6	5	8	24	26	54	8
10	Norwich City	38	7	10	2	24	14	6	4	9	20	28	53	2
11	Queens Park Rangers	38	9	4	6	27	22	4	7	8	18	22	50	1
12	Coventry City	38	11	2	6	24	25	3	5	11	15	34	49	–20
13	MANCHESTER UNITED	38	8	6	5	26	14	5	3	11	20	33	48	–1
14	Manchester City	38	9	4	6	26	21	3	8	8	17	31	48	–9
15	Crystal Palace	38	8	7	4	27	23	5	2	12	15	43	48	–24
16	Derby County	38	9	1	9	29	21	4	6	9	14	19	46	3
17	Luton Town	38	8	8	3	24	18	2	5	12	19	39	43	–14
18	Sheffield Wednesday	38	8	6	5	21	17	3	4	12	14	34	43	–16
19	Charlton Athletic	38	4	6	9	18	25	3	3	13	13	32	30	–26
20	Millwall	38	4	6	9	23	25	1	5	13	16	40	26	–26

SEASON 1990/91

Match # 4012	Saturday 18/08/90 FA Charity Shield	at Wembley	Attendance 66558
Result:	**Manchester United 1 Liverpool 1 (TROPHY SHARED)**		
Teamsheet:	Sealey, Irwin, Donaghy, Bruce, Phelan, Pallister, Blackmore, Ince, McClair, Hughes, Wallace		
Substitute(s):	Robins Scorer(s): Blackmore		

Match # 4013	Saturday 25/08/90 Football League Division 1	at Old Trafford	Attendance 46715
Result:	**Manchester United 2 Coventry City 0**		
Teamsheet:	Sealey, Irwin, Donaghy, Bruce, Phelan, Pallister, Webb, Ince, McClair, Hughes, Blackmore		
Scorer(s):	Bruce, Webb		

Match # 4014	Tuesday 28/08/90 Football League Division 1	at Elland Road	Attendance 29174
Result:	**Leeds United 0 Manchester United 0**		
Teamsheet:	Sealey, Irwin, Donaghy, Bruce, Phelan, Pallister, Webb, Ince, McClair, Hughes, Blackmore		
Substitute(s):	Beardsmore		

Match # 4015	Saturday 01/09/90 Football League Division 1	at Roker Park	Attendance 26105
Result:	**Sunderland 2 Manchester United 1**		
Teamsheet:	Sealey, Irwin, Donaghy, Bruce, Phelan, Pallister, Webb, Ince, McClair, Hughes, Blackmore		
Substitute(s):	Beardsmore, Robins Scorer(s): McClair		

Match # 4016	Tuesday 04/09/90 Football League Division 1	at Kenilworth Road	Attendance 12576
Result:	**Luton Town 0 Manchester United 1**		
Teamsheet:	Sealey, Irwin, Blackmore, Bruce, Phelan, Pallister, Webb, Ince, McClair, Robins, Beardsmore		
Substitute(s):	Donaghy, Hughes Scorer(s): Robins		

Match # 4017	Saturday 08/09/90 Football League Division 1	at Old Trafford	Attendance 43427
Result:	**Manchester United 3 Queens Park Rangers 1**		
Teamsheet:	Sealey, Irwin, Blackmore, Bruce, Phelan, Pallister, Webb, Ince, McClair, Robins, Beardsmore		
Scorer(s):	Robins 2, McClair		

Match # 4018	Sunday 16/09/90 Football League Division 1	at Anfield	Attendance 35726
Result:	**Liverpool 4 Manchester United 0**		
Teamsheet:	Sealey, Irwin, Blackmore, Bruce, Phelan, Pallister, Webb, Ince, McClair, Hughes, Robins		
Substitute(s):	Beardsmore, Donaghy		

Match # 4019	Wednesday 19/09/90 European CWC 1st Round 1st Leg	at Old Trafford	Attendance 28411
Result:	**Manchester United 2 Pecsi Munkas 0**		
Teamsheet:	Sealey, Irwin, Blackmore, Bruce, Phelan, Pallister, Webb, Ince, McClair, Robins, Beardsmore		
Substitute(s):	Hughes, Sharpe Scorer(s): Blackmore, Webb		

Match # 4020	Saturday 22/09/90 Football League Division 1	at Old Trafford	Attendance 41288
Result:	**Manchester United 3 Southampton 2**		
Teamsheet:	Sealey, Irwin, Donaghy, Anderson, Phelan, Pallister, Webb, Robins, McClair, Hughes, Blackmore		
Substitute(s):	Beardsmore, Sharpe Scorer(s): Blackmore, Hughes, McClair		

Match # 4021	Wednesday 26/09/90 League Cup 2nd Round 1st Leg	at The Shay	Attendance 6841
Result:	**Halifax Town 1 Manchester United 3**		
Teamsheet:	Leighton, Irwin, Blackmore, Donaghy, Phelan, Pallister, Webb, Ince, McClair, Hughes, Beardsmore		
Substitute(s):	Martin, Robins Scorer(s): Blackmore, McClair, Webb		

Match # 4022	Saturday 29/09/90 Football League Division 1	at Old Trafford	Attendance 46766
Result:	**Manchester United 0 Nottingham Forest 1**		
Teamsheet:	Sealey, Irwin, Blackmore, Donaghy, Phelan, Pallister, Webb, Ince, McClair, Robins, Beardsmore		
Substitute(s):	Hughes, Martin		

Match # 4023	Wednesday 03/10/90 European CWC 1st Round 2nd Leg	at PMSC Stadion	Attendance 17000
Result:	**Pecsi Munkas 0 Manchester United 1**		
Teamsheet:	Sealey, Anderson, Donaghy, Bruce, Phelan, Pallister, Webb, Blackmore, McClair, Hughes, Martin		
Substitute(s):	Sharpe Scorer(s): McClair		

Match # 4024	Wednesday 10/10/90 League Cup 2nd Round 2nd Leg	at Old Trafford	Attendance 22295
Result:	**Manchester United 2 Halifax Town 1**		
Teamsheet:	Sealey, Anderson, Blackmore, Bruce, Phelan, Pallister, Webb, Irwin, McClair, Hughes, Martin		
Substitute(s):	Robins, Wallace Scorer(s): Anderson, Bruce		

Match # 4025	Saturday 20/10/90 Football League Division 1	at Old Trafford	Attendance 47232
Result:	**Manchester United 0 Arsenal 1**		
Teamsheet:	Sealey, Irwin, Blackmore, Bruce, Phelan, Pallister, Webb, Ince, McClair, Hughes, Sharpe		
Substitute(s):	Martin, Robins		

Match # 4026	Tuesday 23/10/90 European CWC 2nd Round 1st Leg	at Old Trafford	Attendance 29405
Result:	**Manchester United 3 Wrexham 0**		
Teamsheet:	Sealey, Blackmore, Martin, Bruce, Sharpe, Pallister, Webb, Ince, McClair, Hughes, Wallace		
Substitute(s):	Beardsmore, Robins Scorer(s): Bruce, McClair, Pallister		

Match # 4027	Saturday 27/10/90 Football League Division 1	at Maine Road	Attendance 36427
Result:	**Manchester City 3 Manchester United 3**		
Teamsheet:	Sealey, Irwin, Martin, Bruce, Blackmore, Pallister, Webb, Ince, McClair, Hughes, Sharpe		
Substitute(s):	Wallace Scorer(s): McClair 2, Hughes		

Match # 4028	Wednesday 31/10/90 League Cup 3rd Round	at Old Trafford	Attendance 42033
Result:	**Manchester United 3 Liverpool 1**		
Teamsheet:	Sealey, Irwin, Blackmore, Bruce, Phelan, Pallister, Webb, Ince, McClair, Hughes, Sharpe		
Substitute(s):	Donaghy, Wallace Scorer(s): Bruce, Hughes, Sharpe		

Match # 4029	Saturday 03/11/90 Football League Division 1	at Old Trafford	Attendance 45724
Result:	**Manchester United 2 Crystal Palace 0**		
Teamsheet:	Sealey, Irwin, Blackmore, Bruce, Phelan, Pallister, Webb, Ince, McClair, Wallace, Sharpe		
Substitute(s):	Martin Scorer(s): Wallace, Webb		

SEASON 1990/91 (continued)

Match # 4030   Wednesday 07/11/90   European CWC 2nd Round 2nd Leg   at Racecourse Ground   Attendance 13327
Result: **Wrexham 0 Manchester United 2**
Teamsheet: Sealey, Irwin, Blackmore, Bruce, Phelan, Pallister, Webb, Ince, McClair, Robins, Wallace
Substitute(s):   Donaghy, Martin   Scorer(s):   Bruce, Robins

Match # 4031   Saturday 10/11/90   Football League Division 1   at Baseball Ground   Attendance 21115
Result: **Derby County 0 Manchester United 0**
Teamsheet: Sealey, Irwin, Blackmore, Bruce, Phelan, Pallister, Webb, Ince, McClair, Hughes, Sharpe
Substitute(s):   Donaghy, Wallace

Match # 4032   Saturday 17/11/90   Football League Division 1   at Old Trafford   Attendance 45903
Result: **Manchester United 2 Sheffield United 0**
Teamsheet: Sealey, Irwin, Blackmore, Bruce, Phelan, Pallister, Webb, Ince, McClair, Hughes, Sharpe
Substitute(s):   Wallace   Scorer(s):   Bruce, Hughes

Match # 4033   Sunday 25/11/90   Football League Division 1   at Old Trafford   Attendance 37836
Result: **Manchester United 2 Chelsea 3**
Teamsheet: Sealey, Irwin, Blackmore, Bruce, Phelan, Pallister, Webb, Ince, McClair, Hughes, Wallace
Substitute(s):   Martin, Sharpe   Scorer(s):   Hughes, Wallace

Match # 4034   Wednesday 28/11/90   League Cup 4th Round   at Highbury   Attendance 40844
Result: **Arsenal 2 Manchester United 6**
Teamsheet: Sealey, Irwin, Blackmore, Bruce, Phelan, Pallister, Sharpe, Ince, McClair, Hughes, Wallace
Substitute(s):   Donaghy   Scorer(s):   Sharpe 3, Blackmore, Hughes, Wallace

Match # 4035   Saturday 01/12/90   Football League Division 1   at Goodison Park   Attendance 32400
Result: **Everton 0 Manchester United 1**
Teamsheet: Sealey, Irwin, Blackmore, Donaghy, Phelan, Pallister, Sharpe, Ince, McClair, Hughes, Wallace
Substitute(s):   Martin, Webb   Scorer(s):   Sharpe

Match # 4036   Saturday 08/12/90   Football League Division 1   at Old Trafford   Attendance 40927
Result: **Manchester United 1 Leeds United 1**
Teamsheet: Sealey, Irwin, Blackmore, Bruce, Phelan, Pallister, Sharpe, Webb, McClair, Hughes, Wallace
Substitute(s):   Donaghy, Robson   Scorer(s):   Webb

Match # 4037   Saturday 15/12/90   Football League Division 1   at Highfield Road   Attendance 17106
Result: **Coventry City 2 Manchester United 2**
Teamsheet: Sealey, Blackmore, Sharpe, Bruce, Phelan, Pallister, Webb, Ince, McClair, Hughes, Wallace
Substitute(s):   Irwin, Robson   Scorer(s):   Hughes, Wallace

Match # 4038   Saturday 22/12/90   Football League Division 1   at Plough Lane   Attendance 9644
Result: **Wimbledon 1 Manchester United 3**
Teamsheet: Sealey, Blackmore, Donaghy, Bruce, Phelan, Pallister, Robson, Ince, McClair, Hughes, Webb
Substitute(s):   Wallace   Scorer(s):   Bruce 2, Hughes

Match # 4039   Wednesday 26/12/90   Football League Division 1   at Old Trafford   Attendance 39801
Result: **Manchester United 3 Norwich City 0**
Teamsheet: Sealey, Irwin, Blackmore, Bruce, Webb, Pallister, Robson, Ince, McClair, Hughes, Sharpe
Substitute(s):   Donaghy, Phelan   Scorer(s):   McClair 2, Hughes

Match # 4040   Saturday 29/12/90   Football League Division 1   at Old Trafford   Attendance 47485
Result: **Manchester United 1 Aston Villa 1**
Teamsheet: Sealey, Irwin, Blackmore, Bruce, Webb, Pallister, Robson, Ince, McClair, Hughes, Sharpe
Substitute(s):   Phelan   Scorer(s):   Bruce

Match # 4041   Tuesday 01/01/91   Football League Division 1   at White Hart Lane   Attendance 29399
Result: **Tottenham Hotspur 1 Manchester United 2**
Teamsheet: Sealey, Irwin, Blackmore, Bruce, Phelan, Pallister, Webb, Ince, McClair, Hughes, Sharpe
Substitute(s):   Martin, Robins   Scorer(s):   Bruce, McClair

Match # 4042   Monday 07/01/91   FA Cup 3rd Round   at Old Trafford   Attendance 35065
Result: **Manchester United 2 Queens Park Rangers 1**
Teamsheet: Sealey, Irwin, Blackmore, Bruce, Webb, Pallister, Robson, Ince, McClair, Hughes, Sharpe
Scorer(s):   Hughes, McClair

Match # 4043   Saturday 12/01/91   Football League Division 1   at Old Trafford   Attendance 45934
Result: **Manchester United 3 Sunderland 0**
Teamsheet: Sealey, Irwin, Blackmore, Bruce, Webb, Pallister, Robson, Ince, McClair, Hughes, Sharpe
Substitute(s):   Phelan, Robins   Scorer(s):   Hughes 2, McClair

Match # 4044   Wednesday 16/01/91   League Cup 5th Round   at The Dell   Attendance 21011
Result: **Southampton 1 Manchester United 1**
Teamsheet: Sealey, Donaghy, Blackmore, Bruce, Phelan, Pallister, Robson, Webb, McClair, Hughes, Sharpe
Substitute(s):   Irwin   Scorer(s):   Hughes

Match # 4045   Saturday 19/01/91   Football League Division 1   at Loftus Road   Attendance 18544
Result: **Queens Park Rangers 1 Manchester United 1**
Teamsheet: Sealey, Irwin, Martin, Bruce, Phelan, Donaghy, Beardsmore, Webb, McClair, Hughes, Blackmore
Substitute(s):   Robins, Sharpe   Scorer(s):   Phelan

Match # 4046   Wednesday 23/01/91   League Cup 5th Round Replay   at Old Trafford   Attendance 41903
Result: **Manchester United 3 Southampton 2**
Teamsheet: Sealey, Irwin, Blackmore, Bruce, Phelan, Pallister, Robson, Webb, McClair, Hughes, Sharpe
Substitute(s):   Donaghy, Robins   Scorer(s):   Hughes 3

Match # 4047   Saturday 26/01/91   FA Cup 4th Round   at Old Trafford   Attendance 43293
Result: **Manchester United 1 Bolton Wanderers 0**
Teamsheet: Sealey, Irwin, Blackmore, Bruce, Phelan, Pallister, Robson, Webb, McClair, Hughes, Sharpe
Substitute(s):   Robins   Scorer(s):   Hughes

SEASON 1990/91 (continued)

Match # 4048 Sunday 03/02/91 Football League Division 1 at Old Trafford Attendance 43690
Result: **Manchester United 1 Liverpool 1**
Teamsheet: Sealey, Irwin, Blackmore, Bruce, Phelan, Pallister, Robson, Webb, McClair, Hughes, Sharpe
Substitute(s): Martin, Wallace Scorer(s): Bruce

Match # 4049 Sunday 10/02/91 League Cup Semi-Final 1st Leg at Old Trafford Attendance 34050
Result: **Manchester United 2 Leeds United 1**
Teamsheet: Sealey, Irwin, Martin, Bruce, Blackmore, Pallister, Robson, Ince, McClair, Hughes, Sharpe
Substitute(s): Donaghy, Wallace Scorer(s): McClair, Sharpe

Match # 4050 Monday 18/02/91 FA Cup 5th Round at Carrow Road Attendance 23058
Result: **Norwich City 2 Manchester United 1**
Teamsheet: Sealey, Irwin, Martin, Bruce, Blackmore, Pallister, Robson, Ince, McClair, Hughes, Sharpe
Substitute(s): Wallace Scorer(s): McClair

Match # 4051 Sunday 24/02/91 League Cup Semi-Final 2nd Leg at Elland Road Attendance 32014
Result: **Leeds United 0 Manchester United 1**
Teamsheet: Sealey, Donaghy, Blackmore, Webb, Phelan, Pallister, Robson, Ince, McClair, Hughes, Sharpe
Substitute(s): Martin Scorer(s): Sharpe

Match # 4052 Tuesday 26/02/91 Football League Division 1 at Bramall Lane Attendance 27570
Result: **Sheffield United 2 Manchester United 1**
Teamsheet: Walsh, Irwin, Martin, Webb, Donaghy, Pallister, Robson, Ince, McClair, Blackmore, Wallace
Substitute(s): Ferguson, Robins Scorer(s): Blackmore

Match # 4053 Saturday 02/03/91 Football League Division 1 at Old Trafford Attendance 45656
Result: **Manchester United 0 Everton 2**
Teamsheet: Sealey, Irwin, Martin, Ferguson, Donaghy, Pallister, Sharpe, Ince, McClair, Blackmore, Wallace
Substitute(s): Beardsmore, Giggs

Match # 4054 Wednesday 06/03/91 European CWC 3rd Round 1st Leg at Old Trafford Attendance 41942
Result: **Manchester United 1 Montpellier Herault 1**
Teamsheet: Sealey, Blackmore, Martin, Donaghy, Phelan, Pallister, Robson, Ince, McClair, Hughes, Sharpe
Substitute(s): Wallace Scorer(s): McClair

Match # 4055 Sunday 10/03/91 Football League Division 1 at Stamford Bridge Attendance 22818
Result: **Chelsea 3 Manchester United 2**
Teamsheet: Sealey, Blackmore, Martin, Donaghy, Phelan, Pallister, Robson, Ince, McClair, Hughes, Sharpe
Substitute(s): Wallace Scorer(s): Hughes, McClair

Match # 4056 Wednesday 13/03/91 Football League Division 1 at The Dell Attendance 15701
Result: **Southampton 1 Manchester United 1**
Teamsheet: Sealey, Whitworth, Martin, Donaghy, Phelan, Pallister, Beardsmore, Ince, McClair, Wallace, Sharpe
Substitute(s): Ferguson, Robins Scorer(s): Ince

Match # 4057 Saturday 16/03/91 Football League Division 1 at City Ground Attendance 23859
Result: **Nottingham Forest 1 Manchester United 1**
Teamsheet: Sealey, Irwin, Martin, Bruce, Phelan, Pallister, Robson, Ince, Blackmore, Hughes, Wallace
Substitute(s): Donaghy Scorer(s): Blackmore

Match # 4058 Tuesday 19/03/91 European CWC 3rd Round 2nd Leg at Stade de la Masson Attendance 18000
Result: **Montpellier Herault 0 Manchester United 2**
Teamsheet: Sealey, Irwin, Blackmore, Bruce, Phelan, Pallister, Robson, Ince, McClair, Hughes, Sharpe
Substitute(s): Martin Scorer(s): Blackmore, Bruce

Match # 4059 Saturday 23/03/91 Football League Division 1 at Old Trafford Attendance 41752
Result: **Manchester United 4 Luton Town 1**
Teamsheet: Sealey, Irwin, Blackmore, Bruce, Phelan, Pallister, Robson, Wallace, McClair, Hughes, Sharpe
Substitute(s): Robins Scorer(s): Bruce 2, McClair, Robins

Match # 4060 Saturday 30/03/91 Football League Division 1 at Carrow Road Attendance 18282
Result: **Norwich City 0 Manchester United 3**
Teamsheet: Sealey, Irwin, Blackmore, Bruce, Phelan, Pallister, Robson, Ince, Webb, Hughes, Sharpe
Substitute(s): McClair, Robins Scorer(s): Bruce 2, Ince

Match # 4061 Tuesday 02/04/91 Football League Division 1 at Old Trafford Attendance 36660
Result: **Manchester United 2 Wimbledon 1**
Teamsheet: Walsh, Irwin, Donaghy, Bruce, Phelan, Pallister, Webb, Ince, McClair, Blackmore, Sharpe
Substitute(s): Robins, Wrattan Scorer(s): Bruce, McClair

Match # 4062 Saturday 06/04/91 Football League Division 1 at Villa Park Attendance 33307
Result: **Aston Villa 1 Manchester United 1**
Teamsheet: Sealey, Irwin, Donaghy, Bruce, Phelan, Pallister, Robson, Webb, McClair, Hughes, Sharpe
Substitute(s): Robins Scorer(s): Sharpe

Match # 4063 Wednesday 10/04/91 European CWC Semi-Final 1st Leg at Wojska Polskiego Attendance 20000
Result: **Legia Warsaw 1 Manchester United 3**
Teamsheet: Sealey, Irwin, Blackmore, Bruce, Phelan, Pallister, Webb, Ince, McClair, Hughes, Sharpe
Substitute(s): Donaghy Scorer(s): Bruce, Hughes, McClair

Match # 4064 Tuesday 16/04/91 Football League Division 1 at Old Trafford Attendance 32776
Result: **Manchester United 3 Derby County 1**
Teamsheet: Bosnich, Irwin, Donaghy, Bruce, Webb, Pallister, Robson, Ince, Blackmore, Hughes, Wallace
Substitute(s): McClair Scorer(s): Blackmore, McClair, Robson

Match # 4065 Sunday 21/04/91 League Cup Final at Wembley Attendance 77612
Result: **Manchester United 0 Sheffield Wednesday 1**
Teamsheet: Sealey, Irwin, Blackmore, Bruce, Webb, Pallister, Robson, Ince, McClair, Hughes, Sharpe
Substitute(s): Phelan

SEASON 1990/91 (continued)

Match # 4066   Wednesday 24/04/91   European CWC Semi-Final 2nd Leg   at Old Trafford   Attendance 44269
Result: **Manchester United 1   Legia Warsaw 1**
Teamsheet: Walsh, Irwin, Blackmore, Bruce, Phelan, Pallister, Robson, Webb, McClair, Hughes, Sharpe
Substitute(s):   Donaghy   Scorer(s):   Sharpe

Match # 4067   Saturday 04/05/91   Football League Division 1   at Old Trafford   Attendance 45286
Result: **Manchester United 1   Manchester City 0**
Teamsheet: Walsh, Irwin, Blackmore, Bruce, Phelan, Pallister, Robson, Webb, McClair, Hughes, Giggs
Substitute(s):   Donaghy   Scorer(s):   Giggs

Match # 4068   Monday 06/05/91   Football League Division 1   at Highbury   Attendance 40229
Result: **Arsenal 3   Manchester United 1**
Teamsheet: Walsh, Phelan, Blackmore, Bruce, Webb, Donaghy, Robson, Ince, McClair, Hughes, Robins
Substitute(s):   Beardsmore, Ferguson   Scorer(s):   Bruce

Match # 4069   Saturday 11/05/91   Football League Division 1   at Selhurst Park   Attendance 25301
Result: **Crystal Palace 3   Manchester United 0**
Teamsheet: Walsh, Irwin, Donaghy, Bruce, Webb, Pallister, Kanchelskis, Ince, Robins, Ferguson, Wallace
Substitute(s):   Beardsmore, Wrattan

Match # 4070   Wednesday 15/05/91   European Cup-Winners' Cup Final   at Feyenoord Stadion   Attendance 50000
Result: **Manchester United 2   Barcelona 1**
Teamsheet: Sealey, Irwin, Blackmore, Bruce, Phelan, Pallister, Robson, Ince, McClair, Hughes, Sharpe
Scorer(s):   Hughes 2

Match # 4071   Monday 20/05/91   Football League Division 1   at Old Trafford   Attendance 46791
Result: **Manchester United 1   Tottenham Hotspur 1**
Teamsheet: Bosnich, Irwin, Blackmore, Bruce, Phelan, Pallister, Robson, Ince, McClair, Hughes, Wallace
Substitute(s):   Donaghy, Robins   Scorer(s):   Ince

SEASON 1990/91 SUMMARY

APPEARANCES

PLAYER	LGE	FAC	LC	ECWC	CS	TOTAL
Pallister	36	3	9	9	1	58
Blackmore	35	3	9	9	1	57
McClair	34 (2)	3	9	9	1	56 (2)
Sealey	31	3	8	8	1	51
Irwin	33 (1)	3	7 (1)	6	1	50 (2)
Bruce	31	3	7	8	1	50
Hughes	29 (2)	3	9	7 (1)	1	49 (3)
Phelan	30 (3)	1	7 (1)	8	1	47 (4)
Ince	31	2	6	7	1	47
Webb	31 (1)	2	7	6	–	46 (1)
Sharpe	20 (3)	3	7	6 (2)	–	36 (5)
Robson	15 (2)	3	5	4	–	27 (2)
Donaghy	17 (8)	–	3 (4)	2 (3)	1	23 (15)
Wallace	13 (6)	– (1)	1 (3)	2 (1)	1	17 (11)
Martin	7 (7)	1	2 (2)	3 (2)	–	13 (11)
Robins	7 (12)	– (1)	– (3)	2 (1)	– (1)	9 (18)
Beardsmore	5 (7)	–	1	1 (1)	–	7 (8)
Walsh	5	–	–	1	–	6
Anderson	1	–	1	1	–	3
Ferguson	2 (3)	–	–	–	–	2 (3)
Bosnich	2	–	–	–	–	2
Giggs	1 (1)	–	–	–	–	1 (1)
Kanchelskis	1	–	–	–	–	1
Leighton	–	–	1	–	–	1
Whitworth	1	–	–	–	–	1
Wrattan	– (2)	–	–	–	–	– (2)

GOALSCORERS

PLAYER	LGE	FAC	LC	ECWC	CS	TOTAL
McClair	13	2	2	4	–	21
Hughes	10	2	6	3	–	21
Bruce	13	–	2	4	–	19
Blackmore	4	–	2	2	1	9
Sharpe	2	–	6	1	–	9
Robins	4	–	–	1	–	5
Webb	3	–	1	1	–	5
Wallace	3	–	1	–	–	4
Ince	3	–	–	–	–	3
Giggs	1	–	–	–	–	1
Phelan	1	–	–	–	–	1
Robson	1	–	–	–	–	1
Anderson	–	–	1	–	–	1
Pallister	–	–	–	1	–	1

RESULTS & ATTENDANCES SUMMARY

		P	W	D	L	F	A	TOTAL	AVGE
League	H	19	11	4	4	34	17	821649	43245
	A	19	5	8	6	24	28	475283	25015
TOTAL		38	16	12	10	58	45	1296932	34130
FA Cup	H	2	2	0	0	3	1	78358	39179
	A	1	0	0	1	1	2	23058	23058
TOTAL		3	2	0	1	4	3	101416	33805
League	H	4	4	0	0	10	5	140281	35070
Cup	A	4	3	1	0	11	4	100710	25178
	N	1	0	0	1	0	1	77612	77612
TOTAL		9	7	1	1	21	10	318603	35400
European	H	4	2	2	0	7	2	144027	36007
CWC	A	4	4	0	0	8	1	68327	17082
	N	1	1	0	0	2	1	50000	50000
TOTAL		9	7	2	0	17	4	262354	29150
Charity	H	0	0	0	0	0	0	0	n/a
Shield	A	0	0	0	0	0	0	0	n/a
	N	1	0	1	0	1	1	66558	66558
TOTAL		1	0	1	0	1	1	66558	66558
Overall	H	29	19	6	4	54	25	1184315	40838
	A	28	12	9	7	44	35	667378	23835
	N	3	1	1	1	3	3	194170	64723
TOTAL		60	32	16	12	101	63	2045863	34098

FINAL TABLE – LEAGUE DIVISION ONE

		P	W	D	L	F	A	W	D	L	F	A	PTS	GD
				HOME						AWAY				
1	Arsenal **	38	15	4	0	51	10	9	9	1	23	8	83	56
2	Liverpool	38	14	3	2	42	13	9	4	6	35	27	76	37
3	Crystal Palace	38	11	6	2	26	17	9	3	7	24	24	69	9
4	Leeds United	38	12	2	5	46	23	7	5	7	19	24	64	18
5	Manchester City	38	12	3	4	35	25	5	8	6	29	28	62	11
6	MANCHESTER UNITED *	38	11	4	4	34	17	5	8	6	24	28	59	13
7	Wimbledon	38	8	6	5	28	22	6	8	5	25	24	56	7
8	Nottingham Forest	38	11	4	4	42	21	3	8	8	23	29	54	15
9	Everton	38	9	5	5	26	15	4	7	8	24	31	51	4
10	Tottenham Hotspur	38	8	9	2	35	22	3	7	9	16	28	49	1
11	Chelsea	38	10	6	3	33	25	3	4	12	25	44	49	-11
12	Queens Park Rangers	38	8	5	6	27	22	4	5	10	17	31	46	-9
13	Sheffield United	38	9	3	7	23	23	4	4	11	13	32	46	-19
14	Southampton	38	9	6	4	33	22	3	3	13	25	47	45	-11
15	Norwich City	38	9	3	7	27	32	4	3	12	14	32	45	-23
16	Coventry City	38	10	6	3	30	16	1	5	13	12	33	44	-7
17	Aston Villa	38	7	9	3	29	25	2	5	12	17	33	41	-12
18	Luton Town	38	7	5	7	22	18	3	2	14	20	43	37	-19
19	Sunderland	38	6	6	7	15	16	2	4	13	23	44	34	-22
20	Derby County	38	3	8	8	25	36	2	1	16	12	39	24	-38

* Manchester United deducted 1 point for disciplinary reasons
** Arsenal deducted 2 points for disciplinary reasons

SEASON 1991/92

Match # 4072 Saturday 17/08/91   Football League Division 1   at Old Trafford   Attendance 46278
Result: **Manchester United 2 Notts County 0**
Teamsheet: Schmeichel, Irwin, Blackmore, Bruce, Ferguson, Parker, Robson, Ince, McClair, Hughes, Kanchelskis
Substitute(s):   Giggs, Pallister   Scorer(s):   Hughes, Robson

Match # 4073 Wednesday 21/08/91   Football League Division 1   at Villa Park   Attendance 39995
Result: **Aston Villa 0 Manchester United 1**
Teamsheet: Schmeichel, Irwin, Blackmore, Bruce, Donaghy, Parker, Robson, Ince, McClair, Hughes, Kanchelskis
Scorer(s):   Bruce

Match # 4074 Saturday 24/08/91   Football League Division 1   at Goodison Park   Attendance 36085
Result: **Everton 0 Manchester United 0**
Teamsheet: Schmeichel, Irwin, Blackmore, Bruce, Donaghy, Parker, Robson, Ince, McClair, Hughes, Giggs
Substitute(s):   Pallister, Webb

Match # 4075 Wednesday 28/08/91   Football League Division 1   at Old Trafford   Attendance 42078
Result: **Manchester United 1 Oldham Athletic 0**
Teamsheet: Schmeichel, Parker, Irwin, Bruce, Webb, Pallister, Robson, Ince, McClair, Hughes, Giggs
Substitute(s):   Blackmore, Ferguson   Scorer(s):   McClair

Match # 4076 Saturday 31/08/91   Football League Division 1   at Old Trafford   Attendance 43778
Result: **Manchester United 1 Leeds United 1**
Teamsheet: Schmeichel, Parker, Irwin, Bruce, Webb, Pallister, Robson, Ince, McClair, Hughes, Blackmore
Substitute(s):   Giggs, Phelan   Scorer(s):   Robson

Match # 4077 Tuesday 03/09/91   Football League Division 1   at Selhurst Park   Attendance 13824
Result: **Wimbledon 1 Manchester United 2**
Teamsheet: Schmeichel, Parker, Donaghy, Bruce, Phelan, Pallister, Robson, Webb, McClair, Hughes, Blackmore
Substitute(s):   Irwin   Scorer(s):   Blackmore, Pallister

Match # 4078 Saturday 07/09/91   Football League Division 1   at Old Trafford   Attendance 44946
Result: **Manchester United 3 Norwich City 0**
Teamsheet: Schmeichel, Parker, Irwin, Bruce, Webb, Pallister, Robson, Kanchelskis, McClair, Hughes, Giggs
Substitute(s):   Blackmore, Phelan   Scorer(s):   Giggs, Irwin, McClair

Match # 4079 Saturday 14/09/91   Football League Division 1   at The Dell   Attendance 19264
Result: **Southampton 0 Manchester United 1**
Teamsheet: Schmeichel, Phelan, Irwin, Bruce, Webb, Pallister, Robson, Kanchelskis, McClair, Hughes, Giggs
Substitute(s):   Ince   Scorer(s):   Hughes

Match # 4080 Wednesday 18/09/91   European CWC 1st Round 1st Leg   at Apostolos Nikolaidis   Attendance 5400
Result: **Athinaikos 0 Manchester United 0**
Teamsheet: Schmeichel, Phelan, Irwin, Bruce, Webb, Pallister, Robins, Ince, McClair, Hughes, Beardsmore
Substitute(s):   Wallace

Match # 4081 Saturday 21/09/91   Football League Division 1   at Old Trafford   Attendance 46491
Result: **Manchester United 5 Luton Town 0**
Teamsheet: Schmeichel, Phelan, Irwin, Bruce, Webb, Pallister, Robson, Ince, Blackmore, Hughes, Giggs
Substitute(s):   McClair   Scorer(s):   McClair 2, Bruce, Hughes, Ince

Match # 4082 Wednesday 25/09/91   League Cup 2nd Round 1st Leg   at Old Trafford   Attendance 30934
Result: **Manchester United 3 Cambridge United 0**
Teamsheet: Walsh, Phelan, Irwin, Bruce, Webb, Pallister, Robson, Ince, McClair, Hughes, Blackmore
Substitute(s):   Giggs   Scorer(s):   Bruce, Giggs, McClair

Match # 4083 Saturday 28/09/91   Football League Division 1   at White Hart Lane   Attendance 35087
Result: **Tottenham Hotspur 1 Manchester United 2**
Teamsheet: Schmeichel, Phelan, Irwin, Bruce, Kanchelskis, Pallister, Robson, Ince, McClair, Hughes, Giggs
Substitute(s):   Blackmore   Scorer(s):   Hughes, Robson

Match # 4084 Wednesday 02/10/91   European CWC 1st Round 2nd Leg   at Old Trafford   Attendance 35023
Result: **Manchester United 2 Athinaikos 0**
Teamsheet: Schmeichel, Phelan, Martin, Bruce, Kanchelskis, Pallister, Robson, Ince, McClair, Hughes, Wallace
Substitute(s):   Beardsmore, Robins   Scorer(s):   Hughes, McClair

Match # 4085 Sunday 06/10/91   Football League Division 1   at Old Trafford   Attendance 44997
Result: **Manchester United 0 Liverpool 0**
Teamsheet: Schmeichel, Phelan, Irwin, Bruce, Blackmore, Pallister, Robson, Ince, McClair, Hughes, Giggs
Substitute(s):   Donaghy, Kanchelskis

Match # 4086 Wednesday 09/10/91   League Cup 2nd Round 2nd Leg   at Abbey Stadium   Attendance 9248
Result: **Cambridge United 1 Manchester United 1**
Teamsheet: Wilkinson, Donaghy, Irwin, Bruce, Blackmore, Pallister, Robson, Ince, McClair, Hughes, Martin
Substitute(s):   Giggs, Robins   Scorer(s):   McClair

Match # 4087 Saturday 19/10/91   Football League Division 1   at Old Trafford   Attendance 46594
Result: **Manchester United 1 Arsenal 1**
Teamsheet: Schmeichel, Blackmore, Irwin, Bruce, Webb, Pallister, Robson, Ince, McClair, Hughes, Giggs
Substitute(s):   Kanchelskis   Scorer(s):   Bruce

Match # 4088 Wednesday 23/10/91   European CWC 2nd Round 1st Leg   at Vincente Calderon   Attendance 40000
Result: **Athletico Madrid 3 Manchester United 0**
Teamsheet: Schmeichel, Parker, Irwin, Bruce, Webb, Pallister, Robson, Ince, McClair, Hughes, Phelan
Substitute(s):   Beardsmore, Martin

Match # 4089 Saturday 26/10/91   Football League Division 1   at Hillsborough   Attendance 38260
Result: **Sheffield Wednesday 3 Manchester United 2**
Teamsheet: Schmeichel, Parker, Irwin, Bruce, Webb, Pallister, Robson, Kanchelskis, McClair, Blackmore, Giggs
Substitute(s):   Martin   Scorer(s):   McClair 2

SEASON 1991/92 (continued)

Match # 4090 Wednesday 30/10/91   League Cup 3rd Round   at Old Trafford   Attendance 29543
Result: **Manchester United 3 Portsmouth 1**
Teamsheet: Schmeichel, Parker, Irwin, Bruce, Webb, Pallister, Donaghy, Kanchelskis, McClair, Blackmore, Giggs
Substitute(s): Robins, Robson   Scorer(s): Robins 2, Robson

Match # 4091 Saturday 02/11/91   Football League Division 1   at Old Trafford   Attendance 42942
Result: **Manchester United 2 Sheffield United 0**
Teamsheet: Schmeichel, Parker, Blackmore, Bruce, Webb, Donaghy, Kanchelskis, Ince, McClair, Robins, Giggs
Substitute(s): Pallister, Robson   Scorer(s): Kanchelskis, own goal

Match # 4092 Wednesday 06/11/91   European CWC 2nd Round 2nd Leg   at Old Trafford   Attendance 39654
Result: **Manchester United 1 Athletico Madrid 1**
Teamsheet: Walsh, Parker, Blackmore, Bruce, Webb, Phelan, Robson, Robins, McClair, Hughes, Giggs
Substitute(s): Martin, Pallister   Scorer(s): Hughes

Match # 4093 Saturday 16/11/91   Football League Division 1   at Maine Road   Attendance 38180
Result: **Manchester City 0 Manchester United 0**
Teamsheet: Schmeichel, Parker, Irwin, Bruce, Webb, Pallister, Robson, Blackmore, McClair, Hughes, Giggs
Substitute(s): Ince

Match # 4094 Tuesday 19/11/91   European Super Cup Final   at Old Trafford   Attendance 22110
Result: **Manchester United 1 Red Star Belgrade 0**
Teamsheet: Schmeichel, Martin, Irwin, Bruce, Webb, Pallister, Kanchelskis, Ince, McClair, Hughes, Blackmore
Substitute(s): Giggs   Scorer(s): McClair

Match # 4095 Saturday 23/11/91   Football League Division 1   at Old Trafford   Attendance 47185
Result: **Manchester United 2 West Ham United 1**
Teamsheet: Schmeichel, Parker, Irwin, Bruce, Webb, Pallister, Robson, Kanchelskis, McClair, Hughes, Giggs
Substitute(s): Blackmore   Scorer(s): Giggs, Robson

Match # 4096 Saturday 30/11/91   Football League Division 1   at Selhurst Park   Attendance 29017
Result: **Crystal Palace 1 Manchester United 3**
Teamsheet: Schmeichel, Parker, Irwin, Bruce, Webb, Pallister, Robson, Kanchelskis, McClair, Hughes, Giggs
Substitute(s): Blackmore   Scorer(s): Kanchelskis, McClair, Webb

Match # 4097 Wednesday 04/12/91   League Cup 4th Round   at Old Trafford   Attendance 38550
Result: **Manchester United 2 Oldham Athletic 0**
Teamsheet: Schmeichel, Parker, Irwin, Bruce, Webb, Pallister, Robson, Kanchelskis, McClair, Hughes, Giggs
Substitute(s): Blackmore, Ince   Scorer(s): Kanchelskis, McClair

Match # 4098 Saturday 07/12/91   Football League Division 1   at Old Trafford   Attendance 42549
Result: **Manchester United 4 Coventry City 0**
Teamsheet: Schmeichel, Parker, Irwin, Bruce, Webb, Pallister, Kanchelskis, Ince, McClair, Hughes, Giggs
Substitute(s): Blackmore   Scorer(s): Bruce, Hughes, McClair, Webb

Match # 4099 Sunday 15/12/91   Football League Division 1   at Stamford Bridge   Attendance 23120
Result: **Chelsea 1 Manchester United 3**
Teamsheet: Schmeichel, Parker, Irwin, Bruce, Webb, Pallister, Kanchelskis, Ince, McClair, Hughes, Giggs
Substitute(s): Blackmore   Scorer(s): Bruce, Irwin, McClair

Match # 4100 Thursday 26/12/91   Football League Division 1   at Boundary Park   Attendance 18947
Result: **Oldham Athletic 3 Manchester United 6**
Teamsheet: Schmeichel, Parker, Irwin, Bruce, Webb, Pallister, Robson, Ince, McClair, Hughes, Kanchelskis
Substitute(s): Blackmore, Giggs   Scorer(s): Irwin 2, McClair 2, Giggs, Kanchelskis

Match # 4101 Sunday 29/12/91   Football League Division 1   at Elland Road   Attendance 32638
Result: **Leeds United 1 Manchester United 1**
Teamsheet: Schmeichel, Parker, Blackmore, Bruce, Webb, Pallister, Kanchelskis, Ince, McClair, Hughes, Giggs
Substitute(s): Donaghy, Sharpe   Scorer(s): Webb

Match # 4102 Wednesday 01/01/92   Football League Division 1   at Old Trafford   Attendance 38554
Result: **Manchester United 1 Queens Park Rangers 4**
Teamsheet: Schmeichel, Parker, Blackmore, Bruce, Webb, Pallister, Phelan, Ince, McClair, Hughes, Sharpe
Substitute(s): Giggs   Scorer(s): McClair

Match # 4103 Wednesday 08/01/92   League Cup 5th Round   at Elland Road   Attendance 28886
Result: **Leeds United 1 Manchester United 3**
Teamsheet: Schmeichel, Parker, Blackmore, Bruce, Webb, Pallister, Kanchelskis, Ince, McClair, Hughes, Giggs
Substitute(s): Donaghy, Sharpe   Scorer(s): Blackmore, Giggs, Kanchelskis

Match # 4104 Saturday 11/01/92   Football League Division 1   at Old Trafford   Attendance 46619
Result: **Manchester United 1 Everton 0**
Teamsheet: Schmeichel, Parker, Blackmore, Bruce, Webb, Pallister, Kanchelskis, Ince, McClair, Hughes, Giggs
Substitute(s): Donaghy   Scorer(s): Kanchelskis

Match # 4105 Wednesday 15/01/92   FA Cup 3rd Round   at Elland Road   Attendance 31819
Result: **Leeds United 0 Manchester United 1**
Teamsheet: Schmeichel, Parker, Irwin, Bruce, Webb, Pallister, Kanchelskis, Ince, McClair, Hughes, Giggs
Scorer(s): Hughes

Match # 4106 Saturday 18/01/92   Football League Division 1   at Meadow Lane   Attendance 21055
Result: **Notts County 1 Manchester United 1**
Teamsheet: Schmeichel, Parker, Irwin, Bruce, Webb, Pallister, Kanchelskis, Ince, McClair, Hughes, Giggs
Substitute(s): Blackmore, Robins   Scorer(s): Blackmore

Match # 4107 Wednesday 22/01/92   Football League Division 1   at Old Trafford   Attendance 45022
Result: **Manchester United 1 Aston Villa 0**
Teamsheet: Schmeichel, Donaghy, Irwin, Bruce, Webb, Pallister, Robson, Ince, McClair, Hughes, Kanchelskis
Scorer(s): Hughes

SEASON 1991/92 (continued)

Match # 4108 Monday 27/01/92   FA Cup 4th Round   at The Dell   Attendance 19506
Result: **Southampton 0 Manchester United 0**
Teamsheet: Schmeichel, Parker, Irwin, Donaghy, Webb, Pallister, Robson, Ince, McClair, Hughes, Blackmore
Substitute(s): Giggs

Match # 4109 Saturday 01/02/92   Football League Division 1   at Highbury   Attendance 41703
Result: **Arsenal 1 Manchester United 1**
Teamsheet: Schmeichel, Parker, Irwin, Donaghy, Webb, Pallister, Robson, Ince, McClair, Hughes, Kanchelskis
Substitute(s): Giggs   Scorer(s): McClair

Match # 4110 Wednesday 05/02/92   FA Cup 4th Round Replay   at Old Trafford   Attendance 33414
Result: **Manchester United 2 Southampton 2   (United lost the tie 2-4 on penalty kicks)**
Teamsheet: Schmeichel, Parker, Irwin, Donaghy, Webb, Pallister, Robson, Ince, McClair, Giggs, Kanchelskis
Substitute(s): Hughes, Sharpe   Scorer(s): Kanchelskis, McClair

Match # 4111 Saturday 08/02/92   Football League Division 1   at Old Trafford   Attendance 47074
Result: **Manchester United 1 Sheffield Wednesday 1**
Teamsheet: Schmeichel, Giggs, Irwin, Donaghy, Webb, Pallister, Robson, Ince, McClair, Hughes, Kanchelskis
Substitute(s): Phelan, Sharpe   Scorer(s): McClair

Match # 4112 Saturday 22/02/92   Football League Division 1   at Old Trafford   Attendance 46347
Result: **Manchester United 2 Crystal Palace 0**
Teamsheet: Schmeichel, Donaghy, Irwin, Giggs, Webb, Pallister, Robson, Ince, McClair, Hughes, Kanchelskis
Substitute(s): Parker, Sharpe   Scorer(s): Hughes 2

Match # 4113 Wednesday 26/02/92   Football League Division 1   at Old Trafford   Attendance 44872
Result: **Manchester United 1 Chelsea 1**
Teamsheet: Walsh, Donaghy, Irwin, Giggs, Webb, Pallister, Robson, Ince, McClair, Hughes, Kanchelskis
Substitute(s): Blackmore, Parker   Scorer(s): Hughes

Match # 4114 Saturday 29/02/92   Football League Division 1   at Highfield Road   Attendance 23967
Result: **Coventry City 0 Manchester United 0**
Teamsheet: Walsh, Parker, Irwin, Donaghy, Webb, Pallister, Kanchelskis, Ince, McClair, Hughes, Giggs
Substitute(s): Blackmore

Match # 4115 Wednesday 04/03/92   League Cup Semi-Final 1st Leg   at Ayresome Park   Attendance 25572
Result: **Middlesbrough 0 Manchester United 0**
Teamsheet: Schmeichel, Parker, Irwin, Donaghy, Webb, Pallister, Robson, Ince, McClair, Hughes, Giggs
Substitute(s): Phelan, Sharpe

Match # 4116 Wednesday 11/03/92   League Cup Semi-Final 2nd Leg   at Old Trafford   Attendance 45875
Result: **Manchester United 2 Middlesbrough 1**
Teamsheet: Schmeichel, Parker, Irwin, Bruce, Webb, Pallister, Robson, Ince, McClair, Sharpe, Giggs
Substitute(s): Robins   Scorer(s): Giggs, Sharpe

Match # 4117 Saturday 14/03/92   Football League Division 1   at Bramall Lane   Attendance 30183
Result: **Sheffield United 1 Manchester United 2**
Teamsheet: Schmeichel, Parker, Irwin, Bruce, Phelan, Pallister, Robson, Ince, McClair, Sharpe, Kanchelskis
Substitute(s): Blackmore   Scorer(s): Blackmore, McClair

Match # 4118 Wednesday 18/03/92   Football League Division 1   at City Ground   Attendance 28062
Result: **Nottingham Forest 1 Manchester United 0**
Teamsheet: Schmeichel, Blackmore, Irwin, Bruce, Webb, Pallister, Phelan, Ince, McClair, Hughes, Sharpe
Substitute(s): Giggs, Kanchelskis

Match # 4119 Saturday 21/03/92   Football League Division 1   at Old Trafford   Attendance 45428
Result: **Manchester United 0 Wimbledon 0**
Teamsheet: Schmeichel, Blackmore, Irwin, Bruce, Webb, Pallister, Kanchelskis, Ince, McClair, Hughes, Giggs
Substitute(s): Sharpe

Match # 4120 Saturday 28/03/92   Football League Division 1   at Loftus Road   Attendance 22603
Result: **Queens Park Rangers 0 Manchester United 0**
Teamsheet: Schmeichel, Donaghy, Irwin, Bruce, Phelan, Pallister, Robson, Kanchelskis, McClair, Hughes, Giggs
Substitute(s): Sharpe

Match # 4121 Tuesday 31/03/92   Football League Division 1   at Carrow Road   Attendance 17489
Result: **Norwich City 1 Manchester United 3**
Teamsheet: Schmeichel, Donaghy, Irwin, Bruce, Giggs, Pallister, Robson, Ince, McClair, Hughes, Sharpe
Substitute(s): Blackmore   Scorer(s): Ince 2, McClair

Match # 4122 Tuesday 07/04/92   Football League Division 1   at Old Trafford   Attendance 46781
Result: **Manchester United 1 Manchester City 1**
Teamsheet: Schmeichel, Donaghy, Irwin, Bruce, Blackmore, Pallister, Giggs, Ince, McClair, Hughes, Sharpe
Substitute(s): Kanchelskis   Scorer(s): Giggs

Match # 4123 Sunday 12/04/92   League Cup Final   at Wembley   Attendance 76810
Result: **Manchester United 1 Nottingham Forest 0**
Teamsheet: Schmeichel, Parker, Irwin, Bruce, Phelan, Pallister, Kanchelskis, Ince, McClair, Hughes, Giggs
Substitute(s): Sharpe   Scorer(s): McClair

Match # 4124 Thursday 16/04/92   Football League Division 1   at Old Trafford   Attendance 43972
Result: **Manchester United 1 Southampton 0**
Teamsheet: Schmeichel, Parker, Irwin, Bruce, Phelan, Pallister, Kanchelskis, Ince, McClair, Hughes, Giggs
Substitute(s): Webb   Scorer(s): Kanchelskis

Match # 4125 Saturday 18/04/92   Football League Division 1   at Kenilworth Road   Attendance 13410
Result: **Luton Town 1 Manchester United 1**
Teamsheet: Schmeichel, Parker, Irwin, Bruce, Phelan, Pallister, Giggs, Webb, McClair, Hughes, Sharpe
Substitute(s): Blackmore, Kanchelskis   Scorer(s): Sharpe

SEASON 1991/92 (continued)

Match # 4126	Monday 20/04/92 Football League Division 1 at Old Trafford Attendance 47576
Result:	**Manchester United 1 Nottingham Forest 2**
Teamsheet:	Schmeichel, Blackmore, Irwin, Bruce, Phelan, Pallister, Kanchelskis, Webb, McClair, Giggs, Sharpe
Substitute(s):	Donaghy, Hughes Scorer(s): McClair

Match # 4127	Wednesday 22/04/92 Football League Division 1 at Upton Park Attendance 24197
Result:	**West Ham United 1 Manchester United 0**
Teamsheet:	Schmeichel, Donaghy, Irwin, Bruce, Phelan, Pallister, Blackmore, Giggs, McClair, Hughes, Sharpe
Substitute(s):	Ferguson, Kanchelskis

Match # 4128	Sunday 26/04/92 Football League Division 1 at Anfield Attendance 38669
Result:	**Liverpool 2 Manchester United 0**
Teamsheet:	Schmeichel, Donaghy, Irwin, Bruce, Kanchelskis, Pallister, Robson, Ince, McClair, Hughes, Giggs
Substitute(s):	Phelan

Match # 4129	Saturday 02/05/92 Football League Division 1 at Old Trafford Attendance 44595
Result:	**Manchester United 3 Tottenham Hotspur 1**
Teamsheet:	Schmeichel, Ferguson, Irwin, Bruce, Phelan, Donaghy, Kanchelskis, Ince, McClair, Hughes, Giggs
Substitute(s):	Sharpe Scorer(s): Hughes 2, McClair

SEASON 1991/92 SUMMARY

APPEARANCES

PLAYER	LGE	FAC	LC	ECWC	ESC	TOTAL
McClair	41 (1)	3	8	4	1	57 (1)
Schmeichel	40	3	6	3	1	53
Pallister	37 (3)	3	8	3 (1)	1	52 (4)
Hughes	38 (1)	2 (1)	6	4	1	51 (2)
Irwin	37 (1)	3	7	2	1	50 (1)
Bruce	37	1	7	4	1	50
Ince	31 (2)	3	6 (1)	3	1	44 (3)
Webb	29 (2)	3	6	3	1	42 (2)
Giggs	32 (6)	2 (1)	6 (2)	1	- (1)	41 (10)
Kanchelskis	28 (6)	2	4	1	1	36 (6)
Robson	26 (1)	2	5 (1)	3	-	36 (2)
Parker	24 (2)	3	6	2	-	35 (2)
Blackmore	19 (14)	1	4 (1)	1	1	26 (15)
Donaghy	16 (4)	2	3 (1)	-	-	21 (5)
Phelan	14 (4)	-	2 (1)	4	-	20 (5)
Sharpe	8 (6)	- (1)	1 (3)	-	-	9 (10)
Walsh	2	-	1	1	-	4
Robins	1 (1)	-	- (3)	2 (1)	-	3 (5)
Martin	- (1)	-	1	1 (2)	1	3 (3)
Ferguson	2 (2)	-	-	-	-	2 (2)
Beardsmore	-	-	-	1 (2)	-	1 (2)
Wallace	-	-	-	1 (1)	-	1 (1)
Wilkinson	-	-	1	-	-	1

GOALSCORERS

PLAYER	LGE	FAC	LC	ECWC	ESC	TOTAL
McClair	18	1	4	1	1	25
Hughes	11	1	-	2	-	14
Kanchelskis	5	1	2	-	-	8
Giggs	4	-	3	-	-	7
Bruce	5	-	1	-	-	6
Robson	4	-	1	-	-	5
Irwin	4	-	-	-	-	4
Blackmore	3	-	1	-	-	4
Ince	3	-	-	-	-	3
Webb	3	-	-	-	-	3
Sharpe	1	-	1	-	-	2
Robins	-	-	2	-	-	2
Pallister	1	-	-	-	-	1
own goal	1	-	-	-	-	1

RESULTS & ATTENDANCES SUMMARY

		P	W	D	L	F	A	TOTAL	AVGE
League	H	21	12	7	2	34	13	944678	44985
	A	21	9	8	4	29	20	585755	27893
	TOTAL	42	21	15	6	63	33	1530433	36439
FA Cup	H	1	0	1	0	2	2	33414	33414
	A	2	1	1	0	1	0	51325	25663
	TOTAL	3	1	2	0	3	2	84739	28246
League	H	4	4	0	0	10	2	144902	36226
Cup	A	3	1	2	0	4	2	63706	21235
	N	1	1	0	0	1	0	76810	76810
	TOTAL	8	6	2	0	15	4	285418	35677
European	H	2	1	1	0	3	1	74677	37339
CWC	A	2	0	1	1	0	3	45400	22700
	TOTAL	4	1	2	1	3	4	120077	30019
European	H	1	1	0	0	1	0	22110	22110
Super Cup	A	0	0	0	0	0	0	0	n/a
	TOTAL	1	1	0	0	1	0	22110	22110
Overall	H	29	18	9	2	50	18	1219781	42061
	A	28	11	12	5	34	25	746186	26650
	N	1	1	0	0	1	0	76810	76810
	TOTAL	58	30	21	7	85	43	2042777	35220

FINAL TABLE - LEAGUE DIVISION ONE

		P	W	D	L	F	A	W	D	L	F	A	PTS	GD
			HOME						AWAY					
1	Leeds United	42	13	8	0	38	13	9	8	4	36	24	82	37
2	MANCHESTER UNITED	42	12	7	2	34	13	9	8	4	29	20	78	30
3	Sheffield Wednesday	42	13	5	3	39	24	8	7	6	23	25	75	13
4	Arsenal	42	12	7	2	51	22	7	8	6	30	24	72	35
5	Manchester City	42	13	4	4	32	14	7	6	8	29	34	70	13
6	Liverpool	42	13	5	3	34	17	3	11	7	13	23	64	7
7	Aston Villa	42	13	3	5	31	16	4	6	11	17	28	60	4
8	Nottingham Forest	42	10	7	4	36	27	6	4	11	24	31	59	2
9	Sheffield United	42	9	6	6	29	23	7	3	11	36	40	57	2
10	Crystal Palace	42	7	8	6	24	25	7	7	7	29	36	57	-8
11	Queens Park Rangers	42	6	10	5	25	21	6	8	7	23	26	54	1
12	Everton	42	8	8	5	28	19	5	6	10	24	32	53	1
13	Wimbledon	42	10	5	6	32	20	3	9	9	21	33	53	0
14	Chelsea	42	7	8	6	31	30	6	6	9	19	30	53	-10
15	Tottenham Hotspur	42	7	3	11	33	35	8	4	9	25	28	52	-5
16	Southampton	42	7	5	9	17	28	7	5	9	22	27	52	-16
17	Oldham Athletic	42	11	5	5	46	36	3	4	14	17	31	51	-4
18	Norwich City	42	8	6	7	29	28	3	6	12	18	35	45	-16
19	Coventry City	42	6	7	8	18	15	5	4	12	17	29	44	-9
20	Luton Town	42	10	7	4	25	17	0	5	16	13	54	42	-33
21	Notts County	42	7	5	9	24	29	3	5	13	16	33	40	-22
22	West Ham United	42	6	6	9	22	24	3	5	13	15	35	38	-22

SEASON 1992/93

Match # 4130 Saturday 15/08/92   FA Premiership   at Bramall Lane   Attendance 28070
Result: **Sheffield United 2   Manchester United 1**
Teamsheet: Schmeichel, Irwin, Blackmore, Bruce, Ferguson, Pallister, Kanchelskis, Ince, McClair, Hughes, Giggs
Substitute(s):   Dublin, Phelan   Scorer(s):   Hughes

Match # 4131 Wednesday 19/08/92   FA Premiership   at Old Trafford   Attendance 31901
Result: **Manchester United 0   Everton 3**
Teamsheet: Schmeichel, Irwin, Blackmore, Bruce, Ferguson, Pallister, Kanchelskis, Ince, McClair, Hughes, Giggs
Substitute(s):   Dublin, Phelan

Match # 4132 Saturday 22/08/92   FA Premiership   at Old Trafford   Attendance 31704
Result: **Manchester United 1   Ipswich Town 1**
Teamsheet: Schmeichel, Irwin, Blackmore, Bruce, Ferguson, Pallister, Kanchelskis, Phelan, McClair, Hughes, Giggs
Substitute(s):   Dublin, Webb   Scorer(s):   Irwin

Match # 4133 Monday 24/08/92   FA Premiership   at The Dell   Attendance 15623
Result: **Southampton 0   Manchester United 1**
Teamsheet: Schmeichel, Phelan, Irwin, Bruce, Ferguson, Pallister, Dublin, Ince, McClair, Hughes, Giggs
Scorer(s):   Dublin

Match # 4134 Saturday 29/08/92   FA Premiership   at City Ground   Attendance 19694
Result: **Nottingham Forest 0   Manchester United 2**
Teamsheet: Schmeichel, Phelan, Irwin, Bruce, Ferguson, Pallister, Dublin, Ince, McClair, Hughes, Giggs
Substitute(s):   Blackmore, Kanchelskis   Scorer(s):   Giggs, Hughes

Match # 4135 Wednesday 02/09/92   FA Premiership   at Old Trafford   Attendance 29736
Result: **Manchester United 1   Crystal Palace 0**
Teamsheet: Schmeichel, Blackmore, Irwin, Bruce, Ferguson, Pallister, Dublin, Ince, McClair, Hughes, Giggs
Substitute(s):   Kanchelskis   Scorer(s):   Hughes

Match # 4136 Sunday 06/09/92   FA Premiership   at Old Trafford   Attendance 31296
Result: **Manchester United 2   Leeds United 0**
Teamsheet: Schmeichel, Blackmore, Irwin, Bruce, Ferguson, Pallister, Kanchelskis, Ince, McClair, Hughes, Giggs
Scorer(s):   Bruce, Kanchelskis

Match # 4137 Saturday 12/09/92   FA Premiership   at Goodison Park   Attendance 30002
Result: **Everton 0   Manchester United 2**
Teamsheet: Schmeichel, Irwin, Blackmore, Bruce, Ferguson, Pallister, Kanchelskis, Ince, McClair, Hughes, Giggs
Scorer(s):   Bruce, McClair

Match # 4138 Wednesday 16/09/92   UEFA Cup 1st Round 1st Leg   at Old Trafford   Attendance 19998
Result: **Manchester United 0   Torpedo Moscow 0**
Teamsheet: Walsh, Irwin, Martin, Bruce, Blackmore, Pallister, Kanchelskis, Webb, McClair, Hughes, Wallace
Substitute(s):   Neville

Match # 4139 Saturday 19/09/92   FA Premiership   at White Hart Lane   Attendance 33296
Result: **Tottenham Hotspur 1   Manchester United 1**
Teamsheet: Schmeichel, Irwin, Blackmore, Bruce, Ferguson, Pallister, Kanchelskis, Ince, McClair, Hughes, Giggs
Substitute(s):   Wallace   Scorer(s):   Giggs

Match # 4140 Wednesday 23/09/92   League Cup 2nd Round 1st Leg   at Goldstone Ground   Attendance 16649
Result: **Brighton 1   Manchester United 1**
Teamsheet: Walsh, Irwin, Martin, Bruce, Webb, Pallister, Kanchelskis, Ince, McClair, Hughes, Wallace
Substitute(s):   Beckham   Scorer(s):   Wallace

Match # 4141 Saturday 26/09/92   FA Premiership   at Old Trafford   Attendance 33287
Result: **Manchester United 0   Queens Park Rangers 0**
Teamsheet: Schmeichel, Irwin, Blackmore, Bruce, Ferguson, Pallister, Kanchelskis, Ince, McClair, Hughes, Giggs
Substitute(s):   Wallace

Match # 4142 Tuesday 29/09/92   UEFA Cup 1st Round 2nd Leg   at Torpedo Stadion   Attendance 11357
Result: **Torpedo Moscow 0   Manchester United 0**   (United lost the tie 3-4 on penalty kicks)
Teamsheet: Schmeichel, Irwin, Phelan, Bruce, Webb, Pallister, Wallace, Ince, McClair, Hughes, Giggs
Substitute(s):   Parker, Robson

Match # 4143 Saturday 03/10/92   FA Premiership   at Ayresome Park   Attendance 24172
Result: **Middlesbrough 1   Manchester United 1**
Teamsheet: Schmeichel, Irwin, Phelan, Bruce, Ferguson, Pallister, Blackmore, Ince, McClair, Hughes, Giggs
Substitute(s):   Kanchelskis, Robson   Scorer(s):   Bruce

Match # 4144 Wednesday 07/10/92   League Cup 2nd Round 2nd Leg   at Old Trafford   Attendance 25405
Result: **Manchester United 1   Brighton 0**
Teamsheet: Schmeichel, Parker, Irwin, Bruce, Kanchelskis, Pallister, Robson, Ince, McClair, Hughes, Giggs
Scorer(s):   Hughes

Match # 4145 Sunday 18/10/92   FA Premiership   at Old Trafford   Attendance 33243
Result: **Manchester United 2   Liverpool 2**
Teamsheet: Schmeichel, Parker, Irwin, Bruce, Ferguson, Pallister, Kanchelskis, Ince, McClair, Hughes, Giggs
Substitute(s):   Blackmore   Scorer(s):   Hughes 2

Match # 4146 Saturday 24/10/92   FA Premiership   at Ewood Park   Attendance 20305
Result: **Blackburn Rovers 0   Manchester United 0**
Teamsheet: Schmeichel, Parker, Irwin, Bruce, Ferguson, Pallister, Blackmore, Ince, McClair, Hughes, Giggs
Substitute(s):   Kanchelskis

Match # 4147 Wednesday 28/10/92   League Cup 3rd Round   at Villa Park   Attendance 35964
Result: **Aston Villa 1   Manchester United 0**
Teamsheet: Schmeichel, Parker, Irwin, Bruce, Ferguson, Pallister, Blackmore, Ince, McClair, Hughes, Giggs
Substitute(s):   Kanchelskis

SEASON 1992/93 (continued)

Match # 4148	Saturday 31/10/92		FA Premiership				at Old Trafford					Attendance 32622
Result:		**Manchester United 0 Wimbledon 1**
Teamsheet:	Schmeichel, Parker, Blackmore, Bruce, Ferguson, Pallister, Kanchelskis, Ince, McClair, Hughes, Giggs
Substitute(s):	Robson

Match # 4149	Saturday 07/11/92		FA Premiership				at Villa Park					Attendance 39063
Result:		**Aston Villa 1 Manchester United 0**
Teamsheet:	Schmeichel, Parker, Blackmore, Bruce, Ferguson, Pallister, Robson, Ince, Sharpe, Hughes, Giggs
Substitute(s):	McClair

Match # 4150	Saturday 21/11/92		FA Premiership				at Old Trafford					Attendance 33497
Result:		**Manchester United 3 Oldham Athletic 0**
Teamsheet:	Schmeichel, Parker, Irwin, Bruce, Sharpe, Pallister, Robson, Ince, McClair, Hughes, Giggs
Substitute(s):	Butt, Phelan		Scorer(s):	McClair 2, Hughes

Match # 4151	Saturday 28/11/92		FA Premiership				at Highbury					Attendance 29739
Result:		**Arsenal 0 Manchester United 1**
Teamsheet:	Schmeichel, Parker, Irwin, Bruce, Sharpe, Pallister, Robson, Ince, McClair, Hughes, Giggs
Scorer(s):	Hughes

Match # 4152	Sunday 06/12/92		FA Premiership				at Old Trafford					Attendance 35408
Result:		**Manchester United 2 Manchester City 1**
Teamsheet:	Schmeichel, Parker, Irwin, Bruce, Sharpe, Pallister, Robson, Ince, McClair, Hughes, Giggs
Substitute(s):	Cantona		Scorer(s):	Hughes, Ince

Match # 4153	Saturday 12/12/92		FA Premiership				at Old Trafford					Attendance 34500
Result:		**Manchester United 1 Norwich City 0**
Teamsheet:	Schmeichel, Parker, Irwin, Bruce, Sharpe, Pallister, Cantona, Ince, McClair, Hughes, Giggs
Scorer(s):	Hughes

Match # 4154	Saturday 19/12/92		FA Premiership				at Stamford Bridge				Attendance 34464
Result:		**Chelsea 1 Manchester United 1**
Teamsheet:	Schmeichel, Parker, Irwin, Bruce, Phelan, Pallister, Cantona, Ince, McClair, Hughes, Sharpe
Substitute(s):	Kanchelskis		Scorer(s):	Cantona

Match # 4155	Saturday 26/12/92		FA Premiership				at Hillsborough					Attendance 37708
Result:		**Sheffield Wednesday 3 Manchester United 3**
Teamsheet:	Schmeichel, Parker, Irwin, Bruce, Sharpe, Pallister, Cantona, Ince, McClair, Hughes, Giggs
Substitute(s):	Kanchelskis		Scorer(s):	McClair 2, Cantona

Match # 4156	Monday 28/12/92		FA Premiership				at Old Trafford					Attendance 36025
Result:		**Manchester United 5 Coventry City 0**
Teamsheet:	Schmeichel, Parker, Irwin, Bruce, Sharpe, Pallister, Cantona, Ince, McClair, Hughes, Giggs
Substitute(s):	Kanchelskis, Phelan		Scorer(s):	Cantona, Giggs, Hughes, Irwin, Sharpe

Match # 4157	Tuesday 05/01/93		FA Cup 3rd Round			at Old Trafford					Attendance 30668
Result:		**Manchester United 2 Bury 0**
Teamsheet:	Schmeichel, Parker, Irwin, Bruce, Sharpe, Pallister, Cantona, Phelan, McClair, Hughes, Gillespie
Substitute(s):	Blackmore, Robson		Scorer(s):	Gillespie, Phelan

Match # 4158	Saturday 09/01/93		FA Premiership				at Old Trafford					Attendance 35648
Result:		**Manchester United 4 Tottenham Hotspur 1**
Teamsheet:	Schmeichel, Parker, Irwin, Bruce, Sharpe, Pallister, Cantona, Ince, McClair, Hughes, Giggs
Substitute(s):	Kanchelskis, Phelan		Scorer(s):	Cantona, Irwin, McClair, Parker

Match # 4159	Monday 18/01/93		FA Premiership				at Loftus Road					Attendance 21117
Result:		**Queens Park Rangers 1 Manchester United 3**
Teamsheet:	Schmeichel, Parker, Irwin, Bruce, Sharpe, Pallister, Kanchelskis, Ince, McClair, Hughes, Giggs
Substitute(s):	Phelan		Scorer(s):	Giggs, Ince, Kanchelskis

Match # 4160	Saturday 23/01/93		FA Cup 4th Round			at Old Trafford					Attendance 33600
Result:		**Manchester United 1 Brighton 0**
Teamsheet:	Schmeichel, Parker, Irwin, Bruce, Sharpe, Pallister, Wallace, Ince, McClair, Phelan, Giggs
Substitute(s):	Gillespie		Scorer(s):	Giggs

Match # 4161	Wednesday 27/01/93		FA Premiership				at Old Trafford					Attendance 36085
Result:		**Manchester United 2 Nottingham Forest 0**
Teamsheet:	Schmeichel, Parker, Irwin, Bruce, Sharpe, Pallister, Cantona, Ince, McClair, Hughes, Giggs
Scorer(s):	Hughes, Ince

Match # 4162	Saturday 30/01/93		FA Premiership				at Portman Road					Attendance 22068
Result:		**Ipswich Town 2 Manchester United 1**
Teamsheet:	Schmeichel, Parker, Irwin, Bruce, Sharpe, Pallister, Cantona, Ince, McClair, Hughes, Giggs
Substitute(s):	Kanchelskis		Scorer(s):	McClair

Match # 4163	Saturday 06/02/93		FA Premiership				at Old Trafford					Attendance 36156
Result:		**Manchester United 2 Sheffield United 1**
Teamsheet:	Schmeichel, Parker, Irwin, Bruce, Sharpe, Pallister, Cantona, Ince, McClair, Hughes, Giggs
Substitute(s):	Kanchelskis		Scorer(s):	Cantona, McClair

Match # 4164	Monday 08/02/93		FA Premiership				at Elland Road					Attendance 34166
Result:		**Leeds United 0 Manchester United 0**
Teamsheet:	Schmeichel, Parker, Irwin, Bruce, Sharpe, Pallister, Cantona, Ince, McClair, Hughes, Giggs
Substitute(s):	Kanchelskis

Match # 4165	Sunday 14/02/93		FA Cup 5th Round			at Bramall Lane					Attendance 27150
Result:		**Sheffield United 2 Manchester United 1**
Teamsheet:	Schmeichel, Parker, Irwin, Bruce, Sharpe, Pallister, Kanchelskis, Ince, McClair, Hughes, Giggs
Scorer(s):	Giggs

SEASON 1992/93 (continued)

Match # 4166 Saturday 20/02/93   FA Premiership   at Old Trafford   Attendance 36257
Result: **Manchester United 2 Southampton 1**
Teamsheet: Schmeichel, Parker, Irwin, Bruce, Sharpe, Pallister, Cantona, Ince, McClair, Hughes, Giggs
Scorer(s):   Giggs 2

Match # 4167 Saturday 27/02/93   FA Premiership   at Old Trafford   Attendance 36251
Result: **Manchester United 3 Middlesbrough 0**
Teamsheet: Schmeichel, Parker, Irwin, Bruce, Sharpe, Pallister, Cantona, Ince, McClair, Hughes, Giggs
Scorer(s):   Cantona, Giggs, Irwin

Match # 4168 Saturday 06/03/93   FA Premiership   at Anfield   Attendance 44374
Result: **Liverpool 1 Manchester United 2**
Teamsheet: Schmeichel, Parker, Irwin, Bruce, Sharpe, Pallister, Kanchelskis, Ince, McClair, Hughes, Giggs
Scorer(s):   Hughes, McClair

Match # 4169 Tuesday 09/03/93   FA Premiership   at Boundary Park   Attendance 17106
Result: **Oldham Athletic 1 Manchester United 0**
Teamsheet: Schmeichel, Parker, Irwin, Bruce, Sharpe, Pallister, Kanchelskis, Ince, McClair, Hughes, Giggs
Substitute(s):   Dublin

Match # 4170 Tuesday 14/03/93   FA Premiership   at Old Trafford   Attendance 36163
Result: **Manchester United 1 Aston Villa 1**
Teamsheet: Schmeichel, Parker, Irwin, Bruce, Sharpe, Pallister, Cantona, Ince, McClair, Hughes, Giggs
Scorer(s):   Hughes

Match # 4171 Saturday 20/03/93   FA Premiership   at Maine Road   Attendance 37136
Result: **Manchester City 1 Manchester United 1**
Teamsheet: Schmeichel, Parker, Irwin, Bruce, Sharpe, Pallister, Cantona, Ince, McClair, Hughes, Giggs
Scorer(s):   Cantona

Match # 4172 Wednesday 24/03/93   FA Premiership   at Old Trafford   Attendance 37301
Result: **Manchester United 0 Arsenal 0**
Teamsheet: Schmeichel, Parker, Irwin, Bruce, Sharpe, Pallister, Cantona, Ince, McClair, Hughes, Giggs
Substitute(s):   Robson

Match # 4173 Monday 05/04/93   FA Premiership   at Carrow Road   Attendance 20582
Result: **Norwich City 1 Manchester United 3**
Teamsheet: Schmeichel, Parker, Irwin, Bruce, Sharpe, Pallister, Cantona, Ince, McClair, Kanchelskis, Giggs
Substitute(s):   Robson   Scorer(s):   Cantona, Giggs, Kanchelskis

Match # 4174 Saturday 10/04/93   FA Premiership   at Old Trafford   Attendance 40102
Result: **Manchester United 2 Sheffield Wednesday 1**
Teamsheet: Schmeichel, Parker, Irwin, Bruce, Sharpe, Pallister, Cantona, Ince, McClair, Hughes, Giggs
Substitute(s):   Robson   Scorer(s):   Bruce 2

Match # 4175 Monday 12/04/93   FA Premiership   at Highfield Road   Attendance 24249
Result: **Coventry City 0 Manchester United 1**
Teamsheet: Schmeichel, Parker, Irwin, Bruce, Sharpe, Pallister, Cantona, Ince, McClair, Hughes, Giggs
Substitute(s):   Robson   Scorer(s):   Irwin

Match # 4176 Saturday 17/04/93   FA Premiership   at Old Trafford   Attendance 40139
Result: **Manchester United 3 Chelsea 0**
Teamsheet: Schmeichel, Parker, Irwin, Bruce, Sharpe, Pallister, Cantona, Ince, McClair, Hughes, Giggs
Substitute(s):   Kanchelskis, Robson   Scorer(s):   Cantona, Hughes, own goal

Match # 4177 Wednesday 21/04/93   FA Premiership   at Selhurst Park   Attendance 30115
Result: **Crystal Palace 0 Manchester United 2**
Teamsheet: Schmeichel, Parker, Irwin, Bruce, Kanchelskis, Pallister, Cantona, Ince, McClair, Hughes, Giggs
Substitute(s):   Robson   Scorer(s):   Hughes, Ince

Match # 4178 Monday 03/05/93   FA Premiership   at Old Trafford   Attendance 40447
Result: **Manchester United 3 Blackburn Rovers 1**
Teamsheet: Schmeichel, Parker, Irwin, Bruce, Sharpe, Pallister, Cantona, Ince, McClair, Hughes, Giggs
Substitute(s):   Kanchelskis, Robson   Scorer(s):   Giggs, Ince, Pallister

Match # 4179 Sunday 09/05/93   FA Premiership   at Selhurst Park   Attendance 30115
Result: **Wimbledon 1 Manchester United 2**
Teamsheet: Schmeichel, Parker, Irwin, Bruce, Sharpe, Pallister, Robson, Ince, McClair, Hughes, Cantona
Substitute(s):   Giggs   Scorer(s):   Ince, Robson

SEASON 1992/93 SUMMARY

APPEARANCES

PLAYER	LGE	FAC	LC	UC	TOTAL
Bruce	42	3	3	2	50
Pallister	42	3	3	2	50
McClair	41 (1)	3	3	2	49 (1)
Hughes	41	2	3	2	48
Irwin	40	3	3	2	48
Schmeichel	42	3	2	1	48
Ince	41	2	3	1	47
Giggs	40 (1)	2	2	1	45 (1)
Parker	31	3	2	- (1)	36 (1)
Sharpe	27	3	-	-	30
Cantona	21 (1)	1	-	-	22 (1)
Kanchelskis	14 (13)	1	2 (1)	1	18 (14)
Ferguson	15	-	1	-	16
Blackmore	12 (2)	- (1)	1	1	14 (3)
Phelan	5 (6)	2	-	1	8 (6)
Robson	5 (9)	- (1)	1	- (1)	6 (11)
Wallace	- (2)	1	1	2	4 (2)
Dublin	3 (4)	-	-	-	3 (4)
Webb	- (1)	-	1	2	3 (1)
Martin	-	-	1	1	2
Walsh	-	-	1	1	2
Gillespie	-	1 (1)	-	-	1 (1)
Beckham	-	-	- (1)	-	- (1)
Butt	- (1)	-	-	-	- (1)
Neville	-	-	-	- (1)	- (1)

GOALSCORERS

PLAYER	LGE	FAC	LC	UC	TOT
Hughes	15	-	1	-	16
Giggs	9	2	-	-	11
Cantona	9	-	-	-	9
McClair	9	-	-	-	9
Ince	6	-	-	-	6
Bruce	5	-	-	-	5
Irwin	5	-	-	-	5
Kanchelskis	3	-	-	-	3
Dublin	1	-	-	-	1
Pallister	1	-	-	-	1
Parker	1	-	-	-	1
Robson	1	-	-	-	1
Sharpe	1	-	-	-	1
Gillespie	-	1	-	-	1
Phelan	-	1	-	-	1
Wallace	-	-	1	-	1
own goal	1	-	-	-	1

RESULTS & ATTENDANCES SUMMARY

		P	W	D	L	F	A	TOTAL	AVGE
League	H	21	14	5	2	39	14	737768	35132
	A	21	10	7	4	28	17	593164	28246
	TOTAL	42	24	12	6	67	31	1330932	31689
FA Cup	H	2	2	0	0	3	0	64268	32134
	A	1	0	0	1	1	2	27150	27150
	TOTAL	3	2	0	1	4	2	91418	30473
League	H	1	1	0	0	1	0	25405	25405
Cup	A	2	0	1	1	1	2	52613	26307
	TOTAL	3	1	1	1	2	2	78018	26006
UEFA	H	1	0	1	0	0	0	19998	19998
Cup	A	1	0	1	0	0	0	11357	11357
	TOTAL	2	0	2	0	0	0	31355	15678
Overall	H	25	17	6	2	43	14	847439	33898
	A	25	10	9	6	30	21	684284	27371
	TOTAL	50	27	15	8	73	35	1531723	30634

FINAL TABLE – FA PREMIERSHIP

		P	W	D	L	F	A	W	D	L	F	A	PTS	GD
				HOME						AWAY				
1	MANCHESTER UNITED	42	14	5	2	39	14	10	7	4	28	17	84	36
2	Aston Villa	42	13	5	3	36	16	8	6	7	21	24	74	17
3	Norwich City	42	13	6	2	31	19	8	3	10	30	46	72	-4
4	Blackburn Rovers	42	13	4	4	38	18	7	7	7	30	28	71	22
5	Queens Park Rangers	42	11	5	5	41	32	6	7	8	22	23	63	8
6	Liverpool	42	13	4	4	41	18	3	7	11	21	37	59	7
7	Sheffield Wednesday	42	9	8	4	34	26	6	6	9	21	25	59	4
8	Tottenham Hotspur	42	11	5	5	40	25	5	6	10	20	41	59	-6
9	Manchester City	42	7	8	6	30	25	8	4	9	26	26	57	5
10	Arsenal	42	8	6	7	25	20	7	5	9	15	18	56	2
11	Chelsea	42	9	7	5	29	22	5	7	9	22	32	56	-3
12	Wimbledon	42	9	4	8	32	23	5	8	8	24	32	54	1
13	Everton	42	7	6	8	26	27	8	2	11	27	28	53	-2
14	Sheffield United	42	10	6	5	33	19	4	4	13	21	34	52	1
15	Coventry City	42	7	4	10	29	28	6	9	6	23	29	52	-5
16	Ipswich Town	42	8	9	4	29	22	4	7	10	21	33	52	-5
17	Leeds United	42	12	8	1	40	17	0	7	14	17	45	51	-5
18	Southampton	42	10	6	5	30	21	3	5	13	24	40	50	-7
19	Oldham Athletic	42	10	6	5	43	30	3	4	14	20	44	49	-11
20	Crystal Palace	42	6	9	6	27	25	5	7	9	21	36	49	-13
21	Middlesbrough	42	8	5	8	33	27	3	6	12	21	48	44	-21
22	Nottingham Forest	42	6	4	11	17	25	4	6	11	24	37	40	-21

SEASON 1993/94

Match # 4180	Saturday 07/08/93	FA Charity Shield	at Wembley	Attendance 66519
Result:	**Manchester United 1 Arsenal 1 (United won the tie 5-4 on penalty kicks)**			
Teamsheet:	Schmeichel, Parker, Irwin, Bruce, Kanchelskis, Pallister, Cantona, Ince, Keane, Hughes, Giggs			
Substitute(s):	Robson	Scorer(s): Hughes		

Match # 4181	Sunday 15/08/93	FA Premiership	at Carrow Road	Attendance 19705
Result:	**Norwich City 0 Manchester United 2**			
Teamsheet:	Schmeichel, Parker, Irwin, Bruce, Kanchelskis, Pallister, Robson, Ince, Keane, Hughes, Giggs			
Scorer(s):	Giggs, Robson			

Match # 4182	Wednesday 18/08/93	FA Premiership	at Old Trafford	Attendance 41949
Result:	**Manchester United 3 Sheffield United 0**			
Teamsheet:	Schmeichel, Parker, Irwin, Bruce, Kanchelskis, Pallister, Robson, Ince, Keane, Hughes, Giggs			
Substitute(s):	McClair	Scorer(s): Keane 2, Hughes		

Match # 4183	Saturday 21/08/93	FA Premiership	at Old Trafford	Attendance 41829
Result:	**Manchester United 1 Newcastle United 1**			
Teamsheet:	Schmeichel, Parker, Irwin, Bruce, Kanchelskis, Pallister, Robson, Ince, Keane, Hughes, Giggs			
Substitute(s):	McClair, Sharpe	Scorer(s): Giggs		

Match # 4184	Monday 23/08/93	FA Premiership	at Villa Park	Attendance 39624
Result:	**Aston Villa 1 Manchester United 2**			
Teamsheet:	Schmeichel, Parker, Irwin, Bruce, Sharpe, Pallister, Kanchelskis, Ince, Keane, Hughes, Giggs			
Scorer(s):	Sharpe 2			

Match # 4185	Saturday 28/08/93	FA Premiership	at The Dell	Attendance 16189
Result:	**Southampton 1 Manchester United 3**			
Teamsheet:	Schmeichel, Parker, Irwin, Bruce, Sharpe, Pallister, Cantona, Ince, Keane, Hughes, Giggs			
Substitute(s):	Kanchelskis, McClair	Scorer(s): Cantona, Irwin, Sharpe		

Match # 4186	Wednesday 01/09/93	FA Premiership	at Old Trafford	Attendance 44613
Result:	**Manchester United 3 West Ham United 0**			
Teamsheet:	Schmeichel, Parker, Irwin, Bruce, Sharpe, Pallister, Cantona, Ince, Keane, Kanchelskis, Giggs			
Substitute(s):	McClair, Robson	Scorer(s): Bruce, Cantona, Sharpe		

Match # 4187	Saturday 11/09/93	FA Premiership	at Stamford Bridge	Attendance 37064
Result:	**Chelsea 1 Manchester United 0**			
Teamsheet:	Schmeichel, Parker, Irwin, Bruce, Sharpe, Pallister, Cantona, Ince, Keane, Robson, Giggs			
Substitute(s):	McClair			

Match # 4188	Wednesday 15/09/93	European Cup 1st Round 1st Leg	at Jozsef Bozsik Stadium	Attendance 9000
Result:	**Honved 2 Manchester United 3**			
Teamsheet:	Schmeichel, Parker, Irwin, Bruce, Sharpe, Pallister, Robson, Ince, Cantona, Keane, Giggs			
Substitute(s):	Phelan	Scorer(s): Keane 2, Cantona		

Match # 4189	Sunday 19/09/93	FA Premiership	at Old Trafford	Attendance 44009
Result:	**Manchester United 1 Arsenal 0**			
Teamsheet:	Schmeichel, Parker, Irwin, Bruce, Sharpe, Pallister, Cantona, Ince, Keane, Hughes, Giggs			
Substitute(s):	McClair	Scorer(s): Cantona		

Match # 4190	Wednesday 22/09/93	League Cup 2nd Round 1st Leg	at Victoria Ground	Attendance 23327
Result:	**Stoke City 2 Manchester United 1**			
Teamsheet:	Schmeichel, Martin, Irwin, Phelan, Kanchelskis, Pallister, Robson, Ferguson, McClair, Hughes, Dublin			
Substitute(s):	Bruce, Sharpe	Scorer(s): Dublin		

Match # 4191	Saturday 25/09/93	FA Premiership	at Old Trafford	Attendance 44583
Result:	**Manchester United 4 Swindon Town 2**			
Teamsheet:	Schmeichel, Parker, Irwin, Bruce, Sharpe, Pallister, Cantona, Ince, Keane, Hughes, Kanchelskis			
Substitute(s):	Giggs, McClair	Scorer(s): Hughes 2, Cantona, Kanchelskis		

Match # 4192	Wednesday 29/09/93	European Cup 1st Round 2nd Leg	at Old Trafford	Attendance 35781
Result:	**Manchester United 2 Honved 1**			
Teamsheet:	Schmeichel, Parker, Irwin, Bruce, Sharpe, Pallister, Robson, Ince, Cantona, Hughes, Giggs			
Substitute(s):	Martin, Phelan	Scorer(s): Bruce 2		

Match # 4193	Saturday 02/10/93	FA Premiership	at Hillsborough	Attendance 34548
Result:	**Sheffield Wednesday 2 Manchester United 3**			
Teamsheet:	Schmeichel, Parker, Irwin, Bruce, Sharpe, Pallister, Cantona, Ince, Keane, Hughes, Giggs			
Substitute(s):	Kanchelskis	Scorer(s): Hughes 2, Giggs		

Match # 4194	Wednesday 06/10/93	League Cup 2nd Round 2nd Leg	at Old Trafford	Attendance 41387
Result:	**Manchester United 2 Stoke City 0**			
Teamsheet:	Schmeichel, Martin, Irwin, Bruce, Sharpe, Pallister, Robson, Kanchelskis, McClair, Hughes, Keane			
Substitute(s):	Giggs	Scorer(s): McClair, Sharpe		

Match # 4195	Saturday 16/10/93	FA Premiership	at Old Trafford	Attendance 44655
Result:	**Manchester United 2 Tottenham Hotspur 1**			
Teamsheet:	Schmeichel, Parker, Irwin, Bruce, Sharpe, Pallister, Cantona, Robson, Keane, Hughes, Giggs			
Substitute(s):	Butt, McClair	Scorer(s): Keane, Sharpe		

Match # 4196	Wednesday 20/10/93	European Cup 2nd Round 1st Leg	at Old Trafford	Attendance 39346
Result:	**Manchester United 3 Galatasaray 3**			
Teamsheet:	Schmeichel, Martin, Sharpe, Bruce, Keane, Pallister, Robson, Ince, Cantona, Hughes, Giggs			
Substitute(s):	Phelan	Scorer(s): Cantona, Robson, own goal		

Match # 4197	Saturday 23/10/93	FA Premiership	at Goodison Park	Attendance 35430
Result:	**Everton 0 Manchester United 1**			
Teamsheet:	Schmeichel, Martin, Irwin, Bruce, Sharpe, Pallister, Cantona, Ince, McClair, Hughes, Keane			
Scorer(s):	Sharpe			

SEASON 1993/94 (continued)

Match # 4198 Wednesday 27/10/93   League Cup 3rd Round   at Old Trafford   Attendance 41344
Result: **Manchester United 5 Leicester City 1**
Teamsheet: Schmeichel, Phelan, Martin, Bruce, Sharpe, Pallister, Robson, Kanchelskis, McClair, Hughes, Keane
Substitute(s): Giggs, Irwin   Scorer(s):   Bruce 2, Hughes, McClair, Sharpe

Match # 4199 Saturday 30/10/93   FA Premiership   at Old Trafford   Attendance 44663
Result: **Manchester United 2 Queens Park Rangers 1**
Teamsheet: Schmeichel, Parker, Irwin, Bruce, Sharpe, Phelan, Cantona, Ince, Keane, Hughes, Giggs
Scorer(s):   Cantona, Hughes

Match # 4200 Wednesday 03/11/93   European Cup 2nd Round 2nd Leg   at Ali Sami Yen   Attendance 40000
Result: **Galatasaray 0 Manchester United 0   (United lost the tie on away goals rule)**
Teamsheet: Schmeichel, Parker, Irwin, Bruce, Sharpe, Phelan, Robson, Ince, Cantona, Keane, Giggs
Substitute(s): Dublin, Neville

Match # 4201 Sunday 07/11/93   FA Premiership   at Maine Road   Attendance 35155
Result: **Manchester City 2 Manchester United 3**
Teamsheet: Schmeichel, Parker, Irwin, Bruce, Sharpe, Pallister, Cantona, Ince, Keane, Hughes, Kanchelskis
Substitute(s): Giggs   Scorer(s):   Cantona 2, Keane

Match # 4202 Saturday 20/11/93   FA Premiership   at Old Trafford   Attendance 44748
Result: **Manchester United 3 Wimbledon 1**
Teamsheet: Schmeichel, Parker, Irwin, Bruce, Sharpe, Pallister, Cantona, Ince, Robson, Hughes, Kanchelskis
Substitute(s): Phelan   Scorer(s):   Hughes, Kanchelskis, Pallister

Match # 4203 Wednesday 24/11/93   FA Premiership   at Old Trafford   Attendance 43300
Result: **Manchester United 0 Ipswich Town 0**
Teamsheet: Schmeichel, Parker, Irwin, Bruce, Sharpe, Pallister, Cantona, Ince, Robson, Hughes, Kanchelskis
Substitute(s): Ferguson, Giggs

Match # 4204 Saturday 27/11/93   FA Premiership   at Highfield Road   Attendance 17020
Result: **Coventry City 0 Manchester United 1**
Teamsheet: Schmeichel, Parker, Irwin, Bruce, Sharpe, Pallister, Cantona, Ince, Ferguson, Hughes, Giggs
Scorer(s):   Cantona

Match # 4205 Tuesday 30/11/93   League Cup 4th Round   at Goodison Park   Attendance 34052
Result: **Everton 0 Manchester United 2**
Teamsheet: Schmeichel, Parker, Irwin, Bruce, Kanchelskis, Pallister, Cantona, Ince, Robson, Hughes, Giggs
Substitute(s): Ferguson   Scorer(s):   Giggs, Hughes

Match # 4206 Saturday 04/12/93   FA Premiership   at Old Trafford   Attendance 44694
Result: **Manchester United 2 Norwich City 2**
Teamsheet: Schmeichel, Parker, Irwin, Bruce, Kanchelskis, Pallister, Cantona, Ince, McClair, Hughes, Giggs
Substitute(s): Sharpe   Scorer(s):   Giggs, McClair

Match # 4207 Tuesday 07/12/93   FA Premiership   at Bramall Lane   Attendance 26746
Result: **Sheffield United 0 Manchester United 3**
Teamsheet: Schmeichel, Parker, Irwin, Bruce, Sharpe, Pallister, Cantona, Ince, McClair, Hughes, Giggs
Substitute(s): Keane   Scorer(s):   Cantona, Hughes, Sharpe

Match # 4208 Saturday 11/12/93   FA Premiership   at St James' Park   Attendance 36388
Result: **Newcastle United 1 Manchester United 1**
Teamsheet: Schmeichel, Parker, Irwin, Bruce, Sharpe, Pallister, Cantona, Ince, McClair, Hughes, Giggs
Substitute(s): Kanchelskis, Keane   Scorer(s):   Ince

Match # 4209 Sunday 19/12/93   FA Premiership   at Old Trafford   Attendance 44499
Result: **Manchester United 3 Aston Villa 1**
Teamsheet: Schmeichel, Parker, Irwin, Bruce, Sharpe, Pallister, Cantona, Ince, Keane, Hughes, Kanchelskis
Substitute(s): Giggs   Scorer(s):   Cantona 2, Ince

Match # 4210 Sunday 26/12/93   FA Premiership   at Old Trafford   Attendance 44511
Result: **Manchester United 1 Blackburn Rovers 1**
Teamsheet: Schmeichel, Parker, Irwin, Bruce, Sharpe, Pallister, Cantona, Ince, Keane, Hughes, Giggs
Substitute(s): Ferguson, McClair   Scorer(s):   Ince

Match # 4211 Wednesday 29/12/93   FA Premiership   at Boundary Park   Attendance 16708
Result: **Oldham Athletic 2 Manchester United 5**
Teamsheet: Schmeichel, Parker, Irwin, Bruce, Sharpe, Pallister, Cantona, Ince, Keane, Kanchelskis, Giggs
Substitute(s): McClair, Robson   Scorer(s):   Giggs 2, Bruce, Cantona, Kanchelskis

Match # 4212 Saturday 01/01/94   FA Premiership   at Old Trafford   Attendance 44724
Result: **Manchester United 0 Leeds United 0**
Teamsheet: Schmeichel, Parker, Irwin, Bruce, Robson, Pallister, Cantona, Keane, McClair, Kanchelskis, Giggs

Match # 4213 Tuesday 04/01/94   FA Premiership   at Anfield   Attendance 42795
Result: **Liverpool 3 Manchester United 3**
Teamsheet: Schmeichel, Parker, Irwin, Bruce, Keane, Pallister, Cantona, Ince, McClair, Kanchelskis, Giggs
Scorer(s):   Bruce, Giggs, Irwin

Match # 4214 Sunday 09/01/94   FA Cup 3rd Round   at Bramall Lane   Attendance 22019
Result: **Sheffield United 0 Manchester United 1**
Teamsheet: Schmeichel, Parker, Irwin, Bruce, Kanchelskis, Pallister, Cantona, Ince, Keane, Hughes, Giggs
Substitute(s): McClair   Scorer(s):   Hughes

Match # 4215 Wednesday 12/01/94   League Cup 5th Round   at Old Trafford   Attendance 43794
Result: **Manchester United 2 Portsmouth 2**
Teamsheet: Schmeichel, Parker, Irwin, Bruce, Kanchelskis, Pallister, Cantona, Robson, McClair, Hughes, Giggs
Substitute(s): Dublin, Keane   Scorer(s):   Cantona, Giggs

SEASON 1993/94 (continued)

Match # 4216   Saturday 15/01/94   FA Premiership   at White Hart Lane   Attendance 31343
Result: **Tottenham Hotspur 0 Manchester United 1**
Teamsheet: Schmeichel, Parker, Irwin, Bruce, Kanchelskis, Pallister, Cantona, Ince, Keane, Hughes, Giggs
Substitute(s):   McClair   Scorer(s):   Hughes

Match # 4217   Saturday 22/01/94   FA Premiership   at Old Trafford   Attendance 44750
Result: **Manchester United 1 Everton 0**
Teamsheet: Schmeichel, Parker, Irwin, Bruce, Kanchelskis, Pallister, Cantona, Ince, Keane, Hughes, Giggs
Scorer(s):   Giggs

Match # 4218   Wednesday 26/01/94   League Cup 5th Round Replay   at Fratton Park   Attendance 24950
Result: **Portsmouth 0 Manchester United 1**
Teamsheet: Schmeichel, Parker, Irwin, Bruce, Kanchelskis, Pallister, Cantona, Ince, Keane, McClair, Giggs
Scorer(s):   McClair

Match # 4219   Sunday 30/01/94   FA Cup 4th Round   at Carrow Road   Attendance 21060
Result: **Norwich City 0 Manchester United 2**
Teamsheet: Schmeichel, Parker, Irwin, Bruce, Kanchelskis, Pallister, Cantona, Ince, Keane, Hughes, Giggs
Scorer(s):   Cantona, Keane

Match # 4220   Saturday 05/02/94   FA Premiership   at Loftus Road   Attendance 21267
Result: **Queens Park Rangers 2 Manchester United 3**
Teamsheet: Schmeichel, Parker, Irwin, Bruce, Kanchelskis, Pallister, Cantona, Ince, Keane, Hughes, Giggs
Scorer(s):   Cantona, Giggs, Kanchelskis

Match # 4221   Sunday 13/02/94   League Cup Semi-Final 1st Leg   at Old Trafford   Attendance 43294
Result: **Manchester United 1 Sheffield Wednesday 0**
Teamsheet: Schmeichel, Parker, Irwin, Bruce, Kanchelskis, Pallister, Cantona, Ince, Keane, Hughes, Giggs
Scorer(s):   Giggs

Match # 4222   Sunday 20/02/94   FA Cup 5th Round   at Selhurst Park   Attendance 27511
Result: **Wimbledon 0 Manchester United 3**
Teamsheet: Schmeichel, Parker, Irwin, Bruce, Kanchelskis, Pallister, Cantona, Ince, Keane, Hughes, Giggs
Substitute(s):   Dublin, McClair   Scorer(s):   Cantona, Ince, Irwin

Match # 4223   Saturday 26/02/94   FA Premiership   at Upton Park   Attendance 28832
Result: **West Ham United 2 Manchester United 2**
Teamsheet: Schmeichel, Parker, Irwin, Bruce, Kanchelskis, Pallister, Cantona, Ince, McClair, Hughes, Keane
Substitute(s):   Dublin, Thornley   Scorer(s):   Hughes, Ince

Match # 4224   Wednesday 02/03/94   League Cup Semi-Final 2nd Leg   at Hillsborough   Attendance 34878
Result: **Sheffield Wednesday 1 Manchester United 4**
Teamsheet: Schmeichel, Parker, Irwin, Bruce, Kanchelskis, Pallister, Keane, Ince, McClair, Hughes, Giggs
Scorer(s):   Hughes 2, Kanchelskis, McClair

Match # 4225   Saturday 05/03/94   FA Premiership   at Old Trafford   Attendance 44745
Result: **Manchester United 0 Chelsea 1**
Teamsheet: Schmeichel, Parker, Irwin, Bruce, Kanchelskis, Pallister, Keane, Ince, McClair, Hughes, Giggs
Substitute(s):   Dublin, Robson

Match # 4226   Saturday 12/03/94   FA Cup 6th Round   at Old Trafford   Attendance 44347
Result: **Manchester United 3 Charlton Athletic 1**
Teamsheet: Schmeichel, Parker, Irwin, Bruce, Kanchelskis, Pallister, Cantona, Ince, Keane, Hughes, Giggs
Substitute(s):   Sealey   Scorer(s):   Kanchelskis 2, Hughes

Match # 4227   Wednesday 16/03/94   FA Premiership   at Old Trafford   Attendance 43669
Result: **Manchester United 5 Sheffield Wednesday 0**
Teamsheet: Schmeichel, Parker, Irwin, Bruce, Kanchelskis, Pallister, Cantona, Ince, Keane, Hughes, Giggs
Substitute(s):   McClair, Robson   Scorer(s):   Cantona 2, Giggs, Hughes, Ince

Match # 4228   Saturday 19/03/94   FA Premiership   at County Ground   Attendance 18102
Result: **Swindon Town 2 Manchester United 2**
Teamsheet: Schmeichel, Parker, Irwin, Bruce, Keane, Pallister, Cantona, Ince, McClair, Hughes, Giggs
Scorer(s):   Ince, Keane

Match # 4229   Tuesday 22/03/94   FA Premiership   at Highbury   Attendance 36203
Result: **Arsenal 2 Manchester United 2**
Teamsheet: Schmeichel, Parker, Irwin, Bruce, Sharpe, Pallister, Cantona, Ince, Keane, Hughes, Giggs
Substitute(s):   McClair   Scorer(s):   Sharpe 2

Match # 4230   Sunday 27/03/94   League Cup Final   at Wembley   Attendance 77231
Result: **Manchester United 1 Aston Villa 3**
Teamsheet: Sealey, Parker, Irwin, Bruce, Kanchelskis, Pallister, Cantona, Ince, Keane, Hughes, Giggs
Substitute(s):   McClair, Sharpe   Scorer(s):   Hughes

Match # 4231   Wednesday 30/03/94   FA Premiership   at Old Trafford   Attendance 44751
Result: **Manchester United 1 Liverpool 0**
Teamsheet: Schmeichel, Parker, Irwin, Bruce, Sharpe, Pallister, Cantona, Ince, Keane, Hughes, Kanchelskis
Substitute(s):   Giggs, Robson   Scorer(s):   Ince

Match # 4232   Saturday 02/04/94   FA Premiership   at Ewood Park   Attendance 20886
Result: **Blackburn Rovers 2 Manchester United 0**
Teamsheet: Schmeichel, Parker, Irwin, Bruce, Sharpe, Pallister, Kanchelskis, Ince, Keane, Hughes, Giggs
Substitute(s):   McClair

Match # 4233   Monday 04/04/94   FA Premiership   at Old Trafford   Attendance 44686
Result: **Manchester United 3 Oldham Athletic 2**
Teamsheet: Schmeichel, Irwin, Sharpe, Bruce, Kanchelskis, Pallister, Keane, Ince, McClair, Hughes, Giggs
Substitute(s):   Dublin   Scorer(s):   Dublin, Giggs, Ince

SEASON 1993/94 (continued)

Match # 4234	Sunday 10/04/94	FA Cup Semi-Final	at Wembley	Attendance 56399

Result: **Manchester United 1 Oldham Athletic 1**
Teamsheet: Schmeichel, Parker, Irwin, Bruce, Sharpe, Pallister, Dublin, Ince, McClair, Hughes, Giggs
Substitute(s): Butt, Robson   Scorer(s): Hughes

Match # 4235 Wednesday 13/04/94   FA Cup Semi-Final Replay   at Maine Road   Attendance 32311
Result: **Manchester United 4 Oldham Athletic 1**
Teamsheet: Schmeichel, Parker, Irwin, Bruce, Kanchelskis, Pallister, Robson, Ince, Keane, Hughes, Giggs
Substitute(s): McClair, Sharpe   Scorer(s): Giggs, Irwin, Kanchelskis, Robson

Match # 4236 Saturday 16/04/94   FA Premiership   at Selhurst Park   Attendance 28553
Result: **Wimbledon 1 Manchester United 0**
Teamsheet: Schmeichel, Parker, Irwin, Bruce, Kanchelskis, Pallister, Robson, Ince, McClair, Hughes, Giggs
Substitute(s): Dublin, Sharpe

Match # 4237 Saturday 23/04/94   FA Premiership   at Old Trafford   Attendance 44333
Result: **Manchester United 2 Manchester City 0**
Teamsheet: Schmeichel, Parker, Irwin, Bruce, Sharpe, Pallister, Cantona, Ince, Keane, Hughes, Kanchelskis
Substitute(s): Giggs   Scorer(s): Cantona 2

Match # 4238 Wednesday 27/04/94   FA Premiership   at Elland Road   Attendance 41125
Result: **Leeds United 0 Manchester United 2**
Teamsheet: Schmeichel, Parker, Irwin, Bruce, Kanchelskis, Pallister, Cantona, Ince, Keane, Hughes, Giggs
Scorer(s): Giggs, Kanchelskis

Match # 4239 Sunday 01/05/94   FA Premiership   at Portman Road   Attendance 22559
Result: **Ipswich Town 1 Manchester United 2**
Teamsheet: Schmeichel, Parker, Irwin, Bruce, Kanchelskis, Pallister, Cantona, Ince, Keane, Hughes, Giggs
Substitute(s): Sharpe, Walsh   Scorer(s): Cantona, Giggs

Match # 4240 Wednesday 04/05/94   FA Premiership   at Old Trafford   Attendance 44705
Result: **Manchester United 2 Southampton 0**
Teamsheet: Walsh, Parker, Irwin, Keane, Sharpe, Pallister, Cantona, Ince, Kanchelskis, Hughes, Giggs
Scorer(s): Hughes, Kanchelskis

Match # 4241 Sunday 08/05/94   FA Premiership   at Old Trafford   Attendance 44717
Result: **Manchester United 0 Coventry City 0**
Teamsheet: Walsh, Neville, Irwin, Bruce, Sharpe, Pallister, Cantona, Robson, McKee, Dublin, McClair
Substitute(s): Keane, Parker

Match # 4242 Saturday 14/05/94   FA Cup Final   at Wembley   Attendance 79634
Result: **Manchester United 4 Chelsea 0**
Teamsheet: Schmeichel, Parker, Irwin, Bruce, Kanchelskis, Pallister, Cantona, Ince, Keane, Hughes, Giggs
Substitute(s): McClair, Sharpe   Scorer(s): Cantona 2, Hughes, McClair

SEASON 1993/94 SUMMARY

APPEARANCES

PLAYER	LGE	FAC	LC	EC	CS	TOTAL
Bruce	41	7	8 (1)	4	1	61 (1)
Irwin	42	7	8 (1)	3	1	61 (1)
Pallister	41	7	9	3	1	61
Schmeichel	40	7	8	4	1	60
Parker	39 (1)	7	6	3	1	56 (1)
Ince	39	7	5	4	1	56
Hughes	36	7	8	2	1	54
Giggs	32 (6)	7	6 (2)	4	1	50 (8)
Keane	34 (3)	6	6 (1)	3	1	50 (4)
Cantona	34	5	5	4	1	49
Kanchelskis	28 (3)	6	9	–	1	44 (3)
Sharpe	26 (4)	1 (2)	2 (2)	4	–	33 (8)
McClair	12 (14)	1 (4)	6 (1)	–	–	19 (19)
Robson	10 (5)	1 (1)	5	4	– (1)	20 (7)
Martin	1	–	3	1 (1)	–	5 (1)
Phelan	1 (1)	–	2	1 (3)	–	4 (4)
Dublin	1 (4)	1 (1)	1 (1)	– (1)	–	3 (7)
Ferguson	1 (2)	–	1 (1)	–	–	2 (3)
Walsh	2 (1)	–	–	–	–	2 (1)
Neville	1	–	–	– (1)	–	1 (1)
Sealey	–	– (1)	1	–	–	1 (1)
McKee	1	–	–	–	–	1
Butt	– (1)	– (1)	–	–	–	– (2)
Thornley	– (1)	–	–	–	–	– (1)

GOALSCORERS

PLAYER	LGE	FAC	LC	EC	CS	TOTAL
Cantona	18	4	1	2	–	25
Hughes	12	4	5	–	1	22
Giggs	13	1	3	–	–	17
Sharpe L	9	–	2	–	–	11
Kanchelskis	6	3	1	–	–	10
Ince	8	1	–	–	–	9
Keane	5	1	–	2	–	8
Bruce	3	–	2	2	–	7
McClair	1	1	4	–	–	6
Irwin	2	2	–	–	–	4
Robson	1	1	–	1	–	3
Dublin	1	–	1	–	–	2
Pallister	1	–	–	–	–	1
own goal	–	–	–	1	–	1

RESULTS & ATTENDANCES SUMMARY

		P	W	D	L	F	A	TOTAL	AVGE
League	H	21	14	6	1	39	13	929133	44244
	A	21	13	5	3	41	25	606242	28869
	TOTAL	42	27	11	4	80	38	1535375	36557
FA Cup	H	1	1	0	0	3	1	44347	44347
	A	3	3	0	0	6	0	70590	23530
	N	3	2	1	0	9	2	168344	56115
	TOTAL	7	6	1	0	18	3	283281	40469
League Cup	H	4	3	1	0	10	3	169819	42455
	A	4	3	0	1	8	3	117207	29302
	N	1	0	0	1	1	3	77231	77231
	TOTAL	9	6	1	2	19	9	364257	40473
European Cup	H	2	1	1	0	5	4	75127	37564
	A	2	1	1	0	3	2	49000	24500
	TOTAL	4	2	2	0	8	6	124127	31032
Charity Shield	H	0	0	0	0	0	0	0	n/a
	A	0	0	0	0	0	0	0	n/a
	N	1	0	1	0	1	1	66519	66519
	TOTAL	1	0	1	0	1	1	66519	66519
Overall	H	28	19	8	1	57	21	1218426	43515
	A	30	20	6	4	58	30	843039	28101
	N	5	2	2	1	11	6	312094	62419
	TOTAL	63	41	16	6	126	57	2373559	37676

FINAL TABLE – FA PREMIERSHIP

		P	W	D	L	F	A	W	D	L	F	A	PTS	GD
			HOME						AWAY					
1	MANCHESTER UNITED	42	14	6	1	39	13	13	5	3	41	25	92	42
2	Blackburn Rovers	42	14	5	2	31	11	11	4	6	32	25	84	27
3	Newcastle United	42	14	4	3	51	14	9	4	8	31	27	77	41
4	Arsenal	42	10	8	3	25	15	8	9	4	28	13	71	25
5	Leeds United	42	13	6	2	37	18	5	10	6	28	21	70	26
6	Wimbledon	42	12	5	4	35	21	6	6	9	21	32	65	3
7	Sheffield Wednesday	42	10	7	4	48	24	6	9	6	28	30	64	22
8	Liverpool	42	12	4	5	33	23	5	5	11	26	32	60	4
9	Queens Park Rangers	42	8	7	6	32	29	8	5	8	30	32	60	1
10	Aston Villa	42	8	5	8	23	18	7	7	7	23	32	57	-4
11	Coventry City	42	9	7	5	23	17	5	7	9	20	28	56	-2
12	Norwich City	42	4	9	8	26	29	8	8	5	39	32	53	4
13	West Ham United	42	6	7	8	26	31	7	6	8	21	27	52	-11
14	Chelsea	42	11	5	5	31	20	2	7	12	18	33	51	-4
15	Tottenham Hotspur	42	4	8	9	29	33	7	4	10	25	26	45	-5
16	Manchester City	42	6	10	5	24	22	3	8	10	14	27	45	-11
17	Everton	42	8	4	9	26	30	4	4	13	16	33	44	-21
18	Southampton	42	9	2	10	30	31	3	5	13	19	35	43	-17
19	Ipswich Town	42	5	8	8	21	32	4	8	9	14	26	43	-23
20	Sheffield United	42	6	10	5	24	23	2	8	11	18	37	42	-18
21	Oldham Athletic	42	5	8	8	24	33	4	5	12	18	35	40	-26
22	Swindon Town	42	4	7	10	25	45	1	8	12	22	55	30	-53

SEASON 1994/95

Match # 4243	Sunday 14/08/94	FA Charity Shield	at Wembley	Attendance 60402
Result:	**Manchester United 2 Blackburn Rovers 0**			
Teamsheet:	Schmeichel, May, Kanchelskis, Bruce, Sharpe, Pallister, Cantona, Ince, McClair, Hughes, Giggs			
Scorer(s):	Cantona, Ince			

Match # 4244	Saturday 20/08/94	FA Premiership	at Old Trafford	Attendance 43214
Result:	**Manchester United 2 Queens Park Rangers 0**			
Teamsheet:	Schmeichel, May, Irwin, Bruce, Sharpe, Pallister, Kanchelskis, Ince, McClair, Hughes, Giggs			
Substitute(s):	Keane, Parker	Scorer(s): Hughes, McClair		

Match # 4245	Monday 22/08/94	FA Premiership	at City Ground	Attendance 22072
Result:	**Nottingham Forest 1 Manchester United 1**			
Teamsheet:	Schmeichel, May, Irwin, Bruce, Sharpe, Pallister, Kanchelskis, Ince, McClair, Hughes, Giggs			
Substitute(s):	Keane	Scorer(s): Kanchelskis		

Match # 4246	Saturday 27/08/94	FA Premiership	at White Hart Lane	Attendance 24502
Result:	**Tottenham Hotspur 0 Manchester United 1**			
Teamsheet:	Schmeichel, May, Irwin, Bruce, Sharpe, Pallister, Kanchelskis, Ince, McClair, Hughes, Giggs			
Scorer(s):	Bruce			

Match # 4247	Wednesday 31/08/94	FA Premiership	at Old Trafford	Attendance 43440
Result:	**Manchester United 3 Wimbledon 0**			
Teamsheet:	Schmeichel, May, Irwin, Bruce, Sharpe, Pallister, Cantona, Kanchelskis, McClair, Hughes, Giggs			
Scorer(s):	Cantona, Giggs, McClair			

Match # 4248	Sunday 11/09/94	FA Premiership	at Elland Road	Attendance 39396
Result:	**Leeds United 2 Manchester United 1**			
Teamsheet:	Schmeichel, May, Irwin, Bruce, Kanchelskis, Pallister, Cantona, Ince, McClair, Hughes, Giggs			
Substitute(s):	Butt, Sharpe	Scorer(s): Cantona		

Match # 4249	Wednesday 14/09/94	Champions League Phase 1 Match 1	at Old Trafford	Attendance 33625
Result:	**Manchester United 4 Gothenburg 2**			
Teamsheet:	Schmeichel, May, Irwin, Bruce, Sharpe, Pallister, Kanchelskis, Ince, Butt, Hughes, Giggs			
Scorer(s):	Giggs 2, Kanchelskis, Sharpe			

Match # 4250	Saturday 17/09/94	FA Premiership	at Old Trafford	Attendance 43740
Result:	**Manchester United 2 Liverpool 0**			
Teamsheet:	Schmeichel, May, Irwin, Bruce, Sharpe, Pallister, Kanchelskis, Ince, Cantona, Hughes, Giggs			
Substitute(s):	McClair	Scorer(s): Kanchelskis, McClair		

Match # 4251	Wednesday 21/09/94	League Cup 2nd Round 1st Leg	at Vale Park	Attendance 18605
Result:	**Port Vale 1 Manchester United 2**			
Teamsheet:	Walsh, Neville G, Irwin, Butt, May, Keane, Gillespie, Beckham, McClair, Scholes, Davies			
Substitute(s):	O'Kane, Sharpe	Scorer(s): Scholes 2		

Match # 4252	Saturday 24/09/94	FA Premiership	at Portman Road	Attendance 22559
Result:	**Ipswich Town 3 Manchester United 2**			
Teamsheet:	Walsh, Irwin, Sharpe, Bruce, Keane, Pallister, Kanchelskis, Ince, McClair, Cantona, Giggs			
Substitute(s):	Butt, Scholes	Scorer(s): Cantona, Scholes		

Match # 4253	Wednesday 28/09/94	Champions League Phase 1 Match 2	at Ali Sami Yen	Attendance 28605
Result:	**Galatasaray 0 Manchester United 0**			
Teamsheet:	Schmeichel, May, Sharpe, Bruce, Kanchelskis, Pallister, Butt, Ince, Keane, Hughes, Giggs			
Substitute(s):	Parker			

Match # 4254	Saturday 01/10/94	FA Premiership	at Old Trafford	Attendance 43803
Result:	**Manchester United 2 Everton 0**			
Teamsheet:	Schmeichel, May, Irwin, Bruce, Sharpe, Pallister, Cantona, Ince, Keane, Hughes, Kanchelskis			
Substitute(s):	McClair	Scorer(s): Kanchelskis, Sharpe		

Match # 4255	Wednesday 05/10/94	League Cup 2nd Round 2nd Leg	at Old Trafford	Attendance 31615
Result:	**Manchester United 2 Port Vale 0**			
Teamsheet:	Walsh, Casper, O'Kane, Butt, May, Pallister, Gillespie, Beckham, McClair, Scholes, Davies			
Substitute(s):	Neville G, Tomlinson	Scorer(s): May, McClair		

Match # 4256	Saturday 08/10/94	FA Premiership	at Hillsborough	Attendance 33441
Result:	**Sheffield Wednesday 1 Manchester United 0**			
Teamsheet:	Schmeichel, Parker, Irwin, Bruce, Sharpe, Pallister, Keane, Ince, McClair, Hughes, Gillespie			
Substitute(s):	May, Scholes			

Match # 4257	Saturday 15/10/94	FA Premiership	at Old Trafford	Attendance 43795
Result:	**Manchester United 1 West Ham United 0**			
Teamsheet:	Schmeichel, May, Irwin, Bruce, Sharpe, Pallister, Kanchelskis, Ince, Cantona, Hughes, Giggs			
Substitute(s):	Butt	Scorer(s): Cantona		

Match # 4258	Wednesday 19/10/94	Champions League Phase 1 Match 3	at Old Trafford	Attendance 40064
Result:	**Manchester United 2 Barcelona 2**			
Teamsheet:	Schmeichel, May, Irwin, Parker, Sharpe, Pallister, Kanchelskis, Ince, Keane, Hughes, Butt			
Substitute(s):	Bruce, Scholes	Scorer(s): Hughes, Sharpe		

Match # 4259	Monday 24/10/94	FA Premiership	at Ewood Park	Attendance 30260
Result:	**Blackburn Rovers 2 Manchester United 4**			
Teamsheet:	Schmeichel, Keane, Irwin, Bruce, Sharpe, Pallister, Kanchelskis, Ince, Cantona, Hughes, Butt			
Substitute(s):	McClair	Scorer(s): Kanchelskis 2, Cantona, Hughes		

Match # 4260	Wednesday 26/10/94	League Cup 3rd Round	at St James' Park	Attendance 34178
Result:	**Newcastle United 2 Manchester United 0**			
Teamsheet:	Walsh, Neville G, Irwin, Bruce, Gillespie, Pallister, Beckham, Scholes, McClair, Butt, Davies			
Substitute(s):	Sharpe, Tomlinson			

SEASON 1994/95 (continued)

Match # 4261 Saturday 29/10/94 FA Premiership at Old Trafford Attendance 43795
Result: **Manchester United 2 Newcastle United 0**
Teamsheet: Schmeichel, Keane, Irwin, Bruce, Kanchelskis, Pallister, Cantona, Ince, McClair, Hughes, Giggs
Substitute(s): Gillespie Scorer(s): Gillespie, Pallister

Match # 4262 Wednesday 02/11/94 Champions League Phase 1 Match 4 at Estadio Camp Nou Attendance 114273
Result: **Barcelona 4 Manchester United 0**
Teamsheet: Walsh, Parker, Irwin, Bruce, Kanchelskis, Pallister, Butt, Ince, Keane, Hughes, Giggs
Substitute(s): Scholes

Match # 4263 Sunday 06/11/94 FA Premiership at Villa Park Attendance 32136
Result: **Aston Villa 1 Manchester United 2**
Teamsheet: Walsh, Keane, Irwin, Bruce, Kanchelskis, Pallister, Scholes, Ince, Cantona, Butt, Giggs
Substitute(s): Gillespie, McClair Scorer(s): Ince, Kanchelskis

Match # 4264 Thursday 10/11/94 FA Premiership at Old Trafford Attendance 43738
Result: **Manchester United 5 Manchester City 0**
Teamsheet: Schmeichel, Keane, Irwin, Bruce, Kanchelskis, Pallister, Cantona, Ince, McClair, Hughes, Giggs
Substitute(s): Scholes Scorer(s): Kanchelskis 3, Cantona, Hughes

Match # 4265 Saturday 19/11/94 FA Premiership at Old Trafford Attendance 43788
Result: **Manchester United 3 Crystal Palace 0**
Teamsheet: Schmeichel, Neville G, Irwin, May, Kanchelskis, Pallister, Cantona, Ince, McClair, Hughes, Davies
Substitute(s): Gillespie, Pilkington, Scholes Scorer(s): Cantona, Irwin, Kanchelskis

Match # 4266 Wednesday 23/11/94 Champions League Phase 1 Match 5 at NYA Ullevi Stadium Attendance 36350
Result: **Gothenburg 3 Manchester United 1**
Teamsheet: Walsh, May, Irwin, Bruce, Kanchelskis, Pallister, Cantona, Ince, McClair, Hughes, Davies
Substitute(s): Butt, Neville G Scorer(s): Hughes

Match # 4267 Saturday 26/11/94 FA Premiership at Highbury Attendance 38301
Result: **Arsenal 0 Manchester United 0**
Teamsheet: Walsh, Neville G, Irwin, May, Kanchelskis, Pallister, Cantona, Ince, McClair, Hughes, Gillespie
Substitute(s): Butt, Davies

Match # 4268 Saturday 03/12/94 FA Premiership at Old Trafford Attendance 43789
Result: **Manchester United 1 Norwich City 0**
Teamsheet: Walsh, Neville G, Irwin, May, Kanchelskis, Pallister, Cantona, Ince, McClair, Hughes, Davies
Substitute(s): Butt, Gillespie Scorer(s): Cantona

Match # 4269 Wednesday 07/12/94 Champions League Phase 1 Match 6 at Old Trafford Attendance 39220
Result: **Manchester United 4 Galatasaray 0**
Teamsheet: Walsh, Neville G, Irwin, Bruce, Keane, Pallister, Cantona, Beckham, McClair, Butt, Davies
Scorer(s): Beckham, Davies, Keane, own goal

Match # 4270 Saturday 10/12/94 FA Premiership at Loftus Road Attendance 18948
Result: **Queens Park Rangers 2 Manchester United 3**
Teamsheet: Walsh, Neville G, Irwin, Bruce, Keane, Pallister, Kanchelskis, Ince, McClair, Scholes, Davies
Substitute(s): Butt, Gillespie Scorer(s): Scholes 2, Keane

Match # 4271 Saturday 17/12/94 FA Premiership at Old Trafford Attendance 43744
Result: **Manchester United 1 Nottingham Forest 2**
Teamsheet: Walsh, Keane, Irwin, Bruce, Kanchelskis, Pallister, Cantona, Ince, McClair, Hughes, Giggs
Substitute(s): Butt, Neville G Scorer(s): Cantona

Match # 4272 Monday 26/12/94 FA Premiership at Stamford Bridge Attendance 31161
Result: **Chelsea 2 Manchester United 3**
Teamsheet: Walsh, Keane, Irwin, Bruce, Butt, Pallister, Cantona, Ince, McClair, Hughes, Giggs
Substitute(s): Kanchelskis, Neville G Scorer(s): Cantona, Hughes, McClair

Match # 4273 Wednesday 28/12/94 FA Premiership at Old Trafford Attendance 43789
Result: **Manchester United 1 Leicester City 1**
Teamsheet: Walsh, Neville G, Irwin, Bruce, Kanchelskis, Pallister, Cantona, Keane, McClair, Hughes, Giggs
Substitute(s): Scholes Scorer(s): Kanchelskis

Match # 4274 Saturday 31/12/94 FA Premiership at The Dell Attendance 15204
Result: **Southampton 2 Manchester United 2**
Teamsheet: Walsh, May, Neville G, Bruce, Keane, Pallister, Cantona, Butt, McClair, Hughes, Giggs
Substitute(s): Gillespie Scorer(s): Butt, Pallister

Match # 4275 Tuesday 03/01/95 FA Premiership at Old Trafford Attendance 43130
Result: **Manchester United 2 Coventry City 0**
Teamsheet: Walsh, Neville G, Irwin, Bruce, Gillespie, Pallister, Cantona, Keane, Scholes, Butt, Giggs
Substitute(s): McClair Scorer(s): Cantona, Scholes

Match # 4276 Monday 09/01/95 FA Cup 3rd Round at Bramall Lane Attendance 22322
Result: **Sheffield United 0 Manchester United 2**
Teamsheet: Schmeichel, O'Kane, Irwin, Bruce, Keane, Pallister, Cantona, Butt, McClair, Hughes, Giggs
Substitute(s): Scholes, Sharpe Scorer(s): Cantona, Hughes

Match # 4277 Sunday 15/01/95 FA Premiership at St James' Park Attendance 34471
Result: **Newcastle United 1 Manchester United 1**
Teamsheet: Schmeichel, Keane, Irwin, Bruce, Sharpe, Pallister, Cantona, Butt, McClair, Hughes, Giggs
Substitute(s): May, Scholes Scorer(s): Hughes

Match # 4278 Sunday 22/01/95 FA Premiership at Old Trafford Attendance 43742
Result: **Manchester United 1 Blackburn Rovers 0**
Teamsheet: Schmeichel, Keane, Irwin, Bruce, Sharpe, Pallister, Cantona, Ince, McClair, Cole, Giggs
Substitute(s): Kanchelskis Scorer(s): Cantona

SEASON 1994/95 (continued)

Match # 4279   Wednesday 25/01/95   FA Premiership   at Selhurst Park   Attendance 18224
Result: **Crystal Palace 1 Manchester United 1**
Teamsheet: Schmeichel, Keane, Irwin, May, Sharpe, Pallister, Cantona, Ince, McClair, Cole, Giggs
Substitute(s):   Kanchelskis   Scorer(s):   May

Match # 4280   Saturday 28/01/95   FA Cup 4th Round   at Old Trafford   Attendance 43222
Result: **Manchester United 5 Wrexham 2**
Teamsheet: Schmeichel, Neville P, Irwin, May, Sharpe, Pallister, Keane, Ince, McClair, Scholes, Giggs
Substitute(s):   Beckham, Kanchelskis   Scorer(s):   Irwin 2, Giggs, McClair, own goal

Match # 4281   Saturday 04/02/95   FA Premiership   at Old Trafford   Attendance 43795
Result: **Manchester United 1 Aston Villa 0**
Teamsheet: Schmeichel, Neville G, Irwin, Bruce, Sharpe, Pallister, Scholes, Ince, McClair, Cole, Giggs
Substitute(s):   Kanchelskis, May   Scorer(s):   Cole

Match # 4282   Saturday 11/02/95   FA Premiership   at Maine Road   Attendance 26368
Result: **Manchester City 0 Manchester United 3**
Teamsheet: Schmeichel, Neville P, Irwin, Bruce, Sharpe, Pallister, Kanchelskis, Ince, McClair, Cole, Giggs
Substitute(s):   May, Scholes   Scorer(s):   Cole, Ince, Kanchelskis

Match # 4283   Sunday 19/02/95   FA Cup 5th Round   at Old Trafford   Attendance 42744
Result: **Manchester United 3 Leeds United 1**
Teamsheet: Schmeichel, Keane, Irwin, Bruce, Sharpe, Pallister, Kanchelskis, Ince, McClair, Hughes, Giggs
Scorer(s):   Bruce, Hughes, McClair

Match # 4284   Wednesday 22/02/95   FA Premiership   at Carrow Road   Attendance 21824
Result: **Norwich City 0 Manchester United 2**
Teamsheet: Schmeichel, Keane, Sharpe, Bruce, Kanchelskis, Pallister, Cole, Ince, McClair, Hughes, Giggs
Scorer(s):   Ince, Kanchelskis

Match # 4285   Saturday 25/02/95   FA Premiership   at Goodison Park   Attendance 40011
Result: **Everton 1 Manchester United 0**
Teamsheet: Schmeichel, Irwin, Sharpe, Bruce, Keane, Pallister, Cole, Ince, McClair, Hughes, Giggs
Substitute(s):   Kanchelskis

Match # 4286   Saturday 04/03/95   FA Premiership   at Old Trafford   Attendance 43804
Result: **Manchester United 9 Ipswich Town 0**
Teamsheet: Schmeichel, Keane, Irwin, Bruce, Kanchelskis, Pallister, Cole, Ince, McClair, Hughes, Giggs
Substitute(s):   Butt, Sharpe   Scorer(s):   Cole 5, Hughes 2, Ince, Keane

Match # 4287   Tuesday 07/03/95   FA Premiership   at Selhurst Park   Attendance 18224
Result: **Wimbledon 0 Manchester United 1**
Teamsheet: Schmeichel, Neville G, Irwin, Bruce, Sharpe, Pallister, Cole, Ince, McClair, Hughes, Giggs
Scorer(s):   Bruce

Match # 4288   Sunday 12/03/95   FA Cup 6th Round   at Old Trafford   Attendance 42830
Result: **Manchester United 2 Queens Park Rangers 0**
Teamsheet: Schmeichel, Neville G, Irwin, Bruce, Sharpe, Pallister, Kanchelskis, Ince, McClair, Hughes, Giggs
Substitute(s):   Keane   Scorer(s):   Irwin, Sharpe

Match # 4289   Wednesday 15/03/95   FA Premiership   at Old Trafford   Attendance 43802
Result: **Manchester United 0 Tottenham Hotspur 0**
Teamsheet: Schmeichel, Irwin, Sharpe, Bruce, Kanchelskis, Pallister, Cole, Ince, McClair, Hughes, Giggs
Substitute(s):   Butt

Match # 4290   Sunday 19/03/95   FA Premiership   at Anfield   Attendance 38906
Result: **Liverpool 2 Manchester United 0**
Teamsheet: Schmeichel, Irwin, Sharpe, Bruce, Keane, Pallister, Kanchelskis, Ince, McClair, Hughes, Giggs
Substitute(s):   Butt, Cole

Match # 4291   Wednesday 22/03/95   FA Premiership   at Old Trafford   Attendance 43623
Result: **Manchester United 3 Arsenal 0**
Teamsheet: Schmeichel, Keane, Irwin, Bruce, Sharpe, Pallister, Kanchelskis, Ince, Cole, Hughes, Giggs
Scorer(s):   Hughes, Kanchelskis, Sharpe

Match # 4292   Sunday 02/04/95   FA Premiership   at Old Trafford   Attendance 43712
Result: **Manchester United 0 Leeds United 0**
Teamsheet: Schmeichel, Neville G, Irwin, Beckham, Keane, Pallister, Cole, Ince, McClair, Hughes, Giggs

Match # 4293   Sunday 09/04/95   FA Cup Semi-Final   at Villa Park   Attendance 38256
Result: **Manchester United 2 Crystal Palace 2**
Teamsheet: Schmeichel, Neville G, Irwin, Keane, Sharpe, Pallister, Beckham, Ince, McClair, Hughes, Giggs
Substitute(s):   Butt   Scorer(s):   Irwin, Pallister

Match # 4294   Wednesday 12/04/95   FA Cup Semi-Final Replay   at Villa Park   Attendance 17987
Result: **Manchester United 2 Crystal Palace 0**
Teamsheet: Schmeichel, Neville G, Irwin, Bruce, Sharpe, Pallister, Butt, Ince, Keane, Hughes, Giggs
Substitute(s):   McClair   Scorer(s):   Bruce, Pallister

Match # 4295   Saturday 15/04/95   FA Premiership   at Filbert Street   Attendance 21281
Result: **Leicester City 0 Manchester United 4**
Teamsheet: Schmeichel, Neville G, Irwin, Bruce, Sharpe, Pallister, Cole, Ince, McClair, Hughes, Butt
Substitute(s):   Beckham, Scholes   Scorer(s):   Cole 2, Ince, Sharpe

Match # 4296   Monday 17/04/95   FA Premiership   at Old Trafford   Attendance 43728
Result: **Manchester United 0 Chelsea 0**
Teamsheet: Schmeichel, Neville G, Irwin, Bruce, Beckham, Pallister, Cole, Ince, McClair, Hughes, Butt
Substitute(s):   Davies, Scholes

SEASON 1994/95 (continued)

Match # 4297   Monday 01/05/95   FA Premiership   at Highfield Road   Attendance 21885
Result: **Coventry City 2 Manchester United 3**
Teamsheet: Schmeichel, Neville G, Irwin, May, Sharpe, Pallister, Cole, Butt, McClair, Hughes, Scholes
Substitute(s):   Beckham   Scorer(s):   Cole 2, Scholes

Match # 4298   Sunday 07/05/95   FA Premiership   at Old Trafford   Attendance 43868
Result: **Manchester United 1 Sheffield Wednesday 0**
Teamsheet: Schmeichel, Neville G, Irwin, May, Sharpe, Pallister, Cole, Ince, McClair, Hughes, Scholes
Substitute(s):   Butt, Neville P   Scorer(s):   May

Match # 4299   Wednesday 10/05/95   FA Premiership   at Old Trafford   Attendance 43479
Result: **Manchester United 2 Southampton 1**
Teamsheet: Schmeichel, Neville G, Irwin, Bruce, Sharpe, Pallister, Cole, Ince, McClair, Hughes, Butt
Substitute(s):   Scholes   Scorer(s):   Cole, Irwin

Match # 4300   Sunday 14/05/95   FA Premiership   at Upton Park   Attendance 24783
Result: **West Ham United 1 Manchester United 1**
Teamsheet: Schmeichel, Neville G, Irwin, Bruce, Sharpe, Pallister, Cole, Ince, McClair, Keane, Butt
Substitute(s):   Hughes, Scholes   Scorer(s):   McClair

Match # 4301   Saturday 20/05/95   FA Cup Final   at Wembley   Attendance 79592
Result: **Manchester United 0 Everton 1**
Teamsheet: Schmeichel, Neville G, Irwin, Bruce, Sharpe, Pallister, Keane, Ince, McClair, Hughes, Butt
Substitute(s):   Giggs, Scholes

SEASON 1994/95 SUMMARY

APPEARANCES

PLAYER	LGE	FAC	LC	CL	CS	TOTAL
Pallister	42	7	2	6	1	58
Irwin	40	7	2	5	-	54
Ince	36	6	-	5	1	48
McClair	35 (5)	6 (1)	3	2	1	47 (6)
Bruce	35	5	1	5 (1)	1	47 (1)
Hughes	33 (1)	6	-	5	1	45 (1)
Schmeichel	32	7	-	3	1	43
Giggs	29	6 (1)	-	3	1	39 (1)
Sharpe	26 (2)	6 (1)	- (2)	3	1	36 (5)
Keane	23 (2)	6 (1)	1	4	-	34 (3)
Kanchelskis	25 (5)	2 (1)	-	5	1	33 (6)
Cantona	21	1	-	2	1	25
May	15 (4)	1	2	4	1	23 (4)
Neville G	16 (2)	4	2 (1)	1 (1)	-	23 (4)
Butt	11 (11)	3 (1)	3	5 (1)	-	22 (13)
Cole	17 (1)	-	-	-	-	17 (1)
Walsh	10	-	3	3	-	16
Scholes	6 (11)	1 (2)	3	- (2)	-	10 (15)
Davies	3 (2)	-	3	2	-	8 (2)
Beckham	2 (2)	1 (1)	3	1	-	7 (3)
Gillespie	3 (6)	-	3	-	-	6 (6)
Parker	1 (1)	-	-	2 (1)	-	3 (2)
Neville P	1 (1)	1	-	-	-	2 (1)
O'Kane	-	1	1 (1)	-	-	2 (1)
Casper	-	-	1	-	-	1
Tomlinson	-	-	- (2)	-	-	- (2)
Pilkington	- (1)	-	-	-	-	- (1)

GOALSCORERS

PLAYER	LGE	FAC	LC	CL	CS	TOTAL
Kanchelskis	14	-	-	1	-	15
Cantona	12	1	-	-	1	14
Cole	12	-	-	-	-	12
Hughes	8	2	-	2	-	12
McClair	5	2	1	-	-	8
Scholes	5	-	2	-	-	7
Ince	5	-	-	-	1	6
Sharpe	3	1	-	2	-	6
Irwin	2	4	-	-	-	6
Bruce	2	2	-	-	-	4
Pallister	2	2	-	-	-	4
Giggs	1	1	-	2	-	4
Keane	2	-	-	1	-	3
May	2	-	1	-	-	3
Butt	1	-	-	-	-	1
Gillespie	1	-	-	-	-	1
Beckham	-	-	-	1	-	1
Davies	-	-	-	1	-	1
own goals	-	1	-	1	-	2

RESULTS & ATTENDANCES SUMMARY

		P	W	D	L	F	A	TOTAL	AVGE
League	H	21	16	4	1	42	4	917318	43682
	A	21	10	6	5	35	24	573957	27331
TOTAL		42	26	10	6	77	28	1491275	35507
FA Cup	H	3	3	0	0	10	3	128796	42932
	A	1	1	0	0	2	0	22322	22322
	N	3	1	1	1	4	3	135835	45278
TOTAL		7	5	1	1	16	6	286953	40993
League Cup	H	1	1	0	0	2	0	31615	31615
	A	2	1	0	1	2	3	52783	26392
TOTAL		3	2	0	1	4	3	84398	28133
Champions League	H	3	2	1	0	10	4	112909	37636
	A	3	0	1	2	1	7	179228	59743
TOTAL		6	2	2	2	11	11	292137	48690
Charity Shield	H	0	0	0	0	0	0	0	n/a
	A	0	0	0	0	0	0	0	n/a
	N	1	1	0	0	2	0	60402	60402
TOTAL		1	1	0	0	2	0	60402	60402
Overall	H	28	22	5	1	64	11	1190638	42523
	A	27	12	7	8	40	34	828290	30677
	N	4	2	1	1	6	3	196237	49059
TOTAL		59	36	13	10	110	48	2215165	37545

FINAL TABLE - FA PREMIERSHIP

		P	HOME W	D	L	F	A	AWAY W	D	L	F	A	PTS	GD
1	Blackburn Rovers	42	17	2	2	54	21	10	6	5	26	18	89	41
2	MANCHESTER UNITED	42	16	4	1	42	4	10	6	5	35	24	88	49
3	Nottingham Forest	42	12	6	3	36	18	10	5	6	36	25	77	29
4	Liverpool	42	13	5	3	38	13	8	6	7	27	24	74	28
5	Leeds United	42	13	5	3	35	15	7	8	6	24	23	73	21
6	Newcastle United	42	14	6	1	46	20	6	6	9	21	27	72	20
7	Tottenham Hotspur	42	10	5	6	32	25	6	9	6	34	33	62	8
8	Queens Park Rangers	42	11	3	7	36	26	6	6	9	25	33	60	2
9	Wimbledon	42	9	5	7	26	26	6	6	9	22	39	56	-17
10	Southampton	42	8	9	4	33	27	4	9	8	28	36	54	-2
11	Chelsea	42	7	7	7	25	22	6	8	7	25	33	54	-5
12	Arsenal	42	6	9	6	27	21	7	3	11	25	28	51	3
13	Sheffield Wednesday	42	7	7	7	26	26	6	5	10	23	31	51	-8
14	West Ham United	42	9	6	6	28	19	4	5	12	16	29	50	-4
15	Everton	42	8	9	4	31	23	3	8	10	13	28	50	-7
16	Coventry City	42	7	7	7	23	25	5	7	9	21	37	50	-18
17	Manchester City	42	8	7	6	37	28	4	6	11	16	36	49	-11
18	Aston Villa	42	6	9	6	27	24	5	6	10	24	32	48	-5
19	Crystal Palace	42	6	6	9	16	23	5	6	10	18	26	45	-15
20	Norwich City	42	8	8	5	27	21	2	5	14	10	33	43	-17
21	Leicester City	42	5	6	10	28	37	1	5	15	17	43	29	-35
22	Ipswich Town	42	5	3	13	24	34	2	3	16	12	59	27	-57

SEASON 1995/96

Match # 4302 Saturday 19/08/95 FA Premiership at Villa Park Attendance 34655
Result: **Aston Villa 3 Manchester United 1**
Teamsheet: Schmeichel, Parker, Irwin, Neville G, Pallister, Sharpe, Butt, Keane, McClair, Scholes, Neville P
Substitute(s): Beckham, O'Kane Scorer(s): Beckham

Match # 4303 Wednesday 23/08/95 FA Premiership at Old Trafford Attendance 31966
Result: **Manchester United 2 West Ham United 1**
Teamsheet: Schmeichel, Neville G, Irwin, Bruce, Pallister, Sharpe, Butt, Keane, McClair, Scholes, Beckham
Substitute(s): Cole, Thornley Scorer(s): Keane, Scholes

Match # 4304 Saturday 26/08/95 FA Premiership at Old Trafford Attendance 32226
Result: **Manchester United 3 Wimbledon 1**
Teamsheet: Schmeichel, Neville G, Irwin, Bruce, Pallister, Sharpe, Butt, Keane, Cole, Scholes, Beckham
Substitute(s): Davies, Giggs Scorer(s): Keane 2, Cole

Match # 4305 Sunday 28/08/95 FA Premiership at Ewood Park Attendance 29843
Result: **Blackburn Rovers 1 Manchester United 2**
Teamsheet: Schmeichel, Neville G, Irwin, Bruce, Pallister, Sharpe, Butt, Keane, Cole, Scholes, Beckham
Substitute(s): Davies, Giggs Scorer(s): Beckham, Sharpe

Match # 4306 Saturday 09/09/95 FA Premiership at Goodison Park Attendance 39496
Result: **Everton 2 Manchester United 3**
Teamsheet: Schmeichel, Neville G, Irwin, Bruce, Pallister, Sharpe, Butt, Keane, Cole, Scholes, Beckham
Substitute(s): Davies, Giggs Scorer(s): Sharpe 2, Giggs

Match # 4307 Tuesday 12/09/95 UEFA Cup 1st Round 1st Leg at Central Stadion Attendance 33000
Result: **Rotor Volgograd 0 Manchester United 0**
Teamsheet: Schmeichel, Neville G, Irwin, Bruce, Pallister, Sharpe, Butt, Beckham, Keane, Scholes, Giggs
Substitute(s): Davies, Parker

Match # 4308 Saturday 16/09/95 FA Premiership at Old Trafford Attendance 32812
Result: **Manchester United 3 Bolton Wanderers 0**
Teamsheet: Schmeichel, Parker, Neville P, Bruce, Pallister, Sharpe, Butt, Cooke, Beckham, Scholes, Giggs
Substitute(s): Davies Scorer(s): Scholes 2, Giggs

Match # 4309 Wednesday 20/09/95 League Cup 2nd Round 1st Leg at Old Trafford Attendance 29049
Result: **Manchester United 0 York City 3**
Teamsheet: Pilkington, Parker, Irwin, McGibbon, Pallister, Sharpe, Beckham, Neville P, McClair, Davies, Giggs
Substitute(s): Bruce, Cooke

Match # 4310 Saturday 23/09/95 FA Premiership at Hillsborough Attendance 34101
Result: **Sheffield Wednesday 0 Manchester United 0**
Teamsheet: Schmeichel, Parker, Irwin, Bruce, Pallister, Davies, Butt, Beckham, McClair, Scholes, Giggs
Substitute(s): Cooke

Match # 4311 Tuesday 26/09/95 UEFA Cup 1st Round 2nd Leg at Old Trafford Attendance 29724
Result: **Manchester United 2 Rotor Volgograd 2 (United lost the tie on away goals rule)**
Teamsheet: Schmeichel, O'Kane, Neville P, Bruce, Pallister, Sharpe, Butt, Beckham, Keane, Cole, Giggs
Substitute(s): Cooke, Scholes Scorer(s): Schmeichel, Scholes

Match # 4312 Sunday 01/10/95 FA Premiership at Old Trafford Attendance 34934
Result: **Manchester United 2 Liverpool 2**
Teamsheet: Schmeichel, Neville G, Neville P, Bruce, Pallister, Sharpe, Butt, Keane, Cole, Cantona, Giggs
Substitute(s): Beckham, Scholes Scorer(s): Butt, Cantona

Match # 4313 Tuesday 03/10/95 League Cup 2nd Round 2nd Leg at Bootham Crescent Attendance 9386
Result: **York City 1 Manchester United 3**
Teamsheet: Schmeichel, Neville G, Sharpe, Bruce, Pallister, Beckham, Cooke, Scholes, Cole, Cantona, Giggs
Substitute(s): Keane, Neville P Scorer(s): Scholes 2, Cooke

Match # 4314 Saturday 14/10/95 FA Premiership at Old Trafford Attendance 35707
Result: **Manchester United 1 Manchester City 0**
Teamsheet: Schmeichel, Neville G, Neville P, Bruce, Pallister, Beckham, Butt, Keane, Cole, Scholes, Giggs
Substitute(s): McClair, Sharpe Scorer(s): Scholes

Match # 4315 Saturday 21/10/95 FA Premiership at Stamford Bridge Attendance 31019
Result: **Chelsea 1 Manchester United 4**
Teamsheet: Schmeichel, Neville G, Irwin, Bruce, Pallister, Scholes, Butt, Keane, Cole, Cantona, Giggs
Substitute(s): McClair Scorer(s): Scholes 2, Giggs, McClair

Match # 4316 Saturday 28/10/95 FA Premiership at Old Trafford Attendance 36580
Result: **Manchester United 2 Middlesbrough 0**
Teamsheet: Schmeichel, Neville G, Irwin, Bruce, Pallister, Scholes, Butt, Keane, Cole, Cantona, Giggs
Substitute(s): McClair Scorer(s): Cole, Pallister

Match # 4317 Saturday 04/11/95 FA Premiership at Highbury Attendance 38317
Result: **Arsenal 1 Manchester United 0**
Teamsheet: Schmeichel, Neville G, Irwin, Bruce, Pallister, Scholes, Butt, Keane, Cole, Cantona, Giggs
Substitute(s): Beckham, McClair, Sharpe

Match # 4318 Saturday 18/11/95 FA Premiership at Old Trafford Attendance 39301
Result: **Manchester United 4 Southampton 1**
Teamsheet: Schmeichel, Neville G, Irwin, Bruce, Pallister, Scholes, Butt, Beckham, Cole, Cantona, Giggs
Substitute(s): McClair, Neville P, Sharpe Scorer(s): Giggs 2, Cole, Scholes

Match # 4319 Wednesday 22/11/95 FA Premiership at Highfield Road Attendance 23400
Result: **Coventry City 0 Manchester United 4**
Teamsheet: Schmeichel, Neville G, Irwin, Bruce, Pallister, McClair, Butt, Beckham, Cole, Cantona, Giggs
Substitute(s): May, Neville P, Sharpe Scorer(s): McClair 2, Beckham, Irwin

SEASON 1995/96 (continued)

Match # 4320 Monday 27/11/95   FA Premiership   at City Ground   Attendance 29263
Result: **Nottingham Forest 1 Manchester United 1**
Teamsheet: Schmeichel, Neville G, Irwin, Bruce, Pallister, McClair, Butt, Beckham, Cole, Cantona, Giggs
Substitute(s):   Scholes, Sharpe   Scorer(s):   Cantona

Match # 4321 Saturday 02/12/95   FA Premiership   at Old Trafford   Attendance 42019
Result: **Manchester United 1 Chelsea 1**
Teamsheet: Pilkington, Neville G, Irwin, Bruce, May, Sharpe, McClair, Beckham, Cole, Cantona, Scholes
Substitute(s):   Cooke   Scorer(s):   Beckham

Match # 4322 Saturday 09/12/95   FA Premiership   at Old Trafford   Attendance 41849
Result: **Manchester United 2 Sheffield Wednesday 2**
Teamsheet: Pilkington, Neville G, Neville P, Bruce, May, Sharpe, McClair, Beckham, Cole, Cantona, Scholes
Substitute(s):   Cooke, Davies   Scorer(s):   Cantona 2

Match # 4323 Sunday 17/12/95   FA Premiership   at Anfield   Attendance 40546
Result: **Liverpool 2 Manchester United 0**
Teamsheet: Schmeichel, Neville G, Irwin, Bruce, May, Sharpe, McClair, Beckham, Cole, Cantona, Giggs
Substitute(s):   Scholes

Match # 4324 Sunday 24/12/95   FA Premiership   at Elland Road   Attendance 39801
Result: **Leeds United 3 Manchester United 1**
Teamsheet: Schmeichel, Parker, Irwin, Bruce, Neville G, McClair, Butt, Keane, Cole, Cantona, Beckham
Substitute(s):   May, Neville P, Scholes   Scorer(s):   Cole

Match # 4325 Wednesday 27/12/95   FA Premiership   at Old Trafford   Attendance 42024
Result: **Manchester United 2 Newcastle United 0**
Teamsheet: Schmeichel, Neville P, Irwin, May, Neville G, Beckham, Butt, Keane, Cole, Cantona, Giggs
Substitute(s):   McClair   Scorer(s):   Cole, Keane

Match # 4326 Saturday 30/12/95   FA Premiership   at Old Trafford   Attendance 41890
Result: **Manchester United 2 Queens Park Rangers 1**
Teamsheet: Schmeichel, Neville P, Irwin, Prunier, Neville G, Beckham, Butt, Keane, Cole, Cantona, Giggs
Substitute(s):   McClair, Parker, Sharpe   Scorer(s):   Cole, Giggs

Match # 4327 Monday 01/01/96   FA Premiership   at White Hart Lane   Attendance 32852
Result: **Tottenham Hotspur 4 Manchester United 1**
Teamsheet: Schmeichel, Parker, Neville P, Prunier, Neville G, Beckham, Butt, Keane, Cole, Cantona, Giggs
Substitute(s):   McClair, Pilkington, Sharpe   Scorer(s):   Cole

Match # 4328 Saturday 06/01/96   FA Cup 3rd Round   at Old Trafford   Attendance 41563
Result: **Manchester United 2 Sunderland 2**
Teamsheet: Pilkington, Neville G, Irwin, Bruce, Pallister, Beckham, Butt, Keane, Cole, Cantona, Giggs
Substitute(s):   Neville P, Sharpe   Scorer(s):   Butt, Cantona

Match # 4329 Saturday 13/01/96   FA Premiership   at Old Trafford   Attendance 42667
Result: **Manchester United 0 Aston Villa 0**
Teamsheet: Schmeichel, Neville P, Irwin, Bruce, Neville G, Sharpe, Butt, Keane, Cole, Cantona, Giggs
Substitute(s):   Scholes

Match # 4330 Tuesday 16/01/96   FA Cup 3rd Round Replay   at Roker Park   Attendance 21378
Result: **Sunderland 1 Manchester United 2**
Teamsheet: Schmeichel, Parker, Irwin, Bruce, Neville G, Neville P, Butt, Keane, Cole, Cantona, Giggs
Substitute(s):   Scholes, Sharpe   Scorer(s):   Cole, Scholes

Match # 4331 Monday 22/01/96   FA Premiership   at Upton Park   Attendance 24197
Result: **West Ham United 0 Manchester United 1**
Teamsheet: Schmeichel, Neville P, Irwin, Bruce, Neville G, Sharpe, Butt, Keane, Cole, Cantona, Giggs
Substitute(s):   Beckham   Scorer(s):   Cantona

Match # 4332 Saturday 27/01/96   FA Cup 4th Round   at Elm Park   Attendance 14780
Result: **Reading 0 Manchester United 3**
Teamsheet: Schmeichel, Irwin, Neville P, Bruce, Neville G, Sharpe, Butt, Keane, Cole, Cantona, Giggs
Substitute(s):   Parker   Scorer(s):   Cantona, Giggs, Parker

Match # 4333 Saturday 03/02/96   FA Premiership   at Selhurst Park   Attendance 25380
Result: **Wimbledon 2 Manchester United 4**
Teamsheet: Schmeichel, Neville P, Irwin, Bruce, Neville G, Sharpe, Butt, Keane, Cole, Cantona, Giggs
Substitute(s):   Beckham   Scorer(s):   Cantona 2, Cole, own goal

Match # 4334 Saturday 10/02/96   FA Premiership   at Old Trafford   Attendance 42681
Result: **Manchester United 1 Blackburn Rovers 0**
Teamsheet: Schmeichel, Neville P, Irwin, May, Pallister, Sharpe, Beckham, Keane, Cole, Cantona, Giggs
Scorer(s):   Sharpe

Match # 4335 Sunday 18/02/96   FA Cup 5th Round   at Old Trafford   Attendance 42692
Result: **Manchester United 2 Manchester City 1**
Teamsheet: Schmeichel, Irwin, Neville P, Bruce, Pallister, Sharpe, Butt, Keane, Cole, Cantona, Giggs
Scorer(s):   Cantona, Sharpe

Match # 4336 Wednesday 21/02/96   FA Premiership   at Old Trafford   Attendance 42459
Result: **Manchester United 2 Everton 0**
Teamsheet: Schmeichel, Neville P, Irwin, Bruce, Pallister, Sharpe, Butt, Keane, Cole, Cantona, Giggs
Substitute(s):   Beckham   Scorer(s):   Giggs, Keane

Match # 4337 Sunday 25/02/96   FA Premiership   at Burnden Park   Attendance 21381
Result: **Bolton Wanderers 0 Manchester United 6**
Teamsheet: Schmeichel, Neville P, Irwin, Bruce, Pallister, Beckham, Butt, Keane, Cole, Cantona, Giggs
Substitute(s):   McClair, Scholes   Scorer(s):   Scholes 2, Beckham, Bruce, Butt, Cole

SEASON 1995/96 (continued)

Match # 4338 Monday 04/03/96   FA Premiership   at St James' Park   Attendance 36584
Result: **Newcastle United 0 Manchester United 1**
Teamsheet: Schmeichel, Neville P, Irwin, Bruce, Neville G, Sharpe, Butt, Keane, Cole, Cantona, Giggs
Scorer(s):   Cantona

Match # 4339 Monday 11/03/96   FA Cup 6th Round   at Old Trafford   Attendance 45446
Result: **Manchester United 2 Southampton 0**
Teamsheet: Schmeichel, Irwin, Neville P, Bruce, Neville G, Sharpe, Butt, Keane, Cole, Cantona, Giggs
Scorer(s):   Cantona, Sharpe

Match # 4340 Saturday 16/03/96   FA Premiership   at Loftus Road   Attendance 18817
Result: **Queens Park Rangers 1 Manchester United 1**
Teamsheet: Schmeichel, Neville G, Irwin, Bruce, May, Beckham, McClair, Keane, Cole, Cantona, Giggs
Substitute(s): Butt, Scholes, Sharpe   Scorer(s):   Cantona

Match # 4341 Wednesday 20/03/96   FA Premiership   at Old Trafford   Attendance 50028
Result: **Manchester United 1 Arsenal 0**
Teamsheet: Schmeichel, Neville G, Neville P, Bruce, May, Sharpe, Butt, Keane, Cole, Cantona, Giggs
Substitute(s): Scholes   Scorer(s):   Cantona

Match # 4342 Sunday 24/03/96   FA Premiership   at Old Trafford   Attendance 50157
Result: **Manchester United 1 Tottenham Hotspur 0**
Teamsheet: Schmeichel, Neville G, Neville P, Bruce, May, Sharpe, Butt, Keane, Cole, Cantona, Giggs
Substitute(s): Beckham, McClair   Scorer(s):   Cantona

Match # 4343 Sunday 31/03/96   FA Cup Semi-Final   at Villa Park   Attendance 38421
Result: **Manchester United 2 Chelsea 1**
Teamsheet: Schmeichel, Neville P, Sharpe, May, Neville G, Beckham, Butt, Keane, Cole, Cantona, Giggs
Scorer(s):   Beckham, Cole

Match # 4344 Saturday 06/04/96   FA Premiership   at Maine Road   Attendance 29668
Result: **Manchester City 2 Manchester United 3**
Teamsheet: Schmeichel, Neville P, Irwin, Bruce, Neville G, Beckham, Butt, Keane, Cole, Cantona, Giggs
Substitute(s): May, Sharpe   Scorer(s):   Cantona, Cole, Giggs

Match # 4345 Monday 08/04/96   FA Premiership   at Old Trafford   Attendance 50332
Result: **Manchester United 1 Coventry City 0**
Teamsheet: Schmeichel, Irwin, Sharpe, May, Neville G, Beckham, Butt, McClair, Cole, Cantona, Giggs
Scorer(s):   Cantona

Match # 4346 Saturday 13/04/96   FA Premiership   at The Dell   Attendance 15262
Result: **Southampton 3 Manchester United 1**
Teamsheet: Schmeichel, Irwin, Sharpe, Bruce, Neville G, Beckham, Butt, Keane, Cole, Cantona, Giggs
Substitute(s): May, Scholes   Scorer(s):   Giggs

Match # 4347 Wednesday 17/04/96   FA Premiership   at Old Trafford   Attendance 48382
Result: **Manchester United 1 Leeds United 0**
Teamsheet: Schmeichel, Irwin, Neville P, Bruce, Pallister, Beckham, McClair, Keane, Cole, Cantona, Giggs
Substitute(s): May, Scholes, Sharpe   Scorer(s):   Keane

Match # 4348 Sunday 28/04/96   FA Premiership   at Old Trafford   Attendance 53926
Result: **Manchester United 5 Nottingham Forest 0**
Teamsheet: Schmeichel, Irwin, Neville P, May, Pallister, Beckham, Sharpe, Keane, Scholes, Cantona, Giggs
Substitute(s): Neville G   Scorer(s):   Beckham 2, Cantona, Giggs, Scholes

Match # 4349 Sunday 05/05/96   FA Premiership   at Riverside Stadium   Attendance 29921
Result: **Middlesbrough 0 Manchester United 3**
Teamsheet: Schmeichel, Irwin, Neville P, May, Pallister, Beckham, Butt, Keane, Scholes, Cantona, Giggs
Substitute(s): Cole   Scorer(s):   Cole, Giggs, May

Match # 4350 Saturday 11/05/96   FA Cup Final   at Wembley   Attendance 79007
Result: **Manchester United 1 Liverpool 0**
Teamsheet: Schmeichel, Irwin, Neville P, May, Pallister, Beckham, Butt, Keane, Cole, Cantona, Giggs
Substitute(s): Neville G, Scholes   Scorer(s):   Cantona

SEASON 1995/96 SUMMARY

APPEARANCES

PLAYER	LGE	FAC	LC	UC	TOTAL
Schmeichel	36	6	1	2	45
Giggs	30 (3)	7	2	2	41 (3)
Cole	32 (2)	7	1	1	41 (2)
Butt	31 (1)	7	–	2	40 (1)
Irwin	31	6	1	1	39
Bruce	30	5	1 (1)	2	38 (1)
Keane	29	7	– (1)	2	38 (1)
Cantona	30	7	1	–	38
Neville G	30 (1)	5 (1)	1	1	37 (2)
Beckham	26 (7)	3	2	2	33 (7)
Sharpe	21 (10)	4 (2)	2	2	29 (12)
Neville P	21 (3)	6 (1)	1 (1)	1	29 (5)
Pallister	21	3	2	2	28
Scholes	16 (10)	– (2)	1	1 (1)	18 (13)
McClair	12 (10)	–	1	–	13 (10)
May	11 (5)	2	–	–	13 (5)
Parker	5 (1)	1 (1)	1	– (1)	7 (3)
Pilkington	2 (1)	1	1	–	4 (1)
Davies	1 (5)	–	1	– (1)	2 (6)
Cooke	1 (3)	–	1 (1)	– (1)	2 (5)
Prunier	2	–	–	–	2
O'Kane	– (1)	–	–	1	1 (1)
McGibbon	–	–	1	–	1
Thornley	– (1)	–	–	–	– (1)

GOALSCORERS

PLAYER	LGE	FAC	LC	UC	TOT
Cantona	14	5	–	–	19
Scholes	10	1	2	1	14
Cole	11	2	–	–	13
Giggs	11	1	–	–	12
Beckham	7	1	–	–	8
Keane	6	–	–	–	6
Sharpe	4	2	–	–	6
McClair	3	–	–	–	3
Butt	2	1	–	–	3
Bruce	1	–	–	–	1
Irwin	1	–	–	–	1
May	1	–	–	–	1
Pallister	1	–	–	–	1
Cooke	–	–	1	–	1
Parker	–	1	–	–	1
Schmeichel	–	–	–	1	1
own goal	1	–	–	–	1

RESULTS & ATTENDANCES SUMMARY

		P	W	D	L	F	A	TOTAL	AVGE
League	H	19	15	4	0	36	9	791940	41681
	A	19	10	3	6	37	26	574503	30237
TOTAL		38	25	7	6	73	35	1366443	35959
FA Cup	H	3	2	1	0	6	3	129701	43234
	A	2	2	0	0	5	1	36158	18079
	N	2	2	0	0	3	1	117428	58714
TOTAL		7	6	1	0	14	5	283287	40470
League Cup	H	1	0	0	1	0	3	29049	29049
	A	1	1	0	0	3	1	9386	9386
TOTAL		2	1	0	1	3	4	38435	19218
UEFA Cup	H	1	0	1	0	2	2	29724	29724
	A	1	0	1	0	0	0	33000	33000
TOTAL		2	0	2	0	2	2	62724	31362
Overall	H	24	17	6	1	44	17	980414	40851
	A	23	13	4	6	45	28	653047	28393
	N	2	2	0	0	3	1	117428	58714
TOTAL		49	32	10	7	92	46	1750889	35732

FINAL TABLE – FA PREMIERSHIP

		P	HOME					AWAY					PTS	GD
			W	D	L	F	A	W	D	L	F	A		
1	MANCHESTER UNITED	38	15	4	0	36	9	10	3	6	37	26	82	38
2	Newcastle United	38	17	1	1	38	9	7	5	7	28	28	78	29
3	Liverpool	38	14	4	1	46	13	6	7	6	24	21	71	36
4	Aston Villa	38	11	5	3	32	15	7	4	8	20	20	63	17
5	Arsenal	38	10	7	2	30	16	7	5	7	19	16	63	17
6	Everton	38	10	5	4	35	19	7	5	7	29	25	61	20
7	Blackburn Rovers	38	14	2	3	44	19	4	5	10	17	28	61	14
8	Tottenham Hotspur	38	9	5	5	26	19	7	8	4	24	19	61	12
9	Nottingham Forest	38	11	6	2	29	17	4	7	8	21	37	58	-4
10	West Ham United	38	9	5	5	25	21	5	4	10	18	31	51	-9
11	Chelsea	38	7	7	5	30	22	5	7	7	16	22	50	2
12	Middlesbrough	38	8	3	8	27	27	3	7	9	8	23	43	-15
13	Leeds United	38	8	3	8	21	21	4	4	11	19	36	43	-17
14	Wimbledon	38	5	6	8	27	33	5	5	9	28	37	41	-15
15	Sheffield Wednesday	38	7	5	7	30	31	3	5	11	18	30	40	-13
16	Coventry City	38	6	7	6	21	23	2	7	10	21	37	38	-18
17	Southampton	38	7	7	5	21	18	2	4	13	13	34	38	-18
18	Manchester City	38	7	7	5	21	19	2	4	13	12	39	38	-25
19	Queens Park Rangers	38	6	5	8	25	26	3	1	15	13	31	33	-19
20	Bolton Wanderers	38	5	4	10	16	31	3	1	15	23	40	29	-32

SEASON 1996/97

Match # 4351 Sunday 11/08/96   FA Charity Shield   at Wembley   Attendance 73214
Result: **Manchester United 4   Newcastle United 0**
Teamsheet: Schmeichel, Irwin, Neville P, May, Keane, Pallister, Cantona, Butt, Scholes, Beckham, Giggs
Substitute(s):   Cruyff, Neville G, Poborsky   Scorer(s):   Beckham, Butt, Cantona, Keane

Match # 4352 Saturday 17/08/96   FA Premiership   at Selhurst Park   Attendance 25786
Result: **Wimbledon 0   Manchester United 3**
Teamsheet: Schmeichel, Irwin, Neville P, May, Keane, Pallister, Cantona, Butt, Scholes, Beckham, Cruyff
Substitute(s):   Johnsen, McClair   Scorer(s):   Beckham, Cantona, Irwin

Match # 4353 Wednesday 21/08/96   FA Premiership   at Old Trafford   Attendance 54943
Result: **Manchester United 2   Everton 2**
Teamsheet: Schmeichel, Irwin, Neville P, May, Poborsky, Pallister, Cantona, Butt, Cruyff, Beckham, Giggs
Substitute(s):   McClair   Scorer(s):   Cruyff, own goal

Match # 4354 Sunday 25/08/96   FA Premiership   at Old Trafford   Attendance 54178
Result: **Manchester United 2   Blackburn Rovers 2**
Teamsheet: Schmeichel, Irwin, Neville P, May, Johnsen, Pallister, Cantona, McClair, Cruyff, Beckham, Giggs
Substitute(s):   Neville G, Solskjaer   Scorer(s):   Cruyff, Solskjaer

Match # 4355 Wednesday 04/09/96   FA Premiership   at Baseball Ground   Attendance 18026
Result: **Derby County 1   Manchester United 1**
Teamsheet: Schmeichel, Neville G, Irwin, May, Johnsen, Pallister, Cantona, Butt, Cruyff, Beckham, Giggs
Substitute(s):   Scholes, Solskjaer   Scorer(s):   Beckham

Match # 4356 Saturday 07/09/96   FA Premiership   at Elland Road   Attendance 39694
Result: **Leeds United 0   Manchester United 4**
Teamsheet: Schmeichel, Neville G, Irwin, May, Poborsky, Johnsen, Cantona, Butt, Cruyff, Beckham, Giggs
Substitute(s):   Cole, McClair, Solskjaer   Scorer(s):   Butt, Cantona, Poborsky, own goal

Match # 4357 Wednesday 11/09/96   Champions League Phase 1 Match 1   at Stadio Delle Alpi   Attendance 54000
Result: **Juventus 1   Manchester United 0**
Teamsheet: Schmeichel, Neville G, Irwin, Johnsen, Poborsky, Pallister, Cantona, Butt, Cruyff, Beckham, Giggs
Substitute(s):   Cole, McClair, Solskjaer

Match # 4358 Saturday 14/09/96   FA Premiership   at Old Trafford   Attendance 54984
Result: **Manchester United 4   Nottingham Forest 1**
Teamsheet: Schmeichel, Neville G, Irwin, Johnsen, Poborsky, Pallister, Cantona, Butt, Solskjaer, Beckham, Giggs
Substitute(s):   Cole, McClair   Scorer(s):   Cantona 2, Giggs, Solskjaer

Match # 4359 Saturday 21/09/96   FA Premiership   at Villa Park   Attendance 39339
Result: **Aston Villa 0   Manchester United 0**
Teamsheet: van der Gouw, Neville G, Irwin, Johnsen, Keane, Pallister, Cantona, Solskjaer, Cruyff, Beckham, Giggs
Substitute(s):   Cole, Poborsky

Match # 4360 Wednesday 25/09/96   Champions League Phase 1 Match 2   at Old Trafford   Attendance 51831
Result: **Manchester United 2   Rapid Vienna 0**
Teamsheet: Schmeichel, Neville G, Irwin, Johnsen, Keane, Pallister, Cantona, Poborsky, Solskjaer, Beckham, Giggs
Substitute(s):   Butt, Cole, May   Scorer(s):   Beckham, Solskjaer

Match # 4361 Sunday 29/09/96   FA Premiership   at Old Trafford   Attendance 54943
Result: **Manchester United 2   Tottenham Hotspur 0**
Teamsheet: Schmeichel, Neville G, Irwin, May, Poborsky, Pallister, Cantona, Butt, Solskjaer, Beckham, Giggs
Substitute(s):   Cruyff, Scholes   Scorer(s):   Solskjaer 2

Match # 4362 Saturday 12/10/96   FA Premiership   at Old Trafford   Attendance 55128
Result: **Manchester United 1   Liverpool 0**
Teamsheet: Schmeichel, Neville G, Irwin, May, Poborsky, Johnsen, Cantona, Butt, Solskjaer, Beckham, Cruyff
Substitute(s):   Giggs, Scholes   Scorer(s):   Beckham

Match # 4363 Wednesday 16/10/96   Champions League Phase 1 Match 3   at Fenerbahce   Attendance 26200
Result: **Fenerbahce 0   Manchester United 2**
Teamsheet: Schmeichel, Neville G, Irwin, May, Johnsen, Pallister, Cantona, Butt, Solskjaer, Beckham, Cruyff
Substitute(s):   Poborsky   Scorer(s):   Beckham, Cantona

Match # 4364 Sunday 20/10/96   FA Premiership   at St James' Park   Attendance 35579
Result: **Newcastle United 5   Manchester United 0**
Teamsheet: Schmeichel, Neville G, Irwin, May, Johnsen, Pallister, Cantona, Butt, Solskjaer, Beckham, Poborsky
Substitute(s):   Cruyff, McClair, Scholes

Match # 4365 Wednesday 23/10/96   League Cup 3rd Round   at Old Trafford   Attendance 49305
Result: **Manchester United 2   Swindon Town 1**
Teamsheet: van der Gouw, Neville G, Neville P, May, Keane, Casper, Thornley, Appleton, McClair, Scholes, Poborsky
Substitute(s):   Davies   Scorer(s):   Poborsky, Scholes

Match # 4366 Saturday 26/10/96   FA Premiership   at The Dell   Attendance 15253
Result: **Southampton 6   Manchester United 3**
Teamsheet: Schmeichel, Neville G, Neville P, May, Keane, Pallister, Cantona, Butt, Scholes, Beckham, Cruyff
Substitute(s):   Irwin, McClair, Solskjaer   Scorer(s):   Beckham, May, Scholes

Match # 4367 Wednesday 30/10/96   Champions League Phase 1 Match 4   at Old Trafford   Attendance 53297
Result: **Manchester United 0   Fenerbahce 1**
Teamsheet: Schmeichel, Neville G, Irwin, May, Keane, Johnsen, Cantona, Butt, Poborsky, Beckham, Cruyff
Substitute(s):   Neville P, Scholes, Solskjaer

Match # 4368 Saturday 02/11/96   FA Premiership   at Old Trafford   Attendance 55198
Result: **Manchester United 1   Chelsea 2**
Teamsheet: Schmeichel, Irwin, Neville P, May, Keane, Johnsen, Cantona, Butt, Scholes, Beckham, Solskjaer
Substitute(s):   Poborsky   Scorer(s):   May

SEASON 1996/97 (continued)

Match # 4369   Saturday 16/11/96   FA Premiership   at Old Trafford   Attendance 55210
Result: **Manchester United 1   Arsenal 0**
Teamsheet: Schmeichel, Neville G, Neville P, May, Poborsky, Johnsen, Cantona, Butt, Solskjaer, Beckham, Giggs
Scorer(s):   own goal

Match # 4370   Wednesday 20/11/96   Champions League Phase 1 Match 5   at Old Trafford   Attendance 53529
Result: **Manchester United 0   Juventus 1**
Teamsheet: Schmeichel, Neville G, Neville P, May, Keane, Johnsen, Cantona, Butt, Solskjaer, Beckham, Giggs
Substitute(s):   Cruyff, McClair

Match # 4371   Saturday 23/11/96   FA Premiership   at Riverside Stadium   Attendance 30063
Result: **Middlesbrough 2   Manchester United 2**
Teamsheet: Schmeichel, Clegg, O'Kane, May, Keane, Johnsen, Cantona, Butt, Scholes, Beckham, Thornley
Substitute(s):   Cruyff, McClair   Scorer(s):   Keane, May

Match # 4372   Wednesday 27/11/96   League Cup 4th Round   at Filbert Street   Attendance 20428
Result: **Leicester City 2   Manchester United 0**
Teamsheet: van der Gouw, O'Kane, Clegg, May, Keane, Casper, Cruyff, McClair, Scholes, Poborsky, Thornley
Substitute(s):   Appleton, Cooke, Davies

Match # 4373   Saturday 30/11/96   FA Premiership   at Old Trafford   Attendance 55196
Result: **Manchester United 3   Leicester City 1**
Teamsheet: Schmeichel, Neville G, Irwin, May, Keane, Pallister, Cantona, Butt, Cruyff, Beckham, Giggs
Substitute(s):   Poborsky, Solskjaer   Scorer(s):   Butt 2, Solskjaer

Match # 4374   Wednesday 04/12/96   Champions League Phase 1 Match 6   at Ernst Happel Stadion   Attendance 45000
Result: **Rapid Vienna 0   Manchester United 2**
Teamsheet: Schmeichel, Neville G, Irwin, May, Keane, Pallister, Cantona, Butt, Solskjaer, Beckham, Giggs
Substitute(s):   Casper, McClair, Poborsky   Scorer(s):   Cantona, Giggs

Match # 4375   Sunday 08/12/96   FA Premiership   at Upton Park   Attendance 25045
Result: **West Ham United 2   Manchester United 2**
Teamsheet: Schmeichel, Johnsen, Irwin, May, McClair, Pallister, Cantona, Poborsky, Beckham, Giggs
Substitute(s):   Neville P   Scorer(s):   Beckham, Solskjaer

Match # 4376   Wednesday 18/12/96   FA Premiership   at Hillsborough   Attendance 37671
Result: **Sheffield Wednesday 1   Manchester United 1**
Teamsheet: Schmeichel, Neville G, Irwin, May, Johnsen, Pallister, Cantona, Butt, Scholes, Solskjaer, Giggs
Substitute(s):   Beckham, Neville P   Scorer(s):   Scholes

Match # 4377   Saturday 21/12/96   FA Premiership   at Old Trafford   Attendance 55081
Result: **Manchester United 5   Sunderland 0**
Teamsheet: Schmeichel, Neville G, Neville P, May, Irwin, Pallister, Cantona, Butt, Solskjaer, Scholes, Giggs
Substitute(s):   McClair, Poborsky, Thornley   Scorer(s):   Cantona 2, Solskjaer 2, Butt

Match # 4378   Thursday 26/12/96   FA Premiership   at City Ground   Attendance 29032
Result: **Nottingham Forest 0   Manchester United 4**
Teamsheet: Schmeichel, Neville G, Irwin, May, Scholes, Johnsen, Cantona, Butt, Solskjaer, Beckham, Giggs
Substitute(s):   Cole, McClair, Poborsky   Scorer(s):   Beckham, Butt, Cole, Solskjaer

Match # 4379   Saturday 28/12/96   FA Premiership   at Old Trafford   Attendance 55256
Result: **Manchester United 1   Leeds United 0**
Teamsheet: Schmeichel, Neville G, Irwin, May, Keane, Johnsen, Cantona, Scholes, Solskjaer, Beckham, Giggs
Substitute(s):   Butt, Cole   Scorer(s):   Cantona

Match # 4380   Wednesday 01/01/97   FA Premiership   at Old Trafford   Attendance 55133
Result: **Manchester United 0   Aston Villa 0**
Teamsheet: Schmeichel, Neville G, Irwin, May, Keane, Johnsen, Cantona, Butt, Solskjaer, Beckham, Giggs
Substitute(s):   Cole, Scholes

Match # 4381   Sunday 05/01/97   FA Cup 3rd Round   at Old Trafford   Attendance 52445
Result: **Manchester United 2   Tottenham Hotspur 0**
Teamsheet: Schmeichel, Neville G, Irwin, May, Keane, Johnsen, Cantona, Scholes, Cole, Beckham, Giggs
Substitute(s):   McClair, Solskjaer   Scorer(s):   Beckham, Scholes

Match # 4382   Sunday 12/01/97   FA Premiership   at White Hart Lane   Attendance 33026
Result: **Tottenham Hotspur 1   Manchester United 2**
Teamsheet: Schmeichel, Neville G, Johnsen, May, Keane, Pallister, Cantona, Scholes, Solskjaer, Beckham, Giggs
Substitute(s):   Casper, Cole, Poborsky   Scorer(s):   Beckham, Solskjaer

Match # 4383   Saturday 18/01/97   FA Premiership   at Highfield Road   Attendance 23085
Result: **Coventry City 0   Manchester United 2**
Teamsheet: Schmeichel, Neville G, Irwin, Johnsen, Keane, Pallister, Cantona, Scholes, Poborsky, Giggs
Substitute(s):   Casper   Scorer(s):   Giggs, Solskjaer

Match # 4384   Saturday 25/01/97   FA Cup 4th Round   at Old Trafford   Attendance 53342
Result: **Manchester United 1   Wimbledon 1**
Teamsheet: Schmeichel, Clegg, Irwin, Casper, Keane, Neville G, Cantona, McClair, Scholes, Poborsky, Giggs
Substitute(s):   Cole, Solskjaer   Scorer(s):   Scholes

Match # 4385   Wednesday 29/01/97   FA Premiership   at Old Trafford   Attendance 55314
Result: **Manchester United 2   Wimbledon 1**
Teamsheet: Schmeichel, Clegg, Irwin, Neville G, Keane, Pallister, Cantona, Scholes, Solskjaer, Beckham, Giggs
Substitute(s):   Cole   Scorer(s):   Cole, Giggs

Match # 4386   Saturday 01/02/97   FA Premiership   at Old Trafford   Attendance 55269
Result: **Manchester United 2   Southampton 1**
Teamsheet: Schmeichel, Clegg, Irwin, Neville G, Keane, Pallister, Cantona, Poborsky, Solskjaer, Beckham, Giggs
Substitute(s):   Cole, Johnsen   Scorer(s):   Cantona, Pallister

SEASON 1996/97 (continued)

Match # 4387 Tuesday 04/02/97 FA Cup 4th Round Replay at Selhurst Park Attendance 25601
Result: **Wimbledon 1 Manchester United 0**
Teamsheet: Schmeichel, Neville G, Irwin, Johnsen, Keane, Pallister, Cantona, Poborsky, Cole, Beckham, Giggs
Substitute(s): McClair, Solskjaer

Match # 4388 Wednesday 19/02/97 FA Premiership at Highbury Attendance 38172
Result: **Arsenal 1 Manchester United 2**
Teamsheet: Schmeichel, Neville G, Irwin, Johnsen, Keane, Pallister, Solskjaer, Poborsky, Cole, Beckham, Giggs
Substitute(s): Butt, McClair Scorer(s): Cole, Solskjaer

Match # 4389 Saturday 22/02/97 FA Premiership at Stamford Bridge Attendance 28336
Result: **Chelsea 1 Manchester United 1**
Teamsheet: Schmeichel, Neville G, Irwin, Johnsen, Keane, Pallister, Solskjaer, McClair, Cole, Beckham, Giggs
Substitute(s): Cruyff, May Scorer(s): Beckham

Match # 4390 Saturday 01/03/97 FA Premiership at Old Trafford Attendance 55230
Result: **Manchester United 3 Coventry City 1**
Teamsheet: Schmeichel, Neville G, Irwin, May, Poborsky, Pallister, Cantona, Cruyff, Cole, Beckham, Giggs
Substitute(s): Johnsen, McClair, Neville P Scorer(s): Poborsky, own goals 2

Match # 4391 Wednesday 05/03/97 Champions League Quarter-Final 1st Leg at Old Trafford Attendance 53425
Result: **Manchester United 4 Porto 0**
Teamsheet: Schmeichel, Neville G, Irwin, May, Johnsen, Pallister, Cantona, Solskjaer, Cole, Beckham, Giggs
Scorer(s): Cantona, Cole, Giggs, May

Match # 4392 Saturday 08/03/97 FA Premiership at Roker Park Attendance 22225
Result: **Sunderland 2 Manchester United 1**
Teamsheet: Schmeichel, Neville G, Irwin, May, Neville P, Johnsen, Cantona, Poborsky, McClair, Beckham, Cruyff
Substitute(s): Cole, Solskjaer Scorer(s): own goal

Match # 4393 Saturday 15/03/97 FA Premiership at Old Trafford Attendance 55267
Result: **Manchester United 2 Sheffield Wednesday 0**
Teamsheet: Schmeichel, Neville G, Irwin, May, Butt, Pallister, Cantona, Solskjaer, Cole, Beckham, Giggs
Substitute(s): Poborsky, Scholes Scorer(s): Cole, Poborsky

Match # 4394 Wednesday 19/03/97 Champions League Quarter-Final 2nd Leg at Estadio das Antas Attendance 40000
Result: **Porto 0 Manchester United 0**
Teamsheet: Schmeichel, Neville G, Irwin, May, Keane, Pallister, Cantona, Butt, Solskjaer, Beckham, Johnsen
Substitute(s): Neville P, Poborsky, Scholes

Match # 4395 Saturday 22/03/97 FA Premiership at Goodison Park Attendance 40079
Result: **Everton 0 Manchester United 2**
Teamsheet: Schmeichel, Irwin, Neville P, May, Keane, Pallister, Cantona, Butt, Solskjaer, Beckham, Giggs
Substitute(s): Johnsen, McClair Scorer(s): Cantona, Solskjaer

Match # 4396 Saturday 05/04/97 FA Premiership at Old Trafford Attendance 55243
Result: **Manchester United 2 Derby County 3**
Teamsheet: Schmeichel, Neville G, Neville P, Johnsen, Keane, Pallister, Cantona, Butt, Cole, Beckham, Giggs
Substitute(s): Irwin, Scholes, Solskjaer Scorer(s): Cantona, Solskjaer

Match # 4397 Wednesday 09/04/97 Champions League Semi-Final 1st Leg at Westfalenstadion Attendance 48500
Result: **Borussia Dortmund 1 Manchester United 0**
Teamsheet: van der Gouw, Neville G, Irwin, Johnsen, Keane, Pallister, Cantona, Butt, Solskjaer, Beckham, Giggs
Substitute(s): Cole, Scholes

Match # 4398 Saturday 12/04/97 FA Premiership at Ewood Park Attendance 30476
Result: **Blackburn Rovers 2 Manchester United 3**
Teamsheet: van der Gouw, Neville G, Neville P, Johnsen, Keane, Pallister, Cantona, Butt, Cole, Scholes, Solskjaer
Substitute(s): Beckham Scorer(s): Cantona, Cole, Scholes

Match # 4399 Saturday 19/04/97 FA Premiership at Anfield Attendance 40892
Result: **Liverpool 1 Manchester United 3**
Teamsheet: Schmeichel, Neville G, Neville P, Johnsen, Keane, Pallister, Cantona, Butt, Cole, Beckham, Scholes
Substitute(s): McClair Scorer(s): Pallister 2, Cole

Match # 4400 Wednesday 23/04/97 Champions League Semi-Final 2nd Leg at Old Trafford Attendance 53606
Result: **Manchester United 0 Borussia Dortmund 1**
Teamsheet: Schmeichel, Neville G, Neville P, May, Johnsen, Pallister, Cantona, Butt, Cole, Beckham, Solskjaer
Substitute(s): Giggs, Scholes

Match # 4401 Saturday 03/05/97 FA Premiership at Filbert Street Attendance 21068
Result: **Leicester City 2 Manchester United 2**
Teamsheet: Schmeichel, Neville G, Neville P, May, Keane, Pallister, Cantona, Butt, Cole, Solskjaer, Scholes
Substitute(s): Beckham, Johnsen Scorer(s): Solskjaer 2

Match # 4402 Monday 05/05/97 FA Premiership at Old Trafford Attendance 54489
Result: **Manchester United 3 Middlesbrough 3**
Teamsheet: Schmeichel, Neville G, Irwin, May, Johnsen, Pallister, Cantona, Keane, Cole, Beckham, Solskjaer
Substitute(s): Scholes Scorer(s): Keane, Neville G, Solskjaer

Match # 4403 Thursday 08/05/97 FA Premiership at Old Trafford Attendance 55236
Result: **Manchester United 0 Newcastle United 0**
Teamsheet: Schmeichel, Neville G, Neville P, May, Johnsen, Cantona, Poborsky, Cole, Beckham, Scholes
Substitute(s): McClair, Solskjaer

Match # 4404 Sunday 11/05/97 FA Premiership at Old Trafford Attendance 55249
Result: **Manchester United 2 West Ham United 0**
Teamsheet: Schmeichel, Irwin, Neville P, May, Poborsky, Johnsen, Cantona, Butt, Solskjaer, Beckham, Scholes
Substitute(s): Clegg, Cruyff, McClair Scorer(s): Cruyff, Solskjaer

SEASON 1996/97 SUMMARY

APPEARANCES

PLAYER	LGE	FAC	LC	CL	CS	TOTAL
Cantona	36	3	–	10	1	50
Schmeichel	36	3	–	9	1	49
Beckham	33 (3)	2	–	10	1	46 (3)
Neville G	30 (1)	3	1	10	– (1)	44 (2)
Irwin	29 (2)	3	–	8	1	41 (2)
May	28 (1)	1	2	7 (1)	1	39 (2)
Johnsen	26 (5)	2	–	9	–	37 (5)
Pallister	27	1	–	8	1	37
Giggs	25 (1)	3	–	6 (1)	1	35 (2)
Solskjaer	25 (8)	– (3)	–	8 (2)	–	33 (13)
Butt	24 (2)	–	–	8 (1)	1	33 (3)
Keane	21	3	2	6	1	33
Poborsky	15 (7)	2	2	3 (3)	– (1)	22 (11)
Scholes	16 (8)	2	2	– (4)	1	21 (12)
Neville P	15 (3)	–	1	2 (2)	1	19 (5)
Cruyff	11 (5)	–	1	3 (1)	– (1)	15 (7)
Cole	10 (10)	2 (1)	–	2 (3)	–	14 (14)
McClair	4 (15)	1 (2)	2	– (3)	–	7 (20)
Clegg	3 (1)	1	1	–	–	5 (1)
van der Gouw	2	–	2	1	–	5
Casper	– (2)	1	2	– (1)	–	3 (3)
Thornley	1 (1)	–	2	–	–	3 (1)
O'Kane	1	–	1	–	–	2
Appleton	–	–	1 (1)	–	–	1 (1)
Davies	–	–	– (2)	–	–	– (2)
Cooke	–	–	– (1)	–	–	– (1)

GOALSCORERS

PLAYER	LGE	FAC	LC	CL	CS	TOTAL
Solskjaer	18	–	–	1	–	19
Cantona	11	–	–	3	1	15
Beckham	8	1	–	2	1	12
Cole	6	–	–	1	–	7
Butt	5	–	–	–	1	6
Scholes	3	2	1	–	–	6
Giggs	3	–	–	2	–	5
May	3	–	–	1	–	4
Poborsky	3	–	1	–	–	4
Cruyff	3	–	–	–	–	3
Pallister	3	–	–	–	–	3
Keane	2	–	–	–	1	3
Irwin	1	–	–	–	–	1
Neville G	1	–	–	–	–	1
own goals	6	–	–	–	–	6

RESULTS & ATTENDANCES SUMMARY

		P	W	D	L	F	A	TOTAL	AVGE
League	H	19	12	5	2	38	17	1046547	55081
	A	19	9	7	3	38	27	572847	30150
TOTAL		38	21	12	5	76	44	1619394	42616
FA Cup	H	2	1	1	0	3	1	105787	52894
	A	1	0	0	1	0	1	25601	25601
TOTAL		3	1	1	1	3	2	131388	43796
League	H	1	1	0	0	2	1	49305	49305
Cup	A	1	0	0	1	0	2	20428	20428
TOTAL		2	1	0	1	2	3	69733	34867
Champions	H	5	2	0	3	6	3	265688	53138
League	A	5	2	1	2	4	2	213700	42740
TOTAL		10	4	1	5	10	5	479388	47939
Charity	H	0	0	0	0	0	0	0	n/a
Shield	A	0	0	0	0	0	0	0	n/a
	N	1	1	0	0	4	0	73214	73214
TOTAL		1	1	0	0	4	0	73214	73214
Overall	H	27	16	6	5	49	22	1467327	54345
	A	26	11	8	7	42	32	832576	32022
	N	1	1	0	0	4	0	73214	73214
TOTAL		54	28	14	12	95	54	2373117	43947

FINAL TABLE – FA PREMIERSHIP

		P	W	D	L	F	A	W	D	L	F	A	PTS	GD
			HOME						AWAY					
1	MANCHESTER UNITED	38	12	5	2	38	17	9	7	3	38	27	75	32
2	Newcastle United	38	13	3	3	54	20	6	8	5	19	20	68	33
3	Arsenal	38	10	5	4	36	18	9	6	4	26	14	68	30
4	Liverpool	38	10	6	3	38	19	9	5	5	24	18	68	25
5	Aston Villa	38	11	5	3	27	13	6	5	8	20	21	61	13
6	Chelsea	38	9	8	2	33	22	7	3	9	25	33	59	3
7	Sheffield Wednesday	38	8	10	1	25	16	6	5	8	25	35	57	-1
8	Wimbledon	38	9	6	4	28	21	6	5	8	21	25	56	3
9	Leicester City	38	7	5	7	22	26	5	6	8	24	28	47	-8
10	Tottenham Hotspur	38	8	4	7	19	17	5	3	11	25	34	46	-7
11	Leeds United	38	7	7	5	15	13	4	6	9	13	25	46	-10
12	Derby County	38	8	6	5	25	22	3	7	9	20	36	46	-13
13	Blackburn Rovers	38	8	4	7	28	23	1	11	7	14	20	42	-1
14	West Ham United	38	7	6	6	27	25	3	6	10	12	23	42	-9
15	Everton	38	7	4	8	24	22	3	8	8	20	35	42	-13
16	Southampton	38	6	7	6	32	24	4	4	11	18	32	41	-6
17	Coventry City	38	4	8	7	19	23	5	6	8	19	31	41	-16
18	Sunderland	38	7	6	6	20	18	3	4	12	15	35	40	-18
19	Middlesbrough *	38	8	5	6	34	25	2	7	10	17	35	39	-9
20	Nottingham Forest	38	3	9	7	15	27	3	7	9	16	32	34	-28

* Middlesbrough deducted 3 points for failure to fulfil fixture

SEASON 1997/98

Match # 4405 Sunday 03/08/97   FA Charity Shield   at Wembley   Attendance 73636
Result: **Manchester United 1   Chelsea 1   (United won the tie 4-2 on penalty kicks)**
Teamsheet: Schmeichel, Irwin, Neville P, Keane, Johnsen, Pallister, Scholes, Butt, Cole, Sheringham, Giggs
Substitute(s): Beckham, Cruyff   Scorer(s):   Johnsen

Match # 4406 Sunday 10/08/97   FA Premiership   at White Hart Lane Attendance 26359
Result: **Tottenham Hotspur 0   Manchester United 2**
Teamsheet: Schmeichel, Irwin, Neville P, Johnsen, Butt, Pallister, Keane, Scholes, Cruyff, Sheringham, Giggs
Substitute(s): Beckham   Scorer(s):   Butt, own goal

Match # 4407 Wednesday 13/08/97   FA Premiership   at Old Trafford   Attendance 55008
Result: **Manchester United 1   Southampton 0**
Teamsheet: Schmeichel, Irwin, Neville P, Johnsen, Butt, Pallister, Keane, Scholes, Cruyff, Sheringham, Giggs
Substitute(s): Beckham, Berg   Scorer(s):   Beckham

Match # 4408 Saturday 23/08/97   FA Premiership   at Filbert Street   Attendance 21221
Result: **Leicester City 0   Manchester United 0**
Teamsheet: Schmeichel, Neville G, Irwin, Berg, Butt, Pallister, Keane, Beckham, Cruyff, Sheringham, Giggs
Substitute(s): Scholes

Match # 4409 Wednesday 27/08/97   FA Premiership   at Goodison Park   Attendance 40079
Result: **Everton 0   Manchester United 2**
Teamsheet: Schmeichel, Neville G, Irwin, Berg, Butt, Pallister, Keane, Beckham, Scholes, Sheringham, Giggs
Substitute(s): Cole   Scorer(s):   Beckham, Sheringham

Match # 4410 Saturday 30/08/97   FA Premiership   at Old Trafford   Attendance 55074
Result: **Manchester United 3   Coventry City 0**
Teamsheet: Schmeichel, Neville G, Neville P, Berg, Butt, Pallister, Keane, Beckham, Cole, Sheringham, Giggs
Substitute(s): Irwin, Poborsky   Scorer(s):   Cole, Keane, Poborsky

Match # 4411 Saturday 13/09/97   FA Premiership   at Old Trafford   Attendance 55068
Result: **Manchester United 2   West Ham United 1**
Teamsheet: Schmeichel, Neville G, Pallister, Berg, Butt, Beckham, Keane, Neville P, Cole, Scholes, Giggs
Substitute(s): McClair, Poborsky   Scorer(s):   Keane, Scholes

Match # 4412 Wednesday 17/09/97   Champions League Phase 1 Match 1   at TJ Lokomotive Stadium   Attendance 9950
Result: **Kosice 0   Manchester United 3**
Teamsheet: Schmeichel, Neville G, Irwin, Berg, Butt, Pallister, Keane, Beckham, Cole, Scholes, Poborsky
Substitute(s): McClair   Scorer(s):   Berg, Cole, Irwin

Match # 4413 Saturday 20/09/97   FA Premiership   at Reebok Stadium   Attendance 25000
Result: **Bolton Wanderers 0   Manchester United 0**
Teamsheet: Schmeichel, Neville G, Irwin, Berg, Butt, Pallister, Keane, Beckham, Cole, Scholes, Poborsky
Substitute(s): Neville P, Solskjaer

Match # 4414 Wednesday 24/09/97   FA Premiership   at Old Trafford   Attendance 55163
Result: **Manchester United 2   Chelsea 2**
Teamsheet: Schmeichel, Neville G, Irwin, Berg, Butt, Pallister, Keane, Beckham, Cole, Scholes, Poborsky
Substitute(s): Giggs, Sheringham, Solskjaer   Scorer(s):   Scholes, Solskjaer

Match # 4415 Saturday 27/09/97   FA Premiership   at Elland Road   Attendance 39952
Result: **Leeds United 1   Manchester United 0**
Teamsheet: Schmeichel, Neville G, Irwin, Berg, Beckham, Pallister, Keane, Scholes, Poborsky, Sheringham, Solskjaer
Substitute(s): Johnsen, Neville P, Thornley

Match # 4416 Wednesday 01/10/97   Champions League Phase 1 Match 2   at Old Trafford   Attendance 53428
Result: **Manchester United 3   Juventus 2**
Teamsheet: Schmeichel, Neville G, Irwin, Berg, Butt, Pallister, Johnsen, Beckham, Solskjaer, Sheringham, Giggs
Substitute(s): Neville P, Scholes   Scorer(s):   Giggs, Sheringham, Scholes

Match # 4417 Saturday 04/10/97   FA Premiership   at Old Trafford   Attendance 55143
Result: **Manchester United 2   Crystal Palace 0**
Teamsheet: Schmeichel, Neville G, Johnsen, Berg, Butt, Pallister, Beckham, Neville P, Scholes, Sheringham, Giggs
Substitute(s): Irwin, Poborsky   Scorer(s):   Sheringham, own goal

Match # 4418 Tuesday 14/10/97   League Cup 3rd Round   at Portman Road   Attendance 22173
Result: **Ipswich Town 2   Manchester United 0**
Teamsheet: van der Gouw, Curtis, Neville P, May, Johnsen, Mulryne, Thornley, McClair, Cole, Cruyff, Poborsky
Substitute(s): Irwin, Nevland, Scholes

Match # 4419 Saturday 18/10/97   FA Premiership   at Pride Park   Attendance 30014
Result: **Derby County 2   Manchester United 2**
Teamsheet: Schmeichel, Neville G, Irwin, Berg, Butt, Pallister, Beckham, Scholes, Solskjaer, Sheringham, Giggs
Substitute(s): Cole, Johnsen, Neville P   Scorer(s):   Cole, Sheringham

Match # 4420 Wednesday 22/10/97   Champions League Phase 1 Match 3   at Old Trafford   Attendance 53188
Result: **Manchester United 2   Feyenoord 1**
Teamsheet: Schmeichel, Neville G, Irwin, Neville P, Butt, Pallister, Beckham, Scholes, Cole, Sheringham, Giggs
Substitute(s): Solskjaer   Scorer(s):   Irwin, Scholes

Match # 4421 Saturday 25/10/97   FA Premiership   at Old Trafford   Attendance 55142
Result: **Manchester United 7   Barnsley 0**
Teamsheet: Schmeichel, Neville G, Neville P, Curtis, Butt, Pallister, Beckham, Scholes, Cole, Solskjaer, Giggs
Substitute(s): Cruyff, Poborsky, Wallwork   Scorer(s):   Cole 3, Giggs 2, Poborsky, Scholes

Match # 4422 Saturday 01/11/97   FA Premiership   at Old Trafford   Attendance 55259
Result: **Manchester United 6   Sheffield Wednesday 1**
Teamsheet: Schmeichel, Neville G, Neville P, Berg, Butt, Pallister, Beckham, Scholes, Cole, Sheringham, Solskjaer
Substitute(s): Curtis, McClair, Poborsky   Scorer(s):   Sheringham 2, Solskjaer 2, Cole, own goal

SEASON 1997/98 (continued)

Match # 4423 Wednesday 05/11/97   Champions League Phase 1 Match 4   at Feyenoord Stadion   Attendance 51000
Result: **Feyenoord 1 Manchester United 3**
Teamsheet: Schmeichel, Neville G, Irwin, Berg, Butt, Pallister, Beckham, Scholes, Cole, Sheringham, Giggs
Substitute(s): Neville P, Poborsky, Solskjaer   Scorer(s):   Cole 3

Match # 4424 Sunday 09/11/97   FA Premiership   at Highbury   Attendance 38205
Result: **Arsenal 3 Manchester United 2**
Teamsheet: Schmeichel, Neville G, Neville P, Berg, Butt, Pallister, Beckham, Scholes, Cole, Sheringham, Giggs
Substitute(s): Johnsen, Solskjaer   Scorer(s):   Sheringham 2

Match # 4425 Saturday 22/11/97   FA Premiership   at Selhurst Park   Attendance 26309
Result: **Wimbledon 2 Manchester United 5**
Teamsheet: Schmeichel, Neville G, Johnsen, Berg, Butt, Pallister, Neville P, Scholes, Cole, Sheringham, Giggs
Substitute(s): Beckham   Scorer(s):   Beckham 2, Butt, Cole, Scholes

Match # 4426 Thursday 27/11/97   Champions League Phase 1 Match 5   at Old Trafford   Attendance 53535
Result: **Manchester United 3 Kosice 0**
Teamsheet: Schmeichel, Neville G, Johnsen, Neville P, Butt, Pallister, Beckham, Scholes, Cole, Sheringham, Giggs
Substitute(s): Berg, Poborsky, Solskjaer   Scorer(s):   Cole, Sheringham, own goal

Match # 4427 Sunday 30/11/97   FA Premiership   at Old Trafford   Attendance 55175
Result: **Manchester United 4 Blackburn Rovers 0**
Teamsheet: Schmeichel, Neville G, Neville P, Berg, Butt, Pallister, Beckham, Solskjaer, Cole, Sheringham, Giggs
Substitute(s): Johnsen, McClair, Poborsky   Scorer(s):   Solskjaer 2, own goals 2

Match # 4428 Saturday 06/12/97   FA Premiership   at Anfield   Attendance 41027
Result: **Liverpool 1 Manchester United 3**
Teamsheet: Schmeichel, Neville G, Johnsen, Berg, Butt, Pallister, Beckham, Neville P, Cole, Sheringham, Giggs
Scorer(s):   Cole 2, Beckham

Match # 4429 Wednesday 10/12/97   Champions League Phase 1 Match 6   at Stadio Delle Alpi   Attendance 47786
Result: **Juventus 1 Manchester United 0**
Teamsheet: Schmeichel, Neville G, Neville P, Berg, Johnsen, Pallister, Beckham, Poborsky, Solskjaer, Sheringham, Giggs
Substitute(s): Cole, McClair

Match # 4430 Monday 15/12/97   FA Premiership   at Old Trafford   Attendance 55151
Result: **Manchester United 1 Aston Villa 0**
Teamsheet: Schmeichel, Neville G, Johnsen, Neville P, Butt, Pallister, Beckham, Solskjaer, Cole, Sheringham, Giggs
Substitute(s): McClair   Scorer(s):   Giggs

Match # 4431 Sunday 21/12/97   FA Premiership   at St James' Park   Attendance 36767
Result: **Newcastle United 0 Manchester United 1**
Teamsheet: Schmeichel, Neville G, Johnsen, Neville P, Butt, Pallister, Beckham, Scholes, Cole, Sheringham, Giggs
Substitute(s): McClair, Solskjaer   Scorer(s):   Cole

Match # 4432 Friday 26/12/97   FA Premiership   at Old Trafford   Attendance 55167
Result: **Manchester United 2 Everton 0**
Teamsheet: Pilkington, Neville G, Johnsen, Berg, Butt, Pallister, Beckham, Neville P, Cole, Scholes, Solskjaer
Substitute(s): Curtis, McClair, Poborsky   Scorer(s):   Berg, Cole

Match # 4433 Sunday 28/12/97   FA Premiership   at Highfield Road   Attendance 23054
Result: **Coventry City 3 Manchester United 2**
Teamsheet: Pilkington, Neville G, Johnsen, Berg, Beckham, Pallister, Scholes, Solskjaer, Cole, Sheringham, Giggs
Substitute(s): Butt, Curtis   Scorer(s):   Sheringham, Solskjaer

Match # 4434 Sunday 04/01/98   FA Cup 3rd Round   at Stamford Bridge   Attendance 34792
Result: **Chelsea 3 Manchester United 5**
Teamsheet: Schmeichel, Neville G, Irwin, Johnsen, Butt, Pallister, Beckham, Scholes, Cole, Sheringham, Giggs
Substitute(s): Solskjaer   Scorer(s):   Beckham 2, Cole 2, Sheringham

Match # 4435 Saturday 10/01/98   FA Premiership   at Old Trafford   Attendance 55281
Result: **Manchester United 2 Tottenham Hotspur 0**
Teamsheet: Schmeichel, Neville G, Irwin, Johnsen, Beckham, Pallister, Scholes, Solskjaer, Cole, Sheringham, Giggs
Scorer(s):   Giggs 2

Match # 4436 Monday 19/01/98   FA Premiership   at The Dell   Attendance 15241
Result: **Southampton 1 Manchester United 0**
Teamsheet: Schmeichel, Neville G, Irwin, Johnsen, Butt, Pallister, Beckham, Solskjaer, Cole, Scholes, Giggs
Substitute(s): McClair, Nevland

Match # 4437 Saturday 24/01/98   FA Cup 4th Round   at Old Trafford   Attendance 54669
Result: **Manchester United 5 Walsall 1**
Teamsheet: Schmeichel, Neville P, Irwin, Berg, Johnsen, Thornley, Beckham, McClair, Cole, Scholes, Solskjaer
Substitute(s): Clegg, Mulryne, Nevland   Scorer(s):   Cole 2, Solskjaer 2, Johnsen

Match # 4438 Saturday 31/01/98   FA Premiership   at Old Trafford   Attendance 55156
Result: **Manchester United 0 Leicester City 1**
Teamsheet: Schmeichel, Neville G, Irwin, Johnsen, Butt, Pallister, Beckham, Solskjaer, Cole, Scholes, Giggs
Substitute(s): Berg, Neville P, Sheringham

Match # 4439 Saturday 07/02/98   FA Premiership   at Old Trafford   Attendance 55156
Result: **Manchester United 1 Bolton Wanderers 1**
Teamsheet: Schmeichel, Neville G, Irwin, Neville P, Beckham, Pallister, Scholes, Solskjaer, Cole, Sheringham, Giggs
Substitute(s): Berg   Scorer(s):   Cole

Match # 4440 Sunday 15/02/98   FA Cup 5th Round   at Old Trafford   Attendance 54700
Result: **Manchester United 1 Barnsley 1**
Teamsheet: Schmeichel, Clegg, Irwin, Berg, Johnsen, Pallister, Nevland, Neville P, McClair, Sheringham, Giggs
Substitute(s): Beckham, Cruyff, Neville G   Scorer(s):   Sheringham

SEASON 1997/98 (continued)

Match # 4441	Wednesday 18/02/98	FA Premiership	at Villa Park	Attendance 39372
Result:	**Aston Villa 0 Manchester United 2**			
Teamsheet:	Schmeichel, Neville G, Irwin, Berg, Butt, Pallister, Beckham, McClair, Cole, Sheringham, Giggs			
Substitute(s):	Neville P Scorer(s): Beckham, Giggs			

Match # 4442	Saturday 21/02/98	FA Premiership	at Old Trafford	Attendance 55170
Result:	**Manchester United 2 Derby County 0**			
Teamsheet:	Schmeichel, Neville G, Irwin, Berg, Butt, Pallister, Neville P, Cole, Sheringham, Giggs			
Substitute(s):	Clegg, Cruyff, McClair Scorer(s): Giggs, Irwin			

Match # 4443	Wednesday 25/02/98	FA Cup 5th Round Replay	at Oakwell	Attendance 18655
Result:	**Barnsley 3 Manchester United 2**			
Teamsheet:	Schmeichel, Neville G, May, Neville P, Clegg, Pallister, Beckham, Nevland, Cole, McClair, Thornley			
Substitute(s):	Irwin, Sheringham, Twiss Scorer(s): Cole, Sheringham			

Match # 4444	Saturday 28/02/98	FA Premiership	at Stamford Bridge	Attendance 35411
Result:	**Chelsea 0 Manchester United 1**			
Teamsheet:	Schmeichel, Neville G, Irwin, Johnsen, Butt, Pallister, Beckham, Neville P, Cole, Sheringham, Scholes			
Substitute(s):	Berg Scorer(s): Neville P			

Match # 4445	Wednesday 04/03/98	Champions League Quarter-Final 1st Leg	at Stade Louis II	Attendance 15000
Result:	**Monaco 0 Manchester United 0**			
Teamsheet:	Schmeichel, Neville G, Irwin, Berg, Johnsen, Butt, Beckham, Neville P, Cole, Sheringham, Scholes			
Substitute(s):	McClair			

Match # 4446	Saturday 07/03/98	FA Premiership	at Hillsborough	Attendance 39427
Result:	**Sheffield Wednesday 2 Manchester United 0**			
Teamsheet:	van der Gouw, Neville G, May, Berg, Butt, Johnsen, Beckham, Neville P, Cole, Sheringham, Solskjaer			
Substitute(s):	Curtis, McClair, Scholes			

Match # 4447	Wednesday 11/03/98	FA Premiership	at Upton Park	Attendance 25892
Result:	**West Ham United 1 Manchester United 1**			
Teamsheet:	Schmeichel, Neville G, Irwin, Berg, Butt, May, Beckham, McClair, Cole, Sheringham, Scholes			
Substitute(s):	Curtis, Solskjaer, Thornley Scorer(s): Scholes			

Match # 4448	Saturday 14/03/98	FA Premiership	at Old Trafford	Attendance 55174
Result:	**Manchester United 0 Arsenal 1**			
Teamsheet:	Schmeichel, Neville G, Irwin, Berg, Curtis, Johnsen, Beckham, Neville P, Cole, Sheringham, Scholes			
Substitute(s):	May, Solskjaer, Thornley			

Match # 4449	Wednesday 18/03/98	Champions League Quarter-Final 2nd Leg	at Old Trafford	Attendance 53683
Result:	**Manchester United 1 Monaco 1 (United lost the tie on away goals rule)**			
Teamsheet:	van der Gouw, Neville G, Irwin, Neville P, Johnsen, Butt, Beckham, Scholes, Cole, Sheringham, Solskjaer			
Substitute(s):	Berg, Clegg Scorer(s): Solskjaer			

Match # 4450	Saturday 28/03/98	FA Premiership	at Old Trafford	Attendance 55306
Result:	**Manchester United 2 Wimbledon 0**			
Teamsheet:	van der Gouw, Neville G, Irwin, Berg, May, Johnsen, Beckham, Neville P, Cole, Scholes, Solskjaer			
Substitute(s):	McClair, Thornley Scorer(s): Johnsen, Scholes			

Match # 4451	Monday 06/04/98	FA Premiership	at Ewood Park	Attendance 30547
Result:	**Blackburn Rovers 1 Manchester United 3**			
Teamsheet:	Schmeichel, Neville G, Irwin, Johnsen, Neville P, Pallister, Beckham, Scholes, Cole, Solskjaer, Giggs			
Substitute(s):	Butt Scorer(s): Beckham, Cole, Scholes			

Match # 4452	Friday 10/04/98	FA Premiership	at Old Trafford	Attendance 55171
Result:	**Manchester United 1 Liverpool 1**			
Teamsheet:	Schmeichel, Neville G, Irwin, Johnsen, Butt, Pallister, Beckham, Neville P, Cole, Scholes, Giggs			
Substitute(s):	May, Sheringham, Thornley Scorer(s): Johnsen			

Match # 4453	Saturday 18/04/98	FA Premiership	at Old Trafford	Attendance 55194
Result:	**Manchester United 1 Newcastle United 1**			
Teamsheet:	Schmeichel, Neville G, Irwin, May, Butt, Pallister, Beckham, Neville P, Cole, Sheringham, Giggs			
Substitute(s):	Scholes, Solskjaer, van der Gouw Scorer(s): Beckham			

Match # 4454	Monday 27/04/98	FA Premiership	at Selhurst Park	Attendance 26180
Result:	**Crystal Palace 0 Manchester United 3**			
Teamsheet:	Schmeichel, Irwin, May, Neville P, Butt, Pallister, Beckham, Scholes, Cole, Sheringham, Giggs			
Substitute(s):	Clegg Scorer(s): Butt, Cole, Scholes			

Match # 4455	Monday 04/05/98	FA Premiership	at Old Trafford	Attendance 55167
Result:	**Manchester United 3 Leeds United 0**			
Teamsheet:	van der Gouw, Neville G, Irwin, May, Butt, Pallister, Beckham, Scholes, Cole, Sheringham, Giggs			
Substitute(s):	Brown, McClair, Neville P Scorer(s): Beckham, Giggs, Irwin			

Match # 4456	Sunday 10/05/98	FA Premiership	at Oakwell	Attendance 18694
Result:	**Barnsley 0 Manchester United 2**			
Teamsheet:	van der Gouw, May, Curtis, Berg, Butt, Clegg, Brown, Mulryne, Cole, Sheringham, Giggs			
Substitute(s):	Higginbotham Scorer(s): Cole, Sheringham			

SEASON 1997/98 SUMMARY

APPEARANCES

PLAYER	LGE	FAC	LC	CL	CS	TOTAL
Beckham	34 (3)	3 (1)	–	8	– (1)	45 (5)
Neville G	34	2 (1)	–	8	–	44 (1)
Schmeichel	32	4	–	7	1	44
Pallister	33	3	–	6	1	43
Cole	31 (2)	3	1	6 (1)	1	42 (3)
Butt	31 (2)	1	–	7	1	40 (2)
Sheringham	28 (3)	2 (1)	–	7	1	38 (4)
Scholes	28 (3)	2	– (1)	6 (1)	1	37 (5)
Giggs	28 (1)	2	–	5	1	36 (1)
Neville P	24 (6)	3	1	5 (2)	1	34 (8)
Irwin	23 (2)	3 (1)	– (1)	6	1	33 (4)
Berg	23 (4)	2	–	5 (2)	–	30 (6)
Johnsen	18 (4)	3	1	5	1	28 (4)
Solskjaer	15 (7)	1 (1)	–	3 (3)	–	19 (11)
Keane	9	–	–	1	1	11
May	7 (2)	1	1	–	–	9 (2)
McClair	2 (11)	3	–	– (3)	–	6 (14)
Poborsky	3 (7)	–	1	2 (2)	–	6 (9)
van der Gouw	4 (1)	–	1	1	–	6 (1)
Curtis	3 (5)	–	1	–	–	4 (5)
Cruyff	3 (2)	– (1)	1	–	– (1)	4 (4)
Thornley	– (5)	2	1	–	–	3 (5)
Clegg	1 (2)	2 (1)	–	– (1)	–	3 (4)
Nevland	– (1)	2 (1)	– (1)	–	–	2 (3)
Mulryne	1	– (1)	1	–	–	2 (1)
Pilkington	2	–	–	–	–	2
Brown	1 (1)	–	–	–	–	1 (1)
Higginbotham	– (1)	–	–	–	–	– (1)
Twiss	–	– (1)	–	–	–	– (1)
Wallwork	– (1)	–	–	–	–	– (1)

GOALSCORERS

PLAYER	LGE	FAC	LC	CL	CS	TOTAL
Cole	15	5	–	5	–	25
Sheringham	9	3	–	2	–	14
Beckham	9	2	–	–	–	11
Scholes	8	–	–	2	–	10
Giggs	8	–	–	1	–	9
Solskjaer	6	2	–	1	–	9
Irwin	2	–	–	2	–	4
Johnsen	2	1	–	–	1	4
Butt	3	–	–	–	–	3
Keane	2	–	–	–	–	2
Poborsky	2	–	–	–	–	2
Berg	1	–	–	1	–	2
Neville P	1	–	–	–	–	1
own goals	5	–	–	1	–	6

RESULTS & ATTENDANCES SUMMARY

		P	W	D	L	F	A	TOTAL	AVGE
League	H	19	13	4	2	42	9	1048125	55164
	A	19	10	4	5	31	17	578751	30461
	TOTAL	38	23	8	7	73	26	1626876	42813
FA Cup	H	2	1	1	0	6	2	109369	54685
	A	2	1	0	1	7	6	53447	26724
	TOTAL	4	2	1	1	13	8	162816	40704
League	H	0	0	0	0	0	0	0	n/a
Cup	A	1	0	0	1	0	2	22173	22173
	TOTAL	1	0	0	1	0	2	22173	22173
Champions	H	4	3	1	0	9	4	213834	53459
League	A	4	2	1	1	6	2	123736	30934
	TOTAL	8	5	2	1	15	6	337570	42196
Charity	H	0	0	0	0	0	0	0	n/a
Shield	A	0	0	0	0	0	0	0	n/a
	N	1	0	1	0	1	1	73636	73636
	TOTAL	1	0	1	0	1	1	73636	73636
Overall	H	25	17	6	2	57	15	1371328	54853
	A	26	13	5	8	44	27	778107	29927
	N	1	0	1	0	1	1	73636	73636
	TOTAL	52	30	12	10	102	43	2223071	42751

FINAL TABLE - FA PREMIERSHIP

		P	W	D	L	F	A	W	D	L	F	A	PTS	GD
				HOME						AWAY				
1	Arsenal	38	15	2	2	43	10	8	7	4	25	23	78	35
2	MANCHESTER UNITED	38	13	4	2	42	9	10	4	5	31	17	77	47
3	Liverpool	38	13	2	4	42	16	5	9	5	26	26	65	26
4	Chelsea	38	13	2	4	37	14	7	1	11	34	29	63	28
5	Leeds United	38	9	5	5	31	21	8	3	8	26	25	59	11
6	Blackburn Rovers	38	11	4	4	40	26	5	6	8	17	26	58	5
7	Aston Villa	38	9	3	7	26	24	8	3	8	23	24	57	1
8	West Ham United	38	13	4	2	40	18	3	4	12	16	39	56	-1
9	Derby County	38	12	3	4	33	18	4	4	11	19	31	55	3
10	Leicester City	38	6	10	3	21	15	7	4	8	30	26	53	10
11	Coventry City	38	8	9	2	26	17	4	7	8	20	27	52	2
12	Southampton	38	10	1	8	28	23	4	5	10	22	32	48	-5
13	Newcastle United	38	8	5	6	22	20	3	6	10	13	24	44	-9
14	Tottenham Hotspur	38	7	8	4	23	22	4	3	12	21	34	44	-12
15	Wimbledon	38	5	6	8	18	25	5	8	6	16	21	44	-12
16	Sheffield Wednesday	38	9	5	5	30	26	3	3	13	22	41	44	-15
17	Everton	38	7	5	7	25	27	2	8	9	16	29	40	-15
18	Bolton Wanderers	38	7	8	4	25	22	2	5	12	16	39	40	-20
19	Barnsley	38	7	4	8	25	35	3	1	15	12	47	35	-45
20	Crystal Palace	38	2	5	12	15	39	6	4	9	22	32	33	-34

SEASON 1998/99

Match # 4457 Sunday 09/08/98   FA Charity Shield   at Wembley   Attendance 67342
Result: **Manchester United 0 Arsenal 3**
Teamsheet: Schmeichel, Neville G, Irwin, Keane, Johnsen, Stam, Beckham, Butt, Cole, Scholes, Giggs
Substitute(s): Berg, Cruyff, Neville P, Sheringham, Solskjaer

Match # 4458 Wednesday 12/08/98   Champions League Qualifying Round 1st Leg   at Old Trafford   Attendance 50906
Result: **Manchester United 2 LKS Lodz 0**
Teamsheet: Schmeichel, Neville G, Irwin, Keane, Johnsen, Stam, Beckham, Butt, Cole, Scholes, Giggs
Substitute(s): Solskjaer   Scorer(s):   Cole, Giggs

Match # 4459 Saturday 15/08/98   FA Premiership   at Old Trafford   Attendance 55052
Result: **Manchester United 2 Leicester City 2**
Teamsheet: Schmeichel, Neville G, Irwin, Keane, Johnsen, Stam, Beckham, Butt, Cole, Scholes, Giggs
Substitute(s): Berg, Sheringham   Scorer(s):   Beckham, Sheringham

Match # 4460 Saturday 22/08/98   FA Premiership   at Upton Park   Attendance 26039
Result: **West Ham United 0 Manchester United 0**
Teamsheet: Schmeichel, Neville G, Irwin, Keane, Johnsen, Berg, Beckham, Butt, Cole, Yorke, Giggs
Substitute(s): Neville P, Sheringham

Match # 4461 Wednesday 26/08/98   Champions League Qualifying Round 2nd Leg   at LKS Stadion   Attendance 8700
Result: **LKS Lodz 0 Manchester United 0**
Teamsheet: Schmeichel, Neville P, Irwin, Keane, Johnsen, Stam, Beckham, Butt, Scholes, Sheringham, Giggs
Substitute(s): Solskjaer

Match # 4462 Wednesday 09/09/98   FA Premiership   at Old Trafford   Attendance 55147
Result: **Manchester United 4 Charlton Athletic 1**
Teamsheet: Schmeichel, Neville P, Irwin, Keane, Johnsen, Stam, Beckham, Scholes, Solskjaer, Yorke, Blomqvist
Substitute(s): Berg, Cole, Sheringham   Scorer(s):   Solskjaer 2, Yorke 2

Match # 4463 Saturday 12/09/98   FA Premiership   at Old Trafford   Attendance 55198
Result: **Manchester United 2 Coventry City 0**
Teamsheet: Schmeichel, Neville G, Neville P, Keane, Johnsen, Stam, Beckham, Scholes, Solskjaer, Yorke, Giggs
Substitute(s): Berg, Blomqvist, Butt   Scorer(s):   Johnsen, Yorke

Match # 4464 Wednesday 16/09/98   Champions League Phase 1 Match 1   at Old Trafford   Attendance 53601
Result: **Manchester United 3 Barcelona 3**
Teamsheet: Schmeichel, Neville G, Irwin, Keane, Berg, Stam, Beckham, Scholes, Solskjaer, Yorke, Giggs
Substitute(s): Blomqvist, Butt, Neville P   Scorer(s):   Beckham, Scholes, Giggs

Match # 4465 Sunday 20/09/98   FA Premiership   at Highbury   Attendance 38142
Result: **Arsenal 3 Manchester United 0**
Teamsheet: Schmeichel, Neville G, Irwin, Keane, Berg, Stam, Beckham, Butt, Blomqvist, Yorke, Giggs

Match # 4466 Thursday 24/09/98   FA Premiership   at Old Trafford   Attendance 55181
Result: **Manchester United 2 Liverpool 0**
Teamsheet: Schmeichel, Neville G, Irwin, Keane, Neville P, Stam, Beckham, Scholes, Solskjaer, Yorke, Giggs
Substitute(s): Butt, Cole   Scorer(s):   Irwin, Scholes

Match # 4467 Wednesday 30/09/98   Champions League Phase 1 Match 2   at Olympic Stadium   Attendance 53000
Result: **Bayern Munich 2 Manchester United 2**
Teamsheet: Schmeichel, Neville G, Irwin, Keane, Neville P, Stam, Beckham, Scholes, Yorke, Sheringham, Blomqvist
Substitute(s): Cruyff   Scorer(s):   Scholes, Yorke

Match # 4468 Saturday 03/10/98   FA Premiership   at The Dell   Attendance 15251
Result: **Southampton 0 Manchester United 3**
Teamsheet: van der Gouw, Neville G, Irwin, Keane, Neville P, Stam, Beckham, Butt, Cole, Yorke, Blomqvist
Substitute(s): Brown, Cruyff, Sheringham   Scorer(s):   Cole, Cruyff, Yorke

Match # 4469 Saturday 17/10/98   FA Premiership   at Old Trafford   Attendance 55265
Result: **Manchester United 5 Wimbledon 1**
Teamsheet: van der Gouw, Neville G, Neville P, Keane, Brown, Stam, Beckham, Blomqvist, Cole, Yorke, Giggs
Substitute(s): Cruyff, Curtis, Scholes   Scorer(s):   Cole 2, Beckham, Giggs, Yorke

Match # 4470 Wednesday 21/10/98   Champions League Phase 1 Match 3   at Parken Stadion   Attendance 40530
Result: **Brondby 2 Manchester United 6**
Teamsheet: Schmeichel, Neville G, Neville P, Keane, Brown, Stam, Blomqvist, Scholes, Cole, Yorke, Giggs
Substitute(s): Cruyff, Solskjaer, Wilson   Scorer(s):   Giggs 2, Cole, Keane, Solskjaer, Yorke

Match # 4471 Saturday 24/10/98   FA Premiership   at Pride Park   Attendance 30867
Result: **Derby County 1 Manchester United 1**
Teamsheet: Schmeichel, Neville G, Neville P, Keane, Brown, Stam, Beckham, Butt, Cole, Yorke, Giggs
Substitute(s): Blomqvist, Cruyff, Scholes   Scorer(s):   Cruyff

Match # 4472 Wednesday 28/10/98   League Cup 3rd Round   at Old Trafford   Attendance 52495
Result: **Manchester United 2 Bury 0**
Teamsheet: van der Gouw, Clegg, Curtis, May, Neville P, Berg, Wilson, Mulryne, Solskjaer, Cruyff, Greening
Substitute(s): Brown, Nevland, Scholes   Scorer(s):   Nevland, Solskjaer

Match # 4473 Saturday 31/10/98   FA Premiership   at Goodison Park   Attendance 40079
Result: **Everton 1 Manchester United 4**
Teamsheet: Schmeichel, Neville G, Neville P, Keane, Brown, Stam, Beckham, Scholes, Cole, Yorke, Blomqvist
Substitute(s): Irwin   Scorer(s):   Blomqvist, Cole, Yorke, own goal

Match # 4474 Wednesday 04/11/98   Champions League Phase 1 Match 4   at Old Trafford   Attendance 53250
Result: **Manchester United 5 Brondby 0**
Teamsheet: Schmeichel, Neville G, Irwin, Keane, Neville P, Stam, Beckham, Scholes, Cole, Yorke, Blomqvist
Substitute(s): Brown, Cruyff, Solskjaer   Scorer(s):   Beckham, Cole, Neville P, Scholes, Yorke

SEASON 1998/99 (continued)

Match # 4475	Sunday 08/11/98	FA Premiership	at Old Trafford	Attendance 55174
Result:	**Manchester United 0 Newcastle United 0**			
Teamsheet:	Schmeichel, Neville G, Irwin, Keane, Brown, Stam, Beckham, Scholes, Cole, Yorke, Blomqvist			
Substitute(s):	Butt, Johnsen, Solskjaer			

Match # 4476	Wednesday 11/11/98	League Cup 4th Round	at Old Trafford	Attendance 37337
Result:	**Manchester United 2 Nottingham Forest 1**			
Teamsheet:	van der Gouw, Clegg, Curtis, May, Berg, Wilson, Greening, Butt, Solskjaer, Cruyff, Mulryne			
Substitute(s):	Wallwork	Scorer(s): Solskjaer 2		

Match # 4477	Saturday 14/11/98	FA Premiership	at Old Trafford	Attendance 55198
Result:	**Manchester United 3 Blackburn Rovers 2**			
Teamsheet:	Schmeichel, Neville G, Curtis, Scholes, Neville P, Stam, Beckham, Butt, Cole, Yorke, Blomqvist			
Substitute(s):	Cruyff, Keane, Solskjaer	Scorer(s): Scholes 2, Yorke		

Match # 4478	Saturday 21/11/98	FA Premiership	at Hillsborough	Attendance 39475
Result:	**Sheffield Wednesday 3 Manchester United 1**			
Teamsheet:	Schmeichel, Neville G, Irwin, Keane, Neville P, Stam, Beckham, Scholes, Cole, Yorke, Blomqvist			
Substitute(s):	Brown, Butt, Solskjaer	Scorer(s): Cole		

Match # 4479	Wednesday 25/11/98	Champions League Phase 1 Match 5	at Estadio Camp Nou	Attendance 67648
Result:	**Barcelona 3 Manchester United 3**			
Teamsheet:	Schmeichel, Neville G, Irwin, Keane, Brown, Stam, Beckham, Scholes, Cole, Yorke, Blomqvist			
Substitute(s):	Butt	Scorer(s): Yorke 2, Cole		

Match # 4480	Sunday 29/11/98	FA Premiership	at Old Trafford	Attendance 55172
Result:	**Manchester United 3 Leeds United 2**			
Teamsheet:	Schmeichel, Neville G, Neville P, Keane, Brown, Stam, Scholes, Butt, Cole, Yorke, Solskjaer			
Substitute(s):	Berg, Giggs, Sheringham	Scorer(s): Butt, Keane, Solskjaer		

Match # 4481	Wednesday 02/12/98	League Cup 5th Round	at White Hart Lane	Attendance 35702
Result:	**Tottenham Hotspur 3 Manchester United 1**			
Teamsheet:	van der Gouw, Clegg, Curtis, Neville P, Johnsen, Berg, Greening, Butt, Solskjaer, Sheringham, Giggs			
Substitute(s):	Beckham, Blomqvist, Notman	Scorer(s): Sheringham		

Match # 4482	Saturday 05/12/98	FA Premiership	at Villa Park	Attendance 39241
Result:	**Aston Villa 1 Manchester United 1**			
Teamsheet:	Schmeichel, Neville G, Irwin, Keane, Brown, Stam, Beckham, Scholes, Cole, Yorke, Blomqvist			
Substitute(s):	Butt, Giggs	Scorer(s): Scholes		

Match # 4483	Wednesday 09/12/98	Champions League Phase 1 Match 6	at Old Trafford	Attendance 54434
Result:	**Manchester United 1 Bayern Munich 1**			
Teamsheet:	Schmeichel, Neville G, Irwin, Keane, Brown, Stam, Beckham, Scholes, Cole, Yorke, Giggs			
Substitute(s):	Butt, Johnsen	Scorer(s): Keane		

Match # 4484	Saturday 12/12/98	FA Premiership	at White Hart Lane	Attendance 36079
Result:	**Tottenham Hotspur 2 Manchester United 2**			
Teamsheet:	Schmeichel, Neville G, Neville P, Keane, Johnsen, Stam, Beckham, Butt, Solskjaer, Sheringham, Giggs			
Substitute(s):	Berg, Blomqvist, Cole	Scorer(s): Solskjaer 2		

Match # 4485	Wednesday 16/12/98	FA Premiership	at Old Trafford	Attendance 55159
Result:	**Manchester United 1 Chelsea 1**			
Teamsheet:	Schmeichel, Neville G, Irwin, Keane, Brown, Stam, Scholes, Butt, Cole, Yorke, Blomqvist			
Substitute(s):	Beckham, Giggs, Sheringham	Scorer(s): Cole		

Match # 4486	Saturday 19/12/98	FA Premiership	at Old Trafford	Attendance 55152
Result:	**Manchester United 2 Middlesbrough 3**			
Teamsheet:	Schmeichel, Neville G, Irwin, Keane, Johnsen, Neville P, Beckham, Butt, Cole, Sheringham, Giggs			
Substitute(s):	Scholes, Solskjaer	Scorer(s): Butt, Scholes		

Match # 4487	Saturday 26/12/98	FA Premiership	at Old Trafford	Attendance 55216
Result:	**Manchester United 3 Nottingham Forest 0**			
Teamsheet:	Schmeichel, Neville P, Irwin, Keane, Johnsen, Berg, Beckham, Butt, Scholes, Sheringham, Giggs			
Substitute(s):	Blomqvist, Greening, Solskjaer	Scorer(s): Johnsen 2, Giggs		

Match # 4488	Tuesday 29/12/98	FA Premiership	at Stamford Bridge	Attendance 34741
Result:	**Chelsea 0 Manchester United 0**			
Teamsheet:	Schmeichel, Neville G, Irwin, Keane, Johnsen, Stam, Beckham, Butt, Cole, Scholes, Giggs			
Substitute(s):	Sheringham			

Match # 4489	Sunday 03/01/99	FA Cup 3rd Round	at Old Trafford	Attendance 52232
Result:	**Manchester United 3 Middlesbrough 1**			
Teamsheet:	Schmeichel, Brown, Irwin, Keane, Berg, Stam, Blomqvist, Butt, Cole, Yorke, Giggs			
Substitute(s):	Neville P, Sheringham, Solskjaer	Scorer(s): Cole, Irwin, Giggs		

Match # 4490	Sunday 10/01/99	FA Premiership	at Old Trafford	Attendance 55180
Result:	**Manchester United 4 West Ham United 1**			
Teamsheet:	van der Gouw, Brown, Irwin, Keane, Berg, Stam, Blomqvist, Butt, Cole, Yorke, Giggs			
Substitute(s):	Cruyff, Johnsen, Solskjaer	Scorer(s): Cole 2, Solskjaer, Yorke		

Match # 4491	Saturday 16/01/99	FA Premiership	at Filbert Street	Attendance 22091
Result:	**Leicester City 2 Manchester United 6**			
Teamsheet:	Schmeichel, Brown, Irwin, Keane, Berg, Stam, Beckham, Blomqvist, Cole, Yorke, Giggs			
Substitute(s):	Neville P	Scorer(s): Yorke 3, Cole 2, Stam		

Match # 4492	Sunday 24/01/99	FA Cup 4th Round	at Old Trafford	Attendance 54591
Result:	**Manchester United 2 Liverpool 1**			
Teamsheet:	Schmeichel, Neville G, Irwin, Keane, Berg, Stam, Beckham, Butt, Cole, Yorke, Giggs			
Substitute(s):	Johnsen, Scholes, Solskjaer	Scorer(s): Solskjaer, Yorke		

SEASON 1998/99 (continued)

Match # 4493 Sunday 31/01/99 FA Premiership at The Valley Attendance 20043
Result: **Charlton Athletic 0 Manchester United 1**
Teamsheet: Schmeichel, Neville G, Irwin, Keane, Berg, Stam, Beckham, Butt, Cole, Yorke, Giggs
Substitute(s): Scholes, Solskjaer Scorer(s): Yorke

Match # 4494 Wednesday 03/02/99 FA Premiership at Old Trafford Attendance 55174
Result: **Manchester United 1 Derby County 0**
Teamsheet: Schmeichel, Neville G, Irwin, Keane, Johnsen, Stam, Scholes, Butt, Solskjaer, Yorke, Giggs
Substitute(s): Blomqvist Scorer(s): Yorke

Match # 4495 Saturday 06/02/99 FA Premiership at City Ground Attendance 30025
Result: **Nottingham Forest 1 Manchester United 8**
Teamsheet: Schmeichel, Neville G, Neville P, Keane, Johnsen, Stam, Beckham, Scholes, Cole, Yorke, Blomqvist
Substitute(s): Butt, Curtis, Solskjaer Scorer(s): Solskjaer 4, Cole 2, Yorke 2

Match # 4496 Sunday 14/02/99 FA Cup 5th Round at Old Trafford Attendance 54798
Result: **Manchester United 1 Fulham 0**
Teamsheet: Schmeichel, Neville G, Irwin, Neville P, Berg, Stam, Beckham, Butt, Cole, Yorke, Solskjaer
Substitute(s): Blomqvist, Greening, Johnsen Scorer(s): Cole

Match # 4497 Wednesday 17/02/99 FA Premiership at Old Trafford Attendance 55171
Result: **Manchester United 1 Arsenal 1**
Teamsheet: Schmeichel, Neville G, Neville P, Keane, Johnsen, Stam, Beckham, Butt, Cole, Yorke, Blomqvist
Substitute(s): Giggs, Scholes Scorer(s): Cole

Match # 4498 Saturday 20/02/99 FA Premiership at Highfield Road Attendance 22596
Result: **Coventry City 0 Manchester United 1**
Teamsheet: Schmeichel, Neville G, Irwin, Keane, Johnsen, Stam, Beckham, Scholes, Cole, Yorke, Giggs
Substitute(s): Berg, Neville P, Solskjaer Scorer(s): Giggs

Match # 4499 Saturday 27/02/99 FA Premiership at Old Trafford Attendance 55316
Result: **Manchester United 2 Southampton 1**
Teamsheet: Schmeichel, Neville G, Neville P, Scholes, Johnsen, Berg, Beckham, Butt, Solskjaer, Yorke, Giggs
Substitute(s): Cole, Irwin, Keane Scorer(s): Keane, Yorke

Match # 4500 Wednesday 03/03/99 Champions League Quarter-Final 1st Leg at Old Trafford Attendance 54430
Result: **Manchester United 2 Internazionale 0**
Teamsheet: Schmeichel, Neville G, Irwin, Keane, Johnsen, Stam, Beckham, Scholes, Cole, Yorke, Giggs
Substitute(s): Berg, Butt Scorer(s): Yorke 2

Match # 4501 Sunday 07/03/99 FA Cup 6th Round at Old Trafford Attendance 54587
Result: **Manchester United 0 Chelsea 0**
Teamsheet: Schmeichel, Neville G, Irwin, Keane, Brown, Berg, Beckham, Scholes, Solskjaer, Neville P, Blomqvist
Substitute(s): Cole, Sheringham, Yorke

Match # 4502 Wednesday 10/03/99 FA Cup 6th Round Replay at Stamford Bridge Attendance 33075
Result: **Chelsea 0 Manchester United 2**
Teamsheet: Schmeichel, Neville G, Irwin, Keane, Berg, Stam, Beckham, Scholes, Cole, Yorke, Giggs
Substitute(s): Blomqvist, Neville P, Solskjaer Scorer(s): Yorke 2

Match # 4503 Saturday 13/03/99 FA Premiership at St James' Park Attendance 36776
Result: **Newcastle United 1 Manchester United 2**
Teamsheet: Schmeichel, Neville G, Irwin, Keane, Berg, Stam, Beckham, Scholes, Cole, Yorke, Giggs
Substitute(s): Neville P, Johnsen, van der Gouw Scorer(s): Cole 2

Match # 4504 Wednesday 17/03/99 Champions League Quarter-Final 2nd Leg at Stadio San Siro Attendance 79528
Result: **Internazionale 1 Manchester United 1**
Teamsheet: Schmeichel, Neville G, Irwin, Keane, Johnsen, Stam, Beckham, Berg, Cole, Yorke, Giggs
Substitute(s): Neville P, Scholes Scorer(s): Scholes

Match # 4505 Sunday 21/03/99 FA Premiership at Old Trafford Attendance 55182
Result: **Manchester United 3 Everton 1**
Teamsheet: Schmeichel, Neville G, Neville P, Berg, Johnsen, Stam, Beckham, Butt, Cole, Yorke, Solskjaer
Substitute(s): Curtis, Greening, Sheringham Scorer(s): Beckham, Neville G, Solskjaer

Match # 4506 Saturday 03/04/99 FA Premiership at Selhurst Park Attendance 26121
Result: **Wimbledon 1 Manchester United 1**
Teamsheet: Schmeichel, Neville G, Irwin, Keane, Johnsen, Berg, Beckham, Scholes, Cole, Yorke, Blomqvist
Substitute(s): Solskjaer Scorer(s): Beckham

Match # 4507 Wednesday 07/04/99 Champions League Semi-Final 1st Leg at Old Trafford Attendance 54487
Result: **Manchester United 1 Juventus 1**
Teamsheet: Schmeichel, Neville G, Irwin, Keane, Berg, Stam, Beckham, Scholes, Cole, Yorke, Giggs
Substitute(s): Johnsen, Sheringham Scorer(s): Giggs

Match # 4508 Sunday 11/04/99 FA Cup Semi-Final at Villa Park Attendance 39217
Result: **Manchester United 0 Arsenal 0**
Teamsheet: Schmeichel, Neville G, Irwin, Keane, Johnsen, Stam, Beckham, Butt, Cole, Yorke, Giggs
Substitute(s): Neville P, Scholes, Solskjaer

Match # 4509 Wednesday 14/04/99 FA Cup Semi-Final Replay at Villa Park Attendance 30223
Result: **Manchester United 2 Arsenal 1**
Teamsheet: Schmeichel, Neville G, Neville P, Keane, Johnsen, Stam, Beckham, Butt, Solskjaer, Sheringham, Blomqvist
Substitute(s): Giggs, Scholes, Yorke Scorer(s): Beckham, Giggs

Match # 4510 Saturday 17/04/99 FA Premiership at Old Trafford Attendance 55270
Result: **Manchester United 3 Sheffield Wednesday 0**
Teamsheet: van der Gouw, Neville G, Neville P, Keane, Brown, Stam, Scholes, Butt, Solskjaer, Sheringham, Blomqvist
Substitute(s): Greening, Irwin, May Scorer(s): Scholes, Sheringham, Solskjaer

SEASON 1998/99 (continued)

Match # 4511	Wednesday 21/04/99 Champions League Semi-Final 2nd Leg at Stadio Delle Alpi
Result:	**Juventus 2 Manchester United 3**
Teamsheet:	Schmeichel, Neville G, Irwin, Keane, Johnsen, Stam, Beckham, Butt, Cole, Yorke, Blomqvist
Substitute(s):	Scholes Scorer(s): Cole, Keane, Yorke

Attendance 64500

Match # 4512	Sunday 25/04/99 FA Premiership at Elland Road
Result:	**Leeds United 1 Manchester United 1**
Teamsheet:	Schmeichel, Neville G, Irwin, May, Brown, Keane, Beckham, Butt, Cole, Yorke, Blomqvist
Substitute(s):	Neville P, Scholes, Sheringham Scorer(s): Cole

Attendance 40255

Match # 4513	Saturday 01/05/99 FA Premiership at Old Trafford
Result:	**Manchester United 2 Aston Villa 1**
Teamsheet:	Schmeichel, Neville G, Irwin, May, Johnsen, Scholes, Beckham, Butt, Yorke, Sheringham, Blomqvist
Substitute(s):	Brown, Neville P Scorer(s): Beckham, own goal

Attendance 55189

Match # 4514	Wednesday 05/05/99 FA Premiership at Anfield
Result:	**Liverpool 2 Manchester United 2**
Teamsheet:	Schmeichel, Neville G, Irwin, Keane, Johnsen, Stam, Beckham, Scholes, Cole, Yorke, Blomqvist
Substitute(s):	Butt, Neville P Scorer(s): Irwin, Yorke

Attendance 44702

Match # 4515	Sunday 09/05/99 FA Premiership at Riverside Stadium
Result:	**Middlesbrough 0 Manchester United 1**
Teamsheet:	Schmeichel, Neville G, Irwin, May, Keane, Johnsen, Stam, Beckham, Scholes, Yorke, Sheringham, Blomqvist
Substitute(s):	Butt, Cole, Neville P Scorer(s): Yorke

Attendance 34665

Match # 4516	Wednesday 12/05/99 FA Premiership at Ewood Park
Result:	**Blackburn Rovers 0 Manchester United 0**
Teamsheet:	Schmeichel, Neville G, Irwin, Neville P, Johnsen, Stam, Beckham, Butt, Cole, Yorke, Giggs
Substitute(s):	May, Scholes, Sheringham

Attendance 30436

Match # 4517	Sunday 16/05/99 FA Premiership at Old Trafford
Result:	**Manchester United 2 Tottenham Hotspur 1**
Teamsheet:	Schmeichel, Neville G, Irwin, May, Johnsen, Keane, Beckham, Scholes, Sheringham, Yorke, Giggs
Substitute(s):	Butt, Cole, Neville P Scorer(s): Beckham, Cole

Attendance 55189

Match # 4518	Saturday 22/05/99 FA Cup Final at Wembley
Result:	**Manchester United 2 Newcastle United 0**
Teamsheet:	Schmeichel, Neville G, Johnsen, May, Neville P, Keane, Beckham, Scholes, Cole, Solskjaer, Giggs
Substitute(s):	Sheringham, Stam, Yorke Scorer(s): Scholes, Sheringham

Attendance 79101

Match # 4519	Wednesday 26/05/99 Champions League Final at Estadio Camp Nou
Result:	**Manchester United 2 Bayern Munich 1**
Teamsheet:	Schmeichel, Neville G, Irwin, Johnsen, Stam, Beckham, Butt, Blomqvist, Cole, Yorke, Giggs
Substitute(s):	Sheringham, Solskjaer Scorer(s): Sheringham, Solskjaer

Attendance 90000

SEASON 1998/99 SUMMARY

APPEARANCES

PLAYER	LGE	FAC	LC	CL	CS	TOTAL
Schmeichel	34	8	–	13	1	56
Neville G	34	7	–	12	1	54
Beckham	33 (1)	7	– (1)	12	1	53 (2)
Keane	33 (2)	7	–	12	1	53 (2)
Stam	30	6 (1)	–	13	1	50 (1)
Yorke	32	5 (3)	–	11	–	48 (3)
Irwin	26 (3)	6	–	12	1	45 (3)
Cole	26 (6)	6 (1)	–	10	1	43 (7)
Scholes	24 (7)	3 (3)	– (1)	10 (2)	1	38 (13)
Giggs	20 (4)	5 (1)	1	9	1	36 (5)
Butt	22 (9)	5	2	4 (4)	1	34 (13)
Johnsen	19 (3)	3 (2)	1	6 (2)	1	30 (7)
Neville P	19 (9)	4 (3)	2	4 (2)	– (1)	29 (15)
Blomqvist	20 (5)	3 (2)	– (1)	6 (1)	–	29 (9)
Berg	10 (6)	5	3	3 (1)	– (1)	21 (8)
Solskjaer	9 (10)	4 (4)	3	1 (5)	– (1)	17 (20)
Brown	11 (3)	2	– (1)	3 (1)	–	16 (5)
Sheringham	7 (10)	1 (3)	1	2 (2)	– (1)	11 (16)
May	4 (2)	1	2	–	–	7 (2)
van der Gouw	4 (1)	–	3	–	–	7 (1)
Curtis	1 (3)	–	3	–	–	4 (3)
Greening	– (3)	– (1)	3	–	–	3 (4)
Clegg	–	–	3	–	–	3
Cruyff	– (5)	–	2	– (3)	– (1)	2 (9)
Wilson	–	–	2	– (1)	–	2 (1)
Mulryne	–	–	2	–	–	2
Nevland	–	–	– (1)	–	–	– (1)
Notman	–	–	– (1)	–	–	– (1)
Wallwork	–	–	– (1)	–	–	– (1)

GOALSCORERS

PLAYER	LGE	FAC	LC	CL	CS	TOTAL
Yorke	18	3	–	8	–	29
Cole	17	2	–	5	–	24
Solskjaer	12	1	3	2	–	18
Scholes	6	1	–	4	–	11
Giggs	3	2	–	5	–	10
Beckham	6	1	–	2	–	9
Keane	2	–	–	3	–	5
Sheringham	2	1	1	1	–	5
Johnsen	3	–	–	–	–	3
Irwin	2	1	–	–	–	3
Butt	2	–	–	–	–	2
Cruyff	2	–	–	–	–	2
Blomqvist	1	–	–	–	–	1
Neville G	1	–	–	–	–	1
Stam	1	–	–	–	–	1
Neville P	–	–	–	1	–	1
Nevland	–	–	1	–	–	1
own goals	2	–	–	–	–	2

RESULTS & ATTENDANCES SUMMARY

		P	W	D	L	F	A	TOTAL	AVGE
League	H	19	14	4	1	45	18	1048585	55189
	A	19	8	9	2	35	19	607624	31980
TOTAL		38	22	13	3	80	37	1656209	43584
FA Cup	H	4	3	1	0	6	2	216208	54052
	A	1	1	0	0	2	0	33075	33075
	N	3	2	1	0	4	1	148541	49514
TOTAL		8	6	2	0	12	3	397824	49728
League	H	2	2	0	0	4	1	89832	44916
Cup	A	1	0	0	1	1	3	35702	35702
TOTAL		3	2	0	1	5	4	125534	41845
Champions	H	6	3	3	0	14	5	321108	53518
League	A	6	2	4	0	15	10	313906	52318
	N	1	1	0	0	2	1	90000	90000
TOTAL		13	6	7	0	31	16	725014	55770
Charity	H	0	0	0	0	0	0	0	n/a
Shield	A	0	0	0	0	0	0	0	n/a
	N	1	0	0	1	0	3	67342	67342
TOTAL		1	0	0	1	0	3	67342	67342
Overall	H	31	22	8	1	69	26	1675733	54056
	A	27	11	13	3	53	32	990307	36678
	N	5	3	1	1	6	5	305883	61177
TOTAL		63	36	22	5	128	63	2971923	47173

FINAL TABLE – FA PREMIERSHIP

		P	W	D	L	F	A	W	D	L	F	A	PTS	GD
				HOME						AWAY				
1	MANCHESTER UNITED	38	14	4	1	45	18	8	9	2	35	19	79	43
2	Arsenal	38	14	5	0	34	5	8	7	4	25	12	78	42
3	Chelsea	38	12	6	1	29	13	8	9	2	28	17	75	27
4	Leeds United	38	12	5	2	32	9	6	8	5	30	25	67	28
5	West Ham United	38	11	3	5	32	26	5	6	8	14	27	57	-7
6	Aston Villa	38	10	3	6	33	28	5	7	7	18	18	55	5
7	Liverpool	38	10	5	4	44	24	5	4	10	24	25	54	19
8	Derby County	38	8	7	4	22	19	5	6	8	18	26	52	-5
9	Middlesbrough	38	7	9	3	25	18	5	6	8	23	36	51	-6
10	Leicester City	38	7	6	6	25	25	5	7	7	15	21	49	-6
11	Tottenham Hotspur	38	7	7	5	28	26	4	7	8	19	24	47	-3
12	Sheffield Wednesday	38	7	5	7	20	15	6	2	11	21	27	46	-1
13	Newcastle United	38	7	6	6	26	25	4	7	8	22	29	46	-6
14	Everton	38	6	8	5	22	12	5	2	12	20	35	43	-5
15	Coventry City	38	8	6	5	26	21	3	3	13	13	30	42	-12
16	Wimbledon	38	7	7	5	22	21	3	5	11	18	42	42	-23
17	Southampton	38	9	4	6	29	26	2	4	13	8	38	41	-27
18	Charlton Athletic	38	4	7	8	20	20	4	5	10	21	36	36	-15
19	Blackburn Rovers	38	6	5	8	21	24	1	9	9	17	28	35	-14
20	Nottingham Forest	38	3	7	9	18	31	4	2	13	17	38	30	-34

SEASON 1999/2000

Match # 4520   Sunday 01/08/99   FA Charity Shield   at Wembley   Attendance 70185
Result: **Manchester United 1   Arsenal 2**
Teamsheet: Bosnich, Neville P, Irwin, Berg, Scholes, Stam, Beckham, Butt, Cole, Yorke, Cruyff
Substitute(s):   May, Sheringham, Solskjaer   Scorer(s):   Yorke

Match # 4521   Sunday 08/08/99   FA Premiership   at Goodison Park   Attendance 39141
Result: **Everton 1   Manchester United 1**
Teamsheet: Bosnich, Neville P, Irwin, Keane, Berg, Stam, Beckham, Scholes, Cole, Yorke, Solskjaer
Substitute(s):   Butt   Scorer(s):   Yorke

Match # 4522   Wednesday 11/08/99   FA Premiership   at Old Trafford   Attendance 54941
Result: **Manchester United 4   Sheffield Wednesday 0**
Teamsheet: Bosnich, Neville P, Irwin, Keane, Berg, Stam, Beckham, Scholes, Cole, Yorke, Giggs
Substitute(s):   Butt, Sheringham, Solskjaer   Scorer(s):   Cole, Scholes, Solskjaer, Yorke

Match # 4523   Saturday 14/08/99   FA Premiership   at Old Trafford   Attendance 55187
Result: **Manchester United 2   Leeds United 0**
Teamsheet: Bosnich, Neville P, Irwin, Keane, Berg, Stam, Beckham, Scholes, Cole, Yorke, Giggs
Substitute(s):   Butt, Sheringham, van der Gouw   Scorer(s):   Yorke 2

Match # 4524   Sunday 22/08/99   FA Premiership   at Highbury   Attendance 38147
Result: **Arsenal 1   Manchester United 2**
Teamsheet: van der Gouw, Neville P, Irwin, Keane, Berg, Stam, Beckham, Scholes, Cole, Yorke, Giggs
Substitute(s):   Butt, Culkin, Sheringham   Scorer(s):   Keane 2

Match # 4525   Wednesday 25/08/99   FA Premiership   at Highfield Road   Attendance 22024
Result: **Coventry City 1   Manchester United 2**
Teamsheet: van der Gouw, Neville P, Irwin, Keane, Berg, Stam, Beckham, Butt, Yorke, Sheringham, Giggs
Substitute(s):   Curtis, Scholes, Solskjaer   Scorer(s):   Scholes, Yorke

Match # 4526   Friday 27/08/99   European Super Cup   at Stade Louis II   Attendance 14461
Result: **Manchester United 0   Lazio 1**
Teamsheet: van der Gouw, Neville G, Neville P, Keane, Berg, Stam, Beckham, Scholes, Cole, Sheringham, Solskjaer
Substitute(s):   Cruyff, Curtis, Greening

Match # 4527   Monday 30/08/99   FA Premiership   at Old Trafford   Attendance 55190
Result: **Manchester United 5   Newcastle United 1**
Teamsheet: van der Gouw, Neville G, Neville P, Scholes, Berg, Stam, Beckham, Butt, Cole, Yorke, Giggs
Substitute(s):   Clegg, Fortune, Sheringham   Scorer(s):   Cole 4, Giggs

Match # 4528   Saturday 11/09/99   FA Premiership   at Anfield   Attendance 44929
Result: **Liverpool 2   Manchester United 3**
Teamsheet: Taibi, Neville P, Silvestre, Scholes, Berg, Stam, Beckham, Butt, Cole, Yorke, Giggs
Substitute(s):   Clegg, Wallwork   Scorer(s):   Cole, own goals 2

Match # 4529   Tuesday 14/09/99   Champions League Phase 1 Match 1   at Old Trafford   Attendance 53250
Result: **Manchester United 0   Croatia Zagreb 0**
Teamsheet: van der Gouw, Clegg, Neville P, Scholes, Berg, Stam, Beckham, Wilson, Cole, Yorke, Giggs
Substitute(s):   Fortune, Sheringham

Match # 4530   Saturday 18/09/99   FA Premiership   at Old Trafford   Attendance 55189
Result: **Manchester United 1   Wimbledon 1**
Teamsheet: Taibi, Silvestre, Irwin, Scholes, Berg, Stam, Neville P, Solskjaer, Yorke, Sheringham, Giggs
Substitute(s):   Cole, Cruyff   Scorer(s):   Cruyff

Match # 4531   Wednesday 22/09/99   Champions League Phase 1 Match 2   at Schwarzenegger Stadium   Attendance 16480
Result: **Sturm Graz 0   Manchester United 3**
Teamsheet: van der Gouw, Neville P, Irwin, Keane, Berg, Stam, Beckham, Scholes, Cole, Yorke, Cruyff
Substitute(s):   Sheringham, Solskjaer, Wilson   Scorer(s):   Cole, Keane, Yorke

Match # 4532   Saturday 25/09/99   FA Premiership   at Old Trafford   Attendance 55249
Result: **Manchester United 3   Southampton 3**
Teamsheet: Taibi, Silvestre, Irwin, Scholes, Berg, Stam, Beckham, Butt, Yorke, Sheringham, Solskjaer
Scorer(s):   Yorke 2, Sheringham

Match # 4533   Wednesday 29/09/99   Champions League Phase 1 Match 3   at Old Trafford   Attendance 53993
Result: **Manchester United 2   Olympique Marseille 1**
Teamsheet: van der Gouw, Neville P, Irwin, Scholes, Berg, Stam, Beckham, Butt, Cole, Yorke, Solskjaer
Substitute(s):   Clegg, Fortune, Sheringham   Scorer(s):   Cole, Scholes

Match # 4534   Sunday 03/10/99   FA Premiership   at Stamford Bridge   Attendance 34909
Result: **Chelsea 5   Manchester United 0**
Teamsheet: Taibi, Silvestre, Irwin, Scholes, Berg, Stam, Beckham, Butt, Cole, Yorke, Neville P
Substitute(s):   Sheringham, Solskjaer, Wilson

Match # 4535   Wednesday 13/10/99   League Cup 3rd Round   at Villa Park   Attendance 33815
Result: **Aston Villa 3   Manchester United 0**
Teamsheet: Bosnich, Clegg, Higginbotham, Wallwork, O'Shea, Curtis, Cruyff, Twiss, Solskjaer, Greening, Chadwick
Substitute(s):   Healy, Wellens

Match # 4536   Saturday 16/10/99   FA Premiership   at Old Trafford   Attendance 55188
Result: **Manchester United 4   Watford 1**
Teamsheet: Bosnich, Neville P, Irwin, Scholes, Silvestre, Stam, Beckham, Butt, Cole, Yorke, Giggs
Substitute(s):   Greening, Keane, Solskjaer   Scorer(s):   Cole 2, Irwin, Yorke

Match # 4537   Tuesday 19/10/99   Champions League Phase 1 Match 4   at Stade Velodrome   Attendance 56732
Result: **Olympique Marseille 1   Manchester United 0**
Teamsheet: Bosnich, Neville P, Irwin, Keane, Berg, Stam, Beckham, Scholes, Cole, Yorke, Giggs
Substitute(s):   Solskjaer

SEASON 1999/2000 (continued)

Match # 4538 Saturday 23/10/99   FA Premiership   at White Hart Lane   Attendance 36072
Result: **Tottenham Hotspur 3 Manchester United 1**
Teamsheet: Bosnich, Neville P, Irwin, Keane, Silvestre, Stam, Beckham, Scholes, Cole, Yorke, Giggs
Substitute(s): Greening, Solskjaer   Scorer(s): Giggs

Match # 4539 Wednesday 27/10/99   Champions League Phase 1 Match 5   at Maksimir Stadium   Attendance 27500
Result: **Croatia Zagreb 1 Manchester United 2**
Teamsheet: Bosnich, Neville P, Irwin, Keane, Berg, Stam, Beckham, Scholes, Cole, Yorke, Giggs
Substitute(s): Cruyff, Greening, Solskjaer   Scorer(s): Beckham, Keane

Match # 4540 Saturday 30/10/99   FA Premiership   at Old Trafford   Attendance 55211
Result: **Manchester United 3 Aston Villa 0**
Teamsheet: Bosnich, Neville P, Irwin, Keane, Silvestre, Stam, Beckham, Scholes, Cole, Yorke, Giggs
Substitute(s): Cruyff, Solskjaer, Wilson   Scorer(s): Cole, Keane, Scholes

Match # 4541 Tuesday 02/11/99   Champions League Phase 1 Match 6   at Old Trafford   Attendance 53745
Result: **Manchester United 2 Sturm Graz 1**
Teamsheet: Bosnich, Neville G, Irwin, May, Berg, Keane, Greening, Wilson, Cole, Solskjaer, Giggs
Substitute(s): Cruyff, Higginbotham, Neville P   Scorer(s): Keane, Solskjaer

Match # 4542 Saturday 06/11/99   FA Premiership   at Old Trafford   Attendance 55191
Result: **Manchester United 2 Leicester City 0**
Teamsheet: Bosnich, Neville P, Higginbotham, Keane, Silvestre, Stam, Scholes, Solskjaer, Cole, Yorke, Giggs
Substitute(s): Berg, May   Scorer(s): Cole 2

Match # 4543 Saturday 20/11/99   FA Premiership   at Pride Park   Attendance 33370
Result: **Derby County 1 Manchester United 2**
Teamsheet: van der Gouw, Neville G, Neville P, Keane, Silvestre, Stam, Beckham, Butt, Cole, Yorke, Giggs
Substitute(s): Berg, Solskjaer   Scorer(s): Butt, Cole

Match # 4544 Tuesday 23/11/99   Champions League Phase 2 Match 1   at Artemio Franchi   Attendance 36002
Result: **Fiorentina 2 Manchester United 0**
Teamsheet: Bosnich, Neville G, Irwin, Keane, Berg, Stam, Beckham, Scholes, Cole, Yorke, Giggs
Substitute(s): Neville P, Sheringham, Solskjaer

Match # 4545 Tuesday 30/11/99   Inter-Continental Cup Final   at Olympic Stadium, Tokyo   Attendance 53372
Result: **Manchester United 1 Palmeiras 0**
Teamsheet: Bosnich, Neville G, Irwin, Keane, Silvestre, Stam, Beckham, Butt, Solskjaer, Scholes, Giggs
Substitute(s): Sheringham, Yorke   Scorer(s): Keane

Match # 4546 Saturday 04/12/99   FA Premiership   at Old Trafford   Attendance 55193
Result: **Manchester United 5 Everton 1**
Teamsheet: Bosnich, Neville G, Irwin, Keane, Silvestre, Stam, Scholes, Butt, Solskjaer, Sheringham, Giggs
Substitute(s): Cole, Neville P, van der Gouw   Scorer(s): Solskjaer 4, Irwin

Match # 4547 Wednesday 08/12/99   Champions League Phase 2 Match 2   at Old Trafford   Attendance 54606
Result: **Manchester United 3 Valencia 0**
Teamsheet: van der Gouw, Neville G, Irwin, Keane, Neville P, Stam, Beckham, Scholes, Cole, Solskjaer, Giggs
Substitute(s): Butt, Yorke   Scorer(s): Keane, Scholes, Solskjaer

Match # 4548 Saturday 18/12/99   FA Premiership   at Upton Park   Attendance 26037
Result: **West Ham United 2 Manchester United 4**
Teamsheet: van der Gouw, Neville G, Irwin, Keane, Silvestre, Stam, Beckham, Scholes, Yorke, Sheringham, Giggs
Substitute(s): Butt, Neville P   Scorer(s): Giggs 2, Yorke 2

Match # 4549 Sunday 26/12/99   FA Premiership   at Old Trafford   Attendance 55188
Result: **Manchester United 4 Bradford City 0**
Teamsheet: Bosnich, Neville G, Neville P, Keane, Silvestre, Stam, Scholes, Butt, Solskjaer, Sheringham, Fortune
Substitute(s): Cole, Wallwork, Yorke   Scorer(s): Cole, Fortune, Keane, Yorke

Match # 4550 Tuesday 28/12/99   FA Premiership   at Stadium of Light   Attendance 42026
Result: **Sunderland 2 Manchester United 2**
Teamsheet: Bosnich, Neville G, Irwin, Keane, Silvestre, Stam, Beckham, Butt, Cole, Yorke, Giggs
Substitute(s): Neville P, Sheringham, Solskjaer   Scorer(s): Butt, Keane

Match # 4551 Thursday 06/01/00   Club World Championship   at Maracana Stadium   Attendance 50000
Result: **Manchester United 1 Rayos del Necaxa 1**
Teamsheet: Bosnich, Neville G, Irwin, Keane, Silvestre, Stam, Beckham, Butt, Cole, Yorke, Giggs
Substitute(s): Neville P, Sheringham, Solskjaer   Scorer(s): Yorke

Match # 4552 Saturday 08/01/00   Club World Championship   at Maracana Stadium   Attendance 73000
Result: **Manchester United 1 Vasco da Gama 3**
Teamsheet: Bosnich, Neville G, Irwin, Keane, Silvestre, Stam, Neville P, Butt, Solskjaer, Yorke, Giggs
Substitute(s): Cruyff, Fortune, Sheringham   Scorer(s): Butt

Match # 4553 Tuesday 11/01/00   Club World Championship   at Maracana Stadium   Attendance 25000
Result: **Manchester United 2 South Melbourne 0**
Teamsheet: van der Gouw, Neville P, Wallwork, Higginbotham, Wilson, Berg, Greening, Cruyff, Cole, Solskjaer, Fortune
Substitute(s): Beckham, Rachubka   Scorer(s): Fortune 2

Match # 4554 Monday 24/01/00   FA Premiership   at Old Trafford   Attendance 58293
Result: **Manchester United 1 Arsenal 1**
Teamsheet: Bosnich, Neville G, Irwin, Keane, Silvestre, Stam, Beckham, Butt, Cole, Yorke, Giggs
Substitute(s): Neville P, Sheringham   Scorer(s): Sheringham

Match # 4555 Saturday 29/01/00   FA Premiership   at Old Trafford   Attendance 61267
Result: **Manchester United 1 Middlesbrough 0**
Teamsheet: Bosnich, Neville G, Irwin, Keane, Silvestre, Stam, Beckham, Butt, Yorke, Sheringham, Giggs
Substitute(s): Cole, Scholes, Solskjaer   Scorer(s): Beckham

SEASON 1999/2000 (continued)

Match # 4556 Wednesday 02/02/00   FA Premiership   at Hillsborough   Attendance 39640
Result: **Sheffield Wednesday 0 Manchester United 1**
Teamsheet: Bosnich, Neville G, Irwin, Keane, Silvestre, Stam, Beckham, Butt, Yorke, Sheringham, Giggs
Substitute(s): Scholes   Scorer(s):   Sheringham

Match # 4557 Saturday 05/02/00   FA Premiership   at Old Trafford   Attendance 61380
Result: **Manchester United 3 Coventry City 2**
Teamsheet: Bosnich, Neville G, Neville P, Keane, Silvestre, Stam, Beckham, Scholes, Cole, Sheringham, Solskjaer
Substitute(s): Butt, Cruyff   Scorer(s):   Cole 2, Scholes

Match # 4558 Saturday 12/02/00   FA Premiership   at St James' Park   Attendance 36470
Result: **Newcastle United 3 Manchester United 0**
Teamsheet: Bosnich, Neville G, Irwin, Keane, Silvestre, Stam, Beckham, Scholes, Cole, Sheringham, Giggs
Substitute(s): Butt, Solskjaer

Match # 4559 Sunday 20/02/00   FA Premiership   at Elland Road   Attendance 40160
Result: **Leeds United 0 Manchester United 1**
Teamsheet: Bosnich, Neville G, Irwin, Keane, Silvestre, Stam, Scholes, Butt, Cole, Yorke, Giggs
Substitute(s): Sheringham   Scorer(s):   Cole

Match # 4560 Saturday 26/02/00   FA Premiership   at Selhurst Park   Attendance 26129
Result: **Wimbledon 2 Manchester United 2**
Teamsheet: Bosnich, Neville G, Neville P, Cruyff, Silvestre, Stam, Beckham, Butt, Cole, Sheringham, Giggs
Substitute(s): Berg, Solskjaer   Scorer(s):   Cole, Cruyff

Match # 4561 Wednesday 01/03/00   Champions League Phase 2 Match 3   at Old Trafford   Attendance 59786
Result: **Manchester United 2 Girondins Bordeaux 0**
Teamsheet: van der Gouw, Neville G, Irwin, Keane, Silvestre, Stam, Beckham, Butt, Cole, Sheringham, Giggs
Substitute(s): Fortune, Neville P, Solskjaer Scorer(s):   Giggs, Sheringham

Match # 4562 Saturday 04/03/00   FA Premiership   at Old Trafford   Attendance 61592
Result: **Manchester United 1 Liverpool 1**
Teamsheet: van der Gouw, Neville G, Irwin, Keane, Silvestre, Stam, Beckham, Butt, Solskjaer, Yorke, Giggs
Substitute(s): Cole, Sheringham   Scorer(s):   Solskjaer

Match # 4563 Tuesday 07/03/00   Champions League Phase 2 Match 4   at Stade Lescure   Attendance 30130
Result: **Girondins Bordeaux 1 Manchester United 2**
Teamsheet: van der Gouw, Neville G, Irwin, Keane, Silvestre, Stam, Beckham, Butt, Cole, Sheringham, Giggs
Substitute(s): Berg, Solskjaer, Yorke   Scorer(s):   Keane, Solskjaer

Match # 4564 Saturday 11/03/00   FA Premiership   at Old Trafford   Attendance 61619
Result: **Manchester United 3 Derby County 1**
Teamsheet: Bosnich, Neville G, Neville P, Keane, Silvestre, Berg, Beckham, Scholes, Solskjaer, Yorke, Fortune
Substitute(s): Butt, Wallwork   Scorer(s):   Yorke 3

Match # 4565 Wednesday 15/03/00   Champions League Phase 2 Match 5   at Old Trafford   Attendance 59926
Result: **Manchester United 3 Fiorentina 1**
Teamsheet: Bosnich, Neville G, Irwin, Keane, Berg, Stam, Beckham, Scholes, Cole, Yorke, Giggs
Scorer(s): Cole, Keane, Yorke

Match # 4566 Saturday 18/03/00   FA Premiership   at Filbert Street   Attendance 22170
Result: **Leicester City 0 Manchester United 2**
Teamsheet: Bosnich, Neville G, Irwin, Keane, Berg, Stam, Beckham, Scholes, Cole, Yorke, Giggs
Substitute(s): Butt, Sheringham   Scorer(s):   Beckham, Yorke

Match # 4567 Tuesday 21/03/00   Champions League Phase 2 Match 6   at Mestalla   Attendance 40419
Result: **Valencia 0 Manchester United 0**
Teamsheet: Bosnich, Neville G, Irwin, Keane, Berg, Stam, Scholes, Butt, Solskjaer, Sheringham, Fortune
Substitute(s): Cruyff

Match # 4568 Saturday 25/03/00   FA Premiership   at Valley Parade   Attendance 18276
Result: **Bradford City 0 Manchester United 4**
Teamsheet: Bosnich, Neville G, Neville P, Keane, Berg, Silvestre, Beckham, Scholes, Cole, Yorke, Giggs
Substitute(s): Solskjaer, Wallwork   Scorer(s):   Yorke 2, Beckham, Scholes

Match # 4569 Saturday 01/04/00   FA Premiership   at Old Trafford   Attendance 61611
Result: **Manchester United 7 West Ham United 1**
Teamsheet: Bosnich, Neville G, Irwin, Keane, Silvestre, Stam, Beckham, Scholes, Cole, Yorke, Fortune
Substitute(s): Butt, Sheringham, Solskjaer   Scorer(s):   Scholes 3, Beckham, Cole, Irwin, Solskjaer

Match # 4570 Tuesday 04/04/00   Champions League Quarter-Final 1st Leg   at Bernabeu Stadium   Attendance 64119
Result: **Real Madrid 0 Manchester United 0**
Teamsheet: Bosnich, Neville G, Irwin, Keane, Berg, Stam, Beckham, Scholes, Cole, Yorke, Giggs
Substitute(s): Butt, Sheringham, Silvestre

Match # 4571 Monday 10/04/00   FA Premiership   at Riverside Stadium   Attendance 34775
Result: **Middlesbrough 3 Manchester United 4**
Teamsheet: Bosnich, Neville G, Irwin, Keane, Berg, Stam, Beckham, Scholes, Cole, Yorke, Giggs
Substitute(s): Butt, Fortune, Silvestre   Scorer(s):   Cole, Giggs, Fortune, Scholes

Match # 4572 Saturday 15/04/00   FA Premiership   at Old Trafford   Attendance 61612
Result: **Manchester United 4 Sunderland 0**
Teamsheet: Bosnich, Neville G, Neville P, Keane, Silvestre, Stam, Scholes, Butt, Solskjaer, Sheringham, Fortune
Substitute(s): Beckham, Berg, van der Gouw   Scorer(s):   Solskjaer 2, Berg, Butt

Match # 4573 Wednesday 19/04/00   Champions League Quarter-Final 2nd Leg   at Old Trafford   Attendance 59178
Result: **Manchester United 2 Real Madrid 3**
Teamsheet: van der Gouw, Neville G, Irwin, Keane, Berg, Stam, Beckham, Scholes, Cole, Yorke, Giggs
Substitute(s): Sheringham, Silvestre, Solskjaer   Scorer(s):   Beckham, Scholes

SEASON 1999/2000 (continued)

Match # 4574	Saturday 22/04/00 FA Premiership		at The Dell	Attendance 15245
Result:	**Southampton 1 Manchester United 3**			
Teamsheet:	van der Gouw, Neville G, Neville P, Keane, Silvestre, Stam, Beckham, Butt, Cole, Solskjaer, Giggs			
Substitute(s):	Johnsen, Sheringham, Yorke	Scorer(s): Beckham, Solskjaer, own goal		

Match # 4575	Monday 24/04/00 FA Premiership		at Old Trafford	Attendance 61593
Result:	**Manchester United 3 Chelsea 2**			
Teamsheet:	van der Gouw, Neville G, Neville P, Keane, Johnsen, Silvestre, Beckham, Butt, Solskjaer, Yorke, Giggs			
Substitute(s):	Berg, Cruyff, Scholes	Scorer(s): Yorke 2, Solskjaer		

Match # 4576	Saturday 29/04/00 FA Premiership		at Vicarage Road	Attendance 20250
Result:	**Watford 2 Manchester United 3**			
Teamsheet:	van der Gouw, Neville P, Silvestre, Wilson, Johnsen, Berg, Greening, Butt, Solskjaer, Sheringham, Giggs			
Substitute(s):	Cruyff, Higginbotham, Yorke	Scorer(s): Cruyff, Giggs, Yorke		

Match # 4577	Saturday 06/05/00 FA Premiership		at Old Trafford	Attendance 61629
Result:	**Manchester United 3 Tottenham Hotspur 1**			
Teamsheet:	van der Gouw, Neville P, Irwin, Scholes, Silvestre, Stam, Beckham, Butt, Solskjaer, Sheringham, Giggs			
Substitute(s):	Berg, Cruyff, Greening	Scorer(s): Beckham, Sheringham, Solskjaer		

Match # 4578	Sunday 14/05/00 FA Premiership		at Villa Park	Attendance 39217
Result:	**Aston Villa 0 Manchester United 1**			
Teamsheet:	van der Gouw, Higginbotham, Irwin, Neville P, Silvestre, Berg, Yorke, Scholes, Solskjaer, Sheringham, Giggs			
Substitute(s):	Cruyff, Wallwork	Scorer(s): Sheringham		

SEASON 1999/2000 SUMMARY

APPEARANCES

PLAYER	LGE	LC	CL	CS	ESC	ICC	CWC	TOTAL
Stam	33	–	13	1	1	1	2	51
Beckham	30 (1)	–	12	1	1	1	1 (1)	46 (2)
Keane	28 (1)	–	12	–	1	1	2	44 (1)
Giggs	30	–	11	–	–	1	2	44
Irwin	25	–	13	1	–	1	2	42
Yorke	29 (3)	–	9 (2)	1	–	– (1)	2	41 (6)
Scholes	27 (4)	–	11	1	1	1	–	41 (4)
Cole	23 (5)	–	13	1	1	–	2	40 (5)
Neville P	25 (4)	–	6 (3)	1	1	–	2 (1)	35 (8)
Silvestre	30 (1)	–	2 (2)	–	–	1	2	35 (3)
Bosnich	23	1	7	1	–	1	2	35
Neville G	22	–	9	–	1	1	2	35
Berg	16 (6)	–	11 (1)	1	1	–	1	30 (7)
Butt	21 (11)	–	4 (2)	1	–	1	2	29 (13)
Solskjaer	15 (13)	1	4 (7)	– (1)	1	1	2 (1)	24 (22)
Sheringham	15 (12)	–	3 (6)	– (1)	1	– (1)	– (2)	19 (22)
van der Gouw	11 (3)	–	7	–	1	–	1	20 (3)
Fortune	4 (2)	–	1 (3)	–	–	–	1 (1)	6 (6)
Cruyff	1 (7)	–	1 (3)	1	– (1)	–	1 (1)	5 (12)
Greening	1 (3)	1	1 (1)	–	– (1)	–	1	4 (5)
Wilson	1 (2)	–	2 (1)	–	–	–	1	4 (3)
Higginbotham	2 (1)	1	– (1)	–	–	–	1	4 (2)
Taibi	4	–	–	–	–	–	–	4
Wallwork	– (5)	1	–	–	–	–	1	2 (5)
Clegg	– (2)	1	1 (1)	–	–	–	–	2 (3)
Johnsen	2 (1)	–	–	–	–	–	–	2 (1)
Curtis	– (1)	1	–	–	– (1)	–	–	1 (2)
May	– (1)	–	1	– (1)	–	–	–	1 (2)
Chadwick	–	1	–	–	–	–	–	1
O'Shea	–	1	–	–	–	–	–	1
Twiss	–	1	–	–	–	–	–	1
Culkin	– (1)	–	–	–	–	–	–	– (1)
Healy	–	– (1)	–	–	–	–	–	– (1)
Rachubka	–	–	–	–	–	– (1)	–	– (1)
Wellens	–	– (1)	–	–	–	–	–	– (1)

GOALSCORERS

PLAYER	LGE	LC	CL	CS	ESC	ICC	CWC	TOTAL
Yorke	20	–	2	1	–	–	1	24
Cole	19	–	3	–	–	–	–	22
Solskjaer	12	–	3	–	–	–	–	15
Scholes	9	–	3	–	–	–	–	12
Keane	5	–	6	–	–	1	–	12
Beckham	6	–	2	–	–	–	–	8
Giggs	6	–	1	–	–	–	–	7
Sheringham	5	–	1	–	–	–	–	6
Butt	3	–	–	–	–	–	1	4
Fortune	2	–	–	–	–	–	2	4
Cruyff	3	–	–	–	–	–	–	3
Irwin	3	–	–	–	–	–	–	3
Berg	1	–	–	–	–	–	–	1
own goals	3	–	–	–	–	–	–	3

RESULTS & ATTENDANCES SUMMARY

		P	W	D	L	F	A	TOTAL	AVGE
League	H	19	15	4	0	59	16	1102323	58017
	A	19	13	3	3	38	29	608987	32052
	TOTAL	38	28	7	3	97	45	1711310	45034
FA Cup	Did not compete								
League	H	0	0	0	0	0	0	0	n/a
Cup	A	1	0	0	1	0	3	33815	33815
	TOTAL	1	0	0	1	0	3	33815	33815
Champions	H	7	5	1	1	14	6	394484	56355
League	A	7	3	2	2	7	5	271382	38769
	TOTAL	14	8	3	3	21	11	665866	47562
Charity	H	0	0	0	0	0	0	0	n/a
Shield	A	0	0	0	0	0	0	0	n/a
	N	1	0	0	1	1	2	70185	70185
	TOTAL	1	0	0	1	1	2	70185	70185
European	H	0	0	0	0	0	0	0	n/a
Super Cup	A	0	0	0	0	0	0	0	n/a
	N	1	0	0	1	0	1	14461	14461
	TOTAL	1	0	0	1	0	1	14461	14461
ICC	H	0	0	0	0	0	0	0	n/a
	A	0	0	0	0	0	0	0	n/a
	N	1	1	0	0	1	0	53372	53372
	TOTAL	1	1	0	0	1	0	53372	53372
Club WC	H	0	0	0	0	0	0	0	n/a
	A	0	0	0	0	0	0	0	n/a
	N	3	1	1	1	4	4	148000	49333
	TOTAL	3	1	1	1	4	4	148000	49333
Overall	H	26	20	5	1	73	22	1496807	57570
	A	27	16	5	6	45	37	914184	33859
	N	6	2	1	3	6	7	286018	47670
	TOTAL	59	38	11	10	124	66	2697009	45712

FINAL TABLE - FA PREMIERSHIP

		P	HOME					AWAY					PTS	GD
			W	D	L	F	A	W	D	L	F	A		
1	MANCHESTER UNITED	38	15	4	0	59	16	13	3	3	38	29	91	52
2	Arsenal	38	14	3	2	42	17	8	4	7	31	26	73	30
3	Leeds United	38	12	2	5	29	18	9	4	6	29	25	69	15
4	Liverpool	38	11	4	4	28	13	8	6	5	23	17	67	21
5	Chelsea	38	12	5	2	35	12	6	6	7	18	22	65	19
6	Aston Villa	38	8	8	3	23	12	7	5	7	23	23	58	11
7	Sunderland	38	10	6	3	28	17	6	4	9	29	39	58	1
8	Leicester City	38	10	3	6	31	24	6	4	9	24	31	55	0
9	West Ham United	38	11	5	3	32	23	4	5	10	20	30	55	-1
10	Tottenham Hotspur	38	10	3	6	40	26	5	5	9	17	23	53	8
11	Newcastle United	38	10	5	4	42	20	4	5	10	21	34	52	9
12	Middlesbrough	38	8	5	6	23	26	6	5	8	23	26	52	-6
13	Everton	38	7	9	3	36	21	5	5	9	23	28	50	10
14	Coventry City	38	12	1	6	38	22	0	7	12	9	32	44	-7
15	Southampton	38	8	4	7	26	22	4	4	11	19	40	44	-17
16	Derby County	38	6	3	10	22	25	3	8	8	22	32	38	-13
17	Bradford City	38	6	8	5	26	29	3	1	15	12	39	36	-30
18	Wimbledon	38	6	7	6	30	28	1	5	13	16	46	33	-28
19	Sheffield Wednesday	38	6	3	10	21	23	2	4	13	17	47	31	-32
20	Watford	38	5	4	10	24	31	1	2	16	11	46	24	-42

SEASON 2000/01

Match # 4579 Sunday 13/08/00   FA Charity Shield   at Wembley   Attendance 65148
Result: **Manchester United 0 Chelsea 2**
Teamsheet: Barthez, Neville G, Irwin, Keane, Johnsen, Silvestre, Beckham, Scholes, Solskjaer, Sheringham, Giggs
Substitute(s): Cole, Fortune, Stam, Yorke

Match # 4580 Sunday 20/08/00   FA Premiership   at Old Trafford   Attendance 67477
Result: **Manchester United 2 Newcastle United 0**
Teamsheet: Barthez, Neville G, Neville P, Keane, Johnsen, Stam, Beckham, Scholes, Cole, Sheringham, Giggs
Substitute(s): Solskjaer, Wallwork, Yorke   Scorer(s): Cole, Johnsen

Match # 4581 Tuesday 22/08/00   FA Premiership   at Portman Road   Attendance 22007
Result: **Ipswich Town 1 Manchester United 1**
Teamsheet: Barthez, Neville G, Neville P, Keane, Wallwork, Stam, Beckham, Scholes, Solskjaer, Yorke, Giggs
Substitute(s): Cole, Sheringham, Silvestre   Scorer(s): Beckham

Match # 4582 Saturday 26/08/00   FA Premiership   at Upton Park   Attendance 25998
Result: **West Ham United 2 Manchester United 2**
Teamsheet: Barthez, Neville G, Neville P, Keane, Silvestre, Stam, Beckham, Scholes, Cole, Sheringham, Giggs
Substitute(s): Berg   Scorer(s): Beckham, Cole

Match # 4583 Tuesday 05/09/00   FA Premiership   at Old Trafford   Attendance 67447
Result: **Manchester United 6 Bradford City 0**
Teamsheet: Barthez, Neville G, Silvestre, Greening, Johnsen, Wallwork, Beckham, Butt, Cole, Sheringham, Fortune
Substitute(s): Neville P, Scholes, Solskjaer   Scorer(s): Fortune 2, Sheringham 2, Beckham, Cole

Match # 4584 Saturday 09/09/00   FA Premiership   at Old Trafford   Attendance 67503
Result: **Manchester United 3 Sunderland 0**
Teamsheet: Barthez, Neville G, Silvestre, Scholes, Johnsen, Stam, Beckham, Butt, Cole, Sheringham, Giggs
Substitute(s): Irwin, Solskjaer   Scorer(s): Scholes 2, Sheringham

Match # 4585 Wednesday 13/09/00   Champions League Phase 1 Match 1   at Old Trafford   Attendance 62749
Result: **Manchester United 5 Anderlecht 1**
Teamsheet: Barthez, Neville G, Irwin, Keane, Johnsen, Silvestre, Beckham, Scholes, Cole, Sheringham, Giggs
Substitute(s): Neville P, Solskjaer, Yorke   Scorer(s): Cole 3, Irwin, Sheringham

Match # 4586 Saturday 16/09/00   FA Premiership   at Goodison Park   Attendance 38541
Result: **Everton 1 Manchester United 3**
Teamsheet: Barthez, Neville G, Irwin, Scholes, Brown, Silvestre, Beckham, Butt, Solskjaer, Sheringham, Giggs
Substitute(s): Neville P, van der Gouw, Yorke   Scorer(s): Butt, Giggs, Solskjaer

Match # 4587 Tuesday 19/09/00   Champions League Phase 1 Match 2   at Republican Stadium   Attendance 65000
Result: **Dynamo Kiev 0 Manchester United 0**
Teamsheet: van der Gouw, Neville G, Irwin, Keane, Johnsen, Silvestre, Beckham, Butt, Cole, Yorke, Giggs
Substitute(s): Sheringham, Solskjaer

Match # 4588 Saturday 23/09/00   FA Premiership   at Old Trafford   Attendance 67568
Result: **Manchester United 3 Chelsea 3**
Teamsheet: van der Gouw, Neville G, Irwin, Keane, Johnsen, Silvestre, Beckham, Scholes, Cole, Sheringham, Giggs
Substitute(s): Brown, Butt, Solskjaer   Scorer(s): Beckham, Scholes, Sheringham

Match # 4589 Tuesday 26/09/00   Champions League Phase 1 Match 3   at Philipstadion   Attendance 30500
Result: **PSV Eindhoven 3 Manchester United 1**
Teamsheet: van der Gouw, Neville G, Neville P, Keane, Brown, Silvestre, Greening, Butt, Solskjaer, Yorke, Scholes
Substitute(s): Beckham, Giggs, Wallwork   Scorer(s): Scholes

Match # 4590 Sunday 01/10/00   FA Premiership   at Highbury   Attendance 38146
Result: **Arsenal 1 Manchester United 0**
Teamsheet: Barthez, Neville G, Irwin, Keane, Johnsen, Silvestre, Beckham, Scholes, Cole, Sheringham, Giggs
Substitute(s): Solskjaer, Yorke

Match # 4591 Saturday 14/10/00   FA Premiership   at Filbert Street   Attendance 22132
Result: **Leicester City 0 Manchester United 3**
Teamsheet: Barthez, Silvestre, Irwin, Keane, Johnsen, Brown, Solskjaer, Butt, Yorke, Sheringham, Fortune
Substitute(s): Giggs   Scorer(s): Sheringham 2, Solskjaer

Match # 4592 Wednesday 18/10/00   Champions League Phase 1 Match 4   at Old Trafford   Attendance 66313
Result: **Manchester United 3 PSV Eindhoven 1**
Teamsheet: Barthez, Neville G, Irwin, Keane, Johnsen, Silvestre, Beckham, Scholes, Cole, Sheringham, Giggs
Substitute(s): Brown, Butt, Yorke   Scorer(s): Scholes, Sheringham, Yorke

Match # 4593 Saturday 21/10/00   FA Premiership   at Old Trafford   Attendance 67523
Result: **Manchester United 3 Leeds United 0**
Teamsheet: Barthez, Neville G, Neville P, Keane, Johnsen, Silvestre, Scholes, Butt, Solskjaer, Yorke, Fortune
Substitute(s): Beckham, Brown   Scorer(s): Beckham, Yorke, own goal

Match # 4594 Tuesday 24/10/00   Champions League Phase 1 Match 5   at Vanden Stock   Attendance 22506
Result: **Anderlecht 2 Manchester United 1**
Teamsheet: Barthez, Neville G, Irwin, Scholes, Johnsen, Silvestre, Beckham, Butt, Cole, Yorke, Giggs
Substitute(s): Brown, Solskjaer   Scorer(s): Irwin

Match # 4595 Saturday 28/10/00   FA Premiership   at Old Trafford   Attendance 67581
Result: **Manchester United 5 Southampton 0**
Teamsheet: Barthez, Neville G, Irwin, Scholes, Brown, Neville P, Beckham, Butt, Cole, Sheringham, Giggs
Substitute(s): Solskjaer, Wallwork, Yorke   Scorer(s): Sheringham 3, Cole 2

Match # 4596 Tuesday 31/10/00   League Cup 3rd Round   at Vicarage Road   Attendance 18871
Result: **Watford 0 Manchester United 3**
Teamsheet: van der Gouw, Clegg, Neville P, Wallwork, Brown, O'Shea, Chadwick, Greening, Solskjaer, Yorke, Fortune
Substitute(s): Rachubka, Stewart   Scorer(s): Solskjaer 2, Yorke

SEASON 2000/01 (continued)

Match # 4597 Saturday 04/11/00   FA Premiership   at Highfield Road   Attendance 21079
Result: **Coventry City 1 Manchester United 2**
Teamsheet: Barthez, Neville G, Irwin, Keane, Brown, Neville P, Beckham, Scholes, Cole, Sheringham, Giggs
Substitute(s): Solskjaer, Yorke   Scorer(s):   Beckham, Cole

Match # 4598 Wednesday 08/11/00   Champions League Phase 1 Match 6   at Old Trafford   Attendance 66776
Result: **Manchester United 1 Dynamo Kiev 0**
Teamsheet: Barthez, Neville G, Irwin, Keane, Brown, Neville P, Beckham, Butt, Cole, Sheringham, Giggs
Substitute(s): Fortune, Silvestre, Yorke   Scorer(s):   Sheringham

Match # 4599 Saturday 11/11/00   FA Premiership   at Old Trafford   Attendance 67576
Result: **Manchester United 2 Middlesbrough 1**
Teamsheet: Barthez, Neville G, Silvestre, Keane, Brown, Neville P, Beckham, Butt, Solskjaer, Yorke, Scholes
Substitute(s): Chadwick, Sheringham, Wallwork   Scorer(s):   Butt, Sheringham

Match # 4600 Saturday 18/11/00   FA Premiership   at Maine Road   Attendance 34429
Result: **Manchester City 0 Manchester United 1**
Teamsheet: Barthez, Neville G, Irwin, Keane, Brown, Neville P, Beckham, Butt, Yorke, Sheringham, Scholes
Substitute(s): Giggs   Scorer(s):   Beckham

Match # 4601 Tuesday 21/11/00   Champions League Phase 2 Match 1   at Old Trafford   Attendance 65024
Result: **Manchester United 3 Panathinaikos 1**
Teamsheet: Barthez, Neville G, Silvestre, Keane, Brown, Neville P, Beckham, Butt, Yorke, Sheringham, Scholes
Scorer(s):   Scholes 2, Sheringham

Match # 4602 Saturday 25/11/00   FA Premiership   at Pride Park   Attendance 32910
Result: **Derby County 0 Manchester United 3**
Teamsheet: Barthez, Neville G, Irwin, Keane, Brown, Silvestre, Chadwick, Butt, Yorke, Sheringham, Scholes
Substitute(s): Fortune, Solskjaer, van der Gouw   Scorer(s):   Butt, Sheringham, Yorke

Match # 4603 Tuesday 28/11/00   League Cup 4th Round   at Stadium of Light   Attendance 47543
Result: **Sunderland 2 Manchester United 1**
Teamsheet: van der Gouw, Clegg, Neville P, Wallwork, Johnsen, O'Shea, Chadwick, Greening, Yorke, Solskjaer, Fortune
Substitute(s): Healy, Stewart, Webber   Scorer(s):   Yorke

Match # 4604 Saturday 02/12/00   FA Premiership   at Old Trafford   Attendance 67583
Result: **Manchester United 2 Tottenham Hotspur 0**
Teamsheet: Barthez, Neville G, Silvestre, Keane, Brown, Neville P, Beckham, Butt, Yorke, Sheringham, Scholes
Substitute(s): Giggs, Solskjaer   Scorer(s):   Scholes, Solskjaer

Match # 4605 Wednesday 06/12/00   Champions League Phase 2 Match 2   at Schwarzenegger Stadium   Attendance 16500
Result: **Sturm Graz 0 Manchester United 2**
Teamsheet: Barthez, Neville G, Irwin, Keane, Brown, Silvestre, Beckham, Butt, Yorke, Sheringham, Scholes
Substitute(s): Giggs, Neville P, Solskjaer   Scorer(s):   Giggs, Scholes

Match # 4606 Saturday 09/12/00   FA Premiership   at The Valley   Attendance 20043
Result: **Charlton Athletic 3 Manchester United 3**
Teamsheet: van der Gouw, Neville G, Silvestre, Keane, Brown, Neville P, Beckham, Butt, Solskjaer, Chadwick, Giggs
Substitute(s): Greening, Scholes, Sheringham   Scorer(s):   Giggs, Keane, Solskjaer

Match # 4607 Sunday 17/12/00   FA Premiership   at Old Trafford   Attendance 67533
Result: **Manchester United 0 Liverpool 1**
Teamsheet: Barthez, Neville G, Irwin, Keane, Brown, Silvestre, Beckham, Butt, Solskjaer, Scholes, Giggs
Substitute(s): Chadwick, Greening

Match # 4608 Saturday 23/12/00   FA Premiership   at Old Trafford   Attendance 67597
Result: **Manchester United 2 Ipswich Town 0**
Teamsheet: Barthez, Neville G, Silvestre, Keane, Brown, Neville P, Beckham, Scholes, Solskjaer, Fortune, Giggs
Substitute(s): Greening, Healy, Wallwork   Scorer(s):   Solskjaer 2

Match # 4609 Tuesday 26/12/00   FA Premiership   at Villa Park   Attendance 40889
Result: **Aston Villa 0 Manchester United 1**
Teamsheet: Barthez, Neville G, Irwin, Keane, Brown, Silvestre, Beckham, Butt, Solskjaer, Scholes, Giggs
Substitute(s): Neville P, Wallwork   Scorer(s):   Solskjaer

Match # 4610 Saturday 30/12/00   FA Premiership   at St James' Park   Attendance 52134
Result: **Newcastle United 1 Manchester United 1**
Teamsheet: Barthez, Neville G, Silvestre, Keane, Brown, Neville P, Beckham, Butt, Solskjaer, Yorke, Giggs
Substitute(s): Chadwick, Scholes, Wallwork   Scorer(s):   Beckham

Match # 4611 Monday 01/01/01   FA Premiership   at Old Trafford   Attendance 67603
Result: **Manchester United 3 West Ham United 1**
Teamsheet: Barthez, Neville G, Silvestre, Keane, Brown, Neville P, Beckham, Scholes, Solskjaer, Yorke, Giggs
Substitute(s): Butt, Greening, Wallwork   Scorer(s):   Solskjaer, Yorke, own goal

Match # 4612 Sunday 07/01/01   FA Cup 3rd Round   at Craven Cottage   Attendance 19178
Result: **Fulham 1 Manchester United 2**
Teamsheet: van der Gouw, Neville G, Silvestre, Keane, Brown, Neville P, Beckham, Butt, Solskjaer, Yorke, Giggs
Substitute(s): Chadwick, Sheringham, Wallwork   Scorer(s):   Sheringham, Solskjaer

Match # 4613 Saturday 13/01/01   FA Premiership   at Valley Parade   Attendance 20551
Result: **Bradford City 0 Manchester United 3**
Teamsheet: Barthez, Neville G, Irwin, Keane, Silvestre, Stam, Beckham, Neville P, Solskjaer, Sheringham, Giggs
Substitute(s): Brown, Chadwick, Cole   Scorer(s):   Chadwick, Giggs, Sheringham

Match # 4614 Saturday 20/01/01   FA Premiership   at Old Trafford   Attendance 67533
Result: **Manchester United 2 Aston Villa 0**
Teamsheet: Barthez, Neville G, Irwin, Keane, Neville P, Stam, Greening, Butt, Solskjaer, Sheringham, Giggs
Substitute(s): Chadwick, Cole   Scorer(s):   Neville G, Sheringham

SEASON 2000/01 (continued)

Match # 4615 Sunday 28/01/01 FA Cup 4th Round at Old Trafford Attendance 67029
Result: **Manchester United 0 West Ham United 1**
Teamsheet: Barthez, Neville G, Irwin, Keane, Silvestre, Stam, Beckham, Butt, Cole, Sheringham, Giggs
Substitute(s): Solskjaer, Yorke

Match # 4616 Wednesday 31/01/01 FA Premiership at Stadium of Light Attendance 48260
Result: **Sunderland 0 Manchester United 1**
Teamsheet: Barthez, Neville G, Silvestre, Keane, Brown, Stam, Beckham, Scholes, Cole, Sheringham, Giggs
Substitute(s): Butt, Neville P, Solskjaer Scorer(s): Cole

Match # 4617 Saturday 03/02/01 FA Premiership at Old Trafford Attendance 67528
Result: **Manchester United 1 Everton 0**
Teamsheet: Barthez, Silvestre, Irwin, Neville P, Brown, Stam, Beckham, Scholes, Cole, Yorke, Chadwick
Substitute(s): Giggs, Sheringham, Wallwork Scorer(s): own goal

Match # 4618 Saturday 10/02/01 FA Premiership at Stamford Bridge Attendance 34690
Result: **Chelsea 1 Manchester United 1**
Teamsheet: van der Gouw, Neville G, Silvestre, Keane, Brown, Stam, Beckham, Scholes, Cole, Solskjaer, Giggs
Scorer(s): Cole

Match # 4619 Wednesday 14/02/01 Champions League Phase 2 Match 3 at Mestalla Attendance 49541
Result: **Valencia 0 Manchester United 0**
Teamsheet: Barthez, Neville G, Silvestre, Keane, Brown, Stam, Beckham, Scholes, Cole, Sheringham, Giggs
Substitute(s): Butt, Solskjaer

Match # 4620 Tuesday 20/02/01 Champions League Phase 2 Match 4 at Old Trafford Attendance 66715
Result: **Manchester United 1 Valencia 1**
Teamsheet: Barthez, Neville G, Silvestre, Keane, Brown, Stam, Beckham, Scholes, Cole, Sheringham, Giggs
Substitute(s): Butt, Solskjaer Scorer(s): Cole

Match # 4621 Sunday 25/02/01 FA Premiership at Old Trafford Attendance 67535
Result: **Manchester United 6 Arsenal 1**
Teamsheet: Barthez, Neville G, Silvestre, Keane, Brown, Stam, Beckham, Butt, Solskjaer, Yorke, Scholes
Substitute(s): Chadwick, Sheringham Scorer(s): Yorke 3, Keane, Sheringham, Solskjaer

Match # 4622 Saturday 03/03/01 FA Premiership at Elland Road Attendance 40055
Result: **Leeds United 1 Manchester United 1**
Teamsheet: Barthez, Neville G, Irwin, Neville P, Brown, Stam, Beckham, Butt, Solskjaer, Sheringham, Scholes
Substitute(s): Chadwick, Yorke Scorer(s): Chadwick

Match # 4623 Wednesday 07/03/01 Champions League Phase 2 Match 5 at Olympic Stadium Attendance 27231
Result: **Panathinaikos 1 Manchester United 1**
Teamsheet: Barthez, Neville G, Silvestre, Keane, Brown, Stam, Beckham, Scholes, Cole, Yorke, Neville P
Substitute(s): Chadwick, Sheringham, Solskjaer Scorer(s): Scholes

Match # 4624 Tuesday 13/03/01 Champions League Phase 2 Match 6 at Old Trafford Attendance 66404
Result: **Manchester United 3 Sturm Graz 0**
Teamsheet: Barthez, Neville G, Irwin, Keane, Silvestre, Stam, Chadwick, Butt, Solskjaer, Sheringham, Scholes
Substitute(s): Greening Scorer(s): Butt, Keane, Sheringham

Match # 4625 Saturday 17/03/01 FA Premiership at Old Trafford Attendance 67516
Result: **Manchester United 2 Leicester City 0**
Teamsheet: Rachubka, Neville G, Irwin, Keane, Neville P, Stam, Greening, Butt, Solskjaer, Sheringham, Scholes
Substitute(s): Chadwick, Silvestre, Yorke Scorer(s): Silvestre, Yorke

Match # 4626 Saturday 31/03/01 FA Premiership at Anfield Attendance 44806
Result: **Liverpool 2 Manchester United 0**
Teamsheet: Barthez, Neville G, Irwin, Keane, Brown, Neville P, Beckham, Butt, Yorke, Sheringham, Giggs
Substitute(s): Chadwick, Scholes, Silvestre

Match # 4627 Tuesday 03/04/01 Champions League Quarter-Final 1st Leg at Old Trafford Attendance 66584
Result: **Manchester United 0 Bayern Munich 1**
Teamsheet: Barthez, Neville G, Silvestre, Keane, Brown, Stam, Beckham, Scholes, Cole, Solskjaer, Giggs
Substitute(s): Yorke

Match # 4628 Tuesday 10/04/01 FA Premiership at Old Trafford Attendance 67505
Result: **Manchester United 2 Charlton Athletic 1**
Teamsheet: Barthez, Neville G, Irwin, Keane, Brown, Silvestre, Scholes, Butt, Cole, Yorke, Giggs
Substitute(s): Neville P, Sheringham, Solskjaer Scorer(s): Cole, Solskjaer

Match # 4629 Saturday 14/04/01 FA Premiership at Old Trafford Attendance 67637
Result: **Manchester United 4 Coventry City 2**
Teamsheet: Goram, Neville G, Silvestre, Keane, Brown, Stam, Scholes, Butt, Cole, Yorke, Giggs
Substitute(s): Beckham, Solskjaer, van der Gouw Scorer(s): Yorke 2, Giggs, Scholes

Match # 4630 Wednesday 18/04/01 Champions League Quarter-Final 2nd Leg at Olympic Stadium Attendance 60000
Result: **Bayern Munich 2 Manchester United 1**
Teamsheet: Barthez, Neville G, Silvestre, Keane, Brown, Stam, Scholes, Butt, Cole, Yorke, Giggs
Substitute(s): Chadwick, Sheringham, Solskjaer Scorer(s): Giggs

Match # 4631 Saturday 21/04/01 FA Premiership at Old Trafford Attendance 67535
Result: **Manchester United 1 Manchester City 1**
Teamsheet: Barthez, Neville G, Neville P, Keane, Brown, Stam, Beckham, Scholes, Solskjaer, Sheringham, Chadwick
Substitute(s): Butt, Giggs, Silvestre Scorer(s): Sheringham

Match # 4632 Saturday 28/04/01 FA Premiership at Riverside Stadium Attendance 34417
Result: **Middlesbrough 0 Manchester United 2**
Teamsheet: van der Gouw, Brown, Neville P, Stewart, Johnsen, Stam, Beckham, Butt, Solskjaer, Sheringham, Fortune
Substitute(s): Chadwick, Cole, Giggs Scorer(s): Beckham, Neville P

SEASON 2000/01 (continued)

Match # 4633   Saturday 05/05/01   FA Premiership   at Old Trafford   Attendance 67526
Result: **Manchester United 0   Derby County 1**
Teamsheet: Barthez, Neville P, Irwin, Stewart, Johnsen, Wallwork, Beckham, Butt, Cole, Sheringham, Chadwick
Substitute(s):   Giggs, Silvestre, van der Gouw

Match # 4634   Sunday 13/05/01   FA Premiership   at The Dell   Attendance 15526
Result: **Southampton 2   Manchester United 1**
Teamsheet: Goram, Neville P, Irwin, Stewart, Johnsen, Brown, Chadwick, Wallwork, Fortune, Yorke, Giggs
Substitute(s):   May, van der Gouw   Scorer(s):   Giggs

Match # 4635   Saturday 19/05/01   FA Premiership   at White Hart Lane   Attendance 36072
Result: **Tottenham Hotspur 3   Manchester United 1**
Teamsheet: van der Gouw, Neville P, Irwin, May, Johnsen, Silvestre, Scholes, Butt, Cole, Sheringham, Giggs
Substitute(s):   Djordjic   Scorer(s):   Scholes

SEASON 2000/01 SUMMARY

APPEARANCES

PLAYER	LGE	FAC	LC	CL	CS	TOTAL
Neville G	32	2	–	14	1	49
Barthez	30	1	–	12	1	44
Keane	28	2	–	13	1	44
Beckham	29 (2)	2	–	11 (1)	1	43 (3)
Silvestre	25 (5)	2	–	13 (1)	1	41 (6)
Scholes	28 (4)	–	–	12	1	41 (4)
Giggs	24 (7)	2	–	9 (2)	1	36 (9)
Brown	25 (3)	1	1	9 (2)	–	36 (5)
Butt	24 (4)	2	–	8 (3)	–	34 (7)
Sheringham	23 (6)	1 (1)	–	8 (3)	1	33 (10)
Neville P	24 (5)	1	2	4 (2)	–	31 (7)
Irwin	20 (1)	1	–	7	1	29 (1)
Solskjaer	19 (12)	1 (1)	2	3 (8)	1	26 (21)
Cole	15 (4)	1	–	10	– (1)	26 (5)
Yorke	15 (7)	1 (1)	2	7 (4)	– (1)	25 (13)
Stam	15	1	–	6	– (1)	22 (1)
Johnsen	11	–	1	4	1	17
van der Gouw	5 (5)	1	2	2	–	10 (5)
Chadwick	6 (10)	– (1)	2	1 (2)	–	9 (13)
Fortune	6 (1)	–	2	– (1)	– (1)	8 (3)
Wallwork	4 (8)	– (1)	2	– (1)	–	6 (10)
Greening	3 (4)	–	2	1 (1)	–	6 (5)
Stewart	3	–	– (2)	–	–	3 (2)
Clegg	–	–	2	–	–	2
Goram	2	–	–	–	–	2
O'Shea	–	–	2	–	–	2
May	1 (1)	–	–	–	–	1 (1)
Rachubka	1	–	– (1)	–	–	1 (1)
Healy	– (1)	–	– (1)	–	–	– (2)
Berg	– (1)	–	–	–	–	– (1)
Djordjic	– (1)	–	–	–	–	– (1)
Webber	–	–	– (1)	–	–	– (1)

GOALSCORERS

PLAYER	LGE	FAC	LC	CL	CS	TOTAL
Sheringham	15	1	–	5	–	21
Solskjaer	10	1	2	–	–	13
Cole	9	–	–	4	–	13
Yorke	9	–	2	1	–	12
Scholes	6	–	–	6	–	12
Beckham	9	–	–	–	–	9
Giggs	5	–	–	2	–	7
Butt	3	–	–	1	–	4
Keane	2	–	–	1	–	3
Chadwick	2	–	–	–	–	2
Fortune	2	–	–	–	–	2
Irwin	–	–	–	2	–	2
Johnsen	1	–	–	–	–	1
Neville G	1	–	–	–	–	1
Neville P	1	–	–	–	–	1
Silvestre	1	–	–	–	–	1
own goals	3	–	–	–	–	3

RESULTS & ATTENDANCES SUMMARY

		P	W	D	L	F	A	TOTAL	AVGE
League	H	19	15	2	2	49	12	1283306	67542
	A	19	9	6	4	30	19	622685	32773
	TOTAL	38	24	8	6	79	31	1905991	50158
FA Cup	H	1	0	0	1	0	1	67029	67029
	A	1	1	0	0	2	1	19178	19178
	TOTAL	2	1	0	1	2	2	86207	43104
League	H	0	0	0	0	0	0	0	n/a
Cup	A	2	1	0	1	4	2	66414	33207
	TOTAL	2	1	0	1	4	2	66414	33207
Champions	H	7	5	1	1	16	5	460565	65795
League	A	7	1	3	3	6	8	271278	38754
	TOTAL	14	6	4	4	22	13	731843	52275
Charity	H	0	0	0	0	0	0	0	n/a
Shield	A	0	0	0	0	0	0	0	n/a
	N	1	0	0	1	0	2	65148	65148
	TOTAL	1	0	0	1	0	2	65148	65148
Overall	H	27	20	3	4	65	18	1810900	67070
	A	29	12	9	8	42	30	979555	33778
	N	1	0	0	1	0	2	65148	65148
	TOTAL	57	32	12	13	107	50	2855603	50098

FINAL TABLE - FA PREMIERSHIP

		P	W	D	L	F	A	W	D	L	F	A	PTS	GD
			HOME						AWAY					
1	MANCHESTER UNITED	38	15	2	2	49	12	9	6	4	30	19	80	48
2	Arsenal	38	15	3	1	45	13	5	7	7	18	25	70	25
3	Liverpool	38	13	4	2	40	14	7	5	7	31	25	69	32
4	Leeds United	38	11	3	5	36	21	9	5	5	28	22	68	21
5	Ipswich Town	38	11	5	3	31	15	9	1	9	26	27	66	15
6	Chelsea	38	13	3	3	44	20	4	7	8	24	25	61	23
7	Sunderland	38	9	7	3	24	16	6	5	8	22	25	57	5
8	Aston Villa	38	8	8	3	27	20	5	7	7	19	23	54	3
9	Charlton Athletic	38	11	5	3	31	19	3	5	11	19	38	52	-7
10	Southampton	38	11	2	6	27	22	3	8	8	13	26	52	-8
11	Newcastle United	38	10	4	5	26	17	4	5	10	18	33	51	-6
12	Tottenham Hotspur	38	11	6	2	31	16	2	4	13	16	38	49	-7
13	Leicester City	38	10	4	5	28	23	4	2	13	11	28	48	-12
14	Middlesbrough	38	4	7	8	18	23	5	8	6	26	21	42	0
15	West Ham United	38	6	6	7	24	20	4	6	9	21	30	42	-5
16	Everton	38	6	8	5	29	27	5	1	13	16	32	42	-14
17	Derby County	38	8	7	4	23	24	2	5	12	14	35	42	-12
18	Manchester City	38	4	3	12	20	31	4	7	8	21	34	34	-24
19	Coventry City	38	4	7	8	14	23	4	3	12	22	40	34	-27
20	Bradford City	38	4	7	8	20	29	1	4	14	10	41	26	-40

SEASON 2001/02

Match # 4636   Sunday 12/08/01   FA Charity Shield   at Millennium Stadium   Attendance 70227
Result: **Manchester United 1 Liverpool 2**
Teamsheet: Barthez, Neville G, Irwin, Keane, Silvestre, Stam, Beckham, Butt, Scholes, van Nistelrooy, Giggs
Substitute(s):   Yorke   Scorer(s):   van Nistelrooy

Match # 4637   Sunday 19/08/01   FA Premiership   at Old Trafford   Attendance 67534
Result: **Manchester United 3 Fulham 2**
Teamsheet: Barthez, Neville G, Irwin, Veron, Silvestre, Stam, Beckham, Scholes, Neville P, van Nistelrooy, Giggs
Substitute(s):   Brown, Chadwick, Cole   Scorer(s):   van Nistelrooy 2, Beckham

Match # 4638   Wednesday 22/08/01   FA Premiership   at Ewood Park   Attendance 29836
Result: **Blackburn Rovers 2 Manchester United 2**
Teamsheet: Barthez, Silvestre, Irwin, Veron, Johnsen, Brown, Beckham, Scholes, Keane, van Nistelrooy, Giggs
Substitute(s):   Cole, Neville G, Yorke   Scorer(s):   Beckham, Giggs

Match # 4639   Sunday 26/08/01   FA Premiership   at Villa Park   Attendance 42632
Result: **Aston Villa 1 Manchester United 1**
Teamsheet: Carroll, Neville G, Silvestre, Veron, Johnsen, Brown, Beckham, Scholes, Keane, van Nistelrooy, Giggs
Substitute(s):   Cole, Neville P, Solskjaer   Scorer(s):   own goal

Match # 4640   Saturday 08/09/01   FA Premiership   at Old Trafford   Attendance 67534
Result: **Manchester United 4 Everton 1**
Teamsheet: Barthez, Neville G, Neville P, Veron, Brown, Blanc, Chadwick, Keane, Cole, Yorke, Fortune
Substitute(s):   Beckham, Silvestre, van Nistelrooy   Scorer(s):   Beckham, Cole, Fortune, Veron

Match # 4641   Saturday 15/09/01   FA Premiership   at St James' Park   Attendance 52056
Result: **Newcastle United 4 Manchester United 3**
Teamsheet: Barthez, Neville G, Neville P, Veron, Brown, Blanc, Beckham, Keane, Cole, van Nistelrooy, Giggs
Substitute(s):   Scholes   Scorer(s):   Giggs, van Nistelrooy, Veron

Match # 4642   Tuesday 18/09/01   Champions League Phase 1 Match 1   at Old Trafford   Attendance 64827
Result: **Manchester United 1 Lille Metropole 0**
Teamsheet: Barthez, Neville G, Irwin, Veron, Brown, Blanc, Beckham, Scholes, Keane, van Nistelrooy, Giggs
Substitute(s):   Silvestre, Solskjaer   Scorer(s):   Beckham

Match # 4643   Saturday 22/09/01   FA Premiership   at Old Trafford   Attendance 67551
Result: **Manchester United 4 Ipswich Town 0**
Teamsheet: Barthez, Neville P, Silvestre, Keane, Johnsen, May, Chadwick, Butt, Cole, Solskjaer, Fortune
Substitute(s):   Scholes, Veron   Scorer(s):   Solskjaer 2, Cole, Johnsen

Match # 4644   Tuesday 25/09/01   Champions League Phase 1 Match 2   at Estadio de Riazor   Attendance 33108
Result: **Deportivo La Coruna 2 Manchester United 1**
Teamsheet: Barthez, Neville G, Irwin, Veron, Johnsen, Blanc, Beckham, Scholes, Keane, van Nistelrooy, Giggs
Substitute(s):   Cole, Solskjaer   Scorer(s):   Scholes

Match # 4645   Saturday 29/09/01   FA Premiership   at White Hart Lane   Attendance 36038
Result: **Tottenham Hotspur 3 Manchester United 5**
Teamsheet: Barthez, Neville G, Irwin, Veron, Johnsen, Blanc, Beckham, Butt, Cole, van Nistelrooy, Scholes
Substitute(s):   Silvestre, Solskjaer   Scorer(s):   Beckham, Blanc, Cole, van Nistelrooy, Veron

Match # 4646   Wednesday 10/10/01   Champions League Phase 1 Match 3   at Olympic Stadium   Attendance 73537
Result: **Olympiakos Piraeus 0 Manchester United 2**
Teamsheet: Barthez, Neville G, Irwin, Veron, Johnsen, Blanc, Beckham, Scholes, Keane, van Nistelrooy, Giggs
Substitute(s):   Cole, Silvestre, Solskjaer   Scorer(s):   Beckham, Cole

Match # 4647   Saturday 13/10/01   FA Premiership   at Stadium of Light   Attendance 48305
Result: **Sunderland 1 Manchester United 3**
Teamsheet: Carroll, Neville G, Silvestre, Scholes, Brown, Blanc, Chadwick, Butt, Cole, Solskjaer, Giggs
Substitute(s):   Neville P, Stewart, Yorke   Scorer(s):   Cole, Giggs, own goal

Match # 4648   Wednesday 17/10/01   Champions League Phase 1 Match 4   at Old Trafford   Attendance 65585
Result: **Manchester United 2 Deportivo La Coruna 3**
Teamsheet: Barthez, Neville G, Irwin, Veron, Johnsen, Blanc, Beckham, Scholes, Keane, van Nistelrooy, Giggs
Substitute(s):   Brown, Cole, Solskjaer   Scorer(s):   van Nistelrooy 2

Match # 4649   Saturday 20/10/01   FA Premiership   at Old Trafford   Attendance 67559
Result: **Manchester United 1 Bolton Wanderers 2**
Teamsheet: Barthez, Neville P, Silvestre, Veron, Brown, May, Scholes, Butt, Cole, Yorke, Solskjaer
Substitute(s):   Chadwick, Giggs, Neville G   Scorer(s):   Veron

Match # 4650   Tuesday 23/10/01   Champions League Phase 1 Match 5   at Old Trafford   Attendance 66769
Result: **Manchester United 3 Olympiakos Piraeus 0**
Teamsheet: Barthez, Neville G, Irwin, Veron, Brown, Blanc, Beckham, Butt, Scholes, van Nistelrooy, Giggs
Substitute(s):   Solskjaer   Scorer(s):   Giggs, Solskjaer, van Nistelrooy

Match # 4651   Saturday 27/10/01   FA Premiership   at Old Trafford   Attendance 67555
Result: **Manchester United 1 Leeds United 1**
Teamsheet: Barthez, Neville G, Silvestre, Veron, Brown, Blanc, Beckham, Butt, Scholes, van Nistelrooy, Giggs
Substitute(s):   Solskjaer   Scorer(s):   Solskjaer

Match # 4652   Wednesday 31/10/01   Champions League Phase 1 Match 6   at Stade Felix Bollaert   Attendance 38402
Result: **Lille Metropole 1 Manchester United 1**
Teamsheet: Carroll, Neville P, Irwin, Scholes, Silvestre, May, Beckham, Butt, Cole, Solskjaer, Fortune
Substitute(s):   O'Shea, Yorke   Scorer(s):   Solskjaer

Match # 4653   Sunday 04/11/01   FA Premiership   at Anfield   Attendance 44361
Result: **Liverpool 3 Manchester United 1**
Teamsheet: Barthez, Neville G, Irwin, Veron, Brown, Silvestre, Beckham, Butt, Solskjaer, van Nistelrooy, Fortune
Substitute(s):   O'Shea, Scholes, Yorke   Scorer(s):   Beckham

SEASON 2001/02 (continued)

Match # 4654	Monday 05/11/01 League Cup 3rd Round	at Highbury	Attendance 30693
Result:	**Arsenal 4 Manchester United 0**		
Teamsheet:	Carroll, Roche, Neville P, Stewart, O'Shea, Wallwork, Chadwick, Davis, Webber, Yorke, Djordjic		
Substitute(s):	Clegg, Nardiello, van der Gouw		

Match # 4655	Saturday 17/11/01 FA Premiership	at Old Trafford	Attendance 67651
Result:	**Manchester United 2 Leicester City 0**		
Teamsheet:	Barthez, Neville G, Irwin, Keane, Brown, Blanc, Beckham, Scholes, Yorke, van Nistelrooy, Giggs		
Substitute(s):	Fortune, Silvestre Scorer(s): van Nistelrooy, Yorke		

Match # 4656	Tuesday 20/11/01 Champions League Phase 2 Match 1	at Olympic Stadium	Attendance 59000
Result:	**Bayern Munich 1 Manchester United 1**		
Teamsheet:	Barthez, Neville G, Irwin, Veron, Brown, Blanc, Beckham, Scholes, Keane, van Nistelrooy, Fortune		
Substitute(s):	Silvestre, Yorke Scorer(s): van Nistelrooy		

Match # 4657	Sunday 25/11/01 FA Premiership	at Highbury	Attendance 38174
Result:	**Arsenal 3 Manchester United 1**		
Teamsheet:	Barthez, Neville G, Silvestre, Veron, Brown, Blanc, Beckham, Scholes, Keane, van Nistelrooy, Fortune		
Substitute(s):	Neville P, Solskjaer, Yorke Scorer(s): Scholes		

Match # 4658	Saturday 01/12/01 FA Premiership	at Old Trafford	Attendance 67544
Result:	**Manchester United 0 Chelsea 3**		
Teamsheet:	Barthez, Brown, Neville P, Veron, Keane, Blanc, Beckham, Scholes, Cole, van Nistelrooy, Fortune		
Substitute(s):	Chadwick, Neville G, Solskjaer		

Match # 4659	Wednesday 05/12/01 Champions League Phase 2 Match 2	at Old Trafford	Attendance 66274
Result:	**Manchester United 3 Boavista 0**		
Teamsheet:	Barthez, Neville G, Silvestre, Veron, Neville P, Blanc, Keane, Butt, Yorke, van Nistelrooy, Scholes		
Substitute(s):	Fortune, O'Shea, Solskjaer Scorer(s): van Nistelrooy 2, Blanc		

Match # 4660	Saturday 08/12/01 FA Premiership	at Old Trafford	Attendance 67582
Result:	**Manchester United 0 West Ham United 1**		
Teamsheet:	Barthez, Neville G, Silvestre, Keane, Neville P, O'Shea, Chadwick, Butt, Yorke, Solskjaer, Scholes		
Substitute(s):	Beckham, Cole, Fortune		

Match # 4661	Wednesday 12/12/01 FA Premiership	at Old Trafford	Attendance 67577
Result:	**Manchester United 5 Derby County 0**		
Teamsheet:	Barthez, Neville G, Silvestre, Veron, O'Shea, Blanc, Keane, Butt, Solskjaer, van Nistelrooy, Scholes		
Substitute(s):	Carroll, Yorke Scorer(s): Solskjaer 2, Keane, Scholes, van Nistelrooy		

Match # 4662	Saturday 15/12/01 FA Premiership	at Riverside Stadium	Attendance 34358
Result:	**Middlesbrough 0 Manchester United 1**		
Teamsheet:	Carroll, Neville G, Silvestre, Veron, O'Shea, Blanc, Keane, Butt, Solskjaer, van Nistelrooy, Scholes		
Substitute(s):	Giggs, Neville P Scorer(s): van Nistelrooy		

Match # 4663	Saturday 22/12/01 FA Premiership	at Old Trafford	Attendance 67638
Result:	**Manchester United 6 Southampton 1**		
Teamsheet:	Barthez, Neville G, Silvestre, Veron, Neville P, Blanc, Keane, Butt, Solskjaer, van Nistelrooy, Scholes		
Substitute(s):	Beckham, Giggs, Wallwork Scorer(s): van Nistelrooy 3, Keane, Neville P, Solskjaer		

Match # 4664	Wednesday 26/12/01 FA Premiership	at Goodison Park	Attendance 39948
Result:	**Everton 0 Manchester United 2**		
Teamsheet:	Barthez, Neville G, Silvestre, Veron, Neville P, Blanc, Keane, Butt, Solskjaer, van Nistelrooy, Giggs		
Substitute(s):	Beckham Scorer(s): Giggs, van Nistelrooy		

Match # 4665	Sunday 30/12/01 FA Premiership	at Craven Cottage	Attendance 21159
Result:	**Fulham 2 Manchester United 3**		
Teamsheet:	Barthez, Neville G, Silvestre, Keane, Neville P, Blanc, Beckham, Butt, Scholes, van Nistelrooy, Giggs		
Scorer(s):	Giggs 2, van Nistelrooy		

Match # 4666	Wednesday 02/01/02 FA Premiership	at Old Trafford	Attendance 67646
Result:	**Manchester United 3 Newcastle United 1**		
Teamsheet:	Barthez, Neville G, Silvestre, Veron, Neville P, Blanc, Keane, Butt, van Nistelrooy, Scholes		
Substitute(s):	Beckham, Yorke Scorer(s): Scholes 2, van Nistelrooy		

Match # 4667	Sunday 06/01/02 FA Cup 3rd Round	at Villa Park	Attendance 38444
Result:	**Aston Villa 2 Manchester United 3**		
Teamsheet:	Carroll, Neville G, Silvestre, Veron, Neville P, Blanc, Beckham, Butt, Solskjaer, Keane, Scholes		
Substitute(s):	Chadwick, van Nistelrooy Scorer(s): van Nistelrooy 2, Solskjaer		

Match # 4668	Sunday 13/01/02 FA Premiership	at St Mary's Stadium	Attendance 31858
Result:	**Southampton 1 Manchester United 3**		
Teamsheet:	Barthez, Neville G, Silvestre, Veron, Neville P, Blanc, Beckham, Keane, Solskjaer, van Nistelrooy, Scholes		
Substitute(s):	Giggs, Irwin Scorer(s): Beckham, Solskjaer, van Nistelrooy		

Match # 4669	Saturday 19/01/02 FA Premiership	at Old Trafford	Attendance 67552
Result:	**Manchester United 2 Blackburn Rovers 1**		
Teamsheet:	Barthez, Neville G, Silvestre, Veron, Neville P, Blanc, Beckham, Keane, Solskjaer, van Nistelrooy, Scholes		
Substitute(s):	Butt, Giggs, Irwin Scorer(s): Keane, van Nistelrooy		

Match # 4670	Tuesday 22/01/02 FA Premiership	at Old Trafford	Attendance 67599
Result:	**Manchester United 0 Liverpool 1**		
Teamsheet:	Barthez, Neville G, Silvestre, Veron, Neville P, Blanc, Beckham, Keane, Scholes, van Nistelrooy, Giggs		
Substitute(s):	Solskjaer		

Match # 4671	Saturday 26/01/02 FA Cup 4th Round	at Riverside Stadium	Attendance 17624
Result:	**Middlesbrough 2 Manchester United 0**		
Teamsheet:	Barthez, Neville G, Silvestre, Wallwork, Neville P, Blanc, Chadwick, Butt, Solskjaer, Keane, Scholes		
Substitute(s):	Giggs, van Nistelrooy, Yorke		

SEASON 2001/02 (continued)

Match # 4672   Tuesday 29/01/02   FA Premiership   at Reebok Stadium   Attendance 27350
Result: **Bolton Wanderers 0   Manchester United 4**
Teamsheet: Barthez, Neville G, Silvestre, Keane, Neville P, Blanc, Beckham, Scholes, Solskjaer, van Nistelrooy, Giggs
Substitute(s):   Butt, Forlan, O'Shea   Scorer(s):   Solskjaer 3, van Nistelrooy

Match # 4673   Saturday 02/02/02   FA Premiership   at Old Trafford   Attendance 67587
Result: **Manchester United 4   Sunderland 1**
Teamsheet: Barthez, Neville G, Silvestre, Keane, Neville P, Blanc, Beckham, Scholes, Solskjaer, van Nistelrooy, Giggs
Substitute(s):   Butt, Forlan, O'Shea   Scorer(s):   van Nistelrooy 2, Beckham, Neville P

Match # 4674   Sunday 10/02/02   FA Premiership   at The Valley   Attendance 26475
Result: **Charlton Athletic 0   Manchester United 2**
Teamsheet: Carroll, Neville G, Silvestre, Keane, Neville P, Blanc, Beckham, Scholes, Solskjaer, van Nistelrooy, Giggs
Substitute(s):   Butt, Forlan, Veron   Scorer(s):   Solskjaer 2

Match # 4675   Wednesday 20/02/02   Champions League Phase 2 Match 3   at Stade Beaujoire   Attendance 38285
Result: **Nantes Atlantique 1   Manchester United 1**
Teamsheet: Barthez, Neville G, Silvestre, Veron, Neville P, Blanc, Beckham, Scholes, Keane, van Nistelrooy, Giggs
Substitute(s):   Forlan, Solskjaer   Scorer(s):   van Nistelrooy

Match # 4676   Saturday 23/02/02   FA Premiership   at Old Trafford   Attendance 67592
Result: **Manchester United 1   Aston Villa 0**
Teamsheet: Barthez, Neville G, Irwin, Veron, Silvestre, Blanc, Beckham, Butt, Solskjaer, van Nistelrooy, Keane
Substitute(s):   Johnsen   Scorer(s):   van Nistelrooy

Match # 4677   Tuesday 26/02/02   Champions League Phase 2 Match 4   at Old Trafford   Attendance 66492
Result: **Manchester United 5   Nantes Atlantique 1**
Teamsheet: Barthez, Neville G, Irwin, Veron, Silvestre, Blanc, Beckham, Keane, Solskjaer, van Nistelrooy, Giggs
Substitute(s):   Butt, Forlan, Johnsen   Scorer(s):   Solskjaer 2, Beckham, Silvestre, van Nistelrooy

Match # 4678   Sunday 03/03/02   FA Premiership   at Pride Park   Attendance 33041
Result: **Derby County 2   Manchester United 2**
Teamsheet: Barthez, Neville G, Irwin, Veron, Johnsen, Silvestre, Beckham, Scholes, Solskjaer, van Nistelrooy, Giggs
Substitute(s):   O'Shea, Forlan   Scorer(s):   Scholes, Veron

Match # 4679   Wednesday 06/03/02   FA Premiership   at Old Trafford   Attendance 67599
Result: **Manchester United 4   Tottenham Hotspur 0**
Teamsheet: Barthez, Neville G, Silvestre, Veron, Johnsen, Blanc, Beckham, Scholes, Forlan, van Nistelrooy, Keane
Substitute(s):   Butt, Fortune, Neville P   Scorer(s):   Beckham 2, van Nistelrooy 2

Match # 4680   Wednesday 13/03/02   Champions League Phase 2 Match 5   at Old Trafford   Attendance 66818
Result: **Manchester United 0   Bayern Munich 0**
Teamsheet: Barthez, Neville G, Silvestre, Veron, Johnsen, Blanc, Beckham, Keane, Solskjaer, van Nistelrooy, Giggs
Substitute(s):   Forlan

Match # 4681   Saturday 16/03/02   FA Premiership   at Upton Park   Attendance 35281
Result: **West Ham United 3   Manchester United 5**
Teamsheet: Barthez, Neville G, Silvestre, Keane, Johnsen, Blanc, Beckham, Butt, Solskjaer, van Nistelrooy, Scholes
Substitute(s):   Forlan, Fortune   Scorer(s):   Beckham 2, Butt, Scholes, Solskjaer

Match # 4682   Tuesday 19/03/02   Champions League Phase 2 Match 6   at Estadio do Bessa   Attendance 13223
Result: **Boavista 0   Manchester United 3**
Teamsheet: Barthez, Neville G, Silvestre, Scholes, Johnsen, Blanc, Beckham, Butt, Solskjaer, Forlan, Giggs
Substitute(s):   Neville P, O'Shea, Stewart   Scorer(s):   Beckham, Blanc, Solskjaer

Match # 4683   Saturday 23/03/02   FA Premiership   at Old Trafford   Attendance 67683
Result: **Manchester United 0   Middlesbrough 1**
Teamsheet: Barthez, Neville G, Silvestre, Veron, Johnsen, Blanc, Beckham, Butt, Forlan, van Nistelrooy, Giggs
Substitute(s):   Fortune, Scholes

Match # 4684   Saturday 30/03/02   FA Premiership   at Elland Road   Attendance 40058
Result: **Leeds United 3   Manchester United 4**
Teamsheet: Barthez, Neville G, Silvestre, Keane, Johnsen, Blanc, Beckham, Butt, Solskjaer, Scholes, Giggs
Substitute(s):   Forlan, Neville P   Scorer(s):   Solskjaer 2, Giggs, Scholes

Match # 4685   Tuesday 02/04/02   Champions League Quarter-Final 1st Leg   at Estadio de Riazor   Attendance 32351
Result: **Deportivo La Coruna 0   Manchester United 2**
Teamsheet: Barthez, Neville G, Silvestre, Keane, Johnsen, Blanc, Beckham, Butt, Scholes, van Nistelrooy, Giggs
Substitute(s):   Fortune, Neville P, Solskjaer   Scorer(s):   Beckham, van Nistelrooy

Match # 4686   Saturday 06/04/02   FA Premiership   at Filbert Street   Attendance 21447
Result: **Leicester City 0   Manchester United 1**
Teamsheet: Carroll, Neville G, Irwin, Neville P, Silvestre, Blanc, Scholes, Butt, Solskjaer, Forlan, Fortune
Substitute(s):   Brown, Giggs, van Nistelrooy   Scorer(s):   Solskjaer

Match # 4687   Wednesday 10/04/02   Champions League Quarter-Final 2nd Leg   at Old Trafford   Attendance 65875
Result: **Manchester United 3   Deportivo La Coruna 2**
Teamsheet: Barthez, Neville G, Silvestre, Veron, Johnsen, Blanc, Beckham, Butt, Fortune, van Nistelrooy, Giggs
Substitute(s):   Brown, Neville P, Solskjaer   Scorer(s):   Solskjaer 2, Giggs

Match # 4688   Saturday 20/04/02   FA Premiership   at Stamford Bridge   Attendance 41725
Result: **Chelsea 0   Manchester United 3**
Teamsheet: Barthez, Neville G, Silvestre, Scholes, Brown, Blanc, Fortune, Butt, Solskjaer, van Nistelrooy, Giggs
Substitute(s):   Forlan, Neville P   Scorer(s):   Scholes, Solskjaer, van Nistelrooy

Match # 4689   Wednesday 24/04/02   Champions League Semi-Final 1st Leg   at Old Trafford   Attendance 66534
Result: **Manchester United 2   Bayer Leverkusen 2**
Teamsheet: Barthez, Neville G, Silvestre, Veron, Brown, Blanc, Scholes, Butt, Solskjaer, van Nistelrooy, Giggs
Substitute(s):   Irwin, Keane, Neville P   Scorer(s):   van Nistelrooy, own goal

SEASON 2001/02 (continued)

Match # 4690	Saturday 27/04/02 FA Premiership	at Portman Road	Attendance 28433
Result:	**Ipswich Town 0 Manchester United 1**		
Teamsheet:	Carroll, Neville P, Irwin, Keane, Brown, O'Shea, Stewart, Butt, Forlan, van Nistelrooy, Chadwick		
Substitute(s):	Scholes, Silvestre, Solskjaer Scorer(s): van Nistelrooy		

Match # 4691	Tuesday 30/04/02 Champions League Semi-Final 2nd Leg	at Bayarena	Attendance 22500
Result:	**Bayer Leverkusen 1 Manchester United 1 (United lost the tie on away goals rule)**		
Teamsheet:	Barthez, Brown, Silvestre, Veron, Johnsen, Blanc, Scholes, Butt, Keane, van Nistelrooy, Giggs		
Substitute(s):	Forlan, Irwin, Solskjaer Scorer(s): Keane		

Match # 4692	Wednesday 08/05/02 FA Premiership	at Old Trafford	Attendance 67580
Result:	**Manchester United 0 Arsenal 1**		
Teamsheet:	Barthez, Neville P, Silvestre, Veron, Brown, Blanc, Scholes, Keane, Solskjaer, Forlan, Giggs		
Substitute(s):	Fortune, van Nistelrooy		

Match # 4693	Saturday 11/05/02 FA Premiership	at Old Trafford	Attendance 67571
Result:	**Manchester United 0 Charlton Athletic 0**		
Teamsheet:	Barthez, Neville P, Irwin, Keane, Brown, Blanc, Scholes, Stewart, Solskjaer, Forlan, Fortune		
Substitute(s):	Giggs, O'Shea, van der Gouw		

SEASON 2001/02 SUMMARY

APPEARANCES

PLAYER	LGE	FAC	LC	CL	CS	TOTAL
Barthez	32	1	–	15	1	49
Neville G	31 (3)	2	–	14	1	48 (3)
Scholes	30 (5)	2	–	13	1	46 (5)
Blanc	29	2	–	15	–	46
Silvestre	31 (4)	2	–	10 (3)	1	44 (7)
van Nistelrooy	29 (3)	– (2)	–	14	1	44 (5)
Keane	28	2	–	11 (1)	1	42 (1)
Beckham	23 (5)	1	–	13	1	38 (5)
Veron	24 (2)	1	–	13	–	38 (2)
Giggs	18 (7)	– (1)	–	13	1	32 (8)
Butt	20 (5)	2	–	8 (1)	1	31 (6)
Solskjaer	23 (7)	2	–	5 (10)	–	30 (17)
Neville P	21 (7)	2	1	3 (4)	–	27 (11)
Brown	15 (2)	–	–	5 (2)	–	20 (4)
Irwin	10 (2)	–	–	8 (2)	1	19 (4)
Johnsen	9 (1)	–	–	8 (1)	–	17 (2)
Fortune	8 (6)	–	–	3 (2)	–	11 (8)
Carroll	6 (1)	1	1	1	–	9 (1)
Cole	7 (4)	–	–	1 (3)	–	8 (7)
Forlan	6 (7)	–	–	1 (4)	–	7 (11)
Chadwick	5 (3)	1 (1)	1	–	–	7 (4)
Yorke	4 (6)	– (1)	–	1 (2)	– (1)	6 (10)
O'Shea	4 (5)	–	1	– (3)	–	5 (8)
Stewart	2 (1)	–	1	– (1)	–	3 (2)
May	2	–	–	1	–	3
Wallwork	– (1)	1	1	–	–	2 (1)
Stam	1	–	–	–	1	2
Davis	–	–	1	–	–	1
Djordjic	–	–	1	–	–	1
Roche	–	–	1	–	–	1
Webber	–	–	1	–	–	1
van der Gouw	– (1)	–	– (1)	–	–	– (2)
Clegg	–	–	– (1)	–	–	– (1)
Nardiello	–	–	– (1)	–	–	– (1)

GOALSCORERS

PLAYER	LGE	FAC	LC	CL	CS	TOTAL
van Nistelrooy	23	2	–	10	1	36
Solskjaer	17	1	–	7	–	25
Beckham	11	–	–	5	–	16
Scholes	8	–	–	1	–	9
Giggs	7	–	–	2	–	9
Veron	5	–	–	–	–	5
Cole	4	–	–	1	–	5
Keane	3	–	–	1	–	4
Blanc	1	–	–	2	–	3
Neville P	2	–	–	–	–	2
Butt	1	–	–	–	–	1
Fortune	1	–	–	–	–	1
Johnsen	1	–	–	–	–	1
Yorke	1	–	–	–	–	1
Silvestre	–	–	–	1	–	1
own goals	2	–	–	1	–	3

RESULTS & ATTENDANCES SUMMARY

		P	W	D	L	F	A	TOTAL	AVGE
League	H	19	11	2	6	40	17	1284134	67586
	A	19	13	3	3	47	28	672535	35397
TOTAL		38	24	5	9	87	45	1956669	51491
FA Cup	H	0	0	0	0	0	0	0	n/a
	A	2	1	0	1	3	4	56068	28034
TOTAL		2	1	0	1	3	4	56068	28034
League Cup	H	0	0	0	0	0	0	0	n/a
	A	1	0	0	1	0	4	30693	30693
TOTAL		1	0	0	1	0	4	30693	30693
Champions League	H	8	5	2	1	19	8	529174	66147
	A	8	3	4	1	12	6	310406	38801
TOTAL		16	8	6	2	31	14	839580	52474
Charity Shield	H	0	0	0	0	0	0	0	n/a
	A	0	0	0	0	0	0	0	n/a
	N	1	0	0	1	1	2	70227	70227
TOTAL		1	0	0	1	1	2	70227	70227
Overall	H	27	16	4	7	59	25	1813308	67160
	A	30	17	7	6	62	42	1069702	35657
	N	1	0	0	1	1	2	70227	70227
TOTAL		58	33	11	14	122	69	2953237	50918

FINAL TABLE – FA PREMIERSHIP

		P	HOME					AWAY					PTS	GD
			W	D	L	F	A	W	D	L	F	A		
1	Arsenal	38	12	4	3	42	25	14	5	0	37	11	87	43
2	Liverpool	38	12	5	2	33	14	12	3	4	34	16	80	37
3	MANCHESTER UNITED	38	11	2	6	40	17	13	3	3	47	28	77	42
4	Newcastle United	38	12	3	4	40	23	9	5	5	34	29	71	22
5	Leeds United	38	9	6	4	31	21	9	6	4	22	16	66	16
6	Chelsea	38	11	4	4	43	21	6	9	4	23	17	64	28
7	West Ham United	38	12	4	3	32	14	3	4	12	16	43	53	-9
8	Aston Villa	38	8	7	4	22	17	4	7	8	24	30	50	-1
9	Tottenham Hotspur	38	10	4	5	32	24	4	4	11	17	29	50	-4
10	Blackburn Rovers	38	8	6	5	33	20	4	4	11	22	31	46	4
11	Southampton	38	7	5	7	23	22	5	4	10	23	32	45	-8
12	Middlesbrough	38	7	5	7	23	26	5	4	10	12	21	45	-12
13	Fulham	38	7	7	5	21	16	3	7	9	15	28	44	-8
14	Charlton Athletic	38	5	6	8	23	30	5	8	6	15	19	44	-11
15	Everton	38	8	4	7	26	23	3	6	10	19	34	43	-12
16	Bolton Wanderers	38	5	7	7	20	31	4	6	9	24	31	40	-18
17	Sunderland	38	7	7	5	18	16	3	3	13	11	35	40	-22
18	Ipswich Town	38	6	4	9	20	24	3	5	11	21	40	36	-23
19	Derby County	38	5	4	10	20	26	3	2	14	13	37	30	-30
20	Leicester City	38	3	7	9	15	34	2	6	11	15	30	28	-34

SEASON 2002/03

Match # 4694
Wednesday 14/08/02   Champions League Qualifying Round 1st Leg   at Ferenc Puskas Stadium   Attendance 40000
Result: **Zalaegerszeg 1 Manchester United 0**
Teamsheet: Carroll, Brown, Silvestre, Veron, O'Shea, Blanc, Beckham, Keane, Solskjaer, van Nistelrooy, Giggs
Substitute(s): Forlan, Neville P

Match # 4695
Saturday 17/08/02   FA Premiership   at Old Trafford   Attendance 67645
Result: **Manchester United 1 West Bromwich Albion 0**
Teamsheet: Carroll, Neville P, Silvestre, Veron, O'Shea, Blanc, Beckham, Keane, Butt, van Nistelrooy, Giggs
Substitute(s): Forlan, Scholes, Solskjaer   Scorer(s): Solskjaer

Match # 4696
Friday 23/08/02   FA Premiership   at Stamford Bridge   Attendance 41541
Result: **Chelsea 2 Manchester United 2**
Teamsheet: Carroll, Neville P, Silvestre, Keane, O'Shea, Blanc, Beckham, Butt, Scholes, van Nistelrooy, Giggs
Substitute(s): Forlan, Solskjaer, Veron   Scorer(s): Beckham, Giggs

Match # 4697
Tuesday 27/08/02   Champions League Qualifying Round 2nd Leg   at Old Trafford   Attendance 66814
Result: **Manchester United 5 Zalaegerszeg 0**
Teamsheet: Carroll, Neville P, Silvestre, Veron, Ferdinand, Blanc, Beckham, Keane, Scholes, van Nistelrooy, Giggs
Substitute(s): Forlan, O'Shea, Solskjaer   Scorer(s): van Nistelrooy 2, Beckham, Scholes, Solskjaer

Match # 4698
Saturday 31/08/02   FA Premiership   at Stadium of Light   Attendance 47586
Result: **Sunderland 1 Manchester United 1**
Teamsheet: Carroll, Neville P, Silvestre, Veron, Ferdinand, Blanc, Beckham, Keane, Solskjaer, van Nistelrooy, Giggs
Substitute(s): Forlan, O'Shea   Scorer(s): Giggs

Match # 4699
Tuesday 03/09/02   FA Premiership   at Old Trafford   Attendance 67464
Result: **Manchester United 1 Middlesbrough 0**
Teamsheet: Barthez, Neville P, Silvestre, Veron, Ferdinand, Blanc, Beckham, Butt, Scholes, van Nistelrooy, Giggs
Substitute(s): Forlan, O'Shea, Solskjaer   Scorer(s): van Nistelrooy

Match # 4700
Wednesday 11/09/02   FA Premiership   at Old Trafford   Attendance 67623
Result: **Manchester United 0 Bolton Wanderers 1**
Teamsheet: Barthez, Neville P, Silvestre, Veron, Ferdinand, Blanc, Beckham, Butt, Solskjaer, van Nistelrooy, Giggs
Substitute(s): Forlan

Match # 4701
Saturday 14/09/02   FA Premiership   at Elland Road   Attendance 39622
Result: **Leeds United 1 Manchester United 0**
Teamsheet: Barthez, O'Shea, Silvestre, Neville P, Ferdinand, Blanc, Beckham, Butt, Solskjaer, van Nistelrooy, Giggs
Substitute(s): Chadwick, Forlan

Match # 4702
Wednesday 18/09/02   Champions League Phase 1 Match 1   at Old Trafford   Attendance 63439
Result: **Manchester United 5 Maccabi Haifa 2**
Teamsheet: Barthez, O'Shea, Silvestre, Veron, Ferdinand, Blanc, Beckham, Neville P, Solskjaer, van Nistelrooy, Giggs
Substitute(s): Forlan, Pugh, Ricardo   Scorer(s): Giggs, Forlan, Solskjaer, van Nistelrooy, Veron

Match # 4703
Saturday 21/09/02   FA Premiership   at Old Trafford   Attendance 67611
Result: **Manchester United 1 Tottenham Hotspur 0**
Teamsheet: Barthez, Neville P, Silvestre, Veron, Ferdinand, O'Shea, Beckham, Butt, Solskjaer, van Nistelrooy, Giggs
Substitute(s): Forlan, Neville G, Pugh   Scorer(s): van Nistelrooy

Match # 4704
Tuesday 24/09/02   Champions League Phase 1 Match 2   at Bayarena   Attendance 22500
Result: **Bayer Leverkusen 1 Manchester United 2**
Teamsheet: Barthez, O'Shea, Silvestre, Neville P, Ferdinand, Blanc, Beckham, Butt, Veron, van Nistelrooy, Giggs
Substitute(s): Forlan, Neville G, Solskjaer   Scorer(s): van Nistelrooy 2

Match # 4705
Saturday 28/09/02   FA Premiership   at The Valley   Attendance 26630
Result: **Charlton Athletic 1 Manchester United 3**
Teamsheet: Barthez, O'Shea, Neville P, Scholes, Ferdinand, Blanc, Beckham, Butt, Solskjaer, Forlan, Giggs
Substitute(s): Neville G, van Nistelrooy   Scorer(s): Giggs, Scholes, van Nistelrooy

Match # 4706
Tuesday 01/10/02   Champions League Phase 1 Match 3   at Old Trafford   Attendance 66902
Result: **Manchester United 4 Olympiakos Piraeus 0**
Teamsheet: Barthez, Neville G, Silvestre, Veron, Ferdinand, Blanc, Beckham, Butt, Solskjaer, Scholes, Giggs
Substitute(s): Forlan, Fortune, O'Shea   Scorer(s): Giggs, Solskjaer, Veron, own goal

Match # 4707
Monday 07/10/02   FA Premiership   at Old Trafford   Attendance 67629
Result: **Manchester United 3 Everton 0**
Teamsheet: Barthez, Neville G, Silvestre, Veron, O'Shea, Blanc, Beckham, Butt, Scholes, van Nistelrooy, Giggs
Substitute(s): Forlan, Neville P, Solskjaer   Scorer(s): Scholes 2, van Nistelrooy

Match # 4708
Saturday 19/10/02   FA Premiership   at Loftus Road   Attendance 18103
Result: **Fulham 1 Manchester United 1**
Teamsheet: Barthez, Neville G, Silvestre, Veron, O'Shea, Blanc, Beckham, Neville P, Solskjaer, Scholes, Giggs
Substitute(s): Forlan, Fortune   Scorer(s): Solskjaer

Match # 4709
Wednesday 23/10/02   Champions League Phase 1 Match 4   at Rizoupoli   Attendance 13200
Result: **Olympiakos Piraeus 2 Manchester United 3**
Teamsheet: Barthez, Neville G, Silvestre, Veron, O'Shea, Blanc, Beckham, Neville P, Scholes, Forlan, Giggs
Substitute(s): Chadwick, Fortune, Richardson   Scorer(s): Blanc, Scholes, Veron

Match # 4710
Saturday 26/10/02   FA Premiership   at Old Trafford   Attendance 67619
Result: **Manchester United 1 Aston Villa 1**
Teamsheet: Barthez, Neville G, Silvestre, Veron, Ferdinand, Blanc, Beckham, Neville P, Solskjaer, Forlan, Scholes
Substitute(s): Fortune   Scorer(s): Forlan

Match # 4711
Tuesday 29/10/02   Champions League Phase 1 Match 5   at Neo GSP Stadium, Cyprus   Attendance 22000
Result: **Maccabi Haifa 3 Manchester United 0**
Teamsheet: Ricardo, Neville G, Silvestre, Neville P, Ferdinand, O'Shea, Richardson, Scholes, Solskjaer, Forlan, Fortune
Substitute(s): Nardiello, Timm

SEASON 2002/03 (continued)

Match # 4712 Saturday 02/11/02   FA Premiership   at Old Trafford   Attendance 67691
Result: **Manchester United 2 Southampton 1**
Teamsheet: Barthez, Neville G, Silvestre, Veron, Ferdinand, Blanc, Beckham, Neville P, Scholes, van Nistelrooy, Giggs
Substitute(s): Forlan, O'Shea, Solskjaer   Scorer(s):   Forlan, Neville P

Match # 4713 Tuesday 05/11/02   League Cup 3rd Round   at Old Trafford   Attendance 47848
Result: **Manchester United 2 Leicester City 0**
Teamsheet: Carroll, Neville G, Neville P, May, Ferdinand, O'Shea, Beckham, Nardiello, Solskjaer, Forlan, Fortune
Substitute(s): Richardson, Scholes, Veron   Scorer(s):   Beckham, Richardson

Match # 4714 Saturday 09/11/02   FA Premiership   at Maine Road   Attendance 34649
Result: **Manchester City 3 Manchester United 1**
Teamsheet: Barthez, Neville G, Silvestre, Veron, Ferdinand, Blanc, Scholes, Neville P, Solskjaer, van Nistelrooy, Giggs
Substitute(s): Forlan, O'Shea   Scorer(s):   Solskjaer

Match # 4715 Wednesday 13/11/02   Champions League Phase 1 Match 6   at Old Trafford   Attendance 66185
Result: **Manchester United 2 Bayer Leverkusen 0**
Teamsheet: Ricardo, O'Shea, Silvestre, Veron, Ferdinand, Blanc, Beckham, Fortune, Scholes, van Nistelrooy, Giggs
Substitute(s): Chadwick, Neville G, Solskjaer   Scorer(s):   van Nistelrooy, Veron

Match # 4716 Sunday 17/11/02   FA Premiership   at Upton Park   Attendance 35049
Result: **West Ham United 1 Manchester United 1**
Teamsheet: Barthez, O'Shea, Silvestre, Veron, Brown, Blanc, Scholes, Fortune, Solskjaer, van Nistelrooy, Giggs
Scorer(s):   van Nistelrooy

Match # 4717 Saturday 23/11/02   FA Premiership   at Old Trafford   Attendance 67625
Result: **Manchester United 5 Newcastle United 3**
Teamsheet: Barthez, O'Shea, Silvestre, Fortune, Brown, Blanc, Scholes, Forlan, Solskjaer, van Nistelrooy, Giggs
Substitute(s): Richardson, Roche, Veron   Scorer(s):   van Nistelrooy 3, Scholes, Solskjaer

Match # 4718 Tuesday 26/11/02   Champions League Phase 2 Match 1   at St Jakob Stadium   Attendance 29501
Result: **Basel 1 Manchester United 3**
Teamsheet: Barthez, Neville P, Silvestre, Veron, Brown, O'Shea, Scholes, Fortune, Solskjaer, van Nistelrooy, Giggs
Substitute(s): Chadwick, Forlan, May   Scorer(s):   van Nistelrooy 2, Solskjaer

Match # 4719 Sunday 01/12/02   FA Premiership   at Anfield   Attendance 44250
Result: **Liverpool 1 Manchester United 2**
Teamsheet: Barthez, Neville G, Silvestre, Fortune, Brown, O'Shea, Scholes, Forlan, Solskjaer, van Nistelrooy, Giggs
Substitute(s): May, Neville P, Stewart   Scorer(s):   Forlan 2

Match # 4720 Tuesday 03/12/02   League Cup 4th Round   at Turf Moor   Attendance 22034
Result: **Burnley 0 Manchester United 2**
Teamsheet: Carroll, Neville P, Silvestre, O'Shea, Brown, May, Chadwick, Stewart, Forlan, van Nistelrooy, Pugh
Substitute(s): Giggs, Scholes, Solskjaer   Scorer(s):   Forlan, Solskjaer

Match # 4721 Saturday 07/12/02   FA Premiership   at Old Trafford   Attendance 67650
Result: **Manchester United 2 Arsenal 0**
Teamsheet: Barthez, Neville G, Silvestre, Veron, Brown, O'Shea, Scholes, Neville P, Solskjaer, van Nistelrooy, Giggs
Scorer(s):   Scholes, Veron

Match # 4722 Wednesday 11/12/02   Champions League Phase 2 Match 2   at Old Trafford   Attendance 67014
Result: **Manchester United 2 Deportivo La Coruna 0**
Teamsheet: Barthez, Neville G, Silvestre, Veron, Brown, O'Shea, Scholes, Neville P, Solskjaer, van Nistelrooy, Giggs
Substitute(s): Beckham, Forlan, Richardson   Scorer(s):   van Nistelrooy 2

Match # 4723 Saturday 14/12/02   FA Premiership   at Old Trafford   Attendance 67555
Result: **Manchester United 3 West Ham United 0**
Teamsheet: Barthez, Neville G, Silvestre, Veron, Brown, O'Shea, Scholes, Neville P, Solskjaer, van Nistelrooy, Giggs
Substitute(s): Beckham, Blanc, Forlan   Scorer(s):   Solskjaer, Veron, own goal

Match # 4724 Tuesday 17/12/02   League Cup 5th Round   at Old Trafford   Attendance 57985
Result: **Manchester United 1 Chelsea 0**
Teamsheet: Barthez, Neville G, Silvestre, Veron, Brown, O'Shea, Beckham, Neville P, Scholes, Forlan, Giggs
Scorer(s):   Forlan

Match # 4725 Sunday 22/12/02   FA Premiership   at Ewood Park   Attendance 30475
Result: **Blackburn Rovers 1 Manchester United 0**
Teamsheet: Barthez, Neville G, Silvestre, Neville P, Brown, O'Shea, Scholes, Forlan, Solskjaer, van Nistelrooy, Giggs
Substitute(s): Beckham, Blanc, Keane

Match # 4726 Thursday 26/12/02   FA Premiership   at Riverside Stadium   Attendance 34673
Result: **Middlesbrough 3 Manchester United 1**
Teamsheet: Barthez, Neville G, O'Shea, Veron, Brown, Blanc, Scholes, Keane, Solskjaer, van Nistelrooy, Giggs
Substitute(s): Beckham, Ferdinand   Scorer(s):   Giggs

Match # 4727 Saturday 28/12/02   FA Premiership   at Old Trafford   Attendance 67640
Result: **Manchester United 2 Birmingham City 0**
Teamsheet: Barthez, O'Shea, Silvestre, Veron, Brown, Ferdinand, Beckham, Keane, Solskjaer, Forlan, Scholes
Substitute(s): Giggs, Neville P, Richardson   Scorer(s):   Beckham, Forlan

Match # 4728 Wednesday 01/01/03   FA Premiership   at Old Trafford   Attendance 67609
Result: **Manchester United 2 Sunderland 1**
Teamsheet: Barthez, O'Shea, Silvestre, Veron, Brown, Ferdinand, Beckham, Keane, Solskjaer, Forlan, Scholes
Substitute(s): Carroll, Giggs, Neville G   Scorer(s):   Beckham, Scholes

Match # 4729 Saturday 04/01/03   FA Cup 3rd Round   at Old Trafford   Attendance 67222
Result: **Manchester United 4 Portsmouth 1**
Teamsheet: Carroll, Neville G, Silvestre, Neville P, Ferdinand, Blanc, Beckham, Keane, Giggs, van Nistelrooy, Richardson
Substitute(s): Brown, Scholes, Stewart   Scorer(s):   van Nistelrooy 2, Beckham, Scholes

SEASON 2002/03 (continued)

Match # 4730 Tuesday 07/01/03 League Cup Semi-Final 1st Leg at Old Trafford Attendance 62740
Result: **Manchester United 1 Blackburn Rovers 1**
Teamsheet: Barthez, Neville G, Silvestre, Veron, Brown, Ferdinand, Beckham, Neville P, Scholes, van Nistelrooy, Giggs
Substitute(s): Forlan, Solskjaer Scorer(s): Scholes

Match # 4731 Saturday 11/01/03 FA Premiership at The Hawthorns Attendance 27129
Result: **West Bromwich Albion 1 Manchester United 3**
Teamsheet: Barthez, Neville G, Silvestre, Neville P, Brown, Ferdinand, Beckham, Keane, Solskjaer, van Nistelrooy, Scholes
Substitute(s): Forlan, O'Shea Scorer(s): Scholes, Solskjaer, van Nistelrooy

Match # 4732 Saturday 18/01/03 FA Premiership at Old Trafford Attendance 67606
Result: **Manchester United 2 Chelsea 1**
Teamsheet: Barthez, Neville G, Silvestre, Neville P, Brown, Ferdinand, Beckham, Keane, Solskjaer, van Nistelrooy, Scholes
Substitute(s): Forlan, Giggs, Veron Scorer(s): Forlan, Scholes

Match # 4733 Wednesday 22/01/03 League Cup Semi-Final 2nd Leg at Ewood Park Attendance 29048
Result: **Blackburn Rovers 1 Manchester United 3**
Teamsheet: Barthez, Neville G, Silvestre, Veron, Brown, Ferdinand, Beckham, Keane, Scholes, van Nistelrooy, Giggs
Substitute(s): Butt, Forlan Scorer(s): Scholes 2, van Nistelrooy

Match # 4734 Sunday 26/01/03 FA Cup 4th Round at Old Trafford Attendance 67181
Result: **Manchester United 6 West Ham United 0**
Teamsheet: Barthez, Neville G, Neville P, Veron, O'Shea, Ferdinand, Beckham, Keane, Scholes, van Nistelrooy, Giggs
Substitute(s): Butt, Forlan, Solskjaer Scorer(s): Giggs 2, van Nistelrooy 2, Neville P, Solskjaer

Match # 4735 Saturday 01/02/03 FA Premiership at St Mary's Stadium Attendance 32085
Result: **Southampton 0 Manchester United 2**
Teamsheet: Barthez, Neville G, Silvestre, Veron, O'Shea, Ferdinand, Beckham, Keane, Solskjaer, van Nistelrooy, Giggs
Substitute(s): Carroll, Forlan, Scholes Scorer(s): Giggs, van Nistelrooy

Match # 4736 Tuesday 04/02/03 FA Premiership at St Andrews Attendance 29475
Result: **Birmingham City 0 Manchester United 1**
Teamsheet: Carroll, Neville G, Silvestre, Veron, Brown, Ferdinand, Beckham, Keane, Scholes, van Nistelrooy, Giggs
Substitute(s): Solskjaer Scorer(s): van Nistelrooy

Match # 4737 Sunday 09/02/03 FA Premiership at Old Trafford Attendance 67646
Result: **Manchester United 1 Manchester City 1**
Teamsheet: Carroll, Neville G, Silvestre, Veron, Brown, Ferdinand, Beckham, Keane, Scholes, van Nistelrooy, Giggs
Substitute(s): Butt, Solskjaer Scorer(s): van Nistelrooy

Match # 4738 Saturday 15/02/03 FA Cup 5th Round at Old Trafford Attendance 67209
Result: **Manchester United 0 Arsenal 2**
Teamsheet: Barthez, Neville G, Silvestre, Scholes, Brown, Ferdinand, Beckham, Keane, Solskjaer, van Nistelrooy, Giggs
Substitute(s): Butt, Forlan

Match # 4739 Wednesday 19/02/03 Champions League Phase 2 Match 3 at Old Trafford Attendance 66703
Result: **Manchester United 2 Juventus 1**
Teamsheet: Barthez, Neville G, Silvestre, Butt, Brown, Ferdinand, Beckham, Keane, Scholes, van Nistelrooy, Giggs
Substitute(s): Forlan, O'Shea, Solskjaer Scorer(s): Brown, van Nistelrooy

Match # 4740 Saturday 22/02/03 FA Premiership at Reebok Stadium Attendance 27409
Result: **Bolton Wanderers 1 Manchester United 1**
Teamsheet: Barthez, Neville G, O'Shea, Veron, Brown, Ferdinand, Beckham, Keane, Solskjaer, van Nistelrooy, Giggs
Substitute(s): Butt, Forlan, Neville P Scorer(s): Solskjaer

Match # 4741 Tuesday 25/02/03 Champions League Phase 2 Match 4 at Stadio Delle Alpi Attendance 59111
Result: **Juventus 0 Manchester United 3**
Teamsheet: Barthez, Neville G, O'Shea, Veron, Keane, Ferdinand, Beckham, Neville P, Solskjaer, Forlan, Butt
Substitute(s): Giggs, Pugh, van Nistelrooy Scorer(s): Giggs 2, van Nistelrooy

Match # 4742 Sunday 02/03/03 League Cup Final at Millennium Stadium Attendance 74500
Result: **Manchester United 0 Liverpool 2**
Teamsheet: Barthez, Neville G, Silvestre, Veron, Brown, Ferdinand, Beckham, Keane, Scholes, van Nistelrooy, Giggs
Substitute(s): Solskjaer

Match # 4743 Wednesday 05/03/03 FA Premiership at Old Trafford Attendance 67135
Result: **Manchester United 2 Leeds United 1**
Teamsheet: Barthez, O'Shea, Silvestre, Veron, Keane, Ferdinand, Beckham, Butt, Scholes, van Nistelrooy, Fortune
Substitute(s): Giggs, Neville G, Neville P Scorer(s): Silvestre, own goal

Match # 4744 Wednesday 12/03/03 Champions League Phase 2 Match 5 at Old Trafford Attendance 66870
Result: **Manchester United 1 Basel 1**
Teamsheet: Carroll, Neville G, O'Shea, Butt, Blanc, Ferdinand, Fletcher, Neville P, Solskjaer, Forlan, Richardson
Substitute(s): Beckham, Giggs, Scholes Scorer(s): Neville G

Match # 4745 Saturday 15/03/03 FA Premiership at Villa Park Attendance 42602
Result: **Aston Villa 0 Manchester United 1**
Teamsheet: Barthez, Neville G, Silvestre, Butt, O'Shea, Ferdinand, Beckham, Scholes, Solskjaer, van Nistelrooy, Giggs
Scorer(s): Beckham

Match # 4746 Tuesday 18/03/03 Champions League Phase 2 Match 6 at Estadio de Riazor Attendance 25000
Result: **Deportivo La Coruna 2 Manchester United 0**
Teamsheet: Ricardo, Roche, Lynch, Pugh, Blanc, O'Shea, Fletcher, Neville P, Forlan, Butt, Giggs
Substitute(s): Richardson, Stewart, Webber

Match # 4747 Saturday 22/03/03 FA Premiership at Old Trafford Attendance 67706
Result: **Manchester United 3 Fulham 0**
Teamsheet: Barthez, Neville G, O'Shea, Butt, Brown, Ferdinand, Beckham, Scholes, Solskjaer, van Nistelrooy, Giggs
Scorer(s): van Nistelrooy 3

SEASON 2002/03 (continued)

Match # 4748 Saturday 05/04/03 FA Premiership at Old Trafford Attendance 67639
Result: **Manchester United 4 Liverpool 0**
Teamsheet: Barthez, Neville G, Silvestre, Neville P, Brown, Ferdinand, Scholes, Keane, Solskjaer, van Nistelrooy, Giggs
Substitute(s): Beckham, Butt, O'Shea Scorer(s): van Nistelrooy 2, Giggs, Solskjaer

Match # 4749 Tuesday 08/04/03 Champions League Quarter-Final 1st Leg at Bernabeu Stadium Attendance 75000
Result: **Real Madrid 3 Manchester United 1**
Teamsheet: Barthez, Neville G, Silvestre, Butt, Brown, Ferdinand, Beckham, Keane, Scholes, van Nistelrooy, Giggs
Substitute(s): O'Shea, Solskjaer Scorer(s): van Nistelrooy

Match # 4750 Saturday 12/04/03 FA Premiership at St James' Park Attendance 52164
Result: **Newcastle United 2 Manchester United 6**
Teamsheet: Barthez, O'Shea, Silvestre, Butt, Brown, Ferdinand, Scholes, Keane, Solskjaer, van Nistelrooy, Giggs
Substitute(s): Blanc, Forlan, Neville G Scorer(s): Scholes 3, Giggs, Solskjaer, van Nistelrooy

Match # 4751 Wednesday 16/04/03 FA Premiership at Highbury Attendance 38164
Result: **Arsenal 2 Manchester United 2**
Teamsheet: Barthez, O'Shea, Silvestre, Butt, Brown, Ferdinand, Scholes, Keane, Solskjaer, van Nistelrooy, Giggs
Substitute(s): Neville G Scorer(s): Giggs, van Nistelrooy

Match # 4752 Saturday 19/04/03 FA Premiership at Old Trafford Attendance 67626
Result: **Manchester United 3 Blackburn Rovers 1**
Teamsheet: Barthez, Neville P, Silvestre, Butt, Brown, Ferdinand, Beckham, Fortune, Scholes, van Nistelrooy, Giggs
Substitute(s): Keane, Ricardo, Solskjaer Scorer(s): Scholes 2, van Nistelrooy

Match # 4753 Wednesday 23/04/03 Champions League Quarter-Final 2nd Leg at Old Trafford Attendance 66708
Result: **Manchester United 4 Real Madrid 3**
Teamsheet: Barthez, O'Shea, Silvestre, Butt, Brown, Ferdinand, Veron, Keane, Solskjaer, van Nistelrooy, Giggs
Substitute(s): Beckham, Fortune, Neville P Scorer(s): Beckham 2, van Nistelrooy, own goal

Match # 4754 Sunday 27/04/03 FA Premiership at White Hart Lane Attendance 36073
Result: **Tottenham Hotspur 0 Manchester United 2**
Teamsheet: Carroll, O'Shea, Silvestre, Scholes, Brown, Ferdinand, Beckham, Keane, Solskjaer, van Nistelrooy, Giggs
Substitute(s): Fortune, Neville G Scorer(s): Scholes, van Nistelrooy

Match # 4755 Saturday 03/05/03 FA Premiership at Old Trafford Attendance 67721
Result: **Manchester United 4 Charlton Athletic 1**
Teamsheet: Carroll, O'Shea, Silvestre, Scholes, Brown, Ferdinand, Beckham, Keane, Solskjaer, van Nistelrooy, Giggs
Substitute(s): Butt, Forlan, Veron Scorer(s): van Nistelrooy 3, Beckham

Match # 4756 Sunday 11/05/03 FA Premiership at Goodison Park Attendance 40168
Result: **Everton 1 Manchester United 2**
Teamsheet: Carroll, O'Shea, Silvestre, Scholes, Brown, Ferdinand, Beckham, Keane, Solskjaer, van Nistelrooy, Giggs
Substitute(s): Blanc, Fortune, Neville P Scorer(s): Beckham, van Nistelrooy

SEASON 2002/03 SUMMARY

APPEARANCES

PLAYER	LGE	FAC	LC	CL	TOTAL
Silvestre	34	2	5	13	54
Giggs	32 (4)	3	4 (1)	13 (2)	52 (7)
van Nistelrooy	33 (1)	3	4	10 (1)	50 (2)
Scholes	31 (2)	2 (1)	4 (2)	9 (1)	46 (6)
Barthez	30	2	4	10	46
Beckham	27 (4)	3	5	10 (3)	45 (7)
Ferdinand	27 (1)	3	4	11	45 (1)
O'Shea	26 (6)	1	3	12 (4)	42 (10)
Solskjaer	29 (8)	1 (1)	1 (3)	9 (5)	40 (17)
Veron	21 (4)	1	4 (1)	11	37 (5)
Neville G	19 (7)	3	5	8 (2)	35 (9)
Neville P	19 (6)	2	4	10 (2)	35 (8)
Brown	22	1 (1)	5	6	34 (1)
Keane	19 (2)	3	2	6	30 (2)
Blanc	15 (4)	1	–	9	25 (4)
Butt	14 (4)	– (2)	– (1)	8	22 (7)
Forlan	7 (18)	– (2)	3 (2)	5 (8)	15 (30)
Carroll	8 (2)	1	2	3	14 (2)
Fortune	5 (4)	–	1	3 (3)	9 (7)
Richardson	– (2)	1	– (1)	2 (3)	3 (6)
Ricardo	– (1)	–	–	3 (1)	3 (2)
Pugh	– (1)	–	1	1 (2)	2 (3)
May	– (1)	–	2	– (1)	2 (2)
Fletcher	–	–	–	2	2
Chadwick	– (1)	–	1	– (3)	1 (4)
Stewart	– (1)	– (1)	1	– (1)	1 (3)
Nardiello	–	–	1	– (1)	1 (1)
Roche	– (1)	–	–	1	1 (1)
Lynch	–	–	–	1	1
Timm	–	–	–	– (1)	– (1)
Webber	–	–	–	– (1)	– (1)

GOALSCORERS

PLAYER	LGE	FAC	LC	CL	TOTAL
van Nistelrooy	25	4	1	14	44
Scholes	14	1	3	2	20
Solskjaer	9	1	1	4	15
Giggs	8	2	–	4	14
Beckham	6	1	1	3	11
Forlan	6	–	2	1	9
Veron	2	–	–	4	6
Neville	1	1	–	–	2
Silvestre	1	–	–	–	1
Blanc	–	–	–	1	1
Brown	–	–	–	1	1
Neville G	–	–	–	1	1
Richardson	–	–	1	–	1
own goals	2	–	–	2	4

RESULTS & ATTENDANCES SUMMARY

		P	W	D	L	F	A	TOTAL	AVGE
League	H	19	16	2	1	42	12	1284440	67602
	A	19	9	6	4	32	22	677847	35676
TOTAL		38	25	8	5	74	34	1962287	51639
FA Cup	H	3	2	0	1	10	3	201612	67204
	A	0	0	0	0	0	0	0	n/a
TOTAL		3	2	0	1	10	3	201612	67204
League	H	3	2	1	0	4	1	168573	56191
Cup	A	2	2	0	0	5	1	51082	25541
	N	1	0	0	1	0	2	74500	74500
TOTAL		6	4	1	1	9	4	294155	49026
Champions	H	8	7	1	0	25	7	530635	66329
League	A	8	4	0	4	12	13	286312	35789
TOTAL		16	11	1	4	37	20	816947	51059
Overall	H	33	27	4	2	81	23	2185260	66220
	A	29	15	6	8	49	36	1015241	35008
	N	1	0	0	1	0	2	74500	74500
TOTAL		63	42	10	11	130	61	3275001	51984

FINAL TABLE - FA PREMIERSHIP

		P	W	D	L	F	A	W	D	L	F	A	PTS	GD
			HOME					AWAY						
1	MANCHESTER UNITED	38	16	2	1	42	12	9	6	4	32	22	83	40
2	Arsenal	38	15	2	2	47	20	8	7	4	38	22	78	43
3	Newcastle United	38	15	2	2	36	17	6	4	9	27	31	69	15
4	Chelsea	38	12	5	2	41	15	7	5	7	27	23	67	30
5	Liverpool	38	9	8	2	30	16	9	2	8	31	25	64	20
6	Blackburn Rovers	38	9	7	3	24	15	7	5	7	28	28	60	9
7	Everton	38	11	5	3	28	19	6	3	10	20	30	59	-1
8	Southampton	38	9	8	2	25	16	4	5	10	18	30	52	-3
9	Manchester City	38	9	2	8	28	26	6	4	9	19	28	51	-7
10	Tottenham Hotspur	38	9	4	6	30	29	5	4	10	21	33	50	-11
11	Middlesbrough	38	10	7	2	36	21	3	3	13	12	23	49	4
12	Charlton Athletic	38	8	3	8	26	30	6	4	9	19	26	49	-11
13	Birmingham City	38	8	5	6	25	23	5	4	10	16	26	48	-8
14	Fulham	38	11	3	5	26	18	2	6	11	15	32	48	-9
15	Leeds United	38	7	3	9	25	26	7	2	10	33	31	47	1
16	Aston Villa	38	11	2	6	25	14	1	7	11	17	33	45	-5
17	Bolton Wanderers	38	7	8	4	27	24	3	6	10	14	27	44	-10
18	West Ham United	38	5	7	7	21	24	5	5	9	21	35	42	-17
19	West Bromwich Albion	38	3	5	11	17	34	3	3	13	12	31	26	-36
20	Sunderland	38	3	2	14	11	31	1	5	13	10	34	19	-44

SEASON 2003/04

Match # 4757   Sunday 10/08/03   FA Charity Shield   at Millennium Stadium   Attendance 59293
Result: **Manchester United 1   Arsenal 1   (United won the tie 4-3 on penalty kicks)**
Teamsheet: Howard, Neville P, Fortune, Keane, Ferdinand, Silvestre, Scholes, Butt, Solskjaer, van Nistelrooy, Giggs
Substitute(s):   Djemba-Djemba, Forlan, O'Shea   Scorer(s):   Silvestre

Match # 4758   Saturday 16/08/03   FA Premiership   at Old Trafford   Attendance 67647
Result: **Manchester United 4   Bolton Wanderers 0**
Teamsheet: Howard, Neville P, Fortune, Butt, Ferdinand, Silvestre, Solskjaer, Keane, Scholes, van Nistelrooy, Giggs
Substitute(s):   Djemba-Djemba, Forlan, Ronaldo   Scorer(s):   Giggs 2, Scholes, van Nistelrooy

Match # 4759   Saturday 23/08/03   FA Premiership   at St James' Park   Attendance 52165
Result: **Newcastle United 1   Manchester United 2**
Teamsheet: Howard, Neville P, O'Shea, Djemba-Djemba, Ferdinand, Silvestre, Solskjaer, Keane, Scholes, van Nistelrooy, Giggs
Substitute(s):   Forlan, Ronaldo   Scorer(s):   Scholes, van Nistelrooy

Match # 4760   Wednesday 27/08/03   FA Premiership   at Old Trafford   Attendance 67648
Result: **Manchester United 1   Wolverhampton Wanderers 0**
Teamsheet: Howard, Neville G, Neville P, Djemba-Djemba, O'Shea, Keane, Ronaldo, Kleberson, Solskjaer, van Nistelrooy, Forlan
Substitute(s):   Bellion, Giggs, Scholes   Scorer(s):   O'Shea

Match # 4761   Sunday 31/08/03   FA Premiership   at St Mary's Stadium   Attendance 32066
Result: **Southampton 1   Manchester United 0**
Teamsheet: Howard, Neville G, Neville P, Djemba-Djemba, O'Shea, Silvestre, Kleberson, Keane, Forlan, van Nistelrooy, Giggs
Substitute(s):   Butt, Fortune, Ronaldo

Match # 4762   Saturday 13/09/03   FA Premiership   at The Valley   Attendance 26078
Result: **Charlton Athletic 0   Manchester United 2**
Teamsheet: Howard, Neville G, Neville P, Butt, Ferdinand, O'Shea, Fortune, Keane, Ronaldo, van Nistelrooy, Giggs
Substitute(s):   Silvestre, Solskjaer   Scorer(s):   van Nistelrooy 2

Match # 4763   Tuesday 16/09/03   Champions League Phase 1 Match 1   at Old Trafford   Attendance 66520
Result: **Manchester United 5   Panathinaikos 0**
Teamsheet: Howard, Neville G, O'Shea, Neville P, Silvestre, Fortune, Butt, Solskjaer, van Nistelrooy, Giggs
Substitute(s):   Bellion, Djemba-Djemba, Fletcher   Scorer(s):   Butt, Djemba-Djemba, Fortune, Silvestre, Solskjaer

Match # 4764   Sunday 21/09/03   FA Premiership   at Old Trafford   Attendance 67639
Result: **Manchester United 0   Arsenal 0**
Teamsheet: Howard, Neville G, O'Shea, Neville P, Ferdinand, Silvestre, Ronaldo, Keane, Fortune, van Nistelrooy, Giggs
Substitute(s):   Forlan

Match # 4765   Saturday 27/09/03   FA Premiership   at Walkers Stadium   Attendance 32044
Result: **Leicester City 1   Manchester United 4**
Teamsheet: Howard, Neville G, Fortune, Neville P, Ferdinand, O'Shea, Fletcher, Keane, Scholes, van Nistelrooy, Giggs
Substitute(s):   Butt, Djemba-Djemba, Forlan   Scorer(s):   van Nistelrooy 3, Keane

Match # 4766   Wednesday 01/10/03   Champions League Phase 1 Match 2   at Gottlieb-Daimler Stadium   Attendance 53000
Result: **Stuttgart 2   Manchester United 1**
Teamsheet: Howard, Neville G, O'Shea, Neville P, Ferdinand, Silvestre, Ronaldo, Keane, Scholes, van Nistelrooy, Giggs
Substitute(s):   Fletcher, Forlan, Fortune   Scorer(s):   van Nistelrooy

Match # 4767   Saturday 04/10/03   FA Premiership   at Old Trafford   Attendance 67633
Result: **Manchester United 3   Birmingham City 0**
Teamsheet: Howard, Neville G, Fortune, Neville P, Ferdinand, Silvestre, Fletcher, Keane, Scholes, van Nistelrooy, Giggs
Substitute(s):   Butt, Forlan   Scorer(s):   Giggs, Scholes, van Nistelrooy

Match # 4768   Saturday 18/10/03   FA Premiership   at Elland Road   Attendance 40153
Result: **Leeds United 0   Manchester United 1**
Teamsheet: Howard, Neville G, Fortune, Neville P, Ferdinand, Silvestre, Fletcher, Keane, Scholes, van Nistelrooy, Ronaldo
Substitute(s):   Butt, Forlan, O'Shea   Scorer(s):   Keane

Match # 4769   Wednesday 22/10/03   Champions League Phase 1 Match 3   at Ibrox Stadium   Attendance 48730
Result: **Glasgow Rangers 0   Manchester United 1**
Teamsheet: Howard, Neville G, O'Shea, Neville P, Ferdinand, Silvestre, Fortune, Keane, Scholes, van Nistelrooy, Giggs
Substitute(s):   Butt, Djemba-Djemba   Scorer(s):   Neville P

Match # 4770   Saturday 25/10/03   FA Premiership   at Old Trafford   Attendance 67727
Result: **Manchester United 1   Fulham 3**
Teamsheet: Howard, Neville G, O'Shea, Djemba-Djemba, Ferdinand, Silvestre, Ronaldo, Butt, Forlan, van Nistelrooy, Giggs
Substitute(s):   Bellion, Fortune, Scholes   Scorer(s):   Forlan

Match # 4771   Tuesday 28/10/03   League Cup 3rd Round   at Elland Road   Attendance 37546
Result: **Leeds United 2   Manchester United 3**
Teamsheet: Carroll, Neville P, Fortune, Djemba-Djemba, Neville G, O'Shea, Fletcher, Butt, Forlan, Bellion, Richardson
Substitute(s):   Eagles, Johnson   Scorer(s):   Bellion, Djemba-Djemba, Forlan

Match # 4772   Saturday 01/11/03   FA Premiership   at Old Trafford   Attendance 67639
Result: **Manchester United 3   Portsmouth 0**
Teamsheet: Howard, Neville G, Fortune, Djemba-Djemba, Ferdinand, O'Shea, Fletcher, Butt, Forlan, van Nistelrooy, Giggs
Substitute(s):   Bellion, Keane, Ronaldo   Scorer(s):   Forlan, Keane, Ronaldo

Match # 4773   Tuesday 04/11/03   Champions League Phase 1 Match 4   at Old Trafford   Attendance 66707
Result: **Manchester United 3   Glasgow Rangers 0**
Teamsheet: Howard, Neville G, Fortune, Neville P, Ferdinand, Silvestre, Ronaldo, Keane, Forlan, van Nistelrooy, Giggs
Substitute(s):   Bellion, Fletcher, Kleberson   Scorer(s):   van Nistelrooy 2, Forlan

Match # 4774   Sunday 09/11/03   FA Premiership   at Anfield   Attendance 44159
Result: **Liverpool 1   Manchester United 2**
Teamsheet: Howard, Neville G, O'Shea, Neville P, Ferdinand, Silvestre, Fortune, Keane, Forlan, van Nistelrooy, Giggs
Substitute(s):   Fletcher   Scorer(s):   Giggs 2

SEASON 2003/04 (continued)

Match # 4775   Saturday 22/11/03   FA Premiership   at Old Trafford   Attendance 67748
Result: **Manchester United 2 Blackburn Rovers 1**
Teamsheet: Howard, Neville G, O'Shea, Neville P, Ferdinand, Silvestre, Kleberson, Keane, Fortune, van Nistelrooy, Bellion
Substitute(s):   Forlan, Giggs, Ronaldo   Scorer(s):   Kleberson, van Nistelrooy

Match # 4776   Wednesday 26/11/03   Champions League Phase 1 Match 5   at Apostolos Nikolaidis   Attendance 6890
Result: **Panathinaikos 0 Manchester United 1**
Teamsheet: Howard, O'Shea, Fortune, Butt, Ferdinand, Silvestre, Ronaldo, Kleberson, Forlan, Fletcher, Giggs
Substitute(s):   Bellion   Scorer(s):   Forlan

Match # 4777   Sunday 30/11/03   FA Premiership   at Stamford Bridge   Attendance 41932
Result: **Chelsea 1 Manchester United 0**
Teamsheet: Howard, Neville G, O'Shea, Neville P, Ferdinand, Silvestre, Fortune, Keane, Forlan, van Nistelrooy, Giggs
Substitute(s):   Kleberson, Ronaldo

Match # 4778   Wednesday 03/12/03   League Cup 4th Round   at The Hawthorns   Attendance 25282
Result: **West Bromwich Albion 2 Manchester United 0**
Teamsheet: Carroll, Bardsley, Pugh, Tierney, O'Shea, Butt, Ronaldo, Kleberson, Bellion, Fletcher, Richardson
Substitute(s):   Eagles, Nardiello

Match # 4779   Saturday 06/12/03   FA Premiership   at Old Trafford   Attendance 67621
Result: **Manchester United 4 Aston Villa 0**
Teamsheet: Howard, Neville G, Fortune, Neville P, Ferdinand, Silvestre, Ronaldo, Keane, Kleberson, van Nistelrooy, Giggs
Substitute(s):   Bellion, Forlan, Scholes   Scorer(s):   Forlan 2, van Nistelrooy 2

Match # 4780   Tuesday 09/12/03   Champions League Phase 1 Match 6   at Old Trafford   Attendance 67141
Result: **Manchester United 2 Stuttgart 0**
Teamsheet: Carroll, Neville G, O'Shea, Neville P, Ferdinand, Silvestre, Fletcher, Fortune, Scholes, van Nistelrooy, Giggs
Substitute(s):   Bellion, Djemba-Djemba, Forlan   Scorer(s):   Giggs, van Nistelrooy

Match # 4781   Saturday 13/12/03   FA Premiership   at Old Trafford   Attendance 67643
Result: **Manchester United 3 Manchester City 1**
Teamsheet: Howard, Neville G, O'Shea, Neville P, Ferdinand, Silvestre, Kleberson, Keane, Scholes, van Nistelrooy, Giggs
Substitute(s):   Ronaldo   Scorer(s):   Scholes 2, van Nistelrooy

Match # 4782   Sunday 21/12/03   FA Premiership   at White Hart Lane   Attendance 35910
Result: **Tottenham Hotspur 1 Manchester United 2**
Teamsheet: Howard, Neville G, O'Shea, Neville P, Ferdinand, Silvestre, Fletcher, Keane, Scholes, van Nistelrooy, Giggs
Substitute(s):   Butt, Ronaldo   Scorer(s):   O'Shea, van Nistelrooy

Match # 4783   Friday 26/12/03   FA Premiership   at Old Trafford   Attendance 67642
Result: **Manchester United 3 Everton 2**
Teamsheet: Howard, Neville G, O'Shea, Butt, Ferdinand, Silvestre, Kleberson, Fortune, Forlan, Bellion, Ronaldo
Substitute(s):   Djemba-Djemba, Scholes   Scorer(s):   Bellion, Butt, Kleberson

Match # 4784   Sunday 28/12/03   FA Premiership   at Riverside Stadium   Attendance 34738
Result: **Middlesbrough 0 Manchester United 2**
Teamsheet: Howard, Neville G, Fortune, Neville P, Ferdinand, Silvestre, Fletcher, Keane, Scholes, van Nistelrooy, Giggs
Substitute(s):   Butt   Scorer(s):   Fortune

Match # 4785   Sunday 04/01/04   FA Cup 3rd Round   at Villa Park   Attendance 40371
Result: **Aston Villa 1 Manchester United 2**
Teamsheet: Howard, Neville G, O'Shea, Butt, Brown, Silvestre, Kleberson, Fortune, Scholes, Forlan, Giggs
Substitute(s):   Fletcher, Keane, van Nistelrooy   Scorer(s):   Scholes 2

Match # 4786   Wednesday 07/01/04   FA Premiership   at Reebok Stadium   Attendance 27668
Result: **Bolton Wanderers 1 Manchester United 2**
Teamsheet: Howard, Neville G, O'Shea, Neville P, Ferdinand, Silvestre, Fletcher, Keane, Scholes, van Nistelrooy, Giggs
Substitute(s):   Butt, Fortune   Scorer(s):   Scholes, van Nistelrooy

Match # 4787   Sunday 11/01/04   FA Premiership   at Old Trafford   Attendance 67622
Result: **Manchester United 0 Newcastle United 0**
Teamsheet: Howard, Neville G, O'Shea, Neville P, Ferdinand, Silvestre, Kleberson, Keane, Scholes, van Nistelrooy, Giggs
Substitute(s):   Bellion, Forlan, Fortune

Match # 4788   Saturday 17/01/04   FA Premiership   at Molineux   Attendance 29396
Result: **Wolverhampton Wanderers 1 Manchester United 0**
Teamsheet: Howard, O'Shea, Fortune, Neville P, Ferdinand, Silvestre, Fletcher, Keane, Scholes, van Nistelrooy, Ronaldo
Substitute(s):   Bellion, Brown, Forlan

Match # 4789   Sunday 25/01/04   FA Cup 4th Round   at Sixfields Stadium   Attendance 7356
Result: **Northampton Town 0 Manchester United 3**
Teamsheet: Carroll, O'Shea, Fortune, Butt, Brown, Silvestre, Fletcher, Bellion, Scholes, Forlan, Ronaldo
Substitute(s):   Bardsley, Pugh, Richardson   Scorer(s):   Forlan, Silvestre, own goal

Match # 4790   Saturday 31/01/04   FA Premiership   at Old Trafford   Attendance 67758
Result: **Manchester United 3 Southampton 2**
Teamsheet: Howard, O'Shea, Fortune, Neville P, Brown, Silvestre, Scholes, Keane, Saha, van Nistelrooy, Ronaldo
Substitute(s):   Butt, Fletcher   Scorer(s):   Saha, Scholes, van Nistelrooy

Match # 4791   Saturday 07/02/04   FA Premiership   at Goodison Park   Attendance 40190
Result: **Everton 3 Manchester United 4**
Teamsheet: Howard, Neville G, O'Shea, Keane, Brown, Silvestre, Fletcher, Scholes, Saha, van Nistelrooy, Giggs
Substitute(s):   Fortune, Ronaldo   Scorer(s):   Saha 2, van Nistelrooy 2

Match # 4792   Wednesday 11/02/04   FA Premiership   at Old Trafford   Attendance 67346
Result: **Manchester United 2 Middlesbrough 3**
Teamsheet: Howard, O'Shea, Fortune, Butt, Brown, Silvestre, Kleberson, Scholes, Saha, van Nistelrooy, Giggs
Substitute(s):   Forlan, Neville P, Ronaldo   Scorer(s):   Giggs, van Nistelrooy

SEASON 2003/04 (continued)

Match # 4793 Saturday 14/02/04   FA Cup 5th Round   at Old Trafford   Attendance 67228
Result: **Manchester United 4 Manchester City 2**
Teamsheet: Howard, Neville G, Fortune, Neville P, O'Shea, Silvestre, Ronaldo, Keane, Scholes, van Nistelrooy, Giggs
Substitute(s): Brown, Butt   Scorer(s): van Nistelrooy 2, Ronaldo, Scholes

Match # 4794 Saturday 21/02/04   FA Premiership   at Old Trafford   Attendance 67744
Result: **Manchester United 1 Leeds United 1**
Teamsheet: Howard, Neville G, Fortune, Neville P, O'Shea, Silvestre, Kleberson, Butt, Scholes, van Nistelrooy, Giggs
Substitute(s): Brown, Keane, Solskjaer   Scorer(s): Scholes

Match # 4795 Wednesday 25/02/04   Champions League 2nd Round 1st Leg   at Estadio da Dragao   Attendance 49977
Result: **Porto 2 Manchester United 1**
Teamsheet: Howard, Neville P, Fortune, Butt, Brown, Neville G, Scholes, Keane, Saha, van Nistelrooy, Giggs
Substitute(s): O'Shea, Ronaldo   Scorer(s): Fortune

Match # 4796 Saturday 28/02/04   FA Premiership   at Loftus Road   Attendance 18306
Result: **Fulham 1 Manchester United 1**
Teamsheet: Carroll, O'Shea, Fortune, Neville P, Brown, Keane, Fletcher, Scholes, Saha, Forlan, Ronaldo
Substitute(s): Giggs, van Nistelrooy   Scorer(s): Saha

Match # 4797 Saturday 06/03/04   FA Cup 6th Round   at Old Trafford   Attendance 67614
Result: **Manchester United 2 Fulham 1**
Teamsheet: Howard, Neville P, O'Shea, Butt, Brown, Keane, Fletcher, Scholes, Ronaldo, van Nistelrooy, Giggs
Substitute(s): Djemba-Djemba, Solskjaer   Scorer(s): van Nistelrooy 2

Match # 4798 Tuesday 09/03/04   Champions League 2nd Round 2nd Leg   at Old Trafford   Attendance 67029
Result: **Manchester United 1 Porto 1**
Teamsheet: Howard, Neville P, O'Shea, Butt, Brown, Neville G, Fletcher, Djemba-Djemba, Scholes, van Nistelrooy, Giggs
Substitute(s): Ronaldo, Saha, Solskjaer   Scorer(s): Scholes

Match # 4799 Sunday 14/03/04   FA Premiership   at Eastlands Stadium   Attendance 47284
Result: **Manchester City 4 Manchester United 1**
Teamsheet: Howard, Neville P, O'Shea, Butt, Brown, Silvestre, Ronaldo, Fletcher, Scholes, van Nistelrooy, Giggs
Substitute(s): Forlan, Solskjaer   Scorer(s): Scholes

Match # 4800 Saturday 20/03/04   FA Premiership   at Old Trafford   Attendance 67644
Result: **Manchester United 3 Tottenham Hotspur 0**
Teamsheet: Carroll, Neville P, O'Shea, Keane, Brown, Silvestre, Solskjaer, Scholes, Forlan, van Nistelrooy, Giggs
Substitute(s): Bellion, Butt, Ronaldo   Scorer(s): Bellion, Giggs, Ronaldo

Match # 4801 Sunday 28/03/04   FA Premiership   at Highbury   Attendance 38184
Result: **Arsenal 1 Manchester United 1**
Teamsheet: Carroll, Neville G, O'Shea, Keane, Brown, Silvestre, Fletcher, Djemba-Djemba, Scholes, van Nistelrooy, Giggs
Substitute(s): Saha, Solskjaer   Scorer(s): Saha

Match # 4802 Saturday 03/04/04   FA Cup Semi-Final   at Villa Park   Attendance 39939
Result: **Manchester United 1 Arsenal 0**
Teamsheet: Carroll, Neville G, O'Shea, Keane, Brown, Silvestre, Fletcher, Ronaldo, Scholes, Solskjaer, Giggs
Substitute(s): Bellion, Neville P   Scorer(s): Scholes

Match # 4803 Saturday 10/04/04   FA Premiership   at St Andrews   Attendance 29548
Result: **Birmingham City 1 Manchester United 2**
Teamsheet: Carroll, Neville G, O'Shea, Djemba-Djemba, Brown, Silvestre, Fletcher, Scholes, Saha, Solskjaer, Giggs
Substitute(s): Forlan, Neville P, Ronaldo   Scorer(s): Ronaldo, Saha

Match # 4804 Tuesday 13/04/04   FA Premiership   at Old Trafford   Attendance 67749
Result: **Manchester United 1 Leicester City 0**
Teamsheet: Carroll, Neville G, O'Shea, Butt, Brown, Silvestre, Bellion, Scholes, Saha, Forlan, Ronaldo
Substitute(s): Djemba-Djemba, Fletcher   Scorer(s): Neville G

Match # 4805 Saturday 17/04/04   FA Premiership   at Fratton Park   Attendance 20140
Result: **Portsmouth 1 Manchester United 0**
Teamsheet: Carroll, Neville G, O'Shea, Butt, Brown, Silvestre, Scholes, Djemba-Djemba, Saha, Solskjaer, Giggs
Substitute(s): Bellion, Fletcher, Ronaldo

Match # 4806 Tuesday 20/04/04   FA Premiership   at Old Trafford   Attendance 67477
Result: **Manchester United 2 Charlton Athletic 0**
Teamsheet: Howard, Neville G, Neville P, Butt, Brown, Silvestre, Fletcher, Djemba-Djemba, Saha, van Nistelrooy, Bellion
Substitute(s): Giggs, Keane, Ronaldo   Scorer(s): Neville G, Saha

Match # 4807 Saturday 24/04/04   FA Premiership   at Old Trafford   Attendance 67647
Result: **Manchester United 0 Liverpool 1**
Teamsheet: Howard, Neville G, O'Shea, Neville P, Brown, Silvestre, Fletcher, Keane, Saha, Ronaldo, Giggs
Substitute(s): Bellion, Solskjaer

Match # 4808 Saturday 01/05/04   FA Premiership   at Ewood Park   Attendance 29616
Result: **Blackburn Rovers 1 Manchester United 0**
Teamsheet: Howard, Neville G, O'Shea, Neville P, Brown, Silvestre, Djemba-Djemba, Butt, Solskjaer, Kleberson, Giggs
Substitute(s): Bellion, Fletcher, Forlan

Match # 4809 Saturday 08/05/04   FA Premiership   at Old Trafford   Attendance 67609
Result: **Manchester United 1 Chelsea 1**
Teamsheet: Howard, Neville G, O'Shea, Neville P, Brown, Silvestre, Ronaldo, Fletcher, Scholes, van Nistelrooy, Giggs
Substitute(s): Kleberson, Saha, Solskjaer   Scorer(s): van Nistelrooy

Match # 4810 Saturday 15/05/04   FA Premiership   at Villa Park   Attendance 42573
Result: **Aston Villa 0 Manchester United 2**
Teamsheet: Howard, Neville G, O'Shea, Neville P, Brown, Silvestre, Ronaldo, Fletcher, Scholes, van Nistelrooy, Giggs
Substitute(s): Djemba-Djemba, Saha   Scorer(s): Ronaldo, van Nistelrooy

SEASON 2003/04 (continued)

Match # 4811	Saturday 22/05/04	FA Cup Final	at Millennium Stadium	Attendance 71350
Result:	**Manchester United 3 Millwall 0**			
Teamsheet:	Howard, Neville G, O'Shea, Keane, Brown, Silvestre, Ronaldo, Fletcher, Scholes, van Nistelrooy, Giggs			
Substitute(s):	Butt, Carroll, Solskjaer	Scorer(s): van Nistelrooy 2, Ronaldo		

SEASON 2003/04 SUMMARY

APPEARANCES

PLAYER	LGE	FAC	LC	CL	CS	TOTAL
O'Shea	32 (1)	6	2	6 (1)	– (1)	46 (3)
Silvestre	33 (1)	5	–	6	1	45 (1)
Howard	32	4	–	7	1	44
Giggs	29 (4)	5	–	8	1	43 (4)
van Nistelrooy	31 (1)	3 (1)	–	7	1	42 (2)
Neville G	30	4	1	7	–	42
Neville P	29 (2)	2 (1)	1	7	1	40 (3)
Scholes	24 (4)	6	–	5	1	36 (4)
Keane	25 (3)	4 (1)	–	4	1	34 (4)
Fortune	18 (5)	3	1	6 (1)	1	29 (6)
Ferdinand	20	–	–	6	1	27
Fletcher	17 (5)	4 (1)	2	3 (3)	–	26 (9)
Ronaldo	15 (14)	5	1	3 (2)	–	24 (16)
Butt	12 (9)	3 (2)	2	4 (1)	1	22 (12)
Brown	15 (4)	5 (1)	–	2	–	22 (3)
Forlan	10 (14)	2	1	2 (2)	– (1)	15 (17)
Kleberson	10 (2)	1	–	1 (1)	–	13 (3)
Djemba-Djemba	10 (5)	– (1)	1	1 (3)	– (1)	12 (10)
Carroll	6	2 (1)	2	1	–	11 (1)
Solskjaer	7 (6)	1 (2)	–	1 (1)	1	10 (9)
Saha	9 (3)	–	–	1 (1)	–	10 (4)
Bellion	4 (10)	1 (1)	2	– (4)	–	7 (15)
Richardson	–	– (1)	2	–	–	2 (1)
Bardsley	–	– (1)	1	–	–	1 (1)
Pugh	–	– (1)	1	–	–	1 (1)
Tierney	–	–	1	–	–	1
Eagles	–	–	– (2)	–	–	– (2)
Johnson	–	–	– (1)	–	–	– (1)
Nardiello	–	–	– (1)	–	–	– (1)

GOALSCORERS

PLAYER	LGE	FAC	LC	CL	CS	TOTAL
van Nistelrooy	20	6	–	4	–	30
Scholes	9	4	–	1	–	14
Giggs	7	–	–	1	–	8
Forlan	4	1	1	2	–	8
Saha	7	–	–	–	–	7
Ronaldo	4	2	–	–	–	6
Keane	3	–	–	–	–	3
Bellion	2	–	1	–	–	3
Fortune	1	–	–	2	–	3
Silvestre	–	1	–	1	1	3
Kleberson	2	–	–	–	–	2
Neville G	2	–	–	–	–	2
O'Shea	2	–	–	–	–	2
Butt	1	–	–	1	–	2
Djemba-Djemba	–	–	1	1	–	2
Neville P	–	–	–	1	–	1
Solskjaer	–	–	–	1	–	1
own goal	–	1	–	–	–	1

RESULTS & ATTENDANCES SUMMARY

		P	W	D	L	F	A	TOTAL	AVGE
League	H	19	12	4	3	37	15	1285183	67641
	A	19	11	2	6	27	20	662150	34850
	TOTAL	38	23	6	9	64	35	1947333	51246
FA Cup	H	2	2	0	0	6	3	134842	67421
	A	2	2	0	0	5	1	47727	23864
	N	2	2	0	0	4	0	111289	55645
	TOTAL	6	6	0	0	15	4	293858	48976
League	H	0	0	0	0	0	0	0	n/a
Cup	A	2	1	0	1	3	4	62828	31414
	TOTAL	2	1	0	1	3	4	62828	31414
Champions	H	4	3	1	0	11	1	267397	66849
League	A	4	2	0	2	4	4	158597	39649
	TOTAL	8	5	1	2	15	5	425994	53249
Charity	H	0	0	0	0	0	0	0	n/a
Shield	A	0	0	0	0	0	0	0	n/a
	N	1	0	1	0	1	1	59293	59293
	TOTAL	1	0	1	0	1	1	59293	59293
Overall	H	25	17	5	3	54	19	1687422	67497
	A	27	16	2	9	39	29	931302	34493
	N	3	2	1	0	5	1	170582	56861
	TOTAL	55	35	8	12	98	49	2789306	50715

FINAL TABLE - FA PREMIERSHIP

		P	W	D	L	F	A	W	D	L	F	A	PTS	GD
				HOME						AWAY				
1	Arsenal	38	15	4	0	40	14	11	8	0	33	12	90	47
2	Chelsea	38	12	4	3	34	13	12	3	4	33	17	79	37
3	MANCHESTER UNITED	38	12	4	3	37	15	11	2	6	27	20	75	29
4	Liverpool	38	10	4	5	29	15	6	8	5	26	22	60	18
5	Newcastle United	38	11	5	3	33	14	2	12	5	19	26	56	12
6	Aston Villa	38	9	6	4	24	19	6	5	8	24	25	56	4
7	Charlton Athletic	38	7	6	6	29	29	7	5	7	22	22	53	0
8	Bolton Wanderers	38	6	8	5	24	21	8	3	8	24	35	53	-8
9	Fulham	38	9	4	6	29	21	5	6	8	23	25	52	6
10	Birmingham City	38	8	5	6	26	24	4	9	6	17	24	50	-5
11	Middlesbrough	38	8	4	7	25	23	5	5	9	19	29	48	-8
12	Southampton	38	8	6	5	24	17	4	5	10	20	28	47	-1
13	Portsmouth	38	10	4	5	35	19	2	5	12	12	35	45	-7
14	Tottenham Hotspur	38	9	4	6	33	27	4	2	13	14	30	45	-10
15	Blackburn Rovers	38	5	4	10	25	31	7	4	8	26	28	44	-8
16	Manchester City	38	5	9	5	31	24	4	5	10	24	30	41	1
17	Everton	38	8	5	6	27	20	1	7	11	18	37	39	-12
18	Leicester City	38	3	10	6	19	28	3	5	11	29	37	33	-17
19	Leeds United	38	5	7	7	25	31	3	2	14	15	48	33	-39
20	Wolverhampton Wanderers	38	7	5	7	23	35	0	7	12	15	42	33	-39

SEASON 2004/05

Match # 4812   Sunday 08/08/04   FA Charity Shield   at Millennium Stadium   Attendance 63317
Result: **Manchester United 1   Arsenal 3**
Teamsheet: Howard, Neville G, Fortune, Djemba-Djemba, O'Shea, Silvestre, Bellion, Keane, Smith, Scholes, Giggs
Substitute(s): Eagles, Fletcher, Forlan, Neville P, Spector, Richardson   Scorer(s):   Smith

Match # 4813   Wednesday 11/08/04   Champions League Qualifying Round 1st Leg   at National Stadium   Attendance 58000
Result: **Dinamo Bucharest 1   Manchester United 2**
Teamsheet: Howard, Neville G, Fortune, Keane, O'Shea, Silvestre, Fletcher, Djemba-Djemba, Scholes, Smith, Giggs
Substitute(s): Forlan, Miller, Neville P   Scorer(s):   Giggs, own goal

Match # 4814   Sunday 15/08/04   FA Premiership   at Stamford Bridge   Attendance 41813
Result: **Chelsea 1   Manchester United 0**
Teamsheet: Howard, Neville G, Fortune, Keane, Silvestre, O'Shea, Miller, Djemba-Djemba, Scholes, Smith, Giggs
Substitute(s): Bellion, Forlan, Richardson

Match # 4815   Saturday 21/08/04   FA Premiership   at Old Trafford   Attendance 67812
Result: **Manchester United 2   Norwich City 1**
Teamsheet: Howard, Neville G, O'Shea, Keane, Silvestre, Miller, Bellion, Djemba-Djemba, Scholes, Smith, Giggs
Substitute(s): Neville P, Richardson, Ronaldo   Scorer(s):   Bellion, Smith

Match # 4816   Wednesday 25/08/04   Champions League Qualifying Round 2nd Leg   at Old Trafford   Attendance 61041
Result: **Manchester United 3   Dinamo Bucharest 0**
Teamsheet: Howard, Neville G, Spector, Djemba-Djemba, Silvestre, O'Shea, Fletcher, Kleberson, Eagles, Smith, Ronaldo
Substitute(s): Bellion, Neville P, Richardson   Scorer(s):   Smith 2, Bellion

Match # 4817   Saturday 28/08/04   FA Premiership   at Ewood Park   Attendance 26155
Result: **Blackburn Rovers 1   Manchester United 1**
Teamsheet: Howard, Neville G, Spector, Kleberson, Silvestre, O'Shea, Ronaldo, Djemba-Djemba, Scholes, Smith, Giggs
Substitute(s): Bellion, Miller, Saha   Scorer(s):   Smith

Match # 4818   Monday 30/08/04   FA Premiership   at Old Trafford   Attendance 67803
Result: **Manchester United 0   Everton 0**
Teamsheet: Howard, Neville G, Spector, Kleberson, Silvestre, O'Shea, Fletcher, Scholes, Saha, Smith, Ronaldo
Substitute(s): Bellion, Djemba-Djemba, Giggs

Match # 4819   Saturday 11/09/04   FA Premiership   at Reebok Stadium   Attendance 27766
Result: **Bolton Wanderers 2   Manchester United 2**
Teamsheet: Howard, Neville P, Heinze, Keane, Silvestre, Brown, Kleberson, Scholes, Smith, van Nistelrooy, Giggs
Substitute(s): Bellion, Ronaldo   Scorer(s):   Bellion, Heinze

Match # 4820   Wednesday 15/09/04   Champions League Phase 1 Match 1   at Stade de Gerland   Attendance 40000
Result: **Olympique Lyonnais 2   Manchester United 2**
Teamsheet: Howard, O'Shea, Heinze, Keane, Silvestre, Brown, Ronaldo, Djemba-Djemba, Scholes, van Nistelrooy, Giggs
Substitute(s): Neville P, Smith   Scorer(s):   van Nistelrooy 2

Match # 4821   Monday 20/09/04   FA Premiership   at Old Trafford   Attendance 67857
Result: **Manchester United 2   Liverpool 1**
Teamsheet: Carroll, Brown, Heinze, O'Shea, Silvestre, Ferdinand, Ronaldo, Keane, Scholes, van Nistelrooy, Giggs
Substitute(s): Smith   Scorer(s):   Silvestre 2

Match # 4822   Saturday 25/09/04   FA Premiership   at White Hart Lane   Attendance 36103
Result: **Tottenham Hotspur 0   Manchester United 1**
Teamsheet: Carroll, Brown, Heinze, O'Shea, Silvestre, Ferdinand, Ronaldo, Keane, Smith, van Nistelrooy, Giggs
Substitute(s): Bellion, Miller   Scorer(s):   van Nistelrooy

Match # 4823   Tuesday 28/09/04   Champions League Phase 1 Match 2   at Old Trafford   Attendance 67128
Result: **Manchester United 6   Fenerbahce 2**
Teamsheet: Carroll, Neville G, Heinze, Kleberson, Silvestre, Ferdinand, Bellion, Djemba-Djemba, Rooney, van Nistelrooy, Giggs
Substitute(s): Fletcher, Miller, Neville P   Scorer(s):   Rooney 3, Bellion, Giggs, van Nistelrooy

Match # 4824   Sunday 03/10/04   FA Premiership   at Old Trafford   Attendance 67988
Result: **Manchester United 1   Middlesbrough 1**
Teamsheet: Carroll, Neville G, Heinze, O'Shea, Silvestre, Ferdinand, Ronaldo, Keane, Rooney, van Nistelrooy, Giggs
Substitute(s): Smith   Scorer(s):   Smith

Match # 4825   Saturday 16/10/04   FA Premiership   at St Andrews   Attendance 29221
Result: **Birmingham City 0   Manchester United 0**
Teamsheet: Carroll, Neville G, Fortune, Kleberson, Brown, Ferdinand, Ronaldo, Keane, Smith, van Nistelrooy, Saha
Substitute(s): Rooney, Scholes

Match # 4826   Tuesday 19/10/04   Champions League Phase 1 Match 3   at Toyota Arena   Attendance 20654
Result: **Sparta Prague 0   Manchester United 0**
Teamsheet: Carroll, Neville G, Heinze, O'Shea, Silvestre, Brown, Miller, Scholes, Rooney, van Nistelrooy, Giggs
Substitute(s): Ronaldo, Saha

Match # 4827   Sunday 24/10/04   FA Premiership   at Old Trafford   Attendance 67862
Result: **Manchester United 2   Arsenal 0**
Teamsheet: Carroll, Neville G, Heinze, Neville P, Silvestre, Ferdinand, Ronaldo, Scholes, Rooney, van Nistelrooy, Giggs
Substitute(s): Saha, Smith   Scorer(s):   Rooney, van Nistelrooy

Match # 4828   Tuesday 26/10/04   League Cup 3rd Round   at Gresty Road   Attendance 10103
Result: **Crewe Alexandra 0   Manchester United 3**
Teamsheet: Howard, Richardson, O'Shea, Kleberson, Brown, Djemba-Djemba, Fletcher, Miller, Saha, Smith, Bellion
Substitute(s): Ebanks-Blake, Eagles, Pique   Scorer(s):   Miller, Smith, own goal

Match # 4829   Saturday 30/10/04   FA Premiership   at Fratton Park   Attendance 20190
Result: **Portsmouth 2   Manchester United 0**
Teamsheet: Carroll, Neville G, Heinze, Neville P, Silvestre, Ferdinand, Ronaldo, Scholes, Rooney, Smith, Giggs
Substitute(s): Brown, Keane, Saha

SEASON 2004/05 (continued)

Match # 4830   Wednesday 03/11/04   Champions League Phase 1 Match 4   at Old Trafford   Attendance 66706
Result: **Manchester United 4 Sparta Prague 1**
Teamsheet: Carroll, Neville G, Heinze, Keane, Brown, Ferdinand, Miller, Scholes, Rooney, van Nistelrooy, Ronaldo
Substitute(s):   Neville P, Kleberson   Scorer(s):   van Nistelrooy 4

Match # 4831   Sunday 07/11/04   FA Premiership   at Old Trafford   Attendance 67863
Result: **Manchester United 0 Manchester City 0**
Teamsheet: Carroll, Neville G, Heinze, Keane, Silvestre, Ferdinand, Miller, Scholes, Saha, Smith, Ronaldo
Substitute(s):   Giggs, Rooney

Match # 4832   Wednesday 10/11/04   League Cup 4th Round   at Old Trafford   Attendance 48891
Result: **Manchester United 2 Crystal Palace 0**
Teamsheet: Howard, Neville P, Fortune, Kleberson, Brown, O'Shea, Fletcher, Djemba-Djemba, Saha, Bellion, Richardson
Substitute(s):   Eagles, Rossi, Spector   Scorer(s):   Richardson, Saha

Match # 4833   Sunday 14/11/04   FA Premiership   at St James' Park   Attendance 52320
Result: **Newcastle United 1 Manchester United 3**
Teamsheet: Carroll, Neville G, Heinze, Keane, Silvestre, Ferdinand, Fletcher, Scholes, Rooney, van Nistelrooy, Ronaldo
Substitute(s):   Brown, Giggs, Smith   Scorer(s):   Rooney 2, van Nistelrooy

Match # 4834   Saturday 20/11/04   FA Premiership   at Old Trafford   Attendance 67704
Result: **Manchester United 2 Charlton Athletic 0**
Teamsheet: Carroll, Brown, Fortune, Keane, Silvestre, Ferdinand, Fletcher, Scholes, Rooney, van Nistelrooy, Giggs
Substitute(s):   Neville P, O'Shea, Smith   Scorer(s):   Giggs, Scholes

Match # 4835   Tuesday 23/11/04   Champions League Phase 1 Match 5   at Old Trafford   Attendance 66398
Result: **Manchester United 2 Olympique Lyonnais 1**
Teamsheet: Carroll, Neville G, Heinze, Keane, Silvestre, Ferdinand, Ronaldo, Scholes, Rooney, van Nistelrooy, Smith
Substitute(s):   Brown, Fletcher, Fortune   Scorer(s):   Neville G, van Nistelrooy

Match # 4836   Saturday 27/11/04   FA Premiership   at The Hawthorns   Attendance 27709
Result: **West Bromwich Albion 0 Manchester United 3**
Teamsheet: Carroll, Brown, Heinze, Keane, Silvestre, Ferdinand, Fletcher, Scholes, Rooney, van Nistelrooy, Giggs
Substitute(s):   Ronaldo, Smith   Scorer(s):   Scholes 2, van Nistelrooy

Match # 4837   Wednesday 01/12/04   League Cup 5th Round   at Old Trafford   Attendance 67103
Result: **Manchester United 1 Arsenal 0**
Teamsheet: Howard, Neville P, Fortune, Kleberson, Brown, O'Shea, Miller, Djemba-Djemba, Bellion, Eagles, Richardson
Substitute(s):   Jones, Rossi   Scorer(s):   Bellion

Match # 4838   Saturday 04/12/04   FA Premiership   at Old Trafford   Attendance 67921
Result: **Manchester United 3 Southampton 0**
Teamsheet: Carroll, Neville G, Heinze, Keane, Silvestre, Ferdinand, Ronaldo, Scholes, Rooney, Smith, Giggs
Substitute(s):   Bellion   Scorer(s):   Ronaldo, Rooney, Scholes

Match # 4839   Wednesday 08/12/04   Champions League Phase 1 Match 6   at Sukru Saracoglu   Attendance 35000
Result: **Fenerbahce 3 Manchester United 0**
Teamsheet: Howard, Neville P, Fortune, Fletcher, Brown, O'Shea, Ronaldo, Djemba-Djemba, Bellion, Miller, Richardson
Substitute(s):   Eagles, Pique, Spector

Match # 4840   Monday 13/12/04   FA Premiership   at Craven Cottage   Attendance 21940
Result: **Fulham 1 Manchester United 1**
Teamsheet: Carroll, Neville G, Heinze, Keane, Silvestre, Ferdinand, Ronaldo, Scholes, Rooney, Smith, Giggs
Scorer(s):   Smith

Match # 4841   Saturday 18/12/04   FA Premiership   at Old Trafford   Attendance 67814
Result: **Manchester United 5 Crystal Palace 2**
Teamsheet: Carroll, Neville G, Fortune, Keane, Silvestre, Ferdinand, Fletcher, Scholes, Rooney, Smith, Giggs
Substitute(s):   O'Shea   Scorer(s):   Scholes 2, O'Shea, Smith, own goal

Match # 4842   Sunday 26/12/04   FA Premiership   at Old Trafford   Attendance 67867
Result: **Manchester United 2 Bolton Wanderers 0**
Teamsheet: Carroll, O'Shea, Heinze, Keane, Silvestre, Ferdinand, Ronaldo, Fletcher, Rooney, Smith, Giggs
Substitute(s):   Miller, Scholes   Scorer(s):   Giggs, Scholes

Match # 4843   Tuesday 28/12/04   FA Premiership   at Villa Park   Attendance 42593
Result: **Aston Villa 0 Manchester United 1**
Teamsheet: Carroll, O'Shea, Heinze, Neville P, Silvestre, Ferdinand, Fletcher, Scholes, Rooney, Smith, Giggs
Substitute(s):   Keane, Ronaldo   Scorer(s):   Giggs

Match # 4844   Saturday 01/01/05   FA Premiership   at Riverside Stadium   Attendance 34199
Result: **Middlesbrough 0 Manchester United 2**
Teamsheet: Carroll, Neville P, Heinze, Keane, Silvestre, Ferdinand, Fletcher, Scholes, Ronaldo, Smith, Giggs
Substitute(s):   Bellion, Djemba-Djemba   Scorer(s):   Fletcher, Giggs

Match # 4845   Tuesday 04/01/05   FA Premiership   at Old Trafford   Attendance 67962
Result: **Manchester United 0 Tottenham Hotspur 0**
Teamsheet: Carroll, Neville P, Heinze, Keane, Silvestre, Ferdinand, Fletcher, Scholes, Ronaldo, Smith, Giggs
Substitute(s):   Bellion, Miller, Spector

Match # 4846   Saturday 08/01/05   FA Cup 3rd Round   at Old Trafford   Attendance 67551
Result: **Manchester United 0 Exeter City 0**
Teamsheet: Howard, Neville P, Spector, Jones, Brown, Pique, Djemba-Djemba, Eagles, Bellion, Miller, Richardson
Substitute(s):   Ronaldo, Scholes, Smith

Match # 4847   Wednesday 12/01/05   League Cup Semi-Final 1st Leg   at Stamford Bridge   Attendance 41492
Result: **Chelsea 0 Manchester United 0**
Teamsheet: Howard, Neville P, Heinze, Djemba-Djemba, Silvestre, O'Shea, Ronaldo, Fletcher, Rooney, Saha, Fortune
Substitute(s):   Scholes, Smith

SEASON 2004/05 (continued)

Match # 4848   Saturday 15/01/05   FA Premiership   at Anfield   Attendance 44183
Result: **Liverpool 0   Manchester United 1**
Teamsheet: Carroll, Neville P, Heinze, Keane, Silvestre, Brown, Fletcher, Scholes, Rooney, Saha, Ronaldo
Substitute(s):   Bellion, Fortune, O'Shea   Scorer(s):   Rooney

Match # 4849   Wednesday 19/01/05   FA Cup 3rd Round Replay   at St James' Park   Attendance 9033
Result: **Exeter City 0   Manchester United 2**
Teamsheet: Howard, Neville P, Fortune, Djemba-Djemba, Neville G, O'Shea, Ronaldo, Miller, Rooney, Scholes, Giggs
Substitute(s):   Fletcher, Saha, Silvestre   Scorer(s):   Ronaldo, Rooney

Match # 4850   Saturday 22/01/05   FA Premiership   at Old Trafford   Attendance 67859
Result: **Manchester United 3   Aston Villa 1**
Teamsheet: Carroll, Neville G, Heinze, Keane, Silvestre, Ferdinand, Fletcher, Saha, Rooney, Scholes, Ronaldo
Substitute(s):   Fortune, Giggs, O'Shea   Scorer(s):   Ronaldo, Saha, Scholes

Match # 4851   Wednesday 26/01/05   League Cup Semi-Final 2nd Leg   at Old Trafford   Attendance 67000
Result: **Manchester United 1   Chelsea 2**
Teamsheet: Howard, Neville G, Heinze, Keane, Silvestre, Ferdinand, Ronaldo, Scholes, Saha, Fortune, Giggs
Substitute(s):   Rooney   Scorer(s):   Giggs

Match # 4852   Saturday 29/01/05   FA Cup 4th Round   at Old Trafford   Attendance 67251
Result: **Manchester United 3   Middlesbrough 0**
Teamsheet: Carroll, Neville G, Heinze, O'Shea, Brown, Ferdinand, Ronaldo, Neville P, Rooney, Fortune, Giggs
Substitute(s):   Miller, Saha, Silvestre   Scorer(s):   Rooney 2, O'Shea

Match # 4853   Tuesday 01/02/05   FA Premiership   at Highbury   Attendance 38164
Result: **Arsenal 2   Manchester United 4**
Teamsheet: Carroll, Neville G, Heinze, Keane, Silvestre, Ferdinand, Ronaldo, Fletcher, Rooney, Scholes, Giggs
Substitute(s):   Brown, O'Shea, Saha   Scorer(s):   Ronaldo 2, O'Shea, own goal

Match # 4854   Saturday 05/02/05   FA Premiership   at Old Trafford   Attendance 67838
Result: **Manchester United 2   Birmingham City 0**
Teamsheet: Carroll, Neville G, Heinze, O'Shea, Brown, Ferdinand, Ronaldo, Keane, Rooney, Saha, Giggs
Substitute(s):   Fortune, Miller, Neville P   Scorer(s):   Keane, Rooney

Match # 4855   Sunday 13/02/05   FA Premiership   at Eastlands Stadium   Attendance 47111
Result: **Manchester City 0   Manchester United 2**
Teamsheet: Carroll, Neville G, Heinze, O'Shea, Brown, Ferdinand, Fletcher, Keane, Rooney, Scholes, Fortune
Substitute(s):   Giggs, Neville P, Ronaldo   Scorer(s):   Rooney, own goal

Match # 4856   Saturday 19/02/05   FA Cup 5th Round   at Goodison Park   Attendance 38664
Result: **Everton 0   Manchester United 2**
Teamsheet: Carroll, Neville G, Heinze, Neville P, Brown, Ferdinand, Ronaldo, Keane, Rooney, Scholes, Fortune
Substitute(s):   Miller   Scorer(s):   Fortune, Ronaldo

Match # 4857   Wednesday 23/02/05   Champions League 2nd Round 1st Leg   at Old Trafford   Attendance 67162
Result: **Manchester United 0   AC Milan 1**
Teamsheet: Carroll, Neville G, Heinze, Keane, Brown, Ferdinand, Ronaldo, Fortune, Rooney, Scholes, Giggs
Substitute(s):   Saha, Silvestre, van Nistelrooy

Match # 4858   Saturday 26/02/05   FA Premiership   at Old Trafford   Attendance 67989
Result: **Manchester United 2   Portsmouth 1**
Teamsheet: Howard, Neville G, Heinze, O'Shea, Brown, Silvestre, Ronaldo, Neville P, Rooney, van Nistelrooy, Scholes
Substitute(s):   Fortune, Giggs, Smith   Scorer(s):   Rooney 2

Match # 4859   Saturday 05/03/05   FA Premiership   at Selhurst Park   Attendance 26021
Result: **Crystal Palace 0   Manchester United 0**
Teamsheet: Howard, Brown, Heinze, Neville P, Silvestre, Ferdinand, Fortune, Keane, Smith, van Nistelrooy, Giggs
Substitute(s):   Ronaldo, Rooney, Scholes

Match # 4860   Tuesday 08/03/05   Champions League 2nd Round 2nd Leg   at Stadio San Siro   Attendance 78957
Result: **AC Milan 1   Manchester United 0**
Teamsheet: Howard, Brown, Heinze, Keane, Silvestre, Ferdinand, Ronaldo, Scholes, Rooney, van Nistelrooy, Giggs
Substitute(s):   Fortune, Smith

Match # 4861   Saturday 12/03/05   FA Cup 6th Round   at St Mary's Stadium   Attendance 30971
Result: **Southampton 0   Manchester United 4**
Teamsheet: Howard, Brown, Heinze, Keane, Silvestre, Ferdinand, Ronaldo, Scholes, Rooney, van Nistelrooy, Fortune
Substitute(s):   Neville P, O'Shea, Smith   Scorer(s):   Scholes 2, Keane, Ronaldo

Match # 4862   Saturday 19/03/05   FA Premiership   at Old Trafford   Attendance 67959
Result: **Manchester United 1   Fulham 0**
Teamsheet: Howard, Brown, Heinze, Keane, Silvestre, Ferdinand, Ronaldo, Scholes, Rooney, van Nistelrooy, Fortune
Substitute(s):   Neville P, O'Shea, Smith   Scorer(s):   Ronaldo

Match # 4863   Saturday 02/04/05   FA Premiership   at Old Trafford   Attendance 67939
Result: **Manchester United 0   Blackburn Rovers 0**
Teamsheet: Howard, Neville G, Fortune, O'Shea, Silvestre, Ferdinand, Ronaldo, Scholes, Rooney, van Nistelrooy, Giggs
Substitute(s):   Keane, Smith

Match # 4864   Saturday 09/04/05   FA Premiership   at Carrow Road   Attendance 25522
Result: **Norwich City 2   Manchester United 0**
Teamsheet: Howard, Neville G, Heinze, Neville P, Silvestre, Ferdinand, Kleberson, Scholes, Smith, Saha, Fortune
Substitute(s):   Ronaldo, Rooney, van Nistelrooy

Match # 4865   Sunday 17/04/05   FA Cup Semi-Final   at Millennium Stadium   Attendance 69280
Result: **Manchester United 4   Newcastle United 1**
Teamsheet: Howard, Neville G, Heinze, Keane, Brown, Ferdinand, Ronaldo, Scholes, Rooney, van Nistelrooy, Fortune
Substitute(s):   Fletcher, Giggs, Smith   Scorer(s):   van Nistelrooy 2, Ronaldo, Scholes

SEASON 2004/05 (continued)

Match # 4866 Wednesday 20/04/05   FA Premiership   at Goodison Park   Attendance 37160
Result: **Everton 1 Manchester United 0**
Teamsheet: Howard, Neville G, Heinze, Keane, Brown, Ferdinand, Fletcher, Scholes, Rooney, van Nistelrooy, Ronaldo
Substitute(s): O'Shea, Silvestre

Match # 4867 Sunday 24/04/05   FA Premiership   at Old Trafford   Attendance 67845
Result: **Manchester United 2 Newcastle United 1**
Teamsheet: Howard, Neville P, Heinze, Keane, Brown, Ferdinand, Fletcher, Fortune, Rooney, Smith, Giggs
Substitute(s): Kleberson, Ronaldo, Silvestre   Scorer(s):   Brown, Rooney

Match # 4868 Sunday 01/05/05   FA Premiership   at The Valley   Attendance 26789
Result: **Charlton Athletic 0 Manchester United 4**
Teamsheet: Carroll, Brown, O'Shea, Keane, Silvestre, Ferdinand, Fletcher, Scholes, Rooney, Smith, Giggs
Substitute(s): Fortune, Kleberson, Neville P   Scorer(s):   Fletcher, Scholes, Smith, Rooney

Match # 4869 Saturday 07/05/05   FA Premiership   at Old Trafford   Attendance 67827
Result: **Manchester United 1 West Bromwich Albion 1**
Teamsheet: Carroll, Brown, O'Shea, Kleberson, Silvestre, Ferdinand, Ronaldo, Neville P, Smith, Fortune, Giggs
Substitute(s): Rooney, Saha, Scholes   Scorer(s):   Giggs

Match # 4870 Tuesday 10/05/05   FA Premiership   at Old Trafford   Attendance 67832
Result: **Manchester United 1 Chelsea 3**
Teamsheet: Carroll, Neville G, Brown, Keane, Silvestre, Ferdinand, Ronaldo, Scholes, Rooney, van Nistelrooy, Fletcher
Substitute(s): Saha   Scorer(s):   van Nistelrooy

Match # 4871 Sunday 15/05/05   FA Premiership   at St Mary's Stadium   Attendance 32066
Result: **Southampton 1 Manchester United 2**
Teamsheet: Carroll, Brown, O'Shea, Fortune, Silvestre, Ferdinand, Fletcher, Smith, Rooney, van Nistelrooy, Giggs
Substitute(s): Neville P, Saha   Scorer(s):   Fletcher, van Nistelrooy

Match # 4872 Saturday 21/05/05   FA Cup Final   at Millennium Stadium   Attendance 71876
Result: **Manchester United 0 Arsenal 0   (United lost the tie 4-5 on penalty kicks)**
Teamsheet: Carroll, Brown, O'Shea, Keane, Silvestre, Ferdinand, Fletcher, Scholes, Rooney, van Nistelrooy, Ronaldo
Substitute(s): Fortune, Giggs

SEASON 2004/05 SUMMARY

APPEARANCES

PLAYER	LGE	FAC	LC	CL	CS	TOTAL
Silvestre	33 (2)	2 (2)	2	7 (1)	1	45 (5)
Scholes	29 (4)	5 (1)	1 (1)	7	1	43 (6)
Ferdinand	31	5	1	5	–	42
Ronaldo	25 (8)	6 (1)	2	7 (1)	–	40 (10)
Keane	28 (3)	4	1	6	1	40 (3)
Heinze	26	4	2	7	–	39
Rooney	24 (5)	6	1 (1)	6	–	37 (6)
Giggs	26 (6)	2 (2)	1	6	1	36 (8)
Neville G	22	4	1	7	1	35
Carroll	26	3	–	5	–	34
Brown	18 (3)	6	3	6 (1)	–	33 (4)
O'Shea	16 (7)	3 (1)	4	5	1	29 (8)
Smith	22 (9)	– (3)	1 (1)	3 (2)	1	27 (15)
Howard	12	4	5	5	1	27
Fortune	12 (5)	5 (1)	4	3 (2)	1	25 (8)
Fletcher	18	1 (2)	3	3 (2)	– (1)	25 (5)
van Nistelrooy	16 (1)	3	–	6 (1)	–	25 (2)
Neville P	12 (7)	4 (1)	3	1 (5)	– (1)	20 (14)
Djemba	3 (2)	2	4	5	1	15 (2)
Saha	7 (7)	– (2)	4	– (2)	–	11 (11)
Kleberson	6 (2)	–	3	2 (1)	–	11 (3)
Miller	3 (5)	2 (2)	2	3 (2)	–	10 (9)
Bellion	1 (9)	1	3	2 (1)	1	8 (10)
Richardson	– (2)	1	3	1 (1)	– (1)	5 (4)
Spector	2 (1)	1	– (1)	1 (1)	– (1)	4 (4)
Eagles	–	1	1 (2)	1 (1)	– (1)	3 (4)
Pique	–	1	– (1)	– (1)	–	1 (2)
Jones	–	1	– (1)	–	–	1 (1)
Forlan	– (1)	–	–	– (1)	– (1)	– (3)
Rossi	–	–	– (2)	–	–	– (2)
Ebanks–Blake	–	–	– (1)	–	–	– (1)

GOALSCORERS

PLAYER	LGE	FAC	LC	CL	CS	TOTAL
Rooney	11	3	–	3	–	17
van Nistelrooy	6	2	–	8	–	16
Scholes	9	3	–	–	–	12
Smith	6	–	1	2	1	10
Ronaldo	5	4	–	–	–	9
Giggs	5	–	1	2	–	8
Bellion	2	–	1	2	–	5
Fletcher	3	–	–	–	–	3
O'Shea	2	1	–	–	–	3
Silvestre	2	–	–	–	–	2
Keane	1	1	–	–	–	2
Saha	1	–	1	–	–	2
Brown	1	–	–	–	–	1
Heinze	1	–	–	–	–	1
Fortune	–	1	–	–	–	1
Miller	–	–	1	–	–	1
Neville G	–	–	–	1	–	1
Richardson	–	–	1	1	–	1
own goals	3	–	1	1	–	5

RESULTS & ATTENDANCES SUMMARY

		P	W	D	L	F	A	TOTAL	AVGE
League	H	19	12	6	1	31	12	1289541	67871
	A	19	10	5	4	27	14	637025	33528
TOTAL		38	22	11	5	58	26	1926566	50699
FA Cup	H	2	1	1	0	3	0	134802	67401
	A	3	3	0	0	8	0	78668	26223
	N	2	1	1	0	4	1	141156	70578
TOTAL		7	5	2	0	15	1	354626	50661
League	H	3	2	0	1	4	2	182994	60998
Cup	A	2	1	1	0	3	0	51595	25798
TOTAL		5	3	1	1	7	2	234589	46918
Champions	H	5	4	0	1	15	5	328435	65687
League	A	5	1	2	2	4	7	232611	46522
TOTAL		10	5	2	3	19	12	561046	56105
Charity	H	0	0	0	0	0	0	0	n/a
Shield	A	0	0	0	0	0	0	0	n/a
	N	1	0	0	1	1	3	63317	63317
TOTAL		1	0	0	1	1	3	63317	63317
Overall	H	29	19	7	3	53	19	1935772	66751
	A	29	15	8	6	42	21	999899	34479
	N	3	1	1	1	5	4	204473	68158
TOTAL		61	35	16	10	100	44	3140144	51478

FINAL TABLE – FA PREMIERSHIP

		P	W	D	L	F	A	W	D	L	F	A	PTS	GD
			HOME						AWAY					
1	Chelsea	38	14	5	0	35	6	15	3	1	37	9	95	57
2	Arsenal	38	13	5	1	54	19	12	3	4	33	17	83	51
3	MANCHESTER UNITED	38	12	6	1	31	12	10	5	4	27	14	77	32
4	Everton	38	12	2	5	24	15	6	5	8	21	31	61	-1
5	Liverpool	38	12	4	3	31	15	5	3	11	21	26	58	11
6	Bolton Wanderers	38	9	5	5	25	18	7	5	7	24	26	58	5
7	Middlesbrough	38	9	6	4	29	19	5	8	6	24	25	56	9
8	Manchester City	38	8	6	5	24	14	5	7	7	23	25	52	8
9	Tottenham Hotspur	38	9	5	5	36	22	5	5	9	11	19	52	6
10	Aston Villa	38	8	4	7	29	29	4	6	9	13	29	46	-16
11	Charlton Athletic	38	8	6	5	24	15	3	6	10	16	31	45	-6
12	Birmingham City	38	7	7	5	24	17	4	5	10	19	35	45	-9
13	Fulham	38	8	4	7	29	26	4	4	11	23	34	44	-8
14	Newcastle United	38	7	7	5	25	25	3	7	9	22	32	44	-10
15	Blackburn Rovers	38	5	8	6	21	22	4	7	8	11	21	42	-11
16	Portsmouth	38	8	4	7	30	26	2	5	12	13	33	39	-16
17	West Bromwich Albion	38	5	8	6	17	24	1	8	10	19	37	34	-25
18	Crystal Palace	38	6	5	8	21	19	1	7	11	20	43	33	-21
19	Norwich City	38	7	5	7	29	32	0	7	12	13	45	33	-35
20	Southampton	38	5	9	5	30	30	1	5	13	15	36	32	-21

SEASON 2005/06

Match # 4873   Tuesday 09/08/05   Champions League Qualifying Round 1st Leg   at Old Trafford   Attendance 51701
Result: **Manchester United 3   Debreceni 0**
Teamsheet: van der Sar, Neville G, O'Shea, Keane, Ferdinand, Silvestre, Fletcher, Scholes, Rooney, van Nistelrooy, Ronaldo
Substitute(s):   Park, Rossi, Smith   Scorer(s):   Ronaldo, Rooney, van Nistelrooy

Match # 4874   Saturday 13/08/05   FA Premiership   at Goodison Park   Attendance 38610
Result: **Everton 0   Manchester United 2**
Teamsheet: van der Sar, Neville G, O'Shea, Keane, Ferdinand, Silvestre, Fletcher, Scholes, Rooney, van Nistelrooy, Park
Substitute(s):   Heinze, Richardson, Smith   Scorer(s):   Rooney, van Nistelrooy

Match # 4875   Saturday 20/08/05   FA Premiership   at Old Trafford   Attendance 67934
Result: **Manchester United 1   Aston Villa 0**
Teamsheet: van der Sar, Neville G, O'Shea, Keane, Ferdinand, Silvestre, Fletcher, Scholes, Rooney, van Nistelrooy, Park
Substitute(s):   Heinze, Ronaldo, Smith   Scorer(s):   van Nistelrooy

Match # 4876   Wednesday 24/08/05   Champions League Qualifying Round 2nd Leg   at Ferenc Puskas Stadium   Attendance 27000
Result: **Debreceni 0   Manchester United 3**
Teamsheet: van der Sar, Neville G, Heinze, Fletcher, Ferdinand, Brown, Ronaldo, Scholes, Smith, van Nistelrooy, Giggs
Substitute(s):   Bardsley, Miller, Richardson   Scorer(s):   Heinze 2, Richardson

Match # 4877   Sunday 28/08/05   FA Premiership   at St James' Park   Attendance 52327
Result: **Newcastle United 0   Manchester United 2**
Teamsheet: van der Sar, O'Shea, Heinze, Keane, Ferdinand, Silvestre, Fletcher, Scholes, Rooney, van Nistelrooy, Ronaldo
Substitute(s):   Park, Smith   Scorer(s):   Rooney, van Nistelrooy

Match # 4878   Saturday 10/09/05   FA Premiership   at Old Trafford   Attendance 67839
Result: **Manchester United 1   Manchester City 1**
Teamsheet: van der Sar, O'Shea, Heinze, Fletcher, Ferdinand, Silvestre, Smith, Scholes, Rooney, van Nistelrooy, Park
Substitute(s):   Giggs, Keane, Richardson   Scorer(s):   van Nistelrooy

Match # 4879   Wednesday 14/09/05   Champions League Phase 1 Match 1   at El Madrigal Stadium   Attendance 22000
Result: **Villarreal 0   Manchester United 0**
Teamsheet: van der Sar, O'Shea, Heinze, Fletcher, Ferdinand, Silvestre, Smith, Scholes, Rooney, van Nistelrooy, Ronaldo
Substitute(s):   Giggs, Park, Richardson

Match # 4880   Sunday 18/09/05   FA Premiership   at Anfield   Attendance 44917
Result: **Liverpool 0   Manchester United 0**
Teamsheet: van der Sar, O'Shea, Richardson, Keane, Ferdinand, Silvestre, Smith, Scholes, Rooney, van Nistelrooy, Ronaldo
Substitute(s):   Fletcher, Giggs, Park

Match # 4881   Saturday 24/09/05   FA Premiership   at Old Trafford   Attendance 67765
Result: **Manchester United 1   Blackburn Rovers 2**
Teamsheet: van der Sar, O'Shea, Richardson, Fletcher, Ferdinand, Silvestre, Ronaldo, Scholes, Smith, van Nistelrooy, Park
Substitute(s):   Bardsley, Giggs, Rooney   Scorer(s):   van Nistelrooy

Match # 4882   Tuesday 27/09/05   Champions League Phase 1 Match 2   at Old Trafford   Attendance 66112
Result: **Manchester United 2   Benfica 1**
Teamsheet: van der Sar, Bardsley, Richardson, Fletcher, Ferdinand, O'Shea, Ronaldo, Scholes, Smith, van Nistelrooy, Giggs
Scorer(s):   Giggs, van Nistelrooy

Match # 4883   Saturday 01/10/05   FA Premiership   at Craven Cottage   Attendance 21862
Result: **Fulham 2   Manchester United 3**
Teamsheet: van der Sar, O'Shea, Richardson, Fletcher, Ferdinand, Silvestre, Park, Smith, Rooney, van Nistelrooy, Giggs
Substitute(s):   Bardsley, Ronaldo, Scholes   Scorer(s):   van Nistelrooy 2, Rooney

Match # 4884   Saturday 15/10/05   FA Premiership   at Stadium of Light   Attendance 39085
Result: **Sunderland 1   Manchester United 3**
Teamsheet: van der Sar, Bardsley, O'Shea, Smith, Ferdinand, Silvestre, Ronaldo, Scholes, Rooney, van Nistelrooy, Park
Substitute(s):   Miller, Pique, Rossi   Scorer(s):   Rooney, Rossi, van Nistelrooy

Match # 4885   Tuesday 18/10/05   Champions League Phase 1 Match 3   at Old Trafford   Attendance 60626
Result: **Manchester United 0   Lille Metropole 0**
Teamsheet: van der Sar, Bardsley, O'Shea, Fletcher, Ferdinand, Silvestre, Ronaldo, Scholes, Smith, van Nistelrooy, Giggs
Substitute(s):   Park

Match # 4886   Saturday 22/10/05   FA Premiership   at Old Trafford   Attendance 67856
Result: **Manchester United 1   Tottenham Hotspur 1**
Teamsheet: van der Sar, Bardsley, O'Shea, Fletcher, Ferdinand, Silvestre, Smith, Scholes, Rooney, van Nistelrooy, Park
Substitute(s):   Ronaldo, Rossi   Scorer(s):   Silvestre

Match # 4887   Wednesday 26/10/05   League Cup 3rd Round   at Old Trafford   Attendance 43673
Result: **Manchester United 4   Barnet 1**
Teamsheet: Howard, Bardsley, Eckersley, Martin, Brown, Pique, Jones, Miller, Rossi, Ebanks-Blake, Richardson
Substitute(s):   Gibson   Scorer(s):   Ebanks-Blake, Miller, Richardson, Rossi

Match # 4888   Saturday 29/10/05   FA Premiership   at Riverside Stadium   Attendance 30579
Result: **Middlesbrough 4   Manchester United 1**
Teamsheet: van der Sar, Bardsley, O'Shea, Fletcher, Ferdinand, Silvestre, Smith, Scholes, Rooney, van Nistelrooy, Park
Substitute(s):   Brown, Richardson, Ronaldo   Scorer(s):   Rooney

Match # 4889   Wednesday 02/11/05   Champions League Phase 1 Match 4   at Stade de France   Attendance 65000
Result: **Lille Metropole 1   Manchester United 0**
Teamsheet: van der Sar, O'Shea, Brown, Fletcher, Ferdinand, Silvestre, Ronaldo, Smith, Rooney, van Nistelrooy, Richardson
Substitute(s):   Park, Rossi

Match # 4890   Sunday 06/11/05   FA Premiership   at Old Trafford   Attendance 67864
Result: **Manchester United 1   Chelsea 0**
Teamsheet: van der Sar, O'Shea, Brown, Fletcher, Ferdinand, Silvestre, Smith, Scholes, Rooney, van Nistelrooy, Ronaldo
Substitute(s):   Park   Scorer(s):   Fletcher

SEASON 2005/06 (continued)

Match # 4891   Saturday 19/11/05   FA Premiership   at The Valley   Attendance 26730
Result: **Charlton Athletic 1   Manchester United 3**
Teamsheet: van der Sar, O'Shea, Brown, Fletcher, Ferdinand, Silvestre, Smith, Scholes, Rooney, van Nistelrooy, Ronaldo
Substitute(s): Bardsley, Park, Richardson   Scorer(s):   van Nistelrooy 2, Smith

Match # 4892   Tuesday 22/11/05   Champions League Phase 1 Match 5   at Old Trafford   Attendance 67471
Result: **Manchester United 0   Villarreal 0**
Teamsheet: van der Sar, O'Shea, Brown, Fletcher, Ferdinand, Silvestre, Smith, Scholes, Rooney, van Nistelrooy, Ronaldo
Substitute(s): Neville G, Park, Saha

Match # 4893   Sunday 27/11/05   FA Premiership   at Upton Park   Attendance 34755
Result: **West Ham United 1   Manchester United 2**
Teamsheet: van der Sar, O'Shea, Brown, Fletcher, Ferdinand, Silvestre, Smith, Scholes, Rooney, van Nistelrooy, Park
Substitute(s): Neville G, Richardson   Scorer(s):   O'Shea, Rooney

Match # 4894   Wednesday 30/11/05   League Cup 4th Round   at Old Trafford   Attendance 48924
Result: **Manchester United 3   West Bromwich Albion 1**
Teamsheet: Howard, Neville G, O'Shea, Fletcher, Ferdinand, Silvestre, Ronaldo, Richardson, Saha, Rossi, Park
Substitute(s): Bardsley, Jones, Pique   Scorer(s):   O'Shea, Ronaldo, Saha

Match # 4895   Saturday 03/12/05   FA Premiership   at Old Trafford   Attendance 67684
Result: **Manchester United 3   Portsmouth 0**
Teamsheet: van der Sar, Brown, O'Shea, Smith, Ferdinand, Silvestre, Park, Scholes, Rooney, van Nistelrooy, Giggs
Substitute(s): Richardson, Ronaldo, Saha   Scorer(s):   Rooney, Scholes, van Nistelrooy

Match # 4896   Wednesday 07/12/05   Champions League Phase 1 Match 6   at Estadio da Luz   Attendance 61000
Result: **Benfica 2   Manchester United 1**
Teamsheet: van der Sar, Neville G, O'Shea, Smith, Ferdinand, Silvestre, Ronaldo, Scholes, Rooney, van Nistelrooy, Giggs
Substitute(s): Park, Richardson, Saha   Scorer(s):   Scholes

Match # 4897   Sunday 11/12/05   FA Premiership   at Old Trafford   Attendance 67831
Result: **Manchester United 1   Everton 1**
Teamsheet: van der Sar, Neville G, Richardson, Smith, Ferdinand, Silvestre, Park, Scholes, Rooney, Saha, Giggs
Substitute(s): Fletcher, Ronaldo, Rossi   Scorer(s):   Giggs

Match # 4898   Wednesday 14/12/05   FA Premiership   at Old Trafford   Attendance 67793
Result: **Manchester United 4   Wigan Athletic 0**
Teamsheet: van der Sar, Neville G, O'Shea, Smith, Ferdinand, Brown, Fletcher, Scholes, Rooney, van Nistelrooy, Giggs
Substitute(s): Bardsley, Park, Ronaldo   Scorer(s):   Rooney 2, Ferdinand, van Nistelrooy

Match # 4899   Saturday 17/12/05   FA Premiership   at Villa Park   Attendance 37128
Result: **Aston Villa 0   Manchester United 2**
Teamsheet: van der Sar, Neville G, O'Shea, Fletcher, Ferdinand, Brown, Park, Scholes, Rooney, van Nistelrooy, Giggs
Substitute(s): Ronaldo   Scorer(s):   Rooney, van Nistelrooy

Match # 4900   Tuesday 20/12/05   League Cup 5th Round   at St Andrews   Attendance 20454
Result: **Birmingham City 1   Manchester United 3**
Teamsheet: Howard, Neville G, O'Shea, Fletcher, Brown, Silvestre, Ronaldo, Park, Saha, Rossi, Richardson
Substitute(s): Ferdinand, Jones, Rooney   Scorer(s):   Saha 2, Park

Match # 4901   Monday 26/12/05   FA Premiership   at Old Trafford   Attendance 67972
Result: **Manchester United 3   West Bromwich Albion 0**
Teamsheet: van der Sar, Neville G, O'Shea, Fletcher, Ferdinand, Brown, Park, Scholes, Rooney, van Nistelrooy, Giggs
Substitute(s): Richardson, Saha, Smith   Scorer(s):   Ferdinand, Scholes, van Nistelrooy

Match # 4902   Wednesday 28/12/05   FA Premiership   at St Andrews   Attendance 28459
Result: **Birmingham City 2   Manchester United 2**
Teamsheet: van der Sar, Neville G, Richardson, Fletcher, Ferdinand, O'Shea, Smith, Scholes, Rooney, van Nistelrooy, Ronaldo
Substitute(s): Giggs, Park, Solskjaer   Scorer(s):   Rooney, van Nistelrooy

Match # 4903   Saturday 31/12/05   FA Premiership   at Old Trafford   Attendance 67858
Result: **Manchester United 4   Bolton Wanderers 1**
Teamsheet: van der Sar, Neville G, Richardson, O'Shea, Ferdinand, Silvestre, Ronaldo, Fletcher, Rooney, Saha, Giggs
Substitute(s): Park, Pique, van Nistelrooy   Scorer(s):   Ronaldo 2, Saha, own goal

Match # 4904   Tuesday 03/01/06   FA Premiership   at Highbury   Attendance 38313
Result: **Arsenal 0   Manchester United 0**
Teamsheet: van der Sar, Neville G, Silvestre, O'Shea, Ferdinand, Brown, Ronaldo, Fletcher, Rooney, van Nistelrooy, Giggs
Substitute(s): Park

Match # 4905   Sunday 08/01/06   FA Cup 3rd Round   at Pirelli Stadium   Attendance 6191
Result: **Burton Albion 0   Manchester United 0**
Teamsheet: Howard, Bardsley, Richardson, Brown, Silvestre, Pique, Jones, O'Shea, Solskjaer, Saha, Rossi
Substitute(s): Ronaldo, Rooney

Match # 4906   Wednesday 11/01/06   League Cup Semi-Final 1st Leg   at Ewood Park   Attendance 24348
Result: **Blackburn Rovers 1   Manchester United 1**
Teamsheet: van der Sar, Neville G, Silvestre, Smith, Ferdinand, Brown, Ronaldo, Fletcher, Rooney, Saha, Giggs
Substitute(s): O'Shea, van Nistelrooy   Scorer(s):   Saha

Match # 4907   Saturday 14/01/06   FA Premiership   at Eastlands Stadium   Attendance 47192
Result: **Manchester City 3   Manchester United 1**
Teamsheet: van der Sar, Neville G, Evra, O'Shea, Ferdinand, Silvestre, Ronaldo, Fletcher, Rooney, van Nistelrooy, Giggs
Substitute(s): Richardson, Saha, Smith   Scorer(s):   van Nistelrooy

Match # 4908   Wednesday 18/01/06   FA Cup 3rd Round Replay   at Old Trafford   Attendance 53564
Result: **Manchester United 5   Burton Albion 0**
Teamsheet: Howard, Bardsley, Silvestre, O'Shea, Brown, Pique, Solskjaer, Fletcher, Saha, Rossi, Richardson
Substitute(s): Ferdinand, Giggs, Neville G   Scorer(s):   Rossi 2, Giggs, Richardson, Saha

SEASON 2005/06 (continued)

Match # 4909   Sunday 22/01/06   FA Premiership   at Old Trafford   Attendance 67874
Result: **Manchester United 1 Liverpool 0**
Teamsheet: van der Sar, Neville G, Evra, O'Shea, Ferdinand, Brown, Richardson, Fletcher, Rooney, van Nistelrooy, Giggs
Substitute(s):   Saha   Scorer(s):   Ferdinand

Match # 4910   Wednesday 25/01/06   League Cup Semi-Final 2nd Leg   at Old Trafford   Attendance 61636
Result: **Manchester United 2 Blackburn Rovers 1**
Teamsheet: van der Sar, Neville G, Evra, Fletcher, Ferdinand, Brown, Richardson, Rooney, Saha, van Nistelrooy, Giggs
Substitute(s):   Silvestre, Smith, Vidic   Scorer(s):   Saha, van Nistelrooy

Match # 4911   Sunday 29/01/06   FA Cup 4th Round   at Molineux   Attendance 28333
Result: **Wolverhampton Wanderers 0 Manchester United 3**
Teamsheet: van der Sar, Neville G, Silvestre, Brown, Ferdinand, Vidic, Park, Rooney, Saha, van Nistelrooy, Richardson
Substitute(s):   Evra, Fletcher, Smith   Scorer(s):   Richardson 2, Saha

Match # 4912   Wednesday 01/02/06   FA Premiership   at Ewood Park   Attendance 25484
Result: **Blackburn Rovers 4 Manchester United 3**
Teamsheet: van der Sar, Neville G, Evra, Brown, Ferdinand, Vidic, Ronaldo, Rooney, Saha, Fletcher, Richardson
Substitute(s):   Park, Silvestre, van Nistelrooy   Scorer(s):   van Nistelrooy 2, Saha

Match # 4913   Saturday 04/02/06   FA Premiership   at Old Trafford   Attendance 67884
Result: **Manchester United 4 Fulham 2**
Teamsheet: van der Sar, Neville G, Evra, Smith, Brown, Silvestre, Ronaldo, Park, Saha, van Nistelrooy, Richardson
Substitute(s):   Bardsley, Rooney, Vidic   Scorer(s):   Ronaldo 2, Saha, own goal

Match # 4914   Saturday 11/02/06   FA Premiership   at Fratton Park   Attendance 20206
Result: **Portsmouth 1 Manchester United 3**
Teamsheet: van der Sar, Brown, Silvestre, Fletcher, Ferdinand, Vidic, Ronaldo, Park, Rooney, van Nistelrooy, Giggs
Substitute(s):   Howard, Saha, Smith   Scorer(s):   Ronaldo 2, van Nistelrooy

Match # 4915   Saturday 18/02/06   FA Cup 5th Round   at Anfield   Attendance 44039
Result: **Liverpool 1 Manchester United 0**
Teamsheet: van der Sar, Neville G, Silvestre, Fletcher, Brown, Vidic, Richardson, Ronaldo, Rooney, van Nistelrooy, Giggs
Substitute(s):   Park, Saha, Smith

Match # 4916   Sunday 26/02/06   League Cup Final   at Millennium Stadium   Attendance 66866
Result: **Manchester United 4 Wigan Athletic 0**
Teamsheet: van der Sar, Neville G, Silvestre, O'Shea, Ferdinand, Brown, Ronaldo, Park, Rooney, Saha, Giggs
Substitute(s):   Evra, Richardson, Vidic   Scorer(s):   Rooney 2, Ronaldo, Saha

Match # 4917   Monday 06/03/06   FA Premiership   at JJB Stadium   Attendance 23574
Result: **Wigan Athletic 1 Manchester United 2**
Teamsheet: van der Sar, Neville G, Silvestre, O'Shea, Ferdinand, Brown, Ronaldo, Park, Rooney, Saha, Giggs
Substitute(s):   Evra, van Nistelrooy   Scorer(s):   Ronaldo, own goal

Match # 4918   Sunday 12/03/06   FA Premiership   at Old Trafford   Attendance 67858
Result: **Manchester United 2 Newcastle United 0**
Teamsheet: van der Sar, Neville G, Silvestre, O'Shea, Ferdinand, Brown, Ronaldo, Park, Rooney, Saha, Giggs
Substitute(s):   Evra, van Nistelrooy   Scorer(s):   Rooney 2

Match # 4919   Saturday 18/03/06   FA Premiership   at The Hawthorns   Attendance 27623
Result: **West Bromwich Albion 1 Manchester United 2**
Teamsheet: van der Sar, Neville G, Silvestre, O'Shea, Ferdinand, Vidic, Ronaldo, Richardson, Rooney, Saha, Giggs
Substitute(s):   Fletcher   Scorer(s):   Saha 2

Match # 4920   Sunday 26/03/06   FA Premiership   at Old Trafford   Attendance 69070
Result: **Manchester United 3 Birmingham City 0**
Teamsheet: van der Sar, Neville G, Silvestre, O'Shea, Ferdinand, Vidic, Ronaldo, Richardson, Rooney, Saha, Giggs
Substitute(s):   Fletcher, Park, van Nistelrooy   Scorer(s):   Giggs 2, Rooney

Match # 4921   Wednesday 29/03/06   FA Premiership   at Old Trafford   Attendance 69522
Result: **Manchester United 1 West Ham United 0**
Teamsheet: van der Sar, Pique, Evra, O'Shea, Ferdinand, Vidic, Ronaldo, Fletcher, Rooney, van Nistelrooy, Park
Substitute(s):   Giggs, Saha, Silvestre   Scorer(s):   van Nistelrooy

Match # 4922   Saturday 01/04/06   FA Premiership   at Reebok Stadium   Attendance 27718
Result: **Bolton Wanderers 1 Manchester United 2**
Teamsheet: van der Sar, Neville G, Silvestre, O'Shea, Ferdinand, Vidic, Ronaldo, Fletcher, Rooney, Saha, Giggs
Substitute(s):   Park, van Nistelrooy   Scorer(s):   Saha, van Nistelrooy

Match # 4923   Sunday 09/04/06   FA Premiership   at Old Trafford   Attendance 70908
Result: **Manchester United 2 Arsenal 0**
Teamsheet: van der Sar, Neville G, Silvestre, O'Shea, Ferdinand, Vidic, Ronaldo, Park, Rooney, van Nistelrooy, Giggs
Substitute(s):   Evra, Saha   Scorer(s):   Park, Rooney

Match # 4924   Friday 14/04/06   FA Premiership   at Old Trafford   Attendance 72519
Result: **Manchester United 0 Sunderland 0**
Teamsheet: van der Sar, Neville G, Evra, O'Shea, Ferdinand, Brown, Ronaldo, Park, Rooney, van Nistelrooy, Giggs
Substitute(s):   Silvestre, Solskjaer

Match # 4925   Monday 17/04/06   FA Premiership   at White Hart Lane   Attendance 36141
Result: **Tottenham Hotspur 1 Manchester United 2**
Teamsheet: van der Sar, Neville G, Silvestre, O'Shea, Ferdinand, Vidic, Ronaldo, Park, Rooney, van Nistelrooy, Giggs
Substitute(s):   Brown   Scorer(s):   Rooney 2

Match # 4926   Saturday 29/04/06   FA Premiership   at Stamford Bridge   Attendance 42219
Result: **Chelsea 3 Manchester United 0**
Teamsheet: van der Sar, Neville G, Silvestre, O'Shea, Ferdinand, Vidic, Ronaldo, Park, Rooney, Saha, Giggs
Substitute(s):   Evra, Richardson, van Nistelrooy

SEASON 2005/06 (continued)

Match # 4927 Monday 01/05/06   FA Premiership   at Old Trafford   Attendance 69531
Result: **Manchester United 0   Middlesbrough 0**
Teamsheet: van der Sar, Neville G, Evra, Silvestre, Ferdinand, Brown, Park, O'Shea, Saha, van Nistelrooy, Giggs
Substitute(s): Richardson, Ronaldo, Rossi

Match # 4928 Sunday 07/05/06   FA Premiership   at Old Trafford   Attendance 73006
Result: **Manchester United 4   Charlton Athletic 0**
Teamsheet: van der Sar, Neville G, Silvestre, O'Shea, Ferdinand, Brown, Ronaldo, Richardson, Saha, Rossi, Giggs
Substitute(s): Scholes, Solskjaer, Vidic   Scorer(s):   Richardson, Ronaldo, Saha, own goal

SEASON 2005/06 SUMMARY

APPEARANCES

PLAYER	LGE	FAC	LC	CL	TOTAL
van der Sar	38	2	3	8	51
Ferdinand	37	1 (1)	4 (1)	8	50 (2)
O'Shea	34	2	3 (1)	7	46 (1)
Rooney	34 (2)	2 (1)	3 (1)	5	44 (4)
Silvestre	30 (3)	4	4 (1)	6	44 (4)
van Nistelrooy	28 (7)	2	1 (1)	8	39 (8)
Ronaldo	24 (9)	1 (1)	4	8	37 (10)
Fletcher	23 (4)	2 (1)	4	7	36 (5)
Neville	24 (1)	2 (1)	5	3 (1)	34 (3)
Giggs	22 (5)	1 (1)	3	4 (1)	30 (7)
Brown	17 (2)	4	5	3	29 (2)
Park	23 (11)	1 (1)	3	– (6)	27 (18)
Scholes	18 (2)	–	–	7	25 (2)
Smith	15 (6)	– (2)	1 (1)	7 (1)	23 (10)
Richardson	12 (10)	4	4 (1)	2 (3)	22 (14)
Saha	12 (7)	3 (1)	5	– (2)	20 (10)
Vidic	9 (2)	2	– (2)	–	11 (4)
Bardsley	3 (5)	2	1 (1)	2 (1)	8 (7)
Evra	7 (4)	– (1)	1 (1)	–	8 (6)
Rossi	1 (4)	2	3	– (2)	6 (6)
Howard	– (1)	2	3	–	5 (1)
Keane	4 (1)	–	–	1	5 (1)
Pique	1 (2)	2	1 (1)	–	4 (3)
Heinze	2 (2)	–	–	2	4 (2)
Solskjaer	– (3)	2	–	–	2 (3)
Jones	–	1	1 (2)	–	2 (2)
Miller	– (1)	–	1	– (1)	1 (2)
Ebanks–Blake	–	–	1	–	1
Eckersley	–	–	1	–	1
Martin	–	–	1	–	1
Gibson	–	–	– (1)	–	– (1)

RESULTS & ATTENDANCES SUMMARY

		P	W	D	L	F	A	TOTAL	AVGE
League	H	19	13	5	1	37	8	1306568	68767
	A	19	12	3	4	35	26	642922	33838
	TOTAL	38	25	8	5	72	34	1949490	51302
FA Cup	H	1	1	0	0	5	0	53564	53564
	A	3	1	1	1	3	1	78563	26188
	TOTAL	4	2	1	1	8	1	132127	33032
League	H	3	3	0	0	9	3	154233	51411
Cup	A	2	1	1	0	4	2	44802	22401
	N	1	1	0	0	4	0	66866	66866
	TOTAL	6	5	1	0	17	5	265901	44317
Champions	H	4	2	2	0	5	1	245910	61478
League	A	4	1	1	2	4	3	175000	43750
	TOTAL	8	3	3	2	9	4	420910	52614
Overall	H	27	19	7	1	56	12	1760275	65195
	A	28	15	6	7	46	32	941287	33617
	N	1	1	0	0	4	0	66866	66866
	TOTAL	56	35	13	8	106	44	2768428	49436

GOALSCORERS

PLAYER	LGE	FAC	LC	CL	TOTAL
van Nistelrooy	21	–	1	2	24
Rooney	16	–	2	1	19
Saha	7	2	6	–	15
Ronaldo	9	–	2	1	12
Richardson	1	3	1	1	6
Giggs	3	1	–	1	5
Rossi	1	2	1	–	4
Ferdinand	3	–	–	–	3
Scholes	2	–	–	1	3
O'Shea	1	–	1	–	2
Park	1	–	1	–	2
Heinze	–	–	–	2	2
Fletcher	1	–	–	–	1
Silvestre	1	–	–	–	1
Smith	1	–	–	–	1
Ebanks–Blake	–	–	1	–	1
Miller	–	–	1	–	1
own goals	4	–	–	–	4

FINAL TABLE – FA PREMIERSHIP

		P	W	D	L	F	A	W	D	L	F	A	PTS	GD
				HOME					AWAY					
1	Chelsea	38	18	1	0	47	9	11	3	5	25	13	91	50
2	MANCHESTER UNITED	38	13	5	1	37	8	12	3	4	35	26	83	38
3	Liverpool	38	15	3	1	32	8	10	4	5	25	17	82	32
4	Arsenal	38	14	3	2	48	13	6	4	9	20	18	67	37
5	Tottenham Hotspur	38	12	5	2	31	16	6	6	7	22	22	65	15
6	Blackburn Rovers	38	13	3	3	31	18	6	3	10	20	25	63	8
7	Newcastle United	38	11	5	3	28	15	6	2	11	19	27	58	5
8	Bolton Wanderers	38	11	5	3	29	13	4	6	9	20	28	56	8
9	West Ham United	38	9	3	7	30	25	7	4	8	22	30	55	–3
10	Wigan Athletic	38	7	3	9	24	26	8	3	8	21	26	51	–7
11	Everton	38	8	4	7	22	22	6	4	9	12	27	50	–15
12	Fulham	38	13	2	4	31	21	1	4	14	17	37	48	–10
13	Charlton Athletic	38	8	4	7	22	21	5	4	10	19	34	47	–14
14	Middlesbrough	38	7	5	7	28	30	5	4	10	20	28	45	–10
15	Manchester City	38	9	2	8	26	20	4	2	13	17	28	43	–5
16	Aston Villa	38	6	6	7	20	20	4	6	9	23	35	42	–12
17	Portsmouth	38	5	7	7	17	24	5	1	13	20	38	38	–25
18	Birmingham City	38	6	5	8	19	20	2	5	12	9	30	34	–22
19	West Bromwich Albion	38	6	2	11	21	24	1	7	11	10	34	30	–27
20	Sunderland	38	1	4	14	12	37	2	2	15	14	32	15	–43

SEASON 2006/07

Match # 4929   Sunday 20/08/06   FA Premiership   at Old Trafford   Attendance 75115
Result: **Manchester United 5 Fulham 1**
Teamsheet: van der Sar, Neville G, Evra, O'Shea, Ferdinand, Brown, Ronaldo, Scholes, Rooney, Saha, Giggs
Substitute(s):   Park, Silvestre, Solskjaer   Scorer(s):   Rooney 2, Ronaldo, Saha, own goal

Match # 4930   Wednesday 23/08/06   FA Premiership   at The Valley   Attendance 25422
Result: **Charlton Athletic 0 Manchester United 3**
Teamsheet: van der Sar, Brown, Evra, O'Shea, Ferdinand, Silvestre, Ronaldo, Fletcher, Saha, Park, Giggs
Substitute(s):   Carrick, Solskjaer   Scorer(s):   Fletcher, Saha, Solskjaer

Match # 4931   Saturday 26/08/06   FA Premiership   at Vicarage Road   Attendance 19453
Result: **Watford 1 Manchester United 2**
Teamsheet: van der Sar, Brown, O'Shea, Fletcher, Ferdinand, Silvestre, Ronaldo, Carrick, Saha, Solskjaer, Giggs
Substitute(s):   Park, Richardson   Scorer(s):   Giggs, Silvestre

Match # 4932   Saturday 09/09/06   FA Premiership   at Old Trafford   Attendance 75453
Result: **Manchester United 1 Tottenham Hotspur 0**
Teamsheet: van der Sar, Neville G, Evra, O'Shea, Ferdinand, Brown, Ronaldo, Carrick, Saha, Richardson, Giggs
Substitute(s):   Fletcher, Park, Silvestre   Scorer(s):   Giggs

Match # 4933   Wednesday 13/09/06   Champions League Phase 1 Match 1   at Old Trafford   Attendance 74031
Result: **Manchester United 3 Glasgow Celtic 2**
Teamsheet: van der Sar, Neville G, Silvestre, Carrick, Ferdinand, Brown, Fletcher, Scholes, Saha, Rooney, Giggs
Substitute(s):   O'Shea, Richardson, Solskjaer   Scorer(s):   Saha 2, Solskjaer

Match # 4934   Sunday 17/09/06   FA Premiership   at Old Trafford   Attendance 75595
Result: **Manchester United 0 Arsenal 1**
Teamsheet: Kuszczak, Neville G, Silvestre, O'Shea, Ferdinand, Brown, Fletcher, Scholes, Saha, Rooney, Ronaldo
Substitute(s):   Carrick, Evra, Solskjaer

Match # 4935   Saturday 23/09/06   FA Premiership   at Madejski Stadium   Attendance 24098
Result: **Reading 1 Manchester United 1**
Teamsheet: van der Sar, Neville G, Heinze, Fletcher, Ferdinand, Vidic, Ronaldo, Carrick, Scholes, Rooney, Richardson
Substitute(s):   O'Shea, Saha, Solskjaer   Scorer(s):   Ronaldo

Match # 4936   Tuesday 26/09/06   Champions League Phase 1 Match 2   at Estadio da Luz   Attendance 61000
Result: **Benfica 0 Manchester United 1**
Teamsheet: van der Sar, Neville G, Heinze, O'Shea, Ferdinand, Vidic, Ronaldo, Carrick, Saha, Rooney, Scholes
Substitute(s):   Fletcher, Smith   Scorer(s):   Saha

Match # 4937   Sunday 01/10/06   FA Premiership   at Old Trafford   Attendance 75664
Result: **Manchester United 2 Newcastle United 0**
Teamsheet: van der Sar, Neville G, Heinze, Carrick, Ferdinand, Vidic, Fletcher, Scholes, Rooney, Solskjaer, Ronaldo
Substitute(s):   Evra   Scorer(s):   Solskjaer 2

Match # 4938   Saturday 14/10/06   FA Premiership   at JJB Stadium   Attendance 20631
Result: **Wigan Athletic 1 Manchester United 3**
Teamsheet: van der Sar, Brown, Evra, O'Shea, Ferdinand, Vidic, Carrick, Scholes, Rooney, Saha, Solskjaer
Substitute(s):   Giggs   Scorer(s):   Saha, Solskjaer, Vidic

Match # 4939   Tuesday 17/10/06   Champions League Phase 1 Match 3   at Old Trafford   Attendance 72020
Result: **Manchester United 3 Copenhagen 0**
Teamsheet: van der Sar, O'Shea, Evra, Carrick, Brown, Vidic, Fletcher, Scholes, Rooney, Saha, Ronaldo
Substitute(s):   Richardson, Smith, Solskjaer   Scorer(s):   O'Shea, Richardson, Scholes

Match # 4940   Sunday 22/10/06   FA Premiership   at Old Trafford   Attendance 75828
Result: **Manchester United 2 Liverpool 0**
Teamsheet: van der Sar, Neville G, Evra, Carrick, Ferdinand, Vidic, Fletcher, Scholes, Rooney, Saha, Giggs
Substitute(s):   Brown, O'Shea   Scorer(s):   Ferdinand, Scholes

Match # 4941   Wednesday 25/10/06   League Cup 3rd Round   at Gresty Road   Attendance 10046
Result: **Crewe Alexandra 1 Manchester United 2**
Teamsheet: Kuszczak, Gray, Heinze, Jones D, Brown, Silvestre, Marsh, Jones R, Smith, Solskjaer, Richardson
Substitute(s):   Barnes, Lee, Shawcross   Scorer(s):   Lee, Solskjaer

Match # 4942   Saturday 28/10/06   FA Premiership   at Reebok Stadium   Attendance 27229
Result: **Bolton Wanderers 0 Manchester United 4**
Teamsheet: van der Sar, Neville G, Evra, Carrick, Ferdinand, Vidic, Ronaldo, Scholes, Rooney, Saha, Giggs
Substitute(s):   Fletcher, Heinze, O'Shea   Scorer(s):   Rooney 3, Ronaldo

Match # 4943   Wednesday 01/11/06   Champions League Phase 1 Match 4   at Parken Stadion   Attendance 40000
Result: **Copenhagen 1 Manchester United 0**
Teamsheet: van der Sar, Brown, Heinze, O'Shea, Silvestre, Vidic, Fletcher, Carrick, Rooney, Solskjaer, Ronaldo
Substitute(s):   Evra, Ferdinand, Scholes

Match # 4944   Saturday 04/11/06   FA Premiership   at Old Trafford   Attendance 76004
Result: **Manchester United 3 Portsmouth 0**
Teamsheet: van der Sar, Neville G, Evra, Carrick, Ferdinand, Vidic, Ronaldo, Scholes, Rooney, Saha, Giggs
Substitute(s):   Fletcher, O'Shea, Silvestre   Scorer(s):   Ronaldo, Saha, Vidic

Match # 4945   Tuesday 07/11/06   League Cup 4th Round   at Roots Hall   Attendance 11532
Result: **Southend United 1 Manchester United 0**
Teamsheet: Kuszczak, O'Shea, Heinze, Fletcher, Brown, Silvestre, Ronaldo, Jones D, Smith, Rooney, Richardson
Substitute(s):   Evra, Lee, Shawcross

Match # 4946   Saturday 11/11/06   FA Premiership   at Ewood Park   Attendance 26162
Result: **Blackburn Rovers 0 Manchester United 1**
Teamsheet: van der Sar, Neville G, Evra, Carrick, Ferdinand, Vidic, Ronaldo, Scholes, Rooney, Saha, Giggs
Substitute(s):   Fletcher, O'Shea, Silvestre   Scorer(s):   Saha

SEASON 2006/07 (continued)

Match # 4947 Saturday 18/11/06   FA Premiership   at Bramall Lane   Attendance 32584
Result: **Sheffield United 1   Manchester United 2**
Teamsheet: van der Sar, Neville G, Evra, Carrick, Ferdinand, Vidic, Ronaldo, Scholes, Rooney, Saha, Giggs
Substitute(s):   Heinze   Scorer(s):   Rooney 2

Match # 4948 Tuesday 21/11/06   Champions League Phase 1 Match 5   at Celtic Park   Attendance 60632
Result: **Glasgow Celtic 1   Manchester United 0**
Teamsheet: van der Sar, Neville G, Heinze, Carrick, Ferdinand, Vidic, Ronaldo, Scholes, Rooney, Saha, Giggs
Substitute(s):   Evra, O'Shea

Match # 4949 Sunday 26/11/06   FA Premiership   at Old Trafford   Attendance 75948
Result: **Manchester United 1   Chelsea 1**
Teamsheet: van der Sar, Neville G, Heinze, Carrick, Ferdinand, Vidic, Ronaldo, Scholes, Rooney, Saha, Giggs
Substitute(s):   Fletcher, O'Shea   Scorer(s):   Saha

Match # 4950 Wednesday 29/11/06   FA Premiership   at Old Trafford   Attendance 75723
Result: **Manchester United 3   Everton 0**
Teamsheet: van der Sar, Neville G, Evra, Carrick, Ferdinand, Silvestre, Ronaldo, Fletcher, Rooney, O'Shea, Richardson
Substitute(s):   Brown, Heinze   Scorer(s):   Evra, O'Shea, Ronaldo

Match # 4951 Saturday 02/12/06   FA Premiership   at Riverside Stadium   Attendance 31238
Result: **Middlesbrough 1   Manchester United 2**
Teamsheet: van der Sar, Neville G, Heinze, Fletcher, Ferdinand, Vidic, Ronaldo, Scholes, Rooney, Saha, Giggs
Substitute(s):   Brown, O'Shea   Scorer(s):   Fletcher, Saha

Match # 4952 Wednesday 06/12/06   Champions League Phase 1 Match 6   at Old Trafford   Attendance 74955
Result: **Manchester United 3   Benfica 1**
Teamsheet: van der Sar, Neville G, Evra, Carrick, Ferdinand, Vidic, Ronaldo, Scholes, Rooney, Saha, Giggs
Substitute(s):   Fletcher, Heinze, Solskjaer   Scorer(s):   Giggs, Saha, Vidic

Match # 4953 Saturday 09/12/06   FA Premiership   at Old Trafford   Attendance 75858
Result: **Manchester United 3   Manchester City 1**
Teamsheet: van der Sar, Neville G, Heinze, Carrick, Ferdinand, Vidic, Ronaldo, Scholes, Rooney, Saha, Giggs
Substitute(s):   O'Shea   Scorer(s):   Ronaldo, Rooney, Saha

Match # 4954 Sunday 17/12/06   FA Premiership   at Upton Park   Attendance 34966
Result: **West Ham United 1   Manchester United 0**
Teamsheet: van der Sar, Neville G, Heinze, Carrick, Ferdinand, Vidic, Ronaldo, Scholes, Rooney, Saha, Giggs
Substitute(s):   O'Shea, Park, Solskjaer

Match # 4955 Saturday 23/12/06   FA Premiership   at Villa Park   Attendance 42551
Result: **Aston Villa 0   Manchester United 3**
Teamsheet: van der Sar, Neville G, Evra, Fletcher, Ferdinand, Vidic, Ronaldo, Scholes, Giggs, Saha, Park
Substitute(s):   O'Shea, Rooney, Silvestre   Scorer(s):   Ronaldo 2, Scholes

Match # 4956 Tuesday 26/12/06   FA Premiership   at Old Trafford   Attendance 76018
Result: **Manchester United 3   Wigan Athletic 1**
Teamsheet: van der Sar, Brown, Evra, O'Shea, Silvestre, Vidic, Fletcher, Scholes, Rooney, Solskjaer, Park
Substitute(s):   Heinze, Richardson, Ronaldo   Scorer(s):   Ronaldo 2, Solskjaer

Match # 4957 Saturday 30/12/06   FA Premiership   at Old Trafford   Attendance 75910
Result: **Manchester United 3   Reading 2**
Teamsheet: van der Sar, Brown, Heinze, O'Shea, Ferdinand, Silvestre, Ronaldo, Carrick, Rooney, Solskjaer, Park
Substitute(s):   Fletcher, Giggs, Richardson   Scorer(s):   Ronaldo 2, Solskjaer

Match # 4958 Monday 01/01/07   FA Premiership   at St James' Park   Attendance 52302
Result: **Newcastle United 2   Manchester United 2**
Teamsheet: van der Sar, Neville G, Evra, Fletcher, Ferdinand, Vidic, Ronaldo, Scholes, Rooney, Saha, Giggs
Substitute(s):   Carrick, Park   Scorer(s):   Scholes 2

Match # 4959 Sunday 07/01/07   FA Cup 3rd Round   at Old Trafford   Attendance 74924
Result: **Manchester United 2   Aston Villa 1**
Teamsheet: Kuszczak, Neville G, Evra, Carrick, Ferdinand, Brown, Ronaldo, Larsson, Rooney, Park, Giggs
Substitute(s):   Fletcher, O'Shea, Solskjaer   Scorer(s):   Larsson, Solskjaer

Match # 4960 Saturday 13/01/07   FA Premiership   at Old Trafford   Attendance 76073
Result: **Manchester United 3   Aston Villa 1**
Teamsheet: van der Sar, Neville G, Evra, Carrick, Ferdinand, Vidic, Ronaldo, Scholes, Rooney, Larsson, Park
Substitute(s):   O'Shea, Saha, Solskjaer   Scorer(s):   Carrick, Park, Ronaldo

Match # 4961 Sunday 21/01/07   FA Premiership   at Emirates Stadium   Attendance 60128
Result: **Arsenal 2   Manchester United 1**
Teamsheet: van der Sar, Neville G, Evra, Carrick, Ferdinand, Vidic, Ronaldo, Scholes, Rooney, Larsson, Giggs
Substitute(s):   Heinze, Saha   Scorer(s):   Rooney

Match # 4962 Saturday 27/01/07   FA Cup 4th Round   at Old Trafford   Attendance 71137
Result: **Manchester United 2   Portsmouth 1**
Teamsheet: Kuszczak, Neville G, Evra, Carrick, Ferdinand, Vidic, Park, Scholes, Solskjaer, Larsson, Giggs
Substitute(s):   Fletcher, Rooney   Scorer(s):   Rooney 2

Match # 4963 Wednesday 31/01/07   FA Premiership   at Old Trafford   Attendance 76032
Result: **Manchester United 4   Watford 0**
Teamsheet: Kuszczak, Neville G, Heinze, O'Shea, Ferdinand, Vidic, Ronaldo, Carrick, Rooney, Solskjaer, Richardson
Substitute(s):   Brown, Larsson, Silvestre   Scorer(s):   Larsson, Ronaldo, Rooney, own goal

Match # 4964 Sunday 04/02/07   FA Premiership   at White Hart Lane   Attendance 36146
Result: **Tottenham Hotspur 0   Manchester United 4**
Teamsheet: van der Sar, Neville G, Evra, Carrick, Ferdinand, Vidic, Ronaldo, Scholes, Rooney, Larsson, Giggs
Substitute(s):   O'Shea, Park, Saha   Scorer(s):   Giggs, Ronaldo, Scholes, Vidic

SEASON 2006/07 (continued)

Match # 4965 Saturday 10/02/07   FA Premiership   at Old Trafford   Attendance 75883
Result: **Manchester United 2 Charlton Athletic 0**
Teamsheet: Kuszczak, Neville G, Evra, Fletcher, Ferdinand, Vidic, Park, Scholes, Rooney, Saha, Giggs
Substitute(s):   Larsson, Richardson   Scorer(s):   Fletcher, Park

Match # 4966 Saturday 17/02/07   FA Cup 5th Round   at Old Trafford   Attendance 70608
Result: **Manchester United 1 Reading 1**
Teamsheet: Kuszczak, Brown, Heinze, Fletcher, Silvestre, Vidic, Ronaldo, Carrick, Solskjaer, Saha, Park
Substitute(s):   Evra, Larsson, Scholes   Scorer(s):   Carrick

Match # 4967 Tuesday 20/02/07   Champions League 2nd Round 1st Leg   at Stade Felix Bollaert   Attendance 41000
Result: **Lille Metropole 0 Manchester United 1**
Teamsheet: van der Sar, Neville G, Evra, Carrick, Ferdinand, Vidic, Ronaldo, Scholes, Rooney, Larsson, Giggs
Substitute(s):   O'Shea, Saha   Scorer(s):   Giggs

Match # 4968 Saturday 24/02/07   FA Premiership   at Craven Cottage   Attendance 24459
Result: **Fulham 1 Manchester United 2**
Teamsheet: van der Sar, Brown, Evra, Carrick, Ferdinand, Vidic, Ronaldo, Scholes, Rooney, Larsson, Giggs
Substitute(s):   O'Shea, Saha, Silvestre   Scorer(s):   Giggs, Ronaldo

Match # 4969 Tuesday 27/02/07   FA Cup 5th Round Replay   at Madejski Stadium   Attendance 23821
Result: **Reading 2 Manchester United 3**
Teamsheet: van der Sar, Brown, Heinze, O'Shea, Ferdinand, Silvestre, Park, Fletcher, Solskjaer, Saha, Richardson
Substitute(s):   Ronaldo, Rooney   Scorer(s):   Heinze, Saha, Solskjaer

Match # 4970 Saturday 03/03/07   FA Premiership   at Anfield   Attendance 44403
Result: **Liverpool 0 Manchester United 1**
Teamsheet: van der Sar, Neville G, Evra, Carrick, Ferdinand, Vidic, Ronaldo, Scholes, Rooney, Larsson, Giggs
Substitute(s):   O'Shea, Saha, Silvestre   Scorer(s):   O'Shea

Match # 4971 Wednesday 07/03/07   Champions League 2nd Round 2nd Leg   at Old Trafford   Attendance 75182
Result: **Manchester United 1 Lille Metropole 0**
Teamsheet: van der Sar, Neville G, Silvestre, O'Shea, Ferdinand, Vidic, Carrick, Scholes, Rooney, Larsson, Ronaldo
Substitute(s):   Park, Richardson, Smith   Scorer(s):   Larsson

Match # 4972 Saturday 10/03/07   FA Cup 6th Round   at Riverside Stadium   Attendance 33308
Result: **Middlesbrough 2 Manchester United 2**
Teamsheet: Kuszczak, Neville G, Heinze, O'Shea, Ferdinand, Vidic, Ronaldo, Carrick, Rooney, Larsson, Giggs
Scorer(s):   Ronaldo, Rooney

Match # 4973 Saturday 17/03/07   FA Premiership   at Old Trafford   Attendance 76058
Result: **Manchester United 4 Bolton Wanderers 1**
Teamsheet: Kuszczak, Neville G, Heinze, O'Shea, Ferdinand, Vidic, Ronaldo, Carrick, Rooney, Park, Giggs
Substitute(s):   Brown, Richardson, Smith   Scorer(s):   Park 2, Rooney 2

Match # 4974 Monday 19/03/07   FA Cup 6th Round Replay   at Old Trafford   Attendance 71325
Result: **Manchester United 1 Middlesbrough 0**
Teamsheet: Kuszczak, Brown, Heinze, Carrick, Ferdinand, Vidic, Ronaldo, Smith, Rooney, Giggs, Richardson
Substitute(s):   O'Shea, Park   Scorer(s):   Ronaldo

Match # 4975 Saturday 31/03/07   FA Premiership   at Old Trafford   Attendance 76098
Result: **Manchester United 4 Blackburn Rovers 1**
Teamsheet: van der Sar, Brown, Heinze, Carrick, Ferdinand, Vidic, Ronaldo, Scholes, Rooney, Park, Giggs
Substitute(s):   O'Shea, Smith, Solskjaer   Scorer(s):   Carrick, Park, Scholes, Solskjaer

Match # 4976 Wednesday 04/04/07   Champions League Quarter-Final 1st Leg   at Olympic Stadium   Attendance 77000
Result: **Roma 2 Manchester United 1**
Teamsheet: van der Sar, O'Shea, Heinze, Carrick, Ferdinand, Brown, Ronaldo, Scholes, Rooney, Solskjaer, Giggs
Substitute(s):   Fletcher, Saha   Scorer(s):   Rooney

Match # 4977 Saturday 07/04/07   FA Premiership   at Fratton Park   Attendance 20223
Result: **Portsmouth 2 Manchester United 1**
Teamsheet: van der Sar, O'Shea, Heinze, Carrick, Ferdinand, Brown, Ronaldo, Scholes, Rooney, Fletcher, Richardson
Substitute(s):   Giggs, Smith, Solskjaer   Scorer(s):   O'Shea

Match # 4978 Tuesday 10/04/07   Champions League Quarter-Final 2nd Leg   at Old Trafford   Attendance 74476
Result: **Manchester United 7 Roma 1**
Teamsheet: van der Sar, O'Shea, Heinze, Carrick, Ferdinand, Brown, Ronaldo, Smith, Rooney, Fletcher, Giggs
Substitute(s):   Evra, Richardson, Solskjaer   Scorer(s):   Carrick 2, Ronaldo 2, Evra, Rooney, Smith

Match # 4979 Saturday 14/04/07   FA Cup Semi-Final   at Villa Park   Attendance 37425
Result: **Manchester United 4 Watford 1**
Teamsheet: van der Sar, Evra, Heinze, Carrick, Ferdinand, Brown, Ronaldo, Scholes, Rooney, Smith, Giggs
Substitute(s):   Fletcher, Richardson, Solskjaer   Scorer(s):   Rooney 2, Richardson, Ronaldo

Match # 4980 Tuesday 17/04/07   FA Premiership   at Old Trafford   Attendance 75540
Result: **Manchester United 2 Sheffield United 0**
Teamsheet: Kuszczak, Fletcher, Evra, Carrick, Heinze, Brown, Ronaldo, Scholes, Rooney, Smith, Giggs
Substitute(s):   Richardson, Solskjaer   Scorer(s):   Carrick, Rooney

Match # 4981 Saturday 21/04/07   FA Premiership   at Old Trafford   Attendance 75967
Result: **Manchester United 1 Middlesbrough 1**
Teamsheet: van der Sar, O'Shea, Heinze, Carrick, Ferdinand, Brown, Ronaldo, Scholes, Rooney, Smith, Richardson
Substitute(s):   Fletcher, Giggs, Solskjaer   Scorer(s):   Richardson

Match # 4982 Tuesday 24/04/07   Champions League Semi-Final 1st Leg   at Old Trafford   Attendance 73820
Result: **Manchester United 3 AC Milan 2**
Teamsheet: van der Sar, O'Shea, Evra, Carrick, Heinze, Brown, Ronaldo, Scholes, Rooney, Fletcher, Giggs
Scorer(s):   Rooney 2, Ronaldo

SEASON 2006/07 (continued)

Match # 4983	Saturday 28/04/07 FA Premiership	at Goodison Park	Attendance 39682

Match # 4983   Saturday 28/04/07   FA Premiership   at Goodison Park   Attendance 39682
Result: **Everton 2   Manchester United 4**
Teamsheet: van der Sar, O'Shea, Evra, Carrick, Heinze, Brown, Solskjaer, Scholes, Rooney, Smith, Giggs
Substitute(s):   Eagles, Richardson, Ronaldo   Scorer(s):   Eagles, O'Shea, Rooney, own goal

Match # 4984   Wednesday 02/05/07   Champions League Semi-Final 2nd Leg   at Stadio San Siro   Attendance 78500
Result: **AC Milan 3   Manchester United 0**
Teamsheet: van der Sar, O'Shea, Heinze, Carrick, Brown, Vidic, Ronaldo, Scholes, Rooney, Fletcher, Giggs
Substitute(s):   Saha

Match # 4985   Saturday 05/05/07   FA Premiership   at Eastlands Stadium   Attendance 47244
Result: **Manchester City 0   Manchester United 1**
Teamsheet: van der Sar, Brown, Heinze, Carrick, Vidic, Ronaldo, Scholes, Rooney, Smith, Giggs
Substitute(s):   Fletcher, O'Shea   Scorer(s):   Ronaldo

Match # 4986   Wednesday 09/05/07   FA Premiership   at Stamford Bridge   Attendance 41794
Result: **Chelsea 0   Manchester United 0**
Teamsheet: Kuszczak, Lee, Heinze, Eagles, Brown, O'Shea, Solskjaer, Fletcher, Dong, Smith, Richardson
Substitute(s):   Carrick, Rooney

Match # 4987   Sunday 13/05/07   FA Premiership   at Old Trafford   Attendance 75927
Result: **Manchester United 0   West Ham United 1**
Teamsheet: van der Sar, O'Shea, Evra, Carrick, Heinze, Brown, Solskjaer, Fletcher, Rooney, Smith, Richardson
Substitute(s):   Giggs, Ronaldo, Scholes

Match # 4988   Saturday 19/05/07   FA Cup Final   at Wembley   Attendance 89826
Result: **Manchester United 0   Chelsea 1**
Teamsheet: van der Sar, Brown, Heinze, Carrick, Ferdinand, Vidic, Ronaldo, Scholes, Rooney, Fletcher, Giggs
Substitute(s):   O'Shea, Smith, Solskjaer

SEASON 2006/07 SUMMARY

APPEARANCES

PLAYER	LGE	FAC	LC	CL	TOTAL
Rooney	33 (2)	5 (2)	1	12	51 (4)
Ronaldo	31 (3)	6 (1)	1	11	49 (4)
Carrick	29 (4)	7	–	12	48 (4)
Ferdinand	33	7	–	8 (1)	48 (1)
van der Sar	32	3	–	12	47
Scholes	29 (1)	3 (1)	–	10 (1)	42 (3)
Giggs	25 (5)	6	–	8	39 (5)
Vidic	25	5	–	8	38
Neville	24	3	–	6	33
Heinze	17 (5)	6	2	7 (1)	32 (6)
Brown	17 (5)	6	2	7	32 (5)
Evra	22 (2)	3 (1)	– (1)	4 (3)	29 (7)
O'Shea	16 (16)	2 (3)	1	8 (3)	27 (22)
Fletcher	16 (8)	3 (3)	1	6 (3)	26 (14)
Saha	18 (6)	2	–	5 (3)	25 (9)
Solskjaer	9 (10)	3 (3)	1	2 (4)	15 (17)
Silvestre	6 (8)	2	2	3	13 (8)
Richardson	8 (7)	2 (1)	2	– (4)	12 (12)
Kuszczak	6	5	2	–	13
Park	8 (6)	4 (1)	–	– (1)	12 (8)
Smith	6 (3)	2 (1)	2	1 (3)	11 (7)
Larsson	5 (2)	3 (1)	–	2	10 (3)
Jones D	–	–	2	–	2
Lee	1	–	– (2)	–	1 (2)
Eagles	1 (1)	–	–	–	1 (1)
Dong	1	–	–	–	1
Gray	–	–	1	–	1
Jones R	–	–	1	–	1
Marsh	–	–	1	–	1
Shawcross	–	–	– (2)	–	– (2)
Barnes	–	–	– (1)	–	– (1)

GOALSCORERS

PLAYER	LGE	FAC	LC	CL	TOTAL
Ronaldo	17	3	–	3	23
Rooney	14	5	–	4	23
Saha	8	1	–	4	13
Solskjaer	7	2	1	1	11
Scholes	6	–	–	1	7
Giggs	4	–	–	2	6
Carrick	3	1	–	2	6
Park	5	–	–	–	5
O'Shea	4	–	–	1	5
Vidic	3	–	–	1	4
Fletcher	3	–	–	–	3
Larsson	1	1	–	1	3
Richardson	1	–	–	1	3
Evra	1	–	–	1	2
Eagles	1	–	–	–	1
Ferdinand	1	–	–	–	1
Silvestre	1	–	–	–	1
Heinze	–	1	–	–	1
Lee	–	–	1	–	1
Smith	–	–	–	1	1
own goals	3	–	–	–	3

RESULTS & ATTENDANCES SUMMARY

		P	W	D	L	F	A	TOTAL	AVGE
League	H	19	15	2	2	46	12	1440694	75826
	A	19	13	3	3	37	15	650715	34248
TOTAL		38	28	5	5	83	27	2091409	55037
FA Cup	H	4	3	1	0	6	3	287994	71999
	A	2	1	1	0	5	4	57129	28565
	N	2	1	0	1	4	2	127251	63626
TOTAL		8	5	2	1	15	9	472374	59047
League	H	0	0	0	0	0	0	0	n/a
Cup	A	2	1	0	1	2	2	21578	10789
TOTAL		2	1	0	1	2	2	21578	10789
Champions	H	6	6	0	0	20	6	444484	74081
League	A	6	2	0	4	3	7	358132	59689
TOTAL		12	8	0	4	23	13	802616	66885
Overall	H	29	24	3	2	72	21	2173172	74937
	A	29	17	4	8	47	28	1087554	37502
	N	2	1	0	1	4	2	127251	63626
TOTAL		60	42	7	11	123	51	3387977	56466

FINAL TABLE – FA PREMIERSHIP

		P	HOME					AWAY					PTS	GD
			W	D	L	F	A	W	D	L	F	A		
1	MANCHESTER UNITED	38	15	2	2	46	12	13	3	3	37	15	89	56
2	Chelsea	38	12	7	0	37	11	12	4	3	27	13	83	40
3	Liverpool	38	14	4	1	39	7	6	4	9	18	20	68	30
4	Arsenal	38	12	6	1	43	16	7	5	7	20	19	68	28
5	Tottenham Hotspur	38	12	3	4	34	22	5	6	8	23	32	60	3
6	Everton	38	11	4	4	33	17	4	9	6	19	19	58	16
7	Bolton Wanderers	38	9	5	5	26	20	7	3	9	21	32	56	-5
8	Reading	38	11	2	6	29	20	5	5	9	23	27	55	5
9	Portsmouth	38	11	5	3	28	15	3	7	9	17	27	54	3
10	Blackburn Rovers	38	9	3	7	31	25	6	4	9	21	29	52	-2
11	Aston Villa	38	7	8	4	20	14	4	9	6	23	27	50	2
12	Middlesbrough	38	10	3	6	31	24	2	7	10	13	25	46	-5
13	Newcastle United	38	7	7	5	23	20	4	3	12	15	27	43	-9
14	Manchester City	38	5	6	8	10	16	6	3	10	19	28	42	-15
15	West Ham United	38	8	2	9	24	26	4	3	12	11	33	41	-24
16	Fulham	38	7	7	5	18	18	1	8	10	20	42	39	-22
17	Wigan Athletic	38	5	4	10	18	30	5	4	10	19	29	38	-22
18	Sheffield United	38	7	6	6	24	21	3	2	14	8	34	38	-23
19	Charlton Athletic	38	7	5	7	19	20	1	5	13	15	40	34	-26
20	Watford	38	3	9	7	19	25	2	4	13	10	34	28	-30

SEASON 2007/08

Match # 4989 Sunday 05/08/07 FA Charity Shield at Wembley Attendance 80731
Result: **Manchester United 1 Chelsea 1 (United won the tie 3-0 on penalty kicks)**
Teamsheet: van der Sar, Brown, Evra, Silvestre, Ferdinand, Vidic, Ronaldo, O'Shea, Rooney, Carrick, Giggs
Substitute(s): Fletcher, Nani Scorer(s): Giggs

Match # 4990 Sunday 12/08/07 FA Premiership at Old Trafford Attendance 75655
Result: **Manchester United 0 Reading 0**
Teamsheet: van der Sar, Brown, Evra, Silvestre, Ferdinand, Vidic, Ronaldo, Scholes, Rooney, Carrick, Giggs
Substitute(s): Fletcher, Nani, O'Shea

Match # 4991 Wednesday 15/08/07 FA Premiership at Fratton Park Attendance 20510
Result: **Portsmouth 1 Manchester United 1**
Teamsheet: van der Sar, Brown, Evra, Carrick, Ferdinand, Vidic, Ronaldo, Scholes, Tevez, Nani, Giggs
Substitute(s): Eagles, O'Shea Scorer(s): Scholes

Match # 4992 Sunday 19/08/07 FA Premiership at Eastlands Stadium Attendance 44955
Result: **Manchester City 1 Manchester United 0**
Teamsheet: van der Sar, Brown, Evra, Hargreaves, Ferdinand, Vidic, Nani, Scholes, Tevez, Carrick, Giggs
Substitute(s): Campbell, Eagles, O'Shea

Match # 4993 Sunday 26/08/07 FA Premiership at Old Trafford Attendance 75696
Result: **Manchester United 1 Tottenham Hotspur 0**
Teamsheet: van der Sar, Brown, Evra, Hargreaves, Ferdinand, Vidic, Nani, Scholes, Tevez, Carrick, Giggs
Substitute(s): Eagles, Fletcher Scorer(s): Nani

Match # 4994 Saturday 01/09/07 FA Premiership at Old Trafford Attendance 75648
Result: **Manchester United 1 Sunderland 0**
Teamsheet: van der Sar, Brown, Evra, Hargreaves, Ferdinand, Vidic, Nani, Scholes, Tevez, Anderson, Eagles
Substitute(s): Fletcher, O'Shea, Saha Scorer(s): Saha

Match # 4995 Saturday 15/09/07 FA Premiership at Goodison Park Attendance 39364
Result: **Everton 0 Manchester United 1**
Teamsheet: van der Sar, Brown, Evra, Silvestre, Ferdinand, Vidic, Ronaldo, Scholes, Tevez, Carrick, Giggs
Substitute(s): Nani, Pique, Saha Scorer(s): Vidic

Match # 4996 Wednesday 19/09/07 Champions League Phase 1 Match 1 at de Jose Alvalade Attendance 39514
Result: **Sporting Lisbon 0 Manchester United 1**
Teamsheet: van der Sar, Brown, Evra, Carrick, Ferdinand, Vidic, Ronaldo, Scholes, Rooney, Nani, Giggs
Substitute(s): Anderson, Saha, Tevez Scorer(s): Ronaldo

Match # 4997 Sunday 23/09/07 FA Premiership at Old Trafford Attendance 75663
Result: **Manchester United 2 Chelsea 0**
Teamsheet: van der Sar, Brown, Evra, Carrick, Ferdinand, Vidic, Ronaldo, Scholes, Rooney, Tevez, Giggs
Substitute(s): Saha Scorer(s): Saha, Tevez

Match # 4998 Wednesday 26/09/07 League Cup 3rd Round at Old Trafford Attendance 74055
Result: **Manchester United 0 Coventry City 2**
Teamsheet: Kuszczak, Bardsley, Simpson, O'Shea, Pique, Evans, Martin, Anderson, Dong, Nani, Eagles
Substitute(s): Brown, Campbell, Carrick

Match # 4999 Saturday 29/09/07 FA Premiership at St Andrews Attendance 26526
Result: **Birmingham City 0 Manchester United 1**
Teamsheet: van der Sar, Brown, Evra, Carrick, Ferdinand, Vidic, Ronaldo, Scholes, Rooney, Tevez, Giggs
Substitute(s): Kuszczak, O'Shea, Saha Scorer(s): Ronaldo

Match # 5000 Tuesday 02/10/07 Champions League Phase 1 Match 2 at Old Trafford Attendance 73652
Result: **Manchester United 1 Roma 0**
Teamsheet: Kuszczak, O'Shea, Evra, Carrick, Ferdinand, Vidic, Ronaldo, Scholes, Saha, Rooney, Nani
Substitute(s): Anderson, Giggs, Tevez Scorer(s): Rooney

Match # 5001 Saturday 06/10/07 FA Premiership at Old Trafford Attendance 75300
Result: **Manchester United 4 Wigan Athletic 0**
Teamsheet: Kuszczak, Pique, Evra, O'Shea, Ferdinand, Vidic, Ronaldo, Scholes, Rooney, Tevez, Giggs
Substitute(s): Anderson, Nani, Simpson Scorer(s): Ronaldo 2, Rooney, Tevez

Match # 5002 Saturday 20/10/07 FA Premiership at Villa Park Attendance 42640
Result: **Aston Villa 1 Manchester United 4**
Teamsheet: van der Sar, Brown, Evra, Anderson, Ferdinand, Pique, Nani, Scholes, Rooney, Tevez, Giggs
Substitute(s): Fletcher, O'Shea, Ronaldo Scorer(s): Rooney 2, Ferdinand, Giggs

Match # 5003 Tuesday 23/10/07 Champions League Phase 1 Match 3 at Olympic Stadium Attendance 43000
Result: **Dynamo Kiev 2 Manchester United 4**
Teamsheet: van der Sar, Brown, O'Shea, Fletcher, Ferdinand, Vidic, Ronaldo, Anderson, Rooney, Tevez, Giggs
Substitute(s): Kuszczak, Nani, Simpson Scorer(s): Ronaldo 2, Ferdinand, Rooney

Match # 5004 Saturday 27/10/07 FA Premiership at Old Trafford Attendance 75720
Result: **Manchester United 4 Middlesbrough 1**
Teamsheet: van der Sar, Brown, O'Shea, Hargreaves, Ferdinand, Vidic, Ronaldo, Anderson, Rooney, Tevez, Nani
Substitute(s): Fletcher, Giggs, Pique Scorer(s): Tevez 2, Nani, Rooney

Match # 5005 Saturday 03/11/07 FA Premiership at Emirates Stadium Attendance 60161
Result: **Arsenal 2 Manchester United 2**
Teamsheet: van der Sar, Brown, Evra, Hargreaves, Ferdinand, Vidic, Ronaldo, Anderson, Rooney, Tevez, Giggs
Substitute(s): Carrick, O'Shea, Saha Scorer(s): Ronaldo, own goal

Match # 5006 Wednesday 07/11/07 Champions League Phase 1 Match 4 at Old Trafford Attendance 75017
Result: **Manchester United 4 Dynamo Kiev 0**
Teamsheet: van der Sar, Simpson, Evra, Fletcher, Pique, Vidic, Ronaldo, Carrick, Rooney, Tevez, Nani
Substitute(s): Evans, Kuszczak, Saha Scorer(s): Pique, Ronaldo, Rooney, Tevez

SEASON 2007/08 (continued)

Match # 5007	Sunday 11/11/07	FA Premiership	at Old Trafford	Attendance 75710
Result:	**Manchester United 2 Blackburn Rovers 0**			
Teamsheet:	van der Sar, Brown, Evra, Hargreaves, Ferdinand, Vidic, Ronaldo, Anderson, Saha, Tevez, Giggs			
Substitute(s):	Carrick, Nani	Scorer(s): Ronaldo 2		

Match # 5008	Saturday 24/11/07	FA Premiership	at Reebok Stadium	Attendance 25028
Result:	**Bolton Wanderers 1 Manchester United 0**			
Teamsheet:	van der Sar, Brown, Evra, Hargreaves, Ferdinand, Pique, Nani, Carrick, Saha, Tevez, Giggs			
Substitute(s):	Anderson, O'Shea			

Match # 5009	Tuesday 27/11/07	Champions League Phase 1 Match 5	at Old Trafford	Attendance 75162
Result:	**Manchester United 2 Sporting Lisbon 1**			
Teamsheet:	Kuszczak, O'Shea, Evra, Fletcher, Ferdinand, Vidic, Ronaldo, Carrick, Saha, Anderson, Nani			
Substitute(s):	Giggs, Hargreaves, Tevez	Scorer(s): Ronaldo, Tevez		

Match # 5010	Monday 03/12/07	FA Premiership	at Old Trafford	Attendance 75055
Result:	**Manchester United 2 Fulham 0**			
Teamsheet:	van der Sar, Brown, Evra, Hargreaves, Ferdinand, Vidic, Ronaldo, Anderson, Rooney, Tevez, Giggs			
Substitute(s):	Carrick, O'Shea, Saha	Scorer(s): Ronaldo 2		

Match # 5011	Saturday 08/12/07	FA Premiership	at Old Trafford	Attendance 75725
Result:	**Manchester United 4 Derby County 1**			
Teamsheet:	van der Sar, Brown, Evra, Carrick, Ferdinand, Vidic, Ronaldo, Anderson, Rooney, Tevez, Giggs			
Substitute(s):	Fletcher, O'Shea, Saha	Scorer(s): Tevez 2, Giggs, Ronaldo		

Match # 5012	Wednesday 12/12/07	Champions League Phase 1 Match 6	at Olympic Stadium	Attendance 29490
Result:	**Roma 1 Manchester United 1**			
Teamsheet:	Kuszczak, Simpson, O'Shea, Fletcher, Pique, Evans, Eagles, Carrick, Rooney, Saha, Nani			
Substitute(s):	Brown, Dong	Scorer(s): Pique		

Match # 5013	Sunday 16/12/07	FA Premiership	at Anfield	Attendance 44459
Result:	**Liverpool 0 Manchester United 1**			
Teamsheet:	van der Sar, Brown, Evra, Hargreaves, Ferdinand, Vidic, Ronaldo, Anderson, Rooney, Tevez, Giggs			
Substitute(s):	Carrick, O'Shea	Scorer(s): Tevez		

Match # 5014	Sunday 23/12/07	FA Premiership	at Old Trafford	Attendance 75749
Result:	**Manchester United 2 Everton 1**			
Teamsheet:	Kuszczak, Simpson, Evra, Carrick, Brown, Vidic, Ronaldo, Anderson, Rooney, Tevez, Giggs			
Substitute(s):	Fletcher, O'Shea, Saha	Scorer(s): Ronaldo 2		

Match # 5015	Wednesday 26/12/07	FA Premiership	at Stadium of Light	Attendance 47360
Result:	**Sunderland 0 Manchester United 4**			
Teamsheet:	Kuszczak, Brown, O'Shea, Fletcher, Ferdinand, Vidic, Ronaldo, Carrick, Rooney, Saha, Nani			
Substitute(s):	Park, Pique	Scorer(s): Saha 2, Ronaldo, Rooney		

Match # 5016	Saturday 29/12/07	FA Premiership	at Upton Park	Attendance 34966
Result:	**West Ham United 2 Manchester United 1**			
Teamsheet:	Kuszczak, Brown, Evra, Fletcher, Ferdinand, Vidic, Ronaldo, Hargreaves, Saha, Tevez, Giggs			
Substitute(s):	Anderson, Nani, O'Shea	Scorer(s): Ronaldo		

Match # 5017	Tuesday 01/01/08	FA Premiership	at Old Trafford	Attendance 75459
Result:	**Manchester United 1 Birmingham City 0**			
Teamsheet:	Kuszczak, O'Shea, Evra, Carrick, Ferdinand, Vidic, Ronaldo, Anderson, Tevez, Park, Nani			
Substitute(s):	Brown, Hargreaves, Saha	Scorer(s): Tevez		

Match # 5018	Saturday 05/01/08	FA Cup 3rd Round	at Villa Park	Attendance 33630
Result:	**Aston Villa 0 Manchester United 2**			
Teamsheet:	van der Sar, Brown, Evra, Carrick, Ferdinand, Vidic, Ronaldo, Anderson, Saha, Park, Giggs			
Substitute(s):	Hargreaves, O'Shea, Rooney	Scorer(s): Ronaldo, Rooney		

Match # 5019	Saturday 12/01/08	FA Premiership	at Old Trafford	Attendance 75965
Result:	**Manchester United 6 Newcastle United 0**			
Teamsheet:	van der Sar, O'Shea, Evra, Carrick, Ferdinand, Vidic, Ronaldo, Anderson, Rooney, Tevez, Giggs			
Substitute(s):	Fletcher, Nani, Simpson	Scorer(s): Ronaldo 3, Tevez 2, Ferdinand		

Match # 5020	Saturday 19/01/08	FA Premiership	at Madejski Stadium	Attendance 24135
Result:	**Reading 0 Manchester United 2**			
Teamsheet:	van der Sar, Brown, Evra, Hargreaves, Ferdinand, Vidic, Ronaldo, Carrick, Rooney, Tevez, Park			
Substitute(s):	Fletcher, Giggs, Nani	Scorer(s): Ronaldo, Rooney		

Match # 5021	Sunday 27/01/08	FA Cup 4th Round	at Old Trafford	Attendance 75369
Result:	**Manchester United 3 Tottenham Hotspur 1**			
Teamsheet:	van der Sar, O'Shea, Evra, Hargreaves, Ferdinand, Brown, Ronaldo, Carrick, Rooney, Tevez, Giggs			
Substitute(s):	Anderson, Scholes, Simpson	Scorer(s): Ronaldo 2, Tevez		

Match # 5022	Wednesday 30/01/08	FA Premiership	at Old Trafford	Attendance 75415
Result:	**Manchester United 2 Portsmouth 0**			
Teamsheet:	van der Sar, Brown, Evra, Carrick, Ferdinand, Vidic, Ronaldo, Scholes, Rooney, Park, Nani			
Substitute(s):	Anderson, Hargreaves, Tevez	Scorer(s): Ronaldo 2		

Match # 5023	Saturday 02/02/08	FA Premiership	at White Hart Lane	Attendance 36075
Result:	**Tottenham Hotspur 1 Manchester United 1**			
Teamsheet:	van der Sar, Brown, Evra, Hargreaves, Ferdinand, Vidic, Ronaldo, Scholes, Rooney, Tevez, Giggs			
Substitute(s):	Anderson, Carrick, Nani	Scorer(s): Tevez		

Match # 5024	Sunday 10/02/08	FA Premiership	at Old Trafford	Attendance 75970
Result:	**Manchester United 1 Manchester City 2**			
Teamsheet:	van der Sar, Brown, O'Shea, Anderson, Ferdinand, Vidic, Ronaldo, Scholes, Tevez, Nani, Giggs			
Substitute(s):	Carrick, Hargreaves, Park	Scorer(s): Carrick		

SEASON 2007/08 (continued)

Match # 5025 Saturday 16/02/08   FA Cup 5th Round   at Old Trafford   Attendance 75550
Result: **Manchester United 4 Arsenal 0**
Teamsheet: van der Sar, Brown, Evra, Carrick, Ferdinand, Vidic, Fletcher, Anderson, Rooney, Nani, Park
Substitute(s): Saha, Scholes   Scorer(s): Fletcher 2, Nani, Rooney

Match # 5026 Wednesday 20/02/08   Champions League 2nd Round 1st Leg   at Stade de Gerland   Attendance 39230
Result: **Olympique Lyonnais 1 Manchester United 1**
Teamsheet: van der Sar, Brown, Evra, Hargreaves, Ferdinand, Vidic, Ronaldo, Scholes, Rooney, Anderson, Giggs
Substitute(s): Carrick, Nani, Tevez   Scorer(s): Tevez

Match # 5027 Saturday 23/02/08   FA Premiership   at St James' Park   Attendance 52291
Result: **Newcastle United 1 Manchester United 5**
Teamsheet: van der Sar, Brown, Evra, Fletcher, Ferdinand, Vidic, Ronaldo, Carrick, Rooney, Tevez, Nani
Substitute(s): O'Shea, Saha, Scholes   Scorer(s): Ronaldo 2, Rooney 2, Saha

Match # 5028 Saturday 01/03/08   FA Premiership   at Craven Cottage   Attendance 25314
Result: **Fulham 0 Manchester United 3**
Teamsheet: van der Sar, O'Shea, Evra, Hargreaves, Ferdinand, Brown, Nani, Scholes, Saha, Tevez, Park
Substitute(s): Anderson, Ronaldo, Rooney   Scorer(s): Hargreaves, Park, own goal

Match # 5029 Tuesday 04/03/08   Champions League 2nd Round 2nd Leg   at Old Trafford   Attendance 75520
Result: **Manchester United 1 Olympique Lyonnais 0**
Teamsheet: van der Sar, Brown, Evra, Fletcher, Ferdinand, Vidic, Ronaldo, Carrick, Rooney, Anderson, Nani
Substitute(s): Hargreaves, Tevez   Scorer(s): Ronaldo

Match # 5030 Saturday 08/03/08   FA Cup 6th Round   at Old Trafford   Attendance 75463
Result: **Manchester United 0 Portsmouth 1**
Teamsheet: van der Sar, Brown, Evra, Hargreaves, Ferdinand, Vidic, Ronaldo, Scholes, Rooney, Tevez, Nani
Substitute(s): Anderson, Carrick, Kuszczak

Match # 5031 Saturday 15/03/08   FA Premiership   at Pride Park   Attendance 33072
Result: **Derby County 0 Manchester United 1**
Teamsheet: Foster, O'Shea, Evra, Anderson, Brown, Vidic, Ronaldo, Scholes, Rooney, Park, Giggs
Substitute(s): Carrick, Fletcher, Saha   Scorer(s): Ronaldo

Match # 5032 Wednesday 19/03/08   FA Premiership   at Old Trafford   Attendance 75476
Result: **Manchester United 2 Bolton Wanderers 0**
Teamsheet: Kuszczak, Hargreaves, O'Shea, Fletcher, Pique, Vidic, Ronaldo, Anderson, Saha, Tevez, Nani
Substitute(s): Brown, Rooney, Scholes   Scorer(s): Ronaldo 2

Match # 5033 Sunday 23/03/08   FA Premiership   at Old Trafford   Attendance 76000
Result: **Manchester United 3 Liverpool 0**
Teamsheet: van der Sar, Brown, Evra, Carrick, Ferdinand, Vidic, Ronaldo, Scholes, Rooney, Anderson, Giggs
Substitute(s): Nani, Tevez   Scorer(s): Brown, Nani, Ronaldo

Match # 5034 Saturday 29/03/08   FA Premiership   at Old Trafford   Attendance 75932
Result: **Manchester United 4 Aston Villa 0**
Teamsheet: Kuszczak, Brown, Evra, Carrick, Ferdinand, Vidic, Ronaldo, Scholes, Rooney, Tevez, Giggs
Substitute(s): Anderson, Hargreaves, O'Shea   Scorer(s): Rooney 2, Ronaldo, Tevez

Match # 5035 Tuesday 01/04/08   Champions League Quarter-Final 1st Leg   at Olympic Stadium   Attendance 60931
Result: **Roma 0 Manchester United 2**
Teamsheet: van der Sar, Brown, Evra, Carrick, Ferdinand, Vidic, Ronaldo, Scholes, Rooney, Anderson, Park
Substitute(s): Hargreaves, O'Shea, Tevez   Scorer(s): Ronaldo, Rooney

Match # 5036 Sunday 06/04/08   FA Premiership   at Riverside Stadium   Attendance 33952
Result: **Middlesbrough 2 Manchester United 2**
Teamsheet: van der Sar, O'Shea, Evra, Carrick, Ferdinand, Brown, Ronaldo, Scholes, Rooney, Tevez, Giggs
Substitute(s): Hargreaves, Park, Pique   Scorer(s): Ronaldo, Rooney

Match # 5037 Wednesday 09/04/08   Champions League Quarter-Final 2nd Leg   at Old Trafford   Attendance 74423
Result: **Manchester United 1 Roma 0**
Teamsheet: van der Sar, Brown, Silvestre, Hargreaves, Ferdinand, Pique, Park, Carrick, Tevez, Anderson, Giggs
Substitute(s): Neville G, O'Shea, Rooney   Scorer(s): Tevez

Match # 5038 Sunday 13/04/08   FA Premiership   at Old Trafford   Attendance 75985
Result: **Manchester United 2 Arsenal 1**
Teamsheet: van der Sar, Brown, Evra, Hargreaves, Ferdinand, Pique, Ronaldo, Scholes, Rooney, Carrick, Park
Substitute(s): Anderson, Giggs, Tevez   Scorer(s): Hargreaves, Ronaldo

Match # 5039 Saturday 19/04/08   FA Premiership   at Ewood Park   Attendance 30316
Result: **Blackburn Rovers 1 Manchester United 1**
Teamsheet: Kuszczak, Brown, Evra, Carrick, Ferdinand, Vidic, Ronaldo, Scholes, Rooney, Tevez, Giggs
Substitute(s): Nani, O'Shea, Park   Scorer(s): Tevez

Match # 5040 Wednesday 23/04/08   Champions League Semi-Final 1st Leg   at Estadio Camp Nou   Attendance 95949
Result: **Barcelona 0 Manchester United 0**
Teamsheet: van der Sar, Hargreaves, Evra, Carrick, Ferdinand, Vidic, Ronaldo, Scholes, Rooney, Tevez, Park
Substitute(s): Giggs, Nani

Match # 5041 Saturday 26/04/08   FA Premiership   at Stamford Bridge   Attendance 41828
Result: **Chelsea 2 Manchester United 1**
Teamsheet: van der Sar, Brown, Silvestre, Carrick, Ferdinand, Vidic, Fletcher, Anderson, Rooney, Nani, Giggs
Substitute(s): Hargreaves, O'Shea, Ronaldo   Scorer(s): Rooney

Match # 5042 Tuesday 29/04/08   Champions League Semi-Final 2nd Leg   at Old Trafford   Attendance 75061
Result: **Manchester United 1 Barcelona 0**
Teamsheet: van der Sar, Hargreaves, Evra, Carrick, Ferdinand, Brown, Ronaldo, Scholes, Tevez, Nani, Park
Substitute(s): Fletcher, Giggs, Silvestre   Scorer(s): Scholes

SEASON 2007/08 (continued)

Match # 5043	Saturday 03/05/08	FA Premiership	at Old Trafford	Attendance 76013
Result:	**Manchester United 4 West Ham United 1**		
Teamsheet:	van der Sar, Hargreaves, Evra, Carrick, Ferdinand, Brown, Ronaldo, Scholes, Tevez, Nani, Park		
Substitute(s):	Fletcher, Giggs, O'Shea	Scorer(s): Ronaldo 2, Carrick, Tevez	

Match # 5044	Sunday 11/05/08	FA Premiership	at JJB Stadium	Attendance 25133
Result:	**Wigan Athletic 0 Manchester United 2**		
Teamsheet:	van der Sar, Brown, Evra, Carrick, Ferdinand, Vidic, Ronaldo, Scholes, Rooney, Tevez, Park		
Substitute(s):	Giggs, Hargreaves	Scorer(s): Giggs, Ronaldo	

Match # 5045	Wednesday 21/05/08	Chmapions League Final	at Luzhniki Stadium	Attendance 67310
Result:	**Manchester United 1 Chelsea 1 (United won the tie 6-5 on penalty kicks)**		
Teamsheet:	van der Sar, Brown, Evra, Carrick, Ferdinand, Vidic, Ronaldo, Scholes, Rooney, Tevez, Hargreaves		
Substitute(s):	Anderson, Giggs, Nani	Scorer(s): Ronaldo	

SEASON 2007/08 SUMMARY

APPEARANCES

PLAYER	LGE	FAC	LC	CL	CS	TOTAL
Ferdinand	35	4	–	11	1	51
Brown	34 (2)	4	– (1)	9 (1)	1	48 (4)
Evra	33	4	–	10	1	48
Ronaldo	31 (3)	3	–	11	1	46 (3)
Vidic	32	3	–	9	1	45
van der Sar	29	4	–	10	1	44
Carrick	24 (7)	3 (1)	– (1)	11 (1)	1	39 (10)
Tevez	31 (3)	2	–	6 (6)	–	39 (9)
Rooney	25 (2)	3 (1)	–	10 (1)	1	39 (4)
Giggs	26 (5)	2	–	4 (5)	1	33 (10)
Scholes	22 (2)	1 (2)	–	7	–	30 (4)
Nani	16 (10)	2	1	7 (4)	– (1)	26 (15)
Anderson	16 (8)	2 (2)	1	6 (3)	–	25 (13)
Hargreaves	16 (7)	2 (1)	–	5 (3)	–	23 (11)
O'Shea	10 (18)	1 (1)	1	4 (2)	1	17 (21)
Park	8 (4)	2	–	4	–	14 (4)
Kuszczak	8 (1)	– (1)	1	3 (2)	–	12 (4)
Fletcher	5 (11)	1	–	5 (1)	– (1)	11 (13)
Saha	6 (11)	1 (1)	–	3 (2)	–	10 (14)
Pique	5 (4)	–	1	3	–	9 (4)
Silvestre	3	–	–	1 (1)	1	5 (1)
Simpson	1 (2)	– (1)	1	2 (1)	–	4 (4)
Eagles	1 (3)	–	1	1	–	3 (3)
Evans	–	–	1	1 (1)	–	2 (1)
Dong	–	–	1	– (1)	–	1 (1)
Bardsley	–	–	1	–	–	1
Foster	1	–	–	–	–	1
Martin	–	–	1	–	–	1
Campbell	– (1)	–	– (1)	–	–	– (2)
Neville	–	–	–	– (1)	–	– (1)

GOALSCORERS

PLAYER	LGE	FAC	LC	CL	CS	TOTAL
Ronaldo	31	3	–	8	–	42
Tevez	14	1	–	4	–	19
Rooney	12	2	–	4	–	18
Saha	5	–	–	–	–	5
Giggs	3	–	–	–	1	4
Nani	3	1	–	–	–	4
Ferdinand	2	–	–	1	–	3
Carrick	2	–	–	–	–	2
Hargreaves	2	–	–	–	–	2
Scholes	1	–	–	1	–	2
Fletcher	–	2	–	–	–	2
Pique	–	–	–	2	–	2
Brown	1	–	–	–	–	1
Park	1	–	–	–	–	1
Vidic	1	–	–	–	–	1
own goals	2	–	–	–	–	2

RESULTS & ATTENDANCES SUMMARY

		P	W	D	L	F	A	TOTAL	AVGE
League	H	19	17	1	1	47	7	1438136	75691
	A	19	10	5	4	33	15	688085	36215
TOTAL		38	27	6	5	80	22	2126221	55953
FA Cup	H	3	2	0	1	7	2	226382	75461
	A	1	1	0	0	2	0	33630	33630
TOTAL		4	3	0	1	9	2	260012	65003
League	H	1	0	0	1	0	2	74055	74055
Cup	A	0	0	0	0	0	0	0	n/a
TOTAL		1	0	0	1	0	2	74055	74055
Champions	H	6	6	0	0	10	1	448835	74806
League	A	6	3	3	0	9	4	308114	51352
	N	1	0	1	0	1	1	67310	67310
TOTAL		13	9	4	0	20	6	824259	63405
Charity	H	0	0	0	0	0	0	0	n/a
Shield	A	0	0	0	0	0	0	0	n/a
	N	1	0	1	0	1	1	80731	80731
TOTAL		1	0	1	0	1	1	80731	80731
Overall	H	29	25	1	3	64	12	2187408	75428
	A	26	14	8	4	44	19	1029829	39609
	N	2	0	2	0	2	2	148041	74021
TOTAL		57	39	11	7	110	33	3365278	59040

FINAL TABLE – FA PREMIERSHIP

		P	W	D	L	F	A	W	D	L	F	A	PTS	GD
			HOME						AWAY					
1	MANCHESTER UNITED	38	17	1	1	47	7	10	5	4	33	15	87	58
2	Chelsea	38	12	7	0	36	13	13	3	3	29	13	85	39
3	Arsenal	38	14	5	0	37	11	10	6	3	37	20	83	43
4	Liverpool	38	12	6	1	43	13	9	7	3	24	15	76	39
5	Everton	38	11	4	4	34	17	8	4	7	21	16	65	22
6	Aston Villa	38	10	3	6	34	22	6	9	4	37	29	60	20
7	Blackburn Rovers	38	8	7	4	26	19	7	6	6	24	29	58	2
8	Portsmouth	38	7	8	4	24	14	9	1	9	24	26	57	8
9	Manchester City	38	11	4	4	28	20	4	6	9	17	33	55	-8
10	West Ham United	38	7	7	5	24	24	6	3	10	18	26	49	-8
11	Tottenham Hotspur	38	8	5	6	46	34	3	8	8	20	27	46	5
12	Newcastle United	38	8	5	6	25	26	3	5	11	20	39	43	-20
13	Middlesbrough	38	7	5	7	27	23	3	7	9	16	30	42	-10
14	Wigan Athletic	38	8	5	6	21	17	2	5	12	13	34	40	-17
15	Sunderland	38	9	3	7	23	21	2	3	14	13	38	39	-23
16	Bolton Wanderers	38	7	5	7	23	18	2	5	12	13	36	37	-18
17	Fulham	38	5	5	9	22	31	3	7	9	6	29	36	-22
18	Reading	38	8	2	9	19	25	2	4	13	22	41	36	-25
19	Birmingham City	38	6	8	5	30	23	2	3	14	16	39	35	-16
20	Derby County	38	1	5	13	12	43	0	3	16	8	46	11	-69

The Premiership

COMBINED PREMIERSHIP TABLE SINCE DAY ONE - ENOUGH SAID

#	TEAM	P	HOME					AWAY					PTS	GD	
			W	D	L	F	A	W	D	L	F	A			
1	MANCHESTER UNITED	620	224	60	26	669	195	170	77	63	551	343	1319	682	(16 seasons)
2	Arsenal	620	197	77	36	618	253	135	91	84	430	294	1164	501	(16 seasons)
3	Chelsea	620	184	83	43	566	255	126	85	99	411	351	1098	371	(16 seasons)
4	Liverpool	620	193	72	45	587	241	113	85	112	405	366	1075	385	(16 seasons)
5	Aston Villa	620	143	89	78	425	293	87	98	125	357	431	877	58	(16 seasons)
6	Newcastle United	578	164	68	57	515	285	76	84	129	329	433	872	126	(15 seasons)
7	Tottenham Hotspur	620	146	81	83	510	383	77	84	149	329	464	834	-8	(16 seasons)
8	Blackburn Rovers	544	140	64	68	447	291	80	81	111	305	364	805	97	(14 seasons)
9	Everton	620	135	86	89	448	341	76	81	153	310	467	800	-50	(16 seasons)
10	Leeds United	468	118	60	56	357	231	71	65	98	284	342	692	68	(12 seasons)
11	West Ham United	502	113	65	73	365	296	60	61	130	226	403	645	-108	(13 seasons)
12	Middlesbrough	498	101	69	79	359	312	52	76	121	234	372	601	-91	(13 seasons)
13	Southampton	506	107	70	76	358	299	43	67	143	240	439	587	-140	(13 seasons)
14	Manchester City	430	79	64	72	279	245	50	56	109	208	334	507	-92	(11 seasons)
15	Bolton Wanderers	342	66	55	50	215	198	40	40	91	179	294	413	-98	(9 seasons)
16	Coventry City	354	65	56	56	219	199	34	56	87	168	291	409	-103	(9 seasons)
17	Sheffield Wednesday	316	63	50	45	234	187	38	39	81	175	266	392	-44	(8 seasons)
18	Wimbledon	316	62	46	50	218	198	37	48	73	166	274	391	-88	(8 seasons)
19	Charlton Athletic	304	58	40	54	199	198	35	42	75	143	244	361	-100	(8 seasons)
20	Leicester City	308	51	51	52	189	212	33	39	82	165	244	342	-102	(8 seasons)
21	Fulham	266	60	32	41	176	151	19	42	72	129	227	311	-73	(7 seasons)
22	Derby County	266	48	35	50	157	177	20	35	78	114	243	274	-149	(7 seasons)
23	Sunderland	266	46	35	52	136	156	23	26	84	114	238	268	-144	(7 seasons)
24	Nottingham Forest	198	35	32	32	115	118	25	19	47	114	169	239	-58	(5 seasons)
25	Portsmouth	190	41	28	26	134	98	21	19	55	86	159	233	-37	(5 seasons)
26	Ipswich Town	202	35	29	37	125	127	22	24	55	94	185	224	-93	(5 seasons)
27	Queens Park Rangers	164	36	26	26	134	113	23	19	40	90	119	216	-8	(4 seasons)
28	Birmingham City	190	36	29	30	124	105	16	27	52	74	150	212	-57	(5 seasons)
29	Norwich City	164	32	28	22	113	101	18	23	41	92	156	201	-52	(4 seasons)
30	Crystal Palace	160	20	25	35	79	106	17	24	39	81	137	160	-83	(4 seasons)
31	Sheffield United	122	23	22	16	81	63	9	14	38	47	105	132	-40	(3 seasons)
32	Wigan Athletic	114	20	12	25	63	73	15	12	30	53	89	129	-46	(3 seasons)
33	Reading	76	19	4	15	48	45	7	9	22	45	68	91	-20	(2 seasons)
34	West Bromwich Albion	114	14	15	28	55	82	5	18	34	41	102	90	-88	(3 seasons)
35	Oldham Athletic	84	15	14	13	67	63	7	9	26	38	79	89	-37	(2 seasons)
36	Bradford City	76	10	15	13	46	58	4	5	29	22	80	62	-70	(2 seasons)
37	Watford	76	8	13	17	43	56	3	6	29	21	80	52	-72	(2 seasons)
38	Barnsley	38	7	4	8	25	35	3	1	15	12	47	35	-45	(1 season)
39	Wolverhampton Wanderers	38	7	5	7	23	35	0	7	12	15	42	33	-39	(1 season)
40	Swindon Town	42	4	7	10	25	45	1	8	12	22	55	30	-53	(1 season)

MANCHESTER UNITED
The Complete Record

Chapter 1.2
The Opponents

UNITED v ACCRINGTON STANLEY

ALL COMPETITIVE MATCHES						LEAGUE DIVISION ONE						FA CUP					
VENUE	P	W	D	L	F	A	VENUE	P	W	D	L	F	A	VENUE	P	W	D	L	F	A
HOME	3	2	1	0	15	4	HOME	1	0	1	0	3	3	HOME	2	2	0	0	12	1
AWAY	2	0	2	0	4	4	AWAY	1	0	1	0	2	2	AWAY	1	0	1	0	2	2
TOTAL	5	2	3	0	19	8	TOTAL	2	0	2	0	5	5	TOTAL	3	2	1	0	14	3

#	SEASON	DATE	COMPETITION / ROUND	MATCH RESULT	VENUE	ATT
1	1892/93	26/11/92	Football League Division 1	Accrington Stanley 2 Newton Heath 2	Thornleyholme Road	3000
2	1892/93	08/04/93	Football League Division 1	Newton Heath 3 Accrington Stanley 3	North Road	3000
3	1902/03	01/11/02	FA Cup 3rd Qualifying Round	Manchester United 7 Accrington Stanley 0	Bank Street	6000
4	1945/46	05/01/46	FA Cup 3rd Round 1st Leg	Accrington Stanley 2 Manchester United 2	Peel Park	9968
5	1945/46	09/01/46	FA Cup 3rd Round 2nd Leg	Manchester United 5 Accrington Stanley 1	Maine Road	15339

UNITED v AC MILAN

EUROPEAN CUP / CHAMPIONS LEAGUE						
VENUE	P	W	D	L	F	A
HOME	4	3	0	1	6	4
AWAY	4	0	0	4	0	10
TOTAL	8	3	0	5	6	14

#	SEASON	DATE	COMPETITION / ROUND	MATCH RESULT	VENUE	ATT
1	1957/58	08/05/58	European Cup Semi-Final 1st Leg	Manchester United 2 AC Milan 1	Old Trafford	44880
2	1957/58	14/05/58	European Cup Semi-Final 2nd Leg	AC Milan 4 Manchester United 0	Stadio San Siro	80000
3	1968/69	23/04/69	European Cup Semi-Final 1st Leg	AC Milan 2 Manchester United 0	Stadio San Siro	80000
4	1968/69	15/05/69	European Cup Semi-Final 2nd Leg	Manchester United 1 AC Milan 0	Old Trafford	63103
5	2004/05	23/02/05	Champions League 2nd Round 1st Leg	Manchester United 0 AC Milan 1	Old Trafford	67162
6	2004/05	08/03/05	Champions League 2nd Round 2nd Leg	AC Milan 1 Manchester United 0	Stadio San Siro	78957
7	2006/07	24/04/07	Champions League Semi-Final 1st Leg	Manchester United 3 AC Milan 2	Old Trafford	73820
8	2006/07	02/05/07	Champions League Semi-Final 2nd Leg	AC Milan 3 Manchester United 0	Stadio San Siro	78500

UNITED v AJAX

UEFA CUP						
VENUE	P	W	D	L	F	A
HOME	1	1	0	0	2	0
AWAY	1	0	0	1	0	1
TOTAL	2	1	0	1	2	1

#	SEASON	DATE	COMPETITION / ROUND	MATCH RESULT	VENUE	ATT
1	1976/77	15/09/76	UEFA Cup 1st Round 1st Leg	Ajax 1 Manchester United 0	Olympisch Stadion	30000
2	1976/77	29/09/76	UEFA Cup 1st Round 2nd Leg	Manchester United 2 Ajax 0	Old Trafford	58918

UNITED v ALDERSHOT

LEAGUE CUP						
VENUE	P	W	D	L	F	A
HOME	0	0	0	0	0	0
AWAY	1	1	0	0	3	1
TOTAL	1	1	0	0	3	1

#	SEASON	DATE	COMPETITION / ROUND	MATCH RESULT	VENUE	ATT
1	1970/71	09/09/70	League Cup 2nd Round	Aldershot 1 Manchester United 3	Recreation Ground	18509

UNITED v ANDERLECHT

EUROPEAN CUP / CHAMPIONS LEAGUE

VENUE	P	W	D	L	F	A
HOME	3	3	0	0	18	1
AWAY	3	1	0	2	4	5
TOTAL	6	4	0	2	22	6

#	SEASON	DATE	COMPETITION / ROUND	MATCH RESULT	VENUE	ATT
1	1956/57	12/09/56	European Cup Prel Round 1st Leg	Anderlecht 0 Manchester United 2	Park Astrid	35000
2	1956/57	26/09/56	European Cup Prel Round 2nd Leg	Manchester United 10 Anderlecht 0	Maine Road	40000
3	1968/69	13/11/68	European Cup 2nd Round 1st Leg	Manchester United 3 Anderlecht 0	Old Trafford	51000
4	1968/69	27/11/68	European Cup 2nd Round 2nd Leg	Anderlecht 3 Manchester United 1	Park Astrid	40000
5	2000/01	13/09/00	Champions League Phase 1 Match 1	Manchester United 5 Anderlecht 1	Old Trafford	62749
6	2000/01	24/10/00	Champions League Phase 1 Match 5	Anderlecht 2 Manchester United 1	Vanden Stock	22506

UNITED v ARSENAL

ALL COMPETITIVE MATCHES

VENUE	P	W	D	L	F	A
HOME	96	55	24	17	176	83
AWAY	96	24	17	55	120	197
NEUTRAL	11	3	4	4	11	15
TOTAL	203	82	45	76	307	295

ALL LEAGUE MATCHES

VENUE	P	W	D	L	F	A
HOME	89	50	24	15	165	77
AWAY	89	22	17	50	104	175
TOTAL	178	72	41	65	269	252

ALL CUP MATCHES

VENUE	P	W	D	L	F	A
HOME	7	5	0	2	11	6
AWAY	6	2	0	4	13	18
NEUTRAL	6	3	2	1	7	5
TOTAL	19	10	2	7	31	29

PREMIERSHIP

VENUE	P	W	D	L	F	A
HOME	16	9	4	3	22	7
AWAY	16	4	6	6	20	24
TOTAL	32	13	10	9	42	31

LEAGUE DIVISION ONE

VENUE	P	W	D	L	F	A
HOME	63	35	17	11	120	61
AWAY	63	16	11	36	74	126
TOTAL	126	51	28	47	194	187

LEAGUE DIVISION TWO

VENUE	P	W	D	L	F	A
HOME	10	6	3	1	23	9
AWAY	10	2	0	8	10	25
TOTAL	20	8	3	9	33	34

FA CUP

VENUE	P	W	D	L	F	A
HOME	5	3	0	2	8	5
AWAY	2	0	0	2	1	7
NEUTRAL	6	3	2	1	7	5
TOTAL	13	6	2	5	16	17

LEAGUE CUP

VENUE	P	W	D	L	F	A
HOME	2	2	0	0	3	1
AWAY	4	2	0	2	12	11
NEUTRAL	0	0	0	0	0	0
TOTAL	6	4	0	2	15	12

CHARITY SHIELD

VENUE	P	W	D	L	F	A
HOME	0	0	0	0	0	0
AWAY	1	0	0	1	3	4
NEUTRAL	5	0	2	3	4	10
TOTAL	6	0	2	4	7	14

#	SEASON	DATE	COMPETITION / ROUND	MATCH RESULT	VENUE	ATT
1	1894/95	13/10/94	Football League Division 2	Newton Heath 3 Arsenal 3	Bank Street	4000
2	1894/95	30/03/95	Football League Division 2	Arsenal 3 Newton Heath 2	Manor Field	6000
3	1895/96	09/11/95	Football League Division 2	Arsenal 2 Newton Heath 1	Manor Field	9000
4	1895/96	30/11/95	Football League Division 2	Newton Heath 5 Arsenal 1	Bank Street	6000
5	1896/97	22/03/97	Football League Division 2	Newton Heath 1 Arsenal 1	Bank Street	3000
6	1896/97	03/04/97	Football League Division 2	Arsenal 0 Newton Heath 2	Manor Field	6000
7	1897/98	08/01/98	Football League Division 2	Arsenal 5 Newton Heath 1	Manor Field	8000
8	1897/98	26/02/98	Football League Division 2	Newton Heath 5 Arsenal 1	Bank Street	6000
9	1898/99	03/12/98	Football League Division 2	Arsenal 5 Newton Heath 1	Manor Field	7000
10	1898/99	01/04/99	Football League Division 2	Newton Heath 2 Arsenal 2	Bank Street	5000
11	1899/00	04/11/99	Football League Division 2	Newton Heath 2 Arsenal 0	Bank Street	5000
12	1899/00	10/03/00	Football League Division 2	Arsenal 2 Newton Heath 1	Manor Field	3000
13	1900/01	10/11/00	Football League Division 2	Arsenal 2 Newton Heath 1	Manor Field	8000
14	1900/01	16/03/01	Football League Division 2	Newton Heath 1 Arsenal 0	Bank Street	5000
15	1901/02	16/11/01	Football League Division 2	Arsenal 2 Newton Heath 0	Manor Field	3000
16	1901/02	15/03/02	Football League Division 2	Newton Heath 0 Arsenal 1	Bank Street	4000
17	1902/03	25/10/02	Football League Division 2	Arsenal 0 Manchester United 1	Manor Field	12000
18	1902/03	09/03/03	Football League Division 2	Manchester United 3 Arsenal 0	Bank Street	5000
19	1903/04	03/10/03	Football League Division 2	Arsenal 4 Manchester United 0	Manor Field	20000
20	1903/04	30/01/04	Football League Division 2	Manchester United 1 Arsenal 0	Bank Street	40000
21	1905/06	10/03/06	FA Cup 4th Round	Manchester United 2 Arsenal 3	Bank Street	26500
22	1906/07	10/11/06	Football League Division 1	Manchester United 1 Arsenal 0	Bank Street	20000
23	1906/07	16/03/07	Football League Division 1	Arsenal 4 Manchester United 0	Manor Field	6000
24	1907/08	23/11/07	Football League Division 1	Manchester United 4 Arsenal 2	Bank Street	10000
25	1907/08	21/03/08	Football League Division 1	Arsenal 1 Manchester United 0	Manor Field	20000
26	1908/09	19/12/08	Football League Division 1	Arsenal 0 Manchester United 1	Manor Field	10000
27	1908/09	27/04/09	Football League Division 1	Manchester United 1 Arsenal 4	Bank Street	10000

UNITED v ARSENAL (continued)

#	SEASON	DATE	COMPETITION / ROUND	MATCH RESULT	VENUE	ATT
28	1909/10	30/10/09	Football League Division 1	Manchester United 1 Arsenal 0	Bank Street	20000
29	1909/10	12/03/10	Football League Division 1	Arsenal 0 Manchester United 0	Manor Field	4000
30	1910/11	01/09/10	Football League Division 1	Arsenal 1 Manchester United 2	Manor Field	15000
31	1910/11	26/12/10	Football League Division 1	Manchester United 5 Arsenal 0	Old Trafford	40000
32	1911/12	01/01/12	Football League Division 1	Manchester United 2 Arsenal 0	Old Trafford	20000
33	1911/12	05/04/12	Football League Division 1	Arsenal 2 Manchester United 1	Manor Field	14000
34	1912/13	02/09/12	Football League Division 1	Arsenal 0 Manchester United 0	Manor Field	11000
35	1912/13	21/03/13	Football League Division 1	Manchester United 2 Arsenal 0	Old Trafford	20000
36	1919/20	21/02/20	Football League Division 1	Arsenal 0 Manchester United 3	Highbury	25000
37	1919/20	28/02/20	Football League Division 1	Manchester United 0 Arsenal 1	Old Trafford	20000
38	1920/21	30/08/20	Football League Division 1	Arsenal 2 Manchester United 0	Highbury	40000
39	1920/21	06/09/20	Football League Division 1	Manchester United 1 Arsenal 1	Old Trafford	45000
40	1921/22	11/03/22	Football League Division 1	Manchester United 1 Arsenal 0	Old Trafford	30000
41	1921/22	05/04/22	Football League Division 1	Arsenal 3 Manchester United 1	Highbury	25000
42	1925/26	05/09/25	Football League Division 1	Manchester United 0 Arsenal 1	Old Trafford	32288
43	1925/26	16/01/26	Football League Division 1	Arsenal 3 Manchester United 2	Highbury	25252
44	1926/27	15/09/26	Football League Division 1	Manchester United 2 Arsenal 2	Old Trafford	15259
45	1926/27	28/12/26	Football League Division 1	Arsenal 1 Manchester United 0	Highbury	30111
46	1927/28	17/12/27	Football League Division 1	Manchester United 4 Arsenal 1	Old Trafford	18120
47	1927/28	28/04/28	Football League Division 1	Arsenal 0 Manchester United 1	Highbury	22452
48	1928/29	08/12/28	Football League Division 1	Arsenal 3 Manchester United 1	Highbury	18923
49	1928/29	20/04/29	Football League Division 1	Manchester United 4 Arsenal 1	Old Trafford	22858
50	1929/30	26/10/29	Football League Division 1	Manchester United 1 Arsenal 0	Old Trafford	12662
51	1929/30	12/03/30	Football League Division 1	Arsenal 4 Manchester United 2	Highbury	18082
52	1930/31	18/10/30	Football League Division 1	Manchester United 1 Arsenal 2	Old Trafford	23406
53	1930/31	21/02/31	Football League Division 1	Arsenal 4 Manchester United 1	Highbury	41510
54	1936/37	03/10/36	Football League Division 1	Manchester United 2 Arsenal 0	Old Trafford	55884
55	1936/37	30/01/37	FA Cup 4th Round	Arsenal 5 Manchester United 0	Highbury	45637
56	1936/37	06/02/37	Football League Division 1	Arsenal 1 Manchester United 1	Highbury	37236
57	1938/39	10/12/38	Football League Division 1	Manchester United 1 Arsenal 0	Old Trafford	42008
58	1938/39	15/04/39	Football League Division 1	Arsenal 2 Manchester United 1	Highbury	25741
59	1946/47	28/09/46	Football League Division 1	Manchester United 5 Arsenal 2	Maine Road	62718
60	1946/47	01/02/47	Football League Division 1	Arsenal 6 Manchester United 2	Highbury	29415
61	1947/48	06/09/47	Football League Division 1	Arsenal 2 Manchester United 1	Highbury	64905
62	1947/48	17/01/48	Football League Division 1	Manchester United 1 Arsenal 1	Maine Road	81962
63	1948/49	28/08/48	Football League Division 1	Arsenal 0 Manchester United 1	Highbury	64150
64	1948/49	06/10/48	FA Charity Shield	Arsenal 4 Manchester United 3	Highbury	31000
65	1948/49	01/01/49	Football League Division 1	Manchester United 2 Arsenal 0	Maine Road	58688
66	1949/50	26/12/49	Football League Division 1	Manchester United 2 Arsenal 0	Old Trafford	53928
67	1949/50	27/12/49	Football League Division 1	Arsenal 0 Manchester United 0	Highbury	65133
68	1950/51	14/10/50	Football League Division 1	Arsenal 3 Manchester United 0	Highbury	66150
69	1950/51	10/02/51	FA Cup 5th Round	Manchester United 1 Arsenal 0	Old Trafford	55058
70	1950/51	03/03/51	Football League Division 1	Manchester United 3 Arsenal 1	Old Trafford	46202
71	1951/52	08/12/51	Football League Division 1	Arsenal 1 Manchester United 3	Highbury	55451
72	1951/52	26/04/52	Football League Division 1	Manchester United 6 Arsenal 1	Old Trafford	53651
73	1952/53	27/08/52	Football League Division 1	Arsenal 2 Manchester United 1	Highbury	58831
74	1952/53	03/09/52	Football League Division 1	Manchester United 0 Arsenal 0	Old Trafford	39193
75	1953/54	07/11/53	Football League Division 1	Manchester United 2 Arsenal 2	Old Trafford	28141
76	1953/54	27/03/54	Football League Division 1	Arsenal 3 Manchester United 1	Highbury	42753
77	1954/55	20/11/54	Football League Division 1	Manchester United 2 Arsenal 1	Old Trafford	33373
78	1954/55	23/04/55	Football League Division 1	Arsenal 2 Manchester United 3	Highbury	42754
79	1955/56	05/11/55	Football League Division 1	Manchester United 1 Arsenal 1	Old Trafford	41586
80	1955/56	17/03/56	Football League Division 1	Arsenal 1 Manchester United 1	Highbury	50758
81	1956/57	29/09/56	Football League Division 1	Arsenal 1 Manchester United 2	Highbury	62479
82	1956/57	09/02/57	Football League Division 1	Manchester United 6 Arsenal 2	Old Trafford	60384
83	1957/58	21/09/57	Football League Division 1	Manchester United 4 Arsenal 2	Old Trafford	47142
84	1957/58	01/02/58	Football League Division 1	Arsenal 4 Manchester United 5	Highbury	63578
85	1958/59	11/10/58	Football League Division 1	Manchester United 1 Arsenal 1	Old Trafford	56148
86	1958/59	28/02/59	Football League Division 1	Arsenal 3 Manchester United 2	Highbury	67162
87	1959/60	10/10/59	Football League Division 1	Manchester United 4 Arsenal 2	Old Trafford	51626
88	1959/60	23/04/60	Football League Division 1	Arsenal 5 Manchester United 2	Highbury	41057

UNITED v ARSENAL (continued)

#	SEASON	DATE	COMPETITION / ROUND	MATCH RESULT	VENUE	ATT
89	1960/61	29/10/60	Football League Division 1	Arsenal 2 Manchester United 1	Highbury	45715
90	1960/61	18/03/61	Football League Division 1	Manchester United 1 Arsenal 1	Old Trafford	29732
91	1961/62	21/10/61	Football League Division 1	Arsenal 5 Manchester United 1	Highbury	54245
92	1961/62	31/01/62	FA Cup 4th Round	Manchester United 1 Arsenal 0	Old Trafford	54082
93	1961/62	16/04/62	Football League Division 1	Manchester United 2 Arsenal 3	Old Trafford	24258
94	1962/63	25/08/62	Football League Division 1	Arsenal 1 Manchester United 3	Highbury	62308
95	1962/63	06/05/63	Football League Division 1	Manchester United 2 Arsenal 3	Old Trafford	35999
96	1963/64	21/09/63	Football League Division 1	Arsenal 2 Manchester United 1	Highbury	56776
97	1963/64	01/02/64	Football League Division 1	Manchester United 3 Arsenal 1	Old Trafford	48340
98	1964/65	28/11/64	Football League Division 1	Arsenal 2 Manchester United 3	Highbury	59627
99	1964/65	26/04/65	Football League Division 1	Manchester United 3 Arsenal 1	Old Trafford	51625
100	1965/66	25/09/65	Football League Division 1	Arsenal 4 Manchester United 2	Highbury	56757
101	1965/66	19/03/66	Football League Division 1	Manchester United 2 Arsenal 1	Old Trafford	47246
102	1966/67	29/10/66	Football League Division 1	Manchester United 1 Arsenal 0	Old Trafford	45387
103	1966/67	03/03/67	Football League Division 1	Arsenal 1 Manchester United 1	Highbury	63363
104	1967/68	07/10/67	Football League Division 1	Manchester United 1 Arsenal 0	Old Trafford	60197
105	1967/68	24/02/68	Football League Division 1	Arsenal 0 Manchester United 2	Highbury	46417
106	1968/69	05/10/68	Football League Division 1	Manchester United 0 Arsenal 0	Old Trafford	61843
107	1968/69	26/12/68	Football League Division 1	Arsenal 3 Manchester United 0	Highbury	62300
108	1969/70	20/09/69	Football League Division 1	Arsenal 2 Manchester United 2	Highbury	59498
109	1969/70	10/01/70	Football League Division 1	Manchester United 2 Arsenal 1	Old Trafford	41055
110	1970/71	22/08/70	Football League Division 1	Arsenal 4 Manchester United 0	Highbury	54117
111	1970/71	19/12/70	Football League Division 1	Manchester United 1 Arsenal 3	Old Trafford	33182
112	1971/72	20/08/71	Football League Division 1	Manchester United 3 Arsenal 1	Anfield	27649
113	1971/72	25/04/72	Football League Division 1	Arsenal 3 Manchester United 0	Highbury	49125
114	1972/73	26/08/72	Football League Division 1	Manchester United 0 Arsenal 0	Old Trafford	48108
115	1972/73	06/01/73	Football League Division 1	Arsenal 3 Manchester United 1	Highbury	51194
116	1973/74	25/08/73	Football League Division 1	Arsenal 3 Manchester United 0	Highbury	51501
117	1973/74	19/01/74	Football League Division 1	Manchester United 1 Arsenal 1	Old Trafford	38589
118	1975/76	18/10/75	Football League Division 1	Manchester United 3 Arsenal 1	Old Trafford	53885
119	1975/76	22/11/75	Football League Division 1	Arsenal 3 Manchester United 1	Highbury	40102
120	1976/77	18/12/76	Football League Division 1	Arsenal 3 Manchester United 1	Highbury	39572
121	1976/77	14/05/77	Football League Division 1	Manchester United 3 Arsenal 2	Old Trafford	53232
122	1977/78	30/08/77	League Cup 2nd Round	Arsenal 3 Manchester United 2	Highbury	36171
123	1977/78	05/11/77	Football League Division 1	Manchester United 1 Arsenal 2	Old Trafford	53055
124	1977/78	01/04/78	Football League Division 1	Arsenal 3 Manchester United 1	Highbury	40829
125	1978/79	23/09/78	Football League Division 1	Arsenal 1 Manchester United 1	Highbury	45393
126	1978/79	03/02/79	Football League Division 1	Manchester United 0 Arsenal 2	Old Trafford	45460
127	1978/79	12/05/79	FA Cup Final	Manchester United 2 Arsenal 3	Wembley	100000
128	1979/80	25/08/79	Football League Division 1	Arsenal 0 Manchester United 0	Highbury	44380
129	1979/80	29/12/79	Football League Division 1	Manchester United 3 Arsenal 0	Old Trafford	54295
130	1980/81	11/10/80	Football League Division 1	Manchester United 0 Arsenal 0	Old Trafford	49036
131	1980/81	20/12/80	Football League Division 1	Arsenal 2 Manchester United 1	Highbury	33730
132	1981/82	26/09/81	Football League Division 1	Arsenal 0 Manchester United 0	Highbury	39795
133	1981/82	20/02/82	Football League Division 1	Manchester United 0 Arsenal 0	Old Trafford	43833
134	1982/83	25/09/82	Football League Division 1	Manchester United 0 Arsenal 0	Old Trafford	43198
135	1982/83	15/02/83	League Cup Semi-Final 1st Leg	Arsenal 2 Manchester United 4	Highbury	43136
136	1982/83	23/02/83	League Cup Semi-Final 2nd Leg	Manchester United 2 Arsenal 1	Old Trafford	56635
137	1982/83	16/04/83	FA Cup Semi-Final	Manchester United 2 Arsenal 1	Villa Park	46535
138	1982/83	02/05/83	Football League Division 1	Arsenal 3 Manchester United 0	Highbury	23602
139	1983/84	06/09/83	Football League Division 1	Arsenal 2 Manchester United 3	Highbury	42703
140	1983/84	17/03/84	Football League Division 1	Manchester United 4 Arsenal 0	Old Trafford	48942
141	1984/85	02/11/84	Football League Division 1	Manchester United 4 Arsenal 2	Old Trafford	32279
142	1984/85	23/02/85	Football League Division 1	Arsenal 0 Manchester United 1	Highbury	48612
143	1985/86	24/08/85	Football League Division 1	Arsenal 1 Manchester United 2	Highbury	37145
144	1985/86	21/12/85	Football League Division 1	Manchester United 0 Arsenal 1	Old Trafford	44386
145	1986/87	23/08/86	Football League Division 1	Arsenal 1 Manchester United 0	Highbury	41382
146	1986/87	24/01/87	Football League Division 1	Manchester United 2 Arsenal 0	Old Trafford	51367
147	1987/88	19/08/87	Football League Division 1	Manchester United 0 Arsenal 0	Old Trafford	43893
148	1987/88	24/01/88	Football League Division 1	Arsenal 1 Manchester United 2	Highbury	29392
149	1987/88	20/02/88	FA Cup 5th Round	Arsenal 2 Manchester United 1	Highbury	54161
150	1988/89	17/12/88	Football League Division 1	Arsenal 2 Manchester United 1	Highbury	37422
151	1988/89	02/04/89	Football League Division 1	Manchester United 1 Arsenal 1	Old Trafford	37977

UNITED v ARSENAL (continued)

#	SEASON	DATE	COMPETITION / ROUND	MATCH RESULT	VENUE	ATT
152	1989/90	19/08/89	Football League Division 1	Manchester United 4 Arsenal 1	Old Trafford	47245
153	1989/90	03/12/89	Football League Division 1	Arsenal 1 Manchester United 0	Highbury	34484
154	1990/91	20/10/90	Football League Division 1	Manchester United 0 Arsenal 1	Old Trafford	47232
155	1990/91	28/11/90	League Cup 4th Round	Arsenal 2 Manchester United 6	Highbury	40844
156	1990/91	06/05/91	Football League Division 1	Arsenal 3 Manchester United 1	Highbury	40229
157	1991/92	19/10/91	Football League Division 1	Manchester United 1 Arsenal 1	Old Trafford	46594
158	1991/92	01/02/92	Football League Division 1	Arsenal 1 Manchester United 1	Highbury	41703
159	1992/93	28/11/92	FA Premiership	Arsenal 0 Manchester United 1	Highbury	29739
160	1992/93	24/03/93	FA Premiership	Manchester United 0 Arsenal 0	Old Trafford	37301
161	1993/94	07/08/93	FA Charity Shield	Manchester United 1 Arsenal 1	Wembley	66519
				(United won the tie 5-4 on penalty kicks)		
162	1993/94	19/09/93	FA Premiership	Manchester United 1 Arsenal 0	Old Trafford	44009
163	1993/94	22/03/94	FA Premiership	Arsenal 2 Manchester United 2	Highbury	36203
164	1994/95	26/11/94	FA Premiership	Arsenal 0 Manchester United 0	Highbury	38301
165	1994/95	22/03/95	FA Premiership	Manchester United 3 Arsenal 0	Old Trafford	43623
166	1995/96	04/11/95	FA Premiership	Arsenal 1 Manchester United 0	Highbury	38317
167	1995/96	20/03/96	FA Premiership	Manchester United 1 Arsenal 0	Old Trafford	50028
168	1996/97	16/11/96	FA Premiership	Manchester United 1 Arsenal 0	Old Trafford	55210
169	1996/97	19/02/97	FA Premiership	Arsenal 1 Manchester United 2	Highbury	38172
170	1997/98	09/11/97	FA Premiership	Arsenal 3 Manchester United 2	Highbury	38205
171	1997/98	14/03/98	FA Premiership	Manchester United 0 Arsenal 1	Old Trafford	55174
172	1998/99	09/08/98	FA Charity Shield	Manchester United 0 Arsenal 3	Wembley	67342
173	1998/99	20/09/98	FA Premiership	Arsenal 3 Manchester United 0	Highbury	38142
174	1998/99	17/02/99	FA Premiership	Manchester United 1 Arsenal 1	Old Trafford	55171
175	1998/99	11/04/99	FA Cup Semi-Final	Manchester United 0 Arsenal 0	Villa Park	39217
176	1998/99	14/04/99	FA Cup Semi-Final Replay	Manchester United 2 Arsenal 1	Villa Park	30223
177	1999/00	01/08/99	FA Charity Shield	Manchester United 1 Arsenal 2	Wembley	70185
178	1999/00	22/08/99	FA Premiership	Arsenal 1 Manchester United 2	Highbury	38147
179	1999/00	24/01/00	FA Premiership	Manchester United 1 Arsenal 1	Old Trafford	58293
180	2000/01	01/10/00	FA Premiership	Arsenal 1 Manchester United 0	Highbury	38146
181	2000/01	25/02/01	FA Premiership	Manchester United 6 Arsenal 1	Old Trafford	67535
182	2001/02	05/11/01	League Cup 3rd Round	Arsenal 4 Manchester United 0	Highbury	30693
183	2001/02	25/11/01	FA Premiership	Arsenal 3 Manchester United 1	Highbury	38174
184	2001/02	08/05/02	FA Premiership	Manchester United 0 Arsenal 1	Old Trafford	67580
185	2002/03	07/12/02	FA Premiership	Manchester United 2 Arsenal 0	Old Trafford	67650
186	2002/03	15/02/03	FA Cup 5th Round	Manchester United 0 Arsenal 2	Old Trafford	67209
187	2002/03	16/04/03	FA Premiership	Arsenal 2 Manchester United 2	Highbury	38164
188	2003/04	10/08/03	FA Charity Shield	Manchester United 1 Arsenal 1	Millennium Stadium	59293
				(United won the tie 4-3 on penalty kicks)		
189	2003/04	21/09/03	FA Premiership	Manchester United 0 Arsenal 0	Old Trafford	67639
190	2003/04	28/03/04	FA Premiership	Arsenal 1 Manchester United 1	Highbury	38184
191	2003/04	03/04/04	FA Cup Semi-Final	Manchester United 1 Arsenal 0	Villa Park	39939
192	2004/05	08/08/04	FA Charity Shield	Manchester United 1 Arsenal 3	Millennium Stadium	63317
193	2004/05	24/10/04	FA Premiership	Manchester United 2 Arsenal 0	Old Trafford	67862
194	2004/05	01/12/04	League Cup 5th Round	Manchester United 1 Arsenal 0	Old Trafford	67103
195	2004/05	01/02/05	FA Premiership	Arsenal 2 Manchester United 4	Highbury	38164
196	2004/05	21/05/05	FA Cup Final	Manchester United 0 Arsenal 0	Millennium Stadium	71876
				(United lost the tie 4-5 on penalty kicks)		
197	2005/06	03/01/06	FA Premiership	Arsenal 0 Manchester United 0	Highbury	38313
198	2005/06	09/04/06	FA Premiership	Manchester United 2 Arsenal 0	Old Trafford	70908
199	2006/07	17/09/06	FA Premiership	Manchester United 0 Arsenal 1	Old Trafford	75595
200	2006/07	21/01/07	FA Premiership	Arsenal 2 Manchester United 1	Emirates Stadium	60128
201	2007/08	03/11/07	FA Premiership	Arsenal 2 Manchester United 2	Emirates Stadium	60161
202	2007/08	16/02/08	FA Cup 5th Round	Manchester United 4 Arsenal 0	Old Trafford	75550
203	2007/08	13/04/08	FA Premiership	Manchester United 2 Arsenal 1	Old Trafford	75985

UNITED v ASK VORWAERTS

EUROPEAN CUP						
VENUE	P	W	D	L	F	A
HOME	1	1	0	0	3	1
AWAY	1	1	0	0	2	0
TOTAL	2	2	0	0	5	1

#	SEASON	DATE	COMPETITION / ROUND	MATCH RESULT	VENUE	ATT
1	1965/66	17/11/65	European Cup 1st Round 1st Leg	ASK Vorwaerts 0 Manchester United 2	Walter Ulbricht Stadium	40000
2	1965/66	01/12/65	European Cup 1st Round 2nd Leg	Manchester United 3 ASK Vorwaerts 1	Old Trafford	30082

UNITED v ASTON VILLA

ALL COMPETITIVE MATCHES

VENUE	P	W	D	L	F	A
HOME	83	55	17	11	175	72
AWAY	84	31	18	35	130	151
NEUTRAL	2	0	0	2	2	5
TOTAL	169	86	35	48	307	228

ALL LEAGUE MATCHES

VENUE	P	W	D	L	F	A
HOME	75	49	16	10	157	65
AWAY	75	25	18	32	112	137
TOTAL	150	74	34	42	269	202

ALL CUP MATCHES

VENUE	P	W	D	L	F	A
HOME	7	5	1	1	14	7
AWAY	9	6	0	3	18	15
NEUTRAL	2	0	0	2	2	5
TOTAL	18	11	1	6	34	27

PREMIERSHIP

VENUE	P	W	D	L	F	A
HOME	16	12	4	0	30	6
AWAY	16	11	3	2	24	9
TOTAL	32	23	7	2	54	15

LEAGUE DIVISION ONE

VENUE	P	W	D	L	F	A
HOME	57	35	12	10	122	57
AWAY	57	14	15	28	88	123
TOTAL	114	49	27	38	210	180

LEAGUE DIVISION TWO

VENUE	P	W	D	L	F	A
HOME	2	2	0	0	5	2
AWAY	2	0	0	2	0	5
TOTAL	4	2	0	2	5	7

FA CUP

VENUE	P	W	D	L	F	A
HOME	6	5	0	1	13	6
AWAY	5	5	0	0	15	8
NEUTRAL	1	0	0	1	1	2
TOTAL	12	10	0	2	29	16

LEAGUE CUP

VENUE	P	W	D	L	F	A
HOME	1	0	1	0	1	1
AWAY	4	1	0	3	3	7
NEUTRAL	1	0	0	1	1	3
TOTAL	6	1	1	4	5	11

CHARITY SHIELD

VENUE	P	W	D	L	F	A
HOME	1	1	0	0	4	0
AWAY	0	0	0	0	0	0
NEUTRAL	0	0	0	0	0	0
TOTAL	1	1	0	0	4	0

#	SEASON	DATE	COMPETITION / ROUND	MATCH RESULT	VENUE	ATT
1	1892/93	19/11/92	Football League Division 1	Newton Heath 2 Aston Villa 0	North Road	7000
2	1892/93	06/03/93	Football League Division 1	Aston Villa 2 Newton Heath 0	Perry Barr	4000
3	1893/94	16/12/93	Football League Division 1	Newton Heath 1 Aston Villa 3	Bank Street	8000
4	1893/94	03/02/94	Football League Division 1	Aston Villa 5 Newton Heath 1	Perry Barr	5000
5	1905/06	24/02/06	FA Cup 3rd Round	Manchester United 5 Aston Villa 1	Bank Street	35500
6	1906/07	26/12/06	Football League Division 1	Aston Villa 2 Manchester United 0	Perry Barr	20000
7	1906/07	01/01/07	Football League Division 1	Manchester United 1 Aston Villa 0	Bank Street	40000
8	1907/08	02/09/07	Football League Division 1	Aston Villa 1 Manchester United 4	Villa Park	20000
9	1907/08	22/02/08	FA Cup 3rd Round	Aston Villa 0 Manchester United 2	Villa Park	12777
10	1907/08	20/04/08	Football League Division 1	Manchester United 1 Aston Villa 2	Bank Street	10000
11	1908/09	17/10/08	Football League Division 1	Aston Villa 3 Manchester United 1	Villa Park	40000
12	1908/09	31/03/09	Football League Division 1	Manchester United 0 Aston Villa 2	Bank Street	10000
13	1909/10	16/10/09	Football League Division 1	Manchester United 2 Aston Villa 0	Bank Street	20000
14	1909/10	26/02/10	Football League Division 1	Aston Villa 7 Manchester United 1	Villa Park	20000
15	1910/11	17/12/10	Football League Division 1	Manchester United 2 Aston Villa 0	Old Trafford	20000
16	1910/11	04/02/11	FA Cup 2nd Round	Manchester United 2 Aston Villa 1	Old Trafford	65101
17	1910/11	22/04/11	Football League Division 1	Aston Villa 4 Manchester United 2	Villa Park	50000
18	1911/12	25/11/11	Football League Division 1	Manchester United 3 Aston Villa 1	Old Trafford	20000
19	1911/12	30/03/12	Football League Division 1	Aston Villa 6 Manchester United 0	Villa Park	15000
20	1912/13	16/11/12	Football League Division 1	Aston Villa 4 Manchester United 2	Villa Park	20000
21	1912/13	22/03/13	Football League Division 1	Manchester United 4 Aston Villa 0	Old Trafford	30000
22	1913/14	08/11/13	Football League Division 1	Aston Villa 3 Manchester United 1	Villa Park	20000
23	1913/14	14/03/14	Football League Division 1	Manchester United 0 Aston Villa 6	Old Trafford	30000
24	1914/15	19/12/14	Football League Division 1	Aston Villa 3 Manchester United 3	Villa Park	10000
25	1914/15	26/04/15	Football League Division 1	Manchester United 1 Aston Villa 0	Old Trafford	8000
26	1919/20	06/12/19	Football League Division 1	Aston Villa 2 Manchester United 0	Villa Park	40000
27	1919/20	13/12/19	Football League Division 1	Manchester United 1 Aston Villa 2	Old Trafford	30000
28	1919/20	31/01/20	FA Cup 2nd Round	Manchester United 1 Aston Villa 2	Old Trafford	48600
29	1920/21	25/12/20	Football League Division 1	Aston Villa 3 Manchester United 4	Villa Park	38000
30	1920/21	27/12/20	Football League Division 1	Manchester United 1 Aston Villa 3	Old Trafford	70504
31	1921/22	19/11/21	Football League Division 1	Aston Villa 3 Manchester United 1	Villa Park	30000
32	1921/22	26/11/21	Football League Division 1	Manchester United 1 Aston Villa 0	Old Trafford	33000
33	1925/26	02/09/25	Football League Division 1	Manchester United 3 Aston Villa 0	Old Trafford	41717
34	1925/26	07/09/25	Football League Division 1	Aston Villa 2 Manchester United 2	Villa Park	27701
35	1926/27	02/10/26	Football League Division 1	Manchester United 2 Aston Villa 1	Old Trafford	31234
36	1926/27	19/02/27	Football League Division 1	Aston Villa 2 Manchester United 0	Villa Park	32467
37	1927/28	19/11/27	Football League Division 1	Manchester United 5 Aston Villa 1	Old Trafford	25991
38	1927/28	31/03/28	Football League Division 1	Aston Villa 3 Manchester United 1	Villa Park	24691
39	1928/29	27/08/28	Football League Division 1	Aston Villa 0 Manchester United 0	Villa Park	30356
40	1928/29	01/01/29	Football League Division 1	Manchester United 2 Aston Villa 2	Old Trafford	25935
41	1929/30	02/11/29	Football League Division 1	Aston Villa 1 Manchester United 0	Villa Park	24292
42	1929/30	08/03/30	Football League Division 1	Manchester United 2 Aston Villa 3	Old Trafford	25407
43	1930/31	30/08/30	Football League Division 1	Manchester United 3 Aston Villa 4	Old Trafford	18004
44	1930/31	27/12/30	Football League Division 1	Aston Villa 7 Manchester United 0	Villa Park	32505

UNITED v ASTON VILLA (continued)

#	SEASON	DATE	COMPETITION / ROUND	MATCH RESULT	VENUE	ATT
45	1937/38	20/11/37	Football League Division 2	Manchester United 3 Aston Villa 1	Old Trafford	33193
46	1937/38	02/04/38	Football League Division 2	Aston Villa 3 Manchester United 0	Villa Park	54654
47	1938/39	05/11/38	Football League Division 1	Aston Villa 0 Manchester United 2	Villa Park	38357
48	1938/39	11/03/39	Football League Division 1	Manchester United 1 Aston Villa 1	Old Trafford	28292
49	1946/47	02/11/46	Football League Division 1	Aston Villa 0 Manchester United 0	Villa Park	53668
50	1946/47	08/03/47	Football League Division 1	Manchester United 2 Aston Villa 1	Maine Road	36965
51	1947/48	25/10/47	Football League Division 1	Manchester United 2 Aston Villa 0	Maine Road	47078
52	1947/48	10/01/48	FA Cup 3rd Round	Aston Villa 4 Manchester United 6	Villa Park	58683
53	1947/48	22/03/48	Football League Division 1	Aston Villa 0 Manchester United 1	Villa Park	52368
54	1948/49	25/09/48	Football League Division 1	Manchester United 3 Aston Villa 1	Maine Road	53820
55	1948/49	19/02/49	Football League Division 1	Aston Villa 2 Manchester United 1	Villa Park	68354
56	1949/50	15/10/49	Football League Division 1	Aston Villa 0 Manchester United 4	Villa Park	47483
57	1949/50	08/03/50	Football League Division 1	Manchester United 7 Aston Villa 0	Old Trafford	22149
58	1950/51	04/09/50	Football League Division 1	Aston Villa 1 Manchester United 3	Villa Park	42724
59	1950/51	13/09/50	Football League Division 1	Manchester United 0 Aston Villa 0	Old Trafford	33021
60	1951/52	13/10/51	Football League Division 1	Aston Villa 2 Manchester United 5	Villa Park	47795
61	1951/52	01/03/52	Football League Division 1	Manchester United 1 Aston Villa 1	Old Trafford	38910
62	1952/53	20/09/52	Football League Division 1	Aston Villa 3 Manchester United 3	Villa Park	43490
63	1952/53	07/02/53	Football League Division 1	Manchester United 3 Aston Villa 1	Old Trafford	34339
64	1953/54	24/10/53	Football League Division 1	Manchester United 1 Aston Villa 0	Old Trafford	30266
65	1953/54	13/03/54	Football League Division 1	Aston Villa 2 Manchester United 2	Villa Park	26023
66	1954/55	27/12/54	Football League Division 1	Manchester United 0 Aston Villa 1	Old Trafford	49136
67	1954/55	28/12/54	Football League Division 1	Aston Villa 2 Manchester United 1	Villa Park	48718
68	1955/56	15/10/55	Football League Division 1	Aston Villa 4 Manchester United 4	Villa Park	29478
69	1955/56	25/02/56	Football League Division 1	Manchester United 1 Aston Villa 0	Old Trafford	36277
70	1956/57	08/12/56	Football League Division 1	Aston Villa 1 Manchester United 3	Villa Park	42530
71	1956/57	09/03/57	Football League Division 1	Manchester United 1 Aston Villa 1	Old Trafford	55484
72	1956/57	04/05/57	FA Cup Final	Manchester United 1 Aston Villa 2	Wembley	100000
73	1957/58	05/10/57	Football League Division 1	Manchester United 4 Aston Villa 1	Old Trafford	43102
74	1957/58	22/10/57	FA Charity Shield	Manchester United 4 Aston Villa 0	Old Trafford	27293
75	1957/58	31/03/58	Football League Division 1	Aston Villa 3 Manchester United 2	Villa Park	16631
76	1958/59	26/12/58	Football League Division 1	Manchester United 2 Aston Villa 1	Old Trafford	63098
77	1958/59	27/12/58	Football League Division 1	Aston Villa 0 Manchester United 2	Villa Park	56450
78	1960/61	17/09/60	Football League Division 1	Aston Villa 3 Manchester United 1	Villa Park	43593
79	1960/61	04/02/61	Football League Division 1	Manchester United 1 Aston Villa 1	Old Trafford	33525
80	1961/62	18/09/61	Football League Division 1	Aston Villa 1 Manchester United 1	Villa Park	38837
81	1961/62	15/01/62	Football League Division 1	Manchester United 2 Aston Villa 0	Old Trafford	20807
82	1962/63	24/11/62	Football League Division 1	Manchester United 2 Aston Villa 2	Old Trafford	36852
83	1962/63	11/03/63	FA Cup 4th Round	Manchester United 1 Aston Villa 0	Old Trafford	52265
84	1962/63	09/04/63	Football League Division 1	Aston Villa 1 Manchester United 2	Villa Park	26867
85	1963/64	16/11/63	Football League Division 1	Aston Villa 4 Manchester United 0	Villa Park	36276
86	1963/64	06/04/64	Football League Division 1	Manchester United 1 Aston Villa 0	Old Trafford	25848
87	1964/65	24/10/64	Football League Division 1	Manchester United 7 Aston Villa 0	Old Trafford	35807
88	1964/65	28/04/65	Football League Division 1	Aston Villa 2 Manchester United 1	Villa Park	36081
89	1965/66	06/04/66	Football League Division 1	Aston Villa 1 Manchester United 1	Villa Park	28211
90	1965/66	09/05/66	Football League Division 1	Manchester United 6 Aston Villa 1	Old Trafford	23039
91	1966/67	03/12/66	Football League Division 1	Aston Villa 1 Manchester United 1	Villa Park	39937
92	1966/67	29/04/67	Football League Division 1	Manchester United 3 Aston Villa 1	Old Trafford	55782
93	1970/71	16/12/70	League Cup Semi-Final 1st Leg	Manchester United 1 Aston Villa 1	Old Trafford	48889
94	1970/71	23/12/70	League Cup Semi-Final 2nd Leg	Aston Villa 2 Manchester United 1	Villa Park	58667
95	1974/75	16/11/74	Football League Division 2	Manchester United 2 Aston Villa 1	Old Trafford	55615
96	1974/75	22/02/75	Football League Division 2	Aston Villa 2 Manchester United 0	Villa Park	39156
97	1975/76	08/10/75	League Cup 3rd Round	Aston Villa 1 Manchester United 2	Villa Park	41447
98	1975/76	15/11/75	Football League Division 1	Manchester United 2 Aston Villa 0	Old Trafford	51682
99	1975/76	21/02/76	Football League Division 1	Aston Villa 2 Manchester United 1	Villa Park	50094
100	1976/77	06/11/76	Football League Division 1	Aston Villa 3 Manchester United 2	Villa Park	44789
101	1976/77	01/01/77	Football League Division 1	Manchester United 2 Aston Villa 0	Old Trafford	55446
102	1976/77	19/03/77	FA Cup 6th Round	Manchester United 2 Aston Villa 1	Old Trafford	57089
103	1977/78	29/10/77	Football League Division 1	Aston Villa 2 Manchester United 1	Villa Park	39144
104	1977/78	29/03/78	Football League Division 1	Manchester United 1 Aston Villa 1	Old Trafford	41625
105	1978/79	14/10/78	Football League Division 1	Aston Villa 2 Manchester United 2	Villa Park	36204
106	1978/79	24/02/79	Football League Division 1	Manchester United 1 Aston Villa 1	Old Trafford	44437

UNITED v ASTON VILLA (continued)

#	SEASON	DATE	COMPETITION / ROUND	MATCH RESULT	VENUE	ATT
107	1979/80	08/09/79	Football League Division 1	Aston Villa 0 Manchester United 3	Villa Park	34859
108	1979/80	23/04/80	Football League Division 1	Manchester United 2 Aston Villa 1	Old Trafford	45201
109	1980/81	08/10/80	Football League Division 1	Manchester United 3 Aston Villa 3	Old Trafford	38831
110	1980/81	14/03/81	Football League Division 1	Aston Villa 3 Manchester United 3	Villa Park	42182
111	1981/82	12/09/81	Football League Division 1	Aston Villa 1 Manchester United 1	Villa Park	37661
112	1981/82	06/02/82	Football League Division 1	Manchester United 4 Aston Villa 1	Old Trafford	43184
113	1982/83	20/11/82	Football League Division 1	Aston Villa 2 Manchester United 1	Villa Park	35487
114	1982/83	01/01/83	Football League Division 1	Manchester United 3 Aston Villa 1	Old Trafford	41545
115	1983/84	05/11/83	Football League Division 1	Manchester United 1 Aston Villa 2	Old Trafford	45077
116	1983/84	03/03/84	Football League Division 1	Aston Villa 0 Manchester United 3	Villa Park	32874
117	1984/85	06/10/84	Football League Division 1	Aston Villa 3 Manchester United 0	Villa Park	37131
118	1984/85	23/03/85	Football League Division 1	Manchester United 4 Aston Villa 0	Old Trafford	40941
119	1985/86	17/08/85	Football League Division 1	Manchester United 4 Aston Villa 0	Old Trafford	49743
120	1985/86	14/12/85	Football League Division 1	Aston Villa 1 Manchester United 3	Villa Park	27626
121	1986/87	13/12/86	Football League Division 1	Aston Villa 3 Manchester United 3	Villa Park	29205
122	1986/87	09/05/87	Football League Division 1	Manchester United 3 Aston Villa 1	Old Trafford	35179
123	1988/89	05/11/88	Football League Division 1	Manchester United 1 Aston Villa 1	Old Trafford	44804
124	1988/89	12/03/89	Football League Division 1	Aston Villa 0 Manchester United 0	Villa Park	28332
125	1989/90	26/12/89	Football League Division 1	Aston Villa 3 Manchester United 0	Villa Park	41247
126	1989/90	17/04/90	Football League Division 1	Manchester United 2 Aston Villa 0	Old Trafford	44080
127	1990/91	29/12/90	Football League Division 1	Manchester United 1 Aston Villa 1	Old Trafford	47485
128	1990/91	06/04/91	Football League Division 1	Aston Villa 1 Manchester United 1	Villa Park	33307
129	1991/92	21/08/91	Football League Division 1	Aston Villa 0 Manchester United 1	Villa Park	39995
130	1991/92	22/01/92	Football League Division 1	Manchester United 1 Aston Villa 0	Old Trafford	45022
131	1992/93	28/10/92	League Cup 3rd Round	Aston Villa 1 Manchester United 0	Villa Park	35964
132	1992/93	07/11/92	FA Premiership	Aston Villa 1 Manchester United 0	Villa Park	39063
133	1992/93	14/03/93	FA Premiership	Manchester United 1 Aston Villa 1	Old Trafford	36163
134	1993/94	23/08/93	FA Premiership	Aston Villa 1 Manchester United 2	Villa Park	39624
135	1993/94	19/12/93	FA Premiership	Manchester United 3 Aston Villa 1	Old Trafford	44499
136	1993/94	27/03/94	League Cup Final	Manchester United 1 Aston Villa 3	Wembley	77231
137	1994/95	06/11/94	FA Premiership	Aston Villa 1 Manchester United 2	Villa Park	32136
138	1994/95	04/02/95	FA Premiership	Manchester United 1 Aston Villa 0	Old Trafford	43795
139	1995/96	19/08/95	FA Premiership	Aston Villa 3 Manchester United 1	Villa Park	34655
140	1995/96	13/01/96	FA Premiership	Manchester United 0 Aston Villa 0	Old Trafford	42667
141	1996/97	21/09/96	FA Premiership	Aston Villa 0 Manchester United 0	Villa Park	39339
142	1996/97	01/01/97	FA Premiership	Manchester United 0 Aston Villa 0	Old Trafford	55133
143	1997/98	15/12/97	FA Premiership	Manchester United 1 Aston Villa 0	Old Trafford	55151
144	1997/98	18/02/98	FA Premiership	Aston Villa 0 Manchester United 2	Villa Park	39372
145	1998/99	05/12/98	FA Premiership	Aston Villa 1 Manchester United 1	Villa Park	39241
146	1998/99	01/05/99	FA Premiership	Manchester United 2 Aston Villa 1	Old Trafford	55189
147	1999/00	13/10/99	League Cup 3rd Round	Aston Villa 3 Manchester United 0	Villa Park	33815
148	1999/00	30/10/99	FA Premiership	Manchester United 3 Aston Villa 0	Old Trafford	55211
149	1999/00	14/05/00	FA Premiership	Aston Villa 0 Manchester United 1	Villa Park	39217
150	2000/01	26/12/00	FA Premiership	Aston Villa 0 Manchester United 1	Villa Park	40889
151	2000/01	20/01/01	FA Premiership	Manchester United 2 Aston Villa 0	Old Trafford	67533
152	2001/02	26/08/01	FA Premiership	Aston Villa 1 Manchester United 1	Villa Park	42632
153	2001/02	06/01/02	FA Cup 3rd Round	Aston Villa 2 Manchester United 3	Villa Park	38444
154	2001/02	23/02/02	FA Premiership	Manchester United 1 Aston Villa 0	Old Trafford	67592
155	2002/03	26/10/02	FA Premiership	Manchester United 1 Aston Villa 1	Old Trafford	67619
156	2002/03	15/03/03	FA Premiership	Aston Villa 0 Manchester United 1	Villa Park	42602
157	2003/04	06/12/03	FA Premiership	Manchester United 4 Aston Villa 0	Old Trafford	67621
158	2003/04	04/01/04	FA Cup 3rd Round	Aston Villa 1 Manchester United 2	Villa Park	40371
159	2003/04	15/05/04	FA Premiership	Aston Villa 0 Manchester United 2	Villa Park	42573
160	2004/05	28/12/04	FA Premiership	Aston Villa 0 Manchester United 1	Villa Park	42593
161	2004/05	22/01/05	FA Premiership	Manchester United 3 Aston Villa 1	Old Trafford	67859
162	2005/06	20/08/05	FA Premiership	Manchester United 1 Aston Villa 0	Old Trafford	67934
163	2005/06	17/12/05	FA Premiership	Aston Villa 0 Manchester United 2	Villa Park	37128
164	2006/07	23/12/06	FA Premiership	Aston Villa 0 Manchester United 3	Villa Park	42551
165	2006/07	07/01/07	FA Cup 3rd Round	Manchester United 2 Aston Villa 1	Old Trafford	74924
166	2006/07	13/01/07	FA Premiership	Manchester United 3 Aston Villa 1	Old Trafford	76073
167	2007/08	20/10/07	FA Premiership	Aston Villa 1 Manchester United 4	Villa Park	42640
168	2007/08	05/01/08	FA Cup 3rd Round	Aston Villa 0 Manchester United 2	Villa Park	33630
169	2007/08	29/03/08	FA Premiership	Manchester United 4 Aston Villa 0	Old Trafford	75932

UNITED v ATHINAIKOS

EUROPEAN CUP-WINNERS' CUP

VENUE	P	W	D	L	F	A
HOME	1	1	0	0	2	0
AWAY	1	0	1	0	0	0
TOTAL	2	1	1	0	2	0

#	SEASON	DATE	COMPETITION / ROUND	MATCH RESULT	VENUE	ATT
1	1991/92	18/09/91	European CWC 1st Round 1st Leg	Athinaikos 0 Manchester United 0	Apostolos Nikolaidis	5400
2	1991/92	02/10/91	European CWC 1st Round 2nd Leg	Manchester United 2 Athinaikos 0	Old Trafford	35023

UNITED v ATHLETIC BILBAO

EUROPEAN CUP

VENUE	P	W	D	L	F	A
HOME	1	1	0	0	3	0
AWAY	1	0	0	1	3	5
TOTAL	2	1	0	1	6	5

#	SEASON	DATE	COMPETITION / ROUND	MATCH RESULT	VENUE	ATT
1	1956/57	16/01/57	European Cup Quarter-Final 1st Leg	Athletic Bilbao 5 Manchester United 3	Estadio San Mames	60000
2	1956/57	06/02/57	European Cup Quarter-Final 2nd Leg	Manchester United 3 Athletic Bilbao 0	Maine Road	70000

UNITED v ATLETICO MADRID

EUROPEAN CUP-WINNERS' CUP

VENUE	P	W	D	L	F	A
HOME	1	0	1	0	1	1
AWAY	1	0	0	1	0	3
TOTAL	2	0	1	1	1	4

#	SEASON	DATE	COMPETITION / ROUND	MATCH RESULT	VENUE	ATT
1	1991/92	23/10/91	European CWC 2nd Round 1st Leg	Athletico Madrid 3 Manchester United 0	Vincente Calderon	40000
2	1991/92	06/11/91	European CWC 2nd Round 2nd Leg	Manchester United 1 Athletico Madrid 1	Old Trafford	39654

UNITED v BARCELONA

ALL COMPETITIVE MATCHES							CHAMPIONS LEAGUE							EUROPEAN CUP-WINNERS' CUP						
VENUE	P	W	D	L	F	A	VENUE	P	W	D	L	F	A	VENUE	P	W	D	L	F	A
HOME	4	2	2	0	9	5	HOME	3	1	2	0	6	5	HOME	1	1	0	0	3	0
AWAY	4	0	2	2	3	9	AWAY	3	0	2	1	3	7	AWAY	1	0	0	1	0	2
NEUTRAL	1	1	0	0	2	1								NEUTRAL	1	1	0	0	2	1
TOTAL	9	3	4	2	14	15	TOTAL	6	1	4	1	9	12	TOTAL	3	2	0	1	5	3

#	SEASON	DATE	COMPETITION / ROUND	MATCH RESULT	VENUE	ATT
1	1983/84	07/03/84	European CWC 3rd Round 1st Leg	Barcelona 2 Manchester United 0	Estadio Camp Nou	70000
2	1983/84	21/03/84	European CWC 3rd Round 2nd Leg	Manchester United 3 Barcelona 0	Old Trafford	58547
3	1990/91	15/05/91	European CWC Final	Manchester United 2 Barcelona 1	Feyenoord Stadion	50000
4	1994/95	19/10/94	Champions League Phase 1 Match 3	Manchester United 2 Barcelona 2	Old Trafford	40064
5	1994/95	02/11/94	Champions League Phase 1 Match 4	Barcelona 4 Manchester United 0	Estadio Camp Nou	114273
6	1998/99	16/09/98	Champions League Phase 1 Match 1	Manchester United 3 Barcelona 3	Old Trafford	53601
7	1998/99	25/11/98	Champions League Phase 1 Match 5	Barcelona 3 Manchester United 3	Estadio Camp Nou	67648
8	2007/08	23/04/08	Champions League Semi-Final 1st Leg	Barcelona 0 Manchester United 0	Estadio Camp Nou	95949
9	2007/08	29/04/08	Champions League Semi-Final 2nd Leg	Manchester United 1 Barcelona 0	Old Trafford	75061

UNITED v BARNET

LEAGUE CUP

VENUE	P	W	D	L	F	A
HOME	1	1	0	0	4	1
AWAY	0	0	0	0	0	0
TOTAL	1	1	0	0	4	1

#	SEASON	DATE	COMPETITION / ROUND	MATCH RESULT	VENUE	ATT
1	2005/06	26/10/05	League Cup 3rd Round	Manchester United 4 Barnet 1	Old Trafford	43673

UNITED v BARNSLEY

ALL COMPETITIVE MATCHES							ALL LEAGUE MATCHES							FA CUP						
VENUE	P	W	D	L	F	A	VENUE	P	W	D	L	F	A	VENUE	P	W	D	L	F	A
HOME	18	14	3	1	44	8	HOME	16	13	2	1	42	7	HOME	2	1	1	0	2	1
AWAY	19	7	8	4	30	19	AWAY	16	6	7	3	22	14	AWAY	3	1	1	1	8	5
TOTAL	37	21	11	5	74	27	TOTAL	32	19	9	4	64	21	TOTAL	5	2	2	1	10	6

PREMIERSHIP							LEAGUE DIVISION TWO						
VENUE	P	W	D	L	F	A	VENUE	P	W	D	L	F	A
HOME	1	1	0	0	7	0	HOME	15	12	2	1	35	7
AWAY	1	1	0	0	2	0	AWAY	15	5	7	3	20	14
TOTAL	2	2	0	0	9	0	TOTAL	30	17	9	4	55	21

#	SEASON	DATE	COMPETITION / ROUND	MATCH RESULT	VENUE	ATT
1	1898/99	12/11/98	Football League Division 2	Newton Heath 0 Barnsley 0	Bank Street	5000
2	1898/99	04/04/99	Football League Division 2	Barnsley 0 Newton Heath 2	Oakwell	4000
3	1899/00	11/11/99	Football League Division 2	Barnsley 0 Newton Heath 0	Oakwell	3000
4	1899/00	17/03/00	Football League Division 2	Newton Heath 3 Barnsley 0	Bank Street	6000
5	1900/01	13/03/01	Football League Division 2	Newton Heath 1 Barnsley 0	Bank Street	6000
6	1900/01	09/04/01	Football League Division 2	Barnsley 6 Newton Heath 2	Oakwell	3000
7	1901/02	23/11/01	Football League Division 2	Newton Heath 1 Barnsley 0	Bank Street	4000
8	1901/02	22/03/02	Football League Division 2	Barnsley 3 Newton Heath 2	Oakwell	2500
9	1902/03	27/12/02	Football League Division 2	Manchester United 2 Barnsley 1	Bank Street	9000
10	1902/03	25/04/03	Football League Division 2	Barnsley 0 Manchester United 0	Oakwell	2000
11	1903/04	10/10/03	Football League Division 2	Manchester United 4 Barnsley 0	Bank Street	20000
12	1903/04	05/04/04	Football League Division 2	Barnsley 0 Manchester United 2	Oakwell	5000
13	1904/05	29/10/04	Football League Division 2	Manchester United 4 Barnsley 0	Bank Street	15000
14	1904/05	25/02/05	Football League Division 2	Barnsley 0 Manchester United 0	Oakwell	5000
15	1905/06	25/11/05	Football League Division 2	Barnsley 0 Manchester United 3	Oakwell	3000
16	1905/06	31/03/06	Football League Division 2	Manchester United 5 Barnsley 1	Bank Street	15000
17	1922/23	01/01/23	Football League Division 2	Manchester United 1 Barnsley 0	Old Trafford	29000
18	1922/23	28/04/23	Football League Division 2	Barnsley 2 Manchester United 2	Oakwell	8000
19	1923/24	25/12/23	Football League Division 2	Manchester United 1 Barnsley 2	Old Trafford	34000
20	1923/24	26/12/23	Football League Division 2	Barnsley 1 Manchester United 0	Oakwell	12000
21	1924/25	08/09/24	Football League Division 2	Manchester United 1 Barnsley 0	Old Trafford	9500
22	1924/25	02/05/25	Football League Division 2	Barnsley 0 Manchester United 0	Oakwell	11250
23	1931/32	17/10/31	Football League Division 2	Barnsley 0 Manchester United 0	Oakwell	4052
24	1931/32	27/02/32	Football League Division 2	Manchester United 3 Barnsley 0	Old Trafford	18223
25	1934/35	08/09/34	Football League Division 2	Manchester United 4 Barnsley 1	Old Trafford	22315
26	1934/35	19/01/35	Football League Division 2	Barnsley 0 Manchester United 2	Oakwell	10177
27	1935/36	26/12/35	Football League Division 2	Manchester United 1 Barnsley 1	Old Trafford	20993
28	1935/36	01/01/36	Football League Division 2	Barnsley 0 Manchester United 3	Oakwell	20957
29	1937/38	11/09/37	Football League Division 2	Manchester United 4 Barnsley 1	Old Trafford	22934
30	1937/38	22/01/38	FA Cup 4th Round	Barnsley 2 Manchester United 2	Oakwell	35549
31	1937/38	26/01/38	FA Cup 4th Round Replay	Manchester United 1 Barnsley 0	Old Trafford	33601
32	1937/38	02/02/38	Football League Division 2	Barnsley 2 Manchester United 2	Oakwell	7859
33	1963/64	15/02/64	FA Cup 5th Round	Barnsley 0 Manchester United 4	Oakwell	38076
34	1997/98	25/10/97	FA Premiership	Manchester United 7 Barnsley 0	Old Trafford	55142
35	1997/98	15/02/98	FA Cup 5th Round	Manchester United 1 Barnsley 1	Old Trafford	54700
36	1997/98	25/02/98	FA Cup 5th Round Replay	Barnsley 3 Manchester United 2	Oakwell	18655
37	1997/98	10/05/98	FA Premiership	Barnsley 0 Manchester United 2	Oakwell	18694

UNITED v BASEL

CHAMPIONS LEAGUE						
VENUE	P	W	D	L	F	A
HOME	1	0	1	0	1	1
AWAY	1	1	0	0	3	1
TOTAL	2	1	1	0	4	2

#	SEASON	DATE	COMPETITION / ROUND	MATCH RESULT	VENUE	ATT
1	2002/03	26/11/02	Champions League Phase 2 Match 1	Basel 1 Manchester United 3	St Jakob Stadium	29501
2	2002/03	12/03/03	Champions League Phase 2 Match 5	Manchester United 1 Basel 1	Old Trafford	66870

UNITED v BAYER LEVERKUSEN

CHAMPIONS LEAGUE

VENUE	P	W	D	L	F	A
HOME	2	1	1	0	4	2
AWAY	2	1	1	0	3	2
TOTAL	4	2	2	0	7	4

#	SEASON	DATE	COMPETITION / ROUND	MATCH RESULT	VENUE	ATT
1	2001/02	24/04/02	Champions League Semi-Final 1st Leg	Manchester United 2 Bayer Leverkusen 2	Old Trafford	66534
2	2001/02	30/04/02	Champions League Semi-Final 2nd Leg	Bayer Leverkusen 1 Manchester United 1 (United lost the tie on away goals rule)	Bayarena	22500
3	2002/03	24/09/02	Champions League Phase 1 Match 2	Bayer Leverkusen 1 Manchester United 2	Bayarena	22500
4	2002/03	13/11/02	Champions League Phase 1 Match 6	Manchester United 2 Bayer Leverkusen 0	Old Trafford	66185

UNITED v BAYERN MUNICH

CHAMPIONS LEAGUE

VENUE	P	W	D	L	F	A
HOME	3	0	2	1	1	2
AWAY	3	0	2	1	4	5
NEUTRAL	1	1	0	0	2	1
TOTAL	7	1	4	2	7	8

#	SEASON	DATE	COMPETITION / ROUND	MATCH RESULT	VENUE	ATT
1	1998/99	30/09/98	Champions League Phase 1 Match 2	Bayern Munich 2 Manchester United 2	Olympic Stadium	53000
2	1998/99	09/12/98	Champions League Phase 1 Match 6	Manchester United 1 Bayern Munich 1	Old Trafford	54434
3	1998/99	26/05/99	Champions League Final	Manchester United 2 Bayern Munich 1	Estadio Camp Nou	90000
4	2000/01	03/04/01	Champions League Quarter-Final 1st Leg	Manchester United 0 Bayern Munich 1	Old Trafford	66584
5	2000/01	18/04/01	Champions League Quarter-Final 2nd Leg	Bayern Munich 2 Manchester United 1	Olympic Stadium	60000
6	2001/02	20/11/01	Champions League Phase 2 Match 1	Bayern Munich 1 Manchester United 1	Olympic Stadium	59000
7	2001/02	13/03/02	Champions League Phase 2 Match 5	Manchester United 0 Bayern Munich 0	Old Trafford	66818

UNITED v BENFICA

EUROPEAN CUP / CHAMPIONS LEAGUE

VENUE	P	W	D	L	F	A
HOME	3	3	0	0	8	4
AWAY	3	2	0	1	7	3
NEUTRAL	1	1	0	0	4	1
TOTAL	7	6	0	1	19	8

#	SEASON	DATE	COMPETITION / ROUND	MATCH RESULT	VENUE	ATT
1	1965/66	02/02/66	European Cup Quarter-Final 1st Leg	Manchester United 3 Benfica 2	Old Trafford	64035
2	1965/66	09/03/66	European Cup Quarter-Final 2nd Leg	Benfica 1 Manchester United 5	Estadio da Luz	75000
3	1967/68	29/05/68	European Cup Final	Manchester United 4 Benfica 1	Wembley	100000
4	2005/06	27/09/05	Champions League Phase 1 Match 2	Manchester United 2 Benfica 1	Old Trafford	66112
5	2005/06	07/12/05	Champions League Phase 1 Match 6	Benfica 2 Manchester United 1	Estadio da Luz	61000
6	2006/07	26/09/06	Champions League Phase 1 Match 2	Benfica 0 Manchester United 1	Estadio da Luz	61000
7	2006/07	06/12/06	Champions League Phase 1 Match 6	Manchester United 3 Benfica 1	Old Trafford	74955

UNITED v BIRMINGHAM CITY

ALL COMPETITIVE MATCHES

VENUE	P	W	D	L	F	A
HOME	48	30	9	9	79	37
AWAY	49	14	19	16	65	70
NEUTRAL	5	3	2	0	12	5
TOTAL	102	47	30	25	156	112

ALL LEAGUE MATCHES

VENUE	P	W	D	L	F	A
HOME	45	28	8	9	71	34
AWAY	45	13	17	15	59	65
TOTAL	90	41	25	24	130	99

ALL CUP MATCHES

VENUE	P	W	D	L	F	A
HOME	3	2	1	0	8	3
AWAY	4	1	2	1	6	5
NEUTRAL	3	2	1	0	6	2
TOTAL	10	5	4	1	20	10

PREMIERSHIP

VENUE	P	W	D	L	F	A
HOME	5	5	0	0	11	0
AWAY	5	3	2	0	6	3
TOTAL	10	8	2	0	17	3

LEAGUE DIVISION ONE

VENUE	P	W	D	L	F	A
HOME	34	20	7	7	51	28
AWAY	34	10	15	9	50	51
TOTAL	68	30	22	16	101	79

LEAGUE DIVISION TWO

VENUE	P	W	D	L	F	A
HOME	6	3	1	2	9	6
AWAY	6	0	0	6	3	11
TOTAL	12	3	1	8	12	17

FA CUP

VENUE	P	W	D	L	F	A
HOME	3	2	1	0	8	3
AWAY	3	0	2	1	3	4
NEUTRAL	3	2	1	0	6	2
TOTAL	9	4	4	1	17	9

LEAGUE CUP

VENUE	P	W	D	L	F	A
HOME	0	0	0	0	0	0
AWAY	1	1	0	0	3	1
NEUTRAL	0	0	0	0	0	0
TOTAL	1	1	0	0	3	1

OTHER MATCHES

VENUE	P	W	D	L	F	A
HOME	0	0	0	0	0	0
AWAY	0	0	0	0	0	0
NEUTRAL	2	1	1	0	6	3
TOTAL	2	1	1	0	6	3

#	SEASON	DATE	COMPETITION / ROUND	MATCH RESULT	VENUE	ATT
1	1892/93	22/04/93	Football League Test Match	Newton Heath 1 Birmingham City 1	Victoria Ground	4000
2	1892/93	27/04/93	Football League Test Match Replay	Newton Heath 5 Birmingham City 2	Bramall Lane	6000
3	1896/97	10/10/96	Football League Division 2	Newton Heath 1 Birmingham City 1	Bank Street	7000
4	1896/97	28/11/96	Football League Division 2	Birmingham City 1 Newton Heath 0	Muntz Street	4000
5	1897/98	23/10/97	Football League Division 2	Birmingham City 2 Newton Heath 1	Muntz Street	6000
6	1897/98	09/04/98	Football League Division 2	Newton Heath 3 Birmingham City 1	Bank Street	4000
7	1898/99	15/10/98	Football League Division 2	Birmingham City 4 Newton Heath 1	Muntz Street	5000
8	1898/99	25/02/99	Football League Division 2	Newton Heath 2 Birmingham City 0	Bank Street	12000
9	1899/00	14/10/99	Football League Division 2	Birmingham City 1 Newton Heath 0	Muntz Street	10000
10	1899/00	17/02/00	Football League Division 2	Newton Heath 3 Birmingham City 2	Bank Street	10000
11	1900/01	01/12/00	Football League Division 2	Newton Heath 0 Birmingham City 1	Bank Street	5000
12	1900/01	06/04/01	Football League Division 2	Birmingham City 1 Newton Heath 0	Muntz Street	6000
13	1902/03	15/11/02	Football League Division 2	Manchester United 0 Birmingham City 1	Bank Street	25000
14	1902/03	20/04/03	Football League Division 2	Birmingham City 2 Manchester United 1	St Andrews	6000
15	1903/04	12/12/03	FA Cup Intermediate Round	Manchester United 1 Birmingham City 1	Bank Street	10000
16	1903/04	16/12/03	FA Cup Intermediate Round Replay	Birmingham City 1 Manchester United 1	Muntz Street	5000
17	1903/04	21/12/03	FA Cup Intermediate Round 2nd Replay	Manchester United 1 Birmingham City 1	Bramall Lane	3000
18	1903/04	11/01/04	FA Cup Intermediate Round 3rd Replay	Manchester United 3 Birmingham City 1	Hyde Road	9372
19	1906/07	27/10/06	Football League Division 1	Manchester United 2 Birmingham City 1	Bank Street	14000
20	1906/07	02/03/07	Football League Division 1	Birmingham City 1 Manchester United 0	St Andrews	20000
21	1907/08	02/11/07	Football League Division 1	Birmingham City 3 Manchester United 4	St Andrews	20000
22	1907/08	29/02/08	Football League Division 1	Manchester United 1 Birmingham City 0	Bank Street	12000
23	1921/22	18/02/22	Football League Division 1	Birmingham City 0 Manchester United 1	St Andrews	20000
24	1921/22	25/02/22	Football League Division 1	Manchester United 1 Birmingham City 1	Old Trafford	35000
25	1925/26	14/11/25	Football League Division 1	Manchester United 3 Birmingham City 1	Old Trafford	23559
26	1925/26	19/04/26	Football League Division 1	Birmingham City 2 Manchester United 1	St Andrews	8948
27	1926/27	23/10/26	Football League Division 1	Manchester United 0 Birmingham City 1	Old Trafford	32010
28	1926/27	12/03/27	Football League Division 1	Birmingham City 4 Manchester United 0	St Andrews	14392
29	1927/28	03/09/27	Football League Division 1	Birmingham City 0 Manchester United 0	St Andrews	25863
30	1927/28	07/01/28	Football League Division 1	Manchester United 1 Birmingham City 1	Old Trafford	16853
31	1927/28	18/02/28	FA Cup 5th Round	Manchester United 1 Birmingham City 0	Old Trafford	52568
32	1928/29	20/10/28	Football League Division 1	Manchester United 1 Birmingham City 0	Old Trafford	17522
33	1928/29	02/03/29	Football League Division 1	Birmingham City 1 Manchester United 1	St Andrews	16738
34	1929/30	25/12/29	Football League Division 1	Manchester United 0 Birmingham City 0	Old Trafford	18626
35	1929/30	26/12/29	Football League Division 1	Birmingham City 0 Manchester United 1	St Andrews	35682
36	1930/31	01/11/30	Football League Division 1	Manchester United 2 Birmingham City 0	Old Trafford	11479
37	1930/31	07/03/31	Football League Division 1	Birmingham City 0 Manchester United 0	St Andrews	17678
38	1936/37	05/12/36	Football League Division 1	Manchester United 1 Birmingham City 2	Old Trafford	16544
39	1936/37	10/04/37	Football League Division 1	Birmingham City 2 Manchester United 2	St Andrews	19130
40	1938/39	03/09/38	Football League Division 1	Manchester United 4 Birmingham City 1	Old Trafford	22228
41	1938/39	31/12/38	Football League Division 1	Birmingham City 3 Manchester United 3	St Andrews	20787
42	1948/49	20/11/48	Football League Division 1	Manchester United 3 Birmingham City 0	Maine Road	45482
43	1948/49	19/03/49	Football League Division 1	Birmingham City 1 Manchester United 0	St Andrews	46819

UNITED v BIRMINGHAM CITY (continued)

#	SEASON	DATE	COMPETITION / ROUND	MATCH RESULT	VENUE	ATT
44	1949/50	07/04/50	Football League Division 1	Manchester United 0 Birmingham City 2	Old Trafford	47170
45	1949/50	10/04/50	Football League Division 1	Birmingham City 0 Manchester United 0	St Andrews	35863
46	1950/51	24/02/51	FA Cup 6th Round	Birmingham City 1 Manchester United 0	St Andrews	50000
47	1955/56	20/08/55	Football League Division 1	Birmingham City 2 Manchester United 2	St Andrews	37994
48	1955/56	17/12/55	Football League Division 1	Manchester United 2 Birmingham City 1	Old Trafford	27704
49	1956/57	18/08/56	Football League Division 1	Manchester United 2 Birmingham City 2	Old Trafford	32752
50	1956/57	15/12/56	Football League Division 1	Birmingham City 3 Manchester United 1	St Andrews	36146
51	1956/57	23/03/57	FA Cup Semi-Final	Manchester United 2 Birmingham City 0	Hillsborough	65107
52	1957/58	07/12/57	Football League Division 1	Birmingham City 3 Manchester United 3	St Andrews	35791
53	1957/58	19/04/58	Football League Division 1	Manchester United 0 Birmingham City 2	Old Trafford	38991
54	1958/59	29/11/58	Football League Division 1	Birmingham City 0 Manchester United 4	St Andrews	28658
55	1958/59	18/04/59	Football League Division 1	Manchester United 1 Birmingham City 0	Old Trafford	43006
56	1959/60	05/09/59	Football League Division 1	Birmingham City 1 Manchester United 1	St Andrews	38220
57	1959/60	16/01/60	Football League Division 1	Manchester United 2 Birmingham City 1	Old Trafford	47361
58	1960/61	12/11/60	Football League Division 1	Birmingham City 3 Manchester United 1	St Andrews	31549
59	1960/61	15/04/61	Football League Division 1	Manchester United 4 Birmingham City 1	Old Trafford	28376
60	1961/62	14/10/61	Football League Division 1	Manchester United 0 Birmingham City 2	Old Trafford	30674
61	1961/62	03/03/62	Football League Division 1	Birmingham City 1 Manchester United 1	St Andrews	25817
62	1962/63	01/09/62	Football League Division 1	Manchester United 2 Birmingham City 0	Old Trafford	39847
63	1962/63	10/05/63	Football League Division 1	Birmingham City 2 Manchester United 1	St Andrews	21814
64	1963/64	07/09/63	Football League Division 1	Birmingham City 1 Manchester United 1	St Andrews	36874
65	1963/64	11/01/64	Football League Division 1	Manchester United 1 Birmingham City 2	Old Trafford	44695
66	1964/65	16/12/64	Football League Division 1	Manchester United 1 Birmingham City 1	Old Trafford	25721
67	1964/65	19/04/65	Football League Division 1	Birmingham City 2 Manchester United 4	St Andrews	28907
68	1968/69	08/02/69	FA Cup 5th Round	Birmingham City 2 Manchester United 2	St Andrews	52500
69	1968/69	24/02/69	FA Cup 5th Round Replay	Manchester United 6 Birmingham City 2	Old Trafford	61932
70	1972/73	14/10/72	Football League Division 1	Manchester United 1 Birmingham City 0	Old Trafford	52104
71	1972/73	10/03/73	Football League Division 1	Birmingham City 3 Manchester United 1	St Andrews	51278
72	1973/74	20/10/73	Football League Division 1	Manchester United 1 Birmingham City 0	Old Trafford	48937
73	1973/74	16/03/74	Football League Division 1	Birmingham City 1 Manchester United 0	St Andrews	37768
74	1975/76	19/08/75	Football League Division 1	Birmingham City 0 Manchester United 2	St Andrews	33177
75	1975/76	31/01/76	Football League Division 1	Manchester United 3 Birmingham City 1	Old Trafford	50724
76	1976/77	21/08/76	Football League Division 1	Manchester United 2 Birmingham City 2	Old Trafford	58898
77	1976/77	22/01/77	Football League Division 1	Birmingham City 2 Manchester United 3	St Andrews	35316
78	1977/78	20/08/77	Football League Division 1	Birmingham City 1 Manchester United 4	St Andrews	28005
79	1977/78	02/01/78	Football League Division 1	Manchester United 1 Birmingham City 2	Old Trafford	53501
80	1978/79	19/08/78	Football League Division 1	Manchester United 1 Birmingham City 0	Old Trafford	56139
81	1978/79	11/11/78	Football League Division 1	Birmingham City 5 Manchester United 1	St Andrews	23550
82	1980/81	23/08/80	Football League Division 1	Birmingham City 0 Manchester United 0	St Andrews	28661
83	1980/81	31/01/81	Football League Division 1	Manchester United 2 Birmingham City 0	Old Trafford	39081
84	1981/82	17/10/81	Football League Division 1	Manchester United 1 Birmingham City 1	Old Trafford	48800
85	1981/82	06/03/82	Football League Division 1	Birmingham City 0 Manchester United 1	St Andrews	19637
86	1982/83	28/08/82	Football League Division 1	Manchester United 3 Birmingham City 0	Old Trafford	48673
87	1982/83	15/01/83	Football League Division 1	Birmingham City 1 Manchester United 2	St Andrews	19333
88	1983/84	07/02/84	Football League Division 1	Birmingham City 2 Manchester United 2	St Andrews	19957
89	1983/84	07/04/84	Football League Division 1	Manchester United 1 Birmingham City 0	Old Trafford	39896
90	1985/86	01/01/86	Football League Division 1	Manchester United 1 Birmingham City 0	Old Trafford	43095
91	1985/86	29/03/86	Football League Division 1	Birmingham City 1 Manchester United 1	St Andrews	22551
92	2002/03	28/12/02	FA Premiership	Manchester United 2 Birmingham City 0	Old Trafford	67640
93	2002/03	04/02/03	FA Premiership	Birmingham City 0 Manchester United 1	St Andrews	29475
94	2003/04	04/10/03	FA Premiership	Manchester United 3 Birmingham City 0	Old Trafford	67633
95	2003/04	10/04/04	FA Premiership	Birmingham City 1 Manchester United 2	St Andrews	29548
96	2004/05	16/10/04	FA Premiership	Birmingham City 0 Manchester United 0	St Andrews	29221
97	2004/05	05/02/05	FA Premiership	Manchester United 2 Birmingham City 0	Old Trafford	67838
98	2005/06	20/12/05	League Cup 5th Round	Birmingham City 1 Manchester United 3	St Andrews	20454
99	2005/06	28/12/05	FA Premiership	Birmingham City 2 Manchester United 2	St Andrews	28459
100	2005/06	26/03/06	FA Premiership	Manchester United 3 Birmingham City 0	Old Trafford	69070
101	2007/08	29/09/07	FA Premiership	Birmingham City 0 Manchester United 1	St Andrews	26526
102	2007/08	01/01/08	FA Premiership	Manchester United 1 Birmingham City 0	Old Trafford	75459

UNITED v BLACKBURN ROVERS

ALL COMPETITIVE MATCHES						
VENUE	P	W	D	L	F	A
HOME	50	27	14	9	100	54
AWAY	52	17	13	22	84	101
NEUTRAL	1	1	0	0	2	0
TOTAL	103	45	27	31	186	155

ALL LEAGUE MATCHES						
VENUE	P	W	D	L	F	A
HOME	45	25	11	9	90	50
AWAY	45	15	12	18	75	84
TOTAL	90	40	23	27	165	134

ALL CUP MATCHES						
VENUE	P	W	D	L	F	A
HOME	5	2	3	0	10	4
AWAY	7	2	1	4	9	17
TOTAL	12	4	4	4	19	21

PREMIERSHIP						
VENUE	P	W	D	L	F	A
HOME	14	10	3	1	29	12
AWAY	14	5	5	4	20	18
TOTAL	28	15	8	5	49	30

LEAGUE DIVISION ONE						
VENUE	P	W	D	L	F	A
HOME	30	14	8	8	59	37
AWAY	30	10	6	14	54	65
TOTAL	60	24	14	22	113	102

LEAGUE DIVISION TWO						
VENUE	P	W	D	L	F	A
HOME	1	1	0	0	2	1
AWAY	1	0	1	0	1	1
TOTAL	2	1	1	0	3	2

FA CUP						
VENUE	P	W	D	L	F	A
HOME	3	1	2	0	7	2
AWAY	5	1	0	4	5	15
TOTAL	8	2	2	4	12	17

LEAGUE CUP						
VENUE	P	W	D	L	F	A
HOME	2	1	1	0	3	2
AWAY	2	1	1	0	4	2
TOTAL	4	2	2	0	7	4

CHARITY SHIELD						
VENUE	P	W	D	L	F	A
HOME	0	0	0	0	0	0
AWAY	0	0	0	0	0	0
NEUTRAL	1	1	0	0	2	0
TOTAL	1	1	0	0	2	0

#	SEASON	DATE	COMPETITION / ROUND	MATCH RESULT	VENUE	ATT
1	1892/93	03/09/92	Football League Division 1	Blackburn Rovers 4 Newton Heath 3	Ewood Park	8000
2	1892/93	05/11/92	Football League Division 1	Newton Heath 4 Blackburn Rovers 4	North Road	12000
3	1892/93	21/01/93	FA Cup 1st Round	Blackburn Rovers 4 Newton Heath 0	Ewood Park	7000
4	1893/94	10/02/94	FA Cup 2nd Round	Newton Heath 0 Blackburn Rovers 0	Bank Street	18000
5	1893/94	17/02/94	FA Cup 2nd Round Replay	Blackburn Rovers 5 Newton Heath 1	Ewood Park	5000
6	1893/94	12/03/94	Football League Division 1	Newton Heath 5 Blackburn Rovers 1	Bank Street	5000
7	1893/94	26/03/94	Football League Division 1	Blackburn Rovers 4 Newton Heath 0	Ewood Park	5000
8	1906/07	13/10/06	Football League Division 1	Manchester United 1 Blackburn Rovers 1	Bank Street	20000
9	1906/07	16/02/07	Football League Division 1	Blackburn Rovers 2 Manchester United 4	Ewood Park	5000
10	1907/08	19/10/07	Football League Division 1	Blackburn Rovers 1 Manchester United 5	Ewood Park	30000
11	1907/08	15/02/08	Football League Division 1	Manchester United 1 Blackburn Rovers 2	Bank Street	15000
12	1908/09	14/11/08	Football League Division 1	Blackburn Rovers 1 Manchester United 3	Ewood Park	25000
13	1908/09	20/02/09	FA Cup 3rd Round	Manchester United 6 Blackburn Rovers 1	Bank Street	38500
14	1908/09	20/03/09	Football League Division 1	Manchester United 0 Blackburn Rovers 3	Bank Street	11000
15	1909/10	20/11/09	Football League Division 1	Blackburn Rovers 3 Manchester United 2	Ewood Park	40000
16	1909/10	02/04/10	Football League Division 1	Manchester United 2 Blackburn Rovers 0	Old Trafford	20000
17	1910/11	03/09/10	Football League Division 1	Manchester United 3 Blackburn Rovers 2	Old Trafford	40000
18	1910/11	31/12/10	Football League Division 1	Blackburn Rovers 1 Manchester United 0	Ewood Park	20000
19	1911/12	30/09/11	Football League Division 1	Blackburn Rovers 2 Manchester United 2	Ewood Park	30000
20	1911/12	09/03/12	FA Cup 4th Round	Manchester United 1 Blackburn Rovers 1	Old Trafford	59300
21	1911/12	14/03/12	FA Cup 4th Round Replay	Blackburn Rovers 4 Manchester United 2	Ewood Park	39296
22	1911/12	29/04/12	Football League Division 1	Manchester United 3 Blackburn Rovers 1	Old Trafford	20000
23	1912/13	05/10/12	Football League Division 1	Manchester United 1 Blackburn Rovers 1	Old Trafford	45000
24	1912/13	08/02/13	Football League Division 1	Blackburn Rovers 0 Manchester United 0	Ewood Park	38000
25	1913/14	20/12/13	Football League Division 1	Blackburn Rovers 0 Manchester United 1	Ewood Park	35000
26	1913/14	25/04/14	Football League Division 1	Manchester United 0 Blackburn Rovers 0	Old Trafford	20000
27	1914/15	19/09/14	Football League Division 1	Manchester United 2 Blackburn Rovers 0	Old Trafford	15000
28	1914/15	23/01/15	Football League Division 1	Blackburn Rovers 3 Manchester United 3	Ewood Park	7000
29	1919/20	17/04/20	Football League Division 1	Manchester United 1 Blackburn Rovers 1	Old Trafford	40000
30	1919/20	24/04/20	Football League Division 1	Blackburn Rovers 5 Manchester United 0	Ewood Park	30000
31	1920/21	23/04/21	Football League Division 1	Blackburn Rovers 2 Manchester United 0	Ewood Park	18000
32	1920/21	30/04/21	Football League Division 1	Manchester United 0 Blackburn Rovers 1	Old Trafford	20000
33	1921/22	18/03/22	Football League Division 1	Manchester United 0 Blackburn Rovers 1	Old Trafford	30000
34	1921/22	25/03/22	Football League Division 1	Blackburn Rovers 3 Manchester United 0	Ewood Park	15000
35	1925/26	28/11/25	Football League Division 1	Manchester United 2 Blackburn Rovers 0	Old Trafford	33660
36	1925/26	10/04/26	Football League Division 1	Blackburn Rovers 7 Manchester United 0	Ewood Park	15870
37	1926/27	27/11/26	Football League Division 1	Blackburn Rovers 2 Manchester United 1	Ewood Park	17280
38	1926/27	16/04/27	Football League Division 1	Manchester United 2 Blackburn Rovers 0	Old Trafford	24845
39	1927/28	19/09/27	Football League Division 1	Blackburn Rovers 3 Manchester United 0	Ewood Park	18243
40	1927/28	26/12/27	Football League Division 1	Manchester United 1 Blackburn Rovers 1	Old Trafford	31131
41	1927/28	03/03/28	FA Cup 6th Round	Blackburn Rovers 2 Manchester United 0	Ewood Park	42312
42	1928/29	01/12/28	Football League Division 1	Manchester United 1 Blackburn Rovers 4	Old Trafford	19589
43	1928/29	13/04/29	Football League Division 1	Blackburn Rovers 0 Manchester United 3	Ewood Park	8193
44	1929/30	07/09/29	Football League Division 1	Manchester United 1 Blackburn Rovers 0	Old Trafford	22362
45	1929/30	04/01/30	Football League Division 1	Blackburn Rovers 5 Manchester United 4	Ewood Park	23923

UNITED v BLACKBURN ROVERS (continued)

#	SEASON	DATE	COMPETITION / ROUND	MATCH RESULT	VENUE	ATT
46	1930/31	06/12/30	Football League Division 1	Blackburn Rovers 4 Manchester United 1	Ewood Park	10802
47	1930/31	11/04/31	Football League Division 1	Manchester United 0 Blackburn Rovers 1	Old Trafford	6414
48	1937/38	16/10/37	Football League Division 2	Blackburn Rovers 1 Manchester United 1	Ewood Park	19580
49	1937/38	26/02/38	Football League Division 2	Manchester United 2 Blackburn Rovers 1	Old Trafford	30892
50	1946/47	14/12/46	Football League Division 1	Blackburn Rovers 2 Manchester United 1	Ewood Park	21455
51	1946/47	19/04/47	Football League Division 1	Manchester United 4 Blackburn Rovers 0	Maine Road	46196
52	1947/48	13/12/47	Football League Division 1	Blackburn Rovers 1 Manchester United 1	Ewood Park	22784
53	1947/48	01/05/48	Football League Division 1	Manchester United 4 Blackburn Rovers 1	Maine Road	44484
54	1958/59	06/09/58	Football League Division 1	Manchester United 6 Blackburn Rovers 1	Old Trafford	65187
55	1958/59	02/03/59	Football League Division 1	Blackburn Rovers 1 Manchester United 3	Ewood Park	40401
56	1959/60	31/10/59	Football League Division 1	Blackburn Rovers 1 Manchester United 1	Ewood Park	39621
57	1959/60	16/04/60	Football League Division 1	Manchester United 1 Blackburn Rovers 0	Old Trafford	45945
58	1960/61	20/08/60	Football League Division 1	Manchester United 1 Blackburn Rovers 3	Old Trafford	47778
59	1960/61	17/12/60	Football League Division 1	Blackburn Rovers 1 Manchester United 2	Ewood Park	17285
60	1961/62	26/08/61	Football League Division 1	Manchester United 6 Blackburn Rovers 1	Old Trafford	45302
61	1961/62	10/04/62	Football League Division 1	Blackburn Rovers 3 Manchester United 0	Ewood Park	14623
62	1962/63	13/10/62	Football League Division 1	Manchester United 0 Blackburn Rovers 3	Old Trafford	42252
63	1962/63	02/03/63	Football League Division 1	Blackburn Rovers 2 Manchester United 2	Ewood Park	27924
64	1963/64	28/10/63	Football League Division 1	Manchester United 2 Blackburn Rovers 2	Old Trafford	41169
65	1963/64	22/02/64	Football League Division 1	Blackburn Rovers 1 Manchester United 3	Ewood Park	36726
66	1964/65	21/11/64	Football League Division 1	Manchester United 3 Blackburn Rovers 0	Old Trafford	49633
67	1964/65	03/04/65	Football League Division 1	Blackburn Rovers 0 Manchester United 5	Ewood Park	29363
68	1965/66	06/11/65	Football League Division 1	Manchester United 2 Blackburn Rovers 2	Old Trafford	38823
69	1965/66	07/05/66	Football League Division 1	Blackburn Rovers 1 Manchester United 4	Ewood Park	14513
70	1984/85	15/02/85	FA Cup 5th Round	Blackburn Rovers 0 Manchester United 2	Ewood Park	22692
71	1992/93	24/10/92	FA Premiership	Blackburn Rovers 0 Manchester United 0	Ewood Park	20305
72	1992/93	03/05/93	FA Premiership	Manchester United 3 Blackburn Rovers 1	Old Trafford	40447
73	1993/94	26/12/93	FA Premiership	Manchester United 1 Blackburn Rovers 1	Old Trafford	44511
74	1993/94	02/04/94	FA Premiership	Blackburn Rovers 2 Manchester United 0	Ewood Park	20886
75	1994/95	14/08/94	FA Charity Shield	Manchester United 2 Blackburn Rovers 0	Wembley	60402
76	1994/95	24/10/94	FA Premiership	Blackburn Rovers 2 Manchester United 4	Ewood Park	30260
77	1994/95	22/01/95	FA Premiership	Manchester United 1 Blackburn Rovers 0	Old Trafford	43742
78	1995/96	28/08/95	FA Premiership	Blackburn Rovers 1 Manchester United 2	Ewood Park	29843
79	1995/96	10/02/96	FA Premiership	Manchester United 1 Blackburn Rovers 0	Old Trafford	42681
80	1996/97	25/08/96	FA Premiership	Manchester United 2 Blackburn Rovers 2	Old Trafford	54178
81	1996/97	12/04/97	FA Premiership	Blackburn Rovers 2 Manchester United 3	Ewood Park	30476
82	1997/98	30/11/97	FA Premiership	Manchester United 4 Blackburn Rovers 0	Old Trafford	55175
83	1997/98	06/04/98	FA Premiership	Blackburn Rovers 1 Manchester United 3	Ewood Park	30547
84	1998/99	14/11/98	FA Premiership	Manchester United 3 Blackburn Rovers 2	Old Trafford	55198
85	1998/99	12/05/99	FA Premiership	Blackburn Rovers 0 Manchester United 0	Ewood Park	30436
86	2001/02	22/08/01	FA Premiership	Blackburn Rovers 2 Manchester United 2	Ewood Park	29836
87	2001/02	19/01/02	FA Premiership	Manchester United 2 Blackburn Rovers 1	Old Trafford	67552
88	2002/03	22/12/02	FA Premiership	Blackburn Rovers 1 Manchester United 0	Ewood Park	30475
89	2002/03	07/01/03	League Cup Semi-Final 1st Leg	Manchester United 1 Blackburn Rovers 1	Old Trafford	62740
90	2002/03	22/01/03	League Cup Semi-Final 2nd Leg	Blackburn Rovers 1 Manchester United 3	Ewood Park	29048
91	2002/03	19/04/03	FA Premiership	Manchester United 3 Blackburn Rovers 1	Old Trafford	67626
92	2003/04	22/11/03	FA Premiership	Manchester United 2 Blackburn Rovers 1	Old Trafford	67748
93	2003/04	01/05/04	FA Premiership	Blackburn Rovers 1 Manchester United 0	Ewood Park	29616
94	2004/05	28/08/04	FA Premiership	Blackburn Rovers 1 Manchester United 1	Ewood Park	26155
95	2004/05	02/04/05	FA Premiership	Manchester United 0 Blackburn Rovers 0	Old Trafford	67939
96	2005/06	24/09/05	FA Premiership	Manchester United 1 Blackburn Rovers 2	Old Trafford	67765
97	2005/06	11/01/06	League Cup Semi-Final 1st Leg	Blackburn Rovers 1 Manchester United 1	Ewood Park	24348
98	2005/06	25/01/06	League Cup Semi-Final 2nd Leg	Manchester United 2 Blackburn Rovers 1	Old Trafford	61636
99	2005/06	01/02/06	FA Premiership	Blackburn Rovers 4 Manchester United 3	Ewood Park	25484
100	2006/07	11/11/06	FA Premiership	Blackburn Rovers 0 Manchester United 1	Ewood Park	26162
101	2006/07	31/03/07	FA Premiership	Manchester United 4 Blackburn Rovers 1	Old Trafford	76098
102	2007/08	11/11/07	FA Premiership	Manchester United 2 Blackburn Rovers 0	Old Trafford	75710
103	2007/08	19/04/08	FA Premiership	Blackburn Rovers 1 Manchester United 1	Ewood Park	30316

UNITED v BLACKPOOL

ALL COMPETITIVE MATCHES

VENUE	P	W	D	L	F	A
HOME	43	27	9	7	91	41
AWAY	43	19	9	15	71	67
NEUTRAL	1	1	0	0	4	2
TOTAL	87	47	18	22	166	110

ALL LEAGUE MATCHES

VENUE	P	W	D	L	F	A
HOME	40	26	8	6	83	34
AWAY	40	17	9	14	66	60
TOTAL	80	43	17	20	149	94

ALL CUP MATCHES

VENUE	P	W	D	L	F	A
HOME	3	1	1	1	8	7
AWAY	3	2	0	1	5	7
NEUTRAL	1	1	0	0	4	2
TOTAL	7	4	1	2	17	16

LEAGUE DIVISION ONE

VENUE	P	W	D	L	F	A
HOME	24	14	5	5	46	22
AWAY	24	9	8	7	45	38
TOTAL	48	23	13	12	91	60

LEAGUE DIVISION TWO

VENUE	P	W	D	L	F	A
HOME	16	12	3	1	37	12
AWAY	16	8	1	7	21	22
TOTAL	32	20	4	8	58	34

FA CUP

VENUE	P	W	D	L	F	A
HOME	3	1	1	1	8	7
AWAY	2	2	0	0	4	2
NEUTRAL	1	1	0	0	4	2
TOTAL	6	4	1	1	16	11

LEAGUE CUP

VENUE	P	W	D	L	F	A
HOME	0	0	0	0	0	0
AWAY	1	0	0	1	1	5
NEUTRAL	0	0	0	0	0	0
TOTAL	1	0	0	1	1	5

#	SEASON	DATE	COMPETITION / ROUND	MATCH RESULT	VENUE	ATT
1	1891/92	05/12/91	FA Cup 4th Qualifying Round	Newton Heath 3 Blackpool 4	North Road	4000
2	1896/97	17/10/96	Football League Division 2	Blackpool 4 Newton Heath 2	Raikes Hall Gardens	5000
3	1896/97	26/12/96	Football League Division 2	Newton Heath 2 Blackpool 0	Bank Street	9000
4	1896/97	16/01/97	FA Cup 5th Qualifying Round	Newton Heath 2 Blackpool 2	Bank Street	1500
5	1896/97	20/01/97	FA Cup 5th Qualifying Round Replay	Blackpool 1 Newton Heath 2	Raikes Hall Gardens	5000
6	1897/98	25/09/97	Football League Division 2	Blackpool 0 Newton Heath 1	Raikes Hall Gardens	2000
7	1897/98	15/01/98	Football League Division 2	Newton Heath 4 Blackpool 0	Bank Street	4000
8	1898/99	10/12/98	Football League Division 2	Newton Heath 3 Blackpool 1	Bank Street	5000
9	1898/99	03/04/99	Football League Division 2	Blackpool 0 Newton Heath 1	Raikes Hall Gardens	3000
10	1900/01	26/12/00	Football League Division 2	Newton Heath 4 Blackpool 0	Bank Street	10000
11	1900/01	23/03/01	Football League Division 2	Blackpool 1 Newton Heath 2	Bloomfield Road	2000
12	1901/02	28/09/01	Football League Division 2	Blackpool 2 Newton Heath 4	Bloomfield Road	3000
13	1901/02	25/01/02	Football League Division 2	Newton Heath 0 Blackpool 1	Bank Street	2500
14	1902/03	26/12/02	Football League Division 2	Manchester United 2 Blackpool 2	Bank Street	10000
15	1902/03	14/02/03	Football League Division 2	Blackpool 2 Manchester United 0	Bloomfield Road	3000
16	1903/04	09/03/04	Football League Division 2	Blackpool 2 Manchester United 1	Bloomfield Road	3000
17	1903/04	09/04/04	Football League Division 2	Manchester United 3 Blackpool 1	Bank Street	10000
18	1904/05	25/03/05	Football League Division 2	Blackpool 0 Manchester United 1	Bloomfield Road	6000
19	1904/05	24/04/05	Football League Division 2	Manchester United 3 Blackpool 1	Bank Street	4000
20	1905/06	04/09/05	Football League Division 2	Manchester United 2 Blackpool 1	Bank Street	7000
21	1905/06	30/09/05	Football League Division 2	Blackpool 0 Manchester United 1	Bloomfield Road	7000
22	1907/08	11/01/08	FA Cup 1st Round	Manchester United 3 Blackpool 1	Bank Street	11747
23	1910/11	14/01/11	FA Cup 1st Round	Blackpool 1 Manchester United 2	Bloomfield Road	12000
24	1922/23	31/03/23	Football League Division 2	Blackpool 1 Manchester United 0	Bloomfield Road	21000
25	1922/23	07/04/23	Football League Division 2	Manchester United 2 Blackpool 1	Old Trafford	20000
26	1923/24	06/02/24	Football League Division 2	Blackpool 1 Manchester United 0	Bloomfield Road	6000
27	1923/24	09/02/24	Football League Division 2	Manchester United 0 Blackpool 0	Old Trafford	13000
28	1924/25	22/11/24	Football League Division 2	Blackpool 1 Manchester United 1	Bloomfield Road	9500
29	1924/25	28/03/25	Football League Division 2	Manchester United 0 Blackpool 0	Old Trafford	26250
30	1930/31	15/11/30	Football League Division 1	Manchester United 0 Blackpool 0	Old Trafford	14765
31	1930/31	21/03/31	Football League Division 1	Blackpool 5 Manchester United 1	Bloomfield Road	13162
32	1933/34	18/11/33	Football League Division 2	Blackpool 3 Manchester United 1	Bloomfield Road	14384
33	1933/34	31/03/34	Football League Division 2	Manchester United 2 Blackpool 0	Old Trafford	20038
34	1934/35	03/11/34	Football League Division 2	Blackpool 1 Manchester United 2	Bloomfield Road	15663
35	1934/35	16/03/35	Football League Division 2	Manchester United 3 Blackpool 2	Old Trafford	25704
36	1935/36	07/12/35	Football League Division 2	Blackpool 4 Manchester United 1	Bloomfield Road	13218
37	1935/36	29/02/36	Football League Division 2	Manchester United 3 Blackpool 2	Old Trafford	18423
38	1938/39	15/10/38	Football League Division 1	Manchester United 0 Blackpool 0	Old Trafford	39723
39	1938/39	18/02/39	Football League Division 1	Blackpool 3 Manchester United 5	Bloomfield Road	15253
40	1946/47	19/10/46	Football League Division 1	Blackpool 3 Manchester United 1	Bloomfield Road	26307
41	1946/47	22/02/47	Football League Division 1	Manchester United 3 Blackpool 0	Maine Road	29993

UNITED v BLACKPOOL (continued)

#	SEASON	DATE	COMPETITION / ROUND	MATCH RESULT	VENUE	ATT
42	1947/48	06/12/47	Football League Division 1	Manchester United 1 Blackpool 1	Maine Road	63683
43	1947/48	24/04/48	FA Cup Final	Manchester United 4 Blackpool 2	Wembley	99000
44	1947/48	28/04/48	Football League Division 1	Blackpool 1 Manchester United 0	Bloomfield Road	32236
45	1948/49	23/08/48	Football League Division 1	Blackpool 0 Manchester United 3	Bloomfield Road	36880
46	1948/49	01/09/48	Football League Division 1	Manchester United 3 Blackpool 4	Maine Road	51187
47	1949/50	26/11/49	Football League Division 1	Blackpool 3 Manchester United 3	Bloomfield Road	27742
48	1949/50	18/03/50	Football League Division 1	Manchester United 1 Blackpool 2	Old Trafford	53688
49	1950/51	02/09/50	Football League Division 1	Manchester United 1 Blackpool 0	Old Trafford	53260
50	1950/51	05/05/51	Football League Division 1	Blackpool 1 Manchester United 1	Bloomfield Road	22864
51	1951/52	01/12/51	Football League Division 1	Manchester United 3 Blackpool 1	Old Trafford	34154
52	1951/52	19/04/52	Football League Division 1	Blackpool 2 Manchester United 2	Bloomfield Road	29118
53	1952/53	25/12/52	Football League Division 1	Blackpool 0 Manchester United 0	Bloomfield Road	27778
54	1952/53	26/12/52	Football League Division 1	Manchester United 2 Blackpool 1	Old Trafford	48077
55	1953/54	21/11/53	Football League Division 1	Manchester United 4 Blackpool 1	Old Trafford	49853
56	1953/54	10/04/54	Football League Division 1	Blackpool 2 Manchester United 0	Bloomfield Road	25996
57	1954/55	28/08/54	Football League Division 1	Blackpool 2 Manchester United 4	Bloomfield Road	31855
58	1954/55	01/01/55	Football League Division 1	Manchester United 4 Blackpool 1	Old Trafford	51918
59	1955/56	26/11/55	Football League Division 1	Blackpool 0 Manchester United 0	Bloomfield Road	26240
60	1955/56	07/04/56	Football League Division 1	Manchester United 2 Blackpool 1	Old Trafford	62277
61	1956/57	27/10/56	Football League Division 1	Blackpool 2 Manchester United 2	Bloomfield Road	32632
62	1956/57	23/02/57	Football League Division 1	Manchester United 0 Blackpool 2	Old Trafford	42602
63	1957/58	09/09/57	Football League Division 1	Blackpool 1 Manchester United 4	Bloomfield Road	34181
64	1957/58	18/09/57	Football League Division 1	Manchester United 1 Blackpool 2	Old Trafford	40763
65	1958/59	30/08/58	Football League Division 1	Blackpool 2 Manchester United 1	Bloomfield Road	26719
66	1958/59	03/01/59	Football League Division 1	Manchester United 3 Blackpool 1	Old Trafford	61961
67	1959/60	05/12/59	Football League Division 1	Manchester United 3 Blackpool 1	Old Trafford	45558
68	1959/60	27/02/60	Football League Division 1	Blackpool 0 Manchester United 6	Bloomfield Road	23996
69	1960/61	31/03/61	Football League Division 1	Blackpool 2 Manchester United 0	Bloomfield Road	30835
70	1960/61	03/04/61	Football League Division 1	Manchester United 2 Blackpool 0	Old Trafford	39169
71	1961/62	02/09/61	Football League Division 1	Blackpool 2 Manchester United 3	Bloomfield Road	28156
72	1961/62	13/01/62	Football League Division 1	Manchester United 0 Blackpool 1	Old Trafford	26999
73	1962/63	06/10/62	Football League Division 1	Blackpool 2 Manchester United 2	Bloomfield Road	33242
74	1962/63	23/02/63	Football League Division 1	Manchester United 1 Blackpool 1	Old Trafford	43121
75	1963/64	11/09/63	Football League Division 1	Manchester United 3 Blackpool 0	Old Trafford	47400
76	1963/64	16/09/63	Football League Division 1	Blackpool 1 Manchester United 0	Bloomfield Road	29806
77	1964/65	14/11/64	Football League Division 1	Blackpool 1 Manchester United 2	Bloomfield Road	31129
78	1964/65	22/03/65	Football League Division 1	Manchester United 2 Blackpool 0	Old Trafford	42318
79	1965/66	30/10/65	Football League Division 1	Blackpool 1 Manchester United 2	Bloomfield Road	24703
80	1965/66	27/04/66	Football League Division 1	Manchester United 2 Blackpool 1	Old Trafford	26953
81	1966/67	14/09/66	League Cup 2nd Round	Blackpool 5 Manchester United 1	Bloomfield Road	15570
82	1966/67	08/10/66	Football League Division 1	Blackpool 1 Manchester United 2	Bloomfield Road	33555
83	1966/67	25/02/67	Football League Division 1	Manchester United 4 Blackpool 0	Old Trafford	47158
84	1970/71	26/09/70	Football League Division 1	Manchester United 1 Blackpool 1	Old Trafford	46647
85	1970/71	01/05/71	Football League Division 1	Blackpool 1 Manchester United 1	Bloomfield Road	29857
86	1974/75	19/10/74	Football League Division 2	Blackpool 0 Manchester United 3	Bloomfield Road	25370
87	1974/75	26/04/75	Football League Division 2	Manchester United 4 Blackpool 0	Old Trafford	58769

UNITED v BOAVISTA

CHAMPIONS LEAGUE						
VENUE	P	W	D	L	F	A
HOME	1	1	0	0	3	0
AWAY	1	1	0	0	3	0
TOTAL	2	2	0	0	6	0

#	SEASON	DATE	COMPETITION / ROUND	MATCH RESULT	VENUE	ATT
1	2001/02	05/12/01	Champions League Phase 2 Match 2	Manchester United 3 Boavista 0	Old Trafford	66274
2	2001/02	19/03/02	Champions League Phase 2 Match 6	Boavista 0 Manchester United 3	Estadio Do Bessa	13223

UNITED v BOLTON WANDERERS

ALL COMPETITIVE MATCHES

VENUE	P	W	D	L	F	A
HOME	57	31	10	16	102	60
AWAY	55	16	14	25	73	94
NEUTRAL	1	0	0	1	0	2
TOTAL	113	47	24	42	175	156

ALL LEAGUE MATCHES

VENUE	P	W	D	L	F	A
HOME	55	29	10	16	99	59
AWAY	55	16	14	25	73	94
TOTAL	108	44	24	40	172	153

FA CUP

VENUE	P	W	D	L	F	A
HOME	2	2	0	0	3	1
AWAY	0	0	0	0	0	0
NEUTRAL	1	0	0	1	0	2
TOTAL	3	2	0	1	3	3

PREMIERSHIP

VENUE	P	W	D	L	F	A
HOME	9	6	1	2	21	6
AWAY	9	5	3	1	21	6
TOTAL	18	11	4	3	42	12

LEAGUE DIVISION ONE

VENUE	P	W	D	L	F	A
HOME	40	22	8	10	72	41
AWAY	40	9	10	21	44	78
TOTAL	80	31	18	31	116	119

LEAGUE DIVISION TWO

VENUE	P	W	D	L	F	A
HOME	6	1	1	4	6	12
AWAY	6	2	1	3	8	10
TOTAL	12	3	2	7	14	22

#	SEASON	DATE	COMPETITION / ROUND	MATCH RESULT	VENUE	ATT
1	1892/93	03/12/92	Football League Division 1	Bolton Wanderers 4 Newton Heath 1	Pikes Lane	3000
2	1892/93	10/12/92	Football League Division 1	Newton Heath 1 Bolton Wanderers 0	North Road	4000
3	1893/94	09/12/93	Football League Division 1	Bolton Wanderers 2 Newton Heath 0	Pikes Lane	5000
4	1893/94	24/03/94	Football League Division 1	Newton Heath 2 Bolton Wanderers 2	Bank Street	10000
5	1899/00	09/09/99	Football League Division 2	Bolton Wanderers 2 Newton Heath 1	Burnden Park	5000
6	1899/00	06/01/00	Football League Division 2	Newton Heath 1 Bolton Wanderers 2	Bank Street	5000
7	1903/04	07/11/03	Football League Division 2	Manchester United 0 Bolton Wanderers 0	Bank Street	30000
8	1903/04	25/04/04	Football League Division 2	Bolton Wanderers 0 Manchester United 0	Burnden Park	10000
9	1904/05	17/09/04	Football League Division 2	Manchester United 1 Bolton Wanderers 2	Bank Street	25000
10	1904/05	03/01/05	Football League Division 2	Bolton Wanderers 2 Manchester United 4	Burnden Park	35000
11	1906/07	22/09/06	Football League Division 1	Manchester United 1 Bolton Wanderers 2	Bank Street	45000
12	1906/07	26/01/07	Football League Division 1	Bolton Wanderers 0 Manchester United 1	Burnden Park	25000
13	1907/08	26/10/07	Football League Division 1	Manchester United 2 Bolton Wanderers 1	Bank Street	35000
14	1907/08	22/04/08	Football League Division 1	Bolton Wanderers 2 Manchester United 2	Burnden Park	18000
15	1909/10	06/11/09	Football League Division 1	Bolton Wanderers 2 Manchester United 3	Burnden Park	20000
16	1909/10	19/03/10	Football League Division 1	Manchester United 5 Bolton Wanderers 0	Old Trafford	20000
17	1911/12	23/12/11	Football League Division 1	Manchester United 2 Bolton Wanderers 0	Old Trafford	20000
18	1911/12	27/04/12	Football League Division 1	Bolton Wanderers 1 Manchester United 1	Burnden Park	20000
19	1912/13	30/11/12	Football League Division 1	Bolton Wanderers 2 Manchester United 1	Burnden Park	25000
20	1912/13	05/04/13	Football League Division 1	Manchester United 2 Bolton Wanderers 1	Old Trafford	30000
21	1913/14	13/09/13	Football League Division 1	Manchester United 0 Bolton Wanderers 1	Old Trafford	45000
22	1913/14	03/01/14	Football League Division 1	Bolton Wanderers 6 Manchester United 1	Burnden Park	35000
23	1914/15	12/09/14	Football League Division 1	Bolton Wanderers 3 Manchester United 0	Burnden Park	10000
24	1914/15	16/01/15	Football League Division 1	Manchester United 4 Bolton Wanderers 1	Old Trafford	8000
25	1919/20	03/04/20	Football League Division 1	Manchester United 1 Bolton Wanderers 1	Old Trafford	39000
26	1919/20	10/04/20	Football League Division 1	Bolton Wanderers 3 Manchester United 5	Burnden Park	25000
27	1920/21	28/08/20	Football League Division 1	Manchester United 2 Bolton Wanderers 3	Old Trafford	50000
28	1920/21	04/09/20	Football League Division 1	Bolton Wanderers 1 Manchester United 1	Burnden Park	35000
29	1921/22	01/04/22	Football League Division 1	Manchester United 0 Bolton Wanderers 1	Old Trafford	28000
30	1921/22	08/04/22	Football League Division 1	Bolton Wanderers 1 Manchester United 0	Burnden Park	28000
31	1925/26	25/12/25	Football League Division 1	Manchester United 2 Bolton Wanderers 1	Old Trafford	38503
32	1925/26	17/03/26	Football League Division 1	Bolton Wanderers 3 Manchester United 1	Burnden Park	10794
33	1926/27	09/10/26	Football League Division 1	Bolton Wanderers 4 Manchester United 0	Burnden Park	17869
34	1926/27	26/02/27	Football League Division 1	Manchester United 0 Bolton Wanderers 0	Old Trafford	29618
35	1927/28	06/04/28	Football League Division 1	Bolton Wanderers 3 Manchester United 2	Burnden Park	23795
36	1927/28	09/04/28	Football League Division 1	Manchester United 2 Bolton Wanderers 1	Old Trafford	28590
37	1928/29	03/11/28	Football League Division 1	Manchester United 1 Bolton Wanderers 1	Old Trafford	31185
38	1928/29	16/03/29	Football League Division 1	Bolton Wanderers 1 Manchester United 1	Burnden Park	17354
39	1929/30	07/12/29	Football League Division 1	Manchester United 1 Bolton Wanderers 1	Old Trafford	5656
40	1929/30	01/03/30	Football League Division 1	Bolton Wanderers 4 Manchester United 1	Burnden Park	17714
41	1930/31	25/12/30	Football League Division 1	Bolton Wanderers 3 Manchester United 1	Burnden Park	22662
42	1930/31	26/12/30	Football League Division 1	Manchester United 1 Bolton Wanderers 1	Old Trafford	12741
43	1933/34	09/09/33	Football League Division 2	Manchester United 1 Bolton Wanderers 5	Old Trafford	21779
44	1933/34	20/01/34	Football League Division 2	Bolton Wanderers 3 Manchester United 1	Burnden Park	11887
45	1934/35	03/09/34	Football League Division 2	Bolton Wanderers 3 Manchester United 1	Burnden Park	16238
46	1934/35	12/09/34	Football League Division 2	Manchester United 0 Bolton Wanderers 3	Old Trafford	24760
47	1936/37	25/12/36	Football League Division 1	Manchester United 1 Bolton Wanderers 0	Old Trafford	47658
48	1936/37	28/12/36	Football League Division 1	Bolton Wanderers 0 Manchester United 4	Burnden Park	11801

UNITED v BOLTON WANDERERS (continued)

#	SEASON	DATE	COMPETITION / ROUND	MATCH RESULT	VENUE	ATT
49	1938/39	31/08/38	Football League Division 1	Manchester United 2 Bolton Wanderers 2	Old Trafford	37950
50	1938/39	29/04/39	Football League Division 1	Bolton Wanderers 0 Manchester United 0	Burnden Park	10314
51	1946/47	25/12/46	Football League Division 1	Bolton Wanderers 2 Manchester United 2	Burnden Park	28505
52	1946/47	26/12/46	Football League Division 1	Manchester United 1 Bolton Wanderers 0	Maine Road	57186
53	1947/48	26/03/48	Football League Division 1	Manchester United 0 Bolton Wanderers 2	Maine Road	71623
54	1947/48	29/03/48	Football League Division 1	Bolton Wanderers 0 Manchester United 1	Burnden Park	44225
55	1948/49	15/04/49	Football League Division 1	Bolton Wanderers 0 Manchester United 1	Burnden Park	44999
56	1948/49	18/04/49	Football League Division 1	Manchester United 3 Bolton Wanderers 0	Maine Road	47653
57	1949/50	24/08/49	Football League Division 1	Manchester United 3 Bolton Wanderers 0	Old Trafford	41748
58	1949/50	31/08/49	Football League Division 1	Bolton Wanderers 1 Manchester United 2	Burnden Park	36277
59	1950/51	26/08/50	Football League Division 1	Bolton Wanderers 1 Manchester United 0	Burnden Park	40431
60	1950/51	23/12/50	Football League Division 1	Manchester United 2 Bolton Wanderers 3	Old Trafford	35382
61	1951/52	01/09/51	Football League Division 1	Bolton Wanderers 1 Manchester United 0	Burnden Park	52239
62	1951/52	29/12/51	Football League Division 1	Manchester United 1 Bolton Wanderers 0	Old Trafford	53205
63	1952/53	13/09/52	Football League Division 1	Manchester United 1 Bolton Wanderers 0	Old Trafford	40531
64	1952/53	24/01/53	Football League Division 1	Bolton Wanderers 2 Manchester United 1	Burnden Park	43638
65	1953/54	12/09/53	Football League Division 1	Bolton Wanderers 0 Manchester United 0	Burnden Park	43544
66	1953/54	23/01/54	Football League Division 1	Manchester United 1 Bolton Wanderers 5	Old Trafford	46663
67	1954/55	11/09/54	Football League Division 1	Bolton Wanderers 1 Manchester United 1	Burnden Park	44661
68	1954/55	22/01/55	Football League Division 1	Manchester United 1 Bolton Wanderers 1	Old Trafford	39873
69	1955/56	12/11/55	Football League Division 1	Bolton Wanderers 3 Manchester United 1	Burnden Park	38109
70	1955/56	24/03/56	Football League Division 1	Manchester United 1 Bolton Wanderers 0	Old Trafford	46114
71	1956/57	10/11/56	Football League Division 1	Bolton Wanderers 2 Manchester United 0	Burnden Park	39922
72	1956/57	25/03/57	Football League Division 1	Manchester United 0 Bolton Wanderers 2	Old Trafford	60862
73	1957/58	14/09/57	Football League Division 1	Bolton Wanderers 4 Manchester United 0	Burnden Park	48003
74	1957/58	18/01/58	Football League Division 1	Manchester United 7 Bolton Wanderers 2	Old Trafford	41141
75	1957/58	03/05/58	FA Cup Final	Manchester United 0 Bolton Wanderers 2	Wembley	100000
76	1958/59	15/11/58	Football League Division 1	Bolton Wanderers 6 Manchester United 3	Burnden Park	33358
77	1958/59	04/04/59	Football League Division 1	Manchester United 3 Bolton Wanderers 0	Old Trafford	61528
78	1959/60	14/11/59	Football League Division 1	Bolton Wanderers 1 Manchester United 1	Burnden Park	37892
79	1959/60	02/04/60	Football League Division 1	Manchester United 2 Bolton Wanderers 0	Old Trafford	45298
80	1960/61	01/10/60	Football League Division 1	Bolton Wanderers 1 Manchester United 1	Burnden Park	39197
81	1960/61	18/02/61	Football League Division 1	Manchester United 3 Bolton Wanderers 1	Old Trafford	37558
82	1961/62	28/10/61	Football League Division 1	Manchester United 0 Bolton Wanderers 3	Old Trafford	31442
83	1961/62	06/01/62	FA Cup 3rd Round	Manchester United 2 Bolton Wanderers 1	Old Trafford	42202
84	1961/62	17/03/62	Football League Division 1	Bolton Wanderers 1 Manchester United 0	Burnden Park	34366
85	1962/63	05/09/62	Football League Division 1	Bolton Wanderers 3 Manchester United 0	Burnden Park	44859
86	1962/63	12/09/62	Football League Division 1	Manchester United 3 Bolton Wanderers 0	Old Trafford	37721
87	1963/64	05/10/63	Football League Division 1	Bolton Wanderers 0 Manchester United 1	Burnden Park	35872
88	1963/64	19/02/64	Football League Division 1	Manchester United 5 Bolton Wanderers 0	Old Trafford	33926
89	1974/75	25/09/74	Football League Division 2	Manchester United 3 Bolton Wanderers 0	Old Trafford	47084
90	1974/75	08/03/75	Football League Division 2	Bolton Wanderers 0 Manchester United 1	Burnden Park	38152
91	1978/79	22/12/78	Football League Division 1	Bolton Wanderers 3 Manchester United 0	Burnden Park	32390
92	1978/79	11/04/79	Football League Division 1	Manchester United 1 Bolton Wanderers 2	Old Trafford	49617
93	1979/80	27/02/80	Football League Division 1	Manchester United 2 Bolton Wanderers 0	Old Trafford	47546
94	1979/80	07/04/80	Football League Division 1	Bolton Wanderers 1 Manchester United 3	Burnden Park	31902
95	1990/91	26/01/91	FA Cup 4th Round	Manchester United 1 Bolton Wanderers 0	Old Trafford	43293
96	1995/96	16/09/95	FA Premiership	Manchester United 3 Bolton Wanderers 0	Old Trafford	32812
97	1995/96	25/02/96	FA Premiership	Bolton Wanderers 0 Manchester United 6	Burnden Park	21381
98	1997/98	20/09/97	FA Premiership	Bolton Wanderers 0 Manchester United 0	Reebok Stadium	25000
99	1997/98	07/02/98	FA Premiership	Manchester United 1 Bolton Wanderers 1	Old Trafford	55156
100	2001/02	20/10/01	FA Premiership	Manchester United 1 Bolton Wanderers 2	Old Trafford	67559
101	2001/02	29/01/02	FA Premiership	Bolton Wanderers 0 Manchester United 4	Reebok Stadium	27350
102	2002/03	11/09/02	FA Premiership	Manchester United 0 Bolton Wanderers 1	Old Trafford	67623
103	2002/03	22/02/03	FA Premiership	Bolton Wanderers 1 Manchester United 1	Reebok Stadium	27409
104	2003/04	16/08/03	FA Premiership	Manchester United 4 Bolton Wanderers 0	Old Trafford	67647
105	2003/04	07/01/04	FA Premiership	Bolton Wanderers 1 Manchester United 2	Reebok Stadium	27668
106	2004/05	11/09/04	FA Premiership	Bolton Wanderers 2 Manchester United 2	Reebok Stadium	27766
107	2004/05	26/12/04	FA Premiership	Manchester United 2 Bolton Wanderers 0	Old Trafford	67867
108	2005/06	31/12/05	FA Premiership	Manchester United 4 Bolton Wanderers 1	Old Trafford	67858
109	2005/06	01/04/06	FA Premiership	Bolton Wanderers 1 Manchester United 2	Reebok Stadium	27718

UNITED v BOLTON WANDERERS (continued)

#	SEASON	DATE	COMPETITION / ROUND	MATCH RESULT	VENUE	ATT
110	2006/07	28/10/06	FA Premiership	Bolton Wanderers 0 Manchester United 4	Reebok Stadium	27229
111	2006/07	17/03/07	FA Premiership	Manchester United 4 Bolton Wanderers 1	Old Trafford	76058
112	2007/08	24/11/07	FA Premiership	Bolton Wanderers 1 Manchester United 0	Reebok Stadium	25028
113	2007/08	19/03/08	FA Premiership	Manchester United 2 Bolton Wanderers 0	Old Trafford	75476

UNITED v BOOTLE RESERVES

FA CUP						
VENUE	P	W	D	L	F	A
HOME	0	0	0	0	0	0
AWAY	1	0	0	1	0	1
TOTAL	1	0	0	1	0	1

#	SEASON	DATE	COMPETITION / ROUND	MATCH RESULT	VENUE	ATT
1	1890/91	25/10/90	FA Cup 2nd Qualifying Round	Bootle Reserves 1 Newton Heath 0	Bootle Park	500

UNITED v BORUSSIA DORTMUND

ALL COMPETITIVE MATCHES							EUROPEAN CUP / CHAMPIONS LEAGUE							INTER-CITIES' FAIRS CUP						
VENUE	P	W	D	L	F	A	VENUE	P	W	D	L	F	A	VENUE	P	W	D	L	F	A
HOME	3	2	0	1	7	3	HOME	2	1	0	1	3	3	HOME	1	1	0	0	4	0
AWAY	3	1	1	1	6	2	AWAY	2	0	1	1	0	1	AWAY	1	1	0	0	6	1
TOTAL	6	3	1	2	13	5	TOTAL	2	1	1	2	3	4	TOTAL	2	2	0	0	10	1

#	SEASON	DATE	COMPETITION / ROUND	MATCH RESULT	VENUE	ATT
1	1956/57	17/10/56	European Cup 1st Round 1st Leg	Manchester United 3 Borussia Dortmund 2	Maine Road	75598
2	1956/57	21/11/56	European Cup 1st Round 2nd Leg	Borussia Dortmund 0 Manchester United 0	Rote Erde Stadion	44570
3	1964/65	11/11/64	Inter-Cities Fairs Cup 2nd Round 1st Leg	Borussia Dortmund 1 Manchester United 6	Rote Erde Stadion	25000
4	1964/65	02/12/64	Inter-Cities Fairs Cup 2nd Round 2nd Leg	Manchester United 4 Borussia Dortmund 0	Old Trafford	31896
5	1996/97	09/04/97	Champions League Semi-Final 1st Leg	Borussia Dortmund 1 Manchester United 0	Westfalenstadion	48500
6	1996/97	23/04/97	Champions League Semi-Final 2nd Leg	Manchester United 0 Borussia Dortmund 1	Old Trafford	53606

UNITED v BOURNEMOUTH

ALL COMPETITIVE MATCHES							FA CUP							LEAGUE CUP						
VENUE	P	W	D	L	F	A	VENUE	P	W	D	L	F	A	VENUE	P	W	D	L	F	A
HOME	4	4	0	0	12	0	HOME	3	3	0	0	10	0	HOME	1	1	0	0	2	0
AWAY	4	1	2	1	5	6	AWAY	3	1	1	1	3	4	AWAY	1	0	1	0	2	2
TOTAL	8	5	2	1	17	6	TOTAL	6	4	1	1	13	4	TOTAL	2	1	1	0	4	2

#	SEASON	DATE	COMPETITION / ROUND	MATCH RESULT	VENUE	ATT
1	1948/49	08/01/49	FA Cup 3rd Round	Manchester United 6 Bournemouth 0	Maine Road	55012
2	1956/57	02/03/57	FA Cup 6th Round	Bournemouth 1 Manchester United 2	Dean Court	28799
3	1982/83	06/10/82	League Cup 2nd Round 1st Leg	Manchester United 2 Bournemouth 0	Old Trafford	22091
4	1982/83	26/10/82	League Cup 2nd Round 2nd Leg	Bournemouth 2 Manchester United 2	Dean Court	13226
5	1983/84	07/01/84	FA Cup 3rd Round	Bournemouth 2 Manchester United 0	Dean Court	14782
6	1984/85	05/01/85	FA Cup 3rd Round	Manchester United 3 Bournemouth 0	Old Trafford	32080
7	1988/89	18/02/89	FA Cup 5th Round	Bournemouth 1 Manchester United 1	Dean Court	12708
8	1988/89	22/02/89	FA Cup 5th Round Replay	Manchester United 1 Bournemouth 0	Old Trafford	52422

UNITED v BRADFORD CITY

ALL COMPETITIVE MATCHES						
VENUE	P	W	D	L	F	A
HOME	25	17	6	2	51	10
AWAY	26	7	9	10	35	31
TOTAL	51	24	15	12	86	41

ALL LEAGUE MATCHES						
VENUE	P	W	D	L	F	A
HOME	23	15	6	2	45	9
AWAY	23	7	7	9	33	28
TOTAL	46	22	13	11	78	37

ALL CUP MATCHES						
VENUE	P	W	D	L	F	A
HOME	2	2	0	0	6	1
AWAY	3	0	2	1	2	3
TOTAL	5	2	2	1	8	4

PREMIERSHIP						
VENUE	P	W	D	L	F	A
HOME	2	2	0	0	10	0
AWAY	2	2	0	0	7	0
TOTAL	4	4	0	0	17	0

LEAGUE DIVISION ONE						
VENUE	P	W	D	L	F	A
HOME	10	5	4	1	10	4
AWAY	10	2	2	6	9	13
TOTAL	20	7	6	7	19	17

LEAGUE DIVISION TWO						
VENUE	P	W	D	L	F	A
HOME	11	8	2	1	25	5
AWAY	11	3	5	3	17	15
TOTAL	22	11	7	4	42	20

FA CUP						
VENUE	P	W	D	L	F	A
HOME	1	1	0	0	2	0
AWAY	1	0	1	0	1	1
TOTAL	2	1	1	0	3	1

LEAGUE CUP						
VENUE	P	W	D	L	F	A
HOME	1	1	0	0	4	1
AWAY	2	0	1	1	1	2
TOTAL	3	1	1	1	5	3

#	SEASON	DATE	COMPETITION / ROUND	MATCH RESULT	VENUE	ATT
1	1903/04	26/09/03	Football League Division 2	Manchester United 3 Bradford City 1	Bank Street	30000
2	1903/04	23/01/04	Football League Division 2	Bradford City 3 Manchester United 3	Valley Parade	12000
3	1904/05	08/10/04	Football League Division 2	Bradford City 1 Manchester United 1	Valley Parade	12000
4	1904/05	02/01/05	Football League Division 2	Manchester United 7 Bradford City 0	Bank Street	10000
5	1905/06	07/10/05	Football League Division 2	Manchester United 0 Bradford City 0	Bank Street	17000
6	1905/06	10/02/06	Football League Division 2	Bradford City 1 Manchester United 5	Valley Parade	8000
7	1908/09	21/11/08	Football League Division 1	Manchester United 2 Bradford City 0	Bank Street	15000
8	1908/09	29/04/09	Football League Division 1	Bradford City 1 Manchester United 0	Valley Parade	30000
9	1909/10	01/09/09	Football League Division 1	Manchester United 1 Bradford City 0	Bank Street	12000
10	1909/10	01/01/10	Football League Division 1	Bradford City 0 Manchester United 2	Valley Parade	25000
11	1910/11	27/12/10	Football League Division 1	Bradford City 1 Manchester United 0	Valley Parade	35000
12	1910/11	02/01/11	Football League Division 1	Manchester United 1 Bradford City 0	Old Trafford	40000
13	1911/12	25/12/11	Football League Division 1	Manchester United 0 Bradford City 1	Old Trafford	50000
14	1911/12	26/12/11	Football League Division 1	Bradford City 0 Manchester United 1	Valley Parade	40000
15	1912/13	01/01/13	Football League Division 1	Manchester United 2 Bradford City 0	Old Trafford	30000
16	1912/13	25/03/13	Football League Division 1	Bradford City 1 Manchester United 0	Valley Parade	25000
17	1913/14	13/12/13	Football League Division 1	Manchester United 1 Bradford City 1	Old Trafford	18000
18	1913/14	18/04/14	Football League Division 1	Bradford City 1 Manchester United 1	Valley Parade	10000
19	1914/15	07/11/14	Football League Division 1	Bradford City 4 Manchester United 2	Valley Parade	12000
20	1914/15	13/03/15	Football League Division 1	Manchester United 1 Bradford City 0	Old Trafford	14000
21	1919/20	20/03/20	Football League Division 1	Manchester United 0 Bradford City 0	Old Trafford	25000
22	1919/20	27/03/20	Football League Division 1	Bradford City 2 Manchester United 1	Valley Parade	18000
23	1920/21	12/03/21	Football League Division 1	Manchester United 1 Bradford City 1	Old Trafford	30000
24	1920/21	19/03/21	Football League Division 1	Bradford City 1 Manchester United 1	Valley Parade	25000
25	1921/22	03/12/21	Football League Division 1	Bradford City 2 Manchester United 1	Valley Parade	15000
26	1921/22	10/12/21	Football League Division 1	Manchester United 1 Bradford City 1	Old Trafford	9000
27	1922/23	13/01/23	FA Cup 1st Round	Bradford City 1 Manchester United 1	Valley Parade	27000
28	1922/23	17/01/23	FA Cup 1st Round Replay	Manchester United 2 Bradford City 0	Old Trafford	27791
29	1922/23	17/03/23	Football League Division 2	Bradford City 1 Manchester United 1	Valley Parade	10000
30	1922/23	21/03/23	Football League Division 2	Manchester United 1 Bradford City 1	Old Trafford	15000
31	1923/24	29/12/23	Football League Division 2	Bradford City 0 Manchester United 0	Valley Parade	11500
32	1923/24	05/01/24	Football League Division 2	Manchester United 3 Bradford City 0	Old Trafford	18000
33	1924/25	13/12/24	Football League Division 2	Manchester United 3 Bradford City 0	Old Trafford	18250
34	1924/25	18/04/25	Football League Division 2	Bradford City 0 Manchester United 1	Valley Parade	13250
35	1931/32	12/12/31	Football League Division 2	Bradford City 4 Manchester United 3	Valley Parade	13215
36	1931/32	23/04/32	Football League Division 2	Manchester United 1 Bradford City 0	Old Trafford	17765
37	1932/33	03/12/32	Football League Division 2	Manchester United 0 Bradford City 1	Old Trafford	28513
38	1932/33	15/04/33	Football League Division 2	Bradford City 1 Manchester United 2	Valley Parade	11195
39	1933/34	25/11/33	Football League Division 2	Manchester United 2 Bradford City 1	Old Trafford	20902
40	1933/34	07/04/34	Football League Division 2	Bradford City 1 Manchester United 1	Valley Parade	9258
41	1934/35	25/08/34	Football League Division 2	Manchester United 2 Bradford City 0	Old Trafford	27573
42	1934/35	29/12/34	Football League Division 2	Bradford City 2 Manchester United 0	Valley Parade	11908
43	1935/36	07/09/35	Football League Division 2	Manchester United 3 Bradford City 1	Old Trafford	30754
44	1935/36	04/01/36	Football League Division 2	Bradford City 1 Manchester United 0	Valley Parade	11286
45	1960/61	02/11/60	League Cup 2nd Round	Bradford City 2 Manchester United 1	Valley Parade	4670

UNITED v BRADFORD CITY (continued)

#	SEASON	DATE	COMPETITION / ROUND	MATCH RESULT	VENUE	ATT
46	1982/83	10/11/82	League Cup 3rd Round	Bradford City 0 Manchester United 0	Valley Parade	15568
47	1982/83	24/11/82	League Cup 3rd Round Replay	Manchester United 4 Bradford City 1	Old Trafford	24507
48	1999/00	26/12/99	FA Premiership	Manchester United 4 Bradford City 0	Old Trafford	55188
49	1999/00	25/03/00	FA Premiership	Bradford City 0 Manchester United 4	Valley Parade	18276
50	2000/01	05/09/00	FA Premiership	Manchester United 6 Bradford City 0	Old Trafford	67447
51	2000/01	13/01/01	FA Premiership	Bradford City 0 Manchester United 3	Valley Parade	20551

UNITED v BRADFORD PARK AVENUE

ALL COMPETITIVE MATCHES							ALL LEAGUE MATCHES							FA CUP						
VENUE	P	W	D	L	F	A	VENUE	P	W	D	L	F	A	VENUE	P	W	D	L	F	A
HOME	11	6	1	4	23	13	HOME	9	5	0	4	17	12	HOME	2	1	1	0	6	1
AWAY	11	4	2	5	17	25	AWAY	9	3	1	5	13	24	AWAY	2	1	1	0	4	1
TOTAL	22	10	3	9	40	38	TOTAL	18	8	1	9	30	36	TOTAL	4	2	2	0	10	2

LEAGUE DIVISION ONE							LEAGUE DIVISION TWO						
VENUE	P	W	D	L	F	A	VENUE	P	W	D	L	F	A
HOME	3	1	0	2	6	4	HOME	6	4	0	2	11	8
AWAY	3	2	0	1	8	8	AWAY	6	1	1	4	5	16
TOTAL	6	3	0	3	14	12	TOTAL	12	5	1	6	16	24

#	SEASON	DATE	COMPETITION / ROUND	MATCH RESULT	VENUE	ATT
1	1914/15	01/01/15	Football League Division 1	Manchester United 1 Bradford Park Avenue 2	Old Trafford	8000
2	1914/15	05/04/15	Football League Division 1	Bradford Park Avenue 5 Manchester United 0	Park Avenue	15000
3	1919/20	02/04/20	Football League Division 1	Manchester United 0 Bradford Park Avenue 1	Old Trafford	30000
4	1919/20	06/04/20	Football League Division 1	Bradford Park Avenue 1 Manchester United 4	Park Avenue	14000
5	1920/21	04/12/20	Football League Division 1	Manchester United 5 Bradford Park Avenue 1	Old Trafford	25000
6	1920/21	11/12/20	Football League Division 1	Bradford Park Avenue 2 Manchester United 4	Park Avenue	10000
7	1931/32	29/08/31	Football League Division 2	Bradford Park Avenue 3 Manchester United 1	Park Avenue	16239
8	1931/32	02/01/32	Football League Division 2	Manchester United 0 Bradford Park Avenue 2	Old Trafford	6056
9	1932/33	15/10/32	Football League Division 2	Manchester United 2 Bradford Park Avenue 1	Old Trafford	18918
10	1932/33	05/04/33	Football League Division 2	Bradford Park Avenue 1 Manchester United 1	Park Avenue	6314
11	1933/34	14/10/33	Football League Division 2	Bradford Park Avenue 6 Manchester United 1	Park Avenue	11033
12	1933/34	24/02/34	Football League Division 2	Manchester United 0 Bradford Park Avenue 4	Old Trafford	13389
13	1934/35	15/12/34	Football League Division 2	Bradford Park Avenue 1 Manchester United 2	Park Avenue	8405
14	1934/35	27/04/35	Football League Division 2	Manchester United 2 Bradford Park Avenue 0	Old Trafford	8606
15	1935/36	26/10/35	Football League Division 2	Bradford Park Avenue 1 Manchester United 0	Park Avenue	12216
16	1935/36	11/04/36	Football League Division 2	Manchester United 4 Bradford Park Avenue 0	Old Trafford	33517
17	1937/38	11/12/37	Football League Division 2	Bradford Park Avenue 4 Manchester United 0	Park Avenue	12004
18	1937/38	23/04/38	Football League Division 2	Manchester United 3 Bradford Park Avenue 1	Old Trafford	28919
19	1946/47	11/01/47	FA Cup 3rd Round	Bradford Park Avenue 0 Manchester United 3	Park Avenue	26990
20	1948/49	29/01/49	FA Cup 4th Round	Manchester United 1 Bradford Park Avenue 1	Maine Road	82771
21	1948/49	05/02/49	FA Cup 4th Round Replay	Bradford Park Avenue 1 Manchester United 1	Park Avenue	30000
22	1948/49	07/02/49	FA Cup 4th Round 2nd Replay	Manchester United 5 Bradford Park Avenue 0	Maine Road	70434

UNITED v BRENTFORD

ALL COMPETITIVE MATCHES							ALL LEAGUE MATCHES							ALL CUP MATCHES					
VENUE	P	W	D	L	F	A	VENUE	P	W	D	L	F	A	VENUE	P	W	D	L	F	A
HOME	7	4	1	2	18	9	HOME	5	2	1	2	9	7	HOME	2	2	0	0	9	2
AWAY	6	2	1	3	10	14	AWAY	5	2	1	2	10	12	AWAY	1	0	0	1	0	2
TOTAL	13	6	2	5	28	23	TOTAL	10	4	2	4	19	19	TOTAL	3	2	0	1	9	4

LEAGUE DIVISION ONE							LEAGUE DIVISION TWO						
VENUE	P	W	D	L	F	A	VENUE	P	W	D	L	F	A
HOME	3	2	0	1	8	4	HOME	2	0	1	1	1	3
AWAY	3	1	1	1	5	6	AWAY	2	1	0	1	5	6
TOTAL	6	3	1	2	13	10	TOTAL	4	1	1	2	6	9

FA CUP							LEAGUE CUP						
VENUE	P	W	D	L	F	A	VENUE	P	W	D	L	F	A
HOME	1	1	0	0	7	1	HOME	1	1	0	0	2	1
AWAY	1	0	0	1	0	2	AWAY	0	0	0	0	0	0
TOTAL	2	1	0	1	7	3	TOTAL	1	1	0	0	2	1

#	SEASON	DATE	COMPETITION / ROUND	MATCH RESULT	VENUE	ATT
1	1927/28	14/01/28	FA Cup 3rd Round	Manchester United 7 Brentford 1	Old Trafford	18538
2	1933/34	16/09/33	Football League Division 2	Brentford 3 Manchester United 4	Griffin Park	17180
3	1933/34	27/01/34	Football League Division 2	Manchester United 1 Brentford 3	Old Trafford	16891
4	1934/35	01/12/34	Football League Division 2	Brentford 3 Manchester United 1	Griffin Park	21744
5	1934/35	13/04/35	Football League Division 2	Manchester United 0 Brentford 0	Old Trafford	32969
6	1936/37	10/10/36	Football League Division 1	Brentford 4 Manchester United 0	Griffin Park	28019
7	1936/37	13/02/37	Football League Division 1	Manchester United 1 Brentford 3	Old Trafford	31942
8	1937/38	12/02/38	FA Cup 5th Round	Brentford 2 Manchester United 0	Griffin Park	24147
9	1938/39	17/12/38	Football League Division 1	Brentford 2 Manchester United 5	Griffin Park	14919
10	1938/39	22/04/39	Football League Division 1	Manchester United 3 Brentford 0	Old Trafford	15353
11	1946/47	07/12/46	Football League Division 1	Manchester United 4 Brentford 1	Maine Road	31962
12	1946/47	12/04/47	Football League Division 1	Brentford 0 Manchester United 0	Griffin Park	21714
13	1975/76	10/09/75	League Cup 2nd Round	Manchester United 2 Brentford 1	Old Trafford	25286

UNITED v BRIGHTON & HOVE ALBION

ALL COMPETITIVE MATCHES							LEAGUE DIVISION ONE							ALL CUP MATCHES					
VENUE	P	W	D	L	F	A	VENUE	P	W	D	L	F	A	VENUE	P	W	D	L	F	A
HOME	8	6	2	0	12	4	HOME	4	3	1	0	7	2	HOME	4	3	1	0	5	2
AWAY	6	3	2	1	8	3	AWAY	4	2	1	1	5	2	AWAY	2	1	1	0	3	1
NEUTRAL	2	1	1	0	6	2								NEUTRAL	2	1	1	0	6	2
TOTAL	16	10	5	1	26	9	TOTAL	8	5	2	1	12	4	TOTAL	8	5	3	0	14	5

FA CUP							LEAGUE CUP						
VENUE	P	W	D	L	F	A	VENUE	P	W	D	L	F	A
HOME	3	2	1	0	4	2	HOME	1	1	0	0	1	0
AWAY	1	1	0	0	2	0	AWAY	1	0	1	0	1	1
NEUTRAL	2	1	1	0	6	2							
TOTAL	6	4	2	0	12	4	TOTAL	2	1	1	0	2	1

#	SEASON	DATE	COMPETITION / ROUND	MATCH RESULT	VENUE	ATT
1	1908/09	16/01/09	FA Cup 1st Round	Manchester United 1 Brighton 0	Bank Street	8300
2	1979/80	06/10/79	Football League Division 1	Manchester United 2 Brighton 0	Old Trafford	52641
3	1979/80	15/03/80	Football League Division 1	Brighton 0 Manchester United 0	Goldstone Ground	29621
4	1980/81	22/11/80	Football League Division 1	Brighton 1 Manchester United 4	Goldstone Ground	23923
5	1980/81	03/01/81	FA Cup 3rd Round	Manchester United 2 Brighton 2	Old Trafford	42199
6	1980/81	07/01/81	FA Cup 3rd Round Replay	Brighton 0 Manchester United 2	Goldstone Ground	26915
7	1980/81	10/01/81	Football League Division 1	Manchester United 2 Brighton 1	Old Trafford	42208
8	1981/82	28/11/81	Football League Division 1	Manchester United 2 Brighton 0	Old Trafford	41911
9	1981/82	24/04/82	Football League Division 1	Brighton 0 Manchester United 1	Goldstone Ground	20750
10	1982/83	06/11/82	Football League Division 1	Brighton 1 Manchester United 0	Goldstone Ground	18379
11	1982/83	19/03/83	Football League Division 1	Manchester United 1 Brighton 1	Old Trafford	36264
12	1982/83	21/05/83	FA Cup Final	Manchester United 2 Brighton 2	Wembley	100000
13	1982/83	26/05/83	FA Cup Final Replay	Manchester United 4 Brighton 0	Wembley	92000
14	1992/93	23/09/92	League Cup 2nd Round 1st Leg	Brighton 1 Manchester United 1	Goldstone Ground	16649
15	1992/93	07/10/92	League Cup 2nd Round 2nd Leg	Manchester United 1 Brighton 0	Old Trafford	25405
16	1992/93	23/01/93	FA Cup 4th Round	Manchester United 1 Brighton 0	Old Trafford	33600

UNITED v BRISTOL CITY

ALL COMPETITIVE MATCHES							ALL LEAGUE MATCHES							FA CUP					
VENUE	P	W	D	L	F	A	VENUE	P	W	D	L	F	A	VENUE	P	W	D	L	F	A
HOME	17	9	3	5	30	18	HOME	17	9	3	5	30	18	HOME	0	0	0	0	0	0
AWAY	17	5	7	5	17	21	AWAY	17	5	7	5	17	21	AWAY	0	0	0	0	0	0
NEUTRAL	1	1	0	0	1	0								NEUTRAL	1	1	0	0	1	0
TOTAL	35	15	10	10	48	39	TOTAL	34	14	10	10	47	39	TOTAL	1	1	0	0	1	0

LEAGUE DIVISION ONE							LEAGUE DIVISION TWO						
VENUE	P	W	D	L	F	A	VENUE	P	W	D	L	F	A
HOME	9	5	2	2	15	9	HOME	8	4	1	3	15	9
AWAY	9	4	4	1	10	7	AWAY	8	1	3	4	7	14
TOTAL	18	9	6	3	25	16	TOTAL	16	5	4	7	22	23

#	SEASON	DATE	COMPETITION / ROUND	MATCH RESULT	VENUE	ATT
1	1901/02	21/09/01	Football League Division 2	Newton Heath 1 Bristol City 0	Bank Street	5000
2	1901/02	18/01/02	Football League Division 2	Bristol City 4 Newton Heath 0	Ashton Gate	6000
3	1902/03	20/09/02	Football League Division 2	Bristol City 3 Manchester United 1	Ashton Gate	6000
4	1902/03	17/01/03	Football League Division 2	Manchester United 1 Bristol City 2	Bank Street	12000
5	1903/04	05/09/03	Football League Division 2	Manchester United 2 Bristol City 2	Bank Street	40000
6	1903/04	02/01/04	Football League Division 2	Bristol City 1 Manchester United 1	Ashton Gate	8000
7	1904/05	10/09/04	Football League Division 2	Manchester United 4 Bristol City 1	Bank Street	20000
8	1904/05	07/01/05	Football League Division 2	Bristol City 1 Manchester United 1	Ashton Gate	12000
9	1905/06	02/09/05	Football League Division 2	Manchester United 5 Bristol City 1	Bank Street	25000
10	1905/06	30/12/05	Football League Division 2	Bristol City 1 Manchester United 1	Ashton Gate	18000
11	1906/07	01/09/06	Football League Division 1	Bristol City 1 Manchester United 2	Ashton Gate	5000
12	1906/07	29/12/06	Football League Division 1	Manchester United 0 Bristol City 0	Bank Street	10000
13	1907/08	07/12/07	Football League Division 1	Manchester United 2 Bristol City 1	Bank Street	20000
14	1907/08	04/04/08	Football League Division 1	Bristol City 1 Manchester United 1	Ashton Gate	12000
15	1908/09	09/04/09	Football League Division 1	Manchester United 0 Bristol City 0	Bank Street	18000
16	1908/09	12/04/09	Football League Division 1	Bristol City 0 Manchester United 0	Ashton Gate	18000
17	1908/09	24/04/09	FA Cup Final	Manchester United 1 Bristol City 0	Crystal Palace	71401
18	1909/10	25/03/10	Football League Division 1	Manchester United 2 Bristol City 1	Old Trafford	50000
19	1909/10	28/03/10	Football League Division 1	Bristol City 2 Manchester United 1	Ashton Gate	18000
20	1910/11	08/10/10	Football League Division 1	Bristol City 0 Manchester United 1	Ashton Gate	20000
21	1910/11	11/02/11	Football League Division 1	Manchester United 3 Bristol City 1	Old Trafford	14000
22	1923/24	25/08/23	Football League Division 2	Bristol City 1 Manchester United 2	Ashton Gate	20500
23	1923/24	01/09/23	Football League Division 2	Manchester United 2 Bristol City 1	Old Trafford	21000
24	1931/32	19/12/31	Football League Division 2	Manchester United 0 Bristol City 1	Old Trafford	4697
25	1931/32	30/04/32	Football League Division 2	Bristol City 2 Manchester United 1	Ashton Gate	5874
26	1974/75	09/11/74	Football League Division 2	Bristol City 1 Manchester United 0	Ashton Gate	28104
27	1974/75	01/02/75	Football League Division 2	Manchester United 0 Bristol City 1	Old Trafford	47118
28	1976/77	19/01/77	Football League Division 1	Manchester United 2 Bristol City 1	Old Trafford	43051
29	1976/77	07/05/77	Football League Division 1	Bristol City 1 Manchester United 1	Ashton Gate	28864
30	1977/78	08/02/78	Football League Division 1	Manchester United 1 Bristol City 1	Old Trafford	43457
31	1977/78	25/04/78	Football League Division 1	Bristol City 0 Manchester United 1	Ashton Gate	26035
32	1978/79	21/10/78	Football League Division 1	Manchester United 1 Bristol City 3	Old Trafford	47211
33	1978/79	03/03/79	Football League Division 1	Bristol City 1 Manchester United 2	Ashton Gate	24583
34	1979/80	13/10/79	Football League Division 1	Bristol City 1 Manchester United 1	Ashton Gate	28305
35	1979/80	23/02/80	Football League Division 1	Manchester United 4 Bristol City 0	Old Trafford	43329

UNITED v BRISTOL ROVERS

ALL COMPETITIVE MATCHES							LEAGUE DIVISION TWO							ALL CUP MATCHES					
VENUE	P	W	D	L	F	A	VENUE	P	W	D	L	F	A	VENUE	P	W	D	L	F	A
HOME	3	2	0	1	7	3	HOME	1	1	0	0	2	0	HOME	2	1	0	1	5	3
AWAY	4	1	2	1	5	7	AWAY	1	0	1	0	1	1	AWAY	3	1	1	1	4	6
TOTAL	7	3	2	2	12	10	TOTAL	2	1	1	0	3	1	TOTAL	5	2	1	2	9	9

FA CUP							LEAGUE CUP						
VENUE	P	W	D	L	F	A	VENUE	P	W	D	L	F	A
HOME	1	1	0	0	4	1	HOME	1	0	0	1	1	2
AWAY	2	1	0	1	3	5	AWAY	1	0	1	0	1	1
TOTAL	3	2	0	1	7	6	TOTAL	2	0	1	1	2	3

#	SEASON	DATE	COMPETITION / ROUND	MATCH RESULT	VENUE	ATT
1	1934/35	12/01/35	FA Cup 3rd Round	Bristol Rovers 1 Manchester United 3	Eastville	20400
2	1955/56	07/01/56	FA Cup 3rd Round	Bristol Rovers 4 Manchester United 0	Eastville	35872
3	1963/64	25/01/64	FA Cup 4th Round	Manchester United 4 Bristol Rovers 1	Old Trafford	55772
4	1972/73	03/10/72	League Cup 3rd Round	Bristol Rovers 1 Manchester United 1	Eastville	33957
5	1972/73	11/10/72	League Cup 3rd Round Replay	Manchester United 1 Bristol Rovers 2	Old Trafford	29349
6	1974/75	21/09/74	Football League Division 2	Manchester United 2 Bristol Rovers 0	Old Trafford	42948
7	1974/75	28/03/75	Football League Division 2	Bristol Rovers 1 Manchester United 1	Eastville	19337

UNITED v BRONDBY

CHAMPIONS LEAGUE						
VENUE	P	W	D	L	F	A
HOME	1	1	0	0	5	0
AWAY	1	1	0	0	6	2
TOTAL	2	2	0	0	11	2

#	SEASON	DATE	COMPETITION / ROUND	MATCH RESULT	VENUE	ATT
1	1998/99	21/10/98	Champions League Phase 1 Match 3	Brondby 2 Manchester United 6	Parken Stadion	40530
2	1998/99	04/11/98	Champions League Phase 1 Match 4	Manchester United 5 Brondby 0	Old Trafford	53250

UNITED v BURNLEY

ALL COMPETITIVE MATCHES							ALL LEAGUE MATCHES							ALL CUP MATCHES					
VENUE	P	W	D	L	F	A	VENUE	P	W	D	L	F	A	VENUE	P	W	D	L	F	A
HOME	58	35	10	13	129	70	HOME	51	30	8	13	116	66	HOME	6	4	2	0	11	4
AWAY	60	21	9	30	77	109	AWAY	51	17	8	26	64	91	AWAY	8	4	1	3	13	16
TOTAL	118	56	19	43	206	179	TOTAL	102	47	16	39	180	157	TOTAL	14	8	3	3	24	20

LEAGUE DIVISION ONE							LEAGUE DIVISION TWO							FA CUP					
VENUE	P	W	D	L	F	A	VENUE	P	W	D	L	F	A	VENUE	P	W	D	L	F	A
HOME	38	20	7	11	82	56	HOME	13	10	1	2	34	10	HOME	2	1	1	0	2	1
AWAY	38	12	7	19	45	69	AWAY	13	5	1	7	19	22	AWAY	4	1	0	3	7	16
TOTAL	76	32	14	30	127	125	TOTAL	26	15	2	9	53	32	TOTAL	6	2	1	3	9	17

LEAGUE CUP							OTHER MATCHES						
VENUE	P	W	D	L	F	A	VENUE	P	W	D	L	F	A
HOME	4	3	1	0	9	3	HOME	1	1	0	0	2	0
AWAY	4	3	1	0	6	0	AWAY	1	0	0	1	0	2
TOTAL	8	6	2	0	15	3	TOTAL	2	1	0	1	2	2

#	SEASON	DATE	COMPETITION / ROUND	MATCH RESULT	VENUE	ATT
1	1892/93	10/09/92	Football League Division 1	Newton Heath 1 Burnley 1	North Road	10000
2	1892/93	17/09/92	Football League Division 1	Burnley 4 Newton Heath 1	Turf Moor	7000
3	1893/94	02/09/93	Football League Division 1	Newton Heath 3 Burnley 2	North Road	10000
4	1893/94	21/10/93	Football League Division 1	Burnley 4 Newton Heath 1	Turf Moor	7000
5	1896/97	19/04/97	Football League Test Match	Burnley 2 Newton Heath 0	Turf Moor	10000
6	1896/97	21/04/97	Football League Test Match	Newton Heath 2 Burnley 0	Bank Street	7000
7	1897/98	12/01/98	Football League Division 2	Newton Heath 0 Burnley 0	Bank Street	7000
8	1897/98	07/03/98	Football League Division 2	Burnley 6 Newton Heath 3	Turf Moor	3000

UNITED v BURNLEY (continued)

#	SEASON	DATE	COMPETITION / ROUND	MATCH RESULT	VENUE	ATT
9	1900/01	15/09/00	Football League Division 2	Burnley 1 Newton Heath 0	Turf Moor	4000
10	1900/01	12/01/01	Football League Division 2	Newton Heath 0 Burnley 1	Bank Street	10000
11	1900/01	09/02/01	FA Cup 1st Round	Newton Heath 0 Burnley 0	Bank Street	8000
12	1900/01	13/02/01	FA Cup 1st Round Replay	Burnley 7 Newton Heath 1	Turf Moor	4000
13	1901/02	11/02/02	Football League Division 2	Newton Heath 2 Burnley 0	Bank Street	1000
14	1901/02	28/03/02	Football League Division 2	Burnley 1 Newton Heath 0	Turf Moor	3000
15	1902/03	06/12/02	Football League Division 2	Burnley 0 Manchester United 2	Turf Moor	4000
16	1902/03	04/04/03	Football League Division 2	Manchester United 4 Burnley 0	Bank Street	5000
17	1903/04	07/09/03	Football League Division 2	Burnley 2 Manchester United 0	Turf Moor	5000
18	1903/04	12/03/04	Football League Division 2	Manchester United 3 Burnley 1	Bank Street	14000
19	1904/05	12/11/04	Football League Division 2	Manchester United 1 Burnley 0	Bank Street	15000
20	1904/05	11/03/05	Football League Division 2	Burnley 2 Manchester United 0	Turf Moor	7000
21	1905/06	09/12/05	Football League Division 2	Burnley 1 Manchester United 3	Turf Moor	8000
22	1905/06	14/04/06	Football League Division 2	Manchester United 1 Burnley 0	Bank Street	12000
23	1908/09	10/03/09	FA Cup 4th Round	Burnley 2 Manchester United 3	Turf Moor	16850
24	1909/10	15/01/10	FA Cup 1st Round	Burnley 2 Manchester United 0	Turf Moor	16628
25	1913/14	11/10/13	Football League Division 1	Burnley 1 Manchester United 2	Turf Moor	30000
26	1913/14	14/02/14	Football League Division 1	Manchester United 0 Burnley 1	Old Trafford	35000
27	1914/15	14/11/14	Football League Division 1	Manchester United 0 Burnley 2	Old Trafford	12000
28	1914/15	20/03/15	Football League Division 1	Burnley 3 Manchester United 0	Turf Moor	12000
29	1919/20	08/11/19	Football League Division 1	Burnley 2 Manchester United 1	Turf Moor	15000
30	1919/20	15/11/19	Football League Division 1	Manchester United 0 Burnley 1	Old Trafford	25000
31	1920/21	25/03/21	Football League Division 1	Burnley 1 Manchester United 0	Turf Moor	20000
32	1920/21	28/03/21	Football League Division 1	Manchester United 0 Burnley 3	Old Trafford	28000
33	1921/22	26/12/21	Football League Division 1	Manchester United 0 Burnley 1	Old Trafford	15000
34	1921/22	27/12/21	Football League Division 1	Burnley 4 Manchester United 2	Turf Moor	10000
35	1925/26	26/09/25	Football League Division 1	Manchester United 6 Burnley 1	Old Trafford	17259
36	1925/26	06/02/26	Football League Division 1	Burnley 0 Manchester United 1	Turf Moor	17141
37	1926/27	18/09/26	Football League Division 1	Manchester United 2 Burnley 1	Old Trafford	32593
38	1926/27	05/02/27	Football League Division 1	Burnley 1 Manchester United 0	Turf Moor	22010
39	1927/28	26/11/27	Football League Division 1	Burnley 4 Manchester United 0	Turf Moor	18509
40	1927/28	07/04/28	Football League Division 1	Manchester United 4 Burnley 3	Old Trafford	28311
41	1928/29	06/10/28	Football League Division 1	Burnley 3 Manchester United 4	Turf Moor	17493
42	1928/29	16/02/29	Football League Division 1	Manchester United 1 Burnley 0	Old Trafford	12516
43	1929/30	23/11/29	Football League Division 1	Manchester United 1 Burnley 0	Old Trafford	9060
44	1929/30	29/03/30	Football League Division 1	Burnley 4 Manchester United 0	Turf Moor	11659
45	1931/32	03/10/31	Football League Division 2	Burnley 2 Manchester United 0	Turf Moor	9719
46	1931/32	17/02/32	Football League Division 2	Manchester United 5 Burnley 1	Old Trafford	11036
47	1932/33	08/10/32	Football League Division 2	Burnley 2 Manchester United 3	Turf Moor	5314
48	1932/33	22/02/33	Football League Division 2	Manchester United 2 Burnley 1	Old Trafford	18533
49	1933/34	23/09/33	Football League Division 2	Manchester United 5 Burnley 2	Old Trafford	18411
50	1933/34	03/02/34	Football League Division 2	Burnley 1 Manchester United 4	Turf Moor	9906
51	1934/35	06/10/34	Football League Division 2	Burnley 1 Manchester United 2	Turf Moor	16757
52	1934/35	27/03/35	Football League Division 2	Manchester United 3 Burnley 4	Old Trafford	10247
53	1935/36	10/04/36	Football League Division 2	Burnley 2 Manchester United 2	Turf Moor	27245
54	1935/36	13/04/36	Football League Division 2	Manchester United 4 Burnley 0	Old Trafford	39855
55	1937/38	15/04/38	Football League Division 2	Burnley 1 Manchester United 0	Turf Moor	28459
56	1937/38	18/04/38	Football League Division 2	Manchester United 4 Burnley 0	Old Trafford	35808
57	1947/48	08/09/47	Football League Division 1	Burnley 0 Manchester United 0	Turf Moor	37517
58	1947/48	01/01/48	Football League Division 1	Manchester United 5 Burnley 0	Maine Road	59838
59	1948/49	23/10/48	Football League Division 1	Manchester United 1 Burnley 1	Maine Road	47093
60	1948/49	16/04/49	Football League Division 1	Burnley 0 Manchester United 2	Turf Moor	37722
61	1949/50	24/09/49	Football League Division 1	Burnley 1 Manchester United 0	Turf Moor	41072
62	1949/50	04/02/50	Football League Division 1	Manchester United 3 Burnley 2	Old Trafford	46702
63	1950/51	04/11/50	Football League Division 1	Manchester United 1 Burnley 1	Old Trafford	39454
64	1950/51	24/03/51	Football League Division 1	Burnley 1 Manchester United 2	Turf Moor	36656
65	1951/52	11/04/52	Football League Division 1	Burnley 1 Manchester United 1	Turf Moor	38907
66	1951/52	14/04/52	Football League Division 1	Manchester United 6 Burnley 1	Old Trafford	44508
67	1952/53	25/10/52	Football League Division 1	Manchester United 1 Burnley 3	Old Trafford	36913
68	1952/53	14/03/53	Football League Division 1	Burnley 2 Manchester United 1	Turf Moor	45682

UNITED v BURNLEY (continued)

#	SEASON	DATE	COMPETITION / ROUND	MATCH RESULT	VENUE	ATT
69	1953/54	03/10/53	Football League Division 1	Manchester United 1 Burnley 2	Old Trafford	37696
70	1953/54	09/01/54	FA Cup 3rd Round	Burnley 5 Manchester United 3	Turf Moor	54000
71	1953/54	20/02/54	Football League Division 1	Burnley 2 Manchester United 0	Turf Moor	29576
72	1954/55	11/12/54	Football League Division 1	Burnley 2 Manchester United 4	Turf Moor	24977
73	1954/55	05/03/55	Football League Division 1	Manchester United 1 Burnley 0	Old Trafford	31729
74	1955/56	24/09/55	Football League Division 1	Burnley 0 Manchester United 0	Turf Moor	26873
75	1955/56	04/02/56	Football League Division 1	Manchester United 2 Burnley 0	Old Trafford	27342
76	1956/57	19/04/57	Football League Division 1	Burnley 1 Manchester United 3	Turf Moor	41321
77	1956/57	22/04/57	Football League Division 1	Manchester United 2 Burnley 0	Old Trafford	41321
78	1957/58	02/11/57	Football League Division 1	Manchester United 1 Burnley 0	Old Trafford	49449
79	1957/58	15/03/58	Football League Division 1	Burnley 3 Manchester United 0	Turf Moor	37247
80	1958/59	08/11/58	Football League Division 1	Manchester United 1 Burnley 3	Old Trafford	48509
81	1958/59	28/03/59	Football League Division 1	Burnley 4 Manchester United 2	Turf Moor	44577
82	1959/60	26/12/59	Football League Division 1	Manchester United 1 Burnley 2	Old Trafford	62376
83	1959/60	28/12/59	Football League Division 1	Burnley 1 Manchester United 4	Turf Moor	47253
84	1960/61	15/10/60	Football League Division 1	Burnley 5 Manchester United 3	Turf Moor	32011
85	1960/61	12/04/61	Football League Division 1	Manchester United 6 Burnley 0	Old Trafford	25019
86	1961/62	25/11/61	Football League Division 1	Manchester United 1 Burnley 4	Old Trafford	41029
87	1961/62	14/04/62	Football League Division 1	Burnley 1 Manchester United 3	Turf Moor	36240
88	1962/63	22/09/62	Football League Division 1	Manchester United 2 Burnley 5	Old Trafford	45954
89	1962/63	04/05/63	Football League Division 1	Burnley 0 Manchester United 1	Turf Moor	30266
90	1963/64	26/12/63	Football League Division 1	Burnley 6 Manchester United 1	Turf Moor	35764
91	1963/64	28/12/63	Football League Division 1	Manchester United 5 Burnley 1	Old Trafford	47834
92	1964/65	03/10/64	Football League Division 1	Burnley 0 Manchester United 0	Turf Moor	30761
93	1964/65	13/02/65	Football League Division 1	Manchester United 3 Burnley 2	Old Trafford	38865
94	1964/65	20/02/65	FA Cup 5th Round	Manchester United 2 Burnley 1	Old Trafford	54000
95	1965/66	11/09/65	Football League Division 1	Burnley 3 Manchester United 0	Turf Moor	30235
96	1965/66	26/02/66	Football League Division 1	Manchester United 4 Burnley 2	Old Trafford	49892
97	1966/67	24/09/66	Football League Division 1	Manchester United 4 Burnley 1	Old Trafford	52697
98	1966/67	04/02/67	Football League Division 1	Burnley 1 Manchester United 1	Turf Moor	40165
99	1967/68	09/09/67	Football League Division 1	Manchester United 2 Burnley 2	Old Trafford	55809
100	1967/68	17/02/68	Football League Division 1	Burnley 2 Manchester United 1	Turf Moor	31965
101	1968/69	14/09/68	Football League Division 1	Burnley 1 Manchester United 0	Turf Moor	32935
102	1968/69	19/04/69	Football League Division 1	Manchester United 2 Burnley 0	Old Trafford	52626
103	1969/70	14/10/69	League Cup 4th Round	Burnley 0 Manchester United 0	Turf Moor	27959
104	1969/70	20/10/69	League Cup 4th Round Replay	Manchester United 1 Burnley 0	Old Trafford	50275
105	1969/70	29/11/69	Football League Division 1	Burnley 1 Manchester United 1	Turf Moor	23770
106	1969/70	17/03/70	Football League Division 1	Manchester United 3 Burnley 3	Old Trafford	38377
107	1970/71	25/08/70	Football League Division 1	Burnley 0 Manchester United 2	Turf Moor	29385
108	1970/71	16/01/71	Football League Division 1	Manchester United 1 Burnley 1	Old Trafford	40135
109	1971/72	06/10/71	League Cup 3rd Round	Manchester United 1 Burnley 1	Old Trafford	44600
110	1971/72	18/10/71	League Cup 3rd Round Replay	Burnley 0 Manchester United 1	Turf Moor	27511
111	1973/74	27/10/73	Football League Division 1	Burnley 0 Manchester United 0	Turf Moor	31976
112	1973/74	03/04/74	Football League Division 1	Manchester United 3 Burnley 3	Old Trafford	33336
113	1974/75	13/11/74	League Cup 4th Round	Manchester United 3 Burnley 2	Old Trafford	46275
114	1975/76	27/12/75	Football League Division 1	Manchester United 2 Burnley 1	Old Trafford	59726
115	1975/76	19/04/76	Football League Division 1	Burnley 0 Manchester United 1	Turf Moor	27418
116	1984/85	26/09/84	League Cup 2nd Round 1st Leg	Manchester United 4 Burnley 0	Old Trafford	28383
117	1984/85	09/10/84	League Cup 2nd Round 2nd Leg	Burnley 0 Manchester United 3	Turf Moor	12690
118	2002/03	03/12/02	League Cup 4th Round	Burnley 0 Manchester United 2	Turf Moor	22034

UNITED v BURTON ALBION

FA CUP						
VENUE	P	W	D	L	F	A
HOME	1	1	0	0	5	0
AWAY	1	0	1	0	0	0
TOTAL	2	1	1	0	5	0

#	SEASON	DATE	COMPETITION / ROUND	MATCH RESULT	VENUE	ATT
1	2005/06	08/01/06	FA Cup 3rd Round	Burton Albion 0 Manchester United 0	Pirelli Stadium	6191
2	2005/06	18/01/06	FA Cup 3rd Round Replay	Manchester United 5 Burton Albion 0	Old Trafford	53564

UNITED v BURTON SWIFTS

LEAGUE DIVISION TWO

VENUE	P	W	D	L	F	A
HOME	7	4	3	0	22	5
AWAY	7	3	1	3	14	16
TOTAL	14	7	4	3	36	21

#	SEASON	DATE	COMPETITION / ROUND	MATCH RESULT	VENUE	ATT
1	1894/95	20/10/94	Football League Division 2	Burton Swifts 1 Newton Heath 2	Peel Croft	5000
2	1894/95	08/12/94	Football League Division 2	Newton Heath 5 Burton Swifts 1	Bank Street	4000
3	1895/96	21/09/95	Football League Division 2	Newton Heath 5 Burton Swifts 0	Bank Street	9000
4	1895/96	08/02/96	Football League Division 2	Burton Swifts 4 Newton Heath 1	Peel Croft	2000
5	1896/97	05/09/96	Football League Division 2	Burton Swifts 3 Newton Heath 5	Peel Croft	3000
6	1896/97	09/01/97	Football League Division 2	Newton Heath 1 Burton Swifts 1	Bank Street	3000
7	1897/98	11/09/97	Football League Division 2	Burton Swifts 0 Newton Heath 4	Peel Croft	2000
8	1897/98	01/01/98	Football League Division 2	Newton Heath 4 Burton Swifts 0	Bank Street	6000
9	1898/99	01/10/98	Football League Division 2	Burton Swifts 5 Newton Heath 1	Peel Croft	2000
10	1898/99	02/01/99	Football League Division 2	Newton Heath 2 Burton Swifts 2	Bank Street	6000
11	1899/00	23/09/99	Football League Division 2	Burton Swifts 0 Newton Heath 0	Peel Croft	2000
12	1899/00	20/01/00	Football League Division 2	Newton Heath 4 Burton Swifts 0	Bank Street	4000
13	1900/01	27/10/00	Football League Division 2	Burton Swifts 3 Newton Heath 1	Peel Croft	2000
14	1900/01	02/03/01	Football League Division 2	Newton Heath 1 Burton Swifts 1	Bank Street	5000

UNITED v BURTON UNITED

ALL COMPETITIVE MATCHES							LEAGUE DIVISION TWO							FA CUP						
VENUE	P	W	D	L	F	A	VENUE	P	W	D	L	F	A	VENUE	P	W	D	L	F	A
HOME	6	5	1	0	18	2	HOME	5	5	0	0	17	1	HOME	1	0	1	0	1	1
AWAY	6	3	2	1	11	8	AWAY	5	2	2	1	8	7	AWAY	1	1	0	0	3	1
TOTAL	12	8	3	1	29	10	TOTAL	10	7	2	1	25	8	TOTAL	2	1	1	0	4	2

#	SEASON	DATE	COMPETITION / ROUND	MATCH RESULT	VENUE	ATT
1	1901/02	12/10/01	Football League Division 2	Burton United 0 Newton Heath 0	Peel Croft	3000
2	1901/02	21/04/02	Football League Division 2	Newton Heath 3 Burton United 1	Bank Street	500
3	1902/03	13/09/02	Football League Division 2	Manchester United 1 Burton United 0	Bank Street	15000
4	1902/03	13/12/02	FA Cup Intermediate Round	Manchester United 1 Burton United 1	Bank Street	6000
5	1902/03	17/12/02	FA Cup Intermediate Round Replay	Burton United 1 Manchester United 3 (Replay venue switched to Bank Street)	Bank Street	7000
6	1902/03	10/01/03	Football League Division 2	Burton United 3 Manchester United 1	Peel Croft	3000
7	1903/04	26/12/03	Football League Division 2	Burton United 2 Manchester United 2	Peel Croft	4000
8	1903/04	23/04/04	Football League Division 2	Manchester United 2 Burton United 0	Bank Street	8000
9	1904/05	17/12/04	Football League Division 2	Burton United 2 Manchester United 3	Peel Croft	3000
10	1904/05	15/04/05	Football League Division 2	Manchester United 5 Burton United 0	Bank Street	16000
11	1905/06	23/12/05	Football League Division 2	Burton United 0 Manchester United 2	Peel Croft	5000
12	1905/06	28/04/06	Football League Division 2	Manchester United 6 Burton United 0	Bank Street	16000

UNITED v BURTON WANDERERS

LEAGUE DIVISION TWO

VENUE	P	W	D	L	F	A
HOME	3	1	1	1	5	3
AWAY	3	1	0	2	3	7
TOTAL	6	2	1	3	8	10

#	SEASON	DATE	COMPETITION / ROUND	MATCH RESULT	VENUE	ATT
1	1894/95	08/09/94	Football League Division 2	Burton Wanderers 1 Newton Heath 0	Derby Turn	3000
2	1894/95	02/03/95	Football League Division 2	Newton Heath 1 Burton Wanderers 1	Bank Street	6000
3	1895/96	29/02/96	Football League Division 2	Newton Heath 1 Burton Wanderers 2	Bank Street	1000
4	1895/96	18/03/96	Football League Division 2	Burton Wanderers 5 Newton Heath 1	Derby Turn	2000
5	1896/97	24/10/96	Football League Division 2	Newton Heath 3 Burton Wanderers 0	Bank Street	4000
6	1896/97	20/03/97	Football League Division 2	Burton Wanderers 1 Newton Heath 2	Derby Turn	3000

UNITED v BURY

ALL COMPETITIVE MATCHES						
VENUE	P	W	D	L	F	A
HOME	23	12	2	9	29	24
AWAY	21	11	6	4	37	25
TOTAL	44	23	8	13	66	49

ALL LEAGUE MATCHES						
VENUE	P	W	D	L	F	A
HOME	19	9	2	8	24	23
AWAY	19	10	5	4	34	23
TOTAL	38	19	7	12	58	46

ALL CUP MATCHES						
VENUE	P	W	D	L	F	A
HOME	4	3	0	1	5	1
AWAY	2	1	1	0	3	2
TOTAL	6	4	1	1	8	3

LEAGUE DIVISION ONE						
VENUE	P	W	D	L	F	A
HOME	10	5	1	4	13	12
AWAY	10	7	2	1	22	10
TOTAL	20	12	3	5	35	22

LEAGUE DIVISION TWO						
VENUE	P	W	D	L	F	A
HOME	9	4	1	4	11	11
AWAY	9	3	3	3	12	13
TOTAL	18	7	4	7	23	24

FA CUP						
VENUE	P	W	D	L	F	A
HOME	3	2	0	1	3	1
AWAY	1	0	1	0	1	1
TOTAL	4	2	1	1	4	2

LEAGUE CUP						
VENUE	P	W	D	L	F	A
HOME	1	1	0	0	2	0
AWAY	1	1	0	0	2	1
TOTAL	2	2	0	0	4	1

#	SEASON	DATE	COMPETITION / ROUND	MATCH RESULT	VENUE	ATT
1	1894/95	12/04/95	Football League Division 2	Newton Heath 2 Bury 2	Bank Street	15000
2	1894/95	15/04/95	Football League Division 2	Bury 2 Newton Heath 1	Gigg Lane	10000
3	1906/07	24/11/06	Football League Division 1	Manchester United 2 Bury 4	Bank Street	30000
4	1906/07	30/03/07	Football League Division 1	Bury 1 Manchester United 2	Gigg Lane	25000
5	1907/08	25/12/07	Football League Division 1	Manchester United 2 Bury 1	Bank Street	45000
6	1907/08	01/01/08	Football League Division 1	Bury 0 Manchester United 1	Gigg Lane	29500
7	1908/09	07/09/08	Football League Division 1	Manchester United 2 Bury 1	Bank Street	16000
8	1908/09	03/10/08	Football League Division 1	Bury 2 Manchester United 2	Gigg Lane	25000
9	1909/10	04/09/09	Football League Division 1	Manchester United 2 Bury 0	Bank Street	12000
10	1909/10	08/01/10	Football League Division 1	Bury 1 Manchester United 1	Gigg Lane	10000
11	1910/11	03/12/10	Football League Division 1	Manchester United 3 Bury 2	Old Trafford	7000
12	1910/11	08/04/11	Football League Division 1	Bury 0 Manchester United 3	Gigg Lane	20000
13	1911/12	14/10/11	Football League Division 1	Bury 0 Manchester United 1	Gigg Lane	18000
14	1911/12	17/02/12	Football League Division 1	Manchester United 0 Bury 0	Old Trafford	6000
15	1922/23	18/11/22	Football League Division 2	Bury 2 Manchester United 2	Gigg Lane	21000
16	1922/23	25/11/22	Football League Division 2	Manchester United 0 Bury 1	Old Trafford	28000
17	1923/24	08/09/23	Football League Division 2	Bury 2 Manchester United 0	Gigg Lane	19000
18	1923/24	15/09/23	Football League Division 2	Manchester United 0 Bury 1	Old Trafford	43000
19	1925/26	21/11/25	Football League Division 1	Bury 1 Manchester United 3	Gigg Lane	16591
20	1925/26	03/04/26	Football League Division 1	Manchester United 0 Bury 1	Old Trafford	41085
21	1926/27	16/10/26	Football League Division 1	Bury 0 Manchester United 3	Gigg Lane	22728
22	1926/27	05/03/27	Football League Division 1	Manchester United 1 Bury 2	Old Trafford	14709
23	1927/28	03/12/27	Football League Division 1	Manchester United 0 Bury 1	Old Trafford	23581
24	1927/28	28/01/28	FA Cup 4th Round	Bury 1 Manchester United 1	Gigg Lane	25000
25	1927/28	01/02/28	FA Cup 4th Round Replay	Manchester United 1 Bury 0	Old Trafford	48001
26	1927/28	14/04/28	Football League Division 1	Bury 4 Manchester United 3	Gigg Lane	17440
27	1928/29	26/01/29	FA Cup 4th Round	Manchester United 0 Bury 1	Old Trafford	40558
28	1928/29	29/03/29	Football League Division 1	Bury 1 Manchester United 3	Gigg Lane	27167
29	1928/29	01/04/29	Football League Division 1	Manchester United 1 Bury 0	Old Trafford	29742
30	1931/32	21/11/31	Football League Division 2	Manchester United 1 Bury 2	Old Trafford	11745
31	1931/32	02/04/32	Football League Division 2	Bury 0 Manchester United 0	Gigg Lane	12592
32	1932/33	12/11/32	Football League Division 2	Bury 2 Manchester United 2	Gigg Lane	21663
33	1932/33	25/03/33	Football League Division 2	Manchester United 1 Bury 3	Old Trafford	27687
34	1933/34	21/10/33	Football League Division 2	Bury 2 Manchester United 1	Gigg Lane	15008
35	1933/34	03/03/34	Football League Division 2	Manchester United 2 Bury 1	Old Trafford	11176
36	1934/35	10/11/34	Football League Division 2	Manchester United 1 Bury 0	Old Trafford	41415
37	1934/35	23/03/35	Football League Division 2	Bury 0 Manchester United 1	Gigg Lane	7229
38	1935/36	25/04/36	Football League Division 2	Manchester United 2 Bury 1	Old Trafford	35027
39	1935/36	29/04/36	Football League Division 2	Bury 2 Manchester United 3	Gigg Lane	31562
40	1937/38	13/09/37	Football League Division 2	Bury 1 Manchester United 2	Gigg Lane	9954
41	1937/38	07/05/38	Football League Division 2	Manchester United 2 Bury 0	Old Trafford	53604
42	1987/88	18/11/87	League Cup 4th Round	Bury 1 Manchester United 2 (United drawn away – tie switched to Old Trafford)	Old Trafford	33519
43	1992/93	05/01/93	FA Cup 3rd Round	Manchester United 2 Bury 0	Old Trafford	30668
44	1998/99	28/10/98	League Cup 3rd Round	Manchester United 2 Bury 0	Old Trafford	52495

UNITED v CAMBRIDGE UNITED

LEAGUE CUP

VENUE	P	W	D	L	F	A
HOME	1	1	0	0	3	0
AWAY	1	0	1	0	1	1
TOTAL	2	1	1	0	4	1

#	SEASON	DATE	COMPETITION / ROUND	MATCH RESULT	VENUE	ATT
1	1991/92	25/09/91	League Cup 2nd Round 1st Leg	Manchester United 3 Cambridge United 0	Old Trafford	30934
2	1991/92	09/10/91	League Cup 2nd Round 2nd Leg	Cambridge United 1 Manchester United 1	Abbey Stadium	9248

UNITED v CARDIFF CITY

ALL COMPETITIVE MATCHES							ALL LEAGUE MATCHES							FA CUP						
VENUE	P	W	D	L	F	A	VENUE	P	W	D	L	F	A	VENUE	P	W	D	L	F	A
HOME	14	5	6	3	29	23	HOME	13	5	6	2	28	19	HOME	1	0	0	1	1	4
AWAY	13	8	1	4	22	18	AWAY	13	8	1	4	22	18	AWAY	0	0	0	0	0	0
TOTAL	27	13	7	7	51	41	TOTAL	26	13	7	6	50	37	TOTAL	1	0	0	1	1	4

LEAGUE DIVISION ONE							LEAGUE DIVISION TWO						
VENUE	P	W	D	L	F	A	VENUE	P	W	D	L	F	A
HOME	12	4	6	2	24	19	HOME	1	1	0	0	4	0
AWAY	12	7	1	4	21	18	AWAY	1	1	0	0	1	0
TOTAL	24	11	7	6	45	37	TOTAL	2	2	0	0	5	0

#	SEASON	DATE	COMPETITION / ROUND	MATCH RESULT	VENUE	ATT
1	1921/22	07/01/22	FA Cup 1st Round	Manchester United 1 Cardiff City 4	Old Trafford	25726
2	1921/22	29/04/22	Football League Division 1	Manchester United 1 Cardiff City 1	Old Trafford	18000
3	1921/22	06/05/22	Football League Division 1	Cardiff City 3 Manchester United 1	Ninian Park	16000
4	1925/26	24/10/25	Football League Division 1	Cardiff City 0 Manchester United 2	Ninian Park	15846
5	1925/26	28/04/26	Football League Division 1	Manchester United 1 Cardiff City 0	Old Trafford	9116
6	1926/27	25/09/26	Football League Division 1	Cardiff City 0 Manchester United 2	Ninian Park	17267
7	1926/27	12/02/27	Football League Division 1	Manchester United 1 Cardiff City 1	Old Trafford	26213
8	1927/28	15/10/27	Football League Division 1	Manchester United 2 Cardiff City 2	Old Trafford	31090
9	1927/28	25/02/28	Football League Division 1	Cardiff City 2 Manchester United 0	Ninian Park	15579
10	1928/29	13/10/28	Football League Division 1	Manchester United 1 Cardiff City 1	Old Trafford	26010
11	1928/29	23/02/29	Football League Division 1	Cardiff City 2 Manchester United 2	Ninian Park	13070
12	1952/53	15/11/52	Football League Division 1	Cardiff City 1 Manchester United 2	Ninian Park	40096
13	1952/53	04/04/53	Football League Division 1	Manchester United 1 Cardiff City 4	Old Trafford	37163
14	1953/54	14/11/53	Football League Division 1	Cardiff City 1 Manchester United 6	Ninian Park	26844
15	1953/54	03/04/54	Football League Division 1	Manchester United 2 Cardiff City 3	Old Trafford	22832
16	1954/55	09/10/54	Football League Division 1	Manchester United 5 Cardiff City 2	Old Trafford	39378
17	1954/55	26/02/55	Football League Division 1	Cardiff City 3 Manchester United 0	Ninian Park	16329
18	1955/56	29/10/55	Football League Division 1	Cardiff City 0 Manchester United 1	Ninian Park	27795
19	1955/56	10/03/56	Football League Division 1	Manchester United 1 Cardiff City 1	Old Trafford	44693
20	1956/57	26/12/56	Football League Division 1	Manchester United 3 Cardiff City 1	Old Trafford	28607
21	1956/57	27/04/57	Football League Division 1	Cardiff City 2 Manchester United 3	Ninian Park	17708
22	1960/61	26/11/60	Football League Division 1	Cardiff City 3 Manchester United 0	Ninian Park	21122
23	1960/61	29/04/61	Football League Division 1	Manchester United 3 Cardiff City 3	Old Trafford	30320
24	1961/62	16/09/61	Football League Division 1	Cardiff City 1 Manchester United 2	Ninian Park	29251
25	1961/62	03/02/62	Football League Division 1	Manchester United 3 Cardiff City 0	Old Trafford	29200
26	1974/75	31/08/74	Football League Division 2	Cardiff City 0 Manchester United 1	Ninian Park	22344
27	1974/75	01/03/75	Football League Division 2	Manchester United 4 Cardiff City 0	Old Trafford	43601

UNITED v CARLISLE UNITED

FA CUP

VENUE	P	W	D	L	F	A
HOME	1	1	0	0	4	2
AWAY	1	0	1	0	1	1
TOTAL	2	1	1	0	5	2

#	SEASON	DATE	COMPETITION / ROUND	MATCH RESULT	VENUE	ATT
1	1977/78	07/01/78	FA Cup 3rd Round	Carlisle United 1 Manchester United 1	Brunton Park	21710
2	1977/78	11/01/78	FA Cup 3rd Round Replay	Manchester United 4 Carlisle United 2	Old Trafford	54156

UNITED v CHARLTON ATHLETIC

ALL COMPETITIVE MATCHES

VENUE	P	W	D	L	F	A
HOME	31	23	5	3	75	25
AWAY	28	15	6	7	48	36
TOTAL	59	38	11	10	123	61

ALL LEAGUE MATCHES

VENUE	P	W	D	L	F	A
HOME	28	20	5	3	65	23
AWAY	28	15	6	7	48	36
TOTAL	56	35	11	10	113	59

ALL CUP MATCHES

VENUE	P	W	D	L	F	A
HOME	3	3	0	0	10	2
AWAY	0	0	0	0	0	0
TOTAL	3	3	0	0	10	2

PREMIERSHIP

VENUE	P	W	D	L	F	A
HOME	8	7	1	0	20	3
AWAY	8	7	1	0	21	5
TOTAL	16	14	2	0	41	8

LEAGUE DIVISION ONE

VENUE	P	W	D	L	F	A
HOME	17	12	3	2	41	17
AWAY	17	7	4	6	26	30
TOTAL	34	19	7	8	67	47

LEAGUE DIVISION TWO

VENUE	P	W	D	L	F	A
HOME	3	1	1	1	4	3
AWAY	3	1	1	1	1	1
TOTAL	6	2	2	2	5	4

FA CUP

VENUE	P	W	D	L	F	A
HOME	2	2	0	0	5	1
AWAY	0	0	0	0	0	0
TOTAL	2	2	0	0	5	1

LEAGUE CUP

VENUE	P	W	D	L	F	A
HOME	1	1	0	0	5	1
AWAY	0	0	0	0	0	0
TOTAL	1	1	0	0	5	1

#	SEASON	DATE	COMPETITION / ROUND	MATCH RESULT	VENUE	ATT
1	1931/32	25/03/32	Football League Division 2	Manchester United 0 Charlton Athletic 2	Old Trafford	37012
2	1931/32	28/03/32	Football League Division 2	Charlton Athletic 1 Manchester United 0	The Valley	16256
3	1932/33	29/08/32	Football League Division 2	Charlton Athletic 0 Manchester United 1	The Valley	12946
4	1932/33	07/09/32	Football League Division 2	Manchester United 1 Charlton Athletic 1	Old Trafford	9480
5	1935/36	04/09/35	Football League Division 2	Manchester United 3 Charlton Athletic 0	Old Trafford	21211
6	1935/36	09/09/35	Football League Division 2	Charlton Athletic 0 Manchester United 0	The Valley	13178
7	1936/37	07/11/36	Football League Division 1	Manchester United 0 Charlton Athletic 0	Old Trafford	26084
8	1936/37	13/03/37	Football League Division 1	Charlton Athletic 3 Manchester United 0	The Valley	25943
9	1938/39	08/10/38	Football League Division 1	Manchester United 0 Charlton Athletic 2	Old Trafford	35730
10	1938/39	11/02/39	Football League Division 1	Charlton Athletic 7 Manchester United 1	The Valley	23721
11	1946/47	07/09/46	Football League Division 1	Charlton Athletic 1 Manchester United 3	The Valley	44088
12	1946/47	04/01/47	Football League Division 1	Manchester United 4 Charlton Athletic 1	Maine Road	43406
13	1947/48	30/08/47	Football League Division 1	Manchester United 6 Charlton Athletic 2	Maine Road	52659
14	1947/48	03/01/48	Football League Division 1	Charlton Athletic 1 Manchester United 2	The Valley	40484
15	1947/48	07/02/48	FA Cup 5th Round	Manchester United 2 Charlton Athletic 0	Leeds Road	33312
16	1948/49	09/10/48	Football League Division 1	Manchester United 1 Charlton Athletic 1	Maine Road	46964
17	1948/49	05/03/49	Football League Division 1	Charlton Athletic 2 Manchester United 3	The Valley	55291
18	1949/50	08/10/49	Football League Division 1	Manchester United 3 Charlton Athletic 2	Old Trafford	43809
19	1949/50	25/02/50	Football League Division 1	Charlton Athletic 1 Manchester United 0	The Valley	44920
20	1950/51	16/09/50	Football League Division 1	Manchester United 3 Charlton Athletic 0	Old Trafford	36619
21	1950/51	20/01/51	Football League Division 1	Charlton Athletic 1 Manchester United 2	The Valley	31978
22	1951/52	05/09/51	Football League Division 1	Manchester United 3 Charlton Athletic 2	Old Trafford	26773
23	1951/52	12/09/51	Football League Division 1	Charlton Athletic 2 Manchester United 2	The Valley	28806
24	1952/53	03/04/53	Football League Division 1	Charlton Athletic 2 Manchester United 2	The Valley	41814
25	1952/53	06/04/53	Football League Division 1	Manchester United 3 Charlton Athletic 2	Old Trafford	30105
26	1953/54	16/04/54	Football League Division 1	Manchester United 2 Charlton Athletic 0	Old Trafford	31876
27	1953/54	19/04/54	Football League Division 1	Charlton Athletic 1 Manchester United 0	The Valley	19111
28	1954/55	04/09/54	Football League Division 1	Manchester United 3 Charlton Athletic 1	Old Trafford	38105
29	1954/55	26/04/55	Football League Division 1	Charlton Athletic 1 Manchester United 1	The Valley	18149
30	1955/56	26/12/55	Football League Division 1	Manchester United 5 Charlton Athletic 1	Old Trafford	44611
31	1955/56	27/12/55	Football League Division 1	Charlton Athletic 3 Manchester United 0	The Valley	42040
32	1956/57	06/10/56	Football League Division 1	Manchester United 4 Charlton Athletic 2	Old Trafford	41439
33	1956/57	18/02/57	Football League Division 1	Charlton Athletic 1 Manchester United 5	The Valley	16308
34	1974/75	11/09/74	League Cup 2nd Round	Manchester United 5 Charlton Athletic 1	Old Trafford	21616
35	1986/87	30/08/86	Football League Division 1	Manchester United 0 Charlton Athletic 1	Old Trafford	37544
36	1986/87	07/02/87	Football League Division 1	Charlton Athletic 0 Manchester United 0	Selhurst Park	15482
37	1987/88	29/08/87	Football League Division 1	Charlton Athletic 1 Manchester United 3	Selhurst Park	14046
38	1987/88	01/01/88	Football League Division 1	Manchester United 0 Charlton Athletic 0	Old Trafford	37257
39	1988/89	03/12/88	Football League Division 1	Manchester United 3 Charlton Athletic 0	Old Trafford	31173
40	1988/89	22/04/89	Football League Division 1	Charlton Athletic 1 Manchester United 0	Selhurst Park	12055
41	1989/90	04/11/89	Football League Division 1	Charlton Athletic 2 Manchester United 0	Selhurst Park	16065
42	1989/90	05/05/90	Football League Division 1	Manchester United 1 Charlton Athletic 0	Old Trafford	35389
43	1993/94	12/03/94	FA Cup 6th Round	Manchester United 3 Charlton Athletic 1	Old Trafford	44347

UNITED v CHARLTON ATHLETIC (continued)

#	SEASON	DATE	COMPETITION / ROUND	MATCH RESULT	VENUE	ATT
44	1998/99	09/09/98	FA Premiership	Manchester United 4 Charlton Athletic 1	Old Trafford	55147
45	1998/99	31/01/99	FA Premiership	Charlton Athletic 0 Manchester United 1	The Valley	20043
46	2000/01	09/12/00	FA Premiership	Charlton Athletic 3 Manchester United 3	The Valley	20043
47	2000/01	10/04/01	FA Premiership	Manchester United 2 Charlton Athletic 1	Old Trafford	67505
48	2001/02	10/02/02	FA Premiership	Charlton Athletic 0 Manchester United 2	The Valley	26475
49	2001/02	11/05/02	FA Premiership	Manchester United 0 Charlton Athletic 0	Old Trafford	67571
50	2002/03	28/09/02	FA Premiership	Charlton Athletic 1 Manchester United 3	The Valley	26630
51	2002/03	03/05/03	FA Premiership	Manchester United 4 Charlton Athletic 1	Old Trafford	67721
52	2003/04	13/09/03	FA Premiership	Charlton Athletic 0 Manchester United 2	The Valley	26078
53	2003/04	20/04/04	FA Premiership	Manchester United 2 Charlton Athletic 0	Old Trafford	67477
54	2004/05	20/11/04	FA Premiership	Manchester United 2 Charlton Athletic 0	Old Trafford	67704
55	2004/05	01/05/05	FA Premiership	Charlton Athletic 0 Manchester United 4	The Valley	26789
56	2005/06	19/11/05	FA Premiership	Charlton Athletic 1 Manchester United 3	The Valley	26730
57	2005/06	07/05/06	FA Premiership	Manchester United 4 Charlton Athletic 0	Old Trafford	73006
58	2006/07	23/08/06	FA Premiership	Charlton Athletic 0 Manchester United 3	The Valley	25422
59	2006/07	10/02/07	FA Premiership	Manchester United 2 Charlton Athletic 0	Old Trafford	75883

UNITED v CHELSEA

ALL COMPETITIVE MATCHES

VENUE	P	W	D	L	F	A
HOME	74	32	24	18	115	72
AWAY	70	31	18	21	120	100
NEUTRAL	7	2	3	2	9	7
TOTAL	151	65	45	41	244	179

ALL LEAGUE MATCHES

VENUE	P	W	D	L	F	A
HOME	66	26	23	17	103	68
AWAY	66	29	17	20	113	95
TOTAL	132	55	40	37	216	163

ALL CUP MATCHES

VENUE	P	W	D	L	F	A
HOME	8	6	1	1	12	4
AWAY	4	2	1	1	7	5
NEUTRAL	4	2	1	1	7	3
TOTAL	16	10	3	3	26	12

PREMIERSHIP

VENUE	P	W	D	L	F	A
HOME	16	5	7	4	22	21
AWAY	16	4	6	6	17	21
TOTAL	32	9	13	10	39	42

LEAGUE DIVISION ONE

VENUE	P	W	D	L	F	A
HOME	48	20	15	13	80	47
AWAY	48	25	9	14	95	73
TOTAL	96	45	24	27	175	120

LEAGUE DIVISION TWO

VENUE	P	W	D	L	F	A
HOME	2	1	1	0	1	0
AWAY	2	0	2	0	1	1
TOTAL	4	1	3	0	2	1

FA CUP

VENUE	P	W	D	L	F	A
HOME	5	4	1	0	8	1
AWAY	3	2	0	1	7	5
NEUTRAL	3	2	0	1	6	2
TOTAL	11	8	1	2	21	8

LEAGUE CUP

VENUE	P	W	D	L	F	A
HOME	3	2	0	1	4	3
AWAY	1	0	1	0	0	0
TOTAL	4	2	1	1	4	3

CHAMPIONS LEAGUE

VENUE	P	W	D	L	F	A
HOME	0	0	0	0	0	0
AWAY	0	0	0	0	0	0
NEUTRAL	1	0	1	0	1	1
TOTAL	1	0	1	0	1	1

CHARITY SHIELD

VENUE	P	W	D	L	F	A
HOME	0	0	0	0	0	0
AWAY	0	0	0	0	0	0
NEUTRAL	3	0	2	1	2	4
TOTAL	3	0	2	1	2	4

#	SEASON	DATE	COMPETITION / ROUND	MATCH RESULT	VENUE	ATT
1	1905/06	25/12/05	Football League Division 2	Manchester United 0 Chelsea 0	Bank Street	35000
2	1905/06	13/04/06	Football League Division 2	Chelsea 1 Manchester United 1	Stamford Bridge	60000
3	1907/08	28/09/07	Football League Division 1	Chelsea 1 Manchester United 4	Stamford Bridge	40000
4	1907/08	25/01/08	Football League Division 1	Manchester United 1 Chelsea 0	Bank Street	20000
5	1907/08	01/02/08	FA Cup 2nd Round	Manchester United 1 Chelsea 0	Bank Street	25184
6	1908/09	07/11/08	Football League Division 1	Manchester United 0 Chelsea 1	Bank Street	15000
7	1908/09	13/03/09	Football League Division 1	Chelsea 1 Manchester United 1	Stamford Bridge	30000
8	1909/10	13/11/09	Football League Division 1	Manchester United 2 Chelsea 0	Bank Street	10000
9	1909/10	26/03/10	Football League Division 1	Chelsea 1 Manchester United 1	Stamford Bridge	25000
10	1912/13	25/12/12	Football League Division 1	Chelsea 1 Manchester United 4	Stamford Bridge	33000
11	1912/13	26/12/12	Football League Division 1	Manchester United 4 Chelsea 2	Old Trafford	20000
12	1913/14	20/09/13	Football League Division 1	Chelsea 0 Manchester United 2	Stamford Bridge	40000
13	1913/14	17/01/14	Football League Division 1	Manchester United 0 Chelsea 1	Old Trafford	20000
14	1914/15	31/10/14	Football League Division 1	Manchester United 2 Chelsea 2	Old Trafford	15000
15	1914/15	19/04/15	Football League Division 1	Chelsea 1 Manchester United 3	Stamford Bridge	13000
16	1919/20	03/01/20	Football League Division 1	Manchester United 0 Chelsea 2	Old Trafford	25000
17	1919/20	17/01/20	Football League Division 1	Chelsea 1 Manchester United 0	Stamford Bridge	40000

UNITED v CHELSEA (continued)

#	SEASON	DATE	COMPETITION / ROUND	MATCH RESULT	VENUE	ATT
18	1920/21	11/09/20	Football League Division 1	Manchester United 3 Chelsea 1	Old Trafford	40000
19	1920/21	18/09/20	Football League Division 1	Chelsea 1 Manchester United 2	Stamford Bridge	35000
20	1921/22	10/09/21	Football League Division 1	Chelsea 0 Manchester United 0	Stamford Bridge	35000
21	1921/22	17/09/21	Football League Division 1	Manchester United 0 Chelsea 0	Old Trafford	28000
22	1924/25	01/01/25	Football League Division 2	Manchester United 1 Chelsea 0	Old Trafford	30500
23	1924/25	13/04/25	Football League Division 2	Chelsea 0 Manchester United 0	Stamford Bridge	16500
24	1930/31	06/09/30	Football League Division 1	Chelsea 6 Manchester United 2	Stamford Bridge	68648
25	1930/31	03/01/31	Football League Division 1	Manchester United 1 Chelsea 0	Old Trafford	8966
26	1936/37	24/10/36	Football League Division 1	Manchester United 0 Chelsea 0	Old Trafford	29859
27	1936/37	27/02/37	Football League Division 1	Chelsea 4 Manchester United 2	Stamford Bridge	16382
28	1938/39	24/09/38	Football League Division 1	Manchester United 5 Chelsea 1	Old Trafford	34557
29	1938/39	28/01/39	Football League Division 1	Chelsea 0 Manchester United 1	Stamford Bridge	31265
30	1946/47	04/09/46	Football League Division 1	Chelsea 0 Manchester United 3	Stamford Bridge	27750
31	1946/47	18/09/46	Football League Division 1	Manchester United 1 Chelsea 1	Maine Road	30275
32	1947/48	29/11/47	Football League Division 1	Chelsea 0 Manchester United 4	Stamford Bridge	43617
33	1947/48	17/04/48	Football League Division 1	Manchester United 5 Chelsea 0	Maine Road	43225
34	1948/49	13/11/48	Football League Division 1	Chelsea 1 Manchester United 1	Stamford Bridge	62542
35	1948/49	09/04/49	Football League Division 1	Manchester United 1 Chelsea 1	Maine Road	27304
36	1949/50	10/09/49	Football League Division 1	Chelsea 1 Manchester United 1	Stamford Bridge	61357
37	1949/50	14/01/50	Football League Division 1	Manchester United 1 Chelsea 0	Old Trafford	46954
38	1949/50	04/03/50	FA Cup 6th Round	Chelsea 2 Manchester United 0	Stamford Bridge	70362
39	1950/51	11/11/50	Football League Division 1	Chelsea 1 Manchester United 0	Stamford Bridge	51882
40	1950/51	31/03/51	Football League Division 1	Manchester United 4 Chelsea 1	Old Trafford	25779
41	1951/52	10/11/51	Football League Division 1	Chelsea 4 Manchester United 2	Stamford Bridge	48960
42	1951/52	21/04/52	Football League Division 1	Manchester United 3 Chelsea 0	Old Trafford	37436
43	1952/53	23/08/52	Football League Division 1	Manchester United 2 Chelsea 0	Old Trafford	43629
44	1952/53	20/12/52	Football League Division 1	Chelsea 2 Manchester United 3	Stamford Bridge	23261
45	1953/54	19/08/53	Football League Division 1	Manchester United 1 Chelsea 1	Old Trafford	28936
46	1953/54	12/12/53	Football League Division 1	Chelsea 3 Manchester United 1	Stamford Bridge	37153
47	1954/55	16/10/54	Football League Division 1	Chelsea 5 Manchester United 6	Stamford Bridge	55966
48	1954/55	30/04/55	Football League Division 1	Manchester United 2 Chelsea 1	Old Trafford	34933
49	1955/56	19/11/55	Football League Division 1	Manchester United 3 Chelsea 0	Old Trafford	22192
50	1955/56	03/03/56	Football League Division 1	Chelsea 2 Manchester United 4	Stamford Bridge	32050
51	1956/57	05/09/56	Football League Division 1	Chelsea 1 Manchester United 2	Stamford Bridge	29082
52	1956/57	01/01/57	Football League Division 1	Manchester United 3 Chelsea 0	Old Trafford	42116
53	1957/58	14/12/57	Football League Division 1	Manchester United 0 Chelsea 1	Old Trafford	36853
54	1957/58	26/04/58	Football League Division 1	Chelsea 2 Manchester United 1	Stamford Bridge	45011
55	1958/59	23/08/58	Football League Division 1	Manchester United 5 Chelsea 2	Old Trafford	52382
56	1958/59	20/12/58	Football League Division 1	Chelsea 2 Manchester United 3	Stamford Bridge	48550
57	1959/60	26/08/59	Football League Division 1	Manchester United 0 Chelsea 1	Old Trafford	57674
58	1959/60	02/09/59	Football League Division 1	Chelsea 3 Manchester United 6	Stamford Bridge	66579
59	1960/61	24/12/60	Football League Division 1	Chelsea 1 Manchester United 2	Stamford Bridge	37601
60	1960/61	26/12/60	Football League Division 1	Manchester United 6 Chelsea 0	Old Trafford	50164
61	1961/62	23/08/61	Football League Division 1	Manchester United 3 Chelsea 2	Old Trafford	45847
62	1961/62	30/08/61	Football League Division 1	Chelsea 2 Manchester United 0	Stamford Bridge	42248
63	1962/63	16/03/63	FA Cup 5th Round	Manchester United 2 Chelsea 1	Old Trafford	48298
64	1963/64	02/10/63	Football League Division 1	Chelsea 1 Manchester United 1	Stamford Bridge	45351
65	1963/64	23/03/64	Football League Division 1	Manchester United 1 Chelsea 1	Old Trafford	42931
66	1964/65	30/09/64	Football League Division 1	Chelsea 0 Manchester United 2	Stamford Bridge	60769
67	1964/65	13/03/65	Football League Division 1	Manchester United 4 Chelsea 0	Old Trafford	56261
68	1965/66	18/09/65	Football League Division 1	Manchester United 4 Chelsea 1	Old Trafford	37917
69	1965/66	12/03/66	Football League Division 1	Chelsea 2 Manchester United 0	Stamford Bridge	60269
70	1966/67	15/10/66	Football League Division 1	Manchester United 1 Chelsea 1	Old Trafford	56789
71	1966/67	05/11/66	Football League Division 1	Chelsea 1 Manchester United 3	Stamford Bridge	55958
72	1967/68	25/11/67	Football League Division 1	Chelsea 1 Manchester United 1	Stamford Bridge	54712
73	1967/68	02/03/68	Football League Division 1	Manchester United 1 Chelsea 3	Old Trafford	62978
74	1968/69	24/08/68	Football League Division 1	Manchester United 0 Chelsea 4	Old Trafford	55114
75	1968/69	15/03/69	Football League Division 1	Chelsea 3 Manchester United 2	Stamford Bridge	60436
76	1969/70	06/12/69	Football League Division 1	Manchester United 0 Chelsea 2	Old Trafford	49344
77	1969/70	21/03/70	Football League Division 1	Chelsea 2 Manchester United 1	Stamford Bridge	61479

UNITED v CHELSEA (continued)

#	SEASON	DATE	COMPETITION / ROUND	MATCH RESULT	VENUE	ATT
78	1970/71	19/08/70	Football League Division 1	Manchester United 0 Chelsea 0	Old Trafford	50979
79	1970/71	28/10/70	League Cup 4th Round	Manchester United 2 Chelsea 1	Old Trafford	47565
80	1970/71	09/01/71	Football League Division 1	Chelsea 1 Manchester United 2	Stamford Bridge	53482
81	1971/72	18/08/71	Football League Division 1	Chelsea 2 Manchester United 3	Stamford Bridge	54763
82	1971/72	22/01/72	Football League Division 1	Manchester United 0 Chelsea 1	Old Trafford	55927
83	1972/73	30/08/72	Football League Division 1	Manchester United 0 Chelsea 0	Old Trafford	44482
84	1972/73	28/04/73	Football League Division 1	Chelsea 1 Manchester United 0	Stamford Bridge	44184
85	1973/74	03/11/73	Football League Division 1	Manchester United 2 Chelsea 2	Old Trafford	48036
86	1973/74	30/03/74	Football League Division 1	Chelsea 1 Manchester United 3	Stamford Bridge	29602
87	1977/78	17/09/77	Football League Division 1	Manchester United 0 Chelsea 1	Old Trafford	54951
88	1977/78	11/02/78	Football League Division 1	Chelsea 2 Manchester United 2	Stamford Bridge	32849
89	1978/79	25/11/78	Football League Division 1	Chelsea 0 Manchester United 1	Stamford Bridge	28162
90	1978/79	15/01/79	FA Cup 3rd Round	Manchester United 3 Chelsea 0	Old Trafford	38743
91	1978/79	16/05/79	Football League Division 1	Manchester United 1 Chelsea 1	Old Trafford	38109
92	1984/85	05/09/84	Football League Division 1	Manchester United 1 Chelsea 1	Old Trafford	48398
93	1984/85	29/12/84	Football League Division 1	Chelsea 1 Manchester United 3	Stamford Bridge	42197
94	1985/86	26/10/85	Football League Division 1	Chelsea 1 Manchester United 2	Stamford Bridge	42485
95	1985/86	09/04/86	Football League Division 1	Manchester United 1 Chelsea 2	Old Trafford	45355
96	1986/87	28/09/86	Football League Division 1	Manchester United 0 Chelsea 1	Old Trafford	33340
97	1986/87	21/02/87	Football League Division 1	Chelsea 1 Manchester United 1	Stamford Bridge	26516
98	1987/88	31/08/87	Football League Division 1	Manchester United 3 Chelsea 1	Old Trafford	46616
99	1987/88	30/01/88	FA Cup 4th Round	Manchester United 2 Chelsea 0	Old Trafford	50716
100	1987/88	13/02/88	Football League Division 1	Chelsea 1 Manchester United 2	Stamford Bridge	25014
101	1989/90	25/11/89	Football League Division 1	Manchester United 0 Chelsea 0	Old Trafford	46975
102	1989/90	24/02/90	Football League Division 1	Chelsea 1 Manchester United 0	Stamford Bridge	29979
103	1990/91	25/11/90	Football League Division 1	Manchester United 2 Chelsea 3	Old Trafford	37836
104	1990/91	10/03/91	Football League Division 1	Chelsea 3 Manchester United 2	Stamford Bridge	22818
105	1991/92	15/12/91	Football League Division 1	Chelsea 1 Manchester United 3	Stamford Bridge	23120
106	1991/92	26/02/92	Football League Division 1	Manchester United 1 Chelsea 1	Old Trafford	44872
107	1992/93	19/12/92	FA Premiership	Chelsea 1 Manchester United 1	Stamford Bridge	34464
108	1992/93	17/04/93	FA Premiership	Manchester United 3 Chelsea 0	Old Trafford	40139
109	1993/94	11/09/93	FA Premiership	Chelsea 1 Manchester United 0	Stamford Bridge	37064
110	1993/94	05/03/94	FA Premiership	Manchester United 0 Chelsea 1	Old Trafford	44745
111	1993/94	14/05/94	FA Cup Final	Manchester United 4 Chelsea 0	Wembley	79634
112	1994/95	26/12/94	FA Premiership	Chelsea 2 Manchester United 3	Stamford Bridge	31161
113	1994/95	17/04/95	FA Premiership	Manchester United 0 Chelsea 0	Old Trafford	43728
114	1995/96	21/10/95	FA Premiership	Chelsea 1 Manchester United 4	Stamford Bridge	31019
115	1995/96	02/12/95	FA Premiership	Manchester United 1 Chelsea 1	Old Trafford	42019
116	1995/96	31/03/96	FA Cup Semi-Final	Manchester United 2 Chelsea 1	Villa Park	38421
117	1996/97	02/11/96	FA Premiership	Manchester United 1 Chelsea 2	Old Trafford	55198
118	1996/97	22/02/97	FA Premiership	Chelsea 1 Manchester United 1	Stamford Bridge	28336
119	1997/98	03/08/97	FA Charity Shield	Manchester United 1 Chelsea 1 (United won the tie 4-2 on penalty kicks)	Wembley	73636
120	1997/98	24/09/97	FA Premiership	Manchester United 2 Chelsea 2	Old Trafford	55163
121	1997/98	04/01/98	FA Cup 3rd Round	Chelsea 3 Manchester United 5	Stamford Bridge	34792
122	1997/98	28/02/98	FA Premiership	Chelsea 0 Manchester United 1	Stamford Bridge	35411
123	1998/99	16/12/98	FA Premiership	Manchester United 1 Chelsea 1	Old Trafford	55159
124	1998/99	29/12/98	FA Premiership	Chelsea 0 Manchester United 0	Stamford Bridge	34741
125	1998/99	07/03/99	FA Cup 6th Round	Manchester United 0 Chelsea 0	Old Trafford	54587
126	1998/99	10/03/99	FA Cup 6th Round Replay	Chelsea 0 Manchester United 2	Stamford Bridge	33075
127	1999/00	03/10/99	FA Premiership	Chelsea 5 Manchester United 0	Stamford Bridge	34909
128	1999/00	24/04/00	FA Premiership	Manchester United 3 Chelsea 2	Old Trafford	61593
129	2000/01	13/08/00	FA Charity Shield	Manchester United 0 Chelsea 2	Wembley	65148
130	2000/01	23/09/00	FA Premiership	Manchester United 3 Chelsea 3	Old Trafford	67568
131	2000/01	10/02/01	FA Premiership	Chelsea 1 Manchester United 1	Stamford Bridge	34690
132	2001/02	01/12/01	FA Premiership	Manchester United 0 Chelsea 3	Old Trafford	67544
133	2001/02	20/04/02	FA Premiership	Chelsea 0 Manchester United 3	Stamford Bridge	41725
134	2002/03	23/08/02	FA Premiership	Chelsea 2 Manchester United 2	Stamford Bridge	41541
135	2002/03	17/12/02	League Cup 5th Round	Manchester United 1 Chelsea 0	Old Trafford	57985
136	2002/03	18/01/03	FA Premiership	Manchester United 2 Chelsea 1	Old Trafford	67606
137	2003/04	30/11/03	FA Premiership	Chelsea 1 Manchester United 0	Stamford Bridge	41932
138	2003/04	08/05/04	FA Premiership	Manchester United 1 Chelsea 1	Old Trafford	67609
139	2004/05	15/08/04	FA Premiership	Chelsea 1 Manchester United 0	Stamford Bridge	41813
140	2004/05	12/01/05	League Cup Semi-Final 1st Leg	Chelsea 0 Manchester United 0	Stamford Bridge	41492
141	2004/05	26/01/05	League Cup Semi-Final 2nd Leg	Manchester United 1 Chelsea 2	Old Trafford	67000
142	2004/05	10/05/05	FA Premiership	Manchester United 1 Chelsea 3	Old Trafford	67832

UNITED v CHELSEA (continued)

#	SEASON	DATE	COMPETITION / ROUND	MATCH RESULT	VENUE	ATT
143	2005/06	06/11/05	FA Premiership	Manchester United 1 Chelsea 0	Old Trafford	67864
144	2005/06	29/04/06	FA Premiership	Chelsea 3 Manchester United 0	Stamford Bridge	42219
145	2006/07	26/11/06	FA Premiership	Manchester United 1 Chelsea 1	Old Trafford	75948
146	2006/07	09/05/07	FA Premiership	Chelsea 0 Manchester United 0	Stamford Bridge	41794
147	2006/07	19/05/07	FA Cup Final	Manchester United 0 Chelsea 1	Wembley	89826
148	2007/08	05/08/07	FA Charity Shield	Manchester United 1 Chelsea 1 (United won the tie 3-0 on penalty kicks)	Wembley	80731
149	2007/08	23/09/07	FA Premiership	Manchester United 2 Chelsea 0	Old Trafford	75663
150	2007/08	26/04/08	FA Premiership	Chelsea 2 Manchester United 1	Stamford Bridge	41828
151	2007/08	21/05/08	Champions League Final	Manchester United 1 Chelsea 1 (United won the tie 6-5 on penalty kicks)	Luzhniki Stadium	67310

UNITED v CHESTER CITY

FA CUP						
VENUE	P	W	D	L	F	A
HOME	1	1	0	0	2	1
AWAY	0	0	0	0	0	0
TOTAL	1	1	0	0	2	1

#	SEASON	DATE	COMPETITION / ROUND	MATCH RESULT	VENUE	ATT
1	1964/65	09/01/65	FA Cup 3rd Round	Manchester United 2 Chester City 1	Old Trafford	40000

UNITED v CHESTERFIELD

LEAGUE DIVISION TWO						
VENUE	P	W	D	L	F	A
HOME	10	10	0	0	26	7
AWAY	10	3	1	6	15	15
TOTAL	20	13	1	6	41	22

#	SEASON	DATE	COMPETITION / ROUND	MATCH RESULT	VENUE	ATT
1	1899/00	23/12/99	Football League Division 2	Chesterfield 2 Newton Heath 1	Saltergate	2000
2	1899/00	28/04/00	Football League Division 2	Newton Heath 2 Chesterfield 1	Bank Street	6000
3	1900/01	22/12/00	Football League Division 2	Chesterfield 2 Newton Heath 1	Saltergate	4000
4	1900/01	27/04/01	Football League Division 2	Newton Heath 1 Chesterfield 0	Bank Street	1000
5	1901/02	17/03/02	Football League Division 2	Chesterfield 3 Newton Heath 0	Saltergate	2000
6	1901/02	23/04/02	Football League Division 2	Newton Heath 2 Chesterfield 0	Bank Street	2000
7	1902/03	04/10/02	Football League Division 2	Manchester United 2 Chesterfield 1	Bank Street	12000
8	1902/03	31/01/03	Football League Division 2	Chesterfield 2 Manchester United 0	Saltergate	6000
9	1903/04	25/12/03	Football League Division 2	Manchester United 3 Chesterfield 1	Bank Street	15000
10	1903/04	01/04/04	Football League Division 2	Chesterfield 0 Manchester United 2	Saltergate	5000
11	1904/05	26/12/04	Football League Division 2	Manchester United 3 Chesterfield 0	Bank Street	20000
12	1904/05	21/04/05	Football League Division 2	Chesterfield 2 Manchester United 0	Saltergate	10000
13	1905/06	11/11/05	Football League Division 2	Chesterfield 1 Manchester United 0	Saltergate	3000
14	1905/06	17/03/06	Football League Division 2	Manchester United 4 Chesterfield 1	Bank Street	16000
15	1931/32	26/09/31	Football League Division 2	Manchester United 3 Chesterfield 1	Old Trafford	10834
16	1931/32	06/02/32	Football League Division 2	Chesterfield 1 Manchester United 3	Saltergate	9457
17	1932/33	26/11/32	Football League Division 2	Chesterfield 1 Manchester United 1	Saltergate	10277
18	1932/33	08/04/33	Football League Division 2	Manchester United 2 Chesterfield 1	Old Trafford	16031
19	1937/38	13/11/37	Football League Division 2	Chesterfield 1 Manchester United 7	Saltergate	17407
20	1937/38	26/03/38	Football League Division 2	Manchester United 4 Chesterfield 1	Old Trafford	27311

UNITED v COLCHESTER UNITED

ALL COMPETITIVE MATCHES							FA CUP							LEAGUE CUP						
VENUE	P	W	D	L	F	A	VENUE	P	W	D	L	F	A	VENUE	P	W	D	L	F	A
HOME	0	0	0	0	0	0	HOME	0	0	0	0	0	0	HOME	0	0	0	0	0	0
AWAY	2	2	0	0	3	0	AWAY	1	1	0	0	1	0	AWAY	1	1	0	0	2	0
TOTAL	2	2	0	0	3	0	TOTAL	1	1	0	0	1	0	TOTAL	1	1	0	0	2	0

#	SEASON	DATE	COMPETITION / ROUND	MATCH RESULT	VENUE	ATT
1	1978/79	20/02/79	FA Cup 5th Round	Colchester United 0 Manchester United 1	Layer Road	13171
2	1983/84	08/11/83	League Cup 3rd Round	Colchester United 0 Manchester United 2	Layer Road	13031

UNITED v COPENHAGEN

CHAMPIONS LEAGUE

VENUE	P	W	D	L	F	A
HOME	1	1	0	0	3	0
AWAY	1	0	0	1	0	1
TOTAL	2	1	0	1	3	1

#	SEASON	DATE	COMPETITION / ROUND	MATCH RESULT	VENUE	ATT
1	2006/07	17/10/06	Champions League Phase 1 Match 3	Manchester United 3 Copenhagen 0	Old Trafford	72020
2	2006/07	01/11/06	Champions League Phase 1 Match 4	Copenhagen 1 Manchester United 0	Parken Stadion	40000

UNITED v COVENTRY CITY

ALL COMPETITIVE MATCHES

VENUE	P	W	D	L	F	A
HOME	42	24	9	9	75	32
AWAY	41	19	8	14	62	48
TOTAL	83	43	17	23	137	80

ALL LEAGUE MATCHES

VENUE	P	W	D	L	F	A
HOME	37	23	8	6	72	26
AWAY	37	16	8	13	52	44
TOTAL	74	39	16	19	124	70

ALL CUP MATCHES

VENUE	P	W	D	L	F	A
HOME	5	1	1	3	3	6
AWAY	4	3	0	1	10	4
TOTAL	9	4	1	4	13	10

PREMIERSHIP

VENUE	P	W	D	L	F	A
HOME	9	8	1	0	23	5
AWAY	9	8	0	1	18	7
TOTAL	18	16	1	1	41	12

LEAGUE DIVISION ONE

VENUE	P	W	D	L	F	A
HOME	24	13	6	5	39	15
AWAY	24	8	7	9	33	32
TOTAL	48	21	13	14	72	47

LEAGUE DIVISION TWO

VENUE	P	W	D	L	F	A
HOME	4	2	1	1	10	6
AWAY	4	0	1	3	1	5
TOTAL	8	2	2	4	11	11

FA CUP

VENUE	P	W	D	L	F	A
HOME	3	1	1	1	3	3
AWAY	3	3	0	0	10	3
TOTAL	6	4	1	1	13	6

LEAGUE CUP

VENUE	P	W	D	L	F	A
HOME	2	0	0	2	0	3
AWAY	1	0	0	1	0	1
TOTAL	3	0	0	3	0	4

#	SEASON	DATE	COMPETITION / ROUND	MATCH RESULT	VENUE	ATT
1	1911/12	03/02/12	FA Cup 2nd Round	Coventry City 1 Manchester United 5	Highfield Road	17130
2	1912/13	11/01/13	FA Cup 1st Round	Manchester United 1 Coventry City 1	Old Trafford	11500
3	1912/13	16/01/13	FA Cup 1st Round Replay	Coventry City 1 Manchester United 2	Highfield Road	20042
4	1922/23	23/09/22	Football League Division 2	Coventry City 2 Manchester United 0	Highfield Road	19000
5	1922/23	30/09/22	Football League Division 2	Manchester United 2 Coventry City 1	Old Trafford	25000
6	1923/24	17/11/23	Football League Division 2	Coventry City 1 Manchester United 1	Highfield Road	13580
7	1923/24	02/01/24	Football League Division 2	Manchester United 1 Coventry City 2	Old Trafford	7000
8	1924/25	13/09/24	Football League Division 2	Manchester United 5 Coventry City 1	Old Trafford	12000
9	1924/25	17/01/25	Football League Division 2	Coventry City 1 Manchester United 0	Highfield Road	9000
10	1937/38	30/08/37	Football League Division 2	Coventry City 1 Manchester United 0	Highfield Road	30575
11	1937/38	08/09/37	Football League Division 2	Manchester United 2 Coventry City 2	Old Trafford	17455
12	1962/63	30/03/63	FA Cup 6th Round	Coventry City 1 Manchester United 3	Highfield Road	44000
13	1967/68	25/10/67	Football League Division 1	Manchester United 4 Coventry City 0	Old Trafford	54253
14	1967/68	16/03/68	Football League Division 1	Coventry City 2 Manchester United 0	Highfield Road	47110
15	1968/69	21/08/68	Football League Division 1	Manchester United 1 Coventry City 0	Old Trafford	51201
16	1968/69	08/04/69	Football League Division 1	Coventry City 2 Manchester United 1	Highfield Road	45402
17	1969/70	08/11/69	Football League Division 1	Coventry City 1 Manchester United 2	Highfield Road	43446
18	1969/70	30/03/70	Football League Division 1	Manchester United 1 Coventry City 1	Old Trafford	38647
19	1970/71	12/09/70	Football League Division 1	Manchester United 2 Coventry City 0	Old Trafford	48939
20	1970/71	13/04/71	Football League Division 1	Coventry City 2 Manchester United 1	Highfield Road	33818
21	1971/72	27/12/71	Football League Division 1	Manchester United 2 Coventry City 2	Old Trafford	52117
22	1971/72	01/04/72	Football League Division 1	Coventry City 2 Manchester United 3	Highfield Road	37901
23	1972/73	09/09/72	Football League Division 1	Manchester United 0 Coventry City 1	Old Trafford	37073
24	1972/73	27/01/73	Football League Division 1	Coventry City 1 Manchester United 1	Highfield Road	42767
25	1973/74	15/12/73	Football League Division 1	Manchester United 2 Coventry City 3	Old Trafford	28589
26	1973/74	02/02/74	Football League Division 1	Coventry City 1 Manchester United 0	Highfield Road	25313
27	1975/76	27/08/75	Football League Division 1	Manchester United 1 Coventry City 1	Old Trafford	52169
28	1975/76	07/02/76	Football League Division 1	Coventry City 1 Manchester United 0	Highfield Road	33922
29	1976/77	24/08/76	Football League Division 1	Coventry City 0 Manchester United 2	Highfield Road	26775
30	1976/77	15/01/77	Football League Division 1	Manchester United 2 Coventry City 0	Old Trafford	46567
31	1977/78	24/08/77	Football League Division 1	Manchester United 2 Coventry City 1	Old Trafford	55726
32	1977/78	31/12/77	Football League Division 1	Coventry City 3 Manchester United 0	Highfield Road	24706

UNITED v COVENTRY CITY (continued)

#	SEASON	DATE	COMPETITION / ROUND	MATCH RESULT	VENUE	ATT
33	1978/79	20/03/79	Football League Division 1	Coventry City 4 Manchester United 3	Highfield Road	25382
34	1978/79	16/04/79	Football League Division 1	Manchester United 0 Coventry City 0	Old Trafford	46035
35	1979/80	15/12/79	Football League Division 1	Coventry City 1 Manchester United 2	Highfield Road	25541
36	1979/80	26/04/80	Football League Division 1	Manchester United 2 Coventry City 1	Old Trafford	52154
37	1980/81	27/08/80	League Cup 2nd Round 1st Leg	Manchester United 0 Coventry City 1	Old Trafford	31656
38	1980/81	02/09/80	League Cup 2nd Round 2nd Leg	Coventry City 1 Manchester United 0	Highfield Road	18946
39	1980/81	08/11/80	Football League Division 1	Manchester United 0 Coventry City 0	Old Trafford	42794
40	1980/81	11/04/81	Football League Division 1	Coventry City 0 Manchester United 2	Highfield Road	20201
41	1981/82	29/08/81	Football League Division 1	Coventry City 2 Manchester United 1	Highfield Road	19329
42	1981/82	17/03/82	Football League Division 1	Manchester United 0 Coventry City 1	Old Trafford	34499
43	1982/83	28/12/82	Football League Division 1	Coventry City 3 Manchester United 0	Highfield Road	18945
44	1982/83	02/04/83	Football League Division 1	Manchester United 3 Coventry City 0	Old Trafford	36814
45	1983/84	26/12/83	Football League Division 1	Coventry City 1 Manchester United 1	Highfield Road	21553
46	1983/84	21/04/84	Football League Division 1	Manchester United 4 Coventry City 1	Old Trafford	38524
47	1984/85	15/09/84	Football League Division 1	Coventry City 0 Manchester United 3	Highfield Road	18312
48	1984/85	12/01/85	Football League Division 1	Manchester United 0 Coventry City 1	Old Trafford	35992
49	1984/85	26/01/85	FA Cup 4th Round	Manchester United 2 Coventry City 1	Old Trafford	38039
50	1985/86	02/11/85	Football League Division 1	Manchester United 2 Coventry City 0	Old Trafford	46748
51	1985/86	05/04/86	Football League Division 1	Coventry City 1 Manchester United 3	Highfield Road	17160
52	1986/87	01/11/86	Football League Division 1	Manchester United 1 Coventry City 1	Old Trafford	36946
53	1986/87	31/01/87	FA Cup 4th Round	Manchester United 0 Coventry City 1	Old Trafford	49082
54	1986/87	06/05/87	Football League Division 1	Coventry City 1 Manchester United 1	Highfield Road	23407
55	1987/88	05/09/87	Football League Division 1	Coventry City 0 Manchester United 0	Highfield Road	27125
56	1987/88	06/02/88	Football League Division 1	Manchester United 1 Coventry City 0	Old Trafford	37144
57	1988/89	10/12/88	Football League Division 1	Coventry City 1 Manchester United 0	Highfield Road	19936
58	1988/89	29/04/89	Football League Division 1	Manchester United 0 Coventry City 1	Old Trafford	29799
59	1989/90	21/10/89	Football League Division 1	Coventry City 1 Manchester United 4	Highfield Road	19625
60	1989/90	31/03/90	Football League Division 1	Manchester United 3 Coventry City 0	Old Trafford	39172
61	1990/91	25/08/90	Football League Division 1	Manchester United 2 Coventry City 0	Old Trafford	46715
62	1990/91	15/12/90	Football League Division 1	Coventry City 2 Manchester United 2	Highfield Road	17106
63	1991/92	07/12/91	Football League Division 1	Manchester United 4 Coventry City 0	Old Trafford	42549
64	1991/92	29/02/92	Football League Division 1	Coventry City 0 Manchester United 0	Highfield Road	23967
65	1992/93	28/12/92	FA Premiership	Manchester United 5 Coventry City 0	Old Trafford	36025
66	1992/93	12/04/93	FA Premiership	Coventry City 0 Manchester United 1	Highfield Road	24249
67	1993/94	27/11/93	FA Premiership	Coventry City 0 Manchester United 1	Highfield Road	17020
68	1993/94	08/05/94	FA Premiership	Manchester United 0 Coventry City 0	Old Trafford	44717
69	1994/95	03/01/95	FA Premiership	Manchester United 2 Coventry City 0	Old Trafford	43130
70	1994/95	01/05/95	FA Premiership	Coventry City 2 Manchester United 3	Highfield Road	21885
71	1995/96	22/11/95	FA Premiership	Coventry City 0 Manchester United 4	Highfield Road	23400
72	1995/96	08/04/96	FA Premiership	Manchester United 1 Coventry City 0	Old Trafford	50332
73	1996/97	18/01/97	FA Premiership	Coventry City 0 Manchester United 2	Highfield Road	23085
74	1996/97	01/03/97	FA Premiership	Manchester United 3 Coventry City 1	Old Trafford	55230
75	1997/98	30/08/97	FA Premiership	Manchester United 3 Coventry City 0	Old Trafford	55074
76	1997/98	28/12/97	FA Premiership	Coventry City 3 Manchester United 2	Highfield Road	23054
77	1998/99	12/09/98	FA Premiership	Manchester United 2 Coventry City 0	Old Trafford	55198
78	1998/99	20/02/99	FA Premiership	Coventry City 0 Manchester United 1	Highfield Road	22596
79	1999/00	25/08/99	FA Premiership	Coventry City 1 Manchester United 2	Highfield Road	22024
80	1999/00	05/02/00	FA Premiership	Manchester United 3 Coventry City 2	Old Trafford	61380
81	2000/01	04/11/00	FA Premiership	Coventry City 1 Manchester United 2	Highfield Road	21079
82	2000/01	14/04/01	FA Premiership	Manchester United 4 Coventry City 2	Old Trafford	67637
83	2007/08	26/09/07	League Cup 3rd Round	Manchester United 0 Coventry City 2	Old Trafford	74055

UNITED v CREWE ALEXANDRA

ALL COMPETITIVE MATCHES							LEAGUE DIVISION TWO							LEAGUE CUP						
VENUE	P	W	D	L	F	A	VENUE	P	W	D	L	F	A	VENUE	P	W	D	L	F	A
HOME	2	2	0	0	11	1	HOME	2	2	0	0	11	1	HOME	0	0	0	0	0	0
AWAY	4	4	0	0	9	1	AWAY	2	2	0	0	4	0	AWAY	2	2	0	0	5	1
TOTAL	6	6	0	0	20	2	TOTAL	4	4	0	0	15	1	TOTAL	2	2	0	0	5	1

#	SEASON	DATE	COMPETITION / ROUND	MATCH RESULT	VENUE	ATT
1	1894/95	15/09/94	Football League Division 2	Newton Heath 6 Crewe Alexandra 1	Bank Street	6000
2	1894/95	01/12/94	Football League Division 2	Crewe Alexandra 0 Newton Heath 2	Gresty Road	600
3	1895/96	07/09/95	Football League Division 2	Newton Heath 5 Crewe Alexandra 0	Bank Street	6000
4	1895/96	28/09/95	Football League Division 2	Crewe Alexandra 0 Newton Heath 2	Gresty Road	2000
5	2004/05	26/10/04	League Cup 3rd Round	Crewe Alexandra 0 Manchester United 3	Gresty Road	10103
6	2006/07	25/10/06	League Cup 3rd Round	Crewe Alexandra 1 Manchester United 2	Gresty Road	10046

UNITED v CROATIA ZAGREB

CHAMPIONS LEAGUE						
VENUE	P	W	D	L	F	A
HOME	1	0	1	0	0	0
AWAY	1	1	0	0	2	1
TOTAL	2	1	1	0	2	1

#	SEASON	DATE	COMPETITION / ROUND	MATCH RESULT	VENUE	ATT
1	1999/00	14/09/99	Champions League Phase 1 Match 1	Manchester United 0 Croatia Zagreb 0	Old Trafford	53250
2	1999/00	27/10/99	Champions League Phase 1 Match 5	Croatia Zagreb 1 Manchester United 2	Maksimir Stadium	27500

UNITED v CRYSTAL PALACE

ALL COMPETITIVE MATCHES							ALL LEAGUE MATCHES							ALL CUP MATCHES						
VENUE	P	W	D	L	F	A	VENUE	P	W	D	L	F	A	VENUE	P	W	D	L	F	A
HOME	20	16	2	2	42	12	HOME	16	12	2	2	33	9	HOME	4	4	0	0	9	3
AWAY	17	8	5	4	28	23	AWAY	16	7	5	4	27	23	AWAY	1	1	0	0	1	0
NEUTRAL	4	2	2	0	8	5								NEUTRAL	4	2	2	0	8	5
TOTAL	41	26	9	6	78	40	TOTAL	32	19	7	6	60	32	TOTAL	9	7	2	0	18	8

PREMIERSHIP							LEAGUE DIVISION ONE							LEAGUE DIVISION TWO						
VENUE	P	W	D	L	F	A	VENUE	P	W	D	L	F	A	VENUE	P	W	D	L	F	A
HOME	4	4	0	0	11	2	HOME	9	5	2	2	14	5	HOME	3	3	0	0	8	2
AWAY	4	2	2	0	6	1	AWAY	9	4	2	3	16	17	AWAY	3	1	1	1	5	5
TOTAL	8	6	2	0	17	3	TOTAL	18	9	4	5	30	22	TOTAL	6	4	1	1	13	7

FA CUP							LEAGUE CUP						
VENUE	P	W	D	L	F	A	VENUE	P	W	D	L	F	A
HOME	0	0	0	0	0	0	HOME	4	4	0	0	9	3
AWAY	0	0	0	0	0	0	AWAY	1	1	0	0	1	0
NEUTRAL	4	2	2	0	8	5	NEUTRAL	0	0	0	0	0	0
TOTAL	4	2	2	0	8	5	TOTAL	5	5	0	0	10	3

#	SEASON	DATE	COMPETITION / ROUND	MATCH RESULT	VENUE	ATT
1	1922/23	26/08/22	Football League Division 2	Manchester United 2 Crystal Palace 1	Old Trafford	30000
2	1922/23	02/09/22	Football League Division 2	Crystal Palace 2 Manchester United 3	Sydenham Hill	8500
3	1923/24	12/04/24	Football League Division 2	Manchester United 5 Crystal Palace 1	Old Trafford	8000
4	1923/24	19/04/24	Football League Division 2	Crystal Palace 1 Manchester United 1	Sydenham Hill	7000
5	1924/25	11/10/24	Football League Division 2	Manchester United 1 Crystal Palace 0	Old Trafford	27750
6	1924/25	14/02/25	Football League Division 2	Crystal Palace 2 Manchester United 1	Selhurst Park	11250
7	1969/70	09/08/69	Football League Division 1	Crystal Palace 2 Manchester United 2	Selhurst Park	48610
8	1969/70	14/02/70	Football League Division 1	Manchester United 1 Crystal Palace 1	Old Trafford	54711
9	1970/71	10/10/70	Football League Division 1	Manchester United 0 Crystal Palace 1	Old Trafford	42979
10	1970/71	18/11/70	League Cup 5th Round	Manchester United 4 Crystal Palace 2	Old Trafford	48961
11	1970/71	17/04/71	Football League Division 1	Crystal Palace 3 Manchester United 5	Selhurst Park	39145
12	1971/72	11/09/71	Football League Division 1	Crystal Palace 1 Manchester United 3	Selhurst Park	44020
13	1971/72	25/03/72	Football League Division 1	Manchester United 4 Crystal Palace 0	Old Trafford	41550

UNITED v CRYSTAL PALACE (continued)

#	SEASON	DATE	COMPETITION / ROUND	MATCH RESULT	VENUE	ATT
14	1972/73	16/12/72	Football League Division 1	Crystal Palace 5 Manchester United 0	Selhurst Park	39484
15	1972/73	11/04/73	Football League Division 1	Manchester United 2 Crystal Palace 0	Old Trafford	46891
16	1979/80	17/11/79	Football League Division 1	Manchester United 1 Crystal Palace 1	Old Trafford	52800
17	1979/80	29/03/80	Football League Division 1	Crystal Palace 0 Manchester United 2	Selhurst Park	33056
18	1980/81	01/11/80	Football League Division 1	Crystal Palace 1 Manchester United 0	Selhurst Park	31449
19	1980/81	04/04/81	Football League Division 1	Manchester United 1 Crystal Palace 0	Old Trafford	37954
20	1985/86	24/09/85	League Cup 2nd Round 1st Leg	Crystal Palace 0 Manchester United 1	Selhurst Park	21507
21	1985/86	09/10/85	League Cup 2nd Round 2nd Leg	Manchester United 1 Crystal Palace 0	Old Trafford	26118
22	1987/88	28/10/87	League Cup 3rd Round	Manchester United 2 Crystal Palace 1	Old Trafford	27283
23	1989/90	22/08/89	Football League Division 1	Crystal Palace 1 Manchester United 1	Selhurst Park	22423
24	1989/90	09/12/89	Football League Division 1	Manchester United 1 Crystal Palace 2	Old Trafford	33514
25	1989/90	12/05/90	FA Cup Final	Manchester United 3 Crystal Palace 3	Wembley	80000
26	1989/90	17/05/90	FA Cup Final Replay	Manchester United 1 Crystal Palace 0	Wembley	80000
27	1990/91	03/11/90	Football League Division 1	Manchester United 2 Crystal Palace 0	Old Trafford	45724
28	1990/91	11/05/91	Football League Division 1	Crystal Palace 3 Manchester United 0	Selhurst Park	25301
29	1991/92	30/11/91	Football League Division 1	Crystal Palace 1 Manchester United 3	Selhurst Park	29017
30	1991/92	22/02/92	Football League Division 1	Manchester United 2 Crystal Palace 0	Old Trafford	46347
31	1992/93	02/09/92	FA Premiership	Manchester United 1 Crystal Palace 0	Old Trafford	29736
32	1992/93	21/04/93	FA Premiership	Crystal Palace 0 Manchester United 2	Selhurst Park	30115
33	1994/95	19/11/94	FA Premiership	Manchester United 3 Crystal Palace 0	Old Trafford	43788
34	1994/95	25/01/95	FA Premiership	Crystal Palace 1 Manchester United 1	Selhurst Park	18224
35	1994/95	09/04/95	FA Cup Semi-Final	Manchester United 2 Crystal Palace 2	Villa Park	38256
36	1994/95	12/04/95	FA Cup Semi-Final Replay	Manchester United 2 Crystal Palace 0	Villa Park	17987
37	1997/98	04/10/97	FA Premiership	Manchester United 2 Crystal Palace 0	Old Trafford	55143
38	1997/98	27/04/98	FA Premiership	Crystal Palace 0 Manchester United 3	Selhurst Park	26180
39	2004/05	10/11/04	League Cup 4th Round	Manchester United 2 Crystal Palace 0	Old Trafford	48891
40	2004/05	18/12/04	FA Premiership	Manchester United 5 Crystal Palace 2	Old Trafford	67814
41	2004/05	05/03/05	FA Premiership	Crystal Palace 0 Manchester United 0	Selhurst Park	26021

UNITED v DARWEN

ALL COMPETITIVE MATCHES							LEAGUE DIVISION ONE							LEAGUE DIVISION TWO						
VENUE	P	W	D	L	F	A	VENUE	P	W	D	L	F	A	VENUE	P	W	D	L	F	A
HOME	6	4	1	1	20	5	HOME	1	0	0	1	0	1	HOME	5	4	1	0	20	4
AWAY	6	2	2	2	7	8	AWAY	1	0	0	1	0	1	AWAY	5	2	2	1	7	7
TOTAL	12	6	3	3	27	13	TOTAL	2	0	0	2	0	2	TOTAL	10	6	3	1	27	11

#	SEASON	DATE	COMPETITION / ROUND	MATCH RESULT	VENUE	ATT
1	1893/94	30/09/93	Football League Division 1	Darwen 1 Newton Heath 0	Barley Bank	4000
2	1893/94	04/11/93	Football League Division 1	Newton Heath 0 Darwen 1	Bank Street	8000
3	1894/95	06/10/94	Football League Division 2	Darwen 1 Newton Heath 1	Barley Bank	6000
4	1894/95	24/11/94	Football League Division 2	Newton Heath 1 Darwen 1	Bank Street	5000
5	1895/96	21/12/95	Football League Division 2	Darwen 3 Newton Heath 0	Barley Bank	3000
6	1895/96	03/04/96	Football League Division 2	Newton Heath 4 Darwen 0	Bank Street	1000
7	1896/97	02/03/97	Football League Division 2	Newton Heath 3 Darwen 1	Bank Street	3000
8	1896/97	13/03/97	Football League Division 2	Darwen 0 Newton Heath 2	Barley Bank	2000
9	1897/98	19/03/98	Football League Division 2	Darwen 2 Newton Heath 3	Barley Bank	2000
10	1897/98	23/04/98	Football League Division 2	Newton Heath 3 Darwen 2	Bank Street	4000
11	1898/99	24/12/98	Football League Division 2	Newton Heath 9 Darwen 0	Bank Street	2000
12	1898/99	22/04/99	Football League Division 2	Darwen 1 Newton Heath 1	Barley Bank	1000

UNITED v DEBRECENI

CHAMPIONS LEAGUE					
VENUE	P	W	D	L	F	A
HOME	1	1	0	0	3	0
AWAY	1	1	0	0	3	0
TOTAL	2	2	0	0	6	0

#	SEASON	DATE	COMPETITION / ROUND	MATCH RESULT	VENUE	ATT
1	2005/06	09/08/05	Champions League Qualifying Round 1st Leg	Manchester United 3 Debreceni 0	Old Trafford	51701
2	2005/06	24/08/05	Champions League Qualifying Round 2nd Leg	Debreceni 0 Manchester United 3	Ferenc Puskas Stadion	27000

UNITED v DEPORTIVO LA CORUÑA

CHAMPIONS LEAGUE

VENUE	P	W	D	L	F	A
HOME	3	2	0	1	7	5
AWAY	3	1	0	2	3	4
TOTAL	6	3	0	3	10	9

#	SEASON	DATE	COMPETITION / ROUND	MATCH RESULT	VENUE	ATT
1	2001/02	25/09/01	Champions League Phase 1 Match 2	Deportivo La Coruna 2 Manchester United 1	Estadio de Riazor	33108
2	2001/02	17/10/01	Champions League Phase 1 Match 4	Manchester United 2 Deportivo La Coruna 3	Old Trafford	65585
3	2001/02	02/04/02	Champions League Quarter-Final 1st Leg	Deportivo La Coruna 0 Manchester United 2	Estadio de Riazor	32351
4	2001/02	10/04/02	Champions League Quarter-Final 2nd Leg	Manchester United 3 Deportivo La Coruna 2	Old Trafford	65875
5	2002/03	11/12/02	Champions League Phase 2 Match 2	Manchester United 2 Deportivo La Coruna 0	Old Trafford	67014
6	2002/03	18/03/03	Champions League Phase 2 Match 6	Deportivo La Coruna 2 Manchester United 0	Estadio de Riazor	25000

UNITED v DERBY COUNTY

ALL COMPETITIVE MATCHES

VENUE	P	W	D	L	F	A
HOME	47	25	11	11	89	46
AWAY	51	15	18	18	81	102
NEUTRAL	2	2	0	0	5	1
TOTAL	100	42	29	29	175	149

ALL LEAGUE MATCHES

VENUE	P	W	D	L	F	A
HOME	45	24	10	11	87	45
AWAY	45	12	17	16	70	91
TOTAL	90	36	27	27	157	136

ALL CUP MATCHES

VENUE	P	W	D	L	F	A
HOME	2	1	1	0	2	1
AWAY	6	3	1	2	11	11
NEUTRAL	2	2	0	0	5	1
TOTAL	10	6	2	2	18	13

PREMIERSHIP

VENUE	P	W	D	L	F	A
HOME	7	5	0	2	17	6
AWAY	7	3	4	0	12	7
TOTAL	14	8	4	2	29	13

LEAGUE DIVISION ONE

VENUE	P	W	D	L	F	A
HOME	35	19	7	9	69	38
AWAY	35	9	12	14	57	79
TOTAL	70	28	19	23	126	117

LEAGUE DIVISION TWO

VENUE	P	W	D	L	F	A
HOME	3	0	3	0	1	1
AWAY	3	0	1	2	1	5
TOTAL	6	0	4	2	2	6

FA CUP

VENUE	P	W	D	L	F	A
HOME	1	0	1	0	1	1
AWAY	5	3	0	2	11	11
NEUTRAL	2	2	0	0	5	1
TOTAL	8	5	1	2	17	13

LEAGUE CUP

VENUE	P	W	D	L	F	A
HOME	1	1	0	0	1	0
AWAY	1	0	1	0	0	0
NEUTRAL	0	0	0	0	0	0
TOTAL	2	1	1	0	1	0

#	SEASON	DATE	COMPETITION / ROUND	MATCH RESULT	VENUE	ATT
1	1892/93	31/12/92	Football League Division 1	Newton Heath 7 Derby County 1	North Road	3000
2	1892/93	11/02/93	Football League Division 1	Derby County 5 Newton Heath 1	Racecourse Ground	5000
3	1893/94	07/10/93	Football League Division 1	Derby County 2 Newton Heath 0	Racecourse Ground	7000
4	1893/94	17/03/94	Football League Division 1	Newton Heath 2 Derby County 6	Bank Street	7000
5	1895/96	15/02/96	FA Cup 2nd Round	Newton Heath 1 Derby County 1	Bank Street	20000
6	1895/96	19/02/96	FA Cup 2nd Round Replay	Derby County 5 Newton Heath 1	Baseball Ground	6000
7	1896/97	27/02/97	FA Cup 3rd Round	Derby County 2 Newton Heath 0	Baseball Ground	12000
8	1906/07	03/09/06	Football League Division 1	Derby County 2 Manchester United 2	Baseball Ground	5000
9	1906/07	29/09/06	Football League Division 1	Manchester United 1 Derby County 1	Bank Street	25000
10	1912/13	12/10/12	Football League Division 1	Derby County 2 Manchester United 1	Baseball Ground	15000
11	1912/13	15/02/13	Football League Division 1	Manchester United 4 Derby County 0	Old Trafford	30000
12	1913/14	29/11/13	Football League Division 1	Manchester United 3 Derby County 3	Old Trafford	20000
13	1913/14	04/04/14	Football League Division 1	Derby County 4 Manchester United 2	Baseball Ground	7000
14	1919/20	30/08/19	Football League Division 1	Derby County 1 Manchester United 1	Baseball Ground	12000
15	1919/20	06/09/19	Football League Division 1	Manchester United 0 Derby County 2	Old Trafford	15000
16	1920/21	02/05/21	Football League Division 1	Derby County 1 Manchester United 1	Baseball Ground	8000
17	1920/21	07/05/21	Football League Division 1	Manchester United 3 Derby County 0	Old Trafford	10000
18	1922/23	17/02/23	Football League Division 2	Manchester United 0 Derby County 0	Old Trafford	27500
19	1922/23	14/03/23	Football League Division 2	Derby County 1 Manchester United 1	Baseball Ground	12000
20	1923/24	16/02/24	Football League Division 2	Derby County 3 Manchester United 0	Baseball Ground	12000
21	1923/24	23/02/24	Football League Division 2	Manchester United 0 Derby County 0	Old Trafford	25000
22	1924/25	29/11/24	Football League Division 2	Manchester United 1 Derby County 1	Old Trafford	59500
23	1924/25	04/04/25	Football League Division 2	Derby County 1 Manchester United 0	Baseball Ground	24000
24	1926/27	15/04/27	Football League Division 1	Manchester United 2 Derby County 2	Old Trafford	31110
25	1926/27	18/04/27	Football League Division 1	Derby County 2 Manchester United 2	Baseball Ground	17306
26	1927/28	22/10/27	Football League Division 1	Manchester United 5 Derby County 0	Old Trafford	18304
27	1927/28	28/03/28	Football League Division 1	Derby County 5 Manchester United 0	Baseball Ground	8323

UNITED v DERBY COUNTY (continued)

#	SEASON	DATE	COMPETITION / ROUND	MATCH RESULT	VENUE	ATT
28	1928/29	17/11/28	Football League Division 1	Manchester United 0 Derby County 1	Old Trafford	26122
29	1928/29	30/03/29	Football League Division 1	Derby County 6 Manchester United 1	Baseball Ground	14619
30	1929/30	09/11/29	Football League Division 1	Manchester United 3 Derby County 2	Old Trafford	15174
31	1929/30	15/03/30	Football League Division 1	Derby County 1 Manchester United 1	Baseball Ground	9102
32	1930/31	13/12/30	Football League Division 1	Manchester United 2 Derby County 1	Old Trafford	9701
33	1930/31	18/04/31	Football League Division 1	Derby County 6 Manchester United 1	Baseball Ground	6610
34	1936/37	05/09/36	Football League Division 1	Derby County 5 Manchester United 4	Baseball Ground	21194
35	1936/37	02/01/37	Football League Division 1	Manchester United 2 Derby County 2	Old Trafford	31883
36	1938/39	22/10/38	Football League Division 1	Derby County 5 Manchester United 1	Baseball Ground	26612
37	1938/39	25/02/39	Football League Division 1	Manchester United 1 Derby County 1	Old Trafford	37166
38	1946/47	09/11/46	Football League Division 1	Manchester United 4 Derby County 1	Maine Road	57340
39	1946/47	15/03/47	Football League Division 1	Derby County 4 Manchester United 3	Baseball Ground	19579
40	1947/48	15/11/47	Football League Division 1	Derby County 1 Manchester United 1	Baseball Ground	32990
41	1947/48	13/03/48	FA Cup Semi-Final	Manchester United 3 Derby County 1	Hillsborough	60000
42	1947/48	03/04/48	Football League Division 1	Manchester United 1 Derby County 0	Maine Road	49609
43	1948/49	21/08/48	Football League Division 1	Manchester United 1 Derby County 2	Maine Road	52620
44	1948/49	18/12/48	Football League Division 1	Derby County 1 Manchester United 3	Baseball Ground	31498
45	1949/50	20/08/49	Football League Division 1	Derby County 0 Manchester United 1	Baseball Ground	35687
46	1949/50	17/12/49	Football League Division 1	Manchester United 0 Derby County 1	Old Trafford	33753
47	1950/51	23/03/51	Football League Division 1	Manchester United 2 Derby County 0	Old Trafford	42009
48	1950/51	26/03/51	Football League Division 1	Derby County 2 Manchester United 4	Baseball Ground	25860
49	1951/52	06/10/51	Football League Division 1	Manchester United 2 Derby County 1	Old Trafford	39767
50	1951/52	16/02/52	Football League Division 1	Derby County 0 Manchester United 3	Baseball Ground	27693
51	1952/53	10/09/52	Football League Division 1	Derby County 2 Manchester United 3	Baseball Ground	20226
52	1952/53	01/01/53	Football League Division 1	Manchester United 1 Derby County 0	Old Trafford	34813
53	1959/60	09/01/60	FA Cup 3rd Round	Derby County 2 Manchester United 4	Baseball Ground	33297
54	1965/66	22/01/66	FA Cup 3rd Round	Derby County 2 Manchester United 5	Baseball Ground	33827
55	1969/70	04/10/69	Football League Division 1	Derby County 2 Manchester United 0	Baseball Ground	40724
56	1969/70	12/11/69	League Cup 5th Round	Derby County 0 Manchester United 0	Baseball Ground	38895
57	1969/70	19/11/69	League Cup 5th Round Replay	Manchester United 1 Derby County 0	Old Trafford	57393
58	1969/70	31/01/70	Football League Division 1	Manchester United 1 Derby County 0	Old Trafford	59315
59	1970/71	26/12/70	Football League Division 1	Derby County 4 Manchester United 4	Baseball Ground	34068
60	1970/71	10/04/71	Football League Division 1	Manchester United 1 Derby County 2	Old Trafford	45691
61	1971/72	14/08/71	Football League Division 1	Derby County 2 Manchester United 2	Baseball Ground	35886
62	1971/72	16/10/71	Football League Division 1	Manchester United 1 Derby County 0	Old Trafford	53247
63	1972/73	23/09/72	Football League Division 1	Manchester United 3 Derby County 0	Old Trafford	48255
64	1972/73	26/12/72	Football League Division 1	Derby County 3 Manchester United 1	Baseball Ground	35098
65	1973/74	13/10/73	Football League Division 1	Manchester United 0 Derby County 1	Old Trafford	43724
66	1973/74	16/02/74	Football League Division 1	Derby County 2 Manchester United 2	Baseball Ground	29987
67	1975/76	24/09/75	Football League Division 1	Derby County 2 Manchester United 1	Baseball Ground	33187
68	1975/76	25/02/76	Football League Division 1	Manchester United 1 Derby County 1	Old Trafford	59632
69	1975/76	03/04/76	FA Cup Semi-Final	Manchester United 2 Derby County 0	Hillsborough	55000
70	1976/77	28/08/76	Football League Division 1	Derby County 0 Manchester United 0	Baseball Ground	30054
71	1976/77	05/02/77	Football League Division 1	Manchester United 3 Derby County 1	Old Trafford	54044
72	1977/78	03/09/77	Football League Division 1	Derby County 0 Manchester United 1	Baseball Ground	21279
73	1977/78	21/01/78	Football League Division 1	Manchester United 4 Derby County 0	Old Trafford	57115
74	1978/79	09/12/78	Football League Division 1	Derby County 1 Manchester United 3	Baseball Ground	23180
75	1978/79	28/04/79	Football League Division 1	Manchester United 0 Derby County 0	Old Trafford	42546
76	1979/80	15/09/79	Football League Division 1	Manchester United 1 Derby County 0	Old Trafford	54308
77	1979/80	02/02/80	Football League Division 1	Derby County 1 Manchester United 3	Baseball Ground	27783
78	1982/83	19/02/83	FA Cup 5th Round	Derby County 0 Manchester United 1	Baseball Ground	33022
79	1987/88	10/02/88	Football League Division 1	Derby County 1 Manchester United 2	Baseball Ground	20016
80	1987/88	02/04/88	Football League Division 1	Manchester United 4 Derby County 1	Old Trafford	40146
81	1988/89	12/11/88	Football League Division 1	Derby County 2 Manchester United 2	Baseball Ground	24080
82	1988/89	15/04/89	Football League Division 1	Manchester United 0 Derby County 2	Old Trafford	34145
83	1989/90	26/08/89	Football League Division 1	Derby County 2 Manchester United 0	Baseball Ground	22175
84	1989/90	13/01/90	Football League Division 1	Manchester United 1 Derby County 2	Old Trafford	38985
85	1990/91	10/11/90	Football League Division 1	Derby County 0 Manchester United 0	Baseball Ground	21115
86	1990/91	16/04/91	Football League Division 1	Manchester United 3 Derby County 1	Old Trafford	32776
87	1996/97	04/09/96	FA Premiership	Derby County 1 Manchester United 1	Baseball Ground	18026
88	1996/97	05/04/97	FA Premiership	Manchester United 2 Derby County 3	Old Trafford	55243

UNITED v DERBY COUNTY (continued)

#	SEASON	DATE	COMPETITION / ROUND	MATCH RESULT	VENUE	ATT
89	1997/98	18/10/97	FA Premiership	Derby County 2 Manchester United 2	Pride Park	30014
90	1997/98	21/02/98	FA Premiership	Manchester United 2 Derby County 0	Old Trafford	55170
91	1998/99	24/10/98	FA Premiership	Derby County 1 Manchester United 1	Pride Park	30867
92	1998/99	03/02/99	FA Premiership	Manchester United 1 Derby County 0	Old Trafford	55174
93	1999/00	20/11/99	FA Premiership	Derby County 1 Manchester United 2	Pride Park	33370
94	1999/00	11/03/00	FA Premiership	Manchester United 3 Derby County 1	Old Trafford	61619
95	2000/01	25/11/00	FA Premiership	Derby County 0 Manchester United 3	Pride Park	32910
96	2000/01	05/05/01	FA Premiership	Manchester United 0 Derby County 1	Old Trafford	67526
97	2001/02	12/12/01	FA Premiership	Manchester United 5 Derby County 0	Old Trafford	67577
98	2001/02	03/03/02	FA Premiership	Derby County 2 Manchester United 2	Pride Park	33041
99	2007/08	08/12/07	FA Premiership	Manchester United 4 Derby County 1	Old Trafford	75725
100	2007/08	15/03/08	FA Premiership	Derby County 0 Manchester United 1	Pride Park	33072

UNITED v DINAMO BUCHAREST

CHAMPIONS LEAGUE						
VENUE	P	W	D	L	F	A
HOME	1	1	0	0	3	0
AWAY	1	1	0	0	2	1
TOTAL	2	2	0	0	5	1

#	SEASON	DATE	COMPETITION / ROUND	MATCH RESULT	VENUE	ATT
1	2004/05	11/08/04	Champions League Qualifying Round 1st Leg	Dinamo Bucharest 1 Manchester United 2	National Stadium	58000
2	2004/05	25/08/04	Champions League Qualifying Round 2nd Leg	Manchester United 3 Dinamo Bucharest 0	Old Trafford	61041

UNITED v DJURGARDENS

INTER-CITIES' FAIRS CUP						
VENUE	P	W	D	L	F	A
HOME	1	1	0	0	6	1
AWAY	1	0	1	0	1	1
TOTAL	2	1	1	0	7	2

#	SEASON	DATE	COMPETITION / ROUND	MATCH RESULT	VENUE	ATT
1	1964/65	23/09/64	Inter-Cities' Fairs Cup 1st Round 1st Leg	Djurgardens 1 Manchester United 1	Roasunda Stadion	6537
2	1964/65	27/10/64	Inter-Cities' Fairs Cup 1st Round 2nd Leg	Manchester United 6 Djurgardens 1	Old Trafford	38437

UNITED v DONCASTER ROVERS

LEAGUE DIVISION TWO						
VENUE	P	W	D	L	F	A
HOME	4	3	1	0	16	0
AWAY	4	1	2	1	3	6
TOTAL	8	4	3	1	19	6

#	SEASON	DATE	COMPETITION / ROUND	MATCH RESULT	VENUE	ATT
1	1901/02	26/10/01	Football League Division 2	Newton Heath 6 Doncaster Rovers 0	Bank Street	7000
2	1901/02	22/02/02	Football League Division 2	Doncaster Rovers 4 Newton Heath 0	Town Moor Avenue	3000
3	1902/03	28/02/03	Football League Division 2	Doncaster Rovers 2 Manchester United 2	Town Moor Avenue	4000
4	1902/03	13/04/03	Football League Division 2	Manchester United 4 Doncaster Rovers 0	Bank Street	6000
5	1904/05	03/12/04	Football League Division 2	Doncaster Rovers 0 Manchester United 1	Town Moor Avenue	10000
6	1904/05	01/04/05	Football League Division 2	Manchester United 6 Doncaster Rovers 0	Bank Street	6000
7	1935/36	30/11/35	Football League Division 2	Manchester United 0 Doncaster Rovers 0	Old Trafford	23569
8	1935/36	04/04/36	Football League Division 2	Doncaster Rovers 0 Manchester United 0	Belle Vue Stadium	13474

UNITED v DUKLA PRAGUE

ALL COMPETITIVE MATCHES							EUROPEAN CUP							EUROPEAN CUP-WINNERS' CUP					
VENUE	P	W	D	L	F	A	VENUE	P	W	D	L	F	A	VENUE	P	W	D	L	F	A
HOME	2	1	1	0	4	1	HOME	1	1	0	0	3	0	HOME	1	0	1	0	1	1
AWAY	2	0	1	1	2	3	AWAY	1	0	0	1	0	1	AWAY	1	0	1	0	2	2
TOTAL	4	1	2	1	6	4	TOTAL	2	1	0	1	3	1	TOTAL	2	0	2	0	3	3

#	SEASON	DATE	COMPETITION / ROUND	MATCH RESULT	VENUE	ATT
1	1957/58	20/11/57	European Cup 1st Round 1st Leg	Manchester United 3 Dukla Prague 0	Old Trafford	60000
2	1957/58	04/12/57	European Cup 1st Round 2nd Leg	Dukla Prague 1 Manchester United 0	Stadium Strahov	35000
3	1983/84	14/09/83	European CWC 1st Round 1st Leg	Manchester United 1 Dukla Prague 1	Old Trafford	39745
4	1983/84	27/09/83	European CWC 1st Round 2nd Leg	Dukla Prague 2 Manchester United 2 (United won the tie on away goals rule)	Stadion Juliska	28850

UNITED v DUNDEE UNITED

UEFA CUP						
VENUE	P	W	D	L	F	A
HOME	1	0	1	0	2	2
AWAY	1	1	0	0	3	2
TOTAL	2	1	1	0	5	4

#	SEASON	DATE	COMPETITION / ROUND	MATCH RESULT	VENUE	ATT
1	1984/85	28/11/84	UEFA Cup 3rd Round 1st Leg	Manchester United 2 Dundee United 2	Old Trafford	48278
2	1984/85	12/12/84	UEFA Cup 3rd Round 2nd Leg	Dundee United 2 Manchester United 3	Tannadice Park	21821

UNITED v DYNAMO KIEV

CHAMPIONS LEAGUE						
VENUE	P	W	D	L	F	A
HOME	2	2	0	0	5	0
AWAY	2	1	1	0	4	2
TOTAL	4	3	1	0	9	2

#	SEASON	DATE	COMPETITION / ROUND	MATCH RESULT	VENUE	ATT
1	2000/01	19/09/00	Champions League Phase 1 Match 2	Dynamo Kiev 0 Manchester United 0	Republican Stadium	65000
2	2000/01	08/11/00	Champions League Phase 1 Match 6	Manchester United 1 Dynamo Kiev 0	Old Trafford	66776
3	2007/08	23/10/07	Champions League Phase 1 Match 3	Dynamo Kiev 2 Manchester United 4	Olympic Stadium	43000
4	2007/08	07/11/07	Champions League Phase 1 Match 4	Manchester United 4 Dynamo Kiev 0	Old Trafford	75017

UNITED v ESTUDIANTES de la PLATA

INTER-CONTINENTAL CUP						
VENUE	P	W	D	L	F	A
HOME	1	0	1	0	1	1
AWAY	1	0	0	1	0	1
TOTAL	2	0	1	1	1	2

#	SEASON	DATE	COMPETITION / ROUND	MATCH RESULT	VENUE	ATT
1	1968/69	25/09/68	Inter-Continental Cup Final 1st Leg	Estudiantes de la Plata 1 Manchester United 0	Boca Juniors Stadium	55000
2	1968/69	16/10/68	Inter-Continental Cup Final 2nd Leg	Manchester United 1 Estudiantes de la Plata 1	Old Trafford	63500

UNITED v EVERTON

ALL COMPETITIVE MATCHES

VENUE	P	W	D	L	F	A
HOME	86	47	21	18	146	83
AWAY	85	28	17	40	112	163
NEUTRAL	4	1	0	3	1	4
TOTAL	175	76	38	61	259	250

ALL LEAGUE MATCHES

VENUE	P	W	D	L	F	A
HOME	79	44	20	15	141	76
AWAY	79	25	17	37	104	153
TOTAL	158	69	37	52	245	229

ALL CUP MATCHES

VENUE	P	W	D	L	F	A
HOME	7	3	1	3	5	7
AWAY	5	3	0	2	8	6
NEUTRAL	3	1	0	2	1	2
TOTAL	15	7	1	7	14	15

PREMIERSHIP

VENUE	P	W	D	L	F	A
HOME	16	12	3	1	34	12
AWAY	16	13	1	2	33	13
TOTAL	32	25	4	3	67	25

LEAGUE DIVISION ONE

VENUE	P	W	D	L	F	A
HOME	63	32	17	14	107	64
AWAY	63	12	16	35	71	140
TOTAL	126	44	33	49	178	204

INTER-CITIES' FAIRS CUP

VENUE	P	W	D	L	F	A
HOME	1	0	1	0	1	1
AWAY	1	1	0	0	2	1
TOTAL	2	1	1	0	3	2

FA CUP

VENUE	P	W	D	L	F	A
HOME	4	3	0	1	3	1
AWAY	3	1	0	2	4	5
NEUTRAL	3	1	0	2	1	2
TOTAL	10	5	0	5	8	8

LEAGUE CUP

VENUE	P	W	D	L	F	A
HOME	2	0	0	2	1	5
AWAY	1	1	0	0	2	0
NEUTRAL	0	0	0	0	0	0
TOTAL	3	1	0	2	3	5

CHARITY SHIELD

VENUE	P	W	D	L	F	A
HOME	0	0	0	0	0	0
AWAY	1	0	0	1	0	4
NEUTRAL	1	0	0	1	0	2
TOTAL	2	0	0	2	0	6

#	SEASON	DATE	COMPETITION / ROUND	MATCH RESULT	VENUE	ATT
1	1892/93	24/09/92	Football League Division 1	Everton 6 Newton Heath 0	Goodison Park	10000
2	1892/93	19/10/92	Football League Division 1	Newton Heath 3 Everton 4	North Road	4000
3	1893/94	02/12/93	Football League Division 1	Newton Heath 0 Everton 3	Bank Street	6000
4	1893/94	06/01/94	Football League Division 1	Everton 2 Newton Heath 0	Goodison Park	8000
5	1902/03	21/02/03	FA Cup 2nd Round	Everton 3 Manchester United 1	Goodison Park	15000
6	1906/07	03/11/06	Football League Division 1	Everton 3 Manchester United 0	Goodison Park	20000
7	1906/07	22/04/07	Football League Division 1	Manchester United 3 Everton 0	Bank Street	10000
8	1907/08	09/11/07	Football League Division 1	Manchester United 4 Everton 3	Bank Street	30000
9	1907/08	08/04/08	Football League Division 1	Everton 1 Manchester United 3	Goodison Park	17000
10	1908/09	05/12/08	Football League Division 1	Everton 3 Manchester United 2	Goodison Park	35000
11	1908/09	06/02/09	FA Cup 2nd Round	Manchester United 1 Everton 0	Bank Street	35217
12	1908/09	10/04/09	Football League Division 1	Manchester United 2 Everton 2	Bank Street	8000
13	1909/10	06/04/10	Football League Division 1	Manchester United 3 Everton 2	Old Trafford	5500
14	1909/10	23/04/10	Football League Division 1	Everton 3 Manchester United 3	Goodison Park	10000
15	1910/11	24/09/10	Football League Division 1	Everton 0 Manchester United 1	Goodison Park	25000
16	1910/11	28/01/11	Football League Division 1	Manchester United 2 Everton 2	Old Trafford	45000
17	1911/12	09/09/11	Football League Division 1	Manchester United 2 Everton 1	Old Trafford	20000
18	1911/12	06/01/12	Football League Division 1	Everton 4 Manchester United 0	Goodison Park	12000
19	1912/13	21/09/12	Football League Division 1	Manchester United 2 Everton 0	Old Trafford	40000
20	1912/13	18/01/13	Football League Division 1	Everton 4 Manchester United 1	Goodison Park	20000
21	1913/14	25/12/13	Football League Division 1	Manchester United 0 Everton 1	Old Trafford	25000
22	1913/14	26/12/13	Football League Division 1	Everton 5 Manchester United 0	Goodison Park	40000
23	1914/15	24/10/14	Football League Division 1	Everton 4 Manchester United 2	Goodison Park	15000
24	1914/15	27/02/15	Football League Division 1	Manchester United 1 Everton 2	Old Trafford	10000
25	1919/20	06/03/20	Football League Division 1	Manchester United 1 Everton 0	Old Trafford	25000
26	1919/20	13/03/20	Football League Division 1	Everton 0 Manchester United 0	Goodison Park	30000
27	1920/21	12/02/21	Football League Division 1	Manchester United 1 Everton 2	Old Trafford	30000
28	1920/21	09/03/21	Football League Division 1	Everton 2 Manchester United 0	Goodison Park	38000
29	1921/22	27/08/21	Football League Division 1	Everton 5 Manchester United 0	Goodison Park	30000
30	1921/22	03/09/21	Football League Division 1	Manchester United 2 Everton 1	Old Trafford	25000
31	1925/26	07/11/25	Football League Division 1	Everton 1 Manchester United 3	Goodison Park	12387
32	1925/26	20/03/26	Football League Division 1	Manchester United 0 Everton 0	Old Trafford	30058
33	1926/27	20/11/26	Football League Division 1	Manchester United 2 Everton 1	Old Trafford	24361
34	1926/27	09/04/27	Football League Division 1	Everton 0 Manchester United 0	Goodison Park	22564
35	1927/28	08/10/27	Football League Division 1	Everton 5 Manchester United 2	Goodison Park	40000
36	1927/28	14/03/28	Football League Division 1	Manchester United 1 Everton 0	Old Trafford	25667
37	1928/29	15/12/28	Football League Division 1	Manchester United 1 Everton 1	Old Trafford	17080
38	1928/29	27/04/29	Football League Division 1	Everton 2 Manchester United 4	Goodison Park	19442
39	1929/30	14/12/29	Football League Division 1	Everton 0 Manchester United 0	Goodison Park	18182
40	1929/30	19/04/30	Football League Division 1	Manchester United 3 Everton 3	Old Trafford	13320
41	1936/37	26/03/37	Football League Division 1	Manchester United 2 Everton 1	Old Trafford	30071
42	1936/37	29/03/37	Football League Division 1	Everton 2 Manchester United 3	Goodison Park	28395

UNITED v EVERTON (continued)

#	SEASON	DATE	COMPETITION / ROUND	MATCH RESULT	VENUE	ATT
43	1938/39	19/11/38	Football League Division 1	Everton 3 Manchester United 0	Goodison Park	31809
44	1938/39	29/03/39	Football League Division 1	Manchester United 0 Everton 2	Old Trafford	18438
45	1946/47	16/11/46	Football League Division 1	Everton 2 Manchester United 2	Goodison Park	45832
46	1946/47	22/03/47	Football League Division 1	Manchester United 3 Everton 0	Maine Road	43441
47	1947/48	22/11/47	Football League Division 1	Manchester United 2 Everton 2	Maine Road	35509
48	1947/48	10/04/48	Football League Division 1	Everton 2 Manchester United 0	Goodison Park	44198
49	1948/49	06/11/48	Football League Division 1	Manchester United 2 Everton 0	Maine Road	42789
50	1948/49	27/04/49	Football League Division 1	Everton 2 Manchester United 0	Goodison Park	39106
51	1949/50	12/11/49	Football League Division 1	Everton 0 Manchester United 0	Goodison Park	46672
52	1949/50	01/04/50	Football League Division 1	Manchester United 1 Everton 1	Old Trafford	35381
53	1950/51	28/10/50	Football League Division 1	Everton 1 Manchester United 4	Goodison Park	51142
54	1950/51	17/03/51	Football League Division 1	Manchester United 3 Everton 0	Old Trafford	29317
55	1952/53	14/02/53	FA Cup 5th Round	Everton 2 Manchester United 1	Goodison Park	77920
56	1954/55	30/10/54	Football League Division 1	Everton 4 Manchester United 2	Goodison Park	63021
57	1954/55	19/03/55	Football League Division 1	Manchester United 1 Everton 2	Old Trafford	32295
58	1955/56	07/09/55	Football League Division 1	Manchester United 2 Everton 1	Old Trafford	27843
59	1955/56	14/09/55	Football League Division 1	Everton 4 Manchester United 2	Goodison Park	34897
60	1956/57	20/10/56	Football League Division 1	Manchester United 2 Everton 5	Old Trafford	43151
61	1956/57	16/02/57	FA Cup 5th Round	Manchester United 1 Everton 0	Old Trafford	61803
62	1956/57	06/03/57	Football League Division 1	Everton 1 Manchester United 2	Goodison Park	34029
63	1957/58	28/08/57	Football League Division 1	Manchester United 3 Everton 0	Old Trafford	59103
64	1957/58	04/09/57	Football League Division 1	Everton 3 Manchester United 3	Goodison Park	72077
65	1958/59	18/10/58	Football League Division 1	Everton 3 Manchester United 2	Goodison Park	64079
66	1958/59	07/03/59	Football League Division 1	Manchester United 2 Everton 1	Old Trafford	51254
67	1959/60	28/11/59	Football League Division 1	Everton 2 Manchester United 1	Goodison Park	46095
68	1959/60	30/04/60	Football League Division 1	Manchester United 5 Everton 0	Old Trafford	43823
69	1960/61	24/08/60	Football League Division 1	Everton 4 Manchester United 0	Goodison Park	51602
70	1960/61	31/08/60	Football League Division 1	Manchester United 4 Everton 0	Old Trafford	51818
71	1961/62	02/12/61	Football League Division 1	Everton 5 Manchester United 1	Goodison Park	48099
72	1961/62	21/04/62	Football League Division 1	Manchester United 1 Everton 1	Old Trafford	31926
73	1962/63	22/08/62	Football League Division 1	Everton 3 Manchester United 1	Goodison Park	69501
74	1962/63	29/08/62	Football League Division 1	Manchester United 0 Everton 1	Old Trafford	63437
75	1963/64	17/08/63	FA Charity Shield	Everton 4 Manchester United 0	Goodison Park	54840
76	1963/64	31/08/63	Football League Division 1	Manchester United 5 Everton 1	Old Trafford	62965
77	1963/64	21/12/63	Football League Division 1	Everton 4 Manchester United 0	Goodison Park	48027
78	1964/65	08/09/64	Football League Division 1	Everton 3 Manchester United 3	Goodison Park	63024
79	1964/65	16/09/64	Football League Division 1	Manchester United 2 Everton 1	Old Trafford	49968
80	1964/65	20/01/65	Inter-Cities Fairs Cup 3rd Round 1st Leg	Manchester United 1 Everton 1	Old Trafford	50000
81	1964/65	09/02/65	Inter-Cities Fairs Cup 3rd Round 2nd Leg	Everton 1 Manchester United 2	Goodison Park	54397
82	1965/66	15/12/65	Football League Division 1	Manchester United 3 Everton 0	Old Trafford	32624
83	1965/66	23/04/66	FA Cup Semi-Final	Manchester United 0 Everton 1	Burnden Park	60000
84	1965/66	25/04/66	Football League Division 1	Everton 0 Manchester United 0	Goodison Park	50843
85	1966/67	23/08/66	Football League Division 1	Everton 1 Manchester United 2	Goodison Park	60657
86	1966/67	31/08/66	Football League Division 1	Manchester United 3 Everton 0	Old Trafford	61114
87	1967/68	19/08/67	Football League Division 1	Everton 3 Manchester United 1	Goodison Park	61452
88	1967/68	16/12/67	Football League Division 1	Manchester United 3 Everton 1	Old Trafford	60736
89	1968/69	10/08/68	Football League Division 1	Manchester United 2 Everton 1	Old Trafford	61311
90	1968/69	01/03/69	FA Cup 6th Round	Manchester United 0 Everton 1	Old Trafford	63464
91	1968/69	10/03/69	Football League Division 1	Everton 0 Manchester United 0	Goodison Park	57514
92	1969/70	13/08/69	Football League Division 1	Manchester United 0 Everton 2	Old Trafford	57752
93	1969/70	19/08/69	Football League Division 1	Everton 3 Manchester United 0	Goodison Park	53185
94	1970/71	02/09/70	Football League Division 1	Manchester United 2 Everton 0	Old Trafford	51346
95	1970/71	23/02/71	Football League Division 1	Everton 1 Manchester United 0	Goodison Park	52544
96	1971/72	31/08/71	Football League Division 1	Everton 1 Manchester United 0	Goodison Park	52151
97	1971/72	08/03/72	Football League Division 1	Manchester United 0 Everton 0	Old Trafford	38415
98	1972/73	19/08/72	Football League Division 1	Everton 2 Manchester United 0	Goodison Park	52348
99	1972/73	24/01/73	Football League Division 1	Manchester United 0 Everton 0	Old Trafford	58970
100	1973/74	15/04/74	Football League Division 1	Manchester United 3 Everton 0	Old Trafford	48424
101	1973/74	23/04/74	Football League Division 1	Everton 1 Manchester United 0	Goodison Park	46093
102	1975/76	23/12/75	Football League Division 1	Everton 1 Manchester United 1	Goodison Park	41732
103	1975/76	17/04/76	Football League Division 1	Manchester United 2 Everton 1	Old Trafford	61879

UNITED v EVERTON (continued)

#	SEASON	DATE	COMPETITION / ROUND	MATCH RESULT	VENUE	ATT
104	1976/77	01/12/76	League Cup 5th Round	Manchester United 0 Everton 3	Old Trafford	57738
105	1976/77	27/12/76	Football League Division 1	Manchester United 4 Everton 0	Old Trafford	56786
106	1976/77	05/04/77	Football League Division 1	Everton 1 Manchester United 2	Goodison Park	38216
107	1977/78	26/12/77	Football League Division 1	Everton 2 Manchester United 6	Goodison Park	48335
108	1977/78	27/03/78	Football League Division 1	Manchester United 1 Everton 2	Old Trafford	55277
109	1978/79	02/09/78	Football League Division 1	Manchester United 1 Everton 1	Old Trafford	53982
110	1978/79	21/11/78	Football League Division 1	Everton 3 Manchester United 0	Goodison Park	42126
111	1979/80	27/10/79	Football League Division 1	Everton 0 Manchester United 0	Goodison Park	37708
112	1979/80	12/03/80	Football League Division 1	Manchester United 0 Everton 0	Old Trafford	45515
113	1980/81	25/10/80	Football League Division 1	Manchester United 2 Everton 0	Old Trafford	54260
114	1980/81	28/03/81	Football League Division 1	Everton 0 Manchester United 1	Goodison Park	25856
115	1981/82	06/01/82	Football League Division 1	Manchester United 1 Everton 1	Old Trafford	40451
116	1981/82	10/04/82	Football League Division 1	Everton 3 Manchester United 3	Goodison Park	29306
117	1982/83	08/09/82	Football League Division 1	Manchester United 2 Everton 1	Old Trafford	43186
118	1982/83	12/03/83	FA Cup 6th Round	Manchester United 1 Everton 0	Old Trafford	58198
119	1982/83	19/04/83	Football League Division 1	Everton 2 Manchester United 0	Goodison Park	21715
120	1983/84	03/12/83	Football League Division 1	Manchester United 0 Everton 1	Old Trafford	43664
121	1983/84	05/05/84	Football League Division 1	Everton 1 Manchester United 1	Goodison Park	28802
122	1984/85	27/10/84	Football League Division 1	Everton 5 Manchester United 0	Goodison Park	40742
123	1984/85	30/10/84	League Cup 3rd Round	Manchester United 1 Everton 2	Old Trafford	50918
124	1984/85	02/03/85	Football League Division 1	Manchester United 1 Everton 1	Old Trafford	51150
125	1984/85	18/05/85	FA Cup Final	Manchester United 1 Everton 0	Wembley	100000
126	1985/86	10/08/85	FA Charity Shield	Manchester United 0 Everton 2	Wembley	82000
127	1985/86	26/12/85	Football League Division 1	Everton 3 Manchester United 1	Goodison Park	42551
128	1985/86	31/03/86	Football League Division 1	Manchester United 0 Everton 0	Old Trafford	51189
129	1986/87	21/09/86	Football League Division 1	Everton 3 Manchester United 1	Goodison Park	25843
130	1986/87	28/02/87	Football League Division 1	Manchester United 0 Everton 0	Old Trafford	47421
131	1987/88	19/09/87	Football League Division 1	Everton 2 Manchester United 1	Goodison Park	38439
132	1987/88	28/12/87	Football League Division 1	Manchester United 2 Everton 1	Old Trafford	47024
133	1988/89	30/10/88	Football League Division 1	Everton 1 Manchester United 1	Goodison Park	27005
134	1988/89	10/05/89	Football League Division 1	Manchester United 1 Everton 2	Old Trafford	26722
135	1989/90	09/09/89	Football League Division 1	Everton 3 Manchester United 2	Goodison Park	37916
136	1989/90	14/03/90	Football League Division 1	Manchester United 0 Everton 0	Old Trafford	37398
137	1990/91	01/12/90	Football League Division 1	Everton 0 Manchester United 1	Goodison Park	32400
138	1990/91	02/03/91	Football League Division 1	Manchester United 0 Everton 2	Old Trafford	45656
139	1991/92	24/08/91	Football League Division 1	Everton 0 Manchester United 0	Goodison Park	36085
140	1991/92	11/01/92	Football League Division 1	Manchester United 1 Everton 0	Old Trafford	46619
141	1992/93	19/08/92	FA Premiership	Manchester United 0 Everton 3	Old Trafford	31901
142	1992/93	12/09/92	FA Premiership	Everton 0 Manchester United 2	Goodison Park	30002
143	1993/94	23/10/93	FA Premiership	Everton 0 Manchester United 1	Goodison Park	35430
144	1993/94	30/11/93	League Cup 4th Round	Everton 0 Manchester United 2	Goodison Park	34052
145	1993/94	22/01/94	FA Premiership	Manchester United 1 Everton 0	Old Trafford	44750
146	1994/95	01/10/94	FA Premiership	Manchester United 2 Everton 0	Old Trafford	43803
147	1994/95	25/02/95	FA Premiership	Everton 1 Manchester United 0	Goodison Park	40011
148	1994/95	20/05/95	FA Cup Final	Manchester United 0 Everton 1	Wembley	79592
149	1995/96	09/09/95	FA Premiership	Everton 2 Manchester United 3	Goodison Park	39496
150	1995/96	21/02/96	FA Premiership	Manchester United 2 Everton 0	Old Trafford	42459
151	1996/97	21/08/96	FA Premiership	Manchester United 2 Everton 2	Old Trafford	54943
152	1996/97	22/03/97	FA Premiership	Everton 0 Manchester United 2	Goodison Park	40079
153	1997/98	27/08/97	FA Premiership	Everton 0 Manchester United 2	Goodison Park	40079
154	1997/98	26/12/97	FA Premiership	Manchester United 2 Everton 0	Old Trafford	55167
155	1998/99	31/10/98	FA Premiership	Everton 1 Manchester United 4	Goodison Park	40079
156	1998/99	21/03/99	FA Premiership	Manchester United 3 Everton 1	Old Trafford	55182
157	1999/00	08/08/99	FA Premiership	Everton 1 Manchester United 1	Goodison Park	39141
158	1999/00	04/12/99	FA Premiership	Manchester United 5 Everton 1	Old Trafford	55193
159	2000/01	16/09/00	FA Premiership	Everton 1 Manchester United 3	Goodison Park	38541
160	2000/01	03/02/01	FA Premiership	Manchester United 1 Everton 0	Old Trafford	67528
161	2001/02	08/09/01	FA Premiership	Manchester United 4 Everton 1	Old Trafford	67534
162	2001/02	26/12/01	FA Premiership	Everton 0 Manchester United 2	Goodison Park	39948
163	2002/03	07/10/02	FA Premiership	Manchester United 3 Everton 0	Old Trafford	67629
164	2002/03	11/05/03	FA Premiership	Everton 1 Manchester United 2	Goodison Park	40168
165	2003/04	26/12/03	FA Premiership	Manchester United 3 Everton 2	Old Trafford	67642
166	2003/04	07/02/04	FA Premiership	Everton 3 Manchester United 4	Goodison Park	40190

UNITED v EVERTON (continued)

#	SEASON	DATE	COMPETITION / ROUND	MATCH RESULT	VENUE	ATT
167	2004/05	30/08/04	FA Premiership	Manchester United 0 Everton 0	Old Trafford	67803
168	2004/05	19/02/05	FA Cup 5th Round	Everton 0 Manchester United 2	Goodison Park	38664
169	2004/05	20/04/05	FA Premiership	Everton 1 Manchester United 0	Goodison Park	37160
170	2005/06	13/08/05	FA Premiership	Everton 0 Manchester United 2	Goodison Park	38610
171	2005/06	11/12/05	FA Premiership	Manchester United 1 Everton 1	Old Trafford	67831
172	2006/07	29/11/06	FA Premiership	Manchester United 3 Everton 0	Old Trafford	75723
173	2006/07	28/04/07	FA Premiership	Everton 2 Manchester United 4	Goodison Park	39682
174	2007/08	15/09/07	FA Premiership	Everton 0 Manchester United 1	Goodison Park	39364
175	2007/08	23/12/07	FA Premiership	Manchester United 2 Everton 1	Old Trafford	75749

UNITED v EXETER CITY

ALL COMPETITIVE MATCHES							FA CUP							LEAGUE CUP						
VENUE	P	W	D	L	F	A	VENUE	P	W	D	L	F	A	VENUE	P	W	D	L	F	A
HOME	2	1	1	0	4	1	HOME	1	0	1	0	0	0	HOME	1	1	0	0	4	1
AWAY	3	2	1	0	6	2	AWAY	2	2	0	0	5	1	AWAY	1	0	1	0	1	1
TOTAL	5	3	2	0	10	3	TOTAL	3	2	1	0	5	1	TOTAL	2	1	1	0	5	2

#	SEASON	DATE	COMPETITION / ROUND	MATCH RESULT	VENUE	ATT
1	1960/61	19/10/60	League Cup 1st Round	Exeter City 1 Manchester United 1	St James' Park	14494
2	1960/61	26/10/60	League Cup 1st Round Replay	Manchester United 4 Exeter City 1	Old Trafford	15662
3	1968/69	04/01/69	FA Cup 3rd Round	Exeter City 1 Manchester United 3	St James' Park	18500
4	2004/05	08/01/05	FA Cup 3rd Round	Manchester United 0 Exeter City 0	Old Trafford	67551
5	2004/05	19/01/05	FA Cup 3rd Round Replay	Exeter City 0 Manchester United 2	St James' Park	9033

UNITED v FENERBAHCE

CHAMPIONS LEAGUE						
VENUE	P	W	D	L	F	A
HOME	2	1	0	1	6	3
AWAY	2	1	0	1	2	3
TOTAL	4	2	0	2	8	6

#	SEASON	DATE	COMPETITION / ROUND	MATCH RESULT	VENUE	ATT
1	1996/97	16/10/96	Champions League Phase 1 Match 3	Fenerbahce 0 Manchester United 2	Fenerbahce Stadium	26200
2	1996/97	30/10/96	Champions League Phase 1 Match 4	Manchester United 0 Fenerbahce 1	Old Trafford	53297
3	2004/05	28/09/04	Champions League Phase 1 Match 2	Manchester United 6 Fenerbahce 2	Old Trafford	67128
4	2004/05	08/12/04	Champions League Phase 1 Match 6	Fenerbahce 3 Manchester United 0	Sukru Saracoglu	35000

UNITED v FERENCVAROS

INTER-CITIES' FAIRS CUP						
VENUE	P	W	D	L	F	A
HOME	1	1	0	0	3	2
AWAY	2	0	0	2	1	3
TOTAL	3	1	0	2	4	5

#	SEASON	DATE	COMPETITION / ROUND	MATCH RESULT	VENUE	ATT
1	1964/65	31/05/65	Inter-Cities' Fairs Cup Semi-Final 1st Leg	Manchester United 3 Ferencvaros 2	Old Trafford	39902
2	1964/65	06/06/65	Inter-Cities' Fairs Cup Semi-Final 2nd Leg	Ferencvaros 1 Manchester United 0	Nep Stadion	50000
3	1964/65	16/06/65	Inter-Cities' Fairs Cup Semi-Final Replay	Ferencvaros 2 Manchester United 1	Nep Stadion	60000

UNITED v FEYENOORD

CHAMPIONS LEAGUE						
VENUE	P	W	D	L	F	A
HOME	1	1	0	0	2	1
AWAY	1	1	0	0	3	1
TOTAL	2	2	0	0	5	2

#	SEASON	DATE	COMPETITION / ROUND	MATCH RESULT	VENUE	ATT
1	1997/98	22/10/97	Champions League Phase 1 Match 3	Manchester United 2 Feyenoord 1	Old Trafford	53188
2	1997/98	05/11/97	Champions League Phase 1 Match 4	Feyenoord 1 Manchester United 3	Feyenoord Stadium	51000

UNITED v FIORENTINA

CHAMPIONS LEAGUE

VENUE	P	W	D	L	F	A
HOME	1	1	0	0	3	1
AWAY	1	0	0	1	0	2
TOTAL	2	1	0	1	3	3

#	SEASON	DATE	COMPETITION / ROUND	MATCH RESULT	VENUE	ATT
1	1999/00	23/11/99	Champions League Phase 2 Match 1	Fiorentina 2 Manchester United 0	Artemio Franchi	36002
2	1999/00	15/03/00	Champions League Phase 2 Match 5	Manchester United 3 Fiorentina 1	Old Trafford	59926

UNITED v FLEETWOOD RANGERS

FA CUP

VENUE	P	W	D	L	F	A
HOME	0	0	0	0	0	0
AWAY	1	0	1	0	2	2
TOTAL	1	0	1	0	2	2

#	SEASON	DATE	COMPETITION / ROUND	MATCH RESULT	VENUE	ATT
1	1886/87	30/10/86	FA Cup 1st Round	Fleetwood Rangers 2 Newton Heath 2 (Fleetwood awarded tie – see page 2)	Fleetwood Park	2000

UNITED v FULHAM

ALL COMPETITIVE MATCHES

VENUE	P	W	D	L	F	A
HOME	32	26	4	2	69	26
AWAY	33	12	12	9	54	45
NEUTRAL	3	1	1	1	7	6
TOTAL	68	39	17	12	130	77

ALL LEAGUE MATCHES

VENUE	P	W	D	L	F	A
HOME	28	23	3	2	63	23
AWAY	28	10	10	8	48	40
TOTAL	56	33	13	10	111	63

FA CUP

VENUE	P	W	D	L	F	A
HOME	4	3	1	0	6	3
AWAY	5	2	2	1	6	5
NEUTRAL	3	1	1	1	7	6
TOTAL	12	6	4	2	19	14

PREMIERSHIP

VENUE	P	W	D	L	F	A
HOME	7	6	0	1	19	8
AWAY	7	4	3	0	14	8
TOTAL	14	10	3	1	33	16

LEAGUE DIVISION ONE

VENUE	P	W	D	L	F	A
HOME	12	10	1	1	32	11
AWAY	12	4	5	3	25	18
TOTAL	24	14	6	4	57	29

LEAGUE DIVISION TWO

VENUE	P	W	D	L	F	A
HOME	9	7	2	0	12	4
AWAY	9	2	2	5	9	14
TOTAL	18	9	4	5	21	18

#	SEASON	DATE	COMPETITION / ROUND	MATCH RESULT	VENUE	ATT
1	1904/05	14/01/05	FA Cup Intermediate Round	Manchester United 2 Fulham 2	Bank Street	17000
2	1904/05	18/01/05	FA Cup Intermediate Round Replay	Fulham 0 Manchester United 0	Craven Cottage	15000
3	1904/05	23/01/05	FA Cup Intermediate Round 2nd Replay	Manchester United 0 Fulham 1	Villa Park	6000
4	1907/08	07/03/08	FA Cup 4th Round	Fulham 2 Manchester United 1	Craven Cottage	41000
5	1922/23	21/10/22	Football League Division 2	Manchester United 1 Fulham 1	Old Trafford	18000
6	1922/23	28/10/22	Football League Division 2	Fulham 0 Manchester United 0	Craven Cottage	20000
7	1923/24	19/01/24	Football League Division 2	Fulham 3 Manchester United 1	Craven Cottage	15500
8	1923/24	26/01/24	Football League Division 2	Manchester United 0 Fulham 0	Old Trafford	25000
9	1924/25	01/11/24	Football League Division 2	Manchester United 2 Fulham 0	Old Trafford	24000
10	1924/25	07/03/25	Football League Division 2	Fulham 1 Manchester United 0	Craven Cottage	16000
11	1925/26	06/03/26	FA Cup 6th Round	Fulham 1 Manchester United 2	Craven Cottage	28699
12	1932/33	19/11/32	Football League Division 2	Manchester United 4 Fulham 3	Old Trafford	28803
13	1932/33	01/04/33	Football League Division 2	Fulham 3 Manchester United 1	Craven Cottage	21477
14	1933/34	04/11/33	Football League Division 2	Fulham 0 Manchester United 2	Craven Cottage	17049
15	1933/34	17/03/34	Football League Division 2	Manchester United 1 Fulham 0	Old Trafford	17565
16	1934/35	08/12/34	Football League Division 2	Manchester United 1 Fulham 0	Old Trafford	25706
17	1934/35	20/04/35	Football League Division 2	Fulham 3 Manchester United 1	Craven Cottage	11059
18	1935/36	12/10/35	Football League Division 2	Manchester United 1 Fulham 0	Old Trafford	22723
19	1935/36	01/04/36	Football League Division 2	Fulham 2 Manchester United 2	Craven Cottage	11137
20	1937/38	30/10/37	Football League Division 2	Fulham 1 Manchester United 0	Craven Cottage	17350
21	1937/38	12/03/38	Football League Division 2	Manchester United 1 Fulham 0	Old Trafford	30636
22	1949/50	10/12/49	Football League Division 1	Fulham 1 Manchester United 0	Craven Cottage	35362
23	1949/50	29/04/50	Football League Division 1	Manchester United 3 Fulham 0	Old Trafford	11968
24	1950/51	19/08/50	Football League Division 1	Manchester United 1 Fulham 0	Old Trafford	44042
25	1950/51	16/12/50	Football League Division 1	Fulham 2 Manchester United 2	Craven Cottage	19649

UNITED v FULHAM (continued)

#	SEASON	DATE	COMPETITION / ROUND	MATCH RESULT	VENUE	ATT
26	1951/52	25/12/51	Football League Division 1	Manchester United 3 Fulham 2	Old Trafford	33802
27	1951/52	26/12/51	Football League Division 1	Fulham 3 Manchester United 3	Craven Cottage	32671
28	1957/58	22/03/58	FA Cup Semi-Final	Manchester United 2 Fulham 2	Villa Park	69745
29	1957/58	26/03/58	FA Cup Semi-Final Replay	Manchester United 5 Fulham 3	Highbury	38000
30	1959/60	07/11/59	Football League Division 1	Manchester United 3 Fulham 3	Old Trafford	44063
31	1959/60	26/03/60	Football League Division 1	Fulham 0 Manchester United 5	Craven Cottage	38250
32	1960/61	10/12/60	Football League Division 1	Fulham 4 Manchester United 4	Craven Cottage	23625
33	1960/61	01/04/61	Football League Division 1	Manchester United 3 Fulham 1	Old Trafford	24654
34	1961/62	09/12/61	Football League Division 1	Manchester United 3 Fulham 0	Old Trafford	22193
35	1961/62	28/04/62	Football League Division 1	Fulham 2 Manchester United 0	Craven Cottage	40113
36	1962/63	26/12/62	Football League Division 1	Fulham 0 Manchester United 1	Craven Cottage	23928
37	1962/63	01/04/63	Football League Division 1	Manchester United 0 Fulham 2	Old Trafford	28124
38	1963/64	27/03/64	Football League Division 1	Fulham 2 Manchester United 2	Craven Cottage	41769
39	1963/64	30/03/64	Football League Division 1	Manchester United 3 Fulham 0	Old Trafford	42279
40	1964/65	05/09/64	Football League Division 1	Fulham 2 Manchester United 1	Craven Cottage	36291
41	1964/65	15/03/65	Football League Division 1	Manchester United 4 Fulham 1	Old Trafford	45402
42	1965/66	23/10/65	Football League Division 1	Manchester United 4 Fulham 1	Old Trafford	32716
43	1965/66	15/01/66	Football League Division 1	Fulham 0 Manchester United 1	Craven Cottage	33018
44	1966/67	27/03/67	Football League Division 1	Fulham 2 Manchester United 2	Craven Cottage	47290
45	1966/67	28/03/67	Football League Division 1	Manchester United 2 Fulham 1	Old Trafford	51673
46	1967/68	12/04/68	Football League Division 1	Fulham 0 Manchester United 4	Craven Cottage	40152
47	1967/68	15/04/68	Football League Division 1	Manchester United 3 Fulham 0	Old Trafford	60465
48	1974/75	05/10/74	Football League Division 2	Fulham 1 Manchester United 2	Craven Cottage	26513
49	1974/75	12/04/75	Football League Division 2	Manchester United 1 Fulham 0	Old Trafford	52971
50	1978/79	31/01/79	FA Cup 4th Round	Fulham 1 Manchester United 1	Craven Cottage	25229
51	1978/79	12/02/79	FA Cup 4th Round Replay	Manchester United 1 Fulham 0	Old Trafford	41200
52	1998/99	14/02/99	FA Cup 5th Round	Manchester United 1 Fulham 0	Old Trafford	54798
53	2000/01	07/01/01	FA Cup 3rd Round	Fulham 1 Manchester United 2	Craven Cottage	19178
54	2001/02	19/08/01	FA Premiership	Manchester United 3 Fulham 2	Old Trafford	67534
55	2001/02	30/12/01	FA Premiership	Fulham 2 Manchester United 3	Craven Cottage	21159
56	2002/03	19/10/02	FA Premiership	Fulham 1 Manchester United 1	Loftus Road	18103
57	2002/03	22/03/03	FA Premiership	Manchester United 3 Fulham 0	Old Trafford	67706
58	2003/04	25/10/03	FA Premiership	Manchester United 1 Fulham 3	Old Trafford	67727
59	2003/04	28/02/04	FA Premiership	Fulham 1 Manchester United 1	Loftus Road	18306
60	2003/04	06/03/04	FA Cup 6th Round	Manchester United 2 Fulham 1	Old Trafford	67614
61	2004/05	13/12/04	FA Premiership	Fulham 1 Manchester United 1	Craven Cottage	21940
62	2004/05	19/03/05	FA Premiership	Manchester United 1 Fulham 0	Old Trafford	67959
63	2005/06	01/10/05	FA Premiership	Fulham 2 Manchester United 3	Craven Cottage	21862
64	2005/06	04/02/06	FA Premiership	Manchester United 4 Fulham 2	Old Trafford	67884
65	2006/07	20/08/06	FA Premiership	Manchester United 5 Fulham 1	Old Trafford	75115
66	2006/07	24/02/07	FA Premiership	Fulham 1 Manchester United 2	Craven Cottage	24459
67	2007/08	03/12/07	FA Premiership	Manchester United 2 Fulham 0	Old Trafford	75055
68	2007/08	01/03/08	FA Premiership	Fulham 0 Manchester United 3	Craven Cottage	25314

UNITED v GAINSBOROUGH TRINITY

LEAGUE DIVISION TWO

VENUE	P	W	D	L	F	A
HOME	10	8	2	0	26	7
AWAY	10	5	3	2	10	7
TOTAL	20	13	5	2	36	14

#	SEASON	DATE	COMPETITION / ROUND	MATCH RESULT	VENUE	ATT
1	1896/97	01/09/96	Football League Division 2	Newton Heath 2 Gainsborough Trinity 0	Bank Street	4000
2	1896/97	21/10/96	Football League Division 2	Gainsborough Trinity 2 Newton Heath 0	The Northolme	4000
3	1897/98	27/12/97	Football League Division 2	Gainsborough Trinity 2 Newton Heath 1	The Northolme	3000
4	1897/98	08/04/98	Football League Division 2	Newton Heath 1 Gainsborough Trinity 0	Bank Street	5000
5	1898/99	03/09/98	Football League Division 2	Gainsborough Trinity 0 Newton Heath 2	The Northolme	2000
6	1898/99	31/12/98	Football League Division 2	Newton Heath 6 Gainsborough Trinity 1	Bank Street	2000
7	1899/00	02/09/99	Football League Division 2	Newton Heath 2 Gainsborough Trinity 2	Bank Street	8000
8	1899/00	30/12/99	Football League Division 2	Gainsborough Trinity 0 Newton Heath 1	The Northolme	2000

UNITED v GAINSBOROUGH TRINITY (continued)

#	SEASON	DATE	COMPETITION / ROUND	MATCH RESULT	VENUE	ATT
9	1900/01	13/10/00	Football League Division 2	Gainsborough Trinity 0 Newton Heath 1	The Northolme	2000
10	1900/01	16/02/01	Football League Division 2	Newton Heath 0 Gainsborough Trinity 0	Bank Street	7000
11	1901/02	07/09/01	Football League Division 2	Newton Heath 3 Gainsborough Trinity 0	Bank Street	3000
12	1901/02	04/01/02	Football League Division 2	Gainsborough Trinity 1 Newton Heath 1	The Northolme	2000
13	1902/03	06/09/02	Football League Division 2	Gainsborough Trinity 0 Manchester United 1	The Northolme	4000
14	1902/03	03/01/03	Football League Division 2	Manchester United 3 Gainsborough Trinity 1	Bank Street	8000
15	1903/04	19/12/03	Football League Division 2	Manchester United 4 Gainsborough Trinity 2	Bank Street	6000
16	1903/04	16/04/04	Football League Division 2	Gainsborough Trinity 0 Manchester United 1	The Northolme	4000
17	1904/05	10/12/04	Football League Division 2	Manchester United 3 Gainsborough Trinity 1	Bank Street	12000
18	1904/05	08/04/05	Football League Division 2	Gainsborough Trinity 0 Manchester United 0	The Northolme	6000
19	1905/06	25/10/05	Football League Division 2	Gainsborough Trinity 2 Manchester United 2	The Northolme	4000
20	1905/06	16/04/06	Football League Division 2	Manchester United 2 Gainsborough Trinity 0	Bank Street	20000

UNITED v GALATASARAY

EUROPEAN CUP / CHAMPIONS LEAGUE

VENUE	P	W	D	L	F	A
HOME	2	1	1	0	7	3
AWAY	2	0	2	0	0	0
TOTAL	4	1	3	0	7	3

#	SEASON	DATE	COMPETITION / ROUND	MATCH RESULT	VENUE	ATT
1	1993/94	20/10/93	European Cup 2nd Round 1st Leg	Manchester United 3 Galatasaray 3	Old Trafford	39346
2	1993/94	03/11/93	European Cup 2nd Round 2nd Leg	Galatasaray 0 Manchester United 0 (United lost the tie on away goals rule)	Ali Sami Yen	40000
3	1994/95	28/09/94	Champions League Phase 1 Match 2	Galatasaray 0 Manchester United 0	Ali Sami Yen	28605
4	1994/95	07/12/94	Champions League Phase 1 Match 6	Manchester United 4 Galatasaray 0	Old Trafford	39220

UNITED v GIRONDINS BORDEAUX

CHAMPIONS LEAGUE

VENUE	P	W	D	L	F	A
HOME	1	1	0	0	2	0
AWAY	1	1	0	0	2	1
TOTAL	2	2	0	0	4	1

#	SEASON	DATE	COMPETITION / ROUND	MATCH RESULT	VENUE	ATT
1	1999/00	01/03/00	Champions League Phase 2 Match 3	Manchester United 2 Girondins Bordeaux 0	Old Trafford	59786
2	1999/00	07/03/00	Champions League Phase 2 Match 4	Girondins Bordeaux 1 Manchester United 2	Stade Lescure	30130

UNITED v GLASGOW CELTIC

CHAMPIONS LEAGUE

VENUE	P	W	D	L	F	A
HOME	1	1	0	0	3	2
AWAY	1	0	0	1	0	1
TOTAL	2	1	0	1	3	3

#	SEASON	DATE	COMPETITION / ROUND	MATCH RESULT	VENUE	ATT
1	2006/07	13/09/06	Champions League Phase 1 Match 1	Manchester United 3 Glasgow Celtic 2	Old Trafford	74031
2	2006/07	21/11/06	Champions League Phase 1 Match 5	Glasgow Celtic 1 Manchester United 0	Celtic Park	60632

UNITED v GLASGOW RANGERS

CHAMPIONS LEAGUE						
VENUE	P	W	D	L	F	A
HOME	1	1	0	0	3	0
AWAY	1	1	0	0	1	0
TOTAL	2	2	0	0	4	0

#	SEASON	DATE	COMPETITION / ROUND	MATCH RESULT	VENUE	ATT
1	2003/04	22/10/03	Champions League Phase 1 Match 3	Glasgow Rangers 0 Manchester United 1	Ibrox Stadium	48730
2	2003/04	04/11/03	Champions League Phase 1 Match 4	Manchester United 3 Glasgow Rangers 0	Old Trafford	66707

UNITED v GLOSSOP

LEAGUE DIVISION TWO						
VENUE	P	W	D	L	F	A
HOME	7	6	1	0	20	5
AWAY	7	5	1	1	14	5
TOTAL	14	11	2	1	34	10

#	SEASON	DATE	COMPETITION / ROUND	MATCH RESULT	VENUE	ATT
1	1898/99	17/09/98	Football League Division 2	Glossop 1 Newton Heath 2	North Road	6000
2	1898/99	14/01/99	Football League Division 2	Newton Heath 3 Glossop 0	Bank Street	12000
3	1900/01	01/09/00	Football League Division 2	Glossop 1 Newton Heath 0	North Road	8000
4	1900/01	29/12/00	Football League Division 2	Newton Heath 3 Glossop 0	Bank Street	8000
5	1901/02	19/10/01	Football League Division 2	Glossop 0 Newton Heath 0	North Road	7000
6	1901/02	15/02/02	Football League Division 2	Newton Heath 1 Glossop 0	Bank Street	5000
7	1902/03	27/09/02	Football League Division 2	Manchester United 1 Glossop 1	Bank Street	12000
8	1902/03	24/01/03	Football League Division 2	Glossop 1 Manchester United 3	North Road	5000
9	1903/04	19/09/03	Football League Division 2	Glossop 0 Manchester United 5	North Road	3000
10	1903/04	16/01/04	Football League Division 2	Manchester United 3 Glossop 1	Bank Street	10000
11	1904/05	24/09/04	Football League Division 2	Glossop 1 Manchester United 2	North Road	6000
12	1904/05	21/01/05	Football League Division 2	Manchester United 4 Glossop 1	Bank Street	20000
13	1905/06	16/09/05	Football League Division 2	Glossop 1 Manchester United 2	North Road	7000
14	1905/06	20/01/06	Football League Division 2	Manchester United 5 Glossop 2	Bank Street	7000

UNITED v GORNIK ZABRBE

EUROPEAN CUP						
VENUE	P	W	D	L	F	A
HOME	1	1	0	0	2	0
AWAY	1	0	0	1	0	1
TOTAL	2	1	0	1	2	1

#	SEASON	DATE	COMPETITION / ROUND	MATCH RESULT	VENUE	ATT
1	1967/68	28/02/68	European Cup Quarter-Final 1st Leg	Manchester United 2 Gornik Zabrze 0	Old Trafford	63456
2	1967/68	13/03/68	European Cup Quarter-Final 2nd Leg	Gornik Zabrze 1 Manchester United 0	Stadion Slaski	105000

UNITED v GOTHENBURG

CHAMPIONS LEAGUE						
VENUE	P	W	D	L	F	A
HOME	1	1	0	0	4	2
AWAY	1	0	0	1	1	3
TOTAL	2	1	0	1	5	5

#	SEASON	DATE	COMPETITION / ROUND	MATCH RESULT	VENUE	ATT
1	1994/95	14/09/94	Champions League Phase 1 Match 1	Manchester United 4 Gothenburg 2	Old Trafford	33625
2	1994/95	23/11/94	Champions League Phase 1 Match 5	Gothenburg 3 Manchester United 1	NYA Ullevi Stadium	36350

UNITED v GRIMSBY TOWN

ALL COMPETITIVE MATCHES							ALL LEAGUE MATCHES							FA CUP					
VENUE	P	W	D	L	F	A	VENUE	P	W	D	L	F	A	VENUE	P	W	D	L	F	A
HOME	18	12	2	4	38	26	HOME	18	12	2	4	38	26	HOME	0	0	0	0	0	0
AWAY	19	4	4	11	26	38	AWAY	18	4	4	10	26	37	AWAY	1	0	0	1	0	1
TOTAL	37	16	6	15	64	64	TOTAL	36	16	6	14	64	63	TOTAL	1	0	0	1	0	1

LEAGUE DIVISION ONE							LEAGUE DIVISION TWO						
VENUE	P	W	D	L	F	A	VENUE	P	W	D	L	F	A
HOME	6	2	1	3	11	14	HOME	12	10	1	1	27	12
AWAY	6	0	3	3	6	12	AWAY	12	4	1	7	20	25
TOTAL	12	2	4	6	17	26	TOTAL	24	14	2	8	47	37

#	SEASON	DATE	COMPETITION / ROUND	MATCH RESULT	VENUE	ATT
1	1894/95	17/11/94	Football League Division 2	Grimsby Town 2 Newton Heath 1	Abbey Park	3000
2	1894/95	23/03/95	Football League Division 2	Newton Heath 2 Grimsby Town 0	Bank Street	9000
3	1895/96	01/01/96	Football League Division 2	Newton Heath 3 Grimsby Town 2	Bank Street	8000
4	1895/96	14/03/96	Football League Division 2	Grimsby Town 4 Newton Heath 2	Abbey Park	2000
5	1896/97	19/09/96	Football League Division 2	Grimsby Town 2 Newton Heath 0	Abbey Park	3000
6	1896/97	07/11/96	Football League Division 2	Newton Heath 4 Grimsby Town 2	Bank Street	5000
7	1897/98	27/11/97	Football League Division 2	Newton Heath 2 Grimsby Town 1	Bank Street	5000
8	1897/98	02/04/98	Football League Division 2	Grimsby Town 1 Newton Heath 3	Abbey Park	2000
9	1898/99	05/11/98	Football League Division 2	Newton Heath 3 Grimsby Town 2	Bank Street	5000
10	1898/99	04/03/99	Football League Division 2	Grimsby Town 3 Newton Heath 0	Abbey Park	4000
11	1899/00	26/12/99	Football League Division 2	Grimsby Town 0 Newton Heath 7	Blundell Park	2000
12	1899/00	03/03/00	Football League Division 2	Newton Heath 1 Grimsby Town 0	Bank Street	4000
13	1900/01	08/12/00	Football League Division 2	Grimsby Town 2 Newton Heath 0	Blundell Park	4000
14	1900/01	13/04/01	Football League Division 2	Newton Heath 1 Grimsby Town 0	Bank Street	3000
15	1903/04	26/03/04	Football League Division 2	Manchester United 2 Grimsby Town 0	Bank Street	12000
16	1903/04	12/04/04	Football League Division 2	Grimsby Town 3 Manchester United 1	Blundell Park	8000
17	1904/05	19/11/04	Football League Division 2	Grimsby Town 0 Manchester United 1	Blundell Park	4000
18	1904/05	18/03/05	Football League Division 2	Manchester United 2 Grimsby Town 1	Bank Street	12000
19	1905/06	09/09/05	Football League Division 2	Grimsby Town 0 Manchester United 1	Blundell Park	6000
20	1905/06	06/01/06	Football League Division 2	Manchester United 5 Grimsby Town 0	Bank Street	10000
21	1929/30	12/10/29	Football League Division 1	Manchester United 2 Grimsby Town 5	Old Trafford	21494
22	1929/30	15/02/30	Football League Division 1	Grimsby Town 2 Manchester United 2	Blundell Park	9337
23	1930/31	27/09/30	Football League Division 1	Manchester United 0 Grimsby Town 2	Old Trafford	14695
24	1930/31	24/01/31	FA Cup 4th Round	Grimsby Town 1 Manchester United 0	Blundell Park	15000
25	1930/31	31/01/31	Football League Division 1	Grimsby Town 2 Manchester United 1	Blundell Park	9305
26	1932/33	17/09/32	Football League Division 2	Manchester United 1 Grimsby Town 1	Old Trafford	17662
27	1932/33	31/01/33	Football League Division 2	Grimsby Town 1 Manchester United 1	Blundell Park	4020
28	1933/34	25/12/33	Football League Division 2	Manchester United 1 Grimsby Town 3	Old Trafford	29443
29	1933/34	26/12/33	Football League Division 2	Grimsby Town 7 Manchester United 3	Blundell Park	15801
30	1936/37	14/11/36	Football League Division 1	Grimsby Town 6 Manchester United 2	Blundell Park	9844
31	1936/37	20/03/37	Football League Division 1	Manchester United 1 Grimsby Town 1	Old Trafford	26636
32	1938/39	10/09/38	Football League Division 1	Grimsby Town 1 Manchester United 0	Blundell Park	14077
33	1938/39	14/01/39	Football League Division 1	Manchester United 3 Grimsby Town 1	Old Trafford	25654
34	1946/47	31/08/46	Football League Division 1	Manchester United 2 Grimsby Town 1	Maine Road	41025
35	1946/47	28/12/46	Football League Division 1	Grimsby Town 0 Manchester United 0	Blundell Park	17183
36	1947/48	11/10/47	Football League Division 1	Manchester United 3 Grimsby Town 4	Maine Road	40035
37	1947/48	17/03/48	Football League Division 1	Grimsby Town 1 Manchester United 1	Blundell Park	12284

UNITED v HALIFAX TOWN

LEAGUE CUP					
VENUE	P	W	D	L	F	A
HOME	1	1	0	0	2	1
AWAY	1	1	0	0	3	1
TOTAL	2	2	0	0	5	2

#	SEASON	DATE	COMPETITION / ROUND	MATCH RESULT	VENUE	ATT
1	1990/91	26/09/90	League Cup 2nd Round 1st Leg	Halifax Town 1 Manchester United 3	The Shay	6841
2	1990/91	10/10/90	League Cup 2nd Round 2nd Leg	Manchester United 2 Halifax Town 1	Old Trafford	22295

UNITED v HARTLEPOOL UNITED

FA CUP

VENUE	P	W	D	L	F	A
HOME	0	0	0	0	0	0
AWAY	1	1	0	0	4	3
TOTAL	1	1	0	0	4	3

#	SEASON	DATE	COMPETITION / ROUND	MATCH RESULT	VENUE	ATT
1	1956/57	05/01/57	FA Cup 3rd Round	Hartlepool United 3 Manchester United 4	Victoria Ground	17264

UNITED v HEREFORD UNITED

FA CUP

VENUE	P	W	D	L	F	A
HOME	0	0	0	0	0	0
AWAY	1	1	0	0	1	0
TOTAL	1	1	0	0	1	0

#	SEASON	DATE	COMPETITION / ROUND	MATCH RESULT	VENUE	ATT
1	1989/90	28/01/90	FA Cup 4th Round	Hereford United 0 Manchester United 1	Edgar Street	13777

UNITED v HIBERNIANS MALTA

EUROPEAN CUP

VENUE	P	W	D	L	F	A
HOME	1	1	0	0	4	0
AWAY	1	0	1	0	0	0
TOTAL	2	1	1	0	4	0

#	SEASON	DATE	COMPETITION / ROUND	MATCH RESULT	VENUE	ATT
1	1967/68	20/09/67	European Cup 1st Round 1st Leg	Manchester United 4 Hibernians Malta 0	Old Trafford	43912
2	1967/68	27/09/67	European Cup 1st Round 2nd Leg	Hibernians Malta 0 Manchester United 0	Empire Stadium	25000

UNITED v HIGHER WALTON

FA CUP

VENUE	P	W	D	L	F	A
HOME	1	1	0	0	2	0
AWAY	0	0	0	0	0	0
TOTAL	1	1	0	0	2	0

#	SEASON	DATE	COMPETITION / ROUND	MATCH RESULT	VENUE	ATT
1	1890/91	04/10/90	FA Cup 1st Qualifying Round	Newton Heath 2 Higher Walton 0	North Road	3000

UNITED v HJK HELSINKI

EUROPEAN CUP

VENUE	P	W	D	L	F	A
HOME	1	1	0	0	6	0
AWAY	1	1	0	0	3	2
TOTAL	2	2	0	0	9	2

#	SEASON	DATE	COMPETITION / ROUND	MATCH RESULT	VENUE	ATT
1	1965/66	22/09/65	European Cup Preliminary Round 1st Leg	HJK Helsinki 2 Manchester United 3	Olympiastadion	25000
2	1965/66	06/10/65	European Cup Preliminary Round 2nd Leg	Manchester United 6 HJK Helsinki 0	Old Trafford	30388

UNITED v HONVED

EUROPEAN CUP

VENUE	P	W	D	L	F	A
HOME	1	1	0	0	2	1
AWAY	1	1	0	0	3	2
TOTAL	2	2	0	0	5	3

#	SEASON	DATE	COMPETITION / ROUND	MATCH RESULT	VENUE	ATT
1	1993/94	15/09/93	European Cup 1st Round 1st Leg	Honved 2 Manchester United 3	Jozsef Bozsik Stadium	9000
2	1993/94	29/09/93	European Cup 1st Round 2nd Leg	Manchester United 2 Honved 1	Old Trafford	35781

UNITED v HUDDERSFIELD TOWN

ALL COMPETITIVE MATCHES							LEAGUE DIVISION ONE							FA CUP						
VENUE	P	W	D	L	F	A	VENUE	P	W	D	L	F	A	VENUE	P	W	D	L	F	A
HOME	24	13	9	2	54	25	HOME	21	11	9	1	46	21	HOME	3	2	0	1	8	4
AWAY	21	7	6	8	32	39	AWAY	21	7	6	8	32	39	AWAY	0	0	0	0	0	0
TOTAL	45	20	15	10	86	64	TOTAL	42	18	15	9	78	60	TOTAL	3	2	0	1	8	4

#	SEASON	DATE	COMPETITION / ROUND	MATCH RESULT	VENUE	ATT
1	1911/12	13/01/12	FA Cup 1st Round	Manchester United 3 Huddersfield Town 1	Old Trafford	19579
2	1920/21	26/03/21	Football League Division 1	Huddersfield Town 5 Manchester United 2	Leeds Road	17000
3	1920/21	02/04/21	Football League Division 1	Manchester United 2 Huddersfield Town 0	Old Trafford	30000
4	1921/22	11/02/22	Football League Division 1	Manchester United 1 Huddersfield Town 1	Old Trafford	30000
5	1921/22	27/02/22	Football League Division 1	Huddersfield Town 1 Manchester United 1	Leeds Road	30000
6	1923/24	02/02/24	FA Cup 2nd Round	Manchester United 0 Huddersfield Town 3	Old Trafford	66673
7	1925/26	31/10/25	Football League Division 1	Manchester United 1 Huddersfield Town 1	Old Trafford	37213
8	1925/26	13/03/26	Football League Division 1	Huddersfield Town 5 Manchester United 0	Leeds Road	27842
9	1926/27	04/12/26	Football League Division 1	Manchester United 0 Huddersfield Town 0	Old Trafford	33135
10	1926/27	23/04/27	Football League Division 1	Huddersfield Town 0 Manchester United 0	Leeds Road	13870
11	1927/28	17/09/27	Football League Division 1	Huddersfield Town 4 Manchester United 2	Leeds Road	17307
12	1927/28	07/03/28	Football League Division 1	Manchester United 0 Huddersfield Town 0	Old Trafford	35413
13	1928/29	27/10/28	Football League Division 1	Huddersfield Town 1 Manchester United 2	Leeds Road	13648
14	1928/29	09/03/29	Football League Division 1	Manchester United 1 Huddersfield Town 0	Old Trafford	28183
15	1929/30	18/04/30	Football League Division 1	Manchester United 1 Huddersfield Town 0	Old Trafford	26496
16	1929/30	22/04/30	Football League Division 1	Huddersfield Town 2 Manchester United 2	Leeds Road	20716
17	1930/31	10/09/30	Football League Division 1	Manchester United 0 Huddersfield Town 6	Old Trafford	11836
18	1930/31	15/09/30	Football League Division 1	Huddersfield Town 3 Manchester United 1	Leeds Road	14028
19	1936/37	02/09/36	Football League Division 1	Huddersfield Town 3 Manchester United 1	Leeds Road	12612
20	1936/37	09/09/36	Football League Division 1	Manchester United 3 Huddersfield Town 1	Old Trafford	26839
21	1938/39	26/11/38	Football League Division 1	Manchester United 1 Huddersfield Town 1	Old Trafford	23164
22	1938/39	01/04/39	Football League Division 1	Huddersfield Town 1 Manchester United 1	Leeds Road	14007
23	1946/47	23/11/46	Football League Division 1	Manchester United 5 Huddersfield Town 2	Maine Road	39216
24	1946/47	29/03/47	Football League Division 1	Huddersfield Town 2 Manchester United 2	Leeds Road	18509
25	1947/48	08/11/47	Football League Division 1	Manchester United 4 Huddersfield Town 4	Maine Road	59772
26	1947/48	27/03/48	Football League Division 1	Huddersfield Town 0 Manchester United 2	Leeds Road	38266
27	1948/49	04/09/48	Football League Division 1	Manchester United 4 Huddersfield Town 1	Maine Road	57714
28	1948/49	06/04/49	Football League Division 1	Huddersfield Town 2 Manchester United 1	Leeds Road	17256
29	1949/50	05/11/49	Football League Division 1	Manchester United 6 Huddersfield Town 0	Old Trafford	40295
30	1949/50	25/03/50	Football League Division 1	Huddersfield Town 3 Manchester United 1	Leeds Road	34348
31	1950/51	09/12/50	Football League Division 1	Huddersfield Town 2 Manchester United 3	Leeds Road	26713
32	1950/51	28/04/51	Football League Division 1	Manchester United 6 Huddersfield Town 0	Old Trafford	25560
33	1951/52	03/11/51	Football League Division 1	Manchester United 1 Huddersfield Town 1	Old Trafford	25616
34	1951/52	22/03/52	Football League Division 1	Huddersfield Town 3 Manchester United 2	Leeds Road	30316
35	1953/54	31/10/53	Football League Division 1	Huddersfield Town 0 Manchester United 0	Leeds Road	34175
36	1953/54	20/03/54	Football League Division 1	Manchester United 3 Huddersfield Town 1	Old Trafford	40181
37	1954/55	18/09/54	Football League Division 1	Manchester United 1 Huddersfield Town 1	Old Trafford	45648
38	1954/55	05/02/55	Football League Division 1	Huddersfield Town 1 Manchester United 3	Leeds Road	31408
39	1955/56	22/10/55	Football League Division 1	Manchester United 3 Huddersfield Town 0	Old Trafford	34150
40	1955/56	31/03/56	Football League Division 1	Huddersfield Town 0 Manchester United 2	Leeds Road	37780
41	1962/63	04/03/63	FA Cup 3rd Round	Manchester United 5 Huddersfield Town 0	Old Trafford	47703

UNITED v HUDDERSFIELD TOWN (continued)

#	SEASON	DATE	COMPETITION / ROUND	MATCH RESULT	VENUE	ATT
42	1970/71	28/11/70	Football League Division 1	Manchester United 1 Huddersfield Town 1	Old Trafford	45306
43	1970/71	30/01/71	Football League Division 1	Huddersfield Town 1 Manchester United 2	Leeds Road	41464
44	1971/72	09/10/71	Football League Division 1	Huddersfield Town 0 Manchester United 3	Leeds Road	33458
45	1971/72	11/03/72	Football League Division 1	Manchester United 2 Huddersfield Town 0	Old Trafford	53581

UNITED v HULL CITY

ALL COMPETITIVE MATCHES							LEAGUE DIVISION TWO							ALL CUP MATCHES					
VENUE	P	W	D	L	F	A	VENUE	P	W	D	L	F	A	VENUE	P	W	D	L	F	A
HOME	10	8	1	1	27	6	HOME	8	7	1	0	22	4	HOME	2	1	0	1	5	2
AWAY	10	4	2	4	10	13	AWAY	8	2	2	4	8	13	AWAY	2	2	0	0	2	0
TOTAL	20	12	3	5	37	19	TOTAL	16	9	3	4	30	17	TOTAL	4	3	0	1	7	2

FA CUP							LEAGUE CUP						
VENUE	P	W	D	L	F	A	VENUE	P	W	D	L	F	A
HOME	1	0	0	1	0	2	HOME	1	1	0	0	5	0
AWAY	1	1	0	0	1	0	AWAY	1	1	0	0	1	0
TOTAL	2	1	0	1	1	2	TOTAL	2	2	0	0	6	0

#	SEASON	DATE	COMPETITION / ROUND	MATCH RESULT	VENUE	ATT
1	1905/06	28/10/05	Football League Division 2	Hull City 0 Manchester United 1	Anlaby Road	14000
2	1905/06	03/03/06	Football League Division 2	Manchester United 5 Hull City 0	Bank Street	16000
3	1922/23	30/12/22	Football League Division 2	Hull City 2 Manchester United 1	Anlaby Road	6750
4	1922/23	06/01/23	Football League Division 2	Manchester United 3 Hull City 2	Old Trafford	15000
5	1923/24	15/03/24	Football League Division 2	Manchester United 1 Hull City 1	Old Trafford	13000
6	1923/24	22/03/24	Football League Division 2	Hull City 1 Manchester United 1	Anlaby Road	6250
7	1924/25	15/11/24	Football League Division 2	Manchester United 2 Hull City 0	Old Trafford	29750
8	1924/25	21/03/25	Football League Division 2	Hull City 0 Manchester United 1	Anlaby Road	6250
9	1933/34	28/10/33	Football League Division 2	Manchester United 4 Hull City 1	Old Trafford	16269
10	1933/34	10/03/34	Football League Division 2	Hull City 4 Manchester United 1	Anlaby Road	5771
11	1934/35	17/11/34	Football League Division 2	Hull City 3 Manchester United 2	Anlaby Road	6494
12	1934/35	30/03/35	Football League Division 2	Manchester United 3 Hull City 0	Old Trafford	15358
13	1935/36	18/09/35	Football League Division 2	Manchester United 2 Hull City 0	Old Trafford	15739
14	1935/36	02/05/36	Football League Division 2	Hull City 1 Manchester United 1	Anlaby Road	4540
15	1948/49	26/02/49	FA Cup 6th Round	Hull City 0 Manchester United 1	Boothferry Park	55000
16	1951/52	12/01/52	FA Cup 3rd Round	Manchester United 0 Hull City 2	Old Trafford	43517
17	1974/75	23/11/74	Football League Division 2	Hull City 2 Manchester United 0	Boothferry Park	23287
18	1974/75	15/02/75	Football League Division 2	Manchester United 2 Hull City 0	Old Trafford	44712
19	1987/88	23/09/87	League Cup 2nd Round 1st Leg	Manchester United 5 Hull City 0	Old Trafford	25041
20	1987/88	07/10/87	League Cup 2nd Round 2nd Leg	Hull City 0 Manchester United 1	Boothferry Park	13586

UNITED v INTERNAZIONALE

CHAMPIONS LEAGUE						
VENUE	P	W	D	L	F	A
HOME	1	1	0	0	2	0
AWAY	1	0	1	0	1	1
TOTAL	2	1	1	0	3	1

#	SEASON	DATE	COMPETITION / ROUND	MATCH RESULT	VENUE	ATT
1	1998/99	03/03/99	Champions League Quarter-Final 1st Leg	Manchester United 2 Internazionale 0	Old Trafford	54430
2	1998/99	17/03/99	Champions League Quarter-Final 2nd Leg	Internazionale 1 Manchester United 1	Stadio San Siro	79528

UNITED v IPSWICH TOWN

ALL COMPETITIVE MATCHES							ALL LEAGUE MATCHES							ALL CUP MATCHES						
VENUE	P	W	D	L	F	A	VENUE	P	W	D	L	F	A	VENUE	P	W	D	L	F	A
HOME	27	17	4	6	49	15	HOME	25	16	4	5	47	14	HOME	2	1	0	1	2	1
AWAY	29	11	5	13	39	51	AWAY	25	8	5	12	33	47	AWAY	4	3	0	1	6	4
TOTAL	56	28	9	19	88	66	TOTAL	50	24	9	17	80	61	TOTAL	6	4	0	2	8	5

PREMIERSHIP							LEAGUE DIVISION ONE						
VENUE	P	W	D	L	F	A	VENUE	P	W	D	L	F	A
HOME	5	3	2	0	16	1	HOME	20	13	2	5	31	13
AWAY	5	2	1	2	7	7	AWAY	20	6	4	10	26	40
TOTAL	10	5	3	2	23	8	TOTAL	40	19	6	15	57	53

FA CUP							LEAGUE CUP						
VENUE	P	W	D	L	F	A	VENUE	P	W	D	L	F	A
HOME	2	1	0	1	2	1	HOME	0	0	0	0	0	0
AWAY	2	2	0	0	3	1	AWAY	2	1	0	1	3	3
TOTAL	4	3	0	1	5	2	TOTAL	2	1	0	1	3	3

#	SEASON	DATE	COMPETITION / ROUND	MATCH RESULT	VENUE	ATT
1	1957/58	25/01/58	FA Cup 4th Round	Manchester United 2 Ipswich Town 0	Old Trafford	53550
2	1961/62	18/11/61	Football League Division 1	Ipswich Town 4 Manchester United 1	Portman Road	25755
3	1961/62	07/04/62	Football League Division 1	Manchester United 5 Ipswich Town 0	Old Trafford	24976
4	1962/63	03/11/62	Football League Division 1	Ipswich Town 3 Manchester United 5	Portman Road	18483
5	1962/63	23/03/63	Football League Division 1	Manchester United 0 Ipswich Town 1	Old Trafford	32792
6	1963/64	28/08/63	Football League Division 1	Manchester United 2 Ipswich Town 0	Old Trafford	39921
7	1963/64	03/09/63	Football League Division 1	Ipswich Town 2 Manchester United 7	Portman Road	28113
8	1968/69	16/11/68	Football League Division 1	Manchester United 0 Ipswich Town 0	Old Trafford	45796
9	1968/69	01/02/69	Football League Division 1	Ipswich Town 1 Manchester United 0	Portman Road	30837
10	1969/70	11/10/69	Football League Division 1	Manchester United 2 Ipswich Town 1	Old Trafford	52281
11	1969/70	03/01/70	FA Cup 3rd Round	Ipswich Town 0 Manchester United 1	Portman Road	29552
12	1969/70	10/02/70	Football League Division 1	Ipswich Town 0 Manchester United 1	Portman Road	29755
13	1970/71	19/09/70	Football League Division 1	Ipswich Town 4 Manchester United 0	Portman Road	27776
14	1970/71	24/04/71	Football League Division 1	Manchester United 3 Ipswich Town 2	Old Trafford	33566
15	1971/72	04/09/71	Football League Division 1	Manchester United 1 Ipswich Town 0	Old Trafford	45656
16	1971/72	07/09/71	League Cup 2nd Round	Ipswich Town 1 Manchester United 3	Portman Road	28143
17	1971/72	18/12/71	Football League Division 1	Ipswich Town 0 Manchester United 0	Portman Road	29229
18	1972/73	12/08/72	Football League Division 1	Manchester United 1 Ipswich Town 2	Old Trafford	51459
19	1972/73	17/02/73	Football League Division 1	Ipswich Town 4 Manchester United 1	Portman Road	31918
20	1973/74	08/09/73	Football League Division 1	Ipswich Town 2 Manchester United 1	Portman Road	22023
21	1973/74	29/12/73	Football League Division 1	Manchester United 2 Ipswich Town 0	Old Trafford	36365
22	1973/74	26/01/74	FA Cup 4th Round	Manchester United 0 Ipswich Town 1	Old Trafford	37177
23	1975/76	20/09/75	Football League Division 1	Manchester United 1 Ipswich Town 0	Old Trafford	50513
24	1975/76	10/04/76	Football League Division 1	Ipswich Town 3 Manchester United 0	Portman Road	34886
25	1976/77	30/10/76	Football League Division 1	Manchester United 0 Ipswich Town 1	Old Trafford	57416
26	1976/77	03/01/77	Football League Division 1	Ipswich Town 2 Manchester United 1	Portman Road	30105
27	1977/78	27/08/77	Football League Division 1	Manchester United 0 Ipswich Town 0	Old Trafford	57904
28	1977/78	14/01/78	Football League Division 1	Ipswich Town 1 Manchester United 2	Portman Road	23321
29	1978/79	26/08/78	Football League Division 1	Ipswich Town 3 Manchester United 0	Portman Road	21802
30	1978/79	18/11/78	Football League Division 1	Manchester United 2 Ipswich Town 0	Old Trafford	42109
31	1979/80	20/10/79	Football League Division 1	Manchester United 1 Ipswich Town 0	Old Trafford	50826
32	1979/80	01/03/80	Football League Division 1	Ipswich Town 6 Manchester United 0	Portman Road	30229
33	1980/81	18/10/80	Football League Division 1	Ipswich Town 1 Manchester United 1	Portman Road	28572
34	1980/81	21/03/81	Football League Division 1	Manchester United 2 Ipswich Town 1	Old Trafford	46685
35	1981/82	05/09/81	Football League Division 1	Manchester United 1 Ipswich Town 2	Old Trafford	45555
36	1981/82	20/04/82	Football League Division 1	Ipswich Town 2 Manchester United 1	Portman Road	25744
37	1982/83	11/09/82	Football League Division 1	Manchester United 3 Ipswich Town 1	Old Trafford	43140
38	1982/83	05/02/83	Football League Division 1	Ipswich Town 1 Manchester United 1	Portman Road	23804
39	1983/84	10/12/83	Football League Division 1	Ipswich Town 0 Manchester United 2	Portman Road	19779
40	1983/84	07/05/84	Football League Division 1	Manchester United 1 Ipswich Town 2	Old Trafford	44257
41	1984/85	01/09/84	Football League Division 1	Ipswich Town 1 Manchester United 1	Portman Road	20876
42	1984/85	22/12/84	Football League Division 1	Manchester United 3 Ipswich Town 0	Old Trafford	35168
43	1985/86	20/08/85	Football League Division 1	Ipswich Town 0 Manchester United 1	Portman Road	18777
44	1985/86	07/12/85	Football League Division 1	Manchester United 1 Ipswich Town 0	Old Trafford	37981
45	1987/88	10/01/88	FA Cup 3rd Round	Ipswich Town 1 Manchester United 2	Portman Road	23012

UNITED v IPSWICH TOWN (continued)

#	SEASON	DATE	COMPETITION / ROUND	MATCH RESULT	VENUE	ATT
46	1992/93	22/08/92	FA Premiership	Manchester United 1 Ipswich Town 1	Old Trafford	31704
47	1992/93	30/01/93	FA Premiership	Ipswich Town 2 Manchester United 1	Portman Road	22068
48	1993/94	24/11/93	FA Premiership	Manchester United 0 Ipswich Town 0	Old Trafford	43300
49	1993/94	01/05/94	FA Premiership	Ipswich Town 1 Manchester United 2	Portman Road	22559
50	1994/95	24/09/94	FA Premiership	Ipswich Town 3 Manchester United 2	Portman Road	22559
51	1994/95	04/03/95	FA Premiership	Manchester United 9 Ipswich Town 0	Old Trafford	43804
52	1997/98	14/10/97	League Cup 3rd Round	Ipswich Town 2 Manchester United 0	Portman Road	22173
53	2000/01	22/08/00	FA Premiership	Ipswich Town 1 Manchester United 1	Portman Road	22007
54	2000/01	23/12/00	FA Premiership	Manchester United 2 Ipswich Town 0	Old Trafford	67597
55	2001/02	22/09/01	FA Premiership	Manchester United 4 Ipswich Town 0	Old Trafford	67551
56	2001/02	27/04/02	FA Premiership	Ipswich Town 0 Manchester United 1	Portman Road	28433

UNITED v JUVENTUS

ALL COMPETITIVE MATCHES						
VENUE	P	W	D	L	F	A
HOME	6	3	2	1	8	6
AWAY	6	2	0	4	7	9
TOTAL	12	5	2	5	15	15

CHAMPIONS LEAGUE							EUROPEAN CUP-WINNERS' CUP							UEFA CUP						
VENUE	P	W	D	L	F	A	VENUE	P	W	D	L	F	A	VENUE	P	W	D	L	F	A
HOME	4	2	1	1	6	5	HOME	1	0	1	0	1	1	HOME	1	1	0	0	1	0
AWAY	4	2	0	2	6	4	AWAY	1	0	0	1	1	2	AWAY	1	0	0	1	0	3
TOTAL	8	4	1	3	12	9	TOTAL	2	0	1	1	2	3	TOTAL	2	1	0	1	1	3

#	SEASON	DATE	COMPETITION / ROUND	MATCH RESULT	VENUE	ATT
1	1976/77	20/10/76	UEFA Cup 2nd Round 1st Leg	Manchester United 1 Juventus 0	Old Trafford	59000
2	1976/77	03/11/76	UEFA Cup 2nd Round 2nd Leg	Juventus 3 Manchester United 0	Stadio Comunale	66632
3	1983/84	11/04/84	European CWC Semi-Final 1st Leg	Manchester United 1 Juventus 1	Old Trafford	58171
4	1983/84	25/04/84	European CWC Semi-Final 2nd Leg	Juventus 2 Manchester United 1	Stadio Comunale	64655
5	1996/97	11/09/96	Champions League Phase 1 Match 1	Juventus 1 Manchester United 0	Stadio Delle Alpi	54000
6	1996/97	20/11/96	Champions League Phase 1 Match 5	Manchester United 0 Juventus 1	Old Trafford	53529
7	1997/98	01/10/97	Champions League Phase 1 Match 2	Manchester United 3 Juventus 2	Old Trafford	53428
8	1997/98	10/12/97	Champions League Phase 1 Match 6	Juventus 1 Manchester United 0	Stadio Delle Alpi	47786
9	1998/99	07/04/99	Champions League Semi-Final 1st Leg	Manchester United 1 Juventus 1	Old Trafford	54487
10	1998/99	21/04/99	Champions League Semi-Final 2nd Leg	Juventus 2 Manchester United 3	Stadio Delle Alpi	64500
11	2002/03	19/02/03	Champions League Phase 2 Match 3	Manchester United 2 Juventus 1	Old Trafford	66703
12	2002/03	25/02/03	Champions League Phase 2 Match 4	Juventus 0 Manchester United 3	Stadio Delle Alpi	59111

UNITED v KETTERING

FA CUP						
VENUE	P	W	D	L	F	A
HOME	2	2	0	0	7	2
AWAY	0	0	0	0	0	0
TOTAL	2	2	0	0	7	2

#	SEASON	DATE	COMPETITION / ROUND	MATCH RESULT	VENUE	ATT
1	1895/96	01/02/96	FA Cup 1st Round	Newton Heath 2 Kettering 1	Bank Street	6000
2	1896/97	30/01/97	FA Cup 1st Round	Newton Heath 5 Kettering 1	Bank Street	1500

UNITED v KOSICE

CHAMPIONS LEAGUE

VENUE	P	W	D	L	F	A
HOME	1	1	0	0	3	0
AWAY	1	1	0	0	3	0
TOTAL	2	2	0	0	6	0

#	SEASON	DATE	COMPETITION / ROUND	MATCH RESULT	VENUE	ATT
1	1997/98	17/09/97	Champions League Phase 1 Match 1	Kosice 0 Manchester United 3	TJ Lokomotive Stadium	9950
2	1997/98	27/11/97	Champions League Phase 1 Match 5	Manchester United 3 Kosice 0	Old Trafford	53535

UNITED v LAZIO

EUROPEAN SUPER CUP

VENUE	P	W	D	L	F	A
HOME	0	0	0	0	0	0
AWAY	0	0	0	0	0	0
NEUTRAL	1	0	0	1	0	1
TOTAL	1	0	0	1	0	1

#	SEASON	DATE	COMPETITION / ROUND	MATCH RESULT	VENUE	ATT
1	1999/00	27/08/99	European Super Cup Final	Manchester United 0 Lazio 1	Stade Louis II	14461

UNITED v LEEDS UNITED

ALL COMPETITIVE MATCHES

VENUE	P	W	D	L	F	A
HOME	50	24	17	9	79	42
AWAY	51	21	15	15	68	65
NEUTRAL	6	1	3	2	2	3
TOTAL	107	46	35	26	149	110

ALL LEAGUE MATCHES

VENUE	P	W	D	L	F	A
HOME	47	21	17	9	70	40
AWAY	47	17	15	15	60	62
TOTAL	94	38	32	24	130	102

ALL CUP MATCHES

VENUE	P	W	D	L	F	A
HOME	3	3	0	0	9	2
AWAY	4	4	0	0	8	3
NEUTRAL	6	1	3	2	2	3
TOTAL	13	8	3	2	19	8

PREMIERSHIP

VENUE	P	W	D	L	F	A
HOME	12	8	4	0	19	5
AWAY	12	5	3	4	16	12
TOTAL	24	13	7	4	35	17

LEAGUE DIVISION ONE

VENUE	P	W	D	L	F	A
HOME	31	12	12	7	46	26
AWAY	31	9	11	11	36	48
TOTAL	62	21	23	18	82	74

LEAGUE DIVISION TWO

VENUE	P	W	D	L	F	A
HOME	4	1	1	2	5	9
AWAY	4	3	1	0	8	2
TOTAL	8	4	2	2	13	11

FA CUP

VENUE	P	W	D	L	F	A
HOME	2	2	0	0	7	1
AWAY	1	1	0	0	1	0
NEUTRAL	6	1	3	2	2	3
TOTAL	9	4	3	2	10	4

LEAGUE CUP

VENUE	P	W	D	L	F	A
HOME	1	1	0	0	2	1
AWAY	3	3	0	0	7	3
NEUTRAL	0	0	0	0	0	0
TOTAL	4	4	0	0	9	4

#	SEASON	DATE	COMPETITION / ROUND	MATCH RESULT	VENUE	ATT
1	1905/06	15/01/06	Football League Division 2	Manchester United 0 Leeds United 3	Bank Street	6000
2	1905/06	21/04/06	Football League Division 2	Leeds United 1 Manchester United 3	Elland Road	15000
3	1922/23	20/01/23	Football League Division 2	Manchester United 0 Leeds United 0	Old Trafford	25000
4	1922/23	27/01/23	Football League Division 2	Leeds United 0 Manchester United 1	Elland Road	24500
5	1923/24	01/12/23	Football League Division 2	Leeds United 0 Manchester United 0	Elland Road	20000
6	1923/24	08/12/23	Football League Division 2	Manchester United 3 Leeds United 1	Old Trafford	22250
7	1925/26	03/10/25	Football League Division 1	Leeds United 2 Manchester United 0	Elland Road	26265
8	1925/26	13/02/26	Football League Division 1	Manchester United 2 Leeds United 1	Old Trafford	29584
9	1926/27	04/09/26	Football League Division 1	Manchester United 2 Leeds United 2	Old Trafford	26338
10	1926/27	22/01/27	Football League Division 1	Leeds United 2 Manchester United 3	Elland Road	16816
11	1928/29	08/09/28	Football League Division 1	Leeds United 3 Manchester United 2	Elland Road	28723
12	1928/29	19/01/29	Football League Division 1	Manchester United 1 Leeds United 2	Old Trafford	21995
13	1929/30	21/12/29	Football League Division 1	Manchester United 3 Leeds United 1	Old Trafford	15054
14	1929/30	26/04/30	Football League Division 1	Leeds United 3 Manchester United 1	Elland Road	10596
15	1930/31	20/12/30	Football League Division 1	Leeds United 5 Manchester United 0	Elland Road	11282
16	1930/31	01/01/31	Football League Division 1	Manchester United 0 Leeds United 0	Old Trafford	9875
17	1931/32	07/11/31	Football League Division 2	Manchester United 2 Leeds United 5	Old Trafford	9512
18	1931/32	19/03/32	Football League Division 2	Leeds United 1 Manchester United 4	Elland Road	13644

UNITED v LEEDS UNITED (continued)

#	SEASON	DATE	COMPETITION / ROUND	MATCH RESULT	VENUE	ATT
19	1936/37	28/11/36	Football League Division 1	Leeds United 2 Manchester United 1	Elland Road	17610
20	1936/37	03/04/37	Football League Division 1	Manchester United 0 Leeds United 0	Old Trafford	34429
21	1938/39	07/04/39	Football League Division 1	Manchester United 0 Leeds United 0	Old Trafford	35564
22	1938/39	10/04/39	Football League Division 1	Leeds United 3 Manchester United 1	Elland Road	13771
23	1946/47	07/04/47	Football League Division 1	Manchester United 3 Leeds United 1	Maine Road	41772
24	1946/47	08/04/47	Football League Division 1	Leeds United 0 Manchester United 2	Elland Road	15528
25	1950/51	27/01/51	FA Cup 4th Round	Manchester United 4 Leeds United 0	Old Trafford	55434
26	1956/57	17/11/56	Football League Division 1	Manchester United 3 Leeds United 2	Old Trafford	51131
27	1956/57	30/03/57	Football League Division 1	Leeds United 1 Manchester United 2	Elland Road	47216
28	1957/58	07/09/57	Football League Division 1	Manchester United 5 Leeds United 0	Old Trafford	50842
29	1957/58	11/01/58	Football League Division 1	Leeds United 1 Manchester United 1	Elland Road	39401
30	1958/59	01/11/58	Football League Division 1	Leeds United 1 Manchester United 2	Elland Road	48574
31	1958/59	21/03/59	Football League Division 1	Manchester United 4 Leeds United 0	Old Trafford	45473
32	1959/60	09/09/59	Football League Division 1	Manchester United 6 Leeds United 0	Old Trafford	48407
33	1959/60	16/09/59	Football League Division 1	Leeds United 2 Manchester United 2	Elland Road	34048
34	1964/65	05/12/64	Football League Division 1	Manchester United 0 Leeds United 1	Old Trafford	53374
35	1964/65	27/03/65	FA Cup Semi-Final	Manchester United 0 Leeds United 0	Hillsborough	65000
36	1964/65	31/03/65	FA Cup Semi-Final Replay	Manchester United 0 Leeds United 1	City Ground	46300
37	1964/65	17/04/65	Football League Division 1	Leeds United 0 Manchester United 1	Elland Road	52368
38	1965/66	12/01/66	Football League Division 1	Leeds United 1 Manchester United 1	Elland Road	49672
39	1965/66	19/05/66	Football League Division 1	Manchester United 1 Leeds United 1	Old Trafford	35008
40	1966/67	27/08/66	Football League Division 1	Leeds United 3 Manchester United 1	Elland Road	45092
41	1966/67	31/12/66	Football League Division 1	Manchester United 0 Leeds United 0	Old Trafford	53486
42	1967/68	23/08/67	Football League Division 1	Manchester United 1 Leeds United 0	Old Trafford	53016
43	1967/68	08/11/67	Football League Division 1	Leeds United 1 Manchester United 0	Elland Road	43999
44	1968/69	02/11/68	Football League Division 1	Manchester United 0 Leeds United 0	Old Trafford	53839
45	1968/69	11/01/69	Football League Division 1	Leeds United 2 Manchester United 1	Elland Road	48145
46	1969/70	06/09/69	Football League Division 1	Leeds United 2 Manchester United 2	Elland Road	44271
47	1969/70	26/01/70	Football League Division 1	Manchester United 2 Leeds United 2	Old Trafford	59879
48	1969/70	14/03/70	FA Cup Semi-Final	Leeds United 0 Manchester United 0	Hillsborough	55000
49	1969/70	23/03/70	FA Cup Semi-Final Replay	Leeds United 0 Manchester United 0	Villa Park	62500
50	1969/70	26/03/70	FA Cup Semi-Final 2nd Replay	Leeds United 1 Manchester United 0	Burnden Park	56000
51	1970/71	15/08/70	Football League Division 1	Manchester United 0 Leeds United 1	Old Trafford	59365
52	1970/71	17/10/70	Football League Division 1	Leeds United 2 Manchester United 2	Elland Road	50190
53	1971/72	30/10/71	Football League Division 1	Manchester United 0 Leeds United 1	Old Trafford	53960
54	1971/72	19/02/72	Football League Division 1	Leeds United 5 Manchester United 1	Elland Road	45399
55	1972/73	23/12/72	Football League Division 1	Manchester United 1 Leeds United 1	Old Trafford	46382
56	1972/73	18/04/73	Football League Division 1	Leeds United 0 Manchester United 1	Elland Road	45450
57	1973/74	22/09/73	Football League Division 1	Leeds United 0 Manchester United 0	Elland Road	47058
58	1973/74	09/02/74	Football League Division 1	Manchester United 0 Leeds United 2	Old Trafford	60025
59	1975/76	11/10/75	Football League Division 1	Leeds United 1 Manchester United 2	Elland Road	40264
60	1975/76	13/03/76	Football League Division 1	Manchester United 3 Leeds United 2	Old Trafford	59429
61	1976/77	02/10/76	Football League Division 1	Leeds United 0 Manchester United 2	Elland Road	44512
62	1976/77	12/03/77	Football League Division 1	Manchester United 1 Leeds United 0	Old Trafford	60612
63	1976/77	23/04/77	FA Cup Semi-Final	Manchester United 2 Leeds United 1	Hillsborough	55000
64	1977/78	24/09/77	Football League Division 1	Leeds United 1 Manchester United 1	Elland Road	33517
65	1977/78	01/03/78	Football League Division 1	Manchester United 0 Leeds United 1	Old Trafford	49101
66	1978/79	23/08/78	Football League Division 1	Leeds United 2 Manchester United 3	Elland Road	36845
67	1978/79	24/03/79	Football League Division 1	Manchester United 4 Leeds United 1	Old Trafford	51191
68	1979/80	08/12/79	Football League Division 1	Manchester United 1 Leeds United 1	Old Trafford	58348
69	1979/80	03/05/80	Football League Division 1	Leeds United 2 Manchester United 0	Elland Road	39625
70	1980/81	20/09/80	Football League Division 1	Leeds United 0 Manchester United 0	Elland Road	32539
71	1980/81	28/02/81	Football League Division 1	Manchester United 0 Leeds United 1	Old Trafford	45733
72	1981/82	30/09/81	Football League Division 1	Manchester United 1 Leeds United 0	Old Trafford	47019
73	1981/82	03/04/82	Football League Division 1	Leeds United 0 Manchester United 0	Elland Road	30953
74	1990/91	28/08/90	Football League Division 1	Leeds United 0 Manchester United 0	Elland Road	29174
75	1990/91	08/12/90	Football League Division 1	Manchester United 1 Leeds United 1	Old Trafford	40927
76	1990/91	10/02/91	League Cup Semi-Final 1st Leg	Manchester United 2 Leeds United 1	Old Trafford	34050
77	1990/91	24/02/91	League Cup Semi-Final 2nd Leg	Leeds United 0 Manchester United 1	Elland Road	32014
78	1991/92	31/08/91	Football League Division 1	Manchester United 1 Leeds United 1	Old Trafford	43778
79	1991/92	29/12/91	Football League Division 1	Leeds United 1 Manchester United 1	Elland Road	32638
80	1991/92	08/01/92	League Cup 5th Round	Leeds United 1 Manchester United 3	Elland Road	28886
81	1991/92	15/01/92	FA Cup 3rd Round	Leeds United 0 Manchester United 1	Elland Road	31819

UNITED v LEEDS UNITED (continued)

#	SEASON	DATE	COMPETITION / ROUND	MATCH RESULT	VENUE	ATT
82	1992/93	06/09/92	FA Premiership	Manchester United 2 Leeds United 0	Old Trafford	31296
83	1992/93	08/02/93	FA Premiership	Leeds United 0 Manchester United 0	Elland Road	34166
84	1993/94	01/01/94	FA Premiership	Manchester United 0 Leeds United 0	Old Trafford	44724
85	1993/94	27/04/94	FA Premiership	Leeds United 0 Manchester United 2	Elland Road	41125
86	1994/95	11/09/94	FA Premiership	Leeds United 2 Manchester United 1	Elland Road	39396
87	1994/95	19/02/95	FA Cup 5th Round	Manchester United 3 Leeds United 1	Old Trafford	42744
88	1994/95	02/04/95	FA Premiership	Manchester United 0 Leeds United 0	Old Trafford	43712
89	1995/96	24/12/95	FA Premiership	Leeds United 3 Manchester United 1	Elland Road	39801
90	1995/96	17/04/96	FA Premiership	Manchester United 1 Leeds United 0	Old Trafford	48382
91	1996/97	07/09/96	FA Premiership	Leeds United 0 Manchester United 4	Elland Road	39694
92	1996/97	28/12/96	FA Premiership	Manchester United 1 Leeds United 0	Old Trafford	55256
93	1997/98	27/09/97	FA Premiership	Leeds United 1 Manchester United 0	Elland Road	39952
94	1997/98	04/05/98	FA Premiership	Manchester United 3 Leeds United 0	Old Trafford	55167
95	1998/99	29/11/98	FA Premiership	Manchester United 3 Leeds United 2	Old Trafford	55172
96	1998/99	25/04/99	FA Premiership	Leeds United 1 Manchester United 1	Elland Road	40255
97	1999/00	14/08/99	FA Premiership	Manchester United 2 Leeds United 0	Old Trafford	55187
98	1999/00	20/02/00	FA Premiership	Leeds United 0 Manchester United 1	Elland Road	40160
99	2000/01	21/10/00	FA Premiership	Manchester United 3 Leeds United 0	Old Trafford	67523
100	2000/01	03/03/01	FA Premiership	Leeds United 1 Manchester United 1	Elland Road	40055
101	2001/02	27/10/01	FA Premiership	Manchester United 1 Leeds United 1	Old Trafford	67555
102	2001/02	30/03/02	FA Premiership	Leeds United 3 Manchester United 4	Elland Road	40058
103	2002/03	14/09/02	FA Premiership	Leeds United 1 Manchester United 0	Elland Road	39622
104	2002/03	05/03/03	FA Premiership	Manchester United 2 Leeds United 1	Old Trafford	67135
105	2003/04	18/10/03	FA Premiership	Leeds United 0 Manchester United 1	Elland Road	40153
106	2003/04	28/10/03	League Cup 3rd Round	Leeds United 2 Manchester United 3	Elland Road	37546
107	2003/04	21/02/04	FA Premiership	Manchester United 1 Leeds United 1	Old Trafford	67744

UNITED v LEGIA WARSAW

EUROPEAN CUP-WINNERS' CUP

VENUE	P	W	D	L	F	A
HOME	1	0	1	0	1	1
AWAY	1	1	0	0	3	1
TOTAL	2	1	1	0	4	2

#	SEASON	DATE	COMPETITION / ROUND	MATCH RESULT	VENUE	ATT
1	1990/91	10/04/91	European CWC Semi-Final 1st Leg	Legia Warsaw 1 Manchester United 3	Wojska Polskiego	20000
2	1990/91	24/04/91	European CWC Semi-Final 2nd Leg	Manchester United 1 Legia Warsaw 1	Old Trafford	44269

UNITED v LEICESTER CITY

ALL COMPETITIVE MATCHES

VENUE	P	W	D	L	F	A
HOME	58	39	13	6	135	57
AWAY	58	19	13	26	96	98
NEUTRAL	1	1	0	0	3	1
TOTAL	117	59	26	32	234	156

ALL LEAGUE MATCHES

VENUE	P	W	D	L	F	A
HOME	56	37	13	6	128	56
AWAY	56	18	13	25	94	95
TOTAL	112	55	26	31	222	151

ALL CUP MATCHES

VENUE	P	W	D	L	F	A
HOME	2	2	0	0	7	1
AWAY	2	1	0	1	2	3
NEUTRAL	1	1	0	0	3	1
TOTAL	5	4	0	1	12	5

PREMIERSHIP

VENUE	P	W	D	L	F	A
HOME	8	5	2	1	13	5
AWAY	8	6	2	0	22	5
TOTAL	16	11	4	1	35	10

LEAGUE DIVISION ONE

VENUE	P	W	D	L	F	A
HOME	32	21	9	2	77	32
AWAY	32	7	7	18	52	67
TOTAL	64	28	16	20	129	99

LEAGUE DIVISION TWO

VENUE	P	W	D	L	F	A
HOME	16	11	2	3	38	19
AWAY	16	5	4	7	20	23
TOTAL	32	16	6	10	58	42

FA CUP

VENUE	P	W	D	L	F	A
HOME	0	0	0	0	0	0
AWAY	1	1	0	0	2	1
NEUTRAL	1	1	0	0	3	1
TOTAL	2	2	0	0	5	2

LEAGUE CUP

VENUE	P	W	D	L	F	A
HOME	2	2	0	0	7	1
AWAY	1	0	0	1	0	2
NEUTRAL	0	0	0	0	0	0
TOTAL	3	2	0	1	7	3

#	SEASON	DATE	COMPETITION / ROUND	MATCH RESULT	VENUE	ATT
1	1894/95	22/09/94	Football League Division 2	Leicester City 2 Newton Heath 3	Filbert Street	6000
2	1894/95	27/10/94	Football League Division 2	Newton Heath 2 Leicester City 2	Bank Street	3000
3	1895/96	04/01/96	Football League Division 2	Leicester City 3 Newton Heath 0	Filbert Street	7000
4	1895/96	03/02/96	Football League Division 2	Newton Heath 2 Leicester City 0	Bank Street	1000
5	1896/97	28/12/96	Football League Division 2	Leicester City 1 Newton Heath 0	Filbert Street	8000
6	1896/97	20/02/97	Football League Division 2	Newton Heath 2 Leicester City 1	Bank Street	8000
7	1897/98	02/10/97	Football League Division 2	Newton Heath 2 Leicester City 0	Bank Street	6000
8	1897/98	20/11/97	Football League Division 2	Leicester City 1 Newton Heath 1	Filbert Street	6000
9	1898/99	17/12/98	Football League Division 2	Leicester City 1 Newton Heath 0	Filbert Street	8000
10	1898/99	15/04/99	Football League Division 2	Newton Heath 2 Leicester City 2	Bank Street	6000
11	1899/00	24/03/00	Football League Division 2	Leicester City 2 Newton Heath 0	Filbert Street	8000
12	1899/00	13/04/00	Football League Division 2	Newton Heath 3 Leicester City 2	Bank Street	10000
13	1900/01	29/09/00	Football League Division 2	Leicester City 1 Newton Heath 0	Filbert Street	6000
14	1900/01	20/03/01	Football League Division 2	Newton Heath 2 Leicester City 3	Bank Street	2000
15	1901/02	30/11/01	Football League Division 2	Leicester City 3 Newton Heath 2	Filbert Street	4000
16	1901/02	29/03/02	Football League Division 2	Newton Heath 2 Leicester City 0	Bank Street	2000
17	1902/03	22/11/02	Football League Division 2	Leicester City 1 Manchester United 1	Filbert Street	5000
18	1902/03	21/03/03	Football League Division 2	Manchester United 5 Leicester City 1	Bank Street	8000
19	1903/04	02/04/04	Football League Division 2	Leicester City 0 Manchester United 1	Filbert Street	4000
20	1903/04	30/04/04	Football League Division 2	Manchester United 5 Leicester City 2	Bank Street	7000
21	1904/05	22/10/04	Football League Division 2	Leicester City 0 Manchester United 3	Filbert Street	7000
22	1904/05	18/02/05	Football League Division 2	Manchester United 4 Leicester City 1	Bank Street	7000
23	1905/06	21/10/05	Football League Division 2	Manchester United 3 Leicester City 2	Bank Street	12000
24	1905/06	29/03/06	Football League Division 2	Leicester City 2 Manchester United 5	Filbert Street	5000
25	1908/09	12/12/08	Football League Division 1	Manchester United 4 Leicester City 2	Bank Street	10000
26	1908/09	17/04/09	Football League Division 1	Leicester City 3 Manchester United 2	Filbert Street	8000
27	1922/23	14/04/23	Football League Division 2	Leicester City 0 Manchester United 1	Filbert Street	25000
28	1922/23	21/04/23	Football League Division 2	Manchester United 0 Leicester City 2	Old Trafford	30000
29	1923/24	03/11/23	Football League Division 2	Leicester City 2 Manchester United 0	Filbert Street	17000
30	1923/24	10/11/23	Football League Division 2	Manchester United 3 Leicester City 0	Old Trafford	20000
31	1924/25	30/08/24	Football League Division 2	Manchester United 1 Leicester City 0	Old Trafford	21250
32	1924/25	27/12/24	Football League Division 2	Leicester City 3 Manchester United 0	Filbert Street	18250
33	1925/26	16/09/25	Football League Division 1	Manchester United 3 Leicester City 2	Old Trafford	21275
34	1925/26	28/12/25	Football League Division 1	Leicester City 1 Manchester United 3	Filbert Street	28367
35	1926/27	13/11/26	Football League Division 1	Leicester City 2 Manchester United 3	Filbert Street	18521
36	1926/27	02/04/27	Football League Division 1	Manchester United 1 Leicester City 0	Old Trafford	17119
37	1927/28	01/10/27	Football League Division 1	Leicester City 1 Manchester United 0	Filbert Street	22385
38	1927/28	11/02/28	Football League Division 1	Manchester United 5 Leicester City 2	Old Trafford	16640
39	1928/29	25/08/28	Football League Division 1	Manchester United 1 Leicester City 1	Old Trafford	20129
40	1928/29	29/12/28	Football League Division 1	Leicester City 2 Manchester United 1	Filbert Street	21535
41	1929/30	02/09/29	Football League Division 1	Leicester City 4 Manchester United 1	Filbert Street	20490
42	1929/30	11/09/29	Football League Division 1	Manchester United 2 Leicester City 1	Old Trafford	16445

UNITED v LEICESTER CITY (continued)

#	SEASON	DATE	COMPETITION / ROUND	MATCH RESULT	VENUE	ATT
43	1930/31	08/11/30	Football League Division 1	Leicester City 5 Manchester United 4	Filbert Street	17466
44	1930/31	25/03/31	Football League Division 1	Manchester United 0 Leicester City 0	Old Trafford	3679
45	1935/36	02/11/35	Football League Division 2	Manchester United 0 Leicester City 1	Old Trafford	39074
46	1935/36	21/03/36	Football League Division 2	Leicester City 1 Manchester United 1	Filbert Street	18200
47	1938/39	26/12/38	Football League Division 1	Manchester United 3 Leicester City 0	Old Trafford	26332
48	1938/39	27/12/38	Football League Division 1	Leicester City 1 Manchester United 1	Filbert Street	21434
49	1954/55	04/12/54	Football League Division 1	Manchester United 3 Leicester City 1	Old Trafford	19369
50	1954/55	09/04/55	Football League Division 1	Leicester City 1 Manchester United 0	Filbert Street	34362
51	1957/58	24/08/57	Football League Division 1	Leicester City 0 Manchester United 3	Filbert Street	40214
52	1957/58	21/12/57	Football League Division 1	Manchester United 4 Leicester City 0	Old Trafford	41631
53	1958/59	06/12/58	Football League Division 1	Manchester United 4 Leicester City 1	Old Trafford	38482
54	1958/59	25/04/59	Football League Division 1	Leicester City 2 Manchester United 1	Filbert Street	38466
55	1959/60	03/10/59	Football League Division 1	Manchester United 4 Leicester City 1	Old Trafford	41637
56	1959/60	24/02/60	Football League Division 1	Leicester City 3 Manchester United 1	Filbert Street	33191
57	1960/61	10/09/60	Football League Division 1	Manchester United 1 Leicester City 1	Old Trafford	35493
58	1960/61	21/01/61	Football League Division 1	Leicester City 6 Manchester United 0	Filbert Street	31308
59	1961/62	11/11/61	Football League Division 1	Manchester United 2 Leicester City 2	Old Trafford	21567
60	1961/62	04/04/62	Football League Division 1	Leicester City 4 Manchester United 3	Filbert Street	15318
61	1962/63	15/04/63	Football League Division 1	Manchester United 2 Leicester City 2	Old Trafford	50005
62	1962/63	16/04/63	Football League Division 1	Leicester City 4 Manchester United 3	Filbert Street	37002
63	1962/63	25/05/63	FA Cup Final	Manchester United 3 Leicester City 1	Wembley	100000
64	1963/64	28/09/63	Football League Division 1	Manchester United 3 Leicester City 1	Old Trafford	41374
65	1963/64	08/02/64	Football League Division 1	Leicester City 3 Manchester United 2	Filbert Street	35538
66	1964/65	29/08/64	Football League Division 1	Leicester City 2 Manchester United 2	Filbert Street	32373
67	1964/65	12/04/65	Football League Division 1	Manchester United 1 Leicester City 0	Old Trafford	34114
68	1965/66	13/11/65	Football League Division 1	Leicester City 0 Manchester United 5	Filbert Street	34551
69	1965/66	09/04/66	Football League Division 1	Manchester United 1 Leicester City 2	Old Trafford	42593
70	1966/67	30/11/66	Football League Division 1	Leicester City 1 Manchester United 2	Filbert Street	39014
71	1966/67	18/03/67	Football League Division 1	Manchester United 5 Leicester City 2	Old Trafford	50281
72	1967/68	26/08/67	Football League Division 1	Manchester United 1 Leicester City 1	Old Trafford	51256
73	1967/68	23/12/67	Football League Division 1	Leicester City 2 Manchester United 2	Filbert Street	40104
74	1968/69	07/12/68	Football League Division 1	Leicester City 2 Manchester United 1	Filbert Street	36303
75	1968/69	17/05/69	Football League Division 1	Manchester United 3 Leicester City 2	Old Trafford	45860
76	1971/72	20/11/71	Football League Division 1	Manchester United 3 Leicester City 2	Old Trafford	48757
77	1971/72	08/04/72	Football League Division 1	Leicester City 2 Manchester United 0	Filbert Street	35970
78	1972/73	23/08/72	Football League Division 1	Manchester United 1 Leicester City 1	Old Trafford	40067
79	1972/73	04/11/72	Football League Division 1	Leicester City 2 Manchester United 2	Filbert Street	32575
80	1973/74	05/09/73	Football League Division 1	Leicester City 1 Manchester United 0	Filbert Street	29152
81	1973/74	12/09/73	Football League Division 1	Manchester United 1 Leicester City 2	Old Trafford	40793
82	1975/76	04/10/75	Football League Division 1	Manchester United 0 Leicester City 0	Old Trafford	47878
83	1975/76	14/02/76	FA Cup 5th Round	Leicester City 1 Manchester United 2	Filbert Street	34000
84	1975/76	24/04/76	Football League Division 1	Leicester City 2 Manchester United 1	Filbert Street	31053
85	1976/77	20/11/76	Football League Division 1	Leicester City 1 Manchester United 1	Filbert Street	26421
86	1976/77	16/04/77	Football League Division 1	Manchester United 1 Leicester City 1	Old Trafford	49161
87	1977/78	27/12/77	Football League Division 1	Manchester United 3 Leicester City 1	Old Trafford	57396
88	1977/78	25/03/78	Football League Division 1	Leicester City 2 Manchester United 3	Filbert Street	20299
89	1980/81	13/09/80	Football League Division 1	Manchester United 5 Leicester City 0	Old Trafford	43229
90	1980/81	07/02/81	Football League Division 1	Leicester City 1 Manchester United 0	Filbert Street	26085
91	1983/84	12/11/83	Football League Division 1	Leicester City 1 Manchester United 1	Filbert Street	24409
92	1983/84	10/03/84	Football League Division 1	Manchester United 2 Leicester City 0	Old Trafford	39473
93	1984/85	10/11/84	Football League Division 1	Leicester City 2 Manchester United 3	Filbert Street	23840
94	1984/85	03/04/85	Football League Division 1	Manchester United 2 Leicester City 1	Old Trafford	35950
95	1985/86	23/11/85	Football League Division 1	Leicester City 3 Manchester United 0	Filbert Street	22008
96	1985/86	26/04/86	Football League Division 1	Manchester United 4 Leicester City 0	Old Trafford	38840
97	1986/87	06/09/86	Football League Division 1	Leicester City 1 Manchester United 1	Filbert Street	16785
98	1986/87	20/12/86	Football League Division 1	Manchester United 2 Leicester City 0	Old Trafford	34150
99	1993/94	27/10/93	League Cup 3rd Round	Manchester United 5 Leicester City 1	Old Trafford	41344
100	1994/95	28/12/94	FA Premiership	Manchester United 1 Leicester City 1	Old Trafford	43789
101	1994/95	15/04/95	FA Premiership	Leicester City 0 Manchester United 4	Filbert Street	21281
102	1996/97	27/11/96	League Cup 4th Round	Leicester City 2 Manchester United 0	Filbert Street	20428
103	1996/97	30/11/96	FA Premiership	Manchester United 3 Leicester City 1	Old Trafford	55196
104	1996/97	03/05/97	FA Premiership	Leicester City 2 Manchester United 2	Filbert Street	21068

UNITED v LEICESTER CITY (continued)

#	SEASON	DATE	COMPETITION / ROUND	MATCH RESULT	VENUE	ATT
105	1997/98	23/08/97	FA Premiership	Leicester City 0 Manchester United 0	Filbert Street	21221
106	1997/98	31/01/98	FA Premiership	Manchester United 0 Leicester City 1	Old Trafford	55156
107	1998/99	15/08/98	FA Premiership	Manchester United 2 Leicester City 2	Old Trafford	55052
108	1998/99	16/01/99	FA Premiership	Leicester City 2 Manchester United 6	Filbert Street	22091
109	1999/00	06/11/99	FA Premiership	Manchester United 2 Leicester City 0	Old Trafford	55191
110	1999/00	18/03/00	FA Premiership	Leicester City 0 Manchester United 2	Filbert Street	22170
111	2000/01	14/10/00	FA Premiership	Leicester City 0 Manchester United 3	Filbert Street	22132
112	2000/01	17/03/01	FA Premiership	Manchester United 2 Leicester City 0	Old Trafford	67516
113	2001/02	17/11/01	FA Premiership	Manchester United 2 Leicester City 0	Old Trafford	67651
114	2001/02	06/04/02	FA Premiership	Leicester City 0 Manchester United 1	Filbert Street	21447
115	2002/03	05/11/02	League Cup 3rd Round	Manchester United 2 Leicester City 0	Old Trafford	47848
116	2003/04	27/09/03	FA Premiership	Leicester City 1 Manchester United 4	Walkers Stadium	32044
117	2003/04	13/04/04	FA Premiership	Manchester United 1 Leicester City 0	Old Trafford	67749

UNITED v LEYTON ORIENT

ALL COMPETITIVE MATCHES						LEAGUE DIVISION ONE						LEAGUE DIVISION TWO					
VENUE	P	W	D	L	F	A	VENUE	P	W	D	L	F	A	VENUE	P	W	D	L	F	A
HOME	6	3	3	0	13	5	HOME	1	1	0	0	3	1	HOME	5	2	3	0	10	4
AWAY	6	3	1	2	5	3	AWAY	1	0	0	1	0	1	AWAY	5	3	1	1	5	2
TOTAL	12	6	4	2	18	8	TOTAL	2	1	0	1	3	2	TOTAL	10	5	4	1	15	6

#	SEASON	DATE	COMPETITION / ROUND	MATCH RESULT	VENUE	ATT
1	1905/06	02/12/05	Football League Division 2	Manchester United 4 Leyton Orient 0	Bank Street	12000
2	1905/06	07/04/06	Football League Division 2	Leyton Orient 0 Manchester United 1	Millfields Road	8000
3	1922/23	04/11/22	Football League Division 2	Manchester United 0 Leyton Orient 0	Old Trafford	16500
4	1922/23	11/11/22	Football League Division 2	Leyton Orient 1 Manchester United 1	Millfields Road	11000
5	1923/24	18/04/24	Football League Division 2	Leyton Orient 1 Manchester United 0	Millfields Road	18000
6	1923/24	21/04/24	Football League Division 2	Manchester United 2 Leyton Orient 2	Old Trafford	11000
7	1924/25	04/10/24	Football League Division 2	Leyton Orient 0 Manchester United 1	Millfields Road	15000
8	1924/25	07/02/25	Football League Division 2	Manchester United 4 Leyton Orient 2	Old Trafford	18250
9	1962/63	08/09/62	Football League Division 1	Leyton Orient 1 Manchester United 0	Brisbane Road	24901
10	1962/63	18/05/63	Football League Division 1	Manchester United 3 Leyton Orient 1	Old Trafford	32759
11	1974/75	17/08/74	Football League Division 2	Leyton Orient 0 Manchester United 2	Brisbane Road	17772
12	1974/75	14/12/74	Football League Division 2	Manchester United 0 Leyton Orient 0	Old Trafford	41200

UNITED v LILLE METROPOLE

CHAMPIONS LEAGUE					
VENUE	P	W	D	L	F	A
HOME	3	2	1	0	2	0
AWAY	3	1	1	1	2	2
TOTAL	6	3	2	1	4	2

#	SEASON	DATE	COMPETITION / ROUND	MATCH RESULT	VENUE	ATT
1	2001/02	18/09/01	Champions League Phase 1 Match 1	Manchester United 1 Lille Metropole 0	Old Trafford	64827
2	2001/02	31/10/01	Champions League Phase 1 Match 6	Lille Metropole 1 Manchester United 1	Stade Felix Bollaert	38402
3	2005/06	18/10/05	Champions League Phase 1 Match 3	Manchester United 0 Lille Metropole 0	Old Trafford	60626
4	2005/06	02/11/05	Champions League Phase 1 Match 4	Lille Metropole 1 Manchester United 0	Stade de France	65000
5	2006/07	20/02/07	Champions League 2nd Round 1st Leg	Lille Metropole 0 Manchester United 1	Stade Felix Bollaert	41000
6	2006/07	07/03/07	Champions League 2nd Round 2nd Leg	Manchester United 1 Lille Metropole 0	Old Trafford	75182

UNITED v LINCOLN CITY

ALL COMPETITIVE MATCHES							LEAGUE DIVISION TWO							FA CUP					
VENUE	P	W	D	L	F	A	VENUE	P	W	D	L	F	A	VENUE	P	W	D	L	F	A
HOME	15	10	3	2	35	14	HOME	14	10	3	1	34	12	HOME	1	0	0	1	1	2
AWAY	14	3	1	10	12	28	AWAY	14	3	1	10	12	28	AWAY	0	0	0	0	0	0
TOTAL	29	13	4	12	47	42	TOTAL	28	13	4	11	46	40	TOTAL	1	0	0	1	1	2

#	SEASON	DATE	COMPETITION / ROUND	MATCH RESULT	VENUE	ATT
1	1894/95	22/12/94	Football League Division 2	Newton Heath 3 Lincoln City 0	Bank Street	2000
2	1894/95	29/12/94	Football League Division 2	Lincoln City 3 Newton Heath 0	John O'Gaunts	3000
3	1895/96	16/11/95	Football League Division 2	Newton Heath 5 Lincoln City 5	Bank Street	8000
4	1895/96	11/04/96	Football League Division 2	Lincoln City 2 Newton Heath 0	Sincil Bank	2000
5	1896/97	12/09/96	Football League Division 2	Newton Heath 3 Lincoln City 1	Bank Street	7000
6	1896/97	01/04/97	Football League Division 2	Lincoln City 1 Newton Heath 3	Sincil Bank	1000
7	1897/98	04/09/97	Football League Division 2	Newton Heath 5 Lincoln City 0	Bank Street	5000
8	1897/98	06/11/97	Football League Division 2	Lincoln City 1 Newton Heath 0	Sincil Bank	2000
9	1898/99	26/11/98	Football League Division 2	Newton Heath 1 Lincoln City 0	Bank Street	4000
10	1898/99	25/03/99	Football League Division 2	Lincoln City 2 Newton Heath 0	Sincil Bank	3000
11	1899/00	07/10/99	Football League Division 2	Newton Heath 1 Lincoln City 0	Bank Street	5000
12	1899/00	10/02/00	Football League Division 2	Lincoln City 1 Newton Heath 0	Sincil Bank	2000
13	1900/01	15/12/00	Football League Division 2	Newton Heath 4 Lincoln City 1	Bank Street	4000
14	1900/01	05/04/01	Football League Division 2	Lincoln City 2 Newton Heath 0	Sincil Bank	5000
15	1901/02	14/12/01	FA Cup Intermediate Round	Newton Heath 1 Lincoln City 2	Bank Street	4000
16	1901/02	26/12/01	Football League Division 2	Lincoln City 2 Newton Heath 0	Sincil Bank	4000
17	1901/02	01/03/02	Football League Division 2	Newton Heath 0 Lincoln City 0	Bank Street	6000
18	1902/03	08/11/02	Football League Division 2	Lincoln City 1 Manchester United 3	Sincil Bank	3000
19	1902/03	07/03/03	Football League Division 2	Manchester United 1 Lincoln City 2	Bank Street	4000
20	1903/04	17/10/03	Football League Division 2	Lincoln City 0 Manchester United 0	Sincil Bank	5000
21	1903/04	13/02/04	Football League Division 2	Manchester United 2 Lincoln City 0	Bank Street	8000
22	1904/05	15/10/04	Football League Division 2	Manchester United 2 Lincoln City 0	Bank Street	15000
23	1904/05	11/02/05	Football League Division 2	Lincoln City 3 Manchester United 0	Sincil Bank	2000
24	1905/06	04/11/05	Football League Division 2	Manchester United 2 Lincoln City 1	Bank Street	15000
25	1905/06	25/04/06	Football League Division 2	Lincoln City 2 Manchester United 3	Sincil Bank	1500
26	1932/33	17/12/32	Football League Division 2	Manchester United 4 Lincoln City 1	Old Trafford	18021
27	1932/33	29/04/33	Football League Division 2	Lincoln City 3 Manchester United 2	Sincil Bank	8507
28	1933/34	02/09/33	Football League Division 2	Manchester United 1 Lincoln City 1	Old Trafford	16987
29	1933/34	06/01/34	Football League Division 2	Lincoln City 5 Manchester United 1	Sincil Bank	6075

UNITED v LIVERPOOL

ALL COMPETITIVE MATCHES

VENUE	P	W	D	L	F	A
HOME	82	40	27	15	137	72
AWAY	80	23	19	38	91	134
NEUTRAL	13	5	4	4	15	15
TOTAL	175	68	50	57	243	221

ALL LEAGUE MATCHES

VENUE	P	W	D	L	F	A
HOME	75	36	25	14	124	65
AWAY	75	22	18	35	85	127
TOTAL	150	58	43	49	209	192

ALL CUP MATCHES

VENUE	P	W	D	L	F	A
HOME	6	4	1	1	11	5
AWAY	5	1	1	3	6	7
NEUTRAL	8	4	2	2	11	10
TOTAL	19	9	4	6	28	22

PREMIERSHIP

VENUE	P	W	D	L	F	A
HOME	16	9	4	3	24	10
AWAY	16	9	3	4	24	21
TOTAL	32	18	7	7	48	31

LEAGUE DIVISION ONE

VENUE	P	W	D	L	F	A
HOME	57	25	21	11	92	52
AWAY	57	13	15	29	60	95
TOTAL	114	38	36	40	152	147

LEAGUE DIVISION TWO

VENUE	P	W	D	L	F	A
HOME	2	2	0	0	8	3
AWAY	2	0	0	2	1	11
TOTAL	4	2	0	2	9	14

FA CUP

VENUE	P	W	D	L	F	A
HOME	5	3	1	1	8	4
AWAY	4	1	1	2	5	5
NEUTRAL	6	4	2	0	10	6
TOTAL	15	8	4	3	23	15

LEAGUE CUP

VENUE	P	W	D	L	F	A
HOME	1	1	0	0	3	1
AWAY	1	0	0	1	1	2
NEUTRAL	2	0	0	2	1	4
TOTAL	4	1	0	3	5	7

CHARITY SHIELD

VENUE	P	W	D	L	F	A
HOME	1	0	1	0	2	2
AWAY	0	0	0	0	0	0
NEUTRAL	4	1	2	1	4	3
TOTAL	5	1	3	1	6	5

OTHER MATCHES

VENUE	P	W	D	L	F	A
HOME	0	0	0	0	0	0
AWAY	0	0	0	0	0	0
NEUTRAL	1	0	0	1	0	2
TOTAL	1	0	0	1	0	2

#	SEASON	DATE	COMPETITION / ROUND	MATCH RESULT	VENUE	ATT
1	1893/94	28/04/94	Football League Test Match	Newton Heath 0 Liverpool 2	Ewood Park	3000
2	1895/96	12/10/95	Football League Division 2	Liverpool 7 Newton Heath 1	Anfield	7000
3	1895/96	02/11/95	Football League Division 2	Newton Heath 5 Liverpool 2	Bank Street	10000
4	1897/98	12/02/98	FA Cup 2nd Round	Newton Heath 0 Liverpool 0	Bank Street	12000
5	1897/98	16/02/98	FA Cup 2nd Round Replay	Liverpool 2 Newton Heath 1	Anfield	6000
6	1902/03	07/02/03	FA Cup 1st Round	Manchester United 2 Liverpool 1	Bank Street	15000
7	1904/05	24/12/04	Football League Division 2	Manchester United 3 Liverpool 1	Bank Street	40000
8	1904/05	22/04/05	Football League Division 2	Liverpool 4 Manchester United 0	Anfield	28000
9	1906/07	25/12/06	Football League Division 1	Manchester United 0 Liverpool 0	Bank Street	20000
10	1906/07	01/04/07	Football League Division 1	Liverpool 0 Manchester United 1	Anfield	20000
11	1907/08	07/09/07	Football League Division 1	Manchester United 4 Liverpool 0	Bank Street	24000
12	1907/08	25/03/08	Football League Division 1	Liverpool 7 Manchester United 4	Anfield	10000
13	1908/09	26/09/08	Football League Division 1	Manchester United 3 Liverpool 2	Bank Street	25000
14	1908/09	30/01/09	Football League Division 1	Liverpool 3 Manchester United 1	Anfield	30000
15	1909/10	09/10/09	Football League Division 1	Liverpool 3 Manchester United 2	Anfield	30000
16	1909/10	19/02/10	Football League Division 1	Manchester United 3 Liverpool 4	Old Trafford	45000
17	1910/11	26/11/10	Football League Division 1	Liverpool 3 Manchester United 2	Anfield	8000
18	1910/11	01/04/11	Football League Division 1	Manchester United 2 Liverpool 0	Old Trafford	20000
19	1911/12	18/11/11	Football League Division 1	Liverpool 3 Manchester United 2	Anfield	15000
20	1911/12	23/03/12	Football League Division 1	Manchester United 1 Liverpool 1	Old Trafford	10000
21	1912/13	23/11/12	Football League Division 1	Manchester United 3 Liverpool 1	Old Trafford	8000
22	1912/13	29/03/13	Football League Division 1	Liverpool 0 Manchester United 2	Anfield	12000
23	1913/14	01/11/13	Football League Division 1	Manchester United 3 Liverpool 0	Old Trafford	30000
24	1913/14	15/04/14	Football League Division 1	Liverpool 1 Manchester United 2	Anfield	28000
25	1914/15	26/12/14	Football League Division 1	Liverpool 1 Manchester United 1	Anfield	25000
26	1914/15	02/04/15	Football League Division 1	Manchester United 2 Liverpool 0	Old Trafford	18000
27	1919/20	26/12/19	Football League Division 1	Manchester United 0 Liverpool 0	Old Trafford	45000
28	1919/20	01/01/20	Football League Division 1	Liverpool 0 Manchester United 0	Anfield	30000
29	1920/21	08/01/21	FA Cup 1st Round	Liverpool 1 Manchester United 1	Anfield	40000
30	1920/21	12/01/21	FA Cup 1st Round Replay	Manchester United 1 Liverpool 2	Old Trafford	30000
31	1920/21	05/02/21	Football League Division 1	Manchester United 1 Liverpool 1	Old Trafford	30000
32	1920/21	09/02/21	Football League Division 1	Liverpool 2 Manchester United 0	Anfield	35000
33	1921/22	17/12/21	Football League Division 1	Liverpool 2 Manchester United 1	Anfield	40000
34	1921/22	24/12/21	Football League Division 1	Manchester United 0 Liverpool 0	Old Trafford	30000
35	1925/26	19/09/25	Football League Division 1	Liverpool 5 Manchester United 0	Anfield	18824
36	1925/26	10/03/26	Football League Division 1	Manchester United 3 Liverpool 3	Old Trafford	9214

UNITED v LIVERPOOL (continued)

#	SEASON	DATE	COMPETITION / ROUND	MATCH RESULT	VENUE	ATT
37	1926/27	28/08/26	Football League Division 1	Liverpool 4 Manchester United 2	Anfield	34795
38	1926/27	15/01/27	Football League Division 1	Manchester United 0 Liverpool 1	Old Trafford	30304
39	1927/28	24/12/27	Football League Division 1	Liverpool 2 Manchester United 0	Anfield	14971
40	1927/28	05/05/28	Football League Division 1	Manchester United 6 Liverpool 1	Old Trafford	30625
41	1928/29	15/09/28	Football League Division 1	Manchester United 2 Liverpool 2	Old Trafford	24077
42	1928/29	13/02/29	Football League Division 1	Liverpool 2 Manchester United 3	Anfield	8852
43	1929/30	21/09/29	Football League Division 1	Manchester United 1 Liverpool 2	Old Trafford	20788
44	1929/30	25/01/30	Football League Division 1	Liverpool 1 Manchester United 0	Anfield	28592
45	1930/31	03/04/31	Football League Division 1	Liverpool 1 Manchester United 1	Anfield	27782
46	1930/31	06/04/31	Football League Division 1	Manchester United 4 Liverpool 1	Old Trafford	8058
47	1936/37	21/11/36	Football League Division 1	Manchester United 2 Liverpool 5	Old Trafford	26419
48	1936/37	27/03/37	Football League Division 1	Liverpool 2 Manchester United 0	Anfield	25319
49	1938/39	07/09/38	Football League Division 1	Liverpool 1 Manchester United 0	Anfield	25070
50	1938/39	06/05/39	Football League Division 1	Manchester United 2 Liverpool 0	Old Trafford	12073
51	1946/47	11/09/46	Football League Division 1	Manchester United 5 Liverpool 0	Maine Road	41657
52	1946/47	03/05/47	Football League Division 1	Liverpool 1 Manchester United 0	Anfield	48800
53	1947/48	27/08/47	Football League Division 1	Manchester United 2 Liverpool 0	Maine Road	52385
54	1947/48	03/09/47	Football League Division 1	Liverpool 2 Manchester United 2	Anfield	48081
55	1947/48	24/01/48	FA Cup 4th Round	Manchester United 3 Liverpool 0	Goodison Park	74000
56	1948/49	25/12/48	Football League Division 1	Manchester United 0 Liverpool 0	Maine Road	47788
57	1948/49	26/12/48	Football League Division 1	Liverpool 0 Manchester United 2	Anfield	53325
58	1949/50	07/09/49	Football League Division 1	Liverpool 1 Manchester United 1	Anfield	51587
59	1949/50	15/03/50	Football League Division 1	Manchester United 0 Liverpool 0	Old Trafford	43456
60	1950/51	23/08/50	Football League Division 1	Liverpool 2 Manchester United 1	Anfield	30211
61	1950/51	30/08/50	Football League Division 1	Manchester United 1 Liverpool 0	Old Trafford	34835
62	1951/52	24/11/51	Football League Division 1	Liverpool 0 Manchester United 0	Anfield	42378
63	1951/52	12/04/52	Football League Division 1	Manchester United 4 Liverpool 0	Old Trafford	42970
64	1952/53	13/12/52	Football League Division 1	Liverpool 1 Manchester United 2	Anfield	34450
65	1952/53	20/04/53	Football League Division 1	Manchester United 3 Liverpool 1	Old Trafford	20869
66	1953/54	22/08/53	Football League Division 1	Liverpool 4 Manchester United 4	Anfield	48422
67	1953/54	19/12/53	Football League Division 1	Manchester United 5 Liverpool 1	Old Trafford	26074
68	1959/60	30/01/60	FA Cup 4th Round	Liverpool 1 Manchester United 3	Anfield	56736
69	1962/63	10/11/62	Football League Division 1	Manchester United 3 Liverpool 3	Old Trafford	43810
70	1962/63	13/04/63	Football League Division 1	Liverpool 1 Manchester United 0	Anfield	51529
71	1963/64	23/11/63	Football League Division 1	Manchester United 0 Liverpool 1	Old Trafford	54654
72	1963/64	04/04/64	Football League Division 1	Liverpool 3 Manchester United 0	Anfield	52559
73	1964/65	31/10/64	Football League Division 1	Liverpool 0 Manchester United 2	Anfield	52402
74	1964/65	24/04/65	Football League Division 1	Manchester United 3 Liverpool 0	Old Trafford	55772
75	1965/66	14/08/65	FA Charity Shield	Manchester United 2 Liverpool 2 (Trophy Shared)	Old Trafford	48502
76	1965/66	09/10/65	Football League Division 1	Manchester United 2 Liverpool 0	Old Trafford	58161
77	1965/66	01/01/66	Football League Division 1	Liverpool 2 Manchester United 1	Anfield	53790
78	1966/67	10/12/66	Football League Division 1	Manchester United 2 Liverpool 2	Old Trafford	61768
79	1966/67	25/03/67	Football League Division 1	Liverpool 0 Manchester United 0	Anfield	53813
80	1967/68	11/11/67	Football League Division 1	Liverpool 1 Manchester United 2	Anfield	54515
81	1967/68	06/04/68	Football League Division 1	Manchester United 1 Liverpool 2	Old Trafford	63059
82	1968/69	12/10/68	Football League Division 1	Liverpool 2 Manchester United 0	Anfield	53392
83	1968/69	14/12/68	Football League Division 1	Manchester United 1 Liverpool 0	Old Trafford	55354
84	1969/70	13/09/69	Football League Division 1	Manchester United 1 Liverpool 0	Old Trafford	56509
85	1969/70	13/12/69	Football League Division 1	Liverpool 1 Manchester United 4	Anfield	47682
86	1970/71	05/09/70	Football League Division 1	Liverpool 1 Manchester United 1	Anfield	52542
87	1970/71	19/04/71	Football League Division 1	Manchester United 0 Liverpool 2	Old Trafford	44004
88	1971/72	25/09/71	Football League Division 1	Liverpool 2 Manchester United 2	Anfield	55634
89	1971/72	03/04/72	Football League Division 1	Manchester United 0 Liverpool 3	Old Trafford	53826
90	1972/73	15/08/72	Football League Division 1	Liverpool 2 Manchester United 0	Anfield	54789
91	1972/73	11/11/72	Football League Division 1	Manchester United 2 Liverpool 0	Old Trafford	53944
92	1973/74	29/09/73	Football League Division 1	Manchester United 0 Liverpool 0	Old Trafford	53862
93	1973/74	22/12/73	Football League Division 1	Liverpool 2 Manchester United 0	Anfield	40420
94	1975/76	08/11/75	Football League Division 1	Liverpool 3 Manchester United 1	Anfield	49136
95	1975/76	18/02/76	Football League Division 1	Manchester United 0 Liverpool 0	Old Trafford	59709

UNITED v LIVERPOOL (continued)

#	SEASON	DATE	COMPETITION / ROUND	MATCH RESULT	VENUE	ATT
96	1976/77	16/02/77	Football League Division 1	Manchester United 0 Liverpool 0	Old Trafford	57487
97	1976/77	03/05/77	Football League Division 1	Liverpool 1 Manchester United 0	Anfield	53046
98	1976/77	21/05/77	FA Cup Final	Manchester United 2 Liverpool 1	Wembley	100000
99	1977/78	13/08/77	FA Charity Shield	Manchester United 0 Liverpool 0 (Trophy Shared)	Wembley	82000
100	1977/78	01/10/77	Football League Division 1	Manchester United 2 Liverpool 0	Old Trafford	55089
101	1977/78	25/02/78	Football League Division 1	Liverpool 3 Manchester United 1	Anfield	49095
102	1978/79	26/12/78	Football League Division 1	Manchester United 0 Liverpool 3	Old Trafford	54910
103	1978/79	31/03/79	FA Cup Semi-Final	Manchester United 2 Liverpool 2	Maine Road	52524
104	1978/79	04/04/79	FA Cup Semi-Final Replay	Manchester United 1 Liverpool 0	Goodison Park	53069
105	1978/79	14/04/79	Football League Division 1	Liverpool 2 Manchester United 0	Anfield	46608
106	1979/80	26/12/79	Football League Division 1	Liverpool 2 Manchester United 0	Anfield	51073
107	1979/80	05/04/80	Football League Division 1	Manchester United 2 Liverpool 1	Old Trafford	57342
108	1980/81	26/12/80	Football League Division 1	Manchester United 0 Liverpool 0	Old Trafford	57049
109	1980/81	14/04/81	Football League Division 1	Liverpool 0 Manchester United 1	Anfield	31276
110	1981/82	24/10/81	Football League Division 1	Liverpool 1 Manchester United 2	Anfield	41438
111	1981/82	07/04/82	Football League Division 1	Manchester United 0 Liverpool 1	Old Trafford	48317
112	1982/83	16/10/82	Football League Division 1	Liverpool 0 Manchester United 0	Anfield	40853
113	1982/83	26/02/83	Football League Division 1	Manchester United 1 Liverpool 1	Old Trafford	57397
114	1982/83	26/03/83	League Cup Final	Manchester United 1 Liverpool 2	Wembley	100000
115	1983/84	20/08/83	FA Charity Shield	Manchester United 2 Liverpool 0	Wembley	92000
116	1983/84	24/09/83	Football League Division 1	Manchester United 1 Liverpool 0	Old Trafford	56121
117	1983/84	02/01/84	Football League Division 1	Liverpool 1 Manchester United 1	Anfield	44622
118	1984/85	22/09/84	Football League Division 1	Manchester United 1 Liverpool 1	Old Trafford	56638
119	1984/85	31/03/85	Football League Division 1	Liverpool 0 Manchester United 1	Anfield	34886
120	1984/85	13/04/85	FA Cup Semi-Final	Manchester United 2 Liverpool 2	Goodison Park	51690
121	1984/85	17/04/85	FA Cup Semi-Final Replay	Manchester United 2 Liverpool 1	Maine Road	45775
122	1985/86	19/10/85	Football League Division 1	Manchester United 1 Liverpool 1	Old Trafford	54492
123	1985/86	26/11/85	League Cup 4th Round	Liverpool 2 Manchester United 1	Anfield	41291
124	1985/86	09/02/86	Football League Division 1	Liverpool 1 Manchester United 1	Anfield	35064
125	1986/87	26/12/86	Football League Division 1	Liverpool 0 Manchester United 1	Anfield	40663
126	1986/87	20/04/87	Football League Division 1	Manchester United 1 Liverpool 0	Old Trafford	54103
127	1987/88	15/11/87	Football League Division 1	Manchester United 1 Liverpool 1	Old Trafford	47106
128	1987/88	04/04/88	Football League Division 1	Liverpool 3 Manchester United 3	Anfield	43497
129	1988/89	03/09/88	Football League Division 1	Liverpool 1 Manchester United 0	Anfield	42026
130	1988/89	01/01/89	Football League Division 1	Manchester United 3 Liverpool 1	Old Trafford	44745
131	1989/90	23/12/89	Football League Division 1	Liverpool 0 Manchester United 0	Anfield	37426
132	1989/90	18/03/90	Football League Division 1	Manchester United 1 Liverpool 2	Old Trafford	46629
133	1990/91	18/08/90	FA Charity Shield	Manchester United 1 Liverpool 1 (Trophy Shared)	Wembley	66558
134	1990/91	16/09/90	Football League Division 1	Liverpool 4 Manchester United 0	Anfield	35726
135	1990/91	31/10/90	League Cup 3rd Round	Manchester United 3 Liverpool 1	Old Trafford	42033
136	1990/91	03/02/91	Football League Division 1	Manchester United 1 Liverpool 1	Old Trafford	43690
137	1991/92	06/10/91	Football League Division 1	Manchester United 0 Liverpool 0	Old Trafford	44997
138	1991/92	26/04/92	Football League Division 1	Liverpool 2 Manchester United 0	Anfield	38669
139	1992/93	18/10/92	FA Premiership	Manchester United 2 Liverpool 2	Old Trafford	33243
140	1992/93	06/03/93	FA Premiership	Liverpool 1 Manchester United 2	Anfield	44374
141	1993/94	04/01/94	FA Premiership	Liverpool 3 Manchester United 3	Anfield	42795
142	1993/94	30/03/94	FA Premiership	Manchester United 1 Liverpool 0	Old Trafford	44751
143	1994/95	17/09/94	FA Premiership	Manchester United 2 Liverpool 0	Old Trafford	43740
144	1994/95	19/03/95	FA Premiership	Liverpool 2 Manchester United 0	Anfield	38906
145	1995/96	01/10/95	FA Premiership	Manchester United 2 Liverpool 2	Old Trafford	34934
146	1995/96	17/12/95	FA Premiership	Liverpool 2 Manchester United 0	Anfield	40546
147	1995/96	11/05/96	FA Cup Final	Manchester United 1 Liverpool 0	Wembley	79007
148	1996/97	12/10/96	FA Premiership	Manchester United 1 Liverpool 0	Old Trafford	55128
149	1996/97	19/04/97	FA Premiership	Liverpool 1 Manchester United 3	Anfield	40892
150	1997/98	06/12/97	FA Premiership	Liverpool 1 Manchester United 3	Anfield	41027
151	1997/98	10/04/98	FA Premiership	Manchester United 1 Liverpool 1	Old Trafford	55171
152	1998/99	24/09/98	FA Premiership	Manchester United 2 Liverpool 0	Old Trafford	55181
153	1998/99	24/01/99	FA Cup 4th Round	Manchester United 2 Liverpool 1	Old Trafford	54591
154	1998/99	05/05/99	FA Premiership	Liverpool 2 Manchester United 2	Anfield	44702
155	1999/00	11/09/99	FA Premiership	Liverpool 2 Manchester United 3	Anfield	44929
156	1999/00	04/03/00	FA Premiership	Manchester United 1 Liverpool 1	Old Trafford	61592
157	2000/01	17/12/00	FA Premiership	Manchester United 0 Liverpool 1	Old Trafford	67533
158	2000/01	31/03/01	FA Premiership	Liverpool 2 Manchester United 0	Anfield	44806

UNITED v LIVERPOOL (continued)

#	SEASON	DATE	COMPETITION / ROUND	MATCH RESULT	VENUE	ATT
159	2001/02	12/08/01	FA Charity Shield	Manchester United 1 Liverpool 2	Millennium Stadium	70227
160	2001/02	04/11/01	FA Premiership	Liverpool 3 Manchester United 1	Anfield	44361
161	2001/02	22/01/02	FA Premiership	Manchester United 0 Liverpool 1	Old Trafford	67599
162	2002/03	01/12/02	FA Premiership	Liverpool 1 Manchester United 2	Anfield	44250
163	2002/03	02/03/03	League Cup Final	Manchester United 0 Liverpool 2	Millennium Stadium	74500
164	2002/03	05/04/03	FA Premiership	Manchester United 4 Liverpool 0	Old Trafford	67639
165	2003/04	09/11/03	FA Premiership	Liverpool 1 Manchester United 2	Anfield	44159
166	2003/04	24/04/04	FA Premiership	Manchester United 0 Liverpool 1	Old Trafford	67647
167	2004/05	20/09/04	FA Premiership	Manchester United 2 Liverpool 1	Old Trafford	67857
168	2004/05	15/01/05	FA Premiership	Liverpool 0 Manchester United 1	Anfield	44183
169	2005/06	18/09/05	FA Premiership	Liverpool 0 Manchester United 0	Anfield	44917
170	2005/06	22/01/06	FA Premiership	Manchester United 1 Liverpool 0	Old Trafford	67874
171	2005/06	18/02/06	FA Cup 5th Round	Liverpool 1 Manchester United 0	Anfield	44039
172	2006/07	22/10/06	FA Premiership	Manchester United 2 Liverpool 0	Old Trafford	75828
173	2006/07	03/03/07	FA Premiership	Liverpool 0 Manchester United 1	Anfield	44403
174	2007/08	16/12/07	FA Premiership	Liverpool 0 Manchester United 1	Anfield	44459
175	2007/08	23/03/08	FA Premiership	Manchester United 3 Liverpool 0	Old Trafford	76000

UNITED v LKS LODZ

CHAMPIONS LEAGUE						
VENUE	P	W	D	L	F	A
HOME	1	1	0	0	2	0
AWAY	1	0	1	0	0	0
TOTAL	2	1	1	0	2	0

#	SEASON	DATE	COMPETITION / ROUND	MATCH RESULT	VENUE	ATT
1	1998/99	12/08/98	Champions League Qualifying Round 1st Leg	Manchester United 2 LKS Lodz 0	Old Trafford	50906
2	1998/99	26/08/98	Champions League Qualifying Round 2nd Leg	LKS Lodz 0 Manchester United 0	LKS Stadion	8700

UNITED v LOUGHBOROUGH TOWN

LEAGUE DIVISION TWO						
VENUE	P	W	D	L	F	A
HOME	5	5	0	0	23	2
AWAY	5	2	2	1	6	5
TOTAL	10	7	2	1	29	7

#	SEASON	DATE	COMPETITION / ROUND	MATCH RESULT	VENUE	ATT
1	1895/96	14/09/95	Football League Division 2	Loughborough Town 3 Newton Heath 3	The Athletic Ground	3000
2	1895/96	04/04/96	Football League Division 2	Newton Heath 2 Loughborough Town 0	Bank Street	4000
3	1896/97	06/02/97	Football League Division 2	Newton Heath 6 Loughborough Town 0	Bank Street	5000
4	1896/97	10/04/97	Football League Division 2	Loughborough Town 2 Newton Heath 0	The Athletic Ground	3000
5	1897/98	29/03/98	Football League Division 2	Newton Heath 5 Loughborough Town 1	Bank Street	2000
6	1897/98	16/04/98	Football League Division 2	Loughborough Town 0 Newton Heath 0	The Athletic Ground	1000
7	1898/99	22/10/98	Football League Division 2	Newton Heath 6 Loughborough Town 1	Bank Street	2000
8	1898/99	18/02/99	Football League Division 2	Loughborough Town 0 Newton Heath 1	The Athletic Ground	1500
9	1899/00	16/09/99	Football League Division 2	Newton Heath 4 Loughborough Town 0	Bank Street	6000
10	1899/00	13/01/00	Football League Division 2	Loughborough Town 0 Newton Heath 2	The Athletic Ground	1000

UNITED v LUTON TOWN

ALL COMPETITIVE MATCHES								ALL LEAGUE MATCHES								FA CUP					
VENUE	P	W	D	L	F	A		VENUE	P	W	D	L	F	A		VENUE	P	W	D	L	F	A
HOME	19	18	0	1	58	10		HOME	19	18	0	1	58	10		HOME	0	0	0	0	0	0
AWAY	20	10	7	3	32	16		AWAY	19	9	7	3	30	16		AWAY	1	1	0	0	2	0
TOTAL	39	28	7	4	90	26		TOTAL	38	27	7	4	88	26		TOTAL	1	1	0	0	2	0

LEAGUE DIVISION ONE							LEAGUE DIVISION TWO						
VENUE	P	W	D	L	F	A	VENUE	P	W	D	L	F	A
HOME	15	15	0	0	43	6	HOME	4	3	0	1	15	4
AWAY	15	7	6	2	26	13	AWAY	4	2	1	1	4	3
TOTAL	30	22	6	2	69	19	TOTAL	8	5	1	2	19	7

#	SEASON	DATE	COMPETITION / ROUND	MATCH RESULT	VENUE	ATT
1	1897/98	18/09/97	Football League Division 2	Newton Heath 1 Luton Town 2	Bank Street	8000
2	1897/98	21/03/98	Football League Division 2	Luton Town 2 Newton Heath 2	Dunstable Road	2000
3	1898/99	08/04/99	Football League Division 2	Luton Town 0 Newton Heath 1	Dunstable Road	1000
4	1898/99	12/04/99	Football League Division 2	Newton Heath 5 Luton Town 0	Bank Street	3000
5	1899/00	25/11/99	Football League Division 2	Luton Town 0 Newton Heath 1	Dunstable Road	3000
6	1899/00	31/03/00	Football League Division 2	Newton Heath 5 Luton Town 0	Bank Street	6000
7	1937/38	04/09/37	Football League Division 2	Luton Town 1 Manchester United 0	Kenilworth Road	20610
8	1937/38	15/01/38	Football League Division 2	Manchester United 4 Luton Town 2	Old Trafford	16845
9	1955/56	01/10/55	Football League Division 1	Manchester United 3 Luton Town 1	Old Trafford	34409
10	1955/56	11/02/56	Football League Division 1	Luton Town 0 Manchester United 2	Kenilworth Road	16354
11	1956/57	01/12/56	Football League Division 1	Manchester United 3 Luton Town 1	Old Trafford	34736
12	1956/57	13/04/57	Football League Division 1	Luton Town 0 Manchester United 2	Kenilworth Road	21227
13	1957/58	25/12/57	Football League Division 1	Manchester United 3 Luton Town 0	Old Trafford	39444
14	1957/58	26/12/57	Football League Division 1	Luton Town 2 Manchester United 2	Kenilworth Road	26458
15	1958/59	22/11/58	Football League Division 1	Manchester United 2 Luton Town 1	Old Trafford	42428
16	1958/59	11/04/59	Football League Division 1	Luton Town 0 Manchester United 0	Kenilworth Road	27025
17	1959/60	21/11/59	Football League Division 1	Manchester United 4 Luton Town 1	Old Trafford	40572
18	1959/60	09/04/60	Football League Division 1	Luton Town 2 Manchester United 3	Kenilworth Road	21242
19	1982/83	02/10/82	Football League Division 1	Luton Town 1 Manchester United 1	Kenilworth Road	17009
20	1982/83	29/01/83	FA Cup 4th Round	Luton Town 0 Manchester United 2	Kenilworth Road	20516
21	1982/83	09/05/83	Football League Division 1	Manchester United 3 Luton Town 0	Old Trafford	34213
22	1983/84	10/09/83	Football League Division 1	Manchester United 2 Luton Town 0	Old Trafford	41013
23	1983/84	12/02/84	Football League Division 1	Luton Town 0 Manchester United 5	Kenilworth Road	11265
24	1984/85	17/11/84	Football League Division 1	Manchester United 2 Luton Town 0	Old Trafford	41630
25	1984/85	21/04/85	Football League Division 1	Luton Town 2 Manchester United 1	Kenilworth Road	10320
26	1985/86	05/10/85	Football League Division 1	Luton Town 1 Manchester United 1	Kenilworth Road	17454
27	1985/86	19/03/86	Football League Division 1	Manchester United 2 Luton Town 0	Old Trafford	33668
28	1986/87	18/10/86	Football League Division 1	Manchester United 1 Luton Town 0	Old Trafford	39927
29	1986/87	14/03/87	Football League Division 1	Luton Town 2 Manchester United 1	Kenilworth Road	12509
30	1987/88	03/10/87	Football League Division 1	Luton Town 1 Manchester United 1	Kenilworth Road	9137
31	1987/88	12/04/88	Football League Division 1	Manchester United 3 Luton Town 0	Old Trafford	28830
32	1988/89	17/09/88	Football League Division 1	Luton Town 0 Manchester United 2	Kenilworth Road	11010
33	1988/89	25/03/89	Football League Division 1	Manchester United 2 Luton Town 0	Old Trafford	36335
34	1989/90	18/11/89	Football League Division 1	Luton Town 1 Manchester United 3	Kenilworth Road	11141
35	1989/90	03/03/90	Football League Division 1	Manchester United 4 Luton Town 1	Old Trafford	35327
36	1990/91	04/09/90	Football League Division 1	Luton Town 0 Manchester United 1	Kenilworth Road	12576
37	1990/91	23/03/91	Football League Division 1	Manchester United 4 Luton Town 1	Old Trafford	41752
38	1991/92	21/09/91	Football League Division 1	Manchester United 5 Luton Town 0	Old Trafford	46491
39	1991/92	18/04/92	Football League Division 1	Luton Town 1 Manchester United 1	Kenilworth Road	13410

UNITED v MACCABI HAIFA

CHAMPIONS LEAGUE					
VENUE	P	W	D	L	F	A
HOME	1	1	0	0	5	2
AWAY	1	0	0	1	0	3
TOTAL	2	1	0	1	5	5

#	SEASON	DATE	COMPETITION / ROUND	MATCH RESULT	VENUE	ATT
1	2002/03	18/09/02	Champions League Phase 1 Match 1	Manchester United 5 Maccabi Haifa 2	Old Trafford	63439
2	2002/03	29/10/02	Champions League Phase 1 Match 5	Maccabi Haifa 3 Manchester United 0	GSP Stadion Cyprus	22000

UNITED v MANCHESTER CITY

ALL COMPETITIVE MATCHES

VENUE	P	W	D	L	F	A
HOME	76	35	26	15	125	88
AWAY	73	25	23	25	94	110
NEUTRAL	1	0	0	1	0	3
TOTAL	150	60	49	41	219	201

ALL LEAGUE MATCHES

VENUE	P	W	D	L	F	A
HOME	69	29	25	15	107	82
AWAY	69	24	23	22	92	102
TOTAL	138	53	48	37	199	184

ALL CUP MATCHES

VENUE	P	W	D	L	F	A
HOME	7	6	1	0	18	6
AWAY	3	0	0	3	1	8
NEUTRAL	1	0	0	1	0	3
TOTAL	11	6	1	4	19	17

PREMIERSHIP

VENUE	P	W	D	L	F	A
HOME	11	6	4	1	20	8
AWAY	11	6	1	4	17	16
TOTAL	22	12	5	5	37	24

LEAGUE DIVISION ONE

VENUE	P	W	D	L	F	A
HOME	52	20	18	14	75	69
AWAY	52	15	21	16	66	78
TOTAL	104	35	39	30	141	147

LEAGUE DIVISION TWO

VENUE	P	W	D	L	F	A
HOME	6	3	3	0	12	5
AWAY	6	3	1	2	9	8
TOTAL	12	6	4	2	21	13

FA CUP

VENUE	P	W	D	L	F	A
HOME	5	5	0	0	15	4
AWAY	1	0	0	1	0	2
NEUTRAL	1	0	0	1	0	3
TOTAL	7	5	0	2	15	9

LEAGUE CUP

VENUE	P	W	D	L	F	A
HOME	2	1	1	0	3	2
AWAY	2	0	0	2	1	6
NEUTRAL	0	0	0	0	0	0
TOTAL	4	1	1	2	4	8

CHARITY SHIELD

VENUE	P	W	D	L	F	A
HOME	0	0	0	0	0	0
AWAY	1	1	0	0	1	0
NEUTRAL	0	0	0	0	0	0
TOTAL	1	1	0	0	1	0

#	SEASON	DATE	COMPETITION / ROUND	MATCH RESULT	VENUE	ATT
1	1891/92	03/10/91	FA Cup 1st Qualifying Round	Newton Heath 5 Manchester City 1	North Road	11000
2	1894/95	03/11/94	Football League Division 2	Manchester City 2 Newton Heath 5	Hyde Road	14000
3	1894/95	05/01/95	Football League Division 2	Newton Heath 4 Manchester City 1	Bank Street	12000
4	1895/96	05/10/95	Football League Division 2	Newton Heath 1 Manchester City 1	Bank Street	12000
5	1895/96	07/12/95	Football League Division 2	Manchester City 2 Newton Heath 1	Hyde Road	18000
6	1896/97	03/10/96	Football League Division 2	Manchester City 0 Newton Heath 0	Hyde Road	20000
7	1896/97	25/12/96	Football League Division 2	Newton Heath 2 Manchester City 1	Bank Street	18000
8	1897/98	16/10/97	Football League Division 2	Newton Heath 1 Manchester City 1	Bank Street	20000
9	1897/98	25/12/97	Football League Division 2	Manchester City 0 Newton Heath 1	Hyde Road	16000
10	1898/99	10/09/98	Football League Division 2	Newton Heath 3 Manchester City 0	Bank Street	20000
11	1898/99	26/12/98	Football League Division 2	Manchester City 4 Newton Heath 0	Hyde Road	25000
12	1902/03	25/12/02	Football League Division 2	Manchester United 1 Manchester City 1	Bank Street	40000
13	1902/03	10/04/03	Football League Division 2	Manchester City 0 Manchester United 2	Hyde Road	30000
14	1906/07	01/12/06	Football League Division 1	Manchester City 3 Manchester United 0	Hyde Road	40000
15	1906/07	06/04/07	Football League Division 1	Manchester United 1 Manchester City 1	Bank Street	40000
16	1907/08	21/12/07	Football League Division 1	Manchester United 3 Manchester City 1	Bank Street	35000
17	1907/08	18/04/08	Football League Division 1	Manchester City 0 Manchester United 0	Hyde Road	40000
18	1908/09	19/09/08	Football League Division 1	Manchester City 1 Manchester United 2	Hyde Road	40000
19	1908/09	23/01/09	Football League Division 1	Manchester United 3 Manchester City 1	Bank Street	40000
20	1910/11	17/09/10	Football League Division 1	Manchester United 2 Manchester City 1	Old Trafford	60000
21	1910/11	21/01/11	Football League Division 1	Manchester City 1 Manchester United 1	Hyde Road	40000
22	1911/12	02/09/11	Football League Division 1	Manchester City 0 Manchester United 0	Hyde Road	35000
23	1911/12	30/12/11	Football League Division 1	Manchester United 0 Manchester City 0	Old Trafford	50000
24	1912/13	07/09/12	Football League Division 1	Manchester United 0 Manchester City 1	Old Trafford	40000
25	1912/13	28/12/12	Football League Division 1	Manchester City 0 Manchester United 2	Hyde Road	38000
26	1913/14	06/12/13	Football League Division 1	Manchester City 0 Manchester United 2	Hyde Road	40000
27	1913/14	11/04/14	Football League Division 1	Manchester United 0 Manchester City 1	Old Trafford	36000
28	1914/15	05/09/14	Football League Division 1	Manchester United 0 Manchester City 0	Old Trafford	20000
29	1914/15	02/01/15	Football League Division 1	Manchester City 1 Manchester United 1	Hyde Road	30000
30	1919/20	11/10/19	Football League Division 1	Manchester City 3 Manchester United 3	Hyde Road	30000
31	1919/20	18/10/19	Football League Division 1	Manchester United 1 Manchester City 0	Old Trafford	40000
32	1920/21	20/11/20	Football League Division 1	Manchester United 1 Manchester City 1	Old Trafford	63000
33	1920/21	27/11/20	Football League Division 1	Manchester City 3 Manchester United 0	Hyde Road	35000
34	1921/22	22/10/21	Football League Division 1	Manchester City 4 Manchester United 1	Hyde Road	24000
35	1921/22	29/10/21	Football League Division 1	Manchester United 3 Manchester City 1	Old Trafford	56000
36	1925/26	12/09/25	Football League Division 1	Manchester City 1 Manchester United 1	Maine Road	62994
37	1925/26	23/01/26	Football League Division 1	Manchester United 1 Manchester City 6	Old Trafford	48657
38	1925/26	27/03/26	FA Cup Semi-Final	Manchester United 0 Manchester City 3	Bramall Lane	46450
39	1928/29	01/09/28	Football League Division 1	Manchester City 2 Manchester United 2	Maine Road	61007
40	1928/29	05/01/29	Football League Division 1	Manchester United 1 Manchester City 2	Old Trafford	42555
41	1929/30	05/10/29	Football League Division 1	Manchester United 1 Manchester City 3	Old Trafford	57201
42	1929/30	08/02/30	Football League Division 1	Manchester City 0 Manchester United 1	Maine Road	64472

UNITED v MANCHESTER CITY (continued)

#	SEASON	DATE	COMPETITION / ROUND	MATCH RESULT	VENUE	ATT
43	1930/31	04/10/30	Football League Division 1	Manchester City 4 Manchester United 1	Maine Road	41757
44	1930/31	07/02/31	Football League Division 1	Manchester United 1 Manchester City 3	Old Trafford	39876
45	1936/37	12/09/36	Football League Division 1	Manchester United 3 Manchester City 2	Old Trafford	68796
46	1936/37	09/01/37	Football League Division 1	Manchester City 1 Manchester United 0	Maine Road	64862
47	1947/48	20/09/47	Football League Division 1	Manchester City 0 Manchester United 0	Maine Road	71364
48	1947/48	07/04/48	Football League Division 1	Manchester United 1 Manchester City 1	Maine Road	71690
49	1948/49	11/09/48	Football League Division 1	Manchester City 0 Manchester United 0	Maine Road	64502
50	1948/49	22/01/49	Football League Division 1	Manchester United 0 Manchester City 0	Maine Road	66485
51	1949/50	03/09/49	Football League Division 1	Manchester United 2 Manchester City 1	Old Trafford	47760
52	1949/50	31/12/49	Football League Division 1	Manchester City 1 Manchester United 2	Maine Road	63704
53	1951/52	15/09/51	Football League Division 1	Manchester City 1 Manchester United 2	Maine Road	52571
54	1951/52	19/01/52	Football League Division 1	Manchester United 1 Manchester City 1	Old Trafford	54245
55	1952/53	30/08/52	Football League Division 1	Manchester City 2 Manchester United 1	Maine Road	56140
56	1952/53	03/01/53	Football League Division 1	Manchester United 1 Manchester City 1	Old Trafford	47883
57	1953/54	05/09/53	Football League Division 1	Manchester City 2 Manchester United 0	Maine Road	53097
58	1953/54	16/01/54	Football League Division 1	Manchester United 1 Manchester City 1	Old Trafford	46379
59	1954/55	25/09/54	Football League Division 1	Manchester City 3 Manchester United 2	Maine Road	54105
60	1954/55	12/02/55	Football League Division 1	Manchester United 0 Manchester City 5	Old Trafford	47914
61	1954/55	19/02/55	FA Cup 4th Round	Manchester City 2 Manchester United 0	Maine Road	75000
62	1955/56	03/09/55	Football League Division 1	Manchester City 1 Manchester United 0	Maine Road	59162
63	1955/56	31/12/55	Football League Division 1	Manchester United 2 Manchester City 1	Old Trafford	60956
64	1956/57	22/09/56	Football League Division 1	Manchester United 2 Manchester City 0	Old Trafford	53525
65	1956/57	24/10/56	FA Charity Shield	Manchester City 0 Manchester United 1	Maine Road	30495
66	1956/57	02/02/57	Football League Division 1	Manchester City 2 Manchester United 4	Maine Road	63872
67	1957/58	31/08/57	Football League Division 1	Manchester United 4 Manchester City 1	Old Trafford	63347
68	1957/58	28/12/57	Football League Division 1	Manchester City 2 Manchester United 2	Maine Road	70483
69	1958/59	27/09/58	Football League Division 1	Manchester City 1 Manchester United 1	Maine Road	62912
70	1958/59	16/02/59	Football League Division 1	Manchester United 4 Manchester City 1	Old Trafford	59846
71	1959/60	19/09/59	Football League Division 1	Manchester City 3 Manchester United 0	Maine Road	58300
72	1959/60	06/02/60	Football League Division 1	Manchester United 0 Manchester City 0	Old Trafford	59450
73	1960/61	31/12/60	Football League Division 1	Manchester United 5 Manchester City 1	Old Trafford	61213
74	1960/61	04/03/61	Football League Division 1	Manchester City 1 Manchester United 3	Maine Road	50479
75	1961/62	23/09/61	Football League Division 1	Manchester United 3 Manchester City 2	Old Trafford	56345
76	1961/62	10/02/62	Football League Division 1	Manchester City 0 Manchester United 2	Maine Road	49959
77	1962/63	15/09/62	Football League Division 1	Manchester United 2 Manchester City 3	Old Trafford	49193
78	1962/63	15/05/63	Football League Division 1	Manchester City 1 Manchester United 1	Maine Road	52424
79	1966/67	17/09/66	Football League Division 1	Manchester United 1 Manchester City 0	Old Trafford	62085
80	1966/67	21/01/67	Football League Division 1	Manchester City 1 Manchester United 1	Maine Road	62983
81	1967/68	30/09/67	Football League Division 1	Manchester City 1 Manchester United 2	Maine Road	62942
82	1967/68	27/03/68	Football League Division 1	Manchester United 1 Manchester City 3	Old Trafford	63004
83	1968/69	17/08/68	Football League Division 1	Manchester City 0 Manchester United 0	Maine Road	63052
84	1968/69	08/03/69	Football League Division 1	Manchester United 0 Manchester City 1	Old Trafford	63264
85	1969/70	15/11/69	Football League Division 1	Manchester City 4 Manchester United 0	Maine Road	63013
86	1969/70	03/12/69	League Cup Semi-Final 1st Leg	Manchester City 2 Manchester United 1	Maine Road	55799
87	1969/70	17/12/69	League Cup Semi-Final 2nd Leg	Manchester United 2 Manchester City 2	Old Trafford	63418
88	1969/70	24/01/70	FA Cup 4th Round	Manchester United 3 Manchester City 0	Old Trafford	63417
89	1969/70	28/03/70	Football League Division 1	Manchester United 1 Manchester City 2	Old Trafford	59777
90	1970/71	12/12/70	Football League Division 1	Manchester United 1 Manchester City 4	Old Trafford	52636
91	1970/71	05/05/71	Football League Division 1	Manchester City 3 Manchester United 4	Maine Road	43626
92	1971/72	06/11/71	Football League Division 1	Manchester City 3 Manchester United 3	Maine Road	63326
93	1971/72	12/04/72	Football League Division 1	Manchester United 1 Manchester City 3	Old Trafford	56362
94	1972/73	18/11/72	Football League Division 1	Manchester City 3 Manchester United 0	Maine Road	52050
95	1972/73	21/04/73	Football League Division 1	Manchester United 0 Manchester City 0	Old Trafford	61676
96	1973/74	13/03/74	Football League Division 1	Manchester City 0 Manchester United 0	Maine Road	51331
97	1973/74	27/04/74	Football League Division 1	Manchester United 0 Manchester City 1	Old Trafford	56996
98	1974/75	09/10/74	League Cup 3rd Round	Manchester United 1 Manchester City 0	Old Trafford	55169
99	1975/76	27/09/75	Football League Division 1	Manchester City 2 Manchester United 2	Maine Road	46931
100	1975/76	12/11/75	League Cup 4th Round	Manchester City 4 Manchester United 0	Maine Road	50182
101	1975/76	04/05/76	Football League Division 1	Manchester United 2 Manchester City 0	Old Trafford	59517
102	1976/77	25/09/76	Football League Division 1	Manchester City 1 Manchester United 3	Maine Road	48861
103	1976/77	05/03/77	Football League Division 1	Manchester United 3 Manchester City 1	Old Trafford	58595
104	1977/78	10/09/77	Football League Division 1	Manchester City 3 Manchester United 1	Maine Road	50856
105	1977/78	15/03/78	Football League Division 1	Manchester United 2 Manchester City 2	Old Trafford	58398

UNITED v MANCHESTER CITY (continued)

#	SEASON	DATE	COMPETITION / ROUND	MATCH RESULT	VENUE	ATT
106	1978/79	30/09/78	Football League Division 1	Manchester United 1 Manchester City 0	Old Trafford	55301
107	1978/79	10/02/79	Football League Division 1	Manchester City 0 Manchester United 3	Maine Road	46151
108	1979/80	10/11/79	Football League Division 1	Manchester City 2 Manchester United 0	Maine Road	50067
109	1979/80	22/03/80	Football League Division 1	Manchester United 1 Manchester City 0	Old Trafford	56387
110	1980/81	27/09/80	Football League Division 1	Manchester United 2 Manchester City 2	Old Trafford	55918
111	1980/81	21/02/81	Football League Division 1	Manchester City 1 Manchester United 0	Maine Road	50114
112	1981/82	10/10/81	Football League Division 1	Manchester City 0 Manchester United 0	Maine Road	52037
113	1981/82	27/02/82	Football League Division 1	Manchester United 1 Manchester City 1	Old Trafford	57830
114	1982/83	23/10/82	Football League Division 1	Manchester United 2 Manchester City 2	Old Trafford	57334
115	1982/83	05/03/83	Football League Division 1	Manchester City 1 Manchester United 2	Maine Road	45400
116	1985/86	14/09/85	Football League Division 1	Manchester City 0 Manchester United 3	Maine Road	48773
117	1985/86	22/03/86	Football League Division 1	Manchester United 2 Manchester City 2	Old Trafford	51274
118	1986/87	25/10/86	Football League Division 1	Manchester City 1 Manchester United 1	Maine Road	32440
119	1986/87	10/01/87	FA Cup 3rd Round	Manchester United 1 Manchester City 0	Old Trafford	54294
120	1986/87	07/03/87	Football League Division 1	Manchester United 2 Manchester City 0	Old Trafford	48619
121	1989/90	23/09/89	Football League Division 1	Manchester City 5 Manchester United 1	Maine Road	43246
122	1989/90	03/02/90	Football League Division 1	Manchester United 1 Manchester City 1	Old Trafford	40274
123	1990/91	27/10/90	Football League Division 1	Manchester City 3 Manchester United 3	Maine Road	36427
124	1990/91	04/05/91	Football League Division 1	Manchester United 1 Manchester City 0	Old Trafford	45286
125	1991/92	16/11/91	Football League Division 1	Manchester City 0 Manchester United 0	Maine Road	38180
126	1991/92	07/04/92	Football League Division 1	Manchester United 1 Manchester City 1	Old Trafford	46781
127	1992/93	06/12/92	FA Premiership	Manchester United 2 Manchester City 1	Old Trafford	35408
128	1992/93	20/03/93	FA Premiership	Manchester City 1 Manchester United 1	Maine Road	37136
129	1993/94	07/11/93	FA Premiership	Manchester City 2 Manchester United 3	Maine Road	35155
130	1993/94	23/04/94	FA Premiership	Manchester United 2 Manchester City 0	Old Trafford	44333
131	1994/95	10/11/94	FA Premiership	Manchester United 5 Manchester City 0	Old Trafford	43738
132	1994/95	11/02/95	FA Premiership	Manchester City 0 Manchester United 3	Maine Road	26368
133	1995/96	14/10/95	FA Premiership	Manchester United 1 Manchester City 0	Old Trafford	35707
134	1995/96	18/02/96	FA Cup 5th Round	Manchester United 2 Manchester City 1	Old Trafford	42692
135	1995/96	06/04/96	FA Premiership	Manchester City 2 Manchester United 3	Maine Road	29668
136	2000/01	18/11/00	FA Premiership	Manchester City 0 Manchester United 1	Maine Road	34429
137	2000/01	21/04/01	FA Premiership	Manchester United 1 Manchester City 1	Old Trafford	67535
138	2002/03	09/11/02	FA Premiership	Manchester City 3 Manchester United 1	Maine Road	34649
139	2002/03	09/02/03	FA Premiership	Manchester United 1 Manchester City 1	Old Trafford	67646
140	2003/04	13/12/03	FA Premiership	Manchester United 3 Manchester City 1	Old Trafford	67643
141	2003/04	14/02/04	FA Cup 5th Round	Manchester United 4 Manchester City 2	Old Trafford	67228
142	2003/04	14/03/04	FA Premiership	Manchester City 4 Manchester United 1	Eastlands Stadium	47284
143	2004/05	07/11/04	FA Premiership	Manchester United 0 Manchester City 0	Old Trafford	67863
144	2004/05	13/02/05	FA Premiership	Manchester City 0 Manchester United 2	Eastlands Stadium	47111
145	2005/06	10/09/05	FA Premiership	Manchester United 1 Manchester City 1	Old Trafford	67839
146	2005/06	14/01/06	FA Premiership	Manchester City 3 Manchester United 1	Eastlands Stadium	47192
147	2006/07	09/12/06	FA Premiership	Manchester United 3 Manchester City 1	Old Trafford	75858
148	2006/07	05/05/07	FA Premiership	Manchester City 0 Manchester United 1	Eastlands Stadium	47244
149	2007/08	19/08/07	FA Premiership	Manchester City 1 Manchester United 0	Eastlands Stadium	44955
150	2007/08	10/02/08	FA Premiership	Manchester United 1 Manchester City 2	Old Trafford	75970

UNITED v MIDDLESBROUGH

ALL COMPETITIVE MATCHES						
VENUE	P	W	D	L	F	A
HOME	63	38	12	13	122	69
AWAY	57	21	16	20	86	96
TOTAL	120	59	28	33	208	165

ALL LEAGUE MATCHES						
VENUE	P	W	D	L	F	A
HOME	50	29	10	11	99	61
AWAY	50	20	12	18	79	89
TOTAL	100	49	22	29	178	150

ALL CUP MATCHES						
VENUE	P	W	D	L	F	A
HOME	13	9	2	2	23	8
AWAY	7	1	4	2	7	7
TOTAL	20	10	6	4	30	15

PREMIERSHIP						
VENUE	P	W	D	L	F	A
HOME	13	6	4	3	22	14
AWAY	13	8	3	2	23	16
TOTAL	26	14	7	5	45	30

LEAGUE DIVISION ONE						
VENUE	P	W	D	L	F	A
HOME	33	20	6	7	68	44
AWAY	33	11	8	14	53	64
TOTAL	66	31	14	21	121	108

LEAGUE DIVISION TWO						
VENUE	P	W	D	L	F	A
HOME	4	3	0	1	9	3
AWAY	4	1	1	2	3	9
TOTAL	8	4	1	3	12	12

FA CUP						
VENUE	P	W	D	L	F	A
HOME	9	6	2	1	17	6
AWAY	5	1	2	2	7	7
TOTAL	14	7	4	3	24	13

LEAGUE CUP						
VENUE	P	W	D	L	F	A
HOME	4	3	0	1	6	2
AWAY	2	0	2	0	0	0
TOTAL	6	3	2	1	6	2

#	SEASON	DATE	COMPETITION / ROUND	MATCH RESULT	VENUE	ATT
1	1893/94	27/01/94	FA Cup 1st Round	Newton Heath 4 Middlesbrough 0	Bank Street	5000
2	1899/00	16/12/99	Football League Division 2	Newton Heath 2 Middlesbrough 1	Bank Street	4000
3	1899/00	21/04/00	Football League Division 2	Middlesbrough 2 Newton Heath 0	Linthorpe Road	8000
4	1900/01	08/09/00	Football League Division 2	Newton Heath 4 Middlesbrough 0	Bank Street	5500
5	1900/01	01/01/01	Football League Division 2	Middlesbrough 1 Newton Heath 2	Linthorpe Road	12000
6	1901/02	14/09/01	Football League Division 2	Middlesbrough 5 Newton Heath 0	Linthorpe Road	12000
7	1901/02	07/04/02	Football League Division 2	Newton Heath 1 Middlesbrough 2	Bank Street	2000
8	1906/07	08/12/06	Football League Division 1	Manchester United 3 Middlesbrough 1	Bank Street	12000
9	1906/07	13/04/07	Football League Division 1	Middlesbrough 2 Manchester United 0	Ayresome Park	15000
10	1907/08	09/09/07	Football League Division 1	Manchester United 2 Middlesbrough 1	Bank Street	20000
11	1907/08	14/09/07	Football League Division 1	Middlesbrough 2 Manchester United 1	Ayresome Park	18000
12	1908/09	12/09/08	Football League Division 1	Manchester United 6 Middlesbrough 3	Bank Street	25000
13	1908/09	09/01/09	Football League Division 1	Middlesbrough 5 Manchester United 0	Ayresome Park	15000
14	1909/10	18/12/09	Football League Division 1	Middlesbrough 1 Manchester United 2	Ayresome Park	10000
15	1909/10	30/04/10	Football League Division 1	Manchester United 4 Middlesbrough 1	Old Trafford	10000
16	1910/11	29/10/10	Football League Division 1	Manchester United 1 Middlesbrough 2	Old Trafford	35000
17	1910/11	04/03/11	Football League Division 1	Middlesbrough 2 Manchester United 2	Ayresome Park	8000
18	1911/12	21/10/11	Football League Division 1	Manchester United 3 Middlesbrough 4	Old Trafford	20000
19	1911/12	17/04/12	Football League Division 1	Middlesbrough 3 Manchester United 0	Ayresome Park	5000
20	1912/13	26/10/12	Football League Division 1	Middlesbrough 3 Manchester United 2	Ayresome Park	10000
21	1912/13	01/03/13	Football League Division 1	Manchester United 2 Middlesbrough 3	Old Trafford	15000
22	1913/14	15/11/13	Football League Division 1	Manchester United 0 Middlesbrough 1	Old Trafford	15000
23	1913/14	21/02/14	Football League Division 1	Middlesbrough 3 Manchester United 1	Ayresome Park	12000
24	1914/15	05/12/14	Football League Division 1	Middlesbrough 1 Manchester United 1	Ayresome Park	7000
25	1914/15	10/04/15	Football League Division 1	Manchester United 2 Middlesbrough 2	Old Trafford	15000
26	1919/20	27/09/19	Football League Division 1	Middlesbrough 1 Manchester United 1	Ayresome Park	20000
27	1919/20	04/10/19	Football League Division 1	Manchester United 1 Middlesbrough 1	Old Trafford	28000
28	1920/21	09/04/21	Football League Division 1	Middlesbrough 2 Manchester United 4	Ayresome Park	15000
29	1920/21	16/04/21	Football League Division 1	Manchester United 0 Middlesbrough 1	Old Trafford	25000
30	1921/22	05/11/21	Football League Division 1	Manchester United 3 Middlesbrough 5	Old Trafford	30000
31	1921/22	12/11/21	Football League Division 1	Middlesbrough 2 Manchester United 0	Ayresome Park	18000
32	1924/25	25/12/24	Football League Division 2	Middlesbrough 1 Manchester United 1	Ayresome Park	18500
33	1924/25	26/12/24	Football League Division 2	Manchester United 2 Middlesbrough 0	Old Trafford	44000
34	1927/28	27/08/27	Football League Division 1	Manchester United 3 Middlesbrough 0	Old Trafford	44957
35	1927/28	31/12/27	Football League Division 1	Middlesbrough 1 Manchester United 2	Ayresome Park	19652
36	1929/30	14/09/29	Football League Division 1	Middlesbrough 2 Manchester United 3	Ayresome Park	26428
37	1929/30	18/01/30	Football League Division 1	Manchester United 0 Middlesbrough 3	Old Trafford	21028
38	1930/31	03/09/30	Football League Division 1	Middlesbrough 3 Manchester United 1	Ayresome Park	15712
39	1930/31	02/05/31	Football League Division 1	Manchester United 4 Middlesbrough 4	Old Trafford	3969
40	1932/33	14/01/33	FA Cup 3rd Round	Manchester United 1 Middlesbrough 4	Old Trafford	36991
41	1936/37	12/12/36	Football League Division 1	Middlesbrough 3 Manchester United 2	Ayresome Park	11970
42	1936/37	17/04/37	Football League Division 1	Manchester United 2 Middlesbrough 1	Old Trafford	17656
43	1938/39	27/08/38	Football League Division 1	Middlesbrough 3 Manchester United 1	Ayresome Park	25539
44	1938/39	24/12/38	Football League Division 1	Manchester United 1 Middlesbrough 1	Old Trafford	33235

UNITED v MIDDLESBROUGH (continued)

#	SEASON	DATE	COMPETITION / ROUND	MATCH RESULT	VENUE	ATT
45	1946/47	14/09/46	Football League Division 1	Manchester United 1 Middlesbrough 0	Maine Road	65112
46	1946/47	18/01/47	Football League Division 1	Middlesbrough 2 Manchester United 4	Ayresome Park	37435
47	1947/48	23/08/47	Football League Division 1	Middlesbrough 2 Manchester United 2	Ayresome Park	39554
48	1947/48	20/12/47	Football League Division 1	Manchester United 2 Middlesbrough 1	Maine Road	46666
49	1948/49	27/11/48	Football League Division 1	Middlesbrough 1 Manchester United 4	Ayresome Park	31331
50	1948/49	02/05/49	Football League Division 1	Manchester United 1 Middlesbrough 0	Maine Road	20158
51	1949/50	19/11/49	Football League Division 1	Manchester United 2 Middlesbrough 0	Old Trafford	42626
52	1949/50	11/03/50	Football League Division 1	Middlesbrough 2 Manchester United 3	Ayresome Park	46702
53	1950/51	23/09/50	Football League Division 1	Middlesbrough 1 Manchester United 2	Ayresome Park	48051
54	1950/51	03/02/51	Football League Division 1	Manchester United 1 Middlesbrough 0	Old Trafford	44633
55	1951/52	22/08/51	Football League Division 1	Manchester United 4 Middlesbrough 2	Old Trafford	37339
56	1951/52	29/08/51	Football League Division 1	Middlesbrough 1 Manchester United 4	Ayresome Park	44212
57	1952/53	06/12/52	Football League Division 1	Manchester United 3 Middlesbrough 2	Old Trafford	27617
58	1952/53	25/04/53	Football League Division 1	Middlesbrough 5 Manchester United 0	Ayresome Park	34344
59	1953/54	09/09/53	Football League Division 1	Manchester United 2 Middlesbrough 2	Old Trafford	18161
60	1953/54	16/09/53	Football League Division 1	Middlesbrough 1 Manchester United 4	Ayresome Park	23607
61	1960/61	07/01/61	FA Cup 3rd Round	Manchester United 3 Middlesbrough 0	Old Trafford	49184
62	1969/70	03/09/69	League Cup 2nd Round	Manchester United 1 Middlesbrough 0	Old Trafford	38938
63	1969/70	21/02/70	FA Cup 6th Round	Middlesbrough 1 Manchester United 1	Ayresome Park	40000
64	1969/70	25/02/70	FA Cup 6th Round Replay	Manchester United 2 Middlesbrough 1	Old Trafford	63418
65	1970/71	02/01/71	FA Cup 3rd Round	Manchester United 0 Middlesbrough 0	Old Trafford	47824
66	1970/71	05/01/71	FA Cup 3rd Round Replay	Middlesbrough 2 Manchester United 1	Ayresome Park	41000
67	1971/72	26/02/72	FA Cup 5th Round	Manchester United 0 Middlesbrough 0	Old Trafford	53850
68	1971/72	29/02/72	FA Cup 5th Round Replay	Middlesbrough 0 Manchester United 3	Ayresome Park	39683
69	1973/74	08/10/73	League Cup 2nd Round	Manchester United 0 Middlesbrough 1	Old Trafford	23906
70	1974/75	04/12/74	League Cup 5th Round	Middlesbrough 0 Manchester United 0	Ayresome Park	36005
71	1974/75	18/12/74	League Cup 5th Round Replay	Manchester United 3 Middlesbrough 0	Old Trafford	49501
72	1975/76	06/12/75	Football League Division 1	Middlesbrough 0 Manchester United 0	Ayresome Park	32454
73	1975/76	27/03/76	Football League Division 1	Manchester United 3 Middlesbrough 0	Old Trafford	58527
74	1976/77	18/09/76	Football League Division 1	Manchester United 2 Middlesbrough 0	Old Trafford	56712
75	1976/77	26/04/77	Football League Division 1	Middlesbrough 3 Manchester United 0	Ayresome Park	21744
76	1977/78	08/10/77	Football League Division 1	Middlesbrough 2 Manchester United 1	Ayresome Park	26882
77	1977/78	04/03/78	Football League Division 1	Manchester United 0 Middlesbrough 0	Old Trafford	46322
78	1978/79	07/10/78	Football League Division 1	Manchester United 3 Middlesbrough 2	Old Trafford	45402
79	1978/79	27/03/79	Football League Division 1	Middlesbrough 2 Manchester United 2	Ayresome Park	20138
80	1979/80	01/09/79	Football League Division 1	Manchester United 2 Middlesbrough 1	Old Trafford	51015
81	1979/80	12/01/80	Football League Division 1	Middlesbrough 1 Manchester United 1	Ayresome Park	30587
82	1980/81	16/08/80	Football League Division 1	Manchester United 3 Middlesbrough 0	Old Trafford	54394
83	1980/81	15/11/80	Football League Division 1	Middlesbrough 1 Manchester United 1	Ayresome Park	20606
84	1981/82	22/09/81	Football League Division 1	Middlesbrough 0 Manchester United 2	Ayresome Park	19895
85	1981/82	21/10/81	Football League Division 1	Manchester United 1 Middlesbrough 0	Old Trafford	38342
86	1988/89	10/09/88	Football League Division 1	Manchester United 1 Middlesbrough 0	Old Trafford	40422
87	1988/89	02/01/89	Football League Division 1	Middlesbrough 1 Manchester United 0	Ayresome Park	24411
88	1991/92	04/03/92	League Cup Semi-Final 1st Leg	Middlesbrough 0 Manchester United 0	Ayresome Park	25572
89	1991/92	11/03/92	League Cup Semi-Final 2nd Leg	Manchester United 2 Middlesbrough 1	Old Trafford	45875
90	1992/93	03/10/92	FA Premiership	Middlesbrough 1 Manchester United 1	Ayresome Park	24172
91	1992/93	27/02/93	FA Premiership	Manchester United 3 Middlesbrough 0	Old Trafford	36251
92	1995/96	28/10/95	FA Premiership	Manchester United 2 Middlesbrough 0	Old Trafford	36580
93	1995/96	05/05/96	FA Premiership	Middlesbrough 0 Manchester United 3	Riverside Stadium	29921
94	1996/97	23/11/96	FA Premiership	Middlesbrough 2 Manchester United 2	Riverside Stadium	30063
95	1996/97	05/05/97	FA Premiership	Manchester United 3 Middlesbrough 3	Old Trafford	54489
96	1998/99	19/12/98	FA Premiership	Manchester United 2 Middlesbrough 3	Old Trafford	55152
97	1998/99	03/01/99	FA Cup 3rd Round	Manchester United 3 Middlesbrough 1	Old Trafford	52232
98	1998/99	09/05/99	FA Premiership	Middlesbrough 0 Manchester United 1	Riverside Stadium	34665
99	1999/00	29/01/00	FA Premiership	Manchester United 1 Middlesbrough 0	Old Trafford	61267
100	1999/00	10/04/00	FA Premiership	Middlesbrough 3 Manchester United 4	Riverside Stadium	34775
101	2000/01	11/11/00	FA Premiership	Manchester United 2 Middlesbrough 1	Old Trafford	67576
102	2000/01	28/04/01	FA Premiership	Middlesbrough 0 Manchester United 2	Riverside Stadium	34417
103	2001/02	15/12/01	FA Premiership	Middlesbrough 0 Manchester United 1	Riverside Stadium	34358
104	2001/02	26/01/02	FA Cup 4th Round	Middlesbrough 2 Manchester United 0	Riverside Stadium	17624
105	2001/02	23/03/02	FA Premiership	Manchester United 0 Middlesbrough 1	Old Trafford	67683

UNITED v MIDDLESBROUGH (continued)

#	SEASON	DATE	COMPETITION / ROUND	MATCH RESULT	VENUE	ATT
106	2002/03	03/09/02	FA Premiership	Manchester United 1 Middlesbrough 0	Old Trafford	67464
107	2002/03	26/12/02	FA Premiership	Middlesbrough 3 Manchester United 1	Riverside Stadium	34673
108	2003/04	28/12/03	FA Premiership	Middlesbrough 0 Manchester United 1	Riverside Stadium	34738
109	2003/04	11/02/04	FA Premiership	Manchester United 2 Middlesbrough 3	Old Trafford	67346
110	2004/05	03/10/04	FA Premiership	Manchester United 1 Middlesbrough 1	Old Trafford	67988
111	2004/05	01/01/05	FA Premiership	Middlesbrough 0 Manchester United 2	Riverside Stadium	34199
112	2004/05	29/01/05	FA Cup 4th Round	Manchester United 3 Middlesbrough 0	Old Trafford	67251
113	2005/06	29/10/05	FA Premiership	Middlesbrough 4 Manchester United 1	Riverside Stadium	30579
114	2005/06	01/05/06	FA Premiership	Manchester United 0 Middlesbrough 0	Old Trafford	69531
115	2006/07	02/12/06	FA Premiership	Middlesbrough 1 Manchester United 2	Riverside Stadium	31238
116	2006/07	10/03/07	FA Cup 6th Round	Middlesbrough 2 Manchester United 2	Riverside Stadium	33308
117	2006/07	19/03/07	FA Cup 6th Round Replay	Manchester United 1 Middlesbrough 0	Old Trafford	71325
118	2006/07	21/04/07	FA Premiership	Manchester United 1 Middlesbrough 1	Old Trafford	75967
119	2007/08	27/10/07	FA Premiership	Manchester United 4 Middlesbrough 1	Old Trafford	75720
120	2007/08	06/04/08	FA Premiership	Middlesbrough 2 Manchester United 2	Riverside Stadium	33952

UNITED v MILLWALL

ALL COMPETITIVE MATCHES							ALL LEAGUE MATCHES							FA CUP					
VENUE	P	W	D	L	F	A	VENUE	P	W	D	L	F	A	VENUE	P	W	D	L	F	A
HOME	6	5	1	0	22	3	HOME	6	5	1	0	22	3	HOME	0	0	0	0	0	0
AWAY	7	4	2	1	7	4	AWAY	6	3	2	1	6	4	AWAY	1	1	0	0	1	0
NEUTRAL	1	1	0	0	3	0								NEUTRAL	1	1	0	0	3	0
TOTAL	14	10	3	1	32	7	TOTAL	12	8	3	1	28	7	TOTAL	2	2	0	0	4	0

LEAGUE DIVISION ONE							LEAGUE DIVISION TWO						
VENUE	P	W	D	L	F	A	VENUE	P	W	D	L	F	A
HOME	2	2	0	0	8	1	HOME	4	3	1	0	14	2
AWAY	2	1	1	0	2	1	AWAY	4	2	1	1	4	3
TOTAL	4	3	1	0	10	2	TOTAL	8	5	2	1	18	5

#	SEASON	DATE	COMPETITION / ROUND	MATCH RESULT	VENUE	ATT
1	1931/32	05/12/31	Football League Division 2	Manchester United 2 Millwall 0	Old Trafford	6396
2	1931/32	16/04/32	Football League Division 2	Millwall 1 Manchester United 1	The Den	9087
3	1932/33	22/10/32	Football League Division 2	Manchester United 7 Millwall 1	Old Trafford	15860
4	1932/33	04/03/33	Football League Division 2	Millwall 2 Manchester United 0	The Den	22587
5	1933/34	23/12/33	Football League Division 2	Manchester United 1 Millwall 1	Old Trafford	12043
6	1933/34	05/05/34	Football League Division 2	Millwall 0 Manchester United 2	The Den	24003
7	1952/53	10/01/53	FA Cup 3rd Round	Millwall 0 Manchester United 1	The Den	35652
8	1974/75	24/08/74	Football League Division 2	Manchester United 4 Millwall 0	Old Trafford	44756
9	1974/75	16/09/74	Football League Division 2	Millwall 0 Manchester United 1	The Den	16988
10	1988/89	14/01/89	Football League Division 1	Manchester United 3 Millwall 0	Old Trafford	40931
11	1988/89	08/04/89	Football League Division 1	Millwall 0 Manchester United 0	The Den	17523
12	1989/90	16/09/89	Football League Division 1	Manchester United 5 Millwall 1	Old Trafford	42746
13	1989/90	10/02/90	Football League Division 1	Millwall 1 Manchester United 2	The Den	15491
14	2003/04	22/05/04	FA Cup Final	Manchester United 3 Millwall 0	Millennium Stadium	71350

UNITED v MONACO

CHAMPIONS LEAGUE					
VENUE	P	W	D	L	F	A
HOME	1	0	1	0	1	1
AWAY	1	0	1	0	0	0
TOTAL	2	0	2	0	1	1

#	SEASON	DATE	COMPETITION / ROUND	MATCH RESULT	VENUE	ATT
1	1997/98	04/03/98	Champions League Quarter-Final 1st Leg	Monaco 0 Manchester United 0	Stade Louis II	15000
2	1997/98	18/03/98	Champions League Quarter-Final 2nd Leg	Manchester United 1 Monaco 1 (United lost the tie on away goals rule)	Old Trafford	53683

UNITED v MONTPELLIER HERAULT

EUROPEAN CUP-WINNERS' CUP

VENUE	P	W	D	L	F	A
HOME	1	0	1	0	1	1
AWAY	1	1	0	0	2	0
TOTAL	2	1	1	0	3	1

#	SEASON	DATE	COMPETITION / ROUND	MATCH RESULT	VENUE	ATT
1	1990/91	06/03/91	European CWC 3rd Round 1st Leg	Manchester United 1 Montpellier Herault 1	Old Trafford	41942
2	1990/91	19/03/91	European CWC 3rd Round 2nd Leg	Montpellier Herault 0 Manchester United 2	Stade de la Masson	18000

UNITED v NANTES ATLANTIQUE

CHAMPIONS LEAGUE

VENUE	P	W	D	L	F	A
HOME	1	1	0	0	5	1
AWAY	1	0	1	0	1	1
TOTAL	2	1	1	0	6	2

#	SEASON	DATE	COMPETITION / ROUND	MATCH RESULT	VENUE	ATT
1	2001/02	20/02/02	Champions League Phase 2 Match 3	Nantes Atlantique 1 Manchester United 1	Stade Beaujoire	38285
2	2001/02	26/02/02	Champions League Phase 2 Match 4	Manchester United 5 Nantes Atlantique 1	Old Trafford	66492

UNITED v NELSON

ALL COMPETITIVE MATCHES							LEAGUE DIVISION TWO							FA CUP						
VENUE	P	W	D	L	F	A	VENUE	P	W	D	L	F	A	VENUE	P	W	D	L	F	A
HOME	2	1	0	1	3	1	HOME	1	0	0	1	0	1	HOME	1	1	0	0	3	0
AWAY	1	1	0	0	2	0	AWAY	1	1	0	0	2	0	AWAY	0	0	0	0	0	0
TOTAL	3	2	0	1	5	1	TOTAL	2	1	0	1	2	1	TOTAL	1	1	0	0	3	0

#	SEASON	DATE	COMPETITION / ROUND	MATCH RESULT	VENUE	ATT
1	1896/97	02/01/97	FA Cup 4th Qualifying Round	Newton Heath 3 Nelson 0	Bank Street	5000
2	1923/24	01/03/24	Football League Division 2	Nelson 0 Manchester United 2	Seed Hill	2750
3	1923/24	08/03/24	Football League Division 2	Manchester United 0 Nelson 1	Old Trafford	8500

UNITED v NEW BRIGHTON TOWER

LEAGUE DIVISION TWO

VENUE	P	W	D	L	F	A
HOME	3	2	0	1	4	3
AWAY	3	2	0	1	7	3
TOTAL	6	4	0	2	11	6

#	SEASON	DATE	COMPETITION / ROUND	MATCH RESULT	VENUE	ATT
1	1898/99	19/11/98	Football League Division 2	New Brighton Tower 0 Newton Heath 3	Tower Athletic Ground	5000
2	1898/99	18/03/99	Football League Division 2	Newton Heath 1 New Brighton Tower 2	Bank Street	20000
3	1899/00	21/10/99	Football League Division 2	Newton Heath 2 New Brighton Tower 1	Bank Street	5000
4	1899/00	24/02/00	Football League Division 2	New Brighton Tower 1 Newton Heath 4	Tower Athletic Ground	8000
5	1900/01	06/10/00	Football League Division 2	Newton Heath 1 New Brighton Tower 0	Bank Street	5000
6	1900/01	19/02/01	Football League Division 2	New Brighton Tower 2 Newton Heath 0	Tower Athletic Ground	2000

UNITED v NEWCASTLE UNITED

ALL COMPETITIVE MATCHES							ALL LEAGUE MATCHES							ALL CUP MATCHES					
VENUE	P	W	D	L	F	A	VENUE	P	W	D	L	F	A	VENUE	P	W	D	L	F	A
HOME	72	45	18	9	169	79	HOME	70	43	18	9	158	75	HOME	1	1	0	0	7	2
AWAY	72	26	16	30	111	138	AWAY	70	25	16	29	108	134	AWAY	2	1	0	1	3	4
NEUTRAL	4	4	0	0	11	1								NEUTRAL	3	3	0	0	7	1
TOTAL	148	75	34	39	291	218	TOTAL	140	68	34	38	266	209	TOTAL	6	5	0	1	17	7

PREMIERSHIP							LEAGUE DIVISION ONE							LEAGUE DIVISION TWO					
VENUE	P	W	D	L	F	A	VENUE	P	W	D	L	F	A	VENUE	P	W	D	L	F	A
HOME	15	10	5	0	33	8	HOME	48	28	13	7	108	62	HOME	7	5	0	2	17	5
AWAY	15	8	4	3	30	23	AWAY	48	15	11	22	72	100	AWAY	7	2	1	4	6	11
TOTAL	30	18	9	3	63	31	TOTAL	96	43	24	29	180	162	TOTAL	14	7	1	6	23	16

FA CUP							LEAGUE CUP							CHARITY SHIELD					
VENUE	P	W	D	L	F	A	VENUE	P	W	D	L	F	A	VENUE	P	W	D	L	F	A
HOME	0	0	0	0	0	0	HOME	1	1	0	0	7	2	HOME	1	1	0	0	4	2
AWAY	1	1	0	0	3	2	AWAY	1	0	0	1	0	2	AWAY	0	0	0	0	0	0
NEUTRAL	3	3	0	0	7	1	NEUTRAL	0	0	0	0	0	0	NEUTRAL	1	1	0	0	4	0
TOTAL	4	4	0	0	10	3	TOTAL	2	1	0	1	7	4	TOTAL	2	2	0	0	8	2

#	SEASON	DATE	COMPETITION / ROUND	MATCH RESULT	VENUE	ATT
1	1894/95	06/04/95	Football League Division 2	Newton Heath 5 Newcastle United 1	Bank Street	5000
2	1894/95	13/04/95	Football League Division 2	Newcastle United 3 Newton Heath 0	St James' Park	4000
3	1895/96	19/10/95	Football League Division 2	Newton Heath 2 Newcastle United 1	Bank Street	8000
4	1895/96	26/10/95	Football League Division 2	Newcastle United 1 Newton Heath 1	St James' Park	8000
5	1896/97	26/09/96	Football League Division 2	Newton Heath 4 Newcastle United 0	Bank Street	7000
6	1896/97	01/01/97	Football League Division 2	Newcastle United 2 Newton Heath 0	St James' Park	17000
7	1897/98	09/10/97	Football League Division 2	Newcastle United 2 Newton Heath 0	St James' Park	12000
8	1897/98	13/11/97	Football League Division 2	Newton Heath 0 Newcastle United 1	Bank Street	7000
9	1906/07	22/12/06	Football League Division 1	Manchester United 1 Newcastle United 3	Bank Street	18000
10	1906/07	02/02/07	Football League Division 1	Newcastle United 5 Manchester United 0	St James' Park	30000
11	1907/08	12/10/07	Football League Division 1	Newcastle United 1 Manchester United 6	St James' Park	25000
12	1907/08	08/02/08	Football League Division 1	Manchester United 1 Newcastle United 1	Bank Street	50000
13	1908/09	25/12/08	Football League Division 1	Newcastle United 2 Manchester United 1	St James' Park	35000
14	1908/09	26/12/08	Football League Division 1	Manchester United 1 Newcastle United 0	Bank Street	40000
15	1908/09	27/03/09	FA Cup Semi-Final	Manchester United 1 Newcastle United 0	Bramall Lane	40118
16	1909/10	02/10/09	Football League Division 1	Manchester United 1 Newcastle United 1	Bank Street	30000
17	1909/10	12/02/10	Football League Division 1	Newcastle United 3 Manchester United 4	St James' Park	20000
18	1910/11	15/10/10	Football League Division 1	Manchester United 2 Newcastle United 0	Old Trafford	50000
19	1910/11	18/02/11	Football League Division 1	Newcastle United 0 Manchester United 1	St James' Park	45000
20	1911/12	02/12/11	Football League Division 1	Newcastle United 2 Manchester United 3	St James' Park	40000
21	1911/12	06/04/12	Football League Division 1	Manchester United 0 Newcastle United 2	Old Trafford	14000
22	1912/13	14/12/12	Football League Division 1	Newcastle United 1 Manchester United 3	St James' Park	20000
23	1912/13	19/04/13	Football League Division 1	Manchester United 3 Newcastle United 0	Old Trafford	10000
24	1913/14	25/10/13	Football League Division 1	Newcastle United 0 Manchester United 1	St James' Park	35000
25	1913/14	28/02/14	Football League Division 1	Manchester United 2 Newcastle United 2	Old Trafford	30000
26	1914/15	28/11/14	Football League Division 1	Manchester United 1 Newcastle United 0	Old Trafford	5000
27	1914/15	03/04/15	Football League Division 1	Newcastle United 2 Manchester United 0	St James' Park	12000
28	1919/20	20/12/19	Football League Division 1	Manchester United 2 Newcastle United 1	Old Trafford	20000
29	1919/20	27/12/19	Football League Division 1	Newcastle United 2 Manchester United 1	St James' Park	45000
30	1920/21	18/12/20	Football League Division 1	Manchester United 2 Newcastle United 0	Old Trafford	40000
31	1920/21	01/01/21	Football League Division 1	Newcastle United 6 Manchester United 3	St James' Park	40000
32	1921/22	31/12/21	Football League Division 1	Newcastle United 3 Manchester United 0	St James' Park	20000
33	1921/22	14/01/22	Football League Division 1	Manchester United 0 Newcastle United 1	Old Trafford	20000
34	1925/26	10/10/25	Football League Division 1	Manchester United 2 Newcastle United 1	Old Trafford	39651
35	1925/26	14/04/26	Football League Division 1	Newcastle United 4 Manchester United 1	St James' Park	9829
36	1926/27	11/09/26	Football League Division 1	Newcastle United 4 Manchester United 2	St James' Park	28050
37	1926/27	09/02/27	Football League Division 1	Manchester United 3 Newcastle United 3	Old Trafford	25402
38	1927/28	10/09/27	Football League Division 1	Manchester United 1 Newcastle United 7	Old Trafford	50217
39	1927/28	21/01/28	Football League Division 1	Newcastle United 4 Manchester United 1	St James' Park	25912
40	1928/29	29/09/28	Football League Division 1	Manchester United 5 Newcastle United 0	Old Trafford	25243
41	1928/29	09/02/29	Football League Division 1	Newcastle United 5 Manchester United 0	St James' Park	34134
42	1929/30	31/08/29	Football League Division 1	Newcastle United 4 Manchester United 1	St James' Park	43489
43	1929/30	28/12/29	Football League Division 1	Manchester United 5 Newcastle United 0	Old Trafford	14862

UNITED v NEWCASTLE UNITED (continued)

#	SEASON	DATE	COMPETITION / ROUND	MATCH RESULT	VENUE	ATT
44	1930/31	13/09/30	Football League Division 1	Manchester United 4 Newcastle United 7	Old Trafford	10907
45	1930/31	17/01/31	Football League Division 1	Newcastle United 4 Manchester United 3	St James' Park	24835
46	1934/35	20/10/34	Football League Division 2	Newcastle United 0 Manchester United 1	St James' Park	24752
47	1934/35	02/03/35	Football League Division 2	Manchester United 0 Newcastle United 1	Old Trafford	20728
48	1935/36	14/09/35	Football League Division 2	Newcastle United 0 Manchester United 2	St James' Park	28520
49	1935/36	18/01/36	Football League Division 2	Manchester United 3 Newcastle United 1	Old Trafford	22968
50	1937/38	28/08/37	Football League Division 2	Manchester United 3 Newcastle United 0	Old Trafford	29446
51	1937/38	01/01/38	Football League Division 2	Newcastle United 2 Manchester United 2	St James' Park	40088
52	1948/49	04/12/48	Football League Division 1	Manchester United 1 Newcastle United 1	Maine Road	70787
53	1948/49	30/04/49	Football League Division 1	Newcastle United 0 Manchester United 1	St James' Park	38266
54	1949/50	03/12/49	Football League Division 1	Manchester United 1 Newcastle United 1	Old Trafford	30343
55	1949/50	22/04/50	Football League Division 1	Newcastle United 2 Manchester United 1	St James' Park	52203
56	1950/51	02/12/50	Football League Division 1	Manchester United 1 Newcastle United 2	Old Trafford	34502
57	1950/51	21/04/51	Football League Division 1	Newcastle United 0 Manchester United 2	St James' Park	45209
58	1951/52	25/08/51	Football League Division 1	Manchester United 2 Newcastle United 1	Old Trafford	51850
59	1951/52	22/12/51	Football League Division 1	Newcastle United 2 Manchester United 2	St James' Park	45414
60	1952/53	24/09/52	FA Charity Shield	Manchester United 4 Newcastle United 2	Old Trafford	11381
61	1952/53	22/11/52	Football League Division 1	Manchester United 2 Newcastle United 2	Old Trafford	33528
62	1952/53	11/04/53	Football League Division 1	Newcastle United 1 Manchester United 2	St James' Park	38970
63	1953/54	29/08/53	Football League Division 1	Manchester United 1 Newcastle United 1	Old Trafford	27837
64	1953/54	02/01/54	Football League Division 1	Newcastle United 1 Manchester United 2	St James' Park	55780
65	1954/55	23/10/54	Football League Division 1	Manchester United 2 Newcastle United 2	Old Trafford	29217
66	1954/55	18/04/55	Football League Division 1	Newcastle United 2 Manchester United 0	St James' Park	35540
67	1955/56	30/03/56	Football League Division 1	Manchester United 5 Newcastle United 2	Old Trafford	58994
68	1955/56	02/04/56	Football League Division 1	Newcastle United 0 Manchester United 0	St James' Park	37395
69	1956/57	08/09/56	Football League Division 1	Newcastle United 1 Manchester United 1	St James' Park	50130
70	1956/57	12/01/57	Football League Division 1	Manchester United 6 Newcastle United 1	Old Trafford	44911
71	1957/58	23/11/57	Football League Division 1	Newcastle United 1 Manchester United 2	St James' Park	53890
72	1957/58	23/04/58	Football League Division 1	Manchester United 1 Newcastle United 1	Old Trafford	28393
73	1958/59	13/09/58	Football League Division 1	Newcastle United 1 Manchester United 1	St James' Park	60670
74	1958/59	31/01/59	Football League Division 1	Manchester United 4 Newcastle United 4	Old Trafford	49008
75	1959/60	29/08/59	Football League Division 1	Manchester United 3 Newcastle United 2	Old Trafford	53257
76	1959/60	02/01/60	Football League Division 1	Newcastle United 7 Manchester United 3	St James' Park	57200
77	1960/61	22/10/60	Football League Division 1	Manchester United 3 Newcastle United 2	Old Trafford	37516
78	1960/61	11/03/61	Football League Division 1	Newcastle United 1 Manchester United 1	St James' Park	28870
79	1965/66	08/09/65	Football League Division 1	Newcastle United 1 Manchester United 2	St James' Park	57380
80	1965/66	15/09/65	Football League Division 1	Manchester United 1 Newcastle United 1	Old Trafford	30401
81	1966/67	03/09/66	Football League Division 1	Manchester United 3 Newcastle United 2	Old Trafford	44448
82	1966/67	11/03/67	Football League Division 1	Newcastle United 0 Manchester United 0	St James' Park	37430
83	1967/68	09/12/67	Football League Division 1	Newcastle United 2 Manchester United 2	St James' Park	48639
84	1967/68	04/05/68	Football League Division 1	Manchester United 6 Newcastle United 0	Old Trafford	59976
85	1968/69	21/09/68	Football League Division 1	Manchester United 3 Newcastle United 1	Old Trafford	47262
86	1968/69	12/04/69	Football League Division 1	Newcastle United 2 Manchester United 0	St James' Park	46379
87	1969/70	27/08/69	Football League Division 1	Manchester United 0 Newcastle United 0	Old Trafford	52774
88	1969/70	04/04/70	Football League Division 1	Newcastle United 5 Manchester United 1	St James' Park	43094
89	1970/71	31/10/70	Football League Division 1	Newcastle United 1 Manchester United 0	St James' Park	45140
90	1970/71	27/02/71	Football League Division 1	Manchester United 1 Newcastle United 0	Old Trafford	41902
91	1971/72	23/10/71	Football League Division 1	Newcastle United 0 Manchester United 1	St James' Park	52411
92	1971/72	12/02/72	Football League Division 1	Manchester United 0 Newcastle United 2	Old Trafford	44983
93	1972/73	21/10/72	Football League Division 1	Newcastle United 2 Manchester United 1	St James' Park	38170
94	1972/73	17/03/73	Football League Division 1	Manchester United 2 Newcastle United 1	Old Trafford	48426
95	1973/74	17/11/73	Football League Division 1	Newcastle United 3 Manchester United 2	St James' Park	41768
96	1973/74	13/04/74	Football League Division 1	Manchester United 1 Newcastle United 0	Old Trafford	44751
97	1975/76	29/11/75	Football League Division 1	Manchester United 1 Newcastle United 0	Old Trafford	52624
98	1975/76	20/03/76	Football League Division 1	Newcastle United 3 Manchester United 4	St James' Park	45048
99	1976/77	11/09/76	Football League Division 1	Newcastle United 2 Manchester United 2	St James' Park	39037
100	1976/77	27/10/76	League Cup 4th Round	Manchester United 7 Newcastle United 2	Old Trafford	52002
101	1976/77	19/02/77	Football League Division 1	Manchester United 3 Newcastle United 1	Old Trafford	51828
102	1977/78	15/10/77	Football League Division 1	Manchester United 3 Newcastle United 2	Old Trafford	55056
103	1977/78	11/03/78	Football League Division 1	Newcastle United 2 Manchester United 2	St James' Park	25825
104	1984/85	08/09/84	Football League Division 1	Manchester United 5 Newcastle United 0	Old Trafford	54915
105	1984/85	09/02/85	Football League Division 1	Newcastle United 1 Manchester United 1	St James' Park	32555

UNITED v NEWCASTLE UNITED (continued)

#	SEASON	DATE	COMPETITION / ROUND	MATCH RESULT	VENUE	ATT
106	1985/86	04/09/85	Football League Division 1	Manchester United 3 Newcastle United 0	Old Trafford	51102
107	1985/86	16/04/86	Football League Division 1	Newcastle United 2 Manchester United 4	St James' Park	31840
108	1986/87	01/01/87	Football League Division 1	Manchester United 4 Newcastle United 1	Old Trafford	43334
109	1986/87	18/04/87	Football League Division 1	Newcastle United 2 Manchester United 1	St James' Park	32706
110	1987/88	12/09/87	Football League Division 1	Manchester United 2 Newcastle United 2	Old Trafford	45619
111	1987/88	26/12/87	Football League Division 1	Newcastle United 1 Manchester United 0	St James' Park	26461
112	1988/89	27/11/88	Football League Division 1	Newcastle United 0 Manchester United 0	St James' Park	20350
113	1988/89	13/05/89	Football League Division 1	Manchester United 2 Newcastle United 0	Old Trafford	30379
114	1989/90	18/02/90	FA Cup 5th Round	Newcastle United 2 Manchester United 3	St James' Park	31748
115	1993/94	21/08/93	FA Premiership	Manchester United 1 Newcastle United 1	Old Trafford	41829
116	1993/94	11/12/93	FA Premiership	Newcastle United 1 Manchester United 1	St James' Park	36388
117	1994/95	26/10/94	League Cup 3rd Round	Newcastle United 2 Manchester United 0	St James' Park	34178
118	1994/95	29/10/94	FA Premiership	Manchester United 2 Newcastle United 0	Old Trafford	43795
119	1994/95	15/01/95	FA Premiership	Newcastle United 1 Manchester United 1	St James' Park	34471
120	1995/96	27/12/95	FA Premiership	Manchester United 2 Newcastle United 0	Old Trafford	42024
121	1995/96	04/03/96	FA Premiership	Newcastle United 0 Manchester United 1	St James' Park	36584
122	1996/97	11/08/96	FA Charity Shield	Manchester United 4 Newcastle United 0	Wembley	73214
123	1996/97	20/10/96	FA Premiership	Newcastle United 5 Manchester United 0	St James' Park	35579
124	1996/97	08/05/97	FA Premiership	Manchester United 0 Newcastle United 0	Old Trafford	55236
125	1997/98	21/12/97	FA Premiership	Newcastle United 0 Manchester United 1	St James' Park	36767
126	1997/98	18/04/98	FA Premiership	Manchester United 1 Newcastle United 1	Old Trafford	55194
127	1998/99	08/11/98	FA Premiership	Manchester United 0 Newcastle United 0	Old Trafford	55174
128	1998/99	13/03/99	FA Premiership	Newcastle United 1 Manchester United 2	St James' Park	36776
129	1998/99	22/05/99	FA Cup Final	Manchester United 2 Newcastle United 0	Wembley	79101
130	1999/00	30/08/99	FA Premiership	Manchester United 5 Newcastle United 1	Old Trafford	55190
131	1999/00	12/02/00	FA Premiership	Newcastle United 3 Manchester United 0	St James' Park	36470
132	2000/01	20/08/00	FA Premiership	Manchester United 2 Newcastle United 0	Old Trafford	67477
133	2000/01	30/12/00	FA Premiership	Newcastle United 1 Manchester United 1	St James' Park	52134
134	2001/02	15/09/01	FA Premiership	Newcastle United 4 Manchester United 3	St James' Park	52056
135	2001/02	02/01/02	FA Premiership	Manchester United 3 Newcastle United 1	Old Trafford	67646
136	2002/03	23/11/02	FA Premiership	Manchester United 5 Newcastle United 3	Old Trafford	67625
137	2002/03	12/04/03	FA Premiership	Newcastle United 2 Manchester United 6	St James' Park	52164
138	2003/04	23/08/03	FA Premiership	Newcastle United 1 Manchester United 2	St James' Park	52165
139	2003/04	11/01/04	FA Premiership	Manchester United 0 Newcastle United 0	Old Trafford	67622
140	2004/05	14/11/04	FA Premiership	Newcastle United 1 Manchester United 3	St James' Park	52320
141	2004/05	17/04/05	FA Cup Semi-Final	Manchester United 4 Newcastle United 1	Millennium Stadium	69280
142	2004/05	24/04/05	FA Premiership	Manchester United 2 Newcastle United 1	Old Trafford	67845
143	2005/06	28/08/05	FA Premiership	Newcastle United 0 Manchester United 2	St James' Park	52327
144	2005/06	12/03/06	FA Premiership	Manchester United 2 Newcastle United 0	Old Trafford	67858
145	2006/07	01/10/06	FA Premiership	Manchester United 2 Newcastle United 0	Old Trafford	75664
146	2006/07	01/01/07	FA Premiership	Newcastle United 2 Manchester United 2	St James' Park	52302
147	2007/08	12/01/08	FA Premiership	Manchester United 6 Newcastle United 0	Old Trafford	75965
148	2007/08	23/02/08	FA Premiership	Newcastle United 1 Manchester United 5	St James' Park	52291

UNITED v NORTHAMPTON TOWN

ALL COMPETITIVE MATCHES						LEAGUE DIVISION ONE						FA CUP					
VENUE	P	W	D	L	F	A	VENUE	P	W	D	L	F	A	VENUE	P	W	D	L	F	A
HOME	1	1	0	0	6	2	HOME	1	1	0	0	6	2	HOME	0	0	0	0	0	0
AWAY	3	2	1	0	12	3	AWAY	1	0	1	0	1	1	AWAY	2	2	0	0	11	2
TOTAL	4	3	1	0	18	5	TOTAL	2	1	1	0	7	3	TOTAL	2	2	0	0	11	2

#	SEASON	DATE	COMPETITION / ROUND	MATCH RESULT	VENUE	ATT
1	1965/66	28/08/65	Football League Division 1	Northampton Town 1 Manchester United 1	County Ground	21140
2	1965/66	05/02/66	Football League Division 1	Manchester United 6 Northampton Town 2	Old Trafford	34986
3	1969/70	07/02/70	FA Cup 5th Round	Northampton Town 2 Manchester United 8	County Ground	21771
4	2003/04	25/01/04	FA Cup 4th Round	Northampton Town 0 Manchester United 3	Sixfields Stadium	7356

UNITED v NORWICH CITY

ALL COMPETITIVE MATCHES						
VENUE	P	W	D	L	F	A
HOME	28	17	7	4	46	17
AWAY	30	13	6	11	48	41
TOTAL	58	30	13	15	94	58

ALL LEAGUE MATCHES						
VENUE	P	W	D	L	F	A
HOME	25	16	6	3	40	13
AWAY	25	12	6	7	44	31
TOTAL	50	28	12	10	84	44

ALL CUP MATCHES						
VENUE	P	W	D	L	F	A
HOME	3	1	1	1	6	4
AWAY	5	1	0	4	4	10
TOTAL	8	2	1	5	10	14

PREMIERSHIP						
VENUE	P	W	D	L	F	A
HOME	4	3	1	0	6	3
AWAY	4	3	0	1	7	3
TOTAL	8	6	1	1	13	6

LEAGUE DIVISION ONE						
VENUE	P	W	D	L	F	A
HOME	17	11	3	3	26	8
AWAY	17	7	6	4	27	18
TOTAL	34	18	9	7	53	26

LEAGUE DIVISION TWO						
VENUE	P	W	D	L	F	A
HOME	4	2	2	0	8	2
AWAY	4	2	0	2	10	10
TOTAL	8	4	2	2	18	12

FA CUP						
VENUE	P	W	D	L	F	A
HOME	2	1	0	1	4	2
AWAY	3	1	0	2	3	5
TOTAL	5	2	0	3	7	7

LEAGUE CUP						
VENUE	P	W	D	L	F	A
HOME	1	0	1	0	2	2
AWAY	2	0	0	2	1	5
TOTAL	3	0	1	2	3	7

#	SEASON	DATE	COMPETITION / ROUND	MATCH RESULT	VENUE	ATT
1	1905/06	03/02/06	FA Cup 2nd Round	Manchester United 3 Norwich City 0	Bank Street	10000
2	1934/35	22/09/34	Football League Division 2	Manchester United 5 Norwich City 0	Old Trafford	13052
3	1934/35	02/02/35	Football League Division 2	Norwich City 3 Manchester United 2	The Nest	14260
4	1935/36	23/11/35	Football League Division 2	Norwich City 3 Manchester United 5	Carrow Road	17266
5	1935/36	28/03/36	Football League Division 2	Manchester United 2 Norwich City 1	Old Trafford	31596
6	1937/38	27/11/37	Football League Division 2	Norwich City 2 Manchester United 3	Carrow Road	17397
7	1937/38	09/04/38	Football League Division 2	Manchester United 0 Norwich City 0	Old Trafford	25879
8	1958/59	10/01/59	FA Cup 3rd Round	Norwich City 3 Manchester United 0	Carrow Road	38000
9	1966/67	18/02/67	FA Cup 4th Round	Manchester United 1 Norwich City 2	Old Trafford	63409
10	1972/73	02/12/72	Football League Division 1	Norwich City 0 Manchester United 2	Carrow Road	35910
11	1972/73	07/04/73	Football League Division 1	Manchester United 1 Norwich City 0	Old Trafford	48593
12	1973/74	24/11/73	Football League Division 1	Manchester United 0 Norwich City 0	Old Trafford	36338
13	1973/74	06/04/74	Football League Division 1	Norwich City 0 Manchester United 2	Carrow Road	28223
14	1974/75	28/09/74	Football League Division 2	Norwich City 2 Manchester United 0	Carrow Road	24586
15	1974/75	15/01/75	League Cup Semi-Final 1st Leg	Manchester United 2 Norwich City 2	Old Trafford	58010
16	1974/75	22/01/75	League Cup Semi-Final 2nd Leg	Norwich City 1 Manchester United 0	Carrow Road	31621
17	1974/75	15/03/75	Football League Division 2	Manchester United 1 Norwich City 1	Old Trafford	56202
18	1975/76	01/11/75	Football League Division 1	Manchester United 1 Norwich City 0	Old Trafford	50587
19	1975/76	16/03/76	Football League Division 1	Norwich City 1 Manchester United 1	Carrow Road	27787
20	1976/77	23/10/76	Football League Division 1	Manchester United 2 Norwich City 2	Old Trafford	54356
21	1976/77	02/04/77	Football League Division 1	Norwich City 2 Manchester United 1	Carrow Road	24161
22	1977/78	19/11/77	Football League Division 1	Manchester United 1 Norwich City 0	Old Trafford	48729
23	1977/78	15/04/78	Football League Division 1	Norwich City 1 Manchester United 3	Carrow Road	19778
24	1978/79	07/04/79	Football League Division 1	Norwich City 2 Manchester United 2	Carrow Road	19382
25	1978/79	25/04/79	Football League Division 1	Manchester United 1 Norwich City 0	Old Trafford	33678
26	1979/80	26/09/79	League Cup 3rd Round	Norwich City 4 Manchester United 1	Carrow Road	18312
27	1979/80	24/11/79	Football League Division 1	Manchester United 5 Norwich City 0	Old Trafford	46540
28	1979/80	19/04/80	Football League Division 1	Norwich City 0 Manchester United 2	Carrow Road	23274
29	1980/81	06/12/80	Football League Division 1	Norwich City 2 Manchester United 2	Carrow Road	18780
30	1980/81	25/04/81	Football League Division 1	Manchester United 1 Norwich City 0	Old Trafford	40165
31	1982/83	27/11/82	Football League Division 1	Manchester United 3 Norwich City 0	Old Trafford	34579
32	1982/83	30/04/83	Football League Division 1	Norwich City 1 Manchester United 1	Carrow Road	22233
33	1983/84	01/10/83	Football League Division 1	Norwich City 3 Manchester United 3	Carrow Road	19290
34	1983/84	04/02/84	Football League Division 1	Manchester United 0 Norwich City 0	Old Trafford	36851
35	1984/85	01/12/84	Football League Division 1	Manchester United 2 Norwich City 0	Old Trafford	36635
36	1984/85	04/05/85	Football League Division 1	Norwich City 0 Manchester United 1	Carrow Road	15502
37	1986/87	15/11/86	Football League Division 1	Norwich City 0 Manchester United 0	Carrow Road	22684
38	1986/87	27/12/86	Football League Division 1	Manchester United 0 Norwich City 1	Old Trafford	44610
39	1987/88	17/10/87	Football League Division 1	Manchester United 2 Norwich City 1	Old Trafford	39821
40	1987/88	05/03/88	Football League Division 1	Norwich City 1 Manchester United 0	Carrow Road	19129
41	1988/89	26/10/88	Football League Division 1	Manchester United 1 Norwich City 2	Old Trafford	36998
42	1988/89	25/02/89	Football League Division 1	Norwich City 2 Manchester United 1	Carrow Road	23155
43	1989/90	30/08/89	Football League Division 1	Manchester United 0 Norwich City 2	Old Trafford	41610
44	1989/90	21/01/90	Football League Division 1	Norwich City 2 Manchester United 0	Carrow Road	17370

UNITED v NORWICH CITY (continued)

#	SEASON	DATE	COMPETITION / ROUND	MATCH RESULT	VENUE	ATT
45	1990/91	26/12/90	Football League Division 1	Manchester United 3 Norwich City 0	Old Trafford	39801
46	1990/91	18/02/91	FA Cup 5th Round	Norwich City 2 Manchester United 1	Carrow Road	23058
47	1990/91	30/03/91	Football League Division 1	Norwich City 0 Manchester United 3	Carrow Road	18282
48	1991/92	07/09/91	Football League Division 1	Manchester United 3 Norwich City 0	Old Trafford	44946
49	1991/92	31/03/92	Football League Division 1	Norwich City 1 Manchester United 3	Carrow Road	17489
50	1992/93	12/12/92	FA Premiership	Manchester United 1 Norwich City 0	Old Trafford	34500
51	1992/93	05/04/93	FA Premiership	Norwich City 1 Manchester United 3	Carrow Road	20582
52	1993/94	15/08/93	FA Premiership	Norwich City 0 Manchester United 2	Carrow Road	19705
53	1993/94	04/12/93	FA Premiership	Manchester United 2 Norwich City 2	Old Trafford	44694
54	1993/94	30/01/94	FA Cup 4th Round	Norwich City 0 Manchester United 2	Carrow Road	21060
55	1994/95	03/12/94	FA Premiership	Manchester United 1 Norwich City 0	Old Trafford	43789
56	1994/95	22/02/95	FA Premiership	Norwich City 0 Manchester United 2	Carrow Road	21824
57	2004/05	21/08/04	FA Premiership	Manchester United 2 Norwich City 1	Old Trafford	67812
58	2004/05	09/04/05	FA Premiership	Norwich City 2 Manchester United 0	Carrow Road	25522

UNITED v NOTTINGHAM FOREST

ALL COMPETITIVE MATCHES

VENUE	P	W	D	L	F	A
HOME	53	30	11	12	111	64
AWAY	51	17	13	21	72	72
NEUTRAL	1	1	0	0	1	0
TOTAL	105	48	24	33	184	136

ALL LEAGUE MATCHES

VENUE	P	W	D	L	F	A
HOME	48	28	11	9	105	57
AWAY	48	16	12	20	71	71
TOTAL	96	44	23	29	176	128

ALL CUP MATCHES

VENUE	P	W	D	L	F	A
HOME	5	2	0	3	6	7
AWAY	3	1	1	1	1	1
NEUTRAL	1	1	0	0	1	0
TOTAL	9	4	1	4	8	8

PREMIERSHIP

VENUE	P	W	D	L	F	A
HOME	5	4	0	1	15	3
AWAY	5	3	2	0	16	3
TOTAL	10	7	2	1	31	6

LEAGUE DIVISION ONE

VENUE	P	W	D	L	F	A
HOME	36	19	10	7	71	43
AWAY	36	11	7	18	44	57
TOTAL	72	30	17	25	115	100

LEAGUE DIVISION TWO

VENUE	P	W	D	L	F	A
HOME	7	5	1	1	19	11
AWAY	7	2	3	2	11	11
TOTAL	14	7	4	3	30	22

FA CUP

VENUE	P	W	D	L	F	A
HOME	3	0	0	3	0	6
AWAY	3	1	1	1	1	1
NEUTRAL	0	0	0	0	0	0
TOTAL	6	1	1	4	1	7

LEAGUE CUP

VENUE	P	W	D	L	F	A
HOME	2	2	0	0	6	1
AWAY	0	0	0	0	0	0
NEUTRAL	1	1	0	0	1	0
TOTAL	3	3	0	0	7	1

#	SEASON	DATE	COMPETITION / ROUND	MATCH RESULT	VENUE	ATT
1	1892/93	29/10/92	Football League Division 1	Nottingham Forest 1 Newton Heath 1	Town Ground	6000
2	1892/93	14/01/93	Football League Division 1	Newton Heath 1 Nottingham Forest 3	North Road	8000
3	1893/94	23/09/93	Football League Division 1	Newton Heath 1 Nottingham Forest 1	Bank Street	10000
4	1893/94	07/04/94	Football League Division 1	Nottingham Forest 2 Newton Heath 0	Town Ground	4000
5	1907/08	05/10/07	Football League Division 1	Manchester United 4 Nottingham Forest 0	Bank Street	20000
6	1907/08	17/04/08	Football League Division 1	Nottingham Forest 2 Manchester United 0	City Ground	22000
7	1908/09	24/10/08	Football League Division 1	Manchester United 2 Nottingham Forest 2	Bank Street	20000
8	1908/09	27/02/09	Football League Division 1	Nottingham Forest 2 Manchester United 0	City Ground	7000
9	1909/10	27/11/09	Football League Division 1	Manchester United 2 Nottingham Forest 6	Bank Street	12000
10	1909/10	09/04/10	Football League Division 1	Nottingham Forest 2 Manchester United 0	City Ground	7000
11	1910/11	10/09/10	Football League Division 1	Nottingham Forest 2 Manchester United 1	City Ground	20000
12	1910/11	07/01/11	Football League Division 1	Manchester United 4 Nottingham Forest 2	Old Trafford	10000
13	1931/32	19/09/31	Football League Division 2	Nottingham Forest 2 Manchester United 1	City Ground	10166
14	1931/32	30/01/32	Football League Division 2	Manchester United 3 Nottingham Forest 2	Old Trafford	11152
15	1932/33	14/04/33	Football League Division 2	Nottingham Forest 3 Manchester United 2	City Ground	12963
16	1932/33	17/04/33	Football League Division 2	Manchester United 2 Nottingham Forest 1	Old Trafford	16849
17	1933/34	30/08/33	Football League Division 2	Manchester United 0 Nottingham Forest 1	Old Trafford	16934
18	1933/34	07/09/33	Football League Division 2	Nottingham Forest 1 Manchester United 1	City Ground	10650
19	1934/35	24/11/34	Football League Division 2	Manchester United 3 Nottingham Forest 2	Old Trafford	27192
20	1934/35	26/01/35	FA Cup 4th Round	Nottingham Forest 0 Manchester United 0	City Ground	32862
21	1934/35	30/01/35	FA Cup 4th Round Replay	Manchester United 0 Nottingham Forest 3	Old Trafford	33851
22	1934/35	06/04/35	Football League Division 2	Nottingham Forest 2 Manchester United 2	City Ground	8618
23	1935/36	14/12/35	Football League Division 2	Manchester United 5 Nottingham Forest 0	Old Trafford	15284
24	1935/36	18/04/36	Football League Division 2	Nottingham Forest 1 Manchester United 1	City Ground	12156
25	1937/38	27/12/37	Football League Division 2	Manchester United 4 Nottingham Forest 3	Old Trafford	30778
26	1937/38	28/12/37	Football League Division 2	Nottingham Forest 2 Manchester United 3	City Ground	19283

UNITED v NOTTINGHAM FOREST (continued)

#	SEASON	DATE	COMPETITION / ROUND	MATCH RESULT		VENUE	ATT
27	1946/47	25/01/47	FA Cup 4th Round	Manchester United 0	Nottingham Forest 2	Maine Road	34059
28	1957/58	12/10/57	Football League Division 1	Nottingham Forest 1	Manchester United 2	City Ground	47654
29	1957/58	22/02/58	Football League Division 1	Manchester United 1	Nottingham Forest 1	Old Trafford	66124
30	1958/59	27/08/58	Football League Division 1	Nottingham Forest 0	Manchester United 3	City Ground	44971
31	1958/59	03/09/58	Football League Division 1	Manchester United 1	Nottingham Forest 0	Old Trafford	51880
32	1959/60	12/12/59	Football League Division 1	Nottingham Forest 1	Manchester United 5	City Ground	31666
33	1959/60	19/03/60	Football League Division 1	Manchester United 3	Nottingham Forest 1	Old Trafford	35269
34	1960/61	24/10/60	Football League Division 1	Manchester United 2	Nottingham Forest 1	Old Trafford	23628
35	1960/61	25/02/61	Football League Division 1	Nottingham Forest 3	Manchester United 2	City Ground	26850
36	1961/62	26/12/61	Football League Division 1	Manchester United 6	Nottingham Forest 3	Old Trafford	30822
37	1961/62	20/03/62	Football League Division 1	Nottingham Forest 1	Manchester United 0	City Ground	27833
38	1962/63	08/12/62	Football League Division 1	Manchester United 5	Nottingham Forest 1	Old Trafford	27496
39	1962/63	20/05/63	Football League Division 1	Nottingham Forest 3	Manchester United 2	City Ground	16130
40	1963/64	19/10/63	Football League Division 1	Nottingham Forest 1	Manchester United 2	City Ground	41426
41	1963/64	25/04/64	Football League Division 1	Manchester United 3	Nottingham Forest 1	Old Trafford	31671
42	1964/65	12/09/64	Football League Division 1	Manchester United 3	Nottingham Forest 0	Old Trafford	45012
43	1964/65	16/01/65	Football League Division 1	Nottingham Forest 2	Manchester United 2	City Ground	43009
44	1965/66	24/08/65	Football League Division 1	Nottingham Forest 4	Manchester United 2	City Ground	33744
45	1965/66	01/09/65	Football League Division 1	Manchester United 0	Nottingham Forest 0	Old Trafford	38777
46	1966/67	01/10/66	Football League Division 1	Nottingham Forest 4	Manchester United 1	City Ground	41854
47	1966/67	11/02/67	Football League Division 1	Manchester United 1	Nottingham Forest 0	Old Trafford	62727
48	1967/68	28/10/67	Football League Division 1	Nottingham Forest 3	Manchester United 1	City Ground	49946
49	1967/68	23/03/68	Football League Division 1	Manchester United 3	Nottingham Forest 0	Old Trafford	61978
50	1968/69	31/03/69	Football League Division 1	Nottingham Forest 0	Manchester United 1	City Ground	41892
51	1968/69	05/04/69	Football League Division 1	Manchester United 3	Nottingham Forest 0	Old Trafford	51952
52	1969/70	18/10/69	Football League Division 1	Manchester United 1	Nottingham Forest 1	Old Trafford	53702
53	1969/70	31/03/70	Football League Division 1	Nottingham Forest 1	Manchester United 2	City Ground	39228
54	1970/71	14/11/70	Football League Division 1	Nottingham Forest 1	Manchester United 2	City Ground	36364
55	1970/71	13/03/71	Football League Division 1	Manchester United 2	Nottingham Forest 0	Old Trafford	40473
56	1971/72	04/12/71	Football League Division 1	Manchester United 3	Nottingham Forest 2	Old Trafford	45411
57	1971/72	22/04/72	Football League Division 1	Nottingham Forest 0	Manchester United 0	City Ground	35063
58	1974/75	07/09/74	Football League Division 2	Manchester United 2	Nottingham Forest 2	Old Trafford	40671
59	1974/75	22/03/75	Football League Division 2	Nottingham Forest 0	Manchester United 1	City Ground	21893
60	1977/78	12/11/77	Football League Division 1	Nottingham Forest 2	Manchester United 1	City Ground	30183
61	1977/78	17/12/77	Football League Division 1	Manchester United 0	Nottingham Forest 4	Old Trafford	54374
62	1978/79	16/09/78	Football League Division 1	Manchester United 1	Nottingham Forest 1	Old Trafford	53039
63	1978/79	18/04/79	Football League Division 1	Nottingham Forest 1	Manchester United 1	City Ground	33074
64	1979/80	22/12/79	Football League Division 1	Manchester United 3	Nottingham Forest 0	Old Trafford	54607
65	1979/80	02/04/80	Football League Division 1	Nottingham Forest 2	Manchester United 0	City Ground	31417
66	1980/81	04/10/80	Football League Division 1	Nottingham Forest 1	Manchester United 2	City Ground	29801
67	1980/81	24/01/81	FA Cup 4th Round	Nottingham Forest 1	Manchester United 0	City Ground	34110
68	1980/81	18/03/81	Football League Division 1	Manchester United 1	Nottingham Forest 1	Old Trafford	38205
69	1981/82	31/08/81	Football League Division 1	Manchester United 0	Nottingham Forest 0	Old Trafford	51496
70	1981/82	05/05/82	Football League Division 1	Nottingham Forest 0	Manchester United 1	City Ground	18449
71	1982/83	01/09/82	Football League Division 1	Nottingham Forest 0	Manchester United 3	City Ground	23956
72	1982/83	19/01/83	League Cup 5th Round	Manchester United 4	Nottingham Forest 0	Old Trafford	44413
73	1982/83	22/01/83	Football League Division 1	Manchester United 2	Nottingham Forest 0	Old Trafford	38615
74	1983/84	29/08/83	Football League Division 1	Manchester United 1	Nottingham Forest 2	Old Trafford	43005
75	1983/84	16/05/84	Football League Division 1	Nottingham Forest 2	Manchester United 0	City Ground	23651
76	1984/85	08/12/84	Football League Division 1	Nottingham Forest 3	Manchester United 2	City Ground	25902
77	1984/85	06/05/85	Football League Division 1	Manchester United 2	Nottingham Forest 0	Old Trafford	41775
78	1985/86	31/08/85	Football League Division 1	Nottingham Forest 0	Manchester United 3	City Ground	26274
79	1985/86	18/01/86	Football League Division 1	Manchester United 2	Nottingham Forest 3	Old Trafford	46717
80	1986/87	04/10/86	Football League Division 1	Nottingham Forest 1	Manchester United 1	City Ground	34828
81	1986/87	28/03/87	Football League Division 1	Manchester United 2	Nottingham Forest 0	Old Trafford	39182
82	1987/88	31/10/87	Football League Division 1	Manchester United 2	Nottingham Forest 2	Old Trafford	44669
83	1987/88	19/03/88	Football League Division 1	Nottingham Forest 0	Manchester United 0	City Ground	27598
84	1988/89	26/12/88	Football League Division 1	Manchester United 2	Nottingham Forest 0	Old Trafford	39582
85	1988/89	18/03/89	FA Cup 6th Round	Manchester United 0	Nottingham Forest 1	Old Trafford	55040
86	1988/89	27/03/89	Football League Division 1	Nottingham Forest 2	Manchester United 0	City Ground	30092

UNITED v NOTTINGHAM FOREST (continued)

#	SEASON	DATE	COMPETITION / ROUND	MATCH RESULT		VENUE	ATT
87	1989/90	12/11/89	Football League Division 1	Manchester United 1	Nottingham Forest 0	Old Trafford	34182
88	1989/90	07/01/90	FA Cup 3rd Round	Nottingham Forest 0	Manchester United 1	City Ground	23072
89	1989/90	02/05/90	Football League Division 1	Nottingham Forest 4	Manchester United 0	City Ground	21186
90	1990/91	29/09/90	Football League Division 1	Manchester United 0	Nottingham Forest 1	Old Trafford	46766
91	1990/91	16/03/91	Football League Division 1	Nottingham Forest 1	Manchester United 1	City Ground	23859
92	1991/92	18/03/92	Football League Division 1	Nottingham Forest 1	Manchester United 0	City Ground	28062
93	1991/92	12/04/92	League Cup Final	Manchester United 1	Nottingham Forest 0	Wembley	76810
94	1991/92	20/04/92	Football League Division 1	Manchester United 1	Nottingham Forest 2	Old Trafford	47576
95	1992/93	29/08/92	FA Premiership	Nottingham Forest 0	Manchester United 2	City Ground	19694
96	1992/93	27/01/93	FA Premiership	Manchester United 2	Nottingham Forest 0	Old Trafford	36085
97	1994/95	22/08/94	FA Premiership	Nottingham Forest 1	Manchester United 1	City Ground	22072
98	1994/95	17/12/94	FA Premiership	Manchester United 1	Nottingham Forest 2	Old Trafford	43744
99	1995/96	27/11/95	FA Premiership	Nottingham Forest 1	Manchester United 1	City Ground	29263
100	1995/96	28/04/96	FA Premiership	Manchester United 5	Nottingham Forest 0	Old Trafford	53926
101	1996/97	14/09/96	FA Premiership	Manchester United 4	Nottingham Forest 1	Old Trafford	54984
102	1996/97	26/12/96	FA Premiership	Nottingham Forest 0	Manchester United 4	City Ground	29032
103	1998/99	11/11/98	League Cup 4th Round	Manchester United 2	Nottingham Forest 1	Old Trafford	37337
104	1998/99	26/12/98	FA Premiership	Manchester United 3	Nottingham Forest 0	Old Trafford	55216
105	1998/99	06/02/99	FA Premiership	Nottingham Forest 1	Manchester United 8	City Ground	30025

UNITED v NOTTS COUNTY

ALL COMPETITIVE MATCHES						
VENUE	P	W	D	L	F	A
HOME	25	12	9	4	43	28
AWAY	25	9	6	10	36	36
TOTAL	50	21	15	14	79	64

ALL LEAGUE MATCHES						
VENUE	P	W	D	L	F	A
HOME	24	11	9	4	41	27
AWAY	24	9	5	10	33	33
TOTAL	48	20	14	14	74	60

FA CUP						
VENUE	P	W	D	L	F	A
HOME	1	1	0	0	2	1
AWAY	1	0	1	0	3	3
TOTAL	2	1	1	0	5	4

LEAGUE DIVISION ONE						
VENUE	P	W	D	L	F	A
HOME	15	7	5	3	24	16
AWAY	15	6	2	7	20	23
TOTAL	30	13	7	10	44	39

LEAGUE DIVISION TWO						
VENUE	P	W	D	L	F	A
HOME	9	4	4	1	17	11
AWAY	9	3	3	3	13	10
TOTAL	18	7	7	4	30	21

#	SEASON	DATE	COMPETITION / ROUND	MATCH RESULT		VENUE	ATT
1	1892/93	12/11/92	Football League Division 1	Newton Heath 1	Notts County 3	North Road	8000
2	1892/93	26/01/93	Football League Division 1	Notts County 4	Newton Heath 0	Trent Bridge	1000
3	1894/95	15/12/94	Football League Division 2	Notts County 1	Newton Heath 1	Trent Bridge	3000
4	1894/95	20/04/95	Football League Division 2	Newton Heath 3	Notts County 3	Bank Street	12000
5	1895/96	23/11/95	Football League Division 2	Notts County 0	Newton Heath 2	Trent Bridge	3000
6	1895/96	14/12/95	Football League Division 2	Newton Heath 3	Notts County 0	Bank Street	3000
7	1896/97	19/12/96	Football League Division 2	Notts County 3	Newton Heath 0	Trent Bridge	5000
8	1896/97	27/03/97	Football League Division 2	Newton Heath 1	Notts County 1	Bank Street	10000
9	1903/04	06/02/04	FA Cup 1st Round	Notts County 3	Manchester United 3	Trent Bridge	12000
10	1903/04	10/02/04	FA Cup 1st Round Replay	Manchester United 2	Notts County 1	Bank Street	18000
11	1906/07	08/09/06	Football League Division 1	Manchester United 0	Notts County 0	Bank Street	30000
12	1906/07	05/01/07	Football League Division 1	Notts County 3	Manchester United 0	Trent Bridge	10000
13	1907/08	14/12/07	Football League Division 1	Notts County 1	Manchester United 1	Trent Bridge	11000
14	1907/08	11/04/08	Football League Division 1	Manchester United 0	Notts County 1	Bank Street	20000
15	1908/09	01/01/09	Football League Division 1	Manchester United 4	Notts County 3	Bank Street	15000
16	1908/09	13/04/09	Football League Division 1	Notts County 0	Manchester United 1	Trent Bridge	7000
17	1909/10	06/09/09	Football League Division 1	Manchester United 2	Notts County 1	Bank Street	6000
18	1909/10	25/09/09	Football League Division 1	Notts County 3	Manchester United 2	Trent Bridge	11000
19	1910/11	12/11/10	Football League Division 1	Manchester United 0	Notts County 0	Old Trafford	13000
20	1910/11	18/03/11	Football League Division 1	Notts County 1	Manchester United 0	Meadow Lane	12000
21	1911/12	28/10/11	Football League Division 1	Notts County 0	Manchester United 1	Meadow Lane	15000
22	1911/12	02/03/12	Football League Division 1	Manchester United 2	Notts County 0	Old Trafford	10000
23	1912/13	02/11/12	Football League Division 1	Manchester United 2	Notts County 1	Old Trafford	12000
24	1912/13	08/03/13	Football League Division 1	Notts County 1	Manchester United 2	Meadow Lane	10000
25	1914/15	26/09/14	Football League Division 1	Notts County 4	Manchester United 2	Meadow Lane	12000
26	1914/15	30/01/15	Football League Division 1	Manchester United 2	Notts County 2	Old Trafford	7000
27	1919/20	26/04/20	Football League Division 1	Manchester United 0	Notts County 0	Old Trafford	30000
28	1919/20	01/05/20	Football League Division 1	Notts County 0	Manchester United 2	Meadow Lane	20000

UNITED v NOTTS COUNTY (continued)

#	SEASON	DATE	COMPETITION / ROUND	MATCH RESULT	VENUE	ATT
29	1922/23	10/02/23	Football League Division 2	Notts County 1 Manchester United 6	Meadow Lane	10000
30	1922/23	21/02/23	Football League Division 2	Manchester United 1 Notts County 1	Old Trafford	12100
31	1925/26	02/04/26	Football League Division 1	Notts County 0 Manchester United 3	Meadow Lane	18453
32	1925/26	05/04/26	Football League Division 1	Manchester United 0 Notts County 1	Old Trafford	19606
33	1931/32	24/10/31	Football League Division 2	Manchester United 3 Notts County 3	Old Trafford	6694
34	1931/32	05/03/32	Football League Division 2	Notts County 1 Manchester United 2	Meadow Lane	10817
35	1932/33	05/11/32	Football League Division 2	Manchester United 2 Notts County 0	Old Trafford	24178
36	1932/33	18/03/33	Football League Division 2	Notts County 1 Manchester United 0	Meadow Lane	13018
37	1933/34	09/12/33	Football League Division 2	Manchester United 1 Notts County 2	Old Trafford	15564
38	1933/34	21/04/34	Football League Division 2	Notts County 0 Manchester United 0	Meadow Lane	9645
39	1934/35	25/12/34	Football League Division 2	Manchester United 2 Notts County 1	Old Trafford	32965
40	1934/35	26/12/34	Football League Division 2	Notts County 1 Manchester United 0	Meadow Lane	24599
41	1974/75	12/10/74	Football League Division 2	Manchester United 1 Notts County 0	Old Trafford	46565
42	1974/75	19/04/75	Football League Division 2	Notts County 2 Manchester United 2	Meadow Lane	17320
43	1981/82	31/10/81	Football League Division 1	Manchester United 2 Notts County 1	Old Trafford	45928
44	1981/82	20/03/82	Football League Division 1	Notts County 1 Manchester United 3	Meadow Lane	17048
45	1982/83	11/12/82	Football League Division 1	Manchester United 4 Notts County 0	Old Trafford	33618
46	1982/83	14/05/83	Football League Division 1	Notts County 3 Manchester United 2	Meadow Lane	14395
47	1983/84	27/12/83	Football League Division 1	Manchester United 3 Notts County 3	Old Trafford	41544
48	1983/84	14/04/84	Football League Division 1	Notts County 1 Manchester United 0	Meadow Lane	13911
49	1991/92	17/08/91	Football League Division 1	Manchester United 2 Notts County 0	Old Trafford	46278
50	1991/92	18/01/92	Football League Division 1	Notts County 1 Manchester United 1	Meadow Lane	21055

UNITED v OLDHAM ATHLETIC

ALL COMPETITIVE MATCHES

VENUE	P	W	D	L	F	A
HOME	21	13	3	5	45	22
AWAY	19	6	7	6	36	26
NEUTRAL	4	2	2	0	10	6
TOTAL	44	21	12	11	91	54

ALL LEAGUE MATCHES

VENUE	P	W	D	L	F	A
HOME	18	11	3	4	38	19
AWAY	18	6	6	6	36	26
TOTAL	36	17	9	10	74	45

ALL CUP MATCHES

VENUE	P	W	D	L	F	A
HOME	3	2	0	1	7	3
AWAY	1	0	1	0	0	0
NEUTRAL	4	2	2	0	10	6
TOTAL	8	4	3	1	17	9

PREMIERSHIP

VENUE	P	W	D	L	F	A
HOME	2	2	0	0	6	2
AWAY	2	1	0	1	5	3
TOTAL	4	3	0	1	11	5

LEAGUE DIVISION ONE

VENUE	P	W	D	L	F	A
HOME	9	4	3	2	14	10
AWAY	9	3	5	1	19	12
TOTAL	18	7	8	3	33	22

LEAGUE DIVISION TWO

VENUE	P	W	D	L	F	A
HOME	7	5	0	2	18	7
AWAY	7	2	1	4	12	11
TOTAL	14	7	1	6	30	18

FA CUP

VENUE	P	W	D	L	F	A
HOME	2	1	0	1	5	3
AWAY	1	0	1	0	0	0
NEUTRAL	4	2	2	0	10	6
TOTAL	7	3	3	1	15	9

LEAGUE CUP

VENUE	P	W	D	L	F	A
HOME	1	1	0	0	2	0
AWAY	0	0	0	0	0	0
NEUTRAL	0	0	0	0	0	0
TOTAL	1	1	0	0	2	0

#	SEASON	DATE	COMPETITION / ROUND	MATCH RESULT	VENUE	ATT
1	1910/11	19/11/10	Football League Division 1	Oldham Athletic 1 Manchester United 3	Boundary Park	25000
2	1910/11	25/03/11	Football League Division 1	Manchester United 0 Oldham Athletic 0	Old Trafford	35000
3	1911/12	16/12/11	Football League Division 1	Oldham Athletic 2 Manchester United 2	Boundary Park	20000
4	1911/12	20/04/12	Football League Division 1	Manchester United 3 Oldham Athletic 1	Old Trafford	15000
5	1912/13	21/12/12	Football League Division 1	Manchester United 0 Oldham Athletic 0	Old Trafford	30000
6	1912/13	22/02/13	FA Cup 3rd Round	Oldham Athletic 0 Manchester United 0	Boundary Park	26932
7	1912/13	26/02/13	FA Cup 3rd Round Replay	Manchester United 1 Oldham Athletic 2	Old Trafford	31180
8	1912/13	26/04/13	Football League Division 1	Oldham Athletic 0 Manchester United 0	Boundary Park	3000
9	1913/14	27/09/13	Football League Division 1	Manchester United 4 Oldham Athletic 1	Old Trafford	55000
10	1913/14	24/01/14	Football League Division 1	Oldham Athletic 2 Manchester United 2	Boundary Park	10000
11	1914/15	02/09/14	Football League Division 1	Manchester United 1 Oldham Athletic 3	Old Trafford	13000
12	1914/15	06/04/15	Football League Division 1	Oldham Athletic 1 Manchester United 0	Boundary Park	2000
13	1919/20	22/11/19	Football League Division 1	Oldham Athletic 0 Manchester United 3	Boundary Park	15000
14	1919/20	11/02/20	Football League Division 1	Manchester United 1 Oldham Athletic 1	Old Trafford	15000
15	1920/21	09/10/20	Football League Division 1	Manchester United 4 Oldham Athletic 1	Old Trafford	50000
16	1920/21	16/10/20	Football League Division 1	Oldham Athletic 2 Manchester United 2	Boundary Park	20000
17	1921/22	15/04/22	Football League Division 1	Manchester United 0 Oldham Athletic 3	Old Trafford	30000
18	1921/22	22/04/22	Football League Division 1	Oldham Athletic 1 Manchester United 1	Boundary Park	30000

UNITED v OLDHAM ATHLETIC (continued)

#	SEASON	DATE	COMPETITION / ROUND	MATCH RESULT	VENUE	ATT
19	1923/24	06/10/23	Football League Division 2	Oldham Athletic 3 Manchester United 2	Boundary Park	12250
20	1923/24	13/10/23	Football League Division 2	Manchester United 2 Oldham Athletic 0	Old Trafford	26000
21	1924/25	20/09/24	Football League Division 2	Oldham Athletic 0 Manchester United 3	Boundary Park	14500
22	1924/25	24/01/25	Football League Division 2	Manchester United 0 Oldham Athletic 1	Old Trafford	20000
23	1931/32	14/11/31	Football League Division 2	Oldham Athletic 1 Manchester United 5	Boundary Park	10922
24	1931/32	26/03/32	Football League Division 2	Manchester United 5 Oldham Athletic 1	Old Trafford	17886
25	1932/33	24/09/32	Football League Division 2	Oldham Athletic 1 Manchester United 1	Boundary Park	14403
26	1932/33	04/02/33	Football League Division 2	Manchester United 2 Oldham Athletic 0	Old Trafford	15275
27	1933/34	30/09/33	Football League Division 2	Oldham Athletic 2 Manchester United 0	Boundary Park	22736
28	1933/34	10/02/34	Football League Division 2	Manchester United 2 Oldham Athletic 3	Old Trafford	24480
29	1934/35	13/10/34	Football League Division 2	Manchester United 4 Oldham Athletic 0	Old Trafford	29143
30	1934/35	23/02/35	Football League Division 2	Oldham Athletic 3 Manchester United 1	Boundary Park	14432
31	1950/51	06/01/51	FA Cup 3rd Round	Manchester United 4 Oldham Athletic 1	Old Trafford	37161
32	1974/75	28/12/74	Football League Division 2	Oldham Athletic 1 Manchester United 0	Boundary Park	26384
33	1974/75	31/03/75	Football League Division 2	Manchester United 3 Oldham Athletic 2	Old Trafford	56618
34	1989/90	08/04/90	FA Cup Semi-Final	Manchester United 3 Oldham Athletic 3	Maine Road	44026
35	1989/90	11/04/90	FA Cup Semi-Final Replay	Manchester United 2 Oldham Athletic 1	Maine Road	35005
36	1991/92	28/08/91	Football League Division 1	Manchester United 1 Oldham Athletic 0	Old Trafford	42078
37	1991/92	04/12/91	League Cup 4th Round	Manchester United 2 Oldham Athletic 0	Old Trafford	38550
38	1991/92	26/12/91	Football League Division 1	Oldham Athletic 3 Manchester United 6	Boundary Park	18947
39	1992/93	21/11/92	FA Premiership	Manchester United 3 Oldham Athletic 0	Old Trafford	33497
40	1992/93	09/03/93	FA Premiership	Oldham Athletic 1 Manchester United 0	Boundary Park	17106
41	1993/94	29/12/93	FA Premiership	Oldham Athletic 2 Manchester United 5	Boundary Park	16708
42	1993/94	04/04/94	FA Premiership	Manchester United 3 Oldham Athletic 2	Old Trafford	44686
43	1993/94	10/04/94	FA Cup Semi-Final	Manchester United 1 Oldham Athletic 1	Wembley	56399
44	1993/94	13/04/94	FA Cup Semi-Final Replay	Manchester United 4 Oldham Athletic 1	Maine Road	32311

UNITED v OLYMPIAKOS PIRAEUS

CHAMPIONS LEAGUE

VENUE	P	W	D	L	F	A
HOME	2	2	0	0	7	0
AWAY	2	2	0	0	5	2
TOTAL	4	4	0	0	12	2

#	SEASON	DATE	COMPETITION / ROUND	MATCH RESULT	VENUE	ATT
1	2001/02	10/10/01	Champions League Phase 1 Match 3	Olympiakos Piraeus 0 Manchester United 2	Olympic Stadium	73537
2	2001/02	23/10/01	Champions League Phase 1 Match 5	Manchester United 3 Olympiakos Piraeus 0	Old Trafford	66769
3	2002/03	01/10/02	Champions League Phase 1 Match 3	Manchester United 4 Olympiakos Piraeus 0	Old Trafford	66902
4	2002/03	23/10/02	Champions League Phase 1 Match 4	Olympiakos Piraeus 2 Manchester United 3	Rizoupoli	15000

UNITED v OLYMPIQUE LYONNAIS

CHAMPIONS LEAGUE

VENUE	P	W	D	L	F	A
HOME	2	2	0	0	3	1
AWAY	2	0	2	0	3	3
TOTAL	4	2	2	0	6	4

#	SEASON	DATE	COMPETITION / ROUND	MATCH RESULT	VENUE	ATT
1	2004/05	15/09/04	Champions League Phase 1 Match 1	Olympique Lyonnais 2 Manchester United 2	Stade de Gerland	40000
2	2004/05	23/11/04	Champions League Phase 1 Match 5	Manchester United 2 Olympique Lyonnais 1	Old Trafford	66398
3	2007/08	20/02/08	Champions League 2nd Round 1st Leg	Olympique Lyonnais 1 Manchester United 1	Stade de Gerland	39230
4	2007/08	04/03/08	Champions League 2nd Round 2nd Leg	Manchester United 1 Olympique Lyonnais 0	Old Trafford	75520

UNITED v OLYMPIQUE MARSEILLE

CHAMPIONS LEAGUE						
VENUE	P	W	D	L	F	A
HOME	1	1	0	0	2	1
AWAY	1	0	0	1	0	1
TOTAL	2	1	0	1	2	2

#	SEASON	DATE	COMPETITION / ROUND	MATCH RESULT	VENUE	ATT
1	1999/00	29/09/99	Champions League Phase 1 Match 3	Manchester United 2 Olympique Marseille 1	Old Trafford	53993
2	1999/00	19/10/99	Champions League Phase 1 Match 4	Olympique Marseille 1 Manchester United 0	Stade Velodrome	56732

UNITED v OSWALDTWISTLE ROVERS

FA CUP						
VENUE	P	W	D	L	F	A
HOME	1	1	0	0	3	2
AWAY	0	0	0	0	0	0
TOTAL	1	1	0	0	3	2

#	SEASON	DATE	COMPETITION / ROUND	MATCH RESULT	VENUE	ATT
1	1902/03	13/11/02	FA Cup 4th Qualifying Round	Manchester United 3 Oswaldtwistle Rovers 2	Bank Street	5000

UNITED v OXFORD UNITED

ALL COMPETITIVE MATCHES							ALL LEAGUE MATCHES							ALL CUP MATCHES						
VENUE	P	W	D	L	F	A	VENUE	P	W	D	L	F	A	VENUE	P	W	D	L	F	A
HOME	8	7	1	0	23	6	HOME	4	4	0	0	13	3	HOME	4	3	1	0	10	3
AWAY	8	2	2	4	9	11	AWAY	4	2	0	2	5	4	AWAY	4	0	2	2	4	7
TOTAL	16	9	3	4	32	17	TOTAL	8	6	0	2	18	7	TOTAL	8	3	3	2	14	10

LEAGUE DIVISION ONE							LEAGUE DIVISION TWO						
VENUE	P	W	D	L	F	A	VENUE	P	W	D	L	F	A
HOME	3	3	0	0	9	3	HOME	1	1	0	0	4	0
AWAY	3	2	0	1	5	3	AWAY	1	0	0	1	0	1
TOTAL	6	5	0	1	14	6	TOTAL	2	1	0	1	4	1

FA CUP							LEAGUE CUP						
VENUE	P	W	D	L	F	A	VENUE	P	W	D	L	F	A
HOME	2	2	0	0	6	1	HOME	2	1	1	0	4	2
AWAY	0	0	0	0	0	0	AWAY	4	0	2	2	4	7
TOTAL	2	2	0	0	6	1	TOTAL	6	1	3	2	8	9

#	SEASON	DATE	COMPETITION / ROUND	MATCH RESULT	VENUE	ATT
1	1972/73	06/09/72	League Cup 2nd Round	Oxford United 2 Manchester United 2	Manor Ground	16560
2	1972/73	12/09/72	League Cup 2nd Round Replay	Manchester United 3 Oxford United 1	Old Trafford	21486
3	1974/75	02/11/74	Football League Division 2	Manchester United 4 Oxford United 0	Old Trafford	41909
4	1974/75	08/02/75	Football League Division 2	Oxford United 1 Manchester United 0	Manor Ground	15959
5	1975/76	03/01/76	FA Cup 3rd Round	Manchester United 2 Oxford United 1	Old Trafford	41082
6	1983/84	30/11/83	League Cup 4th Round	Oxford United 1 Manchester United 1	Manor Ground	13739
7	1983/84	07/12/83	League Cup 4th Round Replay	Manchester United 1 Oxford United 1	Old Trafford	27459
8	1983/84	19/12/83	League Cup 4th Round 2nd Replay	Oxford United 2 Manchester United 1	Manor Ground	13912
9	1985/86	07/09/85	Football League Division 1	Manchester United 3 Oxford United 0	Old Trafford	51820
10	1985/86	11/01/86	Football League Division 1	Oxford United 1 Manchester United 3	Manor Ground	13280
11	1986/87	08/11/86	Football League Division 1	Oxford United 2 Manchester United 0	Manor Ground	13545
12	1986/87	04/04/87	Football League Division 1	Manchester United 3 Oxford United 2	Old Trafford	32443
13	1987/88	12/12/87	Football League Division 1	Manchester United 3 Oxford United 1	Old Trafford	34709
14	1987/88	20/01/88	League Cup 5th Round	Oxford United 2 Manchester United 0	Manor Ground	12658
15	1987/88	02/05/88	Football League Division 1	Oxford United 0 Manchester United 2	Manor Ground	8966
16	1988/89	28/01/89	FA Cup 4th Round	Manchester United 4 Oxford United 0	Old Trafford	47745

UNITED v PALMEIRAS

INTER-CONTINENTAL CUP

VENUE	P	W	D	L	F	A
HOME	0	0	0	0	0	0
AWAY	0	0	0	0	0	0
NEUTRAL	1	1	0	0	1	0
TOTAL	1	1	0	0	1	0

#	SEASON	DATE	COMPETITION / ROUND	MATCH RESULT	VENUE	ATT
1	1999/00	30/11/99	Inter-Continental Cup Final	Manchester United 1 Palmeiras 0	Olympic Stadium Tokyo	53372

UNITED v PANATHINAIKOS

CHAMPIONS LEAGUE

VENUE	P	W	D	L	F	A
HOME	2	2	0	0	8	1
AWAY	2	1	1	0	2	1
TOTAL	4	3	1	0	10	2

#	SEASON	DATE	COMPETITION / ROUND	MATCH RESULT	VENUE	ATT
1	2000/01	21/11/00	Champions League Phase 2 Match 1	Manchester United 3 Panathinaikos 1	Old Trafford	65024
2	2000/01	07/03/01	Champions League Phase 2 Match 5	Panathinaikos 1 Manchester United 1	Olympic Stadium	27231
3	2003/04	16/09/03	Champions League Phase 1 Match 1	Manchester United 5 Panathinaikos 0	Old Trafford	66520
4	2003/04	26/11/03	Champions League Phase 1 Match 5	Panathinaikos 0 Manchester United 1	Apostolos Nikolaidis	6890

UNITED v PARTIZAN BELGRADE

EUROPEAN CUP

VENUE	P	W	D	L	F	A
HOME	1	1	0	0	1	0
AWAY	1	0	0	1	0	2
TOTAL	2	1	0	1	1	2

#	SEASON	DATE	COMPETITION / ROUND	MATCH RESULT	VENUE	ATT
1	1965/66	13/04/66	European Cup Semi-Final 1st Leg	Partizan Belgrade 2 Manchester United 0	Stadion JNA	60000
2	1965/66	20/04/66	European Cup Semi-Final 2nd Leg	Manchester United 1 Partizan Belgrade 0	Old Trafford	62500

UNITED v PECSI MUNKAS

EUROPEAN CUP-WINNERS' CUP

VENUE	P	W	D	L	F	A
HOME	1	1	0	0	2	0
AWAY	1	1	0	0	1	0
TOTAL	2	2	0	0	3	0

#	SEASON	DATE	COMPETITION / ROUND	MATCH RESULT	VENUE	ATT
1	1990/91	19/09/90	European CWC 1st Round 1st Leg	Manchester United 2 Pecsi Munkas 0	Old Trafford	28411
2	1990/91	03/10/90	European CWC 1st Round 2nd Leg	Pecsi Munkas 0 Manchester United 1	PMSC Stadion	17000

UNITED v PETERBOROUGH UNITED

FA CUP

VENUE	P	W	D	L	F	A
HOME	1	1	0	0	3	1
AWAY	0	0	0	0	0	0
TOTAL	1	1	0	0	3	1

#	SEASON	DATE	COMPETITION / ROUND	MATCH RESULT	VENUE	ATT
1	1975/76	24/01/76	FA Cup 4th Round	Manchester United 3 Peterborough United 1	Old Trafford	56352

UNITED v PLYMOUTH ARGYLE

ALL COMPETITIVE MATCHES

VENUE	P	W	D	L	F	A
HOME	8	6	1	1	14	7
AWAY	8	3	1	4	11	17
TOTAL	16	9	2	5	25	24

LEAGUE DIVISION TWO

VENUE	P	W	D	L	F	A
HOME	6	4	1	1	12	7
AWAY	6	2	1	3	8	13
TOTAL	12	6	2	4	20	20

FA CUP

VENUE	P	W	D	L	F	A
HOME	2	2	0	0	2	0
AWAY	2	1	0	1	3	4
TOTAL	4	3	0	1	5	4

#	SEASON	DATE	COMPETITION / ROUND	MATCH RESULT	VENUE	ATT
1	1912/13	01/02/13	FA Cup 2nd Round	Plymouth Argyle 0 Manchester United 2	Home Park	21700
2	1923/24	12/01/24	FA Cup 1st Round	Manchester United 1 Plymouth Argyle 0	Old Trafford	35700
3	1931/32	31/10/31	Football League Division 2	Plymouth Argyle 3 Manchester United 1	Home Park	22555
4	1931/32	09/01/32	FA Cup 3rd Round	Plymouth Argyle 4 Manchester United 1	Home Park	28000
5	1931/32	12/03/32	Football League Division 2	Manchester United 2 Plymouth Argyle 1	Old Trafford	24827
6	1932/33	26/12/32	Football League Division 2	Plymouth Argyle 2 Manchester United 3	Home Park	33776
7	1932/33	02/01/33	Football League Division 2	Manchester United 4 Plymouth Argyle 0	Old Trafford	30257
8	1933/34	26/08/33	Football League Division 2	Plymouth Argyle 4 Manchester United 0	Home Park	25700
9	1933/34	30/12/33	Football League Division 2	Manchester United 0 Plymouth Argyle 3	Old Trafford	12206
10	1934/35	22/12/34	Football League Division 2	Manchester United 3 Plymouth Argyle 1	Old Trafford	24896
11	1934/35	04/05/35	Football League Division 2	Plymouth Argyle 0 Manchester United 2	Home Park	10767
12	1935/36	31/08/35	Football League Division 2	Plymouth Argyle 3 Manchester United 1	Home Park	22366
13	1935/36	28/12/35	Football League Division 2	Manchester United 3 Plymouth Argyle 2	Old Trafford	20894
14	1937/38	06/11/37	Football League Division 2	Manchester United 0 Plymouth Argyle 0	Old Trafford	18359
15	1937/38	19/03/38	Football League Division 2	Plymouth Argyle 1 Manchester United 1	Home Park	20311
16	1973/74	05/01/74	FA Cup 3rd Round	Manchester United 1 Plymouth Argyle 0	Old Trafford	31810

UNITED v PORT VALE

ALL COMPETITIVE MATCHES

VENUE	P	W	D	L	F	A
HOME	21	19	1	1	58	10
AWAY	24	11	4	9	39	32
TOTAL	45	30	5	10	97	42

LEAGUE DIVISION TWO

VENUE	P	W	D	L	F	A
HOME	18	16	1	1	52	10
AWAY	18	5	4	9	24	27
TOTAL	36	21	5	10	76	37

ALL CUP MATCHES

VENUE	P	W	D	L	F	A
HOME	3	3	0	0	6	0
AWAY	6	6	0	0	15	5
TOTAL	9	9	0	0	21	5

FA CUP

VENUE	P	W	D	L	F	A
HOME	0	0	0	0	0	0
AWAY	3	3	0	0	7	2
TOTAL	3	3	0	0	7	2

LEAGUE CUP

VENUE	P	W	D	L	F	A
HOME	3	3	0	0	6	0
AWAY	3	3	0	0	8	3
TOTAL	6	6	0	0	14	3

#	SEASON	DATE	COMPETITION / ROUND	MATCH RESULT	VENUE	ATT
1	1894/95	24/12/94	Football League Division 2	Port Vale 2 Newton Heath 5	Cobridge Stadium	1000
2	1894/95	01/01/95	Football League Division 2	Newton Heath 3 Port Vale 0	Bank Street	5000
3	1895/96	23/03/96	Football League Division 2	Port Vale 3 Newton Heath 0	Cobridge Stadium	3000
4	1895/96	06/04/96	Football League Division 2	Newton Heath 2 Port Vale 1	Bank Street	5000
5	1898/99	08/10/98	Football League Division 2	Newton Heath 2 Port Vale 1	Bank Street	10000
6	1898/99	04/02/99	Football League Division 2	Port Vale 1 Newton Heath 0	Cobridge Stadium	6000
7	1899/00	02/12/99	Football League Division 2	Newton Heath 3 Port Vale 0	Bank Street	5000
8	1899/00	07/04/00	Football League Division 2	Port Vale 1 Newton Heath 0	Cobridge Stadium	3000
9	1900/01	22/09/00	Football League Division 2	Newton Heath 4 Port Vale 0	Bank Street	6000
10	1900/01	19/01/01	Football League Division 2	Port Vale 2 Newton Heath 0	Cobridge Stadium	1000
11	1901/02	21/12/01	Football League Division 2	Newton Heath 1 Port Vale 0	Bank Street	3000
12	1901/02	19/04/02	Football League Division 2	Port Vale 1 Newton Heath 1	Cobridge Stadium	2000
13	1902/03	20/12/02	Football League Division 2	Port Vale 1 Manchester United 1	Cobridge Stadium	1000
14	1902/03	18/04/03	Football League Division 2	Manchester United 2 Port Vale 1	Bank Street	8000
15	1903/04	12/09/03	Football League Division 2	Port Vale 1 Manchester United 0	Cobridge Stadium	3000
16	1903/04	09/01/04	Football League Division 2	Manchester United 2 Port Vale 0	Bank Street	10000
17	1904/05	03/09/04	Football League Division 2	Port Vale 2 Manchester United 2	Cobridge Stadium	4000
18	1904/05	31/12/04	Football League Division 2	Manchester United 6 Port Vale 1	Bank Street	8000
19	1905/06	18/11/05	Football League Division 2	Manchester United 3 Port Vale 0	Bank Street	8000
20	1905/06	24/03/06	Football League Division 2	Port Vale 1 Manchester United 0	Cobridge Stadium	3000
21	1919/20	10/01/20	FA Cup 1st Round	Port Vale 0 Manchester United 1	Old Recreation Ground	14549
22	1922/23	07/10/22	Football League Division 2	Manchester United 1 Port Vale 2	Old Trafford	25000
23	1922/23	14/10/22	Football League Division 2	Port Vale 1 Manchester United 0	Old Recreation Ground	16000

UNITED v PORT VALE (continued)

#	SEASON	DATE	COMPETITION / ROUND	MATCH RESULT	VENUE	ATT
24	1923/24	15/12/23	Football League Division 2	Port Vale 0 Manchester United 1	Old Recreation Ground	7500
25	1923/24	22/12/23	Football League Division 2	Manchester United 5 Port Vale 0	Old Trafford	11750
26	1924/25	20/12/24	Football League Division 2	Port Vale 2 Manchester United 1	Old Recreation Ground	11000
27	1924/25	25/04/25	Football League Division 2	Manchester United 4 Port Vale 0	Old Trafford	33500
28	1925/26	09/01/26	FA Cup 3rd Round	Port Vale 2 Manchester United 3	Old Recreation Ground	14841
29	1928/29	12/01/29	FA Cup 3rd Round	Port Vale 0 Manchester United 3	Old Recreation Ground	17519
30	1931/32	28/11/31	Football League Division 2	Port Vale 1 Manchester United 2	Old Recreation Ground	6955
31	1931/32	09/04/32	Football League Division 2	Manchester United 2 Port Vale 0	Old Trafford	10916
32	1932/33	29/10/32	Football League Division 2	Port Vale 3 Manchester United 3	Old Recreation Ground	7138
33	1932/33	11/03/33	Football League Division 2	Manchester United 1 Port Vale 1	Old Trafford	24690
34	1933/34	02/12/33	Football League Division 2	Port Vale 2 Manchester United 3	Old Recreation Ground	10316
35	1933/34	14/04/34	Football League Division 2	Manchester United 2 Port Vale 0	Old Trafford	14777
36	1934/35	15/09/34	Football League Division 2	Port Vale 3 Manchester United 2	Old Recreation Ground	9307
37	1934/35	06/02/35	Football League Division 2	Manchester United 2 Port Vale 1	Old Trafford	7372
38	1935/36	05/10/35	Football League Division 2	Port Vale 0 Manchester United 3	Old Recreation Ground	9703
39	1935/36	08/02/36	Football League Division 2	Manchester United 7 Port Vale 2	Old Trafford	22265
40	1983/84	03/10/83	League Cup 2nd Round 1st Leg	Port Vale 0 Manchester United 1	Vale Park	19885
41	1983/84	26/10/83	League Cup 2nd Round 2nd Leg	Manchester United 2 Port Vale 0	Old Trafford	23589
42	1986/87	24/09/86	League Cup 2nd Round 1st Leg	Manchester United 2 Port Vale 0	Old Trafford	18906
43	1986/87	07/10/86	League Cup 2nd Round 2nd Leg	Port Vale 2 Manchester United 5	Vale Park	10486
44	1994/95	21/09/94	League Cup 2nd Round 1st Leg	Port Vale 1 Manchester United 2	Vale Park	18605
45	1994/95	05/10/94	League Cup 2nd Round 2nd Leg	Manchester United 2 Port Vale 0	Old Trafford	31615

UNITED v PORTO

ALL COMPETITIVE MATCHES						CHAMPIONS LEAGUE						EUROPEAN CUP-WINNERS' CUP					
VENUE	P	W	D	L	F	A	VENUE	P	W	D	L	F	A	VENUE	P	W	D	L	F	A

VENUE	P	W	D	L	F	A
HOME	3	2	1	0	10	3
AWAY	3	0	1	2	1	6
TOTAL	6	2	2	2	11	9

VENUE	P	W	D	L	F	A
HOME	2	1	1	0	5	1
AWAY	2	0	1	1	1	2
TOTAL	4	1	2	1	6	3

VENUE	P	W	D	L	F	A
HOME	1	1	0	0	5	2
AWAY	1	0	0	1	0	4
TOTAL	2	1	0	1	5	6

#	SEASON	DATE	COMPETITION / ROUND	MATCH RESULT	VENUE	ATT
1	1977/78	19/10/77	European CWC 2nd Round 1st Leg	Porto 4 Manchester United 0	Estadio das Antas	70000
2	1977/78	02/11/77	European CWC 2nd Round 2nd Leg	Manchester United 5 Porto 2	Old Trafford	51831
3	1996/97	05/03/97	Champions League Quarter-Final 1st Leg	Manchester United 4 Porto 0	Old Trafford	53425
4	1996/97	19/03/97	Champions League Quarter-Final 2nd Leg	Porto 0 Manchester United 0	Estadio das Antas	40000
5	2003/04	25/02/04	Champions League 2nd Round 1st Leg	Porto 2 Manchester United 1	Estadio da Dragao	49977
6	2003/04	09/03/04	Champions League 2nd Round 2nd Leg	Manchester United 1 Porto 1	Old Trafford	67029

UNITED v PORTSMOUTH

ALL COMPETITIVE MATCHES

VENUE	P	W	D	L	F	A
HOME	38	23	7	8	71	34
AWAY	32	9	11	12	38	46
TOTAL	70	32	18	20	109	80

ALL LEAGUE MATCHES

VENUE	P	W	D	L	F	A
HOME	27	18	3	6	51	22
AWAY	27	6	10	11	28	37
TOTAL	54	24	13	17	79	59

ALL CUP MATCHES

VENUE	P	W	D	L	F	A
HOME	11	5	4	2	20	12
AWAY	5	3	1	1	10	9
TOTAL	16	8	5	3	30	21

PREMIERSHIP

VENUE	P	W	D	L	F	A
HOME	5	5	0	0	13	1
AWAY	5	1	1	3	5	7
TOTAL	10	6	1	3	18	8

LEAGUE DIVISION ONE

VENUE	P	W	D	L	F	A
HOME	20	11	3	6	34	20
AWAY	20	5	7	8	22	29
TOTAL	40	16	10	14	56	49

LEAGUE DIVISION TWO

VENUE	P	W	D	L	F	A
HOME	2	2	0	0	4	1
AWAY	2	0	2	0	1	1
TOTAL	4	2	2	0	5	2

FA CUP

VENUE	P	W	D	L	F	A
HOME	7	3	2	2	14	9
AWAY	3	1	1	1	6	7
TOTAL	10	4	3	3	20	16

LEAGUE CUP

VENUE	P	W	D	L	F	A
HOME	4	2	2	0	6	3
AWAY	2	2	0	0	4	2
TOTAL	6	4	2	0	10	5

#	SEASON	DATE	COMPETITION / ROUND	MATCH RESULT	VENUE	ATT
1	1900/01	05/01/01	FA Cup Supplementary Round	Newton Heath 3 Portsmouth 0	Bank Street	5000
2	1906/07	12/01/07	FA Cup 1st Round	Portsmouth 2 Manchester United 2	Fratton Park	24329
3	1906/07	16/01/07	FA Cup 1st Round Replay	Manchester United 1 Portsmouth 2	Bank Street	8000
4	1924/25	08/11/24	Football League Division 2	Portsmouth 1 Manchester United 1	Fratton Park	19500
5	1924/25	14/03/25	Football League Division 2	Manchester United 2 Portsmouth 0	Old Trafford	22000
6	1927/28	05/11/27	Football League Division 1	Manchester United 2 Portsmouth 0	Old Trafford	13119
7	1927/28	17/03/28	Football League Division 1	Portsmouth 1 Manchester United 0	Fratton Park	25400
8	1928/29	22/12/28	Football League Division 1	Portsmouth 3 Manchester United 0	Fratton Park	12836
9	1928/29	04/05/29	Football League Division 1	Manchester United 0 Portsmouth 0	Old Trafford	17728
10	1929/30	19/10/29	Football League Division 1	Portsmouth 3 Manchester United 0	Fratton Park	18070
11	1929/30	22/02/30	Football League Division 1	Manchester United 3 Portsmouth 0	Old Trafford	17317
12	1930/31	25/10/30	Football League Division 1	Portsmouth 4 Manchester United 1	Fratton Park	19262
13	1930/31	16/03/31	Football League Division 1	Manchester United 0 Portsmouth 1	Old Trafford	4808
14	1933/34	13/01/34	FA Cup 3rd Round	Manchester United 1 Portsmouth 1	Old Trafford	23283
15	1933/34	17/01/34	FA Cup 3rd Round Replay	Portsmouth 4 Manchester United 1	Fratton Park	18748
16	1936/37	17/10/36	Football League Division 1	Portsmouth 2 Manchester United 1	Fratton Park	19845
17	1936/37	20/02/37	Football League Division 1	Manchester United 0 Portsmouth 1	Old Trafford	19416
18	1938/39	03/12/38	Football League Division 1	Portsmouth 0 Manchester United 0	Fratton Park	18692
19	1938/39	08/04/39	Football League Division 1	Manchester United 1 Portsmouth 1	Old Trafford	25457
20	1946/47	26/04/47	Football League Division 1	Portsmouth 0 Manchester United 1	Fratton Park	30623
21	1946/47	17/05/47	Football League Division 1	Manchester United 3 Portsmouth 0	Maine Road	37614
22	1947/48	25/12/47	Football League Division 1	Manchester United 3 Portsmouth 2	Maine Road	42776
23	1947/48	27/12/47	Football League Division 1	Portsmouth 1 Manchester United 3	Fratton Park	27674
24	1948/49	11/12/48	Football League Division 1	Portsmouth 2 Manchester United 2	Fratton Park	29966
25	1948/49	07/05/49	Football League Division 1	Manchester United 3 Portsmouth 2	Maine Road	49808
26	1949/50	29/10/49	Football League Division 1	Portsmouth 0 Manchester United 0	Fratton Park	41098
27	1949/50	11/02/50	FA Cup 5th Round	Manchester United 3 Portsmouth 3	Old Trafford	53688
28	1949/50	15/02/50	FA Cup 5th Round Replay	Portsmouth 1 Manchester United 3	Fratton Park	49962
29	1949/50	15/04/50	Football League Division 1	Manchester United 0 Portsmouth 2	Old Trafford	44908
30	1950/51	21/10/50	Football League Division 1	Manchester United 0 Portsmouth 0	Old Trafford	41842
31	1950/51	10/03/51	Football League Division 1	Portsmouth 0 Manchester United 0	Fratton Park	33148
32	1951/52	17/11/51	Football League Division 1	Manchester United 1 Portsmouth 3	Old Trafford	35914
33	1951/52	05/04/52	Football League Division 1	Portsmouth 1 Manchester United 0	Fratton Park	25522
34	1952/53	06/09/52	Football League Division 1	Portsmouth 2 Manchester United 0	Fratton Park	37278
35	1952/53	17/01/53	Football League Division 1	Manchester United 1 Portsmouth 0	Old Trafford	32341
36	1953/54	28/11/53	Football League Division 1	Portsmouth 1 Manchester United 1	Fratton Park	29233
37	1953/54	17/04/54	Football League Division 1	Manchester United 2 Portsmouth 0	Old Trafford	29663
38	1954/55	21/08/54	Football League Division 1	Manchester United 1 Portsmouth 3	Old Trafford	38203
39	1954/55	18/12/54	Football League Division 1	Portsmouth 0 Manchester United 0	Fratton Park	26019
40	1955/56	10/12/55	Football League Division 1	Portsmouth 3 Manchester United 2	Fratton Park	24594
41	1955/56	21/04/56	Football League Division 1	Manchester United 1 Portsmouth 0	Old Trafford	38417
42	1956/57	01/09/56	Football League Division 1	Manchester United 3 Portsmouth 0	Old Trafford	40369
43	1956/57	29/12/56	Football League Division 1	Portsmouth 1 Manchester United 3	Fratton Park	32147
44	1957/58	19/10/57	Football League Division 1	Manchester United 0 Portsmouth 3	Old Trafford	38253
45	1957/58	16/04/58	Football League Division 1	Portsmouth 3 Manchester United 3	Fratton Park	39975

UNITED v PORTSMOUTH (continued)

#	SEASON	DATE	COMPETITION / ROUND	MATCH RESULT	VENUE	ATT
46	1958/59	27/03/59	Football League Division 1	Manchester United 6 Portsmouth 1	Old Trafford	52004
47	1958/59	30/03/59	Football League Division 1	Portsmouth 1 Manchester United 3	Fratton Park	29359
48	1970/71	07/10/70	League Cup 3rd Round	Manchester United 1 Portsmouth 0	Old Trafford	32068
49	1974/75	28/08/74	Football League Division 2	Manchester United 2 Portsmouth 1	Old Trafford	42547
50	1974/75	15/10/74	Football League Division 2	Portsmouth 0 Manchester United 0	Fratton Park	25608
51	1987/88	19/12/87	Football League Division 1	Portsmouth 1 Manchester United 2	Fratton Park	22207
52	1987/88	07/05/88	Football League Division 1	Manchester United 4 Portsmouth 1	Old Trafford	35105
53	1989/90	20/09/89	League Cup 2nd Round 1st Leg	Portsmouth 2 Manchester United 3	Fratton Park	18072
54	1989/90	03/10/89	League Cup 2nd Round 2nd Leg	Manchester United 0 Portsmouth 0	Old Trafford	26698
55	1991/92	30/10/91	League Cup 3rd Round	Manchester United 3 Portsmouth 1	Old Trafford	29543
56	1993/94	12/01/94	League Cup 5th Round	Manchester United 2 Portsmouth 2	Old Trafford	43794
57	1993/94	26/01/94	League Cup 5th Round Replay	Portsmouth 0 Manchester United 1	Fratton Park	24950
58	2002/03	04/01/03	FA Cup 3rd Round	Manchester United 4 Portsmouth 1	Old Trafford	67222
59	2003/04	01/11/03	FA Premiership	Manchester United 3 Portsmouth 0	Old Trafford	67639
60	2003/04	17/04/04	FA Premiership	Portsmouth 1 Manchester United 0	Fratton Park	20140
61	2004/05	30/10/04	FA Premiership	Portsmouth 2 Manchester United 0	Fratton Park	20190
62	2004/05	26/02/05	FA Premiership	Manchester United 2 Portsmouth 1	Old Trafford	67989
63	2005/06	03/12/05	FA Premiership	Manchester United 3 Portsmouth 0	Old Trafford	67684
64	2005/06	11/02/06	FA Premiership	Portsmouth 1 Manchester United 3	Fratton Park	20206
65	2006/07	04/11/06	FA Premiership	Manchester United 3 Portsmouth 0	Old Trafford	76004
66	2006/07	27/01/07	FA Cup 4th Round	Manchester United 2 Portsmouth 1	Old Trafford	71137
67	2006/07	07/04/07	FA Premiership	Portsmouth 2 Manchester United 1	Fratton Park	20223
68	2007/08	15/08/07	FA Premiership	Portsmouth 1 Manchester United 1	Fratton Park	20510
69	2007/08	30/01/08	FA Premiership	Manchester United 2 Portsmouth 0	Old Trafford	75415
70	2007/08	08/03/08	FA Cup 6th Round	Manchester United 0 Portsmouth 1	Old Trafford	75463

UNITED v PRESTON NORTH END

ALL COMPETITIVE MATCHES							ALL LEAGUE MATCHES							FA CUP						
VENUE	P	W	D	L	F	A	VENUE	P	W	D	L	F	A	VENUE	P	W	D	L	F	A
HOME	37	19	11	7	61	39	HOME	33	15	11	7	51	35	HOME	4	4	0	0	10	4
AWAY	38	12	11	15	61	65	AWAY	33	11	9	13	56	55	AWAY	5	1	2	2	5	10
TOTAL	75	31	22	22	122	104	TOTAL	66	26	20	20	107	90	TOTAL	9	5	2	2	15	14

LEAGUE DIVISION ONE							LEAGUE DIVISION TWO						
VENUE	P	W	D	L	F	A	VENUE	P	W	D	L	F	A
HOME	27	13	10	4	47	28	HOME	6	2	1	3	4	7
AWAY	27	11	6	10	48	40	AWAY	6	0	3	3	8	15
TOTAL	54	24	16	14	95	68	TOTAL	12	2	4	6	12	22

#	SEASON	DATE	COMPETITION / ROUND	MATCH RESULT	VENUE	ATT
1	1889/90	18/01/90	FA Cup 1st Round	Preston North End 6 Newton Heath 1	Deepdale	7900
2	1892/93	26/12/92	Football League Division 1	Preston North End 2 Newton Heath 1	Deepdale	4000
3	1892/93	01/04/93	Football League Division 1	Newton Heath 2 Preston North End 1	North Road	9000
4	1893/94	23/12/93	Football League Division 1	Preston North End 2 Newton Heath 0	Deepdale	5000
5	1893/94	14/04/94	Football League Division 1	Newton Heath 1 Preston North End 3	Bank Street	4000
6	1901/02	07/12/01	Football League Division 2	Preston North End 5 Newton Heath 1	Deepdale	2000
7	1901/02	01/01/02	Football League Division 2	Newton Heath 0 Preston North End 2	Bank Street	10000
8	1902/03	30/03/03	Football League Division 2	Manchester United 0 Preston North End 1	Bank Street	3000
9	1902/03	11/04/03	Football League Division 2	Preston North End 3 Manchester United 1	Deepdale	7000
10	1903/04	21/11/03	Football League Division 2	Manchester United 0 Preston North End 2	Bank Street	15000
11	1903/04	19/03/04	Football League Division 2	Preston North End 1 Manchester United 1	Deepdale	7000
12	1906/07	15/12/06	Football League Division 1	Preston North End 2 Manchester United 0	Deepdale	9000
13	1906/07	23/02/07	Football League Division 1	Manchester United 3 Preston North End 0	Bank Street	16000
14	1907/08	28/12/07	Football League Division 1	Preston North End 0 Manchester United 0	Deepdale	12000
15	1907/08	25/04/08	Football League Division 1	Manchester United 2 Preston North End 1	Bank Street	8000
16	1908/09	05/09/08	Football League Division 1	Preston North End 0 Manchester United 3	Deepdale	18000
17	1908/09	02/01/09	Football League Division 1	Manchester United 0 Preston North End 2	Bank Street	18000
18	1909/10	18/09/09	Football League Division 1	Manchester United 1 Preston North End 1	Bank Street	13000
19	1909/10	05/02/10	Football League Division 1	Preston North End 1 Manchester United 0	Deepdale	4000

UNITED v PRESTON NORTH END (continued)

#	SEASON	DATE	COMPETITION / ROUND	MATCH RESULT	VENUE	ATT
20	1910/11	05/11/10	Football League Division 1	Preston North End 0 Manchester United 2	Deepdale	13000
21	1910/11	11/03/11	Football League Division 1	Manchester United 5 Preston North End 0	Old Trafford	25000
22	1911/12	11/11/11	Football League Division 1	Manchester United 0 Preston North End 0	Old Trafford	10000
23	1911/12	16/03/12	Football League Division 1	Preston North End 0 Manchester United 0	Deepdale	7000
24	1913/14	18/10/13	Football League Division 1	Manchester United 3 Preston North End 0	Old Trafford	30000
25	1913/14	05/03/14	Football League Division 1	Preston North End 4 Manchester United 2	Deepdale	12000
26	1919/20	13/09/19	Football League Division 1	Preston North End 2 Manchester United 3	Deepdale	15000
27	1919/20	20/09/19	Football League Division 1	Manchester United 5 Preston North End 1	Old Trafford	18000
28	1920/21	23/10/20	Football League Division 1	Manchester United 1 Preston North End 0	Old Trafford	42000
29	1920/21	30/10/20	Football League Division 1	Preston North End 0 Manchester United 0	Deepdale	25000
30	1921/22	24/09/21	Football League Division 1	Preston North End 3 Manchester United 2	Deepdale	25000
31	1921/22	01/10/21	Football League Division 1	Manchester United 1 Preston North End 1	Old Trafford	30000
32	1931/32	10/10/31	Football League Division 2	Manchester United 3 Preston North End 2	Old Trafford	8496
33	1931/32	20/02/32	Football League Division 2	Preston North End 0 Manchester United 0	Deepdale	13353
34	1932/33	01/10/32	Football League Division 2	Manchester United 0 Preston North End 0	Old Trafford	20800
35	1932/33	11/02/33	Football League Division 2	Preston North End 3 Manchester United 3	Deepdale	15662
36	1933/34	07/10/33	Football League Division 2	Manchester United 1 Preston North End 0	Old Trafford	22303
37	1933/34	21/02/34	Football League Division 2	Preston North End 3 Manchester United 2	Deepdale	9173
38	1936/37	26/09/36	Football League Division 1	Preston North End 3 Manchester United 1	Deepdale	24149
39	1936/37	03/02/37	Football League Division 1	Manchester United 1 Preston North End 1	Old Trafford	13225
40	1938/39	01/10/38	Football League Division 1	Preston North End 1 Manchester United 1	Deepdale	25964
41	1938/39	04/02/39	Football League Division 1	Manchester United 1 Preston North End 1	Old Trafford	41061
42	1945/46	26/01/46	FA Cup 4th Round 1st Leg	Manchester United 1 Preston North End 0	Maine Road	36237
43	1945/46	30/01/46	FA Cup 4th Round 2nd Leg	Preston North End 3 Manchester United 1	Deepdale	21000
44	1946/47	05/10/46	Football League Division 1	Manchester United 1 Preston North End 1	Maine Road	55395
45	1946/47	10/05/47	Football League Division 1	Preston North End 1 Manchester United 1	Deepdale	23278
46	1947/48	27/09/47	Football League Division 1	Preston North End 2 Manchester United 1	Deepdale	34372
47	1947/48	14/02/48	Football League Division 1	Manchester United 1 Preston North End 1	Maine Road	61765
48	1947/48	28/02/48	FA Cup 6th Round	Manchester United 4 Preston North End 2	Maine Road	74213
49	1948/49	30/10/48	Football League Division 1	Preston North End 1 Manchester United 6	Deepdale	37372
50	1948/49	23/04/49	Football League Division 1	Manchester United 2 Preston North End 2	Maine Road	43214
51	1951/52	29/09/51	Football League Division 1	Manchester United 1 Preston North End 2	Old Trafford	53454
52	1951/52	09/02/52	Football League Division 1	Preston North End 1 Manchester United 2	Deepdale	38792
53	1952/53	18/10/52	Football League Division 1	Preston North End 0 Manchester United 5	Deepdale	33502
54	1952/53	07/03/53	Football League Division 1	Manchester United 5 Preston North End 2	Old Trafford	52590
55	1953/54	19/09/53	Football League Division 1	Manchester United 1 Preston North End 0	Old Trafford	41171
56	1953/54	06/02/54	Football League Division 1	Preston North End 1 Manchester United 3	Deepdale	30064
57	1954/55	06/11/54	Football League Division 1	Manchester United 2 Preston North End 1	Old Trafford	30063
58	1954/55	26/03/55	Football League Division 1	Preston North End 0 Manchester United 2	Deepdale	13327
59	1955/56	17/09/55	Football League Division 1	Manchester United 3 Preston North End 2	Old Trafford	33078
60	1955/56	21/01/56	Football League Division 1	Preston North End 3 Manchester United 1	Deepdale	28047
61	1956/57	20/08/56	Football League Division 1	Preston North End 1 Manchester United 3	Deepdale	32569
62	1956/57	29/08/56	Football League Division 1	Manchester United 3 Preston North End 2	Old Trafford	32515
63	1957/58	09/11/57	Football League Division 1	Preston North End 1 Manchester United 1	Deepdale	39063
64	1957/58	05/04/58	Football League Division 1	Manchester United 0 Preston North End 0	Old Trafford	47816
65	1958/59	08/10/58	Football League Division 1	Manchester United 0 Preston North End 2	Old Trafford	46163
66	1958/59	13/12/58	Football League Division 1	Preston North End 3 Manchester United 4	Deepdale	26290
67	1959/60	26/09/59	Football League Division 1	Preston North End 4 Manchester United 0	Deepdale	35016
68	1959/60	13/02/60	Football League Division 1	Manchester United 1 Preston North End 1	Old Trafford	44014
69	1960/61	03/12/60	Football League Division 1	Manchester United 1 Preston North End 0	Old Trafford	24904
70	1960/61	22/04/61	Football League Division 1	Preston North End 2 Manchester United 4	Deepdale	21252
71	1961/62	10/03/62	FA Cup 6th Round	Preston North End 0 Manchester United 0	Deepdale	37521
72	1961/62	14/03/62	FA Cup 6th Round Replay	Manchester United 2 Preston North End 1	Old Trafford	63468
73	1965/66	26/03/66	FA Cup 6th Round	Preston North End 1 Manchester United 1	Deepdale	37876
74	1965/66	30/03/66	FA Cup 6th Round Replay	Manchester United 3 Preston North End 1	Old Trafford	60433
75	1971/72	05/02/72	FA Cup 4th Round	Preston North End 0 Manchester United 2	Deepdale	27025

UNITED v PSV EINDHOVEN

ALL COMPETITIVE MATCHES							CHAMPIONS LEAGUE							UEFA CUP					
VENUE	P	W	D	L	F	A	VENUE	P	W	D	L	F	A	VENUE	P	W	D	L	F	A
HOME	2	2	0	0	4	1	HOME	1	1	0	0	3	1	HOME	1	1	0	0	1	0
AWAY	2	0	1	1	1	3	AWAY	1	0	0	1	1	3	AWAY	1	0	1	0	0	0
TOTAL	4	2	1	1	5	4	TOTAL	2	1	0	1	4	4	TOTAL	2	1	1	0	1	0

#	SEASON	DATE	COMPETITION / ROUND	MATCH RESULT	VENUE	ATT
1	1984/85	24/10/84	UEFA Cup 2nd Round 1st Leg	PSV Eindhoven 0 Manchester United 0	Philipstadion	27500
2	1984/85	07/11/84	UEFA Cup 2nd Round 2nd Leg	Manchester United 1 PSV Eindhoven 0	Old Trafford	39281
3	2000/01	26/09/00	Champions League Phase 1 Match 3	PSV Eindhoven 3 Manchester United 1	Philipstadion	30500
4	2000/01	18/10/00	Champions League Phase 1 Match 4	Manchester United 3 PSV Eindhoven 1	Old Trafford	66313

UNITED v QUEENS PARK RANGERS

ALL COMPETITIVE MATCHES							ALL LEAGUE MATCHES							FA CUP					
VENUE	P	W	D	L	F	A	VENUE	P	W	D	L	F	A	VENUE	P	W	D	L	F	A
HOME	24	19	4	1	47	14	HOME	19	15	3	1	39	13	HOME	5	4	1	0	8	1
AWAY	20	7	8	5	30	30	AWAY	19	7	7	5	28	28	AWAY	1	0	1	0	2	2
NEUTRAL	2	1	1	0	5	1								NEUTRAL	0	0	0	0	0	0
TOTAL	46	27	13	6	82	45	TOTAL	38	22	10	6	67	41	TOTAL	6	4	2	0	10	3

PREMIERSHIP							LEAGUE DIVISION ONE							CHARITY SHIELD					
VENUE	P	W	D	L	F	A	VENUE	P	W	D	L	F	A	VENUE	P	W	D	L	F	A
HOME	4	3	1	0	6	2	HOME	15	12	2	1	33	11	HOME	0	0	0	0	0	0
AWAY	4	3	1	0	10	6	AWAY	15	4	6	5	18	22	AWAY	0	0	0	0	0	0
														NEUTRAL	2	1	1	0	5	1
TOTAL	8	6	2	0	16	8	TOTAL	30	16	8	6	51	33	TOTAL	2	1	1	0	5	1

#	SEASON	DATE	COMPETITION / ROUND	MATCH RESULT	VENUE	ATT
1	1907/08	27/04/08	FA Charity Shield	Manchester United 1 Queens Park Rangers 1	Stamford Bridge	6000
2	1907/08	29/04/08	FA Charity Shield Replay	Manchester United 4 Queens Park Rangers 0	Stamford Bridge	6000
3	1968/69	26/10/68	Football League Division 1	Queens Park Rangers 2 Manchester United 3	Loftus Road	31138
4	1968/69	19/03/69	Football League Division 1	Manchester United 8 Queens Park Rangers 1	Old Trafford	36638
5	1973/74	01/09/73	Football League Division 1	Manchester United 2 Queens Park Rangers 1	Old Trafford	44156
6	1973/74	01/01/74	Football League Division 1	Queens Park Rangers 3 Manchester United 0	Loftus Road	32339
7	1975/76	13/09/75	Football League Division 1	Queens Park Rangers 1 Manchester United 0	Loftus Road	29237
8	1975/76	10/01/76	Football League Division 1	Manchester United 2 Queens Park Rangers 1	Old Trafford	58302
9	1976/77	29/01/77	FA Cup 4th Round	Manchester United 1 Queens Park Rangers 0	Old Trafford	57422
10	1976/77	19/04/77	Football League Division 1	Queens Park Rangers 4 Manchester United 0	Loftus Road	28848
11	1976/77	30/04/77	Football League Division 1	Manchester United 1 Queens Park Rangers 0	Old Trafford	50788
12	1977/78	26/11/77	Football League Division 1	Queens Park Rangers 2 Manchester United 2	Loftus Road	25367
13	1977/78	08/04/78	Football League Division 1	Manchester United 3 Queens Park Rangers 1	Old Trafford	42677
14	1978/79	09/09/78	Football League Division 1	Queens Park Rangers 1 Manchester United 1	Loftus Road	23477
15	1978/79	28/02/79	Football League Division 1	Manchester United 2 Queens Park Rangers 0	Old Trafford	36085
16	1983/84	27/08/83	Football League Division 1	Manchester United 3 Queens Park Rangers 1	Old Trafford	48742
17	1983/84	13/01/84	Football League Division 1	Queens Park Rangers 1 Manchester United 1	Loftus Road	16308
18	1984/85	15/12/84	Football League Division 1	Manchester United 3 Queens Park Rangers 0	Old Trafford	36134
19	1984/85	11/05/85	Football League Division 1	Queens Park Rangers 1 Manchester United 3	Loftus Road	20483
20	1985/86	12/10/85	Football League Division 1	Manchester United 2 Queens Park Rangers 0	Old Trafford	48845
21	1985/86	15/03/86	Football League Division 1	Queens Park Rangers 1 Manchester United 0	Loftus Road	23407
22	1986/87	22/11/86	Football League Division 1	Manchester United 1 Queens Park Rangers 0	Old Trafford	42235
23	1986/87	25/04/87	Football League Division 1	Queens Park Rangers 1 Manchester United 1	Loftus Road	17414
24	1987/88	05/12/87	Football League Division 1	Queens Park Rangers 0 Manchester United 2	Loftus Road	20632
25	1987/88	30/04/88	Football League Division 1	Manchester United 2 Queens Park Rangers 1	Old Trafford	35733
26	1988/89	27/08/88	Football League Division 1	Manchester United 0 Queens Park Rangers 0	Old Trafford	46377
27	1988/89	07/01/89	FA Cup 3rd Round	Manchester United 0 Queens Park Rangers 0	Old Trafford	36222
28	1988/89	11/01/89	FA Cup 3rd Round Replay	Queens Park Rangers 2 Manchester United 2	Loftus Road	22236
29	1988/89	23/01/89	FA Cup 3rd Round 2nd Replay	Manchester United 3 Queens Park Rangers 0	Old Trafford	46257
30	1988/89	08/05/89	Football League Division 1	Queens Park Rangers 3 Manchester United 2	Loftus Road	10017
31	1989/90	01/01/90	Football League Division 1	Manchester United 0 Queens Park Rangers 0	Old Trafford	34824
32	1989/90	14/04/90	Football League Division 1	Queens Park Rangers 1 Manchester United 2	Loftus Road	18997
33	1990/91	08/09/90	Football League Division 1	Manchester United 3 Queens Park Rangers 1	Old Trafford	43427
34	1990/91	07/01/91	FA Cup 3rd Round	Manchester United 2 Queens Park Rangers 1	Old Trafford	35065
35	1990/91	19/01/91	Football League Division 1	Queens Park Rangers 1 Manchester United 1	Loftus Road	18544

UNITED v QUEENS PARK RANGERS (continued)

#	SEASON	DATE	COMPETITION / ROUND	MATCH RESULT	VENUE	ATT
36	1991/92	01/01/92	Football League Division 1	Manchester United 1 Queens Park Rangers 4	Old Trafford	38554
37	1991/92	28/03/92	Football League Division 1	Queens Park Rangers 0 Manchester United 0	Loftus Road	22603
38	1992/93	26/09/92	FA Premiership	Manchester United 0 Queens Park Rangers 0	Old Trafford	33287
39	1992/93	18/01/93	FA Premiership	Queens Park Rangers 1 Manchester United 3	Loftus Road	21117
40	1993/94	30/10/93	FA Premiership	Manchester United 2 Queens Park Rangers 1	Old Trafford	44663
41	1993/94	05/02/94	FA Premiership	Queens Park Rangers 2 Manchester United 3	Loftus Road	21267
42	1994/95	20/08/94	FA Premiership	Manchester United 2 Queens Park Rangers 0	Old Trafford	43214
43	1994/95	10/12/94	FA Premiership	Queens Park Rangers 2 Manchester United 3	Loftus Road	18948
44	1994/95	12/03/95	FA Cup 6th Round	Manchester United 2 Queens Park Rangers 0	Old Trafford	42830
45	1995/96	30/12/95	FA Premiership	Manchester United 2 Queens Park Rangers 1	Old Trafford	41890
46	1995/96	16/03/96	FA Premiership	Queens Park Rangers 1 Manchester United 1	Loftus Road	18817

UNITED v RABA VASAS

UEFA CUP					
VENUE	P	W	D	L	F	A
HOME	1	1	0	0	3	0
AWAY	1	0	1	0	2	2
TOTAL	2	1	1	0	5	2

#	SEASON	DATE	COMPETITION / ROUND	MATCH RESULT	VENUE	ATT
1	1984/85	19/09/84	UEFA Cup 1st Round 1st Leg	Manchester United 3 Raba Vasas 0	Old Trafford	33119
2	1984/85	03/10/84	UEFA Cup 1st Round 2nd Leg	Raba Vasas 2 Manchester United 2	Raba ETO Stadium	26000

UNITED v RAPID VIENNA

EUROPEAN CUP / CHAMPIONS LEAGUE					
VENUE	P	W	D	L	F	A
HOME	2	2	0	0	5	0
AWAY	2	1	1	0	2	0
TOTAL	4	3	1	0	7	0

#	SEASON	DATE	COMPETITION / ROUND	MATCH RESULT	VENUE	ATT
1	1968/69	26/02/69	European Cup Quarter-Final 1st Leg	Manchester United 3 Rapid Vienna 0	Old Trafford	61932
2	1968/69	05/03/69	European Cup Quarter-Final 2nd Leg	Rapid Vienna 0 Manchester United 0	Wiener Stadion	52000
3	1996/97	25/09/96	Champions League Phase 1 Match 2	Manchester United 2 Rapid Vienna 0	Old Trafford	51831
4	1996/97	04/12/96	Champions League Phase 1 Match 6	Rapid Vienna 0 Manchester United 2	Ernst Happel Stadion	45000

UNITED v RAYOS DEL NECAXA

CLUB WORLD CHAMPIONSHIP					
VENUE	P	W	D	L	F	A
HOME	0	0	0	0	0	0
AWAY	0	0	0	0	0	0
NEUTRAL	1	0	1	0	1	1
TOTAL	1	0	1	0	1	1

#	SEASON	DATE	COMPETITION / ROUND	MATCH RESULT	VENUE	ATT
1	1999/00	06/01/00	Club World Championship	Manchester United 1 Rayos del Necaxa 1	Maracana Stadium	50000

UNITED v READING

ALL COMPETITIVE MATCHES	P	W	D	L	F	A	PREMIERSHIP	P	W	D	L	F	A	FA CUP	P	W	D	L	F	A
VENUE							VENUE							VENUE						
HOME	7	4	3	0	14	6	HOME	2	1	1	0	3	2	HOME	5	3	2	0	11	4
AWAY	8	4	4	0	15	7	AWAY	2	1	1	0	3	1	AWAY	6	3	3	0	12	6
NEUTRAL	1	0	0	1	1	2								NEUTRAL	1	0	0	1	1	2
TOTAL	16	8	7	1	30	15	TOTAL	4	2	2	0	6	3	TOTAL	12	6	5	1	24	12

#	SEASON	DATE	COMPETITION / ROUND	MATCH RESULT	VENUE	ATT
1	1911/12	24/02/12	FA Cup 3rd Round	Reading 1 Manchester United 1	Elm Park	24069
2	1911/12	29/02/12	FA Cup 3rd Round Replay	Manchester United 3 Reading 0	Old Trafford	29511
3	1926/27	08/01/27	FA Cup 3rd Round	Reading 1 Manchester United 1	Elm Park	28918
4	1926/27	12/01/27	FA Cup 3rd Round Replay	Manchester United 2 Reading 2	Old Trafford	29122
5	1926/27	17/01/27	FA Cup 3rd Round 2nd Replay	Manchester United 1 Reading 2	Villa Park	16500
6	1935/36	11/01/36	FA Cup 3rd Round	Reading 1 Manchester United 3	Elm Park	25844
7	1936/37	16/01/37	FA Cup 3rd Round	Manchester United 1 Reading 0	Old Trafford	36668
8	1954/55	08/01/55	FA Cup 3rd Round	Reading 1 Manchester United 1	Elm Park	26000
9	1954/55	12/01/55	FA Cup 3rd Round Replay	Manchester United 4 Reading 1	Old Trafford	24578
10	1995/96	27/01/96	FA Cup 4th Round	Reading 0 Manchester United 3	Elm Park	14780
11	2006/07	23/09/06	FA Premiership	Reading 1 Manchester United 1	Madejski Stadium	24098
12	2006/07	30/12/06	FA Premiership	Manchester United 3 Reading 2	Old Trafford	75910
13	2006/07	17/02/07	FA Cup 5th Round	Manchester United 1 Reading 1	Old Trafford	70608
14	2006/07	27/02/07	FA Cup 5th Round Replay	Reading 2 Manchester United 3	Madejski Stadium	23821
15	2007/08	12/08/07	FA Premiership	Manchester United 0 Reading 0	Old Trafford	75655
16	2007/08	19/01/08	FA Premiership	Reading 0 Manchester United 2	Madejski Stadium	24135

UNITED v REAL MADRID

EUROPEAN CUP / CHAMPIONS LEAGUE	P	W	D	L	F	A
VENUE						
HOME	4	2	1	1	9	8
AWAY	4	0	2	2	5	9
TOTAL	8	2	3	3	14	17

#	SEASON	DATE	COMPETITION / ROUND	MATCH RESULT	VENUE	ATT
1	1956/57	11/04/57	European Cup Semi-Final 1st Leg	Real Madrid 3 Manchester United 1	Bernabeu Stadium	135000
2	1956/57	25/04/57	European Cup Semi-Final 2nd Leg	Manchester United 2 Real Madrid 2	Old Trafford	65000
3	1967/68	24/04/68	European Cup Semi-Final 1st Leg	Manchester United 1 Real Madrid 0	Old Trafford	63500
4	1967/68	15/05/68	European Cup Semi-Final 2nd Leg	Real Madrid 3 Manchester United 3	Bernabeu Stadium	125000
5	1999/00	04/04/00	Champions League Quarter-Final 1st Leg	Real Madrid 0 Manchester United 0	Bernabeu Stadium	64119
6	1999/00	19/04/00	Champions League Quarter-Final 2nd Leg	Manchester United 2 Real Madrid 3	Old Trafford	59178
7	2002/03	08/04/03	Champions League Quarter-Final 1st Leg	Real Madrid 3 Manchester United 1	Bernabeu Stadium	75000
8	2002/03	23/04/03	Champions League Quarter-Final 2nd Leg	Manchester United 4 Real Madrid 3	Old Trafford	66708

UNITED v RED STAR BELGRADE

ALL COMPETITIVE MATCHES	P	W	D	L	F	A	EUROPEAN CUP	P	W	D	L	F	A	EUROPEAN SUPER CUP	P	W	D	L	F	A
VENUE							VENUE							VENUE						
HOME	2	2	0	0	3	1	HOME	1	1	0	0	2	1	HOME	1	1	0	0	1	0
AWAY	1	0	1	0	3	3	AWAY	1	0	1	0	3	3	AWAY	0	0	0	0	0	0
TOTAL	3	2	1	0	6	4	TOTAL	2	1	1	0	5	4	TOTAL	1	1	0	0	1	0

#	SEASON	DATE	COMPETITION / ROUND	MATCH RESULT	VENUE	ATT
1	1957/58	14/01/58	European Cup Quarter-Final 1st Leg	Manchester United 2 Red Star Belgrade 1	Old Trafford	60000
2	1957/58	05/02/58	European Cup Quarter-Final 2nd Leg	Red Star Belgrade 3 Manchester United 3	Stadion JNA	55000
3	1991/92	19/11/91	European Super Cup Final	Manchester United 1 Red Star Belgrade 0	Old Trafford	22110

UNITED v ROCHDALE

FA CUP

VENUE	P	W	D	L	F	A
HOME	1	1	0	0	2	0
AWAY	0	0	0	0	0	0
TOTAL	1	1	0	0	2	0

#	SEASON	DATE	COMPETITION / ROUND	MATCH RESULT	VENUE	ATT
1	1985/86	09/01/86	FA Cup 3rd Round	Manchester United 2 Rochdale 0	Old Trafford	40223

UNITED v ROMA

CHAMPIONS LEAGUE

VENUE	P	W	D	L	F	A
HOME	3	3	0	0	9	1
AWAY	3	1	1	1	4	3
TOTAL	6	4	1	1	13	4

#	SEASON	DATE	COMPETITION / ROUND	MATCH RESULT	VENUE	ATT
1	2006/07	04/04/07	Champions League Quarter-Final 1st Leg	Roma 2 Manchester United 1	Olympic Stadium	77000
2	2006/07	10/04/07	Champions League Quarter-Final 2nd Leg	Manchester United 7 Roma 1	Old Trafford	74476
3	2007/08	02/10/07	Champions League Phase 1 Match 2	Manchester United 1 Roma 0	Old Trafford	73652
4	2007/08	12/12/07	Champions League Phase 1 Match 6	Roma 1 Manchester United 1	Olympic Stadium	29490
5	2007/08	01/04/08	Champions League Quarter-Final 1st Leg	Roma 0 Manchester United 2	Olympic Stadium	60931
6	2007/08	09/04/08	Champions League Quarter-Final 2nd Leg	Manchester United 1 Roma 0	Old Trafford	74423

UNITED v ROTHERHAM UNITED

ALL COMPETITIVE MATCHES							LEAGUE DIVISION TWO							ALL CUP MATCHES						
VENUE	P	W	D	L	F	A	VENUE	P	W	D	L	F	A	VENUE	P	W	D	L	F	A
HOME	5	4	1	0	14	2	HOME	3	3	0	0	9	2	HOME	2	1	1	0	5	0
AWAY	5	3	1	1	7	5	AWAY	3	1	1	1	5	5	AWAY	2	2	0	0	2	0
TOTAL	10	7	2	1	21	7	TOTAL	6	4	1	1	14	7	TOTAL	4	3	1	0	7	0

FA CUP							LEAGUE CUP						
VENUE	P	W	D	L	F	A	VENUE	P	W	D	L	F	A
HOME	1	0	1	0	0	0	HOME	1	1	0	0	5	0
AWAY	1	1	0	0	1	0	AWAY	1	1	0	0	1	0
TOTAL	2	1	1	0	1	0	TOTAL	2	2	0	0	6	0

#	SEASON	DATE	COMPETITION / ROUND	MATCH RESULT	VENUE	ATT
1	1894/95	10/11/94	Football League Division 2	Newton Heath 3 Rotherham United 2	Bank Street	4000
2	1894/95	12/01/95	Football League Division 2	Rotherham United 2 Newton Heath 1	Millmoor	2000
3	1895/96	11/01/96	Football League Division 2	Newton Heath 3 Rotherham United 0	Bank Street	3000
4	1895/96	07/03/96	Football League Division 2	Rotherham United 2 Newton Heath 3	Millmoor	1500
5	1922/23	02/12/22	Football League Division 2	Manchester United 3 Rotherham United 0	Old Trafford	13500
6	1922/23	09/12/22	Football League Division 2	Rotherham United 1 Manchester United 1	Millmoor	7500
7	1965/66	12/02/66	FA Cup 4th Round	Manchester United 0 Rotherham United 0	Old Trafford	54263
8	1965/66	15/02/66	FA Cup 4th Round Replay	Rotherham United 0 Manchester United 1	Millmoor	23500
9	1988/89	28/09/88	League Cup 2nd Round 1st Leg	Rotherham United 0 Manchester United 1	Millmoor	12588
10	1988/89	12/10/88	League Cup 2nd Round 2nd Leg	Manchester United 5 Rotherham United 0	Old Trafford	20597

UNITED v ROTOR VOLGOGRAD

UEFA CUP

VENUE	P	W	D	L	F	A
HOME	1	0	1	0	2	2
AWAY	1	0	1	0	0	0
TOTAL	2	0	2	0	2	2

#	SEASON	DATE	COMPETITION / ROUND	MATCH RESULT	VENUE	ATT
1	1995/96	12/09/95	UEFA Cup 1st Round 1st Leg	Rotor Volgograd 0 Manchester United 0	Central Stadion	33000
2	1995/96	26/09/95	UEFA Cup 1st Round 2nd Leg	Manchester United 2 Rotor Volgograd 2	Old Trafford	29724
				(United lost the tie on away goals rule)		

UNITED v SARAJEVO

EUROPEAN CUP						
VENUE	P	W	D	L	F	A
HOME	1	1	0	0	2	1
AWAY	1	0	1	0	0	0
TOTAL	2	1	1	0	2	1

#	SEASON	DATE	COMPETITION / ROUND	MATCH RESULT	VENUE	ATT
1	1967/68	15/11/67	European Cup 2nd Round 1st Leg	Sarajevo 0 Manchester United 0	Stadion Kosevo	45000
2	1967/68	29/11/67	European Cup 2nd Round 2nd Leg	Manchester United 2 Sarajevo 1	Old Trafford	62801

UNITED v SHAMROCK ROVERS

EUROPEAN CUP						
VENUE	P	W	D	L	F	A
HOME	1	1	0	0	3	2
AWAY	1	1	0	0	6	0
TOTAL	2	2	0	0	9	2

#	SEASON	DATE	COMPETITION / ROUND	MATCH RESULT	VENUE	ATT
1	1957/58	25/09/57	European Cup Preliminary Round 1st Leg	Shamrock Rovers 0 Manchester United 6	Dalymount Park	33754
2	1957/58	02/10/57	European Cup Preliminary Round 2nd Leg	Manchester United 3 Shamrock Rovers 2	Old Trafford	45000

UNITED v SHEFFIELD UNITED

ALL COMPETITIVE MATCHES							ALL LEAGUE MATCHES							FA CUP						
VENUE	P	W	D	L	F	A	VENUE	P	W	D	L	F	A	VENUE	P	W	D	L	F	A
HOME	44	27	6	11	90	48	HOME	44	27	6	11	90	48	HOME	0	0	0	0	0	0
AWAY	48	16	9	23	60	79	AWAY	44	13	9	22	55	77	AWAY	4	3	0	1	5	2
TOTAL	92	43	15	34	150	127	TOTAL	88	40	15	33	145	125	TOTAL	4	3	0	1	5	2

PREMIERSHIP							LEAGUE DIVISION ONE							LEAGUE DIVISION TWO						
VENUE	P	W	D	L	F	A	VENUE	P	W	D	L	F	A	VENUE	P	W	D	L	F	A
HOME	3	3	0	0	7	1	HOME	38	23	5	10	77	42	HOME	3	1	1	1	6	5
AWAY	3	2	0	1	6	3	AWAY	38	10	8	20	44	69	AWAY	3	1	1	1	5	5
TOTAL	6	5	0	1	13	4	TOTAL	76	33	13	30	121	111	TOTAL	6	2	2	2	11	10

#	SEASON	DATE	COMPETITION / ROUND	MATCH RESULT	VENUE	ATT
1	1893/94	25/11/93	Football League Division 1	Sheffield United 3 Newton Heath 1	Bramall Lane	2000
2	1893/94	10/03/94	Football League Division 1	Newton Heath 0 Sheffield United 2	Bank Street	5000
3	1906/07	15/09/06	Football League Division 1	Sheffield United 0 Manchester United 2	Bramall Lane	12000
4	1906/07	19/01/07	Football League Division 1	Manchester United 2 Sheffield United 0	Bank Street	15000
5	1907/08	21/09/07	Football League Division 1	Manchester United 2 Sheffield United 1	Bank Street	25000
6	1907/08	18/01/08	Football League Division 1	Sheffield United 2 Manchester United 0	Bramall Lane	17000
7	1908/09	10/10/08	Football League Division 1	Manchester United 2 Sheffield United 1	Bank Street	14000
8	1908/09	13/02/09	Football League Division 1	Sheffield United 0 Manchester United 0	Bramall Lane	12000
9	1909/10	23/10/09	Football League Division 1	Sheffield United 0 Manchester United 1	Bramall Lane	30000
10	1909/10	05/03/10	Football League Division 1	Manchester United 1 Sheffield United 0	Old Trafford	40000
11	1910/11	10/12/10	Football League Division 1	Sheffield United 2 Manchester United 0	Bramall Lane	8000
12	1910/11	15/04/11	Football League Division 1	Manchester United 1 Sheffield United 1	Old Trafford	22000
13	1911/12	09/12/11	Football League Division 1	Manchester United 1 Sheffield United 0	Old Trafford	12000
14	1911/12	13/04/12	Football League Division 1	Sheffield United 6 Manchester United 1	Bramall Lane	7000
15	1912/13	07/12/12	Football League Division 1	Manchester United 4 Sheffield United 0	Old Trafford	12000
16	1912/13	12/04/13	Football League Division 1	Sheffield United 2 Manchester United 1	Bramall Lane	12000
17	1913/14	22/11/13	Football League Division 1	Sheffield United 2 Manchester United 0	Bramall Lane	30000
18	1913/14	22/04/14	Football League Division 1	Manchester United 2 Sheffield United 1	Old Trafford	4500
19	1914/15	12/12/14	Football League Division 1	Manchester United 1 Sheffield United 2	Old Trafford	8000
20	1914/15	17/04/15	Football League Division 1	Sheffield United 3 Manchester United 1	Bramall Lane	14000
21	1919/20	25/10/19	Football League Division 1	Sheffield United 2 Manchester United 2	Bramall Lane	18000
22	1919/20	01/11/19	Football League Division 1	Manchester United 3 Sheffield United 0	Old Trafford	24500
23	1920/21	06/11/20	Football League Division 1	Manchester United 2 Sheffield United 1	Old Trafford	30000
24	1920/21	13/11/20	Football League Division 1	Sheffield United 0 Manchester United 0	Bramall Lane	18000
25	1921/22	02/01/22	Football League Division 1	Sheffield United 3 Manchester United 0	Bramall Lane	18000
26	1921/22	17/04/22	Football League Division 1	Manchester United 3 Sheffield United 2	Old Trafford	28000
27	1925/26	12/12/25	Football League Division 1	Manchester United 1 Sheffield United 2	Old Trafford	31132
28	1925/26	24/04/26	Football League Division 1	Sheffield United 2 Manchester United 0	Bramall Lane	15571

UNITED v SHEFFIELD UNITED (continued)

#	SEASON	DATE	COMPETITION / ROUND	MATCH RESULT	VENUE	ATT
29	1926/27	30/08/26	Football League Division 1	Sheffield United 2 Manchester United 2	Bramall Lane	14844
30	1926/27	01/01/27	Football League Division 1	Manchester United 5 Sheffield United 0	Old Trafford	33593
31	1927/28	10/12/27	Football League Division 1	Sheffield United 2 Manchester United 1	Bramall Lane	11984
32	1927/28	21/04/28	Football League Division 1	Manchester United 2 Sheffield United 3	Old Trafford	27137
33	1928/29	25/12/28	Football League Division 1	Manchester United 1 Sheffield United 1	Old Trafford	22202
34	1928/29	26/12/28	Football League Division 1	Sheffield United 6 Manchester United 1	Bramall Lane	34696
35	1929/30	07/10/29	Football League Division 1	Sheffield United 3 Manchester United 1	Bramall Lane	7987
36	1929/30	03/05/30	Football League Division 1	Manchester United 1 Sheffield United 5	Old Trafford	15268
37	1930/31	22/11/30	Football League Division 1	Sheffield United 3 Manchester United 1	Bramall Lane	12698
38	1930/31	28/03/31	Football League Division 1	Manchester United 1 Sheffield United 2	Old Trafford	5420
39	1934/35	01/09/34	Football League Division 2	Sheffield United 3 Manchester United 2	Bramall Lane	18468
40	1934/35	05/01/35	Football League Division 2	Manchester United 3 Sheffield United 3	Old Trafford	28300
41	1935/36	19/10/35	Football League Division 2	Manchester United 3 Sheffield United 1	Old Trafford	18636
42	1935/36	22/02/36	Football League Division 2	Sheffield United 1 Manchester United 1	Bramall Lane	25852
43	1937/38	02/10/37	Football League Division 2	Manchester United 0 Sheffield United 1	Old Trafford	20105
44	1937/38	17/02/38	Football League Division 2	Sheffield United 1 Manchester United 2	Bramall Lane	17754
45	1946/47	12/10/46	Football League Division 1	Sheffield United 2 Manchester United 2	Bramall Lane	35543
46	1946/47	26/05/47	Football League Division 1	Manchester United 6 Sheffield United 2	Maine Road	34059
47	1947/48	13/09/47	Football League Division 1	Manchester United 0 Sheffield United 1	Maine Road	49808
48	1947/48	31/01/48	Football League Division 1	Sheffield United 2 Manchester United 1	Bramall Lane	45189
49	1948/49	18/09/48	Football League Division 1	Sheffield United 2 Manchester United 2	Bramall Lane	36880
50	1948/49	04/05/49	Football League Division 1	Manchester United 3 Sheffield United 2	Maine Road	20880
51	1953/54	05/12/53	Football League Division 1	Manchester United 2 Sheffield United 2	Old Trafford	31693
52	1953/54	24/04/54	Football League Division 1	Sheffield United 1 Manchester United 3	Bramall Lane	29189
53	1954/55	13/11/54	Football League Division 1	Sheffield United 3 Manchester United 0	Bramall Lane	26257
54	1954/55	02/04/55	Football League Division 1	Manchester United 5 Sheffield United 0	Old Trafford	21158
55	1955/56	10/09/55	Football League Division 1	Sheffield United 1 Manchester United 0	Bramall Lane	28241
56	1955/56	14/01/56	Football League Division 1	Manchester United 3 Sheffield United 1	Old Trafford	30162
57	1961/62	23/04/62	Football League Division 1	Manchester United 0 Sheffield United 1	Old Trafford	30073
58	1961/62	24/04/62	Football League Division 1	Sheffield United 2 Manchester United 3	Bramall Lane	25324
59	1962/63	01/12/62	Football League Division 1	Sheffield United 1 Manchester United 1	Bramall Lane	25173
60	1962/63	20/04/63	Football League Division 1	Manchester United 1 Sheffield United 1	Old Trafford	31179
61	1963/64	30/11/63	Football League Division 1	Sheffield United 1 Manchester United 2	Bramall Lane	30615
62	1963/64	13/04/64	Football League Division 1	Manchester United 2 Sheffield United 1	Old Trafford	27587
63	1964/65	26/12/64	Football League Division 1	Sheffield United 0 Manchester United 1	Bramall Lane	37295
64	1964/65	28/12/64	Football League Division 1	Manchester United 1 Sheffield United 1	Old Trafford	42219
65	1965/66	20/11/65	Football League Division 1	Manchester United 3 Sheffield United 1	Old Trafford	37922
66	1965/66	16/04/66	Football League Division 1	Sheffield United 3 Manchester United 1	Bramall Lane	22330
67	1966/67	26/12/66	Football League Division 1	Sheffield United 2 Manchester United 1	Bramall Lane	42752
68	1966/67	27/12/66	Football League Division 1	Manchester United 2 Sheffield United 0	Old Trafford	59392
69	1967/68	14/10/67	Football League Division 1	Sheffield United 0 Manchester United 3	Bramall Lane	29170
70	1967/68	20/04/68	Football League Division 1	Manchester United 1 Sheffield United 0	Old Trafford	55033
71	1971/72	02/10/71	Football League Division 1	Manchester United 2 Sheffield United 0	Old Trafford	51735
72	1971/72	04/04/72	Football League Division 1	Sheffield United 1 Manchester United 1	Bramall Lane	45045
73	1972/73	30/09/72	Football League Division 1	Sheffield United 1 Manchester United 0	Bramall Lane	37347
74	1972/73	23/04/73	Football League Division 1	Manchester United 1 Sheffield United 2	Old Trafford	57280
75	1973/74	26/12/73	Football League Division 1	Manchester United 1 Sheffield United 2	Old Trafford	38653
76	1973/74	02/03/74	Football League Division 1	Sheffield United 0 Manchester United 1	Bramall Lane	29203
77	1975/76	23/08/75	Football League Division 1	Manchester United 5 Sheffield United 1	Old Trafford	55949
78	1975/76	13/12/75	Football League Division 1	Sheffield United 1 Manchester United 4	Bramall Lane	31741
79	1989/90	11/03/90	FA Cup 6th Round	Sheffield United 0 Manchester United 1	Bramall Lane	34344
80	1990/91	17/11/90	Football League Division 1	Manchester United 2 Sheffield United 0	Old Trafford	45903
81	1990/91	26/02/91	Football League Division 1	Sheffield United 2 Manchester United 1	Bramall Lane	27570
82	1991/92	02/11/91	Football League Division 1	Manchester United 2 Sheffield United 0	Old Trafford	42942
83	1991/92	14/03/92	Football League Division 1	Sheffield United 1 Manchester United 2	Bramall Lane	30183
84	1992/93	15/08/92	FA Premiership	Sheffield United 2 Manchester United 1	Bramall Lane	28070
85	1992/93	06/02/93	FA Premiership	Manchester United 2 Sheffield United 1	Old Trafford	36156
86	1992/93	14/02/93	FA Cup 5th Round	Sheffield United 2 Manchester United 1	Bramall Lane	27150
87	1993/94	18/08/93	FA Premiership	Manchester United 3 Sheffield United 0	Old Trafford	41949
88	1993/94	07/12/93	FA Premiership	Sheffield United 0 Manchester United 3	Bramall Lane	26746
89	1993/94	09/01/94	FA Cup 3rd Round	Sheffield United 0 Manchester United 1	Bramall Lane	22019
90	1994/95	09/01/95	FA Cup 3rd Round	Sheffield United 0 Manchester United 2	Bramall Lane	22322
91	2006/07	18/11/06	FA Premiership	Sheffield United 1 Manchester United 2	Bramall Lane	32584
92	2006/07	17/04/07	FA Premiership	Manchester United 2 Sheffield United 0	Old Trafford	75540

UNITED v SHEFFIELD WEDNESDAY

ALL COMPETITIVE MATCHES

VENUE	P	W	D	L	F	A
HOME	61	39	14	8	122	58
AWAY	62	15	13	34	78	112
NEUTRAL	1	0	0	1	0	1
TOTAL	124	54	27	43	200	171

ALL LEAGUE MATCHES

VENUE	P	W	D	L	F	A
HOME	56	37	13	6	116	50
AWAY	56	13	12	31	71	101
TOTAL	112	50	25	37	187	151

ALL CUP MATCHES

VENUE	P	W	D	L	F	A
HOME	5	2	1	2	6	8
AWAY	6	2	1	3	7	11
NEUTRAL	1	0	0	1	0	1
TOTAL	12	4	2	6	13	20

PREMIERSHIP

VENUE	P	W	D	L	F	A
HOME	8	7	1	0	25	4
AWAY	8	2	3	3	9	12
TOTAL	16	9	4	3	34	16

LEAGUE DIVISION ONE

VENUE	P	W	D	L	F	A
HOME	42	24	12	6	82	46
AWAY	42	10	7	25	53	78
TOTAL	84	34	19	31	135	124

LEAGUE DIVISION TWO

VENUE	P	W	D	L	F	A
HOME	6	6	0	0	9	0
AWAY	6	1	2	3	9	11
TOTAL	12	7	2	3	18	11

FA CUP

VENUE	P	W	D	L	F	A
HOME	4	1	1	2	5	8
AWAY	5	1	1	3	3	10
TOTAL	9	2	2	5	8	18

LEAGUE CUP

VENUE	P	W	D	L	F	A
HOME	1	1	0	0	1	0
AWAY	1	1	0	0	4	1
NEUTRAL	1	0	0	1	0	1
TOTAL	3	2	0	1	5	2

#	SEASON	DATE	COMPETITION / ROUND	MATCH RESULT	VENUE	ATT
1	1892/93	22/10/92	Football League Division 1	Sheffield Wednesday 1 Newton Heath 0	Olive Grove	6000
2	1892/93	24/12/92	Football League Division 1	Newton Heath 1 Sheffield Wednesday 5	North Road	4000
3	1893/94	16/09/93	Football League Division 1	Sheffield Wednesday 0 Newton Heath 1	Olive Grove	7000
4	1893/94	13/01/94	Football League Division 1	Newton Heath 1 Sheffield Wednesday 2	Bank Street	9000
5	1899/00	30/09/99	Football League Division 2	Sheffield Wednesday 2 Newton Heath 1	Hillsborough	8000
6	1899/00	03/02/00	Football League Division 2	Newton Heath 1 Sheffield Wednesday 0	Bank Street	10000
7	1903/04	20/02/04	FA Cup 2nd Round	Sheffield Wednesday 6 Manchester United 0	Hillsborough	22051
8	1906/07	17/11/06	Football League Division 1	Sheffield Wednesday 5 Manchester United 2	Hillsborough	7000
9	1906/07	10/04/07	Football League Division 1	Manchester United 5 Sheffield Wednesday 0	Bank Street	10000
10	1907/08	30/11/07	Football League Division 1	Sheffield Wednesday 2 Manchester United 0	Hillsborough	40000
11	1907/08	28/03/08	Football League Division 1	Manchester United 4 Sheffield Wednesday 1	Bank Street	30000
12	1908/09	28/11/08	Football League Division 1	Manchester United 3 Sheffield Wednesday 1	Bank Street	20000
13	1908/09	03/04/09	Football League Division 1	Sheffield Wednesday 2 Manchester United 0	Hillsborough	15000
14	1909/10	25/12/09	Football League Division 1	Manchester United 0 Sheffield Wednesday 3	Bank Street	25000
15	1909/10	27/12/09	Football League Division 1	Sheffield Wednesday 4 Manchester United 1	Hillsborough	37000
16	1910/11	01/10/10	Football League Division 1	Manchester United 3 Sheffield Wednesday 2	Old Trafford	20000
17	1910/11	17/04/11	Football League Division 1	Sheffield Wednesday 0 Manchester United 0	Hillsborough	25000
18	1911/12	07/10/11	Football League Division 1	Manchester United 3 Sheffield Wednesday 1	Old Trafford	30000
19	1911/12	10/02/12	Football League Division 1	Sheffield Wednesday 3 Manchester United 0	Hillsborough	25000
20	1912/13	28/09/12	Football League Division 1	Sheffield Wednesday 3 Manchester United 3	Hillsborough	30000
21	1912/13	25/01/13	Football League Division 1	Manchester United 2 Sheffield Wednesday 0	Old Trafford	45000
22	1913/14	06/09/13	Football League Division 1	Sheffield Wednesday 1 Manchester United 3	Hillsborough	32000
23	1913/14	27/12/13	Football League Division 1	Manchester United 2 Sheffield Wednesday 1	Old Trafford	10000
24	1914/15	10/10/14	Football League Division 1	Sheffield Wednesday 1 Manchester United 0	Hillsborough	19000
25	1914/15	09/01/15	FA Cup 1st Round	Sheffield Wednesday 1 Manchester United 0	Hillsborough	23248
26	1914/15	13/02/15	Football League Division 1	Manchester United 2 Sheffield Wednesday 0	Old Trafford	7000
27	1919/20	01/09/19	Football League Division 1	Manchester United 0 Sheffield Wednesday 0	Old Trafford	13000
28	1919/20	08/09/19	Football League Division 1	Sheffield Wednesday 1 Manchester United 3	Hillsborough	10000
29	1922/23	28/08/22	Football League Division 2	Sheffield Wednesday 1 Manchester United 0	Hillsborough	12500
30	1922/23	04/09/22	Football League Division 2	Manchester United 1 Sheffield Wednesday 0	Old Trafford	22000
31	1923/24	26/04/24	Football League Division 2	Manchester United 2 Sheffield Wednesday 0	Old Trafford	7500
32	1923/24	03/05/24	Football League Division 2	Sheffield Wednesday 2 Manchester United 0	Hillsborough	7250
33	1924/25	27/09/24	Football League Division 2	Manchester United 2 Sheffield Wednesday 0	Old Trafford	29500
34	1924/25	10/01/25	FA Cup 1st Round	Sheffield Wednesday 2 Manchester United 0	Hillsborough	35079
35	1924/25	23/02/25	Football League Division 2	Sheffield Wednesday 1 Manchester United 1	Hillsborough	3000
36	1926/27	06/11/26	Football League Division 1	Manchester United 0 Sheffield Wednesday 0	Old Trafford	16166
37	1926/27	26/03/27	Football League Division 1	Sheffield Wednesday 2 Manchester United 0	Hillsborough	11997
38	1927/28	29/08/27	Football League Division 1	Sheffield Wednesday 0 Manchester United 2	Hillsborough	17944
39	1927/28	07/09/27	Football League Division 1	Manchester United 1 Sheffield Wednesday 1	Old Trafford	18759
40	1928/29	10/11/28	Football League Division 1	Sheffield Wednesday 2 Manchester United 1	Hillsborough	18113
41	1928/29	23/03/29	Football League Division 1	Manchester United 2 Sheffield Wednesday 1	Old Trafford	27095
42	1929/30	16/11/29	Football League Division 1	Sheffield Wednesday 7 Manchester United 2	Hillsborough	14264
43	1929/30	14/04/30	Football League Division 1	Manchester United 2 Sheffield Wednesday 2	Old Trafford	12806

UNITED v SHEFFIELD WEDNESDAY (continued)

#	SEASON	DATE	COMPETITION / ROUND	MATCH RESULT	VENUE	ATT
44	1930/31	20/09/30	Football League Division 1	Sheffield Wednesday 3 Manchester United 0	Hillsborough	18705
45	1930/31	28/01/31	Football League Division 1	Manchester United 4 Sheffield Wednesday 1	Old Trafford	6077
46	1936/37	19/09/36	Football League Division 1	Manchester United 1 Sheffield Wednesday 1	Old Trafford	40933
47	1936/37	23/01/37	Football League Division 1	Sheffield Wednesday 1 Manchester United 0	Hillsborough	8658
48	1937/38	23/10/37	Football League Division 2	Manchester United 1 Sheffield Wednesday 0	Old Trafford	16379
49	1937/38	05/03/38	Football League Division 2	Sheffield Wednesday 1 Manchester United 3	Hillsborough	37156
50	1950/51	07/10/50	Football League Division 1	Manchester United 3 Sheffield Wednesday 1	Old Trafford	40651
51	1950/51	26/02/51	Football League Division 1	Sheffield Wednesday 0 Manchester United 4	Hillsborough	25693
52	1952/53	08/11/52	Football League Division 1	Manchester United 1 Sheffield Wednesday 1	Old Trafford	48571
53	1952/53	28/03/53	Football League Division 1	Sheffield Wednesday 0 Manchester United 0	Hillsborough	36509
54	1953/54	25/12/53	Football League Division 1	Manchester United 5 Sheffield Wednesday 2	Old Trafford	27123
55	1953/54	26/12/53	Football League Division 1	Sheffield Wednesday 0 Manchester United 1	Hillsborough	44196
56	1954/55	23/08/54	Football League Division 1	Sheffield Wednesday 2 Manchester United 4	Hillsborough	38118
57	1954/55	01/09/54	Football League Division 1	Manchester United 2 Sheffield Wednesday 0	Old Trafford	31371
58	1956/57	15/09/56	Football League Division 1	Manchester United 4 Sheffield Wednesday 1	Old Trafford	48078
59	1956/57	19/01/57	Football League Division 1	Sheffield Wednesday 2 Manchester United 1	Hillsborough	51068
60	1957/58	16/11/57	Football League Division 1	Manchester United 2 Sheffield Wednesday 1	Old Trafford	40366
61	1957/58	19/02/58	FA Cup 5th Round	Manchester United 3 Sheffield Wednesday 0	Old Trafford	59848
62	1957/58	29/03/58	Football League Division 1	Sheffield Wednesday 1 Manchester United 0	Hillsborough	35608
63	1959/60	24/10/59	Football League Division 1	Manchester United 3 Sheffield Wednesday 1	Old Trafford	39259
64	1959/60	20/02/60	FA Cup 5th Round	Manchester United 0 Sheffield Wednesday 1	Old Trafford	66350
65	1959/60	30/03/60	Football League Division 1	Sheffield Wednesday 4 Manchester United 2	Hillsborough	26821
66	1960/61	05/11/60	Football League Division 1	Manchester United 0 Sheffield Wednesday 0	Old Trafford	36855
67	1960/61	28/01/61	FA Cup 4th Round	Sheffield Wednesday 1 Manchester United 1	Hillsborough	58000
68	1960/61	01/02/61	FA Cup 4th Round Replay	Manchester United 2 Sheffield Wednesday 7	Old Trafford	65243
69	1960/61	25/03/61	Football League Division 1	Sheffield Wednesday 5 Manchester United 1	Hillsborough	35901
70	1961/62	04/11/61	Football League Division 1	Sheffield Wednesday 3 Manchester United 1	Hillsborough	35998
71	1961/62	17/02/62	FA Cup 5th Round	Manchester United 0 Sheffield Wednesday 0	Old Trafford	59553
72	1961/62	21/02/62	FA Cup 5th Round Replay	Sheffield Wednesday 0 Manchester United 2	Hillsborough	62969
73	1961/62	24/03/62	Football League Division 1	Manchester United 1 Sheffield Wednesday 1	Old Trafford	31322
74	1962/63	29/09/62	Football League Division 1	Sheffield Wednesday 1 Manchester United 0	Hillsborough	40520
75	1962/63	01/05/63	Football League Division 1	Manchester United 1 Sheffield Wednesday 3	Old Trafford	31878
76	1963/64	24/08/63	Football League Division 1	Sheffield Wednesday 3 Manchester United 3	Hillsborough	32177
77	1963/64	14/12/63	Football League Division 1	Manchester United 3 Sheffield Wednesday 1	Old Trafford	35139
78	1964/65	07/11/64	Football League Division 1	Manchester United 1 Sheffield Wednesday 0	Old Trafford	50178
79	1964/65	20/03/65	Football League Division 1	Sheffield Wednesday 1 Manchester United 0	Hillsborough	33549
80	1965/66	21/08/65	Football League Division 1	Manchester United 1 Sheffield Wednesday 0	Old Trafford	37524
81	1965/66	29/01/66	Football League Division 1	Sheffield Wednesday 0 Manchester United 0	Hillsborough	39281
82	1966/67	12/11/66	Football League Division 1	Manchester United 2 Sheffield Wednesday 0	Old Trafford	46942
83	1966/67	10/04/67	Football League Division 1	Sheffield Wednesday 2 Manchester United 2	Hillsborough	51101
84	1967/68	16/09/67	Football League Division 1	Sheffield Wednesday 1 Manchester United 1	Hillsborough	47274
85	1967/68	20/01/68	Football League Division 1	Manchester United 4 Sheffield Wednesday 2	Old Trafford	55254
86	1968/69	31/08/68	Football League Division 1	Sheffield Wednesday 5 Manchester United 4	Hillsborough	50490
87	1968/69	22/03/69	Football League Division 1	Manchester United 1 Sheffield Wednesday 0	Old Trafford	45527
88	1969/70	17/09/69	Football League Division 1	Sheffield Wednesday 1 Manchester United 3	Hillsborough	39298
89	1969/70	15/04/70	Football League Division 1	Manchester United 2 Sheffield Wednesday 2	Old Trafford	36649
90	1974/75	07/12/74	Football League Division 2	Sheffield Wednesday 4 Manchester United 4	Hillsborough	35230
91	1974/75	11/01/75	Football League Division 2	Manchester United 2 Sheffield Wednesday 0	Old Trafford	45662
92	1984/85	01/01/85	Football League Division 1	Manchester United 1 Sheffield Wednesday 2	Old Trafford	47625
93	1984/85	09/04/85	Football League Division 1	Sheffield Wednesday 1 Manchester United 0	Hillsborough	39380
94	1985/86	09/11/85	Football League Division 1	Sheffield Wednesday 1 Manchester United 0	Hillsborough	48105
95	1985/86	13/04/86	Football League Division 1	Manchester United 0 Sheffield Wednesday 2	Old Trafford	32331
96	1986/87	11/10/86	Football League Division 1	Manchester United 3 Sheffield Wednesday 1	Old Trafford	45890
97	1986/87	21/03/87	Football League Division 1	Sheffield Wednesday 1 Manchester United 0	Hillsborough	29888
98	1987/88	10/10/87	Football League Division 1	Sheffield Wednesday 2 Manchester United 4	Hillsborough	32779
99	1987/88	12/03/88	Football League Division 1	Manchester United 4 Sheffield Wednesday 1	Old Trafford	33318
100	1988/89	23/11/88	Football League Division 1	Manchester United 1 Sheffield Wednesday 1	Old Trafford	30849
101	1988/89	11/02/89	Football League Division 1	Sheffield Wednesday 0 Manchester United 2	Hillsborough	34820
102	1989/90	14/10/89	Football League Division 1	Manchester United 0 Sheffield Wednesday 0	Old Trafford	41492
103	1989/90	21/03/90	Football League Division 1	Sheffield Wednesday 1 Manchester United 0	Hillsborough	33260
104	1990/91	21/04/91	League Cup Final	Manchester United 0 Sheffield Wednesday 1	Wembley	77612
105	1991/92	26/10/91	Football League Division 1	Sheffield Wednesday 3 Manchester United 2	Hillsborough	38260
106	1991/92	08/02/92	Football League Division 1	Manchester United 1 Sheffield Wednesday 1	Old Trafford	47074

UNITED v SHEFFIELD WEDNESDAY (continued)

#	SEASON	DATE	COMPETITION / ROUND	MATCH RESULT	VENUE	ATT
107	1992/93	26/12/92	FA Premiership	Sheffield Wednesday 3 Manchester United 3	Hillsborough	37708
108	1992/93	10/04/93	FA Premiership	Manchester United 2 Sheffield Wednesday 1	Old Trafford	40102
109	1993/94	02/10/93	FA Premiership	Sheffield Wednesday 2 Manchester United 3	Hillsborough	34548
110	1993/94	13/02/94	League Cup Semi-Final 1st Leg	Manchester United 1 Sheffield Wednesday 0	Old Trafford	43294
111	1993/94	02/03/94	League Cup Semi-Final 2nd Leg	Sheffield Wednesday 1 Manchester United 4	Hillsborough	34878
112	1993/94	16/03/94	FA Premiership	Manchester United 5 Sheffield Wednesday 0	Old Trafford	43669
113	1994/95	08/10/94	FA Premiership	Sheffield Wednesday 1 Manchester United 0	Hillsborough	33441
114	1994/95	07/05/95	FA Premiership	Manchester United 1 Sheffield Wednesday 0	Old Trafford	43868
115	1995/96	23/09/95	FA Premiership	Sheffield Wednesday 0 Manchester United 0	Hillsborough	34101
116	1995/96	09/12/95	FA Premiership	Manchester United 2 Sheffield Wednesday 2	Old Trafford	41849
117	1996/97	18/12/96	FA Premiership	Sheffield Wednesday 1 Manchester United 1	Hillsborough	37671
118	1996/97	15/03/97	FA Premiership	Manchester United 2 Sheffield Wednesday 0	Old Trafford	55267
119	1997/98	01/11/97	FA Premiership	Manchester United 6 Sheffield Wednesday 1	Old Trafford	55259
120	1997/98	07/03/98	FA Premiership	Sheffield Wednesday 2 Manchester United 0	Hillsborough	39427
121	1998/99	21/11/98	FA Premiership	Sheffield Wednesday 3 Manchester United 1	Hillsborough	39475
122	1998/99	17/04/99	FA Premiership	Manchester United 3 Sheffield Wednesday 0	Old Trafford	55270
123	1999/00	11/08/99	FA Premiership	Manchester United 4 Sheffield Wednesday 0	Old Trafford	54941
124	1999/00	02/02/00	FA Premiership	Sheffield Wednesday 0 Manchester United 1	Hillsborough	39640

UNITED v SOUTH MELBOURNE

CLUB WORLD CHAMPIONSHIP						
VENUE	P	W	D	L	F	A
HOME	0	0	0	0	0	0
AWAY	0	0	0	0	0	0
NEUTRAL	1	1	0	0	2	0
TOTAL	1	1	0	0	2	0

#	SEASON	DATE	COMPETITION / ROUND	MATCH RESULT	VENUE	ATT
1	1999/00	11/01/00	Club World Championship	Manchester United 2 South Melbourne 0	Maracana Stadium	25000

UNITED v SOUTH SHIELDS

LEAGUE DIVISION TWO						
VENUE	P	W	D	L	F	A
HOME	3	2	1	0	5	1
AWAY	3	2	0	1	5	2
TOTAL	6	4	1	1	10	3

#	SEASON	DATE	COMPETITION / ROUND	MATCH RESULT	VENUE	ATT
1	1922/23	30/03/23	Football League Division 2	Manchester United 3 South Shields 0	Old Trafford	26000
2	1922/23	02/04/23	Football League Division 2	South Shields 0 Manchester United 3	Talbot Road	6500
3	1923/24	22/09/23	Football League Division 2	South Shields 1 Manchester United 0	Talbot Road	9750
4	1923/24	29/09/23	Football League Division 2	Manchester United 1 South Shields 1	Old Trafford	22250
5	1924/25	06/12/24	Football League Division 2	South Shields 1 Manchester United 2	Talbot Road	6500
6	1924/25	11/04/25	Football League Division 2	Manchester United 1 South Shields 0	Old Trafford	24000

UNITED v SOUTH SHORE

FA CUP						
VENUE	P	W	D	L	F	A
HOME	0	0	0	0	0	0
AWAY	2	1	0	1	3	3
TOTAL	2	1	0	1	3	3

#	SEASON	DATE	COMPETITION / ROUND	MATCH RESULT	VENUE	ATT
1	1891/92	14/11/91	FA Cup 3rd Qualifying Round	South Shore 0 Newton Heath 2	Bloomfield Road	2000
2	1899/00	28/10/99	FA Cup 3rd Qualifying Round	South Shore 3 Newton Heath 1	Bloomfield Road	3000

UNITED v SOUTHAMPTON

ALL COMPETITIVE MATCHES						
VENUE	P	W	D	L	F	A
HOME	53	36	10	7	111	54
AWAY	53	18	18	17	75	67
NEUTRAL	2	1	0	1	1	1
TOTAL	108	55	28	25	187	122

ALL LEAGUE MATCHES						
VENUE	P	W	D	L	F	A
HOME	45	30	8	7	93	47
AWAY	45	16	13	16	62	56
TOTAL	90	46	21	23	155	103

ALL CUP MATCHES						
VENUE	P	W	D	L	F	A
HOME	8	6	2	0	18	7
AWAY	8	2	5	1	13	11
NEUTRAL	2	1	0	1	1	1
TOTAL	18	9	7	2	32	19

PREMIERSHIP						
VENUE	P	W	D	L	F	A
HOME	13	12	1	0	37	12
AWAY	13	7	1	5	24	19
TOTAL	26	19	2	5	61	31

LEAGUE DIVISION ONE						
VENUE	P	W	D	L	F	A
HOME	22	13	6	3	40	25
AWAY	22	7	8	7	28	25
TOTAL	44	20	14	10	68	50

LEAGUE DIVISION TWO						
VENUE	P	W	D	L	F	A
HOME	10	5	1	4	16	10
AWAY	10	2	4	4	10	12
TOTAL	20	7	5	8	26	22

FA CUP						
VENUE	P	W	D	L	F	A
HOME	5	4	1	0	13	5
AWAY	6	2	4	0	11	6
NEUTRAL	2	1	0	1	1	1
TOTAL	13	7	5	1	25	12

LEAGUE CUP						
VENUE	P	W	D	L	F	A
HOME	3	2	1	0	5	2
AWAY	2	0	1	1	2	5
TOTAL	5	2	2	1	7	7

#	SEASON	DATE	COMPETITION / ROUND	MATCH RESULT	VENUE	ATT
1	1896/97	13/02/97	FA Cup 2nd Round	Southampton 1 Newton Heath 1	County Cricket Ground	8000
2	1896/97	17/02/97	FA Cup 2nd Round Replay	Newton Heath 3 Southampton 1	Bank Street	7000
3	1922/23	03/03/23	Football League Division 2	Manchester United 1 Southampton 2	Old Trafford	30000
4	1922/23	11/04/23	Football League Division 2	Southampton 0 Manchester United 0	The Dell	5500
5	1923/24	27/08/23	Football League Division 2	Manchester United 1 Southampton 0	Old Trafford	21750
6	1923/24	03/09/23	Football League Division 2	Southampton 0 Manchester United 0	The Dell	11500
7	1924/25	18/10/24	Football League Division 2	Southampton 0 Manchester United 2	The Dell	10000
8	1924/25	22/04/25	Football League Division 2	Manchester United 1 Southampton 1	Old Trafford	26500
9	1931/32	02/09/31	Football League Division 2	Manchester United 2 Southampton 3	Old Trafford	3507
10	1931/32	07/05/32	Football League Division 2	Southampton 1 Manchester United 1	The Dell	6128
11	1932/33	03/09/32	Football League Division 2	Southampton 4 Manchester United 2	The Dell	7978
12	1932/33	07/01/33	Football League Division 2	Manchester United 1 Southampton 2	Old Trafford	21364
13	1933/34	11/11/33	Football League Division 2	Manchester United 1 Southampton 0	Old Trafford	18149
14	1933/34	24/03/34	Football League Division 2	Southampton 1 Manchester United 0	The Dell	4840
15	1934/35	01/01/35	Football League Division 2	Manchester United 3 Southampton 0	Old Trafford	15174
16	1934/35	22/04/35	Football League Division 2	Southampton 1 Manchester United 0	The Dell	12458
17	1935/36	28/09/35	Football League Division 2	Southampton 2 Manchester United 1	The Dell	17678
18	1935/36	01/02/36	Football League Division 2	Manchester United 4 Southampton 0	Old Trafford	23205
19	1937/38	25/09/37	Football League Division 2	Manchester United 1 Southampton 2	Old Trafford	22729
20	1937/38	05/02/38	Football League Division 2	Southampton 3 Manchester United 3	The Dell	20354
21	1962/63	27/04/63	FA Cup Semi-Final	Manchester United 1 Southampton 0	Villa Park	65000
22	1963/64	04/01/64	FA Cup 3rd Round	Southampton 2 Manchester United 3	The Dell	29164
23	1966/67	19/11/66	Football League Division 1	Southampton 1 Manchester United 2	The Dell	29458
24	1966/67	18/04/67	Football League Division 1	Manchester United 3 Southampton 0	Old Trafford	54291
25	1967/68	18/11/67	Football League Division 1	Manchester United 3 Southampton 2	Old Trafford	48732
26	1967/68	13/04/68	Football League Division 1	Southampton 2 Manchester United 2	The Dell	30079
27	1968/69	19/10/68	Football League Division 1	Manchester United 1 Southampton 2	Old Trafford	46526
28	1968/69	21/12/68	Football League Division 1	Southampton 2 Manchester United 0	The Dell	26194
29	1969/70	16/08/69	Football League Division 1	Manchester United 1 Southampton 4	Old Trafford	46328
30	1969/70	08/10/69	Football League Division 1	Southampton 0 Manchester United 3	The Dell	31044
31	1970/71	21/11/70	Football League Division 1	Southampton 1 Manchester United 0	The Dell	30202
32	1970/71	20/02/71	Football League Division 1	Manchester United 5 Southampton 1	Old Trafford	36060
33	1971/72	27/11/71	Football League Division 1	Southampton 2 Manchester United 5	The Dell	30323
34	1971/72	15/01/72	FA Cup 3rd Round	Southampton 1 Manchester United 1	The Dell	30190
35	1971/72	19/01/72	FA Cup 3rd Round Replay	Manchester United 4 Southampton 1	Old Trafford	50960
36	1971/72	15/04/72	Football League Division 1	Manchester United 3 Southampton 2	Old Trafford	38437
37	1972/73	25/11/72	Football League Division 1	Manchester United 2 Southampton 1	Old Trafford	36073
38	1972/73	31/03/73	Football League Division 1	Southampton 0 Manchester United 2	The Dell	23161
39	1973/74	08/12/73	Football League Division 1	Manchester United 0 Southampton 0	Old Trafford	31648
40	1973/74	20/04/74	Football League Division 1	Southampton 1 Manchester United 1	The Dell	30789
41	1974/75	26/10/74	Football League Division 2	Manchester United 1 Southampton 0	Old Trafford	48724
42	1974/75	05/04/75	Football League Division 2	Southampton 0 Manchester United 1	The Dell	21866
43	1975/76	01/05/76	FA Cup Final	Manchester United 0 Southampton 1	Wembley	100000

UNITED v SOUTHAMPTON (continued)

#	SEASON	DATE	COMPETITION / ROUND	MATCH RESULT	VENUE	ATT
44	1976/77	26/02/77	FA Cup 5th Round	Southampton 2 Manchester United 2	The Dell	29137
45	1976/77	08/03/77	FA Cup 5th Round Replay	Manchester United 2 Southampton 1	Old Trafford	58103
46	1978/79	04/11/78	Football League Division 1	Manchester United 1 Southampton 1	Old Trafford	46259
47	1978/79	30/04/79	Football League Division 1	Southampton 1 Manchester United 1	The Dell	21616
48	1979/80	18/08/79	Football League Division 1	Southampton 1 Manchester United 1	The Dell	21768
49	1979/80	03/11/79	Football League Division 1	Manchester United 1 Southampton 0	Old Trafford	50215
50	1980/81	29/11/80	Football League Division 1	Manchester United 1 Southampton 1	Old Trafford	46840
51	1980/81	07/03/81	Football League Division 1	Southampton 1 Manchester United 0	The Dell	22698
52	1981/82	05/12/81	Football League Division 1	Southampton 3 Manchester United 2	The Dell	24404
53	1981/82	01/05/82	Football League Division 1	Manchester United 1 Southampton 0	Old Trafford	40038
54	1982/83	18/09/82	Football League Division 1	Southampton 0 Manchester United 1	The Dell	21700
55	1982/83	01/12/82	League Cup 4th Round	Manchester United 2 Southampton 0	Old Trafford	28378
56	1982/83	09/04/83	Football League Division 1	Manchester United 1 Southampton 1	Old Trafford	37120
57	1983/84	17/09/83	Football League Division 1	Southampton 3 Manchester United 0	The Dell	20674
58	1983/84	21/01/84	Football League Division 1	Manchester United 3 Southampton 2	Old Trafford	40371
59	1984/85	28/08/84	Football League Division 1	Southampton 0 Manchester United 0	The Dell	22183
60	1984/85	24/04/85	Football League Division 1	Manchester United 0 Southampton 0	Old Trafford	31291
61	1985/86	28/09/85	Football League Division 1	Manchester United 1 Southampton 0	Old Trafford	52449
62	1985/86	01/03/86	Football League Division 1	Southampton 1 Manchester United 0	The Dell	19012
63	1986/87	13/09/86	Football League Division 1	Manchester United 5 Southampton 1	Old Trafford	40135
64	1986/87	29/10/86	League Cup 3rd Round	Manchester United 0 Southampton 0	Old Trafford	23639
65	1986/87	04/11/86	League Cup 3rd Round Replay	Southampton 4 Manchester United 1	The Dell	17915
66	1986/87	03/01/87	Football League Division 1	Southampton 1 Manchester United 1	The Dell	20409
67	1987/88	15/08/87	Football League Division 1	Southampton 2 Manchester United 2	The Dell	21214
68	1987/88	16/01/88	Football League Division 1	Manchester United 0 Southampton 2	Old Trafford	35716
69	1988/89	19/11/88	Football League Division 1	Manchester United 2 Southampton 2	Old Trafford	37277
70	1988/89	06/05/89	Football League Division 1	Southampton 2 Manchester United 1	The Dell	17021
71	1989/90	28/10/89	Football League Division 1	Manchester United 2 Southampton 1	Old Trafford	37122
72	1989/90	24/03/90	Football League Division 1	Southampton 0 Manchester United 2	The Dell	20510
73	1990/91	22/09/90	Football League Division 1	Manchester United 3 Southampton 2	Old Trafford	41288
74	1990/91	16/01/91	League Cup 5th Round	Southampton 1 Manchester United 1	The Dell	21011
75	1990/91	23/01/91	League Cup 5th Round Replay	Manchester United 3 Southampton 2	Old Trafford	41903
76	1990/91	13/03/91	Football League Division 1	Southampton 1 Manchester United 1	The Dell	15701
77	1991/92	14/09/91	Football League Division 1	Southampton 0 Manchester United 1	The Dell	19264
78	1991/92	27/01/92	FA Cup 4th Round	Southampton 0 Manchester United 0	The Dell	19506
79	1991/92	05/02/92	FA Cup 4th Round Replay	Manchester United 2 Southampton 2	Old Trafford	33414
				(United lost the tie 2–4 on penalty kicks)		
80	1991/92	16/04/92	Football League Division 1	Manchester United 1 Southampton 0	Old Trafford	43972
81	1992/93	24/08/92	FA Premiership	Southampton 0 Manchester United 1	The Dell	15623
82	1992/93	20/02/93	FA Premiership	Manchester United 2 Southampton 1	Old Trafford	36257
83	1993/94	28/08/93	FA Premiership	Southampton 1 Manchester United 3	The Dell	16189
84	1993/94	04/05/94	FA Premiership	Manchester United 2 Southampton 0	Old Trafford	44705
85	1994/95	31/12/94	FA Premiership	Southampton 2 Manchester United 2	The Dell	15204
86	1994/95	10/05/95	FA Premiership	Manchester United 2 Southampton 1	Old Trafford	43479
87	1995/96	18/11/95	FA Premiership	Manchester United 4 Southampton 1	Old Trafford	39301
88	1995/96	11/03/96	FA Cup 6th Round	Manchester United 2 Southampton 0	Old Trafford	45446
89	1995/96	13/04/96	FA Premiership	Southampton 3 Manchester United 1	The Dell	15262
90	1996/97	26/10/96	FA Premiership	Southampton 6 Manchester United 3	The Dell	15253
91	1996/97	01/02/97	FA Premiership	Manchester United 2 Southampton 1	Old Trafford	55269
92	1997/98	13/08/97	FA Premiership	Manchester United 1 Southampton 0	Old Trafford	55008
93	1997/98	19/01/98	FA Premiership	Southampton 1 Manchester United 0	The Dell	15241
94	1998/99	03/10/98	FA Premiership	Southampton 0 Manchester United 3	The Dell	15251
95	1998/99	27/02/99	FA Premiership	Manchester United 2 Southampton 1	Old Trafford	55316
96	1999/00	25/09/99	FA Premiership	Manchester United 3 Southampton 3	Old Trafford	55249
97	1999/00	22/04/00	FA Premiership	Southampton 1 Manchester United 3	The Dell	15245
98	2000/01	28/10/00	FA Premiership	Manchester United 5 Southampton 0	Old Trafford	67581
99	2000/01	13/05/01	FA Premiership	Southampton 2 Manchester United 1	The Dell	15526
100	2001/02	22/12/01	FA Premiership	Manchester United 6 Southampton 1	Old Trafford	67638
101	2001/02	13/01/02	FA Premiership	Southampton 1 Manchester United 3	St Mary's Stadium	31858
102	2002/03	02/11/02	FA Premiership	Manchester United 2 Southampton 1	Old Trafford	67691
103	2002/03	01/02/03	FA Premiership	Southampton 0 Manchester United 2	St Mary's Stadium	32085
104	2003/04	31/08/03	FA Premiership	Southampton 1 Manchester United 0	St Mary's Stadium	32066
105	2003/04	31/01/04	FA Premiership	Manchester United 3 Southampton 2	Old Trafford	67758
106	2004/05	04/12/04	FA Premiership	Manchester United 3 Southampton 0	Old Trafford	67921
107	2004/05	12/03/05	FA Cup 6th Round	Southampton 0 Manchester United 4	St Mary's Stadium	30971
108	2004/05	15/05/05	FA Premiership	Southampton 1 Manchester United 2	St Mary's Stadium	32066

UNITED v SOUTHEND UNITED

LEAGUE CUP					
VENUE	P	W	D	L	F	A
HOME	0	0	0	0	0	0
AWAY	1	0	0	1	0	1
TOTAL	1	0	0	1	0	1

#	SEASON	DATE	COMPETITION / ROUND	MATCH RESULT	VENUE	ATT
1	2006/07	07/11/06	League Cup 4th Round	Southend United 1 Manchester United 0	Roots Hall	11532

UNITED v SOUTHPORT CENTRAL

FA CUP					
VENUE	P	W	D	L	F	A
HOME	1	1	0	0	4	1
AWAY	0	0	0	0	0	0
TOTAL	1	1	0	0	4	1

#	SEASON	DATE	COMPETITION / ROUND	MATCH RESULT	VENUE	ATT
1	1902/03	29/11/02	FA Cup 5th Qualifying Round	Manchester United 4 Southport Central 1	Bank Street	6000

UNITED v SPARTA PRAGUE

CHAMPIONS LEAGUE					
VENUE	P	W	D	L	F	A
HOME	1	1	0	0	4	1
AWAY	1	0	1	0	0	0
TOTAL	2	1	1	0	4	1

#	SEASON	DATE	COMPETITION / ROUND	MATCH RESULT	VENUE	ATT
1	2004/05	19/10/04	Champions League Phase 1 Match 3	Sparta Prague 0 Manchester United 0	Toyota Stadium	20654
2	2004/05	03/11/04	Champions League Phase 1 Match 4	Manchester United 4 Sparta Prague 1	Old Trafford	66706

UNITED v SPARTAK VARNA

EUROPEAN CUP-WINNERS' CUP					
VENUE	P	W	D	L	F	A
HOME	1	1	0	0	2	0
AWAY	1	1	0	0	2	1
TOTAL	2	2	0	0	4	1

#	SEASON	DATE	COMPETITION / ROUND	MATCH RESULT	VENUE	ATT
1	1983/84	19/10/83	European CWC 2nd Round 1st Leg	Spartak Varna 1 Manchester United 2	Stad Yuri Gargarin	40000
2	1983/84	02/11/83	European CWC 2nd Round 2nd Leg	Manchester United 2 Spartak Varna 0	Old Trafford	39079

UNITED v SPORTING LISBON

ALL COMPETITIVE MATCHES							CHAMPIONS LEAGUE							EUROPEAN CUP-WINNERS' CUP					
VENUE	P	W	D	L	F	A	VENUE	P	W	D	L	F	A	VENUE	P	W	D	L	F	A
HOME	2	2	0	0	6	2	HOME	1	1	0	0	2	1	HOME	1	1	0	0	4	1
AWAY	2	1	0	1	1	5	AWAY	1	1	0	0	1	0	AWAY	1	0	0	1	0	5
TOTAL	4	3	0	1	7	7	TOTAL	2	2	0	0	3	1	TOTAL	2	1	0	1	4	6

#	SEASON	DATE	COMPETITION / ROUND	MATCH RESULT	VENUE	ATT
1	1963/64	26/02/64	European CWC Quarter-Final 1st Leg	Manchester United 4 Sporting Lisbon 1	Old Trafford	60000
2	1963/64	18/03/64	European CWC Quarter-Final 2nd Leg	Sporting Lisbon 5 Manchester United 0	de Jose Alvalade	40000
3	2007/08	19/09/07	Champions League Phase 1 Match 1	Sporting Lisbon 0 Manchester United 1	de Jose Alvalade	39514
4	2007/08	27/11/07	Champions League Phase 1 Match 5	Manchester United 2 Sporting Lisbon 1	Old Trafford	75162

UNITED v ST ETIENNE

EUROPEAN CUP-WINNERS' CUP

VENUE	P	W	D	L	F	A
HOME	1	1	0	0	2	0
AWAY	1	0	1	0	1	1
TOTAL	2	1	1	0	3	1

#	SEASON	DATE	COMPETITION / ROUND	MATCH RESULT	VENUE	ATT
1	1977/78	14/09/77	European CWC 1st Round 1st Leg	St Etienne 1 Manchester United 1	Stade Geoffrey Guichard	33678
2	1977/78	05/10/77	European CWC 1st Round 2nd Leg	Manchester United 2 St Etienne 0	Home Park	31634

UNITED v STAPLE HILL

FA CUP

VENUE	P	W	D	L	F	A
HOME	1	1	0	0	7	2
AWAY	0	0	0	0	0	0
TOTAL	1	1	0	0	7	2

#	SEASON	DATE	COMPETITION / ROUND	MATCH RESULT	VENUE	ATT
1	1905/06	13/01/06	FA Cup 1st Round	Manchester United 7 Staple Hill 2	Bank Street	7560

UNITED v STOCKPORT COUNTY

ALL COMPETITIVE MATCHES							LEAGUE DIVISION TWO							LEAGUE CUP						
VENUE	P	W	D	L	F	A	VENUE	P	W	D	L	F	A	VENUE	P	W	D	L	F	A
HOME	9	7	2	0	21	7	HOME	9	7	2	0	21	7	HOME	0	0	0	0	0	0
AWAY	10	3	0	7	11	13	AWAY	9	2	0	7	8	11	AWAY	1	1	0	0	3	2
TOTAL	19	10	2	7	32	20	TOTAL	18	9	2	7	29	18	TOTAL	1	1	0	0	3	2

#	SEASON	DATE	COMPETITION / ROUND	MATCH RESULT	VENUE	ATT
1	1900/01	24/11/00	Football League Division 2	Stockport County 1 Newton Heath 0	Green Lane	5000
2	1900/01	30/03/01	Football League Division 2	Newton Heath 3 Stockport County 1	Bank Street	4000
3	1901/02	05/10/01	Football League Division 2	Newton Heath 3 Stockport County 3	Bank Street	5000
4	1901/02	01/02/02	Football League Division 2	Stockport County 1 Newton Heath 0	Green Lane	2000
5	1902/03	11/10/02	Football League Division 2	Stockport County 2 Manchester United 1	Edgeley Park	6000
6	1902/03	23/03/03	Football League Division 2	Manchester United 0 Stockport County 0	Bank Street	2000
7	1903/04	24/10/03	Football League Division 2	Manchester United 3 Stockport County 1	Bank Street	15000
8	1903/04	28/03/04	Football League Division 2	Stockport County 0 Manchester United 3	Edgeley Park	2500
9	1905/06	23/09/05	Football League Division 2	Manchester United 3 Stockport County 1	Bank Street	15000
10	1905/06	27/01/06	Football League Division 2	Stockport County 0 Manchester United 1	Edgeley Park	15000
11	1922/23	16/12/22	Football League Division 2	Manchester United 1 Stockport County 0	Old Trafford	24000
12	1922/23	23/12/22	Football League Division 2	Stockport County 1 Manchester United 0	Edgeley Park	15500
13	1923/24	20/10/23	Football League Division 2	Manchester United 3 Stockport County 0	Old Trafford	31500
14	1923/24	27/10/23	Football League Division 2	Stockport County 3 Manchester United 2	Edgeley Park	16500
15	1924/25	01/09/24	Football League Division 2	Stockport County 2 Manchester United 1	Edgeley Park	12500
16	1924/25	10/04/25	Football League Division 2	Manchester United 2 Stockport County 0	Old Trafford	43500
17	1937/38	18/09/37	Football League Division 2	Stockport County 1 Manchester United 0	Edgeley Park	24386
18	1937/38	29/01/38	Football League Division 2	Manchester United 3 Stockport County 1	Old Trafford	31852
19	1978/79	30/08/78	League Cup 2nd Round	Stockport County 2 Manchester United 3 (United drawn away – tie switched to Old Trafford)	Old Trafford	41761

UNITED v STOKE CITY

ALL COMPETITIVE MATCHES						
VENUE	P	W	D	L	F	A
HOME	43	20	16	7	72	36
AWAY	42	9	15	18	46	69
NEUTRAL	2	1	0	1	4	5
TOTAL	87	30	31	26	122	110

ALL LEAGUE MATCHES						
VENUE	P	W	D	L	F	A
HOME	35	17	13	5	63	29
AWAY	35	9	11	15	40	60
TOTAL	70	26	24	20	103	89

ALL CUP MATCHES						
VENUE	P	W	D	L	F	A
HOME	8	3	3	2	9	7
AWAY	7	0	4	3	6	9
NEUTRAL	1	1	0	0	4	2
TOTAL	16	4	7	5	19	18

LEAGUE DIVISION ONE						
VENUE	P	W	D	L	F	A
HOME	31	16	11	4	58	24
AWAY	31	9	9	13	40	54
TOTAL	62	25	20	17	98	78

LEAGUE DIVISION TWO						
VENUE	P	W	D	L	F	A
HOME	4	1	2	1	5	5
AWAY	4	0	2	2	0	6
TOTAL	8	1	4	3	5	11

FA CUP						
VENUE	P	W	D	L	F	A
HOME	6	2	2	2	6	6
AWAY	4	0	3	1	4	5
NEUTRAL	1	1	0	0	4	2
TOTAL	11	3	5	3	14	13

LEAGUE CUP						
VENUE	P	W	D	L	F	A
HOME	2	1	1	0	3	1
AWAY	3	0	1	2	2	4
TOTAL	5	1	2	2	5	5

OTHER MATCHES						
VENUE	P	W	D	L	F	A
HOME	0	0	0	0	0	0
AWAY	0	0	0	0	0	0
NEUTRAL	1	0	0	1	0	3
TOTAL	1	0	0	1	0	3

#	SEASON	DATE	COMPETITION / ROUND	MATCH RESULT	VENUE	ATT
1	1892/93	07/01/93	Football League Division 1	Stoke City 7 Newton Heath 1	Victoria Ground	1000
2	1892/93	31/03/93	Football League Division 1	Newton Heath 1 Stoke City 0	North Road	10000
3	1893/94	23/03/94	Football League Division 1	Newton Heath 6 Stoke City 2	Bank Street	8000
4	1893/94	31/03/94	Football League Division 1	Stoke City 3 Newton Heath 1	Victoria Ground	4000
5	1894/95	02/02/95	FA Cup 1st Round	Newton Heath 2 Stoke City 3	Bank Street	7000
6	1894/95	27/04/95	Football League Test Match	Newton Heath 0 Stoke City 3	Cobridge Stadium	10000
7	1906/07	06/10/06	Football League Division 1	Stoke City 1 Manchester United 2	Victoria Ground	7000
8	1906/07	09/02/07	Football League Division 1	Manchester United 4 Stoke City 1	Bank Street	15000
9	1923/24	29/03/24	Football League Division 2	Manchester United 2 Stoke City 2	Old Trafford	13000
10	1923/24	05/04/24	Football League Division 2	Stoke City 3 Manchester United 0	Victoria Ground	11000
11	1924/25	06/09/24	Football League Division 2	Stoke City 0 Manchester United 0	Victoria Ground	15250
12	1924/25	03/01/25	Football League Division 2	Manchester United 2 Stoke City 0	Old Trafford	24500
13	1930/31	10/01/31	FA Cup 3rd Round	Stoke City 3 Manchester United 3	Victoria Ground	23415
14	1930/31	14/01/31	FA Cup 3rd Round Replay	Manchester United 0 Stoke City 0	Old Trafford	22013
15	1930/31	19/01/31	FA Cup 3rd Round 2nd Replay	Manchester United 4 Stoke City 2	Anfield	11788
16	1931/32	07/09/31	Football League Division 2	Stoke City 3 Manchester United 0	Victoria Ground	10518
17	1931/32	16/09/31	Football League Division 2	Manchester United 1 Stoke City 1	Old Trafford	5025
18	1932/33	27/08/32	Football League Division 2	Manchester United 0 Stoke City 2	Old Trafford	24996
19	1932/33	31/12/32	Football League Division 2	Stoke City 0 Manchester United 0	Victoria Ground	14115
20	1935/36	25/01/36	FA Cup 4th Round	Stoke City 0 Manchester United 0	Victoria Ground	32286
21	1935/36	29/01/36	FA Cup 4th Round Replay	Manchester United 0 Stoke City 2	Old Trafford	34440
22	1936/37	31/10/36	Football League Division 1	Stoke City 3 Manchester United 0	Victoria Ground	22464
23	1936/37	06/03/37	Football League Division 1	Manchester United 2 Stoke City 1	Old Trafford	24660
24	1938/39	17/09/38	Football League Division 1	Stoke City 1 Manchester United 1	Victoria Ground	21526
25	1938/39	21/01/39	Football League Division 1	Manchester United 0 Stoke City 1	Old Trafford	37384
26	1946/47	21/09/46	Football League Division 1	Stoke City 3 Manchester United 2	Victoria Ground	41699
27	1946/47	05/02/47	Football League Division 1	Manchester United 1 Stoke City 1	Maine Road	8456
28	1947/48	04/10/47	Football League Division 1	Manchester United 1 Stoke City 1	Maine Road	45745
29	1947/48	21/02/48	Football League Division 1	Stoke City 0 Manchester United 2	Victoria Ground	36794
30	1948/49	16/10/48	Football League Division 1	Stoke City 2 Manchester United 1	Victoria Ground	45830
31	1948/49	12/03/49	Football League Division 1	Manchester United 3 Stoke City 0	Maine Road	55949
32	1949/50	17/09/49	Football League Division 1	Manchester United 2 Stoke City 2	Old Trafford	43522
33	1949/50	21/01/50	Football League Division 1	Stoke City 3 Manchester United 1	Victoria Ground	38877
34	1950/51	18/11/50	Football League Division 1	Manchester United 0 Stoke City 0	Old Trafford	30031
35	1950/51	07/04/51	Football League Division 1	Stoke City 2 Manchester United 0	Victoria Ground	25690
36	1951/52	08/09/51	Football League Division 1	Manchester United 4 Stoke City 0	Old Trafford	48660
37	1951/52	05/01/52	Football League Division 1	Stoke City 0 Manchester United 0	Victoria Ground	36389
38	1952/53	11/10/52	Football League Division 1	Manchester United 0 Stoke City 2	Old Trafford	28968
39	1952/53	28/02/53	Football League Division 1	Stoke City 3 Manchester United 1	Victoria Ground	30219
40	1963/64	07/12/63	Football League Division 1	Manchester United 5 Stoke City 2	Old Trafford	52232
41	1963/64	18/04/64	Football League Division 1	Stoke City 3 Manchester United 1	Victoria Ground	45670

UNITED v STOKE CITY (continued)

#	SEASON	DATE	COMPETITION / ROUND	MATCH RESULT	VENUE	ATT
42	1964/65	19/09/64	Football League Division 1	Stoke City 1 Manchester United 2	Victoria Ground	40031
43	1964/65	23/01/65	Football League Division 1	Manchester United 1 Stoke City 1	Old Trafford	50392
44	1964/65	30/01/65	FA Cup 4th Round	Stoke City 0 Manchester United 0	Victoria Ground	53009
45	1964/65	03/02/65	FA Cup 4th Round Replay	Manchester United 1 Stoke City 0	Old Trafford	50814
46	1965/66	04/09/65	Football League Division 1	Manchester United 1 Stoke City 1	Old Trafford	37603
47	1965/66	19/02/66	Football League Division 1	Stoke City 2 Manchester United 2	Victoria Ground	36667
48	1966/67	07/09/66	Football League Division 1	Stoke City 3 Manchester United 0	Victoria Ground	44337
49	1966/67	28/01/67	FA Cup 3rd Round	Manchester United 2 Stoke City 0	Old Trafford	63500
50	1966/67	13/05/67	Football League Division 1	Manchester United 0 Stoke City 0	Old Trafford	61071
51	1967/68	04/11/67	Football League Division 1	Manchester United 1 Stoke City 0	Old Trafford	51041
52	1967/68	30/03/68	Football League Division 1	Stoke City 2 Manchester United 4	Victoria Ground	30141
53	1968/69	23/11/68	Football League Division 1	Stoke City 0 Manchester United 0	Victoria Ground	30562
54	1968/69	24/03/69	Football League Division 1	Manchester United 1 Stoke City 1	Old Trafford	39931
55	1969/70	01/11/69	Football League Division 1	Manchester United 1 Stoke City 1	Old Trafford	53406
56	1969/70	28/02/70	Football League Division 1	Stoke City 2 Manchester United 2	Victoria Ground	38917
57	1970/71	07/11/70	Football League Division 1	Manchester United 2 Stoke City 2	Old Trafford	47451
58	1970/71	20/03/71	Football League Division 1	Stoke City 1 Manchester United 2	Victoria Ground	40005
59	1971/72	27/10/71	League Cup 4th Round	Manchester United 1 Stoke City 1	Old Trafford	47062
60	1971/72	08/11/71	League Cup 4th Round Replay	Stoke City 0 Manchester United 0	Victoria Ground	40805
61	1971/72	15/11/71	League Cup 4th Round 2nd Replay	Stoke City 2 Manchester United 1	Victoria Ground	42249
62	1971/72	11/12/71	Football League Division 1	Stoke City 1 Manchester United 1	Victoria Ground	33857
63	1971/72	18/03/72	FA Cup 6th Round	Manchester United 1 Stoke City 1	Old Trafford	54226
64	1971/72	22/03/72	FA Cup 6th Round Replay	Stoke City 2 Manchester United 1	Victoria Ground	49192
65	1971/72	29/04/72	Football League Division 1	Manchester United 3 Stoke City 0	Old Trafford	34959
66	1972/73	09/12/72	Football League Division 1	Manchester United 0 Stoke City 2	Old Trafford	41347
67	1972/73	14/04/73	Football League Division 1	Stoke City 2 Manchester United 2	Victoria Ground	37051
68	1973/74	29/08/73	Football League Division 1	Manchester United 1 Stoke City 0	Old Trafford	43614
69	1973/74	29/04/74	Football League Division 1	Stoke City 1 Manchester United 0	Victoria Ground	27392
70	1975/76	30/08/75	Football League Division 1	Stoke City 0 Manchester United 1	Victoria Ground	33092
71	1975/76	21/04/76	Football League Division 1	Manchester United 0 Stoke City 1	Old Trafford	53879
72	1976/77	09/04/77	Football League Division 1	Manchester United 3 Stoke City 0	Old Trafford	53102
73	1976/77	11/05/77	Football League Division 1	Stoke City 3 Manchester United 3	Victoria Ground	24204
74	1979/80	29/09/79	Football League Division 1	Manchester United 4 Stoke City 0	Old Trafford	52596
75	1979/80	16/02/80	Football League Division 1	Stoke City 1 Manchester United 1	Victoria Ground	28389
76	1980/81	22/10/80	Football League Division 1	Stoke City 1 Manchester United 2	Victoria Ground	24534
77	1980/81	13/12/80	Football League Division 1	Manchester United 2 Stoke City 2	Old Trafford	39568
78	1981/82	23/01/82	Football League Division 1	Stoke City 0 Manchester United 3	Victoria Ground	19793
79	1981/82	15/05/82	Football League Division 1	Manchester United 2 Stoke City 0	Old Trafford	43072
80	1982/83	09/10/82	Football League Division 1	Manchester United 1 Stoke City 0	Old Trafford	43132
81	1982/83	02/03/83	Football League Division 1	Stoke City 1 Manchester United 0	Victoria Ground	21266
82	1983/84	03/09/83	Football League Division 1	Stoke City 0 Manchester United 1	Victoria Ground	23704
83	1983/84	31/12/83	Football League Division 1	Manchester United 1 Stoke City 0	Old Trafford	40164
84	1984/85	26/12/84	Football League Division 1	Stoke City 2 Manchester United 1	Victoria Ground	20985
85	1984/85	06/04/85	Football League Division 1	Manchester United 5 Stoke City 0	Old Trafford	42940
86	1993/94	22/09/93	League Cup 2nd Round 1st Leg	Stoke City 2 Manchester United 1	Victoria Ground	23327
87	1993/94	06/10/93	League Cup 2nd Round 2nd Leg	Manchester United 2 Stoke City 0	Old Trafford	41387

UNITED v STRASBOURG

INTER-CITIES' FAIRS CUP					
VENUE	P	W	D	L	F	A
HOME	1	0	1	0	0	0
AWAY	1	1	0	0	5	0
TOTAL	2	1	1	0	5	0

#	SEASON	DATE	COMPETITION / ROUND	MATCH RESULT	VENUE	ATT
1	1964/65	12/05/65	Inter-Cities' Fairs Cup Quarter-Final 1st Leg	Strasbourg 0 Manchester United 5	Stade de la Meinau	30000
2	1964/65	19/05/65	Inter-Cities' Fairs Cup Quarter-Final 2nd Leg	Manchester United 0 Strasbourg 0	Old Trafford	34188

UNITED v STURM GRAZ

CHAMPIONS LEAGUE

VENUE	P	W	D	L	F	A
HOME	2	2	0	0	5	1
AWAY	2	2	0	0	5	0
TOTAL	4	4	0	0	10	1

#	SEASON	DATE	COMPETITION / ROUND	MATCH RESULT	VENUE	ATT
1	1999/00	22/09/99	Champions League Phase 1 Match 2	Sturm Graz 0 Manchester United 3	Schwarzenegger Stadium	16480
2	1999/00	02/11/99	Champions League Phase 1 Match 6	Manchester United 2 Sturm Graz 1	Old Trafford	53745
3	2000/01	06/12/00	Champions League Phase 2 Match 2	Sturm Graz 0 Manchester United 2	Schwarzenegger Stadium	16500
4	2000/01	13/03/01	Champions League Phase 2 Match 6	Manchester United 3 Sturm Graz 0	Old Trafford	66404

UNITED v STUTTGART

CHAMPIONS LEAGUE

VENUE	P	W	D	L	F	A
HOME	1	1	0	0	2	0
AWAY	1	0	0	1	1	2
TOTAL	2	1	0	1	3	2

#	SEASON	DATE	COMPETITION / ROUND	MATCH RESULT	VENUE	ATT
1	2003/04	01/10/03	Champions League Phase 1 Match 2	Stuttgart 2 Manchester United 1	Gottlieb–Daimler Stadium	53000
2	2003/04	09/12/03	Champions League Phase 1 Match 6	Manchester United 2 Stuttgart 0	Old Trafford	67141

UNITED v SUNDERLAND

ALL COMPETITIVE MATCHES

VENUE	P	W	D	L	F	A
HOME	62	34	17	11	129	71
AWAY	62	17	17	28	86	123
NEUTRAL	1	1	0	0	5	1
TOTAL	125	52	34	39	220	195

ALL LEAGUE MATCHES

VENUE	P	W	D	L	F	A
HOME	55	31	13	11	115	62
AWAY	55	16	13	26	76	111
TOTAL	110	47	26	37	191	173

ALL CUP MATCHES

VENUE	P	W	D	L	F	A
HOME	6	3	3	0	13	8
AWAY	6	1	4	1	10	10
NEUTRAL	1	1	0	0	5	1
TOTAL	13	5	7	1	28	19

PREMIERSHIP

VENUE	P	W	D	L	F	A
HOME	7	6	1	0	19	2
AWAY	7	4	2	1	15	7
TOTAL	14	10	3	1	34	9

LEAGUE DIVISION ONE

VENUE	P	W	D	L	F	A
HOME	47	24	12	11	93	58
AWAY	47	12	10	25	61	104
TOTAL	94	36	22	36	154	162

LEAGUE DIVISION TWO

VENUE	P	W	D	L	F	A
HOME	1	1	0	0	3	2
AWAY	1	0	1	0	0	0
TOTAL	2	1	1	0	3	2

FA CUP

VENUE	P	W	D	L	F	A
HOME	4	2	2	0	10	6
AWAY	4	1	3	0	7	6
NEUTRAL	1	1	0	0	5	1
TOTAL	9	4	5	0	22	13

LEAGUE CUP

VENUE	P	W	D	L	F	A
HOME	2	1	1	0	3	2
AWAY	2	0	1	1	3	4
TOTAL	4	1	2	1	6	6

OTHER MATCHES

VENUE	P	W	D	L	F	A
HOME	1	0	1	0	1	1
AWAY	1	0	0	1	0	2
TOTAL	2	0	1	1	1	3

#	SEASON	DATE	COMPETITION / ROUND	MATCH RESULT	VENUE	ATT
1	1892/93	04/03/93	Football League Division 1	Newton Heath 0 Sunderland 5	North Road	15000
2	1892/93	04/04/93	Football League Division 1	Sunderland 6 Newton Heath 0	Newcastle Road	3500
3	1893/94	06/12/93	Football League Division 1	Sunderland 4 Newton Heath 1	Newcastle Road	5000
4	1893/94	03/03/94	Football League Division 1	Newton Heath 2 Sunderland 4	Bank Street	10000
5	1896/97	24/04/97	Football League Test Match	Newton Heath 1 Sunderland 1	Bank Street	18000
6	1896/97	26/04/97	Football League Test Match	Sunderland 0 Newton Heath 0	Newcastle Road	6000
7	1906/07	20/10/06	Football League Division 1	Sunderland 4 Manchester United 1	Roker Park	18000
8	1906/07	25/03/07	Football League Division 1	Manchester United 2 Sunderland 0	Bank Street	12000
9	1907/08	16/11/07	Football League Division 1	Sunderland 1 Manchester United 2	Roker Park	30000
10	1907/08	14/03/08	Football League Division 1	Manchester United 3 Sunderland 0	Bank Street	15000
11	1908/09	31/10/08	Football League Division 1	Sunderland 6 Manchester United 1	Roker Park	30000
12	1908/09	15/03/09	Football League Division 1	Manchester United 2 Sunderland 2	Bank Street	10000
13	1909/10	04/12/09	Football League Division 1	Sunderland 3 Manchester United 0	Roker Park	12000
14	1909/10	16/04/10	Football League Division 1	Manchester United 2 Sunderland 0	Old Trafford	12000
15	1910/11	24/12/10	Football League Division 1	Sunderland 1 Manchester United 2	Roker Park	30000
16	1910/11	29/04/11	Football League Division 1	Manchester United 5 Sunderland 1	Old Trafford	10000

UNITED v SUNDERLAND (continued)

#	SEASON	DATE	COMPETITION / ROUND	MATCH RESULT	VENUE	ATT
17	1911/12	23/09/11	Football League Division 1	Manchester United 2 Sunderland 2	Old Trafford	20000
18	1911/12	27/01/12	Football League Division 1	Sunderland 5 Manchester United 0	Roker Park	12000
19	1912/13	09/11/12	Football League Division 1	Sunderland 3 Manchester United 1	Roker Park	20000
20	1912/13	15/03/13	Football League Division 1	Manchester United 1 Sunderland 3	Old Trafford	15000
21	1913/14	08/09/13	Football League Division 1	Manchester United 3 Sunderland 1	Old Trafford	25000
22	1913/14	10/04/14	Football League Division 1	Sunderland 2 Manchester United 0	Roker Park	20000
23	1914/15	03/10/14	Football League Division 1	Manchester United 3 Sunderland 0	Old Trafford	16000
24	1914/15	06/02/15	Football League Division 1	Sunderland 1 Manchester United 0	Roker Park	5000
25	1919/20	07/02/20	Football League Division 1	Sunderland 3 Manchester United 0	Roker Park	25000
26	1919/20	14/02/20	Football League Division 1	Manchester United 2 Sunderland 0	Old Trafford	35000
27	1920/21	20/02/21	Football League Division 1	Manchester United 3 Sunderland 0	Old Trafford	40000
28	1920/21	05/03/21	Football League Division 1	Sunderland 2 Manchester United 3	Roker Park	25000
29	1921/22	21/01/22	Football League Division 1	Sunderland 2 Manchester United 1	Roker Park	10000
30	1921/22	28/01/22	Football League Division 1	Manchester United 3 Sunderland 1	Old Trafford	18000
31	1925/26	05/12/25	Football League Division 1	Sunderland 2 Manchester United 1	Roker Park	25507
32	1925/26	20/02/26	FA Cup 5th Round	Sunderland 3 Manchester United 3	Roker Park	50500
33	1925/26	24/02/26	FA Cup 5th Round Replay	Manchester United 2 Sunderland 1	Old Trafford	58661
34	1925/26	21/04/26	Football League Division 1	Manchester United 5 Sunderland 1	Old Trafford	10918
35	1926/27	11/12/26	Football League Division 1	Sunderland 6 Manchester United 0	Roker Park	15385
36	1926/27	30/04/27	Football League Division 1	Manchester United 0 Sunderland 0	Old Trafford	17300
37	1927/28	12/11/27	Football League Division 1	Sunderland 4 Manchester United 1	Roker Park	13319
38	1927/28	25/04/28	Football League Division 1	Manchester United 2 Sunderland 1	Old Trafford	9545
39	1928/29	24/11/28	Football League Division 1	Sunderland 5 Manchester United 1	Roker Park	15932
40	1928/29	06/04/29	Football League Division 1	Manchester United 3 Sunderland 0	Old Trafford	27772
41	1929/30	30/11/29	Football League Division 1	Sunderland 2 Manchester United 4	Roker Park	11508
42	1929/30	05/04/30	Football League Division 1	Manchester United 2 Sunderland 1	Old Trafford	13230
43	1930/31	29/11/30	Football League Division 1	Manchester United 1 Sunderland 1	Old Trafford	10971
44	1930/31	04/04/31	Football League Division 1	Sunderland 1 Manchester United 2	Roker Park	13590
45	1936/37	01/01/37	Football League Division 1	Manchester United 2 Sunderland 1	Old Trafford	46257
46	1936/37	21/04/37	Football League Division 1	Sunderland 1 Manchester United 1	Roker Park	12876
47	1938/39	29/10/38	Football League Division 1	Manchester United 0 Sunderland 1	Old Trafford	33565
48	1938/39	04/03/39	Football League Division 1	Sunderland 5 Manchester United 2	Roker Park	11078
49	1946/47	26/10/46	Football League Division 1	Manchester United 0 Sunderland 3	Maine Road	48385
50	1946/47	01/03/47	Football League Division 1	Sunderland 1 Manchester United 1	Roker Park	25038
51	1947/48	18/10/47	Football League Division 1	Sunderland 1 Manchester United 0	Roker Park	37148
52	1947/48	06/03/48	Football League Division 1	Manchester United 3 Sunderland 1	Maine Road	55160
53	1948/49	02/10/48	Football League Division 1	Sunderland 2 Manchester United 1	Roker Park	54419
54	1948/49	21/04/49	Football League Division 1	Manchester United 1 Sunderland 2	Maine Road	30640
55	1949/50	01/10/49	Football League Division 1	Manchester United 1 Sunderland 3	Old Trafford	49260
56	1949/50	18/02/50	Football League Division 1	Sunderland 2 Manchester United 2	Roker Park	63251
57	1950/51	25/12/50	Football League Division 1	Sunderland 2 Manchester United 1	Roker Park	41215
58	1950/51	26/12/50	Football League Division 1	Manchester United 3 Sunderland 5	Old Trafford	35176
59	1951/52	20/10/51	Football League Division 1	Manchester United 0 Sunderland 1	Old Trafford	40915
60	1951/52	08/03/52	Football League Division 1	Sunderland 1 Manchester United 2	Roker Park	48078
61	1952/53	27/09/52	Football League Division 1	Manchester United 0 Sunderland 1	Old Trafford	28967
62	1952/53	18/02/53	Football League Division 1	Sunderland 2 Manchester United 2	Roker Park	24263
63	1953/54	10/10/53	Football League Division 1	Manchester United 1 Sunderland 0	Old Trafford	34617
64	1953/54	27/02/54	Football League Division 1	Sunderland 0 Manchester United 2	Roker Park	58440
65	1954/55	08/04/55	Football League Division 1	Sunderland 4 Manchester United 3	Roker Park	43882
66	1954/55	11/04/55	Football League Division 1	Manchester United 2 Sunderland 2	Old Trafford	36013
67	1955/56	03/12/55	Football League Division 1	Manchester United 2 Sunderland 1	Old Trafford	39901
68	1955/56	14/04/56	Football League Division 1	Sunderland 2 Manchester United 2	Roker Park	19865
69	1956/57	13/10/56	Football League Division 1	Sunderland 1 Manchester United 3	Roker Park	49487
70	1956/57	20/04/57	Football League Division 1	Manchester United 4 Sunderland 0	Old Trafford	58725
71	1957/58	04/04/58	Football League Division 1	Manchester United 2 Sunderland 2	Old Trafford	47421
72	1957/58	07/04/58	Football League Division 1	Sunderland 1 Manchester United 2	Roker Park	51302
73	1963/64	29/02/64	FA Cup 6th Round	Manchester United 3 Sunderland 3	Old Trafford	63700
74	1963/64	04/03/64	FA Cup 6th Round Replay	Sunderland 2 Manchester United 2	Roker Park	68000
75	1963/64	09/03/64	FA Cup 6th Round 2nd Replay	Manchester United 5 Sunderland 1	Leeds Road	54952
76	1964/65	10/10/64	Football League Division 1	Manchester United 1 Sunderland 0	Old Trafford	48577
77	1964/65	24/02/65	Football League Division 1	Sunderland 1 Manchester United 0	Roker Park	51336

UNITED v SUNDERLAND (continued)

#	SEASON	DATE	COMPETITION / ROUND	MATCH RESULT	VENUE	ATT
78	1965/66	11/12/65	Football League Division 1	Sunderland 2 Manchester United 3	Roker Park	37417
79	1965/66	08/01/66	Football League Division 1	Manchester United 1 Sunderland 1	Old Trafford	39162
80	1966/67	26/11/66	Football League Division 1	Manchester United 5 Sunderland 0	Old Trafford	44687
81	1966/67	22/04/67	Football League Division 1	Sunderland 0 Manchester United 0	Roker Park	43570
82	1967/68	06/09/67	Football League Division 1	Sunderland 1 Manchester United 1	Roker Park	51527
83	1967/68	11/05/68	Football League Division 1	Manchester United 1 Sunderland 2	Old Trafford	62963
84	1968/69	09/11/68	Football League Division 1	Sunderland 1 Manchester United 1	Roker Park	33151
85	1968/69	18/01/69	Football League Division 1	Manchester United 4 Sunderland 1	Old Trafford	45670
86	1969/70	30/08/69	Football League Division 1	Manchester United 3 Sunderland 1	Old Trafford	50570
87	1969/70	27/12/69	Football League Division 1	Sunderland 1 Manchester United 1	Roker Park	36504
88	1974/75	30/11/74	Football League Division 2	Manchester United 3 Sunderland 2	Old Trafford	60585
89	1974/75	18/01/75	Football League Division 2	Sunderland 0 Manchester United 0	Roker Park	45976
90	1976/77	22/09/76	League Cup 3rd Round	Manchester United 2 Sunderland 2	Old Trafford	46170
91	1976/77	04/10/76	League Cup 3rd Round Replay	Sunderland 2 Manchester United 2	Roker Park	46170
92	1976/77	06/10/76	League Cup 3rd Round 2nd Replay	Manchester United 1 Sunderland 0	Old Trafford	47689
93	1976/77	10/11/76	Football League Division 1	Manchester United 3 Sunderland 3	Old Trafford	42685
94	1976/77	11/04/77	Football League Division 1	Sunderland 2 Manchester United 1	Roker Park	38785
95	1980/81	30/08/80	Football League Division 1	Manchester United 1 Sunderland 1	Old Trafford	51498
96	1980/81	28/01/81	Football League Division 1	Sunderland 2 Manchester United 0	Roker Park	31910
97	1981/82	07/11/81	Football League Division 1	Sunderland 1 Manchester United 5	Roker Park	27070
98	1981/82	27/03/82	Football League Division 1	Manchester United 0 Sunderland 0	Old Trafford	40776
99	1982/83	27/12/82	Football League Division 1	Manchester United 0 Sunderland 0	Old Trafford	47783
100	1982/83	04/04/83	Football League Division 1	Sunderland 0 Manchester United 0	Roker Park	31486
101	1983/84	22/10/83	Football League Division 1	Sunderland 0 Manchester United 1	Roker Park	26826
102	1983/84	25/02/84	Football League Division 1	Manchester United 2 Sunderland 1	Old Trafford	40615
103	1984/85	24/11/84	Football League Division 1	Sunderland 3 Manchester United 2	Roker Park	25405
104	1984/85	27/04/85	Football League Division 1	Manchester United 2 Sunderland 2	Old Trafford	38979
105	1985/86	25/01/86	FA Cup 4th Round	Sunderland 0 Manchester United 0	Roker Park	35484
106	1985/86	29/01/86	FA Cup 4th Round Replay	Manchester United 3 Sunderland 0	Old Trafford	43402
107	1990/91	01/09/90	Football League Division 1	Sunderland 2 Manchester United 1	Roker Park	26105
108	1990/91	12/01/91	Football League Division 1	Manchester United 3 Sunderland 0	Old Trafford	45934
109	1995/96	06/01/96	FA Cup 3rd Round	Manchester United 2 Sunderland 2	Old Trafford	41563
110	1995/96	16/01/96	FA Cup 3rd Round Replay	Sunderland 1 Manchester United 2	Roker Park	21378
111	1996/97	21/12/96	FA Premiership	Manchester United 5 Sunderland 0	Old Trafford	55081
112	1996/97	08/03/97	FA Premiership	Sunderland 2 Manchester United 1	Roker Park	22225
113	1999/00	28/12/99	FA Premiership	Sunderland 2 Manchester United 2	Stadium of Light	42026
114	1999/00	15/04/00	FA Premiership	Manchester United 4 Sunderland 0	Old Trafford	61612
115	2000/01	09/09/00	FA Premiership	Manchester United 3 Sunderland 0	Old Trafford	67503
116	2000/01	28/11/00	League Cup 4th Round	Sunderland 2 Manchester United 1	Stadium of Light	47543
117	2000/01	31/01/01	FA Premiership	Sunderland 0 Manchester United 1	Stadium of Light	48260
118	2001/02	13/10/01	FA Premiership	Sunderland 1 Manchester United 3	Stadium of Light	48305
119	2001/02	02/02/02	FA Premiership	Manchester United 4 Sunderland 1	Old Trafford	67587
120	2002/03	31/08/02	FA Premiership	Sunderland 1 Manchester United 1	Stadium of Light	47586
121	2002/03	01/01/03	FA Premiership	Manchester United 2 Sunderland 1	Old Trafford	67609
122	2005/06	15/10/05	FA Premiership	Sunderland 1 Manchester United 3	Stadium of Light	39085
123	2005/06	14/04/06	FA Premiership	Manchester United 0 Sunderland 0	Old Trafford	72519
124	2007/08	01/09/07	FA Premiership	Manchester United 1 Sunderland 0	Old Trafford	75648
125	2007/08	26/12/07	FA Premiership	Sunderland 0 Manchester United 4	Stadium of Light	47360

UNITED v SWANSEA CITY

ALL COMPETITIVE MATCHES							LEAGUE DIVISION ONE							LEAGUE DIVISION TWO					
VENUE	P	W	D	L	F	A	VENUE	P	W	D	L	F	A	VENUE	P	W	D	L	F	A
HOME	8	6	2	0	18	6	HOME	2	2	0	0	3	1	HOME	6	4	2	0	15	5
AWAY	8	0	2	6	6	14	AWAY	2	0	1	1	0	2	AWAY	6	0	1	5	6	12
TOTAL	16	6	4	6	24	20	TOTAL	4	2	1	1	3	3	TOTAL	12	4	3	5	21	17

#	SEASON	DATE	COMPETITION / ROUND	MATCH RESULT	VENUE	ATT
1	1931/32	05/09/31	Football League Division 2	Manchester United 2 Swansea City 1	Old Trafford	6763
2	1931/32	16/01/32	Football League Division 2	Swansea City 3 Manchester United 1	Vetch Field	5888
3	1932/33	24/12/32	Football League Division 2	Swansea City 2 Manchester United 1	Vetch Field	10727
4	1932/33	06/05/33	Football League Division 2	Manchester United 1 Swansea City 1	Old Trafford	65988
5	1933/34	16/12/33	Football League Division 2	Swansea City 2 Manchester United 1	Vetch Field	6591
6	1933/34	28/04/34	Football League Division 2	Manchester United 1 Swansea City 1	Old Trafford	16678
7	1934/35	29/09/34	Football League Division 2	Manchester United 3 Swansea City 1	Old Trafford	14865
8	1934/35	09/02/35	Football League Division 2	Swansea City 1 Manchester United 0	Vetch Field	8876
9	1935/36	09/11/35	Football League Division 2	Swansea City 2 Manchester United 1	Vetch Field	9731
10	1935/36	14/03/36	Football League Division 2	Manchester United 3 Swansea City 0	Old Trafford	27580
11	1937/38	04/12/37	Football League Division 2	Manchester United 5 Swansea City 1	Old Trafford	17782
12	1937/38	16/04/38	Football League Division 2	Swansea City 2 Manchester United 2	Vetch Field	13811
13	1981/82	19/09/81	Football League Division 1	Manchester United 1 Swansea City 0	Old Trafford	47309
14	1981/82	30/01/82	Football League Division 1	Swansea City 2 Manchester United 0	Vetch Field	24115
15	1982/83	18/12/82	Football League Division 1	Swansea City 0 Manchester United 0	Vetch Field	15748
16	1982/83	07/05/83	Football League Division 1	Manchester United 2 Swansea City 1	Old Trafford	35724

UNITED v SWINDON TOWN

ALL COMPETITIVE MATCHES							PREMIERSHIP							ALL CUP MATCHES					
VENUE	P	W	D	L	F	A	VENUE	P	W	D	L	F	A	VENUE	P	W	D	L	F	A
HOME	3	2	0	1	6	5	HOME	1	1	0	0	4	2	HOME	2	1	0	1	2	3
AWAY	2	0	1	1	2	3	AWAY	1	0	1	0	2	2	AWAY	1	0	0	1	0	1
NEUTRAL	1	1	0	0	8	4														
TOTAL	6	3	1	2	16	12	TOTAL	2	1	1	0	6	4	TOTAL	3	1	0	2	2	4

FA CUP							LEAGUE CUP							CHARITY SHIELD					
VENUE	P	W	D	L	F	A	VENUE	P	W	D	L	F	A	VENUE	P	W	D	L	F	A
HOME	1	0	0	1	0	2	HOME	1	1	0	0	2	1	HOME	0	0	0	0	0	0
AWAY	1	0	0	1	0	1	AWAY	0	0	0	0	0	0	AWAY	0	0	0	0	0	0
														NEUTRAL	1	1	0	0	8	4
TOTAL	2	0	0	2	0	3	TOTAL	1	1	0	0	2	1	TOTAL	1	1	0	0	8	4

#	SEASON	DATE	COMPETITION / ROUND	MATCH RESULT	VENUE	ATT
1	1911/12	25/09/11	FA Charity Shield	Manchester United 8 Swindon Town 4	Stamford Bridge	10000
2	1913/14	10/01/14	FA Cup 1st Round	Swindon Town 1 Manchester United 0	County Ground	18187
3	1929/30	11/01/30	FA Cup 3rd Round	Manchester United 0 Swindon Town 2	Old Trafford	33226
4	1993/94	25/09/93	FA Premiership	Manchester United 4 Swindon Town 2	Old Trafford	44583
5	1993/94	19/03/94	FA Premiership	Swindon Town 2 Manchester United 2	County Ground	18102
6	1996/97	23/10/96	League Cup 3rd Round	Manchester United 2 Swindon Town 1	Old Trafford	49305

UNITED v TORPEDO MOSCOW

UEFA CUP					
VENUE	P	W	D	L	F	A
HOME	1	0	1	0	0	0
AWAY	1	0	1	0	0	0
TOTAL	2	0	2	0	0	0

#	SEASON	DATE	COMPETITION / ROUND	MATCH RESULT	VENUE	ATT
1	1992/93	16/09/92	UEFA Cup 1st Round 1st Leg	Manchester United 0 Torpedo Moscow 0	Old Trafford	19998
2	1992/93	29/09/92	UEFA Cup 1st Round 2nd Leg	Torpedo Moscow 0 Manchester United 0	Torpedo Stadion	11357
				(United lost the tie 3–4 on penalty kicks)		

UNITED v TOTTENHAM HOTSPUR

ALL COMPETITIVE MATCHES

VENUE	P	W	D	L	F	A
HOME	83	53	16	14	157	81
AWAY	81	23	27	31	103	137
NEUTRAL	1	0	0	1	1	3
TOTAL	165	76	43	46	261	221

ALL LEAGUE MATCHES

VENUE	P	W	D	L	F	A
HOME	71	47	14	10	133	63
AWAY	71	23	23	25	96	119
TOTAL	142	70	37	35	229	182

ALL CUP MATCHES

VENUE	P	W	D	L	F	A
HOME	11	6	1	4	21	15
AWAY	10	0	4	6	7	18
NEUTRAL	1	0	0	1	1	3
TOTAL	22	6	5	11	29	36

PREMIERSHIP

VENUE	P	W	D	L	F	A
HOME	16	13	3	0	29	5
AWAY	16	10	3	3	29	20
TOTAL	32	23	6	3	58	25

LEAGUE DIVISION ONE

VENUE	P	W	D	L	F	A
HOME	51	33	9	9	101	55
AWAY	51	12	19	20	64	89
TOTAL	102	45	28	29	165	144

LEAGUE DIVISION TWO

VENUE	P	W	D	L	F	A
HOME	4	1	2	1	3	3
AWAY	4	1	1	2	3	10
TOTAL	8	2	3	3	6	13

FA CUP

VENUE	P	W	D	L	F	A
HOME	7	4	1	2	14	9
AWAY	6	0	4	2	5	10
NEUTRAL	1	0	0	1	1	3
TOTAL	14	4	5	5	20	22

LEAGUE CUP

VENUE	P	W	D	L	F	A
HOME	3	1	0	2	3	5
AWAY	3	0	0	3	2	6
NEUTRAL	0	0	0	0	0	0
TOTAL	6	1	0	5	5	11

EUROPEAN CUP-WINNERS' CUP

VENUE	P	W	D	L	F	A
HOME	1	1	0	0	4	1
AWAY	1	0	0	1	0	2
NEUTRAL	0	0	0	0	0	0
TOTAL	2	1	0	1	4	3

CHARITY SHIELD

VENUE	P	W	D	L	F	A
HOME	1	0	1	0	3	3
AWAY	0	0	0	0	0	0
TOTAL	1	0	1	0	3	3

#	SEASON	DATE	COMPETITION / ROUND	MATCH RESULT	VENUE	ATT
1	1898/99	28/01/99	FA Cup 1st Round	Tottenham Hotspur 1 Newton Heath 1	Asplins Farm	15000
2	1898/99	01/02/99	FA Cup 1st Round Replay	Newton Heath 3 Tottenham Hotspur 5	Bank Street	6000
3	1909/10	11/09/09	Football League Division 1	Tottenham Hotspur 2 Manchester United 2	White Hart Lane	40000
4	1909/10	22/01/10	Football League Division 1	Manchester United 5 Tottenham Hotspur 0	Bank Street	7000
5	1910/11	22/10/10	Football League Division 1	Tottenham Hotspur 2 Manchester United 2	White Hart Lane	30000
6	1910/11	15/03/11	Football League Division 1	Manchester United 3 Tottenham Hotspur 2	Old Trafford	10000
7	1911/12	04/11/11	Football League Division 1	Manchester United 1 Tottenham Hotspur 2	Old Trafford	20000
8	1911/12	09/04/12	Football League Division 1	Tottenham Hotspur 1 Manchester United 1	White Hart Lane	20000
9	1912/13	19/10/12	Football League Division 1	Manchester United 2 Tottenham Hotspur 0	Old Trafford	12000
10	1912/13	31/03/13	Football League Division 1	Tottenham Hotspur 1 Manchester United 1	White Hart Lane	12000
11	1913/14	04/10/13	Football League Division 1	Manchester United 3 Tottenham Hotspur 1	Old Trafford	25000
12	1913/14	07/02/14	Football League Division 1	Tottenham Hotspur 2 Manchester United 1	White Hart Lane	22000
13	1914/15	21/11/14	Football League Division 1	Tottenham Hotspur 2 Manchester United 0	White Hart Lane	12000
14	1914/15	27/03/15	Football League Division 1	Manchester United 1 Tottenham Hotspur 0	Old Trafford	15000
15	1920/21	25/09/20	Football League Division 1	Manchester United 0 Tottenham Hotspur 1	Old Trafford	50000
16	1920/21	02/10/20	Football League Division 1	Tottenham Hotspur 4 Manchester United 1	White Hart Lane	45000
17	1921/22	08/10/21	Football League Division 1	Tottenham Hotspur 2 Manchester United 2	White Hart Lane	35000
18	1921/22	15/10/21	Football League Division 1	Manchester United 2 Tottenham Hotspur 1	Old Trafford	30000
19	1922/23	03/02/23	FA Cup 2nd Round	Tottenham Hotspur 4 Manchester United 0	White Hart Lane	38333
20	1925/26	17/10/25	Football League Division 1	Manchester United 0 Tottenham Hotspur 0	Old Trafford	26496
21	1925/26	30/01/26	FA Cup 4th Round	Tottenham Hotspur 2 Manchester United 2	White Hart Lane	40000
22	1925/26	03/02/26	FA Cup 4th Round Replay	Manchester United 2 Tottenham Hotspur 0	Old Trafford	45000
23	1925/26	27/02/26	Football League Division 1	Tottenham Hotspur 0 Manchester United 1	White Hart Lane	25466
24	1926/27	25/12/26	Football League Division 1	Tottenham Hotspur 1 Manchester United 1	White Hart Lane	37287
25	1926/27	27/12/26	Football League Division 1	Manchester United 2 Tottenham Hotspur 1	Old Trafford	50665
26	1927/28	24/09/27	Football League Division 1	Manchester United 3 Tottenham Hotspur 0	Old Trafford	13952
27	1927/28	04/02/28	Football League Division 1	Tottenham Hotspur 4 Manchester United 1	White Hart Lane	23545
28	1931/32	12/09/31	Football League Division 2	Manchester United 1 Tottenham Hotspur 1	Old Trafford	9557
29	1931/32	23/01/32	Football League Division 2	Tottenham Hotspur 4 Manchester United 1	White Hart Lane	19139
30	1932/33	10/09/32	Football League Division 2	Tottenham Hotspur 6 Manchester United 1	White Hart Lane	23333
31	1932/33	21/01/33	Football League Division 2	Manchester United 2 Tottenham Hotspur 1	Old Trafford	20661
32	1935/36	21/09/35	Football League Division 2	Manchester United 0 Tottenham Hotspur 0	Old Trafford	34718
33	1935/36	05/02/36	Football League Division 2	Tottenham Hotspur 0 Manchester United 0	White Hart Lane	20085
34	1937/38	09/10/37	Football League Division 2	Tottenham Hotspur 0 Manchester United 1	White Hart Lane	31189
35	1937/38	19/02/38	Football League Division 2	Manchester United 0 Tottenham Hotspur 1	Old Trafford	34631
36	1950/51	09/09/50	Football League Division 1	Tottenham Hotspur 1 Manchester United 0	White Hart Lane	60621
37	1950/51	13/01/51	Football League Division 1	Manchester United 2 Tottenham Hotspur 1	Old Trafford	43283
38	1951/52	22/09/51	Football League Division 1	Tottenham Hotspur 2 Manchester United 0	White Hart Lane	70882
39	1951/52	26/01/52	Football League Division 1	Manchester United 2 Tottenham Hotspur 0	Old Trafford	40845

UNITED v TOTTENHAM HOTSPUR (continued)

#	SEASON	DATE	COMPETITION / ROUND	MATCH RESULT	VENUE	ATT
40	1952/53	01/11/52	Football League Division 1	Tottenham Hotspur 1 Manchester United 2	White Hart Lane	44300
41	1952/53	25/03/53	Football League Division 1	Manchester United 3 Tottenham Hotspur 2	Old Trafford	18384
42	1953/54	26/09/53	Football League Division 1	Tottenham Hotspur 1 Manchester United 1	White Hart Lane	52837
43	1953/54	13/02/54	Football League Division 1	Manchester United 2 Tottenham Hotspur 0	Old Trafford	35485
44	1954/55	08/09/54	Football League Division 1	Tottenham Hotspur 0 Manchester United 2	White Hart Lane	35162
45	1954/55	15/09/54	Football League Division 1	Manchester United 2 Tottenham Hotspur 1	Old Trafford	29212
46	1955/56	24/08/55	Football League Division 1	Manchester United 2 Tottenham Hotspur 2	Old Trafford	25406
47	1955/56	31/08/55	Football League Division 1	Tottenham Hotspur 1 Manchester United 2	White Hart Lane	27453
48	1956/57	24/11/56	Football League Division 1	Tottenham Hotspur 2 Manchester United 2	White Hart Lane	57724
49	1956/57	06/04/57	Football League Division 1	Manchester United 0 Tottenham Hotspur 0	Old Trafford	60349
50	1957/58	30/11/57	Football League Division 1	Manchester United 3 Tottenham Hotspur 4	Old Trafford	43077
51	1957/58	12/04/58	Football League Division 1	Tottenham Hotspur 1 Manchester United 0	White Hart Lane	59836
52	1958/59	20/09/58	Football League Division 1	Manchester United 2 Tottenham Hotspur 2	Old Trafford	62277
53	1958/59	07/02/59	Football League Division 1	Tottenham Hotspur 1 Manchester United 3	White Hart Lane	48401
54	1959/60	12/09/59	Football League Division 1	Manchester United 1 Tottenham Hotspur 5	Old Trafford	55402
55	1959/60	23/01/60	Football League Division 1	Tottenham Hotspur 2 Manchester United 1	White Hart Lane	62602
56	1960/61	03/09/60	Football League Division 1	Tottenham Hotspur 4 Manchester United 1	White Hart Lane	55445
57	1960/61	14/01/61	Football League Division 1	Manchester United 2 Tottenham Hotspur 0	Old Trafford	65295
58	1961/62	09/09/61	Football League Division 1	Manchester United 1 Tottenham Hotspur 0	Old Trafford	57135
59	1961/62	20/01/62	Football League Division 1	Tottenham Hotspur 2 Manchester United 2	White Hart Lane	55225
60	1961/62	31/03/62	FA Cup Semi-Final	Manchester United 1 Tottenham Hotspur 3	Hillsborough	65000
61	1962/63	24/10/62	Football League Division 1	Tottenham Hotspur 6 Manchester United 2	White Hart Lane	51314
62	1962/63	09/03/63	Football League Division 1	Manchester United 0 Tottenham Hotspur 2	Old Trafford	53416
63	1963/64	09/11/63	Football League Division 1	Manchester United 4 Tottenham Hotspur 1	Old Trafford	57413
64	1963/64	03/12/63	European CWC 2nd Round 1st Leg	Tottenham Hotspur 2 Manchester United 0	White Hart Lane	57447
65	1963/64	10/12/63	European CWC 2nd Round 2nd Leg	Manchester United 4 Tottenham Hotspur 1	Old Trafford	50000
66	1963/64	21/03/64	Football League Division 1	Tottenham Hotspur 2 Manchester United 3	White Hart Lane	56392
67	1964/65	26/09/64	Football League Division 1	Manchester United 4 Tottenham Hotspur 1	Old Trafford	53058
68	1964/65	06/02/65	Football League Division 1	Tottenham Hotspur 1 Manchester United 0	White Hart Lane	58639
69	1965/66	16/10/65	Football League Division 1	Tottenham Hotspur 5 Manchester United 1	White Hart Lane	58051
70	1965/66	18/12/65	Football League Division 1	Manchester United 5 Tottenham Hotspur 1	Old Trafford	39270
71	1966/67	10/09/66	Football League Division 1	Tottenham Hotspur 2 Manchester United 1	White Hart Lane	56295
72	1966/67	14/01/67	Football League Division 1	Manchester United 1 Tottenham Hotspur 0	Old Trafford	57366
73	1967/68	12/08/67	FA Charity Shield	Manchester United 3 Tottenham Hotspur 3 (Trophy Shared)	Old Trafford	54106
74	1967/68	23/09/67	Football League Division 1	Manchester United 3 Tottenham Hotspur 1	Old Trafford	58779
75	1967/68	27/01/68	FA Cup 3rd Round	Manchester United 2 Tottenham Hotspur 2	Old Trafford	63500
76	1967/68	31/01/68	FA Cup 3rd Round Replay	Tottenham Hotspur 1 Manchester United 0	White Hart Lane	57200
77	1967/68	03/02/68	Football League Division 1	Tottenham Hotspur 1 Manchester United 2	White Hart Lane	57790
78	1968/69	28/08/68	Football League Division 1	Manchester United 3 Tottenham Hotspur 1	Old Trafford	62689
79	1968/69	09/10/68	Football League Division 1	Tottenham Hotspur 2 Manchester United 2	White Hart Lane	56205
80	1969/70	22/11/69	Football League Division 1	Manchester United 3 Tottenham Hotspur 1	Old Trafford	50003
81	1969/70	13/04/70	Football League Division 1	Tottenham Hotspur 2 Manchester United 1	White Hart Lane	41808
82	1970/71	05/12/70	Football League Division 1	Tottenham Hotspur 2 Manchester United 2	White Hart Lane	55693
83	1970/71	06/02/71	Football League Division 1	Manchester United 2 Tottenham Hotspur 1	Old Trafford	48965
84	1971/72	13/11/71	Football League Division 1	Manchester United 3 Tottenham Hotspur 1	Old Trafford	54058
85	1971/72	04/03/72	Football League Division 1	Tottenham Hotspur 2 Manchester United 0	White Hart Lane	54814
86	1972/73	28/10/72	Football League Division 1	Manchester United 1 Tottenham Hotspur 4	Old Trafford	52497
87	1972/73	24/03/73	Football League Division 1	Tottenham Hotspur 1 Manchester United 1	White Hart Lane	49751
88	1973/74	10/11/73	Football League Division 1	Tottenham Hotspur 2 Manchester United 1	White Hart Lane	42756
89	1973/74	23/03/74	Football League Division 1	Manchester United 0 Tottenham Hotspur 1	Old Trafford	36278
90	1975/76	06/09/75	Football League Division 1	Manchester United 3 Tottenham Hotspur 2	Old Trafford	51641
91	1975/76	17/01/76	Football League Division 1	Tottenham Hotspur 1 Manchester United 1	White Hart Lane	49189
92	1976/77	04/09/76	Football League Division 1	Manchester United 2 Tottenham Hotspur 3	Old Trafford	60723
93	1976/77	12/02/77	Football League Division 1	Tottenham Hotspur 1 Manchester United 3	White Hart Lane	46946
94	1978/79	16/12/78	Football League Division 1	Manchester United 2 Tottenham Hotspur 0	Old Trafford	52026
95	1978/79	10/03/79	FA Cup 6th Round	Tottenham Hotspur 1 Manchester United 1	White Hart Lane	51800
96	1978/79	14/03/79	FA Cup 6th Round Replay	Manchester United 2 Tottenham Hotspur 0	Old Trafford	55584
97	1978/79	21/04/79	Football League Division 1	Tottenham Hotspur 1 Manchester United 1	White Hart Lane	36665
98	1979/80	29/08/79	League Cup 2nd Round 1st Leg	Tottenham Hotspur 2 Manchester United 1	White Hart Lane	29163
99	1979/80	05/09/79	League Cup 2nd Round 2nd Leg	Manchester United 3 Tottenham Hotspur 1	Old Trafford	48292
100	1979/80	01/12/79	Football League Division 1	Tottenham Hotspur 2 Manchester United 2	White Hart Lane	51389
101	1979/80	05/01/80	FA Cup 3rd Round	Tottenham Hotspur 1 Manchester United 1	White Hart Lane	45207
102	1979/80	09/01/80	FA Cup 3rd Round Replay	Manchester United 0 Tottenham Hotspur 1	Old Trafford	53762
103	1979/80	12/04/80	Football League Division 1	Manchester United 4 Tottenham Hotspur 1	Old Trafford	53151

UNITED v TOTTENHAM HOTSPUR (continued)

#	SEASON	DATE	COMPETITION / ROUND	MATCH RESULT	VENUE	ATT
104	1980/81	06/09/80	Football League Division 1	Tottenham Hotspur 0 Manchester United 0	White Hart Lane	40995
105	1980/81	17/02/81	Football League Division 1	Manchester United 0 Tottenham Hotspur 0	Old Trafford	40642
106	1981/82	07/10/81	League Cup 2nd Round 1st Leg	Tottenham Hotspur 1 Manchester United 0	White Hart Lane	39333
107	1981/82	28/10/81	League Cup 2nd Round 2nd Leg	Manchester United 0 Tottenham Hotspur 1	Old Trafford	55890
108	1981/82	21/11/81	Football League Division 1	Tottenham Hotspur 3 Manchester United 1	White Hart Lane	35534
109	1981/82	17/04/82	Football League Division 1	Manchester United 2 Tottenham Hotspur 0	Old Trafford	50724
110	1982/83	13/11/82	Football League Division 1	Manchester United 1 Tottenham Hotspur 0	Old Trafford	47869
111	1982/83	11/05/83	Football League Division 1	Tottenham Hotspur 2 Manchester United 0	White Hart Lane	32803
112	1983/84	16/12/83	Football League Division 1	Manchester United 4 Tottenham Hotspur 2	Old Trafford	33616
113	1983/84	12/05/84	Football League Division 1	Tottenham Hotspur 1 Manchester United 1	White Hart Lane	39790
114	1984/85	20/10/84	Football League Division 1	Manchester United 1 Tottenham Hotspur 0	Old Trafford	54516
115	1984/85	12/03/85	Football League Division 1	Tottenham Hotspur 1 Manchester United 2	White Hart Lane	42908
116	1985/86	16/11/85	Football League Division 1	Manchester United 0 Tottenham Hotspur 0	Old Trafford	54575
117	1985/86	19/04/86	Football League Division 1	Tottenham Hotspur 0 Manchester United 0	White Hart Lane	32357
118	1986/87	07/12/86	Football League Division 1	Manchester United 3 Tottenham Hotspur 3	Old Trafford	35957
119	1986/87	04/05/87	Football League Division 1	Tottenham Hotspur 4 Manchester United 0	White Hart Lane	36692
120	1987/88	26/09/87	Football League Division 1	Manchester United 1 Tottenham Hotspur 0	Old Trafford	48087
121	1987/88	23/02/88	Football League Division 1	Tottenham Hotspur 1 Manchester United 1	White Hart Lane	25731
122	1988/89	01/10/88	Football League Division 1	Tottenham Hotspur 2 Manchester United 2	White Hart Lane	29318
123	1988/89	05/02/89	Football League Division 1	Manchester United 1 Tottenham Hotspur 0	Old Trafford	41423
124	1989/90	25/10/89	League Cup 3rd Round	Manchester United 0 Tottenham Hotspur 3	Old Trafford	45759
125	1989/90	16/12/89	Football League Division 1	Manchester United 0 Tottenham Hotspur 1	Old Trafford	36230
126	1989/90	21/04/90	Football League Division 1	Tottenham Hotspur 2 Manchester United 1	White Hart Lane	33317
127	1990/91	01/01/91	Football League Division 1	Tottenham Hotspur 1 Manchester United 2	White Hart Lane	29399
128	1990/91	20/05/91	Football League Division 1	Manchester United 1 Tottenham Hotspur 1	Old Trafford	46791
129	1991/92	28/09/91	Football League Division 1	Tottenham Hotspur 1 Manchester United 2	White Hart Lane	35087
130	1991/92	02/05/92	Football League Division 1	Manchester United 3 Tottenham Hotspur 1	Old Trafford	44595
131	1992/93	19/09/92	FA Premiership	Tottenham Hotspur 1 Manchester United 1	White Hart Lane	33296
132	1992/93	09/01/93	FA Premiership	Manchester United 4 Tottenham Hotspur 1	Old Trafford	35648
133	1993/94	16/10/93	FA Premiership	Manchester United 2 Tottenham Hotspur 1	Old Trafford	44655
134	1993/94	15/01/94	FA Premiership	Tottenham Hotspur 0 Manchester United 1	White Hart Lane	31343
135	1994/95	27/08/94	FA Premiership	Tottenham Hotspur 0 Manchester United 1	White Hart Lane	24502
136	1994/95	15/03/95	FA Premiership	Manchester United 0 Tottenham Hotspur 0	Old Trafford	43802
137	1995/96	01/01/96	FA Premiership	Tottenham Hotspur 4 Manchester United 1	White Hart Lane	32852
138	1995/96	24/03/96	FA Premiership	Manchester United 1 Tottenham Hotspur 0	Old Trafford	50157
139	1996/97	29/09/96	FA Premiership	Manchester United 2 Tottenham Hotspur 0	Old Trafford	54943
140	1996/97	05/01/97	FA Cup 3rd Round	Manchester United 2 Tottenham Hotspur 0	Old Trafford	52445
141	1996/97	12/01/97	FA Premiership	Tottenham Hotspur 1 Manchester United 2	White Hart Lane	33026
142	1997/98	10/08/97	FA Premiership	Tottenham Hotspur 0 Manchester United 2	White Hart Lane	26359
143	1997/98	10/01/98	FA Premiership	Manchester United 2 Tottenham Hotspur 0	Old Trafford	55281
144	1998/99	02/12/98	League Cup 5th Round	Tottenham Hotspur 3 Manchester United 1	White Hart Lane	35702
145	1998/99	12/12/98	FA Premiership	Tottenham Hotspur 2 Manchester United 2	White Hart Lane	36079
146	1998/99	16/05/99	FA Premiership	Manchester United 2 Tottenham Hotspur 1	Old Trafford	55189
147	1999/00	23/10/99	FA Premiership	Tottenham Hotspur 3 Manchester United 1	White Hart Lane	36072
148	1999/00	06/05/00	FA Premiership	Manchester United 3 Tottenham Hotspur 1	Old Trafford	61629
149	2000/01	02/12/00	FA Premiership	Manchester United 2 Tottenham Hotspur 0	Old Trafford	67583
150	2000/01	19/05/01	FA Premiership	Tottenham Hotspur 3 Manchester United 1	White Hart Lane	36072
151	2001/02	29/09/01	FA Premiership	Tottenham Hotspur 3 Manchester United 5	White Hart Lane	36038
152	2001/02	06/03/02	FA Premiership	Manchester United 4 Tottenham Hotspur 0	Old Trafford	67599
153	2002/03	21/09/02	FA Premiership	Manchester United 1 Tottenham Hotspur 0	Old Trafford	67611
154	2002/03	27/04/03	FA Premiership	Tottenham Hotspur 0 Manchester United 2	White Hart Lane	36073
155	2003/04	21/12/03	FA Premiership	Tottenham Hotspur 1 Manchester United 2	White Hart Lane	35910
156	2003/04	20/03/04	FA Premiership	Manchester United 3 Tottenham Hotspur 0	Old Trafford	67644
157	2004/05	25/09/04	FA Premiership	Tottenham Hotspur 0 Manchester United 1	White Hart Lane	36103
158	2004/05	04/01/05	FA Premiership	Manchester United 0 Tottenham Hotspur 0	Old Trafford	67962
159	2005/06	22/10/05	FA Premiership	Manchester United 1 Tottenham Hotspur 1	Old Trafford	67856
160	2005/06	17/04/06	FA Premiership	Tottenham Hotspur 1 Manchester United 2	White Hart Lane	36141
161	2006/07	09/09/06	FA Premiership	Manchester United 1 Tottenham Hotspur 0	Old Trafford	75453
162	2006/07	04/02/07	FA Premiership	Tottenham Hotspur 0 Manchester United 4	White Hart Lane	36146
163	2007/08	26/08/07	FA Premiership	Manchester United 1 Tottenham Hotspur 0	Old Trafford	75696
164	2007/08	27/01/08	FA Cup 4th Round	Manchester United 3 Tottenham Hotspur 1	Old Trafford	75369
165	2007/08	02/02/08	FA Premiership	Tottenham Hotspur 1 Manchester United 1	White Hart Lane	36075

UNITED v TRANMERE ROVERS

LEAGUE CUP					
VENUE	P	W	D	L	F	A
HOME	1	1	0	0	5	0
AWAY	0	0	0	0	0	0
TOTAL	1	1	0	0	5	0

#	SEASON	DATE	COMPETITION / ROUND	MATCH RESULT	VENUE	ATT
1	1976/77	01/09/76	League Cup 2nd Round	Manchester United 5 Tranmere Rovers 0	Old Trafford	37586

UNITED v VALENCIA

ALL COMPETITIVE MATCHES							CHAMPIONS LEAGUE							UEFA CUP					
VENUE	P	W	D	L	F	A	VENUE	P	W	D	L	F	A	VENUE	P	W	D	L	F	A
HOME	3	1	2	0	4	1	HOME	2	1	1	0	4	1	HOME	1	0	1	0	0	0
AWAY	3	0	2	1	1	2	AWAY	2	0	2	0	0	0	AWAY	1	0	0	1	1	2
TOTAL	6	1	4	1	5	3	TOTAL	4	1	3	0	4	1	TOTAL	2	0	1	1	1	2

#	SEASON	DATE	COMPETITION / ROUND	MATCH RESULT	VENUE	ATT
1	1982/83	15/09/82	UEFA Cup 1st Round 1st Leg	Manchester United 0 Valencia 0	Old Trafford	46588
2	1982/83	29/09/82	UEFA Cup 1st Round 2nd Leg	Valencia 2 Manchester United 1	Luis Casanova	35000
3	1999/00	08/12/99	Champions League Phase 2 Match 2	Manchester United 3 Valencia 0	Old Trafford	54606
4	1999/00	21/03/00	Champions League Phase 2 Match 6	Valencia 0 Manchester United 0	Mestalla	40419
5	2000/01	14/02/01	Champions League Phase 2 Match 3	Valencia 0 Manchester United 0	Mestalla	49541
6	2000/01	20/02/01	Champions League Phase 2 Match 4	Manchester United 1 Valencia 1	Old Trafford	66715

UNITED v VASCO DA GAMA

CLUB WORLD CHAMPIONSHIP					
VENUE	P	W	D	L	F	A
HOME	0	0	0	0	0	0
AWAY	0	0	0	0	0	0
NEUTRAL	1	0	0	1	1	3
TOTAL	1	0	0	1	1	3

#	SEASON	DATE	COMPETITION / ROUND	MATCH RESULT	VENUE	ATT
1	1999/00	08/01/00	Club World Championship	Manchester United 1 Vasco da Gama 3	Maracana Stadium	73000

UNITED v VIDEOTON

UEFA CUP					
VENUE	P	W	D	L	F	A
HOME	1	1	0	0	1	0
AWAY	1	0	0	1	0	1
TOTAL	2	1	0	1	1	1

#	SEASON	DATE	COMPETITION / ROUND	MATCH RESULT	VENUE	ATT
1	1984/85	06/03/85	UEFA Cup Quarter-Final 1st Leg	Manchester United 1 Videoton 0	Old Trafford	35432
2	1984/85	20/03/85	UEFA Cup Quarter-Final 2nd Leg	Videoton 1 Manchester United 0	Sostoi Stadion	25000
				(United lost the tie 4–5 on penalty kicks)		

UNITED v VILLARREAL

CHAMPIONS LEAGUE					
VENUE	P	W	D	L	F	A
HOME	1	0	1	0	0	0
AWAY	1	0	1	0	0	0
TOTAL	2	0	2	0	0	0

#	SEASON	DATE	COMPETITION / ROUND	MATCH RESULT	VENUE	ATT
1	2005/06	14/09/05	Champions League Phase 1 Match 1	Villarreal 0 Manchester United 0	El Madrigal Stadium	22000
2	2005/06	22/11/05	Champions League Phase 1 Match 5	Manchester United 0 Villarreal 0	Old Trafford	67471

UNITED v WALSALL

ALL COMPETITIVE MATCHES						LEAGUE DIVISION TWO						FA CUP					
VENUE	P	W	D	L	F	A	VENUE	P	W	D	L	F	A	VENUE	P	W	D	L	F	A

VENUE	P	W	D	L	F	A
HOME	10	8	2	0	31	2
AWAY	7	2	3	2	9	10
TOTAL	17	10	5	2	40	12

VENUE	P	W	D	L	F	A
HOME	6	5	1	0	24	1
AWAY	6	2	3	1	7	7
TOTAL	12	7	4	1	31	8

VENUE	P	W	D	L	F	A
HOME	4	3	1	0	7	1
AWAY	1	0	0	1	2	3
TOTAL	5	3	1	1	9	4

#	SEASON	DATE	COMPETITION / ROUND	MATCH RESULT	VENUE	ATT
1	1894/95	26/12/94	Football League Division 2	Walsall 1 Newton Heath 2	West Bromwich Road	1000
2	1894/95	03/04/95	Football League Division 2	Newton Heath 9 Walsall 0	Bank Street	6000
3	1896/97	07/09/96	Football League Division 2	Newton Heath 2 Walsall 0	Bank Street	7000
4	1896/97	21/09/96	Football League Division 2	Walsall 2 Newton Heath 3	Fellows Park	7000
5	1897/98	30/10/97	Football League Division 2	Newton Heath 6 Walsall 0	Bank Street	6000
6	1897/98	11/12/97	Football League Division 2	Walsall 1 Newton Heath 1	Fellows Park	2000
7	1897/98	29/01/98	FA Cup 1st Round	Newton Heath 1 Walsall 0	Bank Street	6000
8	1898/99	24/09/98	Football League Division 2	Newton Heath 1 Walsall 0	Bank Street	8000
9	1898/99	21/01/99	Football League Division 2	Walsall 2 Newton Heath 0	Fellows Park	3000
10	1899/00	14/04/00	Football League Division 2	Newton Heath 5 Walsall 0	Bank Street	4000
11	1899/00	17/04/00	Football League Division 2	Walsall 0 Newton Heath 0	Fellows Park	3000
12	1900/01	20/10/00	Football League Division 2	Newton Heath 1 Walsall 1	Bank Street	8000
13	1900/01	25/02/01	Football League Division 2	Walsall 1 Newton Heath 1	West Bromwich Road	2000
14	1974/75	04/01/75	FA Cup 3rd Round	Manchester United 0 Walsall 0	Old Trafford	43353
15	1974/75	07/01/75	FA Cup 3rd Round Replay	Walsall 3 Manchester United 2	Fellows Park	18105
16	1976/77	08/01/77	FA Cup 3rd Round	Manchester United 1 Walsall 0	Old Trafford	48870
17	1997/98	24/01/98	FA Cup 4th Round	Manchester United 5 Walsall 1	Old Trafford	54669

UNITED v WALTHAMSTOW AVENUE

FA CUP					
VENUE	P	W	D	L	F	A

VENUE	P	W	D	L	F	A
HOME	1	0	1	0	1	1
AWAY	1	1	0	0	5	2
TOTAL	2	1	1	0	6	3

#	SEASON	DATE	COMPETITION / ROUND	MATCH RESULT	VENUE	ATT
1	1952/53	31/01/53	FA Cup 4th Round	Manchester United 1 Walthamstow Avenue 1	Old Trafford	34748
2	1952/53	05/02/53	FA Cup 4th Round Replay	Walthamstow Avenue 2 Manchester United 5	Highbury	49119

UNITED v WATERFORD

EUROPEAN CUP					
VENUE	P	W	D	L	F	A

VENUE	P	W	D	L	F	A
HOME	1	1	0	0	7	1
AWAY	1	1	0	0	3	1
TOTAL	2	2	0	0	10	2

#	SEASON	DATE	COMPETITION / ROUND	MATCH RESULT	VENUE	ATT
1	1968/69	18/09/68	European Cup 1st Round 1st Leg	Waterford 1 Manchester United 3	Lansdowne Road	48000
2	1968/69	02/10/68	European Cup 1st Round 2nd Leg	Manchester United 7 Waterford 1	Old Trafford	41750

UNITED v WATFORD

ALL COMPETITIVE MATCHES

VENUE	P	W	D	L	F	A
HOME	10	6	3	1	23	8
AWAY	12	7	2	3	15	11
NEUTRAL	2	2	0	0	6	1
TOTAL	24	15	5	4	44	20

ALL LEAGUE MATCHES

VENUE	P	W	D	L	F	A
HOME	8	6	2	0	21	5
AWAY	8	4	2	2	9	10
TOTAL	16	10	4	2	30	15

ALL CUP MATCHES

VENUE	P	W	D	L	F	A
HOME	2	0	1	1	2	3
AWAY	4	3	0	1	6	1
NEUTRAL	2	2	0	0	6	1
TOTAL	8	5	1	2	14	5

PREMIERSHIP

VENUE	P	W	D	L	F	A
HOME	2	2	0	0	8	1
AWAY	2	2	0	0	5	3
TOTAL	4	4	0	0	13	4

LEAGUE DIVISION ONE

VENUE	P	W	D	L	F	A
HOME	6	4	2	0	13	4
AWAY	6	2	2	2	4	7
TOTAL	12	6	4	2	17	11

FA CUP

VENUE	P	W	D	L	F	A
HOME	1	0	1	0	1	1
AWAY	3	2	0	1	3	1
NEUTRAL	2	2	0	0	6	1
TOTAL	6	4	1	1	10	3

LEAGUE CUP

VENUE	P	W	D	L	F	A
HOME	1	0	0	1	1	2
AWAY	1	1	0	0	3	0
NEUTRAL	0	0	0	0	0	0
TOTAL	2	1	0	1	4	2

#	SEASON	DATE	COMPETITION / ROUND	MATCH RESULT	VENUE	ATT
1	1949/50	28/01/50	FA Cup 4th Round	Watford 0 Manchester United 1	Vicarage Road	32800
2	1968/69	25/01/69	FA Cup 4th Round	Manchester United 1 Watford 1	Old Trafford	63498
3	1968/69	03/02/69	FA Cup 4th Round Replay	Watford 0 Manchester United 2	Vicarage Road	34000
4	1969/70	10/04/70	FA Cup 3rd Place Play-Off	Manchester United 2 Watford 0	Highbury	15105
5	1978/79	04/10/78	League Cup 3rd Round	Manchester United 1 Watford 2	Old Trafford	40534
6	1981/82	02/01/82	FA Cup 3rd Round	Watford 1 Manchester United 0	Vicarage Road	26104
7	1982/83	04/12/82	Football League Division 1	Watford 0 Manchester United 1	Vicarage Road	25669
8	1982/83	23/04/83	Football League Division 1	Manchester United 2 Watford 0	Old Trafford	43048
9	1983/84	19/11/83	Football League Division 1	Manchester United 4 Watford 1	Old Trafford	43111
10	1983/84	17/04/84	Football League Division 1	Watford 0 Manchester United 0	Vicarage Road	20764
11	1984/85	25/08/84	Football League Division 1	Manchester United 1 Watford 1	Old Trafford	53668
12	1984/85	13/05/85	Football League Division 1	Watford 5 Manchester United 1	Vicarage Road	20500
13	1985/86	30/11/85	Football League Division 1	Manchester United 1 Watford 1	Old Trafford	42181
14	1985/86	03/05/86	Football League Division 1	Watford 1 Manchester United 1	Vicarage Road	18414
15	1986/87	16/09/86	Football League Division 1	Watford 1 Manchester United 0	Vicarage Road	21650
16	1986/87	14/02/87	Football League Division 1	Manchester United 3 Watford 1	Old Trafford	35763
17	1987/88	22/08/87	Football League Division 1	Manchester United 2 Watford 0	Old Trafford	38769
18	1987/88	02/01/88	Football League Division 1	Watford 0 Manchester United 1	Vicarage Road	18038
19	1999/00	16/10/99	FA Premiership	Manchester United 4 Watford 1	Old Trafford	55188
20	1999/00	29/04/00	FA Premiership	Watford 2 Manchester United 3	Vicarage Road	20250
21	2000/01	31/10/00	League Cup 3rd Round	Watford 0 Manchester United 3	Vicarage Road	18871
22	2006/07	26/08/06	FA Premiership	Watford 1 Manchester United 2	Vicarage Road	19453
23	2006/07	31/01/07	FA Premiership	Manchester United 4 Watford 0	Old Trafford	76032
24	2006/07	14/04/07	FA Cup Semi-Final	Manchester United 4 Watford 1	Villa Park	37425

UNITED v WEST BROMWICH ALBION

ALL COMPETITIVE MATCHES

VENUE	P	W	D	L	F	A
HOME	57	30	15	12	113	73
AWAY	57	16	13	28	84	107
TOTAL	114	46	28	40	197	180

ALL LEAGUE MATCHES

VENUE	P	W	D	L	F	A
HOME	53	28	14	11	107	66
AWAY	53	16	11	26	80	100
TOTAL	106	44	25	37	187	166

ALL CUP MATCHES

VENUE	P	W	D	L	F	A
HOME	4	2	1	1	6	7
AWAY	4	0	2	2	4	7
TOTAL	8	2	3	3	10	14

PREMIERSHIP

VENUE	P	W	D	L	F	A
HOME	3	2	1	0	5	1
AWAY	3	3	0	0	8	2
TOTAL	6	5	1	0	13	3

LEAGUE DIVISION ONE

VENUE	P	W	D	L	F	A
HOME	46	24	12	10	97	62
AWAY	46	12	10	24	69	92
TOTAL	92	36	22	34	166	154

LEAGUE DIVISION TWO

VENUE	P	W	D	L	F	A
HOME	4	2	1	1	5	3
AWAY	4	1	1	2	3	6
TOTAL	8	3	2	3	8	9

FA CUP

VENUE	P	W	D	L	F	A
HOME	3	1	1	1	3	6
AWAY	3	0	2	1	4	5
TOTAL	6	1	3	2	7	11

LEAGUE CUP

VENUE	P	W	D	L	F	A
HOME	1	1	0	0	3	1
AWAY	1	0	0	1	0	2
TOTAL	2	1	0	1	3	3

#	SEASON	DATE	COMPETITION / ROUND	MATCH RESULT	VENUE	ATT
1	1892/93	01/10/92	Football League Division 1	West Bromwich Albion 0 Newton Heath 0	Stoney Lane	4000
2	1892/93	08/10/92	Football League Division 1	Newton Heath 2 West Bromwich Albion 4	North Road	9000
3	1893/94	09/09/93	Football League Division 1	West Bromwich Albion 3 Newton Heath 1	Stoney Lane	4500
4	1893/94	14/10/93	Football League Division 1	Newton Heath 4 West Bromwich Albion 1	Bank Street	8000
5	1901/02	09/11/01	Football League Division 2	Newton Heath 1 West Bromwich Albion 2	Bank Street	13000
6	1901/02	08/03/02	Football League Division 2	West Bromwich Albion 4 Newton Heath 0	The Hawthorns	10000
7	1904/05	05/11/04	Football League Division 2	West Bromwich Albion 0 Manchester United 2	The Hawthorns	5000
8	1904/05	04/03/05	Football League Division 2	Manchester United 2 West Bromwich Albion 0	Bank Street	8000
9	1905/06	14/10/05	Football League Division 2	West Bromwich Albion 1 Manchester United 0	The Hawthorns	15000
10	1905/06	17/02/06	Football League Division 2	Manchester United 0 West Bromwich Albion 0	Bank Street	30000
11	1911/12	16/09/11	Football League Division 1	West Bromwich Albion 1 Manchester United 0	The Hawthorns	35000
12	1911/12	20/01/12	Football League Division 1	Manchester United 1 West Bromwich Albion 2	Old Trafford	8000
13	1912/13	14/09/12	Football League Division 1	West Bromwich Albion 1 Manchester United 2	The Hawthorns	25000
14	1912/13	04/01/13	Football League Division 1	Manchester United 1 West Bromwich Albion 1	Old Trafford	25000
15	1913/14	01/01/14	Football League Division 1	Manchester United 1 West Bromwich Albion 0	Old Trafford	35000
16	1913/14	13/04/14	Football League Division 1	West Bromwich Albion 2 Manchester United 1	The Hawthorns	20000
17	1914/15	17/10/14	Football League Division 1	Manchester United 0 West Bromwich Albion 0	Old Trafford	18000
18	1914/15	20/02/15	Football League Division 1	West Bromwich Albion 0 Manchester United 0	The Hawthorns	10000
19	1919/20	24/01/20	Football League Division 1	West Bromwich Albion 2 Manchester United 1	The Hawthorns	20000
20	1919/20	25/02/20	Football League Division 1	Manchester United 1 West Bromwich Albion 2	Old Trafford	20000
21	1920/21	15/01/21	Football League Division 1	Manchester United 1 West Bromwich Albion 4	Old Trafford	30000
22	1920/21	22/01/21	Football League Division 1	West Bromwich Albion 0 Manchester United 2	The Hawthorns	30000
23	1921/22	29/08/21	Football League Division 1	Manchester United 2 West Bromwich Albion 3	Old Trafford	20000
24	1921/22	07/09/21	Football League Division 1	West Bromwich Albion 0 Manchester United 0	The Hawthorns	15000
25	1925/26	19/12/25	Football League Division 1	West Bromwich Albion 5 Manchester United 1	The Hawthorns	17651
26	1925/26	01/05/26	Football League Division 1	Manchester United 3 West Bromwich Albion 2	Old Trafford	9974
27	1926/27	18/12/26	Football League Division 1	Manchester United 2 West Bromwich Albion 0	Old Trafford	18585
28	1926/27	07/05/27	Football League Division 1	West Bromwich Albion 2 Manchester United 2	The Hawthorns	6668
29	1936/37	19/12/36	Football League Division 1	Manchester United 2 West Bromwich Albion 2	Old Trafford	21051
30	1936/37	24/04/37	Football League Division 1	West Bromwich Albion 1 Manchester United 0	The Hawthorns	16234
31	1938/39	07/01/39	FA Cup 3rd Round	West Bromwich Albion 0 Manchester United 0	The Hawthorns	23900
32	1938/39	11/01/39	FA Cup 3rd Round Replay	Manchester United 1 West Bromwich Albion 5	Old Trafford	17641
33	1949/50	27/08/49	Football League Division 1	Manchester United 1 West Bromwich Albion 1	Old Trafford	44655
34	1949/50	24/12/49	Football League Division 1	West Bromwich Albion 1 Manchester United 2	The Hawthorns	46973
35	1950/51	25/11/50	Football League Division 1	West Bromwich Albion 0 Manchester United 1	The Hawthorns	28146
36	1950/51	14/04/51	Football League Division 1	Manchester United 3 West Bromwich Albion 0	Old Trafford	24764
37	1951/52	18/08/51	Football League Division 1	West Bromwich Albion 3 Manchester United 3	The Hawthorns	27486
38	1951/52	15/12/51	Football League Division 1	Manchester United 5 West Bromwich Albion 1	Old Trafford	27584
39	1952/53	29/11/52	Football League Division 1	West Bromwich Albion 3 Manchester United 1	The Hawthorns	23499
40	1952/53	18/04/53	Football League Division 1	Manchester United 2 West Bromwich Albion 2	Old Trafford	31380
41	1953/54	26/08/53	Football League Division 1	Manchester United 1 West Bromwich Albion 3	Old Trafford	31806
42	1953/54	02/09/53	Football League Division 1	West Bromwich Albion 2 Manchester United 0	The Hawthorns	28892
43	1954/55	27/11/54	Football League Division 1	West Bromwich Albion 2 Manchester United 0	The Hawthorns	33931
44	1954/55	16/04/55	Football League Division 1	Manchester United 3 West Bromwich Albion 0	Old Trafford	24765

UNITED v WEST BROMWICH ALBION (continued)

#	SEASON	DATE	COMPETITION / ROUND	MATCH RESULT	VENUE	ATT
45	1955/56	27/08/55	Football League Division 1	Manchester United 3 West Bromwich Albion 1	Old Trafford	31996
46	1955/56	24/12/55	Football League Division 1	West Bromwich Albion 1 Manchester United 4	The Hawthorns	25168
47	1956/57	25/08/56	Football League Division 1	West Bromwich Albion 2 Manchester United 3	The Hawthorns	26387
48	1956/57	29/04/57	Football League Division 1	Manchester United 1 West Bromwich Albion 1	Old Trafford	20357
49	1957/58	26/10/57	Football League Division 1	West Bromwich Albion 4 Manchester United 3	The Hawthorns	52160
50	1957/58	01/03/58	FA Cup 6th Round	West Bromwich Albion 2 Manchester United 2	The Hawthorns	58250
51	1957/58	05/03/58	FA Cup 6th Round Replay	Manchester United 1 West Bromwich Albion 0	Old Trafford	60000
52	1957/58	08/03/58	Football League Division 1	Manchester United 4 West Bromwich Albion 0	Old Trafford	63278
53	1958/59	25/10/58	Football League Division 1	Manchester United 1 West Bromwich Albion 1	Old Trafford	51721
54	1958/59	14/03/59	Football League Division 1	West Bromwich Albion 1 Manchester United 3	The Hawthorns	35463
55	1959/60	22/08/59	Football League Division 1	West Bromwich Albion 3 Manchester United 2	The Hawthorns	40076
56	1959/60	19/12/59	Football League Division 1	Manchester United 2 West Bromwich Albion 3	Old Trafford	33677
57	1960/61	19/11/60	Football League Division 1	Manchester United 3 West Bromwich Albion 0	Old Trafford	32756
58	1960/61	08/04/61	Football League Division 1	West Bromwich Albion 1 Manchester United 1	The Hawthorns	27750
59	1961/62	07/10/61	Football League Division 1	West Bromwich Albion 1 Manchester United 1	The Hawthorns	25645
60	1961/62	24/02/62	Football League Division 1	Manchester United 4 West Bromwich Albion 1	Old Trafford	32456
61	1962/63	18/08/62	Football League Division 1	Manchester United 2 West Bromwich Albion 2	Old Trafford	51685
62	1962/63	15/12/62	Football League Division 1	West Bromwich Albion 3 Manchester United 0	The Hawthorns	18113
63	1963/64	14/09/63	Football League Division 1	Manchester United 1 West Bromwich Albion 0	Old Trafford	50453
64	1963/64	18/01/64	Football League Division 1	West Bromwich Albion 1 Manchester United 4	The Hawthorns	25624
65	1964/65	22/08/64	Football League Division 1	Manchester United 2 West Bromwich Albion 2	Old Trafford	52007
66	1964/65	12/12/64	Football League Division 1	West Bromwich Albion 1 Manchester United 1	The Hawthorns	28126
67	1965/66	27/12/65	Football League Division 1	Manchester United 1 West Bromwich Albion 1	Old Trafford	54102
68	1965/66	04/05/66	Football League Division 1	West Bromwich Albion 3 Manchester United 3	The Hawthorns	22609
69	1966/67	20/08/66	Football League Division 1	Manchester United 5 West Bromwich Albion 3	Old Trafford	41343
70	1966/67	17/12/66	Football League Division 1	West Bromwich Albion 3 Manchester United 4	The Hawthorns	32080
71	1967/68	02/12/67	Football League Division 1	Manchester United 2 West Bromwich Albion 1	Old Trafford	52568
72	1967/68	27/04/68	Football League Division 1	West Bromwich Albion 6 Manchester United 3	The Hawthorns	43412
73	1968/69	14/08/68	Football League Division 1	West Bromwich Albion 3 Manchester United 1	The Hawthorns	38299
74	1968/69	02/04/69	Football League Division 1	Manchester United 2 West Bromwich Albion 1	Old Trafford	38846
75	1969/70	25/10/69	Football League Division 1	West Bromwich Albion 2 Manchester United 1	The Hawthorns	45120
76	1969/70	08/04/70	Football League Division 1	Manchester United 7 West Bromwich Albion 0	Old Trafford	26582
77	1970/71	24/10/70	Football League Division 1	Manchester United 2 West Bromwich Albion 1	Old Trafford	43278
78	1970/71	06/03/71	Football League Division 1	West Bromwich Albion 4 Manchester United 3	The Hawthorns	41112
79	1971/72	23/08/71	Football League Division 1	Manchester United 3 West Bromwich Albion 1	Victoria Ground	23146
80	1971/72	29/01/72	Football League Division 1	West Bromwich Albion 2 Manchester United 1	The Hawthorns	47012
81	1972/73	07/10/72	Football League Division 1	West Bromwich Albion 2 Manchester United 2	The Hawthorns	32909
82	1972/73	03/03/73	Football League Division 1	Manchester United 2 West Bromwich Albion 1	Old Trafford	46735
83	1974/75	14/09/74	Football League Division 2	West Bromwich Albion 1 Manchester United 1	The Hawthorns	23721
84	1974/75	26/12/74	Football League Division 2	Manchester United 2 West Bromwich Albion 1	Old Trafford	51104
85	1976/77	16/10/76	Football League Division 1	West Bromwich Albion 4 Manchester United 0	The Hawthorns	36615
86	1976/77	23/03/77	Football League Division 1	Manchester United 2 West Bromwich Albion 2	Old Trafford	51053
87	1977/78	22/10/77	Football League Division 1	West Bromwich Albion 4 Manchester United 0	The Hawthorns	27526
88	1977/78	28/01/78	FA Cup 4th Round	Manchester United 1 West Bromwich Albion 1	Old Trafford	57056
89	1977/78	01/02/78	FA Cup 4th Round Replay	West Bromwich Albion 3 Manchester United 2	The Hawthorns	37086
90	1977/78	18/03/78	Football League Division 1	Manchester United 1 West Bromwich Albion 1	Old Trafford	46329
91	1978/79	30/12/78	Football League Division 1	Manchester United 3 West Bromwich Albion 5	Old Trafford	45091
92	1978/79	05/05/79	Football League Division 1	West Bromwich Albion 1 Manchester United 0	The Hawthorns	27960
93	1979/80	22/08/79	Football League Division 1	Manchester United 2 West Bromwich Albion 0	Old Trafford	53377
94	1979/80	10/10/79	Football League Division 1	West Bromwich Albion 2 Manchester United 0	The Hawthorns	27713
95	1980/81	27/12/80	Football League Division 1	West Bromwich Albion 3 Manchester United 1	The Hawthorns	30326
96	1980/81	18/04/81	Football League Division 1	Manchester United 2 West Bromwich Albion 1	Old Trafford	44442
97	1981/82	12/04/82	Football League Division 1	Manchester United 1 West Bromwich Albion 0	Old Trafford	38717
98	1981/82	12/05/82	Football League Division 1	West Bromwich Albion 0 Manchester United 3	The Hawthorns	19707
99	1982/83	04/09/82	Football League Division 1	West Bromwich Albion 3 Manchester United 1	The Hawthorns	24928
100	1982/83	03/01/83	Football League Division 1	Manchester United 0 West Bromwich Albion 0	Old Trafford	39123
101	1983/84	15/10/83	Football League Division 1	Manchester United 3 West Bromwich Albion 0	Old Trafford	42221
102	1983/84	31/03/84	Football League Division 1	West Bromwich Albion 2 Manchester United 0	The Hawthorns	28104
103	1984/85	29/09/84	Football League Division 1	West Bromwich Albion 1 Manchester United 2	The Hawthorns	26292
104	1984/85	02/02/85	Football League Division 1	Manchester United 2 West Bromwich Albion 0	Old Trafford	36681
105	1985/86	21/09/85	Football League Division 1	West Bromwich Albion 1 Manchester United 5	The Hawthorns	25068
106	1985/86	22/02/86	Football League Division 1	Manchester United 3 West Bromwich Albion 0	Old Trafford	45193

UNITED v WEST BROMWICH ALBION (continued)

#	SEASON	DATE	COMPETITION / ROUND	MATCH RESULT	VENUE	ATT
107	2002/03	17/08/02	FA Premiership	Manchester United 1 West Bromwich Albion 0	Old Trafford	67645
108	2002/03	11/01/03	FA Premiership	West Bromwich Albion 1 Manchester United 3	The Hawthorns	27129
109	2003/04	03/12/03	League Cup 4th Round	West Bromwich Albion 2 Manchester United 0	The Hawthorns	25282
110	2004/05	27/11/04	FA Premiership	West Bromwich Albion 0 Manchester United 3	The Hawthorns	27709
111	2004/05	07/05/05	FA Premiership	Manchester United 1 West Bromwich Albion 1	Old Trafford	67827
112	2005/06	30/11/05	League Cup 4th Round	Manchester United 3 West Bromwich Albion 1	Old Trafford	48924
113	2005/06	26/12/05	FA Premiership	Manchester United 3 West Bromwich Albion 0	Old Trafford	67972
114	2005/06	18/03/06	FA Premiership	West Bromwich Albion 1 Manchester United 2	The Hawthorns	27623

UNITED v WEST HAM UNITED

ALL COMPETITIVE MATCHES							ALL LEAGUE MATCHES							ALL CUP MATCHES					
VENUE	P	W	D	L	F	A	VENUE	P	W	D	L	F	A	VENUE	P	W	D	L	F	A
HOME	59	39	6	14	136	61	HOME	53	35	6	12	123	56	HOME	6	4	0	2	13	5
AWAY	55	11	18	26	73	92	AWAY	53	11	17	25	71	89	AWAY	2	0	1	1	2	3
NEUTRAL	1	0	0	1	1	3								NEUTRAL	1	0	0	1	1	3
TOTAL	115	50	24	41	210	156	TOTAL	106	46	23	37	194	145	TOTAL	9	4	1	4	16	11

PREMIERSHIP							LEAGUE DIVISION ONE							LEAGUE DIVISION TWO					
VENUE	P	W	D	L	F	A	VENUE	P	W	D	L	F	A	VENUE	P	W	D	L	F	A
HOME	13	11	0	2	32	8	HOME	34	22	6	6	80	39	HOME	6	2	0	4	11	9
AWAY	13	4	7	2	22	18	AWAY	34	5	9	20	43	64	AWAY	6	2	1	3	6	7
TOTAL	26	15	7	4	54	26	TOTAL	68	27	15	26	123	103	TOTAL	12	4	1	7	17	16

FA CUP							LEAGUE CUP					
VENUE	P	W	D	L	F	A	VENUE	P	W	D	L	F	A
HOME	5	3	0	2	12	5	HOME	1	1	0	0	1	0
AWAY	2	0	1	1	2	3	AWAY	0	0	0	0	0	0
NEUTRAL	1	0	0	1	1	3	NEUTRAL	0	0	0	0	0	0
TOTAL	8	3	1	4	15	11	TOTAL	1	1	0	0	1	0

#	SEASON	DATE	COMPETITION / ROUND	MATCH RESULT	VENUE	ATT
1	1910/11	25/02/11	FA Cup 3rd Round	West Ham United 2 Manchester United 1	Upton Park	26000
2	1922/23	25/12/22	Football League Division 2	Manchester United 1 West Ham United 2	Old Trafford	17500
3	1922/23	26/12/22	Football League Division 2	West Ham United 0 Manchester United 2	Upton Park	25000
4	1925/26	29/08/25	Football League Division 1	West Ham United 1 Manchester United 0	Upton Park	25630
5	1925/26	02/01/26	Football League Division 1	Manchester United 2 West Ham United 1	Old Trafford	29612
6	1926/27	30/10/26	Football League Division 1	West Ham United 4 Manchester United 0	Upton Park	19733
7	1926/27	19/03/27	Football League Division 1	Manchester United 0 West Ham United 3	Old Trafford	18347
8	1927/28	29/10/27	Football League Division 1	West Ham United 1 Manchester United 2	Upton Park	21972
9	1927/28	10/03/28	Football League Division 1	Manchester United 1 West Ham United 1	Old Trafford	21577
10	1928/29	22/09/28	Football League Division 1	West Ham United 3 Manchester United 1	Upton Park	20788
11	1928/29	02/02/29	Football League Division 1	Manchester United 2 West Ham United 3	Old Trafford	12020
12	1929/30	28/09/29	Football League Division 1	West Ham United 2 Manchester United 1	Upton Park	20695
13	1929/30	01/02/30	Football League Division 1	Manchester United 4 West Ham United 2	Old Trafford	15424
14	1930/31	11/10/30	Football League Division 1	West Ham United 5 Manchester United 1	Upton Park	20003
15	1930/31	14/02/31	Football League Division 1	Manchester United 1 West Ham United 0	Old Trafford	9745
16	1932/33	10/12/32	Football League Division 2	West Ham United 3 Manchester United 1	Upton Park	13435
17	1932/33	22/04/33	Football League Division 2	Manchester United 1 West Ham United 2	Old Trafford	14958
18	1933/34	30/03/34	Football League Division 2	Manchester United 0 West Ham United 1	Old Trafford	29114
19	1933/34	02/04/34	Football League Division 2	West Ham United 2 Manchester United 1	Upton Park	20085
20	1934/35	27/10/34	Football League Division 2	Manchester United 3 West Ham United 1	Old Trafford	31950
21	1934/35	09/03/35	Football League Division 2	West Ham United 0 Manchester United 0	Upton Park	19718
22	1935/36	16/11/35	Football League Division 2	Manchester United 2 West Ham United 3	Old Trafford	24440
23	1935/36	07/03/36	Football League Division 2	West Ham United 1 Manchester United 2	Upton Park	29684
24	1937/38	23/02/38	Football League Division 2	Manchester United 4 West Ham United 0	Old Trafford	14572
25	1937/38	30/04/38	Football League Division 2	West Ham United 1 Manchester United 0	Upton Park	14816
26	1958/59	08/09/58	Football League Division 1	West Ham United 3 Manchester United 2	Upton Park	35672
27	1958/59	17/09/58	Football League Division 1	Manchester United 4 West Ham United 1	Old Trafford	53276
28	1959/60	15/04/60	Football League Division 1	West Ham United 2 Manchester United 1	Upton Park	34969
29	1959/60	18/04/60	Football League Division 1	Manchester United 5 West Ham United 3	Old Trafford	34676

UNITED v WEST HAM UNITED (continued)

#	SEASON	DATE	COMPETITION / ROUND	MATCH RESULT	VENUE	ATT
30	1960/61	05/09/60	Football League Division 1	West Ham United 2 Manchester United 1	Upton Park	30506
31	1960/61	14/09/60	Football League Division 1	Manchester United 6 West Ham United 1	Old Trafford	33695
32	1961/62	19/08/61	Football League Division 1	West Ham United 1 Manchester United 1	Upton Park	32628
33	1961/62	16/12/61	Football League Division 1	Manchester United 1 West Ham United 2	Old Trafford	29472
34	1962/63	27/10/62	Football League Division 1	Manchester United 3 West Ham United 1	Old Trafford	29204
35	1962/63	18/03/63	Football League Division 1	West Ham United 3 Manchester United 1	Upton Park	28950
36	1963/64	26/10/63	Football League Division 1	Manchester United 0 West Ham United 1	Old Trafford	45120
37	1963/64	07/03/64	Football League Division 1	West Ham United 0 Manchester United 2	Upton Park	27027
38	1963/64	14/03/64	FA Cup Semi-Final	Manchester United 1 West Ham United 3	Hillsborough	65000
39	1964/65	24/08/64	Football League Division 1	West Ham United 3 Manchester United 1	Upton Park	37070
40	1964/65	02/09/64	Football League Division 1	Manchester United 3 West Ham United 1	Old Trafford	45123
41	1965/66	04/12/65	Football League Division 1	Manchester United 0 West Ham United 0	Old Trafford	32924
42	1965/66	30/04/66	Football League Division 1	West Ham United 3 Manchester United 2	Upton Park	36416
43	1966/67	01/04/67	Football League Division 1	Manchester United 3 West Ham United 0	Old Trafford	61308
44	1966/67	06/05/67	Football League Division 1	West Ham United 1 Manchester United 6	Upton Park	38424
45	1967/68	02/09/67	Football League Division 1	West Ham United 1 Manchester United 3	Upton Park	36562
46	1967/68	06/01/68	Football League Division 1	Manchester United 3 West Ham United 1	Old Trafford	54498
47	1968/69	07/09/68	Football League Division 1	Manchester United 1 West Ham United 1	Old Trafford	63274
48	1968/69	29/03/69	Football League Division 1	West Ham United 0 Manchester United 0	Upton Park	41546
49	1969/70	27/09/69	Football League Division 1	Manchester United 5 West Ham United 2	Old Trafford	58579
50	1969/70	17/01/70	Football League Division 1	West Ham United 0 Manchester United 0	Upton Park	41643
51	1970/71	29/08/70	Football League Division 1	Manchester United 1 West Ham United 1	Old Trafford	50643
52	1970/71	03/04/71	Football League Division 1	West Ham United 2 Manchester United 1	Upton Park	38507
53	1971/72	18/09/71	Football League Division 1	Manchester United 4 West Ham United 2	Old Trafford	55339
54	1971/72	01/01/72	Football League Division 1	West Ham United 3 Manchester United 0	Upton Park	41892
55	1972/73	02/09/72	Football League Division 1	West Ham United 2 Manchester United 2	Upton Park	31939
56	1972/73	20/01/73	Football League Division 1	Manchester United 2 West Ham United 2	Old Trafford	50878
57	1973/74	15/09/73	Football League Division 1	Manchester United 3 West Ham United 1	Old Trafford	44757
58	1973/74	12/01/74	Football League Division 1	West Ham United 2 Manchester United 1	Upton Park	34147
59	1975/76	25/10/75	Football League Division 1	West Ham United 2 Manchester United 1	Upton Park	38528
60	1975/76	28/02/76	Football League Division 1	Manchester United 4 West Ham United 0	Old Trafford	57220
61	1976/77	27/11/76	Football League Division 1	Manchester United 0 West Ham United 2	Old Trafford	55366
62	1976/77	16/05/77	Football League Division 1	West Ham United 4 Manchester United 2	Upton Park	29904
63	1977/78	10/12/77	Football League Division 1	West Ham United 2 Manchester United 1	Upton Park	20242
64	1977/78	22/04/78	Football League Division 1	Manchester United 3 West Ham United 0	Old Trafford	54089
65	1981/82	27/01/82	Football League Division 1	Manchester United 1 West Ham United 0	Old Trafford	41291
66	1981/82	08/05/82	Football League Division 1	West Ham United 1 Manchester United 1	Upton Park	26337
67	1982/83	30/10/82	Football League Division 1	West Ham United 3 Manchester United 1	Upton Park	31684
68	1982/83	08/01/83	FA Cup 3rd Round	Manchester United 2 West Ham United 0	Old Trafford	44143
69	1982/83	22/03/83	Football League Division 1	Manchester United 2 West Ham United 1	Old Trafford	30227
70	1983/84	27/11/83	Football League Division 1	West Ham United 1 Manchester United 1	Upton Park	23355
71	1983/84	28/04/84	Football League Division 1	Manchester United 0 West Ham United 0	Old Trafford	44124
72	1984/85	13/10/84	Football League Division 1	Manchester United 5 West Ham United 1	Old Trafford	47559
73	1984/85	09/03/85	FA Cup 6th Round	Manchester United 4 West Ham United 2	Old Trafford	46769
74	1984/85	15/03/85	Football League Division 1	West Ham United 2 Manchester United 2	Upton Park	16674
75	1985/86	26/08/85	Football League Division 1	Manchester United 2 West Ham United 0	Old Trafford	50773
76	1985/86	29/10/85	League Cup 3rd Round	Manchester United 1 West Ham United 0	Old Trafford	32056
77	1985/86	02/02/86	Football League Division 1	West Ham United 2 Manchester United 1	Upton Park	22642
78	1985/86	05/03/86	FA Cup 5th Round	West Ham United 1 Manchester United 1	Upton Park	26441
79	1985/86	09/03/86	FA Cup 5th Round Replay	Manchester United 0 West Ham United 2	Old Trafford	30441
80	1986/87	25/08/86	Football League Division 1	Manchester United 2 West Ham United 3	Old Trafford	43306
81	1986/87	14/04/87	Football League Division 1	West Ham United 0 Manchester United 0	Upton Park	23486
82	1987/88	24/10/87	Football League Division 1	West Ham United 1 Manchester United 1	Upton Park	19863
83	1987/88	26/03/88	Football League Division 1	Manchester United 3 West Ham United 1	Old Trafford	37269
84	1988/89	24/09/88	Football League Division 1	Manchester United 2 West Ham United 0	Old Trafford	39941
85	1988/89	21/01/89	Football League Division 1	West Ham United 1 Manchester United 3	Upton Park	29822
86	1991/92	23/11/91	Football League Division 1	Manchester United 2 West Ham United 1	Old Trafford	47185
87	1991/92	22/04/92	Football League Division 1	West Ham United 1 Manchester United 0	Upton Park	24197
88	1993/94	01/09/93	FA Premiership	Manchester United 3 West Ham United 0	Old Trafford	44613
89	1993/94	26/02/94	FA Premiership	West Ham United 2 Manchester United 2	Upton Park	28832
90	1994/95	15/10/94	FA Premiership	Manchester United 1 West Ham United 0	Old Trafford	43795
91	1994/95	14/05/95	FA Premiership	West Ham United 1 Manchester United 1	Upton Park	24783

UNITED v WEST HAM UNITED (continued)

#	SEASON	DATE	COMPETITION / ROUND	MATCH RESULT	VENUE	ATT
92	1995/96	23/08/95	FA Premiership	Manchester United 2 West Ham United 1	Old Trafford	31966
93	1995/96	22/01/96	FA Premiership	West Ham United 0 Manchester United 1	Upton Park	24197
94	1996/97	08/12/96	FA Premiership	West Ham United 2 Manchester United 2	Upton Park	25045
95	1996/97	11/05/97	FA Premiership	Manchester United 2 West Ham United 0	Old Trafford	55249
96	1997/98	13/09/97	FA Premiership	Manchester United 2 West Ham United 1	Old Trafford	55068
97	1997/98	11/03/98	FA Premiership	West Ham United 1 Manchester United 1	Upton Park	25892
98	1998/99	22/08/98	FA Premiership	West Ham United 0 Manchester United 0	Upton Park	26039
99	1998/99	10/01/99	FA Premiership	Manchester United 4 West Ham United 1	Old Trafford	55180
100	1999/00	18/12/99	FA Premiership	West Ham United 2 Manchester United 4	Upton Park	26037
101	1999/00	01/04/00	FA Premiership	Manchester United 7 West Ham United 1	Old Trafford	61611
102	2000/01	26/08/00	FA Premiership	West Ham United 2 Manchester United 2	Upton Park	25998
103	2000/01	01/01/01	FA Premiership	Manchester United 3 West Ham United 1	Old Trafford	67603
104	2000/01	28/01/01	FA Cup 4th Round	Manchester United 0 West Ham United 1	Old Trafford	67029
105	2001/02	08/12/01	FA Premiership	Manchester United 0 West Ham United 1	Old Trafford	67582
106	2001/02	16/03/02	FA Premiership	West Ham United 3 Manchester United 5	Upton Park	35281
107	2002/03	17/11/02	FA Premiership	West Ham United 1 Manchester United 1	Upton Park	35049
108	2002/03	14/12/02	FA Premiership	Manchester United 3 West Ham United 0	Old Trafford	67555
109	2002/03	26/01/03	FA Cup 4th Round	Manchester United 6 West Ham United 0	Old Trafford	67181
110	2005/06	27/11/05	FA Premiership	West Ham United 1 Manchester United 2	Upton Park	34755
111	2005/06	29/03/06	FA Premiership	Manchester United 1 West Ham United 0	Old Trafford	69522
112	2006/07	17/12/06	FA Premiership	West Ham United 1 Manchester United 0	Upton Park	34966
113	2006/07	13/05/07	FA Premiership	Manchester United 0 West Ham United 1	Old Trafford	75927
114	2007/08	29/12/07	FA Premiership	West Ham United 2 Manchester United 1	Upton Park	34966
115	2007/08	03/05/08	FA Premiership	Manchester United 4 West Ham United 1	Old Trafford	76013

UNITED v WEST MANCHESTER

FA CUP						
VENUE	P	W	D	L	F	A
HOME	1	1	0	0	7	0
AWAY	0	0	0	0	0	0
TOTAL	1	1	0	0	7	0

#	SEASON	DATE	COMPETITION / ROUND	MATCH RESULT	VENUE	ATT
1	1896/97	12/12/96	FA Cup 3rd Qualifying Round	Newton Heath 7 West Manchester 0	Bank Street	6000

UNITED v WEYMOUTH TOWN

FA CUP						
VENUE	P	W	D	L	F	A
HOME	1	1	0	0	4	0
AWAY	0	0	0	0	0	0
TOTAL	1	1	0	0	4	0

#	SEASON	DATE	COMPETITION / ROUND	MATCH RESULT	VENUE	ATT
1	1949/50	07/01/50	FA Cup 3rd Round	Manchester United 4 Weymouth Town 0	Old Trafford	38284

UNITED v WIDZEW LODZ

UEFA CUP						
VENUE	P	W	D	L	F	A
HOME	1	0	1	0	1	1
AWAY	1	0	1	0	0	0
TOTAL	2	0	2	0	1	1

#	SEASON	DATE	COMPETITION / ROUND	MATCH RESULT	VENUE	ATT
1	1980/81	17/09/80	UEFA Cup 1st Round 1st Leg	Manchester United 1 Widzew Lodz 1	Old Trafford	38037
2	1980/81	01/10/80	UEFA Cup 1st Round 2nd Leg	Widzew Lodz 0 Manchester United 0	Stadio TKS	40000
				(United lost the tie on away goals rule)		

UNITED v WIGAN ATHLETIC

ALL COMPETITIVE MATCHES							PREMIERSHIP							LEAGUE CUP						
VENUE	P	W	D	L	F	A	VENUE	P	W	D	L	F	A	VENUE	P	W	D	L	F	A
HOME	3	3	0	0	11	1	HOME	3	3	0	0	11	1	HOME	0	0	0	0	0	0
AWAY	3	3	0	0	7	2	AWAY	3	3	0	0	7	2	AWAY	0	0	0	0	0	0
NEUTRAL	1	1	0	0	4	0								NEUTRAL	1	1	0	0	4	0
TOTAL	7	7	0	0	22	3	TOTAL	6	6	0	0	18	3	TOTAL	1	1	0	0	4	0

#	SEASON	DATE	COMPETITION / ROUND	MATCH RESULT	VENUE	ATT
1	2005/06	14/12/05	FA Premiership	Manchester United 4 Wigan Athletic 0	Old Trafford	67793
2	2005/06	26/02/06	League Cup Final	Manchester United 4 Wigan Athletic 0	Millennium Stadium	66866
3	2005/06	06/03/06	FA Premiership	Wigan Athletic 1 Manchester United 2	JJB Stadium	23574
4	2006/07	14/10/06	FA Premiership	Wigan Athletic 1 Manchester United 3	JJB Stadium	20631
5	2006/07	26/12/06	FA Premiership	Manchester United 3 Wigan Athletic 1	Old Trafford	76018
6	2007/08	06/10/07	FA Premiership	Manchester United 4 Wigan Athletic 0	Old Trafford	75300
7	2007/08	11/05/08	FA Premiership	Wigan Athletic 0 Manchester United 2	JJB Stadium	25133

UNITED v WILLEM II

EUROPEAN CUP-WINNERS' CUP						
VENUE	P	W	D	L	F	A
HOME	1	1	0	0	6	1
AWAY	1	0	1	0	1	1
TOTAL	2	1	1	0	7	2

#	SEASON	DATE	COMPETITION / ROUND	MATCH RESULT	VENUE	ATT
1	1963/64	25/09/63	European CWC 1st Round 1st Leg	Willem II 1 Manchester United 1	Feyenoord Stadion	20000
2	1963/64	15/10/63	European CWC 1st Round 2nd Leg	Manchester United 6 Willem II 1	Old Trafford	46272

UNITED v WIMBLEDON

ALL COMPETITIVE MATCHES							ALL LEAGUE MATCHES							ALL CUP MATCHES						
VENUE	P	W	D	L	F	A	VENUE	P	W	D	L	F	A	VENUE	P	W	D	L	F	A
HOME	15	9	4	2	25	10	HOME	14	9	3	2	24	9	HOME	1	0	1	0	1	1
AWAY	17	8	4	5	31	20	AWAY	14	7	4	3	27	17	AWAY	3	1	0	2	4	3
TOTAL	32	17	8	7	56	30	TOTAL	28	16	7	5	51	26	TOTAL	4	1	1	2	5	4

PREMIERSHIP							LEAGUE DIVISION ONE						
VENUE	P	W	D	L	F	A	VENUE	P	W	D	L	F	A
HOME	8	6	1	1	19	6	HOME	6	3	2	1	5	3
AWAY	8	5	2	1	18	9	AWAY	6	2	2	2	9	8
TOTAL	16	11	3	2	37	15	TOTAL	12	5	4	3	14	11

FA CUP							LEAGUE CUP						
VENUE	P	W	D	L	F	A	VENUE	P	W	D	L	F	A
HOME	1	0	1	0	1	1	HOME	0	0	0	0	0	0
AWAY	2	1	0	1	3	1	AWAY	1	0	0	1	1	2
TOTAL	3	1	1	1	4	2	TOTAL	1	0	0	1	1	2

#	SEASON	DATE	COMPETITION / ROUND	MATCH RESULT	VENUE	ATT
1	1986/87	29/11/86	Football League Division 1	Wimbledon 1 Manchester United 0	Plough Lane	12112
2	1986/87	02/05/87	Football League Division 1	Manchester United 0 Wimbledon 1	Old Trafford	31686
3	1987/88	21/11/87	Football League Division 1	Wimbledon 2 Manchester United 1	Plough Lane	11532
4	1987/88	09/05/88	Football League Division 1	Manchester United 2 Wimbledon 1	Old Trafford	28040
5	1988/89	22/10/88	Football League Division 1	Wimbledon 1 Manchester United 1	Plough Lane	12143
6	1988/89	02/11/88	League Cup 3rd Round	Wimbledon 2 Manchester United 1	Plough Lane	10864
7	1988/89	02/05/89	Football League Division 1	Manchester United 1 Wimbledon 0	Old Trafford	23368
8	1989/90	30/12/89	Football League Division 1	Wimbledon 2 Manchester United 2	Plough Lane	9622
9	1989/90	30/04/90	Football League Division 1	Manchester United 0 Wimbledon 0	Old Trafford	29281
10	1990/91	22/12/90	Football League Division 1	Wimbledon 1 Manchester United 3	Plough Lane	9644
11	1990/91	02/04/91	Football League Division 1	Manchester United 2 Wimbledon 1	Old Trafford	36660
12	1991/92	03/09/91	Football League Division 1	Wimbledon 1 Manchester United 2	Selhurst Park	13824
13	1991/92	21/03/92	Football League Division 1	Manchester United 0 Wimbledon 0	Old Trafford	45428
14	1992/93	31/10/92	FA Premiership	Manchester United 0 Wimbledon 1	Old Trafford	32622
15	1992/93	09/05/93	FA Premiership	Wimbledon 1 Manchester United 2	Selhurst Park	30115

UNITED v WIMBLEDON (continued)

#	SEASON	DATE	COMPETITION / ROUND	MATCH RESULT	VENUE	ATT
16	1993/94	20/11/93	FA Premiership	Manchester United 3 Wimbledon 1	Old Trafford	44748
17	1993/94	20/02/94	FA Cup 5th Round	Wimbledon 0 Manchester United 3	Selhurst Park	27511
18	1993/94	16/04/94	FA Premiership	Wimbledon 1 Manchester United 0	Selhurst Park	28553
19	1994/95	31/08/94	FA Premiership	Manchester United 3 Wimbledon 0	Old Trafford	43440
20	1994/95	07/03/95	FA Premiership	Wimbledon 0 Manchester United 1	Selhurst Park	18224
21	1995/96	26/08/95	FA Premiership	Manchester United 3 Wimbledon 1	Old Trafford	32226
22	1995/96	03/02/96	FA Premiership	Wimbledon 2 Manchester United 4	Selhurst Park	25380
23	1996/97	17/08/96	FA Premiership	Wimbledon 0 Manchester United 3	Selhurst Park	25786
24	1996/97	25/01/97	FA Cup 4th Round	Manchester United 1 Wimbledon 1	Old Trafford	53342
25	1996/97	29/01/97	FA Premiership	Manchester United 2 Wimbledon 1	Old Trafford	55314
26	1996/97	04/02/97	FA Cup 4th Round Replay	Wimbledon 1 Manchester United 0	Selhurst Park	25601
27	1997/98	22/11/97	FA Premiership	Wimbledon 2 Manchester United 5	Selhurst Park	26309
28	1997/98	28/03/98	FA Premiership	Manchester United 2 Wimbledon 0	Old Trafford	55306
29	1998/99	17/10/98	FA Premiership	Manchester United 5 Wimbledon 1	Old Trafford	55265
30	1998/99	03/04/99	FA Premiership	Wimbledon 1 Manchester United 1	Selhurst Park	26121
31	1999/00	18/09/99	FA Premiership	Manchester United 1 Wimbledon 1	Old Trafford	55189
32	1999/00	26/02/00	FA Premiership	Wimbledon 2 Manchester United 2	Selhurst Park	26129

UNITED v WOLVERHAMPTON WANDERERS

ALL COMPETITIVE MATCHES							ALL LEAGUE MATCHES							FA CUP						
VENUE	P	W	D	L	F	A	VENUE	P	W	D	L	F	A	VENUE	P	W	D	L	F	A
HOME	42	27	6	9	82	45	HOME	41	27	5	9	81	44	HOME	1	0	1	0	1	1
AWAY	46	14	9	23	70	90	AWAY	41	10	9	22	55	82	AWAY	5	4	0	1	15	8
NEUTRAL	2	0	1	1	1	2								NEUTRAL	2	0	1	1	1	2
TOTAL	90	41	16	33	153	137	TOTAL	82	37	14	31	136	126	TOTAL	8	4	2	2	17	11

PREMIERSHIP							LEAGUE DIVISION ONE							LEAGUE DIVISION TWO						
VENUE	P	W	D	L	F	A	VENUE	P	W	D	L	F	A	VENUE	P	W	D	L	F	A
HOME	1	1	0	0	1	0	HOME	37	23	5	9	73	42	HOME	3	3	0	0	7	2
AWAY	1	0	0	1	0	1	AWAY	37	9	8	20	54	74	AWAY	3	1	1	1	1	7
TOTAL	2	1	0	1	1	1	TOTAL	74	32	13	29	127	116	TOTAL	6	4	1	1	8	9

#	SEASON	DATE	COMPETITION / ROUND	MATCH RESULT	VENUE	ATT
1	1892/93	15/10/92	Football League Division 1	Newton Heath 10 Wolverhampton Wanderers 1	North Road	4000
2	1892/93	17/12/92	Football League Division 1	Wolverhampton Wanderers 2 Newton Heath 0	Molineux	5000
3	1893/94	28/10/93	Football League Division 1	Wolverhampton Wanderers 2 Newton Heath 0	Molineux	4000
4	1893/94	11/11/93	Football League Division 1	Newton Heath 1 Wolverhampton Wanderers 0	Bank Street	5000
5	1922/23	09/09/22	Football League Division 2	Wolverhampton Wanderers 0 Manchester United 1	Molineux	18000
6	1922/23	16/09/22	Football League Division 2	Manchester United 1 Wolverhampton Wanderers 0	Old Trafford	28000
7	1924/25	25/10/24	Football League Division 2	Wolverhampton Wanderers 0 Manchester United 0	Molineux	17500
8	1924/25	28/02/25	Football League Division 2	Manchester United 3 Wolverhampton Wanderers 0	Old Trafford	21250
9	1931/32	25/12/31	Football League Division 2	Manchester United 3 Wolverhampton Wanderers 2	Old Trafford	33123
10	1931/32	26/12/31	Football League Division 2	Wolverhampton Wanderers 7 Manchester United 0	Molineux	37207
11	1936/37	29/08/36	Football League Division 1	Manchester United 1 Wolverhampton Wanderers 1	Old Trafford	42731
12	1936/37	26/12/36	Football League Division 1	Wolverhampton Wanderers 3 Manchester United 1	Molineux	41525
13	1938/39	12/11/38	Football League Division 1	Manchester United 1 Wolverhampton Wanderers 3	Old Trafford	32821
14	1938/39	18/03/39	Football League Division 1	Wolverhampton Wanderers 3 Manchester United 0	Molineux	31498
15	1946/47	30/11/46	Football League Division 1	Wolverhampton Wanderers 3 Manchester United 2	Molineux	46704
16	1946/47	05/04/47	Football League Division 1	Manchester United 3 Wolverhampton Wanderers 1	Maine Road	66967
17	1947/48	01/11/47	Football League Division 1	Wolverhampton Wanderers 2 Manchester United 6	Molineux	44309
18	1947/48	20/03/48	Football League Division 1	Manchester United 3 Wolverhampton Wanderers 2	Maine Road	50667
19	1948/49	08/09/48	Football League Division 1	Wolverhampton Wanderers 3 Manchester United 2	Molineux	42617
20	1948/49	15/09/48	Football League Division 1	Manchester United 2 Wolverhampton Wanderers 0	Maine Road	33871
21	1948/49	26/03/49	FA Cup Semi-Final	Manchester United 1 Wolverhampton Wanderers 1	Hillsborough	62250
22	1948/49	02/04/49	FA Cup Semi-Final Replay	Manchester United 0 Wolverhampton Wanderers 1	Goodison Park	73000
23	1949/50	22/10/49	Football League Division 1	Manchester United 3 Wolverhampton Wanderers 0	Old Trafford	51427
24	1949/50	08/04/50	Football League Division 1	Wolverhampton Wanderers 1 Manchester United 1	Molineux	54296
25	1950/51	30/09/50	Football League Division 1	Wolverhampton Wanderers 0 Manchester United 0	Molineux	45898
26	1950/51	17/02/51	Football League Division 1	Manchester United 2 Wolverhampton Wanderers 1	Old Trafford	42022
27	1951/52	27/10/51	Football League Division 1	Wolverhampton Wanderers 0 Manchester United 2	Molineux	46167
28	1951/52	15/03/52	Football League Division 1	Manchester United 2 Wolverhampton Wanderers 0	Old Trafford	45109

UNITED v WOLVERHAMPTON WANDERERS (continued)

#	SEASON	DATE	COMPETITION / ROUND	MATCH RESULT	VENUE	ATT
29	1952/53	04/10/52	Football League Division 1	Wolverhampton Wanderers 6 Manchester United 2	Molineux	40132
30	1952/53	21/02/53	Football League Division 1	Manchester United 0 Wolverhampton Wanderers 3	Old Trafford	38269
31	1953/54	17/10/53	Football League Division 1	Wolverhampton Wanderers 3 Manchester United 1	Molineux	40084
32	1953/54	06/03/54	Football League Division 1	Manchester United 1 Wolverhampton Wanderers 0	Old Trafford	38939
33	1954/55	02/10/54	Football League Division 1	Wolverhampton Wanderers 4 Manchester United 2	Molineux	39617
34	1954/55	23/02/55	Football League Division 1	Manchester United 2 Wolverhampton Wanderers 4	Old Trafford	15679
35	1955/56	08/10/55	Football League Division 1	Manchester United 4 Wolverhampton Wanderers 3	Old Trafford	48638
36	1955/56	18/02/56	Football League Division 1	Wolverhampton Wanderers 0 Manchester United 2	Molineux	40014
37	1956/57	03/11/56	Football League Division 1	Manchester United 3 Wolverhampton Wanderers 0	Old Trafford	59835
38	1956/57	16/03/57	Football League Division 1	Wolverhampton Wanderers 1 Manchester United 1	Molineux	53228
39	1957/58	28/09/57	Football League Division 1	Wolverhampton Wanderers 3 Manchester United 1	Molineux	48825
40	1957/58	21/04/58	Football League Division 1	Manchester United 0 Wolverhampton Wanderers 4	Old Trafford	33267
41	1958/59	04/10/58	Football League Division 1	Wolverhampton Wanderers 4 Manchester United 0	Molineux	36840
42	1958/59	21/02/59	Football League Division 1	Manchester United 2 Wolverhampton Wanderers 1	Old Trafford	62794
43	1959/60	17/10/59	Football League Division 1	Wolverhampton Wanderers 3 Manchester United 2	Molineux	45451
44	1959/60	05/03/60	Football League Division 1	Manchester United 0 Wolverhampton Wanderers 2	Old Trafford	60560
45	1960/61	24/09/60	Football League Division 1	Manchester United 1 Wolverhampton Wanderers 3	Old Trafford	44458
46	1960/61	11/02/61	Football League Division 1	Wolverhampton Wanderers 2 Manchester United 1	Molineux	38526
47	1961/62	30/09/61	Football League Division 1	Manchester United 0 Wolverhampton Wanderers 2	Old Trafford	39457
48	1961/62	28/02/62	Football League Division 1	Wolverhampton Wanderers 2 Manchester United 2	Molineux	27565
49	1962/63	17/11/62	Football League Division 1	Wolverhampton Wanderers 2 Manchester United 3	Molineux	27305
50	1962/63	22/04/63	Football League Division 1	Manchester United 2 Wolverhampton Wanderers 1	Old Trafford	36147
51	1963/64	02/11/63	Football League Division 1	Wolverhampton Wanderers 2 Manchester United 0	Molineux	34159
52	1963/64	28/03/64	Football League Division 1	Manchester United 2 Wolverhampton Wanderers 2	Old Trafford	44470
53	1964/65	17/10/64	Football League Division 1	Wolverhampton Wanderers 2 Manchester United 4	Molineux	26763
54	1964/65	27/02/65	Football League Division 1	Manchester United 3 Wolverhampton Wanderers 0	Old Trafford	37018
55	1964/65	10/03/65	FA Cup 6th Round	Wolverhampton Wanderers 3 Manchester United 5	Molineux	53581
56	1965/66	05/03/66	FA Cup 5th Round	Wolverhampton Wanderers 2 Manchester United 4	Molineux	53500
57	1967/68	26/12/67	Football League Division 1	Manchester United 4 Wolverhampton Wanderers 0	Old Trafford	63450
58	1967/68	30/12/67	Football League Division 1	Wolverhampton Wanderers 2 Manchester United 3	Molineux	53940
59	1968/69	30/11/68	Football League Division 1	Manchester United 2 Wolverhampton Wanderers 0	Old Trafford	50165
60	1968/69	15/02/69	Football League Division 1	Wolverhampton Wanderers 2 Manchester United 2	Molineux	44023
61	1969/70	23/08/69	Football League Division 1	Wolverhampton Wanderers 0 Manchester United 0	Molineux	50783
62	1969/70	26/12/69	Football League Division 1	Manchester United 0 Wolverhampton Wanderers 0	Old Trafford	50806
63	1970/71	03/10/70	Football League Division 1	Wolverhampton Wanderers 3 Manchester United 2	Molineux	38629
64	1970/71	12/04/71	Football League Division 1	Manchester United 1 Wolverhampton Wanderers 0	Old Trafford	41886
65	1971/72	28/08/71	Football League Division 1	Wolverhampton Wanderers 1 Manchester United 1	Molineux	46471
66	1971/72	08/01/72	Football League Division 1	Manchester United 1 Wolverhampton Wanderers 3	Old Trafford	46781
67	1972/73	16/09/72	Football League Division 1	Wolverhampton Wanderers 2 Manchester United 0	Molineux	34049
68	1972/73	13/01/73	FA Cup 3rd Round	Wolverhampton Wanderers 1 Manchester United 0	Molineux	40005
69	1972/73	10/02/73	Football League Division 1	Manchester United 2 Wolverhampton Wanderers 1	Old Trafford	52089
70	1973/74	06/10/73	Football League Division 1	Wolverhampton Wanderers 2 Manchester United 1	Molineux	32962
71	1973/74	23/02/74	Football League Division 1	Manchester United 0 Wolverhampton Wanderers 0	Old Trafford	39260
72	1975/76	16/08/75	Football League Division 1	Wolverhampton Wanderers 0 Manchester United 2	Molineux	32348
73	1975/76	20/12/75	Football League Division 1	Manchester United 1 Wolverhampton Wanderers 0	Old Trafford	44269
74	1975/76	06/03/76	FA Cup 6th Round	Manchester United 1 Wolverhampton Wanderers 1	Old Trafford	59433
75	1975/76	09/03/76	FA Cup 6th Round Replay	Wolverhampton Wanderers 2 Manchester United 3	Molineux	44373
76	1977/78	03/12/77	Football League Division 1	Manchester United 3 Wolverhampton Wanderers 1	Old Trafford	48874
77	1977/78	29/04/78	Football League Division 1	Wolverhampton Wanderers 2 Manchester United 1	Molineux	24774
78	1978/79	28/10/78	Football League Division 1	Wolverhampton Wanderers 2 Manchester United 4	Molineux	23141
79	1978/79	07/05/79	Football League Division 1	Manchester United 3 Wolverhampton Wanderers 2	Old Trafford	39402
80	1979/80	22/09/79	Football League Division 1	Wolverhampton Wanderers 3 Manchester United 1	Molineux	35503
81	1979/80	09/02/80	Football League Division 1	Manchester United 0 Wolverhampton Wanderers 1	Old Trafford	51568
82	1980/81	19/08/80	Football League Division 1	Wolverhampton Wanderers 1 Manchester United 0	Molineux	31955
83	1980/81	12/11/80	Football League Division 1	Manchester United 0 Wolverhampton Wanderers 0	Old Trafford	37959
84	1981/82	03/10/81	Football League Division 1	Manchester United 5 Wolverhampton Wanderers 0	Old Trafford	46837
85	1981/82	13/02/82	Football League Division 1	Wolverhampton Wanderers 0 Manchester United 1	Molineux	22481
86	1983/84	29/10/83	Football League Division 1	Manchester United 3 Wolverhampton Wanderers 0	Old Trafford	41880
87	1983/84	18/02/84	Football League Division 1	Wolverhampton Wanderers 1 Manchester United 1	Molineux	20676
88	2003/04	27/08/03	FA Premiership	Manchester United 1 Wolverhampton Wanderers 0	Old Trafford	67648
89	2003/04	17/01/04	FA Premiership	Wolverhampton Wanderers 1 Manchester United 0	Molineux	29396
90	2005/06	29/01/06	FA Cup 4th Round	Wolverhampton Wanderers 0 Manchester United 3	Molineux	28333

UNITED v WORKINGTON

FA CUP						
VENUE	P	W	D	L	F	A
HOME	0	0	0	0	0	0
AWAY	1	1	0	0	3	1
TOTAL	1	1	0	0	3	1

#	SEASON	DATE	COMPETITION / ROUND	MATCH RESULT	VENUE	ATT
1	1957/58	04/01/58	FA Cup 3rd Round	Workington 1 Manchester United 3	Borough Park	21000

UNITED v WREXHAM

ALL COMPETITIVE MATCHES						
VENUE	P	W	D	L	F	A
HOME	3	3	0	0	10	2
AWAY	2	2	0	0	7	0
TOTAL	5	5	0	0	17	2

FA CUP							LEAGUE CUP							EUROPEAN CUP-WINNERS' CUP						
VENUE	P	W	D	L	F	A	VENUE	P	W	D	L	F	A	VENUE	P	W	D	L	F	A
HOME	1	1	0	0	5	2	HOME	1	1	0	0	2	0	HOME	1	1	0	0	3	0
AWAY	1	1	0	0	5	0	AWAY	0	0	0	0	0	0	AWAY	1	1	0	0	2	0
TOTAL	2	2	0	0	10	2	TOTAL	1	1	0	0	2	0	TOTAL	2	2	0	0	5	0

#	SEASON	DATE	COMPETITION / ROUND	MATCH RESULT	VENUE	ATT
1	1956/57	26/01/57	FA Cup 4th Round	Wrexham 0 Manchester United 5	Racecourse Ground	34445
2	1969/70	23/09/69	League Cup 3rd Round	Manchester United 2 Wrexham 0	Old Trafford	48347
3	1990/91	23/10/90	European CWC 2nd Round 1st Leg	Manchester United 3 Wrexham 0	Old Trafford	29405
4	1990/91	07/11/90	European CWC 2nd Round 2nd Leg	Wrexham 0 Manchester United 2	Racecourse Ground	13327
5	1994/95	28/01/95	FA Cup 4th Round	Manchester United 5 Wrexham 2	Old Trafford	43222

UNITED v YEOVIL TOWN

FA CUP						
VENUE	P	W	D	L	F	A
HOME	2	2	0	0	11	0
AWAY	0	0	0	0	0	0
TOTAL	2	2	0	0	11	0

#	SEASON	DATE	COMPETITION / ROUND	MATCH RESULT	VENUE	ATT
1	1937/38	08/01/38	FA Cup 3rd Round	Manchester United 3 Yeovil Town 0	Old Trafford	49004
2	1948/49	12/02/49	FA Cup 5th Round	Manchester United 8 Yeovil Town 0	Maine Road	81565

UNITED v YORK CITY

ALL COMPETITIVE MATCHES							LEAGUE DIVISION TWO							LEAGUE CUP						
VENUE	P	W	D	L	F	A	VENUE	P	W	D	L	F	A	VENUE	P	W	D	L	F	A
HOME	2	1	0	1	2	4	HOME	1	1	0	0	2	1	HOME	1	0	0	1	0	3
AWAY	2	2	0	0	4	1	AWAY	1	1	0	0	1	0	AWAY	1	1	0	0	3	1
TOTAL	4	3	0	1	6	5	TOTAL	2	2	0	0	3	1	TOTAL	2	1	0	1	3	4

#	SEASON	DATE	COMPETITION / ROUND	MATCH RESULT	VENUE	ATT
1	1974/75	21/12/74	Football League Division 2	York City 0 Manchester United 1	Bootham Crescent	15567
2	1974/75	29/03/75	Football League Division 2	Manchester United 2 York City 1	Old Trafford	46802
3	1995/96	20/09/95	League Cup 2nd Round 1st Leg	Manchester United 0 York City 3	Old Trafford	29049
4	1995/96	03/10/95	League Cup 2nd Round 2nd Leg	York City 1 Manchester United 3	Bootham Crescent	9386

UNITED v ZALAERGESZEG

CHAMPIONS LEAGUE					
VENUE	P	W	D	L	F	A
HOME	1	1	0	0	5	0
AWAY	1	0	0	1	0	1
TOTAL	2	1	0	1	5	1

#	SEASON	DATE	COMPETITION / ROUND	MATCH RESULT	VENUE	ATT
1	2002/03	14/08/02	Champions League Qualifying Round 1st Leg	Zalaegerszeg 1 Manchester United 0	Ferenc Puskas Stadion	40000
2	2002/03	27/08/02	Champions League Qualifying Round 2nd Leg	Manchester United 5 Zalaegerszeg 0	Old Trafford	66814

MANCHESTER UNITED
The Complete Record

Chapter 1.3
The Competitions

UNITED in the LEAGUE

OVERALL PLAYING RECORD

VENUE	P	W	D	L	F	A
HOME	2088	1260	470	358	4219	1979
AWAY	2088	702	539	847	2957	3400
TOTAL	4176	1962	1009	1205	7176	5379

PREMIERSHIP

VENUE	P	W	D	L	F	A
HOME	310	224	60	26	669	195
AWAY	310	170	77	63	551	343
TOTAL	620	394	137	89	1220	538

PERFORMANCE (16 SEASONS)

Champions	10 times
Runners-up	3 times
3rd	3 times

LEAGUE DIVISION 1

VENUE	P	W	D	L	F	A
HOME	1370	758	339	273	2614	1440
AWAY	1370	404	365	601	1909	2435
TOTAL	2740	1162	704	874	4523	3875

PERFORMANCE (67 SEASONS)

Champions	7 times	12th	2 times
Runners-up	10 times	13th	4 times
3rd	3 times	14th	2 times
4th	7 times	15th	2 times
5th	2 times	16th	2 times
6th	2 times	17th	1 time
7th	2 times	18th	3 times
8th	6 times	19th	1 time
9th	3 times	21st	2 times
10th	1 time	22nd	2 times
11th	3 times		

LEAGUE DIVISION 2

VENUE	P	W	D	L	F	A
HOME	408	278	71	59	936	344
AWAY	408	128	97	183	497	622
TOTAL	816	406	168	242	1433	966

PERFORMANCE (22 SEASONS)

Champions	2 times	10th	1 time
Runners-up	4 times	12th	1 time
3rd	3 times	14th	1 time
4th	4 times	15th	1 time
5th	2 times	20th	1 time
6th	2 times		

SEASON by SEASON PERFORMANCE

#	SEASON	COMPETITION	P	HOME W	HOME D	HOME L	HOME F	HOME A	AWAY W	AWAY D	AWAY L	AWAY F	AWAY A	PTS	GD	POS
1	1892/93	League Division 1	30	6	3	6	39	35	0	3	12	11	50	18	-35	16th
2	1893/94	League Division 1	30	5	2	8	29	33	1	0	14	7	39	14	-36	16th
3	1894/95	League Division 2	30	9	6	0	52	18	6	2	7	26	26	38	34	3rd
4	1895/96	League Division 2	30	12	2	1	48	15	3	1	11	18	42	33	9	6th
5	1896/97	League Division 2	30	11	4	0	37	10	6	1	8	19	24	39	22	2nd
6	1897/98	League Division 2	30	11	2	2	42	10	5	4	6	22	25	38	29	4th
7	1898/99	League Division 2	34	12	4	1	51	14	7	1	9	16	29	43	24	4th
8	1899/00	League Division 2	34	15	1	1	44	11	5	3	9	19	16	44	36	4th
9	1900/01	League Division 2	34	11	3	3	31	9	3	1	13	11	29	32	4	10th
10	1901/02	League Division 2	34	10	2	5	27	12	1	4	12	11	41	28	-15	15th
11	1902/03	League Division 2	34	9	4	4	32	15	6	4	7	21	23	38	15	5th
12	1903/04	League Division 2	34	14	2	1	42	14	6	6	5	23	19	48	32	3rd
13	1904/05	League Division 2	34	16	0	1	60	10	8	5	4	21	20	53	51	3rd
14	1905/06	League Division 2	38	15	3	1	55	13	13	3	3	35	15	62	62	2nd
15	1906/07	League Division 1	38	10	6	3	33	15	7	2	10	20	41	42	-3	8th
16	1907/08	League Division 1	38	15	1	3	43	19	8	5	6	38	29	52	33	1st
17	1908/09	League Division 1	38	10	3	6	37	33	5	4	10	21	35	37	-10	13th
18	1909/10	League Division 1	38	14	2	3	41	20	5	5	9	28	41	45	8	5th
19	1910/11	League Division 1	38	14	4	1	47	18	8	4	7	25	22	52	32	1st
20	1911/12	League Division 1	38	9	5	5	29	19	4	6	9	16	41	37	-15	13th
21	1912/13	League Division 1	38	13	3	3	41	14	6	5	8	28	29	46	26	4th
22	1913/14	League Division 1	38	8	4	7	27	23	7	2	10	25	39	36	-10	14th
23	1914/15	League Division 1	38	8	6	5	27	19	1	6	12	19	43	30	-16	18th
24	1919/20	League Division 1	42	6	8	7	20	17	7	6	8	34	33	40	4	12th
25	1920/21	League Division 1	42	9	4	8	34	26	6	6	9	30	42	40	-4	13th
26	1921/22	League Division 1	42	7	7	7	25	26	1	5	15	16	47	28	-32	22nd
27	1922/23	League Division 2	42	10	6	5	25	17	7	8	6	26	19	48	15	4th
28	1923/24	League Division 2	42	10	7	4	37	15	3	7	11	15	29	40	8	14th
29	1924/25	League Division 2	42	17	3	1	40	6	6	8	7	17	17	57	34	2nd
30	1925/26	League Division 1	42	12	4	5	40	26	7	2	12	26	47	44	-7	9th
31	1926/27	League Division 1	42	9	8	4	29	19	4	6	11	23	45	40	-12	15th
32	1927/28	League Division 1	42	12	6	3	51	27	4	1	16	21	53	39	-8	18th
33	1928/29	League Division 1	42	8	8	5	32	23	6	5	10	34	53	41	-10	12th
34	1929/30	League Division 1	42	11	4	6	39	34	4	4	13	28	54	38	-21	17th
35	1930/31	League Division 1	42	6	6	9	30	37	1	2	18	23	78	22	-62	22nd

UNITED in the LEAGUE

SEASON by SEASON PERFORMANCE (continued)

#	SEASON	COMPETITION	P	W	D	L	F	A	W	D	L	F	A	PTS	GD	POS
					HOME					AWAY						
36	1931/32	League Division 2	42	12	3	6	44	31	5	5	11	27	41	42	-1	12th
37	1932/33	League Division 2	42	11	5	5	40	24	4	8	9	31	44	43	3	6th
38	1933/34	League Division 2	42	9	3	9	29	33	5	3	13	30	52	34	-26	20th
39	1934/35	League Division 2	42	16	2	3	50	21	7	2	12	26	34	50	21	5th
40	1935/36	League Division 2	42	16	3	2	55	16	6	9	6	30	27	56	42	1st
41	1936/37	League Division 1	42	8	9	4	29	26	2	3	16	26	52	32	-23	21st
42	1937/38	League Division 2	42	15	3	3	50	18	7	6	8	32	32	53	32	2nd
43	1938/39	League Division 1	42	7	9	5	30	20	4	7	10	27	45	38	-8	14th
44	1946/47	League Division 1	42	17	3	1	61	19	5	9	7	34	35	56	41	2nd
45	1947/48	League Division 1	42	11	7	3	50	27	8	7	6	31	21	52	33	2nd
46	1948/49	League Division 1	42	11	7	3	40	20	10	4	7	37	24	53	33	2nd
47	1949/50	League Division 1	42	11	5	5	42	20	7	9	5	27	24	50	25	4th
48	1950/51	League Division 1	42	14	4	3	42	16	10	4	7	32	24	56	34	2nd
49	1951/52	League Division 1	42	15	3	3	55	21	8	8	5	40	31	57	43	1st
50	1952/53	League Division 1	42	11	5	5	35	30	7	5	9	34	42	46	-3	8th
51	1953/54	League Division 1	42	11	6	4	41	27	7	6	8	32	31	48	15	4th
52	1954/55	League Division 1	42	12	4	5	44	30	8	3	10	40	44	47	10	5th
53	1955/56	League Division 1	42	18	3	0	51	20	7	7	7	32	31	60	32	1st
54	1956/57	League Division 1	42	14	4	3	55	25	14	4	3	48	29	64	49	1st
55	1957/58	League Division 1	42	10	4	7	45	31	6	7	8	40	44	43	10	9th
56	1958/59	League Division 1	42	14	4	3	58	27	10	3	8	45	39	55	37	2nd
57	1959/60	League Division 1	42	13	3	5	53	30	6	4	11	49	50	45	22	7th
58	1960/61	League Division 1	42	14	5	2	58	20	4	4	13	30	56	45	12	7th
59	1961/62	League Division 1	42	10	3	8	44	31	5	6	10	28	44	39	-3	15th
60	1962/63	League Division 1	42	6	6	9	36	38	6	4	11	31	43	34	-14	19th
61	1963/64	League Division 1	42	15	3	3	54	19	8	4	9	36	43	53	28	2nd
62	1964/65	League Division 1	42	16	4	1	52	13	10	5	6	37	26	61	50	1st
63	1965/66	League Division 1	42	12	8	1	50	20	6	7	8	34	39	51	25	4th
64	1966/67	League Division 1	42	17	4	0	51	13	7	8	6	33	32	60	39	1st
65	1967/68	League Division 1	42	15	2	4	49	21	9	6	6	40	34	56	34	2nd
66	1968/69	League Division 1	42	13	5	3	38	18	2	7	12	19	35	42	4	11th
67	1969/70	League Division 1	42	8	9	4	37	27	6	8	7	29	34	45	5	8th
68	1970/71	League Division 1	42	9	6	6	29	24	7	5	9	36	42	43	-1	8th
69	1971/72	League Division 1	42	13	2	6	39	26	6	8	7	30	35	48	8	8th
70	1972/73	League Division 1	42	9	7	5	24	19	3	6	12	20	41	37	-16	18th
71	1973/74	League Division 1	42	7	7	7	23	20	3	5	13	15	28	32	-10	21st
72	1974/75	League Division 2	42	17	3	1	45	12	9	6	6	21	18	61	36	1st
73	1975/76	League Division 1	42	16	4	1	40	13	7	6	8	28	29	56	26	3rd
74	1976/77	League Division 1	42	12	6	3	41	22	6	5	10	30	40	47	9	6th
75	1977/78	League Division 1	42	9	6	6	32	23	7	4	10	35	40	42	4	10th
76	1978/79	League Division 1	42	9	7	5	29	25	6	8	7	31	38	45	-3	9th
77	1979/80	League Division 1	42	17	3	1	43	8	7	7	7	22	27	58	30	2nd
78	1980/81	League Division 1	42	9	11	1	30	14	6	7	8	21	22	48	15	8th
79	1981/82	League Division 1	42	12	6	3	27	9	10	6	5	32	20	78	30	3rd
80	1982/83	League Division 1	42	14	7	0	39	10	5	6	10	17	28	70	18	3rd
81	1983/84	League Division 1	42	14	3	4	43	18	6	11	4	28	23	74	30	4th
82	1984/85	League Division 1	42	13	6	2	47	13	9	4	8	30	34	76	30	4th
83	1985/86	League Division 1	42	12	5	4	35	12	10	5	6	35	24	76	34	4th
84	1986/87	League Division 1	42	13	3	5	38	18	1	11	9	14	27	56	7	11th
85	1987/88	League Division 1	40	14	5	1	41	17	9	7	4	30	21	81	33	2nd
86	1988/89	League Division 1	38	10	5	4	27	13	3	7	9	18	22	51	10	11th
87	1989/90	League Division 1	38	8	6	5	26	14	5	3	11	20	33	48	-1	13th
88	1990/91	League Division 1	38	11	4	4	34	17	5	8	6	24	28	59	13	6th
89	1991/92	League Division 1	42	12	7	2	34	13	9	8	4	29	20	78	30	2nd
90	1992/93	Premiership	42	14	5	2	39	14	10	7	4	28	17	84	36	1st
91	1993/94	Premiership	42	14	6	1	39	13	13	5	3	41	25	92	42	1st
92	1994/95	Premiership	42	16	4	1	42	4	10	6	5	35	24	88	49	2nd
93	1995/96	Premiership	38	15	4	0	36	9	10	3	6	37	26	82	38	1st
94	1996/97	Premiership	38	12	5	2	38	17	9	7	3	38	27	75	32	1st
95	1997/98	Premiership	38	13	4	2	42	9	10	4	5	31	17	77	47	2nd
96	1998/99	Premiership	38	14	4	1	45	18	8	9	2	35	19	79	43	1st
97	1999/00	Premiership	38	15	4	0	59	16	13	3	3	38	29	91	52	1st
98	2000/01	Premiership	38	15	2	2	49	12	9	6	4	30	19	80	48	1st
99	2001/02	Premiership	38	11	2	6	40	17	13	3	3	47	28	77	42	3rd
100	2002/03	Premiership	38	16	2	1	42	12	9	6	4	32	22	83	40	1st
101	2003/04	Premiership	38	12	4	3	37	15	11	2	6	27	20	75	29	3rd
102	2004/05	Premiership	38	12	6	1	31	12	10	5	4	27	14	77	32	3rd
103	2005/06	Premiership	38	13	5	1	37	8	12	3	4	35	26	83	38	2nd
104	2006/07	Premiership	38	15	2	2	46	12	13	3	3	37	15	89	56	1st
105	2007/08	Premiership	38	17	1	1	47	7	10	5	4	33	15	87	58	1st

UNITED in the FA CUP

PLAYING RECORD							OVERALL PERFORMANCE RECORD (109 ENTRIES)			

VENUE	P	W	D	L	F	A
HOME	186	119	36	31	390	168
AWAY	166	73	44	49	273	238
NEUTRAL	63	33	15	15	107	66
TOTAL	415	225	95	95	770	472

WINNERS	11 times	Lost in 3rd Round	21 times
		Lost in 2nd Round	8 times
Losing FINALISTS	7 times	Lost in 1st Round	13 times
Losing SEMI-FINALISTS	7 times	Lost in Intermediate Round	2 times
Losing QUARTER-FINALISTS	7 times	Lost in 4th Qualifying Round	1 time
Lost in 5th Round	10 times	Lost in 3rd Qualifying Round	1 time
Lost in 4th Round	20 times	Lost in 2nd Qualifying Round	1 time

#	SEASON	DATE	ROUND	MATCH RESULT	VENUE	ATT
1	1886/87	30/10/86	1st Round	Fleetwood Rangers 2 Newton Heath 2 (Fleetwood awarded tie – see page 2)	Fleetwood Park	2000
2	1889/90	18/01/90	1st Round	Preston North End 6 Newton Heath 1	Deepdale	7900
3	1890/91	04/10/90	1st Qualifying Round	Newton Heath 2 Higher Walton 0	North Road	3000
4	1890/91	25/10/90	2nd Qualifying Round	Bootle Reserves 1 Newton Heath 0	Bootle Park	500
5	1891/92	03/10/91	1st Qualifying Round	Newton Heath 5 Manchester City 1	North Road	11000
6	1891/92	14/11/91	3rd Qualifying Round	South Shore 0 Newton Heath 2	Bloomfield Road	2000
7	1891/92	05/12/91	4th Qualifying Round	Newton Heath 3 Blackpool 4	North Road	4000
8	1892/93	21/01/93	1st Round	Blackburn Rovers 4 Newton Heath 0	Ewood Park	7000
9	1893/94	27/01/94	1st Round	Newton Heath 4 Middlesbrough 0	Bank Street	5000
10	1893/94	10/02/94	2nd Round	Newton Heath 0 Blackburn Rovers 0	Bank Street	18000
11	1893/94	17/02/94	2nd Round Replay	Blackburn Rovers 5 Newton Heath 1	Ewood Park	5000
12	1894/95	02/02/95	1st Round	Newton Heath 2 Stoke City 3	Bank Street	7000
13	1895/96	01/02/96	1st Round	Newton Heath 2 Kettering 1	Bank Street	1000
14	1895/96	15/02/96	2nd Round	Newton Heath 1 Derby County 1	Bank Street	1500
15	1895/96	19/02/96	2nd Round Replay	Derby County 5 Newton Heath 1	Baseball Ground	2000
16	1896/97	12/12/96	3rd Qualifying Round	Newton Heath 7 West Manchester 0	Bank Street	6000
17	1896/97	02/01/97	4th Qualifying Round	Newton Heath 3 Nelson 0	Bank Street	5000
18	1896/97	16/01/97	5th Qualifying Round	Newton Heath 2 Blackpool 2	Bank Street	1500
19	1896/97	20/01/97	5th Qualifying Round Replay	Blackpool 1 Newton Heath 2	Raikes Hall Gardens	5000
20	1896/97	30/01/97	1st Round	Newton Heath 5 Kettering 1	Bank Street	1500
21	1896/97	13/02/97	2nd Round	Southampton 1 Newton Heath 1	County Cricket Ground	8000
22	1896/97	17/02/97	2nd Round Replay	Newton Heath 3 Southampton 1	Bank Street	7000
23	1896/97	27/02/97	3rd Round	Derby County 2 Newton Heath 0	Baseball Ground	12000
24	1897/98	29/01/98	1st Round	Newton Heath 1 Walsall 0	Bank Street	6000
25	1897/98	12/02/98	2nd Round	Newton Heath 0 Liverpool 0	Bank Street	12000
26	1897/98	16/02/98	2nd Round Replay	Liverpool 2 Newton Heath 1	Anfield	6000
27	1898/99	28/01/99	1st Round	Tottenham Hotspur 1 Newton Heath 1	Asplins Farm	15000
28	1898/99	01/02/99	1st Round Replay	Newton Heath 3 Tottenham Hotspur 5	Bank Street	6000
29	1899/00	28/10/99	3rd Qualifying Round	South Shore 3 Newton Heath 1	Bloomfield Road	3000
30	1900/01	05/01/01	Supplementary Round	Newton Heath 3 Portsmouth 0	Bank Street	5000
31	1900/01	09/02/01	1st Round	Newton Heath 0 Burnley 0	Bank Street	8000
32	1900/01	13/02/01	1st Round Replay	Burnley 7 Newton Heath 1	Turf Moor	4000
33	1901/02	14/12/01	Intermediate Round	Newton Heath 1 Lincoln City 2	Bank Street	4000
34	1902/03	01/11/02	3rd Qualifying Round	Manchester United 7 Accrington Stanley 0	Bank Street	6000
35	1902/03	13/11/02	4th Qualifying Round	Manchester United 3 Oswaldtwistle Rovers 2	Bank Street	5000
36	1902/03	29/11/02	5th Qualifying Round	Manchester United 4 Southport Central 1	Bank Street	6000
37	1902/03	13/12/02	Intermediate Round	Manchester United 1 Burton United 1	Bank Street	6000
38	1902/03	17/12/02	Intermediate Round Replay	Burton United 1 Manchester United 3	Bank Street	7000
39	1902/03	07/02/03	1st Round	Manchester United 2 Liverpool 1	Bank Street	15000
40	1902/03	21/02/03	2nd Round	Everton 3 Manchester United 1	Goodison Park	15000
41	1903/04	12/12/03	Intermediate Round	Manchester United 1 Birmingham City 1	Bank Street	10000
42	1903/04	16/12/03	Intermediate Round Replay	Birmingham City 1 Manchester United 1	Muntz Street	5000
43	1903/04	21/12/03	Intermediate Round 2nd Replay	Manchester United 1 Birmingham City 1	Bramall Lane	3000
44	1903/04	11/01/04	Intermediate Round 3rd Replay	Manchester United 3 Birmingham City 1	Hyde Road	9372
45	1903/04	06/02/04	1st Round	Notts County 3 Manchester United 3	Trent Bridge	12000
46	1903/04	10/02/04	1st Round Replay	Manchester United 2 Notts County 1	Bank Street	18000
47	1903/04	20/02/04	2nd Round	Sheffield Wednesday 6 Manchester United 0	Hillsborough	22051
48	1904/05	14/01/05	Intermediate Round	Manchester United 2 Fulham 2	Bank Street	17000
49	1904/05	18/01/05	Intermediate Round Replay	Fulham 0 Manchester United 0	Craven Cottage	15000
50	1904/05	23/01/05	Intermediate Round 2nd Replay	Manchester United 0 Fulham 1	Villa Park	6000
51	1905/06	13/01/06	1st Round	Manchester United 7 Staple Hill 2	Bank Street	7560
52	1905/06	03/02/06	2nd Round	Manchester United 3 Norwich City 0	Bank Street	10000
53	1905/06	24/02/06	3rd Round	Manchester United 5 Aston Villa 1	Bank Street	35500
54	1905/06	10/03/06	4th Round	Manchester United 2 Arsenal 3	Bank Street	26500
55	1906/07	12/01/07	1st Round	Portsmouth 2 Manchester United 2	Fratton Park	24329
56	1906/07	16/01/07	1st Round Replay	Manchester United 1 Portsmouth 2	Bank Street	8000
57	1907/08	11/01/08	1st Round	Manchester United 3 Blackpool 1	Bank Street	11747
58	1907/08	01/02/08	2nd Round	Manchester United 1 Chelsea 0	Bank Street	25184
59	1907/08	22/02/08	3rd Round	Aston Villa 0 Manchester United 2	Villa Park	12777
60	1907/08	07/03/08	4th Round	Fulham 2 Manchester United 1	Craven Cottage	41000

UNITED in the FA CUP

#	SEASON	DATE	ROUND	MATCH RESULT	VENUE	ATT
61	1908/09	16/01/09	1st Round	Manchester United 1 Brighton 0	Bank Street	8300
62	1908/09	06/02/09	2nd Round	Manchester United 1 Everton 0	Bank Street	35217
63	1908/09	20/02/09	3rd Round	Manchester United 6 Blackburn Rovers 1	Bank Street	38500
64	1908/09	10/03/09	4th Round	Burnley 2 Manchester United 3	Turf Moor	16850
65	1908/09	27/03/09	Semi–Final	Manchester United 1 Newcastle United 0	Bramall Lane	40118
66	1908/09	24/04/09	Final	Manchester United 1 Bristol City 0	Crystal Palace	71401
67	1909/10	15/01/10	1st Round	Burnley 2 Manchester United 0	Turf Moor	16628
68	1910/11	14/01/11	1st Round	Blackpool 1 Manchester United 2	Bloomfield Road	12000
69	1910/11	04/02/11	2nd Round	Manchester United 2 Aston Villa 1	Old Trafford	65101
70	1910/11	25/02/11	3rd Round	West Ham United 2 Manchester United 1	Upton Park	26000
71	1911/12	13/01/12	1st Round	Manchester United 3 Huddersfield Town 1	Old Trafford	19579
72	1911/12	03/02/12	2nd Round	Coventry City 1 Manchester United 5	Highfield Road	17130
73	1911/12	24/02/12	3rd Round	Reading 1 Manchester United 1	Elm Park	24069
74	1911/12	29/02/12	3rd Round Replay	Manchester United 3 Reading 0	Old Trafford	29511
75	1911/12	09/03/12	4th Round	Manchester United 1 Blackburn Rovers 1	Old Trafford	59300
76	1911/12	14/03/12	4th Round Replay	Blackburn Rovers 4 Manchester United 2	Ewood Park	39296
77	1912/13	11/01/13	1st Round	Manchester United 1 Coventry City 1	Old Trafford	11500
78	1912/13	16/01/13	1st Round Replay	Coventry City 1 Manchester United 2	Highfield Road	20042
79	1912/13	01/02/13	2nd Round	Plymouth Argyle 0 Manchester United 2	Home Park	21700
80	1912/13	22/02/13	3rd Round	Oldham Athletic 0 Manchester United 0	Boundary Park	26932
81	1912/13	26/02/13	3rd Round Replay	Manchester United 1 Oldham Athletic 2	Old Trafford	31180
82	1913/14	10/01/14	1st Round	Swindon Town 1 Manchester United 0	County Ground	18187
83	1914/15	09/01/15	1st Round	Sheffield Wednesday 1 Manchester United 0	Hillsborough	23248

— The FA Cup was not held from 1915/16 to 1918/19 due to the First World War —

#	SEASON	DATE	ROUND	MATCH RESULT	VENUE	ATT
84	1919/20	10/01/20	1st Round	Port Vale 0 Manchester United 1	Old Recreation Ground	14549
85	1919/20	31/01/20	2nd Round	Manchester United 1 Aston Villa 2	Old Trafford	48600
86	1920/21	08/01/21	1st Round	Liverpool 1 Manchester United 1	Anfield	40000
87	1920/21	12/01/21	1st Round Replay	Manchester United 1 Liverpool 2	Old Trafford	30000
88	1921/22	07/01/22	1st Round	Manchester United 1 Cardiff City 4	Old Trafford	25726
89	1922/23	13/01/23	1st Round	Bradford City 1 Manchester United 1	Valley Parade	27000
90	1922/23	17/01/23	1st Round Replay	Manchester United 2 Bradford City 0	Old Trafford	27791
91	1922/23	03/02/23	2nd Round	Tottenham Hotspur 4 Manchester United 0	White Hart Lane	38333
92	1923/24	12/01/24	1st Round	Manchester United 1 Plymouth Argyle 0	Old Trafford	35700
93	1923/24	02/02/24	2nd Round	Manchester United 0 Huddersfield Town 3	Old Trafford	66673
94	1924/25	10/01/25	1st Round	Sheffield Wednesday 2 Manchester United 0	Hillsborough	35079
95	1925/26	09/01/26	3rd Round	Port Vale 2 Manchester United 3	Old Recreation Ground	14841
96	1925/26	30/01/26	4th Round	Tottenham Hotspur 2 Manchester United 2	White Hart Lane	40000
97	1925/26	03/02/26	4th Round Replay	Manchester United 2 Tottenham Hotspur 0	Old Trafford	45000
98	1925/26	20/02/26	5th Round	Sunderland 3 Manchester United 3	Roker Park	50500
99	1925/26	24/02/26	5th Round Replay	Manchester United 2 Sunderland 1	Old Trafford	58661
100	1925/26	06/03/26	6th Round	Fulham 1 Manchester United 2	Craven Cottage	28699
101	1925/26	27/03/26	Semi–Final	Manchester United 0 Manchester City 3	Bramall Lane	46450
102	1926/27	08/01/27	3rd Round	Reading 1 Manchester United 1	Elm Park	28918
103	1926/27	12/01/27	3rd Round Replay	Manchester United 2 Reading 2	Old Trafford	29122
104	1926/27	17/01/27	3rd Round 2nd Replay	Manchester United 1 Reading 2	Villa Park	16500
105	1927/28	14/01/28	3rd Round	Manchester United 7 Brentford 1	Old Trafford	18538
106	1927/28	28/01/28	4th Round	Bury 1 Manchester United 1	Gigg Lane	25000
107	1927/28	01/02/28	4th Round Replay	Manchester United 1 Bury 0	Old Trafford	48001
108	1927/28	18/02/28	5th Round	Manchester United 1 Birmingham City 0	Old Trafford	52568
109	1927/28	03/03/28	6th Round	Blackburn Rovers 2 Manchester United 0	Ewood Park	42312
110	1928/29	12/01/29	3rd Round	Port Vale 0 Manchester United 3	Old Recreation Ground	17519
111	1928/29	26/01/29	4th Round	Manchester United 0 Bury 1	Old Trafford	40558
112	1929/30	11/01/30	3rd Round	Manchester United 0 Swindon Town 2	Old Trafford	33226
113	1930/31	10/01/31	3rd Round	Stoke City 3 Manchester United 3	Victoria Ground	23415
114	1930/31	14/01/31	3rd Round Replay	Manchester United 0 Stoke City 0	Old Trafford	22013
115	1930/31	19/01/31	3rd Round 2nd Replay	Manchester United 4 Stoke City 2	Anfield	11788
116	1930/31	24/01/31	4th Round	Grimsby Town 1 Manchester United 0	Blundell Park	15000
117	1931/32	09/01/32	3rd Round	Plymouth Argyle 4 Manchester United 1	Home Park	28000
118	1932/33	14/01/33	3rd Round	Manchester United 1 Middlesbrough 4	Old Trafford	36991
119	1933/34	13/01/34	3rd Round	Manchester United 1 Portsmouth 1	Old Trafford	23283
120	1933/34	17/01/34	3rd Round Replay	Portsmouth 4 Manchester United 1	Fratton Park	18748
121	1934/35	12/01/35	3rd Round	Bristol Rovers 1 Manchester United 3	Eastville	20400
122	1934/35	26/01/35	4th Round	Nottingham Forest 0 Manchester United 0	City Ground	32862
123	1934/35	30/01/35	4th Round Replay	Manchester United 0 Nottingham Forest 3	Old Trafford	33851
124	1935/36	11/01/36	3rd Round	Reading 1 Manchester United 3	Elm Park	25844
125	1935/36	25/01/36	4th Round	Stoke City 0 Manchester United 0	Victoria Ground	32286
126	1935/36	29/01/36	4th Round Replay	Manchester United 0 Stoke City 2	Old Trafford	34440

UNITED in the FA CUP

#	SEASON	DATE	ROUND	MATCH RESULT	VENUE	ATT
127	1936/37	16/01/37	3rd Round	Manchester United 1 Reading 0	Old Trafford	36668
128	1936/37	30/01/37	4th Round	Arsenal 5 Manchester United 0	Highbury	45637
129	1937/38	08/01/38	3rd Round	Manchester United 3 Yeovil Town 0	Old Trafford	49004
130	1937/38	22/01/38	4th Round	Barnsley 2 Manchester United 2	Oakwell	35549
131	1937/38	26/01/38	4th Round Replay	Manchester United 1 Barnsley 0	Old Trafford	33601
132	1937/38	12/02/38	5th Round	Brentford 2 Manchester United 0	Griffin Park	24147
133	1938/39	07/01/39	3rd Round	West Bromwich Albion 0 Manchester United 0	The Hawthorns	23900
134	1938/39	11/01/39	3rd Round Replay	Manchester United 1 West Bromwich Albion 5	Old Trafford	17641

The FA Cup was not held from 1939/40 to 1944/45 due to the Second World War

#	SEASON	DATE	ROUND	MATCH RESULT	VENUE	ATT
135	1945/46	05/01/46	3rd Round 1st Leg	Accrington Stanley 2 Manchester United 2	Peel Park	9968
136	1945/46	09/01/46	3rd Round 2nd Leg	Manchester United 5 Accrington Stanley 1	Maine Road	15339
137	1945/46	26/01/46	4th Round 1st Leg	Manchester United 1 Preston North End 0	Maine Road	36237
138	1945/46	30/01/46	4th Round 2nd Leg	Preston North End 3 Manchester United 1	Deepdale	21000

In Season 1945/46 FA Cup ties were played over two legs for the only time in its history

#	SEASON	DATE	ROUND	MATCH RESULT	VENUE	ATT
139	1946/47	11/01/47	3rd Round	Bradford Park Avenue 0 Manchester United 3	Park Avenue	26990
140	1946/47	25/01/47	4th Round	Manchester United 0 Nottingham Forest 2	Maine Road	34059
141	1947/48	10/01/48	3rd Round	Aston Villa 4 Manchester United 6	Villa Park	58683
142	1947/48	24/01/48	4th Round	Manchester United 3 Liverpool 0	Goodison Park	74000
143	1947/48	07/02/48	5th Round	Manchester United 2 Charlton Athletic 0	Leeds Road	33312
144	1947/48	28/02/48	6th Round	Manchester United 4 Preston North End 2	Maine Road	74213
145	1947/48	13/03/48	Semi–Final	Manchester United 3 Derby County 1	Hillsborough	60000
146	1947/48	24/04/48	Final	Manchester United 4 Blackpool 2	Wembley	99000
147	1948/49	08/01/49	3rd Round	Manchester United 6 Bournemouth 0	Maine Road	55012
148	1948/49	29/01/49	4th Round	Manchester United 1 Bradford Park Avenue 1	Maine Road	82771
149	1948/49	05/02/49	4th Round Replay	Bradford Park Avenue 1 Manchester United 1	Park Avenue	30000
150	1948/49	07/02/49	4th Round 2nd Replay	Manchester United 5 Bradford Park Avenue 0	Maine Road	70434
151	1948/49	12/02/49	5th Round	Manchester United 8 Yeovil Town 0	Maine Road	81565
152	1948/49	26/02/49	6th Round	Hull City 0 Manchester United 1	Boothferry Park	55000
153	1948/49	26/03/49	Semi–Final	Manchester United 1 Wolverhampton Wanderers 1	Hillsborough	62250
154	1948/49	02/04/49	Semi–Final Replay	Manchester United 1 Wolverhampton Wanderers 1	Goodison Park	73000
155	1949/50	07/01/50	3rd Round	Manchester United 4 Weymouth Town 0	Old Trafford	38284
156	1949/50	28/01/50	4th Round	Watford 0 Manchester United 1	Vicarage Road	32800
157	1949/50	11/02/50	5th Round	Manchester United 3 Portsmouth 3	Old Trafford	53688
158	1949/50	15/02/50	5th Round Replay	Portsmouth 1 Manchester United 3	Fratton Park	49962
159	1949/50	04/03/50	6th Round	Chelsea 2 Manchester United 0	Stamford Bridge	70362
160	1950/51	06/01/51	3rd Round	Manchester United 4 Oldham Athletic 1	Old Trafford	37161
161	1950/51	27/01/51	4th Round	Manchester United 4 Leeds United 0	Old Trafford	55434
162	1950/51	10/02/51	5th Round	Manchester United 1 Arsenal 0	Old Trafford	55058
163	1950/51	24/02/51	6th Round	Birmingham City 1 Manchester United 0	St Andrews	50000
164	1951/52	12/01/52	3rd Round	Manchester United 0 Hull City 2	Old Trafford	43517
165	1952/53	10/01/53	3rd Round	Millwall 0 Manchester United 1	The Den	35652
166	1952/53	31/01/53	4th Round	Manchester United 1 Walthamstow Avenue 1	Old Trafford	34748
167	1952/53	05/02/53	4th Round Replay	Walthamstow Avenue 2 Manchester United 5	Highbury	49119
168	1952/53	14/02/53	5th Round	Everton 2 Manchester United 1	Goodison Park	77920
169	1953/54	09/01/54	3rd Round	Burnley 5 Manchester United 3	Turf Moor	54000
170	1954/55	08/01/55	3rd Round	Reading 1 Manchester United 1	Elm Park	26000
171	1954/55	12/01/55	3rd Round Replay	Manchester United 4 Reading 1	Old Trafford	24578
172	1954/55	19/02/55	4th Round	Manchester City 2 Manchester United 0	Maine Road	75000
173	1955/56	07/01/56	3rd Round	Bristol Rovers 4 Manchester United 0	Eastville	35872
174	1956/57	05/01/57	3rd Round	Hartlepool United 3 Manchester United 4	Victoria Ground	17264
175	1956/57	26/01/57	4th Round	Wrexham 0 Manchester United 5	Racecourse Ground	34445
176	1956/57	16/02/57	5th Round	Manchester United 1 Everton 0	Old Trafford	61803
177	1956/57	02/03/57	6th Round	Bournemouth 1 Manchester United 2	Dean Court	28799
178	1956/57	23/03/57	Semi–Final	Manchester United 2 Birmingham City 0	Hillsborough	65107
179	1956/57	04/05/57	Final	Manchester United 1 Aston Villa 2	Wembley	100000
180	1957/58	04/01/58	3rd Round	Workington 1 Manchester United 3	Borough Park	21000
181	1957/58	25/01/58	4th Round	Manchester United 2 Ipswich Town 0	Old Trafford	53550
182	1957/58	19/02/58	5th Round	Manchester United 3 Sheffield Wednesday 0	Old Trafford	59848
183	1957/58	01/03/58	6th Round	West Bromwich Albion 2 Manchester United 2	The Hawthorns	58250
184	1957/58	05/03/58	6th Round Replay	Manchester United 1 West Bromwich Albion 0	Old Trafford	60000
185	1957/58	22/03/58	Semi–Final	Manchester United 2 Fulham 2	Villa Park	69745
186	1957/58	26/03/58	Semi–Final Replay	Manchester United 5 Fulham 3	Highbury	38000
187	1957/58	03/05/58	Final	Manchester United 0 Bolton Wanderers 2	Wembley	100000
188	1958/59	10/01/59	3rd Round	Norwich City 3 Manchester United 0	Carrow Road	38000
189	1959/60	09/01/60	3rd Round	Derby County 2 Manchester United 4	Baseball Ground	33297
190	1959/60	30/01/60	4th Round	Liverpool 1 Manchester United 3	Anfield	56736
191	1959/60	20/02/60	5th Round	Manchester United 0 Sheffield Wednesday 1	Old Trafford	66350
192	1960/61	07/01/61	3rd Round	Manchester United 3 Middlesbrough 0	Old Trafford	49184
193	1960/61	28/01/61	4th Round	Sheffield Wednesday 1 Manchester United 1	Hillsborough	58000
194	1960/61	01/02/61	4th Round Replay	Manchester United 2 Sheffield Wednesday 7	Old Trafford	65243

UNITED in the FA CUP

#	SEASON	DATE	ROUND	MATCH RESULT	VENUE	ATT
195	1961/62	06/01/62	3rd Round	Manchester United 2 Bolton Wanderers 1	Old Trafford	42202
196	1961/62	31/01/62	4th Round	Manchester United 1 Arsenal 0	Old Trafford	54082
197	1961/62	17/02/62	5th Round	Manchester United 0 Sheffield Wednesday 0	Old Trafford	59553
198	1961/62	21/02/62	5th Round Replay	Sheffield Wednesday 0 Manchester United 2	Hillsborough	62969
199	1961/62	10/03/62	6th Round	Preston North End 0 Manchester United 0	Deepdale	37521
200	1961/62	14/03/62	6th Round Replay	Manchester United 2 Preston North End 1	Old Trafford	63468
201	1961/62	31/03/62	Semi-Final	Manchester United 1 Tottenham Hotspur 3	Hillsborough	65000
202	1962/63	04/03/63	3rd Round	Manchester United 5 Huddersfield Town 0	Old Trafford	47703
203	1962/63	11/03/63	4th Round	Manchester United 1 Aston Villa 0	Old Trafford	52265
204	1962/63	16/03/63	5th Round	Manchester United 2 Chelsea 1	Old Trafford	48298
205	1962/63	30/03/63	6th Round	Coventry City 1 Manchester United 3	Highfield Road	44000
206	1962/63	27/04/63	Semi-Final	Manchester United 1 Southampton 0	Villa Park	65000
207	1962/63	25/05/63	Final	Manchester United 3 Leicester City 1	Wembley	100000
208	1963/64	04/01/64	3rd Round	Southampton 2 Manchester United 3	The Dell	29164
209	1963/64	25/01/64	4th Round	Manchester United 4 Bristol Rovers 1	Old Trafford	55772
210	1963/64	15/02/64	5th Round	Barnsley 0 Manchester United 4	Oakwell	38076
211	1963/64	29/02/64	6th Round	Manchester United 3 Sunderland 3	Old Trafford	63700
212	1963/64	04/03/64	6th Round Replay	Sunderland 2 Manchester United 2	Roker Park	68000
213	1963/64	09/03/64	6th Round 2nd Replay	Manchester United 5 Sunderland 1	Leeds Road	54952
214	1963/64	14/03/64	Semi-Final	Manchester United 1 West Ham United 3	Hillsborough	65000
215	1964/65	09/01/65	3rd Round	Manchester United 2 Chester City 1	Old Trafford	40000
216	1964/65	30/01/65	4th Round	Stoke City 0 Manchester United 0	Victoria Ground	53009
217	1964/65	03/02/65	4th Round Replay	Manchester United 1 Stoke City 0	Old Trafford	50814
218	1964/65	20/02/65	5th Round	Manchester United 2 Burnley 1	Old Trafford	54000
219	1964/65	10/03/65	6th Round	Wolverhampton Wanderers 3 Manchester United 5	Molineux	53581
220	1964/65	27/03/65	Semi-Final	Manchester United 0 Leeds United 0	Hillsborough	65000
221	1964/65	31/03/65	Semi-Final Replay	Manchester United 0 Leeds United 1	City Ground	46300
222	1965/66	22/01/66	3rd Round	Derby County 2 Manchester United 5	Baseball Ground	33827
223	1965/66	12/02/66	4th Round	Manchester United 0 Rotherham United 0	Old Trafford	54263
224	1965/66	15/02/66	4th Round Replay	Rotherham United 0 Manchester United 1	Millmoor	23500
225	1965/66	05/03/66	5th Round	Wolverhampton Wanderers 2 Manchester United 4	Molineux	53500
226	1965/66	26/03/66	6th Round	Preston North End 1 Manchester United 1	Deepdale	37876
227	1965/66	30/03/66	6th Round Replay	Manchester United 3 Preston North End 1	Old Trafford	60433
228	1965/66	23/04/66	Semi-Final	Manchester United 0 Everton 1	Burnden Park	60000
229	1966/67	28/01/67	3rd Round	Manchester United 2 Stoke City 0	Old Trafford	63500
230	1966/67	18/02/67	4th Round	Manchester United 1 Norwich City 2	Old Trafford	63409
231	1967/68	27/01/68	3rd Round	Manchester United 2 Tottenham Hotspur 2	Old Trafford	63500
232	1967/68	31/01/68	3rd Round Replay	Tottenham Hotspur 1 Manchester United 0	White Hart Lane	57200
233	1968/69	04/01/69	3rd Round	Exeter City 1 Manchester United 3	St James' Park	18500
234	1968/69	25/01/69	4th Round	Manchester United 1 Watford 1	Old Trafford	63498
235	1968/69	03/02/69	4th Round Replay	Watford 0 Manchester United 2	Vicarage Road	34000
236	1968/69	08/02/69	5th Round	Birmingham City 2 Manchester United 2	St Andrews	52500
237	1968/69	24/02/69	5th Round Replay	Manchester United 6 Birmingham City 2	Old Trafford	61932
238	1968/69	01/03/69	6th Round	Manchester United 0 Everton 1	Old Trafford	63464
239	1969/70	03/01/70	3rd Round	Ipswich Town 0 Manchester United 1	Portman Road	29552
240	1969/70	24/01/70	4th Round	Manchester United 3 Manchester City 0	Old Trafford	63417
241	1969/70	07/02/70	5th Round	Northampton Town 2 Manchester United 8	County Ground	21771
242	1969/70	21/02/70	6th Round	Middlesbrough 1 Manchester United 1	Ayresome Park	40000
243	1969/70	25/02/70	6th Round Replay	Manchester United 2 Middlesbrough 1	Old Trafford	63418
244	1969/70	14/03/70	Semi-Final	Manchester United 0 Leeds United 0	Hillsborough	55000
245	1969/70	23/03/70	Semi-Final Replay	Manchester United 0 Leeds United 0	Villa Park	62500
246	1969/70	26/03/70	Semi-Final 2nd Replay	Manchester United 0 Leeds United 1	Burnden Park	56000
247	1969/70	10/04/70	3rd Place Play-Off	Manchester United 2 Watford 0	Highbury	15105

———— In Season 1969/70 the losing Semi-Finalists played a play-off for Third place. This was the only occasion that this occurred ————

#	SEASON	DATE	ROUND	MATCH RESULT	VENUE	ATT
248	1970/71	02/01/71	3rd Round	Manchester United 0 Middlesbrough 0	Old Trafford	47824
249	1970/71	05/01/71	3rd Round Replay	Middlesbrough 2 Manchester United 1	Ayresome Park	41000
250	1971/72	15/01/72	3rd Round	Southampton 1 Manchester United 1	The Dell	30190
251	1971/72	19/01/72	3rd Round Replay	Manchester United 4 Southampton 1	Old Trafford	50960
252	1971/72	05/02/72	4th Round	Preston North End 0 Manchester United 2	Deepdale	27025
253	1971/72	26/02/72	5th Round	Manchester United 0 Middlesbrough 0	Old Trafford	53850
254	1971/72	29/02/72	5th Round Replay	Middlesbrough 0 Manchester United 3	Ayresome Park	39683
255	1971/72	18/03/72	6th Round	Manchester United 1 Stoke City 1	Old Trafford	54226
256	1971/72	22/03/72	6th Round Replay	Stoke City 2 Manchester United 1	Victoria Ground	49192
257	1972/73	13/01/73	3rd Round	Wolverhampton Wanderers 1 Manchester United 0	Molineux	40005
258	1973/74	05/01/74	3rd Round	Manchester United 1 Plymouth Argyle 0	Old Trafford	31810
259	1973/74	26/01/74	4th Round	Manchester United 0 Ipswich Town 1	Old Trafford	37177
260	1974/75	04/01/75	3rd Round	Manchester United 0 Walsall 0	Old Trafford	43353
261	1974/75	07/01/75	3rd Round Replay	Walsall 3 Manchester United 2	Fellows Park	18105
262	1975/76	03/01/76	3rd Round	Manchester United 2 Oxford United 1	Old Trafford	41082
263	1975/76	24/01/76	4th Round	Manchester United 3 Peterborough United 1	Old Trafford	56352
264	1975/76	14/02/76	5th Round	Leicester City 1 Manchester United 2	Filbert Street	34000
265	1975/76	06/03/76	6th Round	Manchester United 1 Wolverhampton Wanderers 1	Old Trafford	59433
266	1975/76	09/03/76	6th Round Replay	Wolverhampton Wanderers 2 Manchester United 3	Molineux	44373
267	1975/76	03/04/76	Semi-Final	Manchester United 2 Derby County 0	Hillsborough	55000
268	1975/76	01/05/76	Final	Manchester United 0 Southampton 1	Wembley	100000

UNITED in the FA CUP

#	SEASON	DATE	ROUND	MATCH RESULT	VENUE	ATT
269	1976/77	08/01/77	3rd Round	Manchester United 1 Walsall 0	Old Trafford	48870
270	1976/77	29/01/77	4th Round	Manchester United 1 Queens Park Rangers 0	Old Trafford	57422
271	1976/77	26/02/77	5th Round	Southampton 2 Manchester United 2	The Dell	29137
272	1976/77	08/03/77	5th Round Replay	Manchester United 2 Southampton 1	Old Trafford	58103
273	1976/77	19/03/77	6th Round	Manchester United 2 Aston Villa 1	Old Trafford	57089
274	1976/77	23/04/77	Semi-Final	Manchester United 2 Leeds United 1	Hillsborough	55000
275	1976/77	21/05/77	Final	Manchester United 2 Liverpool 1	Wembley	100000
276	1977/78	07/01/78	3rd Round	Carlisle United 1 Manchester United 1	Brunton Park	21710
277	1977/78	11/01/78	3rd Round Replay	Manchester United 4 Carlisle United 2	Old Trafford	54156
278	1977/78	28/01/78	4th Round	Manchester United 1 West Bromwich Albion 1	Old Trafford	57056
279	1977/78	01/02/78	4th Round Replay	West Bromwich Albion 3 Manchester United 2	The Hawthorns	37086
280	1978/79	15/01/79	3rd Round	Manchester United 3 Chelsea 0	Old Trafford	38743
281	1978/79	31/01/79	4th Round	Fulham 1 Manchester United 1	Craven Cottage	25229
282	1978/79	12/02/79	4th Round Replay	Manchester United 1 Fulham 0	Old Trafford	41200
283	1978/79	20/02/79	5th Round	Colchester United 0 Manchester United 1	Layer Road	13171
284	1978/79	10/03/79	6th Round	Tottenham Hotspur 1 Manchester United 1	White Hart Lane	51800
285	1978/79	14/03/79	6th Round Replay	Manchester United 2 Tottenham Hotspur 0	Old Trafford	55584
286	1978/79	31/03/79	Semi-Final	Manchester United 2 Liverpool 2	Maine Road	52524
287	1978/79	04/04/79	Semi-Final Replay	Manchester United 1 Liverpool 0	Goodison Park	53069
288	1978/79	12/05/79	Final	Manchester United 2 Arsenal 3	Wembley	100000
289	1979/80	05/01/80	3rd Round	Tottenham Hotspur 1 Manchester United 1	White Hart Lane	45207
290	1979/80	09/01/80	3rd Round Replay	Manchester United 0 Tottenham Hotspur 1	Old Trafford	53762
291	1980/81	03/01/81	3rd Round	Manchester United 2 Brighton 2	Old Trafford	42199
292	1980/81	07/01/81	3rd Round Replay	Brighton 0 Manchester United 2	Goldstone Ground	26915
293	1980/81	24/01/81	4th Round	Nottingham Forest 1 Manchester United 0	City Ground	34110
294	1981/82	02/01/82	3rd Round	Watford 1 Manchester United 0	Vicarage Road	26104
295	1982/83	08/01/83	3rd Round	Manchester United 2 West Ham United 0	Old Trafford	44143
296	1982/83	29/01/83	4th Round	Luton Town 0 Manchester United 2	Kenilworth Road	20516
297	1982/83	19/02/83	5th Round	Derby County 0 Manchester United 1	Baseball Ground	33022
298	1982/83	12/03/83	6th Round	Manchester United 1 Everton 0	Old Trafford	58198
299	1982/83	16/04/83	Semi-Final	Manchester United 2 Arsenal 1	Villa Park	46535
300	1982/83	21/05/83	Final	Manchester United 2 Brighton 2	Wembley	100000
301	1982/83	26/05/83	Final Replay	Manchester United 4 Brighton 0	Wembley	92000
302	1983/84	07/01/84	3rd Round	Bournemouth 2 Manchester United 0	Dean Court	14782
303	1984/85	05/01/85	3rd Round	Manchester United 3 Bournemouth 0	Old Trafford	32080
304	1984/85	26/01/85	4th Round	Manchester United 2 Coventry City 1	Old Trafford	38039
305	1984/85	15/02/85	5th Round	Blackburn Rovers 0 Manchester United 2	Ewood Park	22692
306	1984/85	09/03/85	6th Round	Manchester United 4 West Ham United 2	Old Trafford	46769
307	1984/85	13/04/85	Semi-Final	Manchester United 2 Liverpool 2	Goodison Park	51690
308	1984/85	17/04/85	Semi-Final Replay	Manchester United 2 Liverpool 1	Maine Road	45775
309	1984/85	18/05/85	Final	Manchester United 1 Everton 0	Wembley	100000
310	1985/86	09/01/86	3rd Round	Manchester United 2 Rochdale 0	Old Trafford	40223
311	1985/86	25/01/86	4th Round	Sunderland 0 Manchester United 0	Roker Park	35484
312	1985/86	29/01/86	4th Round Replay	Manchester United 3 Sunderland 0	Old Trafford	43402
313	1985/86	05/03/86	5th Round	West Ham United 1 Manchester United 1	Upton Park	26441
314	1985/86	09/03/86	5th Round Replay	Manchester United 0 West Ham United 2	Old Trafford	30441
315	1986/87	10/01/87	3rd Round	Manchester United 1 Manchester City 0	Old Trafford	54294
316	1986/87	31/01/87	4th Round	Manchester United 0 Coventry City 1	Old Trafford	49082
317	1987/88	10/01/88	3rd Round	Ipswich Town 1 Manchester United 2	Portman Road	23012
318	1987/88	30/01/88	4th Round	Manchester United 2 Chelsea 0	Old Trafford	50716
319	1987/88	20/02/88	5th Round	Arsenal 2 Manchester United 1	Highbury	54161
320	1988/89	07/01/89	3rd Round	Manchester United 0 Queens Park Rangers 0	Old Trafford	36222
321	1988/89	11/01/89	3rd Round Replay	Queens Park Rangers 2 Manchester United 2	Loftus Road	22236
322	1988/89	23/01/89	3rd Round 2nd Replay	Manchester United 3 Queens Park Rangers 0	Old Trafford	46257
323	1988/89	28/01/89	4th Round	Manchester United 4 Oxford United 0	Old Trafford	47745
324	1988/89	18/02/89	5th Round	Bournemouth 1 Manchester United 1	Dean Court	12708
325	1988/89	22/02/89	5th Round Replay	Manchester United 1 Bournemouth 0	Old Trafford	52422
326	1988/89	18/03/89	6th Round	Manchester United 0 Nottingham Forest 1	Old Trafford	55040
327	1989/90	07/01/90	3rd Round	Nottingham Forest 0 Manchester United 1	City Ground	23072
328	1989/90	28/01/90	4th Round	Hereford United 0 Manchester United 1	Edgar Street	13777
329	1989/90	18/02/90	5th Round	Newcastle United 2 Manchester United 3	St James' Park	31748
330	1989/90	11/03/90	6th Round	Sheffield United 0 Manchester United 1	Bramall Lane	34344
331	1989/90	08/04/90	Semi-Final	Manchester United 3 Oldham Athletic 3	Maine Road	44026
332	1989/90	11/04/90	Semi-Final Replay	Manchester United 2 Oldham Athletic 1	Maine Road	35005
333	1989/90	12/05/90	Final	Manchester United 3 Crystal Palace 3	Wembley	80000
334	1989/90	17/05/90	Final Replay	Manchester United 1 Crystal Palace 0	Wembley	80000
335	1990/91	07/01/91	3rd Round	Manchester United 2 Queens Park Rangers 1	Old Trafford	35065
336	1990/91	26/01/91	4th Round	Manchester United 1 Bolton Wanderers 0	Old Trafford	43293
337	1990/91	16/02/91	5th Round	Norwich City 2 Manchester United 1	Carrow Road	23058
338	1991/92	15/01/92	3rd Round	Leeds United 0 Manchester United 1	Elland Road	31819
339	1991/92	27/01/92	4th Round	Southampton 0 Manchester United 0	The Dell	19506
340	1991/92	05/02/92	4th Round Replay	Manchester United 2 Southampton 2	Old Trafford	33414

(United lost the tie 2-4 on penalty kicks)

UNITED in the FA CUP

#	SEASON	DATE	ROUND	MATCH RESULT	VENUE	ATT
341	1992/93	05/01/93	3rd Round	Manchester United 2 Bury 0	Old Trafford	30668
342	1992/93	23/01/93	4th Round	Manchester United 1 Brighton 0	Old Trafford	33600
343	1992/93	14/02/93	5th Round	Sheffield United 2 Manchester United 1	Bramall Lane	27150
344	1993/94	09/01/94	3rd Round	Sheffield United 0 Manchester United 1	Bramall Lane	22019
345	1993/94	30/01/94	4th Round	Norwich City 0 Manchester United 2	Carrow Road	21060
346	1993/94	20/02/94	5th Round	Wimbledon 0 Manchester United 3	Selhurst Park	27511
347	1993/94	12/03/94	6th Round	Manchester United 3 Charlton Athletic 1	Old Trafford	44347
348	1993/94	10/04/94	Semi-Final	Manchester United 1 Oldham Athletic 1	Wembley	56399
349	1993/94	13/04/94	Semi-Final Replay	Manchester United 4 Oldham Athletic 1	Maine Road	32311
350	1993/94	14/05/94	Final	Manchester United 4 Chelsea 0	Wembley	79634
351	1994/95	09/01/95	3rd Round	Sheffield United 0 Manchester United 2	Bramall Lane	22322
352	1994/95	28/01/95	4th Round	Manchester United 5 Wrexham 2	Old Trafford	43222
353	1994/95	19/02/95	5th Round	Manchester United 3 Leeds United 1	Old Trafford	42744
354	1994/95	12/03/95	6th Round	Manchester United 2 Queens Park Rangers 0	Old Trafford	42830
355	1994/95	09/04/95	Semi-Final	Manchester United 2 Crystal Palace 2	Villa Park	38256
356	1994/95	12/04/95	Semi-Final Replay	Manchester United 2 Crystal Palace 0	Villa Park	17987
357	1994/95	20/05/95	Final	Manchester United 0 Everton 1	Wembley	79592
358	1995/96	06/01/96	3rd Round	Manchester United 2 Sunderland 2	Old Trafford	41563
359	1995/96	16/01/96	3rd Round Replay	Sunderland 1 Manchester United 2	Roker Park	21378
360	1995/96	27/01/96	4th Round	Reading 0 Manchester United 3	Elm Park	14780
361	1995/96	18/02/96	5th Round	Manchester United 2 Manchester City 1	Old Trafford	42692
362	1995/96	11/03/96	6th Round	Manchester United 2 Southampton 0	Old Trafford	45446
363	1995/96	31/03/96	Semi-Final	Manchester United 2 Chelsea 1	Villa Park	38421
364	1995/96	11/05/96	Final	Manchester United 1 Liverpool 0	Wembley	79007
365	1996/97	05/01/97	3rd Round	Manchester United 2 Tottenham Hotspur 0	Old Trafford	52445
366	1996/97	25/01/97	4th Round	Manchester United 1 Wimbledon 1	Old Trafford	53342
367	1996/97	04/02/97	4th Round Replay	Wimbledon 1 Manchester United 0	Selhurst Park	25601
368	1997/98	04/01/98	3rd Round	Chelsea 3 Manchester United 5	Stamford Bridge	34792
369	1997/98	24/01/98	4th Round	Manchester United 5 Walsall 1	Old Trafford	54669
370	1997/98	15/02/98	5th Round	Manchester United 1 Barnsley 1	Old Trafford	54700
371	1997/98	25/02/98	5th Round Replay	Barnsley 3 Manchester United 2	Oakwell	18655
372	1998/99	03/01/99	3rd Round	Manchester United 3 Middlesbrough 1	Old Trafford	52232
373	1998/99	24/01/99	4th Round	Manchester United 2 Liverpool 1	Old Trafford	54591
374	1998/99	14/02/99	5th Round	Manchester United 1 Fulham 0	Old Trafford	54798
375	1998/99	07/03/99	6th Round	Manchester United 0 Chelsea 0	Old Trafford	54587
376	1998/99	10/03/99	6th Round Replay	Chelsea 0 Manchester United 2	Stamford Bridge	33075
377	1998/99	11/04/99	Semi-Final	Manchester United 0 Arsenal 0	Villa Park	39217
378	1998/99	14/04/99	Semi-Final Replay	Manchester United 2 Arsenal 1	Villa Park	30223
379	1998/99	22/05/99	Final	Manchester United 2 Newcastle United 0	Wembley	79101
380	2000/01	07/01/01	3rd Round	Fulham 1 Manchester United 2	Craven Cottage	19178
381	2000/01	28/01/01	4th Round	Manchester United 0 West Ham United 1	Old Trafford	67029
382	2001/02	06/01/02	3rd Round	Aston Villa 2 Manchester United 3	Villa Park	38444
383	2001/02	26/01/02	4th Round	Middlesbrough 2 Manchester United 0	Riverside Stadium	17624
384	2002/03	04/01/03	3rd Round	Manchester United 4 Portsmouth 1	Old Trafford	67222
385	2002/03	26/01/03	4th Round	Manchester United 6 West Ham United 0	Old Trafford	67181
386	2002/03	15/02/03	5th Round	Manchester United 0 Arsenal 2	Old Trafford	67209
387	2003/04	04/01/04	3rd Round	Aston Villa 1 Manchester United 2	Villa Park	40371
388	2003/04	25/01/04	4th Round	Northampton Town 0 Manchester United 3	Sixfields Stadium	7356
389	2003/04	14/02/04	5th Round	Manchester United 4 Manchester City 2	Old Trafford	67228
390	2003/04	06/03/04	6th Round	Manchester United 2 Fulham 1	Old Trafford	67614
391	2003/04	03/04/04	Semi-Final	Manchester United 1 Arsenal 0	Villa Park	39939
392	2003/04	22/05/04	Final	Manchester United 3 Millwall 0	Millennium Stadium	71350
393	2004/05	08/01/05	3rd Round	Manchester United 0 Exeter City 0	Old Trafford	67551
394	2004/05	19/01/05	3rd Round Replay	Exeter City 0 Manchester United 2	St James' Park	9033
395	2004/05	29/01/05	4th Round	Manchester United 3 Middlesbrough 0	Old Trafford	67251
396	2004/05	19/02/05	5th Round	Everton 0 Manchester United 2	Goodison Park	38664
397	2004/05	12/03/05	6th Round	Southampton 0 Manchester United 4	St Mary's Stadium	30971
398	2004/05	17/04/05	Semi-Final	Manchester United 4 Newcastle United 1	Millennium Stadium	69280
399	2004/05	21/05/05	Final	Manchester United 0 Arsenal 0 (United lost the tie 4–5 on penalty kicks)	Millennium Stadium	71876
400	2005/06	08/01/06	3rd Round	Burton Albion 0 Manchester United 0	Pirelli Stadium	6191
401	2005/06	18/01/06	3rd Round Replay	Manchester United 5 Burton Albion 0	Old Trafford	53564
402	2005/06	29/01/06	4th Round	Wolverhampton Wanderers 0 Manchester United 3	Molineux	28333
403	2005/06	18/02/06	5th Round	Liverpool 1 Manchester United 0	Anfield	44039
404	2006/07	07/01/07	3rd Round	Manchester United 2 Aston Villa 1	Old Trafford	74924
405	2006/07	27/01/07	4th Round	Manchester United 2 Portsmouth 1	Old Trafford	71137
406	2006/07	17/02/07	5th Round	Manchester United 1 Reading 1	Old Trafford	70608
407	2006/07	27/02/07	5th Round Replay	Reading 2 Manchester United 3	Madejski Stadium	23821
408	2006/07	10/03/07	6th Round	Middlesbrough 2 Manchester United 2	Riverside Stadium	33308
409	2006/07	19/03/07	6th Round Replay	Manchester United 1 Middlesbrough 0	Old Trafford	71325
410	2006/07	14/04/07	Semi-Final	Manchester United 4 Watford 1	Villa Park	37425
411	2006/07	19/05/07	Final	Manchester United 0 Chelsea 1	Wembley	89826
412	2007/08	05/01/08	3rd Round	Aston Villa 0 Manchester United 2	Villa Park	33630
413	2007/08	27/01/08	4th Round	Manchester United 3 Tottenham Hotspur 1	Old Trafford	75369
414	2007/08	16/02/08	5th Round	Manchester United 4 Arsenal 0	Old Trafford	75550
415	2007/08	08/03/08	6th Round	Manchester United 0 Portsmouth 1	Old Trafford	75463

UNITED in the LEAGUE CUP

PLAYING RECORD							OVERALL PERFORMANCE RECORD (41 ENTRIES)			

VENUE	P	W	D	L	F	A
HOME	76	54	11	11	154	63
AWAY	76	31	17	28	108	102
NEUTRAL	6	2	0	4	7	8
TOTAL	158	87	28	43	269	173

WINNERS	2 times	Lost in 5th Round	3 times
		Lost in 4th Round	8 times
Losing FINALISTS	4 times	Lost in 3rd Round	13 times
Losing SEMI-FINALISTS	4 times	Lost in 2nd Round	7 times

#	SEASON	DATE	ROUND	MATCH RESULT	VENUE	ATT
1	1960/61	19/10/60	1st Round	Exeter City 1 Manchester United 1	St James' Park	14494
2	1960/61	26/10/60	1st Round Replay	Manchester United 4 Exeter City 1	Old Trafford	15662
3	1960/61	02/11/60	2nd Round	Bradford City 2 Manchester United 1	Valley Parade	4670
4	1966/67	14/09/66	2nd Round	Blackpool 5 Manchester United 1	Bloomfield Road	15570
5	1969/70	03/09/69	2nd Round	Manchester United 1 Middlesbrough 0	Old Trafford	38938
6	1969/70	23/09/69	3rd Round	Manchester United 2 Wrexham 0	Old Trafford	48347
7	1969/70	14/10/69	4th Round	Burnley 0 Manchester United 0	Turf Moor	27959
8	1969/70	20/10/69	4th Round Replay	Manchester United 1 Burnley 0	Old Trafford	50275
9	1969/70	12/11/69	5th Round	Derby County 0 Manchester United 0	Baseball Ground	38895
10	1969/70	19/11/69	5th Round Replay	Manchester United 1 Derby County 0	Old Trafford	57393
11	1969/70	03/12/69	Semi-Final 1st Leg	Manchester City 2 Manchester United 1	Maine Road	55799
12	1969/70	17/12/69	Semi-Final 2nd Leg	Manchester United 2 Manchester City 2	Old Trafford	63418
13	1970/71	09/09/70	2nd Round	Aldershot 1 Manchester United 3	Recreation Ground	18509
14	1970/71	07/10/70	3rd Round	Manchester United 1 Portsmouth 0	Old Trafford	32068
15	1970/71	28/10/70	4th Round	Manchester United 2 Chelsea 1	Old Trafford	47565
16	1970/71	18/11/70	5th Round	Manchester United 4 Crystal Palace 2	Old Trafford	48961
17	1970/71	16/12/70	Semi-Final 1st Leg	Manchester United 1 Aston Villa 1	Old Trafford	48889
18	1970/71	23/12/70	Semi-Final 2nd Leg	Aston Villa 2 Manchester United 1	Villa Park	58667
19	1971/72	07/09/71	2nd Round	Ipswich Town 1 Manchester United 3	Portman Road	28143
20	1971/72	06/10/71	3rd Round	Manchester United 1 Burnley 1	Old Trafford	44600
21	1971/72	18/10/71	3rd Round Replay	Burnley 0 Manchester United 1	Turf Moor	27511
22	1971/72	27/10/71	4th Round	Manchester United 1 Stoke City 1	Old Trafford	47062
23	1971/72	08/11/71	4th Round Replay	Stoke City 0 Manchester United 0	Victoria Ground	40805
24	1971/72	15/11/71	4th Round 2nd Replay	Stoke City 2 Manchester United 1	Victoria Ground	42249
25	1972/73	06/09/72	2nd Round	Oxford United 2 Manchester United 2	Manor Ground	16560
26	1972/73	12/09/72	2nd Round Replay	Manchester United 3 Oxford United 1	Old Trafford	21486
27	1972/73	03/10/72	3rd Round	Bristol Rovers 1 Manchester United 1	Eastville	33957
28	1972/73	11/10/72	3rd Round Replay	Manchester United 1 Bristol Rovers 2	Old Trafford	29349
29	1973/74	08/10/73	2nd Round	Manchester United 0 Middlesbrough 1	Old Trafford	23906
30	1974/75	11/09/74	2nd Round	Manchester United 5 Charlton Athletic 1	Old Trafford	21616
31	1974/75	09/10/74	3rd Round	Manchester United 1 Manchester City 0	Old Trafford	55169
32	1974/75	13/11/74	4th Round	Manchester United 3 Burnley 2	Old Trafford	46275
33	1974/75	04/12/74	5th Round	Middlesbrough 0 Manchester United 0	Ayresome Park	36005
34	1974/75	18/12/74	5th Round Replay	Manchester United 3 Middlesbrough 0	Old Trafford	49501
35	1974/75	15/01/75	Semi-Final 1st Leg	Manchester United 2 Norwich City 2	Old Trafford	58010
36	1974/75	22/01/75	Semi-Final 2nd Leg	Norwich City 1 Manchester United 0	Carrow Road	31621
37	1975/76	10/09/75	2nd Round	Manchester United 2 Brentford 1	Old Trafford	25286
38	1975/76	08/10/75	3rd Round	Aston Villa 1 Manchester United 2	Villa Park	41447
39	1975/76	12/11/75	4th Round	Manchester City 4 Manchester United 0	Maine Road	50182
40	1976/77	01/09/76	2nd Round	Manchester United 5 Tranmere Rovers 0	Old Trafford	37586
41	1976/77	22/09/76	3rd Round	Manchester United 2 Sunderland 2	Old Trafford	46170
42	1976/77	04/10/76	3rd Round Replay	Sunderland 2 Manchester United 2	Roker Park	46170
43	1976/77	06/10/76	3rd Round 2nd Replay	Manchester United 1 Sunderland 0	Old Trafford	47689
44	1976/77	27/10/76	4th Round	Manchester United 7 Newcastle United 2	Old Trafford	52002
45	1976/77	01/12/76	5th Round	Manchester United 0 Everton 3	Old Trafford	57738
46	1977/78	30/08/77	2nd Round	Arsenal 3 Manchester United 2	Highbury	36171
47	1978/79	30/08/78	2nd Round	Stockport County 2 Manchester United 3	Old Trafford	41761
				(United drawn away – tie switched to Old Trafford)		
48	1978/79	04/10/78	3rd Round	Manchester United 1 Watford 2	Old Trafford	40534
49	1979/80	29/08/79	2nd Round 1st Leg	Tottenham Hotspur 2 Manchester United 1	White Hart Lane	29163
50	1979/80	05/09/79	2nd Round 2nd Leg	Manchester United 3 Tottenham Hotspur 1	Old Trafford	48292
51	1979/80	26/09/79	3rd Round	Norwich City 4 Manchester United 1	Carrow Road	18312
52	1980/81	27/08/80	2nd Round 1st Leg	Manchester United 0 Coventry City 1	Old Trafford	31656
53	1980/81	02/09/80	2nd Round 2nd Leg	Coventry City 1 Manchester United 0	Highfield Road	18946
54	1981/82	07/10/81	2nd Round 1st Leg	Tottenham Hotspur 1 Manchester United 0	White Hart Lane	39333
55	1981/82	28/10/81	2nd Round 2nd Leg	Manchester United 0 Tottenham Hotspur 1	Old Trafford	55890
56	1982/83	06/10/82	2nd Round 1st Leg	Manchester United 2 Bournemouth 0	Old Trafford	22091
57	1982/83	26/10/82	2nd Round 2nd Leg	Bournemouth 2 Manchester United 2	Dean Court	13226
58	1982/83	10/11/82	3rd Round	Bradford City 0 Manchester United 0	Valley Parade	15568
59	1982/83	24/11/82	3rd Round Replay	Manchester United 4 Bradford City 1	Old Trafford	24507
60	1982/83	01/12/82	4th Round	Manchester United 2 Southampton 0	Old Trafford	28378
61	1982/83	19/01/83	5th Round	Manchester United 4 Nottingham Forest 0	Old Trafford	44413
62	1982/83	15/02/83	Semi-Final 1st Leg	Arsenal 2 Manchester United 4	Highbury	43136
63	1982/83	23/02/83	Semi-Final 2nd Leg	Manchester United 2 Arsenal 1	Old Trafford	56635
64	1982/83	26/03/83	Final	Manchester United 1 Liverpool 2	Wembley	100000

UNITED in the LEAGUE CUP

#	SEASON	DATE	ROUND	MATCH RESULT	VENUE	ATT
65	1983/84	03/10/83	2nd Round 1st Leg	Port Vale 0 Manchester United 1	Vale Park	19885
66	1983/84	26/10/83	2nd Round 2nd Leg	Manchester United 2 Port Vale 0	Old Trafford	23589
67	1983/84	08/11/83	3rd Round	Colchester United 0 Manchester United 2	Layer Road	13031
68	1983/84	30/11/83	4th Round	Oxford United 1 Manchester United 1	Manor Ground	13739
69	1983/84	07/12/83	4th Round Replay	Manchester United 1 Oxford United 1	Old Trafford	27459
70	1983/84	19/12/83	4th Round 2nd Replay	Oxford United 2 Manchester United 1	Manor Ground	13912
71	1984/85	26/09/84	2nd Round 1st Leg	Manchester United 4 Burnley 0	Old Trafford	28383
72	1984/85	09/10/84	2nd Round 2nd Leg	Burnley 0 Manchester United 3	Turf Moor	12690
73	1984/85	30/10/84	3rd Round	Manchester United 1 Everton 2	Old Trafford	50918
74	1985/86	24/09/85	2nd Round 1st Leg	Crystal Palace 0 Manchester United 1	Selhurst Park	21507
75	1985/86	09/10/85	2nd Round 2nd Leg	Manchester United 1 Crystal Palace 0	Old Trafford	26118
76	1985/86	29/10/85	3rd Round	Manchester United 1 West Ham United 0	Old Trafford	32056
77	1985/86	26/11/85	4th Round	Liverpool 2 Manchester United 1	Anfield	41291
78	1986/87	24/09/86	2nd Round 1st Leg	Manchester United 2 Port Vale 0	Old Trafford	18906
79	1986/87	07/10/86	2nd Round 2nd Leg	Port Vale 2 Manchester United 5	Vale Park	10486
80	1986/87	29/10/86	3rd Round	Manchester United 0 Southampton 0	Old Trafford	23639
81	1986/87	04/11/86	3rd Round Replay	Southampton 4 Manchester United 1	The Dell	17915
82	1987/88	23/09/87	2nd Round 1st Leg	Manchester United 5 Hull City 0	Old Trafford	25041
83	1987/88	07/10/87	2nd Round 2nd Leg	Hull City 0 Manchester United 1	Boothferry Park	13586
84	1987/88	28/10/87	3rd Round	Manchester United 2 Crystal Palace 1	Old Trafford	27283
85	1987/88	18/11/87	4th Round	Bury 1 Manchester United 2	Old Trafford	33519
				(United drawn away – tie switched to Old Trafford)		
86	1987/88	20/01/88	5th Round	Oxford United 2 Manchester United 0	Manor Ground	12658
87	1988/89	28/09/88	2nd Round 1st Leg	Rotherham United 0 Manchester United 1	Millmoor	12588
88	1988/89	12/10/88	2nd Round 2nd Leg	Manchester United 5 Rotherham United 0	Old Trafford	20597
89	1988/89	02/11/88	3rd Round	Wimbledon 2 Manchester United 1	Plough Lane	10864
90	1989/90	20/09/89	2nd Round 1st Leg	Portsmouth 2 Manchester United 3	Fratton Park	18072
91	1989/90	03/10/89	2nd Round 2nd Leg	Manchester United 0 Portsmouth 0	Old Trafford	26698
92	1989/90	25/10/89	3rd Round	Manchester United 0 Tottenham Hotspur 3	Old Trafford	45759
93	1990/91	26/09/90	2nd Round 1st Leg	Halifax Town 1 Manchester United 3	The Shay	6841
94	1990/91	10/10/90	2nd Round 2nd Leg	Manchester United 2 Halifax Town 1	Old Trafford	22295
95	1990/91	31/10/90	3rd Round	Manchester United 3 Liverpool 1	Old Trafford	42033
96	1990/91	28/11/90	4th Round	Arsenal 2 Manchester United 6	Highbury	40844
97	1990/91	16/01/91	5th Round	Southampton 1 Manchester United 1	The Dell	21011
98	1990/91	23/01/91	5th Round Replay	Manchester United 3 Southampton 2	Old Trafford	41903
99	1990/91	10/02/91	Semi-Final 1st Leg	Manchester United 2 Leeds United 1	Old Trafford	34050
100	1990/91	24/02/91	Semi-Final 2nd Leg	Leeds United 0 Manchester United 1	Elland Road	32014
101	1990/91	21/04/91	Final	Manchester United 0 Sheffield Wednesday 1	Wembley	77612
102	1991/92	25/09/91	2nd Round 1st Leg	Manchester United 3 Cambridge United 0	Old Trafford	30934
103	1991/92	09/10/91	2nd Round 2nd Leg	Cambridge United 1 Manchester United 1	Abbey Stadium	9248
104	1991/92	30/10/91	3rd Round	Manchester United 3 Portsmouth 1	Old Trafford	29543
105	1991/92	04/12/91	4th Round	Manchester United 2 Oldham Athletic 0	Old Trafford	38550
106	1991/92	08/01/92	5th Round	Leeds United 1 Manchester United 3	Elland Road	28886
107	1991/92	04/03/92	Semi-Final 1st Leg	Middlesbrough 0 Manchester United 0	Ayresome Park	25572
108	1991/92	11/03/92	Semi-Final 2nd Leg	Manchester United 2 Middlesbrough 1	Old Trafford	45875
109	1991/92	12/04/92	Final	Manchester United 1 Nottingham Forest 0	Wembley	76810
110	1992/93	23/09/92	2nd Round 1st Leg	Brighton 1 Manchester United 1	Goldstone Ground	16649
111	1992/93	07/10/92	2nd Round 2nd Leg	Manchester United 1 Brighton 0	Old Trafford	25405
112	1992/93	28/10/92	3rd Round	Aston Villa 1 Manchester United 0	Villa Park	35964
113	1993/94	22/09/93	2nd Round 1st Leg	Stoke City 2 Manchester United 1	Victoria Ground	23327
114	1993/94	06/10/93	2nd Round 2nd Leg	Manchester United 2 Stoke City 0	Old Trafford	41387
115	1993/94	27/10/93	3rd Round	Manchester United 5 Leicester City 1	Old Trafford	41344
116	1993/94	30/11/93	4th Round	Everton 0 Manchester United 2	Goodison Park	34052
117	1993/94	12/01/94	5th Round	Manchester United 2 Portsmouth 2	Old Trafford	43794
118	1993/94	26/01/94	5th Round Replay	Portsmouth 0 Manchester United 1	Fratton Park	24950
119	1993/94	13/02/94	Semi-Final 1st Leg	Manchester United 1 Sheffield Wednesday 0	Old Trafford	43294
120	1993/94	02/03/94	Semi-Final 2nd Leg	Sheffield Wednesday 1 Manchester United 4	Hillsborough	34878
121	1993/94	27/03/94	Final	Manchester United 1 Aston Villa 3	Wembley	77231
122	1994/95	21/09/94	2nd Round 1st Leg	Port Vale 1 Manchester United 2	Vale Park	18605
123	1994/95	05/10/94	2nd Round 2nd Leg	Manchester United 2 Port Vale 0	Old Trafford	31615
124	1994/95	26/10/94	3rd Round	Newcastle United 2 Manchester United 0	St James' Park	34178
125	1995/96	20/09/95	2nd Round 1st Leg	Manchester United 0 York City 3	Old Trafford	29049
126	1995/96	03/10/95	2nd Round 2nd Leg	York City 1 Manchester United 3	Bootham Crescent	9386
127	1996/97	23/10/96	3rd Round	Manchester United 2 Swindon Town 1	Old Trafford	49305
128	1996/97	27/11/96	4th Round	Leicester City 2 Manchester United 0	Filbert Street	20428
129	1997/98	14/10/97	3rd Round	Ipswich Town 2 Manchester United 0	Portman Road	22173
130	1998/99	28/10/98	3rd Round	Manchester United 2 Bury 0	Old Trafford	52495
131	1998/99	11/11/98	4th Round	Manchester United 2 Nottingham Forest 1	Old Trafford	37337
132	1998/99	02/12/98	5th Round	Tottenham Hotspur 3 Manchester United 1	White Hart Lane	35702
133	1999/00	13/10/99	3rd Round	Aston Villa 3 Manchester United 0	Villa Park	33815
134	2000/01	31/10/00	3rd Round	Watford 0 Manchester United 3	Vicarage Road	18871
135	2000/01	28/11/00	4th Round	Sunderland 2 Manchester United 1	Stadium of Light	47543
136	2001/02	05/11/01	3rd Round	Arsenal 4 Manchester United 0	Highbury	30693

UNITED in the LEAGUE CUP

#	SEASON	DATE	ROUND	MATCH RESULT	VENUE	ATT
137	2002/03	05/11/02	3rd Round	Manchester United 2 Leicester City 0	Old Trafford	47848
138	2002/03	03/12/02	4th Round	Burnley 0 Manchester United 2	Turf Moor	22034
139	2002/03	17/12/02	5th Round	Manchester United 1 Chelsea 0	Old Trafford	57985
140	2002/03	07/01/03	Semi-Final 1st Leg	Manchester United 1 Blackburn Rovers 1	Old Trafford	62740
141	2002/03	22/01/03	Semi-Final 2nd Leg	Blackburn Rovers 1 Manchester United 3	Ewood Park	29048
142	2002/03	02/03/03	Final	Manchester United 0 Liverpool 2	Millennium Stadium	74500
143	2003/04	28/10/03	3rd Round	Leeds United 2 Manchester United 3	Elland Road	37546
144	2003/04	03/12/03	4th Round	West Bromwich Albion 2 Manchester United 0	The Hawthorns	25282
145	2004/05	26/10/04	3rd Round	Crewe Alexandra 0 Manchester United 3	Gresty Road	10103
146	2004/05	10/11/04	4th Round	Manchester United 2 Crystal Palace 0	Old Trafford	48891
147	2004/05	01/12/04	5th Round	Manchester United 1 Arsenal 0	Old Trafford	67103
148	2004/05	12/01/05	Semi-Final 1st Leg	Chelsea 0 Manchester United 0	Stamford Bridge	41492
149	2004/05	26/01/05	Semi-Final 2nd Leg	Manchester United 1 Chelsea 2	Old Trafford	67000
150	2005/06	25/10/05	3rd Round	Manchester United 4 Barnet 1	Old Trafford	43673
151	2005/06	30/11/05	4th Round	Manchester United 3 West Bromwich Albion 1	Old Trafford	48924
152	2005/06	20/12/05	5th Round	Birmingham City 1 Manchester United 3	St Andrews	20454
153	2005/06	11/01/06	Semi-Final 1st Leg	Blackburn Rovers 1 Manchester United 1	Ewood Park	24348
154	2005/06	25/01/06	Semi-Final 2nd Leg	Manchester United 2 Blackburn Rovers 1	Old Trafford	61636
155	2005/06	26/02/06	Final	Manchester United 4 Wigan Athletic 0	Millennium Stadium	66866
156	2006/07	25/10/06	3rd Round	Crewe Alexandra 1 Manchester United 2	Gresty Road	10046
157	2006/07	07/11/06	4th Round	Southend United 1 Manchester United 0	Roots Hall	11532
158	2007/08	26/09/07	3rd Round	Manchester United 0 Coventry City 2	Old Trafford	74055

UNITED in the EUROPEAN CUP / CHAMPIONS LEAGUE

PLAYING RECORD

VENUE	P	W	D	L	F	A
HOME	95	73	15	7	243	73
AWAY	95	33	29	33	122	111
NEUTRAL	3	2	1	0	7	3
TOTAL	193	108	45	40	372	187

OVERALL PERFORMANCE RECORD (19 ENTRIES)

WINNERS	3 times (including once after penalty kicks)
Losing SEMI-FINALISTS	7 times
Losing QUARTER-FINALISTS	4 times
Lost in 2nd Round	3 times
Eliminated in Group Phase	2 times

#	SEASON	DATE	ROUND	MATCH RESULT	VENUE	ATT
1	1956/57	12/09/56	Preliminary Round 1st Leg	Anderlecht 0 Manchester United 2	Park Astrid	35000
2	1956/57	26/09/56	Preliminary Round 2nd Leg	Manchester United 10 Anderlecht 0	Maine Road	40000
3	1956/57	17/10/56	1st Round 1st Leg	Manchester United 3 Borussia Dortmund 2	Maine Road	75598
4	1956/57	21/11/56	1st Round 2nd Leg	Borussia Dortmund 0 Manchester United 0	Rote Erde Stadion	44570
5	1956/57	16/01/57	Quarter-Final 1st Leg	Athletic Bilbao 5 Manchester United 3	Estadio San Mames	60000
6	1956/57	06/02/57	Quarter-Final 2nd Leg	Manchester United 3 Athletic Bilbao 0	Maine Road	70000
7	1956/57	11/04/57	Semi-Final 1st Leg	Real Madrid 3 Manchester United 1	Bernabeu Stadium	135000
8	1956/57	25/04/57	Semi-Final 2nd Leg	Manchester United 2 Real Madrid 2	Old Trafford	65000
9	1957/58	25/09/57	Preliminary Round 1st Leg	Shamrock Rovers 0 Manchester United 6	Dalymount Park	33754
10	1957/58	02/10/57	Preliminary Round 2nd Leg	Manchester United 3 Shamrock Rovers 2	Old Trafford	45000
11	1957/58	20/11/57	1st Round 1st Leg	Manchester United 3 Dukla Prague 0	Old Trafford	60000
12	1957/58	04/12/57	1st Round 2nd Leg	Dukla Prague 1 Manchester United 0	Stadium Strahov	35000
13	1957/58	14/01/58	Quarter-Final 1st Leg	Manchester United 2 Red Star Belgrade 1	Old Trafford	60000
14	1957/58	05/02/58	Quarter-Final 2nd Leg	Red Star Belgrade 3 Manchester United 3	Stadion JNA	55000
15	1957/58	08/05/58	Semi-Final 1st Leg	Manchester United 2 AC Milan 1	Old Trafford	44880
16	1957/58	14/05/58	Semi-Final 2nd Leg	AC Milan 4 Manchester United 0	Stadio San Siro	80000
17	1965/66	22/09/65	Preliminary Round 1st Leg	HJK Helsinki 2 Manchester United 3	Olympiastadion	25000
18	1965/66	06/10/65	Preliminary Round 2nd Leg	Manchester United 6 HJK Helsinki 0	Old Trafford	30388
19	1965/66	17/11/65	1st Round 1st Leg	ASK Vorwaerts 0 Manchester United 2	Walter Ulbricht Stadium	40000
20	1965/66	01/12/65	1st Round 2nd Leg	Manchester United 3 ASK Vorwaerts 1	Old Trafford	30082
21	1965/66	02/02/66	Quarter-Final 1st Leg	Manchester United 3 Benfica 2	Old Trafford	64035
22	1965/66	09/03/66	Quarter-Final 2nd Leg	Benfica 1 Manchester United 5	Estadio da Luz	75000
23	1965/66	13/04/66	Semi-Final 1st Leg	Partizan Belgrade 2 Manchester United 0	Stadion JNA	60000
24	1965/66	20/04/66	Semi-Final 2nd Leg	Manchester United 1 Partizan Belgrade 0	Old Trafford	62500
25	1967/68	20/09/67	1st Round 1st Leg	Manchester United 4 Hibernians Malta 0	Old Trafford	43912
26	1967/68	27/09/67	1st Round 2nd Leg	Hibernians Malta 0 Manchester United 0	Empire Stadium	25000
27	1967/68	15/11/67	2nd Round 1st Leg	Sarajevo 0 Manchester United 0	Stadion Kosevo	45000
28	1967/68	29/11/67	2nd Round 2nd Leg	Manchester United 2 Sarajevo 1	Old Trafford	62801
29	1967/68	28/02/68	Quarter-Final 1st Leg	Manchester United 2 Gornik Zabrze 0	Old Trafford	63456
30	1967/68	13/03/68	Quarter-Final 2nd Leg	Gornik Zabrze 1 Manchester United 0	Stadion Slaski	105000
31	1967/68	24/04/68	Semi-Final 1st Leg	Manchester United 1 Real Madrid 0	Old Trafford	63500
32	1967/68	15/05/68	Semi-Final 2nd Leg	Real Madrid 3 Manchester United 3	Bernabeu Stadium	125000
33	1967/68	29/05/68	Final	Manchester United 4 Benfica 1	Wembley	100000

UNITED in the EUROPEAN CUP / CHAMPIONS LEAGUE

#	SEASON	DATE	ROUND	MATCH RESULT	VENUE	ATT
34	1968/69	18/09/68	1st Round 1st Leg	Waterford 1 Manchester United 3	Lansdowne Road	48000
35	1968/69	02/10/68	1st Round 2nd Leg	Manchester United 7 Waterford 1	Old Trafford	41750
36	1968/69	13/11/68	2nd Round 1st Leg	Manchester United 3 Anderlecht 0	Old Trafford	51000
37	1968/69	27/11/68	2nd Round 2nd Leg	Anderlecht 3 Manchester United 1	Park Astrid	40000
38	1968/69	26/02/69	Quarter-Final 1st Leg	Manchester United 3 Rapid Vienna 0	Old Trafford	61932
39	1968/69	05/03/69	Quarter-Final 2nd Leg	Rapid Vienna 0 Manchester United 0	Wiener Stadion	52000
40	1968/69	23/04/69	Semi-Final 1st Leg	AC Milan 2 Manchester United 0	Stadio San Siro	80000
41	1968/69	15/05/69	Semi-Final 2nd Leg	Manchester United 1 AC Milan 0	Old Trafford	63103
42	1993/94	15/09/93	1st Round 1st Leg	Honved 2 Manchester United 3	Jozsef Bozsik Stadium	9000
43	1993/94	29/09/93	1st Round 2nd Leg	Manchester United 2 Honved 1	Old Trafford	35781
44	1993/94	20/10/93	2nd Round 1st Leg	Manchester United 3 Galatasaray 3	Old Trafford	39346
45	1993/94	03/11/93	2nd Round 2nd Leg	Galatasaray 0 Manchester United 0	Ali Sami Yen	40000
				(United lost the tie on away goals rule)		
46	1994/95	14/09/94	Phase 1 Match 1	Manchester United 4 Gothenburg 2	Old Trafford	33625
47	1994/95	28/09/94	Phase 1 Match 2	Galatasaray 0 Manchester United 0	Ali Sami Yen	28605
48	1994/95	19/10/94	Phase 1 Match 3	Manchester United 2 Barcelona 2	Old Trafford	40064
49	1994/95	02/11/94	Phase 1 Match 4	Barcelona 4 Manchester United 0	Estadio Camp Nou	114273
50	1994/95	23/11/94	Phase 1 Match 5	Gothenburg 3 Manchester United 1	NYA Ullevi Stadium	36350
51	1994/95	07/12/94	Phase 1 Match 6	Manchester United 4 Galatasaray 0	Old Trafford	39220
				(United failed to qualify from the Group Phase)		
52	1996/97	11/09/96	Phase 1 Match 1	Juventus 1 Manchester United 0	Stadio Delle Alpi	54000
53	1996/97	25/09/96	Phase 1 Match 2	Manchester United 2 Rapid Vienna 0	Old Trafford	51831
54	1996/97	16/10/96	Phase 1 Match 3	Fenerbahce 0 Manchester United 2	Fenerbahce Stadium	26200
55	1996/97	30/10/96	Phase 1 Match 4	Manchester United 0 Fenerbahce 1	Old Trafford	53297
56	1996/97	20/11/96	Phase 1 Match 5	Manchester United 0 Juventus 1	Old Trafford	53529
57	1996/97	04/12/96	Phase 1 Match 6	Rapid Vienna 0 Manchester United 2	Ernst Happel Stadion	45000
58	1996/97	05/03/97	Quarter-Final 1st Leg	Manchester United 4 Porto 0	Old Trafford	53425
59	1996/97	19/03/97	Quarter-Final 2nd Leg	Porto 0 Manchester United 0	Estadio das Antas	40000
60	1996/97	09/04/97	Semi-Final 1st Leg	Borussia Dortmund 1 Manchester United 0	Westfalenstadion	48500
61	1996/97	23/04/97	Semi-Final 2nd Leg	Manchester United 0 Borussia Dortmund 1	Old Trafford	53606
62	1997/98	17/09/97	Phase 1 Match 1	Kosice 0 Manchester United 3	TJ Lokomotive Stadium	9950
63	1997/98	01/10/97	Phase 1 Match 2	Manchester United 3 Juventus 2	Old Trafford	53428
64	1997/98	22/10/97	Phase 1 Match 3	Manchester United 2 Feyenoord 1	Old Trafford	53188
65	1997/98	05/11/97	Phase 1 Match 4	Feyenoord 1 Manchester United 3	Feyenoord Stadion	51000
66	1997/98	27/11/97	Phase 1 Match 5	Manchester United 3 Kosice 0	Old Trafford	53535
67	1997/98	10/12/97	Phase 1 Match 6	Juventus 1 Manchester United 0	Stadio Delle Alpi	47786
68	1997/98	04/03/98	Quarter-Final 1st Leg	Monaco 0 Manchester United 0	Stade Louis II	15000
69	1997/98	18/03/98	Quarter-Final 2nd Leg	Manchester United 1 Monaco 1	Old Trafford	53683
				(United lost the tie on away goals rule)		
70	1998/99	12/08/98	Qualifying Round 1st Leg	Manchester United 2 LKS Lodz 0	Old Trafford	50906
71	1998/99	26/08/98	Qualifying Round 2nd Leg	LKS Lodz 0 Manchester United 0	LKS Stadion	8700
72	1998/99	16/09/98	Phase 1 Match 1	Manchester United 3 Barcelona 3	Old Trafford	53601
73	1998/99	30/09/98	Phase 1 Match 2	Bayern Munich 2 Manchester United 2	Olympic Stadium	53000
74	1998/99	21/10/98	Phase 1 Match 3	Brondby 2 Manchester United 6	Parken Stadion	40530
75	1998/99	04/11/98	Phase 1 Match 4	Manchester United 5 Brondby 0	Old Trafford	53250
76	1998/99	25/11/98	Phase 1 Match 5	Barcelona 3 Manchester United 3	Estadio Camp Nou	67648
77	1998/99	09/12/98	Phase 1 Match 6	Manchester United 1 Bayern Munich 1	Old Trafford	54434
78	1998/99	03/03/99	Quarter-Final 1st Leg	Manchester United 2 Internazionale 0	Old Trafford	54430
79	1998/99	17/03/99	Quarter-Final 2nd Leg	Internazionale 1 Manchester United 1	Stadio San Siro	79528
80	1998/99	07/04/99	Semi-Final 1st Leg	Manchester United 1 Juventus 1	Old Trafford	54487
81	1998/99	21/04/99	Semi-Final 2nd Leg	Juventus 2 Manchester United 3	Stadio Delle Alpi	64500
82	1998/99	26/05/99	Final	Manchester United 2 Bayern Munich 1	Estadio Camp Nou	90000
83	1999/00	14/09/99	Phase 1 Match 1	Manchester United 0 Croatia Zagreb 0	Old Trafford	53250
84	1999/00	22/09/99	Phase 1 Match 2	Sturm Graz 0 Manchester United 3	Schwarzenegger Stadium	16480
85	1999/00	29/09/99	Phase 1 Match 3	Manchester United 2 Olympique Marseille 1	Old Trafford	53993
86	1999/00	19/10/99	Phase 1 Match 4	Olympique Marseille 1 Manchester United 0	Stade Velodrome	56732
87	1999/00	27/10/99	Phase 1 Match 5	Croatia Zagreb 1 Manchester United 2	Maksimir Stadium	27500
88	1999/00	02/11/99	Phase 1 Match 6	Manchester United 2 Sturm Graz 1	Old Trafford	53745
89	1999/00	23/11/99	Phase 2 Match 1	Fiorentina 2 Manchester United 0	Artemio Franchi	36002
90	1999/00	08/12/99	Phase 2 Match 2	Manchester United 3 Valencia 0	Old Trafford	54606
91	1999/00	01/03/00	Phase 2 Match 3	Manchester United 2 Girondins Bordeaux 0	Old Trafford	59786
92	1999/00	07/03/00	Phase 2 Match 4	Girondins Bordeaux 1 Manchester United 2	Stade Lescure	30130
93	1999/00	15/03/00	Phase 2 Match 5	Manchester United 3 Fiorentina 1	Old Trafford	59926
94	1999/00	21/03/00	Phase 2 Match 6	Valencia 0 Manchester United 0	Mestalla	40419
95	1999/00	04/04/00	Quarter-Final 1st Leg	Real Madrid 0 Manchester United 0	Bernabeu Stadium	64119
96	1999/00	19/04/00	Quarter-Final 2nd Leg	Manchester United 2 Real Madrid 3	Old Trafford	59178
97	2000/01	13/09/00	Phase 1 Match 1	Manchester United 5 Anderlecht 1	Old Trafford	62749
98	2000/01	19/09/00	Phase 1 Match 2	Dynamo Kiev 0 Manchester United 0	Republican Stadium	65000
99	2000/01	26/09/00	Phase 1 Match 3	PSV Eindhoven 3 Manchester United 1	Philipstadion	30500
100	2000/01	18/10/00	Phase 1 Match 4	Manchester United 3 PSV Eindhoven 1	Old Trafford	66313
101	2000/01	24/10/00	Phase 1 Match 5	Anderlecht 2 Manchester United 1	Vanden Stock	22506
102	2000/01	08/11/00	Phase 1 Match 6	Manchester United 1 Dynamo Kiev 0	Old Trafford	66776
103	2000/01	21/11/00	Phase 2 Match 1	Manchester United 3 Panathinaikos 1	Old Trafford	65024
104	2000/01	06/12/00	Phase 2 Match 2	Sturm Graz 0 Manchester United 2	Schwarzenegger Stadium	16500
105	2000/01	14/02/01	Phase 2 Match 3	Valencia 0 Manchester United 0	Mestalla	49541
106	2000/01	20/02/01	Phase 2 Match 4	Manchester United 1 Valencia 1	Old Trafford	66715
107	2000/01	07/03/01	Phase 2 Match 5	Panathinaikos 1 Manchester United 1	Olympic Stadium	27231
108	2000/01	13/03/01	Phase 2 Match 6	Manchester United 3 Sturm Graz 0	Old Trafford	66404
109	2000/01	03/04/01	Quarter-Final 1st Leg	Manchester United 0 Bayern Munich 1	Old Trafford	66584
110	2000/01	18/04/01	Quarter-Final 2nd Leg	Bayern Munich 2 Manchester United 1	Olympic Stadium	60000

UNITED in the EUROPEAN CUP / CHAMPIONS LEAGUE

#	SEASON	DATE	ROUND	MATCH RESULT	VENUE	ATT
111	2001/02	18/09/01	Phase 1 Match 1	Manchester United 1 Lille Metropole 0	Old Trafford	64827
112	2001/02	25/09/01	Phase 1 Match 2	Deportivo La Coruna 2 Manchester United 1	Estadio de Riazor	33108
113	2001/02	10/10/01	Phase 1 Match 3	Olympiakos Piraeus 0 Manchester United 2	Olympic Stadium	73537
114	2001/02	17/10/01	Phase 1 Match 4	Manchester United 2 Deportivo La Coruna 3	Old Trafford	65585
115	2001/02	23/10/01	Phase 1 Match 5	Manchester United 3 Olympiakos Piraeus 0	Old Trafford	66769
116	2001/02	31/10/01	Phase 1 Match 6	Lille Metropole 1 Manchester United 1	Stade Felix Bollaert	38402
117	2001/02	20/11/01	Phase 2 Match 1	Bayern Munich 1 Manchester United 1	Olympic Stadium	59000
118	2001/02	05/12/01	Phase 2 Match 2	Manchester United 3 Boavista 0	Old Trafford	66274
119	2001/02	20/02/02	Phase 2 Match 3	Nantes Atlantique 1 Manchester United 1	Stade Beaujoire	38285
120	2001/02	26/02/02	Phase 2 Match 4	Manchester United 5 Nantes Atlantique 1	Old Trafford	66492
121	2001/02	13/03/02	Phase 2 Match 5	Manchester United 0 Bayern Munich 0	Old Trafford	66818
122	2001/02	19/03/02	Phase 2 Match 6	Boavista 0 Manchester United 3	Estadio Do Bessa	13223
123	2001/02	02/04/02	Quarter-Final 1st Leg	Deportivo La Coruna 0 Manchester United 2	Estadio de Riazor	32351
124	2001/02	10/04/02	Quarter-Final 2nd Leg	Manchester United 3 Deportivo La Coruna 2	Old Trafford	65875
125	2001/02	24/04/02	Semi-Final 1st Leg	Manchester United 2 Bayer Leverkusen 2	Old Trafford	66534
126	2001/02	30/04/02	Semi-Final 2nd Leg	Bayer Leverkusen 1 Manchester United 1	Bayarena	22500
				(United lost the tie on away goals rule)		
127	2002/03	14/08/02	Qualifying Round 1st Leg	Zalaegerszeg 1 Manchester United 0	Ferenc Puskas Stadion	40000
128	2002/03	27/08/02	Qualifying Round 2nd Leg	Manchester United 5 Zalaegerszeg 0	Old Trafford	66814
129	2002/03	18/09/02	Phase 1 Match 1	Manchester United 5 Maccabi Haifa 2	Old Trafford	63439
130	2002/03	24/09/02	Phase 1 Match 2	Bayer Leverkusen 1 Manchester United 2	Bayarena	22500
131	2002/03	01/10/02	Phase 1 Match 3	Manchester United 4 Olympiakos Piraeus 0	Old Trafford	66902
132	2002/03	23/10/02	Phase 1 Match 4	Olympiakos Piraeus 2 Manchester United 3	Rizoupoli	15000
133	2002/03	29/10/02	Phase 1 Match 5	Maccabi Haifa 3 Manchester United 0	GSP Stadion Cyprus	22000
134	2002/03	13/11/02	Phase 1 Match 6	Manchester United 2 Bayer Leverkusen 0	Old Trafford	66185
135	2002/03	26/11/02	Phase 2 Match 1	Basel 1 Manchester United 3	St Jakob Stadium	29501
136	2002/03	11/12/02	Phase 2 Match 2	Manchester United 2 Deportivo La Coruna 0	Old Trafford	67014
137	2002/03	19/02/03	Phase 2 Match 3	Manchester United 2 Juventus 1	Old Trafford	66703
138	2002/03	25/02/03	Phase 2 Match 4	Juventus 0 Manchester United 3	Stadio Delle Alpi	59111
139	2002/03	12/03/03	Phase 2 Match 5	Manchester United 1 Basel 1	Old Trafford	66870
140	2002/03	18/03/03	Phase 2 Match 6	Deportivo La Coruna 2 Manchester United 0	Estadio de Riazor	25000
141	2002/03	08/04/03	Quarter-Final 1st Leg	Real Madrid 3 Manchester United 1	Bernabeu Stadium	75000
142	2002/03	23/04/03	Quarter-Final 2nd Leg	Manchester United 4 Real Madrid 3	Old Trafford	66708
143	2003/04	16/09/03	Phase 1 Match 1	Manchester United 5 Panathinaikos 0	Old Trafford	66520
144	2003/04	01/10/03	Phase 1 Match 2	Stuttgart 2 Manchester United 1	Gottlieb-Daimler Stadium	53000
145	2003/04	22/10/03	Phase 1 Match 3	Glasgow Rangers 0 Manchester United 1	Ibrox Stadium	48730
146	2003/04	04/11/03	Phase 1 Match 4	Manchester United 3 Glasgow Rangers 0	Old Trafford	66707
147	2003/04	26/11/03	Phase 1 Match 5	Panathinaikos 0 Manchester United 1	Apostolos Nikolaidis	6890
148	2003/04	09/12/03	Phase 1 Match 6	Manchester United 2 Stuttgart 0	Old Trafford	67141
149	2003/04	25/02/04	2nd Round 1st Leg	Porto 2 Manchester United 1	Estadio da Dragao	49977
150	2003/04	09/03/04	2nd Round 2nd Leg	Manchester United 1 Porto 1	Old Trafford	67029
151	2004/05	11/08/04	Qualifying Round 1st Leg	Dinamo Bucharest 1 Manchester United 2	National Stadium	58000
152	2004/05	25/08/04	Qualifying Round 2nd Leg	Manchester United 3 Dinamo Bucharest 0	Old Trafford	61041
153	2004/05	15/09/04	Phase 1 Match 1	Olympique Lyonnais 2 Manchester United 2	Stade de Gerland	40000
154	2004/05	28/09/04	Phase 1 Match 2	Manchester United 6 Fenerbahce 2	Old Trafford	67128
155	2004/05	19/10/04	Phase 1 Match 3	Sparta Prague 0 Manchester United 0	Toyota Stadium	20654
156	2004/05	03/11/04	Phase 1 Match 4	Manchester United 4 Sparta Prague 1	Old Trafford	66706
157	2004/05	23/11/04	Phase 1 Match 5	Manchester United 2 Olympique Lyonnais 1	Old Trafford	66398
158	2004/05	08/12/04	Phase 1 Match 6	Fenerbahce 3 Manchester United 0	Sukru Saracoglu	35000
159	2004/05	23/02/05	2nd Round 1st Leg	Manchester United 0 AC Milan 1	Old Trafford	67162
160	2004/05	08/03/05	2nd Round 2nd Leg	AC Milan 1 Manchester United 0	Stadio San Siro	78957
161	2005/06	09/08/05	Qualifying Round 1st Leg	Manchester United 3 Debreceni 0	Old Trafford	51701
162	2005/06	24/08/05	Qualifying Round 2nd Leg	Debreceni 0 Manchester United 3	Ferenc Puskas Stadium	27000
163	2005/06	14/09/05	Phase 1 Match 1	Villarreal 0 Manchester United 0	El Madrigal Stadium	22000
164	2005/06	27/09/05	Phase 1 Match 2	Manchester United 2 Benfica 1	Old Trafford	66112
165	2005/06	18/10/05	Phase 1 Match 3	Manchester United 0 Lille Metropole 0	Old Trafford	60626
166	2005/06	02/11/05	Phase 1 Match 4	Lille Metropole 1 Manchester United 0	Stade de France	65000
167	2005/06	22/11/05	Phase 1 Match 5	Manchester United 0 Villarreal 0	Old Trafford	67471
168	2005/06	07/12/05	Phase 1 Match 6	Benfica 2 Manchester United 1	Estadio da Luz	61000
169	2006/07	13/09/06	Phase 1 Match 1	Manchester United 3 Glasgow Celtic 2	Old Trafford	74031
170	2006/07	26/09/06	Phase 1 Match 2	Benfica 0 Manchester United 1	Estadio da Luz	61000
171	2006/07	17/10/06	Phase 1 Match 3	Manchester United 3 Copenhagen 0	Old Trafford	72020
172	2006/07	01/11/06	Phase 1 Match 4	Copenhagen 1 Manchester United 0	Parken Stadion	40000
173	2006/07	21/11/06	Phase 1 Match 5	Glasgow Celtic 1 Manchester United 0	Celtic Park	60632
174	2006/07	06/12/06	Phase 1 Match 6	Manchester United 2 Benfica 1	Old Trafford	74955
175	2006/07	20/02/07	2nd Round 1st Leg	Lille Metropole 0 Manchester United 1	Stade Felix Bollaert	41000
176	2006/07	07/03/07	2nd Round 2nd Leg	Manchester United 1 Lille Metropole 0	Old Trafford	75182
177	2006/07	04/04/07	Quarter-Final 1st Leg	Roma 2 Manchester United 1	Olympic Stadium	77000
178	2006/07	10/04/07	Quarter-Final 2nd Leg	Manchester United 7 Roma 1	Old Trafford	74476
179	2006/07	24/04/07	Semi-Final 1st Leg	Manchester United 3 AC Milan 2	Old Trafford	73820
180	2006/07	02/05/07	Semi-Final 2nd Leg	AC Milan 3 Manchester United 0	Stadio San Siro	78500
181	2007/08	19/09/07	Phase 1 Match 1	Sporting Lisbon 0 Manchester United 1	de Jose Alvalade	39514
182	2007/08	02/10/07	Phase 1 Match 2	Manchester United 1 Roma 0	Old Trafford	73652
183	2007/08	23/10/07	Phase 1 Match 3	Dynamo Kiev 2 Manchester United 4	Olympic Stadium	43000
184	2007/08	07/11/07	Phase 1 Match 4	Manchester United 4 Dynamo Kiev 0	Old Trafford	75017
185	2007/08	27/11/07	Phase 1 Match 5	Manchester United 2 Sporting Lisbon 1	Old Trafford	75162
186	2007/08	12/12/07	Phase 1 Match 6	Roma 1 Manchester United 1	Olympic Stadium	29490
187	2007/08	20/02/08	2nd Round 1st Leg	Olympique Lyonnais 1 Manchester United 1	Stade de Gerland	39230
188	2007/08	04/03/08	2nd Round 2nd Leg	Manchester United 1 Olympique Lyonnais 0	Old Trafford	75520
189	2007/08	01/04/08	Quarter-Final 1st Leg	Roma 0 Manchester United 2	Olympic Stadium	80023
190	2007/08	09/04/08	Quarter-Final 2nd Leg	Manchester United 1 Roma 0	Old Trafford	74423
191	2007/08	23/04/08	Semi-Final 1st Leg	Barcelona 0 Manchester United 0	Estadio Camp Nou	95949
192	2007/08	29/04/08	Semi-Final 2nd Leg	Manchester United 1 Barcelona 0	Old Trafford	75061
193	2007/08	21/05/08	Final	Manchester United 1 Chelsea 1	Luzhniki Stadium	67310
				(United won the tie 6-5 on penalty kicks)		

UNITED in the EUROPEAN CUP-WINNERS' CUP

		PLAYING RECORD					OVERALL PERFORMANCE RECORD (5 ENTRIES)		

VENUE	P	W	D	L	F	A
HOME	15	10	5	0	38	10
AWAY	15	5	4	6	15	24
NEUTRAL	1	1	0	0	2	1
TOTAL	31	16	9	6	55	35

WINNERS	1 time
Losing SEMI-FINALISTS	1 time
Losing QUARTER-FINALISTS	1 time
Lost in 2nd Round	2 times

#	SEASON	DATE	ROUND	MATCH RESULT	VENUE	ATT
1	1963/64	25/09/63	1st Round 1st Leg	Willem II 1 Manchester United 1	Feyenoord Stadion	20000
2	1963/64	15/10/63	1st Round 2nd Leg	Manchester United 6 Willem II 1	Old Trafford	46272
3	1963/64	03/12/63	2nd Round 1st Leg	Tottenham Hotspur 2 Manchester United 0	White Hart Lane	57447
4	1963/64	10/12/63	2nd Round 2nd Leg	Manchester United 4 Tottenham Hotspur 1	Old Trafford	50000
5	1963/64	26/02/64	Quarter-Final 1st Leg	Manchester United 4 Sporting Lisbon 1	Old Trafford	60000
6	1963/64	18/03/64	Quarter-Final 2nd Leg	Sporting Lisbon 5 Manchester United 0	de Jose Alvalade	40000
7	1977/78	14/09/77	1st Round 1st Leg	St Etienne 1 Manchester United 1	Stade Geoffrey Guichard	33678
8	1977/78	05/10/77	1st Round 2nd Leg	Manchester United 2 St Etienne 0	Home Park	31634
9	1977/78	19/10/77	2nd Round 1st Leg	Porto 4 Manchester United 0	Estadio das Antas	70000
10	1977/78	02/11/77	2nd Round 2nd Leg	Manchester United 5 Porto 2	Old Trafford	51831
11	1983/84	14/09/83	1st Round 1st Leg	Manchester United 1 Dukla Prague 1	Old Trafford	39745
12	1983/84	27/09/83	1st Round 2nd Leg	Dukla Prague 2 Manchester United 2	Stadion Juliska	28850
				(United won the tie on away goals rule)		
13	1983/84	19/10/83	2nd Round 1st Leg	Spartak Varna 1 Manchester United 2	Stad Yuri Gargarin	40000
14	1983/84	02/11/83	2nd Round 2nd Leg	Manchester United 2 Spartak Varna 0	Old Trafford	39079
15	1983/84	07/03/84	3rd Round 1st Leg	Barcelona 2 Manchester United 0	Estadio Camp Nou	70000
16	1983/84	21/03/84	3rd Round 2nd Leg	Manchester United 3 Barcelona 0	Old Trafford	58547
17	1983/84	11/04/84	Semi-Final 1st Leg	Manchester United 1 Juventus 1	Old Trafford	58171
18	1983/84	25/04/84	Semi-Final 2nd Leg	Juventus 2 Manchester United 1	Stadio Comunale	64655
19	1990/91	19/09/90	1st Round 1st Leg	Manchester United 2 Pecsi Munkas 0	Old Trafford	28411
20	1990/91	03/10/90	1st Round 2nd Leg	Pecsi Munkas 0 Manchester United 1	PMSC Stadion	17000
21	1990/91	23/10/90	2nd Round 1st Leg	Manchester United 3 Wrexham 0	Old Trafford	29405
22	1990/91	07/11/90	2nd Round 2nd Leg	Wrexham 0 Manchester United 2	Racecourse Ground	13327
23	1990/91	06/03/91	3rd Round 1st Leg	Manchester United 1 Montpellier Herault 1	Old Trafford	41942
24	1990/91	19/03/91	3rd Round 2nd Leg	Montpellier Herault 0 Manchester United 2	Stade de la Masson	18000
25	1990/91	10/04/91	Semi-Final 1st Leg	Legia Warsaw 1 Manchester United 3	Wojska Polskiego	20000
26	1990/91	24/04/91	Semi-Final 2nd Leg	Manchester United 1 Legia Warsaw 1	Old Trafford	44269
27	1990/91	15/05/91	Final	Manchester United 2 Barcelona 1	Feyenoord Stadion	50000
28	1991/92	18/09/91	1st Round 1st Leg	Athinaikos 0 Manchester United 0	Apostolos Nikolaidis	5400
29	1991/92	02/10/91	1st Round 2nd Leg	Manchester United 2 Athinaikos 0	Old Trafford	35023
30	1991/92	23/10/91	2nd Round 1st Leg	Athletico Madrid 3 Manchester United 0	Vincente Calderon	40000
31	1991/92	06/11/91	2nd Round 2nd Leg	Manchester United 1 Athletico Madrid 1	Old Trafford	39654

UNITED in the INTER-CITIES' FAIRS CUP / UEFA CUP

PLAYING RECORD						
VENUE	P	W	D	L	F	A
HOME	15	9	6	0	32	9
AWAY	16	3	7	6	16	17
TOTAL	31	12	13	6	48	26

OVERALL PERFORMANCE RECORD (7 ENTRIES)

Losing SEMI-FINALISTS	1 time
Losing QUARTER-FINALISTS	1 time
Lost in 2nd Round	1 time
Lost in 1st Round	4 times

#	SEASON	DATE	ROUND	MATCH RESULT	VENUE	ATT
1	1964/65	23/09/64	1st Round 1st Leg	Djurgardens 1 Manchester United 1	Roasunda Stadion	6537
2	1964/65	27/10/64	1st Round 2nd Leg	Manchester United 6 Djurgardens 1	Old Trafford	38437
3	1964/65	11/11/64	2nd Round 1st Leg	Borussia Dortmund 1 Manchester United 6	Rote Erde Stadion	25000
4	1964/65	02/12/64	2nd Round 2nd Leg	Manchester United 4 Borussia Dortmund 0	Old Trafford	31896
5	1964/65	20/01/65	3rd Round 1st Leg	Manchester United 1 Everton 1	Old Trafford	50000
6	1964/65	09/02/65	3rd Round 2nd Leg	Everton 1 Manchester United 2	Goodison Park	54397
7	1964/65	12/05/65	Quarter-Final 1st Leg	Strasbourg 0 Manchester United 5	Stade de la Meinau	30000
8	1964/65	19/05/65	Quarter-Final 2nd Leg	Manchester United 0 Strasbourg 0	Old Trafford	34188
9	1964/65	31/05/65	Semi-Final 1st Leg	Manchester United 3 Ferencvaros 2	Old Trafford	39902
10	1964/65	06/06/65	Semi-Final 2nd Leg	Ferencvaros 1 Manchester United 0	Nep Stadion	50000
11	1964/65	16/06/65	Semi-Final Replay	Ferencvaros 2 Manchester United 1	Nep Stadion	60000
12	1976/77	15/09/76	1st Round 1st Leg	Ajax 1 Manchester United 0	Olympisch Stadion	30000
13	1976/77	29/09/76	1st Round 2nd Leg	Manchester United 2 Ajax 0	Old Trafford	58918
14	1976/77	20/10/76	2nd Round 1st Leg	Manchester United 1 Juventus 0	Old Trafford	59000
15	1976/77	03/11/76	2nd Round 2nd Leg	Juventus 3 Manchester United 0	Stadio Comunale	66632
16	1980/81	17/09/80	1st Round 1st Leg	Manchester United 1 Widzew Lodz 1	Old Trafford	38037
17	1980/81	01/10/80	1st Round 2nd Leg	Widzew Lodz 0 Manchester United 0	Stadio TKS	40000
				(United lost the tie on away goals rule)		
18	1982/83	15/09/82	1st Round 1st Leg	Manchester United 0 Valencia 0	Old Trafford	46588
19	1982/83	29/09/82	1st Round 2nd Leg	Valencia 2 Manchester United 1	Luis Casanova	35000
20	1984/85	19/09/84	1st Round 1st Leg	Manchester United 3 Raba Vasas 0	Old Trafford	33119
21	1984/85	03/10/84	1st Round 2nd Leg	Raba Vasas 2 Manchester United 2	Raba ETO Stadium	26000
22	1984/85	24/10/84	2nd Round 1st Leg	PSV Eindhoven 0 Manchester United 0	Philipstadion	27500
23	1984/85	07/11/84	2nd Round 2nd Leg	Manchester United 1 PSV Eindhoven 0	Old Trafford	39281
24	1984/85	28/11/84	3rd Round 1st Leg	Manchester United 2 Dundee United 2	Old Trafford	48278
25	1984/85	12/12/84	3rd Round 2nd Leg	Dundee United 2 Manchester United 3	Tannadice Park	21821
26	1984/85	06/03/85	Quarter-Final 1st Leg	Manchester United 1 Videoton 0	Old Trafford	35432
27	1984/85	20/03/85	Quarter-Final 2nd Leg	Videoton 1 Manchester United 0	Sostoi Stadion	25000
				(United lost the tie 4-5 on penalty kicks)		
28	1992/93	16/09/92	1st Round 1st Leg	Manchester United 0 Torpedo Moscow 0	Old Trafford	19998
29	1992/93	29/09/92	1st Round 2nd Leg	Torpedo Moscow 0 Manchester United 0	Torpedo Stadion	11357
				(United lost the tie 3-4 on penalty kicks)		
30	1995/96	12/09/95	1st Round 1st Leg	Rotor Volgograd 0 Manchester United 0	Central Stadion	33000
31	1995/96	26/09/95	1st Round 2nd Leg	Manchester United 2 Rotor Volgograd 2	Old Trafford	29724
				(United lost the tie on away goals rule)		

UNITED in the FA CHARITY SHIELD / COMMUNITY SHIELD

VENUE	P	W	D	L	F	A
HOME	4	2	2	0	13	7
AWAY	3	1	0	2	4	8
NEUTRAL	18	5	7	6	29	24
TOTAL	25	8	9	8	46	39

PLAYING RECORD

OVERALL PERFORMANCE RECORD (24 ENTRIES)

WINNERS	12 times (including once after a replay and 4 times after penalty kicks)
JOINT WINNERS	4 times
LOSERS	8 times

#	SEASON	DATE	ENTERED AS	MATCH RESULT	VENUE	ATT
1	1907/08	27/04/08	League Champions	Manchester United 1 Queens Park Rangers 1	Stamford Bridge	6000
2	1907/08	29/04/08	Replay	Manchester United 4 Queens Park Rangers 0	Stamford Bridge	6000
3	1911/12	25/09/11	League Champions	Manchester United 8 Swindon Town 4	Stamford Bridge	10000
4	1948/49	06/10/48	FA Cup Winners	Arsenal 4 Manchester United 3	Highbury	31000
5	1952/53	24/09/52	League Champions	Manchester United 4 Newcastle United 2	Old Trafford	11381
6	1956/57	24/10/56	League Champions	Manchester City 0 Manchester United 1	Maine Road	30495
7	1957/58	22/10/57	League Champions	Manchester United 4 Aston Villa 0	Old Trafford	27293
8	1963/64	17/08/63	FA Cup Winners	Everton 4 Manchester United 0	Goodison Park	54840
9	1965/66	14/08/65	League Champions	Manchester United 2 Liverpool 2 (TROPHY SHARED)	Old Trafford	48502
10	1967/68	12/08/67	League Champions	Manchester United 3 Tottenham Hotspur 3 (TROPHY SHARED)	Old Trafford	54106
11	1977/78	13/08/77	FA Cup Winners	Manchester United 0 Liverpool 0 (TROPHY SHARED)	Wembley	82000
12	1983/84	20/08/83	FA Cup Winners	Manchester United 2 Liverpool 0	Wembley	92000
13	1985/86	10/08/85	FA Cup Winners	Manchester United 0 Everton 2	Wembley	82000
14	1990/91	18/08/90	FA Cup Winners	Manchester United 1 Liverpool 1 (TROPHY SHARED)	Wembley	66558
15	1993/94	07/08/93	League Champions	Manchester United 1 Arsenal 1 (United won the tie 5-4 on penalty kicks)	Wembley	66519
16	1994/95	14/08/94	League Champions	Manchester United 2 Blackburn Rovers 0	Wembley	60402
17	1996/97	11/08/96	League Champions	Manchester United 4 Newcastle United 0	Wembley	73214
18	1997/98	03/08/97	League Champions	Manchester United 1 Chelsea 1 (United won the tie 4-2 on penalty kicks)	Wembley	73636
19	1998/99	09/08/98	League Runners-Up	Manchester United 0 Arsenal 3	Wembley	67342
20	1999/00	01/08/99	League Champions	Manchester United 1 Arsenal 2	Wembley	70185
21	2000/01	13/08/00	League Champions	Manchester United 0 Chelsea 2	Wembley	65148
22	2001/02	12/08/01	League Champions	Manchester United 1 Liverpool 2	Millennium Stadium	70227
23	2003/04	10/08/03	League Champions	Manchester United 1 Arsenal 1 (United won the tie 4-3 on penalty kicks)	Millennium Stadium	59293
24	2004/05	08/08/04	FA Cup Winners	Manchester United 1 Arsenal 3	Millennium Stadium	63317
25	2007/08	05/08/07	League Champions	Manchester United 1 Chelsea 1 (United won the tie 3-0 on penalty kicks)	Wembley	80731

UNITED in the EUROPEAN SUPER CUP

PLAYING RECORD							OVERALL PERFORMANCE RECORD (2 ENTRIES)	
VENUE	P	W	D	L	F	A		
HOME	1	1	0	0	1	0	WINNERS	1 time
AWAY	0	0	0	0	0	0		
NEUTRAL	1	0	0	1	0	1	LOSERS	1 time
TOTAL	2	1	0	1	1	1		

#	SEASON	DATE	ROUND	MATCH RESULT	VENUE	ATT
1	1991/92	19/11/91	Final	Manchester United 1　Red Star Belgrade 0	Old Trafford	22110
2	1999/00	27/08/99	Final	Manchester United 0　Lazio 1	Stade Louis II	14461

UNITED in the INTER-CONTINENTAL CUP

PLAYING RECORD							OVERALL PERFORMANCE RECORD (2 ENTRIES)	
VENUE	P	W	D	L	F	A		
HOME	1	0	1	0	1	1	WINNERS	1 time
AWAY	1	0	0	1	0	1		
NEUTRAL	1	1	0	0	1	0	LOSERS	1 time
TOTAL	3	1	1	1	2	2		

#	SEASON	DATE	ROUND	MATCH RESULT	VENUE	ATT
1	1968/69	25/09/68	Final 1st Leg	Estudiantes de la Plata 1　Manchester United 0	Boca Juniors Stadium	55000
2	1968/69	16/10/68	Final 2nd Leg	Manchester United 1　Estudiantes de la Plata 1	Old Trafford	63500
3	1999/00	30/11/99	Final	Manchester United 1　Palmeiras 0	Olympic Stadium, Tokyo	53372

UNITED in the CLUB WORLD CHAMPIONSHIP

PLAYING RECORD							OVERALL PERFORMANCE RECORD (1 ENTRY)
VENUE	P	W	D	L	F	A	
HOME	0	0	0	0	0	0	
AWAY	0	0	0	0	0	0	UNITED FAILED TO QUALIFY FROM THE GROUP PHASE
NEUTRAL	3	1	1	1	4	4	
TOTAL	3	1	1	1	4	4	

#	SEASON	DATE	ROUND	MATCH RESULT	VENUE	ATT
1	1999/00	06/01/00	Group Phase Match 1	Manchester United 1　Rayos del Necaxa 1	Maracana Stadium	50000
2	1999/00	08/01/00	Group Phase Match 2	Manchester United 1　Vasco da Gama 3	Maracana Stadium	73000
3	1999/00	11/01/00	Group Phase Match 3	Manchester United 2　South Melbourne 0	Maracana Stadium	25000

MANCHESTER UNITED
The Complete Record

Chapter 1.4
The Scores

ALL COMPETITIVE MATCHES (5045)

MATCH SCORE	ALL RESULTS	HOME MATCHES	AWAY MATCHES	NEUTRAL VENUE
0-0	356	166	184	6
1-0	450	270	170	10
2-0	381	244	129	8
3-0	234	171	62	1
4-0	106	82	19	5
5-0	60	52	8	–
6-0	19	16	3	–
7-0	8	7	1	–
8-0	1	1	–	–
9-0	3	3	–	–
10-0	1	1	–	–
0-1	336	127	199	10
1-1	531	252	267	12
2-1	385	216	160	9
3-1	254	150	101	3
4-1	117	87	26	4
5-1	57	46	10	1
6-1	26	20	6	–
7-1	7	6	1	–
8-1	2	1	1	–
10-1	1	1	–	–
0-2	195	49	141	5
1-2	272	93	174	5
2-2	249	99	145	5
3-2	159	84	75	–
4-2	60	28	30	2
5-2	31	19	11	1
6-2	13	7	6	–
7-2	5	4	1	–
8-2	1	–	1	–
0-3	106	24	79	3
1-3	143	32	106	5
2-3	89	28	60	1
3-3	66	26	38	2
4-3	20	7	13	–
5-3	14	3	10	1
6-3	4	2	2	–
0-4	47	5	42	–
1-4	47	11	36	–
2-4	30	4	26	–
3-4	23	9	14	–
4-4	9	4	5	–
5-4	1	–	1	–
6-4	1	–	1	–
8-4	1	–	–	1
0-5	22	2	20	–
1-5	31	6	25	–
2-5	10	5	5	–
3-5	7	4	3	–
4-5	4	–	4	–
5-5	1	1	–	–
6-5	1	–	1	–
0-6	9	2	7	–
1-6	11	1	10	–
2-6	8	2	6	–
3-6	5	–	5	–
0-7	3	–	3	–
1-7	6	1	5	–
2-7	2	1	1	–
3-7	2	–	2	–
4-7	2	1	1	–

ALL LEAGUE MATCHES (4176)

MATCH SCORE	ALL RESULTS	HOME MATCHES	AWAY MATCHES
0-0	291	145	146
1-0	360	217	143
2-0	306	205	101
3-0	186	139	47
4-0	85	68	17
5-0	49	43	6
6-0	15	13	2
7-0	6	5	1
8-0	–	–	–
9-0	3	3	–
10-0	–	–	–
0-1	278	110	168
1-1	446	217	229
2-1	314	174	140
3-1	213	131	82
4-1	100	75	25
5-1	45	37	8
6-1	22	17	5
7-1	4	3	1
8-1	2	1	1
10-1	1	1	–
0-2	161	42	119
1-2	228	83	145
2-2	209	82	127
3-2	133	73	60
4-2	47	21	26
5-2	24	16	8
6-2	9	5	4
7-2	3	2	1
8-2	–	–	–
0-3	91	19	72
1-3	129	32	97
2-3	80	24	56
3-3	53	21	32
4-3	18	6	12
5-3	11	3	8
6-3	4	2	2
0-4	38	5	33
1-4	41	9	32
2-4	29	4	25
3-4	21	8	13
4-4	9	4	5
5-4	1	–	1
6-4	–	–	–
8-4	–	–	–
0-5	20	2	18
1-5	27	5	22
2-5	10	5	5
3-5	4	3	1
4-5	4	–	4
5-5	1	1	–
6-5	1	–	1
0-6	8	2	6
1-6	10	1	9
2-6	8	2	6
3-6	5	–	5
0-7	3	–	3
1-7	5	1	4
2-7	1	–	1
3-7	2	–	2
4-7	2	1	1

ALL PREMIERSHIP MATCHES (620)

MATCH SCORE	ALL RESULTS	HOME MATCHES	AWAY MATCHES
0-0	37	22	15
1-0	77	39	38
2-0	75	48	27
3-0	43	29	14
4-0	24	14	10
5-0	7	7	–
6-0	3	2	1
7-0	1	1	–
8-0	–	–	–
9-0	1	1	–
10-0	–	–	–
0-1	36	14	22
1-1	64	27	37
2-1	59	29	30
3-1	34	17	17
4-1	19	15	4
5-1	5	4	1
6-1	3	3	–
7-1	1	1	–
8-1	1	–	1
10-1	–	–	–
0-2	7	–	7
1-2	14	5	9
2-2	30	8	22
3-2	22	9	13
4-2	8	3	5
5-2	3	1	2
6-2	2	–	2
7-2	–	–	–
8-2	–	–	–
0-3	5	2	3
1-3	13	2	11
2-3	6	3	3
3-3	6	3	3
4-3	3	–	3
5-3	3	1	2
6-3	–	–	–
0-4	–	–	–
1-4	3	–	3
2-4	–	–	–
3-4	2	–	2
4-4	–	–	–
5-4	–	–	–
6-4	–	–	–
8-4	–	–	–
0-5	2	–	2
1-5	–	–	–
2-5	–	–	–
3-5	–	–	–
4-5	–	–	–
5-5	–	–	–
6-5	–	–	–
0-6	–	–	–
1-6	–	–	–
2-6	–	–	–
3-6	1	–	1
0-7	–	–	–
1-7	–	–	–
2-7	–	–	–
3-7	–	–	–
4-7	–	–	–

ALL DIVISION 1 MATCHES (2740)

MATCH SCORE	ALL RESULTS	HOME MATCHES	AWAY MATCHES
0-0	199	100	99
1-0	205	137	68
2-0	167	116	51
3-0	106	82	24
4-0	34	28	6
5-0	29	24	5
6-0	7	6	1
7-0	3	3	–
8-0	–	–	–
9-0	–	–	–
10-0	–	–	–
0-1	174	76	98
1-1	309	160	149
2-1	198	108	90
3-1	143	86	57
4-1	67	49	18
5-1	25	20	5
6-1	14	10	4
7-1	1	1	–
8-1	1	1	–
10-1	1	1	–
0-2	117	36	81
1-2	166	59	107
2-2	151	62	89
3-2	81	47	34
4-2	33	14	19
5-2	14	11	3
6-2	7	5	2
7-2	2	1	1
8-2	–	–	–
0-3	69	14	55
1-3	95	27	68
2-3	58	17	41
3-3	37	13	24
4-3	12	4	8
5-3	6	2	4
6-3	4	2	2
0-4	29	4	25
1-4	33	9	24
2-4	26	4	22
3-4	17	7	10
4-4	8	4	4
5-4	1	–	1
6-4	–	–	–
8-4	–	–	–
0-5	17	2	15
1-5	20	4	16
2-5	9	4	5
3-5	4	3	1
4-5	4	–	4
5-5	–	–	–
6-5	1	–	1
0-6	8	2	6
1-6	8	1	7
2-6	7	2	5
3-6	3	–	3
0-7	2	–	2
1-7	4	1	3
2-7	1	–	1
3-7	1	–	1
4-7	2	1	1

ALL DIVISION 2 MATCHES (816)

MATCH SCORE	ALL RESULTS	HOME MATCHES	AWAY MATCHES
0-0	55	23	32
1-0	78	41	37
2-0	64	41	23
3-0	37	28	9
4-0	27	26	1
5-0	13	12	1
6-0	5	5	-
7-0	2	1	1
8-0	-	-	-
9-0	2	2	-
10-0	-	-	-
0-1	68	20	48
1-1	73	30	43
2-1	57	37	20
3-1	36	28	8
4-1	14	11	3
5-1	15	13	2
6-1	5	4	1
7-1	2	1	1
8-1	-	-	-
10-1	-	-	-
0-2	37	6	31
1-2	48	19	29
2-2	28	12	16
3-2	30	17	13
4-2	6	4	2
5-2	7	4	3
6-2	-	-	-
7-2	1	1	-
8-2	-	-	-
0-3	17	3	14
1-3	21	3	18
2-3	16	4	12
3-3	10	5	5
4-3	3	2	1
5-3	2	-	2
6-3	-	-	-
0-4	9	1	8
1-4	5	-	5
2-4	3	-	3
3-4	2	1	1
4-4	1	-	1
5-4	-	-	-
6-4	-	-	-
8-4	-	-	-
0-5	1	-	1
1-5	7	1	6
2-5	1	1	-
3-5	-	-	-
4-5	-	-	-
5-5	1	1	-
6-5	-	-	-
0-6	-	-	-
1-6	2	-	2
2-6	1	-	1
3-6	1	-	1
0-7	1	-	1
1-7	1	-	1
2-7	-	-	-
3-7	1	-	1
4-7	-	-	-

ALL FA CUP MATCHES (415)

MATCH SCORE	ALL RESULTS	HOME MATCHES	AWAY MATCHES	NEUTRAL VENUE
0-0	27	12	10	5
1-0	48	27	13	8
2-0	34	14	15	5
3-0	22	14	7	1
4-0	9	5	2	2
5-0	4	3	1	-
6-0	2	2	-	-
7-0	2	2	-	-
8-0	1	1	-	-
9-0	-	-	-	-
10-0	-	-	-	-
0-1	28	9	11	8
1-1	38	15	20	3
2-1	38	21	10	7
3-1	20	9	8	3
4-1	9	6	-	3
5-1	7	5	1	1
6-1	1	1	-	-
7-1	1	1	-	-
8-1	-	-	-	-
10-1	-	-	-	-
0-2	16	6	9	1
1-2	17	6	9	2
2-2	23	7	11	5
3-2	8	1	7	-
4-2	8	4	2	2
5-2	3	1	2	-
6-2	1	1	-	-
7-2	1	1	-	-
8-2	1	-	1	-
0-3	4	2	1	1
1-3	5	-	3	2
2-3	6	2	3	1
3-3	7	2	3	2
4-3	1	-	1	-
5-3	3	-	2	1
6-3	-	-	-	-
0-4	3	-	3	-
1-4	4	2	2	-
2-4	1	-	1	-
3-4	1	1	-	-
4-4	-	-	-	-
5-4	-	-	-	-
6-4	1	-	1	-
8-4	-	-	-	-
0-5	1	-	1	-
1-5	3	1	2	-
2-5	-	-	-	-
3-5	2	1	1	-
4-5	-	-	-	-
5-5	-	-	-	-
6-5	-	-	-	-
0-6	1	-	1	-
1-6	1	-	1	-
2-6	-	-	-	-
3-6	-	-	-	-
0-7	-	-	-	-
1-7	1	-	1	-
2-7	1	1	-	-
3-7	-	-	-	-
4-7	-	-	-	-

ALL LEAGUE CUP MATCHES (158)

MATCH SCORE	ALL RESULTS	HOME MATCHES	AWAY MATCHES	NEUTRAL VENUE
0-0	9	2	7	-
1-0	20	12	7	1
2-0	14	11	3	-
3-0	5	2	3	-
4-0	3	2	-	1
5-0	3	3	-	-
6-0	-	-	-	-
7-0	-	-	-	-
8-0	-	-	-	-
9-0	-	-	-	-
10-0	-	-	-	-
0-1	9	3	5	1
1-1	12	5	7	-
2-1	14	10	4	-
3-1	12	5	7	-
4-1	4	3	1	-
5-1	2	2	-	-
6-1	-	-	-	-
7-1	-	-	-	-
8-1	-	-	-	-
10-1	-	-	-	-
0-2	7	1	5	1
1-2	15	4	10	1
2-2	7	4	3	-
3-2	5	2	3	-
4-2	2	1	1	-
5-2	1	-	1	-
6-2	1	-	1	-
7-2	1	1	-	-
8-2	-	-	-	-
0-3	4	3	1	-
1-3	2	-	1	1
2-3	1	-	1	-
3-3	-	-	-	-
4-3	-	-	-	-
5-3	-	-	-	-
6-3	-	-	-	-
0-4	2	-	2	-
1-4	2	-	2	-
2-4	-	-	-	-
3-4	-	-	-	-
4-4	-	-	-	-
5-4	-	-	-	-
6-4	-	-	-	-
8-4	-	-	-	-
0-5	-	-	-	-
1-5	1	-	1	-
2-5	-	-	-	-
3-5	-	-	-	-
4-5	-	-	-	-
5-5	-	-	-	-
6-5	-	-	-	-
0-6	-	-	-	-
1-6	-	-	-	-
2-6	-	-	-	-
3-6	-	-	-	-
0-7	-	-	-	-
1-7	-	-	-	-
2-7	-	-	-	-
3-7	-	-	-	-
4-7	-	-	-	-

ALL EUROPEAN MATCHES (255)

MATCH SCORE	ALL RESULTS	HOME MATCHES	AWAY MATCHES	NEUTRAL VENUE
0-0	28	7	21	-
1-0	19	13	6	-
2-0	23	13	10	-
3-0	21	16	5	-
4-0	6	6	-	-
5-0	4	3	1	-
6-0	2	1	1	-
7-0	-	-	-	-
8-0	-	-	-	-
9-0	-	-	-	-
10-0	1	1	-	-
0-1	19	5	14	-
1-1	25	13	11	1
2-1	19	11	6	2
3-1	9	5	4	-
4-1	4	3	-	1
5-1	3	2	1	-
6-1	3	2	1	-
7-1	2	2	-	-
8-1	-	-	-	-
10-1	-	-	-	-
0-2	6	-	6	-
1-2	10	-	10	-
2-2	9	5	4	-
3-2	13	8	5	-
4-2	2	1	1	-
5-2	2	2	-	-
6-2	2	1	1	-
7-2	-	-	-	-
8-2	-	-	-	-
0-3	5	-	5	-
1-3	5	-	5	-
2-3	2	2	-	-
3-3	5	2	3	-
4-3	1	1	-	-
5-3	-	-	-	-
6-3	-	-	-	-
0-4	3	-	3	-
1-4	-	-	-	-
2-4	-	-	-	-
3-4	-	-	-	-
4-4	-	-	-	-
5-4	-	-	-	-
6-4	-	-	-	-
8-4	-	-	-	-
0-5	1	-	1	-
1-5	-	-	-	-
2-5	-	-	-	-
3-5	1	-	1	-
4-5	-	-	-	-
5-5	-	-	-	-
6-5	-	-	-	-
0-6	-	-	-	-
1-6	-	-	-	-
2-6	-	-	-	-
3-6	-	-	-	-
0-7	-	-	-	-
1-7	-	-	-	-
2-7	-	-	-	-
3-7	-	-	-	-
4-7	-	-	-	-

ALL EUROPEAN CUP MATCHES (193)

MATCH SCORE	ALL RESULTS	HOME MATCHES	AWAY MATCHES	NEUTRAL VENUE
0-0	20	4	16	-
1-0	15	10	5	-
2-0	16	8	8	-
3-0	18	13	5	-
4-0	5	5	-	-
5-0	3	3	-	-
6-0	2	1	1	-
7-0	-	-	-	-
8-0	-	-	-	-
9-0	-	-	-	-
10-0	1	1	-	-
0-1	16	5	11	-
1-1	15	6	8	1
2-1	16	11	4	1
3-1	8	5	3	-
4-1	2	1	-	1
5-1	3	2	1	-
6-1	-	-	-	-
7-1	2	2	-	-
8-1	-	-	-	-
10-1	-	-	-	-
0-2	4	-	4	-
1-2	7	-	7	-
2-2	5	3	2	-
3-2	11	7	4	-
4-2	2	1	1	-
5-2	1	1	-	-
6-2	2	1	1	-
7-2	-	-	-	-
8-2	-	-	-	-
0-3	3	-	3	-
1-3	5	-	5	-
2-3	2	2	-	-
3-3	5	2	3	-
4-3	1	1	-	-
5-3	-	-	-	-
6-3	-	-	-	-
0-4	2	-	2	-
1-4	-	-	-	-
2-4	-	-	-	-
3-4	-	-	-	-
4-4	-	-	-	-
5-4	-	-	-	-
6-4	-	-	-	-
8-4	-	-	-	-
0-5	-	-	-	-
1-5	-	-	-	-
2-5	-	-	-	-
3-5	1	-	1	-
4-5	-	-	-	-
5-5	-	-	-	-
6-5	-	-	-	-
0-6	-	-	-	-
1-6	-	-	-	-
2-6	-	-	-	-
3-6	-	-	-	-
0-7	-	-	-	-
1-7	-	-	-	-
2-7	-	-	-	-
3-7	-	-	-	-
4-7	-	-	-	-

ALL CUP-WINNERS CUP MATCHES (31)

MATCH SCORE	ALL RESULTS	HOME MATCHES	AWAY MATCHES	NEUTRAL VENUE
0-0	1	-	1	-
1-0	1	-	1	-
2-0	6	4	2	-
3-0	2	2	-	-
4-0	-	-	-	-
5-0	-	-	-	-
6-0	-	-	-	-
7-0	-	-	-	-
8-0	-	-	-	-
9-0	-	-	-	-
10-0	-	-	-	-
0-1	-	-	-	-
1-1	7	5	2	-
2-1	2	-	1	1
3-1	1	-	1	-
4-1	2	2	-	-
5-1	-	-	-	-
6-1	1	1	-	-
7-1	-	-	-	-
8-1	-	-	-	-
10-1	-	-	-	-
0-2	2	-	2	-
1-2	1	-	1	-
2-2	1	-	1	-
3-2	-	-	-	-
4-2	-	-	-	-
5-2	1	1	-	-
6-2	-	-	-	-
7-2	-	-	-	-
8-2	-	-	-	-
0-3	1	-	1	-
1-3	-	-	-	-
2-3	-	-	-	-
3-3	-	-	-	-
4-3	-	-	-	-
5-3	-	-	-	-
6-3	-	-	-	-
0-4	1	-	1	-
1-4	-	-	-	-
2-4	-	-	-	-
3-4	-	-	-	-
4-4	-	-	-	-
5-4	-	-	-	-
6-4	-	-	-	-
8-4	-	-	-	-
0-5	1	-	1	-
1-5	-	-	-	-
2-5	-	-	-	-
3-5	-	-	-	-
4-5	-	-	-	-
5-5	-	-	-	-
6-5	-	-	-	-
0-6	-	-	-	-
1-6	-	-	-	-
2-6	-	-	-	-
3-6	-	-	-	-
0-7	-	-	-	-
1-7	-	-	-	-
2-7	-	-	-	-
3-7	-	-	-	-
4-7	-	-	-	-

ALL UEFA CUP MATCHES (31)

MATCH SCORE	ALL RESULTS	HOME MATCHES	AWAY MATCHES	NEUTRAL VENUE
0-0	7	3	4	-
1-0	3	3	-	-
2-0	1	1	-	-
3-0	1	1	-	-
4-0	1	1	-	-
5-0	1	-	1	-
6-0	-	-	-	-
7-0	-	-	-	-
8-0	-	-	-	-
9-0	-	-	-	-
10-0	-	-	-	-
0-1	3	-	3	-
1-1	3	2	1	-
2-1	1	-	1	-
3-1	-	-	-	-
4-1	-	-	-	-
5-1	-	-	-	-
6-1	2	1	1	-
7-1	-	-	-	-
8-1	-	-	-	-
10-1	-	-	-	-
0-2	-	-	-	-
1-2	2	-	2	-
2-2	3	2	1	-
3-2	2	1	1	-
4-2	-	-	-	-
5-2	-	-	-	-
6-2	-	-	-	-
7-2	-	-	-	-
8-2	-	-	-	-
0-3	1	-	1	-
1-3	-	-	-	-
2-3	-	-	-	-
3-3	-	-	-	-
4-3	-	-	-	-
5-3	-	-	-	-
6-3	-	-	-	-
0-4	-	-	-	-
1-4	-	-	-	-
2-4	-	-	-	-
3-4	-	-	-	-
4-4	-	-	-	-
5-4	-	-	-	-
6-4	-	-	-	-
8-4	-	-	-	-
0-5	-	-	-	-
1-5	-	-	-	-
2-5	-	-	-	-
3-5	-	-	-	-
4-5	-	-	-	-
5-5	-	-	-	-
6-5	-	-	-	-
0-6	-	-	-	-
1-6	-	-	-	-
2-6	-	-	-	-
3-6	-	-	-	-
0-7	-	-	-	-
1-7	-	-	-	-
2-7	-	-	-	-
3-7	-	-	-	-
4-7	-	-	-	-

ALL OTHER MATCHES (41)

MATCH SCORE	ALL RESULTS	HOME MATCHES	AWAY MATCHES	NEUTRAL VENUE
0-0	1	-	-	1
1-0	3	1	1	1
2-0	4	1	-	3
3-0	-	-	-	-
4-0	3	1	-	2
5-0	-	-	-	-
6-0	-	-	-	-
7-0	-	-	-	-
8-0	-	-	-	-
9-0	-	-	-	-
10-0	-	-	-	-
0-1	2	-	1	1
1-1	10	2	-	8
2-1	-	-	-	-
3-1	-	-	-	-
4-1	-	-	-	-
5-1	-	-	-	-
6-1	-	-	-	-
7-1	-	-	-	-
8-1	-	-	-	-
10-1	-	-	-	-
0-2	5	-	2	3
1-2	2	-	-	2
2-2	1	1	-	-
3-2	-	-	-	-
4-2	1	1	-	-
5-2	1	-	-	1
6-2	-	-	-	-
7-2	-	-	-	-
8-2	-	-	-	-
0-3	2	-	-	2
1-3	2	-	-	2
2-3	-	-	-	-
3-3	1	1	-	-
4-3	-	-	-	-
5-3	-	-	-	-
6-3	-	-	-	-
0-4	1	-	1	-
1-4	-	-	-	-
2-4	-	-	-	-
3-4	1	-	1	-
4-4	-	-	-	-
5-4	-	-	-	-
6-4	-	-	-	-
8-4	1	-	-	1
0-5	-	-	-	-
1-5	-	-	-	-
2-5	-	-	-	-
3-5	-	-	-	-
4-5	-	-	-	-
5-5	-	-	-	-
6-5	-	-	-	-
0-6	-	-	-	-
1-6	-	-	-	-
2-6	-	-	-	-
3-6	-	-	-	-
0-7	-	-	-	-
1-7	-	-	-	-
2-7	-	-	-	-
3-7	-	-	-	-
4-7	-	-	-	-

MANCHESTER UNITED
The Complete Record

Chapter 1.5
The Attendances

TOP 25 ATTENDANCES - ALL COMPETITIVE MATCHES - HOME

#	ATT	SEASON	DATE	COMPETITION / ROUND	MATCH RESULT	VENUE
1	82771	1948/49	29/01/49	FA Cup 4th Round	Manchester United 1 Bradford Park Avenue 1	Maine Road
2	81962	1947/48	17/01/48	Football League Division 1	Manchester United 1 Arsenal 1	Maine Road
3	81565	1948/49	12/02/49	FA Cup 5th Round	Manchester United 8 Yeovil Town 0	Maine Road
4	76098	2006/07	31/03/07	FA Premiership	Manchester United 4 Blackburn Rovers 1	Old Trafford
5	76073	2006/07	13/01/07	FA Premiership	Manchester United 3 Aston Villa 1	Old Trafford
6	76058	2006/07	17/03/07	FA Premiership	Manchester United 4 Bolton Wanderers 1	Old Trafford
7	76032	2006/07	31/01/07	FA Premiership	Manchester United 4 Watford 0	Old Trafford
8	76018	2006/07	26/12/06	FA Premiership	Manchester United 3 Wigan Athletic 1	Old Trafford
9	76013	2007/08	03/05/08	FA Premiership	Manchester United 4 West Ham United 1	Old Trafford
10	76004	2006/07	04/11/06	FA Premiership	Manchester United 3 Portsmouth 0	Old Trafford
11	76000	2007/08	23/03/08	FA Premiership	Manchester United 3 Liverpool 0	Old Trafford
12	75985	2007/08	13/04/08	FA Premiership	Manchester United 2 Arsenal 1	Old Trafford
13	75970	2007/08	10/02/08	FA Premiership	Manchester United 1 Manchester City 2	Old Trafford
14	75967	2006/07	21/04/07	FA Premiership	Manchester United 1 Middlesbrough 1	Old Trafford
15	75965	2007/08	12/01/08	FA Premiership	Manchester United 6 Newcastle United 0	Old Trafford
16	75948	2006/07	26/11/06	FA Premiership	Manchester United 1 Chelsea 1	Old Trafford
17	75932	2007/08	29/03/08	FA Premiership	Manchester United 4 Aston Villa 0	Old Trafford
18	75927	2006/07	13/05/07	FA Premiership	Manchester United 0 West Ham United 1	Old Trafford
19	75910	2006/07	30/12/06	FA Premiership	Manchester United 3 Reading 2	Old Trafford
20	75883	2006/07	10/02/07	FA Premiership	Manchester United 2 Charlton Athletic 0	Old Trafford
21	75858	2006/07	09/12/06	FA Premiership	Manchester United 3 Manchester City 1	Old Trafford
22	75828	2006/07	22/10/06	FA Premiership	Manchester United 2 Liverpool 0	Old Trafford
23	75749	2007/08	23/12/07	FA Premiership	Manchester United 2 Everton 1	Old Trafford
24	75725	2007/08	08/12/07	FA Premiership	Manchester United 4 Derby County 1	Old Trafford
25	75723	2006/07	29/11/06	FA Premiership	Manchester United 3 Everton 0	Old Trafford

TOP 25 ATTENDANCES - ALL COMPETITIVE MATCHES - AWAY

#	ATT	SEASON	DATE	COMPETITION / ROUND	MATCH RESULT	VENUE
1	135000	1956/57	11/04/57	European Cup Semi-Final 1st Leg	Real Madrid 3 Manchester United 1	Bernabeu Stadium
2	125000	1967/68	15/05/68	European Cup Semi-Final 2nd Leg	Real Madrid 3 Manchester United 3	Bernabeu Stadium
3	114273	1994/95	02/11/94	Champions League Phase 1 Match 4	Barcelona 4 Manchester United 0	Estadio Camp Nou
4	105000	1967/68	13/03/68	European Cup Quarter-Final 2nd Leg	Gornik Zabrze 1 Manchester United 0	Stadion Slaski
5	95949	2007/08	23/04/08	Champions League Semi-Final 1st Leg	Barcelona 0 Manchester United 0	Estadio Camp Nou
6	80000	1957/58	14/05/58	European Cup Semi-Final 2nd Leg	AC Milan 4 Manchester United 0	Stadio San Siro
7	80000	1968/69	23/04/69	European Cup Semi-Final 1st Leg	AC Milan 2 Manchester United 0	Stadio San Siro
8	79528	1998/99	17/03/99	Champions League Qtr-Final 2nd Leg	Internazionale 1 Manchester United 1	Stadio San Siro
9	78957	2004/05	08/03/05	Champions League 2nd Round 1st Leg	AC Milan 1 Manchester United 0	San Siro Stadium
10	78500	2006/07	02/05/07	Champions League Semi-Final 2nd Leg	AC Milan 3 Manchester United 0	Stadio San Siro
11	77920	1952/53	14/02/53	FA Cup 5th Round	Everton 2 Manchester United 1	Goodison Park
12	77000	2006/07	04/04/07	Champions League Qtr-Final 1st Leg	Roma 2 Manchester United 1	Olympic Stadium
13	75000	1954/55	19/02/55	FA Cup 4th Round	Manchester City 2 Manchester United 0	Maine Road
14	75000	1965/66	09/03/66	European Cup Quarter-Final 2nd Leg	Benfica 1 Manchester United 5	Estadio da Luz
15	75000	2002/03	08/04/03	Champions League Qtr-Final 1st Leg	Real Madrid 3 Manchester United 1	Bernabeu Stadium
16	73537	2001/02	10/10/01	Champions League Phase 1 Match 3	Olympiakos Piraeus 0 Manchester United 2	Olympic Stadium
17	72077	1957/58	04/09/57	Football League Division 1	Everton 3 Manchester United 3	Goodison Park
18	71364	1947/48	20/09/47	Football League Division 1	Manchester City 0 Manchester United 0	Maine Road
19	70882	1951/52	22/09/51	Football League Division 1	Tottenham Hotspur 2 Manchester United 0	White Hart Lane
20	70483	1957/58	28/12/57	Football League Division 1	Manchester City 2 Manchester United 2	Maine Road
21	70362	1949/50	04/03/50	FA Cup 6th Round	Chelsea 2 Manchester United 0	Stamford Bridge
22	70000	1977/78	19/10/77	European CWC 2nd Round 1st Leg	Porto 4 Manchester United 0	Estadio das Antas
23	70000	1983/84	07/03/84	European CWC 3rd Round 1st Leg	Barcelona 2 Manchester United 0	Estadio Camp Nou
24	69501	1962/63	22/08/62	Football League Division 1	Everton 3 Manchester United 1	Goodison Park
25	68648	1930/31	06/09/30	Football League Division 1	Chelsea 6 Manchester United 2	Stamford Bridge

TOP 25 ATTENDANCES - ALL COMPETITIVE MATCHES - ANY VENUE

#	ATT	SEASON	DATE	COMPETITION / ROUND	MATCH RESULT	VENUE
1	135000	1956/57	11/04/57	European Cup Semi-Final 1st Leg	Real Madrid 3 Manchester United 1	Bernabeu Stadium
2	125000	1967/68	15/05/68	European Cup Semi-Final 2nd Leg	Real Madrid 3 Manchester United 3	Bernabeu Stadium
3	114273	1994/95	02/11/94	Champions League Phase 1 Match 4	Barcelona 4 Manchester United 0	Estadio Camp Nou
4	105000	1967/68	13/03/68	European Cup Quarter-Final 2nd Leg	Gornik Zabrze 1 Manchester United 0	Stadion Slaski
5	100000	1956/57	04/05/57	FA Cup Final	Manchester United 1 Aston Villa 2	Wembley
6	100000	1957/58	03/05/58	FA Cup Final	Manchester United 0 Bolton Wanderers 2	Wembley
7	100000	1962/63	25/05/63	FA Cup Final	Manchester United 3 Leicester City 1	Wembley
8	100000	1967/68	29/05/68	European Cup Final	Manchester United 4 Benfica 1	Wembley
9	100000	1975/76	01/05/76	FA Cup Final	Manchester United 0 Southampton 1	Wembley
10	100000	1976/77	21/05/77	FA Cup Final	Manchester United 2 Liverpool 1	Wembley
11	100000	1978/79	12/05/79	FA Cup Final	Manchester United 2 Arsenal 3	Wembley
12	100000	1982/83	26/03/83	League Cup Final	Manchester United 1 Liverpool 2	Wembley
13	100000	1982/83	21/05/83	FA Cup Final	Manchester United 2 Brighton 2	Wembley
14	100000	1984/85	18/05/85	FA Cup Final	Manchester United 1 Everton 0	Wembley
15	99000	1947/48	24/04/48	FA Cup Final	Manchester United 4 Blackpool 2	Wembley
16	95949	2007/08	23/04/08	Champions League Semi-Final 1st Leg	Barcelona 0 Manchester United 0	Estadio Camp Nou
17	92000	1982/83	26/05/83	FA Cup Final Replay	Manchester United 4 Brighton 0	Wembley
18	92000	1983/84	20/08/83	FA Charity Shield	Manchester United 2 Liverpool 0	Wembley
19	90000	1998/99	26/05/99	Champions League Final	Manchester United 2 Bayern Munich 1	Estadio Camp Nou
20	89826	2006/07	19/05/07	FA Cup Final	Manchester United 0 Chelsea 1	Wembley
21	82771	1948/49	29/01/49	FA Cup 4th Round	Manchester United 1 Bradford Park Avenue 1	Maine Road
22	82000	1977/78	13/08/77	FA Charity Shield	Manchester United 0 Liverpool 0	Wembley
23	82000	1985/86	10/08/85	FA Charity Shield	Manchester United 0 Everton 2	Wembley
24	81962	1947/48	17/01/48	Football League Division 1	Manchester United 1 Arsenal 1	Maine Road
25	81565	1948/49	12/02/49	FA Cup 5th Round	Manchester United 8 Yeovil Town 0	Maine Road

TOP 25 ATTENDANCES - ALL LEAGUE MATCHES - HOME

#	ATT	SEASON	DATE	COMPETITION	MATCH RESULT	VENUE
1	81962	1947/48	17/01/48	Football League Division 1	Manchester United 1 Arsenal 1	Maine Road
2	76098	2006/07	31/03/07	FA Premiership	Manchester United 4 Blackburn Rovers 1	Old Trafford
3	76073	2006/07	13/01/07	FA Premiership	Manchester United 3 Aston Villa 1	Old Trafford
4	76058	2006/07	17/03/07	FA Premiership	Manchester United 4 Bolton Wanderers 1	Old Trafford
5	76032	2006/07	31/01/07	FA Premiership	Manchester United 4 Watford 0	Old Trafford
6	76018	2006/07	26/12/06	FA Premiership	Manchester United 3 Wigan Athletic 1	Old Trafford
7	76013	2007/08	03/05/08	FA Premiership	Manchester United 4 West Ham United 1	Old Trafford
8	76004	2006/07	04/11/06	FA Premiership	Manchester United 3 Portsmouth 0	Old Trafford
9	76000	2007/08	23/03/08	FA Premiership	Manchester United 3 Liverpool 0	Old Trafford
10	75985	2007/08	13/04/08	FA Premiership	Manchester United 2 Arsenal 1	Old Trafford
11	75970	2007/08	10/02/08	FA Premiership	Manchester United 1 Manchester City 2	Old Trafford
12	75967	2006/07	21/04/07	FA Premiership	Manchester United 1 Middlesbrough 1	Old Trafford
13	75965	2007/08	12/01/08	FA Premiership	Manchester United 6 Newcastle United 0	Old Trafford
14	75948	2006/07	26/11/06	FA Premiership	Manchester United 1 Chelsea 1	Old Trafford
15	75932	2007/08	29/03/08	FA Premiership	Manchester United 4 Aston Villa 0	Old Trafford
16	75927	2006/07	13/05/07	FA Premiership	Manchester United 0 West Ham United 1	Old Trafford
17	75910	2006/07	30/12/06	FA Premiership	Manchester United 3 Reading 2	Old Trafford
18	75883	2006/07	10/02/07	FA Premiership	Manchester United 2 Charlton Athletic 0	Old Trafford
19	75858	2006/07	09/12/06	FA Premiership	Manchester United 3 Manchester City 1	Old Trafford
20	75828	2006/07	22/10/06	FA Premiership	Manchester United 2 Liverpool 0	Old Trafford
21	75749	2007/08	23/12/07	FA Premiership	Manchester United 2 Everton 1	Old Trafford
22	75725	2007/08	08/12/07	FA Premiership	Manchester United 4 Derby County 1	Old Trafford
23	75723	2006/07	29/11/06	FA Premiership	Manchester United 3 Everton 0	Old Trafford
24	75720	2007/08	27/10/07	FA Premiership	Manchester United 4 Middlesbrough 1	Old Trafford
25	75710	2007/08	11/11/07	FA Premiership	Manchester United 2 Blackburn Rovers 0	Old Trafford

TOP 25 ATTENDANCES - ALL LEAGUE MATCHES - AWAY

#	ATT	SEASON	DATE	COMPETITION	MATCH RESULT	VENUE
1	72077	1957/58	04/09/57	Football League Division 1	Everton 3 Manchester United 3	Goodison Park
2	71364	1947/48	20/09/47	Football League Division 1	Manchester City 0 Manchester United 0	Maine Road
3	70882	1951/52	22/09/51	Football League Division 1	Tottenham Hotspur 2 Manchester United 0	White Hart Lane
4	70483	1957/58	28/12/57	Football League Division 1	Manchester City 2 Manchester United 2	Maine Road
5	69501	1962/63	22/08/62	Football League Division 1	Everton 3 Manchester United 1	Goodison Park
6	68648	1930/31	06/09/30	Football League Division 1	Chelsea 6 Manchester United 2	Stamford Bridge
7	68354	1948/49	19/02/49	Football League Division 1	Aston Villa 2 Manchester United 1	Villa Park
8	67162	1958/59	28/02/59	Football League Division 1	Arsenal 3 Manchester United 2	Highbury
9	66579	1959/60	02/09/59	Football League Division 1	Chelsea 3 Manchester United 6	Stamford Bridge
10	66150	1950/51	14/10/50	Football League Division 1	Arsenal 3 Manchester United 0	Highbury
11	65133	1949/50	27/12/49	Football League Division 1	Arsenal 0 Manchester United 0	Highbury
12	64905	1947/48	06/09/47	Football League Division 1	Arsenal 2 Manchester United 1	Highbury
13	64862	1936/37	09/01/37	Football League Division 1	Manchester City 1 Manchester United 0	Maine Road
14	64502	1948/49	11/09/48	Football League Division 1	Manchester City 0 Manchester United 0	Maine Road
15	64472	1929/30	08/02/30	Football League Division 1	Manchester City 0 Manchester United 1	Maine Road
16	64150	1948/49	28/08/48	Football League Division 1	Arsenal 0 Manchester United 1	Highbury
17	64079	1958/59	18/10/58	Football League Division 1	Everton 3 Manchester United 2	Goodison Park
18	63872	1956/57	02/02/57	Football League Division 1	Manchester City 2 Manchester United 4	Maine Road
19	63704	1949/50	31/12/49	Football League Division 1	Manchester City 1 Manchester United 2	Maine Road
20	63578	1957/58	01/02/58	Football League Division 1	Arsenal 4 Manchester United 5	Highbury
21	63363	1966/67	03/06/67	Football League Division 1	Arsenal 1 Manchester United 1	Highbury
22	63326	1971/72	06/11/71	Football League Division 1	Manchester City 3 Manchester United 3	Maine Road
23	63251	1949/50	18/02/50	Football League Division 1	Sunderland 2 Manchester United 2	Roker Park
24	63052	1968/69	17/08/68	Football League Division 1	Manchester City 0 Manchester United 0	Maine Road
25	63024	1964/65	08/09/64	Football League Division 1	Everton 3 Manchester United 3	Goodison Park

TOP 25 ATTENDANCES - ALL LEAGUE MATCHES - ANY VENUE

#	ATT	SEASON	DATE	COMPETITION	MATCH RESULT	VENUE
1	81962	1947/48	17/01/48	Football League Division 1	Manchester United 1 Arsenal 1	Maine Road
2	76098	2006/07	31/03/07	FA Premiership	Manchester United 4 Blackburn Rovers 1	Old Trafford
3	76073	2006/07	13/01/07	FA Premiership	Manchester United 3 Aston Villa 1	Old Trafford
4	76058	2006/07	17/03/07	FA Premiership	Manchester United 4 Bolton Wanderers 1	Old Trafford
5	76032	2006/07	31/01/07	FA Premiership	Manchester United 4 Watford 0	Old Trafford
6	76018	2006/07	26/12/06	FA Premiership	Manchester United 3 Wigan Athletic 1	Old Trafford
7	76013	2007/08	03/05/08	FA Premiership	Manchester United 4 West Ham United 1	Old Trafford
8	76004	2006/07	04/11/06	FA Premiership	Manchester United 3 Portsmouth 0	Old Trafford
9	76000	2007/08	23/03/08	FA Premiership	Manchester United 3 Liverpool 0	Old Trafford
10	75985	2007/08	13/04/08	FA Premiership	Manchester United 2 Arsenal 1	Old Trafford
11	75970	2007/08	10/02/08	FA Premiership	Manchester United 1 Manchester City 2	Old Trafford
12	75967	2006/07	21/04/07	FA Premiership	Manchester United 1 Middlesbrough 1	Old Trafford
13	75965	2007/08	12/01/08	FA Premiership	Manchester United 6 Newcastle United 0	Old Trafford
14	75948	2006/07	26/11/06	FA Premiership	Manchester United 1 Chelsea 1	Old Trafford
15	75932	2007/08	29/03/08	FA Premiership	Manchester United 4 Aston Villa 0	Old Trafford
16	75927	2006/07	13/05/07	FA Premiership	Manchester United 0 West Ham United 1	Old Trafford
17	75910	2006/07	30/12/06	FA Premiership	Manchester United 3 Reading 2	Old Trafford
18	75883	2006/07	10/02/07	FA Premiership	Manchester United 2 Charlton Athletic 0	Old Trafford
19	75858	2006/07	09/12/06	FA Premiership	Manchester United 3 Manchester City 1	Old Trafford
20	75828	2006/07	22/10/06	FA Premiership	Manchester United 2 Liverpool 0	Old Trafford
21	75749	2007/08	23/12/07	FA Premiership	Manchester United 2 Everton 1	Old Trafford
22	75725	2007/08	08/12/07	FA Premiership	Manchester United 4 Derby County 1	Old Trafford
23	75723	2006/07	29/11/06	FA Premiership	Manchester United 3 Everton 0	Old Trafford
24	75720	2007/08	27/10/07	FA Premiership	Manchester United 4 Middlesbrough 1	Old Trafford
25	75710	2007/08	11/11/07	FA Premiership	Manchester United 2 Blackburn Rovers 0	Old Trafford

TOP 25 ATTENDANCES - ALL PREMIERSHIP MATCHES - HOME

#	ATT	SEASON	DATE	COMPETITION	MATCH RESULT	VENUE
1	76098	2006/07	31/03/07	FA Premiership	Manchester United 4 Blackburn Rovers 1	Old Trafford
2	76073	2006/07	13/01/07	FA Premiership	Manchester United 3 Aston Villa 1	Old Trafford
3	76058	2006/07	17/03/07	FA Premiership	Manchester United 4 Bolton Wanderers 1	Old Trafford
4	76032	2006/07	31/01/07	FA Premiership	Manchester United 4 Watford 0	Old Trafford
5	76018	2006/07	26/12/06	FA Premiership	Manchester United 3 Wigan Athletic 1	Old Trafford
6	76013	2007/08	03/05/08	FA Premiership	Manchester United 4 West Ham United 1	Old Trafford
7	76004	2006/07	04/11/06	FA Premiership	Manchester United 3 Portsmouth 0	Old Trafford
8	76000	2007/08	23/03/08	FA Premiership	Manchester United 3 Liverpool 0	Old Trafford
9	75985	2007/08	13/04/08	FA Premiership	Manchester United 2 Arsenal 1	Old Trafford
10	75970	2007/08	10/02/08	FA Premiership	Manchester United 1 Manchester City 2	Old Trafford
11	75967	2006/07	21/04/07	FA Premiership	Manchester United 1 Middlesbrough 1	Old Trafford
12	75965	2007/08	12/01/08	FA Premiership	Manchester United 6 Newcastle United 0	Old Trafford
13	75948	2006/07	26/11/06	FA Premiership	Manchester United 1 Chelsea 1	Old Trafford
14	75932	2007/08	29/03/08	FA Premiership	Manchester United 4 Aston Villa 0	Old Trafford
15	75927	2006/07	13/05/07	FA Premiership	Manchester United 0 West Ham United 1	Old Trafford
16	75910	2006/07	30/12/06	FA Premiership	Manchester United 3 Reading 2	Old Trafford
17	75883	2007/08	10/02/07	FA Premiership	Manchester United 2 Charlton Athletic 0	Old Trafford
18	75858	2006/07	09/12/06	FA Premiership	Manchester United 3 Manchester City 1	Old Trafford
19	75828	2006/07	22/10/06	FA Premiership	Manchester United 2 Liverpool 0	Old Trafford
20	75749	2007/08	23/12/07	FA Premiership	Manchester United 2 Everton 1	Old Trafford
21	75725	2007/08	08/12/07	FA Premiership	Manchester United 4 Derby County 1	Old Trafford
22	75723	2006/07	29/11/06	FA Premiership	Manchester United 3 Everton 0	Old Trafford
23	75720	2007/08	27/10/07	FA Premiership	Manchester United 4 Middlesbrough 1	Old Trafford
24	75710	2007/08	11/11/07	FA Premiership	Manchester United 2 Blackburn Rovers 0	Old Trafford
25	75696	2007/08	26/08/07	FA Premiership	Manchester United 1 Tottenham Hotspur 0	Old Trafford

TOP 25 ATTENDANCES - ALL PREMIERHIP MATCHES - AWAY

#	ATT	SEASON	DATE	COMPETITION	MATCH RESULT	VENUE
1	60161	2007/08	03/11/07	FA Premiership	Arsenal 2 Manchester United 2	Emirates Stadium
2	60128	2006/07	21/01/07	FA Premiership	Arsenal 2 Manchester United 1	Emirates Stadium
3	52327	2005/06	28/08/05	FA Premiership	Newcastle United 0 Manchester United 2	St James' Park
4	52320	2004/05	14/11/04	FA Premiership	Newcastle United 1 Manchester United 3	St James' Park
5	52302	2006/07	01/01/07	FA Premiership	Newcastle United 2 Manchester United 2	St James' Park
6	52291	2007/08	23/02/08	FA Premiership	Newcastle United 1 Manchester United 5	St James' Park
7	52165	2003/04	23/08/03	FA Premiership	Newcastle United 1 Manchester United 2	St James' Park
8	52164	2002/03	12/04/03	FA Premiership	Newcastle United 2 Manchester United 6	St James' Park
9	52134	2000/01	30/12/00	FA Premiership	Newcastle United 1 Manchester United 1	St James' Park
10	52056	2001/02	15/09/01	FA Premiership	Newcastle United 4 Manchester United 3	St James' Park
11	48305	2001/02	13/10/01	FA Premiership	Sunderland 1 Manchester United 3	Stadium of Light
12	48260	2000/01	31/01/01	FA Premiership	Sunderland 0 Manchester United 1	Stadium of Light
13	47586	2002/03	31/08/02	FA Premiership	Sunderland 1 Manchester United 1	Stadium of Light
14	47360	2007/08	26/12/07	FA Premiership	Sunderland 0 Manchester United 4	Stadium of Light
15	47284	2003/04	14/03/04	FA Premiership	Manchester City 4 Manchester United 1	Eastlands Stadium
16	47244	2006/07	05/05/07	FA Premiership	Manchester City 0 Manchester United 1	Eastlands Stadium
17	47192	2005/06	14/01/06	FA Premiership	Manchester City 3 Manchester United 1	Eastlands Stadium
18	47111	2004/05	13/02/05	FA Premiership	Manchester City 0 Manchester United 2	Eastlands Stadium
19	44955	2007/08	19/08/07	FA Premiership	Manchester City 1 Manchester United 0	Eastlands Stadium
20	44929	1999/00	11/09/99	FA Premiership	Liverpool 2 Manchester United 3	Anfield
21	44917	2005/06	18/09/05	FA Premiership	Liverpool 0 Manchester United 0	Anfield
22	44806	2000/01	31/03/01	FA Premiership	Liverpool 2 Manchester United 0	Anfield
23	44702	1998/99	05/05/99	FA Premiership	Liverpool 2 Manchester United 2	Anfield
24	44459	2007/08	16/12/07	FA Premiership	Liverpool 0 Manchester United 1	Anfield
25	44403	2006/07	03/03/07	FA Premiership	Liverpool 0 Manchester United 1	Anfield

TOP 25 ATTENDANCES - ALL LEAGUE DIVISION ONE MATCHES - HOME

#	ATT	SEASON	DATE	COMPETITION	MATCH RESULT	VENUE
1	81962	1947/48	17/01/48	Football League Division 1	Manchester United 1 Arsenal 1	Maine Road
2	71690	1947/48	07/04/48	Football League Division 1	Manchester United 1 Manchester City 1	Maine Road
3	71623	1947/48	26/03/48	Football League Division 1	Manchester United 0 Bolton Wanderers 2	Maine Road
4	70787	1948/49	04/12/48	Football League Division 1	Manchester United 1 Newcastle United 1	Maine Road
5	70504	1920/21	27/12/20	Football League Division 1	Manchester United 1 Aston Villa 3	Old Trafford
6	68796	1936/37	12/09/36	Football League Division 1	Manchester United 3 Manchester City 2	Old Trafford
7	66967	1946/47	05/04/47	Football League Division 1	Manchester United 3 Wolverhampton Wanderers 1	Maine Road
8	66485	1948/49	22/01/49	Football League Division 1	Manchester United 0 Manchester City 0	Maine Road
9	66124	1957/58	22/02/58	Football League Division 1	Manchester United 1 Nottingham Forest 1	Old Trafford
10	65295	1960/61	14/01/61	Football League Division 1	Manchester United 2 Tottenham Hotspur 0	Old Trafford
11	65187	1958/59	06/09/58	Football League Division 1	Manchester United 6 Blackburn Rovers 1	Old Trafford
12	65112	1946/47	14/09/46	Football League Division 1	Manchester United 1 Middlesbrough 0	Maine Road
13	63683	1947/48	06/12/47	Football League Division 1	Manchester United 1 Blackpool 1	Maine Road
14	63450	1967/68	26/12/67	Football League Division 1	Manchester United 4 Wolverhampton Wanderers 0	Old Trafford
15	63437	1962/63	29/08/62	Football League Division 1	Manchester United 0 Everton 1	Old Trafford
16	63347	1957/58	31/08/57	Football League Division 1	Manchester United 4 Manchester City 1	Old Trafford
17	63278	1957/58	08/03/58	Football League Division 1	Manchester United 0 West Bromwich Albion 4	Old Trafford
18	63274	1968/69	07/09/68	Football League Division 1	Manchester United 1 West Ham United 1	Old Trafford
19	63264	1968/69	08/03/69	Football League Division 1	Manchester United 0 Manchester City 1	Old Trafford
20	63098	1958/59	26/12/58	Football League Division 1	Manchester United 2 Aston Villa 1	Old Trafford
21	63059	1967/68	06/04/68	Football League Division 1	Manchester United 1 Liverpool 2	Old Trafford
22	63004	1967/68	27/03/68	Football League Division 1	Manchester United 1 Manchester City 3	Old Trafford
23	63000	1920/21	20/11/20	Football League Division 1	Manchester United 1 Manchester City 1	Old Trafford
24	62978	1967/68	02/03/68	Football League Division 1	Manchester United 1 Chelsea 3	Old Trafford
25	62965	1963/64	31/08/63	Football League Division 1	Manchester United 5 Everton 1	Old Trafford

TOP 25 ATTENDANCES - ALL LEAGUE DIVISION ONE MATCHES - AWAY

#	ATT	SEASON	DATE	COMPETITION	MATCH RESULT	VENUE
1	72077	1957/58	04/09/57	Football League Division 1	Everton 3 Manchester United 3	Goodison Park
2	71364	1947/48	20/09/47	Football League Division 1	Manchester City 0 Manchester United 0	Maine Road
3	70882	1951/52	22/09/51	Football League Division 1	Tottenham Hotspur 2 Manchester United 0	White Hart Lane
4	70483	1957/58	28/12/57	Football League Division 1	Manchester City 2 Manchester United 2	Maine Road
5	69501	1962/63	22/08/62	Football League Division 1	Everton 3 Manchester United 1	Goodison Park
6	68648	1930/31	06/09/30	Football League Division 1	Chelsea 6 Manchester United 2	Stamford Bridge
7	68354	1948/49	19/02/49	Football League Division 1	Aston Villa 2 Manchester United 1	Villa Park
8	67162	1958/59	28/02/59	Football League Division 1	Arsenal 3 Manchester United 2	Highbury
9	66579	1959/60	02/09/59	Football League Division 1	Chelsea 3 Manchester United 6	Stamford Bridge
10	66150	1950/51	14/10/50	Football League Division 1	Arsenal 3 Manchester United 0	Highbury
11	65133	1949/50	27/12/49	Football League Division 1	Arsenal 0 Manchester United 0	Highbury
12	64905	1947/48	06/09/47	Football League Division 1	Arsenal 2 Manchester United 1	Highbury
13	64862	1936/37	09/01/37	Football League Division 1	Manchester City 1 Manchester United 0	Maine Road
14	64502	1948/49	11/09/48	Football League Division 1	Manchester City 0 Manchester United 0	Maine Road
15	64472	1929/30	08/02/30	Football League Division 1	Manchester City 0 Manchester United 1	Maine Road
16	64150	1948/49	28/08/48	Football League Division 1	Arsenal 0 Manchester United 1	Highbury
17	64079	1958/59	18/10/58	Football League Division 1	Everton 3 Manchester United 2	Goodison Park
18	63872	1956/57	02/02/57	Football League Division 1	Manchester City 2 Manchester United 4	Maine Road
19	63704	1949/50	31/12/49	Football League Division 1	Manchester City 1 Manchester United 2	Maine Road
20	63578	1957/58	01/02/58	Football League Division 1	Arsenal 4 Manchester United 5	Highbury
21	63363	1966/67	03/03/67	Football League Division 1	Arsenal 1 Manchester United 1	Highbury
22	63326	1971/72	06/11/71	Football League Division 1	Manchester City 3 Manchester United 3	Maine Road
23	63251	1949/50	18/02/50	Football League Division 1	Sunderland 2 Manchester United 2	Roker Park
24	63052	1968/69	17/08/68	Football League Division 1	Manchester City 0 Manchester United 0	Maine Road
25	63024	1964/65	08/09/64	Football League Division 1	Everton 3 Manchester United 3	Goodison Park

TOP 25 ATTENDANCES - ALL LEAGUE DIVISION TWO MATCHES - HOME

#	ATT	SEASON	DATE	COMPETITION	MATCH RESULT	VENUE
1	65988	1932/33	06/05/33	Football League Division 2	Manchester United 1 Swansea City 1	Old Trafford
2	60585	1974/75	30/11/74	Football League Division 2	Manchester United 3 Sunderland 2	Old Trafford
3	59500	1924/25	29/11/24	Football League Division 2	Manchester United 1 Derby County 1	Old Trafford
4	58769	1974/75	26/04/75	Football League Division 2	Manchester United 4 Blackpool 0	Old Trafford
5	56618	1974/75	31/03/75	Football League Division 2	Manchester United 3 Oldham Athletic 2	Old Trafford
6	56202	1974/75	15/03/75	Football League Division 2	Manchester United 1 Norwich City 1	Old Trafford
7	55615	1974/75	16/11/74	Football League Division 2	Manchester United 2 Aston Villa 1	Old Trafford
8	53604	1937/38	07/05/38	Football League Division 2	Manchester United 2 Bury 0	Old Trafford
9	52971	1974/75	12/04/75	Football League Division 2	Manchester United 1 Fulham 0	Old Trafford
10	51104	1974/75	26/12/74	Football League Division 2	Manchester United 2 West Bromwich Albion 1	Old Trafford
11	48724	1974/75	26/10/74	Football League Division 2	Manchester United 1 Southampton 0	Old Trafford
12	47118	1974/75	01/02/75	Football League Division 2	Manchester United 0 Bristol City 1	Old Trafford
13	47084	1974/75	25/09/74	Football League Division 2	Manchester United 3 Bolton Wanderers 0	Old Trafford
14	46802	1974/75	29/03/75	Football League Division 2	Manchester United 2 York City 1	Old Trafford
15	46565	1974/75	12/10/74	Football League Division 2	Manchester United 1 Notts County 0	Old Trafford
16	45662	1974/75	11/01/75	Football League Division 2	Manchester United 2 Sheffield Wednesday 0	Old Trafford
17	44756	1974/75	24/08/74	Football League Division 2	Manchester United 4 Millwall 0	Old Trafford
18	44712	1974/75	15/02/75	Football League Division 2	Manchester United 2 Hull City 0	Old Trafford
19	44000	1924/25	26/12/24	Football League Division 2	Manchester United 2 Middlesbrough 0	Old Trafford
20	43601	1974/75	01/03/75	Football League Division 2	Manchester United 4 Cardiff City 0	Old Trafford
21	43500	1924/25	10/04/25	Football League Division 2	Manchester United 2 Stockport County 0	Old Trafford
22	43000	1923/24	15/09/23	Football League Division 2	Manchester United 0 Bury 0	Old Trafford
23	42948	1974/75	21/09/74	Football League Division 2	Manchester United 2 Bristol Rovers 0	Old Trafford
24	42547	1974/75	28/08/74	Football League Division 2	Manchester United 2 Portsmouth 1	Old Trafford
25	41909	1974/75	02/11/74	Football League Division 2	Manchester United 4 Oxford United 0	Old Trafford

TOP 25 ATTENDANCES - ALL LEAGUE DIVISION TWO MATCHES - AWAY

#	ATT	SEASON	DATE	COMPETITION	MATCH RESULT	VENUE
1	60000	1905/06	13/04/06	Football League Division 2	Chelsea 1 Manchester United 1	Stamford Bridge
2	54654	1937/38	02/04/38	Football League Division 2	Aston Villa 3 Manchester United 0	Villa Park
3	45976	1974/75	18/01/75	Football League Division 2	Sunderland 0 Manchester United 0	Roker Park
4	40088	1937/38	01/01/38	Football League Division 2	Newcastle United 2 Manchester United 2	St James' Park
5	39156	1974/75	22/02/75	Football League Division 2	Aston Villa 2 Manchester United 0	Villa Park
6	38152	1974/75	08/03/75	Football League Division 2	Bolton Wanderers 0 Manchester United 1	Burnden Park
7	37207	1931/32	26/12/31	Football League Division 2	Wolverhampton Wanderers 7 Manchester United 0	Molineux
8	37156	1937/38	05/03/38	Football League Division 2	Sheffield Wednesday 1 Manchester United 3	Hillsborough
9	35230	1974/75	07/12/74	Football League Division 2	Sheffield Wednesday 4 Manchester United 4	Hillsborough
10	35000	1904/05	03/01/05	Football League Division 2	Bolton Wanderers 2 Manchester United 4	Burnden Park
11	33776	1932/33	26/12/32	Football League Division 2	Plymouth Argyle 2 Manchester United 3	Home Park
12	31562	1935/36	29/04/36	Football League Division 2	Bury 2 Manchester United 3	Gigg Lane
13	31189	1937/38	09/10/37	Football League Division 2	Tottenham Hotspur 0 Manchester United 1	White Hart Lane
14	30575	1937/38	30/08/37	Football League Division 2	Coventry City 1 Manchester United 0	Highfield Road
15	30000	1902/03	10/04/03	Football League Division 2	Manchester City 0 Manchester United 2	Hyde Road
16	29684	1935/36	07/03/36	Football League Division 2	West Ham United 1 Manchester United 2	Upton Park
17	28520	1935/36	14/09/35	Football League Division 2	Newcastle United 0 Manchester United 2	St James' Park
18	28459	1937/38	15/04/38	Football League Division 2	Burnley 1 Manchester United 0	Turf Moor
19	28104	1974/75	09/11/74	Football League Division 2	Bristol City 1 Manchester United 0	Ashton Gate
20	28000	1904/05	22/04/05	Football League Division 2	Liverpool 4 Manchester United 0	Anfield
21	27245	1935/36	10/04/36	Football League Division 2	Burnley 2 Manchester United 2	Turf Moor
22	26513	1974/75	05/10/74	Football League Division 2	Fulham 1 Manchester United 2	Craven Cottage
23	26384	1974/75	28/12/74	Football League Division 2	Oldham Athletic 1 Manchester United 0	Boundary Park
24	25852	1935/36	22/02/36	Football League Division 2	Sheffield United 1 Manchester United 1	Bramall Lane
25	25700	1933/34	26/08/33	Football League Division 2	Plymouth Argyle 4 Manchester United 0	Home Park

TOP 25 ATTENDANCES - ALL FA CUP MATCHES - HOME

#	ATT	SEASON	DATE	COMPETITION / ROUND	MATCH RESULT	VENUE
1	82771	1948/49	29/01/49	FA Cup 4th Round	Manchester United 1 Bradford Park Avenue 1	Maine Road
2	81565	1948/49	12/02/49	FA Cup 5th Round	Manchester United 8 Yeovil Town 0	Maine Road
3	75550	2007/08	16/02/08	FA Cup 5th Round	Manchester United 4 Arsenal 0	Old Trafford
4	75463	2007/08	08/03/08	FA Cup 6th Round	Manchester United 0 Portsmouth 1	Old Trafford
5	75369	2007/08	27/01/08	FA Cup 4th Round	Manchester United 3 Tottenham Hotspur 1	Old Trafford
6	74924	2006/07	07/01/07	FA Cup 3rd Round	Manchester United 2 Aston Villa 1	Old Trafford
7	74213	1947/48	28/02/48	FA Cup 6th Round	Manchester United 4 Preston North End 2	Maine Road
8	74000	1947/48	24/01/48	FA Cup 4th Round	Manchester United 3 Liverpool 0	Goodison Park
9	71325	2006/07	19/03/07	FA Cup 6th Round Replay	Manchester United 1 Middlesbrough 0	Old Trafford
10	71137	2006/07	27/01/07	FA Cup 4th Round	Manchester United 2 Portsmouth 1	Old Trafford
11	70608	2006/07	17/02/07	FA Cup 5th Round	Manchester United 1 Reading 1	Old Trafford
12	70434	1948/49	07/02/49	FA Cup 4th Round 2nd Replay	Manchester United 5 Bradford Park Avenue 0	Maine Road
13	67614	2003/04	06/03/04	FA Cup 6th Round	Manchester United 2 Fulham 1	Old Trafford
14	67551	2004/05	08/01/05	FA Cup 3rd Round	Manchester United 0 Exeter City 0	Old Trafford
15	67251	2004/05	29/01/05	FA Cup 4th Round	Manchester United 3 Middlesbrough 0	Old Trafford
16	67228	2003/04	14/02/04	FA Cup 5th Round	Manchester United 4 Manchester City 2	Old Trafford
17	67222	2002/03	04/01/03	FA Cup 3rd Round	Manchester United 4 Portsmouth 1	Old Trafford
18	67209	2002/03	15/02/03	FA Cup 5th Round	Manchester United 0 Arsenal 2	Old Trafford
19	67181	2002/03	26/01/03	FA Cup 4th Round	Manchester United 6 West Ham United 0	Old Trafford
20	67029	2000/01	28/01/01	FA Cup 4th Round	Manchester United 0 West Ham United 1	Old Trafford
21	66673	1923/24	02/02/24	FA Cup 2nd Round	Manchester United 0 Huddersfield Town 3	Old Trafford
22	66350	1959/60	20/02/60	FA Cup 5th Round	Manchester United 0 Sheffield Wednesday 1	Old Trafford
23	65243	1960/61	01/02/61	FA Cup 4th Round Replay	Manchester United 2 Sheffield Wednesday 7	Old Trafford
24	65101	1910/11	04/02/11	FA Cup 2nd Round	Manchester United 2 Aston Villa 1	Old Trafford
25	63700	1963/64	29/02/64	FA Cup 6th Round	Manchester United 3 Sunderland 3	Old Trafford

TOP 25 ATTENDANCES - ALL FA CUP MATCHES - AWAY

#	ATT	SEASON	DATE	COMPETITION / ROUND	MATCH RESULT	VENUE
1	77920	1952/53	14/02/53	FA Cup 5th Round	Everton 2 Manchester United 1	Goodison Park
2	75000	1954/55	19/02/55	FA Cup 5th Round	Manchester City 2 Manchester United 0	Maine Road
3	70362	1949/50	04/03/50	FA Cup 6th Round	Chelsea 2 Manchester United 0	Stamford Bridge
4	68000	1963/64	04/03/64	FA Cup 6th Round Replay	Sunderland 2 Manchester United 2	Roker Park
5	62969	1961/62	21/02/62	FA Cup 5th Round Replay	Sheffield Wednesday 0 Manchester United 2	Hillsborough
6	58683	1947/48	10/01/48	FA Cup 3rd Round	Aston Villa 4 Manchester United 6	Villa Park
7	58250	1957/58	01/03/58	FA Cup 6th Round	West Bromwich Albion 2 Manchester United 2	The Hawthorns
8	58000	1960/61	28/01/61	FA Cup 4th Round	Sheffield Wednesday 1 Manchester United 1	Hillsborough
9	57200	1967/68	31/01/68	FA Cup 3rd Round Replay	Tottenham Hotspur 1 Manchester United 0	White Hart Lane
10	56736	1959/60	30/01/60	FA Cup 4th Round	Liverpool 1 Manchester United 3	Anfield
11	55000	1948/49	26/02/49	FA Cup 6th Round	Hull City 0 Manchester United 1	Boothferry Park
12	54161	1987/88	20/02/88	FA Cup 5th Round	Arsenal 2 Manchester United 1	Highbury
13	54000	1953/54	09/01/54	FA Cup 3rd Round	Burnley 5 Manchester United 3	Turf Moor
14	53581	1964/65	10/03/65	FA Cup 6th Round	Wolverhampton Wanderers 3 Manchester United 5	Molineux
15	53500	1965/66	05/03/66	FA Cup 5th Round	Wolverhampton Wanderers 2 Manchester United 4	Molineux
16	53009	1964/65	30/01/65	FA Cup 4th Round	Stoke City 0 Manchester United 0	Victoria Ground
17	52500	1968/69	08/02/69	FA Cup 5th Round	Birmingham City 2 Manchester United 2	St Andrews
18	51800	1978/79	10/03/79	FA Cup 6th Round	Tottenham Hotspur 1 Manchester United 1	White Hart Lane
19	50500	1925/26	20/02/26	FA Cup 5th Round	Sunderland 3 Manchester United 3	Roker Park
20	50000	1950/51	24/02/51	FA Cup 5th Round	Birmingham City 1 Manchester United 0	St Andrews
21	49962	1949/50	15/02/50	FA Cup 5th Round Replay	Portsmouth 1 Manchester United 3	Fratton Park
22	49192	1971/72	22/03/72	FA Cup 6th Round Replay	Stoke City 2 Manchester United 1	Victoria Ground
23	49119	1952/53	05/02/53	FA Cup 4th Round Replay	Walthamstow Avenue 2 Manchester United 5	Highbury
24	45637	1936/37	30/01/37	FA Cup 4th Round	Arsenal 5 Manchester United 0	Highbury
25	45207	1979/80	05/01/80	FA Cup 3rd Round	Tottenham Hotspur 1 Manchester United 1	White Hart Lane

TOP 25 ATTENDANCES - ALL FA CUP MATCHES - ANY VENUE

#	ATT	SEASON	DATE	COMPETITION / ROUND	MATCH RESULT	VENUE
1	100000	1956/57	04/05/57	FA Cup Final	Manchester United 1 Aston Villa 2	Wembley
2	100000	1957/58	03/05/58	FA Cup Final	Manchester United 0 Bolton Wanderers 2	Wembley
3	100000	1962/63	25/05/63	FA Cup Final	Manchester United 3 Leicester City 1	Wembley
4	100000	1975/76	01/05/76	FA Cup Final	Manchester United 0 Southampton 1	Wembley
5	100000	1976/77	21/05/77	FA Cup Final	Manchester United 2 Liverpool 1	Wembley
6	100000	1978/79	12/05/79	FA Cup Final	Manchester United 2 Arsenal 3	Wembley
7	100000	1982/83	21/05/83	FA Cup Final	Manchester United 2 Brighton 2	Wembley
8	100000	1984/85	18/05/85	FA Cup Final	Manchester United 1 Everton 0	Wembley
9	99000	1947/48	24/04/48	FA Cup Final	Manchester United 4 Blackpool 2	Wembley
10	92000	1982/83	26/05/83	FA Cup Final Replay	Manchester United 4 Brighton 0	Wembley
11	89826	2006/07	19/05/07	FA Cup Final	Manchester United 0 Chelsea 1	Wembley
12	82771	1948/49	29/01/49	FA Cup 4th Round	Manchester United 1 Bradford Park Avenue 1	Maine Road
13	81565	1948/49	12/02/49	FA Cup 5th Round	Manchester United 8 Yeovil Town 0	Maine Road
14	80000	1989/90	12/05/90	FA Cup Final	Manchester United 3 Crystal Palace 3	Wembley
15	80000	1989/90	17/05/90	FA Cup Final Replay	Manchester United 1 Crystal Palace 0	Wembley
16	79634	1993/94	14/05/94	FA Cup Final	Manchester United 4 Chelsea 0	Wembley
17	79592	1994/95	20/05/95	FA Cup Final	Manchester United 0 Everton 1	Wembley
18	79101	1998/99	22/05/99	FA Cup Final	Manchester United 2 Newcastle United 0	Wembley
19	79007	1995/96	11/05/96	FA Cup Final	Manchester United 1 Liverpool 0	Wembley
20	77920	1952/53	14/02/53	FA Cup 5th Round	Everton 2 Manchester United 1	Goodison Park
21	75550	2007/08	16/02/08	FA Cup 5th Round	Manchester United 4 Arsenal 0	Old Trafford
22	75463	2007/08	08/03/08	FA Cup 6th Round	Manchester United 0 Portsmouth 1	Old Trafford
23	75369	2007/08	27/01/08	FA Cup 4th Round	Manchester United 3 Tottenham Hotspur 1	Old Trafford
24	75000	1954/55	19/02/55	FA Cup 4th Round	Manchester City 2 Manchester United 0	Maine Road
25	74924	2006/07	07/01/07	FA Cup 3rd Round	Manchester United 2 Aston Villa 1	Old Trafford

TOP 25 ATTENDANCES - ALL LEAGUE CUP MATCHES - HOME

#	ATT	SEASON	DATE	COMPETITION / ROUND	MATCH RESULT	VENUE
1	74055	2007/08	26/09/07	League Cup 3rd Round	Manchester United 0 Coventry City 2	Old Trafford
2	67103	2004/05	01/12/04	League Cup 5th Round	Manchester United 1 Arsenal 0	Old Trafford
3	67000	2004/05	26/01/05	League Cup Semi-Final 2nd Leg	Manchester United 1 Chelsea 2	Old Trafford
4	63418	1969/70	17/12/69	League Cup Semi-Final 2nd Leg	Manchester United 2 Manchester City 2	Old Trafford
5	62740	2002/03	07/01/03	League Cup Semi-Final 1st Leg	Manchester United 1 Blackburn Rovers 1	Old Trafford
6	61636	2005/06	25/01/06	League Cup Semi-Final 2nd Leg	Manchester United 2 Blackburn Rovers 1	Old Trafford
7	58010	1974/75	15/01/75	League Cup Semi-Final 1st Leg	Manchester United 2 Norwich City 2	Old Trafford
8	57985	2002/03	17/12/02	League Cup 5th Round	Manchester United 1 Chelsea 0	Old Trafford
9	57738	1976/77	01/12/76	League Cup 5th Round	Manchester United 0 Everton 3	Old Trafford
10	57393	1969/70	19/11/69	League Cup 5th Round Replay	Manchester United 1 Derby County 0	Old Trafford
11	56635	1982/83	23/02/83	League Cup Semi-Final 2nd Leg	Manchester United 2 Arsenal 1	Old Trafford
12	55890	1981/82	28/10/81	League Cup 2nd Round 2nd Leg	Manchester United 0 Tottenham Hotspur 1	Old Trafford
13	55169	1974/75	09/10/74	League Cup 3rd Round	Manchester United 1 Manchester City 0	Old Trafford
14	52495	1998/99	28/10/98	League Cup 3rd Round	Manchester United 2 Bury 0	Old Trafford
15	52002	1976/77	27/10/76	League Cup 4th Round	Manchester United 7 Newcastle United 2	Old Trafford
16	50918	1984/85	30/10/84	League Cup 3rd Round	Manchester United 1 Everton 2	Old Trafford
17	50275	1969/70	20/10/69	League Cup 4th Round Replay	Manchester United 1 Burnley 0	Old Trafford
18	49501	1974/75	18/12/74	League Cup 5th Round Replay	Manchester United 3 Middlesbrough 0	Old Trafford
19	49305	1996/97	23/10/96	League Cup 3rd Round	Manchester United 2 Swindon Town 1	Old Trafford
20	48961	1970/71	18/11/70	League Cup 5th Round	Manchester United 4 Crystal Palace 2	Old Trafford
21	48924	2005/06	30/11/05	League Cup 4th Round	Manchester United 3 West Bromwich Albion 1	Old Trafford
22	48891	2004/05	10/11/04	League Cup 4th Round	Manchester United 2 Crystal Palace 0	Old Trafford
23	48889	1971/72	16/12/70	League Cup Semi-Final 1st Leg	Manchester United 1 Aston Villa 1	Old Trafford
24	48347	1969/70	23/09/69	League Cup 3rd Round	Manchester United 2 Wrexham 0	Old Trafford
25	48292	1979/80	05/09/79	League Cup 2nd Round 2nd Leg	Manchester United 3 Tottenham Hotspur 1	Old Trafford

TOP 25 ATTENDANCES - ALL LEAGUE CUP MATCHES - AWAY

#	ATT	SEASON	DATE	COMPETITION / ROUND	MATCH RESULT	VENUE
1	58667	1970/71	23/12/70	League Cup Semi-Final 2nd Leg	Aston Villa 2 Manchester United 1	Villa Park
2	55799	1969/70	03/12/69	League Cup Semi-Final 1st Leg	Manchester City 2 Manchester United 1	Maine Road
3	50182	1975/76	12/11/75	League Cup 4th Round	Manchester City 4 Manchester United 0	Maine Road
4	47543	2000/01	28/11/00	League Cup 4th Round	Sunderland 2 Manchester United 1	Stadium of Light
5	46170	1976/77	04/10/76	League Cup 3rd Round Replay	Sunderland 2 Manchester United 2	Roker Park
6	43136	1982/83	15/02/83	League Cup Semi-Final 1st Leg	Arsenal 2 Manchester United 4	Highbury
7	42249	1971/72	15/11/71	League Cup 4th Round 2nd Replay	Stoke City 2 Manchester United 1	Victoria Ground
8	41761	1978/79	30/08/78	League Cup 2nd Round	Stockport County 2 Manchester United 3	Old Trafford
9	41492	2004/05	12/01/05	League Cup Semi-Final 1st Leg	Chelsea 0 Manchester United 0	Stamford Bridge
10	41447	1975/76	08/10/75	League Cup 3rd Round	Aston Villa 1 Manchester United 2	Villa Park
11	41291	1985/86	26/11/85	League Cup 4th Round	Liverpool 2 Manchester United 1	Anfield
12	40844	1990/91	28/11/90	League Cup 4th Round	Arsenal 2 Manchester United 6	Highbury
13	40805	1971/72	08/11/71	League Cup 4th Round Replay	Stoke City 0 Manchester United 0	Victoria Ground
14	39333	1981/82	07/10/81	League Cup 2nd Round 1st Leg	Tottenham Hotspur 1 Manchester United 0	White Hart Lane
15	38895	1969/70	12/11/69	League Cup 5th Round	Derby County 0 Manchester United 0	Baseball Ground
16	37546	2003/04	28/10/03	League Cup 3rd Round	Leeds United 2 Manchester United 3	Elland Road
17	36171	1977/78	30/08/77	League Cup 2nd Round	Arsenal 3 Manchester United 2	Highbury
18	36005	1974/75	04/12/74	League Cup 5th Round	Middlesbrough 0 Manchester United 0	Ayresome Park
19	35964	1992/93	28/10/92	League Cup 3rd Round	Aston Villa 1 Manchester United 0	Villa Park
20	35702	1998/99	02/12/98	League Cup 5th Round	Tottenham Hotspur 3 Manchester United 1	White Hart Lane
21	34878	1993/94	02/03/94	League Cup Semi-Final 2nd Leg	Sheffield Wednesday 1 Manchester United 4	Hillsborough
22	34178	1994/95	26/10/94	League Cup 3rd Round	Newcastle United 2 Manchester United 0	St James' Park
23	34052	1993/94	30/11/93	League Cup 4th Round	Everton 0 Manchester United 2	Goodison Park
24	33957	1972/73	03/10/72	League Cup 3rd Round	Bristol Rovers 1 Manchester United 1	Eastville
25	33815	1999/00	13/10/99	League Cup 3rd Round	Aston Villa 3 Manchester United 0	Villa Park

TOP 25 ATTENDANCES - ALL LEAGUE CUP MATCHES - ANY VENUE

#	ATT	SEASON	DATE	COMPETITION / ROUND	MATCH RESULT	VENUE
1	100000	1982/83	26/03/83	League Cup Final	Manchester United 1 Liverpool 2	Wembley
2	77612	1990/91	21/04/91	League Cup Final	Manchester United 0 Sheffield Wednesday 1	Wembley
3	77231	1993/94	27/03/94	League Cup Final	Manchester United 1 Aston Villa 3	Wembley
4	76810	1991/92	12/04/92	League Cup Final	Manchester United 1 Nottingham Forest 0	Wembley
5	74500	2002/03	02/03/03	League Cup Final	Manchester United 0 Liverpool 2	Millennium Stadium
6	74055	2007/08	26/09/07	League Cup 3rd Round	Manchester United 0 Coventry City 2	Old Trafford
7	67103	2004/05	01/12/04	League Cup 5th Round	Manchester United 1 Arsenal 0	Old Trafford
8	67000	2004/05	26/01/05	League Cup Semi-Final 2nd Leg	Manchester United 1 Chelsea 2	Old Trafford
9	66866	2005/06	26/02/06	League Cup Final	Manchester United 4 Wigan Athletic 0	Millennium Stadium
10	63418	1969/70	17/12/69	League Cup Semi-Final 2nd Leg	Manchester United 2 Manchester City 2	Old Trafford
11	62740	2002/03	07/01/03	League Cup Semi-Final 1st Leg	Manchester United 1 Blackburn Rovers 1	Old Trafford
12	61636	2005/06	25/01/06	League Cup Semi-Final 2nd Leg	Manchester United 2 Blackburn Rovers 1	Old Trafford
13	58667	1970/71	23/12/70	League Cup Semi-Final 2nd Leg	Aston Villa 2 Manchester United 1	Villa Park
14	58010	1974/75	15/01/75	League Cup Semi-Final 1st Leg	Manchester United 2 Norwich City 2	Old Trafford
15	57985	2002/03	17/12/02	League Cup 5th Round	Manchester United 1 Chelsea 0	Old Trafford
16	57738	1976/77	01/12/76	League Cup 5th Round	Manchester United 0 Everton 3	Old Trafford
17	57393	1969/70	19/11/69	League Cup 5th Round Replay	Manchester United 1 Derby County 0	Old Trafford
18	56635	1982/83	23/02/83	League Cup Semi-Final 2nd Leg	Manchester United 2 Arsenal 1	Old Trafford
19	55890	1981/82	28/10/81	League Cup 2nd Round 2nd Leg	Manchester United 0 Tottenham Hotspur 1	Old Trafford
20	55799	1969/70	03/12/69	League Cup Semi-Final 1st Leg	Manchester City 2 Manchester United 1	Maine Road
21	55169	1974/75	09/10/74	League Cup 3rd Round	Manchester United 1 Manchester City 0	Old Trafford
22	52495	1998/99	28/10/98	League Cup 3rd Round	Manchester United 2 Bury 0	Old Trafford
23	52002	1976/77	27/10/76	League Cup 4th Round	Manchester United 7 Newcastle United 2	Old Trafford
24	50918	1984/85	30/10/84	League Cup 3rd Round	Manchester United 1 Everton 2	Old Trafford
25	50275	1969/70	20/10/69	League Cup 4th Round Replay	Manchester United 1 Burnley 0	Old Trafford

TOP 25 ATTENDANCES - ALL EUROPEAN MATCHES - HOME

#	ATT	SEASON	DATE	COMPETITION / ROUND	MATCH RESULT			VENUE
1	75598	1956/57	17/10/56	European Cup 1st Round 1st Leg	Manchester United 3	Borussia Dortmund 2		Maine Road
2	75520	2007/08	04/03/08	Champions League 2nd Round 2nd Leg	Manchester United 1	Olympique Lyonnais 0		Old Trafford
3	75182	2006/07	07/03/07	Champions League 2nd Round 2nd Leg	Manchester United 1	Lille Metropole 0		Old Trafford
4	75162	2007/08	27/11/07	Champions League Phase 1 Match 5	Manchester United 2	Sporting Lisbon 1		Old Trafford
5	75061	2007/08	29/04/08	Champions League Semi-Final 2nd Leg	Manchester United 1	Barcelona 0		Old Trafford
6	75017	2007/08	07/11/07	Champions League Phase 1 Match 4	Manchester United 4	Dynamo Kiev 0		Old Trafford
7	74955	2006/07	06/12/06	Champions League Phase 1 Match 6	Manchester United 3	Benfica 1		Old Trafford
8	74476	2006/07	10/04/07	Champions League Quarter-Final 2nd Leg	Manchester United 7	Roma 1		Old Trafford
9	74423	2007/08	09/04/08	Champions League Quarter-Final 2nd Leg	Manchester United 1	Roma 0		Old Trafford
10	74031	2006/07	13/09/06	Champions League Phase 1 Match 1	Manchester United 3	Glasgow Celtic 2		Old Trafford
11	73820	2006/07	24/04/07	Champions League Semi-Final 1st Leg	Manchester United 3	AC Milan 2		Old Trafford
12	73652	2007/08	02/10/07	Champions League Phase 1 Match 2	Manchester United 1	Roma 0		Old Trafford
13	72020	2006/07	17/10/06	Champions League Phase 1 Match 3	Manchester United 3	Copenhagen 0		Old Trafford
14	70000	1956/57	06/02/57	European Cup Quarter-Final 2nd Leg	Manchester United 3	Athletic Bilbao 0		Maine Road
15	67471	2005/06	22/11/05	Champions League Phase 1 Match 5	Manchester United 0	Villarreal 0		Old Trafford
16	67162	2004/05	23/02/05	Champions League 2nd Round 1st Leg	Manchester United 0	AC Milan 1		Old Trafford
17	67141	2003/04	09/12/03	Champions League Phase 1 Match 6	Manchester United 2	Stuttgart 0		Old Trafford
18	67128	2004/05	28/09/04	Champions League Phase 1 Match 2	Manchester United 6	Fenerbahce 2		Old Trafford
19	67029	2003/04	09/03/04	Champions League 2nd Round 2nd Leg	Manchester United 1	Porto 1		Old Trafford
20	67014	2002/03	11/12/02	Champions League Phase 2 Match 2	Manchester United 2	Deportivo La Coruna 0		Old Trafford
21	66902	2002/03	01/10/02	Champions League Phase 1 Match 3	Manchester United 4	Olympiakos Piraeus 0		Old Trafford
22	66870	2002/03	12/03/03	Champions League Phase 2 Match 5	Manchester United 1	Basel 1		Old Trafford
23	66818	2001/02	13/03/02	Champions League Phase 2 Match 5	Manchester United 0	Bayern Munich 0		Old Trafford
24	66814	2002/03	27/08/02	Champions League Qual. Round 2nd Leg	Manchester United 5	Zalaegerszeg 0		Old Trafford
25	66776	2000/01	08/11/00	Champions League Phase 1 Match 6	Manchester United 1	Dynamo Kiev 0		Old Trafford

TOP 25 ATTENDANCES - ALL EUROPEAN MATCHES - AWAY

#	ATT	SEASON	DATE	COMPETITION / ROUND	MATCH RESULT		VENUE
1	135000	1956/57	11/04/57	European Cup Semi-Final 1st Leg	Real Madrid 3 Manchester United 1		Bernabeu Stadium
2	125000	1967/68	15/05/68	European Cup Semi-Final 2nd Leg	Real Madrid 3 Manchester United 3		Bernabeu Stadium
3	114273	1994/95	02/11/94	Champions League Phase 1 Match 4	Barcelona 4 Manchester United 0		Estadio Camp Nou
4	105000	1967/68	13/03/68	European Cup Quarter-Final 2nd Leg	Gornik Zabrze 1 Manchester United 0		Stadion Slaski
5	95949	2007/08	23/04/08	Champions League Semi-Final 1st Leg	Barcelona 0 Manchester United 0		Estadio Camp Nou
6	80000	1957/58	14/05/58	European Cup Semi-Final 2nd Leg	AC Milan 4 Manchester United 0		Stadio San Siro
7	80000	1968/69	23/04/69	European Cup Semi-Final 1st Leg	AC Milan 2 Manchester United 0		Stadio San Siro
8	79528	1998/99	17/03/99	Champions League Quarter-Final 2nd Leg	Internazionale 1 Manchester United 1		Stadio San Siro
9	78957	2004/05	08/03/05	Champions League 2nd Round 1st Leg	AC Milan 1 Manchester United 0		San Siro Stadium
10	78500	2006/07	02/05/07	Champions League Semi-Final 2nd Leg	AC Milan 3 Manchester United 0		Stadio San Siro
11	77000	2006/07	04/04/07	Champions League Quarter-Final 1st Leg	Roma 2 Manchester United 1		Olympic Stadium
12	75000	1965/66	09/03/66	European Cup Quarter-Final 2nd Leg	Benfica 1 Manchester United 5		Estadio da Luz
13	75000	2002/03	08/04/03	Champions League Quarter-Final 1st Leg	Real Madrid 3 Manchester United 1		Bernabeu Stadium
14	73537	2001/02	10/10/01	Champions League Phase 1 Match 3	Olympiakos Piraeus 0 Manchester United 2		Olympic Stadium
15	70000	1977/78	19/10/77	European CWC 2nd Round 1st Leg	Porto 4 Manchester United 0		Estadio das Antas
16	70000	1983/84	07/03/84	European CWC 3rd Round 1st Leg	Barcelona 2 Manchester United 0		Estadio Camp Nou
17	67648	1998/99	25/11/98	Champions League Phase 1 Match 5	Barcelona 3 Manchester United 3		Estadio Camp Nou
18	66632	1976/77	03/11/76	UEFA Cup 2nd Round 2nd Leg	Juventus 3 Manchester United 0		Stadio Comunale
19	65000	2000/01	19/09/00	Champions League Phase 1 Match 2	Dynamo Kiev 0 Manchester United 0		Republican
20	65000	2005/06	02/11/05	Champions League Phase 1 Match 4	Lille Metropole 1 Manchester United 0		Stade de France
21	64655	1983/84	25/04/84	European CWC Semi-Final 2nd Leg	Juventus 2 Manchester United 1		Stadio Comunale
22	64500	1998/99	21/04/99	Champions League Semi-Final 2nd Leg	Juventus 2 Manchester United 3		Stadio Delle Alpi
23	64119	1999/00	04/04/00	Champions League Quarter-Final 1st Leg	Real Madrid 0 Manchester United 0		Bernabeu Stadium
24	61000	2005/06	07/12/05	Champions League Phase 1 Match 6	Benfica 2 Manchester United 1		Estadio da Luz
25	61000	2006/07	26/09/06	Champions League Phase 1 Match 2	Benfica 0 Manchester United 1		Estadio da Luz

TOP 25 ATTENDANCES - ALL EUROPEAN MATCHES - ANY VENUE

#	ATT	SEASON	DATE	COMPETITION / ROUND	MATCH RESULT		VENUE
1	135000	1956/57	11/04/57	European Cup Semi-Final 1st Leg	Real Madrid 3 Manchester United 1		Bernabeu Stadium
2	125000	1967/68	15/05/68	European Cup Semi-Final 2nd Leg	Real Madrid 3 Manchester United 3		Bernabeu Stadium
3	114273	1994/95	02/11/94	Champions League Phase 1 Match 4	Barcelona 4 Manchester United 0		Estadio Camp Nou
4	105000	1967/68	13/03/68	European Cup Quarter-Final 2nd Leg	Gornik Zabrze 1 Manchester United 0		Stadion Slaski
5	100000	1967/68	29/05/68	European Cup Final	Manchester United 4 Benfica 1		Wembley
6	95949	2007/08	23/04/08	Champions League Semi-Final 1st Leg	Barcelona 0 Manchester United 0		Estadio Camp Nou
7	90000	1998/99	26/05/99	Champions League Final	Manchester United 2 Bayern Munich 1		Estadio Camp Nou
8	80000	1957/58	14/05/58	European Cup Semi-Final 2nd Leg	AC Milan 4 Manchester United 0		Stadio San Siro
9	80000	1968/69	23/04/69	European Cup Semi-Final 1st Leg	AC Milan 2 Manchester United 0		Stadio San Siro
10	79528	1998/99	17/03/99	Champions League Quarter-Final 2nd Leg	Internazionale 1 Manchester United 1		Stadio San Siro
11	78957	2004/05	08/03/05	Champions League 2nd Round 1st Leg	AC Milan 1 Manchester United 0		San Siro Stadium
12	78500	2006/07	02/05/07	Champions League Semi-Final 2nd Leg	AC Milan 3 Manchester United 0		Stadio San Siro
13	77000	2006/07	04/04/07	Champions League Quarter-Final 1st Leg	Roma 2 Manchester United 1		Olympic Stadium
14	75598	1956/57	17/10/56	European Cup 1st Round 1st Leg	Manchester United 3 Borussia Dortmund 2		Maine Road
15	75520	2007/08	04/03/08	Champions League 2nd Round 2nd Leg	Manchester United 1 Olympique Lyonnais 0		Old Trafford
16	75182	2006/07	07/03/07	Champions League 2nd Round 2nd Leg	Manchester United 1 Lille Metropole 0		Old Trafford
17	75162	2007/08	27/11/07	Champions League Phase 1 Match 5	Manchester United 2 Sporting Lisbon 1		Old Trafford
18	75061	2007/08	29/04/08	Champions League Semi-Final 2nd Leg	Manchester United 1 Barcelona 0		Old Trafford
19	75017	2007/08	07/11/07	Champions League Phase 1 Match 4	Manchester United 4 Dynamo Kiev 0		Old Trafford
20	75000	1965/66	09/03/66	European Cup Quarter-Final 2nd Leg	Benfica 1 Manchester United 5		Estadio da Luz
21	75000	2002/03	08/04/03	Champions League Quarter-Final 1st Leg	Real Madrid 3 Manchester United 1		Bernabeu Stadium
22	74955	2006/07	06/12/06	Champions League Phase 1 Match 6	Manchester United 3 Benfica 1		Old Trafford
23	74476	2006/07	10/04/07	Champions League Quarter-Final 2nd Leg	Manchester United 7 Roma 1		Old Trafford
24	74423	2007/08	09/04/08	Champions League Quarter-Final 2nd Leg	Manchester United 1 Roma 0		Old Trafford
25	74031	2006/07	13/09/06	Champions League Phase 1 Match 1	Manchester United 3 Glasgow Celtic 2		Old Trafford

TOP 25 ATTENDANCES - ALL EUROPEAN CUP MATCHES - HOME

#	ATT	SEASON	DATE	COMPETITION / ROUND	MATCH RESULT	VENUE
1	75598	1956/57	17/10/56	European Cup 1st Round 1st Leg	Manchester United 3 Borussia Dortmund 2	Maine Road
2	75520	2007/08	04/03/08	Champions League 2nd Round 2nd Leg	Manchester United 1 Olympique Lyonnais 0	Old Trafford
3	75182	2006/07	07/03/07	Champions League 2nd Round 2nd Leg	Manchester United 1 Lille Metropole 0	Old Trafford
4	75162	2007/08	27/11/07	Champions League Phase 1 Match 5	Manchester United 2 Sporting Lisbon 1	Old Trafford
5	75061	2007/08	29/04/08	Champions League Semi-Final 2nd Leg	Manchester United 1 Barcelona 0	Old Trafford
6	75017	2007/08	07/11/07	Champions League Phase 1 Match 4	Manchester United 4 Dynamo Kiev 0	Old Trafford
7	74955	2006/07	06/12/06	Champions League Phase 1 Match 6	Manchester United 3 Benfica 1	Old Trafford
8	74476	2006/07	10/04/07	Champions League Quarter-Final 2nd Leg	Manchester United 7 Roma 1	Old Trafford
9	74423	2007/08	09/04/08	Champions League Quarter-Final 2nd Leg	Manchester United 1 Roma 0	Old Trafford
10	74031	2006/07	13/09/06	Champions League Phase 1 Match 1	Manchester United 3 Glasgow Celtic 2	Old Trafford
11	73820	2006/07	24/04/07	Champions League Semi-Final 1st Leg	Manchester United 3 AC Milan 2	Old Trafford
12	73652	2007/08	02/10/07	Champions League Phase 1 Match 2	Manchester United 1 Roma 0	Old Trafford
13	72020	2006/07	17/10/06	Champions League Phase 1 Match 3	Manchester United 3 Copenhagen 0	Old Trafford
14	70000	1956/57	06/02/57	European Cup Quarter-Final 2nd Leg	Manchester United 3 Athletic Bilbao 0	Maine Road
15	67471	2005/06	22/11/05	Champions League Phase 1 Match 5	Manchester United 0 Villarreal 0	Old Trafford
16	67162	2004/05	23/02/05	Champions League 2nd Round 1st Leg	Manchester United 0 AC Milan 1	Old Trafford
17	67141	2003/04	09/12/03	Champions League Phase 1 Match 6	Manchester United 2 Stuttgart 0	Old Trafford
18	67128	2004/05	28/09/04	Champions League Phase 1 Match 2	Manchester United 6 Fenerbahce 2	Old Trafford
19	67029	2003/04	09/03/04	Champions League 2nd Round 2nd Leg	Manchester United 1 Porto 1	Old Trafford
20	67014	2002/03	11/12/02	Champions League Phase 2 Match 2	Manchester United 2 Deportivo La Coruna 0	Old Trafford
21	66902	2002/03	01/10/02	Champions League Phase 1 Match 3	Manchester United 4 Olympiakos Piraeus 0	Old Trafford
22	66870	2002/03	12/03/03	Champions League Phase 2 Match 5	Manchester United 1 Basel 1	Old Trafford
23	66818	2001/02	13/03/02	Champions League Phase 2 Match 5	Manchester United 0 Bayern Munich 0	Old Trafford
24	66814	2002/03	27/08/02	Champions League Qual. Round 2nd Leg	Manchester United 5 Zalaegerszeg 0	Old Trafford
25	66776	2000/01	08/11/00	Champions League Phase 1 Match 6	Manchester United 1 Dynamo Kiev 0	Old Trafford

TOP 25 ATTENDANCES - ALL EUROPEAN CUP MATCHES - AWAY

#	ATT	SEASON	DATE	COMPETITION / ROUND	MATCH RESULT	VENUE
1	135000	1956/57	11/04/57	European Cup Semi-Final 1st Leg	Real Madrid 3 Manchester United 1	Bernabeu Stadium
2	125000	1967/68	15/05/68	European Cup Semi-Final 2nd Leg	Real Madrid 3 Manchester United 3	Bernabeu Stadium
3	114273	1994/95	02/11/94	Champions League Phase 1 Match 4	Barcelona 4 Manchester United 0	Estadio Camp Nou
4	105000	1967/68	13/03/68	European Cup Quarter-Final 2nd Leg	Gornik Zabrze 1 Manchester United 0	Stadion Slaski
5	95949	2007/08	23/04/08	Champions League Semi-Final 1st Leg	Barcelona 0 Manchester United 0	Estadio Camp Nou
6	80000	1957/58	14/05/58	European Cup Semi-Final 2nd Leg	AC Milan 4 Manchester United 0	Stadio San Siro
7	80000	1968/69	23/04/69	European Cup Semi-Final 1st Leg	AC Milan 2 Manchester United 0	Stadio San Siro
8	79528	1998/99	17/03/99	Champions League Quarter-Final 2nd Leg	Internazionale 1 Manchester United 1	Stadio San Siro
9	78957	2004/05	08/03/05	Champions League 2nd Round 1st Leg	AC Milan 1 Manchester United 0	San Siro Stadium
10	78500	2006/07	02/05/07	Champions League Semi-Final 2nd Leg	AC Milan 3 Manchester United 0	Stadio San Siro
11	77000	2006/07	04/04/07	Champions League Quarter-Final 1st Leg	Roma 2 Manchester United 1	Olympic Stadium
12	75000	1965/66	09/03/66	European Cup Quarter-Final 2nd Leg	Benfica 1 Manchester United 5	Estadio da Luz
13	75000	2002/03	08/04/03	Champions League Quarter-Final 1st Leg	Real Madrid 3 Manchester United 1	Bernabeu Stadium
14	73537	2001/02	10/10/01	Champions League Phase 1 Match 3	Olympiakos Piraeus 0 Manchester United 2	Olympic Stadium
15	67648	1998/99	25/11/98	Champions League Phase 1 Match 5	Barcelona 3 Manchester United 3	Estadio Camp Nou
16	65000	2000/01	19/09/00	Champions League Phase 1 Match 2	Dynamo Kiev 0 Manchester United 0	Republican
17	65000	2005/06	02/11/05	Champions League Phase 1 Match 4	Lille Metropole 1 Manchester United 0	Stade de France
18	64500	1998/99	21/04/99	Champions League Semi-Final 2nd Leg	Juventus 2 Manchester United 3	Stadio Delle Alpi
19	64119	1999/00	04/04/00	Champions League Quarter-Final 1st Leg	Real Madrid 0 Manchester United 0	Bernabeu Stadium
20	61000	2005/06	07/12/05	Champions League Phase 1 Match 6	Benfica 2 Manchester United 1	Estadio da Luz
21	61000	2006/07	26/09/06	Champions League Phase 1 Match 2	Benfica 0 Manchester United 1	Estadio da Luz
22	60931	2007/08	01/04/08	Champions League Quarter-Final 1st Leg	Roma 0 Manchester United 2	Olympic Stadium
23	60632	2006/07	21/11/06	Champions League Phase 1 Match 5	Glasgow Celtic 1 Manchester United 0	Celtic Park
24	60000	1956/57	16/01/57	European Cup Quarter-Final 1st Leg	Athletic Bilbao 5 Manchester United 3	Estadio San Mames
25	60000	1965/66	13/04/66	European Cup Semi-Final 1st Leg	Partizan Belgrade 2 Manchester United 0	Stadion JNA

TOP 25 ATTENDANCES - ALL EUROPEAN CUP MATCHES - ANY VENUE

#	ATT	SEASON	DATE	COMPETITION / ROUND	MATCH RESULT	VENUE
1	135000	1956/57	11/04/57	European Cup Semi-Final 1st Leg	Real Madrid 3 Manchester United 1	Bernabeu Stadium
2	125000	1967/68	15/05/68	European Cup Semi-Final 2nd Leg	Real Madrid 3 Manchester United 3	Bernabeu Stadium
3	114273	1994/95	02/11/94	Champions League Phase 1 Match 4	Barcelona 4 Manchester United 0	Estadio Camp Nou
4	105000	1967/68	13/03/68	European Cup Quarter-Final 2nd Leg	Gornik Zabrze 1 Manchester United 0	Stadion Slaski
5	100000	1967/68	29/05/68	European Cup Final	Manchester United 4 Benfica 1	Wembley
6	95949	2007/08	23/04/08	Champions League Semi-Final 1st Leg	Barcelona 0 Manchester United 0	Estadio Camp Nou
7	90000	1998/99	26/05/99	Champions League Final	Manchester United 2 Bayern Munich 1	Estadio Camp Nou
8	80000	1957/58	14/05/58	European Cup Semi-Final 2nd Leg	AC Milan 4 Manchester United 0	Stadio San Siro
9	80000	1968/69	23/04/69	European Cup Semi-Final 1st Leg	AC Milan 2 Manchester United 0	Stadio San Siro
10	79528	1998/99	17/03/99	Champions League Quarter-Final 2nd Leg	Internazionale 1 Manchester United 1	Stadio San Siro
11	78957	2004/05	08/03/05	Champions League 2nd Round 1st Leg	AC Milan 1 Manchester United 0	San Siro Stadium
12	78500	2006/07	02/05/07	Champions League Semi-Final 2nd Leg	AC Milan 3 Manchester United 0	Stadio San Siro
13	77000	2006/07	04/04/07	Champions League Quarter-Final 1st Leg	Roma 2 Manchester United 1	Olympic Stadium
14	75598	1956/57	17/10/56	European Cup 1st Round 1st Leg	Manchester United 3 Borussia Dortmund 2	Maine Road
15	75520	2007/08	04/03/08	Champions League 2nd Round 2nd Leg	Manchester United 1 Olympique Lyonnais 0	Old Trafford
16	75182	2006/07	07/03/07	Champions League 2nd Round 2nd Leg	Manchester United 1 Lille Metropole 0	Old Trafford
17	75162	2007/08	27/11/07	Champions League Phase 1 Match 5	Manchester United 2 Sporting Lisbon 1	Old Trafford
18	75061	2007/08	29/04/08	Champions League Semi-Final 2nd Leg	Manchester United 1 Barcelona 0	Old Trafford
19	75017	2007/08	07/11/07	Champions League Phase 1 Match 4	Manchester United 4 Dynamo Kiev 0	Old Trafford
20	75000	1965/66	09/03/66	European Cup Quarter-Final 2nd Leg	Benfica 1 Manchester United 5	Estadio da Luz
21	75000	2002/03	08/04/03	Champions League Quarter-Final 1st Leg	Real Madrid 3 Manchester United 1	Bernabeu Stadium
22	74955	2006/07	06/12/06	Champions League Phase 1 Match 6	Manchester United 3 Benfica 1	Old Trafford
23	74476	2006/07	10/04/07	Champions League Quarter-Final 2nd Leg	Manchester United 7 Roma 1	Old Trafford
24	74423	2007/08	09/04/08	Champions League Quarter-Final 2nd Leg	Manchester United 1 Roma 0	Old Trafford
25	74031	2006/07	13/09/06	Champions League Phase 1 Match 1	Manchester United 3 Glasgow Celtic 2	Old Trafford

TOP 25 ATTENDANCES - ALL CUP-WINNERS' CUP MATCHES - ANY VENUE

#	ATT	SEASON	DATE	COMPETITION / ROUND	MATCH RESULT	VENUE
1	70000	1977/78	19/10/77	ECWC 2nd Round 1st Leg	Porto 4 Manchester United 0	Estadio das Antas
2	70000	1983/84	07/03/84	ECWC 3rd Round 1st Leg	Barcelona 2 Manchester United 0	Estadio Camp Nou
3	64655	1983/84	25/04/84	ECWC Semi-Final 2nd Leg	Juventus 2 Manchester United 1	Stadio Comunale
4	60000	1963/64	26/02/64	ECWC Quarter-Final 1st Leg	Manchester United 4 Sporting Lisbon 1	Old Trafford
5	58547	1983/84	21/03/84	ECWC 3rd Round 2nd Leg	Manchester United 3 Barcelona 0	Old Trafford
6	58171	1983/84	11/04/84	ECWC Semi-Final 1st Leg	Manchester United 1 Juventus 1	Old Trafford
7	57447	1963/64	03/12/63	ECWC 2nd Round 1st Leg	Tottenham Hotspur 2 Manchester United 0	White Hart Lane
8	51831	1977/78	02/11/77	ECWC 2nd Round 2nd Leg	Manchester United 5 Porto 2	Old Trafford
9	50000	1963/64	10/12/63	ECWC 2nd Round 2nd Leg	Manchester United 4 Tottenham Hotspur 1	Old Trafford
10	50000	1990/91	15/05/91	ECWC Final	Manchester United 2 Barcelona 1	Feyenoord Stadion
11	46272	1963/64	15/10/63	ECWC 1st Round 2nd Leg	Manchester United 6 Willem II 1	Old Trafford
12	44269	1990/91	24/04/91	ECWC Semi-Final 2nd Leg	Manchester United 1 Legia Warsaw 1	Old Trafford
13	41942	1990/91	06/03/91	ECWC 3rd Round 1st Leg	Manchester United 1 Montpelier 1	Old Trafford
14	40000	1963/64	18/03/64	ECWC Quarter-Final 2nd Leg	Sporting Lisbon 5 Manchester United 0	de Jose Alvalade
15	40000	1983/84	19/10/83	ECWC 2nd Round 1st Leg	Spartak Varna 1 Manchester United 2	Stad Yuri Gargarin
16	40000	1991/92	23/10/91	ECWC 2nd Round 1st Leg	Athletico Madrid 3 Manchester United 0	Vincente Calderon
17	39745	1983/84	14/09/83	ECWC 1st Round 1st Leg	Manchester United 1 Dukla Prague 1	Old Trafford
18	39654	1991/92	06/11/91	ECWC 2nd Round 2nd Leg	Manchester United 1 Athletico Madrid 1	Old Trafford
19	39079	1983/84	02/11/83	ECWC 2nd Round 2nd Leg	Manchester United 2 Spartak Varna 0	Old Trafford
20	35023	1991/92	02/10/91	ECWC 1st Round 2nd Leg	Manchester United 2 Athinaikos 0	Old Trafford
21	33678	1977/78	14/09/77	ECWC 1st Round 1st Leg	St Etienne 1 Manchester United 1	Stade Geoffrey Guichard
22	31634	1977/78	05/10/77	ECWC 1st Round 2nd Leg	Manchester United 2 St Etienne 0	Home Park
23	29405	1990/91	23/10/90	ECWC 2nd Round 1st Leg	Manchester United 3 Wrexham 0	Old Trafford
24	28850	1983/84	27/09/83	ECWC 1st Round 2nd Leg	Dukla Prague 2 Manchester United 2	Stadion Juliska
25	28411	1990/91	19/09/90	ECWC 1st Round 1st Leg	Manchester United 2 Pecsi Munkas 0	Old Trafford

TOP 25 ATTENDANCES - ALL FAIRS CUP / UEFA CUP MATCHES - ANY VENUE

#	ATT	SEASON	DATE	COMPETITION / ROUND	MATCH RESULT	VENUE
1	66632	1976/77	03/11/76	UEFA Cup 2nd Round 2nd Leg	Juventus 3 Manchester United 0	Stadio Comunale
2	60000	1964/65	16/06/65	ICFC Semi-Final Play-Off	Ferencvaros 2 Manchester United 1	Nep Stadion
3	59000	1976/77	20/10/76	UEFA Cup 2nd Round 1st Leg	Manchester United 1 Juventus 0	Old Trafford
4	58918	1976/77	29/09/76	UEFA Cup 1st Round 2nd Leg	Manchester United 2 Ajax 0	Old Trafford
5	54397	1964/65	09/02/65	ICFC 3rd Round 2nd Leg	Everton 1 Manchester United 2	Goodison Park
6	50000	1964/65	20/01/65	ICFC 3rd Round 1st Leg	Manchester United 1 Everton 1	Old Trafford
7	50000	1964/65	06/06/65	ICFC Semi-Final 2nd Leg	Ferencvaros 1 Manchester United 0	Nep Stadion
8	48278	1984/85	28/11/84	UEFA Cup 3rd Round 1st Leg	Manchester United 2 Dundee United 2	Old Trafford
9	46588	1982/83	15/09/82	UEFA Cup 1st Round 1st Leg	Manchester United 0 Valencia 0	Old Trafford
10	40000	1980/81	01/10/80	UEFA Cup 1st Round 2nd Leg	Widzew Lodz 0 Manchester United 0	Stadio TKS
11	39902	1964/65	31/05/65	ICFC Semi-Final 1st Leg	Manchester United 3 Ferencvaros 2	Old Trafford
12	39281	1984/85	07/11/84	UEFA Cup 2nd Round 2nd Leg	Manchester United 1 PSV Eindhoven 0	Old Trafford
13	38437	1964/65	27/10/64	ICFC 1st Round 2nd Leg	Manchester United 6 Djurgardens 1	Old Trafford
14	38037	1980/81	17/09/80	UEFA Cup 1st Round 1st Leg	Manchester United 1 Widzew Lodz 1	Old Trafford
15	35432	1984/85	06/03/85	UEFA Cup Quarter-Final 1st Leg	Manchester United 1 Videoton 0	Old Trafford
16	35000	1982/83	29/09/82	UEFA Cup 1st Round 2nd Leg	Valencia 2 Manchester United 1	Luis Casanova
17	34188	1964/65	19/05/65	ICFC Quarter-Final 2nd Leg	Manchester United 0 Strasbourg 0	Old Trafford
18	33119	1984/85	19/09/84	UEFA Cup 1st Round 1st Leg	Manchester United 3 Raba Vasas 0	Old Trafford
19	33000	1995/96	12/09/95	UEFA Cup 2nd Round 1st Leg	Rotor Volgograd 0 Manchester United 0	Central Stadion
20	31896	1964/65	02/12/64	ICFC 2nd Round 2nd Leg	Manchester United 4 Borussia Dortmund 0	Old Trafford
21	30000	1964/65	12/05/65	ICFC Quarter-Final 1st Leg	Strasbourg 0 Manchester United 5	Stade de la Meinau
22	30000	1976/77	15/09/76	UEFA Cup 1st Round 1st Leg	Ajax 1 Manchester United 0	Olympisch Stadion
23	29724	1995/96	26/09/95	UEFA Cup 2nd Round 2nd Leg	Manchester United 2 Rotor Volgograd 2	Old Trafford
24	27500	1984/85	24/10/84	UEFA Cup 2nd Round 1st Leg	PSV Eindhoven 0 Manchester United 0	Philipstadion
25	26000	1984/85	03/10/84	UEFA Cup 1st Round 2nd Leg	Raba Vasas 2 Manchester United 2	Raba ETO Stadium

TOP 25 ATTENDANCES - ALL OTHER COMPETITIVE MATCHES - ANY VENUE

#	ATT	SEASON	DATE	COMPETITION / ROUND	MATCH RESULT	VENUE
1	92000	1983/84	20/08/83	FA Charity Shield	Manchester United 2 Liverpool 0	Wembley
2	82000	1977/78	13/08/77	FA Charity Shield	Manchester United 0 Liverpool 0	Wembley
3	82000	1985/86	10/08/85	FA Charity Shield	Manchester United 0 Everton 2	Wembley
4	80731	2007/08	05/08/07	FA Charity Shield	Manchester United 1 Chelsea 1	Wembley
5	73636	1997/98	03/08/97	FA Charity Shield	Manchester United 1 Chelsea 1	Wembley
6	73214	1996/97	11/08/96	FA Charity Shield	Manchester United 4 Newcastle United 0	Wembley
7	73000	1999/00	08/01/00	Club World Championship	Manchester United 1 Vasco da Gama 3	Maracana Stadium
8	70227	2001/02	12/08/01	FA Charity Shield	Manchester United 1 Liverpool 2	Millennium Stadium
9	70185	1999/00	01/08/99	FA Charity Shield	Manchester United 1 Arsenal 2	Wembley
10	67342	1998/99	09/08/98	FA Charity Shield	Manchester United 0 Arsenal 3	Wembley
11	66558	1990/91	18/08/90	FA Charity Shield	Manchester United 1 Liverpool 1	Wembley
12	66519	1993/94	07/08/93	FA Charity Shield	Manchester United 1 Arsenal 1	Wembley
13	65148	2000/01	13/08/00	FA Charity Shield	Manchester United 0 Chelsea 2	Wembley
14	63500	1968/69	16/10/68	Inter-Continental Cup 2nd Leg	Manchester United 1 Estudiantes de la Plata 1	Old Trafford
15	63317	2004/05	08/08/04	FA Charity Shield	Manchester United 1 Arsenal 3	Millennium Stadium
16	60402	1994/95	14/08/94	FA Charity Shield	Manchester United 2 Blackburn Rovers 0	Wembley
17	59293	2003/04	10/08/03	FA Charity Shield	Manchester United 1 Arsenal 1	Millennium Stadium
18	55000	1968/69	25/09/68	Inter-Continental Cup 1st Leg	Estudiantes de la Plata 1 Manchester United 0	Boca Juniors Stadium
19	54840	1963/64	17/08/63	FA Charity Shield	Everton 4 Manchester United 0	Goodison Park
20	54106	1967/68	12/08/67	FA Charity Shield	Manchester United 3 Tottenham Hotspur 3	Old Trafford
21	53372	1999/00	30/11/99	Inter-Continental Cup	Manchester United 1 Palmeiras 0	Olympic Stadium
22	50000	1999/00	06/01/00	Club World Championship	Manchester United 1 Rayos del Necaxa 1	Maracana Stadium
23	48502	1965/66	14/08/65	FA Charity Shield	Manchester United 2 Liverpool 2	Old Trafford
24	31000	1948/49	06/10/48	FA Charity Shield	Arsenal 4 Manchester United 3	Highbury
25	30495	1956/57	24/10/56	FA Charity Shield	Manchester City 0 Manchester United 1	Maine Road

MANCHESTER UNITED
The Complete Record

Chapter 2.1
Player Roll Call

ALF AINSWORTH

DEBUT (Full Appearance)

Saturday 03/03/1934
Football League Division 2
at Old Trafford

Manchester United 2 Bury 1

CLUB CAREER RECORD	Apps	Subs	Goals
Premiership	0		0
League Division 1	0		0
League Division 2	2		0
FA Cup	0		0
League Cup	0		0
European Cup / Champions League	0		0
European Cup-Winners' Cup	0		0
UEFA Cup / Inter-Cities' Fairs Cup	0		0
Other Matches	0		0
OVERALL TOTAL	**2**		**0**

Opponents	PREM A S G	FLD 1 A S G	FLD 2 A S G	FAC A S G	LC A S G	EC/CL A S G	ECWC A S G	UEFA A S G	OTHER A S G	TOTAL A S G
1 Bury	– –	– –	1 –	– –	– –	– –	– –	– –	– –	1 –
2 Fulham	– –	– –	1 –	– –	– –	– –	– –	– –	– –	1 –

JOHN AITKEN

DEBUT (Full Appearance, 1 goal)

Saturday 07/09/1895
Football League Division 2
at Bank Street

Manchester United 5 Crewe Alexandra 0

CLUB CAREER RECORD	Apps	Subs	Goals
Premiership	0		0
League Division 1	0		0
League Division 2	2		1
FA Cup	0		0
League Cup	0		0
European Cup / Champions League	0		0
European Cup-Winners' Cup	0		0
UEFA Cup / Inter-Cities' Fairs Cup	0		0
Other Matches	0		0
OVERALL TOTAL	**2**		**1**

Opponents	PREM A S G	FLD 1 A S G	FLD 2 A S G	FAC A S G	LC A S G	EC/CL A S G	ECWC A S G	UEFA A S G	OTHER A S G	TOTAL A S G
1 Crewe Alexandra	– –	– –	2 1	– –	– –	– –	– –	– –	– –	2 1

GEORGE ALBINSON

DEBUT (Full Appearance)

Wednesday 12/01/1921
FA Cup 1st Round Replay
at Old Trafford

Manchester United 1 Liverpool 2

CLUB CAREER RECORD	Apps	Subs	Goals
Premiership	0		0
League Division 1	0		0
League Division 2	0		0
FA Cup	1		0
League Cup	0		0
European Cup / Champions League	0		0
European Cup-Winners' Cup	0		0
UEFA Cup / Inter-Cities' Fairs Cup	0		0
Other Matches	0		0
OVERALL TOTAL	**1**		**0**

Opponents	PREM A S G	FLD 1 A S G	FLD 2 A S G	FAC A S G	LC A S G	EC/CL A S G	ECWC A S G	UEFA A S G	OTHER A S G	TOTAL A S G
1 Liverpool	– –	– –	– –	1 –	– –	– –	– –	– –	– –	1 –

ARTHUR ALBISTON

DEBUT (Full Appearance)

Wednesday 09/10/1974
League Cup 3rd Round
at Old Trafford

Manchester United 1 Manchester City 0

CLUB CAREER RECORD	Apps	Subs	Goals
Premiership	0		0
League Division 1	362	(15)	6
League Division 2	2		0
FA Cup	36		0
League Cup	38	(2)	1
European Cup / Champions League	0		0
European Cup-Winners' Cup	12		0
UEFA Cup / Inter-Cities' Fairs Cup	14	(1)	0
Other Matches	3		0
OVERALL TOTAL	**467**	**(18)**	**7**

Opponents	PREM A S G	FLD 1 A S G	FLD 2 A S G	FAC A S G	LC A S G	EC/CL A S G	ECWC A S G	UEFA A S G	OTHER A S G	TOTAL A S G
1 Liverpool	– –	18 1	– –	5 –	1 –	– –	– –	– –	2 –	26 1
2 Coventry City	– –	19 (1) –	– –	1 –	2 –	– –	– –	– –	– –	22 (1) –
3 Everton	– –	16 (1) –	– –	2 –	2 –	– –	– –	– –	1 –	21 (1) –
4 West Ham United	– –	15 (1) –	– –	4 –	1 –	– –	– –	– –	– –	20 (1) –
5 Arsenal	– –	15 –	– –	2 –	3 –	– –	– –	– –	– –	20 –
6 Tottenham Hotspur	– –	14 –	– –	2 –	4 –	– –	– –	– –	– –	20 –
7 West Bromwich Albion	– –	16 1	– –	2 –	– –	– –	– –	– –	– –	18 1
8 Aston Villa	– –	18 –	– –	– –	– –	– –	– –	– –	– –	18 –
9 Ipswich Town	– –	18 –	– –	– –	– –	– –	– –	– –	– –	18 –
10 Nottingham Forest	– –	15 (1) –	– –	1 –	1 –	– –	– –	– –	– –	17 (1) –

continued../

ARTHUR ALBISTON (continued)

Opponents	PREM A	S	G	FLD 1 A	S	G	FLD 2 A	S	G	FAC A	S	G	LC A	S	G	EC/CL A	S	G	ECWC A	S	G	UEFA A	S	G	OTHER A	S	G	TOTAL A	S	G
11 Southampton	–	–		14 (1)	–		–	–		–	–		3	–		–			–			–			–			17 (1)	–	
12 Manchester City	–	–		14 (1)		2	–	–		–	–		1	–		–			–			–			–			15 (1)		2
13 Sunderland	–	–		10 (1)	–		–	–		2	–		– (2)	–		–			–			–			–			12 (3)	–	
14 Birmingham City	–	–		13 (1)	–		–	–		–	–		–	–		–			–			–			–			13 (1)	–	
15 Leicester City	–	–		13 (1)	–		–	–		–	–		–	–		–			–			–			–			13 (1)	–	
16 Brighton	–	–		8		1	–	–		4	–		–	–		–			–			–			–			12		1
17 Stoke City	–	–		12			–	–		–	–		–	–		–			–			–			–			12		
18 Watford	–	–		9 (1)	–		–	–		1	–		1	–		–			–			–			–			11 (1)	–	
19 Norwich City	–	–		10	–		–	–		–	–		1	–		–			–			–			–			11		
20 Queens Park Rangers	–	–		11	–		–	–		–	–		–	–		–			–			–			–			11		
21 Chelsea	–	–		10	–		–	–		–	–		–	–		–			–			–			–			10		
22 Wolverhampton W.	–	–		10	–		–	–		–	–		–	–		–			–			–			–			10		
23 Luton Town	–	–		8		1	–	–		1	–		–	–		–			–			–			–			9		1
24 Leeds United	–	–		9	–		–	–		–	–		–	–		–			–			–			–			9	–	
25 Middlesbrough	–	–		8	–		–	–		–	–		–	–		–			–			–			–			8	–	
26 Oxford United	–	–		3 (2)	–		–	–		–	–		3	–		–			–			–			–			6 (2)	–	
27 Newcastle United	–	–		5 (1)	–		–	–		–	–		1	–		–			–			–			–			6 (1)	–	
28 Bristol City	–	–		6	–		–	–		–	–		–	–		–			–			–			–			6	–	
29 Notts County	–	–		6	–		–	–		–	–		–	–		–			–			–			–			6	–	
30 Derby County	–	–		4 (1)	–		–	–		1	–		–	–		–			–			–			–			5 (1)	–	
31 Crystal Palace	–	–		3	–		–	–		–	–		2	–		–			–			–			–			5	–	
32 Sheffield Wednesday	–	–		5	–		–	–		–	–		–	–		–			–			–			–			5	–	
33 Bournemouth	–	–		–	–		–	–		2	–		2	–		–			–			–			–			4	–	
34 Juventus	–	–		–	–		–	–		–	–		–	–		2	–		–			2	–		–			4	–	
35 Port Vale	–	–		–	–		–	–		–	–		4	–		–			–			–			–			4	–	
36 Swansea City	–	–		3	–		–	–		–	–		–	–		–			–			–			–			3	–	
37 Bradford City	–	–		–	–		–	–		–	–		2		1	–			–			–			–			2		1
38 Barcelona	–	–		–	–		–	–		–	–		–	–		–			2	–		–			–			2	–	
39 Bolton Wanderers	–	–		2	–		–	–		–	–		–	–		–			–			–			–			2	–	
40 Burnley	–	–		–	–		–	–		–	–		2	–		–			–			–			–			2	–	
41 Carlisle United	–	–		–	–		–	–		2	–		–	–		–			–			–			–			2	–	
42 Colchester United	–	–		–	–		–	–		1	–		1	–		–			–			–			–			2	–	
43 Dukla Prague	–	–		–	–		–	–		–	–		–	–		2	–		–			–			–			2	–	
44 Dundee United	–	–		–	–		–	–		–	–		–	–		–			–			2	–		–			2	–	
45 Porto	–	–		–	–		–	–		–	–		–	–		2	–		–			–			–			2	–	
46 PSV Eindhoven	–	–		–	–		–	–		–	–		–	–		–			–			2	–		–			2	–	
47 Raba Vasas	–	–		–	–		–	–		–	–		–	–		–			–			2	–		–			2	–	
48 Spartak Varna	–	–		–	–		–	–		–	–		–	–		–			2	–		–			–			2	–	
49 St Etienne	–	–		–	–		–	–		–	–		–	–		–			2	–		–			–			2	–	
50 Valencia	–	–		–	–		–	–		–	–		–	–		–			–			2	–		–			2	–	
51 Videoton	–	–		–	–		–	–		–	–		–	–		–			–			2	–		–			2	–	
52 Widzew Lodz	–	–		–	–		–	–		–	–		–	–		–			–			2	–		–			2	–	
53 Wimbledon	–	–		1 (1)	–		–	–		–	–		–	–		–			–			–			–			1 (1)	–	
54 Blackburn Rovers	–	–		–	–		–	–		1	–		–	–		–			–			–			–			1	–	
55 Charlton Athletic	–	–		1	–		–	–		–	–		–	–		–			–			–			–			1	–	
56 Fulham	–	–		–	–		–	–		1	–		–	–		–			–			–			–			1	–	
57 Oldham Athletic	–	–		–	–		1	–		–	–		–	–		–			–			–			–			1	–	
58 Portsmouth	–	–		–	–		1	–		–	–		–	–		–			–			–			–			1	–	
59 Rochdale	–	–		–	–		–	–		1	–		–	–		–			–			–			–			1	–	
60 Stockport County	–	–		–	–		–	–		–	–		1	–		–			–			–			–			1	–	
61 Ajax	–	–		–	–		–	–		–	–		–	–		–			–			– (1)	–		–			– (1)	–	

JACK ALLAN

DEBUT (Full Appearance, 2 goals)

Saturday 03/09/1904
Football League Division 2
at Cobridge Stadium

Port Vale 2 Manchester United 2

CLUB CAREER RECORD	Apps	Subs	Goals
Premiership	0		0
League Division 1	3		0
League Division 2	32		21
FA Cup	1		1
League Cup	0		0
European Cup / Champions League	0		0
European Cup-Winners' Cup	0		0
UEFA Cup / Inter-Cities' Fairs Cup	0		0
Other Matches	0		0
OVERALL TOTAL	36		22

Opponents	PREM A	S	G	FLD 1 A	S	G	FLD 2 A	S	G	FAC A	S	G	LC A	S	G	EC/CL A	S	G	ECWC A	S	G	UEFA A	S	G	OTHER A	S	G	TOTAL A	S	G
1 Lincoln City	–	–		–	–		3		2	–	–		–	–		–			–			–			–			3		2
2 Grimsby Town	–	–		–	–		3		1	–	–		–	–		–			–			–			–			3		1
3 Port Vale	–	–		–	–		2		5	–	–		–	–		–			–			–			–			2		5
4 Gainsborough Trinity	–	–		–	–		2		3	–	–		–	–		–			–			–			–			2		3
5 Bolton Wanderers	–	–		–	–		2		2	–	–		–	–		–			–			–			–			2		2
6 Chesterfield	–	–		–	–		2		2	–	–		–	–		–			–			–			–			2		2
7 Barnsley	–	–		–	–		2		1	–	–		–	–		–			–			–			–			2		1
8 Bradford City	–	–		–	–		2		1	–	–		–	–		–			–			–			–			2		1
9 Leeds United	–	–		–	–		2		1	–	–		–	–		–			–			–			–			2		1
10 Leicester City	–	–		–	–		2		1	–	–		–	–		–			–			–			–			2		1

continued../

JACK ALLAN (continued)

Opponents	PREM			FLD 1			FLD 2			FAC			LC			EC/CL			ECWC			UEFA			OTHER			TOTAL	
	A	S	G	A	S	G	A	S	G	A	S	G	A	S	G	A	S	G	A	S	G	A	S	G	A	S	G	A	G
11 Burnley	–	–	–	–	–	–	2	–	–	–	–	–	–	–	–	–	–	–	–	–	–	–	–	–	–	–	–	2	–
12 West Bromwich Albion	–	–	–	–	–	–	2	–	–	–	–	–	–	–	–	–	–	–	–	–	–	–	–	–	–	–	–	2	–
13 Blackpool	–	–	–	–	–	–	1	–	1	–	–	–	–	–	–	–	–	–	–	–	–	–	–	–	–	–	–	1	1
14 Glossop	–	–	–	–	–	–	1	–	1	–	–	–	–	–	–	–	–	–	–	–	–	–	–	–	–	–	–	1	1
15 Staple Hill	–	–	–	–	–	–	–	–	–	1	–	1	–	–	–	–	–	–	–	–	–	–	–	–	–	–	–	1	1
16 Blackburn Rovers	–	–	–	1	–	–	–	–	–	–	–	–	–	–	–	–	–	–	–	–	–	–	–	–	–	–	–	1	–
17 Bristol City	–	–	–	–	–	–	–	–	–	1	–	–	–	–	–	–	–	–	–	–	–	–	–	–	–	–	–	1	–
18 Burton United	–	–	–	–	–	–	–	–	–	1	–	–	–	–	–	–	–	–	–	–	–	–	–	–	–	–	–	1	–
19 Derby County	–	–	–	1	–	–	–	–	–	–	–	–	–	–	–	–	–	–	–	–	–	–	–	–	–	–	–	1	–
20 Doncaster Rovers	–	–	–	–	–	–	–	–	–	1	–	–	–	–	–	–	–	–	–	–	–	–	–	–	–	–	–	1	–
21 Liverpool	–	–	–	–	–	–	–	–	–	1	–	–	–	–	–	–	–	–	–	–	–	–	–	–	–	–	–	1	–
22 Stoke City	–	–	–	1	–	–	–	–	–	–	–	–	–	–	–	–	–	–	–	–	–	–	–	–	–	–	–	1	–

REG ALLEN

DEBUT (Full Appearance)

Saturday 19/08/1950
Football League Division 1
at Old Trafford

Manchester United 1 Fulham 0

CLUB CAREER RECORD	Apps	Subs	Goals
Premiership	0		0
League Division 1	75		0
League Division 2	0		0
FA Cup	5		0
League Cup	0		0
European Cup / Champions League	0		0
European Cup-Winners' Cup	0		0
UEFA Cup / Inter-Cities' Fairs Cup	0		0
Other Matches	0		0
OVERALL TOTAL	80		0

Opponents	PREM			FLD 1			FLD 2			FAC			LC			EC/CL			ECWC			UEFA			OTHER			TOTAL	
	A	S	G	A	S	G	A	S	G	A	S	G	A	S	G	A	S	G	A	S	G	A	S	G	A	S	G	A	G
1 Bolton Wanderers	–	–	–	5	–	–	–	–	–	–	–	–	–	–	–	–	–	–	–	–	–	–	–	–	–	–	–	5	–
2 Arsenal	–	–	–	3	–	–	–	–	–	1	–	–	–	–	–	–	–	–	–	–	–	–	–	–	–	–	–	4	–
3 Burnley	–	–	–	4	–	–	–	–	–	–	–	–	–	–	–	–	–	–	–	–	–	–	–	–	–	–	–	4	–
4 Chelsea	–	–	–	4	–	–	–	–	–	–	–	–	–	–	–	–	–	–	–	–	–	–	–	–	–	–	–	4	–
5 Fulham	–	–	–	4	–	–	–	–	–	–	–	–	–	–	–	–	–	–	–	–	–	–	–	–	–	–	–	4	–
6 Middlesbrough	–	–	–	4	–	–	–	–	–	–	–	–	–	–	–	–	–	–	–	–	–	–	–	–	–	–	–	4	–
7 Newcastle United	–	–	–	4	–	–	–	–	–	–	–	–	–	–	–	–	–	–	–	–	–	–	–	–	–	–	–	4	–
8 Stoke City	–	–	–	4	–	–	–	–	–	–	–	–	–	–	–	–	–	–	–	–	–	–	–	–	–	–	–	4	–
9 Tottenham Hotspur	–	–	–	4	–	–	–	–	–	–	–	–	–	–	–	–	–	–	–	–	–	–	–	–	–	–	–	4	–
10 West Bromwich Albion	–	–	–	4	–	–	–	–	–	–	–	–	–	–	–	–	–	–	–	–	–	–	–	–	–	–	–	4	–
11 Wolverhampton W.	–	–	–	4	–	–	–	–	–	–	–	–	–	–	–	–	–	–	–	–	–	–	–	–	–	–	–	4	–
12 Aston Villa	–	–	–	3	–	–	–	–	–	–	–	–	–	–	–	–	–	–	–	–	–	–	–	–	–	–	–	3	–
13 Blackpool	–	–	–	3	–	–	–	–	–	–	–	–	–	–	–	–	–	–	–	–	–	–	–	–	–	–	–	3	–
14 Charlton Athletic	–	–	–	3	–	–	–	–	–	–	–	–	–	–	–	–	–	–	–	–	–	–	–	–	–	–	–	3	–
15 Derby County	–	–	–	3	–	–	–	–	–	–	–	–	–	–	–	–	–	–	–	–	–	–	–	–	–	–	–	3	–
16 Huddersfield Town	–	–	–	3	–	–	–	–	–	–	–	–	–	–	–	–	–	–	–	–	–	–	–	–	–	–	–	3	–
17 Liverpool	–	–	–	3	–	–	–	–	–	–	–	–	–	–	–	–	–	–	–	–	–	–	–	–	–	–	–	3	–
18 Portsmouth	–	–	–	3	–	–	–	–	–	–	–	–	–	–	–	–	–	–	–	–	–	–	–	–	–	–	–	3	–
19 Sunderland	–	–	–	3	–	–	–	–	–	–	–	–	–	–	–	–	–	–	–	–	–	–	–	–	–	–	–	3	–
20 Manchester City	–	–	–	2	–	–	–	–	–	–	–	–	–	–	–	–	–	–	–	–	–	–	–	–	–	–	–	2	–
21 Preston North End	–	–	–	2	–	–	–	–	–	–	–	–	–	–	–	–	–	–	–	–	–	–	–	–	–	–	–	2	–
22 Sheffield Wednesday	–	–	–	2	–	–	–	–	–	–	–	–	–	–	–	–	–	–	–	–	–	–	–	–	–	–	–	2	–
23 Birmingham City	–	–	–	–	–	–	–	–	–	1	–	–	–	–	–	–	–	–	–	–	–	–	–	–	–	–	–	1	–
24 Everton	–	–	–	1	–	–	–	–	–	–	–	–	–	–	–	–	–	–	–	–	–	–	–	–	–	–	–	1	–
25 Hull City	–	–	–	–	–	–	–	–	–	1	–	–	–	–	–	–	–	–	–	–	–	–	–	–	–	–	–	1	–
26 Leeds United	–	–	–	–	–	–	–	–	–	1	–	–	–	–	–	–	–	–	–	–	–	–	–	–	–	–	–	1	–
27 Oldham Athletic	–	–	–	–	–	–	–	–	–	1	–	–	–	–	–	–	–	–	–	–	–	–	–	–	–	–	–	1	–

ARTHUR ALLMAN

DEBUT (Full Appearance)

Saturday 13/02/1915
Football League Division 1
at Old Trafford

Manchester United 2 Sheffield Wednesday 0

CLUB CAREER RECORD	Apps	Subs	Goals
Premiership	0		0
League Division 1	12		0
League Division 2	0		0
FA Cup	0		0
League Cup	0		0
European Cup / Champions League	0		0
European Cup-Winners' Cup	0		0
UEFA Cup / Inter-Cities' Fairs Cup	0		0
Other Matches	0		0
OVERALL TOTAL	12		0

Opponents	PREM			FLD 1			FLD 2			FAC			LC			EC/CL			ECWC			UEFA			OTHER			TOTAL	
	A	S	G	A	S	G	A	S	G	A	S	G	A	S	G	A	S	G	A	S	G	A	S	G	A	S	G	A	G
1 Aston Villa	–	–	–	1	–	–	–	–	–	–	–	–	–	–	–	–	–	–	–	–	–	–	–	–	–	–	–	1	–
2 Bradford City	–	–	–	1	–	–	–	–	–	–	–	–	–	–	–	–	–	–	–	–	–	–	–	–	–	–	–	1	–
3 Bradford Park Avenue	–	–	–	1	–	–	–	–	–	–	–	–	–	–	–	–	–	–	–	–	–	–	–	–	–	–	–	1	–
4 Burnley	–	–	–	1	–	–	–	–	–	–	–	–	–	–	–	–	–	–	–	–	–	–	–	–	–	–	–	1	–

continued../

ARTHUR ALLMAN (continued)

Opponents	PREM			FLD 1			FLD 2			FAC			LC			EC/CL			ECWC			UEFA			OTHER			TOTAL		
	A	S	G	A	S	G	A	S	G	A	S	G	A	S	G	A	S	G	A	S	G	A	S	G	A	S	G	A	S	G
5 Chelsea	–	–					1			–	–		–	–		–	–		–	–		–	–		–	–		1		
6 Everton	–	–					1			–	–		–	–		–	–		–	–		–	–		–	–		1		
7 Middlesbrough	–	–					1			–	–		–	–		–	–		–	–		–	–		–	–		1		
8 Oldham Athletic	–	–					1			–	–		–	–		–	–		–	–		–	–		–	–		1		
9 Sheffield United	–	–					1			–	–		–	–		–	–		–	–		–	–		–	–		1		
10 Sheffield Wednesday	–	–					1			–	–		–	–		–	–		–	–		–	–		–	–		1		
11 Tottenham Hotspur	–	–					1			–	–		–	–		–	–		–	–		–	–		–	–		1		
12 West Bromwich Albion	–	–					1			–	–		–	–		–	–		–	–		–	–		–	–		1		

ALFRED AMBLER

DEBUT (Full Appearance)

Saturday 02/09/1899
Football League Division 2
at Bank Street

Newton Heath 2 Gainsborough Trinity 2

CLUB CAREER RECORD	Apps	Subs	Goals
Premiership	0		0
League Division 1	0		0
League Division 2	10		1
FA Cup	0		0
League Cup	0		0
European Cup / Champions League	0		0
European Cup-Winners' Cup	0		0
UEFA Cup / Inter-Cities' Fairs Cup	0		0
Other Matches	0		0
OVERALL TOTAL	10		1

Opponents	PREM			FLD 1			FLD 2			FAC			LC			EC/CL			ECWC			UEFA			OTHER			TOTAL		
	A	S	G	A	S	G	A	S	G	A	S	G	A	S	G	A	S	G	A	S	G	A	S	G	A	S	G	A	S	G
1 Gainsborough Trinity	–	–		–	–		2			–			–			–			–			–			–			2	–	
2 Walsall	–	–		–	–		2			–			–			–			–			–			–			2	–	
3 Bolton Wanderers	–	–		–	–		1		1	–			–			–			–			–			–			1		1
4 Barnsley	–	–		–	–		1			–			–			–			–			–			–			1	–	
5 Leicester City	–	–		–	–		1			–			–			–			–			–			–			1	–	
6 Luton Town	–	–		–	–		1			–			–			–			–			–			–			1	–	
7 Middlesbrough	–	–		–	–		1			–			–			–			–			–			–			1	–	
8 Port Vale	–	–		–	–		1			–			–			–			–			–			–			1	–	

ANDERSON

DEBUT (Full Appearance)

Saturday 01/09/2007
FA Premiership
at Old Trafford

Manchester United 1 Sunderland 0

CLUB CAREER RECORD	Apps	Subs	Goals
Premiership	16	(8)	0
League Division 1	0		0
League Division 2	0		0
FA Cup	2	(2)	0
League Cup	1		0
European Cup / Champions League	6	(3)	0
European Cup-Winners' Cup	0		0
UEFA Cup / Inter-Cities' Fairs Cup	0		0
Other Matches	0		0
OVERALL TOTAL	25	(13)	0

Opponents	PREM			FLD 1			FLD 2			FAC			LC			EC/CL			ECWC			UEFA			OTHER			TOTAL		
	A	S	G	A	S	G	A	S	G	A	S	G	A	S	G	A	S	G	A	S	G	A	S	G	A	S	G	A	S	G
1 Arsenal	1 (1)		–	–		–	–		–	1		–	–		–	–		–	–		–	–		–	–		–	2 (1)		–
2 Aston Villa	1 (1)		–	–		–	–		–	1		–	–		–	–		–	–		–	–		–	–		–	2 (1)		–
3 Roma	–		–	–		–	–		–	–		–	–		–	2 (1)		–	–		–	–		–	–		–	2 (1)		–
4 Derby County	2		–	–		–	–		–	–		–	–		–	–		–	–		–	–		–	–		–	2		
5 Liverpool	2		–	–		–	–		–	–		–	–		–	–		–	–		–	–		–	–		–	2		
6 Olympique Lyonnais	–		–	–		–	–		–	–		–	–		–	2		–	–		–	–		–	–		–	2		
7 Bolton Wanderers	1 (1)		–	–		–	–		–	–		–	–		–	–		–	–		–	–		–	–		–	1 (1)		–
8 Chelsea	1		–	–		–	–		–	–		–	–	(1)	–	–		–	–		–	–		–	–		–	1 (1)		–
9 Fulham	1 (1)		–	–		–	–		–	–		–	–		–	–		–	–		–	–		–	–		–	1 (1)		–
10 Sporting Lisbon	–		–	–		–	–		–	–		–	–		–	1 (1)		–	–		–	–		–	–		–	1 (1)		–
11 Portsmouth	– (1)		–	–		–	–		–	– (1)		–	–		–	–		–	–		–	–		–	–		–	– (2)		–
12 Tottenham Hotspur	– (1)		–	–		–	–		–	– (1)		–	–		–	–		–	–		–	–		–	–		–	– (2)		–
13 Birmingham City	1		–	–		–	–		–	–		–	–		–	–		–	–		–	–		–	–		–	1		
14 Blackburn Rovers	1		–	–		–	–		–	–		–	–		–	–		–	–		–	–		–	–		–	1		
15 Coventry City	–		–	–		–	–		–	–		–	1		–	–		–	–		–	–		–	–		–	1		
16 Dynamo Kiev	–		–	–		–	–		–	–		–	–		–	1		–	–		–	–		–	–		–	1		
17 Everton	1		–	–		–	–		–	–		–	–		–	–		–	–		–	–		–	–		–	1		
18 Manchester City	1		–	–		–	–		–	–		–	–		–	–		–	–		–	–		–	–		–	1		
19 Middlesbrough	1		–	–		–	–		–	–		–	–		–	–		–	–		–	–		–	–		–	1		
20 Newcastle United	1		–	–		–	–		–	–		–	–		–	–		–	–		–	–		–	–		–	1		
21 Sunderland	1		–	–		–	–		–	–		–	–		–	–		–	–		–	–		–	–		–	1		
22 West Ham United	– (1)		–	–		–	–		–	–		–	–		–	–		–	–		–	–		–	–		–	– (1)		–
23 Wigan Athletic	– (1)		–	–		–	–		–	–		–	–		–	–		–	–		–	–		–	–		–	– (1)		–

GEORGE ANDERSON

DEBUT (Full Appearance)

Saturday 09/09/1911
Football League Division 1
at Old Trafford

Manchester United 2 Everton 1

CLUB CAREER RECORD	Apps	Subs	Goals
Premiership	0		0
League Division 1	80		37
League Division 2	0		0
FA Cup	6		2
League Cup	0		0
European Cup / Champions League	0		0
European Cup-Winners' Cup	0		0
UEFA Cup / Inter-Cities' Fairs Cup	0		0
Other Matches	0		0
OVERALL TOTAL	**86**		**39**

Opponents	PREM			FLD 1			FLD 2			FAC			LC			EC/CL			ECWC			UEFA			OTHER			TOTAL		
	A	S	G	A	S	G	A	S	G	A	S	G	A	S	G	A	S	G	A	S	G	A	S	G	A	S	G	A	S	G
1 Aston Villa	–	–		6		2	–	–		–			–			–			–			–			–			6		2
2 Oldham Athletic	–	–		4		1	–	–	2	–			–			–			–			–			–			6		1
3 Chelsea	–	–		5		4	–	–		–			–			–			–			–			–			5		4
4 Liverpool	–	–		5		4	–	–		–			–			–			–			–			–			5		4
5 Sheffield United	–	–		5		4	–	–		–			–			–			–			–			–			5		4
6 Bradford City	–	–		5		2	–	–		–			–			–			–			–			–			5		2
7 Sunderland	–	–		5		2	–	–		–			–			–			–			–			–			5		2
8 Newcastle United	–	–		5		1	–	–		–			–			–			–			–			–			5		1
9 Manchester City	–	–		4		2	–	–		–			–			–			–			–			–			4		2
10 Middlesbrough	–	–		4		2	–	–		–			–			–			–			–			–			4		2
11 Bolton Wanderers	–	–		4		1	–	–		–			–			–			–			–			–			4		1
12 Blackburn Rovers	–	–		4		–	–	–		–			–			–			–			–			–			4		–
13 Sheffield Wednesday	–	–		3		–	–	–		1			–			–			–			–			–			4		–
14 Derby County	–	–		3		2	–	–		–			–			–			–			–			–			3		2
15 Notts County	–	–		3		2	–	–		–			–			–			–			–			–			3		2
16 Everton	–	–		3		1	–	–		–			–			–			–			–			–			3		1
17 Tottenham Hotspur	–	–		3		–	–	–		–			–			–			–			–			–			3		–
18 West Bromwich Albion	–	–		3		–	–	–		–			–			–			–			–			–			3		–
19 Preston North End	–	–		2		3	–	–		–			–			–			–			–			–			2		3
20 Burnley	–	–		2		2	–	–		–			–			–			–			–			–			2		2
21 Coventry City	–	–		–		–	–	–		2		1	–			–			–			–			–			2		1
22 Arsenal	–	–		1		1	–	–		–			–			–			–			–			–			1		1
23 Bradford Park Avenue	–	–		1		1	–	–		–			–			–			–			–			–			1		1
24 Plymouth Argyle	–	–		–		–	–	–		1		1	–			–			–			–			–			1		1

JOHN ANDERSON

DEBUT (Full Appearance)

Saturday 20/12/1947
Football League Division 1
at Maine Road

Manchester United 2 Middlesbrough 1

CLUB CAREER RECORD	Apps	Subs	Goals
Premiership	0		0
League Division 1	33		1
League Division 2	0		0
FA Cup	6		1
League Cup	0		0
European Cup / Champions League	0		0
European Cup-Winners' Cup	0		0
UEFA Cup / Inter-Cities' Fairs Cup	0		0
Other Matches	1		0
OVERALL TOTAL	**40**		**2**

Opponents	PREM			FLD 1			FLD 2			FAC			LC			EC/CL			ECWC			UEFA			OTHER			TOTAL		
	A	S	G	A	S	G	A	S	G	A	S	G	A	S	G	A	S	G	A	S	G	A	S	G	A	S	G	A	S	G
1 Blackpool	–	–		3		–	–	–		1		1	–			–			–			–			–			4		1
2 Wolverhampton W.	–	–		3		–	–	–		1			–			–			–			–			–			4		–
3 Arsenal	–	–		2		–	–	–		–			–			–			–			–			1			3		–
4 Chelsea	–	–		3		–	–	–		–			–			–			–			–			–			3		–
5 Derby County	–	–		2		–	–	–		1			–			–			–			–			–			3		–
6 Bolton Wanderers	–	–		2		1	–	–		–			–			–			–			–			–			2		1
7 Aston Villa	–	–		1		–	–	–		1			–			–			–			–			–			2		–
8 Burnley	–	–		2		–	–	–		–			–			–			–			–			–			2		–
9 Huddersfield Town	–	–		2		–	–	–		–			–			–			–			–			–			2		–
10 Portsmouth	–	–		2		–	–	–		–			–			–			–			–			–			2		–
11 Stoke City	–	–		2		–	–	–		–			–			–			–			–			–			2		–
12 Birmingham City	–	–		1		–	–	–		–			–			–			–			–			–			1		–
13 Blackburn Rovers	–	–		1		–	–	–		–			–			–			–			–			–			1		–
14 Charlton Athletic	–	–		1		–	–	–		–			–			–			–			–			–			1		–
15 Everton	–	–		1		–	–	–		–			–			–			–			–			–			1		–
16 Grimsby Town	–	–		1		–	–	–		–			–			–			–			–			–			1		–
17 Liverpool	–	–		–		–	–	–		1			–			–			–			–			–			1		–
18 Manchester City	–	–		1		–	–	–		–			–			–			–			–			–			1		–
19 Middlesbrough	–	–		1		–	–	–		–			–			–			–			–			–			1		–
20 Preston North End	–	–		–		–	–	–		1			–			–			–			–			–			1		–
21 Sheffield United	–	–		1		–	–	–		–			–			–			–			–			–			1		–
22 Sunderland	–	–		1		–	–	–		–			–			–			–			–			–			1		–

TREVOR ANDERSON

DEBUT (Substitute Appearance)

Saturday 31/03/1973
Football League Division 1
at The Dell

Southampton 0 Manchester United 2

CLUB CAREER RECORD	Apps	Subs	Goals
Premiership	0		0
League Division 1	13	(6)	2
League Division 2	0		0
FA Cup	0		0
League Cup	0		0
European Cup / Champions League	0		0
European Cup-Winners' Cup	0		0
UEFA Cup / Inter-Cities' Fairs Cup	0		0
Other Matches	0		0
OVERALL TOTAL	**13**	**(6)**	**2**

Opponents	PREM A	S	G	FLD 1 A	S	G	FLD 2 A	S	G	FAC A	S	G	LC A	S	G	EC/CL A	S	G	ECWC A	S	G	UEFA A	S	G	OTHER A	S	G	TOTAL A	S	G
1 Leeds United	-	-		2		1	-			-			-			-			-			-			-			2		1
2 Leicester City	-	-		2		-	-			-			-			-			-			-			-			2		-
3 Stoke City	-	-		2		-	-			-			-			-			-			-			-			2		-
4 Southampton	-	-		-	(2)	-	-			-			-			-			-			-			-			-	(2)	-
5 Ipswich Town	-	-		1		1	-			-			-			-			-			-			-			1		1
6 Arsenal	-	-		1		-	-			-			-			-			-			-			-			1		-
7 Derby County	-	-		1		-	-			-			-			-			-			-			-			1		-
8 Liverpool	-	-		1		-	-			-			-			-			-			-			-			1		-
9 Queens Park Rangers	-	-		1		-	-			-			-			-			-			-			-			1		-
10 West Ham United	-	-		1		-	-			-			-			-			-			-			-			1		-
11 Wolverhampton W.	-	-		1		-	-			-			-			-			-			-			-			1		-
12 Chelsea	-	-		-	(1)	-	-			-			-			-			-			-			-			-	(1)	-
13 Crystal Palace	-	-		-	(1)	-	-			-			-			-			-			-			-			-	(1)	-
14 Manchester City	-	-		-	(1)	-	-			-			-			-			-			-			-			-	(1)	-
15 Norwich City	-	-		-	(1)	-	-			-			-			-			-			-			-			-	(1)	-

VIV ANDERSON

DEBUT (Full Appearance)

Saturday 15/08/1987
Football League Division 1
at The Dell

Southampton 2 Manchester United 2

CLUB CAREER RECORD	Apps	Subs	Goals
Premiership	0		0
League Division 1	50	(4)	2
League Division 2	0		0
FA Cup	7		1
League Cup	6	(1)	1
European Cup / Champions League	0		0
European Cup-Winners' Cup	1		0
UEFA Cup / Inter-Cities' Fairs Cup	0		0
Other Matches	0		0
OVERALL TOTAL	**64**	**(5)**	**4**

Opponents	PREM A	S	G	FLD 1 A	S	G	FLD 2 A	S	G	FAC A	S	G	LC A	S	G	EC/CL A	S	G	ECWC A	S	G	UEFA A	S	G	OTHER A	S	G	TOTAL A	S	G
1 Arsenal	-	-		3		-	-			1		-	-			-			-			-			-			4		-
2 Chelsea	-	-		3		-	-			1		-	-			-			-			-			-			4		-
3 Derby County	-	-		4		-	-			-			-			-			-			-			-			4		-
4 Liverpool	-	-		4		-	-			-			-			-			-			-			-			4		-
5 Nottingham Forest	-	-		3		-	-			1		-	-			-			-			-			-			4		-
6 Wimbledon	-	-		3		-	-			-			-	(1)	-	-			-			-			-			3	(1)	-
7 Tottenham Hotspur	-	-		2	(2)	-	-			-			-			-			-			-			-			2	(2)	-
8 Millwall	-	-		3		-	-			-			-			-			-			-			-			3		-
9 Southampton	-	-		3		-	-			-			-			-			-			-			-			3		-
10 Everton	-	-		2	(1)	-	-			-			-			-			-			-			-			2	(1)	-
11 Newcastle United	-	-		1	(1)	-	-			1		-	-			-			-			-			-			2	(1)	-
12 Oxford United	-	-		1		1	-			-			1			-			-			-			-			2		1
13 West Ham United	-	-		2		1	-			-			-			-			-			-			-			2		1
14 Aston Villa	-	-		2		-	-			-			-			-			-			-			-			2		-
15 Charlton Athletic	-	-		2		-	-			-			-			-			-			-			-			2		-
16 Coventry City	-	-		2		-	-			-			-			-			-			-			-			2		-
17 Luton Town	-	-		2		-	-			-			-			-			-			-			-			2		-
18 Manchester City	-	-		2		-	-			-			-			-			-			-			-			2		-
19 Portsmouth	-	-		1		-	-			-			1			-			-			-			-			2		-
20 Queens Park Rangers	-	-		2		-	-			-			-			-			-			-			-			2		-
21 Watford	-	-		2		-	-			-			-			-			-			-			-			2		-
22 Halifax Town	-	-		-		-	-			-			1		1	-			-			-			-			1		1
23 Ipswich Town	-	-		-		-	-			1		1	-			-			-			-			-			1		1
24 Bury	-	-		-		-	-			-			1			-			-			-			-			1		-
25 Crystal Palace	-	-		-		-	-			-			1			-			-			-			-			1		-
26 Hereford United	-	-		-		-	-			1			-			-			-			-			-			1		-
27 Hull City	-	-		-		-	-			-			1			-			-			-			-			1		-
28 Norwich City	-	-		1		-	-			-			-			-			-			-			-			1		-
29 Pecsi Munkas	-	-		-		-	-			-			-			-			1			-			-			1		-
30 Sheffield United	-	-		-		-	-			1			-			-			-			-			-			1		-

WILLIE ANDERSON

DEBUT (Full Appearance)

Saturday 28/12/1963
Football League Division 1
at Old Trafford

Manchester United 5 Burnley 1

CLUB CAREER RECORD	Apps	Subs	Goals
Premiership	0		0
League Division 1	7	(2)	0
League Division 2	0		0
FA Cup	2		0
League Cup	0		0
European Cup / Champions League	1		0
European Cup-Winners' Cup	0		0
UEFA Cup / Inter-Cities' Fairs Cup	0		0
Other Matches	0		0
OVERALL TOTAL	10	(2)	0

Opponents	PREM A S G	FLD 1 A S G	FLD 2 A S G	FAC A S G	LC A S G	EC/CL A S G	ECWC A S G	UEFA A S G	OTHER A S G	TOTAL A S G
1 Everton	- - -	1 - -	- - -	1 - -	- - -	- - -	- - -	- - -	- - -	2 - -
2 Aston Villa	- - -	1 - -	- - -	- - -	- - -	- - -	- - -	- - -	- - -	1 - -
3 Burnley	- - -	1 - -	- - -	- - -	- - -	- - -	- - -	- - -	- - -	1 - -
4 Leicester City	- - -	1 - -	- - -	- - -	- - -	- - -	- - -	- - -	- - -	1 - -
5 Partizan Belgrade	- - -	- - -	- - -	- - -	- - -	1 - -	- - -	- - -	- - -	1 - -
6 Sheffield United	- - -	1 - -	- - -	- - -	- - -	- - -	- - -	- - -	- - -	1 - -
7 Sheffield Wednesday	- - -	1 - -	- - -	- - -	- - -	- - -	- - -	- - -	- - -	1 - -
8 Southampton	- - -	- - -	- - -	1 - -	- - -	- - -	- - -	- - -	- - -	1 - -
9 West Ham United	- - -	1 - -	- - -	- - -	- - -	- - -	- - -	- - -	- - -	1 - -
10 Liverpool	- - -	- (1) -	- - -	- - -	- - -	- - -	- - -	- - -	- - -	- (1) -
11 West Bromwich Albion	- - -	- (1) -	- - -	- - -	- - -	- - -	- - -	- - -	- - -	- (1) -

MICHAEL APPLETON

DEBUT (Full Appearance)

Wednesday 23/10/1996
League Cup 3rd Round
at Old Trafford

Manchester United 2 Swindon Town 1

CLUB CAREER RECORD	Apps	Subs	Goals
Premiership	0		0
League Division 1	0		0
League Division 2	0		0
FA Cup	0		0
League Cup	1	(1)	0
European Cup / Champions League	0		0
European Cup-Winners' Cup	0		0
UEFA Cup / Inter-Cities' Fairs Cup	0		0
Other Matches	0		0
OVERALL TOTAL	1	(1)	0

Opponents	PREM A S G	FLD 1 A S G	FLD 2 A S G	FAC A S G	LC A S G	EC/CL A S G	ECWC A S G	UEFA A S G	OTHER A S G	TOTAL A S G
1 Swindon Town	- - -	- - -	- - -	- - -	1 - -	- - -	- - -	- - -	- - -	1 - -
2 Leicester City	- - -	- - -	- - -	- - -	- (1) -	- - -	- - -	- - -	- - -	- (1) -

TOMMY ARKESDEN

DEBUT (Full Appearance)

Saturday 14/02/1903
Football League Division 2
at Bloomfield Road

Blackpool 2 Manchester United 0

CLUB CAREER RECORD	Apps	Subs	Goals
Premiership	0		0
League Division 1	0		0
League Division 2	70		28
FA Cup	9		5
League Cup	0		0
European Cup / Champions League	0		0
European Cup-Winners' Cup	0		0
UEFA Cup / Inter-Cities' Fairs Cup	0		0
Other Matches	0		0
OVERALL TOTAL	79		33

Opponents	PREM A S G	FLD 1 A S G	FLD 2 A S G	FAC A S G	LC A S G	EC/CL A S G	ECWC A S G	UEFA A S G	OTHER A S G	TOTAL A S G
1 Lincoln City	- - -	- - -	6 1 -	- - -	- - -	- - -	- - -	- - -	- - -	6 1 -
2 Bradford City	- - -	- - -	5 3 -	- - -	- - -	- - -	- - -	- - -	- - -	5 3 -
3 Port Vale	- - -	- - -	5 2 -	- - -	- - -	- - -	- - -	- - -	- - -	5 2 -
4 Blackpool	- - -	- - -	5 1 -	- - -	- - -	- - -	- - -	- - -	- - -	5 1 -
5 Glossop	- - -	- - -	4 4 -	- - -	- - -	- - -	- - -	- - -	- - -	4 4 -
6 Burton United	- - -	- - -	4 3 -	- - -	- - -	- - -	- - -	- - -	- - -	4 3 -
7 Bristol City	- - -	- - -	4 1 -	- - -	- - -	- - -	- - -	- - -	- - -	4 1 -
8 Burnley	- - -	- - -	4 1 -	- - -	- - -	- - -	- - -	- - -	- - -	4 1 -
9 Barnsley	- - -	- - -	4 - -	- - -	- - -	- - -	- - -	- - -	- - -	4 - -
10 Birmingham City	- - -	- - -	- - -	3 3 -	- - -	- - -	- - -	- - -	- - -	3 3 -
11 Chesterfield	- - -	- - -	3 2 -	- - -	- - -	- - -	- - -	- - -	- - -	3 2 -
12 Arsenal	- - -	- - -	3 1 -	- - -	- - -	- - -	- - -	- - -	- - -	3 1 -
13 Doncaster Rovers	- - -	- - -	3 1 -	- - -	- - -	- - -	- - -	- - -	- - -	3 1 -
14 Fulham	- - -	- - -	- - -	3 1 -	- - -	- - -	- - -	- - -	- - -	3 1 -
15 Leicester City	- - -	- - -	3 1 -	- - -	- - -	- - -	- - -	- - -	- - -	3 1 -
16 Preston North End	- - -	- - -	3 1 -	- - -	- - -	- - -	- - -	- - -	- - -	3 1 -
17 Bolton Wanderers	- - -	- - -	3 - -	- - -	- - -	- - -	- - -	- - -	- - -	3 - -
18 Gainsborough Trinity	- - -	- - -	2 3 -	- - -	- - -	- - -	- - -	- - -	- - -	2 3 -
19 Liverpool	- - -	- - -	2 1 -	- - -	- - -	- - -	- - -	- - -	- - -	2 1 -
20 Notts County	- - -	- - -	- - -	2 1 -	- - -	- - -	- - -	- - -	- - -	2 1 -

continued../

TOMMY ARKESDEN (continued)

Opponents	PREM A S G	FLD 1 A S G	FLD 2 A S G	FAC A S G	LC A S G	EC/CL A S G	ECWC A S G	UEFA A S G	OTHER A S G	TOTAL A S G
21 West Bromwich Albion	–	–	2 1	–	–	–	–	–	–	2 1
22 Grimsby Town	–	–	2 –	–	–	–	–	–	–	2 –
23 Stockport County	–	–	1 1	–	–	–	–	–	–	1 1
24 Hull City	–	–	–	1	–	–	–	–	–	1 –
25 Manchester City	–	–	–	1	–	–	–	–	–	1 –
26 Sheffield Wednesday	–	–	–	–	1	–	–	–	–	1 –

JOE ASTLEY

DEBUT (Full Appearance)

Wednesday 17/03/1926
Football League Division 1
at Burnden Park

Bolton Wanderers 3 Manchester United 1

CLUB CAREER RECORD	Apps	Subs	Goals
Premiership	0		0
League Division 1	2		0
League Division 2	0		0
FA Cup	0		0
League Cup	0		0
European Cup / Champions League	0		0
European Cup-Winners' Cup	0		0
UEFA Cup / Inter-Cities' Fairs Cup	0		0
Other Matches	0		0
OVERALL TOTAL	**2**		**0**

Opponents	PREM A S G	FLD 1 A S G	FLD 2 A S G	FAC A S G	LC A S G	EC/CL A S G	ECWC A S G	UEFA A S G	OTHER A S G	TOTAL A S G
1 Bolton Wanderers	–	1	–	–	–	–	–	–	–	1 –
2 Sunderland	–	1	–	–	–	–	–	–	–	1 –

JOHN ASTON (junior)

DEBUT (Full Appearance)

Saturday 12/04/1965
Football League Division 1
at Old Trafford

Manchester United 1 Leicester City 0

CLUB CAREER RECORD	Apps	Subs	Goals
Premiership	0		0
League Division 1	139	(16)	25
League Division 2	0		0
FA Cup	5	(2)	1
League Cup	12	(3)	0
European Cup / Champions League	8		1
European Cup-Winners' Cup	0		0
UEFA Cup / Inter-Cities' Fairs Cup	0		0
Other Matches	2		0
OVERALL TOTAL	**166**	**(21)**	**27**

Opponents	PREM A S G	FLD 1 A S G	FLD 2 A S G	FAC A S G	LC A S G	EC/CL A S G	ECWC A S G	UEFA A S G	OTHER A S G	TOTAL A S G
1 West Bromwich Albion	–	10 2	–	–	–	–	–	–	–	10 2
2 Stoke City	–	8 2	–	–	– (2)	–	–	–	–	8 (2) 2
3 Tottenham Hotspur	–	5 (1) –	–	2	–	–	–	1	–	8 (1) –
4 Southampton	–	6 (2) 1	–	–	– (1) 1	–	–	–	–	6 (3) 2
5 Manchester City	–	4 (3) –	–	1	1	–	–	–	–	6 (3) –
6 West Ham United	–	8 2	–	–	–	–	–	–	–	8 2
7 Nottingham Forest	–	8 1	–	–	–	–	–	–	–	8 1
8 Chelsea	–	6 (1) 2	–	–	1	–	–	–	–	7 (1) 2
9 Burnley	–	4 (1) 1	–	–	3	–	–	–	–	7 (1) 1
10 Everton	–	7 1	–	–	–	–	–	–	–	7 1
11 Leeds United	–	7 –	–	–	–	–	–	–	–	7 –
12 Liverpool	–	6 –	–	–	–	–	–	1	–	7 –
13 Arsenal	–	6 (1) 3	–	–	–	–	–	–	–	6 (1) 3
14 Newcastle United	–	6 (1) –	–	–	–	–	–	–	–	6 (1) –
15 Sheffield Wednesday	–	5 (2) –	–	–	–	–	–	–	–	5 (2) –
16 Fulham	–	6 1	–	–	–	–	–	–	–	6 1
17 Sheffield United	–	6 1	–	–	–	–	–	–	–	6 1
18 Derby County	–	3 –	–	1	2	–	–	–	–	6 –
19 Aston Villa	–	4 1	–	–	1	–	–	–	–	5 1
20 Leicester City	–	5 1	–	–	–	–	–	–	–	5 1
21 Coventry City	–	4 (1) 3	–	–	–	–	–	–	–	4 (1) 3
22 Blackpool	–	3 –	–	–	1	–	–	–	–	4 –
23 Sunderland	–	4 –	–	–	–	–	–	–	–	4 –
24 Ipswich Town	–	1 (1) –	–	–	1 (1) –	–	–	–	–	2 (2) –
25 Crystal Palace	–	1 (1) –	–	–	1	–	–	–	–	2 (1) –
26 Sarajevo	–	–	–	–	–	2 1	–	–	–	2 1
27 Wolverhampton W.	–	2 1	–	–	–	–	–	–	–	2 1
28 Blackburn Rovers	–	2 –	–	–	–	–	–	–	–	2 –
29 HJK Helsinki	–	–	–	–	–	2	–	–	–	2 –
30 Real Madrid	–	–	–	–	–	2	–	–	–	2 –
31 Huddersfield Town	–	1 (1) 1	–	–	–	–	–	–	–	1 (1) 1
32 Queens Park Rangers	–	1 1	–	–	–	–	–	–	–	1 1
33 Benfica	–	–	–	–	–	1	–	–	–	1 –
34 Gornik Zabrze	–	–	–	–	–	1	–	–	–	1 –
35 Preston North End	–	–	–	1	–	–	–	–	–	1 –
36 Wrexham	–	–	–	–	1	–	–	–	–	1 –
37 Portsmouth	–	–	–	–	– (1)	–	–	–	–	– (1) –

JOHN ASTON (senior)

DEBUT (Full Appearance)

Wednesday 18/09/1946
Football League Division 1
at Maine Road

Manchester United 1 Chelsea 1

CLUB CAREER RECORD	Apps	Subs	Goals
Premiership	0		0
League Division 1	253		29
League Division 2	0		0
FA Cup	29		1
League Cup	0		0
European Cup / Champions League	0		0
European Cup-Winners' Cup	0		0
UEFA Cup / Inter-Cities' Fairs Cup	0		0
Other Matches	2		0
OVERALL TOTAL	**284**		**30**

	Opponents	PREM A S G	FLD 1 A S G	FLD 2 A S G	FAC A S G	LC A S G	EC/CL A S G	ECWC A S G	UEFA A S G	OTHER A S G	TOTAL A S G
1	Portsmouth	– –	14 –	– –	2 –	– –	– –	– –	– –	– –	16 –
2	Arsenal	– –	13 2	– –	1 –	– –	– –	– –	– –	1 –	15 2
3	Chelsea	– –	13 1	– –	1 –	– –	– –	– –	– –	– –	14 1
4	Liverpool	– –	13 1	– –	1 –	– –	– –	– –	– –	– –	14 1
5	Wolverhampton W.	– –	12 1	– –	2 –	– –	– –	– –	– –	– –	14 1
6	Charlton Athletic	– –	12 2	– –	1 –	– –	– –	– –	– –	– –	13 2
7	Sunderland	– –	13 2	– –	– –	– –	– –	– –	– –	– –	13 2
8	Blackpool	– –	12 –	– –	1 –	– –	– –	– –	– –	– –	13 –
9	Derby County	– –	11 3	– –	1 –	– –	– –	– –	– –	– –	12 3
10	Burnley	– –	12 2	– –	– –	– –	– –	– –	– –	– –	12 2
11	Aston Villa	– –	11 –	– –	1 –	– –	– –	– –	– –	– –	12 –
12	Middlesbrough	– –	11 1	– –	– –	– –	– –	– –	– –	– –	11 1
13	Stoke City	– –	11 –	– –	– –	– –	– –	– –	– –	– –	11 –
14	Preston North End	– –	9 4	– –	1 –	– –	– –	– –	– –	– –	10 4
15	Bolton Wanderers	– –	10 1	– –	– –	– –	– –	– –	– –	– –	10 1
16	Newcastle United	– –	9 1	– –	– –	– –	– –	– –	1 –	– –	10 1
17	Manchester City	– –	10 –	– –	– –	– –	– –	– –	– –	– –	10 –
18	Huddersfield Town	– –	9 4	– –	– –	– –	– –	– –	– –	– –	9 4
19	Everton	– –	8 2	– –	1 –	– –	– –	– –	– –	– –	9 2
20	West Bromwich Albion	– –	7 –	– –	– –	– –	– –	– –	– –	– –	7 –
21	Sheffield United	– –	6 1	– –	– –	– –	– –	– –	– –	– –	6 1
22	Birmingham City	– –	4 –	– –	1 –	– –	– –	– –	– –	– –	5 –
23	Tottenham Hotspur	– –	5 –	– –	– –	– –	– –	– –	– –	– –	5 –
24	Bradford Park Avenue	– –	– –	– –	4 –	– –	– –	– –	– –	– –	4 –
25	Fulham	– –	4 –	– –	– –	– –	– –	– –	– –	– –	4 –
26	Blackburn Rovers	– –	3 –	– –	– –	– –	– –	– –	– –	– –	3 –
27	Grimsby Town	– –	3 –	– –	– –	– –	– –	– –	– –	– –	3 –
28	Leeds United	– –	2 –	– –	1 –	– –	– –	– –	– –	– –	3 –
29	Sheffield Wednesday	– –	3 –	– –	– –	– –	– –	– –	– –	– –	3 –
30	Cardiff City	– –	2 1	– –	– –	– –	– –	– –	– –	– –	2 1
31	Walthamstow Avenue	– –	– –	– –	2 –	– –	– –	– –	– –	– –	2 –
32	Oldham Athletic	– –	– –	– –	1 1	– –	– –	– –	– –	– –	1 1
33	Bournemouth	– –	– –	– –	1 –	– –	– –	– –	– –	– –	1 –
34	Brentford	– –	1 –	– –	– –	– –	– –	– –	– –	– –	1 –
35	Hull City	– –	– –	– –	1 –	– –	– –	– –	– –	– –	1 –
36	Millwall	– –	– –	– –	1 –	– –	– –	– –	– –	– –	1 –
37	Nottingham Forest	– –	– –	– –	1 –	– –	– –	– –	– –	– –	1 –
38	Watford	– –	– –	– –	1 –	– –	– –	– –	– –	– –	1 –
39	Weymouth Town	– –	– –	– –	1 –	– –	– –	– –	– –	– –	1 –
40	Yeovil Town	– –	– –	– –	1 –	– –	– –	– –	– –	– –	1 –

GARY BAILEY

DEBUT (Full Appearance)

Saturday 18/11/1978
Football League Division 1
at Old Trafford

Manchester United 2 Ipswich Town 0

CLUB CAREER RECORD	Apps	Subs	Goals
Premiership	0		0
League Division 1	294		0
League Division 2	0		0
FA Cup	31		0
League Cup	28		0
European Cup / Champions League	0		0
European Cup-Winners' Cup	8		0
UEFA Cup / Inter-Cities' Fairs Cup	12		0
Other Matches	2		0
OVERALL TOTAL	**375**		**0**

	Opponents	PREM A S G	FLD 1 A S G	FLD 2 A S G	FAC A S G	LC A S G	EC/CL A S G	ECWC A S G	UEFA A S G	OTHER A S G	TOTAL A S G
1	Liverpool	– –	15 –	– –	4 –	2 –	– –	– –	– –	1 –	22 –
2	Tottenham Hotspur	– –	14 –	– –	4 –	4 –	– –	– –	– –	– –	22 –
3	Arsenal	– –	15 –	– –	2 –	2 –	– –	– –	– –	– –	19 –
4	Everton	– –	14 –	– –	2 –	1 –	– –	– –	1 –	– –	18 –
5	Nottingham Forest	– –	15 –	– –	1 –	1 –	– –	– –	– –	– –	17 –
6	Coventry City	– –	13 –	– –	– –	2 –	– –	– –	– –	– –	15 –
7	Ipswich Town	– –	15 –	– –	– –	– –	– –	– –	– –	– –	15 –
8	Aston Villa	– –	14 –	– –	– –	– –	– –	– –	– –	– –	14 –
9	Southampton	– –	13 –	– –	– –	1 –	– –	– –	– –	– –	14 –
10	West Bromwich Albion	– –	14 –	– –	– –	– –	– –	– –	– –	– –	14 –
11	Norwich City	– –	12 –	– –	– –	1 –	– –	– –	– –	– –	13 –

continued../

GARY BAILEY (continued)

Opponents	PREM A S G	FLD 1 A S G	FLD 2 A S G	FAC A S G	LC A S G	EC/CL A S G	ECWC A S G	UEFA A S G	OTHER A S G	TOTAL A S G
12 West Ham United	– –	10 –	– –	2 –	1 –	– –	– –	– –	– –	13 –
13 Brighton	– –	7 –	– –	4 –	– –	– –	– –	– –	– –	11 –
14 Manchester City	– –	11 –	– –	– –	– –	– –	– –	– –	– –	11 –
15 Stoke City	– –	11 –	– –	– –	– –	– –	– –	– –	– –	11 –
16 Sunderland	– –	9 –	– –	2 –	– –	– –	– –	– –	– –	11 –
17 Luton Town	– –	8 –	– –	1 –	– –	– –	– –	– –	– –	9 –
18 Wolverhampton W.	– –	8 –	– –	– –	– –	– –	– –	– –	– –	8 –
19 Birmingham City	– –	7 –	– –	– –	– –	– –	– –	– –	– –	7 –
20 Chelsea	– –	6 –	– –	1 –	– –	– –	– –	– –	– –	7 –
21 Leeds United	– –	7 –	– –	– –	– –	– –	– –	– –	– –	7 –
22 Leicester City	– –	7 –	– –	– –	– –	– –	– –	– –	– –	7 –
23 Middlesbrough	– –	7 –	– –	– –	– –	– –	– –	– –	– –	7 –
24 Watford	– –	6 –	– –	1 –	– –	– –	– –	– –	– –	7 –
25 Crystal Palace	– –	4 –	– –	– –	2 –	– –	– –	– –	– –	6 –
26 Queens Park Rangers	– –	6 –	– –	– –	– –	– –	– –	– –	– –	6 –
27 Derby County	– –	4 –	– –	1 –	– –	– –	– –	– –	– –	5 –
28 Bolton Wanderers	– –	4 –	– –	– –	– –	– –	– –	– –	– –	4 –
29 Bournemouth	– –	– –	– –	2 –	2 –	– –	– –	– –	– –	4 –
30 Notts County	– –	4 –	– –	– –	– –	– –	– –	– –	– –	4 –
31 Oxford United	– –	2 –	– –	– –	2 –	– –	– –	– –	– –	4 –
32 Swansea City	– –	4 –	– –	– –	– –	– –	– –	– –	– –	4 –
33 Bristol City	– –	3 –	– –	– –	– –	– –	– –	– –	– –	3 –
34 Sheffield Wednesday	– –	3 –	– –	– –	– –	– –	– –	– –	– –	3 –
35 Barcelona	– –	– –	– –	– –	– –	– –	2 –	– –	– –	2 –
36 Bradford City	– –	– –	– –	– –	2 –	– –	– –	– –	– –	2 –
37 Burnley	– –	– –	– –	– –	2 –	– –	– –	– –	– –	2 –
38 Colchester United	– –	– –	– –	1 –	1 –	– –	– –	– –	– –	2 –
39 Dukla Prague	– –	– –	– –	– –	– –	2 –	– –	– –	– –	2 –
40 Dundee United	– –	– –	– –	– –	– –	– –	– –	2 –	– –	2 –
41 Fulham	– –	– –	– –	2 –	– –	– –	– –	– –	– –	2 –
42 Juventus	– –	– –	– –	– –	– –	– –	2 –	– –	– –	2 –
43 Newcastle United	– –	2 –	– –	– –	– –	– –	– –	– –	– –	2 –
44 Port Vale	– –	– –	– –	– –	2 –	– –	– –	– –	– –	2 –
45 PSV Eindhoven	– –	– –	– –	– –	– –	– –	– –	2 –	– –	2 –
46 Raba Vasas	– –	– –	– –	– –	– –	– –	– –	2 –	– –	2 –
47 Spartak Varna	– –	– –	– –	– –	– –	– –	2 –	– –	– –	2 –
48 Valencia	– –	– –	– –	– –	– –	– –	– –	2 –	– –	2 –
49 Videoton	– –	– –	– –	– –	– –	– –	– –	2 –	– –	2 –
50 Widzew Lodz	– –	– –	– –	– –	– –	– –	– –	2 –	– –	2 –
51 Blackburn Rovers	– –	– –	– –	1 –	– –	– –	– –	– –	– –	1 –

DAVID BAIN

DEBUT (Full Appearance)

Saturday 14/10/1922
Football League Division 2
at Old Recreation Ground

Port Vale 1 Manchester United 0

CLUB CAREER RECORD	Apps	Subs	Goals
Premiership	0		0
League Division 1	0		0
League Division 2	22		9
FA Cup	1		0
League Cup	0		0
European Cup / Champions League	0		0
European Cup-Winners' Cup	0		0
UEFA Cup / Inter-Cities' Fairs Cup	0		0
Other Matches	0		0
OVERALL TOTAL	**23**		**9**

Opponents	PREM A S G	FLD 1 A S G	FLD 2 A S G	FAC A S G	LC A S G	EC/CL A S G	ECWC A S G	UEFA A S G	OTHER A S G	TOTAL A S G
1 Leicester City	– – –	– – –	4 1	– – –	– – –	– – –	– – –	– – –	– – –	4 1
2 Port Vale	– – –	– – –	3 3	– – –	– – –	– – –	– – –	– – –	– – –	3 3
3 Bradford City	– – –	– – –	2 1	– – –	– – –	– – –	– – –	– – –	– – –	2 1
4 Coventry City	– – –	– – –	2 1	– – –	– – –	– – –	– – –	– – –	– – –	2 1
5 Stockport County	– – –	– – –	2 1	– – –	– – –	– – –	– – –	– – –	– – –	2 1
6 Barnsley	– – –	– – –	2 –	– – –	– – –	– – –	– – –	– – –	– – –	2 –
7 Blackpool	– – –	– – –	2 –	– – –	– – –	– – –	– – –	– – –	– – –	2 –
8 Leeds United	– – –	– – –	2 –	– – –	– – –	– – –	– – –	– – –	– – –	2 –
9 Oldham Athletic	– – –	– – –	1 2	– – –	– – –	– – –	– – –	– – –	– – –	1 2
10 Fulham	– – –	– – –	1 –	– – –	– – –	– – –	– – –	– – –	– – –	1 –
11 Plymouth Argyle	– – –	– – –	– –	1 –	– – –	– – –	– – –	– – –	– – –	1 –
12 Southampton	– – –	– – –	1 –	– – –	– – –	– – –	– – –	– – –	– – –	1 –

JAMES BAIN

DEBUT (Full Appearance, 1 goal)

Saturday 16/09/1899
Football League Division 2
at Bank Street

Newton Heath 4 Loughborough Town 0

CLUB CAREER RECORD	Apps	Subs	Goals
Premiership	0		0
League Division 1	0		0
League Division 2	2		1
FA Cup	0		0
League Cup	0		0
European Cup / Champions League	0		0
European Cup-Winners' Cup	0		0
UEFA Cup / Inter-Cities' Fairs Cup	0		0
Other Matches	0		0
OVERALL TOTAL	2		1

Opponents	PREM A S G	FLD 1 A S G	FLD 2 A S G	FAC A S G	LC A S G	EC/CL A S G	ECWC A S G	UEFA A S G	OTHER A S G	TOTAL A S G
1 Loughborough Town	– –	– –	1 1	– –	– –	– –	– –	– –	– –	1 1
2 Burton Swifts	– –	– –	1 –	– –	– –	– –	– –	– –	– –	1 –

JIMMY BAIN

DEBUT (Full Appearance)

Saturday 07/02/1925
Football League Division 2
at Old Trafford

Manchester United 4 Leyton Orient 2

CLUB CAREER RECORD	Apps	Subs	Goals
Premiership	0		0
League Division 1	3		0
League Division 2	1		0
FA Cup	0		0
League Cup	0		0
European Cup / Champions League	0		0
European Cup-Winners' Cup	0		0
UEFA Cup / Inter-Cities' Fairs Cup	0		0
Other Matches	0		0
OVERALL TOTAL	4		0

Opponents	PREM A S G	FLD 1 A S G	FLD 2 A S G	FAC A S G	LC A S G	EC/CL A S G	ECWC A S G	UEFA A S G	OTHER A S G	TOTAL A S G
1 Blackburn Rovers	– –	1 –	– –	– –	– –	– –	– –	– –	– –	1 –
2 Leyton Orient	– –	– –	1 –	– –	– –	– –	– –	– –	– –	1 –
3 Liverpool	– –	1 –	– –	– –	– –	– –	– –	– –	– –	1 –
4 West Ham United	– –	1 –	– –	– –	– –	– –	– –	– –	– –	1 –

BILL BAINBRIDGE

DEBUT (Full Appearance, 1 goal)

Wednesday 09/01/1946
FA Cup 3rd Round 2nd Leg
at Maine Road

Manchester United 5 Accrington Stanley 1

CLUB CAREER RECORD	Apps	Subs	Goals
Premiership	0		0
League Division 1	0		0
League Division 2	0		0
FA Cup	1		1
League Cup	0		0
European Cup / Champions League	0		0
European Cup-Winners' Cup	0		0
UEFA Cup / Inter-Cities' Fairs Cup	0		0
Other Matches	0		0
OVERALL TOTAL	1		1

Opponents	PREM A S G	FLD 1 A S G	FLD 2 A S G	FAC A S G	LC A S G	EC/CL A S G	ECWC A S G	UEFA A S G	OTHER A S G	TOTAL A S G
1 Accrington Stanley	– –	– –	– –	1 1	– –	– –	– –	– –	– –	1 1

HARRY BAIRD

DEBUT (Full Appearance)

Saturday 23/01/1937
Football League Division 1
at Hillsborough

Sheffield Wednesday 1 Manchester United 0

CLUB CAREER RECORD	Apps	Subs	Goals
Premiership	0		0
League Division 1	14		3
League Division 2	35		12
FA Cup	4		3
League Cup	0		0
European Cup / Champions League	0		0
European Cup-Winners' Cup	0		0
UEFA Cup / Inter-Cities' Fairs Cup	0		0
Other Matches	0		0
OVERALL TOTAL	53		18

Opponents	PREM A S G	FLD 1 A S G	FLD 2 A S G	FAC A S G	LC A S G	EC/CL A S G	ECWC A S G	UEFA A S G	OTHER A S G	TOTAL A S G
1 Barnsley	– –	– –	1 –	2 2	– –	– –	– –	– –	– –	3 2
2 Nottingham Forest	– –	– –	2 2	– –	– –	– –	– –	– –	– –	2 2
3 West Ham United	– –	– –	2 2	– –	– –	– –	– –	– –	– –	2 2
4 Blackburn Rovers	– –	– –	2 1	– –	– –	– –	– –	– –	– –	2 1
5 Bradford Park Avenue	– –	– –	2 1	– –	– –	– –	– –	– –	– –	2 1
6 Brentford	– –	1 1	– –	1 –	– –	– –	– –	– –	– –	2 1
7 Burnley	– –	– –	2 1	– –	– –	– –	– –	– –	– –	2 1
8 Chesterfield	– –	– –	2 1	– –	– –	– –	– –	– –	– –	2 1

continued../

HARRY BAIRD (continued)

Opponents	PREM A S G	FLD 1 A S G	FLD 2 A S G	FAC A S G	LC A S G	EC/CL A S G	ECWC A S G	UEFA A S G	OTHER A S G	TOTAL A S G
9 Everton	– –	2 1	–	–	–	–	–	–	–	2 1
10 Norwich City	– –	– –	2 1	–	–	–	–	–	–	2 1
11 Sheffield Wednesday	– –	1 –	1 1	–	–	–	–	–	–	2 1
12 Aston Villa	– –	– –	2	–	–	–	–	–	–	2 –
13 Coventry City	– –	– –	2	–	–	–	–	–	–	2 –
14 Luton Town	– –	– –	2	–	–	–	–	–	–	2 –
15 Newcastle United	– –	– –	2	–	–	–	–	–	–	2 –
16 Sheffield United	– –	– –	2	–	–	–	–	–	–	2 –
17 Swansea City	– –	– –	2	–	–	–	–	–	–	2 –
18 Tottenham Hotspur	– –	– –	2	–	–	–	–	–	–	2 –
19 Fulham	– –	– –	1 1	–	–	–	–	–	–	1 1
20 Southampton	– –	– –	1 1	–	–	–	–	–	–	1 1
21 Stoke City	– –	1 1	–	–	–	–	–	–	–	1 1
22 Yeovil Town	– –	– –	–	1 1	–	–	–	–	–	1 1
23 Arsenal	– –	1	–	–	–	–	–	–	–	1 –
24 Bury	– –	– –	1	–	–	–	–	–	–	1 –
25 Charlton Athletic	– –	1	–	–	–	–	–	–	–	1 –
26 Chelsea	– –	1	–	–	–	–	–	–	–	1 –
27 Grimsby Town	– –	1	–	–	–	–	–	–	–	1 –
28 Leeds United	– –	1	–	–	–	–	–	–	–	1 –
29 Liverpool	– –	1	–	–	–	–	–	–	–	1 –
30 Plymouth Argyle	– –	– –	1	–	–	–	–	–	–	1 –
31 Portsmouth	– –	1	–	–	–	–	–	–	–	1 –
32 Preston North End	– –	1	–	–	–	–	–	–	–	1 –
33 Stockport County	– –	– –	–	1	–	–	–	–	–	1 –
34 West Bromwich Albion	– –	1	–	–	–	–	–	–	–	1 –

TOMMY BALDWIN

DEBUT (Full Appearance)

Saturday 18/01/1975
Football League Division 2
at Roker Park

Sunderland 0 Manchester United 0

CLUB CAREER RECORD	Apps	Subs	Goals
Premiership	0		0
League Division 1	0		0
League Division 2	2		0
FA Cup	0		0
League Cup	0		0
European Cup / Champions League	0		0
European Cup-Winners' Cup	0		0
UEFA Cup / Inter-Cities' Fairs Cup	0		0
Other Matches	0		0
OVERALL TOTAL	2		0

Opponents	PREM A S G	FLD 1 A S G	FLD 2 A S G	FAC A S G	LC A S G	EC/CL A S G	ECWC A S G	UEFA A S G	OTHER A S G	TOTAL A S G
1 Bristol City	– –	– –	1	–	–	–	–	–	–	1 –
2 Sunderland	– –	– –	1	–	–	–	–	–	–	1 –

JACK BALL

DEBUT (Full Appearance, 1 goal)

Wednesday 11/09/1929
Football League Division 1
at Old Trafford

Manchester United 2 Leicester City 1

CLUB CAREER RECORD	Apps	Subs	Goals
Premiership	0		0
League Division 1	23		11
League Division 2	24		6
FA Cup	3		1
League Cup	0		0
European Cup / Champions League	0		0
European Cup-Winners' Cup	0		0
UEFA Cup / Inter-Cities' Fairs Cup	0		0
Other Matches	0		0
OVERALL TOTAL	50		18

Opponents	PREM A S G	FLD 1 A S G	FLD 2 A S G	FAC A S G	LC A S G	EC/CL A S G	ECWC A S G	UEFA A S G	OTHER A S G	TOTAL A S G
1 Bolton Wanderers	– –	1 1	–	3 1	–	–	–	–	–	4 2
2 Burnley	– –	2 –	1	–	–	–	–	–	–	3 –
3 Arsenal	– –	2 2	–	–	–	–	–	–	–	2 2
4 Leeds United	– –	2 2	–	–	–	–	–	–	–	2 2
5 Derby County	– –	2 1	–	–	–	–	–	–	–	2 1
6 Portsmouth	– –	– –	–	–	2 1	–	–	–	–	2 1
7 Sheffield United	– –	1 1	–	1	–	–	–	–	–	2 1
8 Sunderland	– –	2 1	–	–	–	–	–	–	–	2 1
9 Birmingham City	– –	2	–	–	–	–	–	–	–	2 –
10 Bradford City	– –	– –	2	–	–	–	–	–	–	2 –
11 West Ham United	– –	– –	–	2	–	–	–	–	–	2 –
12 Blackburn Rovers	– –	1 1	–	–	–	–	–	–	–	1 1
13 Brentford	– –	– –	1 1	–	–	–	–	–	–	1 1
14 Bury	– –	– –	1 1	–	–	–	–	–	–	1 1
15 Fulham	– –	– –	1 1	–	–	–	–	–	–	1 1

continued../

JACK BALL (continued)

Opponents	PREM			FLD 1			FLD 2			FAC			LC			EC/CL			ECWC			UEFA			OTHER			TOTAL		
	A	S	G	A	S	G	A	S	G	A	S	G	A	S	G	A	S	G	A	S	G	A	S	G	A	S	G	A	S	G
16 Grimsby Town	-	-	-	1		1	-	-	-	-	-	-	-	-	-	-	-	-	-	-	-	-	-	-	-	-	-	1		1
17 Hull City	-	-	-	-		-	1		1	-	-	-	-	-	-	-	-	-	-	-	-	-	-	-	-	-	-	1		1
18 Leicester City	-	-	-	1		1	-	-	-	-	-	-	-	-	-	-	-	-	-	-	-	-	-	-	-	-	-	1		1
19 Sheffield Wednesday	-	-	-	1		1	-	-	-	-	-	-	-	-	-	-	-	-	-	-	-	-	-	-	-	-	-	1		1
20 Aston Villa	-	-	-	1		-	-	-	-	-	-	-	-	-	-	-	-	-	-	-	-	-	-	-	-	-	-	1		-
21 Barnsley	-	-	-	-		-	-	-	-	1		-	-	-	-	-	-	-	-	-	-	-	-	-	-	-	-	1		-
22 Blackpool	-	-	-	-		-	-	-	-	1		-	-	-	-	-	-	-	-	-	-	-	-	-	-	-	-	1		-
23 Bradford Park Avenue	-	-	-	-		-	-	-	-	1		-	-	-	-	-	-	-	-	-	-	-	-	-	-	-	-	1		-
24 Everton	-	-	-	1		-	-	-	-	-	-	-	-	-	-	-	-	-	-	-	-	-	-	-	-	-	-	1		-
25 Huddersfield Town	-	-	-	1		-	-	-	-	-	-	-	-	-	-	-	-	-	-	-	-	-	-	-	-	-	-	1		-
26 Lincoln City	-	-	-	-		-	-	-	-	1		-	-	-	-	-	-	-	-	-	-	-	-	-	-	-	-	1		-
27 Middlesbrough	-	-	-	1		-	-	-	-	-	-	-	-	-	-	-	-	-	-	-	-	-	-	-	-	-	-	1		-
28 Millwall	-	-	-	-		-	-	-	-	1		-	-	-	-	-	-	-	-	-	-	-	-	-	-	-	-	1		-
29 Newcastle United	-	-	-	1		-	-	-	-	-	-	-	-	-	-	-	-	-	-	-	-	-	-	-	-	-	-	1		-
30 Oldham Athletic	-	-	-	-		-	-	-	-	1		-	-	-	-	-	-	-	-	-	-	-	-	-	-	-	-	1		-
31 Plymouth Argyle	-	-	-	-		-	-	-	-	1		-	-	-	-	-	-	-	-	-	-	-	-	-	-	-	-	1		-
32 Port Vale	-	-	-	-		-	-	-	-	1		-	-	-	-	-	-	-	-	-	-	-	-	-	-	-	-	1		-
33 Preston North End	-	-	-	-		-	-	-	-	1		-	-	-	-	-	-	-	-	-	-	-	-	-	-	-	-	1		-
34 Southampton	-	-	-	-		-	-	-	-	1		-	-	-	-	-	-	-	-	-	-	-	-	-	-	-	-	1		-
35 Swansea City	-	-	-	-		-	-	-	-	1		-	-	-	-	-	-	-	-	-	-	-	-	-	-	-	-	1		-
36 Swindon Town	-	-	-	-		-	-	-	-	1		-	-	-	-	-	-	-	-	-	-	-	-	-	-	-	-	1		-

JOHN BALL

DEBUT (Full Appearance)

Saturday 10/04/1948
Football League Division 1
at Goodison Park

Everton 2 Manchester United 0

CLUB CAREER RECORD	Apps	Subs	Goals
Premiership	0		0
League Division 1	22		0
League Division 2	0		0
FA Cup	1		0
League Cup	0		0
European Cup / Champions League	0		0
European Cup-Winners' Cup	0		0
UEFA Cup / Inter-Cities' Fairs Cup	0		0
Other Matches	0		0
OVERALL TOTAL	23		0

Opponents	PREM			FLD 1			FLD 2			FAC			LC			EC/CL			ECWC			UEFA			OTHER			TOTAL		
	A	S	G	A	S	G	A	S	G	A	S	G	A	S	G	A	S	G	A	S	G	A	S	G	A	S	G	A	S	G
1 Charlton Athletic	-	-	3		-																							3		-
2 Aston Villa	-	-	2		-																							2		-
3 Birmingham City	-	-	2		-																							2		-
4 Bolton Wanderers	-	-	2		-																							2		-
5 Everton	-	-	2		-																							2		-
6 Huddersfield Town	-	-	2		-																							2		-
7 Blackpool	-	-	1		-																							1		-
8 Burnley	-	-	1		-																							1		-
9 Chelsea	-	-	1		-																							1		-
10 Fulham	-	-	1		-																							1		-
11 Hull City	-	-	-		-					1																		1		-
12 Middlesbrough	-	-	1		-																							1		-
13 Newcastle United	-	-	1		-																							1		-
14 Portsmouth	-	-	1		-																							1		-
15 Sunderland	-	-	1		-																							1		-
16 Wolverhampton W.	-	-	1		-																							1		-

WILLIAM BALL

DEBUT (Full Appearance)

Saturday 08/11/1902
Football League Division 2
at Sincil Bank

Lincoln City 1 Manchester United 3

CLUB CAREER RECORD	Apps	Subs	Goals
Premiership	0		0
League Division 1	0		0
League Division 2	4		0
FA Cup	0		0
League Cup	0		0
European Cup / Champions League	0		0
European Cup-Winners' Cup	0		0
UEFA Cup / Inter-Cities' Fairs Cup	0		0
Other Matches	0		0
OVERALL TOTAL	4		0

Opponents	PREM			FLD 1			FLD 2			FAC			LC			EC/CL			ECWC			UEFA			OTHER			TOTAL		
	A	S	G	A	S	G	A	S	G	A	S	G	A	S	G	A	S	G	A	S	G	A	S	G	A	S	G	A	S	G
1 Arsenal	-	-	-		-		-	-	-	1		-	-	-	-	-	-	-	-	-	-	-	-	-	-	-	-	1		-
2 Birmingham City	-	-	-		-		1		-	-	-	-	-	-	-	-	-	-	-	-	-	-	-	-	-	-	-	1		-
3 Gainsborough Trinity	-	-	-		-		1		-	-	-	-	-	-	-	-	-	-	-	-	-	-	-	-	-	-	-	1		-
4 Lincoln City	-	-	-		-		1		-	-	-	-	-	-	-	-	-	-	-	-	-	-	-	-	-	-	-	1		-

TOMMY BAMFORD

DEBUT (Full Appearance, 1 goal)

Saturday 20/10/1934
Football League Division 2
at St James' Park

Newcastle United 0 Manchester United 1

CLUB CAREER RECORD	Apps	Subs	Goals
Premiership	0		0
League Division 1	29		14
League Division 2	69		39
FA Cup	11		4
League Cup	0		0
European Cup / Champions League	0		0
European Cup-Winners' Cup	0		0
UEFA Cup / Inter-Cities' Fairs Cup	0		0
Other Matches	0		0
OVERALL TOTAL	**109**		**57**

Opponents	PREM			FLD 1			FLD 2			FAC			LC			EC/CL			ECWC			UEFA			OTHER			TOTAL		
	A	S	G	A	S	G	A	S	G	A	S	G	A	S	G	A	S	G	A	S	G	A	S	G	A	S	G	A	S	G
1 Nottingham Forest	-	-	-	-	-	-	5	-	4	2	-	-	-	-	-	-	-	-	-	-	-	-	-	-	-	-	-	7		4
2 Barnsley	-	-	-	-	-	-	3	-	3	2	-	-	-	-	-	-	-	-	-	-	-	-	-	-	-	-	-	5		3
3 Newcastle United	-	-	-	-	-	-	5	-	3	-	-	-	-	-	-	-	-	-	-	-	-	-	-	-	-	-	-	5		3
4 Plymouth Argyle	-	-	-	-	-	-	5	-	3	-	-	-	-	-	-	-	-	-	-	-	-	-	-	-	-	-	-	5		3
5 Bradford Park Avenue	-	-	-	-	-	-	5	-	2	-	-	-	-	-	-	-	-	-	-	-	-	-	-	-	-	-	-	5		2
6 Bury	-	-	-	-	-	-	5	-	-	-	-	-	-	-	-	-	-	-	-	-	-	-	-	-	-	-	-	5		-
7 Charlton Athletic	-	-	-	2	-	-	2	-	1	-	-	-	-	-	-	-	-	-	-	-	-	-	-	-	-	-	-	4		1
8 Fulham	-	-	-	-	-	-	4	-	1	-	-	-	-	-	-	-	-	-	-	-	-	-	-	-	-	-	-	4		1
9 Hull City	-	-	-	-	-	-	3	-	5	-	-	-	-	-	-	-	-	-	-	-	-	-	-	-	-	-	-	3		5
10 Blackpool	-	-	-	-	-	-	3	-	1	-	-	-	-	-	-	-	-	-	-	-	-	-	-	-	-	-	-	3		1
11 Brentford	-	-	-	1	-	-	1	-	1	1	-	-	-	-	-	-	-	-	-	-	-	-	-	-	-	-	-	3		1
12 Sheffield Wednesday	-	-	-	2	-	1	1	-	-	-	-	-	-	-	-	-	-	-	-	-	-	-	-	-	-	-	-	3		1
13 Swansea City	-	-	-	-	-	-	3	-	1	-	-	-	-	-	-	-	-	-	-	-	-	-	-	-	-	-	-	3		1
14 Stoke City	-	-	-	2	-	-	-	-	-	1	-	-	-	-	-	-	-	-	-	-	-	-	-	-	-	-	-	3		-
15 Birmingham City	-	-	-	2	-	2	-	-	-	-	-	-	-	-	-	-	-	-	-	-	-	-	-	-	-	-	-	2		2
16 Burnley	-	-	-	-	-	-	2	-	2	-	-	-	-	-	-	-	-	-	-	-	-	-	-	-	-	-	-	2		2
17 Bolton Wanderers	-	-	-	2	-	1	-	-	-	-	-	-	-	-	-	-	-	-	-	-	-	-	-	-	-	-	-	2		1
18 Chelsea	-	-	-	2	-	1	-	-	-	-	-	-	-	-	-	-	-	-	-	-	-	-	-	-	-	-	-	2		1
19 Coventry City	-	-	-	-	-	-	2	-	1	-	-	-	-	-	-	-	-	-	-	-	-	-	-	-	-	-	-	2		1
20 Huddersfield Town	-	-	-	2	-	1	-	-	-	-	-	-	-	-	-	-	-	-	-	-	-	-	-	-	-	-	-	2		1
21 Reading	-	-	-	-	-	-	-	-	-	2	-	1	-	-	-	-	-	-	-	-	-	-	-	-	-	-	-	2		1
22 Stockport County	-	-	-	-	-	-	2	-	1	-	-	-	-	-	-	-	-	-	-	-	-	-	-	-	-	-	-	2		1
23 Sunderland	-	-	-	2	-	1	-	-	-	-	-	-	-	-	-	-	-	-	-	-	-	-	-	-	-	-	-	2		1
24 Wolverhampton W.	-	-	-	2	-	1	-	-	-	-	-	-	-	-	-	-	-	-	-	-	-	-	-	-	-	-	-	2		1
25 Arsenal	-	-	-	1	-	-	-	-	-	1	-	-	-	-	-	-	-	-	-	-	-	-	-	-	-	-	-	2		-
26 Norwich City	-	-	-	-	-	-	2	-	-	-	-	-	-	-	-	-	-	-	-	-	-	-	-	-	-	-	-	2		-
27 Notts County	-	-	-	-	-	-	2	-	-	-	-	-	-	-	-	-	-	-	-	-	-	-	-	-	-	-	-	2		-
28 Sheffield United	-	-	-	-	-	-	2	-	-	-	-	-	-	-	-	-	-	-	-	-	-	-	-	-	-	-	-	2		-
29 Southampton	-	-	-	-	-	-	2	-	-	-	-	-	-	-	-	-	-	-	-	-	-	-	-	-	-	-	-	2		-
30 West Bromwich Albion	-	-	-	2	-	-	-	-	-	-	-	-	-	-	-	-	-	-	-	-	-	-	-	-	-	-	-	2		-
31 Chesterfield	-	-	-	-	-	-	1	-	4	-	-	-	-	-	-	-	-	-	-	-	-	-	-	-	-	-	-	1		4
32 Derby County	-	-	-	1	-	3	-	-	-	-	-	-	-	-	-	-	-	-	-	-	-	-	-	-	-	-	-	1		3
33 Bradford City	-	-	-	-	-	-	1	-	2	-	-	-	-	-	-	-	-	-	-	-	-	-	-	-	-	-	-	1		2
34 Bristol Rovers	-	-	-	-	-	-	-	-	-	1	-	2	-	-	-	-	-	-	-	-	-	-	-	-	-	-	-	1		2
35 Aston Villa	-	-	-	-	-	-	1	-	1	-	-	-	-	-	-	-	-	-	-	-	-	-	-	-	-	-	-	1		1
36 Blackburn Rovers	-	-	-	-	-	-	1	-	1	-	-	-	-	-	-	-	-	-	-	-	-	-	-	-	-	-	-	1		1
37 Luton Town	-	-	-	-	-	-	1	-	1	-	-	-	-	-	-	-	-	-	-	-	-	-	-	-	-	-	-	1		1
38 Manchester City	-	-	-	1	-	1	-	-	-	-	-	-	-	-	-	-	-	-	-	-	-	-	-	-	-	-	-	1		1
39 Middlesbrough	-	-	-	1	-	1	-	-	-	-	-	-	-	-	-	-	-	-	-	-	-	-	-	-	-	-	-	1		1
40 Port Vale	-	-	-	-	-	-	1	-	1	-	-	-	-	-	-	-	-	-	-	-	-	-	-	-	-	-	-	1		1
41 Preston North End	-	-	-	1	-	1	-	-	-	-	-	-	-	-	-	-	-	-	-	-	-	-	-	-	-	-	-	1		1
42 Yeovil Town	-	-	-	-	-	-	-	-	-	1	-	1	-	-	-	-	-	-	-	-	-	-	-	-	-	-	-	1		1
43 Doncaster Rovers	-	-	-	-	-	-	1	-	-	-	-	-	-	-	-	-	-	-	-	-	-	-	-	-	-	-	-	1		-
44 Grimsby Town	-	-	-	1	-	-	-	-	-	-	-	-	-	-	-	-	-	-	-	-	-	-	-	-	-	-	-	1		-
45 Leeds United	-	-	-	1	-	-	-	-	-	-	-	-	-	-	-	-	-	-	-	-	-	-	-	-	-	-	-	1		-
46 Leicester City	-	-	-	-	-	-	1	-	-	-	-	-	-	-	-	-	-	-	-	-	-	-	-	-	-	-	-	1		-
47 Portsmouth	-	-	-	1	-	-	-	-	-	-	-	-	-	-	-	-	-	-	-	-	-	-	-	-	-	-	-	1		-
48 Tottenham Hotspur	-	-	-	-	-	-	1	-	-	-	-	-	-	-	-	-	-	-	-	-	-	-	-	-	-	-	-	1		-
49 West Ham United	-	-	-	-	-	-	1	-	-	-	-	-	-	-	-	-	-	-	-	-	-	-	-	-	-	-	-	1		-

JACK BANKS

DEBUT (Full Appearance)

Saturday 07/09/1901
Football League Division 2
at Bank Street

Newton Heath 3 Gainsborough Trinity 0

CLUB CAREER RECORD	Apps	Subs	Goals
Premiership	0		0
League Division 1	0		0
League Division 2	40		0
FA Cup	4		1
League Cup	0		0
European Cup / Champions League	0		0
European Cup-Winners' Cup	0		0
UEFA Cup / Inter-Cities' Fairs Cup	0		0
Other Matches	0		0
OVERALL TOTAL	**44**		**1**

Opponents	PREM			FLD 1			FLD 2			FAC			LC			EC/CL			ECWC			UEFA			OTHER			TOTAL		
	A	S	G	A	S	G	A	S	G	A	S	G	A	S	G	A	S	G	A	S	G	A	S	G	A	S	G	A	S	G
1 Lincoln City	–	–	–	–	–	–	3	–	–	1	–	–	–	–	–	–	–	–	–	–	–	–	–	–	–	–	–	4	–	–
2 Barnsley	–	–	–	–	–	–	3	–	–	–	–	–	–	–	–	–	–	–	–	–	–	–	–	–	–	–	–	3	–	–
3 Burnley	–	–	–	–	–	–	3	–	–	–	–	–	–	–	–	–	–	–	–	–	–	–	–	–	–	–	–	3	–	–
4 Chesterfield	–	–	–	–	–	–	3	–	–	–	–	–	–	–	–	–	–	–	–	–	–	–	–	–	–	–	–	3	–	–
5 Doncaster Rovers	–	–	–	–	–	–	3	–	–	–	–	–	–	–	–	–	–	–	–	–	–	–	–	–	–	–	–	3	–	–
6 Glossop	–	–	–	–	–	–	3	–	–	–	–	–	–	–	–	–	–	–	–	–	–	–	–	–	–	–	–	3	–	–
7 Leicester City	–	–	–	–	–	–	3	–	–	–	–	–	–	–	–	–	–	–	–	–	–	–	–	–	–	–	–	3	–	–
8 Stockport County	–	–	–	–	–	–	3	–	–	–	–	–	–	–	–	–	–	–	–	–	–	–	–	–	–	–	–	3	–	–
9 Arsenal	–	–	–	–	–	–	2	–	–	–	–	–	–	–	–	–	–	–	–	–	–	–	–	–	–	–	–	2	–	–
10 Birmingham City	–	–	–	–	–	–	2	–	–	–	–	–	–	–	–	–	–	–	–	–	–	–	–	–	–	–	–	2	–	–
11 Blackpool	–	–	–	–	–	–	2	–	–	–	–	–	–	–	–	–	–	–	–	–	–	–	–	–	–	–	–	2	–	–
12 Gainsborough Trinity	–	–	–	–	–	–	2	–	–	–	–	–	–	–	–	–	–	–	–	–	–	–	–	–	–	–	–	2	–	–
13 Preston North End	–	–	–	–	–	–	2	–	–	–	–	–	–	–	–	–	–	–	–	–	–	–	–	–	–	–	–	2	–	–
14 West Bromwich Albion	–	–	–	–	–	–	2	–	–	–	–	–	–	–	–	–	–	–	–	–	–	–	–	–	–	–	–	2	–	–
15 Southport Central	–	–	–	–	–	–	–	–	–	1	–	1	–	–	–	–	–	–	–	–	–	–	–	–	–	–	–	1	–	1
16 Accrington Stanley	–	–	–	–	–	–	–	–	–	1	–	–	–	–	–	–	–	–	–	–	–	–	–	–	–	–	–	1	–	–
17 Bristol City	–	–	–	–	–	–	1	–	–	–	–	–	–	–	–	–	–	–	–	–	–	–	–	–	–	–	–	1	–	–
18 Burton United	–	–	–	–	–	–	1	–	–	–	–	–	–	–	–	–	–	–	–	–	–	–	–	–	–	–	–	1	–	–
19 Middlesbrough	–	–	–	–	–	–	1	–	–	–	–	–	–	–	–	–	–	–	–	–	–	–	–	–	–	–	–	1	–	–
20 Oswaldtwistle Rovers	–	–	–	–	–	–	–	–	–	1	–	–	–	–	–	–	–	–	–	–	–	–	–	–	–	–	–	1	–	–
21 Port Vale	–	–	–	–	–	–	1	–	–	–	–	–	–	–	–	–	–	–	–	–	–	–	–	–	–	–	–	1	–	–

JIMMY BANNISTER

DEBUT (Full Appearance)

Tuesday 01/01/1907
Football League Division 1
at Bank Street

Manchester United 1 Aston Villa 0

CLUB CAREER RECORD	Apps	Subs	Goals
Premiership	0		0
League Division 1	57		7
League Division 2	0		0
FA Cup	4		1
League Cup	0		0
European Cup / Champions League	0		0
European Cup-Winners' Cup	0		0
UEFA Cup / Inter-Cities' Fairs Cup	0		0
Other Matches	2		0
OVERALL TOTAL	**63**		**8**

Opponents	PREM			FLD 1			FLD 2			FAC			LC			EC/CL			ECWC			UEFA			OTHER			TOTAL		
	A	S	G	A	S	G	A	S	G	A	S	G	A	S	G	A	S	G	A	S	G	A	S	G	A	S	G	A	S	G
1 Aston Villa	–	–	–	5	–	1	–	–	–	1	–	–	–	–	–	–	–	–	–	–	–	–	–	–	–	–	–	6	–	1
2 Everton	–	–	–	4	–	2	–	–	–	–	–	–	–	–	–	–	–	–	–	–	–	–	–	–	–	–	–	4	–	2
3 Middlesbrough	–	–	–	4	–	1	–	–	–	–	–	–	–	–	–	–	–	–	–	–	–	–	–	–	–	–	–	4	–	1
4 Arsenal	–	–	–	4	–	–	–	–	–	–	–	–	–	–	–	–	–	–	–	–	–	–	–	–	–	–	–	4	–	–
5 Newcastle United	–	–	–	4	–	–	–	–	–	–	–	–	–	–	–	–	–	–	–	–	–	–	–	–	–	–	–	4	–	–
6 Notts County	–	–	–	4	–	–	–	–	–	–	–	–	–	–	–	–	–	–	–	–	–	–	–	–	–	–	–	4	–	–
7 Chelsea	–	–	–	2	–	1	–	–	–	1	–	–	–	–	–	–	–	–	–	–	–	–	–	–	–	–	–	3	–	1
8 Bristol City	–	–	–	3	–	–	–	–	–	–	–	–	–	–	–	–	–	–	–	–	–	–	–	–	–	–	–	3	–	–
9 Manchester City	–	–	–	3	–	–	–	–	–	–	–	–	–	–	–	–	–	–	–	–	–	–	–	–	–	–	–	3	–	–
10 Preston North End	–	–	–	3	–	–	–	–	–	–	–	–	–	–	–	–	–	–	–	–	–	–	–	–	–	–	–	3	–	–
11 Sheffield United	–	–	–	3	–	–	–	–	–	–	–	–	–	–	–	–	–	–	–	–	–	–	–	–	–	–	–	3	–	–
12 Sheffield Wednesday	–	–	–	3	–	–	–	–	–	–	–	–	–	–	–	–	–	–	–	–	–	–	–	–	–	–	–	3	–	–
13 Liverpool	–	–	–	2	–	1	–	–	–	–	–	–	–	–	–	–	–	–	–	–	–	–	–	–	–	–	–	2	–	1
14 Nottingham Forest	–	–	–	2	–	1	–	–	–	–	–	–	–	–	–	–	–	–	–	–	–	–	–	–	–	–	–	2	–	1
15 Birmingham City	–	–	–	2	–	–	–	–	–	–	–	–	–	–	–	–	–	–	–	–	–	–	–	–	–	–	–	2	–	–
16 Blackburn Rovers	–	–	–	2	–	–	–	–	–	–	–	–	–	–	–	–	–	–	–	–	–	–	–	–	–	–	–	2	–	–
17 Bolton Wanderers	–	–	–	2	–	–	–	–	–	–	–	–	–	–	–	–	–	–	–	–	–	–	–	–	–	–	–	2	–	–
18 Bury	–	–	–	2	–	–	–	–	–	–	–	–	–	–	–	–	–	–	–	–	–	–	–	–	–	–	–	2	–	–
19 Queens Park Rangers	–	–	–	–	–	–	–	–	–	–	–	–	–	–	–	–	–	–	–	–	–	–	–	–	2	–	–	2	–	–
20 Sunderland	–	–	–	2	–	–	–	–	–	–	–	–	–	–	–	–	–	–	–	–	–	–	–	–	–	–	–	2	–	–
21 Blackpool	–	–	–	–	–	–	–	–	–	1	–	1	–	–	–	–	–	–	–	–	–	–	–	–	–	–	–	1	–	1
22 Bradford City	–	–	–	1	–	–	–	–	–	–	–	–	–	–	–	–	–	–	–	–	–	–	–	–	–	–	–	1	–	–
23 Fulham	–	–	–	–	–	–	–	–	–	1	–	–	–	–	–	–	–	–	–	–	–	–	–	–	–	–	–	1	–	–

JACK BARBER

DEBUT (Full Appearance)

Saturday 06/01/1923
Football League Division 2
at Old Trafford

Manchester United 3 Hull City 2

CLUB CAREER RECORD	Apps	Subs	Goals
Premiership	0		0
League Division 1	0		0
League Division 2	3		1
FA Cup	1		1
League Cup	0		0
European Cup / Champions League	0		0
European Cup-Winners' Cup	0		0
UEFA Cup / Inter-Cities' Fairs Cup	0		0
Other Matches	0		0
OVERALL TOTAL	**4**		**2**

Opponents	PREM A S G	FLD 1 A S G	FLD 2 A S G	FAC A S G	LC A S G	EC/CL A S G	ECWC A S G	UEFA A S G	OTHER A S G	TOTAL A S G
1 Bradford City	– – –	– – –	– – –	1 – 1	– – –	– – –	– – –	– – –	– – –	1 – 1
2 Stockport County	– – –	– – –	1 – 1	– – –	– – –	– – –	– – –	– – –	– – –	1 – 1
3 Hull City	– – –	– – –	1 – –	– – –	– – –	– – –	– – –	– – –	– – –	1 – –
4 Leeds United	– – –	– – –	1 – –	– – –	– – –	– – –	– – –	– – –	– – –	1 – –

PHIL BARDSLEY

DEBUT (Full Appearance)

Wednesday 03/12/2003
League Cup 4th Round
at The Hawthorns

West Bromwich Albion 2 Manchester United 0

CLUB CAREER RECORD	Apps	Subs	Goals
Premiership	3	(5)	0
League Division 1	0		0
League Division 2	0		0
FA Cup	2	(1)	0
League Cup	3	(1)	0
European Cup / Champions League	2	(1)	0
European Cup-Winners' Cup	0		0
UEFA Cup / Inter-Cities' Fairs Cup	0		0
Other Matches	0		0
OVERALL TOTAL	**10**	**(8)**	**0**

Opponents	PREM A S G	FLD 1 A S G	FLD 2 A S G	FAC A S G	LC A S G	EC/CL A S G	ECWC A S G	UEFA A S G	OTHER A S G	TOTAL A S G
1 Burton Albion	– – –	– – –	– – –	2 – –	– – –	– – –	– – –	– – –	– – –	2 – –
2 West Bromwich Albion	– – –	– – –	– – –	– – –	1 (1) –	– – –	– – –	– – –	– – –	1 (1) –
3 Fulham	– (2) –	– – –	– – –	– – –	– – –	– – –	– – –	– – –	– – –	– (2) –
4 Barnet	– – –	– – –	– – –	– – –	1 – –	– – –	– – –	– – –	– – –	1 – –
5 Benfica	– – –	– – –	– – –	– – –	– – –	1 – –	– – –	– – –	– – –	1 – –
6 Coventry City	– – –	– – –	– – –	– – –	1 – –	– – –	– – –	– – –	– – –	1 – –
7 Lille Metropole	– – –	– – –	– – –	– – –	– – –	1 – –	– – –	– – –	– – –	1 – –
8 Middlesbrough	1 – –	– – –	– – –	– – –	– – –	– – –	– – –	– – –	– – –	1 – –
9 Sunderland	1 – –	– – –	– – –	– – –	– – –	– – –	– – –	– – –	– – –	1 – –
10 Tottenham Hotspur	1 – –	– – –	– – –	– – –	– – –	– – –	– – –	– – –	– – –	1 – –
11 Blackburn Rovers	– (1) –	– – –	– – –	– – –	– – –	– – –	– – –	– – –	– – –	– (1) –
12 Charlton Athletic	– (1) –	– – –	– – –	– – –	– – –	– – –	– – –	– – –	– – –	– (1) –
13 Debreceni	– – –	– – –	– – –	– – –	– – –	– (1) –	– – –	– – –	– – –	– (1) –
14 Northampton Town	– – –	– – –	– – –	– (1) –	– – –	– – –	– – –	– – –	– – –	– (1) –
15 Wigan Athletic	– (1) –	– – –	– – –	– – –	– – –	– – –	– – –	– – –	– – –	– (1) –

CYRIL BARLOW

DEBUT (Full Appearance)

Saturday 07/02/1920
Football League Division 1
at Roker Park

Sunderland 3 Manchester United 0

CLUB CAREER RECORD	Apps	Subs	Goals
Premiership	0		0
League Division 1	29		0
League Division 2	0		0
FA Cup	1		0
League Cup	0		0
European Cup / Champions League	0		0
European Cup-Winners' Cup	0		0
UEFA Cup / Inter-Cities' Fairs Cup	0		0
Other Matches	0		0
OVERALL TOTAL	**30**		**0**

Opponents	PREM A S G	FLD 1 A S G	FLD 2 A S G	FAC A S G	LC A S G	EC/CL A S G	ECWC A S G	UEFA A S G	OTHER A S G	TOTAL A S G
1 Bolton Wanderers	– – –	3 – –	– – –	– – –	– – –	– – –	– – –	– – –	– – –	3 – –
2 Liverpool	– – –	2 – –	– – –	1 – –	– – –	– – –	– – –	– – –	– – –	3 – –
3 Oldham Athletic	– – –	3 – –	– – –	– – –	– – –	– – –	– – –	– – –	– – –	3 – –
4 Bradford City	– – –	2 – –	– – –	– – –	– – –	– – –	– – –	– – –	– – –	2 – –
5 Chelsea	– – –	2 – –	– – –	– – –	– – –	– – –	– – –	– – –	– – –	2 – –
6 Everton	– – –	2 – –	– – –	– – –	– – –	– – –	– – –	– – –	– – –	2 – –
7 Preston North End	– – –	2 – –	– – –	– – –	– – –	– – –	– – –	– – –	– – –	2 – –
8 Sunderland	– – –	2 – –	– – –	– – –	– – –	– – –	– – –	– – –	– – –	2 – –
9 Tottenham Hotspur	– – –	2 – –	– – –	– – –	– – –	– – –	– – –	– – –	– – –	2 – –
10 West Bromwich Albion	– – –	2 – –	– – –	– – –	– – –	– – –	– – –	– – –	– – –	2 – –
11 Arsenal	– – –	1 – –	– – –	– – –	– – –	– – –	– – –	– – –	– – –	1 – –
12 Aston Villa	– – –	1 – –	– – –	– – –	– – –	– – –	– – –	– – –	– – –	1 – –
13 Bradford Park Avenue	– – –	1 – –	– – –	– – –	– – –	– – –	– – –	– – –	– – –	1 – –
14 Huddersfield Town	– – –	1 – –	– – –	– – –	– – –	– – –	– – –	– – –	– – –	1 – –
15 Middlesbrough	– – –	1 – –	– – –	– – –	– – –	– – –	– – –	– – –	– – –	1 – –
16 Notts County	– – –	1 – –	– – –	– – –	– – –	– – –	– – –	– – –	– – –	1 – –
17 Sheffield United	– – –	1 – –	– – –	– – –	– – –	– – –	– – –	– – –	– – –	1 – –

MICHAEL BARNES

DEBUT (Substitute Appearance)

Wednesday 25/10/2006
League Cup 3rd Round
at Gresty Road

Crewe Alexandra 1 Manchester United 2

CLUB CAREER RECORD	Apps	Subs	Goals
Premiership	0		0
League Division 1	0		0
League Division 2	0		0
FA Cup	0		0
League Cup	0	(1)	0
European Cup / Champions League	0		0
European Cup-Winners' Cup	0		0
UEFA Cup / Inter-Cities' Fairs Cup	0		0
Other Matches	0		0
OVERALL TOTAL	**0**	**(1)**	**0**

Opponents	PREM A S G	FLD 1 A S G	FLD 2 A S G	FAC A S G	LC A S G	EC/CL A S G	ECWC A S G	UEFA A S G	OTHER A S G	TOTAL A S G
1 Crewe Alexandra	– –	– –	– –	– –	– (1) –	– –	– –	– –	– –	– (1) –

PETER BARNES

DEBUT (Full Appearance, 1 goal)

Saturday 31/08/1985
Football League Division 1
at City Ground

Nottingham Forest 1 Manchester United 3

CLUB CAREER RECORD	Apps	Subs	Goals
Premiership	0		0
League Division 1	19	(1)	2
League Division 2	0		0
FA Cup	0		0
League Cup	5		2
European Cup / Champions League	0		0
European Cup-Winners' Cup	0		0
UEFA Cup / Inter-Cities' Fairs Cup	0		0
Other Matches	0		0
OVERALL TOTAL	**24**	**(1)**	**4**

Opponents	PREM A S G	FLD 1 A S G	FLD 2 A S G	FAC A S G	LC A S G	EC/CL A S G	ECWC A S G	UEFA A S G	OTHER A S G	TOTAL A S G
1 Manchester City	– –	3 –	– –	– –	– –	– –	– –	– –	– –	3 –
2 Crystal Palace	– –	– –	– –	– –	2 1	– –	– –	– –	– –	2 1
3 Oxford United	– –	2 1	– –	– –	– –	– –	– –	– –	– –	2 1
4 Luton Town	– –	2 –	– –	– –	– –	– –	– –	– –	– –	2 –
5 Queens Park Rangers	– –	2 –	– –	– –	– –	– –	– –	– –	– –	2 –
6 Sheffield Wednesday	– –	2 –	– –	– –	– –	– –	– –	– –	– –	2 –
7 Southampton	– –	1 –	– –	– –	1 –	– –	– –	– –	– –	2 –
8 Nottingham Forest	– –	1 1	– –	– –	– –	– –	– –	– –	– –	1 1
9 Port Vale	– –	– –	– –	– –	1 1	– –	– –	– –	– –	1 1
10 Chelsea	– –	1 –	– –	– –	– –	– –	– –	– –	– –	1 –
11 Coventry City	– –	1 –	– –	– –	– –	– –	– –	– –	– –	1 –
12 Newcastle United	– –	1 –	– –	– –	– –	– –	– –	– –	– –	1 –
13 Norwich City	– –	1 –	– –	– –	– –	– –	– –	– –	– –	1 –
14 Tottenham Hotspur	– –	1 –	– –	– –	– –	– –	– –	– –	– –	1 –
15 West Ham United	– –	– –	– –	– –	1 –	– –	– –	– –	– –	1 –
16 Wimbledon	– –	1 –	– –	– –	– –	– –	– –	– –	– –	1 –
17 Liverpool	– –	– (1) –	– –	– –	– –	– –	– –	– –	– –	– (1) –

FRANK BARRETT

DEBUT (Full Appearance)

Saturday 26/09/1896
Football League Division 2
at Bank Street

Newton Heath 4 Newcastle United 0

CLUB CAREER RECORD	Apps	Subs	Goals
Premiership	0		0
League Division 1	0		0
League Division 2	118		0
FA Cup	14		0
League Cup	0		0
European Cup / Champions League	0		0
European Cup-Winners' Cup	0		0
UEFA Cup / Inter-Cities' Fairs Cup	0		0
Other Matches	4		0
OVERALL TOTAL	**136**		**0**

Opponents	PREM A S G	FLD 1 A S G	FLD 2 A S G	FAC A S G	LC A S G	EC/CL A S G	ECWC A S G	UEFA A S G	OTHER A S G	TOTAL A S G
1 Arsenal	– –	– –	8 –	– –	– –	– –	– –	– –	– –	8 –
2 Blackpool	– –	– –	6 –	2 –	– –	– –	– –	– –	– –	8 –
3 Leicester City	– –	– –	8 –	– –	– –	– –	– –	– –	– –	8 –
4 Loughborough Town	– –	– –	8 –	– –	– –	– –	– –	– –	– –	8 –
5 Burton Swifts	– –	– –	7 –	– –	– –	– –	– –	– –	– –	7 –
6 Gainsborough Trinity	– –	– –	7 –	– –	– –	– –	– –	– –	– –	7 –
7 Grimsby Town	– –	– –	7 –	– –	– –	– –	– –	– –	– –	7 –
8 Lincoln City	– –	– –	7 –	– –	– –	– –	– –	– –	– –	7 –
9 Walsall	– –	– –	6 –	1 –	– –	– –	– –	– –	– –	7 –
10 Birmingham City	– –	– –	6 –	– –	– –	– –	– –	– –	– –	6 –
11 Manchester City	– –	– –	6 –	– –	– –	– –	– –	– –	– –	6 –
12 Darwen	– –	– –	5 –	– –	– –	– –	– –	– –	– –	5 –
13 Luton Town	– –	– –	5 –	– –	– –	– –	– –	– –	– –	5 –
14 Barnsley	– –	– –	4 –	– –	– –	– –	– –	– –	– –	4 –
15 Burnley	– –	– –	2 –	– –	– –	– –	– –	– –	2 –	4 –
16 New Brighton Tower	– –	– –	4 –	– –	– –	– –	– –	– –	– –	4 –

continued../

FRANK BARRETT (continued)

Opponents	PREM A S G	FLD 1 A S G	FLD 2 A S G	FAC A S G	LC A S G	EC/CL A S G	ECWC A S G	UEFA A S G	OTHER A S G	TOTAL A S G
17 Newcastle United	– –	– –	4 –	– –	– –	– –	– –	– –	– –	4 –
18 Port Vale	– –	– –	4 –	– –	– –	– –	– –	– –	– –	4 –
19 Bolton Wanderers	– –	– –	2 –	– –	– –	– –	– –	– –	– –	2 –
20 Burton Wanderers	– –	– –	2 –	– –	– –	– –	– –	– –	– –	2 –
21 Chesterfield	– –	– –	2 –	– –	– –	– –	– –	– –	– –	2 –
22 Glossop	– –	– –	2 –	– –	– –	– –	– –	– –	– –	2 –
23 Liverpool	– –	– –	– –	2 –	– –	– –	– –	– –	– –	2 –
24 Middlesbrough	– –	– –	2 –	– –	– –	– –	– –	– –	– –	2 –
25 Notts County	– –	– –	2 –	– –	– –	– –	– –	– –	– –	2 –
26 Sheffield Wednesday	– –	– –	2 –	– –	– –	– –	– –	– –	– –	2 –
27 Southampton	– –	– –	– –	2 –	– –	– –	– –	– –	– –	2 –
28 Sunderland	– –	– –	– –	– –	– –	– –	– –	– –	2 –	2 –
29 Tottenham Hotspur	– –	– –	– –	2 –	– –	– –	– –	– –	– –	2 –
30 Derby County	– –	– –	– –	1 –	– –	– –	– –	– –	– –	1 –
31 Kettering	– –	– –	– –	1 –	– –	– –	– –	– –	– –	1 –
32 Nelson	– –	– –	– –	1 –	– –	– –	– –	– –	– –	1 –
33 South Shore	– –	– –	– –	1 –	– –	– –	– –	– –	– –	1 –
34 West Manchester	– –	– –	– –	1 –	– –	– –	– –	– –	– –	1 –

FRANK BARSON

DEBUT (Full Appearance)

Saturday 09/09/1922
Football League Division 2
at Molineux

Wolverhampton Wanderers 0 Manchester United 1

CLUB CAREER RECORD	Apps	Subs	Goals
Premiership	0		0
League Division 1	60		4
League Division 2	80		0
FA Cup	12		0
League Cup	0		0
European Cup / Champions League	0		0
European Cup-Winners' Cup	0		0
UEFA Cup / Inter-Cities' Fairs Cup	0		0
Other Matches	0		0
OVERALL TOTAL	**152**		**4**

Opponents	PREM A S G	FLD 1 A S G	FLD 2 A S G	FAC A S G	LC A S G	EC/CL A S G	ECWC A S G	UEFA A S G	OTHER A S G	TOTAL A S G
1 Bradford City	– –	– –	6 –	2 –	– –	– –	– –	– –	– –	8 –
2 Derby County	– –	2 –	5 –	– –	– –	– –	– –	– –	– –	7 –
3 Bury	– –	2 –	4 –	– –	– –	– –	– –	– –	– –	6 –
4 Fulham	– –	– –	5 –	1 –	– –	– –	– –	– –	– –	6 –
5 Aston Villa	– –	5 2	– –	– –	– –	– –	– –	– –	– –	5 2
6 Leeds United	– –	2 –	3 –	– –	– –	– –	– –	– –	– –	5 –
7 South Shields	– –	– –	5 –	– –	– –	– –	– –	– –	– –	5 –
8 Southampton	– –	– –	5 –	– –	– –	– –	– –	– –	– –	5 –
9 Sunderland	– –	3 –	– –	2 –	– –	– –	– –	– –	– –	5 –
10 West Ham United	– –	4 –	1 –	– –	– –	– –	– –	– –	– –	5 –
11 Blackpool	– –	– –	4 –	– –	– –	– –	– –	– –	– –	4 –
12 Cardiff City	– –	4 –	– –	– –	– –	– –	– –	– –	– –	4 –
13 Coventry City	– –	– –	4 –	– –	– –	– –	– –	– –	– –	4 –
14 Huddersfield Town	– –	3 –	– –	1 –	– –	– –	– –	– –	– –	4 –
15 Leicester City	– –	2 –	2 –	– –	– –	– –	– –	– –	– –	4 –
16 Port Vale	– –	– –	4 –	– –	– –	– –	– –	– –	– –	4 –
17 Stockport County	– –	– –	4 –	– –	– –	– –	– –	– –	– –	4 –
18 Tottenham Hotspur	– –	3 –	– –	1 –	– –	– –	– –	– –	– –	4 –
19 Birmingham City	– –	3 1	– –	– –	– –	– –	– –	– –	– –	3 1
20 Barnsley	– –	– –	3 –	– –	– –	– –	– –	– –	– –	3 –
21 Blackburn Rovers	– –	3 –	– –	– –	– –	– –	– –	– –	– –	3 –
22 Burnley	– –	3 –	– –	– –	– –	– –	– –	– –	– –	3 –
23 Leyton Orient	– –	– –	3 –	– –	– –	– –	– –	– –	– –	3 –
24 Liverpool	– –	3 –	– –	– –	– –	– –	– –	– –	– –	3 –
25 Middlesbrough	– –	1 –	2 –	– –	– –	– –	– –	– –	– –	3 –
26 Notts County	– –	1 –	2 –	– –	– –	– –	– –	– –	– –	3 –
27 Portsmouth	– –	2 –	1 –	– –	– –	– –	– –	– –	– –	3 –
28 Reading	– –	– –	– –	3 –	– –	– –	– –	– –	– –	3 –
29 Sheffield Wednesday	– –	2 –	1 –	– –	– –	– –	– –	– –	– –	3 –
30 Wolverhampton W.	– –	– –	3 –	– –	– –	– –	– –	– –	– –	3 –
31 Sheffield United	– –	2 1	– –	– –	– –	– –	– –	– –	– –	2 1
32 Arsenal	– –	2 –	– –	– –	– –	– –	– –	– –	– –	2 –
33 Bolton Wanderers	– –	2 –	– –	– –	– –	– –	– –	– –	– –	2 –
34 Bristol City	– –	– –	2 –	– –	– –	– –	– –	– –	– –	2 –
35 Chelsea	– –	– –	2 –	– –	– –	– –	– –	– –	– –	2 –
36 Everton	– –	2 –	– –	– –	– –	– –	– –	– –	– –	2 –
37 Hull City	– –	– –	2 –	– –	– –	– –	– –	– –	– –	2 –
38 Manchester City	– –	1 –	– –	– –	1 –	– –	– –	– –	– –	2 –
39 Newcastle United	– –	2 –	– –	– –	– –	– –	– –	– –	– –	2 –
40 Oldham Athletic	– –	– –	2 –	– –	– –	– –	– –	– –	– –	2 –
41 Rotherham United	– –	– –	2 –	– –	– –	– –	– –	– –	– –	2 –
42 Stoke City	– –	– –	2 –	– –	– –	– –	– –	– –	– –	2 –
43 Crystal Palace	– –	– –	1 –	– –	– –	– –	– –	– –	– –	1 –
44 Plymouth Argyle	– –	– –	– –	1 –	– –	– –	– –	– –	– –	1 –
45 West Bromwich Albion	– –	1 –	– –	– –	– –	– –	– –	– –	– –	1 –

FABIEN BARTHEZ

DEBUT (Full Appearance)

Sunday 13/08/2000
FA Charity Shield
at Wembley

Manchester United 0 Chelsea 2

CLUB CAREER RECORD	Apps	Subs	Goals
Premiership	92		0
League Division 1	0		0
League Division 2	0		0
FA Cup	4		0
League Cup	4		0
European Cup / Champions League	37		0
European Cup-Winners' Cup	0		0
UEFA Cup / Inter-Cities' Fairs Cup	0		0
Other Matches	2		0
OVERALL TOTAL	**139**		**0**

Opponents	PREM			FLD 1			FLD 2			FAC			LC			EC/CL			ECWC			UEFA			OTHER			TOTAL		
	A	S	G	A	S	G	A	S	G	A	S	G	A	S	G	A	S	G	A	S	G	A	S	G	A	S	G	A	S	G
1 Liverpool	6	–	–	–	–	–	–	–	–	–	–	–	1	–	–	–	–	–	–	–	–	–	–	–	1	–	–	8	–	–
2 West Ham United	6	–	–	–	–	–	–	–	–	2	–	–	–	–	–	–	–	–	–	–	–	–	–	–	–	–	–	8	–	–
3 Arsenal	6	–	–	–	–	–	–	–	–	1	–	–	–	–	–	–	–	–	–	–	–	–	–	–	–	–	–	7	–	–
4 Blackburn Rovers	4	–	–	–	–	–	–	–	–	2	–	–	–	–	–	–	–	–	–	–	–	–	–	–	–	–	–	6	–	–
5 Leeds United	6	–	–	–	–	–	–	–	–	–	–	–	–	–	–	–	–	–	–	–	–	–	–	–	–	–	–	6	–	–
6 Newcastle United	6	–	–	–	–	–	–	–	–	–	–	–	–	–	–	–	–	–	–	–	–	–	–	–	–	–	–	6	–	–
7 Aston Villa	5	–	–	–	–	–	–	–	–	–	–	–	–	–	–	–	–	–	–	–	–	–	–	–	–	–	–	5	–	–
8 Chelsea	3	–	–	–	–	–	–	–	–	–	–	–	1	–	–	–	–	–	–	–	–	–	–	–	1	–	–	5	–	–
9 Deportivo La Coruna	–	–	–	–	–	–	–	–	–	–	–	–	–	–	–	5	–	–	–	–	–	–	–	–	–	–	–	5	–	–
10 Everton	5	–	–	–	–	–	–	–	–	–	–	–	–	–	–	–	–	–	–	–	–	–	–	–	–	–	–	5	–	–
11 Middlesbrough	4	–	–	–	–	–	–	–	–	1	–	–	–	–	–	–	–	–	–	–	–	–	–	–	–	–	–	5	–	–
12 Southampton	5	–	–	–	–	–	–	–	–	–	–	–	–	–	–	–	–	–	–	–	–	–	–	–	–	–	–	5	–	–
13 Bayern Munich	–	–	–	–	–	–	–	–	–	–	–	–	–	–	–	4	–	–	–	–	–	–	–	–	–	–	–	4	–	–
14 Bolton Wanderers	4	–	–	–	–	–	–	–	–	–	–	–	–	–	–	–	–	–	–	–	–	–	–	–	–	–	–	4	–	–
15 Derby County	4	–	–	–	–	–	–	–	–	–	–	–	–	–	–	–	–	–	–	–	–	–	–	–	–	–	–	4	–	–
16 Fulham	4	–	–	–	–	–	–	–	–	–	–	–	–	–	–	–	–	–	–	–	–	–	–	–	–	–	–	4	–	–
17 Olympiakos Piraeus	–	–	–	–	–	–	–	–	–	–	–	–	–	–	–	4	–	–	–	–	–	–	–	–	–	–	–	4	–	–
18 Sunderland	4	–	–	–	–	–	–	–	–	–	–	–	–	–	–	–	–	–	–	–	–	–	–	–	–	–	–	4	–	–
19 Tottenham Hotspur	4	–	–	–	–	–	–	–	–	–	–	–	–	–	–	–	–	–	–	–	–	–	–	–	–	–	–	4	–	–
20 Bayer Leverkusen	–	–	–	–	–	–	–	–	–	–	–	–	–	–	–	3	–	–	–	–	–	–	–	–	–	–	–	3	–	–
21 Charlton Athletic	3	–	–	–	–	–	–	–	–	–	–	–	–	–	–	–	–	–	–	–	–	–	–	–	–	–	–	3	–	–
22 Ipswich Town	3	–	–	–	–	–	–	–	–	–	–	–	–	–	–	–	–	–	–	–	–	–	–	–	–	–	–	3	–	–
23 Manchester City	3	–	–	–	–	–	–	–	–	–	–	–	–	–	–	–	–	–	–	–	–	–	–	–	–	–	–	3	–	–
24 Anderlecht	–	–	–	–	–	–	–	–	–	–	–	–	–	–	–	2	–	–	–	–	–	–	–	–	–	–	–	2	–	–
25 Boavista	–	–	–	–	–	–	–	–	–	–	–	–	–	–	–	2	–	–	–	–	–	–	–	–	–	–	–	2	–	–
26 Bradford City	2	–	–	–	–	–	–	–	–	–	–	–	–	–	–	–	–	–	–	–	–	–	–	–	–	–	–	2	–	–
27 Juventus	–	–	–	–	–	–	–	–	–	–	–	–	–	–	–	2	–	–	–	–	–	–	–	–	–	–	–	2	–	–
28 Leicester City	2	–	–	–	–	–	–	–	–	–	–	–	–	–	–	–	–	–	–	–	–	–	–	–	–	–	–	2	–	–
29 Nantes Atlantique	–	–	–	–	–	–	–	–	–	–	–	–	–	–	–	2	–	–	–	–	–	–	–	–	–	–	–	2	–	–
30 Panathinaikos	–	–	–	–	–	–	–	–	–	–	–	–	–	–	–	2	–	–	–	–	–	–	–	–	–	–	–	2	–	–
31 Real Madrid	–	–	–	–	–	–	–	–	–	–	–	–	–	–	–	2	–	–	–	–	–	–	–	–	–	–	–	2	–	–
32 Sturm Graz	–	–	–	–	–	–	–	–	–	–	–	–	–	–	–	2	–	–	–	–	–	–	–	–	–	–	–	2	–	–
33 Valencia	–	–	–	–	–	–	–	–	–	–	–	–	–	–	–	2	–	–	–	–	–	–	–	–	–	–	–	2	–	–
34 Basel	–	–	–	–	–	–	–	–	–	–	–	–	–	–	–	1	–	–	–	–	–	–	–	–	–	–	–	1	–	–
35 Birmingham City	1	–	–	–	–	–	–	–	–	–	–	–	–	–	–	–	–	–	–	–	–	–	–	–	–	–	–	1	–	–
36 Coventry City	1	–	–	–	–	–	–	–	–	–	–	–	–	–	–	–	–	–	–	–	–	–	–	–	–	–	–	1	–	–
37 Dynamo Kiev	–	–	–	–	–	–	–	–	–	–	–	–	–	–	–	1	–	–	–	–	–	–	–	–	–	–	–	1	–	–
38 Lille Metropole	–	–	–	–	–	–	–	–	–	–	–	–	–	–	–	1	–	–	–	–	–	–	–	–	–	–	–	1	–	–
39 Maccabi Haifa	–	–	–	–	–	–	–	–	–	–	–	–	–	–	–	1	–	–	–	–	–	–	–	–	–	–	–	1	–	–
40 PSV Eindhoven	–	–	–	–	–	–	–	–	–	–	–	–	–	–	–	1	–	–	–	–	–	–	–	–	–	–	–	1	–	–
41 West Bromwich Albion	1	–	–	–	–	–	–	–	–	–	–	–	–	–	–	–	–	–	–	–	–	–	–	–	–	–	–	1	–	–

ARTHUR BEADSWORTH

DEBUT (Full Appearance, 1 goal)

Saturday 25/10/1902
Football League Division 2
at Manor Field

Arsenal 0 Manchester United 1

CLUB CAREER RECORD	Apps	Subs	Goals
Premiership	0		0
League Division 1	0		0
League Division 2	9		1
FA Cup	3		1
League Cup	0		0
European Cup / Champions League	0		0
European Cup-Winners' Cup	0		0
UEFA Cup / Inter-Cities' Fairs Cup	0		0
Other Matches	0		0
OVERALL TOTAL	**12**		**2**

Opponents	PREM			FLD 1			FLD 2			FAC			LC			EC/CL			ECWC			UEFA			OTHER			TOTAL		
	A	S	G	A	S	G	A	S	G	A	S	G	A	S	G	A	S	G	A	S	G	A	S	G	A	S	G	A	S	G
1 Birmingham City	–	–	–	–	–	–	2	–	–	–	–	–	–	–	–	–	–	–	–	–	–	–	–	–	–	–	–	2	–	–
2 Burton United	–	–	–	–	–	–	1	–	–	1	–	–	–	–	–	–	–	–	–	–	–	–	–	–	–	–	–	2	–	–
3 Arsenal	–	–	–	–	–	–	1	–	1	–	–	–	–	–	–	–	–	–	–	–	–	–	–	–	–	–	–	1	–	1
4 Oswaldtwistle Rovers	–	–	–	–	–	–	–	–	–	1	–	1	–	–	–	–	–	–	–	–	–	–	–	–	–	–	–	1	–	1
5 Barnsley	–	–	–	–	–	–	1	–	–	–	–	–	–	–	–	–	–	–	–	–	–	–	–	–	–	–	–	1	–	–
6 Blackpool	–	–	–	–	–	–	1	–	–	–	–	–	–	–	–	–	–	–	–	–	–	–	–	–	–	–	–	1	–	–
7 Leicester City	–	–	–	–	–	–	1	–	–	–	–	–	–	–	–	–	–	–	–	–	–	–	–	–	–	–	–	1	–	–
8 Lincoln City	–	–	–	–	–	–	1	–	–	–	–	–	–	–	–	–	–	–	–	–	–	–	–	–	–	–	–	1	–	–
9 Manchester City	–	–	–	–	–	–	1	–	–	–	–	–	–	–	–	–	–	–	–	–	–	–	–	–	–	–	–	1	–	–
10 Southport Central	–	–	–	–	–	–	–	–	–	1	–	–	–	–	–	–	–	–	–	–	–	–	–	–	–	–	–	1	–	–

ROBERT BEALE

DEBUT (Full Appearance)

Monday 02/09/1912
Football League Division 1
at Manor Field

Arsenal 0 Manchester United 0

CLUB CAREER RECORD	Apps	Subs	Goals
Premiership	0		0
League Division 1	105		0
League Division 2	0		0
FA Cup	7		0
League Cup	0		0
European Cup / Champions League	0		0
European Cup-Winners' Cup	0		0
UEFA Cup / Inter-Cities' Fairs Cup	0		0
Other Matches	0		0
OVERALL TOTAL	**112**		**0**

	Opponents	PREM A S G	FLD 1 A S G	FLD 2 A S G	FAC A S G	LC A S G	EC/CL A S G	ECWC A S G	UEFA A S G	OTHER A S G	TOTAL A S G
1	Oldham Athletic	– –	6 –	– – –	2 –	– –	– –	– –	– –	– –	8 –
2	Sheffield Wednesday	– –	6 –	– – –	1 –	– –	– –	– –	– –	– –	7 –
3	Aston Villa	– –	6 –	– – –	– –	– –	– –	– –	– –	– –	6 –
4	Blackburn Rovers	– –	6 –	– – –	– –	– –	– –	– –	– –	– –	6 –
5	Bolton Wanderers	– –	6 –	– – –	– –	– –	– –	– –	– –	– –	6 –
6	Chelsea	– –	6 –	– – –	– –	– –	– –	– –	– –	– –	6 –
7	Everton	– –	6 –	– – –	– –	– –	– –	– –	– –	– –	6 –
8	Newcastle United	– –	6 –	– – –	– –	– –	– –	– –	– –	– –	6 –
9	Tottenham Hotspur	– –	6 –	– – –	– –	– –	– –	– –	– –	– –	6 –
10	Bradford City	– –	5 –	– – –	– –	– –	– –	– –	– –	– –	5 –
11	Liverpool	– –	5 –	– – –	– –	– –	– –	– –	– –	– –	5 –
12	Manchester City	– –	5 –	– – –	– –	– –	– –	– –	– –	– –	5 –
13	Middlesbrough	– –	5 –	– – –	– –	– –	– –	– –	– –	– –	5 –
14	Sheffield United	– –	5 –	– – –	– –	– –	– –	– –	– –	– –	5 –
15	Sunderland	– –	5 –	– – –	– –	– –	– –	– –	– –	– –	5 –
16	West Bromwich Albion	– –	5 –	– – –	– –	– –	– –	– –	– –	– –	5 –
17	Notts County	– –	4 –	– – –	– –	– –	– –	– –	– –	– –	4 –
18	Burnley	– –	3 –	– – –	– –	– –	– –	– –	– –	– –	3 –
19	Derby County	– –	3 –	– – –	– –	– –	– –	– –	– –	– –	3 –
20	Arsenal	– –	2 –	– – –	– –	– –	– –	– –	– –	– –	2 –
21	Bradford Park Avenue	– –	2 –	– – –	– –	– –	– –	– –	– –	– –	2 –
22	Coventry City	– –	– –	– – –	2 –	– –	– –	– –	– –	– –	2 –
23	Preston North End	– –	2 –	– – –	– –	– –	– –	– –	– –	– –	2 –
24	Plymouth Argyle	– –	– –	– – –	1 –	– –	– –	– –	– –	– –	1 –
25	Swindon Town	– –	– –	– – –	1 –	– –	– –	– –	– –	– –	1 –

PETER BEARDSLEY

DEBUT (Full Appearance)

Wednesday 06/10/1982
League Cup 2nd Round 1st Leg
at Old Trafford

Manchester United 2 Bournemouth 0

CLUB CAREER RECORD	Apps	Subs	Goals
Premiership	0		0
League Division 1	0		0
League Division 2	0		0
FA Cup	0		0
League Cup	1		0
European Cup / Champions League	0		0
European Cup-Winners' Cup	0		0
UEFA Cup / Inter-Cities' Fairs Cup	0		0
Other Matches	0		0
OVERALL TOTAL	**1**		**0**

	Opponents	PREM A S G	FLD 1 A S G	FLD 2 A S G	FAC A S G	LC A S G	EC/CL A S G	ECWC A S G	UEFA A S G	OTHER A S G	TOTAL A S G
1	Bournemouth	– – –	– – –	– – –	– – –	1 –	– – –	– – –	– – –	– – –	1 –

RUSSELL BEARDSMORE

DEBUT (Substitute Appearance)

Saturday 24/09/1988
Football League Division 1
at Old Trafford

Manchester United 2 West Ham United 0

CLUB CAREER RECORD	Apps	Subs	Goals
Premiership	0		0
League Division 1	30	(26)	4
League Division 2	0		0
FA Cup	4	(4)	0
League Cup	3	(1)	0
European Cup / Champions League	0		0
European Cup-Winners' Cup	2	(3)	0
UEFA Cup / Inter-Cities' Fairs Cup	0		0
Other Matches	0		0
OVERALL TOTAL	**39**	**(34)**	**4**

	Opponents	PREM A S G	FLD 1 A S G	FLD 2 A S G	FAC A S G	LC A S G	EC/CL A S G	ECWC A S G	UEFA A S G	OTHER A S G	TOTAL A S G
1	Queens Park Rangers	– –	3 (1) –	– – –	2 (1) –	– –	– –	– –	– –	– –	5 (2) –
2	Nottingham Forest	– –	4 –	– – –	2 –	– –	– –	– –	– –	– –	6 –
3	Millwall	– –	3 (1) –	– – –	– –	– –	– –	– –	– –	– –	3 (1) –
4	Everton	– –	1 (3) 1	– – –	– –	– –	– –	– –	– –	– –	1 (3) 1
5	Arsenal	– –	1 (3) –	– – –	– –	– –	– –	– –	– –	– –	1 (3) –
6	Southampton	– –	2 (1) 1	– – –	– –	– –	– –	– –	– –	– –	2 (1) 1
7	Luton Town	– –	2 (1) –	– – –	– –	– –	– –	– –	– –	– –	2 (1) –

continued../

RUSSELL BEARDSMORE (continued)

Opponents	PREM A S G	FLD 1 A S G	FLD 2 A S G	FAC A S G	LC A S G	EC/CL A S G	ECWC A S G	UEFA A S G	OTHER A S G	TOTAL A S G
8 Liverpool	– –	1 (2) 1	–	–	–	–	–	–	–	1 (2) 1
9 Tottenham Hotspur	– –	1 (2) –	–	–	–	–	–	–	–	1 (2) –
10 Charlton Athletic	– –	2	–	–	–	–	–	–	–	2 –
11 Derby County	– –	2	–	–	–	–	–	–	–	2 –
12 Crystal Palace	– –	1 (1) 1	–	–	–	–	–	–	–	1 (1) 1
13 Aston Villa	– –	1 (1) –	–	–	–	–	–	–	–	1 (1) –
14 Athinaikos	– –	–	–	–	–	–	1 (1) –	–	–	1 (1) –
15 Manchester City	– –	1 (1) –	–	–	–	–	–	–	–	1 (1) –
16 Newcastle United	– –	1	–	– (1) –	–	–	–	–	–	1 (1) –
17 Rotherham United	– –	–	–	–	1 (1) –	–	–	–	–	1 (1) –
18 Sheffield Wednesday	– –	1 (1) –	–	–	–	–	–	–	–	1 (1) –
19 Wimbledon	– –	1 (1) –	–	–	–	–	–	–	–	1 (1) –
20 Chelsea	– –	– (2) –	–	–	–	–	–	–	–	– (2) –
21 Norwich City	– –	– (2) –	–	–	–	–	–	–	–	– (2) –
22 Coventry City	– –	1	–	–	–	–	–	–	–	1 –
23 Halifax Town	– –	–	–	–	1	–	–	–	–	1 –
24 Middlesbrough	– –	1	–	–	–	–	–	–	–	1 –
25 Pecsi Munkas	– –	–	–	–	–	–	1	–	–	1 –
26 Portsmouth	– –	–	–	–	1	–	–	–	–	1 –
27 Athletico Madrid	– –	–	–	–	–	–	– (1) –	–	–	– (1) –
28 Hereford United	– –	–	–	– (1) –	–	–	–	–	–	– (1) –
29 Leeds United	– –	– (1) –	–	–	–	–	–	–	–	– (1) –
30 Oxford United	– –	–	–	– (1) –	–	–	–	–	–	– (1) –
31 Sunderland	– –	– (1) –	–	–	–	–	–	–	–	– (1) –
32 West Ham United	– –	– (1) –	–	–	–	–	–	–	–	– (1) –
33 Wrexham	– –	–	–	–	–	–	– (1) –	–	–	– (1) –

R BECKETT

DEBUT (Full Appearance)

Saturday 30/10/1886
FA Cup 1st Round
at Fleetwood Park

Fleetwood Rangers 2 Newton Heath 2

CLUB CAREER RECORD	Apps	Subs	Goals
Premiership	0		0
League Division 1	0		0
League Division 2	0		0
FA Cup	1		0
League Cup	0		0
European Cup / Champions League	0		0
European Cup-Winners' Cup	0		0
UEFA Cup / Inter-Cities' Fairs Cup	0		0
Other Matches	0		0
OVERALL TOTAL	**1**		**0**

Opponents	PREM A S G	FLD 1 A S G	FLD 2 A S G	FAC A S G	LC A S G	EC/CL A S G	ECWC A S G	UEFA A S G	OTHER A S G	TOTAL A S G
1 Fleetwood Rangers	–	–	–	1	–	–	–	–	–	1 –

DAVID BECKHAM

DEBUT (Substitute Appearance)

Wednesday 23/09/1992
League Cup 2nd Round 1st Leg
at Goldstone Ground

Brighton 1 Manchester United 1

CLUB CAREER RECORD	Apps	Subs	Goals
Premiership	237	(28)	62
League Division 1	0		0
League Division 2	0		0
FA Cup	22	(2)	6
League Cup	10	(2)	1
European Cup / Champions League	77	(4)	15
European Cup-Winners' Cup	0		0
UEFA Cup / Inter-Cities' Fairs Cup	2		0
Other Matches	8	(2)	1
OVERALL TOTAL	**356**	**(38)**	**85**

Opponents	PREM A S G	FLD 1 A S G	FLD 2 A S G	FAC A S G	LC A S G	EC/CL A S G	ECWC A S G	UEFA A S G	OTHER A S G	TOTAL A S G
1 Chelsea	14 (1) 4	–	–	4 3	1	–	–	1 (1) –	–	20 (2) 7
2 Liverpool	13 (2) 3	–	–	2 –	1	–	–	1 –	–	17 (2) 3
3 Arsenal	11 (1) –	–	–	3 1	–	–	–	2 –	–	16 (1) 1
4 Tottenham Hotspur	13 (2) 6	–	–	1 1	– (1) –	–	–	–	–	14 (3) 7
5 Newcastle United	12 (1) 2	–	–	1 –	1	–	–	1 1	–	15 (1) 3
6 West Ham United	11 (3) 5	–	–	2 –	–	–	–	–	–	13 (3) 5
7 Leeds United	14 (1) 2	–	–	–	–	–	–	–	–	14 (1) 2
8 Southampton	13 (2) 4	–	–	–	–	–	–	–	–	13 (2) 4
9 Everton	12 (3) 4	–	–	–	–	–	–	–	–	12 (3) 4
10 Aston Villa	12 (1) 4	–	–	1 –	–	–	–	–	–	13 (1) 4
11 Blackburn Rovers	10 (2) 3	–	–	–	2	–	–	–	–	12 (2) 3
12 Middlesbrough	11 (1) 2	–	–	–	–	–	–	–	–	11 (1) 2
13 Coventry City	10 (2) 2	–	–	–	–	–	–	–	–	10 (2) 2
14 Wimbledon	7 (2) 5	–	–	1 –	–	–	–	–	–	8 (2) 5
15 Leicester City	7 (2) 2	–	–	–	1 1	–	–	–	–	8 (2) 3
16 Derby County	9 1	–	–	–	–	–	–	–	–	9 1

continued../

DAVID BECKHAM (continued)

Opponents	PREM A	S	G	FLD 1 A	S	G	FLD 2 A	S	G	FAC A	S	G	LC A	S	G	EC/CL A	S	G	ECWC A	S	G	UEFA A	S	G	OTHER A	S	G	TOTAL A	S	G
17 Sunderland	7 (1)		2	–	–	–	–	–	–	1			–	–	–	–	–	–	–	–	–	–	–	–	–	–	–	8 (1)		2
18 Sheffield Wednesday	8 (1)		–	–	–	–	–	–	–	–	–	–	–	–	–	–	–	–	–	–	–	–	–	–	–	–	–	8 (1)		–
19 Juventus	–			–	–	–	–	–	–	–	–	–	–	–	–	8			–	–	–	–	–	–	–	–	–	8		–
20 Bolton Wanderers	7		1	–	–	–	–	–	–	–	–	–	–	–	–	–	–	–	–	–	–	–	–	–	–	–	–	7		1
21 Nottingham Forest	6		3	–	–	–	–	–	–	–	–	–	–	–	–	–	–	–	–	–	–	–	–	–	–	–	–	6		3
22 Charlton Athletic	6		1	–	–	–	–	–	–	–	–	–	–	–	–	–	–	–	–	–	–	–	–	–	–	–	–	6		1
23 Fulham	4		1	–	–	–	–	–	–	2			–	–	–	–	–	–	–	–	–	–	–	–	–	–	–	6		1
24 Bayern Munich	–		–	–	–	–	–	–	–	–	–	–	–	–	–	6			–	–	–	–	–	–	–	–	–	6		–
25 Manchester City	5		1	–	–	–	–	–	–	–	–	–	–	–	–	–	–	–	–	–	–	–	–	–	–	–	–	5		1
26 Deportivo La Coruna	–		–	–	–	–	–	–	–	–	–	–	–	–	–	4 (1)		1	–	–	–	–	–	–	–	–	–	4 (1)		1
27 Olympiakos Piraeus	–		–	–	–	–	–	–	–	–	–	–	–	–	–	4		1	–	–	–	–	–	–	–	–	–	4		1
28 Real Madrid	–		–	–	–	–	–	–	–	–	–	–	–	–	–	3 (1)		3	–	–	–	–	–	–	–	–	–	3 (1)		3
29 Bradford City	3		2	–	–	–	–	–	–	–	–	–	–	–	–	–	–	–	–	–	–	–	–	–	–	–	–	3		2
30 Crystal Palace	2		–	–	–	–	–	–	–	1			–	–	–	–	–	–	–	–	–	–	–	–	–	–	–	3		–
31 Valencia	–		–	–	–	–	–	–	–	–	–	–	–	–	–	3			–	–	–	–	–	–	–	–	–	3		–
32 Barnsley	1		–	–	–	–	–	–	–	1 (1)		–	–	–	–	–	–	–	–	–	–	–	–	–	–	–	–	2 (1)		–
33 Barcelona	–		–	–	–	–	–	–	–	–	–	–	–	–	–	2		1	–	–	–	–	–	–	–	–	–	2		1
34 Birmingham City	2		1	–	–	–	–	–	–	–	–	–	–	–	–	–	–	–	–	–	–	–	–	–	–	–	–	2		1
35 Croatia Zagreb	–		–	–	–	–	–	–	–	–	–	–	–	–	–	2		1	–	–	–	–	–	–	–	–	–	2		1
36 Fenerbahce	–		–	–	–	–	–	–	–	–	–	–	–	–	–	2		1	–	–	–	–	–	–	–	–	–	2		1
37 Ipswich Town	2		1	–	–	–	–	–	–	–	–	–	–	–	–	–	–	–	–	–	–	–	–	–	–	–	–	2		1
38 Lille Metropole	–		–	–	–	–	–	–	–	–	–	–	–	–	–	2		1	–	–	–	–	–	–	–	–	–	2		1
39 Nantes Atlantique	–		–	–	–	–	–	–	–	–	–	–	–	–	–	2		1	–	–	–	–	–	–	–	–	–	2		1
40 Rapid Vienna	–		–	–	–	–	–	–	–	–	–	–	–	–	–	2		1	–	–	–	–	–	–	–	–	–	2		1
41 Zalaegerszeg	–		–	–	–	–	–	–	–	–	–	–	–	–	–	2		1	–	–	–	–	–	–	–	–	–	2		1
42 Anderlecht	–		–	–	–	–	–	–	–	–	–	–	–	–	–	2			–	–	–	–	–	–	–	–	–	2		–
43 Bayer Leverkusen	–		–	–	–	–	–	–	–	–	–	–	–	–	–	2			–	–	–	–	–	–	–	–	–	2		–
44 Borussia Dortmund	–		–	–	–	–	–	–	–	–	–	–	–	–	–	2			–	–	–	–	–	–	–	–	–	2		–
45 Dynamo Kiev	–		–	–	–	–	–	–	–	–	–	–	–	–	–	2			–	–	–	–	–	–	–	–	–	2		–
46 Feyenoord	–		–	–	–	–	–	–	–	–	–	–	–	–	–	2			–	–	–	–	–	–	–	–	–	2		–
47 Fiorentina	–		–	–	–	–	–	–	–	–	–	–	–	–	–	2			–	–	–	–	–	–	–	–	–	2		–
48 Girondins Bordeaux	–		–	–	–	–	–	–	–	–	–	–	–	–	–	2			–	–	–	–	–	–	–	–	–	2		–
49 Internazionale	–		–	–	–	–	–	–	–	–	–	–	–	–	–	2			–	–	–	–	–	–	–	–	–	2		–
50 Kosice	–		–	–	–	–	–	–	–	–	–	–	–	–	–	2			–	–	–	–	–	–	–	–	–	2		–
51 LKS Lodz	–		–	–	–	–	–	–	–	–	–	–	–	–	–	2			–	–	–	–	–	–	–	–	–	2		–
52 Monaco	–		–	–	–	–	–	–	–	–	–	–	–	–	–	2			–	–	–	–	–	–	–	–	–	2		–
53 Olympique Marseille	–		–	–	–	–	–	–	–	–	–	–	–	–	–	2			–	–	–	–	–	–	–	–	–	2		–
54 Panathinaikos	–		–	–	–	–	–	–	–	–	–	–	–	–	–	2			–	–	–	–	–	–	–	–	–	2		–
55 Port Vale	–		–	–	–	–	–	–	–	–	–	–	2			–	–	–	–	–	–	–	–	–	–	–	–	2		–
56 Porto	–		–	–	–	–	–	–	–	–	–	–	–	–	–	2			–	–	–	–	–	–	–	–	–	2		–
57 Queens Park Rangers	2		–	–	–	–	–	–	–	–	–	–	–	–	–	–	–	–	–	–	–	–	–	–	–	–	–	2		–
58 Rotor Volgograd	–		–	–	–	–	–	–	–	–	–	–	–	–	–	–	–	–	–	–	–	2			–	–	–	2		–
59 Sturm Graz	–		–	–	–	–	–	–	–	–	–	–	–	–	–	2			–	–	–	–	–	–	–	–	–	2		–
60 West Bromwich Albion	2		–	–	–	–	–	–	–	–	–	–	–	–	–	–	–	–	–	–	–	–	–	–	–	–	–	2		–
61 York City	–		–	–	–	–	–	–	–	–	–	–	2			–	–	–	–	–	–	–	–	–	–	–	–	2		–
62 PSV Eindhoven	–		–	–	–	–	–	–	–	–	–	–	–	–	–	1 (1)			–	–	–	–	–	–	–	–	–	1 (1)		–
63 Boavista	–		–	–	–	–	–	–	–	–	–	–	–	–	–	1		1	–	–	–	–	–	–	–	–	–	1		1
64 Brondby	–		–	–	–	–	–	–	–	–	–	–	–	–	–	1		1	–	–	–	–	–	–	–	–	–	1		1
65 Galatasaray	–		–	–	–	–	–	–	–	–	–	–	–	–	–	1		1	–	–	–	–	–	–	–	–	–	1		1
66 Portsmouth	–		–	–	–	–	–	–	–	1		1	–	–	–	–	–	–	–	–	–	–	–	–	–	–	–	1		1
67 Lazio	–		–	–	–	–	–	–	–	–	–	–	–	–	–	–	–	–	–	–	–	–	–	–	1			1		–
68 Maccabi Haifa	–		–	–	–	–	–	–	–	–	–	–	–	–	–	1			–	–	–	–	–	–	–	–	–	1		–
69 Palmeiras	–		–	–	–	–	–	–	–	–	–	–	–	–	–	–	–	–	–	–	–	–	–	–	1			1		–
70 Rayos del Necaxa	–		–	–	–	–	–	–	–	–	–	–	–	–	–	–	–	–	–	–	–	–	–	–	1			1		–
71 Walsall	–		–	–	–	–	–	–	–	1			–	–	–	–	–	–	–	–	–	–	–	–	–	–	–	1		–
72 Watford	1		–	–	–	–	–	–	–	–	–	–	–	–	–	–	–	–	–	–	–	–	–	–	–	–	–	1		–
73 Basel	–		–	–	–	–	–	–	–	–	–	–	–	–	–	– (1)			–	–	–	–	–	–	–	–	–	– (1)		–
74 Brighton	–		–	–	–	–	–	–	–	–	–	–	– (1)			–	–	–	–	–	–	–	–	–	–	–	–	– (1)		–
75 South Melbourne	–		–	–	–	–	–	–	–	–	–	–	–	–	–	–	–	–	–	–	–	–	–	–	– (1)			– (1)		–
76 Wrexham	–		–	–	–	–	– (1)			–	–	–	–	–	–	–	–	–	–	–	–	–	–	–	–	–	–	– (1)		–

JOHN BEDDOW

DEBUT (Full Appearance)

Saturday 25/02/1905
Football League Division 2
at Oakwell

Barnsley 0 Manchester United 0

CLUB CAREER RECORD	Apps	Subs	Goals
Premiership	0		0
League Division 1	3		0
League Division 2	30		12
FA Cup	1		3
League Cup	0		0
European Cup / Champions League	0		0
European Cup-Winners' Cup	0		0
UEFA Cup / Inter-Cities' Fairs Cup	0		0
Other Matches	0		0
OVERALL TOTAL	**34**		**15**

	Opponents	PREM A S G	FLD 1 A S G	FLD 2 A S G	FAC A S G	LC A S G	EC/CL A S G	ECWC A S G	UEFA A S G	OTHER A S G	TOTAL A S G
1	Grimsby Town	– – –	– – –	3 – 3	– –	– –	– –	– –	– –	– –	3 – 3
2	Blackpool	– – –	– – –	3 –	– –	– –	– –	– –	– –	– –	3 –
3	West Bromwich Albion	– – –	– – –	3 –	– –	– –	– –	– –	– –	– –	3 –
4	Bradford City	– – –	– – –	2 – 2	– –	– –	– –	– –	– –	– –	2 – 2
5	Glossop	– – –	– – –	2 – 2	– –	– –	– –	– –	– –	– –	2 – 2
6	Barnsley	– – –	– – –	2 – 1	– –	– –	– –	– –	– –	– –	2 – 1
7	Bristol City	– – –	– – –	2 – 1	– –	– –	– –	– –	– –	– –	2 – 1
8	Burnley	– – –	– – –	2 – 1	– –	– –	– –	– –	– –	– –	2 – 1
9	Burton United	– – –	– – –	2 –	– –	– –	– –	– –	– –	– –	2 –
10	Sheffield United	– – –	– 2	– –	– –	– –	– –	– –	– –	– –	2 –
11	Stockport County	– – –	– – –	2 –	– –	– –	– –	– –	– –	– –	2 –
12	Staple Hill	– – –	– – –	– –	1 – 3	– –	– –	– –	– –	– –	1 – 3
13	Doncaster Rovers	– – –	– – –	1 – 1	– –	– –	– –	– –	– –	– –	1 – 1
14	Port Vale	– – –	– – –	1 – 1	– –	– –	– –	– –	– –	– –	1 – 1
15	Chelsea	– – –	– – –	1 –	– –	– –	– –	– –	– –	– –	1 –
16	Chesterfield	– – –	– – –	1 –	– –	– –	– –	– –	– –	– –	1 –
17	Gainsborough Trinity	– – –	– – –	1 –	– –	– –	– –	– –	– –	– –	1 –
18	Leeds United	– – –	– – –	1 –	– –	– –	– –	– –	– –	– –	1 –
19	Leyton Orient	– – –	– – –	1 –	– –	– –	– –	– –	– –	– –	1 –
20	Manchester City	– – –	– 1	– –	– –	– –	– –	– –	– –	– –	1 –

BILLY BEHAN

DEBUT (Full Appearance)

Saturday 03/03/1934
Football League Division 2
at Old Trafford

Manchester United 2 Bury 1

CLUB CAREER RECORD	Apps	Subs	Goals
Premiership	0		0
League Division 1	0		0
League Division 2	1		0
FA Cup	0		0
League Cup	0		0
European Cup / Champions League	0		0
European Cup-Winners' Cup	0		0
UEFA Cup / Inter-Cities' Fairs Cup	0		0
Other Matches	0		0
OVERALL TOTAL	**1**		**0**

	Opponents	PREM A S G	FLD 1 A S G	FLD 2 A S G	FAC A S G	LC A S G	EC/CL A S G	ECWC A S G	UEFA A S G	OTHER A S G	TOTAL A S G
1	Bury	– – –	– – –	1 –	– –	– –	– –	– –	– –	– –	1 –

ALEX BELL

DEBUT (Full Appearance)

Saturday 24/01/1903
Football League Division 2
at North Road

Glossop 1 Manchester United 3

CLUB CAREER RECORD	Apps	Subs	Goals
Premiership	0		0
League Division 1	202		5
League Division 2	76		5
FA Cup	28		0
League Cup	0		0
European Cup / Champions League	0		0
European Cup-Winners' Cup	0		0
UEFA Cup / Inter-Cities' Fairs Cup	0		0
Other Matches	3		0
OVERALL TOTAL	**309**		**10**

	Opponents	PREM A S G	FLD 1 A S G	FLD 2 A S G	FAC A S G	LC A S G	EC/CL A S G	ECWC A S G	UEFA A S G	OTHER A S G	TOTAL A S G
1	Aston Villa	– –	11 –	– –	3 –	– –	– –	– –	– –	– –	14 –
2	Blackburn Rovers	– –	11 –	– –	3 –	– –	– –	– –	– –	– –	14 –
3	Sheffield United	– –	13 3	– –	– –	– –	– –	– –	– –	– –	13 3
4	Newcastle United	– –	12 –	– –	1 –	– –	– –	– –	– –	– –	13 –
5	Bristol City	– –	7 –	4 –	1 –	– –	– –	– –	– –	– –	12 –
6	Everton	– –	11 –	– –	1 –	– –	– –	– –	– –	– –	12 –
7	Sunderland	– –	11 1	– –	– –	– –	– –	– –	– –	– –	11 1
8	Arsenal	– –	10 –	– –	1 –	– –	– –	– –	– –	– –	11 –
9	Bolton Wanderers	– –	10 –	1 –	– –	– –	– –	– –	– –	– –	11 –
10	Liverpool	– –	9 –	2 –	– –	– –	– –	– –	– –	– –	11 –
11	Bradford City	– –	6 –	4 –	– –	– –	– –	– –	– –	– –	10 –
12	Bury	– –	10 –	– –	– –	– –	– –	– –	– –	– –	10 –

continued../

ALEX BELL (continued)

Opponents	PREM (A S G)	FLD 1 (A S G)	FLD 2 (A S G)	FAC (A S G)	LC (A S G)	EC/CL (A S G)	ECWC (A S G)	UEFA (A S G)	OTHER (A S G)	TOTAL (A S G)
13 Middlesbrough	–	10 – –	–	–	–	–	–	–	–	10 – –
14 Notts County	–	10 – –	–	–	–	–	–	–	–	10 – –
15 Sheffield Wednesday	–	10 – –	–	–	–	–	–	–	–	10 – –
16 Manchester City	–	9 – –	–	–	–	–	–	–	–	9 – –
17 Chelsea	–	5 – –	2 – –	1 – –	–	–	–	–	–	8 – –
18 Preston North End	–	8 – –	–	–	–	–	–	–	–	8 – –
19 Blackpool	–	–	5 – –	2 – –	–	–	–	–	–	7 – –
20 Nottingham Forest	–	7 – –	–	–	–	–	–	–	–	7 – –
21 Chesterfield	–	–	6 – 1	–	–	–	–	–	–	6 – 1
22 Leicester City	–	1 – –	5 – –	–	–	–	–	–	–	6 – –
23 West Bromwich Albion	–	3 – –	3 – –	–	–	–	–	–	–	6 – –
24 Glossop	–	–	5 – 1	–	–	–	–	–	–	5 – 1
25 Birmingham City	–	4 – –	1 – –	–	–	–	–	–	–	5 – –
26 Lincoln City	–	–	5 – –	–	–	–	–	–	–	5 – –
27 Oldham Athletic	–	5 – –	–	–	–	–	–	–	–	5 – –
28 Barnsley	–	–	–	4 – 1	–	–	–	–	–	4 – 1
29 Grimsby Town	–	–	–	4 – 1	–	–	–	–	–	4 – 1
30 Burnley	–	–	–	3 – –	1 – –	–	–	–	–	4 – –
31 Fulham	–	–	–	4 – –	–	–	–	–	–	4 – –
32 Gainsborough Trinity	–	–	–	4 – –	–	–	–	–	–	4 – –
33 Port Vale	–	–	–	4 – –	–	–	–	–	–	4 – –
34 Tottenham Hotspur	–	4 – –	–	–	–	–	–	–	–	4 – –
35 Derby County	–	3 – 1	–	–	–	–	–	–	–	3 – 1
36 Doncaster Rovers	–	–	–	3 – 1	–	–	–	–	–	3 – 1
37 Burton United	–	–	–	3 – –	–	–	–	–	–	3 – –
38 Hull City	–	–	–	2 – –	–	–	–	–	–	2 – –
39 Leeds United	–	–	–	2 – –	–	–	–	–	–	2 – –
40 Leyton Orient	–	–	–	2 – –	–	–	–	–	–	2 – –
41 Portsmouth	–	–	–	2 – –	–	–	–	–	–	2 – –
42 Queens Park Rangers	–	–	–	–	–	–	–	–	2 – –	2 – –
43 Reading	–	–	–	2 – –	–	–	–	–	–	2 – –
44 Stockport County	–	–	2 – –	–	–	–	–	–	–	2 – –
45 Stoke City	–	2 – –	–	–	–	–	–	–	–	2 – –
46 Brighton	–	–	–	–	1 – –	–	–	–	–	1 – –
47 Coventry City	–	–	–	–	1 – –	–	–	–	–	1 – –
48 Huddersfield Town	–	–	–	–	1 – –	–	–	–	–	1 – –
49 Norwich City	–	–	–	–	1 – –	–	–	–	–	1 – –
50 Staple Hill	–	–	–	–	1 – –	–	–	–	–	1 – –
51 Swindon Town	–	–	–	–	–	–	–	–	1 – –	1 – –
52 West Ham United	–	–	–	–	1 – –	–	–	–	–	1 – –

DAVID BELLION

DEBUT (Substitute Appearance)

Wednesday 27/08/2003
FA Premiership
at Old Trafford

Manchester United 1 Wolverhampton Wanderers 0

CLUB CAREER RECORD	Apps	Subs	Goals
Premiership	5	(19)	4
League Division 1	0		0
League Division 2	0		0
FA Cup	2	(1)	0
League Cup	5		2
European Cup / Champions League	2	(5)	2
European Cup–Winners' Cup	0		0
UEFA Cup / Inter–Cities' Fairs Cup	0		0
Other Matches	1		0
OVERALL TOTAL	**15**	**(25)**	**8**

Opponents	PREM (A S G)	FLD 1 (A S G)	FLD 2 (A S G)	FAC (A S G)	LC (A S G)	EC/CL (A S G)	ECWC (A S G)	UEFA (A S G)	OTHER (A S G)	TOTAL (A S G)
1 Arsenal	–	–	–	– (1) –	1 – 1	–	–	–	1 – –	2 (1) 1
2 Blackburn Rovers	1 (2) –	–	–	–	–	–	–	–	–	1 (2) –
3 Tottenham Hotspur	– (3) 1	–	–	–	–	–	–	–	–	– (3) 1
4 Fenerbahce	–	–	–	–	–	2 – 1	–	–	–	2 – 1
5 Everton	1 (1) 1	–	–	–	–	–	–	–	–	1 (1) 1
6 Liverpool	– (2) –	–	–	–	–	–	–	–	–	– (2) –
7 Panathinaikos	–	–	–	–	–	– (2) –	–	–	–	– (2) –
8 Portsmouth	– (2) –	–	–	–	–	–	–	–	–	– (2) –
9 Wolverhampton W.	– (2) –	–	–	–	–	–	–	–	–	– (2) –
10 Leeds United	–	–	–	–	1 – 1	–	–	–	–	1 – 1
11 Norwich City	1 – –	–	–	–	–	–	–	–	–	1 – –
12 Charlton Athletic	1 – –	–	–	–	–	–	–	–	–	1 – –
13 Crewe Alexandra	–	–	–	–	1 – –	–	–	–	–	1 – –
14 Crystal Palace	–	–	–	–	1 – –	–	–	–	–	1 – –
15 Exeter City	–	–	–	1 – –	–	–	–	–	–	1 – –
16 Leicester City	1 – –	–	–	–	–	–	–	–	–	1 – –
17 Northampton Town	–	–	–	1 – –	–	–	–	–	–	1 – –
18 West Bromwich Albion	–	–	–	–	1 – –	–	–	–	–	1 – –
19 Bolton Wanderers	– (1) 1	–	–	–	–	–	–	–	–	– (1) 1
20 Dinamo Bucharest	–	–	–	–	–	– (1) 1	–	–	–	– (1) 1
21 Aston Villa	– (1) –	–	–	–	–	–	–	–	–	– (1) –

continued../

DAVID BELLION (continued)

Opponents	PREM A	S	G	FLD 1 A	S	G	FLD 2 A	S	G	FAC A	S	G	LC A	S	G	EC/CL A	S	G	ECWC A	S	G	UEFA A	S	G	OTHER A	S	G	TOTAL A	S	G
22 Chelsea	–	(1)	–	–	–	–	–	–	–	–	–	–	–	–	–	–	–	–	–	–	–	–	–	–	–	–	–	–	(1)	–
23 Fulham	–	(1)	–	–	–	–	–	–	–	–	–	–	–	–	–	–	–	–	–	–	–	–	–	–	–	–	–	–	(1)	–
24 Glasgow Rangers	–	–	–	–	–	–	–	–	–	–	–	–	–	–	–	–	(1)	–	–	–	–	–	–	–	–	–	–	–	(1)	–
25 Middlesbrough	–	(1)	–	–	–	–	–	–	–	–	–	–	–	–	–	–	–	–	–	–	–	–	–	–	–	–	–	–	(1)	–
26 Newcastle United	–	(1)	–	–	–	–	–	–	–	–	–	–	–	–	–	–	–	–	–	–	–	–	–	–	–	–	–	–	(1)	–
27 Southampton	–	(1)	–	–	–	–	–	–	–	–	–	–	–	–	–	–	–	–	–	–	–	–	–	–	–	–	–	–	(1)	–
28 Stuttgart	–	–	–	–	–	–	–	–	–	–	–	–	–	–	–	–	(1)	–	–	–	–	–	–	–	–	–	–	–	(1)	–

RAY BENNION

DEBUT (Full Appearance)

Saturday 27/08/1921
Football League Division 1
at Goodison Park

Everton 5 Manchester United 0

CLUB CAREER RECORD	Apps	Subs	Goals
Premiership	0		0
League Division 1	193		2
League Division 2	93		0
FA Cup	15		1
League Cup	0		0
European Cup / Champions League	0		0
European Cup-Winners' Cup	0		0
UEFA Cup / Inter-Cities' Fairs Cup	0		0
Other Matches	0		0
OVERALL TOTAL	**301**		**3**

Opponents	PREM A	S	G	FLD 1 A	S	G	FLD 2 A	S	G	FAC A	S	G	LC A	S	G	EC/CL A	S	G	ECWC A	S	G	UEFA A	S	G	OTHER A	S	G	TOTAL A	S	G
1 Leicester City	–	–	–	10	–	–	5	–	–	–	–	–	–	–	–	–	–	–	–	–	–	–	–	–	–	–	–	15	–	–
2 Blackburn Rovers	–	–	–	11	–	–	–	–	–	1	–	–	–	–	–	–	–	–	–	–	–	–	–	–	–	–	–	12	–	–
3 Derby County	–	–	–	8	–	–	4	–	–	–	–	–	–	–	–	–	–	–	–	–	–	–	–	–	–	–	–	12	–	–
4 Birmingham City	–	–	–	10	–	–	–	–	–	1	–	–	–	–	–	–	–	–	–	–	–	–	–	–	–	–	–	11	–	–
5 Bury	–	–	–	6	–	–	3	–	–	2	–	–	–	–	–	–	–	–	–	–	–	–	–	–	–	–	–	11	–	–
6 Arsenal	–	–	–	10	–	–	–	–	–	–	–	–	–	–	–	–	–	–	–	–	–	–	–	–	–	–	–	10	–	–
7 Bolton Wanderers	–	–	–	10	–	–	–	–	–	–	–	–	–	–	–	–	–	–	–	–	–	–	–	–	–	–	–	10	–	–
8 Huddersfield Town	–	–	–	9	–	–	–	–	–	1	–	–	–	–	–	–	–	–	–	–	–	–	–	–	–	–	–	10	–	–
9 Sheffield Wednesday	–	–	–	9	–	–	1	–	–	–	–	–	–	–	–	–	–	–	–	–	–	–	–	–	–	–	–	10	–	–
10 Aston Villa	–	–	–	9	–	–	–	–	–	–	–	–	–	–	–	–	–	–	–	–	–	–	–	–	–	–	–	9	–	–
11 Burnley	–	–	–	7	–	–	2	–	–	–	–	–	–	–	–	–	–	–	–	–	–	–	–	–	–	–	–	9	–	–
12 Leeds United	–	–	–	6	–	–	3	–	–	–	–	–	–	–	–	–	–	–	–	–	–	–	–	–	–	–	–	9	–	–
13 Sheffield United	–	–	–	9	–	–	–	–	–	–	–	–	–	–	–	–	–	–	–	–	–	–	–	–	–	–	–	9	–	–
14 Liverpool	–	–	–	8	–	–	–	–	–	–	–	–	–	–	–	–	–	–	–	–	–	–	–	–	–	–	–	8	–	–
15 Manchester City	–	–	–	8	–	–	–	–	–	–	–	–	–	–	–	–	–	–	–	–	–	–	–	–	–	–	–	8	–	–
16 Portsmouth	–	–	–	7	–	–	1	–	–	–	–	–	–	–	–	–	–	–	–	–	–	–	–	–	–	–	–	8	–	–
17 Sunderland	–	–	–	8	–	–	–	–	–	–	–	–	–	–	–	–	–	–	–	–	–	–	–	–	–	–	–	8	–	–
18 West Ham United	–	–	–	7	–	–	1	–	–	–	–	–	–	–	–	–	–	–	–	–	–	–	–	–	–	–	–	8	–	–
19 Everton	–	–	–	7	–	1	–	–	–	–	–	–	–	–	–	–	–	–	–	–	–	–	–	–	–	–	–	7	–	1
20 Newcastle United	–	–	–	7	–	–	–	–	–	–	–	–	–	–	–	–	–	–	–	–	–	–	–	–	–	–	–	7	–	–
21 Tottenham Hotspur	–	–	–	5	–	–	2	–	–	–	–	–	–	–	–	–	–	–	–	–	–	–	–	–	–	–	–	7	–	–
22 Blackpool	–	–	–	2	–	–	4	–	–	–	–	–	–	–	–	–	–	–	–	–	–	–	–	–	–	–	–	6	–	–
23 Stoke City	–	–	–	–	–	–	3	–	–	3	–	–	–	–	–	–	–	–	–	–	–	–	–	–	–	–	–	6	–	–
24 Middlesbrough	–	–	–	5	–	1	–	–	–	–	–	–	–	–	–	–	–	–	–	–	–	–	–	–	–	–	–	5	–	1
25 Barnsley	–	–	–	–	–	–	5	–	–	–	–	–	–	–	–	–	–	–	–	–	–	–	–	–	–	–	–	5	–	–
26 Bradford City	–	–	–	–	–	–	5	–	–	–	–	–	–	–	–	–	–	–	–	–	–	–	–	–	–	–	–	5	–	–
27 Cardiff City	–	–	–	5	–	–	–	–	–	–	–	–	–	–	–	–	–	–	–	–	–	–	–	–	–	–	–	5	–	–
28 Port Vale	–	–	–	–	–	–	5	–	–	–	–	–	–	–	–	–	–	–	–	–	–	–	–	–	–	–	–	5	–	–
29 Southampton	–	–	–	–	–	–	5	–	–	–	–	–	–	–	–	–	–	–	–	–	–	–	–	–	–	–	–	5	–	–
30 Bristol City	–	–	–	–	–	–	4	–	–	–	–	–	–	–	–	–	–	–	–	–	–	–	–	–	–	–	–	4	–	–
31 Grimsby Town	–	–	–	3	–	–	–	–	–	1	–	–	–	–	–	–	–	–	–	–	–	–	–	–	–	–	–	4	–	–
32 Hull City	–	–	–	–	–	–	4	–	–	–	–	–	–	–	–	–	–	–	–	–	–	–	–	–	–	–	–	4	–	–
33 Oldham Athletic	–	–	–	1	–	–	3	–	–	–	–	–	–	–	–	–	–	–	–	–	–	–	–	–	–	–	–	4	–	–
34 Stockport County	–	–	–	–	–	–	4	–	–	–	–	–	–	–	–	–	–	–	–	–	–	–	–	–	–	–	–	4	–	–
35 Reading	–	–	–	–	–	–	–	–	–	3	–	1	–	–	–	–	–	–	–	–	–	–	–	–	–	–	–	3	–	1
36 Chelsea	–	–	–	2	–	–	1	–	–	–	–	–	–	–	–	–	–	–	–	–	–	–	–	–	–	–	–	3	–	–
37 Fulham	–	–	–	–	–	–	3	–	–	–	–	–	–	–	–	–	–	–	–	–	–	–	–	–	–	–	–	3	–	–
38 Notts County	–	–	–	–	–	–	3	–	–	–	–	–	–	–	–	–	–	–	–	–	–	–	–	–	–	–	–	3	–	–
39 Plymouth Argyle	–	–	–	–	–	–	1	–	–	2	–	–	–	–	–	–	–	–	–	–	–	–	–	–	–	–	–	3	–	–
40 West Bromwich Albion	–	–	–	3	–	–	–	–	–	–	–	–	–	–	–	–	–	–	–	–	–	–	–	–	–	–	–	3	–	–
41 Wolverhampton W.	–	–	–	–	–	–	3	–	–	–	–	–	–	–	–	–	–	–	–	–	–	–	–	–	–	–	–	3	–	–
42 Bradford Park Avenue	–	–	–	–	–	–	2	–	–	–	–	–	–	–	–	–	–	–	–	–	–	–	–	–	–	–	–	2	–	–
43 Chesterfield	–	–	–	–	–	–	2	–	–	–	–	–	–	–	–	–	–	–	–	–	–	–	–	–	–	–	–	2	–	–
44 Coventry City	–	–	–	–	–	–	2	–	–	–	–	–	–	–	–	–	–	–	–	–	–	–	–	–	–	–	–	2	–	–
45 Leyton Orient	–	–	–	–	–	–	2	–	–	–	–	–	–	–	–	–	–	–	–	–	–	–	–	–	–	–	–	2	–	–
46 Nelson	–	–	–	–	–	–	2	–	–	–	–	–	–	–	–	–	–	–	–	–	–	–	–	–	–	–	–	2	–	–
47 Nottingham Forest	–	–	–	–	–	–	2	–	–	–	–	–	–	–	–	–	–	–	–	–	–	–	–	–	–	–	–	2	–	–
48 Preston North End	–	–	–	1	–	–	1	–	–	–	–	–	–	–	–	–	–	–	–	–	–	–	–	–	–	–	–	2	–	–
49 South Shields	–	–	–	–	–	–	2	–	–	–	–	–	–	–	–	–	–	–	–	–	–	–	–	–	–	–	–	2	–	–
50 Brentford	–	–	–	–	–	–	–	–	–	1	–	–	–	–	–	–	–	–	–	–	–	–	–	–	–	–	–	1	–	–
51 Charlton Athletic	–	–	–	–	–	–	1	–	–	–	–	–	–	–	–	–	–	–	–	–	–	–	–	–	–	–	–	1	–	–
52 Crystal Palace	–	–	–	–	–	–	1	–	–	–	–	–	–	–	–	–	–	–	–	–	–	–	–	–	–	–	–	1	–	–
53 Swansea City	–	–	–	–	–	–	1	–	–	–	–	–	–	–	–	–	–	–	–	–	–	–	–	–	–	–	–	1	–	–

GEOFF BENT

DEBUT (Full Appearance)

Saturday 11/12/1954
Football League Division 1
at Turf Moor

Burnley 2 Manchester United 4

CLUB CAREER RECORD	Apps	Subs	Goals
Premiership	0		0
League Division 1	12		0
League Division 2	0		0
FA Cup	0		0
League Cup	0		0
European Cup / Champions League	0		0
European Cup–Winners' Cup	0		0
UEFA Cup / Inter–Cities' Fairs Cup	0		0
Other Matches	0		0
OVERALL TOTAL	**12**		**0**

Opponents	PREM A S G	FLD 1 A S G	FLD 2 A S G	FAC A S G	LC A S G	EC/CL A S G	ECWC A S G	UEFA A S G	OTHER A S G	TOTAL A S G
1 Charlton Athletic	– –	2	–	–	–	–	–	–	–	2 –
2 Aston Villa	– –	1	–	–	–	–	–	–	–	1 –
3 Birmingham City	– –	1	–	–	–	–	–	–	–	1
4 Burnley	– –	1	–	–	–	–	–	–	–	1
5 Everton	– –	1	–	–	–	–	–	–	–	1
6 Huddersfield Town	– –	1	–	–	–	–	–	–	–	1
7 Luton Town	– –	1	–	–	–	–	–	–	–	1
8 Sheffield United	– –	1	–	–	–	–	–	–	–	1
9 Sunderland	– –	1	–	–	–	–	–	–	–	1
10 Tottenham Hotspur	– –	1	–	–	–	–	–	–	–	1
11 Wolverhampton W.	– –	1	–	–	–	–	–	–	–	1

HENNING BERG

DEBUT (Substitute Appearance)

Wednesday 13/08/1997
FA Premiership
at Old Trafford

Manchester United 1 Southampton 0

CLUB CAREER RECORD	Apps	Subs	Goals
Premiership	49	(17)	2
League Division 1	0		0
League Division 2	0		0
FA Cup	7		0
League Cup	3		0
European Cup / Champions League	19	(4)	1
European Cup–Winners' Cup	0		0
UEFA Cup / Inter–Cities' Fairs Cup	0		0
Other Matches	3	(1)	0
OVERALL TOTAL	**81**	**(22)**	**3**

Opponents	PREM A S G	FLD 1 A S G	FLD 2 A S G	FAC A S G	LC A S G	EC/CL A S G	ECWC A S G	UEFA A S G	OTHER A S G	TOTAL A S G
1 Arsenal	4 –	–	–	–	–	–	–	–	1 (1) –	5 (1) –
2 Chelsea	2 (2) –	–	–	2	–	–	–	–	–	4 (2) –
3 Leicester City	3 (3) –	–	–	–	–	–	–	–	–	3 (3) –
4 West Ham United	4 (1) –	–	–	–	–	–	–	–	–	4 (1) –
5 Wimbledon	4 (1) –	–	–	–	–	–	–	–	–	4 (1) –
6 Coventry City	3 (2) –	–	–	–	–	–	–	–	–	3 (2) –
7 Everton	4 1	–	–	–	–	–	–	–	–	4 1
8 Derby County	3 (1) –	–	–	–	–	–	–	–	–	3 (1) –
9 Juventus	–	–	–	–	–	3	–	–	–	3
10 Liverpool	2	–	–	1	–	–	–	–	–	3
11 Sheffield Wednesday	3	–	–	–	–	–	–	–	–	3
12 Leeds United	2 (1) –	–	–	–	–	–	–	–	–	2 (1) –
13 Southampton	2 (1) –	–	–	–	–	–	–	–	–	2 (1) –
14 Tottenham Hotspur	– (2) –	–	–	–	1	–	–	–	–	1 (2) –
15 Aston Villa	2	–	–	–	–	–	–	–	–	2
16 Barnsley	1	–	–	1	–	–	–	–	–	2
17 Croatia Zagreb	–	–	–	–	–	2	–	–	–	2
18 Fiorentina	–	–	–	–	–	2	–	–	–	2
19 Middlesbrough	1	–	–	1	–	–	–	–	–	2
20 Newcastle United	2	–	–	–	–	–	–	–	–	2
21 Nottingham Forest	1	–	–	–	1	–	–	–	–	2
22 Olympique Marseille	–	–	–	–	–	2	–	–	–	2
23 Real Madrid	–	–	–	–	–	2	–	–	–	2
24 Sturm Graz	–	–	–	–	–	2	–	–	–	2
25 Kosice	–	–	–	–	–	1 (1) 1	–	–	–	1 (1) 1
26 Bolton Wanderers	1 (1) –	–	–	–	–	–	–	–	–	1 (1) –
27 Charlton Athletic	1 (1) –	–	–	–	–	–	–	–	–	1 (1) –
28 Internazionale	–	–	–	–	–	1 (1) –	–	–	–	1 (1) –
29 Monaco	–	–	–	–	–	1 (1) –	–	–	–	1 (1) –
30 Barcelona	–	–	–	–	–	1	–	–	–	1
31 Blackburn Rovers	1	–	–	–	–	–	–	–	–	1
32 Bradford City	1	–	–	–	–	–	–	–	–	1
33 Bury	–	–	–	–	1	–	–	–	–	1
34 Crystal Palace	1	–	–	–	–	–	–	–	–	1
35 Feyenoord	–	–	–	–	–	1	–	–	–	1
36 Fulham	–	–	–	1	–	–	–	–	–	1
37 Lazio	–	–	–	–	–	–	–	–	1	1
38 South Melbourne	–	–	–	–	–	–	–	–	1	1
39 Valencia	–	–	–	–	–	1	–	–	–	1
40 Walsall	–	–	–	1	–	–	–	–	–	1
41 Watford	1	–	–	–	–	–	–	–	–	1
42 Sunderland	– (1) 1	–	–	–	–	–	–	–	–	– (1) 1
43 Girondins Bordeaux	–	–	–	–	–	– (1) –	–	–	–	– (1) –

JOHNNY BERRY

DEBUT (Full Appearance)

Saturday 01/09/1951
Football League Division 1
at Burnden Park

Bolton Wanderers 1 Manchester United 0

CLUB CAREER RECORD	Apps	Subs	Goals
Premiership	0		0
League Division 1	247		37
League Division 2	0		0
FA Cup	15		4
League Cup	0		0
European Cup / Champions League	11		3
European Cup-Winners' Cup	0		0
UEFA Cup / Inter-Cities' Fairs Cup	0		0
Other Matches	3		1
OVERALL TOTAL	**276**		**45**

Opponents	PREM A	S	G	FLD 1 A	S	G	FLD 2 A	S	G	FAC A	S	G	LC A	S	G	EC/CL A	S	G	ECWC A	S	G	UEFA A	S	G	OTHER A	S	G	TOTAL A	S	G
1 Aston Villa	–	–	–	13	–	2	–	–	–	1	–	–	–	–	–	–	–	–	–	–	–	–	–	–	1	–	1	15	–	3
2 Manchester City	–	–	–	12	–	3	–	–	–	1	–	–	–	–	–	–	–	–	–	–	–	–	–	–	–	1	–	14	–	3
3 Blackpool	–	–	–	14	–	1	–	–	–	–	–	–	–	–	–	–	–	–	–	–	–	–	–	–	–	–	–	14	–	1
4 Arsenal	–	–	–	13	–	3	–	–	–	–	–	–	–	–	–	–	–	–	–	–	–	–	–	–	–	–	–	13	–	3
5 Chelsea	–	–	–	13	–	2	–	–	–	–	–	–	–	–	–	–	–	–	–	–	–	–	–	–	–	–	–	13	–	2
6 Bolton Wanderers	–	–	–	13	–	1	–	–	–	–	–	–	–	–	–	–	–	–	–	–	–	–	–	–	–	–	–	13	–	1
7 Burnley	–	–	–	11	–	–	–	–	–	1	–	–	–	–	–	–	–	–	–	–	–	–	–	–	–	–	–	12	–	–
8 Sunderland	–	–	–	12	–	–	–	–	–	–	–	–	–	–	–	–	–	–	–	–	–	–	–	–	–	–	–	12	–	–
9 Portsmouth	–	–	–	11	–	1	–	–	–	–	–	–	–	–	–	–	–	–	–	–	–	–	–	–	–	–	–	11	–	1
10 Preston North End	–	–	–	11	–	1	–	–	–	–	–	–	–	–	–	–	–	–	–	–	–	–	–	–	–	–	–	11	–	1
11 Wolverhampton W.	–	–	–	11	–	1	–	–	–	–	–	–	–	–	–	–	–	–	–	–	–	–	–	–	–	–	–	11	–	1
12 Newcastle United	–	–	–	10	–	–	–	–	–	–	–	–	–	–	–	–	–	–	–	–	–	–	1	–	–	–	–	11	–	–
13 Tottenham Hotspur	–	–	–	10	–	5	–	–	–	–	–	–	–	–	–	–	–	–	–	–	–	–	–	–	–	–	–	10	–	5
14 Charlton Athletic	–	–	–	10	–	2	–	–	–	–	–	–	–	–	–	–	–	–	–	–	–	–	–	–	–	–	–	10	–	2
15 West Bromwich Albion	–	–	–	10	–	1	–	–	–	–	–	–	–	–	–	–	–	–	–	–	–	–	–	–	–	–	–	10	–	1
16 Sheffield Wednesday	–	–	–	9	–	1	–	–	–	–	–	–	–	–	–	–	–	–	–	–	–	–	–	–	–	–	–	9	–	1
17 Cardiff City	–	–	–	8	–	1	–	–	–	–	–	–	–	–	–	–	–	–	–	–	–	–	–	–	–	–	–	8	–	1
18 Everton	–	–	–	7	–	1	–	–	–	1	–	–	–	–	–	–	–	–	–	–	–	–	–	–	–	–	–	8	–	1
19 Huddersfield Town	–	–	–	7	–	2	–	–	–	–	–	–	–	–	–	–	–	–	–	–	–	–	–	–	–	–	–	7	–	2
20 Sheffield United	–	–	–	6	–	2	–	–	–	–	–	–	–	–	–	–	–	–	–	–	–	–	–	–	–	–	–	6	–	2
21 Liverpool	–	–	–	6	–	1	–	–	–	–	–	–	–	–	–	–	–	–	–	–	–	–	–	–	–	–	–	6	–	1
22 Birmingham City	–	–	–	4	–	–	–	–	–	1	–	1	–	–	–	–	–	–	–	–	–	–	–	–	–	–	–	5	–	1
23 Luton Town	–	–	–	5	–	–	–	–	–	–	–	–	–	–	–	–	–	–	–	–	–	–	–	–	–	–	–	5	–	–
24 Derby County	–	–	–	4	–	1	–	–	–	–	–	–	–	–	–	–	–	–	–	–	–	–	–	–	–	–	–	4	–	1
25 Stoke City	–	–	–	4	–	1	–	–	–	–	–	–	–	–	–	–	–	–	–	–	–	–	–	–	–	–	–	4	–	1
26 Middlesbrough	–	–	–	4	–	–	–	–	–	–	–	–	–	–	–	–	–	–	–	–	–	–	–	–	–	–	–	4	–	–
27 Leeds United	–	–	–	3	–	3	–	–	–	–	–	–	–	–	–	–	–	–	–	–	–	–	–	–	–	–	–	3	–	3
28 Leicester City	–	–	–	3	–	–	–	–	–	–	–	–	–	–	–	–	–	–	–	–	–	–	–	–	–	–	–	3	–	–
29 Anderlecht	–	–	–	–	–	–	–	–	–	–	–	–	–	–	–	2	–	1	–	–	–	–	–	–	–	–	–	2	–	1
30 Athletic Bilbao	–	–	–	–	–	–	–	–	–	–	–	–	–	–	–	2	–	1	–	–	–	–	–	–	–	–	–	2	–	1
31 Fulham	–	–	–	2	–	1	–	–	–	–	–	–	–	–	–	–	–	–	–	–	–	–	–	–	–	–	–	2	–	1
32 Shamrock Rovers	–	–	–	–	–	–	–	–	–	–	–	–	–	–	–	2	–	1	–	–	–	–	–	–	–	–	–	2	–	1
33 Borussia Dortmund	–	–	–	–	–	–	–	–	–	–	–	–	–	–	–	2	–	–	–	–	–	–	–	–	–	–	–	2	–	–
34 Reading	–	–	–	–	–	–	–	–	–	2	–	–	–	–	–	–	–	–	–	–	–	–	–	–	–	–	–	2	–	–
35 Real Madrid	–	–	–	–	–	–	–	–	–	–	–	–	–	–	–	2	–	–	–	–	–	–	–	–	–	–	–	2	–	–
36 Walthamstow Avenue	–	–	–	–	–	–	–	–	–	2	–	–	–	–	–	–	–	–	–	–	–	–	–	–	–	–	–	2	–	–
37 Bournemouth	–	–	–	–	–	–	–	–	–	1	–	2	–	–	–	–	–	–	–	–	–	–	–	–	–	–	–	1	–	2
38 Hartlepool United	–	–	–	–	–	–	–	–	–	1	–	1	–	–	–	–	–	–	–	–	–	–	–	–	–	–	–	1	–	1
39 Bristol Rovers	–	–	–	–	–	–	–	–	–	1	–	–	–	–	–	–	–	–	–	–	–	–	–	–	–	–	–	1	–	–
40 Dukla Prague	–	–	–	–	–	–	–	–	–	–	–	–	–	–	–	1	–	–	–	–	–	–	–	–	–	–	–	1	–	–
41 Hull City	–	–	–	–	–	–	–	–	–	1	–	–	–	–	–	–	–	–	–	–	–	–	–	–	–	–	–	1	–	–
42 Millwall	–	–	–	–	–	–	–	–	–	1	–	–	–	–	–	–	–	–	–	–	–	–	–	–	–	–	–	1	–	–
43 Nottingham Forest	–	–	–	1	–	–	–	–	–	–	–	–	–	–	–	–	–	–	–	–	–	–	–	–	–	–	–	1	–	–
44 Wrexham	–	–	–	–	–	–	–	–	–	1	–	–	–	–	–	–	–	–	–	–	–	–	–	–	–	–	–	1	–	–

WILLIAM BERRY

DEBUT (Full Appearance)

Saturday 17/11/1906
Football League Division 1
at Hillsborough

Sheffield Wednesday 5 Manchester United 2

CLUB CAREER RECORD	Apps	Subs	Goals
Premiership	0		0
League Division 1	13		1
League Division 2	0		0
FA Cup	1		0
League Cup	0		0
European Cup / Champions League	0		0
European Cup-Winners' Cup	0		0
UEFA Cup / Inter-Cities' Fairs Cup	0		0
Other Matches	0		0
OVERALL TOTAL	**14**		**1**

Opponents	PREM A	S	G	FLD 1 A	S	G	FLD 2 A	S	G	FAC A	S	G	LC A	S	G	EC/CL A	S	G	ECWC A	S	G	UEFA A	S	G	OTHER A	S	G	TOTAL A	S	G
1 Aston Villa	–	–	–	1	–	–	–	–	–	1	–	–	–	–	–	–	–	–	–	–	–	–	–	–	–	–	–	2	–	–
2 Sunderland	–	–	–	1	–	1	–	–	–	–	–	–	–	–	–	–	–	–	–	–	–	–	–	–	–	–	–	1	–	1
3 Arsenal	–	–	–	1	–	–	–	–	–	–	–	–	–	–	–	–	–	–	–	–	–	–	–	–	–	–	–	1	–	–
4 Bolton Wanderers	–	–	–	1	–	–	–	–	–	–	–	–	–	–	–	–	–	–	–	–	–	–	–	–	–	–	–	1	–	–
5 Bristol City	–	–	–	1	–	–	–	–	–	–	–	–	–	–	–	–	–	–	–	–	–	–	–	–	–	–	–	1	–	–
6 Bury	–	–	–	1	–	–	–	–	–	–	–	–	–	–	–	–	–	–	–	–	–	–	–	–	–	–	–	1	–	–
7 Liverpool	–	–	–	1	–	–	–	–	–	–	–	–	–	–	–	–	–	–	–	–	–	–	–	–	–	–	–	1	–	–

continued../

WILLIAM BERRY (continued)

Opponents	PREM			FLD 1			FLD 2			FAC			LC			EC/CL			ECWC			UEFA			OTHER			TOTAL		
	A	S	G	A	S	G	A	S	G	A	S	G	A	S	G	A	S	G	A	S	G	A	S	G	A	S	G	A	S	G
8 Middlesbrough	–	–		1			–			–			–			–			–			–			–			1		–
9 Newcastle United	–	–		1			–			–			–			–			–			–			–			1		–
10 Notts County	–	–		1			–			–			–			–			–			–			–			1		–
11 Preston North End	–	–		1			–			–			–			–			–			–			–			1		–
12 Sheffield Wednesday	–	–		1			–			–			–			–			–			–			–			1		–
13 Stoke City	–	–		1			–			–			–			–			–			–			–			1		–

GEORGE BEST

DEBUT (Full Appearance)

Saturday 14/09/1963
Football League Division 1
at Old Trafford

Manchester United 1 West Bromwich Albion 0

CLUB CAREER RECORD	Apps	Subs	Goals
Premiership	0		0
League Division 1	361		137
League Division 2	0		0
FA Cup	46		21
League Cup	25		9
European Cup / Champions League	21		9
European Cup-Winners' Cup	2		0
UEFA Cup / Inter-Cities' Fairs Cup	11		2
Other Matches	4		1
OVERALL TOTAL	**470**		**179**

Opponents	PREM			FLD 1			FLD 2			FAC			LC			EC/CL			ECWC			UEFA			OTHER			TOTAL		
	A	S	G	A	S	G	A	S	G	A	S	G	A	S	G	A	S	G	A	S	G	A	S	G	A	S	G	A	S	G
1 Stoke City	–		–	17		4	–		–	5		2	3		1	–		–	–		–	–		–	–		–	25		7
2 Tottenham Hotspur	–		–	19		6	–		–	2		1	–		–	–		–	–		–	–		–	1		–	22		7
3 Burnley	–		–	15		6	–		–	1		–	4		1	–		–	–		–	–		–	–		–	20		7
4 Liverpool	–		–	19		6	–		–	–		–	–		–	–		–	–		–	1		1	–		–	20		7
5 Everton	–		–	16		4	–		–	1		–	–		–	–		–	–		–	2		–	–		–	19		4
6 West Bromwich Albion	–		–	18		11	–		–	–		–	–		–	–		–	–		–	–		–	–		–	18		11
7 Chelsea	–		–	17		3	–		–	–		–	1		1	–		–	–		–	–		–	–		–	18		4
8 Leeds United	–		–	13		3	–		–	5		–	–		–	–		–	–		–	–		–	–		–	18		3
9 Southampton	–		–	14		7	–		–	3		2	–		–	–		–	–		–	–		–	–		–	17		9
10 West Ham United	–		–	15		11	–		–	1		–	–		–	–		–	–		–	–		–	–		–	16		11
11 Nottingham Forest	–		–	16		6	–		–	–		–	–		–	–		–	–		–	–		–	–		–	16		6
12 Arsenal	–		–	16		3	–		–	–		–	–		–	–		–	–		–	–		–	–		–	16		3
13 Sunderland	–		–	12		6	–		–	3		1	–		–	–		–	–		–	–		–	–		–	15		7
14 Wolverhampton W.	–		–	13		5	–		–	2		2	–		–	–		–	–		–	–		–	–		–	15		7
15 Newcastle United	–		–	15		6	–		–	–		–	–		–	–		–	–		–	–		–	–		–	15		6
16 Leicester City	–		–	15		5	–		–	–		–	–		–	–		–	–		–	–		–	–		–	15		5
17 Manchester City	–		–	13		3	–		–	–		–	2		–	–		–	–		–	–		–	–		–	15		3
18 Sheffield Wednesday	–		–	12		8	–		–	–		–	–		–	–		–	–		–	–		–	–		–	12		8
19 Coventry City	–		–	12		5	–		–	–		–	–		–	–		–	–		–	–		–	–		–	12		5
20 Ipswich Town	–		–	10		3	–		–	1		–	1		2	–		–	–		–	–		–	–		–	12		5
21 Sheffield United	–		–	12		4	–		–	–		–	–		–	–		–	–		–	–		–	–		–	12		4
22 Derby County	–		–	6		2	–		–	1		2	2		–	–		–	–		–	–		–	–		–	9		4
23 Fulham	–		–	9		4	–		–	–		–	–		–	–		–	–		–	–		–	–		–	9		4
24 Birmingham City	–		–	5		2	–		–	2		1	–		–	–		–	–		–	–		–	–		–	7		3
25 Crystal Palace	–		–	6		2	–		–	–		–	1		–	–		–	–		–	–		–	–		–	7		2
26 Middlesbrough	–		–	–		–	–		–	6		2	1		–	–		–	–		–	–		–	–		–	7		2
27 Aston Villa	–		–	5		1	–		–	–		–	2		–	–		–	–		–	–		–	–		–	7		1
28 Blackpool	–		–	6		1	–		–	–		–	1		–	–		–	–		–	–		–	–		–	7		1
29 Huddersfield Town	–		–	4		3	–		–	–		–	–		–	–		–	–		–	–		–	–		–	4		3
30 Blackburn Rovers	–		–	4		1	–		–	–		–	–		–	–		–	–		–	–		–	–		–	4		1
31 Northampton Town	–		–	2		–	–		–	1		6	–		–	–		–	–		–	–		–	–		–	3		6
32 Queens Park Rangers	–		–	3		4	–		–	–		–	–		–	–		–	–		–	–		–	–		–	3		4
33 Benfica	–		–	–		–	–		–	–		–	–		–	3		3	–		–	–		–	–		–	3		3
34 Bristol Rovers	–		–	–		–	–		–	1		–	2		–	–		–	–		–	–		–	–		–	3		–
35 Ferencvaros	–		–	–		–	–		–	–		–	–		–	–		–	–		–	3		–	–		–	3		–
36 Watford	–		–	–		–	–		–	3		–	–		–	–		–	–		–	–		–	–		–	3		–
37 Oxford United	–		–	–		–	–		–	–		–	2		2	–		–	–		–	–		–	–		–	2		2
38 Rapid Vienna	–		–	–		–	–		–	–		–	–		–	2		2	–		–	–		–	–		–	2		2
39 Borussia Dortmund	–		–	–		–	–		–	–		–	–		–	–		–	–		–	2		1	–		–	2		1
40 Djurgardens	–		–	–		–	–		–	–		–	–		–	–		–	–		–	2		1	–		–	2		1
41 Real Madrid	–		–	–		–	–		–	–		–	–		–	2		1	–		–	–		–	–		–	2		1
42 Sarajevo	–		–	–		–	–		–	–		–	–		–	2		1	–		–	–		–	–		–	2		1
43 AC Milan	–		–	–		–	–		–	–		–	–		–	2		–	–		–	–		–	–		–	2		–
44 ASK Vorwaerts	–		–	–		–	–		–	–		–	–		–	2		–	–		–	–		–	–		–	2		–
45 Estudiantes de la Plata	–		–	–		–	–		–	–		–	–		–	–		–	–		–	–		–	2		–	2		–
46 Gornik Zabrze	–		–	–		–	–		–	–		–	–		–	2		–	–		–	–		–	–		–	2		–
47 Hibernians Malta	–		–	–		–	–		–	–		–	–		–	2		–	–		–	–		–	–		–	2		–
48 Norwich City	–		–	1		–	–		–	1		–	–		–	–		–	–		–	–		–	–		–	2		–
49 Preston North End	–		–	–		–	–		–	2		–	–		–	–		–	–		–	–		–	–		–	2		–
50 Rotherham United	–		–	–		–	–		–	2		–	–		–	–		–	–		–	–		–	–		–	2		–
51 Sporting Lisbon	–		–	–		–	–		–	–		–	–		–	–		–	2		–	–		–	–		–	2		–
52 Strasbourg	–		–	–		–	–		–	–		–	–		–	–		–	–		–	2		–	–		–	2		–
53 Waterford	–		–	–		–	–		–	–		–	–		–	2		–	–		–	–		–	–		–	2		–
54 Bolton Wanderers	–		–	1		2	–		–	–		–	–		–	–		–	–		–	–		–	–		–	1		2
55 HJK Helsinki	–		–	–		–	–		–	–		–	–		–	1		2	–		–	–		–	–		–	1		2

continued../

GEORGE BEST (continued)

Opponents	PREM			FLD 1			FLD 2			FAC			LC			EC/CL			ECWC			UEFA			OTHER			TOTAL		
	A	S	G	A	S	G	A	S	G	A	S	G	A	S	G	A	S	G	A	S	G	A	S	G	A	S	G	A	S	G
56 Aldershot	–	–	–	–	–	–	–	–	–	1	–	1	–	–	–	–	–	–	–	–	–	–	–	–	–	–	–	1	–	1
57 Barnsley	–	–	–	1	–	1	–	–	–	–	–	–	–	–	–	–	–	–	–	–	–	–	–	–	–	–	–	1	–	1
58 Chester City	–	–	–	–	–	–	–	–	–	1	–	1	–	–	–	–	–	–	–	–	–	–	–	–	–	–	–	1	–	1
59 Wrexham	–	–	–	–	–	–	–	–	–	–	–	–	1	–	1	–	–	–	–	–	–	–	–	–	–	–	–	1	–	1
60 Exeter City	–	–	–	–	–	–	–	–	–	1	–	–	–	–	–	–	–	–	–	–	–	–	–	–	–	–	–	1	–	–
61 Partizan Belgrade	–	–	–	–	–	–	–	–	–	–	–	–	–	–	–	1	–	–	–	–	–	–	–	–	–	–	–	1	–	–
62 Portsmouth	–	–	–	–	–	–	–	–	–	1	–	–	–	–	–	–	–	–	–	–	–	–	–	–	–	–	–	1	–	–

PAUL BIELBY

DEBUT (Full Appearance)

Wednesday 13/03/1974
Football League Division 1
at Maine Road

Manchester City 0 Manchester United 0

CLUB CAREER RECORD	Apps	Subs	Goals
Premiership	0		0
League Division 1	2	(2)	0
League Division 2	0		0
FA Cup	0		0
League Cup	0		0
European Cup / Champions League	0		0
European Cup-Winners' Cup	0		0
UEFA Cup / Inter-Cities' Fairs Cup	0		0
Other Matches	0		0
OVERALL TOTAL	2	(2)	0

Opponents	PREM			FLD 1			FLD 2			FAC			LC			EC/CL			ECWC			UEFA			OTHER			TOTAL		
	A	S	G	A	S	G	A	S	G	A	S	G	A	S	G	A	S	G	A	S	G	A	S	G	A	S	G	A	S	G
1 Birmingham City	–	–	1	–	–	–	–	–	–	–	–	–	–	–	–	–	–	–	–	–	–	–	–	–	–	–	–	1	–	–
2 Manchester City	–	–	1	–	–	–	–	–	–	–	–	–	–	–	–	–	–	–	–	–	–	–	–	–	–	–	–	1	–	–
3 Chelsea	–	–	–	(1)	–	–	–	–	–	–	–	–	–	–	–	–	–	–	–	–	–	–	–	–	–	–	–	(1)	–	–
4 Tottenham Hotspur	–	–	–	(1)	–	–	–	–	–	–	–	–	–	–	–	–	–	–	–	–	–	–	–	–	–	–	–	(1)	–	–

BRIAN BIRCH

DEBUT (Full Appearance)

Saturday 27/08/1949
Football League Division 1
at Old Trafford

Manchester United 1 West Bromwich Albion 1

CLUB CAREER RECORD	Apps	Subs	Goals
Premiership	0		0
League Division 1	11		4
League Division 2	0		0
FA Cup	4		1
League Cup	0		0
European Cup / Champions League	0		0
European Cup-Winners' Cup	0		0
UEFA Cup / Inter-Cities' Fairs Cup	0		0
Other Matches	0		0
OVERALL TOTAL	15		5

Opponents	PREM			FLD 1			FLD 2			FAC			LC			EC/CL			ECWC			UEFA			OTHER			TOTAL		
	A	S	G	A	S	G	A	S	G	A	S	G	A	S	G	A	S	G	A	S	G	A	S	G	A	S	G	A	S	G
1 West Bromwich Albion	–	–	–	2	–	1	–	–	–	–	–	–	–	–	–	–	–	–	–	–	–	–	–	–	–	–	–	2	–	1
2 Wolverhampton W.	–	–	–	2	–	1	–	–	–	–	–	–	–	–	–	–	–	–	–	–	–	–	–	–	–	–	–	2	–	1
3 Huddersfield Town	–	–	–	2	–	–	–	–	–	–	–	–	–	–	–	–	–	–	–	–	–	–	–	–	–	–	–	2	–	–
4 Newcastle United	–	–	–	1	–	1	–	–	–	–	–	–	–	–	–	–	–	–	–	–	–	–	–	–	–	–	–	1	–	1
5 Oldham Athletic	–	–	–	–	–	–	–	–	–	1	–	1	–	–	–	–	–	–	–	–	–	–	–	–	–	–	–	1	–	1
6 Tottenham Hotspur	–	–	–	1	–	1	–	–	–	–	–	–	–	–	–	–	–	–	–	–	–	–	–	–	–	–	–	1	–	1
7 Arsenal	–	–	–	–	–	–	–	–	–	1	–	–	–	–	–	–	–	–	–	–	–	–	–	–	–	–	–	1	–	–
8 Birmingham City	–	–	–	–	–	–	–	–	–	1	–	–	–	–	–	–	–	–	–	–	–	–	–	–	–	–	–	1	–	–
9 Charlton Athletic	–	–	–	1	–	–	–	–	–	–	–	–	–	–	–	–	–	–	–	–	–	–	–	–	–	–	–	1	–	–
10 Leeds United	–	–	–	–	–	–	–	–	–	1	–	–	–	–	–	–	–	–	–	–	–	–	–	–	–	–	–	1	–	–
11 Stoke City	–	–	–	1	–	–	–	–	–	–	–	–	–	–	–	–	–	–	–	–	–	–	–	–	–	–	–	1	–	–
12 Sunderland	–	–	–	1	–	–	–	–	–	–	–	–	–	–	–	–	–	–	–	–	–	–	–	–	–	–	–	1	–	–

HERBERT BIRCHENOUGH

DEBUT (Full Appearance)

Saturday 25/10/1902
Football League Division 2
at Manor Field

Arsenal 0 Manchester United 1

CLUB CAREER RECORD	Apps	Subs	Goals
Premiership	0		0
League Division 1	0		0
League Division 2	25		0
FA Cup	5		0
League Cup	0		0
European Cup / Champions League	0		0
European Cup-Winners' Cup	0		0
UEFA Cup / Inter-Cities' Fairs Cup	0		0
Other Matches	0		0
OVERALL TOTAL	30		0

Opponents	PREM			FLD 1			FLD 2			FAC			LC			EC/CL			ECWC			UEFA			OTHER			TOTAL		
	A	S	G	A	S	G	A	S	G	A	S	G	A	S	G	A	S	G	A	S	G	A	S	G	A	S	G	A	S	G
1 Burton United	–	–	–	–	–	–	1	–	–	2	–	–	–	–	–	–	–	–	–	–	–	–	–	–	–	–	–	3	–	–
2 Arsenal	–	–	–	–	–	–	2	–	–	–	–	–	–	–	–	–	–	–	–	–	–	–	–	–	–	–	–	2	–	–

continued../

HERBERT BIRCHENOUGH (continued)

Opponents	PREM A S G	FLD 1 A S G	FLD 2 A S G	FAC A S G	LC A S G	EC/CL A S G	ECWC A S G	UEFA A S G	OTHER A S G	TOTAL A S G
3 Birmingham City	– –	– –	2 –	– –	– –	– –	– –	– –	– –	2 –
4 Burnley	– –	– –	2 –	– –	– –	– –	– –	– –	– –	2 –
5 Leicester City	– –	– –	2 –	– –	– –	– –	– –	– –	– –	2 –
6 Lincoln City	– –	– –	2 –	– –	– –	– –	– –	– –	– –	2 –
7 Manchester City	– –	– –	2 –	– –	– –	– –	– –	– –	– –	2 –
8 Port Vale	– –	– –	2 –	– –	– –	– –	– –	– –	– –	2 –
9 Preston North End	– –	– –	2 –	– –	– –	– –	– –	– –	– –	2 –
10 Barnsley	– –	– –	1 –	– –	– –	– –	– –	– –	– –	1 –
11 Blackpool	– –	– –	1 –	– –	– –	– –	– –	– –	– –	1 –
12 Bristol City	– –	– –	1 –	– –	– –	– –	– –	– –	– –	1 –
13 Chesterfield	– –	– –	1 –	– –	– –	– –	– –	– –	– –	1 –
14 Doncaster Rovers	– –	– –	1 –	– –	– –	– –	– –	– –	– –	1 –
15 Everton	– –	– –	– –	1 –	– –	– –	– –	– –	– –	1 –
16 Gainsborough Trinity	– –	– –	1 –	– –	– –	– –	– –	– –	– –	1 –
17 Glossop	– –	– –	1 –	– –	– –	– –	– –	– –	– –	1 –
18 Liverpool	– –	– –	– –	1 –	– –	– –	– –	– –	– –	1 –
19 Southport Central	– –	– –	– –	1 –	– –	– –	– –	– –	– –	1 –
20 Stockport County	– –	– –	1 –	– –	– –	– –	– –	– –	– –	1 –

CLIFF BIRKETT

DEBUT (Full Appearance)

Saturday 02/12/1950
Football League Division 1
at Old Trafford

Manchester United 1 Newcastle United 2

CLUB CAREER RECORD	Apps	Subs	Goals
Premiership	0		0
League Division 1	9		2
League Division 2	0		0
FA Cup	4		0
League Cup	0		0
European Cup / Champions League	0		0
European Cup-Winners' Cup	0		0
UEFA Cup / Inter-Cities' Fairs Cup	0		0
Other Matches	0		0
OVERALL TOTAL	**13**		**2**

Opponents	PREM A S G	FLD 1 A S G	FLD 2 A S G	FAC A S G	LC A S G	EC/CL A S G	ECWC A S G	UEFA A S G	OTHER A S G	TOTAL A S G
1 Charlton Athletic	– –	1 1	– –	– –	– –	– –	– –	– –	– –	1 1
2 Huddersfield Town	– –	1 1	– –	– –	– –	– –	– –	– –	– –	1 1
3 Arsenal	– –	– –	– –	1 –	– –	– –	– –	– –	– –	1 –
4 Birmingham City	– –	– –	– –	1 –	– –	– –	– –	– –	– –	1 –
5 Bolton Wanderers	– –	1 –	– –	– –	– –	– –	– –	– –	– –	1 –
6 Fulham	– –	1 –	– –	– –	– –	– –	– –	– –	– –	1 –
7 Leeds United	– –	– –	– –	1 –	– –	– –	– –	– –	– –	1 –
8 Middlesbrough	– –	1 –	– –	– –	– –	– –	– –	– –	– –	1 –
9 Newcastle United	– –	1 –	– –	– –	– –	– –	– –	– –	– –	1 –
10 Oldham Athletic	– –	– –	– –	1 –	– –	– –	– –	– –	– –	1 –
11 Sunderland	– –	1 –	– –	– –	– –	– –	– –	– –	– –	1 –
12 Tottenham Hotspur	– –	1 –	– –	– –	– –	– –	– –	– –	– –	1 –
13 Wolverhampton W.	– –	1 –	– –	– –	– –	– –	– –	– –	– –	1 –

GARY BIRTLES

DEBUT (Full Appearance)

Wednesday 22/10/1980
Football League Division 1
at Victoria Ground

Stoke City 1 Manchester United 2

CLUB CAREER RECORD	Apps	Subs	Goals
Premiership	0		0
League Division 1	57	(1)	11
League Division 2	0		0
FA Cup	4		1
League Cup	2		0
European Cup / Champions League	0		0
European Cup-Winners' Cup	0		0
UEFA Cup / Inter-Cities' Fairs Cup	0		0
Other Matches	0		0
OVERALL TOTAL	**63**	**(1)**	**12**

Opponents	PREM A S G	FLD 1 A S G	FLD 2 A S G	FAC A S G	LC A S G	EC/CL A S G	ECWC A S G	UEFA A S G	OTHER A S G	TOTAL A S G
1 Brighton	– –	3 1	– –	2 1	– –	– –	– –	– –	– –	5 2
2 Tottenham Hotspur	– –	2 1	– –	– –	2 –	– –	– –	– –	– –	4 1
3 Coventry City	– –	4 –	– –	– –	– –	– –	– –	– –	– –	4 –
4 Wolverhampton W.	– –	3 2	– –	– –	– –	– –	– –	– –	– –	3 2
5 Birmingham City	– –	3 1	– –	– –	– –	– –	– –	– –	– –	3 1
6 Middlesbrough	– –	3 1	– –	– –	– –	– –	– –	– –	– –	3 1
7 Stoke City	– –	3 1	– –	– –	– –	– –	– –	– –	– –	3 1
8 Sunderland	– –	3 1	– –	– –	– –	– –	– –	– –	– –	3 1
9 Aston Villa	– –	3 –	– –	– –	– –	– –	– –	– –	– –	3 –
10 Manchester City	– –	3 –	– –	– –	– –	– –	– –	– –	– –	3 –
11 Nottingham Forest	– –	2 –	– –	– –	1 –	– –	– –	– –	– –	3 –
12 Southampton	– –	3 –	– –	– –	– –	– –	– –	– –	– –	3 –

continued../

GARY BIRTLES (continued)

Opponents	PREM A	S	G	FLD 1 A	S	G	FLD 2 A	S	G	FAC A	S	G	LC A	S	G	EC/CL A	S	G	ECWC A	S	G	UEFA A	S	G	OTHER A	S	G	TOTAL A	S	G
13 Ipswich Town	–	–		2	(1)	–	–	–		–	–		–	–		–	–		–	–		–	–		–	–		2	(1)	–
14 Notts County	–	–		2		1	–	–		–	–		–	–		–	–		–	–		–	–		–	–		2		1
15 Swansea City	–	–		2		1	–	–		–	–		–	–		–	–		–	–		–	–		–	–		2		1
16 West Bromwich Albion	–	–		2		1	–	–		–	–		–	–		–	–		–	–		–	–		–	–		2		1
17 Arsenal	–	–		2		–	–	–		–	–		–	–		–	–		–	–		–	–		–	–		2		–
18 Crystal Palace	–	–		2		–	–	–		–	–		–	–		–	–		–	–		–	–		–	–		2		–
19 Everton	–	–		2		–	–	–		–	–		–	–		–	–		–	–		–	–		–	–		2		–
20 Leeds United	–	–		2		–	–	–		–	–		–	–		–	–		–	–		–	–		–	–		2		–
21 Liverpool	–	–		2		–	–	–		–	–		–	–		–	–		–	–		–	–		–	–		2		–
22 West Ham United	–	–		2		–	–	–		–	–		–	–		–	–		–	–		–	–		–	–		2		–
23 Leicester City	–	–		1			–	–		–	–		–	–		–	–		–	–		–	–		–	–		1		
24 Norwich City	–	–		1			–	–		–	–		–	–		–	–		–	–		–	–		–	–		1		
25 Watford	–	–		–	–		–	–		1			–	–		–	–		–	–		–	–		–	–		1		

GEORGE BISSETT

DEBUT (Full Appearance)

Saturday 15/11/1919
Football League Division 1
at Old Trafford

Manchester United 0 Burnley 1

CLUB CAREER RECORD	Apps	Subs	Goals
Premiership	0		0
League Division 1	40		10
League Division 2	0		0
FA Cup	2		0
League Cup	0		0
European Cup / Champions League	0		0
European Cup–Winners' Cup	0		0
UEFA Cup / Inter–Cities' Fairs Cup	0		0
Other Matches	0		0
OVERALL TOTAL	**42**		**10**

Opponents	PREM A	S	G	FLD 1 A	S	G	FLD 2 A	S	G	FAC A	S	G	LC A	S	G	EC/CL A	S	G	ECWC A	S	G	UEFA A	S	G	OTHER A	S	G	TOTAL A	S	G
1 Blackburn Rovers	–	–		4		–	–	–		–	–		–	–		–	–		–	–		–	–		–	–		4		–
2 Bolton Wanderers	–	–		3		2	–	–		–	–		–	–		–	–		–	–		–	–		–	–		3		2
3 Arsenal	–	–		3		–	–	–		–	–		–	–		–	–		–	–		–	–		–	–		3		–
4 Tottenham Hotspur	–	–		3		–	–	–		–	–		–	–		–	–		–	–		–	–		–	–		3		–
5 West Bromwich Albion	–	–		3		–	–	–		–	–		–	–		–	–		–	–		–	–		–	–		3		–
6 Bradford City	–	–		2		1	–	–		–	–		–	–		–	–		–	–		–	–		–	–		2		1
7 Bradford Park Avenue	–	–		2		1	–	–		–	–		–	–		–	–		–	–		–	–		–	–		2		1
8 Derby County	–	–		2		1	–	–		–	–		–	–		–	–		–	–		–	–		–	–		2		1
9 Everton	–	–		2		1	–	–		–	–		–	–		–	–		–	–		–	–		–	–		2		1
10 Middlesbrough	–	–		2		1	–	–		–	–		–	–		–	–		–	–		–	–		–	–		2		1
11 Oldham Athletic	–	–		2		1	–	–		–	–		–	–		–	–		–	–		–	–		–	–		2		1
12 Aston Villa	–	–		2		–	–	–		–	–		–	–		–	–		–	–		–	–		–	–		2		–
13 Burnley	–	–		2		–	–	–		–	–		–	–		–	–		–	–		–	–		–	–		2		–
14 Liverpool	–	–		–	–		–	–		2			–	–		–	–		–	–		–	–		–	–		2		–
15 Notts County	–	–		2		–	–	–		–	–		–	–		–	–		–	–		–	–		–	–		2		–
16 Sunderland	–	–		2		–	–	–		–	–		–	–		–	–		–	–		–	–		–	–		2		–
17 Huddersfield Town	–	–		1		2	–	–		–	–		–	–		–	–		–	–		–	–		–	–		1		2
18 Chelsea	–	–		1		–	–	–		–	–		–	–		–	–		–	–		–	–		–	–		1		–
19 Manchester City	–	–		1		–	–	–		–	–		–	–		–	–		–	–		–	–		–	–		1		–
20 Newcastle United	–	–		1		–	–	–		–	–		–	–		–	–		–	–		–	–		–	–		1		–

DICK BLACK

DEBUT (Full Appearance)

Saturday 23/04/1932
Football League Division 2
at Old Trafford

Manchester United 1 Bradford City 0

CLUB CAREER RECORD	Apps	Subs	Goals
Premiership	0		0
League Division 1	0		0
League Division 2	8		3
FA Cup	0		0
League Cup	0		0
European Cup / Champions League	0		0
European Cup–Winners' Cup	0		0
UEFA Cup / Inter–Cities' Fairs Cup	0		0
Other Matches	0		0
OVERALL TOTAL	**8**		**3**

Opponents	PREM A	S	G	FLD 1 A	S	G	FLD 2 A	S	G	FAC A	S	G	LC A	S	G	EC/CL A	S	G	ECWC A	S	G	UEFA A	S	G	OTHER A	S	G	TOTAL A	S	G
1 Bradford City	–	–		–	–		2		–	–			–	–		–	–		–	–		–	–		–	–		2		–
2 Bristol City	–	–		–	–		1		1	–			–	–		–	–		–	–		–	–		–	–		1		1
3 Port Vale	–	–		–	–		1		1	–			–	–		–	–		–	–		–	–		–	–		1		1
4 Southampton	–	–		–	–		1		1	–			–	–		–	–		–	–		–	–		–	–		1		1
5 Notts County	–	–		–	–		1		–	–			–	–		–	–		–	–		–	–		–	–		1		–
6 Stoke City	–	–		–	–		1		–	–			–	–		–	–		–	–		–	–		–	–		1		–
7 Swansea City	–	–		–	–		1		–	–			–	–		–	–		–	–		–	–		–	–		1		–

CLAYTON BLACKMORE

DEBUT (Full Appearance)

Wednesday 16/05/1984
Football League Division 1
at City Ground

Nottingham Forest 2 Manchester United 0

CLUB CAREER RECORD	Apps	Subs	Goals
Premiership	12	(2)	0
League Division 1	138	(34)	19
League Division 2	0		0
FA Cup	15	(6)	1
League Cup	23	(2)	3
European Cup / Champions League	0		0
European Cup-Winners' Cup	10		2
UEFA Cup / Inter-Cities' Fairs Cup	1		0
Other Matches	2		1
OVERALL TOTAL	**201**	**(44)**	**26**

Opponents	PREM A S G	FLD 1 A S G	FLD 2 A S G	FAC A S G	LC A S G	EC/CL A S G	ECWC A S G	UEFA A S G	OTHER A S G	TOTAL A S G
1 Queens Park Rangers	1 –	9 1	– –	3 –	–	–	–	–	–	13 1
2 Arsenal	–	10 (1) –	– –	– (1) –	1 1	–	–	–	–	11 (2) 1
3 Nottingham Forest	– (1) –	10 1	– –	1 (1) –	–	–	–	–	–	11 (2) 1
4 Wimbledon	1 –	9 (1) 2	– –	– –	1 –	–	–	–	–	11 (1) 2
5 Liverpool	– (1) –	8 –	– –	– –	2 –	–	–	–	1 1	11 (1) 1
6 Norwich City	– –	8 (3) –	– –	1 –	–	–	–	–	–	9 (3) –
7 Everton	2 –	8 (1) –	– –	– –	–	–	–	–	–	10 (1) –
8 Tottenham Hotspur	1 –	5 (5) –	– –	– –	–	–	–	–	–	6 (5) –
9 Aston Villa	1 –	6 (2) 2	– –	– –	1 –	–	–	–	–	8 (2) 2
10 Luton Town	– –	8 (1) 2	– –	– –	–	–	–	–	–	8 (1) 2
11 Leeds United	1 –	4 –	– –	– –	3 1	–	–	–	–	8 1
12 West Ham United	– –	5 (2) –	– –	– (1) –	–	–	–	–	–	5 (3) –
13 Crystal Palace	1 –	2 (2) –	– –	– (1) –	1 (1) –	–	–	–	–	4 (4) –
14 Sheffield Wednesday	– –	5 (1) 2	– –	– –	1 –	–	–	–	–	6 (1) 2
15 Chelsea	– –	3 (3) –	– –	1 –	–	–	–	–	–	4 (3) –
16 Coventry City	– –	3 (3) –	– –	1 –	–	–	–	–	–	4 (3) –
17 Derby County	– –	6 1	– –	– –	–	–	–	–	–	6 1
18 Southampton	– –	2 (1) 1	– –	1 –	2 –	–	–	–	–	5 (1) 1
19 Manchester City	– –	5 1	– –	– –	–	–	–	–	–	5 1
20 Sheffield United	1 –	3 (1) 2	– –	– –	–	–	–	–	–	4 (1) 2
21 Oxford United	– –	2 (1) –	– –	1 –	1 –	–	–	–	–	4 (1) –
22 Sunderland	– –	2 –	– –	1 (1) –	–	–	–	–	–	3 (1) –
23 Charlton Athletic	– –	2 (2) –	– –	– –	–	–	–	–	–	2 (2) –
24 Newcastle United	– –	3 –	– –	– –	–	–	–	–	–	3 –
25 Oldham Athletic	– –	– (2) –	– –	– –	– (1) –	–	–	–	–	– (3) –
26 Halifax Town	– –	–	– –	– –	2 1	–	–	–	–	2 1
27 Millwall	– –	2 1	– –	– –	–	–	–	–	–	2 1
28 Montpellier Herault	– –	–	– –	– –	–	–	2 1	–	–	2 1
29 Pecsi Munkas	– –	–	– –	– –	–	–	2 1	–	–	2 1
30 West Bromwich Albion	– –	2 1	– –	– –	–	–	–	–	–	2 1
31 Bournemouth	– –	–	– –	2 –	–	–	–	–	–	2 –
32 Cambridge United	– –	–	– –	– –	2 –	–	–	–	–	2 –
33 Legia Warsaw	– –	–	– –	– –	–	–	2 –	–	–	2 –
34 Middlesbrough	1 –	1 –	– –	– –	–	–	–	–	–	2 –
35 Rotherham United	– –	–	– –	– –	2 –	–	–	–	–	2 –
36 Watford	– –	2 –	– –	– –	–	–	–	–	–	2 –
37 Wrexham	– –	–	– –	– –	–	–	2 –	–	–	2 –
38 Notts County	– –	1 (1) 1	– –	– –	–	–	–	–	–	1 (1) 1
39 Bury	– –	–	– –	– (1) –	1 –	–	–	–	–	1 (1) –
40 Portsmouth	– –	– (1) –	– –	– –	1 –	–	–	–	–	1 (1) –
41 Hereford United	– –	–	– –	1 1	–	–	–	–	–	1 1
42 Leicester City	– –	1 1	– –	– –	–	–	–	–	–	1 1
43 Athletico Madrid	– –	–	– –	– –	–	–	1 –	–	–	1 –
44 Barcelona	– –	–	– –	– –	–	–	1 –	–	–	1 –
45 Birmingham City	– –	1 –	– –	– –	–	–	–	–	–	1 –
46 Blackburn Rovers	1 –	–	– –	– –	–	–	–	–	–	1 –
47 Bolton Wanderers	– –	–	– –	1 –	–	–	–	–	–	1 –
48 Burnley	– –	–	– –	– –	1 –	–	–	–	–	1 –
49 Hull City	– –	–	– –	– –	1 –	–	–	–	–	1 –
50 Ipswich Town	1 –	–	– –	– –	–	–	–	–	–	1 –
51 Red Star Belgrade	– –	–	– –	– –	–	–	–	–	1 –	1 –
52 Rochdale	– –	–	– –	1 –	–	–	–	–	–	1 –
53 Torpedo Moscow	– –	–	– –	– –	–	–	–	1 –	–	1 –

PETER BLACKMORE

DEBUT (Full Appearance)

Saturday 21/10/1899
Football League Division 2
at Bank Street

Newton Heath 2 New Brighton Tower 1

CLUB CAREER RECORD	Apps	Subs	Goals
Premiership	0		0
League Division 1	0		0
League Division 2	1		0
FA Cup	1		0
League Cup	0		0
European Cup / Champions League	0		0
European Cup-Winners' Cup	0		0
UEFA Cup / Inter-Cities' Fairs Cup	0		0
Other Matches	0		0
OVERALL TOTAL	2		0

Opponents	PREM A S G	FLD 1 A S G	FLD 2 A S G	FAC A S G	LC A S G	EC/CL A S G	ECWC A S G	UEFA A S G	OTHER A S G	TOTAL A S G
1 New Brighton Tower	– –	– –	1 –	– –	– –	– –	– –	– –	– –	1 –
2 South Shore	– –	– –	–	1 –	– –	– –	– –	– –	– –	1 –

TOMMY BLACKSTOCK

DEBUT (Full Appearance)

Saturday 03/10/1903
Football League Division 2
at Manor Field

Arsenal 4 Manchester United 0

CLUB CAREER RECORD	Apps	Subs	Goals
Premiership	0		0
League Division 1	3		0
League Division 2	31		0
FA Cup	4		0
League Cup	0		0
European Cup / Champions League	0		0
European Cup-Winners' Cup	0		0
UEFA Cup / Inter-Cities' Fairs Cup	0		0
Other Matches	0		0
OVERALL TOTAL	38		0

Opponents	PREM A S G	FLD 1 A S G	FLD 2 A S G	FAC A S G	LC A S G	EC/CL A S G	ECWC A S G	UEFA A S G	OTHER A S G	TOTAL A S G
1 Barnsley	– –	– –	3 –	–	– –	– –	– –	– –	– –	3 –
2 Birmingham City	– –	– –	– –	3 –	– –	– –	– –	– –	– –	3 –
3 Blackpool	– –	– –	3 –	–	– –	– –	– –	– –	– –	3 –
4 Gainsborough Trinity	– –	– –	3 –	–	– –	– –	– –	– –	– –	3 –
5 Lincoln City	– –	– –	3 –	–	– –	– –	– –	– –	– –	3 –
6 Bristol City	– –	– –	2 –	–	– –	– –	– –	– –	– –	2 –
7 Leeds United	– –	– –	2 –	–	– –	– –	– –	– –	– –	2 –
8 Stockport County	– –	– –	2 –	–	– –	– –	– –	– –	– –	2 –
9 Arsenal	– –	– –	1 –	–	– –	– –	– –	– –	– –	1 –
10 Bolton Wanderers	– –	– –	1 –	–	– –	– –	– –	– –	– –	1 –
11 Bradford City	– –	– –	1 –	–	– –	– –	– –	– –	– –	1 –
12 Burton United	– –	– –	1 –	–	– –	– –	– –	– –	– –	1 –
13 Bury	– –	1 –	–	–	– –	– –	– –	– –	– –	1 –
14 Chesterfield	– –	– –	1 –	–	– –	– –	– –	– –	– –	1 –
15 Glossop	– –	– –	1 –	–	– –	– –	– –	– –	– –	1 –
16 Grimsby Town	– –	– –	1 –	–	– –	– –	– –	– –	– –	1 –
17 Hull City	– –	– –	1 –	–	– –	– –	– –	– –	– –	1 –
18 Leicester City	– –	– –	1 –	–	– –	– –	– –	– –	– –	1 –
19 Leyton Orient	– –	– –	1 –	–	– –	– –	– –	– –	– –	1 –
20 Liverpool	– –	1 –	–	–	– –	– –	– –	– –	– –	1 –
21 Port Vale	– –	– –	1 –	–	– –	– –	– –	– –	– –	1 –
22 Portsmouth	– –	– –	–	1 –	– –	– –	– –	– –	– –	1 –
23 Preston North End	– –	– –	1 –	–	– –	– –	– –	– –	– –	1 –
24 Stoke City	– –	1 –	–	–	– –	– –	– –	– –	– –	1 –
25 West Bromwich Albion	– –	– –	1 –	–	– –	– –	– –	– –	– –	1 –

LAURENT BLANC

DEBUT (Full Appearance)

Saturday 08/09/2001
FA Premiership
at Old Trafford

Manchester United 4 Everton 1

CLUB CAREER RECORD	Apps	Subs	Goals
Premiership	44	(4)	1
League Division 1	0		0
League Division 2	0		0
FA Cup	3		0
League Cup	0		0
European Cup / Champions League	24		3
European Cup-Winners' Cup	0		0
UEFA Cup / Inter-Cities' Fairs Cup	0		0
Other Matches	0		0
OVERALL TOTAL	71	(4)	4

Opponents	PREM A S G	FLD 1 A S G	FLD 2 A S G	FAC A S G	LC A S G	EC/CL A S G	ECWC A S G	UEFA A S G	OTHER A S G	TOTAL A S G
1 Deportivo La Coruna	– –	– –	– –	–	– –	5 –	– –	– –	– –	5 –
2 Middlesbrough	4 –	– –	– –	1 –	– –	– –	– –	– –	– –	5 –
3 Olympiakos Piraeus	– –	– –	– –	–	– –	4 1	– –	– –	– –	4 1
4 Bayer Leverkusen	– –	– –	– –	–	– –	4 –	– –	– –	– –	4 –
5 Everton	3 (1) –	– –	– –	–	– –	– –	– –	– –	– –	3 (1) –
6 Newcastle United	3 (1) –	– –	– –	–	– –	– –	– –	– –	– –	3 (1) –

continued../

LAURENT BLANC (continued)

Opponents	PREM A S G	FLD 1 A S G	FLD 2 A S G	FAC A S G	LC A S G	EC/CL A S G	ECWC A S G	UEFA A S G	OTHER A S G	TOTAL A S G
7 Aston Villa	2 -	- - -	- - -	- - -	1 - -	- - -	- - -	- - -	- - -	3 -
8 Charlton Athletic	3 -	- - -	- - -	- - -	- - -	- - -	- - -	- - -	- - -	3 -
9 Chelsea	3 -	- - -	- - -	- - -	- - -	- - -	- - -	- - -	- - -	3 -
10 Leeds United	3 -	- - -	- - -	- - -	- - -	- - -	- - -	- - -	- - -	3 -
11 Southampton	3 -	- - -	- - -	- - -	- - -	- - -	- - -	- - -	- - -	3 -
12 Sunderland	3 -	- - -	- - -	- - -	- - -	- - -	- - -	- - -	- - -	3 -
13 West Ham United	2 (1) -	- - -	- - -	- - -	- - -	- - -	- - -	- - -	- - -	2 (1) -
14 Boavista	- -	- - -	- - -	- - -	- - -	2 2	- - -	- - -	- - -	2 2
15 Tottenham Hotspur	2 1	- - -	- - -	- - -	- - -	- - -	- - -	- - -	- - -	2 1
16 Arsenal	2 -	- - -	- - -	- - -	- - -	- - -	- - -	- - -	- - -	2 -
17 Bayern Munich	- -	- - -	- - -	- - -	- - -	2 -	- - -	- - -	- - -	2 -
18 Bolton Wanderers	2 -	- - -	- - -	- - -	- - -	- - -	- - -	- - -	- - -	2 -
19 Fulham	2 -	- - -	- - -	- - -	- - -	- - -	- - -	- - -	- - -	2 -
20 Leicester City	2 -	- - -	- - -	- - -	- - -	- - -	- - -	- - -	- - -	2 -
21 Nantes Atlantique	- -	- - -	- - -	- - -	- - -	2 -	- - -	- - -	- - -	2 -
22 Zalaegerszeg	- -	- - -	- - -	- - -	- - -	2 -	- - -	- - -	- - -	2 -
23 Blackburn Rovers	1 (1) -	- - -	- - -	- - -	- - -	- - -	- - -	- - -	- - -	1 (1) -
24 Basel	- -	- - -	- - -	- - -	- - -	1 -	- - -	- - -	- - -	1 -
25 Derby County	1 -	- - -	- - -	- - -	- - -	- - -	- - -	- - -	- - -	1 -
26 Lille Metropole	- -	- - -	- - -	- - -	- - -	1 -	- - -	- - -	- - -	1 -
27 Liverpool	1 -	- - -	- - -	- - -	- - -	- - -	- - -	- - -	- - -	1 -
28 Maccabi Haifa	- -	- - -	- - -	- - -	- - -	1 -	- - -	- - -	- - -	1 -
29 Manchester City	1 -	- - -	- - -	- - -	- - -	- - -	- - -	- - -	- - -	1 -
30 Portsmouth	- -	- - -	- - -	1 - -	- - -	- - -	- - -	- - -	- - -	1 -
31 West Bromwich Albion	1 -	- - -	- - -	- - -	- - -	- - -	- - -	- - -	- - -	1 -

JACKIE BLANCHFLOWER

DEBUT (Full Appearance)

Saturday 24/11/1951
Football League Division 1
at Anfield

Liverpool 0 Manchester United 0

CLUB CAREER RECORD	Apps	Subs	Goals
Premiership	0		0
League Division 1	105		26
League Division 2	0		0
FA Cup	6		1
League Cup	0		0
European Cup / Champions League	5		0
European Cup-Winners' Cup	0		0
UEFA Cup / Inter-Cities' Fairs Cup	0		0
Other Matches	1		0
OVERALL TOTAL	117		27

Opponents	PREM A S G	FLD 1 A S G	FLD 2 A S G	FAC A S G	LC A S G	EC/CL A S G	ECWC A S G	UEFA A S G	OTHER A S G	TOTAL A S G
1 Tottenham Hotspur	- -	8 - -	- - -	- - -	- - -	- - -	- - -	- - -	- - -	8 -
2 Arsenal	- -	6 4	- - -	- - -	- - -	- - -	- - -	- - -	- - -	6 4
3 Blackpool	- -	6 3	- - -	- - -	- - -	- - -	- - -	- - -	- - -	6 3
4 Everton	- -	6 2	- - -	- - -	- - -	- - -	- - -	- - -	- - -	6 2
5 Aston Villa	- -	4 1	- - -	1 - -	- - -	- - -	- - -	- - -	1 -	6 1
6 Burnley	- -	5 -	- - -	1 1	- - -	- - -	- - -	- - -	- - -	6 1
7 Manchester City	- -	5 1	- - -	1 - -	- - -	- - -	- - -	- - -	- - -	6 1
8 Bolton Wanderers	- -	6 -	- - -	- - -	- - -	- - -	- - -	- - -	- - -	6 -
9 Sheffield Wednesday	- -	5 3	- - -	- - -	- - -	- - -	- - -	- - -	- - -	5 3
10 Cardiff City	- -	5 1	- - -	- - -	- - -	- - -	- - -	- - -	- - -	5 1
11 Huddersfield Town	- -	5 1	- - -	- - -	- - -	- - -	- - -	- - -	- - -	5 1
12 Portsmouth	- -	5 1	- - -	- - -	- - -	- - -	- - -	- - -	- - -	5 1
13 Charlton Athletic	- -	5 -	- - -	- - -	- - -	- - -	- - -	- - -	- - -	5 -
14 Sheffield United	- -	4 3	- - -	- - -	- - -	- - -	- - -	- - -	- - -	4 3
15 Preston North End	- -	4 1	- - -	- - -	- - -	- - -	- - -	- - -	- - -	4 1
16 Chelsea	- -	3 1	- - -	- - -	- - -	- - -	- - -	- - -	- - -	3 1
17 Newcastle United	- -	3 1	- - -	- - -	- - -	- - -	- - -	- - -	- - -	3 1
18 Sunderland	- -	3 1	- - -	- - -	- - -	- - -	- - -	- - -	- - -	3 1
19 Luton Town	- -	3 -	- - -	- - -	- - -	- - -	- - -	- - -	- - -	3 -
20 West Bromwich Albion	- -	3 -	- - -	- - -	- - -	- - -	- - -	- - -	- - -	3 -
21 Wolverhampton W.	- -	3 -	- - -	- - -	- - -	- - -	- - -	- - -	- - -	3 -
22 Liverpool	- -	2 2	- - -	- - -	- - -	- - -	- - -	- - -	- - -	2 2
23 Birmingham City	- -	1 -	- - -	1 - -	- - -	- - -	- - -	- - -	- - -	2 -
24 Leeds United	- -	2 -	- - -	- - -	- - -	- - -	- - -	- - -	- - -	2 -
25 Leicester City	- -	2 -	- - -	- - -	- - -	- - -	- - -	- - -	- - -	2 -
26 Reading	- -	- - -	- - -	2 - -	- - -	- - -	- - -	- - -	- - -	2 -
27 Real Madrid	- -	- - -	- - -	- - -	- - -	2 -	- - -	- - -	- - -	2 -
28 Anderlecht	- -	- - -	- - -	- - -	- - -	1 -	- - -	- - -	- - -	1 -
29 Dukla Prague	- -	- - -	- - -	- - -	- - -	1 -	- - -	- - -	- - -	1 -
30 Nottingham Forest	- -	1 -	- - -	- - -	- - -	- - -	- - -	- - -	- - -	1 -
31 Shamrock Rovers	- -	- - -	- - -	- - -	- - -	1 -	- - -	- - -	- - -	1 -

HORACE BLEW

DEBUT (Full Appearance)

Friday 13/04/1906
Football League Division 2
at Stamford Bridge

Chelsea 1 Manchester United 1

CLUB CAREER RECORD	Apps	Subs	Goals
Premiership	0		0
League Division 1	0		0
League Division 2	1		0
FA Cup	0		0
League Cup	0		0
European Cup / Champions League	0		0
European Cup-Winners' Cup	0		0
UEFA Cup / Inter-Cities' Fairs Cup	0		0
Other Matches	0		0
OVERALL TOTAL	**1**		**0**

Opponents	PREM A S G	FLD 1 A S G	FLD 2 A S G	FAC A S G	LC A S G	EC/CL A S G	ECWC A S G	UEFA A S G	OTHER A S G	TOTAL A S G
1 Chelsea	- - -	- - -	1 -	- - -	- - -	- - -	- - -	- - -	- - -	1 -

JESPER BLOMQVIST

DEBUT (Full Appearance)

Wednesday 09/09/1998
FA Premiership
at Old Trafford

Manchester United 4 Charlton Athletic 1

CLUB CAREER RECORD	Apps	Subs	Goals
Premiership	20	(5)	1
League Division 1	0		0
League Division 2	0		0
FA Cup	3		0
League Cup	0	(1)	0
European Cup / Champions League	6	(1)	0
European Cup-Winners' Cup	0		0
UEFA Cup / Inter-Cities' Fairs Cup	0		0
Other Matches	0		0
OVERALL TOTAL	**29**	**(9)**	**1**

Opponents	PREM A S G	FLD 1 A S G	FLD 2 A S G	FAC A S G	LC A S G	EC/CL A S G	ECWC A S G	UEFA A S G	OTHER A S G	TOTAL A S G
1 Arsenal	2 -	- - -	- - -	1 -	- - -	- - -	- - -	- - -	- - -	3 -
2 Chelsea	1 -	- - -	- - -	1 (1) -	- - -	- - -	- - -	- - -	- - -	2 (1) -
3 Aston Villa	2 -	- - -	- - -	- - -	- - -	- - -	- - -	- - -	- - -	2 -
4 Bayern Munich	- -	- - -	- - -	- - -	- - -	2 -	- - -	- - -	- - -	2 -
5 Brondby	- -	- - -	- - -	- - -	- - -	2 -	- - -	- - -	- - -	2 -
6 Middlesbrough	1 -	- - -	- - -	1 -	- - -	- - -	- - -	- - -	- - -	2 -
7 Sheffield Wednesday	2 -	- - -	- - -	- - -	- - -	- - -	- - -	- - -	- - -	2 -
8 Wimbledon	2 -	- - -	- - -	- - -	- - -	- - -	- - -	- - -	- - -	2 -
9 Barcelona	- -	- - -	- - -	- - -	- - -	1 (1) -	- - -	- - -	- - -	1 (1) -
10 Nottingham Forest	1 (1) -	- - -	- - -	- - -	- - -	- - -	- - -	- - -	- - -	1 (1) -
11 Derby County	- (2) -	- - -	- - -	- - -	- - -	- - -	- - -	- - -	- - -	- (2) -
12 Tottenham Hotspur	- (1) -	- - -	- - -	- - -	- - - (1) -	- - -	- - -	- - -	- - -	- (2) -
13 Everton	1 1	- - -	- - -	- - -	- - -	- - -	- - -	- - -	- - -	1 1
14 Blackburn Rovers	1 -	- - -	- - -	- - -	- - -	- - -	- - -	- - -	- - -	1 -
15 Charlton Athletic	1 -	- - -	- - -	- - -	- - -	- - -	- - -	- - -	- - -	1 -
16 Juventus	- -	- - -	- - -	- - -	- 1 -	- - -	- - -	- - -	- - -	1 -
17 Leeds United	1 -	- - -	- - -	- - -	- - -	- - -	- - -	- - -	- - -	1 -
18 Leicester City	1 -	- - -	- - -	- - -	- - -	- - -	- - -	- - -	- - -	1 -
19 Liverpool	1 -	- - -	- - -	- - -	- - -	- - -	- - -	- - -	- - -	1 -
20 Newcastle United	1 -	- - -	- - -	- - -	- - -	- - -	- - -	- - -	- - -	1 -
21 Southampton	1 -	- - -	- - -	- - -	- - -	- - -	- - -	- - -	- - -	1 -
22 West Ham United	1 -	- - -	- - -	- - -	- - -	- - -	- - -	- - -	- - -	1 -
23 Coventry City	- (1) -	- - -	- - -	- - -	- - -	- - -	- - -	- - -	- - -	- (1) -
24 Fulham	- -	- - -	- - -	- (1) -	- - -	- - -	- - -	- - -	- - -	- (1) -

SAM BLOTT

DEBUT (Full Appearance)

Wednesday 01/09/1909
Football League Division 1
at Bank Street

Manchester United 1 Bradford City 0

CLUB CAREER RECORD	Apps	Subs	Goals
Premiership	0		0
League Division 1	19		2
League Division 2	0		0
FA Cup	0		0
League Cup	0		0
European Cup / Champions League	0		0
European Cup-Winners' Cup	0		0
UEFA Cup / Inter-Cities' Fairs Cup	0		0
Other Matches	0		0
OVERALL TOTAL	**19**		**2**

Opponents	PREM A S G	FLD 1 A S G	FLD 2 A S G	FAC A S G	LC A S G	EC/CL A S G	ECWC A S G	UEFA A S G	OTHER A S G	TOTAL A S G
1 Tottenham Hotspur	- -	3 1	- - -	- - -	- - -	- - -	- - -	- - -	- - -	3 1
2 Liverpool	- -	2 -	- - -	- - -	- - -	- - -	- - -	- - -	- - -	2 -
3 Notts County	- -	2 -	- - -	- - -	- - -	- - -	- - -	- - -	- - -	2 -
4 Preston North End	- -	2 -	- - -	- - -	- - -	- - -	- - -	- - -	- - -	2 -
5 Sheffield Wednesday	- -	2 -	- - -	- - -	- - -	- - -	- - -	- - -	- - -	2 -
6 Newcastle United	- -	1 1	- - -	- - -	- - -	- - -	- - -	- - -	- - -	1 1
7 Arsenal	- -	1 -	- - -	- - -	- - -	- - -	- - -	- - -	- - -	1 -
8 Aston Villa	- -	1 -	- - -	- - -	- - -	- - -	- - -	- - -	- - -	1 -

continued../

SAM BLOTT (continued)

Opponents	PREM A S G	FLD 1 A S G	FLD 2 A S G	FAC A S G	LC A S G	EC/CL A S G	ECWC A S G	UEFA A S G	OTHER A S G	TOTAL A S G
9 Bradford City	– –	1 –	–	–	–	–	–	–	–	1 –
10 Bristol City	– –	1 –	–	–	–	–	–	–	–	1 –
11 Derby County	– –	1 –	–	–	–	–	–	–	–	1 –
12 Everton	– –	1 –	–	–	–	–	–	–	–	1 –
13 Sunderland	– –	1 –	–	–	–	–	–	–	–	1 –

TOMMY BOGAN

DEBUT (Full Appearance)

Saturday 08/10/1949
Football League Division 1
at Old Trafford

Manchester United 3 Charlton Athletic 2

CLUB CAREER RECORD	Apps	Subs	Goals
Premiership	0		0
League Division 1	29		7
League Division 2	0		0
FA Cup	4		0
League Cup	0		0
European Cup / Champions League	0		0
European Cup-Winners' Cup	0		0
UEFA Cup / Inter–Cities' Fairs Cup	0		0
Other Matches	0		0
OVERALL TOTAL	**33**		**7**

Opponents	PREM A S G	FLD 1 A S G	FLD 2 A S G	FAC A S G	LC A S G	EC/CL A S G	ECWC A S G	UEFA A S G	OTHER A S G	TOTAL A S G
1 Blackpool	– –	3 2	–	–	–	–	–	–	–	3 2
2 Aston Villa	– –	3 1	–	–	–	–	–	–	–	3 1
3 Portsmouth	– –	1 –	–	2 –	–	–	–	–	–	3 –
4 West Bromwich Albion	– –	2 1	–	–	–	–	–	–	–	2 1
5 Arsenal	– –	2 –	–	–	–	–	–	–	–	2 –
6 Burnley	– –	2 –	–	–	–	–	–	–	–	2 –
7 Everton	– –	2 –	–	–	–	–	–	–	–	2 –
8 Middlesbrough	– –	2 –	–	–	–	–	–	–	–	2 –
9 Stoke City	– –	2 –	–	–	–	–	–	–	–	2 –
10 Sunderland	– –	1 2	–	–	–	–	–	–	–	1 2
11 Wolverhampton W.	– –	1 1	–	–	–	–	–	–	–	1 1
12 Charlton Athletic	– –	1 –	–	–	–	–	–	–	–	1 –
13 Derby County	– –	1 –	–	–	–	–	–	–	–	1 –
14 Fulham	– –	1 –	–	–	–	–	–	–	–	1 –
15 Huddersfield Town	– –	1 –	–	–	–	–	–	–	–	1 –
16 Liverpool	– –	1 –	–	–	–	–	–	–	–	1 –
17 Manchester City	– –	1 –	–	–	–	–	–	–	–	1 –
18 Newcastle United	– –	1 –	–	–	–	–	–	–	–	1 –
19 Tottenham Hotspur	– –	1 –	–	–	–	–	–	–	–	1 –
20 Watford	– –	–	–	1 –	–	–	–	–	–	1 –
21 Weymouth Town	– –	–	–	1 –	–	–	–	–	–	1 –

ERNIE BOND

DEBUT (Full Appearance)

Saturday 18/08/1951
Football League Division 1
at The Hawthorns

West Bromwich Albion 3 Manchester United 3

CLUB CAREER RECORD	Apps	Subs	Goals
Premiership	0		0
League Division 1	20		4
League Division 2	0		0
FA Cup	1		0
League Cup	0		0
European Cup / Champions League	0		0
European Cup-Winners' Cup	0		0
UEFA Cup / Inter–Cities' Fairs Cup	0		0
Other Matches	0		0
OVERALL TOTAL	**21**		**4**

Opponents	PREM A S G	FLD 1 A S G	FLD 2 A S G	FAC A S G	LC A S G	EC/CL A S G	ECWC A S G	UEFA A S G	OTHER A S G	TOTAL A S G
1 Fulham	– –	2 2	–	–	–	–	–	–	–	2 2
2 Newcastle United	– –	2 1	–	–	–	–	–	–	–	2 1
3 Arsenal	– –	2 –	–	–	–	–	–	–	–	2 –
4 Bolton Wanderers	– –	2 –	–	–	–	–	–	–	–	2 –
5 Middlesbrough	– –	2 –	–	–	–	–	–	–	–	2 –
6 West Bromwich Albion	– –	2 –	–	–	–	–	–	–	–	2 –
7 Aston Villa	– –	1 1	–	–	–	–	–	–	–	1 1
8 Blackpool	– –	1 –	–	–	–	–	–	–	–	1 –
9 Charlton Athletic	– –	1 –	–	–	–	–	–	–	–	1 –
10 Huddersfield Town	– –	1 –	–	–	–	–	–	–	–	1 –
11 Hull City	– –	–	–	1 –	–	–	–	–	–	1 –
12 Liverpool	– –	1 –	–	–	–	–	–	–	–	1 –
13 Portsmouth	– –	1 –	–	–	–	–	–	–	–	1 –
14 Stoke City	– –	1 –	–	–	–	–	–	–	–	1 –
15 Wolverhampton W.	– –	1 –	–	–	–	–	–	–	–	1 –

BOB BONTHRON

DEBUT (Full Appearance)

Saturday 05/09/1903
Football League Division 2
at Bank Street

Manchester United 2 Bristol City 2

CLUB CAREER RECORD	Apps	Subs	Goals
Premiership	0		0
League Division 1	28		0
League Division 2	91		3
FA Cup	15		0
League Cup	0		0
European Cup / Champions League	0		0
European Cup-Winners' Cup	0		0
UEFA Cup / Inter-Cities' Fairs Cup	0		0
Other Matches	0		0
OVERALL TOTAL	**134**		**3**

Opponents	PREM			FLD 1			FLD 2			FAC			LC			EC/CL			ECWC			UEFA			OTHER			TOTAL		
	A	S	G	A	S	G	A	S	G	A	S	G	A	S	G	A	S	G	A	S	G	A	S	G	A	S	G	A	S	G
1 Bristol City	–	–	–	2	–	–	6	–	–	–	–	–	–	–	–	–	–	–	–	–	–	–	–	–	–	–	–	8	–	–
2 Leicester City	–	–	–	–	–	–	6	–	1	–	–	–	–	–	–	–	–	–	–	–	–	–	–	–	–	–	–	6	–	1
3 Bolton Wanderers	–	–	–	2	–	–	4	–	–	–	–	–	–	–	–	–	–	–	–	–	–	–	–	–	–	–	–	6	–	–
4 Bradford City	–	–	–	–	–	–	6	–	–	–	–	–	–	–	–	–	–	–	–	–	–	–	–	–	–	–	–	6	–	–
5 Burnley	–	–	–	–	–	–	6	–	–	–	–	–	–	–	–	–	–	–	–	–	–	–	–	–	–	–	–	6	–	–
6 Chesterfield	–	–	–	–	–	–	6	–	–	–	–	–	–	–	–	–	–	–	–	–	–	–	–	–	–	–	–	6	–	–
7 Grimsby Town	–	–	–	–	–	–	6	–	–	–	–	–	–	–	–	–	–	–	–	–	–	–	–	–	–	–	–	6	–	–
8 Arsenal	–	–	–	2	–	–	2	–	–	1	–	–	–	–	–	–	–	–	–	–	–	–	–	–	–	–	–	5	–	–
9 Birmingham City	–	–	–	1	–	–	–	–	–	4	–	–	–	–	–	–	–	–	–	–	–	–	–	–	–	–	–	5	–	–
10 Blackpool	–	–	–	–	–	–	5	–	–	–	–	–	–	–	–	–	–	–	–	–	–	–	–	–	–	–	–	5	–	–
11 Burton United	–	–	–	–	–	–	5	–	–	–	–	–	–	–	–	–	–	–	–	–	–	–	–	–	–	–	–	5	–	–
12 Glossop	–	–	–	–	–	–	5	–	–	–	–	–	–	–	–	–	–	–	–	–	–	–	–	–	–	–	–	5	–	–
13 Port Vale	–	–	–	–	–	–	5	–	–	–	–	–	–	–	–	–	–	–	–	–	–	–	–	–	–	–	–	5	–	–
14 Gainsborough Trinity	–	–	–	–	–	–	4	–	2	–	–	–	–	–	–	–	–	–	–	–	–	–	–	–	–	–	–	4	–	2
15 Barnsley	–	–	–	–	–	–	4	–	–	–	–	–	–	–	–	–	–	–	–	–	–	–	–	–	–	–	–	4	–	–
16 Lincoln City	–	–	–	–	–	–	4	–	–	–	–	–	–	–	–	–	–	–	–	–	–	–	–	–	–	–	–	4	–	–
17 Notts County	–	–	–	2	–	–	–	–	–	2	–	–	–	–	–	–	–	–	–	–	–	–	–	–	–	–	–	4	–	–
18 Stockport County	–	–	–	–	–	–	4	–	–	–	–	–	–	–	–	–	–	–	–	–	–	–	–	–	–	–	–	4	–	–
19 West Bromwich Albion	–	–	–	–	–	–	4	–	–	–	–	–	–	–	–	–	–	–	–	–	–	–	–	–	–	–	–	4	–	–
20 Fulham	–	–	–	–	–	–	–	–	–	3	–	–	–	–	–	–	–	–	–	–	–	–	–	–	–	–	–	3	–	–
21 Liverpool	–	–	–	1	–	–	2	–	–	–	–	–	–	–	–	–	–	–	–	–	–	–	–	–	–	–	–	3	–	–
22 Preston North End	–	–	–	1	–	–	2	–	–	–	–	–	–	–	–	–	–	–	–	–	–	–	–	–	–	–	–	3	–	–
23 Sheffield Wednesday	–	–	–	2	–	–	–	–	–	1	–	–	–	–	–	–	–	–	–	–	–	–	–	–	–	–	–	3	–	–
24 Aston Villa	–	–	–	1	–	–	–	–	–	1	–	–	–	–	–	–	–	–	–	–	–	–	–	–	–	–	–	2	–	–
25 Derby County	–	–	–	2	–	–	–	–	–	–	–	–	–	–	–	–	–	–	–	–	–	–	–	–	–	–	–	2	–	–
26 Doncaster Rovers	–	–	–	–	–	–	2	–	–	–	–	–	–	–	–	–	–	–	–	–	–	–	–	–	–	–	–	2	–	–
27 Manchester City	–	–	–	2	–	–	–	–	–	–	–	–	–	–	–	–	–	–	–	–	–	–	–	–	–	–	–	2	–	–
28 Middlesbrough	–	–	–	2	–	–	–	–	–	–	–	–	–	–	–	–	–	–	–	–	–	–	–	–	–	–	–	2	–	–
29 Sheffield United	–	–	–	2	–	–	–	–	–	–	–	–	–	–	–	–	–	–	–	–	–	–	–	–	–	–	–	2	–	–
30 Blackburn Rovers	–	–	–	1	–	–	–	–	–	–	–	–	–	–	–	–	–	–	–	–	–	–	–	–	–	–	–	1	–	–
31 Bury	–	–	–	1	–	–	–	–	–	–	–	–	–	–	–	–	–	–	–	–	–	–	–	–	–	–	–	1	–	–
32 Chelsea	–	–	–	–	–	–	–	–	–	1	–	–	–	–	–	–	–	–	–	–	–	–	–	–	–	–	–	1	–	–
33 Everton	–	–	–	1	–	–	–	–	–	–	–	–	–	–	–	–	–	–	–	–	–	–	–	–	–	–	–	1	–	–
34 Hull City	–	–	–	–	–	–	–	–	–	1	–	–	–	–	–	–	–	–	–	–	–	–	–	–	–	–	–	1	–	–
35 Leyton Orient	–	–	–	–	–	–	–	–	–	1	–	–	–	–	–	–	–	–	–	–	–	–	–	–	–	–	–	1	–	–
36 Newcastle United	–	–	–	1	–	–	–	–	–	–	–	–	–	–	–	–	–	–	–	–	–	–	–	–	–	–	–	1	–	–
37 Norwich City	–	–	–	–	–	–	1	–	–	–	–	–	–	–	–	–	–	–	–	–	–	–	–	–	–	–	–	1	–	–
38 Portsmouth	–	–	–	–	–	–	1	–	–	–	–	–	–	–	–	–	–	–	–	–	–	–	–	–	–	–	–	1	–	–
39 Staple Hill	–	–	–	–	–	–	1	–	–	–	–	–	–	–	–	–	–	–	–	–	–	–	–	–	–	–	–	1	–	–
40 Stoke City	–	–	–	1	–	–	–	–	–	–	–	–	–	–	–	–	–	–	–	–	–	–	–	–	–	–	–	1	–	–
41 Sunderland	–	–	–	1	–	–	–	–	–	–	–	–	–	–	–	–	–	–	–	–	–	–	–	–	–	–	–	1	–	–

WILLIAM BOOTH

DEBUT (Full Appearance)

Wednesday 26/12/1900
Football League Division 2
at Bank Street

Newton Heath 4 Blackpool 0

CLUB CAREER RECORD	Apps	Subs	Goals
Premiership	0		0
League Division 1	0		0
League Division 2	2		0
FA Cup	0		0
League Cup	0		0
European Cup / Champions League	0		0
European Cup-Winners' Cup	0		0
UEFA Cup / Inter-Cities' Fairs Cup	0		0
Other Matches	0		0
OVERALL TOTAL	**2**		**0**

Opponents	PREM			FLD 1			FLD 2			FAC			LC			EC/CL			ECWC			UEFA			OTHER			TOTAL		
	A	S	G	A	S	G	A	S	G	A	S	G	A	S	G	A	S	G	A	S	G	A	S	G	A	S	G	A	S	G
1 Blackpool	–	–	–	–	–	–	1	–	–	–	–	–	–	–	–	–	–	–	–	–	–	–	–	–	–	–	–	1	–	–
2 Glossop	–	–	–	–	–	–	1	–	–	–	–	–	–	–	–	–	–	–	–	–	–	–	–	–	–	–	–	1	–	–

MARK BOSNICH

DEBUT (Full Appearance)

Monday 30/04/1990
Football League Division 1
at Old Trafford

Manchester United 0 Wimbledon 0

CLUB CAREER RECORD	Apps	Subs	Goals
Premiership	23		0
League Division 1	3		0
League Division 2	0		0
FA Cup	0		0
League Cup	1		0
European Cup / Champions League	7		0
European Cup-Winners' Cup	0		0
UEFA Cup / Inter-Cities' Fairs Cup	0		0
Other Matches	4		0
OVERALL TOTAL	**38**		**0**

Opponents	PREM			FLD 1			FLD 2			FAC			LC			EC/CL			ECWC			UEFA			OTHER			TOTAL		
	A	S	G	A	S	G	A	S	G	A	S	G	A	S	G	A	S	G	A	S	G	A	S	G	A	S	G	A	S	G
1 Arsenal	1	–	–	–	–	–	–	–	–	–	–	–	–	–	–	–	–	–	–	–	–	–	–	–	1	–	–	2	–	
2 Aston Villa	1	–	–	–	–	–	–	–	–	–	–	–	1	–	–	–	–	–	–	–	–	–	–	–	–	–	–	2	–	
3 Bradford City	2	–	–	–	–	–	–	–	–	–	–	–	–	–	–	–	–	–	–	–	–	–	–	–	–	–	–	2	–	
4 Derby County	1	–	–	1	–	–	–	–	–	–	–	–	–	–	–	–	–	–	–	–	–	–	–	–	–	–	–	2	–	
5 Everton	2	–	–	–	–	–	–	–	–	–	–	–	–	–	–	–	–	–	–	–	–	–	–	–	–	–	–	2	–	
6 Fiorentina	–	–	–	–	–	–	–	–	–	–	–	–	–	–	–	2	–	–	–	–	–	–	–	–	–	–	–	2	–	
7 Leeds United	2	–	–	–	–	–	–	–	–	–	–	–	–	–	–	–	–	–	–	–	–	–	–	–	–	–	–	2	–	
8 Leicester City	2	–	–	–	–	–	–	–	–	–	–	–	–	–	–	–	–	–	–	–	–	–	–	–	–	–	–	2	–	
9 Middlesbrough	2	–	–	–	–	–	–	–	–	–	–	–	–	–	–	–	–	–	–	–	–	–	–	–	–	–	–	2	–	
10 Sheffield Wednesday	2	–	–	–	–	–	–	–	–	–	–	–	–	–	–	–	–	–	–	–	–	–	–	–	–	–	–	2	–	
11 Sunderland	2	–	–	–	–	–	–	–	–	–	–	–	–	–	–	–	–	–	–	–	–	–	–	–	–	–	–	2	–	
12 Tottenham Hotspur	1	–	–	1	–	–	–	–	–	–	–	–	–	–	–	–	–	–	–	–	–	–	–	–	–	–	–	2	–	
13 Wimbledon	1	–	–	1	–	–	–	–	–	–	–	–	–	–	–	–	–	–	–	–	–	–	–	–	–	–	–	2	–	
14 Coventry City	1	–	–	–	–	–	–	–	–	–	–	–	–	–	–	–	–	–	–	–	–	–	–	–	–	–	–	1	–	
15 Croatia Zagreb	–	–	–	–	–	–	–	–	–	–	–	–	–	–	–	1	–	–	–	–	–	–	–	–	–	–	–	1	–	
16 Newcastle United	1	–	–	–	–	–	–	–	–	–	–	–	–	–	–	–	–	–	–	–	–	–	–	–	–	–	–	1	–	
17 Olympique Marseille	–	–	–	–	–	–	–	–	–	–	–	–	–	–	–	1	–	–	–	–	–	–	–	–	–	–	–	1	–	
18 Palmeiras	–	–	–	–	–	–	–	–	–	–	–	–	–	–	–	–	–	–	–	–	–	–	–	–	1	–	–	1	–	
19 Rayos del Necaxa	–	–	–	–	–	–	–	–	–	–	–	–	–	–	–	–	–	–	–	–	–	–	–	–	1	–	–	1	–	
20 Real Madrid	–	–	–	–	–	–	–	–	–	–	–	–	–	–	–	1	–	–	–	–	–	–	–	–	–	–	–	1	–	
21 Sturm Graz	–	–	–	–	–	–	–	–	–	–	–	–	–	–	–	1	–	–	–	–	–	–	–	–	–	–	–	1	–	
22 Valencia	–	–	–	–	–	–	–	–	–	–	–	–	–	–	–	1	–	–	–	–	–	–	–	–	–	–	–	1	–	
23 Vasco da Gama	–	–	–	–	–	–	–	–	–	–	–	–	–	–	–	–	–	–	–	–	–	–	–	–	1	–	–	1	–	
24 Watford	1	–	–	–	–	–	–	–	–	–	–	–	–	–	–	–	–	–	–	–	–	–	–	–	–	–	–	1	–	
25 West Ham United	1	–	–	–	–	–	–	–	–	–	–	–	–	–	–	–	–	–	–	–	–	–	–	–	–	–	–	1	–	

HENRY BOYD

DEBUT (Full Appearance, 1 goal)

Wednesday 20/01/1897
FA Cup 5th Qualifying Round Replay
at Raikes Hall Gardens

Blackpool 1 Newton Heath 2

CLUB CAREER RECORD	Apps	Subs	Goals
Premiership	0		0
League Division 1	0		0
League Division 2	52		32
FA Cup	7		1
League Cup	0		0
European Cup / Champions League	0		0
European Cup-Winners' Cup	0		0
UEFA Cup / Inter-Cities' Fairs Cup	0		0
Other Matches	3		2
OVERALL TOTAL	**62**		**35**

Opponents	PREM			FLD 1			FLD 2			FAC			LC			EC/CL			ECWC			UEFA			OTHER			TOTAL		
	A	S	G	A	S	G	A	S	G	A	S	G	A	S	G	A	S	G	A	S	G	A	S	G	A	S	G	A	S	G
1 Loughborough Town	–	–	–	–	–	–	5	4		–	–		–			–			–			–			–			5	4	
2 Darwen	–	–	–	–	–	–	5	3		–			–			–			–			–			–			5	3	
3 Burton Swifts	–	–	–	–	–	–	4	6		–			–			–			–			–			–			4	6	
4 Arsenal	–	–	–	–	–	–	4	3		–			–			–			–			–			–			4	3	
5 Walsall	–	–	–	–	–	–	3	1		1			–			–			–			–			–			4	1	
6 Blackpool	–	–	–	–	–	–	2	2		1	1		–			–			–			–			–			3	3	
7 Leicester City	–	–	–	–	–	–	3	3		–			–			–			–			–			–			3	3	
8 Lincoln City	–	–	–	–	–	–	3	3		–			–			–			–			–			–			3	3	
9 Birmingham City	–	–	–	–	–	–	3	2		–			–			–			–			–			–			3	2	
10 Gainsborough Trinity	–	–	–	–	–	–	3	2		–			–			–			–			–			–			3	2	
11 Burnley	–	–	–	–	–	–	2			–			–			–			–			–			1	1		3	1	
12 Grimsby Town	–	–	–	–	–	–	3	1		–			–			–			–			–			–			3	1	
13 Manchester City	–	–	–	–	–	–	3	1		–			–			–			–			–			–			3	1	
14 Luton Town	–	–	–	–	–	–	2	1		–			–			–			–			–			–			2	1	
15 Sunderland	–	–	–	–	–	–	–			–			–			–			–			–			2	1		2	1	
16 Liverpool	–	–	–	–	–	–	–			2			–			–			–			–			–			2		
17 Newcastle United	–	–	–	–	–	–	2			–			–			–			–			–			–			2		
18 Port Vale	–	–	–	–	–	–	2			–			–			–			–			–			–			2		
19 Southampton	–	–	–	–	–	–	–			2			–			–			–			–			–			2		
20 Burton Wanderers	–	–	–	–	–	–	1			–			–			–			–			–			–			1		
21 Derby County	–	–	–	–	–	–	–			1			–			–			–			–			–			1		
22 Glossop	–	–	–	–	–	–	1			–			–			–			–			–			–			1		
23 Notts County	–	–	–	–	–	–	1			–			–			–			–			–			–			1		

WILLIAM BOYD

DEBUT (Full Appearance)

Saturday 09/02/1935
Football League Division 2
at Vetch Field

Swansea City 1 Manchester United 0

CLUB CAREER RECORD	Apps	Subs	Goals
Premiership	0		0
League Division 1	0		0
League Division 2	6		4
FA Cup	0		0
League Cup	0		0
European Cup / Champions League	0		0
European Cup-Winners' Cup	0		0
UEFA Cup / Inter-Cities' Fairs Cup	0		0
Other Matches	0		0
OVERALL TOTAL	**6**		**4**

Opponents	PREM			FLD 1			FLD 2			FAC			LC			EC/CL			ECWC			UEFA			OTHER			TOTAL		
	A	S	G	A	S	G	A	S	G	A	S	G	A	S	G	A	S	G	A	S	G	A	S	G	A	S	G	A	S	G
1 Hull City	-	-	-	-	-	-	1	-	3	-	-	-	-	-	-	-	-	-	-	-	-	-	-	-	-	-	-	1	-	3
2 Burnley	-	-	-	-	-	-	1	-	1	-	-	-	-	-	-	-	-	-	-	-	-	-	-	-	-	-	-	1	-	1
3 Newcastle United	-	-	-	-	-	-	1	-	-	-	-	-	-	-	-	-	-	-	-	-	-	-	-	-	-	-	-	1	-	-
4 Oldham Athletic	-	-	-	-	-	-	1	-	-	-	-	-	-	-	-	-	-	-	-	-	-	-	-	-	-	-	-	1	-	-
5 Swansea City	-	-	-	-	-	-	1	-	-	-	-	-	-	-	-	-	-	-	-	-	-	-	-	-	-	-	-	1	-	-
6 West Ham United	-	-	-	-	-	-	1	-	-	-	-	-	-	-	-	-	-	-	-	-	-	-	-	-	-	-	-	1	-	-

TOMMY BOYLE

DEBUT (Full Appearance)

Saturday 30/03/1929
Football League Division 1
at Baseball Ground

Derby County 6 Manchester United 1

CLUB CAREER RECORD	Apps	Subs	Goals
Premiership	0		0
League Division 1	16		6
League Division 2	0		0
FA Cup	1		0
League Cup	0		0
European Cup / Champions League	0		0
European Cup-Winners' Cup	0		0
UEFA Cup / Inter-Cities' Fairs Cup	0		0
Other Matches	0		0
OVERALL TOTAL	**17**		**6**

Opponents	PREM			FLD 1			FLD 2			FAC			LC			EC/CL			ECWC			UEFA			OTHER			TOTAL		
	A	S	G	A	S	G	A	S	G	A	S	G	A	S	G	A	S	G	A	S	G	A	S	G	A	S	G	A	S	G
1 Portsmouth	-	-	-	2	-	1	-	-	-	-	-	-	-	-	-	-	-	-	-	-	-	-	-	-	-	-	-	2	-	1
2 Derby County	-	-	-	2	-	-	-	-	-	-	-	-	-	-	-	-	-	-	-	-	-	-	-	-	-	-	-	2	-	-
3 Grimsby Town	-	-	-	2	-	-	-	-	-	-	-	-	-	-	-	-	-	-	-	-	-	-	-	-	-	-	-	2	-	-
4 Blackburn Rovers	-	-	-	1	-	2	-	-	-	-	-	-	-	-	-	-	-	-	-	-	-	-	-	-	-	-	-	1	-	2
5 Newcastle United	-	-	-	1	-	2	-	-	-	-	-	-	-	-	-	-	-	-	-	-	-	-	-	-	-	-	-	1	-	2
6 Sheffield United	-	-	-	1	-	1	-	-	-	-	-	-	-	-	-	-	-	-	-	-	-	-	-	-	-	-	-	1	-	1
7 Birmingham City	-	-	-	1	-	-	-	-	-	-	-	-	-	-	-	-	-	-	-	-	-	-	-	-	-	-	-	1	-	-
8 Bolton Wanderers	-	-	-	1	-	-	-	-	-	-	-	-	-	-	-	-	-	-	-	-	-	-	-	-	-	-	-	1	-	-
9 Burnley	-	-	-	1	-	-	-	-	-	-	-	-	-	-	-	-	-	-	-	-	-	-	-	-	-	-	-	1	-	-
10 Liverpool	-	-	-	1	-	-	-	-	-	-	-	-	-	-	-	-	-	-	-	-	-	-	-	-	-	-	-	1	-	-
11 Manchester City	-	-	-	1	-	-	-	-	-	-	-	-	-	-	-	-	-	-	-	-	-	-	-	-	-	-	-	1	-	-
12 Middlesbrough	-	-	-	1	-	-	-	-	-	-	-	-	-	-	-	-	-	-	-	-	-	-	-	-	-	-	-	1	-	-
13 Swindon Town	-	-	-	-	-	-	-	-	-	1	-	-	-	-	-	-	-	-	-	-	-	-	-	-	-	-	-	1	-	-
14 West Ham United	-	-	-	1	-	-	-	-	-	-	-	-	-	-	-	-	-	-	-	-	-	-	-	-	-	-	-	1	-	-

LEN BRADBURY

DEBUT (Full Appearance, 1 goal)

Saturday 28/01/1939
Football League Division 1
at Stamford Bridge

Chelsea 0 Manchester United 1

CLUB CAREER RECORD	Apps	Subs	Goals
Premiership	0		0
League Division 1	2		1
League Division 2	0		0
FA Cup	0		0
League Cup	0		0
European Cup / Champions League	0		0
European Cup-Winners' Cup	0		0
UEFA Cup / Inter-Cities' Fairs Cup	0		0
Other Matches	0		0
OVERALL TOTAL	**2**		**1**

Opponents	PREM			FLD 1			FLD 2			FAC			LC			EC/CL			ECWC			UEFA			OTHER			TOTAL		
	A	S	G	A	S	G	A	S	G	A	S	G	A	S	G	A	S	G	A	S	G	A	S	G	A	S	G	A	S	G
1 Chelsea	-	-	-	1	-	1	-	-	-	-	-	-	-	-	-	-	-	-	-	-	-	-	-	-	-	-	-	1	-	1
2 Charlton Athletic	-	-	-	1	-	-	-	-	-	-	-	-	-	-	-	-	-	-	-	-	-	-	-	-	-	-	-	1	-	-

WARREN BRADLEY

DEBUT (Full Appearance)

Saturday 15/11/1958
Football League Division 1
at Burnden Park

Bolton Wanderers 6 Manchester United 3

CLUB CAREER RECORD	Apps	Subs	Goals
Premiership	0		0
League Division 1	63		20
League Division 2	0		0
FA Cup	3		1
League Cup	0		0
European Cup / Champions League	0		0
European Cup-Winners' Cup	0		0
UEFA Cup / Inter-Cities' Fairs Cup	0		0
Other Matches	0		0
OVERALL TOTAL	**66**		**21**

Opponents	PREM A	S	G	FLD 1 A	S	G	FLD 2 A	S	G	FAC A	S	G	LC A	S	G	EC/CL A	S	G	ECWC A	S	G	UEFA A	S	G	OTHER A	S	G	TOTAL A	S	G
1 Birmingham City	-	-	-	5	-	1	-	-	-	-	-	-	-	-	-	-	-	-	-	-	-	-	-	-	-	-	-	5	-	1
2 Leicester City	-	-	-	4	-	2	-	-	-	-	-	-	-	-	-	-	-	-	-	-	-	-	-	-	-	-	-	4	-	2
3 Luton Town	-	-	-	4	-	1	-	-	-	-	-	-	-	-	-	-	-	-	-	-	-	-	-	-	-	-	-	4	-	1
4 Preston North End	-	-	-	4	-	1	-	-	-	-	-	-	-	-	-	-	-	-	-	-	-	-	-	-	-	-	-	4	-	1
5 Sheffield Wednesday	-	-	-	3	-	1	-	-	-	1	-	-	-	-	-	-	-	-	-	-	-	-	-	-	-	-	-	4	-	1
6 Bolton Wanderers	-	-	-	4	-	-	-	-	-	-	-	-	-	-	-	-	-	-	-	-	-	-	-	-	-	-	-	4	-	-
7 Blackburn Rovers	-	-	-	3	-	2	-	-	-	-	-	-	-	-	-	-	-	-	-	-	-	-	-	-	-	-	-	3	-	2
8 Chelsea	-	-	-	3	-	2	-	-	-	-	-	-	-	-	-	-	-	-	-	-	-	-	-	-	-	-	-	3	-	2
9 Leeds United	-	-	-	3	-	2	-	-	-	-	-	-	-	-	-	-	-	-	-	-	-	-	-	-	-	-	-	3	-	2
10 Manchester City	-	-	-	3	-	2	-	-	-	-	-	-	-	-	-	-	-	-	-	-	-	-	-	-	-	-	-	3	-	2
11 Everton	-	-	-	3	-	1	-	-	-	-	-	-	-	-	-	-	-	-	-	-	-	-	-	-	-	-	-	3	-	1
12 Tottenham Hotspur	-	-	-	3	-	1	-	-	-	-	-	-	-	-	-	-	-	-	-	-	-	-	-	-	-	-	-	3	-	1
13 West Bromwich Albion	-	-	-	3	-	1	-	-	-	-	-	-	-	-	-	-	-	-	-	-	-	-	-	-	-	-	-	3	-	1
14 Portsmouth	-	-	-	2	-	2	-	-	-	-	-	-	-	-	-	-	-	-	-	-	-	-	-	-	-	-	-	2	-	2
15 Arsenal	-	-	-	2	-	1	-	-	-	-	-	-	-	-	-	-	-	-	-	-	-	-	-	-	-	-	-	2	-	1
16 Blackpool	-	-	-	2	-	-	-	-	-	-	-	-	-	-	-	-	-	-	-	-	-	-	-	-	-	-	-	2	-	-
17 Burnley	-	-	-	2	-	-	-	-	-	-	-	-	-	-	-	-	-	-	-	-	-	-	-	-	-	-	-	2	-	-
18 Fulham	-	-	-	2	-	-	-	-	-	-	-	-	-	-	-	-	-	-	-	-	-	-	-	-	-	-	-	2	-	-
19 Newcastle United	-	-	-	2	-	-	-	-	-	-	-	-	-	-	-	-	-	-	-	-	-	-	-	-	-	-	-	2	-	-
20 Wolverhampton W.	-	-	-	2	-	-	-	-	-	-	-	-	-	-	-	-	-	-	-	-	-	-	-	-	-	-	-	2	-	-
21 Liverpool	-	-	-	-	-	-	-	-	-	1	-	1	-	-	-	-	-	-	-	-	-	-	-	-	-	-	-	1	-	1
22 Aston Villa	-	-	-	1	-	-	-	-	-	-	-	-	-	-	-	-	-	-	-	-	-	-	-	-	-	-	-	1	-	-
23 Cardiff City	-	-	-	1	-	-	-	-	-	-	-	-	-	-	-	-	-	-	-	-	-	-	-	-	-	-	-	1	-	-
24 Ipswich Town	-	-	-	1	-	-	-	-	-	-	-	-	-	-	-	-	-	-	-	-	-	-	-	-	-	-	-	1	-	-
25 Norwich City	-	-	-	-	-	-	-	-	-	1	-	-	-	-	-	-	-	-	-	-	-	-	-	-	-	-	-	1	-	-
26 West Ham United	-	-	-	1	-	-	-	-	-	-	-	-	-	-	-	-	-	-	-	-	-	-	-	-	-	-	-	1	-	-

HAROLD BRATT

DEBUT (Full Appearance)

Wednesday 02/11/1960
League Cup 2nd Round
at Valley Parade

Bradford City 2 Manchester United 1

CLUB CAREER RECORD	Apps	Subs	Goals
Premiership	0		0
League Division 1	0		0
League Division 2	0		0
FA Cup	0		0
League Cup	1		0
European Cup / Champions League	0		0
European Cup-Winners' Cup	0		0
UEFA Cup / Inter-Cities' Fairs Cup	0		0
Other Matches	0		0
OVERALL TOTAL	**1**		**0**

Opponents	PREM A	S	G	FLD 1 A	S	G	FLD 2 A	S	G	FAC A	S	G	LC A	S	G	EC/CL A	S	G	ECWC A	S	G	UEFA A	S	G	OTHER A	S	G	TOTAL A	S	G
1 Bradford City	-	-	-	-	-	-	-	-	-	-	-	-	1	-	-	-	-	-	-	-	-	-	-	-	-	-	-	1	-	-

ALAN BRAZIL

DEBUT (Full Appearance)

Saturday 25/08/1984
Football League Division 1
at Old Trafford

Manchester United 1 Watford 1

CLUB CAREER RECORD	Apps	Subs	Goals
Premiership	0		0
League Division 1	18	(13)	8
League Division 2	0		0
FA Cup	0	(1)	0
League Cup	4	(3)	3
European Cup / Champions League	0		0
European Cup-Winners' Cup	0		0
UEFA Cup / Inter-Cities' Fairs Cup	2		1
Other Matches	0		0
OVERALL TOTAL	**24**	**(17)**	**12**

Opponents	PREM A	S	G	FLD 1 A	S	G	FLD 2 A	S	G	FAC A	S	G	LC A	S	G	EC/CL A	S	G	ECWC A	S	G	UEFA A	S	G	OTHER A	S	G	TOTAL A	S	G
1 Everton	-	-	-	2	-	-	-	-	-	-	-	-	1	-	1	-	-	-	-	-	-	-	-	-	-	-	-	3	-	1
2 Watford	-	-	-	2	(1)	1	-	-	-	-	-	-	-	-	-	-	-	-	-	-	-	-	-	-	-	-	-	2	(1)	1
3 Nottingham Forest	-	-	-	2	(1)	-	-	-	-	-	-	-	-	-	-	-	-	-	-	-	-	-	-	-	-	-	-	2	(1)	-
4 Queens Park Rangers	-	-	-	2	-	3	-	-	-	-	-	-	-	-	-	-	-	-	-	-	-	-	-	-	-	-	-	2	-	3
5 West Bromwich Albion	-	-	-	2	-	2	-	-	-	-	-	-	-	-	-	-	-	-	-	-	-	-	-	-	-	-	-	2	-	2
6 Burnley	-	-	-	-	-	-	-	-	-	-	-	-	1	(1)	2	-	-	-	-	-	-	-	-	-	-	-	-	1	(1)	2

continued../

ALAN BRAZIL (continued)

Opponents	PREM A S G	FLD 1 A S G	FLD 2 A S G	FAC A S G	LC A S G	EC/CL A S G	ECWC A S G	UEFA A S G	OTHER A S G	TOTAL A S G
7 Leicester City	– –	1 (1) 1	–	–	–	–	–	–	–	1 (1) 1
8 West Ham United	– –	1 _ 1	–	–	– (1) –	–	–	–	–	1 (1) 1
9 Aston Villa	– –	1 (1) –	–	–	–	–	–	–	–	1 (1) –
10 Crystal Palace	– –	–	–	–	1 (1) –	–	–	–	–	1 (1) –
11 Ipswich Town	– –	1 (1) –	–	–	–	–	–	–	–	1 (1) –
12 Sheffield Wednesday	– –	1 (1) –	–	–	–	–	–	–	–	1 (1) –
13 Southampton	– –	1 (1) –	–	–	–	–	–	–	–	1 (1) –
14 Coventry City	– –	– (1) –	–	– (1) –	–	–	–	–	–	– (2) –
15 Raba Vasas	– –	–	–	–	–	–	–	1 _ 1	–	1 _ 1
16 Liverpool	– –	–	–	–	1	–	–	–	–	1
17 PSV Eindhoven	– –	–	–	–	–	–	–	1	–	1
18 Sunderland	– –	1	–	–	–	–	–	–	–	1
19 Tottenham Hotspur	– –	1	–	–	–	–	–	–	–	1
20 Birmingham City	– –	– (1) –	–	–	–	–	–	–	–	– (1) –
21 Manchester City	– –	– (1) –	–	–	–	–	–	–	–	– (1) –
22 Newcastle United	– –	– (1) –	–	–	–	–	–	–	–	– (1) –
23 Oxford United	– –	– (1) –	–	–	–	–	–	–	–	– (1) –
24 Stoke City	– –	– (1) –	–	–	–	–	–	–	–	– (1) –

DEREK BRAZIL

DEBUT (Substitute Appearance)

Wednesday 10/05/1989
Football League Division 1
at Old Trafford

Manchester United 1 Everton 2

CLUB CAREER RECORD	Apps	Subs	Goals
Premiership	0		0
League Division 1	0	(2)	0
League Division 2	0		0
FA Cup	0		0
League Cup	0		0
European Cup / Champions League	0		0
European Cup–Winners' Cup	0		0
UEFA Cup / Inter–Cities' Fairs Cup	0		0
Other Matches	0		0
OVERALL TOTAL	0	(2)	0

Opponents	PREM A S G	FLD 1 A S G	FLD 2 A S G	FAC A S G	LC A S G	EC/CL A S G	ECWC A S G	UEFA A S G	OTHER A S G	TOTAL A S G
1 Everton	– –	– (1) –	–	–	–	–	–	–	–	– (1) –
2 Millwall	– –	– (1) –	–	–	–	–	–	–	–	– (1) –

JACK BREEDON

DEBUT (Full Appearance)

Saturday 31/08/1935
Football League Division 2
at Home Park

Plymouth Argyle 3 Manchester United 1

CLUB CAREER RECORD	Apps	Subs	Goals
Premiership	0		0
League Division 1	23		0
League Division 2	12		0
FA Cup	0		0
League Cup	0		0
European Cup / Champions League	0		0
European Cup–Winners' Cup	0		0
UEFA Cup / Inter–Cities' Fairs Cup	0		0
Other Matches	0		0
OVERALL TOTAL	35		0

Opponents	PREM A S G	FLD 1 A S G	FLD 2 A S G	FAC A S G	LC A S G	EC/CL A S G	ECWC A S G	UEFA A S G	OTHER A S G	TOTAL A S G
1 Arsenal	– –	2 –	–	–	–	–	–	–	–	2 –
2 Bolton Wanderers	– –	2 –	–	–	–	–	–	–	–	2 –
3 Bradford Park Avenue	– –	–	2 –	–	–	–	–	–	–	2 –
4 Brentford	– –	2 –	–	–	–	–	–	–	–	2 –
5 Derby County	– –	2 –	–	–	–	–	–	–	–	2 –
6 Liverpool	– –	2 –	–	–	–	–	–	–	–	2 –
7 Nottingham Forest	– –	–	2 –	–	–	–	–	–	–	2 –
8 Aston Villa	– –	–	1 –	–	–	–	–	–	–	1 –
9 Birmingham City	– –	1 –	–	–	–	–	–	–	–	1 –
10 Blackpool	– –	1 –	–	–	–	–	–	–	–	1 –
11 Charlton Athletic	– –	1 –	–	–	–	–	–	–	–	1 –
12 Chelsea	– –	1 –	–	–	–	–	–	–	–	1 –
13 Chesterfield	– –	–	1 –	–	–	–	–	–	–	1 –
14 Everton	– –	1 –	–	–	–	–	–	–	–	1 –
15 Grimsby Town	– –	1 –	–	–	–	–	–	–	–	1 –
16 Huddersfield Town	– –	1 –	–	–	–	–	–	–	–	1 –
17 Middlesbrough	– –	1 –	–	–	–	–	–	–	–	1 –
18 Newcastle United	– –	–	1 –	–	–	–	–	–	–	1 –
19 Norwich City	– –	1 –	–	–	–	–	–	–	–	1 –
20 Plymouth Argyle	– –	–	1 –	–	–	–	–	–	–	1 –
21 Portsmouth	– –	1 –	–	–	–	–	–	–	–	1 –
22 Preston North End	– –	1 –	–	–	–	–	–	–	–	1 –

continued../

JACK BREEDON (continued)

Opponents	PREM A	S	G	FLD 1 A	S	G	FLD 2 A	S	G	FAC A	S	G	LC A	S	G	EC/CL A	S	G	ECWC A	S	G	UEFA A	S	G	OTHER A	S	G	TOTAL A	S	G
23 Sheffield Wednesday	-	-	-							1																		1		-
24 Stoke City	-	-		1																								1		-
25 Sunderland	-	-					1																					1		-
26 Swansea City	-	-								1																		1		-
27 Tottenham Hotspur	-	-	-							1																		1		-
28 Wolverhampton W.	-	-		1																								1		-

TOMMY BREEN

DEBUT (Full Appearance)

Saturday 28/11/1936
Football League Division 1
at Elland Road

Leeds United 2 Manchester United 1

CLUB CAREER RECORD	Apps	Subs	Goals
Premiership	0		0
League Division 1	32		0
League Division 2	33		0
FA Cup	6		0
League Cup	0		0
European Cup / Champions League	0		0
European Cup–Winners' Cup	0		0
UEFA Cup / Inter–Cities' Fairs Cup	0		0
Other Matches	0		0
OVERALL TOTAL	**71**		**0**

Opponents	PREM A	S	G	FLD 1 A	S	G	FLD 2 A	S	G	FAC A	S	G	LC A	S	G	EC/CL A	S	G	ECWC A	S	G	UEFA A	S	G	OTHER A	S	G	TOTAL A	S	G
1 Barnsley	-	-					2			2																		4		-
2 Aston Villa	-	-		2			1																					3		-
3 Everton	-	-		3																								3		-
4 Middlesbrough	-	-		3																								3		-
5 Arsenal	-	-		1						1																		2		-
6 Birmingham City	-	-		2																								2		-
7 Blackburn Rovers	-	-								2																		2		-
8 Bolton Wanderers	-	-		2																								2		-
9 Brentford	-	-		1						1																		2		-
10 Burnley	-	-					2																					2		-
11 Bury	-	-					2																					2		-
12 Coventry City	-	-					2																					2		-
13 Fulham	-	-					2																					2		-
14 Leeds United	-	-		2																								2		-
15 Luton Town	-	-					2																					2		-
16 Plymouth Argyle	-	-					2																					2		-
17 Sheffield United	-	-					2																					2		-
18 Sheffield Wednesday	-	-		1			1																					2		-
19 Southampton	-	-					2																					2		-
20 Stockport County	-	-					2																					2		-
21 Sunderland	-	-		2																								2		-
22 Tottenham Hotspur	-	-					2																					2		-
23 West Bromwich Albion	-	-		2																								2		-
24 West Ham United	-	-					2																					2		-
25 Wolverhampton W.	-	-		2																								2		-
26 Bradford Park Avenue	-	-								1																		1		-
27 Charlton Athletic	-	-		1																								1		-
28 Chelsea	-	-		1																								1		-
29 Chesterfield	-	-								1																		1		-
30 Grimsby Town	-	-		1																								1		-
31 Huddersfield Town	-	-		1																								1		-
32 Liverpool	-	-		1																								1		-
33 Manchester City	-	-		1																								1		-
34 Newcastle United	-	-								1																		1		-
35 Norwich City	-	-								1																		1		-
36 Portsmouth	-	-		1																								1		-
37 Preston North End	-	-		1																								1		-
38 Reading	-	-								1																		1		-
39 Stoke City	-	-		1																								1		-
40 Swansea City	-	-					1																					1		-
41 Yeovil Town	-	-								1																		1		-

SHAY BRENNAN

DEBUT (Full Appearance, 2 goals)

Wednesday 19/02/1958
FA Cup 5th Round
at Old Trafford

Manchester United 3 Sheffield Wednesday 0

CLUB CAREER RECORD	Apps	Subs	Goals
Premiership	0		0
League Division 1	291	(1)	3
League Division 2	0		0
FA Cup	36		3
League Cup	4		0
European Cup / Champions League	11		0
European Cup-Winners' Cup	2		0
UEFA Cup / Inter-Cities' Fairs Cup	11		0
Other Matches	3		0
OVERALL TOTAL	**358**	**(1)**	**6**

Opponents	PREM A	PREM S	PREM G	FLD1 A	FLD1 S	FLD1 G	FLD2 A	FLD2 S	FLD2 G	FAC A	FAC S	FAC G	LC A	LC S	LC G	EC/CL A	EC/CL S	EC/CL G	ECWC A	ECWC S	ECWC G	UEFA A	UEFA S	UEFA G	OTHER A	OTHER S	OTHER G	TOTAL A	TOTAL S	TOTAL G
1 Sheffield Wednesday	-	-	-	13	-	-	-	-	-	6	-	2	-	-	-	-	-	-	-	-	-	-	-	-	-	-	-	19	-	2
2 Everton	-	-	-	16	-	-	-	-	-	1	-	-	-	-	-	-	-	-	-	-	-	2	-	-	-	-	-	19	-	-
3 Nottingham Forest	-	-	-	16	-	2	-	-	-	-	-	-	-	-	-	-	-	-	-	-	-	-	-	-	-	-	-	16	-	2
4 West Bromwich Albion	-	-	-	15	-	-	-	-	-	-	-	-	-	-	-	-	-	-	-	-	-	-	-	-	-	-	-	15	-	-
5 Burnley	-	-	-	13	-	1	-	-	-	1	-	-	-	-	-	-	-	-	-	-	-	-	-	-	-	-	-	14	-	1
6 Aston Villa	-	-	-	13	-	-	-	-	-	1	-	-	-	-	-	-	-	-	-	-	-	-	-	-	-	-	-	14	-	-
7 Tottenham Hotspur	-	-	-	13	-	-	-	-	-	-	-	-	-	-	-	-	-	-	-	-	-	1	-	-	-	-	-	14	-	-
8 West Ham United	-	-	-	13	-	-	-	-	-	1	-	-	-	-	-	-	-	-	-	-	-	-	-	-	-	-	-	14	-	-
9 Fulham	-	-	-	12	-	-	-	-	-	1	-	1	-	-	-	-	-	-	-	-	-	-	-	-	-	-	-	13	-	1
10 Blackpool	-	-	-	12	-	-	-	-	-	-	-	-	1	-	-	-	-	-	-	-	-	-	-	-	-	-	-	13	-	-
11 Chelsea	-	-	-	12	-	-	-	-	-	1	-	-	-	-	-	-	-	-	-	-	-	-	-	-	-	-	-	13	-	-
12 Leicester City	-	-	-	13	-	-	-	-	-	-	-	-	-	-	-	-	-	-	-	-	-	-	-	-	-	-	-	13	-	-
13 Wolverhampton W.	-	-	-	11	-	-	-	-	-	2	-	-	-	-	-	-	-	-	-	-	-	-	-	-	-	-	-	13	-	-
14 Arsenal	-	-	-	11	-	-	-	-	-	1	-	-	-	-	-	-	-	-	-	-	-	-	-	-	-	-	-	12	-	-
15 Blackburn Rovers	-	-	-	12	-	-	-	-	-	-	-	-	-	-	-	-	-	-	-	-	-	-	-	-	-	-	-	12	-	-
16 Liverpool	-	-	-	9	-	-	-	-	-	1	-	-	-	-	-	-	-	-	-	-	-	1	-	-	-	-	-	11	-	-
17 Manchester City	-	-	-	11	-	-	-	-	-	-	-	-	-	-	-	-	-	-	-	-	-	-	-	-	-	-	-	11	-	-
18 Stoke City	-	-	-	9	-	-	-	-	-	2	-	-	-	-	-	-	-	-	-	-	-	-	-	-	-	-	-	11	-	-
19 Leeds United	-	-	-	8	-	-	-	-	-	2	-	-	-	-	-	-	-	-	-	-	-	-	-	-	-	-	-	10	-	-
20 Birmingham City	-	-	-	9	-	-	-	-	-	-	-	-	-	-	-	-	-	-	-	-	-	-	-	-	-	-	-	9	-	-
21 Bolton Wanderers	-	-	-	8	-	-	-	-	-	1	-	-	-	-	-	-	-	-	-	-	-	-	-	-	-	-	-	9	-	-
22 Newcastle United	-	-	-	9	-	-	-	-	-	-	-	-	-	-	-	-	-	-	-	-	-	-	-	-	-	-	-	9	-	-
23 Sheffield United	-	-	-	9	-	-	-	-	-	-	-	-	-	-	-	-	-	-	-	-	-	-	-	-	-	-	-	9	-	-
24 Sunderland	-	-	-	6	-	-	-	-	-	3	-	-	-	-	-	-	-	-	-	-	-	-	-	-	-	-	-	9	-	-
25 Preston North End	-	-	-	3	-	-	-	-	-	4	-	-	-	-	-	-	-	-	-	-	-	-	-	-	-	-	-	7	-	-
26 Ipswich Town	-	-	-	5	(1)	-	-	-	-	1	-	-	-	-	-	-	-	-	-	-	-	-	-	-	-	-	-	6	(1)	-
27 Cardiff City	-	-	-	4	-	-	-	-	-	-	-	-	-	-	-	-	-	-	-	-	-	-	-	-	-	-	-	4	-	-
28 Coventry City	-	-	-	2	-	-	-	-	-	1	-	-	-	-	-	-	-	-	-	-	-	-	-	-	-	-	-	3	-	-
29 Ferencvaros	-	-	-	-	-	-	-	-	-	-	-	-	-	-	-	-	-	-	-	-	-	3	-	-	-	-	-	3	-	-
30 AC Milan	-	-	-	-	-	-	-	-	-	-	-	-	-	-	-	2	-	-	-	-	-	-	-	-	-	-	-	2	-	-
31 Benfica	-	-	-	-	-	-	-	-	-	-	-	-	-	-	-	2	-	-	-	-	-	-	-	-	-	-	-	2	-	-
32 Borussia Dortmund	-	-	-	-	-	-	-	-	-	-	-	-	-	-	-	-	-	-	-	-	-	2	-	-	-	-	-	2	-	-
33 Derby County	-	-	-	-	-	-	-	-	-	1	-	-	1	-	-	-	-	-	-	-	-	-	-	-	-	-	-	2	-	-
34 Djurgardens	-	-	-	-	-	-	-	-	-	-	-	-	-	-	-	-	-	-	-	-	-	2	-	-	-	-	-	2	-	-
35 HJK Helsinki	-	-	-	-	-	-	-	-	-	-	-	-	-	-	-	2	-	-	-	-	-	-	-	-	-	-	-	2	-	-
36 Partizan Belgrade	-	-	-	-	-	-	-	-	-	-	-	-	-	-	-	2	-	-	-	-	-	-	-	-	-	-	-	2	-	-
37 Sporting Lisbon	-	-	-	-	-	-	-	-	-	-	-	-	-	-	-	-	-	-	2	-	-	-	-	-	-	-	-	2	-	-
38 Strasbourg	-	-	-	-	-	-	-	-	-	-	-	-	-	-	-	-	-	-	-	-	-	2	-	-	-	-	-	2	-	-
39 Anderlecht	-	-	-	-	-	-	-	-	-	-	-	-	-	-	-	1	-	-	-	-	-	-	-	-	-	-	-	1	-	-
40 Barnsley	-	-	-	-	-	-	-	-	-	1	-	-	-	-	-	-	-	-	-	-	-	-	-	-	-	-	-	1	-	-
41 Bradford City	-	-	-	-	-	-	-	-	-	-	-	-	1	-	-	-	-	-	-	-	-	-	-	-	-	-	-	1	-	-
42 Chester City	-	-	-	-	-	-	-	-	-	1	-	-	-	-	-	-	-	-	-	-	-	-	-	-	-	-	-	1	-	-
43 Estudiantes de la Plata	-	-	-	-	-	-	-	-	-	-	-	-	-	-	-	-	-	-	-	-	-	-	-	-	1	-	-	1	-	-
44 Exeter City	-	-	-	-	-	-	-	-	-	-	-	-	1	-	-	-	-	-	-	-	-	-	-	-	-	-	-	1	-	-
45 Huddersfield Town	-	-	-	-	-	-	-	-	-	1	-	-	-	-	-	-	-	-	-	-	-	-	-	-	-	-	-	1	-	-
46 Leyton Orient	-	-	-	1	-	-	-	-	-	-	-	-	-	-	-	-	-	-	-	-	-	-	-	-	-	-	-	1	-	-
47 Luton Town	-	-	-	1	-	-	-	-	-	-	-	-	-	-	-	-	-	-	-	-	-	-	-	-	-	-	-	1	-	-
48 Middlesbrough	-	-	-	-	-	-	-	-	-	1	-	-	-	-	-	-	-	-	-	-	-	-	-	-	-	-	-	1	-	-
49 Queens Park Rangers	-	-	-	1	-	-	-	-	-	-	-	-	-	-	-	-	-	-	-	-	-	-	-	-	-	-	-	1	-	-
50 Real Madrid	-	-	-	-	-	-	-	-	-	-	-	-	-	-	-	1	-	-	-	-	-	-	-	-	-	-	-	1	-	-
51 Rotherham United	-	-	-	-	-	-	-	-	-	1	-	-	-	-	-	-	-	-	-	-	-	-	-	-	-	-	-	1	-	-
52 Sarajevo	-	-	-	-	-	-	-	-	-	-	-	-	-	-	-	1	-	-	-	-	-	-	-	-	-	-	-	1	-	-
53 Southampton	-	-	-	1	-	-	-	-	-	-	-	-	-	-	-	-	-	-	-	-	-	-	-	-	-	-	-	1	-	-

FRANK BRETT

DEBUT (Full Appearance)

Saturday 27/08/1921
Football League Division 1
at Goodison Park

Everton 5 Manchester United 0

CLUB CAREER RECORD	Apps	Subs	Goals
Premiership	0		0
League Division 1	10		0
League Division 2	0		0
FA Cup	0		0
League Cup	0		0
European Cup / Champions League	0		0
European Cup-Winners' Cup	0		0
UEFA Cup / Inter-Cities' Fairs Cup	0		0
Other Matches	0		0
OVERALL TOTAL	**10**		**0**

Opponents	PREM A S G	FLD 1 A S G	FLD 2 A S G	FAC A S G	LC A S G	EC/CL A S G	ECWC A S G	UEFA A S G	OTHER A S G	TOTAL A S G
1 Chelsea	– –	2	–	–	–	–	–	–	–	2 –
2 Everton	– –	2	–	–	–	–	–	–	–	2 –
3 West Bromwich Albion	– –	2	–	–	–	–	–	–	–	2 –
4 Arsenal	– –	1	–	–	–	–	–	–	–	1 –
5 Bradford City	– –	1	–	–	–	–	–	–	–	1 –
6 Manchester City	– –	1	–	–	–	–	–	–	–	1 –
7 Preston North End	– –	1	–	–	–	–	–	–	–	1 –

RONNIE BRIGGS

DEBUT (Full Appearance)

Saturday 21/01/1961
Football League Division 1
at Filbert Street

Leicester City 6 Manchester United 0

CLUB CAREER RECORD	Apps	Subs	Goals
Premiership	0		0
League Division 1	9		0
League Division 2	0		0
FA Cup	2		0
League Cup	0		0
European Cup / Champions League	0		0
European Cup-Winners' Cup	0		0
UEFA Cup / Inter-Cities' Fairs Cup	0		0
Other Matches	0		0
OVERALL TOTAL	**11**		**0**

Opponents	PREM A S G	FLD 1 A S G	FLD 2 A S G	FAC A S G	LC A S G	EC/CL A S G	ECWC A S G	UEFA A S G	OTHER A S G	TOTAL A S G
1 Sheffield Wednesday	– –	–	–	2	–	–	–	–	–	2 –
2 Arsenal	– –	1	–	–	–	–	–	–	–	1 –
3 Birmingham City	– –	1	–	–	–	–	–	–	–	1 –
4 Bolton Wanderers	– –	1	–	–	–	–	–	–	–	1 –
5 Burnley	– –	1	–	–	–	–	–	–	–	1 –
6 Ipswich Town	– –	1	–	–	–	–	–	–	–	1 –
7 Leicester City	– –	1	–	–	–	–	–	–	–	1 –
8 Nottingham Forest	– –	1	–	–	–	–	–	–	–	1 –
9 West Bromwich Albion	– –	1	–	–	–	–	–	–	–	1 –
10 Wolverhampton W.	– –	1	–	–	–	–	–	–	–	1 –

WILLIAM BROOKS

DEBUT (Full Appearance, 2 goals)

Saturday 22/10/1898
Football League Division 2
at Bank Street

Newton Heath 6 Loughborough Town 1

CLUB CAREER RECORD	Apps	Subs	Goals
Premiership	0		0
League Division 1	0		0
League Division 2	3		3
FA Cup	0		0
League Cup	0		0
European Cup / Champions League	0		0
European Cup-Winners' Cup	0		0
UEFA Cup / Inter-Cities' Fairs Cup	0		0
Other Matches	0		0
OVERALL TOTAL	**3**		**3**

Opponents	PREM A S G	FLD 1 A S G	FLD 2 A S G	FAC A S G	LC A S G	EC/CL A S G	ECWC A S G	UEFA A S G	OTHER A S G	TOTAL A S G
1 Loughborough Town	– –	– –	1 2	–	–	–	–	–	–	1 2
2 Grimsby Town	– –	– –	1 1	–	–	–	–	–	–	1 1
3 Manchester City	– –	– –	1 –	–	–	–	–	–	–	1 –

ALBERT BROOME

DEBUT (Full Appearance)

Saturday 28/04/1923
Football League Division 2
at Oakwell

Barnsley 2 Manchester United 2

CLUB CAREER RECORD	Apps	Subs	Goals
Premiership	0		0
League Division 1	0		0
League Division 2	1		0
FA Cup	0		0
League Cup	0		0
European Cup / Champions League	0		0
European Cup-Winners' Cup	0		0
UEFA Cup / Inter-Cities' Fairs Cup	0		0
Other Matches	0		0
OVERALL TOTAL	**1**		**0**

Opponents	PREM A S G	FLD 1 A S G	FLD 2 A S G	FAC A S G	LC A S G	EC/CL A S G	ECWC A S G	UEFA A S G	OTHER A S G	TOTAL A S G
1 Barnsley	– –	– –	1 –	– –	–	–	–	–	–	1 –

HERBERT BROOMFIELD

DEBUT (Full Appearance)

Saturday 21/03/1908
Football League Division 1
at Manor Field

Arsenal 1 Manchester United 0

CLUB CAREER RECORD	Apps	Subs	Goals
Premiership	0		0
League Division 1	9		0
League Division 2	0		0
FA Cup	0		0
League Cup	0		0
European Cup / Champions League	0		0
European Cup-Winners' Cup	0		0
UEFA Cup / Inter-Cities' Fairs Cup	0		0
Other Matches	0		0
OVERALL TOTAL	**9**		**0**

Opponents	PREM A S G	FLD 1 A S G	FLD 2 A S G	FAC A S G	LC A S G	EC/CL A S G	ECWC A S G	UEFA A S G	OTHER A S G	TOTAL A S G
1 Arsenal	– – 1	–	–	–	–	–	–	–	–	1 –
2 Aston Villa	– – 1	–	–	–	–	–	–	–	–	1 –
3 Bolton Wanderers	– – 1	–	–	–	–	–	–	–	–	1 –
4 Bristol City	– – 1	–	–	–	–	–	–	–	–	1 –
5 Everton	– – 1	–	–	–	–	–	–	–	–	1 –
6 Manchester City	– – 1	–	–	–	–	–	–	–	–	1 –
7 Nottingham Forest	– – 1	–	–	–	–	–	–	–	–	1 –
8 Notts County	– – 1	–	–	–	–	–	–	–	–	1 –
9 Sheffield Wednesday	– – 1	–	–	–	–	–	–	–	–	1 –

JAMES BROWN (1932-34)

DEBUT (Full Appearance, 1 goal)

Saturday 17/09/1932
Football League Division 2
at Old Trafford

Manchester United 1 Grimsby Town 1

CLUB CAREER RECORD	Apps	Subs	Goals
Premiership	0		0
League Division 1	0		0
League Division 2	40		17
FA Cup	1		0
League Cup	0		0
European Cup / Champions League	0		0
European Cup-Winners' Cup	0		0
UEFA Cup / Inter-Cities' Fairs Cup	0		0
Other Matches	0		0
OVERALL TOTAL	**41**		**17**

Opponents	PREM A S G	FLD 1 A S G	FLD 2 A S G	FAC A S G	LC A S G	EC/CL A S G	ECWC A S G	UEFA A S G	OTHER A S G	TOTAL A S G
1 Bradford City	– –	– –	4 1	–	–	–	–	–	–	4 1
2 Port Vale	– –	– –	3 3	–	–	–	–	–	–	3 3
3 Lincoln City	– –	– –	3 1	–	–	–	–	–	–	3 1
4 Swansea City	– –	– –	3 1	–	–	–	–	–	–	3 1
5 Bradford Park Avenue	– –	– –	3 –	–	–	–	–	–	–	3 –
6 Notts County	– –	– –	3 –	–	–	–	–	–	–	3 –
7 Burnley	– –	– –	2 2	–	–	–	–	–	–	2 2
8 Millwall	– –	– –	2 2	–	–	–	–	–	–	2 2
9 Grimsby Town	– –	– –	2 1	–	–	–	–	–	–	2 1
10 Nottingham Forest	– –	– –	2 1	–	–	–	–	–	–	2 1
11 Chesterfield	– –	– –	2 –	–	–	–	–	–	–	2 –
12 Oldham Athletic	– –	– –	2 –	–	–	–	–	–	–	2 –
13 Preston North End	– –	– –	2 –	–	–	–	–	–	–	2 –
14 West Ham United	– –	– –	2 –	–	–	–	–	–	–	2 –
15 Brentford	– –	– –	1 2	–	–	–	–	–	–	1 2
16 Blackpool	– –	– –	1 1	–	–	–	–	–	–	1 1
17 Bury	– –	– –	1 1	–	–	–	–	–	–	1 1
18 Fulham	– –	– –	1 1	–	–	–	–	–	–	1 1
19 Portsmouth	– –	– –	– –	1	–	–	–	–	–	1 –
20 Tottenham Hotspur	– –	– –	1 –	–	–	–	–	–	–	1 –

JIM BROWN (1892-93)

DEBUT (Full Appearance)

Saturday 03/09/1892
Football League Division 1
at Ewood Park

Blackburn Rovers 4 Newton Heath 3

CLUB CAREER RECORD	Apps	Subs	Goals
Premiership	0		0
League Division 1	7		0
League Division 2	0		0
FA Cup	0		0
League Cup	0		0
European Cup / Champions League	0		0
European Cup-Winners' Cup	0		0
UEFA Cup / Inter-Cities' Fairs Cup	0		0
Other Matches	0		0
OVERALL TOTAL	7		0

Opponents	PREM			FLD 1			FLD 2			FAC			LC			EC/CL			ECWC			UEFA			OTHER			TOTAL		
	A	S	G	A	S	G	A	S	G	A	S	G	A	S	G	A	S	G	A	S	G	A	S	G	A	S	G	A	S	G
1 Burnley	-	-	-	2	-	-	-	-	-	-	-	-	-	-	-	-	-	-	-	-	-	-	-	-	-	-	-	2	-	-
2 West Bromwich Albion	-	-	-	2	-	-	-	-	-	-	-	-	-	-	-	-	-	-	-	-	-	-	-	-	-	-	-	2	-	-
3 Blackburn Rovers	-	-	-	1	-	-	-	-	-	-	-	-	-	-	-	-	-	-	-	-	-	-	-	-	-	-	-	1	-	-
4 Everton	-	-	-	1	-	-	-	-	-	-	-	-	-	-	-	-	-	-	-	-	-	-	-	-	-	-	-	1	-	-
5 Notts County	-	-	-	1	-	-	-	-	-	-	-	-	-	-	-	-	-	-	-	-	-	-	-	-	-	-	-	1	-	-

JIMMY BROWN (1935-39)

DEBUT (Full Appearance)

Saturday 31/08/1935
Football League Division 2
at Home Park

Plymouth Argyle 3 Manchester United 1

CLUB CAREER RECORD	Apps	Subs	Goals
Premiership	0		0
League Division 1	34		0
League Division 2	68		1
FA Cup	8		0
League Cup	0		0
European Cup / Champions League	0		0
European Cup-Winners' Cup	0		0
UEFA Cup / Inter-Cities' Fairs Cup	0		0
Other Matches	0		0
OVERALL TOTAL	110		1

Opponents	PREM			FLD 1			FLD 2			FAC			LC			EC/CL			ECWC			UEFA			OTHER			TOTAL		
	A	S	G	A	S	G	A	S	G	A	S	G	A	S	G	A	S	G	A	S	G	A	S	G	A	S	G	A	S	G
1 Sheffield Wednesday	-	-	-	2	-	-	2	-	1	-	-	-	-	-	-	-	-	-	-	-	-	-	-	-	-	-	-	4	-	1
2 Barnsley	-	-	-	-	-	-	3	-	-	1	-	-	-	-	-	-	-	-	-	-	-	-	-	-	-	-	-	4	-	-
3 Burnley	-	-	-	-	-	-	4	-	-	-	-	-	-	-	-	-	-	-	-	-	-	-	-	-	-	-	-	4	-	-
4 Bury	-	-	-	-	-	-	4	-	-	-	-	-	-	-	-	-	-	-	-	-	-	-	-	-	-	-	-	4	-	-
5 Fulham	-	-	-	-	-	-	4	-	-	-	-	-	-	-	-	-	-	-	-	-	-	-	-	-	-	-	-	4	-	-
6 Leicester City	-	-	-	2	-	-	2	-	-	-	-	-	-	-	-	-	-	-	-	-	-	-	-	-	-	-	-	4	-	-
7 Norwich City	-	-	-	-	-	-	4	-	-	-	-	-	-	-	-	-	-	-	-	-	-	-	-	-	-	-	-	4	-	-
8 Plymouth Argyle	-	-	-	-	-	-	4	-	-	-	-	-	-	-	-	-	-	-	-	-	-	-	-	-	-	-	-	4	-	-
9 Sheffield United	-	-	-	-	-	-	4	-	-	-	-	-	-	-	-	-	-	-	-	-	-	-	-	-	-	-	-	4	-	-
10 Southampton	-	-	-	-	-	-	4	-	-	-	-	-	-	-	-	-	-	-	-	-	-	-	-	-	-	-	-	4	-	-
11 Tottenham Hotspur	-	-	-	-	-	-	4	-	-	-	-	-	-	-	-	-	-	-	-	-	-	-	-	-	-	-	-	4	-	-
12 Bradford Park Avenue	-	-	-	-	-	-	3	-	-	-	-	-	-	-	-	-	-	-	-	-	-	-	-	-	-	-	-	3	-	-
13 Charlton Athletic	-	-	-	1	-	-	2	-	-	-	-	-	-	-	-	-	-	-	-	-	-	-	-	-	-	-	-	3	-	-
14 Stoke City	-	-	-	1	-	-	-	-	-	2	-	-	-	-	-	-	-	-	-	-	-	-	-	-	-	-	-	3	-	-
15 West Ham United	-	-	-	-	-	-	3	-	-	-	-	-	-	-	-	-	-	-	-	-	-	-	-	-	-	-	-	3	-	-
16 Arsenal	-	-	-	1	-	-	-	-	-	1	-	-	-	-	-	-	-	-	-	-	-	-	-	-	-	-	-	2	-	-
17 Aston Villa	-	-	-	-	-	-	2	-	-	-	-	-	-	-	-	-	-	-	-	-	-	-	-	-	-	-	-	2	-	-
18 Blackburn Rovers	-	-	-	-	-	-	2	-	-	-	-	-	-	-	-	-	-	-	-	-	-	-	-	-	-	-	-	2	-	-
19 Bolton Wanderers	-	-	-	2	-	-	-	-	-	-	-	-	-	-	-	-	-	-	-	-	-	-	-	-	-	-	-	2	-	-
20 Bradford City	-	-	-	-	-	-	2	-	-	-	-	-	-	-	-	-	-	-	-	-	-	-	-	-	-	-	-	2	-	-
21 Brentford	-	-	-	1	-	-	-	-	-	1	-	-	-	-	-	-	-	-	-	-	-	-	-	-	-	-	-	2	-	-
22 Chesterfield	-	-	-	-	-	-	2	-	-	-	-	-	-	-	-	-	-	-	-	-	-	-	-	-	-	-	-	2	-	-
23 Derby County	-	-	-	2	-	-	-	-	-	-	-	-	-	-	-	-	-	-	-	-	-	-	-	-	-	-	-	2	-	-
24 Everton	-	-	-	2	-	-	-	-	-	-	-	-	-	-	-	-	-	-	-	-	-	-	-	-	-	-	-	2	-	-
25 Grimsby Town	-	-	-	2	-	-	-	-	-	-	-	-	-	-	-	-	-	-	-	-	-	-	-	-	-	-	-	2	-	-
26 Huddersfield Town	-	-	-	2	-	-	-	-	-	-	-	-	-	-	-	-	-	-	-	-	-	-	-	-	-	-	-	2	-	-
27 Hull City	-	-	-	-	-	-	2	-	-	-	-	-	-	-	-	-	-	-	-	-	-	-	-	-	-	-	-	2	-	-
28 Leeds United	-	-	-	2	-	-	-	-	-	-	-	-	-	-	-	-	-	-	-	-	-	-	-	-	-	-	-	2	-	-
29 Liverpool	-	-	-	2	-	-	-	-	-	-	-	-	-	-	-	-	-	-	-	-	-	-	-	-	-	-	-	2	-	-
30 Manchester City	-	-	-	2	-	-	-	-	-	-	-	-	-	-	-	-	-	-	-	-	-	-	-	-	-	-	-	2	-	-
31 Newcastle United	-	-	-	-	-	-	2	-	-	-	-	-	-	-	-	-	-	-	-	-	-	-	-	-	-	-	-	2	-	-
32 Nottingham Forest	-	-	-	-	-	-	2	-	-	-	-	-	-	-	-	-	-	-	-	-	-	-	-	-	-	-	-	2	-	-
33 Port Vale	-	-	-	-	-	-	2	-	-	-	-	-	-	-	-	-	-	-	-	-	-	-	-	-	-	-	-	2	-	-
34 Preston North End	-	-	-	2	-	-	-	-	-	-	-	-	-	-	-	-	-	-	-	-	-	-	-	-	-	-	-	2	-	-
35 Reading	-	-	-	-	-	-	-	-	-	2	-	-	-	-	-	-	-	-	-	-	-	-	-	-	-	-	-	2	-	-
36 Sunderland	-	-	-	2	-	-	-	-	-	-	-	-	-	-	-	-	-	-	-	-	-	-	-	-	-	-	-	2	-	-
37 Swansea City	-	-	-	-	-	-	2	-	-	-	-	-	-	-	-	-	-	-	-	-	-	-	-	-	-	-	-	2	-	-
38 Wolverhampton W.	-	-	-	2	-	-	-	-	-	-	-	-	-	-	-	-	-	-	-	-	-	-	-	-	-	-	-	2	-	-
39 Blackpool	-	-	-	-	-	-	1	-	-	-	-	-	-	-	-	-	-	-	-	-	-	-	-	-	-	-	-	1	-	-
40 Chelsea	-	-	-	1	-	-	-	-	-	-	-	-	-	-	-	-	-	-	-	-	-	-	-	-	-	-	-	1	-	-
41 Doncaster Rovers	-	-	-	-	-	-	-	-	-	1	-	-	-	-	-	-	-	-	-	-	-	-	-	-	-	-	-	1	-	-
42 Middlesbrough	-	-	-	1	-	-	-	-	-	-	-	-	-	-	-	-	-	-	-	-	-	-	-	-	-	-	-	1	-	-
43 Portsmouth	-	-	-	1	-	-	-	-	-	-	-	-	-	-	-	-	-	-	-	-	-	-	-	-	-	-	-	1	-	-
44 Stockport County	-	-	-	-	-	-	-	-	-	1	-	-	-	-	-	-	-	-	-	-	-	-	-	-	-	-	-	1	-	-
45 West Bromwich Albion	-	-	-	1	-	-	-	-	-	-	-	-	-	-	-	-	-	-	-	-	-	-	-	-	-	-	-	1	-	-
46 Yeovil Town	-	-	-	-	-	-	-	-	-	1	-	-	-	-	-	-	-	-	-	-	-	-	-	-	-	-	-	1	-	-

ROBERT BROWN

DEBUT (Full Appearance)

Saturday 31/01/1948
Football League Division 1
at Bramall Lane

Sheffield United 2 Manchester United 1

CLUB CAREER RECORD	Apps	Subs	Goals
Premiership	0		0
League Division 1	4		0
League Division 2	0		0
FA Cup	0		0
League Cup	0		0
European Cup / Champions League	0		0
European Cup-Winners' Cup	0		0
UEFA Cup / Inter-Cities' Fairs Cup	0		0
Other Matches	0		0
OVERALL TOTAL	**4**		**0**

Opponents	PREM A S G	FLD 1 A S G	FLD 2 A S G	FAC A S G	LC A S G	EC/CL A S G	ECWC A S G	UEFA A S G	OTHER A S G	TOTAL A S G
1 Blackpool	– –	1 –	– –	– –	– –	– –	– –	– –	– –	1 –
2 Bolton Wanderers	– –	1 –	– –	– –	– –	– –	– –	– –	– –	1 –
3 Huddersfield Town	– –	1 –	– –	– –	– –	– –	– –	– –	– –	1 –
4 Sheffield United	– –	1 –	– –	– –	– –	– –	– –	– –	– –	1 –

WES BROWN

DEBUT (Substitute Appearance)

Monday 04/05/1998
FA Premiership
at Old Trafford

Manchester United 3 Leeds United 0

CLUB CAREER RECORD	Apps	Subs	Goals
Premiership	175	(23)	2
League Division 1	0		0
League Division 2	0		0
FA Cup	29	(2)	0
League Cup	16	(2)	0
European Cup / Champions League	50	(7)	1
European Cup-Winners' Cup	0		0
UEFA Cup / Inter-Cities' Fairs Cup	0		0
Other Matches	1		0
OVERALL TOTAL	**271**	**(34)**	**3**

Opponents	PREM A S G	FLD 1 A S G	FLD 2 A S G	FAC A S G	LC A S G	EC/CL A S G	ECWC A S G	UEFA A S G	OTHER A S G	TOTAL A S G
1 Chelsea	11 (1) –	–	–	2 –	1 –	1 –	–	–	1 –	16 (1) –
2 Arsenal	10 (1) –	–	–	4 –	1 –	–	–	–	–	15 (1) –
3 Liverpool	11 (1) 1	–	–	1 –	1 –	–	–	–	–	13 (1) 1
4 Middlesbrough	8 (2) –	–	–	3 –	–	–	–	–	–	11 (2) –
5 Blackburn Rovers	8 –	–	–	–	4 –	–	–	–	–	12 –
6 Everton	10 (1) –	–	–	1 –	–	–	–	–	–	11 (1) –
7 Aston Villa	7 (1) –	–	–	3 –	–	–	–	–	–	10 (1) –
8 Fulham	8 (1) –	–	–	2 –	–	–	–	–	–	10 (1) –
9 Charlton Athletic	10 –	–	–	–	–	–	–	–	–	10 –
10 Newcastle United	8 (1) 1	–	–	1 –	–	–	–	–	–	9 (1) 1
11 Portsmouth	7 (1) –	–	–	1 (1) –	–	–	–	–	–	8 (2) –
12 Manchester City	8 –	–	–	– (1) –	–	–	–	–	–	8 (1) –
13 Tottenham Hotspur	7 (1) –	–	–	1 –	–	–	–	–	–	8 (1) –
14 West Ham United	8 –	–	–	–	–	–	–	–	–	8 –
15 Birmingham City	6 (1) –	–	–	–	1 –	–	–	–	–	7 (1) –
16 Leeds United	4 (3) –	–	–	–	–	–	–	–	–	4 (3) –
17 Sunderland	6 –	–	–	–	–	–	–	–	–	6 –
18 Wigan Athletic	5 –	–	–	–	1 –	–	–	–	–	6 –
19 Southampton	4 (1) –	–	–	1 –	–	–	–	–	–	5 (1) –
20 Bolton Wanderers	4 (2) –	–	–	–	–	–	–	–	–	4 (2) –
21 Reading	3 –	–	–	2 –	–	–	–	–	–	5 –
22 Leicester City	4 (1) –	–	–	–	–	–	–	–	–	4 (1) –
23 Roma	–	–	–	–	–	4 (1) –	–	–	–	4 (1) –
24 AC Milan	–	–	–	–	–	4 –	–	–	–	4 –
25 Bayern Munich	–	–	–	–	–	4 –	–	–	–	4 –
26 Derby County	4 –	–	–	–	–	–	–	–	–	4 –
27 West Bromwich Albion	4 –	–	–	–	–	–	–	–	–	4 –
28 Olympique Lyonnais	–	–	–	–	–	3 (1) –	–	–	–	3 (1) –
29 Watford	1 (1) –	–	–	1 –	1 –	–	–	–	–	3 (1) –
30 Barcelona	–	–	–	–	–	3 –	–	–	–	3 –
31 Coventry City	2 –	–	–	–	– (1) –	–	–	–	–	2 (1) –
32 Deportivo La Coruna	–	–	–	–	–	1 (2) –	–	–	–	1 (2) –
33 Bayer Leverkusen	–	–	–	–	–	2 –	–	–	–	2 –
34 Burton Albion	–	–	–	2 –	–	–	–	–	–	2 –
35 Copenhagen	–	–	–	–	–	2 –	–	–	–	2 –
36 Crewe Alexandra	–	–	–	–	2 –	–	–	–	–	2 –
37 Crystal Palace	1 –	–	–	–	1 –	–	–	–	–	2 –
38 Dynamo Kiev	–	–	–	–	–	2 –	–	–	–	2 –
39 Ipswich Town	2 –	–	–	–	–	–	–	–	–	2 –
40 Lille Metropole	–	–	–	–	–	2 –	–	–	–	2 –
41 Panathinaikos	–	–	–	–	–	2 –	–	–	–	2 –
42 Porto	–	–	–	–	–	2 –	–	–	–	2 –
43 Real Madrid	–	–	–	–	–	2 –	–	–	–	2 –
44 Sparta Prague	–	–	–	–	–	2 –	–	–	–	2 –
45 Valencia	–	–	–	–	–	2 –	–	–	–	2 –
46 Brondby	–	–	–	–	–	1 (1) –	–	–	–	1 (1) –
47 PSV Eindhoven	–	–	–	–	–	1 (1) –	–	–	–	1 (1) –

continued../

WES BROWN (continued)

Opponents	PREM A S G	FLD 1 A S G	FLD 2 A S G	FAC A S G	LC A S G	EC/CL A S G	ECWC A S G	UEFA A S G	OTHER A S G	TOTAL A S G
48 Sheffield Wednesday	1 (1) –	– –	– –	– –	– –	– –	– –	– –	– –	1 (1) –
49 Wolverhampton W.	– (1) –	– –	– –	– 1	– –	– –	– –	– –	– –	1 (1) –
50 Juventus	– –	– –	– –	– –	– –	1 1	– –	– –	– –	1 1
51 Barnet	– –	– –	– –	– –	1 –	– –	– –	– –	– –	1 –
52 Barnsley	1 –	– –	– –	– –	– –	– –	– –	– –	– –	1 –
53 Basel	– –	– –	– –	– –	– –	1 –	– –	– –	– –	1 –
54 Burnley	– –	– –	– –	– –	1 –	– –	– –	– –	– –	1 –
55 Debreceni	– –	– –	– –	– –	– –	1 –	– –	– –	– –	1 –
56 Exeter City	– –	– –	– –	– 1	– –	– –	– –	– –	– –	1 –
57 Fenerbahce	– –	– –	– –	– –	– –	1 –	– –	– –	– –	1 –
58 Glasgow Celtic	– –	– –	– –	– –	– –	1 –	– –	– –	– –	1 –
59 Millwall	– –	– –	– –	1 –	– –	– –	– –	– –	– –	1 –
60 Northampton Town	– –	– –	– –	– 1	– –	– –	– –	– –	– –	1 –
61 Olympiakos Piraeus	– –	– –	– –	– –	– –	1 –	– –	– –	– –	1 –
62 Sheffield United	1 –	– –	– –	– –	– –	– –	– –	– –	– –	1 –
63 Southend United	– –	– –	– –	– –	1 –	– –	– –	– –	– –	1 –
64 Sporting Lisbon	– –	– –	– –	– –	– –	1 –	– –	– –	– –	1 –
65 Sturm Graz	– –	– –	– –	– –	– –	1 –	– –	– –	– –	1 –
66 Villarreal	– –	– –	– –	– –	– –	1 –	– –	– –	– –	1 –
67 Wimbledon	1 –	– –	– –	– –	– –	– –	– –	– –	– –	1 –
68 Zalaegerszeg	– –	– –	– –	– –	– –	1 –	– –	– –	– –	1 –
69 Anderlecht	– –	– –	– –	– –	– –	– (1) –	– –	– –	– –	– (1) –
70 Bradford City	– (1) –	– –	– –	– –	– –	– –	– –	– –	– –	– (1) –
71 Bury	– –	– –	– –	– –	– (1) –	– –	– –	– –	– –	– (1) –

WILLIAM BROWN

DEBUT (Full Appearance)

Tuesday 01/09/1896
Football League Division 2
at Bank Street

Newton Heath 2 Gainsborough Trinity 0

CLUB CAREER RECORD	Apps	Subs	Goals
Premiership	0		0
League Division 1	0		0
League Division 2	7		2
FA Cup	0		0
League Cup	0		0
European Cup / Champions League	0		0
European Cup-Winners' Cup	0		0
UEFA Cup / Inter-Cities' Fairs Cup	0		0
Other Matches	0		0
OVERALL TOTAL	**7**		**2**

Opponents	PREM A S G	FLD 1 A S G	FLD 2 A S G	FAC A S G	LC A S G	EC/CL A S G	ECWC A S G	UEFA A S G	OTHER A S G	TOTAL A S G
1 Walsall	– –	– –	2 1	– –	– –	– –	– –	– –	– –	2 1
2 Burton Swifts	– –	– –	1 1	– –	– –	– –	– –	– –	– –	1 1
3 Blackpool	– –	– –	1 –	– –	– –	– –	– –	– –	– –	1 –
4 Gainsborough Trinity	– –	– –	1 –	– –	– –	– –	– –	– –	– –	1 –
5 Grimsby Town	– –	– –	1 –	– –	– –	– –	– –	– –	– –	1 –
6 Lincoln City	– –	– –	1 –	– –	– –	– –	– –	– –	– –	1 –

STEVE BRUCE

DEBUT (Full Appearance)

Saturday 19/12/1987
Football League Division 1
at Fratton Park

Portsmouth 1 Manchester United 2

CLUB CAREER RECORD	Apps	Subs	Goals
Premiership	148		11
League Division 1	161		25
League Division 2	0		0
FA Cup	41		3
League Cup	32	(2)	6
European Cup / Champions League	9	(1)	2
European Cup-Winners' Cup	12		4
UEFA Cup / Inter-Cities' Fairs Cup	4		0
Other Matches	4		0
OVERALL TOTAL	**411**	**(3)**	**51**

Opponents	PREM A S G	FLD 1 A S G	FLD 2 A S G	FAC A S G	LC A S G	EC/CL A S G	ECWC A S G	UEFA A S G	OTHER A S G	TOTAL A S G
1 Queens Park Rangers	7 –	9 2	– –	5 –	– –	– –	– –	– –	– –	21 2
2 Wimbledon	8 1	9 3	– –	1 –	1 –	– –	– –	– –	– –	19 4
3 Liverpool	8 1	9 1	– –	– –	1 1	– –	– –	1 –	– –	19 3
4 Arsenal	7 –	8 3	– –	1 –	1 –	– –	– –	1 –	– –	18 3
5 Tottenham Hotspur	7 1	9 2	– –	– –	1 –	– –	– –	– –	– –	17 3
6 Everton	8 1	7 –	– –	1 –	1 –	– –	– –	– –	– –	17 1
7 Southampton	7 –	7 –	– –	1 –	2 –	– –	– –	– –	– –	17 –
8 Aston Villa	7 –	7 3	– –	– –	2 –	– –	– –	– –	– –	16 3
9 Norwich City	5 –	9 2	– –	2 –	– –	– –	– –	– –	– –	16 2
10 Sheffield Wednesday	7 2	6 –	– –	– –	3 –	– –	– –	– –	– –	16 2
11 Nottingham Forest	5 –	8 –	– –	2 –	1 –	– –	– –	– –	– –	16 –
12 Chelsea	8 –	5 2	– –	2 –	– –	– –	– –	– –	– –	15 2
13 Leeds United	7 1	4 –	– –	2 1	2 –	– –	– –	– –	– –	15 2
14 Coventry City	6 –	8 3	– –	– –	– –	– –	– –	– –	– –	14 3

continued../

STEVE BRUCE (continued)

Opponents	PREM A	PREM S	PREM G	FLD 1 A	FLD 1 S	FLD 1 G	FLD 2 A	FLD 2 S	FLD 2 G	FAC A	FAC S	FAC G	LC A	LC S	LC G	EC/CL A	EC/CL S	EC/CL G	ECWC A	ECWC S	ECWC G	UEFA A	UEFA S	UEFA G	OTHER A	OTHER S	OTHER G	TOTAL A	TOTAL S	TOTAL G
15 Manchester City	8	–	–	4	–	–	–	–	–	–	–	–	–	–	–	–	–	–	–	–	–	–	–	–	–	–	–	13	–	–
16 Oldham Athletic	4	–	1	2	–	–	–	–	–	4	–	–	1	–	–	–	–	–	–	–	–	–	–	–	–	–	–	11	–	1
17 Sheffield United	4	–	–	3	–	1	–	–	–	4	–	–	–	–	–	–	–	–	–	–	–	–	–	–	–	–	–	11	–	1
18 West Ham United	6	–	1	5	–	–	–	–	–	–	–	–	–	–	–	–	–	–	–	–	–	–	–	–	–	–	–	11	–	1
19 Crystal Palace	2	–	–	5	–	–	–	–	–	3	–	1	–	–	–	–	–	–	–	–	–	–	–	–	–	–	–	10	–	1
20 Newcastle United	5	–	–	3	–	–	–	–	–	1	–	–	1	–	–	–	–	–	–	–	–	–	–	–	–	–	–	10	–	–
21 Luton Town	–	–	–	9	–	3	–	–	–	–	–	–	–	–	–	–	–	–	–	–	–	–	–	–	–	–	–	9	–	3
22 Blackburn Rovers	7	–	–	–	–	–	–	–	–	–	–	–	–	–	–	–	–	–	–	–	–	1	–	–	–	–	–	8	–	–
23 Derby County	–	–	–	7	–	–	–	–	–	–	–	–	–	–	–	–	–	–	–	–	–	–	–	–	–	–	–	7	–	–
24 Ipswich Town	6	–	–	–	–	–	–	–	–	1	–	–	–	–	–	–	–	–	–	–	–	–	–	–	–	–	–	7	–	–
25 Middlesbrough	3	–	1	2	–	–	–	–	–	–	–	–	1	–	–	–	–	–	–	–	–	–	–	–	–	–	–	6	–	1
26 Charlton Athletic	–	–	–	5	–	–	–	–	–	1	–	–	–	–	–	–	–	–	–	–	–	–	–	–	–	–	–	6	–	–
27 Portsmouth	–	–	–	2	–	–	–	–	–	–	–	–	4	–	–	–	–	–	–	–	–	–	–	–	–	–	–	6	–	–
28 Galatasaray	–	–	–	–	–	–	–	–	–	–	–	–	–	–	–	4	–	–	–	–	–	–	–	–	–	–	–	4	–	–
29 Sunderland	–	–	–	2	–	–	–	–	–	2	–	–	–	–	–	–	–	–	–	–	–	–	–	–	–	–	–	4	–	–
30 Leicester City	2	–	–	–	–	–	–	–	–	–	–	–	1	–	2	–	–	–	–	–	–	–	–	–	–	–	–	3	–	2
31 Bolton Wanderers	2	–	1	–	–	–	–	–	–	–	–	–	1	–	–	–	–	–	–	–	–	–	–	–	–	–	–	3	–	1
32 Brighton	–	–	–	–	–	–	–	–	–	1	–	–	2	–	–	–	–	–	–	–	–	–	–	–	–	–	–	3	–	–
33 Millwall	–	–	–	3	–	–	–	–	–	–	–	–	–	–	–	–	–	–	–	–	–	–	–	–	–	–	–	3	–	–
34 Barcelona	–	–	–	–	–	–	–	–	–	–	–	–	–	–	–	1	(1)	–	1	–	–	–	–	–	–	–	–	2	(1)	–
35 Honved	–	–	–	–	–	–	–	–	–	–	–	–	–	–	–	2	–	2	–	–	–	–	–	–	–	–	–	2	–	2
36 Wrexham	–	–	–	–	–	–	–	–	–	–	–	–	–	–	–	–	–	–	2	–	2	–	–	–	–	–	–	2	–	2
37 Cambridge United	–	–	–	–	–	–	–	–	–	2	–	1	–	–	–	–	–	–	–	–	–	–	–	–	–	–	–	2	–	1
38 Legia Warsaw	–	–	–	–	–	–	–	–	–	–	–	–	–	–	–	–	–	–	2	–	1	–	–	–	–	–	–	2	–	1
39 Oxford United	–	–	–	1	–	–	–	–	–	1	–	1	–	–	–	–	–	–	–	–	–	–	–	–	–	–	–	2	–	1
40 Rotherham United	–	–	–	–	–	–	–	–	–	2	–	1	–	–	–	–	–	–	–	–	–	–	–	–	–	–	–	2	–	1
41 Athinaikos	–	–	–	–	–	–	–	–	–	–	–	–	–	–	–	–	–	–	2	–	–	–	–	–	–	–	–	2	–	–
42 Athletico Madrid	–	–	–	–	–	–	–	–	–	–	–	–	–	–	–	–	–	–	2	–	–	–	–	–	–	–	–	2	–	–
43 Bournemouth	–	–	–	–	–	–	–	–	–	2	–	–	–	–	–	–	–	–	–	–	–	–	–	–	–	–	–	2	–	–
44 Gothenburg	–	–	–	–	–	–	–	–	–	–	–	–	–	–	–	2	–	–	–	–	–	–	–	–	–	–	–	2	–	–
45 Notts County	–	–	–	2	–	–	–	–	–	–	–	–	–	–	–	–	–	–	–	–	–	–	–	–	–	–	–	2	–	–
46 Pecsi Munkas	–	–	–	–	–	–	–	–	–	–	–	–	–	–	–	–	–	–	2	–	–	–	–	–	–	–	–	2	–	–
47 Rotor Volgograd	–	–	–	–	–	–	–	–	–	–	–	–	–	–	–	–	–	–	–	–	–	2	–	–	–	–	–	2	–	–
48 Swindon Town	2	–	–	–	–	–	–	–	–	–	–	–	–	–	–	–	–	–	–	–	–	–	–	–	–	–	–	2	–	–
49 Torpedo Moscow	–	–	–	–	–	–	–	–	–	–	–	–	–	–	–	–	–	–	–	–	–	2	–	–	–	–	–	2	–	–
50 Stoke City	–	–	–	–	–	–	–	–	–	–	–	–	1	(1)	–	–	–	–	–	–	–	–	–	–	–	–	–	1	(1)	–
51 York City	–	–	–	–	–	–	–	–	–	–	–	–	1	(1)	–	–	–	–	–	–	–	–	–	–	–	–	–	1	(1)	–
52 Halifax Town	–	–	–	–	–	–	–	–	–	–	–	–	1	–	1	–	–	–	–	–	–	–	–	–	–	–	–	1	–	1
53 Montpellier Herault	–	–	–	–	–	–	–	–	–	–	–	–	–	–	–	–	–	–	1	–	1	–	–	–	–	–	–	1	–	1
54 Bury	–	–	–	–	–	–	–	–	–	1	–	–	–	–	–	–	–	–	–	–	–	–	–	–	–	–	–	1	–	–
55 Reading	–	–	–	–	–	–	–	–	–	1	–	–	–	–	–	–	–	–	–	–	–	–	–	–	–	–	–	1	–	–
56 Red Star Belgrade	–	–	–	–	–	–	–	–	–	–	–	–	–	–	–	–	–	–	–	–	–	–	–	–	1	–	–	1	–	–
57 Watford	–	–	–	1	–	–	–	–	–	–	–	–	–	–	–	–	–	–	–	–	–	–	–	–	–	–	–	1	–	–

BILLY BRYANT

DEBUT (Full Appearance, 1 goal)

Saturday 03/11/1934
Football League Division 2
at Bloomfield Road

Blackpool 1 Manchester United 2

CLUB CAREER RECORD	Apps	Subs	Goals
Premiership	0		0
League Division 1	64		16
League Division 2	84		26
FA Cup	9		0
League Cup	0		0
European Cup / Champions League	0		0
European Cup-Winners' Cup	0		0
UEFA Cup / Inter-Cities' Fairs Cup	0		0
Other Matches	0		0
OVERALL TOTAL	157		42

Opponents	PREM A	PREM S	PREM G	FLD 1 A	FLD 1 S	FLD 1 G	FLD 2 A	FLD 2 S	FLD 2 G	FAC A	FAC S	FAC G	LC A	LC S	LC G	EC/CL A	EC/CL S	EC/CL G	ECWC A	ECWC S	ECWC G	UEFA A	UEFA S	UEFA G	OTHER A	OTHER S	OTHER G	TOTAL A	TOTAL S	TOTAL G
1 Brentford	–	–	–	4	–	2	2	–	–	1	–	–	–	–	–	–	–	–	–	–	–	–	–	–	–	–	–	7	–	2
2 Nottingham Forest	–	–	–	–	–	–	4	–	3	1	–	–	–	–	–	–	–	–	–	–	–	–	–	–	–	–	–	5	–	3
3 Arsenal	–	–	–	4	–	2	–	–	–	1	–	–	–	–	–	–	–	–	–	–	–	–	–	–	–	–	–	5	–	2
4 Barnsley	–	–	–	–	–	–	3	–	1	2	–	–	–	–	–	–	–	–	–	–	–	–	–	–	–	–	–	5	–	1
5 Bradford Park Avenue	–	–	–	–	–	–	5	–	1	–	–	–	–	–	–	–	–	–	–	–	–	–	–	–	–	–	–	5	–	1
6 Southampton	–	–	–	–	–	–	5	–	1	–	–	–	–	–	–	–	–	–	–	–	–	–	–	–	–	–	–	5	–	1
7 Bury	–	–	–	–	–	–	5	–	–	–	–	–	–	–	–	–	–	–	–	–	–	–	–	–	–	–	–	5	–	–
8 Stoke City	–	–	–	4	–	–	–	–	–	1	–	–	–	–	–	–	–	–	–	–	–	–	–	–	–	–	–	5	–	–
9 Blackpool	–	–	–	1	–	1	3	–	2	–	–	–	–	–	–	–	–	–	–	–	–	–	–	–	–	–	–	4	–	3
10 Burnley	–	–	–	–	–	–	4	–	3	–	–	–	–	–	–	–	–	–	–	–	–	–	–	–	–	–	–	4	–	3
11 Bolton Wanderers	–	–	–	4	–	2	–	–	–	–	–	–	–	–	–	–	–	–	–	–	–	–	–	–	–	–	–	4	–	2
12 Sheffield United	–	–	–	–	–	–	4	–	2	–	–	–	–	–	–	–	–	–	–	–	–	–	–	–	–	–	–	4	–	2
13 Fulham	–	–	–	–	–	–	4	–	1	–	–	–	–	–	–	–	–	–	–	–	–	–	–	–	–	–	–	4	–	1
14 Grimsby Town	–	–	–	4	–	1	–	–	–	–	–	–	–	–	–	–	–	–	–	–	–	–	–	–	–	–	–	4	–	1
15 Middlesbrough	–	–	–	4	–	1	–	–	–	–	–	–	–	–	–	–	–	–	–	–	–	–	–	–	–	–	–	4	–	1
16 Plymouth Argyle	–	–	–	–	–	–	4	–	1	–	–	–	–	–	–	–	–	–	–	–	–	–	–	–	–	–	–	4	–	1
17 Preston North End	–	–	–	4	–	1	–	–	–	–	–	–	–	–	–	–	–	–	–	–	–	–	–	–	–	–	–	4	–	1
18 Swansea City	–	–	–	–	–	–	4	–	1	–	–	–	–	–	–	–	–	–	–	–	–	–	–	–	–	–	–	4	–	1

continued../

BILLY BRYANT (continued)

Opponents	PREM A S G	FLD 1 A S G	FLD 2 A S G	FAC A S G	LC A S G	EC/CL A S G	ECWC A S G	UEFA A S G	OTHER A S G	TOTAL A S G
19 Charlton Athletic	– –	4 –	– –	–	–	–	–	–	–	4 –
20 Chelsea	– –	4 –	– –	–	–	–	–	–	–	4 –
21 Sheffield Wednesday	– –	2 –	2 –	–	–	–	–	–	–	4 –
22 Tottenham Hotspur	– –	– –	4 –	–	–	–	–	–	–	4 –
23 Huddersfield Town	– –	3 1	– –	–	–	–	–	–	–	3 1
24 Leeds United	– –	3 1	– –	–	–	–	–	–	–	3 1
25 Norwich City	– –	– –	3 1	–	–	–	–	–	–	3 1
26 Sunderland	– –	3 1	– –	–	–	–	–	–	–	3 1
27 West Ham United	– –	– –	3 1	–	–	–	–	–	–	3 1
28 Hull City	– –	– –	3 –	–	–	–	–	–	–	3 –
29 Liverpool	– –	3 –	– –	–	–	–	–	–	–	3 –
30 Wolverhampton W.	– –	3 –	– –	–	–	–	–	–	–	3 –
31 Chesterfield	– –	– –	2 2	–	–	–	–	–	–	2 2
32 Birmingham City	– –	2 1	– –	–	–	–	–	–	–	2 1
33 Blackburn Rovers	– –	– –	2 1	–	–	–	–	–	–	2 1
34 Coventry City	– –	– –	2 1	–	–	–	–	–	–	2 1
35 Luton Town	– –	– –	2 1	–	–	–	–	–	–	2 1
36 Newcastle United	– –	– –	2 1	–	–	–	–	–	–	2 1
37 Stockport County	– –	– –	2 1	–	–	–	–	–	–	2 1
38 Aston Villa	– –	– –	2 –	–	–	–	–	–	–	2 –
39 Derby County	– –	2 –	– –	–	–	–	–	–	–	2 –
40 Notts County	– –	– –	2 –	–	–	–	–	–	–	2 –
41 Port Vale	– –	– –	2 –	–	–	–	–	–	–	2 –
42 Portsmouth	– –	2 –	– –	–	–	–	–	–	–	2 –
43 West Bromwich Albion	– –	2 –	– –	–	–	–	–	–	–	2 –
44 Everton	– –	1 1	– –	–	–	–	–	–	–	1 1
45 Leicester City	– –	– –	1 1	–	–	–	–	–	–	1 1
46 Manchester City	– –	1 1	– –	–	–	–	–	–	–	1 1
47 Bradford City	– –	– –	1 –	–	–	–	–	–	–	1 –
48 Bristol Rovers	– –	– –	– –	1	–	–	–	–	–	1 –
49 Doncaster Rovers	– –	– –	1 –	–	–	–	–	–	–	1 –
50 Oldham Athletic	– –	– –	1 –	–	–	–	–	–	–	1 –
51 Reading	– –	– –	– –	1	–	–	–	–	–	1 –
52 Yeovil Town	– –	– –	– –	1	–	–	–	–	–	1 –

WILLIAM BRYANT

DEBUT (Full Appearance)

Tuesday 01/09/1896
Football League Division 2
at Bank Street

Newton Heath 2 Gainsborough Trinity 0

CLUB CAREER RECORD	Apps	Subs	Goals
Premiership	0		0
League Division 1	0		0
League Division 2	109		27
FA Cup	14		6
League Cup	0		0
European Cup / Champions League	0		0
European Cup-Winners' Cup	0		0
UEFA Cup / Inter-Cities' Fairs Cup	0		0
Other Matches	4		0
OVERALL TOTAL	127		33

Opponents	PREM A S G	FLD 1 A S G	FLD 2 A S G	FAC A S G	LC A S G	EC/CL A S G	ECWC A S G	UEFA A S G	OTHER A S G	TOTAL A S G
1 Arsenal	– –	– –	8 3	–	–	–	–	–	–	8 3
2 Burton Swifts	– –	– –	8 2	–	–	–	–	–	–	8 2
3 Gainsborough Trinity	– –	– –	8 2	–	–	–	–	–	–	8 2
4 Grimsby Town	– –	– –	7 3	–	–	–	–	–	–	7 3
5 Birmingham City	– –	– –	7 1	–	–	–	–	–	–	7 1
6 Blackpool	– –	– –	5 1	2	–	–	–	–	–	7 1
7 Walsall	– –	– –	6 1	1	–	–	–	–	–	7 1
8 Darwen	– –	– –	6 4	–	–	–	–	–	–	6 4
9 Loughborough Town	– –	– –	6 1	–	–	–	–	–	–	6 1
10 Leicester City	– –	– –	6 –	–	–	–	–	–	–	6 –
11 Manchester City	– –	– –	6 –	–	–	–	–	–	–	6 –
12 Lincoln City	– –	– –	5 2	–	–	–	–	–	–	5 2
13 Burnley	– –	– –	2 2	–	–	–	–	–	2 –	4 2
14 Luton Town	– –	– –	4 –	–	–	–	–	–	–	4 –
15 Newcastle United	– –	– –	4 –	–	–	–	–	–	–	4 –
16 Port Vale	– –	– –	3 1	–	–	–	–	–	–	3 1
17 Barnsley	– –	– –	3 –	–	–	–	–	–	–	3 –
18 New Brighton Tower	– –	– –	3 –	–	–	–	–	–	–	3 –
19 Tottenham Hotspur	– –	– –	– –	2 3	–	–	–	–	–	2 3
20 Sheffield Wednesday	– –	– –	2 2	–	–	–	–	–	–	2 2
21 Southampton	– –	– –	– –	2 2	–	–	–	–	–	2 2
22 Glossop	– –	– –	2 1	–	–	–	–	–	–	2 1
23 Notts County	– –	– –	2 1	–	–	–	–	–	–	2 1
24 Bolton Wanderers	– –	– –	2 –	–	–	–	–	–	–	2 –
25 Burton Wanderers	– –	– –	2 –	–	–	–	–	–	–	2 –
26 Liverpool	– –	– –	– –	2	–	–	–	–	–	2 –
27 Sunderland	– –	– –	– –	–	–	–	–	–	2 –	2 –

continued../

WILLIAM BRYANT (continued)

Opponents	PREM A S G	FLD 1 A S G	FLD 2 A S G	FAC A S G	LC A S G	EC/CL A S G	ECWC A S G	UEFA A S G	OTHER A S G	TOTAL A S G
28 West Manchester	– –	– –	– –	1 1	– –	– –	– –	– –	– –	1 1
29 Chesterfield	– –	– –	1 –	– –	– –	– –	– –	– –	– –	1 –
30 Derby County	– –	– –	– –	1 –	– –	– –	– –	– –	– –	1 –
31 Kettering	– –	– –	– –	1 –	– –	– –	– –	– –	– –	1 –
32 Middlesbrough	– –	– –	1 –	– –	– –	– –	– –	– –	– –	1 –
33 Nelson	– –	– –	– –	1 –	– –	– –	– –	– –	– –	1 –
34 South Shore	– –	– –	– –	1 –	– –	– –	– –	– –	– –	1 –

GEORGE BUCHAN

DEBUT (Substitute Appearance)

Saturday 15/09/1973
Football League Division 1
at Old Trafford

Manchester United 3 West Ham United 1

CLUB CAREER RECORD	Apps	Subs	Goals
Premiership	0		0
League Division 1	0	(3)	0
League Division 2	0		0
FA Cup	0		0
League Cup	0	(1)	0
European Cup / Champions League	0		0
European Cup–Winners' Cup	0		0
UEFA Cup / Inter-Cities' Fairs Cup	0		0
Other Matches	0		0
OVERALL TOTAL	**0**	**(4)**	**0**

Opponents	PREM A S G	FLD 1 A S G	FLD 2 A S G	FAC A S G	LC A S G	EC/CL A S G	ECWC A S G	UEFA A S G	OTHER A S G	TOTAL A S G
1 Leeds United	– –	– (1) –	– –	– –	– –	– –	– –	– –	– –	– (1) –
2 Liverpool	– –	– (1) –	– –	– –	– –	– –	– –	– –	– –	– (1) –
3 Middlesbrough	– –	– –	– –	– –	– (1) –	– –	– –	– –	– –	– (1) –
4 West Ham United	– –	– (1) –	– –	– –	– –	– –	– –	– –	– –	– (1) –

MARTIN BUCHAN

DEBUT (Full Appearance)

Saturday 04/03/1972
Football League Division 1
at White Hart Lane

Tottenham Hotspur 2 Manchester United 0

CLUB CAREER RECORD	Apps	Subs	Goals
Premiership	0		0
League Division 1	335		4
League Division 2	41		0
FA Cup	39		0
League Cup	30		0
European Cup / Champions League	0		0
European Cup–Winners' Cup	4		0
UEFA Cup / Inter-Cities' Fairs Cup	6		0
Other Matches	1		0
OVERALL TOTAL	**456**		**4**

Opponents	PREM A S G	FLD 1 A S G	FLD 2 A S G	FAC A S G	LC A S G	EC/CL A S G	ECWC A S G	UEFA A S G	OTHER A S G	TOTAL A S G
1 Tottenham Hotspur	– –	15 –	– –	4 –	4 –	– –	– –	– –	– –	23 –
2 Manchester City	– –	18 1	– –	– –	2 –	– –	– –	– –	– –	20 1
3 Coventry City	– –	18 –	– –	– –	2 –	– –	– –	– –	– –	20 –
4 Liverpool	– –	16 –	– –	3 –	– –	– –	– –	1 –	– –	20 –
5 Norwich City	– –	15 –	2 –	– –	3 –	– –	– –	– –	– –	20 –
6 Arsenal	– –	17 –	– –	1 –	1 –	– –	– –	– –	– –	19 –
7 Leeds United	– –	16 –	– –	1 –	– –	– –	– –	– –	– –	17 –
8 Everton	– –	16 1	– –	– –	– –	– –	– –	– –	– –	16 1
9 Aston Villa	– –	12 –	2 –	1 –	1 –	– –	– –	– –	– –	16 –
10 Birmingham City	– –	16 –	– –	– –	– –	– –	– –	– –	– –	16 –
11 Ipswich Town	– –	15 –	– –	1 –	– –	– –	– –	– –	– –	16 –
12 Wolverhampton W.	– –	13 –	– –	3 –	– –	– –	– –	– –	– –	16 –
13 Middlesbrough	– –	12 –	– –	– –	3 –	– –	– –	– –	– –	15 –
14 Southampton	– –	10 –	2 –	3 –	– –	– –	– –	– –	– –	15 –
15 Derby County	– –	13 1	– –	1 –	– –	– –	– –	– –	– –	14 1
16 Stoke City	– –	11 –	– –	2 –	– –	– –	– –	– –	– –	13 –
17 Leicester City	– –	11 –	– –	1 –	– –	– –	– –	– –	– –	12 –
18 Nottingham Forest	– –	9 –	2 –	1 –	– –	– –	– –	– –	– –	12 –
19 West Bromwich Albion	– –	8 –	2 –	2 –	– –	– –	– –	– –	– –	12 –
20 Queens Park Rangers	– –	9 –	– –	1 –	– –	– –	– –	– –	– –	10 –
21 Sunderland	– –	5 –	2 –	– –	3 –	– –	– –	– –	– –	10 –
22 Bristol City	– –	7 –	2 –	– –	– –	– –	– –	– –	– –	9 –
23 Newcastle United	– –	9 –	– –	– –	– –	– –	– –	– –	– –	9 –
24 West Ham United	– –	9 –	– –	– –	– –	– –	– –	– –	– –	9 –
25 Chelsea	– –	6 –	– –	1 –	– –	– –	– –	– –	– –	7 –
26 Sheffield United	– –	7 –	– –	– –	– –	– –	– –	– –	– –	7 –
27 Bolton Wanderers	– –	4 1	2 –	– –	– –	– –	– –	– –	– –	6 1
28 Crystal Palace	– –	6 –	– –	– –	– –	– –	– –	– –	– –	6 –
29 Burnley	– –	4 –	– –	– –	1 –	– –	– –	– –	– –	5 –
30 Oxford United	– –	– –	2 –	1 –	2 –	– –	– –	– –	– –	5 –
31 Brighton	– –	3 –	– –	1 –	– –	– –	– –	– –	– –	4 –
32 Bristol Rovers	– –	– –	2 –	– –	2 –	– –	– –	– –	– –	4 –

continued../

MARTIN BUCHAN (continued)

Opponents	PREM A S G	FLD 1 A S G	FLD 2 A S G	FAC A S G	LC A S G	EC/CL A S G	ECWC A S G	UEFA A S G	OTHER A S G	TOTAL A S G
33 Notts County	– –	2 –	2 –	–	–	–	–	–	–	4 –
34 Fulham	– –	– – 1 –	2 –	–	–	–	–	–	3 –
35 Walsall	– –	– –	– –	3 –	–	–	–	–	–	3 –
36 Watford	– –	1 –	– –	1 –	1 –	–	–	–	–	3 –
37 Ajax	– –	– –	– –	–	–	–	–	2 –	–	2 –
38 Blackpool	– –	– –	2 –	–	–	–	–	–	–	2 –
39 Cardiff City	– –	– –	2 –	–	–	–	–	–	–	2 –
40 Carlisle United	– –	– –	– –	2 –	–	–	–	–	–	2 –
41 Hull City	– –	– –	2 –	–	–	–	–	–	–	2 –
42 Leyton Orient	– –	– –	2 –	–	–	–	–	–	–	2 –
43 Millwall	– –	– –	2 –	–	–	–	–	–	–	2 –
44 Oldham Athletic	– –	– –	2 –	–	–	–	–	–	–	2 –
45 Porto	– –	– –	– –	–	–	–	2 –	–	–	2 –
46 Portsmouth	– –	– –	2 –	–	–	–	–	–	–	2 –
47 Sheffield Wednesday	– –	– –	2 –	–	–	–	–	–	–	2 –
48 St Etienne	– –	– –	– –	–	–	–	2 –	–	–	2 –
49 Valencia	– –	– –	– –	–	–	–	–	2 –	–	2 –
50 Widzew Lodz	– –	– –	– –	–	–	–	–	2 –	–	2 –
51 York City	– –	– –	2 –	–	–	–	–	–	–	2 –
52 Bournemouth	– –	– –	– –	–	1 –	–	–	–	–	1 –
53 Brentford	– –	– –	– –	–	1 –	–	–	–	–	1 –
54 Charlton Athletic	– –	– –	– –	–	1 –	–	–	–	–	1 –
55 Colchester United	– –	– –	– –	1 –	–	–	–	–	–	1 –
56 Huddersfield Town	– –	1 –	– –	–	–	–	–	–	–	1 –
57 Peterborough United	– –	– –	– –	1 –	–	–	–	–	–	1 –
58 Plymouth Argyle	– –	– –	1 –	–	–	–	–	–	–	1 –
59 Stockport County	– –	– –	– –	–	1 –	–	–	–	–	1 –
60 Swansea City	– –	1 –	– –	–	–	–	–	–	–	1 –
61 Tranmere Rovers	– –	– –	– –	1 –	–	–	–	–	–	1 –

TED BUCKLE

DEBUT (Full Appearance)

Saturday 04/01/1947
Football League Division 1
at Maine Road

Manchester United 4 Charlton Athletic 1

CLUB CAREER RECORD	Apps	Subs	Goals
Premiership	0		0
League Division 1	20		6
League Division 2	0		0
FA Cup	4		1
League Cup	0		0
European Cup / Champions League	0		0
European Cup–Winners' Cup	0		0
UEFA Cup / Inter-Cities' Fairs Cup	0		0
Other Matches	0		0
OVERALL TOTAL	24		7

Opponents	PREM A S G	FLD 1 A S G	FLD 2 A S G	FAC A S G	LC A S G	EC/CL A S G	ECWC A S G	UEFA A S G	OTHER A S G	TOTAL A S G
1 Stoke City	– –	3 2	– –	–	–	–	–	–	–	3 2
2 Bradford Park Avenue	– –	– –	– –	3 1	–	–	–	–	–	3 1
3 Chelsea	– –	2 –	– –	–	–	–	–	–	–	2 –
4 Liverpool	– –	2 –	– –	–	–	–	–	–	–	2 –
5 Sunderland	– –	2 –	– –	–	–	–	–	–	–	2 –
6 Charlton Athletic	– –	1 1	– –	–	–	–	–	–	–	1 1
7 Middlesbrough	– –	1 1	– –	–	–	–	–	–	–	1 1
8 Sheffield United	– –	1 1	– –	–	–	–	–	–	–	1 1
9 Wolverhampton W.	– –	1 1	– –	–	–	–	–	–	–	1 1
10 Arsenal	– –	1 –	– –	–	–	–	–	–	–	1 –
11 Blackpool	– –	1 –	– –	–	–	–	–	–	–	1 –
12 Bolton Wanderers	– –	1 –	– –	–	–	–	–	–	–	1 –
13 Burnley	– –	1 –	– –	–	–	–	–	–	–	1 –
14 Everton	– –	1 –	– –	–	–	–	–	–	–	1 –
15 Manchester City	– –	1 –	– –	–	–	–	–	–	–	1 –
16 Nottingham Forest	– –	– –	– –	1 –	–	–	–	–	–	1 –
17 Portsmouth	– –	1 –	– –	–	–	–	–	–	–	1 –

FRANK BUCKLEY

DEBUT (Full Appearance)

Saturday 29/09/1906
Football League Division 1
at Bank Street

Manchester United 1 Derby County 1

CLUB CAREER RECORD	Apps	Subs	Goals
Premiership	0		0
League Division 1	3		0
League Division 2	0		0
FA Cup	0		0
League Cup	0		0
European Cup / Champions League	0		0
European Cup-Winners' Cup	0		0
UEFA Cup / Inter-Cities' Fairs Cup	0		0
Other Matches	0		0
OVERALL TOTAL	**3**		**0**

Opponents	PREM A S G	FLD 1 A S G	FLD 2 A S G	FAC A S G	LC A S G	EC/CL A S G	ECWC A S G	UEFA A S G	OTHER A S G	TOTAL A S G
1 Birmingham City	– –	1 –	– –	– –	– –	– –	– –	– –	– –	1 –
2 Derby County	– –	1 –	– –	– –	– –	– –	– –	– –	– –	1 –
3 Notts County	– –	1 –	– –	– –	– –	– –	– –	– –	– –	1 –

JIMMY BULLOCK

DEBUT (Full Appearance)

Saturday 20/09/1930
Football League Division 1
at Hillsborough

Sheffield Wednesday 3 Manchester United 0

CLUB CAREER RECORD	Apps	Subs	Goals
Premiership	0		0
League Division 1	10		3
League Division 2	0		0
FA Cup	0		0
League Cup	0		0
European Cup / Champions League	0		0
European Cup-Winners' Cup	0		0
UEFA Cup / Inter-Cities' Fairs Cup	0		0
Other Matches	0		0
OVERALL TOTAL	**10**		**3**

Opponents	PREM A S G	FLD 1 A S G	FLD 2 A S G	FAC A S G	LC A S G	EC/CL A S G	ECWC A S G	UEFA A S G	OTHER A S G	TOTAL A S G
1 Birmingham City	– –	2 –	– –	– –	– –	– –	– –	– –	– –	2 –
2 Leicester City	– –	1 3	– –	– –	– –	– –	– –	– –	– –	1 3
3 Arsenal	– –	1 –	– –	– –	– –	– –	– –	– –	– –	1 –
4 Blackburn Rovers	– –	1 –	– –	– –	– –	– –	– –	– –	– –	1 –
5 Blackpool	– –	1 –	– –	– –	– –	– –	– –	– –	– –	1 –
6 Grimsby Town	– –	1 –	– –	– –	– –	– –	– –	– –	– –	1 –
7 Sheffield United	– –	1 –	– –	– –	– –	– –	– –	– –	– –	1 –
8 Sheffield Wednesday	– –	1 –	– –	– –	– –	– –	– –	– –	– –	1 –
9 Sunderland	– –	1 –	– –	– –	– –	– –	– –	– –	– –	1 –

WILLIAM BUNCE

DEBUT (Full Appearance)

Saturday 04/10/1902
Football League Division 2
at Bank Street

Manchester United 2 Chesterfield 1

CLUB CAREER RECORD	Apps	Subs	Goals
Premiership	0		0
League Division 1	0		0
League Division 2	2		0
FA Cup	0		0
League Cup	0		0
European Cup / Champions League	0		0
European Cup-Winners' Cup	0		0
UEFA Cup / Inter-Cities' Fairs Cup	0		0
Other Matches	0		0
OVERALL TOTAL	**2**		**0**

Opponents	PREM A S G	FLD 1 A S G	FLD 2 A S G	FAC A S G	LC A S G	EC/CL A S G	ECWC A S G	UEFA A S G	OTHER A S G	TOTAL A S G
1 Chesterfield	– – –	– 1	– –	– –	– –	– –	– –	– –	– –	1 –
2 Stockport County	– – –	– 1	– –	– –	– –	– –	– –	– –	– –	1 –

HERBERT BURGESS

DEBUT (Full Appearance)

Tuesday 01/01/1907
Football League Division 1
at Bank Street

Manchester United 1 Aston Villa 0

CLUB CAREER RECORD	Apps	Subs	Goals
Premiership	0		0
League Division 1	49		0
League Division 2	0		0
FA Cup	3		0
League Cup	0		0
European Cup / Champions League	0		0
European Cup-Winners' Cup	0		0
UEFA Cup / Inter-Cities' Fairs Cup	0		0
Other Matches	2		0
OVERALL TOTAL	**54**		**0**

Opponents	PREM A S G	FLD 1 A S G	FLD 2 A S G	FAC A S G	LC A S G	EC/CL A S G	ECWC A S G	UEFA A S G	OTHER A S G	TOTAL A S G
1 Middlesbrough	– –	4 –	– –	– –	– –	– –	– –	– –	– –	4 –
2 Sheffield Wednesday	– –	4 –	– –	– –	– –	– –	– –	– –	– –	4 –

continued../

HERBERT BURGESS (continued)

Opponents	PREM A S G	FLD 1 A S G	FLD 2 A S G	FAC A S G	LC A S G	EC/CL A S G	ECWC A S G	UEFA A S G	OTHER A S G	TOTAL A S G
3 Sunderland	– –	4 – –	– – –	– – –	– – –	– – –	– – –	– – –	– – –	4 –
4 Arsenal	– –	3 – –	– – –	– – –	– – –	– – –	– – –	– – –	– – –	3 –
5 Aston Villa	– –	2 – –	– – –	1 – –	– – –	– – –	– – –	– – –	– – –	3 –
6 Blackburn Rovers	– –	3 – –	– – –	– – –	– – –	– – –	– – –	– – –	– – –	3 –
7 Chelsea	– –	2 – –	– – –	1 – –	– – –	– – –	– – –	– – –	– – –	3 –
8 Everton	– –	3 – –	– – –	– – –	– – –	– – –	– – –	– – –	– – –	3 –
9 Notts County	– –	3 – –	– – –	– – –	– – –	– – –	– – –	– – –	– – –	3 –
10 Sheffield United	– –	3 – –	– – –	– – –	– – –	– – –	– – –	– – –	– – –	3 –
11 Birmingham City	– –	2 – –	– – –	– – –	– – –	– – –	– – –	– – –	– – –	2 –
12 Bolton Wanderers	– –	2 – –	– – –	– – –	– – –	– – –	– – –	– – –	– – –	2 –
13 Bury	– –	2 – –	– – –	– – –	– – –	– – –	– – –	– – –	– – –	2 –
14 Liverpool	– –	2 – –	– – –	– – –	– – –	– – –	– – –	– – –	– – –	2 –
15 Manchester City	– –	2 – –	– – –	– – –	– – –	– – –	– – –	– – –	– – –	2 –
16 Newcastle United	– –	2 – –	– – –	– – –	– – –	– – –	– – –	– – –	– – –	2 –
17 Nottingham Forest	– –	2 – –	– – –	– – –	– – –	– – –	– – –	– – –	– – –	2 –
18 Preston North End	– –	2 – –	– – –	– – –	– – –	– – –	– – –	– – –	– – –	2 –
19 Queens Park Rangers	– –	– – –	– – –	– – –	– – –	– – –	– – –	– – –	2 –	2 –
20 Bristol City	– –	1 – –	– – –	– – –	– – –	– – –	– – –	– – –	– – –	1 –
21 Fulham	– –	– – –	– – –	1 – –	– – –	– – –	– – –	– – –	– – –	1 –
22 Stoke City	– –	1 – –	– – –	– – –	– – –	– – –	– – –	– – –	– – –	1 –

RONNIE BURKE

DEBUT (Full Appearance)

Saturday 26/10/1946
Football League Division 1
at Maine Road

Manchester United 0 Sunderland 3

CLUB CAREER RECORD	Apps	Subs	Goals
Premiership	0		0
League Division 1	28		16
League Division 2	0		0
FA Cup	6		6
League Cup	0		0
European Cup / Champions League	0		0
European Cup-Winners' Cup	0		0
UEFA Cup / Inter-Cities' Fairs Cup	0		0
Other Matches	1		1
OVERALL TOTAL	35		23

Opponents	PREM A S G	FLD 1 A S G	FLD 2 A S G	FAC A S G	LC A S G	EC/CL A S G	ECWC A S G	UEFA A S G	OTHER A S G	TOTAL A S G
1 Huddersfield Town	– –	3 – 1	– – –	– – –	– – –	– – –	– – –	– – –	– – –	3 – 1
2 Liverpool	– –	3 – 1	– – –	– – –	– – –	– – –	– – –	– – –	– – –	3 – 1
3 Derby County	– –	2 – 4	– – –	– – –	– – –	– – –	– – –	– – –	– – –	2 – 4
4 Charlton Athletic	– –	2 – 3	– – –	– – –	– – –	– – –	– – –	– – –	– – –	2 – 3
5 Leeds United	– –	2 – 3	– – –	– – –	– – –	– – –	– – –	– – –	– – –	2 – 3
6 Arsenal	– –	1 – 1	– – –	– – –	– – –	– – –	– – –	– – –	1 – 1	2 – 2
7 Bradford Park Avenue	– –	– – –	– – –	2 – 2	– – –	– – –	– – –	– – –	– – –	2 – 2
8 Aston Villa	– –	2 – 1	– – –	– – –	– – –	– – –	– – –	– – –	– – –	2 – 1
9 Everton	– –	2 – 1	– – –	– – –	– – –	– – –	– – –	– – –	– – –	2 – 1
10 Wolverhampton W.	– –	1 – –	– – –	– – –	1 – –	– – –	– – –	– – –	– – –	2 – –
11 Bournemouth	– –	– – –	– – –	1 – 2	– – –	– – –	– – –	– – –	– – –	1 – 2
12 Yeovil Town	– –	– – –	– – –	1 – 2	– – –	– – –	– – –	– – –	– – –	1 – 2
13 Newcastle United	– –	1 – 1	– – –	– – –	– – –	– – –	– – –	– – –	– – –	1 – 1
14 Blackburn Rovers	– –	1 – –	– – –	– – –	– – –	– – –	– – –	– – –	– – –	1 – –
15 Bolton Wanderers	– –	1 – –	– – –	– – –	– – –	– – –	– – –	– – –	– – –	1 – –
16 Brentford	– –	1 – –	– – –	– – –	– – –	– – –	– – –	– – –	– – –	1 – –
17 Chelsea	– –	1 – –	– – –	– – –	– – –	– – –	– – –	– – –	– – –	1 – –
18 Hull City	– –	– – –	– – –	1 – –	– – –	– – –	– – –	– – –	– – –	1 – –
19 Manchester City	– –	1 – –	– – –	– – –	– – –	– – –	– – –	– – –	– – –	1 – –
20 Portsmouth	– –	1 – –	– – –	– – –	– – –	– – –	– – –	– – –	– – –	1 – –
21 Preston North End	– –	1 – –	– – –	– – –	– – –	– – –	– – –	– – –	– – –	1 – –
22 Sheffield United	– –	1 – –	– – –	– – –	– – –	– – –	– – –	– – –	– – –	1 – –
23 Sunderland	– –	1 – –	– – –	– – –	– – –	– – –	– – –	– – –	– – –	1 – –

TOM BURKE

DEBUT (Full Appearance)

Saturday 30/10/1886
FA Cup 1st Round
at Fleetwood Park

Fleetwood Rangers 2 Newton Heath 2

CLUB CAREER RECORD	Apps	Subs	Goals
Premiership	0		0
League Division 1	0		0
League Division 2	0		0
FA Cup	1		0
League Cup	0		0
European Cup / Champions League	0		0
European Cup-Winners' Cup	0		0
UEFA Cup / Inter-Cities' Fairs Cup	0		0
Other Matches	0		0
OVERALL TOTAL	1		0

Opponents	PREM A S G	FLD 1 A S G	FLD 2 A S G	FAC A S G	LC A S G	EC/CL A S G	ECWC A S G	UEFA A S G	OTHER A S G	TOTAL A S G
1 Fleetwood Rangers	– –	– – –	– – –	1 – –	– – –	– – –	– – –	– – –	– – –	1 – –

FRANCIS BURNS

DEBUT (Full Appearance)

Saturday 02/09/1967
Football League Division 1
at Upton Park

West Ham United 1 Manchester United 3

CLUB CAREER RECORD	Apps	Subs	Goals
Premiership	0		0
League Division 1	111	(10)	6
League Division 2	0		0
FA Cup	11	(1)	0
League Cup	10	(1)	0
European Cup / Champions League	10	(1)	1
European Cup-Winners' Cup	0		0
UEFA Cup / Inter-Cities' Fairs Cup	0		0
Other Matches	1		0
OVERALL TOTAL	**143**	**(13)**	**7**

Opponents	PREM A S G	FLD 1 A S G	FLD 2 A S G	FAC A S G	LC A S G	EC/CL A S G	ECWC A S G	UEFA A S G	OTHER A S G	TOTAL A S G
1 Southampton	- - -	7 1	- - -	2 -	- - -	- - -	- - -	- - -	- - -	9 1
2 Stoke City	- -	5 (1) -	- -	- -	3 -	- -	- -	- -	- -	8 (1) -
3 Tottenham Hotspur	- -	6 1	- -	2 -	- -	- -	- -	- -	- -	8 1
4 Manchester City	- -	5 (1) -	- -	1 -	1 -	- -	- -	- -	- -	7 (1) -
5 Liverpool	- -	7 -	- -	- -	- -	- -	- -	- -	- -	7 -
6 Wolverhampton W.	- -	7 -	- -	- -	- -	- -	- -	- -	- -	7 -
7 West Ham United	- -	6 (1) 1	- -	- -	- -	- -	- -	- -	- -	6 (1) 1
8 Chelsea	- -	6 -	- -	- -	- (1)	- -	- -	- -	- -	6 (1) -
9 Coventry City	- -	6 (1) -	- -	- -	- -	- -	- -	- -	- -	6 (1) -
10 Burnley	- -	4 1	- -	- -	2 -	- -	- -	- -	- -	6 1
11 Leeds United	- -	6 1	- -	- -	- -	- -	- -	- -	- -	6 1
12 Arsenal	- -	6 -	- -	- -	- -	- -	- -	- -	- -	6 -
13 West Bromwich Albion	- -	5 (1) -	- -	- -	- -	- -	- -	- -	- -	5 (1) -
14 Derby County	- -	3 -	- -	- -	2 -	- -	- -	- -	- -	5 -
15 Nottingham Forest	- -	4 (1) 1	- -	- -	- -	- -	- -	- -	- -	4 (1) 1
16 Everton	- -	4 (1) -	- -	- -	- -	- -	- -	- -	- -	4 (1) -
17 Ipswich Town	- -	3 -	- -	1 -	- -	- -	- -	- -	- -	4 -
18 Leicester City	- -	4 -	- -	- -	- -	- -	- -	- -	- -	4 -
19 Newcastle United	- -	4 -	- -	- -	- -	- -	- -	- -	- -	4 -
20 Sheffield Wednesday	- -	3 (1) -	- -	- -	- -	- -	- -	- -	- -	3 (1) -
21 Middlesbrough	- -	- -	- -	3 -	- -	- -	- -	- -	- -	3 -
22 Sunderland	- -	3 -	- -	- -	- -	- -	- -	- -	- -	3 -
23 Waterford	- -	- -	- -	- -	- -	2 1	- -	- -	- -	2 1
24 Blackpool	- -	2 -	- -	- -	- -	- -	- -	- -	- -	2 -
25 Fulham	- -	2 -	- -	- -	- -	- -	- -	- -	- -	2 -
26 Gornik Zabrze	- -	- -	- -	- -	- -	2 -	- -	- -	- -	2 -
27 Hibernians Malta	- -	- -	- -	- -	- -	2 -	- -	- -	- -	2 -
28 Sarajevo	- -	- -	- -	- -	- -	2 -	- -	- -	- -	2 -
29 AC Milan	- -	- -	- -	- -	- -	1 (1) -	- -	- -	- -	1 (1) -
30 Crystal Palace	- -	1 (1) -	- -	- -	- -	- -	- -	- -	- -	1 (1) -
31 Sheffield United	- -	1 (1) -	- -	- -	- -	- -	- -	- -	- -	1 (1) -
32 Estudiantes de la Plata	- -	- -	- -	- -	- -	- -	- -	- -	1 -	1 -
33 Exeter City	- -	- -	- -	1 -	- -	- -	- -	- -	- -	1 -
34 Huddersfield Town	- -	1 -	- -	- -	- -	- -	- -	- -	- -	1 -
35 Portsmouth	- -	- -	- -	- -	1 -	- -	- -	- -	- -	1 -
36 Preston North End	- -	- -	- -	1 -	- -	- -	- -	- -	- -	1 -
37 Real Madrid	- -	- -	- -	- -	- -	1 -	- -	- -	- -	1 -
38 Wrexham	- -	- -	- -	- -	1 -	- -	- -	- -	- -	1 -
39 Northampton Town	- -	- -	- -	- (1) -	- -	- -	- -	- -	- -	- (1) -

NICKY BUTT

DEBUT (Substitute Appearance)

Saturday 21/11/1992
FA Premiership
at Old Trafford

Manchester United 3 Oldham Athletic 0

CLUB CAREER RECORD	Apps	Subs	Goals
Premiership	210	(60)	21
League Division 1	0		0
League Division 2	0		0
FA Cup	23	(6)	1
League Cup	7	(1)	0
European Cup / Champions League	56	(13)	2
European Cup-Winners' Cup	0		0
UEFA Cup / Inter-Cities' Fairs Cup	2		0
Other Matches	9		2
OVERALL TOTAL	**307**	**(80)**	**26**

Opponents	PREM A S G	FLD 1 A S G	FLD 2 A S G	FAC A S G	LC A S G	EC/CL A S G	ECWC A S G	UEFA A S G	OTHER A S G	TOTAL A S G
1 Leeds United	13 (4) 2	- -	- -	- -	1 -	- -	- -	- -	- -	14 (4) 2
2 Arsenal	9 (3) -	- -	- -	2 (1) -	- -	- -	- -	- -	3 -	14 (4) -
3 Liverpool	10 (4) 1	- -	- -	2 -	- -	- -	- -	- -	1 -	13 (4) 1
4 Tottenham Hotspur	10 (6) 1	- -	- -	- -	1 -	- -	- -	- -	- -	11 (6) 1
5 Chelsea	12 (1) -	- -	- -	- -	- -	- -	- -	1 -	- -	15 (1) -
6 Southampton	13 (2) 1	- -	- -	1 -	- -	- -	- -	- -	- -	14 (2) 1
7 Middlesbrough	11 (3) 2	- -	- -	2 -	- -	- -	- -	- -	- -	13 (3) 2
8 West Ham United	10 (4) 1	- -	- -	1 (1) -	- -	- -	- -	- -	- -	11 (5) 1
9 Everton	12 (1) 2	- -	- -	1 -	- -	- -	- -	- -	- -	13 (1) 2
10 Aston Villa	11 (1) -	- -	- -	- -	2 -	- -	- -	- -	- -	13 (1) -
11 Newcastle United	10 (2) -	- -	- -	- -	- -	1 -	- -	- -	1 1	12 (2) 1
12 Leicester City	10 (2) 2	- -	- -	- -	- -	- -	- -	- -	- -	10 (2) 2

continued../

NICKY BUTT (continued)

Opponents	PREM			FLD 1			FLD 2			FAC			LC			EC/CL			ECWC			UEFA			OTHER			TOTAL		
	A	S	G	A	S	G	A	S	G	A	S	G	A	S	G	A	S	G	A	S	G	A	S	G	A	S	G	A	S	G
13 Derby County	10	(1)	2	–	–	–	–	–	–	–	–	–	–	–	–	–	–	–	–	–	–	–	–	–	–	–	–	10	(1)	2
14 Blackburn Rovers	8	(2)	–	–	–	–	–	–	–	–	–	–	–	(1)	–	–	–	–	–	–	–	–	–	–	–	–	–	8	(3)	–
15 Coventry City	7	(3)	–	–	–	–	–	–	–	–	–	–	–	–	–	–	–	–	–	–	–	–	–	–	–	–	–	7	(3)	–
16 Sheffield Wednesday	7	(3)	–	–	–	–	–	–	–	–	–	–	–	–	–	–	–	–	–	–	–	–	–	–	–	–	–	7	(3)	–
17 Sunderland	5	(2)	3	–	–	–	–	–	–	2		1	–	–	–	–	–	–	–	–	–	–	–	–	–	–	–	7	(2)	4
18 Bolton Wanderers	6	(3)	1	–	–	–	–	–	–	–	–	–	–	–	–	–	–	–	–	–	–	–	–	–	–	–	–	6	(3)	1
19 Charlton Athletic	6	(2)	–	–	–	–	–	–	–	–	–	–	–	–	–	–	–	–	–	–	–	–	–	–	–	–	–	6	(2)	–
20 Manchester City	4	(2)	–	–	–	–	–	–	–	1	(1)	–	–	–	–	–	–	–	–	–	–	–	–	–	–	–	–	5	(3)	–
21 Nottingham Forest	4	(2)	1	–	–	–	–	–	–	–	–	–	1			–	–	–	–	–	–	–	–	–	–	–	–	5	(2)	1
22 Fulham	3			–	–	–	–	–	–	3			–	–	–	–	–	–	–	–	–	–	–	–	–	–	–	6		
23 Juventus	–			–	–	–	–	–	–	–	–	–	–	–	–	6			–	–	–	–	–	–	–	–	–	6		–
24 Wimbledon	5		1	–	–	–	–	–	–	–	–	–	–	–	–	–	–	–	–	–	–	–	–	–	–	–	–	5		1
25 Crystal Palace	2		1	–	–	–	–	–	–	1	(1)	–	–	–	–	–	–	–	–	–	–	–	–	–	–	–	–	3	(1)	1
26 Barcelona	–			–	–	–	–	–	–	–	–	–	–	–	–	2	(2)	–	–	–	–	–	–	–	–	–	–	2	(2)	–
27 Ipswich Town	2	(2)	–	–	–	–	–	–	–	–	–	–	–	–	–	–	–	–	–	–	–	–	–	–	–	–	–	2	(2)	–
28 Valencia	–			–	–	–	–	–	–	–	–	–	–	–	–	1	(3)	–	–	–	–	–	–	–	–	–	–	1	(3)	–
29 Panathinaikos	–			–	–	–	–	–	–	–	–	–	–	–	–	3		1	–	–	–	–	–	–	–	–	–	3		1
30 Bayer Leverkusen	–			–	–	–	–	–	–	–	–	–	–	–	–	3			–	–	–	–	–	–	–	–	–	3		
31 Deportivo La Coruna	–			–	–	–	–	–	–	–	–	–	–	–	–	3			–	–	–	–	–	–	–	–	–	3		
32 Porto	–			–	–	–	–	–	–	–	–	–	–	–	–	3			–	–	–	–	–	–	–	–	–	3		
33 Bayern Munich	–			–	–	–	–	–	–	–	–	–	–	–	–	2	(1)	–	–	–	–	–	–	–	–	–	–	2	(1)	–
34 Real Madrid	–			–	–	–	–	–	–	–	–	–	–	–	–	2	(1)	–	–	–	–	–	–	–	–	–	–	2	(1)	–
35 Queens Park Rangers	1	(2)	–	–	–	–	–	–	–	–	–	–	–	–	–	–	–	–	–	–	–	–	–	–	–	–	–	1	(2)	–
36 Sturm Graz	–			–	–	–	–	–	–	–	–	–	–	–	–	2		1	–	–	–	–	–	–	–	–	–	2		1
37 Barnsley	2			–	–	–	–	–	–	–	–	–	–	–	–	–	–	–	–	–	–	–	–	–	–	–	–	2		
38 Boavista	–			–	–	–	–	–	–	–	–	–	–	–	–	2			–	–	–	–	–	–	–	–	–	2		
39 Borussia Dortmund	–			–	–	–	–	–	–	–	–	–	–	–	–	2			–	–	–	–	–	–	–	–	–	2		
40 Bradford City	2			–	–	–	–	–	–	–	–	–	–	–	–	–	–	–	–	–	–	–	–	–	–	–	–	2		
41 Dynamo Kiev	–			–	–	–	–	–	–	–	–	–	–	–	–	2			–	–	–	–	–	–	–	–	–	2		
42 Fenerbahce	–			–	–	–	–	–	–	–	–	–	–	–	–	2			–	–	–	–	–	–	–	–	–	2		–
43 Feyenoord	–			–	–	–	–	–	–	–	–	–	–	–	–	2			–	–	–	–	–	–	–	–	–	2		–
44 Galatasaray	–			–	–	–	–	–	–	–	–	–	–	–	–	2			–	–	–	–	–	–	–	–	–	2		
45 Girondins Bordeaux	–			–	–	–	–	–	–	–	–	–	–	–	–	2			–	–	–	–	–	–	–	–	–	2		
46 Kosice	–			–	–	–	–	–	–	–	–	–	–	–	–	2			–	–	–	–	–	–	–	–	–	2		
47 LKS Lodz	–			–	–	–	–	–	–	–	–	–	–	–	–	2			–	–	–	–	–	–	–	–	–	2		
48 Monaco	–			–	–	–	–	–	–	–	–	–	–	–	–	2			–	–	–	–	–	–	–	–	–	2		
49 Olympiakos Piraeus	–			–	–	–	–	–	–	–	–	–	–	–	–	2			–	–	–	–	–	–	–	–	–	2		
50 Port Vale	–			–	–	–	–	–	–	–	–	–	2			–	–	–	–	–	–	–	–	–	–	–	–	2		
51 Portsmouth	2			–	–	–	–	–	–	–	–	–	–	–	–	–	–	–	–	–	–	–	–	–	–	–	–	2		
52 Rotor Volgograd	–			–	–	–	–	–	–	–	–	–	–	–	–	–	–	–	–	–	–	2			–	–	–	2		
53 Watford	2			–	–	–	–	–	–	–	–	–	–	–	–	–	–	–	–	–	–	–	–	–	–	–	–	2		
54 West Bromwich Albion	1			–	–	–	–	–	–	–	–	–	1			–	–	–	–	–	–	–	–	–	–	–	–	2		–
55 Gothenburg	–			–	–	–	–	–	–	–	–	–	–	–	–	1	(1)	–	–	–	–	–	–	–	–	–	–	1	(1)	–
56 PSV Eindhoven	–			–	–	–	–	–	–	–	–	–	–	–	–	1	(1)	–	–	–	–	–	–	–	–	–	–	1	(1)	–
57 Rapid Vienna	–			–	–	–	–	–	–	–	–	–	–	–	–	1	(1)	–	–	–	–	–	–	–	–	–	–	1	(1)	–
58 Oldham Athletic	–	(1)	–	–	–	–	–	–	–	–	(1)	–	–	–	–	–	–	–	–	–	–	–	–	–	–	–	–	–	(2)	–
59 Vasco da Gama	–			–	–	–	–	–	–	–	–	–	–	–	–	–	–	–	–	–	–	–	–	–	1		1	1		1
60 Anderlecht	–			–	–	–	–	–	–	–	–	–	–	–	–	1			–	–	–	–	–	–	–	–	–	1		
61 Basel	–			–	–	–	–	–	–	–	–	–	–	–	–	1			–	–	–	–	–	–	–	–	–	1		
62 Lille Metropole	–			–	–	–	–	–	–	–	–	–	–	–	–	1			–	–	–	–	–	–	–	–	–	1		
63 Northampton Town	–			–	–	–	–	–	–	1			–	–	–	–	–	–	–	–	–	–	–	–	–	–	–	1		
64 Olympique Marseille	–			–	–	–	–	–	–	–	–	–	–	–	–	1			–	–	–	–	–	–	–	–	–	1		
65 Palmeiras	–			–	–	–	–	–	–	–	–	–	–	–	–	–	–	–	–	–	–	–	–	–	1			1		
66 Rayos del Necaxa	–			–	–	–	–	–	–	–	–	–	–	–	–	–	–	–	–	–	–	–	–	–	1			1		
67 Reading	–			–	–	–	–	–	–	1			–	–	–	–	–	–	–	–	–	–	–	–	–	–	–	1		
68 Sheffield United	–			–	–	–	–	–	–	1			–	–	–	–	–	–	–	–	–	–	–	–	–	–	–	1		
69 Birmingham City	–	(1)	–	–	–	–	–	–	–	–	–	–	–	–	–	–	–	–	–	–	–	–	–	–	–	–	–	–	(1)	–
70 Glasgow Rangers	–			–	–	–	–	–	–	–	–	–	–	–	–	–	(1)	–	–	–	–	–	–	–	–	–	–	–	(1)	–
71 Internazionale	–			–	–	–	–	–	–	–	–	–	–	–	–	–	(1)	–	–	–	–	–	–	–	–	–	–	–	(1)	–
72 Millwall	–			–	–	–	–	–	–	–	(1)	–	–	–	–	–	–	–	–	–	–	–	–	–	–	–	–	–	(1)	–
73 Nantes Atlantique	–			–	–	–	–	–	–	–	–	–	–	–	–	–	(1)	–	–	–	–	–	–	–	–	–	–	–	(1)	–
74 Norwich City	–	(1)	–	–	–	–	–	–	–	–	–	–	–	–	–	–	–	–	–	–	–	–	–	–	–	–	–	–	(1)	–

DAVID BYRNE

DEBUT (Full Appearance, 1 goal)

Saturday 21/10/1933
Football League Division 2
at Gigg Lane

Bury 2 Manchester United 1

CLUB CAREER RECORD	Apps	Subs	Goals
Premiership	0		0
League Division 1	0		0
League Division 2	4		3
FA Cup	0		0
League Cup	0		0
European Cup / Champions League	0		0
European Cup-Winners' Cup	0		0
UEFA Cup / Inter-Cities' Fairs Cup	0		0
Other Matches	0		0
OVERALL TOTAL	4		3

| | PREM | | | FLD 1 | | | FLD 2 | | | FAC | | | LC | | | EC/CL | | | ECWC | | | UEFA | | | OTHER | | | TOTAL | | |
Opponents	A	S	G	A	S	G	A	S	G	A	S	G	A	S	G	A	S	G	A	S	G	A	S	G	A	S	G	A	S	G
1 Grimsby Town	–	–	–	–	–	–	2	2		–			–			–			–			–			–			2		2
2 Bury	–	–	–	–	–	–	1	1		–			–			–			–			–			–			1		1
3 Plymouth Argyle	–	–	–	–	–	–	1			–			–			–			–			–			–			1		

ROGER BYRNE

DEBUT (Full Appearance)

Saturday 24/11/1951
Football League Division 1
at Anfield

Liverpool 0 Manchester United 0

CLUB CAREER RECORD	Apps	Subs	Goals
Premiership	0		0
League Division 1	245		17
League Division 2	0		0
FA Cup	18		2
League Cup	0		0
European Cup / Champions League	14		0
European Cup-Winners' Cup	0		0
UEFA Cup / Inter-Cities' Fairs Cup	0		0
Other Matches	3		1
OVERALL TOTAL	280		20

| | PREM | | | FLD 1 | | | FLD 2 | | | FAC | | | LC | | | EC/CL | | | ECWC | | | UEFA | | | OTHER | | | TOTAL | | |
Opponents	A	S	G	A	S	G	A	S	G	A	S	G	A	S	G	A	S	G	A	S	G	A	S	G	A	S	G	A	S	G
1 Manchester City	–	–	13		–			–		1			–			–			–			–			1		15		
2 Arsenal	–	–	14	1			–			–			–			–			–			–			–		14		1
3 Blackpool	–	–	14	1			–			–			–			–			–			–			–		14		1
4 Newcastle United	–	–	12				–			–			–			–			–			1		1			13		1
5 Aston Villa	–	–	11				–		1			–			–			–			1					13		–
6 Bolton Wanderers	–	–	13		–			–			–			–			–			–			–		13		–
7 Burnley	–	–	11	4			–		1			–			–			–			–			–		12		4
8 Preston North End	–	–	12	2			–			–			–			–			–			–			–		12		2
9 Chelsea	–	–	12	1			–			–			–			–			–			–			–		12		1
10 West Bromwich Albion	–	–	12				–			–			–			–			–			–			–		12		–
11 Portsmouth	–	–	11				–			–			–			–			–			–			–		11		–
12 Tottenham Hotspur	–	–	11				–			–			–			–			–			–			–		11		–
13 Sunderland	–	–	10	1			–			–			–			–			–			–			–		10		1
14 Everton	–	–	8				–		2			–			–			–			–			–		10		–
15 Cardiff City	–	–	9	2			–			–			–			–			–			–			–		9		2
16 Charlton Athletic	–	–	9	1			–			–			–			–			–			–			–		9		1
17 Sheffield Wednesday	–	–	9				–			–			–			–			–			–			–		9		–
18 Wolverhampton W.	–	–	8				–			–			–			–			–			–			–		8		–
19 Liverpool	–	–	6	3			–			–			–			–			–			–			–		6		3
20 Huddersfield Town	–	–	6				–			–			–			–			–			–			–		6		–
21 Birmingham City	–	–	4				–		1			–			–			–			–			–		5		–
22 Luton Town	–	–	5				–			–			–			–			–			–			–		5		–
23 Sheffield United	–	–	5				–			–			–			–			–			–			–		5		–
24 Middlesbrough	–	–	4	1			–			–			–			–			–			–			–		4		1
25 Leeds United	–	–	4				–			–			–			–			–			–			–		4		–
26 Leicester City	–	–	4				–			–			–			–			–			–			–		4		–
27 Derby County	–	–	3				–			–			–			–			–			–			–		3		–
28 Walthamstow Avenue	–	–					–		2	1		–			–			–			–			–			2		1
29 Anderlecht	–	–					–			–			–			2			–			–			–		2		–
30 Athletic Bilbao	–	–					–			–			–			2			–			–			–		2		–
31 Borussia Dortmund	–	–					–			–			–			2			–			–			–		2		–
32 Dukla Prague	–	–					–			–			–			2			–			–			–		2		–
33 Fulham	–	–	2				–			–			–			–			–			–			–		2		–
34 Reading	–	–					–		2			–			–			–			–			–		2		–
35 Real Madrid	–	–					–			–			–			2			–			–			–		2		–
36 Red Star Belgrade	–	–					–			–			–			2			–			–			–		2		–
37 Shamrock Rovers	–	–					–			–			–			2			–			–			–		2		–
38 Stoke City	–	–	2				–			–			–			–			–			–			–		2		–
39 Wrexham	–	–					–		1	1		–			–			–			–			–			1		1
40 Bournemouth	–	–					–		1			–			–			–			–			–		1		–
41 Bristol Rovers	–	–					–		1			–			–			–			–			–		1		–
42 Hartlepool United	–	–					–		1			–			–			–			–			–		1		–
43 Hull City	–	–					–		1			–			–			–			–			–		1		–
44 Ipswich Town	–	–					–		1			–			–			–			–			–		1		–
45 Millwall	–	–					–		1			–			–			–			–			–		1		–
46 Nottingham Forest	–	–	1				–			–			–			–			–			–			–		1		–
47 Workington	–	–					–		1			–			–			–			–			–		1		–

JAMES CAIRNS

DEBUT (Full Appearance)

Monday 15/04/1895
Football League Division 2
at Gigg Lane

Bury 2 Newton Heath 1

CLUB CAREER RECORD	Apps	Subs	Goals
Premiership	0		0
League Division 1	0		0
League Division 2	2		0
FA Cup	0		0
League Cup	0		0
European Cup / Champions League	0		0
European Cup-Winners' Cup	0		0
UEFA Cup / Inter-Cities' Fairs Cup	0		0
Other Matches	0		0
OVERALL TOTAL	**2**		**0**

Opponents	PREM A S G	FLD 1 A S G	FLD 2 A S G	FAC A S G	LC A S G	EC/CL A S G	ECWC A S G	UEFA A S G	OTHER A S G	TOTAL A S G
1 Bury	– –	– –	1 –	–	–	–	–	–	– –	1 –
2 Port Vale	– –	– –	1 –	–	–	–	–	–	– –	1 –

FRAIZER CAMPBELL

DEBUT (Substitute Appearance)

Sunday 19/08/2007
FA Premiership
at Eastlands Stadium

Manchester City 1 Manchester United 0

CLUB CAREER RECORD	Apps	Subs	Goals
Premiership	0	(1)	0
League Division 1	0		0
League Division 2	0		0
FA Cup	0		0
League Cup	0	(1)	0
European Cup / Champions League	0		0
European Cup-Winners' Cup	0		0
UEFA Cup / Inter-Cities' Fairs Cup	0		0
Other Matches	0		0
OVERALL TOTAL	**0**	**(2)**	**0**

Opponents	PREM A S G	FLD 1 A S G	FLD 2 A S G	FAC A S G	LC A S G	EC/CL A S G	ECWC A S G	UEFA A S G	OTHER A S G	TOTAL A S G
1 Coventry City	– –	–	–	–	– (1) –	–	–	–	– –	– (1) –
2 Manchester City	– (1) –	–	–	–	–	–	–	–	– –	– (1) –

WILLIAM CAMPBELL

DEBUT (Full Appearance)

Saturday 25/11/1893
Football League Division 1
at Bramall Lane

Sheffield United 3 Newton Heath 1

CLUB CAREER RECORD	Apps	Subs	Goals
Premiership	0		0
League Division 1	5		1
League Division 2	0		0
FA Cup	0		0
League Cup	0		0
European Cup / Champions League	0		0
European Cup-Winners' Cup	0		0
UEFA Cup / Inter-Cities' Fairs Cup	0		0
Other Matches	0		0
OVERALL TOTAL	**5**		**1**

Opponents	PREM A S G	FLD 1 A S G	FLD 2 A S G	FAC A S G	LC A S G	EC/CL A S G	ECWC A S G	UEFA A S G	OTHER A S G	TOTAL A S G
1 Sunderland	– –	1 1	– –	–	–	–	–	–	– –	1 1
2 Aston Villa	– –	1 –	–	–	–	–	–	–	–	1 –
3 Bolton Wanderers	– –	1 –	–	–	–	–	–	–	– –	1 –
4 Everton	– –	1 –	–	–	–	–	–	–	–	1 –
5 Sheffield United	– –	1 –	–	–	–	–	–	–	– –	1 –

ERIC CANTONA

DEBUT (Substitute Appearance)

Saturday 06/12/1992
FA Premiership
at Old Trafford

Manchester United 2 Manchester City 1

CLUB CAREER RECORD	Apps	Subs	Goals
Premiership	142	(1)	64
League Division 1	0		0
League Division 2	0		0
FA Cup	17		10
League Cup	6		1
European Cup / Champions League	16		5
European Cup-Winners' Cup	0		0
UEFA Cup / Inter-Cities' Fairs Cup	0		0
Other Matches	3		2
OVERALL TOTAL	184	(1)	82

Opponents	PREM A S G			FLD 1 A S G			FLD 2 A S G			FAC A S G			LC A S G			EC/CL A S G			ECWC A S G			UEFA A S G			OTHER A S G			TOTAL A S G		
1 Chelsea	7		3	–	–	–	–	–	–	2		2	–	–	–	–	–	–	–	–	–	–	–	–	–	–	–	9		5
2 Wimbledon	6		4	–	–	–	–	–	–	3		1	–	–	–	–	–	–	–	–	–	–	–	–	–	–	–	9		5
3 Coventry City	9		4	–	–	–	–	–	–	–	–	–	–	–	–	–	–	–	–	–	–	–	–	–	–	–	–	9		4
4 Southampton	8		2	–	–	–	–	–	–	1		1	–	–	–	–	–	–	–	–	–	–	–	–	–	–	–	9		3
5 Sheffield Wednesday	7		5	–	–	–	–	–	–	–	–	–	1			–	–	–	–	–	–	–	–	–	–	–	–	8		5
6 Blackburn Rovers	7		3	–	–	–	–	–	–	–	–	–	–	–	–	–	–	–	–	–	–	–	–	–	1		1	8		4
7 Leeds United	8		3	–	–	–	–	–	–	–	–	–	–	–	–	–	–	–	–	–	–	–	–	–	–	–	–	8		3
8 Arsenal	7		2	–	–	–	–	–	–	–	–	–	–	–	–	–	–	–	–	–	–	1		–	–	–	–	8		2
9 Liverpool	7		1	–	–	–	–	–	–	1		1	–	–	–	–	–	–	–	–	–	–	–	–	–	–	–	8		2
10 Newcastle United	7		1	–	–	–	–	–	–	–	–	–	–	–	–	–	–	–	–	–	–	–	–	–	1		1	8		2
11 Tottenham Hotspur	7		2	–	–	–	–	–	–	–	–	–	1			–	–	–	–	–	–	–	–	–	–	–	–	8		2
12 Aston Villa	6		2	–	–	–	–	–	–	–	–	–	1			–	–	–	–	–	–	–	–	–	–	–	–	7		2
13 Everton	6		1	–	–	–	–	–	–	–	–	–	1			–	–	–	–	–	–	–	–	–	–	–	–	7		1
14 Manchester City	5 (1)		7	–	–	–	–	–	–	1		1	–	–	–	–	–	–	–	–	–	–	–	–	–	–	–	6 (1)		8
15 Nottingham Forest	6		5	–	–	–	–	–	–	–	–	–	–	–	–	–	–	–	–	–	–	–	–	–	–	–	–	6		5
16 West Ham United	6		3	–	–	–	–	–	–	–	–	–	–	–	–	–	–	–	–	–	–	–	–	–	–	–	–	6		3
17 Norwich City	4		2	–	–	–	–	–	–	1		1	–	–	–	–	–	–	–	–	–	–	–	–	–	–	–	5		3
18 Middlesbrough	5		1	–	–	–	–	–	–	–	–	–	–	–	–	–	–	–	–	–	–	–	–	–	–	–	–	5		1
19 Queens Park Rangers	4		3	–	–	–	–	–	–	–	–	–	–	–	–	–	–	–	–	–	–	–	–	–	–	–	–	4		3
20 Sheffield United	2		2	–	–	–	–	–	–	2		1	–	–	–	–	–	–	–	–	–	–	–	–	–	–	–	4		3
21 Sunderland	2		2	–	–	–	–	–	–	2		1	–	–	–	–	–	–	–	–	–	–	–	–	–	–	–	4		3
22 Ipswich Town	4		2	–	–	–	–	–	–	–	–	–	–	–	–	–	–	–	–	–	–	–	–	–	–	–	–	4		2
23 Crystal Palace	3		1	–	–	–	–	–	–	–	–	–	–	–	–	–	–	–	–	–	–	–	–	–	–	–	–	3		1
24 Galatasaray	–		–	–	–	–	–	–	–	–	–	–	–	–	–	3		1	–	–	–	–	–	–	–	–	–	3		1
25 Leicester City	3		–	–	–	–	–	–	–	–	–	–	–	–	–	–	–	–	–	–	–	–	–	–	–	–	–	3		–
26 Derby County	2		1	–	–	–	–	–	–	–	–	–	–	–	–	–	–	–	–	–	–	–	–	–	–	–	–	2		1
27 Fenerbahce	–		–	–	–	–	–	–	–	–	–	–	–	–	–	2		1	–	–	–	–	–	–	–	–	–	2		1
28 Honved	–		–	–	–	–	–	–	–	–	–	–	–	–	–	2		1	–	–	–	–	–	–	–	–	–	2		1
29 Porto	–		–	–	–	–	–	–	–	–	–	–	–	–	–	2		1	–	–	–	–	–	–	–	–	–	2		1
30 Portsmouth	–		–	–	–	–	–	–	–	–	–	–	2		1	–	–	–	–	–	–	–	–	–	–	–	–	2		1
31 Rapid Vienna	–		–	–	–	–	–	–	–	–	–	–	–	–	–	2		1	–	–	–	–	–	–	–	–	–	2		1
32 Swindon Town	2		1	–	–	–	–	–	–	–	–	–	–	–	–	–	–	–	–	–	–	–	–	–	–	–	–	2		1
33 Borussia Dortmund	–		–	–	–	–	–	–	–	–	–	–	–	–	–	2			–	–	–	–	–	–	–	–	–	2		–
34 Juventus	–		–	–	–	–	–	–	–	–	–	–	–	–	–	2			–	–	–	–	–	–	–	–	–	2		–
35 Oldham Athletic	1		1	–	–	–	–	–	–	–	–	–	–	–	–	–	–	–	–	–	–	–	–	–	–	–	–	1		1
36 Reading	–		–	–	–	–	–	–	–	1		1	–	–	–	–	–	–	–	–	–	–	–	–	–	–	–	1		1
37 Bolton Wanderers	1			–	–	–	–	–	–	–	–	–	–	–	–	–	–	–	–	–	–	–	–	–	–	–	–	1		–
38 Bury	–		–	–	–	–	–	–	–	1			–	–	–	–	–	–	–	–	–	–	–	–	–	–	–	1		–
39 Charlton Athletic	–		–	–	–	–	–	–	–	1			–	–	–	–	–	–	–	–	–	–	–	–	–	–	–	1		–
40 Gothenburg	–		–	–	–	–	–	–	–	–	–	–	–	–	–	1			–	–	–	–	–	–	–	–	–	1		–
41 York City	–		–	–	–	–	–	–	–	–	–	–	1			–	–	–	–	–	–	–	–	–	–	–	–	1		–

NOEL CANTWELL

DEBUT (Full Appearance)

Saturday 26/11/1960
Football League Division 1
at Ninian Park

Cardiff City 3 Manchester United 0

CLUB CAREER RECORD	Apps	Subs	Goals
Premiership	0		0
League Division 1	123		6
League Division 2	0		0
FA Cup	14		2
League Cup	0		0
European Cup / Champions League	3		0
European Cup-Winners' Cup	4		0
UEFA Cup / Inter-Cities' Fairs Cup	0		0
Other Matches	2		0
OVERALL TOTAL	146		8

Opponents	PREM A S G			FLD 1 A S G			FLD 2 A S G			FAC A S G			LC A S G			EC/CL A S G			ECWC A S G			UEFA A S G			OTHER A S G			TOTAL A S G		
1 Tottenham Hotspur	–		–	6			–	–	–	1			–	–	–	–	–	–	2			–	–	–	–	–	–	9		–
2 Blackpool	–		–	8			–	–	–	–	–	–	–	–	–	–	–	–	–	–	–	–	–	–	–	–	–	8		–
3 Aston Villa	–		–	6		1	–	–	–	1			–	–	–	–	–	–	–	–	–	–	–	–	–	–	–	7		1
4 Sheffield Wednesday	–		–	5			–	–	–	2		1	–	–	–	–	–	–	–	–	–	–	–	–	–	–	–	7		1
5 Chelsea	–		–	6			–	–	–	1			–	–	–	–	–	–	–	–	–	–	–	–	–	–	–	7		–
6 West Bromwich Albion	–		–	7			–	–	–	–	–	–	–	–	–	–	–	–	–	–	–	–	–	–	–	–	–	7		–
7 Arsenal	–		–	6		1	–	–	–	–	–	–	–	–	–	–	–	–	–	–	–	–	–	–	–	–	–	6		1
8 Birmingham City	–		–	6		1	–	–	–	–	–	–	–	–	–	–	–	–	–	–	–	–	–	–	–	–	–	6		1
9 West Ham United	–		–	6		1	–	–	–	–	–	–	–	–	–	–	–	–	–	–	–	–	–	–	–	–	–	6		1
10 Blackburn Rovers	–		–	6			–	–	–	–	–	–	–	–	–	–	–	–	–	–	–	–	–	–	–	–	–	6		–

continued../

NOEL CANTWELL (continued)

Opponents	PREM A S G	FLD 1 A S G	FLD 2 A S G	FAC A S G	LC A S G	EC/CL A S G	ECWC A S G	UEFA A S G	OTHER A S G	TOTAL A S G
11 Everton	– –	5 –	– –	– –	– –	– –	– –	– –	1 –	6 –
12 Burnley	– –	5 1	– –	– –	– –	– –	– –	– –	– –	5 1
13 Leicester City	– –	4 –	– –	1 –	– –	– –	– –	– –	– –	5 –
14 Liverpool	– –	4 –	– –	– –	– –	– –	– –	1 –	– –	5 –
15 Sheffield United	– –	5 –	– –	– –	– –	– –	– –	– –	– –	5 –
16 Wolverhampton W.	– –	5 –	– –	– –	– –	– –	– –	– –	– –	5 –
17 Fulham	– –	4 –	– –	– –	– –	– –	– –	– –	– –	4 –
18 Ipswich Town	– –	4 –	– –	– –	– –	– –	– –	– –	– –	4 –
19 Manchester City	– –	4 –	– –	– –	– –	– –	– –	– –	– –	4 –
20 Nottingham Forest	– –	4 –	– –	– –	– –	– –	– –	– –	– –	4 –
21 Bolton Wanderers	– –	3 1	– –	– –	– –	– –	– –	– –	– –	3 1
22 Cardiff City	– –	3 –	– –	– –	– –	– –	– –	– –	– –	3 –
23 Southampton	– –	1 –	– –	2 –	– –	– –	– –	– –	– –	3 –
24 ASK Vorwaerts	– –	– –	– –	– –	– –	2 –	– –	– –	– –	2 –
25 Leeds United	– –	2 –	– –	– –	– –	– –	– –	– –	– –	2 –
26 Northampton Town	– –	2 –	– –	– –	– –	– –	– –	– –	– –	2 –
27 Preston North End	– –	1 –	– –	1 –	– –	– –	– –	– –	– –	2 –
28 Sunderland	– –	2 –	– –	– –	– –	– –	– –	– –	– –	2 –
29 Willem II	– –	– –	– –	– –	– –	– –	2 –	– –	– –	2 –
30 Middlesbrough	– –	– –	– –	1 1	– –	– –	– –	– –	– –	1 1
31 Benfica	– –	– –	– –	– –	– –	1 –	– –	– –	– –	1 –
32 Bristol Rovers	– –	– –	– –	1 –	– –	– –	– –	– –	– –	1 –
33 Derby County	– –	– –	– –	1 –	– –	– –	– –	– –	– –	1 –
34 Huddersfield Town	– –	– –	– –	1 –	– –	– –	– –	– –	– –	1 –
35 Leyton Orient	– –	1 –	– –	– –	– –	– –	– –	– –	– –	1 –
36 Newcastle United	– –	1 –	– –	– –	– –	– –	– –	– –	– –	1 –
37 Rotherham United	– –	– –	– –	1 –	– –	– –	– –	– –	– –	1 –
38 Stoke City	– –	1 –	– –	– –	– –	– –	– –	– –	– –	1 –

JACK CAPE

DEBUT (Full Appearance)

Saturday 27/01/1934
Football League Division 2
at Old Trafford

Manchester United 1 Brentford 3

CLUB CAREER RECORD	Apps	Subs	Goals
Premiership	0		0
League Division 1	4		1
League Division 2	55		17
FA Cup	1		0
League Cup	0		0
European Cup / Champions League	0		0
European Cup–Winners' Cup	0		0
UEFA Cup / Inter–Cities' Fairs Cup	0		0
Other Matches	0		0
OVERALL TOTAL	**60**		**18**

Opponents	PREM A S G	FLD 1 A S G	FLD 2 A S G	FAC A S G	LC A S G	EC/CL A S G	ECWC A S G	UEFA A S G	OTHER A S G	TOTAL A S G
1 Bradford City	– –	– –	5 1	– –	– –	– –	– –	– –	– –	5 1
2 Port Vale	– –	– –	4 –	– –	– –	– –	– –	– –	– –	4 –
3 Burnley	– –	– –	3 4	– –	– –	– –	– –	– –	– –	3 4
4 Norwich City	– –	– –	3 1	– –	– –	– –	– –	– –	– –	3 1
5 Sheffield United	– –	– –	3 1	– –	– –	– –	– –	– –	– –	3 1
6 West Ham United	– –	– –	3 1	– –	– –	– –	– –	– –	– –	3 1
7 Barnsley	– –	– –	3 –	– –	– –	– –	– –	– –	– –	3 –
8 Nottingham Forest	– –	– –	2 –	1 –	– –	– –	– –	– –	– –	3 –
9 Southampton	– –	– –	2 2	– –	– –	– –	– –	– –	– –	2 2
10 Swansea City	– –	– –	2 2	– –	– –	– –	– –	– –	– –	2 2
11 Blackpool	– –	– –	2 1	– –	– –	– –	– –	– –	– –	2 1
12 Bury	– –	– –	2 1	– –	– –	– –	– –	– –	– –	2 1
13 Charlton Athletic	– –	– –	2 1	– –	– –	– –	– –	– –	– –	2 1
14 Bolton Wanderers	– –	– –	2 –	– –	– –	– –	– –	– –	– –	2 –
15 Bradford Park Avenue	– –	– –	2 –	– –	– –	– –	– –	– –	– –	2 –
16 Brentford	– –	– –	2 –	– –	– –	– –	– –	– –	– –	2 –
17 Fulham	– –	– –	2 –	– –	– –	– –	– –	– –	– –	2 –
18 Hull City	– –	– –	2 –	– –	– –	– –	– –	– –	– –	2 –
19 Newcastle United	– –	– –	2 –	– –	– –	– –	– –	– –	– –	2 –
20 Grimsby Town	– –	1 1	– –	– –	– –	– –	– –	– –	– –	1 1
21 Millwall	– –	– –	1 1	– –	– –	– –	– –	– –	– –	1 1
22 Oldham Athletic	– –	– –	1 1	– –	– –	– –	– –	– –	– –	1 1
23 Derby County	– –	1 –	– –	– –	– –	– –	– –	– –	– –	1 –
24 Doncaster Rovers	– –	– –	1 –	– –	– –	– –	– –	– –	– –	1 –
25 Everton	– –	1 –	– –	– –	– –	– –	– –	– –	– –	1 –
26 Leicester City	– –	– –	1 –	– –	– –	– –	– –	– –	– –	1 –
27 Liverpool	– –	1 –	– –	– –	– –	– –	– –	– –	– –	1 –
28 Notts County	– –	– –	1 –	– –	– –	– –	– –	– –	– –	1 –
29 Plymouth Argyle	– –	– –	1 –	– –	– –	– –	– –	– –	– –	1 –
30 Preston North End	– –	– –	1 –	– –	– –	– –	– –	– –	– –	1 –

FREDDY CAPPER

DEBUT (Full Appearance)

Saturday 23/03/1912
Football League Division 1
at Old Trafford

Manchester United 1 Liverpool 1

CLUB CAREER RECORD	Apps	Subs	Goals
Premiership	0		0
League Division 1	1		0
League Division 2	0		0
FA Cup	0		0
League Cup	0		0
European Cup / Champions League	0		0
European Cup–Winners' Cup	0		0
UEFA Cup / Inter–Cities' Fairs Cup	0		0
Other Matches	0		0
OVERALL TOTAL	**1**		**0**

Opponents	PREM A S G	FLD 1 A S G	FLD 2 A S G	FAC A S G	LC A S G	EC/CL A S G	ECWC A S G	UEFA A S G	OTHER A S G	TOTAL A S G
1 Liverpool	– – –	1 – –	– – –	– – –	– – –	– – –	– – –	– – –	– – –	1 – –

JOHNNY CAREY

DEBUT (Full Appearance)

Saturday 25/09/1937
Football League Division 2
at Old Trafford

Manchester United 1 Southampton 2

CLUB CAREER RECORD	Apps	Subs	Goals
Premiership	0		0
League Division 1	288		13
League Division 2	16		3
FA Cup	38		1
League Cup	0		0
European Cup / Champions League	0		0
European Cup–Winners' Cup	0		0
UEFA Cup / Inter–Cities' Fairs Cup	0		0
Other Matches	2		0
OVERALL TOTAL	**344**		**17**

Opponents	PREM A S G	FLD 1 A S G	FLD 2 A S G	FAC A S G	LC A S G	EC/CL A S G	ECWC A S G	UEFA A S G	OTHER A S G	TOTAL A S G
1 Wolverhampton W.	– – –	16 – –	– – –	2 – –	– – –	– – –	– – –	– – –	– – –	18 – –
2 Blackpool	– – –	16 – 2	– – –	1 – –	– – –	– – –	– – –	– – –	– – –	17 – 2
3 Chelsea	– – –	15 – 2	– – –	1 – –	– – –	– – –	– – –	– – –	– – –	16 – 2
4 Derby County	– – –	15 – 2	– – –	1 – –	– – –	– – –	– – –	– – –	– – –	16 – 2
5 Arsenal	– – –	14 – –	– – –	1 – –	– – –	– – –	– – –	– 1 –	– – –	16 – –
6 Aston Villa	– – –	14 – 1	– – –	1 – –	– – –	– – –	– – –	– – –	– – –	16 – –
7 Liverpool	– – –	15 – –	– – –	1 – –	– – –	– – –	– – –	– – –	– – –	16 – –
8 Portsmouth	– – –	13 – –	– – –	2 – –	– – –	– – –	– – –	– – –	– – –	15 – –
9 Bolton Wanderers	– – –	14 – 1	– – –	– – –	– – –	– – –	– – –	– – –	– – –	14 – 1
10 Middlesbrough	– – –	14 – –	– – –	– – –	– – –	– – –	– – –	– – –	– – –	14 – –
11 Charlton Athletic	– – –	12 – 1	– – –	1 – –	– – –	– – –	– – –	– – –	– – –	13 – 1
12 Preston North End	– – –	10 – –	– – –	3 – –	– – –	– – –	– – –	– – –	– – –	13 – –
13 Stoke City	– – –	13 – –	– – –	– – –	– – –	– – –	– – –	– – –	– – –	13 – –
14 Sunderland	– – –	13 – –	– – –	– – –	– – –	– – –	– – –	– – –	– – –	13 – –
15 Burnley	– – –	12 – 1	– – –	– – –	– – –	– – –	– – –	– – –	– – –	12 – 1
16 Huddersfield Town	– – –	11 – –	– – –	– – –	– – –	– – –	– – –	– – –	– – –	11 – –
17 Manchester City	– – –	10 – 1	– – –	– – –	– – –	– – –	– – –	– – –	– – –	10 – 1
18 Everton	– – –	9 – –	– – –	1 – –	– – –	– – –	– – –	– – –	– – –	10 – –
19 Newcastle United	– – –	8 – –	1 – –	– – –	– – –	– – –	– – –	– 1 –	– – –	10 – –
20 Sheffield United	– – –	6 – –	2 – –	– – –	– – –	– – –	– – –	– – –	– – –	8 – –
21 West Bromwich Albion	– – –	6 – –	– – –	2 – –	– – –	– – –	– – –	– – –	– – –	8 – –
22 Birmingham City	– – –	5 – –	– – –	1 – –	– – –	– – –	– – –	– – –	– – –	6 – –
23 Brentford	– – –	4 – 1	– – –	1 – –	– – –	– – –	– – –	– – –	– – –	5 – 1
24 Leeds United	– – –	4 – 1	– – –	1 – –	– – –	– – –	– – –	– – –	– – –	5 – 1
25 Tottenham Hotspur	– – –	4 – –	1 – –	– – –	– – –	– – –	– – –	– – –	– – –	5 – –
26 Blackburn Rovers	– – –	4 – –	– – –	– – –	– – –	– – –	– – –	– – –	– – –	4 – –
27 Bradford Park Avenue	– – –	– – –	– – –	4 – –	– – –	– – –	– – –	– – –	– – –	4 – –
28 Grimsby Town	– – –	4 – –	– – –	– – –	– – –	– – –	– – –	– – –	– – –	4 – –
29 Sheffield Wednesday	– – –	3 – –	1 – –	– – –	– – –	– – –	– – –	– – –	– – –	4 – –
30 Barnsley	– – –	– – –	1 – –	2 1 –	– – –	– – –	– – –	– – –	– – –	3 1 –
31 Fulham	– – –	2 – –	1 – –	– – –	– – –	– – –	– – –	– – –	– – –	3 – –
32 Leicester City	– – –	2 1 –	– – –	– – –	– – –	– – –	– – –	– – –	– – –	2 1 –
33 Nottingham Forest	– – –	– – –	1 – 1	1 – –	– – –	– – –	– – –	– – –	– – –	2 – 1
34 Accrington Stanley	– – –	– – –	– – –	2 – –	– – –	– – –	– – –	– – –	– – –	2 – –
35 Southampton	– – –	– – –	2 – –	– – –	– – –	– – –	– – –	– – –	– – –	2 – –
36 Walthamstow Avenue	– – –	– – –	– – –	2 – –	– – –	– – –	– – –	– – –	– – –	2 – –
37 Chesterfield	– – –	– – –	1 – 1	– – –	– – –	– – –	– – –	– – –	– – –	1 – 1
38 Luton Town	– – –	– – –	1 – 1	– – –	– – –	– – –	– – –	– – –	– – –	1 – 1
39 Bournemouth	– – –	– – –	– – –	1 – –	– – –	– – –	– – –	– – –	– – –	1 – –
40 Hull City	– – –	– – –	– – –	1 – –	– – –	– – –	– – –	– – –	– – –	1 – –
41 Millwall	– – –	– – –	– – –	1 – –	– – –	– – –	– – –	– – –	– – –	1 – –
42 Norwich City	– – –	– – –	1 – –	– – –	– – –	– – –	– – –	– – –	– – –	1 – –
43 Oldham Athletic	– – –	– – –	– – –	1 – –	– – –	– – –	– – –	– – –	– – –	1 – –
44 Plymouth Argyle	– – –	– – –	1 – –	– – –	– – –	– – –	– – –	– – –	– – –	1 – –
45 Stockport County	– – –	– – –	1 – –	– – –	– – –	– – –	– – –	– – –	– – –	1 – –
46 Watford	– – –	– – –	– – –	1 – –	– – –	– – –	– – –	– – –	– – –	1 – –
47 Weymouth Town	– – –	– – –	– – –	1 – –	– – –	– – –	– – –	– – –	– – –	1 – –
48 Yeovil Town	– – –	– – –	– – –	1 – –	– – –	– – –	– – –	– – –	– – –	1 – –

JAMES CARMAN

DEBUT (Full Appearance)

Saturday 25/12/1897
Football League Division 2
at Hyde Road

Manchester City 0 Newton Heath 1

CLUB CAREER RECORD	Apps	Subs	Goals
Premiership	0		0
League Division 1	0		0
League Division 2	3		1
FA Cup	0		0
League Cup	0		0
European Cup / Champions League	0		0
European Cup–Winners' Cup	0		0
UEFA Cup / Inter–Cities' Fairs Cup	0		0
Other Matches	0		0
OVERALL TOTAL	**3**		**1**

Opponents	PREM A S G	FLD 1 A S G	FLD 2 A S G	FAC A S G	LC A S G	EC/CL A S G	ECWC A S G	UEFA A S G	OTHER A S G	TOTAL A S G
1 Burton Swifts	– – –	– – –	1 – 1	– – –	– – –	– – –	– – –	– – –	– – –	1 – 1
2 Gainsborough Trinity	– – –	– – –	1 – –	– – –	– – –	– – –	– – –	– – –	– – –	1 – –
3 Manchester City	– – –	– – –	1 – –	– – –	– – –	– – –	– – –	– – –	– – –	1 – –

JOSEPH CAROLAN

DEBUT (Full Appearance)

Saturday 22/11/1958
Football League Division 1
at Old Trafford

Manchester United 2 Luton Town 1

CLUB CAREER RECORD	Apps	Subs	Goals
Premiership	0		0
League Division 1	66		0
League Division 2	0		0
FA Cup	4		0
League Cup	1		0
European Cup / Champions League	0		0
European Cup–Winners' Cup	0		0
UEFA Cup / Inter–Cities' Fairs Cup	0		0
Other Matches	0		0
OVERALL TOTAL	**71**		**0**

Opponents	PREM A S G	FLD 1 A S G	FLD 2 A S G	FAC A S G	LC A S G	EC/CL A S G	ECWC A S G	UEFA A S G	OTHER A S G	TOTAL A S G
1 Birmingham City	– –	4 –	– –	– –	– –	– –	– –	– –	– –	4 –
2 Blackburn Rovers	– –	4 –	– –	– –	– –	– –	– –	– –	– –	4 –
3 Everton	– –	4 –	– –	– –	– –	– –	– –	– –	– –	4 –
4 Leicester City	– –	4 –	– –	– –	– –	– –	– –	– –	– –	4 –
5 Luton Town	– –	4 –	– –	– –	– –	– –	– –	– –	– –	4 –
6 Arsenal	– –	3 –	– –	– –	– –	– –	– –	– –	– –	3 –
7 Blackpool	– –	3 –	– –	– –	– –	– –	– –	– –	– –	3 –
8 Bolton Wanderers	– –	3 –	– –	– –	– –	– –	– –	– –	– –	3 –
9 Burnley	– –	3 –	– –	– –	– –	– –	– –	– –	– –	3 –
10 Chelsea	– –	3 –	– –	– –	– –	– –	– –	– –	– –	3 –
11 Leeds United	– –	3 –	– –	– –	– –	– –	– –	– –	– –	3 –
12 Manchester City	– –	3 –	– –	– –	– –	– –	– –	– –	– –	3 –
13 Newcastle United	– –	3 –	– –	– –	– –	– –	– –	– –	– –	3 –
14 Preston North End	– –	3 –	– –	– –	– –	– –	– –	– –	– –	3 –
15 Tottenham Hotspur	– –	3 –	– –	– –	– –	– –	– –	– –	– –	3 –
16 West Bromwich Albion	– –	3 –	– –	– –	– –	– –	– –	– –	– –	3 –
17 Wolverhampton W.	– –	3 –	– –	– –	– –	– –	– –	– –	– –	3 –
18 Fulham	– –	2 –	– –	– –	– –	– –	– –	– –	– –	2 –
19 Nottingham Forest	– –	2 –	– –	– –	– –	– –	– –	– –	– –	2 –
20 Portsmouth	– –	2 –	– –	– –	– –	– –	– –	– –	– –	2 –
21 Sheffield Wednesday	– –	1 –	– –	1 –	– –	– –	– –	– –	– –	2 –
22 West Ham United	– –	2 –	– –	– –	– –	– –	– –	– –	– –	2 –
23 Aston Villa	– –	1 –	– –	– –	– –	– –	– –	– –	– –	1 –
24 Derby County	– –	– –	– –	1 –	– –	– –	– –	– –	– –	1 –
25 Exeter City	– –	– –	– –	– –	1 –	– –	– –	– –	– –	1 –
26 Liverpool	– –	– –	– –	1 –	– –	– –	– –	– –	– –	1 –
27 Norwich City	– –	– –	– –	1 –	– –	– –	– –	– –	– –	1 –

MICHAEL CARRICK

DEBUT (Substitute Appearance)

Wednesday 23/08/2006
FA Premiership
at The Valley

Charlton Athletic 0 Manchester United 3

CLUB CAREER RECORD	Apps	Subs	Goals
Premiership	53	(11)	5
League Division 1	0		0
League Division 2	0		0
FA Cup	10	(1)	1
League Cup	0	(1)	0
European Cup / Champions League	23	(1)	2
European Cup-Winners' Cup	0		0
UEFA Cup / Inter-Cities' Fairs Cup	0		0
Other Matches	1		0
OVERALL TOTAL	87	(14)	8

Opponents	PREM			FLD 1			FLD 2			FAC			LC			EC/CL			ECWC			UEFA			OTHER			TOTAL		
	A	S	G	A	S	G	A	S	G	A	S	G	A	S	G	A	S	G	A	S	G	A	S	G	A	S	G	A	S	G
1 Chelsea	3	(1)	–	–	–	–	–	–	–	1	–	–	–	–	–	1	–	–	–	–	–	–	–	–	1	–	–	6	(1)	–
2 Roma	–	–	–	–	–	–	–	–	–	–	–	–	–	–	–	6		2	–	–	–	–	–	–	–	–	–	6		2
3 Portsmouth	4	–	–	–	–	–	–	–	–	1	(1)	–	–	–	–	–	–	–	–	–	–	–	–	–	–	–	–	5	(1)	–
4 Reading	4	–	–	–	–	–	–	–	–	1		1	–	–	–	–	–	–	–	–	–	–	–	–	–	–	–	5		1
5 Tottenham Hotspur	3	(1)	–	–	–	–	–	–	–	1	–	–	–	–	–	–	–	–	–	–	–	–	–	–	–	–	–	4	(1)	–
6 Arsenal	2	(2)	–	–	–	–	–	–	–	1	–	–	–	–	–	–	–	–	–	–	–	–	–	–	–	–	–	3	(2)	–
7 Aston Villa	2		1	–	–	–	–	–	–	2	–	–	–	–	–	–	–	–	–	–	–	–	–	–	–	–	–	4		1
8 Everton	4	–	–	–	–	–	–	–	–	–	–	–	–	–	–	–	–	–	–	–	–	–	–	–	–	–	–	4		–
9 Middlesbrough	2	–	–	–	–	–	–	–	–	2	–	–	–	–	–	–	–	–	–	–	–	–	–	–	–	–	–	4		–
10 Blackburn Rovers	3	(1)	1	–	–	–	–	–	–	–	–	–	–	–	–	–	–	–	–	–	–	–	–	–	–	–	–	3	(1)	1
11 Manchester City	3	(1)	1	–	–	–	–	–	–	–	–	–	–	–	–	–	–	–	–	–	–	–	–	–	–	–	–	3	(1)	1
12 Liverpool	3	(1)	–	–	–	–	–	–	–	–	–	–	–	–	–	–	–	–	–	–	–	–	–	–	–	–	–	3	(1)	–
13 Newcastle United	3	(1)	–	–	–	–	–	–	–	–	–	–	–	–	–	–	–	–	–	–	–	–	–	–	–	–	–	3	(1)	–
14 West Ham United	3		1	–	–	–	–	–	–	–	–	–	–	–	–	–	–	–	–	–	–	–	–	–	–	–	–	3		1
15 Bolton Wanderers	3	–	–	–	–	–	–	–	–	–	–	–	–	–	–	–	–	–	–	–	–	–	–	–	–	–	–	3		–
16 Watford	2	–	–	–	–	–	–	–	–	1	–	–	–	–	–	–	–	–	–	–	–	–	–	–	–	–	–	3		–
17 Sheffield United	2		1	–	–	–	–	–	–	–	–	–	–	–	–	–	–	–	–	–	–	–	–	–	–	–	–	2		1
18 AC Milan	–	–	–	–	–	–	–	–	–	–	–	–	–	–	–	2	–	–	–	–	–	–	–	–	–	–	–	2		–
19 Barcelona	–	–	–	–	–	–	–	–	–	–	–	–	–	–	–	2	–	–	–	–	–	–	–	–	–	–	–	2		–
20 Benfica	–	–	–	–	–	–	–	–	–	–	–	–	–	–	–	2	–	–	–	–	–	–	–	–	–	–	–	2		–
21 Birmingham City	2	–	–	–	–	–	–	–	–	–	–	–	–	–	–	–	–	–	–	–	–	–	–	–	–	–	–	2		–
22 Copenhagen	–	–	–	–	–	–	–	–	–	–	–	–	–	–	–	2	–	–	–	–	–	–	–	–	–	–	–	2		–
23 Glasgow Celtic	–	–	–	–	–	–	–	–	–	–	–	–	–	–	–	2	–	–	–	–	–	–	–	–	–	–	–	2		–
24 Lille Metropole	–	–	–	–	–	–	–	–	–	–	–	–	–	–	–	2	–	–	–	–	–	–	–	–	–	–	–	2		–
25 Sporting Lisbon	–	–	–	–	–	–	–	–	–	–	–	–	–	–	–	2	–	–	–	–	–	–	–	–	–	–	–	2		–
26 Wigan Athletic	2	–	–	–	–	–	–	–	–	–	–	–	–	–	–	–	–	–	–	–	–	–	–	–	–	–	–	2		–
27 Derby County	1	(1)	–	–	–	–	–	–	–	–	–	–	–	–	–	–	–	–	–	–	–	–	–	–	–	–	–	1	(1)	–
28 Fulham	1	(1)	–	–	–	–	–	–	–	–	–	–	–	–	–	–	–	–	–	–	–	–	–	–	–	–	–	1	(1)	–
29 Olympique Lyonnais	–	–	–	–	–	–	–	–	–	–	–	–	–	–	–	1	(1)	–	–	–	–	–	–	–	–	–	–	1	(1)	–
30 Dynamo Kiev	–	–	–	–	–	–	–	–	–	–	–	–	–	–	–	1	–	–	–	–	–	–	–	–	–	–	–	1		–
31 Sunderland	1	–	–	–	–	–	–	–	–	–	–	–	–	–	–	–	–	–	–	–	–	–	–	–	–	–	–	1		–
32 Charlton Athletic	–	(1)	–	–	–	–	–	–	–	–	–	–	–	–	–	–	–	–	–	–	–	–	–	–	–	–	–	–	(1)	–
33 Coventry City	–	–	–	–	–	–	–	–	–	–	–	–	–	(1)	–	–	–	–	–	–	–	–	–	–	–	–	–	–	(1)	–

ROY CARROLL

DEBUT (Full Appearance)

Sunday 26/08/2001
FA Premiership
at Villa Park

Aston Villa 1 Manchester United 1

CLUB CAREER RECORD	Apps	Subs	Goals
Premiership	46	(3)	0
League Division 1	0		0
League Division 2	0		0
FA Cup	7	(1)	0
League Cup	5		0
European Cup / Champions League	10		0
European Cup-Winners' Cup	0		0
UEFA Cup / Inter-Cities' Fairs Cup	0		0
Other Matches	0		0
OVERALL TOTAL	68	(4)	0

Opponents	PREM			FLD 1			FLD 2			FAC			LC			EC/CL			ECWC			UEFA			OTHER			TOTAL		
	A	S	G	A	S	G	A	S	G	A	S	G	A	S	G	A	S	G	A	S	G	A	S	G	A	S	G	A	S	G
1 Arsenal	3	–	–	–	–	–	–	–	–	2	–	–	1	–	–	–	–	–	–	–	–	–	–	–	–	–	–	6		–
2 Aston Villa	3	–	–	–	–	–	–	–	–	1	–	–	–	–	–	–	–	–	–	–	–	–	–	–	–	–	–	4		–
3 Birmingham City	4	–	–	–	–	–	–	–	–	–	–	–	–	–	–	–	–	–	–	–	–	–	–	–	–	–	–	4		–
4 Charlton Athletic	4	–	–	–	–	–	–	–	–	–	–	–	–	–	–	–	–	–	–	–	–	–	–	–	–	–	–	4		–
5 Middlesbrough	3	–	–	–	–	–	–	–	–	1	–	–	–	–	–	–	–	–	–	–	–	–	–	–	–	–	–	4		–
6 Tottenham Hotspur	4	–	–	–	–	–	–	–	–	–	–	–	–	–	–	–	–	–	–	–	–	–	–	–	–	–	–	4		–
7 West Bromwich Albion	3	–	–	–	–	–	–	–	–	–	–	–	1	–	–	–	–	–	–	–	–	–	–	–	–	–	–	4		–
8 Leicester City	2	–	–	–	–	–	–	–	–	–	–	–	1	–	–	–	–	–	–	–	–	–	–	–	–	–	–	3		–
9 Manchester City	3	–	–	–	–	–	–	–	–	–	–	–	–	–	–	–	–	–	–	–	–	–	–	–	–	–	–	3		–
10 Portsmouth	2	–	–	–	–	–	–	–	–	1	–	–	–	–	–	–	–	–	–	–	–	–	–	–	–	–	–	3		–
11 Southampton	2	(1)	–	–	–	–	–	–	–	–	–	–	–	–	–	–	–	–	–	–	–	–	–	–	–	–	–	2	(1)	–
12 Sunderland	2	(1)	–	–	–	–	–	–	–	–	–	–	–	–	–	–	–	–	–	–	–	–	–	–	–	–	–	2	(1)	–
13 Chelsea	2	–	–	–	–	–	–	–	–	–	–	–	–	–	–	–	–	–	–	–	–	–	–	–	–	–	–	2		–
14 Everton	1	–	–	–	–	–	–	–	–	1	–	–	–	–	–	–	–	–	–	–	–	–	–	–	–	–	–	2		–
15 Fulham	2	–	–	–	–	–	–	–	–	–	–	–	–	–	–	–	–	–	–	–	–	–	–	–	–	–	–	2		–
16 Liverpool	2	–	–	–	–	–	–	–	–	–	–	–	–	–	–	–	–	–	–	–	–	–	–	–	–	–	–	2		–
17 Sparta Prague	–	–	–	–	–	–	–	–	–	–	–	–	–	–	–	2	–	–	–	–	–	–	–	–	–	–	–	2		–
18 Zalaegerszeg	–	–	–	–	–	–	–	–	–	–	–	–	–	–	–	2	–	–	–	–	–	–	–	–	–	–	–	2		–

continued../

ROY CARROLL (continued)

Opponents	PREM A	S	G	FLD 1 A	S	G	FLD 2 A	S	G	FAC A	S	G	LC A	S	G	EC/CL A	S	G	ECWC A	S	G	UEFA A	S	G	OTHER A	S	G	TOTAL A	S	G
19 AC Milan	–	–	–	–	–	–	–	–	–	–	–	–	–	–	–	1	–	–	–	–	–	–	–	–	–	–	–	1	–	–
20 Basel	–	–	–	–	–	–	–	–	–	–	–	–	–	–	–	1	–	–	–	–	–	–	–	–	–	–	–	1	–	–
21 Bolton Wanderers	1	–	–	–	–	–	–	–	–	–	–	–	–	–	–	–	–	–	–	–	–	–	–	–	–	–	–	1	–	–
22 Burnley	–	–	–	–	–	–	–	–	–	–	–	–	1	–	–	–	–	–	–	–	–	–	–	–	–	–	–	1	–	–
23 Crystal Palace	1	–	–	–	–	–	–	–	–	–	–	–	–	–	–	–	–	–	–	–	–	–	–	–	–	–	–	1	–	–
24 Fenerbahce	–	–	–	–	–	–	–	–	–	–	–	–	–	–	–	1	–	–	–	–	–	–	–	–	–	–	–	1	–	–
25 Ipswich Town	1	–	–	–	–	–	–	–	–	–	–	–	–	–	–	–	–	–	–	–	–	–	–	–	–	–	–	1	–	–
26 Leeds United	–	–	–	–	–	–	–	–	–	–	–	–	1	–	–	–	–	–	–	–	–	–	–	–	–	–	–	1	–	–
27 Lille Metropole	–	–	–	–	–	–	–	–	–	–	–	–	–	–	–	1	–	–	–	–	–	–	–	–	–	–	–	1	–	–
28 Newcastle United	1	–	–	–	–	–	–	–	–	–	–	–	–	–	–	–	–	–	–	–	–	–	–	–	–	–	–	1	–	–
29 Northampton Town	–	–	–	–	–	–	–	–	–	1	–	–	–	–	–	–	–	–	–	–	–	–	–	–	–	–	–	1	–	–
30 Olympique Lyonnais	–	–	–	–	–	–	–	–	–	–	–	–	–	–	–	1	–	–	–	–	–	–	–	–	–	–	–	1	–	–
31 Stuttgart	–	–	–	–	–	–	–	–	–	–	–	–	–	–	–	1	–	–	–	–	–	–	–	–	–	–	–	1	–	–
32 Derby County	–	(1)	–	–	–	–	–	–	–	–	–	–	–	–	–	–	–	–	–	–	–	–	–	–	–	–	–	–	(1)	–
33 Millwall	–	–	–	–	–	–	–	–	–	–	(1)	–	–	–	–	–	–	–	–	–	–	–	–	–	–	–	–	–	(1)	–

ADAM CARSON

DEBUT (Full Appearance)

Saturday 03/09/1892
Football League Division 1
at Ewood Park

Blackburn Rovers 4 Newton Heath 3

CLUB CAREER RECORD	Apps	Subs	Goals
Premiership	0		0
League Division 1	13		3
League Division 2	0		0
FA Cup	0		0
League Cup	0		0
European Cup / Champions League	0		0
European Cup-Winners' Cup	0		0
UEFA Cup / Inter-Cities' Fairs Cup	0		0
Other Matches	0		0
OVERALL TOTAL	13		3

Opponents	PREM A	S	G	FLD 1 A	S	G	FLD 2 A	S	G	FAC A	S	G	LC A	S	G	EC/CL A	S	G	ECWC A	S	G	UEFA A	S	G	OTHER A	S	G	TOTAL A	S	G
1 Blackburn Rovers	–	–		2	1		–	–		–	–		–	–		–	–		–	–		–	–		–	–		2	1	
2 Wolverhampton W.	–	–		2	1		–	–		–	–		–	–		–	–		–	–		–	–		–	–		2	1	
3 Burnley	–	–		2	–		–	–		–	–		–	–		–	–		–	–		–	–		–	–		2	–	
4 Everton	–	–		2	–		–	–		–	–		–	–		–	–		–	–		–	–		–	–		2	–	
5 West Bromwich Albion	–	–		2	–		–	–		–	–		–	–		–	–		–	–		–	–		–	–		2	–	
6 Notts County	–	–		1	1		–	–		–	–		–	–		–	–		–	–		–	–		–	–		1	1	
7 Nottingham Forest	–	–		1	–		–	–		–	–		–	–		–	–		–	–		–	–		–	–		1	–	
8 Sheffield Wednesday	–	–		1	–		–	–		–	–		–	–		–	–		–	–		–	–		–	–		1	–	

BERT CARTMAN

DEBUT (Full Appearance)

Saturday 16/12/1922
Football League Division 2
at Old Trafford

Manchester United 1 Stockport County 0

CLUB CAREER RECORD	Apps	Subs	Goals
Premiership	0		0
League Division 1	0		0
League Division 2	3		0
FA Cup	0		0
League Cup	0		0
European Cup / Champions League	0		0
European Cup-Winners' Cup	0		0
UEFA Cup / Inter-Cities' Fairs Cup	0		0
Other Matches	0		0
OVERALL TOTAL	3		0

Opponents	PREM A	S	G	FLD 1 A	S	G	FLD 2 A	S	G	FAC A	S	G	LC A	S	G	EC/CL A	S	G	ECWC A	S	G	UEFA A	S	G	OTHER A	S	G	TOTAL A	S	G
1 Stockport County	–	–		–	–		2	–		–	–		–	–		–	–		–	–		–	–		–	–		2	–	
2 West Ham United	–	–		–	–		1	–		–	–		–	–		–	–		–	–		–	–		–	–		1	–	

WALTER CARTWRIGHT

DEBUT (Full Appearance)

Saturday 07/09/1895
Football League Division 2
at Bank Street

Newton Heath 5 Crewe Alexandra 0

CLUB CAREER RECORD	Apps	Subs	Goals
Premiership	0		0
League Division 1	0		0
League Division 2	228		8
FA Cup	27		0
League Cup	0		0
European Cup / Champions League	0		0
European Cup-Winners' Cup	0		0
UEFA Cup / Inter-Cities' Fairs Cup	0		0
Other Matches	2		0
OVERALL TOTAL	**257**		**8**

Opponents	PREM A S G	FLD 1 A S G	FLD 2 A S G	FAC A S G	LC A S G	EC/CL A S G	ECWC A S G	UEFA A S G	OTHER A S G	TOTAL A S G
1 Lincoln City	– – –	– – –	16 –	1 –	– – –	– – –	– – –	– – –	– – –	17 –
2 Arsenal	– – –	– – –	16 – 2	– –	– – –	– – –	– – –	– – –	– – –	16 – 2
3 Birmingham City	– – –	– – –	10 –	4 –	– – –	– – –	– – –	– – –	– – –	14 –
4 Gainsborough Trinity	– – –	– – –	13 – 1	– –	– – –	– – –	– – –	– – –	– – –	13 – 1
5 Leicester City	– – –	– – –	13 – 1	– –	– – –	– – –	– – –	– – –	– – –	13 – 1
6 Burnley	– – –	– – –	8 –	2 –	– – –	– – –	– – –	– – –	2 –	12 –
7 Port Vale	– – –	– – –	11 –	– –	– – –	– – –	– – –	– – –	– – –	11 –
8 Barnsley	– – –	– – –	10 – 1	– –	– – –	– – –	– – –	– – –	– – –	10 – 1
9 Blackpool	– – –	– – –	9 – 1	1 –	– – –	– – –	– – –	– – –	– – –	10 – 1
10 Burton Swifts	– – –	– – –	10 –	– –	– – –	– – –	– – –	– – –	– – –	10 –
11 Grimsby Town	– – –	– – –	10 –	– –	– – –	– – –	– – –	– – –	– – –	10 –
12 Manchester City	– – –	– – –	9 –	– –	– – –	– – –	– – –	– – –	– – –	9 –
13 Darwen	– – –	– – –	8 –	– –	– – –	– – –	– – –	– – –	– – –	8 –
14 Glossop	– – –	– – –	7 –	– –	– – –	– – –	– – –	– – –	– – –	7 –
15 Loughborough Town	– – –	– – –	7 –	– –	– – –	– – –	– – –	– – –	– – –	7 –
16 Walsall	– – –	– – –	6 –	1 –	– – –	– – –	– – –	– – –	– – –	7 –
17 Burton United	– – –	– – –	4 – 1	2 –	– – –	– – –	– – –	– – –	– – –	6 – 1
18 Newcastle United	– – –	– – –	6 –	– –	– – –	– – –	– – –	– – –	– – –	6 –
19 Stockport County	– – –	– – –	6 –	– –	– – –	– – –	– – –	– – –	– – –	6 –
20 Luton Town	– – –	– – –	5 – 1	– –	– – –	– – –	– – –	– – –	– – –	5 – 1
21 Chesterfield	– – –	– – –	5 –	– –	– – –	– – –	– – –	– – –	– – –	5 –
22 Liverpool	– – –	– – –	2 –	3 –	– – –	– – –	– – –	– – –	– – –	5 –
23 Middlesbrough	– – –	– – –	5 –	– –	– – –	– – –	– – –	– – –	– – –	5 –
24 New Brighton Tower	– – –	– – –	5 –	– –	– – –	– – –	– – –	– – –	– – –	5 –
25 Notts County	– – –	– – –	4 –	1 –	– – –	– – –	– – –	– – –	– – –	5 –
26 Doncaster Rovers	– – –	– – –	4 –	– –	– – –	– – –	– – –	– – –	– – –	4 –
27 Bolton Wanderers	– – –	– – –	3 –	– –	– – –	– – –	– – –	– – –	– – –	3 –
28 Bristol City	– – –	– – –	3 –	– –	– – –	– – –	– – –	– – –	– – –	3 –
29 Burton Wanderers	– – –	– – –	3 –	– –	– – –	– – –	– – –	– – –	– – –	3 –
30 Derby County	– – –	– – –	– –	3 –	– – –	– – –	– – –	– – –	– – –	3 –
31 Sheffield Wednesday	– – –	– – –	2 –	1 –	– – –	– – –	– – –	– – –	– – –	3 –
32 Kettering	– – –	– – –	– –	2 –	– – –	– – –	– – –	– – –	– – –	2 –
33 Preston North End	– – –	– – –	2 –	– –	– – –	– – –	– – –	– – –	– – –	2 –
34 Rotherham United	– – –	– – –	2 –	– –	– – –	– – –	– – –	– – –	– – –	2 –
35 Southampton	– – –	– – –	– –	2 –	– – –	– – –	– – –	– – –	– – –	2 –
36 West Bromwich Albion	– – –	– – –	2 –	– –	– – –	– – –	– – –	– – –	– – –	2 –
37 Bradford City	– – –	– – –	1 –	– –	– – –	– – –	– – –	– – –	– – –	1 –
38 Crewe Alexandra	– – –	– – –	1 –	– –	– – –	– – –	– – –	– – –	– – –	1 –
39 Everton	– – –	– – –	– –	1 –	– – –	– – –	– – –	– – –	– – –	1 –
40 Portsmouth	– – –	– – –	– –	1 –	– – –	– – –	– – –	– – –	– – –	1 –
41 South Shore	– – –	– – –	– –	1 –	– – –	– – –	– – –	– – –	– – –	1 –
42 Tottenham Hotspur	– – –	– – –	– –	1 –	– – –	– – –	– – –	– – –	– – –	1 –

ARTHUR CASHMORE

DEBUT (Full Appearance)

Saturday 13/09/1913
Football League Division 1
at Old Trafford

Manchester United 0 Bolton Wanderers 1

CLUB CAREER RECORD	Apps	Subs	Goals
Premiership	0		0
League Division 1	3		0
League Division 2	0		0
FA Cup	0		0
League Cup	0		0
European Cup / Champions League	0		0
European Cup-Winners' Cup	0		0
UEFA Cup / Inter-Cities' Fairs Cup	0		0
Other Matches	0		0
OVERALL TOTAL	**3**		**0**

Opponents	PREM A S G	FLD 1 A S G	FLD 2 A S G	FAC A S G	LC A S G	EC/CL A S G	ECWC A S G	UEFA A S G	OTHER A S G	TOTAL A S G
1 Bolton Wanderers	– –	1 –	– –	– –	– – –	– – –	– – –	– – –	– – –	1 –
2 Bradford City	– –	1 –	– –	– –	– – –	– – –	– – –	– – –	– – –	1 –
3 Derby County	– –	1 –	– –	– –	– – –	– – –	– – –	– – –	– – –	1 –

CHRIS CASPER

DEBUT (Full Appearance)

Wednesday 05/10/1994
League Cup 2nd Round 2nd Leg
at Old Trafford

Manchester United 2 Port Vale 0

CLUB CAREER RECORD	Apps	Subs	Goals
Premiership	0	(2)	0
League Division 1	0		0
League Division 2	0		0
FA Cup	1		0
League Cup	3		0
European Cup / Champions League	0	(1)	0
European Cup-Winners' Cup	0		0
UEFA Cup / Inter-Cities' Fairs Cup	0		0
Other Matches	0		0
OVERALL TOTAL	**4**	**(3)**	**0**

Opponents	PREM			FLD 1			FLD 2			FAC			LC			EC/CL			ECWC			UEFA			OTHER			TOTAL		
	A	S	G	A	S	G	A	S	G	A	S	G	A	S	G	A	S	G	A	S	G	A	S	G	A	S	G	A	S	G
1 Leicester City	-	-	-	-	-	-	-	-	-	-	-	-	1	-	-	-	-	-	-	-	-	-	-	-	-	-	-	1	-	-
2 Port Vale	-	-	-	-	-	-	-	-	-	-	-	-	1	-	-	-	-	-	-	-	-	-	-	-	-	-	-	1	-	-
3 Swindon Town	-	-	-	-	-	-	-	-	-	-	-	-	1	-	-	-	-	-	-	-	-	-	-	-	-	-	-	1	-	-
4 Wimbledon	-	-	-	-	-	-	-	-	-	1	-	-	-	-	-	-	-	-	-	-	-	-	-	-	-	-	-	1	-	-
5 Coventry City	-	(1)	-	-	-	-	-	-	-	-	-	-	-	-	-	-	-	-	-	-	-	-	-	-	-	-	-	-	(1)	-
6 Rapid Vienna	-	-	-	-	-	-	-	-	-	-	-	-	-	-	-	-	(1)	-	-	-	-	-	-	-	-	-	-	-	(1)	-
7 Tottenham Hotspur	-	(1)	-	-	-	-	-	-	-	-	-	-	-	-	-	-	-	-	-	-	-	-	-	-	-	-	-	-	(1)	-

JOE CASSIDY

DEBUT (Full Appearance)

Friday 31/03/1893
Football League Division 1
at North Road

Manchester United 1 Stoke City 0

CLUB CAREER RECORD	Apps	Subs	Goals
Premiership	0		0
League Division 1	4		0
League Division 2	148		90
FA Cup	15		9
League Cup	0		0
European Cup / Champions League	0		0
European Cup-Winners' Cup	0		0
UEFA Cup / Inter-Cities' Fairs Cup	0		0
Other Matches	7		1
OVERALL TOTAL	**174**		**100**

Opponents	PREM			FLD 1			FLD 2			FAC			LC			EC/CL			ECWC			UEFA			OTHER			TOTAL		
	A	S	G	A	S	G	A	S	G	A	S	G	A	S	G	A	S	G	A	S	G	A	S	G	A	S	G	A	S	G
1 Arsenal	-	-	-	-	-	-	10		4	-	-	-	-	-	-	-	-	-	-	-	-	-	-	-	-	-	-	10		4
2 Birmingham City	-	-	-	-	-	-	8		2	-	-	-	-	-	-	-	-	-	-	-	-	-	-	-	2		1	10		3
3 Grimsby Town	-	-	-	-	-	-	9		12	-	-	-	-	-	-	-	-	-	-	-	-	-	-	-	-	-	-	9		12
4 Loughborough Town	-	-	-	-	-	-	9		7	-	-	-	-	-	-	-	-	-	-	-	-	-	-	-	-	-	-	9		7
5 Burton Swifts	-	-	-	-	-	-	9		5	-	-	-	-	-	-	-	-	-	-	-	-	-	-	-	-	-	-	9		5
6 Lincoln City	-	-	-	-	-	-	9		5	-	-	-	-	-	-	-	-	-	-	-	-	-	-	-	-	-	-	9		5
7 Walsall	-	-	-	-	-	-	8		5	1	-	-	-	-	-	-	-	-	-	-	-	-	-	-	-	-	-	9		5
8 Leicester City	-	-	-	-	-	-	9		1	-	-	-	-	-	-	-	-	-	-	-	-	-	-	-	-	-	-	9		1
9 Newcastle United	-	-	-	-	-	-	8		6	-	-	-	-	-	-	-	-	-	-	-	-	-	-	-	-	-	-	8		6
10 Gainsborough Trinity	-	-	-	-	-	-	8		3	-	-	-	-	-	-	-	-	-	-	-	-	-	-	-	-	-	-	8		3
11 Manchester City	-	-	-	-	-	-	8		3	-	-	-	-	-	-	-	-	-	-	-	-	-	-	-	-	-	-	8		3
12 Blackpool	-	-	-	-	-	-	5		5	2		1	-	-	-	-	-	-	-	-	-	-	-	-	-	-	-	7		6
13 Darwen	-	-	-	-	-	-	7		6	-	-	-	-	-	-	-	-	-	-	-	-	-	-	-	-	-	-	7		6
14 Luton Town	-	-	-	-	-	-	6		6	-	-	-	-	-	-	-	-	-	-	-	-	-	-	-	-	-	-	6		6
15 Notts County	-	-	-	-	-	-	5		3	-	-	-	-	-	-	-	-	-	-	-	-	-	-	-	-	-	-	5		3
16 Port Vale	-	-	-	-	-	-	4		3	-	-	-	-	-	-	-	-	-	-	-	-	-	-	-	-	-	-	4		3
17 Barnsley	-	-	-	-	-	-	4		2	-	-	-	-	-	-	-	-	-	-	-	-	-	-	-	-	-	-	4		2
18 Liverpool	-	-	-	-	-	-	2		1	2	-	-	-	-	-	-	-	-	-	-	-	-	-	-	-	-	-	4		1
19 Burnley	-	-	-	-	-	-	2		-	-	-	-	-	-	-	-	-	-	-	-	-	-	-	-	2		-	4		-
20 New Brighton Tower	-	-	-	-	-	-	3		4	-	-	-	-	-	-	-	-	-	-	-	-	-	-	-	-	-	-	3		4
21 Sunderland	-	-	-	1		-	-	-	-	-	-	-	-	-	-	-	-	-	-	-	-	-	-	-	2		-	3		-
22 Burton Wanderers	-	-	-	-	-	-	2		3	-	-	-	-	-	-	-	-	-	-	-	-	-	-	-	-	-	-	2		3
23 Kettering	-	-	-	-	-	-	-	-	-	2		3	-	-	-	-	-	-	-	-	-	-	-	-	-	-	-	2		3
24 Crewe Alexandra	-	-	-	-	-	-	2		2	-	-	-	-	-	-	-	-	-	-	-	-	-	-	-	-	-	-	2		2
25 Bury	-	-	-	-	-	-	2		1	-	-	-	-	-	-	-	-	-	-	-	-	-	-	-	-	-	-	2		1
26 Glossop	-	-	-	-	-	-	2		1	-	-	-	-	-	-	-	-	-	-	-	-	-	-	-	-	-	-	2		1
27 Southampton	-	-	-	-	-	-	-	-	-	2		1	-	-	-	-	-	-	-	-	-	-	-	-	-	-	-	2		1
28 Tottenham Hotspur	-	-	-	-	-	-	-	-	-	2		1	-	-	-	-	-	-	-	-	-	-	-	-	-	-	-	2		1
29 Bolton Wanderers	-	-	-	-	-	-	2		-	-	-	-	-	-	-	-	-	-	-	-	-	-	-	-	-	-	-	2		-
30 Sheffield Wednesday	-	-	-	-	-	-	2		-	-	-	-	-	-	-	-	-	-	-	-	-	-	-	-	-	-	-	2		-
31 Stoke City	-	-	-	1		-	-	-	-	-	-	-	-	-	-	-	-	-	-	-	-	-	-	-	1		-	2		-
32 West Manchester	-	-	-	-	-	-	-	-	-	1		2	-	-	-	-	-	-	-	-	-	-	-	-	-	-	-	1		2
33 Nelson	-	-	-	-	-	-	-	-	-	1		1	-	-	-	-	-	-	-	-	-	-	-	-	-	-	-	1		1
34 Accrington Stanley	-	-	-	1		-	-	-	-	-	-	-	-	-	-	-	-	-	-	-	-	-	-	-	-	-	-	1		-
35 Chesterfield	-	-	-	-	-	-	1		-	-	-	-	-	-	-	-	-	-	-	-	-	-	-	-	-	-	-	1		-
36 Derby County	-	-	-	-	-	-	-	-	-	1		-	-	-	-	-	-	-	-	-	-	-	-	-	-	-	-	1		-
37 Middlesbrough	-	-	-	-	-	-	1		-	-	-	-	-	-	-	-	-	-	-	-	-	-	-	-	-	-	-	1		-
38 Preston North End	-	-	-	1		-	-	-	-	-	-	-	-	-	-	-	-	-	-	-	-	-	-	-	-	-	-	1		-
39 Rotherham United	-	-	-	-	-	-	1		-	-	-	-	-	-	-	-	-	-	-	-	-	-	-	-	-	-	-	1		-
40 South Shore	-	-	-	-	-	-	-	-	-	1		-	-	-	-	-	-	-	-	-	-	-	-	-	-	-	-	1		-

LAURIE CASSIDY

DEBUT (Full Appearance)

Saturday 10/04/1948
Football League Division 1
at Goodison Park

Everton 2 Manchester United 0

CLUB CAREER RECORD	Apps	Subs	Goals
Premiership	0		0
League Division 1	4		0
League Division 2	0		0
FA Cup	0		0
League Cup	0		0
European Cup / Champions League	0		0
European Cup-Winners' Cup	0		0
UEFA Cup / Inter-Cities' Fairs Cup	0		0
Other Matches	0		0
OVERALL TOTAL	**4**		**0**

Opponents	PREM			FLD 1			FLD 2			FAC			LC			EC/CL			ECWC			UEFA			OTHER			TOTAL		
	A	S	G	A	S	G	A	S	G	A	S	G	A	S	G	A	S	G	A	S	G	A	S	G	A	S	G	A	S	G
1 Everton	–	–		2																								2		
2 Aston Villa	–	–		1																								1	–	
3 Manchester City	–	–		1																								1	–	

LUKE CHADWICK

DEBUT (Full Appearance)

Wednesday 13/10/1999
League Cup 3rd Round
at Villa Park

Aston Villa 3 Manchester United 0

CLUB CAREER RECORD	Apps	Subs	Goals
Premiership	11	(14)	2
League Division 1	0		0
League Division 2	0		0
FA Cup	1	(2)	0
League Cup	5		0
European Cup / Champions League	1	(5)	0
European Cup-Winners' Cup	0		0
UEFA Cup / Inter-Cities' Fairs Cup	0		0
Other Matches	0		0
OVERALL TOTAL	**18**	**(21)**	**2**

Opponents	PREM			FLD 1			FLD 2			FAC			LC			EC/CL			ECWC			UEFA			OTHER			TOTAL		
	A	S	G	A	S	G	A	S	G	A	S	G	A	S	G	A	S	G	A	S	G	A	S	G	A	S	G	A	S	G
1 Aston Villa	–	(1)	–							–	(1)	–	1															1	(2)	–
2 Middlesbrough	–	(2)	–							1																		1	(2)	–
3 Derby County	2																											2		
4 Everton	2																											2	–	
5 Ipswich Town	2																											2	–	
6 Sunderland	1												1															2	–	
7 Arsenal	–	(1)	–										1															1	(1)	–
8 Leeds United	–	(2)	1																									–	(2)	1
9 Fulham	–	(1)	–							–	(1)	–																–	(2)	–
10 Liverpool	–	(2)	–																									–	(2)	–
11 Burnley													1															1		
12 Charlton Athletic	1																											1	–	
13 Manchester City	1																											1	–	
14 Southampton	1																											1	–	
15 Sturm Graz																1												1	–	
16 Watford													1															1	–	
17 West Ham United	1																											1	–	
18 Bradford City	–	(1)	1																									–	(1)	1
19 Basel																–	(1)	–										–	(1)	–
20 Bayer Leverkusen																–	(1)	–										–	(1)	–
21 Bayern Munich																–	(1)	–										–	(1)	–
22 Bolton Wanderers	–	(1)	–																									–	(1)	–
23 Chelsea	–	(1)	–																									–	(1)	–
24 Leicester City	–	(1)	–																									–	(1)	–
25 Newcastle United	–	(1)	–																									–	(1)	–
26 Olympiakos Piraeus																–	(1)	–										–	(1)	–
27 Panathinaikos																–	(1)	–										–	(1)	–

STEWART CHALMERS

DEBUT (Full Appearance)

Saturday 01/10/1932
Football League Division 2
at Old Trafford

Manchester United 0 Preston North End 0

CLUB CAREER RECORD	Apps	Subs	Goals
Premiership	0		0
League Division 1	0		0
League Division 2	34		1
FA Cup	1		0
League Cup	0		0
European Cup / Champions League	0		0
European Cup-Winners' Cup	0		0
UEFA Cup / Inter-Cities' Fairs Cup	0		0
Other Matches	0		0
OVERALL TOTAL	35		1

Opponents	PREM A S G	FLD 1 A S G	FLD 2 A S G	FAC A S G	LC A S G	EC/CL A S G	ECWC A S G	UEFA A S G	OTHER A S G	TOTAL A S G
1 Plymouth Argyle	– – –	– – –	3 – 1	– – –	– – –	– – –	– – –	– – –	– – –	3 – 1
2 Grimsby Town	– – –	– – –	3 – –	– – –	– – –	– – –	– – –	– – –	– – –	3 – –
3 Preston North End	– – –	– – –	3 – –	– – –	– – –	– – –	– – –	– – –	– – –	3 – –
4 Swansea City	– – –	– – –	3 – –	– – –	– – –	– – –	– – –	– – –	– – –	3 – –
5 Bradford City	– – –	– – –	2 – –	– – –	– – –	– – –	– – –	– – –	– – –	2 – –
6 Chesterfield	– – –	– – –	2 – –	– – –	– – –	– – –	– – –	– – –	– – –	2 – –
7 Millwall	– – –	– – –	2 – –	– – –	– – –	– – –	– – –	– – –	– – –	2 – –
8 Nottingham Forest	– – –	– – –	2 – –	– – –	– – –	– – –	– – –	– – –	– – –	2 – –
9 West Ham United	– – –	– – –	2 – –	– – –	– – –	– – –	– – –	– – –	– – –	2 – –
10 Blackpool	– – –	– – –	1 – –	– – –	– – –	– – –	– – –	– – –	– – –	1 – –
11 Bolton Wanderers	– – –	– – –	1 – –	– – –	– – –	– – –	– – –	– – –	– – –	1 – –
12 Bradford Park Avenue	– – –	– – –	1 – –	– – –	– – –	– – –	– – –	– – –	– – –	1 – –
13 Burnley	– – –	– – –	1 – –	– – –	– – –	– – –	– – –	– – –	– – –	1 – –
14 Fulham	– – –	– – –	1 – –	– – –	– – –	– – –	– – –	– – –	– – –	1 – –
15 Lincoln City	– – –	– – –	1 – –	– – –	– – –	– – –	– – –	– – –	– – –	1 – –
16 Middlesbrough	– – –	– – –	– – –	1 – –	– – –	– – –	– – –	– – –	– – –	1 – –
17 Notts County	– – –	– – –	1 – –	– – –	– – –	– – –	– – –	– – –	– – –	1 – –
18 Oldham Athletic	– – –	– – –	1 – –	– – –	– – –	– – –	– – –	– – –	– – –	1 – –
19 Port Vale	– – –	– – –	1 – –	– – –	– – –	– – –	– – –	– – –	– – –	1 – –
20 Southampton	– – –	– – –	1 – –	– – –	– – –	– – –	– – –	– – –	– – –	1 – –
21 Stoke City	– – –	– – –	1 – –	– – –	– – –	– – –	– – –	– – –	– – –	1 – –
22 Tottenham Hotspur	– – –	– – –	1 – –	– – –	– – –	– – –	– – –	– – –	– – –	1 – –

BILLY CHAPMAN

DEBUT (Full Appearance)

Saturday 18/09/1926
Football League Division 1
at Old Trafford

Manchester United 2 Burnley 1

CLUB CAREER RECORD	Apps	Subs	Goals
Premiership	0		0
League Division 1	26		0
League Division 2	0		0
FA Cup	0		0
League Cup	0		0
European Cup / Champions League	0		0
European Cup-Winners' Cup	0		0
UEFA Cup / Inter-Cities' Fairs Cup	0		0
Other Matches	0		0
OVERALL TOTAL	26		0

Opponents	PREM A S G	FLD 1 A S G	FLD 2 A S G	FAC A S G	LC A S G	EC/CL A S G	ECWC A S G	UEFA A S G	OTHER A S G	TOTAL A S G
1 Birmingham City	– – –	3 – –	– – –	– – –	– – –	– – –	– – –	– – –	– – –	3 – –
2 Sheffield Wednesday	– – –	3 – –	– – –	– – –	– – –	– – –	– – –	– – –	– – –	3 – –
3 Blackburn Rovers	– – –	2 – –	– – –	– – –	– – –	– – –	– – –	– – –	– – –	2 – –
4 Bolton Wanderers	– – –	2 – –	– – –	– – –	– – –	– – –	– – –	– – –	– – –	2 – –
5 Bury	– – –	2 – –	– – –	– – –	– – –	– – –	– – –	– – –	– – –	2 – –
6 Derby County	– – –	2 – –	– – –	– – –	– – –	– – –	– – –	– – –	– – –	2 – –
7 Huddersfield Town	– – –	2 – –	– – –	– – –	– – –	– – –	– – –	– – –	– – –	2 – –
8 Aston Villa	– – –	1 – –	– – –	– – –	– – –	– – –	– – –	– – –	– – –	1 – –
9 Burnley	– – –	1 – –	– – –	– – –	– – –	– – –	– – –	– – –	– – –	1 – –
10 Cardiff City	– – –	1 – –	– – –	– – –	– – –	– – –	– – –	– – –	– – –	1 – –
11 Everton	– – –	1 – –	– – –	– – –	– – –	– – –	– – –	– – –	– – –	1 – –
12 Leicester City	– – –	1 – –	– – –	– – –	– – –	– – –	– – –	– – –	– – –	1 – –
13 Middlesbrough	– – –	1 – –	– – –	– – –	– – –	– – –	– – –	– – –	– – –	1 – –
14 Newcastle United	– – –	1 – –	– – –	– – –	– – –	– – –	– – –	– – –	– – –	1 – –
15 Tottenham Hotspur	– – –	1 – –	– – –	– – –	– – –	– – –	– – –	– – –	– – –	1 – –
16 West Bromwich Albion	– – –	1 – –	– – –	– – –	– – –	– – –	– – –	– – –	– – –	1 – –
17 West Ham United	– – –	1 – –	– – –	– – –	– – –	– – –	– – –	– – –	– – –	1 – –

BOBBY CHARLTON

DEBUT (Full Appearance, 2 goals)

Saturday 06/10/1956
Football League Division 1
at Old Trafford

Manchester United 4 Charlton Athletic 2

CLUB CAREER RECORD	Apps	Subs	Goals
Premiership	0		0
League Division 1	604	(2)	199
League Division 2	0		0
FA Cup	78		19
League Cup	24		7
European Cup / Champions League	28		10
European Cup-Winners' Cup	6		4
UEFA Cup / Inter-Cities' Fairs Cup	11		8
Other Matches	5		2
OVERALL TOTAL	**756**	**(2)**	**249**

Opponents	PREM A	S	G	FLD 1 A	S	G	FLD 2 A	S	G	FAC A	S	G	LC A	S	G	EC/CL A	S	G	ECWC A	S	G	UEFA A	S	G	OTHER A	S	G	TOTAL A	S	G
1 Tottenham Hotspur	–		–	32		10	–		–	3		1	–		–	–		–	2		2	–		–	1		2	38		15
2 Wolverhampton W.	–		–	27		11	–		–	3		–	–		–	–		–	–		–	–		–	–		–	30		11
3 Everton	–		–	25		6	–		–	2		–	–		–	–		–	–		–	2		–	1		–	30		6
4 Chelsea	–		–	27	(1)	9	–		–	1		–	1		1	–		–	–		–	–		–	–		–	29	(1)	10
5 West Ham United	–		–	28		10	–		–	1		–	–		–	–		–	–		–	–		–	–		–	29		10
6 Leeds United	–		–	24		9	–		–	5		–	–		–	–		–	–		–	–		–	–		–	29		9
7 Arsenal	–		–	28		4	–		–	1		–	–		–	–		–	–		–	–		–	–		–	29		4
8 Burnley	–		–	24		2	–		–	1		–	4		2	–		–	–		–	–		–	–		–	29		4
9 West Bromwich Albion	–		–	26		7	–		–	2		–	–		–	–		–	–		–	–		–	–		–	28		7
10 Manchester City	–		–	24		8	–		–	1		–	2		1	–		–	–		–	–		–	–		–	27		9
11 Stoke City	–		–	19		4	–		–	5		–	3		–	–		–	–		–	–		–	–		–	27		4
12 Sheffield Wednesday	–		–	21		11	–		–	5		1	–		–	–		–	–		–	–		–	–		–	26		12
13 Leicester City	–		–	25		7	–		–	1		–	–		–	–		–	–		–	–		–	–		–	26		7
14 Liverpool	–		–	22		2	–		–	1		2	–		–	–		–	–		–	1		–	–		–	24		4
15 Newcastle United	–		–	22	(1)	6	–		–	–		–	–		–	–		–	–		–	–		–	–		–	22	(1)	6
16 Nottingham Forest	–		–	22		10	–		–	–		–	–		–	–		–	–		–	–		–	–		–	22		10
17 Fulham	–		–	18		7	–		–	2		3	–		–	–		–	–		–	–		–	–		–	20		10
18 Blackpool	–		–	19		11	–		–	–		–	–		–	–		–	–		–	–		–	–		–	19		11
19 Aston Villa	–		–	15		6	–		–	2		–	2		–	–		–	–		–	–		–	–		–	19		6
20 Ipswich Town	–		–	16		1	–		–	2		2	1		–	–		–	–		–	–		–	–		–	19		3
21 Sunderland	–		–	15		1	–		–	3		2	–		–	–		–	–		–	–		–	–		–	18		3
22 Southampton	–		–	13		6	–		–	4		1	–		–	–		–	–		–	–		–	–		–	17		7
23 Sheffield United	–		–	17		1	–		–	–		–	–		–	–		–	–		–	–		–	–		–	17		1
24 Blackburn Rovers	–		–	15		10	–		–	–		–	–		–	–		–	–		–	–		–	–		–	15		10
25 Bolton Wanderers	–		–	13		8	–		–	1		–	–		–	–		–	–		–	–		–	–		–	14		8
26 Birmingham City	–		–	11		5	–		–	3		1	–		–	–		–	–		–	–		–	–		–	14		6
27 Coventry City	–		–	11		3	–		–	1		2	–		–	–		–	–		–	–		–	–		–	12		5
28 Preston North End	–		–	7		3	–		–	5		1	–		–	–		–	–		–	–		–	–		–	12		4
29 Derby County	–		–	8		1	–		–	2		1	2		–	–		–	–		–	–		–	–		–	12		2
30 Crystal Palace	–		–	7		2	–		–	–		–	1		1	–		–	–		–	–		–	–		–	8		3
31 Middlesbrough	–		–	–		–	–		–	7		2	1		–	–		–	–		–	–		–	–		–	8		2
32 Luton Town	–		–	5		2	–		–	–		–	–		–	–		–	–		–	–		–	–		–	5		2
33 Huddersfield Town	–		–	4		1	–		–	1		–	–		–	–		–	–		–	–		–	–		–	5		1
34 Cardiff City	–		–	4		2	–		–	–		–	–		–	–		–	–		–	–		–	–		–	4		2
35 Norwich City	–		–	2		–	–		–	2		–	–		–	–		–	–		–	–		–	–		–	4		–
36 Portsmouth	–		–	2		4	–		–	–		–	1		1	–		–	–		–	–		–	–		–	3		5
37 Benfica	–		–	–		–	–		–	–		–	–		–	3		3	–		–	–		–	–		–	3		3
38 Northampton Town	–		–	2		3	–		–	1		–	–		–	–		–	–		–	–		–	–		–	3		3
39 Real Madrid	–		–	–		–	–		–	–		–	–		–	3		1	–		–	–		–	–		–	3		1
40 Bristol Rovers	–		–	–		–	–		–	1		–	2		–	–		–	–		–	–		–	–		–	3		–
41 Ferencvaros	–		–	–		–	–		–	–		–	–		–	–		–	–		–	3		–	–		–	3		–
42 Watford	–		–	–		–	–		–	3		–	–		–	–		–	–		–	–		–	–		–	3		–
43 Borussia Dortmund	–		–	–		–	–		–	–		–	–		–	–		–	–		–	2		5	–		–	2		5
44 Charlton Athletic	–		–	2		5	–		–	–		–	–		–	–		–	–		–	–		–	–		–	2		5
45 Red Star Belgrade	–		–	–		–	–		–	–		–	–		–	2		3	–		–	–		–	–		–	2		3
46 Djurgardens	–		–	–		–	–		–	–		–	–		–	–		–	–		–	2		2	–		–	2		2
47 AC Milan	–		–	–		–	–		–	–		–	–		–	2		1	–		–	–		–	–		–	2		1
48 HJK Helsinki	–		–	–		–	–		–	–		–	–		–	2		1	–		–	–		–	–		–	2		1
49 Oxford United	–		–	–		–	–		–	2		1	–		–	–		–	–		–	–		–	–		–	2		1
50 Sporting Lisbon	–		–	–		–	–		–	–		–	–		–	–		–	2		1	–		–	–		–	2		1
51 Strasbourg	–		–	–		–	–		–	–		–	–		–	–		–	–		–	2		1	–		–	2		1
52 Waterford	–		–	–		–	–		–	–		–	–		–	2		1	–		–	–		–	–		–	2		1
53 Willem II	–		–	–		–	–		–	–		–	–		–	–		–	2		1	–		–	–		–	2		1
54 Anderlecht	–		–	–		–	–		–	–		–	–		–	2		–	–		–	–		–	–		–	2		–
55 ASK Vorwaerts	–		–	–		–	–		–	–		–	–		–	2		–	–		–	–		–	–		–	2		–
56 Estudiantes de la Plata	–		–	–		–	–		–	–		–	–		–	–		–	–		–	–		–	2		–	2		–
57 Gornik Zabrze	–		–	–		–	–		–	–		–	–		–	2		–	–		–	–		–	–		–	2		–
58 Hibernians Malta	–		–	–		–	–		–	–		–	–		–	2		–	–		–	–		–	–		–	2		–
59 Partizan Belgrade	–		–	–		–	–		–	–		–	–		–	2		–	–		–	–		–	–		–	2		–
60 Rapid Vienna	–		–	–		–	–		–	–		–	–		–	2		–	–		–	–		–	–		–	2		–
61 Rotherham United	–		–	–		–	–		–	2		–	–		–	–		–	–		–	–		–	–		–	2		–
62 Sarajevo	–		–	–		–	–		–	–		–	–		–	2		–	–		–	–		–	–		–	2		–
63 Leyton Orient	–		–	1		1	–		–	–		–	–		–	–		–	–		–	–		–	–		–	1		1
64 Aldershot	–		–	–		–	–		–	–		–	1		–	–		–	–		–	–		–	–		–	1		–
65 Barnsley	–		–	–		–	–		–	1		–	–		–	–		–	–		–	–		–	–		–	1		–
66 Chester City	–		–	–		–	–		–	1		–	–		–	–		–	–		–	–		–	–		–	1		–
67 Exeter City	–		–	–		–	–		–	1		–	–		–	–		–	–		–	–		–	–		–	1		–
68 Queens Park Rangers	–		–	1		–	–		–	–		–	–		–	–		–	–		–	–		–	–		–	1		–
69 Workington	–		–	–		–	–		–	1		–	–		–	–		–	–		–	–		–	–		–	1		–
70 Wrexham	–		–	–		–	–		–	–		–	1		–	–		–	–		–	–		–	–		–	1		–

REG CHESTER

DEBUT (Full Appearance)

Saturday 31/08/1935
Football League Division 2
at Home Park

Plymouth Argyle 3 Manchester United 1

CLUB CAREER RECORD	Apps	Subs	Goals
Premiership	0		0
League Division 1	0		0
League Division 2	13		1
FA Cup	0		0
League Cup	0		0
European Cup / Champions League	0		0
European Cup-Winners' Cup	0		0
UEFA Cup / Inter-Cities' Fairs Cup	0		0
Other Matches	0		0
OVERALL TOTAL	13		1

Opponents	PREM			FLD 1			FLD 2			FAC			LC			EC/CL			ECWC			UEFA			OTHER			TOTAL		
	A	S	G	A	S	G	A	S	G	A	S	G	A	S	G	A	S	G	A	S	G	A	S	G	A	S	G	A	S	G
1 Charlton Athletic	–	–	–	–	–	–	2	–	1	–	–	–	–	–	–	–	–	–	–	–	–	–	–	–	–	–	–	2	–	1
2 Bradford City	–	–	–	–	–	–	1	–	–	–	–	–	–	–	–	–	–	–	–	–	–	–	–	–	–	–	–	1	–	–
3 Bradford Park Avenue	–	–	–	–	–	–	1	–	–	–	–	–	–	–	–	–	–	–	–	–	–	–	–	–	–	–	–	1	–	–
4 Fulham	–	–	–	–	–	–	1	–	–	–	–	–	–	–	–	–	–	–	–	–	–	–	–	–	–	–	–	1	–	–
5 Hull City	–	–	–	–	–	–	1	–	–	–	–	–	–	–	–	–	–	–	–	–	–	–	–	–	–	–	–	1	–	–
6 Newcastle United	–	–	–	–	–	–	1	–	–	–	–	–	–	–	–	–	–	–	–	–	–	–	–	–	–	–	–	1	–	–
7 Plymouth Argyle	–	–	–	–	–	–	1	–	–	–	–	–	–	–	–	–	–	–	–	–	–	–	–	–	–	–	–	1	–	–
8 Port Vale	–	–	–	–	–	–	1	–	–	–	–	–	–	–	–	–	–	–	–	–	–	–	–	–	–	–	–	1	–	–
9 Sheffield United	–	–	–	–	–	–	1	–	–	–	–	–	–	–	–	–	–	–	–	–	–	–	–	–	–	–	–	1	–	–
10 Southampton	–	–	–	–	–	–	1	–	–	–	–	–	–	–	–	–	–	–	–	–	–	–	–	–	–	–	–	1	–	–
11 Tottenham Hotspur	–	–	–	–	–	–	1	–	–	–	–	–	–	–	–	–	–	–	–	–	–	–	–	–	–	–	–	1	–	–
12 West Ham United	–	–	–	–	–	–	1	–	–	–	–	–	–	–	–	–	–	–	–	–	–	–	–	–	–	–	–	1	–	–

ARTHUR CHESTERS

DEBUT (Full Appearance)

Saturday 28/12/1929
Football League Division 1
at Old Trafford

Manchester United 5 Newcastle United 0

CLUB CAREER RECORD	Apps	Subs	Goals
Premiership	0		0
League Division 1	7		0
League Division 2	2		0
FA Cup	0		0
League Cup	0		0
European Cup / Champions League	0		0
European Cup-Winners' Cup	0		0
UEFA Cup / Inter-Cities' Fairs Cup	0		0
Other Matches	0		0
OVERALL TOTAL	9		0

Opponents	PREM			FLD 1			FLD 2			FAC			LC			EC/CL			ECWC			UEFA			OTHER			TOTAL		
	A	S	G	A	S	G	A	S	G	A	S	G	A	S	G	A	S	G	A	S	G	A	S	G	A	S	G	A	S	G
1 Newcastle United	–	–	–	2	–	–	–	–	–	–	–	–	–	–	–	–	–	–	–	–	–	–	–	–	–	–	–	2	–	–
2 Bristol City	–	–	–	–	–	–	1	–	–	–	–	–	–	–	–	–	–	–	–	–	–	–	–	–	–	–	–	1	–	–
3 Burnley	–	–	–	1	–	–	–	–	–	–	–	–	–	–	–	–	–	–	–	–	–	–	–	–	–	–	–	1	–	–
4 Chelsea	–	–	–	1	–	–	–	–	–	–	–	–	–	–	–	–	–	–	–	–	–	–	–	–	–	–	–	1	–	–
5 Derby County	–	–	–	1	–	–	–	–	–	–	–	–	–	–	–	–	–	–	–	–	–	–	–	–	–	–	–	1	–	–
6 Huddersfield Town	–	–	–	1	–	–	–	–	–	–	–	–	–	–	–	–	–	–	–	–	–	–	–	–	–	–	–	1	–	–
7 Middlesbrough	–	–	–	1	–	–	–	–	–	–	–	–	–	–	–	–	–	–	–	–	–	–	–	–	–	–	–	1	–	–
8 Wolverhampton W.	–	–	–	–	–	–	1	–	–	–	–	–	–	–	–	–	–	–	–	–	–	–	–	–	–	–	–	1	–	–

ALLENBY CHILTON

DEBUT (Full Appearance)

Saturday 05/01/1946
FA Cup 3rd Round 1st Leg
at Peel Park

Accrington Stanley 2 Manchester United 2

CLUB CAREER RECORD	Apps	Subs	Goals
Premiership	0		0
League Division 1	352		3
League Division 2	0		0
FA Cup	37		0
League Cup	0		0
European Cup / Champions League	0		0
European Cup-Winners' Cup	0		0
UEFA Cup / Inter-Cities' Fairs Cup	0		0
Other Matches	2		0
OVERALL TOTAL	391		3

Opponents	PREM			FLD 1			FLD 2			FAC			LC			EC/CL			ECWC			UEFA			OTHER			TOTAL		
	A	S	G	A	S	G	A	S	G	A	S	G	A	S	G	A	S	G	A	S	G	A	S	G	A	S	G	A	S	G
1 Portsmouth	–	–	–	18	–	–	–	–	–	2	–	–	–	–	–	–	–	–	–	–	–	–	–	–	–	–	–	20	–	–
2 Wolverhampton W.	–	–	–	18	–	–	–	–	–	2	–	–	–	–	–	–	–	–	–	–	–	–	–	–	–	–	–	20	–	–
3 Blackpool	–	–	–	18	–	–	–	–	–	1	–	–	–	–	–	–	–	–	–	–	–	–	–	–	–	–	–	19	–	–
4 Chelsea	–	–	–	17	–	1	–	–	–	1	–	–	–	–	–	–	–	–	–	–	–	–	–	–	–	–	–	18	–	1
5 Arsenal	–	–	–	16	–	–	–	–	–	1	–	–	–	–	–	–	–	–	–	–	–	–	–	–	1	–	–	18	–	–
6 Charlton Athletic	–	–	–	17	–	–	–	–	–	1	–	–	–	–	–	–	–	–	–	–	–	–	–	–	–	–	–	18	–	–
7 Aston Villa	–	–	–	16	–	–	–	–	–	1	–	–	–	–	–	–	–	–	–	–	–	–	–	–	–	–	–	17	–	–
8 Liverpool	–	–	–	16	–	–	–	–	–	1	–	–	–	–	–	–	–	–	–	–	–	–	–	–	–	–	–	17	–	–
9 Sunderland	–	–	–	16	–	1	–	–	–	–	–	–	–	–	–	–	–	–	–	–	–	–	–	–	–	–	–	16	–	1
10 Bolton Wanderers	–	–	–	16	–	–	–	–	–	–	–	–	–	–	–	–	–	–	–	–	–	–	–	–	–	–	–	16	–	–
11 Burnley	–	–	–	15	–	–	–	–	–	1	–	–	–	–	–	–	–	–	–	–	–	–	–	–	–	–	–	16	–	–
12 Middlesbrough	–	–	–	16	–	–	–	–	–	–	–	–	–	–	–	–	–	–	–	–	–	–	–	–	–	–	–	16	–	–
13 Preston North End	–	–	–	13	–	–	–	–	–	3	–	–	–	–	–	–	–	–	–	–	–	–	–	–	–	–	–	16	–	–

continued../

ALLENBY CHILTON (continued)

Opponents	PREM A S G	FLD 1 A S G	FLD 2 A S G	FAC A S G	LC A S G	EC/CL A S G	ECWC A S G	UEFA A S G	OTHER A S G	TOTAL A S G
14 Huddersfield Town	– –	15 – –	– – –	– – –	– – –	– – –	– – –	– – –	– – –	15 –
15 Newcastle United	– –	13 – 1	– – –	– – –	– – –	– – –	– – –	– – –	1 – –	14 – 1
16 Derby County	– –	13 – –	– – –	1 – –	– – –	– – –	– – –	– – –	– – –	14 –
17 Manchester City	– –	13 – –	– – –	1 – –	– – –	– – –	– – –	– – –	– – –	14 –
18 Stoke City	– –	14 – –	– – –	– – –	– – –	– – –	– – –	– – –	– – –	14 –
19 Everton	– –	10 – –	– – –	1 – –	– – –	– – –	– – –	– – –	– – –	11 –
20 Tottenham Hotspur	– –	10 – –	– – –	– – –	– – –	– – –	– – –	– – –	– – –	10 –
21 West Bromwich Albion	– –	10 – –	– – –	– – –	– – –	– – –	– – –	– – –	– – –	10 –
22 Sheffield United	– –	9 – –	– – –	– – –	– – –	– – –	– – –	– – –	– – –	9 –
23 Fulham	– –	6 – –	– – –	– – –	– – –	– – –	– – –	– – –	– – –	6 –
24 Sheffield Wednesday	– –	6 – –	– – –	– – –	– – –	– – –	– – –	– – –	– – –	6 –
25 Birmingham City	– –	4 – –	– – –	1 – –	– – –	– – –	– – –	– – –	– – –	5 –
26 Cardiff City	– –	5 – –	– – –	– – –	– – –	– – –	– – –	– – –	– – –	5 –
27 Bradford Park Avenue	– –	– – –	– – –	4 – –	– – –	– – –	– – –	– – –	– – –	4 –
28 Grimsby Town	– –	4 – –	– – –	– – –	– – –	– – –	– – –	– – –	– – –	4 –
29 Blackburn Rovers	– –	3 – –	– – –	– – –	– – –	– – –	– – –	– – –	– – –	3 –
30 Leeds United	– –	2 – –	– – –	1 – –	– – –	– – –	– – –	– – –	– – –	3 –
31 Brentford	– –	2 – –	– – –	– – –	– – –	– – –	– – –	– – –	– – –	2 –
32 Hull City	– –	– – –	– – –	2 – –	– – –	– – –	– – –	– – –	– – –	2 –
33 Reading	– –	– – –	– – –	2 – –	– – –	– – –	– – –	– – –	– – –	2 –
34 Walthamstow Avenue	– –	– – –	– – –	2 – –	– – –	– – –	– – –	– – –	– – –	2 –
35 Accrington Stanley	– –	– – –	– – –	1 – –	– – –	– – –	– – –	– – –	– – –	1 –
36 Bournemouth	– –	– – –	– – –	1 – –	– – –	– – –	– – –	– – –	– – –	1 –
37 Leicester City	– –	1 – –	– – –	– – –	– – –	– – –	– – –	– – –	– – –	1 –
38 Millwall	– –	– – –	– – –	1 – –	– – –	– – –	– – –	– – –	– – –	1 –
39 Nottingham Forest	– –	– – –	– – –	1 – –	– – –	– – –	– – –	– – –	– – –	1 –
40 Oldham Athletic	– –	– – –	– – –	1 – –	– – –	– – –	– – –	– – –	– – –	1 –
41 Watford	– –	– – –	– – –	1 – –	– – –	– – –	– – –	– – –	– – –	1 –
42 Weymouth Town	– –	– – –	– – –	1 – –	– – –	– – –	– – –	– – –	– – –	1 –
43 Yeovil Town	– –	– – –	– – –	1 – –	– – –	– – –	– – –	– – –	– – –	1 –

PHIL CHISNALL

DEBUT (Full Appearance)

Saturday 02/12/1961
Football League Division 1
at Goodison Park

Everton 5 Manchester United 1

CLUB CAREER RECORD	Apps	Subs	Goals
Premiership	0		0
League Division 1	35		8
League Division 2	0		0
FA Cup	8		1
League Cup	0		0
European Cup / Champions League	0		0
European Cup–Winners' Cup	4		1
UEFA Cup / Inter–Cities' Fairs Cup	0		0
Other Matches	0		0
OVERALL TOTAL	47		10

Opponents	PREM A S G	FLD 1 A S G	FLD 2 A S G	FAC A S G	LC A S G	EC/CL A S G	ECWC A S G	UEFA A S G	OTHER A S G	TOTAL A S G
1 Blackpool	– –	4 – –	– – –	– – –	– – –	– – –	– – –	– – –	– – –	4 –
2 Sheffield Wednesday	– –	3 – –	– – –	1 – –	– – –	– – –	– – –	– – –	– – –	4 –
3 West Ham United	– –	3 – –	– – –	1 – –	– – –	– – –	– – –	– – –	– – –	4 –
4 Everton	– –	3 – 2	– – –	– – –	– – –	– – –	– – –	– – –	– – –	3 2
5 Arsenal	– –	2 – 1	– – –	1 – –	– – –	– – –	– – –	– – –	– – –	3 1
6 Birmingham City	– –	2 – 1	– – –	– – –	– – –	– – –	– – –	– – –	– – –	2 1
7 Blackburn Rovers	– –	2 – 1	– – –	– – –	– – –	– – –	– – –	– – –	– – –	2 1
8 Ipswich Town	– –	2 – 1	– – –	– – –	– – –	– – –	– – –	– – –	– – –	2 1
9 Nottingham Forest	– –	2 – 1	– – –	– – –	– – –	– – –	– – –	– – –	– – –	2 1
10 Sunderland	– –	– – –	– – –	2 – 1	– – –	– – –	– – –	– – –	– – –	2 1
11 Willem II	– –	– – –	– – –	– – –	– – –	– – –	2 – 1	– – –	– – –	2 1
12 Bolton Wanderers	– –	1 – –	– – –	1 – –	– – –	– – –	– – –	– – –	– – –	2 –
13 Fulham	– –	2 – –	– – –	– – –	– – –	– – –	– – –	– – –	– – –	2 –
14 Tottenham Hotspur	– –	1 – –	– – –	– – –	– – –	– – –	– – –	1 – –	– – –	2 –
15 Wolverhampton W.	– –	2 – –	– – –	– – –	– – –	– – –	– – –	– – –	– – –	2 –
16 Manchester City	– –	1 – 1	– – –	– – –	– – –	– – –	– – –	– – –	– – –	1 1
17 Aston Villa	– –	1 – –	– – –	– – –	– – –	– – –	– – –	– – –	– – –	1 –
18 Bristol Rovers	– –	– – –	– – –	1 – –	– – –	– – –	– – –	– – –	– – –	1 –
19 Cardiff City	– –	1 – –	– – –	– – –	– – –	– – –	– – –	– – –	– – –	1 –
20 Chelsea	– –	1 – –	– – –	– – –	– – –	– – –	– – –	– – –	– – –	1 –
21 Leicester City	– –	1 – –	– – –	– – –	– – –	– – –	– – –	– – –	– – –	1 –
22 Preston North End	– –	– – –	– – –	1 – –	– – –	– – –	– – –	– – –	– – –	1 –
23 Sporting Lisbon	– –	– – –	– – –	– – –	– – –	– – –	1 – –	– – –	– – –	1 –
24 West Bromwich Albion	– –	1 – –	– – –	– – –	– – –	– – –	– – –	– – –	– – –	1 –

TOM CHORLTON

DEBUT (Full Appearance)

Saturday 11/10/1913
Football League Division 1
at Turf Moor

Burnley 1 Manchester United 2

CLUB CAREER RECORD	Apps	Subs	Goals
Premiership	0		0
League Division 1	4		0
League Division 2	0		0
FA Cup	0		0
League Cup	0		0
European Cup / Champions League	0		0
European Cup-Winners' Cup	0		0
UEFA Cup / Inter-Cities' Fairs Cup	0		0
Other Matches	0		0
OVERALL TOTAL	4		0

Opponents	PREM A S G	FLD 1 A S G	FLD 2 A S G	FAC A S G	LC A S G	EC/CL A S G	ECWC A S G	UEFA A S G	OTHER A S G	TOTAL A S G
1 Aston Villa	– –	1 –	–	–	–	–	–	–	–	1 –
2 Burnley	– –	1	–	–	–	–	–	–	–	1 –
3 Middlesbrough	– –	1 –	–	–	–	–	–	–	–	1 –
4 Newcastle United	– –	1	–	–	–	–	–	–	–	1 –

DAVID CHRISTIE

DEBUT (Full Appearance)

Monday 07/09/1908
Football League Division 1
at Bank Street

Manchester United 2 Bury 1

CLUB CAREER RECORD	Apps	Subs	Goals
Premiership	0		0
League Division 1	2		0
League Division 2	0		0
FA Cup	0		0
League Cup	0		0
European Cup / Champions League	0		0
European Cup-Winners' Cup	0		0
UEFA Cup / Inter-Cities' Fairs Cup	0		0
Other Matches	0		0
OVERALL TOTAL	2		0

Opponents	PREM A S G	FLD 1 A S G	FLD 2 A S G	FAC A S G	LC A S G	EC/CL A S G	ECWC A S G	UEFA A S G	OTHER A S G	TOTAL A S G
1 Bury	– –	1 –	–	–	–	–	–	–	–	1 –
2 Leicester City	– –	1	–	–	–	–	–	–	–	1 –

JOHN CHRISTIE

DEBUT (Full Appearance)

Saturday 28/02/1903
Football League Division 2
at Town Moor Avenue

Doncaster Rovers 2 Manchester United 2

CLUB CAREER RECORD	Apps	Subs	Goals
Premiership	0		0
League Division 1	0		0
League Division 2	1		0
FA Cup	0		0
League Cup	0		0
European Cup / Champions League	0		0
European Cup-Winners' Cup	0		0
UEFA Cup / Inter-Cities' Fairs Cup	0		0
Other Matches	0		0
OVERALL TOTAL	1		0

Opponents	PREM A S G	FLD 1 A S G	FLD 2 A S G	FAC A S G	LC A S G	EC/CL A S G	ECWC A S G	UEFA A S G	OTHER A S G	TOTAL A S G
1 Doncaster Rovers	– –	– –	1	–	–	–	–	–	–	1 –

JOE CLARK

DEBUT (Full Appearance)

Saturday 30/09/1899
Football League Division 2
at Hillsborough

Sheffield Wednesday 2 Newton Heath 1

CLUB CAREER RECORD	Apps	Subs	Goals
Premiership	0		0
League Division 1	0		0
League Division 2	9		0
FA Cup	0		0
League Cup	0		0
European Cup / Champions League	0		0
European Cup-Winners' Cup	0		0
UEFA Cup / Inter-Cities' Fairs Cup	0		0
Other Matches	0		0
OVERALL TOTAL	9		0

Opponents	PREM A S G	FLD 1 A S G	FLD 2 A S G	FAC A S G	LC A S G	EC/CL A S G	ECWC A S G	UEFA A S G	OTHER A S G	TOTAL A S G
1 Arsenal	– –	– –	1	–	–	–	–	–	–	1 –
2 Barnsley	– –	– –	1	–	–	–	–	–	–	1 –
3 Bolton Wanderers	– –	– –	1	–	–	–	–	–	–	1 –
4 Chesterfield	– –	– –	1	–	–	–	–	–	–	1 –
5 Gainsborough Trinity	– –	– –	1	–	–	–	–	–	–	1 –
6 Grimsby Town	– –	– –	1	–	–	–	–	–	–	1 –
7 Luton Town	– –	– –	1	–	–	–	–	–	–	1 –
8 Port Vale	– –	– –	1	–	–	–	–	–	–	1 –
9 Sheffield Wednesday	– –	– –	1	–	–	–	–	–	–	1 –

JONATHAN CLARK

DEBUT (Substitute Appearance)

Wednesday 10/11/1976
Football League Division 1
at Old Trafford

Manchester United 3 Sunderland 3

CLUB CAREER RECORD	Apps	Subs	Goals
Premiership	0		0
League Division 1	0	(1)	0
League Division 2	0		0
FA Cup	0		0
League Cup	0		0
European Cup / Champions League	0		0
European Cup–Winners' Cup	0		0
UEFA Cup / Inter–Cities' Fairs Cup	0		0
Other Matches	0		0
OVERALL TOTAL	**0**	**(1)**	**0**

Opponents	PREM A S G	FLD 1 A S G	FLD 2 A S G	FAC A S G	LC A S G	EC/CL A S G	ECWC A S G	UEFA A S G	OTHER A S G	TOTAL A S G
1 Sunderland	– –	– (1) –	– –	– –	– –	– –	– –	– –	– –	– (1) –

JOHN CLARKIN

DEBUT (Full Appearance)

Saturday 13/01/1894
Football League Division 1
at Bank Street

Newton Heath 1 Sheffield Wednesday 2

CLUB CAREER RECORD	Apps	Subs	Goals
Premiership	0		0
League Division 1	12		5
League Division 2	55		18
FA Cup	5		0
League Cup	0		0
European Cup / Champions League	0		0
European Cup–Winners' Cup	0		0
UEFA Cup / Inter–Cities' Fairs Cup	0		0
Other Matches	2		0
OVERALL TOTAL	**74**		**23**

Opponents	PREM A S G	FLD 1 A S G	FLD 2 A S G	FAC A S G	LC A S G	EC/CL A S G	ECWC A S G	UEFA A S G	OTHER A S G	TOTAL A S G
1 Manchester City	– –	– –	4 4	– –	– –	– –	– –	– –	– –	4 4
2 Arsenal	– –	– –	4 3	– –	– –	– –	– –	– –	– –	4 3
3 Crewe Alexandra	– –	– –	4 2	– –	– –	– –	– –	– –	– –	4 2
4 Lincoln City	– –	– –	4 2	– –	– –	– –	– –	– –	– –	4 2
5 Notts County	– –	– –	4 2	– –	– –	– –	– –	– –	– –	4 2
6 Port Vale	– –	– –	4 2	– –	– –	– –	– –	– –	– –	4 2
7 Stoke City	– –	2 2	– –	1 –	– –	– –	– –	– –	– –	4 2
8 Blackburn Rovers	– –	2 1	– –	2 –	– –	– –	– –	– –	– –	4 1
9 Grimsby Town	– –	– –	4 1	– –	– –	– –	– –	– –	– –	4 1
10 Darwen	– –	– –	4 –	– –	– –	– –	– –	– –	– –	4 –
11 Newcastle United	– –	– –	4 –	– –	– –	– –	– –	– –	– –	4 –
12 Derby County	– –	1 –	2 –	2 –	– –	– –	– –	– –	– –	3 2
13 Liverpool	– –	– –	2 1	– –	– –	– –	– –	1 –	– –	3 1
14 Burton Swifts	– –	– –	3 –	– –	– –	– –	– –	– –	– –	3 –
15 Burton Wanderers	– –	– –	3 –	– –	– –	– –	– –	– –	– –	3 –
16 Leicester City	– –	– –	3 –	– –	– –	– –	– –	– –	– –	3 –
17 Walsall	– –	– –	2 1	– –	– –	– –	– –	– –	– –	2 1
18 Bury	– –	– –	2 –	– –	– –	– –	– –	– –	– –	2 –
19 Loughborough Town	– –	– –	2 –	– –	– –	– –	– –	– –	– –	2 –
20 Rotherham United	– –	– –	2 –	– –	– –	– –	– –	– –	– –	2 –
21 Aston Villa	– –	1 –	– –	– –	– –	– –	– –	– –	– –	1 –
22 Bolton Wanderers	– –	1 –	– –	– –	– –	– –	– –	– –	– –	1 –
23 Nottingham Forest	– –	1 –	– –	– –	– –	– –	– –	– –	– –	1 –
24 Preston North End	– –	1 –	– –	– –	– –	– –	– –	– –	– –	1 –
25 Sheffield United	– –	1 –	– –	– –	– –	– –	– –	– –	– –	1 –
26 Sheffield Wednesday	– –	1 –	– –	– –	– –	– –	– –	– –	– –	1 –
27 Sunderland	– –	1 –	– –	– –	– –	– –	– –	– –	– –	1 –

GORDON CLAYTON

DEBUT (Full Appearance)

Saturday 16/03/1957
Football League Division 1
at Molineux

Wolverhampton Wanderers 1 Manchester United 1

CLUB CAREER RECORD	Apps	Subs	Goals
Premiership	0		0
League Division 1	2		0
League Division 2	0		0
FA Cup	0		0
League Cup	0		0
European Cup / Champions League	0		0
European Cup–Winners' Cup	0		0
UEFA Cup / Inter–Cities' Fairs Cup	0		0
Other Matches	0		0
OVERALL TOTAL	**2**		**0**

Opponents	PREM A S G	FLD 1 A S G	FLD 2 A S G	FAC A S G	LC A S G	EC/CL A S G	ECWC A S G	UEFA A S G	OTHER A S G	TOTAL A S G
1 West Bromwich Albion	– –	1 –	– –	– –	– –	– –	– –	– –	– –	1 –
2 Wolverhampton W.	– –	1 –	– –	– –	– –	– –	– –	– –	– –	1 –

HARRY CLEAVER

DEBUT (Full Appearance)

Saturday 04/04/1903
Football League Division 2
at Bank Street

Manchester United 4 Burnley 0

CLUB CAREER RECORD	Apps	Subs	Goals
Premiership	0		0
League Division 1	0		0
League Division 2	1		0
FA Cup	0		0
League Cup	0		0
European Cup / Champions League	0		0
European Cup-Winners' Cup	0		0
UEFA Cup / Inter-Cities' Fairs Cup	0		0
Other Matches	0		0
OVERALL TOTAL	**1**		**0**

Opponents	PREM			FLD 1			FLD 2			FAC			LC			EC/CL			ECWC			UEFA			OTHER			TOTAL		
	A	S	G	A	S	G	A	S	G	A	S	G	A	S	G	A	S	G	A	S	G	A	S	G	A	S	G	A	S	G
1 Burnley	-		-	-		-	1		-	-		-	-		-	-		-	-		-	-		-	-		-	1		-

MICHAEL CLEGG

DEBUT (Full Appearance)

Saturday 23/11/1996
FA Premiership
at Riverside Stadium

Middlesbrough 2 Manchester United 2

CLUB CAREER RECORD	Apps	Subs	Goals
Premiership	4	(5)	0
League Division 1	0		0
League Division 2	0		0
FA Cup	3	(1)	0
League Cup	7	(1)	0
European Cup / Champions League	1	(2)	0
European Cup-Winners' Cup	0		0
UEFA Cup / Inter-Cities' Fairs Cup	0		0
Other Matches	0		0
OVERALL TOTAL	**15**	**(9)**	**0**

Opponents	PREM			FLD 1			FLD 2			FAC			LC			EC/CL			ECWC			UEFA			OTHER			TOTAL		
	A	S	G	A	S	G	A	S	G	A	S	G	A	S	G	A	S	G	A	S	G	A	S	G	A	S	G	A	S	G
1 Barnsley	1	-	-	-	-	-	-	-	-	2	-	-	-	-	-	-	-	-	-	-	-	-	-	-	-	-	-	3	-	-
2 Wimbledon	1	-	-	-	-	-	-	-	-	1	-	-	-	-	-	-	-	-	-	-	-	-	-	-	-	-	-	2	-	-
3 Aston Villa	-	-	-	-	-	-	-	-	-	-	-	-	1	-	-	-	-	-	-	-	-	-	-	-	-	-	-	1	-	-
4 Bury	-	-	-	-	-	-	-	-	-	-	-	-	1	-	-	-	-	-	-	-	-	-	-	-	-	-	-	1	-	-
5 Croatia Zagreb	-	-	-	-	-	-	-	-	-	-	-	-	-	-	-	1	-	-	-	-	-	-	-	-	-	-	-	1	-	-
6 Leicester City	-	-	-	-	-	-	-	-	-	-	-	-	1	-	-	-	-	-	-	-	-	-	-	-	-	-	-	1	-	-
7 Middlesbrough	1	-	-	-	-	-	-	-	-	-	-	-	-	-	-	-	-	-	-	-	-	-	-	-	-	-	-	1	-	-
8 Nottingham Forest	-	-	-	-	-	-	-	-	-	-	-	-	1	-	-	-	-	-	-	-	-	-	-	-	-	-	-	1	-	-
9 Southampton	1	-	-	-	-	-	-	-	-	-	-	-	-	-	-	-	-	-	-	-	-	-	-	-	-	-	-	1	-	-
10 Sunderland	-	-	-	-	-	-	-	-	-	-	-	-	1	-	-	-	-	-	-	-	-	-	-	-	-	-	-	1	-	-
11 Tottenham Hotspur	-	-	-	-	-	-	-	-	-	-	-	-	1	-	-	-	-	-	-	-	-	-	-	-	-	-	-	1	-	-
12 Watford	-	-	-	-	-	-	-	-	-	-	-	-	1	-	-	-	-	-	-	-	-	-	-	-	-	-	-	1	-	-
13 Arsenal	-	-	-	-	-	-	-	-	-	-	-	-	-	(1)	-	-	-	-	-	-	-	-	-	-	-	-	-	-	(1)	-
14 Crystal Palace	-	(1)	-	-	-	-	-	-	-	-	-	-	-	-	-	-	-	-	-	-	-	-	-	-	-	-	-	-	(1)	-
15 Derby County	-	(1)	-	-	-	-	-	-	-	-	-	-	-	-	-	-	-	-	-	-	-	-	-	-	-	-	-	-	(1)	-
16 Liverpool	-	(1)	-	-	-	-	-	-	-	-	-	-	-	-	-	-	-	-	-	-	-	-	-	-	-	-	-	-	(1)	-
17 Monaco	-	-	-	-	-	-	-	-	-	-	-	-	-	-	-	-	(1)	-	-	-	-	-	-	-	-	-	-	-	(1)	-
18 Newcastle United	-	(1)	-	-	-	-	-	-	-	-	-	-	-	-	-	-	-	-	-	-	-	-	-	-	-	-	-	-	(1)	-
19 Olympique Marseille	-	-	-	-	-	-	-	-	-	-	-	-	-	-	-	-	(1)	-	-	-	-	-	-	-	-	-	-	-	(1)	-
20 Walsall	-	-	-	-	-	-	-	-	-	-	(1)	-	-	-	-	-	-	-	-	-	-	-	-	-	-	-	-	-	(1)	-
21 West Ham United	-	(1)	-	-	-	-	-	-	-	-	-	-	-	-	-	-	-	-	-	-	-	-	-	-	-	-	-	-	(1)	-

JOHN CLEMENTS

DEBUT (Full Appearance)

Saturday 03/10/1891
FA Cup 1st Qualifying Round
at North Road

Newton Heath 5 Manchester City 1

CLUB CAREER RECORD	Apps	Subs	Goals
Premiership	0		0
League Division 1	36		0
League Division 2	0		0
FA Cup	4		0
League Cup	0		0
European Cup / Champions League	0		0
European Cup-Winners' Cup	0		0
UEFA Cup / Inter-Cities' Fairs Cup	0		0
Other Matches	2		0
OVERALL TOTAL	**42**		**0**

Opponents	PREM			FLD 1			FLD 2			FAC			LC			EC/CL			ECWC			UEFA			OTHER			TOTAL		
	A	S	G	A	S	G	A	S	G	A	S	G	A	S	G	A	S	G	A	S	G	A	S	G	A	S	G	A	S	G
1 Blackburn Rovers	-		-	2		-	-		-	1		-	-		-	-		-	-		-	-		-	-		-	3		-
2 Derby County	-		-	3		-	-		-	-		-	-		-	-		-	-		-	-		-	-		-	3		-
3 Everton	-		-	3		-	-		-	-		-	-		-	-		-	-		-	-		-	-		-	3		-
4 Nottingham Forest	-		-	3		-	-		-	-		-	-		-	-		-	-		-	-		-	-		-	3		-
5 Sheffield Wednesday	-		-	3		-	-		-	-		-	-		-	-		-	-		-	-		-	-		-	3		-
6 Wolverhampton W.	-		-	3		-	-		-	-		-	-		-	-		-	-		-	-		-	-		-	3		-
7 Accrington Stanley	-		-	2		-	-		-	-		-	-		-	-		-	-		-	-		-	-		-	2		-
8 Aston Villa	-		-	2		-	-		-	-		-	-		-	-		-	-		-	-		-	-		-	2		-
9 Birmingham City	-		-	-		-	-		-	-		-	-		-	-		-	-		-	-		-	2		-	2		-
10 Bolton Wanderers	-		-	2		-	-		-	-		-	-		-	-		-	-		-	-		-	-		-	2		-
11 Burnley	-		-	2		-	-		-	-		-	-		-	-		-	-		-	-		-	-		-	2		-

continued../

JOHN CLEMENTS (continued)

Opponents	PREM A	S	G	FLD 1 A	S	G	FLD 2 A	S	G	FAC A	S	G	LC A	S	G	EC/CL A	S	G	ECWC A	S	G	UEFA A	S	G	OTHER A	S	G	TOTAL A	S	G
12 Preston North End	–	–		2	–		–	–		–	–		–	–		–	–		–	–		–	–		–	–		2	–	
13 Stoke City	–	–		2	–		–	–		–	–		–	–		–	–		–	–		–	–		–	–		2	–	
14 Sunderland	–	–		2	–		–	–		–	–		–	–		–	–		–	–		–	–		–	–		2	–	
15 West Bromwich Albion	–	–		2	–		–	–		–	–		–	–		–	–		–	–		–	–		–	–		2	–	
16 Blackpool	–	–		–	–		–	–		1	–		–	–		–	–		–	–		–	–		–	–		1	–	
17 Darwen	–	–		1	–		–	–		–	–		–	–		–	–		–	–		–	–		–	–		1	–	
18 Manchester City	–	–		–	–		–	–		1	–		–	–		–	–		–	–		–	–		–	–		1	–	
19 Notts County	–	–		1	–		–	–		–	–		–	–		–	–		–	–		–	–		–	–		1	–	
20 Sheffield United	–	–		1	–		–	–		–	–		–	–		–	–		–	–		–	–		–	–		1	–	
21 South Shore	–	–		–	–		–	–		1	–		–	–		–	–		–	–		–	–		–	–		1	–	

FRANK CLEMPSON

DEBUT (Full Appearance)

Saturday 18/02/1950
Football League Division 1
at Roker Park

Sunderland 2　Manchester United 2

CLUB CAREER RECORD	Apps	Subs	Goals
Premiership	0		0
League Division 1	15		2
League Division 2	0		0
FA Cup	0		0
League Cup	0		0
European Cup / Champions League	0		0
European Cup-Winners' Cup	0		0
UEFA Cup / Inter-Cities' Fairs Cup	0		0
Other Matches	0		0
OVERALL TOTAL	15		2

Opponents	PREM A	S	G	FLD 1 A	S	G	FLD 2 A	S	G	FAC A	S	G	LC A	S	G	EC/CL A	S	G	ECWC A	S	G	UEFA A	S	G	OTHER A	S	G	TOTAL A	S	G
1 Sunderland	–	–		3	–		–	–		–	–		–	–		–	–		–	–		–	–		–	–		3	–	
2 Derby County	–	–		2	–		–	–		–	–		–	–		–	–		–	–		–	–		–	–		2	–	
3 Portsmouth	–	–		2	–		–	–		–	–		–	–		–	–		–	–		–	–		–	–		2	–	
4 Huddersfield Town	–	–		1	1		–	–		–	–		–	–		–	–		–	–		–	–		–	–		1	1	
5 Wolverhampton W.	–	–		1	1		–	–		–	–		–	–		–	–		–	–		–	–		–	–		1	1	
6 Arsenal	–	–		1	–		–	–		–	–		–	–		–	–		–	–		–	–		–	–		1	–	
7 Aston Villa	–	–		1	–		–	–		–	–		–	–		–	–		–	–		–	–		–	–		1	–	
8 Burnley	–	–		1	–		–	–		–	–		–	–		–	–		–	–		–	–		–	–		1	–	
9 Preston North End	–	–		1	–		–	–		–	–		–	–		–	–		–	–		–	–		–	–		1	–	
10 Stoke City	–	–		1	–		–	–		–	–		–	–		–	–		–	–		–	–		–	–		1	–	
11 Tottenham Hotspur	–	–		1	–		–	–		–	–		–	–		–	–		–	–		–	–		–	–		1	–	

HENRY COCKBURN

DEBUT (Full Appearance)

Saturday 05/01/1946
FA Cup 3rd Round 1st Leg
at Peel Park

Accrington Stanley 2　Manchester United 2

CLUB CAREER RECORD	Apps	Subs	Goals
Premiership	0		0
League Division 1	243		4
League Division 2	0		0
FA Cup	32		0
League Cup	0		0
European Cup / Champions League	0		0
European Cup-Winners' Cup	0		0
UEFA Cup / Inter-Cities' Fairs Cup	0		0
Other Matches	0		0
OVERALL TOTAL	275		4

Opponents	PREM A	S	G	FLD 1 A	S	G	FLD 2 A	S	G	FAC A	S	G	LC A	S	G	EC/CL A	S	G	ECWC A	S	G	UEFA A	S	G	OTHER A	S	G	TOTAL A	S	G
1 Wolverhampton W.	–	–		13	–		–	–		2	–		–	–		–	–		–	–		–	–		–	–		15	–	
2 Aston Villa	–	–		13	–		–	–		1	–		–	–		–	–		–	–		–	–		–	–		14	–	
3 Blackpool	–	–		12	–		–	–		1	–		–	–		–	–		–	–		–	–		–	–		13	–	
4 Bolton Wanderers	–	–		13	–		–	–		–	–		–	–		–	–		–	–		–	–		–	–		13	–	
5 Chelsea	–	–		12	–		–	–		1	–		–	–		–	–		–	–		–	–		–	–		13	–	
6 Sunderland	–	–		12	1		–	–		–	–		–	–		–	–		–	–		–	–		–	–		12	1	
7 Derby County	–	–		11	–		–	–		1	–		–	–		–	–		–	–		–	–		–	–		12	–	
8 Middlesbrough	–	–		12	–		–	–		–	–		–	–		–	–		–	–		–	–		–	–		12	–	
9 Portsmouth	–	–		10	–		–	–		2	–		–	–		–	–		–	–		–	–		–	–		12	–	
10 Preston North End	–	–		9	–		–	–		3	–		–	–		–	–		–	–		–	–		–	–		12	–	
11 Stoke City	–	–		12	–		–	–		–	–		–	–		–	–		–	–		–	–		–	–		12	–	
12 Arsenal	–	–		10	–		–	–		1	–		–	–		–	–		–	–		–	–		–	–		11	–	
13 Newcastle United	–	–		10	1		–	–		–	–		–	–		–	–		–	–		–	–		–	–		10	1	
14 Charlton Athletic	–	–		9	–		–	–		1	–		–	–		–	–		–	–		–	–		–	–		10	–	
15 Huddersfield Town	–	–		10	–		–	–		–	–		–	–		–	–		–	–		–	–		–	–		10	–	
16 Liverpool	–	–		9	–		–	–		1	–		–	–		–	–		–	–		–	–		–	–		10	–	
17 Everton	–	–		8	1		–	–		1	–		–	–		–	–		–	–		–	–		–	–		9	1	
18 Burnley	–	–		9	–		–	–		–	–		–	–		–	–		–	–		–	–		–	–		9	–	
19 West Bromwich Albion	–	–		8	–		–	–		–	–		–	–		–	–		–	–		–	–		–	–		8	–	
20 Manchester City	–	–		7	–		–	–		–	–		–	–		–	–		–	–		–	–		–	–		7	–	
21 Fulham	–	–		6	1		–	–		–	–		–	–		–	–		–	–		–	–		–	–		6	1	
22 Tottenham Hotspur	–	–		6	–		–	–		–	–		–	–		–	–		–	–		–	–		–	–		6	–	
23 Birmingham City	–	–		4	–		–	–		1	–		–	–		–	–		–	–		–	–		–	–		5	–	

continued../

HENRY COCKBURN (continued)

Opponents	PREM A S G	FLD 1 A S G	FLD 2 A S G	FAC A S G	LC A S G	EC/CL A S G	ECWC A S G	UEFA A S G	OTHER A S G	TOTAL A S G
24 Blackburn Rovers	– –	4	–	–	–	–	–	–	–	4 –
25 Sheffield United	– –	4	–	–	–	–	–	–	–	4 –
26 Bradford Park Avenue	– –	–	–	3	–	–	–	–	–	3 –
27 Grimsby Town	– –	3	–	–	–	–	–	–	–	3 –
28 Leeds United	– –	2	–	1	–	–	–	–	–	3 –
29 Accrington Stanley	– –	–	–	2	–	–	–	–	–	2 –
30 Brentford	– –	2	–	–	–	–	–	–	–	2 –
31 Hull City	– –	–	–	2	–	–	–	–	–	2 –
32 Sheffield Wednesday	– –	2	–	–	–	–	–	–	–	2 –
33 Walthamstow Avenue	– –	–	–	2	–	–	–	–	–	2 –
34 Bournemouth	– –	–	–	1	–	–	–	–	–	1 –
35 Cardiff City	– –	1	–	–	–	–	–	–	–	1 –
36 Millwall	– –	–	–	1	–	–	–	–	–	1 –
37 Oldham Athletic	– –	–	–	1	–	–	–	–	–	1 –
38 Watford	– –	–	–	1	–	–	–	–	–	1 –
39 Weymouth Town	– –	–	–	1	–	–	–	–	–	1 –
40 Yeovil Town	– –	–	–	1	–	–	–	–	–	1 –

ANDREW COLE

DEBUT (Full Appearance)

Sunday 22/01/1995
FA Premiership
at Old Trafford

Manchester United 1 Blackburn Rovers 0

CLUB CAREER RECORD	Apps	Subs	Goals
Premiership	161	(34)	93
League Division 1	0		0
League Division 2	0		0
FA Cup	19	(2)	9
League Cup	2		0
European Cup / Champions League	42	(7)	19
European Cup-Winners' Cup	0		0
UEFA Cup / Inter-Cities' Fairs Cup	1		0
Other Matches	6	(1)	0
OVERALL TOTAL	231	(44)	121

Opponents	PREM A S G	FLD 1 A S G	FLD 2 A S G	FAC A S G	LC A S G	EC/CL A S G	ECWC A S G	UEFA A S G	OTHER A S G	TOTAL A S G
1 Chelsea	12 2	–	–	3 (1) 3	–	–	–	–	1 (1) –	16 (2) 5
2 Arsenal	10 2	–	–	1	–	–	–	2	–	13 2
3 Newcastle United	11 9	–	–	1	–	–	–	–	–	12 9
4 Wimbledon	8 (2) 7	–	–	1 (1) –	–	–	–	–	–	9 (3) 7
5 Liverpool	7 (3) 4	–	–	2	–	–	–	–	–	9 (3) 4
6 West Ham United	8 (2) 4	–	–	1	–	–	–	–	–	9 (2) 4
7 Everton	9 (2) 3	–	–	–	–	–	–	–	–	9 (2) 3
8 Tottenham Hotspur	7 (3) 3	–	–	1	–	–	–	–	–	8 (3) 3
9 Coventry City	10 6	–	–	–	–	–	–	–	–	10 6
10 Southampton	7 (2) 5	–	–	1	–	–	–	–	–	8 (2) 5
11 Leeds United	8 (2) 3	–	–	–	–	–	–	–	–	8 (2) 3
12 Aston Villa	6 (4) 2	–	–	–	–	–	–	–	–	6 (4) 2
13 Blackburn Rovers	8 (1) 2	–	–	–	–	–	–	–	–	8 (1) 2
14 Middlesbrough	4 (4) 3	–	–	1 1	–	–	–	–	–	5 (4) 4
15 Leicester City	7 6	–	–	–	–	–	–	–	–	7 6
16 Sheffield Wednesday	7 4	–	–	–	–	–	–	–	–	7 4
17 Sunderland	4 (1) 2	–	–	2 1	–	–	–	–	–	6 (1) 3
18 Derby County	5 (1) 2	–	–	–	–	–	–	–	–	5 (1) 2
19 Bolton Wanderers	4 2	–	–	–	–	–	–	–	–	4 2
20 Manchester City	3 2	–	–	1	–	–	–	–	–	4 2
21 Bayern Munich	– –	–	–	–	–	4	–	–	–	4 –
22 Ipswich Town	2 (1) 6	–	–	–	1	–	–	–	–	3 (1) 6
23 Nottingham Forest	2 (2) 3	–	–	–	–	–	–	–	–	2 (2) 3
24 Bradford City	2 (2) 2	–	–	–	–	–	–	–	–	2 (2) 2
25 Juventus	–	–	–	–	–	2 (2) 1	–	–	–	2 (2) 1
26 Barnsley	2 4	–	–	1 1	–	–	–	–	–	3 5
27 Valencia	– –	–	–	–	–	3 1	–	–	–	3 1
28 Charlton Athletic	2 (1) 1	–	–	–	–	–	–	–	–	2 (1) 1
29 Anderlecht	– –	–	–	–	–	2 3	–	–	–	2 3
30 Feyenoord	–	–	–	–	–	2 3	–	–	–	2 3
31 Brondby	–	–	–	–	–	2 2	–	–	–	2 2
32 Kosice	–	–	–	–	–	2 2	–	–	–	2 2
33 Crystal Palace	2 1	–	–	–	–	–	–	–	–	2 1
34 Fiorentina	–	–	–	–	–	2 1	–	–	–	2 1
35 Olympique Marseille	– –	–	–	–	–	2 1	–	–	–	2 1
36 Queens Park Rangers	2 1	–	–	–	–	–	–	–	–	2 1
37 Sturm Graz	–	–	–	–	–	2 1	–	–	–	2 1
38 Croatia Zagreb	–	–	–	–	–	2	–	–	–	2 –
39 Dynamo Kiev	–	–	–	–	–	2	–	–	–	2 –
40 Girondins Bordeaux	–	–	–	–	–	2	–	–	–	2 –
41 Internazionale	–	–	–	–	–	2	–	–	–	2 –
42 Monaco	–	–	–	–	–	2	–	–	–	2 –
43 Real Madrid	–	–	–	–	–	2	–	–	–	2 –
44 Fulham	– (1) –	–	–	1 1	–	–	–	–	–	1 (1) 1

continued../

ANDREW COLE (continued)

Opponents	PREM A S G	FLD 1 A S G	FLD 2 A S G	FAC A S G	LC A S G	EC/CL A S G	ECWC A S G	UEFA A S G	OTHER A S G	TOTAL A S G
45 Borussia Dortmund	– – –	– – –	– – –	– – –	– – –	1 (1) –	– – –	– – –	– – –	1 (1) –
46 Deportivo La Coruna	– – –	– – –	– – –	– – –	– – –	– (2) –	– – –	– – –	– – –	– (2) –
47 Walsall	– – –	– – –	1 – 2	– – –	– – –	– – –	– – –	– – –	– – –	1 – 2
48 Watford	1 – 2	– – –	– – –	– – –	– – –	– – –	– – –	– – –	– – –	1 – 2
49 Barcelona	– – –	– – –	– – –	– – –	– – –	1 – 1	– – –	– – –	– – –	1 – 1
50 LKS Lodz	– – –	– – –	– – –	– – –	– – –	1 – 1	– – –	– – –	– – –	1 – 1
51 Porto	– – –	– – –	– – –	– – –	– – –	1 – 1	– – –	– – –	– – –	1 – 1
52 Lazio	– – –	– – –	– – –	– – –	– – –	– – –	– – –	– – –	1 – –	1 – –
53 Lille Metropole	– – –	– – –	– – –	– – –	– – –	1 – –	– – –	– – –	– – –	1 – –
54 Norwich City	1 – –	– – –	– – –	– – –	– – –	– – –	– – –	– – –	– – –	1 – –
55 Panathinaikos	– – –	– – –	– – –	– – –	– – –	1 – –	– – –	– – –	– – –	1 – –
56 PSV Eindhoven	– – –	– – –	– – –	– – –	– – –	1 – –	– – –	– – –	– – –	1 – –
57 Rayos del Necaxa	– – –	– – –	– – –	– – –	– – –	– – –	– – –	– – –	1 – –	1 – –
58 Reading	– – –	– – –	– – –	1 – –	– – –	– – –	– – –	– – –	– – –	1 – –
59 Rotor Volgograd	– – –	– – –	– – –	– – –	– – –	– – –	– – –	1 – –	– – –	1 – –
60 South Melbourne	– – –	– – –	– – –	– – –	– – –	– – –	– – –	– – –	1 – –	1 – –
61 York City	– – –	– – –	– – –	– – –	1 – –	– – –	– – –	– – –	– – –	1 – –
62 Olympiakos Piraeus	– – –	– – –	– – –	– – –	– – –	– (1) 1	– – –	– – –	– – –	– (1) 1
63 Rapid Vienna	– – –	– – –	– – –	– – –	– – –	– (1) –	– – –	– – –	– – –	– (1) –

CLIFF COLLINSON

DEBUT (Full Appearance)

Saturday 02/11/1946
Football League Division 1
at Villa Park

Aston Villa 0 Manchester United 0

CLUB CAREER RECORD	Apps	Subs	Goals
Premiership	0		0
League Division 1	7		0
League Division 2	0		0
FA Cup	0		0
League Cup	0		0
European Cup / Champions League	0		0
European Cup-Winners' Cup	0		0
UEFA Cup / Inter-Cities' Fairs Cup	0		0
Other Matches	0		0
OVERALL TOTAL	**7**		**0**

Opponents	PREM A S G	FLD 1 A S G	FLD 2 A S G	FAC A S G	LC A S G	EC/CL A S G	ECWC A S G	UEFA A S G	OTHER A S G	TOTAL A S G
1 Aston Villa	– –	1	– –	– –	– –	– –	– –	– –	– –	1 –
2 Blackburn Rovers	– –	1	– –	– –	– –	– –	– –	– –	– –	1 –
3 Brentford	– –	1	– –	– –	– –	– –	– –	– –	– –	1 –
4 Derby County	– –	1	– –	– –	– –	– –	– –	– –	– –	1 –
5 Everton	– –	1	– –	– –	– –	– –	– –	– –	– –	1 –
6 Huddersfield Town	– –	1	– –	– –	– –	– –	– –	– –	– –	1 –
7 Wolverhampton W.	– –	1	– –	– –	– –	– –	– –	– –	– –	1 –

JIMMY COLLINSON

DEBUT (Full Appearance, 1 goal)

Saturday 16/11/1895
Football League Division 2
at Bank Street

Newton Heath 5 Lincoln City 5

CLUB CAREER RECORD	Apps	Subs	Goals
Premiership	0		0
League Division 1	0		0
League Division 2	62		16
FA Cup	9		1
League Cup	0		0
European Cup / Champions League	0		0
European Cup-Winners' Cup	0		0
UEFA Cup / Inter-Cities' Fairs Cup	0		0
Other Matches	0		0
OVERALL TOTAL	**71**		**17**

Opponents	PREM A S G	FLD 1 A S G	FLD 2 A S G	FAC A S G	LC A S G	EC/CL A S G	ECWC A S G	UEFA A S G	OTHER A S G	TOTAL A S G
1 Grimsby Town	– – –	– – –	5 – –	– – –	– – –	– – –	– – –	– – –	– – –	5 – –
2 Arsenal	– – –	– – –	4 – 2	– – –	– – –	– – –	– – –	– – –	– – –	4 – 2
3 Darwen	– – –	– – –	4 – 2	– – –	– – –	– – –	– – –	– – –	– – –	4 – 2
4 Gainsborough Trinity	– – –	– – –	4 – 2	– – –	– – –	– – –	– – –	– – –	– – –	4 – 2
5 Lincoln City	– – –	– – –	4 – 1	– – –	– – –	– – –	– – –	– – –	– – –	4 – 1
6 Birmingham City	– – –	– – –	4 – –	– – –	– – –	– – –	– – –	– – –	– – –	4 – –
7 Leicester City	– – –	– – –	4 – –	– – –	– – –	– – –	– – –	– – –	– – –	4 – –
8 Walsall	– – –	– – –	3 – –	1 – –	– – –	– – –	– – –	– – –	– – –	4 – –
9 New Brighton Tower	– – –	– – –	3 – 4	– – –	– – –	– – –	– – –	– – –	– – –	3 – 4
10 Blackpool	– – –	– – –	3 – 1	– – –	– – –	– – –	– – –	– – –	– – –	3 – 1
11 Burnley	– – –	– – –	2 – 1	1 – –	– – –	– – –	– – –	– – –	– – –	3 – 1
12 Burton Swifts	– – –	– – –	3 – –	– – –	– – –	– – –	– – –	– – –	– – –	3 – –
13 Port Vale	– – –	– – –	3 – –	– – –	– – –	– – –	– – –	– – –	– – –	3 – –
14 Loughborough Town	– – –	– – –	2 – 2	– – –	– – –	– – –	– – –	– – –	– – –	2 – 2
15 Liverpool	– – –	– – –	– – –	2 – 1	– – –	– – –	– – –	– – –	– – –	2 – 1
16 Manchester City	– – –	– – –	2 – 1	– – –	– – –	– – –	– – –	– – –	– – –	2 – 1
17 Barnsley	– – –	– – –	2 – –	– – –	– – –	– – –	– – –	– – –	– – –	2 – –

continued../

JIMMY COLLINSON (continued)

Opponents	PREM A S G	FLD 1 A S G	FLD 2 A S G	FAC A S G	LC A S G	EC/CL A S G	ECWC A S G	UEFA A S G	OTHER A S G	TOTAL A S G
18 Burton Wanderers	-	-	2 - -	-	-	-	-	-	-	2 -
19 Derby County	-	-	-	2 -	-	-	-	-	-	2 -
20 Glossop	-	-	2 -	-	-	-	-	-	-	2 -
21 Notts County	-	-	-	2 -	-	-	-	-	-	2 -
22 Rotherham United	-	-	2 -	-	-	-	-	-	-	2 -
23 Tottenham Hotspur	-	-	-	2 -	-	-	-	-	-	2 -
24 Kettering	-	-	-	1 -	-	-	-	-	-	1 -
25 Luton Town	-	-	1 -	-	-	-	-	-	-	1 -
26 Stockport County	-	-	1 -	-	-	-	-	-	-	1 -

EDDIE COLMAN

DEBUT (Full Appearance)

Saturday 12/11/1955
Football League Division 1
at Burden Park

Bolton Wanderers 3 Manchester United 1

CLUB CAREER RECORD	Apps	Subs	Goals
Premiership	0		0
League Division 1	85		1
League Division 2	0		0
FA Cup	9		0
League Cup	0		0
European Cup / Champions League	13		1
European Cup-Winners' Cup	0		0
UEFA Cup / Inter-Cities' Fairs Cup	0		0
Other Matches	1		0
OVERALL TOTAL	108		2

Opponents	PREM A S G	FLD 1 A S G	FLD 2 A S G	FAC A S G	LC A S G	EC/CL A S G	ECWC A S G	UEFA A S G	OTHER A S G	TOTAL A S G
1 Blackpool	-	6 -	-	-	-	-	-	-	-	6 -
2 Bolton Wanderers	-	6 -	-	-	-	-	-	-	-	6 -
3 Manchester City	-	5 -	-	-	-	-	-	-	1 -	6 -
4 Arsenal	-	5 -	-	-	-	-	-	-	-	5 -
5 Birmingham City	-	4 -	-	1 -	-	-	-	-	-	5 -
6 Chelsea	-	5 -	-	-	-	-	-	-	-	5 -
7 Newcastle United	-	5 -	-	-	-	-	-	-	-	5 -
8 Portsmouth	-	5 -	-	-	-	-	-	-	-	5 -
9 Aston Villa	-	3 -	-	1 -	-	-	-	-	-	4 -
10 Charlton Athletic	-	4 -	-	-	-	-	-	-	-	4 -
11 Everton	-	3 -	-	1 -	-	-	-	-	-	4 -
12 Leeds United	-	4 -	-	-	-	-	-	-	-	4 -
13 Sunderland	-	4 -	-	-	-	-	-	-	-	4 -
14 Tottenham Hotspur	-	3 - 1	-	-	-	-	-	-	-	3 - 1
15 Cardiff City	-	3 -	-	-	-	-	-	-	-	3 -
16 Luton Town	-	3 -	-	-	-	-	-	-	-	3 -
17 Preston North End	-	3 -	-	-	-	-	-	-	-	3 -
18 Sheffield Wednesday	-	3 -	-	-	-	-	-	-	-	3 -
19 Wolverhampton W.	-	3 -	-	-	-	-	-	-	-	3 -
20 Red Star Belgrade	-	-	-	-	-	2 - 1	-	-	-	2 - 1
21 Anderlecht	-	-	-	-	-	2 -	-	-	-	2 -
22 Athletic Bilbao	-	-	-	-	-	2 -	-	-	-	2 -
23 Borussia Dortmund	-	-	-	-	-	2 -	-	-	-	2 -
24 Dukla Prague	-	-	-	-	-	2 -	-	-	-	2 -
25 Leicester City	-	2 -	-	-	-	-	-	-	-	2 -
26 Real Madrid	-	-	-	-	-	2 -	-	-	-	2 -
27 West Bromwich Albion	-	2 -	-	-	-	-	-	-	-	2 -
28 Bournemouth	-	-	-	1 -	-	-	-	-	-	1 -
29 Bristol Rovers	-	-	-	1 -	-	-	-	-	-	1 -
30 Burnley	-	1 -	-	-	-	-	-	-	-	1 -
31 Hartlepool United	-	-	-	1 -	-	-	-	-	-	1 -
32 Huddersfield Town	-	1 -	-	-	-	-	-	-	-	1 -
33 Ipswich Town	-	-	-	1 -	-	-	-	-	-	1 -
34 Nottingham Forest	-	1 -	-	-	-	-	-	-	-	1 -
35 Shamrock Rovers	-	-	-	-	-	1 -	-	-	-	1 -
36 Sheffield United	-	1 -	-	-	-	-	-	-	-	1 -
37 Workington	-	-	-	1 -	-	-	-	-	-	1 -
38 Wrexham	-	-	-	1 -	-	-	-	-	-	1 -

JAMES COLVILLE

DEBUT (Full Appearance)

Saturday 12/11/1892
Football League Division 1
at North Road

Newton Heath 1 Notts County 3

CLUB CAREER RECORD	Apps	Subs	Goals
Premiership	0		0
League Division 1	9		1
League Division 2	0		0
FA Cup	1		0
League Cup	0		0
European Cup / Champions League	0		0
European Cup-Winners' Cup	0		0
UEFA Cup / Inter-Cities' Fairs Cup	0		0
Other Matches	0		0
OVERALL TOTAL	10		1

Opponents	PREM A S G	FLD 1 A S G	FLD 2 A S G	FAC A S G	LC A S G	EC/CL A S G	ECWC A S G	UEFA A S G	OTHER A S G	TOTAL A S G
1 Aston Villa	– –	2 –	–	–	–	–	–	–	–	2 –
2 Bolton Wanderers	– –	2 –	–	–	–	–	–	–	–	2 –
3 Notts County	– –	2 –	–	–	–	–	–	–	–	2 –
4 Accrington Stanley	– –	1 1	–	–	–	–	–	–	–	1 1
5 Blackburn Rovers	– –	– –	–	1	–	–	–	–	–	1 –
6 Nottingham Forest	– –	1 –	–	–	–	–	–	–	–	1 –
7 Sunderland	– –	1 –	–	–	–	–	–	–	–	1 –

JAMES CONNACHAN

DEBUT (Full Appearance)

Saturday 05/11/1898
Football League Division 2
at Bank Street

Newton Heath 3 Grimsby Town 2

CLUB CAREER RECORD	Apps	Subs	Goals
Premiership	0		0
League Division 1	0		0
League Division 2	4		0
FA Cup	0		0
League Cup	0		0
European Cup / Champions League	0		0
European Cup-Winners' Cup	0		0
UEFA Cup / Inter-Cities' Fairs Cup	0		0
Other Matches	0		0
OVERALL TOTAL	4		0

Opponents	PREM A S G	FLD 1 A S G	FLD 2 A S G	FAC A S G	LC A S G	EC/CL A S G	ECWC A S G	UEFA A S G	OTHER A S G	TOTAL A S G
1 Barnsley	– –	– –	1	–	–	–	–	–	–	1 –
2 Blackpool	– –	– –	1	–	–	–	–	–	–	1 –
3 Grimsby Town	– –	– –	1	–	–	–	–	–	–	1 –
4 Leicester City	– –	– –	1	–	–	–	–	–	–	1 –

JOHN CONNAUGHTON

DEBUT (Full Appearance)

Tuesday 04/04/1972
Football League Division 1
at Bramall Lane

Sheffield United 1 Manchester United 1

CLUB CAREER RECORD	Apps	Subs	Goals
Premiership	0		0
League Division 1	3		0
League Division 2	0		0
FA Cup	0		0
League Cup	0		0
European Cup / Champions League	0		0
European Cup-Winners' Cup	0		0
UEFA Cup / Inter-Cities' Fairs Cup	0		0
Other Matches	0		0
OVERALL TOTAL	3		0

Opponents	PREM A S G	FLD 1 A S G	FLD 2 A S G	FAC A S G	LC A S G	EC/CL A S G	ECWC A S G	UEFA A S G	OTHER A S G	TOTAL A S G
1 Leicester City	– –	1 –	–	–	–	–	–	–	–	1 –
2 Manchester City	– –	1 –	–	–	–	–	–	–	–	1 –
3 Sheffield United	– –	1 –	–	–	–	–	–	–	–	1 –

TOM CONNELL

DEBUT (Full Appearance)

Friday 22/12/1978
Football League Division 1
at Burnden Park

Bolton Wanderers 3 Manchester United 0

CLUB CAREER RECORD	Apps	Subs	Goals
Premiership	0		0
League Division 1	2		0
League Division 2	0		0
FA Cup	0		0
League Cup	0		0
European Cup / Champions League	0		0
European Cup-Winners' Cup	0		0
UEFA Cup / Inter-Cities' Fairs Cup	0		0
Other Matches	0		0
OVERALL TOTAL	2		0

Opponents	PREM A S G	FLD 1 A S G	FLD 2 A S G	FAC A S G	LC A S G	EC/CL A S G	ECWC A S G	UEFA A S G	OTHER A S G	TOTAL A S G
1 Bolton Wanderers	– –	1 –	–	–	–	–	–	–	–	1 –
2 Liverpool	– –	1 –	–	–	–	–	–	–	–	1 –

JOHN CONNELLY

DEBUT (Full Appearance)

Saturday 22/08/1964
Football League Division 1
at Old Trafford

Manchester United 2 West Bromwich Albion 2

CLUB CAREER RECORD	Apps	Subs	Goals
Premiership	0		0
League Division 1	79	(1)	22
League Division 2	0		0
FA Cup	13		2
League Cup	1		0
European Cup / Champions League	8		6
European Cup-Winners' Cup	0		0
UEFA Cup / Inter-Cities' Fairs Cup	11		5
Other Matches	0		0
OVERALL TOTAL	**112**	**(1)**	**35**

Opponents	PREM A S G	FLD 1 A S G	FLD 2 A S G	FAC A S G	LC A S G	EC/CL A S G	ECWC A S G	UEFA A S G	OTHER A S G	TOTAL A S G
1 Everton	– –	5 2	– –	–	– –	–	–	2 2	– –	8 4
2 Stoke City	– –	5 2	– –	2 –	– –	–	–	–	– –	7 2
3 Blackpool	– –	4 1	– –	– –	1 –	–	–	–	– –	5 1
4 Leeds United	– –	3 1	– –	2 –	– –	–	–	–	– –	5 1
5 Burnley	– –	4 –	– –	1 –	– –	–	–	–	– –	5 –
6 Leicester City	– –	4 2	– –	– –	– –	–	–	–	– –	4 2
7 Arsenal	– –	4 1	– –	– –	– –	–	–	–	– –	4 1
8 Liverpool	– –	4 1	– –	– –	– –	–	–	–	– –	4 1
9 Nottingham Forest	– –	4 1	– –	– –	– –	–	–	–	– –	4 1
10 West Ham United	– –	4 1	– –	– –	– –	–	–	–	– –	4 1
11 Wolverhampton W.	– –	2 1	– –	2 –	– –	–	–	–	– –	4 1
12 Chelsea	– –	4 –	– –	– –	– –	–	–	–	– –	4 –
13 Sheffield United	– –	4 –	– –	– –	– –	–	–	–	– –	4 –
14 Tottenham Hotspur	– –	4 –	– –	– –	– –	–	–	–	– –	4 –
15 West Bromwich Albion	– –	4 –	– –	– –	– –	–	–	–	– –	4 –
16 Fulham	– –	3 3	– –	– –	– –	–	–	–	– –	3 3
17 Aston Villa	– –	3 1	– –	– –	– –	–	–	–	– –	3 1
18 Ferencvaros	– –	– –	– –	– –	– –	–	–	3 1	– –	3 1
19 Newcastle United	– –	3 1	– –	– –	– –	–	–	–	– –	3 1
20 Sunderland	– –	3 –	– –	– –	– –	–	–	–	– –	3 –
21 Blackburn Rovers	– –	2 (1) 2	– –	– –	– –	–	–	–	– –	2 (1) 2
22 HJK Helsinki	– –	– –	– –	– –	– –	2 4	–	–	– –	2 4
23 Northampton Town	– –	2 2	– –	– –	– –	–	–	–	– –	2 2
24 ASK Vorwaerts	– –	– –	– –	– –	– –	2 1	–	–	– –	2 1
25 Benfica	– –	– –	– –	– –	– –	2 1	–	–	– –	2 1
26 Borussia Dortmund	– –	– –	– –	– –	– –	–	–	2 1	– –	2 1
27 Preston North End	– –	– –	– –	2 1	– –	–	–	–	– –	2 1
28 Rotherham United	– –	– –	– –	2 1	– –	–	–	–	– –	2 1
29 Strasbourg	– –	– –	– –	– –	– –	–	–	2 1	– –	2 1
30 Birmingham City	– –	2 –	– –	– –	– –	–	–	–	– –	2 –
31 Djurgardens	– –	– –	– –	– –	– –	–	–	2 –	– –	2 –
32 Partizan Belgrade	– –	– –	– –	– –	– –	2 –	–	–	– –	2 –
33 Sheffield Wednesday	– –	2 –	– –	– –	– –	–	–	–	– –	2 –
34 Chester City	– –	– –	– –	1 –	– –	–	–	–	– –	1 –

TED CONNOR

DEBUT (Full Appearance)

Monday 27/12/1909
Football League Division 1
at Hillsborough

Sheffield Wednesday 4 Manchester United 1

CLUB CAREER RECORD	Apps	Subs	Goals
Premiership	0		0
League Division 1	15		2
League Division 2	0		0
FA Cup	0		0
League Cup	0		0
European Cup / Champions League	0		0
European Cup-Winners' Cup	0		0
UEFA Cup / Inter-Cities' Fairs Cup	0		0
Other Matches	0		0
OVERALL TOTAL	**15**		**2**

Opponents	PREM A S G	FLD 1 A S G	FLD 2 A S G	FAC A S G	LC A S G	EC/CL A S G	ECWC A S G	UEFA A S G	OTHER A S G	TOTAL A S G
1 Tottenham Hotspur	– –	3 1	– –	– –	– –	–	–	–	– –	3 1
2 Preston North End	– –	2 1	– –	– –	– –	–	–	–	– –	2 1
3 Aston Villa	– –	2 –	– –	– –	– –	–	–	–	– –	2 –
4 Middlesbrough	– –	2 –	– –	– –	– –	–	–	–	– –	2 –
5 Blackburn Rovers	– –	1 –	– –	– –	– –	–	–	–	– –	1 –
6 Bury	– –	1 –	– –	– –	– –	–	–	–	– –	1 –
7 Everton	– –	1 –	– –	– –	– –	–	–	–	– –	1 –
8 Notts County	– –	1 –	– –	– –	– –	–	–	–	– –	1 –
9 Sheffield United	– –	1 –	– –	– –	– –	–	–	–	– –	1 –
10 Sheffield Wednesday	– –	1 –	– –	– –	– –	–	–	–	– –	1 –

TERRY COOKE

DEBUT (Full Appearance)

Saturday 16/09/1995
FA Premiership
at Old Trafford

Manchester United 3 Bolton Wanderers 0

CLUB CAREER RECORD	Apps	Subs	Goals
Premiership	1	(3)	0
League Division 1	0		0
League Division 2	0		0
FA Cup	0		0
League Cup	1	(2)	1
European Cup / Champions League	0		0
European Cup-Winners' Cup	0		0
UEFA Cup / Inter-Cities' Fairs Cup	0	(1)	0
Other Matches	0		0
OVERALL TOTAL	**2**	**(6)**	**1**

Opponents	PREM A S G	FLD 1 A S G	FLD 2 A S G	FAC A S G	LC A S G	EC/CL A S G	ECWC A S G	UEFA A S G	OTHER A S G	TOTAL A S G
1 York City	– – –	– – –	– – –	– – –	1 (1) 1	– – –	– – –	– – –	– – –	1 (1) 1
2 Sheffield Wednesday	– (2) –	– – –	– – –	– – –	– – –	– – –	– – –	– – –	– – –	– (2) –
3 Bolton Wanderers	1 – –	– – –	– – –	– – –	– – –	– – –	– – –	– – –	– – –	1 – –
4 Chelsea	– (1) –	– – –	– – –	– – –	– – –	– – –	– – –	– – –	– – –	– (1) –
5 Leicester City	– – –	– – –	– – –	– – –	– (1) –	– – –	– – –	– – –	– – –	– (1) –
6 Rotor Volgograd	– – –	– – –	– – –	– – –	– – –	– – –	– – –	– (1) –	– – –	– (1) –

SAM COOOKSON

DEBUT (Full Appearance)

Saturday 26/12/1914
Football League Division 1
at Anfield

Liverpool 1 Manchester United 1

CLUB CAREER RECORD	Apps	Subs	Goals
Premiership	0		0
League Division 1	12		0
League Division 2	0		0
FA Cup	1		0
League Cup	0		0
European Cup / Champions League	0		0
European Cup-Winners' Cup	0		0
UEFA Cup / Inter-Cities' Fairs Cup	0		0
Other Matches	0		0
OVERALL TOTAL	**13**		**0**

Opponents	PREM A S G	FLD 1 A S G	FLD 2 A S G	FAC A S G	LC A S G	EC/CL A S G	ECWC A S G	UEFA A S G	OTHER A S G	TOTAL A S G
1 Bradford Park Avenue	– – –	2 – –	– – –	– – –	– – –	– – –	– – –	– – –	– – –	2 – –
2 Sheffield Wednesday	– – –	1 – –	– – –	1 – –	– – –	– – –	– – –	– – –	– – –	2 – –
3 Blackburn Rovers	– – –	1 – –	– – –	– – –	– – –	– – –	– – –	– – –	– – –	1 – –
4 Bolton Wanderers	– – –	1 – –	– – –	– – –	– – –	– – –	– – –	– – –	– – –	1 – –
5 Bradford City	– – –	1 – –	– – –	– – –	– – –	– – –	– – –	– – –	– – –	1 – –
6 Burnley	– – –	1 – –	– – –	– – –	– – –	– – –	– – –	– – –	– – –	1 – –
7 Liverpool	– – –	1 – –	– – –	– – –	– – –	– – –	– – –	– – –	– – –	1 – –
8 Manchester City	– – –	1 – –	– – –	– – –	– – –	– – –	– – –	– – –	– – –	1 – –
9 Notts County	– – –	1 – –	– – –	– – –	– – –	– – –	– – –	– – –	– – –	1 – –
10 Sunderland	– – –	1 – –	– – –	– – –	– – –	– – –	– – –	– – –	– – –	1 – –
11 West Bromwich Albion	– – –	1 – –	– – –	– – –	– – –	– – –	– – –	– – –	– – –	1 – –

RONNIE COPE

DEBUT (Full Appearance)

Saturday 29/09/1956
Football League Division 1
at Highbury

Arsenal 1 Manchester United 2

CLUB CAREER RECORD	Apps	Subs	Goals
Premiership	0		0
League Division 1	93		2
League Division 2	0		0
FA Cup	10		0
League Cup	1		0
European Cup / Champions League	2		0
European Cup-Winners' Cup	0		0
UEFA Cup / Inter-Cities' Fairs Cup	0		0
Other Matches	0		0
OVERALL TOTAL	**106**		**2**

Opponents	PREM A S G	FLD 1 A S G	FLD 2 A S G	FAC A S G	LC A S G	EC/CL A S G	ECWC A S G	UEFA A S G	OTHER A S G	TOTAL A S G
1 West Ham United	– – –	6 – –	– – –	– – –	– – –	– – –	– – –	– – –	– – –	6 – –
2 Arsenal	– – –	5 – –	– – –	– – –	– – –	– – –	– – –	– – –	– – –	5 – –
3 Blackburn Rovers	– – –	5 – –	– – –	– – –	– – –	– – –	– – –	– – –	– – –	5 – –
4 Burnley	– – –	5 – –	– – –	– – –	– – –	– – –	– – –	– – –	– – –	5 – –
5 Nottingham Forest	– – –	5 – –	– – –	– – –	– – –	– – –	– – –	– – –	– – –	5 – –
6 Preston North End	– – –	5 – –	– – –	– – –	– – –	– – –	– – –	– – –	– – –	5 – –
7 Sheffield Wednesday	– – –	3 – –	– – –	2 – –	– – –	– – –	– – –	– – –	– – –	5 – –
8 Tottenham Hotspur	– – –	5 – –	– – –	– – –	– – –	– – –	– – –	– – –	– – –	5 – –
9 West Bromwich Albion	– – –	3 – –	– – –	2 – –	– – –	– – –	– – –	– – –	– – –	5 – –
10 Wolverhampton W.	– – –	5 – –	– – –	– – –	– – –	– – –	– – –	– – –	– – –	5 – –
11 Everton	– – –	4 – 2	– – –	– – –	– – –	– – –	– – –	– – –	– – –	4 – 2
12 Aston Villa	– – –	4 – –	– – –	– – –	– – –	– – –	– – –	– – –	– – –	4 – –
13 Birmingham City	– – –	4 – –	– – –	– – –	– – –	– – –	– – –	– – –	– – –	4 – –
14 Blackpool	– – –	4 – –	– – –	– – –	– – –	– – –	– – –	– – –	– – –	4 – –
15 Bolton Wanderers	– – –	3 – –	– – –	1 – –	– – –	– – –	– – –	– – –	– – –	4 – –
16 Chelsea	– – –	4 – –	– – –	– – –	– – –	– – –	– – –	– – –	– – –	4 – –

continued../

RONNIE COPE (continued)

Opponents	PREM A S G	FLD 1 A S G	FLD 2 A S G	FAC A S G	LC A S G	EC/CL A S G	ECWC A S G	UEFA A S G	OTHER A S G	TOTAL A S G
17 Fulham	− −	2 −	− −	2 −	− −	− −	− −	− −	− −	4 −
18 Leicester City	− −	4 −	− −	− −	− −	− −	− −	− −	− −	4 −
19 Manchester City	− −	4 −	− −	− −	− −	− −	− −	− −	− −	4 −
20 Newcastle United	− −	4 −	− −	− −	− −	− −	− −	− −	− −	4 −
21 Leeds United	− −	3 −	− −	− −	− −	− −	− −	− −	− −	3 −
22 Luton Town	− −	3 −	− −	− −	− −	− −	− −	− −	− −	3 −
23 AC Milan	− −	− −	− −	− −	− −	2 −	− −	− −	− −	2 −
24 Portsmouth	− −	2 −	− −	− −	− −	− −	− −	− −	− −	2 −
25 Derby County	− −	− −	− −	1 −	− −	− −	− −	− −	− −	1 −
26 Exeter City	− −	− −	− −	− −	1 −	− −	− −	− −	− −	1 −
27 Liverpool	− −	− −	− −	1 −	− −	− −	− −	− −	− −	1 −
28 Norwich City	− −	− −	− −	1 −	− −	− −	− −	− −	− −	1 −
29 Sunderland	− −	1 −	− −	− −	− −	− −	− −	− −	− −	1 −

STEVE COPPELL

DEBUT (Substitute Appearance)

Saturday 01/03/1975
Football League Division 2
at Old Trafford

Manchester United 4 Cardiff City 0

CLUB CAREER RECORD	Apps	Subs	Goals
Premiership	0		0
League Division 1	311	(1)	53
League Division 2	9	(1)	1
FA Cup	36		4
League Cup	25		9
European Cup / Champions League	0		0
European Cup-Winners' Cup	4		3
UEFA Cup / Inter-Cities' Fairs Cup	7	(1)	0
Other Matches	1		0
OVERALL TOTAL	393	(3)	70

Opponents	PREM A S G	FLD 1 A S G	FLD 2 A S G	FAC A S G	LC A S G	EC/CL A S G	ECWC A S G	UEFA A S G	OTHER A S G	TOTAL A S G
1 Liverpool	− −	16 1	− −	3 −	1 −	− −	− −	1 −	− −	21 1
2 Tottenham Hotspur	− −	12 3	− −	4 −	3 1	− −	− −	− −	− −	19 4
3 Aston Villa	− −	16 5	− −	1 −	1 1	− −	− −	− −	− −	18 6
4 Arsenal	− −	13 3	− −	1 −	3 3	− −	− −	− −	− −	17 6
5 Everton	− −	15 4	− −	1 −	1 −	− −	− −	− −	− −	17 4
6 Coventry City	− −	15 2	− −	− −	2 −	− −	− −	− −	− −	17 2
7 Manchester City	− −	15 (1) 5	− −	− −	1 −	− −	− −	− −	− −	16 (1) 5
8 West Bromwich Albion	− −	14 3	− −	2 1	− −	− −	− −	− −	− −	16 4
9 Norwich City	− −	13 3	1 −	− −	1 −	− −	− −	− −	− −	15 3
10 Nottingham Forest	− −	12 2	1 −	1 −	1 1	− −	− −	− −	− −	15 3
11 Leeds United	− −	14 1	− −	1 1	− −	− −	− −	− −	− −	15 2
12 Birmingham City	− −	14 3	− −	− −	− −	− −	− −	− −	− −	14 3
13 Ipswich Town	− −	14 2	− −	− −	− −	− −	− −	− −	− −	14 2
14 Middlesbrough	− −	14 2	− −	− −	− −	− −	− −	− −	− −	14 2
15 Wolverhampton W.	− −	12 2	− −	2 −	− −	− −	− −	− −	− −	14 2
16 Derby County	− −	10 −	− −	2 −	− −	− −	− −	− −	− −	12 −
17 West Ham United	− −	10 −	− −	1 1	− −	− −	− −	− −	− −	11 1
18 Southampton	− −	7 −	− −	3 −	1 −	− −	− −	− −	− −	11 −
19 Stoke City	− −	10 2	− −	− −	− −	− −	− −	− −	− −	10 2
20 Sunderland	− −	8 −	− −	− −	2 −	− −	− −	− −	− −	10 −
21 Queens Park Rangers	− −	8 1	− −	1 −	− −	− −	− −	− −	− −	9 1
22 Leicester City	− −	7 2	− −	1 −	− −	− −	− −	− −	− −	8 2
23 Brighton	− −	6 1	− −	2 −	− −	− −	− −	− −	− −	8 1
24 Bristol City	− −	8 −	− −	− −	− −	− −	− −	− −	− −	8 −
25 Newcastle United	− −	6 1	− −	− −	1 1	− −	− −	− −	− −	7 2
26 Bolton Wanderers	− −	4 2	1 −	− −	− −	− −	− −	− −	− −	5 2
27 Chelsea	− −	4 1	− −	− −	1 1	− −	− −	− −	− −	5 2
28 Notts County	− −	3 2	1 −	− −	− −	− −	− −	− −	− −	4 2
29 Crystal Palace	− −	4 −	− −	− −	− −	− −	− −	− −	− −	4 −
30 Fulham	− −	− −	1 −	2 −	− −	− −	− −	− −	− −	3 −
31 Swansea City	− −	3 −	− −	− −	− −	− −	− −	− −	− −	3 −
32 Porto	− −	− −	− −	− −	− −	− −	2 2	− −	− −	2 2
33 Bradford City	− −	− −	− −	− −	2 1	− −	− −	− −	− −	2 1
34 St Etienne	− −	− −	− −	− −	− −	− −	2 1	− −	− −	2 1
35 Ajax	− −	− −	− −	− −	− −	− −	− −	2 −	− −	2 −
36 Carlisle United	− −	− −	− −	2 −	− −	− −	− −	− −	− −	2 −
37 Juventus	− −	− −	− −	− −	− −	− −	− −	2 −	− −	2 −
38 Sheffield United	− −	2 −	− −	− −	− −	− −	− −	− −	− −	2 −
39 Watford	− −	1 −	− −	− −	1 −	− −	− −	− −	− −	2 −
40 Widzew Lodz	− −	− −	− −	− −	− −	− −	− −	2 −	− −	2 −
41 Valencia	− −	− −	− −	− −	− −	− −	− −	1 (1) −	− −	1 (1) −
42 Bournemouth	− −	− −	− −	− −	1 1	− −	− −	− −	− −	1 1
43 Oldham Athletic	− −	− −	1 1	− −	− −	− −	− −	− −	− −	1 1
44 Blackpool	− −	− −	1 −	− −	− −	− −	− −	− −	− −	1 −
45 Brentford	− −	− −	− −	− −	1 −	− −	− −	− −	− −	1 −
46 Bristol Rovers	− −	− −	1 −	− −	− −	− −	− −	− −	− −	1 −
47 Burnley	− −	1 −	− −	− −	− −	− −	− −	− −	− −	1 −
48 Colchester United	− −	− −	− −	1 −	− −	− −	− −	− −	− −	1 −

continued../

STEVE COPPELL (continued)

Opponents	PREM			FLD 1			FLD 2			FAC			LC			EC/CL			ECWC			UEFA			OTHER			TOTAL		
	A	S	G	A	S	G	A	S	G	A	S	G	A	S	G	A	S	G	A	S	G	A	S	G	A	S	G	A	S	G
49 Luton Town	–	–	–	–	–	–	1	–	–	–	–	–	–	–	–	–	–	–	–	–	–	–	–	–	–	–	–	1	–	–
50 Oxford United	–	–	–	–	–	–	1	–	–	–	–	–	–	–	–	–	–	–	–	–	–	–	–	–	–	–	–	1	–	–
51 Peterborough United	–	–	–	–	–	–	1	–	–	–	–	–	–	–	–	–	–	–	–	–	–	–	–	–	–	–	–	1	–	–
52 Stockport County	–	–	–	–	–	–	–	–	–	–	–	–	1	–	–	–	–	–	–	–	–	–	–	–	–	–	–	1	–	–
53 Tranmere Rovers	–	–	–	–	–	–	–	–	–	–	–	–	1	–	–	–	–	–	–	–	–	–	–	–	–	–	–	1	–	–
54 Walsall	–	–	–	–	–	–	–	–	–	1	–	–	–	–	–	–	–	–	–	–	–	–	–	–	–	–	–	1	–	–
55 York City	–	–	–	–	–	–	1	–	–	–	–	–	–	–	–	–	–	–	–	–	–	–	–	–	–	–	–	1	–	–
56 Cardiff City	–	–	–	–	–	–	– (1)	–	–	–	–	–	–	–	–	–	–	–	–	–	–	–	–	–	–	–	–	– (1)	–	–

JIMMY COUPAR

DEBUT (Full Appearance, 1 goal)

Saturday 03/09/1892
Football League Division 1
at Ewood Park

Blackburn Rovers 4 Newton Heath 3

CLUB CAREER RECORD	Apps	Subs	Goals
Premiership	0		0
League Division 1	21		5
League Division 2	11		4
FA Cup	0		0
League Cup	0		0
European Cup / Champions League	0		0
European Cup-Winners' Cup	0		0
UEFA Cup / Inter-Cities' Fairs Cup	0		0
Other Matches	2		1
OVERALL TOTAL	**34**		**10**

Opponents	PREM			FLD 1			FLD 2			FAC			LC			EC/CL			ECWC			UEFA			OTHER			TOTAL		
	A	S	G	A	S	G	A	S	G	A	S	G	A	S	G	A	S	G	A	S	G	A	S	G	A	S	G	A	S	G
1 Preston North End	–	–	–	2	1	–	1	–	–	–	–	–	–	–	–	–	–	–	–	–	–	–	–	–	–	–	–	3	–	1
2 Burnley	–	–	–	2	–	–	1	–	–	–	–	–	–	–	–	–	–	–	–	–	–	–	–	–	–	–	–	3	–	–
3 West Bromwich Albion	–	–	–	2	–	–	1	–	–	–	–	–	–	–	–	–	–	–	–	–	–	–	–	–	–	–	–	3	–	–
4 Aston Villa	–	–	–	2	1	–	–	–	–	–	–	–	–	–	–	–	–	–	–	–	–	–	–	–	–	–	–	2	–	1
5 Birmingham City	–	–	–	–	–	–	–	–	–	–	–	–	–	–	–	–	–	–	–	–	–	2	1	–	–	–	–	2	–	1
6 Chesterfield	–	–	–	–	–	–	2	1	–	–	–	–	–	–	–	–	–	–	–	–	–	–	–	–	–	–	–	2	–	1
7 Stoke City	–	–	–	2	1	–	–	–	–	–	–	–	–	–	–	–	–	–	–	–	–	–	–	–	–	–	–	2	–	1
8 Accrington Stanley	–	–	–	2	–	–	–	–	–	–	–	–	–	–	–	–	–	–	–	–	–	–	–	–	–	–	–	2	–	–
9 Derby County	–	–	–	2	–	–	–	–	–	–	–	–	–	–	–	–	–	–	–	–	–	–	–	–	–	–	–	2	–	–
10 Sunderland	–	–	–	2	–	–	–	–	–	–	–	–	–	–	–	–	–	–	–	–	–	–	–	–	–	–	–	2	–	–
11 Doncaster Rovers	–	–	–	–	–	–	1	3	–	–	–	–	–	–	–	–	–	–	–	–	–	–	–	–	–	–	–	1	–	3
12 Blackburn Rovers	–	–	–	1	1	–	–	–	–	–	–	–	–	–	–	–	–	–	–	–	–	–	–	–	–	–	–	1	–	1
13 Bolton Wanderers	–	–	–	1	1	–	–	–	–	–	–	–	–	–	–	–	–	–	–	–	–	–	–	–	–	–	–	1	–	1
14 Barnsley	–	–	–	–	–	–	1	–	–	–	–	–	–	–	–	–	–	–	–	–	–	–	–	–	–	–	–	1	–	–
15 Burton United	–	–	–	–	–	–	1	–	–	–	–	–	–	–	–	–	–	–	–	–	–	–	–	–	–	–	–	1	–	–
16 Everton	–	–	–	1	–	–	–	–	–	–	–	–	–	–	–	–	–	–	–	–	–	–	–	–	–	–	–	1	–	–
17 Glossop	–	–	–	–	–	–	1	–	–	–	–	–	–	–	–	–	–	–	–	–	–	–	–	–	–	–	–	1	–	–
18 Notts County	–	–	–	1	–	–	–	–	–	–	–	–	–	–	–	–	–	–	–	–	–	–	–	–	–	–	–	1	–	–
19 Port Vale	–	–	–	–	–	–	1	–	–	–	–	–	–	–	–	–	–	–	–	–	–	–	–	–	–	–	–	1	–	–
20 Sheffield Wednesday	–	–	–	1	–	–	–	–	–	–	–	–	–	–	–	–	–	–	–	–	–	–	–	–	–	–	–	1	–	–
21 Stockport County	–	–	–	–	–	–	1	–	–	–	–	–	–	–	–	–	–	–	–	–	–	–	–	–	–	–	–	1	–	–

PETER COYNE

DEBUT (Substitute Appearance)

Saturday 21/02/1976
Football League Division 1
at Villa Park

Aston Villa 2 Manchester United 1

CLUB CAREER RECORD	Apps	Subs	Goals
Premiership	0		0
League Division 1	1	(1)	1
League Division 2	0		0
FA Cup	0		0
League Cup	0		0
European Cup / Champions League	0		0
European Cup-Winners' Cup	0		0
UEFA Cup / Inter-Cities' Fairs Cup	0		0
Other Matches	0		0
OVERALL TOTAL	**1**	**(1)**	**1**

Opponents	PREM			FLD 1			FLD 2			FAC			LC			EC/CL			ECWC			UEFA			OTHER			TOTAL		
	A	S	G	A	S	G	A	S	G	A	S	G	A	S	G	A	S	G	A	S	G	A	S	G	A	S	G	A	S	G
1 Leicester City	–	–	–	1	1	–	–	–	–	–	–	–	–	–	–	–	–	–	–	–	–	–	–	–	–	–	–	1	–	1
2 Aston Villa	–	–	–	– (1)	–	–	–	–	–	–	–	–	–	–	–	–	–	–	–	–	–	–	–	–	–	–	–	– (1)	–	–

T CRAIG

DEBUT (Full Appearance, 1 goal)

Saturday 18/01/1889
FA Cup 1st Round
at Deepdale

Preston North End 6 Newton Heath 1

CLUB CAREER RECORD	Apps	Subs	Goals
Premiership	0		0
League Division 1	0		0
League Division 2	0		0
FA Cup	2		1
League Cup	0		0
European Cup / Champions League	0		0
European Cup-Winners' Cup	0		0
UEFA Cup / Inter-Cities' Fairs Cup	0		0
Other Matches	0		0
OVERALL TOTAL	2		1

Opponents	PREM			FLD 1			FLD 2			FAC			LC			EC/CL			ECWC			UEFA			OTHER			TOTAL		
	A	S	G	A	S	G	A	S	G	A	S	G	A	S	G	A	S	G	A	S	G	A	S	G	A	S	G	A	S	G
1 Preston North End	–	–		–	–		–	–		1		1	–	–		–	–		–	–		–	–		–	–		1		1
2 Bootle Reserves	–	–		–	–		–	–		1		–	–	–		–	–		–	–		–	–		–	–		1		–

CHARLIE CRAVEN

DEBUT (Full Appearance)

Saturday 27/08/1938
Football League Division 1
at Ayresome Park

Middlesbrough 3 Manchester United 1

CLUB CAREER RECORD	Apps	Subs	Goals
Premiership	0		0
League Division 1	11		2
League Division 2	0		0
FA Cup	0		0
League Cup	0		0
European Cup / Champions League	0		0
European Cup-Winners' Cup	0		0
UEFA Cup / Inter-Cities' Fairs Cup	0		0
Other Matches	0		0
OVERALL TOTAL	11		2

Opponents	PREM			FLD 1			FLD 2			FAC			LC			EC/CL			ECWC			UEFA			OTHER			TOTAL		
	A	S	G	A	S	G	A	S	G	A	S	G	A	S	G	A	S	G	A	S	G	A	S	G	A	S	G	A	S	G
1 Birmingham City	–	–		1		1	–			–			–			–			–			–			–			1		1
2 Bolton Wanderers	–	–		1		1	–			–			–			–			–			–			–			1		1
3 Charlton Athletic	–	–		1		–	–			–			–			–			–			–			–			1		–
4 Chelsea	–	–		1		–	–			–			–			–			–			–			–			1		–
5 Grimsby Town	–	–		1		–	–			–			–			–			–			–			–			1		–
6 Huddersfield Town	–	–		1		–	–			–			–			–			–			–			–			1		–
7 Liverpool	–	–		1		–	–			–			–			–			–			–			–			1		–
8 Middlesbrough	–	–		1		–	–			–			–			–			–			–			–			1		–
9 Portsmouth	–	–		1		–	–			–			–			–			–			–			–			1		–
10 Preston North End	–	–		1		–	–			–			–			–			–			–			–			1		–
11 Stoke City	–	–		1		–	–			–			–			–			–			–			–			1		–

PAT CRERAND

DEBUT (Full Appearance)

Saturday 23/02/1963
Football League Division 1
at Old Trafford

Manchester United 1 Blackpool 1

CLUB CAREER RECORD	Apps	Subs	Goals
Premiership	0		0
League Division 1	304		10
League Division 2	0		0
FA Cup	43		4
League Cup	4		0
European Cup / Champions League	24		1
European Cup-Winners' Cup	6		0
UEFA Cup / Inter-Cities' Fairs Cup	11		0
Other Matches	5		0
OVERALL TOTAL	397		15

Opponents	PREM			FLD 1			FLD 2			FAC			LC			EC/CL			ECWC			UEFA			OTHER			TOTAL		
	A	S	G	A	S	G	A	S	G	A	S	G	A	S	G	A	S	G	A	S	G	A	S	G	A	S	G	A	S	G
1 Tottenham Hotspur	–	–		14		3	–	–		2		–	–	–		–	–		2	–		–	–		1		–	19		3
2 Everton	–	–		14		–	–	–		2		–	–	–		–	–		–	–		2	–		1		–	19		–
3 Stoke City	–	–		14		–	–	–		3		–	–	–		–	–		–	–		–	–		–		–	17		–
4 Liverpool	–	–		15		1	–	–		–		–	–	–		–	–		–	–		–	–		1		–	16		1
5 Leeds United	–	–		11		–	–	–		5		–	–	–		–	–		–	–		–	–		–		–	16		–
6 Burnley	–	–		14		3	–	–		1		1	–	–		–	–		–	–		–	–		–		–	15		4
7 Arsenal	–	–		15		–	–	–		–		–	–	–		–	–		–	–		–	–		–		–	15		–
8 Chelsea	–	–		15		–	–	–		–		–	–	–		–	–		–	–		–	–		–		–	15		–
9 Nottingham Forest	–	–		15		–	–	–		–		–	–	–		–	–		–	–		–	–		–		–	15		–
10 West Ham United	–	–		13		1	–	–		1		–	–	–		–	–		–	–		–	–		–		–	14		1
11 Wolverhampton W.	–	–		12		–	–	–		2		1	–	–		–	–		–	–		–	–		–		–	14		1
12 Leicester City	–	–		13		–	–	–		1		–	–	–		–	–		–	–		–	–		–		–	14		–
13 Sunderland	–	–		11		–	–	–		3		–	–	–		–	–		–	–		–	–		–		–	14		–
14 Sheffield Wednesday	–	–		13		–	–	–		–		–	–	–		–	–		–	–		–	–		–		–	13		–
15 West Bromwich Albion	–	–		12		–	–	–		–		–	–	–		–	–		–	–		–	–		–		–	12		–
16 Fulham	–	–		11		1	–	–		–		–	–	–		–	–		–	–		–	–		–		–	11		1
17 Blackpool	–	–		10		–	–	–		–		1	–	–		–	–		–	–		–	–		–		–	11		–
18 Newcastle United	–	–		11		–	–	–		–		–	–	–		–	–		–	–		–	–		–		–	11		–
19 Sheffield United	–	–		10		1	–	–		–		–	–	–		–	–		–	–		–	–		–		–	10		1
20 Southampton	–	–		8		–	–	–		2		1	–	–		–	–		–	–		–	–		–		–	10		1

continued../

PAT CRERAND (continued)

Opponents	PREM A S G	FLD 1 A S G	FLD 2 A S G	FAC A S G	LC A S G	EC/CL A S G	ECWC A S G	UEFA A S G	OTHER A S G	TOTAL A S G
21 Manchester City	– –	8 –	– –	1 –	1 –	– –	– –	– –	– –	10 –
22 Aston Villa	– –	8 –	– –	– –	1 –	– –	– –	– –	– –	9 –
23 Ipswich Town	– –	7 –	– –	1 –	– –	– –	– –	– –	– –	8 –
24 Birmingham City	– –	5 –	– –	2 1	– –	– –	– –	– –	– –	7 1
25 Blackburn Rovers	– –	7 –	– –	– –	– –	– –	– –	– –	– –	7 –
26 Coventry City	– –	4 –	– –	1 –	– –	– –	– –	– –	– –	5 –
27 Middlesbrough	– –	– –	– –	4 –	1 –	– –	– –	– –	– –	5 –
28 Derby County	– –	3 –	– –	1 –	– –	– –	– –	– –	– –	4 –
29 Benfica	– –	– –	– –	– –	– –	3 1	– –	– –	– –	3 1
30 Crystal Palace	– –	3 –	– –	– –	– –	– –	– –	– –	– –	3 –
31 Ferencvaros	– –	– –	– –	– –	– –	– –	– –	3 –	– –	3 –
32 Northampton Town	– –	2 –	– –	1 –	– –	– –	– –	– –	– –	3 –
33 AC Milan	– –	– –	– –	– –	– –	2 –	– –	– –	– –	2 –
34 Anderlecht	– –	– –	– –	– –	– –	2 –	– –	– –	– –	2 –
35 ASK Vorwaerts	– –	– –	– –	– –	– –	2 –	– –	– –	– –	2 –
36 Bolton Wanderers	– –	2 –	– –	– –	– –	– –	– –	– –	– –	2 –
37 Borussia Dortmund	– –	– –	– –	– –	– –	– –	– –	2 –	– –	2 –
38 Djurgardens	– –	– –	– –	– –	– –	– –	– –	2 –	– –	2 –
39 Estudiantes de la Plata	– –	– –	– –	– –	– –	– –	– –	– –	2 –	2 –
40 Gornik Zabrze	– –	– –	– –	– –	– –	2 –	– –	– –	– –	2 –
41 Hibernians Malta	– –	– –	– –	– –	– –	2 –	– –	– –	– –	2 –
42 Partizan Belgrade	– –	– –	– –	– –	– –	2 –	– –	– –	– –	2 –
43 Preston North End	– –	– –	– –	2 –	– –	– –	– –	– –	– –	2 –
44 Queens Park Rangers	– –	2 –	– –	– –	– –	– –	– –	– –	– –	2 –
45 Rapid Vienna	– –	– –	– –	– –	– –	2 –	– –	– –	– –	2 –
46 Real Madrid	– –	– –	– –	– –	– –	2 –	– –	– –	– –	2 –
47 Rotherham United	– –	– –	– –	2 –	– –	– –	– –	– –	– –	2 –
48 Sarajevo	– –	– –	– –	– –	– –	2 –	– –	– –	– –	2 –
49 Sporting Lisbon	– –	– –	– –	– –	– –	– –	2 –	– –	– –	2 –
50 Strasbourg	– –	– –	– –	– –	– –	– –	– –	2 –	– –	2 –
51 Waterford	– –	– –	– –	– –	– –	2 –	– –	– –	– –	2 –
52 Watford	– –	– –	– –	2 –	– –	– –	– –	– –	– –	2 –
53 Willem II	– –	– –	– –	– –	– –	– –	2 –	– –	– –	2 –
54 Barnsley	– –	– –	– –	1 –	– –	– –	– –	– –	– –	1 –
55 Bristol Rovers	– –	– –	– –	1 –	– –	– –	– –	– –	– –	1 –
56 Chester City	– –	– –	– –	1 –	– –	– –	– –	– –	– –	1 –
57 HJK Helsinki	– –	– –	– –	– –	– –	1 –	– –	– –	– –	1 –
58 Huddersfield Town	– –	1 –	– –	– –	– –	– –	– –	– –	– –	1 –
59 Leyton Orient	– –	1 –	– –	– –	– –	– –	– –	– –	– –	1 –
60 Norwich City	– –	– –	– –	1 –	– –	– –	– –	– –	– –	1 –

JACK CROMPTON

DEBUT (Full Appearance)

Saturday 05/01/1946
FA Cup 3rd Round 1st Leg
at Peel Park

Accrington Stanley 2 Manchester United 2

CLUB CAREER RECORD	Apps	Subs	Goals
Premiership	0		0
League Division 1	191		0
League Division 2	0		0
FA Cup	20		0
League Cup	0		0
European Cup / Champions League	0		0
European Cup-Winners' Cup	0		0
UEFA Cup / Inter-Cities' Fairs Cup	0		0
Other Matches	1		0
OVERALL TOTAL	212		0

Opponents	PREM A S G	FLD 1 A S G	FLD 2 A S G	FAC A S G	LC A S G	EC/CL A S G	ECWC A S G	UEFA A S G	OTHER A S G	TOTAL A S G
1 Charlton Athletic	– –	13 –	– –	1 –	– –	– –	– –	– –	– –	14 –
2 Liverpool	– –	12 –	– –	1 –	– –	– –	– –	– –	– –	13 –
3 Preston North End	– –	9 –	– –	3 –	– –	– –	– –	– –	– –	12 –
4 Portsmouth	– –	11 –	– –	– –	– –	– –	– –	– –	– –	11 –
5 Wolverhampton W.	– –	9 –	– –	2 –	– –	– –	– –	– –	– –	11 –
6 Arsenal	– –	9 –	– –	– –	– –	– –	– –	– –	1 –	10 –
7 Chelsea	– –	9 –	– –	1 –	– –	– –	– –	– –	– –	10 –
8 Middlesbrough	– –	10 –	– –	– –	– –	– –	– –	– –	– –	10 –
9 Aston Villa	– –	8 –	– –	1 –	– –	– –	– –	– –	– –	9 –
10 Blackpool	– –	7 –	– –	1 –	– –	– –	– –	– –	– –	8 –
11 Burnley	– –	8 –	– –	– –	– –	– –	– –	– –	– –	8 –
12 Huddersfield Town	– –	8 –	– –	– –	– –	– –	– –	– –	– –	8 –
13 Sunderland	– –	8 –	– –	– –	– –	– –	– –	– –	– –	8 –
14 Bolton Wanderers	– –	7 –	– –	– –	– –	– –	– –	– –	– –	7 –
15 Derby County	– –	6 –	– –	1 –	– –	– –	– –	– –	– –	7 –
16 Stoke City	– –	7 –	– –	– –	– –	– –	– –	– –	– –	7 –
17 Everton	– –	6 –	– –	– –	– –	– –	– –	– –	– –	6 –
18 Manchester City	– –	6 –	– –	– –	– –	– –	– –	– –	– –	6 –
19 Sheffield United	– –	6 –	– –	– –	– –	– –	– –	– –	– –	6 –
20 Newcastle United	– –	5 –	– –	– –	– –	– –	– –	– –	– –	5 –
21 Bradford Park Avenue	– –	– –	– –	4 –	– –	– –	– –	– –	– –	4 –

continued../

JACK CROMPTON (continued)

Opponents	PREM			FLD 1			FLD 2			FAC			LC			EC/CL			ECWC			UEFA			OTHER			TOTAL		
	A	S	G	A	S	G	A	S	G	A	S	G	A	S	G	A	S	G	A	S	G	A	S	G	A	S	G	A	S	G
22 Grimsby Town	-		-	4			-			-			-			-			-			-			-			4		-
23 West Bromwich Albion	-		-	4			-			-			-			-			-			-			-			4		-
24 Birmingham City	-		-	3			-			-			-			-			-			-			-			3		-
25 Blackburn Rovers	-		-	3			-			-			-			-			-			-			-			3		-
26 Cardiff City	-		-	3			-			-			-			-			-			-			-			3		-
27 Tottenham Hotspur	-		-	3			-			-			-			-			-			-			-			3		-
28 Accrington Stanley	-		-	-			-			2			-			-			-			-			-			2		-
29 Leeds United	-		-	2			-			-			-			-			-			-			-			2		-
30 Sheffield Wednesday	-		-	2			-			-			-			-			-			-			-			2		-
31 Bournemouth	-		-	-			-			1			-			-			-			-			-			1		-
32 Brentford	-		-	1			-			-			-			-			-			-			-			1		-
33 Fulham	-		-	1			-			-			-			-			-			-			-			1		-
34 Hull City	-		-	-			-			1			-			-			-			-			-			1		-
35 Leicester City	-		-	1			-			-			-			-			-			-			-			1		-
36 Yeovil Town	-		-	-			-			1			-			-			-			-			-			1		-

GARTH CROOKS

DEBUT (Full Appearance)

Saturday 19/11/1983
Football League Division 1
at Old Trafford

Manchester United 4 Watford 1

CLUB CAREER RECORD	Apps	Subs	Goals
Premiership	0		0
League Division 1	6	(1)	2
League Division 2	0		0
FA Cup	0		0
League Cup	0		0
European Cup / Champions League	0		0
European Cup-Winners' Cup	0		0
UEFA Cup / Inter-Cities' Fairs Cup	0		0
Other Matches	0		0
OVERALL TOTAL	6	(1)	2

Opponents	PREM			FLD 1			FLD 2			FAC			LC			EC/CL			ECWC			UEFA			OTHER			TOTAL		
	A	S	G	A	S	G	A	S	G	A	S	G	A	S	G	A	S	G	A	S	G	A	S	G	A	S	G	A	S	G
1 Ipswich Town	-		-	1		1	-			-			-			-			-			-			-			1		1
2 Notts County	-		-	1		1	-			-			-			-			-			-			-			1		1
3 Coventry City	-		-	1			-			-			-			-			-			-			-			1		-
4 Everton	-		-	1			-			-			-			-			-			-			-			1		
5 Watford	-		-	1			-			-			-			-			-			-			-			1		
6 West Ham United	-		-	1			-			-			-			-			-			-			-			1		
7 Liverpool	-		-	-	(1)		-			-			-			-			-			-			-			-	(1)	-

STAN CROWTHER

DEBUT (Full Appearance)

Wednesday 19/02/1958
FA Cup 5th Round
at Old Trafford

Manchester United 3 Sheffield Wednesday 0

CLUB CAREER RECORD	Apps	Subs	Goals
Premiership	0		0
League Division 1	13		0
League Division 2	0		0
FA Cup	5		0
League Cup	0		0
European Cup / Champions League	2		0
European Cup-Winners' Cup	0		0
UEFA Cup / Inter-Cities' Fairs Cup	0		0
Other Matches	0		0
OVERALL TOTAL	20		0

Opponents	PREM			FLD 1			FLD 2			FAC			LC			EC/CL			ECWC			UEFA			OTHER			TOTAL		
	A	S	G	A	S	G	A	S	G	A	S	G	A	S	G	A	S	G	A	S	G	A	S	G	A	S	G	A	S	G
1 AC Milan	-		-	-			-			-			-			2			-			-			-			2		-
2 Fulham	-		-	-			-			2			-			-			-			-			-			2		-
3 Newcastle United	-		-	2			-			-			-			-			-			-			-			2		-
4 Sheffield Wednesday	-		-	1			-			1			-			-			-			-			-			2		-
5 Aston Villa	-		-	1			-			-			-			-			-			-			-			1		-
6 Birmingham City	-		-	1			-			-			-			-			-			-			-			1		-
7 Bolton Wanderers	-		-	-			-			1			-			-			-			-			-			1		-
8 Burnley	-		-	1			-			-			-			-			-			-			-			1		-
9 Chelsea	-		-	1			-			-			-			-			-			-			-			1		-
10 Nottingham Forest	-		-	1			-			-			-			-			-			-			-			1		-
11 Portsmouth	-		-	1			-			-			-			-			-			-			-			1		-
12 Preston North End	-		-	1			-			-			-			-			-			-			-			1		-
13 Sunderland	-		-	1			-			-			-			-			-			-			-			1		-
14 Tottenham Hotspur	-		-	1			-			-			-			-			-			-			-			1		-
15 West Bromwich Albion	-		-	-			-			1			-			-			-			-			-			1		-
16 Wolverhampton W.	-		-	1			-			-			-			-			-			-			-			1		-

JORDI CRUYFF

DEBUT (Full Appearance)

Saturday 17/08/1996
FA Premiership
at Selhurst Park

Wimbledon 0 Manchester United 3

CLUB CAREER RECORD	Apps	Subs	Goals
Premiership	15	(19)	8
League Division 1	0		0
League Division 2	0		0
FA Cup	0	(1)	0
League Cup	5		0
European Cup / Champions League	4	(7)	0
European Cup-Winners' Cup	0		0
UEFA Cup / Inter–Cities' Fairs Cup	0		0
Other Matches	2	(5)	0
OVERALL TOTAL	26	(32)	8

Opponents	PREM A S G	FLD 1 A S G	FLD 2 A S G	FAC A S G	LC A S G	EC/CL A S G	ECWC A S G	UEFA A S G	OTHER A S G	TOTAL A S G
1 Wimbledon	2 (2) 2	–	–	–	–	–	–	–	–	2 (2) 2
2 Aston Villa	1 (2) –	–	–	–	1	–	–	–	–	2 (2) –
3 Leicester City	2	–	–	–	1	–	–	–	–	3 –
4 Southampton	2 (1) 1	–	–	–	–	–	–	–	–	2 (1) 1
5 Derby County	1 (2) 1	–	–	–	–	–	–	–	–	1 (2) 1
6 Tottenham Hotspur	1 (2) –	–	–	–	–	–	–	–	–	1 (2) –
7 Chelsea	– (2) –	–	–	–	–	–	–	–	– (1) –	– (3) –
8 Fenerbahce	–	–	–	–	–	2	–	–	–	2 –
9 Blackburn Rovers	1 (1) 1	–	–	–	–	–	–	–	–	1 (1) 1
10 Arsenal	–	–	–	–	–	–	–	1 (1) –	–	1 (1) –
11 Coventry City	1 (1) –	–	–	–	–	–	–	–	–	1 (1) –
12 Juventus	–	–	–	–	–	1 (1) –	–	–	–	1 (1) –
13 Sturm Graz	–	–	–	–	–	1 (1) –	–	–	–	1 (1) –
14 West Ham United	– (2) 1	–	–	–	–	–	–	–	–	– (2) 1
15 Barnsley	– (1) –	–	–	– (1) –	–	–	–	–	–	– (2) –
16 Brondby	–	–	–	–	–	– (2) –	–	–	–	– (2) –
17 Newcastle United	– (1) –	–	–	–	–	–	–	–	– (1) –	– (2) –
18 Everton	1 1	–	–	–	–	–	–	–	–	1 1
19 Bury	–	–	–	–	1	–	–	–	–	1 –
20 Ipswich Town	–	–	–	–	1	–	–	–	–	1 –
21 Leeds United	1	–	–	–	–	–	–	–	–	1 –
22 Liverpool	1	–	–	–	–	–	–	–	–	1 –
23 Nottingham Forest	–	–	–	–	1	–	–	–	–	1 –
24 South Melbourne	–	–	–	–	–	–	–	–	1	1 –
25 Sunderland	1	–	–	–	–	–	–	–	–	1 –
26 Watford	– (1) 1	–	–	–	–	–	–	–	–	– (1) 1
27 Bayern Munich	–	–	–	–	–	– (1) –	–	–	–	– (1) –
28 Croatia Zagreb	–	–	–	–	–	– (1) –	–	–	–	– (1) –
29 Lazio	–	–	–	–	–	–	–	–	– (1) –	– (1) –
30 Middlesbrough	– (1) –	–	–	–	–	–	–	–	–	– (1) –
31 Valencia	–	–	–	–	–	– (1) –	–	–	–	– (1) –
32 Vasco da Gama	–	–	–	–	–	–	–	–	– (1) –	– (1) –

NICK CULKIN

DEBUT (Substitute Appearance)

Sunday 22/08/1999
FA Premiership
at Highbury

Arsenal 1 Manchester United 2

CLUB CAREER RECORD	Apps	Subs	Goals
Premiership	0	(1)	0
League Division 1	0		0
League Division 2	0		0
FA Cup	0		0
League Cup	0		0
European Cup / Champions League	0		0
European Cup–Winners' Cup	0		0
UEFA Cup / Inter–Cities' Fairs Cup	0		0
Other Matches	0		0
OVERALL TOTAL	0	(1)	0

Opponents	PREM A S G	FLD 1 A S G	FLD 2 A S G	FAC A S G	LC A S G	EC/CL A S G	ECWC A S G	UEFA A S G	OTHER A S G	TOTAL A S G
1 Arsenal	– (1) –	–	–	–	–	–	–	–	–	– (1) –

JOHN CUNNINGHAM

DEBUT (Full Appearance)

Saturday 05/11/1898
Football League Division 2
at Bank Street

Newton Heath 3 Grimsby Town 2

CLUB CAREER RECORD	Apps	Subs	Goals
Premiership	0		0
League Division 1	0		0
League Division 2	15		2
FA Cup	2		0
League Cup	0		0
European Cup / Champions League	0		0
European Cup-Winners' Cup	0		0
UEFA Cup / Inter-Cities' Fairs Cup	0		0
Other Matches	0		0
OVERALL TOTAL	17		2

Opponents	PREM A S G	FLD 1 A S G	FLD 2 A S G	FAC A S G	LC A S G	EC/CL A S G	ECWC A S G	UEFA A S G	OTHER A S G	TOTAL A S G
1 Grimsby Town	– – –	– – –	2 – –	– – –	– – –	– – –	– – –	– – –	– – –	2 – –
2 Tottenham Hotspur	– – –	– – –	– – –	2 – –	– – –	– – –	– – –	– – –	– – –	2 – –
3 Blackpool	– – –	– – –	1 – 1	– – –	– – –	– – –	– – –	– – –	– – –	1 – 1
4 Glossop	– – –	– – –	1 – 1	– – –	– – –	– – –	– – –	– – –	– – –	1 – 1
5 Arsenal	– – –	– – –	1 – –	– – –	– – –	– – –	– – –	– – –	– – –	1 – –
6 Barnsley	– – –	– – –	1 – –	– – –	– – –	– – –	– – –	– – –	– – –	1 – –
7 Birmingham City	– – –	– – –	1 – –	– – –	– – –	– – –	– – –	– – –	– – –	1 – –
8 Burton Swifts	– – –	– – –	1 – –	– – –	– – –	– – –	– – –	– – –	– – –	1 – –
9 Gainsborough Trinity	– – –	– – –	1 – –	– – –	– – –	– – –	– – –	– – –	– – –	1 – –
10 Leicester City	– – –	– – –	1 – –	– – –	– – –	– – –	– – –	– – –	– – –	1 – –
11 Lincoln City	– – –	– – –	1 – –	– – –	– – –	– – –	– – –	– – –	– – –	1 – –
12 Loughborough Town	– – –	– – –	1 – –	– – –	– – –	– – –	– – –	– – –	– – –	1 – –
13 New Brighton Tower	– – –	– – –	1 – –	– – –	– – –	– – –	– – –	– – –	– – –	1 – –
14 Port Vale	– – –	– – –	1 – –	– – –	– – –	– – –	– – –	– – –	– – –	1 – –
15 Walsall	– – –	– – –	1 – –	– – –	– – –	– – –	– – –	– – –	– – –	1 – –

LAURIE CUNNINGHAM

DEBUT (Substitute Appearance)

Tuesday 19/04/1983
Football League Division 1
at Goodison Park

Everton 2 Manchester United 0

CLUB CAREER RECORD	Apps	Subs	Goals
Premiership	0		0
League Division 1	3	(2)	1
League Division 2	0		0
FA Cup	0		0
League Cup	0		0
European Cup / Champions League	0		0
European Cup-Winners' Cup	0		0
UEFA Cup / Inter-Cities' Fairs Cup	0		0
Other Matches	0		0
OVERALL TOTAL	3	(2)	1

Opponents	PREM A S G	FLD 1 A S G	FLD 2 A S G	FAC A S G	LC A S G	EC/CL A S G	ECWC A S G	UEFA A S G	OTHER A S G	TOTAL A S G
1 Arsenal	– – –	1 – –	– – –	– – –	– – –	– – –	– – –	– – –	– – –	1 – –
2 Norwich City	– – –	1 – –	– – –	– – –	– – –	– – –	– – –	– – –	– – –	1 – –
3 Swansea City	– – –	1 – –	– – –	– – –	– – –	– – –	– – –	– – –	– – –	1 – –
4 Watford	– – –	– (1) 1	– – –	– – –	– – –	– – –	– – –	– – –	– – –	– (1) 1
5 Everton	– – –	– (1) –	– – –	– – –	– – –	– – –	– – –	– – –	– – –	– (1) –

JOE CURRY

DEBUT (Full Appearance)

Saturday 21/11/1908
Football League Division 1
at Bank Street

Manchester United 2 Bradford City 0

CLUB CAREER RECORD	Apps	Subs	Goals
Premiership	0		0
League Division 1	13		0
League Division 2	0		0
FA Cup	1		0
League Cup	0		0
European Cup / Champions League	0		0
European Cup-Winners' Cup	0		0
UEFA Cup / Inter-Cities' Fairs Cup	0		0
Other Matches	0		0
OVERALL TOTAL	14		0

Opponents	PREM A S G	FLD 1 A S G	FLD 2 A S G	FAC A S G	LC A S G	EC/CL A S G	ECWC A S G	UEFA A S G	OTHER A S G	TOTAL A S G
1 Leicester City	– – –	2 – –	– – –	– – –	– – –	– – –	– – –	– – –	– – –	2 – –
2 Blackburn Rovers	– – –	1 – –	– – –	– – –	– – –	– – –	– – –	– – –	– – –	1 – –
3 Bradford City	– – –	1 – –	– – –	– – –	– – –	– – –	– – –	– – –	– – –	1 – –
4 Burnley	– – –	– – –	– – –	1 – –	– – –	– – –	– – –	– – –	– – –	1 – –
5 Bury	– – –	1 – –	– – –	– – –	– – –	– – –	– – –	– – –	– – –	1 – –
6 Everton	– – –	1 – –	– – –	– – –	– – –	– – –	– – –	– – –	– – –	1 – –
7 Liverpool	– – –	1 – –	– – –	– – –	– – –	– – –	– – –	– – –	– – –	1 – –
8 Nottingham Forest	– – –	1 – –	– – –	– – –	– – –	– – –	– – –	– – –	– – –	1 – –
9 Notts County	– – –	1 – –	– – –	– – –	– – –	– – –	– – –	– – –	– – –	1 – –
10 Oldham Athletic	– – –	1 – –	– – –	– – –	– – –	– – –	– – –	– – –	– – –	1 – –
11 Preston North End	– – –	1 – –	– – –	– – –	– – –	– – –	– – –	– – –	– – –	1 – –
12 Sheffield United	– – –	1 – –	– – –	– – –	– – –	– – –	– – –	– – –	– – –	1 – –
13 Sheffield Wednesday	– – –	1 – –	– – –	– – –	– – –	– – –	– – –	– – –	– – –	1 – –

JOHN CURTIS

DEBUT (Full Appearance)

Tuesday 14/10/1997
League Cup 3rd Round
at Portman Road

Ipswich Town 2 Manchester United 0

CLUB CAREER RECORD	Apps	Subs	Goals
Premiership	4	(9)	0
League Division 1	0		0
League Division 2	0		0
FA Cup	0		0
League Cup	5		0
European Cup / Champions League	0		0
European Cup-Winners' Cup	0		0
UEFA Cup / Inter-Cities' Fairs Cup	0		0
Other Matches	0		0
OVERALL TOTAL	**9**	**(9)**	**0**

Opponents	PREM A S G	FLD 1 A S G	FLD 2 A S G	FAC A S G	LC A S G	EC/CL A S G	ECWC A S G	UEFA A S G	OTHER A S G	TOTAL A S G
1 Barnsley	2 – –	– – –	– – –	– – –	– – –	– – –	– – –	– – –	– – –	2 – –
2 Nottingham Forest	– (1) –	– – –	– – –	– – –	1 – –	– – –	– – –	– – –	– – –	1 (1) –
3 Coventry City	– (2) –	– – –	– – –	– – –	– – –	– – –	– – –	– – –	– – –	– (2) –
4 Everton	– (2) –	– – –	– – –	– – –	– – –	– – –	– – –	– – –	– – –	– (2) –
5 Sheffield Wednesday	– (2) –	– – –	– – –	– – –	– – –	– – –	– – –	– – –	– – –	– (2) –
6 Arsenal	1 – –	– – –	– – –	– – –	– – –	– – –	– – –	– – –	– – –	1 – –
7 Aston Villa	– – –	– – –	– – –	– – –	1 – –	– – –	– – –	– – –	– – –	1 – –
8 Blackburn Rovers	1 – –	– – –	– – –	– – –	– – –	– – –	– – –	– – –	– – –	1 – –
9 Bury	– – –	– – –	– – –	– – –	1 – –	– – –	– – –	– – –	– – –	1 – –
10 Ipswich Town	– – –	– – –	– – –	– – –	1 – –	– – –	– – –	– – –	– – –	1 – –
11 Tottenham Hotspur	– – –	– – –	– – –	– – –	1 – –	– – –	– – –	– – –	– – –	1 – –
12 West Ham United	– (1) –	– – –	– – –	– – –	– – –	– – –	– – –	– – –	– – –	– (1) –
13 Wimbledon	– (1) –	– – –	– – –	– – –	– – –	– – –	– – –	– – –	– – –	– (1) –

BILLY DALE

DEBUT (Full Appearance)

Saturday 25/08/1928
Football League Division 1
at Old Trafford

Manchester United 1 Leicester City 1

CLUB CAREER RECORD	Apps	Subs	Goals
Premiership	0		0
League Division 1	60		0
League Division 2	4		0
FA Cup	4		0
League Cup	0		0
European Cup / Champions League	0		0
European Cup-Winners' Cup	0		0
UEFA Cup / Inter-Cities' Fairs Cup	0		0
Other Matches	0		0
OVERALL TOTAL	**68**		**0**

Opponents	PREM A S G	FLD 1 A S G	FLD 2 A S G	FAC A S G	LC A S G	EC/CL A S G	ECWC A S G	UEFA A S G	OTHER A S G	TOTAL A S G
1 Arsenal	– – –	5 – –	– – –	– – –	– – –	– – –	– – –	– – –	– – –	5 – –
2 West Ham United	– – –	5 – –	– – –	– – –	– – –	– – –	– – –	– – –	– – –	5 – –
3 Grimsby Town	– – –	3 – –	– – –	1 – –	– – –	– – –	– – –	– – –	– – –	4 – –
4 Leicester City	– – –	4 – –	– – –	– – –	– – –	– – –	– – –	– – –	– – –	4 – –
5 Portsmouth	– – –	4 – –	– – –	– – –	– – –	– – –	– – –	– – –	– – –	4 – –
6 Sheffield United	– – –	4 – –	– – –	– – –	– – –	– – –	– – –	– – –	– – –	4 – –
7 Aston Villa	– – –	3 – –	– – –	– – –	– – –	– – –	– – –	– – –	– – –	3 – –
8 Everton	– – –	3 – –	– – –	– – –	– – –	– – –	– – –	– – –	– – –	3 – –
9 Huddersfield Town	– – –	3 – –	– – –	– – –	– – –	– – –	– – –	– – –	– – –	3 – –
10 Sheffield Wednesday	– – –	3 – –	– – –	– – –	– – –	– – –	– – –	– – –	– – –	3 – –
11 Stoke City	– – –	– – –	– – –	3 – –	– – –	– – –	– – –	– – –	– – –	3 – –
12 Birmingham City	– – –	2 – –	– – –	– – –	– – –	– – –	– – –	– – –	– – –	2 – –
13 Bolton Wanderers	– – –	2 – –	– – –	– – –	– – –	– – –	– – –	– – –	– – –	2 – –
14 Burnley	– – –	2 – –	– – –	– – –	– – –	– – –	– – –	– – –	– – –	2 – –
15 Bury	– – –	1 – –	1 – –	– – –	– – –	– – –	– – –	– – –	– – –	2 – –
16 Chelsea	– – –	2 – –	– – –	– – –	– – –	– – –	– – –	– – –	– – –	2 – –
17 Liverpool	– – –	2 – –	– – –	– – –	– – –	– – –	– – –	– – –	– – –	2 – –
18 Middlesbrough	– – –	2 – –	– – –	– – –	– – –	– – –	– – –	– – –	– – –	2 – –
19 Newcastle United	– – –	2 – –	– – –	– – –	– – –	– – –	– – –	– – –	– – –	2 – –
20 Sunderland	– – –	2 – –	– – –	– – –	– – –	– – –	– – –	– – –	– – –	2 – –
21 Blackburn Rovers	– – –	1 – –	– – –	– – –	– – –	– – –	– – –	– – –	– – –	1 – –
22 Blackpool	– – –	1 – –	– – –	– – –	– – –	– – –	– – –	– – –	– – –	1 – –
23 Cardiff City	– – –	1 – –	– – –	– – –	– – –	– – –	– – –	– – –	– – –	1 – –
24 Derby County	– – –	1 – –	– – –	– – –	– – –	– – –	– – –	– – –	– – –	1 – –
25 Leeds United	– – –	1 – –	– – –	– – –	– – –	– – –	– – –	– – –	– – –	1 – –
26 Manchester City	– – –	1 – –	– – –	– – –	– – –	– – –	– – –	– – –	– – –	1 – –
27 Millwall	– – –	– – –	1 – –	– – –	– – –	– – –	– – –	– – –	– – –	1 – –
28 Oldham Athletic	– – –	– – –	1 – –	– – –	– – –	– – –	– – –	– – –	– – –	1 – –
29 Port Vale	– – –	– – –	1 – –	– – –	– – –	– – –	– – –	– – –	– – –	1 – –

HERBERT DALE

DEBUT (Full Appearance)

Saturday 25/10/1890
FA Cup 2nd Qualifying Round
at Bootle Park

Bootle Reserves 1   Newton Heath 0

CLUB CAREER RECORD	Apps	Subs	Goals
Premiership	0		0
League Division 1	0		0
League Division 2	0		0
FA Cup	1		0
League Cup	0		0
European Cup / Champions League	0		0
European Cup-Winners' Cup	0		0
UEFA Cup / Inter-Cities' Fairs Cup	0		0
Other Matches	0		0
OVERALL TOTAL	**1**		**0**

Opponents	PREM A S G	FLD 1 A S G	FLD 2 A S G	FAC A S G	LC A S G	EC/CL A S G	ECWC A S G	UEFA A S G	OTHER A S G	TOTAL A S G
1 Bootle Reserves	– –	– –	–	1	–	–	–	–	– –	1 –

JOE DALE

DEBUT (Full Appearance)

Saturday 27/09/1947
Football League Division 1
at Deepdale

Preston North End 2   Manchester United 1

CLUB CAREER RECORD	Apps	Subs	Goals
Premiership	0		0
League Division 1	2		0
League Division 2	0		0
FA Cup	0		0
League Cup	0		0
European Cup / Champions League	0		0
European Cup-Winners' Cup	0		0
UEFA Cup / Inter-Cities' Fairs Cup	0		0
Other Matches	0		0
OVERALL TOTAL	**2**		**0**

Opponents	PREM A S G	FLD 1 A S G	FLD 2 A S G	FAC A S G	LC A S G	EC/CL A S G	ECWC A S G	UEFA A S G	OTHER A S G	TOTAL A S G
1 Preston North End	– –	1 –	–	–	–	–	–	–	–	1 –
2 Stoke City	– –	1 –	–	–	–	–	–	–	–	1 –

TED DALTON

DEBUT (Full Appearance)

Wednesday 25/03/1908
Football League Division 1
at Anfield

Liverpool 7   Manchester United 4

CLUB CAREER RECORD	Apps	Subs	Goals
Premiership	0		0
League Division 1	1		0
League Division 2	0		0
FA Cup	0		0
League Cup	0		0
European Cup / Champions League	0		0
European Cup-Winners' Cup	0		0
UEFA Cup / Inter-Cities' Fairs Cup	0		0
Other Matches	0		0
OVERALL TOTAL	**1**		**0**

Opponents	PREM A S G	FLD 1 A S G	FLD 2 A S G	FAC A S G	LC A S G	EC/CL A S G	ECWC A S G	UEFA A S G	OTHER A S G	TOTAL A S G
1 Liverpool	– –	1 –	–	–	–	–	–	–	–	1 –

GERRY DALY

DEBUT (Full Appearance)

Saturday 25/08/1973
Football League Division 1
at Highbury

Arsenal 3   Manchester United 0

CLUB CAREER RECORD	Apps	Subs	Goals
Premiership	0		0
League Division 1	71	(3)	12
League Division 2	36	(1)	11
FA Cup	9	(1)	5
League Cup	17		4
European Cup / Champions League	0		0
European Cup-Winners' Cup	0		0
UEFA Cup / Inter-Cities' Fairs Cup	4		0
Other Matches	0		0
OVERALL TOTAL	**137**	**(5)**	**32**

Opponents	PREM A S G	FLD 1 A S G	FLD 2 A S G	FAC A S G	LC A S G	EC/CL A S G	ECWC A S G	UEFA A S G	OTHER A S G	TOTAL A S G
1 Norwich City	– –	4 1	2 –	– –	2	–	–	–	–	8 1
2 Manchester City	– –	5 1	– –	– –	2 1	–	–	–	–	7 2
3 Middlesbrough	– –	3 1	– –	– –	3	–	–	–	–	6 1
4 Derby County	– –	4 (1) 1	– –	1	–	–	–	–	–	5 (1) 1
5 Aston Villa	– –	3 –	1 2	– –	1	–	–	–	–	5 2
6 Newcastle United	– –	4 1	– –	– –	1	–	–	–	–	5 1
7 Sunderland	– –	1 –	1	– –	3 1	–	–	–	–	5 1
8 Everton	– –	4 –	– –	– –	1	–	–	–	–	5 –
9 Wolverhampton W.	– –	2 (1) –	– –	2 1	–	–	–	–	–	4 (1) 1
10 Leicester City	– –	3 1	– –	1 1	–	–	–	–	–	4 2

continued../

GERRY DALY (continued)

Opponents	PREM A S G	FLD 1 A S G	FLD 2 A S G	FAC A S G	LC A S G	EC/CL A S G	ECWC A S G	UEFA A S G	OTHER A S G	TOTAL A S G
11 Tottenham Hotspur	– –	4 2	–	–	–	–	–	–	–	4 2
12 Burnley	– –	3 –	–	–	1	–	–	–	–	4 –
13 Ipswich Town	– –	4 –	–	–	–	–	–	–	–	4 –
14 Southampton	– –	1 –	2 –	1 –	–	–	–	–	–	4 –
15 Birmingham City	– –	3 (1) –	–	–	–	–	–	–	–	3 (1) –
16 Leeds United	– –	3 2	–	–	–	–	–	–	–	3 2
17 Sheffield United	– –	3 1	–	–	–	–	–	–	–	3 1
18 West Bromwich Albion	– –	1 –	2 1	–	–	–	–	–	–	3 1
19 Arsenal	– –	3 –	–	–	–	–	–	–	–	3 –
20 Coventry City	– –	3 –	–	–	–	–	–	–	–	3 –
21 West Ham United	– –	3 –	–	–	–	–	–	–	–	3 –
22 Walsall	– –	–	–	2 (1) 1	–	–	–	–	–	2 (1) 1
23 Millwall	– –	–	2 4	–	–	–	–	–	–	2 4
24 Oxford United	– –	–	1 –	1 2	–	–	–	–	–	2 2
25 Cardiff City	– –	–	2 1	–	–	–	–	–	–	2 1
26 Fulham	– –	–	2 1	–	–	–	–	–	–	2 1
27 Nottingham Forest	– –	–	2 1	–	–	–	–	–	–	2 1
28 Portsmouth	– –	–	2 1	–	–	–	–	–	–	2 1
29 Ajax	– –	–	–	–	–	–	–	2 –	–	2 –
30 Blackpool	– –	–	2 –	–	–	–	–	–	–	2 –
31 Bolton Wanderers	– –	–	2 –	–	–	–	–	–	–	2 –
32 Bristol City	– –	–	2 –	–	–	–	–	–	–	2 –
33 Bristol Rovers	– –	–	2 –	–	–	–	–	–	–	2 –
34 Juventus	– –	–	–	–	–	–	–	2 –	–	2 –
35 Leyton Orient	– –	–	2 –	–	–	–	–	–	–	2 –
36 Liverpool	– –	2 –	–	–	–	–	–	–	–	2 –
37 Notts County	– –	–	2 –	–	–	–	–	–	–	2 –
38 Oldham Athletic	– –	–	2 –	–	–	–	–	–	–	2 –
39 Queens Park Rangers	– –	2 –	–	–	–	–	–	–	–	2 –
40 Stoke City	– –	2 –	–	–	–	–	–	–	–	2 –
41 York City	– –	–	2 –	–	–	–	–	–	–	2 –
42 Tranmere Rovers	– –	–	–	–	1 2	–	–	–	–	1 2
43 Chelsea	– –	1 1	–	–	–	–	–	–	–	1 1
44 Brentford	– –	–	–	–	1 –	–	–	–	–	1 –
45 Charlton Athletic	– –	–	–	–	1 –	–	–	–	–	1 –
46 Hull City	– –	–	–	1 –	–	–	–	–	–	1 –
47 Peterborough United	– –	–	–	–	1 –	–	–	–	–	1 –
48 Sheffield Wednesday	– –	–	– (1) –	–	–	–	–	–	–	– (1) –

PETER DAVENPORT

DEBUT (Full Appearance)

Saturday 15/03/1986
Football League Division 1
at Loftus Road

Queens Park Rangers 1 Manchester United 0

CLUB CAREER RECORD	Apps	Subs	Goals
Premiership	0		0
League Division 1	73	(19)	22
League Division 2	0		0
FA Cup	2	(2)	0
League Cup	8	(2)	4
European Cup / Champions League	0		0
European Cup-Winners' Cup	0		0
UEFA Cup / Inter–Cities' Fairs Cup	0		0
Other Matches	0		0
OVERALL TOTAL	83	(23)	26

Opponents	PREM A S G	FLD 1 A S G	FLD 2 A S G	FAC A S G	LC A S G	EC/CL A S G	ECWC A S G	UEFA A S G	OTHER A S G	TOTAL A S G
1 Queens Park Rangers	– –	6 1	–	–	–	–	–	–	–	6 1
2 Southampton	– –	2 (2) 1	–	–	2 1	–	–	–	–	4 (2) 2
3 West Ham United	– –	5 2	–	–	–	–	–	–	–	5 2
4 Norwich City	– –	5 1	–	–	–	–	–	–	–	5 1
5 Sheffield Wednesday	– –	4 (1) 3	–	–	–	–	–	–	–	4 (1) 3
6 Luton Town	– –	4 (1) 2	–	–	–	–	–	–	–	4 (1) 2
7 Oxford United	– –	4 2	–	–	– (1) –	–	–	–	–	4 (1) 2
8 Tottenham Hotspur	– –	4 (1) 2	–	–	–	–	–	–	–	4 (1) 2
9 Coventry City	– –	3 (1) 1	–	– (1) –	–	–	–	–	–	3 (2) 1
10 Liverpool	– –	3 (2) 1	–	–	–	–	–	–	–	3 (2) 1
11 Watford	– –	3 (2) 1	–	–	–	–	–	–	–	3 (2) 1
12 Everton	– –	3 (2) –	–	–	–	–	–	–	–	3 (2) –
13 Chelsea	– –	4 1	–	–	–	–	–	–	–	4 1
14 Wimbledon	– –	4 –	–	–	–	–	–	–	–	4 –
15 Manchester City	– –	2 (1) –	–	1	–	–	–	–	–	3 (1) –
16 Newcastle United	– –	3 (1) –	–	–	–	–	–	–	–	3 (1) –
17 Charlton Athletic	– –	2 (2) –	–	–	–	–	–	–	–	2 (2) –
18 Nottingham Forest	– –	3 –	–	–	–	–	–	–	–	3 –
19 Leicester City	– –	2 (1) 1	–	–	–	–	–	–	–	2 (1) 1
20 Aston Villa	– –	2 2	–	–	–	–	–	–	–	2 2
21 Port Vale	– –	–	–	–	2 1	–	–	–	–	2 1
22 Arsenal	– –	1 –	–	1 –	–	–	–	–	–	2 –
23 Portsmouth	– –	1 (1) 1	–	–	–	–	–	–	–	1 (1) 1

continued../

PETER DAVENPORT (continued)

Opponents	PREM A S G	FLD 1 A S G	FLD 2 A S G	FAC A S G	LC A S G	EC/CL A S G	ECWC A S G	UEFA A S G	OTHER A S G	TOTAL A S G
24 Rotherham United	– –	– –	– –	– –	1 (1) 1	– –	– –	– –	– –	1 (1) 1
25 Derby County	– –	1 (1) –	– –	– –	– –	– –	– –	– –	– –	1 (1) –
26 Hull City	– –	– –	– –	– –	1 1	– –	– –	– –	– –	1 1
27 Birmingham City	– –	1 –	– –	– –	– –	– –	– –	– –	– –	1 –
28 Bury	– –	– –	– –	– –	1 –	– –	– –	– –	– –	1 –
29 Crystal Palace	– –	– –	– –	– –	1 –	– –	– –	– –	– –	1 –
30 Middlesbrough	– –	1 –	– –	– –	– –	– –	– –	– –	– –	1 –
31 Ipswich Town	– –	– –	– –	– (1) –	– –	– –	– –	– –	– –	– (1) –

WILL DAVIDSON

DEBUT (Full Appearance)

Saturday 02/09/1893
Football League Division 1
at North Road

Newton Heath 3 Burnley 2

CLUB CAREER RECORD	Apps	Subs	Goals
Premiership	0		0
League Division 1	28		1
League Division 2	12		1
FA Cup	3		0
League Cup	0		0
European Cup / Champions League	0		0
European Cup-Winners' Cup	0		0
UEFA Cup / Inter-Cities' Fairs Cup	0		0
Other Matches	1		0
OVERALL TOTAL	44		2

Opponents	PREM A S G	FLD 1 A S G	FLD 2 A S G	FAC A S G	LC A S G	EC/CL A S G	ECWC A S G	UEFA A S G	OTHER A S G	TOTAL A S G
1 Darwen	– –	2 –	2 –	– –	– –	– –	– –	– –	– –	4 –
2 Blackburn Rovers	– –	1 –	– –	2 –	– –	– –	– –	– –	– –	3 –
3 Wolverhampton W.	– –	2 1	– –	– –	– –	– –	– –	– –	– –	2 1
4 Aston Villa	– –	2 –	– –	– –	– –	– –	– –	– –	– –	2 –
5 Bolton Wanderers	– –	2 –	– –	– –	– –	– –	– –	– –	– –	2 –
6 Burnley	– –	2 –	– –	– –	– –	– –	– –	– –	– –	2 –
7 Crewe Alexandra	– –	– –	2 –	– –	– –	– –	– –	– –	– –	2 –
8 Everton	– –	2 –	– –	– –	– –	– –	– –	– –	– –	2 –
9 Leicester City	– –	– –	2 –	– –	– –	– –	– –	– –	– –	2 –
10 Nottingham Forest	– –	2 –	– –	– –	– –	– –	– –	– –	– –	2 –
11 Preston North End	– –	2 –	– –	– –	– –	– –	– –	– –	– –	2 –
12 Sheffield United	– –	2 –	– –	– –	– –	– –	– –	– –	– –	2 –
13 Sheffield Wednesday	– –	2 –	– –	– –	– –	– –	– –	– –	– –	2 –
14 Stoke City	– –	2 –	– –	– –	– –	– –	– –	– –	– –	2 –
15 Sunderland	– –	2 –	– –	– –	– –	– –	– –	– –	– –	2 –
16 West Bromwich Albion	– –	2 –	– –	– –	– –	– –	– –	– –	– –	2 –
17 Rotherham United	– –	– –	– –	1 1	– –	– –	– –	– –	– –	1 1
18 Arsenal	– –	– –	– –	1 –	– –	– –	– –	– –	– –	1 –
19 Burton Swifts	– –	– –	– –	1 –	– –	– –	– –	– –	– –	1 –
20 Burton Wanderers	– –	– –	– –	1 –	– –	– –	– –	– –	– –	1 –
21 Derby County	– –	1 –	– –	– –	– –	– –	– –	– –	– –	1 –
22 Grimsby Town	– –	– –	– –	1 –	– –	– –	– –	– –	– –	1 –
23 Liverpool	– –	– –	– –	– –	– –	– –	– –	1 –	– –	1 –
24 Manchester City	– –	– –	– –	1 –	– –	– –	– –	– –	– –	1 –
25 Middlesbrough	– –	– –	– –	1 –	– –	– –	– –	– –	– –	1 –

ALAN DAVIES

DEBUT (Full Appearance)

Saturday 01/05/1982
Football League Division 1
at Old Trafford

Manchester United 1 Southampton 0

CLUB CAREER RECORD	Apps	Subs	Goals
Premiership	0		0
League Division 1	6	(1)	0
League Division 2	0		0
FA Cup	2		0
League Cup	0		0
European Cup / Champions League	0		0
European Cup-Winners' Cup	0	(1)	1
UEFA Cup / Inter-Cities' Fairs Cup	0		0
Other Matches	0		0
OVERALL TOTAL	8	(2)	1

Opponents	PREM A S G	FLD 1 A S G	FLD 2 A S G	FAC A S G	LC A S G	EC/CL A S G	ECWC A S G	UEFA A S G	OTHER A S G	TOTAL A S G
1 Brighton	– –	– –	– –	2 –	– –	– –	– –	– –	– –	2 –
2 Notts County	– –	2 –	– –	– –	– –	– –	– –	– –	– –	2 –
3 Everton	– –	1 –	– –	– –	– –	– –	– –	– –	– –	1 –
4 Luton Town	– –	1 –	– –	– –	– –	– –	– –	– –	– –	1 –
5 Southampton	– –	1 –	– –	– –	– –	– –	– –	– –	– –	1 –
6 Watford	– –	1 –	– –	– –	– –	– –	– –	– –	– –	1 –
7 Juventus	– –	– –	– –	– –	– –	– –	– (1) 1	– –	– –	– (1) 1
8 Swansea City	– –	– (1) –	– –	– –	– –	– –	– –	– –	– –	– (1) –

JOE DAVIES

DEBUT (Full Appearance)

Saturday 30/10/1886
FA Cup 1st Round
at Fleetwood Park

Fleetwood Rangers 2 Newton Heath 2

CLUB CAREER RECORD	Apps	Subs	Goals
Premiership	0		0
League Division 1	0		0
League Division 2	0		0
FA Cup	2		0
League Cup	0		0
European Cup / Champions League	0		0
European Cup-Winners' Cup	0		0
UEFA Cup / Inter-Cities' Fairs Cup	0		0
Other Matches	0		0
OVERALL TOTAL	2		0

Opponents	PREM A S G	FLD 1 A S G	FLD 2 A S G	FAC A S G	LC A S G	EC/CL A S G	ECWC A S G	UEFA A S G	OTHER A S G	TOTAL A S G
1 Fleetwood Rangers	– – –	– – –	– – –	1 –	– – –	– – –	– – –	– – –	– – –	1 –
2 Preston North End	– – –	– – –	– – –	1 –	– – –	– – –	– – –	– – –	– – –	1 –

JOHN DAVIES

DEBUT (Full Appearance)

Saturday 14/01/1893
Football League Division 1
at North Road

Newton Heath 1 Nottingham Forest 3

CLUB CAREER RECORD	Apps	Subs	Goals
Premiership	0		0
League Division 1	7		0
League Division 2	0		0
FA Cup	1		0
League Cup	0		0
European Cup / Champions League	0		0
European Cup-Winners' Cup	0		0
UEFA Cup / Inter-Cities' Fairs Cup	0		0
Other Matches	2		0
OVERALL TOTAL	10		0

Opponents	PREM A S G	FLD 1 A S G	FLD 2 A S G	FAC A S G	LC A S G	EC/CL A S G	ECWC A S G	UEFA A S G	OTHER A S G	TOTAL A S G
1 Birmingham City	– – –	– – –	– – –	– – –	– – –	– – –	– – –	– – –	2 –	2 –
2 Accrington Stanley	– – –	1 –	– – –	– – –	– – –	– – –	– – –	– – –	– – –	1 –
3 Aston Villa	– – –	1 –	– – –	– – –	– – –	– – –	– – –	– – –	– – –	1 –
4 Blackburn Rovers	– – –	– – –	– – –	1 –	– – –	– – –	– – –	– – –	– – –	1 –
5 Nottingham Forest	– – –	1 –	– – –	– – –	– – –	– – –	– – –	– – –	– – –	1 –
6 Notts County	– – –	1 –	– – –	– – –	– – –	– – –	– – –	– – –	– – –	1 –
7 Preston North End	– – –	1 –	– – –	– – –	– – –	– – –	– – –	– – –	– – –	1 –
8 Stoke City	– – –	1 –	– – –	– – –	– – –	– – –	– – –	– – –	– – –	1 –
9 Sunderland	– – –	1 –	– – –	– – –	– – –	– – –	– – –	– – –	– – –	1 –

L DAVIES

DEBUT (Full Appearance)

Saturday 30/10/1886
FA Cup 1st Round
at Fleetwood Park

Fleetwood Rangers 2 Newton Heath 2

CLUB CAREER RECORD	Apps	Subs	Goals
Premiership	0		0
League Division 1	0		0
League Division 2	0		0
FA Cup	1		0
League Cup	0		0
European Cup / Champions League	0		0
European Cup-Winners' Cup	0		0
UEFA Cup / Inter-Cities' Fairs Cup	0		0
Other Matches	0		0
OVERALL TOTAL	1		0

Opponents	PREM A S G	FLD 1 A S G	FLD 2 A S G	FAC A S G	LC A S G	EC/CL A S G	ECWC A S G	UEFA A S G	OTHER A S G	TOTAL A S G
1 Fleetwood Rangers	– – –	– – –	– – –	1 –	– – –	– – –	– – –	– – –	– – –	1 –

RON DAVIES

DEBUT (Substitute Appearance)

Saturday 30/11/1974
Football League Division 2
at Old Trafford

Manchester United 3 Sunderland 2

CLUB CAREER RECORD	Apps	Subs	Goals
Premiership	0		0
League Division 1	0		0
League Division 2	0	(8)	0
FA Cup	0	(2)	0
League Cup	0		0
European Cup / Champions League	0		0
European Cup-Winners' Cup	0		0
UEFA Cup / Inter-Cities' Fairs Cup	0		0
Other Matches	0		0
OVERALL TOTAL	**0**	**(10)**	**0**

Opponents	PREM A S G	FLD 1 A S G	FLD 2 A S G	FAC A S G	LC A S G	EC/CL A S G	ECWC A S G	UEFA A S G	OTHER A S G	TOTAL A S G
1 Walsall	– – –	– – –	– – –	– (2) –	– – –	– – –	– – –	– – –	– – –	– (2) –
2 Aston Villa	– – –	– – –	– (1) –	– – –	– – –	– – –	– – –	– – –	– – –	– (1) –
3 Hull City	– – –	– – –	– (1) –	– – –	– – –	– – –	– – –	– – –	– – –	– (1) –
4 Leyton Orient	– – –	– – –	– (1) –	– – –	– – –	– – –	– – –	– – –	– – –	– (1) –
5 Oldham Athletic	– – –	– – –	– (1) –	– – –	– – –	– – –	– – –	– – –	– – –	– (1) –
6 Oxford United	– – –	– – –	– (1) –	– – –	– – –	– – –	– – –	– – –	– – –	– (1) –
7 Sheffield Wednesday	– – –	– – –	– (1) –	– – –	– – –	– – –	– – –	– – –	– – –	– (1) –
8 Sunderland	– – –	– – –	– (1) –	– – –	– – –	– – –	– – –	– – –	– – –	– (1) –
9 York City	– – –	– – –	– (1) –	– – –	– – –	– – –	– – –	– – –	– – –	– (1) –

SIMON DAVIES

DEBUT (Full Appearance)

Wednesday 21/09/1994
League Cup 2nd Round 1st Leg
at Vale Park

Port Vale 1 Manchester United 2

CLUB CAREER RECORD	Apps	Subs	Goals
Premiership	4	(7)	0
League Division 1	0		0
League Division 2	0		0
FA Cup	0		0
League Cup	4	(2)	0
European Cup / Champions League	2		1
European Cup-Winners' Cup	0		0
UEFA Cup / Inter-Cities' Fairs Cup	0	(1)	0
Other Matches	0		0
OVERALL TOTAL	**10**	**(10)**	**1**

Opponents	PREM A S G	FLD 1 A S G	FLD 2 A S G	FAC A S G	LC A S G	EC/CL A S G	ECWC A S G	UEFA A S G	OTHER A S G	TOTAL A S G
1 Port Vale	– – –	– – –	– – –	– – –	2 – –	– – –	– – –	– – –	– – –	2 – –
2 Sheffield Wednesday	1 (1) –	– – –	– – –	– – –	– – –	– – –	– – –	– – –	– – –	1 (1) –
3 Galatasaray	– – –	– – –	– – –	– – –	– – –	1 – 1	– – –	– – –	– – –	1 – 1
4 Crystal Palace	1 – –	– – –	– – –	– – –	– – –	– – –	– – –	– – –	– – –	1 – –
5 Gothenburg	– – –	– – –	– – –	– – –	– – –	1 – –	– – –	– – –	– – –	1 – –
6 Newcastle United	– – –	– – –	– – –	– – –	1 – –	– – –	– – –	– – –	– – –	1 – –
7 Norwich City	1 – –	– – –	– – –	– – –	– – –	– – –	– – –	– – –	– – –	1 – –
8 Queens Park Rangers	1 – –	– – –	– – –	– – –	– – –	– – –	– – –	– – –	– – –	1 – –
9 York City	– – –	– – –	– – –	– – –	1 – –	– – –	– – –	– – –	– – –	1 – –
10 Arsenal	– (1) –	– – –	– – –	– – –	– – –	– – –	– – –	– – –	– – –	– (1) –
11 Blackburn Rovers	– (1) –	– – –	– – –	– – –	– – –	– – –	– – –	– – –	– – –	– (1) –
12 Bolton Wanderers	– (1) –	– – –	– – –	– – –	– – –	– – –	– – –	– – –	– – –	– (1) –
13 Chelsea	– (1) –	– – –	– – –	– – –	– – –	– – –	– – –	– – –	– – –	– (1) –
14 Everton	– (1) –	– – –	– – –	– – –	– – –	– – –	– – –	– – –	– – –	– (1) –
15 Leicester City	– – –	– – –	– – –	– – –	– (1) –	– – –	– – –	– – –	– – –	– (1) –
16 Rotor Volgograd	– – –	– – –	– – –	– – –	– – –	– – –	– – –	– (1) –	– – –	– (1) –
17 Swindon Town	– – –	– – –	– – –	– – –	– (1) –	– – –	– – –	– – –	– – –	– (1) –
18 Wimbledon	– (1) –	– – –	– – –	– – –	– – –	– – –	– – –	– – –	– – –	– (1) –

WYN DAVIES

DEBUT (Full Appearance, 1 goal)

Saturday 23/09/1972
Football League Division 1
at Old Trafford

Manchester United 3 Derby County 0

CLUB CAREER RECORD	Apps	Subs	Goals
Premiership	0		0
League Division 1	15	(1)	4
League Division 2	0		0
FA Cup	1		0
League Cup	0		0
European Cup / Champions League	0		0
European Cup-Winners' Cup	0		0
UEFA Cup / Inter-Cities' Fairs Cup	0		0
Other Matches	0		0
OVERALL TOTAL	**16**	**(1)**	**4**

Opponents	PREM A S G	FLD 1 A S G	FLD 2 A S G	FAC A S G	LC A S G	EC/CL A S G	ECWC A S G	UEFA A S G	OTHER A S G	TOTAL A S G
1 Derby County	– – –	2 – 1	– – –	– – –	– – –	– – –	– – –	– – –	– – –	2 – 1
2 Leicester City	– – –	1 – 1	– – –	– – –	– – –	– – –	– – –	– – –	– – –	1 – 1
3 Liverpool	– – –	1 – 1	– – –	– – –	– – –	– – –	– – –	– – –	– – –	1 – 1
4 Southampton	– – –	1 – 1	– – –	– – –	– – –	– – –	– – –	– – –	– – –	1 – 1
5 Birmingham City	– – –	1 – –	– – –	– – –	– – –	– – –	– – –	– – –	– – –	1 – –
6 Crystal Palace	– – –	1 – –	– – –	– – –	– – –	– – –	– – –	– – –	– – –	1 – –

continued../

WYN DAVIES (continued)

Opponents	PREM A	S	G	FLD 1 A	S	G	FLD 2 A	S	G	FAC A	S	G	LC A	S	G	EC/CL A	S	G	ECWC A	S	G	UEFA A	S	G	OTHER A	S	G	TOTAL A	S	G
7 Leeds United	–	–		1	–		–	–		–	–		–	–		–	–		–	–		–	–		–	–		1	–	
8 Manchester City	–	–		1	–		–	–		–	–		–	–		–	–		–	–		–	–		–	–		1	–	
9 Newcastle United	–	–		1	–		–	–		–	–		–	–		–	–		–	–		–	–		–	–		1	–	
10 Norwich City	–	–		1	–		–	–		–	–		–	–		–	–		–	–		–	–		–	–		1	–	
11 Sheffield United	–	–		1	–		–	–		–	–		–	–		–	–		–	–		–	–		–	–		1	–	
12 Stoke City	–	–		1	–		–	–		–	–		–	–		–	–		–	–		–	–		–	–		1	–	
13 Tottenham Hotspur	–	–		1	–		–	–		–	–		–	–		–	–		–	–		–	–		–	–		1	–	
14 West Bromwich Albion	–	–		1	–		–	–		–	–		–	–		–	–		–	–		–	–		–	–		1	–	
15 Wolverhampton W.	–	–		–	–		–	–		–	–		1	–		–	–		–	–		–	–		–	–		1	–	
16 West Ham United	–	–		– (1)	–		–	–		–	–		–	–		–	–		–	–		–	–		–	–		– (1)	–	

JIMMY DAVIS

DEBUT (Full Appearance)

Monday 05/11/2001
League Cup 3rd Round
at Highbury

Arsenal 4 Manchester United 0

CLUB CAREER RECORD	Apps	Subs	Goals
Premiership	0		0
League Division 1	0		0
League Division 2	0		0
FA Cup	0		0
League Cup	1		0
European Cup / Champions League	0		0
European Cup-Winners' Cup	0		0
UEFA Cup / Inter-Cities' Fairs Cup	0		0
Other Matches	0		0
OVERALL TOTAL	1		0

Opponents	PREM A	S	G	FLD 1 A	S	G	FLD 2 A	S	G	FAC A	S	G	LC A	S	G	EC/CL A	S	G	ECWC A	S	G	UEFA A	S	G	OTHER A	S	G	TOTAL A	S	G
1 Arsenal	–	–		–	–		–	–		–	–		1	–		–	–		–	–		–	–		–	–		1	–	

ALEX DAWSON

DEBUT (Full Appearance, 1 goal)

Monday 22/04/1957
Football League Division 1
at Old Trafford

Manchester United 2 Burnley 0

CLUB CAREER RECORD	Apps	Subs	Goals
Premiership	0		0
League Division 1	80		45
League Division 2	0		0
FA Cup	10		8
League Cup	3		1
European Cup / Champions League	0		0
European Cup-Winners' Cup	0		0
UEFA Cup / Inter-Cities' Fairs Cup	0		0
Other Matches	0		0
OVERALL TOTAL	93		54

Opponents	PREM A	S	G	FLD 1 A	S	G	FLD 2 A	S	G	FAC A	S	G	LC A	S	G	EC/CL A	S	G	ECWC A	S	G	UEFA A	S	G	OTHER A	S	G	TOTAL A	S	G
1 West Bromwich Albion	–	–		6	4		–	–		2	1		–	–		–	–		–	–		–	–		–	–		8	5	
2 Nottingham Forest	–	–		7	3		–	–		–	–		–	–		–	–		–	–		–	–		–	–		7	3	
3 Sheffield Wednesday	–	–		4	–		–	–		3	2		–	–		–	–		–	–		–	–		–	–		7	2	
4 Bolton Wanderers	–	–		5	5		–	–		1	–		–	–		–	–		–	–		–	–		–	–		6	5	
5 Chelsea	–	–		5	6		–	–		–	–		–	–		–	–		–	–		–	–		–	–		5	6	
6 Burnley	–	–		5	1		–	–		–	–		–	–		–	–		–	–		–	–		–	–		5	1	
7 Fulham	–	–		2	2		–	–		2	3		–	–		–	–		–	–		–	–		–	–		4	5	
8 West Ham United	–	–		4	3		–	–		–	–		–	–		–	–		–	–		–	–		–	–		4	3	
9 Blackpool	–	–		4	–		–	–		–	–		–	–		–	–		–	–		–	–		–	–		4	–	
10 Wolverhampton W.	–	–		4	–		–	–		–	–		–	–		–	–		–	–		–	–		–	–		4	–	
11 Newcastle United	–	–		3	3		–	–		–	–		–	–		–	–		–	–		–	–		–	–		3	3	
12 Cardiff City	–	–		3	2		–	–		–	–		–	–		–	–		–	–		–	–		–	–		3	2	
13 Preston North End	–	–		3	1		–	–		–	–		–	–		–	–		–	–		–	–		–	–		3	1	
14 Arsenal	–	–		3	–		–	–		–	–		–	–		–	–		–	–		–	–		–	–		3	–	
15 Birmingham City	–	–		3	–		–	–		–	–		–	–		–	–		–	–		–	–		–	–		3	–	
16 Leicester City	–	–		3	–		–	–		–	–		–	–		–	–		–	–		–	–		–	–		3	–	
17 Tottenham Hotspur	–	–		3	–		–	–		–	–		–	–		–	–		–	–		–	–		–	–		3	–	
18 Everton	–	–		2	5		–	–		–	–		–	–		–	–		–	–		–	–		–	–		2	5	
19 Manchester City	–	–		2	4		–	–		–	–		–	–		–	–		–	–		–	–		–	–		2	4	
20 Aston Villa	–	–		2	1		–	–		–	–		–	–		–	–		–	–		–	–		–	–		2	1	
21 Blackburn Rovers	–	–		2	1		–	–		–	–		–	–		–	–		–	–		–	–		–	–		2	1	
22 Exeter City	–	–		–	–		–	–		–	–		2	1		–	–		–	–		–	–		–	–		2	1	
23 Portsmouth	–	–		2	1		–	–		–	–		–	–		–	–		–	–		–	–		–	–		2	1	
24 Luton Town	–	–		1	2		–	–		–	–		–	–		–	–		–	–		–	–		–	–		1	2	
25 Middlesbrough	–	–		–	–		–	–		1	2		–	–		–	–		–	–		–	–		–	–		1	2	
26 Sunderland	–	–		1	1		–	–		–	–		–	–		–	–		–	–		–	–		–	–		1	1	
27 Bradford City	–	–		–	–		–	–		–	–		1	–		–	–		–	–		–	–		–	–		1	–	
28 Derby County	–	–		–	–		–	–		1	–		–	–		–	–		–	–		–	–		–	–		1	–	
29 Leeds United	–	–		1	–		–	–		–	–		–	–		–	–		–	–		–	–		–	–		1	–	

HAROLD DEAN

DEBUT (Full Appearance)

Saturday 26/09/1931
Football League Division 2
at Old Trafford

Manchester United 3 Chesterfield 1

CLUB CAREER RECORD	Apps	Subs	Goals
Premiership	0		0
League Division 1	0		0
League Division 2	2		0
FA Cup	0		0
League Cup	0		0
European Cup / Champions League	0		0
European Cup-Winners' Cup	0		0
UEFA Cup / Inter-Cities' Fairs Cup	0		0
Other Matches	0		0
OVERALL TOTAL	2		0

Opponents	PREM A S G	FLD 1 A S G	FLD 2 A S G	FAC A S G	LC A S G	EC/CL A S G	ECWC A S G	UEFA A S G	OTHER A S G	TOTAL A S G
1 Burnley	- - -	- - -	- - -	1 - -	- - -	- - -	- - -	- - -	- - -	1 - -
2 Chesterfield	- - -	- - -	- - -	1 - -	- - -	- - -	- - -	- - -	- - -	1 - -

JIMMY DELANEY

DEBUT (Full Appearance)

Saturday 31/08/1946
Football League Division 1
at Maine Road

Manchester United 2 Grimsby Town 1

CLUB CAREER RECORD	Apps	Subs	Goals
Premiership	0		0
League Division 1	164		25
League Division 2	0		0
FA Cup	19		3
League Cup	0		0
European Cup / Champions League	0		0
European Cup-Winners' Cup	0		0
UEFA Cup / Inter-Cities' Fairs Cup	0		0
Other Matches	1		0
OVERALL TOTAL	184		28

Opponents	PREM A S G	FLD 1 A S G	FLD 2 A S G	FAC A S G	LC A S G	EC/CL A S G	ECWC A S G	UEFA A S G	OTHER A S G	TOTAL A S G
1 Portsmouth	- -	8 2	- -	2 1	- -	- -	- -	- -	- -	10 3
2 Wolverhampton W.	- -	8 3	- -	2 -	- -	- -	- -	- -	- -	10 3
3 Aston Villa	- -	9 1	- -	1 1	- -	- -	- -	- -	- -	10 2
4 Charlton Athletic	- -	9 1	- -	1 -	- -	- -	- -	- -	- -	10 1
5 Arsenal	- -	9 -	- -	- -	- -	- -	- -	1 -	- -	10 -
6 Chelsea	- -	8 1	- -	1 -	- -	- -	- -	- -	- -	9 1
7 Middlesbrough	- -	9 1	- -	- -	- -	- -	- -	- -	- -	9 1
8 Derby County	- -	8 -	- -	1 -	- -	- -	- -	- -	- -	9 -
9 Liverpool	- -	8 -	- -	1 -	- -	- -	- -	- -	- -	9 -
10 Blackpool	- -	7 3	- -	1 -	- -	- -	- -	- -	- -	8 3
11 Everton	- -	8 3	- -	- -	- -	- -	- -	- -	- -	8 3
12 Huddersfield Town	- -	8 3	- -	- -	- -	- -	- -	- -	- -	8 3
13 Sunderland	- -	8 2	- -	- -	- -	- -	- -	- -	- -	8 2
14 Stoke City	- -	7 1	- -	- -	- -	- -	- -	- -	- -	7 1
15 Bolton Wanderers	- -	7 -	- -	- -	- -	- -	- -	- -	- -	7 -
16 Preston North End	- -	5 1	- -	1 -	- -	- -	- -	- -	- -	6 1
17 Burnley	- -	6 -	- -	- -	- -	- -	- -	- -	- -	6 -
18 Manchester City	- -	5 1	- -	- -	- -	- -	- -	- -	- -	5 1
19 Birmingham City	- -	4 -	- -	- -	- -	- -	- -	- -	- -	4 -
20 Grimsby Town	- -	4 -	- -	- -	- -	- -	- -	- -	- -	4 -
21 Newcastle United	- -	4 -	- -	- -	- -	- -	- -	- -	- -	4 -
22 Sheffield United	- -	4 -	- -	- -	- -	- -	- -	- -	- -	4 -
23 Blackburn Rovers	- -	3 1	- -	- -	- -	- -	- -	- -	- -	3 1
24 Fulham	- -	3 -	- -	- -	- -	- -	- -	- -	- -	3 -
25 Leeds United	- -	2 1	- -	- -	- -	- -	- -	- -	- -	2 1
26 Bradford Park Avenue	- -	- -	- -	2 -	- -	- -	- -	- -	- -	2 -
27 West Bromwich Albion	- -	2 -	- -	- -	- -	- -	- -	- -	- -	2 -
28 Weymouth Town	- -	- -	- -	1 1	- -	- -	- -	- -	- -	1 1
29 Bournemouth	- -	- -	- -	1 -	- -	- -	- -	- -	- -	1 -
30 Hull City	- -	- -	- -	1 -	- -	- -	- -	- -	- -	1 -
31 Nottingham Forest	- -	- -	- -	1 -	- -	- -	- -	- -	- -	1 -
32 Sheffield Wednesday	- -	1 -	- -	- -	- -	- -	- -	- -	- -	1 -
33 Watford	- -	- -	- -	1 -	- -	- -	- -	- -	- -	1 -
34 Yeovil Town	- -	- -	- -	1 -	- -	- -	- -	- -	- -	1 -

MARK DEMPSEY

DEBUT (Substitute Appearance)

Wednesday 02/11/1983
European Cup-Winners' Cup 2nd Round 2nd Leg
at Old Trafford

Manchester United 2 Spartak Varna 0

CLUB CAREER RECORD	Apps	Subs	Goals
Premiership	0		0
League Division 1	1		0
League Division 2	0		0
FA Cup	0		0
League Cup	0		0
European Cup / Champions League	0		0
European Cup-Winners' Cup	0	(1)	0
UEFA Cup / Inter-Cities' Fairs Cup	0		0
Other Matches	0		0
OVERALL TOTAL	1	(1)	0

Opponents	PREM A S G	FLD 1 A S G	FLD 2 A S G	FAC A S G	LC A S G	EC/CL A S G	ECWC A S G	UEFA A S G	OTHER A S G	TOTAL A S G
1 Ipswich Town	- -	1 -	- -	- -	- -	- -	- -	- -	- -	1 -
2 Spartak Varna	- -	- -	- -	- -	- -	- -	- (1) -	- -	- -	- (1) -

J DENMAN

DEBUT (Full Appearance)

Saturday 05/12/1891
FA Cup 4th Qualifying Round
at North Road

Newton Heath 3 Blackpool 4

CLUB CAREER RECORD	Apps	Subs	Goals
Premiership	0		0
League Division 1	0		0
League Division 2	0		0
FA Cup	1		0
League Cup	0		0
European Cup / Champions League	0		0
European Cup-Winners' Cup	0		0
UEFA Cup / Inter-Cities' Fairs Cup	0		0
Other Matches	0		0
OVERALL TOTAL	1		0

Opponents	PREM A S G	FLD 1 A S G	FLD 2 A S G	FAC A S G	LC A S G	EC/CL A S G	ECWC A S G	UEFA A S G	OTHER A S G	TOTAL A S G
1 Blackpool	- - -	- - -	- - -	1	- - -	- - -	- - -	- - -	- - -	1 -

BILLY DENNIS

DEBUT (Full Appearance)

Saturday 13/10/1923
Football League Division 2
at Old Trafford

Manchester United 2 Oldham Athletic 0

CLUB CAREER RECORD	Apps	Subs	Goals
Premiership	0		0
League Division 1	0		0
League Division 2	3		0
FA Cup	0		0
League Cup	0		0
European Cup / Champions League	0		0
European Cup-Winners' Cup	0		0
UEFA Cup / Inter-Cities' Fairs Cup	0		0
Other Matches	0		0
OVERALL TOTAL	3		0

Opponents	PREM A S G	FLD 1 A S G	FLD 2 A S G	FAC A S G	LC A S G	EC/CL A S G	ECWC A S G	UEFA A S G	OTHER A S G	TOTAL A S G
1 Stockport County	- - -	- - -	2	- - -	- - -	- - -	- - -	- - -	- - -	2 -
2 Oldham Athletic	- - -	- - -	1	- - -	- - -	- - -	- - -	- - -	- - -	1 -

NEIL DEWAR

DEBUT (Full Appearance, 1 goal)

Saturday 11/02/1933
Football League Division 2
at Deepdale

Preston North End 3 Manchester United 3

CLUB CAREER RECORD	Apps	Subs	Goals
Premiership	0		0
League Division 1	0		0
League Division 2	36		14
FA Cup	0		0
League Cup	0		0
European Cup / Champions League	0		0
European Cup-Winners' Cup	0		0
UEFA Cup / Inter-Cities' Fairs Cup	0		0
Other Matches	0		0
OVERALL TOTAL	36		14

Opponents	PREM A S G	FLD 1 A S G	FLD 2 A S G	FAC A S G	LC A S G	EC/CL A S G	ECWC A S G	UEFA A S G	OTHER A S G	TOTAL A S G
1 Nottingham Forest	- - -	- - -	4 1	- - -	- - -	- - -	- - -	- - -	- - -	4 1
2 Burnley	- -	- -	2 4	- -	- -	- -	- -	- -	- -	2 4
3 Bradford City	- - -	- - -	2 1	- - -	- - -	- - -	- - -	- - -	- - -	2 1
4 Fulham	- -	- -	2 1	- -	- -	- -	- -	- -	- -	2 1
5 Lincoln City	- - -	- - -	2 1	- - -	- - -	- - -	- - -	- - -	- - -	2 1
6 Millwall	- -	- -	2 1	- -	- -	- -	- -	- -	- -	2 1
7 Notts County	- - -	- - -	2 1	- - -	- - -	- - -	- - -	- - -	- - -	2 1
8 Port Vale	- -	- -	2 1	- -	- -	- -	- -	- -	- -	2 1
9 Preston North End	- - -	- - -	2 1	- - -	- - -	- - -	- - -	- - -	- - -	2 1

continued../

NEIL DEWAR (continued)

Opponents	PREM A S G	FLD 1 A S G	FLD 2 A S G	FAC A S G	LC A S G	EC/CL A S G	ECWC A S G	UEFA A S G	OTHER A S G	TOTAL A S G
10 Bradford Park Avenue	– – –	– – –	2 – –	– – –	– – –	– – –	– – –	– – –	– – –	2 – –
11 Bury	– – –	– – –	2 – –	– – –	– – –	– – –	– – –	– – –	– – –	2 – –
12 Swansea City	– – –	– – –	2 – –	– – –	– – –	– – –	– – –	– – –	– – –	2 – –
13 Chesterfield	– – –	– – –	1 – 1	– – –	– – –	– – –	– – –	– – –	– – –	1 – 1
14 West Ham United	– – –	– – –	1 – 1	– – –	– – –	– – –	– – –	– – –	– – –	1 – 1
15 Blackpool	– – –	– – –	1 – –	– – –	– – –	– – –	– – –	– – –	– – –	1 – –
16 Bolton Wanderers	– – –	– – –	1 – –	– – –	– – –	– – –	– – –	– – –	– – –	1 – –
17 Brentford	– – –	– – –	1 – –	– – –	– – –	– – –	– – –	– – –	– – –	1 – –
18 Grimsby Town	– – –	– – –	1 – –	– – –	– – –	– – –	– – –	– – –	– – –	1 – –
19 Hull City	– – –	– – –	1 – –	– – –	– – –	– – –	– – –	– – –	– – –	1 – –
20 Oldham Athletic	– – –	– – –	1 – –	– – –	– – –	– – –	– – –	– – –	– – –	1 – –
21 Plymouth Argyle	– – –	– – –	1 – –	– – –	– – –	– – –	– – –	– – –	– – –	1 – –
22 Southampton	– – –	– – –	1 – –	– – –	– – –	– – –	– – –	– – –	– – –	1 – –

ERIC DJEMBA-DJEMBA

DEBUT (Substitute Appearance)

Sunday 10/08/2003
FA Charity Shield
at Millennium Stadium

Manchester United 1 Arsenal 1

CLUB CAREER RECORD	Apps	Subs	Goals
Premiership	13	(7)	0
League Division 1	0		0
League Division 2	0		0
FA Cup	2	(1)	0
League Cup	5		1
European Cup / Champions League	6	(3)	1
European Cup-Winners' Cup	0		0
UEFA Cup / Inter-Cities' Fairs Cup	0		0
Other Matches	1	(1)	0
OVERALL TOTAL	27	(12)	2

Opponents	PREM A S G	FLD 1 A S G	FLD 2 A S G	FAC A S G	LC A S G	EC/CL A S G	ECWC A S G	UEFA A S G	OTHER A S G	TOTAL A S G
1 Arsenal	1 – –	– – –	– – –	– – –	1 – –	– – –	– – –	– – –	1 (1) –	3 (1) –
2 Blackburn Rovers	2 – –	– – –	– – –	– – –	– – –	– – –	– – –	– – –	– – –	2 – –
3 Chelsea	1 – –	– – –	– – –	– – –	1 – –	– – –	– – –	– – –	– – –	2 – –
4 Dinamo Bucharest	– – –	– – –	– – –	– – –	– – –	2 – –	– – –	– – –	– – –	2 – –
5 Exeter City	– – –	– – –	– – –	2 – –	– – –	– – –	– – –	– – –	– – –	2 – –
6 Fenerbahce	– – –	– – –	– – –	– – –	– – –	2 – –	– – –	– – –	– – –	2 – –
7 Portsmouth	2 – –	– – –	– – –	– – –	– – –	– – –	– – –	– – –	– – –	2 – –
8 Fulham	1 – –	– – –	– – –	– (1) –	– – –	– – –	– – –	– – –	– – –	1 (1) –
9 Everton	– (2) –	– – –	– – –	– – –	– – –	– – –	– – –	– – –	– – –	– (2) –
10 Leicester City	– (2) –	– – –	– – –	– – –	– – –	– – –	– – –	– – –	– – –	– (2) –
11 Leeds United	– – –	– – –	– – –	– – –	1 – 1	– – –	– – –	– – –	– – –	1 – 1
12 Birmingham City	1 – –	– – –	– – –	– – –	– – –	– – –	– – –	– – –	– – –	1 – –
13 Charlton Athletic	1 – –	– – –	– – –	– – –	– – –	– – –	– – –	– – –	– – –	1 – –
14 Crewe Alexandra	– – –	– – –	– – –	– – –	1 – –	– – –	– – –	– – –	– – –	1 – –
15 Crystal Palace	– – –	– – –	– – –	– – –	1 – –	– – –	– – –	– – –	– – –	1 – –
16 Newcastle United	1 – –	– – –	– – –	– – –	– – –	– – –	– – –	– – –	– – –	1 – –
17 Norwich City	1 – –	– – –	– – –	– – –	– – –	– – –	– – –	– – –	– – –	1 – –
18 Olympique Lyonnais	– – –	– – –	– – –	– – –	– – –	1 – –	– – –	– – –	– – –	1 – –
19 Porto	– – –	– – –	– – –	– – –	– – –	1 – –	– – –	– – –	– – –	1 – –
20 Southampton	1 – –	– – –	– – –	– – –	– – –	– – –	– – –	– – –	– – –	1 – –
21 Wolverhampton W.	1 – –	– – –	– – –	– – –	– – –	– – –	– – –	– – –	– – –	1 – –
22 Panathinaikos	– – –	– – –	– – –	– – –	– – –	– (1) 1	– – –	– – –	– – –	– (1) 1
23 Aston Villa	– (1) –	– – –	– – –	– – –	– – –	– – –	– – –	– – –	– – –	– (1) –
24 Bolton Wanderers	– (1) –	– – –	– – –	– – –	– – –	– – –	– – –	– – –	– – –	– (1) –
25 Glasgow Rangers	– – –	– – –	– – –	– – –	– – –	– (1) –	– – –	– – –	– – –	– (1) –
26 Middlesbrough	– (1) –	– – –	– – –	– – –	– – –	– – –	– – –	– – –	– – –	– (1) –
27 Stuttgart	– – –	– – –	– – –	– – –	– – –	– (1) –	– – –	– – –	– – –	– (1) –

BOJAN DJORDJIC

DEBUT (Substitute Appearance)

Saturday 19/05/2001
FA Premiership
at White Hart Lane

Tottenham Hotspur 3 Manchester United 1

CLUB CAREER RECORD	Apps	Subs	Goals
Premiership	0	(1)	0
League Division 1	0		0
League Division 2	0		0
FA Cup	0		0
League Cup	1		0
European Cup / Champions League	0		0
European Cup-Winners' Cup	0		0
UEFA Cup / Inter-Cities' Fairs Cup	0		0
Other Matches	0		0
OVERALL TOTAL	1	(1)	0

Opponents	PREM A S G	FLD 1 A S G	FLD 2 A S G	FAC A S G	LC A S G	EC/CL A S G	ECWC A S G	UEFA A S G	OTHER A S G	TOTAL A S G
1 Arsenal	– – –	– – –	– – –	– – –	1 – –	– – –	– – –	– – –	– – –	1 – –
2 Tottenham Hotspur	– (1) –	– – –	– – –	– – –	– – –	– – –	– – –	– – –	– – –	– (1) –

JOHN DOHERTY

DEBUT (Full Appearance)

Saturday 06/12/1952
Football League Division 1
at Old Trafford

Manchester United 3 Middlesbrough 2

CLUB CAREER RECORD	Apps	Subs	Goals
Premiership	0		0
League Division 1	25		7
League Division 2	0		0
FA Cup	1		0
League Cup	0		0
European Cup / Champions League	0		0
European Cup-Winners' Cup	0		0
UEFA Cup / Inter-Cities' Fairs Cup	0		0
Other Matches	0		0
OVERALL TOTAL	**26**		**7**

Opponents	PREM			FLD 1			FLD 2			FAC			LC			EC/CL			ECWC			UEFA			OTHER			TOTAL		
	A	S	G	A	S	G	A	S	G	A	S	G	A	S	G	A	S	G	A	S	G	A	S	G	A	S	G	A	S	G
1 Blackpool	–	–		3	–		–	–		–	–		–	–		–	–		–	–		–	–		–	–		3	–	
2 Chelsea	–	–		2	–	2	–	–		–	–		–	–		–	–		–	–		–	–		–	–		2	–	2
3 Wolverhampton W.	–	–		2	–	2	–	–		–	–		–	–		–	–		–	–		–	–		–	–		2	–	2
4 Charlton Athletic	–	–		2	–	1	–	–		–	–		–	–		–	–		–	–		–	–		–	–		2	–	1
5 Newcastle United	–	–		2	–	1	–	–		–	–		–	–		–	–		–	–		–	–		–	–		2	–	1
6 Everton	–	–		2	–		–	–		–	–		–	–		–	–		–	–		–	–		–	–		2	–	
7 Manchester City	–	–		2	–		–	–		–	–		–	–		–	–		–	–		–	–		–	–		2	–	
8 Portsmouth	–	–		2	–		–	–		–	–		–	–		–	–		–	–		–	–		–	–		2	–	
9 West Bromwich Albion	–	–		2	–		–	–		–	–		–	–		–	–		–	–		–	–		–	–		2	–	
10 Sunderland	–	–		1	–	1	–	–		–	–		–	–		–	–		–	–		–	–		–	–		1	–	1
11 Birmingham City	–	–		1	–		–	–		–	–		–	–		–	–		–	–		–	–		–	–		1	–	
12 Bristol Rovers	–	–		–	–		–	–		1	–		–	–		–	–		–	–		–	–		–	–		1	–	
13 Burnley	–	–		1	–		–	–		–	–		–	–		–	–		–	–		–	–		–	–		1	–	
14 Huddersfield Town	–	–		1	–		–	–		–	–		–	–		–	–		–	–		–	–		–	–		1	–	
15 Liverpool	–	–		1	–		–	–		–	–		–	–		–	–		–	–		–	–		–	–		1	–	
16 Middlesbrough	–	–		1	–		–	–		–	–		–	–		–	–		–	–		–	–		–	–		1	–	

BERNARD DONAGHY

DEBUT (Full Appearance)

Saturday 04/11/1905
Football League Division 2
at Bank Street

Manchester United 2 Lincoln City 1

CLUB CAREER RECORD	Apps	Subs	Goals
Premiership	0		0
League Division 1	0		0
League Division 2	3		0
FA Cup	0		0
League Cup	0		0
European Cup / Champions League	0		0
European Cup-Winners' Cup	0		0
UEFA Cup / Inter-Cities' Fairs Cup	0		0
Other Matches	0		0
OVERALL TOTAL	**3**		**0**

Opponents	PREM			FLD 1			FLD 2			FAC			LC			EC/CL			ECWC			UEFA			OTHER			TOTAL		
	A	S	G	A	S	G	A	S	G	A	S	G	A	S	G	A	S	G	A	S	G	A	S	G	A	S	G	A	S	G
1 Lincoln City	–	–		–	–		2	–		–	–		–	–		–	–		–	–		–	–		–	–		2	–	
2 Chesterfield	–	–		–	–		1	–		–	–		–	–		–	–		–	–		–	–		–	–		1	–	

MAL DONAGHY

DEBUT (Full Appearance)

Sunday 30/10/1988
Football League Division 1
at Goodison Park

Everton 1 Manchester United 1

CLUB CAREER RECORD	Apps	Subs	Goals
Premiership	0		0
League Division 1	76	(13)	0
League Division 2	0		0
FA Cup	10		0
League Cup	9	(5)	0
European Cup / Champions League	0		0
European Cup-Winners' Cup	2	(3)	0
UEFA Cup / Inter-Cities' Fairs Cup	0		0
Other Matches	1		0
OVERALL TOTAL	**98**	**(21)**	**0**

Opponents	PREM			FLD 1			FLD 2			FAC			LC			EC/CL			ECWC			UEFA			OTHER			TOTAL		
	A	S	G	A	S	G	A	S	G	A	S	G	A	S	G	A	S	G	A	S	G	A	S	G	A	S	G	A	S	G
1 Southampton	–	–		6	–		–	–		2	–		1	(1)		–	–		–	–		–	–		–	–		9	(1)	
2 Everton	–	–		6	(1)		–	–		–	–		–	–		–	–		–	–		–	–		–	–		6	(1)	
3 Coventry City	–	–		6	–		–	–		–	–		–	–		–	–		–	–		–	–		–	–		6	–	
4 Queens Park Rangers	–	–		3	–		–	–		3	–		–	–		–	–		–	–		–	–		–	–		6	–	
5 Arsenal	–	–		5	–		–	–		–	–		–	(1)		–	–		–	–		–	–		–	–		5	(1)	
6 Nottingham Forest	–	–		3	(2)		–	–		1	–		–	–		–	–		–	–		–	–		–	–		4	(2)	
7 Liverpool	–	–		2	(2)		–	–		–	–		–	(1)		–	–		–	–		–	–		1	–		3	(3)	
8 Leeds United	–	–		1	(2)		–	–		–	–		1	(2)		–	–		–	–		–	–		–	–		2	(4)	
9 Aston Villa	–	–		5	–		–	–		–	–		–	–		–	–		–	–		–	–		–	–		5	–	
10 Sheffield Wednesday	–	–		5	–		–	–		–	–		–	–		–	–		–	–		–	–		–	–		5	–	
11 Wimbledon	–	–		4	–		–	–		–	–		–	–		–	–		–	–		–	–		–	–		4	–	
12 Derby County	–	–		3	(1)		–	–		–	–		–	–		–	–		–	–		–	–		–	–		3	(1)	
13 Manchester City	–	–		3	(1)		–	–		–	–		–	–		–	–		–	–		–	–		–	–		3	(1)	
14 Tottenham Hotspur	–	–		2	(1)		–	–		–	–		1	–		–	–		–	–		–	–		–	–		3	(1)	
15 Charlton Athletic	–	–		3	–		–	–		–	–		–	–		–	–		–	–		–	–		–	–		3	–	

continued../

MAL DONAGHY (continued)

Opponents	PREM A S G	FLD 1 A S G	FLD 2 A S G	FAC A S G	LC A S G	EC/CL A S G	ECWC A S G	UEFA A S G	OTHER A S G	TOTAL A S G
16 Crystal Palace	– –	3 –	–	–	–	–	–	–	–	3 –
17 Millwall	– –	3 –	–	–	–	–	–	–	–	3 –
18 Portsmouth	– –	–	–	–	3	–	–	–	–	3 –
19 Chelsea	– –	2 (1) –	–	–	–	–	–	–	–	2 (1) –
20 Norwich City	– –	2 (1) –	–	–	–	–	–	–	–	2 (1) –
21 Bournemouth	– –	–	–	2	–	–	–	–	–	2 –
22 Middlesbrough	– –	1 –	–	–	1	–	–	–	–	2 –
23 Newcastle United	– –	2	–	–	–	–	–	–	–	2 –
24 Sheffield United	– –	2	–	–	–	–	–	–	–	2 –
25 West Ham United	– –	2	–	–	–	–	–	–	–	2 –
26 Luton Town	– –	1 (1) –	–	–	–	–	–	–	–	1 (1) –
27 Legia Warsaw	– –	–	–	–	–	– (2) –	–	–	–	– (2) –
28 Cambridge United	– –	–	–	–	1	–	–	–	–	1 –
29 Halifax Town	– –	–	–	–	1	–	–	–	–	1 –
30 Hereford United	– –	–	–	1	–	–	–	–	–	1 –
31 Montpellier Herault	– –	–	–	–	–	–	–	1	–	1 –
32 Oxford United	– –	–	–	1	–	–	–	–	–	1 –
33 Pecsi Munkas	– –	–	–	–	–	–	–	1	–	1 –
34 Sunderland	– –	1	–	–	–	–	–	–	–	1 –
35 Wrexham	– –	–	–	–	–	–	– (1) –	–	–	– (1) –

IAN DONALD

DEBUT (Full Appearance)

Wednesday 07/10/1970
League Cup 3rd Round
at Old Trafford

Manchester United 1 Portsmouth 0

CLUB CAREER RECORD	Apps	Subs	Goals
Premiership	0		0
League Division 1	4		0
League Division 2	0		0
FA Cup	0		0
League Cup	2		0
European Cup / Champions League	0		0
European Cup-Winners' Cup	0		0
UEFA Cup / Inter-Cities' Fairs Cup	0		0
Other Matches	0		0
OVERALL TOTAL	6		0

Opponents	PREM A S G	FLD 1 A S G	FLD 2 A S G	FAC A S G	LC A S G	EC/CL A S G	ECWC A S G	UEFA A S G	OTHER A S G	TOTAL A S G
1 Bristol Rovers	– –	–	–	–	1	–	–	–	–	1 –
2 Derby County	– –	1	–	–	–	–	–	–	–	1 –
3 Leicester City	– –	1	–	–	–	–	–	–	–	1 –
4 Portsmouth	– –	–	–	–	1	–	–	–	–	1 –
5 Sheffield United	– –	1	–	–	–	–	–	–	–	1 –
6 West Bromwich Albion	– –	1	–	–	–	–	–	–	–	1 –

BOB DONALDSON

DEBUT (Full Appearance, 1 goal)

Saturday 03/09/1892
Football League Division 1
at Ewood Park

Blackburn Rovers 4 Newton Heath 3

CLUB CAREER RECORD	Apps	Subs	Goals
Premiership	0		0
League Division 1	50		23
League Division 2	81		33
FA Cup	16		10
League Cup	0		0
European Cup / Champions League	0		0
European Cup-Winners' Cup	0		0
UEFA Cup / Inter-Cities' Fairs Cup	0		0
Other Matches	8		0
OVERALL TOTAL	155		66

Opponents	PREM A S G	FLD 1 A S G	FLD 2 A S G	FAC A S G	LC A S G	EC/CL A S G	ECWC A S G	UEFA A S G	OTHER A S G	TOTAL A S G
1 Derby County	– –	4 3	–	3 1	–	–	–	–	–	7 4
2 Darwen	– –	1	6 2	–	–	–	–	–	–	7 2
3 Leicester City	– –	–	7 1	–	–	–	–	–	–	7 1
4 Blackburn Rovers	– –	3 4	–	3 1	–	–	–	–	–	6 5
5 Burton Swifts	– –	–	6 5	–	–	–	–	–	–	6 5
6 Burnley	– –	4 2	–	–	–	–	–	–	2 –	6 2
7 Lincoln City	– –	–	6 2	–	–	–	–	–	–	6 2
8 Notts County	– –	1 –	5 2	–	–	–	–	–	–	6 2
9 Grimsby Town	– –	–	6 1	–	–	–	–	–	–	6 1
10 Newcastle United	– –	–	6 1	–	–	–	–	–	–	6 1
11 Stoke City	– –	4 –	–	1	–	–	–	–	1 –	6 –
12 Walsall	– –	–	5 5	–	–	–	–	–	–	5 5
13 Manchester City	– –	–	5 2	–	–	–	–	–	–	5 2
14 Blackpool	– –	–	3 –	2 1	–	–	–	–	–	5 1
15 Birmingham City	– –	–	3 –	–	–	–	–	–	2 –	5 –
16 Arsenal	– –	–	–	4 4	–	–	–	–	–	4 4
17 Rotherham United	– –	–	–	4 4	–	–	–	–	–	4 4

continued../

BOB DONALDSON (continued)

Opponents	PREM A S G	FLD 1 A S G	FLD 2 A S G	FAC A S G	LC A S G	EC/CL A S G	ECWC A S G	UEFA A S G	OTHER A S G	TOTAL A S G
18 West Bromwich Albion	– –	4 3	–	–	–	–	–	–	–	4 3
19 Bolton Wanderers	–	4 2	–	–	–	–	–	–	–	4 2
20 Nottingham Forest	– –	4 2	–	–	–	–	–	–	–	4 2
21 Preston North End	–	4 2	–	–	–	–	–	–	–	4 2
22 Port Vale	– –	–	4 1	–	–	–	–	–	–	4 1
23 Burton Wanderers	–	–	4	–	–	–	–	–	–	4 –
24 Sunderland	–	2	–	–	–	–	–	–	2	4 –
25 Wolverhampton W.	– –	3 3	–	–	–	–	–	–	–	3 3
26 Loughborough Town	– –	–	3 2	–	–	–	–	–	–	3 2
27 Everton	– –	3 1	–	–	–	–	–	–	–	3 1
28 Aston Villa	–	3 –	–	–	–	–	–	–	–	3 –
29 Sheffield Wednesday	– –	3	–	–	–	–	–	–	–	3 –
30 Kettering	– –	–	–	2 3	–	–	–	–	–	2 3
31 Southampton	–	–	–	2 1	–	–	–	–	–	2 1
32 Gainsborough Trinity	– –	–	2	–	–	–	–	–	–	2 –
33 Sheffield United	–	2	–	–	–	–	–	–	–	2 –
34 Middlesbrough	– –	–	–	1 2	–	–	–	–	–	1 2
35 Accrington Stanley	– –	1 1	–	–	–	–	–	–	–	1 1
36 Bury	– –	–	–	1 1	–	–	–	–	–	1 1
37 Nelson	–	–	–	1 1	–	–	–	–	–	1 1
38 Crewe Alexandra	– –	–	1	–	–	–	–	–	–	1 –
39 Liverpool	–	–	–	–	–	–	–	1	–	1 –
40 West Manchester	–	–	–	1	–	–	–	–	–	1 –

DONG FANGZHUO

DEBUT (Full Appearance)

Wednesday 09/05/2007
FA Premiership
at Stamford Bridge

Chelsea 0 Manchester United 0

CLUB CAREER RECORD	Apps	Subs	Goals
Premiership	1		0
League Division 1	0		0
League Division 2	0		0
FA Cup	0		0
League Cup	1		0
European Cup / Champions League	0	(1)	0
European Cup-Winners' Cup	0		0
UEFA Cup / Inter-Cities' Fairs Cup	0		0
Other Matches	0		0
OVERALL TOTAL	2	(1)	0

Opponents	PREM A S G	FLD 1 A S G	FLD 2 A S G	FAC A S G	LC A S G	EC/CL A S G	ECWC A S G	UEFA A S G	OTHER A S G	TOTAL A S G
1 Chelsea	1 –	–	–	–	–	–	–	–	–	1 –
2 Coventry City	–	–	–	–	1 –	–	–	–	–	1 –
3 Roma	–	–	–	–	–	– (1) –	–	–	–	– (1) –

TONY DONNELLY

DEBUT (Full Appearance)

Monday 15/03/1909
Football League Division 1
at Bank Street

Manchester United 2 Sunderland 2

CLUB CAREER RECORD	Apps	Subs	Goals
Premiership	0		0
League Division 1	34		0
League Division 2	0		0
FA Cup	3		0
League Cup	0		0
European Cup / Champions League	0		0
European Cup-Winners' Cup	0		0
UEFA Cup / Inter-Cities' Fairs Cup	0		0
Other Matches	0		0
OVERALL TOTAL	37		0

Opponents	PREM A S G	FLD 1 A S G	FLD 2 A S G	FAC A S G	LC A S G	EC/CL A S G	ECWC A S G	UEFA A S G	OTHER A S G	TOTAL A S G
1 Sunderland	– –	4	–	–	–	–	–	–	–	4 –
2 Aston Villa	– –	2	–	1	–	–	–	–	–	3 –
3 Everton	– –	3	–	–	–	–	–	–	–	3 –
4 Middlesbrough	– –	3	–	–	–	–	–	–	–	3 –
5 Arsenal	– –	2	–	–	–	–	–	–	–	2 –
6 Bradford City	– –	2	–	–	–	–	–	–	–	2 –
7 Liverpool	– –	2	–	–	–	–	–	–	–	2 –
8 Newcastle United	– –	2	–	–	–	–	–	–	–	2 –
9 Notts County	– –	2	–	–	–	–	–	–	–	2 –
10 Preston North End	– –	2	–	–	–	–	–	–	–	2 –
11 Sheffield Wednesday	– –	2	–	–	–	–	–	–	–	2 –
12 Tottenham Hotspur	– –	2	–	–	–	–	–	–	–	2 –
13 Blackburn Rovers	– –	1	–	–	–	–	–	–	–	1 –
14 Blackpool	– –	–	–	1	–	–	–	–	–	1 –
15 Bristol City	– –	1	–	–	–	–	–	–	–	1 –
16 Derby County	– –	1	–	–	–	–	–	–	–	1 –
17 Manchester City	– –	1	–	–	–	–	–	–	–	1 –
18 Nottingham Forest	– –	1	–	–	–	–	–	–	–	1 –
19 Sheffield United	– –	1	–	–	–	–	–	–	–	1 –
20 West Ham United	– –	–	–	1	–	–	–	–	–	1 –

DONNELLY (FIRST NAME NOT KNOWN)

DEBUT (Full Appearance)

Saturday 25/10/1890
FA Cup 2nd Qualifying Round
at Bootle Park

Bootle Reserves 1 Newton Heath 0

CLUB CAREER RECORD	Apps	Subs	Goals
Premiership	0		0
League Division 1	0		0
League Division 2	0		0
FA Cup	1		0
League Cup	0		0
European Cup / Champions League	0		0
European Cup-Winners' Cup	0		0
UEFA Cup / Inter-Cities' Fairs Cup	0		0
Other Matches	0		0
OVERALL TOTAL	1		0

Opponents	PREM A S G	FLD 1 A S G	FLD 2 A S G	FAC A S G	LC A S G	EC/CL A S G	ECWC A S G	UEFA A S G	OTHER A S G	TOTAL A S G
1 Bootle Reserves	– –	– –	– –	1	– –	– –	– –	– –	– –	1 –

TOMMY DOUGAN

DEBUT (Full Appearance)

Wednesday 29/03/1939
Football League Division 1
at Old Trafford

Manchester United 0 Everton 2

CLUB CAREER RECORD	Apps	Subs	Goals
Premiership	0		0
League Division 1	4		0
League Division 2	0		0
FA Cup	0		0
League Cup	0		0
European Cup / Champions League	0		0
European Cup-Winners' Cup	0		0
UEFA Cup / Inter-Cities' Fairs Cup	0		0
Other Matches	0		0
OVERALL TOTAL	4		0

Opponents	PREM A S G	FLD 1 A S G	FLD 2 A S G	FAC A S G	LC A S G	EC/CL A S G	ECWC A S G	UEFA A S G	OTHER A S G	TOTAL A S G
1 Everton	– –	1	– –	– –	– –	– –	– –	– –	– –	1 –
2 Huddersfield Town	– –	1	– –	– –	– –	– –	– –	– –	– –	1 –
3 Leeds United	– –	1	– –	– –	– –	– –	– –	– –	– –	1 –
4 Portsmouth	– –	1	– –	– –	– –	– –	– –	– –	– –	1 –

JACK DOUGHTY

DEBUT (Full Appearance, 2 goals)

Saturday 30/10/1886
FA Cup 1st Round
at Fleetwood Park

Fleetwood Rangers 2 Newton Heath 2

CLUB CAREER RECORD	Apps	Subs	Goals
Premiership	0		0
League Division 1	0		0
League Division 2	0		0
FA Cup	3		3
League Cup	0		0
European Cup / Champions League	0		0
European Cup-Winners' Cup	0		0
UEFA Cup / Inter-Cities' Fairs Cup	0		0
Other Matches	0		0
OVERALL TOTAL	3		3

Opponents	PREM A S G	FLD 1 A S G	FLD 2 A S G	FAC A S G	LC A S G	EC/CL A S G	ECWC A S G	UEFA A S G	OTHER A S G	TOTAL A S G
1 Fleetwood Rangers	– –	– –	– –	1 2	– –	– –	– –	– –	– –	1 2
2 South Shore	– –	– –	– –	1 1	– –	– –	– –	– –	– –	1 1
3 Preston North End	– –	– –	– –	1	– –	– –	– –	– –	– –	1 –

ROGER DOUGHTY

DEBUT (Full Appearance)

Saturday 18/01/1889
FA Cup 1st Round
at Deepdale

Preston North End 6 Newton Heath 1

CLUB CAREER RECORD	Apps	Subs	Goals
Premiership	0		0
League Division 1	0		0
League Division 2	0		0
FA Cup	5		1
League Cup	0		0
European Cup / Champions League	0		0
European Cup-Winners' Cup	0		0
UEFA Cup / Inter-Cities' Fairs Cup	0		0
Other Matches	3		0
OVERALL TOTAL	8		1

Opponents	PREM A S G	FLD 1 A S G	FLD 2 A S G	FAC A S G	LC A S G	EC/CL A S G	ECWC A S G	UEFA A S G	OTHER A S G	TOTAL A S G
1 Sunderland	– –	– –	– –	– –	– –	– –	– –	– –	2 –	2 –
2 Manchester City	– –	– –	– –	1 1	– –	– –	– –	– –	– –	1 1
3 Blackpool	– –	– –	– –	1	– –	– –	– –	– –	– –	1 –
4 Burnley	– –	– –	– –	– –	– –	– –	– –	– –	1 –	1 –
5 Higher Walton	– –	– –	– –	1	– –	– –	– –	– –	– –	1 –
6 Preston North End	– –	– –	– –	1	– –	– –	– –	– –	– –	1 –
7 South Shore	– –	– –	– –	1	– –	– –	– –	– –	– –	1 –

WILLIAM DOUGLAS

DEBUT (Full Appearance)

Saturday 03/02/1894
Football League Division 1
at Perry Barr

Aston Villa 5 Newton Heath 1

CLUB CAREER RECORD	Apps	Subs	Goals
Premiership	0		0
League Division 1	7		0
League Division 2	48		0
FA Cup	1		0
League Cup	0		0
European Cup / Champions League	0		0
European Cup-Winners' Cup	0		0
UEFA Cup / Inter-Cities' Fairs Cup	0		0
Other Matches	1		0
OVERALL TOTAL	**57**		**0**

Opponents	PREM A S G	FLD 1 A S G	FLD 2 A S G	FAC A S G	LC A S G	EC/CL A S G	ECWC A S G	UEFA A S G	OTHER A S G	TOTAL A S G
1 Arsenal	– –	– –	– 4 –	–	–	–	–	–	–	4 –
2 Crewe Alexandra	– –	– –	4	–	–	–	–	–	–	4 –
3 Manchester City	– –	– –	– 4	–	–	–	–	–	–	4 –
4 Newcastle United	– –	– –	– 4 –	–	–	–	–	–	–	4 –
5 Notts County	– –	– –	4	–	–	–	–	–	–	4 –
6 Stoke City	– –	2 –	– –	1 –	–	–	–	–	1 –	4 –
7 Burton Swifts	– –	– –	– 3 –	–	–	–	–	–	–	3 –
8 Darwen	– –	– –	3	–	–	–	–	–	–	3 –
9 Grimsby Town	– –	– –	– 3 –	–	–	–	–	–	–	3 –
10 Leicester City	– –	– –	3	–	–	–	–	–	–	3 –
11 Lincoln City	– –	– –	– 3 –	–	–	–	–	–	–	3 –
12 Burton Wanderers	– –	– –	2	–	–	–	–	–	–	2 –
13 Bury	– –	– –	– 2 –	–	–	–	–	–	–	2 –
14 Liverpool	– –	– –	2	–	–	–	–	–	–	2 –
15 Port Vale	– –	– –	– 2 –	–	–	–	–	–	–	2 –
16 Rotherham United	– –	– –	2	–	–	–	–	–	–	2 –
17 Walsall	– –	– –	– 2 –	–	–	–	–	–	–	2 –
18 Aston Villa	– –	1 –	– –	–	–	–	–	–	–	1 –
19 Blackburn Rovers	– –	1 –	– –	–	–	–	–	–	–	1 –
20 Bolton Wanderers	– –	1 –	– –	–	–	–	–	–	–	1 –
21 Loughborough Town	– –	– –	– 1 –	–	–	–	–	–	–	1 –
22 Nottingham Forest	– –	1 –	– –	–	–	–	–	–	–	1 –
23 Sheffield United	– –	1 –	– –	–	–	–	–	–	–	1 –

JOHN DOW

DEBUT (Full Appearance)

Saturday 24/03/1894
Football League Division 1
at Bank Street

Newton Heath 2 Bolton Wanderers 2

CLUB CAREER RECORD	Apps	Subs	Goals
Premiership	0		0
League Division 1	2		0
League Division 2	46		6
FA Cup	1		0
League Cup	0		0
European Cup / Champions League	0		0
European Cup-Winners' Cup	0		0
UEFA Cup / Inter-Cities' Fairs Cup	0		0
Other Matches	1		0
OVERALL TOTAL	**50**		**6**

Opponents	PREM A S G	FLD 1 A S G	FLD 2 A S G	FAC A S G	LC A S G	EC/CL A S G	ECWC A S G	UEFA A S G	OTHER A S G	TOTAL A S G
1 Crewe Alexandra	– –	– –	– 4 2	–	–	–	–	–	–	4 2
2 Burton Swifts	– –	– –	4 1	–	–	–	–	–	–	4 1
3 Arsenal	– –	– –	– 4 –	–	–	–	–	–	–	4 –
4 Manchester City	– –	– –	4	–	–	–	–	–	–	4 –
5 Newcastle United	– –	– –	– 4 –	–	–	–	–	–	–	4 –
6 Leicester City	– –	– –	3 2	–	–	–	–	–	–	3 2
7 Burton Wanderers	– –	– –	– 3 1	–	–	–	–	–	–	3 1
8 Grimsby Town	– –	– –	3	–	–	–	–	–	–	3 –
9 Lincoln City	– –	– –	– 3 –	–	–	–	–	–	–	3 –
10 Rotherham United	– –	– –	3	–	–	–	–	–	–	3 –
11 Bury	– –	– –	– 2 –	–	–	–	–	–	–	2 –
12 Darwen	– –	– –	2	–	–	–	–	–	–	2 –
13 Liverpool	– –	– –	– 2 –	–	–	–	–	–	–	2 –
14 Notts County	– –	– –	2	–	–	–	–	–	–	2 –
15 Walsall	– –	– –	– 2 –	–	–	–	–	–	–	2 –
16 Blackburn Rovers	– –	1 –	– –	–	–	–	–	–	–	1 –
17 Bolton Wanderers	– –	1 –	– –	–	–	–	–	–	–	1 –
18 Kettering	– –	– –	– –	1 –	–	–	–	–	–	1 –
19 Loughborough Town	– –	– –	– 1 –	–	–	–	–	–	–	1 –
20 Stoke City	– –	– –	– –	–	–	–	–	–	1 –	1 –

ALEX DOWNIE

DEBUT (Full Appearance, 1 goal)

Saturday 22/11/1902
Football League Division 2
at Filbert Street

Leicester City 1 Manchester United 1

CLUB CAREER RECORD	Apps	Subs	Goals
Premiership	0		0
League Division 1	55		2
League Division 2	117		10
FA Cup	19		2
League Cup	0		0
European Cup / Champions League	0		0
European Cup-Winners' Cup	0		0
UEFA Cup / Inter-Cities' Fairs Cup	0		0
Other Matches	0		0
OVERALL TOTAL	**191**		**14**

Opponents	PREM A S G	FLD 1 A S G	FLD 2 A S G	FAC A S G	LC A S G	EC/CL A S G	ECWC A S G	UEFA A S G	OTHER A S G	TOTAL A S G
1 Bristol City	– –	4 –	6 –	–	–	–	–	–	–	10 –
2 Leicester City	– –	2 –	6 1	–	–	–	–	–	–	8 1
3 Burton United	– –	– –	6 –	2 –	–	–	–	–	–	8 –
4 Glossop	– –	– –	7 3	–	–	–	–	–	–	7 3
5 Lincoln City	– –	– –	7 2	–	–	–	–	–	–	7 2
6 Barnsley	– –	– –	7 1	–	–	–	–	–	–	7 1
7 Blackpool	– –	– –	7 1	–	–	–	–	–	–	7 1
8 Bradford City	– –	1 –	6 1	–	–	–	–	–	–	7 1
9 Burnley	– –	– –	7 –	–	–	–	–	–	–	7 –
10 Manchester City	– –	5 –	2 –	–	–	–	–	–	–	7 –
11 Gainsborough Trinity	– –	– –	6 1	–	–	–	–	–	–	6 1
12 Notts County	– –	4 –	– –	2 1	–	–	–	–	–	6 1
13 Bolton Wanderers	– –	2 –	4 –	–	–	–	–	–	–	6 –
14 Chesterfield	– –	– –	6 –	–	–	–	–	–	–	6 –
15 Grimsby Town	– –	– –	6 –	–	–	–	–	–	–	6 –
16 Liverpool	– –	3 –	2 –	1 –	–	–	–	–	–	6 –
17 Port Vale	– –	– –	6 –	–	–	–	–	–	–	6 –
18 Preston North End	– –	2 –	4 –	–	–	–	–	–	–	6 –
19 Arsenal	– –	2 1	2 –	1 –	–	–	–	–	–	5 1
20 Birmingham City	– –	1 –	1 –	3 –	–	–	–	–	–	5 –
21 Sheffield Wednesday	– –	4 –	– –	1 –	–	–	–	–	–	5 –
22 Aston Villa	– –	3 –	– –	1 –	–	–	–	–	–	4 –
23 Chelsea	– –	2 –	2 –	–	–	–	–	–	–	4 –
24 Doncaster Rovers	– –	– –	4 –	–	–	–	–	–	–	4 –
25 Everton	– –	3 –	– –	1 –	–	–	–	–	–	4 –
26 Stockport County	– –	– –	4 –	–	–	–	–	–	–	4 –
27 West Bromwich Albion	– –	– –	4 –	–	–	–	–	–	–	4 –
28 Blackburn Rovers	– –	3 –	– –	–	–	–	–	–	–	3 –
29 Fulham	– –	– –	– –	3 –	–	–	–	–	–	3 –
30 Sunderland	– –	3 –	– –	–	–	–	–	–	–	3 –
31 Sheffield United	– –	2 1	– –	–	–	–	–	–	–	2 1
32 Bury	– –	2 –	– –	–	–	–	–	–	–	2 –
33 Derby County	– –	2 –	– –	–	–	–	–	–	–	2 –
34 Hull City	– –	– –	2 –	–	–	–	–	–	–	2 –
35 Leeds United	– –	– –	2 –	–	–	–	–	–	–	2 –
36 Nottingham Forest	– –	2 –	– –	–	–	–	–	–	–	2 –
37 Norwich City	– –	– –	– –	1 1	–	–	–	–	–	1 1
38 Leyton Orient	– –	– –	1 –	–	–	–	–	–	–	1 –
39 Newcastle United	– –	1 –	– –	–	–	–	–	–	–	1 –
40 Portsmouth	– –	– –	– –	1 –	–	–	–	–	–	1 –
41 Southport Central	– –	– –	– –	1 –	–	–	–	–	–	1 –
42 Staple Hill	– –	– –	– –	1 –	–	–	–	–	–	1 –
43 Stoke City	– –	1 –	– –	–	–	–	–	–	–	1 –
44 Tottenham Hotspur	– –	1 –	– –	–	–	–	–	–	–	1 –

JOHN DOWNIE

DEBUT (Full Appearance, 1 goal)

Saturday 05/03/1949
Football League Division 1
at The Valley

Charlton Athletic 2 Manchester United 3

CLUB CAREER RECORD	Apps	Subs	Goals
Premiership	0		0
League Division 1	110		35
League Division 2	0		0
FA Cup	5		1
League Cup	0		0
European Cup / Champions League	0		0
European Cup-Winners' Cup	0		0
UEFA Cup / Inter-Cities' Fairs Cup	0		0
Other Matches	1		1
OVERALL TOTAL	**116**		**37**

Opponents	PREM A S G	FLD 1 A S G	FLD 2 A S G	FAC A S G	LC A S G	EC/CL A S G	ECWC A S G	UEFA A S G	OTHER A S G	TOTAL A S G
1 Newcastle United	– –	7 2	– –	–	–	–	–	–	1 1	8 3
2 Portsmouth	– –	7 1	– –	1 1	–	–	–	–	–	8 2
3 Chelsea	– –	7 1	– –	1 –	–	–	–	–	–	8 1
4 Bolton Wanderers	– –	8 –	– –	–	–	–	–	–	–	8 –
5 Liverpool	– –	6 2	– –	–	–	–	–	–	–	6 2
6 Stoke City	– –	6 1	– –	–	–	–	–	–	–	6 1
7 Charlton Athletic	– –	5 4	– –	–	–	–	–	–	–	5 4

continued../

JOHN DOWNIE (continued)

Opponents	PREM A S G	FLD 1 A S G	FLD 2 A S G	FAC A S G	LC A S G	EC/CL A S G	ECWC A S G	UEFA A S G	OTHER A S G	TOTAL A S G
8 Blackpool	– –	5 3	– –	– –	– –	– –	– –	– –	– –	5 3
9 Middlesbrough	– –	5 2	– –	– –	– –	– –	– –	– –	– –	5 2
10 Arsenal	– –	5 1	– –	– –	– –	– –	– –	– –	– –	5 1
11 Burnley	– –	5 1	– –	– –	– –	– –	– –	– –	– –	5 1
12 Fulham	– –	5 –	– –	– –	– –	– –	– –	– –	– –	5 –
13 Aston Villa	– –	4 3	– –	– –	– –	– –	– –	– –	– –	4 3
14 West Bromwich Albion	– –	4 3	– –	– –	– –	– –	– –	– –	– –	4 3
15 Derby County	– –	4 2	– –	– –	– –	– –	– –	– –	– –	4 2
16 Huddersfield Town	– –	3 2	– –	– –	– –	– –	– –	– –	– –	3 2
17 Sheffield Wednesday	– –	3 2	– –	– –	– –	– –	– –	– –	– –	3 2
18 Everton	– –	3 1	– –	– –	– –	– –	– –	– –	– –	3 1
19 Manchester City	– –	3 1	– –	– –	– –	– –	– –	– –	– –	3 1
20 Sunderland	– –	3 –	– –	– –	– –	– –	– –	– –	– –	3 –
21 Tottenham Hotspur	– –	3 –	– –	– –	– –	– –	– –	– –	– –	3 –
22 Wolverhampton W.	– –	3 –	– –	– –	– –	– –	– –	– –	– –	3 –
23 Preston North End	– –	2 2	– –	– –	– –	– –	– –	– –	– –	2 2
24 Birmingham City	– –	2 –	– –	– –	– –	– –	– –	– –	– –	2 –
25 Sheffield United	– –	1 1	– –	– –	– –	– –	– –	– –	– –	1 1
26 Cardiff City	– –	1 –	– –	– –	– –	– –	– –	– –	– –	1 –
27 Hull City	– –	– –	– –	1 –	– –	– –	– –	– –	– –	1 –
28 Millwall	– –	– –	– –	1 –	– –	– –	– –	– –	– –	1 –
29 Walthamstow Avenue	– –	– –	– –	1 –	– –	– –	– –	– –	– –	1 –

BILLY DRAYCOTT

DEBUT (Full Appearance)

Tuesday 01/09/1896
Football League Division 2
at Bank Street

Newton Heath 2 Gainsborough Trinity 0

CLUB CAREER RECORD	Apps	Subs	Goals
Premiership	0		0
League Division 1	0		0
League Division 2	81		6
FA Cup	10		0
League Cup	0		0
European Cup / Champions League	0		0
European Cup-Winners' Cup	0		0
UEFA Cup / Inter-Cities' Fairs Cup	0		0
Other Matches	4		0
OVERALL TOTAL	**95**		**6**

Opponents	PREM A S G	FLD 1 A S G	FLD 2 A S G	FAC A S G	LC A S G	EC/CL A S G	ECWC A S G	UEFA A S G	OTHER A S G	TOTAL A S G
1 Walsall	– –	– –	6 1	1 –	– –	– –	– –	– –	– –	7 1
2 Blackpool	– –	– –	5 1	1 –	– –	– –	– –	– –	– –	6 1
3 Gainsborough Trinity	– –	– –	6 1	– –	– –	– –	– –	– –	– –	6 1
4 Arsenal	– –	– –	6 –	– –	– –	– –	– –	– –	– –	6 –
5 Darwen	– –	– –	6 –	– –	– –	– –	– –	– –	– –	6 –
6 Birmingham City	– –	– –	5 1	– –	– –	– –	– –	– –	– –	5 1
7 Burton Swifts	– –	– –	5 1	– –	– –	– –	– –	– –	– –	5 1
8 Loughborough Town	– –	– –	5 1	– –	– –	– –	– –	– –	– –	5 1
9 Grimsby Town	– –	– –	5 –	– –	– –	– –	– –	– –	– –	5 –
10 Leicester City	– –	– –	5 –	– –	– –	– –	– –	– –	– –	5 –
11 Manchester City	– –	– –	5 –	– –	– –	– –	– –	– –	– –	5 –
12 Burnley	– –	– –	2 –	– –	– –	– –	– –	– –	2 –	4 –
13 Lincoln City	– –	– –	3 –	– –	– –	– –	– –	– –	– –	3 –
14 Luton Town	– –	– –	3 –	– –	– –	– –	– –	– –	– –	3 –
15 Newcastle United	– –	– –	3 –	– –	– –	– –	– –	– –	– –	3 –
16 Barnsley	– –	– –	2 –	– –	– –	– –	– –	– –	– –	2 –
17 Burton Wanderers	– –	– –	2 –	– –	– –	– –	– –	– –	– –	2 –
18 Glossop	– –	– –	2 –	– –	– –	– –	– –	– –	– –	2 –
19 Liverpool	– –	– –	– –	2 –	– –	– –	– –	– –	– –	2 –
20 New Brighton Tower	– –	– –	2 –	– –	– –	– –	– –	– –	– –	2 –
21 Notts County	– –	– –	2 –	– –	– –	– –	– –	– –	– –	2 –
22 Sunderland	– –	– –	– –	– –	– –	– –	– –	– –	2 –	2 –
23 Tottenham Hotspur	– –	– –	– –	2 –	– –	– –	– –	– –	– –	2 –
24 Derby County	– –	– –	– –	1 –	– –	– –	– –	– –	– –	1 –
25 Kettering	– –	– –	– –	1 –	– –	– –	– –	– –	– –	1 –
26 Nelson	– –	– –	– –	1 –	– –	– –	– –	– –	– –	1 –
27 Port Vale	– –	– –	1 –	– –	– –	– –	– –	– –	– –	1 –
28 West Manchester	– –	– –	– –	1 –	– –	– –	– –	– –	– –	1 –

DION DUBLIN

DEBUT (Substitute Appearance)

Saturday 15/08/1992
FA Premiership
at Bramall Lane

Sheffield United 2 Manchester United 1

CLUB CAREER RECORD	Apps	Subs	Goals
Premiership	4	(8)	2
League Division 1	0		0
League Division 2	0		0
FA Cup	1	(1)	0
League Cup	1	(1)	1
European Cup / Champions League	0	(1)	0
European Cup-Winners' Cup	0		0
UEFA Cup / Inter-Cities' Fairs Cup	0		0
Other Matches	0		0
OVERALL TOTAL	**6**	**(11)**	**3**

Opponents	PREM A S G	FLD 1 A S G	FLD 2 A S G	FAC A S G	LC A S G	EC/CL A S G	ECWC A S G	UEFA A S G	OTHER A S G	TOTAL A S G
1 Oldham Athletic	– (2) 1	–	–	1 –	–	–	–	–	–	1 (2) 1
2 Wimbledon	– (1) –	–	–	– (1) –	–	–	–	–	–	– (2) –
3 Southampton	1 – 1	–	–	–	–	–	–	–	–	1 – 1
4 Stoke City	–	–	–	–	1 – 1	–	–	–	–	1 – 1
5 Coventry City	1 – –	–	–	–	–	–	–	–	–	1 – –
6 Crystal Palace	1 –	–	–	–	–	–	–	–	–	1 – –
7 Nottingham Forest	1 – –	–	–	–	–	–	–	–	–	1 – –
8 Chelsea	– (1) –	–	–	–	–	–	–	–	–	– (1) –
9 Everton	– (1) –	–	–	–	–	–	–	–	–	– (1) –
10 Galatasaray	–	–	–	–	–	– (1) –	–	–	–	– (1) –
11 Ipswich Town	– (1) –	–	–	–	–	–	–	–	–	– (1) –
12 Portsmouth	–	–	–	–	– (1) –	–	–	–	–	– (1) –
13 Sheffield United	– (1) –	–	–	–	–	–	–	–	–	– (1) –
14 West Ham United	– (1) –	–	–	–	–	–	–	–	–	– (1) –

DICK DUCKWORTH

DEBUT (Full Appearance, 1 goal)

Saturday 19/12/1903
Football League Division 2
at Bank Street

Manchester United 4 Gainsborough Trinity 2

CLUB CAREER RECORD	Apps	Subs	Goals
Premiership	0		0
League Division 1	206		4
League Division 2	19		7
FA Cup	26		0
League Cup	0		0
European Cup / Champions League	0		0
European Cup-Winners' Cup	0		0
UEFA Cup / Inter-Cities' Fairs Cup	0		0
Other Matches	3		0
OVERALL TOTAL	**254**		**11**

Opponents	PREM A S G	FLD 1 A S G	FLD 2 A S G	FAC A S G	LC A S G	EC/CL A S G	ECWC A S G	UEFA A S G	OTHER A S G	TOTAL A S G
1 Blackburn Rovers	– –	12 – –	–	3 –	–	–	–	–	–	15 – –
2 Everton	– –	13 1	–	1 –	–	–	–	–	–	14 1
3 Middlesbrough	– –	14 – –	–	–	–	–	–	–	–	14 – –
4 Aston Villa	– –	12 – –	–	1 –	–	–	–	–	–	13 – –
5 Liverpool	– –	11 –	1 –	–	–	–	–	–	–	12 – –
6 Newcastle United	– –	11 –	–	1 –	–	–	–	–	–	12 – –
7 Preston North End	– –	11 1	–	–	–	–	–	–	–	11 1
8 Arsenal	– –	11 –	–	–	–	–	–	–	–	11 –
9 Manchester City	– –	11 –	–	–	–	–	–	–	–	11 –
10 Notts County	– –	11 –	–	–	–	–	–	–	–	11 –
11 Sheffield Wednesday	– –	11 –	–	–	–	–	–	–	–	11 –
12 Sunderland	– –	10 –	–	–	–	–	–	–	–	10 –
13 Bristol City	– –	8 –	–	1 –	–	–	–	–	–	9 –
14 Chelsea	– –	7 –	1 –	1 –	–	–	–	–	–	9 –
15 Bolton Wanderers	– –	8 –	–	–	–	–	–	–	–	8 –
16 Bury	– –	7 –	–	–	–	–	–	–	–	7 –
17 Sheffield United	– –	7 –	–	–	–	–	–	–	–	7 –
18 Bradford City	– –	6 –	–	–	–	–	–	–	–	6 –
19 Oldham Athletic	– –	4 –	–	2 –	–	–	–	–	–	6 –
20 Burnley	– –	1 –	2 –	2 –	–	–	–	–	–	5 –
21 Nottingham Forest	– –	5 –	–	–	–	–	–	–	–	5 –
22 Blackpool	– –	–	2 –	2 –	–	–	–	–	–	4 –
23 Tottenham Hotspur	– –	4 –	–	–	–	–	–	–	–	4 –
24 Gainsborough Trinity	– –	–	3 1	–	–	–	–	–	–	3 1
25 Birmingham City	– –	3 –	–	–	–	–	–	–	–	3 –
26 Coventry City	– –	–	–	3 –	–	–	–	–	–	3 –
27 West Bromwich Albion	– –	3 –	–	–	–	–	–	–	–	3 –
28 Burton United	– –	–	2 2	–	–	–	–	–	–	2 2
29 Stoke City	– –	2 2	–	–	–	–	–	–	–	2 2
30 Derby County	– –	2 –	–	–	–	–	–	–	–	2 –
31 Leicester City	– –	1 –	–	1 –	–	–	–	–	–	2 –
32 Portsmouth	– –	–	–	2 –	–	–	–	–	–	2 –
33 Queens Park Rangers	– –	–	–	–	–	–	–	–	2 –	2 –
34 Reading	– –	–	–	2 –	–	–	–	–	–	2 –
35 Doncaster Rovers	– –	–	1 3	–	–	–	–	–	–	1 3
36 Grimsby Town	– –	–	1 1	–	–	–	–	–	–	1 1
37 Barnsley	– –	–	1 –	–	–	–	–	–	–	1 –
38 Brighton	– –	–	–	1 –	–	–	–	–	–	1 –

continued../

DICK DUCKWORTH (continued)

Opponents	PREM			FLD 1			FLD 2			FAC			LC			EC/CL			ECWC			UEFA			OTHER			TOTAL		
	A	S	G	A	S	G	A	S	G	A	S	G	A	S	G	A	S	G	A	S	G	A	S	G	A	S	G	A	S	G
39 Fulham	-	-	-	-	-	-	-	-	-	1	-	-	-	-	-	-	-	-	-	-	-	-	-	-	-	-	-	1	-	-
40 Glossop	-	-	-	-	-	-	1	-	-	-	-	-	-	-	-	-	-	-	-	-	-	-	-	-	-	-	-	1	-	-
41 Huddersfield Town	-	-	-	-	-	-	-	-	-	1	-	-	-	-	-	-	-	-	-	-	-	-	-	-	-	-	-	1	-	-
42 Leyton Orient	-	-	-	-	-	-	1	-	-	-	-	-	-	-	-	-	-	-	-	-	-	-	-	-	-	-	-	1	-	-
43 Lincoln City	-	-	-	-	-	-	1	-	-	-	-	-	-	-	-	-	-	-	-	-	-	-	-	-	-	-	-	1	-	-
44 Plymouth Argyle	-	-	-	-	-	-	-	-	-	-	-	-	1	-	-	-	-	-	-	-	-	-	-	-	-	-	-	1	-	-
45 Port Vale	-	-	-	-	-	-	1	-	-	-	-	-	-	-	-	-	-	-	-	-	-	-	-	-	-	-	-	1	-	-
46 Swindon Town	-	-	-	-	-	-	-	-	-	-	-	-	-	-	-	-	-	-	-	-	-	-	-	-	1	-	-	1	-	-
47 West Ham United	-	-	-	-	-	-	1	-	-	-	-	-	-	-	-	-	-	-	-	-	-	-	-	-	-	-	-	1	-	-

WILLIAM DUNN

DEBUT (Full Appearance)

Saturday 04/09/1897
Football League Division 2
at Bank Street

Newton Heath 5 Lincoln City 0

CLUB CAREER RECORD	Apps	Subs	Goals
Premiership	0		0
League Division 1	0		0
League Division 2	10		0
FA Cup	2		0
League Cup	0		0
European Cup / Champions League	0		0
European Cup-Winners' Cup	0		0
UEFA Cup / Inter-Cities' Fairs Cup	0		0
Other Matches	0		0
OVERALL TOTAL	12		0

Opponents	PREM			FLD 1			FLD 2			FAC			LC			EC/CL			ECWC			UEFA			OTHER			TOTAL		
	A	S	G	A	S	G	A	S	G	A	S	G	A	S	G	A	S	G	A	S	G	A	S	G	A	S	G	A	S	G
1 Burton Swifts	-	-	-	-	-	-	2	-	-	-	-	-	-	-	-	-	-	-	-	-	-	-	-	-	-	-	-	2	-	-
2 Lincoln City	-	-	-	-	-	-	2	-	-	-	-	-	-	-	-	-	-	-	-	-	-	-	-	-	-	-	-	2	-	-
3 Walsall	-	-	-	-	-	-	1	-	-	1	-	-	-	-	-	-	-	-	-	-	-	-	-	-	-	-	-	2	-	-
4 Gainsborough Trinity	-	-	-	-	-	-	1	-	-	-	-	-	-	-	-	-	-	-	-	-	-	-	-	-	-	-	-	1	-	-
5 Grimsby Town	-	-	-	-	-	-	1	-	-	-	-	-	-	-	-	-	-	-	-	-	-	-	-	-	-	-	-	1	-	-
6 Leicester City	-	-	-	-	-	-	1	-	-	-	-	-	-	-	-	-	-	-	-	-	-	-	-	-	-	-	-	1	-	-
7 Liverpool	-	-	-	-	-	-	-	-	-	1	-	-	-	-	-	-	-	-	-	-	-	-	-	-	-	-	-	1	-	-
8 Luton Town	-	-	-	-	-	-	1	-	-	-	-	-	-	-	-	-	-	-	-	-	-	-	-	-	-	-	-	1	-	-
9 Manchester City	-	-	-	-	-	-	1	-	-	-	-	-	-	-	-	-	-	-	-	-	-	-	-	-	-	-	-	1	-	-

PAT DUNNE

DEBUT (Full Appearance)

Tuesday 08/09/1964
Football League Division 1
at Goodison Park

Everton 3 Manchester United 3

CLUB CAREER RECORD	Apps	Subs	Goals
Premiership	0		0
League Division 1	45		0
League Division 2	0		0
FA Cup	7		0
League Cup	1		0
European Cup / Champions League	2		0
European Cup-Winners' Cup	0		0
UEFA Cup / Inter-Cities' Fairs Cup	11		0
Other Matches	1		0
OVERALL TOTAL	67		0

Opponents	PREM			FLD 1			FLD 2			FAC			LC			EC/CL			ECWC			UEFA			OTHER			TOTAL		
	A	S	G	A	S	G	A	S	G	A	S	G	A	S	G	A	S	G	A	S	G	A	S	G	A	S	G	A	S	G
1 Everton	-	-	-	2	-	-	-	-	-	-	-	-	-	-	-	-	-	-	-	-	-	2	-	-	-	-	-	4	-	-
2 Leeds United	-	-	-	2	-	-	-	-	-	2	-	-	-	-	-	-	-	-	-	-	-	-	-	-	-	-	-	4	-	-
3 Liverpool	-	-	-	3	-	-	-	-	-	-	-	-	-	-	-	-	-	-	-	-	-	-	-	-	1	-	-	4	-	-
4 Stoke City	-	-	-	2	-	-	-	-	-	2	-	-	-	-	-	-	-	-	-	-	-	-	-	-	-	-	-	4	-	-
5 Arsenal	-	-	-	3	-	-	-	-	-	-	-	-	-	-	-	-	-	-	-	-	-	-	-	-	-	-	-	3	-	-
6 Blackpool	-	-	-	2	-	-	-	-	-	-	-	-	1	-	-	-	-	-	-	-	-	-	-	-	-	-	-	3	-	-
7 Burnley	-	-	-	2	-	-	-	-	-	1	-	-	-	-	-	-	-	-	-	-	-	-	-	-	-	-	-	3	-	-
8 Ferencvaros	-	-	-	-	-	-	-	-	-	-	-	-	-	-	-	-	-	-	-	-	-	3	-	-	-	-	-	3	-	-
9 Nottingham Forest	-	-	-	3	-	-	-	-	-	-	-	-	-	-	-	-	-	-	-	-	-	-	-	-	-	-	-	3	-	-
10 Sheffield Wednesday	-	-	-	3	-	-	-	-	-	-	-	-	-	-	-	-	-	-	-	-	-	-	-	-	-	-	-	3	-	-
11 Sunderland	-	-	-	3	-	-	-	-	-	-	-	-	-	-	-	-	-	-	-	-	-	-	-	-	-	-	-	3	-	-
12 Tottenham Hotspur	-	-	-	3	-	-	-	-	-	-	-	-	-	-	-	-	-	-	-	-	-	-	-	-	-	-	-	3	-	-
13 Wolverhampton W.	-	-	-	2	-	-	-	-	-	1	-	-	-	-	-	-	-	-	-	-	-	-	-	-	-	-	-	3	-	-
14 Aston Villa	-	-	-	2	-	-	-	-	-	-	-	-	-	-	-	-	-	-	-	-	-	-	-	-	-	-	-	2	-	-
15 Birmingham City	-	-	-	2	-	-	-	-	-	-	-	-	-	-	-	-	-	-	-	-	-	-	-	-	-	-	-	2	-	-
16 Blackburn Rovers	-	-	-	2	-	-	-	-	-	-	-	-	-	-	-	-	-	-	-	-	-	-	-	-	-	-	-	2	-	-
17 Borussia Dortmund	-	-	-	-	-	-	-	-	-	-	-	-	-	-	-	-	-	-	-	-	-	2	-	-	-	-	-	2	-	-
18 Chelsea	-	-	-	2	-	-	-	-	-	-	-	-	-	-	-	-	-	-	-	-	-	-	-	-	-	-	-	2	-	-
19 Djurgardens	-	-	-	-	-	-	-	-	-	-	-	-	-	-	-	-	-	-	-	-	-	2	-	-	-	-	-	2	-	-
20 Fulham	-	-	-	2	-	-	-	-	-	-	-	-	-	-	-	-	-	-	-	-	-	-	-	-	-	-	-	2	-	-
21 Sheffield United	-	-	-	2	-	-	-	-	-	-	-	-	-	-	-	-	-	-	-	-	-	-	-	-	-	-	-	2	-	-
22 Strasbourg	-	-	-	-	-	-	-	-	-	-	-	-	-	-	-	-	-	-	-	-	-	2	-	-	-	-	-	2	-	-
23 ASK Vorwaerts	-	-	-	-	-	-	-	-	-	-	-	-	-	-	-	1	-	-	-	-	-	-	-	-	-	-	-	1	-	-
24 Chester City	-	-	-	-	-	-	-	-	-	-	-	-	1	-	-	-	-	-	-	-	-	-	-	-	-	-	-	1	-	-
25 HJK Helsinki	-	-	-	-	-	-	-	-	-	-	-	-	-	-	-	1	-	-	-	-	-	-	-	-	-	-	-	1	-	-
26 Leicester City	-	-	-	1	-	-	-	-	-	-	-	-	-	-	-	-	-	-	-	-	-	-	-	-	-	-	-	1	-	-
27 West Bromwich Albion	-	-	-	1	-	-	-	-	-	-	-	-	-	-	-	-	-	-	-	-	-	-	-	-	-	-	-	1	-	-
28 West Ham United	-	-	-	1	-	-	-	-	-	-	-	-	-	-	-	-	-	-	-	-	-	-	-	-	-	-	-	1	-	-

TONY DUNNE

DEBUT (Full Appearance)

Saturday 15/10/1960
Football League Division 1
at Turf Moor

Burnley 5 Manchester United 3

CLUB CAREER RECORD	Apps	Subs	Goals
Premiership	0		0
League Division 1	414		2
League Division 2	0		0
FA Cup	54	(1)	0
League Cup	21		0
European Cup / Champions League	23		0
European Cup–Winners' Cup	6		0
UEFA Cup / Inter-Cities' Fairs Cup	11		0
Other Matches	5		0
OVERALL TOTAL	**534**	**(1)**	**2**

Opponents	PREM			FLD 1			FLD 2			FAC			LC			EC/CL			ECWC			UEFA			OTHER			TOTAL		
	A	S	G	A	S	G	A	S	G	A	S	G	A	S	G	A	S	G	A	S	G	A	S	G	A	S	G	A	S	G
1 Everton	–	–	–	21	–	–	–	–	–	2	–	–	–	–	–	–	–	–	–	–	–	2	–	–	1	–	–	26	–	–
2 Burnley	–	–	–	20	–	–	–	–	–	1	–	–	4	–	–	–	–	–	–	–	–	–	–	–	–	–	–	25	–	–
3 Tottenham Hotspur	–	–	–	18	–	–	–	–	–	3	–	–	–	–	–	–	–	–	2	–	–	–	–	–	1	–	–	24	–	–
4 Arsenal	–	–	–	21	–	–	–	–	–	1	–	–	–	–	–	–	–	–	–	–	–	–	–	–	–	–	–	22	–	–
5 Leeds United	–	–	–	16	–	–	–	–	–	5	–	–	–	–	–	–	–	–	–	–	–	–	–	–	–	–	–	21	–	–
6 Stoke City	–	–	–	16	–	–	–	–	–	5	–	–	–	–	–	–	–	–	–	–	–	–	–	–	–	–	–	21	–	–
7 Liverpool	–	–	–	19	–	–	–	–	–	–	–	–	–	–	–	–	–	–	–	–	–	–	–	–	1	–	–	20	–	–
8 West Ham United	–	–	–	19	–	–	–	–	–	1	–	–	–	–	–	–	–	–	–	–	–	–	–	–	–	–	–	20	–	–
9 West Bromwich Albion	–	–	–	19	–	1	–	–	–	–	–	–	–	–	–	–	–	–	–	–	–	–	–	–	–	–	–	19	–	1
10 Sheffield Wednesday	–	–	–	16	–	–	–	–	–	2	–	–	–	–	–	–	–	–	–	–	–	–	–	–	–	–	–	18	–	–
11 Chelsea	–	–	–	16	–	–	–	–	–	–	–	–	1	–	–	–	–	–	–	–	–	–	–	–	–	–	–	17	–	–
12 Leicester City	–	–	–	16	–	–	–	–	–	1	–	–	–	–	–	–	–	–	–	–	–	–	–	–	–	–	–	17	–	–
13 Nottingham Forest	–	–	–	17	–	–	–	–	–	–	–	–	–	–	–	–	–	–	–	–	–	–	–	–	–	–	–	17	–	–
14 Wolverhampton W.	–	–	–	14	–	–	–	–	–	2	(1)	–	–	–	–	–	–	–	–	–	–	–	–	–	–	–	–	16	(1)	–
15 Manchester City	–	–	–	14	–	–	–	–	–	–	–	–	2	–	–	–	–	–	–	–	–	–	–	–	–	–	–	16	–	–
16 Ipswich Town	–	–	–	14	–	–	–	–	–	–	–	–	1	–	–	–	–	–	–	–	–	–	–	–	–	–	–	15	–	–
17 Sheffield United	–	–	–	14	–	–	–	–	–	–	–	–	–	–	–	–	–	–	–	–	–	–	–	–	–	–	–	14	–	–
18 Sunderland	–	–	–	11	–	–	–	–	–	3	–	–	–	–	–	–	–	–	–	–	–	–	–	–	–	–	–	14	–	–
19 Newcastle United	–	–	–	13	–	1	–	–	–	–	–	–	–	–	–	–	–	–	–	–	–	–	–	–	–	–	–	13	–	1
20 Fulham	–	–	–	13	–	–	–	–	–	–	–	–	–	–	–	–	–	–	–	–	–	–	–	–	–	–	–	13	–	–
21 Aston Villa	–	–	–	10	–	–	–	–	–	–	–	–	2	–	–	–	–	–	–	–	–	–	–	–	–	–	–	12	–	–
22 Blackpool	–	–	–	11	–	–	–	–	–	–	–	–	1	–	–	–	–	–	–	–	–	–	–	–	–	–	–	12	–	–
23 Southampton	–	–	–	10	–	–	–	–	–	2	–	–	–	–	–	–	–	–	–	–	–	–	–	–	–	–	–	12	–	–
24 Birmingham City	–	–	–	8	–	–	–	–	–	2	–	–	–	–	–	–	–	–	–	–	–	–	–	–	–	–	–	10	–	–
25 Derby County	–	–	–	7	–	–	–	–	–	1	–	–	2	–	–	–	–	–	–	–	–	–	–	–	–	–	–	10	–	–
26 Coventry City	–	–	–	8	–	–	–	–	–	1	–	–	–	–	–	–	–	–	–	–	–	–	–	–	–	–	–	9	–	–
27 Blackburn Rovers	–	–	–	8	–	–	–	–	–	–	–	–	–	–	–	–	–	–	–	–	–	–	–	–	–	–	–	8	–	–
28 Crystal Palace	–	–	–	7	–	–	–	–	–	–	–	–	1	–	–	–	–	–	–	–	–	–	–	–	–	–	–	8	–	–
29 Bolton Wanderers	–	–	–	6	–	–	–	–	–	1	–	–	–	–	–	–	–	–	–	–	–	–	–	–	–	–	–	7	–	–
30 Middlesbrough	–	–	–	–	–	–	–	–	–	6	–	–	1	–	–	–	–	–	–	–	–	–	–	–	–	–	–	7	–	–
31 Preston North End	–	–	–	1	–	–	–	–	–	4	–	–	–	–	–	–	–	–	–	–	–	–	–	–	–	–	–	5	–	–
32 Benfica	–	–	–	–	–	–	–	–	–	–	–	–	–	–	–	3	–	–	–	–	–	–	–	–	–	–	–	3	–	–
33 Bristol Rovers	–	–	–	–	–	–	–	–	–	1	–	–	2	–	–	–	–	–	–	–	–	–	–	–	–	–	–	3	–	–
34 Ferencvaros	–	–	–	–	–	–	–	–	–	–	–	–	–	–	–	–	–	–	–	–	–	3	–	–	–	–	–	3	–	–
35 Huddersfield Town	–	–	–	3	–	–	–	–	–	–	–	–	–	–	–	–	–	–	–	–	–	–	–	–	–	–	–	3	–	–
36 Northampton Town	–	–	–	2	–	–	–	–	–	1	–	–	–	–	–	–	–	–	–	–	–	–	–	–	–	–	–	3	–	–
37 Watford	–	–	–	–	–	–	–	–	–	3	–	–	–	–	–	–	–	–	–	–	–	–	–	–	–	–	–	3	–	–
38 Anderlecht	–	–	–	–	–	–	–	–	–	–	–	–	–	–	–	2	–	–	–	–	–	–	–	–	–	–	–	2	–	–
39 ASK Vorwaerts	–	–	–	–	–	–	–	–	–	–	–	–	–	–	–	2	–	–	–	–	–	–	–	–	–	–	–	2	–	–
40 Borussia Dortmund	–	–	–	–	–	–	–	–	–	–	–	–	–	–	–	–	–	–	–	–	–	2	–	–	–	–	–	2	–	–
41 Djurgardens	–	–	–	–	–	–	–	–	–	–	–	–	–	–	–	–	–	–	–	–	–	2	–	–	–	–	–	2	–	–
42 Estudiantes de la Plata	–	–	–	–	–	–	–	–	–	–	–	–	–	–	–	–	–	–	–	–	–	–	–	–	2	–	–	2	–	–
43 Exeter City	–	–	–	–	–	–	–	–	–	1	–	–	1	–	–	–	–	–	–	–	–	–	–	–	–	–	–	2	–	–
44 Gornik Zabrze	–	–	–	–	–	–	–	–	–	–	–	–	–	–	–	2	–	–	–	–	–	–	–	–	–	–	–	2	–	–
45 Hibernians Malta	–	–	–	–	–	–	–	–	–	–	–	–	–	–	–	2	–	–	–	–	–	–	–	–	–	–	–	2	–	–
46 HJK Helsinki	–	–	–	–	–	–	–	–	–	–	–	–	–	–	–	2	–	–	–	–	–	–	–	–	–	–	–	2	–	–
47 Leyton Orient	–	–	–	2	–	–	–	–	–	–	–	–	–	–	–	–	–	–	–	–	–	–	–	–	–	–	–	2	–	–
48 Norwich City	–	–	–	1	–	–	–	–	–	1	–	–	–	–	–	–	–	–	–	–	–	–	–	–	–	–	–	2	–	–
49 Partizan Belgrade	–	–	–	–	–	–	–	–	–	–	–	–	–	–	–	2	–	–	–	–	–	–	–	–	–	–	–	2	–	–
50 Queens Park Rangers	–	–	–	2	–	–	–	–	–	–	–	–	–	–	–	–	–	–	–	–	–	–	–	–	–	–	–	2	–	–
51 Rapid Vienna	–	–	–	–	–	–	–	–	–	–	–	–	–	–	–	2	–	–	–	–	–	–	–	–	–	–	–	2	–	–
52 Real Madrid	–	–	–	–	–	–	–	–	–	–	–	–	–	–	–	2	–	–	–	–	–	–	–	–	–	–	–	2	–	–
53 Rotherham United	–	–	–	–	–	–	–	–	–	2	–	–	–	–	–	–	–	–	–	–	–	–	–	–	–	–	–	2	–	–
54 Sarajevo	–	–	–	–	–	–	–	–	–	–	–	–	–	–	–	2	–	–	–	–	–	–	–	–	–	–	–	2	–	–
55 Sporting Lisbon	–	–	–	–	–	–	–	–	–	–	–	–	–	–	–	–	–	–	2	–	–	–	–	–	–	–	–	2	–	–
56 Strasbourg	–	–	–	–	–	–	–	–	–	–	–	–	–	–	–	–	–	–	–	–	–	2	–	–	–	–	–	2	–	–
57 Waterford	–	–	–	–	–	–	–	–	–	–	–	–	–	–	–	2	–	–	–	–	–	–	–	–	–	–	–	2	–	–
58 Willem II	–	–	–	–	–	–	–	–	–	–	–	–	–	–	–	–	–	–	2	–	–	–	–	–	–	–	–	2	–	–
59 Aldershot	–	–	–	–	–	–	–	–	–	–	–	–	1	–	–	–	–	–	–	–	–	–	–	–	–	–	–	1	–	–
60 Barnsley	–	–	–	–	–	–	–	–	–	1	–	–	–	–	–	–	–	–	–	–	–	–	–	–	–	–	–	1	–	–
61 Cardiff City	–	–	–	1	–	–	–	–	–	–	–	–	–	–	–	–	–	–	–	–	–	–	–	–	–	–	–	1	–	–
62 Chester City	–	–	–	–	–	–	–	–	–	1	–	–	–	–	–	–	–	–	–	–	–	–	–	–	–	–	–	1	–	–
63 Oxford United	–	–	–	–	–	–	–	–	–	–	–	–	1	–	–	–	–	–	–	–	–	–	–	–	–	–	–	1	–	–
64 Wrexham	–	–	–	–	–	–	–	–	–	–	–	–	1	–	–	–	–	–	–	–	–	–	–	–	–	–	–	1	–	–

MIKE DUXBURY

DEBUT (Substitute Appearance)

Saturday 23/08/1980
Football League Division 1
at St Andrews

Birmingham City 0 Manchester United 0

CLUB CAREER RECORD	Apps	Subs	Goals
Premiership	0		0
League Division 1	274	(25)	6
League Division 2	0		0
FA Cup	20	(5)	1
League Cup	32	(2)	0
European Cup / Champions League	0		0
European Cup-Winners' Cup	8		0
UEFA Cup / Inter-Cities' Fairs Cup	9	(1)	0
Other Matches	2		0
OVERALL TOTAL	**345**	**(33)**	**7**

Opponents	PREM A S G	FLD 1 A S G	FLD 2 A S G	FAC A S G	LC A S G	EC/CL A S G	ECWC A S G	UEFA A S G	OTHER A S G	TOTAL A S G
1 West Ham United	– –	14 –	– – –	4 –	1 –	– –	– –	– –	– –	19 –
2 Everton	– –	15 –	– – –	1 (1) –	– –	– –	– –	– –	1 –	17 (1) –
3 Arsenal	– –	13 –	– – –	2 –	2 –	– –	– –	– –	– –	17 –
4 Liverpool	– –	14 (1) –	– – –	– –	1 –	– –	– –	– –	1 –	16 (1) –
5 Southampton	– –	13 (1) –	– – –	– –	3 –	– –	– –	– –	– –	16 (1) –
6 Nottingham Forest	– –	12 (1) –	– – –	– (1) –	1 –	– –	– –	– –	– –	13 (2) –
7 Tottenham Hotspur	– –	13 (1) –	– – –	– –	– (1) –	– –	– –	– –	– –	13 (2) –
8 Coventry City	– –	11 (2) –	– – –	1 –	– –	– –	– –	– –	– –	12 (2) –
9 Norwich City	– –	13 –	– – –	– –	– –	– –	– –	– –	– –	13 –
10 Queens Park Rangers	– –	11 (1) 1	– – –	– –	– –	– –	– –	– –	– –	11 (1) 1
11 Ipswich Town	– –	9 (2) –	– – –	1 –	– –	– –	– –	– –	– –	10 (2) –
12 Aston Villa	– –	9 (3) 1	– – –	– –	– –	– –	– –	– –	– –	9 (3) 1
13 Manchester City	– –	10 1	– – –	1 –	– –	– –	– –	– –	– –	11 1
14 Luton Town	– –	10 –	– – –	1 –	– –	– –	– –	– –	– –	11 –
15 Watford	– –	10 –	– – –	– –	– –	– –	– –	– –	– –	10 –
16 Oxford United	5 –	– –	– – –	4 –	– –	– –	– –	– –	– –	9 –
17 Chelsea	– –	7 (1) –	– – –	– –	1 –	– –	– –	– –	– –	8 (1) –
18 Brighton	– –	4 (1) 1	– – –	2 (2) 1	– –	– –	– –	– –	– –	6 (3) 2
19 Newcastle United	– –	7 –	– – –	1 –	– –	– –	– –	– –	– –	8 –
20 West Bromwich Albion	– –	8 –	– – –	– –	– –	– –	– –	– –	– –	8 –
21 Stoke City	– –	6 (2) –	– – –	– –	– –	– –	– –	– –	– –	6 (2) –
22 Sunderland	– –	6 (2) –	– – –	– –	– –	– –	– –	– –	– –	6 (2) –
23 Sheffield Wednesday	– –	7 –	– – –	– –	– –	– –	– –	– –	– –	7 –
24 Wimbledon	– –	6 –	– – –	– –	1 –	– –	– –	– –	– –	7 –
25 Birmingham City	– –	6 (1) –	– – –	– –	– –	– –	– –	– –	– –	6 (1) –
26 Derby County	– –	4 (2) –	– – –	1 –	– –	– –	– –	– –	– –	5 (2) –
27 Crystal Palace	– –	2 1	– – –	– –	3 –	– –	– –	– –	– –	5 1
28 Notts County	– –	5 1	– – –	– –	– –	– –	– –	– –	– –	5 1
29 Charlton Athletic	– –	5 –	– – –	– –	– –	– –	– –	– –	– –	5 –
30 Leicester City	5 –	– –	– – –	– –	– –	– –	– –	– –	– –	5 –
31 Bournemouth	– –	– –	– – –	2 –	2 –	– –	– –	– –	– –	4 –
32 Wolverhampton W.	– –	4 –	– – –	– –	– –	– –	– –	– –	– –	4 –
33 Middlesbrough	– –	3 (1) –	– – –	– –	– –	– –	– –	– –	– –	3 (1) –
34 Portsmouth	– –	2 –	– – –	– –	1 (1) –	– –	– –	– –	– –	3 (1) –
35 Port Vale	– –	– –	– – –	– –	3 –	– –	– –	– –	– –	3 –
36 Swansea City	– –	3 –	– – –	– –	– –	– –	– –	– –	– –	3 –
37 Leeds United	– –	1 (2) –	– – –	– –	– –	– –	– –	– –	– –	1 (2) –
38 Barcelona	– –	– –	– – –	– –	– –	– –	2 –	– –	– –	2 –
39 Bradford City	– –	– –	– – –	– –	2 –	– –	– –	– –	– –	2 –
40 Burnley	– –	– –	– – –	– –	2 –	– –	– –	– –	– –	2 –
41 Dukla Prague	– –	– –	– – –	– –	– –	– –	2 –	– –	– –	2 –
42 Dundee United	– –	– –	– – –	– –	– –	– –	– –	2 –	– –	2 –
43 Hull City	– –	– –	– – –	– –	2 –	– –	– –	– –	– –	2 –
44 Juventus	– –	– –	– – –	– –	– –	– –	2 –	– –	– –	2 –
45 Raba Vasas	– –	– –	– – –	– –	– –	– –	– –	2 –	– –	2 –
46 Rotherham United	– –	– –	– – –	– –	2 –	– –	– –	– –	– –	2 –
47 Spartak Varna	– –	– –	– – –	– –	– –	– –	2 –	– –	– –	2 –
48 Valencia	– –	– –	– – –	– –	– –	– –	– –	2 –	– –	2 –
49 Videoton	– –	– –	– – –	– –	– –	– –	– –	2 –	– –	2 –
50 Millwall	– –	1 (1) –	– – –	– –	– –	– –	– –	– –	– –	1 (1) –
51 Widzew Lodz	– –	– –	– – –	– –	– –	– –	– –	1 (1) –	– –	1 (1) –
52 Bury	– –	– –	– – –	– –	1 –	– –	– –	– –	– –	1 –
53 Colchester United	– –	– –	– – –	– –	1 –	– –	– –	– –	– –	1 –
54 Hereford United	– –	– –	– – –	1 –	– –	– –	– –	– –	– –	1 –
55 Rochdale	– –	– –	– – –	1 –	– –	– –	– –	– –	– –	1 –
56 Sheffield United	– –	– –	– – –	– (1) –	– –	– –	– –	– –	– –	– (1) –

JIMMY DYER

DEBUT (Full Appearance)

Saturday 14/10/1905
Football League Division 2
at The Hawthorns

West Bromwich Albion 1 Manchester United 0

CLUB CAREER RECORD	Apps	Subs	Goals
Premiership	0		0
League Division 1	0		0
League Division 2	1		0
FA Cup	0		0
League Cup	0		0
European Cup / Champions League	0		0
European Cup-Winners' Cup	0		0
UEFA Cup / Inter-Cities' Fairs Cup	0		0
Other Matches	0		0
OVERALL TOTAL	1		0

Opponents	PREM A S G	FLD 1 A S G	FLD 2 A S G	FAC A S G	LC A S G	EC/CL A S G	ECWC A S G	UEFA A S G	OTHER A S G	TOTAL A S G
1 West Bromwich Albion	– – –	– – –	1 – –	– – –	– – –	– – –	– – –	– – –	– – –	1 – –

CHRIS EAGLES

DEBUT (Substitute Appearance)

Tuesday 28/10/2003
League Cup 3rd Round
at Elland Road

Leeds United 2 Manchester United 3

CLUB CAREER RECORD	Apps	Subs	Goals
Premiership	2	(4)	1
League Division 1	0		0
League Division 2	0		0
FA Cup	1		0
League Cup	2	(4)	0
European Cup / Champions League	2	(1)	0
European Cup-Winners' Cup	0		0
UEFA Cup / Inter-Cities' Fairs Cup	0		0
Other Matches	0	(1)	0
OVERALL TOTAL	7	(10)	1

Opponents	PREM A S G	FLD 1 A S G	FLD 2 A S G	FAC A S G	LC A S G	EC/CL A S G	ECWC A S G	UEFA A S G	OTHER A S G	TOTAL A S G
1 Arsenal	– – –	– – –	– – –	– – –	1 – –	– – –	– – –	– – –	– (1) –	1 (1) –
2 Chelsea	1 – –	– – –	– – –	– – –	– – –	– – –	– – –	– – –	– – –	1 – –
3 Coventry City	– – –	– – –	– – –	– – –	1 – –	– – –	– – –	– – –	– – –	1 – –
4 Dinamo Bucharest	– – –	– – –	– – –	– – –	– – –	1 – –	– – –	– – –	– – –	1 – –
5 Exeter City	– – –	– – –	– – –	1 – –	– – –	– – –	– – –	– – –	– – –	1 – –
6 Roma	– – –	– – –	– – –	– – –	– – –	1 – –	– – –	– – –	– – –	1 – –
7 Sunderland	1 – –	– – –	– – –	– – –	– – –	– – –	– – –	– – –	– – –	1 – –
8 Everton	– (1) 1	– – –	– – –	– – –	– – –	– – –	– – –	– – –	– – –	– (1) 1
9 Crewe Alexandra	– – –	– – –	– – –	– – –	– (1) –	– – –	– – –	– – –	– – –	– (1) –
10 Crystal Palace	– – –	– – –	– – –	– – –	– (1) –	– – –	– – –	– – –	– – –	– (1) –
11 Fenerbahce	– – –	– – –	– – –	– – –	– – –	– (1) –	– – –	– – –	– – –	– (1) –
12 Leeds United	– – –	– – –	– – –	– – –	– (1) –	– – –	– – –	– – –	– – –	– (1) –
13 Manchester City	– (1) –	– – –	– – –	– – –	– – –	– – –	– – –	– – –	– – –	– (1) –
14 Portsmouth	– (1) –	– – –	– – –	– – –	– – –	– – –	– – –	– – –	– – –	– (1) –
15 Tottenham Hotspur	– (1) –	– – –	– – –	– – –	– – –	– – –	– – –	– – –	– – –	– (1) –
16 West Bromwich Albion	– – –	– – –	– – –	– – –	– (1) –	– – –	– – –	– – –	– – –	– (1) –

JOHN EARP

DEBUT (Full Appearance)

Saturday 30/10/1886
FA Cup 1st Round
at Fleetwood Park

Fleetwood Rangers 2 Newton Heath 2

CLUB CAREER RECORD	Apps	Subs	Goals
Premiership	0		0
League Division 1	0		0
League Division 2	0		0
FA Cup	1		0
League Cup	0		0
European Cup / Champions League	0		0
European Cup-Winners' Cup	0		0
UEFA Cup / Inter-Cities' Fairs Cup	0		0
Other Matches	0		0
OVERALL TOTAL	1		0

Opponents	PREM A S G	FLD 1 A S G	FLD 2 A S G	FAC A S G	LC A S G	EC/CL A S G	ECWC A S G	UEFA A S G	OTHER A S G	TOTAL A S G
1 Fleetwood Rangers	– – –	– – –	– – –	1 – –	– – –	– – –	– – –	– – –	– – –	1 – –

SYLVAN EBANKS-BLAKE

DEBUT (Substitute Appearance)

Tuesday 26/10/2004
League Cup 3rd Round
at Gresty Road

Crewe Alexandra 0 Manchester United 3

CLUB CAREER RECORD	Apps	Subs	Goals
Premiership	0		0
League Division 1	0		0
League Division 2	0		0
FA Cup	0		0
League Cup	1	(1)	1
European Cup / Champions League	0		0
European Cup-Winners' Cup	0		0
UEFA Cup / Inter-Cities' Fairs Cup	0		0
Other Matches	0		0
OVERALL TOTAL	**1**	**(1)**	**1**

Opponents	PREM A S G	FLD 1 A S G	FLD 2 A S G	FAC A S G	LC A S G	EC/CL A S G	ECWC A S G	UEFA A S G	OTHER A S G	TOTAL A S G
1 Barnet	- - -	- - -	- - -	- - -	1 - 1	- - -	- - -	- - -	- - -	1 - 1
2 Crewe Alexandra	- - -	- - -	- - -	- - -	- (1) -	- - -	- - -	- - -	- - -	- (1) -

ADAM ECKERSLEY

DEBUT (Full Appearance)

Wednesday 26/10/2005
League Cup 3rd Round
at Old Trafford

Manchester United 4 Barnet 1

CLUB CAREER RECORD	Apps	Subs	Goals
Premiership	0		0
League Division 1	0		0
League Division 2	0		0
FA Cup	0		0
League Cup	1		0
European Cup / Champions League	0		0
European Cup-Winners' Cup	0		0
UEFA Cup / Inter-Cities' Fairs Cup	0		0
Other Matches	0		0
OVERALL TOTAL	**1**		**0**

Opponents	PREM A S G	FLD 1 A S G	FLD 2 A S G	FAC A S G	LC A S G	EC/CL A S G	ECWC A S G	UEFA A S G	OTHER A S G	TOTAL A S G
1 Barnet	- - -	- - -	- - -	- - -	1 - -	- - -	- - -	- - -	- - -	1 - -

ALF EDGE

DEBUT (Full Appearance)

Saturday 03/10/1891
FA Cup 1st Qualifying Round
at North Road

Newton Heath 5 Manchester City 1

CLUB CAREER RECORD	Apps	Subs	Goals
Premiership	0		0
League Division 1	0		0
League Division 2	0		0
FA Cup	3		3
League Cup	0		0
European Cup / Champions League	0		0
European Cup-Winners' Cup	0		0
UEFA Cup / Inter-Cities' Fairs Cup	0		0
Other Matches	0		0
OVERALL TOTAL	**3**		**3**

Opponents	PREM A S G	FLD 1 A S G	FLD 2 A S G	FAC A S G	LC A S G	EC/CL A S G	ECWC A S G	UEFA A S G	OTHER A S G	TOTAL A S G
1 Blackpool	- - -	- - -	- - -	1 - 2	- - -	- - -	- - -	- - -	- - -	1 - 2
2 Manchester City	- - -	- - -	- - -	1 - 1	- - -	- - -	- - -	- - -	- - -	1 - 1
3 South Shore	- - -	- - -	- - -	1 - -	- - -	- - -	- - -	- - -	- - -	1 - -

HUGH EDMONDS

DEBUT (Full Appearance)

Saturday 11/02/1911
Football League Division 1
at Old Trafford

Manchester United 3 Bristol City 1

CLUB CAREER RECORD	Apps	Subs	Goals
Premiership	0		0
League Division 1	43		0
League Division 2	0		0
FA Cup	7		0
League Cup	0		0
European Cup / Champions League	0		0
European Cup-Winners' Cup	0		0
UEFA Cup / Inter-Cities' Fairs Cup	0		0
Other Matches	1		0
OVERALL TOTAL	**51**		**0**

Opponents	PREM A S G	FLD 1 A S G	FLD 2 A S G	FAC A S G	LC A S G	EC/CL A S G	ECWC A S G	UEFA A S G	OTHER A S G	TOTAL A S G
1 Blackburn Rovers	- - -	1 - -	- - -	2 - -	- - -	- - -	- - -	- - -	- - -	3 - -
2 Bury	- - -	3 - -	- - -	- - -	- - -	- - -	- - -	- - -	- - -	3 - -
3 Notts County	- - -	3 - -	- - -	- - -	- - -	- - -	- - -	- - -	- - -	3 - -
4 Preston North End	- - -	3 - -	- - -	- - -	- - -	- - -	- - -	- - -	- - -	3 - -
5 Sheffield United	- - -	3 - -	- - -	- - -	- - -	- - -	- - -	- - -	- - -	3 - -
6 Sheffield Wednesday	- - -	3 - -	- - -	- - -	- - -	- - -	- - -	- - -	- - -	3 - -
7 Sunderland	- - -	3 - -	- - -	- - -	- - -	- - -	- - -	- - -	- - -	3 - -
8 Tottenham Hotspur	- - -	3 - -	- - -	- - -	- - -	- - -	- - -	- - -	- - -	3 - -
9 Arsenal	- - -	2 - -	- - -	- - -	- - -	- - -	- - -	- - -	- - -	2 - -

continued../

HUGH EDMONDS (continued)

Opponents	PREM A	PREM S	PREM G	FLD 1 A	FLD 1 S	FLD 1 G	FLD 2 A	FLD 2 S	FLD 2 G	FAC A	FAC S	FAC G	LC A	LC S	LC G	EC/CL A	EC/CL S	EC/CL G	ECWC A	ECWC S	ECWC G	UEFA A	UEFA S	UEFA G	OTHER A	OTHER S	OTHER G	TOTAL A	TOTAL S	TOTAL G
10 Bradford City	-	-	2	-	-	-	-	-	-	-	-	-	-	-	-	-	-	-	-	-	-	-	-	-	-	-	-	2	-	-
11 Everton	-	-	2	-	-	-	-	-	-	-	-	-	-	-	-	-	-	-	-	-	-	-	-	-	-	-	-	2	-	-
12 Liverpool	-	-	2	-	-	-	-	-	-	-	-	-	-	-	-	-	-	-	-	-	-	-	-	-	-	-	-	2	-	-
13 Manchester City	-	-	2	-	-	-	-	-	-	-	-	-	-	-	-	-	-	-	-	-	-	-	-	-	-	-	-	2	-	-
14 Middlesbrough	-	-	2	-	-	-	-	-	-	-	-	-	-	-	-	-	-	-	-	-	-	-	-	-	-	-	-	2	-	-
15 Newcastle United	-	-	2	-	-	-	-	-	-	-	-	-	-	-	-	-	-	-	-	-	-	-	-	-	-	-	-	2	-	-
16 Oldham Athletic	-	-	2	-	-	-	-	-	-	-	-	-	-	-	-	-	-	-	-	-	-	-	-	-	-	-	-	2	-	-
17 Reading	-	-	-	-	-	-	-	-	-	2	-	-	-	-	-	-	-	-	-	-	-	-	-	-	-	-	-	2	-	-
18 West Bromwich Albion	-	-	2	-	-	-	-	-	-	-	-	-	-	-	-	-	-	-	-	-	-	-	-	-	-	-	-	2	-	-
19 Aston Villa	-	-	1	-	-	-	-	-	-	-	-	-	-	-	-	-	-	-	-	-	-	-	-	-	-	-	-	1	-	-
20 Bolton Wanderers	-	-	1	-	-	-	-	-	-	-	-	-	-	-	-	-	-	-	-	-	-	-	-	-	-	-	-	1	-	-
21 Bristol City	-	-	1	-	-	-	-	-	-	-	-	-	-	-	-	-	-	-	-	-	-	-	-	-	-	-	-	1	-	-
22 Coventry City	-	-	-	-	-	-	-	-	-	1	-	-	-	-	-	-	-	-	-	-	-	-	-	-	-	-	-	1	-	-
23 Huddersfield Town	-	-	-	-	-	-	-	-	-	1	-	-	-	-	-	-	-	-	-	-	-	-	-	-	-	-	-	1	-	-
24 Swindon Town	-	-	-	-	-	-	-	-	-	-	-	-	-	-	-	-	-	-	-	-	-	-	-	-	1	-	-	1	-	-
25 West Ham United	-	-	-	-	-	-	-	-	-	1	-	-	-	-	-	-	-	-	-	-	-	-	-	-	-	-	-	1	-	-

DUNCAN EDWARDS

DEBUT (Full Appearance)

Saturday 04/04/1953
Football League Division 1
at Old Trafford

Manchester United 1 Cardiff City 4

CLUB CAREER RECORD	Apps	Subs	Goals
Premiership	0		0
League Division 1	151		20
League Division 2	0		0
FA Cup	12		1
League Cup	0		0
European Cup / Champions League	12		0
European Cup-Winners' Cup	0		0
UEFA Cup / Inter-Cities' Fairs Cup	0		0
Other Matches	2		0
OVERALL TOTAL	177		21

Opponents	PREM A	PREM S	PREM G	FLD 1 A	FLD 1 S	FLD 1 G	FLD 2 A	FLD 2 S	FLD 2 G	FAC A	FAC S	FAC G	LC A	LC S	LC G	EC/CL A	EC/CL S	EC/CL G	ECWC A	ECWC S	ECWC G	UEFA A	UEFA S	UEFA G	OTHER A	OTHER S	OTHER G	TOTAL A	TOTAL S	TOTAL G
1 Manchester City	-	-	9	2	-	-	1	-	-	-	-	-	-	-	-	-	-	-	-	-	-	1	-	-	-	-	-	11	-	2
2 Blackpool	-	-	10	2	-	-	-	-	-	-	-	-	-	-	-	-	-	-	-	-	-	-	-	-	-	-	-	10	-	2
3 Bolton Wanderers	-	-	9	1	-	-	-	-	-	-	-	-	-	-	-	-	-	-	-	-	-	-	-	-	-	-	-	9	-	1
4 Arsenal	-	-	8	2	-	-	-	-	-	-	-	-	-	-	-	-	-	-	-	-	-	-	-	-	-	-	-	8	-	2
5 Portsmouth	-	-	8	1	-	-	-	-	-	-	-	-	-	-	-	-	-	-	-	-	-	-	-	-	-	-	-	8	-	1
6 Cardiff City	-	-	8	-	-	-	-	-	-	-	-	-	-	-	-	-	-	-	-	-	-	-	-	-	-	-	-	8	-	-
7 Everton	-	-	6	1	-	-	1	1	-	-	-	-	-	-	-	-	-	-	-	-	-	-	-	-	-	-	-	7	-	2
8 Tottenham Hotspur	-	-	7	2	-	-	-	-	-	-	-	-	-	-	-	-	-	-	-	-	-	-	-	-	-	-	-	7	-	2
9 Newcastle United	-	-	7	1	-	-	-	-	-	-	-	-	-	-	-	-	-	-	-	-	-	-	-	-	-	-	-	7	-	1
10 Wolverhampton W.	-	-	7	1	-	-	-	-	-	-	-	-	-	-	-	-	-	-	-	-	-	-	-	-	-	-	-	7	-	1
11 Aston Villa	-	-	5	-	-	-	1	-	-	-	-	-	-	-	-	-	-	-	-	1	-	-	-	-	-	-	-	7	-	-
12 Chelsea	-	-	7	-	-	-	-	-	-	-	-	-	-	-	-	-	-	-	-	-	-	-	-	-	-	-	-	7	-	-
13 Preston North End	-	-	7	-	-	-	-	-	-	-	-	-	-	-	-	-	-	-	-	-	-	-	-	-	-	-	-	7	-	-
14 Sheffield Wednesday	-	-	7	-	-	-	-	-	-	-	-	-	-	-	-	-	-	-	-	-	-	-	-	-	-	-	-	7	-	-
15 Sunderland	-	-	6	3	-	-	-	-	-	-	-	-	-	-	-	-	-	-	-	-	-	-	-	-	-	-	-	6	-	3
16 Burnley	-	-	5	1	-	-	1	-	-	-	-	-	-	-	-	-	-	-	-	-	-	-	-	-	-	-	-	6	-	1
17 Huddersfield Town	-	-	6	1	-	-	-	-	-	-	-	-	-	-	-	-	-	-	-	-	-	-	-	-	-	-	-	6	-	1
18 Birmingham City	-	-	5	-	-	-	1	-	-	-	-	-	-	-	-	-	-	-	-	-	-	-	-	-	-	-	-	6	-	-
19 West Bromwich Albion	-	-	5	-	-	-	-	-	-	-	-	-	-	-	-	-	-	-	-	-	-	-	-	-	-	-	-	5	-	-
20 Luton Town	-	-	4	2	-	-	-	-	-	-	-	-	-	-	-	-	-	-	-	-	-	-	-	-	-	-	-	4	-	2
21 Charlton Athletic	-	-	4	-	-	-	-	-	-	-	-	-	-	-	-	-	-	-	-	-	-	-	-	-	-	-	-	4	-	-
22 Leeds United	-	-	3	-	-	-	-	-	-	-	-	-	-	-	-	-	-	-	-	-	-	-	-	-	-	-	-	3	-	-
23 Leicester City	-	-	3	-	-	-	-	-	-	-	-	-	-	-	-	-	-	-	-	-	-	-	-	-	-	-	-	3	-	-
24 Sheffield United	-	-	3	-	-	-	-	-	-	-	-	-	-	-	-	-	-	-	-	-	-	-	-	-	-	-	-	3	-	-
25 Athletic Bilbao	-	-	-	-	-	-	-	-	-	-	-	-	-	-	-	2	-	-	-	-	-	-	-	-	-	-	-	2	-	-
26 Borussia Dortmund	-	-	-	-	-	-	-	-	-	-	-	-	-	-	-	2	-	-	-	-	-	-	-	-	-	-	-	2	-	-
27 Dukla Prague	-	-	-	-	-	-	-	-	-	-	-	-	-	-	-	2	-	-	-	-	-	-	-	-	-	-	-	2	-	-
28 Reading	-	-	-	-	-	-	-	-	-	2	-	-	-	-	-	-	-	-	-	-	-	-	-	-	-	-	-	2	-	-
29 Real Madrid	-	-	-	-	-	-	-	-	-	-	-	-	-	-	-	2	-	-	-	-	-	-	-	-	-	-	-	2	-	-
30 Red Star Belgrade	-	-	-	-	-	-	-	-	-	-	-	-	-	-	-	2	-	-	-	-	-	-	-	-	-	-	-	2	-	-
31 Anderlecht	-	-	-	-	-	-	-	-	-	-	-	-	-	-	-	1	-	-	-	-	-	-	-	-	-	-	-	1	-	-
32 Bournemouth	-	-	-	-	-	-	1	-	-	-	-	-	-	-	-	-	-	-	-	-	-	-	-	-	-	-	-	1	-	-
33 Hartlepool United	-	-	-	-	-	-	1	-	-	-	-	-	-	-	-	-	-	-	-	-	-	-	-	-	-	-	-	1	-	-
34 Ipswich Town	-	-	-	-	-	-	-	-	-	1	-	-	-	-	-	-	-	-	-	-	-	-	-	-	-	-	-	1	-	-
35 Liverpool	-	-	1	-	-	-	-	-	-	-	-	-	-	-	-	-	-	-	-	-	-	-	-	-	-	-	-	1	-	-
36 Nottingham Forest	-	-	1	-	-	-	-	-	-	-	-	-	-	-	-	-	-	-	-	-	-	-	-	-	-	-	-	1	-	-
37 Shamrock Rovers	-	-	-	-	-	-	-	-	-	-	-	-	-	-	-	1	-	-	-	-	-	-	-	-	-	-	-	1	-	-
38 Workington	-	-	-	-	-	-	-	-	-	1	-	-	-	-	-	-	-	-	-	-	-	-	-	-	-	-	-	1	-	-
39 Wrexham	-	-	-	-	-	-	-	-	-	1	-	-	-	-	-	-	-	-	-	-	-	-	-	-	-	-	-	1	-	-

PAUL EDWARDS

DEBUT (Full Appearance)

Tuesday 19/08/1969
Football League Division 1
at Goodison Park

Everton 3 Manchester United 0

CLUB CAREER RECORD	Apps	Subs	Goals
Premiership	0		0
League Division 1	52	(2)	0
League Division 2	0		0
FA Cup	10		0
League Cup	4		1
European Cup / Champions League	0		0
European Cup-Winners' Cup	0		0
UEFA Cup / Inter-Cities' Fairs Cup	0		0
Other Matches	0		0
OVERALL TOTAL	66	(2)	1

Opponents	PREM A S G	FLD 1 A S G	FLD 2 A S G	FAC A S G	LC A S G	EC/CL A S G	ECWC A S G	UEFA A S G	OTHER A S G	TOTAL A S G
1 Chelsea	– –	5 –	– –	– –	1 –	– –	– –	– –	– –	6 –
2 Leeds United	– –	3 –	– –	3 –	– –	– –	– –	– –	– –	6 –
3 Manchester City	– –	1 –	– –	1 –	2 1	– –	– –	– –	– –	4 1
4 Burnley	– –	4 –	– –	– –	– –	– –	– –	– –	– –	4 –
5 Southampton	– –	2 –	– –	2 –	– –	– –	– –	– –	– –	4 –
6 West Ham United	– –	4 –	– –	– –	– –	– –	– –	– –	– –	4 –
7 Coventry City	– –	3 –	– –	– –	– –	– –	– –	– –	– –	3 –
8 Crystal Palace	– –	3 –	– –	– –	– –	– –	– –	– –	– –	3 –
9 Everton	– –	3 –	– –	– –	– –	– –	– –	– –	– –	3 –
10 Ipswich Town	– –	2 –	– –	1 –	– –	– –	– –	– –	– –	3 –
11 Stoke City	– –	3 –	– –	– –	– –	– –	– –	– –	– –	3 –
12 Wolverhampton W.	– –	3 –	– –	– –	– –	– –	– –	– –	– –	3 –
13 Tottenham Hotspur	– –	2 (1) –	– –	– –	– –	– –	– –	– –	– –	2 (1) –
14 Derby County	– –	2 –	– –	– –	– –	– –	– –	– –	– –	2 –
15 Liverpool	– –	2 –	– –	– –	– –	– –	– –	– –	– –	2 –
16 Middlesbrough	– –	– –	– –	2 –	– –	– –	– –	– –	– –	2 –
17 Newcastle United	– –	2 –	– –	– –	– –	– –	– –	– –	– –	2 –
18 West Bromwich Albion	– –	2 –	– –	– –	– –	– –	– –	– –	– –	2 –
19 Arsenal	– –	1 (1) –	– –	– –	– –	– –	– –	– –	– –	1 (1) –
20 Aldershot	– –	– –	– –	– –	1 –	– –	– –	– –	– –	1 –
21 Huddersfield Town	– –	1 –	– –	– –	– –	– –	– –	– –	– –	1 –
22 Leicester City	– –	1 –	– –	– –	– –	– –	– –	– –	– –	1 –
23 Northampton Town	– –	– –	– –	1 –	– –	– –	– –	– –	– –	1 –
24 Nottingham Forest	– –	1 –	– –	– –	– –	– –	– –	– –	– –	1 –
25 Sheffield Wednesday	– –	1 –	– –	– –	– –	– –	– –	– –	– –	1 –
26 Sunderland	– –	1 –	– –	– –	– –	– –	– –	– –	– –	1 –

DAVID ELLIS

DEBUT (Full Appearance)

Saturday 25/08/1923
Football League Division 2
at Ashton Gate

Bristol City 1 Manchester United 2

CLUB CAREER RECORD	Apps	Subs	Goals
Premiership	0		0
League Division 1	0		0
League Division 2	11		0
FA Cup	0		0
League Cup	0		0
European Cup / Champions League	0		0
European Cup-Winners' Cup	0		0
UEFA Cup / Inter-Cities' Fairs Cup	0		0
Other Matches	0		0
OVERALL TOTAL	11		0

Opponents	PREM A S G	FLD 1 A S G	FLD 2 A S G	FAC A S G	LC A S G	EC/CL A S G	ECWC A S G	UEFA A S G	OTHER A S G	TOTAL A S G
1 Bristol City	– –	– –	2 –	– –	– –	– –	– –	– –	– –	2 –
2 Bury	– –	– –	2 –	– –	– –	– –	– –	– –	– –	2 –
3 Derby County	– –	– –	2 –	– –	– –	– –	– –	– –	– –	2 –
4 South Shields	– –	– –	2 –	– –	– –	– –	– –	– –	– –	2 –
5 Southampton	– –	– –	2 –	– –	– –	– –	– –	– –	– –	2 –
6 Nelson	– –	– –	1 –	– –	– –	– –	– –	– –	– –	1 –

FRED ERENTZ

DEBUT (Full Appearance)

Saturday 03/09/1892
Football League Division 1
at Ewood Park

Blackburn Rovers 4 Newton Heath 3

CLUB CAREER RECORD	Apps	Subs	Goals
Premiership	0		0
League Division 1	51	2	
League Division 2	229		7
FA Cup	23		0
League Cup	0		0
European Cup / Champions League	0		0
European Cup–Winners' Cup	0		0
UEFA Cup / Inter–Cities' Fairs Cup	0		0
Other Matches	7		0
OVERALL TOTAL	**310**		**9**

Opponents	PREM			FLD 1			FLD 2			FAC			LC			EC/CL			ECWC			UEFA			OTHER			TOTAL		
	A	S	G	A	S	G	A	S	G	A	S	G	A	S	G	A	S	G	A	S	G	A	S	G	A	S	G	A	S	G
1 Lincoln City	–	–	–	–	–	–	15	–	–	1	–	–	–	–	–	–	–	–	–	–	–	–	–	–	–	–	–	16	–	–
2 Arsenal	–	–	–	–	–	–	15	–	1	–	–	–	–	–	–	–	–	–	–	–	–	–	–	–	–	–	–	15	–	1
3 Burton Swifts	–	–	–	–	–	–	14	–	–	–	–	–	–	–	–	–	–	–	–	–	–	–	–	–	–	–	–	14	–	–
4 Walsall	–	–	–	–	–	–	12	–	1	1	–	–	–	–	–	–	–	–	–	–	–	–	–	–	–	–	–	13	–	1
5 Birmingham City	–	–	–	–	–	–	10	–	–	–	–	–	–	–	–	–	–	–	–	–	–	–	–	–	2	–	–	12	–	–
6 Burnley	–	–	–	2	–	–	6	–	–	2	–	–	–	–	–	–	–	–	–	–	–	–	–	–	2	–	–	12	–	–
7 Grimsby Town	–	–	–	–	–	–	12	–	–	–	–	–	–	–	–	–	–	–	–	–	–	–	–	–	–	–	–	12	–	–
8 Blackpool	–	–	–	–	–	–	9	–	–	2	–	–	–	–	–	–	–	–	–	–	–	–	–	–	–	–	–	11	–	–
9 Gainsborough Trinity	–	–	–	–	–	–	11	–	–	–	–	–	–	–	–	–	–	–	–	–	–	–	–	–	–	–	–	11	–	–
10 Leicester City	–	–	–	–	–	–	11	–	–	–	–	–	–	–	–	–	–	–	–	–	–	–	–	–	–	–	–	11	–	–
11 Port Vale	–	–	–	–	–	–	11	–	–	–	–	–	–	–	–	–	–	–	–	–	–	–	–	–	–	–	–	11	–	–
12 Darwen	–	–	–	1	–	–	9	–	–	–	–	–	–	–	–	–	–	–	–	–	–	–	–	–	–	–	–	10	–	–
13 Manchester City	–	–	–	–	–	–	10	–	–	–	–	–	–	–	–	–	–	–	–	–	–	–	–	–	–	–	–	10	–	–
14 Loughborough Town	–	–	–	–	–	–	8	–	–	–	–	–	–	–	–	–	–	–	–	–	–	–	–	–	–	–	–	8	–	–
15 Notts County	–	–	–	2	–	–	6	–	–	–	–	–	–	–	–	–	–	–	–	–	–	–	–	–	–	–	–	8	–	–
16 Middlesbrough	–	–	–	–	–	–	6	–	2	1	–	–	–	–	–	–	–	–	–	–	–	–	–	–	–	–	–	7	–	2
17 Barnsley	–	–	–	–	–	–	7	–	–	–	–	–	–	–	–	–	–	–	–	–	–	–	–	–	–	–	–	7	–	–
18 Blackburn Rovers	–	–	–	4	–	–	–	–	–	3	–	–	–	–	–	–	–	–	–	–	–	–	–	–	–	–	–	7	–	–
19 Bolton Wanderers	–	–	–	4	–	–	2	–	–	–	–	–	–	–	–	–	–	–	–	–	–	–	–	–	–	–	–	6	–	–
20 Burton Wanderers	–	–	–	–	–	–	6	–	–	–	–	–	–	–	–	–	–	–	–	–	–	–	–	–	–	–	–	6	–	–
21 Chesterfield	–	–	–	–	–	–	6	–	–	–	–	–	–	–	–	–	–	–	–	–	–	–	–	–	–	–	–	6	–	–
22 Luton Town	–	–	–	–	–	–	6	–	–	–	–	–	–	–	–	–	–	–	–	–	–	–	–	–	–	–	–	6	–	–
23 New Brighton Tower	–	–	–	–	–	–	6	–	–	–	–	–	–	–	–	–	–	–	–	–	–	–	–	–	–	–	–	6	–	–
24 Newcastle United	–	–	–	–	–	–	6	–	–	–	–	–	–	–	–	–	–	–	–	–	–	–	–	–	–	–	–	6	–	–
25 Sheffield Wednesday	–	–	–	4	–	–	2	–	–	–	–	–	–	–	–	–	–	–	–	–	–	–	–	–	–	–	–	6	–	–
26 Sunderland	–	–	–	4	–	–	–	–	–	–	–	–	–	–	–	–	–	–	–	–	–	–	–	–	2	–	–	6	–	–
27 Glossop	–	–	–	–	–	–	5	–	2	–	–	–	–	–	–	–	–	–	–	–	–	–	–	–	–	–	–	5	–	2
28 Stoke City	–	–	–	4	–	1	–	–	–	1	–	–	–	–	–	–	–	–	–	–	–	–	–	–	–	–	–	5	–	1
29 Derby County	–	–	–	3	–	–	–	–	–	2	–	–	–	–	–	–	–	–	–	–	–	–	–	–	–	–	–	5	–	–
30 Liverpool	–	–	–	–	–	–	2	–	–	2	–	–	–	–	–	–	–	–	–	–	–	–	–	–	1	–	–	5	–	–
31 West Bromwich Albion	–	–	–	3	–	1	1	–	–	–	–	–	–	–	–	–	–	–	–	–	–	–	–	–	–	–	–	4	–	1
32 Aston Villa	–	–	–	4	–	–	–	–	–	–	–	–	–	–	–	–	–	–	–	–	–	–	–	–	–	–	–	4	–	–
33 Crewe Alexandra	–	–	–	–	–	–	4	–	–	–	–	–	–	–	–	–	–	–	–	–	–	–	–	–	–	–	–	4	–	–
34 Nottingham Forest	–	–	–	4	–	–	–	–	–	–	–	–	–	–	–	–	–	–	–	–	–	–	–	–	–	–	–	4	–	–
35 Preston North End	–	–	–	3	–	–	1	–	–	–	–	–	–	–	–	–	–	–	–	–	–	–	–	–	–	–	–	4	–	–
36 Rotherham United	–	–	–	–	–	–	3	–	1	–	–	–	–	–	–	–	–	–	–	–	–	–	–	–	–	–	–	3	–	1
37 Everton	–	–	–	3	–	–	–	–	–	–	–	–	–	–	–	–	–	–	–	–	–	–	–	–	–	–	–	3	–	–
38 Wolverhampton W.	–	–	–	3	–	–	–	–	–	–	–	–	–	–	–	–	–	–	–	–	–	–	–	–	–	–	–	3	–	–
39 Accrington Stanley	–	–	–	2	–	–	–	–	–	–	–	–	–	–	–	–	–	–	–	–	–	–	–	–	–	–	–	2	–	–
40 Bristol City	–	–	–	–	–	–	2	–	–	–	–	–	–	–	–	–	–	–	–	–	–	–	–	–	–	–	–	2	–	–
41 Stockport County	–	–	–	–	–	–	2	–	–	–	–	–	–	–	–	–	–	–	–	–	–	–	–	–	–	–	–	2	–	–
42 Tottenham Hotspur	–	–	–	–	–	–	–	–	–	2	–	–	–	–	–	–	–	–	–	–	–	–	–	–	–	–	–	2	–	–
43 Burton United	–	–	–	–	–	–	1	–	–	–	–	–	–	–	–	–	–	–	–	–	–	–	–	–	–	–	–	1	–	–
44 Bury	–	–	–	–	–	–	1	–	–	–	–	–	–	–	–	–	–	–	–	–	–	–	–	–	–	–	–	1	–	–
45 Doncaster Rovers	–	–	–	–	–	–	1	–	–	–	–	–	–	–	–	–	–	–	–	–	–	–	–	–	–	–	–	1	–	–
46 Kettering	–	–	–	–	–	–	–	–	–	1	–	–	–	–	–	–	–	–	–	–	–	–	–	–	–	–	–	1	–	–
47 Nelson	–	–	–	–	–	–	–	–	–	1	–	–	–	–	–	–	–	–	–	–	–	–	–	–	–	–	–	1	–	–
48 Portsmouth	–	–	–	–	–	–	–	–	–	1	–	–	–	–	–	–	–	–	–	–	–	–	–	–	–	–	–	1	–	–
49 Sheffield United	–	–	–	1	–	–	–	–	–	–	–	–	–	–	–	–	–	–	–	–	–	–	–	–	–	–	–	1	–	–
50 South Shore	–	–	–	–	–	–	–	–	–	1	–	–	–	–	–	–	–	–	–	–	–	–	–	–	–	–	–	1	–	–
51 Southampton	–	–	–	–	–	–	–	–	–	1	–	–	–	–	–	–	–	–	–	–	–	–	–	–	–	–	–	1	–	–
52 West Manchester	–	–	–	–	–	–	–	–	–	1	–	–	–	–	–	–	–	–	–	–	–	–	–	–	–	–	–	1	–	–

HARRY ERENTZ

DEBUT (Full Appearance)

Saturday 08/01/1898
Football League Division 2
at Manor Field

Arsenal 5 Newton Heath 1

CLUB CAREER RECORD	Apps	Subs	Goals
Premiership	0		0
League Division 1	0		0
League Division 2	6		0
FA Cup	3		0
League Cup	0		0
European Cup / Champions League	0		0
European Cup-Winners' Cup	0		0
UEFA Cup / Inter-Cities' Fairs Cup	0		0
Other Matches	0		0
OVERALL TOTAL	**9**		**0**

Opponents	PREM A	S	G	FLD 1 A	S	G	FLD 2 A	S	G	FAC A	S	G	LC A	S	G	EC/CL A	S	G	ECWC A	S	G	UEFA A	S	G	OTHER A	S	G	TOTAL A	S	G
1 Liverpool	-	-	-	-	-	-	-	-	-	2	-	-	-	-	-	-	-	-	-	-	-	-	-	-	-	-	-	2	-	-
2 Loughborough Town	-	-	-	-	-	-	2	-	-	-	-	-	-	-	-	-	-	-	-	-	-	-	-	-	-	-	-	2	-	-
3 Arsenal	-	-	-	-	-	-	1	-	-	-	-	-	-	-	-	-	-	-	-	-	-	-	-	-	-	-	-	1	-	-
4 Blackpool	-	-	-	-	-	-	1	-	-	-	-	-	-	-	-	-	-	-	-	-	-	-	-	-	-	-	-	1	-	-
5 Gainsborough Trinity	-	-	-	-	-	-	1	-	-	-	-	-	-	-	-	-	-	-	-	-	-	-	-	-	-	-	-	1	-	-
6 Grimsby Town	-	-	-	-	-	-	1	-	-	-	-	-	-	-	-	-	-	-	-	-	-	-	-	-	-	-	-	1	-	-
7 Walsall	-	-	-	-	-	-	-	-	-	1	-	-	-	-	-	-	-	-	-	-	-	-	-	-	-	-	-	1	-	-

GEORGE EVANS

DEBUT (Full Appearance, 1 goal)

Saturday 04/10/1890
FA Cup 1st Qualifying Round
at North Road

Newton Heath 2 Higher Walton 0

CLUB CAREER RECORD	Apps	Subs	Goals
Premiership	0		0
League Division 1	0		0
League Division 2	0		0
FA Cup	1		1
League Cup	0		0
European Cup / Champions League	0		0
European Cup-Winners' Cup	0		0
UEFA Cup / Inter-Cities' Fairs Cup	0		0
Other Matches	0		0
OVERALL TOTAL	**1**		**1**

Opponents	PREM A	S	G	FLD 1 A	S	G	FLD 2 A	S	G	FAC A	S	G	LC A	S	G	EC/CL A	S	G	ECWC A	S	G	UEFA A	S	G	OTHER A	S	G	TOTAL A	S	G
1 Higher Walton	-	-	-	-	-	-	-	-	-	1	-	1	-	-	-	-	-	-	-	-	-	-	-	-	-	-	-	1	-	1

SIDNEY EVANS

DEBUT (Full Appearance)

Saturday 12/04/1924
Football League Division 2
at Old Trafford

Manchester United 5 Crystal Palace 1

CLUB CAREER RECORD	Apps	Subs	Goals
Premiership	0		0
League Division 1	0		0
League Division 2	6		2
FA Cup	0		0
League Cup	0		0
European Cup / Champions League	0		0
European Cup-Winners' Cup	0		0
UEFA Cup / Inter-Cities' Fairs Cup	0		0
Other Matches	0		0
OVERALL TOTAL	**6**		**2**

Opponents	PREM A	S	G	FLD 1 A	S	G	FLD 2 A	S	G	FAC A	S	G	LC A	S	G	EC/CL A	S	G	ECWC A	S	G	UEFA A	S	G	OTHER A	S	G	TOTAL A	S	G
1 Leyton Orient	-	-	-	-	-	-	2	-	2	-	-	-	-	-	-	-	-	-	-	-	-	-	-	-	-	-	-	2	-	2
2 Crystal Palace	-	-	-	-	-	-	2	-	-	-	-	-	-	-	-	-	-	-	-	-	-	-	-	-	-	-	-	2	-	-
3 Sheffield Wednesday	-	-	-	-	-	-	2	-	-	-	-	-	-	-	-	-	-	-	-	-	-	-	-	-	-	-	-	2	-	-

JONNY EVANS

DEBUT (Full Appearance)

Wednesday 26/09/2007
League Cup 3rd Round
at Old Trafford

Manchester United 0 Coventry City 2

CLUB CAREER RECORD	Apps	Subs	Goals
Premiership	0		0
League Division 1	0		0
League Division 2	0		0
FA Cup	0		0
League Cup	1		0
European Cup / Champions League	1	(1)	0
European Cup-Winners' Cup	0		0
UEFA Cup / Inter-Cities' Fairs Cup	0		0
Other Matches	0		0
OVERALL TOTAL	**2**	**(1)**	**0**

Opponents	PREM A	S	G	FLD 1 A	S	G	FLD 2 A	S	G	FAC A	S	G	LC A	S	G	EC/CL A	S	G	ECWC A	S	G	UEFA A	S	G	OTHER A	S	G	TOTAL A	S	G
1 Coventry City	-	-	-	-	-	-	-	-	-	-	-	-	1	-	-	-	-	-	-	-	-	-	-	-	-	-	-	1	-	-
2 Roma	-	-	-	-	-	-	-	-	-	-	-	-	-	-	-	1	-	-	-	-	-	-	-	-	-	-	-	1	-	-
3 Dynamo Kiev	-	-	-	-	-	-	-	-	-	-	-	-	-	-	-	-	(1)	-	-	-	-	-	-	-	-	-	-	-	(1)	-

PATRICE EVRA

DEBUT (Full Appearance)

Saturday 14/01/2006
FA Premiership
at Eastlands Stadium

Manchester City 3 Manchester United 1

CLUB CAREER RECORD	Apps	Subs	Goals
Premiership	62	(6)	1
League Division 1	0		0
League Division 2	0		0
FA Cup	7	(2)	0
League Cup	1	(2)	0
European Cup / Champions League	14	(3)	1
European Cup-Winners' Cup	0		0
UEFA Cup / Inter-Cities' Fairs Cup	0		0
Other Matches	1		0
OVERALL TOTAL	**85**	**(13)**	**2**

	Opponents	PREM A S G	FLD 1 A S G	FLD 2 A S G	FAC A S G	LC A S G	EC/CL A S G	ECWC A S G	UEFA A S G	OTHER A S G	TOTAL A S G
1	Aston Villa	4 – –	– – –	– – –	2 – –	– – –	– – –	– – –	– – –	– – –	6 – –
2	Arsenal	3 (2) –	– – –	– – –	– – –	1 – –	– – –	– – –	– – –	– – –	4 (2) –
3	Wigan Athletic	4 (1) –	– – –	– – –	– – –	– (1) –	– – –	– – –	– – –	– – –	4 (2) –
4	Blackburn Rovers	4 – –	– – –	– – –	– – –	1 – –	– – –	– – –	– – –	– – –	5 – –
5	Fulham	5 – –	– – –	– – –	– – –	– – –	– – –	– – –	– – –	– – –	5 – –
6	Liverpool	5 – –	– – –	– – –	– – –	– – –	– – –	– – –	– – –	– – –	5 – –
7	Portsmouth	3 – –	– – –	– – –	– – –	2 – –	– – –	– – –	– – –	– – –	5 – –
8	Tottenham Hotspur	4 – –	– – –	– – –	– – –	1 – –	– – –	– – –	– – –	– – –	5 – –
9	Newcastle United	3 (2) –	– – –	– – –	– – –	– – –	– – –	– – –	– – –	– – –	3 (2) –
10	Everton	4 1	– – –	– – –	– – –	– – –	– – –	– – –	– – –	– – –	4 1
11	West Ham United	4 – –	– – –	– – –	– – –	– – –	– – –	– – –	– – –	– – –	4 – –
12	Chelsea	1 (1) –	– – –	– – –	– – –	– – –	1 – –	– – –	1 – –	– – –	3 (1) –
13	Roma	– – –	– – –	– – –	– – –	– – –	2 (1) 1	– – –	– – –	– – –	2 (1) 1
14	Reading	2 – –	– – –	– – –	– (1) –	– – –	– – –	– – –	– – –	– – –	2 (1) –
15	Barcelona	– – –	– – –	– – –	– – –	– – –	2 – –	– – –	– – –	– – –	2 – –
16	Birmingham City	2 – –	– – –	– – –	– – –	– – –	– – –	– – –	– – –	– – –	2 – –
17	Bolton Wanderers	2 – –	– – –	– – –	– – –	– – –	– – –	– – –	– – –	– – –	2 – –
18	Charlton Athletic	2 – –	– – –	– – –	– – –	– – –	– – –	– – –	– – –	– – –	2 – –
19	Derby County	2 – –	– – –	– – –	– – –	– – –	– – –	– – –	– – –	– – –	2 – –
20	Manchester City	2 – –	– – –	– – –	– – –	– – –	– – –	– – –	– – –	– – –	2 – –
21	Middlesbrough	2 – –	– – –	– – –	– – –	– – –	– – –	– – –	– – –	– – –	2 – –
22	Olympique Lyonnais	– – –	– – –	– – –	– – –	– – –	2 – –	– – –	– – –	– – –	2 – –
23	Sheffield United	2 – –	– – –	– – –	– – –	– – –	– – –	– – –	– – –	– – –	2 – –
24	Sporting Lisbon	– – –	– – –	– – –	– – –	– – –	2 – –	– – –	– – –	– – –	2 – –
25	Sunderland	2 – –	– – –	– – –	– – –	– – –	– – –	– – –	– – –	– – –	2 – –
26	Copenhagen	– – –	– – –	– – –	– – –	– – –	1 (1) –	– – –	– – –	– – –	1 (1) –
27	AC Milan	– – –	– – –	– – –	– – –	– – –	1 – –	– – –	– – –	– – –	1 – –
28	Benfica	– – –	– – –	– – –	– – –	– – –	1 – –	– – –	– – –	– – –	1 – –
29	Dynamo Kiev	– – –	– – –	– – –	– – –	– – –	1 – –	– – –	– – –	– – –	1 – –
30	Lille Metropole	– – –	– – –	– – –	– – –	– – –	1 – –	– – –	– – –	– – –	1 – –
31	Watford	– – –	– – –	– – –	– – –	1 – –	– – –	– – –	– – –	– – –	1 – –
32	Glasgow Celtic	– – –	– – –	– – –	– – –	– – –	– (1) –	– – –	– – –	– – –	– (1) –
33	Southend United	– – –	– – –	– – –	– – –	– (1) –	– – –	– – –	– – –	– – –	– (1) –
34	Wolverhampton W.	– – –	– – –	– – –	– (1) –	– – –	– – –	– – –	– – –	– – –	– (1) –

JOE FALL

DEBUT (Full Appearance)

Saturday 02/09/1893
Football League Division 1
at North Road

Newton Heath 3 Burnley 2

CLUB CAREER RECORD	Apps	Subs	Goals
Premiership	0		0
League Division 1	23		0
League Division 2	0		0
FA Cup	3		0
League Cup	0		0
European Cup / Champions League	0		0
European Cup-Winners' Cup	0		0
UEFA Cup / Inter-Cities' Fairs Cup	0		0
Other Matches	1		0
OVERALL TOTAL	**27**		**0**

	Opponents	PREM A S G	FLD 1 A S G	FLD 2 A S G	FAC A S G	LC A S G	EC/CL A S G	ECWC A S G	UEFA A S G	OTHER A S G	TOTAL A S G
1	Blackburn Rovers	– –	1 – –	– – –	2 – –	– – –	– – –	– – –	– – –	– – –	3 –
2	Burnley	– –	2 – –	– – –	– – –	– – –	– – –	– – –	– – –	– – –	2 –
3	Darwen	– –	2 – –	– – –	– – –	– – –	– – –	– – –	– – –	– – –	2 –
4	Derby County	– –	2 – –	– – –	– – –	– – –	– – –	– – –	– – –	– – –	2 –
5	Everton	– –	2 – –	– – –	– – –	– – –	– – –	– – –	– – –	– – –	2 –
6	Preston North End	– –	2 – –	– – –	– – –	– – –	– – –	– – –	– – –	– – –	2 –
7	Sheffield Wednesday	– –	2 – –	– – –	– – –	– – –	– – –	– – –	– – –	– – –	2 –
8	Sunderland	– –	2 – –	– – –	– – –	– – –	– – –	– – –	– – –	– – –	2 –
9	West Bromwich Albion	– –	2 – –	– – –	– – –	– – –	– – –	– – –	– – –	– – –	2 –
10	Wolverhampton W.	– –	2 – –	– – –	– – –	– – –	– – –	– – –	– – –	– – –	2 –
11	Aston Villa	– –	1 – –	– – –	– – –	– – –	– – –	– – –	– – –	– – –	1 –
12	Bolton Wanderers	– –	1 – –	– – –	– – –	– – –	– – –	– – –	– – –	– – –	1 –
13	Liverpool	– –	– – –	– – –	– – –	– – –	– – –	– – –	1 – –	– – –	1 –
14	Middlesbrough	– –	– – –	– – –	1 – –	– – –	– – –	– – –	– – –	– – –	1 –
15	Nottingham Forest	– –	1 – –	– – –	– – –	– – –	– – –	– – –	– – –	– – –	1 –
16	Sheffield United	– –	1 – –	– – –	– – –	– – –	– – –	– – –	– – –	– – –	1 –

ALF FARMAN

DEBUT (Full Appearance)

Saturday 18/01/1889
FA Cup 1st Round
at Deepdale

Preston North End 6 Newton Heath 1

CLUB CAREER RECORD	Apps	Subs	Goals
Premiership	0		0
League Division 1	46		18
League Division 2	5		0
FA Cup	7		6
League Cup	0		0
European Cup / Champions League	0		0
European Cup-Winners' Cup	0		0
UEFA Cup / Inter-Cities' Fairs Cup	0		0
Other Matches	3		4
OVERALL TOTAL	61		28

Opponents	PREM A S G	FLD 1 A S G	FLD 2 A S G	FAC A S G	LC A S G	EC/CL A S G	ECWC A S G	UEFA A S G	OTHER A S G	TOTAL A S G
1 Blackburn Rovers	– –	4 4	– –	1 –	–	–	–	–	– –	5 4
2 Stoke City	– –	4 3	–	–	–	–	–	–	– –	4 3
3 Bolton Wanderers	– –	4 1	–	–	–	–	–	–	– –	4 1
4 Nottingham Forest	– –	4 1	–	–	–	–	–	–	– –	4 1
5 Preston North End	– –	3 –	–	1 –	–	–	–	–	– –	4 –
6 Burnley	– –	3 3	–	–	–	–	–	–	– –	3 3
7 Derby County	– –	3 3	–	–	–	–	–	–	– –	3 3
8 Everton	– –	3 1	–	–	–	–	–	–	– –	3 1
9 Sheffield Wednesday	– –	3 1	–	–	–	–	–	–	– –	3 1
10 Wolverhampton W.	– –	3 1	–	–	–	–	–	–	– –	3 1
11 Aston Villa	– –	3 –	–	–	–	–	–	–	– –	3 –
12 Sunderland	– –	3 –	–	–	–	–	–	–	– –	3 –
13 Birmingham City	– –	– –	–	–	–	–	–	–	2 4	2 4
14 Accrington Stanley	– –	2 –	–	–	–	–	–	–	– –	2 –
15 Notts County	– –	2 –	–	–	–	–	–	–	– –	2 –
16 Manchester City	– –	– –	–	1 2	–	–	–	–	– –	1 2
17 Blackpool	– –	– –	–	1 1	–	–	–	–	– –	1 1
18 Higher Walton	– –	– –	–	1 1	–	–	–	–	– –	1 1
19 Middlesbrough	– –	– –	–	1 1	–	–	–	–	– –	1 1
20 South Shore	– –	– –	–	1 1	–	–	–	–	– –	1 1
21 Burton Wanderers	– –	– –	1	–	–	–	–	–	– –	1 –
22 Crewe Alexandra	– –	– –	1	–	–	–	–	–	– –	1 –
23 Darwen	– –	1 –	–	–	–	–	–	–	– –	1 –
24 Grimsby Town	– –	– –	1	–	–	–	–	–	– –	1 –
25 Liverpool	– –	– –	–	–	–	–	–	1 –	– –	1 –
26 Rotherham United	– –	– –	1	–	–	–	–	–	– –	1 –
27 Walsall	– –	– –	1	–	–	–	–	–	– –	1 –
28 West Bromwich Albion	– –	1 –	–	–	–	–	–	–	– –	1 –

JOHN FEEHAN

DEBUT (Full Appearance)

Saturday 05/11/1949
Football League Division 1
at Old Trafford

Manchester United 6 Huddersfield Town 0

CLUB CAREER RECORD	Apps	Subs	Goals
Premiership	0		0
League Division 1	12		0
League Division 2	0		0
FA Cup	2		0
League Cup	0		0
European Cup / Champions League	0		0
European Cup-Winners' Cup	0		0
UEFA Cup / Inter-Cities' Fairs Cup	0		0
Other Matches	0		0
OVERALL TOTAL	14		0

Opponents	PREM A S G	FLD 1 A S G	FLD 2 A S G	FAC A S G	LC A S G	EC/CL A S G	ECWC A S G	UEFA A S G	OTHER A S G	TOTAL A S G
1 Arsenal	– –	2 –	–	–	–	–	–	–	– –	2 –
2 Birmingham City	– –	1 –	–	–	–	–	–	–	– –	1 –
3 Blackpool	– –	1 –	–	–	–	–	–	–	– –	1 –
4 Derby County	– –	1 –	–	–	–	–	–	–	– –	1 –
5 Everton	– –	1 –	–	–	–	–	–	–	– –	1 –
6 Fulham	– –	1 –	–	–	–	–	–	–	– –	1 –
7 Huddersfield Town	– –	1 –	–	–	–	–	–	–	– –	1 –
8 Manchester City	– –	1 –	–	–	–	–	–	–	– –	1 –
9 Portsmouth	– –	– –	–	1 –	–	–	–	–	– –	1 –
10 Stoke City	– –	1 –	–	–	–	–	–	–	– –	1 –
11 Sunderland	– –	1 –	–	–	–	–	–	–	– –	1 –
12 West Bromwich Albion	– –	1 –	–	–	–	–	–	–	– –	1 –
13 Weymouth Town	– –	– –	–	1 –	–	–	–	–	– –	1 –

G FELTON

DEBUT (Full Appearance)

Saturday 25/10/1890
FA Cup 2nd Qualifying Round
at Bootle Park

Bootle Reserves 1 Newton Heath 0

CLUB CAREER RECORD	Apps	Subs	Goals
Premiership	0		0
League Division 1	0		0
League Division 2	0		0
FA Cup	1		0
League Cup	0		0
European Cup / Champions League	0		0
European Cup-Winners' Cup	0		0
UEFA Cup / Inter-Cities' Fairs Cup	0		0
Other Matches	0		0
OVERALL TOTAL	**1**		**0**

Opponents	PREM A S G	FLD 1 A S G	FLD 2 A S G	FAC A S G	LC A S G	EC/CL A S G	ECWC A S G	UEFA A S G	OTHER A S G	TOTAL A S G
1 Bootle Reserves	– – –	– – –	– – –	1 – –	– – –	– – –	– – –	– – –	– – –	1 – –

RIO FERDINAND

DEBUT (Full Appearance)

Tuesday 27/08/2002
Champions League Qualifying Round 2nd Leg
at Old Trafford

Manchester United 5 Zalaegerszeg 0

CLUB CAREER RECORD	Apps	Subs	Goals
Premiership	183	(1)	6
League Division 1	0		0
League Division 2	0		0
FA Cup	20	(1)	0
League Cup	9	(1)	0
European Cup / Champions League	49	(1)	1
European Cup-Winners' Cup	0		0
UEFA Cup / Inter-Cities' Fairs Cup	0		0
Other Matches	2		0
OVERALL TOTAL	**263**	**(4)**	**7**

Opponents	PREM A S G	FLD 1 A S G	FLD 2 A S G	FAC A S G	LC A S G	EC/CL A S G	ECWC A S G	UEFA A S G	OTHER A S G	TOTAL A S G
1 Arsenal	10 – –	– – –	– – –	3 – –	– – –	– – –	– – –	– – –	1 – –	14 – –
2 Middlesbrough	10 (1) –	– – –	– – –	3 – –	– – –	– – –	– – –	– – –	– – –	13 (1) –
3 Aston Villa	11 – 1	– – –	– – –	2 – –	– – –	– – –	– – –	– – –	– – –	13 – 1
4 Blackburn Rovers	9 – –	– – –	– – –	– – –	4 – –	– – –	– – –	– – –	– – –	13 – –
5 Newcastle United	11 – 1	– – –	– – –	– – –	1 – –	– – –	– – –	– – –	– – –	12 – 1
6 Chelsea	8 – –	– – –	– – –	1 – –	1 – –	1 – –	– – –	– – –	1 – –	12 – –
7 Tottenham Hotspur	11 – –	– – –	– – –	– – –	1 – –	– – –	– – –	– – –	– – –	12 – –
8 Manchester City	11 – –	– – –	– – –	– – –	– – –	– – –	– – –	– – –	– – –	11 – –
9 Portsmouth	8 – –	– – –	– – –	3 – –	– – –	– – –	– – –	– – –	– – –	11 – –
10 Liverpool	9 – 2	– – –	– – –	– – –	1 – –	– – –	– – –	– – –	– – –	10 – 2
11 Bolton Wanderers	10 – –	– – –	– – –	– – –	– – –	– – –	– – –	– – –	– – –	10 – –
12 Birmingham City	9 – –	– – –	– – –	– – –	– (1) –	– – –	– – –	– – –	– – –	9 (1) –
13 Charlton Athletic	9 – –	– – –	– – –	– – –	– – –	– – –	– – –	– – –	– – –	9 – –
14 Fulham	9 – –	– – –	– – –	– – –	– – –	– – –	– – –	– – –	– – –	9 – –
15 Everton	7 – –	– – –	– – –	1 – –	– – –	– – –	– – –	– – –	– – –	8 – –
16 West Bromwich Albion	5 – 1	– – –	– – –	– – –	1 – –	– – –	– – –	– – –	– – –	6 – 1
17 Wigan Athletic	5 – 1	– – –	– – –	– – –	1 – –	– – –	– – –	– – –	– – –	6 – 1
18 Sunderland	6 – –	– – –	– – –	– – –	– – –	– – –	– – –	– – –	– – –	6 – –
19 West Ham United	5 – –	– – –	– – –	1 – –	– – –	– – –	– – –	– – –	– – –	6 – –
20 Reading	4 – –	– – –	– – –	1 – –	– – –	– – –	– – –	– – –	– – –	5 – –
21 Roma	– – –	– – –	– – –	– – –	– – –	5 – –	– – –	– – –	– – –	5 – –
22 Southampton	4 – –	– – –	– – –	1 – –	– – –	– – –	– – –	– – –	– – –	5 – –
23 Benfica	– – –	– – –	– – –	– – –	– – –	4 – –	– – –	– – –	– – –	4 – –
24 Lille Metropole	– – –	– – –	– – –	– – –	– – –	4 – –	– – –	– – –	– – –	4 – –
25 Leeds United	3 – –	– – –	– – –	– – –	– – –	– – –	– – –	– – –	– – –	3 – –
26 Olympique Lyonnais	– – –	– – –	– – –	– – –	– – –	3 – –	– – –	– – –	– – –	3 – –
27 Watford	2 – –	– – –	– – –	1 – –	– – –	– – –	– – –	– – –	– – –	3 – –
28 AC Milan	– – –	– – –	– – –	– – –	– – –	2 – –	– – –	– – –	– – –	2 – –
29 Barcelona	– – –	– – –	– – –	– – –	– – –	2 – –	– – –	– – –	– – –	2 – –
30 Bayer Leverkusen	– – –	– – –	– – –	– – –	– – –	2 – –	– – –	– – –	– – –	2 – –
31 Crystal Palace	2 – –	– – –	– – –	– – –	– – –	– – –	– – –	– – –	– – –	2 – –
32 Debreceni	– – –	– – –	– – –	– – –	– – –	2 – –	– – –	– – –	– – –	2 – –
33 Glasgow Celtic	– – –	– – –	– – –	– – –	– – –	2 – –	– – –	– – –	– – –	2 – –
34 Glasgow Rangers	– – –	– – –	– – –	– – –	– – –	2 – –	– – –	– – –	– – –	2 – –
35 Juventus	– – –	– – –	– – –	– – –	– – –	2 – –	– – –	– – –	– – –	2 – –
36 Leicester City	1 – –	– – –	– – –	– – –	1 – –	– – –	– – –	– – –	– – –	2 – –
37 Maccabi Haifa	– – –	– – –	– – –	– – –	– – –	2 – –	– – –	– – –	– – –	2 – –
38 Panathinaikos	– – –	– – –	– – –	– – –	– – –	2 – –	– – –	– – –	– – –	2 – –
39 Real Madrid	– – –	– – –	– – –	– – –	– – –	2 – –	– – –	– – –	– – –	2 – –
40 Sporting Lisbon	– – –	– – –	– – –	– – –	– – –	2 – –	– – –	– – –	– – –	2 – –
41 Stuttgart	– – –	– – –	– – –	– – –	– – –	2 – –	– – –	– – –	– – –	2 – –
42 Villarreal	– – –	– – –	– – –	– – –	– – –	2 – –	– – –	– – –	– – –	2 – –
43 Wolverhampton W.	1 – –	– – –	– – –	1 – –	– – –	– – –	– – –	– – –	– – –	2 – –
44 Dynamo Kiev	– – –	– – –	– – –	– – –	– – –	1 – 1	– – –	– – –	– – –	1 – 1
45 Basel	– – –	– – –	– – –	– – –	– – –	1 – –	– – –	– – –	– – –	1 – –
46 Derby County	1 – –	– – –	– – –	– – –	– – –	– – –	– – –	– – –	– – –	1 – –
47 Fenerbahce	– – –	– – –	– – –	– – –	– – –	1 – –	– – –	– – –	– – –	1 – –
48 Norwich City	1 – –	– – –	– – –	– – –	– – –	– – –	– – –	– – –	– – –	1 – –
49 Olympiakos Piraeus	– – –	– – –	– – –	– – –	– – –	1 – –	– – –	– – –	– – –	1 – –
50 Sheffield United	1 – –	– – –	– – –	– – –	– – –	– – –	– – –	– – –	– – –	1 – –

continued../

RIO FERDINAND (continued)

Opponents	PREM			FLD 1			FLD 2			FAC			LC			EC/CL			ECWC			UEFA			OTHER			TOTAL		
	A	S	G	A	S	G	A	S	G	A	S	G	A	S	G	A	S	G	A	S	G	A	S	G	A	S	G	A	S	G
51 Sparta Prague	–	–	–	–	–	–	–	–	–	–	–	–	–	–	–	1	–	–	–	–	–	–	–	–	–	–	–	1	–	
52 Zalaegerszeg	–	–	–	–	–	–	–	–	–	–	–	–	–	–	–	1	–	–	–	–	–	–	–	–	–	–	–	1	–	
53 Burton Albion	–	–	–	–	–	–	–	–	–	– (1)	–		–	–	–	–	–	–	–	–	–	–	–	–	–	–	–	– (1)	–	
54 Copenhagen	–	–	–	–	–	–	–	–	–	–	–	–	– (1)	–		–	–	–	–	–	–	–	–	–	–	–	–	– (1)	–	

DANNY FERGUSON

DEBUT (Full Appearance)

Saturday 07/04/1928
Football League Division 1
at Old Trafford

Manchester United 4 Burnley 3

CLUB CAREER RECORD	Apps	Subs	Goals
Premiership	0		0
League Division 1	4		0
League Division 2	0		0
FA Cup	0		0
League Cup	0		0
European Cup / Champions League	0		0
European Cup-Winners' Cup	0		0
UEFA Cup / Inter-Cities' Fairs Cup	0		0
Other Matches	0		0
OVERALL TOTAL	**4**		**0**

Opponents	PREM			FLD 1			FLD 2			FAC			LC			EC/CL			ECWC			UEFA			OTHER			TOTAL		
	A	S	G	A	S	G	A	S	G	A	S	G	A	S	G	A	S	G	A	S	G	A	S	G	A	S	G	A	S	G
1 Bolton Wanderers	–	–	–	1	–	–	–	–	–	–	–	–	–	–	–	–	–	–	–	–	–	–	–	–	–	–	–	1	–	
2 Burnley	–	–	–	1	–	–	–	–	–	–	–	–	–	–	–	–	–	–	–	–	–	–	–	–	–	–	–	1	–	
3 Bury	–	–	–	1	–	–	–	–	–	–	–	–	–	–	–	–	–	–	–	–	–	–	–	–	–	–	–	1	–	
4 Sheffield United	–	–	–	1	–	–	–	–	–	–	–	–	–	–	–	–	–	–	–	–	–	–	–	–	–	–	–	1	–	

DARREN FERGUSON

DEBUT (Substitute Appearance)

Tuesday 26/02/1991
Football League Division 1
at Bramall Lane

Sheffield United 2 Manchester United 1

CLUB CAREER RECORD	Apps	Subs	Goals
Premiership	16	(2)	0
League Division 1	4	(5)	0
League Division 2	0		0
FA Cup	0		0
League Cup	2	(1)	0
European Cup / Champions League	0		0
European Cup-Winners' Cup	0		0
UEFA Cup / Inter-Cities' Fairs Cup	0		0
Other Matches	0		0
OVERALL TOTAL	**22**	**(8)**	**0**

Opponents	PREM			FLD 1			FLD 2			FAC			LC			EC/CL			ECWC			UEFA			OTHER			TOTAL		
	A	S	G	A	S	G	A	S	G	A	S	G	A	S	G	A	S	G	A	S	G	A	S	G	A	S	G	A	S	G
1 Everton	2	–		1	–		–	–	–	–	–	–	– (1)	–		–	–	–	–	–	–	–	–	–	–	–	–	3 (1)	–	
2 Aston Villa	1	–		–	–	–	–	–	–	–	–	–	1	–		–	–	–	–	–	–	–	–	–	–	–	–	2	–	
3 Crystal Palace	1	–		1	–		–	–	–	–	–	–	–	–	–	–	–	–	–	–	–	–	–	–	–	–	–	2	–	
4 Tottenham Hotspur	1	–		1	–		–	–	–	–	–	–	–	–	–	–	–	–	–	–	–	–	–	–	–	–	–	2	–	
5 Blackburn Rovers	1 (1)	–		–	–	–	–	–	–	–	–	–	–	–	–	–	–	–	–	–	–	–	–	–	–	–	–	1 (1)	–	
6 Ipswich Town	1 (1)	–		–	–	–	–	–	–	–	–	–	–	–	–	–	–	–	–	–	–	–	–	–	–	–	–	1 (1)	–	
7 Sheffield United	1	–		– (1)	–		–	–	–	–	–	–	–	–	–	–	–	–	–	–	–	–	–	–	–	–	–	1 (1)	–	
8 Southampton	1	–		– (1)	–		–	–	–	–	–	–	–	–	–	–	–	–	–	–	–	–	–	–	–	–	–	1 (1)	–	
9 Coventry City	1	–		–	–	–	–	–	–	–	–	–	–	–	–	–	–	–	–	–	–	–	–	–	–	–	–	1	–	
10 Leeds United	1	–		–	–	–	–	–	–	–	–	–	–	–	–	–	–	–	–	–	–	–	–	–	–	–	–	1	–	
11 Liverpool	1	–		–	–	–	–	–	–	–	–	–	–	–	–	–	–	–	–	–	–	–	–	–	–	–	–	1	–	
12 Middlesbrough	1	–		–	–	–	–	–	–	–	–	–	–	–	–	–	–	–	–	–	–	–	–	–	–	–	–	1	–	
13 Nottingham Forest	1	–		–	–	–	–	–	–	–	–	–	–	–	–	–	–	–	–	–	–	–	–	–	–	–	–	1	–	
14 Notts County	–	–	–	1	–		–	–	–	–	–	–	–	–	–	–	–	–	–	–	–	–	–	–	–	–	–	1	–	
15 Queens Park Rangers	1	–		–	–	–	–	–	–	–	–	–	–	–	–	–	–	–	–	–	–	–	–	–	–	–	–	1	–	
16 Stoke City	–	–	–	–	–	–	–	–	–	–	–	–	1	–		–	–	–	–	–	–	–	–	–	–	–	–	1	–	
17 Wimbledon	1	–		–	–	–	–	–	–	–	–	–	–	–	–	–	–	–	–	–	–	–	–	–	–	–	–	1	–	
18 Arsenal	–	–	–	– (1)	–		–	–	–	–	–	–	–	–	–	–	–	–	–	–	–	–	–	–	–	–	–	– (1)	–	
19 Oldham Athletic	–	–	–	– (1)	–		–	–	–	–	–	–	–	–	–	–	–	–	–	–	–	–	–	–	–	–	–	– (1)	–	
20 West Ham United	–	–	–	– (1)	–		–	–	–	–	–	–	–	–	–	–	–	–	–	–	–	–	–	–	–	–	–	– (1)	–	

JOHN FERGUSON

DEBUT (Full Appearance)

Saturday 29/08/1931
Football League Division 2
at Park Avenue

Bradford Park Avenue 3 Manchester United 1

CLUB CAREER RECORD	Apps	Subs	Goals
Premiership	0		0
League Division 1	0		0
League Division 2	8		1
FA Cup	0		0
League Cup	0		0
European Cup / Champions League	0		0
European Cup-Winners' Cup	0		0
UEFA Cup / Inter-Cities' Fairs Cup	0		0
Other Matches	0		0
OVERALL TOTAL	8		1

Opponents	PREM A S G	FLD 1 A S G	FLD 2 A S G	FAC A S G	LC A S G	EC/CL A S G	ECWC A S G	UEFA A S G	OTHER A S G	TOTAL A S G
1 Southampton	– –	– –	1 1	–	–	–	–	–	–	1 1
2 Bradford Park Avenue	– –	– –	1 –	–	–	–	–	–	–	1 –
3 Burnley	– –	– –	1 –	–	–	–	–	–	–	1 –
4 Chesterfield	– –	– –	1 –	–	–	–	–	–	–	1 –
5 Nottingham Forest	– –	– –	1 –	–	–	–	–	–	–	1 –
6 Stoke City	– –	– –	1 –	–	–	–	–	–	–	1 –
7 Swansea City	– –	– –	1 –	–	–	–	–	–	–	1 –
8 Tottenham Hotspur	– –	– –	1 –	–	–	–	–	–	–	1 –

RON FERRIER

DEBUT (Full Appearance)

Wednesday 04/09/1935
Football League Division 2
at Old Trafford

Manchester United 3 Charlton Athletic 0

CLUB CAREER RECORD	Apps	Subs	Goals
Premiership	0		0
League Division 1	6		1
League Division 2	12		3
FA Cup	1		0
League Cup	0		0
European Cup / Champions League	0		0
European Cup-Winners' Cup	0		0
UEFA Cup / Inter-Cities' Fairs Cup	0		0
Other Matches	0		0
OVERALL TOTAL	19		4

Opponents	PREM A S G	FLD 1 A S G	FLD 2 A S G	FAC A S G	LC A S G	EC/CL A S G	ECWC A S G	UEFA A S G	OTHER A S G	TOTAL A S G
1 Charlton Athletic	– –	1 –	2 –	–	–	–	–	–	–	3 –
2 Barnsley	– –	– –	2 –	–	–	–	–	–	–	2 –
3 Tottenham Hotspur	– –	– –	2 –	–	–	–	–	–	–	2 –
4 Bury	– –	– –	1 2	–	–	–	–	–	–	1 2
5 Everton	– –	1 1	– –	–	–	–	–	–	–	1 1
6 Sheffield Wednesday	– –	– –	1 1	–	–	–	–	–	–	1 1
7 Bradford City	– –	– –	1 –	–	–	–	–	–	–	1 –
8 Derby County	– –	1 –	– –	–	–	–	–	–	–	1 –
9 Fulham	– –	– –	1 –	–	–	–	–	–	–	1 –
10 Grimsby Town	– –	1 –	– –	–	–	–	–	–	–	1 –
11 Liverpool	– –	1 –	– –	–	–	–	–	–	–	1 –
12 Norwich City	– –	– –	1 –	–	–	–	–	–	–	1 –
13 Preston North End	– –	1 –	– –	–	–	–	–	–	–	1 –
14 Stockport County	– –	– –	1 –	–	–	–	–	–	–	1 –
15 Stoke City	– –	– –	– –	1	–	–	–	–	–	1 –

BILL FIELDING

DEBUT (Full Appearance)

Saturday 25/01/1947
FA Cup 4th Round
at Maine Road

Manchester United 0 Nottingham Forest 2

CLUB CAREER RECORD	Apps	Subs	Goals
Premiership	0		0
League Division 1	6		0
League Division 2	0		0
FA Cup	1		0
League Cup	0		0
European Cup / Champions League	0		0
European Cup-Winners' Cup	0		0
UEFA Cup / Inter-Cities' Fairs Cup	0		0
Other Matches	0		0
OVERALL TOTAL	7		0

Opponents	PREM A S G	FLD 1 A S G	FLD 2 A S G	FAC A S G	LC A S G	EC/CL A S G	ECWC A S G	UEFA A S G	OTHER A S G	TOTAL A S G
1 Arsenal	– –	1 –	–	–	–	–	–	–	–	1 –
2 Aston Villa	– –	1 –	–	–	–	–	–	–	–	1 –
3 Blackpool	– –	1 –	–	–	–	–	–	–	–	1 –
4 Derby County	– –	1 –	–	–	–	–	–	–	–	1 –
5 Nottingham Forest	– –	– –	–	1	–	–	–	–	–	1 –
6 Stoke City	– –	1 –	–	–	–	–	–	–	–	1 –
7 Sunderland	– –	1 –	–	–	–	–	–	–	–	1 –

JAMES FISHER

DEBUT (Full Appearance)

Saturday 20/10/1900
Football League Division 2
at Bank Street

Newton Heath 1 Walsall 1

CLUB CAREER RECORD	Apps	Subs	Goals
Premiership	0		0
League Division 1	0		0
League Division 2	42		2
FA Cup	4		1
League Cup	0		0
European Cup / Champions League	0		0
European Cup-Winners' Cup	0		0
UEFA Cup / Inter-Cities' Fairs Cup	0		0
Other Matches	0		0
OVERALL TOTAL	**46**		**3**

Opponents	PREM A S G	FLD 1 A S G	FLD 2 A S G	FAC A S G	LC A S G	EC/CL A S G	ECWC A S G	UEFA A S G	OTHER A S G	TOTAL A S G
1 Lincoln City	– –	– –	3 –	1 1	– –	– –	– –	– –	– –	4 1
2 Arsenal	– –	– –	3 –	– –	– –	– –	– –	– –	– –	3 –
3 Barnsley	– –	– –	3 –	– –	– –	– –	– –	– –	– –	3 –
4 Burnley	– –	– –	1 –	2 –	– –	– –	– –	– –	– –	3 –
5 Gainsborough Trinity	– –	– –	3 –	– –	– –	– –	– –	– –	– –	3 –
6 Stockport County	– –	– –	3 –	– –	– –	– –	– –	– –	– –	3 –
7 Leicester City	– –	– –	2 1	– –	– –	– –	– –	– –	– –	2 1
8 Birmingham City	– –	– –	2 –	– –	– –	– –	– –	– –	– –	2 –
9 Blackpool	– –	– –	2 –	– –	– –	– –	– –	– –	– –	2 –
10 Burton Swifts	– –	– –	2 –	– –	– –	– –	– –	– –	– –	2 –
11 Chesterfield	– –	– –	2 –	– –	– –	– –	– –	– –	– –	2 –
12 Grimsby Town	– –	– –	2 –	– –	– –	– –	– –	– –	– –	2 –
13 Middlesbrough	– –	– –	2 –	– –	– –	– –	– –	– –	– –	2 –
14 Port Vale	– –	– –	2 –	– –	– –	– –	– –	– –	– –	2 –
15 Preston North End	– –	– –	2 –	– –	– –	– –	– –	– –	– –	2 –
16 Walsall	– –	– –	2 –	– –	– –	– –	– –	– –	– –	2 –
17 West Bromwich Albion	– –	– –	1 1	– –	– –	– –	– –	– –	– –	1 1
18 Bristol City	– –	– –	1 –	– –	– –	– –	– –	– –	– –	1 –
19 Burton United	– –	– –	1 –	– –	– –	– –	– –	– –	– –	1 –
20 Doncaster Rovers	– –	– –	1 –	– –	– –	– –	– –	– –	– –	1 –
21 Glossop	– –	– –	1 –	– –	– –	– –	– –	– –	– –	1 –
22 New Brighton Tower	– –	– –	1 –	– –	– –	– –	– –	– –	– –	1 –
23 Portsmouth	– –	– –	– –	1 –	– –	– –	– –	– –	– –	1 –

JOHN FITCHETT

DEBUT (Full Appearance)

Saturday 21/03/1903
Football League Division 2
at Bank Street

Manchester United 5 Leicester City 1

CLUB CAREER RECORD	Apps	Subs	Goals
Premiership	0		0
League Division 1	0		0
League Division 2	16		1
FA Cup	2		0
League Cup	0		0
European Cup / Champions League	0		0
European Cup-Winners' Cup	0		0
UEFA Cup / Inter-Cities' Fairs Cup	0		0
Other Matches	0		0
OVERALL TOTAL	**18**		**1**

Opponents	PREM A S G	FLD 1 A S G	FLD 2 A S G	FAC A S G	LC A S G	EC/CL A S G	ECWC A S G	UEFA A S G	OTHER A S G	TOTAL A S G
1 Barnsley	– –	– –	2 –	– –	– –	– –	– –	– –	– –	2 –
2 Fulham	– –	– –	– –	2 –	– –	– –	– –	– –	– –	2 –
3 Preston North End	– –	– –	2 –	– –	– –	– –	– –	– –	– –	2 –
4 Leicester City	– –	– –	1 1	– –	– –	– –	– –	– –	– –	1 1
5 Blackpool	– –	– –	1 –	– –	– –	– –	– –	– –	– –	1 –
6 Burnley	– –	– –	1 –	– –	– –	– –	– –	– –	– –	1 –
7 Burton United	– –	– –	1 –	– –	– –	– –	– –	– –	– –	1 –
8 Chesterfield	– –	– –	1 –	– –	– –	– –	– –	– –	– –	1 –
9 Doncaster Rovers	– –	– –	1 –	– –	– –	– –	– –	– –	– –	1 –
10 Gainsborough Trinity	– –	– –	1 –	– –	– –	– –	– –	– –	– –	1 –
11 Glossop	– –	– –	1 –	– –	– –	– –	– –	– –	– –	1 –
12 Grimsby Town	– –	– –	1 –	– –	– –	– –	– –	– –	– –	1 –
13 Liverpool	– –	– –	1 –	– –	– –	– –	– –	– –	– –	1 –
14 Stockport County	– –	– –	1 –	– –	– –	– –	– –	– –	– –	1 –
15 West Bromwich Albion	– –	– –	1 –	– –	– –	– –	– –	– –	– –	1 –

ARTHUR FITTON

DEBUT (Full Appearance, 1 goal)

Saturday 26/03/1932
Football League Division 2
at Old Trafford

Manchester United 5 Oldham Athletic 1

CLUB CAREER RECORD	Apps	Subs	Goals
Premiership	0		0
League Division 1	0		0
League Division 2	12		2
FA Cup	0		0
League Cup	0		0
European Cup / Champions League	0		0
European Cup-Winners' Cup	0		0
UEFA Cup / Inter-Cities' Fairs Cup	0		0
Other Matches	0		0
OVERALL TOTAL	**12**		**2**

Opponents	PREM			FLD 1			FLD 2			FAC			LC			EC/CL			ECWC			UEFA			OTHER			TOTAL		
	A	S	G	A	S	G	A	S	G	A	S	G	A	S	G	A	S	G	A	S	G	A	S	G	A	S	G	A	S	G
1 Bury	–		–	–		–	2		–	–		–	–		–	–		–	–		–	–		–	–		–	2		–
2 Charlton Athletic	–		–	–		–	2		–	–		–	–		–	–		–	–		–	–		–	–		–	2		–
3 Bradford City	–		–	–		–	1		1	–		–	–		–	–		–	–		–	–		–	–		–	1		1
4 Oldham Athletic	–		–	–		–	1		1	–		–	–		–	–		–	–		–	–		–	–		–	1		1
5 Bristol City	–		–	–		–	1		–	–		–	–		–	–		–	–		–	–		–	–		–	1		–
6 Grimsby Town	–		–	–		–	1		–	–		–	–		–	–		–	–		–	–		–	–		–	1		–
7 Millwall	–		–	–		–	1		–	–		–	–		–	–		–	–		–	–		–	–		–	1		–
8 Port Vale	–		–	–		–	1		–	–		–	–		–	–		–	–		–	–		–	–		–	1		–
9 Southampton	–		–	–		–	1		–	–		–	–		–	–		–	–		–	–		–	–		–	1		–
10 Tottenham Hotspur	–		–	–		–	1		–	–		–	–		–	–		–	–		–	–		–	–		–	1		–

JOHN FITZPATRICK

DEBUT (Full Appearance)

Wednesday 24/02/1965
Football League Division 1
at Roker Park

Sunderland 1 Manchester United 0

CLUB CAREER RECORD	Apps	Subs	Goals
Premiership	0		0
League Division 1	111	(6)	8
League Division 2	0		0
FA Cup	11		1
League Cup	12		1
European Cup / Champions League	7		0
European Cup-Winners' Cup	0		0
UEFA Cup / Inter-Cities' Fairs Cup	0		0
Other Matches	0		0
OVERALL TOTAL	**141**	**(6)**	**10**

Opponents	PREM			FLD 1			FLD 2			FAC			LC			EC/CL			ECWC			UEFA			OTHER			TOTAL		
	A	S	G	A	S	G	A	S	G	A	S	G	A	S	G	A	S	G	A	S	G	A	S	G	A	S	G	A	S	G
1 Tottenham Hotspur	–		–	7 (1)		3	–		–	2		–	–		–	–		–	–		–	–		–	–		–	9 (1)		3
2 Nottingham Forest	–		–	8		–	–		–	–		–	–		–	–		–	–		–	–		–	–		–	8		–
3 Coventry City	–		–	7		1	–		–	–		–	–		–	–		–	–		–	–		–	–		–	7		1
4 Burnley	–		–	5		–	–		–	–		–	2		–	–		–	–		–	–		–	–		–	7		–
5 Everton	–		–	6		–	–		–	1		–	–		–	–		–	–		–	–		–	–		–	7		–
6 West Bromwich Albion	–		–	6		2	–		–	–		–	–		–	–		–	–		–	–		–	–		–	6		2
7 West Ham United	–		–	6		1	–		–	–		–	–		–	–		–	–		–	–		–	–		–	6		1
8 Chelsea	–		–	5		–	–		–	–		–	1		–	–		–	–		–	–		–	–		–	6		–
9 Newcastle United	–		–	6		–	–		–	–		–	–		–	–		–	–		–	–		–	–		–	6		–
10 Leeds United	–		–	5 (1)		1	–		–	–		–	–		–	–		–	–		–	–		–	–		–	5 (1)		1
11 Arsenal	–		–	5		–	–		–	–		–	–		–	–		–	–		–	–		–	–		–	5		–
12 Liverpool	–		–	5		–	–		–	–		–	–		–	–		–	–		–	–		–	–		–	5		–
13 Sheffield Wednesday	–		–	5		–	–		–	–		–	–		–	–		–	–		–	–		–	–		–	5		–
14 Stoke City	–		–	5		–	–		–	–		–	–		–	–		–	–		–	–		–	–		–	5		–
15 Southampton	–		–	4 (1)		–	–		–	–		–	–		–	–		–	–		–	–		–	–		–	4 (1)		–
16 Wolverhampton W.	–		–	4 (1)		–	–		–	–		–	–		–	–		–	–		–	–		–	–		–	4 (1)		–
17 Aston Villa	–		–	2		–	–		–	–		–	2		–	–		–	–		–	–		–	–		–	4		–
18 Manchester City	–		–	4		–	–		–	–		–	–		–	–		–	–		–	–		–	–		–	4		–
19 Sunderland	–		–	3 (1)		–	–		–	–		–	–		–	–		–	–		–	–		–	–		–	3 (1)		–
20 Crystal Palace	–		–	2		–	–		–	–		–	1		1	–		–	–		–	–		–	–		–	3		1
21 Derby County	–		–	2		–	–		–	–		–	1		–	–		–	–		–	–		–	–		–	3		–
22 Ipswich Town	–		–	3		–	–		–	–		–	–		–	–		–	–		–	–		–	–		–	3		–
23 Middlesbrough	–		–	–		–	–		–	2		–	1		–	–		–	–		–	–		–	–		–	3		–
24 Watford	–		–	–		–	–		–	3		–	–		–	–		–	–		–	–		–	–		–	3		–
25 Birmingham City	–		–	–		–	–		–	2		–	–		–	–		–	–		–	–		–	–		–	2		–
26 Huddersfield Town	–		–	2		–	–		–	–		–	–		–	–		–	–		–	–		–	–		–	2		–
27 Rapid Vienna	–		–	–		–	–		–	–		–	–		–	2		–	–		–	–		–	–		–	2		–
28 Sheffield United	–		–	1 (1)		–	–		–	–		–	–		–	–		–	–		–	–		–	–		–	1 (1)		–
29 Exeter City	–		–	–		–	–		–	1		1	–		–	–		–	–		–	–		–	–		–	1		1
30 AC Milan	–		–	–		–	–		–	–		–	–		–	1		–	–		–	–		–	–		–	1		–
31 Aldershot	–		–	–		–	–		–	–		–	1		–	–		–	–		–	–		–	–		–	1		–
32 Anderlecht	–		–	–		–	–		–	–		–	–		–	1		–	–		–	–		–	–		–	1		–
33 Blackpool	–		–	1		–	–		–	–		–	–		–	–		–	–		–	–		–	–		–	1		–
34 Gornik Zabrze	–		–	–		–	–		–	–		–	–		–	1		–	–		–	–		–	–		–	1		–
35 HJK Helsinki	–		–	–		–	–		–	–		–	–		–	1		–	–		–	–		–	–		–	1		–
36 Leicester City	–		–	1		–	–		–	–		–	–		–	–		–	–		–	–		–	–		–	1		–
37 Oxford United	–		–	–		–	–		–	–		–	1		–	–		–	–		–	–		–	–		–	1		–
38 Portsmouth	–		–	–		–	–		–	–		–	1		–	–		–	–		–	–		–	–		–	1		–
39 Queens Park Rangers	–		–	1		–	–		–	–		–	–		–	–		–	–		–	–		–	–		–	1		–
40 Sarajevo	–		–	–		–	–		–	–		–	–		–	1		–	–		–	–		–	–		–	1		–
41 Wrexham	–		–	–		–	–		–	–		–	1		–	–		–	–		–	–		–	–		–	1		–

DAVID FITZSIMMONS

DEBUT (Full Appearance)

Saturday 07/09/1895
Football League Division 2
at Bank Street

Newton Heath 5 Crewe Alexandra 0

CLUB CAREER RECORD	Apps	Subs	Goals
Premiership	0		0
League Division 1	0		0
League Division 2	28		0
FA Cup	3		0
League Cup	0		0
European Cup / Champions League	0		0
European Cup-Winners' Cup	0		0
UEFA Cup / Inter-Cities' Fairs Cup	0		0
Other Matches	0		0
OVERALL TOTAL	**31**		**0**

Opponents	PREM			FLD 1			FLD 2			FAC			LC			EC/CL			ECWC			UEFA			OTHER			TOTAL		
	A	S	G	A	S	G	A	S	G	A	S	G	A	S	G	A	S	G	A	S	G	A	S	G	A	S	G	A	S	G
1 Arsenal	-	-	-	-	-	-	2	-	-	-	-	-	-	-	-	-	-	-	-	-	-	-	-	-	-	-	-	2	-	-
2 Burton Swifts	-	-	-	-	-	-	2	-	-	-	-	-	-	-	-	-	-	-	-	-	-	-	-	-	-	-	-	2	-	-
3 Burton Wanderers	-	-	-	-	-	-	2	-	-	-	-	-	-	-	-	-	-	-	-	-	-	-	-	-	-	-	-	2	-	-
4 Crewe Alexandra	-	-	-	-	-	-	2	-	-	-	-	-	-	-	-	-	-	-	-	-	-	-	-	-	-	-	-	2	-	-
5 Darwen	-	-	-	-	-	-	2	-	-	-	-	-	-	-	-	-	-	-	-	-	-	-	-	-	-	-	-	2	-	-
6 Derby County	-	-	-	-	-	-	-	-	-	2	-	-	-	-	-	-	-	-	-	-	-	-	-	-	-	-	-	2	-	-
7 Grimsby Town	-	-	-	-	-	-	2	-	-	-	-	-	-	-	-	-	-	-	-	-	-	-	-	-	-	-	-	2	-	-
8 Leicester City	-	-	-	-	-	-	2	-	-	-	-	-	-	-	-	-	-	-	-	-	-	-	-	-	-	-	-	2	-	-
9 Lincoln City	-	-	-	-	-	-	2	-	-	-	-	-	-	-	-	-	-	-	-	-	-	-	-	-	-	-	-	2	-	-
10 Loughborough Town	-	-	-	-	-	-	2	-	-	-	-	-	-	-	-	-	-	-	-	-	-	-	-	-	-	-	-	2	-	-
11 Notts County	-	-	-	-	-	-	2	-	-	-	-	-	-	-	-	-	-	-	-	-	-	-	-	-	-	-	-	2	-	-
12 Port Vale	-	-	-	-	-	-	2	-	-	-	-	-	-	-	-	-	-	-	-	-	-	-	-	-	-	-	-	2	-	-
13 Gainsborough Trinity	-	-	-	-	-	-	1	-	-	-	-	-	-	-	-	-	-	-	-	-	-	-	-	-	-	-	-	1	-	-
14 Kettering	-	-	-	-	-	-	-	-	-	1	-	-	-	-	-	-	-	-	-	-	-	-	-	-	-	-	-	1	-	-
15 Liverpool	-	-	-	-	-	-	1	-	-	-	-	-	-	-	-	-	-	-	-	-	-	-	-	-	-	-	-	1	-	-
16 Manchester City	-	-	-	-	-	-	1	-	-	-	-	-	-	-	-	-	-	-	-	-	-	-	-	-	-	-	-	1	-	-
17 New Brighton Tower	-	-	-	-	-	-	1	-	-	-	-	-	-	-	-	-	-	-	-	-	-	-	-	-	-	-	-	1	-	-
18 Newcastle United	-	-	-	-	-	-	1	-	-	-	-	-	-	-	-	-	-	-	-	-	-	-	-	-	-	-	-	1	-	-
19 Rotherham United	-	-	-	-	-	-	1	-	-	-	-	-	-	-	-	-	-	-	-	-	-	-	-	-	-	-	-	1	-	-

TOMMY FITZSIMMONS

DEBUT (Full Appearance, 1 goal)

Saturday 19/11/1892
Football League Division 1
at North Road

Newton Heath 2 Aston Villa 0

CLUB CAREER RECORD	Apps	Subs	Goals
Premiership	0		0
League Division 1	27		6
League Division 2	0		0
FA Cup	1		0
League Cup	0		0
European Cup / Champions League	0		0
European Cup-Winners' Cup	0		0
UEFA Cup / Inter-Cities' Fairs Cup	0		0
Other Matches	2		0
OVERALL TOTAL	**30**		**6**

Opponents	PREM			FLD 1			FLD 2			FAC			LC			EC/CL			ECWC			UEFA			OTHER			TOTAL		
	A	S	G	A	S	G	A	S	G	A	S	G	A	S	G	A	S	G	A	S	G	A	S	G	A	S	G	A	S	G
1 Derby County	-	-	-	3	-	2	-	-	-	-	-	-	-	-	-	-	-	-	-	-	-	-	-	-	-	-	-	3	-	2
2 Wolverhampton W.	-	-	-	3	-	-	-	-	-	-	-	-	-	-	-	-	-	-	-	-	-	-	-	-	-	-	-	3	-	-
3 Accrington Stanley	-	-	-	2	-	2	-	-	-	-	-	-	-	-	-	-	-	-	-	-	-	-	-	-	-	-	-	2	-	2
4 Aston Villa	-	-	-	2	-	1	-	-	-	-	-	-	-	-	-	-	-	-	-	-	-	-	-	-	-	-	-	2	-	1
5 Birmingham City	-	-	-	-	-	-	-	-	-	-	-	-	-	-	-	-	-	-	-	-	-	-	-	-	2	-	-	2	-	-
6 Bolton Wanderers	-	-	-	2	-	-	-	-	-	-	-	-	-	-	-	-	-	-	-	-	-	-	-	-	-	-	-	2	-	-
7 Darwen	-	-	-	2	-	-	-	-	-	-	-	-	-	-	-	-	-	-	-	-	-	-	-	-	-	-	-	2	-	-
8 Preston North End	-	-	-	2	-	-	-	-	-	-	-	-	-	-	-	-	-	-	-	-	-	-	-	-	-	-	-	2	-	-
9 Stoke City	-	-	-	2	-	-	-	-	-	-	-	-	-	-	-	-	-	-	-	-	-	-	-	-	-	-	-	2	-	-
10 Sunderland	-	-	-	2	-	-	-	-	-	-	-	-	-	-	-	-	-	-	-	-	-	-	-	-	-	-	-	2	-	-
11 West Bromwich Albion	-	-	-	2	-	-	-	-	-	-	-	-	-	-	-	-	-	-	-	-	-	-	-	-	-	-	-	2	-	-
12 Sheffield United	-	-	-	1	-	1	-	-	-	-	-	-	-	-	-	-	-	-	-	-	-	-	-	-	-	-	-	1	-	1
13 Blackburn Rovers	-	-	-	-	-	-	-	-	-	1	-	-	-	-	-	-	-	-	-	-	-	-	-	-	-	-	-	1	-	-
14 Burnley	-	-	-	1	-	-	-	-	-	-	-	-	-	-	-	-	-	-	-	-	-	-	-	-	-	-	-	1	-	-
15 Nottingham Forest	-	-	-	1	-	-	-	-	-	-	-	-	-	-	-	-	-	-	-	-	-	-	-	-	-	-	-	1	-	-
16 Notts County	-	-	-	1	-	-	-	-	-	-	-	-	-	-	-	-	-	-	-	-	-	-	-	-	-	-	-	1	-	-
17 Sheffield Wednesday	-	-	-	1	-	-	-	-	-	-	-	-	-	-	-	-	-	-	-	-	-	-	-	-	-	-	-	1	-	-

DARREN FLETCHER

DEBUT (Full Appearance)

Wednesday 12/03/2003
Champions League Phase 2 Match 5
at Old Trafford

Manchester United 1 Basel 1

CLUB CAREER RECORD	Apps	Subs	Goals
Premiership	79	(28)	7
League Division 1	0		0
League Division 2	0		0
FA Cup	11	(7)	2
League Cup	10		0
European Cup / Champions League	26	(9)	0
European Cup-Winners' Cup	0		0
UEFA Cup / Inter-Cities' Fairs Cup	0		0
Other Matches	0	(2)	0
OVERALL TOTAL	**126**	**(46)**	**9**

Opponents	PREM A S G	FLD 1 A S G	FLD 2 A S G	FAC A S G	LC A S G	EC/CL A S G	ECWC A S G	UEFA A S G	OTHER A S G	TOTAL A S G
1 Chelsea	5 (1) 1	–	–	1 –	1 –	–	–	–	– (1) –	7 (2) 1
2 Aston Villa	6 (1) –	–	–	– (2) –	–	–	–	–	–	6 (3) –
3 Arsenal	4 –	–	–	3 2	–	–	–	–	– (1) –	7 (1) 2
4 Newcastle United	6 (1) –	–	–	– (1) –	–	–	–	–	–	6 (2) –
5 Everton	5 (2) –	–	–	–	–	–	–	–	–	5 (2) –
6 Liverpool	4 (2) –	–	–	1 –	–	–	–	–	–	5 (2) –
7 Charlton Athletic	6 3	–	–	–	–	–	–	–	–	6 3
8 Bolton Wanderers	5 (1) –	–	–	–	–	–	–	–	–	5 (1) –
9 Middlesbrough	4 (2) 2	–	–	–	–	–	–	–	–	4 (2) 2
10 Blackburn Rovers	2 (2) –	–	–	–	2 –	–	–	–	–	4 (2) –
11 Portsmouth	3 (2) –	–	–	– (1) –	–	–	–	–	–	3 (3) –
12 Reading	1 (3) –	–	–	2 –	–	–	–	–	–	3 (3) –
13 Birmingham City	3 (1) –	–	–	–	1 –	–	–	–	–	4 (1) –
14 Manchester City	4 (1) –	–	–	–	–	–	–	–	–	4 (1) –
15 West Bromwich Albion	2 (1) –	–	–	–	2 –	–	–	–	–	4 (1) –
16 West Ham United	4 (1) –	–	–	–	–	–	–	–	–	4 (1) –
17 Tottenham Hotspur	3 (2) –	–	–	–	–	–	–	–	–	3 (2) –
18 Fulham	2 –	–	–	1 –	–	–	–	–	–	3 –
19 Roma	–	–	–	–	–	2 (1) –	–	–	–	2 (1) –
20 Benfica	–	–	–	–	–	1 (2) –	–	–	–	1 (2) –
21 AC Milan	–	–	–	–	–	2 –	–	–	–	2 –
22 Copenhagen	–	–	–	–	–	2 –	–	–	–	2 –
23 Crystal Palace	1 –	–	–	–	1 –	–	–	–	–	2 –
24 Debreceni	–	–	–	–	–	2 –	–	–	–	2 –
25 Dinamo Bucharest	–	–	–	–	–	2 –	–	–	–	2 –
26 Dynamo Kiev	–	–	–	–	–	2 –	–	–	–	2 –
27 Leeds United	1 –	–	–	–	1 –	–	–	–	–	2 –
28 Lille Metropole	–	–	–	–	–	2 –	–	–	–	2 –
29 Villarreal	–	–	–	–	–	2 –	–	–	–	2 –
30 Wigan Athletic	2 –	–	–	–	–	–	–	–	–	2 –
31 Southampton	1 (1) 1	–	–	–	–	–	–	–	–	1 (1) 1
32 Fenerbahce	–	–	–	–	–	1 (1) –	–	–	–	1 (1) –
33 Leicester City	1 (1) –	–	–	–	–	–	–	–	–	1 (1) –
34 Olympique Lyonnais	–	–	–	–	–	1 (1) –	–	–	–	1 (1) –
35 Panathinaikos	–	–	–	–	–	1 (1) –	–	–	–	1 (1) –
36 Stuttgart	–	–	–	–	–	1 (1) –	–	–	–	1 (1) –
37 Sunderland	1 (1) –	–	–	–	–	–	–	–	–	1 (1) –
38 Watford	1 –	–	–	– (1) –	–	–	–	–	–	1 (1) –
39 Wolverhampton W.	1 –	–	–	– (1) –	–	–	–	–	–	1 (1) –
40 Derby County	– (2) –	–	–	–	–	–	–	–	–	– (2) –
41 Basel	–	–	–	–	–	1 –	–	–	–	1 –
42 Burton Albion	–	–	–	1 –	–	–	–	–	–	1 –
43 Crewe Alexandra	–	–	–	–	1 –	–	–	–	–	1 –
44 Deportivo La Coruna	–	–	–	–	–	1 –	–	–	–	1 –
45 Glasgow Celtic	–	–	–	–	–	1 –	–	–	–	1 –
46 Millwall	–	–	–	1 –	–	–	–	–	–	1 –
47 Northampton Town	–	–	–	1 –	–	–	–	–	–	1 –
48 Porto	–	–	–	–	–	1 –	–	–	–	1 –
49 Sheffield United	1 –	–	–	–	–	–	–	–	–	1 –
50 Southend United	–	–	–	–	1 –	–	–	–	–	1 –
51 Sporting Lisbon	–	–	–	–	–	1 –	–	–	–	1 –
52 Barcelona	–	–	–	–	–	– (1) –	–	–	–	– (1) –
53 Exeter City	–	–	–	– (1) –	–	–	–	–	–	– (1) –
54 Glasgow Rangers	–	–	–	–	–	– (1) –	–	–	–	– (1) –

PETER FLETCHER

DEBUT (Substitute Appearance)

Saturday 14/04/1973
Football League Division 1
at Victoria Ground

Stoke City 2 Manchester United 2

CLUB CAREER RECORD	Apps	Subs	Goals
Premiership	0		0
League Division 1	2	(5)	0
League Division 2	0		0
FA Cup	0		0
League Cup	0		0
European Cup / Champions League	0		0
European Cup-Winners' Cup	0		0
UEFA Cup / Inter-Cities' Fairs Cup	0		0
Other Matches	0		0
OVERALL TOTAL	2	(5)	0

Opponents	PREM A S G	FLD 1 A S G	FLD 2 A S G	FAC A S G	LC A S G	EC/CL A S G	ECWC A S G	UEFA A S G	OTHER A S G	TOTAL A S G
1 Stoke City	– –	– (2) –	– –	– –	– –	– –	– –	– –	– –	– (2) –
2 Derby County	– –	1 –	– –	– –	– –	– –	– –	– –	– –	1 –
3 Wolverhampton W.	– –	1 –	– –	– –	– –	– –	– –	– –	– –	1 –
4 Leeds United	– –	– (1) –	– –	– –	– –	– –	– –	– –	– –	– (1) –
5 Norwich City	– –	– (1) –	– –	– –	– –	– –	– –	– –	– –	– (1) –
6 Queens Park Rangers	– –	– (1) –	– –	– –	– –	– –	– –	– –	– –	– (1) –

ALAN FOGGON

DEBUT (Substitute Appearance)

Saturday 21/08/1976
Football League Division 1
at Old Trafford

Manchester United 2 Birmingham City 2

CLUB CAREER RECORD	Apps	Subs	Goals
Premiership	0		0
League Division 1	0	(3)	0
League Division 2	0		0
FA Cup	0		0
League Cup	0		0
European Cup / Champions League	0		0
European Cup-Winners' Cup	0		0
UEFA Cup / Inter-Cities' Fairs Cup	0		0
Other Matches	0		0
OVERALL TOTAL	0	(3)	0

Opponents	PREM A S G	FLD 1 A S G	FLD 2 A S G	FAC A S G	LC A S G	EC/CL A S G	ECWC A S G	UEFA A S G	OTHER A S G	TOTAL A S G
1 Birmingham City	– –	– (1) –	– –	– –	– –	– –	– –	– –	– –	– (1) –
2 Middlesbrough	– –	– (1) –	– –	– –	– –	– –	– –	– –	– –	– (1) –
3 Newcastle United	– –	– (1) –	– –	– –	– –	– –	– –	– –	– –	– (1) –

G FOLEY

DEBUT (Full Appearance)

Saturday 17/03/1900
Football League Division 2
at Bank Street

Newton Heath 3 Barnsley 0

CLUB CAREER RECORD	Apps	Subs	Goals
Premiership	0		0
League Division 1	0		0
League Division 2	7		1
FA Cup	0		0
League Cup	0		0
European Cup / Champions League	0		0
European Cup-Winners' Cup	0		0
UEFA Cup / Inter-Cities' Fairs Cup	0		0
Other Matches	0		0
OVERALL TOTAL	7		1

Opponents	PREM A S G	FLD 1 A S G	FLD 2 A S G	FAC A S G	LC A S G	EC/CL A S G	ECWC A S G	UEFA A S G	OTHER A S G	TOTAL A S G
1 Walsall	– –	– –	2 1	– –	– –	– –	– –	– –	– –	2 1
2 Leicester City	– –	– –	2 –	– –	– –	– –	– –	– –	– –	2 –
3 Barnsley	– –	– –	1 –	– –	– –	– –	– –	– –	– –	1 –
4 Middlesbrough	– –	– –	1 –	– –	– –	– –	– –	– –	– –	1 –
5 Port Vale	– –	– –	1 –	– –	– –	– –	– –	– –	– –	1 –

JOE FORD

DEBUT (Full Appearance)

Wednesday 31/03/1909
Football League Division 1
at Bank Street

Manchester United 0 Aston Villa 2

CLUB CAREER RECORD	Apps	Subs	Goals
Premiership	0		0
League Division 1	5		0
League Division 2	0		0
FA Cup	0		0
League Cup	0		0
European Cup / Champions League	0		0
European Cup-Winners' Cup	0		0
UEFA Cup / Inter-Cities' Fairs Cup	0		0
Other Matches	0		0
OVERALL TOTAL	5		0

Opponents	PREM A S G	FLD 1 A S G	FLD 2 A S G	FAC A S G	LC A S G	EC/CL A S G	ECWC A S G	UEFA A S G	OTHER A S G	TOTAL A S G
1 Aston Villa	– –	1 –	– –	– –	– –	– –	– –	– –	– –	1 –
2 Everton	– –	1 –	– –	– –	– –	– –	– –	– –	– –	1 –
3 Liverpool	– –	1 –	– –	– –	– –	– –	– –	– –	– –	1 –
4 Notts County	– –	1 –	– –	– –	– –	– –	– –	– –	– –	1 –
5 Sheffield Wednesday	– –	1 –	– –	– –	– –	– –	– –	– –	– –	1 –

DIEGO FORLAN

DEBUT (Substitute Appearance)

Tuesday 29/01/2002
FA Premiership
at Reebok Stadium

Bolton Wanderers 0 Manchester United 4

CLUB CAREER RECORD	Apps	Subs	Goals
Premiership	23	(40)	10
League Division 1	0		0
League Division 2	0		0
FA Cup	2	(2)	1
League Cup	4	(2)	3
European Cup / Champions League	8	(15)	3
European Cup-Winners' Cup	0		0
UEFA Cup / Inter-Cities' Fairs Cup	0		0
Other Matches	0	(2)	0
OVERALL TOTAL	37	(61)	17

Opponents	PREM			FLD 1			FLD 2			FAC			LC			EC/CL			ECWC			UEFA			OTHER			TOTAL		
	A	S	G	A	S	G	A	S	G	A	S	G	A	S	G	A	S	G	A	S	G	A	S	G	A	S	G	A	S	G
1 Chelsea	1	(4)	1										1	–	1													2	(4)	2
2 Arsenal	1	(1)	–							–	(1)	–													–	(2)	–	1	(4)	–
3 Blackburn Rovers	1	(2)	–										–	(2)	–													1	(4)	–
4 Leicester City	2	(1)	–										1	–	–													3	(1)	–
5 Charlton Athletic	2	(2)	–																									2	(2)	–
6 Leeds United	–	(3)	–										1	–	1													1	(3)	1
7 Newcastle United	1	(3)	–																									1	(3)	–
8 Bolton Wanderers	–	(4)	–																									–	(4)	–
9 Aston Villa	1	(1)	3							1	–	–																2	(1)	3
10 Fulham	2	(1)	1																									2	(1)	1
11 Tottenham Hotspur	2	(1)	–																									2	(1)	–
12 Birmingham City	1	(2)	1																									1	(2)	1
13 Southampton	1	(2)	1																									1	(2)	1
14 Middlesbrough	1	(2)	–																									1	(2)	–
15 Sunderland	1	(2)	–																									1	(2)	–
16 West Ham United	–	(2)	–							–	(1)	–																–	(3)	–
17 Liverpool	2		2																									2		2
18 Maccabi Haifa																1	(1)	1										1	(1)	1
19 Basel																1	(1)	–										1	(1)	–
20 Deportivo La Coruna																1	(1)	–										1	(1)	–
21 Everton	1	(1)	–																									1	(1)	–
22 Juventus																1	(1)	–										1	(1)	–
23 Olympiakos Piraeus																1	(1)	–										1	(1)	–
24 Wolverhampton W.	1	(1)	–																									1	(1)	–
25 Bayer Leverkusen																–	(2)	–										–	(2)	–
26 Manchester City	–	(2)	–																									–	(2)	–
27 Nantes Atlantique																–	(2)	–										–	(2)	–
28 Stuttgart																–	(2)	–										–	(2)	–
29 West Bromwich Albion	–	(2)	–																									–	(2)	–
30 Zalaegerszeg																–	(2)	–										–	(2)	–
31 Burnley													1	–	1													1		1
32 Glasgow Rangers																1	–	1										1		1
33 Northampton Town										1	–	1																1		1
34 Panathinaikos																1	–	1										1		1
35 Portsmouth	1	–	1																									1		1
36 Boavista																1	–	–										1		–
37 Ipswich Town	1	–	–																									1		–
38 Bayern Munich																–	(1)	–										–	(1)	–
39 Derby County	–	(1)	–																									–	(1)	–
40 Dinamo Bucharest																–	(1)	–										–	(1)	–

TOMMY FORSTER

DEBUT (Full Appearance)

Saturday 08/11/1919
Football League Division 1
at Turf Moor

Burnley 2 Manchester United 1

CLUB CAREER RECORD	Apps	Subs	Goals
Premiership	0		0
League Division 1	35		0
League Division 2	0		0
FA Cup	1		0
League Cup	0		0
European Cup / Champions League	0		0
European Cup-Winners' Cup	0		0
UEFA Cup / Inter-Cities' Fairs Cup	0		0
Other Matches	0		0
OVERALL TOTAL	36		0

Opponents	PREM			FLD 1			FLD 2			FAC			LC			EC/CL			ECWC			UEFA			OTHER			TOTAL		
	A	S	G	A	S	G	A	S	G	A	S	G	A	S	G	A	S	G	A	S	G	A	S	G	A	S	G	A	S	G
1 Burnley				4	–																							4		–
2 Middlesbrough				4	–																							4		–
3 Liverpool				2	–					1	–																	3		–
4 Aston Villa				2	–																							2		–
5 Blackburn Rovers				2	–																							2		–
6 Bradford City				2	–																							2		–
7 Bradford Park Avenue				2	–																							2		–
8 Huddersfield Town				2	–																							2		–
9 Manchester City				2	–																							2		–
10 Notts County				2	–																							2		–
11 Oldham Athletic				2	–																							2		–

continued../

TOMMY FORSTER (continued)

Opponents	PREM A S G	FLD 1 A S G	FLD 2 A S G	FAC A S G	LC A S G	EC/CL A S G	ECWC A S G	UEFA A S G	OTHER A S G	TOTAL A S G
12 Sheffield United	– –	2 –	–	–	–	–	–	–	–	2 –
13 Sunderland	– –	2 –	–	–	–	–	–	–	–	2 –
14 West Bromwich Albion	– –	2 –	–	–	–	–	–	–	–	2 –
15 Derby County	– –	1 –	–	–	–	–	–	–	–	1 –
16 Everton	– –	1 –	–	–	–	–	–	–	–	1 –
17 Newcastle United	– –	1 –	–	–	–	–	–	–	–	1 –

ALEX FORSYTH

DEBUT (Full Appearance)

Saturday 06/01/1973
Football League Division 1
at Highbury

Arsenal 3 Manchester United 1

CLUB CAREER RECORD	Apps	Subs	Goals
Premiership	0		0
League Division 1	60	(2)	3
League Division 2	39		1
FA Cup	10		1
League Cup	7		0
European Cup / Champions League	0		0
European Cup-Winners' Cup	0	(1)	0
UEFA Cup / Inter-Cities' Fairs Cup	0		0
Other Matches	0		0
OVERALL TOTAL	116	(3)	5

Opponents	PREM A S G	FLD 1 A S G	FLD 2 A S G	FAC A S G	LC A S G	EC/CL A S G	ECWC A S G	UEFA A S G	OTHER A S G	TOTAL A S G
1 Wolverhampton W.	– –	4 –	–	3 –	–	–	–	–	–	7 –
2 Norwich City	– –	2 –	2 –	–	2 –	–	–	–	–	6 –
3 Derby County	– –	4 –	–	1 –	–	–	–	–	–	5 –
4 Everton	– –	4 –	–	–	1 –	–	–	–	–	5 –
5 Manchester City	– –	4 –	–	–	1 –	–	–	–	–	5 –
6 Coventry City	– –	4 (1) –	–	–	–	–	–	–	–	4 (1) –
7 Birmingham City	– –	4 1	–	–	–	–	–	–	–	4 1
8 Burnley	– –	3 1	–	–	1 –	–	–	–	–	4 1
9 West Ham United	– –	4 1	–	–	–	–	–	–	–	4 1
10 Southampton	– –	1 –	2 –	1 –	–	–	–	–	–	4 –
11 Aston Villa	– –	1 –	2 –	–	–	–	–	–	–	3 –
12 Ipswich Town	– –	2 –	–	1 –	–	–	–	–	–	3 –
13 Middlesbrough	– –	2 –	–	–	1 –	–	–	–	–	3 –
14 Oxford United	– –	–	2 –	1 –	–	–	–	–	–	3 –
15 Sheffield United	– –	3 –	–	–	–	–	–	–	–	3 –
16 Stoke City	– –	3 –	–	–	–	–	–	–	–	3 –
17 West Bromwich Albion	– –	2 –	–	1 –	–	–	–	–	–	3 –
18 Blackpool	– –	–	2 1	–	–	–	–	–	–	2 1
19 Arsenal	– –	2 –	–	–	–	–	–	–	–	2 –
20 Bolton Wanderers	– –	–	2 –	–	–	–	–	–	–	2 –
21 Bristol City	– –	–	2 –	–	–	–	–	–	–	2 –
22 Bristol Rovers	– –	–	2 –	–	–	–	–	–	–	2 –
23 Cardiff City	– –	–	2 –	–	–	–	–	–	–	2 –
24 Fulham	– –	–	2 –	–	–	–	–	–	–	2 –
25 Hull City	– –	–	2 –	–	–	–	–	–	–	2 –
26 Leeds United	– –	2 –	–	–	–	–	–	–	–	2 –
27 Leicester City	– –	1 –	–	1 –	–	–	–	–	–	2 –
28 Leyton Orient	– –	–	2 –	–	–	–	–	–	–	2 –
29 Liverpool	– –	2 –	–	–	–	–	–	–	–	2 –
30 Millwall	– –	–	2 –	–	–	–	–	–	–	2 –
31 Newcastle United	– –	2 –	–	–	–	–	–	–	–	2 –
32 Nottingham Forest	– –	–	2 –	–	–	–	–	–	–	2 –
33 Notts County	– –	–	2 –	–	–	–	–	–	–	2 –
34 Portsmouth	– –	–	2 –	–	–	–	–	–	–	2 –
35 Sheffield Wednesday	– –	–	2 –	–	–	–	–	–	–	2 –
36 Sunderland	– –	–	2 –	–	–	–	–	–	–	2 –
37 Tottenham Hotspur	– –	2 –	–	–	–	–	–	–	–	2 –
38 Queens Park Rangers	– –	1 (1) –	–	–	–	–	–	–	–	1 (1) –
39 Peterborough United	– –	–	–	1 1	–	–	–	–	–	1 1
40 Charlton Athletic	– –	–	–	–	1 –	–	–	–	–	1 –
41 Chelsea	– –	1 –	–	–	–	–	–	–	–	1 –
42 Oldham Athletic	– –	–	1 –	–	–	–	–	–	–	1 –
43 Plymouth Argyle	– –	–	–	1 –	–	–	–	–	–	1 –
44 York City	– –	–	1 –	–	–	–	–	–	–	1 –
45 Porto	– –	–	–	–	–	–	– (1) –	–	–	– (1) –

QUINTON FORTUNE

DEBUT (Substitute Appearance)

Monday 30/08/1999
FA Premiership
at Old Trafford

Manchester United 5 Newcastle United 1

CLUB CAREER RECORD	Apps	Subs	Goals
Premiership	53	(23)	6
League Division 1	0		0
League Division 2	0		0
FA Cup	8	(1)	1
League Cup	8		0
European Cup / Champions League	16	(12)	2
European Cup-Winners' Cup	0		0
UEFA Cup / Inter-Cities' Fairs Cup	0		0
Other Matches	3	(2)	2
OVERALL TOTAL	**88**	**(38)**	**11**

Opponents	PREM A	S	G	FLD1 A	S	G	FLD2 A	S	G	FAC A	S	G	LC A	S	G	EC/CL A	S	G	ECWC A	S	G	UEFA A	S	G	OTHER A	S	G	TOTAL A	S	G
1 Chelsea	4	–	–	–	–	–	–	–	–	–	–	–	2	–	–	–	–	–	–	–	–	–	–	–	–	(1)	–	6	(1)	–
2 Arsenal	2	(1)	–	–	–	–	–	–	–	–	(1)	–	1	–	–	–	–	–	–	–	–	–	–	–	2	–	–	5	(2)	–
3 Middlesbrough	3	(2)	2	–	–	–	–	–	–	1	–	–	–	–	–	–	–	–	–	–	–	–	–	–	–	–	–	4	(2)	2
4 Leeds United	4	–	–	–	–	–	–	–	–	1	–	–	–	–	–	–	–	–	–	–	–	–	–	–	–	–	–	5	–	–
5 Leicester City	3	(1)	–	–	–	–	–	–	–	1	–	–	–	–	–	–	–	–	–	–	–	–	–	–	–	–	–	4	(1)	–
6 Southampton	3	(1)	–	–	–	–	–	–	–	1	–	–	–	–	–	–	–	–	–	–	–	–	–	–	–	–	–	4	(1)	–
7 Everton	2	(2)	1	–	–	–	–	–	–	1	–	1	–	–	–	–	–	–	–	–	–	–	–	–	–	–	–	3	(2)	2
8 Newcastle United	2	(2)	–	–	–	–	–	–	–	–	–	–	1	–	–	–	–	–	–	–	–	–	–	–	–	–	–	3	(2)	–
9 Charlton Athletic	3	(1)	–	–	–	–	–	–	–	–	–	–	–	–	–	–	–	–	–	–	–	–	–	–	–	–	–	3	(1)	–
10 Liverpool	3	(1)	–	–	–	–	–	–	–	–	–	–	–	–	–	–	–	–	–	–	–	–	–	–	–	–	–	3	(1)	–
11 Aston Villa	1	(2)	–	–	–	–	–	–	–	–	–	–	1	–	–	–	–	–	–	–	–	–	–	–	–	–	–	2	(2)	–
12 Fulham	2	(2)	–	–	–	–	–	–	–	–	–	–	–	–	–	–	–	–	–	–	–	–	–	–	–	–	–	2	(2)	–
13 West Ham United	2	(2)	–	–	–	–	–	–	–	–	–	–	–	–	–	–	–	–	–	–	–	–	–	–	–	–	–	2	(2)	–
14 Blackburn Rovers	3	–	–	–	–	–	–	–	–	–	–	–	–	–	–	–	–	–	–	–	–	–	–	–	–	–	–	3	–	–
15 Crystal Palace	2	–	–	–	–	–	–	–	–	–	–	–	1	–	–	–	–	–	–	–	–	–	–	–	–	–	–	3	–	–
16 Birmingham City	2	(1)	–	–	–	–	–	–	–	–	–	–	–	–	–	–	–	–	–	–	–	–	–	–	–	–	–	2	(1)	–
17 Bradford City	2	–	3	–	–	–	–	–	–	–	–	–	–	–	–	–	–	–	–	–	–	–	–	–	–	–	–	2	–	3
18 Panathinaikos	–	–	–	–	–	–	–	–	–	–	–	–	–	–	–	2	–	1	–	–	–	–	–	–	–	–	–	2	–	1
19 Glasgow Rangers	–	–	–	–	–	–	–	–	–	–	–	–	–	–	–	2	–	–	–	–	–	–	–	–	–	–	–	2	–	–
20 Ipswich Town	2	–	–	–	–	–	–	–	–	–	–	–	–	–	–	–	–	–	–	–	–	–	–	–	–	–	–	2	–	–
21 Manchester City	1	–	–	–	–	–	–	–	–	1	–	–	–	–	–	–	–	–	–	–	–	–	–	–	–	–	–	2	–	–
22 Sunderland	1	–	–	–	–	–	–	–	–	–	–	–	1	–	–	–	–	–	–	–	–	–	–	–	–	–	–	2	–	–
23 AC Milan	–	–	–	–	–	–	–	–	–	–	–	–	–	–	–	1	(1)	–	–	–	–	–	–	–	–	–	–	1	(1)	–
24 Bolton Wanderers	1	(1)	–	–	–	–	–	–	–	–	–	–	–	–	–	–	–	–	–	–	–	–	–	–	–	–	–	1	(1)	–
25 Deportivo La Coruna	–	–	–	–	–	–	–	–	–	–	–	–	–	–	–	1	(1)	–	–	–	–	–	–	–	–	–	–	1	(1)	–
26 Derby County	1	(1)	–	–	–	–	–	–	–	–	–	–	–	–	–	–	–	–	–	–	–	–	–	–	–	–	–	1	(1)	–
27 Portsmouth	1	(1)	–	–	–	–	–	–	–	–	–	–	–	–	–	–	–	–	–	–	–	–	–	–	–	–	–	1	(1)	–
28 Stuttgart	–	–	–	–	–	–	–	–	–	–	–	–	–	–	–	1	(1)	–	–	–	–	–	–	–	–	–	–	1	(1)	–
29 Olympiakos Piraeus	–	–	–	–	–	–	–	–	–	–	–	–	–	–	–	–	(2)	–	–	–	–	–	–	–	–	–	–	–	(2)	–
30 Tottenham Hotspur	–	(2)	–	–	–	–	–	–	–	–	–	–	–	–	–	–	–	–	–	–	–	–	–	–	–	–	–	–	(2)	–
31 South Melbourne	–	–	–	–	–	–	–	–	–	–	–	–	–	–	–	–	–	–	–	–	–	–	–	–	1	–	2	1	–	2
32 Porto	–	–	–	–	–	–	–	–	–	–	–	–	–	–	–	1	–	1	–	–	–	–	–	–	–	–	–	1	–	1
33 Basel	–	–	–	–	–	–	–	–	–	–	–	–	–	–	–	1	–	–	–	–	–	–	–	–	–	–	–	1	–	–
34 Bayer Leverkusen	–	–	–	–	–	–	–	–	–	–	–	–	–	–	–	1	–	–	–	–	–	–	–	–	–	–	–	1	–	–
35 Bayern Munich	–	–	–	–	–	–	–	–	–	–	–	–	–	–	–	1	–	–	–	–	–	–	–	–	–	–	–	1	–	–
36 Dinamo Bucharest	–	–	–	–	–	–	–	–	–	–	–	–	–	–	–	1	–	–	–	–	–	–	–	–	–	–	–	1	–	–
37 Exeter City	–	–	–	–	–	–	–	–	–	1	–	–	–	–	–	–	–	–	–	–	–	–	–	–	–	–	–	1	–	–
38 Fenerbahce	–	–	–	–	–	–	–	–	–	–	–	–	–	–	–	1	–	–	–	–	–	–	–	–	–	–	–	1	–	–
39 Lille Metropole	–	–	–	–	–	–	–	–	–	–	–	–	–	–	–	1	–	–	–	–	–	–	–	–	–	–	–	1	–	–
40 Maccabi Haifa	–	–	–	–	–	–	–	–	–	–	–	–	–	–	–	1	–	–	–	–	–	–	–	–	–	–	–	1	–	–
41 Northampton Town	–	–	–	–	–	–	–	–	–	1	–	–	–	–	–	–	–	–	–	–	–	–	–	–	–	–	–	1	–	–
42 Norwich City	1	–	–	–	–	–	–	–	–	–	–	–	–	–	–	–	–	–	–	–	–	–	–	–	–	–	–	1	–	–
43 Valencia	–	–	–	–	–	–	–	–	–	–	–	–	–	–	–	1	–	–	–	–	–	–	–	–	–	–	–	1	–	–
44 Watford	–	–	–	–	–	–	–	–	–	–	–	–	1	–	–	–	–	–	–	–	–	–	–	–	–	–	–	1	–	–
45 West Bromwich Albion	1	–	–	–	–	–	–	–	–	–	–	–	–	–	–	–	–	–	–	–	–	–	–	–	–	–	–	1	–	–
46 Wolverhampton W.	1	–	–	–	–	–	–	–	–	–	–	–	–	–	–	–	–	–	–	–	–	–	–	–	–	–	–	1	–	–
47 Boavista	–	–	–	–	–	–	–	–	–	–	–	–	–	–	–	–	(1)	–	–	–	–	–	–	–	–	–	–	–	(1)	–
48 Croatia Zagreb	–	–	–	–	–	–	–	–	–	–	–	–	–	–	–	–	(1)	–	–	–	–	–	–	–	–	–	–	–	(1)	–
49 Dynamo Kiev	–	–	–	–	–	–	–	–	–	–	–	–	–	–	–	–	(1)	–	–	–	–	–	–	–	–	–	–	–	(1)	–
50 Girondins Bordeaux	–	–	–	–	–	–	–	–	–	–	–	–	–	–	–	–	(1)	–	–	–	–	–	–	–	–	–	–	–	(1)	–
51 Olympique Lyonnais	–	–	–	–	–	–	–	–	–	–	–	–	–	–	–	–	(1)	–	–	–	–	–	–	–	–	–	–	–	(1)	–
52 Olympique Marseille	–	–	–	–	–	–	–	–	–	–	–	–	–	–	–	–	(1)	–	–	–	–	–	–	–	–	–	–	–	(1)	–
53 Real Madrid	–	–	–	–	–	–	–	–	–	–	–	–	–	–	–	–	(1)	–	–	–	–	–	–	–	–	–	–	–	(1)	–
54 Vasco da Gama	–	–	–	–	–	–	–	–	–	–	–	–	–	–	–	–	–	–	–	–	–	–	–	–	–	(1)	–	–	(1)	–

BEN FOSTER

DEBUT (Full Appearance)

Saturday 15/03/2008
FA Premiership
at Pride Park

Derby County 0 Manchester United 1

CLUB CAREER RECORD	Apps	Subs	Goals
Premiership	1		0
League Division 1	0		0
League Division 2	0		0
FA Cup	0		0
League Cup	0		0
European Cup / Champions League	0		0
European Cup-Winners' Cup	0		0
UEFA Cup / Inter-Cities' Fairs Cup	0		0
Other Matches	0		0
OVERALL TOTAL	**1**		**0**

Opponents	PREM			FLD 1			FLD 2			FAC			LC			EC/CL			ECWC			UEFA			OTHER			TOTAL		
	A	S	G	A	S	G	A	S	G	A	S	G	A	S	G	A	S	G	A	S	G	A	S	G	A	S	G	A	S	G
1 Derby County	1	–		–	–		–	–		–	–		–	–		–	–		–	–		–	–		–	–		1	–	

BILL FOULKES

DEBUT (Full Appearance)

Saturday 13/12/1952
Football League Division 1
at Anfield

Liverpool 1 Manchester United 2

CLUB CAREER RECORD	Apps	Subs	Goals
Premiership	0		0
League Division 1	563	(3)	7
League Division 2	0		0
FA Cup	61		0
League Cup	3		0
European Cup / Champions League	35		2
European Cup-Winners' Cup	6		0
UEFA Cup / Inter-Cities' Fairs Cup	11		0
Other Matches	6		0
OVERALL TOTAL	**685**	**(3)**	**9**

Opponents	PREM			FLD 1			FLD 2			FAC			LC			EC/CL			ECWC			UEFA			OTHER			TOTAL		
	A	S	G	A	S	G	A	S	G	A	S	G	A	S	G	A	S	G	A	S	G	A	S	G	A	S	G	A	S	G
1 Tottenham Hotspur	–	–		29	–		–	–		1	–		–	–		–	–	2	–	–		–	–		1	–		33	–	
2 Everton	–	–		26	(1)	1	–	–		2	–		–	–		–	–		–	–		2	–		1	–		31	(1)	1
3 Burnley	–	–		29	–		–	–		2	–		–	–		–	–		–	–		–	–		–	–		31	–	
4 Sheffield Wednesday	–	–		25	–		–	–		6	–		–	–		–	–		–	–		–	–		–	–		31	–	
5 Arsenal	–	–		26	–		–	–		1	–		–	–		–	–		–	–		–	–		–	–		27	–	
6 West Bromwich Albion	–	–		24	(1)	–	–	–		2	–		–	–		–	–		–	–		–	–		–	–		26	(1)	–
7 Aston Villa	–	–		23	–		–	–		2	–		–	–		–	–		–	–		–	–		1	–		26	–	
8 Chelsea	–	–		25	–		–	–		1	–		–	–		–	–		–	–		–	–		–	–		26	–	
9 Blackpool	–	–		24	–		–	–		–	–		1	–		–	–		–	–		–	–		–	–		25	–	
10 Wolverhampton W.	–	–		22	(1)	–	–	–		2	–		–	–		–	–		–	–		–	–		–	–		24	(1)	–
11 Leicester City	–	–		23	–	1	–	–		1	–		–	–		–	–		–	–		–	–		–	–		24	–	1
12 Manchester City	–	–		21	–	1	–	–		1	–		–	–		–	–		–	–		1	–		–	–		23	–	1
13 Bolton Wanderers	–	–		20	–		–	–		2	–		–	–		–	–		–	–		–	–		–	–		22	–	
14 Birmingham City	–	–		19	–		–	–		1	–		–	–		–	–		–	–		–	–		–	–		20	–	
15 Preston North End	–	–		16	–		–	–		4	–		–	–		–	–		–	–		–	–		–	–		20	–	
16 Fulham	–	–		17	–	2	–	–		2	–		–	–		–	–		–	–		–	–		–	–		19	–	2
17 Newcastle United	–	–		19	–	1	–	–		–	–		–	–		–	–		–	–		–	–		–	–		19	–	1
18 West Ham United	–	–		18	–	1	–	–		1	–		–	–		–	–		–	–		–	–		–	–		19	–	1
19 Nottingham Forest	–	–		19	–		–	–		–	–		–	–		–	–		–	–		–	–		–	–		19	–	
20 Sunderland	–	–		15	–		–	–		3	–		–	–		–	–		–	–		–	–		–	–		18	–	
21 Sheffield United	–	–		17	–		–	–		–	–		–	–		–	–		–	–		–	–		–	–		17	–	
22 Leeds United	–	–		14	–		–	–		2	–		–	–		–	–		–	–		–	–		–	–		16	–	
23 Blackburn Rovers	–	–		13	–		–	–		–	–		–	–		–	–		–	–		–	–		–	–		13	–	
24 Liverpool	–	–		12	–		–	–		1	–		–	–		–	–		–	–		–	–		–	–		13	–	
25 Stoke City	–	–		9	–		–	–		3	–		–	–		–	–		–	–		–	–		–	–		12	–	
26 Cardiff City	–	–		11	–		–	–		–	–		–	–		–	–		–	–		–	–		–	–		11	–	
27 Portsmouth	–	–		10	–		–	–		–	–		–	–		–	–		–	–		–	–		–	–		10	–	
28 Luton Town	–	–		9	–		–	–		–	–		–	–		–	–		–	–		–	–		–	–		9	–	
29 Charlton Athletic	–	–		7	–		–	–		–	–		–	–		–	–		–	–		–	–		–	–		7	–	
30 Ipswich Town	–	–		6	–		–	–		1	–		–	–		–	–		–	–		–	–		–	–		7	–	
31 Southampton	–	–		5	–		–	–		2	–		–	–		–	–		–	–		–	–		–	–		7	–	
32 Huddersfield Town	–	–		5	–		–	–		1	–		–	–		–	–		–	–		–	–		–	–		6	–	
33 AC Milan	–	–		–	–		–	–		–	–		–	–		4	–		–	–		–	–		–	–		4	–	
34 Borussia Dortmund	–	–		–	–		–	–		–	–		–	–		2	–		–	–		2	–		–	–		4	–	
35 Benfica	–	–		–	–		–	–		–	–		–	–		3	–	1	–	–		–	–		–	–		3	–	1
36 Real Madrid	–	–		–	–		–	–		–	–		–	–		3	–	1	–	–		–	–		–	–		3	–	1
37 Anderlecht	–	–		–	–		–	–		–	–		–	–		3	–		–	–		–	–		–	–		3	–	
38 Ferencvaros	–	–		–	–		–	–		–	–		–	–		–	–		–	–		3	–		–	–		3	–	
39 ASK Vorwaerts	–	–		–	–		–	–		–	–		–	–		2	–		–	–		–	–		–	–		2	–	
40 Athletic Bilbao	–	–		–	–		–	–		–	–		–	–		2	–		–	–		–	–		–	–		2	–	
41 Bristol Rovers	–	–		–	–		–	–		2	–		–	–		–	–		–	–		–	–		–	–		2	–	
42 Derby County	–	–		–	–		–	–		2	–		–	–		–	–		–	–		–	–		–	–		2	–	
43 Djurgardens	–	–		–	–		–	–		–	–		–	–		–	–		–	–		2	–		–	–		2	–	
44 Dukla Prague	–	–		–	–		–	–		–	–		–	–		2	–		–	–		–	–		–	–		2	–	
45 Estudiantes de la Plata	–	–		–	–		–	–		–	–		–	–		–	–		–	–		–	–		2	–		2	–	
46 Hibernians Malta	–	–		–	–		–	–		–	–		–	–		2	–		–	–		–	–		–	–		2	–	
47 HJK Helsinki	–	–		–	–		–	–		–	–		–	–		2	–		–	–		–	–		–	–		2	–	
48 Leyton Orient	–	–		2	–		–	–		–	–		–	–		–	–		–	–		–	–		–	–		2	–	
49 Northampton Town	–	–		2	–		–	–		–	–		–	–		–	–		–	–		–	–		–	–		2	–	
50 Partizan Belgrade	–	–		–	–		–	–		–	–		–	–		2	–		–	–		–	–		–	–		2	–	

continued../

BILL FOULKES (continued)

Opponents	PREM A S G	FLD 1 A S G	FLD 2 A S G	FAC A S G	LC A S G	EC/CL A S G	ECWC A S G	UEFA A S G	OTHER A S G	TOTAL A S G
51 Reading	– – –	– – –	– – –	2 – –	– – –	– – –	– – –	– – –	– – –	2 –
52 Red Star Belgrade	– – –	– – –	– – –	– – –	– – –	2 – –	– – –	– – –	– – –	2 –
53 Rotherham United	– – –	– – –	– – –	2 – –	– – –	– – –	– – –	– – –	– – –	2 –
54 Sarajevo	– – –	– – –	– – –	– – –	– – –	2 – –	– – –	– – –	– – –	2 –
55 Shamrock Rovers	– – –	– – –	– – –	– – –	– – –	2 – –	– – –	– – –	– – –	2 –
56 Sporting Lisbon	– – –	– – –	– – –	– – –	– – –	– – –	2 – –	– – –	– – –	2 –
57 Strasbourg	– – –	– – –	– – –	– – –	– – –	– – –	– – –	2 – –	– – –	2 –
58 Waterford	– – –	– – –	– – –	– – –	– – –	2 – –	– – –	– – –	– – –	2 –
59 Willem II	– – –	– – –	– – –	– – –	– – –	– – –	2 – –	– – –	– – –	2 –
60 Barnsley	– – –	– – –	– – –	1 – –	– – –	– – –	– – –	– – –	– – –	1 –
61 Bournemouth	– – –	– – –	– – –	1 – –	– – –	– – –	– – –	– – –	– – –	1 –
62 Bradford City	– – –	– – –	– – –	– – –	1 – –	– – –	– – –	– – –	– – –	1 –
63 Chester City	– – –	– – –	– – –	1 – –	– – –	– – –	– – –	– – –	– – –	1 –
64 Coventry City	– – –	– – –	– – –	1 – –	– – –	– – –	– – –	– – –	– – –	1 –
65 Crystal Palace	– – –	– 1 –	– – –	– – –	– – –	– – –	– – –	– – –	– – –	1 –
66 Exeter City	– – –	– – –	– – –	– – –	1 – –	– – –	– – –	– – –	– – –	1 –
67 Hartlepool United	– – –	– – –	– – –	1 – –	– – –	– – –	– – –	– – –	– – –	1 –
68 Middlesbrough	– – –	– – –	– – –	1 – –	– – –	– – –	– – –	– – –	– – –	1 –
69 Norwich City	– – –	– – –	– – –	1 – –	– – –	– – –	– – –	– – –	– – –	1 –
70 Workington	– – –	– – –	– – –	1 – –	– – –	– – –	– – –	– – –	– – –	1 –
71 Wrexham	– – –	– – –	– – –	1 – –	– – –	– – –	– – –	– – –	– – –	1 –

FOX (FIRST NAME NOT KNOWN)

DEBUT (Full Appearance)

Saturday 09/01/1915
FA Cup 1st Round
at Hillsborough

Sheffield Wednesday 1 Manchester United 0

CLUB CAREER RECORD	Apps	Subs	Goals
Premiership	0		0
League Division 1	0		0
League Division 2	0		0
FA Cup	1		0
League Cup	0		0
European Cup / Champions League	0		0
European Cup-Winners' Cup	0		0
UEFA Cup / Inter-Cities' Fairs Cup	0		0
Other Matches	0		0
OVERALL TOTAL	**1**		**0**

Opponents	PREM A S G	FLD 1 A S G	FLD 2 A S G	FAC A S G	LC A S G	EC/CL A S G	ECWC A S G	UEFA A S G	OTHER A S G	TOTAL A S G
1 Sheffield Wednesday	– – –	– – –	– – –	1 – –	– – –	– – –	– – –	– – –	– – –	1 –

TOMMY FRAME

DEBUT (Full Appearance)

Saturday 01/10/1932
Football League Division 2
at Old Trafford

Manchester United 0 Preston North End 0

CLUB CAREER RECORD	Apps	Subs	Goals
Premiership	0		0
League Division 1	0		0
League Division 2	51		4
FA Cup	1		0
League Cup	0		0
European Cup / Champions League	0		0
European Cup-Winners' Cup	0		0
UEFA Cup / Inter-Cities' Fairs Cup	0		0
Other Matches	0		0
OVERALL TOTAL	**52**		**4**

Opponents	PREM A S G	FLD 1 A S G	FLD 2 A S G	FAC A S G	LC A S G	EC/CL A S G	ECWC A S G	UEFA A S G	OTHER A S G	TOTAL A S G
1 Lincoln City	– – –	– – –	4 – –	– – –	– – –	– – –	– – –	– – –	– – –	4 –
2 Grimsby Town	– – –	– – –	3 – 1	– – –	– – –	– – –	– – –	– – –	– – –	3 1
3 Bradford Park Avenue	– – –	– – –	3 – –	– – –	– – –	– – –	– – –	– – –	– – –	3 –
4 Burnley	– – –	– – –	3 – –	– – –	– – –	– – –	– – –	– – –	– – –	3 –
5 Fulham	– – –	– – –	3 – –	– – –	– – –	– – –	– – –	– – –	– – –	3 –
6 Millwall	– – –	– – –	3 – –	– – –	– – –	– – –	– – –	– – –	– – –	3 –
7 Nottingham Forest	– – –	– – –	3 – –	– – –	– – –	– – –	– – –	– – –	– – –	3 –
8 Plymouth Argyle	– – –	– – –	3 – –	– – –	– – –	– – –	– – –	– – –	– – –	3 –
9 Preston North End	– – –	– – –	3 – –	– – –	– – –	– – –	– – –	– – –	– – –	3 –
10 West Ham United	– – –	– – –	3 – –	– – –	– – –	– – –	– – –	– – –	– – –	3 –
11 Chesterfield	– – –	– – –	2 – 1	– – –	– – –	– – –	– – –	– – –	– – –	2 1
12 Bolton Wanderers	– – –	– – –	2 – –	– – –	– – –	– – –	– – –	– – –	– – –	2 –
13 Bradford City	– – –	– – –	2 – –	– – –	– – –	– – –	– – –	– – –	– – –	2 –
14 Notts County	– – –	– – –	2 – –	– – –	– – –	– – –	– – –	– – –	– – –	2 –
15 Oldham Athletic	– – –	– – –	2 – –	– – –	– – –	– – –	– – –	– – –	– – –	2 –
16 Port Vale	– – –	– – –	2 – –	– – –	– – –	– – –	– – –	– – –	– – –	2 –
17 Swansea City	– – –	– – –	2 – –	– – –	– – –	– – –	– – –	– – –	– – –	2 –
18 Brentford	– – –	– – –	1 – 1	– – –	– – –	– – –	– – –	– – –	– – –	1 1
19 Tottenham Hotspur	– – –	– – –	1 – 1	– – –	– – –	– – –	– – –	– – –	– – –	1 1
20 Blackpool	– – –	– – –	1 – –	– – –	– – –	– – –	– – –	– – –	– – –	1 –
21 Bury	– – –	– – –	1 – –	– – –	– – –	– – –	– – –	– – –	– – –	1 –
22 Middlesbrough	– – –	– – –	– – –	1 – –	– – –	– – –	– – –	– – –	– – –	1 –
23 Southampton	– – –	– – –	1 – –	– – –	– – –	– – –	– – –	– – –	– – –	1 –
24 Stoke City	– – –	– – –	1 – –	– – –	– – –	– – –	– – –	– – –	– – –	1 –

STANLEY GALLIMORE

DEBUT (Full Appearance)

Saturday 11/10/1930
Football League Division 1
at Upton Park

West Ham United 5 Manchester United 1

CLUB CAREER RECORD	Apps	Subs	Goals
Premiership	0		0
League Division 1	28		5
League Division 2	44		14
FA Cup	4		1
League Cup	0		0
European Cup / Champions League	0		0
European Cup-Winners' Cup	0		0
UEFA Cup / Inter-Cities' Fairs Cup	0		0
Other Matches	0		0
OVERALL TOTAL	**76**		**20**

Opponents	PREM			FLD 1			FLD 2			FAC			LC			EC/CL			ECWC			UEFA			OTHER			TOTAL		
	A	S	G	A	S	G	A	S	G	A	S	G	A	S	G	A	S	G	A	S	G	A	S	G	A	S	G	A	S	G
1 Preston North End	-	-	-	-	-	-	4	-	3	-	-	-	-	-	-	-	-	-	-	-	-	-	-	-	-	-	-	4	-	3
2 Stoke City	-	-	-	-	-	-	1	-	-	3	-	1	-	-	-	-	-	-	-	-	-	-	-	-	-	-	-	4	-	1
3 West Ham United	-	-	-	2	-	1	2	-	-	-	-	-	-	-	-	-	-	-	-	-	-	-	-	-	-	-	-	4	-	1
4 Notts County	-	-	-	-	-	-	3	-	2	-	-	-	-	-	-	-	-	-	-	-	-	-	-	-	-	-	-	3	-	2
5 Bradford Park Avenue	-	-	-	-	-	-	3	-	-	-	-	-	-	-	-	-	-	-	-	-	-	-	-	-	-	-	-	3	-	-
6 Chesterfield	-	-	-	-	-	-	3	-	-	-	-	-	-	-	-	-	-	-	-	-	-	-	-	-	-	-	-	3	-	-
7 Leeds United	-	-	-	2	-	-	1	-	-	-	-	-	-	-	-	-	-	-	-	-	-	-	-	-	-	-	-	3	-	-
8 Tottenham Hotspur	-	-	-	-	-	-	3	-	-	-	-	-	-	-	-	-	-	-	-	-	-	-	-	-	-	-	-	3	-	-
9 Burnley	-	-	-	-	-	-	2	-	2	-	-	-	-	-	-	-	-	-	-	-	-	-	-	-	-	-	-	2	-	2
10 Fulham	-	-	-	-	-	-	2	-	2	-	-	-	-	-	-	-	-	-	-	-	-	-	-	-	-	-	-	2	-	2
11 Millwall	-	-	-	-	-	-	2	-	2	-	-	-	-	-	-	-	-	-	-	-	-	-	-	-	-	-	-	2	-	2
12 Barnsley	-	-	-	-	-	-	2	-	1	-	-	-	-	-	-	-	-	-	-	-	-	-	-	-	-	-	-	2	-	1
13 Birmingham City	-	-	-	2	-	1	-	-	-	-	-	-	-	-	-	-	-	-	-	-	-	-	-	-	-	-	-	2	-	1
14 Bury	-	-	-	-	-	-	2	-	1	-	-	-	-	-	-	-	-	-	-	-	-	-	-	-	-	-	-	2	-	1
15 Nottingham Forest	-	-	-	-	-	-	2	-	1	-	-	-	-	-	-	-	-	-	-	-	-	-	-	-	-	-	-	2	-	1
16 Sheffield United	-	-	-	2	-	1	-	-	-	-	-	-	-	-	-	-	-	-	-	-	-	-	-	-	-	-	-	2	-	1
17 Sunderland	-	-	-	2	-	1	-	-	-	-	-	-	-	-	-	-	-	-	-	-	-	-	-	-	-	-	-	2	-	1
18 Arsenal	-	-	-	2	-	-	-	-	-	-	-	-	-	-	-	-	-	-	-	-	-	-	-	-	-	-	-	2	-	-
19 Blackpool	-	-	-	2	-	-	-	-	-	-	-	-	-	-	-	-	-	-	-	-	-	-	-	-	-	-	-	2	-	-
20 Bolton Wanderers	-	-	-	2	-	-	-	-	-	-	-	-	-	-	-	-	-	-	-	-	-	-	-	-	-	-	-	2	-	-
21 Derby County	-	-	-	2	-	-	-	-	-	-	-	-	-	-	-	-	-	-	-	-	-	-	-	-	-	-	-	2	-	-
22 Leicester City	-	-	-	2	-	-	-	-	-	-	-	-	-	-	-	-	-	-	-	-	-	-	-	-	-	-	-	2	-	-
23 Oldham Athletic	-	-	-	-	-	-	2	-	-	-	-	-	-	-	-	-	-	-	-	-	-	-	-	-	-	-	-	2	-	-
24 Port Vale	-	-	-	-	-	-	2	-	-	-	-	-	-	-	-	-	-	-	-	-	-	-	-	-	-	-	-	2	-	-
25 Portsmouth	-	-	-	2	-	-	-	-	-	-	-	-	-	-	-	-	-	-	-	-	-	-	-	-	-	-	-	2	-	-
26 Wolverhampton W.	-	-	-	-	-	-	2	-	-	-	-	-	-	-	-	-	-	-	-	-	-	-	-	-	-	-	-	2	-	-
27 Middlesbrough	-	-	-	1	-	1	-	-	-	-	-	-	-	-	-	-	-	-	-	-	-	-	-	-	-	-	-	1	-	1
28 Aston Villa	-	-	-	1	-	-	-	-	-	-	-	-	-	-	-	-	-	-	-	-	-	-	-	-	-	-	-	1	-	-
29 Blackburn Rovers	-	-	-	1	-	-	-	-	-	-	-	-	-	-	-	-	-	-	-	-	-	-	-	-	-	-	-	1	-	-
30 Bradford City	-	-	-	-	-	-	1	-	-	-	-	-	-	-	-	-	-	-	-	-	-	-	-	-	-	-	-	1	-	-
31 Bristol City	-	-	-	-	-	-	1	-	-	-	-	-	-	-	-	-	-	-	-	-	-	-	-	-	-	-	-	1	-	-
32 Charlton Athletic	-	-	-	-	-	-	1	-	-	-	-	-	-	-	-	-	-	-	-	-	-	-	-	-	-	-	-	1	-	-
33 Chelsea	-	-	-	1	-	-	-	-	-	-	-	-	-	-	-	-	-	-	-	-	-	-	-	-	-	-	-	1	-	-
34 Grimsby Town	-	-	-	-	-	-	-	-	-	1	-	-	-	-	-	-	-	-	-	-	-	-	-	-	-	-	-	1	-	-
35 Hull City	-	-	-	-	-	-	1	-	-	-	-	-	-	-	-	-	-	-	-	-	-	-	-	-	-	-	-	1	-	-
36 Manchester City	-	-	-	1	-	-	-	-	-	-	-	-	-	-	-	-	-	-	-	-	-	-	-	-	-	-	-	1	-	-
37 Newcastle United	-	-	-	1	-	-	-	-	-	-	-	-	-	-	-	-	-	-	-	-	-	-	-	-	-	-	-	1	-	-
38 Plymouth Argyle	-	-	-	-	-	-	1	-	-	-	-	-	-	-	-	-	-	-	-	-	-	-	-	-	-	-	-	1	-	-
39 Southampton	-	-	-	-	-	-	1	-	-	-	-	-	-	-	-	-	-	-	-	-	-	-	-	-	-	-	-	1	-	-

DICK GARDNER

DEBUT (Full Appearance)

Saturday 28/12/1935
Football League Division 2
at Old Trafford

Manchester United 3 Plymouth Argyle 2

CLUB CAREER RECORD	Apps	Subs	Goals
Premiership	0		0
League Division 1	4		0
League Division 2	12		1
FA Cup	2		0
League Cup	0		0
European Cup / Champions League	0		0
European Cup-Winners' Cup	0		0
UEFA Cup / Inter-Cities' Fairs Cup	0		0
Other Matches	0		0
OVERALL TOTAL	**18**		**1**

Opponents	PREM			FLD 1			FLD 2			FAC			LC			EC/CL			ECWC			UEFA			OTHER			TOTAL		
	A	S	G	A	S	G	A	S	G	A	S	G	A	S	G	A	S	G	A	S	G	A	S	G	A	S	G	A	S	G
1 Barnsley	-	-	-	-	-	-	1	-	1	-	-	-	-	-	-	-	-	-	-	-	-	-	-	-	-	-	-	1	-	1
2 Birmingham City	-	-	-	1	-	-	-	-	-	-	-	-	-	-	-	-	-	-	-	-	-	-	-	-	-	-	-	1	-	-
3 Blackpool	-	-	-	-	-	-	1	-	-	-	-	-	-	-	-	-	-	-	-	-	-	-	-	-	-	-	-	1	-	-
4 Bradford City	-	-	-	-	-	-	1	-	-	-	-	-	-	-	-	-	-	-	-	-	-	-	-	-	-	-	-	1	-	-
5 Doncaster Rovers	-	-	-	-	-	-	1	-	-	-	-	-	-	-	-	-	-	-	-	-	-	-	-	-	-	-	-	1	-	-
6 Leicester City	-	-	-	-	-	-	1	-	-	-	-	-	-	-	-	-	-	-	-	-	-	-	-	-	-	-	-	1	-	-
7 Middlesbrough	-	-	-	1	-	-	-	-	-	-	-	-	-	-	-	-	-	-	-	-	-	-	-	-	-	-	-	1	-	-
8 Newcastle United	-	-	-	-	-	-	1	-	-	-	-	-	-	-	-	-	-	-	-	-	-	-	-	-	-	-	-	1	-	-
9 Plymouth Argyle	-	-	-	-	-	-	1	-	-	-	-	-	-	-	-	-	-	-	-	-	-	-	-	-	-	-	-	1	-	-
10 Port Vale	-	-	-	-	-	-	1	-	-	-	-	-	-	-	-	-	-	-	-	-	-	-	-	-	-	-	-	1	-	-
11 Reading	-	-	-	-	-	-	-	-	-	1	-	-	-	-	-	-	-	-	-	-	-	-	-	-	-	-	-	1	-	-
12 Sheffield United	-	-	-	-	-	-	1	-	-	-	-	-	-	-	-	-	-	-	-	-	-	-	-	-	-	-	-	1	-	-

continued../

DICK GARDNER (continued)

Opponents	PREM A S G	FLD 1 A S G	FLD 2 A S G	FAC A S G	LC A S G	EC/CL A S G	ECWC A S G	UEFA A S G	OTHER A S G	TOTAL A S G
13 Southampton	- -	- -	1 -	- -	- -	- -	- -	- -	- -	1 -
14 Stoke City	- -	- -	- -	1 -	- -	- -	- -	- -	- -	1 -
15 Sunderland	- -	1 -	- -	- -	- -	- -	- -	- -	- -	1 -
16 Swansea City	- -	- -	- -	1 -	- -	- -	- -	- -	- -	1 -
17 West Bromwich Albion	- -	1 -	- -	- -	- -	- -	- -	- -	- -	1 -
18 West Ham United	- -	- -	- -	1 -	- -	- -	- -	- -	- -	1 -

BILLY GARTON

DEBUT (Full Appearance)

Wednesday 26/09/1984
League Cup 2nd Round 1st Leg
at Old Trafford

Manchester United 4 Burnley 0

CLUB CAREER RECORD	Apps	Subs	Goals
Premiership	0		0
League Division 1	39	(2)	0
League Division 2	0		0
FA Cup	3		0
League Cup	5	(1)	0
European Cup / Champions League	0		0
European Cup-Winners' Cup	0		0
UEFA Cup / Inter-Cities' Fairs Cup	0	(1)	0
Other Matches	0		0
OVERALL TOTAL	47	(4)	0

Opponents	PREM A S G	FLD 1 A S G	FLD 2 A S G	FAC A S G	LC A S G	EC/CL A S G	ECWC A S G	UEFA A S G	OTHER A S G	TOTAL A S G
1 Coventry City	- -	3 -	- -	- -	1 -	- -	- -	- -	- -	4 -
2 Newcastle United	- -	3 -	- -	- -	- -	- -	- -	- -	- -	3 -
3 Norwich City	- -	3 -	- -	- -	- -	- -	- -	- -	- -	3 -
4 Sheffield Wednesday	- -	3 -	- -	- -	- -	- -	- -	- -	- -	3 -
5 Tottenham Hotspur	- -	3 -	- -	- -	- -	- -	- -	- -	- -	3 -
6 Arsenal	- -	2 -	- -	- -	- -	- -	- -	- -	- -	2 -
7 Aston Villa	- -	2 -	- -	- -	- -	- -	- -	- -	- -	2 -
8 Charlton Athletic	- -	2 -	- -	- -	- -	- -	- -	- -	- -	2 -
9 Leicester City	- -	2 -	- -	- -	- -	- -	- -	- -	- -	2 -
10 Luton Town	- -	2 -	- -	- -	- -	- -	- -	- -	- -	2 -
11 Nottingham Forest	- -	2 -	- -	- -	- -	- -	- -	- -	- -	2 -
12 Southampton	- -	2 -	- -	- -	- -	- -	- -	- -	- -	2 -
13 Watford	- -	2 -	- -	- -	- -	- -	- -	- -	- -	2 -
14 Wimbledon	- -	1 -	- -	- -	1 -	- -	- -	- -	- -	2 -
15 Everton	- -	1 (1) -	- -	- -	- -	- -	- -	- -	- -	1 (1) -
16 Hull City	- -	- -	- -	- -	1 (1) -	- -	- -	- -	- -	1 (1) -
17 Birmingham City	- -	1 -	- -	- -	- -	- -	- -	- -	- -	1 -
18 Burnley	- -	- -	- -	- -	1 -	- -	- -	- -	- -	1 -
19 Crystal Palace	- -	- -	- -	- -	1 -	- -	- -	- -	- -	1 -
20 Derby County	- -	1 -	- -	- -	- -	- -	- -	- -	- -	1 -
21 Manchester City	- -	- -	- -	1 -	- -	- -	- -	- -	- -	1 -
22 Middlesbrough	- -	1 -	- -	- -	- -	- -	- -	- -	- -	1 -
23 Oxford United	- -	1 -	- -	- -	- -	- -	- -	- -	- -	1 -
24 Rochdale	- -	- -	- -	1 -	- -	- -	- -	- -	- -	1 -
25 Rotherham United	- -	- -	- -	- -	1 -	- -	- -	- -	- -	1 -
26 Sunderland	- -	1 -	- -	- -	- -	- -	- -	- -	- -	1 -
27 West Ham United	- -	1 -	- -	- -	- -	- -	- -	- -	- -	1 -
28 Liverpool	- -	- (1) -	- -	- -	- -	- -	- -	- -	- -	- (1) -
29 PSV Eindhoven	- -	- -	- -	- -	- -	- -	- -	- (1) -	- -	- (1) -

JAMES GARVEY

DEBUT (Full Appearance)

Saturday 01/09/1900
Football League Division 2
at North Road

Glossop 1 Newton Heath 0

CLUB CAREER RECORD	Apps	Subs	Goals
Premiership	0		0
League Division 1	0		0
League Division 2	6		0
FA Cup	0		0
League Cup	0		0
European Cup / Champions League	0		0
European Cup-Winners' Cup	0		0
UEFA Cup / Inter-Cities' Fairs Cup	0		0
Other Matches	0		0
OVERALL TOTAL	6		0

Opponents	PREM A S G	FLD 1 A S G	FLD 2 A S G	FAC A S G	LC A S G	EC/CL A S G	ECWC A S G	UEFA A S G	OTHER A S G	TOTAL A S G
1 Barnsley	- -	- -	1 -	- -	- -	- -	- -	- -	- -	1 -
2 Glossop	- -	- -	1 -	- -	- -	- -	- -	- -	- -	1 -
3 Leicester City	- -	- -	1 -	- -	- -	- -	- -	- -	- -	1 -
4 Lincoln City	- -	- -	1 -	- -	- -	- -	- -	- -	- -	1 -
5 Middlesbrough	- -	- -	1 -	- -	- -	- -	- -	- -	- -	1 -
6 Walsall	- -	- -	1 -	- -	- -	- -	- -	- -	- -	1 -

DAVID GASKELL

DEBUT (Full Appearance)

Saturday 30/11/1957
Football League Division 1
at Old Trafford

Manchester United 3 Tottenham Hotspur 4

CLUB CAREER RECORD	Apps	Subs	Goals
Premiership	0		0
League Division 1	96		0
League Division 2	0		0
FA Cup	16		0
League Cup	1		0
European Cup / Champions League	1		0
European Cup-Winners' Cup	4		0
UEFA Cup / Inter-Cities' Fairs Cup	0		0
Other Matches	1		0
OVERALL TOTAL	**119**		**0**

Opponents	PREM A	S	G	FLD 1 A	S	G	FLD 2 A	S	G	FAC A	S	G	LC A	S	G	EC/CL A	S	G	ECWC A	S	G	UEFA A	S	G	OTHER A	S	G	TOTAL A	S	G
1 Burnley	–	–	9	–	–	–	–	–	–	–	–	–	–	–	–	–	–	–	–	–	–	–	–	–	–	–	–	9	–
2 Everton	–	–	7	–	–	–	–	–	–	–	–	–	–	–	–	–	–	–	–	–	–	–	1	–	–	–	8	–
3 Sheffield Wednesday	–	–	5	–	–	–	2	–	–	–	–	–	–	–	–	–	–	–	–	–	–	–	–	–	–	–	7	–
4 Tottenham Hotspur	–	–	4	–	–	–	1	–	–	–	–	–	–	–	–	–	2	–	–	–	–	–	–	–	–	–	7	–
5 West Bromwich Albion	–	–	7	–	–	–	–	–	–	–	–	–	–	–	–	–	–	–	–	–	–	–	–	–	–	–	7	–
6 Leicester City	–	–	5	–	–	–	1	–	–	–	–	–	–	–	–	–	–	–	–	–	–	–	–	–	–	–	6	–
7 Arsenal	–	–	4	–	–	–	1	–	–	–	–	–	–	–	–	–	–	–	–	–	–	–	–	–	–	–	5	–
8 Bolton Wanderers	–	–	4	–	–	–	1	–	–	–	–	–	–	–	–	–	–	–	–	–	–	–	–	–	–	–	5	–
9 Fulham	–	–	5	–	–	–	–	–	–	–	–	–	–	–	–	–	–	–	–	–	–	–	–	–	–	–	5	–
10 Nottingham Forest	–	–	5	–	–	–	–	–	–	–	–	–	–	–	–	–	–	–	–	–	–	–	–	–	–	–	5	–
11 West Ham United	–	–	4	–	–	–	1	–	–	–	–	–	–	–	–	–	–	–	–	–	–	–	–	–	–	–	5	–
12 Birmingham City	–	–	4	–	–	–	–	–	–	–	–	–	–	–	–	–	–	–	–	–	–	–	–	–	–	–	4	–
13 Blackpool	–	–	4	–	–	–	–	–	–	–	–	–	–	–	–	–	–	–	–	–	–	–	–	–	–	–	4	–
14 Aston Villa	–	–	3	–	–	–	–	–	–	–	–	–	–	–	–	–	–	–	–	–	–	–	–	–	–	–	3	–
15 Manchester City	–	–	3	–	–	–	–	–	–	–	–	–	–	–	–	–	–	–	–	–	–	–	–	–	–	–	3	–
16 Newcastle United	–	–	3	–	–	–	–	–	–	–	–	–	–	–	–	–	–	–	–	–	–	–	–	–	–	–	3	–
17 Preston North End	–	–	1	–	–	–	2	–	–	–	–	–	–	–	–	–	–	–	–	–	–	–	–	–	–	–	3	–
18 Sheffield United	–	–	3	–	–	–	–	–	–	–	–	–	–	–	–	–	–	–	–	–	–	–	–	–	–	–	3	–
19 Sunderland	–	–	–	–	–	–	3	–	–	–	–	–	–	–	–	–	–	–	–	–	–	–	–	–	–	–	3	–
20 Blackburn Rovers	–	–	2	–	–	–	–	–	–	–	–	–	–	–	–	–	–	–	–	–	–	–	–	–	–	–	2	–
21 Cardiff City	–	–	2	–	–	–	–	–	–	–	–	–	–	–	–	–	–	–	–	–	–	–	–	–	–	–	2	–
22 Chelsea	–	–	2	–	–	–	–	–	–	–	–	–	–	–	–	–	–	–	–	–	–	–	–	–	–	–	2	–
23 Leyton Orient	–	–	2	–	–	–	–	–	–	–	–	–	–	–	–	–	–	–	–	–	–	–	–	–	–	–	2	–
24 Southampton	–	–	–	–	–	–	2	–	–	–	–	–	–	–	–	–	–	–	–	–	–	–	–	–	–	–	2	–
25 Sporting Lisbon	–	–	–	–	–	–	–	–	–	–	–	–	–	–	–	–	2	–	–	–	–	–	–	–	–	–	2	–
26 Stoke City	–	–	2	–	–	–	–	–	–	–	–	–	–	–	–	–	–	–	–	–	–	–	–	–	–	–	2	–
27 Wolverhampton W.	–	–	2	–	–	–	–	–	–	–	–	–	–	–	–	–	–	–	–	–	–	–	–	–	–	–	2	–
28 Barnsley	–	–	–	–	–	–	1	–	–	–	–	–	–	–	–	–	–	–	–	–	–	–	–	–	–	–	1	–
29 Bristol Rovers	–	–	–	–	–	–	1	–	–	–	–	–	–	–	–	–	–	–	–	–	–	–	–	–	–	–	1	–
30 Exeter City	–	–	–	–	–	–	–	–	1	–	–	–	–	–	–	–	–	–	–	–	–	–	–	–	–	–	1	–
31 HJK Helsinki	–	–	–	–	–	–	–	–	–	–	1	–	–	–	–	–	–	–	–	–	–	–	–	–	–	–	1	–
32 Ipswich Town	–	–	1	–	–	–	–	–	–	–	–	–	–	–	–	–	–	–	–	–	–	–	–	–	–	–	1	–
33 Leeds United	–	–	1	–	–	–	–	–	–	–	–	–	–	–	–	–	–	–	–	–	–	–	–	–	–	–	1	–
34 Northampton Town	–	–	1	–	–	–	–	–	–	–	–	–	–	–	–	–	–	–	–	–	–	–	–	–	–	–	1	–
35 Portsmouth	–	–	1	–	–	–	–	–	–	–	–	–	–	–	–	–	–	–	–	–	–	–	–	–	–	–	1	–

RALPH GAUDIE

DEBUT (Full Appearance)

Saturday 05/09/1903
Football League Division 2
at Bank Street

Manchester United 2 Bristol City 2

CLUB CAREER RECORD	Apps	Subs	Goals
Premiership	0		0
League Division 1	0		0
League Division 2	7		0
FA Cup	1		0
League Cup	0		0
European Cup / Champions League	0		0
European Cup-Winners' Cup	0		0
UEFA Cup / Inter-Cities' Fairs Cup	0		0
Other Matches	0		0
OVERALL TOTAL	**8**		**0**

Opponents	PREM A	S	G	FLD 1 A	S	G	FLD 2 A	S	G	FAC A	S	G	LC A	S	G	EC/CL A	S	G	ECWC A	S	G	UEFA A	S	G	OTHER A	S	G	TOTAL A	S	G
1 Birmingham City	–	–	–	–	–	–	–	–	–	1	–	–	–	–	–	–	–	–	–	–	–	–	–	–	–	–	1	–
2 Bradford City	–	–	–	–	–	–	1	–	–	–	–	–	–	–	–	–	–	–	–	–	–	–	–	–	–	–	1	–
3 Bristol City	–	–	–	–	–	–	1	–	–	–	–	–	–	–	–	–	–	–	–	–	–	–	–	–	–	–	1	–
4 Burnley	–	–	–	–	–	–	1	–	–	–	–	–	–	–	–	–	–	–	–	–	–	–	–	–	–	–	1	–
5 Burton United	–	–	–	–	–	–	1	–	–	–	–	–	–	–	–	–	–	–	–	–	–	–	–	–	–	–	1	–
6 Chesterfield	–	–	–	–	–	–	1	–	–	–	–	–	–	–	–	–	–	–	–	–	–	–	–	–	–	–	1	–
7 Glossop	–	–	–	–	–	–	1	–	–	–	–	–	–	–	–	–	–	–	–	–	–	–	–	–	–	–	1	–
8 Port Vale	–	–	–	–	–	–	1	–	–	–	–	–	–	–	–	–	–	–	–	–	–	–	–	–	–	–	1	–

COLIN GIBSON

DEBUT (Full Appearance)

Saturday 30/11/1985
Football League Division 1
at Old Trafford

Manchester United 1 Watford 1

CLUB CAREER RECORD	Apps	Subs	Goals
Premiership	0		0
League Division 1	74	(5)	9
League Division 2	0		0
FA Cup	8	(1)	0
League Cup	7		0
European Cup / Champions League	0		0
European Cup-Winners' Cup	0		0
UEFA Cup / Inter-Cities' Fairs Cup	0		0
Other Matches	0		0
OVERALL TOTAL	89	(6)	9

Opponents	PREM			FLD 1			FLD 2			FAC			LC			EC/CL			ECWC			UEFA			OTHER			TOTAL		
	A	S	G	A	S	G	A	S	G	A	S	G	A	S	G	A	S	G	A	S	G	A	S	G	A	S	G	A	S	G
1 West Ham United	-	-		5		1	-	-		2	-		-	-		-	-		-	-		-	-		-	-		7		1
2 Liverpool	-	-		5		1	-	-		-	-		-	-		-	-		-	-		-	-		-	-		5		1
3 Oxford United	-	-		4		1	-	-		-	-		1	-		-	-		-	-		-	-		-	-		5		1
4 Southampton	-	-		4		1	-	-		-	-		1	-		-	-		-	-		-	-		-	-		5		1
5 Everton	-	-		4	(1)	-	-	-		-	-		-	-		-	-		-	-		-	-		-	-		4	(1)	-
6 Aston Villa	-	-		4		-	-	-		-	-		-	-		-	-		-	-		-	-		-	-		4		-
7 Luton Town	-	-		4		-	-	-		-	-		-	-		-	-		-	-		-	-		-	-		4		-
8 Nottingham Forest	-	-		4		-	-	-		-	-		-	-		-	-		-	-		-	-		-	-		4		-
9 Sheffield Wednesday	-	-		4		-	-	-		-	-		-	-		-	-		-	-		-	-		-	-		4		-
10 Wimbledon	-	-		3		-	-	-		-	-		1	-		-	-		-	-		-	-		-	-		4		-
11 Coventry City	-	-		3	(1)	1	-	-		-	-		-	-		-	-		-	-		-	-		-	-		3	(1)	1
12 Manchester City	-	-		2		1	-	-		1	-		-	-		-	-		-	-		-	-		-	-		3		1
13 Arsenal	-	-		2		-	-	-		1	-		-	-		-	-		-	-		-	-		-	-		3		-
14 Newcastle United	-	-		3		-	-	-		-	-		-	-		-	-		-	-		-	-		-	-		3		-
15 Norwich City	-	-		3		-	-	-		-	-		-	-		-	-		-	-		-	-		-	-		3		-
16 Tottenham Hotspur	-	-		3		-	-	-		-	-		-	-		-	-		-	-		-	-		-	-		3		-
17 Watford	-	-		3		-	-	-		-	-		-	-		-	-		-	-		-	-		-	-		3		-
18 Charlton Athletic	-	-		2	(1)	-	-	-		-	-		-	-		-	-		-	-		-	-		-	-		2	(1)	-
19 Chelsea	-	-		2	(1)	-	-	-		-	-		-	-		-	-		-	-		-	-		-	-		2	(1)	-
20 Queens Park Rangers	-	-		2	(1)	-	-	-		-	-		-	-		-	-		-	-		-	-		-	-		2	(1)	-
21 Birmingham City	-	-		2		1	-	-		-	-		-	-		-	-		-	-		-	-		-	-		2		1
22 Hull City	-	-		-		-	-	-		-	-		2	-		-	-		-	-		-	-		-	-		2		-
23 Ipswich Town	-	-		1		-	-	-		1	-		-	-		-	-		-	-		-	-		-	-		2		-
24 Portsmouth	-	-		2		-	-	-		-	-		-	-		-	-		-	-		-	-		-	-		2		-
25 Oldham Athletic	-	-		-		-	-	-		1	(1)	-	-	-		-	-		-	-		-	-		-	-		1	(1)	-
26 Derby County	-	-		1		1	-	-		-	-		-	-		-	-		-	-		-	-		-	-		1		1
27 Leicester City	-	-		1		1	-	-		-	-		-	-		-	-		-	-		-	-		-	-		1		1
28 Bury	-	-		-		-	-	-		-	-		1	-		-	-		-	-		-	-		-	-		1		-
29 Crystal Palace	-	-		-		-	-	-		-	-		1	-		-	-		-	-		-	-		-	-		1		-
30 Rochdale	-	-		-		-	-	-		1	-		-	-		-	-		-	-		-	-		-	-		1		-
31 Sunderland	-	-		-		-	-	-		1	-		-	-		-	-		-	-		-	-		-	-		1		-
32 West Bromwich Albion	-	-		1		-	-	-		-	-		-	-		-	-		-	-		-	-		-	-		1		-

DARRON GIBSON

DEBUT (Substitute Appearance)

Wednesday 26/10/2005
League Cup 3rd Round
at Old Trafford

Manchester United 4 Barnet 1

CLUB CAREER RECORD	Apps	Subs	Goals
Premiership	0		0
League Division 1	0		0
League Division 2	0		0
FA Cup	0		0
League Cup	0	(1)	0
European Cup / Champions League	0		0
European Cup-Winners' Cup	0		0
UEFA Cup / Inter-Cities' Fairs Cup	0		0
Other Matches	0		0
OVERALL TOTAL	0	(1)	0

Opponents	PREM			FLD 1			FLD 2			FAC			LC			EC/CL			ECWC			UEFA			OTHER			TOTAL		
	A	S	G	A	S	G	A	S	G	A	S	G	A	S	G	A	S	G	A	S	G	A	S	G	A	S	G	A	S	G
1 Barnet	-	-		-	-		-	-		-	-		-	(1)	-	-	-		-	-		-	-		-	-		-	(1)	-

DON GIBSON

DEBUT (Full Appearance)

Saturday 26/08/1950
Football League Division 1
at Burnden Park

Bolton Wanderers 1 Manchester United 0

CLUB CAREER RECORD	Apps	Subs	Goals
Premiership	0		0
League Division 1	108		0
League Division 2	0		0
FA Cup	6		0
League Cup	0		0
European Cup / Champions League	0		0
European Cup-Winners' Cup	0		0
UEFA Cup / Inter-Cities' Fairs Cup	0		0
Other Matches	1		0
OVERALL TOTAL	**115**		**0**

Opponents	PREM A	S	G	FLD 1 A	S	G	FLD 2 A	S	G	FAC A	S	G	LC A	S	G	EC/CL A	S	G	ECWC A	S	G	UEFA A	S	G	OTHER A	S	G	TOTAL A	S	G
1 Charlton Athletic	-	-	-	7	-	-	-	-	-	-	-	-	-	-	-	-	-	-	-	-	-	-	-	-	-	-	-	7	-	-
2 Sunderland	-	-	-	7	-	-	-	-	-	-	-	-	-	-	-	-	-	-	-	-	-	-	-	-	-	-	-	7	-	-
3 Arsenal	-	-	-	5	-	-	-	-	-	1	-	-	-	-	-	-	-	-	-	-	-	-	-	-	-	-	-	6	-	-
4 Aston Villa	-	-	-	6	-	-	-	-	-	-	-	-	-	-	-	-	-	-	-	-	-	-	-	-	-	-	-	6	-	-
5 Chelsea	-	-	-	6	-	-	-	-	-	-	-	-	-	-	-	-	-	-	-	-	-	-	-	-	-	-	-	6	-	-
6 Newcastle United	-	-	-	5	-	-	-	-	-	-	-	-	-	-	-	-	-	-	-	-	-	-	-	-	1	-	-	6	-	-
7 Wolverhampton W.	-	-	-	6	-	-	-	-	-	-	-	-	-	-	-	-	-	-	-	-	-	-	-	-	-	-	-	6	-	-
8 Bolton Wanderers	-	-	-	5	-	-	-	-	-	-	-	-	-	-	-	-	-	-	-	-	-	-	-	-	-	-	-	5	-	-
9 Burnley	-	-	-	5	-	-	-	-	-	-	-	-	-	-	-	-	-	-	-	-	-	-	-	-	-	-	-	5	-	-
10 Portsmouth	-	-	-	5	-	-	-	-	-	-	-	-	-	-	-	-	-	-	-	-	-	-	-	-	-	-	-	5	-	-
11 Tottenham Hotspur	-	-	-	5	-	-	-	-	-	-	-	-	-	-	-	-	-	-	-	-	-	-	-	-	-	-	-	5	-	-
12 West Bromwich Albion	-	-	-	5	-	-	-	-	-	-	-	-	-	-	-	-	-	-	-	-	-	-	-	-	-	-	-	5	-	-
13 Cardiff City	-	-	-	4	-	-	-	-	-	-	-	-	-	-	-	-	-	-	-	-	-	-	-	-	-	-	-	4	-	-
14 Everton	-	-	-	4	-	-	-	-	-	-	-	-	-	-	-	-	-	-	-	-	-	-	-	-	-	-	-	4	-	-
15 Manchester City	-	-	-	3	-	-	-	-	-	1	-	-	-	-	-	-	-	-	-	-	-	-	-	-	-	-	-	4	-	-
16 Middlesbrough	-	-	-	4	-	-	-	-	-	-	-	-	-	-	-	-	-	-	-	-	-	-	-	-	-	-	-	4	-	-
17 Preston North End	-	-	-	4	-	-	-	-	-	-	-	-	-	-	-	-	-	-	-	-	-	-	-	-	-	-	-	4	-	-
18 Stoke City	-	-	-	4	-	-	-	-	-	-	-	-	-	-	-	-	-	-	-	-	-	-	-	-	-	-	-	4	-	-
19 Derby County	-	-	-	3	-	-	-	-	-	-	-	-	-	-	-	-	-	-	-	-	-	-	-	-	-	-	-	3	-	-
20 Huddersfield Town	-	-	-	3	-	-	-	-	-	-	-	-	-	-	-	-	-	-	-	-	-	-	-	-	-	-	-	3	-	-
21 Sheffield Wednesday	-	-	-	3	-	-	-	-	-	-	-	-	-	-	-	-	-	-	-	-	-	-	-	-	-	-	-	3	-	-
22 Blackpool	-	-	-	2	-	-	-	-	-	-	-	-	-	-	-	-	-	-	-	-	-	-	-	-	-	-	-	2	-	-
23 Leicester City	-	-	-	2	-	-	-	-	-	-	-	-	-	-	-	-	-	-	-	-	-	-	-	-	-	-	-	2	-	-
24 Liverpool	-	-	-	2	-	-	-	-	-	-	-	-	-	-	-	-	-	-	-	-	-	-	-	-	-	-	-	2	-	-
25 Reading	-	-	-	-	-	-	-	-	-	2	-	-	-	-	-	-	-	-	-	-	-	-	-	-	-	-	-	2	-	-
26 Sheffield United	-	-	-	2	-	-	-	-	-	-	-	-	-	-	-	-	-	-	-	-	-	-	-	-	-	-	-	2	-	-
27 Birmingham City	-	-	-	-	-	-	-	-	-	1	-	-	-	-	-	-	-	-	-	-	-	-	-	-	-	-	-	1	-	-
28 Fulham	-	-	-	1	-	-	-	-	-	-	-	-	-	-	-	-	-	-	-	-	-	-	-	-	-	-	-	1	-	-
29 Leeds United	-	-	-	-	-	-	-	-	-	1	-	-	-	-	-	-	-	-	-	-	-	-	-	-	-	-	-	1	-	-

RICHARD GIBSON

DEBUT (Full Appearance)

Saturday 27/08/1921
Football League Division 1
at Goodison Park

Everton 5 Manchester United 0

CLUB CAREER RECORD	Apps	Subs	Goals
Premiership	0		0
League Division 1	11		0
League Division 2	0		0
FA Cup	1		0
League Cup	0		0
European Cup / Champions League	0		0
European Cup-Winners' Cup	0		0
UEFA Cup / Inter-Cities' Fairs Cup	0		0
Other Matches	0		0
OVERALL TOTAL	**12**		**0**

Opponents	PREM A	S	G	FLD 1 A	S	G	FLD 2 A	S	G	FAC A	S	G	LC A	S	G	EC/CL A	S	G	ECWC A	S	G	UEFA A	S	G	OTHER A	S	G	TOTAL A	S	G
1 Burnley	-	-	-	2	-	-	-	-	-	-	-	-	-	-	-	-	-	-	-	-	-	-	-	-	-	-	-	2	-	-
2 Liverpool	-	-	-	2	-	-	-	-	-	-	-	-	-	-	-	-	-	-	-	-	-	-	-	-	-	-	-	2	-	-
3 Newcastle United	-	-	-	2	-	-	-	-	-	-	-	-	-	-	-	-	-	-	-	-	-	-	-	-	-	-	-	2	-	-
4 Blackburn Rovers	-	-	-	1	-	-	-	-	-	-	-	-	-	-	-	-	-	-	-	-	-	-	-	-	-	-	-	1	-	-
5 Bolton Wanderers	-	-	-	1	-	-	-	-	-	-	-	-	-	-	-	-	-	-	-	-	-	-	-	-	-	-	-	1	-	-
6 Bradford City	-	-	-	1	-	-	-	-	-	-	-	-	-	-	-	-	-	-	-	-	-	-	-	-	-	-	-	1	-	-
7 Cardiff City	-	-	-	-	-	-	-	-	-	1	-	-	-	-	-	-	-	-	-	-	-	-	-	-	-	-	-	1	-	-
8 Everton	-	-	-	1	-	-	-	-	-	-	-	-	-	-	-	-	-	-	-	-	-	-	-	-	-	-	-	1	-	-
9 Middlesbrough	-	-	-	1	-	-	-	-	-	-	-	-	-	-	-	-	-	-	-	-	-	-	-	-	-	-	-	1	-	-

TERRY GIBSON

DEBUT (Substitute Appearance)

Sunday 02/02/1986
Football League Division 1
at Upton Park

West Ham United 2 Manchester United 1

CLUB CAREER RECORD	Apps	Subs	Goals
Premiership	0		0
League Division 1	14	(9)	1
League Division 2	0		0
FA Cup	1	(1)	0
League Cup	0	(2)	0
European Cup / Champions League	0		0
European Cup-Winners' Cup	0		0
UEFA Cup / Inter-Cities' Fairs Cup	0		0
Other Matches	0		0
OVERALL TOTAL	**15**	**(12)**	**1**

Opponents	PREM A	S	G	FLD 1 A	S	G	FLD 2 A	S	G	FAC A	S	G	LC A	S	G	EC/CL A	S	G	ECWC A	S	G	UEFA A	S	G	OTHER A	S	G	TOTAL A	S	G
1 Southampton	-	-		1	(2)	-	-	-	-	-	-	-	-	(1)	-	-	-		-	-		-	-		-	-		1	(3)	-
2 Newcastle United	-	-		2			-	-		-	-		-	-		-			-			-			-			2		-
3 Charlton Athletic	-	-		1	(1)	-	-	-		-	-		-	-		-			-			-			-			1	(1)	-
4 Luton Town	-	-		1	(1)	-	-	-		-	-		-	-		-			-			-			-			1	(1)	-
5 Manchester City	-	-		1			-	-		-	-		-	(1)	-	-			-			-			-			1	(1)	-
6 West Ham United	-	-		1	(1)	-	-	-		-	-		-	-		-			-			-			-			1	(1)	-
7 Sheffield Wednesday	-	-		-	(2)	-	-	-		-	-		-	-		-			-			-			-			-	(2)	-
8 Arsenal	-	-		1		1	-	-		-	-		-	-		-			-			-			-			1		1
9 Chelsea	-	-		1			-	-		-	-		-	-		-			-			-			-			1		-
10 Coventry City	-	-		-			-	-		1			-	-		-			-			-			-			1		-
11 Everton	-	-		1			-	-		-	-		-	-		-			-			-			-			1		-
12 Leicester City	-	-		1			-	-		-	-		-	-		-			-			-			-			1		-
13 Liverpool	-	-		1			-	-		-	-		-	-		-			-			-			-			1		-
14 Tottenham Hotspur	-	-		1			-	-		-	-		-	-		-			-			-			-			1		-
15 Watford	-	-		1			-	-		-	-		-	-		-			-			-			-			1		-
16 Port Vale	-	-		-			-	-		-	-		-	(1)	-	-			-			-			-			-	(1)	-
17 Queens Park Rangers	-	-		-	(1)	-	-	-		-	-		-	-		-			-			-			-			-	(1)	-
18 West Bromwich Albion	-	-		-	(1)	-	-	-		-	-		-	-		-			-			-			-			-	(1)	-

JOHN GIDMAN

DEBUT (Full Appearance)

Saturday 29/08/1981
Football League Division 1
at Highfield Road

Coventry City 2 Manchester United 1

CLUB CAREER RECORD	Apps	Subs	Goals
Premiership	0		0
League Division 1	94	(1)	4
League Division 2	0		0
FA Cup	9		0
League Cup	5		0
European Cup / Champions League	0		0
European Cup-Winners' Cup	1	(1)	0
UEFA Cup / Inter-Cities' Fairs Cup	6	(1)	0
Other Matches	1	(1)	0
OVERALL TOTAL	**116**	**(4)**	**4**

Opponents	PREM A	S	G	FLD 1 A	S	G	FLD 2 A	S	G	FAC A	S	G	LC A	S	G	EC/CL A	S	G	ECWC A	S	G	UEFA A	S	G	OTHER A	S	G	TOTAL A	S	G
1 Everton	-	-		5	-	-	-			1	-		1			-			-			-			1	-		8		-
2 Tottenham Hotspur	-	-		5	-		-	-		-	-		2			-			-			-			-			7		-
3 Liverpool	-	-		3	-		-	-		2	-		1			-			-			-	(1)	-	-			6	(1)	-
4 Arsenal	-	-		6	-		-	-		-	-		-			-			-			-			-			6		-
5 Sunderland	-	-		4	-		-	-		2	-		-			-			-			-			-			6		-
6 Ipswich Town	-	-		5	2		-	-		-	-		-			-			-			-			-			5		2
7 Aston Villa	-	-		5	-		-	-		-	-		-			-			-			-			-			5		-
8 West Ham United	-	-		4	-		-	-		1	-		-			-			-			-			-			5		-
9 Nottingham Forest	-	-		4	1		-	-		-	-		-			-			-			-			-			4		1
10 Birmingham City	-	-		4	-		-	-		-	-		-			-			-			-			-			4		-
11 Coventry City	-	-		3	-		-	-		1	-		-			-			-			-			-			4		-
12 Leicester City	-	-		4	-		-	-		-	-		-			-			-			-			-			4		-
13 Stoke City	-	-		4	-		-	-		-	-		-			-			-			-			-			4		-
14 West Bromwich Albion	-	-		4	-		-	-		-	-		-			-			-			-			-			4		-
15 Brighton	-	-		3	-		-	-		-	-		-			-			-			-			-			3		-
16 Luton Town	-	-		3	-		-	-		-	-		-			-			-			-			-			3		-
17 Notts County	-	-		3	-		-	-		-	-		-			-			-			-			-			3		-
18 Sheffield Wednesday	-	-		3	-		-	-		-	-		-			-			-			-			-			3		-
19 Southampton	-	-		3	-		-	-		-	-		-			-			-			-			-			3		-
20 Watford	-	-		2	-		-	-		1	-		-			-			-			-			-			3		-
21 Wolverhampton W.	-	-		3	-		-	-		-	-		-			-			-			-			-			3		-
22 Queens Park Rangers	-	-		2	1		-	-		-	-		-			-			-			-			-			2		1
23 Dundee United	-	-		-	-		-	-		-	-		-			-			-			2			-			2		-
24 Manchester City	-	-		2	-		-	-		-	-		-			-			-			-			-			2		-
25 Middlesbrough	-	-		2	-		-	-		-	-		-			-			-			-			-			2		-
26 Newcastle United	-	-		2	-		-	-		-	-		-			-			-			-			-			2		-
27 Norwich City	-	-		2	-		-	-		-	-		-			-			-			-			-			2		-
28 PSV Eindhoven	-	-		-	-		-	-		-	-		-			-			-			2			-			2		-
29 Videoton	-	-		-	-		-	-		-	-		-			-			-			2			-			2		-
30 Swansea City	-	-		1	(1)	-	-	-		-	-		-			-			-			-			-			1	(1)	-
31 Blackburn Rovers	-	-		-	-		-	-		1	-		-			-			-			-			-			1		-
32 Chelsea	-	-		1	-		-	-		-	-		-			-			-			-			-			1		-
33 Juventus	-	-		-	-		-	-		-	-		-			-			1			-			-			1		-

continued../

JOHN GIDMAN (continued)

Opponents	PREM A	S	G	FLD 1 A	S	G	FLD 2 A	S	G	FAC A	S	G	LC A	S	G	EC/CL A	S	G	ECWC A	S	G	UEFA A	S	G	OTHER A	S	G	TOTAL A	S	G
34 Leeds United	-	-	-	1	-	-	-	-	-	-	-	-	-	-	-	-	-	-	-	-	-	-	-	-	-	-	-	1	-	-
35 Oxford United	-	-	-	1	-	-	-	-	-	-	-	-	-	-	-	-	-	-	-	-	-	-	-	-	-	-	-	1	-	-
36 Port Vale	-	-	-	-	-	-	-	-	-	1	-	-	-	-	-	-	-	-	-	-	-	-	-	-	-	-	-	1	-	-
37 Dukla Prague	-	-	-	-	-	-	-	-	-	-	-	-	-	-	-	-	-	-	-	(1)	-	-	-	-	-	-	-	-	(1)	-
38 Raba Vasas	-	-	-	-	-	-	-	-	-	-	-	-	-	-	-	-	-	-	-	(1)	-	-	-	-	-	-	-	-	(1)	-

---

RYAN GIGGS

DEBUT (Substitute Appearance)

Saturday 02/03/1991
Football League Division 1
at Old Trafford

Manchester United 0   Everton 2

CLUB CAREER RECORD	Apps	Subs	Goals
Premiership	436	(59)	96
League Division 1	33	(7)	5
League Division 2	0		0
FA Cup	55	(7)	10
League Cup	25	(5)	7
European Cup / Champions League	103	(11)	25
European Cup-Winners' Cup	1		0
UEFA Cup / Inter–Cities' Fairs Cup	3		0
Other Matches	13	(1)	1
OVERALL TOTAL	669	(90)	144

Opponents	PREM A	S	G	FLD 1 A	S	G	FLD 2 A	S	G	FAC A	S	G	LC A	S	G	EC/CL A	S	G	ECWC A	S	G	UEFA A	S	G	OTHER A	S	G	TOTAL A	S	G
1 Arsenal	25	(2)	1	1	(1)	-	-	-	-	3	(2)	1	-	-	-	-	-	-	-	-	-	-	-	-	4	-	-	33	(5)	2
2 Liverpool	25	(3)	4	2	-	-	-	-	-	3	-	-	1	-	-	-	-	-	-	-	-	-	-	-	1	-	-	32	(3)	4
3 Chelsea	19	(3)	2	2	-	-	-	-	-	5	-	-	2	-	1	-	(1)	-	-	-	-	-	-	-	3	-	1	31	(4)	4
4 Tottenham Hotspur	28	(1)	7	2	-	-	-	-	-	2	-	-	1	-	-	-	-	-	-	-	-	-	-	-	-	-	-	33	(1)	7
5 Aston Villa	23	(3)	4	-	-	-	-	-	-	3	-	-	2	-	-	-	-	-	-	-	-	-	-	-	-	-	-	28	(3)	4
6 Blackburn Rovers	20	(4)	2	-	-	-	-	-	-	-	-	-	4	-	-	-	-	-	-	-	-	1	-	-	-	-	-	25	(4)	2
7 Middlesbrough	17	(4)	6	-	-	-	-	-	-	4	(1)	1	2	-	1	-	-	-	-	-	-	-	-	-	-	-	-	23	(5)	8
8 Manchester City	15	(7)	1	3	-	-	2	-	-	2	-	-	-	-	-	-	-	-	-	-	-	-	-	-	-	-	-	20	(7)	3
9 Newcastle United	22	(1)	4	-	-	-	-	-	-	1	(1)	-	-	-	-	-	-	-	-	-	-	1	-	-	-	-	-	24	(2)	4
10 Southampton	19	(2)	7	2	-	-	-	-	-	2	(1)	-	-	-	-	-	-	-	-	-	-	-	-	-	-	-	-	23	(3)	7
11 Everton	18	(3)	6	2	(1)	-	-	-	-	-	(1)	-	1	-	1	-	-	-	-	-	-	-	-	-	-	-	-	21	(5)	7
12 Leeds United	16	(2)	3	1	(1)	-	-	-	-	2	-	-	1	-	1	-	-	-	-	-	-	-	-	-	-	-	-	20	(3)	4
13 West Ham United	14	(3)	2	2	-	1	-	-	-	2	-	2	-	-	-	-	-	-	-	-	-	-	-	-	-	-	-	18	(3)	5
14 Coventry City	15	-	4	2	-	-	-	-	-	-	-	-	-	-	-	-	-	-	-	-	-	-	-	-	-	-	-	17	-	4
15 Bolton Wanderers	15	(1)	4	-	-	-	-	-	-	-	-	-	-	-	-	-	-	-	-	-	-	-	-	-	-	-	-	15	(1)	4
16 Wimbledon	10	(2)	3	1	-	-	-	-	-	3	-	-	-	-	-	-	-	-	-	-	-	-	-	-	-	-	-	14	(2)	3
17 Charlton Athletic	12	(2)	3	-	-	-	-	-	-	1	-	-	-	-	-	-	-	-	-	-	-	-	-	-	-	-	-	13	(2)	3
18 Portsmouth	7	(2)	-	-	-	-	-	-	-	2	-	-	3	-	1	-	-	-	-	-	-	-	-	-	-	-	-	12	(2)	1
19 Sheffield Wednesday	9	-	2	2	-	-	-	-	-	2	-	-	2	-	1	-	-	-	-	-	-	-	-	-	-	-	-	13	-	3
20 Fulham	10	(1)	3	-	-	-	-	-	-	2	-	-	-	-	-	-	-	-	-	-	-	-	-	-	-	-	-	12	(1)	3
21 Leicester City	10	(2)	-	-	-	-	-	-	-	-	-	-	-	-	-	-	(1)	-	-	-	-	-	-	-	-	-	-	10	(3)	-
22 Nottingham Forest	9	-	4	1	(1)	-	-	-	-	-	-	-	1	-	-	-	-	-	-	-	-	-	-	-	-	-	-	11	(1)	4
23 Crystal Palace	7	-	-	2	-	-	-	-	-	2	-	-	-	-	-	-	-	-	-	-	-	-	-	-	-	-	-	11	-	-
24 Derby County	10	(1)	2	-	-	-	-	-	-	-	-	-	-	-	-	-	-	-	-	-	-	-	-	-	-	-	-	10	(1)	2
25 Sunderland	8	(1)	2	-	-	-	-	-	-	2	-	-	-	-	-	-	-	-	-	-	-	-	-	-	-	-	-	10	(1)	2
26 Sheffield United	6	-	-	1	-	-	-	-	-	3	-	1	-	-	-	-	-	-	-	-	-	-	-	-	-	-	-	10	-	1
27 Queens Park Rangers	7	-	3	1	(1)	-	-	-	-	1	-	-	-	-	-	-	-	-	-	-	-	-	-	-	-	-	-	9	(1)	3
28 Norwich City	6	-	3	2	-	1	-	-	-	1	-	-	-	-	-	-	-	-	-	-	-	-	-	-	-	-	-	9	-	4
29 Oldham Athletic	4	-	3	1	(1)	1	-	-	-	2	-	1	1	-	-	-	-	-	-	-	-	-	-	-	-	-	-	8	(1)	5
30 Ipswich Town	7	(1)	1	-	-	-	-	-	-	-	-	-	-	-	-	-	-	-	-	-	-	-	-	-	-	-	-	7	(1)	1
31 Birmingham City	6	(2)	3	-	-	-	-	-	-	-	-	-	-	-	-	-	-	-	-	-	-	-	-	-	-	-	-	6	(2)	3
32 Juventus	-	-	-	-	-	-	-	-	-	-	-	-	-	-	-	6	(1)	4	-	-	-	-	-	-	-	-	-	6	(1)	4
33 Deportivo La Coruna	-	-	-	-	-	-	-	-	-	-	-	-	-	-	-	6	-	1	-	-	-	-	-	-	-	-	-	6	-	1
34 Wigan Athletic	3	(2)	1	-	-	-	-	-	-	-	-	-	1	-	-	-	-	-	-	-	-	-	-	-	-	-	-	4	(2)	1
35 Bayern Munich	-	-	-	-	-	-	-	-	-	-	-	-	-	-	-	5	-	1	-	-	-	-	-	-	-	-	-	5	-	1
36 West Bromwich Albion	5	-	1	-	-	-	-	-	-	-	-	-	-	-	-	-	-	-	-	-	-	-	-	-	-	-	-	5	-	1
37 Olympiakos Piraeus	-	-	-	-	-	-	-	-	-	-	-	-	-	-	-	4	-	2	-	-	-	-	-	-	-	-	-	4	-	2
38 Watford	3	-	2	-	-	-	-	-	-	1	-	-	-	-	-	-	-	-	-	-	-	-	-	-	-	-	-	4	-	2
39 AC Milan	-	-	-	-	-	-	-	-	-	-	-	-	-	-	-	4	-	-	-	-	-	-	-	-	-	-	-	4	-	-
40 Bayer Leverkusen	-	-	-	-	-	-	-	-	-	-	-	-	-	-	-	4	-	-	-	-	-	-	-	-	-	-	-	4	-	-
41 Real Madrid	-	-	-	-	-	-	-	-	-	-	-	-	-	-	-	4	-	-	-	-	-	-	-	-	-	-	-	4	-	-
42 Roma	-	-	-	-	-	-	-	-	-	-	-	-	-	-	-	3	(1)	-	-	-	-	-	-	-	-	-	-	3	(1)	-
43 Barcelona	-	-	-	-	-	-	-	-	-	-	-	-	-	-	-	2	(2)	1	-	-	-	-	-	-	-	-	-	2	(2)	1
44 Reading	1	(2)	-	-	-	-	-	-	-	1	-	1	-	-	-	-	-	-	-	-	-	-	-	-	-	-	-	2	(2)	1
45 Barnsley	2	-	2	-	-	-	-	-	-	1	-	-	-	-	-	-	-	-	-	-	-	-	-	-	-	-	-	3	-	2
46 Benfica	-	-	-	-	-	-	-	-	-	-	-	-	-	-	-	3	-	2	-	-	-	-	-	-	-	-	-	3	-	2
47 Lille Metropole	-	-	-	-	-	-	-	-	-	-	-	-	-	-	-	3	-	1	-	-	-	-	-	-	-	-	-	3	-	1
48 Porto	-	-	-	-	-	-	-	-	-	-	-	-	-	-	-	3	-	1	-	-	-	-	-	-	-	-	-	3	-	1
49 Dynamo Kiev	-	-	-	-	-	-	-	-	-	-	-	-	-	-	-	3	-	-	-	-	-	-	-	-	-	-	-	3	-	-
50 Galatasaray	-	-	-	-	-	-	-	-	-	-	-	-	-	-	-	3	-	-	-	-	-	-	-	-	-	-	-	3	-	-
51 Valencia	-	-	-	-	-	-	-	-	-	-	-	-	-	-	-	3	-	-	-	-	-	-	-	-	-	-	-	3	-	-
52 Bradford City	2	-	1	-	-	-	-	-	-	-	-	-	-	-	-	-	-	-	-	-	-	-	-	-	-	-	-	2	-	1
53 Brighton	-	-	-	-	-	-	1	-	1	1	-	-	-	-	-	-	-	-	-	-	-	-	-	-	-	-	-	2	-	1
54 Girondins Bordeaux	-	-	-	-	-	-	-	-	-	-	-	-	-	-	-	2	-	1	-	-	-	-	-	-	-	-	-	2	-	1
55 LKS Lodz	-	-	-	-	-	-	-	-	-	-	-	-	-	-	-	2	-	1	-	-	-	-	-	-	-	-	-	2	-	1
56 Rapid Vienna	-	-	-	-	-	-	-	-	-	-	-	-	-	-	-	2	-	1	-	-	-	-	-	-	-	-	-	2	-	1

continued../

RYAN GIGGS (continued)

Opponents	PREM A S G	FLD 1 A S G	FLD 2 A S G	FAC A S G	LC A S G	EC/CL A S G	ECWC A S G	UEFA A S G	OTHER A S G	TOTAL A S G
57 Stuttgart	- - -	- - -	- - -	- - -	- - -	2 1 -	- - -	- - -	- - -	2 1
58 Anderlecht	- - -	- - -	- - -	- - -	- - -	2 -	- - -	- - -	- - -	2 -
59 Croatia Zagreb	- - -	- - -	- - -	- - -	- - -	2 -	- - -	- - -	- - -	2 -
60 Feyenoord	- - -	- - -	- - -	- - -	- - -	2 -	- - -	- - -	- - -	2 -
61 Fiorentina	- - -	- - -	- - -	- - -	- - -	2 -	- - -	- - -	- - -	2 -
62 Glasgow Celtic	- - -	- - -	- - -	- - -	- - -	2 -	- - -	- - -	- - -	2 -
63 Glasgow Rangers	- - -	- - -	- - -	- - -	- - -	2 -	- - -	- - -	- - -	2 -
64 Honved	- - -	- - -	- - -	- - -	- - -	2 -	- - -	- - -	- - -	2 -
65 Internazionale	- - -	- - -	- - -	- - -	- - -	2 -	- - -	- - -	- - -	2 -
66 Luton Town	- - -	2 -	- - -	- - -	- - -	- - -	- - -	- - -	- - -	2 -
67 Nantes Atlantique	- - -	- - -	- - -	- - -	- - -	2 -	- - -	- - -	- - -	2 -
68 Olympique Lyonnais	- - -	- - -	- - -	- - -	- - -	2 -	- - -	- - -	- - -	2 -
69 Panathinaikos	- - -	- - -	- - -	- - -	- - -	2 -	- - -	- - -	- - -	2 -
70 Rotor Volgograd	- - -	- - -	- - -	- - -	- - -	- - -	- - -	2 -	- - -	2 -
71 York City	- - -	- - -	- - -	- - -	2 -	- - -	- - -	- - -	- - -	2 -
72 Zalaegerszeg	- - -	- - -	- - -	- - -	- - -	2 -	- - -	- - -	- - -	2 -
73 Sturm Graz	- - -	- - -	- - -	- - -	- - -	1 (1) 1	- - -	- - -	- - -	1 (1) 1
74 Basel	- - -	- - -	- - -	- - -	- - -	1 (1) -	- - -	- - -	- - -	1 (1) -
75 Borussia Dortmund	- - -	- - -	- - -	- - -	- - -	1 (1) -	- - -	- - -	- - -	1 (1) -
76 Notts County	- - -	1 (1) -	- - -	- - -	- - -	- - -	- - -	- - -	- - -	1 (1) -
77 PSV Eindhoven	- - -	- - -	- - -	- - -	- - -	1 (1) -	- - -	- - -	- - -	1 (1) -
78 Sporting Lisbon	- - -	- - -	- - -	- - -	- - -	1 (1) -	- - -	- - -	- - -	1 (1) -
79 Swindon Town	1 (1) -	- - -	- - -	- - -	- - -	- - -	- - -	- - -	- - -	1 (1) -
80 Cambridge United	- - -	- - -	- - -	- - -	- (2) 1	- - -	- - -	- - -	- - -	- (2) 1
81 Brondby	- - -	- - -	- - -	- - -	- - -	1 2	- - -	- - -	- - -	1 2
82 Gothenburg	- - -	- - -	- - -	- - -	- - -	1 2	- - -	- - -	- - -	1 2
83 Dinamo Bucharest	- - -	- - -	- - -	- - -	- - -	1 1	- - -	- - -	- - -	1 1
84 Fenerbahce	- - -	- - -	- - -	- - -	- - -	1 1	- - -	- - -	- - -	1 1
85 Maccabi Haifa	- - -	- - -	- - -	- - -	- - -	1 1	- - -	- - -	- - -	1 1
86 Wrexham	- - -	- - -	- - -	1 1	- - -	- - -	- - -	- - -	- - -	1 1
87 Athletico Madrid	- - -	- - -	- - -	- - -	- - -	- - -	1 -	- - -	- - -	1 -
88 Boavista	- - -	- - -	- - -	- - -	- - -	1 -	- - -	- - -	- - -	1 -
89 Debreceni	- - -	- - -	- - -	- - -	- - -	1 -	- - -	- - -	- - -	1 -
90 Exeter City	- - -	- - -	- - -	1 -	- - -	- - -	- - -	- - -	- - -	1 -
91 Kosice	- - -	- - -	- - -	- - -	- - -	1 -	- - -	- - -	- - -	1 -
92 Millwall	- - -	- - -	- - -	1 -	- - -	- - -	- - -	- - -	- - -	1 -
93 Olympique Marseille	- - -	- - -	- - -	- - -	- - -	1 -	- - -	- - -	- - -	1 -
94 Palmeiras	- - -	- - -	- - -	- - -	- - -	- - -	- - -	- - -	1 -	1 -
95 Rayos del Necaxa	- - -	- - -	- - -	- - -	- - -	- - -	- - -	- - -	1 -	1 -
96 Sparta Prague	- - -	- - -	- - -	- - -	- - -	1 -	- - -	- - -	- - -	1 -
97 Torpedo Moscow	- - -	- - -	- - -	- - -	- - -	- - -	- - -	1 -	- - -	1 -
98 Vasco da Gama	- - -	- - -	- - -	- - -	- - -	- - -	- - -	- - -	1 -	1 -
99 Burton Albion	- - -	- - -	- - -	- (1) 1	- - -	- - -	- - -	- - -	- - -	- (1) 1
100 Burnley	- - -	- - -	- - -	- - -	- (1) -	- - -	- - -	- - -	- - -	- (1) -
101 Red Star Belgrade	- - -	- - -	- - -	- - -	- - -	- - -	- - -	- - -	- (1) -	- (1) -
102 Stoke City	- - -	- - -	- - -	- - -	- (1) -	- - -	- - -	- - -	- - -	- (1) -
103 Villarreal	- - -	- - -	- - -	- - -	- - -	- (1) -	- - -	- - -	- - -	- (1) -
104 Wolverhampton W.	- (1) -	- - -	- - -	- - -	- - -	- - -	- - -	- - -	- - -	- (1) -

JOHNNY GILES

DEBUT (Full Appearance)

Saturday 12/09/1959
Football League Division 1
at Old Trafford

Manchester United 1 Tottenham Hotspur 5

CLUB CAREER RECORD	Apps	Subs	Goals
Premiership	0		0
League Division 1	99		10
League Division 2	0		0
FA Cup	13		2
League Cup	2		1
European Cup / Champions League	0		0
European Cup-Winners' Cup	0		0
UEFA Cup / Inter-Cities' Fairs Cup	0		0
Other Matches	1		0
OVERALL TOTAL	**115**		**13**

Opponents	PREM A	S	G	FLD 1 A	S	G	FLD 2 A	S	G	FAC A	S	G	LC A	S	G	EC/CL A	S	G	ECWC A	S	G	UEFA A	S	G	OTHER A	S	G	TOTAL A	S	G
1 Arsenal	–	–		6		1	–	–		1	–		–															7		1
2 Everton	–	–		6	–		–			–	–		–										1	–		–		7		–
3 West Ham United	–	–		7	–		–			–	–		–															7		–
4 Nottingham Forest	–	–		6		2	–			–	–		–															6		2
5 Birmingham City	–	–		6		1	–			–	–		–															6		1
6 Bolton Wanderers	–	–		5		1	–	–		1	–		–															6		1
7 Fulham	–	–		6		1	–			–	–		–															6		1
8 Sheffield Wednesday	–	–		4	–		–	–		2		1	–															6		1
9 Burnley	–	–		6	–		–			–	–		–															6		–
10 Tottenham Hotspur	–	–		5	–		–	–		1	–		–															6		–
11 Aston Villa	–	–		4	–		–	–		1	–		–															5		–
12 Blackburn Rovers	–	–		5	–		–			–	–		–															5		–
13 West Bromwich Albion	–	–		5	–		–			–	–		–															5		–
14 Blackpool	–	–		4	–		–			–	–		–															4		–
15 Ipswich Town	–	–		4	–		–			–	–		–															4		–
16 Wolverhampton W.	–	–		4	–		–			–	–		–															4		–
17 Leicester City	–	–		2		2	–	–		1	–		–															3		2
18 Manchester City	–	–		3	–		–			–	–		–															3		–
19 Preston North End	–	–		1	–		–	–		2	–		–															3		–
20 Sheffield United	–	–		3	–		–			–	–		–															3		–
21 Cardiff City	–	–		2		1	–	–		–	–		–															2		1
22 Liverpool	–	–		2		1	–			–	–		–															2		1
23 Exeter City	–	–		–	–		–	–		–	–		1		1													1		1
24 Huddersfield Town	–	–		–	–		–	–		1		1	–															1		1
25 Bradford City	–	–		–	–		–	–		–	–		1															1		–
26 Chelsea	–	–		–	–		–	–		1	–		–															1		–
27 Coventry City	–	–		–	–		–	–		1	–		–															1		–
28 Leyton Orient	–	–		1	–		–			–	–		–															1		–
29 Luton Town	–	–		1	–		–			–	–		–															1		–
30 Newcastle United	–	–		1	–		–			–	–		–															1		–
31 Southampton	–	–		–	–		–	–		1	–		–															1		–

TONY GILL

DEBUT (Full Appearance)

Saturday 03/01/1987
Football League Division 1
at The Dell

Southampton 1 Manchester United 1

CLUB CAREER RECORD	Apps	Subs	Goals
Premiership	0		0
League Division 1	5	(5)	1
League Division 2	0		0
FA Cup	2	(2)	1
League Cup	0		0
European Cup / Champions League	0		0
European Cup-Winners' Cup	0		0
UEFA Cup / Inter-Cities' Fairs Cup	0		0
Other Matches	0		0
OVERALL TOTAL	**7**	**(7)**	**2**

Opponents	PREM A	S	G	FLD 1 A	S	G	FLD 2 A	S	G	FAC A	S	G	LC A	S	G	EC/CL A	S	G	ECWC A	S	G	UEFA A	S	G	OTHER A	S	G	TOTAL A	S	G
1 Queens Park Rangers	–	–		–	–		–	–		2		1	–															2		1
2 Southampton	–	–		1	(1)		–			–	–		–															1	(1)	
3 Millwall	–	–		1		1	–			–	–		–															1		1
4 Middlesbrough	–	–		1	–		–			–	–		–															1		–
5 Newcastle United	–	–		1	–		–			–	–		–															1		–
6 West Ham United	–	–		1	–		–			–	–		–															1		–
7 Arsenal	–	–		–	(1)		–			–	–		–															–	(1)	
8 Bournemouth	–	–		–	–		–	–		–	(1)		–															–	(1)	
9 Coventry City	–	–		–	(1)		–			–	–		–															–	(1)	
10 Nottingham Forest	–	–		–	(1)		–			–	–		–															–	(1)	
11 Oxford United	–	–		–	–		–	–		–	(1)		–															–	(1)	
12 Sheffield Wednesday	–	–		–	(1)		–			–	–		–															–	(1)	

KEITH GILLESPIE

DEBUT (Full Appearance, 1 goal)

Tuesday 05/01/1993
FA Cup 3rd Round
at Old Trafford

Manchester United 2 Bury 0

CLUB CAREER RECORD	Apps	Subs	Goals
Premiership	3	(6)	1
League Division 1	0		0
League Division 2	0		0
FA Cup	1	(1)	1
League Cup	3		0
European Cup / Champions League	0		0
European Cup-Winners' Cup	0		0
UEFA Cup / Inter-Cities' Fairs Cup	0		0
Other Matches	0		0
OVERALL TOTAL	**7**	**(7)**	**2**

Opponents	PREM			FLD 1			FLD 2			FAC			LC			EC/CL			ECWC			UEFA			OTHER			TOTAL		
	A	S	G	A	S	G	A	S	G	A	S	G	A	S	G	A	S	G	A	S	G	A	S	G	A	S	G	A	S	G
1 Port Vale	-	-	-	-	-	-	-	-	-	-	-	-	2	-	-	-	-	-	-	-	-	-	-	-	-	-	-	2	-	-
2 Newcastle United	-	(1)	1	-	-	-	-	-	-	-	-	-	1	-	-	-	-	-	-	-	-	-	-	-	-	-	-	1	(1)	1
3 Bury	-	-	-	-	-	-	-	-	-	1	-	1	-	-	-	-	-	-	-	-	-	-	-	-	-	-	-	1	-	1
4 Arsenal	1	-	-	-	-	-	-	-	-	-	-	-	-	-	-	-	-	-	-	-	-	-	-	-	-	-	-	1	-	-
5 Coventry City	1	-	-	-	-	-	-	-	-	-	-	-	-	-	-	-	-	-	-	-	-	-	-	-	-	-	-	1	-	-
6 Sheffield Wednesday	1	-	-	-	-	-	-	-	-	-	-	-	-	-	-	-	-	-	-	-	-	-	-	-	-	-	-	1	-	-
7 Aston Villa	-	(1)	-	-	-	-	-	-	-	-	-	-	-	-	-	-	-	-	-	-	-	-	-	-	-	-	-	-	(1)	-
8 Brighton	-	-	-	-	-	-	-	-	-	-	(1)	-	-	-	-	-	-	-	-	-	-	-	-	-	-	-	-	-	(1)	-
9 Crystal Palace	-	(1)	-	-	-	-	-	-	-	-	-	-	-	-	-	-	-	-	-	-	-	-	-	-	-	-	-	-	(1)	-
10 Norwich City	-	(1)	-	-	-	-	-	-	-	-	-	-	-	-	-	-	-	-	-	-	-	-	-	-	-	-	-	-	(1)	-
11 Queens Park Rangers	-	(1)	-	-	-	-	-	-	-	-	-	-	-	-	-	-	-	-	-	-	-	-	-	-	-	-	-	-	(1)	-
12 Southampton	-	(1)	-	-	-	-	-	-	-	-	-	-	-	-	-	-	-	-	-	-	-	-	-	-	-	-	-	-	(1)	-

MATTHEW GILLESPIE

DEBUT (Full Appearance)

Saturday 28/11/1896
Football League Division 2
at Muntz Street

Birmingham City 1 Newton Heath 0

CLUB CAREER RECORD	Apps	Subs	Goals
Premiership	0		0
League Division 1	0		0
League Division 2	74		17
FA Cup	11		4
League Cup	0		0
European Cup / Champions League	0		0
European Cup-Winners' Cup	0		0
UEFA Cup / Inter-Cities' Fairs Cup	0		0
Other Matches	4		0
OVERALL TOTAL	**89**		**21**

Opponents	PREM			FLD 1			FLD 2			FAC			LC			EC/CL			ECWC			UEFA			OTHER			TOTAL		
	A	S	G	A	S	G	A	S	G	A	S	G	A	S	G	A	S	G	A	S	G	A	S	G	A	S	G	A	S	G
1 Lincoln City	-	-	-	-	-	-	7	-	-	-	-	-	-	-	-	-	-	-	-	-	-	-	-	-	-	-	-	7	-	-
2 Darwen	-	-	-	-	-	-	6	-	3	-	-	-	-	-	-	-	-	-	-	-	-	-	-	-	-	-	-	6	-	3
3 Arsenal	-	-	-	-	-	-	6	-	-	-	-	-	-	-	-	-	-	-	-	-	-	-	-	-	-	-	-	6	-	-
4 Loughborough Town	-	-	-	-	-	-	6	-	-	-	-	-	-	-	-	-	-	-	-	-	-	-	-	-	-	-	-	6	-	-
5 Walsall	-	-	-	-	-	-	5	-	3	-	-	-	-	-	-	-	-	-	-	-	-	-	-	-	-	-	-	5	-	3
6 Leicester City	-	-	-	-	-	-	5	-	2	-	-	-	-	-	-	-	-	-	-	-	-	-	-	-	-	-	-	5	-	2
7 Birmingham City	-	-	-	-	-	-	5	-	1	-	-	-	-	-	-	-	-	-	-	-	-	-	-	-	-	-	-	5	-	1
8 Blackpool	-	-	-	-	-	-	3	-	-	2	-	1	-	-	-	-	-	-	-	-	-	-	-	-	-	-	-	5	-	1
9 Burton Swifts	-	-	-	-	-	-	4	-	3	-	-	-	-	-	-	-	-	-	-	-	-	-	-	-	-	-	-	4	-	3
10 Luton Town	-	-	-	-	-	-	4	-	1	-	-	-	-	-	-	-	-	-	-	-	-	-	-	-	-	-	-	4	-	1
11 Manchester City	-	-	-	-	-	-	4	-	1	-	-	-	-	-	-	-	-	-	-	-	-	-	-	-	-	-	-	4	-	1
12 Burnley	-	-	-	-	-	-	1	-	-	-	-	-	-	-	-	-	-	-	-	-	-	-	-	-	2	-	-	3	-	-
13 Glossop	-	-	-	-	-	-	2	-	1	-	-	-	-	-	-	-	-	-	-	-	-	-	-	-	-	-	-	2	-	1
14 Grimsby Town	-	-	-	-	-	-	2	-	1	-	-	-	-	-	-	-	-	-	-	-	-	-	-	-	-	-	-	2	-	1
15 Barnsley	-	-	-	-	-	-	2	-	-	-	-	-	-	-	-	-	-	-	-	-	-	-	-	-	-	-	-	2	-	-
16 Gainsborough Trinity	-	-	-	-	-	-	2	-	-	-	-	-	-	-	-	-	-	-	-	-	-	-	-	-	-	-	-	2	-	-
17 New Brighton Tower	-	-	-	-	-	-	2	-	-	-	-	-	-	-	-	-	-	-	-	-	-	-	-	-	-	-	-	2	-	-
18 Newcastle United	-	-	-	-	-	-	2	-	-	-	-	-	-	-	-	-	-	-	-	-	-	-	-	-	-	-	-	2	-	-
19 Notts County	-	-	-	-	-	-	2	-	-	-	-	-	-	-	-	-	-	-	-	-	-	-	-	-	-	-	-	2	-	-
20 Southampton	-	-	-	-	-	-	-	-	-	2	-	-	-	-	-	-	-	-	-	-	-	-	-	-	-	-	-	2	-	-
21 Sunderland	-	-	-	-	-	-	-	-	-	-	-	-	-	-	-	-	-	-	-	-	-	-	-	-	2	-	-	2	-	-
22 Tottenham Hotspur	-	-	-	-	-	-	-	-	-	2	-	-	-	-	-	-	-	-	-	-	-	-	-	-	-	-	-	2	-	-
23 West Manchester	-	-	-	-	-	-	-	-	-	1	-	2	-	-	-	-	-	-	-	-	-	-	-	-	-	-	-	1	-	2
24 Burton Wanderers	-	-	-	-	-	-	1	-	1	-	-	-	-	-	-	-	-	-	-	-	-	-	-	-	-	-	-	1	-	1
25 Nelson	-	-	-	-	-	-	-	-	-	1	-	1	-	-	-	-	-	-	-	-	-	-	-	-	-	-	-	1	-	1
26 Chesterfield	-	-	-	-	-	-	1	-	-	-	-	-	-	-	-	-	-	-	-	-	-	-	-	-	-	-	-	1	-	-
27 Derby County	-	-	-	-	-	-	-	-	-	1	-	-	-	-	-	-	-	-	-	-	-	-	-	-	-	-	-	1	-	-
28 Kettering	-	-	-	-	-	-	-	-	-	1	-	-	-	-	-	-	-	-	-	-	-	-	-	-	-	-	-	1	-	-
29 Liverpool	-	-	-	-	-	-	-	-	-	1	-	-	-	-	-	-	-	-	-	-	-	-	-	-	-	-	-	1	-	-
30 Middlesbrough	-	-	-	-	-	-	1	-	-	-	-	-	-	-	-	-	-	-	-	-	-	-	-	-	-	-	-	1	-	-
31 Port Vale	-	-	-	-	-	-	1	-	-	-	-	-	-	-	-	-	-	-	-	-	-	-	-	-	-	-	-	1	-	-

TOMMY GIPPS

DEBUT (Full Appearance)

Wednesday 25/12/1912
Football League Division 1
at Stamford Bridge

Chelsea 1 Manchester United 4

CLUB CAREER RECORD	Apps	Subs	Goals
Premiership	0		0
League Division 1	23		0
League Division 2	0		0
FA Cup	0		0
League Cup	0		0
European Cup / Champions League	0		0
European Cup-Winners' Cup	0		0
UEFA Cup / Inter-Cities' Fairs Cup	0		0
Other Matches	0		0
OVERALL TOTAL	**23**		**0**

Opponents	PREM A S G	FLD 1 A S G	FLD 2 A S G	FAC A S G	LC A S G	EC/CL A S G	ECWC A S G	UEFA A S G	OTHER A S G	TOTAL A S G
1 Chelsea	– –	3 – –	– – –	– – –	– – –	– – –	– – –	– – –	– – –	3 –
2 West Bromwich Albion	– –	3 – –	– – –	– – –	– – –	– – –	– – –	– – –	– – –	3 –
3 Aston Villa	– –	2 – –	– – –	– – –	– – –	– – –	– – –	– – –	– – –	2 –
4 Liverpool	– –	2 – –	– – –	– – –	– – –	– – –	– – –	– – –	– – –	2 –
5 Manchester City	– –	2 – –	– – –	– – –	– – –	– – –	– – –	– – –	– – –	2 –
6 Sheffield United	– –	2 – –	– – –	– – –	– – –	– – –	– – –	– – –	– – –	2 –
7 Blackburn Rovers	– –	1 – –	– – –	– – –	– – –	– – –	– – –	– – –	– – –	1 –
8 Bolton Wanderers	– –	1 – –	– – –	– – –	– – –	– – –	– – –	– – –	– – –	1 –
9 Bradford City	– –	1 – –	– – –	– – –	– – –	– – –	– – –	– – –	– – –	1 –
10 Bradford Park Avenue	– –	1 – –	– – –	– – –	– – –	– – –	– – –	– – –	– – –	1 –
11 Derby County	– –	1 – –	– – –	– – –	– – –	– – –	– – –	– – –	– – –	1 –
12 Everton	– –	1 – –	– – –	– – –	– – –	– – –	– – –	– – –	– – –	1 –
13 Newcastle United	– –	1 – –	– – –	– – –	– – –	– – –	– – –	– – –	– – –	1 –
14 Notts County	– –	1 – –	– – –	– – –	– – –	– – –	– – –	– – –	– – –	1 –
15 Sunderland	– –	1 – –	– – –	– – –	– – –	– – –	– – –	– – –	– – –	1 –

DON GIVENS

DEBUT (Substitute Appearance)

Saturday 09/08/1969
Football League Division 1
at Selhurst Park

Crystal Palace 2 Manchester United 2

CLUB CAREER RECORD	Apps	Subs	Goals
Premiership	0		0
League Division 1	4	(4)	1
League Division 2	0		0
FA Cup	0		0
League Cup	1		0
European Cup / Champions League	0		0
European Cup-Winners' Cup	0		0
UEFA Cup / Inter-Cities' Fairs Cup	0		0
Other Matches	0		0
OVERALL TOTAL	**5**	**(4)**	**1**

Opponents	PREM A S G	FLD 1 A S G	FLD 2 A S G	FAC A S G	LC A S G	EC/CL A S G	ECWC A S G	UEFA A S G	OTHER A S G	TOTAL A S G
1 Everton	– –	1 (1) –	– – –	– – –	– – –	– – –	– – –	– – –	– – –	1 (1) –
2 Sunderland	– –	1 – 1	– – –	– – –	– – –	– – –	– – –	– – –	– – –	1 – 1
3 Leeds United	– –	1 – –	– – –	– – –	– – –	– – –	– – –	– – –	– – –	1 – –
4 Middlesbrough	– –	– – –	– – –	– – –	1 – –	– – –	– – –	– – –	– – –	1 – –
5 Newcastle United	– –	1 – –	– – –	– – –	– – –	– – –	– – –	– – –	– – –	1 – –
6 Crystal Palace	– –	– (1) –	– – –	– – –	– – –	– – –	– – –	– – –	– – –	– (1) –
7 West Bromwich Albion	– –	– (1) –	– – –	– – –	– – –	– – –	– – –	– – –	– – –	– (1) –
8 Wolverhampton W.	– –	– (1) –	– – –	– – –	– – –	– – –	– – –	– – –	– – –	– (1) –

GEORGE GLADWIN

DEBUT (Full Appearance, 1 goal)

Saturday 27/02/1937
Football League Division 1
at Stamford Bridge

Chelsea 4 Manchester United 2

CLUB CAREER RECORD	Apps	Subs	Goals
Premiership	0		0
League Division 1	20		1
League Division 2	7		0
FA Cup	1		0
League Cup	0		0
European Cup / Champions League	0		0
European Cup-Winners' Cup	0		0
UEFA Cup / Inter-Cities' Fairs Cup	0		0
Other Matches	0		0
OVERALL TOTAL	**28**		**1**

Opponents	PREM A S G	FLD 1 A S G	FLD 2 A S G	FAC A S G	LC A S G	EC/CL A S G	ECWC A S G	UEFA A S G	OTHER A S G	TOTAL A S G
1 Chelsea	– –	2 – 1	– – –	– – –	– – –	– – –	– – –	– – –	– – –	2 – 1
2 Birmingham City	– –	2 – –	– – –	– – –	– – –	– – –	– – –	– – –	– – –	2 –
3 Coventry City	– –	– – –	2 – –	– – –	– – –	– – –	– – –	– – –	– – –	2 –
4 Everton	– –	2 – –	– – –	– – –	– – –	– – –	– – –	– – –	– – –	2 –
5 Grimsby Town	– –	2 – –	– – –	– – –	– – –	– – –	– – –	– – –	– – –	2 –
6 Liverpool	– –	2 – –	– – –	– – –	– – –	– – –	– – –	– – –	– – –	2 –
7 Middlesbrough	– –	2 – –	– – –	– – –	– – –	– – –	– – –	– – –	– – –	2 –
8 West Bromwich Albion	– –	1 – –	– – –	1 – –	– – –	– – –	– – –	– – –	– – –	2 –
9 Blackpool	– –	1 – –	– – –	– – –	– – –	– – –	– – –	– – –	– – –	1 –
10 Bolton Wanderers	– –	1 – –	– – –	– – –	– – –	– – –	– – –	– – –	– – –	1 –

continued../

GEORGE GLADWIN (continued)

Opponents	PREM A S G	FLD 1 A S G	FLD 2 A S G	FAC A S G	LC A S G	EC/CL A S G	ECWC A S G	UEFA A S G	OTHER A S G	TOTAL A S G
11 Charlton Athletic	- - -	1 - -	- - -	- - -	- - -	- - -	- - -	- - -	- - -	1 - -
12 Derby County	- - -	1 - -	- - -	- - -	- - -	- - -	- - -	- - -	- - -	1 - -
13 Luton Town	- - -	- - -	1 - -	- - -	- - -	- - -	- - -	- - -	- - -	1 - -
14 Newcastle United	- - -	- - -	- - -	1 - -	- - -	- - -	- - -	- - -	- - -	1 - -
15 Preston North End	- - -	1 - -	- - -	- - -	- - -	- - -	- - -	- - -	- - -	1 - -
16 Southampton	- - -	- - -	- - -	1 - -	- - -	- - -	- - -	- - -	- - -	1 - -
17 Stoke City	- - -	1 - -	- - -	- - -	- - -	- - -	- - -	- - -	- - -	1 - -
18 Sunderland	- - -	1 - -	- - -	- - -	- - -	- - -	- - -	- - -	- - -	1 - -
19 Swansea City	- - -	- - -	1 - -	- - -	- - -	- - -	- - -	- - -	- - -	1 - -
20 West Ham United	- - -	- - -	- - -	1 - -	- - -	- - -	- - -	- - -	- - -	1 - -

GILBERT GODSMARK

DEBUT (Full Appearance)

Saturday 03/02/1900
Football League Division 2
at Bank Street

Newton Heath 1 Sheffield Wednesday 0

CLUB CAREER RECORD	Apps	Subs	Goals
Premiership	0		0
League Division 1	0		0
League Division 2	9		4
FA Cup	0		0
League Cup	0		0
European Cup / Champions League	0		0
European Cup-Winners' Cup	0		0
UEFA Cup / Inter-Cities' Fairs Cup	0		0
Other Matches	0		0
OVERALL TOTAL	9		4

Opponents	PREM A S G	FLD 1 A S G	FLD 2 A S G	FAC A S G	LC A S G	EC/CL A S G	ECWC A S G	UEFA A S G	OTHER A S G	TOTAL A S G
1 Luton Town	- - -	- - -	1 - 2	- - -	- - -	- - -	- - -	- - -	- - -	1 - 2
2 Birmingham City	- - -	- - -	1 - 1	- - -	- - -	- - -	- - -	- - -	- - -	1 - 1
3 New Brighton Tower	- - -	- - -	1 - 1	- - -	- - -	- - -	- - -	- - -	- - -	1 - 1
4 Arsenal	- - -	- - -	1 - -	- - -	- - -	- - -	- - -	- - -	- - -	1 - -
5 Barnsley	- - -	- - -	1 - -	- - -	- - -	- - -	- - -	- - -	- - -	1 - -
6 Grimsby Town	- - -	- - -	1 - -	- - -	- - -	- - -	- - -	- - -	- - -	1 - -
7 Leicester City	- - -	- - -	1 - -	- - -	- - -	- - -	- - -	- - -	- - -	1 - -
8 Lincoln City	- - -	- - -	1 - -	- - -	- - -	- - -	- - -	- - -	- - -	1 - -
9 Sheffield Wednesday	- - -	- - -	1 - -	- - -	- - -	- - -	- - -	- - -	- - -	1 - -

ERNIE GOLDTHORPE

DEBUT (Full Appearance, 1 goal)

Saturday 11/11/1922
Football League Division 2
at Millfields Road

Leyton Orient 1 Manchester United 1

CLUB CAREER RECORD	Apps	Subs	Goals
Premiership	0		0
League Division 1	0		0
League Division 2	27		15
FA Cup	3		1
League Cup	0		0
European Cup / Champions League	0		0
European Cup-Winners' Cup	0		0
UEFA Cup / Inter-Cities' Fairs Cup	0		0
Other Matches	0		0
OVERALL TOTAL	30		16

Opponents	PREM A S G	FLD 1 A S G	FLD 2 A S G	FAC A S G	LC A S G	EC/CL A S G	ECWC A S G	UEFA A S G	OTHER A S G	TOTAL A S G
1 Bradford City	- - -	- - -	2 - 1	2 - 1	- - -	- - -	- - -	- - -	- - -	4 - 2
2 South Shields	- - -	- - -	3 - 3	- - -	- - -	- - -	- - -	- - -	- - -	3 - 3
3 Bury	- - -	- - -	3 - 2	- - -	- - -	- - -	- - -	- - -	- - -	3 - 2
4 Notts County	- - -	- - -	2 - 4	- - -	- - -	- - -	- - -	- - -	- - -	2 - 4
5 Hull City	- - -	- - -	2 - 1	- - -	- - -	- - -	- - -	- - -	- - -	2 - 1
6 Blackpool	- - -	- - -	2 - -	- - -	- - -	- - -	- - -	- - -	- - -	2 - -
7 Leeds United	- - -	- - -	2 - -	- - -	- - -	- - -	- - -	- - -	- - -	2 - -
8 Stockport County	- - -	- - -	2 - -	- - -	- - -	- - -	- - -	- - -	- - -	2 - -
9 West Ham United	- - -	- - -	2 - -	- - -	- - -	- - -	- - -	- - -	- - -	2 - -
10 Leicester City	- - -	- - -	1 - 1	- - -	- - -	- - -	- - -	- - -	- - -	1 - 1
11 Leyton Orient	- - -	- - -	1 - 1	- - -	- - -	- - -	- - -	- - -	- - -	1 - 1
12 Rotherham United	- - -	- - -	1 - 1	- - -	- - -	- - -	- - -	- - -	- - -	1 - 1
13 Southampton	- - -	- - -	1 - 1	- - -	- - -	- - -	- - -	- - -	- - -	1 - 1
14 Barnsley	- - -	- - -	1 - -	- - -	- - -	- - -	- - -	- - -	- - -	1 - -
15 Bristol City	- - -	- - -	1 - -	- - -	- - -	- - -	- - -	- - -	- - -	1 - -
16 Derby County	- - -	- - -	1 - -	- - -	- - -	- - -	- - -	- - -	- - -	1 - -
17 Tottenham Hotspur	- - -	- - -	- - -	1 - -	- - -	- - -	- - -	- - -	- - -	1 - -

BILLY GOODWIN

DEBUT (Full Appearance)

Saturday 28/08/1920
Football League Division 1
at Old Trafford

Manchester United 2 Bolton Wanderers 3

CLUB CAREER RECORD	Apps	Subs	Goals
Premiership	0		0
League Division 1	7		1
League Division 2	0		0
FA Cup	0		0
League Cup	0		0
European Cup / Champions League	0		0
European Cup-Winners' Cup	0		0
UEFA Cup / Inter-Cities' Fairs Cup	0		0
Other Matches	0		0
OVERALL TOTAL	**7**		**1**

Opponents	PREM A S G	FLD 1 A S G	FLD 2 A S G	FAC A S G	LC A S G	EC/CL A S G	ECWC A S G	UEFA A S G	OTHER A S G	TOTAL A S G
1 Sunderland	– –	2 1	– –	– –	– –	– –	– –	– –	– –	2 1
2 Everton	– –	2	– –	– –	– –	– –	– –	– –	– –	2 –
3 Bolton Wanderers	– –	1	– –	– –	– –	– –	– –	– –	– –	1 –
4 Bradford City	– –	1	– –	– –	– –	– –	– –	– –	– –	1 –
5 West Bromwich Albion	– –	1	– –	– –	– –	– –	– –	– –	– –	1 –

FRED GOODWIN

DEBUT (Full Appearance)

Saturday 20/11/1954
Football League Division 1
at Old Trafford

Manchester United 2 Arsenal 1

CLUB CAREER RECORD	Apps	Subs	Goals
Premiership	0		0
League Division 1	95		7
League Division 2	0		0
FA Cup	8		1
League Cup	0		0
European Cup / Champions League	3		0
European Cup-Winners' Cup	0		0
UEFA Cup / Inter-Cities' Fairs Cup	0		0
Other Matches	1		0
OVERALL TOTAL	**107**		**8**

Opponents	PREM A S G	FLD 1 A S G	FLD 2 A S G	FAC A S G	LC A S G	EC/CL A S G	ECWC A S G	UEFA A S G	OTHER A S G	TOTAL A S G
1 West Bromwich Albion	– –	8 1	– –	2 –	– –	– –	– –	– –	– –	10 1
2 Burnley	– –	9 1	– –	– –	– –	– –	– –	– –	– –	9 1
3 Everton	– –	6 1	– –	– –	– –	– –	– –	– –	– –	6 1
4 Luton Town	– –	6 1	– –	– –	– –	– –	– –	– –	– –	6 1
5 Chelsea	– –	5 1	– –	– –	– –	– –	– –	– –	– –	5 1
6 Arsenal	– –	5	– –	– –	– –	– –	– –	– –	– –	5 –
7 Aston Villa	– –	4	– –	– –	– –	– –	– –	1 –	– –	5 –
8 Preston North End	– –	5	– –	– –	– –	– –	– –	– –	– –	5 –
9 Wolverhampton W.	– –	5	– –	– –	– –	– –	– –	– –	– –	5 –
10 Bolton Wanderers	– –	3	– –	1 –	– –	– –	– –	– –	– –	4 –
11 Nottingham Forest	– –	4	– –	– –	– –	– –	– –	– –	– –	4 –
12 Tottenham Hotspur	– –	4	– –	– –	– –	– –	– –	– –	– –	4 –
13 Manchester City	– –	3 1	– –	– –	– –	– –	– –	– –	– –	3 1
14 Birmingham City	– –	3	– –	– –	– –	– –	– –	– –	– –	3 –
15 Blackburn Rovers	– –	3	– –	– –	– –	– –	– –	– –	– –	3 –
16 Blackpool	– –	3	– –	– –	– –	– –	– –	– –	– –	3 –
17 Fulham	– –	1	– –	2 –	– –	– –	– –	– –	– –	3 –
18 Leicester City	– –	3	– –	– –	– –	– –	– –	– –	– –	3 –
19 Newcastle United	– –	3	– –	– –	– –	– –	– –	– –	– –	3 –
20 Sheffield Wednesday	– –	2	– –	1 –	– –	– –	– –	– –	– –	3 –
21 Leeds United	– –	2 1	– –	– –	– –	– –	– –	– –	– –	2 1
22 AC Milan	– –	–	– –	– –	– –	2 –	– –	– –	– –	2 –
23 Portsmouth	– –	2	– –	– –	– –	– –	– –	– –	– –	2 –
24 Sunderland	– –	2	– –	– –	– –	– –	– –	– –	– –	2 –
25 West Ham United	– –	2	– –	– –	– –	– –	– –	– –	– –	2 –
26 Derby County	– –	–	– –	1 1	– –	– –	– –	– –	– –	1 1
27 Charlton Athletic	– –	1	– –	– –	– –	– –	– –	– –	– –	1 –
28 Norwich City	– –	–	– –	1 –	– –	– –	– –	– –	– –	1 –
29 Shamrock Rovers	– –	–	– –	– –	– –	1 –	– –	– –	– –	1 –
30 Sheffield United	– –	1	– –	– –	– –	– –	– –	– –	– –	1 –

ANDY GORAM

DEBUT (Full Appearance)

Saturday 14/04/2001
FA Premiership
at Old Trafford

Manchester United 4 Coventry City 2

CLUB CAREER RECORD	Apps	Subs	Goals
Premiership	2		0
League Division 1	0		0
League Division 2	0		0
FA Cup	0		0
League Cup	0		0
European Cup / Champions League	0		0
European Cup-Winners' Cup	0		0
UEFA Cup / Inter-Cities' Fairs Cup	0		0
Other Matches	0		0
OVERALL TOTAL	**2**		**0**

Opponents	PREM A S G	FLD 1 A S G	FLD 2 A S G	FAC A S G	LC A S G	EC/CL A S G	ECWC A S G	UEFA A S G	OTHER A S G	TOTAL A S G
1 Coventry City	1 –	– –	– –	– –	– –	– –	– –	– –	– –	1 –
2 Southampton	1 –	– –	– –	– –	– –	– –	– –	– –	– –	1 –

JAMES GOTHERIDGE

DEBUT (Full Appearance)

Saturday 30/10/1886
FA Cup 1st Round
at Fleetwood Park

Fleetwood Rangers 2 Newton Heath 2

CLUB CAREER RECORD	Apps	Subs	Goals
Premiership	0		0
League Division 1	0		0
League Division 2	0		0
FA Cup	1		0
League Cup	0		0
European Cup / Champions League	0		0
European Cup-Winners' Cup	0		0
UEFA Cup / Inter-Cities' Fairs Cup	0		0
Other Matches	0		0
OVERALL TOTAL	1		0

Opponents	PREM A S G	FLD 1 A S G	FLD 2 A S G	FAC A S G	LC A S G	EC/CL A S G	ECWC A S G	UEFA A S G	OTHER A S G	TOTAL A S G
1 Fleetwood Rangers	– – –	– – –	– – –	1 –	– – –	– – –	– – –	– – –	– – –	1 –

JOHN GOURLAY

DEBUT (Full Appearance)

Saturday 18/02/1899
Football League Division 2
at The Athletic Ground

Loughborough Town 0 Newton Heath 1

CLUB CAREER RECORD	Apps	Subs	Goals
Premiership	0		0
League Division 1	0		0
League Division 2	1		0
FA Cup	0		0
League Cup	0		0
European Cup / Champions League	0		0
European Cup-Winners' Cup	0		0
UEFA Cup / Inter-Cities' Fairs Cup	0		0
Other Matches	0		0
OVERALL TOTAL	1		0

Opponents	PREM A S G	FLD 1 A S G	FLD 2 A S G	FAC A S G	LC A S G	EC/CL A S G	ECWC A S G	UEFA A S G	OTHER A S G	TOTAL A S G
1 Loughborough Town	– – –	– –	1 –	– – –	– – –	– – –	– – –	– – –	– – –	1 –

ALAN GOWLING

DEBUT (Full Appearance, 1 goal)

Saturday 30/03/1968
Football League Division 1
at Victoria Ground

Stoke City 2 Manchester United 4

CLUB CAREER RECORD	Apps	Subs	Goals
Premiership	0		0
League Division 1	64	(7)	18
League Division 2	0		0
FA Cup	6	(2)	2
League Cup	7	(1)	1
European Cup / Champions League	0		0
European Cup-Winners' Cup	0		0
UEFA Cup / Inter-Cities' Fairs Cup	0		0
Other Matches	0		0
OVERALL TOTAL	77	(10)	21

Opponents	PREM A S G	FLD 1 A S G	FLD 2 A S G	FAC A S G	LC A S G	EC/CL A S G	ECWC A S G	UEFA A S G	OTHER A S G	TOTAL A S G
1 Stoke City	– –	2 (1) 1	– –	1 (1) –	3 1	– – –	– – –	– – –	– – –	6 (2) 2
2 Liverpool	– –	6 –	– –	– – –	– –	– – –	– – –	– – –	– – –	6 –
3 Southampton	– –	3 4	– –	2 –	– –	– – –	– – –	– – –	– – –	5 4
4 Ipswich Town	– –	4 –	– –	– – –	1 –	– – –	– – –	– – –	– – –	5 –
5 Wolverhampton W.	– –	4 2	– –	– – –	– –	– – –	– – –	– – –	– – –	4 2
6 Manchester City	– –	4 1	– –	– – –	– –	– – –	– – –	– – –	– – –	4 1
7 Newcastle United	– –	4 –	– –	– – –	– –	– – –	– – –	– – –	– – –	4 –
8 Burnley	– –	1 (1) –	– –	– – –	2 –	– – –	– – –	– – –	– – –	3 (1) –
9 Leeds United	– –	3 (1) –	– –	– – –	– –	– – –	– – –	– – –	– – –	3 (1) –
10 Tottenham Hotspur	– –	3 (1) –	– –	– – –	– –	– – –	– – –	– – –	– – –	3 (1) –
11 Middlesbrough	– –	– –	– –	2 (1) –	– (1) –	– – –	– – –	– – –	– – –	2 (2) –
12 Nottingham Forest	– –	3 2	– –	– – –	– –	– – –	– – –	– – –	– – –	3 2
13 Chelsea	– –	3 1	– –	– – –	– –	– – –	– – –	– – –	– – –	3 1
14 Crystal Palace	– –	3 1	– –	– – –	– –	– – –	– – –	– – –	– – –	3 1
15 Coventry City	– –	3 –	– –	– – –	– –	– – –	– – –	– – –	– – –	3 –
16 Everton	– –	3 –	– –	– – –	– –	– – –	– – –	– – –	– – –	3 –
17 Derby County	– –	2 (1) 1	– –	– – –	– –	– – –	– – –	– – –	– – –	2 (1) 1
18 West Bromwich Albion	– –	2 3	– –	– – –	– –	– – –	– – –	– – –	– – –	2 3
19 Arsenal	– –	2 1	– –	– – –	– –	– – –	– – –	– – –	– – –	2 1
20 Blackpool	– –	2 –	– –	– – –	– –	– – –	– – –	– – –	– – –	2 –
21 Huddersfield Town	– –	2 –	– –	– – –	– –	– – –	– – –	– – –	– – –	2 –
22 West Ham United	– –	2 –	– –	– – –	– –	– – –	– – –	– – –	– – –	2 –
23 Leicester City	– –	1 (1) –	– –	– – –	– –	– – –	– – –	– – –	– – –	1 (1) –
24 Preston North End	– –	– –	– –	1 2	– –	– – –	– – –	– – –	– – –	1 2
25 Sheffield United	– –	1 1	– –	– – –	– –	– – –	– – –	– – –	– – –	1 1
26 Portsmouth	– –	– –	– –	– – –	1 –	– – –	– – –	– – –	– – –	1 –
27 Sheffield Wednesday	– –	1 –	– –	– – –	– –	– – –	– – –	– – –	– – –	1 –
28 Sunderland	– –	– (1) –	– –	– – –	– –	– – –	– – –	– – –	– – –	– (1) –

ARTHUR GRAHAM

DEBUT (Full Appearance)

Saturday 20/08/1983
FA Charity Shield
at Wembley

Manchester United 2 Liverpool 0

CLUB CAREER RECORD	Apps	Subs	Goals
Premiership	0		0
League Division 1	33	(4)	5
League Division 2	0		0
FA Cup	1		0
League Cup	6		1
European Cup / Champions League	0		0
European Cup-Winners' Cup	6	(1)	1
UEFA Cup / Inter-Cities' Fairs Cup	0		0
Other Matches	1		0
OVERALL TOTAL	**47**	**(5)**	**7**

Opponents	PREM			FLD 1			FLD 2			FAC			LC			EC/CL			ECWC			UEFA			OTHER			TOTAL		
	A	S	G	A	S	G	A	S	G	A	S	G	A	S	G	A	S	G	A	S	G	A	S	G	A	S	G	A	S	G
1 Liverpool	–	–		2	–	–	–	–	–	–	–	–	–	–	–	–	–	–	–	–	–	–	–	–	–	1	–	3	–	
2 Tottenham Hotspur	–	–		2		2	–	–		–	–		–	–		–	–		–	–		–	–		–	–		2		2
3 Ipswich Town	–	–		2		1	–	–		–	–		–	–		–	–		–	–		–	–		–	–		2		1
4 Oxford United	–	–		–	–		–	–		–	–		2		1	–	–		–	–		–	–		–	–		2		1
5 Spartak Varna	–	–		–	–		–	–		–	–		–	–		–	–		2		1	–	–		–	–		2		1
6 Stoke City	–	–		2		1	–	–		–	–		–	–		–	–		–	–		–	–		–	–		2		1
7 West Bromwich Albion	–	–		2		1	–	–		–	–		–	–		–	–		–	–		–	–		–	–		2		1
8 Birmingham City	–	–		2			–	–		–	–		–	–		–	–		–	–		–	–		–	–		2	–	
9 Coventry City	–	–		2			–	–		–	–		–	–		–	–		–	–		–	–		–	–		2	–	
10 Dukla Prague	–	–		–	–		–	–		–	–		–	–		–	–		2			–	–		–	–		2	–	
11 Juventus	–	–		–	–		–	–		–	–		–	–		–	–		2			–	–		–	–		2	–	
12 Norwich City	–	–		2			–	–		–	–		–	–		–	–		–	–		–	–		–	–		2	–	
13 Nottingham Forest	–	–		2			–	–		–	–		–	–		–	–		–	–		–	–		–	–		2	–	
14 Port Vale	–	–		–	–		–	–		–	–		2			–	–		–	–		–	–		–	–		2	–	
15 Queens Park Rangers	–	–		2			–	–		–	–		–	–		–	–		–	–		–	–		–	–		2	–	
16 Southampton	–	–		2			–	–		–	–		–	–		–	–		–	–		–	–		–	–		2	–	
17 Watford	–	–		2			–	–		–	–		–	–		–	–		–	–		–	–		–	–		2	–	
18 West Ham United	–	–		2			–	–		–	–		–	–		–	–		–	–		–	–		–	–		2	–	
19 Aston Villa	–	–		1	(1)	–	–	–		–	–		–	–		–	–		–	–		–	–		–	–		1	(1)	–
20 Luton Town	–	–		1	(1)	–	–	–		–	–		–	–		–	–		–	–		–	–		–	–		1	(1)	–
21 Sunderland	–	–		1	(1)	–	–	–		–	–		–	–		–	–		–	–		–	–		–	–		1	(1)	–
22 Wolverhampton W.	–	–		1	(1)	–	–	–		–	–		–	–		–	–		–	–		–	–		–	–		1	(1)	–
23 Arsenal	–	–		1			–	–		–	–		–	–		–	–		–	–		–	–		–	–		1		–
24 Bournemouth	–	–		–	–		–	–		1			–	–		–	–		–	–		–	–		–	–		1		–
25 Burnley	–	–		–	–		–	–		–	–		1			–	–		–	–		–	–		–	–		1		–
26 Colchester United	–	–		–	–		–	–		–	–		1			–	–		–	–		–	–		–	–		1		–
27 Leicester City	–	–		1			–	–		–	–		–	–		–	–		–	–		–	–		–	–		1		–
28 Notts County	–	–		1			–	–		–	–		–	–		–	–		–	–		–	–		–	–		1		–
29 Barcelona	–	–		–	–		–	–		–	–		–	–		–	–		–	(1)	–	–	–		–	–		–	(1)	–

DEINIOL GRAHAM

DEBUT (Substitute Appearance)

Wednesday 07/10/1987
League Cup 2nd Round 2nd Leg
at Boothferry Park

Hull City 0 Manchester United 1

CLUB CAREER RECORD	Apps	Subs	Goals
Premiership	0		0
League Division 1	1	(1)	0
League Division 2	0		0
FA Cup	0	(1)	1
League Cup	0	(1)	0
European Cup / Champions League	0		0
European Cup-Winners' Cup	0		0
UEFA Cup / Inter-Cities' Fairs Cup	0		0
Other Matches	0		0
OVERALL TOTAL	**1**	**(3)**	**1**

Opponents	PREM			FLD 1			FLD 2			FAC			LC			EC/CL			ECWC			UEFA			OTHER			TOTAL		
	A	S	G	A	S	G	A	S	G	A	S	G	A	S	G	A	S	G	A	S	G	A	S	G	A	S	G	A	S	G
1 Wimbledon	–	–		1			–	–		–	–		–	–		–	–		–	–		–	–		–	–		1		–
2 Queens Park Rangers	–	–		–	–		–	–		–	(1)	1	–	–		–	–		–	–		–	–		–	–		–	(1)	1
3 Derby County	–	–		–	(1)	–	–	–		–	–		–	–		–	–		–	–		–	–		–	–		–	(1)	–
4 Hull City	–	–		–	–		–	–		–	–		–	(1)	–	–	–		–	–		–	–		–	–		–	(1)	–

GEORGE GRAHAM

DEBUT (Full Appearance)

Saturday 06/01/1973
Football League Division 1
at Highbury

Arsenal 3 Manchester United 1

CLUB CAREER RECORD	Apps	Subs	Goals
Premiership	0		0
League Division 1	41	(1)	2
League Division 2	0	(1)	0
FA Cup	2		0
League Cup	1		0
European Cup / Champions League	0		0
European Cup-Winners' Cup	0		0
UEFA Cup / Inter-Cities' Fairs Cup	0		0
Other Matches	0		0
OVERALL TOTAL	**44**	**(2)**	**2**

Opponents	PREM A S G	FLD 1 A S G	FLD 2 A S G	FAC A S G	LC A S G	EC/CL A S G	ECWC A S G	UEFA A S G	OTHER A S G	TOTAL A S G
1 Birmingham City	– –	3 –	– –	– –	– –	– –	– –	– –	– –	3 –
2 Ipswich Town	– –	3 –	– –	– –	– –	– –	– –	– –	– –	3 –
3 West Ham United	– –	3 –	– –	– –	– –	– –	– –	– –	– –	3 –
4 Wolverhampton W.	– –	2 –	– –	1 –	– –	– –	– –	– –	– –	3 –
5 Newcastle United	– –	2 1	– –	– –	– –	– –	– –	– –	– –	2 1
6 Tottenham Hotspur	– –	2 1	– –	– –	– –	– –	– –	– –	– –	2 1
7 Arsenal	– –	2 –	– –	– –	– –	– –	– –	– –	– –	2 –
8 Chelsea	– –	2 –	– –	– –	– –	– –	– –	– –	– –	2 –
9 Leeds United	– –	2 –	– –	– –	– –	– –	– –	– –	– –	2 –
10 Leicester City	– –	2 –	– –	– –	– –	– –	– –	– –	– –	2 –
11 Liverpool	– –	2 –	– –	– –	– –	– –	– –	– –	– –	2 –
12 Norwich City	– –	2 –	– –	– –	– –	– –	– –	– –	– –	2 –
13 Queens Park Rangers	– –	2 –	– –	– –	– –	– –	– –	– –	– –	2 –
14 Sheffield United	– –	2 –	– –	– –	– –	– –	– –	– –	– –	2 –
15 Stoke City	– –	2 –	– –	– –	– –	– –	– –	– –	– –	2 –
16 Manchester City	– –	1 (1) –	– –	– –	– –	– –	– –	– –	– –	1 (1) –
17 Burnley	– –	1 –	– –	– –	– –	– –	– –	– –	– –	1 –
18 Coventry City	– –	1 –	– –	– –	– –	– –	– –	– –	– –	1 –
19 Crystal Palace	– –	1 –	– –	– –	– –	– –	– –	– –	– –	1 –
20 Derby County	– –	1 –	– –	– –	– –	– –	– –	– –	– –	1 –
21 Everton	– –	1 –	– –	– –	– –	– –	– –	– –	– –	1 –
22 Middlesbrough	– –	– –	– –	– –	1 –	– –	– –	– –	– –	1 –
23 Plymouth Argyle	– –	– –	– –	1 –	– –	– –	– –	– –	– –	1 –
24 Southampton	– –	1 –	– –	– –	– –	– –	– –	– –	– –	1 –
25 West Bromwich Albion	– –	1 –	– –	– –	– –	– –	– –	– –	– –	1 –
26 Bristol City	– –	– –	– (1)	– –	– –	– –	– –	– –	– –	– (1) –

JOHN GRAHAM

DEBUT (Full Appearance)

Saturday 11/11/1893
Football League Division 1
at Bank Street

Newton Heath 1 Wolverhampton Wanderers 0

CLUB CAREER RECORD	Apps	Subs	Goals
Premiership	0		0
League Division 1	4		0
League Division 2	0		0
FA Cup	0		0
League Cup	0		0
European Cup / Champions League	0		0
European Cup-Winners' Cup	0		0
UEFA Cup / Inter-Cities' Fairs Cup	0		0
Other Matches	0		0
OVERALL TOTAL	**4**		**0**

Opponents	PREM A S G	FLD 1 A S G	FLD 2 A S G	FAC A S G	LC A S G	EC/CL A S G	ECWC A S G	UEFA A S G	OTHER A S G	TOTAL A S G
1 Everton	– –	1 –	– –	– –	– –	– –	– –	– –	– –	1 –
2 Sheffield Wednesday	– –	1 –	– –	– –	– –	– –	– –	– –	– –	1 –
3 Sunderland	– –	1 –	– –	– –	– –	– –	– –	– –	– –	1 –
4 Wolverhampton W.	– –	1 –	– –	– –	– –	– –	– –	– –	– –	1 –

BILLY GRASSAM

DEBUT (Full Appearance)

Saturday 03/10/1903
Football League Division 2
at Manor Field

Arsenal 4 Manchester United 0

CLUB CAREER RECORD	Apps	Subs	Goals
Premiership	0		0
League Division 1	0		0
League Division 2	29		13
FA Cup	8		1
League Cup	0		0
European Cup / Champions League	0		0
European Cup-Winners' Cup	0		0
UEFA Cup / Inter-Cities' Fairs Cup	0		0
Other Matches	0		0
OVERALL TOTAL	**37**		**14**

Opponents	PREM A S G	FLD 1 A S G	FLD 2 A S G	FAC A S G	LC A S G	EC/CL A S G	ECWC A S G	UEFA A S G	OTHER A S G	TOTAL A S G
1 Birmingham City	– –	– –	– –	4 1	– –	– –	– –	– –	– –	4 1
2 Blackpool	– –	– –	3 4	– –	– –	– –	– –	– –	– –	3 4
3 Gainsborough Trinity	– –	– –	3 1	– –	– –	– –	– –	– –	– –	3 1

continued../

BILLY GRASSAM (continued)

Opponents	PREM			FLD 1			FLD 2			FAC			LC			EC/CL			ECWC			UEFA			OTHER			TOTAL		
	A	S	G	A	S	G	A	S	G	A	S	G	A	S	G	A	S	G	A	S	G	A	S	G	A	S	G	A	S	G
4 Chesterfield	-	-	-	-	-	-	3	-	-	-	-	-	-	-	-	-	-	-	-	-	-	-	-	-	-	-	-	3	-	-
5 Fulham	-	-	-	-	-	-	3	-	-	-	-	-	-	-	-	-	-	-	-	-	-	-	-	-	-	-	-	3	-	-
6 Barnsley	-	-	-	-	-	-	-	-	-	2	-	1	-	-	-	-	-	-	-	-	-	-	-	-	-	-	-	2	-	1
7 Burton United	-	-	-	-	-	-	-	-	-	2	-	1	-	-	-	-	-	-	-	-	-	-	-	-	-	-	-	2	-	1
8 Glossop	-	-	-	-	-	-	-	-	-	2	-	1	-	-	-	-	-	-	-	-	-	-	-	-	-	-	-	2	-	1
9 Arsenal	-	-	-	-	-	-	-	-	-	2	-	-	-	-	-	-	-	-	-	-	-	-	-	-	-	-	-	2	-	-
10 Bristol City	-	-	-	-	-	-	-	-	-	2	-	-	-	-	-	-	-	-	-	-	-	-	-	-	-	-	-	2	-	-
11 Burnley	-	-	-	-	-	-	-	-	-	1	-	2	-	-	-	-	-	-	-	-	-	-	-	-	-	-	-	1	-	2
12 Grimsby Town	-	-	-	-	-	-	-	-	-	1	-	1	-	-	-	-	-	-	-	-	-	-	-	-	-	-	-	1	-	1
13 Port Vale	-	-	-	-	-	-	-	-	-	1	-	1	-	-	-	-	-	-	-	-	-	-	-	-	-	-	-	1	-	1
14 Stockport County	-	-	-	-	-	-	-	-	-	1	-	1	-	-	-	-	-	-	-	-	-	-	-	-	-	-	-	1	-	1
15 Bolton Wanderers	-	-	-	-	-	-	-	-	-	1	-	-	-	-	-	-	-	-	-	-	-	-	-	-	-	-	-	1	-	-
16 Bradford City	-	-	-	-	-	-	-	-	-	1	-	-	-	-	-	-	-	-	-	-	-	-	-	-	-	-	-	1	-	-
17 Doncaster Rovers	-	-	-	-	-	-	-	-	-	1	-	-	-	-	-	-	-	-	-	-	-	-	-	-	-	-	-	1	-	-
18 Leicester City	-	-	-	-	-	-	-	-	-	1	-	-	-	-	-	-	-	-	-	-	-	-	-	-	-	-	-	1	-	-
19 Lincoln City	-	-	-	-	-	-	-	-	-	1	-	-	-	-	-	-	-	-	-	-	-	-	-	-	-	-	-	1	-	-
20 Notts County	-	-	-	-	-	-	-	-	-	-	-	-	1	-	-	-	-	-	-	-	-	-	-	-	-	-	-	1	-	-
21 Preston North End	-	-	-	-	-	-	-	-	-	1	-	-	-	-	-	-	-	-	-	-	-	-	-	-	-	-	-	1	-	-

DAVID GRAY

DEBUT (Full Appearance)

Wednesday 25/10/2006
League Cup 3rd Round
at Gresty Road

Crewe Alexandra 1 Manchester United 2

CLUB CAREER RECORD	Apps	Subs	Goals
Premiership	0		0
League Division 1	0		0
League Division 2	0		0
FA Cup	0		0
League Cup	1		0
European Cup / Champions League	0		0
European Cup-Winners' Cup	0		0
UEFA Cup / Inter-Cities' Fairs Cup	0		0
Other Matches	0		0
OVERALL TOTAL	**1**		**0**

Opponents	PREM			FLD 1			FLD 2			FAC			LC			EC/CL			ECWC			UEFA			OTHER			TOTAL		
	A	S	G	A	S	G	A	S	G	A	S	G	A	S	G	A	S	G	A	S	G	A	S	G	A	S	G	A	S	G
1 Crewe Alexandra	-	-	-	-	-	-	-	-	-	-	-	-	1	-	-	-	-	-	-	-	-	-	-	-	-	-	-	1	-	-

IAN GREAVES

DEBUT (Full Appearance)

Saturday 02/10/1954
Football League Division 1
at Molineux

Wolverhampton Wanderers 4 Manchester United 2

CLUB CAREER RECORD	Apps	Subs	Goals
Premiership	0		0
League Division 1	67		0
League Division 2	0		0
FA Cup	6		0
League Cup	0		0
European Cup / Champions League	2		0
European Cup-Winners' Cup	0		0
UEFA Cup / Inter-Cities' Fairs Cup	0		0
Other Matches	0		0
OVERALL TOTAL	**75**		**0**

Opponents	PREM			FLD 1			FLD 2			FAC			LC			EC/CL			ECWC			UEFA			OTHER			TOTAL		
	A	S	G	A	S	G	A	S	G	A	S	G	A	S	G	A	S	G	A	S	G	A	S	G	A	S	G	A	S	G
1 West Bromwich Albion	-	-	-	5	-	-	-	-	-	2	-	-	-	-	-	-	-	-	-	-	-	-	-	-	-	-	-	7	-	-
2 Burnley	-	-	-	5	-	-	-	-	-	-	-	-	-	-	-	-	-	-	-	-	-	-	-	-	-	-	-	5	-	-
3 Wolverhampton W.	-	-	-	5	-	-	-	-	-	-	-	-	-	-	-	-	-	-	-	-	-	-	-	-	-	-	-	5	-	-
4 Bolton Wanderers	-	-	-	3	-	-	-	-	-	1	-	-	-	-	-	-	-	-	-	-	-	-	-	-	-	-	-	4	-	-
5 Chelsea	-	-	-	4	-	-	-	-	-	-	-	-	-	-	-	-	-	-	-	-	-	-	-	-	-	-	-	4	-	-
6 Newcastle United	-	-	-	4	-	-	-	-	-	-	-	-	-	-	-	-	-	-	-	-	-	-	-	-	-	-	-	4	-	-
7 Portsmouth	-	-	-	4	-	-	-	-	-	-	-	-	-	-	-	-	-	-	-	-	-	-	-	-	-	-	-	4	-	-
8 Arsenal	-	-	-	3	-	-	-	-	-	-	-	-	-	-	-	-	-	-	-	-	-	-	-	-	-	-	-	3	-	-
9 Blackpool	-	-	-	3	-	-	-	-	-	-	-	-	-	-	-	-	-	-	-	-	-	-	-	-	-	-	-	3	-	-
10 Nottingham Forest	-	-	-	3	-	-	-	-	-	-	-	-	-	-	-	-	-	-	-	-	-	-	-	-	-	-	-	3	-	-
11 Sunderland	-	-	-	3	-	-	-	-	-	-	-	-	-	-	-	-	-	-	-	-	-	-	-	-	-	-	-	3	-	-
12 Tottenham Hotspur	-	-	-	3	-	-	-	-	-	-	-	-	-	-	-	-	-	-	-	-	-	-	-	-	-	-	-	3	-	-
13 AC Milan	-	-	-	-	-	-	-	-	-	-	-	-	-	-	-	2	-	-	-	-	-	-	-	-	-	-	-	2	-	-
14 Aston Villa	-	-	-	2	-	-	-	-	-	-	-	-	-	-	-	-	-	-	-	-	-	-	-	-	-	-	-	2	-	-
15 Birmingham City	-	-	-	2	-	-	-	-	-	-	-	-	-	-	-	-	-	-	-	-	-	-	-	-	-	-	-	2	-	-
16 Blackburn Rovers	-	-	-	2	-	-	-	-	-	-	-	-	-	-	-	-	-	-	-	-	-	-	-	-	-	-	-	2	-	-
17 Cardiff City	-	-	-	2	-	-	-	-	-	-	-	-	-	-	-	-	-	-	-	-	-	-	-	-	-	-	-	2	-	-
18 Everton	-	-	-	2	-	-	-	-	-	-	-	-	-	-	-	-	-	-	-	-	-	-	-	-	-	-	-	2	-	-
19 Fulham	-	-	-	-	-	-	-	-	-	2	-	-	-	-	-	-	-	-	-	-	-	-	-	-	-	-	-	2	-	-
20 Leeds United	-	-	-	2	-	-	-	-	-	-	-	-	-	-	-	-	-	-	-	-	-	-	-	-	-	-	-	2	-	-
21 Luton Town	-	-	-	2	-	-	-	-	-	-	-	-	-	-	-	-	-	-	-	-	-	-	-	-	-	-	-	2	-	-
22 Manchester City	-	-	-	2	-	-	-	-	-	-	-	-	-	-	-	-	-	-	-	-	-	-	-	-	-	-	-	2	-	-
23 Preston North End	-	-	-	2	-	-	-	-	-	-	-	-	-	-	-	-	-	-	-	-	-	-	-	-	-	-	-	2	-	-
24 West Ham United	-	-	-	2	-	-	-	-	-	-	-	-	-	-	-	-	-	-	-	-	-	-	-	-	-	-	-	2	-	-
25 Huddersfield Town	-	-	-	1	-	-	-	-	-	-	-	-	-	-	-	-	-	-	-	-	-	-	-	-	-	-	-	1	-	-
26 Leicester City	-	-	-	1	-	-	-	-	-	-	-	-	-	-	-	-	-	-	-	-	-	-	-	-	-	-	-	1	-	-
27 Sheffield Wednesday	-	-	-	-	-	-	-	-	-	1	-	-	-	-	-	-	-	-	-	-	-	-	-	-	-	-	-	1	-	-

EDDIE GREEN

DEBUT (Full Appearance)

Saturday 26/08/1933
Football League Division 2
at Home Park

Plymouth Argyle 4 Manchester United 0

CLUB CAREER RECORD	Apps	Subs	Goals
Premiership	0		0
League Division 1	0		0
League Division 2	9		4
FA Cup	0		0
League Cup	0		0
European Cup / Champions League	0		0
European Cup–Winners' Cup	0		0
UEFA Cup / Inter–Cities' Fairs Cup	0		0
Other Matches	0		0
OVERALL TOTAL	**9**		**4**

Opponents	PREM			FLD 1			FLD 2			FAC			LC			EC/CL			ECWC			UEFA			OTHER			TOTAL		
	A	S	G	A	S	G	A	S	G	A	S	G	A	S	G	A	S	G	A	S	G	A	S	G	A	S	G	A	S	G
1 Burnley	–	–	–	–			1		1	–	–	–	–	–	–	–	–	–	–	–	–	–	–	–	–	–	–	1		1
2 Hull City	–	–	–	–			1		1	–	–	–	–	–	–	–	–	–	–	–	–	–	–	–	–	–	–	1		1
3 Lincoln City	–	–	–	–			1		1	–	–	–	–	–	–	–	–	–	–	–	–	–	–	–	–	–	–	1		1
4 Oldham Athletic	–	–	–	–			1		1	–	–	–	–	–	–	–	–	–	–	–	–	–	–	–	–	–	–	1		1
5 Blackpool	–	–	–	–			1		–	–	–	–	–	–	–	–	–	–	–	–	–	–	–	–	–	–	–	1		–
6 Fulham	–	–	–	–			1		–	–	–	–	–	–	–	–	–	–	–	–	–	–	–	–	–	–	–	1		–
7 Nottingham Forest	–	–	–	–			1		–	–	–	–	–	–	–	–	–	–	–	–	–	–	–	–	–	–	–	1		–
8 Plymouth Argyle	–	–	–	–			1		–	–	–	–	–	–	–	–	–	–	–	–	–	–	–	–	–	–	–	1		–
9 Southampton	–	–	–	–			1		–	–	–	–	–	–	–	–	–	–	–	–	–	–	–	–	–	–	–	1		–

BRIAN GREENHOFF

DEBUT (Full Appearance)

Saturday 08/09/1973
Football League Division 1
at Portman Road

Ipswich Town 2 Manchester United 1

CLUB CAREER RECORD	Apps	Subs	Goals
Premiership	0		0
League Division 1	179	(1)	9
League Division 2	39	(2)	4
FA Cup	24		2
League Cup	19		2
European Cup / Champions League	0		0
European Cup-Winners' Cup	2		0
UEFA Cup / Inter-Cities' Fairs Cup	4		0
Other Matches	1		0
OVERALL TOTAL	**268**	**(3)**	**17**

Opponents	PREM			FLD 1			FLD 2			FAC			LC			EC/CL			ECWC			UEFA			OTHER			TOTAL		
	A	S	G	A	S	G	A	S	G	A	S	G	A	S	G	A	S	G	A	S	G	A	S	G	A	S	G	A	S	G
1 Norwich City	-	-	-	8	-	1	2	-	-	-	-	-	2	-	-	-	-	-	-	-	-	-	-	-	-	-	-	12	-	1
2 Liverpool	-	-	-	8	-	-	-	-	-	2	-	1	-	-	-	-	-	-	-	-	-	-	-	-	1	-	-	11	-	1
3 Everton	-	-	-	10	-	-	-	-	-	-	-	-	1	-	-	-	-	-	-	-	-	-	-	-	-	-	-	11	-	-
4 Leeds United	-	-	-	10	-	-	-	-	-	1	-	-	-	-	-	-	-	-	-	-	-	-	-	-	-	-	-	11	-	-
5 Wolverhampton W.	-	-	-	8	-	2	-	-	-	2	-	1	-	-	-	-	-	-	-	-	-	-	-	-	-	-	-	10	-	3
6 Birmingham City	-	-	-	10	-	-	-	-	-	-	-	-	-	-	-	-	-	-	-	-	-	-	-	-	-	-	-	10	-	-
7 Coventry City	-	-	-	10	-	-	-	-	-	-	-	-	-	-	-	-	-	-	-	-	-	-	-	-	-	-	-	10	-	-
8 Ipswich Town	-	-	-	9	-	-	-	-	-	1	-	-	-	-	-	-	-	-	-	-	-	-	-	-	-	-	-	10	-	-
9 Manchester City	-	-	-	8	-	-	-	-	-	-	-	-	2	-	-	-	-	-	-	-	-	-	-	-	-	-	-	10	-	-
10 Middlesbrough	-	-	-	7	-	-	-	-	-	-	-	-	3	-	-	-	-	-	-	-	-	-	-	-	-	-	-	10	-	-
11 Aston Villa	-	-	-	6	-	-	1	(1)	-	1	-	-	1	-	-	-	-	-	-	-	-	-	-	-	-	-	-	9	(1)	-
12 Arsenal	-	-	-	8	-	-	-	-	-	-	-	-	1	-	-	-	-	-	-	-	-	-	-	-	-	-	-	9	-	-
13 Queens Park Rangers	-	-	-	8	-	-	-	-	-	1	-	-	-	-	-	-	-	-	-	-	-	-	-	-	-	-	-	9	-	-
14 Derby County	-	-	-	7	-	1	-	-	-	1	-	-	-	-	-	-	-	-	-	-	-	-	-	-	-	-	-	8	-	1
15 Newcastle United	-	-	-	7	-	1	-	-	-	-	-	-	1	-	-	-	-	-	-	-	-	-	-	-	-	-	-	8	-	1
16 Southampton	-	-	-	3	-	-	2	-	-	3	-	-	-	-	-	-	-	-	-	-	-	-	-	-	-	-	-	8	-	-
17 Tottenham Hotspur	-	-	-	8	-	-	-	-	-	-	-	-	-	-	-	-	-	-	-	-	-	-	-	-	-	-	-	8	-	-
18 Sunderland	-	-	-	2	-	1	2	-	-	-	-	-	3	-	2	-	-	-	-	-	-	-	-	-	-	-	-	7	-	3
19 West Ham United	-	-	-	7	-	-	-	-	-	-	-	-	-	-	-	-	-	-	-	-	-	-	-	-	-	-	-	7	-	-
20 Chelsea	-	-	-	5	-	1	-	-	-	1	-	-	-	-	-	-	-	-	-	-	-	-	-	-	-	-	-	6	-	1
21 Nottingham Forest	-	-	-	4	-	-	2	-	1	-	-	-	-	-	-	-	-	-	-	-	-	-	-	-	-	-	-	6	-	1
22 Leicester City	-	-	-	5	-	-	-	-	-	1	-	-	-	-	-	-	-	-	-	-	-	-	-	-	-	-	-	6	-	-
23 West Bromwich Albion	-	-	-	4	-	1	1	(1)	-	-	-	-	-	-	-	-	-	-	-	-	-	-	-	-	-	-	-	5	(1)	1
24 Burnley	-	-	-	4	-	-	-	-	-	-	-	-	1	-	-	-	-	-	-	-	-	-	-	-	-	-	-	5	-	-
25 Stoke City	-	-	-	5	-	-	-	-	-	-	-	-	-	-	-	-	-	-	-	-	-	-	-	-	-	-	-	5	-	-
26 Bristol City	-	-	-	3	(1)	1	1	-	-	-	-	-	-	-	-	-	-	-	-	-	-	-	-	-	-	-	-	4	(1)	1
27 Fulham	-	-	-	-	-	-	2	-	-	2	-	-	-	-	-	-	-	-	-	-	-	-	-	-	-	-	-	4	-	-
28 Sheffield United	-	-	-	4	-	-	-	-	-	-	-	-	-	-	-	-	-	-	-	-	-	-	-	-	-	-	-	4	-	-
29 Bolton Wanderers	-	-	-	1	-	-	2	-	-	-	-	-	-	-	-	-	-	-	-	-	-	-	-	-	-	-	-	3	-	-
30 Oxford United	-	-	-	-	-	-	2	-	-	1	-	-	-	-	-	-	-	-	-	-	-	-	-	-	-	-	-	3	-	-
31 Walsall	-	-	-	-	-	-	-	-	-	3	-	-	-	-	-	-	-	-	-	-	-	-	-	-	-	-	-	3	-	-
32 Blackpool	-	-	-	-	-	-	2	-	1	-	-	-	-	-	-	-	-	-	-	-	-	-	-	-	-	-	-	2	-	1
33 Bristol Rovers	-	-	-	-	-	-	2	-	1	-	-	-	-	-	-	-	-	-	-	-	-	-	-	-	-	-	-	2	-	1
34 Notts County	-	-	-	-	-	-	2	-	1	-	-	-	-	-	-	-	-	-	-	-	-	-	-	-	-	-	-	2	-	1
35 Ajax	-	-	-	-	-	-	-	-	-	-	-	-	-	-	-	-	-	-	-	-	-	2	-	-	-	-	-	2	-	-
36 Cardiff City	-	-	-	-	-	-	2	-	-	-	-	-	-	-	-	-	-	-	-	-	-	-	-	-	-	-	-	2	-	-
37 Hull City	-	-	-	-	-	-	2	-	-	-	-	-	-	-	-	-	-	-	-	-	-	-	-	-	-	-	-	2	-	-
38 Juventus	-	-	-	-	-	-	-	-	-	-	-	-	-	-	-	-	-	-	-	-	-	2	-	-	-	-	-	2	-	-
39 Leyton Orient	-	-	-	-	-	-	2	-	-	-	-	-	-	-	-	-	-	-	-	-	-	-	-	-	-	-	-	2	-	-
40 Millwall	-	-	-	-	-	-	2	-	-	-	-	-	-	-	-	-	-	-	-	-	-	-	-	-	-	-	-	2	-	-
41 Oldham Athletic	-	-	-	-	-	-	2	-	-	-	-	-	-	-	-	-	-	-	-	-	-	-	-	-	-	-	-	2	-	-
42 Portsmouth	-	-	-	-	-	-	2	-	-	-	-	-	-	-	-	-	-	-	-	-	-	-	-	-	-	-	-	2	-	-
43 Sheffield Wednesday	-	-	-	-	-	-	2	-	-	-	-	-	-	-	-	-	-	-	-	-	-	-	-	-	-	-	-	2	-	-
44 St Etienne	-	-	-	-	-	-	-	-	-	-	-	-	-	-	-	-	-	-	2	-	-	-	-	-	-	-	-	2	-	-
45 York City	-	-	-	-	-	-	2	-	-	-	-	-	-	-	-	-	-	-	-	-	-	-	-	-	-	-	-	2	-	-
46 Brentford	-	-	-	-	-	-	-	-	-	-	-	-	1	-	-	-	-	-	-	-	-	-	-	-	-	-	-	1	-	-
47 Carlisle United	-	-	-	-	-	-	-	-	-	1	-	-	-	-	-	-	-	-	-	-	-	-	-	-	-	-	-	1	-	-
48 Colchester United	-	-	-	-	-	-	-	-	-	1	-	-	-	-	-	-	-	-	-	-	-	-	-	-	-	-	-	1	-	-
49 Peterborough United	-	-	-	-	-	-	-	-	-	1	-	-	-	-	-	-	-	-	-	-	-	-	-	-	-	-	-	1	-	-
50 Plymouth Argyle	-	-	-	-	-	-	-	-	-	1	-	-	-	-	-	-	-	-	-	-	-	-	-	-	-	-	-	1	-	-
51 Stockport County	-	-	-	-	-	-	-	-	-	-	-	-	1	-	-	-	-	-	-	-	-	-	-	-	-	-	-	1	-	-
52 Tranmere Rovers	-	-	-	-	-	-	-	-	-	-	-	-	1	-	-	-	-	-	-	-	-	-	-	-	-	-	-	1	-	-
53 Watford	-	-	-	-	-	-	-	-	-	-	-	-	1	-	-	-	-	-	-	-	-	-	-	-	-	-	-	1	-	-

JIMMY GREENHOFF

DEBUT (Full Appearance)

Saturday 20/11/1976
Football League Division 1
at Filbert Street

Leicester City 1 Manchester United 1

CLUB CAREER RECORD	Apps	Subs	Goals
Premiership	0		0
League Division 1	94	(3)	26
League Division 2	0		0
FA Cup	18	(1)	9
League Cup	4		1
European Cup / Champions League	0		0
European Cup-Winners' Cup	1		0
UEFA Cup / Inter-Cities' Fairs Cup	1		0
Other Matches	1		0
OVERALL TOTAL	**119**	**(4)**	**36**

	PREM			FLD 1			FLD 2			FAC			LC			EC/CL			ECWC			UEFA			OTHER			TOTAL		
Opponents	A	S	G	A	S	G	A	S	G	A	S	G	A	S	G	A	S	G	A	S	G	A	S	G	A	S	G	A	S	G
1 Liverpool	–	–		5		1	–	–	–	3		2	–	–		–	–		–	–		–	–		–		1	9		3
2 Leeds United	–	–		6		–	–	–	–	1		1	–	–		–	–		–	–		–	–		–	–		7		1
3 Everton	–	–		6 (1)		2	–	–	–	–		–	–	–		–	–		–	–		–	–		–	–		6 (1)		2
4 Aston Villa	–	–		5 (1)		1	–	–	–	1		–	–	–		–	–		–	–		–	–		–	–		6 (1)		1
5 Queens Park Rangers	–	–		5		2	–	–	–	1		–	–	–		–	–		–	–		–	–		–	–		6		2
6 Coventry City	–	–		4		–	–	–	–	–		–	2			–	–		–	–		–	–		–	–		6		–
7 Middlesbrough	–	–		6		–	–	–	–	–		–	–	–		–	–		–	–		–	–		–	–		6		–
8 Leicester City	–	–		5		3	–	–	–	–		–	–	–		–	–		–	–		–	–		–	–		5		3
9 Arsenal	–	–		4		1	–	–	–	1		–	–	–		–	–		–	–		–	–		–	–		5		1
10 Manchester City	–	–		5		–	–	–	–	–		–	–	–		–	–		–	–		–	–		–	–		5		–
11 Tottenham Hotspur	–	–		3		–	–	–	–	2		–	–	–		–	–		–	–		–	–		–	–		5		–
12 Bristol City	–	–		4 (1)		2	–	–	–	–		–	–	–		–	–		–	–		–	–		–	–		4 (1)		2
13 West Bromwich Albion	–	–		4		–	–	–	–	– (1)		–	–	–		–	–		–	–		–	–		–	–		4 (1)		–
14 Birmingham City	–	–		4		2	–	–	–	–		–	–	–		–	–		–	–		–	–		–	–		4		2
15 Ipswich Town	–	–		4		1	–	–	–	–		–	–	–		–	–		–	–		–	–		–	–		4		1
16 Norwich City	–	–		4		–	–	–	–	–		–	–	–		–	–		–	–		–	–		–	–		4		–
17 Newcastle United	–	–		3		4	–	–	–	–		–	–	–		–	–		–	–		–	–		–	–		3		4
18 Southampton	–	–		1		1	–	–	–	2		2	–	–		–	–		–	–		–	–		–	–		3		3
19 Wolverhampton W.	–	–		3		3	–	–	–	–		–	–	–		–	–		–	–		–	–		–	–		3		3
20 Chelsea	–	–		2		1	–	–	–	1		1	–	–		–	–		–	–		–	–		–	–		3		2
21 Derby County	–	–		3		1	–	–	–	–		–	–	–		–	–		–	–		–	–		–	–		3		1
22 West Ham United	–	–		3		–	–	–	–	–		–	–	–		–	–		–	–		–	–		–	–		3		–
23 Fulham	–	–		–		–	–	–	–	2		2	–	–		–	–		–	–		–	–		–	–		2		2
24 Nottingham Forest	–	–		2		1	–	–	–	–		–	–	–		–	–		–	–		–	–		–	–		2		1
25 Carlisle United	–	–		–		–	–	–	–	2		–	–	–		–	–		–	–		–	–		–	–		2		–
26 Colchester United	–	–		–		–	–	–	–	1		1	–	–		–	–		–	–		–	–		–	–		1		1
27 Stockport County	–	–		–		–	–	–	–	–		–	1		1	–	–		–	–		–	–		–	–		1		1
28 Bolton Wanderers	–	–		1		–	–	–	–	–		–	–	–		–	–		–	–		–	–		–	–		1		–
29 St Etienne	–	–		–		–	–	–	–	–		–	–	–		–	–		1			–	–		–	–		1		–
30 Stoke City	–	–		1		–	–	–	–	–		–	–	–		–	–		–	–		–	–		–	–		1		–
31 Sunderland	–	–		1		–	–	–	–	–		–	–	–		–	–		–	–		–	–		–	–		1		–
32 Walsall	–	–		–		–	–	–	–	1		–	–	–		–	–		–	–		–	–		–	–		1		–
33 Watford	–	–		–		–	–	–	–	–		–	1			–	–		–	–		–	–		–	–		1		–
34 Widzew Lodz	–	–		–		–	–	–	–	–		–	–	–		–	–		–	–		1			–	–		1		–

JONATHAN GREENING

DEBUT (Full Appearance)

Wednesday 28/10/1998
League Cup 3rd Round
at Old Trafford

Manchester United 2 Bury 0

CLUB CAREER RECORD	Apps	Subs	Goals
Premiership	4	(10)	0
League Division 1	0		0
League Division 2	0		0
FA Cup	0	(1)	0
League Cup	6		0
European Cup / Champions League	2	(2)	0
European Cup-Winners' Cup	0		0
UEFA Cup / Inter-Cities' Fairs Cup	0		0
Other Matches	1		0
OVERALL TOTAL	**13**	**(13)**	**0**

	PREM			FLD 1			FLD 2			FAC			LC			EC/CL			ECWC			UEFA			OTHER			TOTAL		
Opponents	A	S	G	A	S	G	A	S	G	A	S	G	A	S	G	A	S	G	A	S	G	A	S	G	A	S	G	A	S	G
1 Watford	1 (1)		–	–	–	–	–	–	–	–	–	–	1			–	–	–	–	–	–	–	–	–	–	–	–	2 (1)		–
2 Tottenham Hotspur	– (2)		–	–	–	–	–	–	–	–	–	–	1			–	–	–	–	–	–	–	–	–	–	–	–	1 (2)		–
3 Aston Villa	1		–	–	–	–	–	–	–	–	–	–	1			–	–	–	–	–	–	–	–	–	–	–	–	2		–
4 Nottingham Forest	– (1)		–	–	–	–	–	–	–	–	–	–	1			–	–	–	–	–	–	–	–	–	–	–	–	1 (1)		–
5 Sturm Graz	–		–	–	–	–	–	–	–	–	–	–	–	–		1 (1)		–	–	–	–	–	–	–	–	–	–	1 (1)		–
6 Bradford City	1		–	–	–	–	–	–	–	–	–	–	–	–		–	–	–	–	–	–	–	–	–	–	–	–	1		–
7 Bury	–		–	–	–	–	–	–	–	–	–	–	1			–	–	–	–	–	–	–	–	–	–	–	–	1		–
8 Leicester City	1		–	–	–	–	–	–	–	–	–	–	–	–		–	–	–	–	–	–	–	–	–	–	–	–	1		–
9 PSV Eindhoven	–		–	–	–	–	–	–	–	–	–	–	–	–		1		–	–	–	–	–	–	–	–	–	–	1		–
10 South Melbourne	–		–	–	–	–	–	–	–	–	–	–	–	–		–	–	–	–	–	–	–	–	–	1		–	1		–
11 Sunderland	–		–	–	–	–	–	–	–	–	–	–	1			–	–	–	–	–	–	–	–	–	–	–	–	1		–
12 Charlton Athletic	– (1)		–	–	–	–	–	–	–	–	–	–	–	–		–	–	–	–	–	–	–	–	–	–	–	–	– (1)		–
13 Croatia Zagreb	–		–	–	–	–	–	–	–	–	–	–	–	–		– (1)		–	–	–	–	–	–	–	–	–	–	– (1)		–
14 Everton	– (1)		–	–	–	–	–	–	–	–	–	–	–	–		–	–	–	–	–	–	–	–	–	–	–	–	– (1)		–
15 Fulham	–		–	–	–	–	–	–	–	– (1)		–	–	–		–	–	–	–	–	–	–	–	–	–	–	–	– (1)		–
16 Ipswich Town	– (1)		–	–	–	–	–	–	–	–	–	–	–	–		–	–	–	–	–	–	–	–	–	–	–	–	– (1)		–
17 Liverpool	– (1)		–	–	–	–	–	–	–	–	–	–	–	–		–	–	–	–	–	–	–	–	–	–	–	–	– (1)		–
18 Sheffield Wednesday	– (1)		–	–	–	–	–	–	–	–	–	–	–	–		–	–	–	–	–	–	–	–	–	–	–	–	– (1)		–
19 West Ham United	– (1)		–	–	–	–	–	–	–	–	–	–	–	–		–	–	–	–	–	–	–	–	–	–	–	–	– (1)		–

WILSON GREENWOOD

DEBUT (Full Appearance)

Saturday 20/10/1900
Football League Division 2
at Bank Street

Newton Heath 1 Walsall 1

CLUB CAREER RECORD	Apps	Subs	Goals
Premiership	0		0
League Division 1	0		0
League Division 2	3		0
FA Cup	0		0
League Cup	0		0
European Cup / Champions League	0		0
European Cup-Winners' Cup	0		0
UEFA Cup / Inter-Cities' Fairs Cup	0		0
Other Matches	0		0
OVERALL TOTAL	3		0

Opponents	PREM A S G	FLD 1 A S G	FLD 2 A S G	FAC A S G	LC A S G	EC/CL A S G	ECWC A S G	UEFA A S G	OTHER A S G	TOTAL A S G
1 Birmingham City	– – –	– – –	1 – –	– – –	– – –	– – –	– – –	– – –	– – –	1 – –
2 Burton Swifts	– – –	– – –	1 – –	– – –	– – –	– – –	– – –	– – –	– – –	1 – –
3 Walsall	– – –	– – –	1 – –	– – –	– – –	– – –	– – –	– – –	– – –	1 – –

HARRY GREGG

DEBUT (Full Appearance)

SaturdSaturday 21/12/1957
Football League Division 1
at Old Trafford

Manchester United 4 Leicester City 0

CLUB CAREER RECORD	Apps	Subs	Goals
Premiership	0		0
League Division 1	210		0
League Division 2	0		0
FA Cup	24		0
League Cup	2		0
European Cup / Champions League	9		0
European Cup-Winners' Cup	2		0
UEFA Cup / Inter-Cities' Fairs Cup	0		0
Other Matches	0		0
OVERALL TOTAL	247		0

Opponents	PREM A S G	FLD 1 A S G	FLD 2 A S G	FAC A S G	LC A S G	EC/CL A S G	ECWC A S G	UEFA A S G	OTHER A S G	TOTAL A S G
1 Blackburn Rovers	– –	12 –	– –	– –	– –	– –	– –	– –	– –	12 –
2 Chelsea	– –	11 –	– –	1 –	– –	– –	– –	– –	– –	12 –
3 Tottenham Hotspur	– –	12 –	– –	– –	– –	– –	– –	– –	– –	12 –
4 West Bromwich Albion	– –	9 –	– –	2 –	– –	– –	– –	– –	– –	11 –
5 West Ham United	– –	11 –	– –	– –	– –	– –	– –	– –	– –	11 –
6 Aston Villa	– –	9 –	– –	1 –	– –	– –	– –	– –	– –	10 –
7 Blackpool	– –	10 –	– –	– –	– –	– –	– –	– –	– –	10 –
8 Everton	– –	9 –	– –	1 –	– –	– –	– –	– –	– –	10 –
9 Leicester City	– –	10 –	– –	– –	– –	– –	– –	– –	– –	10 –
10 Arsenal	– –	9 –	– –	– –	– –	– –	– –	– –	– –	9 –
11 Fulham	– –	7 –	– –	2 –	– –	– –	– –	– –	– –	9 –
12 Sheffield Wednesday	– –	7 –	– –	2 –	– –	– –	– –	– –	– –	9 –
13 Wolverhampton W.	– –	8 –	– –	1 –	– –	– –	– –	– –	– –	9 –
14 Birmingham City	– –	8 –	– –	– –	– –	– –	– –	– –	– –	8 –
15 Bolton Wanderers	– –	7 –	– –	1 –	– –	– –	– –	– –	– –	8 –
16 Manchester City	– –	8 –	– –	– –	– –	– –	– –	– –	– –	8 –
17 Nottingham Forest	– –	8 –	– –	– –	– –	– –	– –	– –	– –	8 –
18 Preston North End	– –	6 –	– –	2 –	– –	– –	– –	– –	– –	8 –
19 Leeds United	– –	7 –	– –	– –	– –	– –	– –	– –	– –	7 –
20 Liverpool	– –	5 –	– –	1 –	– –	– –	– –	– –	– –	6 –
21 Luton Town	– –	6 –	– –	– –	– –	– –	– –	– –	– –	6 –
22 Newcastle United	– –	6 –	– –	– –	– –	– –	– –	– –	– –	6 –
23 Burnley	– –	5 –	– –	– –	– –	– –	– –	– –	– –	5 –
24 Ipswich Town	– –	4 –	– –	1 –	– –	– –	– –	– –	– –	5 –
25 Sheffield United	– –	5 –	– –	– –	– –	– –	– –	– –	– –	5 –
26 Stoke City	– –	3 –	– –	– –	– –	– –	– –	– –	– –	3 –
27 Sunderland	– –	3 –	– –	– –	– –	– –	– –	– –	– –	3 –
28 AC Milan	– –	– –	– –	– –	– –	2 –	– –	– –	– –	2 –
29 Benfica	– –	– –	– –	– –	– –	2 –	– –	– –	– –	2 –
30 Cardiff City	– –	2 –	– –	– –	– –	– –	– –	– –	– –	2 –
31 Derby County	– –	– –	– –	2 –	– –	– –	– –	– –	– –	2 –
32 Partizan Belgrade	– –	– –	– –	– –	– –	2 –	– –	– –	– –	2 –
33 Portsmouth	– –	– –	2 –	– –	– –	– –	– –	– –	– –	2 –
34 Red Star Belgrade	– –	– –	– –	– –	– –	2 –	– –	– –	– –	2 –
35 Rotherham United	– –	– –	– –	2 –	– –	– –	– –	– –	– –	2 –
36 Willem II	– –	– –	– –	– –	– –	– –	2 –	– –	– –	2 –
37 ASK Vorwaerts	– –	– –	– –	– –	– –	1 –	– –	– –	– –	1 –
38 Bradford City	– –	– –	– –	– –	1 –	– –	– –	– –	– –	1 –
39 Coventry City	– –	– –	– –	1 –	– –	– –	– –	– –	– –	1 –
40 Exeter City	– –	– –	– –	– –	1 –	– –	– –	– –	– –	1 –
41 Huddersfield Town	– –	– –	– –	1 –	– –	– –	– –	– –	– –	1 –
42 Middlesbrough	– –	– –	– –	1 –	– –	– –	– –	– –	– –	1 –
43 Northampton Town	– –	1 –	– –	– –	– –	– –	– –	– –	– –	1 –
44 Norwich City	– –	– –	– –	1 –	– –	– –	– –	– –	– –	1 –
45 Workington	– –	– –	– –	1 –	– –	– –	– –	– –	– –	1 –

BILLY GRIFFITHS

DEBUT (Full Appearance)

Saturday 01/04/1899
Football League Division 2
at Bank Street

Newton Heath 2 Arsenal 2

CLUB CAREER RECORD	Apps	Subs	Goals
Premiership	0		0
League Division 1	0		0
League Division 2	157		27
FA Cup	18		3
League Cup	0		0
European Cup / Champions League	0		0
European Cup-Winners' Cup	0		0
UEFA Cup / Inter-Cities' Fairs Cup	0		0
Other Matches	0		0
OVERALL TOTAL	**175**		**30**

Opponents	PREM A S G	FLD 1 A S G	FLD 2 A S G	FAC A S G	LC A S G	EC/CL A S G	ECWC A S G	UEFA A S G	OTHER A S G	TOTAL A S G
1 Barnsley	- - -	- - -	12 - 2	- - -	- - -	- - -	- - -	- - -	- - -	12 - 2
2 Arsenal	- - -	- - -	11 - -	- - -	- - -	- - -	- - -	- - -	- - -	11 - -
3 Burnley	- - -	- - -	9 - 2	1 - -	- - -	- - -	- - -	- - -	- - -	10 - 2
4 Lincoln City	- - -	- - -	9 - 1	1 - -	- - -	- - -	- - -	- - -	- - -	10 - 1
5 Leicester City	- - -	- - -	9 - 4	- - -	- - -	- - -	- - -	- - -	- - -	9 - 4
6 Port Vale	- - -	- - -	9 - -	- - -	- - -	- - -	- - -	- - -	- - -	9 - -
7 Blackpool	- - -	- - -	8 - 3	- - -	- - -	- - -	- - -	- - -	- - -	8 - 3
8 Glossop	- - -	- - -	8 - 3	- - -	- - -	- - -	- - -	- - -	- - -	8 - 3
9 Chesterfield	- - -	- - -	8 - 1	- - -	- - -	- - -	- - -	- - -	- - -	8 - 1
10 Birmingham City	- - -	- - -	4 - -	4 - -	- - -	- - -	- - -	- - -	- - -	8 - -
11 Stockport County	- - -	- - -	7 - -	- - -	- - -	- - -	- - -	- - -	- - -	7 - -
12 Burton United	- - -	- - -	4 - 1	2 - 1	- - -	- - -	- - -	- - -	- - -	6 - 2
13 Gainsborough Trinity	- - -	- - -	6 - -	- - -	- - -	- - -	- - -	- - -	- - -	6 - -
14 Grimsby Town	- - -	- - -	6 - -	- - -	- - -	- - -	- - -	- - -	- - -	6 - -
15 Preston North End	- - -	- - -	6 - -	- - -	- - -	- - -	- - -	- - -	- - -	6 - -
16 Middlesbrough	- - -	- - -	5 - 1	- - -	- - -	- - -	- - -	- - -	- - -	5 - 1
17 Bristol City	- - -	- - -	4 - 4	- - -	- - -	- - -	- - -	- - -	- - -	4 - 4
18 Doncaster Rovers	- - -	- - -	4 - 2	- - -	- - -	- - -	- - -	- - -	- - -	4 - 2
19 Burton Swifts	- - -	- - -	4 - -	- - -	- - -	- - -	- - -	- - -	- - -	4 - -
20 Luton Town	- - -	- - -	4 - -	- - -	- - -	- - -	- - -	- - -	- - -	4 - -
21 Bolton Wanderers	- - -	- - -	3 - -	- - -	- - -	- - -	- - -	- - -	- - -	3 - -
22 New Brighton Tower	- - -	- - -	3 - -	- - -	- - -	- - -	- - -	- - -	- - -	3 - -
23 Sheffield Wednesday	- - -	- - -	2 - -	1 - -	- - -	- - -	- - -	- - -	- - -	3 - -
24 Walsall	- - -	- - -	3 - -	- - -	- - -	- - -	- - -	- - -	- - -	3 - -
25 Bradford City	- - -	- - -	2 - 2	- - -	- - -	- - -	- - -	- - -	- - -	2 - 2
26 Loughborough Town	- - -	- - -	2 - 1	- - -	- - -	- - -	- - -	- - -	- - -	2 - 1
27 Manchester City	- - -	- - -	2 - -	- - -	- - -	- - -	- - -	- - -	- - -	2 - -
28 Notts County	- - -	- - -	- - -	2 - -	- - -	- - -	- - -	- - -	- - -	2 - -
29 West Bromwich Albion	- - -	- - -	2 - -	- - -	- - -	- - -	- - -	- - -	- - -	2 - -
30 Everton	- - -	- - -	- - -	1 - 1	- - -	- - -	- - -	- - -	- - -	1 - 1
31 Portsmouth	- - -	- - -	- - -	1 - 1	- - -	- - -	- - -	- - -	- - -	1 - 1
32 Accrington Stanley	- - -	- - -	- - -	1 - -	- - -	- - -	- - -	- - -	- - -	1 - -
33 Darwen	- - -	- - -	1 - -	- - -	- - -	- - -	- - -	- - -	- - -	1 - -
34 Liverpool	- - -	- - -	- - -	1 - -	- - -	- - -	- - -	- - -	- - -	1 - -
35 Oswaldtwistle Rovers	- - -	- - -	- - -	1 - -	- - -	- - -	- - -	- - -	- - -	1 - -
36 South Shore	- - -	- - -	- - -	1 - -	- - -	- - -	- - -	- - -	- - -	1 - -
37 Southport Central	- - -	- - -	- - -	1 - -	- - -	- - -	- - -	- - -	- - -	1 - -

CLIVE GRIFFITHS

DEBUT (Full Appearance)

Saturday 27/10/1973
Football League Division 1
at Turf Moor

Burnley 0 Manchester United 0

CLUB CAREER RECORD	Apps	Subs	Goals
Premiership	0		0
League Division 1	7		0
League Division 2	0		0
FA Cup	0		0
League Cup	0		0
European Cup / Champions League	0		0
European Cup-Winners' Cup	0		0
UEFA Cup / Inter-Cities' Fairs Cup	0		0
Other Matches	0		0
OVERALL TOTAL	**7**		**0**

Opponents	PREM A S G	FLD 1 A S G	FLD 2 A S G	FAC A S G	LC A S G	EC/CL A S G	ECWC A S G	UEFA A S G	OTHER A S G	TOTAL A S G
1 Burnley	- - -	1 - -	- - -	- - -	- - -	- - -	- - -	- - -	- - -	1 - -
2 Chelsea	- - -	1 - -	- - -	- - -	- - -	- - -	- - -	- - -	- - -	1 - -
3 Coventry City	- - -	1 - -	- - -	- - -	- - -	- - -	- - -	- - -	- - -	1 - -
4 Ipswich Town	- - -	1 - -	- - -	- - -	- - -	- - -	- - -	- - -	- - -	1 - -
5 Liverpool	- - -	1 - -	- - -	- - -	- - -	- - -	- - -	- - -	- - -	1 - -
6 Sheffield United	- - -	1 - -	- - -	- - -	- - -	- - -	- - -	- - -	- - -	1 - -
7 Southampton	- - -	1 - -	- - -	- - -	- - -	- - -	- - -	- - -	- - -	1 - -

JACK GRIFFITHS

DEBUT (Full Appearance)

Saturday 17/03/1934
Football League Division 2
at Old Trafford

Manchester United 1 Fulham 0

CLUB CAREER RECORD	Apps	Subs	Goals
Premiership	0		0
League Division 1	56		0
League Division 2	109		1
FA Cup	8		0
League Cup	0		0
European Cup / Champions League	0		0
European Cup-Winners' Cup	0		0
UEFA Cup / Inter-Cities' Fairs Cup	0		0
Other Matches	0		0
OVERALL TOTAL	173		1

Opponents	PREM A S G	FLD 1 A S G	FLD 2 A S G	FAC A S G	LC A S G	EC/CL A S G	ECWC A S G	UEFA A S G	OTHER A S G	TOTAL A S G
1 Blackpool	– –	2 –	5 –	– –	– –	– –	– –	– –	– –	7 –
2 Nottingham Forest	– –	– –	5 –	2 –	– –	– –	– –	– –	– –	7 –
3 Southampton	– –	– –	7 –	– –	– –	– –	– –	– –	– –	7 –
4 Fulham	– –	– –	6 1	– –	– –	– –	– –	– –	– –	6 1
5 Barnsley	– –	– –	6 –	– –	– –	– –	– –	– –	– –	6 –
6 Charlton Athletic	– –	4 –	2 –	– –	– –	– –	– –	– –	– –	6 –
7 Newcastle United	– –	– –	6 –	– –	– –	– –	– –	– –	– –	6 –
8 West Ham United	– –	– –	6 –	– –	– –	– –	– –	– –	– –	6 –
9 Bradford City	– –	– –	5 –	– –	– –	– –	– –	– –	– –	5 –
10 Brentford	– –	3 –	2 –	– –	– –	– –	– –	– –	– –	5 –
11 Bury	– –	– –	5 –	– –	– –	– –	– –	– –	– –	5 –
12 Sheffield United	– –	– –	5 –	– –	– –	– –	– –	– –	– –	5 –
13 Stoke City	– –	3 –	– –	2 –	– –	– –	– –	– –	– –	5 –
14 Swansea City	– –	– –	5 –	– –	– –	– –	– –	– –	– –	5 –
15 Bradford Park Avenue	– –	– –	4 –	– –	– –	– –	– –	– –	– –	4 –
16 Burnley	– –	– –	4 –	– –	– –	– –	– –	– –	– –	4 –
17 Chelsea	– –	4 –	– –	– –	– –	– –	– –	– –	– –	4 –
18 Grimsby Town	– –	4 –	– –	– –	– –	– –	– –	– –	– –	4 –
19 Hull City	– –	– –	4 –	– –	– –	– –	– –	– –	– –	4 –
20 Leicester City	– –	2 –	2 –	– –	– –	– –	– –	– –	– –	4 –
21 Plymouth Argyle	– –	– –	4 –	– –	– –	– –	– –	– –	– –	4 –
22 Port Vale	– –	– –	4 –	– –	– –	– –	– –	– –	– –	4 –
23 Portsmouth	– –	4 –	– –	– –	– –	– –	– –	– –	– –	4 –
24 Arsenal	– –	3 –	– –	– –	– –	– –	– –	– –	– –	3 –
25 Birmingham City	– –	3 –	– –	– –	– –	– –	– –	– –	– –	3 –
26 Everton	– –	3 –	– –	– –	– –	– –	– –	– –	– –	3 –
27 Leeds United	– –	3 –	– –	– –	– –	– –	– –	– –	– –	3 –
28 Liverpool	– –	3 –	– –	– –	– –	– –	– –	– –	– –	3 –
29 Norwich City	– –	– –	3 –	– –	– –	– –	– –	– –	– –	3 –
30 Notts County	– –	– –	3 –	– –	– –	– –	– –	– –	– –	3 –
31 West Bromwich Albion	– –	1 –	– –	2 –	– –	– –	– –	– –	– –	3 –
32 Aston Villa	– –	2 –	– –	– –	– –	– –	– –	– –	– –	2 –
33 Bolton Wanderers	– –	– –	2 –	– –	– –	– –	– –	– –	– –	2 –
34 Coventry City	– –	– –	2 –	– –	– –	– –	– –	– –	– –	2 –
35 Derby County	– –	2 –	– –	– –	– –	– –	– –	– –	– –	2 –
36 Doncaster Rovers	– –	– –	2 –	– –	– –	– –	– –	– –	– –	2 –
37 Huddersfield Town	– –	2 –	– –	– –	– –	– –	– –	– –	– –	2 –
38 Middlesbrough	– –	2 –	– –	– –	– –	– –	– –	– –	– –	2 –
39 Oldham Athletic	– –	– –	2 –	– –	– –	– –	– –	– –	– –	2 –
40 Preston North End	– –	2 –	– –	– –	– –	– –	– –	– –	– –	2 –
41 Stockport County	– –	– –	2 –	– –	– –	– –	– –	– –	– –	2 –
42 Sunderland	– –	2 –	– –	– –	– –	– –	– –	– –	– –	2 –
43 Tottenham Hotspur	– –	– –	2 –	– –	– –	– –	– –	– –	– –	2 –
44 Wolverhampton W.	– –	2 –	– –	– –	– –	– –	– –	– –	– –	2 –
45 Blackburn Rovers	– –	– –	1 –	– –	– –	– –	– –	– –	– –	1 –
46 Bristol Rovers	– –	– –	– –	1 –	– –	– –	– –	– –	– –	1 –
47 Luton Town	– –	– –	1 –	– –	– –	– –	– –	– –	– –	1 –
48 Millwall	– –	– –	1 –	– –	– –	– –	– –	– –	– –	1 –
49 Reading	– –	– –	– –	1 –	– –	– –	– –	– –	– –	1 –
50 Sheffield Wednesday	– –	– –	1 –	– –	– –	– –	– –	– –	– –	1 –

ASHLEY GRIMES

DEBUT (Substitute Appearance)

Saturday 20/08/1977
Football League Division 1
at St Andrews

Birmingham City 1 Manchester United 4

CLUB CAREER RECORD	Apps	Subs	Goals
Premiership	0		0
League Division 1	62	(28)	10
League Division 2	0		0
FA Cup	5		1
League Cup	6		0
European Cup / Champions League	0		0
European Cup–Winners' Cup	0	(2)	0
UEFA Cup / Inter-Cities' Fairs Cup	4		0
Other Matches	0		0
OVERALL TOTAL	**77**	**(30)**	**11**

Opponents	PREM A S G	FLD 1 A S G	FLD 2 A S G	FAC A S G	LC A S G	EC/CL A S G	ECWC A S G	UEFA A S G	OTHER A S G	TOTAL A S G
1 Wolverhampton W.	– –	4 (3) –	– –	– –	– –	– –	– –	– –	– –	4 (3) –
2 Southampton	– –	6 –	– –	– –	– –	– –	– –	– –	– –	6 –
3 Arsenal	– –	3 (1) –	– –	1 –	1	– –	– –	– –	– –	5 (1) –
4 Tottenham Hotspur	– –	3 (1) –	– –	2	– –	– –	– –	– –	– –	5 (1) –
5 Everton	– –	3 (3) 1	– –	– –	– –	– –	– –	– –	– –	3 (3) 1
6 Bristol City	– –	5 –	– –	– –	– –	– –	– –	– –	– –	5 –
7 Brighton	– –	4 (1) –	– –	– –	– –	– –	– –	– –	– –	4 (1) –
8 West Ham United	– –	4 1	– –	– –	– –	– –	– –	– –	– –	4 1
9 Stoke City	– –	4 –	– –	– –	– –	– –	– –	– –	– –	4 –
10 Ipswich Town	– –	3 (1) 1	– –	– –	– –	– –	– –	– –	– –	3 (1) 1
11 Norwich City	– –	2 (1) –	– –	– –	1	– –	– –	– –	– –	3 (1) –
12 West Bromwich Albion	– –	3 (1) –	– –	– –	– –	– –	– –	– –	– –	3 (1) –
13 Nottingham Forest	– –	1 (3) –	– –	– –	– –	– –	– –	– –	– –	1 (3) –
14 Manchester City	– –	2 (1) –	– –	– –	– –	– –	– –	– –	– –	2 (1) –
15 Aston Villa	– –	1 (2) 1	– –	– –	– –	– –	– –	– –	– –	1 (2) 1
16 Derby County	– –	1 (2) 1	– –	– –	– –	– –	– –	– –	– –	1 (2) 1
17 Liverpool	– –	1 (2) –	– –	– –	– –	– –	– –	– –	– –	1 (2) –
18 Luton Town	– –	2 1	– –	– –	– –	– –	– –	– –	– –	2 1
19 Queens Park Rangers	– –	2 1	– –	– –	– –	– –	– –	– –	– –	2 1
20 Watford	– –	1 1	– –	– –	1	– –	– –	– –	– –	2 1
21 Bolton Wanderers	– –	2	– –	– –	– –	– –	– –	– –	– –	2 –
22 Bournemouth	– –	– –	– –	– –	2	– –	– –	– –	– –	2 –
23 Leeds United	– –	2	– –	– –	– –	– –	– –	– –	– –	2 –
24 Valencia	– –	– –	– –	– –	– –	– –	– –	2	– –	2 –
25 Widzew Lodz	– –	– –	– –	– –	– –	– –	– –	2	– –	2 –
26 Chelsea	– –	– (1) –	– –	1 1	– –	– –	– –	– –	– –	1 (1) 1
27 Middlesbrough	– –	– (2) 1	– –	– –	– –	– –	– –	– –	– –	– (2) 1
28 Leicester City	– –	1 1	– –	– –	– –	– –	– –	– –	– –	1 1
29 Carlisle United	– –	– –	– –	1	– –	– –	– –	– –	– –	1 –
30 Coventry City	– –	1	– –	– –	– –	– –	– –	– –	– –	1 –
31 Stockport County	– –	– –	– –	– –	1	– –	– –	– –	– –	1 –
32 Swansea City	– –	1	– –	– –	– –	– –	– –	– –	– –	1 –
33 Birmingham City	– –	– (1) –	– –	– –	– –	– –	– –	– –	– –	– (1) –
34 Crystal Palace	– –	– (1) –	– –	– –	– –	– –	– –	– –	– –	– (1) –
35 Notts County	– –	– (1) –	– –	– –	– –	– –	– –	– –	– –	– (1) –
36 Porto	– –	– –	– –	– –	– –	– –	– (1) –	– –	– –	– (1) –
37 St Etienne	– –	– –	– –	– –	– –	– –	– (1) –	– –	– –	– (1) –

TONY GRIMSHAW

DEBUT (Substitute Appearance)

Wednesday 10/09/1975
League Cup 2nd Round
at Old Trafford

Manchester United 2 Brentford 1

CLUB CAREER RECORD	Apps	Subs	Goals
Premiership	0		0
League Division 1	0	(1)	0
League Division 2	0		0
FA Cup	0		0
League Cup	0	(1)	0
European Cup / Champions League	0		0
European Cup-Winners' Cup	0		0
UEFA Cup / Inter-Cities' Fairs Cup	0		0
Other Matches	0		0
OVERALL TOTAL	**0**	**(2)**	**0**

Opponents	PREM A S G	FLD 1 A S G	FLD 2 A S G	FAC A S G	LC A S G	EC/CL A S G	ECWC A S G	UEFA A S G	OTHER A S G	TOTAL A S G
1 Brentford	– –	– –	– –	– –	– (1) –	– –	– –	– –	– –	– (1) –
2 Leeds United	– –	– (1) –	– –	– –	– –	– –	– –	– –	– –	– (1) –

JOHN GRIMWOOD

DEBUT (Full Appearance)

Saturday 11/10/1919
Football League Division 1
at Hyde Road

Manchester City 3 Manchester United 3

CLUB CAREER RECORD	Apps	Subs	Goals
Premiership	0		0
League Division 1	99		5
League Division 2	97		3
FA Cup	9		0
League Cup	0		0
European Cup / Champions League	0		0
European Cup–Winners' Cup	0		0
UEFA Cup / Inter–Cities' Fairs Cup	0		0
Other Matches	0		0
OVERALL TOTAL	205		8

Opponents	PREM A	S	G	FLD 1 A	S	G	FLD 2 A	S	G	FAC A	S	G	LC A	S	G	EC/CL A	S	G	ECWC A	S	G	UEFA A	S	G	OTHER A	S	G	TOTAL A	S	G
1 Liverpool	–	–		7	–	1	–	–		2	–		–	–		–	–		–	–		–	–		–	–		9		1
2 Bradford City	–	–		3	–		4	–		2	–		–	–		–	–		–	–		–	–		–	–		9		–
3 Derby County	–	–		3	–		6	–		–	–		–	–		–	–		–	–		–	–		–	–		9		–
4 Newcastle United	–	–		8	–		–	–		–	–		–	–		–	–		–	–		–	–		–	–		8		–
5 West Bromwich Albion	–	–		8	–		–	–		–	–		–	–		–	–		–	–		–	–		–	–		8		–
6 Bolton Wanderers	–	–		7	–		–	–		–	–		–	–		–	–		–	–		–	–		–	–		7		–
7 Everton	–	–		7	–		–	–		–	–		–	–		–	–		–	–		–	–		–	–		7		–
8 Sunderland	–	–		7	–		–	–		–	–		–	–		–	–		–	–		–	–		–	–		7		–
9 Barnsley	–	–		–	–		6	–	1	–	–		–	–		–	–		–	–		–	–		–	–		6		1
10 Chelsea	–	–		4	–		2	–	1	–	–		–	–		–	–		–	–		–	–		–	–		6		1
11 Port Vale	–	–		–	–		4	–	1	2	–		–	–		–	–		–	–		–	–		–	–		6		1
12 Arsenal	–	–		6	–		–	–		–	–		–	–		–	–		–	–		–	–		–	–		6		–
13 Crystal Palace	–	–		–	–		6	–		–	–		–	–		–	–		–	–		–	–		–	–		6		–
14 Hull City	–	–		–	–		6	–		–	–		–	–		–	–		–	–		–	–		–	–		6		–
15 Oldham Athletic	–	–		3	–		3	–		–	–		–	–		–	–		–	–		–	–		–	–		6		–
16 Sheffield Wednesday	–	–		1	–		4	–		1	–		–	–		–	–		–	–		–	–		–	–		6		–
17 South Shields	–	–		–	–		6	–		–	–		–	–		–	–		–	–		–	–		–	–		6		–
18 Blackburn Rovers	–	–		5	–		–	–		–	–		–	–		–	–		–	–		–	–		–	–		5		–
19 Huddersfield Town	–	–		5	–		–	–		–	–		–	–		–	–		–	–		–	–		–	–		5		–
20 Leeds United	–	–		2	–		3	–		–	–		–	–		–	–		–	–		–	–		–	–		5		–
21 Leicester City	–	–		1	–		4	–		–	–		–	–		–	–		–	–		–	–		–	–		5		–
22 Leyton Orient	–	–		–	–		5	–		–	–		–	–		–	–		–	–		–	–		–	–		5		–
23 Aston Villa	–	–		3	–	2	–	–		1	–		–	–		–	–		–	–		–	–		–	–		4		2
24 Bradford Park Avenue	–	–		4	–	1	–	–		–	–		–	–		–	–		–	–		–	–		–	–		4		1
25 Middlesbrough	–	–		2	–	1	2	–		–	–		–	–		–	–		–	–		–	–		–	–		4		1
26 Blackpool	–	–		–	–		4	–		–	–		–	–		–	–		–	–		–	–		–	–		4		–
27 Bury	–	–		1	–		3	–		–	–		–	–		–	–		–	–		–	–		–	–		4		–
28 Cardiff City	–	–		4	–		–	–		–	–		–	–		–	–		–	–		–	–		–	–		4		–
29 Fulham	–	–		–	–		4	–		–	–		–	–		–	–		–	–		–	–		–	–		4		–
30 Southampton	–	–		–	–		4	–		–	–		–	–		–	–		–	–		–	–		–	–		4		–
31 Coventry City	–	–		–	–		3	–		–	–		–	–		–	–		–	–		–	–		–	–		3		–
32 Stockport County	–	–		–	–		3	–		–	–		–	–		–	–		–	–		–	–		–	–		3		–
33 Stoke City	–	–		–	–		3	–		–	–		–	–		–	–		–	–		–	–		–	–		3		–
34 West Ham United	–	–		1	–		2	–		–	–		–	–		–	–		–	–		–	–		–	–		3		–
35 Burnley	–	–		2	–		–	–		–	–		–	–		–	–		–	–		–	–		–	–		2		–
36 Nelson	–	–		–	–		2	–		–	–		–	–		–	–		–	–		–	–		–	–		2		–
37 Notts County	–	–		–	–		2	–		–	–		–	–		–	–		–	–		–	–		–	–		2		–
38 Portsmouth	–	–		–	–		2	–		–	–		–	–		–	–		–	–		–	–		–	–		2		–
39 Rotherham United	–	–		–	–		2	–		–	–		–	–		–	–		–	–		–	–		–	–		2		–
40 Tottenham Hotspur	–	–		1	–		–	–		1	–		–	–		–	–		–	–		–	–		–	–		2		–
41 Wolverhampton W.	–	–		–	–		2	–		–	–		–	–		–	–		–	–		–	–		–	–		2		–
42 Birmingham City	–	–		1	–		–	–		–	–		–	–		–	–		–	–		–	–		–	–		1		–
43 Manchester City	–	–		1	–		–	–		–	–		–	–		–	–		–	–		–	–		–	–		1		–
44 Preston North End	–	–		1	–		–	–		–	–		–	–		–	–		–	–		–	–		–	–		1		–
45 Sheffield United	–	–		1	–		–	–		–	–		–	–		–	–		–	–		–	–		–	–		1		–

JOHN GRUNDY

DEBUT (Full Appearance, 1 goal)

Saturday 28/04/1900
Football League Division 2
at Bank Street

Newton Heath 2 Chesterfield 1

CLUB CAREER RECORD	Apps	Subs	Goals
Premiership	0		0
League Division 1	0		0
League Division 2	11		3
FA Cup	0		0
League Cup	0		0
European Cup / Champions League	0		0
European Cup-Winners' Cup	0		0
UEFA Cup / Inter-Cities' Fairs Cup	0		0
Other Matches	0		0
OVERALL TOTAL	11		3

Opponents	PREM A S G	FLD 1 A S G	FLD 2 A S G	FAC A S G	LC A S G	EC/CL A S G	ECWC A S G	UEFA A S G	OTHER A S G	TOTAL A S G
1 Chesterfield	– – –	– – –	1 1	– – –	–	–	–	–	–	1 1
2 Middlesbrough	– – –	– – –	1 1	–	–	–	–	–	–	1 1
3 Port Vale	– – –	– – –	1 1	–	–	–	–	–	–	1 1
4 Burnley	– – –	– – –	1	–	–	–	–	–	–	1 –
5 Burton Swifts	–	–	1	–	–	–	–	–	–	1 –
6 Gainsborough Trinity	– –	– –	1	–	–	–	–	–	–	1 –
7 Glossop	–	–	1	–	–	–	–	–	–	1 –
8 Grimsby Town	–	–	1	–	–	–	–	–	–	1 –
9 Leicester City	–	–	1	–	–	–	–	–	–	1 –
10 New Brighton Tower	–	–	1	–	–	–	–	–	–	1 –
11 Stockport County	–	–	1	–	–	–	–	–	–	1 –

WILLIAM GYVES

DEBUT (Full Appearance)

Saturday 25/10/1890
FA Cup 2nd Qualifying Round
at Bootle Park

Bootle Reserves 1 Newton Heath 0

CLUB CAREER RECORD	Apps	Subs	Goals
Premiership	0		0
League Division 1	0		0
League Division 2	0		0
FA Cup	1		0
League Cup	0		0
European Cup / Champions League	0		0
European Cup-Winners' Cup	0		0
UEFA Cup / Inter-Cities' Fairs Cup	0		0
Other Matches	0		0
OVERALL TOTAL	1		0

Opponents	PREM A S G	FLD 1 A S G	FLD 2 A S G	FAC A S G	LC A S G	EC/CL A S G	ECWC A S G	UEFA A S G	OTHER A S G	TOTAL A S G
1 Bootle Reserves	–	–	–	1	–	–	–	–	–	1 –

JACK HACKING

DEBUT (Full Appearance)

Saturday 17/03/1934
Football League Division 2
at Old Trafford

Manchester United 1 Fulham 0

CLUB CAREER RECORD	Apps	Subs	Goals
Premiership	0		0
League Division 1	0		0
League Division 2	32		0
FA Cup	2		0
League Cup	0		0
European Cup / Champions League	0		0
European Cup-Winners' Cup	0		0
UEFA Cup / Inter-Cities' Fairs Cup	0		0
Other Matches	0		0
OVERALL TOTAL	34		0

Opponents	PREM A S G	FLD 1 A S G	FLD 2 A S G	FAC A S G	LC A S G	EC/CL A S G	ECWC A S G	UEFA A S G	OTHER A S G	TOTAL A S G
1 Nottingham Forest	–	–	1 –	2	–	–	–	–	–	3 –
2 Notts County	–	–	3	–	–	–	–	–	–	3 –
3 West Ham United	–	–	3	–	–	–	–	–	–	3 –
4 Barnsley	–	–	2	–	–	–	–	–	–	2 –
5 Blackpool	–	–	2	–	–	–	–	–	–	2 –
6 Bolton Wanderers	–	–	2	–	–	–	–	–	–	2 –
7 Bradford City	–	–	2	–	–	–	–	–	–	2 –
8 Fulham	–	–	2	–	–	–	–	–	–	2 –
9 Port Vale	–	–	2	–	–	–	–	–	–	2 –
10 Bradford Park Avenue	–	–	1	–	–	–	–	–	–	1 –
11 Brentford	–	–	1	–	–	–	–	–	–	1 –
12 Burnley	–	–	1	–	–	–	–	–	–	1 –
13 Bury	–	–	1	–	–	–	–	–	–	1 –
14 Hull City	–	–	1	–	–	–	–	–	–	1 –
15 Millwall	–	–	1	–	–	–	–	–	–	1 –
16 Newcastle United	–	–	1	–	–	–	–	–	–	1 –
17 Norwich City	–	–	1	–	–	–	–	–	–	1 –
18 Oldham Athletic	–	–	1	–	–	–	–	–	–	1 –
19 Plymouth Argyle	–	–	1	–	–	–	–	–	–	1 –
20 Sheffield United	–	–	1	–	–	–	–	–	–	1 –
21 Southampton	–	–	1	–	–	–	–	–	–	1 –
22 Swansea City	–	–	1	–	–	–	–	–	–	1 –

JACK HALL (1920s)

DEBUT (Full Appearance)

Saturday 06/02/1926
Football League Division 1
at Turf Moor

Burnley 0 Manchester United 1

CLUB CAREER RECORD	Apps	Subs	Goals
Premiership	0		0
League Division 1	3		0
League Division 2	0		0
FA Cup	0		0
League Cup	0		0
European Cup / Champions League	0		0
European Cup-Winners' Cup	0		0
UEFA Cup / Inter-Cities' Fairs Cup	0		0
Other Matches	0		0
OVERALL TOTAL	**3**		**0**

Opponents	PREM A S G	FLD 1 A S G	FLD 2 A S G	FAC A S G	LC A S G	EC/CL A S G	ECWC A S G	UEFA A S G	OTHER A S G	TOTAL A S G
1 Burnley	– –	1	– – –	– – –	– – –	– – –	– – –	– – –	– – –	1 –
2 Leeds United	– –	1	–	– – –	– – –	– – –	– – –	– – –	– – –	1 –
3 Tottenham Hotspur	– –	1	–	– – –	– – –	– – –	– – –	– – –	– – –	1 –

JACK HALL (1930s)

DEBUT (Full Appearance)

Saturday 30/09/1933
Football League Division 2
at Boundary Park

Oldham Athletic 2 Manchester United 0

CLUB CAREER RECORD	Apps	Subs	Goals
Premiership	0		0
League Division 1	0		0
League Division 2	67		0
FA Cup	6		0
League Cup	0		0
European Cup / Champions League	0		0
European Cup-Winners' Cup	0		0
UEFA Cup / Inter-Cities' Fairs Cup	0		0
Other Matches	0		0
OVERALL TOTAL	**73**		**0**

Opponents	PREM A S G	FLD 1 A S G	FLD 2 A S G	FAC A S G	LC A S G	EC/CL A S G	ECWC A S G	UEFA A S G	OTHER A S G	TOTAL A S G
1 Southampton	– –	– –	5	–	– – –	– – –	– – –	– – –	– – –	5 –
2 Bradford Park Avenue	– –	– –	4	–	– – –	– – –	– – –	– – –	– – –	4 –
3 Port Vale	– –	– –	4	–	– – –	– – –	– – –	– – –	– – –	4 –
4 Swansea City	– –	– –	4	–	– – –	– – –	– – –	– – –	– – –	4 –
5 Bradford City	– –	– –	3	–	– – –	– – –	– – –	– – –	– – –	3 –
6 Burnley	– –	– –	3	–	– – –	– – –	– – –	– – –	– – –	3 –
7 Bury	– –	– –	3	–	– – –	– – –	– – –	– – –	– – –	3 –
8 Fulham	– –	– –	3	–	– – –	– – –	– – –	– – –	– – –	3 –
9 Hull City	– –	– –	3	–	– – –	– – –	– – –	– – –	– – –	3 –
10 Oldham Athletic	– –	– –	3	–	– – –	– – –	– – –	– – –	– – –	3 –
11 Plymouth Argyle	– –	– –	3	–	– – –	– – –	– – –	– – –	– – –	3 –
12 Sheffield United	– –	– –	3	–	– – –	– – –	– – –	– – –	– – –	3 –
13 Barnsley	– –	– –	2	–	– – –	– – –	– – –	– – –	– – –	2 –
14 Blackpool	– –	– –	2	–	– – –	– – –	– – –	– – –	– – –	2 –
15 Charlton Athletic	– –	– –	2	–	– – –	– – –	– – –	– – –	– – –	2 –
16 Grimsby Town	– –	– –	2	–	– – –	– – –	– – –	– – –	– – –	2 –
17 Leicester City	– –	– –	2	–	– – –	– – –	– – –	– – –	– – –	2 –
18 Newcastle United	– –	– –	2	–	– – –	– – –	– – –	– – –	– – –	2 –
19 Nottingham Forest	– –	– –	2	–	– – –	– – –	– – –	– – –	– – –	2 –
20 Portsmouth	– –	– –	– –	2	– – –	– – –	– – –	– – –	– – –	2 –
21 Preston North End	– –	– –	2	–	– – –	– – –	– – –	– – –	– – –	2 –
22 Stoke City	– –	– –	– –	2	– – –	– – –	– – –	– – –	– – –	2 –
23 West Ham United	– –	– –	2	–	– – –	– – –	– – –	– – –	– – –	2 –
24 Bolton Wanderers	– –	– –	1	–	– – –	– – –	– – –	– – –	– – –	1 –
25 Brentford	– –	– –	1	–	– – –	– – –	– – –	– – –	– – –	1 –
26 Bristol Rovers	– –	– –	– –	1	– – –	– – –	– – –	– – –	– – –	1 –
27 Doncaster Rovers	– –	– –	1	–	– – –	– – –	– – –	– – –	– – –	1 –
28 Lincoln City	– –	– –	1	–	– – –	– – –	– – –	– – –	– – –	1 –
29 Millwall	– –	– –	1	–	– – –	– – –	– – –	– – –	– – –	1 –
30 Norwich City	– –	– –	1	–	– – –	– – –	– – –	– – –	– – –	1 –
31 Notts County	– –	– –	1	–	– – –	– – –	– – –	– – –	– – –	1 –
32 Reading	– –	– –	– –	1	– – –	– – –	– – –	– – –	– – –	1 –
33 Tottenham Hotspur	– –	– –	1	–	– – –	– – –	– – –	– – –	– – –	1 –

PROCTOR HALL

DEBUT (Full Appearance)

Saturday 26/03/1904
Football League Division 2
at Bank Street

Manchester United 2 Grimsby Town 0

CLUB CAREER RECORD	Apps	Subs	Goals
Premiership	0		0
League Division 1	0		0
League Division 2	8		2
FA Cup	0		0
League Cup	0		0
European Cup / Champions League	0		0
European Cup-Winners' Cup	0		0
UEFA Cup / Inter-Cities' Fairs Cup	0		0
Other Matches	0		0
OVERALL TOTAL	**8**		**2**

Opponents	PREM A S G	FLD 1 A S G	FLD 2 A S G	FAC A S G	LC A S G	EC/CL A S G	ECWC A S G	UEFA A S G	OTHER A S G	TOTAL A S G
1 Grimsby Town	– –	– –	2 –	–	–	–	–	–	–	2 –
2 Chesterfield	– –	– –	1 1	–	–	–	–	–	–	1 1
3 Stockport County	– –	– –	1 1	–	–	–	–	–	–	1 1
4 Barnsley	– –	– –	1 –	–	–	–	–	–	–	1 –
5 Blackpool	– –	– –	1 –	–	–	–	–	–	–	1 –
6 Gainsborough Trinity	– –	– –	1 –	–	–	–	–	–	–	1 –
7 Leicester City	– –	– –	1 –	–	–	–	–	–	–	1 –

HAROLD HALSE

DEBUT (Full Appearance, 1 goal)

Saturday 28/03/1908
Football League Division 1
at Bank Street

Manchester United 4 Sheffield Wednesday 1

CLUB CAREER RECORD	Apps	Subs	Goals
Premiership	0		0
League Division 1	109		41
League Division 2	0		0
FA Cup	15		9
League Cup	0		0
European Cup / Champions League	0		0
European Cup-Winners' Cup	0		0
UEFA Cup / Inter-Cities' Fairs Cup	0		0
Other Matches	1		6
OVERALL TOTAL	**125**		**56**

Opponents	PREM A S G	FLD 1 A S G	FLD 2 A S G	FAC A S G	LC A S G	EC/CL A S G	ECWC A S G	UEFA A S G	OTHER A S G	TOTAL A S G
1 Newcastle United	– –	7 4	– –	1 1	–	–	–	–	–	8 5
2 Everton	– –	7 3	– –	1 1	–	–	–	–	–	8 4
3 Blackburn Rovers	– –	5 3	– –	3 –	–	–	–	–	–	8 3
4 Aston Villa	– –	6 4	– –	1 1	–	–	–	–	–	7 5
5 Liverpool	– –	7 2	– –	–	–	–	–	–	–	7 2
6 Notts County	– –	7 2	– –	–	–	–	–	–	–	7 2
7 Preston North End	– –	7 2	– –	–	–	–	–	–	–	7 2
8 Bury	– –	6 2	– –	–	–	–	–	–	–	6 2
9 Bristol City	– –	5 1	– –	1 –	–	–	–	–	–	6 1
10 Sheffield Wednesday	– –	5 4	– –	–	–	–	–	–	–	5 4
11 Arsenal	– –	5 2	– –	–	–	–	–	–	–	5 2
12 Manchester City	– –	5 1	– –	–	–	–	–	–	–	5 1
13 Nottingham Forest	– –	5 1	– –	–	–	–	–	–	–	5 1
14 Sheffield United	– –	5 1	– –	–	–	–	–	–	–	5 1
15 Bolton Wanderers	– –	4 4	– –	–	–	–	–	–	–	4 4
16 Tottenham Hotspur	– –	4 1	– –	–	–	–	–	–	–	4 1
17 Bradford City	– –	4 –	– –	–	–	–	–	–	–	4 –
18 Chelsea	– –	4 –	– –	–	–	–	–	–	–	4 –
19 Middlesbrough	– –	3 2	– –	–	–	–	–	–	–	3 2
20 Sunderland	– –	3 2	– –	–	–	–	–	–	–	3 2
21 Burnley	– –	– –	– –	2 1	–	–	–	–	–	2 1
22 Reading	– –	– –	– –	2 1	–	–	–	–	–	2 1
23 Oldham Athletic	– –	2 –	– –	–	–	–	–	–	–	2 –
24 West Bromwich Albion	– –	2 –	– –	–	–	–	–	–	–	2 –
25 Swindon Town	– –	– –	– –	–	–	–	–	–	1 6	1 6
26 Coventry City	– –	– –	– –	1 2	–	–	–	–	–	1 2
27 Brighton	– –	– –	– –	1 1	–	–	–	–	–	1 1
28 Huddersfield Town	– –	– –	– –	1 1	–	–	–	–	–	1 1
29 Leicester City	– –	1 –	– –	–	–	–	–	–	–	1 –
30 West Ham United	– –	– –	– –	1 –	–	–	–	–	–	1 –

REG HALTON

DEBUT (Full Appearance, 1 goal)

Saturday 12/12/1936
Football League Division 1
at Ayresome Park

Middlesbrough 3 Manchester United 2

CLUB CAREER RECORD	Apps	Subs	Goals
Premiership	0		0
League Division 1	4		1
League Division 2	0		0
FA Cup	0		0
League Cup	0		0
European Cup / Champions League	0		0
European Cup-Winners' Cup	0		0
UEFA Cup / Inter-Cities' Fairs Cup	0		0
Other Matches	0		0
OVERALL TOTAL	**4**		**1**

Opponents	PREM A S G	FLD 1 A S G	FLD 2 A S G	FAC A S G	LC A S G	EC/CL A S G	ECWC A S G	UEFA A S G	OTHER A S G	TOTAL A S G
1 Middlesbrough	– –	1 1	– –	– –	– –	– –	– –	– –	– –	1 1
2 Bolton Wanderers	– –	1 –	– –	– –	– –	– –	– –	– –	– –	1 –
3 West Bromwich Albion	– –	1 –	– –	– –	– –	– –	– –	– –	– –	1 –
4 Wolverhampton W.	– –	1 –	– –	– –	– –	– –	– –	– –	– –	1 –

MICKEY HAMILL

DEBUT (Full Appearance)

Saturday 16/09/1911
Football League Division 1
at The Hawthorns

West Bromwich Albion 1 Manchester United 0

CLUB CAREER RECORD	Apps	Subs	Goals
Premiership	0		0
League Division 1	57		2
League Division 2	0		0
FA Cup	2		0
League Cup	0		0
European Cup / Champions League	0		0
European Cup-Winners' Cup	0		0
UEFA Cup / Inter-Cities' Fairs Cup	0		0
Other Matches	1		0
OVERALL TOTAL	**60**		**2**

Opponents	PREM A S G	FLD 1 A S G	FLD 2 A S G	FAC A S G	LC A S G	EC/CL A S G	ECWC A S G	UEFA A S G	OTHER A S G	TOTAL A S G
1 Everton	– –	4 1	– –	– –	– –	– –	– –	– –	– –	4 1
2 Arsenal	– –	4 –	– –	– –	– –	– –	– –	– –	– –	4 –
3 Bradford City	– –	4 –	– –	– –	– –	– –	– –	– –	– –	4 –
4 Liverpool	– –	4 –	– –	– –	– –	– –	– –	– –	– –	4 –
5 Oldham Athletic	– –	3 –	– –	1 –	– –	– –	– –	– –	– –	4 –
6 Tottenham Hotspur	– –	4 –	– –	– –	– –	– –	– –	– –	– –	4 –
7 Blackburn Rovers	– –	3 1	– –	– –	– –	– –	– –	– –	– –	3 1
8 Chelsea	– –	3 –	– –	– –	– –	– –	– –	– –	– –	3 –
9 Manchester City	– –	3 –	– –	– –	– –	– –	– –	– –	– –	3 –
10 Middlesbrough	– –	3 –	– –	– –	– –	– –	– –	– –	– –	3 –
11 Newcastle United	– –	3 –	– –	– –	– –	– –	– –	– –	– –	3 –
12 Preston North End	– –	3 –	– –	– –	– –	– –	– –	– –	– –	3 –
13 Sheffield Wednesday	– –	3 –	– –	– –	– –	– –	– –	– –	– –	3 –
14 Sunderland	– –	3 –	– –	– –	– –	– –	– –	– –	– –	3 –
15 Aston Villa	– –	2 –	– –	– –	– –	– –	– –	– –	– –	2 –
16 Bolton Wanderers	– –	2 –	– –	– –	– –	– –	– –	– –	– –	2 –
17 Sheffield United	– –	2 –	– –	– –	– –	– –	– –	– –	– –	2 –
18 West Bromwich Albion	– –	2 –	– –	– –	– –	– –	– –	– –	– –	2 –
19 Burnley	– –	1 –	– –	– –	– –	– –	– –	– –	– –	1 –
20 Derby County	– –	1 –	– –	– –	– –	– –	– –	– –	– –	1 –
21 Plymouth Argyle	– –	– –	– –	1 –	– –	– –	– –	– –	– –	1 –
22 Swindon Town	– –	– –	– –	– –	– –	– –	– –	– –	1 –	1 –

JIMMY HANLON

DEBUT (Full Appearance, 1 goal)

Saturday 26/11/1938
Football League Division 1
at Old Trafford

Manchester United 1 Huddersfield Town 1

CLUB CAREER RECORD	Apps	Subs	Goals
Premiership	0		0
League Division 1	63		20
League Division 2	0		0
FA Cup	6		2
League Cup	0		0
European Cup / Champions League	0		0
European Cup-Winners' Cup	0		0
UEFA Cup / Inter-Cities' Fairs Cup	0		0
Other Matches	0		0
OVERALL TOTAL	**69**		**22**

Opponents	PREM A S G	FLD 1 A S G	FLD 2 A S G	FAC A S G	LC A S G	EC/CL A S G	ECWC A S G	UEFA A S G	OTHER A S G	TOTAL A S G
1 Preston North End	– –	3 –	– –	2 2	– –	– –	– –	– –	– –	5 2
2 Blackpool	– –	4 4	– –	– –	– –	– –	– –	– –	– –	4 4
3 Arsenal	– –	4 3	– –	– –	– –	– –	– –	– –	– –	4 3
4 Brentford	– –	4 2	– –	– –	– –	– –	– –	– –	– –	4 2
5 Stoke City	– –	4 2	– –	– –	– –	– –	– –	– –	– –	4 2
6 Grimsby Town	– –	4 –	– –	– –	– –	– –	– –	– –	– –	4 –
7 Leeds United	– –	4 –	– –	– –	– –	– –	– –	– –	– –	4 –

continued../

JIMMY HANLON (continued)

Opponents	PREM A S G	FLD 1 A S G	FLD 2 A S G	FAC A S G	LC A S G	EC/CL A S G	ECWC A S G	UEFA A S G	OTHER A S G	TOTAL A S G
8 Liverpool	– –	3 2	– –	– –	– –	– –	– –	– –	– –	3 2
9 Wolverhampton W.	– –	3 2	– –	– –	– –	– –	– –	– –	– –	3 2
10 Huddersfield Town	– –	3 1	– –	– –	– –	– –	– –	– –	– –	3 1
11 Chelsea	– –	3 –	– –	– –	– –	– –	– –	– –	– –	3 –
12 Portsmouth	– –	3 –	– –	– –	– –	– –	– –	– –	– –	3 –
13 Sunderland	– –	3 –	– –	– –	– –	– –	– –	– –	– –	3 –
14 Charlton Athletic	– –	2 2	– –	– –	– –	– –	– –	– –	– –	2 2
15 Leicester City	– –	2 1	– –	– –	– –	– –	– –	– –	– –	2 1
16 Accrington Stanley	– –	– –	– –	2 –	– –	– –	– –	– –	– –	2 –
17 Aston Villa	– –	2 –	– –	– –	– –	– –	– –	– –	– –	2 –
18 Blackburn Rovers	– –	2 –	– –	– –	– –	– –	– –	– –	– –	2 –
19 Bolton Wanderers	– –	2 –	– –	– –	– –	– –	– –	– –	– –	2 –
20 Middlesbrough	– –	2 –	– –	– –	– –	– –	– –	– –	– –	2 –
21 Sheffield United	– –	2 –	– –	– –	– –	– –	– –	– –	– –	2 –
22 West Bromwich Albion	– –	– –	– –	2 –	– –	– –	– –	– –	– –	2 –
23 Birmingham City	– –	1 1	– –	– –	– –	– –	– –	– –	– –	1 1
24 Derby County	– –	1 –	– –	– –	– –	– –	– –	– –	– –	1 –
25 Everton	– –	1 –	– –	– –	– –	– –	– –	– –	– –	1 –
26 Manchester City	– –	1 –	– –	– –	– –	– –	– –	– –	– –	1 –

CHARLIE HANNAFORD

DEBUT (Full Appearance)

Monday 28/12/1925
Football League Division 1
at Filbert Street

Leicester City 1 Manchester United 3

CLUB CAREER RECORD	Apps	Subs	Goals
Premiership	0		0
League Division 1	11		0
League Division 2	0		0
FA Cup	1		0
League Cup	0		0
European Cup / Champions League	0		0
European Cup-Winners' Cup	0		0
UEFA Cup / Inter-Cities' Fairs Cup	0		0
Other Matches	0		0
OVERALL TOTAL	12		0

Opponents	PREM A S G	FLD 1 A S G	FLD 2 A S G	FAC A S G	LC A S G	EC/CL A S G	ECWC A S G	UEFA A S G	OTHER A S G	TOTAL A S G
1 Bolton Wanderers	– –	2 –	– –	– –	– –	– –	– –	– –	– –	2 –
2 Aston Villa	– –	1 –	– –	– –	– –	– –	– –	– –	– –	1 –
3 Birmingham City	– –	1 –	– –	– –	– –	– –	– –	– –	– –	1 –
4 Blackburn Rovers	– –	1 –	– –	– –	– –	– –	– –	– –	– –	1 –
5 Burnley	– –	1 –	– –	– –	– –	– –	– –	– –	– –	1 –
6 Cardiff City	– –	1 –	– –	– –	– –	– –	– –	– –	– –	1 –
7 Fulham	– –	– –	– –	1 –	– –	– –	– –	– –	– –	1 –
8 Leeds United	– –	1 –	– –	– –	– –	– –	– –	– –	– –	1 –
9 Leicester City	– –	1 –	– –	– –	– –	– –	– –	– –	– –	1 –
10 Sheffield Wednesday	– –	1 –	– –	– –	– –	– –	– –	– –	– –	1 –
11 West Ham United	– –	1 –	– –	– –	– –	– –	– –	– –	– –	1 –

JIMMY HANSON

DEBUT (Full Appearance, 1 goal)

Saturday 15/11/1924
Football League Division 2
at Old Trafford

Manchester United 2 Hull City 0

CLUB CAREER RECORD	Apps	Subs	Goals
Premiership	0		0
League Division 1	135		44
League Division 2	3		3
FA Cup	9		5
League Cup	0		0
European Cup / Champions League	0		0
European Cup-Winners' Cup	0		0
UEFA Cup / Inter-Cities' Fairs Cup	0		0
Other Matches	0		0
OVERALL TOTAL	147		52

Opponents	PREM A S G	FLD 1 A S G	FLD 2 A S G	FAC A S G	LC A S G	EC/CL A S G	ECWC A S G	UEFA A S G	OTHER A S G	TOTAL A S G
1 Newcastle United	– –	9 3	– –	– –	– –	– –	– –	– –	– –	9 3
2 Blackburn Rovers	– –	7 1	– –	1 –	– –	– –	– –	– –	– –	8 1
3 Arsenal	– –	7 4	– –	– –	– –	– –	– –	– –	– –	7 4
4 Derby County	– –	6 2	1 1	– –	– –	– –	– –	– –	– –	7 3
5 Everton	– –	7 3	– –	– –	– –	– –	– –	– –	– –	7 3
6 Liverpool	– –	7 3	– –	– –	– –	– –	– –	– –	– –	7 3
7 Sunderland	– –	7 3	– –	– –	– –	– –	– –	– –	– –	7 3
8 Birmingham City	– –	6 2	– –	1 –	– –	– –	– –	– –	– –	7 2
9 Cardiff City	– –	7 2	– –	– –	– –	– –	– –	– –	– –	7 2
10 Leicester City	– –	7 2	– –	– –	– –	– –	– –	– –	– –	7 2
11 West Ham United	– –	7 1	– –	– –	– –	– –	– –	– –	– –	7 1
12 Bolton Wanderers	– –	6 3	– –	– –	– –	– –	– –	– –	– –	6 3

continued../

JIMMY HANSON (continued)

Opponents	PREM A S G	FLD 1 A S G	FLD 2 A S G	FAC A S G	LC A S G	EC/CL A S G	ECWC A S G	UEFA A S G	OTHER A S G	TOTAL A S G
13 Sheffield Wednesday	– –	6 3	– –	– –	– –	– –	– –	– –	– –	6 3
14 Huddersfield Town	– –	6 2	– –	– –	– –	– –	– –	– –	– –	6 2
15 Aston Villa	– –	6 1	– –	– –	– –	– –	– –	– –	– –	6 1
16 Leeds United	– –	6 1	– –	– –	– –	– –	– –	– –	– –	6 1
17 Burnley	– –	5 3	– –	– –	– –	– –	– –	– –	– –	5 3
18 Tottenham Hotspur	– –	3 2	– –	2	– –	– –	– –	– –	– –	5 2
19 Bury	– –	3 –	– –	2	– –	– –	– –	– –	– –	5 –
20 Manchester City	– –	4 –	– –	– –	– –	– –	– –	– –	– –	4 –
21 Portsmouth	– –	4 –	– –	– –	– –	– –	– –	– –	– –	4 –
22 Middlesbrough	– –	3 2	– –	– –	– –	– –	– –	– –	– –	3 2
23 Sheffield United	– –	3 –	– –	– –	– –	– –	– –	– –	– –	3 –
24 West Bromwich Albion	– –	2 1	– –	– –	– –	– –	– –	– –	– –	2 1
25 Brentford	– –	– –	– –	1 4	– –	– –	– –	– –	– –	1 4
26 Blackpool	– –	– –	1 1	– –	– –	– –	– –	– –	– –	1 1
27 Hull City	– –	– –	1 1	– –	– –	– –	– –	– –	– –	1 1
28 Port Vale	– –	– –	– –	1 1	– –	– –	– –	– –	– –	1 1
29 Notts County	– –	1 –	– –	– –	– –	– –	– –	– –	– –	1 –
30 Reading	– –	– –	– –	1	– –	– –	– –	– –	– –	1 –

HAROLD HARDMAN

DEBUT (Full Appearance)

Saturday 19/09/1908
Football League Division 1
at Hyde Road

Manchester City 1 Manchester United 2

CLUB CAREER RECORD	Apps	Subs	Goals
Premiership	0		0
League Division 1	4		0
League Division 2	0		0
FA Cup	0		0
League Cup	0		0
European Cup / Champions League	0		0
European Cup-Winners' Cup	0		0
UEFA Cup / Inter-Cities' Fairs Cup	0		0
Other Matches	0		0
OVERALL TOTAL	**4**		**0**

Opponents	PREM A S G	FLD 1 A S G	FLD 2 A S G	FAC A S G	LC A S G	EC/CL A S G	ECWC A S G	UEFA A S G	OTHER A S G	TOTAL A S G
1 Blackburn Rovers	– –	1	– –	– –	– –	– –	– –	– –	– –	1 –
2 Everton	– –	1	– –	– –	– –	– –	– –	– –	– –	1 –
3 Leicester City	– –	1	– –	– –	– –	– –	– –	– –	– –	1 –
4 Manchester City	– –	1	– –	– –	– –	– –	– –	– –	– –	1 –

OWEN HARGREAVES

DEBUT (Full Appearance)

Saturday 19/08/2007
FA Premiership
at Eastlands Stadium

Manchester City 1 Manchester United 0

CLUB CAREER RECORD	Apps	Subs	Goals
Premiership	16	(7)	2
League Division 1	0		0
League Division 2	0		0
FA Cup	2	(1)	0
League Cup	0		0
European Cup / Champions League	5	(3)	0
European Cup-Winners' Cup	0		0
UEFA Cup / Inter-Cities' Fairs Cup	0		0
Other Matches	0		0
OVERALL TOTAL	**23**	**(11)**	**2**

Opponents	PREM A S G	FLD 1 A S G	FLD 2 A S G	FAC A S G	LC A S G	EC/CL A S G	ECWC A S G	UEFA A S G	OTHER A S G	TOTAL A S G
1 Tottenham Hotspur	2 –	– –	– –	1	– –	– –	– –	– –	– –	3 –
2 Arsenal	2 1	– –	– –	– –	– –	– –	– –	– –	– –	2 1
3 Fulham	2 1	– –	– –	– –	– –	– –	– –	– –	– –	2 1
4 Barcelona	– –	– –	– –	– –	– –	2 –	– –	– –	– –	2 –
5 Bolton Wanderers	2 –	– –	– –	– –	– –	– –	– –	– –	– –	2 –
6 West Ham United	2 –	– –	– –	– –	– –	– –	– –	– –	– –	2 –
7 Chelsea	– (1) –	– –	– –	– –	– –	1 –	– –	– –	– –	1 (1) –
8 Manchester City	1 (1) –	– –	– –	– –	– –	– –	– –	– –	– –	1 (1) –
9 Middlesbrough	1 (1) –	– –	– –	– –	– –	– –	– –	– –	– –	1 (1) –
10 Olympique Lyonnais	– –	– –	– –	– –	– –	1 (1) –	– –	– –	– –	1 (1) –
11 Portsmouth	– (1) –	– –	– –	1	– –	– –	– –	– –	– –	1 (1) –
12 Roma	– –	– –	– –	– –	– –	1 (1) –	– –	– –	– –	1 (1) –
13 Aston Villa	– (1) –	– –	– –	– (1) –	– –	– –	– –	– –	– –	– (2) –
14 Blackburn Rovers	1 –	– –	– –	– –	– –	– –	– –	– –	– –	1 –
15 Liverpool	1 –	– –	– –	– –	– –	– –	– –	– –	– –	1 –
16 Reading	1 –	– –	– –	– –	– –	– –	– –	– –	– –	1 –
17 Sunderland	1 –	– –	– –	– –	– –	– –	– –	– –	– –	1 –
18 Birmingham City	– (1) –	– –	– –	– –	– –	– –	– –	– –	– –	– (1) –
19 Sporting Lisbon	– –	– –	– –	– –	– –	– (1) –	– –	– –	– –	– (1) –
20 Wigan Athletic	– (1) –	– –	– –	– –	– –	– –	– –	– –	– –	– (1) –

FRANK HARRIS

DEBUT (Full Appearance, 1 goal)

Saturday 14/02/1920
Football League Division 1
at Old Trafford

Manchester United 2 Sunderland 0

CLUB CAREER RECORD	Apps	Subs	Goals
Premiership	0		0
League Division 1	46		2
League Division 2	0		0
FA Cup	3		0
League Cup	0		0
European Cup / Champions League	0		0
European Cup-Winners' Cup	0		0
UEFA Cup / Inter–Cities' Fairs Cup	0		0
Other Matches	0		0
OVERALL TOTAL	49		2

Opponents	PREM (A S G)	FLD 1 (A S G)	FLD 2 (A S G)	FAC (A S G)	LC (A S G)	EC/CL (A S G)	ECWC (A S G)	UEFA (A S G)	OTHER (A S G)	TOTAL (A S G)
1 Aston Villa	– – –	4 – –	– – –	– – –	– – –	– – –	– – –	– – –	– – –	4 – –
2 Burnley	– – –	4 – –	– – –	– – –	– – –	– – –	– – –	– – –	– – –	4 – –
3 West Bromwich Albion	– – –	4 – –	– – –	– – –	– – –	– – –	– – –	– – –	– – –	4 – –
4 Arsenal	– – –	3 – –	– – –	– – –	– – –	– – –	– – –	– – –	– – –	3 – –
5 Bradford City	– – –	3 – –	– – –	– – –	– – –	– – –	– – –	– – –	– – –	3 – –
6 Bradford Park Avenue	– – –	3 – –	– – –	– – –	– – –	– – –	– – –	– – –	– – –	3 – –
7 Cardiff City	– – –	2 – –	– – –	1 – –	– – –	– – –	– – –	– – –	– – –	3 – –
8 Chelsea	– – –	3 – –	– – –	– – –	– – –	– – –	– – –	– – –	– – –	3 – –
9 Everton	– – –	3 – –	– – –	– – –	– – –	– – –	– – –	– – –	– – –	3 – –
10 Sheffield United	– – –	3 – –	– – –	– – –	– – –	– – –	– – –	– – –	– – –	3 – –
11 Liverpool	– – –	– – –	– – –	2 – –	– – –	– – –	– – –	– – –	– – –	2 – –
12 Manchester City	– – –	2 – –	– – –	– – –	– – –	– – –	– – –	– – –	– – –	2 – –
13 Newcastle United	– – –	2 – –	– – –	– – –	– – –	– – –	– – –	– – –	– – –	2 – –
14 Oldham Athletic	– – –	2 – –	– – –	– – –	– – –	– – –	– – –	– – –	– – –	2 – –
15 Preston North End	– – –	2 – –	– – –	– – –	– – –	– – –	– – –	– – –	– – –	2 – –
16 Tottenham Hotspur	– – –	2 – –	– – –	– – –	– – –	– – –	– – –	– – –	– – –	2 – –
17 Huddersfield Town	– – –	1 – 1	– – –	– – –	– – –	– – –	– – –	– – –	– – –	1 – 1
18 Sunderland	– – –	1 – 1	– – –	– – –	– – –	– – –	– – –	– – –	– – –	1 – 1
19 Blackburn Rovers	– – –	1 – –	– – –	– – –	– – –	– – –	– – –	– – –	– – –	1 – –
20 Derby County	– – –	1 – –	– – –	– – –	– – –	– – –	– – –	– – –	– – –	1 – –

TOM HARRIS

DEBUT (Full Appearance)

Saturday 30/10/1926
Football League Division 1
at Upton Park

West Ham United 4 Manchester United 0

CLUB CAREER RECORD	Apps	Subs	Goals
Premiership	0		0
League Division 1	4		1
League Division 2	0		0
FA Cup	0		0
League Cup	0		0
European Cup / Champions League	0		0
European Cup-Winners' Cup	0		0
UEFA Cup / Inter–Cities' Fairs Cup	0		0
Other Matches	0		0
OVERALL TOTAL	4		1

Opponents	PREM (A S G)	FLD 1 (A S G)	FLD 2 (A S G)	FAC (A S G)	LC (A S G)	EC/CL (A S G)	ECWC (A S G)	UEFA (A S G)	OTHER (A S G)	TOTAL (A S G)
1 Newcastle United	– – –	1 – 1	– – –	– – –	– – –	– – –	– – –	– – –	– – –	1 – 1
2 Aston Villa	– – –	1 – –	– – –	– – –	– – –	– – –	– – –	– – –	– – –	1 – –
3 Cardiff City	– – –	1 – –	– – –	– – –	– – –	– – –	– – –	– – –	– – –	1 – –
4 West Ham United	– – –	1 – –	– – –	– – –	– – –	– – –	– – –	– – –	– – –	1 – –

CHARLIE HARRISON

DEBUT (Full Appearance)

Saturday 18/01/1889
FA Cup 1st Round
at Deepdale

Preston North End 6 Newton Heath 1

CLUB CAREER RECORD	Apps	Subs	Goals
Premiership	0		0
League Division 1	0		0
League Division 2	0		0
FA Cup	1		0
League Cup	0		0
European Cup / Champions League	0		0
European Cup-Winners' Cup	0		0
UEFA Cup / Inter–Cities' Fairs Cup	0		0
Other Matches	0		0
OVERALL TOTAL	1		0

Opponents	PREM (A S G)	FLD 1 (A S G)	FLD 2 (A S G)	FAC (A S G)	LC (A S G)	EC/CL (A S G)	ECWC (A S G)	UEFA (A S G)	OTHER (A S G)	TOTAL (A S G)
1 Preston North End	– – –	– – –	– – –	1 – –	– – –	– – –	– – –	– – –	– – –	1 – –

WILLIAM HARRISON

DEBUT (Full Appearance)

Saturday 23/10/1920
Football League Division 1
at Old Trafford

Manchester United 1 Preston North End 0

CLUB CAREER RECORD	Apps	Subs	Goals
Premiership	0		0
League Division 1	44		5
League Division 2	0		0
FA Cup	2		0
League Cup	0		0
European Cup / Champions League	0		0
European Cup-Winners' Cup	0		0
UEFA Cup / Inter-Cities' Fairs Cup	0		0
Other Matches	0		0
OVERALL TOTAL	**46**		**5**

Opponents	PREM A S G	FLD 1 A S G	FLD 2 A S G	FAC A S G	LC A S G	EC/CL A S G	ECWC A S G	UEFA A S G	OTHER A S G	TOTAL A S G
1 Preston North End	– –	4 –	–	–	–	–	–	–	–	4 –
2 West Bromwich Albion	– –	4 –	–	–	–	–	–	–	–	4 –
3 Aston Villa	– –	3 2	–	–	–	–	–	–	–	3 2
4 Sheffield United	– –	3 1	–	–	–	–	–	–	–	3 1
5 Liverpool	– –	1 –	–	2	–	–	–	–	–	3 –
6 Manchester City	– –	3 –	–	–	–	–	–	–	–	3 –
7 Everton	– –	2 1	–	–	–	–	–	–	–	2 1
8 Sunderland	– –	2 1	–	–	–	–	–	–	–	2 1
9 Arsenal	– –	2 –	–	–	–	–	–	–	–	2 –
10 Blackburn Rovers	– –	2 –	–	–	–	–	–	–	–	2 –
11 Bradford City	– –	2 –	–	–	–	–	–	–	–	2 –
12 Bradford Park Avenue	– –	2 –	–	–	–	–	–	–	–	2 –
13 Burnley	– –	2 –	–	–	–	–	–	–	–	2 –
14 Cardiff City	– –	2 –	–	–	–	–	–	–	–	2 –
15 Chelsea	– –	2 –	–	–	–	–	–	–	–	2 –
16 Newcastle United	– –	2 –	–	–	–	–	–	–	–	2 –
17 Oldham Athletic	– –	2 –	–	–	–	–	–	–	–	2 –
18 Birmingham City	– –	1 –	–	–	–	–	–	–	–	1 –
19 Bolton Wanderers	– –	1 –	–	–	–	–	–	–	–	1 –
20 Huddersfield Town	– –	1 –	–	–	–	–	–	–	–	1 –
21 Middlesbrough	– –	1 –	–	–	–	–	–	–	–	1 –

BOBBY HARROP

DEBUT (Full Appearance)

Wednesday 05/03/1958
FA Cup 6th Round Replay
at Old Trafford

Manchester United 1 West Bromwich Albion 0

CLUB CAREER RECORD	Apps	Subs	Goals
Premiership	0		0
League Division 1	10		0
League Division 2	0		0
FA Cup	1		0
League Cup	0		0
European Cup / Champions League	0		0
European Cup-Winners' Cup	0		0
UEFA Cup / Inter-Cities' Fairs Cup	0		0
Other Matches	0		0
OVERALL TOTAL	**11**		**0**

Opponents	PREM A S G	FLD 1 A S G	FLD 2 A S G	FAC A S G	LC A S G	EC/CL A S G	ECWC A S G	UEFA A S G	OTHER A S G	TOTAL A S G
1 West Bromwich Albion	– –	2 –	–	1 –	–	–	–	–	–	3 –
2 Burnley	– –	2 –	–	–	–	–	–	–	–	2 –
3 Aston Villa	– –	1 –	–	–	–	–	–	–	–	1 –
4 Leeds United	– –	1 –	–	–	–	–	–	–	–	1 –
5 Newcastle United	– –	1 –	–	–	–	–	–	–	–	1 –
6 Sheffield Wednesday	– –	1 –	–	–	–	–	–	–	–	1 –
7 Sunderland	– –	1 –	–	–	–	–	–	–	–	1 –
8 Wolverhampton W.	– –	1 –	–	–	–	–	–	–	–	1 –

WILLIAM HARTWELL

DEBUT (Full Appearance)

Saturday 30/04/1904
Football League Division 2
at Bank Street

Manchester United 5 Leicester City 2

CLUB CAREER RECORD	Apps	Subs	Goals
Premiership	0		0
League Division 1	0		0
League Division 2	3		0
FA Cup	1		0
League Cup	0		0
European Cup / Champions League	0		0
European Cup-Winners' Cup	0		0
UEFA Cup / Inter-Cities' Fairs Cup	0		0
Other Matches	0		0
OVERALL TOTAL	**4**		**0**

Opponents	PREM A S G	FLD 1 A S G	FLD 2 A S G	FAC A S G	LC A S G	EC/CL A S G	ECWC A S G	UEFA A S G	OTHER A S G	TOTAL A S G
1 Bradford City	– –	– –	1 –	–	–	–	–	–	–	1 –
2 Burton United	– –	– –	1 –	–	–	–	–	–	–	1 –
3 Fulham	– –	– –	– –	1 –	–	–	–	–	–	1 –
4 Leicester City	– –	– –	1 –	–	–	–	–	–	–	1 –

GEORGE HASLAM

DEBUT (Full Appearance)

Saturday 25/02/1922
Football League Division 1
at Old Trafford

Manchester United 1 Birmingham City 1

CLUB CAREER RECORD	Apps	Subs	Goals
Premiership	0		0
League Division 1	17		0
League Division 2	8		0
FA Cup	2		0
League Cup	0		0
European Cup / Champions League	0		0
European Cup-Winners' Cup	0		0
UEFA Cup / Inter-Cities' Fairs Cup	0		0
Other Matches	0		0
OVERALL TOTAL	**27**		**0**

Opponents	PREM A S G	FLD 1 A S G	FLD 2 A S G	FAC A S G	LC A S G	EC/CL A S G	ECWC A S G	UEFA A S G	OTHER A S G	TOTAL A S G
1 Tottenham Hotspur	– –	2 –	– –	2 –	– –	– –	– –	– –	– –	4 –
2 Birmingham City	– –	3 –	– –	– –	– –	– –	– –	– –	– –	3 –
3 Bolton Wanderers	– –	2 –	– –	– –	– –	– –	– –	– –	– –	2 –
4 Sheffield United	– –	2 –	– –	– –	– –	– –	– –	– –	– –	2 –
5 Sheffield Wednesday	– –	– –	2 –	– –	– –	– –	– –	– –	– –	2 –
6 Stockport County	– –	– –	2 –	– –	– –	– –	– –	– –	– –	2 –
7 Blackburn Rovers	– –	1 –	– –	– –	– –	– –	– –	– –	– –	1 –
8 Burnley	– –	1 –	– –	– –	– –	– –	– –	– –	– –	1 –
9 Bury	– –	1 –	– –	– –	– –	– –	– –	– –	– –	1 –
10 Coventry City	– –	– –	1 –	– –	– –	– –	– –	– –	– –	1 –
11 Everton	– –	1 –	– –	– –	– –	– –	– –	– –	– –	1 –
12 Huddersfield Town	– –	1 –	– –	– –	– –	– –	– –	– –	– –	1 –
13 Leeds United	– –	1 –	– –	– –	– –	– –	– –	– –	– –	1 –
14 Leicester City	– –	– –	1 –	– –	– –	– –	– –	– –	– –	1 –
15 Leyton Orient	– –	1 –	– –	– –	– –	– –	– –	– –	– –	1 –
16 Oldham Athletic	– –	– –	1 –	– –	– –	– –	– –	– –	– –	1 –
17 Sunderland	– –	1 –	– –	– –	– –	– –	– –	– –	– –	1 –
18 West Bromwich Albion	– –	1 –	– –	– –	– –	– –	– –	– –	– –	1 –

TONY HAWKSWORTH

DEBUT (Full Appearance)

Saturday 27/10/1956
Football League Division 1
at Bloomfield Road

Blackpool 2 Manchester United 2

CLUB CAREER RECORD	Apps	Subs	Goals
Premiership	0		0
League Division 1	1		0
League Division 2	0		0
FA Cup	0		0
League Cup	0		0
European Cup / Champions League	0		0
European Cup-Winners' Cup	0		0
UEFA Cup / Inter-Cities' Fairs Cup	0		0
Other Matches	0		0
OVERALL TOTAL	**1**		**0**

Opponents	PREM A S G	FLD 1 A S G	FLD 2 A S G	FAC A S G	LC A S G	EC/CL A S G	ECWC A S G	UEFA A S G	OTHER A S G	TOTAL A S G
1 Blackpool	– –	1 –	– –	– –	– –	– –	– –	– –	– –	1 –

RONALD HAWORTH

DEBUT (Full Appearance)

Saturday 28/08/1926
Football League Division 1
at Anfield

Liverpool 4 Manchester United 2

CLUB CAREER RECORD	Apps	Subs	Goals
Premiership	0		0
League Division 1	2		0
League Division 2	0		0
FA Cup	0		0
League Cup	0		0
European Cup / Champions League	0		0
European Cup-Winners' Cup	0		0
UEFA Cup / Inter-Cities' Fairs Cup	0		0
Other Matches	0		0
OVERALL TOTAL	**2**		**0**

Opponents	PREM A S G	FLD 1 A S G	FLD 2 A S G	FAC A S G	LC A S G	EC/CL A S G	ECWC A S G	UEFA A S G	OTHER A S G	TOTAL A S G
1 Liverpool	– –	1 –	– –	– –	– –	– –	– –	– –	– –	1 –
2 Sheffield United	– –	1 –	– –	– –	– –	– –	– –	– –	– –	1 –

TOM HAY

DEBUT (Full Appearance)

Saturday 18/01/1889
FA Cup 1st Round
at Deepdale

Preston North End 6 Newton Heath 1

CLUB CAREER RECORD	Apps	Subs	Goals
Premiership	0		0
League Division 1	0		0
League Division 2	0		0
FA Cup	1		0
League Cup	0		0
European Cup / Champions League	0		0
European Cup-Winners' Cup	0		0
UEFA Cup / Inter-Cities' Fairs Cup	0		0
Other Matches	0		0
OVERALL TOTAL	**1**		**0**

Opponents	PREM A S G	FLD 1 A S G	FLD 2 A S G	FAC A S G	LC A S G	EC/CL A S G	ECWC A S G	UEFA A S G	OTHER A S G	TOTAL A S G
1 Preston North End	– –	– –	– –	1	– –	– –	– –	– –	– –	1 –

FRANK HAYDOCK

DEBUT (Full Appearance)

Saturday 20/08/1960
Football League Division 1
at Old Trafford

Manchester United 1 Blackburn Rovers 3

CLUB CAREER RECORD	Apps	Subs	Goals
Premiership	0		0
League Division 1	6		0
League Division 2	0		0
FA Cup	0		0
League Cup	0		0
European Cup / Champions League	0		0
European Cup-Winners' Cup	0		0
UEFA Cup / Inter-Cities' Fairs Cup	0		0
Other Matches	0		0
OVERALL TOTAL	**6**		**0**

Opponents	PREM A S G	FLD 1 A S G	FLD 2 A S G	FAC A S G	LC A S G	EC/CL A S G	ECWC A S G	UEFA A S G	OTHER A S G	TOTAL A S G
1 Everton	– –	2	– –	– –	– –	– –	– –	– –	– –	2 –
2 Birmingham City	– –	1	– –	– –	– –	– –	– –	– –	– –	1 –
3 Blackburn Rovers	– –	1	– –	– –	– –	– –	– –	– –	– –	1 –
4 Nottingham Forest	– –	1	– –	– –	– –	– –	– –	– –	– –	1 –
5 Tottenham Hotspur	– –	1	– –	– –	– –	– –	– –	– –	– –	1 –

VINCE HAYES

DEBUT (Full Appearance)

Saturday 25/02/1901
Football League Division 2
at West Bromwich Road

Walsall 1 Newton Heath 1

CLUB CAREER RECORD	Apps	Subs	Goals
Premiership	0		0
League Division 1	53		0
League Division 2	62		2
FA Cup	13		0
League Cup	0		0
European Cup / Champions League	0		0
European Cup-Winners' Cup	0		0
UEFA Cup / Inter-Cities' Fairs Cup	0		0
Other Matches	0		0
OVERALL TOTAL	**128**		**2**

Opponents	PREM A S G	FLD 1 A S G	FLD 2 A S G	FAC A S G	LC A S G	EC/CL A S G	ECWC A S G	UEFA A S G	OTHER A S G	TOTAL A S G
1 Leicester City	– –	2	5 1	– –	– –	– –	– –	– –	– –	7 1
2 Arsenal	– –	3	3	– –	– –	– –	– –	– –	– –	6 –
3 Bradford City	– –	3	3	– –	– –	– –	– –	– –	– –	6 –
4 Bristol City	– –	3	2	1	– –	– –	– –	– –	– –	6 –
5 Burnley	– –	– –	4	2	– –	– –	– –	– –	– –	6 –
6 Chesterfield	– –	– –	5	– –	– –	– –	– –	– –	– –	5 –
7 Newcastle United	– –	4	– –	1	– –	– –	– –	– –	– –	5 –
8 Notts County	– –	3	– –	2	– –	– –	– –	– –	– –	5 –
9 Bolton Wanderers	– –	1	3	– –	– –	– –	– –	– –	– –	4 –
10 Burton United	– –	– –	4	– –	– –	– –	– –	– –	– –	4 –
11 Chelsea	– –	4	– –	– –	– –	– –	– –	– –	– –	4 –
12 Everton	– –	3	– –	1	– –	– –	– –	– –	– –	4 –
13 Glossop	– –	– –	4	– –	– –	– –	– –	– –	– –	4 –
14 Lincoln City	– –	– –	4	– –	– –	– –	– –	– –	– –	4 –
15 Liverpool	– –	3	1	– –	– –	– –	– –	– –	– –	4 –
16 Nottingham Forest	– –	4	– –	– –	– –	– –	– –	– –	– –	4 –
17 Preston North End	– –	3	1	– –	– –	– –	– –	– –	– –	4 –
18 Port Vale	– –	– –	3 1	– –	– –	– –	– –	– –	– –	3 1
19 Barnsley	– –	– –	3	– –	– –	– –	– –	– –	– –	3 –
20 Blackburn Rovers	– –	2	– –	1	– –	– –	– –	– –	– –	3 –
21 Blackpool	– –	– –	3	– –	– –	– –	– –	– –	– –	3 –
22 Fulham	– –	– –	– –	3	– –	– –	– –	– –	– –	3 –
23 Grimsby Town	– –	– –	3	– –	– –	– –	– –	– –	– –	3 –
24 Middlesbrough	– –	2	1	– –	– –	– –	– –	– –	– –	3 –
25 Sheffield United	– –	3	– –	– –	– –	– –	– –	– –	– –	3 –
26 Stockport County	– –	– –	3	– –	– –	– –	– –	– –	– –	3 –
27 Aston Villa	– –	2	– –	– –	– –	– –	– –	– –	– –	2 –

continued../

VINCE HAYES (continued)

Opponents	PREM			FLD 1			FLD 2			FAC			LC			EC/CL			ECWC			UEFA			OTHER			TOTAL		
	A	S	G	A	S	G	A	S	G	A	S	G	A	S	G	A	S	G	A	S	G	A	S	G	A	S	G	A	S	G
28 Bury	–	–		2	–		–	–		–	–		–	–		–	–		–	–		–	–		–	–		2	–	
29 Doncaster Rovers	–	–		–	–		2	–		–	–		–	–		–	–		–	–		–	–		–	–		2	–	
30 Gainsborough Trinity	–	–		–	–		2	–		–	–		–	–		–	–		–	–		–	–		–	–		2	–	
31 Sheffield Wednesday	–	–		1	–		–	–		1	–		–	–		–	–		–	–		–	–		–	–		2	–	
32 Sunderland	–	–		2	–		–	–		–	–		–	–		–	–		–	–		–	–		–	–		2	–	
33 Tottenham Hotspur	–	–		2	–		–	–		–	–		–	–		–	–		–	–		–	–		–	–		2	–	
34 West Bromwich Albion	–	–		–	–		2	–		–	–		–	–		–	–		–	–		–	–		–	–		2	–	
35 Brighton	–	–		–	–		–	–		1	–		–	–		–	–		–	–		–	–		–	–		1	–	
36 Manchester City	–	–		1	–		–	–		–	–		–	–		–	–		–	–		–	–		–	–		1	–	
37 Walsall	–	–		–	–		–	–		1	–		–	–		–	–		–	–		–	–		–	–		1	–	

JOE HAYWOOD

DEBUT (Full Appearance)

Saturday 22/11/1913
Football League Division 1
at Bramall Lane

Sheffield United 2 Manchester United 0

CLUB CAREER RECORD	Apps	Subs	Goals
Premiership	0		0
League Division 1	26		0
League Division 2	0		0
FA Cup	0		0
League Cup	0		0
European Cup / Champions League	0		0
European Cup-Winners' Cup	0		0
UEFA Cup / Inter-Cities' Fairs Cup	0		0
Other Matches	0		0
OVERALL TOTAL	**26**		**0**

Opponents	PREM			FLD 1			FLD 2			FAC			LC			EC/CL			ECWC			UEFA			OTHER			TOTAL		
	A	S	G	A	S	G	A	S	G	A	S	G	A	S	G	A	S	G	A	S	G	A	S	G	A	S	G	A	S	G
1 Aston Villa	–	–		2	–		–	–		–	–		–	–		–	–		–	–		–	–		–	–		2	–	
2 Blackburn Rovers	–	–		2	–		–	–		–	–		–	–		–	–		–	–		–	–		–	–		2	–	
3 Derby County	–	–		2	–		–	–		–	–		–	–		–	–		–	–		–	–		–	–		2	–	
4 Middlesbrough	–	–		2	–		–	–		–	–		–	–		–	–		–	–		–	–		–	–		2	–	
5 Newcastle United	–	–		2	–		–	–		–	–		–	–		–	–		–	–		–	–		–	–		2	–	
6 Sheffield United	–	–		2	–		–	–		–	–		–	–		–	–		–	–		–	–		–	–		2	–	
7 Sunderland	–	–		2	–		–	–		–	–		–	–		–	–		–	–		–	–		–	–		2	–	
8 West Bromwich Albion	–	–		2	–		–	–		–	–		–	–		–	–		–	–		–	–		–	–		2	–	
9 Bolton Wanderers	–	–		1	–		–	–		–	–		–	–		–	–		–	–		–	–		–	–		1	–	
10 Bradford City	–	–		1	–		–	–		–	–		–	–		–	–		–	–		–	–		–	–		1	–	
11 Bradford Park Avenue	–	–		1	–		–	–		–	–		–	–		–	–		–	–		–	–		–	–		1	–	
12 Burnley	–	–		1	–		–	–		–	–		–	–		–	–		–	–		–	–		–	–		1	–	
13 Chelsea	–	–		1	–		–	–		–	–		–	–		–	–		–	–		–	–		–	–		1	–	
14 Everton	–	–		1	–		–	–		–	–		–	–		–	–		–	–		–	–		–	–		1	–	
15 Liverpool	–	–		1	–		–	–		–	–		–	–		–	–		–	–		–	–		–	–		1	–	
16 Preston North End	–	–		1	–		–	–		–	–		–	–		–	–		–	–		–	–		–	–		1	–	
17 Sheffield Wednesday	–	–		1	–		–	–		–	–		–	–		–	–		–	–		–	–		–	–		1	–	
18 Tottenham Hotspur	–	–		1	–		–	–		–	–		–	–		–	–		–	–		–	–		–	–		1	–	

DAVID HEALY

DEBUT (Substitute Appearance)

Wednesday 13/10/1999
League Cup 3rd Round
at Villa Park

Aston Villa 3 Manchester United 0

CLUB CAREER RECORD	Apps	Subs	Goals
Premiership	0	(1)	0
League Division 1	0		0
League Division 2	0		0
FA Cup	0		0
League Cup	0	(2)	0
European Cup / Champions League	0		0
European Cup-Winners' Cup	0		0
UEFA Cup / Inter-Cities' Fairs Cup	0		0
Other Matches	0		0
OVERALL TOTAL	**0**	**(3)**	**0**

Opponents	PREM			FLD 1			FLD 2			FAC			LC			EC/CL			ECWC			UEFA			OTHER			TOTAL		
	A	S	G	A	S	G	A	S	G	A	S	G	A	S	G	A	S	G	A	S	G	A	S	G	A	S	G	A	S	G
1 Aston Villa	–	–		–	–		–	–		–	–		–	(1)	–	–	–		–	–		–	–		–	–		–	(1)	–
2 Ipswich Town	–	(1)	–	–	–		–	–		–	–		–	–		–	–		–	–		–	–		–	–		–	(1)	–
3 Sunderland	–	–		–	–		–	–		–	–		–	(1)	–	–	–		–	–		–	–		–	–		–	(1)	–

JOE HEATHCOTE

DEBUT (Full Appearance)

Saturday 16/12/1899
Football League Division 2
at Bank Street

Newton Heath 2 Middlesbrough 1

CLUB CAREER RECORD	Apps	Subs	Goals
Premiership	0		0
League Division 1	0		0
League Division 2	7		0
FA Cup	1		0
League Cup	0		0
European Cup / Champions League	0		0
European Cup-Winners' Cup	0		0
UEFA Cup / Inter-Cities' Fairs Cup	0		0
Other Matches	0		0
OVERALL TOTAL	8		0

Opponents	PREM			FLD 1			FLD 2			FAC			LC			EC/CL			ECWC			UEFA			OTHER			TOTAL		
	A	S	G	A	S	G	A	S	G	A	S	G	A	S	G	A	S	G	A	S	G	A	S	G	A	S	G	A	S	G
1 Burnley	–	–	–	–	–	–	–	–	–	1	–	–	–	–	–	–	–	–	–	–	–	–	–	–	–	–	–	1	–	–
2 Burton Swifts	–	–	–	–	–	–	1	–	–	–	–	–	–	–	–	–	–	–	–	–	–	–	–	–	–	–	–	1	–	–
3 Gainsborough Trinity	–	–	–	–	–	–	1	–	–	–	–	–	–	–	–	–	–	–	–	–	–	–	–	–	–	–	–	1	–	–
4 Lincoln City	–	–	–	–	–	–	1	–	–	–	–	–	–	–	–	–	–	–	–	–	–	–	–	–	–	–	–	1	–	–
5 Middlesbrough	–	–	–	–	–	–	1	–	–	–	–	–	–	–	–	–	–	–	–	–	–	–	–	–	–	–	–	1	–	–
6 New Brighton Tower	–	–	–	–	–	–	1	–	–	–	–	–	–	–	–	–	–	–	–	–	–	–	–	–	–	–	–	1	–	–
7 Port Vale	–	–	–	–	–	–	1	–	–	–	–	–	–	–	–	–	–	–	–	–	–	–	–	–	–	–	–	1	–	–
8 Preston North End	–	–	–	–	–	–	1	–	–	–	–	–	–	–	–	–	–	–	–	–	–	–	–	–	–	–	–	1	–	–

GABRIEL HEINZE

DEBUT (Full Appearance, 1 goal)

Saturday 11/09/2004
FA Premiership
at Reebok Stadium

Bolton Wanderers 2 Manchester United 2

CLUB CAREER RECORD	Apps	Subs	Goals
Premiership	45	(7)	1
League Division 1	0		0
League Division 2	0		0
FA Cup	10		1
League Cup	4		0
European Cup / Champions League	16	(1)	2
European Cup-Winners' Cup	0		0
UEFA Cup / Inter-Cities' Fairs Cup	0		0
Other Matches	0		0
OVERALL TOTAL	75	(8)	4

Opponents	PREM			FLD 1			FLD 2			FAC			LC			EC/CL			ECWC			UEFA			OTHER			TOTAL		
	A	S	G	A	S	G	A	S	G	A	S	G	A	S	G	A	S	G	A	S	G	A	S	G	A	S	G	A	S	G
1 Middlesbrough	4	–	–	–	–	–	–	–	–	3	–	–	–	–	–	–	–	–	–	–	–	–	–	–	–	–	–	7	–	–
2 Chelsea	2	–	–	–	–	–	–	–	–	1	–	–	2	–	–	–	–	–	–	–	–	–	–	–	–	–	–	5	–	–
3 Manchester City	5	–	–	–	–	–	–	–	–	–	–	–	–	–	–	–	–	–	–	–	–	–	–	–	–	–	–	5	–	–
4 Newcastle United	4	–	–	–	–	–	–	–	–	1	–	–	–	–	–	–	–	–	–	–	–	–	–	–	–	–	–	5	–	–
5 Everton	2	(2)	–	–	–	–	–	–	–	1	–	–	–	–	–	–	–	–	–	–	–	–	–	–	–	–	–	3	(2)	–
6 Reading	2	–	–	–	–	–	–	–	–	2	–	1	–	–	–	–	–	–	–	–	–	–	–	–	–	–	–	4	–	1
7 AC Milan	–	–	–	–	–	–	–	–	–	–	–	–	–	–	–	4	–	–	–	–	–	–	–	–	–	–	–	4	–	–
8 Bolton Wanderers	3	(1)	1	–	–	–	–	–	–	–	–	–	–	–	–	–	–	–	–	–	–	–	–	–	–	–	–	3	(1)	1
9 Portsmouth	3	–	–	–	–	–	–	–	–	–	–	–	–	–	–	–	–	–	–	–	–	–	–	–	–	–	–	3	–	–
10 Arsenal	2	(1)	–	–	–	–	–	–	–	–	–	–	–	–	–	–	–	–	–	–	–	–	–	–	–	–	–	2	(1)	–
11 Aston Villa	2	(1)	–	–	–	–	–	–	–	–	–	–	–	–	–	–	–	–	–	–	–	–	–	–	–	–	–	2	(1)	–
12 Fulham	2	–	–	–	–	–	–	–	–	–	–	–	–	–	–	–	–	–	–	–	–	–	–	–	–	–	–	2	–	–
13 Liverpool	2	–	–	–	–	–	–	–	–	–	–	–	–	–	–	–	–	–	–	–	–	–	–	–	–	–	–	2	–	–
14 Olympique Lyonnais	–	–	–	–	–	–	–	–	–	–	–	–	–	–	–	2	–	–	–	–	–	–	–	–	–	–	–	2	–	–
15 Roma	–	–	–	–	–	–	–	–	–	–	–	–	–	–	–	2	–	–	–	–	–	–	–	–	–	–	–	2	–	–
16 Southampton	1	–	–	–	–	–	–	–	–	1	–	–	–	–	–	–	–	–	–	–	–	–	–	–	–	–	–	2	–	–
17 Sparta Prague	–	–	–	–	–	–	–	–	–	–	–	–	–	–	–	2	–	–	–	–	–	–	–	–	–	–	–	2	–	–
18 Tottenham Hotspur	2	–	–	–	–	–	–	–	–	–	–	–	–	–	–	–	–	–	–	–	–	–	–	–	–	–	–	2	–	–
19 Watford	1	–	–	–	–	–	–	–	–	1	–	–	–	–	–	–	–	–	–	–	–	–	–	–	–	–	–	2	–	–
20 West Ham United	2	–	–	–	–	–	–	–	–	–	–	–	–	–	–	–	–	–	–	–	–	–	–	–	–	–	–	2	–	–
21 Benfica	–	–	–	–	–	–	–	–	–	–	–	–	–	–	–	1	(1)	–	–	–	–	–	–	–	–	–	–	1	(1)	–
22 Sheffield United	1	(1)	–	–	–	–	–	–	–	–	–	–	–	–	–	–	–	–	–	–	–	–	–	–	–	–	–	1	(1)	–
23 Debreceni	–	–	–	–	–	–	–	–	–	–	–	–	–	–	–	1	–	2	–	–	–	–	–	–	–	–	–	1	–	2
24 Birmingham City	1	–	–	–	–	–	–	–	–	–	–	–	–	–	–	–	–	–	–	–	–	–	–	–	–	–	–	1	–	–
25 Blackburn Rovers	1	–	–	–	–	–	–	–	–	–	–	–	–	–	–	–	–	–	–	–	–	–	–	–	–	–	–	1	–	–
26 Copenhagen	–	–	–	–	–	–	–	–	–	–	–	–	–	–	–	1	–	–	–	–	–	–	–	–	–	–	–	1	–	–
27 Crewe Alexandra	–	–	–	–	–	–	–	–	–	–	–	–	1	–	–	–	–	–	–	–	–	–	–	–	–	–	–	1	–	–
28 Crystal Palace	1	–	–	–	–	–	–	–	–	–	–	–	–	–	–	–	–	–	–	–	–	–	–	–	–	–	–	1	–	–
29 Fenerbahce	–	–	–	–	–	–	–	–	–	–	–	–	–	–	–	1	–	–	–	–	–	–	–	–	–	–	–	1	–	–
30 Glasgow Celtic	–	–	–	–	–	–	–	–	–	–	–	–	–	–	–	1	–	–	–	–	–	–	–	–	–	–	–	1	–	–
31 Norwich City	1	–	–	–	–	–	–	–	–	–	–	–	–	–	–	–	–	–	–	–	–	–	–	–	–	–	–	1	–	–
32 Southend United	–	–	–	–	–	–	–	–	–	–	–	–	1	–	–	–	–	–	–	–	–	–	–	–	–	–	–	1	–	–
33 Villarreal	–	–	–	–	–	–	–	–	–	–	–	–	–	–	–	1	–	–	–	–	–	–	–	–	–	–	–	1	–	–
34 West Bromwich Albion	1	–	–	–	–	–	–	–	–	–	–	–	–	–	–	–	–	–	–	–	–	–	–	–	–	–	–	1	–	–
35 Wigan Athletic	–	(1)	–	–	–	–	–	–	–	–	–	–	–	–	–	–	–	–	–	–	–	–	–	–	–	–	–	–	(1)	–

WILLIAM HENDERSON

DEBUT (Full Appearance, 1 goal)

Saturday 26/11/1921
Football League Division 1
at Old Trafford

Manchester United 1 Aston Villa 0

CLUB CAREER RECORD	Apps	Subs	Goals
Premiership	0		0
League Division 1	10		2
League Division 2	24		15
FA Cup	2		0
League Cup	0		0
European Cup / Champions League	0		0
European Cup-Winners' Cup	0		0
UEFA Cup / Inter-Cities' Fairs Cup	0		0
Other Matches	0		0
OVERALL TOTAL	**36**		**17**

Opponents	PREM A	S	G	FLD 1 A	S	G	FLD 2 A	S	G	FAC A	S	G	LC A	S	G	EC/CL A	S	G	ECWC A	S	G	UEFA A	S	G	OTHER A	S	G	TOTAL A	S	G
1 Bradford City	–	–	–	2	–	1	1	–	2	–	–	–	–	–	–	–	–	–	–	–	–	–	–	–	–	–	–	3	–	3
2 Coventry City	–	–	–	–	–	–	3	–	3	–	–	–	–	–	–	–	–	–	–	–	–	–	–	–	–	–	–	3	–	3
3 Oldham Athletic	–	–	–	–	–	–	2	–	3	–	–	–	–	–	–	–	–	–	–	–	–	–	–	–	–	–	–	2	–	3
4 Middlesbrough	–	–	–	–	–	–	2	–	2	–	–	–	–	–	–	–	–	–	–	–	–	–	–	–	–	–	–	2	–	2
5 Stoke City	–	–	–	–	–	–	2	–	2	–	–	–	–	–	–	–	–	–	–	–	–	–	–	–	–	–	–	2	–	2
6 Burnley	–	–	–	2	–	–	–	–	–	–	–	–	–	–	–	–	–	–	–	–	–	–	–	–	–	–	–	2	–	–
7 Huddersfield Town	–	–	–	1	–	–	–	–	–	1	–	–	–	–	–	–	–	–	–	–	–	–	–	–	–	–	–	2	–	–
8 Port Vale	–	–	–	–	–	–	2	–	–	–	–	–	–	–	–	–	–	–	–	–	–	–	–	–	–	–	–	2	–	–
9 Sheffield Wednesday	–	–	–	–	–	–	1	–	–	1	–	–	–	–	–	–	–	–	–	–	–	–	–	–	–	–	–	2	–	–
10 Sunderland	–	–	–	2	–	–	–	–	–	–	–	–	–	–	–	–	–	–	–	–	–	–	–	–	–	–	–	2	–	–
11 Aston Villa	–	–	–	1	–	1	–	–	–	–	–	–	–	–	–	–	–	–	–	–	–	–	–	–	–	–	–	1	–	1
12 Barnsley	–	–	–	–	–	–	1	–	1	–	–	–	–	–	–	–	–	–	–	–	–	–	–	–	–	–	–	1	–	1
13 Fulham	–	–	–	–	–	–	1	–	1	–	–	–	–	–	–	–	–	–	–	–	–	–	–	–	–	–	–	1	–	1
14 South Shields	–	–	–	–	–	–	1	–	1	–	–	–	–	–	–	–	–	–	–	–	–	–	–	–	–	–	–	1	–	1
15 Chelsea	–	–	–	–	–	–	1	–	–	–	–	–	–	–	–	–	–	–	–	–	–	–	–	–	–	–	–	1	–	–
16 Crystal Palace	–	–	–	–	–	–	1	–	–	–	–	–	–	–	–	–	–	–	–	–	–	–	–	–	–	–	–	1	–	–
17 Leicester City	–	–	–	–	–	–	1	–	–	–	–	–	–	–	–	–	–	–	–	–	–	–	–	–	–	–	–	1	–	–
18 Leyton Orient	–	–	–	–	–	–	1	–	–	–	–	–	–	–	–	–	–	–	–	–	–	–	–	–	–	–	–	1	–	–
19 Newcastle United	–	–	–	1	–	–	–	–	–	–	–	–	–	–	–	–	–	–	–	–	–	–	–	–	–	–	–	1	–	–
20 Portsmouth	–	–	–	–	–	–	1	–	–	–	–	–	–	–	–	–	–	–	–	–	–	–	–	–	–	–	–	1	–	–
21 Sheffield United	–	–	–	1	–	–	–	–	–	–	–	–	–	–	–	–	–	–	–	–	–	–	–	–	–	–	–	1	–	–
22 Southampton	–	–	–	–	–	–	1	–	–	–	–	–	–	–	–	–	–	–	–	–	–	–	–	–	–	–	–	1	–	–
23 Stockport County	–	–	–	–	–	–	1	–	–	–	–	–	–	–	–	–	–	–	–	–	–	–	–	–	–	–	–	1	–	–
24 Wolverhampton W.	–	–	–	–	–	–	1	–	–	–	–	–	–	–	–	–	–	–	–	–	–	–	–	–	–	–	–	1	–	–

JAMES HENDRY

DEBUT (Full Appearance, 1 goal)

Saturday 15/10/1892
Football League Division 1
at North Road

Newton Heath 10 Wolverhampton Wanderers 1

CLUB CAREER RECORD	Apps	Subs	Goals
Premiership	0		0
League Division 1	2		1
League Division 2	0		0
FA Cup	0		0
League Cup	0		0
European Cup / Champions League	0		0
European Cup-Winners' Cup	0		0
UEFA Cup / Inter-Cities' Fairs Cup	0		0
Other Matches	0		0
OVERALL TOTAL	**2**		**1**

Opponents	PREM A	S	G	FLD 1 A	S	G	FLD 2 A	S	G	FAC A	S	G	LC A	S	G	EC/CL A	S	G	ECWC A	S	G	UEFA A	S	G	OTHER A	S	G	TOTAL A	S	G
1 Wolverhampton W.	–	–	–	1	–	1	–	–	–	–	–	–	–	–	–	–	–	–	–	–	–	–	–	–	–	–	–	1	–	1
2 Sheffield Wednesday	–	–	–	1	–	–	–	–	–	–	–	–	–	–	–	–	–	–	–	–	–	–	–	–	–	–	–	1	–	–

ARTHUR HENRYS

DEBUT (Full Appearance)

Saturday 03/10/1891
FA Cup 1st Qualifying Round
at North Road

Newton Heath 5 Manchester City 1

CLUB CAREER RECORD	Apps	Subs	Goals
Premiership	0		0
League Division 1	3		0
League Division 2	0		0
FA Cup	3		0
League Cup	0		0
European Cup / Champions League	0		0
European Cup-Winners' Cup	0		0
UEFA Cup / Inter-Cities' Fairs Cup	0		0
Other Matches	0		0
OVERALL TOTAL	**6**		**0**

Opponents	PREM A	S	G	FLD 1 A	S	G	FLD 2 A	S	G	FAC A	S	G	LC A	S	G	EC/CL A	S	G	ECWC A	S	G	UEFA A	S	G	OTHER A	S	G	TOTAL A	S	G
1 Accrington Stanley	–	–	–	1	–	–	–	–	–	–	–	–	–	–	–	–	–	–	–	–	–	–	–	–	–	–	–	1	–	–
2 Blackpool	–	–	–	–	–	–	–	–	–	1	–	–	–	–	–	–	–	–	–	–	–	–	–	–	–	–	–	1	–	–
3 Derby County	–	–	–	1	–	–	–	–	–	–	–	–	–	–	–	–	–	–	–	–	–	–	–	–	–	–	–	1	–	–
4 Manchester City	–	–	–	–	–	–	–	–	–	1	–	–	–	–	–	–	–	–	–	–	–	–	–	–	–	–	–	1	–	–
5 Nottingham Forest	–	–	–	1	–	–	–	–	–	–	–	–	–	–	–	–	–	–	–	–	–	–	–	–	–	–	–	1	–	–
6 South Shore	–	–	–	–	–	–	–	–	–	1	–	–	–	–	–	–	–	–	–	–	–	–	–	–	–	–	–	1	–	–

DAVID HERD

DEBUT (Full Appearance)

Saturday 19/08/1961
Football League Division 1
at Upton Park

West Ham United 1 Manchester United 1

CLUB CAREER RECORD	Apps	Subs	Goals
Premiership	0		0
League Division 1	201	(1)	114
League Division 2	0		0
FA Cup	35		15
League Cup	1		1
European Cup / Champions League	8		5
European Cup-Winners' Cup	6		3
UEFA Cup / Inter-Cities' Fairs Cup	11		6
Other Matches	2		1
OVERALL TOTAL	**264**	**(1)**	**145**

Opponents	PREM A S G	FLD 1 A S G	FLD 2 A S G	FAC A S G	LC A S G	EC/CL A S G	ECWC A S G	UEFA A S G	OTHER A S G	TOTAL A S G
1 Tottenham Hotspur	– –	10 4	– –	2 1	– –	– –	2 2	– –	– –	14 7
2 Everton	– –	10 4	– –	1 –	– –	– –	– –	2 1	1 –	14 5
3 Burnley	– –	11 10	– –	1 –	– –	– –	– –	– –	– –	12 10
4 Nottingham Forest	– –	12 7	– –	– –	– –	– –	– –	– –	– –	12 7
5 Leicester City	– –	10 8	– –	1 2	– –	– –	– –	– –	– –	11 10
6 Stoke City	– –	8 4	– –	3 2	– –	– –	– –	– –	– –	11 6
7 Sheffield United	– –	11 3	– –	– –	– –	– –	– –	– –	– –	11 3
8 West Bromwich Albion	– –	10 6	– –	– –	– –	– –	– –	– –	– –	10 6
9 Aston Villa	– –	9 5	– –	1 –	– –	– –	– –	– –	– –	10 5
10 Arsenal	– –	10 4	– –	– –	– –	– –	– –	– –	– –	10 4
11 Chelsea	– –	9 3	– –	1 –	– –	– –	– –	– –	– –	10 3
12 West Ham United	– –	8(1) 3	– –	1 –	– –	– –	– –	– –	– –	9(1) 3
13 Blackpool	– –	8 6	– –	– –	1 1	– –	– –	– –	– –	9 7
14 Sheffield Wednesday	– –	7 6	– –	2 –	– –	– –	– –	– –	– –	9 6
15 Sunderland	– –	5 6	– –	3 1	– –	– –	– –	– –	– –	8 7
16 Wolverhampton W.	– –	6 5	– –	2 2	– –	– –	– –	– –	– –	8 7
17 Blackburn Rovers	– –	8 6	– –	– –	– –	– –	– –	– –	– –	8 6
18 Liverpool	– –	7 2	– –	– –	– –	– –	– –	1 1	– –	8 3
19 Leeds United	– –	6 2	– –	2 –	– –	– –	– –	– –	– –	8 2
20 Fulham	– –	7 9	– –	– –	– –	– –	– –	– –	– –	7 9
21 Bolton Wanderers	– –	5 5	– –	1 1	– –	– –	– –	– –	– –	6 6
22 Birmingham City	– –	6 2	– –	– –	– –	– –	– –	– –	– –	6 2
23 Manchester City	– –	6 1	– –	– –	– –	– –	– –	– –	– –	6 1
24 Ferencvaros	– –	– –	– –	– –	– –	– –	– –	3 2	– –	3 2
25 Newcastle United	– –	3 2	– –	– –	– –	– –	– –	– –	– –	3 2
26 Preston North End	– –	– –	– –	3 2	– –	– –	– –	– –	– –	3 2
27 Ipswich Town	– –	3 1	– –	– –	– –	– –	– –	– –	– –	3 1
28 Southampton	– –	1 –	– –	2 1	– –	– –	– –	– –	– –	3 1
29 ASK Vorwaerts	– –	– –	– –	– –	– –	2 3	– –	– –	– –	2 3
30 Benfica	– –	– –	– –	– –	– –	2 1	– –	– –	– –	2 1
31 Borussia Dortmund	– –	– –	– –	– –	– –	– –	2 1	– –	– –	2 1
32 Djurgardens	– –	– –	– –	– –	– –	– –	– –	2 1	– –	2 1
33 Strasbourg	– –	– –	– –	– –	– –	– –	– –	2 1	– –	2 1
34 Willem II	– –	– –	– –	– –	– –	– –	2 1	– –	– –	2 1
35 Coventry City	– –	1 –	– –	1 –	– –	– –	– –	– –	– –	2 –
36 Leyton Orient	– –	2 –	– –	– –	– –	– –	– –	– –	– –	2 –
37 Northampton Town	– –	2 –	– –	– –	– –	– –	– –	– –	– –	2 –
38 Partizan Belgrade	– –	– –	– –	– –	– –	2 –	– –	– –	– –	2 –
39 Rotherham United	– –	– –	– –	2 –	– –	– –	– –	– –	– –	2 –
40 Sporting Lisbon	– –	– –	– –	– –	– –	– –	2 –	– –	– –	2 –
41 Barnsley	– –	– –	– –	1 1	– –	– –	– –	– –	– –	1 1
42 Bristol Rovers	– –	– –	– –	1 1	– –	– –	– –	– –	– –	1 1
43 Derby County	– –	– –	– –	1 1	– –	– –	– –	– –	– –	1 1
44 HJK Helsinki	– –	– –	– –	– –	– –	1 1	– –	– –	– –	1 1
45 Chester City	– –	– –	– –	1 –	– –	– –	– –	– –	– –	1 –
46 Gornik Zabrze	– –	– –	– –	– –	– –	1 –	– –	– –	– –	1 –
47 Huddersfield Town	– –	– –	– –	1 –	– –	– –	– –	– –	– –	1 –
48 Norwich City	– –	– –	– –	1 –	– –	– –	– –	– –	– –	1 –

TOMMY HERON

DEBUT (Full Appearance)

Saturday 05/04/1958
Football League Division 1
at Old Trafford

Manchester United 0 Preston North End 0

CLUB CAREER RECORD	Apps	Subs	Goals
Premiership	0		0
League Division 1	3		0
League Division 2	0		0
FA Cup	0		0
League Cup	0		0
European Cup / Champions League	0		0
European Cup-Winners' Cup	0		0
UEFA Cup / Inter-Cities' Fairs Cup	0		0
Other Matches	0		0
OVERALL TOTAL	**3**		**0**

Opponents	PREM A S G	FLD 1 A S G	FLD 2 A S G	FAC A S G	LC A S G	EC/CL A S G	ECWC A S G	UEFA A S G	OTHER A S G	TOTAL A S G
1 Arsenal	– –	1 –	– –	– –	– –	– –	– –	– –	– –	1 –
2 Preston North End	– –	1 –	– –	– –	– –	– –	– –	– –	– –	1 –
3 Sheffield Wednesday	– –	1 –	– –	– –	– –	– –	– –	– –	– –	1 –

HERBERT HEYWOOD

DEBUT (Full Appearance)

Saturday 06/05/1933
Football League Division 2
at Old Trafford

Manchester United 1 Swansea City 1

CLUB CAREER RECORD	Apps	Subs	Goals
Premiership	0		0
League Division 1	0		0
League Division 2	4		2
FA Cup	0		0
League Cup	0		0
European Cup / Champions League	0		0
European Cup-Winners' Cup	0		0
UEFA Cup / Inter-Cities' Fairs Cup	0		0
Other Matches	0		0
OVERALL TOTAL	**4**		**2**

Opponents	PREM A S G	FLD 1 A S G	FLD 2 A S G	FAC A S G	LC A S G	EC/CL A S G	ECWC A S G	UEFA A S G	OTHER A S G	TOTAL A S G
1 Hull City	– – –	– – –	1 – 2	– – –	– – –	– – –	– – –	– – –	– – –	1 – 2
2 Fulham	– – –	– – –	1 – –	– – –	– – –	– – –	– – –	– – –	– – –	1 – –
3 Southampton	– – –	– – –	1 – –	– – –	– – –	– – –	– – –	– – –	– – –	1 – –
4 Swansea City	– – –	– – –	1 – –	– – –	– – –	– – –	– – –	– – –	– – –	1 – –

DANNY HIGGINBOTHAM

DEBUT (Substitute Appearance)

Sunday 10/05/1998
FA Premiership
at Oakwell

Barnsley 0 Manchester United 2

CLUB CAREER RECORD	Apps	Subs	Goals
Premiership	2	(2)	0
League Division 1	0		0
League Division 2	0		0
FA Cup	0		0
League Cup	1		0
European Cup / Champions League	0	(1)	0
European Cup-Winners' Cup	0		0
UEFA Cup / Inter-Cities' Fairs Cup	0		0
Other Matches	1		0
OVERALL TOTAL	**4**	**(3)**	**0**

Opponents	PREM A S G	FLD 1 A S G	FLD 2 A S G	FAC A S G	LC A S G	EC/CL A S G	ECWC A S G	UEFA A S G	OTHER A S G	TOTAL A S G
1 Aston Villa	1 – –	– – –	– – –	– – –	1 – –	– – –	– – –	– – –	– – –	2 – –
2 Leicester City	1 – –	– – –	– – –	– – –	– – –	– – –	– – –	– – –	– – –	1 – –
3 South Melbourne	– – –	– – –	– – –	– – –	– – –	– – –	– – –	– – –	1 – –	1 – –
4 Barnsley	– (1) –	– – –	– – –	– – –	– – –	– – –	– – –	– – –	– – –	– (1) –
5 Sturm Graz	– – –	– – –	– – –	– – –	– – –	– (1) –	– – –	– – –	– – –	– (1) –
6 Watford	– (1) –	– – –	– – –	– – –	– – –	– – –	– – –	– – –	– – –	– (1) –

ALEXANDER HIGGINS

DEBUT (Full Appearance)

Saturday 12/10/1901
Football League Division 2
at Peel Croft

Burton United 0 Newton Heath 0

CLUB CAREER RECORD	Apps	Subs	Goals
Premiership	0		0
League Division 1	0		0
League Division 2	10		0
FA Cup	0		0
League Cup	0		0
European Cup / Champions League	0		0
European Cup-Winners' Cup	0		0
UEFA Cup / Inter-Cities' Fairs Cup	0		0
Other Matches	0		0
OVERALL TOTAL	**10**		**0**

Opponents	PREM A S G	FLD 1 A S G	FLD 2 A S G	FAC A S G	LC A S G	EC/CL A S G	ECWC A S G	UEFA A S G	OTHER A S G	TOTAL A S G
1 Arsenal	– – –	– – –	1 – –	– – –	– – –	– – –	– – –	– – –	– – –	1 – –
2 Barnsley	– – –	– – –	1 – –	– – –	– – –	– – –	– – –	– – –	– – –	1 – –
3 Blackpool	– – –	– – –	1 – –	– – –	– – –	– – –	– – –	– – –	– – –	1 – –
4 Bristol City	– – –	– – –	1 – –	– – –	– – –	– – –	– – –	– – –	– – –	1 – –
5 Burton United	– – –	– – –	1 – –	– – –	– – –	– – –	– – –	– – –	– – –	1 – –
6 Doncaster Rovers	– – –	– – –	1 – –	– – –	– – –	– – –	– – –	– – –	– – –	1 – –
7 Glossop	– – –	– – –	1 – –	– – –	– – –	– – –	– – –	– – –	– – –	1 – –
8 Leicester City	– – –	– – –	1 – –	– – –	– – –	– – –	– – –	– – –	– – –	1 – –
9 Port Vale	– – –	– – –	1 – –	– – –	– – –	– – –	– – –	– – –	– – –	1 – –
10 West Bromwich Albion	– – –	– – –	1 – –	– – –	– – –	– – –	– – –	– – –	– – –	1 – –

MARK HIGGINS

DEBUT (Full Appearance)

Thursday 09/01/1986
FA Cup 3rd Round
at Old Trafford

Manchester United 2 Rochdale 0

CLUB CAREER RECORD	Apps	Subs	Goals
Premiership	0		0
League Division 1	6		0
League Division 2	0		0
FA Cup	2		0
League Cup	0		0
European Cup / Champions League	0		0
European Cup-Winners' Cup	0		0
UEFA Cup / Inter-Cities' Fairs Cup	0		0
Other Matches	0		0
OVERALL TOTAL	**8**		**0**

	Opponents	PREM A S G	FLD 1 A S G	FLD 2 A S G	FAC A S G	LC A S G	EC/CL A S G	ECWC A S G	UEFA A S G	OTHER A S G	TOTAL A S G
1	Birmingham City	– –	1 –	– –	– –	– –	– –	– –	– –	– –	1 –
2	Chelsea	– –	1 –	– –	– –	– –	– –	– –	– –	– –	1 –
3	Coventry City	– –	1 –	– –	– –	– –	– –	– –	– –	– –	1 –
4	Everton	– –	1 –	– –	– –	– –	– –	– –	– –	– –	1 –
5	Manchester City	– –	1 –	– –	– –	– –	– –	– –	– –	– –	1 –
6	Rochdale	– –	– –	– –	1 –	– –	– –	– –	– –	– –	1 –
7	Sheffield Wednesday	– –	1 –	– –	– –	– –	– –	– –	– –	– –	1 –
8	West Ham United	– –	– –	– –	1 –	– –	– –	– –	– –	– –	1 –

JAMES HIGSON

DEBUT (Full Appearance)

Saturday 01/03/1902
Football League Division 2
at Bank Street

Newton Heath 0 Lincoln City 0

CLUB CAREER RECORD	Apps	Subs	Goals
Premiership	0		0
League Division 1	0		0
League Division 2	5		1
FA Cup	0		0
League Cup	0		0
European Cup / Champions League	0		0
European Cup-Winners' Cup	0		0
UEFA Cup / Inter-Cities' Fairs Cup	0		0
Other Matches	0		0
OVERALL TOTAL	**5**		**1**

	Opponents	PREM A S G	FLD 1 A S G	FLD 2 A S G	FAC A S G	LC A S G	EC/CL A S G	ECWC A S G	UEFA A S G	OTHER A S G	TOTAL A S G
1	Barnsley	– –	– –	1 1	– –	– –	– –	– –	– –	– –	1 1
2	Arsenal	– –	– –	1 –	– –	– –	– –	– –	– –	– –	1 –
3	Lincoln City	– –	– –	1 –	– –	– –	– –	– –	– –	– –	1 –
4	Middlesbrough	– –	– –	1 –	– –	– –	– –	– –	– –	– –	1 –
5	West Bromwich Albion	– –	– –	1 –	– –	– –	– –	– –	– –	– –	1 –

CLARENCE HILDITCH

DEBUT (Full Appearance)

Saturday 30/08/1919
Football League Division 1
at Baseball Ground

Derby County 1 Manchester United 1

CLUB CAREER RECORD	Apps	Subs	Goals
Premiership	0		0
League Division 1	207		6
League Division 2	94		1
FA Cup	21		0
League Cup	0		0
European Cup / Champions League	0		0
European Cup-Winners' Cup	0		0
UEFA Cup / Inter-Cities' Fairs Cup	0		0
Other Matches	0		0
OVERALL TOTAL	**322**		**7**

	Opponents	PREM A S G	FLD 1 A S G	FLD 2 A S G	FAC A S G	LC A S G	EC/CL A S G	ECWC A S G	UEFA A S G	OTHER A S G	TOTAL A S G
1	Newcastle United	– –	12 1	– –	– –	– –	– –	– –	– –	– –	12 1
2	Sunderland	– –	12 1	– –	– –	– –	– –	– –	– –	– –	12 1
3	Sheffield United	– –	12 –	– –	– –	– –	– –	– –	– –	– –	12 –
4	Liverpool	– –	11 –	– –	– –	– –	– –	– –	– –	– –	11 –
5	Burnley	– –	9 1	1 –	– –	– –	– –	– –	– –	– –	10 1
6	Huddersfield Town	– –	9 1	– –	1 –	– –	– –	– –	– –	– –	10 1
7	Arsenal	– –	10 –	– –	– –	– –	– –	– –	– –	– –	10 –
8	Derby County	– –	9 –	1 –	– –	– –	– –	– –	– –	– –	10 –
9	Everton	– –	10 –	– –	– –	– –	– –	– –	– –	– –	10 –
10	Leeds United	– –	5 –	5 –	– –	– –	– –	– –	– –	– –	10 –
11	Sheffield Wednesday	– –	5 –	4 –	1 –	– –	– –	– –	– –	– –	10 –
12	Blackburn Rovers	– –	9 –	– –	– –	– –	– –	– –	– –	– –	9 –
13	Bolton Wanderers	– –	9 –	– –	– –	– –	– –	– –	– –	– –	9 –
14	Bradford City	– –	4 –	3 –	2 –	– –	– –	– –	– –	– –	9 –
15	Leicester City	– –	4 –	5 –	– –	– –	– –	– –	– –	– –	9 –
16	Manchester City	– –	9 –	– –	– –	– –	– –	– –	– –	– –	9 –
17	Bury	– –	3 –	5 –	– –	– –	– –	– –	– –	– –	8 –
18	Middlesbrough	– –	8 –	– –	– –	– –	– –	– –	– –	– –	8 –
19	Oldham Athletic	– –	6 –	2 –	– –	– –	– –	– –	– –	– –	8 –
20	Tottenham Hotspur	– –	4 –	1 –	3 –	– –	– –	– –	– –	– –	8 –

continued../

CLARENCE HILDITCH (continued)

Opponents	PREM			FLD 1			FLD 2			FAC			LC			EC/CL			ECWC			UEFA			OTHER			TOTAL		
	A	S	G	A	S	G	A	S	G	A	S	G	A	S	G	A	S	G	A	S	G	A	S	G	A	S	G	A	S	G
21 Aston Villa	-	-	-	6	-	2	-	-	-	1	-	-	-	-	-	-	-	-	-	-	-	-	-	-	-	-	-	7	-	2
22 Chelsea	-	-	-	7	-	-	-	-	-	-	-	-	-	-	-	-	-	-	-	-	-	-	-	-	-	-	-	7	-	-
23 Port Vale	-	-	-	-	-	-	5	-	-	2	-	-	-	-	-	-	-	-	-	-	-	-	-	-	-	-	-	7	-	-
24 Preston North End	-	-	-	6	-	-	1	-	-	-	-	-	-	-	-	-	-	-	-	-	-	-	-	-	-	-	-	7	-	-
25 Stoke City	-	-	-	-	-	-	4	-	-	3	-	-	-	-	-	-	-	-	-	-	-	-	-	-	-	-	-	7	-	-
26 Birmingham City	-	-	-	6	-	-	-	-	-	-	-	-	-	-	-	-	-	-	-	-	-	-	-	-	-	-	-	6	-	-
27 Cardiff City	-	-	-	5	-	-	-	-	-	1	-	-	-	-	-	-	-	-	-	-	-	-	-	-	-	-	-	6	-	-
28 Barnsley	-	-	-	-	-	-	5	-	-	-	-	-	-	-	-	-	-	-	-	-	-	-	-	-	-	-	-	5	-	-
29 Blackpool	-	-	-	1	-	-	4	-	-	-	-	-	-	-	-	-	-	-	-	-	-	-	-	-	-	-	-	5	-	-
30 Stockport County	-	-	-	-	-	-	5	-	-	-	-	-	-	-	-	-	-	-	-	-	-	-	-	-	-	-	-	5	-	-
31 West Bromwich Albion	-	-	-	5	-	-	-	-	-	-	-	-	-	-	-	-	-	-	-	-	-	-	-	-	-	-	-	5	-	-
32 West Ham United	-	-	-	5	-	-	-	-	-	-	-	-	-	-	-	-	-	-	-	-	-	-	-	-	-	-	-	5	-	-
33 South Shields	-	-	-	-	-	-	-	-	-	4	-	1	-	-	-	-	-	-	-	-	-	-	-	-	-	-	-	4	-	1
34 Coventry City	-	-	-	-	-	-	-	-	-	4	-	-	-	-	-	-	-	-	-	-	-	-	-	-	-	-	-	4	-	-
35 Crystal Palace	-	-	-	-	-	-	-	-	-	4	-	-	-	-	-	-	-	-	-	-	-	-	-	-	-	-	-	4	-	-
36 Fulham	-	-	-	-	-	-	-	-	-	4	-	-	-	-	-	-	-	-	-	-	-	-	-	-	-	-	-	4	-	-
37 Grimsby Town	-	-	-	3	-	-	-	-	-	1	-	-	-	-	-	-	-	-	-	-	-	-	-	-	-	-	-	4	-	-
38 Leyton Orient	-	-	-	-	-	-	-	-	-	4	-	-	-	-	-	-	-	-	-	-	-	-	-	-	-	-	-	4	-	-
39 Southampton	-	-	-	-	-	-	-	-	-	4	-	-	-	-	-	-	-	-	-	-	-	-	-	-	-	-	-	4	-	-
40 Wolverhampton W.	-	-	-	-	-	-	-	-	-	4	-	-	-	-	-	-	-	-	-	-	-	-	-	-	-	-	-	4	-	-
41 Bristol City	-	-	-	-	-	-	-	-	-	3	-	-	-	-	-	-	-	-	-	-	-	-	-	-	-	-	-	3	-	-
42 Hull City	-	-	-	-	-	-	-	-	-	3	-	-	-	-	-	-	-	-	-	-	-	-	-	-	-	-	-	3	-	-
43 Portsmouth	-	-	-	3	-	-	-	-	-	-	-	-	-	-	-	-	-	-	-	-	-	-	-	-	-	-	-	3	-	-
44 Reading	-	-	-	-	-	-	-	-	-	3	-	-	-	-	-	-	-	-	-	-	-	-	-	-	-	-	-	3	-	-
45 Nelson	-	-	-	-	-	-	2	-	-	-	-	-	-	-	-	-	-	-	-	-	-	-	-	-	-	-	-	2	-	-
46 Plymouth Argyle	-	-	-	-	-	-	-	-	-	2	-	-	-	-	-	-	-	-	-	-	-	-	-	-	-	-	-	2	-	-
47 Rotherham United	-	-	-	-	-	-	2	-	-	-	-	-	-	-	-	-	-	-	-	-	-	-	-	-	-	-	-	2	-	-
48 Bradford Park Avenue	-	-	-	-	-	-	1	-	-	-	-	-	-	-	-	-	-	-	-	-	-	-	-	-	-	-	-	1	-	-
49 Chesterfield	-	-	-	-	-	-	1	-	-	-	-	-	-	-	-	-	-	-	-	-	-	-	-	-	-	-	-	1	-	-
50 Millwall	-	-	-	-	-	-	-	-	-	1	-	-	-	-	-	-	-	-	-	-	-	-	-	-	-	-	-	1	-	-
51 Nottingham Forest	-	-	-	-	-	-	1	-	-	-	-	-	-	-	-	-	-	-	-	-	-	-	-	-	-	-	-	1	-	-
52 Notts County	-	-	-	-	-	-	1	-	-	-	-	-	-	-	-	-	-	-	-	-	-	-	-	-	-	-	-	1	-	-
53 Swindon Town	-	-	-	-	-	-	-	-	-	1	-	-	-	-	-	-	-	-	-	-	-	-	-	-	-	-	-	1	-	-

GORDON HILL

DEBUT (Full Appearance)

Saturday 15/11/1975
Football League Division 1
at Old Trafford

Manchester United 2 Aston Villa 0

CLUB CAREER RECORD	Apps	Subs	Goals
Premiership	0		0
League Division 1	100	(1)	39
League Division 2	0		0
FA Cup	17		6
League Cup	7		4
European Cup / Champions League	0		0
European Cup-Winners' Cup	4		1
UEFA Cup / Inter-Cities' Fairs Cup	4		1
Other Matches	1		0
OVERALL TOTAL	133	(1)	51

Opponents	PREM			FLD 1			FLD 2			FAC			LC			EC/CL			ECWC			UEFA			OTHER			TOTAL		
	A	S	G	A	S	G	A	S	G	A	S	G	A	S	G	A	S	G	A	S	G	A	S	G	A	S	G	A	S	G
1 Everton	-	-	-	6	-	5	-	-	-	-	-	-	1	-	-	-	-	-	-	-	-	-	-	-	-	-	-	7	-	5
2 Newcastle United	-	-	-	6	-	1	-	-	-	-	-	-	1	-	3	-	-	-	-	-	-	-	-	-	-	-	-	7	-	4
3 Liverpool	-	-	-	5	-	-	-	-	-	1	-	-	-	-	-	-	-	-	-	-	-	-	-	-	1	-	-	7	-	-
4 Arsenal	-	-	-	5	-	2	-	-	-	-	-	-	1	-	-	-	-	-	-	-	-	-	-	-	-	-	-	6	-	2
5 West Bromwich Albion	-	-	-	4	-	1	-	-	-	2	-	1	-	-	-	-	-	-	-	-	-	-	-	-	-	-	-	6	-	2
6 Aston Villa	-	-	-	5	-	1	-	-	-	1	-	-	-	-	-	-	-	-	-	-	-	-	-	-	-	-	-	6	-	1
7 Leeds United	-	-	-	5	-	1	-	-	-	1	-	-	-	-	-	-	-	-	-	-	-	-	-	-	-	-	-	6	-	1
8 Middlesbrough	-	-	-	6	-	1	-	-	-	-	-	-	-	-	-	-	-	-	-	-	-	-	-	-	-	-	-	6	-	1
9 Leicester City	-	-	-	4	(1)	2	-	-	-	1	-	-	-	-	-	-	-	-	-	-	-	-	-	-	-	-	-	5	(1)	2
10 Derby County	-	-	-	4	-	2	-	-	-	-	-	-	1	-	2	-	-	-	-	-	-	-	-	-	-	-	-	5	-	4
11 Manchester City	-	-	-	5	-	4	-	-	-	-	-	-	-	-	-	-	-	-	-	-	-	-	-	-	-	-	-	5	-	4
12 Coventry City	-	-	-	5	-	2	-	-	-	-	-	-	-	-	-	-	-	-	-	-	-	-	-	-	-	-	-	5	-	2
13 Sunderland	-	-	-	2	-	2	-	-	-	-	-	-	3	-	-	-	-	-	-	-	-	-	-	-	-	-	-	5	-	2
14 Birmingham City	-	-	-	5	-	1	-	-	-	-	-	-	-	-	-	-	-	-	-	-	-	-	-	-	-	-	-	5	-	1
15 Ipswich Town	-	-	-	5	-	-	-	-	-	-	-	-	-	-	-	-	-	-	-	-	-	-	-	-	-	-	-	5	-	-
16 Queens Park Rangers	-	-	-	3	-	3	-	-	-	1	-	-	-	-	-	-	-	-	-	-	-	-	-	-	-	-	-	4	-	3
17 Norwich City	-	-	-	4	-	2	-	-	-	-	-	-	-	-	-	-	-	-	-	-	-	-	-	-	-	-	-	4	-	2
18 West Ham United	-	-	-	4	-	1	-	-	-	-	-	-	-	-	-	-	-	-	-	-	-	-	-	-	-	-	-	4	-	1
19 Wolverhampton W.	-	-	-	2	-	1	-	-	-	2	-	-	-	-	-	-	-	-	-	-	-	-	-	-	-	-	-	4	-	1
20 Stoke City	-	-	-	3	-	2	-	-	-	-	-	-	-	-	-	-	-	-	-	-	-	-	-	-	-	-	-	3	-	2
21 Tottenham Hotspur	-	-	-	3	-	2	-	-	-	-	-	-	-	-	-	-	-	-	-	-	-	-	-	-	-	-	-	3	-	2
22 Southampton	-	-	-	-	-	-	-	-	-	3	-	1	-	-	-	-	-	-	-	-	-	-	-	-	-	-	-	3	-	1
23 Bristol City	-	-	-	2	-	1	-	-	-	-	-	-	-	-	-	-	-	-	-	-	-	-	-	-	-	-	-	2	-	1
24 Chelsea	-	-	-	2	-	1	-	-	-	-	-	-	-	-	-	-	-	-	-	-	-	-	-	-	-	-	-	2	-	1
25 Juventus	-	-	-	-	-	-	-	-	-	-	-	-	-	-	-	-	-	-	-	-	-	2	-	1	-	-	-	2	-	1
26 St Etienne	-	-	-	-	-	-	-	-	-	-	-	-	-	-	-	-	-	-	2	-	1	-	-	-	-	-	-	2	-	1
27 Ajax	-	-	-	-	-	-	-	-	-	-	-	-	-	-	-	-	-	-	-	-	-	2	-	-	-	-	-	2	-	-
28 Burnley	-	-	-	2	-	-	-	-	-	-	-	-	-	-	-	-	-	-	-	-	-	-	-	-	-	-	-	2	-	-

continued../

GORDON HILL (continued)

Opponents	PREM A S G	FLD 1 A S G	FLD 2 A S G	FAC A S G	LC A S G	EC/CL A S G	ECWC A S G	UEFA A S G	OTHER A S G	TOTAL A S G
29 Nottingham Forest	– –	2 –	– –	– –	– –	– –	– –	– –	– –	2 –
30 Porto	– –	– –	– –	– –	– –	– –	2 –	– –	– –	2 –
31 Peterborough United	– –	– –	– –	1 1	– –	– –	– –	– –	– –	1 1
32 Sheffield United	– –	1 1	– –	– –	– –	– –	– –	– –	– –	1 1
33 Tranmere Rovers	– –	– –	– –	– –	1 1	– –	– –	– –	– –	1 1
34 Walsall	– –	– –	– –	1 1	– –	– –	– –	– –	– –	1 1
35 Carlisle United	– –	– –	– –	1 –	– –	– –	– –	– –	– –	1 –
36 Oxford United	– –	– –	– –	1 –	– –	– –	– –	– –	– –	1 –

CHARLIE HILLAM

DEBUT (Full Appearance)

Saturday 26/08/1933
Football League Division 2
at Home Park

Plymouth Argyle 4 Manchester United 0

CLUB CAREER RECORD	Apps	Subs	Goals
Premiership	0		0
League Division 1	0		0
League Division 2	8		0
FA Cup	0		0
League Cup	0		0
European Cup / Champions League	0		0
European Cup-Winners' Cup	0		0
UEFA Cup / Inter-Cities' Fairs Cup	0		0
Other Matches	0		0
OVERALL TOTAL	**8**		**0**

Opponents	PREM A S G	FLD 1 A S G	FLD 2 A S G	FAC A S G	LC A S G	EC/CL A S G	ECWC A S G	UEFA A S G	OTHER A S G	TOTAL A S G
1 Nottingham Forest	– –	– –	2 –	– –	– –	– –	– –	– –	– –	2 –
2 Bolton Wanderers	– –	– –	1 –	– –	– –	– –	– –	– –	– –	1 –
3 Brentford	– –	– –	1 –	– –	– –	– –	– –	– –	– –	1 –
4 Burnley	– –	– –	1 –	– –	– –	– –	– –	– –	– –	1 –
5 Hull City	– –	– –	1 –	– –	– –	– –	– –	– –	– –	1 –
6 Lincoln City	– –	– –	1 –	– –	– –	– –	– –	– –	– –	1 –
7 Plymouth Argyle	– –	– –	1 –	– –	– –	– –	– –	– –	– –	1 –

ERNIE HINE

DEBUT (Full Appearance)

Saturday 11/02/1933
Football League Division 2
at Deepdale

Preston North End 3 Manchester United 3

CLUB CAREER RECORD	Apps	Subs	Goals
Premiership	0		0
League Division 1	0		0
League Division 2	51		12
FA Cup	2		0
League Cup	0		0
European Cup / Champions League	0		0
European Cup-Winners' Cup	0		0
UEFA Cup / Inter-Cities' Fairs Cup	0		0
Other Matches	0		0
OVERALL TOTAL	**53**		**12**

Opponents	PREM A S G	FLD 1 A S G	FLD 2 A S G	FAC A S G	LC A S G	EC/CL A S G	ECWC A S G	UEFA A S G	OTHER A S G	TOTAL A S G
1 Nottingham Forest	– –	– –	5 2	– –	– –	– –	– –	– –	– –	5 2
2 Port Vale	– –	– –	4 1	– –	– –	– –	– –	– –	– –	4 1
3 Swansea City	– –	– –	3 2	– –	– –	– –	– –	– –	– –	3 2
4 Bradford City	– –	– –	3 1	– –	– –	– –	– –	– –	– –	3 1
5 Bradford Park Avenue	– –	– –	3 1	– –	– –	– –	– –	– –	– –	3 1
6 Brentford	– –	– –	3 1	– –	– –	– –	– –	– –	– –	3 1
7 Millwall	– –	– –	3 –	– –	– –	– –	– –	– –	– –	3 –
8 Notts County	– –	– –	3 –	– –	– –	– –	– –	– –	– –	3 –
9 West Ham United	– –	– –	3 –	– –	– –	– –	– –	– –	– –	3 –
10 Blackpool	– –	– –	2 1	– –	– –	– –	– –	– –	– –	2 1
11 Lincoln City	– –	– –	2 1	– –	– –	– –	– –	– –	– –	2 1
12 Preston North End	– –	– –	2 1	– –	– –	– –	– –	– –	– –	2 1
13 Bolton Wanderers	– –	– –	2 –	– –	– –	– –	– –	– –	– –	2 –
14 Burnley	– –	– –	2 –	– –	– –	– –	– –	– –	– –	2 –
15 Bury	– –	– –	2 –	– –	– –	– –	– –	– –	– –	2 –
16 Fulham	– –	– –	2 –	– –	– –	– –	– –	– –	– –	2 –
17 Oldham Athletic	– –	– –	2 –	– –	– –	– –	– –	– –	– –	2 –
18 Plymouth Argyle	– –	– –	2 –	– –	– –	– –	– –	– –	– –	2 –
19 Portsmouth	– –	– –	– –	2 –	– –	– –	– –	– –	– –	2 –
20 Hull City	– –	– –	1 1	– –	– –	– –	– –	– –	– –	1 1
21 Grimsby Town	– –	– –	1 –	– –	– –	– –	– –	– –	– –	1 –
22 Southampton	– –	– –	1 –	– –	– –	– –	– –	– –	– –	1 –

JAMES HODGE

DEBUT (Full Appearance)

Monday 17/04/1911
Football League Division 1
at Hillsborough

Sheffield Wednesday 0 Manchester United 0

CLUB CAREER RECORD	Apps	Subs	Goals
Premiership	0		0
League Division 1	79		2
League Division 2	0		0
FA Cup	7		0
League Cup	0		0
European Cup / Champions League	0		0
European Cup–Winners' Cup	0		0
UEFA Cup / Inter–Cities' Fairs Cup	0		0
Other Matches	0		0
OVERALL TOTAL	**86**		**2**

Opponents	PREM			FLD 1			FLD 2			FAC			LC			EC/CL			ECWC			UEFA			OTHER			TOTAL		
	A	S	G	A	S	G	A	S	G	A	S	G	A	S	G	A	S	G	A	S	G	A	S	G	A	S	G	A	S	G
1 Middlesbrough	–	–	7	–	–	–	–	–	–	–	–	–	–	–	–	–	–	–	–	–	–	–	–	–	–	–	–	7	–	–
2 Oldham Athletic	–	–	5	–	–	–	2	–	–	–	–	–	–	–	–	–	–	–	–	–	–	–	–	–	–	–	–	7	–	–
3 Sheffield Wednesday	–	–	6	–	–	–	1	–	–	–	–	–	–	–	–	–	–	–	–	–	–	–	–	–	–	–	–	7	–	–
4 Sheffield United	–	–	6	–	–	–	–	–	–	–	–	–	–	–	–	–	–	–	–	–	–	–	–	–	–	–	–	6	–	–
5 Tottenham Hotspur	–	–	6	–	–	–	–	–	–	–	–	–	–	–	–	–	–	–	–	–	–	–	–	–	–	–	–	6	–	–
6 Manchester City	–	–	4	1	–	–	–	–	–	–	–	–	–	–	–	–	–	–	–	–	–	–	–	–	–	–	–	4	–	1
7 Aston Villa	–	–	4	–	–	–	–	–	–	–	–	–	–	–	–	–	–	–	–	–	–	–	–	–	–	–	–	4	–	–
8 Derby County	–	–	4	–	–	–	–	–	–	–	–	–	–	–	–	–	–	–	–	–	–	–	–	–	–	–	–	4	–	–
9 Newcastle United	–	–	4	–	–	–	–	–	–	–	–	–	–	–	–	–	–	–	–	–	–	–	–	–	–	–	–	4	–	–
10 Preston North End	–	–	4	–	–	–	–	–	–	–	–	–	–	–	–	–	–	–	–	–	–	–	–	–	–	–	–	4	–	–
11 Sunderland	–	–	4	–	–	–	–	–	–	–	–	–	–	–	–	–	–	–	–	–	–	–	–	–	–	–	–	4	–	–
12 Blackburn Rovers	–	–	3	–	–	–	–	–	–	–	–	–	–	–	–	–	–	–	–	–	–	–	–	–	–	–	–	3	–	–
13 Bolton Wanderers	–	–	3	–	–	–	–	–	–	–	–	–	–	–	–	–	–	–	–	–	–	–	–	–	–	–	–	3	–	–
14 Bradford City	–	–	3	–	–	–	–	–	–	–	–	–	–	–	–	–	–	–	–	–	–	–	–	–	–	–	–	3	–	–
15 Everton	–	–	3	–	–	–	–	–	–	–	–	–	–	–	–	–	–	–	–	–	–	–	–	–	–	–	–	3	–	–
16 Liverpool	–	–	3	–	–	–	–	–	–	–	–	–	–	–	–	–	–	–	–	–	–	–	–	–	–	–	–	3	–	–
17 Burnley	–	–	2	1	–	–	–	–	–	–	–	–	–	–	–	–	–	–	–	–	–	–	–	–	–	–	–	2	–	1
18 Chelsea	–	–	2	–	–	–	–	–	–	–	–	–	–	–	–	–	–	–	–	–	–	–	–	–	–	–	–	2	–	–
19 Coventry City	–	–	–	–	–	–	2	–	–	–	–	–	–	–	–	–	–	–	–	–	–	–	–	–	–	–	–	2	–	–
20 Notts County	–	–	2	–	–	–	–	–	–	–	–	–	–	–	–	–	–	–	–	–	–	–	–	–	–	–	–	2	–	–
21 West Bromwich Albion	–	–	2	–	–	–	–	–	–	–	–	–	–	–	–	–	–	–	–	–	–	–	–	–	–	–	–	2	–	–
22 Arsenal	–	–	1	–	–	–	–	–	–	–	–	–	–	–	–	–	–	–	–	–	–	–	–	–	–	–	–	1	–	–
23 Bury	–	–	1	–	–	–	–	–	–	–	–	–	–	–	–	–	–	–	–	–	–	–	–	–	–	–	–	1	–	–
24 Plymouth Argyle	–	–	–	–	–	–	1	–	–	–	–	–	–	–	–	–	–	–	–	–	–	–	–	–	–	–	–	1	–	–
25 Swindon Town	–	–	–	–	–	–	1	–	–	–	–	–	–	–	–	–	–	–	–	–	–	–	–	–	–	–	–	1	–	–

JOHN HODGE

DEBUT (Full Appearance)

Saturday 27/12/1913
Football League Division 1
at Old Trafford

Manchester United 2 Sheffield Wednesday 1

CLUB CAREER RECORD	Apps	Subs	Goals
Premiership	0		0
League Division 1	30		0
League Division 2	0		0
FA Cup	0		0
League Cup	0		0
European Cup / Champions League	0		0
European Cup–Winners' Cup	0		0
UEFA Cup / Inter–Cities' Fairs Cup	0		0
Other Matches	0		0
OVERALL TOTAL	**30**		**0**

Opponents	PREM			FLD 1			FLD 2			FAC			LC			EC/CL			ECWC			UEFA			OTHER			TOTAL		
	A	S	G	A	S	G	A	S	G	A	S	G	A	S	G	A	S	G	A	S	G	A	S	G	A	S	G	A	S	G
1 Newcastle United	–	–	3	–	–	–	–	–	–	–	–	–	–	–	–	–	–	–	–	–	–	–	–	–	–	–	–	3	–	–
2 Aston Villa	–	–	2	–	–	–	–	–	–	–	–	–	–	–	–	–	–	–	–	–	–	–	–	–	–	–	–	2	–	–
3 Blackburn Rovers	–	–	2	–	–	–	–	–	–	–	–	–	–	–	–	–	–	–	–	–	–	–	–	–	–	–	–	2	–	–
4 Bolton Wanderers	–	–	2	–	–	–	–	–	–	–	–	–	–	–	–	–	–	–	–	–	–	–	–	–	–	–	–	2	–	–
5 Chelsea	–	–	2	–	–	–	–	–	–	–	–	–	–	–	–	–	–	–	–	–	–	–	–	–	–	–	–	2	–	–
6 Liverpool	–	–	2	–	–	–	–	–	–	–	–	–	–	–	–	–	–	–	–	–	–	–	–	–	–	–	–	2	–	–
7 Manchester City	–	–	2	–	–	–	–	–	–	–	–	–	–	–	–	–	–	–	–	–	–	–	–	–	–	–	–	2	–	–
8 Notts County	–	–	2	–	–	–	–	–	–	–	–	–	–	–	–	–	–	–	–	–	–	–	–	–	–	–	–	2	–	–
9 Sheffield Wednesday	–	–	2	–	–	–	–	–	–	–	–	–	–	–	–	–	–	–	–	–	–	–	–	–	–	–	–	2	–	–
10 Bradford City	–	–	1	–	–	–	–	–	–	–	–	–	–	–	–	–	–	–	–	–	–	–	–	–	–	–	–	1	–	–
11 Bradford Park Avenue	–	–	1	–	–	–	–	–	–	–	–	–	–	–	–	–	–	–	–	–	–	–	–	–	–	–	–	1	–	–
12 Burnley	–	–	1	–	–	–	–	–	–	–	–	–	–	–	–	–	–	–	–	–	–	–	–	–	–	–	–	1	–	–
13 Derby County	–	–	1	–	–	–	–	–	–	–	–	–	–	–	–	–	–	–	–	–	–	–	–	–	–	–	–	1	–	–
14 Everton	–	–	1	–	–	–	–	–	–	–	–	–	–	–	–	–	–	–	–	–	–	–	–	–	–	–	–	1	–	–
15 Middlesbrough	–	–	1	–	–	–	–	–	–	–	–	–	–	–	–	–	–	–	–	–	–	–	–	–	–	–	–	1	–	–
16 Oldham Athletic	–	–	1	–	–	–	–	–	–	–	–	–	–	–	–	–	–	–	–	–	–	–	–	–	–	–	–	1	–	–
17 Preston North End	–	–	1	–	–	–	–	–	–	–	–	–	–	–	–	–	–	–	–	–	–	–	–	–	–	–	–	1	–	–
18 Sheffield United	–	–	1	–	–	–	–	–	–	–	–	–	–	–	–	–	–	–	–	–	–	–	–	–	–	–	–	1	–	–
19 Sunderland	–	–	1	–	–	–	–	–	–	–	–	–	–	–	–	–	–	–	–	–	–	–	–	–	–	–	–	1	–	–
20 West Bromwich Albion	–	–	1	–	–	–	–	–	–	–	–	–	–	–	–	–	–	–	–	–	–	–	–	–	–	–	–	1	–	–

FRANK HODGES

DEBUT (Full Appearance)

Saturday 18/10/1919
Football League Division 1
at Old Trafford

Manchester United 1 Manchester City 0

CLUB CAREER RECORD	Apps	Subs	Goals
Premiership	0		0
League Division 1	20		4
League Division 2	0		0
FA Cup	0		0
League Cup	0		0
European Cup / Champions League	0		0
European Cup-Winners' Cup	0		0
UEFA Cup / Inter-Cities' Fairs Cup	0		0
Other Matches	0		0
OVERALL TOTAL	**20**		**4**

Opponents	PREM			FLD 1			FLD 2			FAC			LC			EC/CL			ECWC			UEFA			OTHER			TOTAL		
	A	S	G	A	S	G	A	S	G	A	S	G	A	S	G	A	S	G	A	S	G	A	S	G	A	S	G	A	S	G
1 Newcastle United	–	–		2		1	–			–			–			–			–			–			–		–	2		1
2 Sheffield United	–	–		2		1	–			–			–			–			–			–			–			2		1
3 Arsenal	–	–		2			–			–			–			–			–			–			–			2		–
4 Burnley	–	–		2			–			–			–			–			–			–			–			2		–
5 Chelsea	–	–		2			–			–			–			–			–			–			–			2		–
6 Liverpool	–	–		2		–				–			–			–			–			–			–			2		–
7 Oldham Athletic	–	–		1		1	–			–			–			–			–			–			–			1		1
8 Sunderland	–	–		1		1	–			–			–			–			–			–			–			1		1
9 Aston Villa	–	–		1			–			–			–			–			–			–			–			1		–
10 Blackburn Rovers	–	–		1			–			–			–			–			–			–			–			1		–
11 Bradford Park Avenue	–	–		1			–			–			–			–			–			–			–			1		–
12 Manchester City	–	–		1			–			–			–			–			–			–			–			1		–
13 Preston North End	–	–		1			–			–			–			–			–			–			–			1		–
14 West Bromwich Albion	–	–		1			–			–			–			–			–			–			–			1		–

LESLIE HOFTON

DEBUT (Full Appearance)

Saturday 18/02/1911
Football League Division 1
at St James' Park

Newcastle United 0 Manchester United 1

CLUB CAREER RECORD	Apps	Subs	Goals
Premiership	0		0
League Division 1	17		0
League Division 2	0		0
FA Cup	1		0
League Cup	0		0
European Cup / Champions League	0		0
European Cup-Winners' Cup	0		0
UEFA Cup / Inter-Cities' Fairs Cup	0		0
Other Matches	1		0
OVERALL TOTAL	**19**		**0**

Opponents	PREM			FLD 1			FLD 2			FAC			LC			EC/CL			ECWC			UEFA			OTHER			TOTAL		
	A	S	G	A	S	G	A	S	G	A	S	G	A	S	G	A	S	G	A	S	G	A	S	G	A	S	G	A	S	G
1 Bury	–	–		2		–				–			–			–			–			–			–			2		–
2 Liverpool	–	–		1			–			1			–			–			–			–			–			2		–
3 Sheffield Wednesday	–	–		2			–			–			–			–			–			–			–			2		–
4 Arsenal	–	–		1			–			–			–			–			–			–			–			1		–
5 Aston Villa	–	–		1			–			–			–			–			–			–			–			1		–
6 Blackburn Rovers	–	–		1			–			–			–			–			–			–			–			1		–
7 Everton	–	–		1			–			–			–			–			–			–			–			1		–
8 Manchester City	–	–		1			–			–			–			–			–			–			–			1		–
9 Newcastle United	–	–		1			–			–			–			–			–			–			–			1		–
10 Oldham Athletic	–	–		1			–			–			–			–			–			–			–			1		–
11 Preston North End	–	–		1			–			–			–			–			–			–			–			1		–
12 Sheffield United	–	–		1			–			–			–			–			–			–			–			1		–
13 Sunderland	–	–		1			–			–			–			–			–			–			–			1		–
14 Swindon Town	–	–		–			–			–			–			–			–			–			1		–	1		–
15 Tottenham Hotspur	–	–		1			–			–			–			–			–			–			–			1		–
16 West Bromwich Albion	–	–		1			–			–			–			–			–			–			–			1		–

GRAEME HOGG

DEBUT (Full Appearance)

Saturday 07/01/1984
FA Cup 3rd Round
at Dean Court

Bournemouth 2 Manchester United 0

CLUB CAREER RECORD	Apps	Subs	Goals
Premiership	0		0
League Division 1	82	(1)	1
League Division 2	0		0
FA Cup	8		0
League Cup	7	(1)	0
European Cup / Champions League	0		0
European Cup-Winners' Cup	4		0
UEFA Cup / Inter-Cities' Fairs Cup	6		0
Other Matches	1		0
OVERALL TOTAL	**108**	**(2)**	**1**

Opponents	PREM			FLD 1			FLD 2			FAC			LC			EC/CL			ECWC			UEFA			OTHER			TOTAL		
	A	S	G	A	S	G	A	S	G	A	S	G	A	S	G	A	S	G	A	S	G	A	S	G	A	S	G	A	S	G
1 Everton	–	–		6		–		–		–			1		–				–			–			1		–	8		–
2 Arsenal	–	–		5		–		–		1			–			–			–			–			–			6		–
3 Coventry City	–	–		5		–		–		–			1			–			–			–			–			6		–
4 Leicester City	–	–		6		–		–		–			–			–			–			–			–			6		–

continued../

GRAEME HOGG (continued)

Opponents	PREM A S G	FLD 1 A S G	FLD 2 A S G	FAC A S G	LC A S G	EC/CL A S G	ECWC A S G	UEFA A S G	OTHER A S G	TOTAL A S G
5 Liverpool	– –	3 –	– –	2 –	1 –	– –	– –	– –	– –	6 –
6 West Ham United	– –	4 –	– –	1 –	1 –	– –	– –	– –	– –	6 –
7 Aston Villa	– –	5 –	– –	– –	– –	– –	– –	– –	– –	5 –
8 Southampton	– –	3 –	– –	– –	2 –	– –	– –	– –	– –	5 –
9 Chelsea	– –	3 –	– –	1 –	– –	– –	– –	– –	– –	4 –
10 Watford	– –	4 –	– –	– –	– –	– –	– –	– –	– –	4 –
11 West Bromwich Albion	– –	4 –	– –	– –	– –	– –	– –	– –	– –	4 –
12 Ipswich Town	– –	3 –	– –	– –	– –	– –	– –	– –	– –	3 –
13 Luton Town	– –	3 –	– –	– –	– –	– –	– –	– –	– –	3 –
14 Newcastle United	– –	3 –	– –	– –	– –	– –	– –	– –	– –	3 –
15 Nottingham Forest	– –	3 –	– –	– –	– –	– –	– –	– –	– –	3 –
16 Queens Park Rangers	– –	3 –	– –	– –	– –	– –	– –	– –	– –	3 –
17 Sheffield Wednesday	– –	3 –	– –	– –	– –	– –	– –	– –	– –	3 –
18 Tottenham Hotspur	– –	3 –	– –	– –	– –	– –	– –	– –	– –	3 –
19 Oxford United	– –	2 –	– –	– –	– (1)	– –	– –	– –	– –	2 (1) –
20 Birmingham City	– –	2 1	– –	– –	– –	– –	– –	– –	– –	2 1
21 Barcelona	– –	– –	– –	– –	– –	– –	2 –	– –	– –	2 –
22 Burnley	– –	– –	– –	– –	2 –	– –	– –	– –	– –	2 –
23 Derby County	– –	2 –	– –	– –	– –	– –	– –	– –	– –	2 –
24 Juventus	– –	– –	– –	– –	– –	– –	2 –	– –	– –	2 –
25 Manchester City	– –	2 –	– –	– –	– –	– –	– –	– –	– –	2 –
26 PSV Eindhoven	– –	– –	– –	– –	– –	– –	– –	2 –	– –	2 –
27 Raba Vasas	– –	– –	– –	– –	– –	– –	– –	2 –	– –	2 –
28 Videoton	– –	– –	– –	– –	– –	– –	– –	2 –	– –	2 –
29 Blackburn Rovers	– –	– –	– –	1 –	– –	– –	– –	– –	– –	1 –
30 Bournemouth	– –	– –	– –	1 –	– –	– –	– –	– –	– –	1 –
31 Norwich City	– –	1 –	– –	– –	– –	– –	– –	– –	– –	1 –
32 Notts County	– –	1 –	– –	– –	– –	– –	– –	– –	– –	1 –
33 Stoke City	– –	1 –	– –	– –	– –	– –	– –	– –	– –	1 –
34 Sunderland	– –	1 –	– –	– –	– –	– –	– –	– –	– –	1 –
35 Wolverhampton W.	– –	1 –	– –	– –	– –	– –	– –	– –	– –	1 –
36 Portsmouth	– –	– (1) –	– –	– –	– –	– –	– –	– –	– –	– (1) –

DICK HOLDEN

DEBUT (Full Appearance)

Monday 24/04/1905
Football League Division 2
at Bank Street

Manchester United 3 Blackpool 1

CLUB CAREER RECORD	Apps	Subs	Goals
Premiership	0		0
League Division 1	78		0
League Division 2	28		0
FA Cup	11		0
League Cup	0		0
European Cup / Champions League	0		0
European Cup-Winners' Cup	0		0
UEFA Cup / Inter-Cities' Fairs Cup	0		0
Other Matches	0		0
OVERALL TOTAL	**117**		**0**

Opponents	PREM A S G	FLD 1 A S G	FLD 2 A S G	FAC A S G	LC A S G	EC/CL A S G	ECWC A S G	UEFA A S G	OTHER A S G	TOTAL A S G
1 Blackburn Rovers	– –	7 –	– –	– –	– –	– –	– –	– –	– –	7 –
2 Aston Villa	– –	4 –	– –	2 –	– –	– –	– –	– –	– –	6 –
3 Everton	– –	6 –	– –	– –	– –	– –	– –	– –	– –	6 –
4 Middlesbrough	– –	6 –	– –	– –	– –	– –	– –	– –	– –	6 –
5 Sunderland	– –	6 –	– –	– –	– –	– –	– –	– –	– –	6 –
6 Arsenal	– –	4 –	– –	1 –	– –	– –	– –	– –	– –	5 –
7 Bristol City	– –	4 –	1 –	– –	– –	– –	– –	– –	– –	5 –
8 Chelsea	– –	2 –	2 –	1 –	– –	– –	– –	– –	– –	5 –
9 Newcastle United	– –	5 –	– –	– –	– –	– –	– –	– –	– –	5 –
10 Sheffield United	– –	5 –	– –	– –	– –	– –	– –	– –	– –	5 –
11 Sheffield Wednesday	– –	5 –	– –	– –	– –	– –	– –	– –	– –	5 –
12 Birmingham City	– –	4 –	– –	– –	– –	– –	– –	– –	– –	4 –
13 Bury	– –	4 –	– –	– –	– –	– –	– –	– –	– –	4 –
14 Preston North End	– –	3 –	– –	– –	– –	– –	– –	– –	– –	3 –
15 West Bromwich Albion	– –	2 –	1 –	– –	– –	– –	– –	– –	– –	3 –
16 Barnsley	– –	– –	2 –	– –	– –	– –	– –	– –	– –	2 –
17 Blackpool	– –	– –	1 –	1 –	– –	– –	– –	– –	– –	2 –
18 Bolton Wanderers	– –	2 –	– –	– –	– –	– –	– –	– –	– –	2 –
19 Burnley	– –	– –	2 –	– –	– –	– –	– –	– –	– –	2 –
20 Burton United	– –	– –	2 –	– –	– –	– –	– –	– –	– –	2 –
21 Hull City	– –	– –	2 –	– –	– –	– –	– –	– –	– –	2 –
22 Leeds United	– –	– –	2 –	– –	– –	– –	– –	– –	– –	2 –
23 Leyton Orient	– –	– –	2 –	– –	– –	– –	– –	– –	– –	2 –
24 Lincoln City	– –	– –	2 –	– –	– –	– –	– –	– –	– –	2 –
25 Liverpool	– –	2 –	– –	– –	– –	– –	– –	– –	– –	2 –
26 Notts County	– –	2 –	– –	– –	– –	– –	– –	– –	– –	2 –
27 Port Vale	– –	– –	2 –	– –	– –	– –	– –	– –	– –	2 –
28 Portsmouth	– –	– –	– –	2 –	– –	– –	– –	– –	– –	2 –
29 Bradford City	– –	– –	1 –	– –	– –	– –	– –	– –	– –	1 –
30 Chesterfield	– –	– –	1 –	– –	– –	– –	– –	– –	– –	1 –

continued../

DICK HOLDEN (continued)

Opponents	PREM			FLD 1			FLD 2			FAC			LC			EC/CL			ECWC			UEFA			OTHER			TOTAL		
	A	S	G	A	S	G	A	S	G	A	S	G	A	S	G	A	S	G	A	S	G	A	S	G	A	S	G	A	S	G
31 Coventry City	–	–	–	–	–	–	–	–	–	1	–	–	–	–	–	–	–	–	–	–	–	–	–	–	–	–	–	1	–	–
32 Derby County	–	–	–	1	–	–	–	–	–	–	–	–	–	–	–	–	–	–	–	–	–	–	–	–	–	–	–	1	–	–
33 Gainsborough Trinity	–	–	–	–	–	–	1	–	–	–	–	–	–	–	–	–	–	–	–	–	–	–	–	–	–	–	–	1	–	–
34 Glossop	–	–	–	–	–	–	1	–	–	–	–	–	–	–	–	–	–	–	–	–	–	–	–	–	–	–	–	1	–	–
35 Grimsby Town	–	–	–	–	–	–	1	–	–	–	–	–	–	–	–	–	–	–	–	–	–	–	–	–	–	–	–	1	–	–
36 Huddersfield Town	–	–	–	–	–	–	–	–	–	1	–	–	–	–	–	–	–	–	–	–	–	–	–	–	–	–	–	1	–	–
37 Leicester City	–	–	–	–	–	–	1	–	–	–	–	–	–	–	–	–	–	–	–	–	–	–	–	–	–	–	–	1	–	–
38 Manchester City	–	–	–	1	–	–	–	–	–	–	–	–	–	–	–	–	–	–	–	–	–	–	–	–	–	–	–	1	–	–
39 Norwich City	–	–	–	–	–	–	–	–	–	1	–	–	–	–	–	–	–	–	–	–	–	–	–	–	–	–	–	1	–	–
40 Nottingham Forest	–	–	–	1	–	–	–	–	–	–	–	–	–	–	–	–	–	–	–	–	–	–	–	–	–	–	–	1	–	–
41 Staple Hill	–	–	–	–	–	–	–	–	–	1	–	–	–	–	–	–	–	–	–	–	–	–	–	–	–	–	–	1	–	–
42 Stockport County	–	–	–	–	–	–	1	–	–	–	–	–	–	–	–	–	–	–	–	–	–	–	–	–	–	–	–	1	–	–
43 Stoke City	–	–	–	1	–	–	–	–	–	–	–	–	–	–	–	–	–	–	–	–	–	–	–	–	–	–	–	1	–	–
44 Tottenham Hotspur	–	–	–	1	–	–	–	–	–	–	–	–	–	–	–	–	–	–	–	–	–	–	–	–	–	–	–	1	–	–

EDWARD HOLT

DEBUT (Full Appearance, 1 goal)

Saturday 28/04/1900
Football League Division 2
at Bank Street

Newton Heath 2 Chesterfield 1

CLUB CAREER RECORD	Apps	Subs	Goals
Premiership	0		0
League Division 1	0		0
League Division 2	1		1
FA Cup	0		0
League Cup	0		0
European Cup / Champions League	0		0
European Cup-Winners' Cup	0		0
UEFA Cup / Inter-Cities' Fairs Cup	0		0
Other Matches	0		0
OVERALL TOTAL	**1**		**1**

Opponents	PREM			FLD 1			FLD 2			FAC			LC			EC/CL			ECWC			UEFA			OTHER			TOTAL		
	A	S	G	A	S	G	A	S	G	A	S	G	A	S	G	A	S	G	A	S	G	A	S	G	A	S	G	A	S	G
1 Chesterfield	–	–	–	–	–	–	1	–	1	–	–	–	–	–	–	–	–	–	–	–	–	–	–	–	–	–	–	1	–	1

JIM HOLTON

DEBUT (Full Appearance)

Saturday 20/01/1973
Football League Division 1
at Old Trafford

Manchester United 2 West Ham United 2

CLUB CAREER RECORD	Apps	Subs	Goals
Premiership	0		0
League Division 1	49		5
League Division 2	14		0
FA Cup	2		0
League Cup	4		0
European Cup / Champions League	0		0
European Cup-Winners' Cup	0		0
UEFA Cup / Inter-Cities' Fairs Cup	0		0
Other Matches	0		0
OVERALL TOTAL	**69**		**5**

Opponents	PREM			FLD 1			FLD 2			FAC			LC			EC/CL			ECWC			UEFA			OTHER			TOTAL		
	A	S	G	A	S	G	A	S	G	A	S	G	A	S	G	A	S	G	A	S	G	A	S	G	A	S	G	A	S	G
1 Manchester City	–	–	–	3	–	–	–	–	–	–	–	–	1	–	–	–	–	–	–	–	–	–	–	–	–	–	–	4	–	–
2 Newcastle United	–	–	–	3	1	–	–	–	–	–	–	–	–	–	–	–	–	–	–	–	–	–	–	–	–	–	–	3	–	1
3 Southampton	–	–	–	2	1	1	1	–	–	–	–	–	–	–	–	–	–	–	–	–	–	–	–	–	–	–	–	3	–	1
4 Everton	–	–	–	3	–	–	–	–	–	–	–	–	–	–	–	–	–	–	–	–	–	–	–	–	–	–	–	3	–	–
5 Ipswich Town	–	–	–	2	–	–	–	–	–	1	–	–	–	–	–	–	–	–	–	–	–	–	–	–	–	–	–	3	–	–
6 Leeds United	–	–	–	3	–	–	–	–	–	–	–	–	–	–	–	–	–	–	–	–	–	–	–	–	–	–	–	3	–	–
7 Norwich City	–	–	–	3	–	–	–	–	–	–	–	–	–	–	–	–	–	–	–	–	–	–	–	–	–	–	–	3	–	–
8 Sheffield United	–	–	–	3	–	–	–	–	–	–	–	–	–	–	–	–	–	–	–	–	–	–	–	–	–	–	–	3	–	–
9 Stoke City	–	–	–	3	–	–	–	–	–	–	–	–	–	–	–	–	–	–	–	–	–	–	–	–	–	–	–	3	–	–
10 West Ham United	–	–	–	3	–	–	–	–	–	–	–	–	–	–	–	–	–	–	–	–	–	–	–	–	–	–	–	3	–	–
11 Wolverhampton W.	–	–	–	3	–	–	–	–	–	–	–	–	–	–	–	–	–	–	–	–	–	–	–	–	–	–	–	3	–	–
12 Coventry City	–	–	–	2	1	–	–	–	–	–	–	–	–	–	–	–	–	–	–	–	–	–	–	–	–	–	–	2	–	1
13 Queens Park Rangers	–	–	–	2	1	–	–	–	–	–	–	–	–	–	–	–	–	–	–	–	–	–	–	–	–	–	–	2	–	1
14 Arsenal	–	–	–	2	–	–	–	–	–	–	–	–	–	–	–	–	–	–	–	–	–	–	–	–	–	–	–	2	–	–
15 Birmingham City	–	–	–	2	–	–	–	–	–	–	–	–	–	–	–	–	–	–	–	–	–	–	–	–	–	–	–	2	–	–
16 Derby County	–	–	–	2	–	–	–	–	–	–	–	–	–	–	–	–	–	–	–	–	–	–	–	–	–	–	–	2	–	–
17 Leicester City	–	–	–	2	–	–	–	–	–	–	–	–	–	–	–	–	–	–	–	–	–	–	–	–	–	–	–	2	–	–
18 Middlesbrough	–	–	–	–	–	–	–	–	–	–	–	–	2	–	–	–	–	–	–	–	–	–	–	–	–	–	–	2	–	–
19 Portsmouth	–	–	–	–	–	–	2	–	–	–	–	–	–	–	–	–	–	–	–	–	–	–	–	–	–	–	–	2	–	–
20 Tottenham Hotspur	–	–	–	2	–	–	–	–	–	–	–	–	–	–	–	–	–	–	–	–	–	–	–	–	–	–	–	2	–	–
21 Burnley	–	–	–	1	1	–	–	–	–	–	–	–	–	–	–	–	–	–	–	–	–	–	–	–	–	–	–	1	–	1
22 Blackpool	–	–	–	–	–	–	1	–	–	–	–	–	–	–	–	–	–	–	–	–	–	–	–	–	–	–	–	1	–	–
23 Bristol Rovers	–	–	–	–	–	–	1	–	–	–	–	–	–	–	–	–	–	–	–	–	–	–	–	–	–	–	–	1	–	–
24 Cardiff City	–	–	–	–	–	–	1	–	–	–	–	–	–	–	–	–	–	–	–	–	–	–	–	–	–	–	–	1	–	–
25 Charlton Athletic	–	–	–	–	–	–	–	–	–	–	–	–	1	–	–	–	–	–	–	–	–	–	–	–	–	–	–	1	–	–
26 Chelsea	–	–	–	1	–	–	–	–	–	–	–	–	–	–	–	–	–	–	–	–	–	–	–	–	–	–	–	1	–	–
27 Crystal Palace	–	–	–	1	–	–	–	–	–	–	–	–	–	–	–	–	–	–	–	–	–	–	–	–	–	–	–	1	–	–
28 Fulham	–	–	–	–	–	–	1	–	–	–	–	–	–	–	–	–	–	–	–	–	–	–	–	–	–	–	–	1	–	–
29 Leyton Orient	–	–	–	–	–	–	1	–	–	–	–	–	–	–	–	–	–	–	–	–	–	–	–	–	–	–	–	1	–	–

continued../

JIM HOLTON (continued)

Opponents	PREM A S G	FLD 1 A S G	FLD 2 A S G	FAC A S G	LC A S G	EC/CL A S G	ECWC A S G	UEFA A S G	OTHER A S G	TOTAL A S G
30 Liverpool	– –	1 –	–	–	–	–	–	–	–	1 –
31 Millwall	– –	–	1	–	–	–	–	–	–	1 –
32 Nottingham Forest	– –	–	–	1	–	–	–	–	–	1 –
33 Notts County	– –	–	–	1	–	–	–	–	–	1 –
34 Plymouth Argyle	– –	–	–	–	1	–	–	–	–	1 –
35 Sheffield Wednesday	– –	–	–	1	–	–	–	–	–	1 –
36 Sunderland	– –	–	–	1	–	–	–	–	–	1 –
37 West Bromwich Albion	– –	–	–	1	–	–	–	–	–	1 –

TOM HOMER

DEBUT (Full Appearance)

Saturday 30/10/1909
Football League Division 1
at Bank Street

Manchester United 1 Arsenal 0

CLUB CAREER RECORD	Apps	Subs	Goals
Premiership	0		0
League Division 1	25		14
League Division 2	0		0
FA Cup	0		0
League Cup	0		0
European Cup / Champions League	0		0
European Cup–Winners' Cup	0		0
UEFA Cup / Inter–Cities' Fairs Cup	0		0
Other Matches	0		0
OVERALL TOTAL	25		14

Opponents	PREM A S G	FLD 1 A S G	FLD 2 A S G	FAC A S G	LC A S G	EC/CL A S G	ECWC A S G	UEFA A S G	OTHER A S G	TOTAL A S G
1 Bury	– –	3 5	–	–	–	–	–	–	–	3 5
2 Middlesbrough	– –	3 1	–	–	–	–	–	–	–	3 1
3 Nottingham Forest	– –	2 1	–	–	–	–	–	–	–	2 1
4 Sheffield United	– –	2 –	–	–	–	–	–	–	–	2 –
5 Sheffield Wednesday	– –	2 –	–	–	–	–	–	–	–	2 –
6 Sunderland	– –	2 –	–	–	–	–	–	–	–	2 –
7 Blackburn Rovers	– –	1 2	–	–	–	–	–	–	–	1 2
8 Bolton Wanderers	– –	1 2	–	–	–	–	–	–	–	1 2
9 Bristol City	– –	1 1	–	–	–	–	–	–	–	1 1
10 Everton	– –	1 1	–	–	–	–	–	–	–	1 1
11 Liverpool	– –	1 1	–	–	–	–	–	–	–	1 1
12 Arsenal	– –	1 –	–	–	–	–	–	–	–	1 –
13 Aston Villa	– –	1 –	–	–	–	–	–	–	–	1 –
14 Bradford City	– –	1 –	–	–	–	–	–	–	–	1 –
15 Chelsea	– –	1 –	–	–	–	–	–	–	–	1 –
16 Manchester City	– –	1 –	–	–	–	–	–	–	–	1 –
17 Tottenham Hotspur	– –	1 –	–	–	–	–	–	–	–	1 –

BILLY HOOD

DEBUT (Full Appearance)

Saturday 01/10/1892
Football League Division 1
at Stoney Lane

West Bromwich Albion 0 Manchester United 0

CLUB CAREER RECORD	Apps	Subs	Goals
Premiership	0		0
League Division 1	33		6
League Division 2	0		0
FA Cup	3		0
League Cup	0		0
European Cup / Champions League	0		0
European Cup–Winners' Cup	0		0
UEFA Cup / Inter–Cities' Fairs Cup	0		0
Other Matches	2		0
OVERALL TOTAL	38		6

Opponents	PREM A S G	FLD 1 A S G	FLD 2 A S G	FAC A S G	LC A S G	EC/CL A S G	ECWC A S G	UEFA A S G	OTHER A S G	TOTAL A S G
1 Blackburn Rovers	– –	2 1	–	2 –	–	–	–	–	–	4 1
2 Sheffield Wednesday	– –	3 1	–	–	–	–	–	–	–	3 1
3 Wolverhampton W.	– –	3 1	–	–	–	–	–	–	–	3 1
4 Preston North End	– –	3 –	–	–	–	–	–	–	–	3 –
5 Stoke City	– –	3 –	–	–	–	–	–	–	–	3 –
6 Everton	– –	2 1	–	–	–	–	–	–	–	2 1
7 West Bromwich Albion	– –	2 1	–	–	–	–	–	–	–	2 1
8 Accrington Stanley	– –	2 –	–	–	–	–	–	–	–	2 –
9 Bolton Wanderers	– –	2 –	–	–	–	–	–	–	–	2 –
10 Derby County	– –	2 –	–	–	–	–	–	–	–	2 –
11 Nottingham Forest	– –	2 –	–	–	–	–	–	–	–	2 –
12 Notts County	– –	2 –	–	–	–	–	–	–	–	2 –
13 Burnley	– –	1 1	–	–	–	–	–	–	–	1 1
14 Aston Villa	– –	1 –	–	–	–	–	–	–	–	1 –
15 Birmingham City	– –	–	–	–	–	–	–	–	1 –	1 –
16 Darwen	– –	1 –	–	–	–	–	–	–	–	1 –
17 Liverpool	– –	–	–	–	–	–	–	–	1 –	1 –
18 Middlesbrough	– –	–	–	1 –	–	–	–	–	–	1 –
19 Sheffield United	– –	1 –	–	–	–	–	–	–	–	1 –
20 Sunderland	– –	1 –	–	–	–	–	–	–	–	1 –

ARTHUR HOOPER

DEBUT (Full Appearance, 1 goal)

Saturday 22/01/1910
Football League Division 1
at Bank Street

Manchester United 5 Tottenham Hotspur 0

CLUB CAREER RECORD	Apps	Subs	Goals
Premiership	0		0
League Division 1	7		1
League Division 2	0		0
FA Cup	0		0
League Cup	0		0
European Cup / Champions League	0		0
European Cup-Winners' Cup	0		0
UEFA Cup / Inter-Cities' Fairs Cup	0		0
Other Matches	0		0
OVERALL TOTAL	**7**		**1**

Opponents	PREM A	S	G	FLD 1 A	S	G	FLD 2 A	S	G	FAC A	S	G	LC A	S	G	EC/CL A	S	G	ECWC A	S	G	UEFA A	S	G	OTHER A	S	G	TOTAL A	S	G
1 Tottenham Hotspur	–	–		2		1	–			–			–			–			–			–			–			2		1
2 Sheffield Wednesday	–	–		2			–			–			–			–			–			–			–			2		
3 Liverpool	–	–		1			–			–			–			–			–			–			–			1		–
4 Middlesbrough	–	–		1			–			–			–			–			–			–			–			1		–
5 Preston North End	–	–		1			–			–			–			–			–			–			–			1		–

FRED HOPKIN

DEBUT (Full Appearance)

Saturday 30/08/1919
Football League Division 1
at Baseball Ground

Derby County 1 Manchester United 1

CLUB CAREER RECORD	Apps	Subs	Goals
Premiership	0		0
League Division 1	70		8
League Division 2	0		0
FA Cup	4		0
League Cup	0		0
European Cup / Champions League	0		0
European Cup-Winners' Cup	0		0
UEFA Cup / Inter-Cities' Fairs Cup	0		0
Other Matches	0		0
OVERALL TOTAL	**74**		**8**

Opponents	PREM A	S	G	FLD 1 A	S	G	FLD 2 A	S	G	FAC A	S	G	LC A	S	G	EC/CL A	S	G	ECWC A	S	G	UEFA A	S	G	OTHER A	S	G	TOTAL A	S	G
1 Liverpool	–	–		4	–		–			2			–			–			–			–			–			6		–
2 Aston Villa	–	–		4	–		–			1			–			–			–			–			–			5		–
3 Newcastle United	–	–		4	2		–			–			–			–			–			–			–			4		2
4 Arsenal	–	–		4	1		–			–			–			–			–			–			–			4		1
5 Blackburn Rovers	–	–		4	1		–			–			–			–			–			–			–			4		1
6 Bolton Wanderers	–	–		4	1		–			–			–			–			–			–			–			4		1
7 Manchester City	–	–		4	1		–			–			–			–			–			–			–			4		1
8 Sheffield United	–	–		4	1		–			–			–			–			–			–			–			4		1
9 Derby County	–	–		4	–		–			–			–			–			–			–			–			4		–
10 Middlesbrough	–	–		4			–			–			–			–			–			–			–			4		–
11 West Bromwich Albion	–	–		4			–			–			–			–			–			–			–			4		–
12 Bradford Park Avenue	–	–		3			–			–			–			–			–			–			–			3		–
13 Burnley	–	–		3			–			–			–			–			–			–			–			3		–
14 Chelsea	–	–		3			–			–			–			–			–			–			–			3		–
15 Everton	–	–		3			–			–			–			–			–			–			–			3		–
16 Preston North End	–	–		3			–			–			–			–			–			–			–			3		–
17 Oldham Athletic	–	–		2	1		–			–			–			–			–			–			–			2		1
18 Bradford City	–	–		2			–			–			–			–			–			–			–			2		–
19 Sheffield Wednesday	–	–		2			–			–			–			–			–			–			–			2		–
20 Sunderland	–	–		2			–			–			–			–			–			–			–			2		–
21 Huddersfield Town	–	–		1			–			–			–			–			–			–			–			1		–
22 Notts County	–	–		1			–			–			–			–			–			–			–			1		–
23 Port Vale	–	–		–			–			1			–			–			–			–			–			1		–
24 Tottenham Hotspur	–	–		1			–			–			–			–			–			–			–			1		–

JAMES HOPKINS

DEBUT (Full Appearance)

Saturday 18/03/1899
Football League Division 2
at Bank Street

Newton Heath 1 New Brighton Tower 2

CLUB CAREER RECORD	Apps	Subs	Goals
Premiership	0		0
League Division 1	0		0
League Division 2	1		0
FA Cup	0		0
League Cup	0		0
European Cup / Champions League	0		0
European Cup-Winners' Cup	0		0
UEFA Cup / Inter-Cities' Fairs Cup	0		0
Other Matches	0		0
OVERALL TOTAL	**1**		**0**

Opponents	PREM A	S	G	FLD 1 A	S	G	FLD 2 A	S	G	FAC A	S	G	LC A	S	G	EC/CL A	S	G	ECWC A	S	G	UEFA A	S	G	OTHER A	S	G	TOTAL A	S	G
1 New Brighton Tower	–	–		–	–		1		–	–			–			–			–			–			–			1		–

SAMUEL HOPKINSON

DEBUT (Full Appearance)

Saturday 17/01/1931
Football League Division 1
at St James' Park

Newcastle United 4 Manchester United 3

CLUB CAREER RECORD	Apps	Subs	Goals
Premiership	0		0
League Division 1	17		4
League Division 2	34		6
FA Cup	2		2
League Cup	0		0
European Cup / Champions League	0		0
European Cup-Winners' Cup	0		0
UEFA Cup / Inter-Cities' Fairs Cup	0		0
Other Matches	0		0
OVERALL TOTAL	**53**		**12**

#	Opponents	PREM			FLD 1			FLD 2			FAC			LC			EC/CL			ECWC			UEFA			OTHER			TOTAL		
		A	S	G	A	S	G	A	S	G	A	S	G	A	S	G	A	S	G	A	S	G	A	S	G	A	S	G	A	S	G
1	Preston North End	-	-	-	-	-	-	3	-	1	-	-	-	-	-	-	-	-	-	-	-	-	-	-	-	-	-	-	3	-	1
2	Tottenham Hotspur	-	-	-	-	-	-	3	-	-	-	-	-	-	-	-	-	-	-	-	-	-	-	-	-	-	-	-	3	-	-
3	Stoke City	-	-	-	-	-	-	1	-	-	1	-	2	-	-	-	-	-	-	-	-	-	-	-	-	-	-	-	2	-	2
4	Notts County	-	-	-	-	-	-	2	-	1	-	-	-	-	-	-	-	-	-	-	-	-	-	-	-	-	-	-	2	-	1
5	Swansea City	-	-	-	-	-	-	2	-	1	-	-	-	-	-	-	-	-	-	-	-	-	-	-	-	-	-	-	2	-	1
6	Wolverhampton W.	-	-	-	-	-	-	2	-	1	-	-	-	-	-	-	-	-	-	-	-	-	-	-	-	-	-	-	2	-	1
7	Bradford Park Avenue	-	-	-	-	-	-	2	-	-	-	-	-	-	-	-	-	-	-	-	-	-	-	-	-	-	-	-	2	-	-
8	Grimsby Town	-	-	-	1	-	-	-	-	-	1	-	-	-	-	-	-	-	-	-	-	-	-	-	-	-	-	-	2	-	-
9	Liverpool	-	-	-	2	-	-	-	-	-	-	-	-	-	-	-	-	-	-	-	-	-	-	-	-	-	-	-	2	-	-
10	Millwall	-	-	-	-	-	-	2	-	-	-	-	-	-	-	-	-	-	-	-	-	-	-	-	-	-	-	-	2	-	-
11	Nottingham Forest	-	-	-	-	-	-	2	-	-	-	-	-	-	-	-	-	-	-	-	-	-	-	-	-	-	-	-	2	-	-
12	Southampton	-	-	-	-	-	-	2	-	-	-	-	-	-	-	-	-	-	-	-	-	-	-	-	-	-	-	-	2	-	-
13	Barnsley	-	-	-	-	-	-	1	-	2	-	-	-	-	-	-	-	-	-	-	-	-	-	-	-	-	-	-	1	-	2
14	Blackpool	-	-	-	1	1	-	-	-	-	-	-	-	-	-	-	-	-	-	-	-	-	-	-	-	-	-	-	1	1	-
15	Sheffield United	-	-	-	1	1	-	-	-	-	-	-	-	-	-	-	-	-	-	-	-	-	-	-	-	-	-	-	1	1	-
16	Sheffield Wednesday	-	-	-	1	1	-	-	-	-	-	-	-	-	-	-	-	-	-	-	-	-	-	-	-	-	-	-	1	1	-
17	Sunderland	-	-	-	1	1	-	-	-	-	-	-	-	-	-	-	-	-	-	-	-	-	-	-	-	-	-	-	1	1	-
18	Arsenal	-	-	-	1	-	-	-	-	-	-	-	-	-	-	-	-	-	-	-	-	-	-	-	-	-	-	-	1	-	-
19	Birmingham City	-	-	-	1	-	-	-	-	-	-	-	-	-	-	-	-	-	-	-	-	-	-	-	-	-	-	-	1	-	-
20	Blackburn Rovers	-	-	-	1	-	-	-	-	-	-	-	-	-	-	-	-	-	-	-	-	-	-	-	-	-	-	-	1	-	-
21	Bradford City	-	-	-	-	-	-	-	-	-	1	-	-	-	-	-	-	-	-	-	-	-	-	-	-	-	-	-	1	-	-
22	Burnley	-	-	-	-	-	-	-	-	-	1	-	-	-	-	-	-	-	-	-	-	-	-	-	-	-	-	-	1	-	-
23	Bury	-	-	-	-	-	-	-	-	-	1	-	-	-	-	-	-	-	-	-	-	-	-	-	-	-	-	-	1	-	-
24	Charlton Athletic	-	-	-	-	-	-	-	-	-	1	-	-	-	-	-	-	-	-	-	-	-	-	-	-	-	-	-	1	-	-
25	Chesterfield	-	-	-	-	-	-	-	-	-	1	-	-	-	-	-	-	-	-	-	-	-	-	-	-	-	-	-	1	-	-
26	Derby County	-	-	-	1	-	-	-	-	-	-	-	-	-	-	-	-	-	-	-	-	-	-	-	-	-	-	-	1	-	-
27	Fulham	-	-	-	-	-	-	-	-	-	1	-	-	-	-	-	-	-	-	-	-	-	-	-	-	-	-	-	1	-	-
28	Hull City	-	-	-	-	-	-	-	-	-	1	-	-	-	-	-	-	-	-	-	-	-	-	-	-	-	-	-	1	-	-
29	Leeds United	-	-	-	-	-	-	-	-	-	1	-	-	-	-	-	-	-	-	-	-	-	-	-	-	-	-	-	1	-	-
30	Leicester City	-	-	-	1	-	-	-	-	-	-	-	-	-	-	-	-	-	-	-	-	-	-	-	-	-	-	-	1	-	-
31	Lincoln City	-	-	-	-	-	-	-	-	-	1	-	-	-	-	-	-	-	-	-	-	-	-	-	-	-	-	-	1	-	-
32	Manchester City	-	-	-	1	-	-	-	-	-	-	-	-	-	-	-	-	-	-	-	-	-	-	-	-	-	-	-	1	-	-
33	Middlesbrough	-	-	-	1	-	-	-	-	-	-	-	-	-	-	-	-	-	-	-	-	-	-	-	-	-	-	-	1	-	-
34	Newcastle United	-	-	-	1	-	-	-	-	-	-	-	-	-	-	-	-	-	-	-	-	-	-	-	-	-	-	-	1	-	-
35	Oldham Athletic	-	-	-	-	-	-	-	-	-	1	-	-	-	-	-	-	-	-	-	-	-	-	-	-	-	-	-	1	-	-
36	Plymouth Argyle	-	-	-	-	-	-	-	-	-	1	-	-	-	-	-	-	-	-	-	-	-	-	-	-	-	-	-	1	-	-
37	Port Vale	-	-	-	-	-	-	-	-	-	1	-	-	-	-	-	-	-	-	-	-	-	-	-	-	-	-	-	1	-	-
38	Portsmouth	-	-	-	1	-	-	-	-	-	-	-	-	-	-	-	-	-	-	-	-	-	-	-	-	-	-	-	1	-	-
39	West Ham United	-	-	-	1	-	-	-	-	-	-	-	-	-	-	-	-	-	-	-	-	-	-	-	-	-	-	-	1	-	-

STEWART HOUSTON

DEBUT (Full Appearance)

Tuesday 01/01/1974
Football League Division 1
at Loftus Road

Queens Park Rangers 3 Manchester United 0

CLUB CAREER RECORD	Apps	Subs	Goals
Premiership	0		0
League Division 1	164	(1)	7
League Division 2	40		6
FA Cup	22		1
League Cup	16		2
European Cup / Champions League	0		0
European Cup-Winners' Cup	2	(1)	0
UEFA Cup / Inter-Cities' Fairs Cup	4		0
Other Matches	0		0
OVERALL TOTAL	**248**	**(2)**	**16**

#	Opponents	PREM			FLD 1			FLD 2			FAC			LC			EC/CL			ECWC			UEFA			OTHER			TOTAL		
		A	S	G	A	S	G	A	S	G	A	S	G	A	S	G	A	S	G	A	S	G	A	S	G	A	S	G	A	S	G
1	Norwich City	-	-	-	8	-	-	2	-	-	-	-	-	2	-	-	-	-	-	-	-	-	-	-	-	-	-	-	12	-	-
2	Aston Villa	-	-	-	7	-	-	2	-	-	1	-	1	1	-	-	-	-	-	-	-	-	-	-	-	-	-	-	11	-	1
3	Derby County	-	-	-	9	-	2	-	-	-	1	-	-	-	-	-	-	-	-	-	-	-	-	-	-	-	-	-	10	-	2
4	Manchester City	-	-	-	9	-	-	-	-	-	-	-	-	1	-	-	-	-	-	-	-	-	-	-	-	-	-	-	10	-	-
5	Wolverhampton W.	-	-	-	8	-	-	-	-	-	2	-	-	-	-	-	-	-	-	-	-	-	-	-	-	-	-	-	10	-	-
6	Everton	-	-	-	9	-	1	-	-	-	-	-	-	-	-	-	-	-	-	-	-	-	-	-	-	-	-	-	9	-	1
7	Arsenal	-	-	-	9	-	-	-	-	-	-	-	-	-	-	-	-	-	-	-	-	-	-	-	-	-	-	-	9	-	-
8	Middlesbrough	-	-	-	7	-	-	-	-	-	-	-	-	2	-	-	-	-	-	-	-	-	-	-	-	-	-	-	9	-	-
9	Southampton	-	-	-	4	-	-	2	-	-	3	-	-	-	-	-	-	-	-	-	-	-	-	-	-	-	-	-	9	-	-
10	Tottenham Hotspur	-	-	-	6	-	-	-	-	-	2	-	-	1	-	-	-	-	-	-	-	-	-	-	-	-	-	-	9	-	-
11	West Bromwich Albion	-	-	-	5	-	-	2	-	-	2	-	-	-	-	-	-	-	-	-	-	-	-	-	-	-	-	-	9	-	-
12	Leeds United	-	-	-	7	-	1	-	-	-	1	-	-	-	-	-	-	-	-	-	-	-	-	-	-	-	-	-	8	-	1

continued../

STEWART HOUSTON (continued)

Opponents	PREM A S G	FLD 1 A S G	FLD 2 A S G	FAC A S G	LC A S G	EC/CL A S G	ECWC A S G	UEFA A S G	OTHER A S G	TOTAL A S G
13 Newcastle United	– –	–	–	– –	1 1	–	–	–	–	8 1
14 Bristol City	– –	6 –	2 –	–	–	–	–	–	–	8 –
15 Queens Park Rangers	– –	7 –	–	1 –	–	–	–	–	–	8 –
16 Coventry City	– –	7 –	–	–	–	–	–	–	–	7 –
17 Sunderland	– –	2 –	2 –	–	3 –	–	–	–	–	7 –
18 Liverpool	– –	6 (1) –	–	–	–	–	–	–	–	6 (1) –
19 Birmingham City	– –	6 1	–	1 –	–	–	–	–	–	6 1
20 Ipswich Town	– –	6 1	–	–	–	–	–	–	–	6 1
21 West Ham United	– –	6 –	–	–	–	–	–	–	–	6 –
22 Stoke City	– –	5 1	–	–	–	–	–	–	–	5 1
23 Chelsea	– –	4 –	–	1 –	–	–	–	–	–	5 –
24 Nottingham Forest	– –	3 –	2 –	–	–	–	–	–	–	5 –
25 Burnley	– –	3 –	–	–	1 –	–	–	–	–	4 –
26 Leicester City	– –	3 –	–	1 –	–	–	–	–	–	4 –
27 Bolton Wanderers	– –	1 –	2 1	–	–	–	–	–	–	3 1
28 Fulham	– –	–	2 –	1 –	–	–	–	–	–	3 –
29 Oxford United	– –	–	2 –	1 –	–	–	–	–	–	3 –
30 Sheffield United	– –	3 –	–	–	–	–	–	–	–	3 –
31 Walsall	– –	–	–	3 –	–	–	–	–	–	3 –
32 Cardiff City	– –	–	2 1	–	–	–	–	–	–	2 1
33 Hull City	– –	–	2 1	–	–	–	–	–	–	2 1
34 Leyton Orient	– –	–	2 1	–	–	–	–	–	–	2 1
35 Notts County	– –	–	2 1	–	–	–	–	–	–	2 1
36 Sheffield Wednesday	– –	–	2 1	–	–	–	–	–	–	2 1
37 Ajax	– –	–	–	–	–	–	–	2 –	–	2 –
38 Blackpool	– –	–	2 –	–	–	–	–	–	–	2 –
39 Bristol Rovers	– –	–	2 –	–	–	–	–	–	–	2 –
40 Juventus	– –	–	–	–	–	–	–	2 –	–	2 –
41 Millwall	– –	–	2 –	–	–	–	–	–	–	2 –
42 Porto	– –	–	–	–	–	–	2 –	–	–	2 –
43 York City	– –	–	2 –	–	–	–	–	–	–	2 –
44 Charlton Athletic	– –	–	–	–	1 1	–	–	–	–	1 1
45 Brentford	– –	–	–	–	1 –	–	–	–	–	1 –
46 Carlisle United	– –	–	–	1 –	–	–	–	–	–	1 –
47 Crystal Palace	– –	1 –	–	–	–	–	–	–	–	1 –
48 Oldham Athletic	– –	–	1 –	–	–	–	–	–	–	1 –
49 Peterborough United	– –	–	–	1 –	–	–	–	–	–	1 –
50 Portsmouth	– –	–	1 –	–	–	–	–	–	–	1 –
51 Tranmere Rovers	– –	–	–	–	1 –	–	–	–	–	1 –
52 Watford	– –	–	–	–	1 –	–	–	–	–	1 –
53 St Etienne	– –	–	–	–	–	–	– (1) –	–	–	– (1) –

TIM HOWARD

DEBUT (Full Appearance)

Sunday 10/08/2003
FA Charity Shield
at Millennium Stadium

Manchester United 1 Arsenal 1

CLUB CAREER RECORD	Apps	Subs	Goals
Premiership	44	(1)	0
League Division 1	0		0
League Division 2	0		0
FA Cup	10		0
League Cup	8		0
European Cup / Champions League	12		0
European Cup–Winners' Cup	0		0
UEFA Cup / Inter–Cities' Fairs Cup	0		0
Other Matches	2		0
OVERALL TOTAL	76	(1)	0

Opponents	PREM A S G	FLD 1 A S G	FLD 2 A S G	FAC A S G	LC A S G	EC/CL A S G	ECWC A S G	UEFA A S G	OTHER A S G	TOTAL A S G
1 Chelsea	3 –	–	–	–	2 –	–	–	–	–	5 –
2 Arsenal	1 –	–	–	–	1 –	–	–	–	2 –	4 –
3 Blackburn Rovers	4 –	–	–	–	–	–	–	–	–	4 –
4 Everton	4 –	–	–	–	–	–	–	–	–	4 –
5 Newcastle United	3 –	–	–	1 –	–	–	–	–	–	4 –
6 Aston Villa	2 –	–	–	–	1 –	–	–	–	–	3 –
7 Bolton Wanderers	3 –	–	–	–	–	–	–	–	–	3 –
8 Fulham	2 –	–	–	1 –	–	–	–	–	–	3 –
9 Manchester City	2 –	–	–	1 –	–	–	–	–	–	3 –
10 Southampton	2 –	–	–	–	1 –	–	–	–	–	3 –
11 Portsmouth	2 (1) –	–	–	–	–	–	–	–	–	2 (1) –
12 Birmingham City	1 –	–	–	–	1 –	–	–	–	–	2 –
13 Burton Albion	– –	–	–	2 –	–	–	–	–	–	2 –
14 Charlton Athletic	2 –	–	–	–	–	–	–	–	–	2 –
15 Crystal Palace	1 –	–	–	–	1 –	–	–	–	–	2 –
16 Dinamo Bucharest	– –	–	–	–	–	2 –	–	–	–	2 –
17 Exeter City	– –	–	–	2 –	–	–	–	–	–	2 –
18 Glasgow Rangers	– –	–	–	–	–	2 –	–	–	–	2 –
19 Leeds United	2 –	–	–	–	–	–	–	–	–	2 –
20 Liverpool	2 –	–	–	–	–	–	–	–	–	2 –

continued../

TIM HOWARD (continued)

Opponents	PREM A S G	FLD 1 A S G	FLD 2 A S G	FAC A S G	LC A S G	EC/CL A S G	ECWC A S G	UEFA A S G	OTHER A S G	TOTAL A S G
21 Middlesbrough	2 –	–	–	–	–	–	–	–	–	2 –
22 Norwich City	2 –	–	–	–	–	–	–	–	–	2 –
23 Panathinaikos	–	–	–	–	–	2 –	–	–	–	2 –
24 Porto	–	–	–	–	–	2 –	–	–	–	2 –
25 Wolverhampton W.	2 –	–	–	–	–	–	–	–	–	2 –
26 AC Milan	–	–	–	–	–	–	1 –	–	–	1 –
27 Barnet	–	–	–	–	1	–	–	–	–	1 –
28 Crewe Alexandra	–	–	–	–	1	–	–	–	–	1 –
29 Fenerbahce	–	–	–	–	–	1	–	–	–	1 –
30 Leicester City	1	–	–	–	–	–	–	–	–	1 –
31 Millwall	–	–	–	1	–	–	–	–	–	1 –
32 Olympique Lyonnais	–	–	–	–	–	1	–	–	–	1 –
33 Stuttgart	–	–	–	–	–	1	–	–	–	1 –
34 Tottenham Hotspur	1	–	–	–	–	–	–	–	–	1 –
35 West Bromwich Albion	–	–	–	–	1	–	–	–	–	1 –

JOHN HOWARTH

DEBUT (Full Appearance)

Monday 02/01/1922
Football League Division 1
at Bramall Lane

Sheffield United 3 Manchester United 0

CLUB CAREER RECORD	Apps	Subs	Goals
Premiership	0		0
League Division 1	4		0
League Division 2	0		0
FA Cup	0		0
League Cup	0		0
European Cup / Champions League	0		0
European Cup-Winners' Cup	0		0
UEFA Cup / Inter-Cities' Fairs Cup	0		0
Other Matches	0		0
OVERALL TOTAL	4		0

Opponents	PREM A S G	FLD 1 A S G	FLD 2 A S G	FAC A S G	LC A S G	EC/CL A S G	ECWC A S G	UEFA A S G	OTHER A S G	TOTAL A S G
1 Sheffield United	– –	2	–	–	–	–	–	–	–	2 –
2 Bolton Wanderers	– –	1	–	–	–	–	–	–	–	1 –
3 Oldham Athletic	– –	1	–	–	–	–	–	–	–	1 –

E HOWELLS

DEBUT (Full Appearance)

Saturday 30/10/1886
FA Cup 1st Round
at Fleetwood Park

Fleetwood Rangers 2 Newton Heath 2

CLUB CAREER RECORD	Apps	Subs	Goals
Premiership	0		0
League Division 1	0		0
League Division 2	0		0
FA Cup	1		0
League Cup	0		0
European Cup / Champions League	0		0
European Cup-Winners' Cup	0		0
UEFA Cup / Inter-Cities' Fairs Cup	0		0
Other Matches	0		0
OVERALL TOTAL	1		0

Opponents	PREM A S G	FLD 1 A S G	FLD 2 A S G	FAC A S G	LC A S G	EC/CL A S G	ECWC A S G	UEFA A S G	OTHER A S G	TOTAL A S G
1 Fleetwood Rangers	–	–	–	1	–	–	–	–	–	1 –

EDWARD HUDSON

DEBUT (Full Appearance)

Saturday 24/01/1914
Football League Division 1
at Boundary Park

Oldham Athletic 2 Manchester United 2

CLUB CAREER RECORD	Apps	Subs	Goals
Premiership	0		0
League Division 1	11		0
League Division 2	0		0
FA Cup	0		0
League Cup	0		0
European Cup / Champions League	0		0
European Cup-Winners' Cup	0		0
UEFA Cup / Inter-Cities' Fairs Cup	0		0
Other Matches	0		0
OVERALL TOTAL	11		0

Opponents	PREM A S G	FLD 1 A S G	FLD 2 A S G	FAC A S G	LC A S G	EC/CL A S G	ECWC A S G	UEFA A S G	OTHER A S G	TOTAL A S G
1 Tottenham Hotspur	– –	2	–	–	–	–	–	–	–	2 –
2 Blackburn Rovers	– –	1	–	–	–	–	–	–	–	1 –
3 Bradford City	– –	1	–	–	–	–	–	–	–	1 –
4 Everton	– –	1	–	–	–	–	–	–	–	1 –
5 Liverpool	– –	1	–	–	–	–	–	–	–	1 –
6 Manchester City	– –	1	–	–	–	–	–	–	–	1 –
7 Oldham Athletic	– –	1	–	–	–	–	–	–	–	1 –
8 Sheffield United	– –	1	–	–	–	–	–	–	–	1 –
9 Sunderland	– –	1	–	–	–	–	–	–	–	1 –
10 West Bromwich Albion	– –	1	–	–	–	–	–	–	–	1 –

MARK HUGHES

DEBUT (Substitute Appearance)

Wednesday 26/10/1983
League Cup 2nd Round 2nd Leg
at Old Trafford

Manchester United 2　Port Vale 0

CLUB CAREER RECORD	Apps	Subs	Goals
Premiership	110	(1)	35
League Division 1	226	(8)	85
League Division 2	0		0
FA Cup	45	(1)	17
League Cup	37	(1)	16
European Cup / Champions League	7		2
European Cup-Winners' Cup	13	(3)	5
UEFA Cup / Inter-Cities' Fairs Cup	10		2
Other Matches	5		1
OVERALL TOTAL	453	(14)	163

Opponents	PREM A	S	G	FLD 1 A	S	G	FLD 2 A	S	G	FAC A	S	G	LC A	S	G	EC/CL A	S	G	ECWC A	S	G	UEFA A	S	G	OTHER A	S	G	TOTAL A	S	G
1 Everton	6	–	–	12		2	–	–	–	2		–	2		1	–		–	–		–	–		–	1		–	23		3
2 Southampton	6		1	11	(1)	4	–	–	–	1	(1)	–	2		4	–		–	–		–	–		–	–		–	20	(2)	9
3 Liverpool	5		3	12		1	–	–	–	2		1	1		1	–		–	–		–	–		–	1		–	21		6
4 Arsenal	6		2	12	(1)	4	–	–	–	–		–	1		1	–		–	–		–	–		–	1		1	20	(1)	8
5 Tottenham Hotspur	6		1	13		6	–	–	–	–		–	1		–	–		–	–		–	–		–	–		–	20		7
6 Coventry City	4		1	13		8	–	–	–	1		1	–		–	–		–	–		–	–		–	–		–	18		10
7 Aston Villa	4		1	12		7	–	–	–	–		–	2		1	–		–	–		–	–		–	–		–	18		9
8 Sheffield Wednesday	6		3	9		2	–	–	–	–		–	3		2	–		–	–		–	–		–	–		–	18		7
9 Queens Park Rangers	5		2	8		1	–	–	–	5		1	–		–	–		–	–		–	–		–	–		–	18		4
10 Norwich City	5		1	10		3	–	–	–	2		–	–		–	–		–	–		–	–		–	–		–	17		4
11 Nottingham Forest	4		2	8	(2)	2	–	–	–	2		–	1		–	–		–	–		–	–		–	–		–	15	(2)	4
12 Chelsea	5		2	10		5	–	–	–	1		1	–		–	–		–	–		–	–		–	–		–	16		8
13 West Ham United	2	(1)	1	9		3	–	–	–	3		–	1		–	–		–	–		–	–		–	–		–	15	(1)	5
14 Wimbledon	6		1	7		3	–	–	–	1		–	1		–	–		–	–		–	–		–	–		–	15		4
15 Leeds United	5		–	4		–	–	–	–	2		2	3		–	–		–	–		–	–		–	–		–	14		2
16 Manchester City	5		2	8		2	–	–	–	–		–	–		–	–		–	–		–	–		–	–		–	13		4
17 Crystal Palace	3		2	3	(1)	2	–	–	–	4		2	1		–	–		–	–		–	–		–	–		–	11	(1)	6
18 Luton Town	–		–	11	(1)	5	–	–	–	–		–	–		–	–		–	–		–	–		–	–		–	11	(1)	5
19 Newcastle United	4		1	6		4	–	–	–	1		–	–		–	–		–	–		–	–		–	–		–	11		5
20 Ipswich Town	5		2	5		2	–	–	–	–		–	–		–	–		–	–		–	–		–	–		–	10		4
21 Oldham Athletic	3		1	2		–	–	–	–	4		1	1		–	–		–	–		–	–		–	–		–	10		2
22 Sheffield United	4		3	1		1	–	–	–	4		2	–		–	–		–	–		–	–		–	–		–	9		6
23 Leicester City	2		–	5		3	–	–	–	–		–	1		1	–		–	–		–	–		–	–		–	8		4
24 Blackburn Rovers	5		1	–		–	–	–	–	1		–	–		–	–		–	–		–	1		–	–		–	7		1
25 Derby County	–		–	6		1	–	–	–	–		–	–		–	–		–	–		–	–		–	–		–	6		1
26 Charlton Athletic	–		–	4		1	–	–	–	1		1	–		–	–		–	–		–	–		–	–		–	5		2
27 Middlesbrough	2		–	2		–	–	–	–	–		–	1		–	–		–	–		–	–		–	–		–	5		–
28 Barcelona	–		–	–		–	–	–	–	–		–	–		–	2		1	2	(1)	2	–		–	–		–	4	(1)	3
29 Millwall	–		–	4		5	–	–	–	–		–	–		–	–		–	–		–	–		–	–		–	4		5
30 Oxford United	–		–	2		1	–	–	–	1		1	1		1	–		–	–		–	–		–	–		–	4		3
31 Sunderland	–		–	4		3	–	–	–	–		–	–		–	–		–	–		–	–		–	–		–	4		3
32 Stoke City	–		–	2		2	–	–	–	–		–	2		–	–		–	–		–	–		–	–		–	4		2
33 Watford	–		–	4		1	–	–	–	–		–	–		–	–		–	–		–	–		–	–		–	4		1
34 Bournemouth	–		–	–		–	–	–	–	3		1	–		–	–		–	–		–	–		–	–		–	3		1
35 Portsmouth	–		–	–		–	–	–	–	–		–	3		–	–		–	–		–	–		–	–		–	3		–
36 West Bromwich Albion	–		–	3		–	–	–	–	–		–	–		–	–		–	–		–	–		–	–		–	3		–
37 Notts County	–		–	2	(1)	1	–	–	–	–		–	–		–	–		–	–		–	–		–	–		–	2	(1)	1
38 Birmingham City	–		–	2	(1)	–	–	–	–	–		–	–		–	–		–	–		–	–		–	–		–	2	(1)	–
39 Swindon Town	2		2	–		–	–	–	–	–		–	–		–	–		–	–		–	–		–	–		–	2		2
40 Athinaikos	–		–	–		–	–	–	–	–		–	–		–	–		–	2		1	–		–	–		–	2		1
41 Athletico Madrid	–		–	–		–	–	–	–	–		–	–		–	–		–	2		1	–		–	–		–	2		1
42 Brighton	–		–	–		–	–	–	–	–		–	2		1	–		–	–		–	–		–	–		–	2		1
43 Dundee United	–		–	–		–	–	–	–	–		–	–		–	–		–	–		–	2		1	–		–	2		1
44 Gothenburg	–		–	–		–	–	–	–	–		–	–		–	2		1	–		–	–		–	–		–	2		1
45 Legia Warsaw	–		–	–		–	–	–	–	–		–	–		–	–		–	2		1	–		–	–		–	2		1
46 Raba Vasas	–		–	–		–	–	–	–	–		–	–		–	–		–	–		–	2		1	–		–	2		1
47 Cambridge United	–		–	–		–	–	–	–	–		–	2		–	–		–	–		–	–		–	–		–	2		–
48 Galatasaray	–		–	–		–	–	–	–	–		–	–		–	2		–	–		–	–		–	–		–	2		–
49 Halifax Town	–		–	–		–	–	–	–	–		–	2		–	–		–	–		–	–		–	–		–	2		–
50 Montpellier Herault	–		–	–		–	–	–	–	–		–	–		–	–		–	2		–	–		–	–		–	2		–
51 PSV Eindhoven	–		–	–		–	–	–	–	–		–	–		–	–		–	–		–	2		–	–		–	2		–
52 Rotherham United	–		–	–		–	–	–	–	–		–	2		–	–		–	–		–	–		–	–		–	2		–
53 Torpedo Moscow	–		–	–		–	–	–	–	–		–	–		–	–		–	–		–	2		–	–		–	2		–
54 Videoton	–		–	–		–	–	–	–	–		–	–		–	–		–	–		–	2		–	–		–	2		–
55 Pecsi Munkas	–		–	–		–	–	–	–	–		–	–		–	–		–	1	(1)	–	–		–	–		–	1	(1)	–
56 Burnley	–		–	–		–	–	–	–	–		–	1		3	–		–	–		–	–		–	–		–	1		3
57 Bolton Wanderers	–		–	–		–	–	–	–	1		1	–		–	–		–	–		–	–		–	–		–	1		1
58 Rochdale	–		–	–		–	–	–	–	1		1	–		–	–		–	–		–	–		–	–		–	1		1
59 Bury	–		–	–		–	–	–	–	1		–	–		–	–		–	–		–	–		–	–		–	1		–
60 Hereford United	–		–	–		–	–	–	–	1		–	–		–	–		–	–		–	–		–	–		–	1		–
61 Honved	–		–	–		–	–	–	–	–		–	–		–	1		–	–		–	–		–	–		–	1		–
62 Juventus	–		–	–		–	–	–	–	–		–	–		–	1		–	–		–	–		–	–		–	1		–
63 Red Star Belgrade	–		–	–		–	–	–	–	–		–	–		–	–		–	–		–	1		–	–		–	1		–
64 Wrexham	–		–	–		–	–	–	–	–		–	–		–	–		–	1		–	–		–	–		–	1		–
65 Port Vale	–		–	–		–	–	–	–	–		–	–	(1)	–	–		–	–		–	–		–	–		–	–	(1)	–
66 Spartak Varna	–		–	–		–	–	–	–	–		–	–		–	–		–	–	(1)	–	–		–	–		–	–	(1)	–

AARON HULME

DEBUT (Full Appearance)

Saturday 25/04/1908
Football League Division 1
at Bank Street

Manchester United 2 Preston North End 1

CLUB CAREER RECORD	Apps	Subs	Goals
Premiership	0		0
League Division 1	4		0
League Division 2	0		0
FA Cup	0		0
League Cup	0		0
European Cup / Champions League	0		0
European Cup-Winners' Cup	0		0
UEFA Cup / Inter-Cities' Fairs Cup	0		0
Other Matches	0		0
OVERALL TOTAL	**4**		**0**

Opponents	PREM A S G	FLD 1 A S G	FLD 2 A S G	FAC A S G	LC A S G	EC/CL A S G	ECWC A S G	UEFA A S G	OTHER A S G	TOTAL A S G
1 Aston Villa	– –	1	– –	–	–	–	–	–	– –	1 –
2 Bury	– –	1	–	–	–	–	–	–	–	1 –
3 Preston North End	– –	1	– –	–	–	–	–	–	– –	1 –
4 Sheffield United	– –	1	–	–	–	–	–	–	–	1 –

GEORGE HUNTER

DEBUT (Full Appearance)

Saturday 14/03/1914
Football League Division 1
at Old Trafford

Manchester United 0 Aston Villa 6

CLUB CAREER RECORD	Apps	Subs	Goals
Premiership	0		0
League Division 1	22		2
League Division 2	0		0
FA Cup	1		0
League Cup	0		0
European Cup / Champions League	0		0
European Cup-Winners' Cup	0		0
UEFA Cup / Inter-Cities' Fairs Cup	0		0
Other Matches	0		0
OVERALL TOTAL	**23**		**2**

Opponents	PREM A S G	FLD 1 A S G	FLD 2 A S G	FAC A S G	LC A S G	EC/CL A S G	ECWC A S G	UEFA A S G	OTHER A S G	TOTAL A S G
1 Bradford City	– –	2 1	–	–	–	–	–	–	–	2 1
2 Aston Villa	– –	2	–	–	–	–	–	–	–	2 –
3 Manchester City	– –	2	–	–	–	–	–	–	–	2 –
4 Sheffield Wednesday	– –	1	–	– 1	–	–	–	–	–	2 –
5 Sunderland	– –	2	–	–	–	–	–	–	–	2 –
6 Chelsea	– –	1 1	–	–	–	–	–	–	–	1 1
7 Blackburn Rovers	– –	1	–	–	–	–	–	–	–	1 –
8 Bolton Wanderers	– –	1	–	–	–	–	–	–	–	1 –
9 Burnley	– –	1	–	–	–	–	–	–	–	1 –
10 Derby County	– –	1	–	–	–	–	–	–	–	1 –
11 Liverpool	– –	1	–	–	–	–	–	–	–	1 –
12 Middlesbrough	– –	1	–	–	–	–	–	–	–	1 –
13 Newcastle United	– –	1	–	–	–	–	–	–	–	1 –
14 Notts County	– –	1	–	–	–	–	–	–	–	1 –
15 Oldham Athletic	– –	1	–	–	–	–	–	–	–	1 –
16 Sheffield United	– –	1	–	–	–	–	–	–	–	1 –
17 Tottenham Hotspur	– –	1	–	–	–	–	–	–	–	1 –
18 West Bromwich Albion	– –	1	–	–	–	–	–	–	–	1 –

REG HUNTER

DEBUT (Full Appearance)

Saturday 27/12/1958
Football League Division 1
at Villa Park

Aston Villa 0 Manchester United 2

CLUB CAREER RECORD	Apps	Subs	Goals
Premiership	0		0
League Division 1	1		0
League Division 2	0		0
FA Cup	0		0
League Cup	0		0
European Cup / Champions League	0		0
European Cup-Winners' Cup	0		0
UEFA Cup / Inter-Cities' Fairs Cup	0		0
Other Matches	0		0
OVERALL TOTAL	**1**		**0**

Opponents	PREM A S G	FLD 1 A S G	FLD 2 A S G	FAC A S G	LC A S G	EC/CL A S G	ECWC A S G	UEFA A S G	OTHER A S G	TOTAL A S G
1 Aston Villa	– –	1	–	–	–	–	–	–	–	1 –

WILLIAM HUNTER

DEBUT (Full Appearance)

Saturday 29/03/1913
Football League Division 1
at Anfield

Liverpool 0 Manchester United 2

CLUB CAREER RECORD	Apps	Subs	Goals
Premiership	0		0
League Division 1	3		2
League Division 2	0		0
FA Cup	0		0
League Cup	0		0
European Cup / Champions League	0		0
European Cup–Winners' Cup	0		0
UEFA Cup / Inter–Cities' Fairs Cup	0		0
Other Matches	0		0
OVERALL TOTAL	**3**		**2**

Opponents	PREM A S G	FLD 1 A S G	FLD 2 A S G	FAC A S G	LC A S G	EC/CL A S G	ECWC A S G	UEFA A S G	OTHER A S G	TOTAL A S G
1 Newcastle United	– –	1 2	– –	– –	– –	– –	– –	– –	– –	1 2
2 Liverpool	– –	1 –	– –	– –	– –	– –	– –	– –	– –	1 –
3 Oldham Athletic	– –	1 –	– –	– –	– –	– –	– –	– –	– –	1 –

DANIEL HURST

DEBUT (Full Appearance)

Saturday 06/09/1902
Football League Division 2
at The Northolme

Gainsborough Trinity 0 Manchester United 1

CLUB CAREER RECORD	Apps	Subs	Goals
Premiership	0		0
League Division 1	0		0
League Division 2	16		4
FA Cup	5		0
League Cup	0		0
European Cup / Champions League	0		0
European Cup–Winners' Cup	0		0
UEFA Cup / Inter–Cities' Fairs Cup	0		0
Other Matches	0		0
OVERALL TOTAL	**21**		**4**

Opponents	PREM A S G	FLD 1 A S G	FLD 2 A S G	FAC A S G	LC A S G	EC/CL A S G	ECWC A S G	UEFA A S G	OTHER A S G	TOTAL A S G
1 Burton United	– –	– –	1 1	2 –	– –	– –	– –	– –	– –	3 1
2 Bristol City	– –	– –	2 1	– –	– –	– –	– –	– –	– –	2 1
3 Glossop	– –	– –	2 1	– –	– –	– –	– –	– –	– –	2 1
4 Lincoln City	– –	– –	2 1	– –	– –	– –	– –	– –	– –	2 1
5 Chesterfield	– –	– –	2 –	– –	– –	– –	– –	– –	– –	2 –
6 Accrington Stanley	– –	– –	– –	1 –	– –	– –	– –	– –	– –	1 –
7 Arsenal	– –	– –	1 –	– –	– –	– –	– –	– –	– –	1 –
8 Birmingham City	– –	– –	1 –	– –	– –	– –	– –	– –	– –	1 –
9 Blackpool	– –	– –	1 –	– –	– –	– –	– –	– –	– –	1 –
10 Burnley	– –	– –	1 –	– –	– –	– –	– –	– –	– –	1 –
11 Everton	– –	– –	– –	1 –	– –	– –	– –	– –	– –	1 –
12 Gainsborough Trinity	– –	– –	1 –	– –	– –	– –	– –	– –	– –	1 –
13 Liverpool	– –	– –	– –	1 –	– –	– –	– –	– –	– –	1 –
14 Preston North End	– –	– –	1 –	– –	– –	– –	– –	– –	– –	1 –
15 Stockport County	– –	– –	1 –	– –	– –	– –	– –	– –	– –	1 –

RICHARD IDDON

DEBUT (Full Appearance)

Saturday 29/08/1925
Football League Division 1
at Upton Park

West Ham United 1 Manchester United 0

CLUB CAREER RECORD	Apps	Subs	Goals
Premiership	0		0
League Division 1	2		0
League Division 2	0		0
FA Cup	0		0
League Cup	0		0
European Cup / Champions League	0		0
European Cup–Winners' Cup	0		0
UEFA Cup / Inter–Cities' Fairs Cup	0		0
Other Matches	0		0
OVERALL TOTAL	**2**		**0**

Opponents	PREM A S G	FLD 1 A S G	FLD 2 A S G	FAC A S G	LC A S G	EC/CL A S G	ECWC A S G	UEFA A S G	OTHER A S G	TOTAL A S G
1 Burnley	– –	1 –	– –	– –	– –	– –	– –	– –	– –	1 –
2 West Ham United	– –	1 –	– –	– –	– –	– –	– –	– –	– –	1 –

PAUL INCE

DEBUT (Full Appearance)

Saturday 16/09/1989
Football League Division 1
at Old Trafford

Manchester United 5 Millwall 1

CLUB CAREER RECORD	Apps	Subs	Goals
Premiership	116		19
League Division 1	87	(3)	6
League Division 2	0		0
FA Cup	26	(1)	1
League Cup	23	(1)	2
European Cup / Champions League	9		0
European Cup-Winners' Cup	10		0
UEFA Cup / Inter-Cities' Fairs Cup	1		0
Other Matches	4		1
OVERALL TOTAL	**276**	**(5)**	**29**

Opponents	PREM A	S	G	FLD 1 A	S	G	FLD 2 A	S	G	FAC A	S	G	LC A	S	G	EC/CL A	S	G	ECWC A	S	G	UEFA A	S	G	OTHER A	S	G	TOTAL A	S	G
1 Liverpool	6		1	5		–							1												1		–	13		1
2 Arsenal	6		–	5									1												1		–	13		
3 Chelsea	6		–	6						1																		13		
4 Everton	6		–	5						1		–	1															13		
5 Leeds United	5		–	3						2			3															13		
6 Norwich City	6		1	4		3				2																		12		4
7 Aston Villa	6		2	4									2															12		2
8 Crystal Palace	4		1	4						4																		12		1
9 Sheffield Wednesday	6		1	2	(1)	–							3															11	(1)	1
10 Southampton	5		–	4	(1)	1				2																		11	(1)	1
11 Wimbledon	5		1	5		–				1		1																11		2
12 Queens Park Rangers	6		1	3		–				2																		11		1
13 Tottenham Hotspur	5		–	5		1							1															11		1
14 Sheffield United	4		–	4						3																		11		–
15 Oldham Athletic	4		1	2						4			–	(1)														10	(1)	1
16 Manchester City	6		2	3	(1)	–																						9	(1)	2
17 Nottingham Forest	4		1	4		–							1															9		1
18 Coventry City	3		–	6																								9		–
19 Blackburn Rovers	6		2																			1		1				7		3
20 Ipswich Town	5		1																									5		1
21 Luton Town			–	4		1																						4		1
22 West Ham United	4		1																									4		1
23 Middlesbrough	2		–										2															4		–
24 Newcastle United	3		1							–	(1)	–																3	(1)	1
25 Portsmouth													3		2													3		2
26 Barcelona																2		–	1									3		–
27 Brighton										1		–	2		–													3		–
28 Charlton Athletic				2		–				1																		3		–
29 Galatasaray																3		–										3		–
30 Wrexham										1		–										2		–				3		–
31 Swindon Town	2		1																									2		1
32 Athinaikos																			2		–							2		–
33 Cambridge United													2		–													2		–
34 Derby County				2		–																						2		–
35 Gothenburg																2		–										2		–
36 Honved																2		–										2		–
37 Montpellier Herault																			2		–							2		–
38 Notts County				2		–																						2		–
39 Sunderland				2		–																						2		–
40 Leicester City	1		1																									1		1
41 Athletico Madrid																			1		–							1		–
42 Halifax Town													1		–													1		–
43 Hereford United										1		–																1		–
44 Legia Warsaw																						1		–				1		–
45 Millwall				1		–																						1		–
46 Pecsi Munkas																			1		–							1		–
47 Red Star Belgrade																									1		–	1		–
48 Torpedo Moscow																						1						1		–

BILL INGLIS

DEBUT (Full Appearance)

Saturday 20/03/1926
Football League Division 1
at Old Trafford

Manchester United 0 Everton 0

CLUB CAREER RECORD	Apps	Subs	Goals
Premiership	0		0
League Division 1	14		1
League Division 2	0		0
FA Cup	0		0
League Cup	0		0
European Cup / Champions League	0		0
European Cup-Winners' Cup	0		0
UEFA Cup / Inter-Cities' Fairs Cup	0		0
Other Matches	0		0
OVERALL TOTAL	**14**		**1**

Opponents	PREM A	S	G	FLD 1 A	S	G	FLD 2 A	S	G	FAC A	S	G	LC A	S	G	EC/CL A	S	G	ECWC A	S	G	UEFA A	S	G	OTHER A	S	G	TOTAL A	S	G
1 Sheffield United			–	3		–																						3		–
2 Newcastle United			–	2		–																						2		–
3 Cardiff City			–	1		1																						1		1

continued../

BILL INGLIS (continued)

Opponents	PREM A S G	FLD 1 A S G	FLD 2 A S G	FAC A S G	LC A S G	EC/CL A S G	ECWC A S G	UEFA A S G	OTHER A S G	TOTAL A S G
4 Arsenal	– –	1	–	–	–	–	–	–	–	1 –
5 Birmingham City	– –	1	–	–	–	–	–	–	–	1 –
6 Burnley	– –	1	–	–	–	–	–	–	–	1 –
7 Everton	– –	1	–	–	–	–	–	–	–	1 –
8 Leeds United	– –	1	–	–	–	–	–	–	–	1 –
9 Liverpool	– –	1	–	–	–	–	–	–	–	1 –
10 Sunderland	– –	1	–	–	–	–	–	–	–	1 –
11 West Bromwich Albion	–	1	–	–	–	–	–	–	–	1 –

DENIS IRWIN

DEBUT (Full Appearance)

Saturday 18/08/1990
FA Charity Shield
at Wembley

Manchester United 1 Liverpool 1

CLUB CAREER RECORD	Apps	Subs	Goals
Premiership	286	(10)	18
League Division 1	70	(2)	4
League Division 2	0		0
FA Cup	42	(1)	7
League Cup	28	(3)	0
European Cup / Champions League	62	(2)	4
European Cup-Winners' Cup	8		0
UEFA Cup / Inter-Cities' Fairs Cup	3		0
Other Matches	12		0
OVERALL TOTAL	**511**	**(18)**	**33**

Opponents	PREM A S G	FLD 1 A S G	FLD 2 A S G	FAC A S G	LC A S G	EC/CL A S G	ECWC A S G	UEFA A S G	OTHER A S G	TOTAL A S G
1 Chelsea	16 –	3 1	–	4 –	–	–	–	–	2 –	25 1
2 Southampton	14 (3) 2	3 –	–	3 –	1 (1) –	–	–	–	–	21 (4) 2
3 Liverpool	15 3	4 –	–	2 –	1 –	–	–	–	2 –	24 3
4 Aston Villa	17 –	4 –	–	–	2 –	–	–	–	–	23 –
5 Leeds United	16 1	3 –	–	2 –	1 –	–	–	–	–	22 1
6 Arsenal	13 –	3 –	–	1 –	1 –	–	–	3 –	–	21 –
7 Everton	15 (1) 1	3 –	–	1 –	1 –	–	–	–	–	20 (1) 1
8 Tottenham Hotspur	14 1	4 –	–	1 –	–	–	–	–	–	19 1
9 Wimbledon	12 1	2 (1) –	–	3 1	–	–	–	–	–	17 (1) 2
10 Sheffield Wednesday	12 (1) –	2 –	–	–	3 –	–	–	–	–	17 (1) –
11 Coventry City	13 (1) 3	3 (1) –	–	–	–	–	–	–	–	16 (2) 3
12 West Ham United	13 1	2 –	–	1 –	–	–	–	–	–	16 1
13 Nottingham Forest	9 –	4 –	–	–	1 –	–	–	–	–	14 –
14 Queens Park Rangers	8 –	3 –	–	2 1	–	–	–	–	–	13 1
15 Manchester City	8 –	4 –	–	1 –	–	–	–	–	–	13 –
16 Newcastle United	11 –	–	–	–	1 –	–	–	1 –	–	13 –
17 Blackburn Rovers	12 (1) –	–	–	–	–	–	–	–	–	12 (1) –
18 Leicester City	12 –	–	–	–	– (1)	–	–	–	–	12 (1) –
19 Middlesbrough	9 1	–	–	1 1	2 –	–	–	–	–	12 2
20 Crystal Palace	5 (1) 1	4 –	–	2 1	–	–	–	–	–	11 (1) 2
21 Norwich City	5 –	4 1	–	2 –	–	–	–	–	–	11 1
22 Sheffield United	4 –	3 –	–	3 –	–	–	–	–	–	10 –
23 Derby County	7 (1) 1	2 –	–	–	–	–	–	–	–	9 (1) 1
24 Oldham Athletic	4 –	2 2	–	2 1	1 –	–	–	–	–	9 3
25 Ipswich Town	7 1	–	–	–	– (1)	–	–	–	–	7 (1) –
26 Sunderland	3 (1) –	2 –	–	2 –	–	–	–	–	–	7 (1) –
27 Barcelona	–	–	–	–	–	4 –	1 –	–	–	5 –
28 Charlton Athletic	4 –	–	–	1 –	–	–	–	–	–	5 –
29 Bayern Munich	–	–	–	–	–	4 –	–	–	–	4 –
30 Bolton Wanderers	3 –	–	–	1 –	–	–	–	–	–	4 –
31 Juventus	–	–	–	–	–	4 –	–	–	–	4 –
32 Luton Town	–	4 –	–	–	–	–	–	–	–	4 –
33 Sturm Graz	–	–	–	–	–	4 –	–	–	–	4 –
34 Brighton	–	–	–	1 –	2 –	–	–	–	–	3 –
35 Portsmouth	–	–	–	–	3 –	–	–	–	–	3 –
36 Anderlecht	–	–	–	–	–	2 2	–	–	–	2 2
37 Wrexham	–	–	–	1 2	–	–	1 –	–	–	2 2
38 Feyenoord	–	–	–	–	–	2 1	–	–	–	2 1
39 Cambridge United	–	–	–	–	2 –	–	–	–	–	2 –
40 Deportivo La Coruna	–	–	–	–	–	2 –	–	–	–	2 –
41 Dynamo Kiev	–	–	–	–	–	2 –	–	–	–	2 –
42 Fenerbahce	–	–	–	–	–	2 –	–	–	–	2 –
43 Fiorentina	–	–	–	–	–	2 –	–	–	–	2 –
44 Fulham	1 –	–	–	1 –	–	–	–	–	–	2 –
45 Galatasaray	–	–	–	–	–	2 –	–	–	–	2 –
46 Girondins Bordeaux	–	–	–	–	–	2 –	–	–	–	2 –
47 Gothenburg	–	–	–	–	–	2 –	–	–	–	2 –
48 Halifax Town	–	–	–	–	2 –	–	–	–	–	2 –
49 Honved	–	–	–	–	–	2 –	–	–	–	2 –
50 Internazionale	–	–	–	–	–	2 –	–	–	–	2 –
51 Legia Warsaw	–	–	–	–	–	–	2 –	–	–	2 –
52 Lille Metropole	–	–	–	–	–	2 –	–	–	–	2 –
53 LKS Lodz	–	–	–	–	–	2 –	–	–	–	2 –

continued../

DENIS IRWIN (continued)

Opponents	PREM A S G	FLD 1 A S G	FLD 2 A S G	FAC A S G	LC A S G	EC/CL A S G	ECWC A S G	UEFA A S G	OTHER A S G	TOTAL A S G
54 Monaco	– –	– –	– –	– –	– –	2 –	– –	– –	– –	2 –
55 Notts County	– –	2 –	– –	– –	– –	– –	– –	– –	– –	2 –
56 Olympiakos Piraeus	– –	– –	– –	– –	– –	2 –	– –	– –	– –	2 –
57 Olympique Marseille	– –	– –	– –	– –	– –	2 –	– –	– –	– –	2 –
58 Porto	– –	– –	– –	– –	– –	2 –	– –	– –	– –	2 –
59 Rapid Vienna	– –	– –	– –	– –	– –	2 –	– –	– –	– –	2 –
60 Real Madrid	– –	– –	– –	– –	– –	2 –	– –	– –	– –	2 –
61 Stoke City	– –	– –	– –	– –	2 –	– –	– –	– –	– –	2 –
62 Swindon Town	2 –	– –	– –	– –	– –	– –	– –	– –	– –	2 –
63 Torpedo Moscow	– –	– –	– –	– –	– –	– –	– –	2 –	– –	2 –
64 Valencia	– –	– –	– –	– –	– –	2 –	– –	– –	– –	2 –
65 Barnsley	– –	– –	– –	1 (1) –	– –	– –	– –	– –	– –	1 (1) –
66 Bayer Leverkusen	– –	– –	– –	– –	– –	– (2) –	– –	– –	– –	– (2) –
67 Kosice	– –	– –	– –	– –	– –	1 1	– –	– –	– –	1 1
68 Watford	1 – 1	– –	– –	– –	– –	– –	– –	– –	– –	1 – 1
69 Athinaikos	– –	– –	– –	– –	– –	– –	1 –	– –	– –	1 –
70 Athletico Madrid	– –	– –	– –	– –	– –	– –	1 –	– –	– –	1 –
71 Borussia Dortmund	– –	– –	– –	– –	– –	1 –	– –	– –	– –	1 –
72 Bradford City	1 –	– –	– –	– –	– –	– –	– –	– –	– –	1 –
73 Brondby	– –	– –	– –	– –	– –	1 –	– –	– –	– –	1 –
74 Bury	– –	– –	– –	1 –	– –	– –	– –	– –	– –	1 –
75 Croatia Zagreb	– –	– –	– –	– –	– –	1 –	– –	– –	– –	1 –
76 Montpellier Herault	– –	– –	– –	– –	– –	– –	1 –	– –	– –	1 –
77 Nantes Atlantique	– –	– –	– –	– –	– –	1 –	– –	– –	– –	1 –
78 Palmeiras	– –	– –	– –	– –	– –	– –	– –	1 –	– –	1 –
79 Pecsi Munkas	– –	– –	– –	– –	– –	– –	1 –	– –	– –	1 –
80 Port Vale	– –	– –	– –	1 –	– –	– –	– –	– –	– –	1 –
81 PSV Eindhoven	– –	– –	– –	– –	– –	1 –	– –	– –	– –	1 –
82 Rayos del Necaxa	– –	– –	– –	– –	– –	– –	– –	1 –	– –	1 –
83 Reading	– –	– –	– –	1 –	– –	– –	– –	– –	– –	1 –
84 Red Star Belgrade	– –	– –	– –	– –	– –	– –	– –	1 –	– –	1 –
85 Rotor Volgograd	– –	– –	– –	– –	– –	– –	– –	1 –	– –	1 –
86 Vasco da Gama	– –	– –	– –	– –	– –	– –	– –	1 –	– –	1 –
87 Walsall	– –	– –	– –	1 –	– –	– –	– –	– –	– –	1 –
88 York City	– –	– –	– –	– –	1 –	– –	– –	– –	– –	1 –

BILL JACKSON

DEBUT (Full Appearance)

Saturday 02/09/1899
Football League Division 2
at Bank Street

Newton Heath 2 Gainsborough Trinity 2

CLUB CAREER RECORD	Apps	Subs	Goals
Premiership	0		0
League Division 1	0		0
League Division 2	61		12
FA Cup	3		2
League Cup	0		0
European Cup / Champions League	0		0
European Cup-Winners' Cup	0		0
UEFA Cup / Inter-Cities' Fairs Cup	0		0
Other Matches	0		0
OVERALL TOTAL	64		14

Opponents	PREM A S G	FLD 1 A S G	FLD 2 A S G	FAC A S G	LC A S G	EC/CL A S G	ECWC A S G	UEFA A S G	OTHER A S G	TOTAL A S G
1 Arsenal	– –	– –	4 2	– –	– –	– –	– –	– –	– –	4 2
2 Grimsby Town	– –	– –	4 1	– –	– –	– –	– –	– –	– –	4 1
3 Leicester City	– –	– –	4 1	– –	– –	– –	– –	– –	– –	4 1
4 Middlesbrough	– –	– –	4 1	– –	– –	– –	– –	– –	– –	4 1
5 Port Vale	– –	– –	4 1	– –	– –	– –	– –	– –	– –	4 1
6 Birmingham City	– –	– –	4 –	– –	– –	– –	– –	– –	– –	4 –
7 Lincoln City	– –	– –	4 –	– –	– –	– –	– –	– –	– –	4 –
8 Walsall	– –	– –	3 2	– –	– –	– –	– –	– –	– –	3 2
9 Barnsley	– –	– –	3 1	– –	– –	– –	– –	– –	– –	3 1
10 New Brighton Tower	– –	– –	3 1	– –	– –	– –	– –	– –	– –	3 1
11 Burnley	– –	– –	2 –	1 –	– –	– –	– –	– –	– –	3 –
12 Burton Swifts	– –	– –	3 –	– –	– –	– –	– –	– –	– –	3 –
13 Gainsborough Trinity	– –	– –	3 –	– –	– –	– –	– –	– –	– –	3 –
14 Loughborough Town	– –	– –	2 1	– –	– –	– –	– –	– –	– –	2 1
15 Luton Town	– –	– –	2 1	– –	– –	– –	– –	– –	– –	2 1
16 Blackpool	– –	– –	2 –	– –	– –	– –	– –	– –	– –	2 –
17 Bolton Wanderers	– –	– –	2 –	– –	– –	– –	– –	– –	– –	2 –
18 Chesterfield	– –	– –	2 –	– –	– –	– –	– –	– –	– –	2 –
19 Glossop	– –	– –	2 –	– –	– –	– –	– –	– –	– –	2 –
20 Sheffield Wednesday	– –	– –	2 –	– –	– –	– –	– –	– –	– –	2 –
21 Stockport County	– –	– –	2 –	– –	– –	– –	– –	– –	– –	2 –
22 Portsmouth	– –	– –	– –	1 1	– –	– –	– –	– –	– –	1 1
23 South Shore	– –	– –	– –	1 1	– –	– –	– –	– –	– –	1 1

TOMMY JACKSON

DEBUT (Full Appearance)

Saturday 16/08/1975
Football League Division 1
at Molineux

Wolverhampton Wanderers 0 Manchester United 2

CLUB CAREER RECORD	Apps	Subs	Goals
Premiership	0		0
League Division 1	18	(1)	0
League Division 2	0		0
FA Cup	0		0
League Cup	4		0
European Cup / Champions League	0		0
European Cup-Winners' Cup	0		0
UEFA Cup / Inter-Cities' Fairs Cup	0		0
Other Matches	0		0
OVERALL TOTAL	22	(1)	0

Opponents	PREM			FLD 1			FLD 2			FAC			LC			EC/CL			ECWC			UEFA			OTHER			TOTAL		
	A	S	G	A	S	G	A	S	G	A	S	G	A	S	G	A	S	G	A	S	G	A	S	G	A	S	G	A	S	G
1 Stoke City	-	-		3	-		-	-		-	-		-	-		-	-		-	-		-	-		-	-		3	-	
2 Leicester City	-	-		2	-		-	-		-	-		-	-		-	-		-	-		-	-		-	-		2	-	
3 Manchester City	-	-		1	-		-	-		-	-		1	-		-	-		-	-		-	-		-	-		2	-	
4 Arsenal	-	-		1	-		-	-		-	-		-	-		-	-		-	-		-	-		-	-		1	-	
5 Aston Villa	-	-		-	-		-	-		-	-		1	-		-	-		-	-		-	-		-	-		1	-	
6 Birmingham City	-	-		1	-		-	-		-	-		-	-		-	-		-	-		-	-		-	-		1	-	
7 Brentford	-	-		-	-		-	-		-	-		1	-		-	-		-	-		-	-		-	-		1	-	
8 Bristol City	-	-		1	-		-	-		-	-		-	-		-	-		-	-		-	-		-	-		1	-	
9 Coventry City	-	-		1	-		-	-		-	-		-	-		-	-		-	-		-	-		-	-		1	-	
10 Everton	-	-		-	-		-	-		-	-		1	-		-	-		-	-		-	-		-	-		1	-	
11 Leeds United	-	-		1	-		-	-		-	-		-	-		-	-		-	-		-	-		-	-		1	-	
12 Liverpool	-	-		1	-		-	-		-	-		-	-		-	-		-	-		-	-		-	-		1	-	
13 Norwich City	-	-		1	-		-	-		-	-		-	-		-	-		-	-		-	-		-	-		1	-	
14 Queens Park Rangers	-	-		1	-		-	-		-	-		-	-		-	-		-	-		-	-		-	-		1	-	
15 Sheffield United	-	-		1	-		-	-		-	-		-	-		-	-		-	-		-	-		-	-		1	-	
16 Tottenham Hotspur	-	-		1	-		-	-		-	-		-	-		-	-		-	-		-	-		-	-		1	-	
17 West Ham United	-	-		1	-		-	-		-	-		-	-		-	-		-	-		-	-		-	-		1	-	
18 Wolverhampton W.	-	-		1	-		-	-		-	-		-	-		-	-		-	-		-	-		-	-		1	-	
19 Burnley	-	-		-	(1)		-	-		-	-		-	-		-	-		-	-		-	-		-	-		-	(1)	

STEVE JAMES

DEBUT (Full Appearance)

Saturday 12/10/1968
Football League Division 1
at Anfield

Liverpool 2 Manchester United 0

CLUB CAREER RECORD	Apps	Subs	Goals
Premiership	0		0
League Division 1	116		4
League Division 2	13		0
FA Cup	12		0
League Cup	17	(1)	0
European Cup / Champions League	2		0
European Cup-Winners' Cup	0		0
UEFA Cup / Inter-Cities' Fairs Cup	0		0
Other Matches	0		0
OVERALL TOTAL	160	(1)	4

Opponents	PREM			FLD 1			FLD 2			FAC			LC			EC/CL			ECWC			UEFA			OTHER			TOTAL		
	A	S	G	A	S	G	A	S	G	A	S	G	A	S	G	A	S	G	A	S	G	A	S	G	A	S	G	A	S	G
1 Stoke City	-	-		7	1		-	-		2	-		3	-		-	-		-	-		-	-		-	-		12	1	
2 Ipswich Town	-	-		6	-		-	-		1	-		1	-		-	-		-	-		-	-		-	-		8	-	
3 Newcastle United	-	-		7	-		-	-		-	-		-	-		-	-		-	-		-	-		-	-		7	-	
4 Nottingham Forest	-	-		6	-		1	-		-	-		-	-		-	-		-	-		-	-		-	-		7	-	
5 Arsenal	-	-		6	1		-	-		-	-		-	-		-	-		-	-		-	-		-	-		6	1	
6 Chelsea	-	-		5	1		-	-		-	-		1	-		-	-		-	-		-	-		-	-		6	1	
7 Coventry City	-	-		6	1		-	-		-	-		-	-		-	-		-	-		-	-		-	-		6	1	
8 Leeds United	-	-		6	-		-	-		-	-		-	-		-	-		-	-		-	-		-	-		6	-	
9 Liverpool	-	-		6	-		-	-		-	-		-	-		-	-		-	-		-	-		-	-		6	-	
10 Southampton	-	-		6	-		-	-		-	-		-	-		-	-		-	-		-	-		-	-		6	-	
11 Tottenham Hotspur	-	-		6	-		-	-		-	-		-	-		-	-		-	-		-	-		-	-		6	-	
12 Everton	-	-		4	-		-	-		1	-		-	-		-	-		-	-		-	-		-	-		5	-	
13 Manchester City	-	-		5	-		-	-		-	-		-	-		-	-		-	-		-	-		-	-		5	-	
14 Norwich City	-	-		2	-		1	-		-	-		2	-		-	-		-	-		-	-		-	-		5	-	
15 West Bromwich Albion	-	-		5	-		-	-		-	-		-	-		-	-		-	-		-	-		-	-		5	-	
16 Wolverhampton W.	-	-		5	-		-	-		-	-		-	-		-	-		-	-		-	-		-	-		5	-	
17 Birmingham City	-	-		2	-		-	-		2	-		-	-		-	-		-	-		-	-		-	-		4	-	
18 Crystal Palace	-	-		3	-		-	-		-	-		1	-		-	-		-	-		-	-		-	-		4	-	
19 Derby County	-	-		4	-		-	-		-	-		-	-		-	-		-	-		-	-		-	-		4	-	
20 Middlesbrough	-	-		-	-		2	-		-	-		2	-		-	-		-	-		-	-		-	-		4	-	
21 West Ham United	-	-		4	-		-	-		-	-		-	-		-	-		-	-		-	-		-	-		4	-	
22 Blackpool	-	-		2	-		1	-		-	-		-	-		-	-		-	-		-	-		-	-		3	-	
23 Bristol Rovers	-	-		-	-		1	-		-	-		2	-		-	-		-	-		-	-		-	-		3	-	
24 Burnley	-	-		1	-		-	-		-	-		2	-		-	-		-	-		-	-		-	-		3	-	
25 Huddersfield Town	-	-		3	-		-	-		-	-		-	-		-	-		-	-		-	-		-	-		3	-	
26 Leicester City	-	-		3	-		-	-		-	-		-	-		-	-		-	-		-	-		-	-		3	-	
27 Oxford United	-	-		-	-		1	-		-	-		2	-		-	-		-	-		-	-		-	-		3	-	
28 Sheffield United	-	-		3	-		-	-		-	-		-	-		-	-		-	-		-	-		-	-		3	-	
29 Rapid Vienna	-	-		-	-		-	-		-	-		-	-		2	-		-	-		-	-		-	-		2	-	
30 Sheffield Wednesday	-	-		1	-		1	-		-	-		-	-		-	-		-	-		-	-		-	-		2	-	
31 Sunderland	-	-		1	-		1	-		-	-		-	-		-	-		-	-		-	-		-	-		2	-	
32 Watford	-	-		-	-		-	-		2	-		-	-		-	-		-	-		-	-		-	-		2	-	
33 Aston Villa	-	-		-	-		-	-		-	-		1	-		-	-		-	-		-	-		-	-		1	-	

continued../

STEVE JAMES (continued)

Opponents	PREM A	S	G	FLD 1 A	S	G	FLD 2 A	S	G	FAC A	S	G	LC A	S	G	EC/CL A	S	G	ECWC A	S	G	UEFA A	S	G	OTHER A	S	G	TOTAL A	S	G
34 Bolton Wanderers	–	–	–	–	–	–	1	–	–	–	–	–	–	–	–	–	–	–	–	–	–	–	–	–	–	–	–	1	–	–
35 Bristol City	–	–	–	–	–	–	1	–	–	–	–	–	–	–	–	–	–	–	–	–	–	–	–	–	–	–	–	1	–	–
36 Cardiff City	–	–	–	–	–	–	1	–	–	–	–	–	–	–	–	–	–	–	–	–	–	–	–	–	–	–	–	1	–	–
37 Exeter City	–	–	–	–	–	–	–	–	–	1	–	–	–	–	–	–	–	–	–	–	–	–	–	–	–	–	–	1	–	–
38 Fulham	–	–	–	–	–	–	1	–	–	–	–	–	–	–	–	–	–	–	–	–	–	–	–	–	–	–	–	1	–	–
39 Hull City	–	–	–	–	–	–	1	–	–	–	–	–	–	–	–	–	–	–	–	–	–	–	–	–	–	–	–	1	–	–
40 Notts County	–	–	–	–	–	–	1	–	–	–	–	–	–	–	–	–	–	–	–	–	–	–	–	–	–	–	–	1	–	–
41 Preston North End	–	–	–	–	–	–	–	–	–	1	–	–	–	–	–	–	–	–	–	–	–	–	–	–	–	–	–	1	–	–
42 Queens Park Rangers	–	–	–	1	–	–	–	–	–	–	–	–	–	–	–	–	–	–	–	–	–	–	–	–	–	–	–	1	–	–
43 Aldershot	–	–	–	–	–	–	–	–	–	–	–	–	– (1)	–	–	–	–	–	–	–	–	–	–	–	–	–	–	– (1)	–

CAESAR JENKYNS

DEBUT (Full Appearance)

Tuesday 01/09/1896
Football League Division 2
at Bank Street

Newton Heath 2 Gainsborough Trinity 0

CLUB CAREER RECORD	Apps	Subs	Goals
Premiership	0		0
League Division 1	0		0
League Division 2	35		5
FA Cup	8		0
League Cup	0		0
European Cup / Champions League	0		0
European Cup-Winners' Cup	0		0
UEFA Cup / Inter-Cities' Fairs Cup	0		0
Other Matches	4		1
OVERALL TOTAL	47		6

Opponents	PREM A	S	G	FLD 1 A	S	G	FLD 2 A	S	G	FAC A	S	G	LC A	S	G	EC/CL A	S	G	ECWC A	S	G	UEFA A	S	G	OTHER A	S	G	TOTAL A	S	G
1 Blackpool	–	–	–	–	–	–	3	–	–	2	–	–	–	–	–	–	–	–	–	–	–	–	–	–	–	–	–	5	–	–
2 Newcastle United	–	–	–	–	–	–	4	–	–	–	–	–	–	–	–	–	–	–	–	–	–	–	–	–	–	–	–	4	–	–
3 Lincoln City	–	–	–	–	–	–	3	–	3	–	–	–	–	–	–	–	–	–	–	–	–	–	–	–	–	–	–	3	–	3
4 Birmingham City	–	–	–	–	–	–	3	–	–	–	–	–	–	–	–	–	–	–	–	–	–	–	–	–	–	–	–	3	–	–
5 Leicester City	–	–	–	–	–	–	3	–	–	–	–	–	–	–	–	–	–	–	–	–	–	–	–	–	–	–	–	3	–	–
6 Manchester City	–	–	–	–	–	–	3	–	–	–	–	–	–	–	–	–	–	–	–	–	–	–	–	–	–	–	–	3	–	–
7 Walsall	–	–	–	–	–	–	3	–	–	–	–	–	–	–	–	–	–	–	–	–	–	–	–	–	–	–	–	3	–	–
8 Burnley	–	–	–	–	–	–	–	–	–	–	–	–	–	–	–	–	–	–	–	–	–	2	–	1	–	–	–	2	–	1
9 Grimsby Town	–	–	–	–	–	–	2	–	1	–	–	–	–	–	–	–	–	–	–	–	–	–	–	–	–	–	–	2	–	1
10 Arsenal	–	–	–	–	–	–	2	–	–	–	–	–	–	–	–	–	–	–	–	–	–	–	–	–	–	–	–	2	–	–
11 Burton Swifts	–	–	–	–	–	–	2	–	–	–	–	–	–	–	–	–	–	–	–	–	–	–	–	–	–	–	–	2	–	–
12 Gainsborough Trinity	–	–	–	–	–	–	2	–	–	–	–	–	–	–	–	–	–	–	–	–	–	–	–	–	–	–	–	2	–	–
13 Notts County	–	–	–	–	–	–	2	–	–	–	–	–	–	–	–	–	–	–	–	–	–	–	–	–	–	–	–	2	–	–
14 Southampton	–	–	–	–	–	–	–	–	–	2	–	–	–	–	–	–	–	–	–	–	–	–	–	–	–	–	–	2	–	–
15 Sunderland	–	–	–	–	–	–	–	–	–	–	–	–	–	–	–	–	–	–	–	–	–	2	–	–	–	–	–	2	–	–
16 Loughborough Town	–	–	–	–	–	–	1	–	1	–	–	–	–	–	–	–	–	–	–	–	–	–	–	–	–	–	–	1	–	1
17 Burton Wanderers	–	–	–	–	–	–	1	–	–	–	–	–	–	–	–	–	–	–	–	–	–	–	–	–	–	–	–	1	–	–
18 Darwen	–	–	–	–	–	–	1	–	–	–	–	–	–	–	–	–	–	–	–	–	–	–	–	–	–	–	–	1	–	–
19 Derby County	–	–	–	–	–	–	–	–	–	1	–	–	–	–	–	–	–	–	–	–	–	–	–	–	–	–	–	1	–	–
20 Kettering	–	–	–	–	–	–	–	–	–	1	–	–	–	–	–	–	–	–	–	–	–	–	–	–	–	–	–	1	–	–
21 Nelson	–	–	–	–	–	–	–	–	–	1	–	–	–	–	–	–	–	–	–	–	–	–	–	–	–	–	–	1	–	–
22 West Manchester	–	–	–	–	–	–	–	–	–	1	–	–	–	–	–	–	–	–	–	–	–	–	–	–	–	–	–	1	–	–

ROY JOHN

DEBUT (Full Appearance)

Saturday 29/08/1936
Football League Division 1
at Old Trafford

Manchester United 1 Wolverhampton Wanderers 1

CLUB CAREER RECORD	Apps	Subs	Goals
Premiership	0		0
League Division 1	15		0
League Division 2	0		0
FA Cup	0		0
League Cup	0		0
European Cup / Champions League	0		0
European Cup-Winners' Cup	0		0
UEFA Cup / Inter-Cities' Fairs Cup	0		0
Other Matches	0		0
OVERALL TOTAL	15		0

Opponents	PREM A	S	G	FLD 1 A	S	G	FLD 2 A	S	G	FAC A	S	G	LC A	S	G	EC/CL A	S	G	ECWC A	S	G	UEFA A	S	G	OTHER A	S	G	TOTAL A	S	G
1 Huddersfield Town	–	–	–	2	–	–	–	–	–	–	–	–	–	–	–	–	–	–	–	–	–	–	–	–	–	–	–	2	–	–
2 Arsenal	–	–	–	1	–	–	–	–	–	–	–	–	–	–	–	–	–	–	–	–	–	–	–	–	–	–	–	1	–	–
3 Brentford	–	–	–	1	–	–	–	–	–	–	–	–	–	–	–	–	–	–	–	–	–	–	–	–	–	–	–	1	–	–
4 Charlton Athletic	–	–	–	1	–	–	–	–	–	–	–	–	–	–	–	–	–	–	–	–	–	–	–	–	–	–	–	1	–	–
5 Chelsea	–	–	–	1	–	–	–	–	–	–	–	–	–	–	–	–	–	–	–	–	–	–	–	–	–	–	–	1	–	–
6 Derby County	–	–	–	1	–	–	–	–	–	–	–	–	–	–	–	–	–	–	–	–	–	–	–	–	–	–	–	1	–	–
7 Grimsby Town	–	–	–	1	–	–	–	–	–	–	–	–	–	–	–	–	–	–	–	–	–	–	–	–	–	–	–	1	–	–
8 Liverpool	–	–	–	1	–	–	–	–	–	–	–	–	–	–	–	–	–	–	–	–	–	–	–	–	–	–	–	1	–	–
9 Manchester City	–	–	–	1	–	–	–	–	–	–	–	–	–	–	–	–	–	–	–	–	–	–	–	–	–	–	–	1	–	–
10 Portsmouth	–	–	–	1	–	–	–	–	–	–	–	–	–	–	–	–	–	–	–	–	–	–	–	–	–	–	–	1	–	–
11 Preston North End	–	–	–	1	–	–	–	–	–	–	–	–	–	–	–	–	–	–	–	–	–	–	–	–	–	–	–	1	–	–
12 Sheffield Wednesday	–	–	–	1	–	–	–	–	–	–	–	–	–	–	–	–	–	–	–	–	–	–	–	–	–	–	–	1	–	–
13 Stoke City	–	–	–	1	–	–	–	–	–	–	–	–	–	–	–	–	–	–	–	–	–	–	–	–	–	–	–	1	–	–
14 Wolverhampton W.	–	–	–	1	–	–	–	–	–	–	–	–	–	–	–	–	–	–	–	–	–	–	–	–	–	–	–	1	–	–

RONNIE JOHNSEN

DEBUT (Substitute Appearance)

Saturday 17/08/1996
FA Premiership
at Selhurst Park

Wimbledon 0 Manchester United 3

CLUB CAREER RECORD	Apps	Subs	Goals
Premiership	85	(14)	7
League Division 1	0		0
League Division 2	0		0
FA Cup	8	(2)	1
League Cup	3		0
European Cup / Champions League	32	(3)	0
European Cup-Winners' Cup	0		0
UEFA Cup / Inter-Cities' Fairs Cup	0		0
Other Matches	3		1
OVERALL TOTAL	**131**	**(19)**	**9**

Opponents	PREM A S G	FLD 1 A S G	FLD 2 A S G	FAC A S G	LC A S G	EC/CL A S G	ECWC A S G	UEFA A S G	OTHER A S G	TOTAL A S G
1 Tottenham Hotspur	8 – –	– – –	– – –	1 –	1 –	– – –	– – –	– – –	– – –	10 –
2 Chelsea	6 –	– – –	– – –	1 –	– –	– – –	– – –	– – –	2 1	9 1
3 Arsenal	5 (1) –	– – –	– – –	2 –	– –	– – –	– – –	– – –	1 –	8 (1) –
4 Newcastle United	4 (2) 1	– – –	– – –	1 –	– –	– – –	– – –	– – –	– – –	5 (2) 1
5 Liverpool	5 1	– – –	– – –	– (1) –	– –	– – –	– – –	– – –	– – –	5 (1) 1
6 Aston Villa	5 (1) –	– – –	– – –	– –	– –	– – –	– – –	– – –	– – –	5 (1) –
7 Blackburn Rovers	5 (1) –	– – –	– – –	– –	– –	– – –	– – –	– – –	– – –	5 (1) –
8 Derby County	5 (1) –	– – –	– – –	– –	– –	– – –	– – –	– – –	– – –	5 (1) –
9 Juventus	–	– – –	– – –	– –	– –	5 (1) –	– – –	– – –	– – –	5 (1) –
10 Southampton	4 (2) –	– – –	– – –	– –	– –	– – –	– – –	– – –	– – –	4 (2) –
11 Middlesbrough	5 –	– – –	– – –	– –	– –	– – –	– – –	– – –	– – –	5 –
12 Coventry City	4 (1) 1	– – –	– – –	– –	– –	– – –	– – –	– – –	– – –	4 (1) 1
13 Wimbledon	3 (1) 1	– – –	– – –	1 –	– –	– – –	– – –	– – –	– – –	4 (1) 1
14 Leeds United	4 (1) –	– – –	– – –	– –	– –	– – –	– – –	– – –	– – –	4 (1) –
15 West Ham United	4 (1) –	– – –	– – –	– –	– –	– – –	– – –	– – –	– – –	4 (1) –
16 Nottingham Forest	4 2	– – –	– – –	– –	– –	– – –	– – –	– – –	– – –	4 2
17 Deportivo La Coruna	–	– – –	– – –	– –	– –	4 –	– – –	– – –	– – –	4 –
18 Leicester City	3 (1) –	– – –	– – –	– –	– –	– – –	– – –	– – –	– – –	3 (1) –
19 Sunderland	2 –	– – –	– – –	– –	1 –	– – –	– – –	– – –	– – –	3 –
20 Bayern Munich	–	– – –	– – –	– –	– –	2 (1) –	– – –	– – –	– – –	2 (1) –
21 Everton	2 (1) –	– – –	– – –	– –	– –	– – –	– – –	– – –	– – –	2 (1) –
22 Ipswich Town	1 1	– – –	– – –	– –	1 –	– – –	– – –	– – –	– – –	2 1
23 Anderlecht	–	– – –	– – –	– –	– –	2 –	– – –	– – –	– – –	2 –
24 Borussia Dortmund	–	– – –	– – –	– –	– –	2 –	– – –	– – –	– – –	2 –
25 Fenerbahce	–	– – –	– – –	– –	– –	2 –	– – –	– – –	– – –	2 –
26 Internazionale	–	– – –	– – –	– –	– –	2 –	– – –	– – –	– – –	2 –
27 LKS Lodz	–	– – –	– – –	– –	– –	2 –	– – –	– – –	– – –	2 –
28 Monaco	–	– – –	– – –	– –	– –	2 –	– – –	– – –	– – –	2 –
29 Porto	–	– – –	– – –	– –	– –	2 –	– – –	– – –	– – –	2 –
30 Sheffield Wednesday	2 –	– – –	– – –	– –	– –	– – –	– – –	– – –	– – –	2 –
31 Walsall	–	– – –	– – –	1 1	– –	– – –	– – –	– – –	– – –	1 1
32 Barnsley	–	– – –	– – –	1 –	– –	– – –	– – –	– – –	– – –	1 –
33 Bayer Leverkusen	–	– – –	– – –	– –	– –	1 –	– – –	– – –	– – –	1 –
34 Boavista	–	– – –	– – –	– –	– –	1 –	– – –	– – –	– – –	1 –
35 Bradford City	1 –	– – –	– – –	– –	– –	– – –	– – –	– – –	– – –	1 –
36 Charlton Athletic	1 –	– – –	– – –	– –	– –	– – –	– – –	– – –	– – –	1 –
37 Crystal Palace	1 –	– – –	– – –	– –	– –	– – –	– – –	– – –	– – –	1 –
38 Dynamo Kiev	–	– – –	– – –	– –	– –	1 –	– – –	– – –	– – –	1 –
39 Kosice	–	– – –	– – –	– –	– –	1 –	– – –	– – –	– – –	1 –
40 Olympiakos Piraeus	–	– – –	– – –	– –	– –	1 –	– – –	– – –	– – –	1 –
41 PSV Eindhoven	–	– – –	– – –	– –	– –	1 –	– – –	– – –	– – –	1 –
42 Rapid Vienna	–	– – –	– – –	– –	– –	1 –	– – –	– – –	– – –	1 –
43 Watford	1 –	– – –	– – –	– –	– –	– – –	– – –	– – –	– – –	1 –
44 Fulham	–	– – –	– – –	– (1) –	– –	– – –	– – –	– – –	– – –	– (1) –
45 Nantes Atlantique	–	– – –	– – –	– –	– –	– (1) –	– – –	– – –	– – –	– (1) –

EDDIE JOHNSON

DEBUT (Substitute Appearance)

Tuesday 28/10/2003
League Cup 3rd Round
at Elland Road

Leeds United 2 Manchester United 3

CLUB CAREER RECORD	Apps	Subs	Goals
Premiership	0		0
League Division 1	0		0
League Division 2	0		0
FA Cup	0		0
League Cup	0	(1)	0
European Cup / Champions League	0		0
European Cup-Winners' Cup	0		0
UEFA Cup / Inter-Cities' Fairs Cup	0		0
Other Matches	0		0
OVERALL TOTAL	**0**	**(1)**	**0**

Opponents	PREM A S G	FLD 1 A S G	FLD 2 A S G	FAC A S G	LC A S G	EC/CL A S G	ECWC A S G	UEFA A S G	OTHER A S G	TOTAL A S G
1 Leeds United	–	– – –	– – –	– –	– (1) –	– – –	– – –	– – –	– – –	– (1) –

SAMUEL JOHNSON

DEBUT (Full Appearance)

Wednesday 20/03/1901
Football League Division 2
at Bank Street

Newton Heath 2 Leicester City 3

CLUB CAREER RECORD	Apps	Subs	Goals
Premiership	0		0
League Division 1	0		0
League Division 2	1		0
FA Cup	0		0
League Cup	0		0
European Cup / Champions League	0		0
European Cup-Winners' Cup	0		0
UEFA Cup / Inter-Cities' Fairs Cup	0		0
Other Matches	0		0
OVERALL TOTAL	**1**		**0**

Opponents	PREM			FLD 1			FLD 2			FAC			LC			EC/CL			ECWC			UEFA			OTHER			TOTAL		
	A	S	G	A	S	G	A	S	G	A	S	G	A	S	G	A	S	G	A	S	G	A	S	G	A	S	G	A	S	G
1 Leicester City	–	–	–	–	–	–	1	–	–	–	–	–	–	–	–	–	–	–	–	–	–	–	–	–	–	–	–	1	–	–

BILLY JOHNSTON

DEBUT (Full Appearance)

Saturday 15/10/1927
Football League Division 1
at Old Trafford

Manchester United 2 Cardiff City 2

CLUB CAREER RECORD	Apps	Subs	Goals
Premiership	0		0
League Division 1	43		13
League Division 2	28		11
FA Cup	6		3
League Cup	0		0
European Cup / Champions League	0		0
European Cup-Winners' Cup	0		0
UEFA Cup / Inter-Cities' Fairs Cup	0		0
Other Matches	0		0
OVERALL TOTAL	**77**		**27**

Opponents	PREM			FLD 1			FLD 2			FAC			LC			EC/CL			ECWC			UEFA			OTHER			TOTAL		
	A	S	G	A	S	G	A	S	G	A	S	G	A	S	G	A	S	G	A	S	G	A	S	G	A	S	G	A	S	G
1 Burnley	–	–	–	3	–	–	2	–	2	–	–	–	–	–	–	–	–	–	–	–	–	–	–	–	–	–	–	5	–	2
2 Bury	–	–	–	2	–	1	1	–	–	2	–	1	–	–	–	–	–	–	–	–	–	–	–	–	–	–	–	5	–	2
3 Birmingham City	–	–	–	2	–	1	–	–	–	1	–	1	–	–	–	–	–	–	–	–	–	–	–	–	–	–	–	3	–	2
4 Leeds United	–	–	–	1	–	1	2	–	1	–	–	–	–	–	–	–	–	–	–	–	–	–	–	–	–	–	–	3	–	2
5 Aston Villa	–	–	–	3	–	1	–	–	–	–	–	–	–	–	–	–	–	–	–	–	–	–	–	–	–	–	–	3	–	1
6 Cardiff City	–	–	–	3	–	1	–	–	–	–	–	–	–	–	–	–	–	–	–	–	–	–	–	–	–	–	–	3	–	1
7 Plymouth Argyle	–	–	–	–	–	–	2	–	1	1	–	–	–	–	–	–	–	–	–	–	–	–	–	–	–	–	–	3	–	1
8 West Ham United	–	–	–	3	–	1	–	–	–	–	–	–	–	–	–	–	–	–	–	–	–	–	–	–	–	–	–	3	–	1
9 Liverpool	–	–	–	3	–	–	–	–	–	–	–	–	–	–	–	–	–	–	–	–	–	–	–	–	–	–	–	3	–	–
10 Sheffield United	–	–	–	3	–	–	–	–	–	–	–	–	–	–	–	–	–	–	–	–	–	–	–	–	–	–	–	3	–	–
11 Tottenham Hotspur	–	–	–	1	–	1	1	–	1	–	–	–	–	–	–	–	–	–	–	–	–	–	–	–	–	–	–	2	–	2
12 Bolton Wanderers	–	–	–	2	–	1	–	–	–	–	–	–	–	–	–	–	–	–	–	–	–	–	–	–	–	–	–	2	–	1
13 Derby County	–	–	–	2	–	1	–	–	–	–	–	–	–	–	–	–	–	–	–	–	–	–	–	–	–	–	–	2	–	1
14 Newcastle United	–	–	–	2	–	1	–	–	–	–	–	–	–	–	–	–	–	–	–	–	–	–	–	–	–	–	–	2	–	1
15 Sunderland	–	–	–	2	–	1	–	–	–	–	–	–	–	–	–	–	–	–	–	–	–	–	–	–	–	–	–	2	–	1
16 Arsenal	–	–	–	2	–	–	–	–	–	–	–	–	–	–	–	–	–	–	–	–	–	–	–	–	–	–	–	2	–	–
17 Barnsley	–	–	–	–	–	–	2	–	–	–	–	–	–	–	–	–	–	–	–	–	–	–	–	–	–	–	–	2	–	–
18 Blackburn Rovers	–	–	–	1	–	–	–	–	–	1	–	–	–	–	–	–	–	–	–	–	–	–	–	–	–	–	–	2	–	–
19 Leicester City	–	–	–	2	–	–	–	–	–	–	–	–	–	–	–	–	–	–	–	–	–	–	–	–	–	–	–	2	–	–
20 Notts County	–	–	–	–	–	–	2	–	–	–	–	–	–	–	–	–	–	–	–	–	–	–	–	–	–	–	–	2	–	–
21 Port Vale	–	–	–	–	–	–	2	–	–	–	–	–	–	–	–	–	–	–	–	–	–	–	–	–	–	–	–	2	–	–
22 Portsmouth	–	–	–	2	–	–	–	–	–	–	–	–	–	–	–	–	–	–	–	–	–	–	–	–	–	–	–	2	–	–
23 Stoke City	–	–	–	–	–	–	2	–	–	–	–	–	–	–	–	–	–	–	–	–	–	–	–	–	–	–	–	2	–	–
24 Swansea City	–	–	–	–	–	–	2	–	–	–	–	–	–	–	–	–	–	–	–	–	–	–	–	–	–	–	–	2	–	–
25 Oldham Athletic	–	–	–	–	–	–	1	–	2	–	–	–	–	–	–	–	–	–	–	–	–	–	–	–	–	–	–	1	–	2
26 Bradford City	–	–	–	–	–	–	1	–	1	–	–	–	–	–	–	–	–	–	–	–	–	–	–	–	–	–	–	1	–	1
27 Brentford	–	–	–	–	–	–	–	–	–	1	–	1	–	–	–	–	–	–	–	–	–	–	–	–	–	–	–	1	–	1
28 Chesterfield	–	–	–	–	–	–	1	–	1	–	–	–	–	–	–	–	–	–	–	–	–	–	–	–	–	–	–	1	–	1
29 Manchester City	–	–	–	1	–	1	–	–	–	–	–	–	–	–	–	–	–	–	–	–	–	–	–	–	–	–	–	1	–	1
30 Middlesbrough	–	–	–	1	–	1	–	–	–	–	–	–	–	–	–	–	–	–	–	–	–	–	–	–	–	–	–	1	–	1
31 Preston North End	–	–	–	–	–	–	1	–	1	–	–	–	–	–	–	–	–	–	–	–	–	–	–	–	–	–	–	1	–	1
32 Southampton	–	–	–	–	–	–	1	–	1	–	–	–	–	–	–	–	–	–	–	–	–	–	–	–	–	–	–	1	–	1
33 Bradford Park Avenue	–	–	–	–	–	–	1	–	–	–	–	–	–	–	–	–	–	–	–	–	–	–	–	–	–	–	–	1	–	–
34 Bristol City	–	–	–	–	–	–	1	–	–	–	–	–	–	–	–	–	–	–	–	–	–	–	–	–	–	–	–	1	–	–
35 Everton	–	–	–	1	–	–	–	–	–	–	–	–	–	–	–	–	–	–	–	–	–	–	–	–	–	–	–	1	–	–
36 Huddersfield Town	–	–	–	1	–	–	–	–	–	–	–	–	–	–	–	–	–	–	–	–	–	–	–	–	–	–	–	1	–	–
37 Millwall	–	–	–	–	–	–	1	–	–	–	–	–	–	–	–	–	–	–	–	–	–	–	–	–	–	–	–	1	–	–
38 Nottingham Forest	–	–	–	–	–	–	1	–	–	–	–	–	–	–	–	–	–	–	–	–	–	–	–	–	–	–	–	1	–	–
39 Wolverhampton W.	–	–	–	–	–	–	1	–	–	–	–	–	–	–	–	–	–	–	–	–	–	–	–	–	–	–	–	1	–	–

DAVID JONES (1937)

DEBUT (Full Appearance)

Saturday 11/12/1937
Football League Division 2
at Park Avenue

Bradford Park Avenue 4 Manchester United 0

CLUB CAREER RECORD	Apps	Subs	Goals
Premiership	0		0
League Division 1	0		0
League Division 2	1		0
FA Cup	0		0
League Cup	0		0
European Cup / Champions League	0		0
European Cup-Winners' Cup	0		0
UEFA Cup / Inter-Cities' Fairs Cup	0		0
Other Matches	0		0
OVERALL TOTAL	**1**		**0**

Opponents	PREM A S G	FLD 1 A S G	FLD 2 A S G	FAC A S G	LC A S G	EC/CL A S G	ECWC A S G	UEFA A S G	OTHER A S G	TOTAL A S G
1 Bradford Park Avenue	–	–	1	–	–	–	–	–	–	1 –

DAVID JONES (2004)

DEBUT (Substitute Appearance)

Wednesday 01/12/2004
League Cup 5th Round
at Old Trafford

Manchester United 1 Arsenal 0

CLUB CAREER RECORD	Apps	Subs	Goals
Premiership	0		0
League Division 1	0		0
League Division 2	0		0
FA Cup	1		0
League Cup	2	(1)	0
European Cup / Champions League	0		0
European Cup-Winners' Cup	0		0
UEFA Cup / Inter-Cities' Fairs Cup	0		0
Other Matches	0		0
OVERALL TOTAL	**3**	**(1)**	**0**

Opponents	PREM A S G	FLD 1 A S G	FLD 2 A S G	FAC A S G	LC A S G	EC/CL A S G	ECWC A S G	UEFA A S G	OTHER A S G	TOTAL A S G
1 Crewe Alexandra	–	–	–	–	1	–	–	–	–	1 –
2 Exeter City	–	–	1	–	–	–	–	–	–	1 –
3 Southend United	–	–	–	–	1	–	–	–	–	1 –
4 Arsenal	–	–	–	–	– (1) –	–	–	–	–	– (1) –

MARK JONES

DEBUT (Full Appearance)

Saturday 07/10/1950
Football League Division 1
at Old Trafford

Manchester United 3 Sheffield Wednesday 1

CLUB CAREER RECORD	Apps	Subs	Goals
Premiership	0		0
League Division 1	103		1
League Division 2	0		0
FA Cup	7		0
League Cup	0		0
European Cup / Champions League	10		0
European Cup-Winners' Cup	0		0
UEFA Cup / Inter-Cities' Fairs Cup	0		0
Other Matches	1		0
OVERALL TOTAL	**121**		**1**

Opponents	PREM A S G	FLD 1 A S G	FLD 2 A S G	FAC A S G	LC A S G	EC/CL A S G	ECWC A S G	UEFA A S G	OTHER A S G	TOTAL A S G
1 Arsenal	– –	6 –	–	–	–	–	–	–	–	6 –
2 Chelsea	– –	6 –	–	–	–	–	–	–	–	6 –
3 Everton	– –	5 –	–	1 –	–	–	–	–	–	6 –
4 Manchester City	– –	5 –	–	–	–	–	–	1 –	–	6 –
5 Sunderland	– –	6 –	–	–	–	–	–	–	–	6 –
6 Birmingham City	– –	5 1	–	–	–	–	–	–	–	5 1
7 Bolton Wanderers	– –	5 –	–	–	–	–	–	–	–	5 –
8 Charlton Athletic	– –	5 –	–	–	–	–	–	–	–	5 –
9 Luton Town	– –	5 –	–	–	–	–	–	–	–	5 –
10 Newcastle United	– –	5 –	–	–	–	–	–	–	–	5 –
11 Preston North End	– –	5 –	–	–	–	–	–	–	–	5 –
12 West Bromwich Albion	– –	5 –	–	–	–	–	–	–	–	5 –
13 Aston Villa	– –	4 –	–	–	–	–	–	–	–	4 –
14 Blackpool	– –	4 –	–	–	–	–	–	–	–	4 –
15 Cardiff City	– –	4 –	–	–	–	–	–	–	–	4 –
16 Portsmouth	– –	4 –	–	–	–	–	–	–	–	4 –
17 Sheffield Wednesday	– –	4 –	–	–	–	–	–	–	–	4 –
18 Burnley	– –	3 –	–	–	–	–	–	–	–	3 –
19 Sheffield United	– –	3 –	–	–	–	–	–	–	–	3 –
20 Wolverhampton W.	– –	3 –	–	–	–	–	–	–	–	3 –
21 Anderlecht	– –	–	–	–	–	2 –	–	–	–	2 –
22 Athletic Bilbao	– –	–	–	–	–	2 –	–	–	–	2 –
23 Borussia Dortmund	– –	–	–	–	–	2 –	–	–	–	2 –
24 Fulham	– –	2 –	–	–	–	–	–	–	–	2 –
25 Huddersfield Town	– –	2 –	–	–	–	–	–	–	–	2 –
26 Leeds United	– –	2 –	–	–	–	–	–	–	–	2 –
27 Leicester City	– –	2 –	–	–	–	–	–	–	–	2 –
28 Red Star Belgrade	– –	–	–	–	–	2 –	–	–	–	2 –

continued../

MARK JONES (continued)

Opponents	PREM A S G	FLD 1 A S G	FLD 2 A S G	FAC A S G	LC A S G	EC/CL A S G	ECWC A S G	UEFA A S G	OTHER A S G	TOTAL A S G
29 Tottenham Hotspur	– – 2	– – –	– – –	– – –	– – –	– – –	– – –	– – –	– – –	2 –
30 Bournemouth	– – –	– – –	– – –	1 –	– – –	– – –	– – –	– – –	– – –	1 –
31 Bristol Rovers	– – –	– – –	– – –	1 –	– – –	– – –	– – –	– – –	– – –	1 –
32 Dukla Prague	– – –	– – –	– – –	– – –	– – –	1 –	– – –	– – –	– – –	1 –
33 Hartlepool United	– – –	– – –	– – –	1 –	– – –	– – –	– – –	– – –	– – –	1 –
34 Ipswich Town	– – –	– – –	– – –	1 –	– – –	– – –	– – –	– – –	– – –	1 –
35 Shamrock Rovers	– – –	– – –	– – –	– – –	– – –	1 –	– – –	– – –	– – –	1 –
36 Stoke City	– – 1	– – –	– – –	– – –	– – –	– – –	– – –	– – –	– – –	1 –
37 Workington	– – –	– – –	– – –	1 –	– – –	– – –	– – –	– – –	– – –	1 –
38 Wrexham	– – –	– – –	– – –	1 –	– – –	– – –	– – –	– – –	– – –	1 –

OWEN JONES

DEBUT (Full Appearance)

Saturday 03/09/1898
Football League Division 2
at The Northolme

Gainsborough Trinity 0 Newton Heath 2

CLUB CAREER RECORD	Apps	Subs	Goals
Premiership	0		0
League Division 1	0		0
League Division 2	2		0
FA Cup	0		0
League Cup	0		0
European Cup / Champions League	0		0
European Cup–Winners' Cup	0		0
UEFA Cup / Inter-Cities' Fairs Cup	0		0
Other Matches	0		0
OVERALL TOTAL	**2**		**0**

Opponents	PREM A S G	FLD 1 A S G	FLD 2 A S G	FAC A S G	LC A S G	EC/CL A S G	ECWC A S G	UEFA A S G	OTHER A S G	TOTAL A S G
1 Burton Swifts	– –	– –	1	– –	– –	– –	– –	– –	– –	1 –
2 Gainsborough Trinity	– –	– –	1	– –	– –	– –	– –	– –	– –	1 –

PETER JONES

DEBUT (Full Appearance)

Saturday 19/10/1957
Football League Division 1
at Old Trafford

Manchester United 0 Portsmouth 3

CLUB CAREER RECORD	Apps	Subs	Goals
Premiership	0		0
League Division 1	1		0
League Division 2	0		0
FA Cup	0		0
League Cup	0		0
European Cup / Champions League	0		0
European Cup–Winners' Cup	0		0
UEFA Cup / Inter-Cities' Fairs Cup	0		0
Other Matches	0		0
OVERALL TOTAL	**1**		**0**

Opponents	PREM A S G	FLD 1 A S G	FLD 2 A S G	FAC A S G	LC A S G	EC/CL A S G	ECWC A S G	UEFA A S G	OTHER A S G	TOTAL A S G
1 Portsmouth	– –	1	– –	– –	– –	– –	– –	– –	– –	1 –

RICHARD JONES

DEBUT (Full Appearance)

Wednesday 26/10/2005
League Cup 3rd Round
at Old Trafford

Manchester United 4 Barnet 1

CLUB CAREER RECORD	Apps	Subs	Goals
Premiership	0		0
League Division 1	0		0
League Division 2	0		0
FA Cup	1		0
League Cup	2	(2)	0
European Cup / Champions League	0		0
European Cup–Winners' Cup	0		0
UEFA Cup / Inter-Cities' Fairs Cup	0		0
Other Matches	0		0
OVERALL TOTAL	**3**	**(2)**	**0**

Opponents	PREM A S G	FLD 1 A S G	FLD 2 A S G	FAC A S G	LC A S G	EC/CL A S G	ECWC A S G	UEFA A S G	OTHER A S G	TOTAL A S G
1 Barnet	– –	– –	– –	– –	1 –	– –	– –	– –	– –	1 –
2 Burton Albion	– –	– –	– –	1 –	– –	– –	– –	– –	– –	1 –
3 Crewe Alexandra	– –	– –	– –	– –	1 –	– –	– –	– –	– –	1 –
4 Birmingham City	– –	– –	– –	– –	– (1) –	– –	– –	– –	– –	– (1) –
5 West Bromwich Albion	– –	– –	– –	– –	– (1) –	– –	– –	– –	– –	– (1) –

TOM JONES

DEBUT (Full Appearance)

Saturday 08/11/1924
Football League Division 2
at Fratton Park

Portsmouth 1 Manchester United 1

CLUB CAREER RECORD	Apps	Subs	Goals
Premiership	0		0
League Division 1	86		0
League Division 2	103		0
FA Cup	11		0
League Cup	0		0
European Cup / Champions League	0		0
European Cup-Winners' Cup	0		0
UEFA Cup / Inter-Cities' Fairs Cup	0		0
Other Matches	0		0
OVERALL TOTAL	**200**		**0**

Opponents	PREM A	S	G	FLD 1 A	S	G	FLD 2 A	S	G	FAC A	S	G	LC A	S	G	EC/CL A	S	G	ECWC A	S	G	UEFA A	S	G	OTHER A	S	G	TOTAL A	S	G
1 Burnley	–	–		5	–		5	–		–	–		–	–		–	–		–	–		–	–		–	–		10	–	
2 Birmingham City	–	–		8	–		–	–		1	–		–	–		–	–		–	–		–	–		–	–		9	–	
3 Bury	–	–		4	–		3	–		2	–		–	–		–	–		–	–		–	–		–	–		9	–	
4 Bradford City	–	–		–	–		7	–		–	–		–	–		–	–		–	–		–	–		–	–		7	–	
5 Port Vale	–	–		–	–		7	–		–	–		–	–		–	–		–	–		–	–		–	–		7	–	
6 Bolton Wanderers	–	–		3	–		3	–		–	–		–	–		–	–		–	–		–	–		–	–		6	–	
7 Notts County	–	–		1	–		5	–		–	–		–	–		–	–		–	–		–	–		–	–		6	–	
8 Plymouth Argyle	–	–		–	–		6	–		–	–		–	–		–	–		–	–		–	–		–	–		6	–	
9 Portsmouth	–	–		2	–		2	–		2	–		–	–		–	–		–	–		–	–		–	–		6	–	
10 Sheffield United	–	–		4	–		2	–		–	–		–	–		–	–		–	–		–	–		–	–		6	–	
11 West Ham United	–	–		3	–		3	–		–	–		–	–		–	–		–	–		–	–		–	–		6	–	
12 Arsenal	–	–		5	–		–	–		–	–		–	–		–	–		–	–		–	–		–	–		5	–	
13 Blackpool	–	–		1	–		4	–		–	–		–	–		–	–		–	–		–	–		–	–		5	–	
14 Fulham	–	–		–	–		5	–		–	–		–	–		–	–		–	–		–	–		–	–		5	–	
15 Huddersfield Town	–	–		5	–		–	–		–	–		–	–		–	–		–	–		–	–		–	–		5	–	
16 Nottingham Forest	–	–		–	–		4	–		1	–		–	–		–	–		–	–		–	–		–	–		5	–	
17 Oldham Athletic	–	–		–	–		5	–		–	–		–	–		–	–		–	–		–	–		–	–		5	–	
18 Sunderland	–	–		5	–		–	–		–	–		–	–		–	–		–	–		–	–		–	–		5	–	
19 Aston Villa	–	–		4	–		–	–		–	–		–	–		–	–		–	–		–	–		–	–		4	–	
20 Blackburn Rovers	–	–		3	–		–	–		1	–		–	–		–	–		–	–		–	–		–	–		4	–	
21 Brentford	–	–		–	–		3	–		1	–		–	–		–	–		–	–		–	–		–	–		4	–	
22 Derby County	–	–		3	–		1	–		–	–		–	–		–	–		–	–		–	–		–	–		4	–	
23 Everton	–	–		4	–		–	–		–	–		–	–		–	–		–	–		–	–		–	–		4	–	
24 Hull City	–	–		–	–		4	–		–	–		–	–		–	–		–	–		–	–		–	–		4	–	
25 Leeds United	–	–		3	–		1	–		–	–		–	–		–	–		–	–		–	–		–	–		4	–	
26 Newcastle United	–	–		3	–		1	–		–	–		–	–		–	–		–	–		–	–		–	–		4	–	
27 Preston North End	–	–		–	–		4	–		–	–		–	–		–	–		–	–		–	–		–	–		4	–	
28 Sheffield Wednesday	–	–		3	–		–	–		1	–		–	–		–	–		–	–		–	–		–	–		4	–	
29 Southampton	–	–		–	–		4	–		–	–		–	–		–	–		–	–		–	–		–	–		4	–	
30 Barnsley	–	–		–	–		3	–		–	–		–	–		–	–		–	–		–	–		–	–		3	–	
31 Bradford Park Avenue	–	–		–	–		3	–		–	–		–	–		–	–		–	–		–	–		–	–		3	–	
32 Chesterfield	–	–		–	–		3	–		–	–		–	–		–	–		–	–		–	–		–	–		3	–	
33 Grimsby Town	–	–		1	–		2	–		–	–		–	–		–	–		–	–		–	–		–	–		3	–	
34 Liverpool	–	–		3	–		–	–		–	–		–	–		–	–		–	–		–	–		–	–		3	–	
35 Manchester City	–	–		3	–		–	–		–	–		–	–		–	–		–	–		–	–		–	–		3	–	
36 Middlesbrough	–	–		3	–		–	–		–	–		–	–		–	–		–	–		–	–		–	–		3	–	
37 Millwall	–	–		–	–		3	–		–	–		–	–		–	–		–	–		–	–		–	–		3	–	
38 Swansea City	–	–		–	–		3	–		–	–		–	–		–	–		–	–		–	–		–	–		3	–	
39 Cardiff City	–	–		2	–		–	–		–	–		–	–		–	–		–	–		–	–		–	–		2	–	
40 Leicester City	–	–		2	–		–	–		–	–		–	–		–	–		–	–		–	–		–	–		2	–	
41 Norwich City	–	–		–	–		2	–		–	–		–	–		–	–		–	–		–	–		–	–		2	–	
42 Tottenham Hotspur	–	–		2	–		–	–		–	–		–	–		–	–		–	–		–	–		–	–		2	–	
43 Bristol Rovers	–	–		–	–		–	–		1	–		–	–		–	–		–	–		–	–		–	–		1	–	
44 Charlton Athletic	–	–		–	–		1	–		–	–		–	–		–	–		–	–		–	–		–	–		1	–	
45 Chelsea	–	–		–	–		–	–		1	–		–	–		–	–		–	–		–	–		–	–		1	–	
46 Lincoln City	–	–		–	–		1	–		–	–		–	–		–	–		–	–		–	–		–	–		1	–	
47 Stockport County	–	–		–	–		1	–		–	–		–	–		–	–		–	–		–	–		–	–		1	–	
48 Swindon Town	–	–		–	–		–	–		1	–		–	–		–	–		–	–		–	–		–	–		1	–	
49 West Bromwich Albion	–	–		1	–		–	–		–	–		–	–		–	–		–	–		–	–		–	–		1	–	
50 Wolverhampton W.	–	–		–	–		1	–		–	–		–	–		–	–		–	–		–	–		–	–		1	–	

TOMMY JONES

DEBUT (Full Appearance)

Saturday 25/08/1934
Football League Division 2
at Old Trafford

Manchester United 2 Bradford City 0

CLUB CAREER RECORD	Apps	Subs	Goals
Premiership	0		0
League Division 1	0		0
League Division 2	20		4
FA Cup	2		0
League Cup	0		0
European Cup / Champions League	0		0
European Cup-Winners' Cup	0		0
UEFA Cup / Inter-Cities' Fairs Cup	0		0
Other Matches	0		0
OVERALL TOTAL	**22**		**4**

Opponents	PREM A S G	FLD 1 A S G	FLD 2 A S G	FAC A S G	LC A S G	EC/CL A S G	ECWC A S G	UEFA A S G	OTHER A S G	TOTAL A S G
1 Port Vale	– –	– –	2 2	– –	– –	– –	– –	– –	– –	2 2
2 Barnsley	– –	– –	2 1	– –	– –	– –	– –	– –	– –	2 1
3 Norwich City	– –	– –	2 1	– –	– –	– –	– –	– –	– –	2 1
4 Bolton Wanderers	– –	– –	2 –	– –	– –	– –	– –	– –	– –	2 –
5 Nottingham Forest	– –	– –	2 –	– –	– –	– –	– –	– –	– –	2 –
6 Oldham Athletic	– –	– –	2 –	– –	– –	– –	– –	– –	– –	2 –
7 Swansea City	– –	– –	2 –	– –	– –	– –	– –	– –	– –	2 –
8 Blackpool	– –	– –	1 –	– –	– –	– –	– –	– –	– –	1 –
9 Bradford City	– –	– –	1 –	– –	– –	– –	– –	– –	– –	1 –
10 Burnley	– –	– –	1 –	– –	– –	– –	– –	– –	– –	1 –
11 Bury	– –	– –	1 –	– –	– –	– –	– –	– –	– –	1 –
12 Fulham	– –	– –	1 –	– –	– –	– –	– –	– –	– –	1 –
13 Newcastle United	– –	– –	1 –	– –	– –	– –	– –	– –	– –	1 –
14 Sheffield United	– –	– –	1 –	– –	– –	– –	– –	– –	– –	1 –
15 West Ham United	– –	– –	1 –	– –	– –	– –	– –	– –	– –	1 –

JOE JORDAN

DEBUT (Full Appearance)

Saturday 28/01/1978
FA Cup 4th Round
at Old Trafford

Manchester United 1 West Bromwich Albion 1

CLUB CAREER RECORD	Apps	Subs	Goals
Premiership	0		0
League Division 1	109		37
League Division 2	0		0
FA Cup	11	(1)	2
League Cup	4		2
European Cup / Champions League	0		0
European Cup-Winners' Cup	0		0
UEFA Cup / Inter-Cities' Fairs Cup	1		0
Other Matches	0		0
OVERALL TOTAL	**125**	**(1)**	**41**

Opponents	PREM A S G	FLD 1 A S G	FLD 2 A S G	FAC A S G	LC A S G	EC/CL A S G	ECWC A S G	UEFA A S G	OTHER A S G	TOTAL A S G
1 Tottenham Hotspur	– –	3 –	– –	3 (1) 1	2 –	– –	– –	– –	– –	8 (1) 1
2 Liverpool	– –	6 –	– –	2 1	– –	– –	– –	– –	– –	8 1
3 Norwich City	– –	7 6	– –	– –	– –	– –	– –	– –	– –	7 6
4 Nottingham Forest	– –	6 3	– –	1 –	– –	– –	– –	– –	– –	7 3
5 Arsenal	– –	6 2	– –	1 –	– –	– –	– –	– –	– –	7 2
6 Middlesbrough	– –	7 2	– –	– –	– –	– –	– –	– –	– –	7 2
7 Aston Villa	– –	6 4	– –	– –	– –	– –	– –	– –	– –	6 4
8 Coventry City	– –	6 2	– –	– –	– –	– –	– –	– –	– –	6 2
9 West Bromwich Albion	– –	4 1	– –	2 –	– –	– –	– –	– –	– –	6 1
10 Brighton	– –	3 2	– –	2 –	– –	– –	– –	– –	– –	5 2
11 Everton	– –	5 2	– –	– –	– –	– –	– –	– –	– –	5 2
12 Wolverhampton W.	– –	5 1	– –	– –	– –	– –	– –	– –	– –	5 1
13 Ipswich Town	– –	5 –	– –	– –	– –	– –	– –	– –	– –	5 –
14 Leeds United	– –	5 –	– –	– –	– –	– –	– –	– –	– –	5 –
15 Bristol City	– –	4 2	– –	– –	– –	– –	– –	– –	– –	4 2
16 Crystal Palace	– –	4 2	– –	– –	– –	– –	– –	– –	– –	4 2
17 Southampton	– –	4 1	– –	– –	– –	– –	– –	– –	– –	4 1
18 Birmingham City	– –	3 3	– –	– –	– –	– –	– –	– –	– –	3 3
19 Stoke City	– –	3 2	– –	– –	– –	– –	– –	– –	– –	3 2
20 Manchester City	– –	3 1	– –	– –	– –	– –	– –	– –	– –	3 1
21 Bolton Wanderers	– –	3 –	– –	– –	– –	– –	– –	– –	– –	3 –
22 Chelsea	– –	3 –	– –	– –	– –	– –	– –	– –	– –	3 –
23 Derby County	– –	2 –	– –	– –	– –	– –	– –	– –	– –	2 –
24 Queens Park Rangers	– –	2 –	– –	– –	– –	– –	– –	– –	– –	2 –
25 Newcastle United	– –	1 1	– –	– –	– –	– –	– –	– –	– –	1 1
26 Stockport County	– –	– –	– –	– –	1 1	– –	– –	– –	– –	1 1
27 Watford	– –	– –	– –	– –	1 1	– –	– –	– –	– –	1 1
28 Leicester City	– –	1 –	– –	– –	– –	– –	– –	– –	– –	1 –
29 Sunderland	– –	1 –	– –	– –	– –	– –	– –	– –	– –	1 –
30 West Ham United	– –	1 –	– –	– –	– –	– –	– –	– –	– –	1 –
31 Widzew Lodz	– –	– –	– –	– –	– –	– –	– –	1 –	– –	1 –

NIKKI JOVANOVIC

DEBUT (Full Appearance)

Saturday 02/02/1980
Football League Division 1
at Baseball Ground

Derby County 1 Manchester United 3

CLUB CAREER RECORD	Apps	Subs	Goals
Premiership	0		0
League Division 1	20	(1)	4
League Division 2	0		0
FA Cup	1		0
League Cup	2		0
European Cup / Champions League	0		0
European Cup-Winners' Cup	0		0
UEFA Cup / Inter-Cities' Fairs Cup	2		0
Other Matches	0		0
OVERALL TOTAL	**25**	**(1)**	**4**

Opponents	PREM A S G	FLD 1 A S G	FLD 2 A S G	FAC A S G	LC A S G	EC/CL A S G	ECWC A S G	UEFA A S G	OTHER A S G	TOTAL A S G
1 Coventry City	–	1	–	–	2	–	–	–	–	3 –
2 Leicester City	–	2 2	–	–	–	–	–	–	–	2 2
3 Arsenal	–	2	–	–	–	–	–	–	–	2 –
4 Brighton	–	1	–	– 1	–	–	–	–	–	2 –
5 Stoke City	–	2	–	–	–	–	–	–	–	2 –
6 Widzew Lodz	–	–	–	–	–	–	–	2	–	2 –
7 Ipswich Town	–	1 (1)	–	–	–	–	–	–	–	1 (1) –
8 Sunderland	–	1 1	–	–	–	–	–	–	–	1 1
9 West Bromwich Albion	–	1 1	–	–	–	–	–	–	–	1 1
10 Aston Villa	–	1	–	–	–	–	–	–	–	1 –
11 Crystal Palace	–	1	–	–	–	–	–	–	–	1 –
12 Derby County	–	1	–	–	–	–	–	–	–	1 –
13 Leeds United	–	1	–	–	–	–	–	–	–	1 –
14 Liverpool	–	1	–	–	–	–	–	–	–	1 –
15 Norwich City	–	1	–	–	–	–	–	–	–	1 –
16 Nottingham Forest	–	1	–	–	–	–	–	–	–	1 –
17 Southampton	–	1	–	–	–	–	–	–	–	1 –
18 Tottenham Hotspur	–	1	–	–	–	–	–	–	–	1 –

ANDREI KANCHELSKIS

DEBUT (Full Appearance)

Saturday 11/05/1991
Football League Division 1
at Selhurst Park

Crystal Palace 3 Manchester United 0

CLUB CAREER RECORD	Apps	Subs	Goals
Premiership	67	(21)	23
League Division 1	29	(6)	5
League Division 2	0		0
FA Cup	11	(1)	4
League Cup	15	(1)	3
European Cup / Champions League	5		1
European Cup-Winners' Cup	1		0
UEFA Cup / Inter-Cities' Fairs Cup	1		0
Other Matches	3		0
OVERALL TOTAL	**132**	**(29)**	**36**

Opponents	PREM A S G	FLD 1 A S G	FLD 2 A S G	FAC A S G	LC A S G	EC/CL A S G	ECWC A S G	UEFA A S G	OTHER A S G	TOTAL A S G
1 Leeds United	4 (1) 2	1 –	–	2 –	1 1	–	–	–	–	8 (1) 3
2 Liverpool	6 1	1 (1) –	–	–	–	–	–	–	–	7 (1) 1
3 Aston Villa	3 (1) 1	2 –	–	–	1 (1) –	–	–	–	–	6 (2) 1
4 Norwich City	5 2	1 –	–	1 –	–	–	–	–	–	7 2
5 Queens Park Rangers	5 2	1 –	–	–	1 –	–	–	–	–	7 2
6 Everton	4 (1) 1	1 1	–	–	1 –	–	–	–	–	6 (1) 2
7 Sheffield United	2 (1) –	2 1	–	2 –	–	–	–	–	–	6 (1) 1
8 Tottenham Hotspur	4 (1) –	2 –	–	–	–	–	–	–	–	6 (1) –
9 Crystal Palace	2 (2) 1	3 1	–	–	–	–	–	–	–	5 (2) 2
10 Sheffield Wednesday	1 (2) –	2 –	–	–	2 1	–	–	–	–	5 (2) 1
11 Chelsea	1 (3) –	2 –	–	1 –	–	–	–	–	–	4 (3) –
12 Oldham Athletic	3 1	1 1	–	1 1	1 1	–	–	–	–	6 4
13 Wimbledon	4 1	1 –	–	1 –	–	–	–	–	–	6 1
14 Ipswich Town	5 (1) –	–	–	–	–	–	–	–	–	5 (1) –
15 Nottingham Forest	2 (1) 1	1 (1) –	–	–	1 –	–	–	–	–	4 (2) 1
16 Blackburn Rovers	2 (3) 2	–	–	–	–	–	–	–	–	3 (3) 2
17 Manchester City	4 4	– (1) –	–	–	–	–	–	–	–	4 (1) 4
18 Southampton	1 (1) 1	2 1	–	1 1	–	–	–	–	–	4 (1) 3
19 Arsenal	2 1	1 (1) –	–	–	–	–	1 –	–	–	4 (1) 1
20 West Ham United	3 –	1 (1) –	–	–	–	–	–	–	–	4 (1) –
21 Portsmouth	–	–	–	–	3 –	–	–	–	–	3 –
22 Coventry City	– (1) –	2 –	–	–	–	–	–	–	–	2 (1) –
23 Newcastle United	2 (1) –	–	–	–	–	–	–	–	–	2 (1) –
24 Gothenburg	–	–	–	–	–	2 1	–	–	–	2 1
25 Leicester City	1 1	–	–	–	1 –	–	–	–	–	2 1
26 Barcelona	–	–	–	–	–	2 –	–	–	–	2 –
27 Brighton	–	–	–	2 –	–	–	–	–	–	2 –
28 Notts County	–	2 –	–	–	–	–	–	–	–	2 –
29 Stoke City	–	–	–	–	2 –	–	–	–	–	2 –
30 Charlton Athletic	–	–	–	1 2	–	–	–	–	–	1 2
31 Swindon Town	1 1	–	–	–	–	–	–	–	–	1 1
32 Athinaikos	–	–	–	–	–	–	1 –	–	–	1 –
33 Galatasaray	–	–	–	–	–	1 –	–	–	–	1 –

continued../

ANDREI KANCHELSKIS (continued)

Opponents	PREM A S G	FLD 1 A S G	FLD 2 A S G	FAC A S G	LC A S G	EC/CL A S G	ECWC A S G	UEFA A S G	OTHER A S G	TOTAL A S G
34 Red Star Belgrade	– – –	– – –	– – –	– – –	– – –	– – –	– – –	– – –	1 – –	1 – –
35 Torpedo Moscow	– – –	– – –	– – –	– – –	– – –	– – –	– – –	1 – –	– – –	1 – –
36 Luton Town	– – –	– – –	– (1) –	– – –	– – –	– – –	– – –	– – –	– – –	– (1) –
37 Middlesbrough	– (1) –	– – –	– – –	– – –	– – –	– – –	– – –	– – –	– – –	– (1) –
38 Wrexham	– – –	– – –	– – –	– (1) –	– – –	– – –	– – –	– – –	– – –	– (1) –

ROY KEANE

DEBUT (Full Appearance)

Saturday 07/08/1993
FA Charity Shield
at Wembley

Manchester United 1 Arsenal 1

CLUB CAREER RECORD	Apps	Subs	Goals
Premiership	309	(17)	33
League Division 1	0		0
League Division 2	0		0
FA Cup	44	(2)	2
League Cup	12	(2)	0
European Cup / Champions League	79	(1)	14
European Cup-Winners' Cup	0		0
UEFA Cup / Inter-Cities' Fairs Cup	2		0
Other Matches	12		2
OVERALL TOTAL	458	(22)	51

Opponents	PREM A S G	FLD 1 A S G	FLD 2 A S G	FAC A S G	LC A S G	EC/CL A S G	ECWC A S G	UEFA A S G	OTHER A S G	TOTAL A S G
1 Arsenal	18 _ 3	– – –	– – –	5 _ –	– – –	– – –	– – –	4 – –	– – –	27 _ 3
2 Chelsea	18 – –	– – –	– – –	4 – –	1 – –	– – –	– – –	2 – –	– – –	25 – –
3 Newcastle United	19(1) _ 1	– – –	– – –	2 – –	– – –	– – –	– – –	1 – 1	– – –	22(1) _ 2
4 Liverpool	17 – –	– – –	– – –	2 – –	1 – –	– – –	– – –	1 – –	– – –	21 – –
5 Aston Villa	16(1) _ 1	– – –	– – –	1(1) _ –	1 – –	– – –	– – –	– – –	– – –	18(2) _ 1
6 Everton	17 – 1	– – –	– – –	2 – –	– – –	– – –	– – –	– – –	– – –	19 – 1
7 Southampton	15(1) _ 2	– – –	– – –	2 _ 1	– – –	– – –	– – –	– – –	– – –	17(1) _ 3
8 Tottenham Hotspur	16 – 1	– – –	– – –	1 – –	– – –	– – –	– – –	– – –	– – –	17 – 1
9 Leeds United	15(1) _ 3	– – –	– – –	1 _ –	– – –	– – –	– – –	– – –	– – –	16(1) _ 3
10 Middlesbrough	14 – 2	– – –	– – –	2 – –	– – –	– – –	– – –	– – –	– – –	16 – 2
11 West Ham United	14 – 2	– – –	– – –	2 – –	– – –	– – –	– – –	– – –	– – –	16 – 2
12 Blackburn Rovers	10(4) _ 1	– – –	– – –	– – –	1 – –	– – –	– – –	– – –	– – –	11(4) _ 1
13 Leicester City	12 – 1	– – –	– – –	– – –	2 – –	– – –	– – –	– – –	– – –	14 – 1
14 Manchester City	11(1) _ 1	– – –	– – –	2 – –	– – –	– – –	– – –	– – –	– – –	13(1) _ 1
15 Charlton Athletic	10(1) _ 1	– – –	– – –	1 _ –	– – –	– – –	– – –	– – –	– – –	11(1) _ 1
16 Coventry City	9(1) _ 1	– – –	– – –	– – –	– – –	– – –	– – –	– – –	– – –	9(1) _ 1
17 Wimbledon	6 – 2	– – –	– – –	3 – –	– – –	– – –	– – –	– – –	– – –	9 – 2
18 Sheffield Wednesday	7 – –	– – –	– – –	– – –	2 – –	– – –	– – –	– – –	– – –	9 – –
19 Sunderland	6 – 1	– – –	– – –	2 – –	– – –	– – –	– – –	– – –	– – –	8 – 1
20 Bolton Wanderers	8 – –	– – –	– – –	– – –	– – –	– – –	– – –	– – –	– – –	8 – –
21 Derby County	7 – 1	– – –	– – –	– – –	– – –	– – –	– – –	– – –	– – –	7 – 1
22 Ipswich Town	7 – 1	– – –	– – –	– – –	– – –	– – –	– – –	– – –	– – –	7 – 1
23 Queens Park Rangers	5(1) _ 1	– – –	– – –	– (1) _ –	– – –	– – –	– – –	– – –	– – –	5(2) _ 1
24 Bayern Munich	– – –	– – –	– – –	– – –	– – –	6 _ 1	– – –	– – –	– – –	6 _ 1
25 Fulham	4 – –	– – –	– – –	2 – –	– – –	– – –	– – –	– – –	– – –	6 – –
26 Birmingham City	5 – 1	– – –	– – –	– – –	– – –	– – –	– – –	– – –	– – –	5 – 1
27 Juventus	– – –	– – –	– – –	– – –	– – –	5 _ 1	– – –	– – –	– – –	5 _ 1
28 Crystal Palace	3 – –	– – –	– – –	2 – –	– – –	– – –	– – –	– – –	– – –	5 – –
29 Nottingham Forest	4(1) _ –	– – –	– – –	– – –	– – –	– – –	– – –	– – –	– – –	4(1) _ –
30 Portsmouth	– (2) _ 1	– – –	– – –	1 – –	1(1) _ –	– – –	– – –	– – –	– – –	2(3) _ 1
31 Sturm Graz	– – –	– – –	– – –	– – –	– – –	4 _ 3	– – –	– – –	– – –	4 _ 3
32 Galatasaray	– – –	– – –	– – –	– – –	– – –	4 _ 1	– – –	– – –	– – –	4 _ 1
33 Norwich City	3 – –	– – –	– – –	1 _ 1	– – –	– – –	– – –	– – –	– – –	4 _ 1
34 Valencia	– – –	– – –	– – –	– – –	– – –	4 _ 1	– – –	– – –	– – –	4 _ 1
35 Barcelona	– – –	– – –	– – –	– – –	– – –	4 _ –	– – –	– – –	– – –	4 _ –
36 Real Madrid	– – –	– – –	– – –	– – –	– – –	4 – –	– – –	– – –	– – –	4 – –
37 Sheffield United	1(1) _ 2	– – –	– – –	2 – –	– – –	– – –	– – –	– – –	– – –	3(1) _ 2
38 Bradford City	3 – 1	– – –	– – –	– – –	– – –	– – –	– – –	– – –	– – –	3 – 1
39 Swindon Town	2 – 1	– – –	– – –	– – –	1 – –	– – –	– – –	– – –	– – –	3 – 1
40 Deportivo La Coruna	– – –	– – –	– – –	– – –	– – –	3 – –	– – –	– – –	– – –	3 – –
41 Oldham Athletic	2 – –	– – –	– – –	1 – –	– – –	– – –	– – –	– – –	– – –	3 – –
42 West Bromwich Albion	3 – –	– – –	– – –	– – –	– – –	– – –	– – –	– – –	– – –	3 – –
43 Brondby	– – –	– – –	– – –	– – –	– – –	2 _ 1	– – –	– – –	– – –	2 _ 1
44 Fiorentina	– – –	– – –	– – –	– – –	– – –	2 _ 1	– – –	– – –	– – –	2 _ 1
45 Girondins Bordeaux	– – –	– – –	– – –	– – –	– – –	2 _ 1	– – –	– – –	– – –	2 _ 1
46 AC Milan	– – –	– – –	– – –	– – –	– – –	2 – –	– – –	– – –	– – –	2 – –
47 Dynamo Kiev	– – –	– – –	– – –	– – –	– – –	2 – –	– – –	– – –	– – –	2 – –
48 Glasgow Rangers	– – –	– – –	– – –	– – –	– – –	2 – –	– – –	– – –	– – –	2 – –
49 Internazionale	– – –	– – –	– – –	– – –	– – –	2 – –	– – –	– – –	– – –	2 – –
50 LKS Lodz	– – –	– – –	– – –	– – –	– – –	2 – –	– – –	– – –	– – –	2 – –
51 Nantes Atlantique	– – –	– – –	– – –	– – –	– – –	2 – –	– – –	– – –	– – –	2 – –
52 Olympique Lyonnais	– – –	– – –	– – –	– – –	– – –	2 – –	– – –	– – –	– – –	2 – –
53 Panathinaikos	– – –	– – –	– – –	– – –	– – –	2 – –	– – –	– – –	– – –	2 – –
54 Porto	– – –	– – –	– – –	– – –	– – –	2 – –	– – –	– – –	– – –	2 – –
55 PSV Eindhoven	– – –	– – –	– – –	– – –	– – –	2 – –	– – –	– – –	– – –	2 – –
56 Rapid Vienna	– – –	– – –	– – –	– – –	– – –	2 – –	– – –	– – –	– – –	2 – –

continued../

ROY KEANE (continued)

Opponents	PREM A S G	FLD 1 A S G	FLD 2 A S G	FAC A S G	LC A S G	EC/CL A S G	ECWC A S G	UEFA A S G	OTHER A S G	TOTAL A S G
57 Rotor Volgograd	– –	– –	– –	– –	– –	– –	– –	2 –	– –	2 –
58 Wolverhampton W.	2 –	– –	– –	– –	– –	– –	– –	– –	– –	2 –
59 Zalaegerszeg	– –	– –	– –	– –	– –	2 –	– –	– –	– –	2 –
60 Bayer Leverkusen	– –	– –	– –	– –	– –	1 (1) 1	– –	– –	– –	1 (1) 1
61 Honved	– –	– –	– –	– –	– –	1 2	– –	– –	– –	1 2
62 Croatia Zagreb	– –	– –	– –	– –	– –	1 1	– –	– –	– –	1 1
63 Palmeiras	– –	– –	– –	– –	– –	– –	– –	– –	1 1	1 1
64 Anderlecht	– –	– –	– –	– –	– –	1 –	– –	– –	– –	1 –
65 Boavista	– –	– –	– –	– –	– –	1 –	– –	– –	– –	1 –
66 Borussia Dortmund	– –	– –	– –	– –	– –	1 –	– –	– –	– –	1 –
67 Debreceni	– –	– –	– –	– –	– –	1 –	– –	– –	– –	1 –
68 Dinamo Bucharest	– –	– –	– –	– –	– –	1 –	– –	– –	– –	1 –
69 Fenerbahce	– –	– –	– –	– –	– –	1 –	– –	– –	– –	1 –
70 Kosice	– –	– –	– –	– –	– –	1 –	– –	– –	– –	1 –
71 Lazio	– –	– –	– –	– –	– –	– –	– –	1 –	– –	1 –
72 Lille Metropole	– –	– –	– –	– –	– –	1 –	– –	– –	– –	1 –
73 Millwall	– –	– –	1 –	– –	– –	– –	– –	– –	– –	1 –
74 Olympiakos Piraeus	– –	– –	– –	– –	– –	1 –	– –	– –	– –	1 –
75 Olympique Marseille	– –	– –	– –	– –	– –	1 –	– –	– –	– –	1 –
76 Port Vale	– –	– –	– –	– –	1 –	– –	– –	– –	– –	1 –
77 Rayos del Necaxa	– –	– –	– –	– –	– –	– –	– –	– –	1 –	1 –
78 Reading	– –	– –	– –	1 –	– –	– –	– –	– –	– –	1 –
79 Sparta Prague	– –	– –	– –	– –	– –	1 –	– –	– –	– –	1 –
80 Stoke City	– –	– –	– –	– –	1 –	– –	– –	– –	– –	1 –
81 Stuttgart	– –	– –	– –	– –	– –	1 –	– –	– –	– –	1 –
82 Vasco da Gama	– –	– –	– –	– –	– –	– –	– –	– –	1 –	1 –
83 Wrexham	– –	– –	– –	1 –	– –	– –	– –	– –	– –	1 –
84 Watford	– (1) –	– –	– –	– –	– –	– –	– –	– –	– –	– (1) –
85 York City	– –	– –	– –	– –	– (1) –	– –	– –	– –	– –	– (1) –

JIMMY KELLY

DEBUT (Substitute Appearance)

Saturday 20/12/1975
Football League Division 1
at Old Trafford

Manchester United 1 Wolverhampton Wanderers 0

CLUB CAREER RECORD	Apps	Subs	Goals
Premiership	0		0
League Division 1	0	(1)	0
League Division 2	0		0
FA Cup	0		0
League Cup	0		0
European Cup / Champions League	0		0
European Cup-Winners' Cup	0		0
UEFA Cup / Inter-Cities' Fairs Cup	0		0
Other Matches	0		0
OVERALL TOTAL	**0**	**(1)**	**0**

Opponents	PREM A S G	FLD 1 A S G	FLD 2 A S G	FAC A S G	LC A S G	EC/CL A S G	ECWC A S G	UEFA A S G	OTHER A S G	TOTAL A S G
1 Wolverhampton W.	– –	– (1) –	– –	– –	– –	– –	– –	– –	– –	– (1) –

FRED KENNEDY

DEBUT (Full Appearance)

Saturday 06/10/1923
Football League Division 2
at Boundary Park

Oldham Athletic 3 Manchester United 2

CLUB CAREER RECORD	Apps	Subs	Goals
Premiership	0		0
League Division 1	0		0
League Division 2	17		4
FA Cup	1		0
League Cup	0		0
European Cup / Champions League	0		0
European Cup-Winners' Cup	0		0
UEFA Cup / Inter-Cities' Fairs Cup	0		0
Other Matches	0		0
OVERALL TOTAL	**18**		**4**

Opponents	PREM A S G	FLD 1 A S G	FLD 2 A S G	FAC A S G	LC A S G	EC/CL A S G	ECWC A S G	UEFA A S G	OTHER A S G	TOTAL A S G
1 Nelson	– –	– –	2 1	– –	– –	– –	– –	– –	– –	2 1
2 Blackpool	– –	– –	2 –	– –	– –	– –	– –	– –	– –	2 –
3 Middlesbrough	– –	– –	2 –	– –	– –	– –	– –	– –	– –	2 –
4 Oldham Athletic	– –	– –	2 –	– –	– –	– –	– –	– –	– –	2 –
5 Sheffield Wednesday	– –	– –	1 –	1 –	– –	– –	– –	– –	– –	2 –
6 Leyton Orient	– –	– –	1 2	– –	– –	– –	– –	– –	– –	1 2
7 Wolverhampton W.	– –	– –	1 1	– –	– –	– –	– –	– –	– –	1 1
8 Chelsea	– –	– –	1 –	– –	– –	– –	– –	– –	– –	1 –
9 Crystal Palace	– –	– –	1 –	– –	– –	– –	– –	– –	– –	1 –
10 Derby County	– –	– –	1 –	– –	– –	– –	– –	– –	– –	1 –
11 Fulham	– –	– –	1 –	– –	– –	– –	– –	– –	– –	1 –
12 Leicester City	– –	– –	1 –	– –	– –	– –	– –	– –	– –	1 –
13 Stoke City	– –	– –	1 –	– –	– –	– –	– –	– –	– –	1 –

PATRICK KENNEDY

DEBUT (Full Appearance)

Saturday 02/10/1954
Football League Division 1
at Molineux

Wolverhampton Wanderers 4 Manchester United 2

CLUB CAREER RECORD	Apps	Subs	Goals
Premiership	0		0
League Division 1	1		0
League Division 2	0		0
FA Cup	0		0
League Cup	0		0
European Cup / Champions League	0		0
European Cup-Winners' Cup	0		0
UEFA Cup / Inter-Cities' Fairs Cup	0		0
Other Matches	0		0
OVERALL TOTAL	1		0

Opponents	PREM A S G	FLD 1 A S G	FLD 2 A S G	FAC A S G	LC A S G	EC/CL A S G	ECWC A S G	UEFA A S G	OTHER A S G	TOTAL A S G
1 Wolverhampton W.	– –	1 –	– –	– –	– –	– –	– –	– –	– –	1 –

WILLIAM KENNEDY

DEBUT (Full Appearance, 1 goal)

Saturday 07/09/1895
Football League Division 2
at Bank Street

Newton Heath 5 Crewe Alexandra 0

CLUB CAREER RECORD	Apps	Subs	Goals
Premiership	0		0
League Division 1	0		0
League Division 2	30		11
FA Cup	3		1
League Cup	0		0
European Cup / Champions League	0		0
European Cup-Winners' Cup	0		0
UEFA Cup / Inter-Cities' Fairs Cup	0		0
Other Matches	0		0
OVERALL TOTAL	33		12

Opponents	PREM A S G	FLD 1 A S G	FLD 2 A S G	FAC A S G	LC A S G	EC/CL A S G	ECWC A S G	UEFA A S G	OTHER A S G	TOTAL A S G
1 Darwen	– – –	– – –	– – –	2 3	– –	– –	– –	– –	– –	2 3
2 Arsenal	– – –	– – –	2 1	– –	– –	– –	– –	– –	– –	2 1
3 Burton Swifts	– – –	– – –	2 1	– –	– –	– –	– –	– –	– –	2 1
4 Crewe Alexandra	– – –	– – –	2 1	– –	– –	– –	– –	– –	– –	2 1
5 Derby County	– – –	– – –	– –	2 1	– –	– –	– –	– –	– –	2 1
6 Grimsby Town	– – –	– – –	2 1	– –	– –	– –	– –	– –	– –	2 1
7 Leicester City	– – –	– – –	2 1	– –	– –	– –	– –	– –	– –	2 1
8 Newcastle United	– – –	– – –	2 1	– –	– –	– –	– –	– –	– –	2 1
9 Notts County	– – –	– – –	2 1	– –	– –	– –	– –	– –	– –	2 1
10 Rotherham United	– – –	– – –	2 1	– –	– –	– –	– –	– –	– –	2 1
11 Burton Wanderers	– – –	– – –	2 –	– –	– –	– –	– –	– –	– –	2 –
12 Liverpool	– – –	– – –	2 –	– –	– –	– –	– –	– –	– –	2 –
13 Loughborough Town	– – –	– – –	2 –	– –	– –	– –	– –	– –	– –	2 –
14 Manchester City	– – –	– – –	2 –	– –	– –	– –	– –	– –	– –	2 –
15 Port Vale	– – –	– – –	2 –	– –	– –	– –	– –	– –	– –	2 –
16 Gainsborough Trinity	– – –	– – –	1 –	– –	– –	– –	– –	– –	– –	1 –
17 Kettering	– – –	– – –	– –	1 –	– –	– –	– –	– –	– –	1 –
18 Lincoln City	– – –	– – –	1 –	– –	– –	– –	– –	– –	– –	1 –

HUGH KERR

DEBUT (Full Appearance)

Wednesday 09/03/1904
Football League Division 2
at Bloomfield Road

Blackpool 2 Manchester United 1

CLUB CAREER RECORD	Apps	Subs	Goals
Premiership	0		0
League Division 1	0		0
League Division 2	2		0
FA Cup	0		0
League Cup	0		0
European Cup / Champions League	0		0
European Cup-Winners' Cup	0		0
UEFA Cup / Inter-Cities' Fairs Cup	0		0
Other Matches	0		0
OVERALL TOTAL	2		0

Opponents	PREM A S G	FLD 1 A S G	FLD 2 A S G	FAC A S G	LC A S G	EC/CL A S G	ECWC A S G	UEFA A S G	OTHER A S G	TOTAL A S G
1 Blackpool	– – –	– –	1 –	– –	– –	– –	– –	– –	– –	1 –
2 Grimsby Town	– – –	– –	1 –	– –	– –	– –	– –	– –	– –	1 –

BRIAN KIDD

DEBUT (Full Appearance)

Saturday 12/08/1967
FA Charity Shield
at Old Trafford

Manchester United 3   Tottenham Hotspur 3

CLUB CAREER RECORD	Apps	Subs	Goals
Premiership	0		0
League Division 1	195	(8)	52
League Division 2	0		0
FA Cup	24	(1)	8
League Cup	20		7
European Cup / Champions League	16		3
European Cup-Winners' Cup	0		0
UEFA Cup / Inter-Cities' Fairs Cup	0		0
Other Matches	2		0
OVERALL TOTAL	**257**	**(9)**	**70**

Opponents	PREM A	S	G	FLD 1 A	S	G	FLD 2 A	S	G	FAC A	S	G	LC A	S	G	EC/CL A	S	G	ECWC A	S	G	UEFA A	S	G	OTHER A	S	G	TOTAL A	S	G
1 Leeds United	–		–	10	(1)	1	–		–	3		–	–		–	–		–	–		–	–		–	–		–	13	(1)	1
2 Tottenham Hotspur	–		–	10		–	–		–	2		–	–		–	–		–	–		–		1	–	–		–	13		–
3 Ipswich Town	–		–	10		3	–		–	1	(1)	–	1		–	–		–	–		–	–		–	–		–	12	(1)	3
4 Manchester City	–		–	9	(2)	3	–		–	1		2	1		–	–		–	–		–	–		–	–		–	11	(2)	5
5 Wolverhampton W.	–		–	10	(2)	3	–		–	1		–	–		–	–		–	–		–	–		–	–		–	11	(2)	3
6 Everton	–		–	10	(1)	–	–		–	1		–	–		–	–		–	–		–	–		–	–		–	11	(1)	–
7 Newcastle United	–		–	10	(1)	4	–		–	–		–	–		–	–		–	–		–	–		–	–		–	10	(1)	4
8 West Bromwich Albion	–		–	10		7	–		–	–		–	–		–	–		–	–		–	–		–	–		–	10		7
9 Southampton	–		–	9		4	–		–	1		–	–		–	–		–	–		–	–		–	–		–	10		4
10 Stoke City	–		–	6		–	–		–	2		–	2		–	–		–	–		–	–		–	–		–	10		–
11 West Ham United	–		–	9		4	–		–	–		–	–		–	–		–	–		–	–		–	–		–	9		4
12 Chelsea	–		–	8		3	–		–	–		–	1		–	–		–	–		–	–		–	–		–	9		3
13 Arsenal	–		–	9		2	–		–	–		–	–		–	–		–	–		–	–		–	–		–	9		2
14 Derby County	–		–	8		1	–		–	–		–	1		1	–		–	–		–	–		–	–		–	9		2
15 Coventry City	–		–	9		1	–		–	–		–	–		–	–		–	–		–	–		–	–		–	9		1
16 Burnley	–		–	5		–	–		–	–		–	4		–	–		–	–		–	–		–	–		–	9		–
17 Crystal Palace	–		–	7		3	–		–	–		–	1		2	–		–	–		–	–		–	–		–	8		5
18 Liverpool	–		–	7		1	–		–	–		–	–		–	–		–	–		–	–		–	–		–	7		1
19 Nottingham Forest	–		–	6		2	–		–	–		–	–		–	–		–	–		–	–		–	–		–	6		2
20 Sheffield Wednesday	–		–	6		2	–		–	–		–	–		–	–		–	–		–	–		–	–		–	6		2
21 Middlesbrough	–		–	–		–	–		–	4		–	2		–	–		–	–		–	–		–	–		–	6		–
22 Leicester City	–		–	5	(1)	1	–		–	–		–	–		–	–		–	–		–	–		–	–		–	5	(1)	1
23 Sunderland	–		–	5		3	–		–	–		–	–		–	–		–	–		–	–		–	–		–	5		3
24 Sheffield United	–		–	4		2	–		–	–		–	–		–	–		–	–		–	–		–	–		–	4		2
25 Birmingham City	–		–	2		–	–		–	2		1	–		–	–		–	–		–	–		–	–		–	4		1
26 Huddersfield Town	–		–	3		–	–		–	–		–	–		–	–		–	–		–	–		–	–		–	3		–
27 Aston Villa	–		–	–		–	–		–	–		–	2		2	–		–	–		–	–		–	–		–	2		2
28 Watford	–		–	–		–	–		–	2		2	–		–	–		–	–		–	–		–	–		–	2		2
29 Fulham	–		–	2		1	–		–	–		–	–		–	–		–	–		–	–		–	–		–	2		1
30 Gornik Zabrze	–		–	–		–	–		–	–		–	–		–	2		1	–		–	–		–	–		–	2		1
31 Queens Park Rangers	–		–	2		1	–		–	–		–	–		–	–		–	–		–	–		–	–		–	2		1
32 AC Milan	–		–	–		–	–		–	–		–	–		–	2		–	–		–	–		–	–		–	2		–
33 Blackpool	–		–	2		–	–		–	–		–	–		–	–		–	–		–	–		–	–		–	2		–
34 Bristol Rovers	–		–	–		–	–		–	–		–	2		–	–		–	–		–	–		–	–		–	2		–
35 Hibernians Malta	–		–	–		–	–		–	–		–	–		–	2		–	–		–	–		–	–		–	2		–
36 Norwich City	–		–	2		–	–		–	–		–	–		–	–		–	–		–	–		–	–		–	2		–
37 Rapid Vienna	–		–	–		–	–		–	–		–	–		–	2		–	–		–	–		–	–		–	2		–
38 Real Madrid	–		–	–		–	–		–	–		–	–		–	2		–	–		–	–		–	–		–	2		–
39 Sarajevo	–		–	–		–	–		–	–		–	–		–	2		–	–		–	–		–	–		–	2		–
40 Waterford	–		–	–		–	–		–	–		–	–		–	2		–	–		–	–		–	–		–	2		–
41 Northampton Town	–		–	–		–	–		–	1		2	–		–	–		–	–		–	–		–	–		–	1		2
42 Aldershot	–		–	–		–	–		–	–		–	1		1	–		–	–		–	–		–	–		–	1		1
43 Anderlecht	–		–	–		–	–		–	–		–	–		–	1		1	–		–	–		–	–		–	1		1
44 Benfica	–		–	–		–	–		–	–		–	–		–	1		1	–		–	–		–	–		–	1		1
45 Exeter City	–		–	–		–	–		–	1		1	–		–	–		–	–		–	–		–	–		–	1		1
46 Wrexham	–		–	–		–	–		–	–		–	1		1	–		–	–		–	–		–	–		–	1		1
47 Estudiantes de la Plata	–		–	–		–	–		–	–		–	–		–	–		–	–		–	–		–	1		–	1		–
48 Plymouth Argyle	–		–	–		–	–		–	1		–	–		–	–		–	–		–	–		–	–		–	1		–
49 Portsmouth	–		–	–		–	–		–	–		–	1		–	–		–	–		–	–		–	–		–	1		–
50 Preston North End	–		–	–		–	–		–	1		–	–		–	–		–	–		–	–		–	–		–	1		–

JOE KINLOCH

DEBUT (Full Appearance)

Saturday 29/10/1892
Football League Division 1
at Town Ground

Nottingham Forest 1   Newton Heath 1

CLUB CAREER RECORD	Apps	Subs	Goals
Premiership	0		0
League Division 1	1		0
League Division 2	0		0
FA Cup	0		0
League Cup	0		0
European Cup / Champions League	0		0
European Cup-Winners' Cup	0		0
UEFA Cup / Inter-Cities' Fairs Cup	0		0
Other Matches	0		0
OVERALL TOTAL	**1**		**0**

Opponents	PREM A	S	G	FLD 1 A	S	G	FLD 2 A	S	G	FAC A	S	G	LC A	S	G	EC/CL A	S	G	ECWC A	S	G	UEFA A	S	G	OTHER A	S	G	TOTAL A	S	G
1 Nottingham Forest	–		–	1		–	–		–	–		–	–		–	–		–	–		–	–		–	–		–	1		–

ALBERT KINSEY

DEBUT (Full Appearance, 1 goal)

Saturday 09/01/1965
FA Cup 3rd Round
at Old Trafford

Manchester United 2 Chester City 1

CLUB CAREER RECORD	Apps	Subs	Goals
Premiership	0		0
League Division 1	0		0
League Division 2	0		0
FA Cup	1		1
League Cup	0		0
European Cup / Champions League	0		0
European Cup-Winners' Cup	0		0
UEFA Cup / Inter-Cities' Fairs Cup	0		0
Other Matches	0		0
OVERALL TOTAL	1		1

Opponents	PREM A S G	FLD 1 A S G	FLD 2 A S G	FAC A S G	LC A S G	EC/CL A S G	ECWC A S G	UEFA A S G	OTHER A S G	TOTAL A S G
1 Chester City	– – –	– – –	– – –	1 1	– – –	– – –	– – –	– – –	– – –	1 1

JOSE KLEBERSON

DEBUT (Full Appearance)

Wednesday 27/08/2003
FA Premiership
at Old Trafford

Manchester United 1 Wolverhampton Wanderers 0

CLUB CAREER RECORD	Apps	Subs	Goals
Premiership	16	(4)	2
League Division 1	0		0
League Division 2	0		0
FA Cup	1		0
League Cup	4		0
European Cup / Champions League	3	(2)	0
European Cup-Winners' Cup	0		0
UEFA Cup / Inter-Cities' Fairs Cup	0		0
Other Matches	0		0
OVERALL TOTAL	24	(6)	2

Opponents	PREM A S G	FLD 1 A S G	FLD 2 A S G	FAC A S G	LC A S G	EC/CL A S G	ECWC A S G	UEFA A S G	OTHER A S G	TOTAL A S G
1 Blackburn Rovers	3 1	– – –	– – –	– – –	– – –	– – –	– – –	– – –	– – –	3 1
2 Everton	2 1	– – –	– – –	– – –	– – –	– – –	– – –	– – –	– – –	2 1
3 Aston Villa	1 – –	– – –	– – –	1 – –	– – –	– – –	– – –	– – –	– – –	2 – –
4 West Bromwich Albion	1 – –	– – –	– – –	– – –	1 – –	– – –	– – –	– – –	– – –	2 – –
5 Newcastle United	1 (1) –	– – –	– – –	– – –	– – –	– – –	– – –	– – –	– – –	1 (1) –
6 Chelsea	– (2) –	– – –	– – –	– – –	– – –	– – –	– – –	– – –	– – –	– (2) –
7 Arsenal	– – –	– – –	– – –	– – –	1 – –	– – –	– – –	– – –	– – –	1 – –
8 Birmingham City	1 – –	– – –	– – –	– – –	– – –	– – –	– – –	– – –	– – –	1 – –
9 Bolton Wanderers	1 – –	– – –	– – –	– – –	– – –	– – –	– – –	– – –	– – –	1 – –
10 Crewe Alexandra	– – –	– – –	– – –	– – –	1 – –	– – –	– – –	– – –	– – –	1 – –
11 Crystal Palace	– – –	– – –	– – –	– – –	1 – –	– – –	– – –	– – –	– – –	1 – –
12 Dinamo Bucharest	– – –	– – –	– – –	– – –	– – –	1 – –	– – –	– – –	– – –	1 – –
13 Fenerbahce	– – –	– – –	– – –	– – –	– – –	1 – –	– – –	– – –	– – –	1 – –
14 Leeds United	1 – –	– – –	– – –	– – –	– – –	– – –	– – –	– – –	– – –	1 – –
15 Manchester City	1 – –	– – –	– – –	– – –	– – –	– – –	– – –	– – –	– – –	1 – –
16 Middlesbrough	1 – –	– – –	– – –	– – –	– – –	– – –	– – –	– – –	– – –	1 – –
17 Norwich City	1 – –	– – –	– – –	– – –	– – –	– – –	– – –	– – –	– – –	1 – –
18 Panathinaikos	– – –	– – –	– – –	– – –	– – –	1 – –	– – –	– – –	– – –	1 – –
19 Southampton	1 – –	– – –	– – –	– – –	– – –	– – –	– – –	– – –	– – –	1 – –
20 Wolverhampton W.	1 – –	– – –	– – –	– – –	– – –	– – –	– – –	– – –	– – –	1 – –
21 Charlton Athletic	– (1) –	– – –	– – –	– – –	– – –	– – –	– – –	– – –	– – –	– (1) –
22 Glasgow Rangers	– – –	– – –	– – –	– – –	– – –	– (1) –	– – –	– – –	– – –	– (1) –
23 Sparta Prague	– – –	– – –	– – –	– – –	– – –	– (1) –	– – –	– – –	– – –	– (1) –

FRANK KNOWLES

DEBUT (Full Appearance)

Saturday 30/03/1912
Football League Division 1
at Villa Park

Aston Villa 6 Manchester United 0

CLUB CAREER RECORD	Apps	Subs	Goals
Premiership	0		0
League Division 1	46		1
League Division 2	0		0
FA Cup	1		0
League Cup	0		0
European Cup / Champions League	0		0
European Cup-Winners' Cup	0		0
UEFA Cup / Inter-Cities' Fairs Cup	0		0
Other Matches	0		0
OVERALL TOTAL	47		1

Opponents	PREM A S G	FLD 1 A S G	FLD 2 A S G	FAC A S G	LC A S G	EC/CL A S G	ECWC A S G	UEFA A S G	OTHER A S G	TOTAL A S G
1 Bolton Wanderers	– – –	6 – –	– – –	– – –	– – –	– – –	– – –	– – –	– – –	6 – –
2 Blackburn Rovers	– – –	5 – –	– – –	– – –	– – –	– – –	– – –	– – –	– – –	5 – –
3 Oldham Athletic	– – –	4 – –	– – –	– – –	– – –	– – –	– – –	– – –	– – –	4 – –
4 Bradford City	– – –	3 – 1	– – –	– – –	– – –	– – –	– – –	– – –	– – –	3 – 1
5 Everton	– – –	3 – –	– – –	– – –	– – –	– – –	– – –	– – –	– – –	3 – –
6 Manchester City	– – –	3 – –	– – –	– – –	– – –	– – –	– – –	– – –	– – –	3 – –
7 Newcastle United	– – –	3 – –	– – –	– – –	– – –	– – –	– – –	– – –	– – –	3 – –
8 Chelsea	– – –	2 – –	– – –	– – –	– – –	– – –	– – –	– – –	– – –	2 – –
9 Liverpool	– – –	2 – –	– – –	– – –	– – –	– – –	– – –	– – –	– – –	2 – –

continued../

FRANK KNOWLES (continued)

Opponents	PREM A S G	FLD 1 A S G	FLD 2 A S G	FAC A S G	LC A S G	EC/CL A S G	ECWC A S G	UEFA A S G	OTHER A S G	TOTAL A S G
10 Middlesbrough	– –	2 –	–	–	–	–	–	–	–	2 –
11 Notts County	– –	2 –	–	–	–	–	–	–	–	2 –
12 Sheffield United	– –	2 –	–	–	–	–	–	–	–	2 –
13 Sheffield Wednesday	– –	2 –	–	–	–	–	–	–	–	2 –
14 West Bromwich Albion	– –	2 –	–	–	–	–	–	–	–	2 –
15 Arsenal	– –	1 –	–	–	–	–	–	–	–	1 –
16 Aston Villa	– –	1 –	–	–	–	–	–	–	–	1 –
17 Burnley	– –	1 –	–	–	–	–	–	–	–	1 –
18 Sunderland	– –	1 –	–	–	–	–	–	–	–	1 –
19 Swindon Town	– –	– –	–	–	1	–	–	–	–	1 –
20 Tottenham Hotspur	– –	1 –	–	–	–	–	–	–	–	1 –

FRANK KOPEL

DEBUT (Substitute Appearance)

Saturday 09/09/1967
Football League Division 1
at Old Trafford

Manchester United 2 Burnley 2

CLUB CAREER RECORD	Apps	Subs	Goals
Premiership	0		0
League Division 1	8	(2)	0
League Division 2	0		0
FA Cup	1		0
League Cup	0		0
European Cup / Champions League	1		0
European Cup–Winners' Cup	0		0
UEFA Cup / Inter-Cities' Fairs Cup	0		0
Other Matches	0		0
OVERALL TOTAL	10	(2)	0

Opponents	PREM A S G	FLD 1 A S G	FLD 2 A S G	FAC A S G	LC A S G	EC/CL A S G	ECWC A S G	UEFA A S G	OTHER A S G	TOTAL A S G
1 Anderlecht	–	–	–	–	–	1	–	–	–	1 –
2 Chelsea	–	1	–	–	–	–	–	–	–	1 –
3 Coventry City	–	1	–	–	–	–	–	–	–	1 –
4 Liverpool	–	1	–	–	–	–	–	–	–	1 –
5 Manchester City	–	1	–	–	–	–	–	–	–	1 –
6 Nottingham Forest	–	1	–	–	–	–	–	–	–	1 –
7 Southampton	–	1	–	–	–	–	–	–	–	1 –
8 Stoke City	–	1	–	–	–	–	–	–	–	1 –
9 Watford	–	–	–	1	–	–	–	–	–	1 –
10 Wolverhampton W.	–	1	–	–	–	–	–	–	–	1 –
11 Burnley	–	– (1) –	–	–	–	–	–	–	–	– (1) –
12 Ipswich Town	–	– (1) –	–	–	–	–	–	–	–	– (1) –

TOMASZ KUSZCZAK

DEBUT (Full Appearance)

Sunday 17/09/2006
FA Premiership
at Old Trafford

Manchester United 0 Arsenal 1

CLUB CAREER RECORD	Apps	Subs	Goals
Premiership	14	(1)	0
League Division 1	0		0
League Division 2	0		0
FA Cup	5	(1)	0
League Cup	3		0
European Cup / Champions League	3	(2)	0
European Cup–Winners' Cup	0		0
UEFA Cup / Inter-Cities' Fairs Cup	0		0
Other Matches	0		0
OVERALL TOTAL	25	(4)	0

Opponents	PREM A S G	FLD 1 A S G	FLD 2 A S G	FAC A S G	LC A S G	EC/CL A S G	ECWC A S G	UEFA A S G	OTHER A S G	TOTAL A S G
1 Aston Villa	1 –	–	–	1	–	–	–	–	–	2 –
2 Bolton Wanderers	2 –	–	–	–	–	–	–	–	–	2 –
3 Middlesbrough	–	–	–	2	–	–	–	–	–	2 –
4 Roma	–	–	–	–	–	2	–	–	–	2 –
5 Birmingham City	1 (1) –	–	–	–	–	–	–	–	–	1 (1) –
6 Portsmouth	–	–	–	–	1 (1) –	–	–	–	–	1 (1) –
7 Dynamo Kiev	–	–	–	–	–	– (2) –	–	–	–	– (2) –
8 Arsenal	1 –	–	–	–	–	–	–	–	–	1 –
9 Blackburn Rovers	1 –	–	–	–	–	–	–	–	–	1 –
10 Charlton Athletic	1 –	–	–	–	–	–	–	–	–	1 –
11 Chelsea	1 –	–	–	–	–	–	–	–	–	1 –
12 Coventry City	–	–	–	–	1	–	–	–	–	1 –
13 Crewe Alexandra	–	–	–	–	1	–	–	–	–	1 –
14 Everton	1 –	–	–	–	–	–	–	–	–	1 –
15 Reading	–	–	–	1	–	–	–	–	–	1 –
16 Sheffield United	1 –	–	–	–	–	–	–	–	–	1 –
17 Southend United	–	–	–	–	1	–	–	–	–	1 –
18 Sporting Lisbon	–	–	–	–	–	1	–	–	–	1 –
19 Sunderland	1 –	–	–	–	–	–	–	–	–	1 –
20 Watford	1 –	–	–	–	–	–	–	–	–	1 –
21 West Ham United	1 –	–	–	–	–	–	–	–	–	1 –
22 Wigan Athletic	1 –	–	–	–	–	–	–	–	–	1 –

JOE LANCASTER

DEBUT (Full Appearance)

Saturday 14/01/1950
Football League Division 1
at Old Trafford

Manchester United 1 Chelsea 0

CLUB CAREER RECORD	Apps	Subs	Goals
Premiership	0		0
League Division 1	2		0
League Division 2	0		0
FA Cup	2		0
League Cup	0		0
European Cup / Champions League	0		0
European Cup-Winners' Cup	0		0
UEFA Cup / Inter-Cities' Fairs Cup	0		0
Other Matches	0		0
OVERALL TOTAL	**4**		**0**

Opponents	PREM A S G	FLD 1 A S G	FLD 2 A S G	FAC A S G	LC A S G	EC/CL A S G	ECWC A S G	UEFA A S G	OTHER A S G	TOTAL A S G
1 Burnley	– –	1 –	– –	– –	– –	– –	– –	– –	– –	1 –
2 Chelsea	– –	1 –	– –	– –	– –	– –	– –	– –	– –	1 –
3 Portsmouth	– –	– –	– –	– –	1 –	– –	– –	– –	– –	1 –
4 Watford	– –	– –	– –	1 –	– –	– –	– –	– –	– –	1 –

TOMMY LANG

DEBUT (Full Appearance)

Saturday 11/04/1936
Football League Division 2
at Old Trafford

Manchester United 4 Bradford Park Avenue 0

CLUB CAREER RECORD	Apps	Subs	Goals
Premiership	0		0
League Division 1	8		0
League Division 2	4		1
FA Cup	1		0
League Cup	0		0
European Cup / Champions League	0		0
European Cup-Winners' Cup	0		0
UEFA Cup / Inter-Cities' Fairs Cup	0		0
Other Matches	0		0
OVERALL TOTAL	**13**		**1**

Opponents	PREM A S G	FLD 1 A S G	FLD 2 A S G	FAC A S G	LC A S G	EC/CL A S G	ECWC A S G	UEFA A S G	OTHER A S G	TOTAL A S G
1 Bury	– –	– –	1 1	– –	– –	– –	– –	– –	– –	1 1
2 Arsenal	– –	1 –	– –	– –	– –	– –	– –	– –	– –	1 –
3 Bolton Wanderers	– –	1 –	– –	– –	– –	– –	– –	– –	– –	1 –
4 Bradford Park Avenue	– –	– –	1 –	– –	– –	– –	– –	– –	– –	1 –
5 Brentford	– –	1 –	– –	– –	– –	– –	– –	– –	– –	1 –
6 Burnley	– –	– –	1 –	– –	– –	– –	– –	– –	– –	1 –
7 Derby County	– –	1 –	– –	– –	– –	– –	– –	– –	– –	1 –
8 Everton	– –	1 –	– –	– –	– –	– –	– –	– –	– –	1 –
9 Leeds United	– –	1 –	– –	– –	– –	– –	– –	– –	– –	1 –
10 Manchester City	– –	1 –	– –	– –	– –	– –	– –	– –	– –	1 –
11 Nottingham Forest	– –	– –	1 –	– –	– –	– –	– –	– –	– –	1 –
12 Reading	– –	– –	– –	1 –	– –	– –	– –	– –	– –	1 –
13 Sunderland	– –	1 –	– –	– –	– –	– –	– –	– –	– –	1 –

LEN LANGFORD

DEBUT (Full Appearance)

Saturday 22/09/1934
Football League Division 2
at Old Trafford

Manchester United 5 Norwich City 0

CLUB CAREER RECORD	Apps	Subs	Goals
Premiership	0		0
League Division 1	0		0
League Division 2	15		0
FA Cup	0		0
League Cup	0		0
European Cup / Champions League	0		0
European Cup-Winners' Cup	0		0
UEFA Cup / Inter-Cities' Fairs Cup	0		0
Other Matches	0		0
OVERALL TOTAL	**15**		**0**

Opponents	PREM A S G	FLD 1 A S G	FLD 2 A S G	FAC A S G	LC A S G	EC/CL A S G	ECWC A S G	UEFA A S G	OTHER A S G	TOTAL A S G
1 Blackpool	– –	– –	2 –	– –	– –	– –	– –	– –	– –	2 –
2 Norwich City	– –	– –	2 –	– –	– –	– –	– –	– –	– –	2 –
3 Bradford City	– –	– –	1 –	– –	– –	– –	– –	– –	– –	1 –
4 Brentford	– –	– –	1 –	– –	– –	– –	– –	– –	– –	1 –
5 Burnley	– –	– –	1 –	– –	– –	– –	– –	– –	– –	1 –
6 Bury	– –	– –	1 –	– –	– –	– –	– –	– –	– –	1 –
7 Doncaster Rovers	– –	– –	1 –	– –	– –	– –	– –	– –	– –	1 –
8 Fulham	– –	– –	1 –	– –	– –	– –	– –	– –	– –	1 –
9 Hull City	– –	– –	1 –	– –	– –	– –	– –	– –	– –	1 –
10 Newcastle United	– –	– –	1 –	– –	– –	– –	– –	– –	– –	1 –
11 Nottingham Forest	– –	– –	1 –	– –	– –	– –	– –	– –	– –	1 –
12 Swansea City	– –	– –	1 –	– –	– –	– –	– –	– –	– –	1 –
13 West Ham United	– –	– –	1 –	– –	– –	– –	– –	– –	– –	1 –

HARRY LAPPIN

DEBUT (Full Appearance)

Saturday 27/04/1901
Football League Division 2
at Bank Street

Newton Heath 1 Chesterfield 0

CLUB CAREER RECORD	Apps	Subs	Goals
Premiership	0		0
League Division 1	0		0
League Division 2	27		4
FA Cup	0		0
League Cup	0		0
European Cup / Champions League	0		0
European Cup-Winners' Cup	0		0
UEFA Cup / Inter-Cities' Fairs Cup	0		0
Other Matches	0		0
OVERALL TOTAL	27		4

Opponents	PREM A	S	G	FLD 1 A	S	G	FLD 2 A	S	G	FAC A	S	G	LC A	S	G	EC/CL A	S	G	ECWC A	S	G	UEFA A	S	G	OTHER A	S	G	TOTAL A	S	G
1 Gainsborough Trinity	–	–	–	–	–	–	3		2	–	–	–	–	–	–	–	–	–	–	–	–	–	–	–	–	–	–	3		2
2 Blackpool	–	–	–	–	–	–	3		–	–	–	–	–	–	–	–	–	–	–	–	–	–	–	–	–	–	–	3		–
3 Chesterfield	–	–	–	–	–	–	3		–	–	–	–	–	–	–	–	–	–	–	–	–	–	–	–	–	–	–	3		–
4 Arsenal	–	–	–	–	–	–	2		–	–	–	–	–	–	–	–	–	–	–	–	–	–	–	–	–	–	–	2		–
5 Bristol City	–	–	–	–	–	–	2		–	–	–	–	–	–	–	–	–	–	–	–	–	–	–	–	–	–	–	2		–
6 Burton United	–	–	–	–	–	–	2		–	–	–	–	–	–	–	–	–	–	–	–	–	–	–	–	–	–	–	2		–
7 Port Vale	–	–	–	–	–	–	2		–	–	–	–	–	–	–	–	–	–	–	–	–	–	–	–	–	–	–	2		–
8 Stockport County	–	–	–	–	–	–	2		–	–	–	–	–	–	–	–	–	–	–	–	–	–	–	–	–	–	–	2		–
9 Barnsley	–	–	–	–	–	–	1		1	–	–	–	–	–	–	–	–	–	–	–	–	–	–	–	–	–	–	1		1
10 Burnley	–	–	–	–	–	–	1		1	–	–	–	–	–	–	–	–	–	–	–	–	–	–	–	–	–	–	1		1
11 Doncaster Rovers	–	–	–	–	–	–	1		–	–	–	–	–	–	–	–	–	–	–	–	–	–	–	–	–	–	–	1		–
12 Glossop	–	–	–	–	–	–	1		–	–	–	–	–	–	–	–	–	–	–	–	–	–	–	–	–	–	–	1		–
13 Leicester City	–	–	–	–	–	–	1		–	–	–	–	–	–	–	–	–	–	–	–	–	–	–	–	–	–	–	1		–
14 Lincoln City	–	–	–	–	–	–	1		–	–	–	–	–	–	–	–	–	–	–	–	–	–	–	–	–	–	–	1		–
15 Middlesbrough	–	–	–	–	–	–	1		–	–	–	–	–	–	–	–	–	–	–	–	–	–	–	–	–	–	–	1		–
16 Preston North End	–	–	–	–	–	–	1		–	–	–	–	–	–	–	–	–	–	–	–	–	–	–	–	–	–	–	1		–

HENRIK LARSSON

DEBUT (Full Appearance, 1 goal)

Sunday 07/01/2007
FA Cup 3rd Round
at Old Trafford

Manchester United 2 Aston Villa 1

CLUB CAREER RECORD	Apps	Subs	Goals
Premiership	5	(2)	1
League Division 1	0		0
League Division 2	0		0
FA Cup	3	(1)	1
League Cup	0		0
European Cup / Champions League	2		1
European Cup-Winners' Cup	0		0
UEFA Cup / Inter-Cities' Fairs Cup	0		0
Other Matches	0		0
OVERALL TOTAL	10	(3)	3

Opponents	PREM A	S	G	FLD 1 A	S	G	FLD 2 A	S	G	FAC A	S	G	LC A	S	G	EC/CL A	S	G	ECWC A	S	G	UEFA A	S	G	OTHER A	S	G	TOTAL A	S	G
1 Aston Villa	1		–	–	–	–	–	–	–	1		1	–	–	–	–	–	–	–	–	–	–	–	–	–	–	–	2		1
2 Lille Metropole	–	–	–	–	–	–	–	–	–	–	–	–	–	–	–	2		1	–	–	–	–	–	–	–	–	–	2		1
3 Arsenal	1		–	–	–	–	–	–	–	–	–	–	–	–	–	–	–	–	–	–	–	–	–	–	–	–	–	1		–
4 Fulham	1		–	–	–	–	–	–	–	–	–	–	–	–	–	–	–	–	–	–	–	–	–	–	–	–	–	1		–
5 Liverpool	1		–	–	–	–	–	–	–	–	–	–	–	–	–	–	–	–	–	–	–	–	–	–	–	–	–	1		–
6 Middlesbrough	–	–	–	–	–	–	–	–	–	1		–	–	–	–	–	–	–	–	–	–	–	–	–	–	–	–	1		–
7 Portsmouth	–	–	–	–	–	–	–	–	–	1		–	–	–	–	–	–	–	–	–	–	–	–	–	–	–	–	1		–
8 Tottenham Hotspur	1		–	–	–	–	–	–	–	–	–	–	–	–	–	–	–	–	–	–	–	–	–	–	–	–	–	1		–
9 Watford	–	(1)	1	–	–	–	–	–	–	–	–	–	–	–	–	–	–	–	–	–	–	–	–	–	–	–	–	–	(1)	1
10 Charlton Athletic	–	(1)	–	–	–	–	–	–	–	–	–	–	–	–	–	–	–	–	–	–	–	–	–	–	–	–	–	–	(1)	–
11 Reading	–	–	–	–	–	–	–	–	–	–	(1)	–	–	–	–	–	–	–	–	–	–	–	–	–	–	–	–	–	(1)	–

DENIS LAW

DEBUT (Full Appearance, 1 goal)

Saturday 18/08/1962
Football League Division 1
at Old Trafford

Manchester United 2 West Bromwich Albion 2

CLUB CAREER RECORD	Apps	Subs	Goals
Premiership	0		0
League Division 1	305	(4)	171
League Division 2	0		0
FA Cup	44	(2)	34
League Cup	11		3
European Cup / Champions League	18		14
European Cup-Winners' Cup	5		6
UEFA Cup / Inter-Cities' Fairs Cup	10		8
Other Matches	5		1
OVERALL TOTAL	398	(6)	237

Opponents	PREM A	S	G	FLD 1 A	S	G	FLD 2 A	S	G	FAC A	S	G	LC A	S	G	EC/CL A	S	G	ECWC A	S	G	UEFA A	S	G	OTHER A	S	G	TOTAL A	S	G
1 Everton	–		–	16		8	–		–	2		–	–	–	–	–	–	–	–	–	–	2		–	1		–	21		8
2 Tottenham Hotspur	–		–	16		14	–		–	1		–	–	–	–	–	–	–	1		–	–		–	1		1	19		15
3 West Ham United	–		–	18		7	–		–	1		1	–	–	–	–	–	–	–	–	–	–		–	–		–	19		8
4 Arsenal	–		–	17		8	–		–	–		–	–	–	–	–	–	–	–	–	–	–		–	–		–	17		8
5 Stoke City	–		–	10	(1)	7	–		–	5		1	1		–	–	–	–	–	–	–	–		–	–		–	16	(1)	8
6 Burnley	–		–	14		6	–		–	1		1	1		–	–	–	–	–	–	–	–		–	–		–	16		7

continued../

DENIS LAW (continued)

Opponents	PREM			FLD 1			FLD 2			FAC			LC			EC/CL			ECWC			UEFA			OTHER			TOTAL		
	A	S	G	A	S	G	A	S	G	A	S	G	A	S	G	A	S	G	A	S	G	A	S	G	A	S	G	A	S	G
7 Wolverhampton W.	–	–		12		6	–		–	3		4	–		–	–		–	–		–	–		–	–		–	15		10
8 Liverpool	–	–		14		6	–		–	–		–	–		–	–		–	–		–	–		–	1		–	15		6
9 Leeds United	–	–		11		–	–		–	2 (2)		–	–		–	–		–	–		–	–		–	–		–	13 (2)		–
10 Chelsea	–	–		12		8	–		–	1		1	1		–	–		–	–		–	–		–	–		–	14		9
11 Leicester City	–	–		12		12	–		–	1		1	–		–	–		–	–		–	–		–	–		–	13		13
12 West Bromwich Albion	–	–		13		11	–		–	–		–	–		–	–		–	–		–	–		–	–		–	13		11
13 Nottingham Forest	–	–		13		8	–		–	–		–	–		–	–		–	–		–	–		–	–		–	13		8
14 Sheffield Wednesday	–	–		12		2	–		–	–		–	–		–	–		–	–		–	–		–	–		–	12		2
15 Ipswich Town	–	–		11		10	–		–	–		–	–		–	–		–	–		–	–		–	–		–	11		10
16 Fulham	–	–		11		2	–		–	–		–	–		–	–		–	–		–	–		–	–		–	11		2
17 Manchester City	–	–		8 (2)		4	–		–	–		–	1		1	–		–	–		–	–		–	–		–	9 (2)		5
18 Sunderland	–	–		7		4	–		–	3		4	–		–	–		–	–		–	–		–	–		–	10		8
19 Aston Villa	–	–		8		6	–		–	1		–	1		–	–		–	–		–	–		–	–		–	10		6
20 Southampton	–	–		6		1	–		–	3		1	–		–	–		–	–		–	–		–	–		–	9		2
21 Blackpool	–	–		8		8	–		–	–		–	–		–	–		–	–		–	–		–	–		–	8		8
22 Sheffield United	–	–		8		7	–		–	–		–	–		–	–		–	–		–	–		–	–		–	8		7
23 Newcastle United	–	–		8		3	–		–	–		–	–		–	–		–	–		–	–		–	–		–	8		3
24 Coventry City	–	–		7		2	–		–	1		–	–		–	–		–	–		–	–		–	–		–	8		2
25 Derby County	–	–		4		4	–		–	1		2	2		–	–		–	–		–	–		–	–		–	7		6
26 Birmingham City	–	–		5		1	–		–	2		4	–		–	–		–	–		–	–		–	–		–	7		5
27 Blackburn Rovers	–	–		7		4	–		–	–		–	–		–	–		–	–		–	–		–	–		–	7		4
28 Crystal Palace	–	–		4 (1)		6	–		–	–		–	1		–	–		–	–		–	–		–	–		–	5 (1)		6
29 Huddersfield Town	–	–		3		2	–		–	1		3	–		–	–		–	–		–	–		–	–		–	4		5
30 Middlesbrough	–	–		–		–	–		–	4		–	–		–	–		–	–		–	–		–	–		–	4		–
31 Preston North End	–	–		–		–	–		–	3		2	–		–	–		–	–		–	–		–	–		–	3		2
32 Ferencvaros	–	–		–		–	–		–	–		–	–		–	–		–	–		–	3		1	–		–	3		1
33 Bolton Wanderers	–	–		3		–	–		–	–		–	–		–	–		–	–		–	–		–	–		–	3		–
34 Waterford	–	–		–		–	–		–	–		–	–		–	2		7	–		–	–		–	–		–	2		7
35 Sporting Lisbon	–	–		–		–	–		–	–		–	–		–	–		–	2		3	–		–	–		–	2		3
36 Watford	–	–		–		–	–		–	2		3	–		–	–		–	–		–	–		–	–		–	2		3
37 Willem II	–	–		–		–	–		–	–		–	–		–	–		–	2		3	–		–	–		–	2		3
38 Anderlecht	–	–		–		–	–		–	–		–	–		–	2		2	–		–	–		–	–		–	2		2
39 Borussia Dortmund	–	–		–		–	–		–	–		–	–		–	–		–	–		–	2		2	–		–	2		2
40 Hibernians Malta	–	–		–		–	–		–	–		–	–		–	2		2	–		–	–		–	–		–	2		2
41 Northampton Town	–	–		2		2	–		–	–		–	–		–	–		–	–		–	–		–	–		–	2		2
42 Strasbourg	–	–		–		–	–		–	–		–	–		–	–		–	–		–	2		2	–		–	2		2
43 ASK Vorwaerts	–	–		–		–	–		–	–		–	–		–	2		1	–		–	–		–	–		–	2		1
44 Benfica	–	–		–		–	–		–	–		–	–		–	2		1	–		–	–		–	–		–	2		1
45 HJK Helsinki	–	–		–		–	–		–	–		–	–		–	2		1	–		–	–		–	–		–	2		1
46 Leyton Orient	–	–		2		1	–		–	–		–	–		–	–		–	–		–	–		–	–		–	2		1
47 Norwich City	–	–		1		–	–		–	1		1	–		–	–		–	–		–	–		–	–		–	2		1
48 Oxford United	–	–		–		–	–		–	–		–	2		1	–		–	–		–	–		–	–		–	2		1
49 Queens Park Rangers	–	–		2		1	–		–	–		–	–		–	–		–	–		–	–		–	–		–	2		1
50 AC Milan	–	–		–		–	–		–	–		–	–		–	2		–	–		–	–		–	–		–	2		–
51 Estudiantes de la Plata	–	–		–		–	–		–	–		–	–		–	–		–	–		–	–		–	2		–	2		–
52 Partizan Belgrade	–	–		–		–	–		–	–		–	–		–	2		–	–		–	–		–	–		–	2		–
53 Rotherham United	–	–		–		–	–		–	2		–	–		–	–		–	–		–	–		–	–		–	2		–
54 Bristol Rovers	–	–		–		–	–		–	1		3	–		–	–		–	–		–	–		–	–		–	1		3
55 Djurgardens	–	–		–		–	–		–	–		–	–		–	–		–	–		–	1		3	–		–	1		3
56 Barnsley	–	–		–		–	–		–	1		2	–		–	–		–	–		–	–		–	–		–	1		2
57 Aldershot	–	–		–		–	–		–	–		–	1		1	–		–	–		–	–		–	–		–	1		1
58 Exeter City	–	–		–		–	–		–	1		–	–		–	–		–	–		–	–		–	–		–	1		–
59 Rapid Vienna	–	–		–		–	–		–	–		–	–		–	1		–	–		–	–		–	–		–	1		–
60 Real Madrid	–	–		–		–	–		–	–		–	–		–	1		–	–		–	–		–	–		–	1		–

REG LAWSON

DEBUT (Full Appearance)

Saturday 01/09/1900
Football League Division 2
at North Road

Glossop 1 Newton Heath 0

CLUB CAREER RECORD	Apps	Subs	Goals
Premiership	0		0
League Division 1	0		0
League Division 2	3		0
FA Cup	0		0
League Cup	0		0
European Cup / Champions League	0		0
European Cup-Winners' Cup	0		0
UEFA Cup / Inter-Cities' Fairs Cup	0		0
Other Matches	0		0
OVERALL TOTAL	3		0

Opponents	PREM			FLD 1			FLD 2			FAC			LC			EC/CL			ECWC			UEFA			OTHER			TOTAL		
	A	S	G	A	S	G	A	S	G	A	S	G	A	S	G	A	S	G	A	S	G	A	S	G	A	S	G	A	S	G
1 Burnley	–	–	–	–	–	–	1		–	–	–	–	–	–	–	–	–	–	–	–	–	–	–	–	–	–	–	1		–
2 Glossop	–	–	–	–	–	–	1		–	–	–	–	–	–	–	–	–	–	–	–	–	–	–	–	–	–	–	1		–
3 Middlesbrough	–	–	–	–	–	–	1		–	–	–	–	–	–	–	–	–	–	–	–	–	–	–	–	–	–	–	1		–

NOBBY LAWTON

DEBUT (Full Appearance)

Saturday 09/04/1960
Football League Division 1
at Kenilworth Road

Luton Town 2 Manchester United 3

CLUB CAREER RECORD	Apps	Subs	Goals
Premiership	0		0
League Division 1	36		6
League Division 2	0		0
FA Cup	7		0
League Cup	1		0
European Cup / Champions League	0		0
European Cup-Winners' Cup	0		0
UEFA Cup / Inter-Cities' Fairs Cup	0		0
Other Matches	0		0
OVERALL TOTAL	**44**		**6**

Opponents	PREM A S G	FLD 1 A S G	FLD 2 A S G	FAC A S G	LC A S G	EC/CL A S G	ECWC A S G	UEFA A S G	OTHER A S G	TOTAL A S G
1 Bolton Wanderers	– –	3 – –	– – –	1 –	– –	– – –	– – –	– – –	– – –	4 –
2 Sheffield Wednesday	– –	2 – –	– – –	2 –	– –	– – –	– – –	– – –	– – –	4 –
3 Nottingham Forest	– –	3 3 –	– – –	– –	– –	– – –	– – –	– – –	– – –	3 3
4 Arsenal	– –	2 – –	– – –	1 –	– –	– – –	– – –	– – –	– – –	3 –
5 Birmingham City	– –	3 – –	– – –	– –	– –	– – –	– – –	– – –	– – –	3 –
6 Wolverhampton W.	– –	2 1 –	– – –	– –	– –	– – –	– – –	– – –	– – –	2 1
7 Blackpool	– –	2 – –	– – –	– –	– –	– – –	– – –	– – –	– – –	2 –
8 Everton	– –	2 – –	– – –	– –	– –	– – –	– – –	– – –	– – –	2 –
9 Manchester City	– –	2 – –	– – –	– –	– –	– – –	– – –	– – –	– – –	2 –
10 Preston North End	– –	– – –	– – –	2 –	– –	– – –	– – –	– – –	– – –	2 –
11 Tottenham Hotspur	– –	1 – –	– – –	1 –	– –	– – –	– – –	– – –	– – –	2 –
12 West Bromwich Albion	– –	2 – –	– – –	– –	– –	– – –	– – –	– – –	– – –	2 –
13 West Ham United	– –	2 – –	– – –	– –	– –	– – –	– – –	– – –	– – –	2 –
14 Cardiff City	– –	1 1 –	– – –	– –	– –	– – –	– – –	– – –	– – –	1 1
15 Fulham	– –	1 1 –	– – –	– –	– –	– – –	– – –	– – –	– – –	1 1
16 Aston Villa	– –	1 – –	– – –	– –	– –	– – –	– – –	– – –	– – –	1 –
17 Blackburn Rovers	– –	1 – –	– – –	– –	– –	– – –	– – –	– – –	– – –	1 –
18 Burnley	– –	1 – –	– – –	– –	– –	– – –	– – –	– – –	– – –	1 –
19 Exeter City	– –	– – –	– – –	– –	1 –	– – –	– – –	– – –	– – –	1 –
20 Leicester City	– –	1 – –	– – –	– –	– –	– – –	– – –	– – –	– – –	1 –
21 Leyton Orient	– –	1 – –	– – –	– –	– –	– – –	– – –	– – –	– – –	1 –
22 Luton Town	– –	1 – –	– – –	– –	– –	– – –	– – –	– – –	– – –	1 –
23 Newcastle United	– –	1 – –	– – –	– –	– –	– – –	– – –	– – –	– – –	1 –
24 Sheffield United	– –	1 – –	– – –	– –	– –	– – –	– – –	– – –	– – –	1 –

EDWIN LEE

DEBUT (Full Appearance)

Saturday 25/03/1899
Football League Division 2
at Sincil Bank

Lincoln City 2 Newton Heath 0

CLUB CAREER RECORD	Apps	Subs	Goals
Premiership	0		0
League Division 1	0		0
League Division 2	11		5
FA Cup	0		0
League Cup	0		0
European Cup / Champions League	0		0
European Cup-Winners' Cup	0		0
UEFA Cup / Inter-Cities' Fairs Cup	0		0
Other Matches	0		0
OVERALL TOTAL	**11**		**5**

Opponents	PREM A S G	FLD 1 A S G	FLD 2 A S G	FAC A S G	LC A S G	EC/CL A S G	ECWC A S G	UEFA A S G	OTHER A S G	TOTAL A S G
1 Luton Town	– – –	– – –	2 2	– –	– –	– – –	– – –	– – –	– – –	2 2
2 Barnsley	– – –	– – –	1 2	– –	– –	– – –	– – –	– – –	– – –	1 2
3 Gainsborough Trinity	– – –	– – –	1 1	– –	– –	– – –	– – –	– – –	– – –	1 1
4 Blackpool	– – –	– – –	1 –	– –	– –	– – –	– – –	– – –	– – –	1 –
5 Bolton Wanderers	– – –	– – –	1 –	– –	– –	– – –	– – –	– – –	– – –	1 –
6 Darwen	– – –	– – –	1 –	– –	– –	– – –	– – –	– – –	– – –	1 –
7 Leicester City	– – –	– – –	1 –	– –	– –	– – –	– – –	– – –	– – –	1 –
8 Lincoln City	– – –	– – –	1 –	– –	– –	– – –	– – –	– – –	– – –	1 –
9 Loughborough Town	– – –	– – –	1 –	– –	– –	– – –	– – –	– – –	– – –	1 –
10 Middlesbrough	– – –	– – –	1 –	– –	– –	– – –	– – –	– – –	– – –	1 –

KIERAN LEE

DEBUT (Substitute Appearance, 1 goal)

Wednesday 25/10/2006
League Cup 3rd Round
at Gresty Road

Crewe Alexandra 1 Manchester United 2

CLUB CAREER RECORD	Apps	Subs	Goals
Premiership	1		0
League Division 1	0		0
League Division 2	0		0
FA Cup	0		0
League Cup	0	(2)	1
European Cup / Champions League	0		0
European Cup-Winners' Cup	0		0
UEFA Cup / Inter-Cities' Fairs Cup	0		0
Other Matches	0		0
OVERALL TOTAL	**1**	**(2)**	**1**

Opponents	PREM A S G	FLD 1 A S G	FLD 2 A S G	FAC A S G	LC A S G	EC/CL A S G	ECWC A S G	UEFA A S G	OTHER A S G	TOTAL A S G
1 Chelsea	1 – –	– – –	– – –	– – –	– – –	– – –	– – –	– – –	– – –	1 – –
2 Crewe Alexandra	– – –	– – –	– – –	– – –	– (1) 1	– – –	– – –	– – –	– – –	– (1) 1
3 Southend United	– – –	– – –	– – –	– – –	– (1) –	– – –	– – –	– – –	– – –	– (1) –

TOM LEIGH

DEBUT (Full Appearance, 1 goal)

Saturday 17/03/1900
Football League Division 2
at Bank Street

Newton Heath 3 Barnsley 0

CLUB CAREER RECORD	Apps	Subs	Goals
Premiership	0		0
League Division 1	0		0
League Division 2	43		15
FA Cup	3		0
League Cup	0		0
European Cup / Champions League	0		0
European Cup-Winners' Cup	0		0
UEFA Cup / Inter-Cities' Fairs Cup	0		0
Other Matches	0		0
OVERALL TOTAL	**46**		**15**

Opponents	PREM			FLD 1			FLD 2			FAC			LC			EC/CL			ECWC			UEFA			OTHER			TOTAL		
	A	S	G	A	S	G	A	S	G	A	S	G	A	S	G	A	S	G	A	S	G	A	S	G	A	S	G	A	S	G
1 Burnley	-	-	-	-	-	-	2	-	-	2	-	-	-	-	-	-	-	-	-	-	-	-	-	-	-	-	-	4	-	-
2 Leicester City	-	-	-	-	-	-	4	-	-	-	-	-	-	-	-	-	-	-	-	-	-	-	-	-	-	-	-	4	-	-
3 Walsall	-	-	-	-	-	-	4	-	-	-	-	-	-	-	-	-	-	-	-	-	-	-	-	-	-	-	-	4	-	-
4 Barnsley	-	-	-	-	-	-	3	-	2	-	-	-	-	-	-	-	-	-	-	-	-	-	-	-	-	-	-	3	-	2
5 Chesterfield	-	-	-	-	-	-	3	-	1	-	-	-	-	-	-	-	-	-	-	-	-	-	-	-	-	-	-	3	-	1
6 Middlesbrough	-	-	-	-	-	-	3	-	1	-	-	-	-	-	-	-	-	-	-	-	-	-	-	-	-	-	-	3	-	1
7 Port Vale	-	-	-	-	-	-	3	-	1	-	-	-	-	-	-	-	-	-	-	-	-	-	-	-	-	-	-	3	-	1
8 Burton Swifts	-	-	-	-	-	-	2	-	2	-	-	-	-	-	-	-	-	-	-	-	-	-	-	-	-	-	-	2	-	2
9 Glossop	-	-	-	-	-	-	2	-	2	-	-	-	-	-	-	-	-	-	-	-	-	-	-	-	-	-	-	2	-	2
10 Lincoln City	-	-	-	-	-	-	2	-	2	-	-	-	-	-	-	-	-	-	-	-	-	-	-	-	-	-	-	2	-	2
11 Arsenal	-	-	-	-	-	-	2	-	1	-	-	-	-	-	-	-	-	-	-	-	-	-	-	-	-	-	-	2	-	1
12 Blackpool	-	-	-	-	-	-	2	-	1	-	-	-	-	-	-	-	-	-	-	-	-	-	-	-	-	-	-	2	-	1
13 Gainsborough Trinity	-	-	-	-	-	-	2	-	1	-	-	-	-	-	-	-	-	-	-	-	-	-	-	-	-	-	-	2	-	1
14 Stockport County	-	-	-	-	-	-	2	-	1	-	-	-	-	-	-	-	-	-	-	-	-	-	-	-	-	-	-	2	-	1
15 Birmingham City	-	-	-	-	-	-	2	-	-	-	-	-	-	-	-	-	-	-	-	-	-	-	-	-	-	-	-	2	-	-
16 Grimsby Town	-	-	-	-	-	-	2	-	-	-	-	-	-	-	-	-	-	-	-	-	-	-	-	-	-	-	-	2	-	-
17 New Brighton Tower	-	-	-	-	-	-	2	-	-	-	-	-	-	-	-	-	-	-	-	-	-	-	-	-	-	-	-	2	-	-
18 Luton Town	-	-	-	-	-	-	1	-	-	-	-	-	-	-	-	-	-	-	-	-	-	-	-	-	-	-	-	1	-	-
19 Portsmouth	-	-	-	-	-	-	-	-	-	1	-	-	-	-	-	-	-	-	-	-	-	-	-	-	-	-	-	1	-	-

JIM LEIGHTON

DEBUT (Full Appearance)

Saturday 27/08/1988
Football League Division 1
at Old Trafford

Manchester United 0 Queens Park Rangers 0

CLUB CAREER RECORD	Apps	Subs	Goals
Premiership	0		0
League Division 1	73		0
League Division 2	0		0
FA Cup	14		0
League Cup	7		0
European Cup / Champions League	0		0
European Cup-Winners' Cup	0		0
UEFA Cup / Inter-Cities' Fairs Cup	0		0
Other Matches	0		0
OVERALL TOTAL	**94**		**0**

Opponents	PREM			FLD 1			FLD 2			FAC			LC			EC/CL			ECWC			UEFA			OTHER			TOTAL		
	A	S	G	A	S	G	A	S	G	A	S	G	A	S	G	A	S	G	A	S	G	A	S	G	A	S	G	A	S	G
1 Nottingham Forest	-	-	-	4	-	-	-	-	-	2	-	-	-	-	-	-	-	-	-	-	-	-	-	-	-	-	-	6	-	-
2 Queens Park Rangers	-	-	-	3	-	-	-	-	-	3	-	-	-	-	-	-	-	-	-	-	-	-	-	-	-	-	-	6	-	-
3 Tottenham Hotspur	-	-	-	4	-	-	-	-	-	-	-	-	1	-	-	-	-	-	-	-	-	-	-	-	-	-	-	5	-	-
4 Arsenal	-	-	-	4	-	-	-	-	-	-	-	-	-	-	-	-	-	-	-	-	-	-	-	-	-	-	-	4	-	-
5 Charlton Athletic	-	-	-	4	-	-	-	-	-	-	-	-	-	-	-	-	-	-	-	-	-	-	-	-	-	-	-	4	-	-
6 Coventry City	-	-	-	4	-	-	-	-	-	-	-	-	-	-	-	-	-	-	-	-	-	-	-	-	-	-	-	4	-	-
7 Derby County	-	-	-	4	-	-	-	-	-	-	-	-	-	-	-	-	-	-	-	-	-	-	-	-	-	-	-	4	-	-
8 Everton	-	-	-	4	-	-	-	-	-	-	-	-	-	-	-	-	-	-	-	-	-	-	-	-	-	-	-	4	-	-
9 Liverpool	-	-	-	4	-	-	-	-	-	-	-	-	-	-	-	-	-	-	-	-	-	-	-	-	-	-	-	4	-	-
10 Luton Town	-	-	-	4	-	-	-	-	-	-	-	-	-	-	-	-	-	-	-	-	-	-	-	-	-	-	-	4	-	-
11 Millwall	-	-	-	4	-	-	-	-	-	-	-	-	-	-	-	-	-	-	-	-	-	-	-	-	-	-	-	4	-	-
12 Norwich City	-	-	-	4	-	-	-	-	-	-	-	-	-	-	-	-	-	-	-	-	-	-	-	-	-	-	-	4	-	-
13 Sheffield Wednesday	-	-	-	4	-	-	-	-	-	-	-	-	-	-	-	-	-	-	-	-	-	-	-	-	-	-	-	4	-	-
14 Southampton	-	-	-	4	-	-	-	-	-	-	-	-	-	-	-	-	-	-	-	-	-	-	-	-	-	-	-	4	-	-
15 Wimbledon	-	-	-	3	-	-	-	-	-	-	-	-	1	-	-	-	-	-	-	-	-	-	-	-	-	-	-	4	-	-
16 Aston Villa	-	-	-	3	-	-	-	-	-	-	-	-	-	-	-	-	-	-	-	-	-	-	-	-	-	-	-	3	-	-
17 Crystal Palace	-	-	-	2	-	-	-	-	-	1	-	-	-	-	-	-	-	-	-	-	-	-	-	-	-	-	-	3	-	-
18 Newcastle United	-	-	-	2	-	-	-	-	-	1	-	-	-	-	-	-	-	-	-	-	-	-	-	-	-	-	-	3	-	-
19 Bournemouth	-	-	-	-	-	-	-	-	-	2	-	-	-	-	-	-	-	-	-	-	-	-	-	-	-	-	-	2	-	-
20 Chelsea	-	-	-	2	-	-	-	-	-	-	-	-	-	-	-	-	-	-	-	-	-	-	-	-	-	-	-	2	-	-
21 Manchester City	-	-	-	2	-	-	-	-	-	-	-	-	-	-	-	-	-	-	-	-	-	-	-	-	-	-	-	2	-	-
22 Middlesbrough	-	-	-	2	-	-	-	-	-	-	-	-	-	-	-	-	-	-	-	-	-	-	-	-	-	-	-	2	-	-
23 Oldham Athletic	-	-	-	-	-	-	-	-	-	2	-	-	-	-	-	-	-	-	-	-	-	-	-	-	-	-	-	2	-	-
24 Portsmouth	-	-	-	-	-	-	-	-	-	-	-	-	2	-	-	-	-	-	-	-	-	-	-	-	-	-	-	2	-	-
25 Rotherham United	-	-	-	-	-	-	-	-	-	-	-	-	2	-	-	-	-	-	-	-	-	-	-	-	-	-	-	2	-	-
26 West Ham United	-	-	-	2	-	-	-	-	-	-	-	-	-	-	-	-	-	-	-	-	-	-	-	-	-	-	-	2	-	-
27 Halifax Town	-	-	-	-	-	-	-	-	-	-	-	-	1	-	-	-	-	-	-	-	-	-	-	-	-	-	-	1	-	-
28 Hereford United	-	-	-	-	-	-	-	-	-	1	-	-	-	-	-	-	-	-	-	-	-	-	-	-	-	-	-	1	-	-
29 Oxford United	-	-	-	-	-	-	-	-	-	1	-	-	-	-	-	-	-	-	-	-	-	-	-	-	-	-	-	1	-	-
30 Sheffield United	-	-	-	-	-	-	-	-	-	1	-	-	-	-	-	-	-	-	-	-	-	-	-	-	-	-	-	1	-	-

HARRY LEONARD

DEBUT (Full Appearance, 1 goal)

Saturday 11/09/1920
Football League Division 1
at Old Trafford

Manchester United 3 Chelsea 1

CLUB CAREER RECORD	Apps	Subs	Goals
Premiership	0		0
League Division 1	10		5
League Division 2	0		0
FA Cup	0		0
League Cup	0		0
European Cup / Champions League	0		0
European Cup-Winners' Cup	0		0
UEFA Cup / Inter-Cities' Fairs Cup	0		0
Other Matches	0		0
OVERALL TOTAL	**10**		**5**

Opponents	PREM A S G	FLD 1 A S G	FLD 2 A S G	FAC A S G	LC A S G	EC/CL A S G	ECWC A S G	UEFA A S G	OTHER A S G	TOTAL A S G
1 Chelsea	– –	2 3	– –	– –	– –	– –	– –	– –	– –	2 3
2 Sheffield United	– –	2 2	– –	– –	– –	– –	– –	– –	– –	2 2
3 Manchester City	– –	2 –	– –	– –	– –	– –	– –	– –	– –	2 –
4 Tottenham Hotspur	– –	2 –	– –	– –	– –	– –	– –	– –	– –	2 –
5 Burnley	– –	1 –	– –	– –	– –	– –	– –	– –	– –	1 –
6 Preston North End	– –	1	– –	– –	– –	– –	– –	– –	– –	1

EDDIE LEWIS

DEBUT (Full Appearance, 1 goal)

Saturday 29/11/1952
Football League Division 1
at The Hawthorns

West Bromwich Albion 3 Manchester United 1

CLUB CAREER RECORD	Apps	Subs	Goals
Premiership	0		0
League Division 1	20		9
League Division 2	0		0
FA Cup	4		2
League Cup	0		0
European Cup / Champions League	0		0
European Cup-Winners' Cup	0		0
UEFA Cup / Inter-Cities' Fairs Cup	0		0
Other Matches	0		0
OVERALL TOTAL	**24**		**11**

Opponents	PREM A S G	FLD 1 A S G	FLD 2 A S G	FAC A S G	LC A S G	EC/CL A S G	ECWC A S G	UEFA A S G	OTHER A S G	TOTAL A S G
1 West Bromwich Albion	– –	4 2	– –	– –	– –	– –	– –	– –	– –	4 2
2 Walthamstow Avenue	– –	– –	– –	2 2	– –	– –	– –	– –	– –	2 2
3 Everton	– –	1 –	– –	1 –	– –	– –	– –	– –	– –	2 –
4 Manchester City	– –	2 –	– –	– –	– –	– –	– –	– –	– –	2 –
5 Aston Villa	– –	1 1	– –	– –	– –	– –	– –	– –	– –	1 1
6 Blackpool	– –	1 1	– –	– –	– –	– –	– –	– –	– –	1 1
7 Bolton Wanderers	– –	1 1	– –	– –	– –	– –	– –	– –	– –	1 1
8 Derby County	– –	1 1	– –	– –	– –	– –	– –	– –	– –	1 1
9 Liverpool	– –	1 1	– –	– –	– –	– –	– –	– –	– –	1 1
10 Portsmouth	– –	1 1	– –	– –	– –	– –	– –	– –	– –	1 1
11 Sunderland	– –	1 1	– –	– –	– –	– –	– –	– –	– –	1 1
12 Cardiff City	– –	1 –	– –	– –	– –	– –	– –	– –	– –	1 –
13 Charlton Athletic	– –	1 –	– –	– –	– –	– –	– –	– –	– –	1 –
14 Middlesbrough	– –	1 –	– –	– –	– –	– –	– –	– –	– –	1 –
15 Millwall	– –	– –	– –	1 –	– –	– –	– –	– –	– –	1 –
16 Newcastle United	– –	1 –	– –	– –	– –	– –	– –	– –	– –	1 –
17 Tottenham Hotspur	– –	1 –	– –	– –	– –	– –	– –	– –	– –	1 –
18 Wolverhampton W.	– –	1	– –	– –	– –	– –	– –	– –	– –	1

LESLIE LIEVESLEY

DEBUT (Full Appearance)

Friday 25/03/1932
Football League Division 2
at Old Trafford

Manchester United 0 Charlton Athletic 2

CLUB CAREER RECORD	Apps	Subs	Goals
Premiership	0		0
League Division 1	0		0
League Division 2	2		0
FA Cup	0		0
League Cup	0		0
European Cup / Champions League	0		0
European Cup-Winners' Cup	0		0
UEFA Cup / Inter-Cities' Fairs Cup	0		0
Other Matches	0		0
OVERALL TOTAL	**2**		**0**

Opponents	PREM A S G	FLD 1 A S G	FLD 2 A S G	FAC A S G	LC A S G	EC/CL A S G	ECWC A S G	UEFA A S G	OTHER A S G	TOTAL A S G
1 Charlton Athletic	– –	– –	1 –	– –	– –	– –	– –	– –	– –	1 –
2 Oldham Athletic	– –	– –	1 –	– –	– –	– –	– –	– –	– –	1 –

WILFRED LIEVESLEY

DEBUT (Full Appearance)

Saturday 20/01/1923
Football League Division 2
at Old Trafford

Manchester United 0 Leeds United 0

CLUB CAREER RECORD	Apps	Subs	Goals
Premiership	0		0
League Division 1	0		0
League Division 2	2		0
FA Cup	1		0
League Cup	0		0
European Cup / Champions League	0		0
European Cup-Winners' Cup	0		0
UEFA Cup / Inter-Cities' Fairs Cup	0		0
Other Matches	0		0
OVERALL TOTAL	**3**		**0**

Opponents	PREM A S G	FLD 1 A S G	FLD 2 A S G	FAC A S G	LC A S G	EC/CL A S G	ECWC A S G	UEFA A S G	OTHER A S G	TOTAL A S G
1 Leeds United	– – –	– – –	2	– – –	– – –	– – –	– – –	– – –	– – –	2 –
2 Tottenham Hotspur	– – –	– – –	– – –	1	– – –	– – –	– – –	– – –	– – –	1 –

OSCAR LINKSON

DEBUT (Full Appearance)

Saturday 24/10/1908
Football League Division 1
at Bank Street

Manchester United 2 Nottingham Forest 2

CLUB CAREER RECORD	Apps	Subs	Goals
Premiership	0		0
League Division 1	55		0
League Division 2	0		0
FA Cup	4		0
League Cup	0		0
European Cup / Champions League	0		0
European Cup-Winners' Cup	0		0
UEFA Cup / Inter-Cities' Fairs Cup	0		0
Other Matches	0		0
OVERALL TOTAL	**59**		**0**

Opponents	PREM A S G	FLD 1 A S G	FLD 2 A S G	FAC A S G	LC A S G	EC/CL A S G	ECWC A S G	UEFA A S G	OTHER A S G	TOTAL A S G
1 Arsenal	– –	6 –	– –	– –	– –	– –	– –	– –	– –	6 –
2 Blackburn Rovers	– –	3 –	– –	2 –	– –	– –	– –	– –	– –	5 –
3 Aston Villa	– –	4 –	– –	– –	– –	– –	– –	– –	– –	4 –
4 Notts County	– –	4 –	– –	– –	– –	– –	– –	– –	– –	4 –
5 Oldham Athletic	– –	4 –	– –	– –	– –	– –	– –	– –	– –	4 –
6 Bradford City	– –	3 –	– –	– –	– –	– –	– –	– –	– –	3 –
7 Manchester City	– –	3 –	– –	– –	– –	– –	– –	– –	– –	3 –
8 Middlesbrough	– –	3 –	– –	– –	– –	– –	– –	– –	– –	3 –
9 Newcastle United	– –	3 –	– –	– –	– –	– –	– –	– –	– –	3 –
10 Sheffield United	– –	3 –	– –	– –	– –	– –	– –	– –	– –	3 –
11 Bolton Wanderers	– –	2 –	– –	– –	– –	– –	– –	– –	– –	2 –
12 Chelsea	– –	2 –	– –	– –	– –	– –	– –	– –	– –	2 –
13 Leicester City	– –	2 –	– –	– –	– –	– –	– –	– –	– –	2 –
14 Liverpool	– –	2 –	– –	– –	– –	– –	– –	– –	– –	2 –
15 Preston North End	– –	2 –	– –	– –	– –	– –	– –	– –	– –	2 –
16 Reading	– –	– –	– –	2 –	– –	– –	– –	– –	– –	2 –
17 Sheffield Wednesday	– –	2 –	– –	– –	– –	– –	– –	– –	– –	2 –
18 Tottenham Hotspur	– –	2 –	– –	– –	– –	– –	– –	– –	– –	2 –
19 Bristol City	– –	1 –	– –	– –	– –	– –	– –	– –	– –	1 –
20 Bury	– –	1 –	– –	– –	– –	– –	– –	– –	– –	1 –
21 Derby County	– –	1 –	– –	– –	– –	– –	– –	– –	– –	1 –
22 Nottingham Forest	– –	1 –	– –	– –	– –	– –	– –	– –	– –	1 –
23 Sunderland	– –	1 –	– –	– –	– –	– –	– –	– –	– –	1 –

GEORGE LIVINGSTONE

DEBUT (Full Appearance, 2 goals)

Saturday 23/01/1909
Football League Division 1
at Bank Street

Manchester United 3 Manchester City 1

CLUB CAREER RECORD	Apps	Subs	Goals
Premiership	0		0
League Division 1	43		4
League Division 2	0		0
FA Cup	3		0
League Cup	0		0
European Cup / Champions League	0		0
European Cup-Winners' Cup	0		0
UEFA Cup / Inter-Cities' Fairs Cup	0		0
Other Matches	0		0
OVERALL TOTAL	**46**		**4**

Opponents	PREM A S G	FLD 1 A S G	FLD 2 A S G	FAC A S G	LC A S G	EC/CL A S G	ECWC A S G	UEFA A S G	OTHER A S G	TOTAL A S G
1 Bury	– –	4 –	– –	– –	– –	– –	– –	– –	– –	4 –
2 Sunderland	– –	4 –	– –	– –	– –	– –	– –	– –	– –	4 –
3 Blackburn Rovers	– –	2 –	– –	1 –	– –	– –	– –	– –	– –	3 –
4 Bradford City	– –	3 –	– –	– –	– –	– –	– –	– –	– –	3 –
5 Bristol City	– –	3 –	– –	– –	– –	– –	– –	– –	– –	3 –
6 Sheffield United	– –	3 –	– –	– –	– –	– –	– –	– –	– –	3 –
7 Tottenham Hotspur	– –	3 –	– –	– –	– –	– –	– –	– –	– –	3 –
8 Notts County	– –	2 1	– –	– –	– –	– –	– –	– –	– –	2 1

continued../

GEORGE LIVINGSTONE (continued)

Opponents	PREM A	S	G	FLD 1 A	S	G	FLD 2 A	S	G	FAC A	S	G	LC A	S	G	EC/CL A	S	G	ECWC A	S	G	UEFA A	S	G	OTHER A	S	G	TOTAL A	S	G
9 Aston Villa	–	–		2	–		–	–		–	–		–	–		–	–		–	–		–	–		–	–		2	–	
10 Everton	–	–		1	–		–	–		1	–		–	–		–	–		–	–		–	–		–	–		2	–	
11 Liverpool	–	–		2	–		–	–		–	–		–	–		–	–		–	–		–	–		–	–		2	–	
12 Middlesbrough	–	–		2	–		–	–		–	–		–	–		–	–		–	–		–	–		–	–		2	–	
13 Newcastle United	–	–		2	–		–	–		–	–		–	–		–	–		–	–		–	–		–	–		2	–	
14 Oldham Athletic	–	–		2	–		–	–		–	–		–	–		–	–		–	–		–	–		–	–		2	–	
15 Manchester City	–	–		1		2	–	–		–	–		–	–		–	–		–	–		–	–		–	–		1		2
16 West Bromwich Albion	–	–		1		1	–	–		–	–		–	–		–	–		–	–		–	–		–	–		1		1
17 Arsenal	–	–		1	–		–	–		–	–		–	–		–	–		–	–		–	–		–	–		1	–	
18 Bolton Wanderers	–	–		1	–		–	–		–	–		–	–		–	–		–	–		–	–		–	–		1	–	
19 Leicester City	–	–		1	–		–	–		–	–		–	–		–	–		–	–		–	–		–	–		1	–	
20 Nottingham Forest	–	–		1	–		–	–		–	–		–	–		–	–		–	–		–	–		–	–		1	–	
21 Preston North End	–	–		1	–		–	–		–	–		–	–		–	–		–	–		–	–		–	–		1	–	
22 Sheffield Wednesday	–	–		1	–		–	–		–	–		–	–		–	–		–	–		–	–		–	–		1	–	
23 Swindon Town	–	–		–	–		–	–		1	–		–	–		–	–		–	–		–	–		–	–		1	–	

ARTHUR LOCHHEAD

DEBUT (Full Appearance)

Saturday 27/08/1921
Football League Division 1
at Goodison Park

Everton 5 Manchester United 0

CLUB CAREER RECORD	Apps	Subs	Goals
Premiership	0		0
League Division 1	36		10
League Division 2	111		40
FA Cup	6		0
League Cup	0		0
European Cup / Champions League	0		0
European Cup-Winners' Cup	0		0
UEFA Cup / Inter-Cities' Fairs Cup	0		0
Other Matches	0		0
OVERALL TOTAL	153		50

Opponents	PREM A	S	G	FLD 1 A	S	G	FLD 2 A	S	G	FAC A	S	G	LC A	S	G	EC/CL A	S	G	ECWC A	S	G	UEFA A	S	G	OTHER A	S	G	TOTAL A	S	G
1 Bradford City	–	–		1	–		6		1	2	–		–	–		–	–		–	–		–	–		–	–		9		1
2 Hull City	–	–		–	–		6		4	–	–		–	–		–	–		–	–		–	–		–	–		6		4
3 Leicester City	–	–		1		1	5		3	–	–		–	–		–	–		–	–		–	–		–	–		6		4
4 South Shields	–	–		–	–		6		3	–	–		–	–		–	–		–	–		–	–		–	–		6		3
5 Southampton	–	–		–	–		6		3	–	–		–	–		–	–		–	–		–	–		–	–		6		3
6 Barnsley	–	–		–	–		6		2	–	–		–	–		–	–		–	–		–	–		–	–		6		2
7 Crystal Palace	–	–		–	–		6		2	–	–		–	–		–	–		–	–		–	–		–	–		6		2
8 Fulham	–	–		–	–		6		2	–	–		–	–		–	–		–	–		–	–		–	–		6		2
9 Sheffield Wednesday	–	–		–	–		6		1	–	–		–	–		–	–		–	–		–	–		–	–		6		1
10 Derby County	–	–		–	–		6	–		–	–		–	–		–	–		–	–		–	–		–	–		6	–	
11 Port Vale	–	–		–	–		5		3	–	–		–	–		–	–		–	–		–	–		–	–		5		3
12 Blackpool	–	–		–	–		5		1	–	–		–	–		–	–		–	–		–	–		–	–		5		1
13 Coventry City	–	–		–	–		5		1	–	–		–	–		–	–		–	–		–	–		–	–		5		1
14 Leeds United	–	–		–	–		4		3	–	–		–	–		–	–		–	–		–	–		–	–		4		3
15 Stockport County	–	–		–	–		4		2	–	–		–	–		–	–		–	–		–	–		–	–		4		2
16 Leyton Orient	–	–		–	–		4		1	–	–		–	–		–	–		–	–		–	–		–	–		4		1
17 Oldham Athletic	–	–		1		1	3	–		–	–		–	–		–	–		–	–		–	–		–	–		4		1
18 Stoke City	–	–		–	–		4	–		–	–		–	–		–	–		–	–		–	–		–	–		4	–	
19 Wolverhampton W.	–	–		–	–		4	–		–	–		–	–		–	–		–	–		–	–		–	–		4	–	
20 West Ham United	–	–		1	–		2		3	–	–		–	–		–	–		–	–		–	–		–	–		3		3
21 Arsenal	–	–		3		1	–	–		–	–		–	–		–	–		–	–		–	–		–	–		3		1
22 Cardiff City	–	–		2		1	–	–		1	–		–	–		–	–		–	–		–	–		–	–		3		1
23 Huddersfield Town	–	–		2	–		–	–		1	–		–	–		–	–		–	–		–	–		–	–		3	–	
24 Tottenham Hotspur	–	–		2	–		–	–		1	–		–	–		–	–		–	–		–	–		–	–		3	–	
25 Bristol City	–	–		–	–		2		2	–	–		–	–		–	–		–	–		–	–		–	–		2		2
26 Aston Villa	–	–		2		1	–	–		–	–		–	–		–	–		–	–		–	–		–	–		2		1
27 Burnley	–	–		2		1	–	–		–	–		–	–		–	–		–	–		–	–		–	–		2		1
28 Middlesbrough	–	–		2		1	–	–		–	–		–	–		–	–		–	–		–	–		–	–		2		1
29 Notts County	–	–		–	–		2		1	–	–		–	–		–	–		–	–		–	–		–	–		2		1
30 Portsmouth	–	–		–	–		2		1	–	–		–	–		–	–		–	–		–	–		–	–		2		1
31 Preston North End	–	–		2		1	–	–		–	–		–	–		–	–		–	–		–	–		–	–		2		1
32 Rotherham United	–	–		–	–		2		1	–	–		–	–		–	–		–	–		–	–		–	–		2		1
33 Sheffield United	–	–		2		1	–	–		–	–		–	–		–	–		–	–		–	–		–	–		2		1
34 Sunderland	–	–		2		1	–	–		–	–		–	–		–	–		–	–		–	–		–	–		2		1
35 Birmingham City	–	–		2	–		–	–		–	–		–	–		–	–		–	–		–	–		–	–		2	–	
36 Bury	–	–		–	–		2	–		–	–		–	–		–	–		–	–		–	–		–	–		2	–	
37 Chelsea	–	–		1	–		1	–		–	–		–	–		–	–		–	–		–	–		–	–		2	–	
38 Liverpool	–	–		2	–		–	–		–	–		–	–		–	–		–	–		–	–		–	–		2	–	
39 Manchester City	–	–		2	–		–	–		–	–		–	–		–	–		–	–		–	–		–	–		2	–	
40 Newcastle United	–	–		2	–		–	–		–	–		–	–		–	–		–	–		–	–		–	–		2	–	
41 Blackburn Rovers	–	–		1	–		–	–		–	–		–	–		–	–		–	–		–	–		–	–		1	–	
42 Everton	–	–		1	–		–	–		–	–		–	–		–	–		–	–		–	–		–	–		1	–	
43 Nelson	–	–		–	–		1	–		–	–		–	–		–	–		–	–		–	–		–	–		1	–	
44 Plymouth Argyle	–	–		–	–		–	–		1	–		–	–		–	–		–	–		–	–		–	–		1	–	

WILLIAM LONGAIR

DEBUT (Full Appearance)

Saturday 20/04/1895
Football League Division 2
at Bank Street

Newton Heath 3 Notts County 3

CLUB CAREER RECORD	Apps	Subs	Goals
Premiership	0		0
League Division 1	0		0
League Division 2	1		0
FA Cup	0		0
League Cup	0		0
European Cup / Champions League	0		0
European Cup-Winners' Cup	0		0
UEFA Cup / Inter-Cities' Fairs Cup	0		0
Other Matches	0		0
OVERALL TOTAL	1		0

Opponents	PREM A S G	FLD 1 A S G	FLD 2 A S G	FAC A S G	LC A S G	EC/CL A S G	ECWC A S G	UEFA A S G	OTHER A S G	TOTAL A S G
1 Notts County	– – –	– – –	1 –	– – –	– – –	– – –	– – –	– – –	– – –	1 –

LONGTON (FIRST NAME NOT KNOWN)

DEBUT (Full Appearance)

Saturday 30/10/1886
FA Cup 1st Round
at Fleetwood Park

Fleetwood Rangers 2 Newton Heath 2

CLUB CAREER RECORD	Apps	Subs	Goals
Premiership	0		0
League Division 1	0		0
League Division 2	0		0
FA Cup	1		0
League Cup	0		0
European Cup / Champions League	0		0
European Cup-Winners' Cup	0		0
UEFA Cup / Inter-Cities' Fairs Cup	0		0
Other Matches	0		0
OVERALL TOTAL	1		0

Opponents	PREM A S G	FLD 1 A S G	FLD 2 A S G	FAC A S G	LC A S G	EC/CL A S G	ECWC A S G	UEFA A S G	OTHER A S G	TOTAL A S G
1 Fleetwood Rangers	– – –	– – –	– – –	1 –	– – –	– – –	– – –	– – –	– – –	1

TOMMY LOWRIE

DEBUT (Full Appearance)

Wednesday 07/04/1948
Football League Division 1
at Maine Road

Manchester United 1 Manchester City 1

CLUB CAREER RECORD	Apps	Subs	Goals
Premiership	0		0
League Division 1	13		0
League Division 2	0		0
FA Cup	1		0
League Cup	0		0
European Cup / Champions League	0		0
European Cup-Winners' Cup	0		0
UEFA Cup / Inter-Cities' Fairs Cup	0		0
Other Matches	0		0
OVERALL TOTAL	14		0

Opponents	PREM A S G	FLD 1 A S G	FLD 2 A S G	FAC A S G	LC A S G	EC/CL A S G	ECWC A S G	UEFA A S G	OTHER A S G	TOTAL A S G
1 Bolton Wanderers	– –	2 –	– –	– – –	– –	– –	– –	– –	– – –	2 –
2 Everton	– –	2 –	– –	– – –	– –	– –	– –	– –	– – –	2 –
3 Sunderland	– –	2 –	– –	– – –	– –	– –	– –	– –	– – –	2 –
4 Burnley	– –	1 –	– –	– – –	– –	– –	– –	– –	– – –	1 –
5 Chelsea	– –	1 –	– –	– – –	– –	– –	– –	– –	– – –	1 –
6 Liverpool	– –	1 –	– –	– – –	– –	– –	– –	– –	– – –	1 –
7 Manchester City	– –	1 –	– –	– – –	– –	– –	– –	– –	– – –	1 –
8 Middlesbrough	– –	1 –	– –	– – –	– –	– –	– –	– –	– – –	1 –
9 Newcastle United	– –	1 –	– –	– – –	– –	– –	– –	– –	– – –	1 –
10 Oldham Athletic	– –	– –	– –	1 –	– –	– –	– –	– –	– – –	1 –
11 Preston North End	– –	1 –	– –	– – –	– –	– –	– –	– –	– – –	1 –

GEORGE LYDON

DEBUT (Full Appearance)

Thursday 25/12/1930
Football League Division 1
at Burnden Park

Bolton Wanderers 3 Manchester United 1

CLUB CAREER RECORD	Apps	Subs	Goals
Premiership	0		0
League Division 1	1		0
League Division 2	2		0
FA Cup	0		0
League Cup	0		0
European Cup / Champions League	0		0
European Cup-Winners' Cup	0		0
UEFA Cup / Inter-Cities' Fairs Cup	0		0
Other Matches	0		0
OVERALL TOTAL	3		0

Opponents	PREM A S G	FLD 1 A S G	FLD 2 A S G	FAC A S G	LC A S G	EC/CL A S G	ECWC A S G	UEFA A S G	OTHER A S G	TOTAL A S G
1 Bolton Wanderers	– –	1 –	– –	– – –	– –	– –	– –	– –	– – –	1 –
2 Bradford City	– –	– –	1 –	– – –	– –	– –	– –	– –	– – –	1 –
3 Millwall	– –	– –	1 –	– – –	– –	– –	– –	– –	– – –	1 –

MARK LYNCH

DEBUT (Full Appearance)

Tuesday 18/03/2003
Champions League Phase 2 Match 6
at Estadio de Riazor

Deportivo La Coruna 2 Manchester United 0

CLUB CAREER RECORD	Apps	Subs	Goals
Premiership	0		0
League Division 1	0		0
League Division 2	0		0
FA Cup	0		0
League Cup	0		0
European Cup / Champions League	1		0
European Cup-Winners' Cup	0		0
UEFA Cup / Inter-Cities' Fairs Cup	0		0
Other Matches	0		0
OVERALL TOTAL	1		0

Opponents	PREM A S G	FLD 1 A S G	FLD 2 A S G	FAC A S G	LC A S G	EC/CL A S G	ECWC A S G	UEFA A S G	OTHER A S G	TOTAL A S G
1 Deportivo La Coruna	– – –	– – –	– – –	– – –	– – –	1 – –	– – –	– – –	– – –	1 –

DAVID LYNER

DEBUT (Full Appearance)

Saturday 23/09/1922
Football League Division 2
at Highfield Road

Coventry City 2 Manchester United 0

CLUB CAREER RECORD	Apps	Subs	Goals
Premiership	0		0
League Division 1	0		0
League Division 2	3		0
FA Cup	0		0
League Cup	0		0
European Cup / Champions League	0		0
European Cup-Winners' Cup	0		0
UEFA Cup / Inter-Cities' Fairs Cup	0		0
Other Matches	0		0
OVERALL TOTAL	3		0

Opponents	PREM A S G	FLD 1 A S G	FLD 2 A S G	FAC A S G	LC A S G	EC/CL A S G	ECWC A S G	UEFA A S G	OTHER A S G	TOTAL A S G
1 Coventry City	– – –	– – –	2 – –	– – –	– – –	– – –	– – –	– – –	– – –	2 –
2 Port Vale	– – –	– – –	1 – –	– – –	– – –	– – –	– – –	– – –	– – –	1 –

SAMMY LYNN

DEBUT (Full Appearance)

Saturday 03/01/1948
Football League Division 1
at The Valley

Charlton Athletic 1 Manchester United 2

CLUB CAREER RECORD	Apps	Subs	Goals
Premiership	0		0
League Division 1	13		0
League Division 2	0		0
FA Cup	0		0
League Cup	0		0
European Cup / Champions League	0		0
European Cup-Winners' Cup	0		0
UEFA Cup / Inter-Cities' Fairs Cup	0		0
Other Matches	0		0
OVERALL TOTAL	13		0

Opponents	PREM A S G	FLD 1 A S G	FLD 2 A S G	FAC A S G	LC A S G	EC/CL A S G	ECWC A S G	UEFA A S G	OTHER A S G	TOTAL A S G
1 Bolton Wanderers	– –	3 – –	– – –	– – –	– – –	– – –	– – –	– – –	– – –	3 –
2 Aston Villa	– –	2 – –	– – –	– – –	– – –	– – –	– – –	– – –	– – –	2 –
3 Burnley	– –	1 – –	– – –	– – –	– – –	– – –	– – –	– – –	– – –	1 –
4 Charlton Athletic	– –	1 – –	– – –	– – –	– – –	– – –	– – –	– – –	– – –	1 –
5 Chelsea	– –	1 – –	– – –	– – –	– – –	– – –	– – –	– – –	– – –	1 –
6 Derby County	– –	1 – –	– – –	– – –	– – –	– – –	– – –	– – –	– – –	1 –
7 Liverpool	– –	1 – –	– – –	– – –	– – –	– – –	– – –	– – –	– – –	1 –
8 Manchester City	– –	1 – –	– – –	– – –	– – –	– – –	– – –	– – –	– – –	1 –
9 Stoke City	– –	1 – –	– – –	– – –	– – –	– – –	– – –	– – –	– – –	1 –
10 West Bromwich Albion	–	1 –								1 –

GEORGE LYONS

DEBUT (Full Appearance)

Saturday 23/04/1904
Football League Division 2
at Bank Street

Manchester United 2 Burton United 0

CLUB CAREER RECORD	Apps	Subs	Goals
Premiership	0		0
League Division 1	0		0
League Division 2	4		0
FA Cup	1		0
League Cup	0		0
European Cup / Champions League	0		0
European Cup-Winners' Cup	0		0
UEFA Cup / Inter-Cities' Fairs Cup	0		0
Other Matches	0		0
OVERALL TOTAL	5		0

Opponents	PREM A S G	FLD 1 A S G	FLD 2 A S G	FAC A S G	LC A S G	EC/CL A S G	ECWC A S G	UEFA A S G	OTHER A S G	TOTAL A S G
1 Bolton Wanderers	– – –	– – –	1 – –	– – –	– – –	– – –	– – –	– – –	– – –	1 –
2 Burton United	– – –	– – –	1 – –	– – –	– – –	– – –	– – –	– – –	– – –	1 –
3 Fulham	– – –	– – –	– – –	1 – –	– – –	– – –	– – –	– – –	– – –	1 –
4 Port Vale	– – –	– – –	1 – –	– – –	– – –	– – –	– – –	– – –	– – –	1 –
5 West Bromwich Albion	– – –	– – –	1 – –	– – –	– – –	– – –	– – –	– – –	– – –	1 –

LOU MACARI

DEBUT (Full Appearance, 1 goal)

Saturday 20/01/1973
Football League Division 1
at Old Trafford

Manchester United 2 West Ham United 2

CLUB CAREER RECORD	Apps	Subs	Goals
Premiership	0		0
League Division 1	275	(16)	67
League Division 2	36	(2)	11
FA Cup	31	(3)	8
League Cup	22	(5)	10
European Cup / Champions League	0		0
European Cup–Winners' Cup	4		0
UEFA Cup / Inter-Cities' Fairs Cup	5	(1)	1
Other Matches	1		0
OVERALL TOTAL	374	(27)	97

Opponents	PREM A S G	FLD 1 A S G	FLD 2 A S G	FAC A S G	LC A S G	EC/CL A S G	ECWC A S G	UEFA A S G	OTHER A S G	TOTAL A S G
1 Liverpool	– –	14 (1) 1	– –	2 –	– (1) –	–	–	–	1 –	17 (2) 1
2 Coventry City	– –	14 (1) 7	– –	– –	2 –	–	–	–	–	16 (1) 7
3 Norwich City	– –	11 4	2 –	– –	3 2	–	–	–	–	16 6
4 Arsenal	– –	14 2	– –	1 –	1 –	–	–	–	–	16 2
5 Aston Villa	– –	11 (1) 2	2 –	1 1	1 1	–	–	–	–	15 (1) 4
6 Tottenham Hotspur	– –	11 (1) 2	– –	2 –	2 –	–	–	–	–	15 (1) 2
7 Manchester City	– –	13 (1) 1	– –	– –	1 (1) –	–	–	–	–	14 (2) 1
8 Everton	– –	12 (2) 4	– –	– (1) –	– –	–	–	–	–	12 (3) 4
9 Middlesbrough	– –	11 5	– –	– –	3 1	–	–	–	–	14 6
10 Leeds United	– –	13 1	– –	1 –	– –	–	–	–	–	14 1
11 Southampton	– –	8 (1) 2	2 1	3 1	– –	–	–	–	–	13 (1) 4
12 Ipswich Town	– –	12 (1) 2	– –	1 –	– –	–	–	–	–	13 (1) 2
13 Birmingham City	– –	13 6	– –	– –	– –	–	–	–	–	13 6
14 Wolverhampton W.	– –	11 3	– –	2 –	– –	–	–	–	–	13 3
15 West Bromwich Albion	– –	10 2	1 –	2 –	– –	–	–	–	–	13 2
16 Stoke City	– –	12 4	– –	– –	– –	–	–	–	–	12 4
17 Derby County	– –	11 2	– –	– –	– –	–	–	–	–	11 2
18 Nottingham Forest	– –	7 (1) 1	1 (1) –	1 –	– –	–	–	–	–	9 (2) 1
19 Queens Park Rangers	– –	8 (1) 1	– –	1 1	– –	–	–	–	–	9 (1) 2
20 Sunderland	– –	5 (1) –	2 –	– –	2 –	–	–	–	–	9 (1) –
21 Leicester City	– –	8 1	– –	1 1	– –	–	–	–	–	9 2
22 Newcastle United	– –	8 2	– –	– –	1 –	–	–	–	–	9 2
23 Bristol City	– –	6 1	2 –	– –	– –	–	–	–	–	8 1
24 West Ham United	– –	6 (1) 4	– –	– –	– –	–	–	–	–	6 (1) 4
25 Brighton	– –	3 (2) 2	– –	2 –	– –	–	–	–	–	5 (2) 2
26 Sheffield United	– –	5 3	– –	– –	– –	–	–	–	–	5 3
27 Bolton Wanderers	– –	3 –	2 1	– –	– –	–	–	–	–	5 1
28 Chelsea	– –	5 –	– –	– –	– –	–	–	–	–	5 –
29 Crystal Palace	– –	5 –	– –	– –	– –	–	–	–	–	5 –
30 Burnley	– –	3 2	– –	– –	1 2	–	–	–	–	4 4
31 Oxford United	– –	– –	2 1	1 –	– (1) –	–	–	–	–	3 (1) 1
32 Fulham	– –	– –	1 (1) –	2 –	– –	–	–	–	–	3 (1) –
33 Walsall	– –	– –	– –	3 –	– –	–	–	–	–	3 –
34 Notts County	– –	– (1) –	2 –	– –	– –	–	–	–	–	2 (1) –
35 Carlisle United	– –	– –	– –	2 3	– –	–	–	–	–	2 3
36 Blackpool	– –	– –	2 2	– –	– –	–	–	–	–	2 2
37 Sheffield Wednesday	– –	– –	2 2	– –	– –	–	–	–	–	2 2
38 Ajax	– –	– –	– –	– –	– –	–	–	2 1	–	2 1
39 Bristol Rovers	– –	– –	– –	2 1	– –	–	–	–	–	2 1
40 Oldham Athletic	– –	– –	– –	2 1	– –	–	–	–	–	2 1
41 York City	– –	– –	– –	2 1	– –	–	–	–	–	2 1
42 Hull City	– –	– –	– –	2 –	– –	–	–	–	–	2 –
43 Juventus	– –	– –	– –	– –	– –	–	–	2 –	–	2 –
44 Leyton Orient	– –	– –	2 –	– –	– –	–	–	–	–	2 –
45 Swansea City	– –	2 –	– –	– –	– –	–	–	–	–	2 –
46 Colchester United	– –	– –	– –	1 –	– (1) –	–	–	–	–	1 (1) –
47 Bournemouth	– –	– –	– –	– (1) –	– (1) –	–	–	–	–	– (2) –
48 Charlton Athletic	– –	– –	– –	– –	1 2	–	–	–	–	1 2
49 Brentford	– –	– –	– –	– –	1 1	–	–	–	–	1 1
50 Cardiff City	– –	– –	1 1	– –	– –	–	–	–	–	1 1
51 Plymouth Argyle	– –	– –	– –	1 1	– –	–	–	–	–	1 1
52 Tranmere Rovers	– –	– –	– –	– –	1 1	–	–	–	–	1 1
53 Bradford City	– –	– –	– –	– –	1 –	–	–	–	–	1 –
54 Dukla Prague	– –	– –	– –	– –	– –	–	1 –	–	–	1 –
55 Millwall	– –	– –	1 –	– –	– –	–	–	–	–	1 –
56 Peterborough United	– –	– –	– –	1 –	– –	–	–	–	–	1 –
57 Porto	– –	– –	– –	– –	– –	–	1 –	–	–	1 –
58 Portsmouth	– –	– –	1 –	– –	– –	–	–	–	–	1 –
59 Spartak Varna	– –	– –	– –	– –	– –	–	1 –	–	–	1 –
60 St Etienne	– –	– –	– –	– –	– –	–	1 –	–	–	1 –
61 Stockport County	– –	– –	– –	– –	1 –	–	–	–	–	1 –
62 Widzew Lodz	– –	– –	– –	– –	– –	–	–	1 –	–	1 –
63 Valencia	– –	– –	– –	– –	– –	–	–	– (1) –	–	– (1) –
64 Watford	– –	– –	– –	– (1) –	– –	–	–	–	–	– (1) –

KEN MACDONALD

DEBUT (Full Appearance)

Saturday 03/03/1923
Football League Division 2
at Old Trafford

Manchester United 1 Southampton 2

CLUB CAREER RECORD	Apps	Subs	Goals
Premiership	0		0
League Division 1	0		0
League Division 2	9		2
FA Cup	0		0
League Cup	0		0
European Cup / Champions League	0		0
European Cup-Winners' Cup	0		0
UEFA Cup / Inter-Cities' Fairs Cup	0		0
Other Matches	0		0
OVERALL TOTAL	**9**		**2**

Opponents	PREM A S G	FLD 1 A S G	FLD 2 A S G	FAC A S G	LC A S G	EC/CL A S G	ECWC A S G	UEFA A S G	OTHER A S G	TOTAL A S G
1 Southampton	– – –	– – –	3 – –	– – –	– – –	– – –	– – –	– – –	– – –	3 – –
2 Bristol City	– – –	– – –	2 1	– – –	– – –	– – –	– – –	– – –	– – –	2 1
3 Derby County	– – –	– – –	1 1	– – –	– – –	– – –	– – –	– – –	– – –	1 1
4 Bury	– – –	– – –	1 –	– – –	– – –	– – –	– – –	– – –	– – –	1 –
5 Oldham Athletic	– – –	– – –	1 –	– – –	– – –	– – –	– – –	– – –	– – –	1 –
6 South Shields	– – –	– – –	1 –	– – –	– – –	– – –	– – –	– – –	– – –	1 –

TED MACDOUGALL

DEBUT (Full Appearance)

Saturday 07/10/1972
Football League Division 1
at The Hawthorns

West Bromwich Albion 2 Manchester United 2

CLUB CAREER RECORD	Apps	Subs	Goals
Premiership	0		0
League Division 1	18		5
League Division 2	0		0
FA Cup	0		0
League Cup	0		0
European Cup / Champions League	0		0
European Cup-Winners' Cup	0		0
UEFA Cup / Inter-Cities' Fairs Cup	0		0
Other Matches	0		0
OVERALL TOTAL	**18**		**5**

Opponents	PREM A S G	FLD 1 A S G	FLD 2 A S G	FAC A S G	LC A S G	EC/CL A S G	ECWC A S G	UEFA A S G	OTHER A S G	TOTAL A S G
1 Birmingham City	– –	1 1	– –	– –	– –	– –	– –	– –	– –	1 1
2 Leeds United	– –	1 1	– –	– –	– –	– –	– –	– –	– –	1 1
3 Liverpool	– –	1 1	– –	– –	– –	– –	– –	– –	– –	1 1
4 Norwich City	– –	1 1	– –	– –	– –	– –	– –	– –	– –	1 1
5 Southampton	– –	1 1	– –	– –	– –	– –	– –	– –	– –	1 1
6 Coventry City	– –	1 –	– –	– –	– –	– –	– –	– –	– –	1 –
7 Crystal Palace	– –	1 –	– –	– –	– –	– –	– –	– –	– –	1 –
8 Derby County	– –	1 –	– –	– –	– –	– –	– –	– –	– –	1 –
9 Everton	– –	1 –	– –	– –	– –	– –	– –	– –	– –	1 –
10 Ipswich Town	– –	1 –	– –	– –	– –	– –	– –	– –	– –	1 –
11 Leicester City	– –	1 –	– –	– –	– –	– –	– –	– –	– –	1 –
12 Manchester City	– –	1 –	– –	– –	– –	– –	– –	– –	– –	1 –
13 Newcastle United	– –	1 –	– –	– –	– –	– –	– –	– –	– –	1 –
14 Stoke City	– –	1 –	– –	– –	– –	– –	– –	– –	– –	1 –
15 Tottenham Hotspur	– –	1 –	– –	– –	– –	– –	– –	– –	– –	1 –
16 West Bromwich Albion	– –	1 –	– –	– –	– –	– –	– –	– –	– –	1 –
17 West Ham United	– –	1 –	– –	– –	– –	– –	– –	– –	– –	1 –
18 Wolverhampton W.	– –	1 –	– –	– –	– –	– –	– –	– –	– –	1 –

CHARLIE MACKIE

DEBUT (Full Appearance)

Saturday 03/09/1904
Football League Division 2
at Cobridge Stadium

Port Vale 2 Manchester United 2

CLUB CAREER RECORD	Apps	Subs	Goals
Premiership	0		0
League Division 1	0		0
League Division 2	5		3
FA Cup	2		1
League Cup	0		0
European Cup / Champions League	0		0
European Cup-Winners' Cup	0		0
UEFA Cup / Inter-Cities' Fairs Cup	0		0
Other Matches	0		0
OVERALL TOTAL	**7**		**4**

Opponents	PREM A S G	FLD 1 A S G	FLD 2 A S G	FAC A S G	LC A S G	EC/CL A S G	ECWC A S G	UEFA A S G	OTHER A S G	TOTAL A S G
1 Glossop	– – –	– – –	2 2	– – –	– – –	– – –	– – –	– – –	– – –	2 2
2 Fulham	– – –	– – –	– – –	2 1	– – –	– – –	– – –	– – –	– – –	2 1
3 Bolton Wanderers	– – –	– – –	1 1	– – –	– – –	– – –	– – –	– – –	– – –	1 1
4 Bristol City	– – –	– – –	1 –	– – –	– – –	– – –	– – –	– – –	– – –	1 –
5 Port Vale	– – –	– – –	1 –	– – –	– – –	– – –	– – –	– – –	– – –	1 –

JULES MAIORANA

DEBUT (Substitute Appearance)

Saturday 14/01/1989
Football League Division 1
at Old Trafford

Manchester United 3 Millwall 0

CLUB CAREER RECORD	Apps	Subs	Goals
Premiership	0		0
League Division 1	2	(5)	0
League Division 2	0		0
FA Cup	0		0
League Cup	0	(1)	0
European Cup / Champions League	0		0
European Cup-Winners' Cup	0		0
UEFA Cup / Inter-Cities' Fairs Cup	0		0
Other Matches	0		0
OVERALL TOTAL	**2**	**(6)**	**0**

Opponents	PREM A S G	FLD 1 A S G	FLD 2 A S G	FAC A S G	LC A S G	EC/CL A S G	ECWC A S G	UEFA A S G	OTHER A S G	TOTAL A S G
1 Millwall	– –	– (2) –	– –	– –	– –	– –	– –	– –	– –	– (2) –
2 Arsenal	– –	1 –	– –	– –	– –	– –	– –	– –	– –	1 –
3 Derby County	– –	1 –	– –	– –	– –	– –	– –	– –	– –	1 –
4 Coventry City	– –	– (1) –	– –	– –	– –	– –	– –	– –	– –	– (1) –
5 Luton Town	– –	– (1) –	– –	– –	– –	– –	– –	– –	– –	– (1) –
6 Tottenham Hotspur	– –	– –	– –	– –	– (1) –	– –	– –	– –	– –	– (1) –
7 Wimbledon	– –	– (1) –	– –	– –	– –	– –	– –	– –	– –	– (1) –

TOM MANLEY

DEBUT (Full Appearance)

Saturday 05/12/1931
Football League Division 2
at Old Trafford

Manchester United 2 Millwall 0

CLUB CAREER RECORD	Apps	Subs	Goals
Premiership	0		0
League Division 1	54		8
League Division 2	134		32
FA Cup	7		1
League Cup	0		0
European Cup / Champions League	0		0
European Cup-Winners' Cup	0		0
UEFA Cup / Inter-Cities' Fairs Cup	0		0
Other Matches	0		0
OVERALL TOTAL	**195**		**41**

Opponents	PREM A S G	FLD 1 A S G	FLD 2 A S G	FAC A S G	LC A S G	EC/CL A S G	ECWC A S G	UEFA A S G	OTHER A S G	TOTAL A S G
1 Bury	– –	– –	7 2	– –	– –	– –	– –	– –	– –	7 2
2 Blackpool	– –	1 –	6 1	– –	– –	– –	– –	– –	– –	7 1
3 Brentford	– –	3 1	3 –	1 –	– –	– –	– –	– –	– –	7 1
4 Burnley	– –	– –	7 1	– –	– –	– –	– –	– –	– –	7 1
5 Plymouth Argyle	– –	– –	7 1	– –	– –	– –	– –	– –	– –	7 1
6 Oldham Athletic	– –	– –	6 2	– –	– –	– –	– –	– –	– –	6 2
7 Southampton	– –	– –	6 2	– –	– –	– –	– –	– –	– –	6 2
8 Nottingham Forest	– –	– –	6 1	– –	– –	– –	– –	– –	– –	6 1
9 Portsmouth	– –	4 1	– –	2 –	– –	– –	– –	– –	– –	6 1
10 Swansea City	– –	– –	6 1	– –	– –	– –	– –	– –	– –	6 1
11 Grimsby Town	– –	2 –	4 –	– –	– –	– –	– –	– –	– –	6 –
12 West Ham United	– –	– –	6 –	– –	– –	– –	– –	– –	– –	6 –
13 Port Vale	– –	– –	5 4	– –	– –	– –	– –	– –	– –	5 4
14 Bradford City	– –	– –	5 2	– –	– –	– –	– –	– –	– –	5 2
15 Newcastle United	– –	– –	5 2	– –	– –	– –	– –	– –	– –	5 2
16 Sheffield United	– –	– –	5 2	– –	– –	– –	– –	– –	– –	5 2
17 Bradford Park Avenue	– –	– –	5 1	– –	– –	– –	– –	– –	– –	5 1
18 Tottenham Hotspur	– –	– –	5 1	– –	– –	– –	– –	– –	– –	5 1
19 Preston North End	– –	2 –	3 –	– –	– –	– –	– –	– –	– –	5 –
20 Stoke City	– –	2 –	1 –	2 –	– –	– –	– –	– –	– –	5 –
21 Barnsley	– –	– –	4 3	– –	– –	– –	– –	– –	– –	4 3
22 Norwich City	– –	– –	4 3	– –	– –	– –	– –	– –	– –	4 3
23 Huddersfield Town	– –	4 1	– –	– –	– –	– –	– –	– –	– –	4 1
24 Bolton Wanderers	– –	1 –	3 –	– –	– –	– –	– –	– –	– –	4 –
25 Everton	– –	4 –	– –	– –	– –	– –	– –	– –	– –	4 –
26 Fulham	– –	– –	4 –	– –	– –	– –	– –	– –	– –	4 –
27 Hull City	– –	– –	4 –	– –	– –	– –	– –	– –	– –	4 –
28 Leeds United	– –	4 –	– –	– –	– –	– –	– –	– –	– –	4 –
29 Liverpool	– –	3 1	– –	– –	– –	– –	– –	– –	– –	3 1
30 Millwall	– –	– –	3 1	– –	– –	– –	– –	– –	– –	3 1
31 Sunderland	– –	3 1	– –	– –	– –	– –	– –	– –	– –	3 1
32 Arsenal	– –	3 –	– –	– –	– –	– –	– –	– –	– –	3 –
33 Birmingham City	– –	3 –	– –	– –	– –	– –	– –	– –	– –	3 –
34 Wolverhampton W.	– –	3 –	– –	– –	– –	– –	– –	– –	– –	3 –
35 Aston Villa	– –	1 –	1 1	– –	– –	– –	– –	– –	– –	2 1
36 Chelsea	– –	2 1	– –	– –	– –	– –	– –	– –	– –	2 1
37 Charlton Athletic	– –	2 –	– –	– –	– –	– –	– –	– –	– –	2 –
38 Coventry City	– –	– –	2 –	– –	– –	– –	– –	– –	– –	2 –
39 Derby County	– –	2 –	– –	– –	– –	– –	– –	– –	– –	2 –
40 Doncaster Rovers	– –	– –	2 –	– –	– –	– –	– –	– –	– –	2 –
41 Lincoln City	– –	– –	2 –	– –	– –	– –	– –	– –	– –	2 –
42 West Bromwich Albion	– –	2 –	– –	– –	– –	– –	– –	– –	– –	2 –
43 Chesterfield	– –	– –	1 1	– –	– –	– –	– –	– –	– –	1 1
44 Manchester City	– –	1 1	– –	– –	– –	– –	– –	– –	– –	1 1

continued../

TOM MANLEY (continued)

Opponents	PREM A	S	G	FLD 1 A	S	G	FLD 2 A	S	G	FAC A	S	G	LC A	S	G	EC/CL A	S	G	ECWC A	S	G	UEFA A	S	G	OTHER A	S	G	TOTAL A	S	G
45 Middlesbrough	–	–		1		1	–	–		–	–		–	–		–	–		–	–		–	–		–	–		1		1
46 Reading	–	–		–	–		–	–		1		1	–	–		–	–		–	–		–	–		–	–		1		1
47 Blackburn Rovers	–	–		–	–		1			–	–		–	–		–	–		–	–		–	–		–	–		1		–
48 Bristol City	–	–		–	–		1			–	–		–	–		–	–		–	–		–	–		–	–		1		–
49 Bristol Rovers	–	–		–	–		–	–		1			–	–		–	–		–	–		–	–		–	–		1		–
50 Leicester City	–	–		–	–		1			–	–		–	–		–	–		–	–		–	–		–	–		1		–
51 Luton Town	–	–		–	–		1			–	–		–	–		–	–		–	–		–	–		–	–		1		–
52 Notts County	–	–		–	–		1			–	–		–	–		–	–		–	–		–	–		–	–		1		–
53 Sheffield Wednesday	–	–		1			–	–		–	–		–	–		–	–		–	–		–	–		–	–		1		–
54 Stockport County	–	–		–	–		1			–	–		–	–		–	–		–	–		–	–		–	–		1		–

FRANK MANN

DEBUT (Full Appearance)

Saturday 17/03/1923
Football League Division 2
at Valley Parade

Bradford City 1 Manchester United 1

CLUB CAREER RECORD	Apps	Subs	Goals
Premiership	0		0
League Division 1	113		2
League Division 2	67		3
FA Cup	17		0
League Cup	0		0
European Cup / Champions League	0		0
European Cup-Winners' Cup	0		0
UEFA Cup / Inter-Cities' Fairs Cup	0		0
Other Matches	0		0
OVERALL TOTAL	197		5

Opponents	PREM A	S	G	FLD 1 A	S	G	FLD 2 A	S	G	FAC A	S	G	LC A	S	G	EC/CL A	S	G	ECWC A	S	G	UEFA A	S	G	OTHER A	S	G	TOTAL A	S	G
1 Leicester City	–	–		7			5		1	–	–		–	–		–	–		–	–		–	–		–	–		12		1
2 Bury	–	–		5			1			3			–	–		–	–		–	–		–	–		–	–		9		–
3 Arsenal	–	–		8			–	–		–	–		–	–		–	–		–	–		–	–		–	–		8		–
4 Liverpool	–	–		8			–	–		–	–		–	–		–	–		–	–		–	–		–	–		8		–
5 Blackburn Rovers	–	–		6		1	–	–		1			–	–		–	–		–	–		–	–		–	–		7		1
6 Sunderland	–	–		5		1	–	–		2			–	–		–	–		–	–		–	–		–	–		7		1
7 Sheffield Wednesday	–	–		2			4			1			–	–		–	–		–	–		–	–		–	–		7		–
8 Aston Villa	–	–		6			–	–		–	–		–	–		–	–		–	–		–	–		–	–		6		–
9 Derby County	–	–		3			3			–	–		–	–		–	–		–	–		–	–		–	–		6		–
10 Huddersfield Town	–	–		5			–	–		1			–	–		–	–		–	–		–	–		–	–		6		–
11 Leeds United	–	–		4			2			–	–		–	–		–	–		–	–		–	–		–	–		6		–
12 Newcastle United	–	–		6			–	–		–	–		–	–		–	–		–	–		–	–		–	–		6		–
13 Sheffield United	–	–		6			–	–		–	–		–	–		–	–		–	–		–	–		–	–		6		–
14 Tottenham Hotspur	–	–		4			–	–		2			–	–		–	–		–	–		–	–		–	–		6		–
15 West Ham United	–	–		6			–	–		–	–		–	–		–	–		–	–		–	–		–	–		6		–
16 Birmingham City	–	–		4			–	–		1			–	–		–	–		–	–		–	–		–	–		5		–
17 Bolton Wanderers	–	–		5			–	–		–	–		–	–		–	–		–	–		–	–		–	–		5		–
18 Bradford City	–	–		–	–		5			–	–		–	–		–	–		–	–		–	–		–	–		5		–
19 Manchester City	–	–		4			–	–		1			–	–		–	–		–	–		–	–		–	–		5		–
20 Port Vale	–	–		–	–		3			2			–	–		–	–		–	–		–	–		–	–		5		–
21 Barnsley	–	–		–	–		4			–	–		–	–		–	–		–	–		–	–		–	–		4		–
22 Blackpool	–	–		–	–		4			–	–		–	–		–	–		–	–		–	–		–	–		4		–
23 Burnley	–	–		4			–	–		–	–		–	–		–	–		–	–		–	–		–	–		4		–
24 Cardiff City	–	–		4			–	–		–	–		–	–		–	–		–	–		–	–		–	–		4		–
25 Coventry City	–	–		–	–		4			–	–		–	–		–	–		–	–		–	–		–	–		4		–
26 Crystal Palace	–	–		–	–		4			–	–		–	–		–	–		–	–		–	–		–	–		4		–
27 Everton	–	–		4			–	–		–	–		–	–		–	–		–	–		–	–		–	–		4		–
28 Fulham	–	–		–	–		3			1			–	–		–	–		–	–		–	–		–	–		4		–
29 Middlesbrough	–	–		2			2			–	–		–	–		–	–		–	–		–	–		–	–		4		–
30 Portsmouth	–	–		2			2			–	–		–	–		–	–		–	–		–	–		–	–		4		–
31 South Shields	–	–		–	–		4			–	–		–	–		–	–		–	–		–	–		–	–		4		–
32 Oldham Athletic	–	–		–	–		3			–	–		–	–		–	–		–	–		–	–		–	–		3		–
33 Hull City	–	–		–	–		2			–	–		–	–		–	–		–	–		–	–		–	–		2		–
34 Leyton Orient	–	–		–	–		2			–	–		–	–		–	–		–	–		–	–		–	–		2		–
35 Nelson	–	–		–	–		2			–	–		–	–		–	–		–	–		–	–		–	–		2		–
36 Notts County	–	–		2			–	–		–	–		–	–		–	–		–	–		–	–		–	–		2		–
37 Southampton	–	–		–	–		2			–	–		–	–		–	–		–	–		–	–		–	–		2		–
38 Stoke City	–	–		–	–		2			–	–		–	–		–	–		–	–		–	–		–	–		2		–
39 Wolverhampton W.	–	–		–	–		2			–	–		–	–		–	–		–	–		–	–		–	–		2		–
40 Stockport County	–	–		–	–		1		2	–	–		–	–		–	–		–	–		–	–		–	–		1		2
41 Brentford	–	–		–	–		–	–		1			–	–		–	–		–	–		–	–		–	–		1		–
42 Chelsea	–	–		–	–		1			–	–		–	–		–	–		–	–		–	–		–	–		1		–
43 Plymouth Argyle	–	–		–	–		–	–		1			–	–		–	–		–	–		–	–		–	–		1		–
44 West Bromwich Albion	–	–		1			–	–		–	–		–	–		–	–		–	–		–	–		–	–		1		–

HERBERT MANN

DEBUT (Full Appearance)

Saturday 29/08/1931
Football League Division 2
at Park Avenue

Bradford Park Avenue 3 Manchester United 1

CLUB CAREER RECORD	Apps	Subs	Goals
Premiership	0		0
League Division 1	0		0
League Division 2	13		2
FA Cup	0		0
League Cup	0		0
European Cup / Champions League	0		0
European Cup–Winners' Cup	0		0
UEFA Cup / Inter-Cities' Fairs Cup	0		0
Other Matches	0		0
OVERALL TOTAL	**13**		**2**

Opponents	PREM A S G	FLD 1 A S G	FLD 2 A S G	FAC A S G	LC A S G	EC/CL A S G	ECWC A S G	UEFA A S G	OTHER A S G	TOTAL A S G
1 Notts County	– –	– –	1 1	–	–	–	–	–	–	1 1
2 Oldham Athletic	– –	– –	1 1	–	–	–	–	–	–	1 1
3 Barnsley	– –	– –	1	–	–	–	–	–	–	1 –
4 Bradford City	– –	– –	1	–	–	–	–	–	–	1 –
5 Bradford Park Avenue	– –	– –	1	–	–	–	–	–	–	1 –
6 Bristol City	– –	– –	1	–	–	–	–	–	–	1 –
7 Bury	– –	– –	1	–	–	–	–	–	–	1 –
8 Leeds United	– –	– –	1	–	–	–	–	–	–	1 –
9 Millwall	– –	– –	1	–	–	–	–	–	–	1 –
10 Plymouth Argyle	– –	– –	1	–	–	–	–	–	–	1 –
11 Port Vale	– –	– –	1	–	–	–	–	–	–	1 –
12 Preston North End	– –	– –	1	–	–	–	–	–	–	1 –
13 Stoke City	– –	– –	1	–	–	–	–	–	–	1 –

TOM MANNS

DEBUT (Full Appearance)

Saturday 03/02/1934
Football League Division 2
at Turf Moor

Burnley 1 Manchester United 4

CLUB CAREER RECORD	Apps	Subs	Goals
Premiership	0		0
League Division 1	0		0
League Division 2	2		0
FA Cup	0		0
League Cup	0		0
European Cup / Champions League	0		0
European Cup–Winners' Cup	0		0
UEFA Cup / Inter-Cities' Fairs Cup	0		0
Other Matches	0		0
OVERALL TOTAL	**2**		**0**

Opponents	PREM A S G	FLD 1 A S G	FLD 2 A S G	FAC A S G	LC A S G	EC/CL A S G	ECWC A S G	UEFA A S G	OTHER A S G	TOTAL A S G
1 Burnley	– –	– –	1	–	–	–	–	–	–	1 –
2 Oldham Athletic	– –	– –	1	–	–	–	–	–	–	1 –

PHILIP MARSH

DEBUT (Full Appearance)

Wednesday 25/10/2006
League Cup 3rd Round
at Gresty Road

Crewe Alexandra 1 Manchester United 2

CLUB CAREER RECORD	Apps	Subs	Goals
Premiership	0		0
League Division 1	0		0
League Division 2	0		0
FA Cup	0		0
League Cup	1		0
European Cup / Champions League	0		0
European Cup–Winners' Cup	0		0
UEFA Cup / Inter-Cities' Fairs Cup	0		0
Other Matches	0		0
OVERALL TOTAL	**1**		**0**

Opponents	PREM A S G	FLD 1 A S G	FLD 2 A S G	FAC A S G	LC A S G	EC/CL A S G	ECWC A S G	UEFA A S G	OTHER A S G	TOTAL A S G
1 Crewe Alexandra	– –	– –	– –	–	1	–	–	–	–	1 –

ARTHUR MARSHALL

DEBUT (Full Appearance)

Monday 09/03/1903
Football League Division 2
at Bank Street

Manchester United 3 Arsenal 0

CLUB CAREER RECORD	Apps	Subs	Goals
Premiership	0		0
League Division 1	0		0
League Division 2	6		0
FA Cup	0		0
League Cup	0		0
European Cup / Champions League	0		0
European Cup-Winners' Cup	0		0
UEFA Cup / Inter-Cities' Fairs Cup	0		0
Other Matches	0		0
OVERALL TOTAL	**6**		**0**

Opponents	PREM A S G	FLD 1 A S G	FLD 2 A S G	FAC A S G	LC A S G	EC/CL A S G	ECWC A S G	UEFA A S G	OTHER A S G	TOTAL A S G
1 Preston North End	– – –	– – –	2 – –	– – –	– – –	– – –	– – –	– – –	– – –	2 – –
2 Arsenal	– – –	1 – –	– – –	– – –	– – –	– – –	– – –	– – –	– – –	1 – –
3 Doncaster Rovers	– – –	– – –	1 – –	– – –	– – –	– – –	– – –	– – –	– – –	1 – –
4 Leicester City	– – –	– – –	1 – –	– – –	– – –	– – –	– – –	– – –	– – –	1 – –
5 Stockport County	– – –	– – –	1 – –	– – –	– – –	– – –	– – –	– – –	– – –	1 – –

LEE MARTIN (1990s)

DEBUT (Substitute Appearance)

Monday 09/05/1988
Football League Division 1
at Old Trafford

Manchester United 2 Wimbledon 1

CLUB CAREER RECORD	Apps	Subs	Goals
Premiership	1		0
League Division 1	55	(17)	1
League Division 2	0		0
FA Cup	13	(1)	1
League Cup	8	(2)	0
European Cup / Champions League	1	(1)	0
European Cup-Winners' Cup	4	(4)	0
UEFA Cup / Inter-Cities' Fairs Cup	1		0
Other Matches	1		0
OVERALL TOTAL	**84**	**(25)**	**2**

Opponents	PREM A S G	FLD 1 A S G	FLD 2 A S G	FAC A S G	LC A S G	EC/CL A S G	ECWC A S G	UEFA A S G	OTHER A S G	TOTAL A S G
1 Queens Park Rangers	– –	5 – –	– – –	3 – –	– – –	– – –	– – –	– – –	– – –	8 – –
2 Nottingham Forest	– –	3 (2) –	– – –	1 (1) –	– – –	– – –	– – –	– – –	– – –	4 (3) –
3 Everton	1 –	4 (1) –	– –	– –	– – –	– – –	– – –	– – –	– – –	5 (1) –
4 Arsenal	– –	2 (3) –	– – –	– – –	– – –	– – –	– – –	– – –	– – –	2 (3) –
5 Southampton	– –	4 – –	– – –	– – –	– – –	– – –	– – –	– – –	– – –	4 – –
6 Crystal Palace	– –	1 (1) –	– –	2 – 1	– – –	– – –	– – –	– – –	– – –	3 (1) 1
7 Chelsea	– –	3 (1) –	– – –	– – –	– – –	– – –	– – –	– – –	– – –	3 (1) –
8 Coventry City	– –	3 (1) –	– – –	– – –	– – –	– – –	– – –	– – –	– – –	3 (1) –
9 Liverpool	– –	3 (1) –	– – –	– – –	– – –	– – –	– – –	– – –	– – –	3 (1) –
10 Tottenham Hotspur	– –	2 (1) –	– – –	– – –	1 – –	– – –	– – –	– – –	– – –	3 (1) –
11 Wimbledon	– –	3 (1) –	– – –	– – –	– – –	– – –	– – –	– – –	– – –	3 (1) –
12 Norwich City	– –	1 (2) –	– – –	1 – –	– – –	– – –	– – –	– – –	– – –	2 (2) –
13 Sheffield Wednesday	– –	2 (2) –	– – –	– – –	– – –	– – –	– – –	– – –	– – –	2 (2) –
14 Charlton Athletic	– –	3 – –	– – –	– – –	– – –	– – –	– – –	– – –	– – –	3 – –
15 Derby County	– –	3 – –	– – –	– – –	– – –	– – –	– – –	– – –	– – –	3 – –
16 Luton Town	– –	3 – –	– – –	– – –	– – –	– – –	– – –	– – –	– – –	3 – –
17 Millwall	– –	3 – –	– – –	– – –	– – –	– – –	– – –	– – –	– – –	3 – –
18 Newcastle United	– –	1 (1) –	– – –	1 – –	– – –	– – –	– – –	– – –	– – –	2 (1) –
19 Aston Villa	– –	2 – –	– – –	– – –	– – –	– – –	– – –	– – –	– – –	2 – –
20 Manchester City	– –	2 – –	– – –	– – –	– – –	– – –	– – –	– – –	– – –	2 – –
21 Oldham Athletic	– –	– – –	– – –	2 – –	– – –	– – –	– – –	– – –	– – –	2 – –
22 Sheffield United	– –	1 – –	– – –	1 – –	– – –	– – –	– – –	– – –	– – –	2 – –
23 Stoke City	– –	– – –	– – –	– – –	2 – –	– – –	– – –	– – –	– – –	2 – –
24 Halifax Town	– –	– – –	– – –	– – –	1 (1) –	– – –	– – –	– – –	– – –	1 (1) –
25 Leeds United	– –	– – –	– – –	– – –	1 (1) –	– – –	– – –	– – –	– – –	1 (1) –
26 Montpellier Herault	– –	– – –	– – –	– – –	– – –	– – –	1 (1) –	– – –	– – –	1 (1) –
27 Wrexham	– –	– – –	– – –	– – –	– – –	– – –	1 (1) –	– – –	– – –	1 (1) –
28 Athletico Madrid	– –	– – –	– – –	– – –	– – –	– – –	– (2) –	– – –	– – –	– (2) –
29 West Ham United	– –	1 – 1	– – –	– – –	– – –	– – –	– – –	– – –	– – –	1 – 1
30 Athinaikos	– –	– – –	– – –	– – –	– – –	– – –	– – –	1 – –	– – –	1 – –
31 Bournemouth	– –	– – –	– – –	1 – –	– – –	– – –	– – –	– – –	– – –	1 – –
32 Brighton	– –	– – –	– – –	– – –	1 – –	– – –	– – –	– – –	– – –	1 – –
33 Cambridge United	– –	– – –	– – –	– – –	1 – –	– – –	– – –	– – –	– – –	1 – –
34 Galatasaray	– –	– – –	– – –	– – –	– – –	1 – –	– – –	– – –	– – –	1 – –
35 Hereford United	– –	– – –	– – –	1 – –	– – –	– – –	– – –	– – –	– – –	1 – –
36 Leicester City	– –	– – –	– – –	– – –	1 – –	– – –	– – –	– – –	– – –	1 – –
37 Pecsi Munkas	– –	– – –	– – –	– – –	– – –	– – –	1 – –	– – –	– – –	1 – –
38 Red Star Belgrade	– –	– – –	– – –	– – –	– – –	– – –	– – –	– – –	1 – –	1 – –
39 Torpedo Moscow	– –	– – –	– – –	– – –	– – –	– – –	– – –	1 – –	– – –	1 – –
40 Honved	– –	– – –	– – –	– – –	– – –	– (1) –	– – –	– – –	– – –	– (1) –

LEE MARTIN (2000s)

DEBUT (Full Appearance)

Wednesday 26/10/2005
League Cup 3rd Round
at Old Trafford

Manchester United 4 Barnet 1

CLUB CAREER RECORD	Apps	Subs	Goals
Premiership	0		0
League Division 1	0		0
League Division 2	0		0
FA Cup	0		0
League Cup	2		0
European Cup / Champions League	0		0
European Cup-Winners' Cup	0		0
UEFA Cup / Inter-Cities' Fairs Cup	0		0
Other Matches	0		0
OVERALL TOTAL	**2**		**0**

Opponents	PREM			FLD 1			FLD 2			FAC			LC			EC/CL			ECWC			UEFA			OTHER			TOTAL		
	A	S	G	A	S	G	A	S	G	A	S	G	A	S	G	A	S	G	A	S	G	A	S	G	A	S	G	A	S	G
1 Barnet	-	-	-	-	-	-	-	-	-	-	-	-	1	-	-	-	-	-	-	-	-	-	-	-	-	-	-	1	-	-
2 Coventry City	-	-	-	-	-	-	-	-	-	-	-	-	1	-	-	-	-	-	-	-	-	-	-	-	-	-	-	1	-	-

MICK MARTIN

DEBUT (Full Appearance)

Wednesday 24/01/1973
Football League Division 1
at Old Trafford

Manchester United 0 Everton 0

CLUB CAREER RECORD	Apps	Subs	Goals
Premiership	0		0
League Division 1	26	(6)	2
League Division 2	7	(1)	0
FA Cup	2		0
League Cup	1		0
European Cup / Champions League	0		0
European Cup-Winners' Cup	0		0
UEFA Cup / Inter-Cities' Fairs Cup	0		0
Other Matches	0		0
OVERALL TOTAL	**36**	**(7)**	**2**

Opponents	PREM			FLD 1			FLD 2			FAC			LC			EC/CL			ECWC			UEFA			OTHER			TOTAL		
	A	S	G	A	S	G	A	S	G	A	S	G	A	S	G	A	S	G	A	S	G	A	S	G	A	S	G	A	S	G
1 Stoke City	-	-	-	3	-	-	-	-	-	-	-	-	-	-	-	-	-	-	-	-	-	-	-	-	-	-	-	3	-	-
2 Birmingham City	-	-	-	1	(2)	-	-	-	-	-	-	-	-	-	-	-	-	-	-	-	-	-	-	-	-	-	-	1	(2)	-
3 Arsenal	-	-	-	2	-	-	-	-	-	-	-	-	-	-	-	-	-	-	-	-	-	-	-	-	-	-	-	2	-	-
4 Chelsea	-	-	-	2	-	-	-	-	-	-	-	-	-	-	-	-	-	-	-	-	-	-	-	-	-	-	-	2	-	-
5 Ipswich Town	-	-	-	1	-	-	-	-	-	1	-	-	-	-	-	-	-	-	-	-	-	-	-	-	-	-	-	2	-	-
6 Manchester City	-	-	-	2	-	-	-	-	-	-	-	-	-	-	-	-	-	-	-	-	-	-	-	-	-	-	-	2	-	-
7 Sheffield United	-	-	-	2	-	-	-	-	-	-	-	-	-	-	-	-	-	-	-	-	-	-	-	-	-	-	-	2	-	-
8 Coventry City	-	-	-	1	(1)	-	-	-	-	-	-	-	-	-	-	-	-	-	-	-	-	-	-	-	-	-	-	1	(1)	-
9 Everton	-	-	-	1	(1)	-	-	-	-	-	-	-	-	-	-	-	-	-	-	-	-	-	-	-	-	-	-	1	(1)	-
10 Leicester City	-	-	-	1	(1)	-	-	-	-	-	-	-	-	-	-	-	-	-	-	-	-	-	-	-	-	-	-	1	(1)	-
11 West Bromwich Albion	-	-	-	-	(1)	-	-	-	-	1	-	-	-	-	-	-	-	-	-	-	-	-	-	-	-	-	-	1	(1)	-
12 Newcastle United	-	-	-	1	-	1	-	-	-	-	-	-	-	-	-	-	-	-	-	-	-	-	-	-	-	-	-	1	-	1
13 Norwich City	-	-	-	1	-	1	-	-	-	-	-	-	-	-	-	-	-	-	-	-	-	-	-	-	-	-	-	1	-	1
14 Aston Villa	-	-	-	-	-	-	1	-	-	-	-	-	-	-	-	-	-	-	-	-	-	-	-	-	-	-	-	1	-	-
15 Burnley	-	-	-	1	-	-	-	-	-	-	-	-	-	-	-	-	-	-	-	-	-	-	-	-	-	-	-	1	-	-
16 Cardiff City	-	-	-	-	-	-	1	-	-	-	-	-	-	-	-	-	-	-	-	-	-	-	-	-	-	-	-	1	-	-
17 Charlton Athletic	-	-	-	-	-	-	-	-	-	-	-	-	1	-	-	-	-	-	-	-	-	-	-	-	-	-	-	1	-	-
18 Crystal Palace	-	-	-	1	-	-	-	-	-	-	-	-	-	-	-	-	-	-	-	-	-	-	-	-	-	-	-	1	-	-
19 Hull City	-	-	-	-	-	-	1	-	-	-	-	-	-	-	-	-	-	-	-	-	-	-	-	-	-	-	-	1	-	-
20 Leeds United	-	-	-	1	-	-	-	-	-	-	-	-	-	-	-	-	-	-	-	-	-	-	-	-	-	-	-	1	-	-
21 Millwall	-	-	-	-	-	-	1	-	-	-	-	-	-	-	-	-	-	-	-	-	-	-	-	-	-	-	-	1	-	-
22 Nottingham Forest	-	-	-	-	-	-	1	-	-	-	-	-	-	-	-	-	-	-	-	-	-	-	-	-	-	-	-	1	-	-
23 Plymouth Argyle	-	-	-	-	-	-	1	-	-	-	-	-	-	-	-	-	-	-	-	-	-	-	-	-	-	-	-	1	-	-
24 Portsmouth	-	-	-	-	-	-	1	-	-	-	-	-	-	-	-	-	-	-	-	-	-	-	-	-	-	-	-	1	-	-
25 Queens Park Rangers	-	-	-	1	-	-	-	-	-	-	-	-	-	-	-	-	-	-	-	-	-	-	-	-	-	-	-	1	-	-
26 Southampton	-	-	-	1	-	-	-	-	-	-	-	-	-	-	-	-	-	-	-	-	-	-	-	-	-	-	-	1	-	-
27 Tottenham Hotspur	-	-	-	1	-	-	-	-	-	-	-	-	-	-	-	-	-	-	-	-	-	-	-	-	-	-	-	1	-	-
28 West Ham United	-	-	-	1	-	-	-	-	-	-	-	-	-	-	-	-	-	-	-	-	-	-	-	-	-	-	-	1	-	-
29 Wolverhampton W.	-	-	-	1	-	-	-	-	-	-	-	-	-	-	-	-	-	-	-	-	-	-	-	-	-	-	-	1	-	-
30 Oldham Athletic	-	-	-	-	-	-	-	(1)	-	-	-	-	-	-	-	-	-	-	-	-	-	-	-	-	-	-	-	-	(1)	-

WILLIAM MATHIESON

DEBUT (Full Appearance)

Saturday 03/09/1892
Football League Division 1
at Ewood Park

Blackburn Rovers 4 Newton Heath 3

CLUB CAREER RECORD	Apps	Subs	Goals
Premiership	0		0
League Division 1	10		2
League Division 2	0		0
FA Cup	0		0
League Cup	0		0
European Cup / Champions League	0		0
European Cup-Winners' Cup	0		0
UEFA Cup / Inter-Cities' Fairs Cup	0		0
Other Matches	0		0
OVERALL TOTAL	**10**		**2**

Opponents	PREM			FLD 1			FLD 2			FAC			LC			EC/CL			ECWC			UEFA			OTHER			TOTAL		
	A	S	G	A	S	G	A	S	G	A	S	G	A	S	G	A	S	G	A	S	G	A	S	G	A	S	G	A	S	G
1 Blackburn Rovers	-	-	-	2	-	-	-	-	-	-	-	-	-	-	-	-	-	-	-	-	-	-	-	-	-	-	-	2	-	-
2 Burnley	-	-	-	2	-	-	-	-	-	-	-	-	-	-	-	-	-	-	-	-	-	-	-	-	-	-	-	2	-	-

continued../

WILLIAM MATHIESON (continued)

Opponents	PREM A	PREM S	PREM G	FLD 1 A	FLD 1 S	FLD 1 G	FLD 2 A	FLD 2 S	FLD 2 G	FAC A	FAC S	FAC G	LC A	LC S	LC G	EC/CL A	EC/CL S	EC/CL G	ECWC A	ECWC S	ECWC G	UEFA A	UEFA S	UEFA G	OTHER A	OTHER S	OTHER G	TOTAL A	TOTAL S	TOTAL G
3 Everton	–	–	–	2	–	–	–	–	–	–	–	–	–	–	–	–	–	–	–	–	–	–	–	–	–	–	–	2	–	–
4 West Bromwich Albion	–	–	–	2	–	–	–	–	–	–	–	–	–	–	–	–	–	–	–	–	–	–	–	–	–	–	–	2	–	–
5 Aston Villa	–	–	–	1	–	1	–	–	–	–	–	–	–	–	–	–	–	–	–	–	–	–	–	–	–	–	–	1	–	1
6 Preston North End	–	–	–	1	–	1	–	–	–	–	–	–	–	–	–	–	–	–	–	–	–	–	–	–	–	–	–	1	–	1

DAVID MAY

DEBUT (Full Appearance)

Saturday 20/08/1994
FA Premiership
at Old Trafford

Manchester United 2 Queens Park Rangers 0

CLUB CAREER RECORD	Apps	Subs	Goals
Premiership	68	(17)	6
League Division 1	0		0
League Division 2	0		0
FA Cup	6		0
League Cup	9		1
European Cup / Champions League	13	(2)	1
European Cup-Winners' Cup	0		0
UEFA Cup / Inter-Cities' Fairs Cup	0		0
Other Matches	2	(1)	0
OVERALL TOTAL	98	(20)	8

Opponents	PREM A	PREM S	PREM G	FLD 1 A	FLD 1 S	FLD 1 G	FLD 2 A	FLD 2 S	FLD 2 G	FAC A	FAC S	FAC G	LC A	LC S	LC G	EC/CL A	EC/CL S	EC/CL G	ECWC A	ECWC S	ECWC G	UEFA A	UEFA S	UEFA G	OTHER A	OTHER S	OTHER G	TOTAL A	TOTAL S	TOTAL G
1 Tottenham Hotspur	6	–	–	–	–	–	–	–	–	1	–	–	–	–	–	–	–	–	–	–	–	–	–	–	–	–	–	7	–	–
2 Newcastle United	4	(1)	–	–	–	–	–	–	–	1	–	–	–	–	–	–	–	–	–	–	–	1	–	–	–	–	–	6	(1)	–
3 Sheffield Wednesday	5	(2)	1	–	–	–	–	–	–	–	–	–	–	–	–	–	–	–	–	–	–	–	–	–	–	–	–	5	(2)	1
4 Leeds United	5	(2)	–	–	–	–	–	–	–	–	–	–	–	–	–	–	–	–	–	–	–	–	–	–	–	–	–	5	(2)	–
5 Liverpool	3	(2)	–	–	–	–	–	–	–	1	–	–	–	–	–	–	–	–	–	–	–	–	–	–	–	–	–	4	(2)	–
6 Leicester City	2	(1)	–	–	–	–	–	–	–	–	–	–	2	–	–	–	–	–	–	–	–	–	–	–	–	–	–	4	(1)	–
7 Arsenal	3	(1)	–	–	–	–	–	–	–	–	–	–	–	–	–	–	–	–	–	–	–	–	(1)	–	–	–	–	3	(2)	–
8 Middlesbrough	4	–	2	–	–	–	–	–	–	–	–	–	–	–	–	–	–	–	–	–	–	–	–	–	–	–	–	4	–	2
9 Nottingham Forest	3	–	–	–	–	–	–	–	–	–	–	–	1	–	–	–	–	–	–	–	–	–	–	–	–	–	–	4	–	–
10 West Ham United	4	–	–	–	–	–	–	–	–	–	–	–	–	–	–	–	–	–	–	–	–	–	–	–	–	–	–	4	–	–
11 Chelsea	2	(1)	1	–	–	–	–	–	–	1	–	–	–	–	–	–	–	–	–	–	–	–	–	–	–	–	–	3	(1)	1
12 Blackburn Rovers	2	(1)	–	–	–	–	–	–	–	–	–	–	–	–	–	–	–	–	–	–	–	1	–	–	–	–	–	3	(1)	–
13 Coventry City	3	(1)	–	–	–	–	–	–	–	–	–	–	–	–	–	–	–	–	–	–	–	–	–	–	–	–	–	3	(1)	–
14 Southampton	2	(2)	1	–	–	–	–	–	–	–	–	–	–	–	–	–	–	–	–	–	–	–	–	–	–	–	–	2	(2)	1
15 Crystal Palace	3	–	1	–	–	–	–	–	–	–	–	–	–	–	–	–	–	–	–	–	–	–	–	–	–	–	–	3	–	1
16 Everton	3	–	–	–	–	–	–	–	–	–	–	–	–	–	–	–	–	–	–	–	–	–	–	–	–	–	–	3	–	–
17 Wimbledon	3	–	–	–	–	–	–	–	–	–	–	–	–	–	–	–	–	–	–	–	–	–	–	–	–	–	–	3	–	–
18 Aston Villa	2	(1)	–	–	–	–	–	–	–	–	–	–	–	–	–	–	–	–	–	–	–	–	–	–	–	–	–	2	(1)	–
19 Port Vale	–	–	–	–	–	–	–	–	–	–	–	–	2	–	1	–	–	–	–	–	–	–	–	–	–	–	–	2	–	1
20 Porto	–	–	–	–	–	–	–	–	–	–	–	–	–	–	–	2	–	1	–	–	–	–	–	–	–	–	–	2	–	1
21 Barnsley	1	–	–	–	–	–	–	–	–	1	–	–	–	–	–	–	–	–	–	–	–	–	–	–	–	–	–	2	–	–
22 Fenerbahce	–	–	–	–	–	–	–	–	–	–	–	–	–	–	–	2	–	–	–	–	–	–	–	–	–	–	–	2	–	–
23 Gothenburg	–	–	–	–	–	–	–	–	–	–	–	–	–	–	–	2	–	–	–	–	–	–	–	–	–	–	–	2	–	–
24 Ipswich Town	1	–	–	–	–	–	–	–	–	–	–	–	1	–	–	–	–	–	–	–	–	–	–	–	–	–	–	2	–	–
25 Queens Park Rangers	2	–	–	–	–	–	–	–	–	–	–	–	–	–	–	–	–	–	–	–	–	–	–	–	–	–	–	2	–	–
26 Sunderland	2	–	–	–	–	–	–	–	–	–	–	–	–	–	–	–	–	–	–	–	–	–	–	–	–	–	–	2	–	–
27 Rapid Vienna	–	–	–	–	–	–	–	–	–	–	–	–	–	–	–	1	(1)	–	–	–	–	–	–	–	–	–	–	1	(1)	–
28 Manchester City	–	(2)	–	–	–	–	–	–	–	–	–	–	–	–	–	–	–	–	–	–	–	–	–	–	–	–	–	–	(2)	–
29 Barcelona	–	–	–	–	–	–	–	–	–	–	–	–	–	–	–	1	–	–	–	–	–	–	–	–	–	–	–	1	–	–
30 Bolton Wanderers	1	–	–	–	–	–	–	–	–	–	–	–	–	–	–	–	–	–	–	–	–	–	–	–	–	–	–	1	–	–
31 Borussia Dortmund	–	–	–	–	–	–	–	–	–	–	–	–	–	–	–	1	–	–	–	–	–	–	–	–	–	–	–	1	–	–
32 Burnley	–	–	–	–	–	–	–	–	–	–	–	–	1	–	–	–	–	–	–	–	–	–	–	–	–	–	–	1	–	–
33 Bury	–	–	–	–	–	–	–	–	–	–	–	–	1	–	–	–	–	–	–	–	–	–	–	–	–	–	–	1	–	–
34 Derby County	1	–	–	–	–	–	–	–	–	–	–	–	–	–	–	–	–	–	–	–	–	–	–	–	–	–	–	1	–	–
35 Galatasaray	–	–	–	–	–	–	–	–	–	–	–	–	–	–	–	1	–	–	–	–	–	–	–	–	–	–	–	1	–	–
36 Juventus	–	–	–	–	–	–	–	–	–	–	–	–	–	–	–	1	–	–	–	–	–	–	–	–	–	–	–	1	–	–
37 Lille Metropole	–	–	–	–	–	–	–	–	–	–	–	–	–	–	–	1	–	–	–	–	–	–	–	–	–	–	–	1	–	–
38 Norwich City	1	–	–	–	–	–	–	–	–	–	–	–	–	–	–	–	–	–	–	–	–	–	–	–	–	–	–	1	–	–
39 Sturm Graz	–	–	–	–	–	–	–	–	–	–	–	–	–	–	–	1	–	–	–	–	–	–	–	–	–	–	–	1	–	–
40 Swindon Town	–	–	–	–	–	–	–	–	–	–	–	–	1	–	–	–	–	–	–	–	–	–	–	–	–	–	–	1	–	–
41 Wrexham	–	–	–	–	–	–	–	–	–	1	–	–	–	–	–	–	–	–	–	–	–	–	–	–	–	–	–	1	–	–
42 Basel	–	–	–	–	–	–	–	–	–	–	–	–	–	–	–	–	(1)	–	–	–	–	–	–	–	–	–	–	–	(1)	–

NEIL McBAIN

DEBUT (Full Appearance)

Saturday 26/11/1921
Football League Division 1
at Old Trafford

Manchester United 1 Aston Villa 0

CLUB CAREER RECORD	Apps	Subs	Goals
Premiership	0		0
League Division 1	21		0
League Division 2	21		2
FA Cup	1		0
League Cup	0		0
European Cup / Champions League	0		0
European Cup-Winners' Cup	0		0
UEFA Cup / Inter-Cities' Fairs Cup	0		0
Other Matches	0		0
OVERALL TOTAL	**43**		**2**

Opponents	PREM			FLD 1			FLD 2			FAC			LC			EC/CL			ECWC			UEFA			OTHER			TOTAL		
	A	S	G	A	S	G	A	S	G	A	S	G	A	S	G	A	S	G	A	S	G	A	S	G	A	S	G	A	S	G
1 Stockport County	–	–	–	–	–	–	2	–	1	–	–	–	–	–	–	–	–	–	–	–	–	–	–	–	–	–	–	2	–	1
2 Birmingham City	–	–	–	2	–	–	–	–	–	–	–	–	–	–	–	–	–	–	–	–	–	–	–	–	–	–	–	2	–	–
3 Blackburn Rovers	–	–	–	2	–	–	–	–	–	–	–	–	–	–	–	–	–	–	–	–	–	–	–	–	–	–	–	2	–	–
4 Bradford City	–	–	–	2	–	–	–	–	–	–	–	–	–	–	–	–	–	–	–	–	–	–	–	–	–	–	–	2	–	–
5 Burnley	–	–	–	2	–	–	–	–	–	–	–	–	–	–	–	–	–	–	–	–	–	–	–	–	–	–	–	2	–	–
6 Bury	–	–	–	–	–	–	2	–	–	–	–	–	–	–	–	–	–	–	–	–	–	–	–	–	–	–	–	2	–	–
7 Coventry City	–	–	–	–	–	–	2	–	–	–	–	–	–	–	–	–	–	–	–	–	–	–	–	–	–	–	–	2	–	–
8 Crystal Palace	–	–	–	–	–	–	2	–	–	–	–	–	–	–	–	–	–	–	–	–	–	–	–	–	–	–	–	2	–	–
9 Huddersfield Town	–	–	–	2	–	–	–	–	–	–	–	–	–	–	–	–	–	–	–	–	–	–	–	–	–	–	–	2	–	–
10 Leyton Orient	–	–	–	–	–	–	2	–	–	–	–	–	–	–	–	–	–	–	–	–	–	–	–	–	–	–	–	2	–	–
11 Liverpool	–	–	–	2	–	–	–	–	–	–	–	–	–	–	–	–	–	–	–	–	–	–	–	–	–	–	–	2	–	–
12 Oldham Athletic	–	–	–	2	–	–	–	–	–	–	–	–	–	–	–	–	–	–	–	–	–	–	–	–	–	–	–	2	–	–
13 Port Vale	–	–	–	–	–	–	2	–	–	–	–	–	–	–	–	–	–	–	–	–	–	–	–	–	–	–	–	2	–	–
14 Sheffield Wednesday	–	–	–	–	–	–	2	–	–	–	–	–	–	–	–	–	–	–	–	–	–	–	–	–	–	–	–	2	–	–
15 Sunderland	–	–	–	2	–	–	–	–	–	–	–	–	–	–	–	–	–	–	–	–	–	–	–	–	–	–	–	2	–	–
16 West Ham United	–	–	–	–	–	–	2	–	–	–	–	–	–	–	–	–	–	–	–	–	–	–	–	–	–	–	–	2	–	–
17 Wolverhampton W.	–	–	–	–	–	–	2	–	–	–	–	–	–	–	–	–	–	–	–	–	–	–	–	–	–	–	–	2	–	–
18 Rotherham United	–	–	–	–	–	–	1	–	1	–	–	–	–	–	–	–	–	–	–	–	–	–	–	–	–	–	–	1	–	1
19 Arsenal	–	–	–	1	–	–	–	–	–	–	–	–	–	–	–	–	–	–	–	–	–	–	–	–	–	–	–	1	–	–
20 Aston Villa	–	–	–	1	–	–	–	–	–	–	–	–	–	–	–	–	–	–	–	–	–	–	–	–	–	–	–	1	–	–
21 Bolton Wanderers	–	–	–	1	–	–	–	–	–	–	–	–	–	–	–	–	–	–	–	–	–	–	–	–	–	–	–	1	–	–
22 Cardiff City	–	–	–	–	–	–	–	–	–	1	–	–	–	–	–	–	–	–	–	–	–	–	–	–	–	–	–	1	–	–
23 Fulham	–	–	–	–	–	–	1	–	–	–	–	–	–	–	–	–	–	–	–	–	–	–	–	–	–	–	–	1	–	–
24 Hull City	–	–	–	–	–	–	1	–	–	–	–	–	–	–	–	–	–	–	–	–	–	–	–	–	–	–	–	1	–	–
25 Newcastle United	–	–	–	1	–	–	–	–	–	–	–	–	–	–	–	–	–	–	–	–	–	–	–	–	–	–	–	1	–	–
26 Sheffield United	–	–	–	1	–	–	–	–	–	–	–	–	–	–	–	–	–	–	–	–	–	–	–	–	–	–	–	1	–	–

JIM McCALLIOG

DEBUT (Full Appearance)

Saturday 16/03/1974
Football League Division 1
at St Andrews

Birmingham City 1 Manchester United 0

CLUB CAREER RECORD	Apps	Subs	Goals
Premiership	0		0
League Division 1	11		4
League Division 2	20		3
FA Cup	1		0
League Cup	5	(1)	0
European Cup / Champions League	0		0
European Cup-Winners' Cup	0		0
UEFA Cup / Inter-Cities' Fairs Cup	0		0
Other Matches	0		0
OVERALL TOTAL	**37**	**(1)**	**7**

Opponents	PREM			FLD 1			FLD 2			FAC			LC			EC/CL			ECWC			UEFA			OTHER			TOTAL		
	A	S	G	A	S	G	A	S	G	A	S	G	A	S	G	A	S	G	A	S	G	A	S	G	A	S	G	A	S	G
1 Norwich City	–	–	–	1	–	–	1	–	–	–	–	–	2	–	–	–	–	–	–	–	–	–	–	–	–	–	–	4	–	–
2 Everton	–	–	–	2	–	2	–	–	–	–	–	–	–	–	–	–	–	–	–	–	–	–	–	–	–	–	–	2	–	2
3 Sheffield Wednesday	–	–	–	–	–	–	2	–	2	–	–	–	–	–	–	–	–	–	–	–	–	–	–	–	–	–	–	2	–	2
4 Southampton	–	–	–	1	–	1	1	–	–	–	–	–	–	–	–	–	–	–	–	–	–	–	–	–	–	–	–	2	–	1
5 Bristol City	–	–	–	–	–	–	2	–	–	–	–	–	–	–	–	–	–	–	–	–	–	–	–	–	–	–	–	2	–	–
6 Burnley	–	–	–	1	–	–	–	–	–	–	–	–	1	–	–	–	–	–	–	–	–	–	–	–	–	–	–	2	–	–
7 Manchester City	–	–	–	1	–	–	–	–	–	–	–	–	1	–	–	–	–	–	–	–	–	–	–	–	–	–	–	2	–	–
8 Blackpool	–	–	–	–	–	–	1	–	1	–	–	–	–	–	–	–	–	–	–	–	–	–	–	–	–	–	–	1	–	1
9 Newcastle United	–	–	–	1	–	1	–	–	–	–	–	–	–	–	–	–	–	–	–	–	–	–	–	–	–	–	–	1	–	1
10 Aston Villa	–	–	–	–	–	–	1	–	–	–	–	–	–	–	–	–	–	–	–	–	–	–	–	–	–	–	–	1	–	–
11 Birmingham City	–	–	–	1	–	–	–	–	–	–	–	–	–	–	–	–	–	–	–	–	–	–	–	–	–	–	–	1	–	–
12 Bolton Wanderers	–	–	–	–	–	–	1	–	–	–	–	–	–	–	–	–	–	–	–	–	–	–	–	–	–	–	–	1	–	–
13 Bristol Rovers	–	–	–	–	–	–	1	–	–	–	–	–	–	–	–	–	–	–	–	–	–	–	–	–	–	–	–	1	–	–
14 Charlton Athletic	–	–	–	–	–	–	–	–	–	–	–	–	1	–	–	–	–	–	–	–	–	–	–	–	–	–	–	1	–	–
15 Chelsea	–	–	–	1	–	–	–	–	–	–	–	–	–	–	–	–	–	–	–	–	–	–	–	–	–	–	–	1	–	–
16 Fulham	–	–	–	–	–	–	1	–	–	–	–	–	–	–	–	–	–	–	–	–	–	–	–	–	–	–	–	1	–	–
17 Hull City	–	–	–	–	–	–	1	–	–	–	–	–	–	–	–	–	–	–	–	–	–	–	–	–	–	–	–	1	–	–
18 Leyton Orient	–	–	–	–	–	–	1	–	–	–	–	–	–	–	–	–	–	–	–	–	–	–	–	–	–	–	–	1	–	–
19 Millwall	–	–	–	–	–	–	1	–	–	–	–	–	–	–	–	–	–	–	–	–	–	–	–	–	–	–	–	1	–	–
20 Nottingham Forest	–	–	–	–	–	–	1	–	–	–	–	–	–	–	–	–	–	–	–	–	–	–	–	–	–	–	–	1	–	–
21 Notts County	–	–	–	–	–	–	1	–	–	–	–	–	–	–	–	–	–	–	–	–	–	–	–	–	–	–	–	1	–	–
22 Oxford United	–	–	–	–	–	–	1	–	–	–	–	–	–	–	–	–	–	–	–	–	–	–	–	–	–	–	–	1	–	–
23 Portsmouth	–	–	–	–	–	–	1	–	–	–	–	–	–	–	–	–	–	–	–	–	–	–	–	–	–	–	–	1	–	–
24 Stoke City	–	–	–	1	–	–	–	–	–	–	–	–	–	–	–	–	–	–	–	–	–	–	–	–	–	–	–	1	–	–
25 Sunderland	–	–	–	–	–	–	1	–	–	–	–	–	–	–	–	–	–	–	–	–	–	–	–	–	–	–	–	1	–	–

continued../

JIM McCALLIOG (continued)

Opponents	PREM A S G	FLD 1 A S G	FLD 2 A S G	FAC A S G	LC A S G	EC/CL A S G	ECWC A S G	UEFA A S G	OTHER A S G	TOTAL A S G
26 Tottenham Hotspur	–	– 1	–	–	–	–	–	–	–	1 –
27 Walsall	–	–	– 1	–	–	–	–	–	–	1 –
28 West Bromwich Albion	–	–	– 1	–	–	–	–	–	–	1 –
29 Middlesbrough	–	–	–	–	– (1) –	–	–	–	–	– (1) –

PAT McCARTHY

DEBUT (Full Appearance)

Saturday 20/01/1912
Football League Division 1
at Old Trafford

Manchester United 1 West Bromwich Albion 2

CLUB CAREER RECORD	Apps	Subs	Goals
Premiership	0		0
League Division 1	1		0
League Division 2	0		0
FA Cup	0		0
League Cup	0		0
European Cup / Champions League	0		0
European Cup-Winners' Cup	0		0
UEFA Cup / Inter-Cities' Fairs Cup	0		0
Other Matches	0		0
OVERALL TOTAL	1		0

Opponents	PREM A S G	FLD 1 A S G	FLD 2 A S G	FAC A S G	LC A S G	EC/CL A S G	ECWC A S G	UEFA A S G	OTHER A S G	TOTAL A S G
1 West Bromwich Albion	–	– 1	–	–	–	–	–	–	–	1 –

JOHN McCARTNEY

DEBUT (Full Appearance)

Saturday 08/09/1894
Football League Division 2
at Derby Turn

Burton Wanderers 1 Newton Heath 0

CLUB CAREER RECORD	Apps	Subs	Goals
Premiership	0		0
League Division 1	0		0
League Division 2	18		1
FA Cup	1		0
League Cup	0		0
European Cup / Champions League	0		0
European Cup-Winners' Cup	0		0
UEFA Cup / Inter-Cities' Fairs Cup	0		0
Other Matches	1		0
OVERALL TOTAL	20		1

Opponents	PREM A S G	FLD 1 A S G	FLD 2 A S G	FAC A S G	LC A S G	EC/CL A S G	ECWC A S G	UEFA A S G	OTHER A S G	TOTAL A S G
1 Crewe Alexandra	–	–	2 1	–	–	–	–	–	–	2 1
2 Burton Wanderers	–	–	2 –	–	–	–	–	–	–	2 –
3 Darwen	–	–	2 –	–	–	–	–	–	–	2 –
4 Leicester City	–	–	2 –	–	–	–	–	–	–	2 –
5 Manchester City	–	–	2 –	–	–	–	–	–	–	2 –
6 Port Vale	–	–	2 –	–	–	–	–	–	–	2 –
7 Rotherham United	–	–	2 –	–	–	–	–	–	–	2 –
8 Stoke City	–	–	–	1 –	–	–	–	–	1 –	2 –
9 Arsenal	–	–	1 –	–	–	–	–	–	–	1 –
10 Burton Swifts	–	–	1 –	–	–	–	–	–	–	1 –
11 Lincoln City	–	–	1 –	–	–	–	–	–	–	1 –
12 Notts County	–	–	1 –	–	–	–	–	–	–	1 –

WILLIAM McCARTNEY

DEBUT (Full Appearance)

Saturday 05/09/1903
Football League Division 2
at Bank Street

Manchester United 2 Bristol City 2

CLUB CAREER RECORD	Apps	Subs	Goals
Premiership	0		0
League Division 1	0		0
League Division 2	13		1
FA Cup	0		0
League Cup	0		0
European Cup / Champions League	0		0
European Cup-Winners' Cup	0		0
UEFA Cup / Inter-Cities' Fairs Cup	0		0
Other Matches	0		0
OVERALL TOTAL	13		1

Opponents	PREM A S G	FLD 1 A S G	FLD 2 A S G	FAC A S G	LC A S G	EC/CL A S G	ECWC A S G	UEFA A S G	OTHER A S G	TOTAL A S G
1 Bristol City	–	–	2 –	–	–	–	–	–	–	2 –
2 Chesterfield	–	–	2 –	–	–	–	–	–	–	2 –
3 Leicester City	–	–	1 1	–	–	–	–	–	–	1 1
4 Barnsley	–	–	1 –	–	–	–	–	–	–	1 –
5 Blackpool	–	–	1 –	–	–	–	–	–	–	1 –
6 Burnley	–	–	1 –	–	–	–	–	–	–	1 –
7 Burton United	–	–	1 –	–	–	–	–	–	–	1 –
8 Gainsborough Trinity	–	–	1 –	–	–	–	–	–	–	1 –
9 Glossop	–	–	1 –	–	–	–	–	–	–	1 –
10 Grimsby Town	–	–	1 –	–	–	–	–	–	–	1 –
11 Port Vale	–	–	1 –	–	–	–	–	–	–	1 –

BRIAN McCLAIR

DEBUT (Full Appearance)

Saturday 15/08/1987
Football League Division 1
at The Dell

Southampton 2 Manchester United 2

CLUB CAREER RECORD	Apps	Subs	Goals
Premiership	106	(56)	18
League Division 1	190	(3)	70
League Division 2	0		0
FA Cup	38	(7)	14
League Cup	44	(1)	19
European Cup / Champions League	2	(6)	0
European Cup-Winners' Cup	13		5
UEFA Cup / Inter-Cities' Fairs Cup	2		0
Other Matches	3		1
OVERALL TOTAL	**398**	**(73)**	**127**

Opponents	PREM A S G	FLD 1 A S G	FLD 2 A S G	FAC A S G	LC A S G	EC/CL A S G	ECWC A S G	UEFA A S G	OTHER A S G	TOTAL A S G
1 Southampton	4 (4) –	10 3	–	2 1	2	–	–	–	–	18 (4) 4
2 Queens Park Rangers	5 (1) 1	10 2	–	5 3	–	–	–	–	–	20 (1) 6
3 Wimbledon	5 (2) –	9 4	–	1 (2) –	1	–	–	–	–	16 (4) 5
4 Tottenham Hotspur	4 (4) 1	10 6	–	– (1) –	1	–	–	–	–	15 (5) 7
5 Liverpool	5 (2) 2	10 1	–	–	1	–	–	–	1	17 (2) 3
6 Nottingham Forest	5 (2) –	9 1	–	2 –	1 1	–	–	–	–	17 (2) 2
7 Sheffield Wednesday	6 (3) 2	8 9	–	–	2 1	–	–	–	–	16 (3) 12
8 Chelsea	7 (2) 2	8 3	–	1 (1) 2	–	–	–	–	–	16 (3) 7
9 Arsenal	3 (4) –	10 3	–	1 1	1	–	–	–	–	15 (4) 4
10 Everton	4 (4) 1	10 3	–	1	–	–	–	–	–	15 (4) 4
11 Coventry City	6 (2) 2	10 1	–	–	–	–	–	–	–	16 (2) 3
12 Leeds United	7 (2) –	4	–	2 1	3 1	–	–	–	–	16 (2) 2
13 Aston Villa	4 (3) –	8 –	–	–	1 (1) –	–	–	–	–	13 (4) –
14 Norwich City	5 1	9 (1) 4	–	1 1	–	–	–	–	–	15 (1) 6
15 Crystal Palace	4 –	5 1	–	3 (1) –	1 2	–	–	–	–	13 (1) 3
16 West Ham United	5 (3) 1	6 1	–	–	–	–	–	–	–	11 (3) 2
17 Newcastle United	3 (5) –	4 2	–	1 1	1	–	–	–	–	9 (5) 3
18 Sheffield United	3 (1) 1	4 1	–	3 (1) 1	–	–	–	–	–	10 (2) 3
19 Manchester City	4 (1) –	6 2	–	–	–	–	–	–	–	10 (1) 2
20 Oldham Athletic	3 (1) 2	2 3	–	3 (1) 1	1 1	–	–	–	–	9 (2) 7
21 Luton Town	–	9 (1) 6	–	–	–	–	–	–	–	9 (1) 6
22 Derby County	– (1) –	7 (1) 5	–	–	–	–	–	–	–	7 (2) 5
23 Blackburn Rovers	4 (4) –	–	–	–	–	–	–	–	1	5 (4) –
24 Middlesbrough	2 (2) –	2 –	–	–	2	–	–	–	–	6 (2) –
25 Portsmouth	–	2 3	–	–	5 1	–	–	–	–	7 4
26 Charlton Athletic	–	6 2	–	–	–	–	–	–	–	6 2
27 Ipswich Town	4 1	–	–	1	1	–	–	–	–	6 1
28 Leicester City	2	–	–	–	2 1	–	–	–	–	4 1
29 Millwall	–	4	–	–	–	–	–	–	–	4
30 Oxford United	–	2	–	1	1	–	–	–	–	4 –
31 Sunderland	1 (1) –	2 2	–	–	–	–	–	–	–	3 (1) 2
32 Wrexham	–	–	–	1 1	–	–	2 1	–	–	3 2
33 Brighton	–	–	–	1	2	–	–	–	–	3 –
34 Swindon Town	1 (1) –	–	–	–	1	–	–	–	–	2 (1) –
35 Juventus	–	–	–	–	–	– (3) –	–	–	–	– (3) –
36 Rotherham United	–	–	–	–	2 3	–	–	–	–	2 3
37 Cambridge United	–	–	–	–	2 2	–	–	–	–	2 2
38 Hull City	–	–	–	–	2 2	–	–	–	–	2 2
39 Watford	–	2 2	–	–	–	–	–	–	–	2 2
40 Athinaikos	–	–	–	–	–	–	–	2 1	–	2 1
41 Bournemouth	–	–	–	2 1	–	–	–	–	–	2 1
42 Bury	–	–	–	1 –	1 1	–	–	–	–	2 1
43 Halifax Town	–	–	–	–	2 1	–	–	–	–	2 1
44 Legia Warsaw	–	–	–	–	–	–	2 1	–	–	2 1
45 Montpellier Herault	–	–	–	–	–	–	2 1	–	–	2 1
46 Pecsi Munkas	–	–	–	–	–	–	2 1	–	–	2 1
47 Port Vale	–	–	–	–	2 1	–	–	–	–	2 1
48 Stoke City	–	–	–	–	2 1	–	–	–	–	2 1
49 Athletico Madrid	–	–	–	–	–	–	2 –	–	–	2 –
50 Barnsley	–	–	–	2	–	–	–	–	–	2 –
51 Notts County	–	2	–	–	–	–	–	–	–	2 –
52 Torpedo Moscow	–	–	–	–	–	–	–	2	–	2 –
53 Bolton Wanderers	– (1) –	–	–	1	–	–	–	–	–	1 (1) –
54 Red Star Belgrade	–	–	–	–	–	–	–	–	1 1	1 1
55 Barcelona	–	–	–	–	–	–	1	–	–	1
56 Galatasaray	–	–	–	–	–	1	–	–	–	1
57 Gothenburg	–	–	–	–	–	1	–	–	–	1
58 Hereford United	–	–	–	1	–	–	–	–	–	1
59 Walsall	–	–	–	1	–	–	–	–	–	1
60 York City	–	–	–	–	1	–	–	–	–	1
61 Kosice	–	–	–	–	–	– (1) –	–	–	–	– (1) –
62 Monaco	–	–	–	–	–	– (1) –	–	–	–	– (1) –
63 Rapid Vienna	–	–	–	–	–	– (1) –	–	–	–	– (1) –

JIMMY McCLELLAND

DEBUT (Full Appearance)

Wednesday 02/09/1936
Football League Division 1
at Leeds Road

Huddersfield Town 3 Manchester United 1

CLUB CAREER RECORD	Apps	Subs	Goals
Premiership	0		0
League Division 1	5		1
League Division 2	0		0
FA Cup	0		0
League Cup	0		0
European Cup / Champions League	0		0
European Cup-Winners' Cup	0		0
UEFA Cup / Inter-Cities' Fairs Cup	0		0
Other Matches	0		0
OVERALL TOTAL	**5**		**1**

Opponents	PREM A S G	FLD 1 A S G	FLD 2 A S G	FAC A S G	LC A S G	EC/CL A S G	ECWC A S G	UEFA A S G	OTHER A S G	TOTAL A S G
1 Stoke City	- -	1 1	- -	- -	- -	- -	- -	- -	- -	1 1
2 Birmingham City	- -	1	- -	- -	- -	- -	- -	- -	- -	1 -
3 Huddersfield Town	- -	1 -	- -	- -	- -	- -	- -	- -	- -	1 -
4 Middlesbrough	- -	1 -	- -	- -	- -	- -	- -	- -	- -	1 -
5 Sunderland	- -	1 -	- -	- -	- -	- -	- -	- -	- -	1 -

JAMES McCRAE

DEBUT (Full Appearance)

Saturday 16/01/1926
Football League Division 1
at Highbury

Arsenal 3 Manchester United 2

CLUB CAREER RECORD	Apps	Subs	Goals
Premiership	0		0
League Division 1	9		0
League Division 2	0		0
FA Cup	4		0
League Cup	0		0
European Cup / Champions League	0		0
European Cup-Winners' Cup	0		0
UEFA Cup / Inter-Cities' Fairs Cup	0		0
Other Matches	0		0
OVERALL TOTAL	**13**		**0**

Opponents	PREM A S G	FLD 1 A S G	FLD 2 A S G	FAC A S G	LC A S G	EC/CL A S G	ECWC A S G	UEFA A S G	OTHER A S G	TOTAL A S G
1 Notts County	- -	2 -	- -	- -	- -	- -	- -	- -	- -	2 -
2 Sunderland	- -	- -	- -	2 -	- -	- -	- -	- -	- -	2 -
3 Arsenal	- -	1 -	- -	- -	- -	- -	- -	- -	- -	1 -
4 Burnley	- -	1 -	- -	- -	- -	- -	- -	- -	- -	1 -
5 Bury	- -	1 -	- -	- -	- -	- -	- -	- -	- -	1 -
6 Everton	- -	1 -	- -	- -	- -	- -	- -	- -	- -	1 -
7 Fulham	- -	- -	- -	1 -	- -	- -	- -	- -	- -	1 -
8 Leeds United	- -	1 -	- -	- -	- -	- -	- -	- -	- -	1 -
9 Manchester City	- -	- -	- -	1 -	- -	- -	- -	- -	- -	1 -
10 Newcastle United	- -	1 -	- -	- -	- -	- -	- -	- -	- -	1 -
11 Tottenham Hotspur	- -	1 -	- -	- -	- -	- -	- -	- -	- -	1 -

DAVID McCREERY

DEBUT (Substitute Appearance)

Tuesday 15/10/1974
Football League Division 2
at Fratton Park

Portsmouth 0 Manchester United 0

CLUB CAREER RECORD	Apps	Subs	Goals
Premiership	0		0
League Division 1	48	(37)	7
League Division 2	0	(2)	0
FA Cup	1	(6)	0
League Cup	4	(4)	1
European Cup / Champions League	0		0
European Cup-Winners' Cup	3		0
UEFA Cup / Inter-Cities' Fairs Cup	1	(3)	0
Other Matches	0	(1)	0
OVERALL TOTAL	57	(53)	8

Opponents	PREM A S G	FLD 1 A S G	FLD 2 A S G	FAC A S G	LC A S G	EC/CL A S G	ECWC A S G	UEFA A S G	OTHER A S G	TOTAL A S G
1 Ipswich Town	– –	5 (1) –	– –	– –	– –	– –	– –	– –	– –	5 (1) –
2 Arsenal	– –	2 (3) –	– –	– –	1 1	– –	– –	– –	– –	3 (3) 1
3 Manchester City	– –	2 (3) 2	– –	– –	– (1) –	– –	– –	– –	– –	2 (4) 2
4 Birmingham City	– –	4 (1) –	– –	– –	– –	– –	– –	– –	– –	4 (1) –
5 Derby County	– –	3 (1) –	– –	1	– –	– –	– –	– –	– –	4 (1) –
6 Norwich City	– –	4 (1) –	– –	– –	– –	– –	– –	– –	– –	4 (1) –
7 Everton	– –	2 (2) 1	– –	– –	– (1) –	– –	– –	– –	– –	2 (3) 1
8 Aston Villa	– –	1 (3) –	– –	– (1) –	– –	– –	– –	– –	– –	1 (4) –
9 Liverpool	– –	– (3) –	– –	– (1) –	– –	– –	– –	– (1) –	– –	– (5) –
10 Sunderland	– –	1 –	– –	– –	3	– –	– –	– –	– –	4 –
11 Queens Park Rangers	– –	3 (1) –	– –	– –	– –	– –	– –	– –	– –	3 (1) –
12 Leeds United	– –	2 (2) –	– –	– –	– –	– –	– –	– –	– –	2 (2) –
13 Leicester City	– –	2 (1) –	– –	– (1) –	– –	– –	– –	– –	– –	2 (2) –
14 West Bromwich Albion	– –	2 (2) –	– –	– –	– –	– –	– –	– –	– –	2 (2) –
15 Coventry City	– –	1 (3) 1	– –	– –	– –	– –	– –	– –	– –	1 (3) 1
16 Middlesbrough	– –	3 1	– –	– –	– –	– –	– –	– –	– –	3 1
17 Nottingham Forest	– –	3	– –	– –	– –	– –	– –	– –	– –	3
18 Stoke City	– –	2 (1) 1	– –	– –	– –	– –	– –	– –	– –	2 (1) 1
19 Tottenham Hotspur	– –	1 (2) –	– –	– –	– –	– –	– –	– –	– –	1 (2) –
20 West Ham United	– –	– (3) 1	– –	– –	– –	– –	– –	– –	– –	– (3) 1
21 Chelsea	– –	2	– –	– –	– –	– –	– –	– –	– –	2
22 Porto	– –	–	– –	– –	– –	2	– –	– –	– –	2
23 Ajax	– –	–	– –	– –	– –	– –	1 (1) –	– –	– –	1 (1) –
24 Bristol City	– –	1 (1) –	– –	– –	– –	– –	– –	– –	– –	1 (1) –
25 Burnley	– –	1 (1) –	– –	– –	– –	– –	– –	– –	– –	1 (1) –
26 Newcastle United	– –	1 (1) –	– –	– –	– –	– –	– –	– –	– –	1 (1) –
27 Juventus	– –	–	– –	– –	– –	– –	– –	– (2) –	– –	– (2) –
28 Southampton	– –	–	– –	– (2) –	– –	– –	– –	– –	– –	– (2) –
29 St Etienne	– –	–	– –	– –	– –	– –	1	– –	– –	1
30 Blackpool	– –	–	– –	– (1) –	– –	– –	– –	– –	– –	– (1) –
31 Carlisle United	– –	–	– –	– (1) –	– –	– –	– –	– –	– –	– (1) –
32 Portsmouth	– –	–	– –	– (1) –	– –	– –	– –	– –	– –	– (1) –
33 Sheffield United	– –	– (1) –	– –	– –	– –	– –	– –	– –	– –	– (1) –
34 Tranmere Rovers	– –	–	– –	– –	– (1) –	– –	– –	– –	– –	– (1) –
35 Watford	– –	–	– –	– –	– (1) –	– –	– –	– –	– –	– (1) –

WILLIE McDONALD

DEBUT (Full Appearance)

Saturday 23/04/1932
Football League Division 2
at Old Trafford

Manchester United 1 Bradford City 0

CLUB CAREER RECORD	Apps	Subs	Goals
Premiership	0		0
League Division 1	0		0
League Division 2	27		4
FA Cup	0		0
League Cup	0		0
European Cup / Champions League	0		0
European Cup-Winners' Cup	0		0
UEFA Cup / Inter-Cities' Fairs Cup	0		0
Other Matches	0		0
OVERALL TOTAL	27		4

Opponents	PREM A S G	FLD 1 A S G	FLD 2 A S G	FAC A S G	LC A S G	EC/CL A S G	ECWC A S G	UEFA A S G	OTHER A S G	TOTAL A S G
1 Southampton	– –	– –	3 1	– –	– –	– –	– –	– –	– –	3 1
2 Bradford City	– –	– –	3 –	– –	– –	– –	– –	– –	– –	3 –
3 Grimsby Town	– –	– –	3 –	– –	– –	– –	– –	– –	– –	3 –
4 Tottenham Hotspur	– –	– –	2 1	– –	– –	– –	– –	– –	– –	2 1
5 Bury	– –	– –	2 –	– –	– –	– –	– –	– –	– –	2 –
6 Charlton Athletic	– –	– –	2 –	– –	– –	– –	– –	– –	– –	2 –
7 Burnley	– –	– –	1 1	– –	– –	– –	– –	– –	– –	1 1
8 Nottingham Forest	– –	– –	1 1	– –	– –	– –	– –	– –	– –	1 1
9 Bolton Wanderers	– –	– –	1 –	– –	– –	– –	– –	– –	– –	1 –
10 Brentford	– –	– –	1	– –	– –	– –	– –	– –	– –	1
11 Hull City	– –	– –	1	– –	– –	– –	– –	– –	– –	1
12 Lincoln City	– –	– –	1	– –	– –	– –	– –	– –	– –	1
13 Millwall	– –	– –	1	– –	– –	– –	– –	– –	– –	1
14 Oldham Athletic	– –	– –	1	– –	– –	– –	– –	– –	– –	1
15 Plymouth Argyle	– –	– –	1	– –	– –	– –	– –	– –	– –	1
16 Preston North End	– –	– –	1	– –	– –	– –	– –	– –	– –	1
17 Stoke City	– –	– –	1	– –	– –	– –	– –	– –	– –	1
18 West Ham United	– –	– –	1	– –	– –	– –	– –	– –	– –	1

BOB McFARLANE

DEBUT (Full Appearance)

Saturday 03/10/1891
FA Cup 1st Qualifying Round
at North Road

Newton Heath 5 Manchester City 1

CLUB CAREER RECORD	Apps	Subs	Goals
Premiership	0		0
League Division 1	0		0
League Division 2	0		0
FA Cup	3		0
League Cup	0		0
European Cup / Champions League	0		0
European Cup-Winners' Cup	0		0
UEFA Cup / Inter-Cities' Fairs Cup	0		0
Other Matches	0		0
OVERALL TOTAL	**3**		**0**

Opponents	PREM A S G	FLD 1 A S G	FLD 2 A S G	FAC A S G	LC A S G	EC/CL A S G	ECWC A S G	UEFA A S G	OTHER A S G	TOTAL A S G
1 Blackpool	– –	– –	– –	1 –	– –	– –	– –	– –	– –	1 –
2 Manchester City	– –	– –	– –	1 –	– –	– –	– –	– –	– –	1 –
3 South Shore	– –	– –	– –	1 –	– –	– –	– –	– –	– –	1 –

NOEL McFARLANE

DEBUT (Full Appearance)

Saturday 13/02/1954
Football League Division 1
at Old Trafford

Manchester United 2 Tottenham Hotspur 0

CLUB CAREER RECORD	Apps	Subs	Goals
Premiership	0		0
League Division 1	1		0
League Division 2	0		0
FA Cup	0		0
League Cup	0		0
European Cup / Champions League	0		0
European Cup-Winners' Cup	0		0
UEFA Cup / Inter-Cities' Fairs Cup	0		0
Other Matches	0		0
OVERALL TOTAL	**1**		**0**

Opponents	PREM A S G	FLD 1 A S G	FLD 2 A S G	FAC A S G	LC A S G	EC/CL A S G	ECWC A S G	UEFA A S G	OTHER A S G	TOTAL A S G
1 Tottenham Hotspur	– –	1 –	– –	– –	– –	– –	– –	– –	– –	1 –

DAVID McFETTERIDGE

DEBUT (Full Appearance)

Saturday 13/04/1895
Football League Division 2
at St James' Park

Newcastle United 3 Newton Heath 0

CLUB CAREER RECORD	Apps	Subs	Goals
Premiership	0		0
League Division 1	0		0
League Division 2	1		0
FA Cup	0		0
League Cup	0		0
European Cup / Champions League	0		0
European Cup-Winners' Cup	0		0
UEFA Cup / Inter-Cities' Fairs Cup	0		0
Other Matches	0		0
OVERALL TOTAL	**1**		**0**

Opponents	PREM A S G	FLD 1 A S G	FLD 2 A S G	FAC A S G	LC A S G	EC/CL A S G	ECWC A S G	UEFA A S G	OTHER A S G	TOTAL A S G
1 Newcastle United	– –	– –	1 –	– –	– –	– –	– –	– –	– –	1 –

SCOTT McGARVEY

DEBUT (Substitute Appearance)

Saturday 13/09/1980
Football League Division 1
at Old Trafford

Manchester United 5 Leicester City 0

CLUB CAREER RECORD	Apps	Subs	Goals
Premiership	0		0
League Division 1	13	(12)	3
League Division 2	0		0
FA Cup	0		0
League Cup	0		0
European Cup / Champions League	0		0
European Cup-Winners' Cup	0		0
UEFA Cup / Inter-Cities' Fairs Cup	0		0
Other Matches	0		0
OVERALL TOTAL	**13**	**(12)**	**3**

Opponents	PREM A S G	FLD 1 A S G	FLD 2 A S G	FAC A S G	LC A S G	EC/CL A S G	ECWC A S G	UEFA A S G	OTHER A S G	TOTAL A S G
1 Everton	– –	2 –	– –	– –	– –	– –	– –	– –	– –	2 –
2 Tottenham Hotspur	– –	1 (1) 1	– –	– –	– –	– –	– –	– –	– –	1 (1) 1
3 West Ham United	– –	1 (1) 1	– –	– –	– –	– –	– –	– –	– –	1 (1) 1
4 Aston Villa	– –	– (2) –	– –	– –	– –	– –	– –	– –	– –	– (2) –
5 Sunderland	– –	– (2) –	– –	– –	– –	– –	– –	– –	– –	– (2) –
6 Southampton	– –	1 1	– –	– –	– –	– –	– –	– –	– –	1 1
7 Arsenal	– –	1 –	– –	– –	– –	– –	– –	– –	– –	1 –
8 Brighton	– –	1 –	– –	– –	– –	– –	– –	– –	– –	1 –
9 Coventry City	– –	1 –	– –	– –	– –	– –	– –	– –	– –	1 –

continued../

SCOTT McGARVEY (continued)

Opponents	PREM A S G	FLD 1 A S G	FLD 2 A S G	FAC A S G	LC A S G	EC/CL A S G	ECWC A S G	UEFA A S G	OTHER A S G	TOTAL A S G
10 Ipswich Town	– –	1	–	–	–	–	–	–	–	1 –
11 Leeds United	– –	1	–	–	–	–	–	–	–	1 –
12 Liverpool	– –	1	–	–	–	–	–	–	–	1 –
13 Nottingham Forest	– –	1	–	–	–	–	–	–	–	1 –
14 West Bromwich Albion	– –	1	–	–	–	–	–	–	–	1 –
15 Birmingham City	– –	– (1) –	–	–	–	–	–	–	–	– (1) –
16 Leicester City	– –	– (1) –	–	–	–	–	–	–	–	– (1) –
17 Luton Town	– –	– (1) –	–	–	–	–	–	–	–	– (1) –
18 Manchester City	– –	– (1) –	–	–	–	–	–	–	–	– (1) –
19 Notts County	– –	– (1) –	–	–	–	–	–	–	–	– (1) –
20 Stoke City	– –	– (1) –	–	–	–	–	–	–	–	– (1) –

PAT McGIBBON

DEBUT (Full Appearance)

Wednesday 20/09/1995
League Cup 2nd Round 1st Leg
at Old Trafford

Manchester United 0 York City 3

CLUB CAREER RECORD	Apps	Subs	Goals
Premiership	0		0
League Division 1	0		0
League Division 2	0		0
FA Cup	0		0
League Cup	1		0
European Cup / Champions League	0		0
European Cup-Winners' Cup	0		0
UEFA Cup / Inter-Cities' Fairs Cup	0		0
Other Matches	0		0
OVERALL TOTAL	**1**		**0**

Opponents	PREM A S G	FLD 1 A S G	FLD 2 A S G	FAC A S G	LC A S G	EC/CL A S G	ECWC A S G	UEFA A S G	OTHER A S G	TOTAL A S G
1 York City	–	–	–	–	1	–	–	–	–	1

CHARLIE McGILLIVRAY

DEBUT (Full Appearance)

Saturday 26/08/1933
Football League Division 2
at Home Park

Plymouth Argyle 4 Manchester United 0

CLUB CAREER RECORD	Apps	Subs	Goals
Premiership	0		0
League Division 1	0		0
League Division 2	8		0
FA Cup	1		0
League Cup	0		0
European Cup / Champions League	0		0
European Cup-Winners' Cup	0		0
UEFA Cup / Inter-Cities' Fairs Cup	0		0
Other Matches	0		0
OVERALL TOTAL	**9**		**0**

Opponents	PREM A S G	FLD 1 A S G	FLD 2 A S G	FAC A S G	LC A S G	EC/CL A S G	ECWC A S G	UEFA A S G	OTHER A S G	TOTAL A S G
1 Bolton Wanderers	– –	– –	2 –	–	–	–	–	–	–	2 –
2 Lincoln City	– –	– –	2 –	–	–	–	–	–	–	2 –
3 Nottingham Forest	– –	– –	2 –	–	–	–	–	–	–	2 –
4 Grimsby Town	– –	– –	1 –	–	–	–	–	–	–	1 –
5 Plymouth Argyle	– –	– –	1 –	–	–	–	–	–	–	1 –
6 Portsmouth	– –	– –	– –	1	–	–	–	–	–	1 –

JOHN McGILLIVRAY

DEBUT (Full Appearance)

Saturday 11/01/1908
FA Cup 1st Round
at Bank Street

Manchester United 3 Blackpool 1

CLUB CAREER RECORD	Apps	Subs	Goals
Premiership	0		0
League Division 1	3		0
League Division 2	0		0
FA Cup	1		0
League Cup	0		0
European Cup / Champions League	0		0
European Cup-Winners' Cup	0		0
UEFA Cup / Inter-Cities' Fairs Cup	0		0
Other Matches	0		0
OVERALL TOTAL	**4**		**0**

Opponents	PREM A S G	FLD 1 A S G	FLD 2 A S G	FAC A S G	LC A S G	EC/CL A S G	ECWC A S G	UEFA A S G	OTHER A S G	TOTAL A S G
1 Aston Villa	– –	1 –	–	–	–	–	–	–	–	1 –
2 Blackpool	– –	– –	–	1 –	–	–	–	–	–	1 –
3 Sheffield United	– –	1 –	–	–	–	–	–	–	–	1 –
4 Sheffield Wednesday	– –	1 –	–	–	–	–	–	–	–	1 –

BILLY McGLEN

DEBUT (Full Appearance)

Saturday 31/08/1946
Football League Division 1
at Maine Road

Manchester United 2 Grimsby Town 1

CLUB CAREER RECORD	Apps	Subs	Goals
Premiership	0		0
League Division 1	110		2
League Division 2	0		0
FA Cup	12		0
League Cup	0		0
European Cup / Champions League	0		0
European Cup-Winners' Cup	0		0
UEFA Cup / Inter-Cities' Fairs Cup	0		0
Other Matches	0		0
OVERALL TOTAL	**122**		**2**

Opponents	PREM			FLD 1			FLD 2			FAC			LC			EC/CL			ECWC			UEFA			OTHER			TOTAL		
	A	S	G	A	S	G	A	S	G	A	S	G	A	S	G	A	S	G	A	S	G	A	S	G	A	S	G	A	S	G
1 Huddersfield Town	–	–		8																								8	–	
2 Liverpool	–	–		8																								8	–	
3 Arsenal	–	–		6																								6	–	
4 Derby County	–	–		6																								6	–	
5 Sunderland	–	–		6																								6	–	
6 Blackpool	–	–		5																								5	–	
7 Charlton Athletic	–	–		5																								5	–	
8 Middlesbrough	–	–		5																								5	–	
9 Sheffield United	–	–		5																								5	–	
10 Stoke City	–	–		5																								5	–	
11 Wolverhampton W.	–	–		3						2																		5	–	
12 Portsmouth	–	–		4	1																							4	1	
13 Aston Villa	–	–		4																								4	–	
14 Bolton Wanderers	–	–		4																								4	–	
15 Bradford Park Avenue	–	–								4																		4	–	
16 Chelsea	–	–		4																								4	–	
17 Manchester City	–	–		4																								4	–	
18 Everton	–	–		3																								3	–	
19 Fulham	–	–		3																								3	–	
20 Newcastle United	–	–		3																								3	–	
21 Preston North End	–	–		3																								3	–	
22 West Bromwich Albion	–	–		3																								3	–	
23 Leeds United	–	–		2	1																							2	1	
24 Birmingham City	–	–		2																								2	–	
25 Burnley	–	–		2																								2	–	
26 Grimsby Town	–	–		2																								2	–	
27 Sheffield Wednesday	–	–		2																								2	–	
28 Blackburn Rovers	–	–		1																								1	–	
29 Bournemouth	–	–								1																		1	–	
30 Brentford	–	–		1																								1	–	
31 Hull City	–	–								1																		1	–	
32 Nottingham Forest	–	–		–	–					1																		1	–	
33 Oldham Athletic	–	–								1																		1	–	
34 Tottenham Hotspur	–	–		1																								1	–	
35 Weymouth Town	–	–								1																		1	–	
36 Yeovil Town	–	–		–	–					1																		1	–	

CHRIS McGRATH

DEBUT (Substitute Appearance)

Saturday 23/10/1976
Football League Division 1
at Old Trafford

Manchester United 2 Norwich City 2

CLUB CAREER RECORD	Apps	Subs	Goals
Premiership	0		0
League Division 1	12	(16)	1
League Division 2	0		0
FA Cup	0		0
League Cup	0	(2)	0
European Cup / Champions League	0		0
European Cup-Winners' Cup	3	(1)	0
UEFA Cup / Inter-Cities' Fairs Cup	0		0
Other Matches	0		0
OVERALL TOTAL	**15**	**(19)**	**1**

Opponents	PREM			FLD 1			FLD 2			FAC			LC			EC/CL			ECWC			UEFA			OTHER			TOTAL		
	A	S	G	A	S	G	A	S	G	A	S	G	A	S	G	A	S	G	A	S	G	A	S	G	A	S	G	A	S	G
1 Ipswich Town	–	–		1 (3)	–																							1 (3)	–	
2 Arsenal	–	–		1 (1)	–								– (1)	–														1 (2)	–	
3 Norwich City	–	–		– (3)	–																							– (3)	–	
4 Aston Villa	–	–		2																								2		
5 Porto	–	–																	2	–								2	–	
6 Leeds United	–	–		1 (1)	–																							1 (1)	–	
7 Middlesbrough	–	–		1 (1)	–																							1 (1)	–	
8 Newcastle United	–	–		1	–								– (1)	–														1 (1)	–	
9 St Etienne	–	–																	1 (1)	–								1 (1)	–	
10 West Bromwich Albion	–	–		– (2)	–																							– (2)	–	
11 West Ham United	–	–		1	1																							1		1
12 Birmingham City	–	–		1																								1		
13 Liverpool	–	–		1																								1		
14 Nottingham Forest	–	–		1																								1		
15 Stoke City	–	–		1																								1		

continued../

CHRIS McGRATH (continued)

Opponents	PREM A S G	FLD 1 A S G	FLD 2 A S G	FAC A S G	LC A S G	EC/CL A S G	ECWC A S G	UEFA A S G	OTHER A S G	TOTAL A S G
16 Chelsea	– –	– (1) –	–	–	–	–	–	–	–	– (1) –
17 Coventry City	– –	– (1) –	–	–	–	–	–	–	–	– (1) –
18 Manchester City	– –	– (1) –	–	–	–	–	–	–	–	– (1) –
19 Queens Park Rangers	– –	– (1) –	–	–	–	–	–	–	–	– (1) –
20 Wolverhampton W.	– –	– (1) –	–	–	–	–	–	–	–	– (1) –

PAUL McGRATH

DEBUT (Full Appearance)

Wednesday 10/11/1982
League Cup 3rd Round
at Valley Parade

Bradford City 0 Manchester United 0

CLUB CAREER RECORD	Apps	Subs	Goals
Premiership	0		0
League Division 1	159	(4)	12
League Division 2	0		0
FA Cup	15	(3)	2
League Cup	13		2
European Cup / Champions League	0		0
European Cup–Winners' Cup	2		0
UEFA Cup / Inter-Cities' Fairs Cup	2		0
Other Matches	1		0
OVERALL TOTAL	**192**	**(7)**	**16**

Opponents	PREM A S G	FLD 1 A S G	FLD 2 A S G	FAC A S G	LC A S G	EC/CL A S G	ECWC A S G	UEFA A S G	OTHER A S G	TOTAL A S G
1 West Ham United	– –	9 –	– –	3 –	1 –	–	–	–	–	13 –
2 Coventry City	– –	9 1	– –	1 (1) 1	–	–	–	–	–	10 (1) 2
3 Tottenham Hotspur	– –	10 (1) –	– –	–	–	–	–	–	–	10 (1) –
4 Luton Town	– –	10 3	– –	–	–	–	–	–	–	10 3
5 Liverpool	– –	6 (1) 1	– –	2 –	1 1	–	–	–	–	9 (1) 2
6 Everton	– –	7 –	– –	1 –	–	–	–	1 –	–	9 –
7 Southampton	– –	7 –	– –	–	2 –	–	–	–	–	9 –
8 Nottingham Forest	– –	7 (1) 1	– –	1 –	–	–	–	–	–	8 (1) 1
9 Arsenal	– –	7 (1) 1	– –	– (1) –	–	–	–	–	–	7 (2) 1
10 Watford	– –	8 2	– –	–	–	–	–	–	–	8 2
11 Sheffield Wednesday	– –	8 –	– –	–	–	–	–	–	–	8 –
12 Queens Park Rangers	– –	7 –	– –	– (1) –	–	–	–	–	–	7 (1) –
13 Norwich City	– –	6 1	– –	–	–	–	–	–	–	6 1
14 Aston Villa	– –	6 –	– –	–	–	–	–	–	–	6 –
15 Chelsea	– –	6 –	– –	–	–	–	–	–	–	6 –
16 Manchester City	– –	5 –	– –	–	–	–	–	–	–	5 –
17 Newcastle United	– –	5 –	– –	–	–	–	–	–	–	5 –
18 Oxford United	– –	4 –	– –	1 –	–	–	–	–	–	5 –
19 Leicester City	– –	4 –	– –	–	–	–	–	–	–	4 –
20 Sunderland	– –	2 –	– –	2 –	–	–	–	–	–	4 –
21 Wimbledon	– –	4 –	– –	–	–	–	–	–	–	4 –
22 Charlton Athletic	– –	3 1	– –	–	–	–	–	–	–	3 1
23 Bournemouth	– –	– –	– –	3 –	–	–	–	–	–	3 –
24 Ipswich Town	– –	3 –	– –	–	–	–	–	–	–	3 –
25 Port Vale	– –	– –	– –	–	3 –	–	–	–	–	3 –
26 West Bromwich Albion	– –	3 –	– –	–	–	–	–	–	–	3 –
27 Hull City	– –	– –	– –	–	2 1	–	–	–	–	2 1
28 Notts County	– –	2 1	– –	–	–	–	–	–	–	2 1
29 Birmingham City	– –	2 –	– –	–	–	–	–	–	–	2 –
30 Crystal Palace	– –	– –	– –	–	2 –	–	–	–	–	2 –
31 Derby County	– –	2 –	– –	–	–	–	–	–	–	2 –
32 Juventus	– –	– –	– –	–	–	2 –	–	–	–	2 –
33 Middlesbrough	– –	2 –	– –	–	–	–	–	–	–	2 –
34 Stoke City	– –	2 –	– –	–	–	–	–	–	–	2 –
35 Videoton	– –	– –	– –	–	–	–	–	2 –	–	2 –
36 Blackburn Rovers	– –	– –	– –	1 1	–	–	–	–	–	1 1
37 Bradford City	– –	– –	– –	–	1 –	–	–	–	–	1 –
38 Brighton	– –	1 –	– –	–	–	–	–	–	–	1 –
39 Millwall	– –	1 –	– –	–	–	–	–	–	–	1 –
40 Portsmouth	– –	1 –	– –	–	–	–	–	–	–	1 –
41 Rotherham United	– –	– –	– –	–	1 –	–	–	–	–	1 –

WILF McGUINNESS

DEBUT (Full Appearance)

Saturday 08/10/1955
Football League Division 1
at Old Trafford

Manchester United 4 Wolverhampton Wanderers 3

CLUB CAREER RECORD	Apps	Subs	Goals
Premiership	0		0
League Division 1	81		2
League Division 2	0		0
FA Cup	2		0
League Cup	0		0
European Cup / Champions League	2		0
European Cup-Winners' Cup	0		0
UEFA Cup / Inter-Cities' Fairs Cup	0		0
Other Matches	0		0
OVERALL TOTAL	**85**		**2**

Opponents	PREM A	S	G	FLD 1 A	S	G	FLD 2 A	S	G	FAC A	S	G	LC A	S	G	EC/CL A	S	G	ECWC A	S	G	UEFA A	S	G	OTHER A	S	G	TOTAL A	S	G
1 Aston Villa	–	–	–	5	–	–	–	–	–	–	–	–	–	–	–	–	–	–	–	–	–	–	–	–	–	–	–	5	–	–
2 Leeds United	–	–	–	5	–	–	–	–	–	–	–	–	–	–	–	–	–	–	–	–	–	–	–	–	–	–	–	5	–	–
3 Portsmouth	–	–	–	5	–	–	–	–	–	–	–	–	–	–	–	–	–	–	–	–	–	–	–	–	–	–	–	5	–	–
4 Tottenham Hotspur	–	–	–	5	–	–	–	–	–	–	–	–	–	–	–	–	–	–	–	–	–	–	–	–	–	–	–	5	–	–
5 Wolverhampton W.	–	–	–	5	–	–	–	–	–	–	–	–	–	–	–	–	–	–	–	–	–	–	–	–	–	–	–	5	–	–
6 Bolton Wanderers	–	–	–	4	–	–	–	–	–	–	–	–	–	–	–	–	–	–	–	–	–	–	–	–	–	–	–	4	–	–
7 Chelsea	–	–	–	4	–	–	–	–	–	–	–	–	–	–	–	–	–	–	–	–	–	–	–	–	–	–	–	4	–	–
8 Everton	–	–	–	4	–	–	–	–	–	–	–	–	–	–	–	–	–	–	–	–	–	–	–	–	–	–	–	4	–	–
9 Luton Town	–	–	–	4	–	–	–	–	–	–	–	–	–	–	–	–	–	–	–	–	–	–	–	–	–	–	–	4	–	–
10 West Bromwich Albion	–	–	–	4	–	–	–	–	–	–	–	–	–	–	–	–	–	–	–	–	–	–	–	–	–	–	–	4	–	–
11 Arsenal	–	–	–	3	–	–	–	–	–	–	–	–	–	–	–	–	–	–	–	–	–	–	–	–	–	–	–	3	–	–
12 Birmingham City	–	–	–	3	–	–	–	–	–	–	–	–	–	–	–	–	–	–	–	–	–	–	–	–	–	–	–	3	–	–
13 Blackburn Rovers	–	–	–	3	–	–	–	–	–	–	–	–	–	–	–	–	–	–	–	–	–	–	–	–	–	–	–	3	–	–
14 Burnley	–	–	–	3	–	–	–	–	–	–	–	–	–	–	–	–	–	–	–	–	–	–	–	–	–	–	–	3	–	–
15 Manchester City	–	–	–	3	–	–	–	–	–	–	–	–	–	–	–	–	–	–	–	–	–	–	–	–	–	–	–	3	–	–
16 Newcastle United	–	–	–	3	–	–	–	–	–	–	–	–	–	–	–	–	–	–	–	–	–	–	–	–	–	–	–	3	–	–
17 Preston North End	–	–	–	3	–	–	–	–	–	–	–	–	–	–	–	–	–	–	–	–	–	–	–	–	–	–	–	3	–	–
18 Sunderland	–	–	–	2	–	1	–	–	–	–	–	–	–	–	–	–	–	–	–	–	–	–	–	–	–	–	–	2	–	1
19 West Ham United	–	–	–	2	–	1	–	–	–	–	–	–	–	–	–	–	–	–	–	–	–	–	–	–	–	–	–	2	–	1
20 Blackpool	–	–	–	2	–	–	–	–	–	–	–	–	–	–	–	–	–	–	–	–	–	–	–	–	–	–	–	2	–	–
21 Charlton Athletic	–	–	–	2	–	–	–	–	–	–	–	–	–	–	–	–	–	–	–	–	–	–	–	–	–	–	–	2	–	–
22 Leicester City	–	–	–	2	–	–	–	–	–	–	–	–	–	–	–	–	–	–	–	–	–	–	–	–	–	–	–	2	–	–
23 Nottingham Forest	–	–	–	2	–	–	–	–	–	–	–	–	–	–	–	–	–	–	–	–	–	–	–	–	–	–	–	2	–	–
24 Borussia Dortmund	–	–	–	–	–	–	–	–	–	–	–	–	–	–	–	1	–	–	–	–	–	–	–	–	–	–	–	1	–	–
25 Bournemouth	–	–	–	–	–	–	–	–	–	1	–	–	–	–	–	–	–	–	–	–	–	–	–	–	–	–	–	1	–	–
26 Cardiff City	–	–	–	1	–	–	–	–	–	–	–	–	–	–	–	–	–	–	–	–	–	–	–	–	–	–	–	1	–	–
27 Fulham	–	–	–	1	–	–	–	–	–	–	–	–	–	–	–	–	–	–	–	–	–	–	–	–	–	–	–	1	–	–
28 Norwich City	–	–	–	–	–	–	–	–	–	1	–	–	–	–	–	–	–	–	–	–	–	–	–	–	–	–	–	1	–	–
29 Shamrock Rovers	–	–	–	–	–	–	–	–	–	–	–	–	–	–	–	1	–	–	–	–	–	–	–	–	–	–	–	1	–	–
30 Sheffield Wednesday	–	–	–	1	–	–	–	–	–	–	–	–	–	–	–	–	–	–	–	–	–	–	–	–	–	–	–	1	–	–

SAMMY McILROY

DEBUT (Full Appearance, 1 goal)

Saturday 06/11/1971
Football League Division 1
at Maine Road

Manchester City 3 Manchester United 3

CLUB CAREER RECORD	Apps	Subs	Goals
Premiership	0		0
League Division 1	279	(21)	50
League Division 2	41	(1)	7
FA Cup	35	(3)	6
League Cup	25	(3)	6
European Cup / Champions League	0		0
European Cup-Winners' Cup	4		0
UEFA Cup / Inter-Cities' Fairs Cup	6		2
Other Matches	1		0
OVERALL TOTAL	**391**	**(28)**	**71**

Opponents	PREM A	S	G	FLD 1 A	S	G	FLD 2 A	S	G	FAC A	S	G	LC A	S	G	EC/CL A	S	G	ECWC A	S	G	UEFA A	S	G	OTHER A	S	G	TOTAL A	S	G
1 Tottenham Hotspur	–	–	–	13		3	–	–	–	4		2	2		–	–	–	–	–	–	–	–	–	–	–	–	–	19		5
2 Coventry City	–	–	–	15	(1)	3	–	–	–	–	–	–	2		–	–	–	–	–	–	–	–	–	–	–	–	–	17	(1)	3
3 Aston Villa	–	–	–	13		6	2		–	1		–	1		–	–	–	–	–	–	–	–	–	–	–	–	–	17		6
4 Manchester City	–	–	–	15		2	–	–	–	–	–	–	2		–	–	–	–	–	–	–	–	–	–	–	–	–	17		2
5 Norwich City	–	–	–	12		1	2		–	–	–	–	3		1	–	–	–	–	–	–	–	–	–	–	–	–	17		2
6 Arsenal	–	–	–	14	(2)	1	–	–	–	1		1	–	–	–	–	–	–	–	–	–	–	–	–	–	–	–	15	(2)	3
7 Everton	–	–	–	14	(2)	1	–	–	–	–	–	–	1		–	–	–	–	–	–	–	–	–	–	–	–	–	15	(2)	1
8 Southampton	–	–	–	9	(1)	1	2		–	4	(1)	–	–	–	–	–	–	–	–	–	–	–	–	–	–	–	–	15	(2)	1
9 Liverpool	–	–	–	10	(3)	2	–	–	–	3		–	–	–	–	–	–	–	–	–	–	1		–	–	–	–	14	(3)	2
10 Wolverhampton W.	–	–	–	13	(1)	6	–	–	–	2		1	–	–	–	–	–	–	–	–	–	–	–	–	–	–	–	15	(1)	7
11 Ipswich Town	–	–	–	14	(1)	3	–	–	–	1		–	–	–	–	–	–	–	–	–	–	–	–	–	–	–	–	15	(1)	3
12 Leeds United	–	–	–	13	(2)	3	–	–	–	1		–	–	–	–	–	–	–	–	–	–	–	–	–	–	–	–	14	(2)	3
13 Stoke City	–	–	–	10	(1)	1	–	–	–	–	(1)	–	2		–	–	–	–	–	–	–	–	–	–	–	–	–	12	(2)	1
14 West Bromwich Albion	–	–	–	9		1	2	1		2		–	–	–	–	–	–	–	–	–	–	–	–	–	–	–	–	13		2
15 Middlesbrough	–	–	–	11		–	–	–	–	–	–	–	2		1	–	–	–	–	–	–	–	–	–	–	–	–	13		1
16 Derby County	–	–	–	11		1	–	–	–	1		–	–	–	–	–	–	–	–	–	–	–	–	–	–	–	–	12		1
17 Nottingham Forest	–	–	–	9		–	2		1	–	–	–	–	–	–	–	–	–	–	–	–	–	–	–	–	–	–	11		1
18 Leicester City	–	–	–	9	(1)	–	–	–	–	1		–	–	–	–	–	–	–	–	–	–	–	–	–	–	–	–	10	(1)	–
19 Queens Park Rangers	–	–	–	9		2	–	–	–	1		–	–	–	–	–	–	–	–	–	–	–	–	–	–	–	–	10		2
20 Birmingham City	–	–	–	9	(1)	3	–	–	–	–	–	–	–	–	–	–	–	–	–	–	–	–	–	–	–	–	–	9	(1)	3
21 Bristol City	–	–	–	7	(1)	1	2		–	–	–	–	–	–	–	–	–	–	–	–	–	–	–	–	–	–	–	9	(1)	1

continued../

SAMMY McILROY (continued)

Opponents	PREM A S G	FLD 1 A S G	FLD 2 A S G	FAC A S G	LC A S G	EC/CL A S G	ECWC A S G	UEFA A S G	OTHER A S G	TOTAL A S G
22 Newcastle United	– –	7 –	– –	– –	1 –	– –	– –	– –	– –	8 –
23 Chelsea	– –	6 2	– –	1 –	– –	– –	– –	– –	– –	7 2
24 Sunderland	– –	2 –	2 1	– –	3 –	– –	– –	– –	– –	7 1
25 West Ham United	– –	5 (2) 2	– –	– –	– –	– –	– –	– –	– –	5 (2) 2
26 Bolton Wanderers	– –	4 –	2 –	– –	– –	– –	– –	– –	– –	6 –
27 Sheffield United	– –	5 (1) 1	– –	– –	– –	– –	– –	– –	– –	5 (1) 1
28 Brighton	– –	4 1	– –	1 –	– –	– –	– –	– –	– –	5 1
29 Oxford United	– –	– –	2 –	1 –	– (2) –	– –	– –	– –	– –	3 (2) –
30 Burnley	– –	3 2	– –	– –	1 –	– –	– –	– –	– –	4 2
31 Fulham	– –	– –	2 –	2 –	– –	– –	– –	– –	– –	4 –
32 Crystal Palace	– –	3 (1) –	– –	– –	– –	– –	– –	– –	– –	3 (1) –
33 Walsall	– –	– –	– –	3 1	– –	– –	– –	– –	– –	3 1
34 Bristol Rovers	– –	– –	2 –	– –	– (1) 1	– –	– –	– –	– –	2 (1) 1
35 Ajax	– –	– –	– –	– –	– –	– –	– –	2 1	– –	2 1
36 Cardiff City	– –	– –	2 1	– –	– –	– –	– –	– –	– –	2 1
37 Notts County	– –	– –	2 1	– –	– –	– –	– –	– –	– –	2 1
38 Oldham Athletic	– –	– –	2 1	– –	– –	– –	– –	– –	– –	2 1
39 Portsmouth	– –	– –	2 1	– –	– –	– –	– –	– –	– –	2 1
40 Widzew Lodz	– –	– –	– –	– –	– –	– –	– –	2 1	– –	2 1
41 Blackpool	– –	– –	2 –	– –	– –	– –	– –	– –	– –	2 –
42 Carlisle United	– –	– –	– –	2 –	– –	– –	– –	– –	– –	2 –
43 Hull City	– –	– –	2 –	– –	– –	– –	– –	– –	– –	2 –
44 Juventus	– –	– –	– –	– –	– –	– –	– –	2 –	– –	2 –
45 Millwall	– –	– –	2 –	– –	– –	– –	– –	– –	– –	2 –
46 Porto	– –	– –	– –	– –	– –	– –	2 –	– –	– –	2 –
47 Sheffield Wednesday	– –	– –	2 –	– –	– –	– –	– –	– –	– –	2 –
48 St Etienne	– –	– –	– –	– –	– –	– –	2 –	– –	– –	2 –
49 Watford	– –	– –	– –	1 –	1 –	– –	– –	– –	– –	2 –
50 York City	– –	– –	2 –	– –	– –	– –	– –	– –	– –	2 –
51 Leyton Orient	– –	– –	1 (1) –	– –	– –	– –	– –	– –	– –	1 (1) –
52 Brentford	– –	– –	– –	– –	1 1	– –	– –	– –	– –	1 1
53 Charlton Athletic	– –	– –	– –	– –	1 1	– –	– –	– –	– –	1 1
54 Peterborough United	– –	– –	– –	1 1	– –	– –	– –	– –	– –	1 1
55 Stockport County	– –	– –	– –	– –	1 1	– –	– –	– –	– –	1 1
56 Colchester United	– –	– –	– –	1 –	– –	– –	– –	– –	– –	1 –
57 Swansea City	– –	1 –	– –	– –	– –	– –	– –	– –	– –	1 –
58 Tranmere Rovers	– –	– –	– –	– –	1 –	– –	– –	– –	– –	1 –
59 Plymouth Argyle	– –	– –	– –	– (1) –	– –	– –	– –	– –	– –	– (1) –

EDDIE McILVENNY

DEBUT (Full Appearance)

Saturday 19/08/1950
Football League Division 1
at Old Trafford

Manchester United 1 Fulham 0

CLUB CAREER RECORD	Apps	Subs	Goals
Premiership	0		0
League Division 1	2		0
League Division 2	0		0
FA Cup	0		0
League Cup	0		0
European Cup / Champions League	0		0
European Cup-Winners' Cup	0		0
UEFA Cup / Inter-Cities' Fairs Cup	0		0
Other Matches	0		0
OVERALL TOTAL	**2**		**0**

Opponents	PREM A S G	FLD 1 A S G	FLD 2 A S G	FAC A S G	LC A S G	EC/CL A S G	ECWC A S G	UEFA A S G	OTHER A S G	TOTAL A S G
1 Fulham	– –	1 –	– –	– –	– –	– –	– –	– –	– –	1 –
2 Liverpool	– –	1 –	– –	– –	– –	– –	– –	– –	– –	1 –

BILL McKAY

DEBUT (Full Appearance)

Saturday 17/03/1934
Football League Division 2
at Old Trafford

Manchester United 1 Fulham 0

CLUB CAREER RECORD	Apps	Subs	Goals
Premiership	0		0
League Division 1	49		5
League Division 2	120		10
FA Cup	13		0
League Cup	0		0
European Cup / Champions League	0		0
European Cup–Winners' Cup	0		0
UEFA Cup / Inter-Cities' Fairs Cup	0		0
Other Matches	0		0
OVERALL TOTAL	182		15

Opponents	PREM A S G	FLD 1 A S G	FLD 2 A S G	FAC A S G	LC A S G	EC/CL A S G	ECWC A S G	UEFA A S G	OTHER A S G	TOTAL A S G
1 West Ham United	– – –	– –	8 1	– –	– – –	– – –	– – –	– – –	– – –	8 1
2 Barnsley	– – –	5 –	2 –	–	– – –	– – –	– – –	– – –	– – –	7 –
3 Fulham	– – –	– –	7 –	– –	– – –	– – –	– – –	– – –	– – –	7 –
4 Bolton Wanderers	– –	4 2	2 –	– –	– – –	– – –	– – –	– – –	– – –	6 2
5 Nottingham Forest	– – –	– –	4 1	2 –	– – –	– – –	– – –	– – –	– – –	6 1
6 Norwich City	– – –	– –	6 –	– –	– – –	– – –	– – –	– – –	– – –	6 –
7 Southampton	– – –	– –	6 –	– –	– – –	– – –	– – –	– – –	– – –	6 –
8 Burnley	– – –	– –	5 2	– –	– – –	– – –	– – –	– – –	– – –	5 2
9 Blackpool	– –	1 –	4 1	– –	– – –	– – –	– – –	– – –	– – –	5 1
10 Bradford Park Avenue	– – –	– –	5 1	– –	– – –	– – –	– – –	– – –	– – –	5 1
11 Bradford City	– – –	– –	5 –	– –	– – –	– – –	– – –	– – –	– – –	5 –
12 Brentford	– –	3 –	2 –	– –	– – –	– – –	– – –	– – –	– – –	5 –
13 Charlton Athletic	– –	3 –	2 –	– –	– – –	– – –	– – –	– – –	– – –	5 –
14 Newcastle United	– – –	– –	5 –	– –	– – –	– – –	– – –	– – –	– – –	5 –
15 Plymouth Argyle	– – –	– –	5 –	– –	– – –	– – –	– – –	– – –	– – –	5 –
16 Port Vale	– – –	– –	5 –	– –	– – –	– – –	– – –	– – –	– – –	5 –
17 Sheffield United	– – –	– –	5 –	– –	– – –	– – –	– – –	– – –	– – –	5 –
18 Swansea City	– – –	– –	5 –	– –	– – –	– – –	– – –	– – –	– – –	5 –
19 Bury	– – –	– –	4 1	– –	– – –	– – –	– – –	– – –	– – –	4 1
20 West Bromwich Albion	– –	2 1	– –	– –	– – –	– – –	– – –	– – –	– – –	4 1
21 Arsenal	– –	3 –	– –	1 –	– – –	– – –	– – –	– – –	– – –	4 –
22 Stoke City	– –	2 –	– –	2 –	– – –	– – –	– – –	– – –	– – –	4 –
23 Sunderland	– –	4 –	– –	– –	– – –	– – –	– – –	– – –	– – –	4 –
24 Tottenham Hotspur	– – –	– –	4 –	– –	– – –	– – –	– – –	– – –	– – –	4 –
25 Wolverhampton W.	– –	3 1	– –	– –	– – –	– – –	– – –	– – –	– – –	3 1
26 Aston Villa	– –	1 –	2 –	– –	– – –	– – –	– – –	– – –	– – –	3 –
27 Derby County	– –	3 –	– –	– –	– – –	– – –	– – –	– – –	– – –	3 –
28 Hull City	– – –	– –	3 –	– –	– – –	– – –	– – –	– – –	– – –	3 –
29 Notts County	– – –	– –	3 –	– –	– – –	– – –	– – –	– – –	– – –	3 –
30 Preston North End	– –	3 –	– –	– –	– – –	– – –	– – –	– – –	– – –	3 –
31 Sheffield Wednesday	– –	1 –	2 –	– –	– – –	– – –	– – –	– – –	– – –	3 –
32 Birmingham City	– –	2 1	– –	– –	– – –	– – –	– – –	– – –	– – –	2 1
33 Luton Town	– – –	– –	2 1	– –	– – –	– – –	– – –	– – –	– – –	2 1
34 Oldham Athletic	– – –	– –	2 1	– –	– – –	– – –	– – –	– – –	– – –	2 1
35 Stockport County	– – –	– –	2 1	– –	– – –	– – –	– – –	– – –	– – –	2 1
36 Blackburn Rovers	– – –	– –	2 –	– –	– – –	– – –	– – –	– – –	– – –	2 –
37 Coventry City	– – –	– –	2 –	– –	– – –	– – –	– – –	– – –	– – –	2 –
38 Doncaster Rovers	– – –	– –	2 –	– –	– – –	– – –	– – –	– – –	– – –	2 –
39 Grimsby Town	– –	2 –	– –	– –	– – –	– – –	– – –	– – –	– – –	2 –
40 Huddersfield Town	– –	2 –	– –	– –	– – –	– – –	– – –	– – –	– – –	2 –
41 Leeds United	– –	2 –	– –	– –	– – –	– – –	– – –	– – –	– – –	2 –
42 Leicester City	– – –	– –	2 –	– –	– – –	– – –	– – –	– – –	– – –	2 –
43 Liverpool	– –	2 –	– –	– –	– – –	– – –	– – –	– – –	– – –	2 –
44 Manchester City	– –	2 –	– –	– –	– – –	– – –	– – –	– – –	– – –	2 –
45 Middlesbrough	– –	2 –	– –	– –	– – –	– – –	– – –	– – –	– – –	2 –
46 Reading	– – –	– –	– –	2 –	– – –	– – –	– – –	– – –	– – –	2 –
47 Bristol Rovers	– – –	– –	– –	1 –	– – –	– – –	– – –	– – –	– – –	1 –
48 Chelsea	– –	1 –	– –	– –	– – –	– – –	– – –	– – –	– – –	1 –
49 Chesterfield	– – –	– –	1 –	– –	– – –	– – –	– – –	– – –	– – –	1 –
50 Millwall	– – –	– –	1 –	– –	– – –	– – –	– – –	– – –	– – –	1 –
51 Portsmouth	– –	1 –	– –	– –	– – –	– – –	– – –	– – –	– – –	1 –
52 Yeovil Town	– – –	– –	– –	1 –	– – –	– – –	– – –	– – –	– – –	1 –

COLIN McKEE

DEBUT (Full Appearance)

Sunday 08/05/1994
FA Premiership
at Old Trafford

Manchester United 0 Coventry City 0

CLUB CAREER RECORD	Apps	Subs	Goals
Premiership	1		0
League Division 1	0		0
League Division 2	0		0
FA Cup	0		0
League Cup	0		0
European Cup / Champions League	0		0
European Cup–Winners' Cup	0		0
UEFA Cup / Inter-Cities' Fairs Cup	0		0
Other Matches	0		0
OVERALL TOTAL	1		0

Opponents	PREM A S G	FLD 1 A S G	FLD 2 A S G	FAC A S G	LC A S G	EC/CL A S G	ECWC A S G	UEFA A S G	OTHER A S G	TOTAL A S G
1 Coventry City	1 – –	– –	– –	– –	– – –	– – –	– – –	– – –	– – –	1 –

GEORGE McLACHLAN

DEBUT (Full Appearance)

Saturday 21/12/1929
Football League Division 1
at Old Trafford

Manchester United 3 Leeds United 1

CLUB CAREER RECORD	Apps	Subs	Goals
Premiership	0		0
League Division 1	65		4
League Division 2	45		0
FA Cup	6		0
League Cup	0		0
European Cup / Champions League	0		0
European Cup-Winners' Cup	0		0
UEFA Cup / Inter-Cities' Fairs Cup	0		0
Other Matches	0		0
OVERALL TOTAL	116		4

#	Opponents	PREM A	S	G	FLD 1 A	S	G	FLD 2 A	S	G	FAC A	S	G	LC A	S	G	EC/CL A	S	G	ECWC A	S	G	UEFA A	S	G	OTHER A	S	G	TOTAL A	S	G
1	Leeds United	-	-	-	4	-	-	2	-	-	-	-	-	-	-	-	-	-	-	-	-	-	-	-	-	-	-	-	6	-	-
2	Grimsby Town	-	-	-	3	-	-	1	-	-	1	-	-	-	-	-	-	-	-	-	-	-	-	-	-	-	-	-	5	-	-
3	Stoke City	-	-	-	-	-	-	2	-	-	3	-	-	-	-	-	-	-	-	-	-	-	-	-	-	-	-	-	5	-	-
4	Birmingham City	-	-	-	4	-	-	-	-	-	-	-	-	-	-	-	-	-	-	-	-	-	-	-	-	-	-	-	4	-	-
5	Charlton Athletic	-	-	-	-	-	-	4	-	-	-	-	-	-	-	-	-	-	-	-	-	-	-	-	-	-	-	-	4	-	-
6	Huddersfield Town	-	-	-	4	-	-	-	-	-	-	-	-	-	-	-	-	-	-	-	-	-	-	-	-	-	-	-	4	-	-
7	Plymouth Argyle	-	-	-	-	-	-	3	-	-	1	-	-	-	-	-	-	-	-	-	-	-	-	-	-	-	-	-	4	-	-
8	West Ham United	-	-	-	3	-	-	1	-	-	-	-	-	-	-	-	-	-	-	-	-	-	-	-	-	-	-	-	4	-	-
9	Arsenal	-	-	-	3	-	1	-	-	-	-	-	-	-	-	-	-	-	-	-	-	-	-	-	-	-	-	-	3	-	1
10	Aston Villa	-	-	-	3	-	1	-	-	-	-	-	-	-	-	-	-	-	-	-	-	-	-	-	-	-	-	-	3	-	1
11	Newcastle United	-	-	-	3	-	1	-	-	-	-	-	-	-	-	-	-	-	-	-	-	-	-	-	-	-	-	-	3	-	1
12	Blackburn Rovers	-	-	-	3	-	-	-	-	-	-	-	-	-	-	-	-	-	-	-	-	-	-	-	-	-	-	-	3	-	-
13	Bolton Wanderers	-	-	-	3	-	-	-	-	-	-	-	-	-	-	-	-	-	-	-	-	-	-	-	-	-	-	-	3	-	-
14	Bradford Park Avenue	-	-	-	-	-	-	-	-	-	3	-	-	-	-	-	-	-	-	-	-	-	-	-	-	-	-	-	3	-	-
15	Derby County	-	-	-	3	-	-	-	-	-	-	-	-	-	-	-	-	-	-	-	-	-	-	-	-	-	-	-	3	-	-
16	Liverpool	-	-	-	3	-	-	-	-	-	-	-	-	-	-	-	-	-	-	-	-	-	-	-	-	-	-	-	3	-	-
17	Manchester City	-	-	-	3	-	-	-	-	-	-	-	-	-	-	-	-	-	-	-	-	-	-	-	-	-	-	-	3	-	-
18	Middlesbrough	-	-	-	3	-	-	-	-	-	-	-	-	-	-	-	-	-	-	-	-	-	-	-	-	-	-	-	3	-	-
19	Nottingham Forest	-	-	-	-	-	-	-	-	-	3	-	-	-	-	-	-	-	-	-	-	-	-	-	-	-	-	-	3	-	-
20	Portsmouth	-	-	-	3	-	-	-	-	-	-	-	-	-	-	-	-	-	-	-	-	-	-	-	-	-	-	-	3	-	-
21	Sheffield United	-	-	-	3	-	-	-	-	-	-	-	-	-	-	-	-	-	-	-	-	-	-	-	-	-	-	-	3	-	-
22	Sheffield Wednesday	-	-	-	3	-	-	-	-	-	-	-	-	-	-	-	-	-	-	-	-	-	-	-	-	-	-	-	3	-	-
23	Southampton	-	-	-	-	-	-	-	-	-	3	-	-	-	-	-	-	-	-	-	-	-	-	-	-	-	-	-	3	-	-
24	Sunderland	-	-	-	3	-	-	-	-	-	-	-	-	-	-	-	-	-	-	-	-	-	-	-	-	-	-	-	3	-	-
25	Leicester City	-	-	-	2	-	1	-	-	-	-	-	-	-	-	-	-	-	-	-	-	-	-	-	-	-	-	-	2	-	1
26	Blackpool	-	-	-	2	-	-	-	-	-	-	-	-	-	-	-	-	-	-	-	-	-	-	-	-	-	-	-	2	-	-
27	Bradford City	-	-	-	-	-	-	2	-	-	-	-	-	-	-	-	-	-	-	-	-	-	-	-	-	-	-	-	2	-	-
28	Burnley	-	-	-	1	-	-	1	-	-	-	-	-	-	-	-	-	-	-	-	-	-	-	-	-	-	-	-	2	-	-
29	Bury	-	-	-	-	-	-	2	-	-	-	-	-	-	-	-	-	-	-	-	-	-	-	-	-	-	-	-	2	-	-
30	Chelsea	-	-	-	2	-	-	-	-	-	-	-	-	-	-	-	-	-	-	-	-	-	-	-	-	-	-	-	2	-	-
31	Chesterfield	-	-	-	-	-	-	2	-	-	-	-	-	-	-	-	-	-	-	-	-	-	-	-	-	-	-	-	2	-	-
32	Millwall	-	-	-	-	-	-	2	-	-	-	-	-	-	-	-	-	-	-	-	-	-	-	-	-	-	-	-	2	-	-
33	Oldham Athletic	-	-	-	-	-	-	2	-	-	-	-	-	-	-	-	-	-	-	-	-	-	-	-	-	-	-	-	2	-	-
34	Swansea City	-	-	-	-	-	-	2	-	-	-	-	-	-	-	-	-	-	-	-	-	-	-	-	-	-	-	-	2	-	-
35	Tottenham Hotspur	-	-	-	-	-	-	2	-	-	-	-	-	-	-	-	-	-	-	-	-	-	-	-	-	-	-	-	2	-	-
36	Wolverhampton W.	-	-	-	-	-	-	2	-	-	-	-	-	-	-	-	-	-	-	-	-	-	-	-	-	-	-	-	2	-	-
37	Barnsley	-	-	-	-	-	-	1	-	-	-	-	-	-	-	-	-	-	-	-	-	-	-	-	-	-	-	-	1	-	-
38	Bristol City	-	-	-	-	-	-	1	-	-	-	-	-	-	-	-	-	-	-	-	-	-	-	-	-	-	-	-	1	-	-
39	Everton	-	-	-	1	-	-	-	-	-	-	-	-	-	-	-	-	-	-	-	-	-	-	-	-	-	-	-	1	-	-
40	Fulham	-	-	-	-	-	-	1	-	-	-	-	-	-	-	-	-	-	-	-	-	-	-	-	-	-	-	-	1	-	-
41	Notts County	-	-	-	-	-	-	1	-	-	-	-	-	-	-	-	-	-	-	-	-	-	-	-	-	-	-	-	1	-	-
42	Port Vale	-	-	-	-	-	-	1	-	-	-	-	-	-	-	-	-	-	-	-	-	-	-	-	-	-	-	-	1	-	-
43	Preston North End	-	-	-	-	-	-	1	-	-	-	-	-	-	-	-	-	-	-	-	-	-	-	-	-	-	-	-	1	-	-
44	Swindon Town	-	-	-	-	-	-	-	-	-	1	-	-	-	-	-	-	-	-	-	-	-	-	-	-	-	-	-	1	-	-

HUGH McLENAHAN

DEBUT (Full Appearance)

Saturday 04/02/1928
Football League Division 1
at White Hart Lane

Tottenham Hotspur 4 Manchester United 1

CLUB CAREER RECORD	Apps	Subs	Goals
Premiership	0		0
League Division 1	45		8
League Division 2	67		3
FA Cup	4		1
League Cup	0		0
European Cup / Champions League	0		0
European Cup-Winners' Cup	0		0
UEFA Cup / Inter-Cities' Fairs Cup	0		0
Other Matches	0		0
OVERALL TOTAL	116		12

#	Opponents	PREM A	S	G	FLD 1 A	S	G	FLD 2 A	S	G	FAC A	S	G	LC A	S	G	EC/CL A	S	G	ECWC A	S	G	UEFA A	S	G	OTHER A	S	G	TOTAL A	S	G
1	Bury	-	-	-	1	-	1	5	-	1	-	-	-	-	-	-	-	-	-	-	-	-	-	-	-	-	-	-	6	-	2
2	Huddersfield Town	-	-	-	5	-	2	-	-	-	-	-	-	-	-	-	-	-	-	-	-	-	-	-	-	-	-	-	5	-	2
3	Bolton Wanderers	-	-	-	3	-	-	2	-	-	-	-	-	-	-	-	-	-	-	-	-	-	-	-	-	-	-	-	5	-	-
4	Southampton	-	-	-	-	-	-	5	-	-	-	-	-	-	-	-	-	-	-	-	-	-	-	-	-	-	-	-	5	-	-
5	Liverpool	-	-	-	4	-	1	-	-	-	-	-	-	-	-	-	-	-	-	-	-	-	-	-	-	-	-	-	4	-	1
6	Burnley	-	-	-	2	-	-	2	-	-	-	-	-	-	-	-	-	-	-	-	-	-	-	-	-	-	-	-	4	-	-
7	Derby County	-	-	-	4	-	-	-	-	-	-	-	-	-	-	-	-	-	-	-	-	-	-	-	-	-	-	-	4	-	-

continued../

HUGH McLENAHAN (continued)

Opponents	PREM A S G	FLD 1 A S G	FLD 2 A S G	FAC A S G	LC A S G	EC/CL A S G	ECWC A S G	UEFA A S G	OTHER A S G	TOTAL A S G
8 Fulham	- - -	- - -	4 - -	- - -	- - -	- - -	- - -	- - -	- - -	4 - -
9 Notts County	- - -	- - -	4 - -	- - -	- - -	- - -	- - -	- - -	- - -	4 - -
10 Preston North End	- - -	- - -	4 - -	- - -	- - -	- - -	- - -	- - -	- - -	4 - -
11 Swansea City	- - -	- - -	4 - -	- - -	- - -	- - -	- - -	- - -	- - -	4 - -
12 Sunderland	- - -	3 - 2	- - -	- - -	- - -	- - -	- - -	- - -	- - -	3 - 2
13 Aston Villa	- - -	3 - -	- - -	- - -	- - -	- - -	- - -	- - -	- - -	3 - -
14 Barnsley	- - -	- - -	3 - -	- - -	- - -	- - -	- - -	- - -	- - -	3 - -
15 Bradford Park Avenue	- - -	- - -	3 - -	- - -	- - -	- - -	- - -	- - -	- - -	3 - -
16 Grimsby Town	- - -	2 - -	1 - -	- - -	- - -	- - -	- - -	- - -	- - -	3 - -
17 Lincoln City	- - -	- - -	3 - -	- - -	- - -	- - -	- - -	- - -	- - -	3 - -
18 Middlesbrough	- - -	2 - -	- - -	- - 1	- - -	- - -	- - -	- - -	- - -	3 - -
19 Millwall	- - -	- - -	3 - -	- - -	- - -	- - -	- - -	- - -	- - -	3 - -
20 Nottingham Forest	- - -	- - -	3 - -	- - -	- - -	- - -	- - -	- - -	- - -	3 - -
21 Oldham Athletic	- - -	- - -	3 - -	- - -	- - -	- - -	- - -	- - -	- - -	3 - -
22 Plymouth Argyle	- - -	- - -	2 - -	1 - -	- - -	- - -	- - -	- - -	- - -	3 - -
23 Port Vale	- - -	- - -	3 - -	- - -	- - -	- - -	- - -	- - -	- - -	3 - -
24 Sheffield United	- - -	3 - -	- - -	- - -	- - -	- - -	- - -	- - -	- - -	3 - -
25 Charlton Athletic	- - -	- - -	2 - 1	- - -	- - -	- - -	- - -	- - -	- - -	2 - 1
26 Portsmouth	- - -	- - -	- - -	- - -	2 - 1	- - -	- - -	- - -	- - -	2 - 1
27 Sheffield Wednesday	- - -	2 - 1	- - -	- - -	- - -	- - -	- - -	- - -	- - -	2 - 1
28 Blackburn Rovers	- - -	2 - -	- - -	- - -	- - -	- - -	- - -	- - -	- - -	2 - -
29 Brentford	- - -	- - -	2 - -	- - -	- - -	- - -	- - -	- - -	- - -	2 - -
30 Leeds United	- - -	2 - -	- - -	- - -	- - -	- - -	- - -	- - -	- - -	2 - -
31 Stoke City	- - -	- - -	2 - -	- - -	- - -	- - -	- - -	- - -	- - -	2 - -
32 Tottenham Hotspur	- - -	1 - -	1 - -	- - -	- - -	- - -	- - -	- - -	- - -	2 - -
33 Everton	- - -	1 - 1	- - -	- - -	- - -	- - -	- - -	- - -	- - -	1 - 1
34 Norwich City	- - -	- - -	1 - 1	- - -	- - -	- - -	- - -	- - -	- - -	1 - 1
35 Arsenal	- - -	1 - -	- - -	- - -	- - -	- - -	- - -	- - -	- - -	1 - -
36 Blackpool	- - -	- - -	1 - -	- - -	- - -	- - -	- - -	- - -	- - -	1 - -
37 Bradford City	- - -	- - -	1 - -	- - -	- - -	- - -	- - -	- - -	- - -	1 - -
38 Chelsea	- - -	1 - -	- - -	- - -	- - -	- - -	- - -	- - -	- - -	1 - -
39 Chesterfield	- - -	- - -	1 - -	- - -	- - -	- - -	- - -	- - -	- - -	1 - -
40 Hull City	- - -	- - -	1 - -	- - -	- - -	- - -	- - -	- - -	- - -	1 - -
41 Leicester City	- - -	1 - -	- - -	- - -	- - -	- - -	- - -	- - -	- - -	1 - -
42 Manchester City	- - -	1 - -	- - -	- - -	- - -	- - -	- - -	- - -	- - -	1 - -
43 Newcastle United	- - -	1 - -	- - -	- - -	- - -	- - -	- - -	- - -	- - -	1 - -
44 West Ham United	- - -	- - -	1 - -	- - -	- - -	- - -	- - -	- - -	- - -	1 - -

SAMMY McMILLAN

DEBUT (Full Appearance)

Saturday 04/11/1961
Football League Division 1
at Hillsborough

Sheffield Wednesday 3 Manchester United 1

CLUB CAREER RECORD	Apps	Subs	Goals
Premiership	0		0
League Division 1	15		6
League Division 2	0		0
FA Cup	0		0
League Cup	0		0
European Cup / Champions League	0		0
European Cup–Winners' Cup	0		0
UEFA Cup / Inter-Cities' Fairs Cup	0		0
Other Matches	0		0
OVERALL TOTAL	15		6

Opponents	PREM A S G	FLD 1 A S G	FLD 2 A S G	FAC A S G	LC A S G	EC/CL A S G	ECWC A S G	UEFA A S G	OTHER A S G	TOTAL A S G
1 Leicester City	- - -	2 - 2	- - -	- - -	- - -	- - -	- - -	- - -	- - -	2 - 2
2 Sheffield United	- - -	2 - 2	- - -	- - -	- - -	- - -	- - -	- - -	- - -	2 - 2
3 Ipswich Town	- - -	2 - 1	- - -	- - -	- - -	- - -	- - -	- - -	- - -	2 - 1
4 Blackburn Rovers	- - -	2 - -	- - -	- - -	- - -	- - -	- - -	- - -	- - -	2 - -
5 Sheffield Wednesday	- - -	2 - -	- - -	- - -	- - -	- - -	- - -	- - -	- - -	2 - -
6 Arsenal	- - -	1 - 1	- - -	- - -	- - -	- - -	- - -	- - -	- - -	1 - 1
7 Blackpool	- - -	1 - -	- - -	- - -	- - -	- - -	- - -	- - -	- - -	1 - -
8 Burnley	- - -	1 - -	- - -	- - -	- - -	- - -	- - -	- - -	- - -	1 - -
9 Fulham	- - -	1 - -	- - -	- - -	- - -	- - -	- - -	- - -	- - -	1 - -
10 Leyton Orient	- - -	1 - -	- - -	- - -	- - -	- - -	- - -	- - -	- - -	1 - -

WALTER McMILLEN

DEBUT (Full Appearance)

Saturday 16/09/1933
Football League Division 2
at Griffin Park

Brentford 3 Manchester United 4

CLUB CAREER RECORD	Apps	Subs	Goals
Premiership	0		0
League Division 1	0		0
League Division 2	27		2
FA Cup	2		0
League Cup	0		0
European Cup / Champions League	0		0
European Cup-Winners' Cup	0		0
UEFA Cup / Inter-Cities' Fairs Cup	0		0
Other Matches	0		0
OVERALL TOTAL	29		2

Opponents	PREM			FLD 1			FLD 2			FAC			LC			EC/CL			ECWC			UEFA			OTHER			TOTAL		
	A	S	G	A	S	G	A	S	G	A	S	G	A	S	G	A	S	G	A	S	G	A	S	G	A	S	G	A	S	G
1 Burnley	-	-	-	-	-	-	2	-	1	-	-	-	-	-	-	-	-	-	-	-	-	-	-	-	-	-	-	2	-	1
2 Blackpool	-	-	-	-	-	-	2	-	-	-	-	-	-	-	-	-	-	-	-	-	-	-	-	-	-	-	-	2	-	-
3 Brentford	-	-	-	-	-	-	2	-	-	-	-	-	-	-	-	-	-	-	-	-	-	-	-	-	-	-	-	2	-	-
4 Bury	-	-	-	-	-	-	2	-	-	-	-	-	-	-	-	-	-	-	-	-	-	-	-	-	-	-	-	2	-	-
5 Grimsby Town	-	-	-	-	-	-	2	-	-	-	-	-	-	-	-	-	-	-	-	-	-	-	-	-	-	-	-	2	-	-
6 Hull City	-	-	-	-	-	-	2	-	-	-	-	-	-	-	-	-	-	-	-	-	-	-	-	-	-	-	-	2	-	-
7 Notts County	-	-	-	-	-	-	2	-	-	-	-	-	-	-	-	-	-	-	-	-	-	-	-	-	-	-	-	2	-	-
8 Portsmouth	-	-	-	-	-	-	-	-	-	2	-	-	-	-	-	-	-	-	-	-	-	-	-	-	-	-	-	2	-	-
9 West Ham United	-	-	-	-	-	-	2	-	-	-	-	-	-	-	-	-	-	-	-	-	-	-	-	-	-	-	-	2	-	-
10 Port Vale	-	-	-	-	-	-	1	-	1	-	-	-	-	-	-	-	-	-	-	-	-	-	-	-	-	-	-	1	-	1
11 Bolton Wanderers	-	-	-	-	-	-	1	-	-	-	-	-	-	-	-	-	-	-	-	-	-	-	-	-	-	-	-	1	-	-
12 Bradford City	-	-	-	-	-	-	1	-	-	-	-	-	-	-	-	-	-	-	-	-	-	-	-	-	-	-	-	1	-	-
13 Fulham	-	-	-	-	-	-	1	-	-	-	-	-	-	-	-	-	-	-	-	-	-	-	-	-	-	-	-	1	-	-
14 Lincoln City	-	-	-	-	-	-	1	-	-	-	-	-	-	-	-	-	-	-	-	-	-	-	-	-	-	-	-	1	-	-
15 Millwall	-	-	-	-	-	-	1	-	-	-	-	-	-	-	-	-	-	-	-	-	-	-	-	-	-	-	-	1	-	-
16 Oldham Athletic	-	-	-	-	-	-	1	-	-	-	-	-	-	-	-	-	-	-	-	-	-	-	-	-	-	-	-	1	-	-
17 Plymouth Argyle	-	-	-	-	-	-	1	-	-	-	-	-	-	-	-	-	-	-	-	-	-	-	-	-	-	-	-	1	-	-
18 Preston North End	-	-	-	-	-	-	1	-	-	-	-	-	-	-	-	-	-	-	-	-	-	-	-	-	-	-	-	1	-	-
19 Southampton	-	-	-	-	-	-	1	-	-	-	-	-	-	-	-	-	-	-	-	-	-	-	-	-	-	-	-	1	-	-
20 Swansea City	-	-	-	-	-	-	1	-	-	-	-	-	-	-	-	-	-	-	-	-	-	-	-	-	-	-	-	1	-	-

JAMES McNAUGHT

DEBUT (Full Appearance)

Saturday 02/09/1893
Football League Division 1
at North Road

Newton Heath 3 Burnley 2

CLUB CAREER RECORD	Apps	Subs	Goals
Premiership	0		0
League Division 1	26		1
League Division 2	114		11
FA Cup	17		0
League Cup	0		0
European Cup / Champions League	0		0
European Cup-Winners' Cup	0		0
UEFA Cup / Inter-Cities' Fairs Cup	0		0
Other Matches	5		0
OVERALL TOTAL	162		12

Opponents	PREM			FLD 1			FLD 2			FAC			LC			EC/CL			ECWC			UEFA			OTHER			TOTAL		
	A	S	G	A	S	G	A	S	G	A	S	G	A	S	G	A	S	G	A	S	G	A	S	G	A	S	G	A	S	G
1 Darwen	-	-	-	2	-	-	8	-	2	-	-	-	-	-	-	-	-	-	-	-	-	-	-	-	-	-	-	10	-	2
2 Burton Swifts	-	-	-	-	-	-	8	-	2	-	-	-	-	-	-	-	-	-	-	-	-	-	-	-	-	-	-	8	-	2
3 Arsenal	-	-	-	-	-	-	8	-	-	-	-	-	-	-	-	-	-	-	-	-	-	-	-	-	-	-	-	8	-	-
4 Grimsby Town	-	-	-	-	-	-	8	-	-	-	-	-	-	-	-	-	-	-	-	-	-	-	-	-	-	-	-	8	-	-
5 Manchester City	-	-	-	-	-	-	8	-	-	-	-	-	-	-	-	-	-	-	-	-	-	-	-	-	-	-	-	8	-	-
6 Leicester City	-	-	-	-	-	-	7	-	1	-	-	-	-	-	-	-	-	-	-	-	-	-	-	-	-	-	-	7	-	1
7 Walsall	-	-	-	-	-	-	6	-	1	1	-	-	-	-	-	-	-	-	-	-	-	-	-	-	-	-	-	7	-	1
8 Lincoln City	-	-	-	-	-	-	7	-	-	-	-	-	-	-	-	-	-	-	-	-	-	-	-	-	-	-	-	7	-	-
9 Newcastle United	-	-	-	-	-	-	7	-	-	-	-	-	-	-	-	-	-	-	-	-	-	-	-	-	-	-	-	7	-	-
10 Burton Wanderers	-	-	-	-	-	-	6	-	1	-	-	-	-	-	-	-	-	-	-	-	-	-	-	-	-	-	-	6	-	1
11 Loughborough Town	-	-	-	-	-	-	6	-	1	-	-	-	-	-	-	-	-	-	-	-	-	-	-	-	-	-	-	6	-	1
12 Blackpool	-	-	-	-	-	-	4	-	-	2	-	-	-	-	-	-	-	-	-	-	-	-	-	-	-	-	-	6	-	-
13 Burnley	-	-	-	2	-	-	2	-	-	-	-	-	-	-	-	-	-	-	-	-	-	-	-	-	2	-	-	6	-	-
14 Derby County	-	-	-	2	-	-	-	-	-	3	-	-	-	-	-	-	-	-	-	-	-	-	-	-	-	-	-	5	-	-
15 Liverpool	-	-	-	-	-	-	2	-	-	2	-	-	-	-	-	-	-	-	-	-	-	-	-	-	1	-	-	5	-	-
16 Notts County	-	-	-	-	-	-	5	-	-	-	-	-	-	-	-	-	-	-	-	-	-	-	-	-	-	-	-	5	-	-
17 Gainsborough Trinity	-	-	-	-	-	-	4	-	2	-	-	-	-	-	-	-	-	-	-	-	-	-	-	-	-	-	-	4	-	2
18 Port Vale	-	-	-	-	-	-	4	-	1	-	-	-	-	-	-	-	-	-	-	-	-	-	-	-	-	-	-	4	-	1
19 Sunderland	-	-	-	2	-	1	-	-	-	-	-	-	-	-	-	-	-	-	-	-	-	-	-	-	2	-	-	4	-	1
20 Birmingham City	-	-	-	-	-	-	4	-	-	-	-	-	-	-	-	-	-	-	-	-	-	-	-	-	-	-	-	4	-	-
21 Crewe Alexandra	-	-	-	-	-	-	4	-	-	-	-	-	-	-	-	-	-	-	-	-	-	-	-	-	-	-	-	4	-	-
22 Blackburn Rovers	-	-	-	1	-	-	-	-	-	2	-	-	-	-	-	-	-	-	-	-	-	-	-	-	-	-	-	3	-	-
23 Rotherham United	-	-	-	-	-	-	3	-	-	-	-	-	-	-	-	-	-	-	-	-	-	-	-	-	-	-	-	3	-	-
24 Stoke City	-	-	-	2	-	-	-	-	-	1	-	-	-	-	-	-	-	-	-	-	-	-	-	-	-	-	-	3	-	-
25 Aston Villa	-	-	-	2	-	-	-	-	-	-	-	-	-	-	-	-	-	-	-	-	-	-	-	-	-	-	-	2	-	-
26 Everton	-	-	-	2	-	-	-	-	-	-	-	-	-	-	-	-	-	-	-	-	-	-	-	-	-	-	-	2	-	-
27 Luton Town	-	-	-	-	-	-	2	-	-	-	-	-	-	-	-	-	-	-	-	-	-	-	-	-	-	-	-	2	-	-
28 Sheffield United	-	-	-	2	-	-	-	-	-	-	-	-	-	-	-	-	-	-	-	-	-	-	-	-	-	-	-	2	-	-
29 Sheffield Wednesday	-	-	-	2	-	-	-	-	-	-	-	-	-	-	-	-	-	-	-	-	-	-	-	-	-	-	-	2	-	-
30 Southampton	-	-	-	-	-	-	-	-	-	2	-	-	-	-	-	-	-	-	-	-	-	-	-	-	-	-	-	2	-	-
31 West Bromwich Albion	-	-	-	2	-	-	-	-	-	-	-	-	-	-	-	-	-	-	-	-	-	-	-	-	-	-	-	2	-	-

continued../

JAMES McNAUGHT (continued)

Opponents	PREM A S G	FLD 1 A S G	FLD 2 A S G	FAC A S G	LC A S G	EC/CL A S G	ECWC A S G	UEFA A S G	OTHER A S G	TOTAL A S G
32 Wolverhampton W.	– –	2 –	–	–	–	–	–	–	–	2 –
33 Bolton Wanderers	– –	1	–	–	–	–	–	–	–	1 –
34 Bury	– –	– –	1	–	–	–	–	–	–	1 –
35 Kettering	– –	–	–	1	–	–	–	–	–	1 –
36 Middlesbrough	– –	–	–	1	–	–	–	–	–	1 –
37 Nelson	– –	–	–	1	–	–	–	–	–	1 –
38 Nottingham Forest	– –	1	–	–	–	–	–	–	–	1 –
39 Preston North End	– –	1	–	–	–	–	–	–	–	1 –
40 West Manchester	– –	–	–	1	–	–	–	–	–	1 –

THOMAS McNULTY

DEBUT (Full Appearance)

Saturday 15/04/1950
Football League Division 1
at Old Trafford

Manchester United 0 Portsmouth 2

CLUB CAREER RECORD	Apps	Subs	Goals
Premiership	0		0
League Division 1	57		0
League Division 2	0		0
FA Cup	2		0
League Cup	0		0
European Cup / Champions League	0		0
European Cup–Winners' Cup	0		0
UEFA Cup / Inter–Cities' Fairs Cup	0		0
Other Matches	1		0
OVERALL TOTAL	60		0

Opponents	PREM A S G	FLD 1 A S G	FLD 2 A S G	FAC A S G	LC A S G	EC/CL A S G	ECWC A S G	UEFA A S G	OTHER A S G	TOTAL A S G
1 Newcastle United	– –	4	–	–	–	–	–	1	–	5 –
2 Blackpool	– –	4	–	–	–	–	–	–	–	4 –
3 Fulham	– –	4	–	–	–	–	–	–	–	4 –
4 Middlesbrough	– –	4	–	–	–	–	–	–	–	4 –
5 West Bromwich Albion	– –	4	–	–	–	–	–	–	–	4 –
6 Arsenal	– –	3	–	–	–	–	–	–	–	3 –
7 Aston Villa	– –	3	–	–	–	–	–	–	–	3 –
8 Bolton Wanderers	– –	3	–	–	–	–	–	–	–	3 –
9 Portsmouth	– –	3	–	–	–	–	–	–	–	3 –
10 Stoke City	– –	3	–	–	–	–	–	–	–	3 –
11 Wolverhampton W.	– –	3	–	–	–	–	–	–	–	3 –
12 Burnley	– –	2	–	–	–	–	–	–	–	2 –
13 Chelsea	– –	2	–	–	–	–	–	–	–	2 –
14 Derby County	– –	2	–	–	–	–	–	–	–	2 –
15 Huddersfield Town	– –	2	–	–	–	–	–	–	–	2 –
16 Manchester City	– –	2	–	–	–	–	–	–	–	2 –
17 Sunderland	– –	2	–	–	–	–	–	–	–	2 –
18 Tottenham Hotspur	– –	2	–	–	–	–	–	–	–	2 –
19 Birmingham City	– –	–	–	1	–	–	–	–	–	1 –
20 Cardiff City	– –	1	–	–	–	–	–	–	–	1 –
21 Charlton Athletic	– –	1	–	–	–	–	–	–	–	1 –
22 Hull City	– –	–	–	1	–	–	–	–	–	1 –
23 Liverpool	– –	1	–	–	–	–	–	–	–	1 –
24 Preston North End	– –	1	–	–	–	–	–	–	–	1 –
25 Sheffield Wednesday	– –	1	–	–	–	–	–	–	–	1 –

FRANK McPHERSON

DEBUT (Full Appearance)

Saturday 25/08/1923
Football League Division 2
at Ashton Gate

Bristol City 1 Manchester United 2

CLUB CAREER RECORD	Apps	Subs	Goals
Premiership	0		0
League Division 1	87		37
League Division 2	72		8
FA Cup	16		7
League Cup	0		0
European Cup / Champions League	0		0
European Cup–Winners' Cup	0		0
UEFA Cup / Inter–Cities' Fairs Cup	0		0
Other Matches	0		0
OVERALL TOTAL	175		52

Opponents	PREM A S G	FLD 1 A S G	FLD 2 A S G	FAC A S G	LC A S G	EC/CL A S G	ECWC A S G	UEFA A S G	OTHER A S G	TOTAL A S G
1 Bury	– –	6 3	2 –	2 –	–	–	–	–	–	10 3
2 Leicester City	– –	5 5	4 –	–	–	–	–	–	–	9 5
3 Sheffield Wednesday	– –	3 1	4 1	1 –	–	–	–	–	–	8 2
4 Tottenham Hotspur	– –	5 2	–	2 –	–	–	–	–	–	7 2
5 West Ham United	– –	6 1	–	–	–	–	–	–	–	6 1
6 Leeds United	– –	3 4	2 –	–	–	–	–	–	–	5 4
7 Arsenal	– –	5 2	–	–	–	–	–	–	–	5 2
8 Everton	– –	5 1	–	–	–	–	–	–	–	5 1
9 Fulham	– –	– –	4 –	1 1	–	–	–	–	–	5 1

continued../

FRANK McPHERSON (continued)

Opponents	PREM A S G	FLD 1 A S G	FLD 2 A S G	FAC A S G	LC A S G	EC/CL A S G	ECWC A S G	UEFA A S G	OTHER A S G	TOTAL A S G
10 Birmingham City	– –	5 –	– –	– –	– –	– –	– –	– –	– –	5 –
11 Bradford City	– –	– –	4 2	– –	– –	– –	– –	– –	– –	4 2
12 Liverpool	– –	4 2	– –	– –	– –	– –	– –	– –	– –	4 2
13 Port Vale	– –	– –	3 1	1 1	– –	– –	– –	– –	– –	4 2
14 Sunderland	– –	2 –	– –	2 2	– –	– –	– –	– –	– –	4 2
15 Aston Villa	– –	4 1	– –	– –	– –	– –	– –	– –	– –	4 1
16 Blackburn Rovers	– –	4 1	– –	– –	– –	– –	– –	– –	– –	4 1
17 Bolton Wanderers	– –	4 1	– –	– –	– –	– –	– –	– –	– –	4 1
18 Burnley	– –	4 1	– –	– –	– –	– –	– –	– –	– –	4 1
19 Coventry City	– –	– –	4 1	– –	– –	– –	– –	– –	– –	4 1
20 Derby County	– –	2 1	2 –	– –	– –	– –	– –	– –	– –	4 1
21 South Shields	– –	– –	4 1	– –	– –	– –	– –	– –	– –	4 1
22 Barnsley	– –	– –	4 –	– –	– –	– –	– –	– –	– –	4 –
23 Huddersfield Town	– –	3 –	– –	1 –	– –	– –	– –	– –	– –	4 –
24 Oldham Athletic	– –	– –	4 –	– –	– –	– –	– –	– –	– –	4 –
25 Southampton	– –	– –	4 –	– –	– –	– –	– –	– –	– –	4 –
26 Stoke City	– –	– –	4 –	– –	– –	– –	– –	– –	– –	4 –
27 Sheffield United	– –	3 5	– –	– –	– –	– –	– –	– –	– –	3 5
28 Cardiff City	– –	3 2	– –	– –	– –	– –	– –	– –	– –	3 2
29 Leyton Orient	– –	– –	3 1	– –	– –	– –	– –	– –	– –	3 1
30 Newcastle United	– –	3 1	– –	– –	– –	– –	– –	– –	– –	3 1
31 Reading	– –	– –	– –	3 1	– –	– –	– –	– –	– –	3 1
32 Blackpool	– –	– –	3 –	– –	– –	– –	– –	– –	– –	3 –
33 Manchester City	– –	2 –	– –	1 –	– –	– –	– –	– –	– –	3 –
34 Middlesbrough	– –	1 –	2 –	– –	– –	– –	– –	– –	– –	3 –
35 Stockport County	– –	– –	3 –	– –	– –	– –	– –	– –	– –	3 –
36 Hull City	– –	– –	2 1	– –	– –	– –	– –	– –	– –	2 1
37 Notts County	– –	2 1	– –	– –	– –	– –	– –	– –	– –	2 1
38 Portsmouth	– –	1 1	1 –	– –	– –	– –	– –	– –	– –	2 1
39 West Bromwich Albion	– –	2 1	– –	– –	– –	– –	– –	– –	– –	2 1
40 Bristol City	– –	– –	2 –	– –	– –	– –	– –	– –	– –	2 –
41 Chelsea	– –	– –	2 –	– –	– –	– –	– –	– –	– –	2 –
42 Crystal Palace	– –	– –	2 –	– –	– –	– –	– –	– –	– –	2 –
43 Nelson	– –	– –	2 –	– –	– –	– –	– –	– –	– –	2 –
44 Brentford	– –	– –	– –	1 1	– –	– –	– –	– –	– –	1 1
45 Plymouth Argyle	– –	– –	– –	1 1	– –	– –	– –	– –	– –	1 1
46 Wolverhampton W.	– –	– –	1 –	– –	– –	– –	– –	– –	– –	1 –

GORDON McQUEEN

DEBUT (Full Appearance)

Saturday 25/02/1978
Football League Division 1
at Anfield

Liverpool 3 Manchester United 1

CLUB CAREER RECORD	Apps	Subs	Goals
Premiership	0		0
League Division 1	184		20
League Division 2	0		0
FA Cup	21		2
League Cup	16		4
European Cup / Champions League	0		0
European Cup–Winners' Cup	4		0
UEFA Cup / Inter–Cities' Fairs Cup	3		0
Other Matches	1		0
OVERALL TOTAL	229		26

Opponents	PREM A S G	FLD 1 A S G	FLD 2 A S G	FAC A S G	LC A S G	EC/CL A S G	ECWC A S G	UEFA A S G	OTHER A S G	TOTAL A S G
1 Arsenal	– –	9 1	– –	2 1	2 –	– –	– –	– –	– –	13 2
2 Liverpool	– –	9 1	– –	2 –	1 –	– –	– –	– –	1 –	13 1
3 Nottingham Forest	– –	9 1	– –	1 –	1 2	– –	– –	– –	– –	11 3
4 West Bromwich Albion	– –	11 3	– –	– –	– –	– –	– –	– –	– –	11 3
5 Ipswich Town	– –	11 –	– –	– –	– –	– –	– –	– –	– –	11 –
6 Tottenham Hotspur	– –	5 1	– –	4 –	1 –	– –	– –	– –	– –	10 1
7 Everton	– –	9 –	– –	– –	1 –	– –	– –	– –	– –	10 –
8 Stoke City	– –	9 2	– –	– –	– –	– –	– –	– –	– –	9 2
9 Brighton	– –	6 1	– –	3 –	– –	– –	– –	– –	– –	9 1
10 Coventry City	– –	9 1	– –	– –	– –	– –	– –	– –	– –	9 1
11 Southampton	– –	7 1	– –	– –	– –	1 1	– –	– –	– –	8 2
12 Norwich City	– –	7 1	– –	– –	1 –	– –	– –	– –	– –	8 1
13 Aston Villa	– –	8 –	– –	– –	– –	– –	– –	– –	– –	8 –
14 Manchester City	– –	7 –	– –	– –	– –	– –	– –	– –	– –	7 –
15 Middlesbrough	– –	6 1	– –	– –	– –	– –	– –	– –	– –	6 1
16 Sunderland	– –	6 –	– –	– –	– –	– –	– –	– –	– –	6 –
17 Bristol City	– –	5 1	– –	– –	– –	– –	– –	– –	– –	5 1
18 West Ham United	– –	4 1	– –	1 –	– –	– –	– –	– –	– –	5 1
19 Luton Town	– –	4 –	– –	– –	1 –	– –	– –	– –	– –	5 –
20 Queens Park Rangers	– –	5 –	– –	– –	– –	– –	– –	– –	– –	5 –
21 Wolverhampton W.	– –	5 –	– –	– –	– –	– –	– –	– –	– –	5 –
22 Bolton Wanderers	– –	4 2	– –	– –	– –	– –	– –	– –	– –	4 2
23 Leeds United	– –	4 1	– –	– –	– –	– –	– –	– –	– –	4 1
24 Birmingham City	– –	4 –	– –	– –	– –	– –	– –	– –	– –	4 –

continued../

GORDON McQUEEN (continued)

Opponents	PREM			FLD 1			FLD 2			FAC			LC			EC/CL			ECWC			UEFA			OTHER			TOTAL		
	A	S	G	A	S	G	A	S	G	A	S	G	A	S	G	A	S	G	A	S	G	A	S	G	A	S	G	A	S	G
25 Chelsea	-	-	-	3	-	-	-	-	-	1	-	-	-	-	-	-	-	-	-	-	-	-	-	-	-	-	-	4	-	-
26 Derby County	-	-	-	3	-	-	-	-	-	1	-	-	-	-	-	-	-	-	-	-	-	-	-	-	-	-	-	4	-	-
27 Swansea City	-	-	-	4	-	-	-	-	-	-	-	-	-	-	-	-	-	-	-	-	-	-	-	-	-	-	-	4	-	-
28 Watford	-	-	-	3	-	-	-	-	-	-	-	-	1	-	-	-	-	-	-	-	-	-	-	-	-	-	-	4	-	-
29 Bournemouth	-	-	-	-	-	-	-	-	-	1	-	1	1	-	-	-	-	-	-	-	-	-	-	-	-	-	-	2	-	1
30 Colchester United	-	-	-	-	-	-	-	-	-	1	-	-	1	-	1	-	-	-	-	-	-	-	-	-	-	-	-	2	-	1
31 Notts County	-	-	-	2	-	1	-	-	-	-	-	-	-	-	-	-	-	-	-	-	-	-	-	-	-	-	-	2	-	1
32 Bradford City	-	-	-	-	-	-	-	-	-	-	-	-	2	-	-	-	-	-	-	-	-	-	-	-	-	-	-	2	-	-
33 Crystal Palace	-	-	-	2	-	-	-	-	-	-	-	-	-	-	-	-	-	-	-	-	-	-	-	-	-	-	-	2	-	-
34 Dukla Prague	-	-	-	-	-	-	-	-	-	-	-	-	-	-	-	-	-	-	2	-	-	-	-	-	-	-	-	2	-	-
35 Dundee United	-	-	-	-	-	-	-	-	-	-	-	-	-	-	-	-	-	-	-	-	-	2	-	-	-	-	-	2	-	-
36 Fulham	-	-	-	-	-	-	-	-	-	2	-	-	-	-	-	-	-	-	-	-	-	-	-	-	-	-	-	2	-	-
37 Leicester City	-	-	-	2	-	-	-	-	-	-	-	-	-	-	-	-	-	-	-	-	-	-	-	-	-	-	-	2	-	-
38 Oxford United	-	-	-	-	-	-	-	-	-	-	-	-	2	-	-	-	-	-	-	-	-	-	-	-	-	-	-	2	-	-
39 Spartak Varna	-	-	-	-	-	-	-	-	-	-	-	-	-	-	-	-	-	-	2	-	-	-	-	-	-	-	-	2	-	-
40 Newcastle United	-	-	-	1	-	-	-	-	-	-	-	-	-	-	-	-	-	-	-	-	-	-	-	-	-	-	-	1	-	-
41 Port Vale	-	-	-	-	-	-	-	-	-	-	-	-	1	-	-	-	-	-	-	-	-	-	-	-	-	-	-	1	-	-
42 Sheffield Wednesday	-	-	-	1	-	-	-	-	-	-	-	-	-	-	-	-	-	-	-	-	-	-	-	-	-	-	-	1	-	-
43 Stockport County	-	-	-	-	-	-	-	-	-	-	-	-	1	-	-	-	-	-	-	-	-	-	-	-	-	-	-	1	-	-
44 Valencia	-	-	-	-	-	-	-	-	-	-	-	-	-	-	-	-	-	-	-	-	-	1	-	-	-	-	-	1	-	-

HARRY McSHANE

DEBUT (Full Appearance)

Wednesday 13/09/1950
Football League Division 1
at Old Trafford

Manchester United 0 Aston Villa 0

CLUB CAREER RECORD	Apps	Subs	Goals
Premiership	0		0
League Division 1	56		8
League Division 2	0		0
FA Cup	1		0
League Cup	0		0
European Cup / Champions League	0		0
European Cup-Winners' Cup	0		0
UEFA Cup / Inter-Cities' Fairs Cup	0		0
Other Matches	0		0
OVERALL TOTAL	**57**		**8**

Opponents	PREM			FLD 1			FLD 2			FAC			LC			EC/CL			ECWC			UEFA			OTHER			TOTAL		
	A	S	G	A	S	G	A	S	G	A	S	G	A	S	G	A	S	G	A	S	G	A	S	G	A	S	G	A	S	G
1 Middlesbrough	-	-	-	5	-	-	-	-	-	-	-	-	-	-	-	-	-	-	-	-	-	-	-	-	-	-	-	5	-	-
2 Newcastle United	-	-	-	4	-	-	-	-	-	-	-	-	-	-	-	-	-	-	-	-	-	-	-	-	-	-	-	4	-	-
3 West Bromwich Albion	-	-	-	4	-	-	-	-	-	-	-	-	-	-	-	-	-	-	-	-	-	-	-	-	-	-	-	4	-	-
4 Burnley	-	-	-	3	-	2	-	-	-	-	-	-	-	-	-	-	-	-	-	-	-	-	-	-	-	-	-	3	-	2
5 Huddersfield Town	-	-	-	3	-	2	-	-	-	-	-	-	-	-	-	-	-	-	-	-	-	-	-	-	-	-	-	3	-	2
6 Sheffield Wednesday	-	-	-	3	-	2	-	-	-	-	-	-	-	-	-	-	-	-	-	-	-	-	-	-	-	-	-	3	-	2
7 Derby County	-	-	-	3	-	-	-	-	-	-	-	-	-	-	-	-	-	-	-	-	-	-	-	-	-	-	-	3	-	-
8 Stoke City	-	-	-	3	-	-	-	-	-	-	-	-	-	-	-	-	-	-	-	-	-	-	-	-	-	-	-	3	-	-
9 Sunderland	-	-	-	3	-	-	-	-	-	-	-	-	-	-	-	-	-	-	-	-	-	-	-	-	-	-	-	3	-	-
10 Tottenham Hotspur	-	-	-	3	-	-	-	-	-	-	-	-	-	-	-	-	-	-	-	-	-	-	-	-	-	-	-	3	-	-
11 Wolverhampton W.	-	-	-	3	-	-	-	-	-	-	-	-	-	-	-	-	-	-	-	-	-	-	-	-	-	-	-	3	-	-
12 Chelsea	-	-	-	2	-	1	-	-	-	-	-	-	-	-	-	-	-	-	-	-	-	-	-	-	-	-	-	2	-	1
13 Arsenal	-	-	-	2	-	-	-	-	-	-	-	-	-	-	-	-	-	-	-	-	-	-	-	-	-	-	-	2	-	-
14 Aston Villa	-	-	-	2	-	-	-	-	-	-	-	-	-	-	-	-	-	-	-	-	-	-	-	-	-	-	-	2	-	-
15 Bolton Wanderers	-	-	-	2	-	-	-	-	-	-	-	-	-	-	-	-	-	-	-	-	-	-	-	-	-	-	-	2	-	-
16 Charlton Athletic	-	-	-	2	-	-	-	-	-	-	-	-	-	-	-	-	-	-	-	-	-	-	-	-	-	-	-	2	-	-
17 Everton	-	-	-	2	-	-	-	-	-	-	-	-	-	-	-	-	-	-	-	-	-	-	-	-	-	-	-	2	-	-
18 Portsmouth	-	-	-	2	-	-	-	-	-	-	-	-	-	-	-	-	-	-	-	-	-	-	-	-	-	-	-	2	-	-
19 Manchester City	-	-	-	1	-	1	-	-	-	-	-	-	-	-	-	-	-	-	-	-	-	-	-	-	-	-	-	1	-	1
20 Blackpool	-	-	-	1	-	-	-	-	-	-	-	-	-	-	-	-	-	-	-	-	-	-	-	-	-	-	-	1	-	-
21 Cardiff City	-	-	-	1	-	-	-	-	-	-	-	-	-	-	-	-	-	-	-	-	-	-	-	-	-	-	-	1	-	-
22 Fulham	-	-	-	1	-	-	-	-	-	-	-	-	-	-	-	-	-	-	-	-	-	-	-	-	-	-	-	1	-	-
23 Oldham Athletic	-	-	-	-	-	-	-	-	-	1	-	-	-	-	-	-	-	-	-	-	-	-	-	-	-	-	-	1	-	-
24 Preston North End	-	-	-	1	-	-	-	-	-	-	-	-	-	-	-	-	-	-	-	-	-	-	-	-	-	-	-	1	-	-

TOMMY MEEHAN

DEBUT (Full Appearance)

Monday 01/09/1919
Football League Division 1
at Old Trafford

Manchester United 0 Sheffield Wednesday 0

CLUB CAREER RECORD	Apps	Subs	Goals
Premiership	0		0
League Division 1	51		6
League Division 2	0		0
FA Cup	2		0
League Cup	0		0
European Cup / Champions League	0		0
European Cup-Winners' Cup	0		0
UEFA Cup / Inter-Cities' Fairs Cup	0		0
Other Matches	0		0
OVERALL TOTAL	**53**		**6**

Opponents	PREM A S G	FLD 1 A S G	FLD 2 A S G	FAC A S G	LC A S G	EC/CL A S G	ECWC A S G	UEFA A S G	OTHER A S G	TOTAL A S G
1 Bolton Wanderers	– –	4 1	– –	– –	– –	– –	– –	– –	– –	4 1
2 Oldham Athletic	– –	4 1	– –	– –	– –	– –	– –	– –	– –	4 1
3 Preston North End	– –	4 1	– –	– –	– –	– –	– –	– –	– –	4 1
4 Arsenal	– –	4 –	– –	– –	– –	– –	– –	– –	– –	4 –
5 Manchester City	– –	4 –	– –	– –	– –	– –	– –	– –	– –	4 –
6 Chelsea	– –	3 2	– –	– –	– –	– –	– –	– –	– –	3 2
7 Aston Villa	– –	2 –	– –	1 –	– –	– –	– –	– –	– –	3 –
8 Sheffield United	– –	3 –	– –	– –	– –	– –	– –	– –	– –	3 –
9 Sheffield Wednesday	– –	2 1	– –	– –	– –	– –	– –	– –	– –	2 1
10 Bradford Park Avenue	– –	2 –	– –	– –	– –	– –	– –	– –	– –	2 –
11 Burnley	– –	2 –	– –	– –	– –	– –	– –	– –	– –	2 –
12 Everton	– –	2 –	– –	– –	– –	– –	– –	– –	– –	2 –
13 Middlesbrough	– –	2 –	– –	– –	– –	– –	– –	– –	– –	2 –
14 Newcastle United	– –	2 –	– –	– –	– –	– –	– –	– –	– –	2 –
15 Notts County	– –	2 –	– –	– –	– –	– –	– –	– –	– –	2 –
16 Sunderland	– –	2 –	– –	– –	– –	– –	– –	– –	– –	2 –
17 Tottenham Hotspur	– –	2 –	– –	– –	– –	– –	– –	– –	– –	2 –
18 Blackburn Rovers	– –	1 –	– –	– –	– –	– –	– –	– –	– –	1 –
19 Bradford City	– –	1 –	– –	– –	– –	– –	– –	– –	– –	1 –
20 Derby County	– –	1 –	– –	– –	– –	– –	– –	– –	– –	1 –
21 Liverpool	– –	1 –	– –	– –	– –	– –	– –	– –	– –	1 –
22 Port Vale	– –	– –	– –	1 –	– –	– –	– –	– –	– –	1 –
23 West Bromwich Albion	– –	1 –	– –	– –	– –	– –	– –	– –	– –	1 –

JACK MELLOR

DEBUT (Full Appearance)

Monday 15/09/1930
Football League Division 1
at Leeds Road

Huddersfield Town 3 Manchester United 0

CLUB CAREER RECORD	Apps	Subs	Goals
Premiership	0		0
League Division 1	37		0
League Division 2	79		0
FA Cup	6		0
League Cup	0		0
European Cup / Champions League	0		0
European Cup-Winners' Cup	0		0
UEFA Cup / Inter-Cities' Fairs Cup	0		0
Other Matches	0		0
OVERALL TOTAL	**122**		**0**

Opponents	PREM A S G	FLD 1 A S G	FLD 2 A S G	FAC A S G	LC A S G	EC/CL A S G	ECWC A S G	UEFA A S G	OTHER A S G	TOTAL A S G
1 Stoke City	– –	– –	4 –	3 –	– –	– –	– –	– –	– –	7 –
2 Grimsby Town	– –	2 –	2 –	1 –	– –	– –	– –	– –	– –	5 –
3 Nottingham Forest	– –	– –	5 –	– –	– –	– –	– –	– –	– –	5 –
4 Bradford City	– –	– –	4 –	– –	– –	– –	– –	– –	– –	4 –
5 Bradford Park Avenue	– –	– –	4 –	– –	– –	– –	– –	– –	– –	4 –
6 Bury	– –	– –	4 –	– –	– –	– –	– –	– –	– –	4 –
7 Millwall	– –	– –	4 –	– –	– –	– –	– –	– –	– –	4 –
8 Notts County	– –	– –	4 –	– –	– –	– –	– –	– –	– –	4 –
9 Plymouth Argyle	– –	– –	3 –	1 –	– –	– –	– –	– –	– –	4 –
10 Port Vale	– –	– –	4 –	– –	– –	– –	– –	– –	– –	4 –
11 Southampton	– –	– –	4 –	– –	– –	– –	– –	– –	– –	4 –
12 Swansea City	– –	– –	4 –	– –	– –	– –	– –	– –	– –	4 –
13 Tottenham Hotspur	– –	– –	4 –	– –	– –	– –	– –	– –	– –	4 –
14 West Ham United	– –	2 –	2 –	– –	– –	– –	– –	– –	– –	4 –
15 Bolton Wanderers	– –	2 –	1 –	– –	– –	– –	– –	– –	– –	3 –
16 Charlton Athletic	– –	– –	3 –	– –	– –	– –	– –	– –	– –	3 –
17 Chesterfield	– –	– –	3 –	– –	– –	– –	– –	– –	– –	3 –
18 Leeds United	– –	2 –	1 –	– –	– –	– –	– –	– –	– –	3 –
19 Lincoln City	– –	– –	3 –	– –	– –	– –	– –	– –	– –	3 –
20 Oldham Athletic	– –	– –	3 –	– –	– –	– –	– –	– –	– –	3 –
21 Preston North End	– –	– –	3 –	– –	– –	– –	– –	– –	– –	3 –
22 Arsenal	– –	2 –	– –	– –	– –	– –	– –	– –	– –	2 –
23 Birmingham City	– –	2 –	– –	– –	– –	– –	– –	– –	– –	2 –
24 Blackburn Rovers	– –	2 –	– –	– –	– –	– –	– –	– –	– –	2 –
25 Blackpool	– –	2 –	– –	– –	– –	– –	– –	– –	– –	2 –
26 Bristol City	– –	– –	2 –	– –	– –	– –	– –	– –	– –	2 –
27 Burnley	– –	– –	2 –	– –	– –	– –	– –	– –	– –	2 –
28 Derby County	– –	2 –	– –	– –	– –	– –	– –	– –	– –	2 –

continued../

JACK MELLOR (continued)

Opponents	PREM A	S	G	FLD 1 A	S	G	FLD 2 A	S	G	FAC A	S	G	LC A	S	G	EC/CL A	S	G	ECWC A	S	G	UEFA A	S	G	OTHER A	S	G	TOTAL A	S	G
29 Fulham	–	–		–	–		2			–	–		–	–		–	–		–	–		–	–		–	–		2	–	
30 Huddersfield Town	–	–		2			–	–		–	–		–	–		–	–		–	–		–	–		–	–		2	–	
31 Leicester City	–	–		2			–	–		–	–		–	–		–	–		–	–		–	–		–	–		2	–	
32 Liverpool	–	–		2			–	–		–	–		–	–		–	–		–	–		–	–		–	–		2	–	
33 Middlesbrough	–	–		1			–	–		1			–	–		–	–		–	–		–	–		–	–		2	–	
34 Portsmouth	–	–		2			–	–		–	–		–	–		–	–		–	–		–	–		–	–		2	–	
35 Sheffield United	–	–		2			–	–		–	–		–	–		–	–		–	–		–	–		–	–		2	–	
36 Sheffield Wednesday	–	–		2			–	–		–	–		–	–		–	–		–	–		–	–		–	–		2	–	
37 Sunderland	–	–		2			–	–		–	–		–	–		–	–		–	–		–	–		–	–		2	–	
38 Wolverhampton W.	–	–		–	–		2			–	–		–	–		–	–		–	–		–	–		–	–		2	–	
39 Aston Villa	–	–		1			–	–		–	–		–	–		–	–		–	–		–	–		–	–		1	–	
40 Barnsley	–	–		–	–		–	–		1			–	–		–	–		–	–		–	–		–	–		1	–	
41 Chelsea	–	–		1			–	–		–	–		–	–		–	–		–	–		–	–		–	–		1	–	
42 Manchester City	–	–		1			–	–		–	–		–	–		–	–		–	–		–	–		–	–		1	–	
43 Newcastle United	–	–		1			–	–		–	–		–	–		–	–		–	–		–	–		–	–		1	–	
44 Norwich City	–	–		–	–		–	–		1			–	–		–	–		–	–		–	–		–	–		1	–	

ALEX MENZIES

DEBUT (Full Appearance)

Saturday 17/11/1906
Football League Division 1
at Hillsborough

Sheffield Wednesday 5 Manchester United 2

CLUB CAREER RECORD	Apps	Subs	Goals
Premiership	0		0
League Division 1	23		4
League Division 2	0		0
FA Cup	2		0
League Cup	0		0
European Cup / Champions League	0		0
European Cup-Winners' Cup	0		0
UEFA Cup / Inter-Cities' Fairs Cup	0		0
Other Matches	0		0
OVERALL TOTAL	25		4

Opponents	PREM A	S	G	FLD 1 A	S	G	FLD 2 A	S	G	FAC A	S	G	LC A	S	G	EC/CL A	S	G	ECWC A	S	G	UEFA A	S	G	OTHER A	S	G	TOTAL A	S	G
1 Aston Villa	–	–		3			–	–		–	–		–	–		–	–		–	–		–	–		–	–		3	–	
2 Liverpool	–	–		3			–	–		–	–		–	–		–	–		–	–		–	–		–	–		3	–	
3 Bury	–	–		2		1	–	–		–	–		–	–		–	–		–	–		–	–		–	–		2		1
4 Newcastle United	–	–		2		1	–	–		–	–		–	–		–	–		–	–		–	–		–	–		2		1
5 Manchester City	–	–		2			–	–		–	–		–	–		–	–		–	–		–	–		–	–		2	–	
6 Middlesbrough	–	–		2			–	–		–	–		–	–		–	–		–	–		–	–		–	–		2	–	
7 Portsmouth	–	–		–	–		–	–		2			–	–		–	–		–	–		–	–		–	–		2	–	
8 Birmingham City	–	–		1		1	–	–		–	–		–	–		–	–		–	–		–	–		–	–		1		1
9 Sheffield Wednesday	–	–		1		1	–	–		–	–		–	–		–	–		–	–		–	–		–	–		1		1
10 Arsenal	–	–		1			–	–		–	–		–	–		–	–		–	–		–	–		–	–		1	–	
11 Bristol City	–	–		1			–	–		–	–		–	–		–	–		–	–		–	–		–	–		1	–	
12 Chelsea	–	–		1			–	–		–	–		–	–		–	–		–	–		–	–		–	–		1	–	
13 Notts County	–	–		1			–	–		–	–		–	–		–	–		–	–		–	–		–	–		1	–	
14 Sheffield United	–	–		1			–	–		–	–		–	–		–	–		–	–		–	–		–	–		1	–	
15 Stoke City	–	–		1			–	–		–	–		–	–		–	–		–	–		–	–		–	–		1	–	
16 Sunderland	–	–		1			–	–		–	–		–	–		–	–		–	–		–	–		–	–				

BILLY MEREDITH

DEBUT (Full Appearance)

Tuesday 01/01/1907
Football League Division 1
at Bank Street

Manchester United 1 Aston Villa 0

CLUB CAREER RECORD	Apps	Subs	Goals
Premiership	0		0
League Division 1	303		35
League Division 2	0		0
FA Cup	29		0
League Cup	0		0
European Cup / Champions League	0		0
European Cup-Winners' Cup	0		0
UEFA Cup / Inter-Cities' Fairs Cup	0		0
Other Matches	3		1
OVERALL TOTAL	335		36

Opponents	PREM A	S	G	FLD 1 A	S	G	FLD 2 A	S	G	FAC A	S	G	LC A	S	G	EC/CL A	S	G	ECWC A	S	G	UEFA A	S	G	OTHER A	S	G	TOTAL A	S	G
1 Liverpool	–	–		19			–	–		–	–		–	–		–	–		–	–		–	–		–	–		19	–	
2 Blackburn Rovers	–	–		16		4	–	–		2			–	–		–	–		–	–		–	–		–	–		18		4
3 Aston Villa	–	–		15		3	–	–		3			–	–		–	–		–	–		–	–		–	–		18		3
4 Middlesbrough	–	–		18		1	–	–		–	–		–	–		–	–		–	–		–	–		–	–		18		1
5 Sheffield Wednesday	–	–		17		1	–	–		1			–	–		–	–		–	–		–	–		–	–		18		1
6 Everton	–	–		16		4	–	–		–	–		–	–		–	–		–	–		–	–		–	–		16		4
7 Newcastle United	–	–		14		1	–	–		1			–	–		–	–		–	–		–	–		–	–		15		1
8 Sunderland	–	–		15		1	–	–		–	–		–	–		–	–		–	–		–	–		–	–		15		1
9 Manchester City	–	–		15			–	–		–	–		–	–		–	–		–	–		–	–		–	–		15	–	
10 Bolton Wanderers	–	–		14		3	–	–		–	–		–	–		–	–		–	–		–	–		–	–		14		3

continued../

BILLY MEREDITH (continued)

Opponents	PREM			FLD 1			FLD 2			FAC			LC			EC/CL			ECWC			UEFA			OTHER			TOTAL		
	A	S	G	A	S	G	A	S	G	A	S	G	A	S	G	A	S	G	A	S	G	A	S	G	A	S	G	A	S	G
11 Chelsea	–	–	–	13	–	2	–	–	–	1	–	–	–	–	–	–	–	–	–	–	–	–	–	–	–	–	–	14	–	2
12 Notts County	–	–	–	13	–	3	–	–	–	–	–	–	–	–	–	–	–	–	–	–	–	–	–	–	–	–	–	13	–	3
13 Arsenal	–	–	–	13	–	2	–	–	–	–	–	–	–	–	–	–	–	–	–	–	–	–	–	–	–	–	–	13	–	2
14 Oldham Athletic	–	–	–	10	–	–	–	–	–	2	–	–	–	–	–	–	–	–	–	–	–	–	–	–	–	–	–	12	–	–
15 Sheffield United	–	–	–	12	–	–	–	–	–	–	–	–	–	–	–	–	–	–	–	–	–	–	–	–	–	–	–	12	–	–
16 Preston North End	–	–	–	11	–	–	–	–	–	–	–	–	–	–	–	–	–	–	–	–	–	–	–	–	–	–	–	11	–	–
17 Bury	–	–	–	10	–	2	–	–	–	–	–	–	–	–	–	–	–	–	–	–	–	–	–	–	–	–	–	10	–	2
18 Tottenham Hotspur	–	–	–	10	–	2	–	–	–	–	–	–	–	–	–	–	–	–	–	–	–	–	–	–	–	–	–	10	–	2
19 Bradford City	–	–	–	9	–	1	–	–	–	–	–	–	–	–	–	–	–	–	–	–	–	–	–	–	–	–	–	9	–	1
20 Bristol City	–	–	–	8	–	1	–	–	–	1	–	–	–	–	–	–	–	–	–	–	–	–	–	–	–	–	–	9	–	1
21 Nottingham Forest	–	–	–	7	–	–	–	–	–	–	–	–	–	–	–	–	–	–	–	–	–	–	–	–	–	–	–	7	–	–
22 West Bromwich Albion	–	–	–	7	–	–	–	–	–	–	–	–	–	–	–	–	–	–	–	–	–	–	–	–	–	–	–	7	–	–
23 Derby County	–	–	–	6	–	1	–	–	–	–	–	–	–	–	–	–	–	–	–	–	–	–	–	–	–	–	–	6	–	1
24 Burnley	–	–	–	3	–	–	–	–	–	2	–	–	–	–	–	–	–	–	–	–	–	–	–	–	–	–	–	5	–	–
25 Bradford Park Avenue	–	–	–	4	–	–	–	–	–	–	–	–	–	–	–	–	–	–	–	–	–	–	–	–	–	–	–	4	–	–
26 Birmingham City	–	–	–	3	–	2	–	–	–	–	–	–	–	–	–	–	–	–	–	–	–	–	–	–	–	–	–	3	–	2
27 Coventry City	–	–	–	–	–	–	–	–	–	3	–	–	–	–	–	–	–	–	–	–	–	–	–	–	–	–	–	3	–	–
28 Huddersfield Town	–	–	–	2	–	–	–	–	–	1	–	–	–	–	–	–	–	–	–	–	–	–	–	–	–	–	–	3	–	–
29 Queens Park Rangers	–	–	–	–	–	–	–	–	–	–	–	–	–	–	–	–	–	–	–	–	–	–	–	–	2	–	1	2	–	1
30 Blackpool	–	–	–	–	–	–	–	–	–	2	–	–	–	–	–	–	–	–	–	–	–	–	–	–	–	–	–	2	–	–
31 Leicester City	–	–	–	2	–	–	–	–	–	–	–	–	–	–	–	–	–	–	–	–	–	–	–	–	–	–	–	2	–	–
32 Portsmouth	–	–	–	–	–	–	–	–	–	2	–	–	–	–	–	–	–	–	–	–	–	–	–	–	–	–	–	2	–	–
33 Reading	–	–	–	–	–	–	–	–	–	2	–	–	–	–	–	–	–	–	–	–	–	–	–	–	–	–	–	2	–	–
34 Swindon Town	–	–	–	–	–	–	–	–	–	1	–	–	–	–	–	–	–	–	–	–	–	–	–	–	1	–	–	2	–	–
35 Stoke City	–	–	–	1	–	1	–	–	–	–	–	–	–	–	–	–	–	–	–	–	–	–	–	–	–	–	–	1	–	1
36 Brighton	–	–	–	–	–	–	–	–	–	1	–	–	–	–	–	–	–	–	–	–	–	–	–	–	–	–	–	1	–	–
37 Fulham	–	–	–	–	–	–	–	–	–	1	–	–	–	–	–	–	–	–	–	–	–	–	–	–	–	–	–	1	–	–
38 Plymouth Argyle	–	–	–	–	–	–	–	–	–	1	–	–	–	–	–	–	–	–	–	–	–	–	–	–	–	–	–	1	–	–
39 Port Vale	–	–	–	–	–	–	–	–	–	1	–	–	–	–	–	–	–	–	–	–	–	–	–	–	–	–	–	1	–	–
40 West Ham United	–	–	–	–	–	–	–	–	–	1	–	–	–	–	–	–	–	–	–	–	–	–	–	–	–	–	–	1	–	–

JACK MEW

DEBUT (Full Appearance)

Saturday 26/10/1912
Football League Division 1
at Ayresome Park

Middlesbrough 3 Manchester United 2

CLUB CAREER RECORD	Apps	Subs	Goals
Premiership	0		0
League Division 1	133		0
League Division 2	53		0
FA Cup	13		0
League Cup	0		0
European Cup / Champions League	0		0
European Cup–Winners' Cup	0		0
UEFA Cup / Inter-Cities' Fairs Cup	0		0
Other Matches	0		0
OVERALL TOTAL	199		0

Opponents	PREM			FLD 1			FLD 2			FAC			LC			EC/CL			ECWC			UEFA			OTHER			TOTAL		
	A	S	G	A	S	G	A	S	G	A	S	G	A	S	G	A	S	G	A	S	G	A	S	G	A	S	G	A	S	G
1 Bradford City	–	–	–	5	–	–	2	–	–	2	–	–	–	–	–	–	–	–	–	–	–	–	–	–	–	–	–	9	–	–
2 Liverpool	–	–	–	7	–	–	–	–	–	2	–	–	–	–	–	–	–	–	–	–	–	–	–	–	–	–	–	9	–	–
3 Burnley	–	–	–	8	–	–	–	–	–	–	–	–	–	–	–	–	–	–	–	–	–	–	–	–	–	–	–	8	–	–
4 Sunderland	–	–	–	6	–	–	–	–	–	2	–	–	–	–	–	–	–	–	–	–	–	–	–	–	–	–	–	8	–	–
5 Tottenham Hotspur	–	–	–	5	–	–	–	–	–	3	–	–	–	–	–	–	–	–	–	–	–	–	–	–	–	–	–	8	–	–
6 Aston Villa	–	–	–	6	–	–	–	–	–	1	–	–	–	–	–	–	–	–	–	–	–	–	–	–	–	–	–	7	–	–
7 Bolton Wanderers	–	–	–	7	–	–	–	–	–	–	–	–	–	–	–	–	–	–	–	–	–	–	–	–	–	–	–	7	–	–
8 Derby County	–	–	–	5	–	–	2	–	–	–	–	–	–	–	–	–	–	–	–	–	–	–	–	–	–	–	–	7	–	–
9 Middlesbrough	–	–	–	7	–	–	–	–	–	–	–	–	–	–	–	–	–	–	–	–	–	–	–	–	–	–	–	7	–	–
10 Oldham Athletic	–	–	–	6	–	–	1	–	–	–	–	–	–	–	–	–	–	–	–	–	–	–	–	–	–	–	–	7	–	–
11 Arsenal	–	–	–	6	–	–	–	–	–	–	–	–	–	–	–	–	–	–	–	–	–	–	–	–	–	–	–	6	–	–
12 Blackburn Rovers	–	–	–	6	–	–	–	–	–	–	–	–	–	–	–	–	–	–	–	–	–	–	–	–	–	–	–	6	–	–
13 Chelsea	–	–	–	6	–	–	–	–	–	–	–	–	–	–	–	–	–	–	–	–	–	–	–	–	–	–	–	6	–	–
14 Everton	–	–	–	6	–	–	–	–	–	–	–	–	–	–	–	–	–	–	–	–	–	–	–	–	–	–	–	6	–	–
15 Manchester City	–	–	–	6	–	–	–	–	–	–	–	–	–	–	–	–	–	–	–	–	–	–	–	–	–	–	–	6	–	–
16 Newcastle United	–	–	–	6	–	–	–	–	–	–	–	–	–	–	–	–	–	–	–	–	–	–	–	–	–	–	–	6	–	–
17 Sheffield United	–	–	–	6	–	–	–	–	–	–	–	–	–	–	–	–	–	–	–	–	–	–	–	–	–	–	–	6	–	–
18 West Bromwich Albion	–	–	–	6	–	–	–	–	–	–	–	–	–	–	–	–	–	–	–	–	–	–	–	–	–	–	–	6	–	–
19 Huddersfield Town	–	–	–	5	–	–	–	–	–	–	–	–	–	–	–	–	–	–	–	–	–	–	–	–	–	–	–	5	–	–
20 Preston North End	–	–	–	5	–	–	–	–	–	–	–	–	–	–	–	–	–	–	–	–	–	–	–	–	–	–	–	5	–	–
21 Bradford Park Avenue	–	–	–	4	–	–	–	–	–	–	–	–	–	–	–	–	–	–	–	–	–	–	–	–	–	–	–	4	–	–
22 Hull City	–	–	–	–	–	–	4	–	–	–	–	–	–	–	–	–	–	–	–	–	–	–	–	–	–	–	–	4	–	–
23 Notts County	–	–	–	2	–	–	2	–	–	–	–	–	–	–	–	–	–	–	–	–	–	–	–	–	–	–	–	4	–	–
24 Sheffield Wednesday	–	–	–	2	–	–	2	–	–	–	–	–	–	–	–	–	–	–	–	–	–	–	–	–	–	–	–	4	–	–
25 South Shields	–	–	–	–	–	–	4	–	–	–	–	–	–	–	–	–	–	–	–	–	–	–	–	–	–	–	–	4	–	–
26 Southampton	–	–	–	–	–	–	4	–	–	–	–	–	–	–	–	–	–	–	–	–	–	–	–	–	–	–	–	4	–	–
27 Bury	–	–	–	–	–	–	3	–	–	–	–	–	–	–	–	–	–	–	–	–	–	–	–	–	–	–	–	3	–	–
28 Cardiff City	–	–	–	2	–	–	–	–	–	1	–	–	–	–	–	–	–	–	–	–	–	–	–	–	–	–	–	3	–	–
29 Fulham	–	–	–	–	–	–	2	–	–	1	–	–	–	–	–	–	–	–	–	–	–	–	–	–	–	–	–	3	–	–
30 Leeds United	–	–	–	1	–	–	2	–	–	–	–	–	–	–	–	–	–	–	–	–	–	–	–	–	–	–	–	3	–	–
31 Port Vale	–	–	–	–	–	–	2	–	–	1	–	–	–	–	–	–	–	–	–	–	–	–	–	–	–	–	–	3	–	–

continued../

JACK MEW (continued)

Opponents	PREM A S G	FLD 1 A S G	FLD 2 A S G	FAC A S G	LC A S G	EC/CL A S G	ECWC A S G	UEFA A S G	OTHER A S G	TOTAL A S G
32 Barnsley	– – –	– – –	2 – –	– – –	– – –	– – –	– – –	– – –	– – –	2 – –
33 Birmingham City	– – –	2 – –	– – –	– – –	– – –	– – –	– – –	– – –	– – –	2 – –
34 Blackpool	– – –	– – –	– – –	2 – –	– – –	– – –	– – –	– – –	– – –	2 – –
35 Bristol City	– – –	– – –	– – –	2 – –	– – –	– – –	– – –	– – –	– – –	2 – –
36 Coventry City	– – –	– – –	– – –	2 – –	– – –	– – –	– – –	– – –	– – –	2 – –
37 Crystal Palace	– – –	– – –	– – –	2 – –	– – –	– – –	– – –	– – –	– – –	2 – –
38 Leyton Orient	– – –	– – –	– – –	2 – –	– – –	– – –	– – –	– – –	– – –	2 – –
39 Rotherham United	– – –	– – –	– – –	2 – –	– – –	– – –	– – –	– – –	– – –	2 – –
40 Stockport County	– – –	– – –	– – –	2 – –	– – –	– – –	– – –	– – –	– – –	2 – –
41 Stoke City	– – –	– – –	– – –	2 – –	– – –	– – –	– – –	– – –	– – –	2 – –
42 West Ham United	– – –	– – –	– – –	2 – –	– – –	– – –	– – –	– – –	– – –	2 – –
43 Wolverhampton W.	– – –	– – –	– – –	2 – –	– – –	– – –	– – –	– – –	– – –	2 – –
44 Leicester City	– – –	– – –	– – –	1 – –	– – –	– – –	– – –	– – –	– – –	1 – –

BOB MILARVIE

DEBUT (Full Appearance)

Saturday 04/10/1890
FA Cup 1st Qualifying Round
at North Road

Newton Heath 2 Higher Walton 0

CLUB CAREER RECORD	Apps	Subs	Goals
Premiership	0		0
League Division 1	0		0
League Division 2	0		0
FA Cup	1		0
League Cup	0		0
European Cup / Champions League	0		0
European Cup-Winners' Cup	0		0
UEFA Cup / Inter-Cities' Fairs Cup	0		0
Other Matches	0		0
OVERALL TOTAL	1		0

Opponents	PREM A S G	FLD 1 A S G	FLD 2 A S G	FAC A S G	LC A S G	EC/CL A S G	ECWC A S G	UEFA A S G	OTHER A S G	TOTAL A S G
1 Higher Walton	– – –	– – –	– – –	1 – –	– – –	– – –	– – –	– – –	– – –	1 – –

GEORGE MILLAR

DEBUT (Full Appearance, 1 goal)

Saturday 22/12/1894
Football League Division 2
at Bank Street

Newton Heath 3 Lincoln City 0

CLUB CAREER RECORD	Apps	Subs	Goals
Premiership	0		0
League Division 1	0		0
League Division 2	6		5
FA Cup	1		0
League Cup	0		0
European Cup / Champions League	0		0
European Cup-Winners' Cup	0		0
UEFA Cup / Inter-Cities' Fairs Cup	0		0
Other Matches	0		0
OVERALL TOTAL	7		5

Opponents	PREM A S G	FLD 1 A S G	FLD 2 A S G	FAC A S G	LC A S G	EC/CL A S G	ECWC A S G	UEFA A S G	OTHER A S G	TOTAL A S G
1 Port Vale	– – –	– – –	2 – 3	– – –	– – –	– – –	– – –	– – –	– – –	2 – 3
2 Lincoln City	– – –	– – –	2 – 1	– – –	– – –	– – –	– – –	– – –	– – –	2 – 1
3 Walsall	– – –	– – –	1 – 1	– – –	– – –	– – –	– – –	– – –	– – –	1 – 1
4 Bury	– – –	– – –	1 – –	– – –	– – –	– – –	– – –	– – –	– – –	1 – –
5 Stoke City	– – –	– – –	– – –	1 – –	– – –	– – –	– – –	– – –	– – –	1 – –

JAMES MILLER

DEBUT (Full Appearance)

Saturday 15/03/1924
Football League Division 2
at Old Trafford

Manchester United 1 Hull City 1

CLUB CAREER RECORD	Apps	Subs	Goals
Premiership	0		0
League Division 1	0		0
League Division 2	4		1
FA Cup	0		0
League Cup	0		0
European Cup / Champions League	0		0
European Cup-Winners' Cup	0		0
UEFA Cup / Inter-Cities' Fairs Cup	0		0
Other Matches	0		0
OVERALL TOTAL	4		1

Opponents	PREM A S G	FLD 1 A S G	FLD 2 A S G	FAC A S G	LC A S G	EC/CL A S G	ECWC A S G	UEFA A S G	OTHER A S G	TOTAL A S G
1 Hull City	– – –	– – –	2 – 1	– – –	– – –	– – –	– – –	– – –	– – –	2 – 1
2 Stoke City	– – –	– – –	2 – –	– – –	– – –	– – –	– – –	– – –	– – –	2 – –

LIAM MILLER

DEBUT (Substitute Appearance)

Wednesday 11/08/2004
Champions League Qualifying Round 1st Leg
at National Stadium

Dinamo Bucharest 1 Manchester United 2

CLUB CAREER RECORD	Apps	Subs	Goals
Premiership	3	(6)	0
League Division 1	0		0
League Division 2	0		0
FA Cup	2	(2)	0
League Cup	3		2
European Cup / Champions League	3	(3)	0
European Cup-Winners' Cup	0		0
UEFA Cup / Inter-Cities' Fairs Cup	0		0
Other Matches	0		0
OVERALL TOTAL	**11**	**(11)**	**2**

	PREM A S G	FLD 1 A S G	FLD 2 A S G	FAC A S G	LC A S G	EC/CL A S G	ECWC A S G	UEFA A S G	OTHER A S G	TOTAL A S G
1 Exeter City	– – –	– – –	– – –	2 – –	– – –	– – –	– – –	– – –	– – –	2 – –
2 Sparta Prague	– – –	– – –	– – –	– – –	– – –	2 – –	– – –	– – –	– – –	2 – –
3 Fenerbahce	– – –	– – –	– – –	– – –	– – –	1 (1) –	– – –	– – –	– – –	1 (1) –
4 Tottenham Hotspur	– (2) –	– – –	– – –	– – –	– – –	– – –	– – –	– – –	– – –	– (2) –
5 Barnet	– – –	– – –	– – –	– – –	1 – 1	– – –	– – –	– – –	– – –	1 – 1
6 Crewe Alexandra	– – –	– – –	– – –	– – –	1 – 1	– – –	– – –	– – –	– – –	1 – 1
7 Arsenal	– – –	– – –	– – –	– – –	1 – –	– – –	– – –	– – –	– – –	1 – –
8 Chelsea	1 – –	– – –	– – –	– – –	– – –	– – –	– – –	– – –	– – –	1 – –
9 Manchester City	1 – –	– – –	– – –	– – –	– – –	– – –	– – –	– – –	– – –	1 – –
10 Norwich City	1 – –	– – –	– – –	– – –	– – –	– – –	– – –	– – –	– – –	1 – –
11 Birmingham City	– (1) –	– – –	– – –	– – –	– – –	– – –	– – –	– – –	– – –	– (1) –
12 Blackburn Rovers	– (1) –	– – –	– – –	– – –	– – –	– – –	– – –	– – –	– – –	– (1) –
13 Bolton Wanderers	– (1) –	– – –	– – –	– – –	– – –	– – –	– – –	– – –	– – –	– (1) –
14 Debreceni	– – –	– – –	– – –	– – –	– – –	– (1) –	– – –	– – –	– – –	– (1) –
15 Dinamo Bucharest	– – –	– – –	– – –	– – –	– – –	– (1) –	– – –	– – –	– – –	– (1) –
16 Everton	– – –	– – –	– – –	– (1) –	– – –	– – –	– – –	– – –	– – –	– (1) –
17 Middlesbrough	– – –	– – –	– – –	– (1) –	– – –	– – –	– – –	– – –	– – –	– (1) –
18 Sunderland	– (1) –	– – –	– – –	– – –	– – –	– – –	– – –	– – –	– – –	– (1) –

TOM MILLER

DEBUT (Full Appearance)

Saturday 25/09/1920
Football League Division 1
at Old Trafford

Manchester United 0 Tottenham Hotspur 1

CLUB CAREER RECORD	Apps	Subs	Goals
Premiership	0		0
League Division 1	25		7
League Division 2	0		0
FA Cup	2		1
League Cup	0		0
European Cup / Champions League	0		0
European Cup-Winners' Cup	0		0
UEFA Cup / Inter-Cities' Fairs Cup	0		0
Other Matches	0		0
OVERALL TOTAL	**27**		**8**

	PREM A S G	FLD 1 A S G	FLD 2 A S G	FAC A S G	LC A S G	EC/CL A S G	ECWC A S G	UEFA A S G	OTHER A S G	TOTAL A S G
1 Liverpool	– – –	1 – –	– – –	2 – 1	– – –	– – –	– – –	– – –	– – –	3 – 1
2 Bradford Park Avenue	– – –	2 – 3	– – –	– – –	– – –	– – –	– – –	– – –	– – –	2 – 3
3 Manchester City	– – –	2 – 1	– – –	– – –	– – –	– – –	– – –	– – –	– – –	2 – 1
4 Oldham Athletic	– – –	2 – 1	– – –	– – –	– – –	– – –	– – –	– – –	– – –	2 – 1
5 Preston North End	– – –	2 – 1	– – –	– – –	– – –	– – –	– – –	– – –	– – –	2 – 1
6 Aston Villa	– – –	2 – –	– – –	– – –	– – –	– – –	– – –	– – –	– – –	2 – –
7 Blackburn Rovers	– – –	2 – –	– – –	– – –	– – –	– – –	– – –	– – –	– – –	2 – –
8 Huddersfield Town	– – –	2 – –	– – –	– – –	– – –	– – –	– – –	– – –	– – –	2 – –
9 Sheffield United	– – –	2 – –	– – –	– – –	– – –	– – –	– – –	– – –	– – –	2 – –
10 Tottenham Hotspur	– – –	2 – –	– – –	– – –	– – –	– – –	– – –	– – –	– – –	2 – –
11 West Bromwich Albion	– – –	2 – –	– – –	– – –	– – –	– – –	– – –	– – –	– – –	2 – –
12 Newcastle United	– – –	1 – 1	– – –	– – –	– – –	– – –	– – –	– – –	– – –	1 – 1
13 Bradford City	– – –	1 – –	– – –	– – –	– – –	– – –	– – –	– – –	– – –	1 – –
14 Burnley	– – –	1 – –	– – –	– – –	– – –	– – –	– – –	– – –	– – –	1 – –
15 Everton	– – –	1 – –	– – –	– – –	– – –	– – –	– – –	– – –	– – –	1 – –

RALPH MILNE

DEBUT (Full Appearance)

Saturday 19/11/1988
Football League Division 1
at Old Trafford

Manchester United 2 Southampton 2

CLUB CAREER RECORD	Apps	Subs	Goals
Premiership	0		0
League Division 1	19	(4)	3
League Division 2	0		0
FA Cup	7		0
League Cup	0		0
European Cup / Champions League	0		0
European Cup-Winners' Cup	0		0
UEFA Cup / Inter-Cities' Fairs Cup	0		0
Other Matches	0		0
OVERALL TOTAL	26	(4)	3

Opponents	PREM A S G	FLD 1 A S G	FLD 2 A S G	FAC A S G	LC A S G	EC/CL A S G	ECWC A S G	UEFA A S G	OTHER A S G	TOTAL A S G
1 Queens Park Rangers	– –	1 –	– –	3 –	–	–	–	–	–	4 –
2 Nottingham Forest	– –	2 1	– –	1 –	–	–	–	–	–	3 1
3 Charlton Athletic	– –	2 1	– –	–	–	–	–	–	–	2 1
4 Bournemouth	– –	– –	– –	2 –	–	–	–	–	–	2 –
5 Newcastle United	– –	2 –	–	–	–	–	–	–	–	2 –
6 Sheffield Wednesday	– –	2 –	–	–	–	–	–	–	–	2 –
7 Southampton	– –	1 (1)	–	–	–	–	–	–	–	1 (1)
8 Luton Town	– –	1 1	–	–	–	–	–	–	–	1 1
9 Arsenal	– –	1 –	–	–	–	–	–	–	–	1 –
10 Everton	– –	1 –	–	–	–	–	–	–	–	1 –
11 Liverpool	– –	1 –	–	–	–	–	–	–	–	1 –
12 Middlesbrough	– –	1 –	–	–	–	–	–	–	–	1 –
13 Millwall	– –	1 –	–	–	–	–	–	–	–	1 –
14 Norwich City	– –	1 –	–	–	–	–	–	–	–	1 –
15 Oxford United	– –	– –	–	–	1	–	–	–	–	1 –
16 Tottenham Hotspur	– –	1 –	–	–	–	–	–	–	–	1 –
17 West Ham United	– –	1 –	–	–	–	–	–	–	–	1 –
18 Aston Villa	– –	– (1) –	–	–	–	–	–	–	–	– (1)
19 Coventry City	– –	– (1) –	–	–	–	–	–	–	–	– (1)
20 Derby County	– –	– (1) –	–	–	–	–	–	–	–	– (1)

ANDREW MITCHELL (1890s)

DEBUT (Full Appearance)

Saturday 30/10/1886
FA Cup 1st Round
at Fleetwood Park

Fleetwood Rangers 2 Newton Heath 2

CLUB CAREER RECORD	Apps	Subs	Goals
Premiership	0		0
League Division 1	54		0
League Division 2	0		0
FA Cup	7		0
League Cup	0		0
European Cup / Champions League	0		0
European Cup-Winners' Cup	0		0
UEFA Cup / Inter-Cities' Fairs Cup	0		0
Other Matches	3		0
OVERALL TOTAL	64		0

Opponents	PREM A S G	FLD 1 A S G	FLD 2 A S G	FAC A S G	LC A S G	EC/CL A S G	ECWC A S G	UEFA A S G	OTHER A S G	TOTAL A S G
1 Blackburn Rovers	– –	2 –	– –	3 –	–	–	–	–	–	5 –
2 Aston Villa	– –	4 –	–	–	–	–	–	–	–	4 –
3 Burnley	– –	4 –	–	–	–	–	–	–	–	4 –
4 Derby County	– –	4 –	–	–	–	–	–	–	–	4 –
5 Nottingham Forest	– –	4 –	–	–	–	–	–	–	–	4 –
6 Preston North End	– –	4 –	–	–	–	–	–	–	–	4 –
7 Sheffield Wednesday	– –	4 –	–	–	–	–	–	–	–	4 –
8 Sunderland	– –	4 –	–	–	–	–	–	–	–	4 –
9 West Bromwich Albion	– –	4 –	–	–	–	–	–	–	–	4 –
10 Wolverhampton W.	– –	4 –	–	–	–	–	–	–	–	4 –
11 Bolton Wanderers	– –	3 –	–	–	–	–	–	–	–	3 –
12 Everton	– –	3 –	–	–	–	–	–	–	–	3 –
13 Accrington Stanley	– –	2 –	–	–	–	–	–	–	–	2 –
14 Birmingham City	– –	– –	–	–	–	–	–	–	2 –	2 –
15 Darwen	– –	2 –	–	–	–	–	–	–	–	2 –
16 Notts County	– –	2 –	–	–	–	–	–	–	–	2 –
17 Sheffield United	– –	2 –	–	–	–	–	–	–	–	2 –
18 Stoke City	– –	2 –	–	–	–	–	–	–	–	2 –
19 Bootle Reserves	– –	– –	–	1 –	–	–	–	–	–	1 –
20 Fleetwood Rangers	– –	– –	–	1 –	–	–	–	–	–	1 –
21 Higher Walton	– –	– –	–	1 –	–	–	–	–	–	1 –
22 Liverpool	– –	– –	–	–	–	–	–	–	1 –	1 –
23 Middlesbrough	– –	– –	–	1 –	–	–	–	–	–	1 –

ANDREW MITCHELL (1930s)

DEBUT (Full Appearance)

Saturday 18/03/1933
Football League Division 2
at Meadow Lane

Notts County 1 Manchester United 0

CLUB CAREER RECORD	Apps	Subs	Goals
Premiership	0		0
League Division 1	0		0
League Division 2	1		0
FA Cup	0		0
League Cup	0		0
European Cup / Champions League	0		0
European Cup-Winners' Cup	0		0
UEFA Cup / Inter-Cities' Fairs Cup	0		0
Other Matches	0		0
OVERALL TOTAL	1		0

Opponents	PREM A S G	FLD 1 A S G	FLD 2 A S G	FAC A S G	LC A S G	EC/CL A S G	ECWC A S G	UEFA A S G	OTHER A S G	TOTAL A S G
1 Notts County	– –	– –	1	– –	– –	– –	– –	– –	– –	1 –

CHARLIE MITTEN

DEBUT (Full Appearance)

Saturday 31/08/1946
Football League Division 1
at Maine Road

Manchester United 2 Grimsby Town 1

CLUB CAREER RECORD	Apps	Subs	Goals
Premiership	0		0
League Division 1	142		50
League Division 2	0		0
FA Cup	19		11
League Cup	0		0
European Cup / Champions League	0		0
European Cup-Winners' Cup	0		0
UEFA Cup / Inter-Cities' Fairs Cup	0		0
Other Matches	1		0
OVERALL TOTAL	162		61

Opponents	PREM A S G	FLD 1 A S G	FLD 2 A S G	FAC A S G	LC A S G	EC/CL A S G	ECWC A S G	UEFA A S G	OTHER A S G	TOTAL A S G
1 Portsmouth	– –	7 3	– –	2 3	– –	– –	– –	– –	– –	9 6
2 Chelsea	– –	8 4	– –	1 –	– –	– –	– –	– –	– –	9 4
3 Wolverhampton W.	– –	7 2	– –	2 1	– –	– –	– –	– –	– –	9 3
4 Aston Villa	– –	7 8	– –	1 –	– –	– –	– –	– –	– –	8 8
5 Liverpool	– –	7 3	– –	1 1	– –	– –	– –	– –	– –	8 4
6 Bolton Wanderers	– –	8 3	– –	– –	– –	– –	– –	– –	– –	8 3
7 Charlton Athletic	– –	7 2	– –	1 1	– –	– –	– –	– –	– –	8 3
8 Derby County	– –	7 1	– –	1 –	– –	– –	– –	– –	– –	8 1
9 Huddersfield Town	– –	7 4	– –	– –	– –	– –	– –	– –	– –	7 4
10 Arsenal	– –	6 2	– –	– –	– –	– –	– –	1 –	– –	7 2
11 Blackpool	– –	6 2	– –	1 –	– –	– –	– –	– –	– –	7 2
12 Everton	– –	7 –	– –	– –	– –	– –	– –	– –	– –	7 –
13 Middlesbrough	– –	7 –	– –	– –	– –	– –	– –	– –	– –	7 –
14 Burnley	– –	6 4	– –	– –	– –	– –	– –	– –	– –	6 4
15 Sunderland	– –	6 2	– –	– –	– –	– –	– –	– –	– –	6 2
16 Manchester City	– –	6 –	– –	– –	– –	– –	– –	– –	– –	6 –
17 Stoke City	– –	5 2	– –	– –	– –	– –	– –	– –	– –	5 2
18 Preston North End	– –	3 2	– –	1 1	– –	– –	– –	– –	– –	4 3
19 Grimsby Town	– –	4 2	– –	– –	– –	– –	– –	– –	– –	4 2
20 Newcastle United	– –	4 2	– –	– –	– –	– –	– –	– –	– –	4 2
21 Sheffield United	– –	4 1	– –	– –	– –	– –	– –	– –	– –	4 1
22 Birmingham City	– –	4 –	– –	– –	– –	– –	– –	– –	– –	4 –
23 Bradford Park Avenue	– –	– –	– –	3 2	– –	– –	– –	– –	– –	3 2
24 Blackburn Rovers	– –	3 –	– –	– –	– –	– –	– –	– –	– –	3 –
25 Brentford	– –	2 1	– –	– –	– –	– –	– –	– –	– –	2 1
26 Fulham	– –	2 –	– –	– –	– –	– –	– –	– –	– –	2 –
27 West Bromwich Albion	– –	2 –	– –	– –	– –	– –	– –	– –	– –	2 –
28 Bournemouth	– –	– –	– –	1 1	– –	– –	– –	– –	– –	1 1
29 Yeovil Town	– –	– –	– –	1 1	– –	– –	– –	– –	– –	1 1
30 Hull City	– –	– –	– –	1 –	– –	– –	– –	– –	– –	1 –
31 Watford	– –	– –	– –	1 –	– –	– –	– –	– –	– –	1 –
32 Weymouth Town	– –	– –	– –	1 –	– –	– –	– –	– –	– –	1 –

HARRY MOGER

DEBUT (Full Appearance)

Saturday 10/10/1903
Football League Division 2
at Bank Street

Manchester United 4 Barnsley 0

CLUB CAREER RECORD	Apps	Subs	Goals
Premiership	0		0
League Division 1	170		0
League Division 2	72		0
FA Cup	22		0
League Cup	0		0
European Cup / Champions League	0		0
European Cup-Winners' Cup	0		0
UEFA Cup / Inter-Cities' Fairs Cup	0		0
Other Matches	2		0
OVERALL TOTAL	266		0

Opponents	PREM A S G	FLD 1 A S G	FLD 2 A S G	FAC A S G	LC A S G	EC/CL A S G	ECWC A S G	UEFA A S G	OTHER A S G	TOTAL A S G
1 Bristol City	- -	8 -	4 -	1 -	-	-	-	-	-	13 -
2 Blackburn Rovers	- -	11 -	- -	1 -	-	-	-	-	-	12 -
3 Aston Villa	- -	8 -	- -	3 -	-	-	-	-	-	11 -
4 Newcastle United	- -	10 -	- -	1 -	-	-	-	-	-	11 -
5 Arsenal	- -	9 -	- -	1 -	-	-	-	-	-	10 -
6 Bradford City	- -	6 -	4 -	- -	-	-	-	-	-	10 -
7 Everton	- -	9 -	- -	1 -	-	-	-	-	-	10 -
8 Liverpool	- -	8 -	2 -	- -	-	-	-	-	-	10 -
9 Middlesbrough	- -	10 -	- -	- -	-	-	-	-	-	10 -
10 Bolton Wanderers	- -	6 -	3 -	- -	-	-	-	-	-	9 -
11 Bury	- -	9 -	- -	- -	-	-	-	-	-	9 -
12 Chelsea	- -	6 -	2 -	1 -	-	-	-	-	-	9 -
13 Preston North End	- -	9 -	- -	- -	-	-	-	-	-	9 -
14 Sheffield United	- -	9 -	- -	- -	-	-	-	-	-	9 -
15 Sunderland	- -	9 -	- -	- -	-	-	-	-	-	9 -
16 Notts County	- -	8 -	- -	- -	-	-	-	-	-	8 -
17 Leicester City	- -	2 -	5 -	- -	-	-	-	-	-	7 -
18 Manchester City	- -	7 -	- -	- -	-	-	-	-	-	7 -
19 Sheffield Wednesday	- -	7 -	- -	- -	-	-	-	-	-	7 -
20 Barnsley	- -	- -	6 -	- -	-	-	-	-	-	6 -
21 Burnley	- -	- -	4 -	2 -	-	-	-	-	-	6 -
22 Burton United	- -	- -	6 -	- -	-	-	-	-	-	6 -
23 Nottingham Forest	- -	6 -	- -	- -	-	-	-	-	-	6 -
24 Grimsby Town	- -	- -	5 -	- -	-	-	-	-	-	5 -
25 Birmingham City	- -	4 -	- -	- -	-	-	-	-	-	4 -
26 Blackpool	- -	- -	2 -	2 -	-	-	-	-	-	4 -
27 Chesterfield	- -	- -	4 -	- -	-	-	-	-	-	4 -
28 Fulham	- -	- -	- -	4 -	-	-	-	-	-	4 -
29 Port Vale	- -	- -	4 -	- -	-	-	-	-	-	4 -
30 Gainsborough Trinity	- -	- -	3 -	- -	-	-	-	-	-	3 -
31 Glossop	- -	- -	3 -	- -	-	-	-	-	-	3 -
32 Lincoln City	- -	- -	3 -	- -	-	-	-	-	-	3 -
33 Tottenham Hotspur	- -	3 -	- -	- -	-	-	-	-	-	3 -
34 West Bromwich Albion	- -	- -	3 -	- -	-	-	-	-	-	3 -
35 Derby County	- -	2 -	- -	- -	-	-	-	-	-	2 -
36 Doncaster Rovers	- -	- -	2 -	- -	-	-	-	-	-	2 -
37 Leeds United	- -	- -	2 -	- -	-	-	-	-	-	2 -
38 Leyton Orient	- -	- -	2 -	- -	-	-	-	-	-	2 -
39 Oldham Athletic	- -	2 -	- -	- -	-	-	-	-	-	2 -
40 Portsmouth	- -	- -	- -	2 -	-	-	-	-	-	2 -
41 Queens Park Rangers	- -	- -	- -	- -	-	-	-	-	2 -	2 -
42 Stockport County	- -	- -	2 -	- -	-	-	-	-	-	2 -
43 Stoke City	- -	2 -	- -	- -	-	-	-	-	-	2 -
44 Brighton	- -	- -	- -	1 -	-	-	-	-	-	1 -
45 Hull City	- -	- -	1 -	- -	-	-	-	-	-	1 -
46 Norwich City	- -	- -	- -	1 -	-	-	-	-	-	1 -
47 Staple Hill	- -	- -	- -	1 -	-	-	-	-	-	1 -

IAN MOIR

DEBUT (Full Appearance)

Saturday 01/10/1960
Football League Division 1
at Burnden Park

Bolton Wanderers 1 Manchester United 1

CLUB CAREER RECORD	Apps	Subs	Goals
Premiership	0		0
League Division 1	45		5
League Division 2	0		0
FA Cup	0		0
League Cup	0		0
European Cup / Champions League	0		0
European Cup-Winners' Cup	0		0
UEFA Cup / Inter-Cities' Fairs Cup	0		0
Other Matches	0		0
OVERALL TOTAL	45		5

Opponents	PREM A S G	FLD 1 A S G	FLD 2 A S G	FAC A S G	LC A S G	EC/CL A S G	ECWC A S G	UEFA A S G	OTHER A S G	TOTAL A S G
1 Everton	- -	4 1	- -	- -	-	-	-	-	-	4 1
2 Birmingham City	- -	4 -	- -	- -	-	-	-	-	-	4 -
3 Blackpool	- -	4 -	- -	- -	-	-	-	-	-	4 -
4 Arsenal	- -	3 1	- -	- -	-	-	-	-	-	3 1

continued../

IAN MOIR (continued)

Opponents	PREM A S G	FLD 1 A S G	FLD 2 A S G	FAC A S G	LC A S G	EC/CL A S G	ECWC A S G	UEFA A S G	OTHER A S G	TOTAL A S G
5 Ipswich Town	– –	3 1	– –	– –	– –	– –	– –	– –	– –	3 1
6 Sheffield Wednesday	– –	3 1	– –	– –	– –	– –	– –	– –	– –	3 1
7 Bolton Wanderers	– –	3 –	– –	– –	– –	– –	– –	– –	– –	3 –
8 West Bromwich Albion	– –	3	– –	– –	– –	– –	– –	– –	– –	3 –
9 Blackburn Rovers	– –	2	– –	– –	– –	– –	– –	– –	– –	2
10 Burnley	– –	2	– –	– –	– –	– –	– –	– –	– –	2 –
11 Leicester City	– –	2	– –	– –	– –	– –	– –	– –	– –	2
12 West Ham United	– –	2	– –	– –	– –	– –	– –	– –	– –	2 –
13 Sheffield United	– –	1 1	– –	– –	– –	– –	– –	– –	– –	1 1
14 Aston Villa	– –	1	– –	– –	– –	– –	– –	– –	– –	1 –
15 Chelsea	– –	1	– –	– –	– –	– –	– –	– –	– –	1
16 Fulham	– –	1	– –	– –	– –	– –	– –	– –	– –	1 –
17 Leyton Orient	– –	1	– –	– –	– –	– –	– –	– –	– –	1
18 Manchester City	– –	1	– –	– –	– –	– –	– –	– –	– –	1 –
19 Newcastle United	– –	1	– –	– –	– –	– –	– –	– –	– –	1
20 Nottingham Forest	– –	1	– –	– –	– –	– –	– –	– –	– –	1 –
21 Stoke City	– –	1	– –	– –	– –	– –	– –	– –	– –	1
22 Wolverhampton W.	– –	1	– –	– –	– –	– –	– –	– –	– –	1 –

ARCHIE MONTGOMERY

DEBUT (Full Appearance)

Saturday 16/09/1905
Football League Division 2
at North Road

Glossop 1 Manchester United 2

CLUB CAREER RECORD	Apps	Subs	Goals
Premiership	0		0
League Division 1	0		0
League Division 2	3		0
FA Cup	0		0
League Cup	0		0
European Cup / Champions League	0		0
European Cup-Winners' Cup	0		0
UEFA Cup / Inter-Cities' Fairs Cup	0		0
Other Matches	0		0
OVERALL TOTAL	3		0

Opponents	PREM A S G	FLD 1 A S G	FLD 2 A S G	FAC A S G	LC A S G	EC/CL A S G	ECWC A S G	UEFA A S G	OTHER A S G	TOTAL A S G
1 Blackpool	– –	– –	1 –	– –	– –	– –	– –	– –	– –	1 –
2 Glossop	– –	– –	1 –	– –	– –	– –	– –	– –	– –	1 –
3 Stockport County	– –	– –	1 –	– –	– –	– –	– –	– –	– –	1 –

JAMES MONTGOMERY

DEBUT (Full Appearance)

Saturday 13/03/1915
Football League Division 1
at Old Trafford

Manchester United 1 Bradford City 0

CLUB CAREER RECORD	Apps	Subs	Goals
Premiership	0		0
League Division 1	27		1
League Division 2	0		0
FA Cup	0		0
League Cup	0		0
European Cup / Champions League	0		0
European Cup-Winners' Cup	0		0
UEFA Cup / Inter-Cities' Fairs Cup	0		0
Other Matches	0		0
OVERALL TOTAL	27		1

Opponents	PREM A S G	FLD 1 A S G	FLD 2 A S G	FAC A S G	LC A S G	EC/CL A S G	ECWC A S G	UEFA A S G	OTHER A S G	TOTAL A S G
1 Preston North End	– –	2 1	– –	– –	– –	– –	– –	– –	– –	2 1
2 Aston Villa	– –	2	– –	– –	– –	– –	– –	– –	– –	2 –
3 Blackburn Rovers	– –	2	– –	– –	– –	– –	– –	– –	– –	2 –
4 Bolton Wanderers	– –	2	– –	– –	– –	– –	– –	– –	– –	2 –
5 Bradford City	– –	2	– –	– –	– –	– –	– –	– –	– –	2 –
6 Bradford Park Avenue	– –	2	– –	– –	– –	– –	– –	– –	– –	2 –
7 Derby County	– –	2	– –	– –	– –	– –	– –	– –	– –	2 –
8 Middlesbrough	– –	2	– –	– –	– –	– –	– –	– –	– –	2 –
9 Sheffield Wednesday	– –	2	– –	– –	– –	– –	– –	– –	– –	2 –
10 Tottenham Hotspur	– –	2	– –	– –	– –	– –	– –	– –	– –	2 –
11 Burnley	– –	1	– –	– –	– –	– –	– –	– –	– –	1 –
12 Chelsea	– –	1	– –	– –	– –	– –	– –	– –	– –	1 –
13 Liverpool	– –	1	– –	– –	– –	– –	– –	– –	– –	1 –
14 Newcastle United	– –	1	– –	– –	– –	– –	– –	– –	– –	1 –
15 Notts County	– –	1	– –	– –	– –	– –	– –	– –	– –	1 –
16 Oldham Athletic	– –	1	– –	– –	– –	– –	– –	– –	– –	1 –
17 Sheffield United	– –	1	– –	– –	– –	– –	– –	– –	– –	1 –

JOHN MOODY

DEBUT (Full Appearance)

Saturday 26/03/1932
Football League Division 2
at Old Trafford

Manchester United 5 Oldham Athletic 1

CLUB CAREER RECORD	Apps	Subs	Goals
Premiership	0		0
League Division 1	0		0
League Division 2	50		0
FA Cup	1		0
League Cup	0		0
European Cup / Champions League	0		0
European Cup–Winners' Cup	0		0
UEFA Cup / Inter-Cities' Fairs Cup	0		0
Other Matches	0		0
OVERALL TOTAL	51		0

Opponents	PREM A	S	G	FLD 1 A	S	G	FLD 2 A	S	G	FAC A	S	G	LC A	S	G	EC/CL A	S	G	ECWC A	S	G	UEFA A	S	G	OTHER A	S	G	TOTAL A	S	G
1 Bradford City	–	–		–	–		3	–		–	–		–	–		–	–		–	–		–	–		–	–		3	–	
2 Bury	–	–		–	–		3	–		–	–		–	–		–	–		–	–		–	–		–	–		3	–	
3 Charlton Athletic	–	–		–	–		3	–		–	–		–	–		–	–		–	–		–	–		–	–		3	–	
4 Millwall	–	–		–	–		3	–		–	–		–	–		–	–		–	–		–	–		–	–		3	–	
5 Oldham Athletic	–	–		–	–		3	–		–	–		–	–		–	–		–	–		–	–		–	–		3	–	
6 Port Vale	–	–		–	–		3	–		–	–		–	–		–	–		–	–		–	–		–	–		3	–	
7 Southampton	–	–		–	–		3	–		–	–		–	–		–	–		–	–		–	–		–	–		3	–	
8 Bradford Park Avenue	–	–		–	–		2	–		–	–		–	–		–	–		–	–		–	–		–	–		2	–	
9 Burnley	–	–		–	–		2	–		–	–		–	–		–	–		–	–		–	–		–	–		2	–	
10 Chesterfield	–	–		–	–		2	–		–	–		–	–		–	–		–	–		–	–		–	–		2	–	
11 Fulham	–	–		–	–		2	–		–	–		–	–		–	–		–	–		–	–		–	–		2	–	
12 Grimsby Town	–	–		–	–		2	–		–	–		–	–		–	–		–	–		–	–		–	–		2	–	
13 Lincoln City	–	–		–	–		2	–		–	–		–	–		–	–		–	–		–	–		–	–		2	–	
14 Nottingham Forest	–	–		–	–		2	–		–	–		–	–		–	–		–	–		–	–		–	–		2	–	
15 Notts County	–	–		–	–		2	–		–	–		–	–		–	–		–	–		–	–		–	–		2	–	
16 Plymouth Argyle	–	–		–	–		2	–		–	–		–	–		–	–		–	–		–	–		–	–		2	–	
17 Preston North End	–	–		–	–		2	–		–	–		–	–		–	–		–	–		–	–		–	–		2	–	
18 Stoke City	–	–		–	–		2	–		–	–		–	–		–	–		–	–		–	–		–	–		2	–	
19 Swansea City	–	–		–	–		2	–		–	–		–	–		–	–		–	–		–	–		–	–		2	–	
20 Tottenham Hotspur	–	–		–	–		2	–		–	–		–	–		–	–		–	–		–	–		–	–		2	–	
21 West Ham United	–	–		–	–		2	–		–	–		–	–		–	–		–	–		–	–		–	–		2	–	
22 Bristol City	–	–		–	–		1	–		–	–		–	–		–	–		–	–		–	–		–	–		1	–	
23 Middlesbrough	–	–		–	–		–	–		1	–		–	–		–	–		–	–		–	–		–	–		1	–	

CHARLIE MOORE

DEBUT (Full Appearance)

Saturday 30/08/1919
Football League Division 1
at Baseball Ground

Derby County 1 Manchester United 1

CLUB CAREER RECORD	Apps	Subs	Goals
Premiership	0		0
League Division 1	215		0
League Division 2	94		0
FA Cup	19		0
League Cup	0		0
European Cup / Champions League	0		0
European Cup–Winners' Cup	0		0
UEFA Cup / Inter-Cities' Fairs Cup	0		0
Other Matches	0		0
OVERALL TOTAL	328		0

Opponents	PREM A	S	G	FLD 1 A	S	G	FLD 2 A	S	G	FAC A	S	G	LC A	S	G	EC/CL A	S	G	ECWC A	S	G	UEFA A	S	G	OTHER A	S	G	TOTAL A	S	G
1 Blackburn Rovers	–	–		14	–		–	–		1	–		–	–		–	–		–	–		–	–		–	–		15	–	
2 Sheffield Wednesday	–	–		8	–		5	–		1	–		–	–		–	–		–	–		–	–		–	–		14	–	
3 Aston Villa	–	–		12	–		–	–		1	–		–	–		–	–		–	–		–	–		–	–		13	–	
4 Derby County	–	–		8	–		4	–		–	–		–	–		–	–		–	–		–	–		–	–		12	–	
5 Leicester City	–	–		8	–		4	–		–	–		–	–		–	–		–	–		–	–		–	–		12	–	
6 Burnley	–	–		11	–		–	–		–	–		–	–		–	–		–	–		–	–		–	–		11	–	
7 Everton	–	–		11	–		–	–		–	–		–	–		–	–		–	–		–	–		–	–		11	–	
8 Newcastle United	–	–		11	–		–	–		–	–		–	–		–	–		–	–		–	–		–	–		11	–	
9 Bolton Wanderers	–	–		10	–		–	–		–	–		–	–		–	–		–	–		–	–		–	–		10	–	
10 Huddersfield Town	–	–		9	–		–	–		1	–		–	–		–	–		–	–		–	–		–	–		10	–	
11 Liverpool	–	–		10	–		–	–		–	–		–	–		–	–		–	–		–	–		–	–		10	–	
12 Middlesbrough	–	–		8	–		2	–		–	–		–	–		–	–		–	–		–	–		–	–		10	–	
13 Sunderland	–	–		8	–		–	–		2	–		–	–		–	–		–	–		–	–		–	–		10	–	
14 Leeds United	–	–		6	–		3	–		–	–		–	–		–	–		–	–		–	–		–	–		9	–	
15 Manchester City	–	–		8	–		–	–		1	–		–	–		–	–		–	–		–	–		–	–		9	–	
16 Tottenham Hotspur	–	–		7	–		–	–		2	–		–	–		–	–		–	–		–	–		–	–		9	–	
17 Arsenal	–	–		8	–		–	–		–	–		–	–		–	–		–	–		–	–		–	–		8	–	
18 Bradford City	–	–		4	–		4	–		–	–		–	–		–	–		–	–		–	–		–	–		8	–	
19 Bury	–	–		5	–		2	–		1	–		–	–		–	–		–	–		–	–		–	–		8	–	
20 Birmingham City	–	–		7	–		–	–		–	–		–	–		–	–		–	–		–	–		–	–		7	–	
21 Port Vale	–	–		–	–		4	–		3	–		–	–		–	–		–	–		–	–		–	–		7	–	
22 Portsmouth	–	–		5	–		2	–		–	–		–	–		–	–		–	–		–	–		–	–		7	–	
23 Sheffield United	–	–		7	–		–	–		–	–		–	–		–	–		–	–		–	–		–	–		7	–	
24 West Ham United	–	–		7	–		–	–		–	–		–	–		–	–		–	–		–	–		–	–		7	–	
25 Coventry City	–	–		–	–		6	–		–	–		–	–		–	–		–	–		–	–		–	–		6	–	
26 Barnsley	–	–		–	–		5	–		–	–		–	–		–	–		–	–		–	–		–	–		5	–	
27 Cardiff City	–	–		5	–		–	–		–	–		–	–		–	–		–	–		–	–		–	–		5	–	
28 Crystal Palace	–	–		–	–		5	–		–	–		–	–		–	–		–	–		–	–		–	–		5	–	

continued../

CHARLIE MOORE (continued)

Opponents	PREM A S G	FLD 1 A S G	FLD 2 A S G	FAC A S G	LC A S G	EC/CL A S G	ECWC A S G	UEFA A S G	OTHER A S G	TOTAL A S G
29 Fulham	– – –	– – –	4 – –	1 – –	– – –	– – –	– – –	– – –	– – –	5 – –
30 Hull City	– – –	– – –	5 – –	– – –	– – –	– – –	– – –	– – –	– – –	5 – –
31 Oldham Athletic	– – –	1 – –	4 – –	– – –	– – –	– – –	– – –	– – –	– – –	5 – –
32 West Bromwich Albion	– – –	5 – –	– – –	– – –	– – –	– – –	– – –	– – –	– – –	5 – –
33 Blackpool	– – –	– – –	4 – –	– – –	– – –	– – –	– – –	– – –	– – –	4 – –
34 Chelsea	– – –	2 – –	2 – –	– – –	– – –	– – –	– – –	– – –	– – –	4 – –
35 Leyton Orient	– – –	– – –	4 – –	– – –	– – –	– – –	– – –	– – –	– – –	4 – –
36 South Shields	– – –	– – –	4 – –	– – –	– – –	– – –	– – –	– – –	– – –	4 – –
37 Southampton	– – –	– – –	4 – –	– – –	– – –	– – –	– – –	– – –	– – –	4 – –
38 Stockport County	– – –	– – –	4 – –	– – –	– – –	– – –	– – –	– – –	– – –	4 – –
39 Stoke City	– – –	– – –	4 – –	– – –	– – –	– – –	– – –	– – –	– – –	4 – –
40 Wolverhampton W.	– – –	– – –	4 – –	– – –	– – –	– – –	– – –	– – –	– – –	4 – –
41 Bradford Park Avenue	– – –	3 – –	– – –	– – –	– – –	– – –	– – –	– – –	– – –	3 – –
42 Notts County	– – –	3 – –	– – –	– – –	– – –	– – –	– – –	– – –	– – –	3 – –
43 Reading	– – –	– – –	– – –	3 – –	– – –	– – –	– – –	– – –	– – –	3 – –
44 Bristol City	– – –	– – –	2 – –	– – –	– – –	– – –	– – –	– – –	– – –	2 – –
45 Grimsby Town	– – –	2 – –	– – –	– – –	– – –	– – –	– – –	– – –	– – –	2 – –
46 Nelson	– – –	– – –	2 – –	– – –	– – –	– – –	– – –	– – –	– – –	2 – –
47 Preston North End	– – –	2 – –	– – –	– – –	– – –	– – –	– – –	– – –	– – –	2 – –
48 Plymouth Argyle	– – –	– – –	– – –	1 – –	– – –	– – –	– – –	– – –	– – –	1 – –
49 Rotherham United	– – –	– – –	1 – –	– – –	– – –	– – –	– – –	– – –	– – –	1 – –
50 Swindon Town	– – –	– – –	– – –	1 – –	– – –	– – –	– – –	– – –	– – –	1 – –

GRAHAM MOORE

DEBUT (Full Appearance)

Saturday 09/11/1963
Football League Division 1
at Old Trafford

Manchester United 4 Tottenham Hotspur 1

CLUB CAREER RECORD	Apps	Subs	Goals
Premiership	0		0
League Division 1	18		4
League Division 2	0		0
FA Cup	1		1
League Cup	0		0
European Cup / Champions League	0		0
European Cup-Winners' Cup	0		0
UEFA Cup / Inter-Cities' Fairs Cup	0		0
Other Matches	0		0
OVERALL TOTAL	19		5

Opponents	PREM A S G	FLD 1 A S G	FLD 2 A S G	FAC A S G	LC A S G	EC/CL A S G	ECWC A S G	UEFA A S G	OTHER A S G	TOTAL A S G
1 Burnley	– – –	2 – 2	– – –	– – –	– – –	– – –	– – –	– – –	– – –	2 – 2
2 Tottenham Hotspur	– – –	2 – 1	– – –	– – –	– – –	– – –	– – –	– – –	– – –	2 – 1
3 Fulham	– – –	2 – –	– – –	– – –	– – –	– – –	– – –	– – –	– – –	2 – –
4 Nottingham Forest	– – –	1 – 1	– – –	– – –	– – –	– – –	– – –	– – –	– – –	1 – 1
5 Southampton	– – –	– – –	– – –	1 – 1	– – –	– – –	– – –	– – –	– – –	1 – 1
6 Arsenal	– – –	1 – –	– – –	– – –	– – –	– – –	– – –	– – –	– – –	1 – –
7 Aston Villa	– – –	1 – –	– – –	– – –	– – –	– – –	– – –	– – –	– – –	1 – –
8 Birmingham City	– – –	1 – –	– – –	– – –	– – –	– – –	– – –	– – –	– – –	1 – –
9 Chelsea	– – –	1 – –	– – –	– – –	– – –	– – –	– – –	– – –	– – –	1 – –
10 Everton	– – –	1 – –	– – –	– – –	– – –	– – –	– – –	– – –	– – –	1 – –
11 Leicester City	– – –	1 – –	– – –	– – –	– – –	– – –	– – –	– – –	– – –	1 – –
12 Liverpool	– – –	1 – –	– – –	– – –	– – –	– – –	– – –	– – –	– – –	1 – –
13 Sheffield United	– – –	1 – –	– – –	– – –	– – –	– – –	– – –	– – –	– – –	1 – –
14 Sheffield Wednesday	– – –	1 – –	– – –	– – –	– – –	– – –	– – –	– – –	– – –	1 – –
15 Stoke City	– – –	1 – –	– – –	– – –	– – –	– – –	– – –	– – –	– – –	1 – –
16 West Bromwich Albion	– – –	1 – –	– – –	– – –	– – –	– – –	– – –	– – –	– – –	1 – –

KEVIN MORAN

DEBUT (Full Appearance)

Monday 30/04/1979
Football League Division 1
at The Dell

Southampton 1 Manchester United 1

CLUB CAREER RECORD	Apps	Subs	Goals
Premiership	0		0
League Division 1	228	(3)	21
League Division 2	0		0
FA Cup	18		1
League Cup	24	(1)	2
European Cup / Champions League	0		0
European Cup-Winners' Cup	8		0
UEFA Cup / Inter-Cities' Fairs Cup	5	(1)	0
Other Matches	1		0
OVERALL TOTAL	284	(5)	24

Opponents	PREM A S G	FLD 1 A S G	FLD 2 A S G	FAC A S G	LC A S G	EC/CL A S G	ECWC A S G	UEFA A S G	OTHER A S G	TOTAL A S G
1 Liverpool	– – –	14 – 1	– – –	– – –	2 – –	– – –	– – –	– – –	1 – –	17 – 1
2 Southampton	– – –	14 – –	– – –	– – –	1 (1) –	– – –	– – –	– – –	– – –	15 (1) –
3 Arsenal	– – –	12 – 1	– – –	1 – –	2 – 1	– – –	– – –	– – –	– – –	15 – 2
4 Everton	– – –	11 – –	– – –	2 – –	1 – –	– – –	– – –	– – –	– – –	14 – –
5 Tottenham Hotspur	– – –	11 – 2	– – –	– – –	2 – –	– – –	– – –	– – –	– – –	13 – 2

continued../

KEVIN MORAN (continued)

Opponents	PREM A S G	FLD 1 A S G	FLD 2 A S G	FAC A S G	LC A S G	EC/CL A S G	ECWC A S G	UEFA A S G	OTHER A S G	TOTAL A S G
6 Coventry City	– –	11 –	–	– – 2 –	–	–	–	–	–	13 –
7 Nottingham Forest	– –	11 1	–	–	– – 1	–	–	–	–	12 1
8 West Bromwich Albion	– –	11 (1) 1	–	–	–	–	–	–	–	11 (1) 1
9 West Ham United	– –	8 2	–	– – 2	– – 1	–	–	–	–	11 2
10 Norwich City	– –	9 (2) 2	–	–	–	–	–	–	–	9 (2) 2
11 Aston Villa	– –	10 2	–	–	–	–	–	–	–	10 2
12 Watford	– –	8 1	–	– – 1	–	–	–	–	–	9 1
13 Ipswich Town	– –	8 –	–	–	– – 1	–	–	–	–	9 –
14 Luton Town	– –	7 –	–	– – 1 1	–	–	–	–	–	8 1
15 Sunderland	– –	5 4	–	– – 2	–	–	–	–	–	7 4
16 Birmingham City	– –	7 1	–	–	–	–	–	–	–	7 1
17 Manchester City	– –	6 1	–	– – 1	–	–	–	–	–	7 1
18 Brighton	– –	4 –	–	– – 3	–	–	–	–	–	7 –
19 Oxford United	– –	3 –	–	–	– – 4	–	–	–	–	7 –
20 Stoke City	– –	7 –	–	–	–	–	–	–	–	7 –
21 Newcastle United	– –	6 1	–	–	–	–	–	–	–	6 1
22 Crystal Palace	– –	3 –	–	–	– – 3	–	–	–	–	6 –
23 Queens Park Rangers	– –	6 –	–	–	–	–	–	–	–	6 –
24 Chelsea	– –	5 –	–	–	–	–	–	–	–	5 –
25 Wolverhampton W.	– –	5 –	–	–	–	–	–	–	–	5 –
26 Notts County	– –	4 1	–	–	–	–	–	–	–	4 1
27 Leicester City	– –	4 –	–	–	–	–	–	–	–	4 –
28 Charlton Athletic	– –	3 –	–	–	–	–	–	–	–	3 –
29 Leeds United	– –	3 –	–	–	–	–	–	–	–	3 –
30 Port Vale	– –	–	–	–	– – 3	–	–	–	–	3 –
31 Sheffield Wednesday	– –	3 –	–	–	–	–	–	–	–	3 –
32 Swansea City	– –	3 –	–	–	–	–	–	–	–	3 –
33 Wimbledon	– –	3 –	–	–	–	–	–	–	–	3 –
34 Barcelona	– –	–	–	–	–	–	2 –	–	–	2 –
35 Dukla Prague	– –	–	–	–	–	–	2 –	–	–	2 –
36 Juventus	– –	–	–	–	–	–	2 –	–	–	2 –
37 Middlesbrough	– –	2 –	–	–	–	–	–	–	–	2 –
38 PSV Eindhoven	– –	–	–	–	–	–	–	2 –	–	2 –
39 Raba Vasas	– –	–	–	–	–	–	–	2 –	–	2 –
40 Spartak Varna	– –	–	–	–	–	–	2 –	–	–	2 –
41 Bradford City	– –	–	–	–	– – 1 1	–	–	–	–	1 1
42 Blackburn Rovers	– –	–	–	– – 1	–	–	–	–	–	1 –
43 Bournemouth	– –	–	–	–	– – 1	–	–	–	–	1 –
44 Burnley	– –	–	–	–	– – 1	–	–	–	–	1 –
45 Colchester United	– –	–	–	–	– – 1	–	–	–	–	1 –
46 Derby County	– –	–	–	– – 1	–	–	–	–	–	1 –
47 Portsmouth	– –	1 –	–	–	–	–	–	–	–	1 –
48 Valencia	– –	–	–	–	–	–	–	1 –	–	1 –
49 Widzew Lodz	– –	–	–	–	–	–	–	– (1) –	–	– (1) –

BILLY MORGAN

DEBUT (Full Appearance)

Tuesday 02/03/1897
Football League Division 2
at Bank Street

Newton Heath 3 Darwen 1

CLUB CAREER RECORD	Apps	Subs	Goals
Premiership	0		0
League Division 1	0		0
League Division 2	143		6
FA Cup	9		1
League Cup	0		0
European Cup / Champions League	0		0
European Cup–Winners' Cup	0		0
UEFA Cup / Inter–Cities' Fairs Cup	0		0
Other Matches	0		0
OVERALL TOTAL	**152**		**7**

Opponents	PREM A S G	FLD 1 A S G	FLD 2 A S G	FAC A S G	LC A S G	EC/CL A S G	ECWC A S G	UEFA A S G	OTHER A S G	TOTAL A S G
1 Lincoln City	– –	–	10 –	– – 1	–	–	–	–	–	11 –
2 Arsenal	– –	–	10 –	–	–	–	–	–	–	10 –
3 Gainsborough Trinity	– –	–	9 –	–	–	–	–	–	–	9 –
4 Birmingham City	– –	–	8 1	–	–	–	–	–	–	8 1
5 Port Vale	– –	–	8 –	–	–	–	–	–	–	8 –
6 Barnsley	– –	–	7 1	–	–	–	–	–	–	7 1
7 Burnley	– –	–	4 –	– – 2	–	–	–	–	–	6 –
8 Chesterfield	– –	–	6 –	–	–	–	–	–	–	6 –
9 Glossop	– –	–	6 –	–	–	–	–	–	–	6 –
10 Grimsby Town	– –	–	6 –	–	–	–	–	–	–	6 –
11 Leicester City	– –	–	6 –	–	–	–	–	–	–	6 –
12 Loughborough Town	– –	–	6 –	–	–	–	–	–	–	6 –
13 New Brighton Tower	– –	–	6 –	–	–	–	–	–	–	6 –
14 Blackpool	– –	–	5 1	–	–	–	–	–	–	5 1
15 Luton Town	– –	–	5 1	–	–	–	–	–	–	5 1
16 Walsall	– –	–	5 1	–	–	–	–	–	–	5 1
17 Burton Swifts	– –	–	5 –	–	–	–	–	–	–	5 –

continued../

BILLY MORGAN (continued)

Opponents	PREM A S G	FLD 1 A S G	FLD 2 A S G	FAC A S G	LC A S G	EC/CL A S G	ECWC A S G	UEFA A S G	OTHER A S G	TOTAL A S G
18 Middlesbrough	– –	– –	5 –	– –	– –	– –	– –	– –	– –	5 –
19 Bristol City	– –	– –	4 –	– –	– –	– –	– –	– –	– –	4 –
20 Burton United	– –	– –	4 –	– –	– –	– –	– –	– –	– –	4 –
21 Stockport County	– –	– –	4 –	– –	– –	– –	– –	– –	– –	4 –
22 Darwen	– –	– –	2 1	– –	– –	– –	– –	– –	– –	2 1
23 Bolton Wanderers	– –	– –	2 –	– –	– –	– –	– –	– –	– –	2 –
24 Doncaster Rovers	– –	– –	2 –	– –	– –	– –	– –	– –	– –	2 –
25 Preston North End	– –	– –	2 –	– –	– –	– –	– –	– –	– –	2 –
26 Sheffield Wednesday	– –	– –	2 –	– –	– –	– –	– –	– –	– –	2 –
27 Tottenham Hotspur	– –	– –	– –	2 –	– –	– –	– –	– –	– –	2 –
28 West Bromwich Albion	– –	– –	2 –	– –	– –	– –	– –	– –	– –	2 –
29 Accrington Stanley	– –	– –	– –	– –	1 1	– –	– –	– –	– –	1 1
30 Burton Wanderers	– –	– –	1 –	– –	– –	– –	– –	– –	– –	1 –
31 Manchester City	– –	– –	1 –	– –	– –	– –	– –	– –	– –	1 –
32 Oswaldtwistle Rovers	– –	– –	– –	– –	1 –	– –	– –	– –	– –	1 –
33 Portsmouth	– –	– –	– –	1 –	– –	– –	– –	– –	– –	1 –
34 South Shore	– –	– –	– –	1 –	– –	– –	– –	– –	– –	1 –

HUGH MORGAN

DEBUT (Full Appearance, 1 goal)

Saturday 15/12/1900
Football League Division 2
at Bank Street

Newton Heath 4 Lincoln City 1

CLUB CAREER RECORD	Apps	Subs	Goals
Premiership	0		0
League Division 1	0		0
League Division 2	20		4
FA Cup	3		0
League Cup	0		0
European Cup / Champions League	0		0
European Cup-Winners' Cup	0		0
UEFA Cup / Inter-Cities' Fairs Cup	0		0
Other Matches	0		0
OVERALL TOTAL	**23**		**4**

Opponents	PREM A S G	FLD 1 A S G	FLD 2 A S G	FAC A S G	LC A S G	EC/CL A S G	ECWC A S G	UEFA A S G	OTHER A S G	TOTAL A S G
1 Burnley	– –	– –	1 –	2 –	– –	– –	– –	– –	– –	3 –
2 Lincoln City	– –	– –	2 1	– –	– –	– –	– –	– –	– –	2 1
3 Barnsley	– –	– –	2 –	– –	– –	– –	– –	– –	– –	2 –
4 Blackpool	– –	– –	2 –	– –	– –	– –	– –	– –	– –	2 –
5 Glossop	– –	– –	1 1	– –	– –	– –	– –	– –	– –	1 1
6 Grimsby Town	– –	– –	1 1	– –	– –	– –	– –	– –	– –	1 1
7 Stockport County	– –	– –	1 1	– –	– –	– –	– –	– –	– –	1 1
8 Arsenal	– –	– –	1 –	– –	– –	– –	– –	– –	– –	1 –
9 Birmingham City	– –	– –	1 –	– –	– –	– –	– –	– –	– –	1 –
10 Burton Swifts	– –	– –	1 –	– –	– –	– –	– –	– –	– –	1 –
11 Chesterfield	– –	– –	1 –	– –	– –	– –	– –	– –	– –	1 –
12 Gainsborough Trinity	– –	– –	1 –	– –	– –	– –	– –	– –	– –	1 –
13 Leicester City	– –	– –	1 –	– –	– –	– –	– –	– –	– –	1 –
14 Middlesbrough	– –	– –	1 –	– –	– –	– –	– –	– –	– –	1 –
15 New Brighton Tower	– –	– –	1 –	– –	– –	– –	– –	– –	– –	1 –
16 Port Vale	– –	– –	1 –	– –	– –	– –	– –	– –	– –	1 –
17 Portsmouth	– –	– –	– –	1 –	– –	– –	– –	– –	– –	1 –
18 Walsall	– –	– –	1 –	– –	– –	– –	– –	– –	– –	1 –

WILLIE MORGAN

DEBUT (Full Appearance)

Wednesday 28/08/1968
Football League Division 1
at Old Trafford

Manchester United 3 Tottenham Hotspur 1

CLUB CAREER RECORD	Apps	Subs	Goals
Premiership	0		0
League Division 1	204		22
League Division 2	32	(2)	3
FA Cup	27		4
League Cup	24	(1)	3
European Cup / Champions League	4		1
European Cup-Winners' Cup	0		0
UEFA Cup / Inter-Cities' Fairs Cup	0		0
Other Matches	2		1
OVERALL TOTAL	**293**	**(3)**	**34**

Opponents	PREM A S G	FLD 1 A S G	FLD 2 A S G	FAC A S G	LC A S G	EC/CL A S G	ECWC A S G	UEFA A S G	OTHER A S G	TOTAL A S G
1 Stoke City	– –	9 2	– –	2 –	3 –	– –	– –	– –	– –	14 2
2 Southampton	– –	9 2	2 –	2 –	– –	– –	– –	– –	– –	13 2
3 Ipswich Town	– –	9 –	– –	2 –	1 1	– –	– –	– –	– –	12 1
4 Leeds United	– –	9 –	– –	3 –	– –	– –	– –	– –	– –	12 –
5 Wolverhampton W.	– –	11 –	– –	1 –	– –	– –	– –	– –	– –	12 –
6 Burnley	– –	7 –	– –	– –	4 (1) 1	– –	– –	– –	– –	11 (1) 1
7 Newcastle United	– –	11 –	– –	– –	– –	– –	– –	– –	– –	11 –
8 West Ham United	– –	11 –	– –	– –	– –	– –	– –	– –	– –	11 –

continued../

WILLIE MORGAN (continued)

Opponents	PREM A	S	G	FLD 1 A	S	G	FLD 2 A	S	G	FAC A	S	G	LC A	S	G	EC/CL A	S	G	ECWC A	S	G	UEFA A	S	G	OTHER A	S	G	TOTAL A	S	G
9 Chelsea	-	-		10		4	-	-		-	-		-	-		-	-		-	-		-	-		-	-		10		4
10 Middlesbrough	-	-		-	-		-	-		6		2	4			-	-		-	-		-	-		-	-		10		2
11 Arsenal	-	-		10		1	-	-		-	-		-	-		-	-		-	-		-	-		-	-		10		1
12 Derby County	-	-		10		1	-	-		-	-		-	-		-	-		-	-		-	-		-	-		10		1
13 Manchester City	-	-		7		-	-	-		1		1	2			-	-		-	-		-	-		-	-		10		1
14 Tottenham Hotspur	-	-		10		1	-	-		-	-		-	-		-	-		-	-		-	-		-	-		10		1
15 Liverpool	-	-		9		2	-	-		-	-		-	-		-	-		-	-		-	-		-	-		9		2
16 Everton	-	-		8		-	-	-		1			-	-		-	-		-	-		-	-		-	-		9		-
17 West Bromwich Albion	-	-		7		-	2			-	-		-	-		-	-		-	-		-	-		-	-		9		-
18 Coventry City	-	-		8		1	-	-		-	-		-	-		-	-		-	-		-	-		-	-		8		1
19 Leicester City	-	-		8		1	-	-		-	-		-	-		-	-		-	-		-	-		-	-		8		1
20 Crystal Palace	-	-		7		2	-	-		-	-		-	-		-	-		-	-		-	-		-	-		7		2
21 Nottingham Forest	-	-		6		2	1			-	-		-	-		-	-		-	-		-	-		-	-		7		2
22 Norwich City	-	-		4		-	-	-		1			2			-	-		-	-		-	-		-	-		7		-
23 Sunderland	-	-		4		-	2		1	-	-		-	-		-	-		-	-		-	-		-	-		6		1
24 Sheffield Wednesday	-	-		4		-	2			-	-		-	-		-	-		-	-		-	-		-	-		6		-
25 Birmingham City	-	-		3		-	-	-		2		1	-	-		-	-		-	-		-	-		-	-		5		1
26 Sheffield United	-	-		5		-	-	-		-	-		-	-		-	-		-	-		-	-		-	-		5		-
27 Queens Park Rangers	-	-		4		3	-	-		-	-		-	-		-	-		-	-		-	-		-	-		4		3
28 Bristol Rovers	-	-		-	-		1	(1)	-	-	-		2		1	-	-		-	-		-	-		-	-		3	(1)	1
29 Oxford United	-	-		-	-		1	(1)	-	-	-		2			-	-		-	-		-	-		-	-		3	(1)	-
30 Huddersfield Town	-	-		3		-	-	-		-	-		-	-		-	-		-	-		-	-		-	-		3		-
31 Portsmouth	-	-		-	-		2			-	-		1			-	-		-	-		-	-		-	-		3		-
32 Watford	-	-		-	-		-	-		3			-	-		-	-		-	-		-	-		-	-		3		-
33 Estudiantes de la Plata	-	-		-	-		-	-		-	-		-	-		-	-		-	-		-	-		2		1	2		1
34 Leyton Orient	-	-		-	-		2		1	-	-		-	-		-	-		-	-		-	-		-	-		2		1
35 Rapid Vienna	-	-		-	-		-	-		-	-		-	-		2		1	-	-		-	-		-	-		2		1
36 York City	-	-		-	-		2		1	-	-		-	-		-	-		-	-		-	-		-	-		2		1
37 AC Milan	-	-		-	-		-	-		-	-		-	-		2			-	-		-	-		-	-		2		-
38 Aston Villa	-	-		-	-		-	-		1			1			-	-		-	-		-	-		-	-		2		-
39 Blackpool	-	-		1			1			-	-		-	-		-	-		-	-		-	-		-	-		2		-
40 Cardiff City	-	-		-	-		2			-	-		-	-		-	-		-	-		-	-		-	-		2		-
41 Fulham	-	-		-	-		2			-	-		-	-		-	-		-	-		-	-		-	-		2		-
42 Millwall	-	-		-	-		2			-	-		-	-		-	-		-	-		-	-		-	-		2		-
43 Oldham Athletic	-	-		-	-		2			-	-		-	-		-	-		-	-		-	-		-	-		2		-
44 Bolton Wanderers	-	-		-	-		1			-	-		-	-		-	-		-	-		-	-		-	-		1		-
45 Bristol City	-	-		-	-		1			-	-		-	-		-	-		-	-		-	-		-	-		1		-
46 Charlton Athletic	-	-		-	-		-	-		-	-		1			-	-		-	-		-	-		-	-		1		-
47 Hull City	-	-		-	-		1			-	-		-	-		-	-		-	-		-	-		-	-		1		-
48 Northampton Town	-	-		-	-		-	-		1			-	-		-	-		-	-		-	-		-	-		1		-
49 Notts County	-	-		-	-		1			-	-		-	-		-	-		-	-		-	-		-	-		1		-
50 Plymouth Argyle	-	-		-	-		-	-		1			-	-		-	-		-	-		-	-		-	-		1		-
51 Preston North End	-	-		-	-		-	-		1			-	-		-	-		-	-		-	-		-	-		1		-
52 Walsall	-	-		-	-		-	-		1			-	-		-	-		-	-		-	-		-	-		1		-
53 Wrexham	-	-		-	-		-	-		-	-		1			-	-		-	-		-	-		-	-		1		-

KENNY MORGANS

DEBUT (Full Appearance)

Saturday 21/12/1957
Football League Division 1
at Old Trafford

Manchester United 4 Leicester City 0

CLUB CAREER RECORD	Apps	Subs	Goals
Premiership	0		0
League Division 1	17		0
League Division 2	0		0
FA Cup	2		0
League Cup	0		0
European Cup / Champions League	4		0
European Cup-Winners' Cup	0		0
UEFA Cup / Inter-Cities' Fairs Cup	0		0
Other Matches	0		0
OVERALL TOTAL	**23**		**0**

Opponents	PREM A	S	G	FLD 1 A	S	G	FLD 2 A	S	G	FAC A	S	G	LC A	S	G	EC/CL A	S	G	ECWC A	S	G	UEFA A	S	G	OTHER A	S	G	TOTAL A	S	G
1 AC Milan	-	-		-	-		-	-		-	-		-	-		2			-	-		-	-		-	-		2		-
2 Bolton Wanderers	-	-		2			-	-		-	-		-	-		-	-		-	-		-	-		-	-		2		-
3 Leeds United	-	-		2			-	-		-	-		-	-		-	-		-	-		-	-		-	-		2		-
4 Red Star Belgrade	-	-		-	-		-	-		-	-		-	-		2			-	-		-	-		-	-		2		-
5 Arsenal	-	-		1			-	-		-	-		-	-		-	-		-	-		-	-		-	-		1		-
6 Birmingham City	-	-		1			-	-		-	-		-	-		-	-		-	-		-	-		-	-		1		-
7 Burnley	-	-		1			-	-		-	-		-	-		-	-		-	-		-	-		-	-		1		-
8 Ipswich Town	-	-		-	-		-	-		1			-	-		-	-		-	-		-	-		-	-		1		-
9 Leicester City	-	-		1			-	-		-	-		-	-		-	-		-	-		-	-		-	-		1		-
10 Luton Town	-	-		1			-	-		-	-		-	-		-	-		-	-		-	-		-	-		1		-
11 Manchester City	-	-		1			-	-		-	-		-	-		-	-		-	-		-	-		-	-		1		-
12 Newcastle United	-	-		1			-	-		-	-		-	-		-	-		-	-		-	-		-	-		1		-
13 Nottingham Forest	-	-		1			-	-		-	-		-	-		-	-		-	-		-	-		-	-		1		-
14 Portsmouth	-	-		1			-	-		-	-		-	-		-	-		-	-		-	-		-	-		1		-
15 Preston North End	-	-		1			-	-		-	-		-	-		-	-		-	-		-	-		-	-		1		-
16 Sunderland	-	-		1			-	-		-	-		-	-		-	-		-	-		-	-		-	-		1		-
17 Tottenham Hotspur	-	-		1			-	-		-	-		-	-		-	-		-	-		-	-		-	-		1		-
18 Wolverhampton W.	-	-		1			-	-		-	-		-	-		-	-		-	-		-	-		-	-		1		-
19 Workington	-	-		-	-		-	-		1			-	-		-	-		-	-		-	-		-	-		1		-

JOHNNY MORRIS

DEBUT (Full Appearance)

Saturday 26/10/1946
Football League Division 1
at Maine Road

Manchester United 0 Sunderland 3

CLUB CAREER RECORD	Apps	Subs	Goals
Premiership	0		0
League Division 1	83		32
League Division 2	0		0
FA Cup	9		3
League Cup	0		0
European Cup / Champions League	0		0
European Cup-Winners' Cup	0		0
UEFA Cup / Inter-Cities' Fairs Cup	0		0
Other Matches	1		0
OVERALL TOTAL	**93**		**35**

Opponents	PREM A	S	G	FLD 1 A	S	G	FLD 2 A	S	G	FAC A	S	G	LC A	S	G	EC/CL A	S	G	ECWC A	S	G	UEFA A	S	G	OTHER A	S	G	TOTAL A	S	G
1 Arsenal	–	–		5		2	–	–		–			–			–			–			–			1		–	6		2
2 Derby County	–	–		5		–	–		–	1		–	–			–			–			–			–			6		–
3 Wolverhampton W.	–	–		5		4	–		–	–		–	–			–			–			–			–			5		4
4 Aston Villa	–	–		4		–	–		–	1		2	–			–			–			–			–			5		2
5 Charlton Athletic	–	–		4		2	–		–	1		–	–			–			–			–			–			5		2
6 Everton	–	–		5		2	–		–	–		–	–			–			–			–			–			5		2
7 Preston North End	–	–		4		2	–		–	1		–	–			–			–			–			–			5		2
8 Blackpool	–	–		4		1	–		–	1		–	–			–			–			–			–			5		1
9 Portsmouth	–	–		4		5	–		–	–		–	–			–			–			–			–			4		5
10 Huddersfield Town	–	–		4		2	–		–	–		–	–			–			–			–			–			4		2
11 Sheffield United	–	–		4		2	–		–	–		–	–			–			–			–			–			4		2
12 Middlesbrough	–	–		4		1	–		–	–		–	–			–			–			–			–			4		1
13 Stoke City	–	–		4		1	–		–	–		–	–			–			–			–			–			4		1
14 Bolton Wanderers	–	–		4		–	–		–	–		–	–			–			–			–			–			4		–
15 Manchester City	–	–		4		–	–		–	–		–	–			–			–			–			–			4		–
16 Chelsea	–	–		3		3	–		–	–		–	–			–			–			–			–			3		3
17 Blackburn Rovers	–	–		3		2	–		–	–		–	–			–			–			–			–			3		2
18 Liverpool	–	–		2		1	–		–	1		1	–			–			–			–			–			3		2
19 Burnley	–	–		3		–	–		–	–		–	–			–			–			–			–			3		–
20 Sunderland	–	–		3		–	–		–	–		–	–			–			–			–			–			3		–
21 Grimsby Town	–	–		2		1	–		–	–		–	–			–			–			–			–			2		1
22 Bradford Park Avenue	–			–		–	–		–	2		–	–			–			–			–			–			2		–
23 Birmingham City	–	–		1		1	–		–	–		–	–			–			–			–			–			1		1
24 Brentford	–	–		1		–	–		–	–		–	–			–			–			–			–			1		–
25 Newcastle United	–	–		1		–	–		–	–		–	–			–			–			–			–			1		–
26 Nottingham Forest	–	–		–		–	–		–	1		–	–			–			–			–			–			1		–

TOMMY MORRISON

DEBUT (Full Appearance)

Thursday 25/12/1902
Football League Division 2
at Bank Street

Manchester United 1 Manchester City 1

CLUB CAREER RECORD	Apps	Subs	Goals
Premiership	0		0
League Division 1	0		0
League Division 2	29		7
FA Cup	7		1
League Cup	0		0
European Cup / Champions League	0		0
European Cup-Winners' Cup	0		0
UEFA Cup / Inter-Cities' Fairs Cup	0		0
Other Matches	0		0
OVERALL TOTAL	**36**		**8**

Opponents	PREM A	S	G	FLD 1 A	S	G	FLD 2 A	S	G	FAC A	S	G	LC A	S	G	EC/CL A	S	G	ECWC A	S	G	UEFA A	S	G	OTHER A	S	G	TOTAL A	S	G
1 Birmingham City	–	–		–		–	–		–	4		–	–			–			–			–			–			4		–
2 Preston North End	–	–		–		–	4		–	–		–	–			–			–			–			–			4		–
3 Arsenal	–	–		–		–	3		–	–		–	–			–			–			–			–			3		–
4 Doncaster Rovers	–	–		–		–	2		3	–		–	–			–			–			–			–			2		3
5 Blackpool	–	–		–		–	2		1	–		–	–			–			–			–			–			2		1
6 Burnley	–	–		–		–	2		1	–		–	–			–			–			–			–			2		1
7 Glossop	–	–		–		–	2		1	–		–	–			–			–			–			–			2		1
8 Notts County	–	–		–		–	–		–	2		1	–			–			–			–			–			2		1
9 Lincoln City	–	–		–		–	2		–	–		–	–			–			–			–			–			2		–
10 Manchester City	–	–		–		–	2		–	–		–	–			–			–			–			–			2		–
11 Leicester City	–	–		–		–	–		–	1		1	–			–			–			–			–			1		1
12 Barnsley	–	–		–		–	1		–	–		–	–			–			–			–			–			1		–
13 Bolton Wanderers	–	–		–		–	1		–	–		–	–			–			–			–			–			1		–
14 Bradford City	–	–		–		–	1		–	–		–	–			–			–			–			–			1		–
15 Bristol City	–	–		–		–	1		–	–		–	–			–			–			–			–			1		–
16 Burton United	–	–		–		–	1		–	–		–	–			–			–			–			–			1		–
17 Chesterfield	–	–		–		–	1		–	–		–	–			–			–			–			–			1		–
18 Gainsborough Trinity	–	–		–		–	1		–	–		–	–			–			–			–			–			1		–
19 Port Vale	–	–		–		–	1		–	–		–	–			–			–			–			–			1		–
20 Sheffield Wednesday	–	–		–		–	–		–	1		–	–			–			–			–			–			1		–
21 Stockport County	–	–		–		–	1		–	–		–	–			–			–			–			–			1		–

BEN MORTON

DEBUT (Full Appearance)

Saturday 16/11/1935
Football League Division 2
at Old Trafford

Manchester United 2 West Ham United 3

CLUB CAREER RECORD	Apps	Subs	Goals
Premiership	0		0
League Division 1	0		0
League Division 2	1		0
FA Cup	0		0
League Cup	0		0
European Cup / Champions League	0		0
European Cup-Winners' Cup	0		0
UEFA Cup / Inter-Cities' Fairs Cup	0		0
Other Matches	0		0
OVERALL TOTAL	**1**		**0**

Opponents	PREM			FLD 1			FLD 2			FAC			LC			EC/CL			ECWC			UEFA			OTHER			TOTAL		
	A	S	G	A	S	G	A	S	G	A	S	G	A	S	G	A	S	G	A	S	G	A	S	G	A	S	G	A	S	G
1 West Ham United	–	–	–	–	–	–	1	–	–	–	–	–	–	–	–	–	–	–	–	–	–	–	–	–	–	–	–	1	–	–

REMI MOSES

DEBUT (Substitute Appearance)

Saturday 19/09/1981
Football League Division 1
at Old Trafford

Manchester United 1 Swansea City 0

CLUB CAREER RECORD	Apps	Subs	Goals
Premiership	0		0
League Division 1	143	(7)	7
League Division 2	0		0
FA Cup	11		1
League Cup	22	(2)	4
European Cup / Champions League	0		0
European Cup-Winners' Cup	5	(1)	0
UEFA Cup / Inter-Cities' Fairs Cup	7		0
Other Matches	0	(1)	0
OVERALL TOTAL	**188**	**(11)**	**12**

Opponents	PREM			FLD 1			FLD 2			FAC			LC			EC/CL			ECWC			UEFA			OTHER			TOTAL		
	A	S	G	A	S	G	A	S	G	A	S	G	A	S	G	A	S	G	A	S	G	A	S	G	A	S	G	A	S	G
1 Southampton	–	–	–	8	–	–	–	–	–	–	–	–	3	–	–	–	–	–	–	–	–	–	–	–	–	–	–	11	–	–
2 Everton	–	–	–	7	(1)	–	–	–	–	1	–	–	1	–	–	–	–	–	–	–	–	–	–	–	–	(1)	–	9	(2)	–
3 Coventry City	–	–	–	8	(1)	–	–	–	–	1	–	–	–	–	–	–	–	–	–	–	–	–	–	–	–	–	–	9	(1)	–
4 Arsenal	–	–	–	5	(1)	–	–	–	–	1	–	–	2	–	–	–	–	–	–	–	–	–	–	–	–	–	–	8	(1)	–
5 Liverpool	–	–	–	7	–	–	–	–	–	–	–	–	1	–	–	–	–	–	–	–	–	–	–	–	–	–	–	8	–	–
6 Tottenham Hotspur	–	–	–	7	–	–	–	–	–	–	–	–	1	–	–	–	–	–	–	–	–	–	–	–	–	–	–	8	–	–
7 Aston Villa	–	–	–	7	–	1	–	–	–	–	–	–	–	–	–	–	–	–	–	–	–	–	–	–	–	–	–	7	–	1
8 West Ham United	–	–	–	6	–	1	–	–	–	1	–	–	–	–	–	–	–	–	–	–	–	–	–	–	–	–	–	7	–	1
9 Sunderland	–	–	–	7	–	–	–	–	–	–	–	–	–	–	–	–	–	–	–	–	–	–	–	–	–	–	–	7	–	–
10 Watford	–	–	–	6	–	–	–	–	–	1	–	–	–	–	–	–	–	–	–	–	–	–	–	–	–	–	–	7	–	–
11 Notts County	–	–	–	6	–	1	–	–	–	–	–	–	–	–	–	–	–	–	–	–	–	–	–	–	–	–	–	6	–	1
12 Ipswich Town	–	–	–	5	–	–	–	–	–	1	–	–	–	–	–	–	–	–	–	–	–	–	–	–	–	–	–	6	–	–
13 Oxford United	–	–	–	3	–	–	–	–	–	–	–	–	3	–	–	–	–	–	–	–	–	–	–	–	–	–	–	6	–	–
14 Luton Town	–	–	–	4	(1)	–	–	–	–	1	–	1	–	–	–	–	–	–	–	–	–	–	–	–	–	–	–	5	(1)	1
15 Norwich City	–	–	–	5	(1)	–	–	–	–	–	–	–	–	–	–	–	–	–	–	–	–	–	–	–	–	–	–	5	(1)	–
16 Newcastle United	–	–	–	5	–	1	–	–	–	–	–	–	–	–	–	–	–	–	–	–	–	–	–	–	–	–	–	5	–	1
17 Queens Park Rangers	–	–	–	5	–	–	–	–	–	–	–	–	–	–	–	–	–	–	–	–	–	–	–	–	–	–	–	5	–	–
18 Chelsea	–	–	–	4	–	1	–	–	–	–	–	–	–	–	–	–	–	–	–	–	–	–	–	–	–	–	–	4	–	1
19 Birmingham City	–	–	–	4	–	–	–	–	–	–	–	–	–	–	–	–	–	–	–	–	–	–	–	–	–	–	–	4	–	–
20 Nottingham Forest	–	–	–	3	–	–	–	–	–	–	–	–	1	–	–	–	–	–	–	–	–	–	–	–	–	–	–	4	–	–
21 Stoke City	–	–	–	4	–	–	–	–	–	–	–	–	–	–	–	–	–	–	–	–	–	–	–	–	–	–	–	4	–	–
22 West Bromwich Albion	–	–	–	4	–	–	–	–	–	–	–	–	–	–	–	–	–	–	–	–	–	–	–	–	–	–	–	4	–	–
23 Wimbledon	–	–	–	4	–	–	–	–	–	–	–	–	–	–	–	–	–	–	–	–	–	–	–	–	–	–	–	4	–	–
24 Port Vale	–	–	–	–	–	–	–	–	–	–	–	–	3	(1)	2	–	–	–	–	–	–	–	–	–	–	–	–	3	(1)	2
25 Leicester City	–	–	–	3	–	1	–	–	–	–	–	–	–	–	–	–	–	–	–	–	–	–	–	–	–	–	–	3	–	1
26 Bournemouth	–	–	–	–	–	–	–	–	–	2	–	–	1	–	–	–	–	–	–	–	–	–	–	–	–	–	–	3	–	–
27 Manchester City	–	–	–	3	–	–	–	–	–	–	–	–	–	–	–	–	–	–	–	–	–	–	–	–	–	–	–	3	–	–
28 Wolverhampton W.	–	–	–	2	(1)	–	–	–	–	–	–	–	–	–	–	–	–	–	–	–	–	–	–	–	–	–	–	2	(1)	–
29 Bradford City	–	–	–	–	–	–	–	–	–	–	–	–	2	–	1	–	–	–	–	–	–	–	–	–	–	–	–	2	–	1
30 Middlesbrough	–	–	–	2	–	1	–	–	–	–	–	–	–	–	–	–	–	–	–	–	–	–	–	–	–	–	–	2	–	1
31 Barcelona	–	–	–	–	–	–	–	–	–	–	–	–	–	–	–	–	–	–	2	–	–	–	–	–	–	–	–	2	–	–
32 Brighton	–	–	–	2	–	–	–	–	–	–	–	–	–	–	–	–	–	–	–	–	–	–	–	–	–	–	–	2	–	–
33 Burnley	–	–	–	–	–	–	–	–	–	–	–	–	2	–	–	–	–	–	–	–	–	–	–	–	–	–	–	2	–	–
34 Charlton Athletic	–	–	–	2	–	–	–	–	–	–	–	–	–	–	–	–	–	–	–	–	–	–	–	–	–	–	–	2	–	–
35 Dundee United	–	–	–	–	–	–	–	–	–	–	–	–	–	–	–	–	–	–	–	–	–	2	–	–	–	–	–	2	–	–
36 Juventus	–	–	–	–	–	–	–	–	–	–	–	–	–	–	–	2	–	–	–	–	–	–	–	–	–	–	–	2	–	–
37 Leeds United	–	–	–	2	–	–	–	–	–	–	–	–	–	–	–	–	–	–	–	–	–	–	–	–	–	–	–	2	–	–
38 PSV Eindhoven	–	–	–	–	–	–	–	–	–	–	–	–	–	–	–	–	–	–	–	–	–	2	–	–	–	–	–	2	–	–
39 Raba Vasas	–	–	–	–	–	–	–	–	–	–	–	–	–	–	–	–	–	–	–	–	–	2	–	–	–	–	–	2	–	–
40 Swansea City	–	–	–	1	(1)	–	–	–	–	–	–	–	–	–	–	–	–	–	–	–	–	–	–	–	–	–	–	1	(1)	–
41 Colchester United	–	–	–	–	–	–	–	–	–	–	–	–	1	–	1	–	–	–	–	–	–	–	–	–	–	–	–	1	–	1
42 Blackburn Rovers	–	–	–	–	–	–	–	–	–	1	–	–	–	–	–	–	–	–	–	–	–	–	–	–	–	–	–	1	–	–
43 Derby County	–	–	–	–	–	–	–	–	–	1	–	–	–	–	–	–	–	–	–	–	–	–	–	–	–	–	–	1	–	–
44 Hull City	–	–	–	–	–	–	–	–	–	–	–	–	1	–	–	–	–	–	–	–	–	–	–	–	–	–	–	1	–	–
45 Portsmouth	–	–	–	1	–	–	–	–	–	–	–	–	–	–	–	–	–	–	–	–	–	–	–	–	–	–	–	1	–	–
46 Sheffield Wednesday	–	–	–	1	–	–	–	–	–	–	–	–	–	–	–	–	–	–	–	–	–	–	–	–	–	–	–	1	–	–
47 Spartak Varna	–	–	–	–	–	–	–	–	–	–	–	–	–	–	–	–	–	–	1	–	–	–	–	–	–	–	–	1	–	–
48 Valencia	–	–	–	–	–	–	–	–	–	–	–	–	–	–	–	–	–	–	–	–	–	1	–	–	–	–	–	1	–	–
49 Bury	–	–	–	–	–	–	–	–	–	–	–	–	–	(1)	–	–	–	–	–	–	–	–	–	–	–	–	–	–	(1)	–
50 Dukla Prague	–	–	–	–	–	–	–	–	–	–	–	–	–	–	–	–	(1)	–	–	–	–	–	–	–	–	–	–	–	(1)	–

ARNOLD MUHREN

DEBUT (Full Appearance, 1 goal)

Saturday 28/08/1982
Football League Division 1
at Old Trafford

Manchester United 3 Birmingham City 0

CLUB CAREER RECORD	Apps	Subs	Goals
Premiership	0		0
League Division 1	65	(5)	13
League Division 2	0		0
FA Cup	8		1
League Cup	11		1
European Cup / Champions League	0		0
European Cup-Winners' Cup	5		0
UEFA Cup / Inter-Cities' Fairs Cup	3		3
Other Matches	1		0
OVERALL TOTAL	**93**	**(5)**	**18**

Opponents	PREM			FLD 1			FLD 2			FAC			LC			EC/CL			ECWC			UEFA			OTHER			TOTAL		
	A	S	G	A	S	G	A	S	G	A	S	G	A	S	G	A	S	G	A	S	G	A	S	G	A	S	G	A	S	G
1 Liverpool	–	–		3	(1)	1	–	–		–	–		1	–		–	–		–	–		–	–		1	–		5	(1)	1
2 Nottingham Forest	–	–		4	(1)	1	–	–		–	–		1	–		–	–		–	–		–	–		–	–		5	(1)	1
3 Luton Town	–	–		4	–	1	–	–		1	–		–	–		–	–		–	–		–	–		–	–		5	–	1
4 Arsenal	–	–		2	–	2	–	–		–	–		2	–		–	–		–	–		–	–		–	–		4	–	2
5 Brighton	–	–		2	–	–	–	–		2	–	1	–	–		–	–		–	–		–	–		–	–		4	–	1
6 Southampton	–	–		3	–	1	–	–		–	–		1	–		–	–		–	–		–	–		–	–		4	–	1
7 Stoke City	–	–		4	–	1	–	–		–	–		–	–		–	–		–	–		–	–		–	–		4	–	1
8 Aston Villa	–	–		4	–	–	–	–		–	–		–	–		–	–		–	–		–	–		–	–		4	–	–
9 West Ham United	–	–		3	–	–	–	–		1	–		–	–		–	–		–	–		–	–		–	–		4	–	–
10 Sunderland	–	–		3	(1)	–	–	–		–	–		–	–		–	–		–	–		–	–		–	–		3	(1)	–
11 Bournemouth	–	–		–	–		–	–		2	–		1	–	1	–	–		–	–		–	–		–	–		3	–	1
12 Coventry City	–	–		3	–	1	–	–		–	–		–	–		–	–		–	–		–	–		–	–		3	–	1
13 Norwich City	–	–		3	–	1	–	–		–	–		–	–		–	–		–	–		–	–		–	–		3	–	1
14 Notts County	–	–		3	–	1	–	–		–	–		–	–		–	–		–	–		–	–		–	–		3	–	1
15 Tottenham Hotspur	–	–		3	–	1	–	–		–	–		–	–		–	–		–	–		–	–		–	–		3	–	1
16 West Bromwich Albion	–	–		3	–	–	–	–		–	–		–	–		–	–		–	–		–	–		–	–		3	–	–
17 Queens Park Rangers	–	–		2	(1)	2	–	–		–	–		–	–		–	–		–	–		–	–		–	–		2	(1)	2
18 Watford	–	–		2	(1)	–	–	–		–	–		–	–		–	–		–	–		–	–		–	–		2	(1)	–
19 Raba Vasas	–	–		–	–		–	–		–	–		–	–		–	–		–	–		2	–	2	–	–		2	–	2
20 Barcelona	–	–		–	–		–	–		–	–		–	–		–	–		2	–		–	–		–	–		2	–	–
21 Birmingham City	–	–		2	–	–	–	–		–	–		–	–		–	–		–	–		–	–		–	–		2	–	–
22 Bradford City	–	–		–	–		–	–		–	–		2	–		–	–		–	–		–	–		–	–		2	–	–
23 Dukla Prague	–	–		–	–		–	–		–	–		–	–		–	–		2	–		–	–		–	–		2	–	–
24 Everton	–	–		1	–	–	–	–		1	–		–	–		–	–		–	–		–	–		–	–		2	–	–
25 Ipswich Town	–	–		2	–	–	–	–		–	–		–	–		–	–		–	–		–	–		–	–		2	–	–
26 Manchester City	–	–		2	–	–	–	–		–	–		–	–		–	–		–	–		–	–		–	–		2	–	–
27 Swansea City	–	–		2	–	–	–	–		–	–		–	–		–	–		–	–		–	–		–	–		2	–	–
28 Wolverhampton W.	–	–		2	–	–	–	–		–	–		–	–		–	–		–	–		–	–		–	–		2	–	–
29 Dundee United	–	–		–	–		–	–		–	–		–	–		–	–		–	–		1	–	1	–	–		1	–	1
30 Burnley	–	–		–	–		–	–		–	–		1	–		–	–		–	–		–	–		–	–		1	–	–
31 Chelsea	–	–		1	–	–	–	–		–	–		–	–		–	–		–	–		–	–		–	–		1	–	–
32 Derby County	–	–		–	–		–	–		1	–		–	–		–	–		–	–		–	–		–	–		1	–	–
33 Leicester City	–	–		1	–	–	–	–		–	–		–	–		–	–		–	–		–	–		–	–		1	–	–
34 Oxford United	–	–		–	–		–	–		–	–		1	–		–	–		–	–		–	–		–	–		1	–	–
35 Port Vale	–	–		–	–		–	–		–	–		1	–		–	–		–	–		–	–		–	–		1	–	–
36 Sheffield Wednesday	–	–		1	–	–	–	–		–	–		–	–		–	–		–	–		–	–		–	–		1	–	–
37 Spartak Varna	–	–		–	–		–	–		–	–		–	–		–	–		1	–		–	–		–	–		1	–	–

PHILIP MULRYNE

DEBUT (Full Appearance)

Tuesday 14/10/1997
League Cup 3rd Round
at Portman Road

Ipswich Town 2 Manchester United 0

CLUB CAREER RECORD	Apps	Subs	Goals
Premiership	1		0
League Division 1	0		0
League Division 2	0		0
FA Cup	0	(1)	0
League Cup	3		0
European Cup / Champions League	0		0
European Cup-Winners' Cup	0		0
UEFA Cup / Inter-Cities' Fairs Cup	0		0
Other Matches	0		0
OVERALL TOTAL	**4**	**(1)**	**0**

Opponents	PREM			FLD 1			FLD 2			FAC			LC			EC/CL			ECWC			UEFA			OTHER			TOTAL		
	A	S	G	A	S	G	A	S	G	A	S	G	A	S	G	A	S	G	A	S	G	A	S	G	A	S	G	A	S	G
1 Barnsley	1	–		–	–		–	–		–	–		–	–		–	–		–	–		–	–		–	–		1	–	
2 Bury	–	–		–	–		–	–		–	–		1	–		–	–		–	–		–	–		–	–		1	–	
3 Ipswich Town	–	–		–	–		–	–		–	–		1	–		–	–		–	–		–	–		–	–		1	–	
4 Nottingham Forest	–	–		–	–		–	–		–	–		1	–		–	–		–	–		–	–		–	–		1	–	
5 Walsall	–	–		–	–		–	–		–	(1)	–	–	–		–	–		–	–		–	–		–	–		–	(1)	–

ROBERT MURRAY

DEBUT (Full Appearance)

Saturday 28/08/1937
Football League Division 2
at Old Trafford

Manchester United 3 Newcastle United 0

CLUB CAREER RECORD	Apps	Subs	Goals
Premiership	0		0
League Division 1	0		0
League Division 2	4		0
FA Cup	0		0
League Cup	0		0
European Cup / Champions League	0		0
European Cup-Winners' Cup	0		0
UEFA Cup / Inter-Cities' Fairs Cup	0		0
Other Matches	0		0
OVERALL TOTAL	4		0

Opponents	PREM			FLD 1			FLD 2			FAC			LC			EC/CL			ECWC			UEFA			OTHER			TOTAL		
	A	S	G	A	S	G	A	S	G	A	S	G	A	S	G	A	S	G	A	S	G	A	S	G	A	S	G	A	S	G
1 Coventry City	-	-	-	-	-	-	1	-	-	-	-	-	-	-	-	-	-	-	-	-	-	-	-	-	-	-	-	1	-	-
2 Luton Town	-	-	-	-	-	-	1	-	-	-	-	-	-	-	-	-	-	-	-	-	-	-	-	-	-	-	-	1	-	-
3 Newcastle United	-	-	-	-	-	-	1	-	-	-	-	-	-	-	-	-	-	-	-	-	-	-	-	-	-	-	-	1	-	-
4 Sheffield Wednesday	-	-	-	-	-	-	1	-	-	-	-	-	-	-	-	-	-	-	-	-	-	-	-	-	-	-	-	1	-	-

GEORGE MUTCH

DEBUT (Full Appearance)

Saturday 25/08/1934
Football League Division 2
at Old Trafford

Manchester United 2 Bradford City 0

CLUB CAREER RECORD	Apps	Subs	Goals
Premiership	0		0
League Division 1	28		7
League Division 2	84		39
FA Cup	8		3
League Cup	0		0
European Cup / Champions League	0		0
European Cup-Winners' Cup	0		0
UEFA Cup / Inter-Cities' Fairs Cup	0		0
Other Matches	0		0
OVERALL TOTAL	120		49

Opponents	PREM			FLD 1			FLD 2			FAC			LC			EC/CL			ECWC			UEFA			OTHER			TOTAL		
	A	S	G	A	S	G	A	S	G	A	S	G	A	S	G	A	S	G	A	S	G	A	S	G	A	S	G	A	S	G
1 Nottingham Forest	-	-	-	-	-	-	4	-	3	2	-	-	-	-	-	-	-	-	-	-	-	-	-	-	-	-	-	6	-	3
2 Barnsley	-	-	-	-	-	-	4	-	5	-	-	-	-	-	-	-	-	-	-	-	-	-	-	-	-	-	-	4	-	5
3 Port Vale	-	-	-	-	-	-	4	-	4	-	-	-	-	-	-	-	-	-	-	-	-	-	-	-	-	-	-	4	-	4
4 Blackpool	-	-	-	-	-	-	4	-	3	-	-	-	-	-	-	-	-	-	-	-	-	-	-	-	-	-	-	4	-	3
5 West Ham United	-	-	-	-	-	-	4	-	3	-	-	-	-	-	-	-	-	-	-	-	-	-	-	-	-	-	-	4	-	3
6 Bury	-	-	-	-	-	-	4	-	2	-	-	-	-	-	-	-	-	-	-	-	-	-	-	-	-	-	-	4	-	2
7 Newcastle United	-	-	-	-	-	-	4	-	2	-	-	-	-	-	-	-	-	-	-	-	-	-	-	-	-	-	-	4	-	2
8 Plymouth Argyle	-	-	-	-	-	-	4	-	2	-	-	-	-	-	-	-	-	-	-	-	-	-	-	-	-	-	-	4	-	2
9 Sheffield United	-	-	-	-	-	-	4	-	2	-	-	-	-	-	-	-	-	-	-	-	-	-	-	-	-	-	-	4	-	2
10 Southampton	-	-	-	-	-	-	4	-	2	-	-	-	-	-	-	-	-	-	-	-	-	-	-	-	-	-	-	4	-	2
11 Swansea City	-	-	-	-	-	-	4	-	2	-	-	-	-	-	-	-	-	-	-	-	-	-	-	-	-	-	-	4	-	2
12 Bradford City	-	-	-	-	-	-	4	-	1	-	-	-	-	-	-	-	-	-	-	-	-	-	-	-	-	-	-	4	-	1
13 Fulham	-	-	-	-	-	-	4	-	1	-	-	-	-	-	-	-	-	-	-	-	-	-	-	-	-	-	-	4	-	1
14 Norwich City	-	-	-	-	-	-	4	-	1	-	-	-	-	-	-	-	-	-	-	-	-	-	-	-	-	-	-	4	-	1
15 Bolton Wanderers	-	-	-	2	-	-	2	-	-	-	-	-	-	-	-	-	-	-	-	-	-	-	-	-	-	-	-	4	-	-
16 Burnley	-	-	-	-	-	-	4	-	-	-	-	-	-	-	-	-	-	-	-	-	-	-	-	-	-	-	-	4	-	-
17 Charlton Athletic	-	-	-	2	-	-	2	-	-	-	-	-	-	-	-	-	-	-	-	-	-	-	-	-	-	-	-	4	-	-
18 Hull City	-	-	-	-	-	-	4	-	-	-	-	-	-	-	-	-	-	-	-	-	-	-	-	-	-	-	-	4	-	-
19 Bradford Park Avenue	-	-	-	-	-	-	3	-	3	-	-	-	-	-	-	-	-	-	-	-	-	-	-	-	-	-	-	3	-	3
20 Stoke City	-	-	-	1	-	-	-	-	-	2	-	-	-	-	-	-	-	-	-	-	-	-	-	-	-	-	-	3	-	-
21 Everton	-	-	-	2	-	2	-	-	-	-	-	-	-	-	-	-	-	-	-	-	-	-	-	-	-	-	-	2	-	2
22 Oldham Athletic	-	-	-	-	-	-	2	-	2	-	-	-	-	-	-	-	-	-	-	-	-	-	-	-	-	-	-	2	-	2
23 Reading	-	-	-	-	-	-	-	-	-	2	-	2	-	-	-	-	-	-	-	-	-	-	-	-	-	-	-	2	-	2
24 Notts County	-	-	-	-	-	-	2	-	1	-	-	-	-	-	-	-	-	-	-	-	-	-	-	-	-	-	-	2	-	1
25 Arsenal	-	-	-	1	-	-	-	-	-	1	-	-	-	-	-	-	-	-	-	-	-	-	-	-	-	-	-	2	-	-
26 Brentford	-	-	-	1	-	-	1	-	-	-	-	-	-	-	-	-	-	-	-	-	-	-	-	-	-	-	-	2	-	-
27 Doncaster Rovers	-	-	-	-	-	-	2	-	-	-	-	-	-	-	-	-	-	-	-	-	-	-	-	-	-	-	-	2	-	-
28 Leeds United	-	-	-	2	-	-	-	-	-	-	-	-	-	-	-	-	-	-	-	-	-	-	-	-	-	-	-	2	-	-
29 Leicester City	-	-	-	-	-	-	2	-	-	-	-	-	-	-	-	-	-	-	-	-	-	-	-	-	-	-	-	2	-	-
30 Liverpool	-	-	-	2	-	-	-	-	-	-	-	-	-	-	-	-	-	-	-	-	-	-	-	-	-	-	-	2	-	-
31 Manchester City	-	-	-	2	-	-	-	-	-	-	-	-	-	-	-	-	-	-	-	-	-	-	-	-	-	-	-	2	-	-
32 Sheffield Wednesday	-	-	-	2	-	-	-	-	-	-	-	-	-	-	-	-	-	-	-	-	-	-	-	-	-	-	-	2	-	-
33 Tottenham Hotspur	-	-	-	-	-	-	2	-	-	-	-	-	-	-	-	-	-	-	-	-	-	-	-	-	-	-	-	2	-	-
34 Wolverhampton W.	-	-	-	2	-	-	-	-	-	-	-	-	-	-	-	-	-	-	-	-	-	-	-	-	-	-	-	2	-	-
35 Birmingham City	-	-	-	1	-	1	-	-	-	-	-	-	-	-	-	-	-	-	-	-	-	-	-	-	-	-	-	1	-	1
36 Bristol Rovers	-	-	-	-	-	-	-	-	-	1	-	1	-	-	-	-	-	-	-	-	-	-	-	-	-	-	-	1	-	1
37 Grimsby Town	-	-	-	1	-	1	-	-	-	-	-	-	-	-	-	-	-	-	-	-	-	-	-	-	-	-	-	1	-	1
38 Huddersfield Town	-	-	-	1	-	1	-	-	-	-	-	-	-	-	-	-	-	-	-	-	-	-	-	-	-	-	-	1	-	1
39 Sunderland	-	-	-	1	-	1	-	-	-	-	-	-	-	-	-	-	-	-	-	-	-	-	-	-	-	-	-	1	-	1
40 West Bromwich Albion	-	-	-	1	-	1	-	-	-	-	-	-	-	-	-	-	-	-	-	-	-	-	-	-	-	-	-	1	-	1
41 Chelsea	-	-	-	1	-	-	-	-	-	-	-	-	-	-	-	-	-	-	-	-	-	-	-	-	-	-	-	1	-	-
42 Derby County	-	-	-	1	-	-	-	-	-	-	-	-	-	-	-	-	-	-	-	-	-	-	-	-	-	-	-	1	-	-
43 Luton Town	-	-	-	-	-	-	1	-	-	-	-	-	-	-	-	-	-	-	-	-	-	-	-	-	-	-	-	1	-	-
44 Middlesbrough	-	-	-	1	-	-	-	-	-	-	-	-	-	-	-	-	-	-	-	-	-	-	-	-	-	-	-	1	-	-
45 Portsmouth	-	-	-	1	-	-	-	-	-	-	-	-	-	-	-	-	-	-	-	-	-	-	-	-	-	-	-	1	-	-
46 Stockport County	-	-	-	-	-	-	1	-	-	-	-	-	-	-	-	-	-	-	-	-	-	-	-	-	-	-	-	1	-	-

JOE MYERSCOUGH

DEBUT (Full Appearance)

Saturday 04/09/1920
Football League Division 1
at Burnden Park

Bolton Wanderers 1 Manchester United 1

CLUB CAREER RECORD	Apps	Subs	Goals
Premiership	0		0
League Division 1	20		5
League Division 2	13		3
FA Cup	1		0
League Cup	0		0
European Cup / Champions League	0		0
European Cup-Winners' Cup	0		0
UEFA Cup / Inter-Cities' Fairs Cup	0		0
Other Matches	0		0
OVERALL TOTAL	**34**		**8**

Opponents	PREM			FLD 1			FLD 2			FAC			LC			EC/CL			ECWC			UEFA			OTHER			TOTAL		
	A	S	G	A	S	G	A	S	G	A	S	G	A	S	G	A	S	G	A	S	G	A	S	G	A	S	G	A	S	G
1 Liverpool	–	–		3	–		–			–			–			–			–			–			–			3	–	
2 Bradford Park Avenue	–	–		2		4	–			–			–			–			–			–			–			2		4
3 Notts County	–	–		–			2		2	–			–			–			–			–			–			2		2
4 Fulham	–	–		–			2		1	–			–			–			–			–			–			2		1
5 Arsenal	–	–		2		–	–			–			–			–			–			–			–			2		–
6 Aston Villa	–	–		2		–	–			–			–			–			–			–			–			2		–
7 Bolton Wanderers	–	–		2		–	–			–			–			–			–			–			–			2		–
8 Bury	–	–		–			2		–	–			–			–			–			–			–			2		–
9 Cardiff City	–	–		2		–	–			–			–			–			–			–			–			2		–
10 Derby County	–	–		–			2		–	–			–			–			–			–			–			2		–
11 Everton	–	–		2		–	–			–			–			–			–			–			–			2		–
12 Leyton Orient	–	–		–			2		–	–			–			–			–			–			–			2		–
13 Newcastle United	–	–		2		–	–			–			–			–			–			–			–			2		–
14 West Bromwich Albion	–	–		1		1	–			–			–			–			–			–			–			1		1
15 Barnsley	–	–		–			1		–	–			–			–			–			–			–			1		–
16 Bradford City	–	–		1		–	–			–			–			–			–			–			–			1		–
17 Leeds United	–	–		–			1		–	–			–			–			–			–			–			1		–
18 Oldham Athletic	–	–		1		–	–			–			–			–			–			–			–			1		–
19 Southampton	–	–		–			1		–	–			–			–			–			–			–			1		–
20 Tottenham Hotspur	–	–		–			–			1			–			–			–			–			–			1		–

NANI

DEBUT (Substitute Appearance)

Sunday 05/08/2007
FA Charity Shield
at Wembley

Manchester United 1 Chelsea 1

CLUB CAREER RECORD	Apps	Subs	Goals
Premiership	16	(10)	3
League Division 1	0		0
League Division 2	0		0
FA Cup	2		1
League Cup	1		0
European Cup / Champions League	7	(4)	0
European Cup-Winners' Cup	0		0
UEFA Cup / Inter-Cities' Fairs Cup	0		0
Other Matches	0	(1)	0
OVERALL TOTAL	**26**	**(15)**	**4**

Opponents	PREM			FLD 1			FLD 2			FAC			LC			EC/CL			ECWC			UEFA			OTHER			TOTAL		
	A	S	G	A	S	G	A	S	G	A	S	G	A	S	G	A	S	G	A	S	G	A	S	G	A	S	G	A	S	G
1 Portsmouth	2	–		–			–			1	–		–			–			–			–			–			3	–	
2 Chelsea	1	–		–			–			–			–			–	(1)	–	–			–			–	(1)	–	1	(2)	–
3 Bolton Wanderers	2	–		–			–			–			–			–			–			–			–			2	–	
4 Manchester City	2	–		–			–			–			–			–			–			–			–			2	–	
5 Roma	–			–			–			–			–			2			–			–			–			2	–	
6 Sporting Lisbon	–			–			–			–			–			2			–			–			–			2	–	
7 Sunderland	2	–		–			–			–			–			–			–			–			–			2	–	
8 Tottenham Hotspur	1	(1)	1	–			–			–			–			–			–			–			–			1	(1)	1
9 Barcelona	–			–			–			–			–			1	(1)	–	–			–			–			1	(1)	–
10 Dynamo Kiev	–			–			–			–			–			1	(1)	–	–			–			–			1	(1)	–
11 Newcastle United	1	(1)	–	–			–			–			–			–			–			–			–			1	(1)	–
12 Olympique Lyonnais	–			–			–			–			–			1	(1)	–	–			–			–			1	(1)	–
13 West Ham United	1	(1)	–	–			–			–			–			–			–			–			–			1	(1)	–
14 Blackburn Rovers	–	(2)	–	–			–			–			–			–			–			–			–			–	(2)	–
15 Reading	–	(2)	–	–			–			–			–			–			–			–			–			–	(2)	–
16 Arsenal	–			–			–			1		1	–			–			–			–			–			1		1
17 Middlesbrough	1		1	–			–			–			–			–			–			–			–			1		1
18 Aston Villa	1	–		–			–			–			–			–			–			–			–			1	–	
19 Birmingham City	1	–		–			–			–			–			–			–			–			–			1	–	
20 Coventry City	–			–			–			–			1			–			–			–			–			1	–	
21 Fulham	1	–		–			–			–			–			–			–			–			–			1	–	
22 Liverpool	–	(1)	1	–			–			–			–			–			–			–			–			–	(1)	1
23 Everton	–	(1)	–	–			–			–			–			–			–			–			–			–	(1)	–
24 Wigan Athletic	–	(1)	–	–			–			–			–			–			–			–			–			–	(1)	–

DANIEL NARDIELLO

DEBUT (Substitute Appearance)

Monday 05/11/2001
League Cup 3rd Round
at Highbury

Arsenal 4 Manchester United 0

CLUB CAREER RECORD	Apps	Subs	Goals
Premiership	0		0
League Division 1	0		0
League Division 2	0		0
FA Cup	0		0
League Cup	1	(2)	0
European Cup / Champions League	0	(1)	0
European Cup-Winners' Cup	0		0
UEFA Cup / Inter-Cities' Fairs Cup	0		0
Other Matches	0		0
OVERALL TOTAL	**1**	**(3)**	**0**

Opponents	PREM			FLD 1			FLD 2			FAC			LC			EC/CL			ECWC			UEFA			OTHER			TOTAL		
	A	S	G	A	S	G	A	S	G	A	S	G	A	S	G	A	S	G	A	S	G	A	S	G	A	S	G	A	S	G
1 Leicester City	–			–			–			–			1			–			–			–			–			1		
2 Arsenal	–			–			–			–			–	(1)		–			–			–			–			–	(1)	
3 Maccabi Haifa	–			–			–			–			–			–	(1)		–			–			–			–	(1)	
4 West Bromwich Albion	–			–			–			–			–	(1)		–			–			–			–			–	(1)	

GARY NEVILLE

DEBUT (Substitute Appearance)

Wednesday 16/09/1992
UEFA Cup 1st Round 1st Leg
at Old Trafford

Manchester United 0 Torpedo Moscow 0

CLUB CAREER RECORD	Apps	Subs	Goals
Premiership	349	(15)	5
League Division 1	0		0
League Division 2	0		0
FA Cup	41	(3)	0
League Cup	16	(1)	0
European Cup / Champions League	99	(6)	2
European Cup-Winners' Cup	0		0
UEFA Cup / Inter-Cities' Fairs Cup	1	(1)	0
Other Matches	8	(1)	0
OVERALL TOTAL	**514**	**(27)**	**7**

Opponents	PREM			FLD 1			FLD 2			FAC			LC			EC/CL			ECWC			UEFA			OTHER			TOTAL		
	A	S	G	A	S	G	A	S	G	A	S	G	A	S	G	A	S	G	A	S	G	A	S	G	A	S	G	A	S	G
1 Arsenal	22	(1)								4															2			28	(1)	
2 Chelsea	19	(2)								4			2												1			26	(2)	
3 Aston Villa	22		1							3																		25		1
4 Liverpool	20									2	(1)		1												1			24	(1)	
5 Newcastle United	19	(1)								2			1									–	(1)					22	(2)	
6 Blackburn Rovers	14	(2)											4															18	(2)	
7 Everton	17		1							2																		19		1
8 Southampton	17									1																		18		
9 Middlesbrough	14		1							3																		17		1
10 Leeds United	15	(1)											1															16	(1)	
11 West Ham United	14	(1)								2																		16	(1)	
12 Tottenham Hotspur	14	(2)								1												–	/					15	(2)	
13 Leicester City	13		1										1															14		1
14 Coventry City	14																											14		
15 Manchester City	11									1																		12		
16 Sunderland	9	(1)								2																		11	(1)	
17 Derby County	11																											11		
18 Wimbledon	9									2																		11		
19 Fulham	8									2																		10		
20 Bolton Wanderers	9	(1)																										9	(1)	
21 Sheffield Wednesday	9																											9		
22 Charlton Athletic	8	(1)	1																									8	(1)	1
23 Birmingham City	7												1															8		
24 Juventus																8												8		
25 Bayern Munich																7												7		
26 Portsmouth	5									2																		7		
27 Nottingham Forest	4	(2)																										4	(2)	
28 Crystal Palace	3									2																		5		
29 Deportivo La Coruna																5												5		
30 Bradford City	4																											4		
31 Olympiakos Piraeus																4												4		
32 Porto																4												4		
33 Queens Park Rangers	3									1																		4		
34 Valencia																4												4		
35 West Bromwich Albion	3												1															4		
36 Benfica																3												3		
37 Fenerbahce																3												3		
38 Lille Metropole																3												3		
39 Norwich City	3																											3		
40 Panathinaikos																3												3		
41 Real Madrid																3												3		
42 Sturm Graz																3												3		
43 Wigan Athletic	2												1															3		
44 Barnsley	1									1	(1)																	2	(1)	
45 Bayer Leverkusen																1	(2)											1	(2)	
46 Anderlecht																2												2		
47 Barcelona																2												2		

continued../

GARY NEVILLE (continued)

Opponents	PREM A S G	FLD 1 A S G	FLD 2 A S G	FAC A S G	LC A S G	EC/CL A S G	ECWC A S G	UEFA A S G	OTHER A S G	TOTAL A S G
48 Boavista	–	–	–	–	–	2 –	–	–	–	2 –
49 Borussia Dortmund	–	–	–	–	–	2 –	–	–	–	2 –
50 Brondby	–	–	–	–	–	2 –	–	–	–	2 –
51 Debreceni	–	–	–	–	–	2 –	–	–	–	2 –
52 Dinamo Bucharest	–	–	–	–	–	2 –	–	–	–	2 –
53 Dynamo Kiev	–	–	–	–	–	2 –	–	–	–	2 –
54 Feyenoord	–	–	–	–	–	2 –	–	–	–	2 –
55 Fiorentina	–	–	–	–	–	2 –	–	–	–	2 –
56 Girondins Bordeaux	–	–	–	–	–	2 –	–	–	–	2 –
57 Glasgow Celtic	–	–	–	–	–	2 –	–	–	–	2 –
58 Glasgow Rangers	–	–	–	–	–	2 –	–	–	–	2 –
59 Internazionale	–	–	–	–	–	2 –	–	–	–	2 –
60 Ipswich Town	2 –	–	–	–	–	–	–	–	–	2 –
61 Kosice	–	–	–	–	–	2 –	–	–	–	2 –
62 Monaco	–	–	–	–	–	2 –	–	–	–	2 –
63 Nantes Atlantique	–	–	–	–	–	2 –	–	–	–	2 –
64 PSV Eindhoven	–	–	–	–	–	2 –	–	–	–	2 –
65 Rapid Vienna	–	–	–	–	–	2 –	–	–	–	2 –
66 Reading	1 –	–	–	1 –	–	–	–	–	–	2 –
67 Sparta Prague	–	–	–	–	–	2 –	–	–	–	2 –
68 Stuttgart	–	–	–	–	–	2 –	–	–	–	2 –
69 Wolverhampton W.	1 –	–	–	1 –	–	–	–	–	–	2 –
70 Galatasaray	–	–	–	–	–	1 (1) –	–	–	–	1 (1) –
71 Port Vale	–	–	–	–	1 (1) –	–	–	–	–	1 (1) –
72 Basel	–	–	–	–	–	1 1	–	–	–	1 1
73 Olympique Lyonnais	–	–	–	–	–	1 1	–	–	–	1 1
74 AC Milan	–	–	–	–	–	1 –	–	–	–	1 –
75 Exeter City	–	–	–	1 –	–	–	–	–	–	1 –
76 Lazio	–	–	–	–	–	–	–	1 –	–	1 –
77 LKS Lodz	–	–	–	–	1 –	–	–	–	–	1 –
78 Maccabi Haifa	–	–	–	–	–	1 –	–	–	–	1 –
79 Millwall	–	–	–	1 –	–	–	–	–	–	1 –
80 Palmeiras	–	–	–	–	–	–	–	–	1 –	1 –
81 Rayos del Necaxa	–	–	–	–	–	–	–	–	1 –	1 –
82 Rotor Volgograd	–	–	–	–	–	–	–	1 –	–	1 –
83 Sheffield United	1 –	–	–	–	–	–	–	–	–	1 –
84 Swindon Town	–	–	–	–	1 –	–	–	–	–	1 –
85 Vasco da Gama	–	–	–	–	–	–	–	–	1 –	1 –
86 Watford	1 –	–	–	–	–	–	–	–	–	1 –
87 York City	–	–	–	–	1 –	–	–	–	–	1 –
88 Burton Albion	–	–	–	– (1) –	–	–	–	–	–	– (1) –
89 Gothenburg	–	–	–	–	–	– (1)	–	–	–	– (1) –
90 Roma	–	–	–	–	–	– (1)	–	–	–	– (1) –
91 Torpedo Moscow	–	–	–	–	–	–	–	– (1) –	–	– (1) –
92 Villarreal	–	–	–	–	–	– (1)	–	–	–	– (1) –

PHILIP NEVILLE

DEBUT (Full Appearance)

Saturday 28/01/1995
FA Cup 4th Round
at Old Trafford

Manchester United 5 Wrexham 2

CLUB CAREER RECORD	Apps	Subs	Goals
Premiership	210	(53)	5
League Division 1	0		0
League Division 2	0		0
FA Cup	25	(6)	1
League Cup	16	(1)	0
European Cup / Champions League	42	(22)	2
European Cup-Winners' Cup	0		0
UEFA Cup / Inter-Cities' Fairs Cup	1		0
Other Matches	7	(3)	0
OVERALL TOTAL	301	(85)	8

Opponents	PREM A S G	FLD 1 A S G	FLD 2 A S G	FAC A S G	LC A S G	EC/CL A S G	ECWC A S G	UEFA A S G	OTHER A S G	TOTAL A S G
1 Arsenal	10 (2) –	–	–	1 (2) –	2	–	–	–	2 (2) –	15 (6) –
2 Newcastle United	13 (1) –	–	–	1	–	–	–	–	1 –	15 (1) –
3 Chelsea	9 (1) 1	–	–	2 (1) –	2	–	–	–	1	14 (2) 1
4 Southampton	12 (2) 2	–	–	1 (1) –	–	–	–	–	–	13 (3) 2
5 Liverpool	12 (2) –	–	–	–	1	–	–	–	–	13 (2) –
6 Tottenham Hotspur	12 (2) –	–	–	–	–	1	–	–	–	13 (2) –
7 Aston Villa	10 (4) –	–	–	1	–	–	–	–	–	11 (4) –
8 Everton	10 (4) –	–	–	1	–	–	–	–	–	11 (4) –
9 Leeds United	8 (6) –	–	–	–	1	–	–	–	–	9 (6) –
10 Blackburn Rovers	12	–	–	–	1	–	–	–	–	13
11 Middlesbrough	7 (3) 1	–	–	2 (1) –	–	–	–	–	–	9 (4) 1
12 Manchester City	8 (1) –	–	–	2	–	–	–	–	–	10 (1) –
13 Bolton Wanderers	9 (2) –	–	–	–	–	–	–	–	–	9 (2) –
14 West Ham United	7 (3) –	–	–	1 1	–	–	–	–	–	8 (3) 1
15 Sunderland	5 (3) 1	–	–	1 (1) –	1	–	–	–	–	7 (4) 1
16 Charlton Athletic	7 (3) –	–	–	–	–	–	–	–	–	7 (3) –

continued../

PHILIP NEVILLE (continued)

Opponents	PREM A	S	G	FLD 1 A	S	G	FLD 2 A	S	G	FAC A	S	G	LC A	S	G	EC/CL A	S	G	ECWC A	S	G	UEFA A	S	G	OTHER A	S	G	TOTAL A	S	G
17 Fulham	4 (1)	–		–	–	–	–	–	–	3	–		–	–		–	–		–	–		–	–		–	–		7 (1)	–	
18 Leicester City	5 (2)	–		–	–	–	–	–	–	–	–		1			–	–		–	–		–	–		–	–		6 (2)	–	
19 Sheffield Wednesday	6 (2)	–		–	–	–	–	–	–	–	–		–			–	–		–	–		–	–		–	–		6 (2)	–	
20 Coventry City	5 (3)	–		–	–	–	–	–	–	–	–		–			–	–		–	–		–	–		–	–		5 (3)	–	
21 Wimbledon	7			–	–	–	–	–	–	–	–		–			–	–		–	–		–	–		–	–		7	–	
22 Derby County	6 (1)	–		–	–	–	–	–	–	–	–		–			–	–		–	–		–	–		–	–		6 (1)	–	
23 Ipswich Town	4			–	–	–	–	–	–	–	–		1			–	–		–	–		–	–		–	–		5	–	
24 Crystal Palace	3			–	–	–	–	–	–	–	–		1			–	–		–	–		–	–		–	–		4	–	
25 Bradford City	3 (1)	–		–	–	–	–	–	–	–	–		–			–	–		–	–		–	–		–	–		3 (1)	–	
26 Juventus	–			–	–	–	–	–	–	–	–		–			3 (1)	–		–	–		–	–		–	–		3 (1)	–	
27 Deportivo La Coruna	–			–	–	–	–	–	–	–	–		–			2 (2)	–		–	–		–	–		–	–		2 (2)	–	
28 Birmingham City	1 (3)	–		–	–	–	–	–	–	–	–		–			–	–		–	–		–	–		–	–		1 (3)	–	
29 Barnsley	1			–	–	–	–	–	–	2	–		–			–	–		–	–		–	–		–	–		3	–	
30 Nottingham Forest	3			–	–	–	–	–	–	–	–		–			–	–		–	–		–	–		–	–		3	–	
31 Panathinaikos	–			–	–	–	–	–	–	–	–		–			3			–	–		–	–		–	–		3	–	
32 Portsmouth	2			–	–	–	–	–	–	1	–		–			–	–		–	–		–	–		–	–		3	–	
33 Watford	2			–	–	–	–	–	–	–	–		1			–	–		–	–		–	–		–	–		3	–	
34 West Bromwich Albion	3			–	–	–	–	–	–	–	–		–			–	–		–	–		–	–		–	–		3	–	
35 Porto	–			–	–	–	–	–	–	–	–		–			2 (1)	–		–	–		–	–		–	–		2 (1)	–	
36 Fenerbahce	–			–	–	–	–	–	–	–	–		–			1 (2)	–		–	–		–	–		–	–		1 (2)	–	
37 Sturm Graz	–			–	–	–	–	–	–	–	–		–			1 (2)	–		–	–		–	–		–	–		1 (2)	–	
38 Brondby	–			–	–	–	–	–	–	–	–		–			2	1		–	–		–	–		–	–		2	1	
39 Glasgow Rangers	–			–	–	–	–	–	–	–	–		–			2	1		–	–		–	–		–	–		2	1	
40 Basel	–			–	–	–	–	–	–	–	–		–			2			–	–		–	–		–	–		2	–	
41 Croatia Zagreb	–			–	–	–	–	–	–	–	–		–			2			–	–		–	–		–	–		2	–	
42 Exeter City	–			–	–	–	–	–	–	2	–		–			–	–		–	–		–	–		–	–		2	–	
43 Maccabi Haifa	–			–	–	–	–	–	–	–	–		–			2			–	–		–	–		–	–		2	–	
44 Monaco	–			–	–	–	–	–	–	–	–		–			2			–	–		–	–		–	–		2	–	
45 Olympique Marseille	–			–	–	–	–	–	–	–	–		–			2			–	–		–	–		–	–		2	–	
46 Stuttgart	–			–	–	–	–	–	–	–	–		–			2			–	–		–	–		–	–		2	–	
47 Wolverhampton W.	2			–	–	–	–	–	–	–	–		–			–	–		–	–		–	–		–	–		2	–	
48 Bayer Leverkusen	–			–	–	–	–	–	–	–	–		–			1 (1)	–		–	–		–	–		–	–		1 (1)	–	
49 Boavista	–			–	–	–	–	–	–	–	–		–			1 (1)	–		–	–		–	–		–	–		1 (1)	–	
50 Feyenoord	–			–	–	–	–	–	–	–	–		–			1 (1)	–		–	–		–	–		–	–		1 (1)	–	
51 Norwich City	1 (1)	–		–	–	–	–	–	–	–	–		–			–	–		–	–		–	–		–	–		1 (1)	–	
52 York City	–			–	–	–	–	–	–	–	–		1 (1)	–		–	–		–	–		–	–		–	–		1 (1)	–	
53 Zalaegerszeg	–			–	–	–	–	–	–	–	–		–			1 (1)	–		–	–		–	–		–	–		1 (1)	–	
54 Dinamo Bucharest	–			–	–	–	–	–	–	–	–		–			– (2)	–		–	–		–	–		–	–		– (2)	–	
55 Bayern Munich	–			–	–	–	–	–	–	–	–		–			1			–	–		–	–		–	–		1	–	
56 Borussia Dortmund	–			–	–	–	–	–	–	–	–		–			1			–	–		–	–		–	–		1	–	
57 Burnley	–			–	–	–	–	–	–	–	–		1			–	–		–	–		–	–		–	–		1	–	
58 Bury	–			–	–	–	–	–	–	–	–		1			–	–		–	–		–	–		–	–		1	–	
59 Dynamo Kiev	–			–	–	–	–	–	–	–	–		–			1			–	–		–	–		–	–		1	–	
60 Kosice	–			–	–	–	–	–	–	–	–		–			1			–	–		–	–		–	–		1	–	
61 Lazio	–			–	–	–	–	–	–	–	–		–			–	–		–	–		1			–	–		1	–	
62 Lille Metropole	–			–	–	–	–	–	–	–	–		–			1			–	–		–	–		–	–		1	–	
63 LKS Lodz	–			–	–	–	–	–	–	–	–		–			1			–	–		–	–		–	–		1	–	
64 Nantes Atlantique	–			–	–	–	–	–	–	–	–		–			1			–	–		–	–		–	–		1	–	
65 Olympiakos Piraeus	–			–	–	–	–	–	–	–	–		–			1			–	–		–	–		–	–		1	–	
66 PSV Eindhoven	–			–	–	–	–	–	–	–	–		–			1			–	–		–	–		–	–		1	–	
67 Queens Park Rangers	1			–	–	–	–	–	–	–	–		–			–	–		–	–		–	–		–	–		1	–	
68 Reading	–			–	–	–	–	–	–	1	–		–			–	–		–	–		–	–		–	–		1	–	
69 Rotor Volgograd	–			–	–	–	–	–	–	–	–		–			–	–		–	–		1			–	–		1	–	
70 South Melbourne	–			–	–	–	–	–	–	–	–		–			–	–		–	–		–	–		1			1	–	
71 Swindon Town	–			–	–	–	–	–	–	–	–		1			–	–		–	–		–	–		–	–		1	–	
72 Valencia	–			–	–	–	–	–	–	–	–		–			1			–	–		–	–		–	–		1	–	
73 Vasco da Gama	–			–	–	–	–	–	–	–	–		–			–	–		–	–		–	–		1			1	–	
74 Walsall	–			–	–	–	–	–	–	1	–		–			–	–		–	–		–	–		–	–		1	–	
75 Wrexham	–			–	–	–	–	–	–	1	–		–			–	–		–	–		–	–		–	–		1	–	
76 Anderlecht	–			–	–	–	–	–	–	–	–		–			– (1)	–		–	–		–	–		–	–		– (1)	–	
77 Barcelona	–			–	–	–	–	–	–	–	–		–			– (1)	–		–	–		–	–		–	–		– (1)	–	
78 Fiorentina	–			–	–	–	–	–	–	–	–		–			– (1)	–		–	–		–	–		–	–		– (1)	–	
79 Girondins Bordeaux	–			–	–	–	–	–	–	–	–		–			– (1)	–		–	–		–	–		–	–		– (1)	–	
80 Internazionale	–			–	–	–	–	–	–	–	–		–			– (1)	–		–	–		–	–		–	–		– (1)	–	
81 Olympique Lyonnais	–			–	–	–	–	–	–	–	–		–			– (1)	–		–	–		–	–		–	–		– (1)	–	
82 Rayos del Necaxa	–			–	–	–	–	–	–	–	–		–			–	–		–	–		–	–		– (1)	–		– (1)	–	
83 Real Madrid	–			–	–	–	–	–	–	–	–		–			– (1)	–		–	–		–	–		–	–		– (1)	–	
84 Sparta Prague	–			–	–	–	–	–	–	–	–		–			– (1)	–		–	–		–	–		–	–		– (1)	–	

GEORGE NEVIN

DEBUT (Full Appearance)

Saturday 06/01/1934
Football League Division 2
at Sincil Bank

Lincoln City 5 Manchester United 1

CLUB CAREER RECORD	Apps	Subs	Goals
Premiership	0		0
League Division 1	0		0
League Division 2	4		0
FA Cup	1		0
League Cup	0		0
European Cup / Champions League	0		0
European Cup-Winners' Cup	0		0
UEFA Cup / Inter-Cities' Fairs Cup	0		0
Other Matches	0		0
OVERALL TOTAL	**5**		**0**

Opponents	PREM A S G	FLD 1 A S G	FLD 2 A S G	FAC A S G	LC A S G	EC/CL A S G	ECWC A S G	UEFA A S G	OTHER A S G	TOTAL A S G
1 Bolton Wanderers	– –	– –	1 –	– –	– –	– –	– –	– –	– –	1 –
2 Burnley	– –	– –	1 –	– –	– –	– –	– –	– –	– –	1 –
3 Lincoln City	– –	– –	1 –	– –	– –	– –	– –	– –	– –	1 –
4 Oldham Athletic	– –	– –	1 –	– –	– –	– –	– –	– –	– –	1 –
5 Portsmouth	– –	– –	– –	1 –	– –	– –	– –	– –	– –	1 –

ERIK NEVLAND

DEBUT (Substitute Appearance)

Tuesday 14/10/1997
League Cup 3rd Round
at Portman Road

Ipswich Town 2 Manchester United 0

CLUB CAREER RECORD	Apps	Subs	Goals
Premiership	0	(1)	0
League Division 1	0		0
League Division 2	0		0
FA Cup	2	(1)	0
League Cup	0	(2)	1
European Cup / Champions League	0		0
European Cup-Winners' Cup	0		0
UEFA Cup / Inter-Cities' Fairs Cup	0		0
Other Matches	0		0
OVERALL TOTAL	**2**	**(4)**	**1**

Opponents	PREM A S G	FLD 1 A S G	FLD 2 A S G	FAC A S G	LC A S G	EC/CL A S G	ECWC A S G	UEFA A S G	OTHER A S G	TOTAL A S G
1 Barnsley	– –	– –	– –	2 –	– –	– –	– –	– –	– –	2 –
2 Bury	– –	– –	– –	– –	– (1) 1	– –	– –	– –	– –	– (1) 1
3 Ipswich Town	– –	– –	– –	– –	– (1) –	– –	– –	– –	– –	– (1) –
4 Southampton	– (1) –	– –	– –	– –	– –	– –	– –	– –	– –	– (1) –
5 Walsall	– –	– –	– –	– (1) –	– –	– –	– –	– –	– –	– (1) –

PERCY NEWTON

DEBUT (Full Appearance)

Saturday 03/02/1934
Football League Division 2
at Turf Moor

Burnley 1 Manchester United 4

CLUB CAREER RECORD	Apps	Subs	Goals
Premiership	0		0
League Division 1	0		0
League Division 2	2		0
FA Cup	0		0
League Cup	0		0
European Cup / Champions League	0		0
European Cup-Winners' Cup	0		0
UEFA Cup / Inter-Cities' Fairs Cup	0		0
Other Matches	0		0
OVERALL TOTAL	**2**		**0**

Opponents	PREM A S G	FLD 1 A S G	FLD 2 A S G	FAC A S G	LC A S G	EC/CL A S G	ECWC A S G	UEFA A S G	OTHER A S G	TOTAL A S G
1 Burnley	– –	– –	1 –	– –	– –	– –	– –	– –	– –	1 –
2 Oldham Athletic	– –	– –	1 –	– –	– –	– –	– –	– –	– –	1 –

JIMMY NICHOLL

DEBUT (Substitute Appearance)

Saturday 05/04/1975
Football League Division 2
at The Dell

Southampton 0 Manchester United 1

CLUB CAREER RECORD	Apps	Subs	Goals
Premiership	0		0
League Division 1	188	(8)	3
League Division 2	0	(1)	0
FA Cup	22	(4)	1
League Cup	14		1
European Cup / Champions League	0		0
European Cup-Winners' Cup	4		1
UEFA Cup / Inter-Cities' Fairs Cup	6		0
Other Matches	1		0
OVERALL TOTAL	**235**	**(13)**	**6**

Opponents	PREM A S G	FLD 1 A S G	FLD 2 A S G	FAC A S G	LC A S G	EC/CL A S G	ECWC A S G	UEFA A S G	OTHER A S G	TOTAL A S G
1 Tottenham Hotspur	– –	8 (1) –	– –	4 –	2 –	– –	– –	– –	– –	14 (1) –
2 Liverpool	– –	9 –	– –	3 –	– –	– –	– –	1 –	– –	13 –
3 Arsenal	– –	9 –	– –	1 –	1 –	– –	– –	– –	– –	11 –
4 Coventry City	– –	9 –	– –	– –	2 –	– –	– –	– –	– –	11 –
5 Leeds United	– –	10 –	– –	1 –	– –	– –	– –	– –	– –	11 –

continued../

JIMMY NICHOLL (continued)

Opponents	PREM			FLD 1			FLD 2			FAC			LC			EC/CL			ECWC			UEFA			OTHER			TOTAL		
	A	S	G	A	S	G	A	S	G	A	S	G	A	S	G	A	S	G	A	S	G	A	S	G	A	S	G	A	S	G
6 Aston Villa	–	–	–	8	(1)	1	–	–	–	1	–	–	1	–	–	–	–	–	–	–	–	–	–	–	–	–	–	10	(1)	1
7 Manchester City	–	–	–	9	–	1	–	–	–	–	–	–	1	–	–	–	–	–	–	–	–	–	–	–	–	–	–	10	–	1
8 Middlesbrough	–	–	–	9	(1)	–	–	–	–	–	–	–	–	–	–	–	–	–	–	–	–	–	–	–	–	–	–	9	(1)	–
9 Wolverhampton W.	–	–	–	8	(1)	–	–	–	–	–	(1)	–	–	–	–	–	–	–	–	–	–	–	–	–	–	–	–	8	(2)	–
10 Ipswich Town	–	–	–	9	–	1	–	–	–	–	–	–	–	–	–	–	–	–	–	–	–	–	–	–	–	–	–	9	–	1
11 Everton	–	–	–	9	–	–	–	–	–	–	–	–	–	–	–	–	–	–	–	–	–	–	–	–	–	–	–	9	–	–
12 Norwich City	–	–	–	8	–	–	–	–	–	–	–	–	1	–	–	–	–	–	–	–	–	–	–	–	–	–	–	9	–	–
13 West Bromwich Albion	–	–	–	7	–	–	–	–	–	2	–	–	–	–	–	–	–	–	–	–	–	–	–	–	–	–	–	9	–	–
14 Derby County	–	–	–	8	–	–	–	–	–	–	–	–	–	–	–	–	–	–	–	–	–	–	–	–	–	–	–	8	–	–
15 Leicester City	–	–	–	8	–	–	–	–	–	–	–	–	–	–	–	–	–	–	–	–	–	–	–	–	–	–	–	8	–	–
16 Nottingham Forest	–	–	–	7	–	–	–	–	–	1	–	–	–	–	–	–	–	–	–	–	–	–	–	–	–	–	–	8	–	–
17 Birmingham City	–	–	–	7	(1)	–	–	–	–	–	–	–	–	–	–	–	–	–	–	–	–	–	–	–	–	–	–	7	(1)	–
18 Bristol City	–	–	–	7	–	–	–	–	–	–	–	–	–	–	–	–	–	–	–	–	–	–	–	–	–	–	–	7	–	–
19 Southampton	–	–	–	4	–	–	–	(1)	–	2	–	–	–	–	–	–	–	–	–	–	–	–	–	–	–	–	–	6	(1)	–
20 Stoke City	–	–	–	6	(1)	–	–	–	–	–	–	–	–	–	–	–	–	–	–	–	–	–	–	–	–	–	–	6	(1)	–
21 Brighton	–	–	–	4	–	–	–	–	–	2	–	1	–	–	–	–	–	–	–	–	–	–	–	–	–	–	–	6	–	1
22 Newcastle United	–	–	–	5	–	–	–	–	–	–	–	–	1	–	1	–	–	–	–	–	–	–	–	–	–	–	–	6	–	1
23 Queens Park Rangers	–	–	–	5	–	–	–	–	–	1	–	–	–	–	–	–	–	–	–	–	–	–	–	–	–	–	–	6	–	–
24 Sunderland	–	–	–	3	–	–	–	–	–	–	–	–	3	–	–	–	–	–	–	–	–	–	–	–	–	–	–	6	–	–
25 Chelsea	–	–	–	3	–	–	–	–	–	1	–	–	–	–	–	–	–	–	–	–	–	–	–	–	–	–	–	4	–	–
26 Bolton Wanderers	–	–	–	3	(1)	–	–	–	–	–	–	–	–	–	–	–	–	–	–	–	–	–	–	–	–	–	–	3	(1)	–
27 Crystal Palace	–	–	–	3	–	–	–	–	–	–	–	–	–	–	–	–	–	–	–	–	–	–	–	–	–	–	–	3	–	–
28 West Ham United	–	–	–	3	–	–	–	–	–	–	–	–	–	–	–	–	–	–	–	–	–	–	–	–	–	–	–	3	–	–
29 Porto	–	–	–	–	–	–	–	–	–	–	–	–	–	–	–	–	–	–	2	–	1	–	–	–	–	–	–	2	–	1
30 Ajax	–	–	–	–	–	–	–	–	–	–	–	–	–	–	–	–	–	–	–	–	–	2	–	–	–	–	–	2	–	–
31 Carlisle United	–	–	–	–	–	–	–	–	–	2	–	–	–	–	–	–	–	–	–	–	–	–	–	–	–	–	–	2	–	–
32 Juventus	–	–	–	–	–	–	–	–	–	–	–	–	–	–	–	–	–	–	–	–	–	2	–	–	–	–	–	2	–	–
33 St Etienne	–	–	–	–	–	–	–	–	–	–	–	–	–	–	–	–	–	–	2	–	–	–	–	–	–	–	–	2	–	–
34 Widzew Lodz	–	–	–	–	–	–	–	–	–	–	–	–	–	–	–	–	–	–	–	–	–	2	–	–	–	–	–	2	–	–
35 Brentford	–	–	–	–	–	–	–	–	–	–	–	–	1	–	–	–	–	–	–	–	–	–	–	–	–	–	–	1	–	–
36 Tranmere Rovers	–	–	–	–	–	–	–	–	–	–	–	–	1	–	–	–	–	–	–	–	–	–	–	–	–	–	–	1	–	–
37 Walsall	–	–	–	–	–	–	–	–	–	1	–	–	–	–	–	–	–	–	–	–	–	–	–	–	–	–	–	1	–	–
38 Colchester United	–	–	–	–	–	–	–	(1)	–	–	–	–	–	–	–	–	–	–	–	–	–	–	–	–	–	–	–	–	(1)	–
39 Fulham	–	–	–	–	–	–	–	(1)	–	–	–	–	–	–	–	–	–	–	–	–	–	–	–	–	–	–	–	–	(1)	–
40 Oxford United	–	–	–	–	–	–	–	(1)	–	–	–	–	–	–	–	–	–	–	–	–	–	–	–	–	–	–	–	–	(1)	–
41 Sheffield United	–	–	–	–	(1)	–	–	–	–	–	–	–	–	–	–	–	–	–	–	–	–	–	–	–	–	–	–	–	(1)	–

JIMMY NICHOLSON

DEBUT (Full Appearance)

Wednesday 24/08/1960
Football League Division 1
at Goodison Park

Everton 4 Manchester United 0

CLUB CAREER RECORD	Apps	Subs	Goals
Premiership	0		0
League Division 1	58		5
League Division 2	0		0
FA Cup	7		1
League Cup	3		0
European Cup / Champions League	0		0
European Cup-Winners' Cup	0		0
UEFA Cup / Inter-Cities' Fairs Cup	0		0
Other Matches	0		0
OVERALL TOTAL	68		6

Opponents	PREM			FLD 1			FLD 2			FAC			LC			EC/CL			ECWC			UEFA			OTHER			TOTAL		
	A	S	G	A	S	G	A	S	G	A	S	G	A	S	G	A	S	G	A	S	G	A	S	G	A	S	G	A	S	G
1 Bolton Wanderers	–	–	–	4	–	–	–	–	–	1	–	1	–	–	–	–	–	–	–	–	–	–	–	–	–	–	–	5	–	1
2 Nottingham Forest	–	–	–	5	–	–	–	–	–	–	–	–	–	–	–	–	–	–	–	–	–	–	–	–	–	–	–	5	–	–
3 Everton	–	–	–	4	–	1	–	–	–	–	–	–	–	–	–	–	–	–	–	–	–	–	–	–	–	–	–	4	–	1
4 Arsenal	–	–	–	3	–	–	–	–	–	1	–	–	–	–	–	–	–	–	–	–	–	–	–	–	–	–	–	4	–	–
5 Fulham	–	–	–	4	–	–	–	–	–	–	–	–	–	–	–	–	–	–	–	–	–	–	–	–	–	–	–	4	–	–
6 Sheffield Wednesday	–	–	–	1	–	–	–	–	–	3	–	–	–	–	–	–	–	–	–	–	–	–	–	–	–	–	–	4	–	–
7 Blackpool	–	–	–	3	–	1	–	–	–	–	–	–	–	–	–	–	–	–	–	–	–	–	–	–	–	–	–	3	–	1
8 Wolverhampton W.	–	–	–	3	–	1	–	–	–	–	–	–	–	–	–	–	–	–	–	–	–	–	–	–	–	–	–	3	–	1
9 Aston Villa	–	–	–	3	–	–	–	–	–	–	–	–	–	–	–	–	–	–	–	–	–	–	–	–	–	–	–	3	–	–
10 Leicester City	–	–	–	3	–	–	–	–	–	–	–	–	–	–	–	–	–	–	–	–	–	–	–	–	–	–	–	3	–	–
11 Manchester City	–	–	–	3	–	–	–	–	–	–	–	–	–	–	–	–	–	–	–	–	–	–	–	–	–	–	–	3	–	–
12 Tottenham Hotspur	–	–	–	3	–	–	–	–	–	–	–	–	–	–	–	–	–	–	–	–	–	–	–	–	–	–	–	3	–	–
13 West Bromwich Albion	–	–	–	3	–	–	–	–	–	–	–	–	–	–	–	–	–	–	–	–	–	–	–	–	–	–	–	3	–	–
14 West Ham United	–	–	–	3	–	–	–	–	–	–	–	–	–	–	–	–	–	–	–	–	–	–	–	–	–	–	–	3	–	–
15 Chelsea	–	–	–	2	–	2	–	–	–	–	–	–	–	–	–	–	–	–	–	–	–	–	–	–	–	–	–	2	–	2
16 Birmingham City	–	–	–	2	–	–	–	–	–	–	–	–	–	–	–	–	–	–	–	–	–	–	–	–	–	–	–	2	–	–
17 Blackburn Rovers	–	–	–	2	–	–	–	–	–	–	–	–	–	–	–	–	–	–	–	–	–	–	–	–	–	–	–	2	–	–
18 Cardiff City	–	–	–	2	–	–	–	–	–	–	–	–	–	–	–	–	–	–	–	–	–	–	–	–	–	–	–	2	–	–
19 Exeter City	–	–	–	–	–	–	–	–	–	–	–	–	2	–	–	–	–	–	–	–	–	–	–	–	–	–	–	2	–	–
20 Preston North End	–	–	–	1	–	–	–	–	–	1	–	–	–	–	–	–	–	–	–	–	–	–	–	–	–	–	–	2	–	–
21 Bradford City	–	–	–	–	–	–	–	–	–	–	–	–	1	–	–	–	–	–	–	–	–	–	–	–	–	–	–	1	–	–
22 Burnley	–	–	–	1	–	–	–	–	–	–	–	–	–	–	–	–	–	–	–	–	–	–	–	–	–	–	–	1	–	–
23 Leyton Orient	–	–	–	1	–	–	–	–	–	–	–	–	–	–	–	–	–	–	–	–	–	–	–	–	–	–	–	1	–	–
24 Middlesbrough	–	–	–	–	–	–	–	–	–	1	–	–	–	–	–	–	–	–	–	–	–	–	–	–	–	–	–	1	–	–
25 Newcastle United	–	–	–	1	–	–	–	–	–	–	–	–	–	–	–	–	–	–	–	–	–	–	–	–	–	–	–	1	–	–
26 Sheffield United	–	–	–	1	–	–	–	–	–	–	–	–	–	–	–	–	–	–	–	–	–	–	–	–	–	–	–	1	–	–

GEORGE NICOL

DEBUT (Full Appearance, 2 goals)

Saturday 11/02/1928
Football League Division 1
at Old Trafford

Manchester United 5 Leicester City 2

CLUB CAREER RECORD	Apps	Subs	Goals
Premiership	0		0
League Division 1	6		2
League Division 2	0		0
FA Cup	1		0
League Cup	0		0
European Cup / Champions League	0		0
European Cup-Winners' Cup	0		0
UEFA Cup / Inter-Cities' Fairs Cup	0		0
Other Matches	0		0
OVERALL TOTAL	7		2

Opponents	PREM A S G	FLD 1 A S G	FLD 2 A S G	FAC A S G	LC A S G	EC/CL A S G	ECWC A S G	UEFA A S G	OTHER A S G	TOTAL A S G
1 Leicester City	- -	1 2	-	-	-	-	-	-	-	1 2
2 Aston Villa	- -	1	-	-	-	-	-	-	-	1 -
3 Birmingham City	- -	-	-	1	-	-	-	-	1 -
4 Bolton Wanderers	- -	1	-	-	-	-	-	-	-	1 -
5 Cardiff City	- -	1	-	-	-	-	-	-	-	1 -
6 Everton	- -	1	-	-	-	-	-	-	-	1 -
7 Portsmouth	- -	1	-	-	-	-	-	-	-	1 -

BOBBY NOBLE

DEBUT (Full Appearance)

Saturday 09/04/1966
Football League Division 1
at Old Trafford

Manchester United 1 Leicester City 2

CLUB CAREER RECORD	Apps	Subs	Goals
Premiership	0		0
League Division 1	31		0
League Division 2	0		0
FA Cup	2		0
League Cup	0		0
European Cup / Champions League	0		0
European Cup-Winners' Cup	0		0
UEFA Cup / Inter-Cities' Fairs Cup	0		0
Other Matches	0		0
OVERALL TOTAL	33		0

Opponents	PREM A S G	FLD 1 A S G	FLD 2 A S G	FAC A S G	LC A S G	EC/CL A S G	ECWC A S G	UEFA A S G	OTHER A S G	TOTAL A S G
1 Leicester City	- -	3	-	-	-	-	-	-	-	3 -
2 Arsenal	- -	2	-	-	-	-	-	-	-	2 -
3 Blackpool	- -	2	-	-	-	-	-	-	-	2 -
4 Chelsea	- -	2	-	-	-	-	-	-	-	2 -
5 Fulham	- -	2	-	-	-	-	-	-	-	2 -
6 Leeds United	- -	2	-	-	-	-	-	-	-	2 -
7 Liverpool	- -	2	-	-	-	-	-	-	-	2 -
8 Sheffield United	- -	2	-	-	-	-	-	-	-	2 -
9 Sheffield Wednesday	- -	2	-	-	-	-	-	-	-	2 -
10 Southampton	- -	2	-	-	-	-	-	-	-	2 -
11 Sunderland	- -	2	-	-	-	-	-	-	-	2 -
12 Aston Villa	- -	1	-	-	-	-	-	-	-	1 -
13 Burnley	- -	1	-	-	-	-	-	-	-	1 -
14 Manchester City	- -	1	-	-	-	-	-	-	-	1 -
15 Newcastle United	- -	1	-	-	-	-	-	-	-	1 -
16 Norwich City	- -	-	-	1	-	-	-	-	-	1 -
17 Nottingham Forest	- -	1	-	-	-	-	-	-	-	1 -
18 Stoke City	- -	-	-	1	-	-	-	-	-	1 -
19 Tottenham Hotspur	- -	1	-	-	-	-	-	-	-	1 -
20 West Bromwich Albion	- -	1	-	-	-	-	-	-	-	1 -
21 West Ham United	- -	1	-	-	-	-	-	-	-	1 -

JOE NORTON

DEBUT (Full Appearance)

Saturday 24/01/1914
Football League Division 1
at Boundary Park

Oldham Athletic 2 Manchester United 2

CLUB CAREER RECORD	Apps	Subs	Goals
Premiership	0		0
League Division 1	37		3
League Division 2	0		0
FA Cup	0		0
League Cup	0		0
European Cup / Champions League	0		0
European Cup-Winners' Cup	0		0
UEFA Cup / Inter-Cities' Fairs Cup	0		0
Other Matches	0		0
OVERALL TOTAL	37		3

Opponents	PREM A S G	FLD 1 A S G	FLD 2 A S G	FAC A S G	LC A S G	EC/CL A S G	ECWC A S G	UEFA A S G	OTHER A S G	TOTAL A S G
1 Newcastle United	- -	3 -	-	-	-	-	-	-	-	3 -
2 Sunderland	- -	3 -	-	-	-	-	-	-	-	3 -
3 Aston Villa	- -	2 2	-	-	-	-	-	-	-	2 2
4 Chelsea	- -	2 1	-	-	-	-	-	-	-	2 1
5 Blackburn Rovers	- -	2 -	-	-	-	-	-	-	-	2 -
6 Bolton Wanderers	- -	2 -	-	-	-	-	-	-	-	2 -

continued../

JOE NORTON (continued)

Opponents	PREM A S G	FLD 1 A S G	FLD 2 A S G	FAC A S G	LC A S G	EC/CL A S G	ECWC A S G	UEFA A S G	OTHER A S G	TOTAL A S G
7 Bradford City	– –	2	– – –	– –	– –	– –	– –	– –	– –	2 –
8 Bradford Park Avenue	– –	2	– – –	– –	– –	– –	– –	– –	– –	2 –
9 Burnley	– –	2	– – –	– –	– –	– –	– –	– –	– –	2 –
10 Everton	– –	2	– – –	– –	– –	– –	– –	– –	– –	2 –
11 Liverpool	– –	2	– – –	– –	– –	– –	– –	– –	– –	2 –
12 Sheffield United	– –	2	– – –	– –	– –	– –	– –	– –	– –	2 –
13 Sheffield Wednesday	– –	2	– – –	– –	– –	– –	– –	– –	– –	2 –
14 West Bromwich Albion	– –	2	– – –	– –	– –	– –	– –	– –	– –	2 –
15 Derby County	– –	1	– – –	– –	– –	– –	– –	– –	– –	1 –
16 Manchester City	– –	1	– – –	– –	– –	– –	– –	– –	– –	1 –
17 Middlesbrough	– –	1	– – –	– –	– –	– –	– –	– –	– –	1 –
18 Notts County	– –	1	– – –	– –	– –	– –	– –	– –	– –	1 –
19 Oldham Athletic	– –	1	– – –	– –	– –	– –	– –	– –	– –	1 –
20 Preston North End	– –	1	– – –	– –	– –	– –	– –	– –	– –	1 –
21 Tottenham Hotspur	– –	1	– – –	– –	– –	– –	– –	– –	– –	1 –

ALEX NOTMAN

DEBUT (Substitute Appearance)

Wednesday 02/12/1998
League Cup 5th Round
at White Hart Lane

Tottenham Hotspur 3 Manchester United 1

CLUB CAREER RECORD	Apps	Subs	Goals
Premiership	0		0
League Division 1	0		0
League Division 2	0		0
FA Cup	0		0
League Cup	0	(1)	0
European Cup / Champions League	0		0
European Cup-Winners' Cup	0		0
UEFA Cup / Inter-Cities' Fairs Cup	0		0
Other Matches	0		0
OVERALL TOTAL	**0**	**(1)**	**0**

Opponents	PREM A S G	FLD 1 A S G	FLD 2 A S G	FAC A S G	LC A S G	EC/CL A S G	ECWC A S G	UEFA A S G	OTHER A S G	TOTAL A S G
1 Tottenham Hotspur	– – –	– – –	– – –	– – –	– (1) –	– – –	– – –	– – –	– – –	– (1) –

TOM NUTTALL

DEBUT (Full Appearance, 1 goal)

Saturday 23/03/1912
Football League Division 1
at Old Trafford

Manchester United 1 Liverpool 1

CLUB CAREER RECORD	Apps	Subs	Goals
Premiership	0		0
League Division 1	16		4
League Division 2	0		0
FA Cup	0		0
League Cup	0		0
European Cup / Champions League	0		0
European Cup-Winners' Cup	0		0
UEFA Cup / Inter-Cities' Fairs Cup	0		0
Other Matches	0		0
OVERALL TOTAL	**16**		**4**

Opponents	PREM A S G	FLD 1 A S G	FLD 2 A S G	FAC A S G	LC A S G	EC/CL A S G	ECWC A S G	UEFA A S G	OTHER A S G	TOTAL A S G
1 Middlesbrough	– –	2 2	– –	– –	– –	– –	– –	– –	– –	2 2
2 Liverpool	– –	2 1	– –	– –	– –	– –	– –	– –	– –	2 1
3 Blackburn Rovers	– –	2	– –	– –	– –	– –	– –	– –	– –	2 –
4 Bolton Wanderers	– –	2	– –	– –	– –	– –	– –	– –	– –	2 –
5 Everton	– –	2	– –	– –	– –	– –	– –	– –	– –	2 –
6 Sheffield United	– –	1 1	– –	– –	– –	– –	– –	– –	– –	1 1
7 Derby County	– –	1	– –	– –	– –	– –	– –	– –	– –	1 –
8 Notts County	– –	1	– –	– –	– –	– –	– –	– –	– –	1 –
9 Oldham Athletic	– –	1	– –	– –	– –	– –	– –	– –	– –	1 –
10 Sheffield Wednesday	– –	1	– –	– –	– –	– –	– –	– –	– –	1 –
11 Tottenham Hotspur	– –	1	– –	– –	– –	– –	– –	– –	– –	1 –

GEORGE O'BRIEN

DEBUT (Full Appearance)

Monday 07/04/1902
Football League Division 2
at Bank Street

Newton Heath 1 Middlesbrough 2

CLUB CAREER RECORD	Apps	Subs	Goals
Premiership	0		0
League Division 1	0		0
League Division 2	1		0
FA Cup	0		0
League Cup	0		0
European Cup / Champions League	0		0
European Cup-Winners' Cup	0		0
UEFA Cup / Inter-Cities' Fairs Cup	0		0
Other Matches	0		0
OVERALL TOTAL	**1**		**0**

Opponents	PREM A S G	FLD 1 A S G	FLD 2 A S G	FAC A S G	LC A S G	EC/CL A S G	ECWC A S G	UEFA A S G	OTHER A S G	TOTAL A S G
1 Middlesbrough	– –	– –	1 –	– –	– –	– –	– –	– –	– –	1 –

LIAM O'BRIEN

DEBUT (Full Appearance)

Saturday 20/12/1986
Football League Division 1
at Old Trafford

Manchester United 2 Leicester City 0

CLUB CAREER RECORD	Apps	Subs	Goals
Premiership	0		0
League Division 1	16	(15)	2
League Division 2	0		0
FA Cup	0	(2)	0
League Cup	1	(2)	0
European Cup / Champions League	0		0
European Cup-Winners' Cup	0		0
UEFA Cup / Inter-Cities' Fairs Cup	0		0
Other Matches	0		0
OVERALL TOTAL	**17**	**(19)**	**2**

Opponents	PREM A	S	G	FLD 1 A	S	G	FLD 2 A	S	G	FAC A	S	G	LC A	S	G	EC/CL A	S	G	ECWC A	S	G	UEFA A	S	G	OTHER A	S	G	TOTAL A	S	G
1 Norwich City	–	–		1	(2)	–	–			–			–			–			–			–			–			1	(2)	–
2 Queens Park Rangers	–	–		1	(2)	–	–			–			–			–			–			–			–			1	(2)	–
3 Newcastle United	–	–		2		–	–			–			–			–			–			–			–			2		–
4 Chelsea	–	–		1		1	–			–	(1)	–	–			–			–			–			–			1	(1)	1
5 Derby County	–	–		1	(1)	–	–			–			–			–			–			–			–			1	(1)	–
6 Luton Town	–	–		1	(1)	–	–			–			–			–			–			–			–			1	(1)	–
7 Nottingham Forest	–	–		1	(1)	–	–			–			–			–			–			–			–			1	(1)	–
8 Sheffield Wednesday	–	–		1	(1)	–	–			–			–			–			–			–			–			1	(1)	–
9 Southampton	–	–		1	(1)	–	–			–			–			–			–			–			–			1	(1)	–
10 Wimbledon	–	–		–	(1)	–	–			–			1			–			–			–			–			1	(1)	–
11 Arsenal	–	–		–	(1)	–	–			–	(1)	–	–			–			–			–			–			–	(2)	–
12 Everton	–	–		–	(2)	–	–			–			–			–			–			–			–			–	(2)	–
13 Coventry City	–	–		1		1	–			–			–			–			–			–			–			1		1
14 Aston Villa	–	–		1			–			–			–			–			–			–			–			1		–
15 Leicester City	–	–		1			–			–			–			–			–			–			–			1		–
16 Manchester City	–	–		1			–			–			–			–			–			–			–			1		–
17 Oxford United	–	–		1			–			–			–			–			–			–			–			1		–
18 Tottenham Hotspur	–	–		1			–			–			–			–			–			–			–			1		–
19 Bury	–	–		–			–			–			–	(1)	–	–			–			–			–			–	(1)	–
20 Charlton Athletic	–	–		–	(1)	–	–			–			–			–			–			–			–			–	(1)	–
21 Hull City	–	–		–			–			–			–	(1)	–	–			–			–			–			–	(1)	–
22 Watford	–	–		–	(1)	–	–			–			–			–			–			–			–			–	(1)	–

PAT O'CONNELL

DEBUT (Full Appearance, 1 goal)

Wednesday 02/09/1914
Football League Division 1
at Old Trafford

Manchester United 1 Oldham Athletic 3

CLUB CAREER RECORD	Apps	Subs	Goals
Premiership	0		0
League Division 1	34		2
League Division 2	0		0
FA Cup	1		0
League Cup	0		0
European Cup / Champions League	0		0
European Cup-Winners' Cup	0		0
UEFA Cup / Inter-Cities' Fairs Cup	0		0
Other Matches	0		0
OVERALL TOTAL	**35**		**2**

Opponents	PREM A	S	G	FLD 1 A	S	G	FLD 2 A	S	G	FAC A	S	G	LC A	S	G	EC/CL A	S	G	ECWC A	S	G	UEFA A	S	G	OTHER A	S	G	TOTAL A	S	G
1 Sheffield Wednesday	–	–		2			–			1			–			–			–			–			–			3		–
2 Middlesbrough	–	–		2		1	–			–			–			–			–			–			–			2		1
3 Oldham Athletic	–	–		2		1	–			–			–			–			–			–			–			2		1
4 Aston Villa	–	–		2			–			–			–			–			–			–			–			2		–
5 Bolton Wanderers	–	–		2			–			–			–			–			–			–			–			2		–
6 Bradford Park Avenue	–	–		2			–			–			–			–			–			–			–			2		–
7 Burnley	–	–		2			–			–			–			–			–			–			–			2		–
8 Everton	–	–		2			–			–			–			–			–			–			–			2		–
9 Liverpool	–	–		2			–			–			–			–			–			–			–			2		–
10 Manchester City	–	–		2			–			–			–			–			–			–			–			2		–
11 Newcastle United	–	–		2			–			–			–			–			–			–			–			2		–
12 Sheffield United	–	–		2			–			–			–			–			–			–			–			2		–
13 Sunderland	–	–		2			–			–			–			–			–			–			–			2		–
14 Tottenham Hotspur	–	–		2			–			–			–			–			–			–			–			2		–
15 West Bromwich Albion	–	–		2			–			–			–			–			–			–			–			2		–
16 Blackburn Rovers	–	–		1			–			–			–			–			–			–			–			1		–
17 Bradford City	–	–		1			–			–			–			–			–			–			–			1		–
18 Chelsea	–	–		1			–			–			–			–			–			–			–			1		–
19 Notts County	–	–		1			–			–			–			–			–			–			–			1		–

JOHN O'KANE

DEBUT (Substitute Appearance)

Wednesday 21/09/1994
League Cup 2nd Round 1st Leg
at Vale Park

Port Vale 1 Manchester United 2

CLUB CAREER RECORD	Apps	Subs	Goals
Premiership	1	(1)	0
League Division 1	0		0
League Division 2	0		0
FA Cup	1		0
League Cup	2	(1)	0
European Cup / Champions League	0		0
European Cup-Winners' Cup	0		0
UEFA Cup / Inter-Cities' Fairs Cup	1		0
Other Matches	0		0
OVERALL TOTAL	**5**	**(2)**	**0**

Opponents	PREM A S G	FLD 1 A S G	FLD 2 A S G	FAC A S G	LC A S G	EC/CL A S G	ECWC A S G	UEFA A S G	OTHER A S G	TOTAL A S G
1 Port Vale	–	–	–	–	1 (1) –	–	–	–	–	1 (1) –
2 Leicester City	–	–	–	–	1	–	–	–	–	1 –
3 Middlesbrough	1	–	–	–	–	–	–	–	–	1 –
4 Rotor Volgograd	–	–	–	–	–	–	–	1	–	1 –
5 Sheffield United	–	–	–	1	–	–	–	–	–	1 –
6 Aston Villa	– (1)	–	–	–	–	–	–	–	–	– (1) –

LES OLIVE

DEBUT (Full Appearance)

Saturday 11/04/1953
Football League Division 1
at St James' Park

Newcastle United 1 Manchester United 2

CLUB CAREER RECORD	Apps	Subs	Goals
Premiership	0		0
League Division 1	2		0
League Division 2	0		0
FA Cup	0		0
League Cup	0		0
European Cup / Champions League	0		0
European Cup-Winners' Cup	0		0
UEFA Cup / Inter-Cities' Fairs Cup	0		0
Other Matches	0		0
OVERALL TOTAL	**2**		**0**

Opponents	PREM A S G	FLD 1 A S G	FLD 2 A S G	FAC A S G	LC A S G	EC/CL A S G	ECWC A S G	UEFA A S G	OTHER A S G	TOTAL A S G
1 Newcastle United	– –	1	–	–	–	–	–	–	–	1 –
2 West Bromwich Albion	– –	1	–	–	–	–	–	–	–	1 –

JESPER OLSEN

DEBUT (Full Appearance)

Saturday 25/08/1984
Football League Division 1
at Old Trafford

Manchester United 1 Watford 1

CLUB CAREER RECORD	Apps	Subs	Goals
Premiership	0		0
League Division 1	119	(20)	21
League Division 2	0		0
FA Cup	13	(3)	2
League Cup	10	(3)	1
European Cup / Champions League	0		0
European Cup-Winners' Cup	0		0
UEFA Cup / Inter-Cities' Fairs Cup	6	(1)	0
Other Matches	1		0
OVERALL TOTAL	**149**	**(27)**	**24**

Opponents	PREM A S G	FLD 1 A S G	FLD 2 A S G	FAC A S G	LC A S G	EC/CL A S G	ECWC A S G	UEFA A S G	OTHER A S G	TOTAL A S G
1 West Ham United	–	5 (3)	–	2 (1) –	1	–	–	–	–	8 (4) –
2 Liverpool	–	7 (1) –	–	2	1	–	–	–	–	10 (1) –
3 Everton	–	6 (1) 1	–	1	1	–	–	–	1	9 (1) 1
4 Southampton	–	7 2	–	–	1 (1) –	–	–	–	–	8 (1) 2
5 Arsenal	–	7 (1) –	–	1	–	–	–	–	–	8 (1) –
6 Tottenham Hotspur	–	6 (3)	–	–	–	–	–	–	–	6 (3) –
7 Queens Park Rangers	–	8 1	–	–	–	–	–	–	–	8 1
8 Coventry City	–	5 2	–	2	–	–	–	–	–	7 2
9 Chelsea	–	5 (1) 3	–	1	–	–	–	–	–	6 (1) 3
10 Aston Villa	–	6 (1) 1	–	–	–	–	–	–	–	6 (1) 1
11 Norwich City	–	5 (2) –	–	–	–	–	–	–	–	5 (2) –
12 Leicester City	–	5 (1) –	–	–	–	–	–	–	–	5 (1) –
13 Luton Town	–	5 (1) –	–	–	–	–	–	–	–	5 (1) –
14 Watford	–	5 (1) –	–	–	–	–	–	–	–	5 (1) –
15 Nottingham Forest	–	5 2	–	–	–	–	–	–	–	5 2
16 Sheffield Wednesday	–	5	–	–	–	–	–	–	–	5
17 Newcastle United	–	4 (1) 3	–	–	–	–	–	–	–	4 (1) 3
18 Ipswich Town	–	4	–	– (1) –	–	–	–	–	–	4 (1) –
19 Sunderland	–	2	–	–	2 2	–	–	–	–	4 2
20 Charlton Athletic	–	4	–	–	–	–	–	–	–	4 –
21 Wimbledon	–	3	–	–	1	–	–	–	–	4 –
22 Oxford United	–	2 (1) 1	–	–	1	–	–	–	–	3 (1) 1
23 West Bromwich Albion	–	3 3	–	–	–	–	–	–	–	3 3
24 Derby County	–	1 (2)	–	–	–	–	–	–	–	1 (2) –
25 Portsmouth	–	2	–	–	–	–	–	–	–	2 –
26 PSV Eindhoven	–	–	–	–	–	–	–	2	–	2 –

continued../

JESPER OLSEN (continued)

Opponents	PREM			FLD 1			FLD 2			FAC			LC			EC/CL			ECWC			UEFA			OTHER			TOTAL		
	A	S	G	A	S	G	A	S	G	A	S	G	A	S	G	A	S	G	A	S	G	A	S	G	A	S	G	A	S	G
27 Raba Vasas	-	-	-	-	-	-	-	-	-	-	-	-	-	-	-	-	-	-	-	-	-	2	-	-	-	-	-	2	-	-
28 Crystal Palace	-	-	-	-	-	-	-	-	-	-	-	-	1	(1)	-	-	-	-	-	-	-	-	-	-	-	-	-	1	(1)	-
29 Videoton	-	-	-	-	-	-	-	-	-	-	-	-	-	-	-	-	-	-	1	(1)	-	-	-	-	-	-	-	1	(1)	-
30 Stoke City	-	-	-	1	-	2	-	-	-	-	-	-	-	-	-	-	-	-	-	-	-	-	-	-	-	-	-	1	-	2
31 Burnley	-	-	-	-	-	-	-	-	-	-	-	-	1	-	1	-	-	-	-	-	-	-	-	-	-	-	-	1	-	1
32 Blackburn Rovers	-	-	-	-	-	-	-	-	-	1	-	-	-	-	-	-	-	-	-	-	-	-	-	-	-	-	-	1	-	-
33 Bury	-	-	-	-	-	-	-	-	-	-	-	-	1	-	-	-	-	-	-	-	-	-	-	-	-	-	-	1	-	-
34 Dundee United	-	-	-	-	-	-	-	-	-	-	-	-	-	-	-	-	-	-	-	-	-	1	-	-	-	-	-	1	-	-
35 Hull City	-	-	-	-	-	-	-	-	-	-	-	-	1	-	-	-	-	-	-	-	-	-	-	-	-	-	-	1	-	-
36 Manchester City	-	-	-	-	-	-	-	-	-	1	-	-	-	-	-	-	-	-	-	-	-	-	-	-	-	-	-	1	-	-
37 Middlesbrough	-	-	-	1	-	-	-	-	-	-	-	-	-	-	-	-	-	-	-	-	-	-	-	-	-	-	-	1	-	-
38 Rochdale	-	-	-	-	-	-	-	-	-	-	(1)	-	-	-	-	-	-	-	-	-	-	-	-	-	-	-	-	-	(1)	-
39 Rotherham United	-	-	-	-	-	-	-	-	-	-	-	-	-	(1)	-	-	-	-	-	-	-	-	-	-	-	-	-	-	(1)	-

TOMMY O'NEIL

DEBUT (Full Appearance)

Wednesday 05/05/1971
Football League Division 1
at Maine Road

Manchester City 3 Manchester United 4

CLUB CAREER RECORD	Apps	Subs	Goals
Premiership	0		0
League Division 1	54		0
League Division 2	0		0
FA Cup	7		0
League Cup	7		0
European Cup / Champions League	0		0
European Cup–Winners' Cup	0		0
UEFA Cup / Inter–Cities' Fairs Cup	0		0
Other Matches	0		0
OVERALL TOTAL	68		0

Opponents	PREM			FLD 1			FLD 2			FAC			LC			EC/CL			ECWC			UEFA			OTHER			TOTAL		
	A	S	G	A	S	G	A	S	G	A	S	G	A	S	G	A	S	G	A	S	G	A	S	G	A	S	G	A	S	G
1 Stoke City	-	-	3	-	-	-	-	-	2	-	3	-	-	-	-	-	-	-	-	-	-	-	-	-	-	-	-	8	-	
2 Southampton	-	-	3	-	-	-	-	-	2	-	-	-	-	-	-	-	-	-	-	-	-	-	-	-	-	-	-	5	-	
3 Liverpool	-	-	4	-	-	-	-	-	-	-	-	-	-	-	-	-	-	-	-	-	-	-	-	-	-	-	-	4	-	
4 Manchester City	-	-	4	-	-	-	-	-	-	-	-	-	-	-	-	-	-	-	-	-	-	-	-	-	-	-	-	4	-	
5 Arsenal	-	-	3	-	-	-	-	-	-	-	-	-	-	-	-	-	-	-	-	-	-	-	-	-	-	-	-	3	-	
6 Crystal Palace	-	-	3	-	-	-	-	-	-	-	-	-	-	-	-	-	-	-	-	-	-	-	-	-	-	-	-	3	-	
7 Derby County	-	-	3	-	-	-	-	-	-	-	-	-	-	-	-	-	-	-	-	-	-	-	-	-	-	-	-	3	-	
8 Everton	-	-	3	-	-	-	-	-	-	-	-	-	-	-	-	-	-	-	-	-	-	-	-	-	-	-	-	3	-	
9 Ipswich Town	-	-	2	-	-	-	-	-	-	-	1	-	-	-	-	-	-	-	-	-	-	-	-	-	-	-	-	3	-	
10 Leeds United	-	-	3	-	-	-	-	-	-	-	-	-	-	-	-	-	-	-	-	-	-	-	-	-	-	-	-	3	-	
11 Leicester City	-	-	3	-	-	-	-	-	-	-	-	-	-	-	-	-	-	-	-	-	-	-	-	-	-	-	-	3	-	
12 Burnley	-	-	-	-	-	-	-	-	-	-	2	-	-	-	-	-	-	-	-	-	-	-	-	-	-	-	-	2	-	
13 Chelsea	-	-	2	-	-	-	-	-	-	-	-	-	-	-	-	-	-	-	-	-	-	-	-	-	-	-	-	2	-	
14 Coventry City	-	-	2	-	-	-	-	-	-	-	-	-	-	-	-	-	-	-	-	-	-	-	-	-	-	-	-	2	-	
15 Huddersfield Town	-	-	2	-	-	-	-	-	-	-	-	-	-	-	-	-	-	-	-	-	-	-	-	-	-	-	-	2	-	
16 Middlesbrough	-	-	-	-	-	-	-	-	2	-	-	-	-	-	-	-	-	-	-	-	-	-	-	-	-	-	-	2	-	
17 Newcastle United	-	-	2	-	-	-	-	-	-	-	-	-	-	-	-	-	-	-	-	-	-	-	-	-	-	-	-	2	-	
18 Nottingham Forest	-	-	2	-	-	-	-	-	-	-	-	-	-	-	-	-	-	-	-	-	-	-	-	-	-	-	-	2	-	
19 Sheffield United	-	-	2	-	-	-	-	-	-	-	-	-	-	-	-	-	-	-	-	-	-	-	-	-	-	-	-	2	-	
20 Tottenham Hotspur	-	-	2	-	-	-	-	-	-	-	-	-	-	-	-	-	-	-	-	-	-	-	-	-	-	-	-	2	-	
21 West Bromwich Albion	-	-	2	-	-	-	-	-	-	-	-	-	-	-	-	-	-	-	-	-	-	-	-	-	-	-	-	2	-	
22 West Ham United	-	-	2	-	-	-	-	-	-	-	-	-	-	-	-	-	-	-	-	-	-	-	-	-	-	-	-	2	-	
23 Norwich City	-	-	1	-	-	-	-	-	-	-	-	-	-	-	-	-	-	-	-	-	-	-	-	-	-	-	-	1	-	
24 Oxford United	-	-	-	-	-	-	-	-	-	-	1	-	-	-	-	-	-	-	-	-	-	-	-	-	-	-	-	1	-	
25 Preston North End	-	-	-	-	-	-	-	-	1	-	-	-	-	-	-	-	-	-	-	-	-	-	-	-	-	-	-	1	-	
26 Wolverhampton W.	-	-	1	-	-	-	-	-	-	-	-	-	-	-	-	-	-	-	-	-	-	-	-	-	-	-	-	1	-	

T O'SHAUGHNESSY

DEBUT (Full Appearance)

Saturday 25/10/1890
FA Cup 2nd Qualifying Round
at Bootle Park

Bootle Reserves 1 Newton Heath 0

CLUB CAREER RECORD	Apps	Subs	Goals
Premiership	0		0
League Division 1	0		0
League Division 2	0		0
FA Cup	1		0
League Cup	0		0
European Cup / Champions League	0		0
European Cup–Winners' Cup	0		0
UEFA Cup / Inter–Cities' Fairs Cup	0		0
Other Matches	0		0
OVERALL TOTAL	1		0

Opponents	PREM			FLD 1			FLD 2			FAC			LC			EC/CL			ECWC			UEFA			OTHER			TOTAL		
	A	S	G	A	S	G	A	S	G	A	S	G	A	S	G	A	S	G	A	S	G	A	S	G	A	S	G	A	S	G
1 Bootle Reserves	-	-	-	-	-	-	-	-	1	-	-	-	-	-	-	-	-	-	-	-	-	-	-	-	-	-	-	1	-	

JOHN O'SHEA

DEBUT (Full Appearance)

Wednesday 13/10/1999
League Cup 3rd Round
at Villa Park

Aston Villa 3 Manchester United 0

CLUB CAREER RECORD	Apps	Subs	Goals
Premiership	138	(53)	9
League Division 1	0		0
League Division 2	0		0
FA Cup	15	(5)	1
League Cup	18	(1)	1
European Cup / Champions League	42	(13)	1
European Cup–Winners' Cup	0		0
UEFA Cup / Inter–Cities' Fairs Cup	0		0
Other Matches	2	(1)	0
OVERALL TOTAL	**215**	**(73)**	**12**

Opponents	PREM A S G	FLD 1 A S G	FLD 2 A S G	FAC A S G	LC A S G	EC/CL A S G	ECWC A S G	UEFA A S G	OTHER A S G	TOTAL A S G
1 Arsenal	7 (2) 1	–	–	2 –	2 –	–	–	–	1 (1) –	12 (3) 1
2 Middlesbrough	9 (2) –	–	–	2 (1) 1	–	–	–	–	–	11 (3) 1
3 Aston Villa	5 (5) –	–	–	1 (2) –	1 –	–	–	–	–	7 (7) –
4 Chelsea	7 (2) –	–	–	– (1) –	2 –	–	–	1 –	–	10 (3) –
5 Liverpool	6 (6) 1	–	–	–	–	–	–	–	–	6 (6) 1
6 Fulham	7 (3) –	–	–	1 –	–	–	–	–	–	8 (3) –
7 Manchester City	6 (4) –	–	–	1 –	–	–	–	–	–	7 (4) –
8 Tottenham Hotspur	8 (1) 1	–	–	1 –	–	–	–	–	–	9 (1) 1
9 Everton	8 (2) 2	–	–	–	–	–	–	–	–	8 (2) 2
10 West Ham United	6 (3) 1	–	–	1 –	–	–	–	–	–	7 (3) 1
11 Bolton Wanderers	7 (3) –	–	–	–	–	–	–	–	–	7 (3) –
12 Blackburn Rovers	6 (3) –	–	–	–	– (1) –	–	–	–	–	6 (4) –
13 Charlton Athletic	7 (2) –	–	–	–	–	–	–	–	–	7 (2) –
14 Birmingham City	6 (1) –	–	–	–	1 –	–	–	–	–	7 (1) –
15 Newcastle United	7 (1) –	–	–	–	–	–	–	–	–	7 (1) –
16 Sunderland	4 (3) –	–	–	–	1 –	–	–	–	–	5 (3) –
17 West Bromwich Albion	4 (1) –	–	–	–	2 1	–	–	–	–	6 (1) 1
18 Portsmouth	5 (2) 1	–	–	–	–	–	–	–	–	5 (2) 1
19 Wigan Athletic	5 –	–	–	–	1 –	–	–	–	–	6 –
20 Roma	–	–	–	–	–	4 (2) –	–	–	–	4 (2) –
21 Southampton	4 (1) –	–	–	– (1) –	–	–	–	–	–	4 (2) –
22 Leeds United	3 (1) –	–	–	–	1 –	–	–	–	–	4 (1) –
23 Lille Metropole	–	–	–	–	–	3 (2) –	–	–	–	3 (2) –
24 Derby County	2 (2) –	–	–	–	–	–	–	–	–	2 (2) –
25 Reading	1 (2) –	–	–	1 –	–	–	–	–	–	2 (2) –
26 Benfica	–	–	–	–	–	3 –	–	–	–	3 –
27 Leicester City	2 –	–	–	–	1 –	–	–	–	–	3 –
28 Watford	2 –	–	–	–	1 –	–	–	–	–	3 –
29 Copenhagen	–	–	–	–	–	2 1	–	–	–	2 1
30 Wolverhampton W.	2 1	–	–	–	–	–	–	–	–	2 1
31 AC Milan	–	–	–	–	–	2 –	–	–	–	2 –
32 Basel	–	–	–	–	–	2 –	–	–	–	2 –
33 Bayer Leverkusen	–	–	–	–	–	2 –	–	–	–	2 –
34 Burton Albion	–	–	–	2 –	–	–	–	–	–	2 –
35 Deportivo La Coruna	–	–	–	–	–	2 –	–	–	–	2 –
36 Dinamo Bucharest	–	–	–	–	–	2 –	–	–	–	2 –
37 Maccabi Haifa	–	–	–	–	–	2 –	–	–	–	2 –
38 Panathinaikos	–	–	–	–	–	2 –	–	–	–	2 –
39 Stuttgart	–	–	–	–	–	2 –	–	–	–	2 –
40 Villarreal	–	–	–	–	–	2 –	–	–	–	2 –
41 Crystal Palace	– (1) 1	–	–	–	1 –	–	–	–	–	1 (1) 1
42 Juventus	–	–	–	–	–	1 (1) –	–	–	–	1 (1) –
43 Olympiakos Piraeus	–	–	–	–	–	1 (1) –	–	–	–	1 (1) –
44 Porto	–	–	–	–	–	1 (1) –	–	–	–	1 (1) –
45 Real Madrid	–	–	–	–	–	1 (1) –	–	–	–	1 (1) –
46 Zalaegerszeg	–	–	–	–	–	1 (1) –	–	–	–	1 (1) –
47 Boavista	–	–	–	–	–	– (2) –	–	–	–	– (2) –
48 Glasgow Celtic	–	–	–	–	–	– (2) –	–	–	–	– (2) –
49 Burnley	–	–	–	–	1 –	–	–	–	–	1 –
50 Coventry City	–	–	–	–	1 –	–	–	–	–	1 –
51 Crewe Alexandra	–	–	–	–	1 –	–	–	–	–	1 –
52 Debreceni	–	–	–	–	–	1 –	–	–	–	1 –
53 Dynamo Kiev	–	–	–	–	–	1 –	–	–	–	1 –
54 Exeter City	–	–	–	1 –	–	–	–	–	–	1 –
55 Fenerbahce	–	–	–	–	–	1 –	–	–	–	1 –
56 Glasgow Rangers	–	–	–	–	–	1 –	–	–	–	1 –
57 Ipswich Town	1 –	–	–	–	–	–	–	–	–	1 –
58 Millwall	–	–	–	1 –	–	–	–	–	–	1 –
59 Northampton Town	–	–	–	1 –	–	–	–	–	–	1 –
60 Norwich City	1 –	–	–	–	–	–	–	–	–	1 –
61 Olympique Lyonnais	–	–	–	–	–	1 –	–	–	–	1 –
62 Southend United	–	–	–	–	1 –	–	–	–	–	1 –
63 Sparta Prague	–	–	–	–	–	1 –	–	–	–	1 –
64 Sporting Lisbon	–	–	–	–	–	1 –	–	–	–	1 –

BILL OWEN

DEBUT (Full Appearance)

Saturday 15/10/1898
Football League Division 2
at Muntz Street

Birmingham City 4 Newton Heath 1

CLUB CAREER RECORD	Apps	Subs	Goals
Premiership	0		0
League Division 1	0		0
League Division 2	1		0
FA Cup	0		0
League Cup	0		0
European Cup / Champions League	0		0
European Cup-Winners' Cup	0		0
UEFA Cup / Inter-Cities' Fairs Cup	0		0
Other Matches	0		0
OVERALL TOTAL	1		0

Opponents	PREM A S G	FLD 1 A S G	FLD 2 A S G	FAC A S G	LC A S G	EC/CL A S G	ECWC A S G	UEFA A S G	OTHER A S G	TOTAL A S G
1 Birmingham City	– – –	– – –	1	– –	– –	– – –	– – –	– – –	– –	1 –

GEORGE OWEN

DEBUT (Full Appearance)

Saturday 18/01/1889
FA Cup 1st Round
at Deepdale

Preston North End 6 Newton Heath 1

CLUB CAREER RECORD	Apps	Subs	Goals
Premiership	0		0
League Division 1	0		0
League Division 2	0		0
FA Cup	1		0
League Cup	0		0
European Cup / Champions League	0		0
European Cup-Winners' Cup	0		0
UEFA Cup / Inter-Cities' Fairs Cup	0		0
Other Matches	0		0
OVERALL TOTAL	1		0

Opponents	PREM A S G	FLD 1 A S G	FLD 2 A S G	FAC A S G	LC A S G	EC/CL A S G	ECWC A S G	UEFA A S G	OTHER A S G	TOTAL A S G
1 Preston North End	– – –	– – –	– – –	1	– –	– – –	– – –	– – –	– –	1 –

JACK OWEN

DEBUT (Full Appearance)

Saturday 18/01/1889
FA Cup 1st Round
at Deepdale

Preston North End 6 Newton Heath 1

CLUB CAREER RECORD	Apps	Subs	Goals
Premiership	0		0
League Division 1	0		0
League Division 2	0		0
FA Cup	6		0
League Cup	0		0
European Cup / Champions League	0		0
European Cup-Winners' Cup	0		0
UEFA Cup / Inter-Cities' Fairs Cup	0		0
Other Matches	0		0
OVERALL TOTAL	6		0

Opponents	PREM A S G	FLD 1 A S G	FLD 2 A S G	FAC A S G	LC A S G	EC/CL A S G	ECWC A S G	UEFA A S G	OTHER A S G	TOTAL A S G
1 Blackpool	– –	– –	– –	1	–	– –	– –	– –	– –	1 –
2 Bootle Reserves	– –	– –	– –	1	–	– –	– –	– –	– –	1 –
3 Higher Walton	– –	– –	– –	1	–	– –	– –	– –	– –	1 –
4 Manchester City	– –	– –	– –	1	–	– –	– –	– –	– –	1 –
5 Preston North End	– –	– –	– –	1	–	– –	– –	– –	– –	1 –
6 South Shore	– –	– –	– –	1	–	– –	– –	– –	– –	1 –

W OWEN

DEBUT (Full Appearance, 1 goal)

Saturday 22/09/1934
Football League Division 2
at Old Trafford

Manchester United 5 Norwich City 0

CLUB CAREER RECORD	Apps	Subs	Goals
Premiership	0		0
League Division 1	0		0
League Division 2	17		1
FA Cup	0		0
League Cup	0		0
European Cup / Champions League	0		0
European Cup-Winners' Cup	0		0
UEFA Cup / Inter-Cities' Fairs Cup	0		0
Other Matches	0		0
OVERALL TOTAL	17		1

Opponents	PREM A S G	FLD 1 A S G	FLD 2 A S G	FAC A S G	LC A S G	EC/CL A S G	ECWC A S G	UEFA A S G	OTHER A S G	TOTAL A S G
1 Hull City	– –	– –	2	–	–	– –	– –	– –	– –	2 –
2 Notts County	– –	– –	2	–	–	– –	– –	– –	– –	2 –
3 Swansea City	– –	– –	2	–	–	– –	– –	– –	– –	2 –
4 Norwich City	– –	– –	1 1	–	–	– –	– –	– –	– –	1 1
5 Bradford City	– –	– –	1	–	–	– –	– –	– –	– –	1 –
6 Bradford Park Avenue	– –	– –	1	–	–	– –	– –	– –	– –	1 –
7 Brentford	– –	– –	1	–	–	– –	– –	– –	– –	1 –
8 Burnley	– –	– –	1	–	–	– –	– –	– –	– –	1 –

continued../

W OWEN (continued)

Opponents	PREM			FLD 1			FLD 2			FAC			LC			EC/CL			ECWC			UEFA			OTHER			TOTAL		
	A	S	G	A	S	G	A	S	G	A	S	G	A	S	G	A	S	G	A	S	G	A	S	G	A	S	G	A	S	G
9 Leicester City										1																		1		
10 Newcastle United										1																		1		
11 Nottingham Forest										1																		1		
12 Oldham Athletic										1																		1		
13 Plymouth Argyle										1																		1		
14 West Ham United										1																		1		

LOUIS PAGE

CLUB CAREER RECORD	Apps	Subs	Goals
Premiership	0		0
League Division 1	0		0
League Division 2	12		0
FA Cup	0		0
League Cup	0		0
European Cup / Champions League	0		0
European Cup-Winners' Cup	0		0
UEFA Cup / Inter-Cities' Fairs Cup	0		0
Other Matches	0		0
OVERALL TOTAL	**12**		**0**

DEBUT (Full Appearance)

Friday 25/03/1932
Football League Division 2
at Old Trafford

Manchester United 0 Charlton Athletic 2

Opponents	PREM			FLD 1			FLD 2			FAC			LC			EC/CL			ECWC			UEFA			OTHER			TOTAL		
	A	S	G	A	S	G	A	S	G	A	S	G	A	S	G	A	S	G	A	S	G	A	S	G	A	S	G	A	S	G
1 Charlton Athletic							3																					3		
2 Bradford City							1																					1		
3 Bristol City							1																					1		
4 Bury							1																					1		
5 Grimsby Town							1																					1		
6 Millwall							1																					1		
7 Oldham Athletic							1																					1		
8 Port Vale							1																					1		
9 Southampton							1																					1		
10 Stoke City							1																					1		

GARY PALLISTER

CLUB CAREER RECORD	Apps	Subs	Goals
Premiership	206		8
League Division 1	108	(3)	4
League Division 2	0		0
FA Cup	38		2
League Cup	36		0
European Cup / Champions League	23		0
European Cup-Winners' Cup	12	(1)	1
UEFA Cup / Inter-Cities' Fairs Cup	4		0
Other Matches	6		0
OVERALL TOTAL	**433**	**(4)**	**15**

DEBUT (Full Appearance)

Wednesday 30/08/1989
Football League Division 1
at Old Trafford

Manchester United 0 Norwich City 2

Opponents	PREM			FLD 1			FLD 2			FAC			LC			EC/CL			ECWC			UEFA			OTHER			TOTAL		
	A	S	G	A	S	G	A	S	G	A	S	G	A	S	G	A	S	G	A	S	G	A	S	G	A	S	G	A	S	G
1 Southampton	11		2	6						2			2															21		2
2 Everton	12			5 (1)						1			1															19 (1)		
3 Liverpool	10		2	6						1			1									1						19		2
4 Chelsea	10			6						2												1						19		
5 Wimbledon	10		1	6		1				2																		18		2
6 Leeds United	9			4						2			3															18		
7 Aston Villa	10			5									2															17		
8 Coventry City	11			6																								17		
9 Sheffield Wednesday	10			4									3															17		
10 Tottenham Hotspur	10			5									1															16		
11 Crystal Palace	6			5						4		2																15		2
12 Nottingham Forest	7			6		1				1			1															15		1
13 Arsenal	9			5																		1						15		
14 Manchester City	7			6						1																		14		
15 Norwich City	6			6						2																		14		
16 Blackburn Rovers	12		1																			1						13		1
17 Queens Park Rangers	5			5						2																		12		
18 Sheffield United	4			3 (1)						4																		11 (1)		
19 Oldham Athletic	4			2						4			1															11		
20 Newcastle United	7		1							1			1									1						10		1
21 West Ham United	7			2																								9		
22 Derby County	4			3		1																						7		1
23 Middlesbrough	5		1																2									7		1
24 Leicester City	6												1															7		
25 Ipswich Town	6																											6		
26 Luton Town				6																								6		
27 Bolton Wanderers	4									1																		5		
28 Portsmouth													5															5		

continued../

GARY PALLISTER (continued)

Opponents	PREM A S G	FLD 1 A S G	FLD 2 A S G	FAC A S G	LC A S G	EC/CL A S G	ECWC A S G	UEFA A S G	OTHER A S G	TOTAL A S G
29 Sunderland	1 –	2 –	– –	1 –	– –	– –	– –	– –	– –	4 –
30 Charlton Athletic	– –	2 1	– –	1 –	– –	– –	– –	– –	– –	3 1
31 Wrexham	– –	– –	– –	– –	1 –	– –	2 1	– –	– –	3 1
32 Barcelona	– –	– –	– –	– –	– –	2 –	1 –	– –	– –	3 –
33 Barnsley	1 –	– –	– –	2 –	– –	– –	– –	– –	– –	3 –
34 Brighton	– –	– –	– –	1 –	2 –	– –	– –	– –	– –	3 –
35 Galatasaray	– –	– –	– –	– –	– –	3 –	– –	– –	– –	3 –
36 Juventus	– –	– –	– –	– –	– –	3 –	– –	– –	– –	3 –
37 Athinaikos	– –	– –	– –	– –	– –	– –	2 –	– –	– –	2 –
38 Borussia Dortmund	– –	– –	– –	– –	– –	2 –	– –	– –	– –	2 –
39 Cambridge United	– –	– –	– –	2 –	– –	– –	– –	– –	– –	2 –
40 Feyenoord	– –	– –	– –	– –	– –	2 –	– –	– –	– –	2 –
41 Gothenburg	– –	– –	– –	– –	– –	2 –	– –	– –	– –	2 –
42 Halifax Town	– –	– –	– –	2 –	– –	– –	– –	– –	– –	2 –
43 Honved	– –	– –	– –	– –	– –	2 –	– –	– –	– –	2 –
44 Kosice	– –	– –	– –	– –	– –	2 –	– –	– –	– –	2 –
45 Legia Warsaw	– –	– –	– –	– –	– –	– –	2 –	– –	– –	2 –
46 Millwall	– –	2 –	– –	– –	– –	– –	– –	– –	– –	2 –
47 Montpellier Herault	– –	– –	– –	– –	– –	– –	2 –	– –	– –	2 –
48 Pecsi Munkas	– –	– –	– –	– –	– –	– –	2 –	– –	– –	2 –
49 Porto	– –	– –	– –	– –	– –	2 –	– –	– –	– –	2 –
50 Rapid Vienna	– –	– –	– –	– –	– –	2 –	– –	– –	– –	2 –
51 Rotor Volgograd	– –	– –	– –	– –	– –	– –	– –	2 –	– –	2 –
52 Stoke City	– –	– –	– –	2 –	– –	– –	– –	– –	– –	2 –
53 Swindon Town	2 –	– –	– –	– –	– –	– –	– –	– –	– –	2 –
54 Torpedo Moscow	– –	– –	– –	– –	– –	– –	– –	2 –	– –	2 –
55 York City	– –	– –	– –	– –	2 –	– –	– –	– –	– –	2 –
56 Athletico Madrid	– –	– –	– –	– –	– –	– –	1 (1) –	– –	– –	1 (1) –
57 Notts County	– –	1 (1) –	– –	– –	– –	– –	– –	– –	– –	1 (1) –
58 Bury	– –	– –	– –	1 –	– –	– –	– –	– –	– –	1 –
59 Fenerbahce	– –	– –	– –	– –	– –	1 –	– –	– –	– –	1 –
60 Hereford United	– –	– –	– –	1 –	– –	– –	– –	– –	– –	1 –
61 Port Vale	– –	– –	– –	– –	1 –	– –	– –	– –	– –	1 –
62 Red Star Belgrade	– –	– –	– –	– –	– –	– –	– –	– –	1 –	1 –

ALBERT PAPE

DEBUT (Full Appearance, 1 goal)

Saturday 07/02/1925
Football League Division 2
at Old Trafford

Manchester United 4 Leyton Orient 2

CLUB CAREER RECORD	Apps	Subs	Goals
Premiership	0		0
League Division 1	2		0
League Division 2	16		5
FA Cup	0		0
League Cup	0		0
European Cup / Champions League	0		0
European Cup-Winners' Cup	0		0
UEFA Cup / Inter-Cities' Fairs Cup	0		0
Other Matches	0		0
OVERALL TOTAL	18		5

Opponents	PREM A S G	FLD 1 A S G	FLD 2 A S G	FAC A S G	LC A S G	EC/CL A S G	ECWC A S G	UEFA A S G	OTHER A S G	TOTAL A S G
1 Stockport County	– –	– –	1 2	– –	– –	– –	– –	– –	– –	1 2
2 Leyton Orient	– –	– –	1 1	– –	– –	– –	– –	– –	– –	1 1
3 Sheffield Wednesday	– –	– –	1 1	– –	– –	– –	– –	– –	– –	1 1
4 Southampton	– –	– –	1 1	– –	– –	– –	– –	– –	– –	1 1
5 Arsenal	– –	1 –	– –	– –	– –	– –	– –	– –	– –	1 –
6 Aston Villa	– –	1 –	– –	– –	– –	– –	– –	– –	– –	1 –
7 Barnsley	– –	– –	1 –	– –	– –	– –	– –	– –	– –	1 –
8 Blackpool	– –	– –	1 –	– –	– –	– –	– –	– –	– –	1 –
9 Bradford City	– –	– –	1 –	– –	– –	– –	– –	– –	– –	1 –
10 Chelsea	– –	– –	1 –	– –	– –	– –	– –	– –	– –	1 –
11 Crystal Palace	– –	– –	1 –	– –	– –	– –	– –	– –	– –	1 –
12 Derby County	– –	– –	1 –	– –	– –	– –	– –	– –	– –	1 –
13 Fulham	– –	– –	1 –	– –	– –	– –	– –	– –	– –	1 –
14 Hull City	– –	– –	1 –	– –	– –	– –	– –	– –	– –	1 –
15 Port Vale	– –	– –	1 –	– –	– –	– –	– –	– –	– –	1 –
16 Portsmouth	– –	– –	1 –	– –	– –	– –	– –	– –	– –	1 –
17 South Shields	– –	– –	1 –	– –	– –	– –	– –	– –	– –	1 –
18 Wolverhampton W.	– –	– –	1 –	– –	– –	– –	– –	– –	– –	1 –

PARK JI-SUNG

DEBUT (Substitute Appearance)

Tuesday 09/08/2005
Champions League Qualifying Round 1st Leg
at Old Trafford

Manchester United 3 Debreceni 0

CLUB CAREER RECORD	Apps	Subs	Goals
Premiership	39	(21)	7
League Division 1	0		0
League Division 2	0		0
FA Cup	7	(2)	0
League Cup	3		1
European Cup / Champions League	4	(7)	0
European Cup–Winners' Cup	0		0
UEFA Cup / Inter-Cities' Fairs Cup	0		0
Other Matches	0		0
OVERALL TOTAL	**53**	**(30)**	**8**

Opponents	PREM A S G	FLD 1 A S G	FLD 2 A S G	FAC A S G	LC A S G	EC/CL A S G	ECWC A S G	UEFA A S G	OTHER A S G	TOTAL A S G
1 Aston Villa	4 – 1	–	–	2 – –	–	–	–	–	–	6 – 1
2 Wigan Athletic	3 (1) –	–	–	–	1 – –	–	–	–	–	4 (1) –
3 Portsmouth	3 – –	–	–	1 – –	–	–	–	–	–	4 – –
4 Reading	2 – –	–	–	2 – –	–	–	–	–	–	4 – –
5 Arsenal	2 (1) 1	–	–	1 – –	–	–	–	–	–	3 (1) 1
6 Fulham	3 (1) 1	–	–	–	–	–	–	–	–	3 (1) 1
7 West Ham United	3 (1) –	–	–	–	–	–	–	–	–	3 (1) –
8 Birmingham City	1 (2) –	–	–	–	1 – 1	–	–	–	–	2 (2) 1
9 Blackburn Rovers	2 (2) 1	–	–	–	–	–	–	–	–	2 (2) 1
10 Middlesbrough	2 (1) –	–	–	– (1) –	–	–	–	–	–	2 (2) –
11 Tottenham Hotspur	2 (2) –	–	–	–	–	–	–	–	–	2 (2) –
12 Charlton Athletic	2 (1) 1	–	–	–	–	–	–	–	–	2 (1) 1
13 Sunderland	2 (1) –	–	–	–	–	–	–	–	–	2 (1) –
14 Bolton Wanderers	1 (2) 2	–	–	–	–	–	–	–	–	1 (2) 2
15 Newcastle United	1 (2) –	–	–	–	–	–	–	–	–	1 (2) –
16 Lille Metropole	–	–	–	–	–	– (3) –	–	–	–	– (3) –
17 Barcelona	–	–	–	–	–	2 – –	–	–	–	2 – –
18 Everton	2 – –	–	–	–	–	–	–	–	–	2 – –
19 Roma	–	–	–	–	–	2 – –	–	–	–	2 – –
20 West Bromwich Albion	1 – –	–	–	–	1 – –	–	–	–	–	2 – –
21 Chelsea	1 (1) –	–	–	–	–	–	–	–	–	1 (1) –
22 Manchester City	1 (1) –	–	–	–	–	–	–	–	–	1 (1) –
23 Liverpool	– (1) –	–	–	– (1) –	–	–	–	–	–	– (2) –
24 Villarreal	–	–	–	–	–	– (2) –	–	–	–	– (2) –
25 Derby County	1 – –	–	–	–	–	–	–	–	–	1 – –
26 Wolverhampton W.	–	–	–	1 – –	–	–	–	–	–	1 – –
27 Benfica	–	–	–	–	–	– (1) –	–	–	–	– (1) –
28 Debreceni	–	–	–	–	–	– (1) –	–	–	–	– (1) –
29 Watford	– (1) –	–	–	–	–	–	–	–	–	– (1) –

PAUL PARKER

DEBUT (Full Appearance)

Saturday 17/08/1991
Football League Division 1
at Old Trafford

Manchester United 2 Notts County 0

CLUB CAREER RECORD	Apps	Subs	Goals
Premiership	76	(3)	1
League Division 1	24	(2)	0
League Division 2	0		0
FA Cup	14	(1)	1
League Cup	15		0
European Cup / Champions League	5	(1)	0
European Cup–Winners' Cup	2		0
UEFA Cup / Inter-Cities' Fairs Cup	0	(2)	0
Other Matches	1		0
OVERALL TOTAL	**137**	**(9)**	**2**

Opponents	PREM A S G	FLD 1 A S G	FLD 2 A S G	FAC A S G	LC A S G	EC/CL A S G	ECWC A S G	UEFA A S G	OTHER A S G	TOTAL A S G
1 Sheffield Wednesday	6 –	1 –	–	–	2 –	–	–	–	–	9 –
2 Aston Villa	5 –	1 –	–	–	2 –	–	–	–	–	8 –
3 Leeds United	4 –	2 –	–	1 –	1 –	–	–	–	–	8 –
4 Oldham Athletic	3 –	2 –	–	2 –	1 –	–	–	–	–	8 –
5 Sheffield United	3 –	2 –	–	2 –	–	–	–	–	–	7 –
6 Chelsea	4 –	1 (1) –	–	1 –	–	–	–	–	–	6 (1) –
7 Arsenal	4 –	1 –	–	–	–	–	–	1 –	–	6 –
8 Norwich City	4 –	1 –	–	1 –	–	–	–	–	–	6 –
9 Southampton	3 –	1 –	–	2 –	–	–	–	–	–	6 –
10 Wimbledon	4 –	1 –	–	1 –	–	–	–	–	–	6 –
11 Coventry City	3 (1) –	2 –	–	–	–	–	–	–	–	5 (1) –
12 Queens Park Rangers	3 (2) –	1 –	–	–	–	–	–	–	–	4 (2) –
13 Manchester City	4 –	1 –	–	–	–	–	–	–	–	5 –
14 Tottenham Hotspur	4 1	–	–	–	–	–	–	–	–	4 1
15 Blackburn Rovers	4 –	–	–	–	–	–	–	–	–	4 –
16 Everton	1 –	2 –	–	–	1 –	–	–	–	–	4 –
17 Liverpool	4 –	–	–	–	–	–	–	–	–	4 –
18 Ipswich Town	3 –	–	–	–	–	–	–	–	–	3 –
19 Middlesbrough	1 –	–	–	–	2 –	–	–	–	–	3 –
20 Portsmouth	–	–	–	–	3 –	–	–	–	–	3 –
21 West Ham United	2 –	1 –	–	–	–	–	–	–	–	3 –
22 Crystal Palace	1 –	1 (1) –	–	–	–	–	–	–	–	2 (1) –

continued../

PAUL PARKER (continued)

Opponents	PREM			FLD 1			FLD 2			FAC			LC			EC/CL			ECWC			UEFA			OTHER			TOTAL		
	A	S	G	A	S	G	A	S	G	A	S	G	A	S	G	A	S	G	A	S	G	A	S	G	A	S	G	A	S	G
23 Athletico Madrid	-	-	-	-	-	-	-	-	-	-	-	-	-	-	-	-	-	-	2	-	-	-	-	-	-	-	-	2	-	-
24 Barcelona	-	-	-	-	-	-	-	-	-	-	-	-	-	-	-	2	-	-	-	-	-	-	-	-	-	-	-	2	-	-
25 Brighton	-	-	-	-	-	-	-	-	-	1	-	-	1	-	-	-	-	-	-	-	-	-	-	-	-	-	-	2	-	-
26 Honved	-	-	-	-	-	-	-	-	-	-	-	-	-	-	-	2	-	-	-	-	-	-	-	-	-	-	-	2	-	-
27 Newcastle United	2	-	-	-	-	-	-	-	-	-	-	-	-	-	-	-	-	-	-	-	-	-	-	-	-	-	-	2	-	-
28 Nottingham Forest	1	-	-	-	-	-	-	-	-	-	-	-	1	-	-	-	-	-	-	-	-	-	-	-	-	-	-	2	-	-
29 Notts County	-	-	-	-	-	-	2	-	-	-	-	-	-	-	-	-	-	-	-	-	-	-	-	-	-	-	-	2	-	-
30 Swindon Town	2	-	-	-	-	-	-	-	-	-	-	-	-	-	-	-	-	-	-	-	-	-	-	-	-	-	-	2	-	-
31 Galatasaray	-	-	-	-	-	-	-	-	-	-	-	-	-	-	-	1	(1)	-	-	-	-	-	-	-	-	-	-	1	(1)	-
32 Bolton Wanderers	1	-	-	-	-	-	-	-	-	-	-	-	-	-	-	-	-	-	-	-	-	-	-	-	-	-	-	1	-	-
33 Bury	-	-	-	-	-	-	-	-	-	1	-	-	-	-	-	-	-	-	-	-	-	-	-	-	-	-	-	1	-	-
34 Charlton Athletic	-	-	-	-	-	-	-	-	-	1	-	-	-	-	-	-	-	-	-	-	-	-	-	-	-	-	-	1	-	-
35 Luton Town	-	-	-	1	-	-	-	-	-	-	-	-	-	-	-	-	-	-	-	-	-	-	-	-	-	-	-	1	-	-
36 Sunderland	-	-	-	-	-	-	-	-	-	1	-	-	-	-	-	-	-	-	-	-	-	-	-	-	-	-	-	1	-	-
37 York City	-	-	-	-	-	-	-	-	-	-	-	-	1	-	-	-	-	-	-	-	-	-	-	-	-	-	-	1	-	-
38 Reading	-	-	-	-	-	-	-	-	-	-	(1)	1	-	-	-	-	-	-	-	-	-	-	-	-	-	-	-	-	(1)	1
39 Rotor Volgograd	-	-	-	-	-	-	-	-	-	-	-	-	-	-	-	-	-	-	-	-	-	-	(1)	-	-	-	-	-	(1)	-
40 Torpedo Moscow	-	-	-	-	-	-	-	-	-	-	-	-	-	-	-	-	-	-	-	-	-	-	(1)	-	-	-	-	-	(1)	-

---

SAMUEL PARKER

DEBUT (Full Appearance)

Saturday 13/01/1894
Football League Division 1
at Bank Street

Manchester United 1 Sheffield Wednesday 2

CLUB CAREER RECORD	Apps	Subs	Goals
Premiership	0		0
League Division 1	11		0
League Division 2	0		0
FA Cup	1		0
League Cup	0		0
European Cup / Champions League	0		0
European Cup-Winners' Cup	0		0
UEFA Cup / Inter-Cities' Fairs Cup	0		0
Other Matches	0		0
OVERALL TOTAL	**12**		**0**

Opponents	PREM			FLD 1			FLD 2			FAC			LC			EC/CL			ECWC			UEFA			OTHER			TOTAL		
	A	S	G	A	S	G	A	S	G	A	S	G	A	S	G	A	S	G	A	S	G	A	S	G	A	S	G	A	S	G
1 Blackburn Rovers	-	-	-	2	-	-	-	-	-	1	-	-	-	-	-	-	-	-	-	-	-	-	-	-	-	-	-	3	-	-
2 Stoke City	-	-	-	2	-	-	-	-	-	-	-	-	-	-	-	-	-	-	-	-	-	-	-	-	-	-	-	2	-	-
3 Aston Villa	-	-	-	1	-	-	-	-	-	-	-	-	-	-	-	-	-	-	-	-	-	-	-	-	-	-	-	1	-	-
4 Bolton Wanderers	-	-	-	1	-	-	-	-	-	-	-	-	-	-	-	-	-	-	-	-	-	-	-	-	-	-	-	1	-	-
5 Derby County	-	-	-	1	-	-	-	-	-	-	-	-	-	-	-	-	-	-	-	-	-	-	-	-	-	-	-	1	-	-
6 Nottingham Forest	-	-	-	1	-	-	-	-	-	-	-	-	-	-	-	-	-	-	-	-	-	-	-	-	-	-	-	1	-	-
7 Sheffield United	-	-	-	1	-	-	-	-	-	-	-	-	-	-	-	-	-	-	-	-	-	-	-	-	-	-	-	1	-	-
8 Sheffield Wednesday	-	-	-	1	-	-	-	-	-	-	-	-	-	-	-	-	-	-	-	-	-	-	-	-	-	-	-	1	-	-
9 Sunderland	-	-	-	1	-	-	-	-	-	-	-	-	-	-	-	-	-	-	-	-	-	-	-	-	-	-	-	1	-	-

---

THOMAS PARKER

DEBUT (Full Appearance)

Saturday 11/10/1930
Football League Division 1
at Upton Park

West Ham United 5 Manchester United 1

CLUB CAREER RECORD	Apps	Subs	Goals
Premiership	0		0
League Division 1	9		0
League Division 2	8		0
FA Cup	0		0
League Cup	0		0
European Cup / Champions League	0		0
European Cup-Winners' Cup	0		0
UEFA Cup / Inter-Cities' Fairs Cup	0		0
Other Matches	0		0
OVERALL TOTAL	**17**		**0**

Opponents	PREM			FLD 1			FLD 2			FAC			LC			EC/CL			ECWC			UEFA			OTHER			TOTAL		
	A	S	G	A	S	G	A	S	G	A	S	G	A	S	G	A	S	G	A	S	G	A	S	G	A	S	G	A	S	G
1 Swansea City	-	-	-	-	-	-	2	-	-	-	-	-	-	-	-	-	-	-	-	-	-	-	-	-	-	-	-	2	-	-
2 Arsenal	-	-	-	1	-	-	-	-	-	-	-	-	-	-	-	-	-	-	-	-	-	-	-	-	-	-	-	1	-	-
3 Birmingham City	-	-	-	1	-	-	-	-	-	-	-	-	-	-	-	-	-	-	-	-	-	-	-	-	-	-	-	1	-	-
4 Blackburn Rovers	-	-	-	1	-	-	-	-	-	-	-	-	-	-	-	-	-	-	-	-	-	-	-	-	-	-	-	1	-	-
5 Blackpool	-	-	-	1	-	-	-	-	-	-	-	-	-	-	-	-	-	-	-	-	-	-	-	-	-	-	-	1	-	-
6 Bradford Park Avenue	-	-	-	-	-	-	-	-	-	1	-	-	-	-	-	-	-	-	-	-	-	-	-	-	-	-	-	1	-	-
7 Leicester City	-	-	-	1	-	-	-	-	-	-	-	-	-	-	-	-	-	-	-	-	-	-	-	-	-	-	-	1	-	-
8 Nottingham Forest	-	-	-	-	-	-	1	-	-	-	-	-	-	-	-	-	-	-	-	-	-	-	-	-	-	-	-	1	-	-
9 Oldham Athletic	-	-	-	-	-	-	1	-	-	-	-	-	-	-	-	-	-	-	-	-	-	-	-	-	-	-	-	1	-	-
10 Portsmouth	-	-	-	1	-	-	-	-	-	-	-	-	-	-	-	-	-	-	-	-	-	-	-	-	-	-	-	1	-	-
11 Sheffield United	-	-	-	1	-	-	-	-	-	-	-	-	-	-	-	-	-	-	-	-	-	-	-	-	-	-	-	1	-	-
12 Southampton	-	-	-	-	-	-	1	-	-	-	-	-	-	-	-	-	-	-	-	-	-	-	-	-	-	-	-	1	-	-
13 Stoke City	-	-	-	-	-	-	1	-	-	-	-	-	-	-	-	-	-	-	-	-	-	-	-	-	-	-	-	1	-	-
14 Sunderland	-	-	-	1	-	-	-	-	-	-	-	-	-	-	-	-	-	-	-	-	-	-	-	-	-	-	-	1	-	-
15 Tottenham Hotspur	-	-	-	-	-	-	1	-	-	-	-	-	-	-	-	-	-	-	-	-	-	-	-	-	-	-	-	1	-	-
16 West Ham United	-	-	-	1	-	-	-	-	-	-	-	-	-	-	-	-	-	-	-	-	-	-	-	-	-	-	-	1	-	-

ROBERT PARKINSON

DEBUT (Full Appearance)

Saturday 11/11/1899
Football League Division 2
at Oakwell

Barnsley 0 Newton Heath 0

CLUB CAREER RECORD	Apps	Subs	Goals
Premiership	0		0
League Division 1	0		0
League Division 2	15		7
FA Cup	0		0
League Cup	0		0
European Cup / Champions League	0		0
European Cup-Winners' Cup	0		0
UEFA Cup / Inter-Cities' Fairs Cup	0		0
Other Matches	0		0
OVERALL TOTAL	**15**		**7**

Opponents	PREM			FLD 1			FLD 2			FAC			LC			EC/CL			ECWC			UEFA			OTHER			TOTAL		
	A	S	G	A	S	G	A	S	G	A	S	G	A	S	G	A	S	G	A	S	G	A	S	G	A	S	G	A	S	G
1 Grimsby Town	–	–	–	–	–	–	2	–	1	–	–	–	–	–	–	–	–	–	–	–	–	–	–	–	–	–	–	2	–	1
2 Birmingham City	–	–	–	–	–	–	1	–	1	–	–	–	–	–	–	–	–	–	–	–	–	–	–	–	–	–	–	1	–	1
3 Bolton Wanderers	–	–	–	–	–	–	1	–	1	–	–	–	–	–	–	–	–	–	–	–	–	–	–	–	–	–	–	1	–	1
4 Burton Swifts	–	–	–	–	–	–	1	–	1	–	–	–	–	–	–	–	–	–	–	–	–	–	–	–	–	–	–	1	–	1
5 Gainsborough Trinity	–	–	–	–	–	–	1	–	1	–	–	–	–	–	–	–	–	–	–	–	–	–	–	–	–	–	–	1	–	1
6 Loughborough Town	–	–	–	–	–	–	1	–	1	–	–	–	–	–	–	–	–	–	–	–	–	–	–	–	–	–	–	1	–	1
7 Middlesbrough	–	–	–	–	–	–	1	–	1	–	–	–	–	–	–	–	–	–	–	–	–	–	–	–	–	–	–	1	–	1
8 Barnsley	–	–	–	–	–	–	1	–	–	–	–	–	–	–	–	–	–	–	–	–	–	–	–	–	–	–	–	1	–	–
9 Chesterfield	–	–	–	–	–	–	1	–	–	–	–	–	–	–	–	–	–	–	–	–	–	–	–	–	–	–	–	1	–	–
10 Lincoln City	–	–	–	–	–	–	1	–	–	–	–	–	–	–	–	–	–	–	–	–	–	–	–	–	–	–	–	1	–	–
11 Luton Town	–	–	–	–	–	–	1	–	–	–	–	–	–	–	–	–	–	–	–	–	–	–	–	–	–	–	–	1	–	–
12 New Brighton Tower	–	–	–	–	–	–	1	–	–	–	–	–	–	–	–	–	–	–	–	–	–	–	–	–	–	–	–	1	–	–
13 Port Vale	–	–	–	–	–	–	1	–	–	–	–	–	–	–	–	–	–	–	–	–	–	–	–	–	–	–	–	1	–	–
14 Sheffield Wednesday	–	–	–	–	–	–	1	–	–	–	–	–	–	–	–	–	–	–	–	–	–	–	–	–	–	–	–	1	–	–

TEDDY PARTRIDGE

DEBUT (Full Appearance)

Saturday 09/10/1920
Football League Division 1
at Old Trafford

Manchester United 4 Oldham Athletic 1

CLUB CAREER RECORD	Apps	Subs	Goals
Premiership	0		0
League Division 1	112		16
League Division 2	36		0
FA Cup	12		2
League Cup	0		0
European Cup / Champions League	0		0
European Cup-Winners' Cup	0		0
UEFA Cup / Inter-Cities' Fairs Cup	0		0
Other Matches	0		0
OVERALL TOTAL	**160**		**18**

Opponents	PREM			FLD 1			FLD 2			FAC			LC			EC/CL			ECWC			UEFA			OTHER			TOTAL		
	A	S	G	A	S	G	A	S	G	A	S	G	A	S	G	A	S	G	A	S	G	A	S	G	A	S	G	A	S	G
1 Liverpool	–	–	–	7	–	–	–	–	–	2	–	1	–	–	–	–	–	–	–	–	–	–	–	–	–	–	–	9	–	1
2 Sheffield United	–	–	–	8	–	1	–	–	–	–	–	–	–	–	–	–	–	–	–	–	–	–	–	–	–	–	–	8	–	1
3 Blackburn Rovers	–	–	–	7	–	–	–	–	–	1	–	–	–	–	–	–	–	–	–	–	–	–	–	–	–	–	–	8	–	–
4 Newcastle United	–	–	–	7	–	2	–	–	–	–	–	–	–	–	–	–	–	–	–	–	–	–	–	–	–	–	–	7	–	2
5 Bradford City	–	–	–	3	–	–	2	–	–	2	–	1	–	–	–	–	–	–	–	–	–	–	–	–	–	–	–	7	–	1
6 Huddersfield Town	–	–	–	7	–	1	–	–	–	–	–	–	–	–	–	–	–	–	–	–	–	–	–	–	–	–	–	7	–	1
7 Everton	–	–	–	7	–	–	–	–	–	–	–	–	–	–	–	–	–	–	–	–	–	–	–	–	–	–	–	7	–	–
8 Aston Villa	–	–	–	6	–	3	–	–	–	–	–	–	–	–	–	–	–	–	–	–	–	–	–	–	–	–	–	6	–	3
9 Leicester City	–	–	–	4	–	–	2	–	–	–	–	–	–	–	–	–	–	–	–	–	–	–	–	–	–	–	–	6	–	–
10 Middlesbrough	–	–	–	6	–	–	–	–	–	–	–	–	–	–	–	–	–	–	–	–	–	–	–	–	–	–	–	6	–	–
11 Tottenham Hotspur	–	–	–	5	–	–	–	–	–	1	–	–	–	–	–	–	–	–	–	–	–	–	–	–	–	–	–	6	–	–
12 West Bromwich Albion	–	–	–	5	–	3	–	–	–	–	–	–	–	–	–	–	–	–	–	–	–	–	–	–	–	–	–	5	–	3
13 Arsenal	–	–	–	5	–	1	–	–	–	–	–	–	–	–	–	–	–	–	–	–	–	–	–	–	–	–	–	5	–	1
14 Burnley	–	–	–	5	–	–	–	–	–	–	–	–	–	–	–	–	–	–	–	–	–	–	–	–	–	–	–	5	–	–
15 Cardiff City	–	–	–	3	–	1	–	–	–	1	–	–	–	–	–	–	–	–	–	–	–	–	–	–	–	–	–	4	–	1
16 Birmingham City	–	–	–	3	–	–	–	–	–	1	–	–	–	–	–	–	–	–	–	–	–	–	–	–	–	–	–	4	–	–
17 Bury	–	–	–	2	–	–	2	–	–	–	–	–	–	–	–	–	–	–	–	–	–	–	–	–	–	–	–	4	–	–
18 Derby County	–	–	–	1	–	–	3	–	–	–	–	–	–	–	–	–	–	–	–	–	–	–	–	–	–	–	–	4	–	–
19 Oldham Athletic	–	–	–	4	–	–	–	–	–	–	–	–	–	–	–	–	–	–	–	–	–	–	–	–	–	–	–	4	–	–
20 Sunderland	–	–	–	4	–	–	–	–	–	–	–	–	–	–	–	–	–	–	–	–	–	–	–	–	–	–	–	4	–	–
21 Preston North End	–	–	–	3	–	1	–	–	–	–	–	–	–	–	–	–	–	–	–	–	–	–	–	–	–	–	–	3	–	1
22 Crystal Palace	–	–	–	–	–	–	3	–	–	–	–	–	–	–	–	–	–	–	–	–	–	–	–	–	–	–	–	3	–	–
23 Leeds United	–	–	–	1	–	–	2	–	–	–	–	–	–	–	–	–	–	–	–	–	–	–	–	–	–	–	–	3	–	–
24 Leyton Orient	–	–	–	–	–	–	3	–	–	–	–	–	–	–	–	–	–	–	–	–	–	–	–	–	–	–	–	3	–	–
25 Reading	–	–	–	–	–	–	–	–	–	3	–	–	–	–	–	–	–	–	–	–	–	–	–	–	–	–	–	3	–	–
26 West Ham United	–	–	–	1	–	–	2	–	–	–	–	–	–	–	–	–	–	–	–	–	–	–	–	–	–	–	–	3	–	–
27 Bradford Park Avenue	–	–	–	2	–	2	–	–	–	–	–	–	–	–	–	–	–	–	–	–	–	–	–	–	–	–	–	2	–	2
28 Sheffield Wednesday	–	–	–	2	–	1	–	–	–	–	–	–	–	–	–	–	–	–	–	–	–	–	–	–	–	–	–	2	–	1
29 Bolton Wanderers	–	–	–	2	–	–	–	–	–	–	–	–	–	–	–	–	–	–	–	–	–	–	–	–	–	–	–	2	–	–
30 Fulham	–	–	–	–	–	–	2	–	–	–	–	–	–	–	–	–	–	–	–	–	–	–	–	–	–	–	–	2	–	–
31 Hull City	–	–	–	–	–	–	2	–	–	–	–	–	–	–	–	–	–	–	–	–	–	–	–	–	–	–	–	2	–	–
32 Manchester City	–	–	–	2	–	–	–	–	–	–	–	–	–	–	–	–	–	–	–	–	–	–	–	–	–	–	–	2	–	–
33 Notts County	–	–	–	–	–	–	2	–	–	–	–	–	–	–	–	–	–	–	–	–	–	–	–	–	–	–	–	2	–	–
34 Rotherham United	–	–	–	–	–	–	2	–	–	–	–	–	–	–	–	–	–	–	–	–	–	–	–	–	–	–	–	2	–	–
35 Stockport County	–	–	–	–	–	–	2	–	–	–	–	–	–	–	–	–	–	–	–	–	–	–	–	–	–	–	–	2	–	–
36 Wolverhampton W.	–	–	–	–	–	–	2	–	–	–	–	–	–	–	–	–	–	–	–	–	–	–	–	–	–	–	–	2	–	–
37 Barnsley	–	–	–	–	–	–	1	–	–	–	–	–	–	–	–	–	–	–	–	–	–	–	–	–	–	–	–	1	–	–

continued../

TEDDY PARTRIDGE (continued)

Opponents	PREM A S G	FLD 1 A S G	FLD 2 A S G	FAC A S G	LC A S G	EC/CL A S G	ECWC A S G	UEFA A S G	OTHER A S G	TOTAL A S G
38 Blackpool	- -	- -	1 -	- -	- -	- -	- -	- -	- -	1 -
39 Brentford	- -	- -	- -	1 -	- -	- -	- -	- -	- -	1 -
40 Coventry City	- -	- -	1 -	- -	- -	- -	- -	- -	- -	1 -
41 Port Vale	- -	- -	1 -	- -	- -	- -	- -	- -	- -	1 -
42 Southampton	- -	- -	1 -	- -	- -	- -	- -	- -	- -	1 -

STEVE PATERSON

DEBUT (Substitute Appearance)

Wednesday 29/09/1976
UEFA Cup 1st Round 2nd Leg
at Old Trafford

Manchester United 2 Ajax 0

CLUB CAREER RECORD	Apps	Subs	Goals
Premiership	0		0
League Division 1	3	(3)	0
League Division 2	0		0
FA Cup	0		0
League Cup	2		0
European Cup / Champions League	0		0
European Cup-Winners' Cup	0		0
UEFA Cup / Inter-Cities' Fairs Cup	0	(2)	0
Other Matches	0		0
OVERALL TOTAL	5	(5)	0

Opponents	PREM A S G	FLD 1 A S G	FLD 2 A S G	FAC A S G	LC A S G	EC/CL A S G	ECWC A S G	UEFA A S G	OTHER A S G	TOTAL A S G
1 Tottenham Hotspur	- -	- (1) -	- -	- -	1 -	- -	- -	- -	- -	1 (1) -
2 Everton	- -	- -	- -	- -	1 -	- -	- -	- -	- -	1 -
3 Leicester City	- -	1 -	- -	- -	- -	- -	- -	- -	- -	1 -
4 Southampton	- -	1 -	- -	- -	- -	- -	- -	- -	- -	1 -
5 Sunderland	- -	1 -	- -	- -	- -	- -	- -	- -	- -	1 -
6 Ajax	- -	- -	- -	- -	- -	- -	- -	- (1) -	- -	- (1) -
7 Arsenal	- -	- (1) -	- -	- -	- -	- -	- -	- -	- -	- (1) -
8 Juventus	- -	- -	- -	- -	- -	- -	- -	- (1) -	- -	- (1) -
9 Leeds United	- -	- (1) -	- -	- -	- -	- -	- -	- -	- -	- (1) -

ERNEST PAYNE

DEBUT (Full Appearance)

Saturday 27/02/1909
Football League Division 1
at City Ground

Nottingham Forest 2 Manchester United 0

CLUB CAREER RECORD	Apps	Subs	Goals
Premiership	0		0
League Division 1	2		1
League Division 2	0		0
FA Cup	0		0
League Cup	0		0
European Cup / Champions League	0		0
European Cup-Winners' Cup	0		0
UEFA Cup / Inter-Cities' Fairs Cup	0		0
Other Matches	0		0
OVERALL TOTAL	2		1

Opponents	PREM A S G	FLD 1 A S G	FLD 2 A S G	FAC A S G	LC A S G	EC/CL A S G	ECWC A S G	UEFA A S G	OTHER A S G	TOTAL A S G
1 Sunderland	- -	1 1	- -	- -	- -	- -	- -	- -	- -	1 1
2 Nottingham Forest	- -	1 -	- -	- -	- -	- -	- -	- -	- -	1 -

STEVE PEARS

DEBUT (Full Appearance)

Saturday 12/01/1985
Football League Division 1
at Old Trafford

Manchester United 0 Coventry City 1

CLUB CAREER RECORD	Apps	Subs	Goals
Premiership	0		0
League Division 1	4		0
League Division 2	0		0
FA Cup	1		0
League Cup	0		0
European Cup / Champions League	0		0
European Cup-Winners' Cup	0		0
UEFA Cup / Inter-Cities' Fairs Cup	0		0
Other Matches	0		0
OVERALL TOTAL	5		0

Opponents	PREM A S G	FLD 1 A S G	FLD 2 A S G	FAC A S G	LC A S G	EC/CL A S G	ECWC A S G	UEFA A S G	OTHER A S G	TOTAL A S G
1 Coventry City	- -	1 -	- -	1 -	- -	- -	- -	- -	- -	2 -
2 Newcastle United	- -	1 -	- -	- -	- -	- -	- -	- -	- -	1 -
3 Sheffield Wednesday	- -	1 -	- -	- -	- -	- -	- -	- -	- -	1 -
4 West Bromwich Albion	- -	1 -	- -	- -	- -	- -	- -	- -	- -	1 -

MARK PEARSON

DEBUT (Full Appearance)

Wednesday 19/02/1958
FA Cup 5th Round
at Old Trafford

Manchester United 3 Sheffield Wednesday 0

CLUB CAREER RECORD	Apps	Subs	Goals
Premiership	0		0
League Division 1	68		12
League Division 2	0		0
FA Cup	7		1
League Cup	3		1
European Cup / Champions League	2		0
European Cup-Winners' Cup	0		0
UEFA Cup / Inter-Cities' Fairs Cup	0		0
Other Matches	0		0
OVERALL TOTAL	80		14

Opponents	PREM A	S	G	FLD 1 A	S	G	FLD 2 A	S	G	FAC A	S	G	LC A	S	G	EC/CL A	S	G	ECWC A	S	G	UEFA A	S	G	OTHER A	S	G	TOTAL A	S	G
1 Aston Villa	–	–		5		1	–			–			–			–			–			–			–			5		1
2 Fulham	–			4		1	–			1			–			–			–			–			–			5		1
3 Sheffield Wednesday	–			2		–	–			3		1	–			–			–			–			–			5		1
4 West Bromwich Albion	–			3		1	–			2			–			–			–			–			–			5		1
5 Burnley	–			5			–			–			–			–			–			–			–			5		–
6 Nottingham Forest	–			5			–			–			–			–			–			–			–			5		–
7 Blackpool	–			4		1	–			–			–			–			–			–			–			4		1
8 Chelsea	–			4		1	–			–			–			–			–			–			–			4		1
9 Wolverhampton W.	–			4			–			–			–			–			–			–			–			4		–
10 Birmingham City	–			3		2	–			–			–			–			–			–			–			3		2
11 Blackburn Rovers	–			3		2	–			–			–			–			–			–			–			3		2
12 Arsenal	–			3		1	–			–			–			–			–			–			–			3		1
13 Manchester City	–			3		1	–			–			–			–			–			–			–			3		1
14 Tottenham Hotspur	–			3		1	–			–			–			–			–			–			–			3		1
15 Everton	–			3			–			–			–			–			–			–			–			3		–
16 Exeter City	–			–			–			2		1	–			–			–			–			–			2		1
17 AC Milan	–			–			–			–			–			2			–			–			–			2		–
18 Bolton Wanderers	–			2			–			–			–			–			–			–			–			2		–
19 Cardiff City	–			2			–			–			–			–			–			–			–			2		–
20 Preston North End	–			2			–			–			–			–			–			–			–			2		–
21 Sheffield United	–			2			–			–			–			–			–			–			–			2		–
22 Bradford City	–			–			–			–			1			–			–			–			–			1		–
23 Leicester City	–			1			–			–			–			–			–			–			–			1		–
24 Luton Town	–			1			–			–			–			–			–			–			–			1		–
25 Middlesbrough	–			–			–			1			–			–			–			–			–			1		–
26 Newcastle United	–			1			–			–			–			–			–			–			–			1		–
27 Portsmouth	–			1			–			–			–			–			–			–			–			1		–
28 Sunderland	–			1			–			–			–			–			–			–			–			1		–
29 West Ham United	–			1			–			–			–			–			–			–			–			1		–

STAN PEARSON

DEBUT (Full Appearance)

Saturday 13/11/1937
Football League Division 2
at Saltergate

Chesterfield 1 Manchester United 7

CLUB CAREER RECORD	Apps	Subs	Goals
Premiership	0		0
League Division 1	301		125
League Division 2	11		2
FA Cup	30		21
League Cup	0		0
European Cup / Champions League	0		0
European Cup-Winners' Cup	0		0
UEFA Cup / Inter-Cities' Fairs Cup	0		0
Other Matches	1		0
OVERALL TOTAL	343		148

Opponents	PREM A	S	G	FLD 1 A	S	G	FLD 2 A	S	G	FAC A	S	G	LC A	S	G	EC/CL A	S	G	ECWC A	S	G	UEFA A	S	G	OTHER A	S	G	TOTAL A	S	G
1 Wolverhampton W.	–			16		6	–			2			–			–			–			–			–			18		6
2 Aston Villa	–			15		6	1		1	1		2	–			–			–			–			–			17		9
3 Liverpool	–			15		8	–			1			–			–			–			–			–			16		8
4 Bolton Wanderers	–			16		4	–			–			–			–			–			–			–			16		4
5 Middlesbrough	–			15		13	–			–			–			–			–			–			–			15		13
6 Chelsea	–			14		9	–			1			–			–			–			–			–			15		9
7 Arsenal	–			14		6	–			1		1	–			–			–			–			–			15		7
8 Blackpool	–			14		3	–			1		1	–			–			–			–			–			15		4
9 Sunderland	–			15		1	–			–			–			–			–			–			–			15		1
10 Derby County	–			13		12	–			1		3	–			–			–			–			–			14		15
11 Charlton Athletic	–			13		6	–			1			–			–			–			–			–			14		6
12 Burnley	–			12		2	2			–			–			–			–			–			–			14		2
13 Portsmouth	–			13			–			1		1	–			–			–			–			–			14		1
14 Huddersfield Town	–			12		8	–			–			–			–			–			–			–			12		8
15 Preston North End	–			11		5	–			1		2	–			–			–			–			–			12		7
16 Stoke City	–			12		2	–			–			–			–			–			–			–			12		2
17 Everton	–			10		3	–			1			–			–			–			–			–			11		3
18 Newcastle United	–			10		2	–			–			–			–			–			–			1			11		2
19 Manchester City	–			10		4	–			–			–			–			–			–			–			10		4
20 West Bromwich Albion	–			8		5	–			–			–			–			–			–			–			8		5
21 Tottenham Hotspur	–			7		3	–			–			–			–			–			–			–			7		3
22 Birmingham City	–			6		2	–			1			–			–			–			–			–			7		2
23 Fulham	–			6		4	–			–			–			–			–			–			–			6		4

continued../

STAN PEARSON (continued)

Opponents	PREM A S G	FLD 1 A S G	FLD 2 A S G	FAC A S G	LC A S G	EC/CL A S G	ECWC A S G	UEFA A S G	OTHER A S G	TOTAL A G
24 Sheffield United	– –	6 – 3	–	–	–	–	–	–	–	6 3
25 Bradford Park Avenue	– –	– –	2 – –	4 – 1	–	–	–	–	–	6 1
26 Blackburn Rovers	– –	4 – 5	–	–	–	–	–	–	–	4 5
27 Sheffield Wednesday	– –	4 – 2	–	–	–	–	–	–	–	4 2
28 Grimsby Town	– –	4 – –	–	–	–	–	–	–	–	4 –
29 Leeds United	– –	2 – –	–	1 – 3	–	–	–	–	–	3 3
30 Cardiff City	– –	2 – 1	–	–	–	–	–	–	–	2 1
31 Hull City	– –	– –	–	2 – 1	–	–	–	–	–	2 1
32 Walthamstow Avenue	– –	– –	–	2 – 1	–	–	–	–	–	2 1
33 Yeovil Town	– –	– –	–	2 – 1	–	–	–	–	–	2 1
34 Brentford	– –	2 – –	–	–	–	–	–	–	–	2 –
35 Nottingham Forest	– –	– –	1 – –	1 – –	–	–	–	–	–	2 –
36 Bournemouth	– –	– –	–	1 – 1	–	–	–	–	–	1 1
37 Millwall	– –	– –	–	1 – 1	–	–	–	–	–	1 1
38 Norwich City	– –	– –	1 – 1	–	–	–	–	–	–	1 1
39 Oldham Athletic	– –	– –	–	1 – 1	–	–	–	–	–	1 1
40 Weymouth Town	– –	– –	–	1 – 1	–	–	–	–	–	1 1
41 Bury	– –	– –	1 – –	–	–	–	–	–	–	1 –
42 Chesterfield	– –	– –	1 – –	–	–	–	–	–	–	1 –
43 Swansea City	– –	– –	1 – –	–	–	–	–	–	–	1 –
44 Watford	– –	– –	–	1 – –	–	–	–	–	–	1 –
45 West Ham United	– –	– –	1 – –	–	–	–	–	–	–	1 –

STUART PEARSON

DEBUT (Full Appearance)

Saturday 17/08/1974
Football League Division 2
at Brisbane Road

Leyton Orient 0 Manchester United 2

CLUB CAREER RECORD	Apps	Subs	Goals
Premiership	0		0
League Division 1	108		38
League Division 2	30	(1)	17
FA Cup	22		5
League Cup	12		5
European Cup / Champions League	0		0
European Cup–Winners' Cup	3		1
UEFA Cup / Inter-Cities' Fairs Cup	3		0
Other Matches	1		0
OVERALL TOTAL	179	(1)	66

Opponents	PREM A S G	FLD 1 A S G	FLD 2 A S G	FAC A S G	LC A S G	EC/CL A S G	ECWC A S G	UEFA A S G	OTHER A S G	TOTAL A G
1 Aston Villa	– –	6 – 3	2 – –	1 – –	1 – –	–	–	–	–	10 3
2 West Bromwich Albion	– –	4 – –	2 – 1	2 – 1	–	–	–	–	–	8 2
3 Arsenal	– –	6 – 2	–	–	1 – 1	–	–	–	–	7 3
4 Derby County	– –	6 – 2	–	1 – –	–	–	–	–	–	7 2
5 Queens Park Rangers	– –	6 – 2	–	–	1 – –	–	–	–	–	7 2
6 Liverpool	– –	5 – –	–	1 – 1	–	–	–	1 – –	–	7 1
7 Manchester City	– –	5 – 1	–	–	2 – –	–	–	–	–	7 1
8 Norwich City	– –	5 – 2	1 – 1	–	–	–	–	–	–	6 3
9 West Ham United	– –	6 – 3	–	–	–	–	–	–	–	6 3
10 Middlesbrough	– –	4 – 1	–	–	2 – 1	–	–	–	–	6 2
11 Wolverhampton W.	– –	4 – 1	–	2 – 1	–	–	–	–	–	6 2
12 Everton	– –	5 – 1	–	–	1 – –	–	–	–	–	6 1
13 Leeds United	– –	5 – 1	–	1 – –	–	–	–	–	–	6 1
14 Newcastle United	– –	4 – 3	–	–	1 – 1	–	–	–	–	5 4
15 Ipswich Town	– –	5 – 2	–	–	–	–	–	–	–	5 2
16 Coventry City	– –	5 – 1	–	–	–	–	–	–	–	5 1
17 Leicester City	– –	4 – 1	–	1 – –	–	–	–	–	–	5 1
18 Southampton	– –	– –	1 (1) 1	3 – –	–	–	–	–	–	4 (1) 1
19 Sunderland	– –	2 – 1	1 – 1	–	1 – 1	–	–	–	–	4 3
20 Birmingham City	– –	4 – 2	–	–	–	–	–	–	–	4 2
21 Bristol City	– –	3 – 2	1 – –	–	–	–	–	–	–	4 2
22 Tottenham Hotspur	– –	4 – 1	–	–	–	–	–	–	–	4 1
23 Oxford United	– –	– –	2 – 3	1 – –	–	–	–	–	–	3 3
24 Fulham	– –	– –	2 – 2	1 – –	–	–	–	–	–	3 2
25 Nottingham Forest	– –	2 – 1	1 – –	–	–	–	–	–	–	3 1
26 Burnley	– –	2 – –	–	–	1 – –	–	–	–	–	3 –
27 Chelsea	– –	2 – –	–	1 – –	–	–	–	–	–	3 –
28 Walsall	– –	– –	–	3 – –	–	–	–	–	–	3 –
29 Sheffield United	– –	2 – 4	–	–	–	–	–	–	–	2 4
30 Carlisle United	– –	– –	–	2 – 2	–	–	–	–	–	2 2
31 Cardiff City	– –	– –	2 – 1	–	–	–	–	–	–	2 1
32 Sheffield Wednesday	– –	– –	2 – 1	–	–	–	–	–	–	2 1
33 St Etienne	– –	– –	–	–	–	–	2 – 1	–	–	2 1
34 Stoke City	– –	2 – 1	–	–	–	–	–	–	–	2 1
35 York City	– –	– –	2 – 1	–	–	–	–	–	–	2 1
36 Juventus	– –	– –	–	–	–	–	–	2 – –	–	2 –
37 Leyton Orient	– –	– –	2 – –	–	–	–	–	–	–	2 –
38 Oldham Athletic	– –	– –	2 – –	–	–	–	–	–	–	2 –
39 Blackpool	– –	– –	1 – 2	–	–	–	–	–	–	1 2

continued../

STUART PEARSON (continued)

Opponents	PREM			FLD 1			FLD 2			FAC			LC			EC/CL			ECWC			UEFA			OTHER			TOTAL		
	A	S	G	A	S	G	A	S	G	A	S	G	A	S	G	A	S	G	A	S	G	A	S	G	A	S	G	A	S	G
40 Bolton Wanderers	–	–	–	–	–	–	–	–	–	1	–	1	–	–	–	–	–	–	–	–	–	–	–	–	–	–	–	1	–	1
41 Hull City	–	–	–	–	–	–	–	–	–	1	–	1	–	–	–	–	–	–	–	–	–	–	–	–	–	–	–	1	–	1
42 Millwall	–	–	–	–	–	–	–	–	–	1	–	1	–	–	–	–	–	–	–	–	–	–	–	–	–	–	–	1	–	1
43 Tranmere Rovers	–	–	–	–	–	–	–	–	–	–	–	–	1	–	1	–	–	–	–	–	–	–	–	–	–	–	–	1	–	1
44 Ajax	–	–	–	–	–	–	–	–	–	–	–	–	–	–	–	–	–	–	–	–	–	1	–	–	–	–	–	1	–	–
45 Brentford	–	–	–	–	–	–	–	–	–	–	–	–	1	–	–	–	–	–	–	–	–	–	–	–	–	–	–	1	–	–
46 Bristol Rovers	–	–	–	–	–	–	–	–	–	1	–	–	–	–	–	–	–	–	–	–	–	–	–	–	–	–	–	1	–	–
47 Notts County	–	–	–	–	–	–	–	–	–	1	–	–	–	–	–	–	–	–	–	–	–	–	–	–	–	–	–	1	–	–
48 Peterborough United	–	–	–	–	–	–	–	–	–	–	–	–	1	–	–	–	–	–	–	–	–	–	–	–	–	–	–	1	–	–
49 Porto	–	–	–	–	–	–	–	–	–	–	–	–	–	–	–	1	–	–	–	–	–	–	–	–	–	–	–	1	–	–
50 Portsmouth	–	–	–	–	–	–	–	–	–	1	–	–	–	–	–	–	–	–	–	–	–	–	–	–	–	–	–	1	–	–

JACK PEDDIE

DEBUT (Full Appearance)

Saturday 06/09/1902
Football League Division 2
at The Northholme

Gainsborough Trinity 0 Manchester United 1

CLUB CAREER RECORD	Apps	Subs	Goals
Premiership	0		0
League Division 1	16		6
League Division 2	96		46
FA Cup	9		6
League Cup	0		0
European Cup / Champions League	0		0
European Cup-Winners' Cup	0		0
UEFA Cup / Inter-Cities' Fairs Cup	0		0
Other Matches	0		0
OVERALL TOTAL	**121**		**58**

Opponents	PREM			FLD 1			FLD 2			FAC			LC			EC/CL			ECWC			UEFA			OTHER			TOTAL		
	A	S	G	A	S	G	A	S	G	A	S	G	A	S	G	A	S	G	A	S	G	A	S	G	A	S	G	A	S	G
1 Burton United	–	–	–	–	–	–	6	–	7	2	–	1	–	–	–	–	–	–	–	–	–	–	–	–	–	–	–	8	–	8
2 Bristol City	–	–	–	1	–	–	6	–	1	–	–	–	–	–	–	–	–	–	–	–	–	–	–	–	–	–	–	7	–	1
3 Leicester City	–	–	–	–	–	–	6	–	9	–	–	–	–	–	–	–	–	–	–	–	–	–	–	–	–	–	–	6	–	9
4 Blackpool	–	–	–	–	–	–	6	–	3	–	–	–	–	–	–	–	–	–	–	–	–	–	–	–	–	–	–	6	–	3
5 Burnley	–	–	–	–	–	–	6	–	3	–	–	–	–	–	–	–	–	–	–	–	–	–	–	–	–	–	–	6	–	3
6 Gainsborough Trinity	–	–	–	–	–	–	6	–	1	–	–	–	–	–	–	–	–	–	–	–	–	–	–	–	–	–	–	6	–	1
7 Chesterfield	–	–	–	–	–	–	6	–	–	–	–	–	–	–	–	–	–	–	–	–	–	–	–	–	–	–	–	6	–	–
8 Barnsley	–	–	–	–	–	–	5	–	2	–	–	–	–	–	–	–	–	–	–	–	–	–	–	–	–	–	–	5	–	2
9 Port Vale	–	–	–	–	–	–	5	–	2	–	–	–	–	–	–	–	–	–	–	–	–	–	–	–	–	–	–	5	–	2
10 Glossop	–	–	–	–	–	–	5	–	1	–	–	–	–	–	–	–	–	–	–	–	–	–	–	–	–	–	–	5	–	1
11 Stockport County	–	–	–	–	–	–	4	–	3	–	–	–	–	–	–	–	–	–	–	–	–	–	–	–	–	–	–	4	–	3
12 Lincoln City	–	–	–	–	–	–	4	–	2	–	–	–	–	–	–	–	–	–	–	–	–	–	–	–	–	–	–	4	–	2
13 Bradford City	–	–	–	–	–	–	4	–	1	–	–	–	–	–	–	–	–	–	–	–	–	–	–	–	–	–	–	4	–	1
14 West Bromwich Albion	–	–	–	–	–	–	4	–	1	–	–	–	–	–	–	–	–	–	–	–	–	–	–	–	–	–	–	4	–	1
15 Birmingham City	–	–	–	1	–	2	2	–	–	–	–	–	–	–	–	–	–	–	–	–	–	–	–	–	–	–	–	3	–	2
16 Arsenal	–	–	–	1	–	–	1	–	1	1	–	1	–	–	–	–	–	–	–	–	–	–	–	–	–	–	–	3	–	2
17 Bolton Wanderers	–	–	–	1	–	1	2	–	1	–	–	–	–	–	–	–	–	–	–	–	–	–	–	–	–	–	–	3	–	2
18 Doncaster Rovers	–	–	–	–	–	–	3	–	2	–	–	–	–	–	–	–	–	–	–	–	–	–	–	–	–	–	–	3	–	2
19 Liverpool	–	–	–	–	–	–	2	–	1	1	–	1	–	–	–	–	–	–	–	–	–	–	–	–	–	–	–	3	–	2
20 Leyton Orient	–	–	–	–	–	–	2	–	2	–	–	–	–	–	–	–	–	–	–	–	–	–	–	–	–	–	–	2	–	2
21 Hull City	–	–	–	–	–	–	2	–	1	–	–	–	–	–	–	–	–	–	–	–	–	–	–	–	–	–	–	2	–	1
22 Manchester City	–	–	–	–	–	–	2	–	1	–	–	–	–	–	–	–	–	–	–	–	–	–	–	–	–	–	–	2	–	1
23 Aston Villa	–	–	–	1	–	–	1	–	–	–	–	–	–	–	–	–	–	–	–	–	–	–	–	–	–	–	–	2	–	–
24 Chelsea	–	–	–	–	–	–	2	–	–	–	–	–	–	–	–	–	–	–	–	–	–	–	–	–	–	–	–	2	–	–
25 Derby County	–	–	–	2	–	–	–	–	–	–	–	–	–	–	–	–	–	–	–	–	–	–	–	–	–	–	–	2	–	–
26 Everton	–	–	–	1	–	–	–	–	–	1	–	–	–	–	–	–	–	–	–	–	–	–	–	–	–	–	–	2	–	–
27 Grimsby Town	–	–	–	–	–	–	2	–	–	–	–	–	–	–	–	–	–	–	–	–	–	–	–	–	–	–	–	2	–	–
28 Preston North End	–	–	–	–	–	–	2	–	–	–	–	–	–	–	–	–	–	–	–	–	–	–	–	–	–	–	–	2	–	–
29 Accrington Stanley	–	–	–	–	–	–	–	–	–	1	–	1	–	–	–	–	–	–	–	–	–	–	–	–	–	–	–	1	–	1
30 Bury	–	–	–	1	–	1	–	–	–	–	–	–	–	–	–	–	–	–	–	–	–	–	–	–	–	–	–	1	–	1
31 Leeds United	–	–	–	–	–	–	–	–	–	1	–	1	–	–	–	–	–	–	–	–	–	–	–	–	–	–	–	1	–	1
32 Norwich City	–	–	–	–	–	–	–	–	–	1	–	1	–	–	–	–	–	–	–	–	–	–	–	–	–	–	–	1	–	1
33 Sheffield Wednesday	–	–	–	1	–	1	–	–	–	–	–	–	–	–	–	–	–	–	–	–	–	–	–	–	–	–	–	1	–	1
34 Sunderland	–	–	–	1	–	1	–	–	–	–	–	–	–	–	–	–	–	–	–	–	–	–	–	–	–	–	–	1	–	1
35 Blackburn Rovers	–	–	–	1	–	–	–	–	–	–	–	–	–	–	–	–	–	–	–	–	–	–	–	–	–	–	–	1	–	–
36 Newcastle United	–	–	–	1	–	–	–	–	–	–	–	–	–	–	–	–	–	–	–	–	–	–	–	–	–	–	–	1	–	–
37 Notts County	–	–	–	1	–	–	–	–	–	–	–	–	–	–	–	–	–	–	–	–	–	–	–	–	–	–	–	1	–	–
38 Sheffield United	–	–	–	1	–	–	–	–	–	–	–	–	–	–	–	–	–	–	–	–	–	–	–	–	–	–	–	1	–	–
39 Southport Central	–	–	–	–	–	–	–	–	–	1	–	–	–	–	–	–	–	–	–	–	–	–	–	–	–	–	–	1	–	–
40 Stoke City	–	–	–	1	–	–	–	–	–	–	–	–	–	–	–	–	–	–	–	–	–	–	–	–	–	–	–	1	–	–

JACK PEDEN

DEBUT (Full Appearance)

Saturday 02/09/1893
Football League Division 1
at North Road

Newton Heath 3 Burnley 2

CLUB CAREER RECORD	Apps	Subs	Goals
Premiership	0		0
League Division 1	28		7
League Division 2	0		0
FA Cup	3		1
League Cup	0		0
European Cup / Champions League	0		0
European Cup-Winners' Cup	0		0
UEFA Cup / Inter-Cities' Fairs Cup	0		0
Other Matches	1		0
OVERALL TOTAL	32		8

Opponents	PREM A	S	G	FLD 1 A	S	G	FLD 2 A	S	G	FAC A	S	G	LC A	S	G	EC/CL A	S	G	ECWC A	S	G	UEFA A	S	G	OTHER A	S	G	TOTAL A	S	G
1 Blackburn Rovers	–	–		2	–	–				2			–															4		–
2 Stoke City	–	–		2		2	–			–			–			–			–			–			–			2		2
3 West Bromwich Albion	–			2		2	–			–			–			–			–			–			–			2		2
4 Sheffield Wednesday	–			2		1	–			–			–			–			–			–			–			2		1
5 Sunderland	–			2		1	–			–			–			–			–			–			–			2		1
6 Bolton Wanderers	–			2		–				–																		2		–
7 Burnley				2		–																						2		
8 Darwen	–			2		–																						2		–
9 Derby County				2		–																						2		
10 Everton	–			2		–																						2		
11 Preston North End	–			2		–																						2		
12 Sheffield United	–			2		–																						2		
13 Wolverhampton W.	–			2		–																						2		–
14 Aston Villa	–			1		1	–			–															–			1		1
15 Middlesbrough	–			–		–	–			1		1																1		1
16 Liverpool	–			–		–				–												–			1		–	1		–
17 Nottingham Forest	–			1		–																						1		–

DAVID PEGG

DEBUT (Full Appearance)

Saturday 06/12/1952
Football League Division 1
at Old Trafford

Manchester United 3 Middlesbrough 2

CLUB CAREER RECORD	Apps	Subs	Goals
Premiership	0		0
League Division 1	127		24
League Division 2	0		0
FA Cup	9		0
League Cup	0		0
European Cup / Champions League	12		4
European Cup-Winners' Cup	0		0
UEFA Cup / Inter-Cities' Fairs Cup	0		0
Other Matches	2		0
OVERALL TOTAL	150		28

Opponents	PREM A	S	G	FLD 1 A	S	G	FLD 2 A	S	G	FAC A	S	G	LC A	S	G	EC/CL A	S	G	ECWC A	S	G	UEFA A	S	G	OTHER A	S	G	TOTAL A	S	G
1 Aston Villa	–			7		3	–			1			–			–			–			–			1		–	9		3
2 Blackpool	–			9		–	–			–			–			–			–			–			–			9		–
3 Manchester City	–			7		–	–			–			–			–			–			–			1		–	8		–
4 Portsmouth	–			7		3	–			–			–			–			–			–			–			7		3
5 Wolverhampton W.	–			7		2	–			–			–			–			–			–			–			7		2
6 Chelsea	–			7		1	–			–			–			–			–			–			–			7		1
7 Bolton Wanderers	–			7		–	–			–			–			–			–			–			–			7		–
8 Charlton Athletic	–			7		–	–			–			–			–			–			–			–			7		–
9 Preston North End	–			6		3	–			–			–			–			–			–			–			6		3
10 Burnley	–			6		–	–			–			–			–			–			–			–			6		–
11 Everton	–			4		–	–			2			–			–			–			–			–			6		–
12 Newcastle United	–			5		3	–			–			–			–			–			–			–			5		3
13 Arsenal	–			5		1	–			–			–			–			–			–			–			5		1
14 Sunderland	–			5		1	–			–			–			–			–			–			–			5		1
15 Birmingham City	–			4		–	–			1			–			–			–			–			–			5		–
16 Cardiff City	–			5		–	–			–			–			–			–			–			–			5		–
17 Sheffield Wednesday	–			4		–	–			–			–			–			–			–			–			4		–
18 West Bromwich Albion	–			4		–	–			–			–			–			–			–			–			4		–
19 Tottenham Hotspur	–			3		3	–			–			–			–			–			–			–			3		3
20 Huddersfield Town	–			3		2	–			–			–			–			–			–			–			3		2
21 Luton Town	–			3		1	–			–			–			–			–			–			–			3		1
22 Leeds United	–			3		–	–			–			–			–			–			–			–			3		–
23 Shamrock Rovers	–			–		–	–			–			–			2		2	–			–			–			2		2
24 Borussia Dortmund	–			–		–	–			–			–			2		1	–			–			–			2		1
25 Dukla Prague	–			–		–	–			–			–			2		1	–			–			–			2		1
26 Sheffield United	–			2		1	–			–			–			–			–			–			–			2		1
27 Anderlecht	–			–		–	–			–			–			2		–	–			–			–			2		–
28 Athletic Bilbao	–			–		–	–			–			–			2		–	–			–			–			2		–
29 Liverpool	–			2		–	–			–			–			–			–			–			–			2		–
30 Real Madrid	–			–		–	–			–			–			2		–	–			–			–			2		–
31 Bournemouth	–			–		–	–			1			–			–			–			–			–			1		–
32 Bristol Rovers	–			–		–	–			1			–			–			–			–			–			1		–
33 Derby County	–			1		–	–			–			–			–			–			–			–			1		–
34 Hartlepool United	–			–		–	–			1			–			–			–			–			–			1		–

continued../

DAVID PEGG (continued)

Opponents	PREM			FLD 1			FLD 2			FAC			LC			EC/CL			ECWC			UEFA			OTHER			TOTAL		
	A	S	G	A	S	G	A	S	G	A	S	G	A	S	G	A	S	G	A	S	G	A	S	G	A	S	G	A	S	G
35 Leicester City	-	-	1	-	-	-	-	-	-	-	-	-	-	-	-	-	-	-	-	-	-	-	-	-	-	-	-	1	-	
36 Middlesbrough	-	-	1	-	-	-	-	-	-	-	-	-	-	-	-	-	-	-	-	-	-	-	-	-	-	-	-	1	-	
37 Nottingham Forest	-	-	1	-	-	-	-	-	-	-	-	-	-	-	-	-	-	-	-	-	-	-	-	-	-	-	-	1	-	
38 Stoke City	-	-	1	-	-	-	-	-	-	-	-	-	-	-	-	-	-	-	-	-	-	-	-	-	-	-	-	1	-	
39 Walthamstow Avenue	-	-	-	-	-	-	1	-	-	-	-	-	-	-	-	-	-	-	-	-	-	-	-	-	-	-	-	1	-	
40 Wrexham	-	-	-	-	-	-	1	-	-	-	-	-	-	-	-	-	-	-	-	-	-	-	-	-	-	-	-	1	-	

DICK PEGG

DEBUT (Full Appearance)

Saturday 06/09/1902
Football League Division 2
at The Northolme

Gainsborough Trinity 0 Manchester United 1

CLUB CAREER RECORD	Apps	Subs	Goals
Premiership	0		0
League Division 1	0		0
League Division 2	41		13
FA Cup	10		7
League Cup	0		0
European Cup / Champions League	0		0
European Cup-Winners' Cup	0		0
UEFA Cup / Inter-Cities' Fairs Cup	0		0
Other Matches	0		0
OVERALL TOTAL	51		20

Opponents	PREM			FLD 1			FLD 2			FAC			LC			EC/CL			ECWC			UEFA			OTHER			TOTAL		
	A	S	G	A	S	G	A	S	G	A	S	G	A	S	G	A	S	G	A	S	G	A	S	G	A	S	G	A	S	G
1 Stockport County	-	-	-	-	-	-	4	-	2	-	-	-	-	-	-	-	-	-	-	-	-	-	-	-	-	-	-	4	-	2
2 Burton United	-	-	-	-	-	-	2	-	-	2	-	1	-	-	-	-	-	-	-	-	-	-	-	-	-	-	-	4	-	1
3 Barnsley	-	-	-	-	-	-	3	-	2	-	-	-	-	-	-	-	-	-	-	-	-	-	-	-	-	-	-	3	-	2
4 Arsenal	-	-	-	-	-	-	3	-	1	-	-	-	-	-	-	-	-	-	-	-	-	-	-	-	-	-	-	3	-	1
5 Gainsborough Trinity	-	-	-	-	-	-	3	-	1	-	-	-	-	-	-	-	-	-	-	-	-	-	-	-	-	-	-	3	-	1
6 Leicester City	-	-	-	-	-	-	3	-	1	-	-	-	-	-	-	-	-	-	-	-	-	-	-	-	-	-	-	3	-	1
7 Birmingham City	-	-	-	-	-	-	2	-	-	1	-	-	-	-	-	-	-	-	-	-	-	-	-	-	-	-	-	3	-	-
8 Chesterfield	-	-	-	-	-	-	3	-	-	-	-	-	-	-	-	-	-	-	-	-	-	-	-	-	-	-	-	3	-	-
9 Lincoln City	-	-	-	-	-	-	3	-	-	-	-	-	-	-	-	-	-	-	-	-	-	-	-	-	-	-	-	3	-	-
10 Manchester City	-	-	-	-	-	-	2	-	1	-	-	-	-	-	-	-	-	-	-	-	-	-	-	-	-	-	-	2	-	1
11 Preston North End	-	-	-	-	-	-	2	-	1	-	-	-	-	-	-	-	-	-	-	-	-	-	-	-	-	-	-	2	-	1
12 Doncaster Rovers	-	-	-	-	-	-	2	-	-	-	-	-	-	-	-	-	-	-	-	-	-	-	-	-	-	-	-	2	-	-
13 Glossop	-	-	-	-	-	-	2	-	-	-	-	-	-	-	-	-	-	-	-	-	-	-	-	-	-	-	-	2	-	-
14 Port Vale	-	-	-	-	-	-	2	-	-	-	-	-	-	-	-	-	-	-	-	-	-	-	-	-	-	-	-	2	-	-
15 Bradford City	-	-	-	-	-	-	1	-	3	-	-	-	-	-	-	-	-	-	-	-	-	-	-	-	-	-	-	1	-	3
16 Southport Central	-	-	-	-	-	-	-	-	-	1	-	3	-	-	-	-	-	-	-	-	-	-	-	-	-	-	-	1	-	3
17 Accrington Stanley	-	-	-	-	-	-	-	-	-	1	-	1	-	-	-	-	-	-	-	-	-	-	-	-	-	-	-	1	-	1
18 Burnley	-	-	-	-	-	-	1	-	1	-	-	-	-	-	-	-	-	-	-	-	-	-	-	-	-	-	-	1	-	1
19 Notts County	-	-	-	-	-	-	-	-	-	1	-	1	-	-	-	-	-	-	-	-	-	-	-	-	-	-	-	1	-	1
20 Oswaldtwistle Rovers	-	-	-	-	-	-	-	-	-	1	-	1	-	-	-	-	-	-	-	-	-	-	-	-	-	-	-	1	-	1
21 Blackpool	-	-	-	-	-	-	1	-	-	-	-	-	-	-	-	-	-	-	-	-	-	-	-	-	-	-	-	1	-	-
22 Bolton Wanderers	-	-	-	-	-	-	1	-	-	-	-	-	-	-	-	-	-	-	-	-	-	-	-	-	-	-	-	1	-	-
23 Bristol City	-	-	-	-	-	-	1	-	-	-	-	-	-	-	-	-	-	-	-	-	-	-	-	-	-	-	-	1	-	-
24 Everton	-	-	-	-	-	-	-	-	-	1	-	-	-	-	-	-	-	-	-	-	-	-	-	-	-	-	-	1	-	-
25 Liverpool	-	-	-	-	-	-	-	-	-	1	-	-	-	-	-	-	-	-	-	-	-	-	-	-	-	-	-	1	-	-
26 Sheffield Wednesday	-	-	-	-	-	-	-	-	-	1	-	-	-	-	-	-	-	-	-	-	-	-	-	-	-	-	-	1	-	-

---

KEN PEGG

DEBUT (Full Appearance)

Saturday 15/11/1947
Football League Division 1
at Baseball Ground

Derby County 1 Manchester United 1

CLUB CAREER RECORD	Apps	Subs	Goals
Premiership	0		0
League Division 1	2		0
League Division 2	0		0
FA Cup	0		0
League Cup	0		0
European Cup / Champions League	0		0
European Cup-Winners' Cup	0		0
UEFA Cup / Inter-Cities' Fairs Cup	0		0
Other Matches	0		0
OVERALL TOTAL	2		0

Opponents	PREM			FLD 1			FLD 2			FAC			LC			EC/CL			ECWC			UEFA			OTHER			TOTAL		
	A	S	G	A	S	G	A	S	G	A	S	G	A	S	G	A	S	G	A	S	G	A	S	G	A	S	G	A	S	G
1 Derby County	-	-	-	1	-	-	-	-	-	-	-	-	-	-	-	-	-	-	-	-	-	-	-	-	-	-	-	1	-	-
2 Everton	-	-	-	1	-	-	-	-	-	-	-	-	-	-	-	-	-	-	-	-	-	-	-	-	-	-	-	1	-	-

FRANK PEPPER

DEBUT (Full Appearance)

Saturday 10/12/1898
Football League Division 2
at Bank Street

Newton Heath 3 Blackpool 1

CLUB CAREER RECORD	Apps	Subs	Goals
Premiership	0		0
League Division 1	0		0
League Division 2	7		0
FA Cup	1		0
League Cup	0		0
European Cup / Champions League	0		0
European Cup-Winners' Cup	0		0
UEFA Cup / Inter-Cities' Fairs Cup	0		0
Other Matches	0		0
OVERALL TOTAL	**8**		**0**

Opponents	PREM A S G	FLD 1 A S G	FLD 2 A S G	FAC A S G	LC A S G	EC/CL A S G	ECWC A S G	UEFA A S G	OTHER A S G	TOTAL A S G
1 Blackpool	- - -	- - -	1 - -	- - -	- - -	- - -	- - -	- - -	- - -	1 - -
2 Burton Swifts	- - -	- - -	1 - -	- - -	- - -	- - -	- - -	- - -	- - -	1 - -
3 Darwen	- - -	- - -	1 - -	- - -	- - -	- - -	- - -	- - -	- - -	1 - -
4 Gainsborough Trinity	- - -	- - -	1 - -	- - -	- - -	- - -	- - -	- - -	- - -	1 - -
5 Leicester City	- - -	- - -	1 - -	- - -	- - -	- - -	- - -	- - -	- - -	1 - -
6 Manchester City	- - -	- - -	1 - -	- - -	- - -	- - -	- - -	- - -	- - -	1 - -
7 Port Vale	- - -	- - -	1 - -	- - -	- - -	- - -	- - -	- - -	- - -	1 - -
8 Tottenham Hotspur	- - -	- - -	- - -	1 - -	- - -	- - -	- - -	- - -	- - -	1 - -

GEORGE PERRINS

DEBUT (Full Appearance)

Saturday 03/09/1892
Football League Division 1
at Ewood Park

Blackburn Rovers 4 Newton Heath 3

CLUB CAREER RECORD	Apps	Subs	Goals
Premiership	0		0
League Division 1	55		0
League Division 2	37		0
FA Cup	6		0
League Cup	0		0
European Cup / Champions League	0		0
European Cup-Winners' Cup	0		0
UEFA Cup / Inter-Cities' Fairs Cup	0		0
Other Matches	4		0
OVERALL TOTAL	**102**		**0**

Opponents	PREM A S G	FLD 1 A S G	FLD 2 A S G	FAC A S G	LC A S G	EC/CL A S G	ECWC A S G	UEFA A S G	OTHER A S G	TOTAL A S G
1 Blackburn Rovers	- - -	4 - -	- - -	3 - -	- - -	- - -	- - -	- - -	- - -	7 - -
2 Stoke City	- - -	4 - -	1 - -	- - -	- - -	- - -	- - -	- - -	1 - -	6 - -
3 Aston Villa	- - -	4 - -	- - -	- - -	- - -	- - -	- - -	- - -	- - -	4 - -
4 Bolton Wanderers	- - -	4 - -	- - -	- - -	- - -	- - -	- - -	- - -	- - -	4 - -
5 Burnley	- - -	4 - -	- - -	- - -	- - -	- - -	- - -	- - -	- - -	4 - -
6 Derby County	- - -	4 - -	- - -	- - -	- - -	- - -	- - -	- - -	- - -	4 - -
7 Everton	- - -	4 - -	- - -	- - -	- - -	- - -	- - -	- - -	- - -	4 - -
8 Newcastle United	- - -	- - -	4 - -	- - -	- - -	- - -	- - -	- - -	- - -	4 - -
9 Notts County	- - -	2 - -	2 - -	- - -	- - -	- - -	- - -	- - -	- - -	4 - -
10 Preston North End	- - -	4 - -	- - -	- - -	- - -	- - -	- - -	- - -	- - -	4 - -
11 Sunderland	- - -	4 - -	- - -	- - -	- - -	- - -	- - -	- - -	- - -	4 - -
12 West Bromwich Albion	- - -	4 - -	- - -	- - -	- - -	- - -	- - -	- - -	- - -	4 - -
13 Burton Swifts	- - -	- - -	3 - -	- - -	- - -	- - -	- - -	- - -	- - -	3 - -
14 Burton Wanderers	- - -	- - -	3 - -	- - -	- - -	- - -	- - -	- - -	- - -	3 - -
15 Darwen	- - -	1 - -	2 - -	- - -	- - -	- - -	- - -	- - -	- - -	3 - -
16 Leicester City	- - -	- - -	3 - -	- - -	- - -	- - -	- - -	- - -	- - -	3 - -
17 Lincoln City	- - -	- - -	3 - -	- - -	- - -	- - -	- - -	- - -	- - -	3 - -
18 Nottingham Forest	- - -	3 - -	- - -	- - -	- - -	- - -	- - -	- - -	- - -	3 - -
19 Rotherham United	- - -	- - -	3 - -	- - -	- - -	- - -	- - -	- - -	- - -	3 - -
20 Sheffield Wednesday	- - -	3 - -	- - -	- - -	- - -	- - -	- - -	- - -	- - -	3 - -
21 Wolverhampton W.	- - -	3 - -	- - -	- - -	- - -	- - -	- - -	- - -	- - -	3 - -
22 Arsenal	- - -	- - -	2 - -	- - -	- - -	- - -	- - -	- - -	- - -	2 - -
23 Birmingham City	- - -	- - -	- - -	- - -	- - -	- - -	- - -	- - -	2 - -	2 - -
24 Bury	- - -	- - -	2 - -	- - -	- - -	- - -	- - -	- - -	- - -	2 - -
25 Crewe Alexandra	- - -	- - -	2 - -	- - -	- - -	- - -	- - -	- - -	- - -	2 - -
26 Grimsby Town	- - -	- - -	2 - -	- - -	- - -	- - -	- - -	- - -	- - -	2 - -
27 Liverpool	- - -	- - -	- - -	1 - -	- - -	- - -	- - -	- - -	1 - -	2 - -
28 Manchester City	- - -	- - -	2 - -	- - -	- - -	- - -	- - -	- - -	- - -	2 - -
29 Sheffield United	- - -	2 - -	- - -	- - -	- - -	- - -	- - -	- - -	- - -	2 - -
30 Walsall	- - -	- - -	2 - -	- - -	- - -	- - -	- - -	- - -	- - -	2 - -
31 Accrington Stanley	- - -	1 - -	- - -	- - -	- - -	- - -	- - -	- - -	- - -	1 - -
32 Kettering	- - -	- - -	- - -	1 - -	- - -	- - -	- - -	- - -	- - -	1 - -
33 Middlesbrough	- - -	- - -	- - -	1 - -	- - -	- - -	- - -	- - -	- - -	1 - -
34 Port Vale	- - -	- - -	1 - -	- - -	- - -	- - -	- - -	- - -	- - -	1 - -

JAMES PETERS

DEBUT (Full Appearance)

Saturday 08/09/1894
Football League Division 2
at Derby Turn

Burton Wanderers 1 Newton Heath 0

CLUB CAREER RECORD	Apps	Subs	Goals
Premiership	0		0
League Division 1	0		0
League Division 2	46		13
FA Cup	4		1
League Cup	0		0
European Cup / Champions League	0		0
European Cup-Winners' Cup	0		0
UEFA Cup / Inter-Cities' Fairs Cup	0		0
Other Matches	1		0
OVERALL TOTAL	**51**		**14**

Opponents	PREM			FLD 1			FLD 2			FAC			LC			EC/CL			ECWC			UEFA			OTHER			TOTAL		
	A	S	G	A	S	G	A	S	G	A	S	G	A	S	G	A	S	G	A	S	G	A	S	G	A	S	G	A	S	G
1 Arsenal	–	–	–	–	–	–	4	–	1	–	–	–	–	–	–	–	–	–	–	–	–	–	–	–	–	–	–	4		1
2 Newcastle United	–	–	–	–	–	–	4	–	1	–	–	–	–	–	–	–	–	–	–	–	–	–	–	–	–	–	–	4		1
3 Rotherham United	–	–	–	–	–	–	4	–	1	–	–	–	–	–	–	–	–	–	–	–	–	–	–	–	–	–	–	4		1
4 Manchester City	–	–	–	–	–	–	4	–	–	–	–	–	–	–	–	–	–	–	–	–	–	–	–	–	–	–	–	4		–
5 Burton Wanderers	–	–	–	–	–	–	3	–	1	–	–	–	–	–	–	–	–	–	–	–	–	–	–	–	–	–	–	3		1
6 Lincoln City	–	–	–	–	–	–	3	–	1	–	–	–	–	–	–	–	–	–	–	–	–	–	–	–	–	–	–	3		1
7 Darwen	–	–	–	–	–	–	3	–	–	–	–	–	–	–	–	–	–	–	–	–	–	–	–	–	–	–	–	3		–
8 Leicester City	–	–	–	–	–	–	3	–	–	–	–	–	–	–	–	–	–	–	–	–	–	–	–	–	–	–	–	3		–
9 Notts County	–	–	–	–	–	–	3	–	–	–	–	–	–	–	–	–	–	–	–	–	–	–	–	–	–	–	–	3		–
10 Liverpool	–	–	–	–	–	–	2	–	3	–	–	–	–	–	–	–	–	–	–	–	–	–	–	–	–	–	–	2		3
11 Burton Swifts	–	–	–	–	–	–	2	–	2	–	–	–	–	–	–	–	–	–	–	–	–	–	–	–	–	–	–	2		2
12 Walsall	–	–	–	–	–	–	2	–	2	–	–	–	–	–	–	–	–	–	–	–	–	–	–	–	–	–	–	2		2
13 Bury	–	–	–	–	–	–	2	–	1	–	–	–	–	–	–	–	–	–	–	–	–	–	–	–	–	–	–	2		1
14 Stoke City	–	–	–	–	–	–	–	–	–	1	–	1	–	–	–	–	–	–	–	–	–	–	–	–	1	–	–	2		1
15 Crewe Alexandra	–	–	–	–	–	–	2	–	–	–	–	–	–	–	–	–	–	–	–	–	–	–	–	–	–	–	–	2		–
16 Derby County	–	–	–	–	–	–	–	–	–	2	–	–	–	–	–	–	–	–	–	–	–	–	–	–	–	–	–	2		–
17 Grimsby Town	–	–	–	–	–	–	2	–	–	–	–	–	–	–	–	–	–	–	–	–	–	–	–	–	–	–	–	2		–
18 Port Vale	–	–	–	–	–	–	2	–	–	–	–	–	–	–	–	–	–	–	–	–	–	–	–	–	–	–	–	2		–
19 Kettering	–	–	–	–	–	–	–	–	–	1	–	–	–	–	–	–	–	–	–	–	–	–	–	–	–	–	–	1		–
20 Loughborough Town	–	–	–	–	–	–	1	–	–	–	–	–	–	–	–	–	–	–	–	–	–	–	–	–	–	–	–	1		–

MIKE PHELAN

DEBUT (Full Appearance)

Saturday 19/08/1989
Football League Division 1
at Old Trafford

Manchester United 4 Arsenal 1

CLUB CAREER RECORD	Apps	Subs	Goals
Premiership	6	(7)	0
League Division 1	82	(7)	2
League Division 2	0		0
FA Cup	10		1
League Cup	14	(2)	0
European Cup / Champions League	1	(3)	0
European Cup-Winners' Cup	12		0
UEFA Cup / Inter-Cities' Fairs Cup	1		0
Other Matches	1		0
OVERALL TOTAL	**127**	**(19)**	**3**

Opponents	PREM			FLD 1			FLD 2			FAC			LC			EC/CL			ECWC			UEFA			OTHER			TOTAL		
	A	S	G	A	S	G	A	S	G	A	S	G	A	S	G	A	S	G	A	S	G	A	S	G	A	S	G	A	S	G
1 Nottingham Forest	1	–	–	6	–	–	–	–	–	1	–	–	1	–	–	–	–	–	–	–	–	–	–	–	–	–	–	9		–
2 Southampton	1	–	–	6	–	–	–	–	–	–	–	–	2	–	–	–	–	–	–	–	–	–	–	–	–	–	–	9		–
3 Queens Park Rangers	1	(1)	–	6	–	1	–	–	–	–	–	–	–	–	–	–	–	–	–	–	–	–	–	–	–	–	–	7	(1)	1
4 Liverpool	–	–	–	5	(1)	–	–	–	–	–	–	–	1	–	–	–	–	–	–	–	–	1	–	–	–	–	–	7	(1)	–
5 Tottenham Hotspur	–	(1)	–	6	–	–	–	–	–	–	–	–	1	–	–	–	–	–	–	–	–	–	–	–	–	–	–	7	(1)	–
6 Luton Town	–	–	–	6	–	–	–	–	–	–	–	–	–	–	–	–	–	–	–	–	–	–	–	–	–	–	–	6		–
7 Wimbledon	–	(1)	–	5	–	–	–	–	–	–	–	–	–	–	–	–	–	–	–	–	–	–	–	–	–	–	–	5	(1)	–
8 Arsenal	–	–	–	4	–	–	–	–	–	–	–	–	1	–	–	–	–	–	–	–	–	–	–	–	–	–	–	5		–
9 Chelsea	1	–	–	4	–	–	–	–	–	–	–	–	–	–	–	–	–	–	–	–	–	–	–	–	–	–	–	5		–
10 Crystal Palace	–	–	–	3	–	–	–	–	–	2	–	–	–	–	–	–	–	–	–	–	–	–	–	–	–	–	–	5		–
11 Coventry City	–	(1)	–	4	–	1	–	–	–	–	–	–	–	–	–	–	–	–	–	–	–	–	–	–	–	–	–	4	(1)	1
12 Norwich City	–	–	–	3	(2)	–	–	–	–	–	–	–	–	–	–	–	–	–	–	–	–	–	–	–	–	–	–	3	(2)	–
13 Aston Villa	–	–	–	3	(1)	–	–	–	–	–	–	–	–	–	–	–	–	–	–	–	–	–	–	–	–	–	–	3	(1)	–
14 Everton	–	(1)	–	3	–	–	–	–	–	–	–	–	–	–	–	–	–	–	–	–	–	–	–	–	–	–	–	3	(1)	–
15 Leeds United	–	–	–	2	(1)	–	–	–	–	–	–	–	1	–	–	–	–	–	–	–	–	–	–	–	–	–	–	3	(1)	–
16 Sheffield United	–	(1)	–	2	–	–	–	–	–	1	–	–	–	–	–	–	–	–	–	–	–	–	–	–	–	–	–	3	(1)	–
17 Sheffield Wednesday	–	–	–	2	(1)	–	–	–	–	–	–	–	–	(1)	–	–	–	–	–	–	–	–	–	–	–	–	–	2	(2)	–
18 Derby County	–	–	–	3	–	–	–	–	–	–	–	–	–	–	–	–	–	–	–	–	–	–	–	–	–	–	–	3		–
19 Manchester City	–	–	–	3	–	–	–	–	–	–	–	–	–	–	–	–	–	–	–	–	–	–	–	–	–	–	–	3		–
20 Oldham Athletic	–	(1)	–	–	–	–	–	–	–	2	–	–	–	–	–	–	–	–	–	–	–	–	–	–	–	–	–	2	(1)	–
21 Athinaikos	–	–	–	–	–	–	–	–	–	–	–	–	–	–	–	–	–	–	2	–	–	–	–	–	–	–	–	2		–
22 Athletico Madrid	–	–	–	–	–	–	–	–	–	–	–	–	–	–	–	–	–	–	2	–	–	–	–	–	–	–	–	2		–
23 Charlton Athletic	–	–	–	2	–	–	–	–	–	–	–	–	–	–	–	–	–	–	–	–	–	–	–	–	–	–	–	2		–
24 Halifax Town	–	–	–	–	–	–	–	–	–	–	–	–	2	–	–	–	–	–	–	–	–	–	–	–	–	–	–	2		–
25 Legia Warsaw	–	–	–	–	–	–	–	–	–	–	–	–	–	–	–	–	–	–	2	–	–	–	–	–	–	–	–	2		–
26 Millwall	–	–	–	2	–	–	–	–	–	–	–	–	–	–	–	–	–	–	–	–	–	–	–	–	–	–	–	2		–
27 Montpellier Herault	–	–	–	–	–	–	–	–	–	–	–	–	–	–	–	–	–	–	2	–	–	–	–	–	–	–	–	2		–
28 Pecsi Munkas	–	–	–	–	–	–	–	–	–	–	–	–	–	–	–	–	–	–	2	–	–	–	–	–	–	–	–	2		–
29 Portsmouth	–	–	–	–	–	–	–	–	–	–	–	–	2	–	–	–	–	–	–	–	–	–	–	–	–	–	–	2		–
30 Galatasaray	–	–	–	–	–	–	–	–	–	–	–	–	–	–	–	1	(1)	–	–	–	–	–	–	–	–	–	–	1	(1)	–
31 Middlesbrough	1	–	–	–	–	–	–	–	–	–	–	–	–	(1)	–	–	–	–	–	–	–	–	–	–	–	–	–	1	(1)	–

continued../

MIKE PHELAN (continued)

Opponents	PREM			FLD 1			FLD 2			FAC			LC			EC/CL			ECWC			UEFA			OTHER			TOTAL		
	A	S	G	A	S	G	A	S	G	A	S	G	A	S	G	A	S	G	A	S	G	A	S	G	A	S	G	A	S	G
32 Sunderland	–	–		1 (1)	–		–			–			–			–			–			–			–			1 (1)	–	
33 Honved	–	–		–	–		–			–			–			– (2)	–		–			–			–			– (2)	–	
34 Bury	–	–		–	–		–			1	1		–			–			–			–			–			1		1
35 Barcelona	–	–		–	–		–			–			–			–			1			–			–			1		
36 Bolton Wanderers	–	–		–	–		–			1			–			–			–			–			–			1		
37 Brighton	–	–		–	–		–			1			–			–			–			–			–			1		
38 Cambridge United	–	–		–	–		–			–			1			–			–			–			–			1		
39 Ipswich Town	1	–		–	–		–			–			–			–			–			–			–			1		
40 Leicester City	–	–		–	–		–			–			1			–			–			–			–			1		
41 Newcastle United	–	–		–	–		–			1			–			–			–			–			–			1		
42 Stoke City	–	–		–	–		–			–			1			–			–			–			–			1		
43 Torpedo Moscow	–	–		–	–		–			–			–			–			–			1			–			1		
44 West Ham United	–	–		1	–		–			–			–			–			–			–			–			1		
45 Wrexham	–	–		–	–		–			–			–			–			1			–			–			1		

JACK PICKEN

DEBUT (Full Appearance, 1 goal)

Saturday 02/09/1905
Football League Division 2
at Bank Street

Manchester United 5 Bristol City 1

CLUB CAREER RECORD	Apps	Subs	Goals
Premiership	0		0
League Division 1	80		19
League Division 2	33		20
FA Cup	8		7
League Cup	0		0
European Cup / Champions League	0		0
European Cup–Winners' Cup	0		0
UEFA Cup / Inter–Cities' Fairs Cup	0		0
Other Matches	1		0
OVERALL TOTAL	122		46

Opponents	PREM			FLD 1			FLD 2			FAC			LC			EC/CL			ECWC			UEFA			OTHER			TOTAL		
	A	S	G	A	S	G	A	S	G	A	S	G	A	S	G	A	S	G	A	S	G	A	S	G	A	S	G	A	S	G
1 Bristol City	–	–		7		3	2		1	–			–			–			–			–			–			9		4
2 Preston North End	–	–		7			–			–			–			–			–			–			–			7		
3 Arsenal	–	–		5		2	–			1			–			–			–			–			–			6		2
4 Bradford City	–	–		4		1	2			–			–			–			–			–			–			6		1
5 Aston Villa	–	–		4		1	–			1		3	–			–			–			–			–			5		4
6 Blackburn Rovers	–	–		5			–			–			–			–			–			–			–			5		
7 Bolton Wanderers	–	–		4		1	–			–			–			–			–			–			–			4		1
8 Nottingham Forest	–	–		4		1	–			–			–			–			–			–			–			4		1
9 Sheffield United	–	–		4		1	–			–			–			–			–			–			–			4		1
10 Notts County	–	–		4			–			–			–			–			–			–			–			4		
11 Middlesbrough	–	–		3		4	–			–			–			–			–			–			–			3		4
12 Leicester City	–	–		1		1	2		1	–			–			–			–			–			–			3		2
13 Sheffield Wednesday	–	–		3		2	–			–			–			–			–			–			–			3		2
14 Blackpool	–	–		–			2			1		1	–			–			–			–			–			3		1
15 Burnley	–	–		–			2		1	1			–			–			–			–			–			3		1
16 Birmingham City	–	–		3			–			–			–			–			–			–			–			3		
17 Chelsea	–	–		2			1			–			–			–			–			–			–			3		
18 Everton	–	–		3			–			–			–			–			–			–			–			3		
19 Newcastle United	–	–		3			–			–			–			–			–			–			–			3		
20 Sunderland	–	–		3			–			–			–			–			–			–			–			3		
21 Chesterfield	–	–		–			2		3	–			–			–			–			–			–			2		3
22 Hull City	–	–		–			2		3	–			–			–			–			–			–			2		3
23 Barnsley	–	–		–			2		2	–			–			–			–			–			–			2		2
24 Glossop	–	–		–			2		2	–			–			–			–			–			–			2		2
25 Grimsby Town	–	–		–			2		2	–			–			–			–			–			–			2		2
26 Leyton Orient	–	–		–			2		2	–			–			–			–			–			–			2		2
27 Stoke City	–	–		2		2	–			–			–			–			–			–			–			2		2
28 Portsmouth	–	–		–			–			2		1	–			–			–			–			–			2		1
29 Bury	–	–		2			–			–			–			–			–			–			–			2		
30 Derby County	–	–		2			–			–			–			–			–			–			–			2		
31 Gainsborough Trinity	–	–		–			2			–			–			–			–			–			–			2		
32 Liverpool	–	–		2			–			–			–			–			–			–			–			2		
33 Manchester City	–	–		2			–			–			–			–			–			–			–			2		
34 Port Vale	–	–		–			2			–			–			–			–			–			–			2		
35 Stockport County	–	–		–			2			–			–			–			–			–			–			2		
36 Burton United	–	–		–			1		2	–			–			–			–			–			–			1		2
37 Staple Hill	–	–		–			–			1		2	–			–			–			–			–			1		2
38 Lincoln City	–	–		–			1		1	–			–			–			–			–			–			1		1
39 Leeds United	–	–		–			1			–			–			–			–			–			–			1		
40 Norwich City	–	–		–			–			1			–			–			–			–			–			1		
41 Queens Park Rangers	–	–		–			–			–			–			–			–			–			1			1		
42 Tottenham Hotspur	–	–		1			–			–			–			–			–			–			–			1		
43 West Bromwich Albion	–	–		–			1			–			–			–			–			–			–			1		

KEVIN PILKINGTON

DEBUT (Substitute Appearance)

Saturday 19/11/1994
FA Premiership
at Old Trafford

Manchester United 3 Crystal Palace 0

CLUB CAREER RECORD	Apps	Subs	Goals
Premiership	4	(2)	0
League Division 1	0		0
League Division 2	0		0
FA Cup	1		0
League Cup	1		0
European Cup / Champions League	0		0
European Cup-Winners' Cup	0		0
UEFA Cup / Inter-Cities' Fairs Cup	0		0
Other Matches	0		0
OVERALL TOTAL	**6**	**(2)**	**0**

Opponents	PREM A	S	G	FLD 1 A	S	G	FLD 2 A	S	G	FAC A	S	G	LC A	S	G	EC/CL A	S	G	ECWC A	S	G	UEFA A	S	G	OTHER A	S	G	TOTAL A	S	G
1 Chelsea	1	–	–	–	–	–	–	–	–	–	–	–	–	–	–	–	–	–	–	–	–	–	–	–	–	–	–	1	–	–
2 Coventry City	1	–	–	–	–	–	–	–	–	–	–	–	–	–	–	–	–	–	–	–	–	–	–	–	–	–	–	1	–	–
3 Everton	1	–	–	–	–	–	–	–	–	–	–	–	–	–	–	–	–	–	–	–	–	–	–	–	–	–	–	1	–	–
4 Sheffield Wednesday	1	–	–	–	–	–	–	–	–	–	–	–	–	–	–	–	–	–	–	–	–	–	–	–	–	–	–	1	–	–
5 Sunderland	–	–	–	–	–	–	–	–	–	1	–	–	–	–	–	–	–	–	–	–	–	–	–	–	–	–	–	1	–	–
6 York City	–	–	–	–	–	–	–	–	–	–	–	–	1	–	–	–	–	–	–	–	–	–	–	–	–	–	–	1	–	–
7 Crystal Palace	–	(1)	–	–	–	–	–	–	–	–	–	–	–	–	–	–	–	–	–	–	–	–	–	–	–	–	–	–	(1)	–
8 Tottenham Hotspur	–	(1)	–	–	–	–	–	–	–	–	–	–	–	–	–	–	–	–	–	–	–	–	–	–	–	–	–	–	(1)	–

MIKE PINNER

DEBUT (Full Appearance)

Saturday 04/02/1961
Football League Division 1
at Old Trafford

Manchester United 1 Aston Villa 1

CLUB CAREER RECORD	Apps	Subs	Goals
Premiership	0		0
League Division 1	4		0
League Division 2	0		0
FA Cup	0		0
League Cup	0		0
European Cup / Champions League	0		0
European Cup-Winners' Cup	0		0
UEFA Cup / Inter-Cities' Fairs Cup	0		0
Other Matches	0		0
OVERALL TOTAL	**4**		**0**

Opponents	PREM A	S	G	FLD 1 A	S	G	FLD 2 A	S	G	FAC A	S	G	LC A	S	G	EC/CL A	S	G	ECWC A	S	G	UEFA A	S	G	OTHER A	S	G	TOTAL A	S	G
1 Aston Villa	–	–	–	1	–	–	–	–	–	–	–	–	–	–	–	–	–	–	–	–	–	–	–	–	–	–	–	1	–	–
2 Bolton Wanderers	–	–	–	1	–	–	–	–	–	–	–	–	–	–	–	–	–	–	–	–	–	–	–	–	–	–	–	1	–	–
3 Newcastle United	–	–	–	1	–	–	–	–	–	–	–	–	–	–	–	–	–	–	–	–	–	–	–	–	–	–	–	1	–	–
4 Wolverhampton W.	–	–	–	1	–	–	–	–	–	–	–	–	–	–	–	–	–	–	–	–	–	–	–	–	–	–	–	1	–	–

GERARD PIQUE

DEBUT (Substitute Appearance)

Tuesday 26/10/2004
League Cup 3rd Round
at Gresty Road

Crewe Alexandra 0 Manchester United 3

CLUB CAREER RECORD	Apps	Subs	Goals
Premiership	6	(6)	0
League Division 1	0		0
League Division 2	0		0
FA Cup	3		0
League Cup	2	(2)	0
European Cup / Champions League	3	(1)	2
European Cup-Winners' Cup	0		0
UEFA Cup / Inter-Cities' Fairs Cup	0		0
Other Matches	0		0
OVERALL TOTAL	**14**	**(9)**	**2**

Opponents	PREM A	S	G	FLD 1 A	S	G	FLD 2 A	S	G	FAC A	S	G	LC A	S	G	EC/CL A	S	G	ECWC A	S	G	UEFA A	S	G	OTHER A	S	G	TOTAL A	S	G
1 Bolton Wanderers	2	(1)	–	–	–	–	–	–	–	–	–	–	–	–	–	–	–	–	–	–	–	–	–	–	–	–	–	2	(1)	–
2 Roma	–	–	–	–	–	–	–	–	–	–	–	–	–	–	–	2		1	–	–	–	–	–	–	–	–	–	2		1
3 Burton Albion	–	–	–	–	–	–	–	–	–	2	–	–	–	–	–	–	–	–	–	–	–	–	–	–	–	–	–	2	–	–
4 Middlesbrough	–	(2)	–	–	–	–	–	–	–	–	–	–	–	–	–	–	–	–	–	–	–	–	–	–	–	–	–	–	(2)	–
5 Sunderland	–	(2)	–	–	–	–	–	–	–	–	–	–	–	–	–	–	–	–	–	–	–	–	–	–	–	–	–	–	(2)	–
6 Dynamo Kiev	–	–	–	–	–	–	–	–	–	–	–	–	–	–	–	1		1	–	–	–	–	–	–	–	–	–	1		1
7 Arsenal	1	–	–	–	–	–	–	–	–	–	–	–	–	–	–	–	–	–	–	–	–	–	–	–	–	–	–	1	–	–
8 Aston Villa	1	–	–	–	–	–	–	–	–	–	–	–	–	–	–	–	–	–	–	–	–	–	–	–	–	–	–	1	–	–
9 Barnet	–	–	–	–	–	–	–	–	–	–	–	–	1	–	–	–	–	–	–	–	–	–	–	–	–	–	–	1	–	–
10 Coventry City	–	–	–	–	–	–	–	–	–	–	–	–	1	–	–	–	–	–	–	–	–	–	–	–	–	–	–	1	–	–
11 Exeter City	–	–	–	–	–	–	–	–	–	1	–	–	–	–	–	–	–	–	–	–	–	–	–	–	–	–	–	1	–	–
12 West Ham United	1	–	–	–	–	–	–	–	–	–	–	–	–	–	–	–	–	–	–	–	–	–	–	–	–	–	–	1	–	–
13 Wigan Athletic	1	–	–	–	–	–	–	–	–	–	–	–	–	–	–	–	–	–	–	–	–	–	–	–	–	–	–	1	–	–
14 Crewe Alexandra	–	–	–	–	–	–	–	–	–	–	–	–	–	(1)	–	–	–	–	–	–	–	–	–	–	–	–	–	–	(1)	–
15 Everton	–	(1)	–	–	–	–	–	–	–	–	–	–	–	–	–	–	–	–	–	–	–	–	–	–	–	–	–	–	(1)	–
16 Fenerbahce	–	–	–	–	–	–	–	–	–	–	–	–	–	–	–	–	(1)	–	–	–	–	–	–	–	–	–	–	–	(1)	–
17 West Bromwich Albion	–	–	–	–	–	–	–	–	–	–	–	–	–	(1)	–	–	–	–	–	–	–	–	–	–	–	–	–	–	(1)	–

KAREL POBORSKY

DEBUT (Full Appearance)

Wednesday 21/08/1996
FA Premiership
at Old Trafford

Manchester United 2 Everton 2

CLUB CAREER RECORD	Apps	Subs	Goals
Premiership	18	(14)	5
League Division 1	0		0
League Division 2	0		0
FA Cup	2		0
League Cup	3		1
European Cup / Champions League	5	(5)	0
European Cup-Winners' Cup	0		0
UEFA Cup / Inter-Cities' Fairs Cup	0		0
Other Matches	0	(1)	0
OVERALL TOTAL	**28**	**(20)**	**6**

Opponents	PREM A S G	FLD 1 A S G	FLD 2 A S G	FAC A S G	LC A S G	EC/CL A S G	ECWC A S G	UEFA A S G	OTHER A S G	TOTAL A S G
1 Coventry City	2 (1) 2	– – –	– – –	– – –	– – –	– – –	– – –	– – –	– – –	2 (1) 2
2 Newcastle United	2 – –	– – –	– – –	– – –	– – –	– – –	– – –	– – –	– (1) –	2 (1) –
3 West Ham United	2 (1) –	– – –	– – –	– – –	– – –	– – –	– – –	– – –	– – –	2 (1) –
4 Leeds United	2 – 1	– – –	– – –	– – –	– – –	– – –	– – –	– – –	– – –	2 – 1
5 Arsenal	2 – –	– – –	– – –	– – –	– – –	– – –	– – –	– – –	– – –	2 – –
6 Juventus	– – –	– – –	– – –	– – –	– – –	2 – –	– – –	– – –	– – –	2 – –
7 Wimbledon	– – –	– – –	– – –	2 – –	– – –	– – –	– – –	– – –	– – –	2 – –
8 Chelsea	1 (1) –	– – –	– – –	– – –	– – –	– – –	– – –	– – –	– – –	1 (1) –
9 Everton	1 (1) –	– – –	– – –	– – –	– – –	– – –	– – –	– – –	– – –	1 (1) –
10 Fenerbahce	– – –	– – –	– – –	– – –	– – –	1 (1) –	– – –	– – –	– – –	1 (1) –
11 Kosice	– – –	– – –	– – –	– – –	– – –	1 (1) –	– – –	– – –	– – –	1 (1) –
12 Leicester City	– (1) –	– – –	– – –	– – –	1 – –	– – –	– – –	– – –	– – –	1 (1) –
13 Nottingham Forest	1 (1) –	– – –	– – –	– – –	– – –	– – –	– – –	– – –	– – –	1 (1) –
14 Rapid Vienna	– – –	– – –	– – –	– – –	– – –	1 (1) –	– – –	– – –	– – –	1 (1) –
15 Sunderland	1 (1) –	– – –	– – –	– – –	– – –	– – –	– – –	– – –	– – –	1 (1) –
16 Tottenham Hotspur	1 (1) –	– – –	– – –	– – –	– – –	– – –	– – –	– – –	– – –	1 (1) –
17 Sheffield Wednesday	– (2) 1	– – –	– – –	– – –	– – –	– – –	– – –	– – –	– – –	– (2) 1
18 Swindon Town	– – –	– – –	– – –	– – –	1 – 1	– – –	– – –	– – –	– – –	1 – 1
19 Bolton Wanderers	1 – –	– – –	– – –	– – –	– – –	– – –	– – –	– – –	– – –	1 – –
20 Ipswich Town	– – –	– – –	– – –	– – –	1 – –	– – –	– – –	– – –	– – –	1 – –
21 Liverpool	1 – –	– – –	– – –	– – –	– – –	– – –	– – –	– – –	– – –	1 – –
22 Southampton	1 – –	– – –	– – –	– – –	– – –	– – –	– – –	– – –	– – –	1 – –
23 Barnsley	– (1) 1	– – –	– – –	– – –	– – –	– – –	– – –	– – –	– – –	– (1) 1
24 Aston Villa	– (1) –	– – –	– – –	– – –	– – –	– – –	– – –	– – –	– – –	– (1) –
25 Blackburn Rovers	– (1) –	– – –	– – –	– – –	– – –	– – –	– – –	– – –	– – –	– (1) –
26 Crystal Palace	– (1) –	– – –	– – –	– – –	– – –	– – –	– – –	– – –	– – –	– (1) –
27 Feyenoord	– – –	– – –	– – –	– – –	– – –	– (1) –	– – –	– – –	– – –	– (1) –
28 Porto	– – –	– – –	– – –	– – –	– – –	– (1) –	– – –	– – –	– – –	– (1) –

BILLY PORTER

DEBUT (Full Appearance)

Saturday 19/01/1935
Football League Division 2
at Oakwell

Barnsley 0 Manchester United 2

CLUB CAREER RECORD	Apps	Subs	Goals
Premiership	0		0
League Division 1	2		0
League Division 2	59		0
FA Cup	4		0
League Cup	0		0
European Cup / Champions League	0		0
European Cup-Winners' Cup	0		0
UEFA Cup / Inter-Cities' Fairs Cup	0		0
Other Matches	0		0
OVERALL TOTAL	**65**		**0**

Opponents	PREM A S G	FLD 1 A S G	FLD 2 A S G	FAC A S G	LC A S G	EC/CL A S G	ECWC A S G	UEFA A S G	OTHER A S G	TOTAL A S G
1 Barnsley	– – –	– – –	4 – –	– – –	– – –	– – –	– – –	– – –	– – –	4 – –
2 Nottingham Forest	– – –	– – –	3 – –	1 – –	– – –	– – –	– – –	– – –	– – –	4 – –
3 Southampton	– – –	– – –	4 – –	– – –	– – –	– – –	– – –	– – –	– – –	4 – –
4 Blackpool	– – –	– – –	3 – –	– – –	– – –	– – –	– – –	– – –	– – –	3 – –
5 Bradford Park Avenue	– – –	– – –	3 – –	– – –	– – –	– – –	– – –	– – –	– – –	3 – –
6 Burnley	– – –	– – –	3 – –	– – –	– – –	– – –	– – –	– – –	– – –	3 – –
7 Bury	– – –	– – –	3 – –	– – –	– – –	– – –	– – –	– – –	– – –	3 – –
8 Fulham	– – –	– – –	3 – –	– – –	– – –	– – –	– – –	– – –	– – –	3 – –
9 Hull City	– – –	– – –	3 – –	– – –	– – –	– – –	– – –	– – –	– – –	3 – –
10 Newcastle United	– – –	– – –	3 – –	– – –	– – –	– – –	– – –	– – –	– – –	3 – –
11 Plymouth Argyle	– – –	– – –	3 – –	– – –	– – –	– – –	– – –	– – –	– – –	3 – –
12 Swansea City	– – –	– – –	3 – –	– – –	– – –	– – –	– – –	– – –	– – –	3 – –
13 West Ham United	– – –	– – –	3 – –	– – –	– – –	– – –	– – –	– – –	– – –	3 – –
14 Bradford City	– – –	– – –	2 – –	– – –	– – –	– – –	– – –	– – –	– – –	2 – –
15 Charlton Athletic	– – –	– – –	2 – –	– – –	– – –	– – –	– – –	– – –	– – –	2 – –
16 Doncaster Rovers	– – –	– – –	2 – –	– – –	– – –	– – –	– – –	– – –	– – –	2 – –
17 Leicester City	– – –	– – –	2 – –	– – –	– – –	– – –	– – –	– – –	– – –	2 – –
18 Norwich City	– – –	– – –	2 – –	– – –	– – –	– – –	– – –	– – –	– – –	2 – –
19 Port Vale	– – –	– – –	2 – –	– – –	– – –	– – –	– – –	– – –	– – –	2 – –
20 Sheffield United	– – –	– – –	2 – –	– – –	– – –	– – –	– – –	– – –	– – –	2 – –
21 Stoke City	– – –	– – –	– – –	2 – –	– – –	– – –	– – –	– – –	– – –	2 – –
22 Tottenham Hotspur	– – –	– – –	2 – –	– – –	– – –	– – –	– – –	– – –	– – –	2 – –
23 Brentford	– – –	– – –	1 – –	– – –	– – –	– – –	– – –	– – –	– – –	1 – –

continued../

BILLY PORTER (continued)

Opponents	PREM A	S	G	FLD 1 A	S	G	FLD 2 A	S	G	FAC A	S	G	LC A	S	G	EC/CL A	S	G	ECWC A	S	G	UEFA A	S	G	OTHER A	S	G	TOTAL A	S	G
24 Leeds United	–	–		1																								1		
25 Oldham Athletic	–	–					1																					1		–
26 Reading	–	–								1																		1		–
27 Wolverhampton W.	–	–		1																								1		–

ARTHUR POTTS

DEBUT (Full Appearance)

Friday 26/12/1913
Football League Division 1
at Goodison Park

Everton 5 Manchester United 0

CLUB CAREER RECORD	Apps	Subs	Goals
Premiership	0		0
League Division 1	27		5
League Division 2	0		0
FA Cup	1		0
League Cup	0		0
European Cup / Champions League	0		0
European Cup-Winners' Cup	0		0
UEFA Cup / Inter–Cities' Fairs Cup	0		0
Other Matches	0		0
OVERALL TOTAL	28		5

Opponents	PREM A	S	G	FLD 1 A	S	G	FLD 2 A	S	G	FAC A	S	G	LC A	S	G	EC/CL A	S	G	ECWC A	S	G	UEFA A	S	G	OTHER A	S	G	TOTAL A	S	G
1 West Bromwich Albion	–	–		4																								4		–
2 Bradford City	–	–		2	1																							2		1
3 Newcastle United	–	–		2	1																							2		1
4 Aston Villa	–	–		1	–					1																		2		–
5 Everton	–	–		2																								2		–
6 Liverpool	–	–		2																								2		–
7 Sheffield Wednesday	–	–		2																								2		–
8 Bolton Wanderers	–	–		1	2																							1		2
9 Notts County	–	–		1	1																							1		1
10 Blackburn Rovers	–	–		1																								1		–
11 Bradford Park Avenue	–	–		1																								1		–
12 Burnley	–	–		1																								1		–
13 Chelsea	–	–		1																								1		–
14 Derby County	–	–		1																								1		–
15 Manchester City	–	–		1																								1		–
16 Preston North End	–	–		1																								1		–
17 Sheffield United	–	–		1																								1		–
18 Sunderland	–	–		1																								1		–
19 Tottenham Hotspur	–	–		1																								1		–

JACK POWELL

DEBUT (Full Appearance)

Saturday 30/10/1886
FA Cup 1st Round
at Fleetwood Park

Fleetwood Rangers 2 Newton Heath 2

CLUB CAREER RECORD	Apps	Subs	Goals
Premiership	0		0
League Division 1	0		0
League Division 2	0		0
FA Cup	4		0
League Cup	0		0
European Cup / Champions League	0		0
European Cup-Winners' Cup	0		0
UEFA Cup / Inter–Cities' Fairs Cup	0		0
Other Matches	0		0
OVERALL TOTAL	4		0

Opponents	PREM A	S	G	FLD 1 A	S	G	FLD 2 A	S	G	FAC A	S	G	LC A	S	G	EC/CL A	S	G	ECWC A	S	G	UEFA A	S	G	OTHER A	S	G	TOTAL A	S	G
1 Bootle Reserves	–	–		–	–					1																		1		–
2 Fleetwood Rangers	–	–		–	–					1																		1		–
3 Higher Walton	–	–		–	–					1																		1		–
4 Preston North End	–	–		–	–					1																		1		–

JOHN PRENTICE

DEBUT (Full Appearance)

Friday 02/04/1920
Football League Division 1
at Old Trafford

Manchester United 0 Bradford Park Avenue 1

CLUB CAREER RECORD	Apps	Subs	Goals
Premiership	0		0
League Division 1	1		0
League Division 2	0		0
FA Cup	0		0
League Cup	0		0
European Cup / Champions League	0		0
European Cup-Winners' Cup	0		0
UEFA Cup / Inter–Cities' Fairs Cup	0		0
Other Matches	0		0
OVERALL TOTAL	1		0

Opponents	PREM A	S	G	FLD 1 A	S	G	FLD 2 A	S	G	FAC A	S	G	LC A	S	G	EC/CL A	S	G	ECWC A	S	G	UEFA A	S	G	OTHER A	S	G	TOTAL A	S	G
1 Bradford Park Avenue	–	–		1																								1		–

STEPHEN PRESTON

DEBUT (Full Appearance, 2 goals)

Friday 07/09/1901
Football League Division 2
at Bank Street

Newton Heath 3 Gainsborough Trinity 0

CLUB CAREER RECORD	Apps	Subs	Goals
Premiership	0		0
League Division 1	0		0
League Division 2	33		14
FA Cup	1		0
League Cup	0		0
European Cup / Champions League	0		0
European Cup-Winners' Cup	0		0
UEFA Cup / Inter-Cities' Fairs Cup	0		0
Other Matches	0		0
OVERALL TOTAL	**34**		**14**

Opponents	PREM A S G	FLD 1 A S G	FLD 2 A S G	FAC A S G	LC A S G	EC/CL A S G	ECWC A S G	UEFA A S G	OTHER A S G	TOTAL A S G
1 Chesterfield	– –	– –	3 3	–	–	–	–	–	–	3 3
2 Gainsborough Trinity	– –	– –	3 2	–	–	–	–	–	–	3 2
3 Bristol City	– –	– –	3 1	–	–	–	–	–	–	3 1
4 Stockport County	– –	– –	3 1	–	–	–	–	–	–	3 1
5 Burnley	– –	– –	2 1	–	–	–	–	–	–	2 1
6 Burton United	– –	– –	2 1	–	–	–	–	–	–	2 1
7 Doncaster Rovers	– –	– –	2 1	–	–	–	–	–	–	2 1
8 Leicester City	– –	– –	2 1	–	–	–	–	–	–	2 1
9 Arsenal	– –	– –	2 –	–	–	–	–	–	–	2 –
10 Glossop	– –	– –	2 –	–	–	–	–	–	–	2 –
11 Lincoln City	– –	– –	1 –	1	–	–	–	–	–	2 –
12 Middlesbrough	– –	– –	2 –	–	–	–	–	–	–	2 –
13 Port Vale	– –	– –	2 –	–	–	–	–	–	–	2 –
14 Blackpool	– –	– –	1 2	–	–	–	–	–	–	1 2
15 Preston North End	– –	– –	1 1	–	–	–	–	–	–	1 1
16 Barnsley	– –	– –	1 –	–	–	–	–	–	–	1 –
17 West Bromwich Albion	– –	– –	1 –	–	–	–	–	–	–	1 –

ALBERT PRINCE

DEBUT (Full Appearance)

Saturday 27/02/1915
Football League Division 1
at Old Trafford

Manchester United 1 Everton 2

CLUB CAREER RECORD	Apps	Subs	Goals
Premiership	0		0
League Division 1	1		0
League Division 2	0		0
FA Cup	0		0
League Cup	0		0
European Cup / Champions League	0		0
European Cup-Winners' Cup	0		0
UEFA Cup / Inter-Cities' Fairs Cup	0		0
Other Matches	0		0
OVERALL TOTAL	**1**		**0**

Opponents	PREM A S G	FLD 1 A S G	FLD 2 A S G	FAC A S G	LC A S G	EC/CL A S G	ECWC A S G	UEFA A S G	OTHER A S G	TOTAL A S G
1 Everton	– –	1 –	–	–	–	–	–	–	–	1 –

D PRINCE

DEBUT (Full Appearance)

Saturday 04/11/1893
Football League Division 1
at Bank Street

Newton Heath 0 Darwen 1

CLUB CAREER RECORD	Apps	Subs	Goals
Premiership	0		0
League Division 1	2		0
League Division 2	0		0
FA Cup	0		0
League Cup	0		0
European Cup / Champions League	0		0
European Cup-Winners' Cup	0		0
UEFA Cup / Inter-Cities' Fairs Cup	0		0
Other Matches	0		0
OVERALL TOTAL	**2**		**0**

Opponents	PREM A S G	FLD 1 A S G	FLD 2 A S G	FAC A S G	LC A S G	EC/CL A S G	ECWC A S G	UEFA A S G	OTHER A S G	TOTAL A S G
1 Darwen	– –	1 –	–	–	–	–	–	–	–	1 –
2 Nottingham Forest	– –	1 –	–	–	–	–	–	–	–	1 –

WILLIAM PRUNIER

DEBUT (Full Appearance)

Saturday 30/12/1995
FA Premiership
at Old Trafford

Manchester United 2 Queens Park Rangers 1

CLUB CAREER RECORD	Apps	Subs	Goals
Premiership	2		0
League Division 1	0		0
League Division 2	0		0
FA Cup	0		0
League Cup	0		0
European Cup / Champions League	0		0
European Cup-Winners' Cup	0		0
UEFA Cup / Inter-Cities' Fairs Cup	0		0
Other Matches	0		0
OVERALL TOTAL	2		0

Opponents	PREM A S G	FLD 1 A S G	FLD 2 A S G	FAC A S G	LC A S G	EC/CL A S G	ECWC A S G	UEFA A S G	OTHER A S G	TOTAL A S G
1 Queens Park Rangers	1 – –	–	–	–	–	–	–	–	–	1 –
2 Tottenham Hotspur	1 –	–	–	–	–	–	–	–	–	1 –

DANNY PUGH

DEBUT (Substitute Appearance)

Wednesday 18/09/2002
Champions League Phase 1 Match 1
at Old Trafford

Manchester United 5 Maccabi Haifa 2

CLUB CAREER RECORD	Apps	Subs	Goals
Premiership	0	(1)	0
League Division 1	0		0
League Division 2	0		0
FA Cup	0	(1)	0
League Cup	2		0
European Cup / Champions League	1	(2)	0
European Cup-Winners' Cup	0		0
UEFA Cup / Inter-Cities' Fairs Cup	0		0
Other Matches	0		0
OVERALL TOTAL	3	(4)	0

Opponents	PREM A S G	FLD 1 A S G	FLD 2 A S G	FAC A S G	LC A S G	EC/CL A S G	ECWC A S G	UEFA A S G	OTHER A S G	TOTAL A S G
1 Burnley	–	–	–	–	1 –	–	–	–	–	1 –
2 Deportivo La Coruna	–	–	–	–	–	1	–	–	–	1 –
3 West Bromwich Albion	–	–	–	–	1 –	–	–	–	–	1 –
4 Juventus	–	–	–	–	–	– (1) –	–	–	–	– (1) –
5 Maccabi Haifa	–	–	–	–	–	– (1) –	–	–	–	– (1) –
6 Northampton Town	–	–	–	– (1) –	–	–	–	–	–	– (1) –
7 Tottenham Hotspur	– (1) –	–	–	–	–	–	–	–	–	– (1) –

JAMES PUGH

DEBUT (Full Appearance)

Saturday 29/04/1922
Football League Division 1
at Old Trafford

Manchester United 1 Cardiff City 1

CLUB CAREER RECORD	Apps	Subs	Goals
Premiership	0		0
League Division 1	1		0
League Division 2	1		0
FA Cup	0		0
League Cup	0		0
European Cup / Champions League	0		0
European Cup-Winners' Cup	0		0
UEFA Cup / Inter-Cities' Fairs Cup	0		0
Other Matches	0		0
OVERALL TOTAL	2		0

Opponents	PREM A S G	FLD 1 A S G	FLD 2 A S G	FAC A S G	LC A S G	EC/CL A S G	ECWC A S G	UEFA A S G	OTHER A S G	TOTAL A S G
1 Cardiff City	–	1 –	–	–	–	–	–	–	–	1 –
2 Fulham	–	–	1 –	–	–	–	–	–	–	1 –

JACK QUINN

DEBUT (Full Appearance)

Saturday 03/04/1909
Football League Division 1
at Hillsborough

Sheffield Wednesday 2 Manchester United 0

CLUB CAREER RECORD	Apps	Subs	Goals
Premiership	0		0
League Division 1	2		0
League Division 2	0		0
FA Cup	0		0
League Cup	0		0
European Cup / Champions League	0		0
European Cup-Winners' Cup	0		0
UEFA Cup / Inter-Cities' Fairs Cup	0		0
Other Matches	0		0
OVERALL TOTAL	2		0

Opponents	PREM A S G	FLD 1 A S G	FLD 2 A S G	FAC A S G	LC A S G	EC/CL A S G	ECWC A S G	UEFA A S G	OTHER A S G	TOTAL A S G
1 Bradford City	–	1 –	–	–	–	–	–	–	–	1 –
2 Sheffield Wednesday	–	1 –	–	–	–	–	–	–	–	1 –

ALBERT QUIXALL

DEBUT (Full Appearance)

Saturday 20/09/1958
Football League Division 1
at Old Trafford

Manchester United 2 Tottenham Hotspur 2

CLUB CAREER RECORD	Apps	Subs	Goals
Premiership	0		0
League Division 1	165		50
League Division 2	0		0
FA Cup	14		4
League Cup	1		2
European Cup / Champions League	0		0
European Cup-Winners' Cup	3		0
UEFA Cup / Inter-Cities' Fairs Cup	0		0
Other Matches	1		0
OVERALL TOTAL	**184**		**56**

Opponents	PREM			FLD 1			FLD 2			FAC			LC			EC/CL			ECWC			UEFA			OTHER			TOTAL		
	A	S	G	A	S	G	A	S	G	A	S	G	A	S	G	A	S	G	A	S	G	A	S	G	A	S	G	A	S	G
1 Tottenham Hotspur	–	–		9		2	–	–		1			–			–			2	–		–			–			12		2
2 Aston Villa	–	–		9		4	–	–		1		1	–			–			–			–			–			10		5
3 West Bromwich Albion	–	–		10		3	–	–		–			–			–			–			–			–			10		3
4 Leicester City	–	–		9		2	–	–		1			–			–			–			–			–			10		2
5 Wolverhampton W.	–	–		10		–	–	–		–			–			–			–			–			–			10		–
6 Burnley	–	–		9		5	–	–		–			–			–			–			–			–			9		5
7 Sheffield Wednesday	–	–		6		–	–	–		3			–			–			–			–			–			9		–
8 Chelsea	–	–		7		1	–	–		1		1	–			–			–			–			–			8		2
9 Manchester City	–	–		8		1	–	–		–			–			–			–			–			–			8		1
10 Blackburn Rovers	–	–		7		5	–	–		–			–			–			–			–			–			7		5
11 Birmingham City	–	–		7		4	–	–		–			–			–			–			–			–			7		4
12 Arsenal	–	–		7		2	–	–		–			–			–			–			–			–			7		2
13 Bolton Wanderers	–	–		7		1	–	–		–			–			–			–			–			–			7		1
14 Everton	–	–		6		1	–	–		–			–			–			–			–			1		–	7		1
15 Nottingham Forest	–	–		6		2	–	–		–			–			–			–			–			–			6		2
16 Blackpool	–	–		6		–	–	–		–			–			–			–			–			–			6		–
17 Preston North End	–	–		5		–	–	–		1			–			–			–			–			–			6		–
18 West Ham United	–	–		5		5	–	–		–			–			–			–			–			–			5		5
19 Fulham	–	–		5		3	–	–		–			–			–			–			–			–			5		3
20 Newcastle United	–	–		4		3	–	–		–			–			–			–			–			–			4		3
21 Liverpool	–	–		3		1	–	–		1			–			–			–			–			–			4		1
22 Leeds United	–	–		4		–	–	–		–			–			–			–			–			–			4		–
23 Ipswich Town	–	–		3		3	–	–		–			–			–			–			–			–			3		3
24 Cardiff City	–	–		3		1	–	–		–			–			–			–			–			–			3		1
25 Luton Town	–	–		3		1	–	–		–			–			–			–			–			–			3		1
26 Sheffield United	–	–		3		–	–	–		–			–			–			–			–			–			3		–
27 Portsmouth	–	–		2		–	–	–		–			–			–			–			–			–			2		–
28 Exeter City	–	–		–		–	–	–		–			1		2	–			–			–			–			1		2
29 Coventry City	–	–		–		–	–	–		1		1	–			–			–			–			–			1		1
30 Huddersfield Town	–	–		–		–	–	–		1		1	–			–			–			–			–			1		1
31 Derby County	–	–		–		–	–	–		1			–			–			–			–			–			1		–
32 Leyton Orient	–	–		1		–	–	–		–			–			–			–			–			–			1		–
33 Middlesbrough	–	–		–		–	–	–		1			–			–			–			–			–			1		–
34 Norwich City	–	–		–		–	–	–		1			–			–			–			–			–			1		–
35 Stoke City	–	–		1		–	–	–		–			–			–			–			–			–			1		–
36 Willem II	–	–		–		–	–	–		–			–			–			1	–		–			–			1		–

PAUL RACHUBKA

DEBUT (Substitute Appearance)

Tuesday 31/10/2000
League Cup 3rd Round
at Vicarage Road

Watford 0 Manchester United 3

CLUB CAREER RECORD	Apps	Subs	Goals
Premiership	1		0
League Division 1	0		0
League Division 2	0		0
FA Cup	0		0
League Cup	0	(1)	0
European Cup / Champions League	0		0
European Cup-Winners' Cup	0		0
UEFA Cup / Inter-Cities' Fairs Cup	0		0
Other Matches	0	(1)	0
OVERALL TOTAL	**1**	**(2)**	**0**

Opponents	PREM			FLD 1			FLD 2			FAC			LC			EC/CL			ECWC			UEFA			OTHER			TOTAL		
	A	S	G	A	S	G	A	S	G	A	S	G	A	S	G	A	S	G	A	S	G	A	S	G	A	S	G	A	S	G
1 Leicester City	1	–		–			–			–			–			–			–			–			–			1		–
2 South Melbourne	–	–		–			–			–			–			–			–			–			–	(1)	–	–	(1)	–
3 Watford	–	–		–			–			–			–	(1)		–			–			–			–			–	(1)	–

GEORGE RADCLIFFE

DEBUT (Full Appearance)

Wednesday 12/04/1899
Football League Division 2
at Bank Street

Newton Heath 5 Luton Town 0

CLUB CAREER RECORD	Apps	Subs	Goals
Premiership	0		0
League Division 1	0		0
League Division 2	1		0
FA Cup	0		0
League Cup	0		0
European Cup / Champions League	0		0
European Cup-Winners' Cup	0		0
UEFA Cup / Inter-Cities' Fairs Cup	0		0
Other Matches	0		0
OVERALL TOTAL	1		0

Opponents	PREM			FLD 1			FLD 2			FAC			LC			EC/CL			ECWC			UEFA			OTHER			TOTAL		
	A	S	G	A	S	G	A	S	G	A	S	G	A	S	G	A	S	G	A	S	G	A	S	G	A	S	G	A	S	G
1 Luton Town	–	–	–	–	–	–	1	–	–	–	–	–	–	–	–	–	–	–	–	–	–	–	–	–	–	–	–	1	–	–

CHARLIE RADFORD

DEBUT (Full Appearance)

Saturday 07/05/1921
Football League Division 1
at Old Trafford

Manchester United 3 Derby County 0

CLUB CAREER RECORD	Apps	Subs	Goals
Premiership	0		0
League Division 1	27		0
League Division 2	64		1
FA Cup	5		0
League Cup	0		0
European Cup / Champions League	0		0
European Cup-Winners' Cup	0		0
UEFA Cup / Inter-Cities' Fairs Cup	0		0
Other Matches	0		0
OVERALL TOTAL	96		1

Opponents	PREM			FLD 1			FLD 2			FAC			LC			EC/CL			ECWC			UEFA			OTHER			TOTAL		
	A	S	G	A	S	G	A	S	G	A	S	G	A	S	G	A	S	G	A	S	G	A	S	G	A	S	G	A	S	G
1 Bradford City	–	–	–	1	–	–	4	–	–	2	–	–	–	–	–	–	–	–	–	–	–	–	–	–	–	–	–	7	–	–
2 Derby County	–	–	–	1	–	–	4	–	–	–	–	–	–	–	–	–	–	–	–	–	–	–	–	–	–	–	–	5	–	–
3 Blackpool	–	–	–	–	–	–	4	–	1	–	–	–	–	–	–	–	–	–	–	–	–	–	–	–	–	–	–	4	–	1
4 Barnsley	–	–	–	–	–	–	4	–	–	–	–	–	–	–	–	–	–	–	–	–	–	–	–	–	–	–	–	4	–	–
5 Bury	–	–	–	–	–	–	4	–	–	–	–	–	–	–	–	–	–	–	–	–	–	–	–	–	–	–	–	4	–	–
6 Fulham	–	–	–	–	–	–	4	–	–	–	–	–	–	–	–	–	–	–	–	–	–	–	–	–	–	–	–	4	–	–
7 Hull City	–	–	–	–	–	–	4	–	–	–	–	–	–	–	–	–	–	–	–	–	–	–	–	–	–	–	–	4	–	–
8 South Shields	–	–	–	–	–	–	4	–	–	–	–	–	–	–	–	–	–	–	–	–	–	–	–	–	–	–	–	4	–	–
9 Southampton	–	–	–	–	–	–	4	–	–	–	–	–	–	–	–	–	–	–	–	–	–	–	–	–	–	–	–	4	–	–
10 Cardiff City	–	–	–	2	–	–	–	–	–	1	–	–	–	–	–	–	–	–	–	–	–	–	–	–	–	–	–	3	–	–
11 Leeds United	–	–	–	–	–	–	3	–	–	–	–	–	–	–	–	–	–	–	–	–	–	–	–	–	–	–	–	3	–	–
12 Leicester City	–	–	–	–	–	–	3	–	–	–	–	–	–	–	–	–	–	–	–	–	–	–	–	–	–	–	–	3	–	–
13 Port Vale	–	–	–	–	–	–	3	–	–	–	–	–	–	–	–	–	–	–	–	–	–	–	–	–	–	–	–	3	–	–
14 Tottenham Hotspur	–	–	–	2	–	–	–	–	–	1	–	–	–	–	–	–	–	–	–	–	–	–	–	–	–	–	–	3	–	–
15 Aston Villa	–	–	–	2	–	–	–	–	–	–	–	–	–	–	–	–	–	–	–	–	–	–	–	–	–	–	–	2	–	–
16 Birmingham City	–	–	–	2	–	–	–	–	–	–	–	–	–	–	–	–	–	–	–	–	–	–	–	–	–	–	–	2	–	–
17 Blackburn Rovers	–	–	–	2	–	–	–	–	–	–	–	–	–	–	–	–	–	–	–	–	–	–	–	–	–	–	–	2	–	–
18 Bristol City	–	–	–	–	–	–	2	–	–	–	–	–	–	–	–	–	–	–	–	–	–	–	–	–	–	–	–	2	–	–
19 Coventry City	–	–	–	–	–	–	2	–	–	–	–	–	–	–	–	–	–	–	–	–	–	–	–	–	–	–	–	2	–	–
20 Leyton Orient	–	–	–	–	–	–	2	–	–	–	–	–	–	–	–	–	–	–	–	–	–	–	–	–	–	–	–	2	–	–
21 Manchester City	–	–	–	2	–	–	–	–	–	–	–	–	–	–	–	–	–	–	–	–	–	–	–	–	–	–	–	2	–	–
22 Middlesbrough	–	–	–	2	–	–	–	–	–	–	–	–	–	–	–	–	–	–	–	–	–	–	–	–	–	–	–	2	–	–
23 Nelson	–	–	–	–	–	–	2	–	–	–	–	–	–	–	–	–	–	–	–	–	–	–	–	–	–	–	–	2	–	–
24 Newcastle United	–	–	–	2	–	–	–	–	–	–	–	–	–	–	–	–	–	–	–	–	–	–	–	–	–	–	–	2	–	–
25 Notts County	–	–	–	–	–	–	2	–	–	–	–	–	–	–	–	–	–	–	–	–	–	–	–	–	–	–	–	2	–	–
26 Oldham Athletic	–	–	–	1	–	–	1	–	–	–	–	–	–	–	–	–	–	–	–	–	–	–	–	–	–	–	–	2	–	–
27 Preston North End	–	–	–	2	–	–	–	–	–	–	–	–	–	–	–	–	–	–	–	–	–	–	–	–	–	–	–	2	–	–
28 Rotherham United	–	–	–	–	–	–	2	–	–	–	–	–	–	–	–	–	–	–	–	–	–	–	–	–	–	–	–	2	–	–
29 Sheffield United	–	–	–	2	–	–	–	–	–	–	–	–	–	–	–	–	–	–	–	–	–	–	–	–	–	–	–	2	–	–
30 Stockport County	–	–	–	–	–	–	2	–	–	–	–	–	–	–	–	–	–	–	–	–	–	–	–	–	–	–	–	2	–	–
31 Sunderland	–	–	–	2	–	–	–	–	–	–	–	–	–	–	–	–	–	–	–	–	–	–	–	–	–	–	–	2	–	–
32 West Ham United	–	–	–	–	–	–	2	–	–	–	–	–	–	–	–	–	–	–	–	–	–	–	–	–	–	–	–	2	–	–
33 Arsenal	–	–	–	1	–	–	–	–	–	–	–	–	–	–	–	–	–	–	–	–	–	–	–	–	–	–	–	1	–	–
34 Crystal Palace	–	–	–	–	–	–	1	–	–	–	–	–	–	–	–	–	–	–	–	–	–	–	–	–	–	–	–	1	–	–
35 Huddersfield Town	–	–	–	1	–	–	–	–	–	–	–	–	–	–	–	–	–	–	–	–	–	–	–	–	–	–	–	1	–	–
36 Plymouth Argyle	–	–	–	–	–	–	–	–	–	1	–	–	–	–	–	–	–	–	–	–	–	–	–	–	–	–	–	1	–	–
37 Sheffield Wednesday	–	–	–	–	–	–	1	–	–	–	–	–	–	–	–	–	–	–	–	–	–	–	–	–	–	–	–	1	–	–

ROBERT RAMSAY

DEBUT (Full Appearance)

Saturday 04/10/1890
FA Cup 1st Qualifying Round
at North Road

Newton Heath 2 Higher Walton 0

CLUB CAREER RECORD	Apps	Subs	Goals
Premiership	0		0
League Division 1	0		0
League Division 2	0		0
FA Cup	1		0
League Cup	0		0
European Cup / Champions League	0		0
European Cup-Winners' Cup	0		0
UEFA Cup / Inter-Cities' Fairs Cup	0		0
Other Matches	0		0
OVERALL TOTAL	1		0

Opponents	PREM A S G	FLD 1 A S G	FLD 2 A S G	FAC A S G	LC A S G	EC/CL A S G	ECWC A S G	UEFA A S G	OTHER A S G	TOTAL A S G
1 Higher Walton	– –	– –	– –	1 –	– –	– –	– –	– –	– –	1 –

CHARLIE RAMSDEN

DEBUT (Full Appearance)

Saturday 24/09/1927
Football League Division 1
at Old Trafford

Manchester United 3 Tottenham Hotspur 0

CLUB CAREER RECORD	Apps	Subs	Goals
Premiership	0		0
League Division 1	14		3
League Division 2	0		0
FA Cup	2		0
League Cup	0		0
European Cup / Champions League	0		0
European Cup-Winners' Cup	0		0
UEFA Cup / Inter-Cities' Fairs Cup	0		0
Other Matches	0		0
OVERALL TOTAL	16		3

Opponents	PREM A S G	FLD 1 A S G	FLD 2 A S G	FAC A S G	LC A S G	EC/CL A S G	ECWC A S G	UEFA A S G	OTHER A S G	TOTAL A S G
1 Blackburn Rovers	– –	3 2	– –	– –	– –	– –	– –	– –	– –	3 2
2 Sheffield United	– –	2 1	– –	– –	– –	– –	– –	– –	– –	2 1
3 Leicester City	– –	2 –	– –	– –	– –	– –	– –	– –	– –	2 –
4 Stoke City	– –	– –	– –	2 –	– –	– –	– –	– –	– –	2 –
5 Aston Villa	– –	1 –	– –	– –	– –	– –	– –	– –	– –	1 –
6 Bolton Wanderers	– –	1 –	– –	– –	– –	– –	– –	– –	– –	1 –
7 Chelsea	– –	1 –	– –	– –	– –	– –	– –	– –	– –	1 –
8 Leeds United	– –	1 –	– –	– –	– –	– –	– –	– –	– –	1 –
9 Middlesbrough	– –	1 –	– –	– –	– –	– –	– –	– –	– –	1 –
10 Sunderland	– –	1 –	– –	– –	– –	– –	– –	– –	– –	1 –
11 Tottenham Hotspur	– –	1 –	– –	– –	– –	– –	– –	– –	– –	1 –

RATTIGAN (FIRST NAME NOT KNOWN)

DEBUT (Full Appearance)

Saturday 25/10/1890
FA Cup 2nd Qualifying Round
at Bootle Park

Bootle Reserves 1 Manchester United 0

CLUB CAREER RECORD	Apps	Subs	Goals
Premiership	0		0
League Division 1	0		0
League Division 2	0		0
FA Cup	1		0
League Cup	0		0
European Cup / Champions League	0		0
European Cup-Winners' Cup	0		0
UEFA Cup / Inter-Cities' Fairs Cup	0		0
Other Matches	0		0
OVERALL TOTAL	1		0

Opponents	PREM A S G	FLD 1 A S G	FLD 2 A S G	FAC A S G	LC A S G	EC/CL A S G	ECWC A S G	UEFA A S G	OTHER A S G	TOTAL A S G
1 Bootle Reserves	– –	– –	– –	1 –	– –	– –	– –	– –	– –	1 –

BILL RAWLINGS

DEBUT (Full Appearance, 1 goal)

Wednesday 14/03/1928
Football League Division 1
at Old Trafford

Manchester United 1 Everton 0

CLUB CAREER RECORD	Apps	Subs	Goals
Premiership	0		0
League Division 1	35		19
League Division 2	0		0
FA Cup	1		0
League Cup	0		0
European Cup / Champions League	0		0
European Cup-Winners' Cup	0		0
UEFA Cup / Inter-Cities' Fairs Cup	0		0
Other Matches	0		0
OVERALL TOTAL	36		19

Opponents	PREM A S G	FLD 1 A S G	FLD 2 A S G	FAC A S G	LC A S G	EC/CL A S G	ECWC A S G	UEFA A S G	OTHER A S G	TOTAL A S G
1 Sheffield United	– –	4 2	– –	– –	– –	– –	– –	– –	– –	4 2
2 Liverpool	– –	3 2	– –	– –	– –	– –	– –	– –	– –	3 2
3 Bolton Wanderers	– –	3 1	– –	– –	– –	– –	– –	– –	– –	3 1
4 Burnley	– –	2 3	– –	– –	– –	– –	– –	– –	– –	2 3

continued../

BILL RAWLINGS (continued)

Opponents	PREM			FLD 1			FLD 2			FAC			LC			EC/CL			ECWC			UEFA			OTHER			TOTAL		
	A	S	G	A	S	G	A	S	G	A	S	G	A	S	G	A	S	G	A	S	G	A	S	G	A	S	G	A	S	G
5 Arsenal	-		-	2		1	-		-	-		-	-		-	-		-	-		-	-		-	-		-	2		1
6 Aston Villa	-		-	2		1	-		-	-		-	-		-	-		-	-		-	-		-	-		-	2		1
7 Manchester City	-		-	2		1	-		-	-		-	-		-	-		-	-		-	-		-	-		-	2		1
8 West Ham United	-		-	2		1	-		-	-		-	-		-	-		-	-		-	-		-	-		-	2		1
9 Bury	-		-	1		-	-		-	1		-	-		-	-		-	-		-	-		-	-		-	2		-
10 Derby County	-		-	2		-	-		-	-		-	-		-	-		-	-		-	-		-	-		-	2		-
11 Sunderland	-		-	2		-	-		-	-		-	-		-	-		-	-		-	-		-	-		-	2		-
12 Middlesbrough	-		-	1		3	-		-	-		-	-		-	-		-	-		-	-		-	-		-	1		3
13 Newcastle United	-		-	1		2	-		-	-		-	-		-	-		-	-		-	-		-	-		-	1		2
14 Everton	-		-	1		1	-		-	-		-	-		-	-		-	-		-	-		-	-		-	1		1
15 Leicester City	-		-	1		1	-		-	-		-	-		-	-		-	-		-	-		-	-		-	1		1
16 Birmingham City	-		-	1		-	-		-	-		-	-		-	-		-	-		-	-		-	-		-	1		-
17 Cardiff City	-		-	1		-	-		-	-		-	-		-	-		-	-		-	-		-	-		-	1		-
18 Huddersfield Town	-		-	1		-	-		-	-		-	-		-	-		-	-		-	-		-	-		-	1		-
19 Leeds United	-		-	1		-	-		-	-		-	-		-	-		-	-		-	-		-	-		-	1		-
20 Portsmouth	-		-	1		-	-		-	-		-	-		-	-		-	-		-	-		-	-		-	1		-
21 Sheffield Wednesday	-		-	1		-	-		-	-		-	-		-	-		-	-		-	-		-	-		-	1		-

BERT READ

DEBUT (Full Appearance)

Saturday 06/09/1902
Football League Division 2
at The Northolme

Gainsborough Trinity 0 Manchester United 1

CLUB CAREER RECORD	Apps	Subs	Goals
Premiership	0		0
League Division 1	0		0
League Division 2	35		0
FA Cup	7		0
League Cup	0		0
European Cup / Champions League	0		0
European Cup-Winners' Cup	0		0
UEFA Cup / Inter-Cities' Fairs Cup	0		0
Other Matches	0		0
OVERALL TOTAL	**42**		**0**

Opponents	PREM			FLD 1			FLD 2			FAC			LC			EC/CL			ECWC			UEFA			OTHER			TOTAL		
	A	S	G	A	S	G	A	S	G	A	S	G	A	S	G	A	S	G	A	S	G	A	S	G	A	S	G	A	S	G
1 Burton United	-		-	-		-	-		-	2		-	2		-	-		-	-		-	-		-	-		-	4		-
2 Glossop	-		-	-		-	4		-	-		-	-		-	-		-	-		-	-		-	-		-	4		-
3 Port Vale	-		-	-		-	4		-	-		-	-		-	-		-	-		-	-		-	-		-	4		-
4 Bristol City	-		-	-		-	3		-	-		-	-		-	-		-	-		-	-		-	-		-	3		-
5 Burnley	-		-	-		-	3		-	-		-	-		-	-		-	-		-	-		-	-		-	3		-
6 Arsenal	-		-	-		-	2		-	-		-	-		-	-		-	-		-	-		-	-		-	2		-
7 Barnsley	-		-	-		-	2		-	-		-	-		-	-		-	-		-	-		-	-		-	2		-
8 Birmingham City	-		-	-		-	1		-	1		-	-		-	-		-	-		-	-		-	-		-	2		-
9 Chesterfield	-		-	-		-	2		-	-		-	-		-	-		-	-		-	-		-	-		-	2		-
10 Doncaster Rovers	-		-	-		-	2		-	-		-	-		-	-		-	-		-	-		-	-		-	2		-
11 Gainsborough Trinity	-		-	-		-	2		-	-		-	-		-	-		-	-		-	-		-	-		-	2		-
12 Manchester City	-		-	-		-	2		-	-		-	-		-	-		-	-		-	-		-	-		-	2		-
13 Preston North End	-		-	-		-	2		-	-		-	-		-	-		-	-		-	-		-	-		-	2		-
14 Accrington Stanley	-		-	-		-	-		-	-		-	1		-	-		-	-		-	-		-	-		-	1		-
15 Blackpool	-		-	-		-	1		-	-		-	-		-	-		-	-		-	-		-	-		-	1		-
16 Bradford City	-		-	-		-	1		-	-		-	-		-	-		-	-		-	-		-	-		-	1		-
17 Everton	-		-	-		-	-		-	1		-	-		-	-		-	-		-	-		-	-		-	1		-
18 Lincoln City	-		-	-		-	1		-	-		-	-		-	-		-	-		-	-		-	-		-	1		-
19 Oswaldtwistle Rovers	-		-	-		-	1		-	-		-	-		-	-		-	-		-	-		-	-		-	1		-
20 Southport Central	-		-	-		-	-		-	-		-	1		-	-		-	-		-	-		-	-		-	1		-
21 Stockport County	-		-	-		-	1		-	-		-	-		-	-		-	-		-	-		-	-		-	1		-

BILLY REDMAN

DEBUT (Full Appearance)

Saturday 07/10/1950
Football League Division 1
at Old Trafford

Manchester United 3 Sheffield Wednesday 1

CLUB CAREER RECORD	Apps	Subs	Goals
Premiership	0		0
League Division 1	36		0
League Division 2	0		0
FA Cup	2		0
League Cup	0		0
European Cup / Champions League	0		0
European Cup-Winners' Cup	0		0
UEFA Cup / Inter-Cities' Fairs Cup	0		0
Other Matches	0		0
OVERALL TOTAL	**38**		**0**

Opponents	PREM			FLD 1			FLD 2			FAC			LC			EC/CL			ECWC			UEFA			OTHER			TOTAL		
	A	S	G	A	S	G	A	S	G	A	S	G	A	S	G	A	S	G	A	S	G	A	S	G	A	S	G	A	S	G
1 Derby County	-		-	4		-	-		-	-		-	-		-	-		-	-		-	-		-	-		-	4		-
2 Charlton Athletic	-		-	3		-	-		-	-		-	-		-	-		-	-		-	-		-	-		-	3		-
3 Middlesbrough	-		-	3		-	-		-	-		-	-		-	-		-	-		-	-		-	-		-	3		-
4 Arsenal	-		-	1		-	-		-	1		-	-		-	-		-	-		-	-		-	-		-	2		-
5 Chelsea	-		-	2		-	-		-	-		-	-		-	-		-	-		-	-		-	-		-	2		-
6 Huddersfield Town	-		-	2		-	-		-	-		-	-		-	-		-	-		-	-		-	-		-	2		-

continued../

BILLY REDMAN (continued)

Opponents	PREM A S G	FLD 1 A S G	FLD 2 A S G	FAC A S G	LC A S G	EC/CL A S G	ECWC A S G	UEFA A S G	OTHER A S G	TOTAL A S G
7 Newcastle United	– –	2 –	–	–	–	–	–	–	–	2 –
8 Portsmouth	– –	2 –	–	–	–	–	–	–	–	2 –
9 Stoke City	– –	2 –	–	–	–	–	–	–	–	2 –
10 Tottenham Hotspur	– –	2 –	–	–	–	–	–	–	–	2 –
11 West Bromwich Albion	– –	2 –	–	–	–	–	–	–	–	2 –
12 Wolverhampton W.	– –	2 –	–	–	–	–	–	–	–	2 –
13 Aston Villa	– –	1 –	–	–	–	–	–	–	–	1 –
14 Blackpool	– –	1 –	–	–	–	–	–	–	–	1 –
15 Bolton Wanderers	– –	1 –	–	–	–	–	–	–	–	1 –
16 Burnley	– –	1 –	–	–	–	–	–	–	–	1 –
17 Everton	– –	1 –	–	–	–	–	–	–	–	1 –
18 Leeds United	– –	–	–	1	–	–	–	–	–	1 –
19 Manchester City	– –	1 –	–	–	–	–	–	–	–	1 –
20 Preston North End	– –	1 –	–	–	–	–	–	–	–	1 –
21 Sheffield Wednesday	– –	1 –	–	–	–	–	–	–	–	1 –
22 Sunderland	– –	1 –	–	–	–	–	–	–	–	1 –

HUBERT REDWOOD

DEBUT (Full Appearance)

Saturday 21/09/1935
Football League Division 2
at Old Trafford

Manchester United 0 Tottenham Hotspur 0

CLUB CAREER RECORD	Apps	Subs	Goals
Premiership	0		0
League Division 1	56		1
League Division 2	30		2
FA Cup	7		1
League Cup	0		0
European Cup / Champions League	0		0
European Cup–Winners' Cup	0		0
UEFA Cup / Inter–Cities' Fairs Cup	0		0
Other Matches	0		0
OVERALL TOTAL	93		4

Opponents	PREM A S G	FLD 1 A S G	FLD 2 A S G	FAC A S G	LC A S G	EC/CL A S G	ECWC A S G	UEFA A S G	OTHER A S G	TOTAL A S G
1 Aston Villa	– –	2 –	2 –	–	–	–	–	–	–	4 –
2 Bolton Wanderers	– –	4 –	–	–	–	–	–	–	–	4 –
3 Middlesbrough	– –	4 –	–	–	–	–	–	–	–	4 –
4 Preston North End	– –	4 –	–	–	–	–	–	–	–	4 –
5 Wolverhampton W.	– –	4 –	–	–	–	–	–	–	–	4 –
6 West Bromwich Albion	– –	1 –	–	2 1	–	–	–	–	–	3 1
7 Arsenal	– –	2 –	–	1	–	–	–	–	–	3 –
8 Barnsley	– –	–	1 –	2	–	–	–	–	–	3 –
9 Birmingham City	– –	3 –	–	–	–	–	–	–	–	3 –
10 Brentford	– –	2 –	–	1	–	–	–	–	–	3 –
11 Derby County	– –	3 –	–	–	–	–	–	–	–	3 –
12 Huddersfield Town	– –	3 –	–	–	–	–	–	–	–	3 –
13 Sheffield Wednesday	– –	2 –	1 –	–	–	–	–	–	–	3 –
14 Sunderland	– –	3 –	–	–	–	–	–	–	–	3 –
15 Chelsea	– –	2 1	–	–	–	–	–	–	–	2 1
16 Blackpool	– –	2 –	–	–	–	–	–	–	–	2 –
17 Bradford Park Avenue	– –	–	2 –	–	–	–	–	–	–	2 –
18 Burnley	– –	–	2 –	–	–	–	–	–	–	2 –
19 Charlton Athletic	– –	2 –	–	–	–	–	–	–	–	2 –
20 Chesterfield	– –	–	2 –	–	–	–	–	–	–	2 –
21 Everton	– –	2 –	–	–	–	–	–	–	–	2 –
22 Grimsby Town	– –	2 –	–	–	–	–	–	–	–	2 –
23 Leicester City	– –	2 –	–	–	–	–	–	–	–	2 –
24 Liverpool	– –	2 –	–	–	–	–	–	–	–	2 –
25 Manchester City	– –	2 –	–	–	–	–	–	–	–	2 –
26 Norwich City	– –	–	2 –	–	–	–	–	–	–	2 –
27 Nottingham Forest	– –	–	2 –	–	–	–	–	–	–	2 –
28 Plymouth Argyle	– –	–	2 –	–	–	–	–	–	–	2 –
29 Stoke City	– –	2 –	–	–	–	–	–	–	–	2 –
30 Swansea City	– –	–	2 –	–	–	–	–	–	–	2 –
31 Tottenham Hotspur	– –	–	2 –	–	–	–	–	–	–	2 –
32 West Ham United	– –	–	2 –	–	–	–	–	–	–	2 –
33 Southampton	– –	–	1 2	–	–	–	–	–	–	1 2
34 Blackburn Rovers	– –	–	1 –	–	–	–	–	–	–	1 –
35 Bury	– –	–	1 –	–	–	–	–	–	–	1 –
36 Fulham	– –	–	1 –	–	–	–	–	–	–	1 –
37 Luton Town	– –	–	1 –	–	–	–	–	–	–	1 –
38 Newcastle United	– –	–	1 –	–	–	–	–	–	–	1 –
39 Portsmouth	– –	1 –	–	–	–	–	–	–	–	1 –
40 Sheffield United	– –	–	1 –	–	–	–	–	–	–	1 –
41 Stockport County	– –	–	1 –	–	–	–	–	–	–	1 –
42 Yeovil Town	– –	–	–	1	–	–	–	–	–	1 –

TOM REID

DEBUT (Full Appearance, 1 goal)

Saturday 02/02/1929
Football League Division 1
at Old Trafford

Manchester United 2 West Ham United 3

CLUB CAREER RECORD	Apps	Subs	Goals
Premiership	0		0
League Division 1	60		36
League Division 2	36		27
FA Cup	5		4
League Cup	0		0
European Cup / Champions League	0		0
European Cup-Winners' Cup	0		0
UEFA Cup / Inter-Cities' Fairs Cup	0		0
Other Matches	0		0
OVERALL TOTAL	**101**		**67**

Opponents	PREM (A S G)	FLD 1 (A S G)	FLD 2 (A S G)	FAC (A S G)	LC (A S G)	EC/CL (A S G)	ECWC (A S G)	UEFA (A S G)	OTHER (A S G)	TOTAL (A S G)
1 Portsmouth	– – –	5 – 2	– – –	– – –	– – –	– – –	– – –	– – –	– – –	5 – 2
2 Newcastle United	– – –	4 – 4	– – –	– – –	– – –	– – –	– – –	– – –	– – –	4 – 4
3 Bolton Wanderers	– – –	4 – 3	– – –	– – –	– – –	– – –	– – –	– – –	– – –	4 – 3
4 Stoke City	– – –	– – –	2 – –	2 – 3	– – –	– – –	– – –	– – –	– – –	4 – 3
5 Grimsby Town	– – –	3 – 2	1 – –	– – –	– – –	– – –	– – –	– – –	– – –	4 – 2
6 West Ham United	– – –	4 – 2	– – –	– – –	– – –	– – –	– – –	– – –	– – –	4 – 2
7 Manchester City	– – –	4 – 1	– – –	– – –	– – –	– – –	– – –	– – –	– – –	4 – 1
8 Charlton Athletic	– – –	– – –	4 – –	– – –	– – –	– – –	– – –	– – –	– – –	4 – –
9 Liverpool	– – –	3 – 4	– – –	– – –	– – –	– – –	– – –	– – –	– – –	3 – 4
10 Millwall	– – –	– – –	3 – 4	– – –	– – –	– – –	– – –	– – –	– – –	3 – 4
11 Bradford Park Avenue	– – –	– – –	3 – 3	– – –	– – –	– – –	– – –	– – –	– – –	3 – 3
12 Blackburn Rovers	– – –	3 – 2	– – –	– – –	– – –	– – –	– – –	– – –	– – –	3 – 2
13 Bury	– – –	2 – 2	1 – –	– – –	– – –	– – –	– – –	– – –	– – –	3 – 2
14 Leeds United	– – –	2 – –	1 – 2	– – –	– – –	– – –	– – –	– – –	– – –	3 – 2
15 Middlesbrough	– – –	2 – 2	1 – –	– – –	– – –	– – –	– – –	– – –	– – –	3 – 2
16 Plymouth Argyle	– – –	– – –	2 – 1	1 – 1	– – –	– – –	– – –	– – –	– – –	3 – 2
17 Sheffield Wednesday	– – –	3 – 2	– – –	– – –	– – –	– – –	– – –	– – –	– – –	3 – 2
18 Aston Villa	– – –	3 – 1	– – –	– – –	– – –	– – –	– – –	– – –	– – –	3 – 1
19 Derby County	– – –	3 – 1	– – –	– – –	– – –	– – –	– – –	– – –	– – –	3 – 1
20 Swansea City	– – –	– – –	3 – 1	– – –	– – –	– – –	– – –	– – –	– – –	3 – 1
21 Huddersfield Town	– – –	3 – –	– – –	– – –	– – –	– – –	– – –	– – –	– – –	3 – –
22 Nottingham Forest	– – –	– – –	2 – 3	– – –	– – –	– – –	– – –	– – –	– – –	2 – 3
23 Arsenal	– – –	2 – 2	– – –	– – –	– – –	– – –	– – –	– – –	– – –	2 – 2
24 Sunderland	– – –	2 – 2	– – –	– – –	– – –	– – –	– – –	– – –	– – –	2 – 2
25 Chelsea	– – –	2 – 1	– – –	– – –	– – –	– – –	– – –	– – –	– – –	2 – 1
26 Southampton	– – –	– – –	2 – 1	– – –	– – –	– – –	– – –	– – –	– – –	2 – 1
27 Bristol City	– – –	– – –	– – –	2 – –	– – –	– – –	– – –	– – –	– – –	2 – –
28 Burnley	– – –	1 – –	1 – –	– – –	– – –	– – –	– – –	– – –	– – –	2 – –
29 Lincoln City	– – –	– – –	1 – 3	– – –	– – –	– – –	– – –	– – –	– – –	1 – 3
30 Oldham Athletic	– – –	– – –	1 – 3	– – –	– – –	– – –	– – –	– – –	– – –	1 – 3
31 Chesterfield	– – –	– – –	1 – 2	– – –	– – –	– – –	– – –	– – –	– – –	1 – 2
32 Everton	– – –	1 – 2	– – –	– – –	– – –	– – –	– – –	– – –	– – –	1 – 2
33 Cardiff City	– – –	1 – 1	– – –	– – –	– – –	– – –	– – –	– – –	– – –	1 – 1
34 Notts County	– – –	– – –	1 – 1	– – –	– – –	– – –	– – –	– – –	– – –	1 – 1
35 Port Vale	– – –	– – –	1 – 1	– – –	– – –	– – –	– – –	– – –	– – –	1 – 1
36 Tottenham Hotspur	– – –	– – –	1 – 1	– – –	– – –	– – –	– – –	– – –	– – –	1 – 1
37 Wolverhampton W.	– – –	– – –	1 – 1	– – –	– – –	– – –	– – –	– – –	– – –	1 – 1
38 Barnsley	– – –	– – –	1 – –	– – –	– – –	– – –	– – –	– – –	– – –	1 – –
39 Birmingham City	– – –	1 – –	– – –	– – –	– – –	– – –	– – –	– – –	– – –	1 – –
40 Blackpool	– – –	1 – –	– – –	– – –	– – –	– – –	– – –	– – –	– – –	1 – –
41 Bradford City	– – –	– – –	1 – –	– – –	– – –	– – –	– – –	– – –	– – –	1 – –
42 Leicester City	– – –	1 – –	– – –	– – –	– – –	– – –	– – –	– – –	– – –	1 – –
43 Preston North End	– – –	– – –	1 – –	– – –	– – –	– – –	– – –	– – –	– – –	1 – –

CHARLIE RENNOX

DEBUT (Full Appearance)

Saturday 14/03/1925
Football League Division 2
at Old Trafford

Manchester United 2 Portsmouth 0

CLUB CAREER RECORD	Apps	Subs	Goals
Premiership	0		0
League Division 1	56		24
League Division 2	4		0
FA Cup	8		1
League Cup	0		0
European Cup / Champions League	0		0
European Cup-Winners' Cup	0		0
UEFA Cup / Inter-Cities' Fairs Cup	0		0
Other Matches	0		0
OVERALL TOTAL	**68**		**25**

Opponents	PREM (A S G)	FLD 1 (A S G)	FLD 2 (A S G)	FAC (A S G)	LC (A S G)	EC/CL (A S G)	ECWC (A S G)	UEFA (A S G)	OTHER (A S G)	TOTAL (A S G)
1 Sunderland	– – –	3 – 1	– – –	2 – –	– – –	– – –	– – –	– – –	– – –	5 – 1
2 Tottenham Hotspur	– – –	3 – –	– – –	2 – 1	– – –	– – –	– – –	– – –	– – –	5 – 1
3 Bolton Wanderers	– – –	4 – –	– – –	– – –	– – –	– – –	– – –	– – –	– – –	4 – –
4 Burnley	– – –	3 – 3	– – –	– – –	– – –	– – –	– – –	– – –	– – –	3 – 3
5 Leicester City	– – –	3 – 3	– – –	– – –	– – –	– – –	– – –	– – –	– – –	3 – 3
6 Aston Villa	– – –	3 – 2	– – –	– – –	– – –	– – –	– – –	– – –	– – –	3 – 2
7 Manchester City	– – –	2 – 2	– – –	1 – –	– – –	– – –	– – –	– – –	– – –	3 – 2
8 Birmingham City	– – –	3 – 1	– – –	– – –	– – –	– – –	– – –	– – –	– – –	3 – 1

continued../

CHARLIE RENNOX (continued)

Opponents	PREM A S G	FLD 1 A S G	FLD 2 A S G	FAC A S G	LC A S G	EC/CL A S G	ECWC A S G	UEFA A S G	OTHER A S G	TOTAL A S G
9 Newcastle United	– –	3 1	–	–	–	–	–	–	–	3 1
10 Sheffield United	– –	3 1	–	–	–	–	–	–	–	3 1
11 Arsenal	– –	3 –	–	–	–	–	–	–	–	3 –
12 Bury	– –	3	–	–	–	–	–	–	–	3 –
13 Huddersfield Town	– –	3	–	–	–	–	–	–	–	3 –
14 Everton	– –	2 3	–	–	–	–	–	–	–	2 3
15 Notts County	– –	2 2	–	–	–	–	–	–	–	2 2
16 West Ham United	– –	2 2	–	–	–	–	–	–	–	2 2
17 Cardiff City	– –	2 1	–	–	–	–	–	–	–	2 1
18 Leeds United	– –	2 1	–	–	–	–	–	–	–	2 1
19 Liverpool	– –	2 1	–	–	–	–	–	–	–	2 1
20 Blackburn Rovers	– –	2 –	–	–	–	–	–	–	–	2 –
21 Sheffield Wednesday	– –	2 –	–	–	–	–	–	–	–	2 –
22 Blackpool	– –	–	–	1	–	–	–	–	–	1 –
23 Derby County	– –	–	–	1	–	–	–	–	–	1 –
24 Fulham	– –	–	–	–	1	–	–	–	–	1 –
25 Hull City	– –	–	–	1	–	–	–	–	–	1 –
26 Port Vale	– –	–	–	–	1	–	–	–	–	1 –
27 Portsmouth	– –	–	–	1	–	–	–	–	–	1 –
28 Reading	– –	–	–	1	–	–	–	–	–	1 –
29 West Bromwich Albion	– –	1	–	–	–	–	–	–	–	1 –

FELIPE RICARDO

DEBUT (Substitute Appearance)

Wednesday 18/09/2002
Champions League Phase 1 Match 1
at Old Trafford

Manchester United 5 Maccabi Haifa 2

CLUB CAREER RECORD	Apps	Subs	Goals
Premiership	0	(1)	0
League Division 1	0		0
League Division 2	0		0
FA Cup	0		0
League Cup	0		0
European Cup / Champions League	3	(1)	0
European Cup-Winners' Cup	0		0
UEFA Cup / Inter-Cities' Fairs Cup	0		0
Other Matches	0		0
OVERALL TOTAL	3	(2)	0

Opponents	PREM A S G	FLD 1 A S G	FLD 2 A S G	FAC A S G	LC A S G	EC/CL A S G	ECWC A S G	UEFA A S G	OTHER A S G	TOTAL A S G
1 Maccabi Haifa	–	–	–	–	–	1 (1) –	–	–	–	1 (1) –
2 Bayer Leverkusen	–	–	–	–	–	1	–	–	–	1 –
3 Deportivo La Coruna	–	–	–	–	–	1	–	–	–	1 –
4 Blackburn Rovers	– (1) –	–	–	–	–	–	–	–	–	– (1) –

BILLY RICHARDS

DEBUT (Full Appearance, 1 goal)

Saturday 21/12/1901
Football League Division 2
at Bank Street

Manchester United 1 Port Vale 0

CLUB CAREER RECORD	Apps	Subs	Goals
Premiership	0		0
League Division 1	0		0
League Division 2	9		1
FA Cup	0		0
League Cup	0		0
European Cup / Champions League	0		0
European Cup-Winners' Cup	0		0
UEFA Cup / Inter-Cities' Fairs Cup	0		0
Other Matches	0		0
OVERALL TOTAL	9		1

Opponents	PREM A S G	FLD 1 A S G	FLD 2 A S G	FAC A S G	LC A S G	EC/CL A S G	ECWC A S G	UEFA A S G	OTHER A S G	TOTAL A S G
1 Port Vale	–	–	1 1	–	–	–	–	–	–	1 1
2 Blackpool	–	–	1	–	–	–	–	–	–	1 –
3 Bristol City	–	–	1	–	–	–	–	–	–	1 –
4 Chesterfield	–	–	1	–	–	–	–	–	–	1 –
5 Gainsborough Trinity	–	–	1	–	–	–	–	–	–	1 –
6 Glossop	–	–	1	–	–	–	–	–	–	1 –
7 Lincoln City	–	–	1	–	–	–	–	–	–	1 –
8 Preston North End	–	–	1	–	–	–	–	–	–	1 –
9 West Bromwich Albion	–	–	1	–	–	–	–	–	–	1 –

CHARLIE RICHARDS

DEBUT (Full Appearance, 1 goal)

Saturday 06/09/1902
Football League Division 2
at The Northolme

Gainsborough Trinity 0 Manchester United 1

CLUB CAREER RECORD	Apps	Subs	Goals
Premiership	0		0
League Division 1	0		0
League Division 2	8		1
FA Cup	3		1
League Cup	0		0
European Cup / Champions League	0		0
European Cup-Winners' Cup	0		0
UEFA Cup / Inter-Cities' Fairs Cup	0		0
Other Matches	0		0
OVERALL TOTAL	11		2

Opponents	PREM A S G	FLD 1 A S G	FLD 2 A S G	FAC A S G	LC A S G	EC/CL A S G	ECWC A S G	UEFA A S G	OTHER A S G	TOTAL A S G
1 Accrington Stanley	- - -	- - -	- - -	1 - 1	- - -	- - -	- - -	- - -	- - -	1 - 1
2 Gainsborough Trinity	- - -	- - -	1 - 1	- - -	- - -	- - -	- - -	- - -	- - -	1 - 1
3 Arsenal	- - -	- - -	- - -	1 - -	- - -	- - -	- - -	- - -	- - -	1 - -
4 Barnsley	- - -	- - -	1 - -	- - -	- - -	- - -	- - -	- - -	- - -	1 - -
5 Bristol City	- - -	- - -	1 - -	- - -	- - -	- - -	- - -	- - -	- - -	1 - -
6 Burnley	- - -	- - -	1 - -	- - -	- - -	- - -	- - -	- - -	- - -	1 - -
7 Burton United	- - -	- - -	- - -	1 - -	- - -	- - -	- - -	- - -	- - -	1 - -
8 Chesterfield	- - -	- - -	1 - -	- - -	- - -	- - -	- - -	- - -	- - -	1 - -
9 Port Vale	- - -	- - -	1 - -	- - -	- - -	- - -	- - -	- - -	- - -	1 - -
10 Southport Central	- - -	- - -	- - -	1 - -	- - -	- - -	- - -	- - -	- - -	1 - -
11 Stockport County	- - -	- - -	1 - -	- - -	- - -	- - -	- - -	- - -	- - -	1 - -

KIERAN RICHARDSON

DEBUT (Substitute Appearance)

Wednesday 23/10/2002
Champions League Phase 1 Match 4
at Rizoupoli

Olympiakos Piraeus 2 Manchester United 3

CLUB CAREER RECORD	Apps	Subs	Goals
Premiership	20	(21)	2
League Division 1	0		0
League Division 2	0		0
FA Cup	8	(2)	4
League Cup	11	(2)	3
European Cup / Champions League	5	(11)	2
European Cup-Winners' Cup	0		0
UEFA Cup / Inter-Cities' Fairs Cup	0		0
Other Matches	0	(1)	0
OVERALL TOTAL	44	(37)	11

Opponents	PREM A S G	FLD 1 A S G	FLD 2 A S G	FAC A S G	LC A S G	EC/CL A S G	ECWC A S G	UEFA A S G	OTHER A S G	TOTAL A S G
1 Birmingham City	2 (1) -	- - -	- - -	- - -	1 - -	- - -	- - -	- - -	- - -	3 (1) -
2 West Bromwich Albion	1 (1) -	- - -	- - -	- - -	2 - -	- - -	- - -	- - -	- - -	3 (1) -
3 Middlesbrough	1 (2) 1	- - -	- - -	1 - -	- - -	- - -	- - -	- - -	- - -	2 (2) 1
4 Everton	2 (2) -	- - -	- - -	- - -	- - -	- - -	- - -	- - -	- - -	2 (2) -
5 Blackburn Rovers	2 - -	- - -	- - -	- - -	1 - -	- - -	- - -	- - -	- - -	3 - -
6 Liverpool	2 - -	- - -	- - -	1 - -	- - -	- - -	- - -	- - -	- - -	3 - -
7 Portsmouth	1 (1) -	- - -	- - -	- - -	1 - -	- - -	- - -	- - -	- - -	2 (1) -
8 Reading	1 (1) -	- - -	- - -	- - -	1 - -	- - -	- - -	- - -	- - -	2 (1) -
9 Charlton Athletic	1 (2) 1	- - -	- - -	- - -	- - -	- - -	- - -	- - -	- - -	1 (2) 1
10 Watford	1 (1) -	- - -	- - -	- (1) 1	- - -	- - -	- - -	- - -	- - -	1 (2) 1
11 Chelsea	1 (2) -	- - -	- - -	- - -	- - -	- - -	- - -	- - -	- - -	1 (2) -
12 Burton Albion	- - -	- - -	- - -	2 1	- - -	- - -	- - -	- - -	- - -	2 - 1
13 Crewe Alexandra	- - -	- - -	- - -	- - -	2 - -	- - -	- - -	- - -	- - -	2 - -
14 Fulham	2 - -	- - -	- - -	- - -	- - -	- - -	- - -	- - -	- - -	2 - -
15 Arsenal	- - -	- - -	- - -	- - -	1 - -	- - -	- - -	- (1) -	- - -	1 (1) -
16 Benfica	- - -	- - -	- - -	- - -	- - -	1 (1) -	- - -	- - -	- - -	1 (1) -
17 Bolton Wanderers	1 (1) -	- - -	- - -	- - -	- - -	- - -	- - -	- - -	- - -	1 (1) -
18 Lille Metropole	- - -	- - -	- - -	- - -	- - -	1 (1) -	- - -	- - -	- - -	1 (1) -
19 West Ham United	1 (1) -	- - -	- - -	- - -	- - -	- - -	- - -	- - -	- - -	1 (1) -
20 Deportivo La Coruna	- - -	- - -	- - -	- - -	- - -	- (2) -	- - -	- - -	- - -	- (2) -
21 Manchester City	- (2) -	- - -	- - -	- - -	- - -	- - -	- - -	- - -	- - -	- (2) -
22 Wigan Athletic	- (1) -	- - -	- - -	- - -	- (1) -	- - -	- - -	- - -	- - -	- (2) -
23 Wolverhampton W.	- - -	- - -	- - -	1 2	- - -	- - -	- - -	- - -	- - -	1 - 2
24 Barnet	- - -	- - -	- - -	- - -	1 1	- - -	- - -	- - -	- - -	1 - 1
25 Crystal Palace	- - -	- - -	- - -	- - -	1 1	- - -	- - -	- - -	- - -	1 - 1
26 Basel	- - -	- - -	- - -	- - -	- - -	1 - -	- - -	- - -	- - -	1 - -
27 Exeter City	- - -	- - -	- - -	1 - -	- - -	- - -	- - -	- - -	- - -	1 - -
28 Fenerbahce	- - -	- - -	- - -	- - -	- - -	1 - -	- - -	- - -	- - -	1 - -
29 Leeds United	- - -	- - -	- - -	- - -	1 - -	- - -	- - -	- - -	- - -	1 - -
30 Maccabi Haifa	- - -	- - -	- - -	- - -	- - -	1 - -	- - -	- - -	- - -	1 - -
31 Southend United	- - -	- - -	- - -	- - -	1 - -	- - -	- - -	- - -	- - -	1 - -
32 Tottenham Hotspur	1 - -	- - -	- - -	- - -	- - -	- - -	- - -	- - -	- - -	1 - -
33 Copenhagen	- - -	- - -	- - -	- - -	- - -	- (1) 1	- - -	- - -	- - -	- (1) 1
34 Debreceni	- - -	- - -	- - -	- - -	- - -	- (1) 1	- - -	- - -	- - -	- (1) 1
35 Leicester City	- - -	- - -	- - -	- - -	- (1) 1	- - -	- - -	- - -	- - -	- (1) 1
36 Dinamo Bucharest	- - -	- - -	- - -	- - -	- - -	- (1) -	- - -	- - -	- - -	- (1) -
37 Glasgow Celtic	- - -	- - -	- - -	- - -	- - -	- (1) -	- - -	- - -	- - -	- (1) -
38 Newcastle United	- (1) -	- - -	- - -	- - -	- - -	- - -	- - -	- - -	- - -	- (1) -
39 Northampton Town	- - -	- - -	- - -	- (1) -	- - -	- - -	- - -	- - -	- - -	- (1) -
40 Norwich City	- (1) -	- - -	- - -	- - -	- - -	- - -	- - -	- - -	- - -	- (1) -

continued../

KIERAN RICHARDSON (continued)

Opponents	PREM			FLD 1			FLD 2			FAC			LC			EC/CL			ECWC			UEFA			OTHER			TOTAL		
	A	S	G	A	S	G	A	S	G	A	S	G	A	S	G	A	S	G	A	S	G	A	S	G	A	S	G	A	S	G
41 Olympiakos Piraeus	–	–	–	–	–	–	–	–	–	–	–	–	–	–	–	–	(1)	–	–	–	–	–	–	–	–	–	–	–	(1)	–
42 Roma	–	–	–	–	–	–	–	–	–	–	–	–	–	–	–	–	(1)	–	–	–	–	–	–	–	–	–	–	–	(1)	–
43 Sheffield United	–	(1)	–	–	–	–	–	–	–	–	–	–	–	–	–	–	–	–	–	–	–	–	–	–	–	–	–	–	(1)	–
44 Villarreal	–	–	–	–	–	–	–	–	–	–	–	–	–	–	–	–	(1)	–	–	–	–	–	–	–	–	–	–	–	(1)	–

LANCE RICHARDSON

DEBUT (Full Appearance)

Saturday 01/05/1926
Football League Division 1
at Old Trafford

Manchester United 3 West Bromwich Albion 2

CLUB CAREER RECORD	Apps	Subs	Goals
Premiership	0		0
League Division 1	38		0
League Division 2	0		0
FA Cup	4		0
League Cup	0		0
European Cup / Champions League	0		0
European Cup-Winners' Cup	0		0
UEFA Cup / Inter-Cities' Fairs Cup	0		0
Other Matches	0		0
OVERALL TOTAL	**42**		**0**

Opponents	PREM			FLD 1			FLD 2			FAC			LC			EC/CL			ECWC			UEFA			OTHER			TOTAL		
	A	S	G	A	S	G	A	S	G	A	S	G	A	S	G	A	S	G	A	S	G	A	S	G	A	S	G	A	S	G
1 Bury	–	–		2	–	–	–	–	–	2	–	–	–	–	–	–	–	–	–	–	–	–	–	–	–	–	–	4	–	
2 Sheffield United	–	–		4	–	–	–	–	–	–	–	–	–	–	–	–	–	–	–	–	–	–	–	–	–	–	–	4	–	
3 Everton	–	–		3	–	–	–	–	–	–	–	–	–	–	–	–	–	–	–	–	–	–	–	–	–	–	–	3	–	
4 Leicester City	–	–		3	–	–	–	–	–	–	–	–	–	–	–	–	–	–	–	–	–	–	–	–	–	–	–	3	–	
5 Portsmouth	–	–		3	–	–	–	–	–	–	–	–	–	–	–	–	–	–	–	–	–	–	–	–	–	–	–	3	–	
6 Aston Villa	–	–		2	–	–	–	–	–	–	–	–	–	–	–	–	–	–	–	–	–	–	–	–	–	–	–	2	–	
7 Blackburn Rovers	–	–		1	–	–	–	–	–	1	–	–	–	–	–	–	–	–	–	–	–	–	–	–	–	–	–	2	–	
8 Bolton Wanderers	–	–		2	–	–	–	–	–	–	–	–	–	–	–	–	–	–	–	–	–	–	–	–	–	–	–	2	–	
9 Burnley	–	–		2	–	–	–	–	–	–	–	–	–	–	–	–	–	–	–	–	–	–	–	–	–	–	–	2	–	
10 Cardiff City	–	–		2	–	–	–	–	–	–	–	–	–	–	–	–	–	–	–	–	–	–	–	–	–	–	–	2	–	
11 Derby County	–	–		2	–	–	–	–	–	–	–	–	–	–	–	–	–	–	–	–	–	–	–	–	–	–	–	2	–	
12 Tottenham Hotspur	–	–		2	–	–	–	–	–	–	–	–	–	–	–	–	–	–	–	–	–	–	–	–	–	–	–	2	–	
13 West Ham United	–	–		2	–	–	–	–	–	–	–	–	–	–	–	–	–	–	–	–	–	–	–	–	–	–	–	2	–	
14 Arsenal	–	–		1	–	–	–	–	–	–	–	–	–	–	–	–	–	–	–	–	–	–	–	–	–	–	–	1	–	
15 Birmingham City	–	–		1	–	–	–	–	–	–	–	–	–	–	–	–	–	–	–	–	–	–	–	–	–	–	–	1	–	
16 Brentford	–	–		–	–	–	–	–	–	1	–	–	–	–	–	–	–	–	–	–	–	–	–	–	–	–	–	1	–	
17 Huddersfield Town	–	–		1	–	–	–	–	–	–	–	–	–	–	–	–	–	–	–	–	–	–	–	–	–	–	–	1	–	
18 Liverpool	–	–		1	–	–	–	–	–	–	–	–	–	–	–	–	–	–	–	–	–	–	–	–	–	–	–	1	–	
19 Middlesbrough	–	–		1	–	–	–	–	–	–	–	–	–	–	–	–	–	–	–	–	–	–	–	–	–	–	–	1	–	
20 Newcastle United	–	–		1	–	–	–	–	–	–	–	–	–	–	–	–	–	–	–	–	–	–	–	–	–	–	–	1	–	
21 Sunderland	–	–		1	–	–	–	–	–	–	–	–	–	–	–	–	–	–	–	–	–	–	–	–	–	–	–	1	–	
22 West Bromwich Albion	–	–		1	–	–	–	–	–	–	–	–	–	–	–	–	–	–	–	–	–	–	–	–	–	–	–	1	–	

BILL RIDDING

DEBUT (Full Appearance)

Friday 25/12/1931
Football League Division 2
at Old Trafford

Manchester United 3 Wolverhampton Wanderers 2

CLUB CAREER RECORD	Apps	Subs	Goals
Premiership	0		0
League Division 1	0		0
League Division 2	42		14
FA Cup	2		0
League Cup	0		0
European Cup / Champions League	0		0
European Cup-Winners' Cup	0		0
UEFA Cup / Inter-Cities' Fairs Cup	0		0
Other Matches	0		0
OVERALL TOTAL	**44**		**14**

Opponents	PREM A S G	FLD 1 A S G	FLD 2 A S G	FAC A S G	LC A S G	EC/CL A S G	ECWC A S G	UEFA A S G	OTHER A S G	TOTAL A S G
1 Plymouth Argyle	- - -	- - -	3 2	1 -	- - -	- - -	- - -	- - -	- - -	4 2
2 Port Vale	- - -	- - -	3 2	- -	- - -	- - -	- - -	- - -	- - -	3 2
3 Bury	- - -	- - -	3 1	- -	- - -	- - -	- - -	- - -	- - -	3 1
4 Notts County	- - -	- - -	3 1	- -	- - -	- - -	- - -	- - -	- - -	3 1
5 Tottenham Hotspur	- - -	- - -	3 1	- -	- - -	- - -	- - -	- - -	- - -	3 1
6 Bradford Park Avenue	- - -	- - -	3 -	- -	- - -	- - -	- - -	- - -	- - -	3 -
7 Chesterfield	- - -	- - -	2 1	- -	- - -	- - -	- - -	- - -	- - -	2 1
8 Fulham	- - -	- - -	2 1	- -	- - -	- - -	- - -	- - -	- - -	2 1
9 Oldham Athletic	- - -	- - -	2 1	- -	- - -	- - -	- - -	- - -	- - -	2 1
10 Bradford City	- - -	- - -	2 -	- -	- - -	- - -	- - -	- - -	- - -	2 -
11 Charlton Athletic	- - -	- - -	2 -	- -	- - -	- - -	- - -	- - -	- - -	2 -
12 Southampton	- - -	- - -	2 -	- -	- - -	- - -	- - -	- - -	- - -	2 -
13 Stoke City	- - -	- - -	2 -	- -	- - -	- - -	- - -	- - -	- - -	2 -
14 Wolverhampton W.	- - -	- - -	2 -	- -	- - -	- - -	- - -	- - -	- - -	2 -
15 Burnley	- - -	- - -	1 2	- -	- - -	- - -	- - -	- - -	- - -	1 2
16 Leeds United	- - -	- - -	1 1	- -	- - -	- - -	- - -	- - -	- - -	1 1
17 West Ham United	- - -	- - -	1 1	- -	- - -	- - -	- - -	- - -	- - -	1 1
18 Grimsby Town	- - -	- - -	1 -	- -	- - -	- - -	- - -	- - -	- - -	1 -
19 Lincoln City	- - -	- - -	1 -	- -	- - -	- - -	- - -	- - -	- - -	1 -
20 Middlesbrough	- - -	- - -	- -	1 -	- - -	- - -	- - -	- - -	- - -	1 -
21 Millwall	- - -	- - -	1 -	- -	- - -	- - -	- - -	- - -	- - -	1 -
22 Preston North End	- - -	- - -	1 -	- -	- - -	- - -	- - -	- - -	- - -	1 -
23 Swansea City	- - -	- - -	1 -	- -	- - -	- - -	- - -	- - -	- - -	1 -

JOE RIDGWAY

DEBUT (Full Appearance)

Saturday 11/01/1896
Football League Division 2
at Bank Street

Newton Heath 3 Rotherham United 0

CLUB CAREER RECORD	Apps	Subs	Goals
Premiership	0		0
League Division 1	0		0
League Division 2	14		0
FA Cup	3		0
League Cup	0		0
European Cup / Champions League	0		0
European Cup-Winners' Cup	0		0
UEFA Cup / Inter-Cities' Fairs Cup	0		0
Other Matches	0		0
OVERALL TOTAL	**17**		**0**

Opponents	PREM A S G	FLD 1 A S G	FLD 2 A S G	FAC A S G	LC A S G	EC/CL A S G	ECWC A S G	UEFA A S G	OTHER A S G	TOTAL A S G
1 Burton Swifts	- - -	- - -	2 -	- -	- - -	- - -	- - -	- - -	- - -	2 -
2 Darwen	- - -	- - -	2 -	- -	- - -	- - -	- - -	- - -	- - -	2 -
3 Derby County	- - -	- - -	- -	2 -	- - -	- - -	- - -	- - -	- - -	2 -
4 Birmingham City	- - -	- - -	1 -	- -	- - -	- - -	- - -	- - -	- - -	1 -
5 Gainsborough Trinity	- - -	- - -	1 -	- -	- - -	- - -	- - -	- - -	- - -	1 -
6 Grimsby Town	- - -	- - -	1 -	- -	- - -	- - -	- - -	- - -	- - -	1 -
7 Kettering	- - -	- - -	- -	1 -	- - -	- - -	- - -	- - -	- - -	1 -
8 Leicester City	- - -	- - -	1 -	- -	- - -	- - -	- - -	- - -	- - -	1 -
9 Lincoln City	- - -	- - -	1 -	- -	- - -	- - -	- - -	- - -	- - -	1 -
10 Loughborough Town	- - -	- - -	1 -	- -	- - -	- - -	- - -	- - -	- - -	1 -
11 Luton Town	- - -	- - -	1 -	- -	- - -	- - -	- - -	- - -	- - -	1 -
12 Port Vale	- - -	- - -	1 -	- -	- - -	- - -	- - -	- - -	- - -	1 -
13 Rotherham United	- - -	- - -	1 -	- -	- - -	- - -	- - -	- - -	- - -	1 -
14 Walsall	- - -	- - -	1 -	- -	- - -	- - -	- - -	- - -	- - -	1 -

JIMMY RIMMER

DEBUT (Full Appearance)

Monday 15/04/1968
Football League Division 1
at Old Trafford

Manchester United 3 Fulham 0

CLUB CAREER RECORD	Apps	Subs	Goals
Premiership	0		0
League Division 1	34		0
League Division 2	0		0
FA Cup	3		0
League Cup	6		0
European Cup / Champions League	2	(1)	0
European Cup-Winners' Cup	0		0
UEFA Cup / Inter-Cities' Fairs Cup	0		0
Other Matches	0		0
OVERALL TOTAL	45	(1)	0

Opponents	PREM			FLD 1			FLD 2			FAC			LC			EC/CL			ECWC			UEFA			OTHER			TOTAL		
	A	S	G	A	S	G	A	S	G	A	S	G	A	S	G	A	S	G	A	S	G	A	S	G	A	S	G	A	S	G
1 Burnley	-	-	-	3	-	-	-	-	-	-	-	-	-	-	-	-	-	-	-	-	-	-	-	-	-	-	-	3	-	-
2 Crystal Palace	-	-	-	2	-	-	-	-	-	-	-	-	1	-	-	-	-	-	-	-	-	-	-	-	-	-	-	3	-	-
3 Newcastle United	-	-	-	3	-	-	-	-	-	-	-	-	-	-	-	-	-	-	-	-	-	-	-	-	-	-	-	3	-	-
4 Southampton	-	-	-	3	-	-	-	-	-	-	-	-	-	-	-	-	-	-	-	-	-	-	-	-	-	-	-	3	-	-
5 AC Milan	-	-	-	-	-	-	-	-	-	-	-	-	-	-	-	2	-	-	-	-	-	-	-	-	-	-	-	2	-	-
6 Aston Villa	-	-	-	-	-	-	-	-	-	-	-	-	2	-	-	-	-	-	-	-	-	-	-	-	-	-	-	2	-	-
7 Everton	-	-	-	2	-	-	-	-	-	-	-	-	-	-	-	-	-	-	-	-	-	-	-	-	-	-	-	2	-	-
8 Middlesbrough	-	-	-	-	-	-	-	-	-	2	-	-	-	-	-	-	-	-	-	-	-	-	-	-	-	-	-	2	-	-
9 Tottenham Hotspur	-	-	-	2	-	-	-	-	-	-	-	-	-	-	-	-	-	-	-	-	-	-	-	-	-	-	-	2	-	-
10 West Ham United	-	-	-	2	-	-	-	-	-	-	-	-	-	-	-	-	-	-	-	-	-	-	-	-	-	-	-	2	-	-
11 Aldershot	-	-	-	-	-	-	-	-	-	-	-	-	1	-	-	-	-	-	-	-	-	-	-	-	-	-	-	1	-	-
12 Arsenal	-	-	-	1	-	-	-	-	-	-	-	-	-	-	-	-	-	-	-	-	-	-	-	-	-	-	-	1	-	-
13 Birmingham City	-	-	-	1	-	-	-	-	-	-	-	-	-	-	-	-	-	-	-	-	-	-	-	-	-	-	-	1	-	-
14 Blackpool	-	-	-	1	-	-	-	-	-	-	-	-	-	-	-	-	-	-	-	-	-	-	-	-	-	-	-	1	-	-
15 Chelsea	-	-	-	-	-	-	-	-	-	-	-	-	1	-	-	-	-	-	-	-	-	-	-	-	-	-	-	1	-	-
16 Coventry City	-	-	-	1	-	-	-	-	-	-	-	-	-	-	-	-	-	-	-	-	-	-	-	-	-	-	-	1	-	-
17 Derby County	-	-	-	1	-	-	-	-	-	-	-	-	-	-	-	-	-	-	-	-	-	-	-	-	-	-	-	1	-	-
18 Fulham	-	-	-	1	-	-	-	-	-	-	-	-	-	-	-	-	-	-	-	-	-	-	-	-	-	-	-	1	-	-
19 Huddersfield Town	-	-	-	1	-	-	-	-	-	-	-	-	-	-	-	-	-	-	-	-	-	-	-	-	-	-	-	1	-	-
20 Ipswich Town	-	-	-	1	-	-	-	-	-	-	-	-	-	-	-	-	-	-	-	-	-	-	-	-	-	-	-	1	-	-
21 Leeds United	-	-	-	1	-	-	-	-	-	-	-	-	-	-	-	-	-	-	-	-	-	-	-	-	-	-	-	1	-	-
22 Leicester City	-	-	-	1	-	-	-	-	-	-	-	-	-	-	-	-	-	-	-	-	-	-	-	-	-	-	-	1	-	-
23 Liverpool	-	-	-	1	-	-	-	-	-	-	-	-	-	-	-	-	-	-	-	-	-	-	-	-	-	-	-	1	-	-
24 Manchester City	-	-	-	1	-	-	-	-	-	-	-	-	-	-	-	-	-	-	-	-	-	-	-	-	-	-	-	1	-	-
25 Nottingham Forest	-	-	-	1	-	-	-	-	-	-	-	-	-	-	-	-	-	-	-	-	-	-	-	-	-	-	-	1	-	-
26 Portsmouth	-	-	-	-	-	-	-	-	-	-	-	-	1	-	-	-	-	-	-	-	-	-	-	-	-	-	-	1	-	-
27 Stoke City	-	-	-	1	-	-	-	-	-	-	-	-	-	-	-	-	-	-	-	-	-	-	-	-	-	-	-	1	-	-
28 Sunderland	-	-	-	1	-	-	-	-	-	-	-	-	-	-	-	-	-	-	-	-	-	-	-	-	-	-	-	1	-	-
29 Watford	-	-	-	-	-	-	-	-	-	1	-	-	-	-	-	-	-	-	-	-	-	-	-	-	-	-	-	1	-	-
30 West Bromwich Albion	-	-	-	1	-	-	-	-	-	-	-	-	-	-	-	-	-	-	-	-	-	-	-	-	-	-	-	1	-	-
31 Wolverhampton W.	-	-	-	1	-	-	-	-	-	-	-	-	-	-	-	-	-	-	-	-	-	-	-	-	-	-	-	1	-	-
32 Waterford	-	-	-	-	-	-	-	-	-	-	-	-	-	-	-	-	(1)	-	-	-	-	-	-	-	-	-	-	-	(1)	-

ANDY RITCHIE

DEBUT (Full Appearance)

Monday 26/12/1977
Football League Division 1
at Goodison Park

Everton 2 Manchester United 6

CLUB CAREER RECORD	Apps	Subs	Goals
Premiership	0		0
League Division 1	26	(7)	13
League Division 2	0		0
FA Cup	3	(1)	0
League Cup	3	(2)	0
European Cup / Champions League	0		0
European Cup-Winners' Cup	0		0
UEFA Cup / Inter-Cities' Fairs Cup	0		0
Other Matches	0		0
OVERALL TOTAL	32	(10)	13

Opponents	PREM			FLD 1			FLD 2			FAC			LC			EC/CL			ECWC			UEFA			OTHER			TOTAL		
	A	S	G	A	S	G	A	S	G	A	S	G	A	S	G	A	S	G	A	S	G	A	S	G	A	S	G	A	S	G
1 Tottenham Hotspur	-	-	-	3	-	4	-	-	-	1	-	-	1	(1)	-	-	-	-	-	-	-	-	-	-	-	-	-	5	(1)	4
2 Coventry City	-	-	-	2	-	-	-	-	-	-	-	-	2	-	-	-	-	-	-	-	-	-	-	-	-	-	-	4	-	-
3 Derby County	-	-	-	3	-	2	-	-	-	-	-	-	-	-	-	-	-	-	-	-	-	-	-	-	-	-	-	3	-	2
4 Bolton Wanderers	-	-	-	2	(1)	-	-	-	-	-	-	-	-	-	-	-	-	-	-	-	-	-	-	-	-	-	-	2	(1)	-
5 Liverpool	-	-	-	2	-	-	-	-	-	-	(1)	-	-	-	-	-	-	-	-	-	-	-	-	-	-	-	-	2	(1)	-
6 Birmingham City	-	-	-	2	-	-	-	-	-	-	-	-	-	-	-	-	-	-	-	-	-	-	-	-	-	-	-	2	-	-
7 Leeds United	-	-	-	1	(1)	3	-	-	-	-	-	-	-	-	-	-	-	-	-	-	-	-	-	-	-	-	-	1	(1)	3
8 Bristol City	-	-	-	1	(1)	1	-	-	-	-	-	-	-	-	-	-	-	-	-	-	-	-	-	-	-	-	-	1	(1)	1
9 Wolverhampton W.	-	-	-	1	(1)	1	-	-	-	-	-	-	-	-	-	-	-	-	-	-	-	-	-	-	-	-	-	1	(1)	1
10 Norwich City	-	-	-	1	-	-	-	-	-	-	-	-	-	(1)	-	-	-	-	-	-	-	-	-	-	-	-	-	1	(1)	-
11 West Bromwich Albion	-	-	-	1	(1)	-	-	-	-	-	-	-	-	-	-	-	-	-	-	-	-	-	-	-	-	-	-	1	(1)	-
12 Manchester City	-	-	-	1	-	1	-	-	-	-	-	-	-	-	-	-	-	-	-	-	-	-	-	-	-	-	-	1	-	1
13 Southampton	-	-	-	1	-	1	-	-	-	-	-	-	-	-	-	-	-	-	-	-	-	-	-	-	-	-	-	1	-	1
14 Aston Villa	-	-	-	1	-	-	-	-	-	-	-	-	-	-	-	-	-	-	-	-	-	-	-	-	-	-	-	1	-	-
15 Colchester United	-	-	-	-	-	-	-	-	-	1	-	-	-	-	-	-	-	-	-	-	-	-	-	-	-	-	-	1	-	-
16 Everton	-	-	-	1	-	-	-	-	-	-	-	-	-	-	-	-	-	-	-	-	-	-	-	-	-	-	-	1	-	-
17 Fulham	-	-	-	-	-	-	-	-	-	1	-	-	-	-	-	-	-	-	-	-	-	-	-	-	-	-	-	1	-	-
18 Leicester City	-	-	-	1	-	-	-	-	-	-	-	-	-	-	-	-	-	-	-	-	-	-	-	-	-	-	-	1	-	-
19 Queens Park Rangers	-	-	-	1	-	-	-	-	-	-	-	-	-	-	-	-	-	-	-	-	-	-	-	-	-	-	-	1	-	-
20 Sunderland	-	-	-	1	-	-	-	-	-	-	-	-	-	-	-	-	-	-	-	-	-	-	-	-	-	-	-	1	-	-
21 Arsenal	-	-	-	-	(1)	-	-	-	-	-	-	-	-	-	-	-	-	-	-	-	-	-	-	-	-	-	-	-	(1)	-
22 Stoke City	-	-	-	-	(1)	-	-	-	-	-	-	-	-	-	-	-	-	-	-	-	-	-	-	-	-	-	-	-	(1)	-

JOHN ROACH

DEBUT (Full Appearance)

Saturday 05/01/1946
FA Cup 3rd Round 1st Leg
at Peel Park

Accrington Stanley 2 Manchester United 2

CLUB CAREER RECORD	Apps	Subs	Goals
Premiership	0		0
League Division 1	0		0
League Division 2	0		0
FA Cup	2		0
League Cup	0		0
European Cup / Champions League	0		0
European Cup-Winners' Cup	0		0
UEFA Cup / Inter-Cities' Fairs Cup	0		0
Other Matches	0		0
OVERALL TOTAL	**2**		**0**

Opponents	PREM A S G	FLD 1 A S G	FLD 2 A S G	FAC A S G	LC A S G	EC/CL A S G	ECWC A S G	UEFA A S G	OTHER A S G	TOTAL A S G
1 Accrington Stanley	– – –	– – –	– – –	2 – –	– – –	– – –	– – –	– – –	– – –	2 –

DAVID ROBBIE

DEBUT (Full Appearance)

Saturday 28/09/1935
Football League Division 2
at The Dell

Southampton 2 Manchester United 1

CLUB CAREER RECORD	Apps	Subs	Goals
Premiership	0		0
League Division 1	0		0
League Division 2	1		0
FA Cup	0		0
League Cup	0		0
European Cup / Champions League	0		0
European Cup-Winners' Cup	0		0
UEFA Cup / Inter-Cities' Fairs Cup	0		0
Other Matches	0		0
OVERALL TOTAL	**1**		**0**

Opponents	PREM A S G	FLD 1 A S G	FLD 2 A S G	FAC A S G	LC A S G	EC/CL A S G	ECWC A S G	UEFA A S G	OTHER A S G	TOTAL A S G
1 Southampton	– – –	– – –	1 – –	– – –	– – –	– – –	– – –	– – –	– – –	1 –

CHARLIE ROBERTS

DEBUT (Full Appearance)

Saturday 23/04/1904
Football League Division 2
at Bank Street

Manchester United 2 Burton United 0

CLUB CAREER RECORD	Apps	Subs	Goals
Premiership	0		0
League Division 1	207		13
League Division 2	64		9
FA Cup	28		1
League Cup	0		0
European Cup / Champions League	0		0
European Cup-Winners' Cup	0		0
UEFA Cup / Inter-Cities' Fairs Cup	0		0
Other Matches	3		0
OVERALL TOTAL	**302**		**23**

Opponents	PREM A S G	FLD 1 A S G	FLD 2 A S G	FAC A S G	LC A S G	EC/CL A S G	ECWC A S G	UEFA A S G	OTHER A S G	TOTAL A S G
1 Liverpool	– –	13 2	2 1	– –	– –	– –	– –	– –	– –	15 3
2 Bristol City	– –	8 1	4 1	1 –	– –	– –	– –	– –	– –	13 2
3 Aston Villa	– –	10 1	– –	3 –	– –	– –	– –	– –	– –	13 1
4 Blackburn Rovers	– –	10 –	– –	3 –	– –	– –	– –	– –	– –	13 –
5 Newcastle United	– –	11 2	– –	1 –	– –	– –	– –	– –	– –	12 2
6 Everton	– –	11 1	– –	1 –	– –	– –	– –	– –	– –	12 1
7 Manchester City	– –	12 1	– –	– –	– –	– –	– –	– –	– –	12 1
8 Middlesbrough	– –	12 –	– –	– –	– –	– –	– –	– –	– –	12 –
9 Notts County	– –	11 1	– –	– –	– –	– –	– –	– –	– –	11 1
10 Preston North End	– –	11 1	– –	– –	– –	– –	– –	– –	– –	11 1
11 Arsenal	– –	10 –	– –	1 –	– –	– –	– –	– –	– –	11 –
12 Sunderland	– –	11 –	– –	– –	– –	– –	– –	– –	– –	11 –
13 Bolton Wanderers	– –	7 –	3 –	– –	– –	– –	– –	– –	– –	10 –
14 Bury	– –	10 –	– –	– –	– –	– –	– –	– –	– –	10 –
15 Sheffield United	– –	10 –	– –	– –	– –	– –	– –	– –	– –	10 –
16 Bradford City	– –	6 –	3 3	– –	– –	– –	– –	– –	– –	9 3
17 West Bromwich Albion	– –	4 1	4 –	– –	– –	– –	– –	– –	– –	8 1
18 Oldham Athletic	– –	6 –	– –	2 –	– –	– –	– –	– –	– –	8 –
19 Sheffield Wednesday	– –	8 –	– –	– –	– –	– –	– –	– –	– –	8 –
20 Nottingham Forest	– –	7 –	– –	– –	– –	– –	– –	– –	– –	7 –
21 Tottenham Hotspur	– –	6 2	– –	– –	– –	– –	– –	– –	– –	6 2
22 Chelsea	– –	4 –	1 –	1 –	– –	– –	– –	– –	– –	6 –
23 Blackpool	– –	– –	4 1	1 –	– –	– –	– –	– –	– –	5 1
24 Burton United	– –	– –	5 –	– –	– –	– –	– –	– –	– –	5 –
25 Port Vale	– –	– –	4 1	– –	– –	– –	– –	– –	– –	4 1
26 Burnley	– –	– –	2 –	2 –	– –	– –	– –	– –	– –	4 –
27 Chesterfield	– –	– –	4 –	– –	– –	– –	– –	– –	– –	4 –
28 Derby County	– –	4 –	– –	– –	– –	– –	– –	– –	– –	4 –
29 Grimsby Town	– –	– –	4 –	– –	– –	– –	– –	– –	– –	4 –
30 Leicester City	– –	– –	4 –	– –	– –	– –	– –	– –	– –	4 –
31 Glossop	– –	– –	3 1	– –	– –	– –	– –	– –	– –	3 1

continued../

CHARLIE ROBERTS (continued)

Opponents	PREM A S G	FLD 1 A S G	FLD 2 A S G	FAC A S G	LC A S G	EC/CL A S G	ECWC A S G	UEFA A S G	OTHER A S G	TOTAL A S G
32 Lincoln City	–	–	3 – 1	–	–	–	–	–	–	3 – 1
33 Birmingham City	–	3 – –	–	–	–	–	–	–	–	3 – –
34 Gainsborough Trinity	–	–	3 – –	–	–	–	–	–	–	3 – –
35 Coventry City	–	–	–	2 – 1	–	–	–	–	–	2 – 1
36 Barnsley	–	–	–	2 – –	–	–	–	–	–	2 – –
37 Hull City	–	–	–	2 – –	–	–	–	–	–	2 – –
38 Leeds United	–	–	–	2 – –	–	–	–	–	–	2 – –
39 Leyton Orient	–	–	–	2 – –	–	–	–	–	–	2 – –
40 Queens Park Rangers	–	–	–	–	–	–	–	–	2 – –	2 – –
41 Reading	–	–	–	–	2 – –	–	–	–	–	2 – –
42 Stockport County	–	–	2 – –	–	–	–	–	–	–	2 – –
43 Stoke City	–	2 – –	–	–	–	–	–	–	–	2 – –
44 Brighton	–	–	–	–	1 – –	–	–	–	–	1 – –
45 Doncaster Rovers	–	–	–	1 – –	–	–	–	–	–	1 – –
46 Fulham	–	–	–	–	1 – –	–	–	–	–	1 – –
47 Huddersfield Town	–	–	–	1 – –	–	–	–	–	–	1 – –
48 Norwich City	–	–	–	–	1 – –	–	–	–	–	1 – –
49 Plymouth Argyle	–	–	–	1 – –	–	–	–	–	–	1 – –
50 Portsmouth	–	–	–	–	1 – –	–	–	–	–	1 – –
51 Staple Hill	–	–	–	1 – –	–	–	–	–	–	1 – –
52 Swindon Town	–	–	–	–	–	–	–	–	1 – –	1 – –
53 West Ham United	–	–	–	1 – –	–	–	–	–	–	1 – –

ROBERT ROBERTS

DEBUT (Full Appearance)

Saturday 27/12/1913
Football League Division 1
at Old Trafford

Manchester United 2 Sheffield Wednesday 1

CLUB CAREER RECORD	Apps	Subs	Goals
Premiership	0		0
League Division 1	2		0
League Division 2	0		0
FA Cup	0		0
League Cup	0		0
European Cup / Champions League	0		0
European Cup-Winners' Cup	0		0
UEFA Cup / Inter-Cities' Fairs Cup	0		0
Other Matches	0		0
OVERALL TOTAL	2		0

Opponents	PREM A S G	FLD 1 A S G	FLD 2 A S G	FAC A S G	LC A S G	EC/CL A S G	ECWC A S G	UEFA A S G	OTHER A S G	TOTAL A S G
1 Bolton Wanderers	–	1 – –	–	–	–	–	–	–	–	1 – –
2 Sheffield Wednesday	–	1 – –	–	–	–	–	–	–	–	1 – –

W ROBERTS

DEBUT (Full Appearance)

Saturday 18/02/1899
Football League Division 2
at The Athletic Ground

Loughborough Town 0 Newton Heath 1

CLUB CAREER RECORD	Apps	Subs	Goals
Premiership	0		0
League Division 1	0		0
League Division 2	9		2
FA Cup	1		0
League Cup	0		0
European Cup / Champions League	0		0
European Cup-Winners' Cup	0		0
UEFA Cup / Inter-Cities' Fairs Cup	0		0
Other Matches	0		0
OVERALL TOTAL	10		2

Opponents	PREM A S G	FLD 1 A S G	FLD 2 A S G	FAC A S G	LC A S G	EC/CL A S G	ECWC A S G	UEFA A S G	OTHER A S G	TOTAL A S G
1 New Brighton Tower	–	–	2 – –	–	–	–	–	–	–	2 – –
2 Arsenal	–	–	1 – 1	–	–	–	–	–	–	1 – 1
3 Birmingham City	–	–	1 – 1	–	–	–	–	–	–	1 – 1
4 Burton Swifts	–	–	1 – –	–	–	–	–	–	–	1 – –
5 Chesterfield	–	–	1 – –	–	–	–	–	–	–	1 – –
6 Lincoln City	–	–	1 – –	–	–	–	–	–	–	1 – –
7 Loughborough Town	–	–	1 – –	–	–	–	–	–	–	1 – –
8 Sheffield Wednesday	–	–	1 – –	–	–	–	–	–	–	1 – –
9 South Shore	–	–	–	1 – –	–	–	–	–	–	1 – –

ALEX ROBERTSON

DEBUT (Full Appearance)

Saturday 05/09/1903
Football League Division 2
at Bank Street

Manchester United 2 Bristol City 2

CLUB CAREER RECORD	Apps	Subs	Goals
Premiership	0		0
League Division 1	0		0
League Division 2	28		10
FA Cup	6		0
League Cup	0		0
European Cup / Champions League	0		0
European Cup-Winners' Cup	0		0
UEFA Cup / Inter-Cities' Fairs Cup	0		0
Other Matches	0		0
OVERALL TOTAL	**34**		**10**

Opponents	PREM A S G	FLD 1 A S G	FLD 2 A S G	FAC A S G	LC A S G	EC/CL A S G	ECWC A S G	UEFA A S G	OTHER A S G	TOTAL A S G
1 Gainsborough Trinity	– – –	– – –	2 2	– – –	– – –	– – –	– – –	– – –	– – –	2 2
2 Grimsby Town	– – –	– – –	2 2	– – –	– – –	– – –	– – –	– – –	– – –	2 2
3 Barnsley	– – –	– – –	2 1	– – –	– – –	– – –	– – –	– – –	– – –	2 1
4 Chesterfield	– – –	– – –	2 1	– – –	– – –	– – –	– – –	– – –	– – –	2 1
5 Leicester City	– – –	– – –	2 1	– – –	– – –	– – –	– – –	– – –	– – –	2 1
6 Birmingham City	– – –	– – –	– –	2 –	– – –	– – –	– – –	– – –	– – –	2 –
7 Bolton Wanderers	– – –	– – –	2 –	– – –	– – –	– – –	– – –	– – –	– – –	2 –
8 Bradford City	– – –	– – –	2 –	– – –	– – –	– – –	– – –	– – –	– – –	2 –
9 Bristol City	– – –	– – –	2 –	– – –	– – –	– – –	– – –	– – –	– – –	2 –
10 Lincoln City	– – –	– – –	2 –	– – –	– – –	– – –	– – –	– – –	– – –	2 –
11 Notts County	– – –	– – –	– –	2 –	– – –	– – –	– – –	– – –	– – –	2 –
12 Port Vale	– – –	– – –	2 –	– – –	– – –	– – –	– – –	– – –	– – –	2 –
13 Stockport County	– – –	– – –	2 –	– – –	– – –	– – –	– – –	– – –	– – –	2 –
14 Arsenal	– – –	– – –	1 1	– – –	– – –	– – –	– – –	– – –	– – –	1 1
15 Burton United	– – –	– – –	1 1	– – –	– – –	– – –	– – –	– – –	– – –	1 1
16 Glossop	– – –	– – –	1 1	– – –	– – –	– – –	– – –	– – –	– – –	1 1
17 Blackpool	– – –	– – –	1 –	– – –	– – –	– – –	– – –	– – –	– – –	1 –
18 Burnley	– – –	– – –	1 –	– – –	– – –	– – –	– – –	– – –	– – –	1 –
19 Fulham	– – –	– – –	– –	1 –	– – –	– – –	– – –	– – –	– – –	1 –
20 Preston North End	– – –	– – –	1 –	– – –	– – –	– – –	– – –	– – –	– – –	1 –
21 Sheffield Wednesday	– – –	– – –	– –	1 –	– – –	– – –	– – –	– – –	– – –	1 –

SANDY ROBERTSON

DEBUT (Full Appearance)

Saturday 05/09/1903
Football League Division 2
at Bank Street

Manchester United 2 Bristol City 2

CLUB CAREER RECORD	Apps	Subs	Goals
Premiership	0		0
League Division 1	0		0
League Division 2	33		1
FA Cup	2		0
League Cup	0		0
European Cup / Champions League	0		0
European Cup-Winners' Cup	0		0
UEFA Cup / Inter-Cities' Fairs Cup	0		0
Other Matches	0		0
OVERALL TOTAL	**35**		**1**

Opponents	PREM A S G	FLD 1 A S G	FLD 2 A S G	FAC A S G	LC A S G	EC/CL A S G	ECWC A S G	UEFA A S G	OTHER A S G	TOTAL A S G
1 Bristol City	– – –	– – –	3 1	– – –	– – –	– – –	– – –	– – –	– – –	3 1
2 Barnsley	– – –	– – –	2 –	– – –	– – –	– – –	– – –	– – –	– – –	2 –
3 Blackpool	– – –	– – –	2 –	– – –	– – –	– – –	– – –	– – –	– – –	2 –
4 Bolton Wanderers	– – –	– – –	2 –	– – –	– – –	– – –	– – –	– – –	– – –	2 –
5 Bradford City	– – –	– – –	2 –	– – –	– – –	– – –	– – –	– – –	– – –	2 –
6 Burnley	– – –	– – –	2 –	– – –	– – –	– – –	– – –	– – –	– – –	2 –
7 Burton United	– – –	– – –	2 –	– – –	– – –	– – –	– – –	– – –	– – –	2 –
8 Gainsborough Trinity	– – –	– – –	2 –	– – –	– – –	– – –	– – –	– – –	– – –	2 –
9 Glossop	– – –	– – –	2 –	– – –	– – –	– – –	– – –	– – –	– – –	2 –
10 Grimsby Town	– – –	– – –	2 –	– – –	– – –	– – –	– – –	– – –	– – –	2 –
11 Leicester City	– – –	– – –	2 –	– – –	– – –	– – –	– – –	– – –	– – –	2 –
12 Port Vale	– – –	– – –	2 –	– – –	– – –	– – –	– – –	– – –	– – –	2 –
13 Preston North End	– – –	– – –	2 –	– – –	– – –	– – –	– – –	– – –	– – –	2 –
14 Stockport County	– – –	– – –	2 –	– – –	– – –	– – –	– – –	– – –	– – –	2 –
15 Arsenal	– – –	– – –	1 –	– – –	– – –	– – –	– – –	– – –	– – –	1 –
16 Birmingham City	– – –	– – –	– –	1 –	– – –	– – –	– – –	– – –	– – –	1 –
17 Chesterfield	– – –	– – –	1 –	– – –	– – –	– – –	– – –	– – –	– – –	1 –
18 Doncaster Rovers	– – –	– – –	1 –	– – –	– – –	– – –	– – –	– – –	– – –	1 –
19 Notts County	– – –	– – –	– –	1 –	– – –	– – –	– – –	– – –	– – –	1 –
20 West Bromwich Albion	– – –	– – –	1 –	– – –	– – –	– – –	– – –	– – –	– – –	1 –

THOMAS ROBERTSON

DEBUT (Full Appearance)

Saturday 05/09/1903
Football League Division 2
at Bank Street

Manchester United 2 Bristol City 2

CLUB CAREER RECORD	Apps	Subs	Goals
Premiership	0		0
League Division 1	0		0
League Division 2	3		0
FA Cup	0		0
League Cup	0		0
European Cup / Champions League	0		0
European Cup-Winners' Cup	0		0
UEFA Cup / Inter-Cities' Fairs Cup	0		0
Other Matches	0		0
OVERALL TOTAL	**3**		**0**

Opponents	PREM A S G	FLD 1 A S G	FLD 2 A S G	FAC A S G	LC A S G	EC/CL A S G	ECWC A S G	UEFA A S G	OTHER A S G	TOTAL A S G
1 Bristol City	– –	– –	1 –	–	–	–	–	–	–	1 –
2 Burnley	– –	– –	1 –	–	–	–	–	–	–	1 –
3 Port Vale	– –	– –	1 –	–	–	–	–	–	–	1 –

WILLIAM ROBERTSON

DEBUT (Full Appearance)

Saturday 17/03/1934
Football League Division 2
at Old Trafford

Manchester United 1 Fulham 0

CLUB CAREER RECORD	Apps	Subs	Goals
Premiership	0		0
League Division 1	0		0
League Division 2	47		1
FA Cup	3		0
League Cup	0		0
European Cup / Champions League	0		0
European Cup-Winners' Cup	0		0
UEFA Cup / Inter-Cities' Fairs Cup	0		0
Other Matches	0		0
OVERALL TOTAL	**50**		**1**

Opponents	PREM A S G	FLD 1 A S G	FLD 2 A S G	FAC A S G	LC A S G	EC/CL A S G	ECWC A S G	UEFA A S G	OTHER A S G	TOTAL A S G
1 Blackpool	– –	– –	4 –	–	–	–	–	–	–	4 –
2 Nottingham Forest	– –	– –	2 –	2 –	–	–	–	–	–	4 –
3 West Ham United	– –	– –	4 –	–	–	–	–	–	–	4 –
4 Bradford City	– –	– –	3 –	–	–	–	–	–	–	3 –
5 Notts County	– –	– –	3 –	–	–	–	–	–	–	3 –
6 Southampton	– –	– –	3 –	–	–	–	–	–	–	3 –
7 Swansea City	– –	– –	3 –	–	–	–	–	–	–	3 –
8 Bradford Park Avenue	– –	– –	2 1	–	–	–	–	–	–	2 1
9 Brentford	– –	– –	2 –	–	–	–	–	–	–	2 –
10 Bury	– –	– –	2 –	–	–	–	–	–	–	2 –
11 Fulham	– –	– –	2 –	–	–	–	–	–	–	2 –
12 Hull City	– –	– –	2 –	–	–	–	–	–	–	2 –
13 Newcastle United	– –	– –	2 –	–	–	–	–	–	–	2 –
14 Norwich City	– –	– –	2 –	–	–	–	–	–	–	2 –
15 Plymouth Argyle	– –	– –	2 –	–	–	–	–	–	–	2 –
16 Port Vale	– –	– –	2 –	–	–	–	–	–	–	2 –
17 Sheffield United	– –	– –	2 –	–	–	–	–	–	–	2 –
18 Barnsley	– –	– –	1 –	–	–	–	–	–	–	1 –
19 Bolton Wanderers	– –	– –	1 –	–	–	–	–	–	–	1 –
20 Bristol Rovers	– –	– –	– –	1 –	–	–	–	–	–	1 –
21 Burnley	– –	– –	1 –	–	–	–	–	–	–	1 –
22 Millwall	– –	– –	1 –	–	–	–	–	–	–	1 –
23 Oldham Athletic	– –	– –	1 –	–	–	–	–	–	–	1 –

MARK ROBINS

DEBUT (Substitute Appearance)

Wednesday 12/10/1988
League Cup 2nd Round 2nd Leg
at Old Trafford

Manchester United 5 Rotherham United 0

CLUB CAREER RECORD	Apps	Subs	Goals
Premiership	0		0
League Division 1	19	(29)	11
League Division 2	0		0
FA Cup	4	(4)	3
League Cup	0	(7)	2
European Cup / Champions League	0		0
European Cup-Winners' Cup	4	(2)	1
UEFA Cup / Inter-Cities' Fairs Cup	0		0
Other Matches	0	(1)	0
OVERALL TOTAL	**27**	**(43)**	**17**

Opponents	PREM A S G	FLD 1 A S G	FLD 2 A S G	FAC A S G	LC A S G	EC/CL A S G	ECWC A S G	UEFA A S G	OTHER A S G	TOTAL A S G
1 Queens Park Rangers	– –	2 (3) 3	– –	1 –	–	–	–	–	–	3 (3) 3
2 Wimbledon	– –	2 (2) 1	– –	–	–	–	–	–	–	2 (2) 1
3 Southampton	– –	1 (2) 1	– –	–	– (1) –	–	–	–	–	1 (3) 1
4 Nottingham Forest	– –	2 –	– –	1 1	–	–	–	–	–	3 1
5 Luton Town	– –	2 (1) 3	– –	–	–	–	–	–	–	2 (1) 3
6 Sheffield United	– –	1 (1) –	– –	1 –	–	–	–	–	–	2 (1) –
7 Aston Villa	– –	1 (2) 2	– –	–	–	–	–	–	–	1 (2) 2
8 Newcastle United	– –	– (2) –	– –	1 1	–	–	–	–	–	1 (2) 1
9 Liverpool	– –	1 (1) –	– –	–	–	–	–	–	– (1) –	1 (2) –

continued../

MARK ROBINS (continued)

Opponents	PREM A S G	FLD 1 A S G	FLD 2 A S G	FAC A S G	LC A S G	EC/CL A S G	ECWC A S G	UEFA A S G	OTHER A S G	TOTAL A S G
10 Norwich City	– –	1 (2) –	–	–	–	–	–	–	–	1 (2) –
11 Tottenham Hotspur	– –	1 (2) –	–	–	–	–	–	–	–	1 (2) –
12 Derby County	– –	2 –	–	–	–	–	–	–	–	2 –
13 Wrexham	– –	–	–	–	–	–	1 (1) 1	–	–	1 (1) 1
14 Arsenal	– –	1 (1) –	–	–	–	–	–	–	–	1 (1) –
15 Athinaikos	– –	–	–	–	–	–	1 (1) –	–	–	1 (1) –
16 Crystal Palace	– –	1 –	–	– (1)	–	–	–	–	–	1 (1) –
17 Everton	– –	1 (1) –	–	–	–	–	–	–	–	1 (1) –
18 Coventry City	– –	– (2) 1	–	–	–	–	–	–	–	– (2) 1
19 Oldham Athletic	– –	–	–	– (2) 1	–	–	–	–	–	– (2) 1
20 Halifax Town	– –	–	–	–	– (2)	–	–	–	–	– (2) –
21 Middlesbrough	– –	– (1) –	–	–	– (1)	–	–	–	–	– (2) –
22 Sunderland	– –	– (2) –	–	–	–	–	–	–	–	– (2) –
23 Athletico Madrid	– –	–	–	–	–	–	1 –	–	–	1 –
24 Pecsi Munkas	– –	–	–	–	–	–	1 –	–	–	1 –
25 Portsmouth	– –	–	–	–	– (1) 2	–	–	–	–	– (1) 2
26 Bolton Wanderers	– –	–	–	– (1) –	–	–	–	–	–	– (1) –
27 Cambridge United	– –	–	–	–	– (1) –	–	–	–	–	– (1) –
28 Charlton Athletic	– –	– (1) –	–	–	–	–	–	–	–	– (1) –
29 Manchester City	– –	– (1) –	–	–	–	–	–	–	–	– (1) –
30 Millwall	– –	– (1) –	–	–	–	–	–	–	–	– (1) –
31 Notts County	– –	– (1) –	–	–	–	–	–	–	–	– (1) –
32 Rotherham United	– –	–	–	–	– (1) –	–	–	–	–	– (1) –

JAMES ROBINSON

DEBUT (Full Appearance)

Saturday 03/01/1920
Football League Division 1
at Old Trafford

Manchester United 0 Chelsea 2

CLUB CAREER RECORD	Apps	Subs	Goals
Premiership	0		0
League Division 1	21		3
League Division 2	0		0
FA Cup	0		0
League Cup	0		0
European Cup / Champions League	0		0
European Cup–Winners' Cup	0		0
UEFA Cup / Inter–Cities' Fairs Cup	0		0
Other Matches	0		0
OVERALL TOTAL	21		3

Opponents	PREM A S G	FLD 1 A S G	FLD 2 A S G	FAC A S G	LC A S G	EC/CL A S G	ECWC A S G	UEFA A S G	OTHER A S G	TOTAL A S G
1 Sunderland	–	3 1	–	–	–	–	–	–	–	3 1
2 Chelsea	–	3 –	–	–	–	–	–	–	–	3 –
3 Bradford City	–	2 1	–	–	–	–	–	–	–	2 1
4 West Bromwich Albion	–	2 1	–	–	–	–	–	–	–	2 1
5 Everton	–	2 –	–	–	–	–	–	–	–	2 –
6 Huddersfield Town	–	2 –	–	–	–	–	–	–	–	2 –
7 Birmingham City	–	1 –	–	–	–	–	–	–	–	1 –
8 Burnley	–	1 –	–	–	–	–	–	–	–	1 –
9 Derby County	–	1 –	–	–	–	–	–	–	–	1 –
10 Liverpool	–	1 –	–	–	–	–	–	–	–	1 –
11 Notts County	–	1 –	–	–	–	–	–	–	–	1 –
12 Preston North End	–	1 –	–	–	–	–	–	–	–	1 –
13 Sheffield United	–	1 –	–	–	–	–	–	–	–	1 –

MATT ROBINSON

DEBUT (Full Appearance)

Saturday 26/09/1931
Football League Division 2
at Old Trafford

Manchester United 3 Chesterfield 1

CLUB CAREER RECORD	Apps	Subs	Goals
Premiership	0		0
League Division 1	0		0
League Division 2	10		0
FA Cup	0		0
League Cup	0		0
European Cup / Champions League	0		0
European Cup–Winners' Cup	0		0
UEFA Cup / Inter–Cities' Fairs Cup	0		0
Other Matches	0		0
OVERALL TOTAL	10		0

Opponents	PREM A S G	FLD 1 A S G	FLD 2 A S G	FAC A S G	LC A S G	EC/CL A S G	ECWC A S G	UEFA A S G	OTHER A S G	TOTAL A S G
1 Barnsley	–	–	1	–	–	–	–	–	–	1 –
2 Burnley	–	–	1	–	–	–	–	–	–	1 –
3 Bury	–	–	1	–	–	–	–	–	–	1 –
4 Chesterfield	–	–	1	–	–	–	–	–	–	1 –
5 Leeds United	–	–	1	–	–	–	–	–	–	1 –
6 Notts County	–	–	1	–	–	–	–	–	–	1 –
7 Oldham Athletic	–	–	1	–	–	–	–	–	–	1 –
8 Plymouth Argyle	–	–	1	–	–	–	–	–	–	1 –
9 Port Vale	–	–	1	–	–	–	–	–	–	1 –
10 Preston North End	–	–	1	–	–	–	–	–	–	1 –

BRYAN ROBSON

DEBUT (Full Appearance)

Wednesday 07/10/1981
League Cup 2nd Round 1st Leg
at White Hart Lane

Tottenham Hotspur 1 Manchester United 0

CLUB CAREER RECORD	Apps	Subs	Goals
Premiership	15	(14)	2
League Division 1	311	(5)	72
League Division 2	0		0
FA Cup	33	(2)	10
League Cup	50	(1)	5
European Cup / Champions League	4		1
European Cup-Winners' Cup	13		4
UEFA Cup / Inter-Cities' Fairs Cup	9	(1)	3
Other Matches	2	(1)	2
OVERALL TOTAL	**437**	**(24)**	**99**

Opponents	PREM			FLD 1			FLD 2			FAC			LC			EC/CL			ECWC			UEFA			OTHER			TOTAL		
	A	S	G	A	S	G	A	S	G	A	S	G	A	S	G	A	S	G	A	S	G	A	S	G	A	S	G	A	S	G
1 Southampton	–		–	16		4	–		–	2		–	4			–			–			–			–			22		4
2 Arsenal	1	(1)	–	15		3	–		–	1		1	2			–			–			–			–	(1)	–	19	(2)	4
3 Tottenham Hotspur	1		–	16		1	–		–	–		–	3			–			–			–			–			20		1
4 Liverpool	–	(1)	–	15		2	–		–	2		2	–			–			–			–			1		2	18	(1)	6
5 Norwich City	1	(1)	1	16		4	–		–	1			–			–			–			–			–			18	(1)	5
6 Everton	–		–	14		2	–		–	1		–	2			–			–			1		–	–			18		2
7 Luton Town	–		–	16		5	–		–	1			–			–			–			–			–			17		5
8 Aston Villa	1		–	16		4	–		–	–		–	–			–			–			–			–			17		4
9 Nottingham Forest	–		–	14		4	–		–	–		–	1		1	–			–			–			–			16		5
10 West Ham United	–	(1)	–	12	(1)	4	–		–	2		–	–			–			–			–			–			14	(2)	4
11 Sheffield Wednesday	–	(2)	–	13		1	–		–	–		–	1			–			–			–			–			14	(2)	1
12 Coventry City	1	(1)	–	11	(1)	2	–		–	–		–	–			–			–			–			–			12	(2)	2
13 Wimbledon	3	(1)	1	8	(1)	–	–		–	–		–	1		1	–			–			–			–			12	(2)	2
14 Queens Park Rangers	–		–	10		2	–		–	3		1	–			–			–			–			–			13		3
15 Chelsea	1	(2)	–	9		–	–		–	1			–			–			–			–			–			11	(2)	–
16 Sunderland	–		–	8		3	–		–	2		–	–			–			–			–			–			10		3
17 Ipswich Town	1		–	8		2	–		–	1			–			–			–			–			–			10		2
18 Crystal Palace	–	(1)	–	4		1	–		–	2		1	3			–			–			–			–			9	(1)	2
19 Oxford United	–		–	4		2	–		–	1		1	4			–			–			–			–			9		3
20 Manchester City	1		–	8		2	–		–	–		–	–			–			–			–			–			9		2
21 Watford	–		–	8		1	–		–	1		–	–			–			–			–			–			9		1
22 Oldham Athletic	1	(1)	–	2		–	–		–	3	(1)	2	1			–			–			–			–			7	(2)	2
23 West Bromwich Albion	–		–	8		3	–		–	–		–	–			–			–			–			–			8		3
24 Newcastle United	1		–	7		2	–		–	–		–	–			–			–			–			–			8		2
25 Stoke City	–		–	6		2	–		–	–		–	2		–				–			–			–			8		2
26 Birmingham City	–		–	7		3	–		–	–		–	–			–			–			–			–			7		3
27 Brighton	–		–	3		–	–		–	2		2	1			–			–			–			–			6		2
28 Leicester City	–		–	5		2	–		–	–		–	1			–			–			–			–			6		2
29 Charlton Athletic	–		–	6		1	–		–	–		–	–			–			–			–			–			6		1
30 Derby County	–		–	5		1	–		–	1		–	–			–			–			–			–			6		1
31 Bournemouth	–		–	–		–	–		–	4		–	2			–			–			–			–			6		–
32 Portsmouth	–		–	2		2	–		–	–		–	3	(1)	1	–			–			–			–			5	(1)	3
33 Leeds United	1		–	2	(1)	1	–		–	–		–	2			–			–			–			–			5	(1)	1
34 Middlesbrough	–	(1)	–	3		1	–		–	–		–	2			–			–			–			–			5	(1)	1
35 Notts County	–		–	4		2	–		–	–		–	–			–			–			–			–			4		2
36 Port Vale	–		–	–		–	–		–	–		–	4			–			–			–			–			4		–
37 Sheffield United	1		–	2	(1)	–	–		–	–		–	–			–			–			–			–			3	(1)	–
38 Barcelona	–		–	–		–	–		–	–		–	–			–			3		2	–			–			3		2
39 Swansea City	–		–	3		1	–		–	–		–	–			–			–			–			–			3		1
40 Wolverhampton W.	–		–	3		1	–		–	–		–	–			–			–			–			–			3		1
41 Dukla Prague	–		–	–		–	–		–	–		–	–			–			2		1	–			–			2		1
42 Dundee United	–		–	–		–	–		–	–		–	–			–			–			2		1	–			2		1
43 Galatasaray	–		–	–		–	–		–	–		–	–			2		1	–			–			–			2		1
44 Millwall	–		–	2		1	–		–	–		–	–			–			–			–			–			2		1
45 Raba Vasas	–		–	–		–	–		–	–		–	–			–			–			2		1	–			2		1
46 Rotherham United	–		–	–		–	–		–	–		–	2		1	–			–			–			–			2		1
47 Spartak Varna	–		–	–		–	–		–	–		–	–			–			2		1	–			–			2		1
48 Valencia	–		–	–		–	–		–	–		–	–			–			–			2		1	–			2		1
49 Athletico Madrid	–		–	–		–	–		–	–		–	–			–			2		–	–			–			2		–
50 Bradford City	–		–	–		–	–		–	–		–	2			–			–			–			–			2		–
51 Cambridge United	–		–	–		–	–		–	–		–	2			–			–			–			–			2		–
52 Honved	–		–	–		–	–		–	–		–	–			2		–	–			–			–			2		–
53 Hull City	–		–	–		–	–		–	–		–	2			–			–			–			–			2		–
54 Montpellier Herault	–		–	–		–	–		–	–		–	–			–			2		–	–			–			2		–
55 PSV Eindhoven	–		–	–		–	–		–	–		–	–			–			–			2		–	–			2		–
56 Bury	–		–	–		–	–		–	–	(1)	–	1			–			–			–			–			1	(1)	–
57 Burnley	–		–	–		–	–		–	–		–	1		1	–			–			–			–			1		1
58 Athinaikos	–		–	–		–	–		–	–		–	–			–			1		–	–			–			1		–
59 Bolton Wanderers	–		–	–		–	–		–	1			–			–			–			–			–			1		–
60 Colchester United	–		–	–		–	–		–	–		–	1			–			–			–			–			1		–
61 Legia Warsaw	–		–	–		–	–		–	–		–	–			–			1		–	–			–			1		–
62 Videoton	–		–	–		–	–		–	–		–	–			–			–			1		–	–			1		–
63 Blackburn Rovers	–	(1)	–	–		–	–		–	–		–	–			–			–			–			–			–	(1)	–
64 Torpedo Moscow	–		–	–		–	–		–	–		–	–			–			–			–	(1)	–	–			–	(1)	–

LEE ROCHE

DEBUT (Full Appearance)

Monday 05/11/2001
League Cup 3rd Round
at Highbury

Arsenal 4 Manchester United 0

CLUB CAREER RECORD	Apps	Subs	Goals
Premiership	0	(1)	0
League Division 1	0		0
League Division 2	0		0
FA Cup	0		0
League Cup	1		0
European Cup / Champions League	1		0
European Cup-Winners' Cup	0		0
UEFA Cup / Inter-Cities' Fairs Cup	0		0
Other Matches	0		0
OVERALL TOTAL	2	(1)	0

Opponents	PREM A S G	FLD 1 A S G	FLD 2 A S G	FAC A S G	LC A S G	EC/CL A S G	ECWC A S G	UEFA A S G	OTHER A S G	TOTAL A S G
1 Arsenal	– –	– –	– –	– –	1 –	– –	– –	– –	– –	1 –
2 Deportivo La Coruna	– –	– –	– –	– –	– –	1 –	– –	– –	– –	1 –
3 Newcastle United	– (1) –	– –	– –	– –	– –	– –	– –	– –	– –	– (1) –

PADDY ROCHE

DEBUT (Full Appearance)

Saturday 08/02/1975
Football League Division 2
at Manor Ground

Oxford United 1 Manchester United 0

CLUB CAREER RECORD	Apps	Subs	Goals
Premiership	0		0
League Division 1	44		0
League Division 2	2		0
FA Cup	4		0
League Cup	3		0
European Cup / Champions League	0		0
European Cup-Winners' Cup	0		0
UEFA Cup / Inter-Cities' Fairs Cup	0		0
Other Matches	0		0
OVERALL TOTAL	53		0

Opponents	PREM A S G	FLD 1 A S G	FLD 2 A S G	FAC A S G	LC A S G	EC/CL A S G	ECWC A S G	UEFA A S G	OTHER A S G	TOTAL A S G
1 Birmingham City	– –	4 –	– –	– –	– –	– –	– –	– –	– –	4 –
2 Bristol City	– –	3 –	– –	– –	– –	– –	– –	– –	– –	3 –
3 Nottingham Forest	– –	3 –	– –	– –	– –	– –	– –	– –	– –	3 –
4 Wolverhampton W.	– –	3 –	– –	– –	– –	– –	– –	– –	– –	3 –
5 Arsenal	– –	2 –	– –	– –	– –	– –	– –	– –	– –	2 –
6 Aston Villa	– –	2 –	– –	– –	– –	– –	– –	– –	– –	2 –
7 Carlisle United	– –	– –	– –	2 –	– –	– –	– –	– –	– –	2 –
8 Everton	– –	2 –	– –	– –	– –	– –	– –	– –	– –	2 –
9 Ipswich Town	– –	2 –	– –	– –	– –	– –	– –	– –	– –	2 –
10 Leeds United	– –	2 –	– –	– –	– –	– –	– –	– –	– –	2 –
11 Liverpool	– –	2 –	– –	– –	– –	– –	– –	– –	– –	2 –
12 Manchester City	– –	1 –	– –	– –	1 –	– –	– –	– –	– –	2 –
13 Middlesbrough	– –	2 –	– –	– –	– –	– –	– –	– –	– –	2 –
14 Norwich City	– –	2 –	– –	– –	– –	– –	– –	– –	– –	2 –
15 Queens Park Rangers	– –	2 –	– –	– –	– –	– –	– –	– –	– –	2 –
16 Southampton	– –	2 –	– –	– –	– –	– –	– –	– –	– –	2 –
17 West Bromwich Albion	– –	– –	– –	2 –	– –	– –	– –	– –	– –	2 –
18 West Ham United	– –	2 –	– –	– –	– –	– –	– –	– –	– –	2 –
19 Brighton	– –	1 –	– –	– –	– –	– –	– –	– –	– –	1 –
20 Chelsea	– –	1 –	– –	– –	– –	– –	– –	– –	– –	1 –
21 Coventry City	– –	1 –	– –	– –	– –	– –	– –	– –	– –	1 –
22 Derby County	– –	1 –	– –	– –	– –	– –	– –	– –	– –	1 –
23 Hull City	– –	– –	– –	1 –	– –	– –	– –	– –	– –	1 –
24 Leicester City	– –	1 –	– –	– –	– –	– –	– –	– –	– –	1 –
25 Newcastle United	– –	1 –	– –	– –	– –	– –	– –	– –	– –	1 –
26 Oxford United	– –	– –	1 –	– –	– –	– –	– –	– –	– –	1 –
27 Stockport County	– –	– –	– –	– –	1 –	– –	– –	– –	– –	1 –
28 Sunderland	– –	1 –	– –	– –	– –	– –	– –	– –	– –	1 –
29 Tottenham Hotspur	– –	1 –	– –	– –	– –	– –	– –	– –	– –	1 –
30 Watford	– –	– –	– –	– –	1 –	– –	– –	– –	– –	1 –

MARTYN ROGERS

DEBUT (Full Appearance)

Saturday 22/10/1977
Football League Division 1
at The Hawthorns

West Bromwich Albion 4 Manchester United 0

CLUB CAREER RECORD	Apps	Subs	Goals
Premiership	0		0
League Division 1	1		0
League Division 2	0		0
FA Cup	0		0
League Cup	0		0
European Cup / Champions League	0		0
European Cup-Winners' Cup	0		0
UEFA Cup / Inter-Cities' Fairs Cup	0		0
Other Matches	0		0
OVERALL TOTAL	1		0

Opponents	PREM A S G	FLD 1 A S G	FLD 2 A S G	FAC A S G	LC A S G	EC/CL A S G	ECWC A S G	UEFA A S G	OTHER A S G	TOTAL A S G
1 West Bromwich Albion	– –	1 –	– –	– –	– –	– –	– –	– –	– –	1 –

CRISTIANO RONALDO

DEBUT (Substitute Appearance)

Saturday 16/08/2003
FA Premiership
at Old Trafford

Manchester United 4 Bolton Wanderers 0

CLUB CAREER RECORD	Apps	Subs	Goals
Premiership	126	(37)	66
League Division 1	0		0
League Division 2	0		0
FA Cup	21	(3)	12
League Cup	8		2
European Cup / Champions League	40	(3)	12
European Cup-Winners' Cup	0		0
UEFA Cup / Inter-Cities' Fairs Cup	0		0
Other Matches	1		0
OVERALL TOTAL	**196**	**(43)**	**92**

Opponents	PREM A S G			FLD 1 A S G			FLD 2 A S G			FAC A S G			LC A S G			EC/CL A S G			ECWC A S G			UEFA A S G			OTHER A S G			TOTAL A S G		
1 Chelsea	6	(2)	–	–	–	–	–	–	–	1		–	2		–	1		1	–		–	–		–	1		–	11	(2)	1
2 Middlesbrough	6	(3)	2	–	–	–	–	–	–	3		2	–		–	–		–	–		–	–		–	–		–	9	(3)	4
3 Aston Villa	6	(4)	6	–	–	–	–	–	–	2		1	–		–	–		–	–		–	–		–	–		–	8	(4)	7
4 Arsenal	9		4	–	–	–	–	–	–	2		–	–		–	–		–	–		–	–		–	–		–	11		4
5 Fulham	8	(2)	7	–	–	–	–	–	–	1		–	–		–	–		–	–		–	–		–	–		–	9	(2)	7
6 Portsmouth	7	(3)	6	–	–	–	–	–	–	1		–	–		–	–		–	–		–	–		–	–		–	8	(3)	6
7 Blackburn Rovers	8	(1)	2	–	–	–	–	–	–	–		–	1		–	–		–	–		–	–		–	–		–	9	(1)	2
8 Newcastle United	7	(2)	5	–	–	–	–	–	–	1		1	–		–	–		–	–		–	–		–	–		–	8	(2)	6
9 Everton	6	(3)	3	–	–	–	–	–	–	1		1	–		–	–		–	–		–	–		–	–		–	7	(3)	4
10 Tottenham Hotspur	6	(3)	2	–	–	–	–	–	–	1		2	–		–	–		–	–		–	–		–	–		–	7	(3)	4
11 Manchester City	6	(2)	2	–	–	–	–	–	–	1		1	–		–	–		–	–		–	–		–	–		–	7	(2)	3
12 Liverpool	7		1	–	–	–	–	–	–	1		–	–		–	–		–	–		–	–		–	–		–	8		1
13 Birmingham City	6	(1)	2	–	–	–	–	–	–	–		–	1		–	–		–	–		–	–		–	–		–	7	(1)	2
14 Bolton Wanderers	6	(2)	5	–	–	–	–	–	–	–		–	–		–	–		–	–		–	–		–	–		–	6	(2)	5
15 Reading	4		4	–	–	–	–	–	–	1	(1)	–	–		–	–		–	–		–	–		–	–		–	5	(1)	4
16 Wigan Athletic	3	(2)	6	–	–	–	–	–	–	–		–	1		1	–		–	–		–	–		–	–		–	4	(2)	7
17 West Ham United	4	(1)	3	–	–	–	–	–	–	–		–	–		–	–		–	–		–	–		–	–		–	4	(1)	3
18 Charlton Athletic	4	(1)	1	–	–	–	–	–	–	–		–	–		–	–		–	–		–	–		–	–		–	4	(1)	1
19 West Bromwich Albion	2	(1)	–	–	–	–	–	–	–	–		–	2		1	–		–	–		–	–		–	–		–	4	(1)	1
20 Roma	–		–	–	–	–	–	–	–	–		–	–		–	4		3	–		–	–		–	–		–	4		3
21 AC Milan	–		–	–	–	–	–	–	–	–		–	–		–	4		1	–		–	–		–	–		–	4		1
22 Olympique Lyonnais	–		–	–	–	–	–	–	–	–		–	–		–	4		1	–		–	–		–	–		–	4		1
23 Benfica	–		–	–	–	–	–	–	–	–		–	–		–	4		–	–		–	–		–	–		–	4		–
24 Lille Metropole	–		–	–	–	–	–	–	–	–		–	–		–	4		–	–		–	–		–	–		–	4		–
25 Southampton	2	(1)	1	–	–	–	–	–	–	1		1	–		–	–		–	–		–	–		–	–		–	3	(1)	2
26 Watford	2		1	–	–	–	–	–	–	1		1	–		–	–		–	–		–	–		–	–		–	3		2
27 Sunderland	3		1	–	–	–	–	–	–	–		–	–		–	–		–	–		–	–		–	–		–	3		1
28 Dynamo Kiev	–		–	–	–	–	–	–	–	–		–	–		–	2		3	–		–	–		–	–		–	2		3
29 Derby County	2		2	–	–	–	–	–	–	–		–	–		–	–		–	–		–	–		–	–		–	2		2
30 Sporting Lisbon	–		–	–	–	–	–	–	–	–		–	–		–	2		2	–		–	–		–	–		–	2		2
31 Debreceni	–		–	–	–	–	–	–	–	–		–	–		–	2		1	–		–	–		–	–		–	2		1
32 Barcelona	–		–	–	–	–	–	–	–	–		–	–		–	2		–	–		–	–		–	–		–	2		–
33 Copenhagen	–		–	–	–	–	–	–	–	–		–	–		–	2		–	–		–	–		–	–		–	2		–
34 Sheffield United	2		–	–	–	–	–	–	–	–		–	–		–	–		–	–		–	–		–	–		–	2		–
35 Villarreal	–		–	–	–	–	–	–	–	–		–	–		–	2		–	–		–	–		–	–		–	2		–
36 Wolverhampton W.	2		–	–	–	–	–	–	–	–		–	–		–	–		–	–		–	–		–	–		–	2		–
37 Exeter City	–		–	–	–	–	–	–	–	1	(1)	1	–		–	–		–	–		–	–		–	–		–	1	(1)	1
38 Sparta Prague	–		–	–	–	–	–	–	–	–		–	–		–	1	(1)	–	–		–	–		–	–		–	1	(1)	–
39 Norwich City	–	(2)	–	–	–	–	–	–	–	–		–	–		–	–		–	–		–	–		–	–		–	–	(2)	–
40 Porto	–		–	–	–	–	–	–	–	–		–	–		–	–	(2)	–	–		–	–		–	–		–	–	(2)	–
41 Millwall	–		–	–	–	–	–	–	–	1		1	–		–	–		–	–		–	–		–	–		–	1		1
42 Dinamo Bucharest	–		–	–	–	–	–	–	–	–		–	–		–	1		–	–		–	–		–	–		–	1		–
43 Fenerbahce	–		–	–	–	–	–	–	–	–		–	–		–	1		–	–		–	–		–	–		–	1		–
44 Glasgow Celtic	–		–	–	–	–	–	–	–	–		–	–		–	1		–	–		–	–		–	–		–	1		–
45 Glasgow Rangers	–		–	–	–	–	–	–	–	–		–	–		–	1		–	–		–	–		–	–		–	1		–
46 Leeds United	1		–	–	–	–	–	–	–	–		–	–		–	–		–	–		–	–		–	–		–	1		–
47 Leicester City	1		–	–	–	–	–	–	–	–		–	–		–	–		–	–		–	–		–	–		–	1		–
48 Northampton Town	–		–	–	–	–	–	–	–	1		–	–		–	–		–	–		–	–		–	–		–	1		–
49 Panathinaikos	–		–	–	–	–	–	–	–	–		–	–		–	1		–	–		–	–		–	–		–	1		–
50 Southend United	–		–	–	–	–	–	–	–	–		–	1		–	–		–	–		–	–		–	–		–	1		–
51 Stuttgart	–		–	–	–	–	–	–	–	–		–	–		–	1		–	–		–	–		–	–		–	1		–
52 Burton Albion	–		–	–	–	–	–	–	–	–	(1)	–	–		–	–		–	–		–	–		–	–		–	–	(1)	–
53 Crystal Palace	–	(1)	–	–	–	–	–	–	–	–		–	–		–	–		–	–		–	–		–	–		–	–	(1)	–

WAYNE ROONEY

DEBUT (Full Appearance, 3 goals)

Tuesday 28/09/2004
Champions League Phase 1 Match 2
at Old Trafford

Manchester United 6 Fenerbahce 2

CLUB CAREER RECORD	Apps	Subs	Goals
Premiership	116	(11)	53
League Division 1	0		0
League Division 2	0		0
FA Cup	16	(4)	10
League Cup	5	(2)	2
European Cup / Champions League	33	(1)	12
European Cup-Winners' Cup	0		0
UEFA Cup / Inter-Cities' Fairs Cup	0		0
Other Matches	1		0
OVERALL TOTAL	171	(18)	77

Opponents	PREM A S G	FLD 1 A S G	FLD 2 A S G	FAC A S G	LC A S G	EC/CL A S G	ECWC A S G	UEFA A S G	OTHER A S G	TOTAL A S G
1 Chelsea	6 (1) 1	–	–	1 –	1 (1) –	1 –	–	–	1 –	10 (2) 1
2 Arsenal	8 3	–	–	2 1	–	–	–	–	–	10 4
3 Aston Villa	7 (1) 5	–	–	1 (1) 1	–	–	–	–	–	8 (2) 6
4 Newcastle United	8 8	–	–	1 –	–	–	–	–	–	9 8
5 Middlesbrough	6 2	–	–	3 3	–	–	–	–	–	9 5
6 Portsmouth	7 3	–	–	1 (1) 2	–	–	–	–	–	8 (1) 5
7 Liverpool	7 1	–	–	1 –	–	–	–	–	–	8 1
8 Blackburn Rovers	5 (1) –	–	–	–	2 –	–	–	–	–	7 (1) –
9 Fulham	6 (2) 3	–	–	–	–	–	–	–	–	6 (2) 3
10 Wigan Athletic	6 3	–	–	–	1 2	–	–	–	–	7 5
11 Everton	6 2	–	–	1 –	–	–	–	–	–	7 2
12 Bolton Wanderers	5 (1) 5	–	–	–	–	–	–	–	–	5 (1) 5
13 Roma	–	–	–	–	–	5 (1) 4	–	–	–	5 (1) 4
14 Manchester City	5 (1) 2	–	–	–	–	–	–	–	–	5 (1) 2
15 Birmingham City	4 (1) 3	–	–	–	– (1) –	–	–	–	–	4 (2) 3
16 Tottenham Hotspur	4 2	–	–	1 –	–	–	–	–	–	5 2
17 Reading	4 1	–	–	– (1) –	–	–	–	–	–	4 (1) 1
18 AC Milan	–	–	–	–	–	4 2	–	–	–	4 2
19 Charlton Athletic	4 1	–	–	–	–	–	–	–	–	4 1
20 West Ham United	4 1	–	–	–	–	–	–	–	–	4 1
21 West Bromwich Albion	3 (1) –	–	–	–	–	–	–	–	–	3 (1) –
22 Sunderland	3 2	–	–	–	–	–	–	–	–	3 2
23 Southampton	2 1	–	–	1 –	–	–	–	–	–	3 1
24 Benfica	–	–	–	–	–	3 –	–	–	–	3 –
25 Lille Metropole	–	–	–	–	–	3 –	–	–	–	3 –
26 Olympique Lyonnais	–	–	–	–	–	3 –	–	–	–	3 –
27 Sheffield United	2 3	–	–	–	–	–	–	–	–	2 3
28 Watford	1 1	–	–	1 2	–	–	–	–	–	2 3
29 Dynamo Kiev	–	–	–	–	–	2 2	–	–	–	2 2
30 Copenhagen	–	–	–	–	–	2 –	–	–	–	2 –
31 Derby County	2 –	–	–	–	–	–	–	–	–	2 –
32 Glasgow Celtic	–	–	–	–	–	2 –	–	–	–	2 –
33 Sparta Prague	–	–	–	–	–	2 –	–	–	–	2 –
34 Villarreal	–	–	–	–	–	2 –	–	–	–	2 –
35 Crystal Palace	1 (1) –	–	–	–	–	–	–	–	–	1 (1) –
36 Fenerbahce	–	–	–	–	–	1 3	–	–	–	1 3
37 Debreceni	–	–	–	–	–	1 1	–	–	–	1 1
38 Exeter City	–	–	–	1 1	–	–	–	–	–	1 1
39 Barcelona	–	–	–	–	–	1 –	–	–	–	1 –
40 Southend United	–	–	–	–	1 –	–	–	–	–	1 –
41 Sporting Lisbon	–	–	–	–	–	1 –	–	–	–	1 –
42 Wolverhampton W.	–	–	–	1 –	–	–	–	–	–	1 –
43 Burton Albion	–	–	–	– (1) –	–	–	–	–	–	– (1) –
44 Norwich City	– (1) –	–	–	–	–	–	–	–	–	– (1) –

GIUSEPPE ROSSI

DEBUT (Substitute Appearance)

Wednesday 10/11/2004
League Cup 4th Round
at Old Trafford

Manchester United 2 Crystal Palace 0

CLUB CAREER RECORD	Apps	Subs	Goals
Premiership	1	(4)	1
League Division 1	0		0
League Division 2	0		0
FA Cup	2		2
League Cup	3	(2)	1
European Cup / Champions League	0	(2)	0
European Cup-Winners' Cup	0		0
UEFA Cup / Inter-Cities' Fairs Cup	0		0
Other Matches	0		0
OVERALL TOTAL	6	(8)	4

Opponents	PREM A S G	FLD 1 A S G	FLD 2 A S G	FAC A S G	LC A S G	EC/CL A S G	ECWC A S G	UEFA A S G	OTHER A S G	TOTAL A S G
1 Burton Albion	–	–	–	2 2	–	–	–	–	–	2 2
2 Barnet	–	–	–	–	1 1	–	–	–	–	1 1
3 Birmingham City	–	–	–	–	1 –	–	–	–	–	1 –
4 Charlton Athletic	1 –	–	–	–	–	–	–	–	–	1 –
5 West Bromwich Albion	–	–	–	–	1 –	–	–	–	–	1 –
6 Sunderland	– (1) 1	–	–	–	–	–	–	–	–	– (1) 1
7 Arsenal	–	–	–	–	– (1) –	–	–	–	–	– (1) –

continued../

GIUSEPPE ROSSI (continued)

Opponents	PREM A S G	FLD 1 A S G	FLD 2 A S G	FAC A S G	LC A S G	EC/CL A S G	ECWC A S G	UEFA A S G	OTHER A S G	TOTAL A S G
8 Crystal Palace	– – –	– – –	– – –	– – –	– (1) –	– – –	– – –	– – –	– – –	– (1) –
9 Debreceni	– – –	– – –	– – –	– – –	– – –	– (1) –	– – –	– – –	– – –	– (1) –
10 Everton	– – –	– (1) –	– – –	– – –	– – –	– – –	– – –	– – –	– – –	– (1) –
11 Lille Metropole	– – –	– – –	– – –	– – –	– – –	– (1) –	– – –	– – –	– – –	– (1) –
12 Middlesbrough	– (1) –	– – –	– – –	– – –	– – –	– – –	– – –	– – –	– – –	– (1) –
13 Tottenham Hotspur	– (1) –	– – –	– – –	– – –	– – –	– – –	– – –	– – –	– – –	– (1) –

CHARLES ROTHWELL

DEBUT (Full Appearance)

Saturday 02/12/1893
Football League Division 1
at Bank Street

Newton Heath 0 Everton 3

CLUB CAREER RECORD	Apps	Subs	Goals
Premiership	0		0
League Division 1	1		0
League Division 2	1		1
FA Cup	1		2
League Cup	0		0
European Cup / Champions League	0		0
European Cup-Winners' Cup	0		0
UEFA Cup / Inter-Cities' Fairs Cup	0		0
Other Matches	0		0
OVERALL TOTAL	**3**		**3**

Opponents	PREM A S G	FLD 1 A S G	FLD 2 A S G	FAC A S G	LC A S G	EC/CL A S G	ECWC A S G	UEFA A S G	OTHER A S G	TOTAL A S G
1 West Manchester	– –	– –	– –	1 2	– –	– –	– –	– –	– –	1 2
2 Port Vale	– –	– –	1 1	– –	– –	– –	– –	– –	– –	1 1
3 Everton	– –	1	– –	– –	– –	– –	– –	– –	– –	1

HERBERT ROTHWELL

DEBUT (Full Appearance)

Saturday 25/10/1902
Football League Division 2
at Manor Field

Arsenal 0 Manchester United 1

CLUB CAREER RECORD	Apps	Subs	Goals
Premiership	0		0
League Division 1	0		0
League Division 2	22		0
FA Cup	6		0
League Cup	0		0
European Cup / Champions League	0		0
European Cup-Winners' Cup	0		0
UEFA Cup / Inter-Cities' Fairs Cup	0		0
Other Matches	0		0
OVERALL TOTAL	**28**		**0**

Opponents	PREM A S G	FLD 1 A S G	FLD 2 A S G	FAC A S G	LC A S G	EC/CL A S G	ECWC A S G	UEFA A S G	OTHER A S G	TOTAL A S G
1 Burton United	– –	– –	1 –	2 –	– –	– –	– –	– –	– –	3 –
2 Birmingham City	– –	– –	2 –	– –	– –	– –	– –	– –	– –	2 –
3 Blackpool	– –	– –	2 –	– –	– –	– –	– –	– –	– –	2 –
4 Burnley	– –	– –	2 –	– –	– –	– –	– –	– –	– –	2 –
5 Leicester City	– –	– –	2 –	– –	– –	– –	– –	– –	– –	2 –
6 Lincoln City	– –	– –	2 –	– –	– –	– –	– –	– –	– –	2 –
7 Manchester City	– –	– –	2 –	– –	– –	– –	– –	– –	– –	2 –
8 Port Vale	– –	– –	2 –	– –	– –	– –	– –	– –	– –	2 –
9 Arsenal	– –	– –	1 –	– –	– –	– –	– –	– –	– –	1 –
10 Bristol City	– –	– –	1 –	– –	– –	– –	– –	– –	– –	1 –
11 Chesterfield	– –	– –	1 –	– –	– –	– –	– –	– –	– –	1 –
12 Everton	– –	– –	– –	1 –	– –	– –	– –	– –	– –	1 –
13 Gainsborough Trinity	– –	– –	1 –	– –	– –	– –	– –	– –	– –	1 –
14 Glossop	– –	– –	1 –	– –	– –	– –	– –	– –	– –	1 –
15 Liverpool	– –	– –	– –	1 –	– –	– –	– –	– –	– –	1 –
16 Oswaldtwistle Rovers	– –	– –	– –	1 –	– –	– –	– –	– –	– –	1 –
17 Preston North End	– –	– –	1 –	– –	– –	– –	– –	– –	– –	1 –
18 Southport Central	– –	– –	– –	1 –	– –	– –	– –	– –	– –	1 –
19 Stockport County	– –	– –	1 –	– –	– –	– –	– –	– –	– –	1 –

GEORGE ROUGHTON

DEBUT (Full Appearance)

Saturday 12/09/1936
Football League Division 1
at Old Trafford

Manchester United 3 Manchester City 2

CLUB CAREER RECORD	Apps	Subs	Goals
Premiership	0		0
League Division 1	47		0
League Division 2	39		0
FA Cup	6		0
League Cup	0		0
European Cup / Champions League	0		0
European Cup-Winners' Cup	0		0
UEFA Cup / Inter-Cities' Fairs Cup	0		0
Other Matches	0		0
OVERALL TOTAL	**92**		**0**

Opponents	PREM A S G	FLD 1 A S G	FLD 2 A S G	FAC A S G	LC A S G	EC/CL A S G	ECWC A S G	UEFA A S G	OTHER A S G	TOTAL A S G
1 Bolton Wanderers	– –	4 –	– –	– –	– –	– –	– –	– –	– –	4 –
2 Leeds United	– –	4 –	– –	– –	– –	– –	– –	– –	– –	4 –
3 Sheffield Wednesday	– –	2 –	2 –	– –	– –	– –	– –	– –	– –	4 –
4 Arsenal	– –	2 –	– –	1 –	– –	– –	– –	– –	– –	3 –
5 Barnsley	– –	– –	1 –	2 –	– –	– –	– –	– –	– –	3 –
6 Brentford	– –	2 –	– –	1 –	– –	– –	– –	– –	– –	3 –
7 Everton	– –	3 –	– –	– –	– –	– –	– –	– –	– –	3 –
8 Liverpool	– –	3 –	– –	– –	– –	– –	– –	– –	– –	3 –
9 Portsmouth	– –	3 –	– –	– –	– –	– –	– –	– –	– –	3 –
10 Stoke City	– –	3 –	– –	– –	– –	– –	– –	– –	– –	3 –
11 Sunderland	– –	3 –	– –	– –	– –	– –	– –	– –	– –	3 –
12 Aston Villa	– –	– –	– –	2 –	– –	– –	– –	– –	– –	2 –
13 Blackburn Rovers	– –	– –	– –	2 –	– –	– –	– –	– –	– –	2 –
14 Bradford Park Avenue	– –	– –	– –	2 –	– –	– –	– –	– –	– –	2 –
15 Burnley	– –	– –	– –	2 –	– –	– –	– –	– –	– –	2 –
16 Bury	– –	– –	– –	2 –	– –	– –	– –	– –	– –	2 –
17 Charlton Athletic	– –	2 –	– –	– –	– –	– –	– –	– –	– –	2 –
18 Chelsea	– –	2 –	– –	– –	– –	– –	– –	– –	– –	2 –
19 Chesterfield	– –	– –	– –	2 –	– –	– –	– –	– –	– –	2 –
20 Coventry City	– –	– –	– –	2 –	– –	– –	– –	– –	– –	2 –
21 Derby County	– –	2 –	– –	– –	– –	– –	– –	– –	– –	2 –
22 Fulham	– –	– –	– –	2 –	– –	– –	– –	– –	– –	2 –
23 Luton Town	– –	– –	– –	2 –	– –	– –	– –	– –	– –	2 –
24 Manchester City	– –	2 –	– –	– –	– –	– –	– –	– –	– –	2 –
25 Middlesbrough	– –	2 –	– –	– –	– –	– –	– –	– –	– –	2 –
26 Newcastle United	– –	– –	– –	2 –	– –	– –	– –	– –	– –	2 –
27 Norwich City	– –	– –	– –	2 –	– –	– –	– –	– –	– –	2 –
28 Nottingham Forest	– –	– –	– –	2 –	– –	– –	– –	– –	– –	2 –
29 Plymouth Argyle	– –	– –	– –	2 –	– –	– –	– –	– –	– –	2 –
30 Preston North End	– –	2 –	– –	– –	– –	– –	– –	– –	– –	2 –
31 Sheffield United	– –	– –	– –	2 –	– –	– –	– –	– –	– –	2 –
32 Swansea City	– –	– –	– –	2 –	– –	– –	– –	– –	– –	2 –
33 Tottenham Hotspur	– –	– –	– –	2 –	– –	– –	– –	– –	– –	2 –
34 West Bromwich Albion	– –	2 –	– –	– –	– –	– –	– –	– –	– –	2 –
35 West Ham United	– –	– –	– –	2 –	– –	– –	– –	– –	– –	2 –
36 Birmingham City	– –	1 –	– –	– –	– –	– –	– –	– –	– –	1 –
37 Grimsby Town	– –	1 –	– –	– –	– –	– –	– –	– –	– –	1 –
38 Huddersfield Town	– –	1 –	– –	– –	– –	– –	– –	– –	– –	1 –
39 Reading	– –	– –	– –	1 –	– –	– –	– –	– –	– –	1 –
40 Southampton	– –	– –	– –	1 –	– –	– –	– –	– –	– –	1 –
41 Stockport County	– –	– –	– –	1 –	– –	– –	– –	– –	– –	1 –
42 Wolverhampton W.	– –	1 –	– –	– –	– –	– –	– –	– –	– –	1 –
43 Yeovil Town	– –	– –	– –	1 –	– –	– –	– –	– –	– –	1 –

ELIJAH ROUND

DEBUT (Full Appearance)

Saturday 09/10/1909
Football League Division 1
at Anfield

Liverpool 3 Manchester United 2

CLUB CAREER RECORD	Apps	Subs	Goals
Premiership	0		0
League Division 1	2		0
League Division 2	0		0
FA Cup	0		0
League Cup	0		0
European Cup / Champions League	0		0
European Cup-Winners' Cup	0		0
UEFA Cup / Inter-Cities' Fairs Cup	0		0
Other Matches	0		0
OVERALL TOTAL	**2**		**0**

Opponents	PREM A S G	FLD 1 A S G	FLD 2 A S G	FAC A S G	LC A S G	EC/CL A S G	ECWC A S G	UEFA A S G	OTHER A S G	TOTAL A S G
1 Aston Villa	– –	1 –	– –	– –	– –	– –	– –	– –	– –	1 –
2 Liverpool	– –	1 –	– –	– –	– –	– –	– –	– –	– –	1 –

JOELYN ROWE

DEBUT (Full Appearance)

Thursday 05/03/1914
Football League Division 1
at Deepdale

Preston North End 4 Manchester United 2

CLUB CAREER RECORD	Apps	Subs	Goals
Premiership	0		0
League Division 1	1		0
League Division 2	0		0
FA Cup	0		0
League Cup	0		0
European Cup / Champions League	0		0
European Cup-Winners' Cup	0		0
UEFA Cup / Inter-Cities' Fairs Cup	0		0
Other Matches	0		0
OVERALL TOTAL	**1**		**0**

Opponents	PREM A S G	FLD 1 A S G	FLD 2 A S G	FAC A S G	LC A S G	EC/CL A S G	ECWC A S G	UEFA A S G	OTHER A S G	TOTAL A S G
1 Preston North End	– –	1 –	– –	– –	– –	– –	– –	– –	– –	1 –

HARRY ROWLEY

DEBUT (Full Appearance)

Saturday 27/10/1928
Football League Division 1
at Leeds Road

Huddersfield Town 1 Manchester United 2

CLUB CAREER RECORD	Apps	Subs	Goals
Premiership	0		0
League Division 1	111		28
League Division 2	62		27
FA Cup	7		0
League Cup	0		0
European Cup / Champions League	0		0
European Cup-Winners' Cup	0		0
UEFA Cup / Inter-Cities' Fairs Cup	0		0
Other Matches	0		0
OVERALL TOTAL	**180**		**55**

Opponents	PREM A S G	FLD 1 A S G	FLD 2 A S G	FAC A S G	LC A S G	EC/CL A S G	ECWC A S G	UEFA A S G	OTHER A S G	TOTAL A S G
1 Newcastle United	– –	4 2	3 2	– –	–	–	–	–	–	7 4
2 West Ham United	– –	4 1	3 2	– –	–	–	–	–	–	7 3
3 Huddersfield Town	– –	7 –	– –	– –	–	–	–	–	–	7 –
4 Burnley	– –	3 2	3 2	– –	–	–	–	–	–	6 4
5 Arsenal	– –	6 2	– –	– –	–	–	–	–	–	6 2
6 Blackburn Rovers	– –	6 2	– –	– –	–	–	–	–	–	6 2
7 Sheffield Wednesday	– –	6 2	– –	– –	–	–	–	–	–	6 2
8 Leicester City	– –	4 1	2 –	– –	–	–	–	–	–	6 1
9 Portsmouth	– –	6 1	– –	– –	–	–	–	–	–	6 1
10 Derby County	– –	5 4	– –	– –	–	–	–	–	–	5 4
11 Sheffield United	– –	2 1	3 2	– –	–	–	–	–	–	5 3
12 Aston Villa	– –	5 2	– –	– –	–	–	–	–	–	5 2
13 Birmingham City	– –	5 2	– –	– –	–	–	–	–	–	5 2
14 Grimsby Town	– –	5 2	– –	– –	–	–	–	–	–	5 2
15 Bury	– –	2 –	3 1	– –	–	–	–	–	–	5 1
16 Liverpool	– –	5 1	– –	– –	–	–	–	–	–	5 1
17 Nottingham Forest	– –	– –	3 1	2 –	–	–	–	–	–	5 1
18 Sunderland	– –	5 1	– –	– –	–	–	–	–	–	5 1
19 Bolton Wanderers	– –	5 –	– –	– –	–	–	–	–	–	5 –
20 Leeds United	– –	5 –	– –	– –	–	–	–	–	–	5 –
21 Manchester City	– –	5 –	– –	– –	–	–	–	–	–	5 –
22 Plymouth Argyle	– –	– –	4 2	– –	–	–	–	–	–	4 2
23 Southampton	– –	– –	4 2	– –	–	–	–	–	–	4 2
24 Blackpool	– –	1 –	3 1	– –	–	–	–	–	–	4 1
25 Middlesbrough	– –	4 1	– –	– –	–	–	–	–	–	4 1
26 Bradford Park Avenue	– –	– –	4 –	– –	–	–	–	–	–	4 –
27 Stoke City	– –	1 –	1 –	2 –	–	–	–	–	–	4 –
28 Norwich City	– –	– –	3 6	– –	–	–	–	–	–	3 6
29 Port Vale	– –	– –	3 3	– –	–	–	–	–	–	3 3
30 Everton	– –	3 1	– –	– –	–	–	–	–	–	3 1
31 Fulham	– –	– –	3 1	– –	–	–	–	–	–	3 1
32 Swansea City	– –	– –	3 1	– –	–	–	–	–	–	3 1
33 Brentford	– –	2 –	1 –	– –	–	–	–	–	–	3 –
34 Hull City	– –	– –	3 –	– –	–	–	–	–	–	3 –
35 Notts County	– –	– –	2 1	– –	–	–	–	–	–	2 1
36 Barnsley	– –	– –	2 –	– –	–	–	–	–	–	2 –
37 Bradford City	– –	– –	2 –	– –	–	–	–	–	–	2 –
38 Chelsea	– –	2 –	– –	– –	–	–	–	–	–	2 –
39 Doncaster Rovers	– –	– –	2 –	– –	–	–	–	–	–	2 –
40 Bristol Rovers	– –	– –	– –	1 –	–	–	–	–	–	1 –
41 Cardiff City	– –	1 –	– –	– –	–	–	–	–	–	1 –
42 Oldham Athletic	– –	– –	1 –	– –	–	–	–	–	–	1 –
43 Preston North End	– –	1 –	– –	– –	–	–	–	–	–	1 –
44 Reading	– –	– –	– –	1 –	–	–	–	–	–	1 –
45 Swindon Town	– –	– –	– –	1 –	–	–	–	–	–	1 –
46 Tottenham Hotspur	– –	– –	1 –	– –	–	–	–	–	–	1 –
47 Wolverhampton W.	– –	1 –	– –	– –	–	–	–	–	–	1 –

JACK ROWLEY

DEBUT (Full Appearance)

Saturday 23/10/1937
Football League Division 2
at Old Trafford

Manchester United 1 Sheffield Wednesday 0

CLUB CAREER RECORD	Apps	Subs	Goals
Premiership	0		0
League Division 1	355		173
League Division 2	25		9
FA Cup	42		26
League Cup	0		0
European Cup / Champions League	0		0
European Cup-Winners' Cup	0		0
UEFA Cup / Inter-Cities' Fairs Cup	0		0
Other Matches	2		3
OVERALL TOTAL	**424**		**211**

Opponents	PREM			FLD 1			FLD 2			FAC			LC			EC/CL			ECWC			UEFA			OTHER			TOTAL		
	A	S	G	A	S	G	A	S	G	A	S	G	A	S	G	A	S	G	A	S	G	A	S	G	A	S	G	A	S	G
1 Aston Villa	–	–	–	19		13	1		–	1		1	–		–	–		–	–		–	–		–	–		–	21		14
2 Wolverhampton W.	–	–	–	18		10	–		–	2		–	–		–	–		–	–		–	–		–	–		–	20		10
3 Portsmouth	–	–	–	17		6	–		–	2		–	–		–	–		–	–		–	–		–	–		–	19		6
4 Chelsea	–	–	–	17		7	–		–	1		–	–		–	–		–	–		–	–		–	–		–	18		7
5 Liverpool	–	–	–	17		5	–		–	1		1	–		–	–		–	–		–	–		–	–		–	18		6
6 Preston North End	–	–	–	15		5	–		–	3		1	–		–	–		–	–		–	–		–	–		–	18		6
7 Middlesbrough	–	–	–	17		17	–		–	–		–	–		–	–		–	–		–	–		–	–		–	17		17
8 Charlton Athletic	–	–	–	16		13	–		–	1		–	–		–	–		–	–		–	–		–	–		–	17		13
9 Arsenal	–	–	–	15		9	–		–	1		–	–		–	–		–	–		–	–		–	1		1	17		10
10 Blackpool	–	–	–	16		6	–		–	1		2	–		–	–		–	–		–	–		–	–		–	17		8
11 Burnley	–	–	–	14		8	2		–	1		–	–		–	–		–	–		–	–		–	–		–	17		8
12 Sunderland	–	–	–	16		6	–		–	–		–	–		–	–		–	–		–	–		–	–		–	16		6
13 Derby County	–	–	–	15		4	–		–	1		–	–		–	–		–	–		–	–		–	–		–	16		4
14 Stoke City	–	–	–	15		6	–		–	–		–	–		–	–		–	–		–	–		–	–		–	15		6
15 Bolton Wanderers	–	–	–	15		5	–		–	–		–	–		–	–		–	–		–	–		–	–		–	15		5
16 Huddersfield Town	–	–	–	14		11	–		–	–		–	–		–	–		–	–		–	–		–	–		–	14		11
17 Everton	–	–	–	11		4	–		–	1		1	–		–	–		–	–		–	–		–	–		–	12		5
18 Newcastle United	–	–	–	10		2	1		1	–		–	–		–	–		–	–		–	–		–	1		2	12		5
19 Manchester City	–	–	–	10		1	–		–	1		–	–		–	–		–	–		–	–		–	–		–	11		1
20 Sheffield United	–	–	–	9		6	1		–	–		–	–		–	–		–	–		–	–		–	–		–	10		6
21 West Bromwich Albion	–	–	–	9		5	–		–	1		–	–		–	–		–	–		–	–		–	–		–	10		5
22 Tottenham Hotspur	–	–	–	9		4	–		–	–		–	–		–	–		–	–		–	–		–	–		–	9		4
23 Sheffield Wednesday	–	–	–	7		2	2		1	–		–	–		–	–		–	–		–	–		–	–		–	9		3
24 Grimsby Town	–	–	–	6		5	–		–	–		–	–		–	–		–	–		–	–		–	–		–	6		5
25 Bradford Park Avenue	–	–	–	–		–	2		–	4		4	–		–	–		–	–		–	–		–	–		–	6		4
26 Fulham	–	–	–	5		4	1		–	–		–	–		–	–		–	–		–	–		–	–		–	6		4
27 Birmingham City	–	–	–	5		1	–		–	1		–	–		–	–		–	–		–	–		–	–		–	6		1
28 Blackburn Rovers	–	–	–	4		1	1		–	–		–	–		–	–		–	–		–	–		–	–		–	5		1
29 Leeds United	–	–	–	4		–	–		–	1		1	–		–	–		–	–		–	–		–	–		–	5		1
30 Brentford	–	–	–	3		4	–		–	1		–	–		–	–		–	–		–	–		–	–		–	4		4
31 Cardiff City	–	–	–	4		2	–		–	–		–	–		–	–		–	–		–	–		–	–		–	4		2
32 Barnsley	–	–	–	–		–	1		1	2		–	–		–	–		–	–		–	–		–	–		–	3		1
33 Leicester City	–	–	–	3		1	–		–	–		–	–		–	–		–	–		–	–		–	–		–	3		1
34 Nottingham Forest	–	–	–	–		–	2		–	1		–	–		–	–		–	–		–	–		–	–		–	3		–
35 Swansea City	–	–	–	–		–	2		5	–		–	–		–	–		–	–		–	–		–	–		–	2		5
36 Yeovil Town	–	–	–	–		–	–		–	2		5	–		–	–		–	–		–	–		–	–		–	2		5
37 Accrington Stanley	–	–	–	–		–	–		–	2		2	–		–	–		–	–		–	–		–	–		–	2		2
38 Walthamstow Avenue	–	–	–	–		–	–		–	2		2	–		–	–		–	–		–	–		–	–		–	2		2
39 Reading	–	–	–	–		–	–		–	2		1	–		–	–		–	–		–	–		–	–		–	2		1
40 Hull City	–	–	–	–		–	–		–	2		–	–		–	–		–	–		–	–		–	–		–	2		–
41 West Ham United	–	–	–	–		–	2		–	–		–	–		–	–		–	–		–	–		–	–		–	2		–
42 Bournemouth	–	–	–	–		–	–		–	1		2	–		–	–		–	–		–	–		–	–		–	1		2
43 Weymouth Town	–	–	–	–		–	–		–	1		2	–		–	–		–	–		–	–		–	–		–	1		2
44 Plymouth Argyle	–	–	–	–		–	1		1	–		–	–		–	–		–	–		–	–		–	–		–	1		1
45 Watford	–	–	–	–		–	–		–	1		1	–		–	–		–	–		–	–		–	–		–	1		1
46 Bury	–	–	–	–		–	1		–	–		–	–		–	–		–	–		–	–		–	–		–	1		–
47 Chesterfield	–	–	–	–		–	1		–	–		–	–		–	–		–	–		–	–		–	–		–	1		–
48 Luton Town	–	–	–	–		–	1		–	–		–	–		–	–		–	–		–	–		–	–		–	1		–
49 Millwall	–	–	–	–		–	–		–	1		–	–		–	–		–	–		–	–		–	–		–	1		–
50 Norwich City	–	–	–	–		–	1		–	–		–	–		–	–		–	–		–	–		–	–		–	1		–
51 Southampton	–	–	–	–		–	1		–	–		–	–		–	–		–	–		–	–		–	–		–	1		–
52 Stockport County	–	–	–	–		–	1		–	–		–	–		–	–		–	–		–	–		–	–		–	1		–

EZRA ROYALS

DEBUT (Full Appearance)

Saturday 23/03/1912
Football League Division 1
at Old Trafford

Manchester United 1 Liverpool 1

CLUB CAREER RECORD	Apps	Subs	Goals
Premiership	0		0
League Division 1	7		0
League Division 2	0		0
FA Cup	0		0
League Cup	0		0
European Cup / Champions League	0		0
European Cup-Winners' Cup	0		0
UEFA Cup / Inter-Cities' Fairs Cup	0		0
Other Matches	0		0
OVERALL TOTAL	**7**		**0**

Opponents	PREM A S G	FLD 1 A S G	FLD 2 A S G	FAC A S G	LC A S G	EC/CL A S G	ECWC A S G	UEFA A S G	OTHER A S G	TOTAL A S G
1 Liverpool	– –	2 –	–	–	–	–	–	–	–	2 –
2 Aston Villa	– –	1 –	–	–	–	–	–	–	–	1 –
3 Bradford City	– –	1 –	–	–	–	–	–	–	–	1 –
4 Manchester City	– –	1 –	–	–	–	–	–	–	–	1 –
5 Sunderland	– –	1 –	–	–	–	–	–	–	–	1 –
6 West Bromwich Albion	– –	1 –	–	–	–	–	–	–	–	1 –

JIMMY RYAN

DEBUT (Full Appearance)

Wednesday 04/05/1966
Football League Division 1
at The Hawthorns

West Bromwich Albion 3 Manchester United 3

CLUB CAREER RECORD	Apps	Subs	Goals
Premiership	0		0
League Division 1	21	(3)	4
League Division 2	0		0
FA Cup	1		0
League Cup	0		0
European Cup / Champions League	2		0
European Cup-Winners' Cup	0		0
UEFA Cup / Inter-Cities' Fairs Cup	0		0
Other Matches	0		0
OVERALL TOTAL	**24**	**(3)**	**4**

Opponents	PREM A S G	FLD 1 A S G	FLD 2 A S G	FAC A S G	LC A S G	EC/CL A S G	ECWC A S G	UEFA A S G	OTHER A S G	TOTAL A S G
1 Leeds United	– –	3 –	–	–	–	–	–	–	–	3 –
2 Stoke City	– –	2 (1) 1	–	–	–	–	–	–	–	2 (1) 1
3 Chelsea	– –	2 (1) –	–	–	–	–	–	–	–	2 (1) –
4 West Ham United	– –	2 1	–	–	–	–	–	–	–	2 1
5 Liverpool	– –	2 –	–	–	–	–	–	–	–	2 –
6 West Bromwich Albion	– –	2 –	–	–	–	–	–	–	–	2 –
7 Nottingham Forest	– –	1 (1) –	–	–	–	–	–	–	–	1 (1) –
8 Aston Villa	– –	1 1	–	–	–	–	–	–	–	1 1
9 Coventry City	– –	1 1	–	–	–	–	–	–	–	1 1
10 Anderlecht	– –	– –	–	–	–	1 –	–	–	–	1 –
11 Blackburn Rovers	– –	1 –	–	–	–	–	–	–	–	1 –
12 Burnley	– –	1 –	–	–	–	–	–	–	–	1 –
13 Gornik Zabrze	– –	– –	–	–	–	1 –	–	–	–	1 –
14 Manchester City	– –	1 –	–	–	–	–	–	–	–	1 –
15 Norwich City	– –	– –	–	1 –	–	–	–	–	–	1 –
16 Sunderland	– –	1 –	–	–	–	–	–	–	–	1 –
17 Tottenham Hotspur	– –	1 –	–	–	–	–	–	–	–	1 –

DAVID SADLER

DEBUT (Full Appearance)

Saturday 24/08/1963
Football League Division 1
at Hillsborough

Sheffield Wednesday 3 Manchester United 3

CLUB CAREER RECORD	Apps	Subs	Goals
Premiership	0		0
League Division 1	266	(6)	22
League Division 2	0		0
FA Cup	22	(1)	1
League Cup	22		1
European Cup / Champions League	14		3
European Cup-Winners' Cup	2		0
UEFA Cup / Inter-Cities' Fairs Cup	0		0
Other Matches	2		0
OVERALL TOTAL	**328**	**(7)**	**27**

Opponents	PREM A S G	FLD 1 A S G	FLD 2 A S G	FAC A S G	LC A S G	EC/CL A S G	ECWC A S G	UEFA A S G	OTHER A S G	TOTAL A S G
1 West Ham United	– –	15 (1) 2	–	–	–	–	–	–	–	15 (1) 2
2 Stoke City	– –	10 (1) 1	–	2 –	3 –	–	–	–	–	15 (1) 1
3 Manchester City	– –	12 –	–	1 –	2 –	–	–	–	–	15 –
4 Tottenham Hotspur	– –	12 –	–	2 –	–	–	1 –	–	–	15 –
5 Southampton	– –	12 1	–	2 1	–	–	–	–	–	14 2
6 Chelsea	– –	13 –	–	–	1 –	–	–	–	–	14 –
7 Arsenal	– –	13 2	–	–	–	–	–	–	–	13 2
8 Leeds United	– –	10 1	–	3 –	–	–	–	–	–	13 1
9 Burnley	– –	8 (1) 2	–	–	4 –	–	–	–	–	12 (1) 2
10 Everton	– –	12 (1) 2	–	–	–	–	–	–	–	12 (1) 2
11 Newcastle United	– –	12 1	–	–	–	–	–	–	–	12 1

continued../

DAVID SADLER (continued)

Opponents	PREM A S G	FLD 1 A S G	FLD 2 A S G	FAC A S G	LC A S G	EC/CL A S G	ECWC A S G	UEFA A S G	OTHER A S G	TOTAL A S G
12 Nottingham Forest	– –	12 –	– –	– –	– –	– –	– –	– –	– –	12 –
13 Leicester City	– –	11 (1) 2	– –	– –	– –	– –	– –	– –	– –	11 (1) 2
14 West Bromwich Albion	– –	11 (1) 1	– –	– –	– –	– –	– –	– –	– –	11 (1) 1
15 Ipswich Town	– –	9 1	– –	1 –	1 –	– –	– –	– –	– –	11 1
16 Liverpool	– –	11 –	– –	– –	– –	– –	– –	– –	– –	11 –
17 Wolverhampton W.	– –	10 –	– –	1 –	– –	– –	– –	– –	– –	11 –
18 Sheffield United	– –	10 2	– –	– –	– –	– –	– –	– –	– –	10 2
19 Coventry City	– –	9 –	– –	– –	– –	– –	– –	– –	– –	9 –
20 Sheffield Wednesday	– –	9 –	– –	– –	– –	– –	– –	– –	– –	9 –
21 Blackpool	– –	7 –	– –	– –	1 –	– –	– –	– –	– –	8 –
22 Derby County	– –	6 –	– –	– –	2 –	– –	– –	– –	– –	8 –
23 Middlesbrough	– –	– –	– –	6 –	1 1	– –	– –	– –	– –	7 1
24 Sunderland	– –	7 –	– –	– –	– –	– –	– –	– –	– –	7 –
25 Crystal Palace	– –	5 –	– –	– –	1 –	– –	– –	– –	– –	6 –
26 Fulham	– –	5 –	– –	– –	– –	– –	– –	– –	– –	5 –
27 Aston Villa	– –	3 2	– –	– –	1 –	– –	– –	– –	– –	4 2
28 Birmingham City	– –	4 1	– –	– –	– –	– –	– –	– –	– –	4 1
29 Huddersfield Town	– –	4 –	– –	– –	– –	– –	– –	– –	– –	4 –
30 Hibernians Malta	– –	– –	– –	– –	– –	2 2	– –	– –	– –	2 2
31 Real Madrid	– –	– –	– –	– –	– –	2 1	– –	– –	– –	2 1
32 Anderlecht	– –	– –	– –	– –	– –	2 –	– –	– –	– –	2 –
33 Estudiantes de la Plata	– –	– –	– –	– –	– –	– –	– –	– –	2 –	2 –
34 Gornik Zabrze	– –	– –	– –	– –	– –	2 –	– –	– –	– –	2 –
35 Norwich City	– –	1 –	– –	1 –	– –	– –	– –	– –	– –	2 –
36 Oxford United	– –	– –	– –	– –	2 –	– –	– –	– –	– –	2 –
37 Sarajevo	– –	– –	– –	– –	– –	– –	2 –	– –	– –	2 –
38 Waterford	– –	– –	– –	– –	– –	2 –	– –	– –	– –	2 –
39 Blackburn Rovers	– –	1 1	– –	– –	– –	– –	– –	– –	– –	1 1
40 Aldershot	– –	– –	– –	– –	1 –	– –	– –	– –	– –	1 –
41 Benfica	– –	– –	– –	– –	– –	1 –	– –	– –	– –	1 –
42 Bolton Wanderers	– –	1 –	– –	– –	– –	– –	– –	– –	– –	1 –
43 Northampton Town	– –	– –	– –	1 –	– –	– –	– –	– –	– –	1 –
44 Portsmouth	– –	– –	– –	– –	1 –	– –	– –	– –	– –	1 –
45 Preston North End	– –	– –	– –	1 –	– –	– –	– –	– –	– –	1 –
46 Queens Park Rangers	– –	1 –	– –	– –	– –	– –	– –	– –	– –	1 –
47 Rapid Vienna	– –	– –	– –	– –	– –	1 –	– –	– –	– –	1 –
48 Watford	– –	– –	– –	1 –	– –	– –	– –	– –	– –	1 –
49 Willem II	– –	– –	– –	– –	– –	– –	– –	1 –	– –	1 –
50 Wrexham	– –	– –	– –	– –	1 –	– –	– –	– –	– –	1 –
51 Exeter City	– –	– –	– –	– (1) –	– –	– –	– –	– –	– –	– (1) –

CHARLES SAGAR

DEBUT (Full Appearance, 3 goals)

Saturday 02/09/1905
Football League Division 2
at Bank Street

Manchester United 5 Bristol City 1

CLUB CAREER RECORD	Apps	Subs	Goals
Premiership	0		0
League Division 1	10		4
League Division 2	20		16
FA Cup	3		4
League Cup	0		0
European Cup / Champions League	0		0
European Cup-Winners' Cup	0		0
UEFA Cup / Inter-Cities' Fairs Cup	0		0
Other Matches	0		0
OVERALL TOTAL	33		24

Opponents	PREM A S G	FLD 1 A S G	FLD 2 A S G	FAC A S G	LC A S G	EC/CL A S G	ECWC A S G	UEFA A S G	OTHER A S G	TOTAL A S G
1 Bristol City	– –	1 –	1 3	– –	– –	– –	– –	– –	– –	2 3
2 Burton United	– –	– –	2 2	– –	– –	– –	– –	– –	– –	2 2
3 Leicester City	– –	– –	2 2	– –	– –	– –	– –	– –	– –	2 2
4 Chelsea	– –	– –	2 1	– –	– –	– –	– –	– –	– –	2 1
5 Middlesbrough	– –	2 1	– –	– –	– –	– –	– –	– –	– –	2 1
6 Preston North End	– –	2 1	– –	– –	– –	– –	– –	– –	– –	2 1
7 Barnsley	– –	– –	1 3	– –	– –	– –	– –	– –	– –	1 3
8 Aston Villa	– –	– –	– –	1 2	– –	– –	– –	– –	– –	1 2
9 Arsenal	– –	– –	– –	1 1	– –	– –	– –	– –	– –	1 1
10 Blackburn Rovers	– –	1 1	– –	– –	– –	– –	– –	– –	– –	1 1
11 Burnley	– –	– –	1 1	– –	– –	– –	– –	– –	– –	1 1
12 Chesterfield	– –	– –	1 1	– –	– –	– –	– –	– –	– –	1 1
13 Grimsby Town	– –	– –	1 1	– –	– –	– –	– –	– –	– –	1 1
14 Hull City	– –	– –	1 1	– –	– –	– –	– –	– –	– –	1 1
15 Norwich City	– –	– –	– –	1 1	– –	– –	– –	– –	– –	1 1
16 Sheffield Wednesday	– –	1 1	– –	– –	– –	– –	– –	– –	– –	1 1
17 Stockport County	– –	– –	1 1	– –	– –	– –	– –	– –	– –	1 1
18 Blackpool	– –	– –	1 –	– –	– –	– –	– –	– –	– –	1 –
19 Bradford City	– –	– –	1 –	– –	– –	– –	– –	– –	– –	1 –
20 Derby County	– –	1 –	– –	– –	– –	– –	– –	– –	– –	1 –
21 Everton	– –	1 –	– –	– –	– –	– –	– –	– –	– –	1 –

continued../

CHARLES SAGAR (continued)

Opponents	PREM A S G	FLD 1 A S G	FLD 2 A S G	FAC A S G	LC A S G	EC/CL A S G	ECWC A S G	UEFA A S G	OTHER A S G	TOTAL A S G
22 Gainsborough Trinity	– –	– –	1 –	– –	– –	– –	– –	– –	– –	1 –
23 Leeds United	– –	– –	1 –	– –	– –	– –	– –	– –	– –	1 –
24 Leyton Orient	– –	– –	1 –	– –	– –	– –	– –	– –	– –	1 –
25 Lincoln City	– –	– –	1 –	– –	– –	– –	– –	– –	– –	1 –
26 Notts County	– –	1 –	– –	– –	– –	– –	– –	– –	– –	1 –
27 Port Vale	– –	– –	– –	1 –	– –	– –	– –	– –	– –	1 –

LOUIS SAHA

DEBUT (Full Appearance, 1 goal)

Saturday 31/01/2004
FA Premiership
at Old Trafford

Manchester United 3 Southampton 2

CLUB CAREER RECORD	Apps	Subs	Goals
Premiership	52	(34)	28
League Division 1	0		0
League Division 2	0		0
FA Cup	6	(4)	3
League Cup	9		7
European Cup / Champions League	9	(10)	4
European Cup-Winners' Cup	0		0
UEFA Cup / Inter-Cities' Fairs Cup	0		0
Other Matches	0		0
OVERALL TOTAL	**76**	**(48)**	**42**

Opponents	PREM A S G	FLD 1 A S G	FLD 2 A S G	FAC A S G	LC A S G	EC/CL A S G	ECWC A S G	UEFA A S G	OTHER A S G	TOTAL A S G
1 Arsenal	1 (6) 1	– –	– –	– (1) –	– –	– –	– –	– –	– –	1 (7) 1
2 Birmingham City	4 (2) 1	– –	– –	– –	1 2	– –	– –	– –	– –	5 (2) 3
3 Chelsea	2 (3) 2	– –	– –	– –	2 –	– –	– –	– –	– –	4 (3) 2
4 Blackburn Rovers	3 (1) 2	– –	– –	– –	2 2	– –	– –	– –	– –	5 (1) 4
5 Fulham	4 (2) 3	– –	– –	– –	– –	– –	– –	– –	– –	4 (2) 3
6 Liverpool	3 (2) –	– –	– –	– (1) –	– –	– –	– –	– –	– –	3 (3) –
7 Bolton Wanderers	5 – 2	– –	– –	– –	– –	– –	– –	– –	– –	5 – 2
8 Everton	3 (2) 2	– –	– –	– –	– –	– –	– –	– –	– –	3 (2) 2
9 Aston Villa	2 (2) 1	– –	– –	1 –	– –	– –	– –	– –	– –	3 (2) 1
10 Portsmouth	2 (3) 1	– –	– –	– –	– –	– –	– –	– –	– –	2 (3) 1
11 Charlton Athletic	4 – 3	– –	– –	– –	– –	– –	– –	– –	– –	4 – 3
12 Middlesbrough	3 – 1	– –	– –	– (1) –	– –	– –	– –	– –	– –	3 (1) 1
13 West Bromwich Albion	1 (2) 2	– –	– –	– –	1 1	– –	– –	– –	– –	2 (2) 3
14 Wigan Athletic	2 – 1	– –	– –	– –	1 1	– –	– –	– –	– –	3 – 2
15 Benfica	– –	– –	– –	– –	– –	2 (1) 2	– –	– –	– –	2 (1) 2
16 Manchester City	2 (1) 1	– –	– –	– –	– –	– –	– –	– –	– –	2 (1) 1
17 Newcastle United	2 (1) 1	– –	– –	– –	– –	– –	– –	– –	– –	2 (1) 1
18 Reading	– (1) –	– –	– –	2 1	– –	– –	– –	– –	– –	2 (1) 1
19 Roma	– –	– –	– –	– –	– –	2 (1) –	– –	– –	– –	2 (1) –
20 West Ham United	2 (1) –	– –	– –	– –	– –	– –	– –	– –	– –	2 (1) –
21 Glasgow Celtic	– –	– –	– –	– –	– –	2 2	– –	– –	– –	2 – 2
22 Burton Albion	– –	– –	– –	2 1	– –	– –	– –	– –	– –	2 – 1
23 Sunderland	1 (1) 3	– –	– –	– –	– –	– –	– –	– –	– –	1 (1) 3
24 Southampton	1 (1) 1	– –	– –	– –	– –	– –	– –	– –	– –	1 (1) 1
25 Porto	– –	– –	– –	– –	– –	1 (1) –	– –	– –	– –	1 (1) –
26 Sporting Lisbon	– –	– –	– –	– –	– –	1 (1) –	– –	– –	– –	1 (1) –
27 Tottenham Hotspur	1 (1) –	– –	– –	– –	– –	– –	– –	– –	– –	1 (1) –
28 AC Milan	– –	– –	– –	– –	– –	– (2) –	– –	– –	– –	– (2) –
29 Derby County	– (2) –	– –	– –	– –	– –	– –	– –	– –	– –	– (2) –
30 Crystal Palace	– –	– –	– –	– –	1 1	– –	– –	– –	– –	1 1
31 Wolverhampton W.	– –	– –	– –	1 1	– –	– –	– –	– –	– –	1 1
32 Copenhagen	– –	– –	– –	– –	– –	1 –	– –	– –	– –	1 –
33 Crewe Alexandra	– –	– –	– –	– –	1 –	– –	– –	– –	– –	1 –
34 Leicester City	1 –	– –	– –	– –	– –	– –	– –	– –	– –	1 –
35 Norwich City	1 –	– –	– –	– –	– –	– –	– –	– –	– –	1 –
36 Sheffield United	1 –	– –	– –	– –	– –	– –	– –	– –	– –	1 –
37 Watford	1 –	– –	– –	– –	– –	– –	– –	– –	– –	1 –
38 Dynamo Kiev	– –	– –	– –	– –	– –	– (1) –	– –	– –	– –	– (1) –
39 Exeter City	– –	– –	– –	– (1) –	– –	– –	– –	– –	– –	– (1) –
40 Lille Metropole	– –	– –	– –	– –	– –	– (1) –	– –	– –	– –	– (1) –
41 Sparta Prague	– –	– –	– –	– –	– –	– (1) –	– –	– –	– –	– (1) –
42 Villarreal	– –	– –	– –	– –	– –	– (1) –	– –	– –	– –	– (1) –

GEORGE SAPSFORD

DEBUT (Full Appearance)

Monday 26/04/1920
Football League Division 1
at Old Trafford

Manchester United 0 Notts County 0

CLUB CAREER RECORD	Apps	Subs	Goals
Premiership	0		0
League Division 1	52		16
League Division 2	0		0
FA Cup	1		1
League Cup	0		0
European Cup / Champions League	0		0
European Cup-Winners' Cup	0		0
UEFA Cup / Inter-Cities' Fairs Cup	0		0
Other Matches	0		0
OVERALL TOTAL	**53**		**17**

Opponents	PREM			FLD 1			FLD 2			FAC			LC			EC/CL			ECWC			UEFA			OTHER			TOTAL		
	A	S	G	A	S	G	A	S	G	A	S	G	A	S	G	A	S	G	A	S	G	A	S	G	A	S	G	A	S	G
1 Sunderland	–	–		4		4	–			–			–			–			–			–			–			4		4
2 Tottenham Hotspur	–	–		4		2	–			–			–			–			–			–			–			4		2
3 Bolton Wanderers	–	–		4		1	–			–			–			–			–			–			–			4		1
4 Bradford City	–	–		4		1	–			–			–			–			–			–			–			4		1
5 Chelsea	–	–		4		–	–			–			–			–			–			–			–			4		–
6 Oldham Athletic	–	–		3		2	–			–			–			–			–			–			–			3		2
7 Arsenal	–	–		3		–	–			–			–			–			–			–			–			3		–
8 Manchester City	–	–		3		–	–			–			–			–			–			–			–			3		–
9 Birmingham City	–	–		2		1	–			–			–			–			–			–			–			2		1
10 Burnley	–	–		2		1	–			–			–			–			–			–			–			2		1
11 Derby County	–	–		2		1	–			–			–			–			–			–			–			2		1
12 Huddersfield Town	–	–		2		1	–			–			–			–			–			–			–			2		1
13 Middlesbrough	–	–		2		1	–			–			–			–			–			–			–			2		1
14 Aston Villa	–	–		2		–	–			–			–			–			–			–			–			2		–
15 Blackburn Rovers	–	–		2		–	–			–			–			–			–			–			–			2		–
16 Everton	–	–		2		–	–			–			–			–			–			–			–			2		–
17 Notts County	–	–		2		–	–			–			–			–			–			–			–			2		–
18 Preston North End	–	–		2		–	–			–			–			–			–			–			–			2		–
19 Cardiff City	–	–		–		–	–			1		1	–			–			–			–			–			1		1
20 Liverpool	–	–		1		1	–			–			–			–			–			–			–			1		1
21 Newcastle United	–	–		1		–	–			–			–			–			–			–			–			1		–
22 West Bromwich Albion	–	–		1		–	–			–			–			–			–			–			–			1		–

CARLO SARTORI

DEBUT (Substitute Appearance)

Wednesday 09/10/1968
Football League Division 1
at White Hart Lane

Tottenham Hotspur 2 Manchester United 2

CLUB CAREER RECORD	Apps	Subs	Goals
Premiership	0		0
League Division 1	26	(13)	4
League Division 2	0		0
FA Cup	9		1
League Cup	3	(2)	0
European Cup / Champions League	2		1
European Cup-Winners' Cup	0		0
UEFA Cup / Inter-Cities' Fairs Cup	0		0
Other Matches	0		0
OVERALL TOTAL	**40**	**(15)**	**6**

Opponents	PREM			FLD 1			FLD 2			FAC			LC			EC/CL			ECWC			UEFA			OTHER			TOTAL		
	A	S	G	A	S	G	A	S	G	A	S	G	A	S	G	A	S	G	A	S	G	A	S	G	A	S	G	A	S	G
1 Leeds United	–	–		2 (2)		–	–			3			–			–			–			–			–			5 (2)		–
2 Manchester City	–	–		2 (1)		–	–			1			–			–			–			–			–			3 (1)		–
3 Derby County	–	–		1 (1)		–	–			–			1 (1)		–	–			–			–			–			2 (2)		–
4 Wolverhampton W.	–	–		2 (2)		–	–			–			–			–			–			–			–			2 (2)		–
5 Stoke City	–	–		2		1	–			–			1			–			–			–			–			3		1
6 Liverpool	–	–		2 (1)		–	–			–			–			–			–			–			–			2 (1)		–
7 Southampton	–	–		2 (1)		–	–			–			–			–			–			–			–			2 (1)		–
8 Arsenal	–	–		1 (2)		2	–			–			–			–			–			–			–			1 (2)		2
9 Anderlecht	–	–		–			–			–			–			2		1	–			–			–			2		1
10 Middlesbrough	–	–		–			–			2		1	–			–			–			–			–			2		1
11 Sunderland	–	–		2		–	–			–			–			–			–			–			–			2		–
12 Burnley	–	–		1		–	–			–			– (1)		–	–			–			–			–			1 (1)		–
13 Ipswich Town	–	–		1 (1)		–	–			–			–			–			–			–			–			1 (1)		–
14 Tottenham Hotspur	–	–		1 (1)		–	–			–			–			–			–			–			–			1 (1)		–
15 Nottingham Forest	–	–		1		1	–			–			–			–			–			–			–			1		1
16 Aston Villa	–	–		–			–			–			1			–			–			–			–			1		–
17 Chelsea	–	–		1		–	–			–			–			–			–			–			–			1		–
18 Coventry City	–	–		1		–	–			–			–			–			–			–			–			1		–
19 Crystal Palace	–	–		1		–	–			–			–			–			–			–			–			1		–
20 Exeter City	–	–		–			–			1			–			–			–			–			–			1		–
21 Leicester City	–	–		1		–	–			–			–			–			–			–			–			1		–
22 Northampton Town	–	–		–			–			1			–			–			–			–			–			1		–
23 Watford	–	–		–			–			1			–			–			–			–			–			1		–
24 West Bromwich Albion	–	–		1		–	–			–			–			–			–			–			–			1		–
25 West Ham United	–	–		1		–	–			–			–			–			–			–			–			1		–
26 Newcastle United	–	–		– (1)		–	–			–			–			–			–			–			–			– (1)		–

WILLIAM SARVIS

DEBUT (Full Appearance)

Saturday 23/09/1922
Football League Division 2
at Highfield Road

Coventry City 2 Manchester United 0

CLUB CAREER RECORD	Apps	Subs	Goals
Premiership	0		0
League Division 1	0		0
League Division 2	1		0
FA Cup	0		0
League Cup	0		0
European Cup / Champions League	0		0
European Cup-Winners' Cup	0		0
UEFA Cup / Inter-Cities' Fairs Cup	0		0
Other Matches	0		0
OVERALL TOTAL	1		0

Opponents	PREM A S G	FLD 1 A S G	FLD 2 A S G	FAC A S G	LC A S G	EC/CL A S G	ECWC A S G	UEFA A S G	OTHER A S G	TOTAL A S G
1 Coventry City	– –	– –	1 –	– –	– –	– –	– –	– –	– –	1 –

JAMES SAUNDERS

DEBUT (Full Appearance)

Thursday 26/12/1901
Football League Division 2
at Sincil Bank

Lincoln City 2 Newton Heath 0

CLUB CAREER RECORD	Apps	Subs	Goals
Premiership	0		0
League Division 1	0		0
League Division 2	12		0
FA Cup	1		0
League Cup	0		0
European Cup / Champions League	0		0
European Cup-Winners' Cup	0		0
UEFA Cup / Inter-Cities' Fairs Cup	0		0
Other Matches	0		0
OVERALL TOTAL	13		0

Opponents	PREM A S G	FLD 1 A S G	FLD 2 A S G	FAC A S G	LC A S G	EC/CL A S G	ECWC A S G	UEFA A S G	OTHER A S G	TOTAL A S G
1 Barnsley	– –	– –	2 –	– –	– –	– –	– –	– –	– –	2 –
2 Lincoln City	– –	– –	2 –	– –	– –	– –	– –	– –	– –	2 –
3 Burnley	– –	– –	1 –	– –	– –	– –	– –	– –	– –	1 –
4 Chesterfield	– –	– –	1 –	– –	– –	– –	– –	– –	– –	1 –
5 Doncaster Rovers	– –	– –	1 –	– –	– –	– –	– –	– –	– –	1 –
6 Gainsborough Trinity	– –	– –	1 –	– –	– –	– –	– –	– –	– –	1 –
7 Glossop	– –	– –	1 –	– –	– –	– –	– –	– –	– –	1 –
8 Leicester City	– –	– –	1 –	– –	– –	– –	– –	– –	– –	1 –
9 Oswaldtwistle Rovers	– –	– –	– –	1 –	– –	– –	– –	– –	– –	1 –
10 Preston North End	– –	– –	1 –	– –	– –	– –	– –	– –	– –	1 –
11 Stockport County	– –	– –	1 –	– –	– –	– –	– –	– –	– –	1 –

TED SAVAGE

DEBUT (Full Appearance)

Saturday 01/01/1938
Football League Division 2
at St James' Park

Newcastle United 2 Manchester United 2

CLUB CAREER RECORD	Apps	Subs	Goals
Premiership	0		0
League Division 1	0		0
League Division 2	4		0
FA Cup	1		0
League Cup	0		0
European Cup / Champions League	0		0
European Cup-Winners' Cup	0		0
UEFA Cup / Inter-Cities' Fairs Cup	0		0
Other Matches	0		0
OVERALL TOTAL	5		0

Opponents	PREM A S G	FLD 1 A S G	FLD 2 A S G	FAC A S G	LC A S G	EC/CL A S G	ECWC A S G	UEFA A S G	OTHER A S G	TOTAL A S G
1 Barnsley	– –	– –	1 –	1 –	– –	– –	– –	– –	– –	2 –
2 Luton Town	– –	– –	1 –	– –	– –	– –	– –	– –	– –	1 –
3 Newcastle United	– –	– –	1 –	– –	– –	– –	– –	– –	– –	1 –
4 Stockport County	– –	– –	1 –	– –	– –	– –	– –	– –	– –	1 –

F SAWYER

DEBUT (Full Appearance)

Saturday 14/10/1899
Football League Division 2
at Muntz Street

Birmingham City 1 Newton Heath 0

CLUB CAREER RECORD	Apps	Subs	Goals
Premiership	0		0
League Division 1	0		0
League Division 2	6		0
FA Cup	0		0
League Cup	0		0
European Cup / Champions League	0		0
European Cup-Winners' Cup	0		0
UEFA Cup / Inter-Cities' Fairs Cup	0		0
Other Matches	0		0
OVERALL TOTAL	**6**		**0**

Opponents	PREM A S G	FLD 1 A S G	FLD 2 A S G	FAC A S G	LC A S G	EC/CL A S G	ECWC A S G	UEFA A S G	OTHER A S G	TOTAL A S G
1 Birmingham City	– – –	– – –	2 – –	– – –	– – –	– – –	– – –	– – –	– – –	2 – –
2 Barnsley	– – –	– – –	1 – –	– – –	– – –	– – –	– – –	– – –	– – –	1 – –
3 Chesterfield	– – –	– – –	1 – –	– – –	– – –	– – –	– – –	– – –	– – –	1 – –
4 Grimsby Town	– – –	– – –	1 – –	– – –	– – –	– – –	– – –	– – –	– – –	1 – –
5 Loughborough Town	– – –	– – –	1 – –	– – –	– – –	– – –	– – –	– – –	– – –	1 – –

ALBERT SCANLON

DEBUT (Full Appearance)

Saturday 20/11/1954
Football League Division 1
at Old Trafford

Manchester United 2 Arsenal 1

CLUB CAREER RECORD	Apps	Subs	Goals
Premiership	0		0
League Division 1	115		34
League Division 2	0		0
FA Cup	6		1
League Cup	3		0
European Cup / Champions League	3		0
European Cup-Winners' Cup	0		0
UEFA Cup / Inter-Cities' Fairs Cup	0		0
Other Matches	0		0
OVERALL TOTAL	**127**		**35**

Opponents	PREM A S G	FLD 1 A S G	FLD 2 A S G	FAC A S G	LC A S G	EC/CL A S G	ECWC A S G	UEFA A S G	OTHER A S G	TOTAL A S G
1 West Bromwich Albion	– – –	8 – 2	– – –	– – –	– – –	– – –	– – –	– – –	– – –	8 – 2
2 Tottenham Hotspur	– – –	8 – 1	– – –	– – –	– – –	– – –	– – –	– – –	– – –	8 – 1
3 Luton Town	– – –	7 – 1	– – –	– – –	– – –	– – –	– – –	– – –	– – –	7 – 1
4 Newcastle United	– – –	7 – 1	– – –	– – –	– – –	– – –	– – –	– – –	– – –	7 – 1
5 Leicester City	– – –	6 – 3	– – –	– – –	– – –	– – –	– – –	– – –	– – –	6 – 3
6 Burnley	– – –	6 – 2	– – –	– – –	– – –	– – –	– – –	– – –	– – –	6 – 2
7 Everton	– – –	6 – 2	– – –	– – –	– – –	– – –	– – –	– – –	– – –	6 – 2
8 Manchester City	– – –	6 – 1	– – –	– – –	– – –	– – –	– – –	– – –	– – –	6 – 1
9 Arsenal	– – –	6 – –	– – –	– – –	– – –	– – –	– – –	– – –	– – –	6 – –
10 Leeds United	– – –	5 – 2	– – –	– – –	– – –	– – –	– – –	– – –	– – –	5 – 2
11 Preston North End	– – –	5 – 2	– – –	– – –	– – –	– – –	– – –	– – –	– – –	5 – 2
12 Birmingham City	– – –	5 – 1	– – –	– – –	– – –	– – –	– – –	– – –	– – –	5 – 1
13 Wolverhampton W.	– – –	5 – –	– – –	– – –	– – –	– – –	– – –	– – –	– – –	5 – –
14 Blackburn Rovers	– – –	4 – 2	– – –	– – –	– – –	– – –	– – –	– – –	– – –	4 – 2
15 Bolton Wanderers	– – –	4 – 2	– – –	– – –	– – –	– – –	– – –	– – –	– – –	4 – 2
16 Nottingham Forest	– – –	4 – 2	– – –	– – –	– – –	– – –	– – –	– – –	– – –	4 – 2
17 Blackpool	– – –	4 – 1	– – –	– – –	– – –	– – –	– – –	– – –	– – –	4 – 1
18 Chelsea	– – –	4 – 1	– – –	– – –	– – –	– – –	– – –	– – –	– – –	4 – 1
19 West Ham United	– – –	3 – 4	– – –	– – –	– – –	– – –	– – –	– – –	– – –	3 – 4
20 Aston Villa	– – –	3 – –	– – –	– – –	– – –	– – –	– – –	– – –	– – –	3 – –
21 Sunderland	– – –	2 – 1	– – –	– – –	– – –	– – –	– – –	– – –	– – –	2 – 1
22 Exeter City	– – –	– – –	– – –	– – –	2 – –	– – –	– – –	– – –	– – –	2 – –
23 Portsmouth	– – –	2 – –	– – –	– – –	– – –	– – –	– – –	– – –	– – –	2 – –
24 Red Star Belgrade	– – –	– – –	– – –	– – –	– – –	2 – –	– – –	– – –	– – –	2 – –
25 Sheffield Wednesday	– – –	1 – –	– – –	1 – –	– – –	– – –	– – –	– – –	– – –	2 – –
26 Cardiff City	– – –	1 – 2	– – –	– – –	– – –	– – –	– – –	– – –	– – –	1 – 2
27 Derby County	– – –	– – –	– – –	1 – 1	– – –	– – –	– – –	– – –	– – –	1 – 1
28 Fulham	– – –	1 – 1	– – –	– – –	– – –	– – –	– – –	– – –	– – –	1 – 1
29 Bradford City	– – –	– – –	– – –	– – –	1 – –	– – –	– – –	– – –	– – –	1 – –
30 Charlton Athletic	– – –	1 – –	– – –	– – –	– – –	– – –	– – –	– – –	– – –	1 – –
31 Dukla Prague	– – –	– – –	– – –	– – –	– – –	1 – –	– – –	– – –	– – –	1 – –
32 Ipswich Town	– – –	– – –	– – –	1 – –	– – –	– – –	– – –	– – –	– – –	1 – –
33 Liverpool	– – –	– – –	– – –	1 – –	– – –	– – –	– – –	– – –	– – –	1 – –
34 Norwich City	– – –	– – –	– – –	1 – –	– – –	– – –	– – –	– – –	– – –	1 – –
35 Sheffield United	– – –	1 – –	– – –	– – –	– – –	– – –	– – –	– – –	– – –	1 – –
36 Workington	– – –	– – –	– – –	1 – –	– – –	– – –	– – –	– – –	– – –	1 – –

PETER SCHMEICHEL

DEBUT (Full Appearance)

Saturday 17/08/1991
Football League Division 1
at Old Trafford

Manchester United 2 Notts County 0

CLUB CAREER RECORD	Apps	Subs	Goals
Premiership	252		0
League Division 1	40		0
League Division 2	0		0
FA Cup	41		0
League Cup	17		0
European Cup / Champions League	36		0
European Cup-Winners' Cup	3		0
UEFA Cup / Inter-Cities' Fairs Cup	3		1
Other Matches	6		0
OVERALL TOTAL	**398**		**1**

Opponents	PREM			FLD 1			FLD 2			FAC			LC			EC/CL			ECWC			UEFA			OTHER			TOTAL		
	A	S	G	A	S	G	A	S	G	A	S	G	A	S	G	A	S	G	A	S	G	A	S	G	A	S	G	A	S	G
1 Arsenal	13	–		2	–		–	–		2	–		–	–		–	–		–	–		–	–		2	–		19	–	
2 Chelsea	12	–		1	–		–	–		5	–		–	–		–	–		–	–		–	–		1	–		19	–	
3 Leeds United	13	–		2	–		–	–		2	–		1	–		–	–		–	–		–	–		–	–		18	–	
4 Liverpool	14	–		2	–		–	–		2	–		–	–		–	–		–	–		–	–		–	–		18	–	
5 Everton	13	–		2	–		–	–		1	–		1	–		–	–		–	–		–	–		–	–		17	–	
6 Tottenham Hotspur	14	–		2	–		–	–		1	–		–	–		–	–		–	–		–	–		–	–		17	–	
7 Wimbledon	12	–		2	–		–	–		3	–		–	–		–	–		–	–		–	–		–	–		17	–	
8 Southampton	11	–		2	–		–	–		3	–		–	–		–	–		–	–		–	–		–	–		16	–	
9 Aston Villa	12	–		2	–		–	–		–	–		1	–		–	–		–	–		–	–		–	–		15	–	
10 Sheffield Wednesday	11	–		2	–		–	–		–	–		2	–		–	–		–	–		–	–		–	–		15	–	
11 Blackburn Rovers	13	–		–	–		–	–		–	–		–	–		–	–		–	–		1	–		–	–		14	–	
12 Newcastle United	12	–		–	–		–	–		1	–		–	–		–	–		–	–		1	–		–	–		14	–	
13 West Ham United	11	–		2	–		–	–		–	–		–	–		–	–		–	–		–	–		–	–		13	–	
14 Coventry City	11	–		1	–		–	–		–	–		–	–		–	–		–	–		–	–		–	–		12	–	
15 Nottingham Forest	9	–		2	–		–	–		–	–		1	–		–	–		–	–		–	–		–	–		12	–	
16 Manchester City	8	–		2	–		–	–		1	–		–	–		–	–		–	–		–	–		–	–		11	–	
17 Middlesbrough	8	–		–	–		–	–		1	–		2	–		–	–		–	–		–	–		–	–		11	–	
18 Crystal Palace	6	–		2	–		–	–		2	–		–	–		–	–		–	–		–	–		–	–		10	–	
19 Queens Park Rangers	7	–		2	–		–	–		1	–		–	–		–	–		–	–		–	–		–	–		10	–	
20 Oldham Athletic	4	–		2	–		–	–		2	–		1	–		–	–		–	–		–	–		–	–		9	–	
21 Sheffield United	4	–		2	–		–	–		3	–		–	–		–	–		–	–		–	–		–	–		9	–	
22 Leicester City	7	–		–	–		–	–		–	–		1	–		–	–		–	–		–	–		–	–		8	–	
23 Norwich City	5	–		2	–		–	–		1	–		–	–		–	–		–	–		–	–		–	–		8	–	
24 Derby County	6	–		–	–		–	–		–	–		–	–		–	–		–	–		–	–		–	–		6	–	
25 Juventus	–	–		–	–		–	–		–	–		–	–		6	–		–	–		–	–		–	–		6	–	
26 Ipswich Town	5	–		–	–		–	–		–	–		–	–		–	–		–	–		–	–		–	–		5	–	
27 Bolton Wanderers	4	–		–	–		–	–		–	–		–	–		–	–		–	–		–	–		–	–		4	–	
28 Barcelona	–	–		–	–		–	–		–	–		–	–		3	–		–	–		–	–		–	–		3	–	
29 Barnsley	1	–		–	–		–	–		2	–		–	–		–	–		–	–		–	–		–	–		3	–	
30 Bayern Munich	–	–		–	–		–	–		–	–		–	–		3	–		–	–		–	–		–	–		3	–	
31 Charlton Athletic	2	–		–	–		–	–		1	–		–	–		–	–		–	–		–	–		–	–		3	–	
32 Galatasaray	–	–		–	–		–	–		–	–		–	–		3	–		–	–		–	–		–	–		3	–	
33 Portsmouth	–	–		–	–		–	–		3	–		–	–		–	–		–	–		–	–		–	–		3	–	
34 Sunderland	2	–		–	–		–	–		1	–		–	–		–	–		–	–		–	–		–	–		3	–	
35 Rotor Volgograd	–	–		–	–		–	–		–	–		–	–		–	–		–	–		2	1		–	–		2		1
36 Athinaikos	–	–		–	–		–	–		–	–		–	–		–	–		2	–		–	–		–	–		2	–	
37 Brighton	–	–		–	–		–	–		1	–		1	–		–	–		–	–		–	–		–	–		2	–	
38 Brondby	–	–		–	–		–	–		–	–		–	–		2	–		–	–		–	–		–	–		2	–	
39 Fenerbahce	–	–		–	–		–	–		–	–		–	–		2	–		–	–		–	–		–	–		2	–	
40 Feyenoord	–	–		–	–		–	–		–	–		–	–		2	–		–	–		–	–		–	–		2	–	
41 Honved	–	–		–	–		–	–		–	–		–	–		2	–		–	–		–	–		–	–		2	–	
42 Internazionale	–	–		–	–		–	–		–	–		–	–		2	–		–	–		–	–		–	–		2	–	
43 Kosice	–	–		–	–		–	–		–	–		–	–		2	–		–	–		–	–		–	–		2	–	
44 LKS Lodz	–	–		–	–		–	–		–	–		–	–		2	–		–	–		–	–		–	–		2	–	
45 Luton Town	–	–		2	–		–	–		–	–		–	–		–	–		–	–		–	–		–	–		2	–	
46 Notts County	–	–		2	–		–	–		–	–		–	–		–	–		–	–		–	–		–	–		2	–	
47 Porto	–	–		–	–		–	–		–	–		–	–		2	–		–	–		–	–		–	–		2	–	
48 Rapid Vienna	–	–		–	–		–	–		–	–		–	–		2	–		–	–		–	–		–	–		2	–	
49 Stoke City	–	–		–	–		–	–		–	–		2	–		–	–		–	–		–	–		–	–		2	–	
50 Swindon Town	2	–		–	–		–	–		–	–		–	–		–	–		–	–		–	–		–	–		2	–	
51 Athletico Madrid	–	–		–	–		–	–		–	–		–	–		–	–		1	–		–	–		–	–		1	–	
52 Borussia Dortmund	–	–		–	–		–	–		–	–		–	–		1	–		–	–		–	–		–	–		1	–	
53 Bury	–	–		–	–		–	–		1	–		–	–		–	–		–	–		–	–		–	–		1	–	
54 Fulham	–	–		–	–		–	–		1	–		–	–		–	–		–	–		–	–		–	–		1	–	
55 Gothenburg	–	–		–	–		–	–		–	–		–	–		1	–		–	–		–	–		–	–		1	–	
56 Monaco	–	–		–	–		–	–		–	–		–	–		1	–		–	–		–	–		–	–		1	–	
57 Reading	–	–		–	–		–	–		1	–		–	–		–	–		–	–		–	–		–	–		1	–	
58 Red Star Belgrade	–	–		–	–		–	–		–	–		–	–		–	–		–	–		1	–		–	–		1	–	
59 Torpedo Moscow	–	–		–	–		–	–		–	–		–	–		–	–		1	–		–	–		–	–		1	–	
60 Walsall	–	–		–	–		–	–		1	–		–	–		–	–		–	–		–	–		–	–		1	–	
61 Wrexham	–	–		–	–		–	–		1	–		–	–		–	–		–	–		–	–		–	–		1	–	
62 York City	–	–		–	–		–	–		–	–		1	–		–	–		–	–		–	–		–	–		1	–	

ALF SCHOFIELD

DEBUT (Full Appearance)

Saturday 01/09/1900
Football League Division 2
at North Road

Glossop 1 Newton Heath 0

CLUB CAREER RECORD	Apps	Subs	Goals
Premiership	0		0
League Division 1	10		2
League Division 2	147		28
FA Cup	22		5
League Cup	0		0
European Cup / Champions League	0		0
European Cup–Winners' Cup	0		0
UEFA Cup / Inter–Cities' Fairs Cup	0		0
Other Matches	0		0
OVERALL TOTAL	179		35

Opponents	PREM			FLD 1			FLD 2			FAC			LC			EC/CL			ECWC			UEFA			OTHER			TOTAL		
	A	S	G	A	S	G	A	S	G	A	S	G	A	S	G	A	S	G	A	S	G	A	S	G	A	S	G	A	S	G
1 Port Vale	–	–	–	–	–	–	10	–	4	–	–	–	–	–	–	–	–	–	–	–	–	–	–	–	–	–	–	10	–	4
2 Leicester City	–	–	–	–	–	–	10	–	3	–	–	–	–	–	–	–	–	–	–	–	–	–	–	–	–	–	–	10	–	3
3 Lincoln City	–	–	–	–	–	–	9	–	2	1	–	–	–	–	–	–	–	–	–	–	–	–	–	–	–	–	–	10	–	2
4 Burnley	–	–	–	–	–	–	8	–	–	2	–	1	–	–	–	–	–	–	–	–	–	–	–	–	–	–	–	10	–	1
5 Burton United	–	–	–	–	–	–	7	–	2	2	–	1	–	–	–	–	–	–	–	–	–	–	–	–	–	–	–	9	–	3
6 Barnsley	–	–	–	–	–	–	9	–	2	–	–	–	–	–	–	–	–	–	–	–	–	–	–	–	–	–	–	9	–	2
7 Gainsborough Trinity	–	–	–	–	–	–	9	–	–	–	–	–	–	–	–	–	–	–	–	–	–	–	–	–	–	–	–	9	–	–
8 Stockport County	–	–	–	–	–	–	8	–	5	–	–	–	–	–	–	–	–	–	–	–	–	–	–	–	–	–	–	8	–	5
9 Arsenal	–	–	–	1	–	–	6	–	–	1	–	–	–	–	–	–	–	–	–	–	–	–	–	–	–	–	–	8	–	–
10 Blackpool	–	–	–	–	–	–	7	–	3	–	–	–	–	–	–	–	–	–	–	–	–	–	–	–	–	–	–	7	–	3
11 Bristol City	–	–	–	1	–	–	6	–	1	–	–	–	–	–	–	–	–	–	–	–	–	–	–	–	–	–	–	7	–	1
12 Chesterfield	–	–	–	–	–	–	7	–	–	–	–	–	–	–	–	–	–	–	–	–	–	–	–	–	–	–	–	7	–	–
13 Glossop	–	–	–	–	–	–	7	–	–	–	–	–	–	–	–	–	–	–	–	–	–	–	–	–	–	–	–	7	–	–
14 Birmingham City	–	–	–	–	–	–	2	–	–	4	–	2	–	–	–	–	–	–	–	–	–	–	–	–	–	–	–	6	–	2
15 Preston North End	–	–	–	1	–	–	5	–	–	–	–	–	–	–	–	–	–	–	–	–	–	–	–	–	–	–	–	6	–	–
16 Bradford City	–	–	–	–	–	–	5	–	1	–	–	–	–	–	–	–	–	–	–	–	–	–	–	–	–	–	–	5	–	1
17 Grimsby Town	–	–	–	–	–	–	5	–	–	–	–	–	–	–	–	–	–	–	–	–	–	–	–	–	–	–	–	5	–	–
18 Middlesbrough	–	–	–	1	–	–	3	–	2	–	–	–	–	–	–	–	–	–	–	–	–	–	–	–	–	–	–	4	–	2
19 Bolton Wanderers	–	–	–	–	–	–	4	–	–	–	–	–	–	–	–	–	–	–	–	–	–	–	–	–	–	–	–	4	–	–
20 West Bromwich Albion	–	–	–	–	–	–	4	–	–	–	–	–	–	–	–	–	–	–	–	–	–	–	–	–	–	–	–	4	–	–
21 Notts County	–	–	–	1	–	–	–	–	–	2	–	1	–	–	–	–	–	–	–	–	–	–	–	–	–	–	–	3	–	1
22 Fulham	–	–	–	–	–	–	–	–	–	3	–	–	–	–	–	–	–	–	–	–	–	–	–	–	–	–	–	3	–	–
23 Liverpool	–	–	–	1	–	–	2	–	–	–	–	–	–	–	–	–	–	–	–	–	–	–	–	–	–	–	–	3	–	–
24 Derby County	–	–	–	2	–	2	–	–	–	–	–	–	–	–	–	–	–	–	–	–	–	–	–	–	–	–	–	2	–	2
25 Hull City	–	–	–	–	–	–	2	–	1	–	–	–	–	–	–	–	–	–	–	–	–	–	–	–	–	–	–	2	–	1
26 Manchester City	–	–	–	–	–	–	2	–	1	–	–	–	–	–	–	–	–	–	–	–	–	–	–	–	–	–	–	2	–	1
27 Walsall	–	–	–	–	–	–	2	–	1	–	–	–	–	–	–	–	–	–	–	–	–	–	–	–	–	–	–	2	–	1
28 Doncaster Rovers	–	–	–	–	–	–	2	–	–	–	–	–	–	–	–	–	–	–	–	–	–	–	–	–	–	–	–	2	–	–
29 New Brighton Tower	–	–	–	–	–	–	2	–	–	–	–	–	–	–	–	–	–	–	–	–	–	–	–	–	–	–	–	2	–	–
30 Aston Villa	–	–	–	–	–	–	–	–	–	1	–	–	–	–	–	–	–	–	–	–	–	–	–	–	–	–	–	1	–	–
31 Blackburn Rovers	–	–	–	1	–	–	–	–	–	–	–	–	–	–	–	–	–	–	–	–	–	–	–	–	–	–	–	1	–	–
32 Burton Swifts	–	–	–	–	–	–	1	–	–	–	–	–	–	–	–	–	–	–	–	–	–	–	–	–	–	–	–	1	–	–
33 Chelsea	–	–	–	–	–	–	1	–	–	–	–	–	–	–	–	–	–	–	–	–	–	–	–	–	–	–	–	1	–	–
34 Leeds United	–	–	–	–	–	–	1	–	–	–	–	–	–	–	–	–	–	–	–	–	–	–	–	–	–	–	–	1	–	–
35 Leyton Orient	–	–	–	–	–	–	1	–	–	–	–	–	–	–	–	–	–	–	–	–	–	–	–	–	–	–	–	1	–	–
36 Newcastle United	–	–	–	1	–	–	–	–	–	–	–	–	–	–	–	–	–	–	–	–	–	–	–	–	–	–	–	1	–	–
37 Norwich City	–	–	–	–	–	–	–	–	–	1	–	–	–	–	–	–	–	–	–	–	–	–	–	–	–	–	–	1	–	–
38 Oswaldtwistle Rovers	–	–	–	–	–	–	–	–	–	1	–	–	–	–	–	–	–	–	–	–	–	–	–	–	–	–	–	1	–	–
39 Portsmouth	–	–	–	–	–	–	–	–	–	1	–	–	–	–	–	–	–	–	–	–	–	–	–	–	–	–	–	1	–	–
40 Sheffield Wednesday	–	–	–	–	–	–	–	–	–	1	–	–	–	–	–	–	–	–	–	–	–	–	–	–	–	–	–	1	–	–
41 Southport Central	–	–	–	–	–	–	–	–	–	1	–	–	–	–	–	–	–	–	–	–	–	–	–	–	–	–	–	1	–	–
42 Staple Hill	–	–	–	–	–	–	–	–	–	1	–	–	–	–	–	–	–	–	–	–	–	–	–	–	–	–	–	1	–	–

GEORGE SCHOFIELD

DEBUT (Full Appearance)

Saturday 04/09/1920
Football League Division 1
at Burnden Park

Bolton Wanderers 1 Manchester United 1

CLUB CAREER RECORD	Apps	Subs	Goals
Premiership	0		0
League Division 1	1		0
League Division 2	0		0
FA Cup	0		0
League Cup	0		0
European Cup / Champions League	0		0
European Cup–Winners' Cup	0		0
UEFA Cup / Inter–Cities' Fairs Cup	0		0
Other Matches	0		0
OVERALL TOTAL	1		0

Opponents	PREM			FLD 1			FLD 2			FAC			LC			EC/CL			ECWC			UEFA			OTHER			TOTAL		
	A	S	G	A	S	G	A	S	G	A	S	G	A	S	G	A	S	G	A	S	G	A	S	G	A	S	G	A	S	G
1 Bolton Wanderers	–	–	–	1	–	–	–	–	–	–	–	–	–	–	–	–	–	–	–	–	–	–	–	–	–	–	–	1	–	–

JOSEPH SCHOFIELD

DEBUT (Full Appearance)

Saturday 26/03/1904
Football League Division 2
at Bank Street

Manchester United 2 Grimsby Town 0

CLUB CAREER RECORD	Apps	Subs	Goals
Premiership	0		0
League Division 1	0		0
League Division 2	2		0
FA Cup	0		0
League Cup	0		0
European Cup / Champions League	0		0
European Cup-Winners' Cup	0		0
UEFA Cup / Inter-Cities' Fairs Cup	0		0
Other Matches	0		0
OVERALL TOTAL	**2**		**0**

Opponents	PREM A S G	FLD 1 A S G	FLD 2 A S G	FAC A S G	LC A S G	EC/CL A S G	ECWC A S G	UEFA A S G	OTHER A S G	TOTAL A S G
1 Grimsby Town	– –	– –	1	– –	– –	– –	– –	– –	– –	1 –
2 Stockport County	– –	– –	1	– –	– –	– –	– –	– –	– –	1 –

PERCY SCHOFIELD

DEBUT (Full Appearance)

Saturday 01/10/1921
Football League Division 1
at Old Trafford

Manchester United 1 Preston North End 1

CLUB CAREER RECORD	Apps	Subs	Goals
Premiership	0		0
League Division 1	1		0
League Division 2	0		0
FA Cup	0		0
League Cup	0		0
European Cup / Champions League	0		0
European Cup-Winners' Cup	0		0
UEFA Cup / Inter-Cities' Fairs Cup	0		0
Other Matches	0		0
OVERALL TOTAL	**1**		**0**

Opponents	PREM A S G	FLD 1 A S G	FLD 2 A S G	FAC A S G	LC A S G	EC/CL A S G	ECWC A S G	UEFA A S G	OTHER A S G	TOTAL A S G
1 Preston North End	– –	1 –	– –	– –	– –	– –	– –	– –	– –	1 –

PAUL SCHOLES

DEBUT (Full Appearance, 2 goals)

Wednesday 21/09/1994
League Cup 2nd Round 1st Leg
at Vale Park

Port Vale 1 Manchester United 2

CLUB CAREER RECORD	Apps	Subs	Goals
Premiership	328	(67)	96
League Division 1	0		0
League Division 2	0		0
FA Cup	27	(12)	12
League Cup	11	(5)	8
European Cup / Champions League	97	(11)	22
European Cup-Winners' Cup	0		0
UEFA Cup / Inter-Cities' Fairs Cup	1	(1)	1
Other Matches	10		0
OVERALL TOTAL	**474**	**(96)**	**139**

Opponents	PREM A S G	FLD 1 A S G	FLD 2 A S G	FAC A S G	LC A S G	EC/CL A S G	ECWC A S G	UEFA A S G	OTHER A S G	TOTAL A S G
1 Chelsea	20 (2) 6	– –	– –	4 –	2 (1) –	1	– –	– –	2 –	29 (3) 6
2 Arsenal	16 (2) 2	– –	– –	3 (3) 1	– –	– –	– –	– –	4 –	23 (5) 3
3 Newcastle United	16 (6) 9	– –	– –	2 2	1 –	– –	– –	– –	1 –	20 (6) 11
4 Aston Villa	20 (3) 4	– –	– –	2 2	– –	– –	– –	– –	– –	22 (3) 6
5 Liverpool	15 (5) 2	– –	– –	– (2) –	1 –	– –	– –	– –	1 –	17 (7) 2
6 Tottenham Hotspur	18 (1) 4	– –	– –	1 (1) 1	– –	– –	– –	– –	– –	19 (2) 5
7 Middlesbrough	16 (4) 2	– –	– –	1 –	– –	– –	– –	– –	– –	17 (4) 2
8 Everton	17 (1) 2	– –	– –	1 (1) –	– –	– –	– –	– –	– –	18 (2) 2
9 West Ham United	15 (2) 7	– –	– –	1 –	– –	– –	– –	– –	– –	16 (2) 7
10 Blackburn Rovers	14 (1) 7	– –	– –	– –	2 3	– –	– –	– –	– –	16 (1) 10
11 Manchester City	14 (2) 4	– –	– –	1 1	– –	– –	– –	– –	– –	15 (2) 5
12 Southampton	12 (3) 4	– –	– –	1 2	– –	– –	– –	– –	– –	13 (3) 6
13 Leeds United	13 (3) 2	– –	– –	– –	– –	– –	– –	– –	– –	13 (3) 2
14 Leicester City	10 (3) –	– –	– –	– –	1 (1) –	– –	– –	– –	– –	11 (4) –
15 Fulham	10 (2) –	– –	– –	1 –	– –	– –	– –	– –	– –	11 (2) –
16 Charlton Athletic	10 (3) 3	– –	– –	– –	– –	– –	– –	– –	– –	10 (3) 3
17 Bolton Wanderers	9 (3) 7	– –	– –	– –	– –	– –	– –	– –	– –	9 (3) 7
18 Sheffield Wednesday	8 (4) 3	– –	– –	– –	– –	– –	– –	– –	– –	8 (4) 3
19 Portsmouth	8 2	– –	– –	2 (1) 1	– –	– –	– –	– –	– –	10 (1) 3
20 Coventry City	9 (1) 5	– –	– –	– –	– –	– –	– –	– –	– –	9 (1) 5
21 Sunderland	9 3	– –	– –	– (1) 1	– –	– –	– –	– –	– –	9 (1) 4
22 Derby County	7 (3) 2	– –	– –	– –	– –	– –	– –	– –	– –	7 (3) 2
23 Wimbledon	7 (1) 2	– –	– –	1 1	– –	– –	– –	– –	– –	8 (1) 3
24 Birmingham City	6 (1) 1	– –	– –	– –	– –	– –	– –	– –	– –	6 (1) 1
25 Barcelona	– –	– –	– –	– –	– –	4 (2) 2	– –	– –	– –	4 (2) 2
26 Ipswich Town	2 (3) 1	– –	– –	– –	– (1) –	– –	– –	– –	– –	2 (4) 1
27 Bayern Munich	– –	– –	– –	– –	– –	5 1	– –	– –	– –	5 1
28 Lille Metropole	– –	– –	– –	– –	– –	5 –	– –	– –	– –	5 –
29 Wigan Athletic	5 –	– –	– –	– –	– –	– –	– –	– –	– –	5 –
30 Nottingham Forest	4 (1) 1	– –	– –	– –	– –	– –	– –	– –	– –	4 (1) 1
31 West Bromwich Albion	3 (2) 4	– –	– –	– –	– –	– –	– –	– –	– –	3 (2) 4
32 Crystal Palace	3 (2) 3	– –	– –	– –	– –	– –	– –	– –	– –	3 (2) 3

continued../

PAUL SCHOLES (continued)

Opponents	PREM A S G	FLD 1 A S G	FLD 2 A S G	FAC A S G	LC A S G	EC/CL A S G	ECWC A S G	UEFA A S G	OTHER A S G	TOTAL A S G
33 Benfica	–	–	–	–	–	4 1	–	–	–	4 1
34 Deportivo La Coruna	–	–	–	–	–	4 1	–	–	–	4 1
35 Olympiakos Piraeus	–	–	–	–	–	4 1	–	–	–	4 1
36 Valencia	–	–	–	–	–	4 1	–	–	–	4 1
37 AC Milan	–	–	–	–	–	4	–	–	–	4
38 Juventus	–	–	–	–	–	2 (2) 1	–	–	–	2 (2) 1
39 Real Madrid	–	–	–	–	–	3 1	–	–	–	3 1
40 Sturm Graz	–	–	–	–	–	3 1	–	–	–	3 1
41 Bayer Leverkusen	–	–	–	–	–	3	–	–	–	3
42 Olympique Lyonnais	–	–	–	–	–	3	–	–	–	3
43 Roma	–	–	–	–	–	3	–	–	–	3
44 Bradford City	2 (1) 1	–	–	–	–	–	–	–	–	2 (1) 1
45 Porto	–	–	–	–	–	2 (1) 1	–	–	–	2 (1) 1
46 Reading	2	–	–	– (1) –	–	–	–	–	–	2 (1) –
47 Sheffield United	2	–	–	– (1) –	–	–	–	–	–	2 (1) –
48 Panathinaikos	–	–	–	–	–	2 3	–	–	–	2 3
49 Port Vale	–	–	–	–	2 2	–	–	–	–	2 2
50 PSV Eindhoven	–	–	–	–	–	2 2	–	–	–	2 2
51 Brondby	–	–	–	–	–	2 1	–	–	–	2 1
52 Feyenoord	–	–	–	–	–	2 1	–	–	–	2 1
53 Olympique Marseille	–	–	–	–	–	2 1	–	–	–	2 1
54 Anderlecht	–	–	–	–	–	2	–	–	–	2
55 Boavista	–	–	–	–	–	2	–	–	–	2
56 Croatia Zagreb	–	–	–	–	–	2	–	–	–	2
57 Debreceni	–	–	–	–	–	2	–	–	–	2
58 Fiorentina	–	–	–	–	–	2	–	–	–	2
59 Glasgow Celtic	–	–	–	–	–	2	–	–	–	2
60 Kosice	–	–	–	–	–	2	–	–	–	2
61 LKS Lodz	–	–	–	–	–	2	–	–	–	2
62 Monaco	–	–	–	–	–	2	–	–	–	2
63 Norwich City	2	–	–	–	–	–	–	–	–	2
64 Sparta Prague	–	–	–	–	–	2	–	–	–	2
65 Stuttgart	–	–	–	–	–	2	–	–	–	2
66 Villarreal	–	–	–	–	–	2	–	–	–	2
67 Watford	1	–	–	1	–	–	–	–	–	2
68 Queens Park Rangers	1 (1) 2	–	–	–	–	–	–	–	–	1 (1) 2
69 Copenhagen	–	–	–	–	–	1 (1) 1	–	–	–	1 (1) 1
70 Internazionale	–	–	–	–	–	1 (1) 1	–	–	–	1 (1) 1
71 Rotor Volgograd	–	–	–	–	–	–	–	1 (1) 1	–	1 (1) 1
72 Basel	–	–	–	–	–	1 (1) –	–	–	–	1 (1) –
73 Exeter City	–	–	–	1 (1) –	–	–	–	–	–	1 (1) –
74 Wolverhampton W.	1 (1) –	–	–	–	–	–	–	–	–	1 (1) –
75 Borussia Dortmund	–	–	–	–	–	– (2) –	–	–	–	– (2) –
76 York City	–	–	–	–	1 2	–	–	–	–	1 2
77 Barnsley	1 1	–	–	–	–	–	–	–	–	1 1
78 Swindon Town	–	–	–	–	1 1	–	–	–	–	1 1
79 Zalaegerszeg	–	–	–	–	–	1 1	–	–	–	1 1
80 Dinamo Bucharest	–	–	–	–	–	1	–	–	–	1
81 Glasgow Rangers	–	–	–	–	–	1	–	–	–	1
82 Lazio	–	–	–	–	–	–	–	1	–	1
83 Maccabi Haifa	–	–	–	–	–	1	–	–	–	1
84 Millwall	–	–	–	1	–	–	–	–	–	1
85 Nantes Atlantique	–	–	–	–	–	1	–	–	–	1
86 Northampton Town	–	–	–	1	–	–	–	–	–	1
87 Palmeiras	–	–	–	–	–	–	–	–	1	1
88 Sporting Lisbon	–	–	–	–	–	1	–	–	–	1
89 Walsall	–	–	–	1	–	–	–	–	–	1
90 Wrexham	–	–	–	1	–	–	–	–	–	1
91 Burnley	–	–	–	–	– (1) –	–	–	–	–	– (1) –
92 Bury	–	–	–	–	– (1) –	–	–	–	–	– (1) –
93 Fenerbahce	–	–	–	–	–	– (1) –	–	–	–	– (1) –

JACK SCOTT

DEBUT (Full Appearance)

Saturday 04/10/1952
Football League Division 1
at Molineux

Wolverhampton Wanderers 6 Manchester United 2

CLUB CAREER RECORD	Apps	Subs	Goals
Premiership	0		0
League Division 1	3		0
League Division 2	0		0
FA Cup	0		0
League Cup	0		0
European Cup / Champions League	0		0
European Cup-Winners' Cup	0		0
UEFA Cup / Inter-Cities' Fairs Cup	0		0
Other Matches	0		0
OVERALL TOTAL	**3**		**0**

Opponents	PREM A S G	FLD 1 A S G	FLD 2 A S G	FAC A S G	LC A S G	EC/CL A S G	ECWC A S G	UEFA A S G	OTHER A S G	TOTAL A S G
1 Preston North End	–	1	–	–	–	–	–	–	–	1 –
2 Stoke City	–	1	–	–	–	–	–	–	–	1 –
3 Wolverhampton W.	–	1	–	–	–	–	–	–	–	1 –

JOHN SCOTT

DEBUT (Full Appearance)

Saturday 27/08/1921
Football League Division 1
at Goodison Park

Everton 5 Manchester United 0

CLUB CAREER RECORD	Apps	Subs	Goals
Premiership	0		0
League Division 1	23		0
League Division 2	0		0
FA Cup	1		0
League Cup	0		0
European Cup / Champions League	0		0
European Cup-Winners' Cup	0		0
UEFA Cup / Inter-Cities' Fairs Cup	0		0
Other Matches	0		0
OVERALL TOTAL	**24**		**0**

Opponents	PREM			FLD 1			FLD 2			FAC			LC			EC/CL			ECWC			UEFA			OTHER			TOTAL		
	A	S	G	A	S	G	A	S	G	A	S	G	A	S	G	A	S	G	A	S	G	A	S	G	A	S	G	A	S	G
1 Aston Villa	-	-	-	2	-	-	-	-	-	-	-	-	-	-	-	-	-	-	-	-	-	-	-	-	-	-	-	2	-	-
2 Bradford City	-	-	-	2	-	-	-	-	-	-	-	-	-	-	-	-	-	-	-	-	-	-	-	-	-	-	-	2	-	-
3 Burnley	-	-	-	2	-	-	-	-	-	-	-	-	-	-	-	-	-	-	-	-	-	-	-	-	-	-	-	2	-	-
4 Chelsea	-	-	-	2	-	-	-	-	-	-	-	-	-	-	-	-	-	-	-	-	-	-	-	-	-	-	-	2	-	-
5 Everton	-	-	-	2	-	-	-	-	-	-	-	-	-	-	-	-	-	-	-	-	-	-	-	-	-	-	-	2	-	-
6 Liverpool	-	-	-	2	-	-	-	-	-	-	-	-	-	-	-	-	-	-	-	-	-	-	-	-	-	-	-	2	-	-
7 Manchester City	-	-	-	2	-	-	-	-	-	-	-	-	-	-	-	-	-	-	-	-	-	-	-	-	-	-	-	2	-	-
8 Middlesbrough	-	-	-	2	-	-	-	-	-	-	-	-	-	-	-	-	-	-	-	-	-	-	-	-	-	-	-	2	-	-
9 Preston North End	-	-	-	2	-	-	-	-	-	-	-	-	-	-	-	-	-	-	-	-	-	-	-	-	-	-	-	2	-	-
10 Tottenham Hotspur	-	-	-	2	-	-	-	-	-	-	-	-	-	-	-	-	-	-	-	-	-	-	-	-	-	-	-	2	-	-
11 West Bromwich Albion	-	-	-	2	-	-	-	-	-	-	-	-	-	-	-	-	-	-	-	-	-	-	-	-	-	-	-	2	-	-
12 Cardiff City	-	-	-	-	-	-	-	-	-	1	-	-	-	-	-	-	-	-	-	-	-	-	-	-	-	-	-	1	-	-
13 Newcastle United	-	-	-	1	-	-	-	-	-	-	-	-	-	-	-	-	-	-	-	-	-	-	-	-	-	-	-	1	-	-

LES SEALEY

DEBUT (Full Appearance)

Saturday 14/04/1990
Football League Division 1
at Loftus Road

Queens Park Rangers 1 Manchester United 2

CLUB CAREER RECORD	Apps	Subs	Goals
Premiership	0		0
League Division 1	33		0
League Division 2	0		0
FA Cup	4	(1)	0
League Cup	9		0
European Cup / Champions League	0		0
European Cup-Winners' Cup	8		0
UEFA Cup / Inter-Cities' Fairs Cup	0		0
Other Matches	1		0
OVERALL TOTAL	**55**	**(1)**	**0**

Opponents	PREM			FLD 1			FLD 2			FAC			LC			EC/CL			ECWC			UEFA			OTHER			TOTAL		
	A	S	G	A	S	G	A	S	G	A	S	G	A	S	G	A	S	G	A	S	G	A	S	G	A	S	G	A	S	G
1 Aston Villa	-	-	-	3	-	-	-	-	-	-	-	-	1	-	-	-	-	-	-	-	-	-	-	-	-	-	-	4	-	-
2 Leeds United	-	-	-	2	-	-	-	-	-	-	-	-	2	-	-	-	-	-	-	-	-	-	-	-	-	-	-	4	-	-
3 Liverpool	-	-	-	2	-	-	-	-	-	-	-	-	1	-	-	-	-	-	-	-	-	-	-	-	1	-	-	4	-	-
4 Queens Park Rangers	-	-	-	3	-	-	-	-	-	1	-	-	-	-	-	-	-	-	-	-	-	-	-	-	-	-	-	4	-	-
5 Southampton	-	-	-	2	-	-	-	-	-	-	-	-	2	-	-	-	-	-	-	-	-	-	-	-	-	-	-	4	-	-
6 Norwich City	-	-	-	2	-	-	-	-	-	1	-	-	-	-	-	-	-	-	-	-	-	-	-	-	-	-	-	3	-	-
7 Arsenal	-	-	-	1	-	-	-	-	-	-	-	-	1	-	-	-	-	-	-	-	-	-	-	-	-	-	-	2	-	-
8 Chelsea	-	-	-	2	-	-	-	-	-	-	-	-	-	-	-	-	-	-	-	-	-	-	-	-	-	-	-	2	-	-
9 Coventry City	-	-	-	2	-	-	-	-	-	-	-	-	-	-	-	-	-	-	-	-	-	-	-	-	-	-	-	2	-	-
10 Crystal Palace	-	-	-	1	-	-	-	-	-	1	-	-	-	-	-	-	-	-	-	-	-	-	-	-	-	-	-	2	-	-
11 Everton	-	-	-	2	-	-	-	-	-	-	-	-	-	-	-	-	-	-	-	-	-	-	-	-	-	-	-	2	-	-
12 Luton Town	-	-	-	2	-	-	-	-	-	-	-	-	-	-	-	-	-	-	-	-	-	-	-	-	-	-	-	2	-	-
13 Montpellier Herault	-	-	-	-	-	-	-	-	-	-	-	-	-	-	-	-	-	-	2	-	-	-	-	-	-	-	-	2	-	-
14 Nottingham Forest	-	-	-	2	-	-	-	-	-	-	-	-	-	-	-	-	-	-	-	-	-	-	-	-	-	-	-	2	-	-
15 Pecsi Munkas	-	-	-	-	-	-	-	-	-	-	-	-	-	-	-	-	-	-	2	-	-	-	-	-	-	-	-	2	-	-
16 Sunderland	-	-	-	2	-	-	-	-	-	-	-	-	-	-	-	-	-	-	-	-	-	-	-	-	-	-	-	2	-	-
17 Wrexham	-	-	-	-	-	-	-	-	-	-	-	-	-	-	-	-	-	-	2	-	-	-	-	-	-	-	-	2	-	-
18 Barcelona	-	-	-	-	-	-	-	-	-	-	-	-	-	-	-	-	-	-	1	-	-	-	-	-	-	-	-	1	-	-
19 Bolton Wanderers	-	-	-	-	-	-	-	-	-	1	-	-	-	-	-	-	-	-	-	-	-	-	-	-	-	-	-	1	-	-
20 Derby County	-	-	-	1	-	-	-	-	-	-	-	-	-	-	-	-	-	-	-	-	-	-	-	-	-	-	-	1	-	-
21 Halifax Town	-	-	-	-	-	-	-	-	-	-	-	-	1	-	-	-	-	-	-	-	-	-	-	-	-	-	-	1	-	-
22 Legia Warsaw	-	-	-	-	-	-	-	-	-	-	-	-	-	-	-	-	-	-	1	-	-	-	-	-	-	-	-	1	-	-
23 Manchester City	-	-	-	1	-	-	-	-	-	-	-	-	-	-	-	-	-	-	-	-	-	-	-	-	-	-	-	1	-	-
24 Sheffield United	-	-	-	1	-	-	-	-	-	-	-	-	-	-	-	-	-	-	-	-	-	-	-	-	-	-	-	1	-	-
25 Sheffield Wednesday	-	-	-	-	-	-	-	-	-	-	-	-	1	-	-	-	-	-	-	-	-	-	-	-	-	-	-	1	-	-
26 Tottenham Hotspur	-	-	-	1	-	-	-	-	-	-	-	-	-	-	-	-	-	-	-	-	-	-	-	-	-	-	-	1	-	-
27 Wimbledon	-	-	-	1	-	-	-	-	-	-	-	-	-	-	-	-	-	-	-	-	-	-	-	-	-	-	-	1	-	-
28 Charlton Athletic	-	-	-	-	-	-	-	-	-	-	(1)	-	-	-	-	-	-	-	-	-	-	-	-	-	-	-	-	-	(1)	-

MAURICE SETTERS

DEBUT (Full Appearance)

Saturday 16/01/1960
Football League Division 1
at Old Trafford

Manchester United 2 Birmingham City 1

CLUB CAREER RECORD	Apps	Subs	Goals
Premiership	0		0
League Division 1	159		12
League Division 2	0		0
FA Cup	25		1
League Cup	2		0
European Cup / Champions League	0		0
European Cup-Winners' Cup	6		1
UEFA Cup / Inter–Cities' Fairs Cup	1		0
Other Matches	1		0
OVERALL TOTAL	**194**		**14**

Opponents	PREM A S G			FLD 1 A S G			FLD 2 A S G			FAC A S G			LC A S G			EC/CL A S G			ECWC A S G			UEFA A S G			OTHER A S G			TOTAL A S G		
1 Sheffield Wednesday	–	–		8	1		–	–		5	–		–	–		–	–		–	–		–	–		–	–		13	1	
2 Leicester City	–	–		9	1		–	–		1	–		–	–		–	–		–	–		–	–		–	–		10	1	
3 Tottenham Hotspur	–	–		7	–		–	–		1	–		–	–		–	–		2	–		–	–		–	–		10	–	
4 West Ham United	–	–		9	–		–	–		1	–		–	–		–	–		–	–		–	–		–	–		10	–	
5 Aston Villa	–	–		8	–		–	–		1	–		–	–		–	–		–	–		–	–		–	–		9	–	
6 Bolton Wanderers	–	–		8	–		–	–		1	–		–	–		–	–		–	–		–	–		–	–		9	–	
7 Blackburn Rovers	–	–		8	1		–	–		–	–		–	–		–	–		–	–		–	–		–	–		8	1	
8 Blackpool	–	–		8	–		–	–		–	–		–	–		–	–		–	–		–	–		–	–		8	–	
9 Everton	–	–		7	–		–	–		–	–		–	–		–	–		–	–		1	–		–	–		8	–	
10 Wolverhampton W.	–	–		8	–		–	–		–	–		–	–		–	–		–	–		–	–		–	–		8	–	
11 Arsenal	–	–		6	1		–	–		1	1		–	–		–	–		–	–		–	–		–	–		7	2	
12 West Bromwich Albion	–	–		7	1		–	–		–	–		–	–		–	–		–	–		–	–		–	–		7	1	
13 Burnley	–	–		7	–		–	–		–	–		–	–		–	–		–	–		–	–		–	–		7	–	
14 Fulham	–	–		7	–		–	–		–	–		–	–		–	–		–	–		–	–		–	–		7	–	
15 Nottingham Forest	–	–		7	–		–	–		–	–		–	–		–	–		–	–		–	–		–	–		7	–	
16 Ipswich Town	–	–		6	2		–	–		–	–		–	–		–	–		–	–		–	–		–	–		6	2	
17 Chelsea	–	–		5	1		–	–		1	–		–	–		–	–		–	–		–	–		–	–		6	1	
18 Birmingham City	–	–		6	–		–	–		–	–		–	–		–	–		–	–		–	–		–	–		6	–	
19 Preston North End	–	–		3	2		–	–		2	–		–	–		–	–		–	–		–	–		–	–		5	2	
20 Liverpool	–	–		4	–		–	–		1	–		–	–		–	–		–	–		–	–		–	–		5	–	
21 Manchester City	–	–		5	–		–	–		–	–		–	–		–	–		–	–		–	–		–	–		5	–	
22 Sheffield United	–	–		5	–		–	–		–	–		–	–		–	–		–	–		–	–		–	–		5	–	
23 Cardiff City	–	–		4	1		–	–		–	–		–	–		–	–		–	–		–	–		–	–		4	1	
24 Sunderland	–	–		–	–		–	–		3	–		–	–		–	–		–	–		–	–		–	–		3	–	
25 Newcastle United	–	–		2	1		–	–		–	–		–	–		–	–		–	–		–	–		–	–		2	1	
26 Willem II	–	–		–	–		–	–		–	–		–	–		–	–		2	1		–	–		–	–		2	1	
27 Leyton Orient	–	–		2	–		–	–		–	–		–	–		–	–		–	–		–	–		–	–		2	–	
28 Southampton	–	–		–	–		–	–		2	–		–	–		–	–		–	–		–	–		–	–		2	–	
29 Sporting Lisbon	–	–		–	–		–	–		–	–		–	–		–	–		2	–		–	–		–	–		2	–	
30 Stoke City	–	–		2	–		–	–		–	–		–	–		–	–		–	–		–	–		–	–		2	–	
31 Barnsley	–	–		–	–		–	–		1	–		–	–		–	–		–	–		–	–		–	–		1	–	
32 Bradford City	–	–		–	–		–	–		–	–		1	–		–	–		–	–		–	–		–	–		1	–	
33 Bristol Rovers	–	–		–	–		–	–		1	–		–	–		–	–		–	–		–	–		–	–		1	–	
34 Coventry City	–	–		–	–		–	–		1	–		–	–		–	–		–	–		–	–		–	–		1	–	
35 Djurgardens	–	–		–	–		–	–		–	–		–	–		–	–		–	–		1	–		–	–		1	–	
36 Exeter City	–	–		–	–		–	–		–	–		1	–		–	–		–	–		–	–		–	–		1	–	
37 Huddersfield Town	–	–		–	–		–	–		1	–		–	–		–	–		–	–		–	–		–	–		1	–	
38 Luton Town	–	–		1	–		–	–		–	–		–	–		–	–		–	–		–	–		–	–		1	–	
39 Middlesbrough	–	–		–	–		–	–		1	–		–	–		–	–		–	–		–	–		–	–		1	–	

LEE SHARPE

DEBUT (Full Appearance)

Saturday 24/09/1988
Football League Division 1
at Old Trafford

Manchester United 2 West Ham United 0

CLUB CAREER RECORD	Apps	Subs	Goals
Premiership	100	(16)	17
League Division 1	60	(17)	4
League Division 2	0		0
FA Cup	22	(7)	3
League Cup	15	(8)	9
European Cup / Champions League	7		2
European Cup-Winners' Cup	6	(2)	1
UEFA Cup / Inter-Cities' Fairs Cup	2		0
Other Matches	1		0
OVERALL TOTAL	**213**	**(50)**	**36**

Opponents	PREM A	S	G	FLD 1 A	S	G	FLD 2 A	S	G	FAC A	S	G	LC A	S	G	EC/CL A	S	G	ECWC A	S	G	UEFA A	S	G	OTHER A	S	G	TOTAL A	S	G
1 Southampton	5	(1)	1	3	(2)	-	-	-	-	1	(1)	1	2	-	-	-	-	-	-	-	-	-	-	-	-	-	-	11	(4)	2
2 Queens Park Rangers	3	(2)	-	3	(2)	-	-	-	-	4		1	-	-	-	-	-	-	-	-	-	-	-	-	-	-	-	10	(4)	1
3 Aston Villa	7		2	4		1	-	-	-	-	-	-	-	(1)	-	-	-	-	-	-	-	-	-	-	-	-	-	11	(1)	3
4 Tottenham Hotspur	5	(1)	1	4	(1)	-	-	-	-	-	-	-	1		-	-	-	-	-	-	-	-	-	-	-	-	-	10	(2)	1
5 Arsenal	6	(1)	3	3		-	-	-	-	-	-	-	1		3	-	-	-	-	-	-	-	-	-	-	-	-	10	(1)	6
6 Norwich City	3	(1)	-	6		-	-	-	-	1		-	-	-	-	-	-	-	-	-	-	-	-	-	-	-	-	10	(1)	-
7 Manchester City	5	(2)	-	2	(1)	-	-	-	-	1		1	-	-	-	-	-	-	-	-	-	-	-	-	-	-	-	8	(3)	1
8 Wimbledon	6	(1)	-	2	(2)	-	-	-	-	-	-	-	-	-	-	-	-	-	-	-	-	-	-	-	-	-	-	8	(3)	-
9 Everton	5		4	4		1	-	-	-	1		-	-	-	-	-	-	-	-	-	-	-	-	-	-	-	-	10		5
10 Coventry City	6	(1)	1	3		-	-	-	-	-	-	-	-	-	-	-	-	-	-	-	-	-	-	-	-	-	-	9	(1)	1
11 Liverpool	6		-	2	(1)	-	-	-	-	-	-	-	1		1	-	-	-	-	-	-	-	-	-	-	-	-	9	(1)	1
12 Sheffield Wednesday	6		-	1	(2)	-	-	-	-	-	-	-	1		-	-	-	-	-	-	-	-	-	-	-	-	-	8	(2)	-
13 Nottingham Forest	3	(1)	-	3	(1)	-	-	-	-	1		-	-	(1)	-	-	-	-	-	-	-	-	-	-	-	-	-	7	(3)	-
14 Leeds United	1	(2)	-	1	(1)	-	-	-	-	1		-	2	(1)	2	-	-	-	-	-	-	-	-	-	-	-	-	5	(4)	2
15 Blackburn Rovers	7		2	-	-	-	-	-	-	-	-	-	-	-	-	-	-	-	-	-	-	1		-	-	-	-	8		2
16 West Ham United	5		1	2	(1)	-	-	-	-	-	-	-	-	-	-	-	-	-	-	-	-	-	-	-	-	-	-	7	(1)	1
17 Chelsea	4		-	1	(1)	-	-	-	-	1	(1)	-	-	-	-	-	-	-	-	-	-	-	-	-	-	-	-	6	(2)	-
18 Crystal Palace	1			3	(1)	-	-	-	-	2		-	-	-	-	-	-	-	-	-	-	-	-	-	-	-	-	6	(1)	-
19 Newcastle United	3	(1)	-	1	(1)	-	-	-	-	-	-	-	-	(1)	-	-	-	-	-	-	-	-	-	-	-	-	-	4	(3)	-
20 Sheffield United	2		1	2		-	-	-	-	1	(1)	-	-	-	-	-	-	-	-	-	-	-	-	-	-	-	-	5	(1)	1
21 Oldham Athletic	4		-	-	-	-	-	-	-	1	(1)	-	-	-	-	-	-	-	-	-	-	-	-	-	-	-	-	5	(1)	-
22 Ipswich Town	3	(2)	-	-	-	-	-	-	-	-	-	-	-	-	-	-	-	-	-	-	-	-	-	-	-	-	-	3	(2)	-
23 Middlesbrough	1			1		-	-	-	-	-	-	-	1	(1)	1	-	-	-	-	-	-	-	-	-	-	-	-	3	(1)	1
24 Derby County	-			3			-	-	-	-	-	-	-	-	-	-	-	-	-	-	-	-	-	-	-	-	-	3		
25 Galatasaray	-			-			-	-	-	-	-	-	-	-	-	3			-	-	-	-	-	-	-	-	-	3		
26 Sunderland	-			1			-	-	-	-	(2)	-	-	-	-	-	-	-	-	-	-	-	-	-	-	-	-	1	(2)	-
27 Leicester City	1		1	-			-	-	-	-	-	-	1		1	-	-	-	-	-	-	-	-	-	-	-	-	2		2
28 Barcelona	-			-			-	-	-	-	-	-	-	-	-	1		1	-	-	-	-	-	-	-	-	-	2		1
29 Legia Warsaw	-			-			-	-	-	-	-	-	-	-	-	-	-	-	2		1	-	-	-	-	-	-	2		1
30 Luton Town	-			2		1	-	-	-	-	-	-	-	-	-	-	-	-	-	-	-	-	-	-	-	-	-	2		1
31 Millwall	-			2		1	-	-	-	-	-	-	-	-	-	-	-	-	-	-	-	-	-	-	-	-	-	2		1
32 Bolton Wanderers	1			-			-	-	-	1			-	-	-	-	-	-	-	-	-	-	-	-	-	-	-	2		
33 Honved	-			-			-	-	-	-	-	-	-	-	-	2			-	-	-	-	-	-	-	-	-	2		
34 Montpellier Herault	-			-			-	-	-	-	-	-	-	-	-	-	-	-	2			-	-	-	-	-	-	2		
35 Rotherham United	-			-			-	-	-	-	-	-	2			-	-	-	-	-	-	-	-	-	-	-	-	2		
36 Rotor Volgograd	-			-			-	-	-	-	-	-	-	-	-	-	-	-	-	-	-	2			-	-	-	2		
37 Wrexham	-			-			-	-	-	1			-	-	-	-	-	-	1			-	-	-	-	-	-	2		
38 York City	-			-			-	-	-	-	-	-	2			-	-	-	-	-	-	-	-	-	-	-	-	2		
39 Stoke City	-			-			-	-	-	-	-	-	1	(1)	1	-	-	-	-	-	-	-	-	-	-	-	-	1	(1)	1
40 Bournemouth	-			-			-	-	-	1	(1)	-	-	-	-	-	-	-	-	-	-	-	-	-	-	-	-	1	(1)	-
41 Pecsi Munkas	-			-			-	-	-	-	-	-	-	-	-	-	-	-	-	(2)	-	-	-	-	-	-	-	-	(2)	-
42 Gothenburg	-			-			-	-	-	-	-	-	-	-	-	1		1	-	-	-	-	-	-	-	-	-	1		1
43 Brighton	-			-			-	-	-	1			-	-	-	-	-	-	-	-	-	-	-	-	-	-	-	1		
44 Bury	-			-			-	-	-	1			-	-	-	-	-	-	-	-	-	-	-	-	-	-	-	1		
45 Charlton Athletic	-			1			-	-	-	-	-	-	-	-	-	-	-	-	-	-	-	-	-	-	-	-	-	1		
46 Oxford United	-			-			-	-	-	1			-	-	-	-	-	-	-	-	-	-	-	-	-	-	-	1		
47 Reading	-			-			-	-	-	1			-	-	-	-	-	-	-	-	-	-	-	-	-	-	-	1		
48 Swindon Town	1			-			-	-	-	-	-	-	-	-	-	-	-	-	-	-	-	-	-	-	-	-	-	1		
49 Port Vale	-			-			-	-	-	-	-	-	-	(1)	-	-	-	-	-	-	-	-	-	-	-	-	-	-	(1)	-
50 Portsmouth	-			-			-	-	-	-	-	-	-	(1)	-	-	-	-	-	-	-	-	-	-	-	-	-	-	(1)	-

WILLIAM SHARPE

DEBUT (Full Appearance)

Saturday 04/10/1890
FA Cup 1st Qualifying Round
at North Road

Newton Heath 2 Higher Walton 0

CLUB CAREER RECORD	Apps	Subs	Goals
Premiership	0		0
League Division 1	0		0
League Division 2	0		0
FA Cup	2		0
League Cup	0		0
European Cup / Champions League	0		0
European Cup-Winners' Cup	0		0
UEFA Cup / Inter-Cities' Fairs Cup	0		0
Other Matches	0		0
OVERALL TOTAL	**2**		**0**

Opponents	PREM A	S	G	FLD 1 A	S	G	FLD 2 A	S	G	FAC A	S	G	LC A	S	G	EC/CL A	S	G	ECWC A	S	G	UEFA A	S	G	OTHER A	S	G	TOTAL A	S	G
1 Higher Walton	-	-	-	-	-	-	-	-	-	1			-	-	-	-	-	-	-	-	-	-	-	-	-	-	-	1		-
2 Manchester City	-	-	-	-	-	-	-	-	-	1			-	-	-	-	-	-	-	-	-	-	-	-	-	-	-	1		-

RYAN SHAWCROSS

DEBUT (Substitute Appearance)

Wednesday 25/10/2006
League Cup 3rd Round
at Gresty Road

Crewe Alexandra 1 Manchester United 2

CLUB CAREER RECORD	Apps	Subs	Goals
Premiership	0		0
League Division 1	0		0
League Division 2	0		0
FA Cup	0		0
League Cup	0	(2)	0
European Cup / Champions League	0		0
European Cup–Winners' Cup	0		0
UEFA Cup / Inter–Cities' Fairs Cup	0		0
Other Matches	0		0
OVERALL TOTAL	**0**	**(2)**	**0**

Opponents	PREM A S G	FLD 1 A S G	FLD 2 A S G	FAC A S G	LC A S G	EC/CL A S G	ECWC A S G	UEFA A S G	OTHER A S G	TOTAL A S G
1 Crewe Alexandra	–	–	–	–	– (1) –	–	–	–	–	– (1) –
2 Southend United	–	–	–	–	– (1) –	–	–	–	–	– (1) –

JOHN SHELDON

DEBUT (Full Appearance)

Tuesday 27/12/1910
Football League Division 1
at Valley Parade

Bradford City 1 Manchester United 0

CLUB CAREER RECORD	Apps	Subs	Goals
Premiership	0		0
League Division 1	26		1
League Division 2	0		0
FA Cup	0		0
League Cup	0		0
European Cup / Champions League	0		0
European Cup–Winners' Cup	0		0
UEFA Cup / Inter–Cities' Fairs Cup	0		0
Other Matches	0		0
OVERALL TOTAL	**26**		**1**

Opponents	PREM A S G	FLD 1 A S G	FLD 2 A S G	FAC A S G	LC A S G	EC/CL A S G	ECWC A S G	UEFA A S G	OTHER A S G	TOTAL A S G
1 Bradford City	– –	3	–	–	–	–	–	–	–	3 –
2 Aston Villa	– –	2	–	–	–	–	–	–	–	2 –
3 Blackburn Rovers	– –	2	–	–	–	–	–	–	–	2 –
4 Chelsea	– –	2	–	–	–	–	–	–	–	2 –
5 Everton	– –	2	–	–	–	–	–	–	–	2 –
6 Liverpool	– –	2	–	–	–	–	–	–	–	2 –
7 Notts County	– –	2	–	–	–	–	–	–	–	2 –
8 Oldham Athletic	– –	2	–	–	–	–	–	–	–	2 –
9 Sheffield United	– –	2	–	–	–	–	–	–	–	2 –
10 Sunderland	– –	1 1	–	–	–	–	–	–	–	1 1
11 Arsenal	– –	1	–	–	–	–	–	–	–	1 –
12 Bolton Wanderers	– –	1	–	–	–	–	–	–	–	1 –
13 Middlesbrough	– –	1	–	–	–	–	–	–	–	1 –
14 Newcastle United	– –	1	–	–	–	–	–	–	–	1 –
15 Sheffield Wednesday	– –	1	–	–	–	–	–	–	–	1 –
16 Tottenham Hotspur	– –	1	–	–	–	–	–	–	–	1 –

TEDDY SHERINGHAM

DEBUT (Full Appearance)

Sunday 10/08/1997
FA Premiership
at White Hart Lane

Tottenham Hotspur 0 Manchester United 2

CLUB CAREER RECORD	Apps	Subs	Goals
Premiership	73	(31)	31
League Division 1	0		0
League Division 2	0		0
FA Cup	4	(5)	5
League Cup	1		1
European Cup / Champions League	20	(11)	9
European Cup–Winners' Cup	0		0
UEFA Cup / Inter–Cities' Fairs Cup	0		0
Other Matches	3	(5)	0
OVERALL TOTAL	**101**	**(52)**	**46**

Opponents	PREM A S G	FLD 1 A S G	FLD 2 A S G	FAC A S G	LC A S G	EC/CL A S G	ECWC A S G	UEFA A S G	OTHER A S G	TOTAL A S G
1 Chelsea	2 (4) 1	–	–	1 (1) 1	–	–	–	–	2 –	5 (5) 2
2 Arsenal	3 (3) 4	–	–	1 –	–	–	–	– (2) –	–	4 (5) 4
3 Tottenham Hotspur	7 1	–	–	–	1 1	–	–	–	–	8 2
4 Leeds United	3 (4) –	–	–	–	–	–	–	–	–	3 (4) –
5 Middlesbrough	4 (1) 1	–	–	– (1) –	–	–	–	–	–	4 (2) 1
6 Newcastle United	4 (1) –	–	–	– (1) 1	–	–	–	–	–	4 (2) 1
7 West Ham United	3 (2) –	–	–	1 –	–	–	–	–	–	4 (2) –
8 Leicester City	3 (3) 3	–	–	–	–	–	–	–	–	3 (3) 3
9 Aston Villa	5 2	–	–	–	–	–	–	–	–	5 2
10 Coventry City	5 1	–	–	–	–	–	–	–	–	5 1
11 Sheffield Wednesday	4 (1) 4	–	–	–	–	–	–	–	–	4 (1) 4
12 Southampton	3 (2) 4	–	–	–	–	–	–	–	–	3 (2) 4
13 Everton	3 (2) 1	–	–	–	–	–	–	–	–	3 (2) 1
14 Derby County	4 2	–	–	–	–	–	–	–	–	4 2
15 Sunderland	3 (1) 1	–	–	–	–	–	–	–	–	3 (1) 1

continued../

TEDDY SHERINGHAM (continued)

Opponents	PREM			FLD 1			FLD 2			FAC			LC			EC/CL			ECWC			UEFA			OTHER			TOTAL		
	A	S	G	A	S	G	A	S	G	A	S	G	A	S	G	A	S	G	A	S	G	A	S	G	A	S	G	A	S	G
16 Liverpool	2	(2)	-	-	-	-	-	-	-	-	-	-	-	-	-	-	-	-	-	-	-	-	-	-	-	-	-	2	(2)	-
17 Bradford City	3	-	3	-	-	-	-	-	-	-	-	-	-	-	-	-	-	-	-	-	-	-	-	-	-	-	-	3	-	3
18 Valencia	-	-	-	-	-	-	-	-	-	-	-	-	-	-	-	3	-	-	-	-	-	-	-	-	-	-	-	3	-	-
19 Wimbledon	3	-	-	-	-	-	-	-	-	-	-	-	-	-	-	-	-	-	-	-	-	-	-	-	-	-	-	3	-	-
20 Barnsley	1	-	1	-	-	-	-	-	-	1	(1)	2	-	-	-	-	-	-	-	-	-	-	-	-	-	-	-	2	(1)	3
21 Juventus	-	-	-	-	-	-	-	-	-	-	-	-	-	-	-	2	(1)	1	-	-	-	-	-	-	-	-	-	2	(1)	1
22 Sturm Graz	-	-	-	-	-	-	-	-	-	-	-	-	-	-	-	2	(1)	1	-	-	-	-	-	-	-	-	-	2	(1)	1
23 Bayern Munich	-	-	-	-	-	-	-	-	-	-	-	-	-	-	-	1	(2)	1	-	-	-	-	-	-	-	-	-	1	(2)	1
24 Charlton Athletic	-	(3)	-	-	-	-	-	-	-	-	-	-	-	-	-	-	-	-	-	-	-	-	-	-	-	-	-	-	(3)	-
25 Crystal Palace	2	-	1	-	-	-	-	-	-	-	-	-	-	-	-	-	-	-	-	-	-	-	-	-	-	-	-	2	-	1
26 Girondins Bordeaux	-	-	-	-	-	-	-	-	-	-	-	-	-	-	-	2	-	1	-	-	-	-	-	-	-	-	-	2	-	1
27 Manchester City	2	-	1	-	-	-	-	-	-	-	-	-	-	-	-	-	-	-	-	-	-	-	-	-	-	-	-	2	-	1
28 Feyenoord	-	-	-	-	-	-	-	-	-	-	-	-	-	-	-	2	-	-	-	-	-	-	-	-	-	-	-	2	-	-
29 Monaco	-	-	-	-	-	-	-	-	-	-	-	-	-	-	-	2	-	-	-	-	-	-	-	-	-	-	-	2	-	-
30 Dynamo Kiev	-	-	-	-	-	-	-	-	-	-	-	-	-	-	-	1	(1)	1	-	-	-	-	-	-	-	-	-	1	(1)	1
31 Panathinaikos	-	-	-	-	-	-	-	-	-	-	-	-	-	-	-	1	(1)	1	-	-	-	-	-	-	-	-	-	1	(1)	1
32 Blackburn Rovers	1	(1)	-	-	-	-	-	-	-	-	-	-	-	-	-	-	-	-	-	-	-	-	-	-	-	-	-	1	(1)	-
33 Real Madrid	-	-	-	-	-	-	-	-	-	-	-	-	-	-	-	-	(2)	-	-	-	-	-	-	-	-	-	-	-	(2)	-
34 Anderlecht	-	-	-	-	-	-	-	-	-	-	-	-	-	-	-	1	-	1	-	-	-	-	-	-	-	-	-	1	-	1
35 Kosice	-	-	-	-	-	-	-	-	-	-	-	-	-	-	-	1	-	1	-	-	-	-	-	-	-	-	-	1	-	1
36 PSV Eindhoven	-	-	-	-	-	-	-	-	-	-	-	-	-	-	-	1	-	1	-	-	-	-	-	-	-	-	-	1	-	1
37 Bolton Wanderers	1	-	-	-	-	-	-	-	-	-	-	-	-	-	-	-	-	-	-	-	-	-	-	-	-	-	-	1	-	-
38 Lazio	-	-	-	-	-	-	-	-	-	-	-	-	-	-	-	-	-	-	-	-	-	-	-	-	1	-	-	1	-	-
39 LKS Lodz	-	-	-	-	-	-	-	-	-	-	-	-	1	-	-	-	-	-	-	-	-	-	-	-	-	-	-	1	-	-
40 Nottingham Forest	1	-	-	-	-	-	-	-	-	-	-	-	-	-	-	-	-	-	-	-	-	-	-	-	-	-	-	1	-	-
41 Watford	1	-	-	-	-	-	-	-	-	-	-	-	-	-	-	-	-	-	-	-	-	-	-	-	-	-	-	1	-	-
42 Fulham	-	-	-	-	-	-	-	-	-	-	(1)	1	-	-	-	-	-	-	-	-	-	-	-	-	-	-	-	-	(1)	1
43 Croatia Zagreb	-	-	-	-	-	-	-	-	-	-	-	-	-	-	-	-	(1)	-	-	-	-	-	-	-	-	-	-	-	(1)	-
44 Fiorentina	-	-	-	-	-	-	-	-	-	-	-	-	-	-	-	-	(1)	-	-	-	-	-	-	-	-	-	-	-	(1)	-
45 Ipswich Town	-	(1)	-	-	-	-	-	-	-	-	-	-	-	-	-	-	-	-	-	-	-	-	-	-	-	-	-	-	(1)	-
46 Olympique Marseille	-	-	-	-	-	-	-	-	-	-	-	-	-	-	-	-	(1)	-	-	-	-	-	-	-	-	-	-	-	(1)	-
47 Palmeiras	-	-	-	-	-	-	-	-	-	-	-	-	-	-	-	-	-	-	-	-	-	-	-	-	-	(1)	-	-	(1)	-
48 Rayos del Necaxa	-	-	-	-	-	-	-	-	-	-	-	-	-	-	-	-	-	-	-	-	-	-	-	-	-	(1)	-	-	(1)	-
49 Vasco da Gama	-	-	-	-	-	-	-	-	-	-	-	-	-	-	-	-	-	-	-	-	-	-	-	-	-	(1)	-	-	(1)	-

ARNOLD SIDEBOTTOM

DEBUT (Full Appearance)

Monday 23/04/1973
Football League Division 1
at Old Trafford

Manchester United 1 Sheffield United 2

CLUB CAREER RECORD	Apps	Subs	Goals
Premiership	0		0
League Division 1	4		0
League Division 2	12		0
FA Cup	2		0
League Cup	2		0
European Cup / Champions League	0		0
European Cup-Winners' Cup	0		0
UEFA Cup / Inter-Cities' Fairs Cup	0		0
Other Matches	0		0
OVERALL TOTAL	20		0

Opponents	PREM			FLD 1			FLD 2			FAC			LC			EC/CL			ECWC			UEFA			OTHER			TOTAL		
	A	S	G	A	S	G	A	S	G	A	S	G	A	S	G	A	S	G	A	S	G	A	S	G	A	S	G	A	S	G
1 Aston Villa	-	-	-	-	-	-	2	-	-	-	-	-	-	-	-	-	-	-	-	-	-	-	-	-	-	-	-	2	-	-
2 Walsall	-	-	-	-	-	-	-	-	-	2	-	-	-	-	-	-	-	-	-	-	-	-	-	-	-	-	-	2	-	-
3 Bolton Wanderers	-	-	-	-	-	-	1	-	-	-	-	-	-	-	-	-	-	-	-	-	-	-	-	-	-	-	-	1	-	-
4 Bristol City	-	-	-	-	-	-	1	-	-	-	-	-	-	-	-	-	-	-	-	-	-	-	-	-	-	-	-	1	-	-
5 Burnley	-	-	-	-	-	-	-	-	-	-	-	-	1	-	-	-	-	-	-	-	-	-	-	-	-	-	-	1	-	-
6 Chelsea	-	-	-	1	-	-	-	-	-	-	-	-	-	-	-	-	-	-	-	-	-	-	-	-	-	-	-	1	-	-
7 Hull City	-	-	-	-	-	-	1	-	-	-	-	-	-	-	-	-	-	-	-	-	-	-	-	-	-	-	-	1	-	-
8 Leyton Orient	-	-	-	-	-	-	1	-	-	-	-	-	-	-	-	-	-	-	-	-	-	-	-	-	-	-	-	1	-	-
9 Liverpool	-	-	-	1	-	-	-	-	-	-	-	-	-	-	-	-	-	-	-	-	-	-	-	-	-	-	-	1	-	-
10 Middlesbrough	-	-	-	-	-	-	-	-	-	-	-	-	1	-	-	-	-	-	-	-	-	-	-	-	-	-	-	1	-	-
11 Millwall	-	-	-	-	-	-	1	-	-	-	-	-	-	-	-	-	-	-	-	-	-	-	-	-	-	-	-	1	-	-
12 Norwich City	-	-	-	-	-	-	1	-	-	-	-	-	-	-	-	-	-	-	-	-	-	-	-	-	-	-	-	1	-	-
13 Oldham Athletic	-	-	-	-	-	-	1	-	-	-	-	-	-	-	-	-	-	-	-	-	-	-	-	-	-	-	-	1	-	-
14 Oxford United	-	-	-	-	-	-	1	-	-	-	-	-	-	-	-	-	-	-	-	-	-	-	-	-	-	-	-	1	-	-
15 Queens Park Rangers	-	-	-	1	-	-	-	-	-	-	-	-	-	-	-	-	-	-	-	-	-	-	-	-	-	-	-	1	-	-
16 Sheffield United	-	-	-	1	-	-	-	-	-	-	-	-	-	-	-	-	-	-	-	-	-	-	-	-	-	-	-	1	-	-
17 West Bromwich Albion	-	-	-	-	-	-	1	-	-	-	-	-	-	-	-	-	-	-	-	-	-	-	-	-	-	-	-	1	-	-
18 York City	-	-	-	-	-	-	1	-	-	-	-	-	-	-	-	-	-	-	-	-	-	-	-	-	-	-	-	1	-	-

JACK SILCOCK

DEBUT (Full Appearance)

Saturday 30/08/1919
Football League Division 1
at Baseball Ground

Derby County 1 Manchester United 1

CLUB CAREER RECORD	Apps	Subs	Goals
Premiership	0		0
League Division 1	271		2
League Division 2	152		0
FA Cup	26		0
League Cup	0		0
European Cup / Champions League	0		0
European Cup-Winners' Cup	0		0
UEFA Cup / Inter-Cities' Fairs Cup	0		0
Other Matches	0		0
OVERALL TOTAL	449		2

Opponents	PREM A S G	FLD 1 A S G	FLD 2 A S G	FAC A S G	LC A S G	EC/CL A S G	ECWC A S G	UEFA A S G	OTHER A S G	TOTAL A S G
1 Liverpool	– – –	14 – 1	– – –	2 – –	– – –	– – –	– – –	– – –	– – –	16 – 1
2 Burnley	– – –	11 – –	5 – –	– – –	– – –	– – –	– – –	– – –	– – –	16 – –
3 Bury	– – –	6 – –	7 – –	3 – –	– – –	– – –	– – –	– – –	– – –	16 – –
4 Derby County	– – –	13 – –	3 – –	– – –	– – –	– – –	– – –	– – –	– – –	16 – –
5 Newcastle United	– – –	15 – 1	– – –	– – –	– – –	– – –	– – –	– – –	– – –	15 – 1
6 Bolton Wanderers	– – –	14 – –	1 – –	– – –	– – –	– – –	– – –	– – –	– – –	15 – –
7 Sheffield Wednesday	– – –	9 – –	6 – –	– – –	– – –	– – –	– – –	– – –	– – –	15 – –
8 Sunderland	– – –	13 – –	– – –	2 – –	– – –	– – –	– – –	– – –	– – –	15 – –
9 Blackburn Rovers	– – –	14 – –	– – –	– – –	– – –	– – –	– – –	– – –	– – –	14 – –
10 Huddersfield Town	– – –	13 – –	– – –	1 – –	– – –	– – –	– – –	– – –	– – –	14 – –
11 Tottenham Hotspur	– – –	7 – –	4 – –	3 – –	– – –	– – –	– – –	– – –	– – –	14 – –
12 Aston Villa	– – –	13 – –	– – –	– – –	– – –	– – –	– – –	– – –	– – –	13 – –
13 Manchester City	– – –	12 – –	– – –	1 – –	– – –	– – –	– – –	– – –	– – –	13 – –
14 Leicester City	– – –	8 – –	4 – –	– – –	– – –	– – –	– – –	– – –	– – –	12 – –
15 Sheffield United	– – –	12 – –	– – –	– – –	– – –	– – –	– – –	– – –	– – –	12 – –
16 Bradford City	– – –	3 – –	6 – –	2 – –	– – –	– – –	– – –	– – –	– – –	11 – –
17 Leeds United	– – –	7 – –	4 – –	– – –	– – –	– – –	– – –	– – –	– – –	11 – –
18 Oldham Athletic	– – –	6 – –	5 – –	– – –	– – –	– – –	– – –	– – –	– – –	11 – –
19 Arsenal	– – –	10 – –	– – –	– – –	– – –	– – –	– – –	– – –	– – –	10 – –
20 Middlesbrough	– – –	7 – –	2 – –	1 – –	– – –	– – –	– – –	– – –	– – –	10 – –
21 West Ham United	– – –	7 – –	3 – –	– – –	– – –	– – –	– – –	– – –	– – –	10 – –
22 Everton	– – –	9 – –	– – –	– – –	– – –	– – –	– – –	– – –	– – –	9 – –
23 Preston North End	– – –	5 – –	4 – –	– – –	– – –	– – –	– – –	– – –	– – –	9 – –
24 West Bromwich Albion	– – –	9 – –	– – –	– – –	– – –	– – –	– – –	– – –	– – –	9 – –
25 Birmingham City	– – –	7 – –	– – –	1 – –	– – –	– – –	– – –	– – –	– – –	8 – –
26 Cardiff City	– – –	8 – –	– – –	– – –	– – –	– – –	– – –	– – –	– – –	8 – –
27 Chelsea	– – –	7 – –	1 – –	– – –	– – –	– – –	– – –	– – –	– – –	8 – –
28 Notts County	– – –	3 – –	5 – –	– – –	– – –	– – –	– – –	– – –	– – –	8 – –
29 Southampton	– – –	– – –	8 – –	– – –	– – –	– – –	– – –	– – –	– – –	8 – –
30 Stoke City	– – –	– – –	8 – –	– – –	– – –	– – –	– – –	– – –	– – –	8 – –
31 Bradford Park Avenue	– – –	4 – –	3 – –	– – –	– – –	– – –	– – –	– – –	– – –	7 – –
32 Port Vale	– – –	– – –	4 – –	3 – –	– – –	– – –	– – –	– – –	– – –	7 – –
33 Crystal Palace	– – –	– – –	6 – –	– – –	– – –	– – –	– – –	– – –	– – –	6 – –
34 Leyton Orient	– – –	– – –	6 – –	– – –	– – –	– – –	– – –	– – –	– – –	6 – –
35 Fulham	– – –	– – –	4 – –	1 – –	– – –	– – –	– – –	– – –	– – –	5 – –
36 Wolverhampton W.	– – –	– – –	5 – –	– – –	– – –	– – –	– – –	– – –	– – –	5 – –
37 Barnsley	– – –	– – –	4 – –	– – –	– – –	– – –	– – –	– – –	– – –	4 – –
38 Blackpool	– – –	– – –	4 – –	– – –	– – –	– – –	– – –	– – –	– – –	4 – –
39 Charlton Athletic	– – –	– – –	4 – –	– – –	– – –	– – –	– – –	– – –	– – –	4 – –
40 Coventry City	– – –	– – –	4 – –	– – –	– – –	– – –	– – –	– – –	– – –	4 – –
41 Hull City	– – –	– – –	4 – –	– – –	– – –	– – –	– – –	– – –	– – –	4 – –
42 Plymouth Argyle	– – –	– – –	3 – –	1 – –	– – –	– – –	– – –	– – –	– – –	4 – –
43 Portsmouth	– – –	3 – –	– – –	1 – –	– – –	– – –	– – –	– – –	– – –	4 – –
44 South Shields	– – –	– – –	4 – –	– – –	– – –	– – –	– – –	– – –	– – –	4 – –
45 Swansea City	– – –	– – –	4 – –	– – –	– – –	– – –	– – –	– – –	– – –	4 – –
46 Brentford	– – –	– – –	2 – –	1 – –	– – –	– – –	– – –	– – –	– – –	3 – –
47 Grimsby Town	– – –	2 – –	1 – –	– – –	– – –	– – –	– – –	– – –	– – –	3 – –
48 Nottingham Forest	– – –	– – –	3 – –	– – –	– – –	– – –	– – –	– – –	– – –	3 – –
49 Reading	– – –	– – –	– – –	3 – –	– – –	– – –	– – –	– – –	– – –	3 – –
50 Stockport County	– – –	– – –	3 – –	– – –	– – –	– – –	– – –	– – –	– – –	3 – –
51 Bristol City	– – –	– – –	2 – –	– – –	– – –	– – –	– – –	– – –	– – –	2 – –
52 Lincoln City	– – –	– – –	2 – –	– – –	– – –	– – –	– – –	– – –	– – –	2 – –
53 Millwall	– – –	– – –	2 – –	– – –	– – –	– – –	– – –	– – –	– – –	2 – –
54 Chesterfield	– – –	– – –	1 – –	– – –	– – –	– – –	– – –	– – –	– – –	1 – –
55 Rotherham United	– – –	– – –	1 – –	– – –	– – –	– – –	– – –	– – –	– – –	1 – –

MIKAEL SILVESTRE

DEBUT (Full Appearance)

Saturday 11/09/1999
FA Premiership
at Anfield

Liverpool 2 Manchester United 3

CLUB CAREER RECORD	Apps	Subs	Goals
Premiership	225	(24)	6
League Division 1	0		0
League Division 2	0		0
FA Cup	19	(2)	1
League Cup	13	(1)	0
European Cup / Champions League	61	(8)	2
European Cup-Winners' Cup	0		0
UEFA Cup / Inter-Cities' Fairs Cup	0		0
Other Matches	8		1
OVERALL TOTAL	**326**	**(35)**	**10**

Opponents	PREM			FLD 1			FLD 2			FAC			LC			EC/CL			ECWC			UEFA			OTHER			TOTAL		
	A	S	G	A	S	G	A	S	G	A	S	G	A	S	G	A	S	G	A	S	G	A	S	G	A	S	G	A	S	G
1 Arsenal	14	–	–	–	–	–	–	–	–	3	–	–	–	–	–	–	–	–	–	–	–	–	–	–	2		1	19		1
2 Chelsea	14	–	–	–	–	–	–	–	–	–	–	–	3	–	–	–	–	–	–	–	–	–	–	–	2		–	19		–
3 Liverpool	12	(2)	2	–	–	–	–	–	–	1	–	–	1	–	–	–	–	–	–	–	–	–	–	–	1		–	15	(2)	2
4 Aston Villa	12	(1)	–	–	–	–	–	–	–	2	–	–	–	–	–	–	–	–	–	–	–	–	–	–	–		–	14	(1)	–
5 Tottenham Hotspur	13	(2)	1	–	–	–	–	–	–	–	–	–	–	–	–	–	–	–	–	–	–	–	–	–	–		–	13	(2)	1
6 Everton	13	(2)	–	–	–	–	–	–	–	–	–	–	–	–	–	–	–	–	–	–	–	–	–	–	–		–	13	(2)	–
7 Blackburn Rovers	9	(2)	–	–	–	–	–	–	–	–	–	–	3	(1)	–	–	–	–	–	–	–	–	–	–	–		–	12	(3)	–
8 Middlesbrough	11	(1)	–	–	–	–	–	–	–	1	(1)	–	–	–	–	–	–	–	–	–	–	–	–	–	–		–	12	(2)	–
9 Southampton	10		–	–	–	–	–	–	–	1	–	–	–	–	–	–	–	–	–	–	–	–	–	–	–		–	11		–
10 Charlton Athletic	10	(1)	–	–	–	–	–	–	–	–	–	–	–	–	–	–	–	–	–	–	–	–	–	–	–		–	10	(1)	–
11 Newcastle United	10	(1)	–	–	–	–	–	–	–	–	–	–	–	–	–	–	–	–	–	–	–	–	–	–	–		–	10	(1)	–
12 West Ham United	9	(1)	–	–	–	–	–	–	–	1	–	–	–	–	–	–	–	–	–	–	–	–	–	–	–		–	10	(1)	–
13 Fulham	8	(2)	–	–	–	–	–	–	–	1	–	–	–	–	–	–	–	–	–	–	–	–	–	–	–		–	9	(2)	–
14 Sunderland	9	(1)	–	–	–	–	–	–	–	–	–	–	–	–	–	–	–	–	–	–	–	–	–	–	–		–	9	(1)	–
15 Bolton Wanderers	9		–	–	–	–	–	–	–	–	–	–	–	–	–	–	–	–	–	–	–	–	–	–	–		–	9		–
16 Manchester City	7	(1)	–	–	–	–	–	–	–	1	–	–	–	–	–	–	–	–	–	–	–	–	–	–	–		–	8	(1)	–
17 Leeds United	8		1	–	–	–	–	–	–	–	–	–	–	–	–	–	–	–	–	–	–	–	–	–	–		–	8		1
18 Portsmouth	5	(1)	–	–	–	–	–	–	–	1	–	–	–	–	–	–	–	–	–	–	–	–	–	–	–		–	6	(1)	–
19 Birmingham City	5		–	–	–	–	–	–	–	–	–	–	1	–	–	–	–	–	–	–	–	–	–	–	–		–	6		–
20 West Bromwich Albion	5		–	–	–	–	–	–	–	–	–	–	1	–	–	–	–	–	–	–	–	–	–	–	–		–	6		–
21 Derby County	5	(1)	–	–	–	–	–	–	–	–	–	–	–	–	–	–	–	–	–	–	–	–	–	–	–		–	5	(1)	–
22 Leicester City	4	(2)	1	–	–	–	–	–	–	–	–	–	–	–	–	–	–	–	–	–	–	–	–	–	–		–	4	(2)	1
23 Lille Metropole	–	–	–	–	–	–	–	–	–	–	–	–	–	–	–	4	(1)	–	–	–	–	–	–	–	–		–	4	(1)	–
24 Panathinaikos	–	–	–	–	–	–	–	–	–	–	–	–	–	–	–	4		1	–	–	–	–	–	–	–		–	4		1
25 Bayer Leverkusen	–	–	–	–	–	–	–	–	–	–	–	–	–	–	–	4		–	–	–	–	–	–	–	–		–	4		–
26 Bradford City	4		–	–	–	–	–	–	–	–	–	–	–	–	–	–	–	–	–	–	–	–	–	–	–		–	4		–
27 Reading	2		–	–	–	–	–	–	–	2	–	–	–	–	–	–	–	–	–	–	–	–	–	–	–		–	4		–
28 Watford	3	(1)	1	–	–	–	–	–	–	–	–	–	–	–	–	–	–	–	–	–	–	–	–	–	–		–	3	(1)	1
29 Bayern Munich	–	–	–	–	–	–	–	–	–	–	–	–	–	–	–	3	(1)	–	–	–	–	–	–	–	–		–	3	(1)	–
30 Ipswich Town	2	(2)	–	–	–	–	–	–	–	–	–	–	–	–	–	–	–	–	–	–	–	–	–	–	–		–	2	(2)	–
31 Real Madrid	–	–	–	–	–	–	–	–	–	–	–	–	–	–	–	2	(2)	–	–	–	–	–	–	–	–		–	2	(2)	–
32 Deportivo La Coruna	–	–	–	–	–	–	–	–	–	–	–	–	–	–	–	3		–	–	–	–	–	–	–	–		–	3		–
33 Wigan Athletic	2		–	–	–	–	–	–	–	–	–	–	1	–	–	–	–	–	–	–	–	–	–	–	–		–	3		–
34 Olympiakos Piraeus	–	–	–	–	–	–	–	–	–	–	–	–	–	–	–	2	(1)	–	–	–	–	–	–	–	–		–	2	(1)	–
35 Nantes Atlantique	–	–	–	–	–	–	–	–	–	–	–	–	–	–	–	2		1	–	–	–	–	–	–	–		–	2		1
36 Anderlecht	–	–	–	–	–	–	–	–	–	–	–	–	–	–	–	2		–	–	–	–	–	–	–	–		–	2		–
37 Boavista	–	–	–	–	–	–	–	–	–	–	–	–	–	–	–	2		–	–	–	–	–	–	–	–		–	2		–
38 Burton Albion	–	–	–	–	–	–	–	–	–	2	–	–	–	–	–	–	–	–	–	–	–	–	–	–	–		–	2		–
39 Coventry City	2		–	–	–	–	–	–	–	–	–	–	–	–	–	–	–	–	–	–	–	–	–	–	–		–	2		–
40 Crystal Palace	2		–	–	–	–	–	–	–	–	–	–	–	–	–	–	–	–	–	–	–	–	–	–	–		–	2		–
41 Dinamo Bucharest	–	–	–	–	–	–	–	–	–	–	–	–	–	–	–	2		–	–	–	–	–	–	–	–		–	2		–
42 Girondins Bordeaux	–	–	–	–	–	–	–	–	–	–	–	–	–	–	–	2		–	–	–	–	–	–	–	–		–	2		–
43 Glasgow Rangers	–	–	–	–	–	–	–	–	–	–	–	–	–	–	–	2		–	–	–	–	–	–	–	–		–	2		–
44 Maccabi Haifa	–	–	–	–	–	–	–	–	–	–	–	–	–	–	–	2		–	–	–	–	–	–	–	–		–	2		–
45 Norwich City	2		–	–	–	–	–	–	–	–	–	–	–	–	–	–	–	–	–	–	–	–	–	–	–		–	2		–
46 Olympique Lyonnais	–	–	–	–	–	–	–	–	–	–	–	–	–	–	–	2		–	–	–	–	–	–	–	–		–	2		–
47 PSV Eindhoven	–	–	–	–	–	–	–	–	–	–	–	–	–	–	–	2		–	–	–	–	–	–	–	–		–	2		–
48 Sturm Graz	–	–	–	–	–	–	–	–	–	–	–	–	–	–	–	2		–	–	–	–	–	–	–	–		–	2		–
49 Stuttgart	–	–	–	–	–	–	–	–	–	–	–	–	–	–	–	2		–	–	–	–	–	–	–	–		–	2		–
50 Valencia	–	–	–	–	–	–	–	–	–	–	–	–	–	–	–	2		–	–	–	–	–	–	–	–		–	2		–
51 Villarreal	–	–	–	–	–	–	–	–	–	–	–	–	–	–	–	2		–	–	–	–	–	–	–	–		–	2		–
52 Wimbledon	2		–	–	–	–	–	–	–	–	–	–	–	–	–	–	–	–	–	–	–	–	–	–	–		–	2		–
53 Wolverhampton W.	1		–	–	–	–	–	–	–	1	–	–	–	–	–	–	–	–	–	–	–	–	–	–	–		–	2		–
54 Zalaegerszeg	–	–	–	–	–	–	–	–	–	–	–	–	–	–	–	2		–	–	–	–	–	–	–	–		–	2		–
55 AC Milan	–	–	–	–	–	–	–	–	–	–	–	–	–	–	–	1	(1)	–	–	–	–	–	–	–	–		–	1	(1)	–
56 Dynamo Kiev	–	–	–	–	–	–	–	–	–	–	–	–	–	–	–	1	(1)	–	–	–	–	–	–	–	–		–	1	(1)	–
57 Northampton Town	–	–	–	–	–	–	–	–	–	1	–	1	–	–	–	–	–	–	–	–	–	–	–	–	–		–	1		1
58 Basel	–	–	–	–	–	–	–	–	–	–	–	–	–	–	–	1		–	–	–	–	–	–	–	–		–	1		–
59 Benfica	–	–	–	–	–	–	–	–	–	–	–	–	–	–	–	1		–	–	–	–	–	–	–	–		–	1		–
60 Burnley	–	–	–	–	–	–	–	–	–	–	–	–	1	–	–	–	–	–	–	–	–	–	–	–	–		–	1		–
61 Copenhagen	–	–	–	–	–	–	–	–	–	–	–	–	–	–	–	1		–	–	–	–	–	–	–	–		–	1		–
62 Crewe Alexandra	–	–	–	–	–	–	–	–	–	–	–	–	1	–	–	–	–	–	–	–	–	–	–	–	–		–	1		–
63 Debreceni	–	–	–	–	–	–	–	–	–	–	–	–	–	–	–	1		–	–	–	–	–	–	–	–		–	1		–
64 Fenerbahce	–	–	–	–	–	–	–	–	–	–	–	–	–	–	–	1		–	–	–	–	–	–	–	–		–	1		–
65 Glasgow Celtic	–	–	–	–	–	–	–	–	–	–	–	–	–	–	–	1		–	–	–	–	–	–	–	–		–	1		–
66 Juventus	–	–	–	–	–	–	–	–	–	–	–	–	–	–	–	1		–	–	–	–	–	–	–	–		–	1		–
67 Millwall	–	–	–	–	–	–	–	–	–	1	–	–	–	–	–	–	–	–	–	–	–	–	–	–	–		–	1		–
68 Palmeiras	–	–	–	–	–	–	–	–	–	–	–	–	–	–	–	–	–	–	–	–	–	–	–	–	1		–	1		–
69 Rayos del Necaxa	–	–	–	–	–	–	–	–	–	–	–	–	–	–	–	–	–	–	–	–	–	–	–	–	1		–	1		–

continued../

MIKAEL SILVESTRE (continued)

Opponents	PREM A S G	FLD 1 A S G	FLD 2 A S G	FAC A S G	LC A S G	EC/CL A S G	ECWC A S G	UEFA A S G	OTHER A S G	TOTAL A S G
70 Roma	-	-	-	-	-	1	-	-	-	1 -
71 Sheffield Wednesday	1	-	-	-	-	-	-	-	-	1 -
72 Southend United	-	-	-	-	1	-	-	-	-	1 -
73 Sparta Prague	-	-	-	-	-	1	-	-	-	1 -
74 Vasco da Gama	-	-	-	-	-	-	-	-	1	1 -
75 Barcelona	-	-	-	-	-	- (1)	-	-	-	- (1) -
76 Exeter City	-	-	-	- (1)	-	-	-	-	-	- (1) -

DANNY SIMPSON

DEBUT (Full Appearance)

Wednesday 26/09/2007
League Cup 3rd Round
at Old Trafford

Manchester United 0 Coventry City 2

CLUB CAREER RECORD	Apps	Subs	Goals
Premiership	1	(2)	0
League Division 1	0		0
League Division 2	0		0
FA Cup	0	(1)	0
League Cup	1		0
European Cup / Champions League	2	(1)	0
European Cup-Winners' Cup	0		0
UEFA Cup / Inter-Cities' Fairs Cup	0		0
Other Matches	0		0
OVERALL TOTAL	4	(4)	0

Opponents	PREM A S G	FLD 1 A S G	FLD 2 A S G	FAC A S G	LC A S G	EC/CL A S G	ECWC A S G	UEFA A S G	OTHER A S G	TOTAL A S G
1 Dynamo Kiev	-	-	-	-	-	1 (1) -	-	-	-	1 (1) -
2 Coventry City	-	-	-	-	1	-	-	-	-	1 -
3 Everton	1	-	-	-	-	-	-	-	-	1 -
4 Roma	-	-	-	-	1	-	-	-	-	1 -
5 Newcastle United	- (1)	-	-	-	-	-	-	-	-	- (1) -
6 Tottenham Hotspur	-	-	-	- (1)	-	-	-	-	-	- (1) -
7 Wigan Athletic	- (1)	-	-	-	-	-	-	-	-	- (1) -

JOHNNY SIVEBAEK

DEBUT (Full Appearance)

Sunday 09/02/1986
Football League Division 1
at Anfield

Liverpool 1 Manchester United 1

CLUB CAREER RECORD	Apps	Subs	Goals
Premiership	0		0
League Division 1	29	(2)	1
League Division 2	0		0
FA Cup	2		0
League Cup	1		0
European Cup / Champions League	0		0
European Cup-Winners' Cup	0		0
UEFA Cup / Inter-Cities' Fairs Cup	0		0
Other Matches	0		0
OVERALL TOTAL	32	(2)	1

Opponents	PREM A S G	FLD 1 A S G	FLD 2 A S G	FAC A S G	LC A S G	EC/CL A S G	ECWC A S G	UEFA A S G	OTHER A S G	TOTAL A S G
1 Liverpool	-	3	-	-	-	-	-	-	-	3 -
2 Manchester City	-	2	-	1	-	-	-	-	-	3 -
3 Coventry City	-	1	-	1	-	-	-	-	-	2 -
4 Leicester City	-	2	-	-	-	-	-	-	-	2 -
5 Luton Town	-	2	-	-	-	-	-	-	-	2 -
6 Norwich City	-	2	-	-	-	-	-	-	-	2 -
7 Nottingham Forest	-	2	-	-	-	-	-	-	-	2 -
8 Sheffield Wednesday	-	2	-	-	-	-	-	-	-	2 -
9 Tottenham Hotspur	-	2	-	-	-	-	-	-	-	2 -
10 Queens Park Rangers	-	1 (1) 1	-	-	-	-	-	-	-	1 (1) 1
11 Newcastle United	-	1 (1) -	-	-	-	-	-	-	-	1 (1) -
12 Arsenal	-	1	-	-	-	-	-	-	-	1 -
13 Aston Villa	-	1	-	-	-	-	-	-	-	1 -
14 Charlton Athletic	-	1	-	-	-	-	-	-	-	1 -
15 Chelsea	-	1	-	-	-	-	-	-	-	1 -
16 Everton	-	1	-	-	-	-	-	-	-	1 -
17 Oxford United	-	1	-	-	-	-	-	-	-	1 -
18 Port Vale	-	-	-	-	1	-	-	-	-	1 -
19 Southampton	-	1	-	-	-	-	-	-	-	1 -
20 Watford	-	1	-	-	-	-	-	-	-	1 -
21 Wimbledon	-	1	-	-	-	-	-	-	-	1 -

J SLATER

DEBUT (Full Appearance)

Saturday 04/10/1890
FA Cup 1st Qualifying Round
at North Road

Newton Heath 2 Higher Walton 0

CLUB CAREER RECORD	Apps	Subs	Goals
Premiership	0		0
League Division 1	0		0
League Division 2	0		0
FA Cup	4		0
League Cup	0		0
European Cup / Champions League	0		0
European Cup-Winners' Cup	0		0
UEFA Cup / Inter-Cities' Fairs Cup	0		0
Other Matches	0		0
OVERALL TOTAL	4		0

Opponents	PREM A S G	FLD 1 A S G	FLD 2 A S G	FAC A S G	LC A S G	EC/CL A S G	ECWC A S G	UEFA A S G	OTHER A S G	TOTAL A S G
1 Blackpool	- - -	- - -	- - -	1 - -	- - -	- - -	- - -	- - -	- - -	1 - -
2 Higher Walton	- - -	- - -	- - -	1 - -	- - -	- - -	- - -	- - -	- - -	1 - -
3 Manchester City	- - -	- - -	- - -	1 - -	- - -	- - -	- - -	- - -	- - -	1 - -
4 South Shore	- - -	- - -	- - -	1 - -	- - -	- - -	- - -	- - -	- - -	1 - -

TOM SLOAN

DEBUT (Full Appearance)

Saturday 18/11/1978
Football League Division 1
at Old Trafford

Manchester United 2 Ipswich Town 0

CLUB CAREER RECORD	Apps	Subs	Goals
Premiership	0		0
League Division 1	4	(7)	0
League Division 2	0		0
FA Cup	0		0
League Cup	0	(1)	0
European Cup / Champions League	0		0
European Cup-Winners' Cup	0		0
UEFA Cup / Inter-Cities' Fairs Cup	0		0
Other Matches	0		0
OVERALL TOTAL	4	(8)	0

Opponents	PREM A S G	FLD 1 A S G	FLD 2 A S G	FAC A S G	LC A S G	EC/CL A S G	ECWC A S G	UEFA A S G	OTHER A S G	TOTAL A S G
1 Coventry City	- - -	- (2) -	- - -	- - -	- (1) -	- - -	- - -	- - -	- - -	- (3) -
2 Ipswich Town	- - -	2 - -	- - -	- - -	- - -	- - -	- - -	- - -	- - -	2 - -
3 Everton	- - -	1 (1) -	- - -	- - -	- - -	- - -	- - -	- - -	- - -	1 (1) -
4 Southampton	- - -	1 - -	- - -	- - -	- - -	- - -	- - -	- - -	- - -	1 - -
5 Bolton Wanderers	- - -	- (1) -	- - -	- - -	- - -	- - -	- - -	- - -	- - -	- (1) -
6 Manchester City	- - -	- (1) -	- - -	- - -	- - -	- - -	- - -	- - -	- - -	- (1) -
7 Stoke City	- - -	- (1) -	- - -	- - -	- - -	- - -	- - -	- - -	- - -	- (1) -
8 West Bromwich Albion	- - -	- (1) -	- - -	- - -	- - -	- - -	- - -	- - -	- - -	- (1) -

ALAN SMITH

DEBUT (Full Appearance, 1 goal)

Sunday 08/08/2004
FA Charity Shield
at Millennium Stadium

Manchester United 1 Arsenal 3

CLUB CAREER RECORD	Apps	Subs	Goals
Premiership	43	(18)	7
League Division 1	0		0
League Division 2	0		0
FA Cup	2	(6)	0
League Cup	4	(2)	1
European Cup / Champions League	11	(6)	3
European Cup-Winners' Cup	0		0
UEFA Cup / Inter-Cities' Fairs Cup	0		0
Other Matches	1		1
OVERALL TOTAL	61	(32)	12

Opponents	PREM A S G	FLD 1 A S G	FLD 2 A S G	FAC A S G	LC A S G	EC/CL A S G	ECWC A S G	UEFA A S G	OTHER A S G	TOTAL A S G
1 Blackburn Rovers	2 (2) 1	- - -	- - -	- - -	1 (1) -	- - -	- - -	- - -	- - -	3 (3) 1
2 Middlesbrough	3 (1) 1	- - -	- - -	1 - -	- - -	- - -	- - -	- - -	- - -	4 (1) 1
3 Chelsea	3 - -	- - -	- - -	- (1) -	- (1) -	- - -	- - -	- - -	- - -	3 (2) -
4 Portsmouth	2 (3) -	- - -	- - -	- - -	- - -	- - -	- - -	- - -	- - -	2 (3) -
5 Fulham	3 (1) 1	- - -	- - -	- - -	- - -	- - -	- - -	- - -	- - -	3 (1) 1
6 Everton	3 (1) -	- - -	- - -	- - -	- - -	- - -	- - -	- - -	- - -	3 (1) -
7 Manchester City	3 (1) -	- - -	- - -	- - -	- - -	- - -	- - -	- - -	- - -	3 (1) -
8 Newcastle United	1 (2) -	- - -	- - -	- - -	- (1) -	- - -	- - -	- - -	- - -	1 (3) -
9 Tottenham Hotspur	3 - -	- - -	- - -	- - -	- - -	- - -	- - -	- - -	- - -	3 - -
10 Charlton Athletic	2 (1) 2	- - -	- - -	- - -	- - -	- - -	- - -	- - -	- - -	2 (1) 2
11 Benfica	- - -	- - -	- - -	- - -	- - -	2 (1) -	- - -	- - -	- - -	2 (1) -
12 Bolton Wanderers	2 (1) -	- - -	- - -	- - -	- - -	- - -	- - -	- - -	- - -	2 (1) -
13 Lille Metropole	- - -	- - -	- - -	- - -	- - -	2 (1) -	- - -	- - -	- - -	2 (1) -
14 Southampton	2 - -	- - -	- - -	- (1) -	- - -	- - -	- - -	- - -	- - -	2 (1) -
15 Liverpool	1 (1) -	- - -	- - -	- (1) -	- - -	- - -	- - -	- - -	- - -	1 (2) -
16 West Bromwich Albion	1 (2) -	- - -	- - -	- - -	- - -	- - -	- - -	- - -	- - -	1 (2) -
17 Dinamo Bucharest	- - -	- - -	- - -	- - -	- - -	2 - 2	- - -	- - -	- - -	2 - 2
18 Crewe Alexandra	- - -	- - -	- - -	- - -	2 - 1	- - -	- - -	- - -	- - -	2 - 1
19 Crystal Palace	2 - 1	- - -	- - -	- - -	- - -	- - -	- - -	- - -	- - -	2 - 1
20 Norwich City	2 - 1	- - -	- - -	- - -	- - -	- - -	- - -	- - -	- - -	2 - 1
21 Birmingham City	2 - -	- - -	- - -	- - -	- - -	- - -	- - -	- - -	- - -	2 - -
22 Villarreal	- - -	- - -	- - -	- - -	- - -	2 - -	- - -	- - -	- - -	2 - -

continued../

ALAN SMITH (continued)

Opponents	PREM			FLD 1			FLD 2			FAC			LC			EC/CL			ECWC			UEFA			OTHER			TOTAL		
	A	S	G	A	S	G	A	S	G	A	S	G	A	S	G	A	S	G	A	S	G	A	S	G	A	S	G	A	S	G
23 West Ham United	2	-	-	-	-	-	-	-	-	-	-	-	-	-	-	-	-	-	-	-	-	-	-	-	-	-	-	2	-	-
24 Arsenal	-	(1)	-	-	-	-	-	-	-	-	-	-	-	-	-	-	-	-	-	-	-	-	-	-	1	-	1	1	(1)	1
25 Aston Villa	1	(1)	-	-	-	-	-	-	-	-	-	-	-	-	-	-	-	-	-	-	-	-	-	-	-	-	-	1	(1)	-
26 Debreceni	-	-	-	-	-	-	-	-	-	-	-	-	-	-	-	1	(1)	-	-	-	-	-	-	-	-	-	-	1	(1)	-
27 Olympique Lyonnais	-	-	-	-	-	-	-	-	-	-	-	-	-	-	-	1	(1)	-	-	-	-	-	-	-	-	-	-	1	(1)	-
28 Roma	-	-	-	-	-	-	-	-	-	-	-	-	1	-	1	-	-	-	-	-	-	-	-	-	-	-	-	1	-	1
29 Sheffield United	1	-	-	-	-	-	-	-	-	-	-	-	-	-	-	-	-	-	-	-	-	-	-	-	-	-	-	1	-	-
30 Southend United	-	-	-	-	-	-	-	-	-	-	-	-	1	-	-	-	-	-	-	-	-	-	-	-	-	-	-	1	-	-
31 Sunderland	1	-	-	-	-	-	-	-	-	-	-	-	-	-	-	-	-	-	-	-	-	-	-	-	-	-	-	1	-	-
32 Watford	-	-	-	-	-	-	-	-	-	1	-	-	-	-	-	-	-	-	-	-	-	-	-	-	-	-	-	1	-	-
33 Wigan Athletic	1	-	-	-	-	-	-	-	-	-	-	-	-	-	-	-	-	-	-	-	-	-	-	-	-	-	-	1	-	-
34 AC Milan	-	-	-	-	-	-	-	-	-	-	-	-	-	-	-	-	(1)	-	-	-	-	-	-	-	-	-	-	-	(1)	-
35 Copenhagen	-	-	-	-	-	-	-	-	-	-	-	-	-	-	-	-	(1)	-	-	-	-	-	-	-	-	-	-	-	(1)	-
36 Exeter City	-	-	-	-	-	-	-	-	-	-	(1)	-	-	-	-	-	-	-	-	-	-	-	-	-	-	-	-	-	(1)	-
37 Wolverhampton W.	-	-	-	-	-	-	-	-	-	-	(1)	-	-	-	-	-	-	-	-	-	-	-	-	-	-	-	-	-	(1)	-

ALBERT SMITH

DEBUT (Full Appearance)

Saturday 22/01/1927
Football League Division 1
at Elland Road

Leeds United 2 Manchester United 3

CLUB CAREER RECORD	Apps	Subs	Goals
Premiership	0		0
League Division 1	5		1
League Division 2	0		0
FA Cup	0		0
League Cup	0		0
European Cup / Champions League	0		0
European Cup-Winners' Cup	0		0
UEFA Cup / Inter-Cities' Fairs Cup	0		0
Other Matches	0		0
OVERALL TOTAL	5		1

Opponents	PREM			FLD 1			FLD 2			FAC			LC			EC/CL			ECWC			UEFA			OTHER			TOTAL		
	A	S	G	A	S	G	A	S	G	A	S	G	A	S	G	A	S	G	A	S	G	A	S	G	A	S	G	A	S	G
1 Bury	-	-	-	1	-	1	-	-	-	-	-	-	-	-	-	-	-	-	-	-	-	-	-	-	-	-	-	1	-	1
2 Birmingham City	-	-	-	1	-	-	-	-	-	-	-	-	-	-	-	-	-	-	-	-	-	-	-	-	-	-	-	1	-	-
3 Burnley	-	-	-	1	-	-	-	-	-	-	-	-	-	-	-	-	-	-	-	-	-	-	-	-	-	-	-	1	-	-
4 Leeds United	-	-	-	1	-	-	-	-	-	-	-	-	-	-	-	-	-	-	-	-	-	-	-	-	-	-	-	1	-	-
5 Sunderland	-	-	-	1	-	-	-	-	-	-	-	-	-	-	-	-	-	-	-	-	-	-	-	-	-	-	-	1	-	-

BILL SMITH

DEBUT (Full Appearance)

Saturday 14/09/1901
Football League Division 2
at Linthorpe Road

Middlesbrough 5 Newton Heath 0

CLUB CAREER RECORD	Apps	Subs	Goals
Premiership	0		0
League Division 1	0		0
League Division 2	16		0
FA Cup	1		0
League Cup	0		0
European Cup / Champions League	0		0
European Cup-Winners' Cup	0		0
UEFA Cup / Inter-Cities' Fairs Cup	0		0
Other Matches	0		0
OVERALL TOTAL	17		0

Opponents	PREM			FLD 1			FLD 2			FAC			LC			EC/CL			ECWC			UEFA			OTHER			TOTAL		
	A	S	G	A	S	G	A	S	G	A	S	G	A	S	G	A	S	G	A	S	G	A	S	G	A	S	G	A	S	G
1 Blackpool	-	-	-	-	-	-	-	-	-	2	-	-	-	-	-	-	-	-	-	-	-	-	-	-	-	-	-	2	-	-
2 Doncaster Rovers	-	-	-	-	-	-	-	-	-	2	-	-	-	-	-	-	-	-	-	-	-	-	-	-	-	-	-	2	-	-
3 Arsenal	-	-	-	-	-	-	1	-	-	-	-	-	-	-	-	-	-	-	-	-	-	-	-	-	-	-	-	1	-	-
4 Barnsley	-	-	-	-	-	-	1	-	-	-	-	-	-	-	-	-	-	-	-	-	-	-	-	-	-	-	-	1	-	-
5 Bristol City	-	-	-	-	-	-	1	-	-	-	-	-	-	-	-	-	-	-	-	-	-	-	-	-	-	-	-	1	-	-
6 Burnley	-	-	-	-	-	-	1	-	-	-	-	-	-	-	-	-	-	-	-	-	-	-	-	-	-	-	-	1	-	-
7 Burton United	-	-	-	-	-	-	1	-	-	-	-	-	-	-	-	-	-	-	-	-	-	-	-	-	-	-	-	1	-	-
8 Chesterfield	-	-	-	-	-	-	1	-	-	-	-	-	-	-	-	-	-	-	-	-	-	-	-	-	-	-	-	1	-	-
9 Glossop	-	-	-	-	-	-	1	-	-	-	-	-	-	-	-	-	-	-	-	-	-	-	-	-	-	-	-	1	-	-
10 Leicester City	-	-	-	-	-	-	1	-	-	-	-	-	-	-	-	-	-	-	-	-	-	-	-	-	-	-	-	1	-	-
11 Lincoln City	-	-	-	-	-	-	-	-	-	-	-	-	1	-	-	-	-	-	-	-	-	-	-	-	-	-	-	1	-	-
12 Middlesbrough	-	-	-	-	-	-	1	-	-	-	-	-	-	-	-	-	-	-	-	-	-	-	-	-	-	-	-	1	-	-
13 Preston North End	-	-	-	-	-	-	1	-	-	-	-	-	-	-	-	-	-	-	-	-	-	-	-	-	-	-	-	1	-	-
14 Stockport County	-	-	-	-	-	-	1	-	-	-	-	-	-	-	-	-	-	-	-	-	-	-	-	-	-	-	-	1	-	-
15 West Bromwich Albion	-	-	-	-	-	-	1	-	-	-	-	-	-	-	-	-	-	-	-	-	-	-	-	-	-	-	-	1	-	-

DICK SMITH

DEBUT (Full Appearance)

Saturday 08/09/1894
Football League Division 2
at Derby Turn

Burton Wanderers 1 Newton Heath 0

CLUB CAREER RECORD	Apps	Subs	Goals
Premiership	0		0
League Division 1	0		0
League Division 2	93		35
FA Cup	7		2
League Cup	0		0
European Cup / Champions League	0		0
European Cup-Winners' Cup	0		0
UEFA Cup / Inter-Cities' Fairs Cup	0		0
Other Matches	1		0
OVERALL TOTAL	**101**		**37**

Opponents	PREM A	S	G	FLD 1 A	S	G	FLD 2 A	S	G	FAC A	S	G	LC A	S	G	EC/CL A	S	G	ECWC A	S	G	UEFA A	S	G	OTHER A	S	G	TOTAL A	S	G
1 Leicester City	-	-	-	-	-	-	9	-	3	-	-	-	-	-	-	-	-	-	-	-	-	-	-	-	-	-	-	9	-	3
2 Grimsby Town	-	-	-	-	-	-	7	-	2	-	-	-	-	-	-	-	-	-	-	-	-	-	-	-	-	-	-	7	-	2
3 Manchester City	-	-	-	-	-	-	6	-	6	-	-	-	-	-	-	-	-	-	-	-	-	-	-	-	-	-	-	6	-	6
4 Port Vale	-	-	-	-	-	-	6	-	3	-	-	-	-	-	-	-	-	-	-	-	-	-	-	-	-	-	-	6	-	3
5 Newcastle United	-	-	-	-	-	-	6	-	2	-	-	-	-	-	-	-	-	-	-	-	-	-	-	-	-	-	-	6	-	2
6 Arsenal	-	-	-	-	-	-	6	-	-	-	-	-	-	-	-	-	-	-	-	-	-	-	-	-	-	-	-	6	-	-
7 Burton Swifts	-	-	-	-	-	-	5	-	2	-	-	-	-	-	-	-	-	-	-	-	-	-	-	-	-	-	-	5	-	2
8 Blackpool	-	-	-	-	-	-	4	-	1	1	-	-	-	-	-	-	-	-	-	-	-	-	-	-	-	-	-	5	-	1
9 Lincoln City	-	-	-	-	-	-	5	-	1	-	-	-	-	-	-	-	-	-	-	-	-	-	-	-	-	-	-	5	-	1
10 Burton Wanderers	-	-	-	-	-	-	5	-	-	-	-	-	-	-	-	-	-	-	-	-	-	-	-	-	-	-	-	5	-	-
11 Crewe Alexandra	-	-	-	-	-	-	4	-	6	-	-	-	-	-	-	-	-	-	-	-	-	-	-	-	-	-	-	4	-	6
12 Walsall	-	-	-	-	-	-	4	-	2	-	-	-	-	-	-	-	-	-	-	-	-	-	-	-	-	-	-	4	-	2
13 Notts County	-	-	-	-	-	-	4	-	1	-	-	-	-	-	-	-	-	-	-	-	-	-	-	-	-	-	-	4	-	1
14 Loughborough Town	-	-	-	-	-	-	3	-	3	-	-	-	-	-	-	-	-	-	-	-	-	-	-	-	-	-	-	3	-	3
15 Rotherham United	-	-	-	-	-	-	3	-	1	-	-	-	-	-	-	-	-	-	-	-	-	-	-	-	-	-	-	3	-	1
16 Darwen	-	-	-	-	-	-	3	-	-	-	-	-	-	-	-	-	-	-	-	-	-	-	-	-	-	-	-	3	-	-
17 Liverpool	-	-	-	-	-	-	2	-	1	-	-	-	-	-	-	-	-	-	-	-	-	-	-	-	-	-	-	2	-	1
18 New Brighton Tower	-	-	-	-	-	-	2	-	1	-	-	-	-	-	-	-	-	-	-	-	-	-	-	-	-	-	-	2	-	1
19 Stoke City	-	-	-	-	-	-	-	-	-	-	-	-	1	-	1	-	-	-	-	-	-	-	-	-	1	-	-	2	-	1
20 Bury	-	-	-	-	-	-	2	-	-	-	-	-	-	-	-	-	-	-	-	-	-	-	-	-	-	-	-	2	-	-
21 Derby County	-	-	-	-	-	-	-	-	-	2	-	-	-	-	-	-	-	-	-	-	-	-	-	-	-	-	-	2	-	-
22 Kettering	-	-	-	-	-	-	-	-	-	-	-	-	1	-	1	-	-	-	-	-	-	-	-	-	-	-	-	1	-	1
23 Barnsley	-	-	-	-	-	-	1	-	-	-	-	-	-	-	-	-	-	-	-	-	-	-	-	-	-	-	-	1	-	-
24 Birmingham City	-	-	-	-	-	-	1	-	-	-	-	-	-	-	-	-	-	-	-	-	-	-	-	-	-	-	-	1	-	-
25 Burnley	-	-	-	-	-	-	1	-	-	-	-	-	-	-	-	-	-	-	-	-	-	-	-	-	-	-	-	1	-	-
26 Chesterfield	-	-	-	-	-	-	1	-	-	-	-	-	-	-	-	-	-	-	-	-	-	-	-	-	-	-	-	1	-	-
27 Gainsborough Trinity	-	-	-	-	-	-	1	-	-	-	-	-	-	-	-	-	-	-	-	-	-	-	-	-	-	-	-	1	-	-
28 Luton Town	-	-	-	-	-	-	1	-	-	-	-	-	-	-	-	-	-	-	-	-	-	-	-	-	-	-	-	1	-	-
29 Middlesbrough	-	-	-	-	-	-	1	-	-	-	-	-	-	-	-	-	-	-	-	-	-	-	-	-	-	-	-	1	-	-
30 Nelson	-	-	-	-	-	-	-	-	-	1	-	-	-	-	-	-	-	-	-	-	-	-	-	-	-	-	-	1	-	-
31 Southampton	-	-	-	-	-	-	-	-	-	1	-	-	-	-	-	-	-	-	-	-	-	-	-	-	-	-	-	1	-	-

JACK SMITH

DEBUT (Full Appearance)

Wednesday 02/02/1938
Football League Division 2
at Oakwell

Barnsley 2 Manchester United 2

CLUB CAREER RECORD	Apps	Subs	Goals
Premiership	0		0
League Division 1	19		6
League Division 2	17		8
FA Cup	5		1
League Cup	0		0
European Cup / Champions League	0		0
European Cup-Winners' Cup	0		0
UEFA Cup / Inter-Cities' Fairs Cup	0		0
Other Matches	0		0
OVERALL TOTAL	**41**		**15**

Opponents	PREM A	S	G	FLD 1 A	S	G	FLD 2 A	S	G	FAC A	S	G	LC A	S	G	EC/CL A	S	G	ECWC A	S	G	UEFA A	S	G	OTHER A	S	G	TOTAL A	S	G
1 Aston Villa	-	-	-	2	-	-	1	-	-	-	-	-	-	-	-	-	-	-	-	-	-	-	-	-	-	-	-	3	-	-
2 Preston North End	-	-	-	1	-	-	-	-	-	2	-	-	-	-	-	-	-	-	-	-	-	-	-	-	-	-	-	3	-	-
3 Accrington Stanley	-	-	-	-	-	-	2	-	1	-	-	-	-	-	-	-	-	-	-	-	-	-	-	-	-	-	-	2	-	1
4 West Ham United	-	-	-	-	-	-	2	-	1	-	-	-	-	-	-	-	-	-	-	-	-	-	-	-	-	-	-	2	-	1
5 Burnley	-	-	-	-	-	-	2	-	-	-	-	-	-	-	-	-	-	-	-	-	-	-	-	-	-	-	-	2	-	-
6 Leeds United	-	-	-	2	-	-	-	-	-	-	-	-	-	-	-	-	-	-	-	-	-	-	-	-	-	-	-	2	-	-
7 Birmingham City	-	-	-	1	-	2	-	-	-	-	-	-	-	-	-	-	-	-	-	-	-	-	-	-	-	-	-	1	-	2
8 Chesterfield	-	-	-	-	-	-	-	-	-	1	-	2	-	-	-	-	-	-	-	-	-	-	-	-	-	-	-	1	-	2
9 Barnsley	-	-	-	-	-	-	1	-	1	-	-	-	-	-	-	-	-	-	-	-	-	-	-	-	-	-	-	1	-	1
10 Bradford Park Avenue	-	-	-	-	-	-	-	-	-	1	-	1	-	-	-	-	-	-	-	-	-	-	-	-	-	-	-	1	-	1
11 Bury	-	-	-	-	-	-	1	-	1	-	-	-	-	-	-	-	-	-	-	-	-	-	-	-	-	-	-	1	-	1
12 Chelsea	-	-	-	1	-	1	-	-	-	-	-	-	-	-	-	-	-	-	-	-	-	-	-	-	-	-	-	1	-	1
13 Derby County	-	-	-	1	-	1	-	-	-	-	-	-	-	-	-	-	-	-	-	-	-	-	-	-	-	-	-	1	-	1
14 Middlesbrough	-	-	-	1	-	1	-	-	-	-	-	-	-	-	-	-	-	-	-	-	-	-	-	-	-	-	-	1	-	1
15 Sheffield United	-	-	-	-	-	-	-	-	-	1	-	1	-	-	-	-	-	-	-	-	-	-	-	-	-	-	-	1	-	1
16 Stoke City	-	-	-	1	-	1	-	-	-	-	-	-	-	-	-	-	-	-	-	-	-	-	-	-	-	-	-	1	-	1
17 Swansea City	-	-	-	-	-	-	-	-	-	1	-	1	-	-	-	-	-	-	-	-	-	-	-	-	-	-	-	1	-	1
18 Blackburn Rovers	-	-	-	-	-	-	1	-	-	-	-	-	-	-	-	-	-	-	-	-	-	-	-	-	-	-	-	1	-	-
19 Blackpool	-	-	-	1	-	-	-	-	-	-	-	-	-	-	-	-	-	-	-	-	-	-	-	-	-	-	-	1	-	-
20 Bolton Wanderers	-	-	-	1	-	-	-	-	-	-	-	-	-	-	-	-	-	-	-	-	-	-	-	-	-	-	-	1	-	-
21 Charlton Athletic	-	-	-	1	-	-	-	-	-	-	-	-	-	-	-	-	-	-	-	-	-	-	-	-	-	-	-	1	-	-

continued../

JACK SMITH (continued)

Opponents	PREM A	S	G	FLD 1 A	S	G	FLD 2 A	S	G	FAC A	S	G	LC A	S	G	EC/CL A	S	G	ECWC A	S	G	UEFA A	S	G	OTHER A	S	G	TOTAL A	S	G
22 Everton	–	–	1	–	–	–	–	–	–	–	–	–	–	–	–	–	–	–	–	–	–	–	–	–	–	–	–	1	–
23 Fulham	–	–	–	–	1	–	–	–	–	–	–	–	–	–	–	–	–	–	–	–	–	–	–	–	–	–	–	1	–
24 Grimsby Town	–	–	1	–	–	–	–	–	–	–	–	–	–	–	–	–	–	–	–	–	–	–	–	–	–	–	–	1	–
25 Huddersfield Town	–	–	1	–	–	–	–	–	–	–	–	–	–	–	–	–	–	–	–	–	–	–	–	–	–	–	–	1	–
26 Liverpool	–	–	1	–	–	–	–	–	–	–	–	–	–	–	–	–	–	–	–	–	–	–	–	–	–	–	–	1	–
27 Norwich City	–	–	–	–	1	–	–	–	–	–	–	–	–	–	–	–	–	–	–	–	–	–	–	–	–	–	–	1	–
28 Sheffield Wednesday	–	–	–	–	–	–	1	–	–	–	–	–	–	–	–	–	–	–	–	–	–	–	–	–	–	–	–	1	–
29 Southampton	–	–	–	–	1	–	–	–	–	–	–	–	–	–	–	–	–	–	–	–	–	–	–	–	–	–	–	1	–
30 Sunderland	–	–	1	–	–	–	–	–	–	–	–	–	–	–	–	–	–	–	–	–	–	–	–	–	–	–	–	1	–
31 Tottenham Hotspur	–	–	–	–	1	–	–	–	–	–	–	–	–	–	–	–	–	–	–	–	–	–	–	–	–	–	–	1	–
32 West Bromwich Albion	–	–	–	–	–	–	–	1	–	–	–	–	–	–	–	–	–	–	–	–	–	–	–	–	–	–	–	1	–
33 Wolverhampton W.	–	–	1	–	–	–	–	–	–	–	–	–	–	–	–	–	–	–	–	–	–	–	–	–	–	–	–	1	–

LAWRENCE SMITH

DEBUT (Full Appearance)

Saturday 12/12/1896
FA Cup 3rd Qualifying Round
at Bank Street

Newton Heath 7 West Manchester 0

CLUB CAREER RECORD	Apps	Subs	Goals
Premiership	0		0
League Division 1	0		0
League Division 2	8		1
FA Cup	2		0
League Cup	0		0
European Cup / Champions League	0		0
European Cup–Winners' Cup	0		0
UEFA Cup / Inter–Cities' Fairs Cup	0		0
Other Matches	0		0
OVERALL TOTAL	10		1

Opponents	PREM A	S	G	FLD 1 A	S	G	FLD 2 A	S	G	FAC A	S	G	LC A	S	G	EC/CL A	S	G	ECWC A	S	G	UEFA A	S	G	OTHER A	S	G	TOTAL A	S	G
1 Leicester City	–	–	–	–	–	–	2	–	1	–	–	–	–	–	–	–	–	–	–	–	–	–	–	–	–	–	–	2	1
2 Doncaster Rovers	–	–	–	–	–	–	2	–	–	–	–	–	–	–	–	–	–	–	–	–	–	–	–	–	–	–	–	2	–
3 Birmingham City	–	–	–	–	–	–	1	–	–	–	–	–	–	–	–	–	–	–	–	–	–	–	–	–	–	–	–	1	–
4 Burnley	–	–	–	–	–	–	1	–	–	–	–	–	–	–	–	–	–	–	–	–	–	–	–	–	–	–	–	1	–
5 Everton	–	–	–	–	–	–	–	–	–	1	–	–	–	–	–	–	–	–	–	–	–	–	–	–	–	–	–	1	–
6 Liverpool	–	–	–	–	–	–	1	–	–	–	–	–	–	–	–	–	–	–	–	–	–	–	–	–	–	–	–	1	–
7 Port Vale	–	–	–	–	–	–	1	–	–	–	–	–	–	–	–	–	–	–	–	–	–	–	–	–	–	–	–	1	–
8 Stockport County	–	–	–	–	–	–	–	–	–	1	–	–	–	–	–	–	–	–	–	–	–	–	–	–	–	–	–	1	–

TOM SMITH

DEBUT (Full Appearance)

Saturday 19/01/1924
Football League Division 2
at Craven Cottage

Fulham 3 Manchester United 1

CLUB CAREER RECORD	Apps	Subs	Goals
Premiership	0		0
League Division 1	40		3
League Division 2	43		9
FA Cup	7		4
League Cup	0		0
European Cup / Champions League	0		0
European Cup–Winners' Cup	0		0
UEFA Cup / Inter–Cities' Fairs Cup	0		0
Other Matches	0		0
OVERALL TOTAL	90		16

Opponents	PREM A	S	G	FLD 1 A	S	G	FLD 2 A	S	G	FAC A	S	G	LC A	S	G	EC/CL A	S	G	ECWC A	S	G	UEFA A	S	G	OTHER A	S	G	TOTAL A	S	G
1 Sheffield Wednesday	–	–	2	–	–	–	3	–	2	1	–	–	–	–	–	–	–	–	–	–	–	–	–	–	–	–	–	6	2
2 Sunderland	–	–	3	1	–	–	2	–	3	–	–	–	–	–	–	–	–	–	–	–	–	–	–	–	–	–	–	5	4
3 Fulham	–	–	–	–	–	–	3	–	1	1	–	–	–	–	–	–	–	–	–	–	–	–	–	–	–	–	–	4	1
4 Leicester City	–	–	2	–	–	–	2	–	–	–	–	–	–	–	–	–	–	–	–	–	–	–	–	–	–	–	–	4	–
5 Stoke City	–	–	–	–	–	–	3	–	2	–	–	–	–	–	–	–	–	–	–	–	–	–	–	–	–	–	–	3	2
6 Crystal Palace	–	–	–	–	–	–	3	–	1	–	–	–	–	–	–	–	–	–	–	–	–	–	–	–	–	–	–	3	1
7 Port Vale	–	–	–	–	–	–	2	–	1	1	–	–	–	–	–	–	–	–	–	–	–	–	–	–	–	–	–	3	1
8 Everton	–	–	3	–	–	–	–	–	–	–	–	–	–	–	–	–	–	–	–	–	–	–	–	–	–	–	–	3	–
9 Hull City	–	–	–	–	–	–	3	–	–	–	–	–	–	–	–	–	–	–	–	–	–	–	–	–	–	–	–	3	–
10 Leyton Orient	–	–	–	–	–	–	3	–	–	–	–	–	–	–	–	–	–	–	–	–	–	–	–	–	–	–	–	3	–
11 Liverpool	–	–	3	–	–	–	–	–	–	–	–	–	–	–	–	–	–	–	–	–	–	–	–	–	–	–	–	3	–
12 Bradford City	–	–	–	–	–	–	2	–	1	–	–	–	–	–	–	–	–	–	–	–	–	–	–	–	–	–	–	2	1
13 Burnley	–	–	2	1	–	–	–	–	–	–	–	–	–	–	–	–	–	–	–	–	–	–	–	–	–	–	–	2	1
14 Middlesbrough	–	–	–	–	–	–	2	–	1	–	–	–	–	–	–	–	–	–	–	–	–	–	–	–	–	–	–	2	1
15 Tottenham Hotspur	–	–	2	1	–	–	–	–	–	–	–	–	–	–	–	–	–	–	–	–	–	–	–	–	–	–	–	2	1
16 Aston Villa	–	–	2	–	–	–	–	–	–	–	–	–	–	–	–	–	–	–	–	–	–	–	–	–	–	–	–	2	–
17 Barnsley	–	–	–	–	–	–	2	–	–	–	–	–	–	–	–	–	–	–	–	–	–	–	–	–	–	–	–	2	–
18 Birmingham City	–	–	2	–	–	–	–	–	–	–	–	–	–	–	–	–	–	–	–	–	–	–	–	–	–	–	–	2	–
19 Blackburn Rovers	–	–	2	–	–	–	–	–	–	–	–	–	–	–	–	–	–	–	–	–	–	–	–	–	–	–	–	2	–
20 Bolton Wanderers	–	–	2	–	–	–	–	–	–	–	–	–	–	–	–	–	–	–	–	–	–	–	–	–	–	–	–	2	–
21 Chelsea	–	–	–	–	–	–	2	–	–	–	–	–	–	–	–	–	–	–	–	–	–	–	–	–	–	–	–	2	–
22 Huddersfield Town	–	–	2	–	–	–	–	–	–	–	–	–	–	–	–	–	–	–	–	–	–	–	–	–	–	–	–	2	–
23 Manchester City	–	–	1	–	–	–	–	–	–	1	–	–	–	–	–	–	–	–	–	–	–	–	–	–	–	–	–	2	–
24 Newcastle United	–	–	2	–	–	–	–	–	–	–	–	–	–	–	–	–	–	–	–	–	–	–	–	–	–	–	–	2	–
25 Notts County	–	–	2	–	–	–	–	–	–	–	–	–	–	–	–	–	–	–	–	–	–	–	–	–	–	–	–	2	–

continued../

TOM SMITH (continued)

Opponents	PREM A S G	FLD 1 A S G	FLD 2 A S G	FAC A S G	LC A S G	EC/CL A S G	ECWC A S G	UEFA A S G	OTHER A S G	TOTAL A S G
26 Oldham Athletic	– –	–	–	2 –	–	–	–	–	–	2 –
27 Sheffield United	– –	2	–	–	–	–	–	–	–	2 –
28 South Shields	– –	–	–	2	–	–	–	–	–	2 –
29 Southampton	– –	–	–	2	–	–	–	–	–	2 –
30 Stockport County	– –	–	–	2	–	–	–	–	–	2 –
31 Portsmouth	– –	–	–	1 1	–	–	–	–	–	1 1
32 Arsenal	– –	1	–	–	–	–	–	–	–	1 –
33 Blackpool	– –	–	–	1	–	–	–	–	–	1 –
34 Bury	– –	1	–	–	–	–	–	–	–	1 –
35 Cardiff City	– –	1	–	–	–	–	–	–	–	1 –
36 Coventry City	– –	–	–	1	–	–	–	–	–	1 –
37 Derby County	– –	–	–	1	–	–	–	–	–	1 –
38 Leeds United	– –	1	–	–	–	–	–	–	–	1 –
39 Reading	– –	–	–	1	–	–	–	–	–	1 –
40 West Bromwich Albion	– –	1	–	–	–	–	–	–	–	1 –
41 West Ham United	– –	1	–	–	–	–	–	–	–	1 –
42 Wolverhampton W.	– –	–	1	–	–	–	–	–	–	1 –

J SNEDDON

DEBUT (Full Appearance, 1 goal)

Saturday 03/10/1891
FA Cup 1st Qualifying Round
at North Road

Newton Heath 5 Manchester City 1

CLUB CAREER RECORD	Apps	Subs	Goals
Premiership	0		0
League Division 1	0		0
League Division 2	0		0
FA Cup	3		1
League Cup	0		0
European Cup / Champions League	0		0
European Cup–Winners' Cup	0		0
UEFA Cup / Inter–Cities' Fairs Cup	0		0
Other Matches	0		0
OVERALL TOTAL	3		1

Opponents	PREM A S G	FLD 1 A S G	FLD 2 A S G	FAC A S G	LC A S G	EC/CL A S G	ECWC A S G	UEFA A S G	OTHER A S G	TOTAL A S G
1 Manchester City	–	–	–	1 1	–	–	–	–	–	1 1
2 Blackpool	–	–	–	1	–	–	–	–	–	1 –
3 South Shore	–	–	–	1	–	–	–	–	–	1 –

OLE GUNNAR SOLSKJAER

DEBUT (Substitute Appearance, 1 goal)

Sunday 25/08/1996
FA Premiership
at Old Trafford

Manchester United 2 Blackburn Rovers 2

CLUB CAREER RECORD	Apps	Subs	Goals
Premiership	151	(84)	91
League Division 1	0		0
League Division 2	0		0
FA Cup	15	(15)	8
League Cup	8	(3)	7
European Cup / Champions League	36	(45)	20
European Cup–Winners' Cup	0		0
UEFA Cup / Inter–Cities' Fairs Cup	0		0
Other Matches	6	(3)	0
OVERALL TOTAL	216	(150)	126

Opponents	PREM A S G	FLD 1 A S G	FLD 2 A S G	FAC A S G	LC A S G	EC/CL A S G	ECWC A S G	UEFA A S G	OTHER A S G	TOTAL A S G
1 Arsenal	6 (6) 2	–	–	3 (1) –	–	–	–	–	1 (2) –	10 (9) 2
2 Chelsea	7 (6) 3	–	–	1 (3) –	–	–	–	–	1 –	9 (9) 3
3 Aston Villa	9 (3) 1	–	–	1 (1) 2	1	–	–	–	–	11 (4) 3
4 West Ham United	8 (4) 7	–	–	– (2) 1	–	–	–	–	–	8 (6) 8
5 Newcastle United	7 (6) 4	–	–	1	–	–	–	–	–	8 (6) 4
6 Tottenham Hotspur	8 (3) 7	–	–	– (1) –	–	–	–	–	–	9 (4) 7
7 Sunderland	6 (5) 4	–	–	–	1	–	–	–	–	7 (5) 4
8 Southampton	8 (3) 3	–	–	–	–	–	–	–	–	8 (3) 3
9 Liverpool	7 (2) 2	–	–	– (1) 1	– (1)	–	–	–	–	7 (4) 3
10 Charlton Athletic	6 (5) 7	–	–	–	–	–	–	–	–	6 (5) 7
11 Blackburn Rovers	6 (4) 4	–	–	–	– (1)	–	–	–	–	6 (5) 4
12 Middlesbrough	5 (4) 1	–	–	1 (1) –	–	–	–	–	–	6 (5) 1
13 Everton	9 (1) 7	–	–	–	–	–	–	–	–	9 (1) 7
14 Leeds United	7 (3) 4	–	–	–	–	–	–	–	–	7 (3) 4
15 Derby County	5 (4) 3	–	–	–	–	–	–	–	–	5 (4) 3
16 Leicester City	6 (1) 5	–	–	–	1	–	–	–	–	7 (1) 5
17 Coventry City	4 (4) 2	–	–	–	–	–	–	–	–	4 (4) 2
18 Bolton Wanderers	6 (1) 4	–	–	–	–	–	–	–	–	6 (1) 4
19 Sheffield Wednesday	5 (2) 4	–	–	–	–	–	–	–	–	5 (2) 4
20 Wimbledon	3 (2) –	–	–	– (2) –	–	–	–	–	–	3 (4) –
21 Fulham	2 (1) 1	–	–	2 (1) 1	–	–	–	–	–	4 (2) 2
22 Watford	3 (1) –	–	–	– (1) –	–	–	–	–	–	4 (2) 2
23 Juventus	–	–	–	–	–	4 (2) –	–	–	–	4 (2) –
24 Nottingham Forest	2 (2) 6	–	–	–	1	2	–	–	–	3 (2) 8
25 Deportivo La Coruna	–	–	–	–	–	1 (4) 2	–	–	–	1 (4) 2

continued../

OLE GUNNAR SOLSKJAER (continued)

Opponents	PREM A S G	FLD 1 A S G	FLD 2 A S G	FAC A S G	LC A S G	EC/CL A S G	ECWC A S G	UEFA A S G	OTHER A S G	TOTAL A S G
26 Ipswich Town	3 (1) 4	–	–	–	–	–	–	–	–	3 (1) 4
27 Reading	1 (1) 1	–	–	2 1	–	–	–	–	–	3 (1) 2
28 Bayern Munich	–	–	–	–	–	2 (2) 1	–	–	–	2 (2) 1
29 Manchester City	2 (2) 1	–	–	–	–	–	–	–	–	2 (2) 1
30 Sturm Graz	–	–	–	–	–	2 (2) 1	–	–	–	2 (2) 1
31 Valencia	–	–	–	–	–	2 (2) 1	–	–	–	2 (2) 1
32 Birmingham City	2 (2) –	–	–	–	–	–	–	–	–	2 (2) –
33 Bradford City	2 (2) –	–	–	–	–	–	–	–	–	2 (2) –
34 Bayer Leverkusen	–	–	–	–	–	1 (3) –	–	–	–	1 (3) –
35 Porto	–	–	–	–	–	2 (1) –	–	–	–	2 (1) –
36 Portsmouth	1 (1) –	–	–	1	–	–	–	–	–	2 (1) –
37 Olympiakos Piraeus	–	–	–	–	–	1 (2) 2	–	–	–	1 (2) 2
38 Real Madrid	–	–	–	–	–	1 (2) –	–	–	–	1 (2) –
39 Wigan Athletic	2 2	–	–	–	–	–	–	–	–	2 2
40 Basel	–	–	–	–	–	2 1	–	–	–	2 1
41 Maccabi Haifa	–	–	–	–	–	2 1	–	–	–	2 1
42 Rapid Vienna	–	–	–	–	–	2 1	–	–	–	2 1
43 Borussia Dortmund	–	–	–	–	–	2	–	–	–	2
44 Burton Albion	–	–	–	2	–	–	–	–	–	2
45 Nantes Atlantique	–	–	–	–	–	1 (1) 2	–	–	–	1 (1) 2
46 West Bromwich Albion	1 (1) 2	–	–	–	–	–	–	–	–	1 (1) 2
47 Boavista	–	–	–	–	–	1 (1) 1	–	–	–	1 (1) 1
48 Lille Metropole	–	–	–	–	–	1 (1) 1	–	–	–	1 (1) 1
49 Panathinaikos	–	–	–	–	–	1 (1) 1	–	–	–	1 (1) 1
50 Zalaegerszeg	–	–	–	–	–	1 (1) 1	–	–	–	1 (1) 1
51 Copenhagen	–	–	–	–	–	1 (1) –	–	–	–	1 (1) –
52 Fenerbahce	–	–	–	–	–	1 (1) –	–	–	–	1 (1) –
53 Olympique Marseille	–	–	–	–	–	1 (1) –	–	–	–	1 (1) –
54 Roma	–	–	–	–	–	1 (1) –	–	–	–	1 (1) –
55 Brondby	–	–	–	–	–	– (2) 1	–	–	–	– (2) 1
56 Girondins Bordeaux	–	–	–	–	–	– (2) 1	–	–	–	– (2) 1
57 Anderlecht	–	–	–	–	–	– (2)	–	–	–	– (2)
58 Feyenoord	–	–	–	–	–	– (2) –	–	–	–	– (2) –
59 LKS Lodz	–	–	–	–	–	– (2) –	–	–	–	– (2) –
60 Walsall	–	–	–	1 2	–	–	–	–	–	1 2
61 Bury	–	–	–	–	1 1	–	–	–	–	1 1
62 Crewe Alexandra	–	–	–	–	1 1	–	–	–	–	1 1
63 Monaco	–	–	–	–	–	1 1	–	–	–	1 1
64 Barcelona	–	–	–	–	–	1	–	–	–	1
65 Barnsley	1	–	–	–	–	–	–	–	–	1
66 Lazio	–	–	–	–	–	–	–	1	–	1
67 Palmeiras	–	–	–	–	–	–	–	–	1	1
68 PSV Eindhoven	–	–	–	–	–	1	–	–	–	1
69 South Melbourne	–	–	–	–	–	–	–	–	1	1
70 Vasco da Gama	–	–	–	–	–	–	–	–	1	1
71 Wolverhampton W.	1	–	–	–	–	–	–	–	–	1
72 Burnley	–	–	–	–	– (1) 1	–	–	–	–	– (1) 1
73 Glasgow Celtic	–	–	–	–	–	– (1) 1	–	–	–	– (1) 1
74 Benfica	–	–	–	–	–	– (1) –	–	–	–	– (1) –
75 Croatia Zagreb	–	–	–	–	–	– (1) –	–	–	–	– (1) –
76 Dynamo Kiev	–	–	–	–	–	– (1) –	–	–	–	– (1) –
77 Fiorentina	–	–	–	–	–	– (1) –	–	–	–	– (1) –
78 Kosice	–	–	–	–	–	– (1) –	–	–	–	– (1) –
79 Millwall	–	–	–	– (1) –	–	–	–	–	–	– (1) –
80 Rayos del Necaxa	–	–	–	–	–	–	–	–	– (1) –	– (1) –
81 Sheffield United	– (1) –	–	–	–	–	–	–	–	–	– (1) –

JONATHAN SPECTOR

DEBUT (Full Appearance)

Wednesday 25/08/2004
Champions League Qualifying Round 2nd Leg
at Old Trafford

Manchester United 3 Dinamo Bucharest 0

CLUB CAREER RECORD	Apps	Subs	Goals
Premiership	2	(1)	0
League Division 1	0		0
League Division 2	0		0
FA Cup	1		0
League Cup	0	(1)	0
European Cup / Champions League	1	(1)	0
European Cup-Winners' Cup	0		0
UEFA Cup / Inter-Cities' Fairs Cup	0		0
Other Matches	0	(1)	0
OVERALL TOTAL	4	(4)	0

Opponents	PREM A S G	FLD 1 A S G	FLD 2 A S G	FAC A S G	LC A S G	EC/CL A S G	ECWC A S G	UEFA A S G	OTHER A S G	TOTAL A S G
1 Blackburn Rovers	1	–	–	–	–	–	–	–	–	1
2 Dinamo Bucharest	–	–	–	–	–	1	–	–	–	1
3 Everton	1	–	–	–	–	–	–	–	–	1
4 Exeter City	–	–	–	1	–	–	–	–	–	1
5 Arsenal	–	–	–	–	–	–	–	–	– (1) –	– (1) –
6 Crystal Palace	–	–	–	–	– (1) –	–	–	–	–	– (1) –
7 Fenerbahce	–	–	–	–	–	– (1) –	–	–	–	– (1) –
8 Tottenham Hotspur	– (1) –	–	–	–	–	–	–	–	–	– (1) –

JOE SPENCE

DEBUT (Full Appearance)

Saturday 30/08/1919
Football League Division 1
at Baseball Ground

Derby County 1 Manchester United 1

CLUB CAREER RECORD	Apps	Subs	Goals
Premiership	0		0
League Division 1	312		106
League Division 2	169		52
FA Cup	29		10
League Cup	0		0
European Cup / Champions League	0		0
European Cup-Winners' Cup	0		0
UEFA Cup / Inter-Cities' Fairs Cup	0		0
Other Matches	0		0
OVERALL TOTAL	**510**		**168**

Opponents	PREM A	S	G	FLD 1 A	S	G	FLD 2 A	S	G	FAC A	S	G	LC A	S	G	EC/CL A	S	G	ECWC A	S	G	UEFA A	S	G	OTHER A	S	G	TOTAL A	S	G
1 Derby County	–		–	13		11	5		–	–		–	–		–	–		–	–		–	–		–	–		–	18		11
2 Arsenal	–		–	17		7	–		–	–		–	–		–	–		–	–		–	–		–	–		–	17		7
3 Newcastle United	–		–	17		7	–		–	–		–	–		–	–		–	–		–	–		–	–		–	17		7
4 Leicester City	–		–	11		4	6		1	–		–	–		–	–		–	–		–	–		–	–		–	17		5
5 Liverpool	–		–	17		5	–		–	–		–	–		–	–		–	–		–	–		–	–		–	17		5
6 Sunderland	–		–	15		4	–		–	2		–	–		–	–		–	–		–	–		–	–		–	17		4
7 Sheffield Wednesday	–		–	12		2	4		1	1		–	–		–	–		–	–		–	–		–	–		–	17		3
8 Huddersfield Town	–		–	15		4	–		–	1		–	–		–	–		–	–		–	–		–	–		–	16		4
9 Aston Villa	–		–	15		3	–		–	1		–	–		–	–		–	–		–	–		–	–		–	16		3
10 Bury	–		–	7		3	5		1	3		1	–		–	–		–	–		–	–		–	–		–	15		5
11 Birmingham City	–		–	14		2	–		–	1		–	–		–	–		–	–		–	–		–	–		–	15		2
12 Manchester City	–		–	13		8	–		–	1		–	–		–	–		–	–		–	–		–	–		–	14		8
13 Middlesbrough	–		–	11		5	2		–	1		1	–		–	–		–	–		–	–		–	–		–	14		6
14 Tottenham Hotspur	–		–	8		5	3		–	2		2	–		–	–		–	–		–	–		–	–		–	13		7
15 Burnley	–		–	11		4	2		1	–		–	–		–	–		–	–		–	–		–	–		–	13		5
16 Bradford City	–		–	3		1	8		3	2		–	–		–	–		–	–		–	–		–	–		–	13		4
17 Blackburn Rovers	–		–	12		3	–		–	1		–	–		–	–		–	–		–	–		–	–		–	13		3
18 Sheffield United	–		–	13		2	–		–	–		–	–		–	–		–	–		–	–		–	–		–	13		2
19 Leeds United	–		–	8		3	4		3	–		–	–		–	–		–	–		–	–		–	–		–	12		6
20 Oldham Athletic	–		–	4		2	8		4	–		–	–		–	–		–	–		–	–		–	–		–	12		6
21 Everton	–		–	12		4	–		–	–		–	–		–	–		–	–		–	–		–	–		–	12		4
22 West Ham United	–		–	10		4	2		–	–		–	–		–	–		–	–		–	–		–	–		–	12		4
23 Port Vale	–		–	–		–	9		6	2		3	–		–	–		–	–		–	–		–	–		–	11		9
24 Bolton Wanderers	–		–	11		2	–		–	–		–	–		–	–		–	–		–	–		–	–		–	11		2
25 Portsmouth	–		–	8		1	2		1	–		–	–		–	–		–	–		–	–		–	–		–	10		1
26 Cardiff City	–		–	8		2	–		–	1		–	–		–	–		–	–		–	–		–	–		–	9		2
27 Stoke City	–		–	–		–	8		1	1		1	–		–	–		–	–		–	–		–	–		–	9		2
28 Barnsley	–		–	–		–	8		1	–		–	–		–	–		–	–		–	–		–	–		–	8		1
29 Chelsea	–		–	6		1	2		–	–		–	–		–	–		–	–		–	–		–	–		–	8		1
30 Blackpool	–		–	2		–	6		–	–		–	–		–	–		–	–		–	–		–	–		–	8		–
31 Southampton	–		–	–		–	8		–	–		–	–		–	–		–	–		–	–		–	–		–	8		–
32 Preston North End	–		–	4		5	3		1	–		–	–		–	–		–	–		–	–		–	–		–	7		6
33 Notts County	–		–	3		1	4		1	–		–	–		–	–		–	–		–	–		–	–		–	7		2
34 West Bromwich Albion	–		–	7		2	–		–	–		–	–		–	–		–	–		–	–		–	–		–	7		2
35 Crystal Palace	–		–	–		–	6		8	–		–	–		–	–		–	–		–	–		–	–		–	6		8
36 Plymouth Argyle	–		–	–		–	4		5	2		–	–		–	–		–	–		–	–		–	–		–	6		5
37 Wolverhampton W.	–		–	–		–	6		4	–		–	–		–	–		–	–		–	–		–	–		–	6		4
38 Coventry City	–		–	–		–	6		2	–		–	–		–	–		–	–		–	–		–	–		–	6		2
39 Fulham	–		–	–		–	5		–	1		–	–		–	–		–	–		–	–		–	–		–	6		–
40 Grimsby Town	–		–	4		–	1		–	1		–	–		–	–		–	–		–	–		–	–		–	6		–
41 Leyton Orient	–		–	–		–	6		–	–		–	–		–	–		–	–		–	–		–	–		–	6		–
42 Stockport County	–		–	–		–	6		–	–		–	–		–	–		–	–		–	–		–	–		–	6		–
43 South Shields	–		–	–		–	5		1	–		–	–		–	–		–	–		–	–		–	–		–	5		1
44 Hull City	–		–	–		–	5		–	–		–	–		–	–		–	–		–	–		–	–		–	5		–
45 Charlton Athletic	–		–	–		–	4		1	–		–	–		–	–		–	–		–	–		–	–		–	4		1
46 Millwall	–		–	–		–	3		2	–		–	–		–	–		–	–		–	–		–	–		–	3		2
47 Bristol City	–		–	–		–	3		1	–		–	–		–	–		–	–		–	–		–	–		–	3		1
48 Reading	–		–	–		–	–		–	3		1	–		–	–		–	–		–	–		–	–		–	3		1
49 Bradford Park Avenue	–		–	1		–	2		–	–		–	–		–	–		–	–		–	–		–	–		–	3		–
50 Nelson	–		–	–		–	2		1	–		–	–		–	–		–	–		–	–		–	–		–	2		1
51 Rotherham United	–		–	–		–	2		1	–		–	–		–	–		–	–		–	–		–	–		–	2		1
52 Swansea City	–		–	–		–	2		–	–		–	–		–	–		–	–		–	–		–	–		–	2		–
53 Brentford	–		–	–		–	–		–	1		1	–		–	–		–	–		–	–		–	–		–	1		1
54 Chesterfield	–		–	–		–	1		1	–		–	–		–	–		–	–		–	–		–	–		–	1		1
55 Nottingham Forest	–		–	–		–	1		–	–		–	–		–	–		–	–		–	–		–	–		–	1		–
56 Swindon Town	–		–	–		–	–		–	1		–	–		–	–		–	–		–	–		–	–		–	1		–

CHARLIE SPENCER

DEBUT (Full Appearance)

Saturday 15/09/1928
Football League Division 1
at Old Trafford

Manchester United 2 Liverpool 2

CLUB CAREER RECORD	Apps	Subs	Goals
Premiership	0		0
League Division 1	46		0
League Division 2	0		0
FA Cup	2		0
League Cup	0		0
European Cup / Champions League	0		0
European Cup-Winners' Cup	0		0
UEFA Cup / Inter-Cities' Fairs Cup	0		0
Other Matches	0		0
OVERALL TOTAL	48		0

Opponents	PREM			FLD 1			FLD 2			FAC			LC			EC/CL			ECWC			UEFA			OTHER			TOTAL		
	A	S	G	A	S	G	A	S	G	A	S	G	A	S	G	A	S	G	A	S	G	A	S	G	A	S	G	A	S	G
1 Arsenal	–	–		3	–		–			–			–			–			–			–			–			3	–	
2 Bury	–	–		2	–		–			1			–			–			–			–			–			3	–	
3 Leicester City	–	–		3	–		–			–			–			–			–			–			–			3	–	
4 Liverpool	–	–		3	–		–			–			–			–			–			–			–			3	–	
5 Newcastle United	–	–		3	–		–			–			–			–			–			–			–			3	–	
6 Sheffield United	–	–		3	–		–			–			–			–			–			–			–			3	–	
7 Aston Villa	–	–		2	–		–			–			–			–			–			–			–			2	–	
8 Birmingham City	–	–		2	–		–			–			–			–			–			–			–			2	–	
9 Blackburn Rovers	–	–		2	–		–			–			–			–			–			–			–			2	–	
10 Bolton Wanderers	–	–		2	–		–			–			–			–			–			–			–			2	–	
11 Burnley	–	–		2	–		–			–			–			–			–			–			–			2	–	
12 Cardiff City	–	–		2	–		–			–			–			–			–			–			–			2	–	
13 Derby County	–	–		2	–		–			–			–			–			–			–			–			2	–	
14 Everton	–	–		2	–		–			–			–			–			–			–			–			2	–	
15 Huddersfield Town	–	–		2	–		–			–			–			–			–			–			–			2	–	
16 Manchester City	–	–		2	–		–			–			–			–			–			–			–			2	–	
17 Portsmouth	–	–		2	–		–			–			–			–			–			–			–			2	–	
18 Sheffield Wednesday	–	–		2	–		–			–			–			–			–			–			–			2	–	
19 West Ham United	–	–		2	–		–			–			–			–			–			–			–			2	–	
20 Leeds United	–	–		1	–		–			–			–			–			–			–			–			1	–	
21 Middlesbrough	–	–		1	–		–			–			–			–			–			–			–			1	–	
22 Port Vale	–	–		–	–		–			1			–			–			–			–			–			1	–	
23 Sunderland	–	–		1	–		–			–			–			–			–			–			–			1	–	

WALTER SPRATT

DEBUT (Full Appearance)

Saturday 06/02/1915
Football League Division 1
at Roker Park

Sunderland 1 Manchester United 0

CLUB CAREER RECORD	Apps	Subs	Goals
Premiership	0		0
League Division 1	13		0
League Division 2	0		0
FA Cup	0		0
League Cup	0		0
European Cup / Champions League	0		0
European Cup-Winners' Cup	0		0
UEFA Cup / Inter-Cities' Fairs Cup	0		0
Other Matches	0		0
OVERALL TOTAL	13		0

Opponents	PREM			FLD 1			FLD 2			FAC			LC			EC/CL			ECWC			UEFA			OTHER			TOTAL		
	A	S	G	A	S	G	A	S	G	A	S	G	A	S	G	A	S	G	A	S	G	A	S	G	A	S	G	A	S	G
1 Arsenal	–	–		1	–		–			–			–			–			–			–			–			1	–	
2 Bradford City	–	–		1	–		–			–			–			–			–			–			–			1	–	
3 Bradford Park Avenue	–	–		1	–		–			–			–			–			–			–			–			1	–	
4 Burnley	–	–		1	–		–			–			–			–			–			–			–			1	–	
5 Everton	–	–		1	–		–			–			–			–			–			–			–			1	–	
6 Liverpool	–	–		1	–		–			–			–			–			–			–			–			1	–	
7 Middlesbrough	–	–		1	–		–			–			–			–			–			–			–			1	–	
8 Newcastle United	–	–		1	–		–			–			–			–			–			–			–			1	–	
9 Sheffield United	–	–		1	–		–			–			–			–			–			–			–			1	–	
10 Sheffield Wednesday	–	–		1	–		–			–			–			–			–			–			–			1	–	
11 Sunderland	–	–		1	–		–			–			–			–			–			–			–			1	–	
12 Tottenham Hotspur	–	–		1	–		–			–			–			–			–			–			–			1	–	
13 West Bromwich Albion	–	–		1	–		–			–			–			–			–			–			–			1	–	

GEORGE STACEY

DEBUT (Full Appearance)

Saturday 12/10/1907
Football League Division 1
at St James' Park

Newcastle United 1 Manchester United 6

CLUB CAREER RECORD	Apps	Subs	Goals
Premiership	0		0
League Division 1	241		9
League Division 2	0		0
FA Cup	26		0
League Cup	0		0
European Cup / Champions League	0		0
European Cup-Winners' Cup	0		0
UEFA Cup / Inter-Cities' Fairs Cup	0		0
Other Matches	3		0
OVERALL TOTAL	**270**		**9**

Opponents	PREM A S G	FLD 1 A S G	FLD 2 A S G	FAC A S G	LC A S G	EC/CL A S G	ECWC A S G	UEFA A S G	OTHER A S G	TOTAL A S G
1 Aston Villa	–	12 1	–	2	–	–	–	–	–	14 1
2 Blackburn Rovers	–	11	–	3	–	–	–	–	–	14
3 Liverpool	–	13 1	–	–	–	–	–	–	–	13 1
4 Notts County	–	13 1	–	–	–	–	–	–	–	13 1
5 Bradford City	–	13	–	–	–	–	–	–	–	13
6 Manchester City	–	13	–	–	–	–	–	–	–	13
7 Newcastle United	–	12	–	1	–	–	–	–	–	13
8 Sunderland	–	12 3	–	–	–	–	–	–	–	12 3
9 Everton	–	11	–	1	–	–	–	–	–	12
10 Oldham Athletic	–	10	–	2	–	–	–	–	–	12
11 Sheffield United	–	12	–	–	–	–	–	–	–	12
12 Sheffield Wednesday	–	11	–	1	–	–	–	–	–	12
13 Preston North End	–	11	–	–	–	–	–	–	–	11
14 Bolton Wanderers	–	10 2	–	–	–	–	–	–	–	10 2
15 Tottenham Hotspur	–	10 1	–	–	–	–	–	–	–	10 1
16 Bury	–	10	–	–	–	–	–	–	–	10
17 Middlesbrough	–	10	–	–	–	–	–	–	–	10
18 Arsenal	–	9	–	–	–	–	–	–	–	9
19 Chelsea	–	9	–	–	–	–	–	–	–	9
20 Bristol City	–	7	–	1	–	–	–	–	–	8
21 Nottingham Forest	–	7	–	–	–	–	–	–	–	7
22 West Bromwich Albion	–	7	–	–	–	–	–	–	–	7
23 Burnley	–	3	–	2	–	–	–	–	–	5
24 Coventry City	–	–	–	3	–	–	–	–	–	3
25 Derby County	–	3	–	–	–	–	–	–	–	3
26 Blackpool	–	–	–	2	–	–	–	–	–	2
27 Queens Park Rangers	–	–	–	–	–	–	–	2	–	2
28 Reading	–	–	–	2	–	–	–	–	–	2
29 Swindon Town	–	–	–	1	–	–	–	1	–	2
30 Birmingham City	–	–	1	–	–	–	–	–	–	1
31 Bradford Park Avenue	–	–	1	–	–	–	–	–	–	1
32 Brighton	–	–	–	1	–	–	–	–	–	1
33 Fulham	–	–	–	1	–	–	–	–	–	1
34 Huddersfield Town	–	–	–	1	–	–	–	–	–	1
35 Plymouth Argyle	–	–	–	1	–	–	–	–	–	1
36 West Ham United	–	–	–	1	–	–	–	–	–	1

HARRY STAFFORD

DEBUT (Full Appearance)

Friday 03/04/1896
Football League Division 2
at Bank Street

Newton Heath 4 Darwen 0

CLUB CAREER RECORD	Apps	Subs	Goals
Premiership	0		0
League Division 1	0		0
League Division 2	183		0
FA Cup	17		1
League Cup	0		0
European Cup / Champions League	0		0
European Cup-Winners' Cup	0		0
UEFA Cup / Inter-Cities' Fairs Cup	0		0
Other Matches	0		0
OVERALL TOTAL	**200**		**1**

Opponents	PREM A S G	FLD 1 A S G	FLD 2 A S G	FAC A S G	LC A S G	EC/CL A S G	ECWC A S G	UEFA A S G	OTHER A S G	TOTAL A S G
1 Lincoln City	–	–	12	1	–	–	–	–	–	13
2 Gainsborough Trinity	–	–	12	–	–	–	–	–	–	12
3 Leicester City	–	–	12	–	–	–	–	–	–	12
4 Blackpool	–	–	9	2	–	–	–	–	–	11
5 Burton Swifts	–	–	10	–	–	–	–	–	–	10
6 Birmingham City	–	–	9	–	–	–	–	–	–	9
7 Grimsby Town	–	–	9	–	–	–	–	–	–	9
8 Arsenal	–	–	8	–	–	–	–	–	–	8
9 Barnsley	–	–	8	–	–	–	–	–	–	8
10 Burnley	–	–	6	2	–	–	–	–	–	8
11 Loughborough Town	–	–	8	–	–	–	–	–	–	8
12 Port Vale	–	–	8	–	–	–	–	–	–	8
13 Walsall	–	–	8	–	–	–	–	–	–	8
14 Chesterfield	–	–	6	–	–	–	–	–	–	6
15 Darwen	–	–	6	–	–	–	–	–	–	6

continued../

HARRY STAFFORD (continued)

Opponents	PREM A S G	FLD 1 A S G	FLD 2 A S G	FAC A S G	LC A S G	EC/CL A S G	ECWC A S G	UEFA A S G	OTHER A S G	TOTAL A S G
16 Glossop	– –	– –	6 –	–	–	–	–	–	–	6 –
17 Luton Town	– –	– –	6 –	–	–	–	–	–	–	6 –
18 Manchester City	– –	– –	6 –	–	–	–	–	–	–	6 –
19 Middlesbrough	– –	– –	6 –	–	–	–	–	–	–	6 –
20 New Brighton Tower	– –	– –	6 –	–	–	–	–	–	–	6 –
21 Bristol City	– –	– –	3 –	–	–	–	–	–	–	3 –
22 Burton United	– –	– –	3 –	–	–	–	–	–	–	3 –
23 Newcastle United	– –	– –	3 –	–	–	–	–	–	–	3 –
24 Stockport County	– –	– –	3 –	–	–	–	–	–	–	3 –
25 Bolton Wanderers	– –	– –	2 –	–	–	–	–	–	–	2 –
26 Preston North End	– –	– –	2 –	–	–	–	–	–	–	2 –
27 Sheffield Wednesday	– –	– –	2 –	–	–	–	–	–	–	2 –
28 Southampton	– –	– –	– –	2 –	–	–	–	–	–	2 –
29 Tottenham Hotspur	– –	– –	– –	2 –	–	–	–	–	–	2 –
30 Portsmouth	– –	– –	– –	1 1	–	–	–	–	–	1 1
31 Accrington Stanley	– –	– –	– –	1 –	–	–	–	–	–	1 –
32 Burton Wanderers	– –	1 –	– –	–	–	–	–	–	–	1 –
33 Derby County	– –	– –	– –	1 –	–	–	–	–	–	1 –
34 Doncaster Rovers	– –	1 –	– –	–	–	–	–	–	–	1 –
35 Kettering	– –	– –	– –	1 –	–	–	–	–	–	1 –
36 Liverpool	– –	– –	– –	1 –	–	–	–	–	–	1 –
37 Nelson	– –	– –	– –	1 –	–	–	–	–	–	1 –
38 Notts County	– –	1 –	– –	–	–	–	–	–	–	1 –
39 South Shore	– –	– –	– –	1 –	–	–	–	–	–	1 –
40 West Bromwich Albion	– –	1 –	– –	–	–	–	–	–	–	1 –
41 West Manchester	– –	– –	– –	1 –	–	–	–	–	–	1 –

JAAP STAM

DEBUT (Full Appearance)

Wednesday 12/08/1998
Champions League Preliminary Round 1st Leg
at Old Trafford

Manchester United 2 LKS Lodz 0

CLUB CAREER RECORD	Apps	Subs	Goals
Premiership	79		1
League Division 1	0		0
League Division 2	0		0
FA Cup	7	(1)	0
League Cup	0		0
European Cup / Champions League	32		0
European Cup-Winners' Cup	0		0
UEFA Cup / Inter-Cities' Fairs Cup	0		0
Other Matches	7	(1)	0
OVERALL TOTAL	125	(2)	1

Opponents	PREM A S G	FLD 1 A S G	FLD 2 A S G	FAC A S G	LC A S G	EC/CL A S G	ECWC A S G	UEFA A S G	OTHER A S G	TOTAL A S G
1 Arsenal	5 –	–	–	2 –	–	–	–	–	2 –	9 –
2 Liverpool	4 –	–	–	1 –	–	–	–	–	1 –	6 –
3 Chelsea	4 –	–	–	1 –	–	–	–	– (1) –	–	5 (1) –
4 Newcastle United	5 –	–	–	– (1) –	–	–	–	–	–	5 (1) –
5 Leicester City	5 1	–	–	–	–	–	–	–	–	5 1
6 Bayern Munich	–	–	–	–	–	5 –	–	–	–	5 –
7 Coventry City	5 –	–	–	–	–	–	–	–	–	5 –
8 Everton	5 –	–	–	–	–	–	–	–	–	5 –
9 Middlesbrough	4 –	–	–	1 –	–	–	–	–	–	5 –
10 West Ham United	4 –	–	–	1 –	–	–	–	–	–	5 –
11 Leeds United	4 –	–	–	–	–	–	–	–	–	4 –
12 Sheffield Wednesday	4 –	–	–	–	–	–	–	–	–	4 –
13 Sunderland	4 –	–	–	–	–	–	–	–	–	4 –
14 Valencia	–	–	–	–	–	4 –	–	–	–	4 –
15 Aston Villa	3 –	–	–	–	–	–	–	–	–	3 –
16 Derby County	3 –	–	–	–	–	–	–	–	–	3 –
17 Southampton	3 –	–	–	–	–	–	–	–	–	3 –
18 Tottenham Hotspur	3 –	–	–	–	–	–	–	–	–	3 –
19 Wimbledon	3 –	–	–	–	–	–	–	–	–	3 –
20 Barcelona	–	–	–	–	–	2 –	–	–	–	2 –
21 Blackburn Rovers	2 –	–	–	–	–	–	–	–	–	2 –
22 Bradford City	2 –	–	–	–	–	–	–	–	–	2 –
23 Brondby	–	–	–	–	–	2 –	–	–	–	2 –
24 Charlton Athletic	2 –	–	–	–	–	–	–	–	–	2 –
25 Croatia Zagreb	–	–	–	–	–	2 –	–	–	–	2 –
26 Fiorentina	–	–	–	–	–	2 –	–	–	–	2 –
27 Fulham	1 –	–	–	1 –	–	–	–	–	–	2 –
28 Girondins Bordeaux	–	–	–	–	–	2 –	–	–	–	2 –
29 Internazionale	–	–	–	–	–	2 –	–	–	–	2 –
30 Juventus	–	–	–	–	–	2 –	–	–	–	2 –
31 LKS Lodz	–	–	–	–	–	2 –	–	–	–	2 –
32 Olympique Marseille	–	–	–	–	–	2 –	–	–	–	2 –
33 Real Madrid	–	–	–	–	–	2 –	–	–	–	2 –
34 Sturm Graz	–	–	–	–	–	2 –	–	–	–	2 –
35 Ipswich Town	1 –	–	–	–	–	–	–	–	–	1 –

continued../

JAAP STAM (continued)

Opponents	PREM			FLD 1			FLD 2			FAC			LC			EC/CL			ECWC			UEFA			OTHER			TOTAL		
	A	S	G	A	S	G	A	S	G	A	S	G	A	S	G	A	S	G	A	S	G	A	S	G	A	S	G	A	S	G
36 Lazio	-	-	-	-	-	-	-	-	-	-	-	-	-	-	-	-	-	-	-	-	-	-	-	-	1	-	-	1	-	-
37 Manchester City	1	-	-	-	-	-	-	-	-	-	-	-	-	-	-	-	-	-	-	-	-	-	-	-	-	-	-	1	-	-
38 Nottingham Forest	1	-	-	-	-	-	-	-	-	-	-	-	-	-	-	-	-	-	-	-	-	-	-	-	-	-	-	1	-	-
39 Palmeiras	-	-	-	-	-	-	-	-	-	-	-	-	-	-	-	-	-	-	-	-	-	-	-	-	1	-	-	1	-	-
40 Panathinaikos	-	-	-	-	-	-	-	-	-	-	-	-	-	-	-	1	-	-	-	-	-	-	-	-	-	-	-	1	-	-
41 Rayos del Necaxa	-	-	-	-	-	-	-	-	-	-	-	-	-	-	-	-	-	-	-	-	-	-	-	-	1	-	-	1	-	-
42 Vasco da Gama	-	-	-	-	-	-	-	-	-	-	-	-	-	-	-	-	-	-	-	-	-	-	-	-	1	-	-	1	-	-
43 Watford	1	-	-	-	-	-	-	-	-	-	-	-	-	-	-	-	-	-	-	-	-	-	-	-	-	-	-	1	-	-

FRANK STAPLETON

DEBUT (Full Appearance)

Saturday 29/08/1981
Football League Division 1
at Highfield Road

Coventry City 2 Manchester United 1

CLUB CAREER RECORD	Apps	Subs	Goals
Premiership	0		0
League Division 1	204	(19)	60
League Division 2	0		0
FA Cup	21		7
League Cup	26	(1)	6
European Cup / Champions League	0		0
European Cup-Winners' Cup	8		4
UEFA Cup / Inter-Cities' Fairs Cup	6	(1)	1
Other Matches	2		0
OVERALL TOTAL	267	(21)	78

Opponents	PREM			FLD 1			FLD 2			FAC			LC			EC/CL			ECWC			UEFA			OTHER			TOTAL		
	A	S	G	A	S	G	A	S	G	A	S	G	A	S	G	A	S	G	A	S	G	A	S	G	A	S	G	A	S	G
1 West Ham United	-	-	-	11	-	3	-	-	-	4	-	2	1	-	-	-	-	-	-	-	-	-	-	-	-	-	-	16	-	5
2 Liverpool	-	-	-	9	(2)	2	-	-	-	2	-	1	2	-	-	-	-	-	-	-	-	1	-	-	-	-	-	14	(2)	3
3 Southampton	-	-	-	11	-	4	-	-	-	-	-	-	3	-	-	-	-	-	-	-	-	-	-	-	-	-	-	14	-	4
4 Arsenal	-	-	-	11	-	2	-	-	-	1	-	-	2	-	1	-	-	-	-	-	-	-	-	-	-	-	-	14	-	3
5 Everton	-	-	-	8	(2)	3	-	-	-	2	-	1	-	(1)	-	-	-	-	-	-	-	1	-	-	-	-	-	11	(3)	4
6 Nottingham Forest	-	-	-	12	-	3	-	-	-	-	-	-	-	-	-	-	-	-	-	-	-	-	-	-	-	-	-	13	-	3
7 Tottenham Hotspur	-	-	-	9	(1)	-	-	-	-	-	-	-	2	-	-	-	-	-	-	-	-	-	-	-	-	-	-	11	(1)	-
8 Coventry City	-	-	-	9	(1)	1	-	-	-	1	-	-	-	-	-	-	-	-	-	-	-	-	-	-	-	-	-	10	(1)	1
9 Aston Villa	-	-	-	9	(1)	4	-	-	-	-	-	-	-	-	-	-	-	-	-	-	-	-	-	-	-	-	-	9	(1)	4
10 Watford	-	-	-	8	(1)	3	-	-	-	1	-	-	-	-	-	-	-	-	-	-	-	-	-	-	-	-	-	9	(1)	3
11 Luton Town	-	-	-	7	(2)	3	-	-	-	1	-	-	-	-	-	-	-	-	-	-	-	-	-	-	-	-	-	8	(2)	3
12 Ipswich Town	-	-	-	9	-	3	-	-	-	-	-	-	-	-	-	-	-	-	-	-	-	-	-	-	-	-	-	9	-	3
13 Sunderland	-	-	-	6	-	2	-	-	-	2	-	-	-	-	-	-	-	-	-	-	-	-	-	-	-	-	-	8	-	2
14 West Bromwich Albion	-	-	-	8	-	1	-	-	-	-	-	-	-	-	-	-	-	-	-	-	-	-	-	-	-	-	-	8	-	1
15 Manchester City	-	-	-	6	(1)	5	-	-	-	1	-	-	-	-	-	-	-	-	-	-	-	-	-	-	-	-	-	7	(1)	5
16 Birmingham City	-	-	-	7	(1)	1	-	-	-	-	-	-	-	-	-	-	-	-	-	-	-	-	-	-	-	-	-	7	(1)	1
17 Stoke City	-	-	-	7	-	2	-	-	-	-	-	-	-	-	-	-	-	-	-	-	-	-	-	-	-	-	-	7	-	2
18 Norwich City	-	-	-	7	-	1	-	-	-	-	-	-	-	-	-	-	-	-	-	-	-	-	-	-	-	-	-	7	-	1
19 Oxford United	-	-	-	4	-	-	-	-	-	-	-	-	3	-	1	-	-	-	-	-	-	-	-	-	-	-	-	7	-	1
20 Queens Park Rangers	-	-	-	7	-	1	-	-	-	-	-	-	-	-	-	-	-	-	-	-	-	-	-	-	-	-	-	7	-	1
21 Leicester City	-	-	-	6	(1)	3	-	-	-	-	-	-	-	-	-	-	-	-	-	-	-	-	-	-	-	-	-	6	(1)	3
22 Brighton	-	-	-	4	-	1	-	-	-	2	-	1	-	-	-	-	-	-	-	-	-	-	-	-	-	-	-	6	-	2
23 Notts County	-	-	-	6	-	2	-	-	-	-	-	-	-	-	-	-	-	-	-	-	-	-	-	-	-	-	-	6	-	2
24 Chelsea	-	-	-	3	(2)	1	-	-	-	-	-	-	-	-	-	-	-	-	-	-	-	-	-	-	-	-	-	3	(2)	1
25 Newcastle United	-	-	-	2	(3)	3	-	-	-	-	-	-	-	-	-	-	-	-	-	-	-	-	-	-	-	-	-	2	(3)	3
26 Port Vale	-	-	-	-	-	-	-	-	-	-	-	-	4	-	3	-	-	-	-	-	-	-	-	-	-	-	-	4	-	3
27 Wolverhampton W.	-	-	-	4	-	3	-	-	-	-	-	-	-	-	-	-	-	-	-	-	-	-	-	-	-	-	-	4	-	3
28 Bournemouth	-	-	-	-	-	-	-	-	-	2	-	1	2	-	1	-	-	-	-	-	-	-	-	-	-	-	-	4	-	2
29 Swansea City	-	-	-	4	-	1	-	-	-	-	-	-	-	-	-	-	-	-	-	-	-	-	-	-	-	-	-	4	-	1
30 Sheffield Wednesday	-	-	-	3	-	-	-	-	-	-	-	-	-	-	-	-	-	-	-	-	-	-	-	-	-	-	-	3	-	-
31 Spartak Varna	-	-	-	-	-	-	-	-	-	-	-	-	-	-	-	-	-	-	2	-	2	-	-	-	-	-	-	2	-	2
32 Barcelona	-	-	-	-	-	-	-	-	-	-	-	-	-	-	-	-	-	-	2	-	1	-	-	-	-	-	-	2	-	1
33 Dukla Prague	-	-	-	-	-	-	-	-	-	-	-	-	-	-	-	-	-	-	2	-	1	-	-	-	-	-	-	2	-	1
34 Leeds United	-	-	-	2	-	1	-	-	-	-	-	-	-	-	-	-	-	-	-	-	-	-	-	-	-	-	-	2	-	1
35 Middlesbrough	-	-	-	2	-	1	-	-	-	-	-	-	-	-	-	-	-	-	-	-	-	-	-	-	-	-	-	2	-	1
36 Videoton	-	-	-	-	-	-	-	-	-	-	-	-	-	-	-	-	-	-	-	-	-	2	-	1	-	-	-	2	-	1
37 Bradford City	-	-	-	-	-	-	-	-	-	-	-	-	2	-	-	-	-	-	-	-	-	-	-	-	-	-	-	2	-	-
38 Charlton Athletic	-	-	-	2	-	-	-	-	-	-	-	-	-	-	-	-	-	-	-	-	-	-	-	-	-	-	-	2	-	-
39 Crystal Palace	-	-	-	-	-	-	-	-	-	-	-	-	2	-	-	-	-	-	-	-	-	-	-	-	-	-	-	2	-	-
40 Juventus	-	-	-	-	-	-	-	-	-	-	-	-	-	-	-	-	-	-	2	-	-	-	-	-	-	-	-	2	-	-
41 Valencia	-	-	-	-	-	-	-	-	-	-	-	-	-	-	-	-	-	-	-	-	-	2	-	-	-	-	-	2	-	-
42 Dundee United	-	-	-	-	-	-	-	-	-	-	-	-	-	-	-	-	-	-	-	-	-	1	(1)	-	-	-	-	1	(1)	-
43 Wimbledon	-	-	-	1	(1)	-	-	-	-	-	-	-	-	-	-	-	-	-	-	-	-	-	-	-	-	-	-	1	(1)	-
44 Rochdale	-	-	-	-	-	-	-	-	-	1	-	1	-	-	-	-	-	-	-	-	-	-	-	-	-	-	-	1	-	1
45 Burnley	-	-	-	-	-	-	-	-	-	-	-	-	1	-	-	-	-	-	-	-	-	-	-	-	-	-	-	1	-	-
46 Colchester United	-	-	-	-	-	-	-	-	-	-	-	-	1	-	-	-	-	-	-	-	-	-	-	-	-	-	-	1	-	-
47 Derby County	-	-	-	-	-	-	-	-	-	1	-	-	-	-	-	-	-	-	-	-	-	-	-	-	-	-	-	1	-	-
48 PSV Eindhoven	-	-	-	-	-	-	-	-	-	-	-	-	-	-	-	1	-	-	-	-	-	-	-	-	-	-	-	1	-	-

R STEPHENSON

DEBUT (Full Appearance, 1 goal)

Saturday 11/01/1896
Football League Division 2
at Bank Street

Newton Heath 3 Rotherham United 0

CLUB CAREER RECORD	Apps	Subs	Goals
Premiership	0		0
League Division 1	0		0
League Division 2	1		1
FA Cup	0		0
League Cup	0		0
European Cup / Champions League	0		0
European Cup-Winners' Cup	0		0
UEFA Cup / Inter-Cities' Fairs Cup	0		0
Other Matches	0		0
OVERALL TOTAL	1		1

Opponents	PREM A S G	FLD 1 A S G	FLD 2 A S G	FAC A S G	LC A S G	EC/CL A S G	ECWC A S G	UEFA A S G	OTHER A S G	TOTAL A S G
1 Rotherham United	– – –	– – –	1 – 1	– – –	– – –	– – –	– – –	– – –	– – –	1 – 1

ALEX STEPNEY

DEBUT (Full Appearance)

Saturday 17/09/1966
Football League Division 1
at Old Trafford

Manchester United 1 Manchester City 0

CLUB CAREER RECORD	Apps	Subs	Goals
Premiership	0		0
League Division 1	393		2
League Division 2	40		0
FA Cup	44		0
League Cup	35		0
European Cup / Champions League	15		0
European Cup-Winners' Cup	4		0
UEFA Cup / Inter-Cities' Fairs Cup	4		0
Other Matches	4		0
OVERALL TOTAL	539		2

Opponents	PREM A S G	FLD 1 A S G	FLD 2 A S G	FAC A S G	LC A S G	EC/CL A S G	ECWC A S G	UEFA A S G	OTHER A S G	TOTAL A S G
1 Manchester City	– – –	20 – –	– – –	1 – –	3 – –	– – –	– – –	– – –	– – –	24 – –
2 Stoke City	– – –	18 – –	– – –	3 – –	3 – –	– – –	– – –	– – –	– – –	24 – –
3 Leeds United	– – –	19 – –	– – –	4 – –	– – –	– – –	– – –	– – –	– – –	23 – –
4 Arsenal	– – –	20 – –	– – –	– – –	1 – –	– – –	– – –	– – –	– – –	21 – –
5 Liverpool	– – –	19 – –	– – –	1 – –	– – –	– – –	– – –	1 – –	– – –	21 – –
6 Southampton	– – –	13 – –	2 – –	5 – –	– – –	– – –	– – –	– – –	– – –	20 – –
7 Tottenham Hotspur	– – –	17 – –	– – –	2 – –	– – –	– – –	– – –	1 – –	– – –	20 – –
8 Everton	– – –	17 – –	– – –	1 – –	1 – –	– – –	– – –	– – –	– – –	19 – –
9 Ipswich Town	– – –	16 – –	– – –	2 – –	1 – –	– – –	– – –	– – –	– – –	19 – –
10 Wolverhampton W.	– – –	16 – –	– – –	3 – –	– – –	– – –	– – –	– – –	– – –	19 – –
11 Coventry City	– – –	18 – –	– – –	– – –	– – –	– – –	– – –	– – –	– – –	18 – –
12 Newcastle United	– – –	17 – –	– – –	– – –	1 – –	– – –	– – –	– – –	– – –	18 – –
13 West Bromwich Albion	– – –	16 – –	2 – –	– – –	– – –	– – –	– – –	– – –	– – –	18 – –
14 West Ham United	– – –	18 – –	– – –	– – –	– – –	– – –	– – –	– – –	– – –	18 – –
15 Chelsea	– – –	17 – –	– – –	– – –	– – –	– – –	– – –	– – –	– – –	17 – –
16 Derby County	– – –	14 – –	– – –	1 – –	2 – –	– – –	– – –	– – –	– – –	17 – –
17 Leicester City	– – –	15 1 –	– – –	1 – –	– – –	– – –	– – –	– – –	– – –	16 1 –
18 Burnley	– – –	11 – –	– – –	– – –	5 – –	– – –	– – –	– – –	– – –	16 – –
19 Middlesbrough	– – –	5 – –	– – –	4 – –	4 – –	– – –	– – –	– – –	– – –	13 – –
20 Norwich City	– – –	8 – –	2 – –	1 – –	2 – –	– – –	– – –	– – –	– – –	13 – –
21 Nottingham Forest	– – –	11 – –	2 – –	– – –	– – –	– – –	– – –	– – –	– – –	13 – –
22 Sunderland	– – –	8 – –	2 – –	– – –	3 – –	– – –	– – –	– – –	– – –	13 – –
23 Aston Villa	– – –	7 – –	2 – –	1 – –	1 – –	– – –	– – –	– – –	– – –	11 – –
24 Sheffield United	– – –	11 – –	– – –	– – –	– – –	– – –	– – –	– – –	– – –	11 – –
25 Birmingham City	– – –	8 1 –	– – –	2 – –	– – –	– – –	– – –	– – –	– – –	10 1 –
26 Queens Park Rangers	– – –	9 – –	– – –	– – –	1 – –	– – –	– – –	– – –	– – –	10 – –
27 Sheffield Wednesday	– – –	8 – –	2 – –	– – –	– – –	– – –	– – –	– – –	– – –	10 – –
28 Crystal Palace	– – –	6 – –	– – –	– – –	– – –	– – –	– – –	– – –	– – –	6 – –
29 Blackpool	– – –	3 – –	2 – –	– – –	– – –	– – –	– – –	– – –	– – –	5 – –
30 Fulham	– – –	3 – –	2 – –	– – –	– – –	– – –	– – –	– – –	– – –	5 – –
31 Bristol City	– – –	2 – –	2 – –	– – –	– – –	– – –	– – –	– – –	– – –	4 – –
32 Bristol Rovers	– – –	– – –	2 – –	– – –	2 – –	– – –	– – –	– – –	– – –	4 – –
33 Oxford United	– – –	– – –	– – –	1 – –	1 – –	2 – –	– – –	– – –	– – –	4 – –
34 Huddersfield Town	– – –	3 – –	– – –	– – –	– – –	– – –	– – –	– – –	– – –	3 – –
35 Walsall	– – –	– – –	– – –	– – –	3 – –	– – –	– – –	– – –	– – –	3 – –
36 Ajax	– – –	– – –	– – –	– – –	– – –	– – –	– – –	2 – –	– – –	2 – –
37 Anderlecht	– – –	– – –	– – –	– – –	– – –	2 – –	– – –	– – –	– – –	2 – –
38 Bolton Wanderers	– – –	– – –	2 – –	– – –	– – –	– – –	– – –	– – –	– – –	2 – –
39 Cardiff City	– – –	– – –	2 – –	– – –	– – –	– – –	– – –	– – –	– – –	2 – –
40 Estudiantes de la Plata	– – –	– – –	– – –	– – –	– – –	– – –	– – –	– – –	2 – –	2 – –
41 Gornik Zabrze	– – –	– – –	– – –	– – –	– – –	2 – –	– – –	– – –	– – –	2 – –
42 Hibernians Malta	– – –	– – –	– – –	– – –	– – –	2 – –	– – –	– – –	– – –	2 – –
43 Juventus	– – –	– – –	– – –	– – –	– – –	– – –	– – –	2 – –	– – –	2 – –
44 Leyton Orient	– – –	– – –	2 – –	– – –	– – –	– – –	– – –	– – –	– – –	2 – –
45 Millwall	– – –	– – –	2 – –	– – –	– – –	– – –	– – –	– – –	– – –	2 – –
46 Notts County	– – –	– – –	2 – –	– – –	– – –	– – –	– – –	– – –	– – –	2 – –
47 Oldham Athletic	– – –	– – –	2 – –	– – –	– – –	– – –	– – –	– – –	– – –	2 – –
48 Porto	– – –	– – –	– – –	– – –	– – –	– – –	2 – –	– – –	– – –	2 – –
49 Portsmouth	– – –	– – –	2 – –	– – –	– – –	– – –	– – –	– – –	– – –	2 – –
50 Rapid Vienna	– – –	– – –	– – –	– – –	– – –	2 – –	– – –	– – –	– – –	2 – –

continued../

ALEX STEPNEY (continued)

Opponents	PREM A S G	FLD 1 A S G	FLD 2 A S G	FAC A S G	LC A S G	EC/CL A S G	ECWC A S G	UEFA A S G	OTHER A S G	TOTAL A S G
51 Real Madrid	- - -	- - -	- - -	- - -	- - -	2 - -	- - -	- - -	- - -	2 -
52 Sarajevo	- - -	- - -	- - -	- - -	- - -	2 -	- - -	- - -	- - -	2 -
53 St Etienne	- - -	- - -	- - -	- - -	- - -	- -	2 -	- - -	- - -	2 -
54 Waterford	- - -	- - -	- - -	- - -	- - -	2 -	- - -	- - -	- - -	2 -
55 Watford	- - -	- - -	- - -	2 -	- - -	- -	- - -	- - -	- - -	2 -
56 York City	- - -	- - -	2 -	- - -	- - -	- -	- - -	- - -	- - -	2 -
57 Benfica	- - -	- - -	- - -	- - -	- - -	1 -	- - -	- - -	- - -	1 -
58 Brentford	- - -	- - -	- - -	- - -	1 -	- -	- - -	- - -	- - -	1 -
59 Charlton Athletic	- - -	- - -	- - -	- - -	1 -	- -	- - -	- - -	- - -	1 -
60 Exeter City	- - -	- - -	- - -	- - 1	- - -	- -	- - -	- - -	- - -	1 -
61 Hull City	- - -	- - 1	- - -	- - -	- - -	- -	- - -	- - -	- - -	1 -
62 Northampton Town	- - -	- - -	- - -	1 -	- - -	- -	- - -	- - -	- - -	1 -
63 Peterborough United	- - -	- - -	- - -	1 -	- - -	- -	- - -	- - -	- - -	1 -
64 Plymouth Argyle	- - -	- - -	- - -	1 -	- - -	- -	- - -	- - -	- - -	1 -
65 Preston North End	- - -	- - -	- - -	1 -	- - -	- -	- - -	- - -	- - -	1 -
66 Tranmere Rovers	- - -	- - -	- - -	- - -	1 -	- -	- - -	- - -	- - -	1 -
67 Wrexham	- - -	- - -	- - -	- - -	1 -	- -	- - -	- - -	- - -	1 -

ALFRED STEWARD

DEBUT (Full Appearance)

Saturday 23/10/1920
Football League Division 1
at Old Trafford

Manchester United 1 Preston North End 0

CLUB CAREER RECORD	Apps	Subs	Goals
Premiership	0		0
League Division 1	204		0
League Division 2	105		0
FA Cup	17		0
League Cup	0		0
European Cup / Champions League	0		0
European Cup-Winners' Cup	0		0
UEFA Cup / Inter-Cities' Fairs Cup	0		0
Other Matches	0		0
OVERALL TOTAL	326		0

Opponents	PREM A S G	FLD 1 A S G	FLD 2 A S G	FAC A S G	LC A S G	EC/CL A S G	ECWC A S G	UEFA A S G	OTHER A S G	TOTAL A S G
1 Sheffield Wednesday	- -	10 -	4 -	1 -	- -	- -	- -	- -	- -	15 -
2 Leicester City	- -	9 -	5 -	- -	- -	- -	- -	- -	- -	14 -
3 Leeds United	- -	9 -	4 -	- -	- -	- -	- -	- -	- -	13 -
4 Birmingham City	- -	11 -	- -	1 -	- -	- -	- -	- -	- -	12 -
5 Arsenal	- -	11 -	- -	- -	- -	- -	- -	- -	- -	11 -
6 Blackburn Rovers	- -	11 -	- -	- -	- -	- -	- -	- -	- -	11 -
7 Derby County	- -	7 -	4 -	- -	- -	- -	- -	- -	- -	11 -
8 Sunderland	- -	11 -	- -	- -	- -	- -	- -	- -	- -	11 -
9 Aston Villa	- -	10 -	- -	- -	- -	- -	- -	- -	- -	10 -
10 Huddersfield Town	- -	9 -	- -	1 -	- -	- -	- -	- -	- -	10 -
11 Liverpool	- -	10 -	- -	- -	- -	- -	- -	- -	- -	10 -
12 West Ham United	- -	10 -	- -	- -	- -	- -	- -	- -	- -	10 -
13 Bolton Wanderers	- -	9 -	- -	- -	- -	- -	- -	- -	- -	9 -
14 Bury	- -	6 -	2 -	1 -	- -	- -	- -	- -	- -	9 -
15 Manchester City	- -	8 -	- -	1 -	- -	- -	- -	- -	- -	9 -
16 Newcastle United	- -	9 -	- -	- -	- -	- -	- -	- -	- -	9 -
17 Sheffield United	- -	9 -	- -	- -	- -	- -	- -	- -	- -	9 -
18 Burnley	- -	6 -	2 -	- -	- -	- -	- -	- -	- -	8 -
19 Everton	- -	7 -	- -	- -	- -	- -	- -	- -	- -	7 -
20 Port Vale	- -	- -	5 -	2 -	- -	- -	- -	- -	- -	7 -
21 Portsmouth	- -	5 -	2 -	- -	- -	- -	- -	- -	- -	7 -
22 Stoke City	- -	- -	4 -	3 -	- -	- -	- -	- -	- -	7 -
23 Barnsley	- -	- -	6 -	- -	- -	- -	- -	- -	- -	6 -
24 Blackpool	- -	2 -	4 -	- -	- -	- -	- -	- -	- -	6 -
25 Bradford City	- -	1 -	5 -	- -	- -	- -	- -	- -	- -	6 -
26 Cardiff City	- -	6 -	- -	- -	- -	- -	- -	- -	- -	6 -
27 Middlesbrough	- -	4 -	2 -	- -	- -	- -	- -	- -	- -	6 -
28 Grimsby Town	- -	4 -	- -	1 -	- -	- -	- -	- -	- -	5 -
29 Tottenham Hotspur	- -	3 -	2 -	- -	- -	- -	- -	- -	- -	5 -
30 Coventry City	- -	- -	4 -	- -	- -	- -	- -	- -	- -	4 -
31 Crystal Palace	- -	- -	4 -	- -	- -	- -	- -	- -	- -	4 -
32 Fulham	- -	- -	4 -	- -	- -	- -	- -	- -	- -	4 -
33 Leyton Orient	- -	- -	4 -	- -	- -	- -	- -	- -	- -	4 -
34 Notts County	- -	2 -	2 -	- -	- -	- -	- -	- -	- -	4 -
35 Oldham Athletic	- -	- -	4 -	- -	- -	- -	- -	- -	- -	4 -
36 Plymouth Argyle	- -	- -	2 -	2 -	- -	- -	- -	- -	- -	4 -
37 Stockport County	- -	- -	4 -	- -	- -	- -	- -	- -	- -	4 -
38 Chelsea	- -	1 -	2 -	- -	- -	- -	- -	- -	- -	3 -
39 Preston North End	- -	1 -	2 -	- -	- -	- -	- -	- -	- -	3 -
40 Reading	- -	- -	- -	3 -	- -	- -	- -	- -	- -	3 -
41 Southampton	- -	- -	3 -	- -	- -	- -	- -	- -	- -	3 -
42 West Bromwich Albion	- -	3 -	- -	- -	- -	- -	- -	- -	- -	3 -
43 Wolverhampton W.	- -	- -	3 -	- -	- -	- -	- -	- -	- -	3 -
44 Bradford Park Avenue	- -	- -	2 -	- -	- -	- -	- -	- -	- -	2 -

continued../

ALFRED STEWARD (continued)

Opponents	PREM A S G	FLD 1 A S G	FLD 2 A S G	FAC A S G	LC A S G	EC/CL A S G	ECWC A S G	UEFA A S G	OTHER A S G	TOTAL A S G
45 Chesterfield	– –	– –	– 2	– –	– –	– –	– –	– –	– –	2 –
46 Hull City	– –	– –	– 2	– –	– –	– –	– –	– –	– –	2 –
47 Nelson	– –	– –	– 2	– –	– –	– –	– –	– –	– –	2 –
48 Nottingham Forest	– –	– –	– 2	– –	– –	– –	– –	– –	– –	2 –
49 South Shields	– –	– –	– 2	– –	– –	– –	– –	– –	– –	2 –
50 Swansea City	– –	– –	– 2	– –	– –	– –	– –	– –	– –	2 –
51 Charlton Athletic	– –	– –	– 1	– –	– –	– –	– –	– –	– –	1 –
52 Millwall	– –	– –	1	– –	– –	– –	– –	– –	– –	1 –
53 Swindon Town	– –	– –	– –	1	– –	– –	– –	– –	– –	1 –

MICHAEL STEWART

DEBUT (Substitute Appearance)

Tuesday 31/10/2000
League Cup 3rd Round
at Vicarage Road

Watford 0 Manchester United 3

CLUB CAREER RECORD	Apps	Subs	Goals
Premiership	5	(2)	0
League Division 1	0		0
League Division 2	0		0
FA Cup	0	(1)	0
League Cup	2	(2)	0
European Cup / Champions League	0	(2)	0
European Cup-Winners' Cup	0		0
UEFA Cup / Inter-Cities' Fairs Cup	0		0
Other Matches	0		0
OVERALL TOTAL	7	(7)	0

Opponents	PREM A S G	FLD 1 A S G	FLD 2 A S G	FAC A S G	LC A S G	EC/CL A S G	ECWC A S G	UEFA A S G	OTHER A S G	TOTAL A S G
1 Sunderland	– (1) –	– –	– –	– –	– (1)	– –	– –	– –	– –	– (2) –
2 Arsenal	– –	– –	– –	– –	1 –	– –	– –	– –	– –	1 –
3 Burnley	– –	– –	– –	– –	1 –	– –	– –	– –	– –	1 –
4 Charlton Athletic	1 –	– –	– –	– –	– –	– –	– –	– –	– –	1 –
5 Derby County	1 –	– –	– –	– –	– –	– –	– –	– –	– –	1
6 Ipswich Town	1 –	– –	– –	– –	– –	– –	– –	– –	– –	1 –
7 Middlesbrough	1 –	– –	– –	– –	– –	– –	– –	– –	– –	1 –
8 Southampton	1 –	– –	– –	– –	– –	– –	– –	– –	– –	1 –
9 Boavista	– –	– –	– –	– –	– –	– (1) –	– –	– –	– –	– (1) –
10 Deportivo La Coruna	– –	– –	– –	– –	– –	– (1) –	– –	– –	– –	– (1) –
11 Liverpool	– (1) –	– –	– –	– –	– –	– –	– –	– –	– –	– (1) –
12 Portsmouth	– –	– –	– –	– (1) –	– –	– –	– –	– –	– –	– (1) –
13 Watford	– –	– –	– –	– –	– (1) –	– –	– –	– –	– –	– (1) –

WILLIAM STEWART

DEBUT (Full Appearance)

Saturday 19/11/1932
Football League Division 2
at Old Trafford

Manchester United 4 Fulham 3

CLUB CAREER RECORD	Apps	Subs	Goals
Premiership	0		0
League Division 1	0		0
League Division 2	46		7
FA Cup	3		0
League Cup	0		0
European Cup / Champions League	0		0
European Cup-Winners' Cup	0		0
UEFA Cup / Inter-Cities' Fairs Cup	0		0
Other Matches	0		0
OVERALL TOTAL	49		7

Opponents	PREM A S G	FLD 1 A S G	FLD 2 A S G	FAC A S G	LC A S G	EC/CL A S G	ECWC A S G	UEFA A S G	OTHER A S G	TOTAL A S G
1 Burnley	– –	– –	3 1	– –	– –	– –	– –	– –	– –	3 1
2 Fulham	– –	– –	3 1	– –	– –	– –	– –	– –	– –	3 1
3 Grimsby Town	– –	– –	3 1	– –	– –	– –	– –	– –	– –	3 1
4 Oldham Athletic	– –	– –	3 1	– –	– –	– –	– –	– –	– –	3 1
5 Bury	– –	– –	3 –	– –	– –	– –	– –	– –	– –	3 –
6 Lincoln City	– –	– –	3	– –	– –	– –	– –	– –	– –	3 –
7 Plymouth Argyle	– –	– –	3	– –	– –	– –	– –	– –	– –	3 –
8 Bolton Wanderers	– –	– –	2 1	– –	– –	– –	– –	– –	– –	2 1
9 Nottingham Forest	– –	– –	2 1	– –	– –	– –	– –	– –	– –	2 1
10 Preston North End	– –	– –	2 1	– –	– –	– –	– –	– –	– –	2 1
11 Bradford Park Avenue	– –	– –	2	– –	– –	– –	– –	– –	– –	2 –
12 Brentford	– –	– –	2	– –	– –	– –	– –	– –	– –	2 –
13 Chesterfield	– –	– –	2	– –	– –	– –	– –	– –	– –	2 –
14 Hull City	– –	– –	2	– –	– –	– –	– –	– –	– –	2 –
15 Portsmouth	– –	– –	– –	2 –	– –	– –	– –	– –	– –	2 –
16 Southampton	– –	– –	2	– –	– –	– –	– –	– –	– –	2 –
17 Blackpool	– –	– –	1	– –	– –	– –	– –	– –	– –	1 –
18 Bradford City	– –	– –	1	– –	– –	– –	– –	– –	– –	1 –
19 Middlesbrough	– –	– –	– –	1	– –	– –	– –	– –	– –	1 –
20 Millwall	– –	– –	1	– –	– –	– –	– –	– –	– –	1 –

continued../

WILLIAM STEWART (continued)

Opponents	PREM A S G	FLD 1 A S G	FLD 2 A S G	FAC A S G	LC A S G	EC/CL A S G	ECWC A S G	UEFA A S G	OTHER A S G	TOTAL A S G
21 Notts County	– –	– –	1 –	– –	– –	– –	– –	– –	– –	1 –
22 Port Vale	– –	– –	1 –	– –	– –	– –	– –	– –	– –	1 –
23 Stoke City	– –	– –	1 –	– –	– –	– –	– –	– –	– –	1 –
24 Swansea City	– –	– –	1 –	– –	– –	– –	– –	– –	– –	1 –
25 Tottenham Hotspur	– –	– –	1 –	– –	– –	– –	– –	– –	– –	1 –
26 West Ham United	– –	– –	1 –	– –	– –	– –	– –	– –	– –	1 –

WILLIE STEWART

DEBUT (Full Appearance)

Saturday 04/10/1890
FA Cup 1st Qualifying Round
at North Road

Newton Heath 2 Higher Walton 0

CLUB CAREER RECORD	Apps	Subs	Goals
Premiership	0		0
League Division 1	54		4
League Division 2	22		1
FA Cup	9		0
League Cup	0		0
European Cup / Champions League	0		0
European Cup-Winners' Cup	0		0
UEFA Cup / Inter-Cities' Fairs Cup	0		0
Other Matches	2		0
OVERALL TOTAL	87		5

Opponents	PREM A S G	FLD 1 A S G	FLD 2 A S G	FAC A S G	LC A S G	EC/CL A S G	ECWC A S G	UEFA A S G	OTHER A S G	TOTAL A S G
1 Blackburn Rovers	– –	3 –	– –	3 –	– –	– –	– –	– –	– –	6 –
2 Wolverhampton W.	– –	4 3	– –	– –	– –	– –	– –	– –	– –	4 3
3 Aston Villa	– –	4 –	– –	– –	– –	– –	– –	– –	– –	4 –
4 Burnley	– –	4 –	– –	– –	– –	– –	– –	– –	– –	4 –
5 Derby County	– –	4 –	– –	– –	– –	– –	– –	– –	– –	4 –
6 Everton	– –	4 –	– –	– –	– –	– –	– –	– –	– –	4 –
7 Nottingham Forest	– –	4 –	– –	– –	– –	– –	– –	– –	– –	4 –
8 Notts County	– –	2 –	2 –	– –	– –	– –	– –	– –	– –	4 –
9 Preston North End	– –	4 –	– –	– –	– –	– –	– –	– –	– –	4 –
10 Sheffield Wednesday	– –	4 –	– –	– –	– –	– –	– –	– –	– –	4 –
11 Stoke City	– –	2 –	– –	1 –	– –	– –	– –	1 –	– –	4 –
12 Sunderland	– –	4 –	– –	– –	– –	– –	– –	– –	– –	4 –
13 West Bromwich Albion	– –	4 –	– –	– –	– –	– –	– –	– –	– –	4 –
14 Bolton Wanderers	– –	3 –	– –	– –	– –	– –	– –	– –	– –	3 –
15 Walsall	– –	– –	2 1	– –	– –	– –	– –	– –	– –	2 1
16 Burton Swifts	– –	– –	2 –	– –	– –	– –	– –	– –	– –	2 –
17 Burton Wanderers	– –	– –	2 –	– –	– –	– –	– –	– –	– –	2 –
18 Bury	– –	– –	2 –	– –	– –	– –	– –	– –	– –	2 –
19 Darwen	– –	2 –	– –	– –	– –	– –	– –	– –	– –	2 –
20 Grimsby Town	– –	– –	2 –	– –	– –	– –	– –	– –	– –	2 –
21 Lincoln City	– –	– –	2 –	– –	– –	– –	– –	– –	– –	2 –
22 Manchester City	– –	– –	1 –	1 –	– –	– –	– –	– –	– –	2 –
23 Newcastle United	– –	– –	2 –	– –	– –	– –	– –	– –	– –	2 –
24 Accrington Stanley	– –	1 1	– –	– –	– –	– –	– –	– –	– –	1 1
25 Arsenal	– –	– –	1 –	– –	– –	– –	– –	– –	– –	1 –
26 Birmingham City	– –	– –	– –	– –	– –	– –	– –	1 –	– –	1 –
27 Blackpool	– –	– –	– –	– –	1 –	– –	– –	– –	– –	1 –
28 Crewe Alexandra	– –	– –	1 –	– –	– –	– –	– –	– –	– –	1 –
29 Higher Walton	– –	– –	– –	1 –	– –	– –	– –	– –	– –	1 –
30 Leicester City	– –	– –	1 –	– –	– –	– –	– –	– –	– –	1 –
31 Middlesbrough	– –	– –	– –	– –	1 –	– –	– –	– –	– –	1 –
32 Port Vale	– –	– –	1 –	– –	– –	– –	– –	– –	– –	1 –
33 Rotherham United	– –	– –	1 –	– –	– –	– –	– –	– –	– –	1 –
34 Sheffield United	– –	1 –	– –	– –	– –	– –	– –	– –	– –	1 –
35 South Shore	– –	– –	– –	1 –	– –	– –	– –	– –	– –	1 –

NOBBY STILES

DEBUT (Full Appearance)

Saturday 01/10/1960
Football League Division 1
at Burnden Park

Bolton Wanderers 1 Manchester United 1

CLUB CAREER RECORD	Apps	Subs	Goals
Premiership	0		0
League Division 1	311		17
League Division 2	0		0
FA Cup	38		0
League Cup	7		0
European Cup / Champions League	23		2
European Cup-Winners' Cup	2		0
UEFA Cup / Inter-Cities' Fairs Cup	11		0
Other Matches	3		0
OVERALL TOTAL	**395**		**19**

Opponents	PREM			FLD 1			FLD 2			FAC			LC			EC/CL			ECWC			UEFA			OTHER			TOTAL		
	A	S	G	A	S	G	A	S	G	A	S	G	A	S	G	A	S	G	A	S	G	A	S	G	A	S	G	A	S	G
1 Burnley	–	–	–	18	–	1	–	–	–	1	–	–	–	–	–	–	–	–	–	–	–	–	–	–	–	–	–	19	–	1
2 Chelsea	–	–	–	18	–	–	–	–	–	1	–	–	–	–	–	–	–	–	–	–	–	–	–	–	–	–	–	19	–	–
3 Sheffield Wednesday	–	–	–	16	–	–	–	–	–	3	–	–	–	–	–	–	–	–	–	–	–	–	–	–	–	–	–	19	–	–
4 Tottenham Hotspur	–	–	–	15	–	2	–	–	–	1	–	–	–	–	–	–	–	–	1	–	–	–	–	–	1	–	–	18	–	2
5 Arsenal	–	–	–	16	–	1	–	–	–	1	–	–	–	–	–	–	–	–	–	–	–	–	–	–	–	–	–	17	–	1
6 Everton	–	–	–	13	–	–	–	–	–	2	–	–	–	–	–	–	–	–	–	–	–	2	–	–	–	–	–	17	–	–
7 Manchester City	–	–	–	13	–	1	–	–	–	–	–	–	2	–	–	–	–	–	–	–	–	–	–	–	–	–	–	15	–	1
8 West Bromwich Albion	–	–	–	15	–	1	–	–	–	–	–	–	–	–	–	–	–	–	–	–	–	–	–	–	–	–	–	15	–	1
9 West Ham United	–	–	–	15	–	1	–	–	–	–	–	–	–	–	–	–	–	–	–	–	–	–	–	–	–	–	–	15	–	1
10 Leicester City	–	–	–	14	–	–	–	–	–	–	–	–	–	–	–	–	–	–	–	–	–	–	–	–	–	–	–	14	–	–
11 Leeds United	–	–	–	9	–	–	–	–	–	4	–	–	–	–	–	–	–	–	–	–	–	–	–	–	–	–	–	13	–	–
12 Nottingham Forest	–	–	–	13	–	–	–	–	–	–	–	–	–	–	–	–	–	–	–	–	–	–	–	–	–	–	–	13	–	–
13 Aston Villa	–	–	–	10	–	2	–	–	–	1	–	–	1	–	–	–	–	–	–	–	–	–	–	–	–	–	–	12	–	2
14 Liverpool	–	–	–	11	–	–	–	–	–	–	–	–	–	–	–	–	–	–	–	–	–	–	–	–	1	–	–	12	–	–
15 Stoke City	–	–	–	9	–	–	–	–	–	3	–	–	–	–	–	–	–	–	–	–	–	–	–	–	–	–	–	12	–	–
16 Wolverhampton W.	–	–	–	10	–	–	–	–	–	2	–	–	–	–	–	–	–	–	–	–	–	–	–	–	–	–	–	12	–	–
17 Fulham	–	–	–	11	–	2	–	–	–	–	–	–	–	–	–	–	–	–	–	–	–	–	–	–	–	–	–	11	–	2
18 Sheffield United	–	–	–	11	–	1	–	–	–	–	–	–	–	–	–	–	–	–	–	–	–	–	–	–	–	–	–	11	–	1
19 Blackpool	–	–	–	10	–	–	–	–	–	–	–	–	1	–	–	–	–	–	–	–	–	–	–	–	–	–	–	11	–	–
20 Sunderland	–	–	–	9	–	–	–	–	–	1	–	–	–	–	–	–	–	–	–	–	–	–	–	–	–	–	–	10	–	–
21 Newcastle United	–	–	–	9	–	2	–	–	–	–	–	–	–	–	–	–	–	–	–	–	–	–	–	–	–	–	–	9	–	2
22 Birmingham City	–	–	–	7	–	–	–	–	–	2	–	–	–	–	–	–	–	–	–	–	–	–	–	–	–	–	–	9	–	–
23 Blackburn Rovers	–	–	–	8	–	–	–	–	–	–	–	–	–	–	–	–	–	–	–	–	–	–	–	–	–	–	–	8	–	–
24 Ipswich Town	–	–	–	6	–	1	–	–	–	–	–	–	–	–	–	–	–	–	–	–	–	–	–	–	–	–	–	6	–	1
25 Bolton Wanderers	–	–	–	6	–	–	–	–	–	–	–	–	–	–	–	–	–	–	–	–	–	–	–	–	–	–	–	6	–	–
26 Coventry City	–	–	–	5	–	–	–	–	–	–	–	–	–	–	–	–	–	–	–	–	–	–	–	–	–	–	–	5	–	–
27 Southampton	–	–	–	4	–	–	–	–	–	1	–	–	–	–	–	–	–	–	–	–	–	–	–	–	–	–	–	5	–	–
28 Preston North End	–	–	–	1	–	–	–	–	–	3	–	–	–	–	–	–	–	–	–	–	–	–	–	–	–	–	–	4	–	–
29 Cardiff City	–	–	–	3	–	1	–	–	–	–	–	–	–	–	–	–	–	–	–	–	–	–	–	–	–	–	–	3	–	1
30 Benfica	–	–	–	–	–	–	–	–	–	–	–	–	–	–	–	3	–	–	–	–	–	–	–	–	–	–	–	3	–	–
31 Exeter City	–	–	–	–	–	–	–	–	–	1	–	–	2	–	–	–	–	–	–	–	–	–	–	–	–	–	–	3	–	–
32 Ferencvaros	–	–	–	–	–	–	–	–	–	–	–	–	–	–	–	–	–	–	–	–	–	3	–	–	–	–	–	3	–	–
33 Watford	–	–	–	–	–	–	–	–	–	3	–	–	–	–	–	–	–	–	–	–	–	–	–	–	–	–	–	3	–	–
34 Partizan Belgrade	–	–	–	–	–	–	–	–	–	–	–	–	–	–	–	2	–	1	–	–	–	–	–	–	–	–	–	2	–	1
35 Queens Park Rangers	–	–	–	2	–	1	–	–	–	–	–	–	–	–	–	–	–	–	–	–	–	–	–	–	–	–	–	2	–	1
36 Waterford	–	–	–	–	–	–	–	–	–	–	–	–	–	–	–	2	–	1	–	–	–	–	–	–	–	–	–	2	–	1
37 AC Milan	–	–	–	–	–	–	–	–	–	–	–	–	–	–	–	2	–	–	–	–	–	–	–	–	–	–	–	2	–	–
38 Anderlecht	–	–	–	–	–	–	–	–	–	–	–	–	–	–	–	2	–	–	–	–	–	–	–	–	–	–	–	2	–	–
39 ASK Vorwaerts	–	–	–	–	–	–	–	–	–	–	–	–	–	–	–	2	–	–	–	–	–	–	–	–	–	–	–	2	–	–
40 Borussia Dortmund	–	–	–	–	–	–	–	–	–	–	–	–	–	–	–	–	–	–	–	–	–	2	–	–	–	–	–	2	–	–
41 Derby County	–	–	–	1	–	–	–	–	–	1	–	–	–	–	–	–	–	–	–	–	–	–	–	–	–	–	–	2	–	–
42 Djurgardens	–	–	–	–	–	–	–	–	–	–	–	–	–	–	–	–	–	–	–	–	–	2	–	–	–	–	–	2	–	–
43 Gornik Zabrze	–	–	–	–	–	–	–	–	–	–	–	–	–	–	–	2	–	–	–	–	–	–	–	–	–	–	–	2	–	–
44 Hibernians Malta	–	–	–	–	–	–	–	–	–	–	–	–	–	–	–	2	–	–	–	–	–	–	–	–	–	–	–	2	–	–
45 HJK Helsinki	–	–	–	–	–	–	–	–	–	–	–	–	–	–	–	2	–	–	–	–	–	–	–	–	–	–	–	2	–	–
46 Northampton Town	–	–	–	2	–	–	–	–	–	–	–	–	–	–	–	–	–	–	–	–	–	–	–	–	–	–	–	2	–	–
47 Rapid Vienna	–	–	–	–	–	–	–	–	–	–	–	–	–	–	–	2	–	–	–	–	–	–	–	–	–	–	–	2	–	–
48 Real Madrid	–	–	–	–	–	–	–	–	–	–	–	–	–	–	–	2	–	–	–	–	–	–	–	–	–	–	–	2	–	–
49 Rotherham United	–	–	–	–	–	–	–	–	–	2	–	–	–	–	–	–	–	–	–	–	–	–	–	–	–	–	–	2	–	–
50 Strasbourg	–	–	–	–	–	–	–	–	–	–	–	–	–	–	–	–	–	–	–	–	–	2	–	–	–	–	–	2	–	–
51 Aldershot	–	–	–	–	–	–	–	–	–	–	–	–	1	–	–	–	–	–	–	–	–	–	–	–	–	–	–	1	–	–
52 Barnsley	–	–	–	–	–	–	–	–	–	1	–	–	–	–	–	–	–	–	–	–	–	–	–	–	–	–	–	1	–	–
53 Chester City	–	–	–	–	–	–	–	–	–	1	–	–	–	–	–	–	–	–	–	–	–	–	–	–	–	–	–	1	–	–
54 Crystal Palace	–	–	–	1	–	–	–	–	–	–	–	–	–	–	–	–	–	–	–	–	–	–	–	–	–	–	–	1	–	–
55 Estudiantes de la Plata	–	–	–	–	–	–	–	–	–	–	–	–	–	–	–	–	–	–	–	–	–	–	–	–	1	–	–	1	–	–
56 Huddersfield Town	–	–	–	–	–	–	–	–	–	1	–	–	–	–	–	–	–	–	–	–	–	–	–	–	–	–	–	1	–	–
57 Middlesbrough	–	–	–	–	–	–	–	–	–	1	–	–	–	–	–	–	–	–	–	–	–	–	–	–	–	–	–	1	–	–
58 Norwich City	–	–	–	–	–	–	–	–	–	1	–	–	–	–	–	–	–	–	–	–	–	–	–	–	–	–	–	1	–	–
59 Sporting Lisbon	–	–	–	–	–	–	–	–	–	–	–	–	–	–	–	–	–	–	1	–	–	–	–	–	–	–	–	1	–	–

HERBERT STONE

DEBUT (Full Appearance)

Monday 26/03/1894
Football League Division 1
at Ewood Park

Blackburn Rovers 4 Newton Heath 0

CLUB CAREER RECORD	Apps	Subs	Goals
Premiership	0		0
League Division 1	2		0
League Division 2	4		0
FA Cup	0		0
League Cup	0		0
European Cup / Champions League	0		0
European Cup-Winners' Cup	0		0
UEFA Cup / Inter-Cities' Fairs Cup	0		0
Other Matches	1		0
OVERALL TOTAL	7		0

Opponents	PREM A	S	G	FLD 1 A	S	G	FLD 2 A	S	G	FAC A	S	G	LC A	S	G	EC/CL A	S	G	ECWC A	S	G	UEFA A	S	G	OTHER A	S	G	TOTAL A	S	G
1 Blackburn Rovers	–	–			1	–	–		–	–		–	–		–	–		–	–		–	–		–	–		–	1	–	
2 Bury	–	–		–	–		1		–	–		–	–		–	–		–	–		–	–		–	–		–	1	–	
3 Manchester City	–	–		–	–		1		–	–		–	–		–	–		–	–		–	–		–	–		–	1	–	
4 Newcastle United	–	–		–	–		–	–		1		–	–		–	–		–	–		–	–		–	–		–	1	–	
5 Port Vale	–	–		–	–		1		–	–		–	–		–	–		–	–		–	–		–	–		–	1	–	
6 Preston North End	–	–		1		–	–		–	–		–	–		–	–		–	–		–	–		–	–		–	1	–	
7 Stoke City	–	–		–	–		–	–		–	–		–	–		–	–		–	–		–	–		1	–		1	–	

IAN STOREY-MOORE

DEBUT (Full Appearance, 1 goal)

Saturday 11/03/1972
Football League Division 1
at Old Trafford

Manchester United 2 Huddersfield Town 0

CLUB CAREER RECORD	Apps	Subs	Goals
Premiership	0		0
League Division 1	39		11
League Division 2	0		0
FA Cup	0		0
League Cup	4		1
European Cup / Champions League	0		0
European Cup-Winners' Cup	0		0
UEFA Cup / Inter-Cities' Fairs Cup	0		0
Other Matches	0		0
OVERALL TOTAL	43		12

Opponents	PREM A	S	G	FLD 1 A	S	G	FLD 2 A	S	G	FAC A	S	G	LC A	S	G	EC/CL A	S	G	ECWC A	S	G	UEFA A	S	G	OTHER A	S	G	TOTAL A	S	G
1 Leicester City	–	–		4		–	–		–	–		–	–		–	–		–	–		–	–		–	–		–	4	–	
2 Arsenal	–	–		3		–	–		–	–		–	–		–	–		–	–		–	–		–	–		–	3	–	
3 Liverpool	–	–		3		–	–		–	–		–	–		–	–		–	–		–	–		–	–		–	3	–	
4 Derby County	–	–		2	2	–	–		–	–		–	–		–	–		–	–		–	–		–	–		–	2	2	
5 West Ham United	–	–		2	2	–	–		–	–		–	–		–	–		–	–		–	–		–	–		–	2	2	
6 Coventry City	–	–		2	1	–	–		–	–		–	–		–	–		–	–		–	–		–	–		–	2	1	
7 Crystal Palace	–	–		2	1	–	–		–	–		–	–		–	–		–	–		–	–		–	–		–	2	1	
8 Oxford United	–	–		–	–		–	–		–	–		2	1	–	–		–	–		–	–		–	–		–	2	1	
9 Southampton	–	–		2	1	–	–		–	–		–	–		–	–		–	–		–	–		–	–		–	2	1	
10 Stoke City	–	–		2	1	–	–		–	–		–	–		–	–		–	–		–	–		–	–		–	2	1	
11 West Bromwich Albion	–	–		2	1	–	–		–	–		–	–		–	–		–	–		–	–		–	–		–	2	1	
12 Birmingham City	–	–		2		–	–		–	–		–	–		–	–		–	–		–	–		–	–		–	2	–	
13 Bristol Rovers	–	–		–	–		–	–		–	–		2		–	–		–	–		–	–		–	–		–	2	–	
14 Manchester City	–	–		2		–	–		–	–		–	–		–	–		–	–		–	–		–	–		–	2	–	
15 Sheffield United	–	–		2		–	–		–	–		–	–		–	–		–	–		–	–		–	–		–	2	–	
16 Huddersfield Town	–	–		1	1	–	–		–	–		–	–		–	–		–	–		–	–		–	–		–	1	1	
17 Norwich City	–	–		1	1	–	–		–	–		–	–		–	–		–	–		–	–		–	–		–	1	1	
18 Chelsea	–	–		1		–	–		–	–		–	–		–	–		–	–		–	–		–	–		–	1	–	
19 Everton	–	–		1		–	–		–	–		–	–		–	–		–	–		–	–		–	–		–	1	–	
20 Ipswich Town	–	–		1		–	–		–	–		–	–		–	–		–	–		–	–		–	–		–	1	–	
21 Leeds United	–	–		1		–	–		–	–		–	–		–	–		–	–		–	–		–	–		–	1	–	
22 Newcastle United	–	–		1		–	–		–	–		–	–		–	–		–	–		–	–		–	–		–	1	–	
23 Nottingham Forest	–	–		1		–	–		–	–		–	–		–	–		–	–		–	–		–	–		–	1	–	
24 Wolverhampton W.	–	–		1		–	–		–	–		–	–		–	–		–	–		–	–		–	–		–	1	–	

GORDON STRACHAN

DEBUT (Full Appearance, 1 goal)

Saturday 25/08/1984
Football League Division 1
at Old Trafford

Manchester United 1 Watford 1

CLUB CAREER RECORD	Apps	Subs	Goals
Premiership	0		0
League Division 1	155	(5)	33
League Division 2	0		0
FA Cup	22		2
League Cup	12	(1)	1
European Cup / Champions League	0		0
European Cup-Winners' Cup	0		0
UEFA Cup / Inter-Cities' Fairs Cup	6		2
Other Matches	0		0
OVERALL TOTAL	**195**	**(6)**	**38**

	Opponents	PREM A S G	FLD 1 A S G	FLD 2 A S G	FAC A S G	LC A S G	EC/CL A S G	ECWC A S G	UEFA A S G	OTHER A S G	TOTAL A S G
1	West Ham United	– –	9 4	– –	3 –						12 4
2	Liverpool	– –	8 2	– –	2 –	1 –					11 2
3	Everton	– –	9 –	– –	1 –	1 –					11 –
4	Arsenal	– –	9 4	– –	1 –						10 4
5	Coventry City	– –	8 1	– –	2 –						10 1
6	Queens Park Rangers	– –	7 (1) 2	– –	1 –						8 (1) 2
7	Sheffield Wednesday	– –	8 (1) –	– –							8 (1) –
8	Tottenham Hotspur	– –	8 (1) –	– –							8 (1) –
9	Nottingham Forest	– –	6 (1) 2	– –	1 –						7 (1) 2
10	Southampton	– –	7 (1) –	– –	– –						7 (1) –
11	Newcastle United	– –	7 3	– –							7 3
12	Chelsea	– –	6 1	– –	1 –						7 1
13	Oxford United	– –	4 3	– –	1 –	1 –					6 3
14	Watford	– –	6 2	– –	– –						6 2
15	Aston Villa	– –	6 1	– –							6 1
16	Luton Town	– –	6 –	– –							6 –
17	Norwich City	– –	6 –	– –							6 –
18	Ipswich Town	– –	4 1	– –	1 –						5 1
19	Leicester City	– –	5 1	– –							5 1
20	Charlton Athletic	– –	5 –	– –							5 –
21	West Bromwich Albion	– –	4 4	– –							4 4
22	Manchester City	– –	3 1	– –	1 –						4 1
23	Sunderland	– –	2 –	– –	2 –						4 –
24	Wimbledon	– –	3 –	– –	– –	– (1) –					3 (1) –
25	Bournemouth	– –	– –	– –	3 1						3 1
26	Derby County	– –	3 1	– –	– –						3 1
27	Dundee United	– –	– –	– –	– –				2 1		2 1
28	Hull City	– –	– –	– –	– –	2 1					2 1
29	PSV Eindhoven	– –	– –	– –	– –				2 1		2 1
30	Birmingham City	– –	2 –	– –							2 –
31	Port Vale	– –	– –	– –	– –	2 –					2 –
32	Portsmouth	– –	2 –	– –							2 –
33	Rotherham United	– –	– –	– –	– –	2 –					2 –
34	Stoke City	– –	2 –	– –							2 –
35	Videoton	– –	– –	– –	– –				2 –		2 –
36	Blackburn Rovers	– –	– –	– –	1 1	– –					1 1
37	Burnley	– –	– –	– –	– –	1 –					1 –
38	Bury	– –	– –	– –	– –	1 –					1 –
39	Crystal Palace	– –	– –	– –	– –	1 –					1 –
40	Rochdale	– –	– –	– –	– –	1 –					1 –

ERNEST STREET

DEBUT (Full Appearance)

Saturday 07/02/1903
FA Cup 1st Round
at Bank Street

Manchester United 2 Liverpool 1

CLUB CAREER RECORD	Apps	Subs	Goals
Premiership	0		0
League Division 1	0		0
League Division 2	1		0
FA Cup	2		0
League Cup	0		0
European Cup / Champions League	0		0
European Cup-Winners' Cup	0		0
UEFA Cup / Inter-Cities' Fairs Cup	0		0
Other Matches	0		0
OVERALL TOTAL	**3**		**0**

	Opponents	PREM A S G	FLD 1 A S G	FLD 2 A S G	FAC A S G	LC A S G	EC/CL A S G	ECWC A S G	UEFA A S G	OTHER A S G	TOTAL A S G
1	Everton	– –	– –	– –	1 –						1 –
2	Lincoln City	– –	– –	1 –	– –						1 –
3	Liverpool	– –	– –	– –	1 –						1 –

JOHN SUTCLIFFE

DEBUT (Full Appearance)

Saturday 05/09/1903
Football League Division 2
at Bank Street

Manchester United 2 Bristol City 2

CLUB CAREER RECORD	Apps	Subs	Goals
Premiership	0		0
League Division 1	0		0
League Division 2	21		0
FA Cup	7		0
League Cup	0		0
European Cup / Champions League	0		0
European Cup-Winners' Cup	0		0
UEFA Cup / Inter-Cities' Fairs Cup	0		0
Other Matches	0		0
OVERALL TOTAL	**28**		**0**

Opponents	PREM A S G	FLD 1 A S G	FLD 2 A S G	FAC A S G	LC A S G	EC/CL A S G	ECWC A S G	UEFA A S G	OTHER A S G	TOTAL A S G
1 Birmingham City	– –	– –	– –	4 –	–	–	–	–	–	4 –
2 Arsenal	– –	– –	2 –	– –	–	–	–	–	–	2 –
3 Bristol City	– –	– –	2 –	– –	–	–	–	–	–	2 –
4 Burnley	– –	– –	2 –	– –	–	–	–	–	–	2 –
5 Glossop	– –	– –	2 –	– –	–	–	–	–	–	2 –
6 Lincoln City	– –	– –	2 –	– –	–	–	–	–	–	2 –
7 Notts County	– –	– –	– –	2 –	–	–	–	–	–	2 –
8 Port Vale	– –	– –	2 –	– –	–	–	–	–	–	2 –
9 Preston North End	– –	– –	2 –	– –	–	–	–	–	–	2 –
10 Blackpool	– –	– –	1 –	– –	–	–	–	–	–	1 –
11 Bolton Wanderers	– –	– –	1 –	– –	–	–	–	–	–	1 –
12 Bradford City	– –	– –	1 –	– –	–	–	–	–	–	1 –
13 Chesterfield	– –	– –	1 –	– –	–	–	–	–	–	1 –
14 Gainsborough Trinity	– –	– –	1 –	– –	–	–	–	–	–	1 –
15 Grimsby Town	– –	– –	1 –	– –	–	–	–	–	–	1 –
16 Sheffield Wednesday	– –	– –	– –	1 –	–	–	–	–	–	1 –
17 Stockport County	– –	– –	1 –	– –	–	–	–	–	–	1 –

ERIC SWEENEY

DEBUT (Full Appearance, 1 goal)

Saturday 13/02/1926
Football League Division 1
at Old Trafford

Manchester United 2 Leeds United 1

CLUB CAREER RECORD	Apps	Subs	Goals
Premiership	0		0
League Division 1	27		6
League Division 2	0		0
FA Cup	5		1
League Cup	0		0
European Cup / Champions League	0		0
European Cup-Winners' Cup	0		0
UEFA Cup / Inter-Cities' Fairs Cup	0		0
Other Matches	0		0
OVERALL TOTAL	**32**		**7**

Opponents	PREM A S G	FLD 1 A S G	FLD 2 A S G	FAC A S G	LC A S G	EC/CL A S G	ECWC A S G	UEFA A S G	OTHER A S G	TOTAL A S G
1 Leeds United	– –	3 2	– –	– –	–	–	–	–	–	3 2
2 Cardiff City	– –	3 1	– –	– –	–	–	–	–	–	3 1
3 Reading	– –	– –	– –	3 1	–	–	–	–	–	3 1
4 Sheffield United	– –	3 1	– –	– –	–	–	–	–	–	3 1
5 Leicester City	– –	3 –	– –	– –	–	–	–	–	–	3 –
6 West Bromwich Albion	– –	2 2	– –	– –	–	–	–	–	–	2 2
7 Bury	– –	1 –	– –	– –	1	–	–	–	–	2 –
8 Tottenham Hotspur	– –	2 –	– –	– –	–	–	–	–	–	2 –
9 Aston Villa	– –	1 –	– –	– –	–	–	–	–	–	1 –
10 Birmingham City	– –	1 –	– –	– –	–	–	–	–	–	1 –
11 Burnley	– –	1 –	– –	– –	–	–	–	–	–	1 –
12 Derby County	– –	1 –	– –	– –	–	–	–	–	–	1 –
13 Everton	– –	1 –	– –	– –	–	–	–	–	–	1 –
14 Huddersfield Town	– –	1 –	– –	– –	–	–	–	–	–	1 –
15 Liverpool	– –	1 –	– –	– –	–	–	–	–	–	1 –
16 Newcastle United	– –	1 –	– –	– –	–	–	–	–	–	1 –
17 Port Vale	– –	– –	– –	1 –	–	–	–	–	–	1 –
18 Portsmouth	– –	1 –	– –	– –	–	–	–	–	–	1 –
19 West Ham United	– –	1 –	– –	– –	–	–	–	–	–	1 –

MASSIMO TAIBI

DEBUT (Full Appearance)

Saturday 11/09/1999
FA Premiership
at Anfield

Liverpool 2 Manchester United 3

CLUB CAREER RECORD	Apps	Subs	Goals
Premiership	4		0
League Division 1	0		0
League Division 2	0		0
FA Cup	0		0
League Cup	0		0
European Cup / Champions League	0		0
European Cup-Winners' Cup	0		0
UEFA Cup / Inter-Cities' Fairs Cup	0		0
Other Matches	0		0
OVERALL TOTAL	**4**		**0**

Opponents	PREM A S G	FLD 1 A S G	FLD 2 A S G	FAC A S G	LC A S G	EC/CL A S G	ECWC A S G	UEFA A S G	OTHER A S G	TOTAL A S G
1 Chelsea	1 - -	- - -	- - -	- - -	- - -	- - -	- - -	- - -	- - -	1 - -
2 Liverpool	1 -	- -	- -	-	-	-	-	-	-	1 -
3 Southampton	1 - -	- - -	- - -	- - -	- - -	- - -	- - -	- - -	- - -	1 - -
4 Wimbledon	1 -	-	-	-	-	-	-	-	-	1 -

NORMAN TAPKEN

DEBUT (Full Appearance)

Monday 26/12/1938
Football League Division 1
at Old Trafford

Manchester United 3 Leicester City 0

CLUB CAREER RECORD	Apps	Subs	Goals
Premiership	0		0
League Division 1	14		0
League Division 2	0		0
FA Cup	2		0
League Cup	0		0
European Cup / Champions League	0		0
European Cup-Winners' Cup	0		0
UEFA Cup / Inter-Cities' Fairs Cup	0		0
Other Matches	0		0
OVERALL TOTAL	**16**		**0**

Opponents	PREM A S G	FLD 1 A S G	FLD 2 A S G	FAC A S G	LC A S G	EC/CL A S G	ECWC A S G	UEFA A S G	OTHER A S G	TOTAL A S G
1 Leeds United	- -	2 -	- -	- -	- -	- -	- -	- -	- -	2 -
2 Leicester City	- -	2 -	- -	- -	- -	- -	- -	- -	- -	2 -
3 West Bromwich Albion	- - -	- - -	- - -	2 - -	- - -	- - -	- - -	- - -	- - -	2 - -
4 Birmingham City	- -	1 -	- -	- -	- -	- -	- -	- -	- -	1 -
5 Blackpool	- -	1 -	- -	- -	- -	- -	- -	- -	- -	1 -
6 Charlton Athletic	- -	1 -	- -	- -	- -	- -	- -	- -	- -	1 -
7 Chelsea	- -	1 -	- -	- -	- -	- -	- -	- -	- -	1 -
8 Derby County	- -	1 -	- -	- -	- -	- -	- -	- -	- -	1 -
9 Grimsby Town	- -	1 -	- -	- -	- -	- -	- -	- -	- -	1 -
10 Portsmouth	- -	1 -	- -	- -	- -	- -	- -	- -	- -	1 -
11 Preston North End	- -	1 -	- -	- -	- -	- -	- -	- -	- -	1 -
12 Stoke City	- -	1 -	- -	- -	- -	- -	- -	- -	- -	1 -
13 Sunderland	- -	1 -	- -	- -	- -	- -	- -	- -	- -	1 -

CHRIS TAYLOR

DEBUT (Full Appearance)

Saturday 17/01/1925
Football League Division 2
at Highfield Road

Coventry City 1 Manchester United 0

CLUB CAREER RECORD	Apps	Subs	Goals
Premiership	0		0
League Division 1	27		6
League Division 2	1		0
FA Cup	2		1
League Cup	0		0
European Cup / Champions League	0		0
European Cup-Winners' Cup	0		0
UEFA Cup / Inter-Cities' Fairs Cup	0		0
Other Matches	0		0
OVERALL TOTAL	**30**		**7**

Opponents	PREM A	S	G	FLD 1 A	S	G	FLD 2 A	S	G	FAC A	S	G	LC A	S	G	EC/CL A	S	G	ECWC A	S	G	UEFA A	S	G	OTHER A	S	G	TOTAL A	S	G
1 Birmingham City	–	–		3	–		–	–		–	–		–	–		–	–		–	–		–	–		–	–		3	–	
2 Sunderland	–	–		2		3	–	–		–	–		–	–		–	–		–	–		–	–		–	–		2		3
3 West Bromwich Albion	–	–		2		3	–	–		–	–		–	–		–	–		–	–		–	–		–	–		2		3
4 Arsenal	–	–		2	–		–	–		–	–		–	–		–	–		–	–		–	–		–	–		2	–	
5 Blackburn Rovers	–	–		2			–	–		–	–		–	–		–	–		–	–		–	–		–	–		2		
6 Leeds United	–	–		2			–	–		–	–		–	–		–	–		–	–		–	–		–	–		2		
7 Middlesbrough	–	–		2			–	–		–	–		–	–		–	–		–	–		–	–		–	–		2		
8 Port Vale	–	–		–	–		–	–		1		1	–	–		–	–		–	–		–	–		–	–		1		1
9 Aston Villa	–	–		1			–	–		–	–		–	–		–	–		–	–		–	–		–	–		1		
10 Bolton Wanderers	–	–		1			–	–		–	–		–	–		–	–		–	–		–	–		–	–		1		
11 Burnley	–	–		1			–	–		–	–		–	–		–	–		–	–		–	–		–	–		1		
12 Coventry City	–	–		–	–		–	–			1		–	–		–	–		–	–		–	–		–	–		1		
13 Derby County	–	–		1			–	–		–	–		–	–		–	–		–	–		–	–		–	–		1		
14 Everton	–	–		1			–	–		–	–		–	–		–	–		–	–		–	–		–	–		1		
15 Grimsby Town	–	–		1			–	–		–	–		–	–		–	–		–	–		–	–		–	–		1		
16 Manchester City	–	–		1			–	–		–	–		–	–		–	–		–	–		–	–		–	–		1		
17 Newcastle United	–	–		1			–	–		–	–		–	–		–	–		–	–		–	–		–	–		1		
18 Portsmouth	–	–		1			–	–		–	–		–	–		–	–		–	–		–	–		–	–		1		
19 Sheffield United	–	–		1			–	–		–	–		–	–		–	–		–	–		–	–		–	–		1		
20 Sheffield Wednesday	–	–		1			–	–		–	–		–	–		–	–		–	–		–	–		–	–		1		
21 Swindon Town	–	–		–			–	–		1			–	–		–	–		–	–		–	–		–	–		1		
22 West Ham United	–	–		1			–	–		–	–		–	–		–	–		–	–		–	–		–	–		1		

ERNIE TAYLOR

DEBUT (Full Appearance)

Wednesday 19/02/1958
FA Cup 5th Round
at Old Trafford

Manchester United 3 Sheffield Wednesday 0

CLUB CAREER RECORD	Apps	Subs	Goals
Premiership	0		0
League Division 1	22		2
League Division 2	0		0
FA Cup	6		1
League Cup	0		0
European Cup / Champions League	2		1
European Cup-Winners' Cup	0		0
UEFA Cup / Inter-Cities' Fairs Cup	0		0
Other Matches	0		0
OVERALL TOTAL	**30**		**4**

Opponents	PREM A	S	G	FLD 1 A	S	G	FLD 2 A	S	G	FAC A	S	G	LC A	S	G	EC/CL A	S	G	ECWC A	S	G	UEFA A	S	G	OTHER A	S	G	TOTAL A	S	G
1 West Bromwich Albion	–	–		1	–		–	–		2		1	–	–		–	–		–	–		–	–		–	–		3		1
2 Nottingham Forest	–	–		3			–	–		–	–		–	–		–	–		–	–		–	–		–	–		3		–
3 AC Milan	–	–		–	–		–	–		–	–		–	–		2		1	–	–		–	–		–	–		2		1
4 Chelsea	–	–		2		1	–	–		–	–		–	–		–	–		–	–		–	–		–	–		2		1
5 Fulham	–	–		–	–		–	–		–	–		2			–	–		–	–		–	–		–	–		2		–
6 Newcastle United	–	–		2			–	–		–	–		–	–		–	–		–	–		–	–		–	–		2		–
7 Preston North End	–	–		2			–	–		–	–		–	–		–	–		–	–		–	–		–	–		2		–
8 Sheffield Wednesday	–	–		1			–	–		1			–	–		–	–		–	–		–	–		–	–		2		–
9 Sunderland	–	–		2			–	–		–	–		–	–		–	–		–	–		–	–		–	–		2		–
10 West Ham United	–	–		2			–	–		–	–		–	–		–	–		–	–		–	–		–	–		2		–
11 Portsmouth	–	–		1		1	–	–		–	–		–	–		–	–		–	–		–	–		–	–		1		1
12 Arsenal	–	–		1			–	–		–	–		–	–		–	–		–	–		–	–		–	–		1		–
13 Birmingham City	–	–		1			–	–		–	–		–	–		–	–		–	–		–	–		–	–		1		–
14 Blackburn Rovers	–	–		1			–	–		–	–		–	–		–	–		–	–		–	–		–	–		1		–
15 Blackpool	–	–		1			–	–		–	–		–	–		–	–		–	–		–	–		–	–		1		–
16 Bolton Wanderers	–	–		–	–		–	–		1			–	–		–	–		–	–		–	–		–	–		1		–
17 Everton	–	–		1			–	–		–	–		–	–		–	–		–	–		–	–		–	–		1		–
18 Tottenham Hotspur	–	–		1			–	–		–	–		–	–		–	–		–	–		–	–		–	–		1		–

TOMMY TAYLOR

DEBUT (Full Appearance, 2 goals)

Saturday 07/03/1953
Football League Division 1
at Old Trafford

Manchester United 5 Preston North End 2

CLUB CAREER RECORD	Apps	Subs	Goals
Premiership	0		0
League Division 1	166		112
League Division 2	0		0
FA Cup	9		5
League Cup	0		0
European Cup / Champions League	14		11
European Cup-Winners' Cup	0		0
UEFA Cup / Inter-Cities' Fairs Cup	0		0
Other Matches	2		3
OVERALL TOTAL	**191**		**131**

Opponents	PREM (A S G)	FLD 1 (A S G)	FLD 2 (A S G)	FAC (A S G)	LC (A S G)	EC/CL (A S G)	ECWC (A S G)	UEFA (A S G)	OTHER (A S G)	TOTAL (A S G)
1 Arsenal	– – –	10 – 7	– – –	– – –	– – –	– – –	– – –	– – –	– – –	10 – 7
2 Newcastle United	– – –	10 – 5	– – –	– – –	– – –	– – –	– – –	– – –	– – –	10 – 5
3 Aston Villa	– – –	7 – 7	– – –	1 – 1	– – –	– – –	– – –	– – –	1 – 3	9 – 11
4 Chelsea	– – –	9 – 9	– – –	– – –	– – –	– – –	– – –	– – –	– – –	9 – 9
5 Preston North End	– – –	9 – 6	– – –	– – –	– – –	– – –	– – –	– – –	– – –	9 – 6
6 Manchester City	– – –	7 – 4	– – –	1 – –	– – –	– – –	– – –	– – –	1 – –	9 – 4
7 Burnley	– – –	8 – 2	– – –	1 – 1	– – –	– – –	– – –	– – –	– – –	9 – 3
8 West Bromwich Albion	– – –	8 – 7	– – –	– – –	– – –	– – –	– – –	– – –	– – –	8 – 7
9 Wolverhampton W.	– – –	8 – 7	– – –	– – –	– – –	– – –	– – –	– – –	– – –	8 – 7
10 Blackpool	– – –	8 – 6	– – –	– – –	– – –	– – –	– – –	– – –	– – –	8 – 6
11 Bolton Wanderers	– – –	8 – 4	– – –	– – –	– – –	– – –	– – –	– – –	– – –	8 – 4
12 Cardiff City	– – –	7 – 7	– – –	– – –	– – –	– – –	– – –	– – –	– – –	7 – 7
13 Charlton Athletic	– – –	7 – 7	– – –	– – –	– – –	– – –	– – –	– – –	– – –	7 – 7
14 Sunderland	– – –	7 – 3	– – –	– – –	– – –	– – –	– – –	– – –	– – –	7 – 3
15 Luton Town	– – –	6 – 7	– – –	– – –	– – –	– – –	– – –	– – –	– – –	6 – 7
16 Sheffield Wednesday	– – –	6 – 5	– – –	– – –	– – –	– – –	– – –	– – –	– – –	6 – 5
17 Everton	– – –	5 – 2	– – –	1 – –	– – –	– – –	– – –	– – –	– – –	6 – 2
18 Tottenham Hotspur	– – –	6 – 1	– – –	– – –	– – –	– – –	– – –	– – –	– – –	6 – 1
19 Huddersfield Town	– – –	5 – 3	– – –	– – –	– – –	– – –	– – –	– – –	– – –	5 – 3
20 Birmingham City	– – –	5 – 1	– – –	– – –	– – –	– – –	– – –	– – –	– – –	5 – 1
21 Sheffield United	– – –	4 – 3	– – –	– – –	– – –	– – –	– – –	– – –	– – –	4 – 3
22 Portsmouth	– – –	4 – 2	– – –	– – –	– – –	– – –	– – –	– – –	– – –	4 – 2
23 Liverpool	– – –	3 – 3	– – –	– – –	– – –	– – –	– – –	– – –	– – –	3 – 3
24 Leeds United	– – –	3 – 2	– – –	– – –	– – –	– – –	– – –	– – –	– – –	3 – 2
25 Leicester City	– – –	3 – –	– – –	– – –	– – –	– – –	– – –	– – –	– – –	3 – –
26 Anderlecht	– – –	– – –	– – –	– – –	– – –	2 – 4	– – –	– – –	– – –	2 – 4
27 Athletic Bilbao	– – –	– – –	– – –	– – –	– – –	2 – 2	– – –	– – –	– – –	2 – 2
28 Middlesbrough	– – –	2 – 2	– – –	– – –	– – –	– – –	– – –	– – –	– – –	2 – 2
29 Real Madrid	– – –	– – –	– – –	– – –	– – –	2 – 2	– – –	– – –	– – –	2 – 2
30 Shamrock Rovers	– – –	– – –	– – –	– – –	– – –	2 – 2	– – –	– – –	– – –	2 – 2
31 Dukla Prague	– – –	– – –	– – –	– – –	– – –	2 – 1	– – –	– – –	– – –	2 – 1
32 Borussia Dortmund	– – –	– – –	– – –	– – –	– – –	2 – –	– – –	– – –	– – –	2 – –
33 Red Star Belgrade	– – –	– – –	– – –	– – –	– – –	2 – –	– – –	– – –	– – –	2 – –
34 Wrexham	– – –	– – –	– – –	1 – 2	– – –	– – –	– – –	– – –	– – –	1 – 2
35 Hartlepool United	– – –	– – –	– – –	1 – 1	– – –	– – –	– – –	– – –	– – –	1 – 1
36 Bristol Rovers	– – –	– – –	– – –	1 – –	– – –	– – –	– – –	– – –	– – –	1 – –
37 Ipswich Town	– – –	– – –	– – –	1 – –	– – –	– – –	– – –	– – –	– – –	1 – –
38 Nottingham Forest	– – –	1 – –	– – –	– – –	– – –	– – –	– – –	– – –	– – –	1 – –
39 Workington	– – –	– – –	– – –	1 – –	– – –	– – –	– – –	– – –	– – –	1 – –

WALTER TAYLOR

DEBUT (Full Appearance)

Monday 02/01/1922
Football League Division 1
at Bramall Lane

Sheffield United 3 Manchester United 0

CLUB CAREER RECORD	Apps	Subs	Goals
Premiership	0		0
League Division 1	1		0
League Division 2	0		0
FA Cup	0		0
League Cup	0		0
European Cup / Champions League	0		0
European Cup-Winners' Cup	0		0
UEFA Cup / Inter-Cities' Fairs Cup	0		0
Other Matches	0		0
OVERALL TOTAL	**1**		**0**

Opponents	PREM (A S G)	FLD 1 (A S G)	FLD 2 (A S G)	FAC (A S G)	LC (A S G)	EC/CL (A S G)	ECWC (A S G)	UEFA (A S G)	OTHER (A S G)	TOTAL (A S G)
1 Sheffield United	– – –	1 – –	– – –	– – –	– – –	– – –	– – –	– – –	– – –	1 – –

CARLOS TEVEZ

DEBUT (Full Appearance)

Wednesday 15/08/2007
FA Premiership
at Fratton Park

Portsmouth 1 Manchester United 1

CLUB CAREER RECORD	Apps	Subs	Goals
Premiership	31	(3)	14
League Division 1	0		0
League Division 2	0		0
FA Cup	2		1
League Cup	0		0
European Cup / Champions League	6	(6)	4
European Cup-Winners' Cup	0		0
UEFA Cup / Inter-Cities' Fairs Cup	0		0
Other Matches	0		0
OVERALL TOTAL	**39**	**(9)**	**19**

Opponents	PREM			FLD 1			FLD 2			FAC			LC			EC/CL			ECWC			UEFA			OTHER			TOTAL		
	A	S	G	A	S	G	A	S	G	A	S	G	A	S	G	A	S	G	A	S	G	A	S	G	A	S	G	A	S	G
1 Tottenham Hotspur	2	–	1	–	–	–	–	–	–	1	–	1	–	–	–	–	–	–	–	–	–	–	–	–	–	–	–	3	–	2
2 Portsmouth	1	(1)	–	–	–	–	–	–	–	1	–		–	–	–	–	–	–	–	–	–	–	–	–	–	–	–	2	(1)	–
3 Roma	–	–	–	–	–	–	–	–	–	–	–	–	–	–	–	1	(2)	1	–	–	–	–	–	–	–	–	–	1	(2)	1
4 Middlesbrough	2	–	2	–	–	–	–	–	–	–	–	–	–	–	–	–	–	–	–	–	–	–	–	–	–	–	–	2	–	2
5 Newcastle United	2	–	2	–	–	–	–	–	–	–	–	–	–	–	–	–	–	–	–	–	–	–	–	–	–	–	–	2	–	2
6 Aston Villa	2	–	1	–	–	–	–	–	–	–	–	–	–	–	–	–	–	–	–	–	–	–	–	–	–	–	–	2	–	1
7 Birmingham City	2	–	1	–	–	–	–	–	–	–	–	–	–	–	–	–	–	–	–	–	–	–	–	–	–	–	–	2	–	1
8 Blackburn Rovers	2	–	1	–	–	–	–	–	–	–	–	–	–	–	–	–	–	–	–	–	–	–	–	–	–	–	–	2	–	1
9 Chelsea	1	–	1	–	–	–	–	–	–	–	–	–	–	–	–	1	–		–	–	–	–	–	–	–	–	–	2	–	1
10 Dynamo Kiev	–	–	–	–	–	–	–	–	–	–	–	–	–	–	–	2	–	1	–	–	–	–	–	–	–	–	–	2	–	1
11 West Ham United	2	–	1	–	–	–	–	–	–	–	–	–	–	–	–	–	–	–	–	–	–	–	–	–	–	–	–	2	–	1
12 Wigan Athletic	2	–	1	–	–	–	–	–	–	–	–	–	–	–	–	–	–	–	–	–	–	–	–	–	–	–	–	2	–	1
13 Barcelona	–	–	–	–	–	–	–	–	–	–	–	–	–	–	–	2	–		–	–	–	–	–	–	–	–	–	2	–	–
14 Bolton Wanderers	2	–	–	–	–	–	–	–	–	–	–	–	–	–	–	–	–	–	–	–	–	–	–	–	–	–	–	2	–	–
15 Everton	2	–		–	–	–	–	–	–	–	–	–	–	–	–	–	–	–	–	–	–	–	–	–	–	–	–	2	–	
16 Fulham	2	–		–	–	–	–	–	–	–	–	–	–	–	–	–	–	–	–	–	–	–	–	–	–	–	–	2	–	
17 Manchester City	2	–		–	–	–	–	–	–	–	–	–	–	–	–	–	–	–	–	–	–	–	–	–	–	–	–	2	–	
18 Liverpool	1	(1)	1	–	–	–	–	–	–	–	–	–	–	–	–	–	–	–	–	–	–	–	–	–	–	–	–	1	(1)	1
19 Arsenal	1	(1)	–	–	–	–	–	–	–	–	–	–	–	–	–	–	–	–	–	–	–	–	–	–	–	–	–	1	(1)	–
20 Olympique Lyonnais	–	–	–	–	–	–	–	–	–	–	–	–	–	–	–	–	(2)	1	–	–	–	–	–	–	–	–	–	–	(2)	1
21 Sporting Lisbon	–	–	–	–	–	–	–	–	–	–	–	–	–	–	–	–	(2)	1	–	–	–	–	–	–	–	–	–	–	(2)	1
22 Derby County	1	–	2	–	–	–	–	–	–	–	–	–	–	–	–	–	–	–	–	–	–	–	–	–	–	–	–	1	–	2
23 Reading	1	–		–	–	–	–	–	–	–	–	–	–	–	–	–	–	–	–	–	–	–	–	–	–	–	–	1	–	
24 Sunderland	1	–		–	–	–	–	–	–	–	–	–	–	–	–	–	–	–	–	–	–	–	–	–	–	–	–	1	–	

HARRY THOMAS

DEBUT (Full Appearance)

Saturday 22/04/1922
Football League Division 1
at Boundary Park

Oldham Athletic 1 Manchester United 1

CLUB CAREER RECORD	Apps	Subs	Goals
Premiership	0		0
League Division 1	101		12
League Division 2	27		0
FA Cup	7		1
League Cup	0		0
European Cup / Champions League	0		0
European Cup–Winners' Cup	0		0
UEFA Cup / Inter–Cities' Fairs Cup	0		0
Other Matches	0		0
OVERALL TOTAL	**135**		**13**

Opponents	PREM A	S	G	FLD 1 A	S	G	FLD 2 A	S	G	FAC A	S	G	LC A	S	G	EC/CL A	S	G	ECWC A	S	G	UEFA A	S	G	OTHER A	S	G	TOTAL A	S	G
1 Sunderland	–	–		7		1	–	–		2	–		–	–		–	–		–	–		–	–		–	–		9		1
2 Huddersfield Town	–	–		7		1	–	–		–	–		–	–		–	–		–	–		–	–		–	–		7		1
3 Blackburn Rovers	–	–		6		1	–	–		–	–		–	–		–	–		–	–		–	–		–	–		6		1
4 Bolton Wanderers	–	–		6		1	–	–		–	–		–	–		–	–		–	–		–	–		–	–		6		1
5 Sheffield United	–	–		6		1	–	–		–	–		–	–		–	–		–	–		–	–		–	–		6		1
6 Derby County	–	–		4		–	2	–		–	–		–	–		–	–		–	–		–	–		–	–		6		–
7 Everton	–	–		6		–	–	–		–	–		–	–		–	–		–	–		–	–		–	–		6		–
8 Sheffield Wednesday	–	–		2		–	4	–		–	–		–	–		–	–		–	–		–	–		–	–		6		–
9 Bury	–	–		4		2	–	–		1	–		–	–		–	–		–	–		–	–		–	–		5		2
10 Arsenal	–	–		5		1	–	–		–	–		–	–		–	–		–	–		–	–		–	–		5		1
11 Newcastle United	–	–		5		1	–	–		–	–		–	–		–	–		–	–		–	–		–	–		5		1
12 Cardiff City	–	–		5		–	–	–		–	–		–	–		–	–		–	–		–	–		–	–		5		–
13 Portsmouth	–	–		4		–	1	–		–	–		–	–		–	–		–	–		–	–		–	–		5		–
14 Liverpool	–	–		4		1	–	–		–	–		–	–		–	–		–	–		–	–		–	–		4		1
15 Tottenham Hotspur	–	–		2		–	–	–		2	–	1	–	–		–	–		–	–		–	–		–	–		4		1
16 Burnley	–	–		4		–	–	–		–	–		–	–		–	–		–	–		–	–		–	–		4		–
17 Leicester City	–	–		4		–	–	–		–	–		–	–		–	–		–	–		–	–		–	–		4		–
18 Port Vale	–	–		–		–	3	–		1	–		–	–		–	–		–	–		–	–		–	–		4		–
19 West Ham United	–	–		4		–	–	–		–	–		–	–		–	–		–	–		–	–		–	–		4		–
20 Birmingham City	–	–		3		1	–	–		–	–		–	–		–	–		–	–		–	–		–	–		3		1
21 Manchester City	–	–		2		1	–	–		1	–		–	–		–	–		–	–		–	–		–	–		3		1
22 Blackpool	–	–		–		–	3	–		–	–		–	–		–	–		–	–		–	–		–	–		3		–
23 Notts County	–	–		2		–	–	–		1	–		–	–		–	–		–	–		–	–		–	–		3		–
24 West Bromwich Albion	–	–		3		–	–	–		–	–		–	–		–	–		–	–		–	–		–	–		3		–
25 Aston Villa	–	–		2		–	–	–		–	–		–	–		–	–		–	–		–	–		–	–		2		–
26 Coventry City	–	–		–		–	2	–		–	–		–	–		–	–		–	–		–	–		–	–		2		–
27 Crystal Palace	–	–		–		–	2	–		–	–		–	–		–	–		–	–		–	–		–	–		2		–
28 Hull City	–	–		–		–	2	–		–	–		–	–		–	–		–	–		–	–		–	–		2		–
29 South Shields	–	–		–		–	2	–		–	–		–	–		–	–		–	–		–	–		–	–		2		–
30 Wolverhampton W.	–	–		–		–	2	–		–	–		–	–		–	–		–	–		–	–		–	–		2		–
31 Barnsley	–	–		–		–	–	–		1	–		–	–		–	–		–	–		–	–		–	–		1		–
32 Grimsby Town	–	–		1		–	–	–		–	–		–	–		–	–		–	–		–	–		–	–		1		–
33 Leeds United	–	–		1		–	–	–		–	–		–	–		–	–		–	–		–	–		–	–		1		–
34 Middlesbrough	–	–		1		–	–	–		–	–		–	–		–	–		–	–		–	–		–	–		1		–
35 Oldham Athletic	–	–		1		–	–	–		–	–		–	–		–	–		–	–		–	–		–	–		1		–
36 Southampton	–	–		–		–	1	–		–	–		–	–		–	–		–	–		–	–		–	–		1		–
37 Stockport County	–	–		–		–	1	–		–	–		–	–		–	–		–	–		–	–		–	–		1		–

MICKEY THOMAS

DEBUT (Full Appearance)

Saturday 25/11/1978
Football League Division 1
at Stamford Bridge

Chelsea 0 Manchester United 1

CLUB CAREER RECORD	Apps	Subs	Goals
Premiership	0		0
League Division 1	90		11
League Division 2	0		0
FA Cup	13		2
League Cup	5		2
European Cup / Champions League	0		0
European Cup–Winners' Cup	0		0
UEFA Cup / Inter–Cities' Fairs Cup	2		0
Other Matches	0		0
OVERALL TOTAL	**110**		**15**

Opponents	PREM A	S	G	FLD 1 A	S	G	FLD 2 A	S	G	FAC A	S	G	LC A	S	G	EC/CL A	S	G	ECWC A	S	G	UEFA A	S	G	OTHER A	S	G	TOTAL A	S	G
1 Tottenham Hotspur	–	–		5		–	–	–		4	–	1	2	–	2	–	–		–	–		–	–		–	–		11		3
2 Liverpool	–	–		5		1	–	–		2	–		–	–		–	–		–	–		–	–		–	–		7		1
3 Coventry City	–	–		5		–	–	–		–	–		2	–		–	–		–	–		–	–		–	–		7		–
4 Arsenal	–	–		5		–	–	–		1	–		–	–		–	–		–	–		–	–		–	–		6		–
5 Middlesbrough	–	–		5		2	–	–		–	–		–	–		–	–		–	–		–	–		–	–		5		2
6 Brighton	–	–		3		–	–	–		2	–	1	–	–		–	–		–	–		–	–		–	–		5		1
7 Norwich City	–	–		4		–	–	–		–	–		1	–		–	–		–	–		–	–		–	–		5		–
8 Nottingham Forest	–	–		4		–	–	–		1	–		–	–		–	–		–	–		–	–		–	–		5		–
9 West Bromwich Albion	–	–		5		–	–	–		–	–		–	–		–	–		–	–		–	–		–	–		5		–
10 Wolverhampton W.	–	–		5		–	–	–		–	–		–	–		–	–		–	–		–	–		–	–		5		–
11 Leeds United	–	–		4		2	–	–		–	–		–	–		–	–		–	–		–	–		–	–		4		2
12 Aston Villa	–	–		4		1	–	–		–	–		–	–		–	–		–	–		–	–		–	–		4		1
13 Crystal Palace	–	–		4		1	–	–		–	–		–	–		–	–		–	–		–	–		–	–		4		1
14 Manchester City	–	–		4		1	–	–		–	–		–	–		–	–		–	–		–	–		–	–		4		1

continued../

MICKEY THOMAS (continued)

Opponents	PREM A S G	FLD 1 A S G	FLD 2 A S G	FAC A S G	LC A S G	EC/CL A S G	ECWC A S G	UEFA A S G	OTHER A S G	TOTAL A S G
15 Bolton Wanderers	– – –	3 – 1	– – –	– – –	– – –	– – –	– – –	– – –	– – –	3 – 1
16 Derby County	– – –	3 – 1	– – –	– – –	– – –	– – –	– – –	– – –	– – –	3 – 1
17 Ipswich Town	– – –	3 – 1	– – –	– – –	– – –	– – –	– – –	– – –	– – –	3 – 1
18 Everton	– – –	3 – –	– – –	– – –	– – –	– – –	– – –	– – –	– – –	3 – –
19 Stoke City	– – –	3 – –	– – –	– – –	– – –	– – –	– – –	– – –	– – –	3 – –
20 Birmingham City	– – –	2 – –	– – –	– – –	– – –	– – –	– – –	– – –	– – –	2 – –
21 Bristol City	– – –	2 – –	– – –	– – –	– – –	– – –	– – –	– – –	– – –	2 – –
22 Chelsea	– – –	2 – –	– – –	– – –	– – –	– – –	– – –	– – –	– – –	2 – –
23 Fulham	– – –	– – –	– – –	2 – –	– – –	– – –	– – –	– – –	– – –	2 – –
24 Leicester City	– – –	2 – –	– – –	– – –	– – –	– – –	– – –	– – –	– – –	2 – –
25 Southampton	– – –	2 – –	– – –	– – –	– – –	– – –	– – –	– – –	– – –	2 – –
26 Sunderland	– – –	2 – –	– – –	– – –	– – –	– – –	– – –	– – –	– – –	2 – –
27 Widzew Lodz	– – –	– – –	– – –	– – –	– – –	– – –	– – –	2 – –	– – –	2 – –
28 Colchester United	– – –	– – –	– – –	– – –	1 – –	– – –	– – –	– – –	– – –	1 – –
29 Queens Park Rangers	– – –	1 – –	– – –	– – –	– – –	– – –	– – –	– – –	– – –	1 – –

JOHN THOMPSON

DEBUT (Full Appearance, 1 goal)

Saturday 21/11/1936
Football League Division 1
at Old Trafford

Manchester United 2 Liverpool 5

CLUB CAREER RECORD	Apps	Subs	Goals
Premiership	0		0
League Division 1	2		1
League Division 2	1		0
FA Cup	0		0
League Cup	0		0
European Cup / Champions League	0		0
European Cup–Winners' Cup	0		0
UEFA Cup / Inter-Cities' Fairs Cup	0		0
Other Matches	0		0
OVERALL TOTAL	3		1

Opponents	PREM A S G	FLD 1 A S G	FLD 2 A S G	FAC A S G	LC A S G	EC/CL A S G	ECWC A S G	UEFA A S G	OTHER A S G	TOTAL A S G
1 Liverpool	– – –	1 – 1	– – –	– – –	– – –	– – –	– – –	– – –	– – –	1 – 1
2 Leeds United	– – –	1 – –	– – –	– – –	– – –	– – –	– – –	– – –	– – –	1 – –
3 Southampton	– – –	– – –	1 – –	– – –	– – –	– – –	– – –	– – –	– – –	1 – –

WILLIAM THOMPSON

DEBUT (Full Appearance)

Saturday 21/10/1893
Football League Division 1
at Turf Moor

Burnley 4 Newton Heath 1

CLUB CAREER RECORD	Apps	Subs	Goals
Premiership	0		0
League Division 1	3		0
League Division 2	0		0
FA Cup	0		0
League Cup	0		0
European Cup / Champions League	0		0
European Cup–Winners' Cup	0		0
UEFA Cup / Inter-Cities' Fairs Cup	0		0
Other Matches	0		0
OVERALL TOTAL	3		0

Opponents	PREM A S G	FLD 1 A S G	FLD 2 A S G	FAC A S G	LC A S G	EC/CL A S G	ECWC A S G	UEFA A S G	OTHER A S G	TOTAL A S G
1 Burnley	– – –	1 – –	– – –	– – –	– – –	– – –	– – –	– – –	– – –	1 – –
2 Darwen	– – –	1 – –	– – –	– – –	– – –	– – –	– – –	– – –	– – –	1 – –
3 Wolverhampton W.	– – –	1 – –	– – –	– – –	– – –	– – –	– – –	– – –	– – –	1 – –

ARTHUR THOMSON

DEBUT (Full Appearance)

Saturday 26/01/1929
FA Cup 4th Round
at Old Trafford

Manchester United 0 Bury 1

CLUB CAREER RECORD	Apps	Subs	Goals
Premiership	0		0
League Division 1	3		1
League Division 2	0		0
FA Cup	2		0
League Cup	0		0
European Cup / Champions League	0		0
European Cup–Winners' Cup	0		0
UEFA Cup / Inter-Cities' Fairs Cup	0		0
Other Matches	0		0
OVERALL TOTAL	5		1

Opponents	PREM A S G	FLD 1 A S G	FLD 2 A S G	FAC A S G	LC A S G	EC/CL A S G	ECWC A S G	UEFA A S G	OTHER A S G	TOTAL A S G
1 Arsenal	– – –	1 – 1	– – –	– – –	– – –	– – –	– – –	– – –	– – –	1 – 1
2 Bury	– – –	– – –	– – –	1 – –	– – –	– – –	– – –	– – –	– – –	1 – –
3 Everton	– – –	1 – –	– – –	– – –	– – –	– – –	– – –	– – –	– – –	1 – –
4 Stoke City	– – –	– – –	– – –	1 – –	– – –	– – –	– – –	– – –	– – –	1 – –
5 West Ham United	– – –	1 – –	– – –	– – –	– – –	– – –	– – –	– – –	– – –	1 – –

ERNEST THOMSON

DEBUT (Full Appearance)

Saturday 14/09/1907
Football League Division 1
at Ayresome Park

Middlesbrough 2 Manchester United 1

CLUB CAREER RECORD	Apps	Subs	Goals
Premiership	0		0
League Division 1	4		0
League Division 2	0		0
FA Cup	0		0
League Cup	0		0
European Cup / Champions League	0		0
European Cup-Winners' Cup	0		0
UEFA Cup / Inter-Cities' Fairs Cup	0		0
Other Matches	0		0
OVERALL TOTAL	**4**		**0**

Opponents	PREM A S G	FLD 1 A S G	FLD 2 A S G	FAC A S G	LC A S G	EC/CL A S G	ECWC A S G	UEFA A S G	OTHER A S G	TOTAL A S G
1 Bolton Wanderers	– –	1 –	– –	– –	– –	– –	– –	– –	– –	1 –
2 Middlesbrough	– –	1 –	– –	– –	– –	– –	– –	– –	– –	1 –
3 Preston North End	– –	1 –	– –	– –	– –	– –	– –	– –	– –	1 –
4 Sunderland	– –	1 –	– –	– –	– –	– –	– –	– –	– –	1 –

JAMES THOMSON

DEBUT (Full Appearance)

Saturday 13/12/1913
Football League Division 1
at Old Trafford

Manchester United 1 Bradford City 1

CLUB CAREER RECORD	Apps	Subs	Goals
Premiership	0		0
League Division 1	6		1
League Division 2	0		0
FA Cup	0		0
League Cup	0		0
European Cup / Champions League	0		0
European Cup-Winners' Cup	0		0
UEFA Cup / Inter-Cities' Fairs Cup	0		0
Other Matches	0		0
OVERALL TOTAL	**6**		**1**

Opponents	PREM A S G	FLD 1 A S G	FLD 2 A S G	FAC A S G	LC A S G	EC/CL A S G	ECWC A S G	UEFA A S G	OTHER A S G	TOTAL A S G
1 Bradford City	– –	2 1	– –	– –	– –	– –	– –	– –	– –	2 1
2 Blackburn Rovers	– –	1 –	– –	– –	– –	– –	– –	– –	– –	1 –
3 Manchester City	– –	1 –	– –	– –	– –	– –	– –	– –	– –	1 –
4 Sunderland	– –	1 –	– –	– –	– –	– –	– –	– –	– –	1 –
5 West Bromwich Albion	– –	1 –	– –	– –	– –	– –	– –	– –	– –	1 –

BEN THORNLEY

DEBUT (Substitute Appearance)

Saturday 26/02/1994
FA Premiership
at Upton Park

West Ham United 2 Manchester United 2

CLUB CAREER RECORD	Apps	Subs	Goals
Premiership	1	(8)	0
League Division 1	0		0
League Division 2	0		0
FA Cup	2		0
League Cup	3		0
European Cup / Champions League	0		0
European Cup-Winners' Cup	0		0
UEFA Cup / Inter-Cities' Fairs Cup	0		0
Other Matches	0		0
OVERALL TOTAL	**6**	**(8)**	**0**

Opponents	PREM A S G	FLD 1 A S G	FLD 2 A S G	FAC A S G	LC A S G	EC/CL A S G	ECWC A S G	UEFA A S G	OTHER A S G	TOTAL A S G
1 West Ham United	– (3) –	– –	– –	– –	– –	– –	– –	– –	– –	– (3) –
2 Barnsley	– –	– –	– –	1 –	– –	– –	– –	– –	– –	1 –
3 Ipswich Town	– –	– –	– –	– –	1 –	– –	– –	– –	– –	1 –
4 Leicester City	– –	– –	– –	– –	1 –	– –	– –	– –	– –	1 –
5 Middlesbrough	1 –	– –	– –	– –	– –	– –	– –	– –	– –	1 –
6 Swindon Town	– –	– –	– –	– –	1 –	– –	– –	– –	– –	1 –
7 Walsall	– –	– –	– –	1 –	– –	– –	– –	– –	– –	1 –
8 Arsenal	– (1) –	– –	– –	– –	– –	– –	– –	– –	– –	– (1) –
9 Leeds United	– (1) –	– –	– –	– –	– –	– –	– –	– –	– –	– (1) –
10 Liverpool	– (1) –	– –	– –	– –	– –	– –	– –	– –	– –	– (1) –
11 Sunderland	– (1) –	– –	– –	– –	– –	– –	– –	– –	– –	– (1) –
12 Wimbledon	– (1) –	– –	– –	– –	– –	– –	– –	– –	– –	– (1) –

PAUL TIERNEY

DEBUT (Full Appearance)

Wednesday 03/12/2003
League Cup 4th Round
at The Hawthorns

West Bromwich Albion 2 Manchester United 0

CLUB CAREER RECORD	Apps	Subs	Goals
Premiership	0		0
League Division 1	0		0
League Division 2	0		0
FA Cup	0		0
League Cup	1		0
European Cup / Champions League	0		0
European Cup-Winners' Cup	0		0
UEFA Cup / Inter-Cities' Fairs Cup	0		0
Other Matches	0		0
OVERALL TOTAL	**1**		**0**

Opponents	PREM A S G	FLD 1 A S G	FLD 2 A S G	FAC A S G	LC A S G	EC/CL A S G	ECWC A S G	UEFA A S G	OTHER A S G	TOTAL A S G
1 West Bromwich Albion	– – –	– – –	– – –	– – –	1 – –	– – –	– – –	– – –	– – –	1 – –

MADS TIMM

DEBUT (Substitute Appearance)

Tuesday 29/10/2002
Champions League Phase 1 Match 5
at Neo GSP Stadium

Maccabi Haifa 3 Manchester United 0

CLUB CAREER RECORD	Apps	Subs	Goals
Premiership	0		0
League Division 1	0		0
League Division 2	0		0
FA Cup	0		0
League Cup	0		0
European Cup / Champions League	0	(1)	0
European Cup-Winners' Cup	0		0
UEFA Cup / Inter-Cities' Fairs Cup	0		0
Other Matches	0		0
OVERALL TOTAL	**0**	**(1)**	**0**

Opponents	PREM A S G	FLD 1 A S G	FLD 2 A S G	FAC A S G	LC A S G	EC/CL A S G	ECWC A S G	UEFA A S G	OTHER A S G	TOTAL A S G
1 Maccabi Haifa	– – –	– – –	– – –	– – –	– – –	– (1) –	– – –	– – –	– – –	– (1) –

GRAEME TOMLINSON

DEBUT (Substitute Appearance)

Wednesday 05/10/1994
League Cup 2nd Round 2nd Leg
at Old Trafford

Manchester United 2 Port Vale 0

CLUB CAREER RECORD	Apps	Subs	Goals
Premiership	0		0
League Division 1	0		0
League Division 2	0		0
FA Cup	0		0
League Cup	0	(2)	0
European Cup / Champions League	0		0
European Cup-Winners' Cup	0		0
UEFA Cup / Inter-Cities' Fairs Cup	0		0
Other Matches	0		0
OVERALL TOTAL	**0**	**(2)**	**0**

Opponents	PREM A S G	FLD 1 A S G	FLD 2 A S G	FAC A S G	LC A S G	EC/CL A S G	ECWC A S G	UEFA A S G	OTHER A S G	TOTAL A S G
1 Newcastle United	– – –	– – –	– – –	– – –	– (1) –	– – –	– – –	– – –	– – –	– (1) –
2 Port Vale	– – –	– – –	– – –	– – –	– (1) –	– – –	– – –	– – –	– – –	– (1) –

BILLY TOMS

DEBUT (Full Appearance)

Saturday 04/10/1919
Football League Division 1
at Old Trafford

Manchester United 1 Middlesbrough 1

CLUB CAREER RECORD	Apps	Subs	Goals
Premiership	0		0
League Division 1	13		3
League Division 2	0		0
FA Cup	1		1
League Cup	0		0
European Cup / Champions League	0		0
European Cup-Winners' Cup	0		0
UEFA Cup / Inter-Cities' Fairs Cup	0		0
Other Matches	0		0
OVERALL TOTAL	**14**		**4**

Opponents	PREM A S G	FLD 1 A S G	FLD 2 A S G	FAC A S G	LC A S G	EC/CL A S G	ECWC A S G	UEFA A S G	OTHER A S G	TOTAL A S G
1 Bolton Wanderers	– – –	2 – 2	– – –	– – –	– – –	– – –	– – –	– – –	– – –	2 – 2
2 Aston Villa	– – –	2 – –	– – –	– – –	– – –	– – –	– – –	– – –	– – –	2 – –
3 Blackburn Rovers	– – –	2 – –	– – –	– – –	– – –	– – –	– – –	– – –	– – –	2 – –
4 Bradford Park Avenue	– – –	1 – 1	– – –	– – –	– – –	– – –	– – –	– – –	– – –	1 – 1
5 Port Vale	– – –	– – –	– – –	1 – 1	– – –	– – –	– – –	– – –	– – –	1 – 1
6 Arsenal	– – –	1 – –	– – –	– – –	– – –	– – –	– – –	– – –	– – –	1 – –
7 Manchester City	– – –	1 – –	– – –	– – –	– – –	– – –	– – –	– – –	– – –	1 – –
8 Middlesbrough	– – –	1 – –	– – –	– – –	– – –	– – –	– – –	– – –	– – –	1 – –
9 Notts County	– – –	1 – –	– – –	– – –	– – –	– – –	– – –	– – –	– – –	1 – –
10 Oldham Athletic	– – –	1 – –	– – –	– – –	– – –	– – –	– – –	– – –	– – –	1 – –
11 West Bromwich Albion	– – –	1 – –	– – –	– – –	– – –	– – –	– – –	– – –	– – –	1 – –

HENRY TOPPING

DEBUT (Full Appearance)

Wednesday 05/04/1933
Football League Division 2
at Park Avenue

Bradford Park Avenue 1 Manchester United 1

CLUB CAREER RECORD	Apps	Subs	Goals
Premiership	0		0
League Division 1	0		0
League Division 2	12		1
FA Cup	0		0
League Cup	0		0
European Cup / Champions League	0		0
European Cup-Winners' Cup	0		0
UEFA Cup / Inter-Cities' Fairs Cup	0		0
Other Matches	0		0
OVERALL TOTAL	12		1

Opponents	PREM A S G	FLD 1 A S G	FLD 2 A S G	FAC A S G	LC A S G	EC/CL A S G	ECWC A S G	UEFA A S G	OTHER A S G	TOTAL A S G
1 Swansea City	– – –	– – –	2 – 1	– – –	– – –	– – –	– – –	– – –	– – –	2 – 1
2 Bradford Park Avenue	– – –	– – –	2 – –	– – –	– – –	– – –	– – –	– – –	– – –	2 – –
3 Port Vale	– – –	– – –	2 – –	– – –	– – –	– – –	– – –	– – –	– – –	2 – –
4 Chesterfield	– – –	– – –	1 – –	– – –	– – –	– – –	– – –	– – –	– – –	1 – –
5 Grimsby Town	– – –	– – –	1 – –	– – –	– – –	– – –	– – –	– – –	– – –	1 – –
6 Lincoln City	– – –	– – –	1 – –	– – –	– – –	– – –	– – –	– – –	– – –	1 – –
7 Nottingham Forest	– – –	– – –	1 – –	– – –	– – –	– – –	– – –	– – –	– – –	1 – –
8 Preston North End	– – –	– – –	1 – –	– – –	– – –	– – –	– – –	– – –	– – –	1 – –
9 West Ham United	– – –	– – –	1 – –	– – –	– – –	– – –	– – –	– – –	– – –	1 – –

WILF TRANTER

DEBUT (Full Appearance)

Saturday 07/03/1964
Football League Division 1
at Upton Park

West Ham United 0 Manchester United 2

CLUB CAREER RECORD	Apps	Subs	Goals
Premiership	0		0
League Division 1	1		0
League Division 2	0		0
FA Cup	0		0
League Cup	0		0
European Cup / Champions League	0		0
European Cup-Winners' Cup	0		0
UEFA Cup / Inter-Cities' Fairs Cup	0		0
Other Matches	0		0
OVERALL TOTAL	1		0

Opponents	PREM A S G	FLD 1 A S G	FLD 2 A S G	FAC A S G	LC A S G	EC/CL A S G	ECWC A S G	UEFA A S G	OTHER A S G	TOTAL A S G
1 West Ham United	– – –	1 – –	– – –	– – –	– – –	– – –	– – –	– – –	– – –	1 – –

GEORGE TRAVERS

DEBUT (Full Appearance)

Saturday 07/02/1914
Football League Division 1
at White Hart Lane

Tottenham Hotspur 2 Manchester United 1

CLUB CAREER RECORD	Apps	Subs	Goals
Premiership	0		0
League Division 1	21		4
League Division 2	0		0
FA Cup	0		0
League Cup	0		0
European Cup / Champions League	0		0
European Cup-Winners' Cup	0		0
UEFA Cup / Inter-Cities' Fairs Cup	0		0
Other Matches	0		0
OVERALL TOTAL	21		4

Opponents	PREM A S G	FLD 1 A S G	FLD 2 A S G	FAC A S G	LC A S G	EC/CL A S G	ECWC A S G	UEFA A S G	OTHER A S G	TOTAL A S G
1 West Bromwich Albion	– – –	2 – 1	– – –	– – –	– – –	– – –	– – –	– – –	– – –	2 – 1
2 Burnley	– – –	2 – –	– – –	– – –	– – –	– – –	– – –	– – –	– – –	2 – –
3 Manchester City	– – –	2 – –	– – –	– – –	– – –	– – –	– – –	– – –	– – –	2 – –
4 Derby County	– – –	1 – 1	– – –	– – –	– – –	– – –	– – –	– – –	– – –	1 – 1
5 Liverpool	– – –	1 – 1	– – –	– – –	– – –	– – –	– – –	– – –	– – –	1 – 1
6 Preston North End	– – –	1 – 1	– – –	– – –	– – –	– – –	– – –	– – –	– – –	1 – 1
7 Aston Villa	– – –	1 – –	– – –	– – –	– – –	– – –	– – –	– – –	– – –	1 – –
8 Blackburn Rovers	– – –	1 – –	– – –	– – –	– – –	– – –	– – –	– – –	– – –	1 – –
9 Bolton Wanderers	– – –	1 – –	– – –	– – –	– – –	– – –	– – –	– – –	– – –	1 – –
10 Bradford City	– – –	1 – –	– – –	– – –	– – –	– – –	– – –	– – –	– – –	1 – –
11 Chelsea	– – –	1 – –	– – –	– – –	– – –	– – –	– – –	– – –	– – –	1 – –
12 Everton	– – –	1 – –	– – –	– – –	– – –	– – –	– – –	– – –	– – –	1 – –
13 Newcastle United	– – –	1 – –	– – –	– – –	– – –	– – –	– – –	– – –	– – –	1 – –
14 Oldham Athletic	– – –	1 – –	– – –	– – –	– – –	– – –	– – –	– – –	– – –	1 – –
15 Sheffield United	– – –	1 – –	– – –	– – –	– – –	– – –	– – –	– – –	– – –	1 – –
16 Sheffield Wednesday	– – –	1 – –	– – –	– – –	– – –	– – –	– – –	– – –	– – –	1 – –
17 Sunderland	– – –	1 – –	– – –	– – –	– – –	– – –	– – –	– – –	– – –	1 – –
18 Tottenham Hotspur	– – –	1 – –	– – –	– – –	– – –	– – –	– – –	– – –	– – –	1 – –

JIMMY TURNBULL

DEBUT (Full Appearance)

Saturday 28/09/1907
Football League Division 1
at Stamford Bridge

Chelsea 1 Manchester United 4

CLUB CAREER RECORD	Apps	Subs	Goals
Premiership	0		0
League Division 1	67		36
League Division 2	0		0
FA Cup	9		6
League Cup	0		0
European Cup / Champions League	0		0
European Cup-Winners' Cup	0		0
UEFA Cup / Inter-Cities' Fairs Cup	0		0
Other Matches	2		3
OVERALL TOTAL	**78**		**45**

Opponents	PREM A	S	G	FLD 1 A	S	G	FLD 2 A	S	G	FAC A	S	G	LC A	S	G	EC/CL A	S	G	ECWC A	S	G	UEFA A	S	G	OTHER A	S	G	TOTAL A	S	G
1 Blackburn Rovers	–	–		5		3	–	–		1		3																6		6
2 Bury	–	–		5		5																						5		5
3 Chelsea	–	–		4		2	–	–		1																		5		2
4 Bristol City	–	–		4		1	–	–		1																		5		1
5 Sheffield United	–	–		5																								5		–
6 Everton	–	–		3		4	–	–		1																		4		4
7 Newcastle United	–	–		3		2	–	–		1																		4		2
8 Nottingham Forest	–	–		4		1																						4		1
9 Notts County	–	–		4		1																						4		1
10 Liverpool	–	–		3		2																						3		2
11 Preston North End	–	–		3		2																						3		2
12 Arsenal	–	–		3		1																						3		1
13 Manchester City	–	–		3		1																						3		1
14 Sheffield Wednesday	–	–		3		1																						3		1
15 Sunderland	–	–		3		1																						3		1
16 Middlesbrough	–	–		2		4																						2		4
17 Queens Park Rangers	–	–		–		–																2		3				2		3
18 Bolton Wanderers	–	–		2		2																						2		2
19 Birmingham City	–	–		2		1																						2		1
20 Aston Villa	–	–		2																								2		–
21 Bradford City	–	–		2		–																						2		–
22 Burnley	–	–		–		–	–	–		1		2																1		2
23 Fulham	–	–		–		–	–	–		1		1																1		1
24 Leicester City	–	–		1		1																						1		1
25 Tottenham Hotspur	–	–		1		1																						1		1
26 Blackpool	–	–		–		–	–	–		1																		1		–
27 Brighton	–	–		–		–	–	–		1																		1		

SANDY TURNBULL

DEBUT (Full Appearance, 1 goal)

Tuesday 01/01/1907
Football League Division 1
at Bank Street

Manchester United 1 Aston Villa 0

CLUB CAREER RECORD	Apps	Subs	Goals
Premiership	0		0
League Division 1	220		90
League Division 2	0		0
FA Cup	25		10
League Cup	0		0
European Cup / Champions League	0		0
European Cup-Winners' Cup	0		0
UEFA Cup / Inter-Cities' Fairs Cup	0		0
Other Matches	2		1
OVERALL TOTAL	**247**		**101**

Opponents	PREM A	S	G	FLD 1 A	S	G	FLD 2 A	S	G	FAC A	S	G	LC A	S	G	EC/CL A	S	G	ECWC A	S	G	UEFA A	S	G	OTHER A	S	G	TOTAL A	S	G
1 Sunderland	–	–		15		8	–	–		–																		15		8
2 Newcastle United	–	–		14		4	–	–		1																		15		4
3 Blackburn Rovers	–	–		11		5	–	–		3		3																14		8
4 Middlesbrough	–	–		14		7	–	–		–																		14		7
5 Aston Villa	–	–		11		4	–	–		2		1																13		5
6 Sheffield United	–	–		13		4	–	–																				13		4
7 Notts County	–	–		12		6	–	–		–																		12		6
8 Everton	–	–		11		5	–	–		1																		12		5
9 Manchester City	–	–		11		4	–	–		–																		11		4
10 Bradford City	–	–		11		1	–	–																				11		1
11 Liverpool	–	–		10		9	–																					10		9
12 Arsenal	–	–		10		5	–	–		–																		10		5
13 Chelsea	–	–		9		4	–	–		1		1																10		5
14 Sheffield Wednesday	–	–		10		3	–	–		–																		10		3
15 Bury	–	–		10		2	–	–		–																		10		2
16 Tottenham Hotspur	–	–		9		2	–	–																				9		2
17 Oldham Athletic	–	–		7		3	–	–		1																		8		3
18 Preston North End	–	–		8		2	–			–																		8		2
19 Bolton Wanderers	–	–		6		3	–	–																				6		3
20 Nottingham Forest	–	–		5		3	–	–																				5		3
21 West Bromwich Albion	–	–		4		1	–	–		–																		4		1
22 Burnley	–	–		2		–	–	–		2																		4		–
23 Derby County	–	–		3		4	–	–		–																		3		4
24 Bristol City	–	–		2		–	–	–		1		1																3		1

continued../

SANDY TURNBULL (continued)

Opponents	PREM A S G	FLD 1 A S G	FLD 2 A S G	FAC A S G	LC A S G	EC/CL A S G	ECWC A S G	UEFA A S G	OTHER A S G	TOTAL A S G
25 Coventry City	– –	– –	– –	3 1	– –	–	–	–	– –	3 1
26 Reading	– –	– –	– –	2 2	–	–	–	–	– –	2 2
27 Birmingham City	– –	2 1	– –	–	–	–	–	–	– –	2 1
28 Swindon Town	– –	– –	– –	1 –	–	–	–	–	1 1 –	2 1
29 Blackpool	– –	– –	– –	2 –	–	–	–	–	– –	2 –
30 West Ham United	– –	– –	– –	1 1	–	–	–	–	– –	1 1
31 Brighton	– –	– –	– –	1 –	–	–	–	–	– –	1 –
32 Fulham	– –	– –	– –	1 –	–	–	–	–	– –	1 –
33 Huddersfield Town	– –	– –	– –	1 –	–	–	–	–	– –	1 –
34 Plymouth Argyle	– –	– –	– –	1 –	–	–	–	–	– –	1 –
35 Queens Park Rangers	–	–	–	–	–	–	–	1 1	–	1 –

CHRIS TURNER

DEBUT (Full Appearance)

Saturday 14/12/1985
Football League Division 1
at Villa Park

Aston Villa 1 Manchester United 3

CLUB CAREER RECORD	Apps	Subs	Goals
Premiership	0		0
League Division 1	64		0
League Division 2	0		0
FA Cup	8		0
League Cup	7		0
European Cup / Champions League	0		0
European Cup-Winners' Cup	0		0
UEFA Cup / Inter-Cities' Fairs Cup	0		0
Other Matches	0		0
OVERALL TOTAL	79		0

Opponents	PREM A S G	FLD 1 A S G	FLD 2 A S G	FAC A S G	LC A S G	EC/CL A S G	ECWC A S G	UEFA A S G	OTHER A S G	TOTAL A S G
1 Southampton	– –	4 –	– –	–	2	–	–	–	–	6 –
2 Arsenal	– –	3 –	– –	1	–	–	–	–	–	4 –
3 Chelsea	– –	3 –	– –	1	–	–	–	–	–	4 –
4 Coventry City	– –	3 –	– –	1	–	–	–	–	–	4 –
5 Oxford United	– –	3 –	– –	–	1	–	–	–	–	4 –
6 Queens Park Rangers	–	4 –	– –	–	–	–	–	–	–	4 –
7 Watford	– –	4 –	– –	–	–	–	–	–	–	4 –
8 West Ham United	– –	2 –	– –	2	–	–	–	–	–	4 –
9 Charlton Athletic	– –	3 –	– –	–	–	–	–	–	–	3 –
10 Everton	– –	3 –	– –	–	–	–	–	–	–	3 –
11 Luton Town	– –	3 –	– –	–	–	–	–	–	–	3 –
12 Manchester City	– –	2 –	– –	1	–	–	–	–	–	3 –
13 Newcastle United	– –	3 –	– –	–	–	–	–	–	–	3 –
14 Sheffield Wednesday	– –	3 –	– –	–	–	–	–	–	–	3 –
15 Tottenham Hotspur	– –	3 –	– –	–	–	–	–	–	–	3 –
16 Birmingham City	– –	2 –	– –	–	–	–	–	–	–	2 –
17 Derby County	– –	2 –	– –	–	–	–	–	–	–	2 –
18 Leicester City	– –	2 –	– –	–	–	–	–	–	–	2 –
19 Liverpool	– –	2 –	– –	–	–	–	–	–	–	2 –
20 Norwich City	– –	2 –	– –	–	–	–	–	–	–	2 –
21 Nottingham Forest	– –	2 –	– –	–	–	–	–	–	–	2 –
22 Port Vale	– –	– –	– –	–	2	–	–	–	–	2 –
23 Portsmouth	– –	2 –	– –	–	–	–	–	–	–	2 –
24 Wimbledon	– –	2 –	– –	–	–	–	–	–	–	2 –
25 Aston Villa	– –	1 –	– –	–	–	–	–	–	–	1 –
26 Crystal Palace	– –	– –	– –	–	1	–	–	–	–	1 –
27 Hull City	– –	– –	– –	–	1	–	–	–	–	1 –
28 Ipswich Town	– –	– –	– –	1	–	–	–	–	–	1 –
29 Rochdale	– –	– –	– –	1	–	–	–	–	–	1 –
30 West Bromwich Albion	–	1 –	– –	–	–	–	–	–	–	1 –

JOHN TURNER

DEBUT (Full Appearance)

Saturday 22/10/1898
Football League Division 2
at Bank Street

Newton Heath 6 Loughborough Town 1

CLUB CAREER RECORD	Apps	Subs	Goals
Premiership	0		0
League Division 1	0		0
League Division 2	3		0
FA Cup	1		0
League Cup	0		0
European Cup / Champions League	0		0
European Cup-Winners' Cup	0		0
UEFA Cup / Inter-Cities' Fairs Cup	0		0
Other Matches	0		0
OVERALL TOTAL	4		0

Opponents	PREM A S G	FLD 1 A S G	FLD 2 A S G	FAC A S G	LC A S G	EC/CL A S G	ECWC A S G	UEFA A S G	OTHER A S G	TOTAL A S G
1 Blackpool	– –	– –	1 –	–	–	–	–	–	–	1 –
2 Grimsby Town	– –	– –	1 –	–	–	–	–	–	–	1 –
3 Loughborough Town	– –	– –	1 –	–	–	–	–	–	–	1 –
4 Oswaldtwistle Rovers	– –	– –	– –	1 –	–	–	–	–	–	1 –

ROBERT TURNER

DEBUT (Full Appearance)

Saturday 08/10/1898
Football League Division 2
at Bank Street

Newton Heath 2 Port Vale 1

CLUB CAREER RECORD	Apps	Subs	Goals
Premiership	0		0
League Division 1	0		0
League Division 2	2		0
FA Cup	0		0
League Cup	0		0
European Cup / Champions League	0		0
European Cup-Winners' Cup	0		0
UEFA Cup / Inter-Cities' Fairs Cup	0		0
Other Matches	0		0
OVERALL TOTAL	2		0

Opponents	PREM A S G	FLD 1 A S G	FLD 2 A S G	FAC A S G	LC A S G	EC/CL A S G	ECWC A S G	UEFA A S G	OTHER A S G	TOTAL A S G
1 Loughborough Town	– –	– –	1 –	–	– –	– –	– –	– –	– –	1 –
2 Port Vale	– –	– –	1 –	–	– –	– –	– –	– –	– –	1 –

TURNER (FIRST NAME NOT KNOWN)

DEBUT (Full Appearance)

Saturday 25/10/1890
FA Cup 2nd Qualifying Round
at Bootle Park

Bootle Reserves 1 Newton Heath 0

CLUB CAREER RECORD	Apps	Subs	Goals
Premiership	0		0
League Division 1	0		0
League Division 2	0		0
FA Cup	1		0
League Cup	0		0
European Cup / Champions League	0		0
European Cup-Winners' Cup	0		0
UEFA Cup / Inter-Cities' Fairs Cup	0		0
Other Matches	0		0
OVERALL TOTAL	1		0

Opponents	PREM A S G	FLD 1 A S G	FLD 2 A S G	FAC A S G	LC A S G	EC/CL A S G	ECWC A S G	UEFA A S G	OTHER A S G	TOTAL A S G
1 Bootle Reserves	– –	– –	– –	1	– –	– –	– –	– –	– –	1 –

MICHAEL TWISS

DEBUT (Substitute Appearance)

Wednesday 25/02/1998
FA Cup 5th Round Replay
at Oakwell

Barnsley 3 Manchester United 2

CLUB CAREER RECORD	Apps	Subs	Goals
Premiership	0		0
League Division 1	0		0
League Division 2	0		0
FA Cup	0	(1)	0
League Cup	1		0
European Cup / Champions League	0		0
European Cup-Winners' Cup	0		0
UEFA Cup / Inter-Cities' Fairs Cup	0		0
Other Matches	0		0
OVERALL TOTAL	1	(1)	0

Opponents	PREM A S G	FLD 1 A S G	FLD 2 A S G	FAC A S G	LC A S G	EC/CL A S G	ECWC A S G	UEFA A S G	OTHER A S G	TOTAL A S G
1 Aston Villa	– –	– –	– –	–	1 –	– –	– –	– –	– –	1 –
2 Barnsley	– –	– –	– –	– (1) –	–	– –	– –	– –	– –	– (1) –

SIDNEY TYLER

DEBUT (Full Appearance)

Saturday 10/11/1923
Football League Division 2
at Old Trafford

Manchester United 3 Leicester City 0

CLUB CAREER RECORD	Apps	Subs	Goals
Premiership	0		0
League Division 1	0		0
League Division 2	1		0
FA Cup	0		0
League Cup	0		0
European Cup / Champions League	0		0
European Cup-Winners' Cup	0		0
UEFA Cup / Inter-Cities' Fairs Cup	0		0
Other Matches	0		0
OVERALL TOTAL	1		0

Opponents	PREM A S G	FLD 1 A S G	FLD 2 A S G	FAC A S G	LC A S G	EC/CL A S G	ECWC A S G	UEFA A S G	OTHER A S G	TOTAL A S G
1 Leicester City	– –	– –	1 –	–	– –	– –	– –	– –	– –	1 –

IAN URE

DEBUT (Full Appearance)

Saturday 23/08/1969
Football League Division 1
at Molineux

Wolverhampton Wanderers 0 Manchester United 0

CLUB CAREER RECORD	Apps	Subs	Goals
Premiership	0		0
League Division 1	47		1
League Division 2	0		0
FA Cup	8		0
League Cup	10		0
European Cup / Champions League	0		0
European Cup–Winners' Cup	0		0
UEFA Cup / Inter-Cities' Fairs Cup	0		0
Other Matches	0		0
OVERALL TOTAL	**65**		**1**

Opponents	PREM A S G	FLD 1 A S G	FLD 2 A S G	FAC A S G	LC A S G	EC/CL A S G	ECWC A S G	UEFA A S G	OTHER A S G	TOTAL A S G
1 Burnley	– – –	3 – –	– – –	– – –	2 – –	– – –	– – –	– – –	– – –	5 – –
2 Derby County	– – –	3 – –	– – –	– – –	2 – –	– – –	– – –	– – –	– – –	5 – –
3 Leeds United	– – –	4 – –	– – –	1 – –	– – –	– – –	– – –	– – –	– – –	5 – –
4 Ipswich Town	– – –	3 – –	– – –	1 – –	– – –	– – –	– – –	– – –	– – –	4 – –
5 Manchester City	– – –	1 – –	– – –	1 – –	2 – –	– – –	– – –	– – –	– – –	4 – –
6 Liverpool	– – –	3 – 1	– – –	– – –	– – –	– – –	– – –	– – –	– – –	3 – 1
7 Arsenal	– – –	3 – –	– – –	– – –	– – –	– – –	– – –	– – –	– – –	3 – –
8 Chelsea	– – –	3 – –	– – –	– – –	– – –	– – –	– – –	– – –	– – –	3 – –
9 Coventry City	– – –	3 – –	– – –	– – –	– – –	– – –	– – –	– – –	– – –	3 – –
10 Middlesbrough	– – –	– – –	– – –	3 – –	– – –	– – –	– – –	– – –	– – –	3 – –
11 West Bromwich Albion	– – –	3 – –	– – –	– – –	– – –	– – –	– – –	– – –	– – –	3 – –
12 West Ham United	– – –	3 – –	– – –	– – –	– – –	– – –	– – –	– – –	– – –	3 – –
13 Crystal Palace	– – –	2 – –	– – –	– – –	– – –	– – –	– – –	– – –	– – –	2 – –
14 Stoke City	– – –	2 – –	– – –	– – –	– – –	– – –	– – –	– – –	– – –	2 – –
15 Sunderland	– – –	2 – –	– – –	– – –	– – –	– – –	– – –	– – –	– – –	2 – –
16 Tottenham Hotspur	– – –	2 – –	– – –	– – –	– – –	– – –	– – –	– – –	– – –	2 – –
17 Wolverhampton W.	– – –	2 – –	– – –	– – –	– – –	– – –	– – –	– – –	– – –	2 – –
18 Aldershot	– – –	– – –	– – –	– – –	1 – –	– – –	– – –	– – –	– – –	1 – –
19 Aston Villa	– – –	– – –	– – –	– – –	1 – –	– – –	– – –	– – –	– – –	1 – –
20 Everton	– – –	1 – –	– – –	– – –	– – –	– – –	– – –	– – –	– – –	1 – –
21 Newcastle United	– – –	1 – –	– – –	– – –	– – –	– – –	– – –	– – –	– – –	1 – –
22 Northampton Town	– – –	– – –	– – –	1 – –	– – –	– – –	– – –	– – –	– – –	1 – –
23 Nottingham Forest	– – –	1 – –	– – –	– – –	– – –	– – –	– – –	– – –	– – –	1 – –
24 Portsmouth	– – –	– – –	– – –	– – –	1 – –	– – –	– – –	– – –	– – –	1 – –
25 Sheffield Wednesday	– – –	1 – –	– – –	– – –	– – –	– – –	– – –	– – –	– – –	1 – –
26 Southampton	– – –	1 – –	– – –	– – –	– – –	– – –	– – –	– – –	– – –	1 – –
27 Watford	– – –	– – –	– – –	1 – –	– – –	– – –	– – –	– – –	– – –	1 – –
28 Wrexham	– – –	– – –	– – –	– – –	1 – –	– – –	– – –	– – –	– – –	1 – –

BOB VALENTINE

DEBUT (Full Appearance)

Saturday 25/03/1905
Football League Division 2
at Bloomfield Road

Blackpool 0 Manchester United 1

CLUB CAREER RECORD	Apps	Subs	Goals
Premiership	0		0
League Division 1	0		0
League Division 2	10		0
FA Cup	0		0
League Cup	0		0
European Cup / Champions League	0		0
European Cup–Winners' Cup	0		0
UEFA Cup / Inter-Cities' Fairs Cup	0		0
Other Matches	0		0
OVERALL TOTAL	**10**		**0**

Opponents	PREM A S G	FLD 1 A S G	FLD 2 A S G	FAC A S G	LC A S G	EC/CL A S G	ECWC A S G	UEFA A S G	OTHER A S G	TOTAL A S G
1 Blackpool	– – –	– – –	2 – –	– – –	– – –	– – –	– – –	– – –	– – –	2 – –
2 Gainsborough Trinity	– – –	– – –	2 – –	– – –	– – –	– – –	– – –	– – –	– – –	2 – –
3 Bradford City	– – –	– – –	1 – –	– – –	– – –	– – –	– – –	– – –	– – –	1 – –
4 Chesterfield	– – –	– – –	1 – –	– – –	– – –	– – –	– – –	– – –	– – –	1 – –
5 Hull City	– – –	– – –	1 – –	– – –	– – –	– – –	– – –	– – –	– – –	1 – –
6 Leicester City	– – –	– – –	1 – –	– – –	– – –	– – –	– – –	– – –	– – –	1 – –
7 Lincoln City	– – –	– – –	1 – –	– – –	– – –	– – –	– – –	– – –	– – –	1 – –
8 West Bromwich Albion	– – –	– – –	1 – –	– – –	– – –	– – –	– – –	– – –	– – –	1 – –

JAMES VANCE

DEBUT (Full Appearance)

Monday 03/02/1896
Football League Division 2
at Bank Street

Newton Heath 2 Leicester City 0

CLUB CAREER RECORD	Apps	Subs	Goals
Premiership	0		0
League Division 1	0		0
League Division 2	11		1
FA Cup	0		0
League Cup	0		0
European Cup / Champions League	0		0
European Cup-Winners' Cup	0		0
UEFA Cup / Inter-Cities' Fairs Cup	0		0
Other Matches	0		0
OVERALL TOTAL	11		1

Opponents	PREM A	S	G	FLD 1 A	S	G	FLD 2 A	S	G	FAC A	S	G	LC A	S	G	EC/CL A	S	G	ECWC A	S	G	UEFA A	S	G	OTHER A	S	G	TOTAL A	S	G
1 Burton Wanderers	–	–	–	–	–	–	2	–	–	–	–	–	–	–	–	–	–	–	–	–	–	–	–	–	–	–	–	2	–	–
2 Port Vale	–	–	–	–	–	–	2	–	–	–	–	–	–	–	–	–	–	–	–	–	–	–	–	–	–	–	–	2	–	–
3 Burton Swifts	–	–	–	–	–	–	1	–	1	–	–	–	–	–	–	–	–	–	–	–	–	–	–	–	–	–	–	1	–	1
4 Darwen	–	–	–	–	–	–	1	–	–	–	–	–	–	–	–	–	–	–	–	–	–	–	–	–	–	–	–	1	–	–
5 Grimsby Town	–	–	–	–	–	–	1	–	–	–	–	–	–	–	–	–	–	–	–	–	–	–	–	–	–	–	–	1	–	–
6 Leicester City	–	–	–	–	–	–	1	–	–	–	–	–	–	–	–	–	–	–	–	–	–	–	–	–	–	–	–	1	–	–
7 Lincoln City	–	–	–	–	–	–	1	–	–	–	–	–	–	–	–	–	–	–	–	–	–	–	–	–	–	–	–	1	–	–
8 Loughborough Town	–	–	–	–	–	–	1	–	–	–	–	–	–	–	–	–	–	–	–	–	–	–	–	–	–	–	–	1	–	–
9 Rotherham United	–	–	–	–	–	–	1	–	–	–	–	–	–	–	–	–	–	–	–	–	–	–	–	–	–	–	–	1	–	–

RAIMOND van der GOUW

DEBUT (Full Appearance)

Saturday 21/09/1996
FA Premiership
at Villa Park

Aston Villa 0 Manchester United 0

CLUB CAREER RECORD	Apps	Subs	Goals
Premiership	26	(11)	0
League Division 1	0		0
League Division 2	0		0
FA Cup	1		0
League Cup	8	(1)	0
European Cup / Champions League	11		0
European Cup-Winners' Cup	0		0
UEFA Cup / Inter-Cities' Fairs Cup	0		0
Other Matches	2		0
OVERALL TOTAL	48	(12)	0

Opponents	PREM A	S	G	FLD 1 A	S	G	FLD 2 A	S	G	FAC A	S	G	LC A	S	G	EC/CL A	S	G	ECWC A	S	G	UEFA A	S	G	OTHER A	S	G	TOTAL A	S	G
1 Chelsea	3	–	–	–	–	–	–	–	–	–	–	–	–	–	–	–	–	–	–	–	–	–	–	–	–	–	–	3	–	–
2 Tottenham Hotspur	2	–	–	–	–	–	–	–	–	–	–	–	1	–	–	–	–	–	–	–	–	–	–	–	–	–	–	3	–	–
3 Southampton	2	(1)	–	–	–	–	–	–	–	–	–	–	–	–	–	–	–	–	–	–	–	–	–	–	–	–	–	2	(1)	–
4 Derby County	1	(2)	–	–	–	–	–	–	–	–	–	–	–	–	–	–	–	–	–	–	–	–	–	–	–	–	–	1	(2)	–
5 Newcastle United	1	(2)	–	–	–	–	–	–	–	–	–	–	–	–	–	–	–	–	–	–	–	–	–	–	–	–	–	1	(2)	–
6 Aston Villa	2	–	–	–	–	–	–	–	–	–	–	–	–	–	–	–	–	–	–	–	–	–	–	–	–	–	–	2	–	–
7 Girondins Bordeaux	–	–	–	–	–	–	–	–	–	–	–	–	–	–	–	2	–	–	–	–	–	–	–	–	–	–	–	2	–	–
8 Sheffield Wednesday	2	–	–	–	–	–	–	–	–	–	–	–	–	–	–	–	–	–	–	–	–	–	–	–	–	–	–	2	–	–
9 Watford	1	–	–	–	–	–	–	–	–	–	–	–	1	–	–	–	–	–	–	–	–	–	–	–	–	–	–	2	–	–
10 West Ham United	2	–	–	–	–	–	–	–	–	–	–	–	–	–	–	–	–	–	–	–	–	–	–	–	–	–	–	2	–	–
11 Wimbledon	2	–	–	–	–	–	–	–	–	–	–	–	–	–	–	–	–	–	–	–	–	–	–	–	–	–	–	2	–	–
12 Arsenal	1	–	–	–	–	–	–	–	–	–	–	–	–	(1)	–	–	–	–	–	–	–	–	–	–	–	–	–	1	(1)	–
13 Charlton Athletic	1	(1)	–	–	–	–	–	–	–	–	–	–	–	–	–	–	–	–	–	–	–	–	–	–	–	–	–	1	(1)	–
14 Coventry City	1	(1)	–	–	–	–	–	–	–	–	–	–	–	–	–	–	–	–	–	–	–	–	–	–	–	–	–	1	(1)	–
15 Leeds United	1	(1)	–	–	–	–	–	–	–	–	–	–	–	–	–	–	–	–	–	–	–	–	–	–	–	–	–	1	(1)	–
16 Sunderland	–	(1)	–	–	–	–	–	–	–	–	–	–	1	–	–	–	–	–	–	–	–	–	–	–	–	–	–	1	(1)	–
17 Everton	–	(2)	–	–	–	–	–	–	–	–	–	–	–	–	–	–	–	–	–	–	–	–	–	–	–	–	–	–	(2)	–
18 Barnsley	1	–	–	–	–	–	–	–	–	–	–	–	–	–	–	–	–	–	–	–	–	–	–	–	–	–	–	1	–	–
19 Blackburn Rovers	1	–	–	–	–	–	–	–	–	–	–	–	–	–	–	–	–	–	–	–	–	–	–	–	–	–	–	1	–	–
20 Borussia Dortmund	–	–	–	–	–	–	–	–	–	–	–	–	–	–	–	1	–	–	–	–	–	–	–	–	–	–	–	1	–	–
21 Bury	–	–	–	–	–	–	–	–	–	–	–	–	1	–	–	–	–	–	–	–	–	–	–	–	–	–	–	1	–	–
22 Croatia Zagreb	–	–	–	–	–	–	–	–	–	–	–	–	–	–	–	1	–	–	–	–	–	–	–	–	–	–	–	1	–	–
23 Dynamo Kiev	–	–	–	–	–	–	–	–	–	–	–	–	–	–	–	1	–	–	–	–	–	–	–	–	–	–	–	1	–	–
24 Fulham	–	–	–	–	–	–	–	–	–	1	–	–	–	–	–	–	–	–	–	–	–	–	–	–	–	–	–	1	–	–
25 Ipswich Town	–	–	–	–	–	–	–	–	–	–	–	–	1	–	–	–	–	–	–	–	–	–	–	–	–	–	–	1	–	–
26 Lazio	–	–	–	–	–	–	–	–	–	–	–	–	–	–	–	–	–	–	–	–	–	1	–	–	–	–	–	1	–	–
27 Leicester City	–	–	–	–	–	–	–	–	–	–	–	–	1	–	–	–	–	–	–	–	–	–	–	–	–	–	–	1	–	–
28 Liverpool	1	–	–	–	–	–	–	–	–	–	–	–	–	–	–	–	–	–	–	–	–	–	–	–	–	–	–	1	–	–
29 Middlesbrough	1	–	–	–	–	–	–	–	–	–	–	–	–	–	–	–	–	–	–	–	–	–	–	–	–	–	–	1	–	–
30 Monaco	–	–	–	–	–	–	–	–	–	–	–	–	–	–	–	1	–	–	–	–	–	–	–	–	–	–	–	1	–	–
31 Nottingham Forest	–	–	–	–	–	–	–	–	–	–	–	–	1	–	–	–	–	–	–	–	–	–	–	–	–	–	–	1	–	–
32 Olympique Marseille	–	–	–	–	–	–	–	–	–	–	–	–	–	–	–	1	–	–	–	–	–	–	–	–	–	–	–	1	–	–
33 PSV Eindhoven	–	–	–	–	–	–	–	–	–	–	–	–	–	–	–	1	–	–	–	–	–	–	–	–	–	–	–	1	–	–
34 Real Madrid	–	–	–	–	–	–	–	–	–	–	–	–	–	–	–	1	–	–	–	–	–	–	–	–	–	–	–	1	–	–
35 South Melbourne	–	–	–	–	–	–	–	–	–	–	–	–	–	–	–	–	–	–	–	–	–	–	–	–	1	–	–	1	–	–
36 Sturm Graz	–	–	–	–	–	–	–	–	–	–	–	–	–	–	–	1	–	–	–	–	–	–	–	–	–	–	–	1	–	–
37 Swindon Town	–	–	–	–	–	–	–	–	–	–	–	–	1	–	–	–	–	–	–	–	–	–	–	–	–	–	–	1	–	–
38 Valencia	–	–	–	–	–	–	–	–	–	–	–	–	–	–	–	1	–	–	–	–	–	–	–	–	–	–	–	1	–	–

EDWIN van der SAR

DEBUT (Full Appearance)

Tuesday 09/08/2005
Champions League Qualifying Round 1st Leg
at Old Trafford

Manchester United 3 Debreceni 0

CLUB CAREER RECORD	Apps	Subs	Goals
Premiership	99		0
League Division 1	0		0
League Division 2	0		0
FA Cup	9		0
League Cup	3		0
European Cup / Champions League	30		0
European Cup-Winners' Cup	0		0
UEFA Cup / Inter-Cities' Fairs Cup	0		0
Other Matches	1		0
OVERALL TOTAL	**142**		**0**

Opponents	PREM A S G	FLD 1 A S G	FLD 2 A S G	FAC A S G	LC A S G	EC/CL A S G	ECWC A S G	UEFA A S G	OTHER A S G	TOTAL A S G
1 Chelsea	5 – –	– – –	– – –	1 – –	1 – –	– – –	– – –	– – –	1 –	8 –
2 Blackburn Rovers	5 –	– – –	– – –	– –	2 –	– –	– –	– –	– –	7 –
3 Liverpool	6 –	– – –	– – –	1 –	– –	– –	– –	– –	– –	7 –
4 Portsmouth	6 –	– – –	– – –	1 –	– –	– –	– –	– –	– –	7 –
5 Tottenham Hotspur	6 –	– – –	– – –	1 –	– –	– –	– –	– –	– –	7 –
6 Arsenal	5 –	– – –	– – –	1 –	– –	– –	– –	– –	– –	6 –
7 Aston Villa	5 –	– – –	– – –	1 –	– –	– –	– –	– –	– –	6 –
8 Fulham	6 –	– – –	– – –	– –	– –	– –	– –	– –	– –	6 –
9 Manchester City	6 –	– – –	– – –	– –	– –	– –	– –	– –	– –	6 –
10 Middlesbrough	6 –	– – –	– – –	– –	– –	– –	– –	– –	– –	6 –
11 Newcastle United	6 –	– – –	– – –	– –	– –	– –	– –	– –	– –	6 –
12 Wigan Athletic	5 –	– – –	– – –	– –	1 –	– –	– –	– –	– –	6 –
13 Everton	5 –	– – –	– – –	– –	– –	– –	– –	– –	– –	5 –
14 Reading	4 –	– – –	– – –	1 –	– –	– –	– –	– –	– –	5 –
15 West Ham United	5 –	– – –	– – –	– –	– –	– –	– –	– –	– –	5 –
16 Benfica	–	– – –	– – –	– –	– –	4 –	– –	– –	– –	4 –
17 Bolton Wanderers	4 –	– – –	– – –	– –	– –	– –	– –	– –	– –	4 –
18 Lille Metropole	–	– – –	– – –	– –	– –	4 –	– –	– –	– –	4 –
19 Roma	–	– – –	– – –	– –	– –	4 –	– –	– –	– –	4 –
20 Birmingham City	3 –	– – –	– – –	– –	– –	– –	– –	– –	– –	3 –
21 Charlton Athletic	3 –	– – –	– – –	– –	– –	– –	– –	– –	– –	3 –
22 Sunderland	3 –	– – –	– – –	– –	– –	– –	– –	– –	– –	3 –
23 AC Milan	–	– – –	– – –	– –	– –	2 –	– –	– –	– –	2 –
24 Barcelona	–	– – –	– – –	– –	– –	2 –	– –	– –	– –	2 –
25 Copenhagen	–	– – –	– – –	– –	– –	2 –	– –	– –	– –	2 –
26 Debreceni	–	– – –	– – –	– –	– –	2 –	– –	– –	– –	2 –
27 Dynamo Kiev	–	– – –	– – –	– –	– –	2 –	– –	– –	– –	2 –
28 Glasgow Celtic	–	– – –	– – –	– –	– –	2 –	– –	– –	– –	2 –
29 Olympique Lyonnais	–	– – –	– – –	– –	– –	2 –	– –	– –	– –	2 –
30 Villarreal	–	– – –	– – –	– –	– –	2 –	– –	– –	– –	2 –
31 Watford	1 –	– – –	– – –	1 –	– –	– –	– –	– –	– –	2 –
32 West Bromwich Albion	2 –	– – –	– – –	– –	– –	– –	– –	– –	– –	2 –
33 Derby County	1 –	– – –	– – –	– –	– –	– –	– –	– –	– –	1 –
34 Sheffield United	1 –	– – –	– – –	– –	– –	– –	– –	– –	– –	1 –
35 Sporting Lisbon	–	– – –	– – –	– –	– –	1 –	– –	– –	– –	1 –
36 Wolverhampton W.	–	– – –	– – –	1 –	– –	– –	– –	– –	– –	1 –

RUUD van NISTELROOY

DEBUT (Full Appearance, 1 goal)

Sunday 12/08/2001
FA Charity Shield
at Millennium Stadium

Manchester United 1 Liverpool 2

CLUB CAREER RECORD	Apps	Subs	Goals
Premiership	137	(13)	95
League Division 1	0		0
League Division 2	0		0
FA Cup	11	(3)	14
League Cup	5	(1)	2
European Cup / Champions League	45	(2)	38
European Cup–Winners' Cup	0		0
UEFA Cup / Inter–Cities' Fairs Cup	0		0
Other Matches	2		1
OVERALL TOTAL	200	(19)	150

Opponents	PREM A S G	FLD 1 A S G	FLD 2 A S G	FAC A S G	LC A S G	EC/CL A S G	ECWC A S G	UEFA A S G	OTHER A S G	TOTAL A S G
1 Arsenal	8 (1) 2	– –	– –	2 –	– –	– –	– –	– –	1 –	11 (1) 2
2 Blackburn Rovers	7 (1) 6	– –	– –	– –	3 (1) 2	– –	– –	– –	– –	10 (2) 8
3 Liverpool	8 2	– –	– –	1 –	1 –	– –	– –	– –	1 1	11 3
4 Newcastle United	8 (1) 9	– –	– –	1 2	– –	– –	– –	– –	– –	9 (1) 11
5 Middlesbrough	9 3	– –	– –	– (1) –	– –	– –	– –	– –	– –	9 (1) 3
6 Tottenham Hotspur	9 7	– –	– –	– –	– –	– –	– –	– –	– –	9 7
7 Fulham	7 (1) 8	– –	– –	1 2	– –	– –	– –	– –	– –	8 (1) 10
8 Chelsea	8 (1) 3	– –	– –	– –	– –	– –	– –	– –	– –	8 (1) 3
9 Aston Villa	7 6	– –	– –	– (2) 2	– –	– –	– –	– –	– –	7 (2) 8
10 Southampton	7 7	– –	– –	1 –	– –	– –	– –	– –	– –	8 7
11 Bolton Wanderers	6 (2) 4	– –	– –	– –	– –	– –	– –	– –	– –	6 (2) 4
12 Manchester City	6 4	– –	– –	1 2	– –	– –	– –	– –	– –	7 6
13 Charlton Athletic	6 (1) 8	– –	– –	– –	– –	– –	– –	– –	– –	6 (1) 8
14 Everton	6 (1) 6	– –	– –	– –	– –	– –	– –	– –	– –	6 (1) 6
15 West Ham United	5 2	– –	– –	1 2	– –	– –	– –	– –	– –	6 4
16 Deportivo La Coruna	– –	– –	– –	– –	– –	5 5	– –	– –	– –	5 5
17 Portsmouth	4 2	– –	– –	1 2	– –	– –	– –	– –	– –	5 4
18 Leeds United	5 –	– –	– –	– –	– –	– –	– –	– –	– –	5 –
19 Birmingham City	4 (1) 3	– –	– –	– –	– –	– –	– –	– –	– –	4 (1) 3
20 Bayer Leverkusen	– –	– –	– –	– –	– –	4 4	– –	– –	– –	4 4
21 Sunderland	4 3	– –	– –	– –	– –	– –	– –	– –	– –	4 3
22 West Bromwich Albion	4 3	– –	– –	– –	– –	– –	– –	– –	– –	4 3
23 Lille Metropole	– –	– –	– –	– –	– –	3 –	– –	– –	– –	3 –
24 Wolverhampton W.	2 –	– –	– –	1 –	– –	– –	– –	– –	– –	3 –
25 Leicester City	2 (1) 4	– –	– –	– –	– –	– –	– –	– –	– –	2 (1) 4
26 Sparta Prague	– –	– –	– –	– –	– –	2 4	– –	– –	– –	2 4
27 Olympique Lyonnais	– –	– –	– –	– –	– –	2 3	– –	– –	– –	2 3
28 Glasgow Rangers	– –	– –	– –	– –	– –	2 2	– –	– –	– –	2 2
29 Nantes Atlantique	– –	– –	– –	– –	– –	2 2	– –	– –	– –	2 2
30 Real Madrid	– –	– –	– –	– –	– –	2 2	– –	– –	– –	2 2
31 Stuttgart	– –	– –	– –	– –	– –	2 2	– –	– –	– –	2 2
32 Zalaegerszeg	– –	– –	– –	– –	– –	2 2	– –	– –	– –	2 2
33 Bayern Munich	– –	– –	– –	– –	– –	2 1	– –	– –	– –	2 1
34 Benfica	– –	– –	– –	– –	– –	2 1	– –	– –	– –	2 1
35 Debreceni	– –	– –	– –	– –	– –	2 1	– –	– –	– –	2 1
36 Derby County	2 1	– –	– –	– –	– –	– –	– –	– –	– –	2 1
37 Olympiakos Piraeus	– –	– –	– –	– –	– –	2 1	– –	– –	– –	2 1
38 Porto	– –	– –	– –	– –	– –	2 –	– –	– –	– –	2 –
39 Villarreal	– –	– –	– –	– –	– –	2 –	– –	– –	– –	2 –
40 Juventus	– –	– –	– –	– –	– –	1 (1) 2	– –	– –	– –	1 (1) 2
41 Wigan Athletic	1 (1) 1	– –	– –	– –	– –	– –	– –	– –	– –	1 (1) 1
42 AC Milan	– –	– –	– –	– –	– –	1 (1) –	– –	– –	– –	1 (1) –
43 Basel	– –	– –	– –	– –	– –	1 2	– –	– –	– –	1 2
44 Boavista	– –	– –	– –	– –	– –	1 2	– –	– –	– –	1 2
45 Millwall	– –	– –	– –	1 2	– –	– –	– –	– –	– –	1 2
46 Fenerbahce	– –	– –	– –	– –	– –	1 1	– –	– –	– –	1 1
47 Ipswich Town	1 1	– –	– –	– –	– –	– –	– –	– –	– –	1 1
48 Maccabi Haifa	– –	– –	– –	– –	– –	1 1	– –	– –	– –	1 1
49 Burnley	– –	– –	– –	– –	1 –	– –	– –	– –	– –	1 –
50 Crystal Palace	1 –	– –	– –	– –	– –	– –	– –	– –	– –	1 –
51 Panathinaikos	– –	– –	– –	– –	– –	1 –	– –	– –	– –	1 –
52 Norwich City	– (1) –	– –	– –	– –	– –	– –	– –	– –	– –	– (1) –

JUAN-SEBASTIAN VERON

DEBUT (Full Appearance)

Sunday 19/08/2001
FA Premiership
at Old Trafford

Manchester United 3 Fulham 2

CLUB CAREER RECORD	Apps	Subs	Goals
Premiership	45	(6)	7
League Division 1	0		0
League Division 2	0		0
FA Cup	2		0
League Cup	4	(1)	0
European Cup / Champions League	24		4
European Cup-Winners' Cup	0		0
UEFA Cup / Inter-Cities' Fairs Cup	0		0
Other Matches	0		0
OVERALL TOTAL	**75**	**(7)**	**11**

Opponents	PREM			FLD 1			FLD 2			FAC			LC			EC/CL			ECWC			UEFA			OTHER			TOTAL		
	A	S	G	A	S	G	A	S	G	A	S	G	A	S	G	A	S	G	A	S	G	A	S	G	A	S	G	A	S	G
1 Olympiakos Piraeus	–	–	–	–	–	–	–	–	–	–	–	–	–	–	–	4		2	–	–	–	–	–	–	–	–	–	4		2
2 Bayer Leverkusen	–	–	–	–	–	–	–	–	–	–	–	–	–	–	–	4		1	–	–	–	–	–	–	–	–	–	4		1
3 Aston Villa	3	–	–	–	–	–	–	–	–	1	–	–	–	–	–	–	–	–	–	–	–	–	–	–	–	–	–	4		–
4 Blackburn Rovers	2	–	–	–	–	–	–	–	–	–	–	–	2	–	–	–	–	–	–	–	–	–	–	–	–	–	–	4		–
5 Deportivo La Coruna	–	–	–	–	–	–	–	–	–	–	–	–	–	–	–	4		–	–	–	–	–	–	–	–	–	–	4		–
6 Middlesbrough	4	–	–	–	–	–	–	–	–	–	–	–	–	–	–	–	–	–	–	–	–	–	–	–	–	–	–	4		–
7 Southampton	4	–	–	–	–	–	–	–	–	–	–	–	–	–	–	–	–	–	–	–	–	–	–	–	–	–	–	4		–
8 Chelsea	1 (2)	–	–	–	–	–	–	–	–	–	–	–	1	–	–	–	–	–	–	–	–	–	–	–	–	–	–	2 (2)		–
9 Arsenal	3		1	–	–	–	–	–	–	–	–	–	–	–	–	–	–	–	–	–	–	–	–	–	–	–	–	3		1
10 Bolton Wanderers	3		1	–	–	–	–	–	–	–	–	–	–	–	–	–	–	–	–	–	–	–	–	–	–	–	–	3		1
11 Everton	3		1	–	–	–	–	–	–	–	–	–	–	–	–	–	–	–	–	–	–	–	–	–	–	–	–	3		1
12 Tottenham Hotspur	3		1	–	–	–	–	–	–	–	–	–	–	–	–	–	–	–	–	–	–	–	–	–	–	–	–	3		1
13 West Ham United	2		1	–	–	–	–	–	–	1	–	–	–	–	–	–	–	–	–	–	–	–	–	–	–	–	–	3		1
14 Liverpool	2	–	–	–	–	–	–	–	–	–	–	–	1	–	–	–	–	–	–	–	–	–	–	–	–	–	–	3		–
15 Newcastle United	2 (1)		1	–	–	–	–	–	–	–	–	–	–	–	–	–	–	–	–	–	–	–	–	–	–	–	–	2 (1)		1
16 Derby County	2		1	–	–	–	–	–	–	–	–	–	–	–	–	–	–	–	–	–	–	–	–	–	–	–	–	2		1
17 Bayern Munich	–	–	–	–	–	–	–	–	–	–	–	–	–	–	–	2		–	–	–	–	–	–	–	–	–	–	2		–
18 Birmingham City	2	–	–	–	–	–	–	–	–	–	–	–	–	–	–	–	–	–	–	–	–	–	–	–	–	–	–	2		–
19 Fulham	2	–	–	–	–	–	–	–	–	–	–	–	–	–	–	–	–	–	–	–	–	–	–	–	–	–	–	2		–
20 Leeds United	2	–	–	–	–	–	–	–	–	–	–	–	–	–	–	–	–	–	–	–	–	–	–	–	–	–	–	2		–
21 Manchester City	2	–	–	–	–	–	–	–	–	–	–	–	–	–	–	–	–	–	–	–	–	–	–	–	–	–	–	2		–
22 Nantes Atlantique	–	–	–	–	–	–	–	–	–	–	–	–	–	–	–	2		–	–	–	–	–	–	–	–	–	–	2		–
23 Sunderland	2	–	–	–	–	–	–	–	–	–	–	–	–	–	–	–	–	–	–	–	–	–	–	–	–	–	–	2		–
24 Zalaegerszeg	–	–	–	–	–	–	–	–	–	–	–	–	–	–	–	2		–	–	–	–	–	–	–	–	–	–	2		–
25 Charlton Athletic	– (2)	–	–	–	–	–	–	–	–	–	–	–	–	–	–	–	–	–	–	–	–	–	–	–	–	–	–	– (2)		–
26 Maccabi Haifa	–	–	–	–	–	–	–	–	–	–	–	–	–	–	–	1		1	–	–	–	–	–	–	–	–	–	1		1
27 Basel	–	–	–	–	–	–	–	–	–	–	–	–	–	–	–	1		–	–	–	–	–	–	–	–	–	–	1		–
28 Boavista	–	–	–	–	–	–	–	–	–	–	–	–	–	–	–	1		–	–	–	–	–	–	–	–	–	–	1		–
29 Juventus	–	–	–	–	–	–	–	–	–	–	–	–	–	–	–	1		–	–	–	–	–	–	–	–	–	–	1		–
30 Lille Metropole	–	–	–	–	–	–	–	–	–	–	–	–	–	–	–	1		–	–	–	–	–	–	–	–	–	–	1		–
31 Real Madrid	–	–	–	–	–	–	–	–	–	–	–	–	–	–	–	1		–	–	–	–	–	–	–	–	–	–	1		–
32 West Bromwich Albion	1	–	–	–	–	–	–	–	–	–	–	–	–	–	–	–	–	–	–	–	–	–	–	–	–	–	–	1		–
33 Ipswich Town	– (1)	–	–	–	–	–	–	–	–	–	–	–	–	–	–	–	–	–	–	–	–	–	–	–	–	–	–	– (1)		–
34 Leicester City	–	–	–	–	–	–	–	–	–	–	–	–	– (1)	–	–	–	–	–	–	–	–	–	–	–	–	–	–	– (1)		–

NEMANJA VIDIC

DEBUT (Substitute Appearance)

Wednesday 25/01/2006
League Cup Semi-Final 2nd Leg
at Old Trafford

Manchester United 2 Blackburn Rovers 1

CLUB CAREER RECORD	Apps	Subs	Goals
Premiership	66	(2)	4
League Division 1	0		0
League Division 2	0		0
FA Cup	10		0
League Cup	0	(2)	0
European Cup / Champions League	17		1
European Cup-Winners' Cup	0		0
UEFA Cup / Inter-Cities' Fairs Cup	0		0
Other Matches	1		0
OVERALL TOTAL	**94**	**(4)**	**5**

Opponents	PREM			FLD 1			FLD 2			FAC			LC			EC/CL			ECWC			UEFA			OTHER			TOTAL		
	A	S	G	A	S	G	A	S	G	A	S	G	A	S	G	A	S	G	A	S	G	A	S	G	A	S	G	A	S	G
1 Chelsea	4	-	-	-	-	-	-	-	-	1	-	-	-	-	-	1	-	-	-	-	-	-	-	-	1	-	-	7	-	
2 Portsmouth	4	1	-	-	-	-	2	-	-	-	-	-	-	-	-	-	-	-	-	-	-	-	-	-	-	-	-	6	1	
3 Blackburn Rovers	5	-	-	-	-	-	-	-	-	-	-	-	-	(1)	-	-	-	-	-	-	-	-	-	-	-	-	-	5	(1)	-
4 Liverpool	4	-	-	-	-	-	-	-	-	1	-	-	-	-	-	-	-	-	-	-	-	-	-	-	-	-	-	5	-	
5 Wigan Athletic	4	1	-	-	-	-	-	-	-	-	-	-	-	(1)	-	-	-	-	-	-	-	-	-	-	-	-	-	4	(1)	1
6 Tottenham Hotspur	4	1	-	-	-	-	-	-	-	-	-	-	-	-	-	-	-	-	-	-	-	-	-	-	-	-	-	4	1	
7 Arsenal	3	-	-	-	-	-	-	-	-	-	-	-	1	-	-	-	-	-	-	-	-	-	-	-	-	-	-	4	-	
8 Aston Villa	3	-	-	-	-	-	-	-	-	-	-	-	1	-	-	-	-	-	-	-	-	-	-	-	-	-	-	4	-	
9 Bolton Wanderers	4	-	-	-	-	-	-	-	-	-	-	-	-	-	-	-	-	-	-	-	-	-	-	-	-	-	-	4	-	
10 Manchester City	4	-	-	-	-	-	-	-	-	-	-	-	-	-	-	-	-	-	-	-	-	-	-	-	-	-	-	4	-	
11 Middlesbrough	2	-	-	-	-	-	-	-	-	2	-	-	-	-	-	-	-	-	-	-	-	-	-	-	-	-	-	4	-	
12 Newcastle United	4	-	-	-	-	-	-	-	-	-	-	-	-	-	-	-	-	-	-	-	-	-	-	-	-	-	-	4	-	
13 Reading	3	-	-	-	-	-	-	-	-	1	-	-	-	-	-	-	-	-	-	-	-	-	-	-	-	-	-	4	-	
14 Birmingham City	3	-	-	-	-	-	-	-	-	-	-	-	-	-	-	-	-	-	-	-	-	-	-	-	-	-	-	3	-	
15 West Ham United	3	-	-	-	-	-	-	-	-	-	-	-	-	-	-	-	-	-	-	-	-	-	-	-	-	-	-	3	-	
16 Fulham	2	(1)	-	-	-	-	-	-	-	-	-	-	-	-	-	-	-	-	-	-	-	-	-	-	-	-	-	2	(1)	-
17 Benfica	-	-	-	-	-	-	-	-	-	-	-	-	-	-	-	2	-	1	-	-	-	-	-	-	-	-	-	2	-	1
18 Everton	2	1	-	-	-	-	-	-	-	-	-	-	-	-	-	-	-	-	-	-	-	-	-	-	-	-	-	2	-	1
19 Copenhagen	-	-	-	-	-	-	-	-	-	-	-	-	-	-	-	2	-	-	-	-	-	-	-	-	-	-	-	2	-	
20 Derby County	2	-	-	-	-	-	-	-	-	-	-	-	-	-	-	-	-	-	-	-	-	-	-	-	-	-	-	2	-	
21 Dynamo Kiev	-	-	-	-	-	-	-	-	-	-	-	-	-	-	-	2	-	-	-	-	-	-	-	-	-	-	-	2	-	
22 Lille Metropole	-	-	-	-	-	-	-	-	-	-	-	-	-	-	-	2	-	-	-	-	-	-	-	-	-	-	-	2	-	
23 Olympique Lyonnais	-	-	-	-	-	-	-	-	-	-	-	-	-	-	-	2	-	-	-	-	-	-	-	-	-	-	-	2	-	
24 Roma	-	-	-	-	-	-	-	-	-	-	-	-	-	-	-	2	-	-	-	-	-	-	-	-	-	-	-	2	-	
25 Sporting Lisbon	-	-	-	-	-	-	-	-	-	-	-	-	-	-	-	2	-	-	-	-	-	-	-	-	-	-	-	2	-	
26 Sunderland	2	-	-	-	-	-	-	-	-	-	-	-	-	-	-	-	-	-	-	-	-	-	-	-	-	-	-	2	-	
27 Charlton Athletic	1	(1)	-	-	-	-	-	-	-	-	-	-	-	-	-	-	-	-	-	-	-	-	-	-	-	-	-	1	(1)	-
28 AC Milan	-	-	-	-	-	-	-	-	-	-	-	-	-	-	-	1	-	-	-	-	-	-	-	-	-	-	-	1	-	
29 Glasgow Celtic	-	-	-	-	-	-	-	-	-	-	-	-	-	-	-	1	-	-	-	-	-	-	-	-	-	-	-	1	-	
30 Sheffield United	1	-	-	-	-	-	-	-	-	-	-	-	-	-	-	-	-	-	-	-	-	-	-	-	-	-	-	1	-	
31 Watford	1	-	-	-	-	-	-	-	-	-	-	-	-	-	-	-	-	-	-	-	-	-	-	-	-	-	-	1	-	
32 West Bromwich Albion	1	-	-	-	-	-	-	-	-	-	-	-	-	-	-	-	-	-	-	-	-	-	-	-	-	-	-	1	-	
33 Wolverhampton W.	-	-	-	-	-	-	-	-	-	1	-	-	-	-	-	-	-	-	-	-	-	-	-	-	-	-	-	1	-	

ERNEST VINCENT

DEBUT (Full Appearance)

Saturday 06/02/1932
Football League Division 2
at Saltergate

Chesterfield 1 Manchester United 3

CLUB CAREER RECORD	Apps	Subs	Goals
Premiership	0		0
League Division 1	0		0
League Division 2	64		1
FA Cup	1		0
League Cup	0		0
European Cup / Champions League	0		0
European Cup-Winners' Cup	0		0
UEFA Cup / Inter-Cities' Fairs Cup	0		0
Other Matches	0		0
OVERALL TOTAL	**65**		**1**

Opponents	PREM			FLD 1			FLD 2			FAC			LC			EC/CL			ECWC			UEFA			OTHER			TOTAL		
	A	S	G	A	S	G	A	S	G	A	S	G	A	S	G	A	S	G	A	S	G	A	S	G	A	S	G	A	S	G
1 Notts County	-	-	-	-	5	-	-	-	-	-	-	-	-	-	-	-	-	-	-	-	-	-	-	-	-	-	-	5	-	
2 Port Vale	-	-	-	-	5	-	-	-	-	-	-	-	-	-	-	-	-	-	-	-	-	-	-	-	-	-	-	5	-	
3 Bradford City	-	-	-	-	4	-	-	-	-	-	-	-	-	-	-	-	-	-	-	-	-	-	-	-	-	-	-	4	-	
4 Charlton Athletic	-	-	-	-	4	-	-	-	-	-	-	-	-	-	-	-	-	-	-	-	-	-	-	-	-	-	-	4	-	
5 Bradford Park Avenue	-	-	-	-	3	1	-	-	-	-	-	-	-	-	-	-	-	-	-	-	-	-	-	-	-	-	-	3	-	1
6 Burnley	-	-	-	-	3	-	-	-	-	-	-	-	-	-	-	-	-	-	-	-	-	-	-	-	-	-	-	3	-	
7 Bury	-	-	-	-	3	-	-	-	-	-	-	-	-	-	-	-	-	-	-	-	-	-	-	-	-	-	-	3	-	
8 Chesterfield	-	-	-	-	3	-	-	-	-	-	-	-	-	-	-	-	-	-	-	-	-	-	-	-	-	-	-	3	-	
9 Lincoln City	-	-	-	-	3	-	-	-	-	-	-	-	-	-	-	-	-	-	-	-	-	-	-	-	-	-	-	3	-	
10 Millwall	-	-	-	-	3	-	-	-	-	-	-	-	-	-	-	-	-	-	-	-	-	-	-	-	-	-	-	3	-	
11 Oldham Athletic	-	-	-	-	3	-	-	-	-	-	-	-	-	-	-	-	-	-	-	-	-	-	-	-	-	-	-	3	-	
12 Plymouth Argyle	-	-	-	-	3	-	-	-	-	-	-	-	-	-	-	-	-	-	-	-	-	-	-	-	-	-	-	3	-	
13 Preston North End	-	-	-	-	3	-	-	-	-	-	-	-	-	-	-	-	-	-	-	-	-	-	-	-	-	-	-	3	-	
14 Southampton	-	-	-	-	3	-	-	-	-	-	-	-	-	-	-	-	-	-	-	-	-	-	-	-	-	-	-	3	-	
15 Fulham	-	-	-	-	2	-	-	-	-	-	-	-	-	-	-	-	-	-	-	-	-	-	-	-	-	-	-	2	-	
16 Nottingham Forest	-	-	-	-	2	-	-	-	-	-	-	-	-	-	-	-	-	-	-	-	-	-	-	-	-	-	-	2	-	
17 Stoke City	-	-	-	-	2	-	-	-	-	-	-	-	-	-	-	-	-	-	-	-	-	-	-	-	-	-	-	2	-	
18 Swansea City	-	-	-	-	2	-	-	-	-	-	-	-	-	-	-	-	-	-	-	-	-	-	-	-	-	-	-	2	-	

continued../

ERNEST VINCENT (continued)

Opponents	PREM			FLD 1			FLD 2			FAC			LC			EC/CL			ECWC			UEFA			OTHER			TOTAL		
	A	S	G	A	S	G	A	S	G	A	S	G	A	S	G	A	S	G	A	S	G	A	S	G	A	S	G	A	S	G
19 West Ham United	–	–		–	–		–	–		2	–		–	–		–	–		–	–		–	–		–	–		2	–	
20 Barnsley	–	–		–	–		1	–		–	–		–	–		–	–		–	–		–	–		–	–		1	–	
21 Bolton Wanderers	–	–		–	–		1	–		–	–		–	–		–	–		–	–		–	–		–	–		1	–	
22 Bristol City	–	–		–	–		1	–		–	–		–	–		–	–		–	–		–	–		–	–		1	–	
23 Grimsby Town	–	–		–	–		1	–		–	–		–	–		–	–		–	–		–	–		–	–		1	–	
24 Leeds United	–	–		–	–		1	–		–	–		–	–		–	–		–	–		–	–		–	–		1	–	
25 Middlesbrough	–	–		–	–		–	–		–	–		1	–		–	–		–	–		–	–		–	–		1	–	
26 Tottenham Hotspur	–	–		–	–		1	–		–	–		–	–		–	–		–	–		–	–		–	–		1	–	

DENNIS VIOLLET

DEBUT (Full Appearance)

Saturday 11/04/1953
Football League Division 1
at St James' Park

Newcastle United 1 Manchester United 2

CLUB CAREER RECORD	Apps	Subs	Goals
Premiership	0		0
League Division 1	259		159
League Division 2	0		0
FA Cup	18		5
League Cup	2		1
European Cup / Champions League	12		13
European Cup-Winners' Cup	0		0
UEFA Cup / Inter-Cities' Fairs Cup	0		0
Other Matches	2		1
OVERALL TOTAL	293		179

Opponents	PREM			FLD 1			FLD 2			FAC			LC			EC/CL			ECWC			UEFA			OTHER			TOTAL		
	A	S	G	A	S	G	A	S	G	A	S	G	A	S	G	A	S	G	A	S	G	A	S	G	A	S	G	A	S	G
1 Blackpool	–		–	15		13	–		–	–		–	–		–	–		–	–		–	–		–	–		–	15		13
2 Chelsea	–		–	15		8	–		–	–		–	–		–	–		–	–		–	–		–	–		–	15		8
3 Manchester City	–		–	13		6	–		–	1		–	–		–	–		–	–		–	–		–	1		1	15		7
4 Arsenal	–		–	15		6	–		–	–		–	–		–	–		–	–		–	–		–	–		–	15		6
5 West Bromwich Albion	–		–	14		11	–		–	–		–	–		–	–		–	–		–	–		–	–		–	14		11
6 Newcastle United	–		–	13		7	–		–	–		–	–		–	–		–	–		–	–		–	–		–	13		7
7 Sheffield Wednesday	–		–	10		11	–		–	2		–	–		–	–		–	–		–	–		–	–		–	12		11
8 Birmingham City	–		–	11		9	–		–	1		–	–		–	–		–	–		–	–		–	–		–	12		9
9 Burnley	–		–	10		11	–		–	1		1	–		–	–		–	–		–	–		–	–		–	11		12
10 Preston North End	–		–	11		8	–		–	–		–	–		–	–		–	–		–	–		–	–		–	11		8
11 Portsmouth	–		–	11		6	–		–	–		–	–		–	–		–	–		–	–		–	–		–	11		6
12 Cardiff City	–		–	11		5	–		–	–		–	–		–	–		–	–		–	–		–	–		–	11		5
13 Tottenham Hotspur	–		–	11		3	–		–	–		–	–		–	–		–	–		–	–		–	–		–	11		3
14 Aston Villa	–		–	9		4	–		–	–		–	–		–	–		–	–		–	1		–	–		–	10		4
15 Bolton Wanderers	–		–	9		3	–		–	1		–	–		–	–		–	–		–	–		–	–		–	10		3
16 Wolverhampton W.	–		–	10		3	–		–	–		–	–		–	–		–	–		–	–		–	–		–	10		3
17 Leicester City	–		–	9		7	–		–	–		–	–		–	–		–	–		–	–		–	–		–	9		7
18 Everton	–		–	8		3	–		–	1		–	–		–	–		–	–		–	–		–	–		–	9		3
19 Charlton Athletic	–		–	7		4	–		–	–		–	–		–	–		–	–		–	–		–	–		–	7		4
20 Luton Town	–		–	7		4	–		–	–		–	–		–	–		–	–		–	–		–	–		–	7		4
21 Nottingham Forest	–		–	6		6	–		–	–		–	–		–	–		–	–		–	–		–	–		–	6		6
22 Leeds United	–		–	5		6	–		–	–		–	–		–	–		–	–		–	–		–	–		–	5		6
23 Blackburn Rovers	–		–	5		2	–		–	–		–	–		–	–		–	–		–	–		–	–		–	5		2
24 Huddersfield Town	–		–	5		2	–		–	–		–	–		–	–		–	–		–	–		–	–		–	5		2
25 Sheffield United	–		–	5		2	–		–	–		–	–		–	–		–	–		–	–		–	–		–	5		2
26 West Ham United	–		–	5		2	–		–	–		–	–		–	–		–	–		–	–		–	–		–	5		2
27 Sunderland	–		–	4		2	–		–	–		–	–		–	–		–	–		–	–		–	–		–	4		2
28 Fulham	–		–	3		4	–		–	–		–	–		–	–		–	–		–	–		–	–		–	3		4
29 Anderlecht	–		–	–		–	–		–	–		–	–		–	2		5	–		–	–		–	–		–	2		5
30 Athletic Bilbao	–		–	–		–	–		–	–		–	–		–	2		2	–		–	–		–	–		–	2		2
31 Shamrock Rovers	–		–	–		–	–		–	–		–	–		–	2		2	–		–	–		–	–		–	2		2
32 AC Milan	–		–	–		–	–		–	–		–	–		–	2		1	–		–	–		–	–		–	2		1
33 Liverpool	–		–	1		1	–		–	1		–	–		–	–		–	–		–	–		–	–		–	2		1
34 Reading	–		–	–		–	–		–	2		1	–		–	–		–	–		–	–		–	–		–	2		1
35 Red Star Belgrade	–		–	–		–	–		–	–		–	–		–	2		1	–		–	–		–	–		–	2		1
36 Workington	–		–	–		–	–		–	1		3	–		–	–		–	–		–	–		–	–		–	1		3
37 Borussia Dortmund	–		–	–		–	–		–	–		–	–		–	1		2	–		–	–		–	–		–	1		2
38 Bradford City	–		–	–		–	–		–	–		–	1		1	–		–	–		–	–		–	–		–	1		1
39 Bournemouth	–		–	–		–	–		–	1		–	–		–	–		–	–		–	–		–	–		–	1		–
40 Bristol Rovers	–		–	–		–	–		–	1		–	–		–	–		–	–		–	–		–	–		–	1		–
41 Derby County	–		–	–		–	–		–	1		–	–		–	–		–	–		–	–		–	–		–	1		–
42 Exeter City	–		–	–		–	–		–	–		–	1		–	–		–	–		–	–		–	–		–	1		–
43 Hartlepool United	–		–	–		–	–		–	1		–	–		–	–		–	–		–	–		–	–		–	1		–
44 Ipswich Town	–		–	–		–	–		–	1		–	–		–	–		–	–		–	–		–	–		–	1		–
45 Middlesbrough	–		–	1		–	–		–	–		–	–		–	–		–	–		–	–		–	–		–	1		–
46 Norwich City	–		–	–		–	–		–	1		–	–		–	–		–	–		–	–		–	–		–	1		–
47 Real Madrid	–		–	–		–	–		–	–		–	–		–	1		–	–		–	–		–	–		–	1		–
48 Wrexham	–		–	–		–	–		–	1		–	–		–	–		–	–		–	–		–	–		–	1		–

GEORGE VOSE

DEBUT (Full Appearance)

Saturday 26/08/1933
Football League Division 2
at Home Park

Plymouth Argyle 4 Manchester United 0

CLUB CAREER RECORD	Apps	Subs	Goals
Premiership	0		0
League Division 1	65		0
League Division 2	130		1
FA Cup	14		0
League Cup	0		0
European Cup / Champions League	0		0
European Cup–Winners' Cup	0		0
UEFA Cup / Inter-Cities' Fairs Cup	0		0
Other Matches	0		0
OVERALL TOTAL	**209**		**1**

Opponents	PREM			FLD 1			FLD 2			FAC			LC			EC/CL			ECWC			UEFA			OTHER			TOTAL		
	A	S	G	A	S	G	A	S	G	A	S	G	A	S	G	A	S	G	A	S	G	A	S	G	A	S	G	A	S	G
1 Nottingham Forest	–	–	–	–	–	–	8	–	–	2	–	–	–	–	–	–	–	–	–	–	–	–	–	–	–	–	–	10	–	–
2 Plymouth Argyle	–	–	–	–	–	–	8	–	–	–	–	–	–	–	–	–	–	–	–	–	–	–	–	–	–	–	–	8	–	–
3 Barnsley	–	–	–	–	–	–	5	–	–	2	–	–	–	–	–	–	–	–	–	–	–	–	–	–	–	–	–	7	–	–
4 Brentford	–	–	–	4	–	–	2	–	–	1	–	–	–	–	–	–	–	–	–	–	–	–	–	–	–	–	–	7	–	–
5 Blackpool	–	–	–	2	–	–	4	–	–	–	–	–	–	–	–	–	–	–	–	–	–	–	–	–	–	–	–	6	–	–
6 Bradford Park Avenue	–	–	–	–	–	–	6	–	–	–	–	–	–	–	–	–	–	–	–	–	–	–	–	–	–	–	–	6	–	–
7 Burnley	–	–	–	–	–	–	6	–	–	–	–	–	–	–	–	–	–	–	–	–	–	–	–	–	–	–	–	6	–	–
8 Fulham	–	–	–	–	–	–	6	–	–	–	–	–	–	–	–	–	–	–	–	–	–	–	–	–	–	–	–	6	–	–
9 Norwich City	–	–	–	–	–	–	6	–	–	–	–	–	–	–	–	–	–	–	–	–	–	–	–	–	–	–	–	6	–	–
10 Portsmouth	–	–	–	4	–	–	–	–	–	2	–	–	–	–	–	–	–	–	–	–	–	–	–	–	–	–	–	6	–	–
11 Sheffield United	–	–	–	–	–	–	6	–	–	–	–	–	–	–	–	–	–	–	–	–	–	–	–	–	–	–	–	6	–	–
12 Swansea City	–	–	–	–	–	–	6	–	–	–	–	–	–	–	–	–	–	–	–	–	–	–	–	–	–	–	–	6	–	–
13 Grimsby Town	–	–	–	3	–	–	2	–	1	–	–	–	–	–	–	–	–	–	–	–	–	–	–	–	–	–	–	5	–	1
14 Bradford City	–	–	–	–	–	–	5	–	–	–	–	–	–	–	–	–	–	–	–	–	–	–	–	–	–	–	–	5	–	–
15 Bury	–	–	–	–	–	–	5	–	–	–	–	–	–	–	–	–	–	–	–	–	–	–	–	–	–	–	–	5	–	–
16 Charlton Athletic	–	–	–	3	–	–	2	–	–	–	–	–	–	–	–	–	–	–	–	–	–	–	–	–	–	–	–	5	–	–
17 Hull City	–	–	–	–	–	–	5	–	–	–	–	–	–	–	–	–	–	–	–	–	–	–	–	–	–	–	–	5	–	–
18 Newcastle United	–	–	–	–	–	–	5	–	–	–	–	–	–	–	–	–	–	–	–	–	–	–	–	–	–	–	–	5	–	–
19 Southampton	–	–	–	–	–	–	5	–	–	–	–	–	–	–	–	–	–	–	–	–	–	–	–	–	–	–	–	5	–	–
20 Stoke City	–	–	–	3	–	–	–	–	–	2	–	–	–	–	–	–	–	–	–	–	–	–	–	–	–	–	–	5	–	–
21 West Ham United	–	–	–	–	–	–	5	–	–	–	–	–	–	–	–	–	–	–	–	–	–	–	–	–	–	–	–	5	–	–
22 Arsenal	–	–	–	4	–	–	–	–	–	–	–	–	–	–	–	–	–	–	–	–	–	–	–	–	–	–	–	4	–	–
23 Aston Villa	–	–	–	2	–	–	2	–	–	–	–	–	–	–	–	–	–	–	–	–	–	–	–	–	–	–	–	4	–	–
24 Birmingham City	–	–	–	4	–	–	–	–	–	–	–	–	–	–	–	–	–	–	–	–	–	–	–	–	–	–	–	4	–	–
25 Bolton Wanderers	–	–	–	2	–	–	2	–	–	–	–	–	–	–	–	–	–	–	–	–	–	–	–	–	–	–	–	4	–	–
26 Chelsea	–	–	–	4	–	–	–	–	–	–	–	–	–	–	–	–	–	–	–	–	–	–	–	–	–	–	–	4	–	–
27 Huddersfield Town	–	–	–	4	–	–	–	–	–	–	–	–	–	–	–	–	–	–	–	–	–	–	–	–	–	–	–	4	–	–
28 Leicester City	–	–	–	2	–	–	2	–	–	–	–	–	–	–	–	–	–	–	–	–	–	–	–	–	–	–	–	4	–	–
29 Port Vale	–	–	–	–	–	–	4	–	–	–	–	–	–	–	–	–	–	–	–	–	–	–	–	–	–	–	–	4	–	–
30 Preston North End	–	–	–	3	–	–	1	–	–	–	–	–	–	–	–	–	–	–	–	–	–	–	–	–	–	–	–	4	–	–
31 Tottenham Hotspur	–	–	–	–	–	–	4	–	–	–	–	–	–	–	–	–	–	–	–	–	–	–	–	–	–	–	–	4	–	–
32 Derby County	–	–	–	3	–	–	–	–	–	–	–	–	–	–	–	–	–	–	–	–	–	–	–	–	–	–	–	3	–	–
33 Middlesbrough	–	–	–	3	–	–	–	–	–	–	–	–	–	–	–	–	–	–	–	–	–	–	–	–	–	–	–	3	–	–
34 Oldham Athletic	–	–	–	–	–	–	3	–	–	–	–	–	–	–	–	–	–	–	–	–	–	–	–	–	–	–	–	3	–	–
35 Sheffield Wednesday	–	–	–	1	–	–	2	–	–	–	–	–	–	–	–	–	–	–	–	–	–	–	–	–	–	–	–	3	–	–
36 Wolverhampton W.	–	–	–	3	–	–	–	–	–	–	–	–	–	–	–	–	–	–	–	–	–	–	–	–	–	–	–	3	–	–
37 Chesterfield	–	–	–	–	–	–	2	–	–	–	–	–	–	–	–	–	–	–	–	–	–	–	–	–	–	–	–	2	–	–
38 Coventry City	–	–	–	–	–	–	2	–	–	–	–	–	–	–	–	–	–	–	–	–	–	–	–	–	–	–	–	2	–	–
39 Doncaster Rovers	–	–	–	–	–	–	2	–	–	–	–	–	–	–	–	–	–	–	–	–	–	–	–	–	–	–	–	2	–	–
40 Everton	–	–	–	2	–	–	–	–	–	–	–	–	–	–	–	–	–	–	–	–	–	–	–	–	–	–	–	2	–	–
41 Leeds United	–	–	–	2	–	–	–	–	–	–	–	–	–	–	–	–	–	–	–	–	–	–	–	–	–	–	–	2	–	–
42 Liverpool	–	–	–	2	–	–	–	–	–	–	–	–	–	–	–	–	–	–	–	–	–	–	–	–	–	–	–	2	–	–
43 Luton Town	–	–	–	–	–	–	2	–	–	–	–	–	–	–	–	–	–	–	–	–	–	–	–	–	–	–	–	2	–	–
44 Manchester City	–	–	–	2	–	–	–	–	–	–	–	–	–	–	–	–	–	–	–	–	–	–	–	–	–	–	–	2	–	–
45 Notts County	–	–	–	–	–	–	2	–	–	–	–	–	–	–	–	–	–	–	–	–	–	–	–	–	–	–	–	2	–	–
46 Reading	–	–	–	–	–	–	–	–	–	2	–	–	–	–	–	–	–	–	–	–	–	–	–	–	–	–	–	2	–	–
47 Sunderland	–	–	–	2	–	–	–	–	–	–	–	–	–	–	–	–	–	–	–	–	–	–	–	–	–	–	–	2	–	–
48 West Bromwich Albion	–	–	–	1	–	–	–	–	–	1	–	–	–	–	–	–	–	–	–	–	–	–	–	–	–	–	–	2	–	–
49 Blackburn Rovers	–	–	–	–	–	–	1	–	–	–	–	–	–	–	–	–	–	–	–	–	–	–	–	–	–	–	–	1	–	–
50 Bristol Rovers	–	–	–	–	–	–	–	–	–	1	–	–	–	–	–	–	–	–	–	–	–	–	–	–	–	–	–	1	–	–
51 Millwall	–	–	–	–	–	–	1	–	–	–	–	–	–	–	–	–	–	–	–	–	–	–	–	–	–	–	–	1	–	–
52 Stockport County	–	–	–	–	–	–	1	–	–	–	–	–	–	–	–	–	–	–	–	–	–	–	–	–	–	–	–	1	–	–
53 Yeovil Town	–	–	–	–	–	–	–	–	–	1	–	–	–	–	–	–	–	–	–	–	–	–	–	–	–	–	–	1	–	–

COLIN WALDRON

DEBUT (Full Appearance)

Monday 04/10/1976
League Cup 3rd Round Replay
at Roker Park

Sunderland 2 Manchester United 2

CLUB CAREER RECORD	Apps	Subs	Goals
Premiership	0		0
League Division 1	3		0
League Division 2	0		0
FA Cup	0		0
League Cup	1		0
European Cup / Champions League	0		0
European Cup–Winners' Cup	0		0
UEFA Cup / Inter-Cities' Fairs Cup	0		0
Other Matches	0		0
OVERALL TOTAL	**4**		**0**

Opponents	PREM			FLD 1			FLD 2			FAC			LC			EC/CL			ECWC			UEFA			OTHER			TOTAL		
	A	S	G	A	S	G	A	S	G	A	S	G	A	S	G	A	S	G	A	S	G	A	S	G	A	S	G	A	S	G
1 Sunderland	–	–		1	–		–	–		–	–		1	–		–	–		–	–		–	–		–	–		2	–	
2 Norwich City	–	–		1	–		–	–		–	–		–	–		–	–		–	–		–	–		–	–		1	–	
3 West Bromwich Albion	–	–		1	–		–	–		–	–		–	–		–	–		–	–		–	–		–	–		1	–	

DENNIS WALKER

DEBUT (Full Appearance)

Monday 20/05/1963
Football League Division 1
at City Ground

Nottingham Forest 3 Manchester United 2

CLUB CAREER RECORD	Apps	Subs	Goals
Premiership	0		0
League Division 1	1		0
League Division 2	0		0
FA Cup	0		0
League Cup	0		0
European Cup / Champions League	0		0
European Cup–Winners' Cup	0		0
UEFA Cup / Inter-Cities' Fairs Cup	0		0
Other Matches	0		0
OVERALL TOTAL	**1**		**0**

Opponents	PREM			FLD 1			FLD 2			FAC			LC			EC/CL			ECWC			UEFA			OTHER			TOTAL		
	A	S	G	A	S	G	A	S	G	A	S	G	A	S	G	A	S	G	A	S	G	A	S	G	A	S	G	A	S	G
1 Nottingham Forest	–	–		1	–		–	–		–	–		–	–		–	–		–	–		–	–		–	–		1	–	

ROBERT WALKER

DEBUT (Full Appearance)

Saturday 14/01/1899
Football League Division 2
at Bank Street

Newton Heath 3 Glossop 0

CLUB CAREER RECORD	Apps	Subs	Goals
Premiership	0		0
League Division 1	0		0
League Division 2	2		0
FA Cup	0		0
League Cup	0		0
European Cup / Champions League	0		0
European Cup–Winners' Cup	0		0
UEFA Cup / Inter-Cities' Fairs Cup	0		0
Other Matches	0		0
OVERALL TOTAL	**2**		**0**

Opponents	PREM			FLD 1			FLD 2			FAC			LC			EC/CL			ECWC			UEFA			OTHER			TOTAL		
	A	S	G	A	S	G	A	S	G	A	S	G	A	S	G	A	S	G	A	S	G	A	S	G	A	S	G	A	S	G
1 Glossop	–	–		–	–		1	–		–	–		–	–		–	–		–	–		–	–		–	–		1	–	
2 Walsall	–	–		–	–		1	–		–	–		–	–		–	–		–	–		–	–		–	–		1	–	

GEORGE WALL

DEBUT (Full Appearance, 1 goal)

Saturday 07/04/1906
Football League Division 2
at Millfields Road

Leyton Orient 0 Manchester United 1

CLUB CAREER RECORD	Apps	Subs	Goals
Premiership	0		0
League Division 1	281		86
League Division 2	6		3
FA Cup	29		9
League Cup	0		0
European Cup / Champions League	0		0
European Cup–Winners' Cup	0		0
UEFA Cup / Inter-Cities' Fairs Cup	0		0
Other Matches	3		2
OVERALL TOTAL	**319**		**100**

Opponents	PREM			FLD 1			FLD 2			FAC			LC			EC/CL			ECWC			UEFA			OTHER			TOTAL		
	A	S	G	A	S	G	A	S	G	A	S	G	A	S	G	A	S	G	A	S	G	A	S	G	A	S	G	A	S	G
1 Newcastle United	–	–		17	4		–	–		1	–		–	–		–	–		–	–		–	–		–	–		18	4	
2 Everton	–	–		16	6		–	–		1	–		–	–		–	–		–	–		–	–		–	–		17	6	
3 Blackburn Rovers	–	–		14	4		–	–		3	–		–	–		–	–		–	–		–	–		–	–		17	4	
4 Sheffield Wednesday	–	–		14	9		–	–		1	–		–	–		–	–		–	–		–	–		–	–		15	9	
5 Sheffield United	–	–		15	4		–	–		–	–		–	–		–	–		–	–		–	–		–	–		15	4	
6 Aston Villa	–	–		12	3		–	–		2	2		–	–		–	–		–	–		–	–		–	–		14	5	
7 Middlesbrough	–	–		14	3		–	–		–	–		–	–		–	–		–	–		–	–		–	–		14	3	
8 Manchester City	–	–		14	2		–	–		–	–		–	–		–	–		–	–		–	–		–	–		14	2	
9 Sunderland	–	–		14	2		–	–		–	–		–	–		–	–		–	–		–	–		–	–		14	2	
10 Chelsea	–	–		11	4		–	–		1	–		1	–		–	–		–	–		–	–		–	–		13	4	

continued../

GEORGE WALL (continued)

Opponents	PREM A S G			FLD 1 A S G			FLD 2 A S G			FAC A S G			LC A S G			EC/CL A S G			ECWC A S G			UEFA A S G			OTHER A S G			TOTAL A S G		
11 Bolton Wanderers	–	–	–	13		3	–	–	–	–	–	–	–	–	–	–	–	–	–	–	–	–	–	–	–	–	–	13		3
12 Arsenal	–	–	–	13		1	–	–	–	–	–	–	–	–	–	–	–	–	–	–	–	–	–	–	–	–	–	13		1
13 Liverpool	–	–	–	12		9	–	–	–	–	–	–	–	–	–	–	–	–	–	–	–	–	–	–	–	–	–	12		9
14 Bradford City	–	–	–	12		3	–	–	–	–	–	–	–	–	–	–	–	–	–	–	–	–	–	–	–	–	–	12		3
15 Notts County	–	–	–	12		2	–	–	–	–	–	–	–	–	–	–	–	–	–	–	–	–	–	–	–	–	–	12		2
16 Oldham Athletic	–	–	–	9		4	–	–	–	2			–	–	–	–	–	–	–	–	–	–	–	–	–	–	–	11		4
17 Bristol City	–	–	–	10		3	–	–	–	1			–	–	–	–	–	–	–	–	–	–	–	–	–	–	–	11		3
18 Preston North End	–	–	–	11		3	–	–	–	–	–	–	–	–	–	–	–	–	–	–	–	–	–	–	–	–	–	11		3
19 Bury	–	–	–	10		3	–	–	–	–	–	–	–	–	–	–	–	–	–	–	–	–	–	–	–	–	–	10		3
20 Tottenham Hotspur	–	–	–	8		4	–	–	–	–	–	–	–	–	–	–	–	–	–	–	–	–	–	–	–	–	–	8		4
21 Nottingham Forest	–	–	–	8		3	–	–	–	–	–	–	–	–	–	–	–	–	–	–	–	–	–	–	–	–	–	8		3
22 Burnley	–	–	–	4		–	1			2			–	–	–	–	–	–	–	–	–	–	–	–	–	–	–	7		–
23 West Bromwich Albion	–	–	–	6		2	–	–	–	–	–	–	–	–	–	–	–	–	–	–	–	–	–	–	–	–	–	6		2
24 Birmingham City	–	–	–	4		1	–	–	–	–	–	–	–	–	–	–	–	–	–	–	–	–	–	–	–	–	–	4		1
25 Derby County	–	–	–	4		–	–	–	–	–	–	–	–	–	–	–	–	–	–	–	–	–	–	–	–	–	–	4		–
26 Coventry City	–	–	–	–	–	–	–	–	–	3		2	–	–	–	–	–	–	–	–	–	–	–	–	–	–	–	3		2
27 Leicester City	–	–	–	2		4	–	–	–	–	–	–	–	–	–	–	–	–	–	–	–	–	–	–	–	–	–	2		4
28 Blackpool	–	–	–	–	–	–	–	–	–	2		2	–	–	–	–	–	–	–	–	–	–	–	–	–	–	–	2		2
29 Portsmouth	–	–	–	–	–	–	–	–	–	2		2	–	–	–	–	–	–	–	–	–	–	–	–	–	–	–	2		2
30 Queens Park Rangers	–	–	–	–	–	–	–	–	–	–	–	–	–	–	–	–	–	–	–	–	–	–	–	–	2		1	2		1
31 Swindon Town	–	–	–	–	–	–	–	–	–	1			–	–	–	–	–	–	–	–	–	–	–	–	1		1	2		1
32 Reading	–	–	–	–	–	–	–	–	–	2			–	–	–	–	–	–	–	–	–	–	–	–	–	–	–	2		–
33 Stoke City	–	–	–	2			–	–	–	–	–	–	–	–	–	–	–	–	–	–	–	–	–	–	–	–	–	2		–
34 Burton United	–	–	–	–	–	–	1		1	–	–	–	–	–	–	–	–	–	–	–	–	–	–	–	–	–	–	1		1
35 Leyton Orient	–	–	–	–	–	–	1		1	–	–	–	–	–	–	–	–	–	–	–	–	–	–	–	–	–	–	1		1
36 Lincoln City	–	–	–	–	–	–	1		1	–	–	–	–	–	–	–	–	–	–	–	–	–	–	–	–	–	–	1		1
37 Plymouth Argyle	–	–	–	–	–	–	–	–	–	1		1	–	–	–	–	–	–	–	–	–	–	–	–	–	–	–	1		1
38 Brighton	–	–	–	–	–	–	–	–	–	1			–	–	–	–	–	–	–	–	–	–	–	–	–	–	–	1		–
39 Fulham	–	–	–	–	–	–	–	–	–	1			–	–	–	–	–	–	–	–	–	–	–	–	–	–	–	1		–
40 Huddersfield Town	–	–	–	–	–	–	–	–	–	1			–	–	–	–	–	–	–	–	–	–	–	–	–	–	–	1		–
41 Leeds United	–	–	–	–	–	–	–	–	–	1			–	–	–	–	–	–	–	–	–	–	–	–	–	–	–	1		–
42 West Ham United	–	–	–	–	–	–	–	–	–	1			–	–	–	–	–	–	–	–	–	–	–	–	–	–	–	1		–

DANNY WALLACE

DEBUT (Full Appearance, 1 goal)

Wednesday 20/09/1989
League Cup 2nd Round 1st Leg
at Fratton Park

Portsmouth 2 Manchester United 3

CLUB CAREER RECORD	Apps	Subs	Goals
Premiership	0	(2)	0
League Division 1	36	(9)	6
League Division 2	0		0
FA Cup	7	(2)	2
League Cup	4	(3)	3
European Cup / Champions League	0		0
European Cup-Winners' Cup	3	(2)	0
UEFA Cup / Inter-Cities' Fairs Cup	2		0
Other Matches	1		0
OVERALL TOTAL	**53**	**(18)**	**11**

Opponents	PREM A S G			FLD 1 A S G			FLD 2 A S G			FAC A S G			LC A S G			EC/CL A S G			ECWC A S G			UEFA A S G			OTHER A S G			TOTAL A S G		
1 Crystal Palace	–	–	–	3		1	–	–	–	2			–	–	–	–	–	–	–	–	–	–	–	–	–	–	–	5		1
2 Liverpool	–	–	–	2	(1)	–	–	–	–	–	–	–	–	(1)	–	–	–	–	–	–	–	1		–	–	–	–	3	(2)	–
3 Chelsea	–	–	–	3	(1)	1	–	–	–	–	–	–	–	–	–	–	–	–	–	–	–	–	–	–	–	–	–	3	(1)	1
4 Tottenham Hotspur	–	(1)	–	3			–	–	–	–	–	–	–	–	–	–	–	–	–	–	–	–	–	–	–	–	–	3	(1)	–
5 Luton Town	–	–	–	3		2	–	–	–	–	–	–	–	–	–	–	–	–	–	–	–	–	–	–	–	–	–	3		2
6 Everton	–	–	–	3			–	–	–	–	–	–	–	–	–	–	–	–	–	–	–	–	–	–	–	–	–	3		–
7 Nottingham Forest	–	–	–	3			–	–	–	–	–	–	–	–	–	–	–	–	–	–	–	–	–	–	–	–	–	3		–
8 Manchester City	–	–	–	2	(1)		–	–	–	–	–	–	–	–	–	–	–	–	–	–	–	–	–	–	–	–	–	2	(1)	–
9 Sheffield United	–	–	–	1	(1)		–	–	–	1			–	–	–	–	–	–	–	–	–	–	–	–	–	–	–	2	(1)	–
10 Arsenal	–	–	–	1			–	–	–	–	–	–	1		1	–	–	–	–	–	–	–	–	–	–	–	–	2		1
11 Brighton	–	–	–	–	–	–	–	–	–	1			1		1	–	–	–	–	–	–	–	–	–	–	–	–	2		1
12 Coventry City	–	–	–	2		1	–	–	–	–	–	–	–	–	–	–	–	–	–	–	–	–	–	–	–	–	–	2		1
13 Portsmouth	–	–	–	–	–	–	–	–	–	–	–	–	2		1	–	–	–	–	–	–	–	–	–	–	–	–	2		1
14 Southampton	–	–	–	2			–	–	–	–	–	–	–	–	–	–	–	–	–	–	–	–	–	–	–	–	–	2		–
15 Torpedo Moscow	–	–	–	–	–	–	–	–	–	–	–	–	–	–	–	–	–	–	–	–	–	2			–	–	–	2		–
16 Wrexham	–	–	–	–	–	–	–	–	–	–	–	–	–	–	–	–	–	–	2			–	–	–	–	–	–	2		–
17 Oldham Athletic	–	–	–	–	–	–	–	–	–	1	(1)	1	–	–	–	–	–	–	–	–	–	–	–	–	–	–	–	1	(1)	1
18 Athinaikos	–	–	–	–	–	–	–	–	–	–	–	–	–	–	–	–	–	–	1	(1)		–	–	–	–	–	–	1	(1)	–
19 Charlton Athletic	–	–	–	1	(1)		–	–	–	–	–	–	–	–	–	–	–	–	–	–	–	–	–	–	–	–	–	1	(1)	–
20 Derby County	–	–	–	1	(1)		–	–	–	–	–	–	–	–	–	–	–	–	–	–	–	–	–	–	–	–	–	1	(1)	–
21 Leeds United	–	–	–	1			–	–	–	–	–	–	–	(1)		–	–	–	–	–	–	–	–	–	–	–	–	1	(1)	–
22 Norwich City	–	–	–	1			–	–	–	–	–	–	–	(1)		–	–	–	–	–	–	–	–	–	–	–	–	1	(1)	–
23 Queens Park Rangers	–	(1)	–	1			–	–	–	–	–	–	–	–	–	–	–	–	–	–	–	–	–	–	–	–	–	1	(1)	–
24 Sheffield Wednesday	–	–	–	1	(1)		–	–	–	–	–	–	–	–	–	–	–	–	–	–	–	–	–	–	–	–	–	1	(1)	–
25 Wimbledon	–	–	–	–	(2)		–	–	–	–	–	–	–	–	–	–	–	–	–	–	–	–	–	–	–	–	–	–	(2)	–
26 Millwall	–	–	–	1		1	–	–	–	–	–	–	–	–	–	–	–	–	–	–	–	–	–	–	–	–	–	1		1
27 Newcastle United	–	–	–	–	–	–	–	–	–	1		1	–	–	–	–	–	–	–	–	–	–	–	–	–	–	–	1		1
28 Aston Villa	–	–	–	1			–	–	–	–	–	–	–	–	–	–	–	–	–	–	–	–	–	–	–	–	–	1		–
29 Hereford United	–	–	–	–	–	–	–	–	–	1			–	–	–	–	–	–	–	–	–	–	–	–	–	–	–	1		–
30 Halifax Town	–	–	–	–	–	–	–	–	–	–	–	–	–	(1)	–	–	–	–	–	–	–	–	–	–	–	–	–	–	(1)	–
31 Montpellier Herault	–	–	–	–	–	–	–	–	–	–	–	–	–	–	–	–	–	–	–	(1)	–	–	–	–	–	–	–	–	(1)	–

RONNIE WALLWORK

DEBUT (Substitute Appearance)

Saturday 25/10/1997
FA Premiership
at Old Trafford

Manchester United 7 Barnsley 0

CLUB CAREER RECORD	Apps	Subs	Goals
Premiership	4	(15)	0
League Division 1	0		0
League Division 2	0		0
FA Cup	1	(1)	0
League Cup	4	(1)	0
European Cup / Champions League	0	(1)	0
European Cup-Winners' Cup	0		0
UEFA Cup / Inter-Cities' Fairs Cup	0		0
Other Matches	1		0
OVERALL TOTAL	**10**	**(18)**	**0**

Opponents	PREM	FLD 1	FLD 2	FAC	LC	EC/CL	ECWC	UEFA	OTHER	TOTAL
	A S G	A S G	A S G	A S G	A S G	A S G	A S G	A S G	A S G	A S G
1 Aston Villa	– (2) –	–	–	–	1	–	–	–	–	1 (2) –
2 Bradford City	1 (2) –	–	–	–	–	–	–	–	–	1 (2) –
3 Southampton	1 (2) –	–	–	–	–	–	–	–	–	1 (2) –
4 Derby County	1 (1) –	–	–	–	–	–	–	–	–	1 (1) –
5 Ipswich Town	1 (1) –	–	–	–	–	–	–	–	–	1 (1) –
6 Middlesbrough	– (1) –	–	–	1	–	–	–	–	–	1 (1) –
7 Newcastle United	– (2) –	–	–	–	–	–	–	–	–	– (2) –
8 Arsenal	–	–	–	–	1	–	–	–	–	1
9 South Melbourne	–	–	–	–	–	–	–	–	1	1
10 Sunderland	–	–	–	–	1	–	–	–	–	1
11 Watford	–	–	–	–	1	–	–	–	–	1
12 Barnsley	– (1) –	–	–	–	–	–	–	–	–	– (1) –
13 Everton	– (1) –	–	–	–	–	–	–	–	–	– (1) –
14 Fulham	–	–	–	– (1) –	–	–	–	–	–	– (1) –
15 Liverpool	– (1) –	–	–	–	–	–	–	–	–	– (1) –
16 Nottingham Forest	–	–	–	–	– (1) –	–	–	–	–	– (1) –
17 PSV Eindhoven	–	–	–	–	–	– (1) –	–	–	–	– (1) –
18 West Ham United	– (1) –	–	–	–	–	–	–	–	–	– (1) –

GARY WALSH

DEBUT (Full Appearance)

Saturday 13/12/1986
Football League Division 1
at Villa Park

Aston Villa 3 Manchester United 3

CLUB CAREER RECORD	Apps	Subs	Goals
Premiership	12	(1)	0
League Division 1	37		0
League Division 2	0		0
FA Cup	0		0
League Cup	7		0
European Cup / Champions League	3		0
European Cup-Winners' Cup	2		0
UEFA Cup / Inter-Cities' Fairs Cup	1		0
Other Matches	0		0
OVERALL TOTAL	**62**	**(1)**	**0**

Opponents	PREM	FLD 1	FLD 2	FAC	LC	EC/CL	ECWC	UEFA	OTHER	TOTAL
	A S G	A S G	A S G	A S G	A S G	A S G	A S G	A S G	A S G	A S G
1 Coventry City	2 –	3 –	–	–	–	–	–	–	–	5 –
2 Arsenal	1 –	2 –	–	–	–	–	–	–	–	3 –
3 Aston Villa	1 –	2 –	–	–	–	–	–	–	–	3 –
4 Chelsea	1 –	2 –	–	–	–	–	–	–	–	3 –
5 Liverpool	–	3 –	–	–	–	–	–	–	–	3 –
6 Newcastle United	–	2 –	–	–	1	–	–	–	–	3 –
7 Norwich City	1 –	2 –	–	–	–	–	–	–	–	3 –
8 Nottingham Forest	1 –	2 –	–	–	–	–	–	–	–	3 –
9 Southampton	2 –	1 –	–	–	–	–	–	–	–	3 –
10 Wimbledon	–	3 –	–	–	–	–	–	–	–	3 –
11 Leicester City	1 –	1 –	–	–	–	–	–	–	–	2 –
12 Port Vale	–	–	–	–	2	–	–	–	–	2 –
13 Queens Park Rangers	1 –	1 –	–	–	–	–	–	–	–	2 –
14 Tottenham Hotspur	–	2 –	–	–	–	–	–	–	–	2 –
15 West Ham United	–	2 –	–	–	–	–	–	–	–	2 –
16 Ipswich Town	1 (1) –	–	–	–	–	–	–	–	–	1 (1) –
17 Athletico Madrid	–	–	–	–	–	–	1	–	–	1 –
18 Barcelona	–	–	–	–	–	1	–	–	–	1 –
19 Brighton	–	–	–	1	–	–	–	–	–	1 –
20 Bury	–	–	–	1	–	–	–	–	–	1 –
21 Cambridge United	–	–	–	1	–	–	–	–	–	1 –
22 Charlton Athletic	–	1 –	–	–	–	–	–	–	–	1 –
23 Crystal Palace	–	1 –	–	–	–	–	–	–	–	1 –
24 Everton	–	1 –	–	–	–	–	–	–	–	1 –
25 Galatasaray	–	–	–	–	–	1	–	–	–	1 –
26 Gothenburg	–	–	–	–	–	1	–	–	–	1 –
27 Hull City	–	–	–	1	–	–	–	–	–	1 –
28 Legia Warsaw	–	–	–	–	–	–	1	–	–	1 –
29 Luton Town	–	1 –	–	–	–	–	–	–	–	1 –
30 Manchester City	–	1 –	–	–	–	–	–	–	–	1 –
31 Oxford United	–	1 –	–	–	–	–	–	–	–	1 –
32 Sheffield United	–	1 –	–	–	–	–	–	–	–	1 –
33 Sheffield Wednesday	–	1 –	–	–	–	–	–	–	–	1 –
34 Torpedo Moscow	–	–	–	–	–	–	–	1	–	1 –
35 Watford	–	1 –	–	–	–	–	–	–	–	1 –

JOE WALTON

DEBUT (Full Appearance)

Saturday 26/01/1946
FA Cup 4th Round 1st Leg
at Maine Road

Manchester United 1 Preston North End 0

CLUB CAREER RECORD	Apps	Subs	Goals
Premiership	0		0
League Division 1	21		0
League Division 2	0		0
FA Cup	2		0
League Cup	0		0
European Cup / Champions League	0		0
European Cup-Winners' Cup	0		0
UEFA Cup / Inter-Cities' Fairs Cup	0		0
Other Matches	0		0
OVERALL TOTAL	**23**		**0**

Opponents	PREM A S G	FLD 1 A S G	FLD 2 A S G	FAC A S G	LC A S G	EC/CL A S G	ECWC A S G	UEFA A S G	OTHER A S G	TOTAL A S G
1 Blackpool	– –	3 –	– –	– –	– –	– –	– –	– –	– –	3 –
2 Preston North End	– –	1 –	– –	2 –	– –	– –	– –	– –	– –	3 –
3 Sunderland	– –	3 –	– –	– –	– –	– –	– –	– –	– –	3 –
4 Aston Villa	– –	2 –	– –	– –	– –	– –	– –	– –	– –	2 –
5 Derby County	– –	2 –	– –	– –	– –	– –	– –	– –	– –	2 –
6 Portsmouth	– –	2 –	– –	– –	– –	– –	– –	– –	– –	2 –
7 Arsenal	– –	1 –	– –	– –	– –	– –	– –	– –	– –	1 –
8 Blackburn Rovers	– –	1 –	– –	– –	– –	– –	– –	– –	– –	1 –
9 Chelsea	– –	1 –	– –	– –	– –	– –	– –	– –	– –	1 –
10 Everton	– –	1 –	– –	– –	– –	– –	– –	– –	– –	1 –
11 Huddersfield Town	– –	1 –	– –	– –	– –	– –	– –	– –	– –	1 –
12 Middlesbrough	– –	1 –	– –	– –	– –	– –	– –	– –	– –	1 –
13 Sheffield United	– –	1 –	– –	– –	– –	– –	– –	– –	– –	1 –
14 Stoke City	– –	1 –	– –	– –	– –	– –	– –	– –	– –	1 –

JOHN WALTON

DEBUT (Full Appearance)

Saturday 29/09/1951
Football League Division 1
at Old Trafford

Manchester United 1 Preston North End 2

CLUB CAREER RECORD	Apps	Subs	Goals
Premiership	0		0
League Division 1	2		0
League Division 2	0		0
FA Cup	0		0
League Cup	0		0
European Cup / Champions League	0		0
European Cup-Winners' Cup	0		0
UEFA Cup / Inter-Cities' Fairs Cup	0		0
Other Matches	0		0
OVERALL TOTAL	**2**		**0**

Opponents	PREM A S G	FLD 1 A S G	FLD 2 A S G	FAC A S G	LC A S G	EC/CL A S G	ECWC A S G	UEFA A S G	OTHER A S G	TOTAL A S G
1 Derby County	– –	1 –	– –	– –	– –	– –	– –	– –	– –	1 –
2 Preston North End	– –	1 –	– –	– –	– –	– –	– –	– –	– –	1 –

ARTHUR WARBURTON

DEBUT (Full Appearance, 1 goal)

Saturday 08/03/1930
Football League Division 1
at Old Trafford

Manchester United 2 Aston Villa 3

CLUB CAREER RECORD	Apps	Subs	Goals
Premiership	0		0
League Division 1	20		6
League Division 2	15		4
FA Cup	4		0
League Cup	0		0
European Cup / Champions League	0		0
European Cup-Winners' Cup	0		0
UEFA Cup / Inter-Cities' Fairs Cup	0		0
Other Matches	0		0
OVERALL TOTAL	**39**		**10**

Opponents	PREM A S G	FLD 1 A S G	FLD 2 A S G	FAC A S G	LC A S G	EC/CL A S G	ECWC A S G	UEFA A S G	OTHER A S G	TOTAL A S G
1 Stoke City	– –	– –	– –	3 –	– –	– –	– –	– –	– –	3 –
2 Aston Villa	– –	2 2	– –	– –	– –	– –	– –	– –	– –	2 2
3 Newcastle United	– –	2 2	– –	– –	– –	– –	– –	– –	– –	2 2
4 Burnley	– –	– –	2 1	– –	– –	– –	– –	– –	– –	2 1
5 Chelsea	– –	2 1	– –	– –	– –	– –	– –	– –	– –	2 1
6 Sheffield Wednesday	– –	2 1	– –	– –	– –	– –	– –	– –	– –	2 1
7 Bury	– –	– –	2 –	– –	– –	– –	– –	– –	– –	2 –
8 Grimsby Town	– –	1 –	– –	1 –	– –	– –	– –	– –	– –	2 –
9 Huddersfield Town	– –	2 –	– –	– –	– –	– –	– –	– –	– –	2 –
10 Manchester City	– –	2 –	– –	– –	– –	– –	– –	– –	– –	2 –
11 Southampton	– –	– –	2 –	– –	– –	– –	– –	– –	– –	2 –
12 Chesterfield	– –	– –	1 2	– –	– –	– –	– –	– –	– –	1 2
13 Swansea City	– –	– –	1 1	– –	– –	– –	– –	– –	– –	1 1
14 Arsenal	– –	1 –	– –	– –	– –	– –	– –	– –	– –	1 –
15 Birmingham City	– –	1 –	– –	– –	– –	– –	– –	– –	– –	1 –
16 Blackpool	– –	1 –	– –	– –	– –	– –	– –	– –	– –	1 –
17 Bradford Park Avenue	– –	– –	1 –	– –	– –	– –	– –	– –	– –	1 –

continued../

ARTHUR WARBURTON (continued)

Opponents	PREM A S G	FLD 1 A S G	FLD 2 A S G	FAC A S G	LC A S G	EC/CL A S G	ECWC A S G	UEFA A S G	OTHER A S G	TOTAL A S G
18 Brentford	- -	- -	1 -	- -	- -	- -	- -	- -	- -	1 -
19 Charlton Athletic	- -	- -	1 -	- -	- -	- -	- -	- -	- -	1 -
20 Leicester City	- -	1 -	- -	- -	- -	- -	- -	- -	- -	1 -
21 Middlesbrough	- -	1 -	- -	- -	- -	- -	- -	- -	- -	1 -
22 Millwall	- -	- -	1 -	- -	- -	- -	- -	- -	- -	1 -
23 Nottingham Forest	- -	- -	1 -	- -	- -	- -	- -	- -	- -	1 -
24 Port Vale	- -	- -	1 -	- -	- -	- -	- -	- -	- -	1 -
25 Portsmouth	- -	1 -	- -	- -	- -	- -	- -	- -	- -	1 -
26 Preston North End	- -	- -	1 -	- -	- -	- -	- -	- -	- -	1 -
27 Sheffield United	- -	1 -	- -	- -	- -	- -	- -	- -	- -	1 -

JACK WARNER

DEBUT (Full Appearance)

Saturday 05/11/1938
Football League Division 1
at Villa Park

Aston Villa 0 Manchester United 2

CLUB CAREER RECORD	Apps	Subs	Goals
Premiership	0		0
League Division 1	102		1
League Division 2	0		0
FA Cup	13		1
League Cup	0		0
European Cup / Champions League	0		0
European Cup-Winners' Cup	0		0
UEFA Cup / Inter-Cities' Fairs Cup	0		0
Other Matches	1		0
OVERALL TOTAL	**116**		**2**

Opponents	PREM A S G	FLD 1 A S G	FLD 2 A S G	FAC A S G	LC A S G	EC/CL A S G	ECWC A S G	UEFA A S G	OTHER A S G	TOTAL A S G
1 Charlton Athletic	- -	7 -	- -	1 1	- -	- -	- -	- -	- -	8 1
2 Arsenal	- -	7 -	- -	- -	- -	- -	- -	- -	1 -	8 -
3 Preston North End	- -	6 -	- -	2 -	- -	- -	- -	- -	- -	8 -
4 Everton	- -	6 1	- -	- -	- -	- -	- -	- -	- -	6 1
5 Aston Villa	- -	6 -	- -	- -	- -	- -	- -	- -	- -	6 -
6 Liverpool	- -	6 -	- -	- -	- -	- -	- -	- -	- -	6 -
7 Portsmouth	- -	4 -	- -	2 -	- -	- -	- -	- -	- -	6 -
8 Bolton Wanderers	- -	5 -	- -	- -	- -	- -	- -	- -	- -	5 -
9 Middlesbrough	- -	5 -	- -	- -	- -	- -	- -	- -	- -	5 -
10 Brentford	- -	4 -	- -	- -	- -	- -	- -	- -	- -	4 -
11 Chelsea	- -	3 -	- -	1 -	- -	- -	- -	- -	- -	4 -
12 Derby County	- -	4 -	- -	- -	- -	- -	- -	- -	- -	4 -
13 Grimsby Town	- -	4 -	- -	- -	- -	- -	- -	- -	- -	4 -
14 Huddersfield Town	- -	4 -	- -	- -	- -	- -	- -	- -	- -	4 -
15 Stoke City	- -	4 -	- -	- -	- -	- -	- -	- -	- -	4 -
16 Sunderland	- -	4 -	- -	- -	- -	- -	- -	- -	- -	4 -
17 Wolverhampton W.	- -	4 -	- -	- -	- -	- -	- -	- -	- -	4 -
18 Blackpool	- -	3 -	- -	- -	- -	- -	- -	- -	- -	3 -
19 Manchester City	- -	3 -	- -	- -	- -	- -	- -	- -	- -	3 -
20 Sheffield United	- -	3 -	- -	- -	- -	- -	- -	- -	- -	3 -
21 West Bromwich Albion	- -	1 -	- -	2 -	- -	- -	- -	- -	- -	3 -
22 Accrington Stanley	- -	- -	- -	2 -	- -	- -	- -	- -	- -	2 -
23 Blackburn Rovers	- -	2 -	- -	- -	- -	- -	- -	- -	- -	2 -
24 Burnley	- -	2 -	- -	- -	- -	- -	- -	- -	- -	2 -
25 Leicester City	- -	2 -	- -	- -	- -	- -	- -	- -	- -	2 -
26 Birmingham City	- -	1 -	- -	- -	- -	- -	- -	- -	- -	1 -
27 Bradford Park Avenue	- -	- -	- -	1 -	- -	- -	- -	- -	- -	1 -
28 Leeds United	- -	1 -	- -	- -	- -	- -	- -	- -	- -	1 -
29 Newcastle United	- -	1 -	- -	- -	- -	- -	- -	- -	- -	1 -
30 Nottingham Forest	- -	- -	- -	1 -	- -	- -	- -	- -	- -	1 -
31 Watford	- -	- -	- -	1 -	- -	- -	- -	- -	- -	1 -

JIMMY WARNER

DEBUT (Full Appearance)

Saturday 03/09/1892
Football League Division 1
at Ewood Park

Blackburn Rovers 4 Newton Heath 3

CLUB CAREER RECORD	Apps	Subs	Goals
Premiership	0		0
League Division 1	22		0
League Division 2	0		0
FA Cup	0		0
League Cup	0		0
European Cup / Champions League	0		0
European Cup-Winners' Cup	0		0
UEFA Cup / Inter-Cities' Fairs Cup	0		0
Other Matches	0		0
OVERALL TOTAL	22		0

Opponents	PREM A S G	FLD 1 A S G	FLD 2 A S G	FAC A S G	LC A S G	EC/CL A S G	ECWC A S G	UEFA A S G	OTHER A S G	TOTAL A S G
1 Blackburn Rovers	– –	2 –	– –	– –	– –	– –	– –	– –	– –	2 –
2 Bolton Wanderers	– –	2 –	– –	– –	– –	– –	– –	– –	– –	2 –
3 Burnley	– –	2 –	– –	– –	– –	– –	– –	– –	– –	2 –
4 Derby County	– –	2 –	– –	– –	– –	– –	– –	– –	– –	2 –
5 Everton	– –	2 –	– –	– –	– –	– –	– –	– –	– –	2 –
6 Sheffield Wednesday	– –	2 –	– –	– –	– –	– –	– –	– –	– –	2 –
7 West Bromwich Albion	– –	2 –	– –	– –	– –	– –	– –	– –	– –	2 –
8 Wolverhampton W.	– –	2 –	– –	– –	– –	– –	– –	– –	– –	2 –
9 Accrington Stanley	– –	1 –	– –	– –	– –	– –	– –	– –	– –	1 –
10 Aston Villa	– –	1 –	– –	– –	– –	– –	– –	– –	– –	1 –
11 Nottingham Forest	– –	1 –	– –	– –	– –	– –	– –	– –	– –	1 –
12 Notts County	– –	1 –	– –	– –	– –	– –	– –	– –	– –	1 –
13 Preston North End	– –	1 –	– –	– –	– –	– –	– –	– –	– –	1 –
14 Sunderland	– –	1 –	– –	– –	– –	– –	– –	– –	– –	1 –

JACKIE WASSALL

DEBUT (Full Appearance)

Saturday 09/11/1935
Football League Division 2
at Vetch Field

Swansea City 2 Manchester United 1

CLUB CAREER RECORD	Apps	Subs	Goals
Premiership	0		0
League Division 1	34		5
League Division 2	11		1
FA Cup	2		0
League Cup	0		0
European Cup / Champions League	0		0
European Cup-Winners' Cup	0		0
UEFA Cup / Inter-Cities' Fairs Cup	0		0
Other Matches	0		0
OVERALL TOTAL	47		6

Opponents	PREM A S G	FLD 1 A S G	FLD 2 A S G	FAC A S G	LC A S G	EC/CL A S G	ECWC A S G	UEFA A S G	OTHER A S G	TOTAL A S G
1 Derby County	– –	3 1	– –	– –	– –	– –	– –	– –	– –	3 1
2 Middlesbrough	– –	3 1	– –	– –	– –	– –	– –	– –	– –	3 1
3 Portsmouth	– –	3 –	– –	– –	– –	– –	– –	– –	– –	3 –
4 Brentford	– –	2 1	– –	– –	– –	– –	– –	– –	– –	2 1
5 West Ham United	– –	– –	2 1	– –	– –	– –	– –	– –	– –	2 1
6 Arsenal	– –	2 –	– –	– –	– –	– –	– –	– –	– –	2 –
7 Blackburn Rovers	– –	– –	2 –	– –	– –	– –	– –	– –	– –	2 –
8 Blackpool	– –	2 –	– –	– –	– –	– –	– –	– –	– –	2 –
9 Huddersfield Town	– –	2 –	– –	– –	– –	– –	– –	– –	– –	2 –
10 Leicester City	– –	2 –	– –	– –	– –	– –	– –	– –	– –	2 –
11 Preston North End	– –	2 –	– –	– –	– –	– –	– –	– –	– –	2 –
12 West Bromwich Albion	– –	– –	– –	2 –	– –	– –	– –	– –	– –	2 –
13 Aston Villa	– –	1 1	– –	– –	– –	– –	– –	– –	– –	1 1
14 Grimsby Town	– –	1 1	– –	– –	– –	– –	– –	– –	– –	1 1
15 Barnsley	– –	– –	1 –	– –	– –	– –	– –	– –	– –	1 –
16 Birmingham City	– –	1 –	– –	– –	– –	– –	– –	– –	– –	1 –
17 Bolton Wanderers	– –	1 –	– –	– –	– –	– –	– –	– –	– –	1 –
18 Bury	– –	– –	– –	1 –	– –	– –	– –	– –	– –	1 –
19 Charlton Athletic	– –	1 –	– –	– –	– –	– –	– –	– –	– –	1 –
20 Chelsea	– –	1 –	– –	– –	– –	– –	– –	– –	– –	1 –
21 Coventry City	– –	– –	1 –	– –	– –	– –	– –	– –	– –	1 –
22 Everton	– –	1 –	– –	– –	– –	– –	– –	– –	– –	1 –
23 Fulham	– –	– –	1 –	– –	– –	– –	– –	– –	– –	1 –
24 Liverpool	– –	1 –	– –	– –	– –	– –	– –	– –	– –	1 –
25 Manchester City	– –	1 –	– –	– –	– –	– –	– –	– –	– –	1 –
26 Plymouth Argyle	– –	– –	– –	1 –	– –	– –	– –	– –	– –	1 –
27 Sheffield Wednesday	– –	1 –	– –	– –	– –	– –	– –	– –	– –	1 –
28 Stoke City	– –	1 –	– –	– –	– –	– –	– –	– –	– –	1 –
29 Sunderland	– –	1 –	– –	– –	– –	– –	– –	– –	– –	1 –
30 Swansea City	– –	– –	1 –	– –	– –	– –	– –	– –	– –	1 –
31 Tottenham Hotspur	– –	– –	1 –	– –	– –	– –	– –	– –	– –	1 –
32 Wolverhampton W.	– –	1 –	– –	– –	– –	– –	– –	– –	– –	1 –

WILLIE WATSON

DEBUT (Full Appearance)

Saturday 26/09/1970
Football League Division 1
at Old Trafford

Manchester United 1 Blackpool 1

CLUB CAREER RECORD	Apps	Subs	Goals
Premiership	0		0
League Division 1	11		0
League Division 2	0		0
FA Cup	0		0
League Cup	3		0
European Cup / Champions League	0		0
European Cup-Winners' Cup	0		0
UEFA Cup / Inter-Cities' Fairs Cup	0		0
Other Matches	0		0
OVERALL TOTAL	**14**		**0**

Opponents	PREM			FLD 1			FLD 2			FAC			LC			EC/CL			ECWC			UEFA			OTHER			TOTAL		
	A	S	G	A	S	G	A	S	G	A	S	G	A	S	G	A	S	G	A	S	G	A	S	G	A	S	G	A	S	G
1 Tottenham Hotspur	–	–		2	–		–	–		–	–		–	–		–	–		–	–		–	–		–	–		2	–	
2 Arsenal	–	–		1	–		–	–		–	–		–	–		–	–		–	–		–	–		–	–		1	–	
3 Aston Villa	–	–		–	–		–	–		–	–		1	–		–	–		–	–		–	–		–	–		1	–	
4 Birmingham City	–	–		1	–		–	–		–	–		–	–		–	–		–	–		–	–		–	–		1	–	
5 Blackpool	–	–		1	–		–	–		–	–		–	–		–	–		–	–		–	–		–	–		1	–	
6 Bristol Rovers	–	–		–	–		–	–		–	–		1	–		–	–		–	–		–	–		–	–		1	–	
7 Crystal Palace	–	–		–	–		–	–		–	–		1	–		–	–		–	–		–	–		–	–		1	–	
8 Huddersfield Town	–	–		1	–		–	–		–	–		–	–		–	–		–	–		–	–		–	–		1	–	
9 Manchester City	–	–		1	–		–	–		–	–		–	–		–	–		–	–		–	–		–	–		1	–	
10 Newcastle United	–	–		1	–		–	–		–	–		–	–		–	–		–	–		–	–		–	–		1	–	
11 Nottingham Forest	–	–		1	–		–	–		–	–		–	–		–	–		–	–		–	–		–	–		1	–	
12 Southampton	–	–		1	–		–	–		–	–		–	–		–	–		–	–		–	–		–	–		1	–	
13 Wolverhampton W.	–	–		1	–		–	–		–	–		–	–		–	–		–	–		–	–		–	–		1	–	

JEFFREY WEALANDS

DEBUT (Full Appearance)

Saturday 02/04/1983
Football League Division 1
at Old Trafford

Manchester United 3 Coventry City 0

CLUB CAREER RECORD	Apps	Subs	Goals
Premiership	0		0
League Division 1	7		0
League Division 2	0		0
FA Cup	0		0
League Cup	1		0
European Cup / Champions League	0		0
European Cup-Winners' Cup	0		0
UEFA Cup / Inter-Cities' Fairs Cup	0		0
Other Matches	0		0
OVERALL TOTAL	**8**		**0**

Opponents	PREM			FLD 1			FLD 2			FAC			LC			EC/CL			ECWC			UEFA			OTHER			TOTAL		
	A	S	G	A	S	G	A	S	G	A	S	G	A	S	G	A	S	G	A	S	G	A	S	G	A	S	G	A	S	G
1 Notts County	–	–		2	–		–	–		–	–		–	–		–	–		–	–		–	–		–	–		2	–	
2 Coventry City	–	–		1	–		–	–		–	–		–	–		–	–		–	–		–	–		–	–		1	–	
3 Everton	–	–		1	–		–	–		–	–		–	–		–	–		–	–		–	–		–	–		1	–	
4 Oxford United	–	–		–	–		–	–		–	–		1	–		–	–		–	–		–	–		–	–		1	–	
5 Stoke City	–	–		1	–		–	–		–	–		–	–		–	–		–	–		–	–		–	–		1	–	
6 Sunderland	–	–		1	–		–	–		–	–		–	–		–	–		–	–		–	–		–	–		1	–	
7 Watford	–	–		1	–		–	–		–	–		–	–		–	–		–	–		–	–		–	–		1	–	

NEIL WEBB

DEBUT (Full Appearance, 1 goal)

Saturday 19/08/1989
Football League Division 1
at Old Trafford

Manchester United 4 Arsenal 1

CLUB CAREER RECORD	Apps	Subs	Goals
Premiership	0	(1)	0
League Division 1	70	(4)	8
League Division 2	0		0
FA Cup	9		1
League Cup	14		1
European Cup / Champions League	0		0
European Cup-Winners' Cup	9		1
UEFA Cup / Inter-Cities' Fairs Cup	2		0
Other Matches	1		0
OVERALL TOTAL	**105**	**(5)**	**11**

Opponents	PREM			FLD 1			FLD 2			FAC			LC			EC/CL			ECWC			UEFA			OTHER			TOTAL		
	A	S	G	A	S	G	A	S	G	A	S	G	A	S	G	A	S	G	A	S	G	A	S	G	A	S	G	A	S	G
1 Southampton	–	–		2	(2)	–	–	–		2	–		2	–		–	–		–	–		–	–		–	–		6	(2)	–
2 Crystal Palace	–	–		5		2	–	–		2	–		–	–		–	–		–	–		–	–		–	–		7		2
3 Leeds United	–	–		4		2	–	–		1	–		2	–		–	–		–	–		–	–		–	–		7		2
4 Coventry City	–	–		5		2	–	–		–	–		–	–		–	–		–	–		–	–		–	–		5		2
5 Arsenal	–	–		5		1	–	–		–	–		–	–		–	–		–	–		–	–		–	–		5		1
6 Oldham Athletic	–	–		2	–		–	–		2	1		1	–		–	–		–	–		–	–		–	–		5		1
7 Queens Park Rangers	–	–		4		1	–	–		1	–		–	–		–	–		–	–		–	–		–	–		5		1
8 Aston Villa	–	–		4	–		–	–		–	–		–	–		–	–		–	–		–	–		–	–		4	–	
9 Norwich City	–	–		4	–		–	–		–	–		–	–		–	–		–	–		–	–		–	–		4	–	
10 Nottingham Forest	–	–		4	–		–	–		–	–		–	–		–	–		–	–		–	–		–	–		4	–	
11 Wimbledon	–	–		4	–		–	–		–	–		–	–		–	–		–	–		–	–		–	–		4	–	
12 Chelsea	–	–		3	–		–	–		–	–		–	–		–	–		–	–		–	–		–	–		3	–	
13 Derby County	–	–		3	–		–	–		–	–		–	–		–	–		–	–		–	–		–	–		3	–	

continued../

NEIL WEBB (continued)

Opponents	PREM A S G	FLD 1 A S G	FLD 2 A S G	FAC A S G	LC A S G	EC/CL A S G	ECWC A S G	UEFA A S G	OTHER A S G	TOTAL A S G
14 Liverpool	– –	2 –	– – –	– –	1 –	– –	– –	– –	– –	3 –
15 Luton Town	– –	3 –	– –	– –	– –	– –	– –	– –	– –	3 –
16 Manchester City	– –	3 –	– –	– –	– –	– –	– –	– –	– –	3 –
17 Sheffield United	– –	3 –	– –	– –	– – –	– –	– –	– –	– –	3 –
18 Sheffield Wednesday	– –	2 –	– –	– –	1 –	– –	– –	– –	– –	3 –
19 Everton	– –	1 (2) –	– –	– –	– –	– –	– –	– –	– –	1 (2) –
20 Halifax Town	– –	– –	– –	– –	2 1	– –	– –	– –	– –	2 1
21 Pecsi Munkas	– –	– –	– –	– –	– –	– –	2 1	– –	– –	2 1
22 Athletico Madrid	– –	– –	– –	– –	– –	– –	2 –	– –	– –	2 –
23 Legia Warsaw	– –	– –	– –	– –	– –	– –	2 –	– –	– –	2 –
24 Middlesbrough	– –	– –	– –	– –	2 –	– –	– –	– –	– –	2 –
25 Sunderland	– –	2 –	– –	– –	– –	– –	– –	– –	– –	2 –
26 Torpedo Moscow	– –	– –	– –	– –	– –	– –	– –	2 –	– –	2 –
27 Tottenham Hotspur	– –	2 –	– –	– –	– –	– –	– –	– –	– –	2 –
28 Wrexham	– –	– –	– –	– –	– –	– –	2 –	– –	– –	2 –
29 Athinaikos	– –	– –	– –	– –	– –	– –	1 –	– –	– –	1 –
30 Bolton Wanderers	– –	– –	– –	1 –	– –	– –	– –	– –	– –	1 –
31 Brighton	– –	– –	– –	– –	1 –	– –	– –	– –	– –	1 –
32 Cambridge United	– –	– –	– –	– –	1 –	– –	– –	– –	– –	1 –
33 Charlton Athletic	– –	1 –	– –	– –	– –	– –	– –	– –	– –	1 –
34 Notts County	– –	1 –	– –	– –	– –	– –	– –	– –	– –	1 –
35 Portsmouth	– –	– –	– –	– –	1 –	– –	– –	– –	– –	1 –
36 Red Star Belgrade	– –	– –	– –	– –	– –	– –	– –	– –	1 –	1 –
37 West Ham United	– –	1 –	– –	– –	– –	– –	– –	– –	– –	1 –
38 Ipswich Town	– (1) –	– –	– –	– –	– –	– –	– –	– –	– –	– (1) –

DANNY WEBBER

DEBUT (Substitute Appearance)

Tuesday 28/11/2000
League Cup 4th Round
at Stadium of Light

Sunderland 2 Manchester United 1

CLUB CAREER RECORD	Apps	Subs	Goals
Premiership	0		0
League Division 1	0		0
League Division 2	0		0
FA Cup	0		0
League Cup	1	(1)	0
European Cup / Champions League	0	(1)	0
European Cup-Winners' Cup	0		0
UEFA Cup / Inter-Cities' Fairs Cup	0		0
Other Matches	0		0
OVERALL TOTAL	1	(2)	0

Opponents	PREM A S G	FLD 1 A S G	FLD 2 A S G	FAC A S G	LC A S G	EC/CL A S G	ECWC A S G	UEFA A S G	OTHER A S G	TOTAL A S G
1 Arsenal	– –	– –	– –	– –	1 –	– –	– –	– –	– –	1 –
2 Deportivo La Coruna	– –	– –	– –	– –	– –	– (1) –	– –	– –	– –	– (1) –
3 Sunderland	– –	– –	– –	– –	– (1) –	– –	– –	– –	– –	– (1) –

COLIN WEBSTER

DEBUT (Full Appearance)

Saturday 28/11/1953
Football League Division 1
at Fratton Park

Portsmouth 1 Manchester United 1

CLUB CAREER RECORD	Apps	Subs	Goals
Premiership	0		0
League Division 1	65		26
League Division 2	0		0
FA Cup	9		4
League Cup	0		0
European Cup / Champions League	5		1
European Cup-Winners' Cup	0		0
UEFA Cup / Inter-Cities' Fairs Cup	0		0
Other Matches	0		0
OVERALL TOTAL	79		31

Opponents	PREM A S G	FLD 1 A S G	FLD 2 A S G	FAC A S G	LC A S G	EC/CL A S G	ECWC A S G	UEFA A S G	OTHER A S G	TOTAL A S G
1 Burnley	– –	6 4	– –	– –	– –	– –	– –	– –	– –	6 4
2 Tottenham Hotspur	– –	6 4	– –	– –	– –	– –	– –	– –	– –	6 4
3 Everton	– –	4 3	– –	1 –	– –	– –	– –	– –	– –	5 3
4 Sheffield Wednesday	– –	4 2	– –	1 –	– –	– –	– –	– –	– –	5 2
5 Wolverhampton W.	– –	5 –	– –	– –	– –	– –	– –	– –	– –	5 –
6 Aston Villa	– –	4 2	– –	– –	– –	– –	– –	– –	– –	4 2
7 Portsmouth	– –	4 1	– –	– –	– –	– –	– –	– –	– –	4 1
8 West Bromwich Albion	– –	2 –	– –	2 1	– –	– –	– –	– –	– –	4 1
9 Manchester City	– –	4 –	– –	– –	– –	– –	– –	– –	– –	4 –
10 Preston North End	– –	4 –	– –	– –	– –	– –	– –	– –	– –	4 –
11 Bolton Wanderers	– –	2 1	– –	1 –	– –	– –	– –	– –	– –	3 1
12 Newcastle United	– –	3 –	– –	– –	– –	– –	– –	– –	– –	3 –
13 Reading	– –	– –	– –	2 3	– –	– –	– –	– –	– –	2 3
14 Sunderland	– –	2 2	– –	– –	– –	– –	– –	– –	– –	2 2

continued../

COLIN WEBSTER (continued)

Opponents	PREM			FLD 1			FLD 2			FAC			LC			EC/CL			ECWC			UEFA			OTHER			TOTAL		
	A	S	G	A	S	G	A	S	G	A	S	G	A	S	G	A	S	G	A	S	G	A	S	G	A	S	G	A	S	G
15 West Ham United	–	–	–	2	–	2	–	–	–	–	–	–	–	–	–	–	–	–	–	–	–	–	–	–	–	–	–	2	–	2
16 Dukla Prague	–	–	–	–	–	–	–	–	–	–	–	–	–	–	–	2	–	1	–	–	–	–	–	–	–	–	–	2	–	1
17 AC Milan	–	–	–	–	–	–	–	–	–	–	–	–	–	–	–	2	–	–	–	–	–	–	–	–	–	–	–	2	–	–
18 Birmingham City	–	–	–	2	–	–	–	–	–	–	–	–	–	–	–	–	–	–	–	–	–	–	–	–	–	–	–	2	–	–
19 Cardiff City	–	–	–	2	–	–	–	–	–	–	–	–	–	–	–	–	–	–	–	–	–	–	–	–	–	–	–	2	–	–
20 Fulham	–	–	–	–	–	–	–	–	–	2	–	–	–	–	–	–	–	–	–	–	–	–	–	–	–	–	–	2	–	–
21 Blackpool	–	–	–	1	–	2	–	–	–	–	–	–	–	–	–	–	–	–	–	–	–	–	–	–	–	–	–	1	–	2
22 Blackburn Rovers	–	–	–	1	–	1	–	–	–	–	–	–	–	–	–	–	–	–	–	–	–	–	–	–	–	–	–	1	–	1
23 Leicester City	–	–	–	1	–	1	–	–	–	–	–	–	–	–	–	–	–	–	–	–	–	–	–	–	–	–	–	1	–	1
24 Luton Town	–	–	–	1	–	1	–	–	–	–	–	–	–	–	–	–	–	–	–	–	–	–	–	–	–	–	–	1	–	1
25 Chelsea	–	–	–	1	–	–	–	–	–	–	–	–	–	–	–	–	–	–	–	–	–	–	–	–	–	–	–	1	–	–
26 Huddersfield Town	–	–	–	1	–	–	–	–	–	–	–	–	–	–	–	–	–	–	–	–	–	–	–	–	–	–	–	1	–	–
27 Leeds United	–	–	–	1	–	–	–	–	–	–	–	–	–	–	–	–	–	–	–	–	–	–	–	–	–	–	–	1	–	–
28 Nottingham Forest	–	–	–	1	–	–	–	–	–	–	–	–	–	–	–	–	–	–	–	–	–	–	–	–	–	–	–	1	–	–
29 Shamrock Rovers	–	–	–	–	–	–	–	–	–	–	–	–	–	–	–	1	–	–	–	–	–	–	–	–	–	–	–	1	–	–
30 Sheffield United	–	–	1	–	–	–	–	–	–	–	–	–	–	–	–	–	–	–	–	–	–	–	–	–	–	–	–	1	–	–

FRANK WEDGE

DEBUT (Full Appearance)

Saturday 20/11/1897
Football League Division 2
at Filbert Street

Leicester City 1 Newton Heath 1

CLUB CAREER RECORD	Apps	Subs	Goals
Premiership	0		0
League Division 1	0		0
League Division 2	2		2
FA Cup	0		0
League Cup	0		0
European Cup / Champions League	0		0
European Cup-Winners' Cup	0		0
UEFA Cup / Inter-Cities' Fairs Cup	0		0
Other Matches	0		0
OVERALL TOTAL	**2**		**2**

Opponents	PREM			FLD 1			FLD 2			FAC			LC			EC/CL			ECWC			UEFA			OTHER			TOTAL		
	A	S	G	A	S	G	A	S	G	A	S	G	A	S	G	A	S	G	A	S	G	A	S	G	A	S	G	A	S	G
1 Grimsby Town	–	–	–	–	–	–	1	–	1	–	–	–	–	–	–	–	–	–	–	–	–	–	–	–	–	–	–	1	–	1
2 Leicester City	–	–	–	–	–	–	1	–	1	–	–	–	–	–	–	–	–	–	–	–	–	–	–	–	–	–	–	1	–	1

RICHARD WELLENS

DEBUT (Substitute Appearance)

Wednesday 13/10/1999
League Cup 3rd Round
at Villa Park

Aston Villa 3 Manchester United 0

CLUB CAREER RECORD	Apps	Subs	Goals
Premiership	0		0
League Division 1	0		0
League Division 2	0		0
FA Cup	0		0
League Cup	0	(1)	0
European Cup / Champions League	0		0
European Cup-Winners' Cup	0		0
UEFA Cup / Inter-Cities' Fairs Cup	0		0
Other Matches	0		0
OVERALL TOTAL	**0**	**(1)**	**0**

Opponents	PREM			FLD 1			FLD 2			FAC			LC			EC/CL			ECWC			UEFA			OTHER			TOTAL		
	A	S	G	A	S	G	A	S	G	A	S	G	A	S	G	A	S	G	A	S	G	A	S	G	A	S	G	A	S	G
1 Aston Villa	–	–	–	–	–	–	–	–	–	–	–	–	–	(1)	–	–	–	–	–	–	–	–	–	–	–	–	–	–	(1)	–

ENOCH WEST

DEBUT (Full Appearance)

Thursday 01/09/1910
Football League Division 1
at Manor Field

Arsenal 1 Manchester United 2

CLUB CAREER RECORD	Apps	Subs	Goals
Premiership	0		0
League Division 1	166		72
League Division 2	0		0
FA Cup	15		8
League Cup	0		0
European Cup / Champions League	0		0
European Cup-Winners' Cup	0		0
UEFA Cup / Inter-Cities' Fairs Cup	0		0
Other Matches	0		0
OVERALL TOTAL	**181**		**80**

Opponents	PREM			FLD 1			FLD 2			FAC			LC			EC/CL			ECWC			UEFA			OTHER			TOTAL		
	A	S	G	A	S	G	A	S	G	A	S	G	A	S	G	A	S	G	A	S	G	A	S	G	A	S	G	A	S	G
1 Blackburn Rovers	–	–	10	–	6	–	–	–	2	2	–	–	–	–	–	–	–	–	–	–	–	–	–	–	–	–	–	12	–	8
2 Oldham Athletic	–	–	10	–	5	–	–	–	2	1	–	–	–	–	–	–	–	–	–	–	–	–	–	–	–	–	–	12	–	6
3 Sheffield Wednesday	–	–	9	–	7	–	–	–	1	–	–	–	–	–	–	–	–	–	–	–	–	–	–	–	–	–	–	10	–	7
4 Aston Villa	–	–	9	–	5	–	–	–	1	–	–	–	–	–	–	–	–	–	–	–	–	–	–	–	–	–	–	10	–	5
5 Tottenham Hotspur	–	–	10	–	4	–	–	–	–	–	–	–	–	–	–	–	–	–	–	–	–	–	–	–	–	–	–	10	–	4

continued../

ENOCH WEST (continued)

Opponents	PREM A S G	FLD 1 A S G	FLD 2 A S G	FAC A S G	LC A S G	EC/CL A S G	ECWC A S G	UEFA A S G	OTHER A S G	TOTAL A S G
6 Newcastle United	– –	9 8	– –	– –	– –	–	–	– –	– –	9 8
7 Manchester City	– –	9 4	– –	–	–	–	–	–	– –	9 4
8 Sheffield United	– –	9 3	– –	– –	– –	–	–	– –	– –	9 3
9 Bradford City	– –	9 2	– –	–	–	–	–	–	– –	9 2
10 Middlesbrough	– –	9 2	– –	– –	– –	–	–	– –	– –	9 2
11 Liverpool	– –	8 5	– –	–	–	–	–	–	– –	8 5
12 Sunderland	– –	8 3	– –	– –	– –	–	–	– –	– –	8 3
13 Bolton Wanderers	– –	8 1	– –	–	–	–	–	–	– –	8 1
14 Everton	– –	7 2	– –	– –	– –	–	–	– –	– –	7 2
15 Notts County	– –	7 2	– –	–	–	–	–	–	– –	7 2
16 Arsenal	– –	6 4	– –	– –	– –	–	–	– –	– –	6 4
17 Chelsea	– –	5 3	– –	–	–	–	–	–	– –	5 3
18 Preston North End	– –	5 3	– –	– –	– –	–	–	– –	– –	5 3
19 West Bromwich Albion	– –	4 –	– –	–	–	–	–	–	– –	4 –
20 Derby County	– –	3 2	– –	– –	– –	–	–	– –	– –	3 2
21 Coventry City	– –	– –	– –	3 1	–	–	–	–	– –	3 1
22 Burnley	– –	3 –	– –	– –	– –	–	–	– –	– –	3 –
23 Bury	– –	3 –	– –	–	–	–	–	–	– –	3 –
24 Bristol City	– –	2 1	– –	– –	– –	–	–	– –	– –	2 1
25 Reading	– –	– –	– –	2 1	–	–	–	–	– –	2 1
26 Bradford Park Avenue	– –	2 –	– –	– –	– –	–	–	– –	– –	2 –
27 Nottingham Forest	– –	2 –	– –	–	–	–	–	–	– –	2 –
28 Huddersfield Town	– –	– –	– –	1 2	– –	–	–	– –	– –	1 2
29 Blackpool	– –	– –	– –	1 1	–	–	–	–	– –	1 1
30 Swindon Town	– –	– –	– –	1 –	– –	–	–	– –	– –	1 –
31 West Ham United	– –	– –	– –	1 –	–	–	–	–	– –	1 –

JOE WETHERELL

DEBUT (Full Appearance)

Monday 21/09/1896
Football League Division 2
at Fellows Park

Walsall 2 Newton Heath 3

CLUB CAREER RECORD	Apps	Subs	Goals
Premiership	0		0
League Division 1	0		0
League Division 2	2		0
FA Cup	0		0
League Cup	0		0
European Cup / Champions League	0		0
European Cup-Winners' Cup	0		0
UEFA Cup / Inter-Cities' Fairs Cup	0		0
Other Matches	0		0
OVERALL TOTAL	2		0

Opponents	PREM A S G	FLD 1 A S G	FLD 2 A S G	FAC A S G	LC A S G	EC/CL A S G	ECWC A S G	UEFA A S G	OTHER A S G	TOTAL A S G
1 Birmingham City	– – –	– –	1 –	–	–	–	–	–	– –	1 –
2 Walsall	– – –	– –	1 –	–	–	–	–	–	– –	1 –

ARTHUR WHALLEY

DEBUT (Full Appearance)

Monday 27/12/1909
Football League Division 1
at Hillsborough

Sheffield Wednesday 4 Manchester United 1

CLUB CAREER RECORD	Apps	Subs	Goals
Premiership	0		0
League Division 1	97		6
League Division 2	0		0
FA Cup	9		0
League Cup	0		0
European Cup / Champions League	0		0
European Cup-Winners' Cup	0		0
UEFA Cup / Inter-Cities' Fairs Cup	0		0
Other Matches	0		0
OVERALL TOTAL	106		6

Opponents	PREM A S G	FLD 1 A S G	FLD 2 A S G	FAC A S G	LC A S G	EC/CL A S G	ECWC A S G	UEFA A S G	OTHER A S G	TOTAL A S G
1 Sheffield Wednesday	– –	8 1	– –	– –	– –	–	–	– –	– –	8 1
2 Chelsea	– –	7 1	– –	–	–	–	–	–	– –	7 1
3 Bradford City	– –	7 –	– –	– –	– –	–	–	– –	– –	7 –
4 Sunderland	– –	6 1	– –	–	–	–	–	–	– –	6 1
5 Aston Villa	– –	5 –	– –	1 –	– –	–	–	– –	– –	6 –
6 Everton	– –	6 –	– –	–	–	–	–	–	– –	6 –
7 Middlesbrough	– –	5 1	– –	– –	– –	–	–	– –	– –	5 1
8 Liverpool	– –	5 –	– –	–	–	–	–	–	– –	5 –
9 Sheffield United	– –	5 –	– –	– –	– –	–	–	– –	– –	5 –
10 Tottenham Hotspur	– –	4 1	– –	–	–	–	–	–	– –	4 1
11 Blackburn Rovers	– –	4 –	– –	– –	– –	–	–	– –	– –	4 –
12 Derby County	– –	4 –	– –	–	–	–	–	–	– –	4 –
13 Manchester City	– –	4 –	– –	– –	– –	–	–	– –	– –	4 –
14 Newcastle United	– –	4 –	– –	–	–	–	–	–	– –	4 –

continued../

ARTHUR WHALLEY (continued)

Opponents	PREM A	S	G	FLD 1 A	S	G	FLD 2 A	S	G	FAC A	S	G	LC A	S	G	EC/CL A	S	G	ECWC A	S	G	UEFA A	S	G	OTHER A	S	G	TOTAL A	S	G
15 Oldham Athletic	–	–		2	–		–	–		2	–		–	–		–	–		–	–		–	–		–	–		4	–	
16 Arsenal	–	–		3	–	1	–	–		–	–		–	–		–	–		–	–		–	–		–	–		3	–	1
17 Bolton Wanderers	–	–		3	–		–	–		–	–		–	–		–	–		–	–		–	–		–	–		3	–	
18 Coventry City	–	–		–	–		–	–		3	–		–	–		–	–		–	–		–	–		–	–		3	–	
19 Notts County	–	–		3	–		–	–		–	–		–	–		–	–		–	–		–	–		–	–		3	–	
20 Preston North End	–	–		3	–		–	–		–	–		–	–		–	–		–	–		–	–		–	–		3	–	
21 West Bromwich Albion	–	–		3	–		–	–		–	–		–	–		–	–		–	–		–	–		–	–		3	–	
22 Bristol City	–	–		2	–		–	–		–	–		–	–		–	–		–	–		–	–		–	–		2	–	
23 Bury	–	–		2	–		–	–		–	–		–	–		–	–		–	–		–	–		–	–		2	–	
24 Burnley	–	–		1	–		–	–		–	–		–	–		–	–		–	–		–	–		–	–		1	–	
25 Nottingham Forest	–	–		1	–		–	–		–	–		–	–		–	–		–	–		–	–		–	–		1	–	
26 Plymouth Argyle	–	–		–	–		–	–		1	–		–	–		–	–		–	–		–	–		–	–		1	–	
27 Port Vale	–	–		–	–		–	–		1	–		–	–		–	–		–	–		–	–		–	–		1	–	
28 Swindon Town	–	–		–	–		–	–		1	–		–	–		–	–		–	–		–	–		–	–		1	–	

BERT WHALLEY

DEBUT (Full Appearance)

Saturday 30/11/1935
Football League Division 2
at Old Trafford

Manchester United 0 Doncaster Rovers 0

CLUB CAREER RECORD	Apps	Subs	Goals
Premiership	0		0
League Division 1	24		0
League Division 2	8		0
FA Cup	6		0
League Cup	0		0
European Cup / Champions League	0		0
European Cup-Winners' Cup	0		0
UEFA Cup / Inter-Cities' Fairs Cup	0		0
Other Matches	0		0
OVERALL TOTAL	**38**		**0**

Opponents	PREM A	S	G	FLD 1 A	S	G	FLD 2 A	S	G	FAC A	S	G	LC A	S	G	EC/CL A	S	G	ECWC A	S	G	UEFA A	S	G	OTHER A	S	G	TOTAL A	S	G
1 Chelsea	–	–		3	–		–	–		–	–		–	–		–	–		–	–		–	–		–	–		3	–	
2 Preston North End	–	–		1	–		–	–		2	–		–	–		–	–		–	–		–	–		–	–		3	–	
3 Accrington Stanley	–	–		–	–		–	–		2	–		–	–		–	–		–	–		–	–		–	–		2	–	
4 Arsenal	–	–		1	–		–	–		1	–		–	–		–	–		–	–		–	–		–	–		2	–	
5 Everton	–	–		2	–		–	–		–	–		–	–		–	–		–	–		–	–		–	–		2	–	
6 Grimsby Town	–	–		2	–		–	–		–	–		–	–		–	–		–	–		–	–		–	–		2	–	
7 Stoke City	–	–		2	–		–	–		–	–		–	–		–	–		–	–		–	–		–	–		2	–	
8 Birmingham City	–	–		1	–		–	–		–	–		–	–		–	–		–	–		–	–		–	–		1	–	
9 Blackburn Rovers	–	–		1	–		–	–		–	–		–	–		–	–		–	–		–	–		–	–		1	–	
10 Bolton Wanderers	–	–		1	–		–	–		–	–		–	–		–	–		–	–		–	–		–	–		1	–	
11 Bradford Park Avenue	–	–		–	–		1	–		–	–		–	–		–	–		–	–		–	–		–	–		1	–	
12 Brentford	–	–		1	–		–	–		–	–		–	–		–	–		–	–		–	–		–	–		1	–	
13 Burnley	–	–		–	–		1	–		–	–		–	–		–	–		–	–		–	–		–	–		1	–	
14 Charlton Athletic	–	–		1	–		–	–		–	–		–	–		–	–		–	–		–	–		–	–		1	–	
15 Chesterfield	–	–		–	–		1	–		–	–		–	–		–	–		–	–		–	–		–	–		1	–	
16 Derby County	–	–		1	–		–	–		–	–		–	–		–	–		–	–		–	–		–	–		1	–	
17 Doncaster Rovers	–	–		–	–		1	–		–	–		–	–		–	–		–	–		–	–		–	–		1	–	
18 Fulham	–	–		–	–		1	–		–	–		–	–		–	–		–	–		–	–		–	–		1	–	
19 Leeds United	–	–		1	–		–	–		–	–		–	–		–	–		–	–		–	–		–	–		1	–	
20 Liverpool	–	–		1	–		–	–		–	–		–	–		–	–		–	–		–	–		–	–		1	–	
21 Manchester City	–	–		1	–		–	–		–	–		–	–		–	–		–	–		–	–		–	–		1	–	
22 Middlesbrough	–	–		1	–		–	–		–	–		–	–		–	–		–	–		–	–		–	–		1	–	
23 Nottingham Forest	–	–		–	–		1	–		–	–		–	–		–	–		–	–		–	–		–	–		1	–	
24 Plymouth Argyle	–	–		–	–		1	–		–	–		–	–		–	–		–	–		–	–		–	–		1	–	
25 Portsmouth	–	–		1	–		–	–		–	–		–	–		–	–		–	–		–	–		–	–		1	–	
26 Reading	–	–		–	–		–	–		1	–		–	–		–	–		–	–		–	–		–	–		1	–	
27 Sheffield Wednesday	–	–		1	–		–	–		–	–		–	–		–	–		–	–		–	–		–	–		1	–	
28 Sunderland	–	–		1	–		–	–		–	–		–	–		–	–		–	–		–	–		–	–		1	–	
29 Swansea City	–	–		–	–		1	–		–	–		–	–		–	–		–	–		–	–		–	–		1	–	

ANTHONY WHELAN

DEBUT (Substitute Appearance)

Saturday 29/11/1980
Football League Division 1
at Old Trafford

Manchester United 1 Southampton 1

CLUB CAREER RECORD	Apps	Subs	Goals
Premiership	0		0
League Division 1	0	(1)	0
League Division 2	0		0
FA Cup	0		0
League Cup	0		0
European Cup / Champions League	0		0
European Cup-Winners' Cup	0		0
UEFA Cup / Inter-Cities' Fairs Cup	0		0
Other Matches	0		0
OVERALL TOTAL	**0**	**(1)**	**0**

Opponents	PREM A	S	G	FLD 1 A	S	G	FLD 2 A	S	G	FAC A	S	G	LC A	S	G	EC/CL A	S	G	ECWC A	S	G	UEFA A	S	G	OTHER A	S	G	TOTAL A	S	G
1 Southampton	–	–		–	(1)	–	–	–		–	–		–	–		–	–		–	–		–	–		–	–		–	(1)	–

WILLIAM WHELAN

DEBUT (Full Appearance)

Saturday 26/03/1955
Football League Division 1
at Deepdale

Preston North End 0 Manchester United 2

CLUB CAREER RECORD	Apps	Subs	Goals
Premiership	0		0
League Division 1	79		43
League Division 2	0		0
FA Cup	6		4
League Cup	0		0
European Cup / Champions League	11		5
European Cup–Winners' Cup	0		0
UEFA Cup / Inter–Cities' Fairs Cup	0		0
Other Matches	2		0
OVERALL TOTAL	**98**		**52**

Opponents	PREM A S G	FLD 1 A S G	FLD 2 A S G	FAC A S G	LC A S G	EC/CL A S G	ECWC A S G	UEFA A S G	OTHER A S G	TOTAL A S G
1 Everton	– –	5 2	– –	1 –	–	–	–	–	–	6 2
2 Aston Villa	– –	4 1	– –	1 –	–	–	–	–	1 –	6 1
3 Sunderland	– –	5 4	–	–	–	–	–	–	–	5 4
4 Preston North End	– –	5 3	–	–	–	–	–	–	–	5 3
5 Arsenal	– –	4 5	–	–	–	–	–	–	–	4 5
6 Newcastle United	– –	4 3	–	–	–	–	–	–	–	4 3
7 Blackpool	– –	4 2	–	–	–	–	–	–	–	4 2
8 Chelsea	– –	4 2	–	–	–	–	–	–	–	4 2
9 Manchester City	– –	3 2	–	–	–	–	–	–	1 –	4 2
10 Birmingham City	– –	3 1	–	1 –	–	–	–	–	–	4 1
11 Bolton Wanderers	– –	4 –	–	–	–	–	–	–	–	4 –
12 Burnley	– –	3 3	–	–	–	–	–	–	–	3 3
13 Leeds United	– –	3 2	–	–	–	–	–	–	–	3 2
14 West Bromwich Albion	– –	3 2	–	–	–	–	–	–	–	3 2
15 Cardiff City	– –	3 1	–	–	–	–	–	–	–	3 1
16 Sheffield United	– –	3 1	–	–	–	–	–	–	–	3 1
17 Sheffield Wednesday	– –	3 1	–	–	–	–	–	–	–	3 1
18 Tottenham Hotspur	– –	3 1	–	–	–	–	–	–	–	3 1
19 Wolverhampton W.	– –	3 1	–	–	–	–	–	–	–	3 1
20 Portsmouth	– –	3 –	–	–	–	–	–	–	–	3 –
21 Leicester City	– –	2 3	–	–	–	–	–	–	–	2 3
22 Anderlecht	– –	–	–	–	–	2 2	–	–	–	2 2
23 Athletic Bilbao	– –	–	–	–	–	2 1	–	–	–	2 1
24 Charlton Athletic	– –	2 1	–	–	–	–	–	–	–	2 1
25 Luton Town	– –	2 1	–	–	–	–	–	–	–	2 1
26 Borussia Dortmund	– –	–	–	–	–	2 –	–	–	–	2 –
27 Dukla Prague	– –	–	–	–	–	2 –	–	–	–	2 –
28 Real Madrid	– –	–	–	–	–	2 –	–	–	–	2 –
29 Hartlepool United	– –	–	–	1 2	–	–	–	–	–	1 2
30 Shamrock Rovers	– –	–	–	–	–	1 2	–	–	–	1 2
31 Wrexham	– –	–	–	1 2	–	–	–	–	–	1 2
32 Nottingham Forest	– –	1 1	–	–	–	–	–	–	–	1 1
33 Bournemouth	– –	–	–	1 –	–	–	–	–	–	1 –

JEFF WHITEFOOT

DEBUT (Full Appearance)

Saturday 15/04/1950
Football League Division 1
at Old Trafford

Manchester United 0 Portsmouth 2

CLUB CAREER RECORD	Apps	Subs	Goals
Premiership	0		0
League Division 1	93		0
League Division 2	0		0
FA Cup	2		0
League Cup	0		0
European Cup / Champions League	0		0
European Cup–Winners' Cup	0		0
UEFA Cup / Inter–Cities' Fairs Cup	0		0
Other Matches	0		0
OVERALL TOTAL	**95**		**0**

Opponents	PREM A S G	FLD 1 A S G	FLD 2 A S G	FAC A S G	LC A S G	EC/CL A S G	ECWC A S G	UEFA A S G	OTHER A S G	TOTAL A S G
1 Burnley	– –	7 –	–	1 –	–	–	–	–	–	8 –
2 Tottenham Hotspur	– –	7 –	–	–	–	–	–	–	–	7 –
3 Portsmouth	– –	6 –	–	–	–	–	–	–	–	6 –
4 Huddersfield Town	– –	5 –	–	–	–	–	–	–	–	5 –
5 Manchester City	– –	5 –	–	–	–	–	–	–	–	5 –
6 Preston North End	– –	5 –	–	–	–	–	–	–	–	5 –
7 Sheffield Wednesday	– –	5 –	–	–	–	–	–	–	–	5 –
8 Cardiff City	– –	4 –	–	–	–	–	–	–	–	4 –
9 Charlton Athletic	– –	4 –	–	–	–	–	–	–	–	4 –
10 Newcastle United	– –	4 –	–	–	–	–	–	–	–	4 –
11 Sheffield United	– –	4 –	–	–	–	–	–	–	–	4 –
12 Sunderland	– –	4 –	–	–	–	–	–	–	–	4 –
13 West Bromwich Albion	– –	4 –	–	–	–	–	–	–	–	4 –
14 Wolverhampton W.	– –	4 –	–	–	–	–	–	–	–	4 –
15 Arsenal	– –	3 –	–	–	–	–	–	–	–	3 –
16 Aston Villa	– –	3 –	–	–	–	–	–	–	–	3 –
17 Blackpool	– –	3 –	–	–	–	–	–	–	–	3 –
18 Bolton Wanderers	– –	3 –	–	–	–	–	–	–	–	3 –

continued../

JEFF WHITEFOOT (continued)

Opponents	PREM			FLD 1			FLD 2			FAC			LC			EC/CL			ECWC			UEFA			OTHER			TOTAL		
	A	S	G	A	S	G	A	S	G	A	S	G	A	S	G	A	S	G	A	S	G	A	S	G	A	S	G	A	S	G
19 Liverpool	–			3			–			–			–			–			–			–			–			3		
20 Middlesbrough	–			3			–			–			–			–			–			–			–			3		
21 Everton	–			2			–			–			–			–			–			–			–			2		
22 Leicester City	–			2			–			–			–			–			–			–			–			2		
23 Birmingham City	–			1			–			–			–			–			–			–			–			1		
24 Bristol Rovers	–			–			–			1			–			–			–			–			–			1		
25 Chelsea	–			1			–			–			–			–			–			–			–			1		
26 Luton Town	–			1			–			–			–			–			–			–			–			1		

JIMMY WHITEHOUSE

DEBUT (Full Appearance)

Saturday 15/09/1900
Football League Division 2
at Turf Moor

Burnley 1 Newton Heath 0

CLUB CAREER RECORD	Apps	Subs	Goals
Premiership	0		0
League Division 1	0		0
League Division 2	59		0
FA Cup	5		0
League Cup	0		0
European Cup / Champions League	0		0
European Cup-Winners' Cup	0		0
UEFA Cup / Inter-Cities' Fairs Cup	0		0
Other Matches	0		0
OVERALL TOTAL	**64**		**0**

Opponents	PREM			FLD 1			FLD 2			FAC			LC			EC/CL			ECWC			UEFA			OTHER			TOTAL		
	A	S	G	A	S	G	A	S	G	A	S	G	A	S	G	A	S	G	A	S	G	A	S	G	A	S	G	A	S	G
1 Blackpool	–			–			5			–			–			–			–			–			–			5		
2 Burnley	–			–			3			2			–			–			–			–			–			5		
3 Arsenal	–			–			4			–			–			–			–			–			–			4		
4 Chesterfield	–			–			4			–			–			–			–			–			–			4		
5 Gainsborough Trinity	–			–			4			–			–			–			–			–			–			4		
6 Port Vale	–			–			4			–			–			–			–			–			–			4		
7 Stockport County	–			–			4			–			–			–			–			–			–			4		
8 Bristol City	–			–			3			–			–			–			–			–			–			3		
9 Burton United	–			–			3			–			–			–			–			–			–			3		
10 Glossop	–			–			3			–			–			–			–			–			–			3		
11 Middlesbrough	–			–			3			–			–			–			–			–			–			3		
12 Barnsley	–			–			2			–			–			–			–			–			–			2		
13 Birmingham City	–			–			2			–			–			–			–			–			–			2		
14 Burton Swifts	–			–			2			–			–			–			–			–			–			2		
15 Grimsby Town	–			–			2			–			–			–			–			–			–			2		
16 Leicester City	–			–			2			–			–			–			–			–			–			2		
17 Lincoln City	–			–			1			1			–			–			–			–			–			2		
18 New Brighton Tower	–			–			2			–			–			–			–			–			–			2		
19 Walsall	–			–			2			–			–			–			–			–			–			2		
20 West Bromwich Albion	–			–			2			–			–			–			–			–			–			2		
21 Accrington Stanley	–			–			–			–			1			–			–			–			–			1		
22 Doncaster Rovers	–			–			–			1			–			–			–			–			–			1		
23 Portsmouth	–			–			–			–			1			–			–			–			–			1		
24 Preston North End	–			–			–			1			–			–			–			–			–			1		

WALTER WHITEHURST

DEBUT (Full Appearance)

Wednesday 14/09/1955
Football League Division 1
at Goodison Park

Everton 4 Manchester United 2

CLUB CAREER RECORD	Apps	Subs	Goals
Premiership	0		0
League Division 1	1		0
League Division 2	0		0
FA Cup	0		0
League Cup	0		0
European Cup / Champions League	0		0
European Cup-Winners' Cup	0		0
UEFA Cup / Inter-Cities' Fairs Cup	0		0
Other Matches	0		0
OVERALL TOTAL	**1**		**0**

Opponents	PREM			FLD 1			FLD 2			FAC			LC			EC/CL			ECWC			UEFA			OTHER			TOTAL		
	A	S	G	A	S	G	A	S	G	A	S	G	A	S	G	A	S	G	A	S	G	A	S	G	A	S	G	A	S	G
1 Everton	–			1			–			–			–			–			–			–			–			1		

KERR WHITESIDE

DEBUT (Full Appearance)

Saturday 18/01/1908
Football League Division 1
at Bramall Lane

Sheffield United 2 Manchester United 0

CLUB CAREER RECORD	Apps	Subs	Goals
Premiership	0		0
League Division 1	1		0
League Division 2	0		0
FA Cup	0		0
League Cup	0		0
European Cup / Champions League	0		0
European Cup-Winners' Cup	0		0
UEFA Cup / Inter-Cities' Fairs Cup	0		0
Other Matches	0		0
OVERALL TOTAL	**1**		**0**

Opponents	PREM A S G	FLD 1 A S G	FLD 2 A S G	FAC A S G	LC A S G	EC/CL A S G	ECWC A S G	UEFA A S G	OTHER A S G	TOTAL A S G
1 Sheffield United	– –	1 –	–	–	–	–	–	–	–	1 –

NORMAN WHITESIDE

DEBUT (Substitute Appearance)

Saturday 24/04/1982
Football League Division 1
at Goldstone Ground

Brighton 0 Manchester United 1

CLUB CAREER RECORD	Apps	Subs	Goals
Premiership	0		0
League Division 1	193	(13)	47
League Division 2	0		0
FA Cup	24		10
League Cup	26	(3)	9
European Cup / Champions League	0		0
European Cup-Winners' Cup	5	(1)	1
UEFA Cup / Inter-Cities' Fairs Cup	6	(1)	0
Other Matches	2		0
OVERALL TOTAL	**256**	**(18)**	**67**

Opponents	PREM A S G	FLD 1 A S G	FLD 2 A S G	FAC A S G	LC A S G	EC/CL A S G	ECWC A S G	UEFA A S G	OTHER A S G	TOTAL A S G
1 Liverpool	– –	11 (1) 3	–	2 –	2 1	–	–	–	1 –	16 (1) 4
2 Arsenal	– –	11 (1) 1	–	2 1	2 1	–	–	–	–	15 (1) 3
3 Everton	– –	10 (1) 2	–	2 1	–	–	–	–	1 –	13 (1) 3
4 Luton Town	– –	11 5	–	1 –	–	–	–	–	–	12 5
5 Southampton	– –	9 3	–	–	3 1	–	–	–	–	12 4
6 Coventry City	– –	9 (1) 3	–	2 –	–	–	–	–	–	11 (1) 3
7 West Ham United	– –	5 (2) –	–	4 3	1 1	–	–	–	–	10 (2) 4
8 Nottingham Forest	– –	10 2	–	–	1 –	–	–	–	–	11 2
9 Tottenham Hotspur	– –	10 (1) 3	–	–	–	–	–	–	–	10 (1) 3
10 Aston Villa	– –	9 4	–	–	–	–	–	–	–	9 4
11 Watford	– –	8 (1) 1	–	–	–	–	–	–	–	8 (1) 1
12 Norwich City	– –	8 3	–	–	–	–	–	–	–	8 3
13 Newcastle United	– –	8 2	–	–	–	–	–	–	–	8 2
14 Chelsea	– –	6 1	–	1 1	–	–	–	–	–	7 2
15 Oxford United	– –	3 2	–	–	4 –	–	–	–	–	7 2
16 Manchester City	– –	6 –	–	1 1	–	–	–	–	–	7 1
17 Sunderland	– –	5 –	–	2 1	–	–	–	–	–	7 1
18 Leicester City	– –	6 (1) 1	–	–	–	–	–	–	–	6 (1) 1
19 Ipswich Town	– –	4 (2) 2	–	–	1 –	–	–	–	–	5 (2) 2
20 Birmingham City	– –	6 2	–	–	–	–	–	–	–	6 2
21 Stoke City	– –	6 2	–	–	–	–	–	–	–	6 2
22 West Bromwich Albion	– –	6 1	–	–	–	–	–	–	–	6 1
23 Queens Park Rangers	– –	5 –	–	–	–	–	–	–	–	5 –
24 Brighton	– –	2 (1) –	–	2 1	–	–	–	–	–	4 (1) 1
25 Sheffield Wednesday	– –	4 1	–	–	–	–	–	–	–	4 1
26 Port Vale	– –	–	–	–	3 (1) 2	–	–	–	–	3 (1) 2
27 Notts County	– –	3 (1) 1	–	–	–	–	–	–	–	3 (1) 1
28 Crystal Palace	– –	–	–	–	3 1	–	–	–	–	3 1
29 Charlton Athletic	– –	3 –	–	–	–	–	–	–	–	3 –
30 Bournemouth	– –	–	–	1 –	1 (1) –	–	–	–	–	2 (1) –
31 Derby County	– –	1 1	–	1 1	–	–	–	–	–	2 2
32 Hull City	– –	–	–	–	2 1	–	–	–	–	2 1
33 Wolverhampton W.	– –	2 1	–	–	–	–	–	–	–	2 1
34 Spartak Varna	– –	–	–	–	–	–	2 –	–	–	2 –
35 Swansea City	– –	2 –	–	–	–	–	–	–	–	2 –
36 Valencia	– –	–	–	–	–	–	–	2 –	–	2 –
37 Videoton	– –	–	–	–	–	–	–	2 –	–	2 –
38 Wimbledon	– –	2 –	–	–	–	–	–	–	–	2 –
39 Juventus	– –	–	–	–	–	–	1 (1) 1	–	–	1 (1) 1
40 Bradford City	– –	–	–	–	1 (1) –	–	–	–	–	1 (1) –
41 Bury	– –	–	–	–	1 1	–	–	–	–	1 1
42 Barcelona	– –	–	–	–	–	–	1 –	–	–	1 –
43 Blackburn Rovers	– –	–	–	1 –	–	–	–	–	–	1 –
44 Burnley	– –	–	–	–	1 –	–	–	–	–	1 –
45 Colchester United	– –	–	–	–	1 –	–	–	–	–	1 –
46 Dukla Prague	– –	–	–	–	–	–	1 –	–	–	1 –
47 Dundee United	– –	–	–	–	–	–	–	1 –	–	1 –
48 Millwall	– –	1 –	–	–	–	–	–	–	–	1 –
49 Portsmouth	– –	1 –	–	–	–	–	–	–	–	1 –
50 Raba Vasas	– –	–	–	–	–	–	–	1 –	–	1 –
51 Rochdale	– –	–	–	1 –	–	–	–	–	–	1 –
52 PSV Eindhoven	– –	–	–	–	–	–	–	– (1) –	–	– (1) –

JOHN WHITNEY

DEBUT (Full Appearance)

Saturday 29/02/1896
Football League Division 2
at Bank Street

Newton Heath 1 Burton Wanderers 2

CLUB CAREER RECORD	Apps	Subs	Goals
Premiership	0		0
League Division 1	0		0
League Division 2	3		0
FA Cup	0		0
League Cup	0		0
European Cup / Champions League	0		0
European Cup-Winners' Cup	0		0
UEFA Cup / Inter-Cities' Fairs Cup	0		0
Other Matches	0		0
OVERALL TOTAL	**3**		**0**

Opponents	PREM A S G	FLD 1 A S G	FLD 2 A S G	FAC A S G	LC A S G	EC/CL A S G	ECWC A S G	UEFA A S G	OTHER A S G	TOTAL A S G
1 Burton Wanderers	– –	– –	1	– – –	–	–	–	–	–	1 –
2 Rotherham United	– –	– –	1	– – –	–	–	–	–	–	1 –
3 Walsall	– –	– –	1	– – –	–	–	–	–	–	1 –

WALTER WHITTAKER

DEBUT (Full Appearance)

Saturday 14/03/1896
Football League Division 2
at Abbey Park

Grimsby Town 4 Newton Heath 2

CLUB CAREER RECORD	Apps	Subs	Goals
Premiership	0		0
League Division 1	0		0
League Division 2	3		0
FA Cup	0		0
League Cup	0		0
European Cup / Champions League	0		0
European Cup-Winners' Cup	0		0
UEFA Cup / Inter-Cities' Fairs Cup	0		0
Other Matches	0		0
OVERALL TOTAL	**3**		**0**

Opponents	PREM A S G	FLD 1 A S G	FLD 2 A S G	FAC A S G	LC A S G	EC/CL A S G	ECWC A S G	UEFA A S G	OTHER A S G	TOTAL A S G
1 Grimsby Town	– –	– –	1	– – –	–	–	–	–	–	1 –
2 Lincoln City	– –	– –	1	– – –	–	–	–	–	–	1 –
3 Port Vale	– –	– –	1	– – –	–	–	–	–	–	1 –

JOHN WHITTLE

DEBUT (Full Appearance)

Saturday 16/01/1932
Football League Division 2
at Vetch Field

Swansea City 3 Manchester United 1

CLUB CAREER RECORD	Apps	Subs	Goals
Premiership	0		0
League Division 1	0		0
League Division 2	1		0
FA Cup	0		0
League Cup	0		0
European Cup / Champions League	0		0
European Cup-Winners' Cup	0		0
UEFA Cup / Inter-Cities' Fairs Cup	0		0
Other Matches	0		0
OVERALL TOTAL	**1**		**0**

Opponents	PREM A S G	FLD 1 A S G	FLD 2 A S G	FAC A S G	LC A S G	EC/CL A S G	ECWC A S G	UEFA A S G	OTHER A S G	TOTAL A S G
1 Swansea City	– –	– –	1	– – –	–	–	–	–	–	1 –

NEIL WHITWORTH

DEBUT (Full Appearance)

Wednesday 13/03/1991
Football League Division 1
at The Dell

Southampton 1 Manchester United 1

CLUB CAREER RECORD	Apps	Subs	Goals
Premiership	0		0
League Division 1	1		0
League Division 2	0		0
FA Cup	0		0
League Cup	0		0
European Cup / Champions League	0		0
European Cup-Winners' Cup	0		0
UEFA Cup / Inter-Cities' Fairs Cup	0		0
Other Matches	0		0
OVERALL TOTAL	**1**		**0**

Opponents	PREM A S G	FLD 1 A S G	FLD 2 A S G	FAC A S G	LC A S G	EC/CL A S G	ECWC A S G	UEFA A S G	OTHER A S G	TOTAL A S G
1 Southampton	– –	1 –	– –	– – –	–	–	–	–	–	1 –

TOM WILCOX

DEBUT (Full Appearance)

Saturday 24/10/1908
Football League Division 1
at Bank Street

Manchester United 2 Nottingham Forest 2

CLUB CAREER RECORD	Apps	Subs	Goals
Premiership	0		0
League Division 1	2		0
League Division 2	0		0
FA Cup	0		0
League Cup	0		0
European Cup / Champions League	0		0
European Cup-Winners' Cup	0		0
UEFA Cup / Inter-Cities' Fairs Cup	0		0
Other Matches	0		0
OVERALL TOTAL	2		0

Opponents	PREM A S G	FLD 1 A S G	FLD 2 A S G	FAC A S G	LC A S G	EC/CL A S G	ECWC A S G	UEFA A S G	OTHER A S G	TOTAL A S G
1 Nottingham Forest	– –	1 –	– –	– –	– –	– –	– –	– –	– –	1 –
2 Sheffield Wednesday	– –	1 –	– –	– –	– –	– –	– –	– –	– –	1 –

RAY WILKINS

DEBUT (Full Appearance)

Saturday 18/08/1979
Football League Division 1
at The Dell

Southampton 1 Manchester United 1

CLUB CAREER RECORD	Apps	Subs	Goals
Premiership	0		0
League Division 1	158	(2)	7
League Division 2	0		0
FA Cup	10		1
League Cup	14	(1)	1
European Cup / Champions League	0		0
European Cup-Winners' Cup	6		1
UEFA Cup / Inter-Cities' Fairs Cup	2		0
Other Matches	1		0
OVERALL TOTAL	191	(3)	10

Opponents	PREM A S G	FLD 1 A S G	FLD 2 A S G	FAC A S G	LC A S G	EC/CL A S G	ECWC A S G	UEFA A S G	OTHER A S G	TOTAL A S G
1 Tottenham Hotspur	– –	7 1	– –	2 –	4 –	– –	– –	– –	– –	13 1
2 Liverpool	– –	9 –	– –	– –	1 –	– –	– –	– –	1 –	11 –
3 Arsenal	– –	8 –	– –	1 –	– (1) –	– –	– –	– –	– –	9 (1) –
4 Brighton	– –	6 1	– –	3 1	– –	– –	– –	– –	– –	9 2
5 Nottingham Forest	– –	8 1	– –	1 –	– –	– –	– –	– –	– –	9 1
6 Everton	– –	8 –	– –	1 –	– –	– –	– –	– –	– –	9 –
7 Southampton	– –	9 –	– –	– –	– –	– –	– –	– –	– –	9 –
8 Coventry City	– –	8 1	– –	– –	– –	– –	– –	– –	– –	8 1
9 Stoke City	– –	8 1	– –	– –	– –	– –	– –	– –	– –	8 1
10 West Bromwich Albion	– –	8 –	– –	– –	– –	– –	– –	– –	– –	8 –
11 Manchester City	– –	7 –	– –	– –	– –	– –	– –	– –	– –	7 –
12 Norwich City	– –	6 –	– –	– –	1 –	– –	– –	– –	– –	7 –
13 Aston Villa	– –	6 –	– –	– –	– –	– –	– –	– –	– –	6 –
14 Ipswich Town	– –	6 –	– –	– –	– –	– –	– –	– –	– –	6 –
15 Wolverhampton W.	– –	6 –	– –	– –	– –	– –	– –	– –	– –	6 –
16 Sunderland	– –	5 1	– –	– –	– –	– –	– –	– –	– –	5 1
17 West Ham United	– –	5 1	– –	– –	– –	– –	– –	– –	– –	5 1
18 Birmingham City	– –	5 –	– –	– –	– –	– –	– –	– –	– –	5 –
19 Notts County	– –	5 –	– –	– –	– –	– –	– –	– –	– –	5 –
20 Leeds United	– –	4 –	– –	– –	– –	– –	– –	– –	– –	4 –
21 Middlesbrough	– –	4 –	– –	– –	– –	– –	– –	– –	– –	4 –
22 Watford	– –	3 –	– –	1 –	– –	– –	– –	– –	– –	4 –
23 Bournemouth	– –	– –	– –	1 –	2 –	– –	– –	– –	– –	3 –
24 Luton Town	– –	3 –	– –	– –	– –	– –	– –	– –	– –	3 –
25 Oxford United	– –	– –	– –	– –	3 –	– –	– –	– –	– –	3 –
26 Swansea City	– –	3 –	– –	– –	– –	– –	– –	– –	– –	3 –
27 Crystal Palace	– –	2 (1) –	– –	– –	– –	– –	– –	– –	– –	2 (1) –
28 Leicester City	– –	2 (1) –	– –	– –	– –	– –	– –	– –	– –	2 (1) –
29 Dukla Prague	– –	– –	– –	– –	– –	– –	2 1	– –	– –	2 1
30 Port Vale	– –	– –	– –	– –	2 1	– –	– –	– –	– –	2 1
31 Barcelona	– –	– –	– –	– –	– –	– –	2 –	– –	– –	2 –
32 Bolton Wanderers	– –	2 –	– –	– –	– –	– –	– –	– –	– –	2 –
33 Bristol City	– –	2 –	– –	– –	– –	– –	– –	– –	– –	2 –
34 Queens Park Rangers	– –	2 –	– –	– –	– –	– –	– –	– –	– –	2 –
35 Valencia	– –	– –	– –	– –	– –	– –	– –	2 –	– –	2 –
36 Colchester United	– –	– –	– –	– –	1 –	– –	– –	– –	– –	1 –
37 Derby County	– –	1 –	– –	– –	– –	– –	– –	– –	– –	1 –
38 Juventus	– –	– –	– –	– –	– –	– –	1 –	– –	– –	1 –
39 Spartak Varna	– –	– –	– –	– –	– –	– –	1 –	– –	– –	1 –

HARRY WILKINSON

DEBUT (Full Appearance)

Saturday 26/12/1903
Football League Division 2
at Peel Croft

Burton United 2 Manchester United 2

CLUB CAREER RECORD	Apps	Subs	Goals
Premiership	0		0
League Division 1	0		0
League Division 2	8		0
FA Cup	1		0
League Cup	0		0
European Cup / Champions League	0		0
European Cup-Winners' Cup	0		0
UEFA Cup / Inter-Cities' Fairs Cup	0		0
Other Matches	0		0
OVERALL TOTAL	**9**		**0**

Opponents	PREM A S G	FLD 1 A S G	FLD 2 A S G	FAC A S G	LC A S G	EC/CL A S G	ECWC A S G	UEFA A S G	OTHER A S G	TOTAL A S G
1 Birmingham City	–	–	–	1 –	–	–	–	–	–	1 –
2 Blackpool	–	–	1 –	–	–	–	–	–	–	1 –
3 Bradford City	–	–	1 –	–	–	–	–	–	–	1 –
4 Bristol City	–	–	1 –	–	–	–	–	–	–	1 –
5 Burnley	–	–	1 –	–	–	–	–	–	–	1 –
6 Burton United	–	–	1 –	–	–	–	–	–	–	1 –
7 Glossop	–	–	1 –	–	–	–	–	–	–	1 –
8 Port Vale	–	–	1 –	–	–	–	–	–	–	1 –
9 Preston North End	–	–	1 –	–	–	–	–	–	–	1 –

IAN WILKINSON

DEBUT (Full Appearance)

Wednesday 09/10/1991
League Cup 2nd Round 2nd Leg
at Abbey Stadium

Cambridge United 1 Manchester United 1

CLUB CAREER RECORD	Apps	Subs	Goals
Premiership	0		0
League Division 1	0		0
League Division 2	0		0
FA Cup	0		0
League Cup	1		0
European Cup / Champions League	0		0
European Cup-Winners' Cup	0		0
UEFA Cup / Inter-Cities' Fairs Cup	0		0
Other Matches	0		0
OVERALL TOTAL	**1**		**0**

Opponents	PREM A S G	FLD 1 A S G	FLD 2 A S G	FAC A S G	LC A S G	EC/CL A S G	ECWC A S G	UEFA A S G	OTHER A S G	TOTAL A S G
1 Cambridge United	–	–	–	–	1 –	–	–	–	–	1 –

BILL WILLIAMS

DEBUT (Full Appearance)

Saturday 07/09/1901
Football League Division 2
at Bank Street

Newton Heath 3 Gainsborough Trinity 0

CLUB CAREER RECORD	Apps	Subs	Goals
Premiership	0		0
League Division 1	0		0
League Division 2	4		0
FA Cup	0		0
League Cup	0		0
European Cup / Champions League	0		0
European Cup-Winners' Cup	0		0
UEFA Cup / Inter-Cities' Fairs Cup	0		0
Other Matches	0		0
OVERALL TOTAL	**4**		**0**

Opponents	PREM A S G	FLD 1 A S G	FLD 2 A S G	FAC A S G	LC A S G	EC/CL A S G	ECWC A S G	UEFA A S G	OTHER A S G	TOTAL A S G
1 Bristol City	–	–	1 –	–	–	–	–	–	–	1 –
2 Gainsborough Trinity	–	–	1 –	–	–	–	–	–	–	1 –
3 Glossop	–	–	1 –	–	–	–	–	–	–	1 –
4 Middlesbrough	–	–	1 –	–	–	–	–	–	–	1 –

FRANK WILLIAMS

DEBUT (Full Appearance)

Saturday 13/09/1930
Football League Division 1
at Old Trafford

Manchester United 4 Newcastle United 7

CLUB CAREER RECORD	Apps	Subs	Goals
Premiership	0		0
League Division 1	3		0
League Division 2	0		0
FA Cup	0		0
League Cup	0		0
European Cup / Champions League	0		0
European Cup-Winners' Cup	0		0
UEFA Cup / Inter-Cities' Fairs Cup	0		0
Other Matches	0		0
OVERALL TOTAL	**3**		**0**

Opponents	PREM A S G	FLD 1 A S G	FLD 2 A S G	FAC A S G	LC A S G	EC/CL A S G	ECWC A S G	UEFA A S G	OTHER A S G	TOTAL A S G
1 Huddersfield Town	–	1 –	–	–	–	–	–	–	–	1 –
2 Newcastle United	–	1 –	–	–	–	–	–	–	–	1 –
3 Sheffield Wednesday	–	1 –	–	–	–	–	–	–	–	1 –

FRED WILLIAMS

DEBUT (Full Appearance)

Saturday 06/09/1902
Football League Division 2
at The Northolme

Gainsborough Trinity 0 Manchester United 1

CLUB CAREER RECORD	Apps	Subs	Goals
Premiership	0		0
League Division 1	0		0
League Division 2	8		0
FA Cup	2		4
League Cup	0		0
European Cup / Champions League	0		0
European Cup-Winners' Cup	0		0
UEFA Cup / Inter-Cities' Fairs Cup	0		0
Other Matches	0		0
OVERALL TOTAL	10		4

Opponents	PREM A S G	FLD 1 A S G	FLD 2 A S G	FAC A S G	LC A S G	EC/CL A S G	ECWC A S G	UEFA A S G	OTHER A S G	TOTAL A S G
1 Accrington Stanley	- - -	- - -	- - -	1 - 3	- - -	- - -	- - -	- - -	- - -	1 - 3
2 Oswaldtwistle Rovers	- - -	- - -	- - -	1 - 1	- - -	- - -	- - -	- - -	- - -	1 - 1
3 Arsenal	- - -	- - -	1 - -	- - -	- - -	- - -	- - -	- - -	- - -	1 - -
4 Birmingham City	- - -	- - -	1 - -	- - -	- - -	- - -	- - -	- - -	- - -	1 - -
5 Bristol City	- - -	- - -	1 - -	- - -	- - -	- - -	- - -	- - -	- - -	1 - -
6 Burton United	- - -	- - -	1 - -	- - -	- - -	- - -	- - -	- - -	- - -	1 - -
7 Gainsborough Trinity	- - -	- - -	1 - -	- - -	- - -	- - -	- - -	- - -	- - -	1 - -
8 Glossop	- - -	- - -	1 - -	- - -	- - -	- - -	- - -	- - -	- - -	1 - -
9 Leicester City	- - -	- - -	1 - -	- - -	- - -	- - -	- - -	- - -	- - -	1 - -
10 Lincoln City	- - -	- - -	1 - -	- - -	- - -	- - -	- - -	- - -	- - -	1 - -

HARRY WILLIAMS (1900s)

DEBUT (Full Appearance, 1 goal)

Saturday 10/09/1904
Football League Division 2
at Bank Street

Manchester United 4 Bristol City 1

CLUB CAREER RECORD	Apps	Subs	Goals
Premiership	0		0
League Division 1	1		0
League Division 2	32		7
FA Cup	4		1
League Cup	0		0
European Cup / Champions League	0		0
European Cup-Winners' Cup	0		0
UEFA Cup / Inter-Cities' Fairs Cup	0		0
Other Matches	0		0
OVERALL TOTAL	37		8

Opponents	PREM A S G	FLD 1 A S G	FLD 2 A S G	FAC A S G	LC A S G	EC/CL A S G	ECWC A S G	UEFA A S G	OTHER A S G	TOTAL A S G
1 Bristol City	- - -	- - -	3 - 1	- - -	- - -	- - -	- - -	- - -	- - -	3 - 1
2 Glossop	- - -	- - -	3 - 1	- - -	- - -	- - -	- - -	- - -	- - -	3 - 1
3 Barnsley	- - -	- - -	3 - -	- - -	- - -	- - -	- - -	- - -	- - -	3 - -
4 Burnley	- - -	- - -	3 - -	- - -	- - -	- - -	- - -	- - -	- - -	3 - -
5 West Bromwich Albion	- - -	- - -	2 - 2	- - -	- - -	- - -	- - -	- - -	- - -	2 - 2
6 Bolton Wanderers	- - -	- - -	2 - 1	- - -	- - -	- - -	- - -	- - -	- - -	2 - 1
7 Fulham	- - -	- - -	- - -	2 - -	- - -	- - -	- - -	- - -	- - -	2 - -
8 Grimsby Town	- - -	- - -	2 - -	- - -	- - -	- - -	- - -	- - -	- - -	2 - -
9 Leicester City	- - -	- - -	2 - -	- - -	- - -	- - -	- - -	- - -	- - -	2 - -
10 Lincoln City	- - -	- - -	2 - -	- - -	- - -	- - -	- - -	- - -	- - -	2 - -
11 Port Vale	- - -	- - -	2 - -	- - -	- - -	- - -	- - -	- - -	- - -	2 - -
12 Chesterfield	- - -	- - -	1 - 1	- - -	- - -	- - -	- - -	- - -	- - -	1 - 1
13 Liverpool	- - -	- - -	1 - 1	- - -	- - -	- - -	- - -	- - -	- - -	1 - 1
14 Staple Hill	- - -	- - -	- - -	1 - 1	- - -	- - -	- - -	- - -	- - -	1 - 1
15 Arsenal	- - -	1 - -	- - -	- - -	- - -	- - -	- - -	- - -	- - -	1 - -
16 Burton United	- - -	- - -	1 - -	- - -	- - -	- - -	- - -	- - -	- - -	1 - -
17 Doncaster Rovers	- - -	- - -	1 - -	- - -	- - -	- - -	- - -	- - -	- - -	1 - -
18 Gainsborough Trinity	- - -	- - -	1 - -	- - -	- - -	- - -	- - -	- - -	- - -	1 - -
19 Leeds United	- - -	- - -	1 - -	- - -	- - -	- - -	- - -	- - -	- - -	1 - -
20 Leyton Orient	- - -	- - -	1 - -	- - -	- - -	- - -	- - -	- - -	- - -	1 - -
21 Norwich City	- - -	- - -	- - -	1 - -	- - -	- - -	- - -	- - -	- - -	1 - -
22 Stockport County	- - -	- - -	1 - -	- - -	- - -	- - -	- - -	- - -	- - -	1 - -

HARRY WILLIAMS (1920s)

DEBUT (Full Appearance)

Monday 28/08/1922
Football League Division 2
at Hillsborough

Sheffield Wednesday 1 Manchester United 0

CLUB CAREER RECORD	Apps	Subs	Goals
Premiership	0		0
League Division 1	0		0
League Division 2	5		2
FA Cup	0		0
League Cup	0		0
European Cup / Champions League	0		0
European Cup-Winners' Cup	0		0
UEFA Cup / Inter-Cities' Fairs Cup	0		0
Other Matches	0		0
OVERALL TOTAL	5		2

Opponents	PREM A S G	FLD 1 A S G	FLD 2 A S G	FAC A S G	LC A S G	EC/CL A S G	ECWC A S G	UEFA A S G	OTHER A S G	TOTAL A S G
1 Sheffield Wednesday	- - -	- - -	2 - -	- - -	- - -	- - -	- - -	- - -	- - -	2 - -
2 Crystal Palace	- - -	- - -	1 - 1	- - -	- - -	- - -	- - -	- - -	- - -	1 - 1
3 Wolverhampton W.	- - -	- - -	1 - 1	- - -	- - -	- - -	- - -	- - -	- - -	1 - 1
4 Fulham	- - -	- - -	1 - -	- - -	- - -	- - -	- - -	- - -	- - -	1 - -

JOE WILLIAMS

DEBUT (Full Appearance, 1 goal)

Monday 25/03/1907
Football League Division 1
at Bank Street

Manchester United 2 Sunderland 0

CLUB CAREER RECORD	Apps	Subs	Goals
Premiership	0		0
League Division 1	3		1
League Division 2	0		0
FA Cup	0		0
League Cup	0		0
European Cup / Champions League	0		0
European Cup–Winners' Cup	0		0
UEFA Cup / Inter-Cities' Fairs Cup	0		0
Other Matches	0		0
OVERALL TOTAL	**3**		**1**

Opponents	PREM A S G	FLD 1 A S G	FLD 2 A S G	FAC A S G	LC A S G	EC/CL A S G	ECWC A S G	UEFA A S G	OTHER A S G	TOTAL A S G
1 Sunderland	– –	1 1	– –	–	–	–	–	–	–	1 1
2 Bury	– –	1	–	–	–	–	–	–	–	1 –
3 Liverpool	– –	1	–	–	–	–	–	–	–	1 –

REES WILLIAMS

DEBUT (Full Appearance)

Saturday 08/10/1927
Football League Division 1
at Goodison Park

Everton 5 Manchester United 2

CLUB CAREER RECORD	Apps	Subs	Goals
Premiership	0		0
League Division 1	31		2
League Division 2	0		0
FA Cup	4		0
League Cup	0		0
European Cup / Champions League	0		0
European Cup–Winners' Cup	0		0
UEFA Cup / Inter-Cities' Fairs Cup	0		0
Other Matches	0		0
OVERALL TOTAL	**35**		**2**

Opponents	PREM A S G	FLD 1 A S G	FLD 2 A S G	FAC A S G	LC A S G	EC/CL A S G	ECWC A S G	UEFA A S G	OTHER A S G	TOTAL A S G
1 Bury	– –	2 1	– –	2 –	–	–	–	–	–	4 1
2 Burnley	– –	3 1	–	–	–	–	–	–	–	3 1
3 Aston Villa	– –	2	–	–	–	–	–	–	–	2 –
4 Blackburn Rovers	– –	1	–	1	–	–	–	–	–	2 –
5 Bolton Wanderers	– –	2	–	–	–	–	–	–	–	2 –
6 Cardiff City	– –	2	–	–	–	–	–	–	–	2 –
7 Derby County	– –	2	–	–	–	–	–	–	–	2 –
8 Leeds United	– –	2	–	–	–	–	–	–	–	2 –
9 Manchester City	– –	2	–	–	–	–	–	–	–	2 –
10 Sunderland	– –	2	–	–	–	–	–	–	–	2 –
11 West Ham United	– –	2	–	–	–	–	–	–	–	2 –
12 Arsenal	– –	1	–	–	–	–	–	–	–	1 –
13 Birmingham City	– –	1	–	–	–	–	–	–	–	1 –
14 Everton	– –	1	–	–	–	–	–	–	–	1 –
15 Leicester City	– –	1	–	–	–	–	–	–	–	1 –
16 Liverpool	– –	1	–	–	–	–	–	–	–	1 –
17 Newcastle United	– –	1	–	–	–	–	–	–	–	1 –
18 Port Vale	– –	–	–	1	–	–	–	–	–	1 –
19 Portsmouth	– –	1	–	–	–	–	–	–	–	1 –
20 Sheffield United	– –	1	–	–	–	–	–	–	–	1 –
21 Sheffield Wednesday	– –	1	–	–	–	–	–	–	–	1 –

JOHN WILLIAMSON

DEBUT (Full Appearance)

Saturday 17/04/1920
Football League Division 1
at Old Trafford

Manchester United 1 Blackburn Rovers 1

CLUB CAREER RECORD	Apps	Subs	Goals
Premiership	0		0
League Division 1	2		0
League Division 2	0		0
FA Cup	0		0
League Cup	0		0
European Cup / Champions League	0		0
European Cup–Winners' Cup	0		0
UEFA Cup / Inter-Cities' Fairs Cup	0		0
Other Matches	0		0
OVERALL TOTAL	**2**		**0**

Opponents	PREM A S G	FLD 1 A S G	FLD 2 A S G	FAC A S G	LC A S G	EC/CL A S G	ECWC A S G	UEFA A S G	OTHER A S G	TOTAL A S G
1 Blackburn Rovers	– –	2	–	–	–	–	–	–	–	2 –

DAVID WILSON

DEBUT (Substitute Appearance)

Wednesday 23/11/1988
Football League Division 1
at Old Trafford

Manchester United 1 Sheffield Wednesday 1

CLUB CAREER RECORD	Apps	Subs	Goals
Premiership	0		0
League Division 1	0	(4)	0
League Division 2	0		0
FA Cup	0	(2)	0
League Cup	0		0
European Cup / Champions League	0		0
European Cup-Winners' Cup	0		0
UEFA Cup / Inter-Cities' Fairs Cup	0		0
Other Matches	0		0
OVERALL TOTAL	**0**	**(6)**	**0**

Opponents	PREM A S G	FLD 1 A S G	FLD 2 A S G	FAC A S G	LC A S G	EC/CL A S G	ECWC A S G	UEFA A S G	OTHER A S G	TOTAL A S G
1 Queens Park Rangers	– – –	– – –	– – –	– (2) –	– – –	– – –	– – –	– – –	– – –	– (2) –
2 Derby County	– – –	– (1) –	– – –	– – –	– – –	– – –	– – –	– – –	– – –	– (1) –
3 Middlesbrough	– – –	– (1) –	– – –	– – –	– – –	– – –	– – –	– – –	– – –	– (1) –
4 Millwall	– – –	– (1) –	– – –	– – –	– – –	– – –	– – –	– – –	– – –	– (1) –
5 Sheffield Wednesday	– – –	– (1) –	– – –	– – –	– – –	– – –	– – –	– – –	– – –	– (1) –

EDGAR WILSON

DEBUT (Full Appearance)

Saturday 18/01/1889
FA Cup 1st Round
at Deepdale

Preston North End 6 Newton Heath 1

CLUB CAREER RECORD	Apps	Subs	Goals
Premiership	0		0
League Division 1	0		0
League Division 2	0		0
FA Cup	1		0
League Cup	0		0
European Cup / Champions League	0		0
European Cup-Winners' Cup	0		0
UEFA Cup / Inter-Cities' Fairs Cup	0		0
Other Matches	0		0
OVERALL TOTAL	**1**		**0**

Opponents	PREM A S G	FLD 1 A S G	FLD 2 A S G	FAC A S G	LC A S G	EC/CL A S G	ECWC A S G	UEFA A S G	OTHER A S G	TOTAL A S G
1 Preston North End	– – –	– – –	– – –	1 – –	– – –	– – –	– – –	– – –	– – –	1 – –

JACK WILSON

DEBUT (Full Appearance)

Saturday 04/09/1926
Football League Division 1
at Old Trafford

Manchester United 2 Leeds United 2

CLUB CAREER RECORD	Apps	Subs	Goals
Premiership	0		0
League Division 1	121		3
League Division 2	9		0
FA Cup	10		0
League Cup	0		0
European Cup / Champions League	0		0
European Cup-Winners' Cup	0		0
UEFA Cup / Inter-Cities' Fairs Cup	0		0
Other Matches	0		0
OVERALL TOTAL	**140**		**3**

Opponents	PREM A S G	FLD 1 A S G	FLD 2 A S G	FAC A S G	LC A S G	EC/CL A S G	ECWC A S G	UEFA A S G	OTHER A S G	TOTAL A S G
1 Birmingham City	– – –	7 – –	– – –	1 – –	– – –	– – –	– – –	– – –	– – –	8 – –
2 Leeds United	– – –	7 – –	1 – –	– – –	– – –	– – –	– – –	– – –	– – –	8 – –
3 West Ham United	– – –	8 – –	– – –	– – –	– – –	– – –	– – –	– – –	– – –	8 – –
4 Sunderland	– – –	7 – –	– – –	– – –	– – –	– – –	– – –	– – –	– – –	7 – –
5 Aston Villa	– – –	6 – –	– – –	– – –	– – –	– – –	– – –	– – –	– – –	6 – –
6 Bolton Wanderers	– – –	6 – –	– – –	– – –	– – –	– – –	– – –	– – –	– – –	6 – –
7 Derby County	– – –	6 – –	– – –	– – –	– – –	– – –	– – –	– – –	– – –	6 – –
8 Everton	– – –	6 – –	– – –	– – –	– – –	– – –	– – –	– – –	– – –	6 – –
9 Sheffield Wednesday	– – –	6 – –	– – –	– – –	– – –	– – –	– – –	– – –	– – –	6 – –
10 Arsenal	– – –	5 – 1	– – –	– – –	– – –	– – –	– – –	– – –	– – –	5 – 1
11 Liverpool	– – –	5 – 1	– – –	– – –	– – –	– – –	– – –	– – –	– – –	5 – 1
12 Burnley	– – –	4 – –	1 – –	– – –	– – –	– – –	– – –	– – –	– – –	5 – –
13 Bury	– – –	2 – –	– – –	3 – –	– – –	– – –	– – –	– – –	– – –	5 – –
14 Huddersfield Town	– – –	5 – –	– – –	– – –	– – –	– – –	– – –	– – –	– – –	5 – –
15 Leicester City	– – –	5 – –	– – –	– – –	– – –	– – –	– – –	– – –	– – –	5 – –
16 Portsmouth	– – –	5 – –	– – –	– – –	– – –	– – –	– – –	– – –	– – –	5 – –
17 Sheffield United	– – –	5 – –	– – –	– – –	– – –	– – –	– – –	– – –	– – –	5 – –
18 Blackburn Rovers	– – –	3 – –	– – –	1 – –	– – –	– – –	– – –	– – –	– – –	4 – –
19 Cardiff City	– – –	4 – –	– – –	– – –	– – –	– – –	– – –	– – –	– – –	4 – –
20 Middlesbrough	– – –	4 – –	– – –	– – –	– – –	– – –	– – –	– – –	– – –	4 – –
21 Newcastle United	– – –	4 – –	– – –	– – –	– – –	– – –	– – –	– – –	– – –	4 – –
22 Tottenham Hotspur	– – –	3 – –	1 – –	– – –	– – –	– – –	– – –	– – –	– – –	4 – –
23 Manchester City	– – –	3 – 1	– – –	– – –	– – –	– – –	– – –	– – –	– – –	3 – 1
24 Stoke City	– – –	– – –	1 – 2	– – –	– – –	– – –	– – –	– – –	– – –	3 – –
25 Plymouth Argyle	– – –	– – –	2 – –	– – –	– – –	– – –	– – –	– – –	– – –	2 – –
26 West Bromwich Albion	– – –	2 – –	– – –	– – –	– – –	– – –	– – –	– – –	– – –	2 – –
27 Blackpool	– – –	1 – –	– – –	– – –	– – –	– – –	– – –	– – –	– – –	1 – –

continued../

JACK WILSON (continued)

Opponents	PREM A S G	FLD 1 A S G	FLD 2 A S G	FAC A S G	LC A S G	EC/CL A S G	ECWC A S G	UEFA A S G	OTHER A S G	TOTAL A S G
28 Brentford	- -	- -	- -	1 -	- -	- -	- -	- -	- -	1 -
29 Chelsea	- -	1 -	- -	- -	- -	- -	- -	- -	- -	1 -
30 Chesterfield	- -	- -	1 -	- -	- -	- -	- -	- -	- -	1 -
31 Grimsby Town	- -	1 -	- -	- -	- -	- -	- -	- -	- -	1 -
32 Nottingham Forest	- -	- -	1 -	- -	- -	- -	- -	- -	- -	1 -
33 Notts County	- -	- -	1 -	- -	- -	- -	- -	- -	- -	1 -
34 Port Vale	- -	- -	- -	1 -	- -	- -	- -	- -	- -	1 -
35 Swindon Town	- -	- -	- -	1 -	- -	- -	- -	- -	- -	1 -

MARK WILSON

DEBUT (Substitute Appearance)

Wednesday 21/10/1998
Champions League Phase 1 Match 3
at Parken Stadion

Brondby 2 Manchester United 6

CLUB CAREER RECORD	Apps	Subs	Goals
Premiership	1	(2)	0
League Division 1	0		0
League Division 2	0		0
FA Cup	0		0
League Cup	2		0
European Cup / Champions League	2	(2)	0
European Cup-Winners' Cup	0		0
UEFA Cup / Inter-Cities' Fairs Cup	0		0
Other Matches	1		0
OVERALL TOTAL	6	(4)	0

Opponents	PREM A S G	FLD 1 A S G	FLD 2 A S G	FAC A S G	LC A S G	EC/CL A S G	ECWC A S G	UEFA A S G	OTHER A S G	TOTAL A S G
1 Sturm Graz	- -	- -	- -	- -	- -	1 (1) -	- -	- -	- -	1 (1) -
2 Bury	- -	- -	- -	- -	1 -	- -	- -	- -	- -	1 -
3 Croatia Zagreb	- -	- -	- -	- -	- -	1 -	- -	- -	- -	1 -
4 Nottingham Forest	- -	- -	- -	- -	1 -	- -	- -	- -	- -	1 -
5 South Melbourne	- -	- -	- -	- -	- -	- -	- -	- -	1 -	1 -
6 Watford	1 -	- -	- -	- -	- -	- -	- -	- -	- -	1 -
7 Aston Villa	- (1) -	- -	- -	- -	- -	- -	- -	- -	- -	- (1) -
8 Brondby	- -	- -	- -	- -	- -	- (1) -	- -	- -	- -	- (1) -
9 Chelsea	- (1) -	- -	- -	- -	- -	- -	- -	- -	- -	- (1) -

TOMMY WILSON

DEBUT (Full Appearance)

Saturday 15/02/1908
Football League Division 1
at Bank Street

Manchester United 1 Blackburn Rovers 2

CLUB CAREER RECORD	Apps	Subs	Goals
Premiership	0		0
League Division 1	1		0
League Division 2	0		0
FA Cup	0		0
League Cup	0		0
European Cup / Champions League	0		0
European Cup-Winners' Cup	0		0
UEFA Cup / Inter-Cities' Fairs Cup	0		0
Other Matches	0		0
OVERALL TOTAL	1		0

Opponents	PREM A S G	FLD 1 A S G	FLD 2 A S G	FAC A S G	LC A S G	EC/CL A S G	ECWC A S G	UEFA A S G	OTHER A S G	TOTAL A S G
1 Blackburn Rovers	- -	1 -	- -	- -	- -	- -	- -	- -	- -	1 -

WALTER WINTERBOTTOM

DEBUT (Full Appearance)

Saturday 28/11/1936
Football League Division 1
at Elland Road

Leeds United 2 Manchester United 1

CLUB CAREER RECORD	Apps	Subs	Goals
Premiership	0		0
League Division 1	21		0
League Division 2	4		0
FA Cup	2		0
League Cup	0		0
European Cup / Champions League	0		0
European Cup-Winners' Cup	0		0
UEFA Cup / Inter-Cities' Fairs Cup	0		0
Other Matches	0		0
OVERALL TOTAL	27		0

Opponents	PREM A S G	FLD 1 A S G	FLD 2 A S G	FAC A S G	LC A S G	EC/CL A S G	ECWC A S G	UEFA A S G	OTHER A S G	TOTAL A S G
1 Arsenal	- -	1 -	- -	1 -	- -	- -	- -	- -	- -	2 -
2 Bolton Wanderers	- -	2 -	- -	- -	- -	- -	- -	- -	- -	2 -
3 Barnsley	- -	- -	1 -	- -	- -	- -	- -	- -	- -	1 -
4 Birmingham City	- -	1 -	- -	- -	- -	- -	- -	- -	- -	1 -
5 Brentford	- -	1 -	- -	- -	- -	- -	- -	- -	- -	1 -
6 Bury	- -	- -	1 -	- -	- -	- -	- -	- -	- -	1 -

continued../

WALTER WINTERBOTTOM (continued)

Opponents	PREM			FLD 1			FLD 2			FAC			LC			EC/CL			ECWC			UEFA			OTHER			TOTAL		
	A	S	G	A	S	G	A	S	G	A	S	G	A	S	G	A	S	G	A	S	G	A	S	G	A	S	G	A	S	G
7 Charlton Athletic	–	–		1																								1	–	
8 Chelsea	–	–		1																								1	–	
9 Derby County	–	–		1																								1	–	
10 Everton	–	–		1																								1	–	
11 Grimsby Town	–	–		1																								1	–	
12 Leeds United	–	–		1																								1	–	
13 Liverpool	–	–		1																								1	–	
14 Manchester City	–	–		1																								1	–	
15 Middlesbrough	–	–		1																								1	–	
16 Portsmouth	–	–		1																								1	–	
17 Preston North End	–	–		1																								1	–	
18 Reading	–	–		–						1																		1	–	
19 Sheffield Wednesday	–	–		1																								1	–	
20 Southampton	–	–		–			1																					1	–	
21 Stockport County	–	–		–						1																		1	–	
22 Stoke City	–	–		1																								1	–	
23 Sunderland	–	–		1																								1	–	
24 West Bromwich Albion	–	–		1																								1	–	
25 Wolverhampton W.	–	–		1																								1	–	

DICK WOMBWELL

DEBUT (Full Appearance)

Saturday 18/03/1905
Football League Division 2
at Bank Street

Manchester United 2 Grimsby Town 1

CLUB CAREER RECORD	Apps	Subs	Goals
Premiership	0		0
League Division 1	14		0
League Division 2	33		3
FA Cup	4		0
League Cup	0		0
European Cup / Champions League	0		0
European Cup-Winners' Cup	0		0
UEFA Cup / Inter-Cities' Fairs Cup	0		0
Other Matches	0		0
OVERALL TOTAL	51		3

Opponents	PREM			FLD 1			FLD 2			FAC			LC			EC/CL			ECWC			UEFA			OTHER			TOTAL		
	A	S	G	A	S	G	A	S	G	A	S	G	A	S	G	A	S	G	A	S	G	A	S	G	A	S	G	A	S	G
1 Blackpool	–	–		–			3																					3	–	
2 Chesterfield	–	–		–			3																					3	–	
3 Gainsborough Trinity	–	–		–			3																					3	–	
4 Arsenal	–	–		1			–			1																		2	–	
5 Aston Villa	–	–		1			–			1																		2	–	
6 Burton United	–	–		–			2																					2	–	
7 Chelsea	–	–		–			2																					2	–	
8 Grimsby Town	–	–		–			2																					2	–	
9 Hull City	–	–		–			2																					2	–	
10 Leicester City	–	–		–			2																					2	–	
11 Lincoln City	–	–		–			2																					2	–	
12 Portsmouth	–	–		–			–			2																		2	–	
13 West Bromwich Albion	–	–		–			2																					2	–	
14 Bradford City	–	–		–			1		1																			1		1
15 Doncaster Rovers	–	–		–			1		1																			1		1
16 Leeds United	–	–		–			1		1																			1		1
17 Barnsley	–	–		–			1																					1	–	
18 Birmingham City	–	–		1																								1	–	
19 Blackburn Rovers	–	–		1																								1	–	
20 Bolton Wanderers	–	–		1																								1	–	
21 Bristol City	–	–		1																								1	–	
22 Burnley	–	–		–			–			1																		1	–	
23 Bury	–	–		1																								1	–	
24 Everton	–	–		1																								1	–	
25 Glossop	–	–		–			1																					1	–	
26 Leyton Orient	–	–		–			1																					1	–	
27 Liverpool	–	–		–			1																					1	–	
28 Manchester City	–	–		1																								1	–	
29 Middlesbrough	–	–		1																								1	–	
30 Port Vale	–	–		–			–			1																		1	–	
31 Preston North End	–	–		1																								1	–	
32 Sheffield United	–	–		1																								1	–	
33 Sheffield Wednesday	–	–		1																								1	–	
34 Stockport County	–	–		–			–			1																		1	–	
35 Sunderland	–	–		1																								1	–	

JOHN WOOD

DEBUT (Full Appearance, 1 goal)

Saturday 26/08/1922
Football League Division 2
at Old Trafford

Manchester United 2 Crystal Palace 1

CLUB CAREER RECORD	Apps	Subs	Goals
Premiership	0		0
League Division 1	0		0
League Division 2	15		1
FA Cup	1		0
League Cup	0		0
European Cup / Champions League	0		0
European Cup-Winners' Cup	0		0
UEFA Cup / Inter-Cities' Fairs Cup	0		0
Other Matches	0		0
OVERALL TOTAL	**16**		**1**

Opponents	PREM A S G	FLD 1 A S G	FLD 2 A S G	FAC A S G	LC A S G	EC/CL A S G	ECWC A S G	UEFA A S G	OTHER A S G	TOTAL A S G
1 Crystal Palace	– –	– –	2 1	– –	– –	– –	– –	– –	– –	2 1
2 Fulham	– –	– –	2 –	– –	– –	– –	– –	– –	– –	2 –
3 Hull City	– –	– –	2 –	– –	– –	– –	– –	– –	– –	2 –
4 Rotherham United	– –	– –	2 –	– –	– –	– –	– –	– –	– –	2 –
5 Sheffield Wednesday	– –	– –	2 –	– –	– –	– –	– –	– –	– –	2 –
6 Wolverhampton W.	– –	– –	2 –	– –	– –	– –	– –	– –	– –	2 –
7 Bradford City	– –	– –	– –	1 –	– –	– –	– –	– –	– –	1 –
8 Leyton Orient	– –	– –	1 –	– –	– –	– –	– –	– –	– –	1 –
9 Port Vale	– –	– –	1 –	– –	– –	– –	– –	– –	– –	1 –
10 West Ham United	– –	– –	1 –	– –	– –	– –	– –	– –	– –	1 –

NICKY WOOD

DEBUT (Substitute Appearance)

Thursday 26/12/1985
Football League Division 1
at Goodison Park

Everton 3 Manchester United 1

CLUB CAREER RECORD	Apps	Subs	Goals
Premiership	0		0
League Division 1	2	(1)	0
League Division 2	0		0
FA Cup	0		0
League Cup	0	(1)	0
European Cup / Champions League	0		0
European Cup-Winners' Cup	0		0
UEFA Cup / Inter-Cities' Fairs Cup	0		0
Other Matches	0		0
OVERALL TOTAL	**2**	**(2)**	**0**

Opponents	PREM A S G	FLD 1 A S G	FLD 2 A S G	FAC A S G	LC A S G	EC/CL A S G	ECWC A S G	UEFA A S G	OTHER A S G	TOTAL A S G
1 Nottingham Forest	– –	1 –	– –	– –	– –	– –	– –	– –	– –	1 –
2 Oxford United	– –	1 –	– –	– –	– –	– –	– –	– –	– –	1 –
3 Everton	– –	– (1) –	– –	– –	– –	– –	– –	– –	– –	– (1) –
4 Southampton	– –	– –	– –	– –	– (1) –	– –	– –	– –	– –	– (1) –

RAY WOOD

DEBUT (Full Appearance)

Saturday 03/12/1949
Football League Division 1
at Old Trafford

Manchester United 1 Newcastle United 1

CLUB CAREER RECORD	Apps	Subs	Goals
Premiership	0		0
League Division 1	178		0
League Division 2	0		0
FA Cup	15		0
League Cup	0		0
European Cup / Champions League	12		0
European Cup-Winners' Cup	0		0
UEFA Cup / Inter-Cities' Fairs Cup	0		0
Other Matches	3		0
OVERALL TOTAL	**208**		**0**

Opponents	PREM A S G	FLD 1 A S G	FLD 2 A S G	FAC A S G	LC A S G	EC/CL A S G	ECWC A S G	UEFA A S G	OTHER A S G	TOTAL A S G
1 Aston Villa	– –	10 –	– –	1 –	– –	– –	– –	– –	1 –	12 –
2 Manchester City	– –	10 –	– –	1 –	– –	– –	– –	– –	1 –	12 –
3 Blackpool	– –	10 –	– –	– –	– –	– –	– –	– –	– –	10 –
4 Bolton Wanderers	– –	10 –	– –	– –	– –	– –	– –	– –	– –	10 –
5 Everton	– –	8 –	– –	2 –	– –	– –	– –	– –	– –	10 –
6 Newcastle United	– –	9 –	– –	– –	– –	– –	– –	– –	1 –	10 –
7 Burnley	– –	8 –	– –	1 –	– –	– –	– –	– –	– –	9 –
8 Chelsea	– –	9 –	– –	– –	– –	– –	– –	– –	– –	9 –
9 Portsmouth	– –	9 –	– –	– –	– –	– –	– –	– –	– –	9 –
10 Wolverhampton W.	– –	9 –	– –	– –	– –	– –	– –	– –	– –	9 –
11 Arsenal	– –	8 –	– –	– –	– –	– –	– –	– –	– –	8 –
12 Preston North End	– –	8 –	– –	– –	– –	– –	– –	– –	– –	8 –
13 Sunderland	– –	8 –	– –	– –	– –	– –	– –	– –	– –	8 –
14 Cardiff City	– –	7 –	– –	– –	– –	– –	– –	– –	– –	7 –
15 Sheffield Wednesday	– –	7 –	– –	– –	– –	– –	– –	– –	– –	7 –
16 Tottenham Hotspur	– –	7 –	– –	– –	– –	– –	– –	– –	– –	7 –
17 Birmingham City	– –	5 –	– –	1 –	– –	– –	– –	– –	– –	6 –
18 Charlton Athletic	– –	6 –	– –	– –	– –	– –	– –	– –	– –	6 –
19 West Bromwich Albion	– –	6 –	– –	– –	– –	– –	– –	– –	– –	6 –

continued../

RAY WOOD (continued)

Opponents	PREM A	S	G	FLD 1 A	S	G	FLD 2 A	S	G	FAC A	S	G	LC A	S	G	EC/CL A	S	G	ECWC A	S	G	UEFA A	S	G	OTHER A	S	G	TOTAL A	S	G
20 Sheffield United	–	–		5	–		–	–		–	–		–	–		–	–		–	–		–	–		–	–		5	–	
21 Huddersfield Town	–	–		4			–	–		–	–		–	–		–	–		–	–		–	–		–	–		4	–	
22 Luton Town	–	–		4			–	–		–	–		–	–		–	–		–	–		–	–		–	–		4	–	
23 Leeds United	–	–		3			–	–		–	–		–	–		–	–		–	–		–	–		–	–		3	–	
24 Anderlecht	–	–		–	–		–	–		–	–		–	–		2			–	–		–	–		–	–		2	–	
25 Athletic Bilbao	–	–		–	–		–	–		–	–		–	–		2			–	–		–	–		–	–		2	–	
26 Borussia Dortmund	–	–		–	–		–	–		–	–		–	–		2			–	–		–	–		–	–		2	–	
27 Dukla Prague	–	–		–	–		–	–		–	–		–	–		2			–	–		–	–		–	–		2	–	
28 Leicester City	–	–		2			–	–		–	–		–	–		–	–		–	–		–	–		–	–		2	–	
29 Middlesbrough	–	–		2			–	–		–	–		–	–		–	–		–	–		–	–		–	–		2	–	
30 Reading	–	–		–	–		–	–		2			–	–		–	–		–	–		–	–		–	–		2	–	
31 Real Madrid	–	–		–	–		–	–		–	–		–	–		2			–	–		–	–		–	–		2	–	
32 Shamrock Rovers	–	–		–	–		–	–		–	–		–	–		2			–	–		–	–		–	–		2	–	
33 Walthamstow Avenue	–	–		–	–		–	–		2			–	–		–	–		–	–		–	–		–	–		2	–	
34 Bournemouth	–	–		–	–		–	–		1			–	–		–	–		–	–		–	–		–	–		1	–	
35 Bristol Rovers	–	–		–	–		–	–		1			–	–		–	–		–	–		–	–		–	–		1	–	
36 Derby County	–	–		1			–	–		–	–		–	–		–	–		–	–		–	–		–	–		1	–	
37 Hartlepool United	–	–		–	–		–	–		1			–	–		–	–		–	–		–	–		–	–		1	–	
38 Liverpool	–	–		1			–	–		–	–		–	–		–	–		–	–		–	–		–	–		1	–	
39 Millwall	–	–		–	–		–	–		1			–	–		–	–		–	–		–	–		–	–		1	–	
40 Nottingham Forest	–	–		1			–	–		–	–		–	–		–	–		–	–		–	–		–	–		1	–	
41 Stoke City	–	–		1			–	–		–	–		–	–		–	–		–	–		–	–		–	–		1	–	
42 Wrexham	–	–		–	–		–	–		1			–	–		–	–		–	–		–	–		–	–		1	–	

WILF WOODCOCK

DEBUT (Full Appearance)

Saturday 01/11/1913
Football League Division 1
at Old Trafford

Manchester United 3 Liverpool 0

CLUB CAREER RECORD	Apps	Subs	Goals
Premiership	0		0
League Division 1	58		20
League Division 2	0		0
FA Cup	3		1
League Cup	0		0
European Cup / Champions League	0		0
European Cup–Winners' Cup	0		0
UEFA Cup / Inter–Cities' Fairs Cup	0		0
Other Matches	0		0
OVERALL TOTAL	61		21

Opponents	PREM A	S	G	FLD 1 A	S	G	FLD 2 A	S	G	FAC A	S	G	LC A	S	G	EC/CL A	S	G	ECWC A	S	G	UEFA A	S	G	OTHER A	S	G	TOTAL A	S	G
1 West Bromwich Albion	–	–		5		1	–	–		–	–		–	–		–	–		–	–		–	–		–	–		5		1
2 Burnley	–	–		5		–	–	–		–	–		–	–		–	–		–	–		–	–		–	–		5		–
3 Aston Villa	–	–		3		1	–	–		1		1	–	–		–	–		–	–		–	–		–	–		4		2
4 Bolton Wanderers	–	–		4		2	–	–		–	–		–	–		–	–		–	–		–	–		–	–		4		2
5 Middlesbrough	–	–		4		2	–	–		–	–		–	–		–	–		–	–		–	–		–	–		4		2
6 Sheffield Wednesday	–	–		4		2	–	–		–	–		–	–		–	–		–	–		–	–		–	–		4		2
7 Chelsea	–	–		4		1	–	–		–	–		–	–		–	–		–	–		–	–		–	–		4		1
8 Sheffield United	–	–		3		2	–	–		–	–		–	–		–	–		–	–		–	–		–	–		3		2
9 Everton	–	–		3		1	–	–		–	–		–	–		–	–		–	–		–	–		–	–		3		1
10 Bradford City	–	–		3		–	–	–		–	–		–	–		–	–		–	–		–	–		–	–		3		–
11 Liverpool	–	–		3		–	–	–		–	–		–	–		–	–		–	–		–	–		–	–		3		–
12 Manchester City	–	–		3		–	–	–		–	–		–	–		–	–		–	–		–	–		–	–		3		–
13 Blackburn Rovers	–	–		2		2	–	–		–	–		–	–		–	–		–	–		–	–		–	–		2		2
14 Preston North End	–	–		2		2	–	–		–	–		–	–		–	–		–	–		–	–		–	–		2		2
15 Bradford Park Avenue	–	–		2		1	–	–		–	–		–	–		–	–		–	–		–	–		–	–		2		1
16 Derby County	–	–		2		1	–	–		–	–		–	–		–	–		–	–		–	–		–	–		2		1
17 Oldham Athletic	–	–		2		1	–	–		–	–		–	–		–	–		–	–		–	–		–	–		2		1
18 Sunderland	–	–		2		–	–	–		–	–		–	–		–	–		–	–		–	–		–	–		2		–
19 Tottenham Hotspur	–	–		1		1	–	–		–	–		–	–		–	–		–	–		–	–		–	–		1		1
20 Notts County	–	–		1		–	–	–		–	–		–	–		–	–		–	–		–	–		–	–		1		–
21 Port Vale	–	–		–	–		–	–		1			–	–		–	–		–	–		–	–		–	–		1		–
22 Swindon Town	–	–		–	–		–	–		1			–	–		–	–		–	–		–	–		–	–		1		

HARRY WORRALL

DEBUT (Full Appearance)

Saturday 30/11/1946
Football League Division 1
at Molineux

Wolverhampton Wanderers 3 Manchester United 2

CLUB CAREER RECORD	Apps	Subs	Goals
Premiership	0		0
League Division 1	6		0
League Division 2	0		0
FA Cup	0		0
League Cup	0		0
European Cup / Champions League	0		0
European Cup–Winners' Cup	0		0
UEFA Cup / Inter–Cities' Fairs Cup	0		0
Other Matches	0		0
OVERALL TOTAL	**6**		**0**

Opponents	PREM A S G	FLD 1 A S G	FLD 2 A S G	FAC A S G	LC A S G	EC/CL A S G	ECWC A S G	UEFA A S G	OTHER A S G	TOTAL A S G
1 Wolverhampton W.	– –	2 – –	–	–	–	–	–	–	–	2 –
2 Aston Villa	– –	1 – –	–	–	–	–	–	–	–	1 –
3 Derby County	– –	1 – –	–	–	–	–	–	–	–	1 –
4 Everton	– –	1 – –	–	–	–	–	–	–	–	1 –
5 Huddersfield Town	– –	1 – –	–	–	–	–	–	–	–	1 –

PAUL WRATTAN

DEBUT (Substitute Appearance)

Tuesday 02/04/1991
Football League Division 1
at Old Trafford

Manchester United 2 Wimbledon 1

CLUB CAREER RECORD	Apps	Subs	Goals
Premiership	0		0
League Division 1	0	(2)	0
League Division 2	0		0
FA Cup	0		0
League Cup	0		0
European Cup / Champions League	0		0
European Cup–Winners' Cup	0		0
UEFA Cup / Inter–Cities' Fairs Cup	0		0
Other Matches	0		0
OVERALL TOTAL	**0**	**(2)**	**0**

Opponents	PREM A S G	FLD 1 A S G	FLD 2 A S G	FAC A S G	LC A S G	EC/CL A S G	ECWC A S G	UEFA A S G	OTHER A S G	TOTAL A S G
1 Crystal Palace	– – –	– (1) –	–	–	–	–	–	–	–	– (1) –
2 Wimbledon	– – –	– (1) –	–	–	–	–	–	–	–	– (1) –

BILLY WRIGGLESWORTH

DEBUT (Full Appearance)

Saturday 23/01/1937
Football League Division 1
at Hillsborough

Sheffield Wednesday 1 Manchester United 0

CLUB CAREER RECORD	Apps	Subs	Goals
Premiership	0		0
League Division 1	23		6
League Division 2	4		1
FA Cup	7		2
League Cup	0		0
European Cup / Champions League	0		0
European Cup–Winners' Cup	0		0
UEFA Cup / Inter–Cities' Fairs Cup	0		0
Other Matches	0		0
OVERALL TOTAL	**34**		**9**

Opponents	PREM A S G	FLD 1 A S G	FLD 2 A S G	FAC A S G	LC A S G	EC/CL A S G	ECWC A S G	UEFA A S G	OTHER A S G	TOTAL A S G
1 Preston North End	– –	2 – 2	– –	2 – –	–	–	–	–	–	4 – 2
2 Accrington Stanley	– –	– – –	2 – 2	– –	–	–	–	–	–	2 – 2
3 Leicester City	– –	2 – 2	– –	– –	–	–	–	–	–	2 – 2
4 Arsenal	– –	1 – 1	– –	1 – –	–	–	–	–	–	2 – 1
5 Birmingham City	– –	2 – –	– –	– –	–	–	–	–	–	2 – –
6 Blackpool	– –	2 – –	– –	– –	–	–	–	–	–	2 – –
7 West Bromwich Albion	– –	– – –	– –	2 – –	–	–	–	–	–	2 – –
8 Aston Villa	– –	1 – 1	– –	– –	–	–	–	–	–	1 – 1
9 Nottingham Forest	– –	– – –	1 – 1	– –	–	–	–	–	–	1 – 1
10 Blackburn Rovers	– –	– – –	1 – –	– –	–	–	–	–	–	1 – –
11 Bolton Wanderers	– –	1 – –	– –	– –	–	–	–	–	–	1 – –
12 Brentford	– –	1 – –	– –	– –	–	–	–	–	–	1 – –
13 Charlton Athletic	– –	1 – –	– –	– –	–	–	–	–	–	1 – –
14 Chelsea	– –	1 – –	– –	– –	–	–	–	–	–	1 – –
15 Derby County	– –	1 – –	– –	– –	–	–	–	–	–	1 – –
16 Everton	– –	1 – –	– –	– –	–	–	–	–	–	1 – –
17 Fulham	– –	– – –	1 – –	– –	–	–	–	–	–	1 – –
18 Middlesbrough	– –	1 – –	– –	– –	–	–	–	–	–	1 – –
19 Plymouth Argyle	– –	– – –	1 – –	– –	–	–	–	–	–	1 – –
20 Portsmouth	– –	1 – –	– –	– –	–	–	–	–	–	1 – –
21 Sheffield United	– –	1 – –	– –	– –	–	–	–	–	–	1 – –
22 Sheffield Wednesday	– –	1 – –	– –	– –	–	–	–	–	–	1 – –
23 Stoke City	– –	1 – –	– –	– –	–	–	–	–	–	1 – –
24 Sunderland	– –	1 – –	– –	– –	–	–	–	–	–	1 – –
25 Wolverhampton W.	– –	1 – –	– –	– –	–	–	–	–	–	1 – –

WILLIAM YATES

DEBUT (Full Appearance)

Saturday 15/09/1906
Football League Division 1
at Bramall Lane

Sheffield United 0 Manchester United 2

CLUB CAREER RECORD	Apps	Subs	Goals
Premiership	0		0
League Division 1	3		0
League Division 2	0		0
FA Cup	0		0
League Cup	0		0
European Cup / Champions League	0		0
European Cup-Winners' Cup	0		0
UEFA Cup / Inter-Cities' Fairs Cup	0		0
Other Matches	0		0
OVERALL TOTAL	**3**		**0**

Opponents	PREM A S G	FLD 1 A S G	FLD 2 A S G	FAC A S G	LC A S G	EC/CL A S G	ECWC A S G	UEFA A S G	OTHER A S G	TOTAL A S G
1 Bolton Wanderers	– –	1	– –	– –	–	–	–	–	–	1 –
2 Everton	– –	1	– –	– –	–	–	–	–	–	1 –
3 Sheffield United	– –	1	– –	– –	–	–	–	–	–	1 –

DWIGHT YORKE

DEBUT (Full Appearance)

Saturday 22/08/1998
FA Premiership
at Upton Park

West Ham United 0 Manchester United 0

CLUB CAREER RECORD	Apps	Subs	Goals
Premiership	80	(16)	48
League Division 1	0		0
League Division 2	0		0
FA Cup	6	(5)	3
League Cup	3		2
European Cup / Champions League	28	(8)	11
European Cup-Winners' Cup	0		0
UEFA Cup / Inter-Cities' Fairs Cup	0		0
Other Matches	3	(3)	2
OVERALL TOTAL	**120**	**(32)**	**66**

Opponents	PREM A S G	FLD 1 A S G	FLD 2 A S G	FAC A S G	LC A S G	EC/CL A S G	ECWC A S G	UEFA A S G	OTHER A S G	TOTAL A S G
1 Arsenal	5 (2) 3	– –	– –	1 (1) –	1	–	–	–	1 1	8 (3) 4
2 Liverpool	5 (1) 1	– –	– –	1 1	–	–	–	–	– (1) –	6 (2) 2
3 West Ham United	6 4	– –	– –	– (1) –	–	–	–	–	–	6 (1) 4
4 Newcastle United	4 (2) –	– –	– –	– (1) –	–	–	–	–	–	4 (3) –
5 Leicester City	5 (1) 6	– –	– –	– –	–	–	–	–	–	5 (1) 6
6 Derby County	5 (1) 5	– –	– –	– –	–	–	–	–	–	5 (1) 5
7 Leeds United	5 (1) 3	– –	– –	– –	–	–	–	–	–	5 (1) 3
8 Everton	5 (1) 2	– –	– –	– –	–	–	–	–	–	5 (1) 2
9 Middlesbrough	4 1	– –	– –	1 (1) –	–	–	–	–	–	5 (1) 1
10 Chelsea	3 2	– –	– –	1 (1) 2	–	–	–	–	– (1) –	4 (2) 4
11 Southampton	4 (2) 4	– –	– –	– –	–	–	–	–	–	4 (2) 4
12 Bayern Munich	–	–	–	–	–	4 (2) 1	–	–	–	4 (2) 1
13 Coventry City	4 (1) 4	– –	– –	– –	–	–	–	–	–	4 (1) 4
14 Aston Villa	4 –	–	–	–	–	–	–	–	–	4 –
15 Charlton Athletic	3 3	–	–	–	–	–	–	–	–	3 3
16 Sheffield Wednesday	3 1	– –	– –	– –	–	–	–	–	–	3 1
17 Wimbledon	3 1	– –	– –	– –	–	–	–	–	–	3 1
18 Tottenham Hotspur	3 –	–	–	–	–	–	–	–	–	3 –
19 Watford	1 (1) 2	– –	– –	– –	1 1	–	–	–	–	2 (1) 3
20 Blackburn Rovers	2 (1) 1	– –	– –	– –	–	–	–	–	–	2 (1) 1
21 Sunderland	1 (1) –	– –	– –	– –	1 1	–	–	–	–	2 (1) 1
22 Barcelona	– –	– –	– –	– –	–	2 2	–	–	–	2 2
23 Brondby	– –	– –	– –	– –	–	2 2	–	–	–	2 2
24 Internazionale	– –	– –	– –	– –	–	2 2	–	–	–	2 2
25 Fiorentina	– –	– –	– –	– –	–	2 1	–	–	–	2 1
26 Juventus	– –	– –	– –	– –	–	2 1	–	–	–	2 1
27 Sturm Graz	– –	– –	– –	– –	–	2 1	–	–	–	2 1
28 Croatia Zagreb	– –	– –	– –	– –	–	2 –	–	–	–	2 –
29 Fulham	– –	– –	– –	2	–	–	–	–	–	2 –
30 Olympique Marseille	– –	– –	– –	– –	–	2	–	–	–	2 –
31 Panathinaikos	– –	– –	– –	– –	–	2	–	–	–	2 –
32 Real Madrid	– –	– –	– –	– –	–	2	–	–	–	2 –
33 Bradford City	1 (1) 3	– –	– –	– –	–	–	–	–	–	1 (1) 3
34 PSV Eindhoven	– –	– –	– –	– –	–	1 (1) 1	–	–	–	1 (1) 1
35 Anderlecht	– –	– –	– –	– –	–	1 (1)	–	–	–	1 (1) –
36 Dynamo Kiev	– –	– –	– –	– –	–	1 (1)	–	–	–	1 (1) –
37 Nottingham Forest	1 2	– –	– –	– –	–	–	–	–	–	1 2
38 Rayos del Necaxa	– –	– –	– –	– –	–	–	–	–	1 1	1 1
39 Boavista	– –	– –	– –	– –	–	1	–	–	–	1 –
40 Bolton Wanderers	1	–	–	–	–	–	–	–	–	1 –
41 Ipswich Town	1	–	–	–	–	–	–	–	–	1 –
42 Manchester City	1	–	–	–	–	–	–	–	–	1 –
43 Vasco da Gama	– –	– –	– –	– –	–	–	–	–	1	1 –
44 Girondins Bordeaux	– –	– –	– –	– –	–	– (1) –	–	–	–	– (1) –
45 Lille Metropole	– –	– –	– –	– –	–	– (1)	–	–	–	– (1) –
46 Palmeiras	– –	– –	– –	– –	–	–	–	–	– (1) –	– (1) –
47 Valencia	– –	– –	– –	– –	–	– (1) –	–	–	–	– (1) –

ARTHUR YOUNG

DEBUT (Full Appearance)

Saturday 27/10/1906
Football League Division 1
at Bank Street

Manchester United 2 Birmingham City 1

CLUB CAREER RECORD	Apps	Subs	Goals
Premiership	0		0
League Division 1	2		0
League Division 2	0		0
FA Cup	0		0
League Cup	0		0
European Cup / Champions League	0		0
European Cup-Winners' Cup	0		0
UEFA Cup / Inter-Cities' Fairs Cup	0		0
Other Matches	0		0
OVERALL TOTAL	**2**		**0**

Opponents	PREM A S G	FLD 1 A S G	FLD 2 A S G	FAC A S G	LC A S G	EC/CL A S G	ECWC A S G	UEFA A S G	OTHER A S G	TOTAL A S G
1 Birmingham City	– –	1 –	– –	– –	– –	– –	– –	– –	– –	1 –
2 Everton	– –	1 –	– –	– –	– –	– –	– –	– –	– –	1 –

TONY YOUNG

DEBUT (Substitute Appearance)

Saturday 29/08/1970
Football League Division 1
at Old Trafford

Manchester United 1 West Ham United 1

CLUB CAREER RECORD	Apps	Subs	Goals
Premiership	0		0
League Division 1	62	(6)	1
League Division 2	7	(8)	0
FA Cup	5		0
League Cup	5	(4)	0
European Cup / Champions League	0		0
European Cup-Winners' Cup	0		0
UEFA Cup / Inter-Cities' Fairs Cup	0		0
Other Matches	0		0
OVERALL TOTAL	**79**	**(18)**	**1**

Opponents	PREM A S G	FLD 1 A S G	FLD 2 A S G	FAC A S G	LC A S G	EC/CL A S G	ECWC A S G	UEFA A S G	OTHER A S G	TOTAL A S G
1 Norwich City	– –	3 –	– (2) –	– –	– (2) –	– –	– –	– –	– –	3 (4) –
2 Arsenal	– –	5 –	– –	– –	– –	– –	– –	– –	– –	5 –
3 Southampton	– –	4 –	1 –	– –	– –	– –	– –	– –	– –	5 –
4 Sheffield United	– –	4 –	– –	– –	– –	– –	– –	– –	– –	4 –
5 Stoke City	– –	4 –	– –	– –	– –	– –	– –	– –	– –	4 –
6 Wolverhampton W.	– –	3 –	– –	1 –	– –	– –	– –	– –	– –	4 –
7 Coventry City	– –	3 (1) –	– –	– –	– –	– –	– –	– –	– –	3 (1) –
8 Liverpool	– –	3 (1) –	– –	– –	– –	– –	– –	– –	– –	3 (1) –
9 West Ham United	– –	3 (1) –	– –	– –	– –	– –	– –	– –	– –	3 (1) –
10 Birmingham City	– –	3 –	– –	– –	– –	– –	– –	– –	– –	3 –
11 Ipswich Town	– –	2 –	– –	1 –	– –	– –	– –	– –	– –	3 –
12 Leeds United	– –	3 –	– –	– –	– –	– –	– –	– –	– –	3 –
13 Leicester City	– –	3 –	– –	– –	– –	– –	– –	– –	– –	3 –
14 Newcastle United	– –	3 –	– –	– –	– –	– –	– –	– –	– –	3 –
15 West Bromwich Albion	– –	2 –	1 –	– –	– –	– –	– –	– –	– –	3 –
16 Bristol Rovers	– –	– –	– (1) –	– –	2 –	– –	– –	– –	– –	2 (1) –
17 Derby County	– –	2 (1) –	– –	– –	– –	– –	– –	– –	– –	2 (1) –
18 Middlesbrough	– –	– –	– –	– –	2 (1) –	– –	– –	– –	– –	2 (1) –
19 Queens Park Rangers	– –	2 (1) –	– –	– –	– –	– –	– –	– –	– –	2 (1) –
20 Chelsea	– –	2 1	– –	– –	– –	– –	– –	– –	– –	2 1
21 Crystal Palace	– –	2 –	– –	– –	– –	– –	– –	– –	– –	2 –
22 Everton	– –	2 –	– –	– –	– –	– –	– –	– –	– –	2 –
23 Oxford United	– –	– –	1 –	– –	1 –	– –	– –	– –	– –	2 –
24 Tottenham Hotspur	– –	2 –	– –	– –	– –	– –	– –	– –	– –	2 –
25 Walsall	– –	– –	– –	2 –	– –	– –	– –	– –	– –	2 –
26 Aston Villa	– –	– –	1 –	– –	– –	– –	– –	– –	– –	1 –
27 Burnley	– –	1 –	– –	– –	– –	– –	– –	– –	– –	1 –
28 Hull City	– –	– –	1 –	– –	– –	– –	– –	– –	– –	1 –
29 Manchester City	– –	1 –	– –	– –	– –	– –	– –	– –	– –	1 –
30 Oldham Athletic	– –	– –	1 –	– –	– –	– –	– –	– –	– –	1 –
31 Plymouth Argyle	– –	– –	– –	1 –	– –	– –	– –	– –	– –	1 –
32 York City	– –	– –	1 –	– –	– –	– –	– –	– –	– –	1 –
33 Bolton Wanderers	– –	– –	– (1) –	– –	– –	– –	– –	– –	– –	– (1) –
34 Bristol City	– –	– –	– (1) –	– –	– –	– –	– –	– –	– –	– (1) –
35 Cardiff City	– –	– –	– (1) –	– –	– –	– –	– –	– –	– –	– (1) –
36 Charlton Athletic	– –	– –	– –	– –	– (1) –	– –	– –	– –	– –	– (1) –
37 Millwall	– –	– –	– (1) –	– –	– –	– –	– –	– –	– –	– (1) –
38 Nottingham Forest	– –	– (1) –	– –	– –	– –	– –	– –	– –	– –	– (1) –
39 Notts County	– –	– –	– (1) –	– –	– –	– –	– –	– –	– –	– (1) –

MANCHESTER UNITED
The Complete Record

Chapter 2.2
The Appearances

ALL COMPETITIVE MATCHES

#	PLAYER	A	S	T
1	Giggs, Ryan	669 (90)		759
2	Charlton, Bobby	756 (2)		758
3	Foulkes, Bill	685 (3)		688
4	Scholes, Paul	474 (96)		570
5	Neville, Gary	514 (27)		541
6	Stepney, Alex	539		539
7	Dunne, Tony	534 (1)		535
8	Irwin, Denis	511 (18)		529
9	Spence, Joe	510		510
10	Albiston, Arthur	467 (18)		485
11	Keane, Roy	458 (22)		480
12	McClair, Brian	398 (73)		471
13	Best, George	470		470
14	Hughes, Mark	453 (14)		467
15	Robson, Bryan	437 (24)		461
16	Buchan, Martin	456		456
17	Silcock, Jack	449		449
18	Pallister, Gary	433 (4)		437
19	Rowley, Jack	424		424
20	McIlroy, Sammy	391 (28)		419
21	Bruce, Steve	411 (3)		414
22	Law, Denis	398 (6)		404
23	Macari, Lou	374 (27)		401
24	Schmeichel, Peter	398		398
25	Crerand, Pat	397		397
26	Coppell, Steve	393 (3)		396
27	Stiles, Nobby	395		395
28	Beckham, David	356 (38)		394
29	Chilton, Allenby	391		391
30	Butt, Nicky	307 (80)		387
31	Neville, Phil	301 (85)		386
32	Duxbury, Mike	345 (33)		378
33	Bailey, Gary	375		375
34	Solskjaer, Ole Gunnar	216 (150)		366
35	Silvestre, Mikael	326 (35)		361
36	Brennan, Shay	358 (1)		359
37	Carey, Johnny	344		344
38	Pearson, Stan	343		343
39	Meredith, Billy	335		335
40	Sadler, David	328 (7)		335
41	Moore, Charlie	328		328
42	Steward, Alfred	326		326
43	Hilditch, Clarence	322		322
44	Wall, George	319		319
45	Erentz, Fred	310		310
46	Bell, Alex	309		309
47	Brown, Wes	271 (34)		305
48	Roberts, Charlie	302		302
49	Bennion, Ray	301		301
50	Morgan, Willie	293 (3)		296
51	Viollet, Dennis	293		293
52	Moran, Kevin	284 (5)		289
53	Stapleton, Frank	267 (21)		288
54	O'Shea, John	215 (73)		288
55	Aston, John (Snr)	284		284
56	Ince, Paul	276 (5)		281
57	Byrne, Roger	280		280
58	Berry, Johnny	276		276
59	Cockburn, Henry	275		275
60	Cole, Andrew	231 (44)		275
61	Whiteside, Norman	256 (18)		274
62	Greenhoff, Brian	268 (3)		271
63	Stacey, George	270		270
64	Ferdinand, Rio	263 (4)		267
65	Moger, Harry	266		266
66	Kidd, Brian	257 (9)		266
67	Herd, David	264 (1)		265
68	Sharpe, Lee	213 (50)		263
69	Cartwright, Walter	257		257
70	Duckworth, Dick	254		254
71	Houston, Stewart	248 (2)		250
72	Nicholl, Jimmy	235 (13)		248
73	Gregg, Harry	247		247
74	Turnbull, Sandy	247		247
75	Blackmore, Clayton	201 (44)		245

#	PLAYER	A	S	T
76	Ronaldo, Cristiano	196 (43)		239
77	McQueen, Gordon	229		229
78	van Nistelrooy, Ruud	200 (19)		219
79	Crompton, Jack	212		212
80	Vose, George	209		209
81	Wood, Ray	208		208
82	Grimwood, John	205		205
83	Strachan, Gordon	195 (6)		201
84	Jones, Tom	200		200
85	Stafford, Harry	200		200
86	Mew, Jack	199		199
87	McGrath, Paul	192 (7)		199
88	Moses, Remi	188 (11)		199
89	Mann, Frank	197		197
90	Manley, Tom	195		195
91	Setters, Maurice	194		194
92	Wilkins, Ray	191 (3)		194
93	Downie, Alex	191		191
94	Taylor, Tommy	191		191
95	Rooney, Wayne	171 (18)		189
96	Aston, John (Jnr)	166 (21)		187
97	Cantona, Eric	184 (1)		185
98	Delaney, Jimmy	184		184
99	Quixall, Albert	184		184
100	McKay, Bill	182		182
101	West, Enoch	181		181
102	Rowley, Harry	180		180
103	Pearson, Stuart	179 (1)		180
104	Schofield, Alf	179		179
105	Edwards, Duncan	177		177
106	Olsen, Jesper	149 (27)		176
107	Griffiths, Billy	175		175
108	McPherson, Frank	175		175
109	Cassidy, Joe	174		174
110	Griffiths, Jack	173		173
111	Fletcher, Darren	126 (46)		172
112	McNaught, James	162		162
113	Mitten, Charlie	162		162
114	James, Steve	160 (1)		161
115	Kanchelskis, Andrei	132 (29)		161
116	Partridge, Teddy	160		160
117	Bryant, Billy	157		157
118	Burns, Francis	143 (13)		156
119	Donaldson, Bob	155		155
120	Lochhead, Arthur	153		153
121	Sheringham, Teddy	101 (52)		153
122	Barson, Frank	152		152
123	Morgan, Billy	152		152
124	Yorke, Dwight	120 (32)		152
125	Pegg, David	150		150
126	Johnsen, Ronny	131 (19)		150
127	Hanson, Jimmy	147		147
128	Fitzpatrick, John	141 (6)		147
129	Cantwell, Noel	146		146
130	Parker, Paul	137 (9)		146
131	Phelan, Mike	127 (19)		146
132	van der Sar, Edwin	142		142
133	Daly, Gerry	137 (5)		142
134	Wilson, Jack	140		140
135	Barthez, Fabien	139		139
136	Barrett, Frank	136		136
137	Thomas, Harry	135		135
138	Bonthron, Bob	134		134
139	Hill, Gordon	133 (1)		134
140	Hayes, Vince	128		128
141	Bryant, William	127		127
142	Scanlon, Albert	127		127
143	Stam, Jaap	125 (2)		127
144	Jordan, Joe	125 (1)		126
145	Fortune, Quinton	88 (38)		126
146	Halse, Harold	125		125
147	Saha, Louis	76 (48)		124
148	Greenhoff, Jimmy	119 (4)		123
149	McGlen, Billy	122		122
150	Mellor, Jack	122		122

#	PLAYER	A	S	T
151	Picken, Jack	122		122
152	Jones, Mark	121		121
153	Peddie, Jack	121		121
154	Mutch, George	120		120
155	Gidman, John	116 (4)		120
156	Gaskell, David	119		119
157	Forsyth, Alex	116 (3)		119
158	Donaghy, Mal	98 (21)		119
159	May, David	98 (20)		118
160	Blanchflower, Jackie	117		117
161	Holden, Dick	117		117
162	Downie, John	116		116
163	McLachlan, George	116		116
164	McLenahan, Hugh	116		116
165	Warner, Jack	116		116
166	Gibson, Don	115		115
167	Giles, Johnny	115		115
168	Connelly, John	112 (1)		113
169	Beale, Robert	112		112
170	Brown, James (1935-39)	110		110
171	Thomas, Mickey	110		110
172	Hogg, Graeme	108 (2)		110
173	Webb, Neil	105 (5)		110
174	McCreery, David	57 (53)		110
175	Bamford, Tommy	109		109
176	Martin, Lee (1990s)	84 (25)		109
177	Colman, Eddie	108		108
178	Goodwin, Fred	107		107
179	Grimes, Ashley	77 (30)		107
180	Cope, Ronnie	106		106
181	Whalley, Arthur	106		106
182	Davenport, Peter	83 (23)		106
183	Berg, Henning	81 (22)		103
184	Perrins, George	102		102
185	Reid, Tom	101		101
186	Smith, Dick	101		101
187	Carrick, Michael	87 (14)		101
188	Whelan, William	98		98
189	Vidic, Nemanja	94 (4)		98
190	Muhren, Arnold	93 (5)		98
191	Evra, Patrice	85 (13)		98
192	Forlan, Diego	37 (61)		98
193	Young, Tony	79 (18)		97
194	Radford, Charlie	96		96
195	Draycott, Billy	95		95
196	Whitefoot, Jeff	95		95
197	Gibson, Colin	89 (6)		95
198	Leighton, Jim	94		94
199	Dawson, Alex	93		93
200	Morris, Johnny	93		93
201	Redwood, Hubert	93		93
202	Smith, Alan	61 (32)		93
203	Roughton, George	92		92
204	Smith, Tom	90		90
205	Gillespie, Matthew	89		89
206	Stewart, Willie	87		87
207	Gowling, Alan	77 (10)		87
208	Anderson, George	86		86
209	Hodge, James	86		86
210	McGuinness, Wilf	85		85
211	Heinze, Gabriel	75 (8)		83
212	Park, Ji-Sung	53 (30)		83
213	Veron, Juan-Sebastian	75 (7)		82
214	Richardson, Kieran	44 (37)		81
215	Allen, Reg	80		80
216	Pearson, Mark	80		80
217	Arkesden, Tommy	79		79
218	Turner, Chris	79		79
219	Webster, Colin	79		79
220	Turnbull, Jimmy	78		78
221	Johnston, Billy	77		77
222	Howard, Tim	76 (1)		77
223	Gallimore, Stanley	76		76
224	Greaves, Ian	75		75
225	Blanc, Laurent	71 (4)		75

continued../

ALL COMPETITIVE MATCHES (continued)

#	PLAYER	A	S	T	#	PLAYER	A	S	T	#	PLAYER	A	S	T
226	Clarkin, John	74		74	301	Moir, Ian	45		45	376	Kuszczak, Tomasz	25	(4)	29
227	Hopkin, Fred	74		74	302	Banks, Jack	44		44	377	Gladwin, George	28		28
228	Hall, Jack (1932–1936)	73		73	303	Davidson, Will	44		44	378	Potts, Arthur	28		28
229	Beardsmore, Russell	39	(34)	73	304	Lawton, Nobby	44		44	379	Rothwell, Herbert	28		28
230	Carroll, Roy	68	(4)	72	305	Ridding, Bill	44		44	380	Sutcliffe, John	28		28
231	Breen, Tommy	71		71	306	McBain, Neil	43		43	381	Wallwork, Ronnie	10	(18)	28
232	Carolan, Joseph	71		71	307	Storey-Moore, Ian	43		43	382	Fall, Joe	27		27
233	Collinson, Jimmy	71		71	308	Martin, Mick	36	(7)	43	383	Haslam, George	27		27
234	Wallace, Danny	53	(18)	71	309	Bissett, George	42		42	384	Lappin, Harry	27		27
235	Robins, Mark	27	(43)	70	310	Clements, John	42		42	385	McDonald, Willie	27		27
236	Hanlon, Jimmy	69		69	311	Read, Bert	42		42	386	Miller, Tom	27		27
237	Holton, Jim	69		69	312	Richardson, Lance	42		42	387	Montgomery, James	27		27
238	Anderson, Viv	64	(5)	69	313	Ritchie, Andy	32	(10)	42	388	Winterbottom, Walter	27		27
239	Dale, Billy	68		68	314	Brown, James (1932-34)	41		41	389	Ryan, Jimmy	24	(3)	27
240	Nicholson, Jimmy	68		68	315	Smith, Jack	41		41	390	Gibson, Terry	15	(12)	27
241	O'Neil, Tommy	68		68	316	Nani	26	(15)	41	391	Greening, Jonathan	13	(14)	27
242	Rennox, Charlie	68		68	317	Brazil, Alan	24	(17)	41	392	Chapman, Billy	26		26
243	Edwards, Paul	66	(2)	68	318	Anderson, John	40		40	393	Doherty, John	26		26
244	Bradley, Warren	67		67	319	Bellion, David	15	(25)	40	394	Haywood, Joe	26		26
245	Dunne, Pat	67		67	320	Warburton, Arthur	39		39	395	Sheldon, John	26		26
246	Porter, Billy	65		65	321	Djemba-Djemba, Eric	27	(12)	39	396	Jovanovic, Nikki	25	(1)	26
247	Ure, Ian	65		65	322	Chadwick, Luke	18	(21)	39	397	Homer, Tom	25		25
248	Vincent, Ernest	65		65	323	Blackstock, Tommy	38		38	398	Menzies, Alex	25		25
249	Jackson, William	64		64	324	Bosnich, Mark	38		38	399	Barnes, Peter	24	(1)	25
250	Mitchell, Andrew (1890s)	64		64	325	Hood, Billy	38		38	400	McGarvey, Scott	13	(12)	25
251	Whitehouse, Jimmy	64		64	326	Redman, Billy	38		38	401	Buckle, Ted	24		24
252	Birtles, Gary	63	(1)	64	327	Whalley, Bert	38		38	402	Lewis, Eddie	24		24
253	Bannister, Jimmy	63		63	328	McCalliog, Jim	37	(1)	38	403	Scott, John	24		24
254	Walsh, Gary	62	(1)	63	329	Blomqvist, Jesper	29	(9)	38	404	Clegg, Michael	15	(9)	24
255	Boyd, Henry	62		62	330	Anderson	25	(13)	38	405	Bain, David	23		23
256	Farman, Alf	61		61	331	Donnelly, Tony	37		37	406	Ball, John	23		23
257	Woodcock, Wilf	61		61	332	Grassam, Billy	37		37	407	Gipps, Tommy	23		23
258	Cape, Jack	60		60	333	Norton, Joe	37		37	408	Hunter, George	23		23
259	Hamill, Mickey	60		60	334	Williams, Harry (1904-06)	37		37	409	Morgan, Hugh	23		23
260	McNulty, Thomas	60		60	335	Allan, Jack	36		36	410	Morgans, Kenny	23		23
261	van der Gouw, Raimond	48	(12)	60	336	Dewar, Neil	36		36	411	Walton, Joe	23		23
262	Linkson, Oscar	59		59	337	Forster, Tommy	36		36	412	Jackson, Tommy	22	(1)	23
263	Cruyff, Jordi	26	(32)	58	338	Henderson, William	36		36	413	Pique, Gerard	14	(9)	23
264	Douglas, William	57		57	339	Morrison, Tommy	36		36	414	Jones, Tommy	22		22
265	McShane, Harry	57		57	340	Rawlings, Bill	36		36	415	Warner, Jimmy	22		22
266	Sealey, Les	55	(1)	56	341	O'Brien, Liam	17	(19)	36	416	Miller, Liam	11	(11)	22
267	Sartori, Carlo	40	(15)	55	342	Breedon, Jack	35		35	417	Bond, Ernie	21		21
268	Burgess, Herbert	54		54	343	Burke, Ronnie	35		35	418	Hurst, Daniel	21		21
269	Baird, Harry	53		53	344	Chalmers, Stewart	35		35	419	Robinson, James	21		21
270	Hine, Ernie	53		53	345	O'Connell, Pat	35		35	420	Travers, George	21		21
271	Hopkinson, Samuel	53		53	346	Robertson, Sandy	35		35	421	Crowther, Stan	20		20
272	Meehan, Tommy	53		53	347	Williams, Rees	35		35	422	Hodges, Frank	20		20
273	Roche, Paddy	53		53	348	Beddow, John	34		34	423	McCartney, John	20		20
274	Sapsford, George	53		53	349	Coupar, Jimmy	34		34	424	Sidebottom, Arnold	20		20
275	Frame, Tommy	52		52	350	Hacking, Jack	34		34	425	Davies, Simon	10	(10)	20
276	Graham, Arthur	47	(5)	52	351	Myerscough, Joe	34		34	426	Blott, Sam	19		19
277	Edmonds, Hugh	51		51	352	Preston, Stephen	34		34	427	Ferrier, Ron	19		19
278	Moody, John	51		51	353	Robertson, Alex	34		34	428	Hofton, Leslie	19		19
279	Pegg, Dick	51		51	354	Wrigglesworth, Billy	34		34	429	Moore, Graham	19		19
280	Peters, James	51		51	355	Sivebaek, Johnny	32	(2)	34	430	Anderson, Trevor	13	(6)	19
281	Wombwell, Dick	51		51	356	Hargreaves, Owen	23	(11)	34	431	Curtis, John	9	(10)	19
282	Garton, Billy	47	(4)	51	357	McGrath, Chris	15	(19)	34	432	Fitchett, John	18		18
283	Ball, Jack	50		50	358	Bogan, Tommy	33		33	433	Gardner, Dick	18		18
284	Dow, John	50		50	359	Kennedy, William	33		33	434	Kennedy, Fred	18		18
285	Robertson, William	50		50	360	Noble, Bobby	33		33	435	MacDougall, Ted	18		18
286	Harris, Frank	49		49	361	Sagar, Charles	33		33	436	Pape, Albert	18		18
287	Stewart, William	49		49	362	Peden, Jack	32		32	437	Bardsley, Phil	10	(8)	18
288	Spencer, Charlie	48		48	363	Sweeney, Eric	32		32	438	Boyle, Tommy	17		17
289	Tevez, Carlos	39	(9)	48	364	Fitzsimmons, David	31		31	439	Cunningham, John	17		17
290	Poborsky, Karel	28	(20)	48	365	Barlow, Cyril	30		30	440	Owen, W	17		17
291	Chisnall, Phil	47		47	366	Birchenough, Herbert	30		30	441	Parker, Thomas	17		17
292	Jenkyns, Caesar	47		47	367	Fitzsimmons, Tommy	30		30	442	Ridgway, Joe	17		17
293	Knowles, Frank	47		47	368	Goldthorpe, Ernie	30		30	443	Smith, William	17		17
294	Wassall, Jackie	47		47	369	Hodge, John	30		30	444	Davies, Wyn	16	(1)	17
295	Fisher, James	46		46	370	Taylor, Chris	30		30	445	Eagles, Chris	7	(10)	17
296	Harrison, William	46		46	371	Taylor, Ernie	30		30	446	Dublin, Dion	6	(11)	17
297	Leigh, Tom	46		46	372	Milne, Ralph	26	(4)	30	447	Nuttall, Tom	16		16
298	Livingstone, George	46		46	373	Kleberson, Jose	24	(6)	30	448	Ramsden, Charlie	16		16
299	Rimmer, Jimmy	45	(1)	46	374	Ferguson, Darren	22	(8)	30	449	Tapken, Norman	16		16
300	Graham, George	44	(2)	46	375	McMillen, Walter	29		29	450	Wood, John	16		16

continued../

ALL COMPETITIVE MATCHES (continued)

#	PLAYER	A	S	T	#	PLAYER	A	S	T	#	PLAYER	A	S	T
451	Birch, Brian	15		15	526	Green, Eddie	9		9	601	Connachan, James	4		4
452	Clempson, Frank	15		15	527	MacDonald, Ken	9		9	602	Dougan, Tommy	4		4
453	Connor, Ted	15		15	528	McGillivray, Charlie	9		9	603	Ferguson, Danny	4		4
454	John, Roy	15		15	529	Richards, Billy	9		9	604	Graham, John	4		4
455	Langford, Len	15		15	530	Wilkinson, Harry	9		9	605	Halton, Reg	4		4
456	McMillan, Sammy	15		15	531	Givens, Don	5	(4)	9	606	Hardman, Harold	4		4
457	Parkinson, Robert	15		15	532	Black, Dick	8		8	607	Harris, Tom	4		4
458	Berry, Bill	14		14	533	Doughty, Roger	8		8	608	Hartwell, William	4		4
459	Curry, Joe	14		14	534	Ferguson, John	8		8	609	Heywood, Herbert	4		4
460	Feehan, John	-	14	14	535	Gaudie, Ralph	8		8	610	Howarth, John	4		4
461	Inglis, Bill	14		14	536	Hall, Proctor	8		8	611	Hulme, Aaron	4		4
462	Lowrie, Tommy	14		14	537	Heathcote, Joe	8		8	612	Lancaster, Joe	4		4
463	Toms, Billy	14		14	538	Higgins, Mark	8		8	613	McGillivray, John	4		4
464	Watson, Willie	14		14	539	Hillam, Charlie	8		8	614	Miller, James	4		4
465	Gill, Tony	7	(7)	14	540	Pepper, Frank	8		8	615	Murray, Robert	4		4
466	Gillespie, Keith	7	(7)	14	541	Wealands, Jeffrey	8		8	616	Pinner, Mike	4		4
467	Stewart, Michael	7	(7)	14	542	Pilkington, Kevin	6	(2)	8	617	Powell, Jack	4		4
468	Rossi, Giuseppe	6	(8)	14	543	Simpson, Danny	4	(4)	8	618	Slater, J.F	4		4
469	Thornley, Ben	6	(8)	14	544	Spector, Jonathan	4	(4)	8	619	Taibi, Massimo	4		4
470	Birkett, Cliff	13		13	545	Cooke, Terry	2	(6)	8	620	Thomson, Ernest	4		4
471	Carson, Adam	13		13	546	Maiorana, Jules	2	(6)	8	621	Turner, John	4		4
472	Chester, Reg	13		13	547	Brown, James (1892-93)	7		7	622	Waldron, Colin	4		4
473	Cookson, Sam	13		13	548	Brown, William	7		7	623	Williams, Bill	4		4
474	Lang, Tommy	13		13	549	Collinson, Cliff	7		7	624	Jones, David (2004)	3	(1)	4
475	Lynn, Sammy	13		13	550	Fielding, Bill	7		7	625	Bielby, Paul	2	(2)	4
476	Mann, Herbert	13		13	551	Foley, G	7		7	626	Wood, Nicky	2	(2)	4
477	McCartney, William	13		13	552	Goodwin, Billy	7		7	627	Graham, Deiniol	1	(3)	4
478	McCrae, James	13		13	553	Griffiths, Clive	7		7	628	Nardiello, Daniel	1	(3)	4
479	Saunders, James	13		13	554	Hooper, Arthur	7		7	629	Buchan, George	-	(4)	4
480	Spratt, Walter	13		13	555	Mackie, Charlie	7		7	630	Brooks, William	3		3
481	Larsson, Henrik	10	(3)	13	556	Millar, George	7		7	631	Buckley, Frank	3		3
482	Allman, Arthur	12		12	557	Nicol, George	7		7	632	Carman, James	3		3
483	Beadsworth, Arthur	12		12	558	Royals, Ezra	7		7	633	Cartman, Bert	3		3
484	Bent, Geoff	12		12	559	Stone, Herbert	7		7	634	Cashmore, Arthur	3		3
485	Dunn, William	12		12	560	Crooks, Garth	6	(1)	7	635	Connaughton, John	3		3
486	Fitton, Arthur	12		12	561	O'Kane, John	5	(2)	7	636	Dennis, Billy	3		3
487	Gibson, Richard	12		12	562	Casper, Chris	4	(3)	7	637	Donaghy, Bernard	3		3
488	Hannaford, Charlie	12		12	563	Higginbotham, Danny	4	(3)	7	638	Doughty, Jack	3		3
489	Page, Louis	12		12	564	Pugh, Danny	3	(4)	7	639	Edge, Alf	3		3
490	Parker, Samuel	12		12	565	Fletcher, Peter	2	(5)	7	640	Greenwood, Wilson	3		3
491	Topping, Henry	12		12	566	Boyd, Billy	6		6	641	Hall, Jack (1925-1926)	3		3
492	Anderson, Willie	10	(2)	12	567	Donald, Ian	6		6	642	Heron, Tommy	3		3
493	Kopel, Frank	10	(2)	12	568	Evans, Sidney	6		6	643	Hunter, William	3		3
494	Sloan, Tom	4	(8)	12	569	Garvey, James	6		6	644	Lawson, Reg	3		3
495	Briggs, Ronnie	11		11	570	Haydock, Frank	6		6	645	Lievesley, Wilfred	3		3
496	Craven, Charlie	11		11	571	Henrys, Arthur	6		6	646	Lydon, George	3		3
497	Ellis, David	11		11	572	Marshall, Arthur	6		6	647	Lyner, David	3		3
498	Grundy, John	11		11	573	Owen, Jack	6		6	648	McFarlane, Bob	3		3
499	Harrop, Bobby	11		11	574	Sawyer, F	6		6	649	Montgomery, Archie	3		3
500	Hudson, Edward	11		11	575	Thomson, James	6		6	650	Robertson, Thomas	3		3
501	Lee, Edwin	11		11	576	Worrall, Harry	6		6	651	Rothwell, Charles	3		3
502	Richards, Charlie	11		11	577	Nevland, Erik	2	(4)	6	652	Scott, Jack	3		3
503	Vance, James	11		11	578	Wilson, David	-	(6)	6	653	Sneddon, J	3		3
504	Ambler, Alfred	10		10	579	Campbell, William	5		5	654	Street, Ernest	3		3
505	Brett, Frank	10		10	580	Ford, Joe	5		5	655	Thompson, John	3		3
506	Bullock, Jimmy	10		10	581	Higson, James	5		5	656	Thompson, William	3		3
507	Colville, James	10		10	582	Lyons, George	5		5	657	Whitney, John	3		3
508	Davies, John	10		10	583	McClelland, Jimmy	5		5	658	Whittaker, Walter	3		3
509	Higgins, Alexander	10		10	584	Nevin, George	5		5	659	Williams, Frank	3		3
510	Leonard, Harry	10		10	585	Pears, Steve	5		5	660	Williams, Joe	3		3
511	Mathieson, William	10		10	586	Savage, Ted	5		5	661	Yates, William	3		3
512	Roberts, W.A	10		10	587	Smith, Albert	5		5	662	Dong, Fangzhuo	2	(1)	3
513	Robinson, Matt	10		10	588	Thomson, Arthur	5		5	663	Evans, Jonny	2	(1)	3
514	Smith, Lawrence	10		10	589	Williams, Harry (1922-23)	5		5	664	Roche, Lee	2	(1)	3
515	Valentine, Bob	10		10	590	Mulryne, Philip	4	(1)	5	665	Lee, Kieran	1	(2)	3
516	Williams, Fred	10		10	591	Cunningham, Laurie	3	(2)	5	666	Rachubka, Paul	1	(2)	3
517	Davies, Alan	8	(2)	10	592	Jones, Richard	3	(2)	5	667	Webber, Danny	1	(2)	3
518	Wilson, Mark	6	(4)	10	593	Ricardo, Felipe	3	(2)	5	668	Foggon, Alan	-	(3)	3
519	Paterson, Steve	5	(5)	10	594	Bain, Jimmy	4		4	669	Healy, David	-	(3)	3
520	Davies, Ron	-	(10)	10	595	Ball, Billy	4		4	670	Ainsworth, Alf	2		2
521	Broomfield, Herbert	9		9	596	Barber, Jack	4		4	671	Aitken, John	2		2
522	Chesters, Arthur	9		9	597	Brown, Robert	4		4	672	Astley, Joe	2		2
523	Clark, Joe	9		9	598	Byrne, David	4		4	673	Bain, James	2		2
524	Erentz, Harry	9		9	599	Cassidy, Laurie	4		4	674	Baldwin, Tommy	2		2
525	Godsmark, Gilbert	9		9	600	Chorlton, Tom	4		4	675	Blackmore, Peter	2		2

continued../

ALL COMPETITIVE MATCHES (continued)

#	PLAYER	A	S	T
676	Booth, William	2		2
677	Bradbury, Len	2		2
678	Bunce, William	2		2
679	Cairns, James	2		2
680	Christie, David	2		2
681	Clayton, Gordon	2		2
682	Connell, Tom	2		2
683	Craig, T	2		2
684	Dale, Joe	2		2
685	Davies, Joe	2		2
686	Dean, Harold	2		2
687	Goram, Andy	2		2
688	Haworth, Ronald	2		2
689	Hendry, James	2		2
690	Iddon, Richard	2		2
691	Jones, Owen	2		2
692	Kerr, Hugh	2		2
693	Lievesley, Leslie	2		2
694	Manns, Tom	2		2
695	Martin, Lee (2005)	2		2
696	McIlvenny, Eddie	2		2
697	Newton, Percy	2		2
698	Olive, Les	2		2
699	Payne, Ernest	2		2
700	Pegg, Ken	2		2
701	Prince, D	2		2
702	Prunier, William	2		2
703	Pugh, James	2		2
704	Quinn, Jack	2		2
705	Roach, John	2		2
706	Roberts, Robert	2		2
707	Round, Elijah	2		2
708	Schofield, Joseph	2		2
709	Sharpe, William	2		2
710	Turner, Robert	2		2
711	Walker, Robert	2		2
712	Walton, John	2		2
713	Wedge, Frank	2		2
714	Wetherell, Joe	2		2
715	Wilcox, Tom	2		2
716	Williamson, John	2		2
717	Young, Arthur	2		2
718	Appleton, Michael	1	(1)	2
719	Coyne, Peter	1	(1)	2
720	Dempsey, Mark	1	(1)	2
721	Djordjic, Bojan	1	(1)	2
722	Ebanks-Blake, Sylvan	1	(1)	2
723	Twiss, Michael	1	(1)	2
724	Brazil, Derek	–	(2)	2
725	Campbell, Fraizer	–	(2)	2
726	Grimshaw, Tony	–	(2)	2
727	Shawcross, Ryan	–	(2)	2
728	Tomlinson, Graeme	–	(2)	2
729	Wrattan, Paul	–	(2)	2
730	Albinson, George	1		1
731	Bainbridge, Bill	1		1
732	Beardsley, Peter	1		1
733	Beckett, R	1		1
734	Behan, Billy	1		1
735	Blew, Horace	1		1
736	Bratt, Harold	1		1
737	Broome, Albert	1		1
738	Burke, Tom	1		1
739	Capper, Freddy	1		1
740	Christie, John	1		1
741	Cleaver, Harry	1		1
742	Dale, Herbert	1		1
743	Dalton, Ted	1		1
744	Davies, L	1		1
745	Davis, Jimmy	1		1
746	Denman, J	1		1
747	Donnelly, not known	1		1
748	Dyer, Jimmy	1		1
749	Earp, John	1		1
750	Eckersley, Adam	1		1
751	Evans, George	1		1
752	Felton, G	1		1
753	Foster, Ben	1		1
754	Fox, not known	1		1
755	Gotheridge, James	1		1
756	Gourlay, John	1		1
757	Gray, David	1		1
758	Gyves, William	1		1
759	Harrison, Charlie	1		1
760	Hawksworth, Tony	1		1
761	Hay, Tom	1		1
762	Holt, Edward	1		1
763	Hopkins, James	1		1
764	Hunter, Reg	1		1
765	Johnson, Samuel	1		1
766	Johnson, Samuel	1		1
767	Jones, David (1937)	1		1
768	Jones, Peter	1		1
769	Kennedy, Patrick	1		1
770	Kinloch, Joe	1		1
771	Kinsey, Albert	1		1
772	Longair, William	1		1
773	Longton, not known	1		1
774	Lynch, Mark	1		1
775	Marsh, Philip	1		1
776	McCarthy, Pat	1		1
777	McFarlane, Noel	1		1
778	McFetteridge, David	1		1
779	McGibbon, Pat	1		1
780	McKee, Colin	1		1
781	Milarvie, Bob	1		1
782	Mitchell, Andrew (1930s)	1		1
783	Morton, Ben	1		1
784	O'Brien, George	1		1
785	O'Shaughnessy, T	1		1
786	Owen, Bill	1		1
787	Owen, George	1		1
788	Prentice, John	1		1
789	Prince, Albert	1		1
790	Radcliffe, George	1		1
791	Ramsay, Robert	1		1
792	Rattigan, not known	1		1
793	Robbie, David	1		1
794	Rogers, Martyn	1		1
795	Rowe, Joelyn	1		1
796	Sarvis, William	1		1
797	Schofield, George	1		1
798	Schofield, Percy	1		1
799	Stephenson, R	1		1
800	Taylor, Walter	1		1
801	Tierney, Paul	1		1
802	Tranter, Wilf	1		1
803	Turner, not known	1		1
804	Tyler, Sidney	1		1
805	Walker, Dennis	1		1
806	Whitehurst, Walter	1		1
807	Whiteside, Kerr	1		1
808	Whittle, John	1		1
809	Whitworth, Neil	1		1
810	Wilkinson, Ian	1		1
811	Wilson, Edgar	1		1
812	Wilson, Tommy	1		1
813	Barnes, Michael	–	(1)	1
814	Clark, Jonathan	–	(1)	1
815	Culkin, Nick	–	(1)	1
816	Gibson, Darron	–	(1)	1
817	Johnson, Eddie	–	(1)	1
818	Kelly, Jimmy	–	(1)	1
819	Notman, Alex	–	(1)	1
820	Timm, Mads	–	(1)	1
821	Wellens, Richard	–	(1)	1
822	Whelan, Anthony	–	(1)	1

ALL LEAGUE MATCHES

#	PLAYER	A	S	T
1	Charlton, Bobby	604 (2)		606
2	Foulkes, Bill	563 (3)		566
3	Giggs, Ryan	469 (66)		535
4	Spence, Joe	481		481
5	Stepney, Alex	433		433
6	Silcock, Jack	423		423
7	Dunne, Tony	414		414
8	Scholes, Paul	328 (67)		395
9	Rowley, Jack	380		380
10	Albiston, Arthur	364 (15)		379
11	Buchan, Martin	376		376
12	Irwin, Denis	356 (12)		368
13	Neville, Gary	349 (15)		364
14	Best, George	361		361
15	McClair, Brian	296 (59)		355
16	Chilton, Allenby	352		352
17	Hughes, Mark	336 (9)		345
18	Robson, Bryan	326 (19)		345
19	McIlroy, Sammy	320 (22)		342
20	Macari, Lou	311 (18)		329
21	Keane, Roy	309 (17)		326
22	Coppell, Steve	320 (2)		322
23	Pallister, Gary	314 (3)		317
24	Pearson, Stan	312		312
25	Stiles, Nobby	311		311
26	Bruce, Steve	309		309
27	Moore, Charlie	309		309
28	Steward, Alfred	309		309
29	Law, Denis	305 (4)		309
30	Carey, Johnny	304		304
31	Crerand, Pat	304		304
32	Meredith, Billy	303		303
33	Hilditch, Clarence	301		301
34	Duxbury, Mike	274 (25)		299
35	Bailey, Gary	294		294
36	Schmeichel, Peter	292		292
37	Brennan, Shay	291 (1)		292
38	Wall, George	287		287
39	Bennion, Ray	286		286
40	Erentz, Fred	280		280
41	Bell, Alex	278		278
42	Sadler, David	266 (6)		272
43	Roberts, Charlie	271		271
44	Butt, Nicky	210 (60)		270
45	Beckham, David	237 (28)		265
46	Neville, Phil	210 (53)		263
47	Viollet, Dennis	259		259
48	Aston, John (Snr)	253		253
49	Silvestre, Mikael	225 (24)		249
50	Berry, Johnny	247		247
51	Byrne, Roger	245		245
52	Cockburn, Henry	243		243
53	Moger, Harry	242		242
54	Stacey, George	241		241
55	Morgan, Willie	236 (2)		238
56	Solskjaer, Ole Gunnar	151 (84)		235
57	Moran, Kevin	228 (3)		231
58	Cartwright, Walter	228		228
59	Duckworth, Dick	225		225
60	Stapleton, Frank	204 (19)		223
61	Greenhoff, Brian	218 (3)		221
62	Turnbull, Sandy	220		220
63	Gregg, Harry	210		210
64	Ince, Paul	203 (3)		206
65	Whiteside, Norman	193 (13)		206
66	Houston, Stewart	204 (1)		205
67	Kidd, Brian	195 (8)		203
68	Herd, David	201 (1)		202
69	Brown, Wes	175 (23)		198
70	Nicholl, Jimmy	188 (9)		197
71	Grimwood, John	196		196
72	Vose, George	195		195
73	Cole, Andrew	161 (34)		195
74	Sharpe, Lee	160 (33)		193
75	Crompton, Jack	191		191
76	O'Shea, John	138 (53)		191
77	Jones, Tom	189		189
78	Manley, Tom	188		188
79	Mew, Jack	186		186
80	Blackmore, Clayton	150 (36)		186
81	McQueen, Gordon	184		184
82	Ferdinand, Rio	183 (1)		184
83	Stafford, Harry	183		183
84	Mann, Frank	180		180
85	Wood, Ray	178		178
86	Rowley, Harry	173		173
87	Downie, Alex	172		172
88	McKay, Bill	169		169
89	Taylor, Tommy	166		166
90	West, Enoch	166		166
91	Griffiths, Jack	165		165
92	Quixall, Albert	165		165
93	Delaney, Jimmy	164		164
94	McGrath, Paul	159 (4)		163
95	Ronaldo, Cristiano	126 (37)		163
96	Wilkins, Ray	158 (2)		160
97	Strachan, Gordon	155 (5)		160
98	McPherson, Frank	159		159
99	Setters, Maurice	159		159
100	Griffiths, Billy	157		157
101	Schofield, Alf	157		157
102	Aston, John (Jnr)	139 (16)		155
103	Cassidy, Joe	152		152
104	Edwards, Duncan	151		151
105	Moses, Remi	143 (7)		150
106	van Nistelrooy, Ruud	137 (13)		150
107	Bryant, Billy	148		148
108	Partridge, Teddy	148		148
109	Lochhead, Arthur	147		147
110	Morgan, Billy	143		143
111	Cantona, Eric	142 (1)		143
112	Mitten, Charlie	142		142
113	Barson, Frank	140		140
114	McNaught, James	140		140
115	Pearson, Stuart	138 (1)		139
116	Olsen, Jesper	119 (20)		139
117	Hanson, Jimmy	138		138
118	Donaldson, Bob	131		131
119	Wilson, Jack	130		130
120	James, Steve	129		129
121	Thomas, Harry	128		128
122	Pegg, David	127		127
123	Rooney, Wayne	116 (11)		127
124	Cantwell, Noel	123		123
125	Kanchelskis, Andrei	96 (27)		123
126	Burns, Francis	111 (10)		121
127	Bonthron, Bob	119		119
128	Barrett, Frank	118		118
129	Fitzpatrick, John	111 (6)		117
130	Mellor, Jack	116		116
131	Hayes, Vince	115		115
132	Scanlon, Albert	115		115
133	Picken, Jack	113		113
134	McLenahan, Hugh	112		112
135	Mutch, George	112		112
136	Peddie, Jack	112		112
137	Daly, Gerry	107 (4)		111
138	Downie, John	110		110
139	McGlen, Billy	110		110
140	McLachlan, George	110		110
141	Bryant, William	109		109
142	Halse, Harold	109		109
143	Jordan, Joe	109		109
144	Gibson, Don	108		108
145	Fletcher, Darren	79 (28)		107
146	Holden, Dick	106		106
147	Beale, Robert	105		105
148	Blanchflower, Jackie	105		105
149	Parker, Paul	100 (5)		105
150	Sheringham, Teddy	73 (31)		104
151	Jones, Mark	103		103
152	Brown, James (1935-39)	102		102
153	Warner, Jack	102		102
154	Phelan, Mike	88 (14)		102
155	Hill, Gordon	100 (1)		101
156	Forsyth, Alex	99 (2)		101
157	Giles, Johnny	99		99
158	van der Sar, Edwin	99		99
159	Johnsen, Ronny	85 (14)		99
160	Bamford, Tommy	98		98
161	Whalley, Arthur	97		97
162	Greenhoff, Jimmy	94 (3)		97
163	Gaskell, David	96		96
164	Reid, Tom	96		96
165	Yorke, Dwight	80 (16)		96
166	Goodwin, Fred	95		95
167	Gidman, John	94 (1)		95
168	Cope, Ronnie	93		93
169	Smith, Dick	93		93
170	Whitefoot, Jeff	93		93
171	Barthez, Fabien	92		92
172	Perrins, George	92		92
173	Davenport, Peter	73 (19)		92
174	Radford, Charlie	91		91
175	Thomas, Mickey	90		90
176	Grimes, Ashley	62 (28)		90
177	Donaghy, Mal	76 (13)		89
178	McCreery, David	48 (39)		87
179	Redwood, Hubert	86		86
180	Roughton, George	86		86
181	Saha, Louis	52 (34)		86
182	Colman, Eddie	85		85
183	May, David	68 (17)		85
184	Morris, Johnny	83		83
185	Smith, Tom	83		83
186	Hogg, Graeme	82 (1)		83
187	Young, Tony	69 (14)		83
188	Draycott, Billy	81		81
189	McGuinness, Wilf	81		81
190	Anderson, George	80		80
191	Dawson, Alex	80		80
192	Connelly, John	79 (1)		80
193	Hodge, James	79		79
194	Stam, Jaap	79		79
195	Whelan, William	79		79
196	Gibson, Colin	74 (5)		79
197	Stewart, Willie	76		76
198	Fortune, Quinton	53 (23)		76
199	Allen, Reg	75		75
200	Webb, Neil	70 (5)		75
201	Gillespie, Matthew	74		74
202	Leighton, Jim	73		73
203	Martin, Lee (1990s)	56 (17)		73
204	Gallimore, Stanley	72		72
205	Johnston, Billy	71		71
206	Gowling, Alan	64 (7)		71
207	Arkesden, Tommy	70		70
208	Hopkin, Fred	70		70
209	Muhren, Arnold	65 (5)		70
210	Pearson, Mark	68		68
211	Vidic, Nemanja	66 (2)		68
212	Evra, Patrice	62 (6)		68
213	Clarkin, John	67		67
214	Greaves, Ian	67		67
215	Hall, Jimmy (1932-1936)	67		67
216	Turnbull, Jimmy	67		67
217	Carolan, Joseph	66		66
218	Berg, Henning	49 (17)		66
219	Breen, Tommy	65		65
220	Webster, Colin	65		65
221	Dale, Billy	64		64
222	Turner, Chris	64		64
223	Vincent, Ernest	64		64
224	Carrick, Michael	53 (11)		64
225	Bradley, Warren	63		63

continued../

ALL LEAGUE MATCHES (continued)

#	PLAYER	A	S	T	#	PLAYER	A	S	T	#	PLAYER	A	S	T
226	Hanlon, Jimmy	63		63	301	Richardson, Lance	38		38	376	Haslam, George	25		25
227	Holton, Jim	63		63	302	Norton, Joe	37		37	377	Homer, Tom	25		25
228	Forlan, Diego	23 (40)		63	303	Graham, Arthur	33 (4)		37	378	Miller, Tom	25		25
229	Collinson, Jimmy	62		62	304	van der Gouw, Raimond	26 (11)		37	379	Winterbottom, Walter	25		25
230	Jackson, William	61		61	305	Clements, John	36		36	380	Blomqvist, Jesper	20 (5)		25
231	Porter, Billy	61		61	306	Dewar, Neil	36		36	381	McGarvey, Scott	13 (12)		25
232	Smith, Alan	43 (18)		61	307	Lawton, Nobby	36		36	382	Chadwick, Luke	11 (14)		25
233	Rennox, Charlie	60		60	308	Redman, Billy	36		36	383	Ryan, Jimmy	21 (3)		24
234	Park, Ji-Sung	39 (21)		60	309	Smith, Jack	36		36	384	Anderson	16 (8)		24
235	Cape, Jack	59		59	310	Allan, Jack	35		35	385	Bellion, David	5 (19)		24
236	Whitehouse, Jimmy	59		59	311	Breedon, Jack	35		35	386	Fall, Joe	23		23
237	Nicholson, Jimmy	58		58	312	Chisnall, Phil	35		35	387	Gipps, Tommy	23		23
238	Woodcock, Wilf	58		58	313	Forster, Tommy	35		35	388	Menzies, Alex	23		23
239	Birtles, Gary	57 (1)		58	314	Jenkyns, Caesar	35		35	389	Scott, John	23		23
240	Bannister, Jimmy	57		57	315	Rawlings, Bill	35		35	390	Milne, Ralph	19 (4)		23
241	Hamill, Mickey	57		57	316	Read, Bert	35		35	391	Hargreaves, Owen	16 (7)		23
242	McNulty, Thomas	57		57	317	Warburton, Arthur	35		35	392	Gibson, Terry	14 (9)		23
243	McShane, Harry	56		56	318	Blackstock, Tommy	34		34	393	Bain, David	22		22
244	Beardsmore, Russell	30 (26)		56	319	Chalmers, Stewart	34		34	394	Ball, John	22		22
245	Douglas, William	55		55	320	Donnelly, Tony	34		34	395	Hunter, George	22		22
246	Linkson, Oscar	55		55	321	Henderson, William	34		34	396	Rothwell, Herbert	22		22
247	Mitchell, Andrew (1890s)	54		54	322	O'Connell, Pat	34		34	397	Taylor, Ernie	22		22
248	O'Neil, Tommy	54		54	323	Rimmer, Jimmy	34		34	398	Warner, Jimmy	22		22
249	Edwards, Paul	52 (2)		54	324	Tevez, Carlos	31 (3)		34	399	Robinson, James	21		21
250	Anderson, Viv	50 (4)		54	325	Cruyff, Jordi	15 (19)		34	400	Sutcliffe, John	21		21
251	Boyd, Henry	52		52	326	Anderson, John	33		33	401	Travers, George	21		21
252	Sapsford, George	52		52	327	Beddow, John	33		33	402	Walton, Joe	21		21
253	Heinze, Gabriel	45 (7)		52	328	Hood, Billy	33		33	403	Jovanovic, Nikki	20 (1)		21
254	Farman, Alf	51		51	329	Myerscough, Joe	33		33	404	Bond, Ernie	20		20
255	Frame, Tommy	51		51	330	Preston, Stephen	33		33	405	Buckle, Ted	20		20
256	Hine, Ernie	51		51	331	Robertson, Sandy	33		33	406	Hodges, Frank	20		20
257	Hopkinson, Samuel	51		51	332	Sealey, Les	33		33	407	Jones, Tommy	20		20
258	Meehan, Tommy	51		51	333	Williams, Harry (1904-06)	33		33	408	Lewis, Eddie	20		20
259	Veron, Juan-Sebastian	45 (6)		51	334	Ritchie, Andy	26 (7)		33	409	Morgan, Hugh	20		20
260	Moody, John	50		50	335	Coupar, Jimmy	32		32	410	Barnes, Peter	19 (1)		20
261	Walsh, Gary	49 (1)		50	336	Hacking, Jack	32		32	411	Kleberson, Jose	16 (4)		20
262	Baird, Harry	49		49	337	Whalley, Bert	32		32	412	Djemba-Djemba, Eric	13 (7)		20
263	Burgess, Herbert	49		49	338	Poborsky, Karel	18 (14)		32	413	Blott, Sam	19		19
264	Carroll, Roy	46 (3)		49	339	McCalliog, Jim	31		31	414	Jackson, Tommy	18 (1)		19
265	Dow, John	48		48	340	Noble, Bobby	31		31	415	Anderson, Trevor	13 (6)		19
266	Blanc, Laurent	44 (4)		48	341	Williams, Rees	31		31	416	Wallwork, Ronnie	4 (15)		19
267	Robins, Mark	19 (29)		48	342	Sivebaek, Johnny	29 (2)		31	417	Ferrier, Ron	18		18
268	Ball, Jack	47		47	343	Brazil, Alan	18 (13)		31	418	MacDougall, Ted	18		18
269	Robertson, William	47		47	344	O'Brien, Liam	16 (15)		31	419	McCartney, John	18		18
270	Ure, Ian	47		47	345	Hodge, John	30		30	420	Moore, Graham	18		18
271	Wombwell, Dick	47		47	346	Kennedy, William	30		30	421	Pape, Albert	18		18
272	Wallace, Danny	36 (11)		47	347	Sagar, Charles	30		30	422	Hofton, Leslie	17		17
273	Harris, Frank	46		46	348	Barlow, Cyril	29		29	423	Kennedy, Fred	17		17
274	Knowles, Frank	46		46	349	Bogan, Tommy	29		29	424	Morgans, Kenny	17		17
275	Peters, James	46		46	350	Grassam, Billy	29		29	425	Owen, W	17		17
276	Roche, Paddy	46		46	351	Morrison, Tommy	29		29	426	Parker, Thomas	17		17
277	Spencer, Charlie	46		46	352	Burke, Ronnie	28		28	427	Boyle, Tommy	16		16
278	Stewart, William	46		46	353	Fitzsimmons, David	28		28	428	Fitchett, John	16		16
279	Dunne, Pat	45		45	354	Peden, Jack	28		28	429	Gardner, Dick	16		16
280	Moir, Ian	45		45	355	Robertson, Alex	28		28	430	Hurst, Daniel	16		16
281	Wassall, Jackie	45		45	356	Taylor, Chris	28		28	431	Nuttall, Tom	16		16
282	Howard, Tim	44 (1)		45	357	McGrath, Chris	12 (16)		28	432	Sidebottom, Arnold	16		16
283	Harrison, William	44		44	358	Fitzsimmons, Tommy	27		27	433	Smith, William	16		16
284	Edmonds, Hugh	43		43	359	Gladwin, George	27		27	434	Davies, Wyn	15 (1)		16
285	Leigh, Tom	43		43	360	Goldthorpe, Ernie	27		27	435	Clempson, Frank	15		15
286	Livingstone, George	43		43	361	Lappin, Harry	27		27	436	Connor, Ted	15		15
287	Graham, George	41 (2)		43	362	McDonald, Willie	27		27	437	Cunningham, John	15		15
288	Fisher, James	42		42	363	McMillen, Walter	27		27	438	John, Roy	15		15
289	McBain, Neil	42		42	364	Montgomery, James	27		27	439	Langford, Len	15		15
290	Ridding, Bill	42		42	365	Potts, Arthur	27		27	440	McMillan, Sammy	15		15
291	Pegg, Dick	41		41	366	Sweeney, Eric	27		27	441	Parkinson, Robert	15		15
292	Garton, Billy	39 (2)		41	367	Wrigglesworth, Billy	27		27	442	Wood, John	15		15
293	Richardson, Kieran	20 (21)		41	368	Ferguson, Darren	20 (7)		27	443	Kuszczak, Tomasz	14 (1)		15
294	Banks, Jack	40		40	369	Bosnich, Mark	26		26	444	Inglis, Bill	14		14
295	Bissett, George	40		40	370	Chapman, Billy	26		26	445	Ramsden, Charlie	14		14
296	Brown, James (1932-34)	40		40	371	Haywood, Joe	26		26	446	Ridgway, Joe	14		14
297	Davidson, Will	40		40	372	Sheldon, John	26		26	447	Tapken, Norman	14		14
298	Martin, Mick	33 (7)		40	373	Nani	16 (10)		26	448	Greening, Jonathan	4 (10)		14
299	Storey-Moore, Ian	39		39	374	Birchenough, Herbert	25		25	449	Berry, Bill	13		13
300	Sartori, Carlo	26 (13)		39	375	Doherty, John	25		25	450	Carson, Adam	13		13

continued../

ALL LEAGUE MATCHES (continued)

#	PLAYER	A	S	T	#	PLAYER	A	S	T	#	PLAYER	A	S	T
451	Chester, Reg	13		13	526	Davies, Ron	–	(8)	8	601	Cooke, Terry	1	(3)	4
452	Crowther, Stan	13		13	527	Brown, James (1892–93)	7		7	602	Wilson, David	–	(4)	4
453	Curry, Joe	13		13	528	Brown, William	7		7	603	Barber, Jack	3		3
454	Lowrie, Tommy	13		13	529	Collinson, Cliff	7		7	604	Brooks, William	3		3
455	Lynn, Sammy	13		13	530	Davies, John	7		7	605	Buckley, Frank	3		3
456	Mann, Herbert	13		13	531	Foley, G	7		7	606	Carman, James	3		3
457	McCartney, William	13		13	532	Gaudie, Ralph	7		7	607	Cartman, Bert	3		3
458	Spratt, Walter	13		13	533	Goodwin, Billy	7		7	608	Cashmore, Arthur	3		3
459	Toms, Billy	13		13	534	Griffiths, Clive	7		7	609	Connaughton, John	3		3
460	Curtis, John	4	(9)	13	535	Heathcote, Joe	7		7	610	Dennis, Billy	3		3
461	Allman, Arthur	12		12	536	Hooper, Arthur	7		7	611	Donaghy, Bernard	3		3
462	Bent, Geoff	12		12	537	Pepper, Frank	7		7	612	Greenwood, Wilson	3		3
463	Cookson, Sam	12		12	538	Royals, Ezra	7		7	613	Hall, Jack (1925–26)	3		3
464	Feehan, John	12		12	539	Wealands, Jeffrey	7		7	614	Hartwell, William	3		3
465	Fitton, Arthur	12		12	540	Crooks, Garth	6	(1)	7	615	Henrys, Arthur	3		3
466	Lang, Tommy	12		12	541	Davies, Alan	6	(1)	7	616	Heron, Tommy	3		3
467	Page, Louis	12		12	542	Larsson, Henrik	5	(2)	7	617	Hunter, William	3		3
468	Saunders, James	12		12	543	Stewart, Michael	5	(2)	7	618	Lawson, Reg	3		3
469	Topping, Henry	12		12	544	Fletcher, Peter	2	(5)	7	619	Lydon, George	3		3
470	Pique, Gerard	6	(6)	12	545	Maiorana, Jules	2	(5)	7	620	Lyner, David	3		3
471	Dublin, Dion	4	(8)	12	546	Boyd, Billy	6		6	621	McGillivray, John	3		3
472	Birch, Brian	11		11	547	Erentz, Harry	6		6	622	Montgomery, Archie	3		3
473	Craven, Charlie	11		11	548	Evans, Sidney	6		6	623	Robertson, Thomas	3		3
474	Ellis, David	11		11	549	Fielding, Bill	6		6	624	Scott, Jack	3		3
475	Gibson, Richard	11		11	550	Garvey, James	6		6	625	Thompson, John	3		3
476	Grundy, John	11		11	551	Haydock, Frank	6		6	626	Thompson, William	3		3
477	Hannaford, Charlie	11		11	552	Higgins, Mark	6		6	627	Thomson, Arthur	3		3
478	Hudson, Edward	11		11	553	Marshall, Arthur	6		6	628	Turner, James	3		3
479	Lee, Edwin	11		11	554	Millar, George	6		6	629	Waldron, Colin	3		3
480	Parker, Samuel	11		11	555	Nicol, George	6		6	630	Whitney, John	3		3
481	Vance, James	11		11	556	Sawyer, F	6		6	631	Whittaker, Walter	3		3
482	Watson, Willie	11		11	557	Stone, Herbert	6		6	632	Williams, Frank	3		3
483	Davies, Simon	4	(7)	11	558	Thomson, James	6		6	633	Williams, Joe	3		3
484	Sloan, Tom	4	(7)	11	559	Worrall, Harry	6		6	634	Yates, William	3		3
485	Ambler, Alfred	10		10	560	Pilkington, Kevin	4	(2)	6	635	Spector, Jonathan	2	(1)	3
486	Brett, Frank	10		10	561	Paterson, Steve	3	(3)	6	636	Wood, Nicky	2	(1)	3
487	Bullock, Jimmy	10		10	562	Eagles, Chris	2	(4)	6	637	Simpson, Danny	1	(2)	3
488	Dunn, William	10		10	563	Campbell, William	5		5	638	Wilson, Mark	1	(2)	3
489	Harrop, Bobby	10		10	564	Ford, Joe	5		5	639	Buchan, George	–	(3)	3
490	Higgins, Alexander	10		10	565	Higson, James	5		5	640	Foggon, Alan	–	(3)	3
491	Leonard, Harry	10		10	566	Mackie, Charlie	5		5	641	Ainsworth, Alf	2		2
492	Mathieson, William	10		10	567	McClelland, Jimmy	5		5	642	Aitken, John	2		2
493	Robinson, Matt	10		10	568	Smith, Albert	5		5	643	Astley, Joe	2		2
494	Valentine, Bob	10		10	569	Williams, Harry (1922–23)	5		5	644	Bain, James	2		2
495	Kopel, Frank	8	(2)	10	570	Cunningham, Laurie	3	(2)	5	645	Baldwin, Tommy	2		2
496	Gill, Tony	5	(5)	10	571	Rossi, Giuseppe	1	(4)	5	646	Booth, William	2		2
497	Beadsworth, Arthur	9		9	572	Bain, Jimmy	4		4	647	Bradbury, Len	2		2
498	Birkett, Cliff	9		9	573	Ball, Billy	4		4	648	Bunce, William	2		2
499	Briggs, Ronnie	9		9	574	Brown, Robert	4		4	649	Cairns, James	2		2
500	Broomfield, Herbert	9		9	575	Byrne, David	4		4	650	Christie, David	2		2
501	Chesters, Arthur	9		9	576	Cassidy, Laurie	4		4	651	Clayton, Gordon	2		2
502	Clark, Joe	9		9	577	Chorlton, Tom	4		4	652	Connell, Tom	2		2
503	Colville, James	9		9	578	Connachan, James	4		4	653	Dale, Joe	2		2
504	Godsmark, Gilbert	9		9	579	Donald, Ian	4		4	654	Dean, Harold	2		2
505	Green, Eddie	9		9	580	Dougan, Tommy	4		4	655	Goram, Andy	2		2
506	MacDonald, Ken	9		9	581	Ferguson, Danny	4		4	656	Haworth, Ronald	2		2
507	McCrae, James	9		9	582	Graham, John	4		4	657	Hendry, James	2		2
508	Richards, Billy	9		9	583	Halton, Reg	4		4	658	Iddon, Richard	2		2
509	Roberts, W.A	9		9	584	Hardman, Harold	4		4	659	Jones, Owen	2		2
510	Anderson, Willie	7	(2)	9	585	Harris, Tom	4		4	660	Kerr, Hugh	2		2
511	Clegg, Michael	4	(5)	9	586	Heywood, Herbert	4		4	661	Lancaster, Joe	2		2
512	Gillespie, Keith	3	(6)	9	587	Howarth, John	4		4	662	Lievesley, Leslie	2		2
513	Miller, Liam	3	(6)	9	588	Hulme, Aaron	4		4	663	Lievesley, Wilfred	2		2
514	Thornley, Ben	1	(8)	9	589	Lyons, George	4		4	664	Manns, Tom	2		2
515	Black, Dick	8		8	590	Miller, James	4		4	665	McIlvenny, Eddie	2		2
516	Ferguson, John	8		8	591	Murray, Robert	4		4	666	Newton, Percy	2		2
517	Hall, Proctor	8		8	592	Nevin, George	4		4	667	Olive, Les	2		2
518	Hillam, Charlie	8		8	593	Pears, Steve	4		4	668	Payne, Ernest	2		2
519	McGillivray, Charlie	8		8	594	Pinner, Mike	4		4	669	Pegg, Ken	2		2
520	Richards, Charlie	8		8	595	Savage, Ted	4		4	670	Prince, D	2		2
521	Smith, Lawrence	8		8	596	Taibi, Massimo	4		4	671	Prunier, William	2		2
522	Wilkinson, Harry	8		8	597	Thomson, Ernest	4		4	672	Pugh, James	2		2
523	Williams, Fred	8		8	598	Williams, Bill	4		4	673	Quinn, Jack	2		2
524	Givens, Don	4	(4)	8	599	Bielby, Paul	2	(2)	4	674	Roberts, Robert	2		2
525	Bardsley, Phil	3	(5)	8	600	Higginbotham, Danny	2	(2)	4	675	Rothwell, Charles	2		2

continued../

ALL LEAGUE MATCHES (continued)

#	PLAYER	A	S	T
676	Round, Elijah	2		2
677	Schofield, Joseph	2		2
678	Turner, Robert	2		2
679	Walker, Robert	2		2
680	Walton, John	2		2
681	Wedge, Frank	2		2
682	Wetherell, Joe	2		2
683	Wilcox, Tom	2		2
684	Williamson, John	2		2
685	Young, Arthur	2		2
686	Coyne, Peter	1	(1)	2
687	Graham, Deiniol	1	(1)	2
688	O'Kane, John	1	(1)	2
689	Brazil, Derek	-	(2)	2
690	Casper, Chris	-	(2)	2
691	Wrattan, Paul	-	(2)	2
692	Behan, Billy	1		1
693	Blackmore, Peter	1		1
694	Blew, Horace	1		1
695	Broome, Albert	1		1
696	Capper, Freddy	1		1
697	Christie, John	1		1
698	Cleaver, Harry	1		1
699	Dalton, Ted	1		1
700	Dempsey, Mark	1		1
701	Dong, Fangzhuo	1		1
702	Dyer, Jimmy	1		1
703	Foster, Ben	1		1
704	Gourlay, John	1		1
705	Hawksworth, Tony	1		1
706	Holt, Edward	1		1
707	Hopkins, James	1		1
708	Hunter, Reg	1		1
709	Johnson, Samuel	1		1
710	Jones, David (1937)	1		1
711	Jones, Peter	1		1
712	Kennedy, Patrick	1		1
713	Kinloch, Joe	1		1
714	Lee, Kieran	1		1
715	Longair, William	1		1
716	McCarthy, Pat	1		1
717	McFarlane, Noel	1		1
718	McFetteridge, David	1		1
719	McKee, Colin	1		1
720	Mitchell, Andrew (1930s)	1		1
721	Morton, Ben	1		1
722	Mulryne, Philip	1		1
723	O'Brien, George	1		1
724	Owen, Bill	1		1
725	Prentice, John	1		1
726	Prince, Albert	1		1
727	Rachubka, Paul	1		1
728	Radcliffe, George	1		1
729	Robbie, David	1		1
730	Rogers, Martyn	1		1
731	Rowe, Joelyn	1		1
732	Sarvis, William	1		1
733	Schofield, George	1		1
734	Schofield, Percy	1		1
735	Stephenson, R	1		1
736	Street, Ernest	1		1
737	Taylor, Walter	1		1
738	Tranter, Wilf	1		1
739	Tyler, Sidney	1		1
740	Walker, Dennis	1		1
741	Whitehurst, Walter	1		1
742	Whiteside, Kerr	1		1
743	Whittle, John	1		1
744	Whitworth, Neil	1		1
745	Wilson, Tommy	1		1
746	Campbell, Fraizer	-	(1)	1
747	Clark, Jonathan	-	(1)	1
748	Culkin, Nick	-	(1)	1
749	Djordjic, Bojan	-	(1)	1
750	Grimshaw, Tony	-	(1)	1
751	Healy, David	-	(1)	1
752	Kelly, Jimmy	-	(1)	1
753	Nevland, Erik	-	(1)	1
754	Pugh, Danny	-	(1)	1
755	Ricardo, Felipe	-	(1)	1
756	Roche, Lee	-	(1)	1
757	Whelan, Anthony	-	(1)	1

ALL PREMIERSHIP MATCHES

#	PLAYER	A	S	T
1	Giggs, Ryan	436	(59)	495
2	Scholes, Paul	328	(67)	395
3	Neville, Gary	349	(15)	364
4	Keane, Roy	309	(17)	326
5	Irwin, Denis	286	(10)	296
6	Butt, Nicky	210	(60)	270
7	Beckham, David	237	(28)	265
8	Neville, Phil	210	(53)	263
9	Schmeichel, Peter	252		252
10	Silvestre, Mikael	225	(24)	249
11	Solskjaer, Ole Gunnar	151	(84)	235
12	Pallister, Gary	206		206
13	Brown, Wes	175	(23)	198
14	Cole, Andrew	161	(34)	195
15	O'Shea, John	138	(53)	191
16	Ferdinand, Rio	183	(1)	184
17	Ronaldo, Cristiano	126	(37)	163
18	McClair, Brian	106	(56)	162
19	van Nistelrooy, Ruud	137	(13)	150
20	Bruce, Steve	148		148
21	Cantona, Eric	142	(1)	143
22	Rooney, Wayne	116	(11)	127
23	Ince, Paul	116		116
24	Sharpe, Lee	100	(16)	116
25	Hughes, Mark	110	(1)	111
26	Fletcher, Darren	79	(28)	107
27	Sheringham, Teddy	73	(31)	104
28	van der Sar, Edwin	99		99
29	Johnsen, Ronny	85	(14)	99
30	Yorke, Dwight	80	(16)	96
31	Barthez, Fabien	92		92
32	Kanchelskis, Andrei	67	(21)	88
33	Saha, Louis	52	(34)	86
34	May, David	68	(17)	85
35	Stam, Jaap	79		79
36	Parker, Paul	76	(3)	79
37	Fortune, Quinton	53	(23)	76
38	Vidic, Nemanja	66	(2)	68
39	Evra, Patrice	62	(6)	68
40	Berg, Henning	49	(17)	66
41	Carrick, Michael	53	(11)	64
42	Forlan, Diego	23	(40)	63
43	Smith, Alan	43	(18)	61
44	Park, Ji-Sung	39	(21)	60
45	Heinze, Gabriel	45	(7)	52
46	Veron, Juan-Sebastian	45	(6)	51
47	Carroll, Roy	46	(3)	49
48	Blanc, Laurent	44	(4)	48
49	Howard, Tim	44	(1)	45
50	Richardson, Kieran	20	(21)	41
51	van der Gouw, Raimond	26	(11)	37
52	Tevez, Carlos	31	(3)	34
53	Cruyff, Jordi	15	(19)	34
54	Poborsky, Karel	18	(14)	32
55	Robson, Bryan	15	(14)	29
56	Nani	16	(10)	26
57	Blomqvist, Jesper	20	(5)	25
58	Chadwick, Luke	11	(14)	25
59	Anderson	16	(8)	24
60	Bellion, David	5	(19)	24
61	Bosnich, Mark	23		23
62	Hargreaves, Owen	16	(7)	23
63	Kleberson, Jose	16	(4)	20
64	Djemba-Djemba, Eric	13	(7)	20
65	Wallwork, Ronnie	4	(15)	19
66	Ferguson, Darren	16	(2)	18
67	Kuszczak, Tomasz	14	(1)	15
68	Blackmore, Clayton	12	(2)	14
69	Greening, Jonathan	4	(10)	14
70	Walsh, Gary	12	(1)	13
71	Phelan, Mike	6	(7)	13
72	Curtis, John	4	(9)	13
73	Pique, Gerard	6	(6)	12
74	Dublin, Dion	4	(8)	12
75	Davies, Simon	4	(7)	11
76	Clegg, Michael	4	(5)	9
77	Gillespie, Keith	3	(6)	9
78	Miller, Liam	3	(6)	9
79	Thornley, Ben	1	(8)	9
80	Bardsley, Phil	3	(5)	8
81	Larsson, Henrik	5	(2)	7
82	Stewart, Michael	5	(2)	7
83	Pilkington, Kevin	4	(2)	6
84	Eagles, Chris	2	(4)	6
85	Rossi, Giuseppe	1	(4)	5
86	Taibi, Massimo	4		4
87	Higginbotham, Danny	2	(2)	4
88	Cooke, Terry	1	(3)	4
89	Spector, Jonathan	2	(1)	3
90	Simpson, Danny	1	(2)	3
91	Wilson, Mark	1	(2)	3
92	Goram, Andy	2		2
93	Prunier, William	2		2
94	O'Kane, John	1	(1)	2
95	Casper, Chris	-	(2)	2
96	Wallace, Danny	-	(2)	2
97	Dong, Fangzhuo	1		1
98	Foster, Ben	1		1
99	Lee, Kieran	1		1
100	Martin, Lee (1990s)	1		1
101	McKee, Colin	1		1
102	Mulryne, Philip	1		1
103	Rachubka, Paul	1		1
104	Campbell, Fraizer	-	(1)	1
105	Culkin, Nick	-	(1)	1
106	Djordjic, Bojan	-	(1)	1
107	Healy, David	-	(1)	1
108	Nevland, Erik	-	(1)	1
109	Pugh, Danny	-	(1)	1
110	Ricardo, Felipe	-	(1)	1
111	Roche, Lee	-	(1)	1
112	Webb, Neil	-	(1)	1

ALL LEAGUE DIVISION 1 MATCHES

#	PLAYER	A	S	T	#	PLAYER	A	S	T	#	PLAYER	A	S	T
1	Charlton, Bobby	604	(2)	606	76	Wilson, Jack	121		121	151	Dale, Billy	60		60
2	Foulkes, Bill	563	(3)	566	77	Burns, Francis	111	(10)	121	152	Reid, Tom	60		60
3	Dunne, Tony	414		414	78	Fitzpatrick, John	111	(6)	117	153	Nicholson, Jimmy	58		58
4	Stepney, Alex	393		393	79	James, Steve	116		116	154	Woodcock, Wilf	58		58
5	Albiston, Arthur	362	(15)	377	80	Scanlon, Albert	115		115	155	Birtles, Gary	57	(1)	58
6	Best, George	361		361	81	Mann, Frank	113		113	156	Bannister, Jimmy	57		57
7	Rowley, Jack	355		355	82	Partridge, Teddy	112		112	157	Hamill, Mickey	57		57
8	Chilton, Allenby	352		352	83	Rowley, Harry	111		111	158	McNulty, Thomas	57		57
9	Buchan, Martin	335		335	84	Pallister, Gary	108	(3)	111	159	Griffiths, Jack	56		56
10	Robson, Bryan	311	(5)	316	85	Downie, John	110		110	160	McShane, Harry	56		56
11	Spence, Joe	312		312	86	McGlen, Billy	110		110	161	Redwood, Hubert	56		56
12	Coppell, Steve	311	(1)	312	87	Halse, Harold	109		109	162	Rennox, Charlie	56		56
13	Stiles, Nobby	311		311	88	Jordan, Joe	109		109	163	Beardsmore, Russell	30	(26)	56
14	Law, Denis	305	(4)	309	89	Gibson, Don	108		108	164	Downie, Alex	55		55
15	Crerand, Pat	304		304	90	Pearson, Stuart	108		108	165	Linkson, Oscar	55		55
16	Meredith, Billy	303		303	91	Beale, Robert	105		105	166	Perrins, George	55		55
17	Pearson, Stan	301		301	92	Blanchflower, Jackie	105		105	167	Manley, Tom	54		54
18	McIlroy, Sammy	279	(21)	300	93	Jones, Mark	103		103	168	Mitchell, Andrew (1890s)	54		54
19	Duxbury, Mike	274	(25)	299	94	Warner, Jack	102		102	169	O'Neil, Tommy	54		54
20	Bailey, Gary	294		294	95	Thomas, Harry	101		101	170	Stewart, Willie	54		54
21	Brennan, Shay	291	(1)	292	96	Hill, Gordon	100	(1)	101	171	Edwards, Paul	52	(2)	54
22	Macari, Lou	275	(16)	291	97	Giles, Johnny	99		99	172	Anderson, Viv	50	(4)	54
23	Carey, Johnny	288		288	98	Grimwood, John	99		99	173	Hayes, Vince	53		53
24	Wall, George	281		281	99	Whalley, Arthur	97		97	174	Sapsford, George	52		52
25	Sadler, David	266	(6)	272	100	Greenhoff, Jimmy	94	(3)	97	175	Erentz, Fred	51		51
26	Silcock, Jack	271		271	101	Gaskell, David	96		96	176	Meehan, Tommy	51		51
27	Viollet, Dennis	259		259	102	Goodwin, Fred	95		95	177	Donaldson, Bob	50		50
28	Aston, John (senior)	253		253	103	Gidman, John	94	(1)	95	178	Burgess, Herbert	49		49
29	Berry, Johnny	247		247	104	Cope, Ronnie	93		93	179	Holton, Jim	49		49
30	Byrne, Roger	245		245	105	Whitefoot, Jeff	93		93	180	McKay, Bill	49		49
31	Cockburn, Henry	243		243	106	Davenport, Peter	73	(19)	92	181	Robins, Mark	19	(29)	48
32	Stacey, George	241		241	107	Thomas, Mickey	90		90	182	Roughton, George	47		47
33	Hughes, Mark	226	(8)	234	108	Ince, Paul	87	(3)	90	183	Ure, Ian	47		47
34	Moran, Kevin	228	(3)	231	109	Grimes, Ashley	62	(28)	90	184	Farman, Alf	46		46
35	Stapleton, Frank	204	(19)	223	110	Phelan, Mike	82	(7)	89	185	Harris, Frank	46		46
36	Turnbull, Sandy	220		220	111	Donaghy, Mal	76	(13)	89	186	Knowles, Frank	46		46
37	Moore, Charlie	215		215	112	McPherson, Frank	87		87	187	Spencer, Charlie	46		46
38	Gregg, Harry	210		210	113	Jones, Tom	86		86	188	Dunne, Pat	45		45
39	Hilditch, Clarence	207		207	114	Colman, Eddie	85		85	189	McLenahan, Hugh	45		45
40	Roberts, Charlie	207		207	115	McCreery, David	48	(37)	85	190	Moir, Ian	45		45
41	Duckworth, Dick	206		206	116	Morris, Johnny	83		83	191	Wallace, Danny	36	(9)	45
42	Whiteside, Norman	193	(13)	206	117	Hogg, Graeme	82	(1)	83	192	Harrison, William	44		44
43	Morgan, Willie	204		204	118	McGuinness, Wilf	81		81	193	Roche, Paddy	44		44
44	Steward, Alfred	204		204	119	Anderson, George	80		80	194	Edmonds, Hugh	43		43
45	Kidd, Brian	195	(8)	203	120	Dawson, Alex	80		80	195	Johnston, Billy	43		43
46	Bell, Alex	202		202	121	Picken, Jack	80		80	196	Livingstone, George	43		43
47	Herd, David	201	(1)	202	122	Connelly, John	79	(1)	80	197	Graham, George	41	(1)	42
48	Nicholl, Jimmy	188	(8)	196	123	Hodge, James	79		79	198	Garton, Billy	39	(2)	41
49	Bennion, Ray	193		193	124	Whelan, William	79		79	199	Bissett, George	40		40
50	McClair, Brian	190	(3)	193	125	Gibson, Colin	74	(5)	79	200	Schmeichel, Peter	40		40
51	Crompton, Jack	191		191	126	Holden, Dick	78		78	201	Smith, Tom	40		40
52	McQueen, Gordon	184		184	127	Sharpe, Lee	60	(17)	77	202	Giggs, Ryan	33	(7)	40
53	Greenhoff, Brian	179	(1)	180	128	Allen, Reg	75		75	203	Storey-Moore, Ian	39		39
54	Wood, Ray	178		178	129	Daly, Gerry	71	(3)	74	204	Sartori, Carlo	26	(13)	39
55	Blackmore, Clayton	138	(34)	172	130	Webb, Neil	70	(4)	74	205	Richardson, Lance	38		38
56	Moger, Harry	170		170	131	Leighton, Jim	73		73	206	Mellor, Jack	37		37
57	Taylor, Tommy	166		166	132	Irwin, Denis	70	(2)	72	207	Norton, Joe	37		37
58	West, Enoch	166		166	133	Martin, Lee (1990s)	55	(17)	72	208	Walsh, Gary	37		37
59	Quixall, Albert	165		165	134	Gowling, Alan	64	(7)	71	209	Graham, Arthur	33	(4)	37
60	Houston, Stewart	164	(1)	165	135	Hopkin, Fred	70		70	210	Clements, John	36		36
61	Delaney, Jimmy	164		164	136	Muhren, Arnold	65	(5)	70	211	Lawton, Nobby	36		36
62	McGrath, Paul	159	(4)	163	137	Pearson, Mark	68		68	212	Lochhead, Arthur	36		36
63	Bruce, Steve	161		161	138	Young, Tony	62	(6)	68	213	Redman, Billy	36		36
64	Wilkins, Ray	158	(2)	160	139	Greaves, Ian	67		67	214	Chisnall, Phil	35		35
65	Strachan, Gordon	155	(5)	160	140	Turnbull, Jimmy	67		67	215	Forster, Tommy	35		35
66	Setters, Maurice	159		159	141	Carolan, Joseph	66		66	216	Rawlings, Bill	35		35
67	Aston, John (junior)	139	(16)	155	142	McLachlan, George	65		65	217	Kanchelskis, Andrei	29	(6)	35
68	Edwards, Duncan	151		151	143	Vose, George	65		65	218	Brown, Jimmy (1935-39)	34		34
69	Moses, Remi	143	(7)	150	144	Webster, Colin	65		65	219	Donnelly, Tony	34		34
70	Mitten, Charlie	142		142	145	Bryant, Billy	64		64	220	O'Connell, Pat	34		34
71	Olsen, Jesper	119	(20)	139	146	Turner, Chris	64		64	221	Rimmer, Jimmy	34		34
72	Hanson, Jimmy	135		135	147	Bradley, Warren	63		63	222	Wassall, Jackie	34		34
73	Mew, Jack	133		133	148	Hanlon, Johnny	63		63	223	Anderson, John	33		33
74	Pegg, David	127		127	149	Forsyth, Alex	60	(2)	62	224	Hood, Billy	33		33
75	Cantwell, Noel	123		123	150	Barson, Frank	60		60	225	Sealey, Les	33		33

continued../

ALL LEAGUE DIVISION 1 MATCHES (continued)

#	PLAYER	A	S	T	#	PLAYER	A	S	T	#	PLAYER	A	S	T
226	Ritchie, Andy	26	(7)	33	301	Nuttall, Tom	16		16	376	Paterson, Steve	3	(3)	6
227	Breen, Tommy	32		32	302	Peddie, Jack	16		16	377	Campbell, William	5		5
228	Martin, Mick	26	(6)	32	303	Davies, Wyn	15	(1)	16	378	Ford, Joe	5		5
229	Noble, Bobby	31		31	304	Clempson, Frank	15		15	379	McClelland, Jimmy	5		5
230	Williams, Rees	31		31	305	Connor, Ted	15		15	380	Smith, Albert	5		5
231	Sivebaek, Johnny	29	(2)	31	306	John, Roy	15		15	381	Cunningham, Laurie	3	(2)	5
232	Brazil, Alan	18	(13)	31	307	McMillan, Sammy	15		15	382	Brown, Robert	4		4
233	O'Brien, Liam	16	(15)	31	308	Baird, Harry	14		14	383	Cape, Jack	4		4
234	Hodge, John	30		30	309	Inglis, Bill	14		14	384	Cassidy, Joe	4		4
235	Bamford, Tommy	29		29	310	Ramsden, Charlie	14		14	385	Cassidy, Laurie	4		4
236	Barlow, Cyril	29		29	311	Tapken, Norman	14		14	386	Chorlton, Tom	4		4
237	Bogan, Tommy	29		29	312	Wombwell, Dick	14		14	387	Donald, Ian	4		4
238	Bonthron, Bob	28		28	313	Berry, Bill	13		13	388	Dougan, Tommy	4		4
239	Burke, Ronnie	28		28	314	Carson, Adam	13		13	389	Ferguson, Danny	4		4
240	Davidson, Will	28		28	315	Crowther, Stan	13		13	390	Gardner, Dick	4		4
241	Gallimore, Stanley	28		28	316	Curry, Joe	13		13	391	Graham, John	4		4
242	Mutch, George	28		28	317	Lowrie, Tommy	13		13	392	Halton, Reg	4		4
243	Peden, Jack	28		28	318	Lynn, Sammy	13		13	393	Hardman, Harold	4		4
244	McGrath, Chris	12	(16)	28	319	Spratt, Walter	13		13	394	Harris, Tom	4		4
245	Fitzsimmons, Tommy	27		27	320	Toms, Billy	13		13	395	Howarth, John	4		4
246	Montgomery, James	27		27	321	Allman, Arthur	12		12	396	Hulme, Aaron	4		4
247	Potts, Arthur	27		27	322	Bent, Geoff	12		12	397	Pears, Steve	4		4
248	Radford, Charlie	27		27	323	Clarkin, John	12		12	398	Pinner, Mike	4		4
249	Sweeney, Eric	27		27	324	Cookson, Sam	12		12	399	Sidebottom, Arnold	4		4
250	Taylor, Chris	27		27	325	Feehan, John	12		12	400	Thomson, Ernest	4		4
251	Chapman, Billy	26		26	326	Birch, Brian	11		11	401	Bielby, Paul	2	(2)	4
252	Haywood, Joe	26		26	327	Craven, Charlie	11		11	402	Wilson, David	–	(4)	4
253	McNaught, James	26		26	328	Gibson, Richard	11		11	403	Allan, Jack	3		3
254	Sheldon, John	26		26	329	Hannaford, Charlie	11		11	404	Bain, Jimmy	3		3
255	Parker, Paul	24	(2)	26	330	Hudson, Edward	11		11	405	Beddow, John	3		3
256	Doherty, John	25		25	331	McCalliog, Jim	11		11	406	Blackstock, Tommy	3		3
257	Homer, Tom	25		25	332	Parker, Samuel	11		11	407	Bosnich, Mark	3		3
258	Miller, Tom	25		25	333	Watson, Willie	11		11	408	Buckley, Frank	3		3
259	McGarvey, Scott	13	(12)	25	334	Sloan, Tom	4	(7)	11	409	Cashmore, Arthur	3		3
260	Whalley, Bert	24		24	335	Brett, Frank	10		10	410	Connaughton, John	3		3
261	Ryan, Jimmy	21	(3)	24	336	Bullock, Jimmy	10		10	411	Hall, Jack (1920s)	3		3
262	Ball, Jack	23		23	337	Harrop, Bobby	10		10	412	Henrys, Arthur	3		3
263	Breedon, Jack	23		23	338	Henderson, William	10		10	413	Heron, Tommy	3		3
264	Fall, Joe	23		23	339	Leonard, Harry	10		10	414	Hunter, William	3		3
265	Gipps, Tommy	23		23	340	Mathieson, William	10		10	415	McGillivray, John	3		3
266	Menzies, Alex	23		23	341	Sagar, Charles	10		10	416	Scott, Jack	3		3
267	Scott, John	23		23	342	Schofield, Alf	10		10	417	Thompson, William	3		3
268	Wrigglesworth, Billy	23		23	343	Kopel, Frank	8	(2)	10	418	Thomson, Arthur	3		3
269	Milne, Ralph	19	(4)	23	344	Gill, Tony	5	(5)	10	419	Waldron, Colin	3		3
270	Gibson, Terry	14	(9)	23	345	Birkett, Cliff	9		9	420	Williams, Frank	3		3
271	Ball, John	22		22	346	Briggs, Ronnie	9		9	421	Williams, Joe	3		3
272	Hunter, George	22		22	347	Broomfield, Herbert	9		9	422	Yates, William	3		3
273	Taylor, Ernie	22		22	348	Colville, James	9		9	423	Wood, Nicky	2	(1)	3
274	Warner, Jimmy	22		22	349	McCrae, James	9		9	424	Buchan, George	–	(3)	3
275	Coupar, Jimmy	21		21	350	Parker, Thomas	9		9	425	Foggon, Alan	–	(3)	3
276	McBain, Neil	21		21	351	Anderson, Willie	7	(2)	9	426	Astley, Joe	2		2
277	Robinson, James	21		21	352	Ferguson, Darren	4	(5)	9	427	Bradbury, Len	2		2
278	Travers, George	21		21	353	Lang, Tommy	8		8	428	Christie, David	2		2
279	Walton, Joe	21		21	354	Givens, Don	4	(4)	8	429	Clayton, Gordon	2		2
280	Winterbottom, Walter	21		21	355	Brown, Jim (1892–93)	7		7	430	Connell, Tom	2		2
281	Jovanovic, Nikki	20	(1)	21	356	Chesters, Arthur	7		7	431	Dale, Joe	2		2
282	Bond, Ernie	20		20	357	Collinson, Cliff	7		7	432	Dow, John	2		2
283	Buckle, Ted	20		20	358	Davies, John	7		7	433	Haworth, Ronald	2		2
284	Gladwin, George	20		20	359	Douglas, William	7		7	434	Hendry, James	2		2
285	Hodges, Frank	20		20	360	Goodwin, Billy	7		7	435	Iddon, Richard	2		2
286	Lewis, Eddie	20		20	361	Griffiths, Clive	7		7	436	Lancaster, Joe	2		2
287	Myerscough, Joe	20		20	362	Hooper, Arthur	7		7	437	McIlvenny, Eddie	2		2
288	Warburton, Arthur	20		20	363	Royals, Ezra	7		7	438	Olive, Les	2		2
289	Barnes, Peter	19	(1)	20	364	Wealands, Jeffrey	7		7	439	Pape, Albert	2		2
290	Blott, Sam	19		19	365	Crooks, Garth	6	(1)	7	440	Payne, Ernest	2		2
291	Smith, Jack	19		19	366	Davies, Alan	6	(1)	7	441	Pegg, Ken	2		2
292	Jackson, Tommy	18	(1)	19	367	Fletcher, Peter	2	(5)	7	442	Porter, Billy	2		2
293	Anderson, Trevor	13	(6)	19	368	Maiorana, Jules	2	(5)	7	443	Prince, D	2		2
294	MacDougall, Ted	18		18	369	Ferrier, Ron	6		6	444	Quinn, Jack	2		2
295	Moore, Graham	18		18	370	Fielding, Bill	6		6	445	Roberts, Ernest	2		2
296	Haslam, George	17		17	371	Haydock, Frank	6		6	446	Round, Elijah	2		2
297	Hofton, Leslie	17		17	372	Higgins, Mark	6		6	447	Stone, Herbert	2		2
298	Hopkinson, Samuel	17		17	373	Nicol, George	6		6	448	Thompson, John	2		2
299	Morgans, Kenny	17		17	374	Thomson, James	6		6	449	Walton, John	2		2
300	Boyle, Tommy	16		16	375	Worrall, Harry	6		6	450	Wilcox, Tom	2		2

continued../

ALL LEAGUE DIVISION 1 MATCHES (continued)

#	PLAYER	A	S	T
451	Williamson, John	2		2
452	Young, Arthur	2		2
453	Coyne, Peter	1	(1)	2
454	Graham, Deiniol	1	(1)	2
455	Brazil, Derek	–	(2)	2
456	Wrattan, Paul	–	(2)	2
457	Capper, Freddy	1		1
458	Dalton, Ted	1		1
459	Dempsey, Mark	1		1
460	Hawksworth, Tony	1		1
461	Hunter, Reg	1		1
462	Jones, Peter	1		1
463	Kennedy, Patrick	1		1
464	Kinloch, Joe	1		1
465	Lydon, George	1		1

#	PLAYER	A	S	T
466	McCarthy, Pat	1		1
467	McFarlane, Noel	1		1
468	Prentice, John	1		1
469	Prince, Albert	1		1
470	Pugh, James	1		1
471	Rogers, Martyn	1		1
472	Rothwell, Charles	1		1
473	Rowe, Joelyn	1		1
474	Schofield, George	1		1
475	Schofield, Percy	1		1
476	Taylor, Walter	1		1
477	Tranter, Wilf	1		1
478	Walker, Dennis	1		1
479	Whitehurst, Walter	1		1
480	Whiteside, Kerr	1		1

#	PLAYER	A	S	T
481	Whitworth, Neil	1		1
482	Williams, Harry (1900s)	1		1
483	Wilson, Tommy	1		1
484	Clark, Jonathan	–	(1)	1
485	Grimshaw, Tony	–	(1)	1
486	Kelly, Jimmy	–	(1)	1
487	Whelan, Anthony	–	(1)	1

ALL LEAGUE DIVISION 2 MATCHES

#	PLAYER	A	S	T	#	PLAYER	A	S	T	#	PLAYER	A	S	T
1	Erentz, Fred	229		229	76	Brown, James (1932–34)	40		40	151	McCartney, William	13		13
2	Cartwright, Walter	228		228	77	Houston, Stewart	40		40	152	Myerscough, Joe	13		13
3	Stafford, Harry	183		183	78	Stepney, Alex	40		40	153	Breedon, Jack	12		12
4	Spence, Joe	169		169	79	Forsyth, Alex	39		39	154	Davidson, Will	12		12
5	Griffiths, Billy	157		157	80	Roughton, George	39		39	155	Ferrier, Ron	12		12
6	Silcock, Jack	152		152	81	Macari, Lou	36	(2)	38	156	Fitton, Arthur	12		12
7	Cassidy, Joe	148		148	82	Perrins, George	37		37	157	Gardner, Dick	12		12
8	Schofield, Alf	147		147	83	Daly, Gerry	36	(1)	37	158	Page, Louis	12		12
9	Morgan, Billy	143		143	84	Dewar, Neil	36		36	159	Saunders, James	12		12
10	Manley, Tom	134		134	85	Partridge, Teddy	36		36	160	Sidebottom, Arnold	12		12
11	Vose, George	130		130	86	Reid, Tom	36		36	161	Topping, Henry	12		12
12	McKay, Bill	120		120	87	Baird, Harry	35		35	162	Coupar, Jimmy	11		11
13	Barrett, Frank	118		118	88	Jenkyns, Caesar	35		35	163	Ellis, David	11		11
14	Downie, Alex	117		117	89	Read, Bert	35		35	164	Grundy, John	11		11
15	McNaught, James	114		114	90	Chalmers, Stewart	34		34	165	Lee, Edwin	11		11
16	Lochhead, Arthur	111		111	91	Hopkinson, Samuel	34		34	166	Pearson, Stan	11		11
17	Bryant, William	109		109	92	Morgan, Willie	32	(2)	34	167	Vance, James	11		11
18	Griffiths, Jack	109		109	93	Breen, Tommy	33		33	168	Wassall, Jackie	11		11
19	Steward, Alfred	105		105	94	Picken, Jack	33		33	169	Ambler, Alfred	10		10
20	Jones, Tom	103		103	95	Preston, Stephen	33		33	170	Dunn, William	10		10
21	Grimwood, John	97		97	96	Robertson, Sandy	33		33	171	Higgins, Alexander	10		10
22	Peddie, Jack	96		96	97	Wombwell, Dick	33		33	172	Robinson, Matt	10		10
23	Hilditch, Clarence	94		94	98	Allan, Jack	32		32	173	Valentine, Bob	10		10
24	Moore, Charlie	94		94	99	Hacking, Jack	32		32	174	Coppell, Steve	9	(1)	10
25	Bennion, Ray	93		93	100	Williams, Harry (1900s)	32		32	175	Beadsworth, Arthur	9		9
26	Smith, Dick	93		93	101	Blackstock, Tommy	31		31	176	Clark, Joe	9		9
27	Bonthron, Bob	91		91	102	Pearson, Stuart	30	(1)	31	177	Godsmark, Gilbert	9		9
28	Bryant, Billy	84		84	103	Beddow, John	30		30	178	Green, Eddie	9		9
29	Mutch, George	84		84	104	Kennedy, William	30		30	179	MacDonald, Ken	9		9
30	Donaldson, Bob	81		81	105	Redwood, Hubert	30		30	180	Richards, Billy	9		9
31	Draycott, Billy	81		81	106	Grassam, Billy	29		29	181	Roberts, W	9		9
32	Barson, Frank	80		80	107	Morrison, Tommy	29		29	182	Wilson, Jack	9		9
33	Mellor, Jack	79		79	108	Fitzsimmons, David	28		28	183	Black, Dick	8		8
34	Bell, Alex	76		76	109	Holden, Dick	28		28	184	Ferguson, John	8		8
35	Gillespie, Matthew	74		74	110	Johnston, Billy	28		28	185	Hall, Proctor	8		8
36	McPherson, Frank	72		72	111	Robertson, Alex	28		28	186	Haslam, George	8		8
37	Moger, Harry	72		72	112	Goldthorpe, Ernie	27		27	187	Hillam, Charlie	8		8
38	Arkesden, Tommy	70		70	113	Lappin, Harry	27		27	188	McGillivray, Charlie	8		8
39	Bamford, Tommy	69		69	114	McDonald, Willie	27		27	189	Parker, Thomas	8		8
40	Brown, Jimmy (1935–39)	68		68	115	McMillen, Walter	27		27	190	Richards, Charlie	8		8
41	Hall, Jack (1930s)	67		67	116	Thomas, Harry	27		27	191	Smith, Lawrence	8		8
42	Mann, Frank	67		67	117	Birchenough, Herbert	25		25	192	Whalley, Bert	8		8
43	McLenahan, Hugh	67		67	118	Rowley, Jack	25		25	193	Wilkinson, Harry	8		8
44	Radford, Charlie	64		64	119	Ball, Jack	24		24	194	Williams, Fred	8		8
45	Roberts, Charlie	64		64	120	Henderson, William	24		24	195	Martin, Mick	7	(1)	8
46	Vincent, Ernest	64		64	121	Bain, David	22		22	196	Davies, Ron	–	(8)	8
47	Collinson, Jimmy	62		62	122	Rothwell, Herbert	22		22	197	Brown, William	7		7
48	Hayes, Vince	62		62	123	Stewart, Willie	22		22	198	Foley, G	7		7
49	Rowley, Harry	62		62	124	McBain, Neil	21		21	199	Gaudie, Ralph	7		7
50	Jackson, Bill	61		61	125	Sutcliffe, John	21		21	200	Gladwin, George	7		7
51	Porter, Billy	59		59	126	Jones, Tommy	20		20	201	Heathcote, Joe	7		7
52	Whitehouse, Jimmy	59		59	127	McCalliog, Jim	20		20	202	Pepper, Frank	7		7
53	Cape, Jack	55		55	128	Morgan, Hugh	20		20	203	Boyd, William	6		6
54	Clarkin, John	55		55	129	Sagar, Charles	20		20	204	Erentz, Harry	6		6
55	Mew, Jack	53		53	130	Duckworth, Dick	19		19	205	Evans, Sidney	6		6
56	Boyd, Henry	52		52	131	McCartney, John	18		18	206	Garvey, James	6		6
57	Frame, Tommy	51		51	132	Kennedy, Fred	17		17	207	Marshall, Arthur	6		6
58	Hine, Ernie	51		51	133	Owen, W	17		17	208	Millar, George	6		6
59	Moody, John	50		50	134	Smith, Jack	17		17	209	Sawyer, F	6		6
60	Douglas, William	48		48	135	Carey, Johnny	16		16	210	Wall, George	6		6
61	Robertson, William	47		47	136	Fitchett, John	16		16	211	Farman, Alf	5		5
62	Dow, John	46		46	137	Hurst, Daniel	16		16	212	Higson, James	5		5
63	Peters, James	46		46	138	Pape, Albert	16		16	213	Mackie, Charlie	5		5
64	Stewart, William	46		46	139	Smith, Bill	16		16	214	Williams, Harry (1920s)	5		5
65	McLachlan, George	45		45	140	Cunningham, John	15		15	215	Ball, William	4		4
66	Gallimore, Stanley	44		44	141	Langford, Len	15		15	216	Byrne, David	4		4
67	Leigh, Tom	43		43	142	Parkinson, Robert	15		15	217	Connachan, James	4		4
68	Smith, Tom	43		43	143	Warburton, Arthur	15		15	218	Dale, Billy	4		4
69	Fisher, James	42		42	144	Wood, John	15		15	219	Heywood, Herbert	4		4
70	Ridding, Bill	42		42	145	Young, Tony	7	(8)	15	220	Lang, Tommy	4		4
71	McIlroy, Sammy	41	(1)	42	146	Holton, Jim	14		14	221	Lyons, George	4		4
72	Buchan, Martin	41		41	147	Ridgway, Joe	14		14	222	Miller, James	4		4
73	Pegg, Dick	41		41	148	Chester, Reg	13		13	223	Murray, Robert	4		4
74	Greenhoff, Brian	39	(2)	41	149	James, Steve	13		13	224	Nevin, George	4		4
75	Banks, Jack	40		40	150	Mann, Herbert	13		13	225	Rennox, Charlie	4		4

continued../

ALL LEAGUE DIVISION 2 MATCHES (continued)

#	PLAYER	A	S	T
226	Savage, Ted	4		4
227	Stone, Herbert	4		4
228	Williams, Bill	4		4
229	Winterbottom, Walter	4		4
230	Wrigglesworth, Billy	4		4
231	Barber, Jack	3		3
232	Brooks, William	3		3
233	Carman, James	3		3
234	Cartman, Bert	3		3
235	Dennis, Billy	3		3
236	Donaghy, Bernard	3		3
237	Greenwood, Wilson	3		3
238	Hanson, Jimmy	3		3
239	Hartwell, William	3		3
240	Lawson, Reg	3		3
241	Lyner, David	3		3
242	Montgomery, Archie	3		3
243	Robertson, Thomas	3		3
244	Turner, John	3		3
245	Whitney, John	3		3
246	Whittaker, Walter	3		3
247	Ainsworth, Alf	2		2
248	Aitken, John	2		2
249	Albiston, Arthur	2		2
250	Bain, James	2		2
251	Baldwin, Tommy	2		2
252	Booth, William	2		2
253	Bunce, William	2		2
254	Cairns, James	2		2
255	Chesters, Arthur	2		2

#	PLAYER	A	S	T
256	Dean, Harold	2		2
257	Jones, Owen	2		2
258	Kerr, Hugh	2		2
259	Lievesley, Leslie	2		2
260	Lievesley, Wilfred	2		2
261	Lydon, George	2		2
262	Manns, Tom	2		2
263	Newton, Percy	2		2
264	Roche, Paddy	2		2
265	Schofield, Joseph	2		2
266	Turner, Robert	2		2
267	Walker, Robert	2		2
268	Wedge, Frank	2		2
269	Wetherell, Joe	2		2
270	McCreery, David	–	(2)	2
271	Bain, Jimmy	1		1
272	Behan, Billy	1		1
273	Blackmore, Peter	1		1
274	Blew, Horace	1		1
275	Broome, Albert	1		1
276	Christie, John	1		1
277	Cleaver, Harry	1		1
278	Dyer, Jimmy	1		1
279	Gourlay, John	1		1
280	Holt, Edward	1		1
281	Hopkins, James	1		1
282	Johnson, Samuel	1		1
283	Jones, David (1937)	1		1
284	Longair, William	1		1
285	McFetteridge, David	1		1

#	PLAYER	A	S	T
286	Mitchell, Andrew (1930s)	1		1
287	Morton, Ben	1		1
288	O'Brien, George	1		1
289	Owen, Bill	1		1
290	Pugh, James	1		1
291	Radcliffe, George	1		1
292	Robbie, David	1		1
293	Rothwell, Charles	1		1
294	Sarvis, William	1		1
295	Stephenson, R	1		1
296	Street, Ernest	1		1
297	Taylor, Chris	1		1
298	Thompson, John	1		1
299	Tyler, Sidney	1		1
300	Whittle, John	1		1
301	Graham, George	–	(1)	1
302	Nicholl, Jimmy	–	(1)	1

ALL FA CUP MATCHES

#	PLAYER	A	S	T	#	PLAYER	A	S	T	#	PLAYER	A	S	T
1	Charlton, Bobby	78		78	76	O'Shea, John	15	(5)	20	151	Johnsen, Ronny	8	(2)	10
2	Giggs, Ryan	55	(7)	62	77	Delaney, Jimmy	19		19	152	Richardson, Kieran	8	(2)	10
3	Foulkes, Bill	61		61	78	Downie, Alex	19		19	153	Saha, Louis	6	(4)	10
4	Dunne, Tony	54	(1)	55	79	Mitten, Charlie	19		19	154	Arkesden, Tommy	9		9
5	Best, George	46		46	80	Moore, Charlie	19		19	155	Bryant, Billy	9		9
6	Hughes, Mark	45	(1)	46	81	Greenhoff, Jimmy	18	(1)	19	156	Collinson, Jimmy	9		9
7	Keane, Roy	44	(2)	46	82	Byrne, Roger	18		18	157	Colman, Eddie	9		9
8	Law, Denis	44	(2)	46	83	Griffiths, Billy	18		18	158	Gidman, John	9		9
9	McClair, Brian	38	(7)	45	84	Moran, Kevin	18		18	159	Grimwood, John	9		9
10	Stepney, Alex	44		44	85	Viollet, Dennis	18		18	160	Hanson, Jimmy	9		9
11	Neville, Gary	41	(3)	44	86	McGrath, Paul	15	(3)	18	161	Morgan, Billy	9		9
12	Crerand, Pat	43		43	87	Fletcher, Darren	11	(7)	18	162	Morris, Johnny	9		9
13	Irwin, Denis	42	(1)	43	88	Cantona, Eric	17		17	163	Peddie, Jack	9		9
14	Rowley, Jack	42		42	89	Hill, Gordon	17		17	164	Pegg, David	9		9
15	Bruce, Steve	41		41	90	Mann, Frank	17		17	165	Sartori, Carlo	9		9
16	Schmeichel, Peter	41		41	91	McNaught, James	17		17	166	Stewart, Willie	9		9
17	Buchan, Martin	39		39	92	Stafford, Harry	17		17	167	Taylor, Tommy	9		9
18	Scholes, Paul	27	(12)	39	93	Steward, Alfred	17		17	168	Turnbull, Jimmy	9		9
19	Carey, Johnny	38		38	94	Donaldson, Bob	16		16	169	van der Sar, Edwin	9		9
20	Pallister, Gary	38		38	95	Gaskell, David	16		16	170	Webb, Neil	9		9
21	Stiles, Nobby	38		38	96	McPherson, Frank	16		16	171	Webster, Colin	9		9
22	McIlroy, Sammy	35	(3)	38	97	Olsen, Jesper	13	(3)	16	172	Whalley, Arthur	9		9
23	Chilton, Allenby	37		37	98	Bennion, Ray	15		15	173	Fortune, Quinton	8	(1)	9
24	Albiston, Arthur	36		36	99	Berry, Johnny	15		15	174	Gibson, Colin	8	(1)	9
25	Brennan, Shay	36		36	100	Bonthron, Bob	15		15	175	Evra, Patrice	7	(2)	9
26	Coppell, Steve	36		36	101	Cassidy, Joe	15		15	176	Park, Ji-Sung	7	(2)	9
27	Herd, David	35		35	102	Halse, Harold	15		15	177	Wallace, Danny	7	(2)	9
28	Robson, Bryan	33	(2)	35	103	West, Enoch	15		15	178	Sheringham, Teddy	4	(5)	9
29	Macari, Lou	31	(3)	34	104	Wood, Ray	15		15	179	Brown, James (1935-39)	8		8
30	Cockburn, Henry	32		32	105	Parker, Paul	14	(1)	15	180	Chisnall, Phil	8		8
31	Bailey, Gary	31		31	106	Barrett, Frank	14		14	181	Goodwin, Fred	8		8
32	Brown, Wes	29	(2)	31	107	Bryant, William	14		14	182	Grassam, Billy	8		8
33	Neville, Phil	25	(6)	31	108	Cantwell, Noel	14		14	183	Griffiths, Jack	8		8
34	Pearson, Stan	30		30	109	Leighton, Jim	14		14	184	Hogg, Graeme	8		8
35	Solskjaer, Ole Gunnar	15	(15)	30	110	Quixall, Albert	14		14	185	Jenkyns, Caesar	8		8
36	Aston, John (Snr)	29		29	111	Vose, George	14		14	186	Muhren, Arnold	8		8
37	Meredith, Billy	29		29	112	Martin, Lee (1990s)	13	(1)	14	187	Mutch, George	8		8
38	Spence, Joe	29		29	113	van Nistelrooy, Ruud	11	(3)	14	188	Picken, Jack	8		8
39	Wall, George	29		29	114	Connelly, John	13		13	189	Rennox, Charlie	8		8
40	Butt, Nicky	23	(6)	29	115	Giles, Johnny	13		13	190	Turner, Chris	8		8
41	Sharpe, Lee	22	(7)	29	116	Hayes, Vince	13		13	191	Ure, Ian	8		8
42	Bell, Alex	28		28	117	McKay, Bill	13		13	192	Carroll, Roy	7	(1)	8
43	Roberts, Charlie	28		28	118	Mew, Jack	13		13	193	Stam, Jaap	7	(1)	8
44	Cartwright, Walter	27		27	119	Thomas, Mickey	13		13	194	Gowling, Alan	6	(2)	8
45	Morgan, Willie	27		27	120	Warner, Jack	13		13	195	Beardsmore, Russell	4	(4)	8
46	Ince, Paul	26	(1)	27	121	Barson, Frank	12		12	196	Robins, Mark	4	(4)	8
47	Duckworth, Dick	26		26	122	Edwards, Duncan	12		12	197	Smith, Alan	2	(6)	8
48	Silcock, Jack	26		26	123	James, Steve	12		12	198	Anderson, Viv	7		7
49	Stacey, George	26		26	124	McGlen, Billy	12		12	199	Beale, Robert	7		7
50	Nicholl, Jimmy	22	(4)	26	125	Partridge, Teddy	12		12	200	Berg, Henning	7		7
51	Setters, Maurice	25		25	126	Burns, Francis	11	(1)	12	201	Boyd, Henry	7		7
52	Turnbull, Sandy	25		25	127	Jordan, Joe	11	(1)	12	202	Dunne, Pat	7		7
53	Kidd, Brian	24	(1)	25	128	Kanchelskis, Andrei	11	(1)	12	203	Edmonds, Hugh	7		7
54	Duxbury, Mike	20	(5)	25	129	Bamford, Tommy	11		11	204	Farman, Alf	7		7
55	Greenhoff, Brian	24		24	130	Fitzpatrick, John	11		11	205	Hodge, James	7		7
56	Gregg, Harry	24		24	131	Gillespie, Matthew	11		11	206	Jones, Mark	7		7
57	Whiteside, Norman	24		24	132	Holden, Dick	11		11	207	Lawton, Nobby	7		7
58	Beckham, David	22	(2)	24	133	Jones, Tom	11		11	208	Manley, Tom	7		7
59	Ronaldo, Cristiano	21	(3)	24	134	Moses, Remi	11		11	209	Milne, Ralph	7		7
60	Erentz, Fred	23		23	135	Carrick, Michael	10	(1)	11	210	Mitchell, Andrew (1890s)	7		7
61	Sadler, David	22	(1)	23	136	Yorke, Dwight	6	(5)	11	211	Morrison, Tommy	7		7
62	Houston, Stewart	22		22	137	Cope, Ronnie	10		10	212	Nicholson, Jimmy	7		7
63	Moger, Harry	22		22	138	Dawson, Alex	10		10	213	O'Neil, Tommy	7		7
64	Pearson, Stuart	22		22	139	Donaghy, Mal	10		10	214	Pearson, Mark	7		7
65	Schofield, Alf	22		22	140	Draycott, Billy	10		10	215	Read, Bert	7		7
66	Strachan, Gordon	22		22	141	Edwards, Paul	10		10	216	Redwood, Hubert	7		7
67	Hilditch, Clarence	21		21	142	Forsyth, Alex	10		10	217	Rowley, Harry	7		7
68	McQueen, Gordon	21		21	143	Heinze, Gabriel	10		10	218	Smith, Dick	7		7
69	Stapleton, Frank	21		21	144	Howard, Tim	10		10	219	Smith, Tom	7		7
70	Ferdinand, Rio	20	(1)	21	145	Pegg, Dick	10		10	220	Sutcliffe, John	7		7
71	Cole, Andrew	19	(2)	21	146	Phelan, Mike	10		10	221	Thomas, Harry	7		7
72	Silvestre, Mikael	19	(2)	21	147	Vidic, Nemanja	10		10	222	Wrigglesworth, Billy	7		7
73	Blackmore, Clayton	15	(6)	21	148	Wilkins, Ray	10		10	223	Aston, John (Jnr)	5	(2)	7
74	Crompton, Jack	20		20	149	Wilson, Jack	10		10	224	McCreery, David	1	(6)	7
75	Rooney, Wayne	16	(4)	20	150	Daly, Gerry	9	(1)	10	225	Anderson, George	6		6

continued../

ALL FA CUP MATCHES (continued)

#	PLAYER	A	S	T	#	PLAYER	A	S	T	#	PLAYER	A	S	T
226	Anderson, John	6		6	301	Forlan, Diego	2	(2)	4	376	Poborsky, Karel	2		2
227	Blanchflower, Jackie	6		6	302	Gill, Tony	2	(2)	4	377	Ramsden, Charlie	2		2
228	Breen, Tommy	6		6	303	Miller, Liam	2	(2)	4	378	Redman, Billy	2		2
229	Burke, Ronnie	6		6	304	Ball, Jack	3		3	379	Ridding, Bill	2		2
230	Gibson, Don	6		6	305	Beadsworth, Arthur	3		3	380	Roach, John	2		2
231	Greaves, Ian	6		6	306	Blanc, Laurent	3		3	381	Robertson, Sandy	2		2
232	Hall, Jack (1932–1936)	6		6	307	Burgess, Herbert	3		3	382	Rossi, Giuseppe	2		2
233	Hanlon, Jimmy	6		6	308	Davidson, Will	3		3	383	Sharpe, William	2		2
234	Johnston, Billy	6		6	309	Donnelly, Tony	3		3	384	Sidebottom, Arnold	2		2
235	Lochhead, Arthur	6		6	310	Doughty, Jack	3		3	385	Sivebaek, Johnny	2		2
236	May, David	6		6	311	Edge, Alf	3		3	386	Smith, Lawrence	2		2
237	McLachlan, George	6		6	312	Erentz, Harry	3		3	387	Spencer, Charlie	2		2
238	Mellor, Jack	6		6	313	Fall, Joe	3		3	388	Street, Ernest	2		2
239	Owen, Jack	6		6	314	Fitzsimmons, David	3		3	389	Tapken, Norman	2		2
240	Perrins, George	6		6	315	Garton, Billy	3		3	390	Taylor, Chris	2		2
241	Robertson, Alex	6		6	316	Goldthorpe, Ernie	3		3	391	Tevez, Carlos	2		2
242	Rothwell, Herbert	6		6	317	Harris, Frank	3		3	392	Thomson, Arthur	2		2
243	Roughton, George	6		6	318	Henrys, Arthur	3		3	393	Thornley, Ben	2		2
244	Scanlon, Albert	6		6	319	Hood, Billy	3		3	394	Veron, Juan–Sebastian	2		2
245	Taylor, Ernie	6		6	320	Jackson, William	3		3	395	Walton, Joe	2		2
246	Whalley, Bert	6		6	321	Kennedy, William	3		3	396	Wassall, Jackie	2		2
247	Whelan, William	6		6	322	Leigh, Tom	3		3	397	Whitefoot, Jeff	2		2
248	Kuszczak, Tomasz	5	(1)	6	323	Livingstone, George	3		3	398	Williams, Fred	2		2
249	Allen, Reg	5		5	324	McFarlane, Bob	3		3	399	Winterbottom, Walter	2		2
250	Birchenough, Herbert	5		5	325	Morgan, Hugh	3		3	400	Dublin, Dion	1	(1)	2
251	Clarkin, John	5		5	326	Peden, Jack	3		3	401	Gibson, Terry	1	(1)	2
252	Crowther, Stan	5		5	327	Pique, Gerard	3		3	402	Gillespie, Keith	1	(1)	2
253	Doughty, Roger	5		5	328	Richards, Charlie	3		3	403	Wallwork, Ronnie	1	(1)	2
254	Downie, John	5		5	329	Ridgway, Joe	3		3	404	Davies, Ron	–	(2)	2
255	Grimes, Ashley	5		5	330	Rimmer, Jimmy	3		3	405	O'Brien, Liam	–	(2)	2
256	Hurst, Daniel	5		5	331	Robertson, William	3		3	406	Wilson, David	–	(2)	2
257	Radford, Charlie	5		5	332	Sagar, Charles	3		3	407	Albinson, George	1		1
258	Reid, Tom	5		5	333	Sneddon, J	3		3	408	Allan, Jack	1		1
259	Smith, Jack	5		5	334	Stewart, William	3		3	409	Bain, David	1		1
260	Sweeney, Eric	5		5	335	Woodcock, Wilf	3		3	410	Bainbridge, Bill	1		1
261	Whitehouse, Jimmy	5		5	336	Bardsley, Phil	2	(1)	3	411	Ball, John	1		1
262	Young, Tony	5		5	337	Bellion, David	2	(1)	3	412	Barber, Jack	1		1
263	Sealey, Les	4	(1)	5	338	Djemba–Djemba, Eric	2	(1)	3	413	Barlow, Cyril	1		1
264	Blomqvist, Jesper	3	(2)	5	339	Hargreaves, Owen	2	(1)	3	414	Beckett, R	1		1
265	Baird, Harry	4		4	340	Nevland, Erik	2	(1)	3	415	Beddow, John	1		1
266	Banks, Jack	4		4	341	Chadwick, Luke	1	(2)	3	416	Berry, Bill	1		1
267	Bannister, Jimmy	4		4	342	Anderson, Willie	2		2	417	Blackmore, Peter	1		1
268	Barthez, Fabien	4		4	343	Bissett, George	2		2	418	Bond, Ernie	1		1
269	Birch, Brian	4		4	344	Briggs, Ronnie	2		2	419	Boyle, Tommy	1		1
270	Birkett, Cliff	4		4	345	Craig, T	2		2	420	Brown, James (1932–34)	1		1
271	Birtles, Gary	4		4	346	Cunningham, John	2		2	421	Burke, Tom	1		1
272	Blackstock, Tommy	4		4	347	Davies, Alan	2		2	422	Cape, Jack	1		1
273	Bogan, Tommy	4		4	348	Davies, Joe	2		2	423	Casper, Chris	1		1
274	Bradley, Warren	4		4	349	Dunn, William	2		2	424	Chalmers, Stewart	1		1
275	Buckle, Ted	4		4	350	Feehan, John	2		2	425	Colville, James	1		1
276	Carolan, Joseph	4		4	351	Fitchett, John	2		2	426	Cookson, Sam	1		1
277	Clements, John	4		4	352	Gardner, Dick	2		2	427	Curry, Joe	1		1
278	Dale, Billy	4		4	353	Graham, George	2		2	428	Dale, Herbert	1		1
279	Fisher, James	4		4	354	Hacking, Jack	2		2	429	Davies, John	1		1
280	Gallimore, Stanley	4		4	355	Hamill, Mickey	2		2	430	Davies, L	1		1
281	Hopkin, Fred	4		4	356	Harrison, William	2		2	431	Davies, Wyn	1		1
282	Lewis, Eddie	4		4	357	Haslam, George	2		2	432	Denman, J	1		1
283	Linkson, Oscar	4		4	358	Henderson, William	2		2	433	Doherty, John	1		1
284	McCrae, James	4		4	359	Higgins, Mark	2		2	434	Donnelly, not known	1		1
285	McLenahan, Hugh	4		4	360	Hine, Ernie	2		2	435	Douglas, William	1		1
286	Peters, James	4		4	361	Holton, Jim	2		2	436	Dow, John	1		1
287	Porter, Billy	4		4	362	Hopkinson, Samuel	2		2	437	Eagles, Chris	1		1
288	Powell, Jack	4		4	363	Jones, Tommy	2		2	438	Earp, John	1		1
289	Richardson, Lance	4		4	364	Lancaster, Joe	2		2	439	Evans, George	1		1
290	Roche, Paddy	4		4	365	Mackie, Charlie	2		2	440	Felton, G	1		1
291	Slater, J.F	4		4	366	Martin, Mick	2		2	441	Ferrier, Ron	1		1
292	Warburton, Arthur	4		4	367	McGuinness, Wilf	2		2	442	Fielding, Bill	1		1
293	Williams, Harry (1904–06)	4		4	368	McMillen, Walter	2		2	443	Fitzsimmons, Tommy	1		1
294	Williams, Rees	4		4	369	McNulty, Thomas	2		2	444	Forster, Tommy	1		1
295	Wombwell, Dick	4		4	370	Meehan, Tommy	2		2	445	Fox, not known	1		1
296	Clegg, Michael	3	(1)	4	371	Menzies, Alex	2		2	446	Frame, Tommy	1		1
297	Larsson, Henrik	3	(1)	4	372	Miller, Tom	2		2	447	Gaudie, Ralph	1		1
298	Ritchie, Andy	3	(1)	4	373	Morgans, Kenny	2		2	448	Gibson, Richard	1		1
299	Anderson	2	(2)	4	374	Nani	2		2	449	Gladwin, George	1		1
300	Davenport, Peter	2	(2)	4	375	Noble, Bobby	2		2	450	Gotheridge, James	1		1

continued../

ALL FA CUP MATCHES (continued)

#	PLAYER	A	S	T	#	PLAYER	A	S	T	#	PLAYER	A	S	T
451	Graham, Arthur	1		1	476	McCalliog, Jim	1		1	501	Roberts, W.A	1		1
452	Gyves, William	1		1	477	McCartney, John	1		1	502	Rothwell, Charles	1		1
453	Hannaford, Charlie	1		1	478	McGillivray, Charlie	1		1	503	Ryan, Jimmy	1		1
454	Harrison, Charlie	1		1	479	McGillivray, John	1		1	504	Sapsford, George	1		1
455	Harrop, Bobby	1		1	480	McShane, Harry	1		1	505	Saunders, James	1		1
456	Hartwell, William	1		1	481	Milarvie, Bob	1		1	506	Savage, Ted	1		1
457	Hay, Tom	1		1	482	Millar, George	1		1	507	Scott, John	1		1
458	Heathcote, Joe	1		1	483	Moody, John	1		1	508	Smith, William	1		1
459	Hofton, Leslie	1		1	484	Moore, Graham	1		1	509	Spector, Jonathan	1		1
460	Howells, E	1		1	485	Myerscough, Joe	1		1	510	Toms, Billy	1		1
461	Hunter, George	1		1	486	Nevin, George	1		1	511	Turner, John	1		1
462	Jones, David (2004)	1		1	487	Nicol, George	1		1	512	Turner, not known	1		1
463	Jones, Richard	1		1	488	O'Connell, Pat	1		1	513	van der Gouw, Raimond	1		1
464	Jovanovic, Nikki	1		1	489	O'Kane, John	1		1	514	Vincent, Ernest	1		1
465	Kennedy, Fred	1		1	490	O'Shaughnessy, T	1		1	515	Wilkinson, Harry	1		1
466	Kinsey, Albert	1		1	491	Owen, George	1		1	516	Wilson, Edgar	1		1
467	Kleberson, Jose	1		1	492	Parker, Samuel	1		1	517	Wood, John	1		1
468	Knowles, Frank	1		1	493	Pears, Steve	1		1	518	Brazil, Alan	–	(1)	1
469	Kopel, Frank	1		1	494	Pepper, Frank	1		1	519	Cruyff, Jordi	–	(1)	1
470	Lang, Tommy	1		1	495	Pilkington, Kevin	1		1	520	Graham, Deiniol	–	(1)	1
471	Lievesley, Wilfred	1		1	496	Potts, Arthur	1		1	521	Greening, Jonathan	–	(1)	1
472	Longton, not known	1		1	497	Preston, Stephen	1		1	522	Mulryne, Philip	–	(1)	1
473	Lowrie, Tommy	1		1	498	Ramsay, Robert	1		1	523	Pugh, Danny	–	(1)	1
474	Lyons, George	1		1	499	Rattigan, not known	1		1	524	Simpson, Danny	–	(1)	1
475	McBain, Neil	1		1	500	Rawlings, Bill	1		1	525	Stewart, Michael	–	(1)	1
										526	Twiss, Michael	–	(1)	1

ALL LEAGUE CUP MATCHES

#	PLAYER	A	S	T
1	Robson, Bryan	50	(1)	51
2	McClair, Brian	44	(1)	45
3	Albiston, Arthur	38	(2)	40
4	Hughes, Mark	37	(1)	38
5	Pallister, Gary	36		36
6	Stepney, Alex	35		35
7	Bruce, Steve	32	(2)	34
8	Duxbury, Mike	32	(2)	34
9	Irwin, Denis	28	(3)	31
10	Buchan, Martin	30		30
11	Giggs, Ryan	25	(5)	30
12	Whiteside, Norman	26	(3)	29
13	Bailey, Gary	28		28
14	McIlroy, Sammy	25	(3)	28
15	Stapleton, Frank	26	(1)	27
16	Macari, Lou	22	(5)	27
17	Best, George	25		25
18	Coppell, Steve	25		25
19	Moran, Kevin	24	(1)	25
20	Morgan, Willie	24	(1)	25
21	Blackmore, Clayton	23	(2)	25
22	Charlton, Bobby	24		24
23	Ince, Paul	23	(1)	24
24	Moses, Remi	22	(2)	24
25	Sharpe, Lee	15	(8)	23
26	Sadler, David	22		22
27	Dunne, Tony	21		21
28	Kidd, Brian	20		20
29	Greenhoff, Brian	19		19
30	O'Shea, John	18	(1)	19
31	James, Steve	17	(1)	18
32	Brown, Wes	16	(2)	18
33	Daly, Gerry	17		17
34	Schmeichel, Peter	17		17
35	Neville, Gary	16	(1)	17
36	Neville, Phil	16	(1)	17
37	Houston, Stewart	16		16
38	McQueen, Gordon	16		16
39	Kanchelskis, Andrei	15	(1)	16
40	Phelan, Mike	14	(2)	16
41	Scholes, Paul	11	(5)	16
42	Parker, Paul	15		15
43	Wilkins, Ray	14	(1)	15
44	Aston, John (Jnr)	12	(3)	15
45	Nicholl, Jimmy	14		14
46	Webb, Neil	14		14
47	Silvestre, Mikael	13	(1)	14
48	Keane, Roy	12	(2)	14
49	Donaghy, Mal	9	(5)	14
50	McGrath, Paul	13		13
51	Strachan, Gordon	12	(1)	13
52	Richardson, Kieran	11	(2)	13
53	Olsen, Jesper	10	(3)	13
54	Fitzpatrick, John	12		12
55	Pearson, Stuart	12		12
56	Beckham, David	10	(2)	12
57	Law, Denis	11		11
58	Muhren, Arnold	11		11
59	Burns, Francis	10	(1)	11
60	Solskjaer, Ole Gunnar	8	(3)	11
61	Fletcher, Darren	10		10
62	Ure, Ian	10		10
63	Ferdinand, Rio	9	(1)	10
64	Davenport, Peter	8	(2)	10
65	Martin, Lee (1990s)	8	(2)	10
66	May, David	9		9
67	Saha, Louis	9		9
68	Sealey, Les	9		9
69	van der Gouw, Raimond	8	(1)	9
70	Young, Tony	5	(4)	9
71	Fortune, Quinton	8		8
72	Howard, Tim	8		8
73	Ronaldo, Cristiano	8		8
74	Butt, Nicky	7	(1)	8
75	Clegg, Michael	7	(1)	8
76	Gowling, Alan	7	(1)	8
77	Hogg, Graeme	7	(1)	8
78	McCreery, David	4	(4)	8
79	Forsyth, Alex	7		7
80	Gibson, Colin	7		7
81	Hill, Gordon	7		7
82	Leighton, Jim	7		7
83	O'Neil, Tommy	7		7
84	Stiles, Nobby	7		7
85	Turner, Chris	7		7
86	Walsh, Gary	7		7
87	Anderson, Viv	6	(1)	7
88	Rooney, Wayne	5	(2)	7
89	Brazil, Alan	4	(3)	7
90	Wallace, Danny	4	(3)	7
91	Robins, Mark	–	(7)	7
92	Cantona, Eric	6		6
93	Graham, Arthur	6		6
94	Greening, Jonathan	6		6
95	Grimes, Ashley	6		6
96	Rimmer, Jimmy	6		6
97	Garton, Billy	5	(1)	6
98	McCalliog, Jim	5	(1)	6
99	van Nistelrooy, Ruud	5	(1)	6
100	Davies, Simon	4	(2)	6
101	Forlan, Diego	4	(2)	6
102	Smith, Alan	4	(2)	6
103	Eagles, Chris	2	(4)	6
104	Barnes, Peter	5		5
105	Bellion, David	5		5
106	Carroll, Roy	5		5
107	Chadwick, Luke	5		5
108	Cruyff, Jordi	5		5
109	Curtis, John	5		5
110	Djemba-Djemba, Eric	5		5
111	Gidman, John	5		5
112	Thomas, Mickey	5		5
113	Veron, Juan-Sebastian	4	(1)	5
114	Wallwork, Ronnie	4	(1)	5
115	Ritchie, Andy	3	(2)	5
116	Rossi, Giuseppe	3	(2)	5
117	Sartori, Carlo	3	(2)	5
118	Barthez, Fabien	4		4
119	Brennan, Shay	4		4
120	Crerand, Pat	4		4
121	Edwards, Paul	4		4
122	Greenhoff, Jimmy	4		4
123	Heinze, Gabriel	4		4
124	Holton, Jim	4		4
125	Jackson, Tommy	4		4
126	Jordan, Joe	4		4
127	Kleberson, Jose	4		4
128	Storey-Moore, Ian	4		4
129	Bardsley, Phil	3	(1)	4
130	Beardsmore, Russell	3	(1)	4
131	Jones, Richard	2	(2)	4
132	Pique, Gerard	2	(2)	4
133	Stewart, Michael	2	(2)	4
134	Berg, Henning	3		3
135	Casper, Chris	3		3
136	Dawson, Alex	3		3
137	Foulkes, Bill	3		3
138	Gillespie, Keith	3		3
139	Johnsen, Ronny	3		3
140	Kuszczak, Tomasz	3		3
141	Miller, Liam	3		3
142	Mulryne, Philip	3		3
143	Nicholson, Jimmy	3		3
144	Park, Ji-Sung	3		3
145	Pearson, Mark	3		3
146	Poborsky, Karel	3		3
147	Roche, Paddy	3		3
148	Scanlon, Albert	3		3
149	Thornley, Ben	3		3
150	van der Sar, Edwin	3		3
151	Watson, Willie	3		3
152	Yorke, Dwight	3		3
153	Ferguson, Darren	2	(1)	3
154	Jones, David (2004)	2	(1)	3
155	O'Kane, John	2	(1)	3
156	Cooke, Terry	1	(2)	3
157	Evra, Patrice	1	(2)	3
158	Nardiello, Daniel	1	(2)	3
159	O'Brien, Liam	1	(2)	3
160	Birtles, Gary	2		2
161	Cole, Andrew	2		2
162	Donald, Ian	2		2
163	Giles, Johnny	2		2
164	Gregg, Harry	2		2
165	Jovanovic, Nikki	2		2
166	Martin, Lee (2005)	2		2
167	Paterson, Steve	2		2
168	Pugh, Danny	2		2
169	Setters, Maurice	2		2
170	Sidebottom, Arnold	2		2
171	Viollet, Dennis	2		2
172	Wilson, Mark	2		2
173	Appleton, Michael	1	(1)	2
174	Dublin, Dion	1	(1)	2
175	Ebanks-Blake, Sylvan	1	(1)	2
176	Webber, Danny	1	(1)	2
177	Gibson, Terry	–	(2)	2
178	Healy, David	–	(2)	2
179	Lee, Kieran	–	(2)	2
180	McGrath, Chris	–	(2)	2
181	Nevland, Erik	–	(2)	2
182	Shawcross, Ryan	–	(2)	2
183	Tomlinson, Graeme	–	(2)	2
184	Vidic, Nemanja	–	(2)	2
185	Anderson	1		1
186	Beardsley, Peter	1		1
187	Bosnich, Mark	1		1
188	Bratt, Harold	1		1
189	Carolan, Joseph	1		1
190	Connelly, John	1		1
191	Cope, Ronnie	1		1
192	Davis, Jimmy	1		1
193	Djordjic, Bojan	1		1
194	Dong, Fangzhuo	1		1
195	Dunne, Pat	1		1
196	Eckersley, Adam	1		1
197	Evans, Jonny	1		1
198	Gaskell, David	1		1
199	Givens, Don	1		1
200	Graham, George	1		1
201	Gray, David	1		1
202	Herd, David	1		1
203	Higginbotham, Danny	1		1
204	Lawton, Nobby	1		1
205	Marsh, Philip	1		1
206	Martin, Mick	1		1
207	McGibbon, Pat	1		1
208	Nani	1		1
209	Pilkington, Kevin	1		1
210	Quixall, Albert	1		1
211	Roche, Lee	1		1
212	Sheringham, Teddy	1		1
213	Simpson, Danny	1		1
214	Sivebaek, Johnny	1		1
215	Tierney, Paul	1		1
216	Twiss, Michael	1		1
217	Waldron, Colin	1		1
218	Wealands, Jeffrey	1		1
219	Wilkinson, Ian	1		1
220	Barnes, Michael	–	(1)	1
221	Blomqvist, Jesper	–	(1)	1
222	Buchan, George	–	(1)	1
223	Campbell, Fraizer	–	(1)	1
224	Carrick, Michael	–	(1)	1
225	Gibson, Darron	–	(1)	1
226	Graham, Deiniol	–	(1)	1
227	Grimshaw, Tony	–	(1)	1
228	Johnson, Eddie	–	(1)	1
229	Maiorana, Jules	–	(1)	1
230	Notman, Alex	–	(1)	1
231	Rachubka, Paul	–	(1)	1
232	Sloan, Tom	–	(1)	1
233	Spector, Jonathan	–	(1)	1
234	Wellens, Richard	–	(1)	1
235	Wood, Nicky	–	(1)	1

ALL EUROPEAN MATCHES

#	PLAYER	A	S	T
1	Giggs, Ryan	107	(11)	118
2	Scholes, Paul	98	(12)	110
3	Neville, Gary	100	(7)	107
4	Beckham, David	79	(4)	83
5	Keane, Roy	81	(1)	82
6	Solskjaer, Ole Gunnar	36	(45)	81
7	Irwin, Denis	73	(2)	75
8	Butt, Nicky	58	(13)	71
9	Silvestre, Mikael	61	(8)	69
10	Neville, Phil	43	(22)	65
11	Brown, Wes	50	(7)	57
12	O'Shea, John	42	(13)	55
13	Foulkes, Bill	52		52
14	Ferdinand, Rio	49	(1)	50
15	Cole, Andrew	43	(7)	50
16	van Nistelrooy, Ruud	45	(2)	47
17	Charlton, Bobby	45		45
18	Ronaldo, Cristiano	40	(3)	43
19	Schmeichel, Peter	42		42
20	Crerand, Pat	41		41
21	Dunne, Tony	40		40
22	Pallister, Gary	39	(1)	40
23	Barthez, Fabien	37		37
24	Stiles, Nobby	36		36
25	Yorke, Dwight	28	(8)	36
26	Johnsen, Ronny	32	(3)	35
27	Fletcher, Darren	26	(9)	35
28	Best, George	34		34
29	Rooney, Wayne	33	(1)	34
30	Law, Denis	33		33
31	Hughes, Mark	30	(3)	33
32	Stam, Jaap	32		32
33	Sheringham, Teddy	20	(11)	31
34	van der Sar, Edwin	30		30
35	Fortune, Quinton	16	(12)	28
36	Albiston, Arthur	26	(1)	27
37	Robson, Bryan	26	(1)	27
38	Bruce, Steve	25	(1)	26
39	Herd, David	25		25
40	Blanc, Laurent	24		24
41	Brennan, Shay	24		24
42	Veron, Juan-Sebastian	24		24
43	Carrick, Michael	23	(1)	24
44	Stepney, Alex	23		23
45	Berg, Henning	19	(4)	23
46	McClair, Brian	17	(6)	23
47	Forlan, Diego	8	(15)	23
48	Bailey, Gary	20		20
49	Ince, Paul	20		20
50	Connelly, John	19		19
51	Saha, Louis	9	(10)	19
52	Duxbury, Mike	17	(1)	18
53	Vidic, Nemanja	17		17
54	Heinze, Gabriel	16	(1)	17
55	Sharpe, Lee	15	(2)	17
56	Evra, Patrice	14	(3)	17
57	Phelan, Mike	14	(3)	17
58	Smith, Alan	11	(6)	17
59	Cantona, Eric	16		16
60	Kidd, Brian	16		16
61	Sadler, David	16		16
62	Richardson, Kieran	5	(11)	16
63	Stapleton, Frank	14	(1)	15
64	May, David	13	(2)	15
65	Byrne, Roger	14		14
66	Taylor, Tommy	14		14
67	Moran, Kevin	13	(1)	14
68	Colman, Eddie	13		13
69	Dunne, Pat	13		13
70	Moses, Remi	12	(1)	13
71	Whiteside, Norman	11	(2)	13
72	Edwards, Duncan	12		12
73	Howard, Tim	12		12
74	Pegg, David	12		12
75	Viollet, Dennis	12		12

#	PLAYER	A	S	T
76	Wood, Ray	12		12
77	Coppell, Steve	11	(1)	12
78	Tevez, Carlos	6	(6)	12
79	Berry, Johnny	11		11
80	Blackmore, Clayton	11		11
81	Gregg, Harry	11		11
82	van der Gouw, Raimond	11		11
83	Webb, Neil	11		11
84	Whelan, William	11		11
85	Burns, Francis	10	(1)	11
86	Nani	7	(4)	11
87	Martin, Lee (1990s)	6	(5)	11
88	Cruyff, Jordi	4	(7)	11
89	Park, Ji-Sung	4	(7)	11
90	Buchan, Martin	10		10
91	Carroll, Roy	10		10
92	Hogg, Graeme	10		10
93	Jones, Mark	10		10
94	McIlroy, Sammy	10		10
95	Nicholl, Jimmy	10		10
96	Macari, Lou	9	(1)	10
97	Parker, Paul	7	(3)	10
98	Poborsky, Karel	5	(5)	10
99	Gidman, John	7	(2)	9
100	Anderson	6	(3)	9
101	Djemba-Djemba, Eric	6	(3)	9
102	Aston, John (Jnr)	8		8
103	Hill, Gordon	8		8
104	Muhren, Arnold	8		8
105	Sealey, Les	8		8
106	Wilkins, Ray	8		8
107	Hargreaves, Owen	5	(3)	8
108	Bosnich, Mark	7		7
109	Cantwell, Noel	7		7
110	Fitzpatrick, John	7		7
111	Kanchelskis, Andrei	7		7
112	McQueen, Gordon	7		7
113	Setters, Maurice	7		7
114	Blomqvist, Jesper	6	(1)	7
115	Graham, Arthur	6	(1)	7
116	Houston, Stewart	6	(1)	7
117	Olsen, Jesper	6	(1)	7
118	Wallace, Danny	5	(2)	7
119	McCreery, David	4	(3)	7
120	Bellion, David	2	(5)	7
121	Greenhoff, Brian	6		6
122	Pearson, Stuart	6		6
123	Strachan, Gordon	6		6
124	Walsh, Gary	6		6
125	Grimes, Ashley	4	(2)	6
126	Robins, Mark	4	(2)	6
127	Miller, Liam	3	(3)	6
128	Chadwick, Luke	1	(5)	6
129	Blanchflower, Jackie	5		5
130	Gaskell, David	5		5
131	Webster, Colin	5		5
132	Kleberson, Jose	3	(2)	5
133	Kuszczak, Tomasz	3	(2)	5
134	Beardsmore, Russell	2	(3)	5
135	Donaghy, Mal	2	(3)	5
136	Chisnall, Phil	4		4
137	Daly, Gerry	4		4
138	McGrath, Paul	4		4
139	Morgan, Willie	4		4
140	Morgans, Kenny	4		4
141	McGrath, Chris	3	(1)	4
142	Pique, Gerard	3	(1)	4
143	Ricardo, Felipe	3	(1)	4
144	Greening, Jonathan	2	(2)	4
145	Wilson, Mark	2	(2)	4
146	Goodwin, Fred	3		3
147	Quixall, Albert	3		3
148	Scanlon, Albert	3		3
149	Bardsley, Phil	2	(1)	3
150	Davies, Simon	2	(1)	3

#	PLAYER	A	S	T
151	Eagles, Chris	2	(1)	3
152	Rimmer, Jimmy	2	(1)	3
153	Simpson, Danny	2	(1)	3
154	Clegg, Michael	1	(2)	3
155	Pugh, Danny	1	(2)	3
156	Brazil, Alan	2		2
157	Cope, Ronnie	2		2
158	Crowther, Stan	2		2
159	Greaves, Ian	2		2
160	Greenhoff, Jimmy	2		2
161	James, Steve	2		2
162	Jovanovic, Nikki	2		2
163	Larsson, Henrik	2		2
164	McGuinness, Wilf	2		2
165	Pearson, Mark	2		2
166	Ryan, Jimmy	2		2
167	Sartori, Carlo	2		2
168	Taylor, Ernie	2		2
169	Thomas, Mickey	2		2
170	Evans, Jonny	1	(1)	2
171	Spector, Jonathan	1	(1)	2
172	Paterson, Steve	–	(2)	2
173	Rossi, Giuseppe	–	(2)	2
174	Stewart, Michael	–	(2)	2
175	Anderson, Viv	1		1
176	Anderson, Willie	1		1
177	Jordan, Joe	1		1
178	Kopel, Frank	1		1
179	Lynch, Mark	1		1
180	O'Kane, John	1		1
181	Roche, Lee	1		1
182	Casper, Chris	–	(1)	1
183	Cooke, Terry	–	(1)	1
184	Davies, Alan	–	(1)	1
185	Dempsey, Mark	–	(1)	1
186	Dong, Fangzhuo	–	(1)	1
187	Dublin, Dion	–	(1)	1
188	Forsyth, Alex	–	(1)	1
189	Garton, Billy	–	(1)	1
190	Higginbotham, Danny	–	(1)	1
191	Nardiello, Daniel	–	(1)	1
192	Timm, Mads	–	(1)	1
193	Wallwork, Ronnie	–	(1)	1
194	Webber, Danny	–	(1)	1

ALL EUROPEAN CUP / CHAMPIONS LEAGUE MATCHES

#	PLAYER	A	S	T
1	Giggs, Ryan	103	(11)	114
2	Scholes, Paul	97	(11)	108
3	Neville, Gary	99	(6)	105
4	Beckham, David	77	(4)	81
5	Solskjaer, Ole Gunnar	36	(45)	81
6	Keane, Roy	79	(1)	80
7	Silvestre, Mikael	61	(8)	69
8	Butt, Nicky	56	(13)	69
9	Irwin, Denis	62	(2)	64
10	Neville, Phil	42	(22)	64
11	Brown, Wes	50	(7)	57
12	O'Shea, John	42	(13)	55
13	Ferdinand, Rio	49	(1)	50
14	Cole, Andrew	42	(7)	49
15	van Nistelrooy, Ruud	45	(2)	47
16	Ronaldo, Cristiano	40	(3)	43
17	Barthez, Fabien	37		37
18	Schmeichel, Peter	36		36
19	Yorke, Dwight	28	(8)	36
20	Foulkes, Bill	35		35
21	Johnsen, Ronny	32	(3)	35
22	Fletcher, Darren	26	(9)	35
23	Rooney, Wayne	33	(1)	34
24	Stam, Jaap	32		32
25	Sheringham, Teddy	20	(11)	31
26	van der Sar, Edwin	30		30
27	Charlton, Bobby	28		28
28	Fortune, Quinton	16	(12)	28
29	Blanc, Laurent	24		24
30	Crerand, Pat	24		24
31	Veron, Juan-Sebastian	24		24
32	Carrick, Michael	23	(1)	24
33	Dunne, Tony	23		23
34	Pallister, Gary	23		23
35	Stiles, Nobby	23		23
36	Berg, Henning	19	(4)	23
37	Forlan, Diego	8	(15)	23
38	Best, George	21		21
39	Saha, Louis	9	(10)	19
40	Law, Denis	18		18
41	Vidic, Nemanja	17		17
42	Heinze, Gabriel	16	(1)	17
43	Evra, Patrice	14	(3)	17
44	Smith, Alan	11	(6)	17
45	Cantona, Eric	16		16
46	Kidd, Brian	16		16
47	Richardson, Kieran	5	(11)	16
48	Stepney, Alex	15		15
49	May, David	13	(2)	15
50	Byrne, Roger	14		14

#	PLAYER	A	S	T
51	Sadler, David	14		14
52	Taylor, Tommy	14		14
53	Colman, Eddie	13		13
54	Edwards, Duncan	12		12
55	Howard, Tim	12		12
56	Pegg, David	12		12
57	Viollet, Dennis	12		12
58	Wood, Ray	12		12
59	Tevez, Carlos	6	(6)	12
60	Berry, Johnny	11		11
61	Brennan, Shay	11		11
62	van der Gouw, Raimond	11		11
63	Whelan, William	11		11
64	Burns, Francis	10	(1)	11
65	Nani	7	(4)	11
66	Cruyff, Jordi	4	(7)	11
67	Park, Ji-Sung	4	(7)	11
68	Carroll, Roy	10		10
69	Jones, Mark	10		10
70	Bruce, Steve	9	(1)	10
71	Poborsky, Karel	5	(5)	10
72	Gregg, Harry	9		9
73	Ince, Paul	9		9
74	Anderson	6	(3)	9
75	Djemba-Djemba, Eric	6	(3)	9
76	Aston, John (Jnr)	8		8
77	Connelly, John	8		8
78	Herd, David	8		8
79	Hargreaves, Owen	5	(3)	8
80	McClair, Brian	2	(6)	8
81	Bosnich, Mark	7		7
82	Fitzpatrick, John	7		7
83	Hughes, Mark	7		7
84	Sharpe, Lee	7		7
85	Blomqvist, Jesper	6	(1)	7
86	Bellion, David	2	(5)	7
87	Parker, Paul	5	(1)	6
88	Miller, Liam	3	(3)	6
89	Chadwick, Luke	1	(5)	6
90	Blanchflower, Jackie	5		5
91	Kanchelskis, Andrei	5		5
92	Webster, Colin	5		5
93	Kleberson, Jose	3	(2)	5
94	Kuszczak, Tomasz	3	(2)	5
95	Morgan, Willie	4		4
96	Morgans, Kenny	4		4
97	Robson, Bryan	4		4
98	Pique, Gerard	3	(1)	4
99	Ricardo, Felipe	3	(1)	4
100	Greening, Jonathan	2	(2)	4

#	PLAYER	A	S	T
101	Wilson, Mark	2	(2)	4
102	Phelan, Mike	1	(3)	4
103	Cantwell, Noel	3		3
104	Goodwin, Fred	3		3
105	Scanlon, Albert	3		3
106	Walsh, Gary	3		3
107	Bardsley, Phil	2	(1)	3
108	Eagles, Chris	2	(1)	3
109	Rimmer, Jimmy	2	(1)	3
110	Simpson, Danny	2	(1)	3
111	Clegg, Michael	1	(2)	3
112	Pugh, Danny	1	(2)	3
113	Cope, Ronnie	2		2
114	Crowther, Stan	2		2
115	Davies, Simon	2		2
116	Dunne, Pat	2		2
117	Greaves, Ian	2		2
118	James, Steve	2		2
119	Larsson, Henrik	2		2
120	McGuinness, Wilf	2		2
121	Pearson, Mark	2		2
122	Ryan, Jimmy	2		2
123	Sartori, Carlo	2		2
124	Taylor, Ernie	2		2
125	Evans, Jonny	1	(1)	2
126	Martin, Lee (1990s)	1	(1)	2
127	Spector, Jonathan	1	(1)	2
128	Rossi, Giuseppe	-	(2)	2
129	Stewart, Michael	-	(2)	2
130	Anderson, Willie	1		1
131	Gaskell, David	1		1
132	Kopel, Frank	1		1
133	Lynch, Mark	1		1
134	Roche, Lee	1		1
135	Casper, Chris	-	(1)	1
136	Dong, Fangzhuo	-	(1)	1
137	Dublin, Dion	-	(1)	1
138	Higginbotham, Danny	-	(1)	1
139	Nardiello, Daniel	-	(1)	1
140	Timm, Mads	-	(1)	1
141	Wallwork, Ronnie	-	(1)	1
142	Webber, Danny	-	(1)	1

ALL EUROPEAN CUP-WINNERS' CUP MATCHES

#	PLAYER	A	S	T	#	PLAYER	A	S	T	#	PLAYER	A	S	T
1	Hughes, Mark	13	(3)	16	26	Wilkins, Ray	6		6	51	Schmeichel, Peter	3		3
2	McClair, Brian	13		13	27	Moses, Remi	5	(1)	6	52	Houston, Stewart	2	(1)	3
3	Robson, Bryan	13		13	28	Whiteside, Norman	5	(1)	6	53	Best, George	2		2
4	Pallister, Gary	12	(1)	13	29	Robins, Mark	4	(2)	6	54	Brennan, Shay	2		2
5	Albiston, Arthur	12		12	30	Law, Denis	5		5	55	Greenhoff, Brian	2		2
6	Bruce, Steve	12		12	31	Muhren, Arnold	5		5	56	Gregg, Harry	2		2
7	Phelan, Mike	12		12	32	Wallace, Danny	3	(2)	5	57	McGrath, Paul	2		2
8	Blackmore, Clayton	10		10	33	Beardsmore, Russell	2	(3)	5	58	Parker, Paul	2		2
9	Ince, Paul	10		10	34	Donaghy, Mal	2	(3)	5	59	Sadler, David	2		2
10	Webb, Neil	9		9	35	Buchan, Martin	4		4	60	Stiles, Nobby	2		2
11	Bailey, Gary	8		8	36	Cantwell, Noel	4		4	61	Walsh, Gary	2		2
12	Duxbury, Mike	8		8	37	Chisnall, Phil	4		4	62	Gidman, John	1	(1)	2
13	Irwin, Denis	8		8	38	Coppell, Steve	4		4	63	Grimes, Ashley	–	(2)	2
14	Moran, Kevin	8		8	39	Gaskell, David	4		4	64	Anderson, Viv	1		1
15	Sealey, Les	8		8	40	Hill, Gordon	4		4	65	Giggs, Ryan	1		1
16	Stapleton, Frank	8		8	41	Hogg, Graeme	4		4	66	Greenhoff, Jimmy	1		1
17	Sharpe, Lee	6	(2)	8	42	Macari, Lou	4		4	67	Kanchelskis, Andrei	1		1
18	Martin, Lee (1990s)	4	(4)	8	43	McIlroy, Sammy	4		4	68	Davies, Alan	–	(1)	1
19	Graham, Arthur	6	(1)	7	44	McQueen, Gordon	4		4	69	Dempsey, Mark	–	(1)	1
20	Charlton, Bobby	6		6	45	Nicholl, Jimmy	4		4	70	Forsyth, Alex	–	(1)	1
21	Crerand, Pat	6		6	46	Stepney, Alex	4		4					
22	Dunne, Tony	6		6	47	McGrath, Chris	3	(1)	4					
23	Foulkes, Bill	6		6	48	McCreery, David	3		3					
24	Herd, David	6		6	49	Pearson, Stuart	3		3					
25	Setters, Maurice	6		6	50	Quixall, Albert	3		3					

ALL UEFA CUP / INTER-CITIES' FAIRS CUP MATCHES

#	PLAYER	A	S	T	#	PLAYER	A	S	T	#	PLAYER	A	S	T
1	Albiston, Arthur	14	(1)	15	26	Nicholl, Jimmy	6		6	51	McGrath, Paul	2		2
2	Bailey, Gary	12		12	27	Strachan, Gordon	6		6	52	Sharpe, Lee	2		2
3	Best, George	11		11	28	Macari, Lou	5	(1)	6	53	Thomas, Mickey	2		2
4	Brennan, Shay	11		11	29	Moran, Kevin	5	(1)	6	54	Wallace, Danny	2		2
5	Charlton, Bobby	11		11	30	Bruce, Steve	4		4	55	Webb, Neil	2		2
6	Connelly, John	11		11	31	Daly, Gerry	4		4	56	Wilkins, Ray	2		2
7	Crerand, Pat	11		11	32	Greenhoff, Brian	4		4	57	Neville, Gary	1	(1)	2
8	Dunne, Pat	11		11	33	Grimes, Ashley	4		4	58	Scholes, Paul	1	(1)	2
9	Dunne, Tony	11		11	34	Hill, Gordon	4		4	59	Parker, Paul	–	(2)	2
10	Foulkes, Bill	11		11	35	Houston, Stewart	4		4	60	Paterson, Steve	–	(2)	2
11	Herd, David	11		11	36	Pallister, Gary	4		4	61	Blackmore, Clayton	1		1
12	Stiles, Nobby	11		11	37	Stepney, Alex	4		4	62	Cole, Andrew	1		1
13	Hughes, Mark	10		10	38	McCreery, David	1	(3)	4	63	Greenhoff, Jimmy	1		1
14	Law, Denis	10		10	39	Giggs, Ryan	3		3	64	Ince, Paul	1		1
15	Duxbury, Mike	9	(1)	10	40	Irwin, Denis	3		3	65	Jordan, Joe	1		1
16	Robson, Bryan	9	(1)	10	41	McQueen, Gordon	3		3	66	Kanchelskis, Andrei	1		1
17	Coppell, Steve	7	(1)	8	42	Muhren, Arnold	3		3	67	Martin, Lee (1990s)	1		1
18	Moses, Remi	7		7	43	Pearson, Stuart	3		3	68	Neville, Philip	1		1
19	Gidman, John	6	(1)	7	44	Schmeichel, Peter	3		3	69	O'Kane, John	1		1
20	Olsen, Jesper	6	(1)	7	45	Beckham, David	2		2	70	Phelan, Mike	1		1
21	Stapleton, Frank	6	(1)	7	46	Brazil, Alan	2		2	71	Setters, Maurice	1		1
22	Whiteside, Norman	6	(1)	7	47	Butt, Nicky	2		2	72	Walsh, Gary	1		1
23	Buchan, Martin	6		6	48	Jovanovic, Nikki	2		2	73	Cooke, Terry	–	(1)	1
24	Hogg, Graeme	6		6	49	Keane, Roy	2		2	74	Davies, Simon	–	(1)	1
25	McIlroy, Sammy	6		6	50	McClair, Brian	2		2	75	Garton, Billy	–	(1)	1

ALL OTHER COMPETITIVE MATCHES

#	PLAYER	A	S	T
1	Giggs, Ryan	13	(1)	14
2	Irwin, Denis	12		12
3	Keane, Roy	12		12
4	Scholes, Paul	10		10
5	Beckham, David	8	(2)	10
6	Neville, Phil	7	(3)	10
7	Butt, Nicky	9		9
8	Neville, Gary	8	(1)	9
9	Solskjaer, Ole Gunnar	6	(3)	9
10	Donaldson, Bob	8		8
11	Silvestre, Mikael	8		8
12	Stam, Jaap	7	(1)	8
13	Sheringham, Teddy	3	(5)	8
14	Cassidy, Joe	7		7
15	Erentz, Fred	7		7
16	Cole, Andrew	6	(1)	7
17	Cruyff, Jordi	2	(5)	7
18	Foulkes, Bill	6		6
19	Pallister, Gary	6		6
20	Schmeichel, Peter	6		6
21	Yorke, Dwight	3	(3)	6
22	Charlton, Bobby	5		5
23	Crerand, Pat	5		5
24	Dunne, Tony	5		5
25	Hughes, Mark	5		5
26	Law, Denis	5		5
27	McNaught, James	5		5
28	Fortune, Quinton	3	(2)	5
29	Barrett, Frank	4		4
30	Best, George	4		4
31	Bosnich, Mark	4		4
32	Bruce, Steve	4		4
33	Bryant, William	4		4
34	Draycott, Billy	4		4
35	Gillespie, Matthew	4		4
36	Ince, Paul	4		4
37	Jenkyns, Caesar	4		4
38	Perrins, George	4		4
39	Stepney, Alex	4		4
40	Berg, Henning	3	(1)	4
41	Albiston, Arthur	3		3
42	Bell, Alex	3		3
43	Berry, Johnny	3		3
44	Boyd, Henry	3		3
45	Brennan, Shay	3		3
46	Byrne, Roger	3		3
47	Cantona, Eric	3		3
48	Doughty, Roger	3		3
49	Duckworth, Dick	3		3
50	Farman, Alf	3		3
51	Johnsen, Ronny	3		3
52	Kanchelskis, Andrei	3		3
53	McClair, Brian	3		3
54	Meredith, Billy	3		3
55	Mitchell, Andrew (1890s)	3		3
56	Roberts, Charlie	3		3
57	Stacey, George	3		3
58	Stiles, Nobby	3		3
59	Wall, George	3		3
60	Wood, Ray	3		3
61	May, David	2	(1)	3
62	O'Shea, John	2	(1)	3
63	Robson, Bryan	2	(1)	3
64	Aston, John (Jnr)	2		2
65	Aston, John (Snr)	2		2
66	Bailey, Gary	2		2
67	Bannister, Jimmy	2		2
68	Barthez, Fabien	2		2
69	Blackmore, Clayton	2		2
70	Burgess, Herbert	2		2
71	Cantwell, Noel	2		2
72	Carey, Johnny	2		2
73	Cartwright, Walter	2		2
74	Chilton, Allenby	2		2
75	Clarkin, John	2		2

#	PLAYER	A	S	T
76	Clements, John	2		2
77	Coupar, Jimmy	2		2
78	Davies, John	2		2
79	Duxbury, Mike	2		2
80	Edwards, Duncan	2		2
81	Ferdinand, Rio	2		2
82	Fitzsimmons, Tommy	2		2
83	Herd, David	2		2
84	Hood, Billy	2		2
85	Howard, Tim	2		2
86	Kidd, Brian	2		2
87	Moger, Harry	2		2
88	Morgan, Willie	2		2
89	Pegg, David	2		2
90	Rowley, Jack	2		2
91	Sadler, David	2		2
92	Stapleton, Frank	2		2
93	Stewart, Willie	2		2
94	Taylor, Tommy	2		2
95	Turnbull, Jimmy	2		2
96	Turnbull, Sandy	2		2
97	van der Gouw, Raimond	2		2
98	van Nistelrooy, Ruud	2		2
99	Viollet, Dennis	2		2
100	Whelan, William	2		2
101	Whiteside, Norman	2		2
102	Djemba-Djemba, Eric	1	(1)	2
103	Gidman, John	1	(1)	2
104	Greening, Jonathan	1	(1)	2
105	Fletcher, Darren	-	(2)	2
106	Forlan, Diego	-	(2)	2
107	Anderson, John	1		1
108	Bellion, David	1		1
109	Blanchflower, Jackie	1		1
110	Brown, Wes	1		1
111	Buchan, Martin	1		1
112	Burke, Ronnie	1		1
113	Burns, Francis	1		1
114	Carrick, Michael	1		1
115	Colman, Eddie	1		1
116	Coppell, Steve	1		1
117	Crompton, Jack	1		1
118	Davidson, Will	1		1
119	Delaney, Jimmy	1		1
120	Donaghy, Mal	1		1
121	Douglas, William	1		1
122	Dow, John	1		1
123	Downie, John	1		1
124	Dunne, Pat	1		1
125	Edmonds, Hugh	1		1
126	Evra, Patrice	1		1
127	Fall, Joe	1		1
128	Gaskell, David	1		1
129	Gibson, Don	1		1
130	Giles, Johnny	1		1
131	Goodwin, Fred	1		1
132	Graham, Arthur	1		1
133	Greenhoff, Brian	1		1
134	Greenhoff, Jimmy	1		1
135	Halse, Harold	1		1
136	Hamill, Mickey	1		1
137	Higginbotham, Danny	1		1
138	Hill, Gordon	1		1
139	Hofton, Leslie	1		1
140	Hogg, Graeme	1		1
141	Jones, Mark	1		1
142	Macari, Lou	1		1
143	Martin, Lee (1990s)	1		1
144	McCartney, John	1		1
145	McGrath, Paul	1		1
146	McIlroy, Sammy	1		1
147	McNulty, Thomas	1		1
148	McQueen, Gordon	1		1
149	Mitten, Charlie	1		1
150	Moran, Kevin	1		1

#	PLAYER	A	S	T
151	Morris, Johnny	1		1
152	Muhren, Arnold	1		1
153	Nicholl, Jimmy	1		1
154	Olsen, Jesper	1		1
155	Parker, Paul	1		1
156	Pearson, Stan	1		1
157	Pearson, Stuart	1		1
158	Peden, Jack	1		1
159	Peters, James	1		1
160	Phelan, Mike	1		1
161	Picken, Jack	1		1
162	Quixall, Albert	1		1
163	Ronaldo, Cristiano	1		1
164	Rooney, Wayne	1		1
165	Sealey, Les	1		1
166	Setters, Maurice	1		1
167	Sharpe, Lee	1		1
168	Smith, Alan	1		1
169	Smith, Dick	1		1
170	Stone, Herbert	1		1
171	van der Sar, Edwin	1		1
172	Vidic, Nemanja	1		1
173	Wallace, Danny	1		1
174	Wallwork, Ronnie	1		1
175	Warner, Jack	1		1
176	Webb, Neil	1		1
177	Wilkins, Ray	1		1
178	Wilson, Mark	1		1
179	Curtis, John	-	(1)	1
180	Eagles, Chris	-	(1)	1
181	McCreery, David	-	(1)	1
182	Moses, Remi	-	(1)	1
183	Nani	-	(1)	1
184	Poborsky, Karel	-	(1)	1
185	Rachubka, Paul	-	(1)	1
186	Richardson, Kieran	-	(1)	1
187	Robins, Mark	-	(1)	1
188	Spector, Jonathan	-	(1)	1

MANCHESTER UNITED
The Complete Record

Chapter 2.3
The Goalscorers

ALL COMPETITIVE MATCHES

#	PLAYER	GOALS	#	PLAYER	GOALS	#	PLAYER	GOALS
1	Charlton, Bobby	249	76	Daly, Gerry	32	151	Hine, Ernie	12
2	Law, Denis	237	77	Webster, Colin	31	152	Hopkinson, Samuel	12
3	Rowley, Jack	211	78	Aston, John (Snr)	30	153	Kennedy, William	12
4	Best, George	179	79	Griffiths, Billy	30	154	McLenahan, Hugh	12
5	Viollet, Dennis	179	80	Ince, Paul	29	155	McNaught, James	12
6	Spence, Joe	168	81	Delaney, Jimmy	28	156	Moses, Remi	12
7	Hughes, Mark	163	82	Farman, Alf	28	157	O'Shea, John	12
8	van Nistelrooy, Ruud	150	83	Pegg, David	28	158	Smith, Alan	12
9	Pearson, Stan	148	84	Aston, John (Jnr)	27	159	Storey-Moore, Ian	12
10	Herd, David	145	85	Blanchflower, Jackie	27	160	Duckworth, Dick	11
11	Giggs, Ryan	144	86	Johnston, Billy	27	161	Fortune, Quinton	11
12	Scholes, Paul	139	87	Sadler, David	27	162	Grimes, Ashley	11
13	Taylor, Tommy	131	88	Blackmore, Clayton	26	163	Lewis, Eddie	11
14	McClair, Brian	127	89	Butt, Nicky	26	164	Richardson, Kieran	11
15	Solskjaer, Ole Gunnar	126	90	Davenport, Peter	26	165	Veron, Juan-Sebastian	11
16	Cole, Andrew	121	91	McQueen, Gordon	26	166	Wallace, Danny	11
17	Turnbull, Sandy	101	92	Rennox, Charlie	25	167	Webb, Neil	11
18	Cassidy, Joe	100	93	Moran, Kevin	24	168	Bell, Alex	10
19	Wall, George	100	94	Olsen, Jesper	24	169	Bissett, George	10
20	Robson, Bryan	99	95	Sagar, Charles	24	170	Chisnall, Phil	10
21	Macari, Lou	97	96	Burke, Ronnie	23	171	Coupar, Jimmy	10
22	Ronaldo, Cristiano	92	97	Clarkin, John	23	172	Fitzpatrick, John	10
23	Beckham, David	85	98	Roberts, Charlie	23	173	Robertson, Alex	10
24	Cantona, Eric	82	99	Allan, Jack	22	174	Silvestre, Mikael	10
25	West, Enoch	80	100	Hanlon, Jimmy	22	175	Warburton, Arthur	10
26	Stapleton, Frank	78	101	Bradley, Warren	21	176	Wilkins, Ray	10
27	Rooney, Wayne	77	102	Edwards, Duncan	21	177	Bain, David	9
28	McIlroy, Sammy	71	103	Gillespie, Matthew	21	178	Erentz, Fred	9
29	Coppell, Steve	70	104	Gowling, Alan	21	179	Fletcher, Darren	9
30	Kidd, Brian	70	105	Woodcock, Wilf	21	180	Foulkes, Bill	9
31	Reid, Tom	67	106	Byrne, Roger	20	181	Gibson, Colin	9
32	Whiteside, Norman	67	107	Gallimore, Stanley	20	182	Johnsen, Ronny	9
33	Donaldson, Bob	66	108	Pegg, Dick	20	183	Stacey, George	9
34	Pearson, Stuart	66	109	Rawlings, Bill	19	184	Wrigglesworth, Billy	9
35	Yorke, Dwight	66	110	Stiles, Nobby	19	185	Bannister, Jimmy	8
36	Mitten, Charlie	61	111	Tevez, Carlos	19	186	Bellion, David	8
37	Peddie, Jack	58	112	Baird, Harry	18	187	Cantwell, Noel	8
38	Bamford, Tommy	57	113	Ball, Jack	18	188	Carrick, Michael	8
39	Halse, Harold	56	114	Cape, Jack	18	189	Cartwright, Walter	8
40	Quixall, Albert	56	115	Muhren, Arnold	18	190	Cruyff, Jordi	8
41	Rowley, Harry	55	116	Partridge, Teddy	18	191	Goodwin, Fred	8
42	Dawson, Alex	54	117	Brown, James (1932–34)	17	192	Grimwood, John	8
43	Hanson, Jimmy	52	118	Carey, Johnny	17	193	Hopkin, Fred	8
44	McPherson, Frank	52	119	Collinson, Jimmy	17	194	May, David	8
45	Whelan, William	52	120	Forlan, Diego	17	195	McCreery, David	8
46	Bruce, Steve	51	121	Greenhoff, Brian	17	196	McShane, Harry	8
47	Hill, Gordon	51	122	Henderson, William	17	197	Miller, Tom	8
48	Keane, Roy	51	123	Robins, Mark	17	198	Morrison, Tommy	8
49	Lochhead, Arthur	50	124	Sapsford, George	17	199	Myerscough, Joe	8
50	Mutch, George	49	125	Goldthorpe, Ernie	16	200	Neville, Phil	8
51	Picken, Jack	46	126	Houston, Stewart	16	201	Park, Ji-Sung	8
52	Sheringham, Teddy	46	127	McGrath, Paul	16	202	Peden, Jack	8
53	Berry, Johnny	45	128	Smith, Tom	16	203	Williams, Harry (1904–06)	8
54	Turnbull, Jimmy	45	129	Beddow, John	15	204	Albiston, Arthur	7
55	Bryant, Billy	42	130	Crerand, Pat	15	205	Bogan, Tommy	7
56	Saha, Louis	42	131	Leigh, Tom	15	206	Buckle, Ted	7
57	Jordan, Joe	41	132	McKay, Bill	15	207	Burns, Francis	7
58	Manley, Tom	41	133	Pallister, Gary	15	208	Doherty, John	7
59	Anderson, George	39	134	Smith, Jack	15	209	Duxbury, Mike	7
60	Strachan, Gordon	38	135	Thomas, Mickey	15	210	Ferdinand, Rio	7
61	Downie, John	37	136	Dewar, Neil	14	211	Graham, Arthur	7
62	Smith, Dick	37	137	Downie, Alex	14	212	Hilditch, Clarence	7
63	Greenhoff, Jimmy	36	138	Grassam, Billy	14	213	McCalliog, Jim	7
64	Kanchelskis, Andrei	36	139	Homer, Tom	14	214	Morgan, Billy	7
65	Meredith, Billy	36	140	Jackson, William	14	215	Neville, Gary	7
66	Sharpe, Lee	36	141	Pearson, Mark	14	216	Parkinson, Robert	7
67	Boyd, Henry	35	142	Peters, James	14	217	Stewart, William	7
68	Connelly, John	35	143	Preston, Stephen	14	218	Sweeney, Eric	7
69	Morris, Johnny	35	144	Ridding, Bill	14	219	Taylor, Chris	7
70	Scanlon, Albert	35	145	Setters, Maurice	14	220	Boyle, Tommy	6
71	Schofield, Alf	35	146	Giles, Johnny	13	221	Brennan, Shay	6
72	Morgan, Willie	34	147	Ritchie, Andy	13	222	Dow, John	6
73	Arkesden, Tommy	33	148	Thomas, Harry	13	223	Draycott, Billy	6
74	Bryant, William	33	149	Birtles, Gary	12	224	Fitzsimmons, Tommy	6
75	Irwin, Denis	33	150	Brazil, Alan	12	225	Hood, Billy	6

continued../

ALL COMPETITIVE MATCHES (continued)

#	PLAYER	GOALS
226	Jenkyns, Caesar	6
227	Lawton, Nobby	6
228	McMillan, Sammy	6
229	Meehan, Tommy	6
230	Nicholl, Jimmy	6
231	Nicholson, Jimmy	6
232	Poborsky, Karel	6
233	Sartori, Carlo	6
234	Wassall, Jackie	6
235	Whalley, Arthur	6
236	Birch, Brian	5
237	Forsyth, Alex	5
238	Harrison, William	5
239	Holton, Jim	5
240	Lee, Edwin	5
241	Leonard, Harry	5
242	MacDougall, Ted	5
243	Mann, Frank	5
244	Millar, George	5
245	Moir, Ian	5
246	Moore, Graham	5
247	Pape, Albert	5
248	Potts, Arthur	5
249	Stewart, Willie	5
250	Vidic, Nemanja	5
251	Anderson, Viv	4
252	Barnes, Peter	4
253	Barson, Frank	4
254	Beardsmore, Russell	4
255	Blanc, Laurent	4
256	Bond, Ernie	4
257	Boyd, Billy	4
258	Buchan, Martin	4
259	Cockburn, Henry	4
260	Davies, Wyn	4
261	Ferrier, Ron	4
262	Frame, Tommy	4
263	Gidman, John	4
264	Godsmark, Gilbert	4
265	Green, Eddie	4
266	Heinze, Gabriel	4
267	Hodges, Frank	4
268	Hurst, Daniel	4
269	James, Steve	4
270	Jones, Tommy	4
271	Jovanovic, Nikki	4
272	Kennedy, Fred	4
273	Lappin, Harry	4
274	Livingstone, George	4
275	Mackie, Charlie	4
276	McDonald, Willie	4
277	McLachlan, George	4
278	Menzies, Alex	4
279	Morgan, Hugh	4
280	Nani	4
281	Nuttall, Tom	4
282	Redwood, Hubert	4
283	Rossi, Giuseppe	4
284	Ryan, Jimmy	4
285	Taylor, Ernie	4
286	Toms, Billy	4
287	Travers, George	4
288	Williams, Fred	4
289	Bennion, Ray	3
290	Berg, Henning	3
291	Black, Dick	3
292	Bonthron, Bob	3
293	Brooks, William	3
294	Brown, Wes	3
295	Bullock, Jimmy	3
296	Byrne, David	3
297	Carson, Adam	3
298	Chilton, Allenby	3
299	Doughty, Jack	3
300	Dublin, Dion	3

#	PLAYER	GOALS
301	Edge, Alf	3
302	Fisher, James	3
303	Grundy, John	3
304	Larsson, Henrik	3
305	McGarvey, Scott	3
306	Milne, Ralph	3
307	Norton, Joe	3
308	Phelan, Mike	3
309	Ramsden, Charlie	3
310	Robinson, James	3
311	Rothwell, Charles	3
312	Wilson, Jack	3
313	Wombwell, Dick	3
314	Anderson, John	2
315	Anderson, Trevor	2
316	Barber, Jack	2
317	Beadsworth, Arthur	2
318	Birkett, Cliff	2
319	Blott, Sam	2
320	Brown, William	2
321	Chadwick, Luke	2
322	Clempson, Frank	2
323	Colman, Eddie	2
324	Connor, Ted	2
325	Cope, Ronnie	2
326	Craven, Charlie	2
327	Crooks, Garth	2
328	Cunningham, John	2
329	Davidson, Will	2
330	Djemba-Djemba, Eric	2
331	Dunne, Tony	2
332	Evans, Sidney	2
333	Evra, Patrice	2
334	Fitton, Arthur	2
335	Gill, Tony	2
336	Gillespie, Keith	2
337	Graham, George	2
338	Hall, Proctor	2
339	Hamill, Mickey	2
340	Hargreaves, Owen	2
341	Harris, Frank	2
342	Hayes, Vince	2
343	Heywood, Herbert	2
344	Hodge, James	2
345	Hunter, George	2
346	Hunter, William	2
347	Kleberson, Jose	2
348	MacDonald, Ken	2
349	Mann, Herbert	2
350	Martin, Lee (1990s)	2
351	Martin, Mick	2
352	Mathieson, William	2
353	McBain, Neil	2
354	McGlen, Billy	2
355	McGuinness, Wilf	2
356	McMillen, Walter	2
357	Miller, Liam	2
358	Nicol, George	2
359	O'Brien, Liam	2
360	O'Connell, Pat	2
361	Parker, Paul	2
362	Pique, Gerard	2
363	Richards, Charlie	2
364	Roberts, W.A	2
365	Silcock, Jack	2
366	Stepney, Alex	2
367	Warner, Jack	2
368	Wedge, Frank	2
369	Williams, Harry (1922-3)	2
370	Williams, Rees	2
371	Aitken, John	1
372	Ambler, Alfred	1
373	Bain, James	1
374	Bainbridge, Bill	1
375	Banks, Jack	1

#	PLAYER	GOALS
376	Berry, Bill	1
377	Blomqvist, Jesper	1
378	Bradbury, Len	1
379	Brown, James (1935-39)	1
380	Campbell, William	1
381	Carman, James	1
382	Chalmers, Stewart	1
383	Chester, Reg	1
384	Colville, James	1
385	Cooke, Terry	1
386	Coyne, Peter	1
387	Craig, T	1
388	Cunningham, Laurie	1
389	Davies, Alan	1
390	Davies, Simon	1
391	Doughty, Roger	1
392	Eagles, Chris	1
393	Ebanks-Blake, Sylvan	1
394	Edwards, Paul	1
395	Evans, George	1
396	Ferguson, John	1
397	Fitchett, John	1
398	Foley, G	1
399	Gardner, Dick	1
400	Gibson, Terry	1
401	Givens, Don	1
402	Gladwin, George	1
403	Goodwin, Billy	1
404	Graham, Deiniol	1
405	Griffiths, Jack	1
406	Halton, Reg	1
407	Harris, Tom	1
408	Hendry, James	1
409	Higson, James	1
410	Hogg, Graeme	1
411	Holt, Edward	1
412	Hooper, Arthur	1
413	Inglis, Bill	1
414	Jones, Mark	1
415	Kinsey, Albert	1
416	Knowles, Frank	1
417	Lang, Tommy	1
418	Lee, Kieran	1
419	McCartney, John	1
420	McCartney, William	1
421	McClelland, Jimmy	1
422	McGrath, Chris	1
423	Miller, James	1
424	Montgomery, James	1
425	Nevland, Erik	1
426	Owen, W	1
427	Payne, Ernest	1
428	Radford, Charlie	1
429	Richards, Billy	1
430	Robertson, Sandy	1
431	Robertson, William	1
432	Schmeichel, Peter	1
433	Sheldon, John	1
434	Sivebaek, Johnny	1
435	Smith, Albert	1
436	Smith, Lawrence	1
437	Sneddon, J	1
438	Stafford, Harry	1
439	Stam, Jaap	1
440	Stephenson, R	1
441	Thompson, John	1
442	Thomson, Arthur	1
443	Thomson, James	1
444	Topping, Henry	1
445	Ure, Ian	1
446	Vance, James	1
447	Vincent, Ernest	1
448	Vose, George	1
449	Williams, Joe	1
450	Wood, John	1
451	Young, Tony	1
	own goals	152

ALL LEAGUE MATCHES

#	PLAYER	GOALS	#	PLAYER	GOALS	#	PLAYER	GOALS
1	Charlton, Bobby	199	76	Aston, John (Jnr)	25	151	Storey-Moore, Ian	11
2	Rowley, Jack	182	77	Delaney, Jimmy	25	152	Thomas, Mickey	11
3	Law, Denis	171	78	Ince, Paul	25	153	Bell, Alex	10
4	Viollet, Dennis	159	79	Morgan, Willie	25	154	Bissett, George	10
5	Spence, Joe	158	80	Johnston, Billy	24	155	Crerand, Pat	10
6	Best, George	137	81	Pegg, David	24	156	Forlan, Diego	10
7	Pearson, Stan	127	82	Rennox, Charlie	24	157	Giles, Johnny	10
8	Hughes, Mark	120	83	Clarkin, John	23	158	Grimes, Ashley	10
9	Herd, David	114	84	Daly, Gerry	23	159	Hopkinson, Samuel	10
10	Taylor, Tommy	112	85	Connelly, John	22	160	Robertson, Alex	10
11	Giggs, Ryan	101	86	Davenport, Peter	22	161	Warburton, Arthur	10
12	Scholes, Paul	96	87	Irwin, Denis	22	162	Bain, David	9
13	van Nistelrooy, Ruud	95	88	Roberts, Charlie	22	163	Coupar, Jimmy	9
14	Cole, Andrew	93	89	Sadler, David	22	164	Erentz, Fred	9
15	Solskjaer, Ole Gunnar	91	90	Allan, Jack	21	165	Gibson, Colin	9
16	Cassidy, Joe	90	91	Butt, Nicky	21	166	Lewis, Eddie	9
17	Turnbull, Sandy	90	92	Moran, Kevin	21	167	O'Shea, John	9
18	Wall, George	89	93	Olsen, Jesper	21	168	Stacey, George	9
19	McClair, Brian	88	94	Sharpe, Lee	21	169	Brazil, Alan	8
20	Macari, Lou	78	95	Bradley, Warren	20	170	Cartwright, Walter	8
21	Robson, Bryan	74	96	Edwards, Duncan	20	171	Chisnall, Phil	8
22	West, Enoch	72	97	Hanlon, Jimmy	20	172	Cruyff, Jordi	8
23	Ronaldo, Cristiano	66	98	McQueen, Gordon	20	173	Fitzpatrick, John	8
24	Cantona, Eric	64	99	Sagar, Charles	20	174	Grimwood, John	8
25	Reid, Tom	63	100	Woodcock, Wilf	20	175	Hopkin, Fred	8
26	Beckham, David	62	101	Blackmore, Clayton	19	176	McShane, Harry	8
27	Stapleton, Frank	60	102	Gallimore, Stanley	19	177	Myerscough, Joe	8
28	McIlroy, Sammy	57	103	Rawlings, Bill	19	178	Webb, Neil	8
29	Donaldson, Bob	56	104	Cape, Jack	18	179	Bannister, Jimmy	7
30	Pearson, Stuart	55	105	Farman, Alf	18	180	Bogan, Tommy	7
31	Rowley, Harry	55	106	Gowling, Alan	18	181	Doherty, John	7
32	Coppell, Steve	54	107	Ball, Jack	17	182	Fletcher, Darren	7
33	Bamford, Tommy	53	108	Brown, James (1932–34)	17	183	Foulkes, Bill	7
34	Rooney, Wayne	53	109	Byrne, Roger	17	184	Goodwin, Fred	7
35	Kidd, Brian	52	110	Gillespie, Matthew	17	185	Hilditch, Clarence	7
36	Peddie, Jack	52	111	Henderson, William	17	186	Johnsen, Ronny	7
37	Lochhead, Arthur	50	112	Stiles, Nobby	17	187	McCalliog, Jim	7
38	Mitten, Charlie	50	113	Burke, Ronnie	16	188	McCreery, David	7
39	Quixall, Albert	50	114	Carey, Johnny	16	189	Miller, Tom	7
40	Yorke, Dwight	48	115	Collinson, Jimmy	16	190	Morrison, Tommy	7
41	Hanson, Jimmy	47	116	Partridge, Teddy	16	191	Moses, Remi	7
42	Whiteside, Norman	47	117	Sapsford, George	16	192	Park, Ji-Sung	7
43	Mutch, George	46	118	Baird, Harry	15	193	Parkinson, Robert	7
44	Dawson, Alex	45	119	Goldthorpe, Ernie	15	194	Peden, Jack	7
45	McPherson, Frank	45	120	Leigh, Tom	15	195	Smith, Alan	7
46	Whelan, William	43	121	McKay, Bill	15	196	Stewart, William	7
47	Bryant, Billy	42	122	Dewar, Neil	14	197	Veron, Juan-Sebastian	7
48	Halse, Harold	41	123	Homer, Tom	14	198	Wilkins, Ray	7
49	Manley, Tom	40	124	Preston, Stephen	14	199	Williams, Harry (1904–06)	7
50	Hill, Gordon	39	125	Ridding, Bill	14	200	Wrigglesworth, Billy	7
51	Picken, Jack	39	126	Smith, Jack	14	201	Albiston, Arthur	6
52	Anderson, George	37	127	Tevez, Carlos	14	202	Boyle, Tommy	6
53	Berry, Johnny	37	128	Grassam, Billy	13	203	Buckle, Ted	6
54	Jordan, Joe	37	129	Greenhoff, Brian	13	204	Burns, Francis	6
55	Bruce, Steve	36	130	Houston, Stewart	13	205	Cantwell, Noel	6
56	Turnbull, Jimmy	36	131	Muhren, Arnold	13	206	Dow, John	6
57	Downie, John	35	132	Pegg, Dick	13	207	Draycott, Billy	6
58	Meredith, Billy	35	133	Peters, James	13	208	Duxbury, Mike	6
59	Smith, Dick	35	134	Ritchie, Andy	13	209	Ferdinand, Rio	6
60	Scanlon, Albert	34	135	Beddow, John	12	210	Fitzsimmons, Tommy	6
61	Keane, Roy	33	136	Downie, Alex	12	211	Fortune, Quinton	6
62	Strachan, Gordon	33	137	Hine, Ernie	12	212	Hood, Billy	6
63	Boyd, Henry	32	138	Jackson, William	12	213	Lawton, Nobby	6
64	Morris, Johnny	32	139	McGrath, Paul	12	214	May, David	6
65	Sheringham, Teddy	31	140	McNaught, James	12	215	McMillan, Sammy	6
66	Schofield, Alf	30	141	Pallister, Gary	12	216	Meehan, Tommy	6
67	Aston, John (Snr)	29	142	Pearson, Mark	12	217	Morgan, Billy	6
68	Arkesden, Tommy	28	143	Setters, Maurice	12	218	Silvestre, Mikael	6
69	Kanchelskis, Andrei	28	144	Smith, Tom	12	219	Sweeney, Eric	6
70	Saha, Louis	28	145	Thomas, Harry	12	220	Taylor, Chris	6
71	Bryant, William	27	146	Birtles, Gary	11	221	Wallace, Danny	6
72	Griffiths, Billy	27	147	Duckworth, Dick	11	222	Wassall, Jackie	6
73	Blanchflower, Jackie	26	148	Kennedy, William	11	223	Whalley, Arthur	6
74	Greenhoff, Jimmy	26	149	McLenahan, Hugh	11	224	Carrick, Michael	5
75	Webster, Colin	26	150	Robins, Mark	11	225	Graham, Arthur	5

continued../

ALL LEAGUE MATCHES (continued)

#	PLAYER	GOALS	#	PLAYER	GOALS	#	PLAYER	GOALS
226	Harrison, William	5	301	Birkett, Cliff	2	376	Gillespie, Keith	1
227	Holton, Jim	5	302	Blott, Sam	2	377	Givens, Don	1
228	Jenkyns, Caesar	5	303	Brown, Wes	2	378	Gladwin, George	1
229	Lee, Edwin	5	304	Brown, William	2	379	Goodwin, Billy	1
230	Leonard, Harry	5	305	Chadwick, Luke	2	380	Griffiths, Jack	1
231	MacDougall, Ted	5	306	Clempson, Frank	2	381	Halton, Reg	1
232	Mann, Frank	5	307	Connor, Ted	2	382	Harris, Tom	1
233	Millar, George	5	308	Cope, Ronnie	2	383	Heinze, Gabriel	1
234	Moir, Ian	5	309	Craven, Charlie	2	384	Hendry, James	1
235	Neville, Gary	5	310	Crooks, Garth	2	385	Higson, James	1
236	Neville, Phil	5	311	Cunningham, John	2	386	Hogg, Graeme	1
237	Nicholson, Jimmy	5	312	Davidson, Will	2	387	Holt, Edward	1
238	Pape, Albert	5	313	Dublin, Dion	2	388	Hooper, Arthur	1
239	Poborsky, Karel	5	314	Dunne, Tony	2	389	Inglis, Bill	1
240	Potts, Arthur	5	315	Evans, Sidney	2	390	Jones, Mark	1
241	Stewart, Willie	5	316	Fisher, James	2	391	Knowles, Frank	1
242	Barson, Frank	4	317	Fitton, Arthur	2	392	Lang, Tommy	1
243	Beardsmore, Russell	4	318	Graham, George	2	393	Larsson, Henrik	1
244	Bellion, David	4	319	Hall, Proctor	2	394	Martin, Lee (1990s)	1
245	Birch, Brian	4	320	Hamill, Mickey	2	395	McCartney, John	1
246	Bond, Ernie	4	321	Hargreaves, Owen	2	396	McCartney, William	1
247	Boyd, Billy	4	322	Harris, Frank	2	397	McClelland, Jimmy	1
248	Buchan, Martin	4	323	Hayes, Vince	2	398	McGrath, Chris	1
249	Cockburn, Henry	4	324	Heywood, Herbert	2	399	Miller, James	1
250	Davies, Wyn	4	325	Hodge, James	2	400	Montgomery, James	1
251	Ferrier, Ron	4	326	Hunter, George	2	401	Owen, W	1
252	Forsyth, Alex	4	327	Hunter, William	2	402	Parker, Paul	1
253	Frame, Tommy	4	328	Kleberson, Jose	2	403	Payne, Ernest	1
254	Gidman, John	4	329	MacDonald, Ken	2	404	Radford, Charlie	1
255	Godsmark, Gilbert	4	330	Mann, Herbert	2	405	Richards, Billy	1
256	Green, Eddie	4	331	Martin, Mick	2	406	Richards, Charlie	1
257	Hodges, Frank	4	332	Mathieson, William	2	407	Robertson, Sandy	1
258	Hurst, Daniel	4	333	McBain, Neil	2	408	Robertson, William	1
259	James, Steve	4	334	McGlen, Billy	2	409	Rossi, Giuseppe	1
260	Jones, Tommy	4	335	McGuinness, Wilf	2	410	Rothwell, Charles	1
261	Jovanovic, Nikki	4	336	McMillen, Walter	2	411	Sheldon, John	1
262	Kennedy, Fred	4	337	Nicol, George	2	412	Sivebaek, Johnny	1
263	Lappin, Harry	4	338	O'Brien, Liam	2	413	Smith, Albert	1
264	Livingstone, George	4	339	O'Connell, Pat	2	414	Smith, Lawrence	1
265	McDonald, Willie	4	340	Phelan, Mike	2	415	Stam, Jaap	1
266	McLachlan, George	4	341	Richardson, Kieran	2	416	Stephenson, R	1
267	Menzies, Alex	4	342	Roberts, W.A	2	417	Thompson, John	1
268	Moore, Graham	4	343	Silcock, Jack	2	418	Thomson, Arthur	1
269	Morgan, Hugh	4	344	Stepney, Alex	2	419	Thomson, James	1
270	Nuttall, Tom	4	345	Taylor, Ernie	2	420	Topping, Henry	1
271	Ryan, Jimmy	4	346	Wedge, Frank	2	421	Ure, Ian	1
272	Sartori, Carlo	4	347	Williams, Harry (1922–3)	2	422	Vance, James	1
273	Travers, George	4	348	Williams, Rees	2	423	Vincent, Ernest	1
274	Vidic, Nemanja	4	349	Aitken, John	1	424	Vose, George	1
275	Black, Dick	3	350	Ambler, Alfred	1	425	Warner, Jack	1
276	Bonthron, Bob	3	351	Anderson, John	1	426	Williams, Joe	1
277	Brennan, Shay	3	352	Bain, James	1	427	Wood, John	1
278	Brooks, William	3	353	Barber, Jack	1	428	Young, Tony	1
279	Bullock, Jimmy	3	354	Beadsworth, Arthur	1		own goals	122
280	Byrne, David	3	355	Berry, Bill	1			
281	Carson, Adam	3	356	Blanc, Laurent	1			
282	Chilton, Allenby	3	357	Blomqvist, Jesper	1			
283	Grundy, John	3	358	Bradbury, Len	1			
284	Mackie, Charlie	3	359	Brown, James (1935–39)	1			
285	McGarvey, Scott	3	360	Campbell, William	1			
286	Milne, Ralph	3	361	Carman, James	1			
287	Nani	3	362	Chalmers, Stewart	1			
288	Nicholl, Jimmy	3	363	Chester, Reg	1			
289	Norton, Joe	3	364	Colman, Eddie	1			
290	Ramsden, Charlie	3	365	Colville, James	1			
291	Redwood, Hubert	3	366	Coyne, Peter	1			
292	Robinson, James	3	367	Cunningham, Laurie	1			
293	Toms, Billy	3	368	Eagles, Chris	1			
294	Wilson, Jack	3	369	Evra, Patrice	1			
295	Wombwell, Dick	3	370	Ferguson, John	1			
296	Anderson, Trevor	2	371	Fitchett, John	1			
297	Anderson, Viv	2	372	Foley, G	1			
298	Barnes, Peter	2	373	Gardner, Dick	1			
299	Bennion, Ray	2	374	Gibson, Terry	1			
300	Berg, Henning	2	375	Gill, Tony	1			

ALL PREMIERSHIP MATCHES

#	PLAYER	GOALS	#	PLAYER	GOALS	#	PLAYER	GOALS
1	Giggs, Ryan	96	26	Pallister, Gary	8	51	Blanc, Laurent	1
2	Scholes, Paul	96	27	Fletcher, Darren	7	52	Blomqvist, Jesper	1
3	van Nistelrooy, Ruud	95	28	Johnsen, Ronny	7	53	Eagles, Chris	1
4	Cole, Andrew	93	29	Park, Ji-Sung	7	54	Evra, Patrice	1
5	Solskjaer, Ole Gunnar	91	30	Smith, Alan	7	55	Gillespie, Keith	1
6	Ronaldo, Cristiano	66	31	Veron, Juan-Sebastian	7	56	Heinze, Gabriel	1
7	Cantona, Eric	64	32	Ferdinand, Rio	6	57	Larsson, Henrik	1
8	Beckham, David	62	33	Fortune, Quinton	6	58	Parker, Paul	1
9	Rooney, Wayne	53	34	May, David	6	59	Rossi, Giuseppe	1
10	Yorke, Dwight	48	35	Silvestre, Mikael	6	60	Stam, Jaap	1
11	Hughes, Mark	35	36	Carrick, Michael	5		own goals	37
12	Keane, Roy	33	37	Neville, Gary	5			
13	Sheringham, Teddy	31	38	Neville, Phil	5			
14	Saha, Louis	28	39	Poborsky, Karel	5			
15	Kanchelskis, Andrei	23	40	Bellion, David	4			
16	Butt, Nicky	21	41	Vidic, Nemanja	4			
17	Ince, Paul	19	42	Nani	3			
18	Irwin, Denis	18	43	Berg, Henning	2			
19	McClair, Brian	18	44	Brown, Wes	2			
20	Sharpe, Lee	17	45	Chadwick, Luke	2			
21	Tevez, Carlos	14	46	Dublin, Dion	2			
22	Bruce, Steve	11	47	Hargreaves, Owen	2			
23	Forlan, Diego	10	48	Kleberson, Jose	2			
24	O'Shea, John	9	49	Richardson, Kieran	2			
25	Cruyff, Jordi	8	50	Robson, Bryan	2			

ALL LEAGUE DIVISION 1 MATCHES

#	PLAYER	GOALS	#	PLAYER	GOALS	#	PLAYER	GOALS
1	Charlton, Bobby	199	76	Carey, Johnny	13	151	Leonard, Harry	5
2	Rowley, Jack	173	77	Johnston, Billy	13	152	MacDougall, Ted	5
3	Law, Denis	171	78	Muhren, Arnold	13	153	McKay, Bill	5
4	Viollet, Dennis	159	79	Ritchie, Andy	13	154	Moir, Ian	5
5	Best, George	137	80	Roberts, Charlie	13	155	Myerscough, Joe	5
6	Pearson, Stan	125	81	Daly, Gerry	12	156	Nicholson, Jimmy	5
7	Herd, David	114	82	McGrath, Paul	12	157	Potts, Arthur	5
8	Taylor, Tommy	112	83	Pearson, Mark	12	158	Wassall, Jackie	5
9	Spence, Joe	106	84	Setters, Maurice	12	159	Barson, Frank	4
10	Turnbull, Sandy	90	85	Thomas, Harry	12	160	Beardsmore, Russell	4
11	Wall, George	86	86	Ball, Jack	11	161	Birch, Brian	4
12	Hughes, Mark	85	87	Birtles, Gary	11	162	Bond, Ernie	4
13	Robson, Bryan	72	88	Robins, Mark	11	163	Buchan, Martin	4
14	West, Enoch	72	89	Storey–Moore, Ian	11	164	Cockburn, Henry	4
15	McClair, Brian	70	90	Thomas, Mickey	11	165	Davies, Wyn	4
16	Macari, Lou	67	91	Bissett, George	10	166	Duckworth, Dick	4
17	Stapleton, Frank	60	92	Crerand, Pat	10	167	Gidman, John	4
18	Coppell, Steve	53	93	Giles, Johnny	10	168	Hodges, Frank	4
19	Kidd, Brian	52	94	Grimes, Ashley	10	169	Hopkinson, Samuel	4
20	McIlroy, Sammy	50	95	Lochhead, Arthur	10	170	Irwin, Denis	4
21	Mitten, Charlie	50	96	Gibson, Colin	9	171	James, Steve	4
22	Quixall, Albert	50	97	Greenhoff, Brian	9	172	Jovanovic, Nikki	4
23	Whiteside, Norman	47	98	Lewis, Eddie	9	173	Livingstone, George	4
24	Dawson, Alex	45	99	Stacey, George	9	174	McCalliog, Jim	4
25	Hanson, Jimmy	44	100	Brazil, Alan	8	175	McLachlan, George	4
26	Whelan, William	43	101	Chisnall, Phil	8	176	Menzies, Alex	4
27	Halse, Harold	41	102	Fitzpatrick, John	8	177	Moore, Graham	4
28	Hill, Gordon	39	103	Hopkin, Fred	8	178	Nuttall, Tom	4
29	Pearson, Stuart	38	104	Manley, Tom	8	179	Pallister, Gary	4
30	Anderson, George	37	105	McLenahan, Hugh	8	180	Ryan, Jimmy	4
31	Berry, Johnny	37	106	McShane, Harry	8	181	Sagar, Charles	4
32	Jordan, Joe	37	107	Webb, Neil	8	182	Sartori, Carlo	4
33	McPherson, Frank	37	108	Bannister, Jimmy	7	183	Sharpe, Lee	4
34	Reid, Tom	36	109	Bogan, Tommy	7	184	Stewart, Willie	4
35	Turnbull, Jimmy	36	110	Doherty, John	7	185	Travers, George	4
36	Downie, John	35	111	Foulkes, Bill	7	186	Baird, Harry	3
37	Meredith, Billy	35	112	Goodwin, Fred	7	187	Brennan, Shay	3
38	Scanlon, Albert	34	113	Houston, Stewart	7	188	Bullock, Jimmy	3
39	Strachan, Gordon	33	114	McCreery, David	7	189	Carson, Adam	3
40	Morris, Johnny	32	115	Miller, Tom	7	190	Chilton, Allenby	3
41	Aston, John (senior)	29	116	Moses, Remi	7	191	Forsyth, Alex	3
42	Rowley, Harry	28	117	Mutch, George	7	192	McGarvey, Scott	3
43	Blanchflower, Jackie	26	118	Peden, Jack	7	193	Milne, Ralph	3
44	Greenhoff, Jimmy	26	119	Wilkins, Ray	7	194	Nicholl, Jimmy	3
45	Webster, Colin	26	120	Albiston, Arthur	6	195	Norton, Joe	3
46	Aston, John (junior)	25	121	Boyle, Tommy	6	196	Ramsden, Charlie	3
47	Bruce, Steve	25	122	Buckle, Ted	6	197	Robinson, James	3
48	Delaney, Jimmy	25	123	Burns, Francis	6	198	Smith, Tom	3
49	Pegg, David	24	124	Cantwell, Noel	6	199	Toms, Billy	3
50	Rennox, Charlie	24	125	Duxbury, Mike	6	200	Wilson, Jack	3
51	Donaldson, Bob	23	126	Fitzsimmons, Tommy	6	201	Anderson, Trevor	2
52	Connelly, John	22	127	Hilditch, Clarence	6	202	Anderson, Viv	2
53	Davenport, Peter	22	128	Hood, Billy	6	203	Barnes, Peter	2
54	Morgan, Willie	22	129	Ince, Paul	6	204	Bennion, Ray	2
55	Sadler, David	22	130	Lawton, Nobby	6	205	Birkett, Cliff	2
56	Moran, Kevin	21	131	McMillan, Sammy	6	206	Blott, Sam	2
57	Olsen, Jesper	21	132	Meehan, Tommy	6	207	Clempson, Frank	2
58	Bradley, Warren	20	133	Peddie, Jack	6	208	Connor, Ted	2
59	Edwards, Duncan	20	134	Smith, Jack	6	209	Cope, Ronnie	2
60	Hanlon, Jimmy	20	135	Sweeney, Eric	6	210	Craven, Charlie	2
61	McQueen, Gordon	20	136	Taylor, Chris	6	211	Crooks, Garth	2
62	Woodcock, Wilf	20	137	Wallace, Danny	6	212	Downie, Alex	2
63	Blackmore, Clayton	19	138	Warburton, Arthur	6	213	Dunne, Tony	2
64	Picken, Jack	19	139	Whalley, Arthur	6	214	Erentz, Fred	2
65	Rawlings, Bill	19	140	Wrigglesworth, Billy	6	215	Graham, George	2
66	Farman, Alf	18	141	Bell, Alex	5	216	Hamill, Mickey	2
67	Gowling, Alan	18	142	Clarkin, John	5	217	Harris, Frank	2
68	Byrne, Roger	17	143	Coupar, Jimmy	5	218	Henderson, William	2
69	Stiles, Nobby	17	144	Gallimore, Stanley	5	219	Hodge, James	2
70	Bryant, Billy	16	145	Giggs, Ryan	5	220	Hunter, George	2
71	Burke, Ronnie	16	146	Graham, Arthur	5	221	Hunter, William	2
72	Partridge, Teddy	16	147	Grimwood, John	5	222	Mann, Frank	2
73	Sapsford, George	16	148	Harrison, William	5	223	Martin, Mick	2
74	Bamford, Tommy	14	149	Holton, Jim	5	224	Mathieson, William	2
75	Homer, Tom	14	150	Kanchelskis, Andrei	5	225	McGlen, Billy	2

continued../

ALL LEAGUE DIVISION 1 MATCHES (continued)

#	PLAYER	GOALS	#	PLAYER	GOALS	#	PLAYER	GOALS
226	McGuinness, Wilf	2	246	Ferrier, Ron	1	266	Redwood, Hubert	1
227	Nicol, George	2	247	Gibson, Terry	1	267	Sheldon, John	1
228	O'Brien, Liam	2	248	Gill, Tony	1	268	Sivebaek, Johnny	1
229	O'Connell, Pat	2	249	Givens, Don	1	269	Smith, Albert	1
230	Phelan, Mike	2	250	Gladwin, George	1	270	Thompson, John	1
231	Schofield, Alf	2	251	Goodwin, Billy	1	271	Thomson, Arthur	1
232	Silcock, Jack	2	252	Halton, Reg	1	272	Thomson, James	1
233	Stepney, Alex	2	253	Harris, Tom	1	273	Ure, Ian	1
234	Taylor, Ernie	2	254	Hendry, James	1	274	Warner, Jack	1
235	Williams, Rees	2	255	Hogg, Graeme	1	275	Williams, Joe	1
236	Anderson, John	1	256	Hooper, Arthur	1	276	Young, Tony	1
237	Berry, Bill	1	257	Inglis, Bill	1		own goals	60
238	Bradbury, Len	1	258	Jones, Mark	1			
239	Campbell, William	1	259	Knowles, Frank	1			
240	Cape, Jack	1	260	Martin, Lee (1990s)	1			
241	Colman, Eddie	1	261	McClelland, Jimmy	1			
242	Colville, James	1	262	McGrath, Chris	1			
243	Coyne, Peter	1	263	McNaught, James	1			
244	Cunningham, Laurie	1	264	Montgomery, James	1			
245	Davidson, Will	1	265	Payne, Ernest	1			

ALL LEAGUE DIVISION 2 MATCHES

#	PLAYER	GOALS	#	PLAYER	GOALS	#	PLAYER	GOALS
1	Cassidy, Joe	90	76	Frame, Tommy	4	151	Rothwell, Charles	1
2	Spence, Joe	52	77	Godsmark, Gilbert	4	152	Smith, Lawrence	1
3	Peddie, Jack	46	78	Green, Eddie	4	153	Stephenson, R	1
4	Lochhead, Arthur	40	79	Greenhoff, Brian	4	154	Stewart, Willie	1
5	Bamford, Tommy	39	80	Hurst, Daniel	4	155	Topping, Henry	1
6	Mutch, George	39	81	Jones, Tommy	4	156	Vance, James	1
7	Smith, Dick	35	82	Kennedy, Fred	4	157	Vincent, Ernest	1
8	Donaldson, Bob	33	83	Lappin, Harry	4	158	Vose, George	1
9	Boyd, Henry	32	84	McDonald, Willie	4	159	Wassall, Jackie	1
10	Manley, Tom	32	85	Morgan, Hugh	4	160	Wood, John	1
11	Arkesden, Tommy	28	86	Warburton, Arthur	4	161	Wrigglesworth, Billy	1
12	Schofield, Alf	28	87	Black, Dick	3		own goals	25
13	Bryant, William	27	88	Bonthron, Bob	3			
14	Griffiths, Billy	27	89	Brooks, William	3			
15	Reid, Tom	27	90	Byrne, David	3			
16	Rowley, Harry	27	91	Carey, Johnny	3			
17	Bryant, Billy	26	92	Ferrier, Ron	3			
18	Allan, Jack	21	93	Grimwood, John	3			
19	Picken, Jack	20	94	Grundy, John	3			
20	Clarkin, John	18	95	Hanson, Jimmy	3			
21	Brown, James (1932–34)	17	96	Mackie, Charlie	3			
22	Cape, Jack	17	97	Mann, Frank	3			
23	Gillespie, Matthew	17	98	McCalliog, Jim	3			
24	Pearson, Stuart	17	99	McLenahan, Hugh	3			
25	Collinson, Jimmy	16	100	Morgan, Willie	3			
26	Sagar, Charles	16	101	Myerscough, Joe	3			
27	Goldthorpe, Ernie	15	102	Wall, George	3			
28	Henderson, William	15	103	Wombwell, Dick	3			
29	Leigh, Tom	15	104	Brown, William	2			
30	Dewar, Neil	14	105	Cunningham, John	2			
31	Gallimore, Stanley	14	106	Evans, Sidney	2			
32	Preston, Stephen	14	107	Fisher, James	2			
33	Ridding, Bill	14	108	Fitton, Arthur	2			
34	Grassam, Billy	13	109	Hall, Proctor	2			
35	Pegg, Dick	13	110	Hayes, Vince	2			
36	Peters, James	13	111	Heywood, Herbert	2			
37	Baird, Harry	12	112	MacDonald, Ken	2			
38	Beddow, John	12	113	Mann, Herbert	2			
39	Hine, Ernie	12	114	McBain, Neil	2			
40	Jackson, Bill	12	115	McMillen, Walter	2			
41	Daly, Gerry	11	116	Pearson, Stan	2			
42	Johnston, Billy	11	117	Redwood, Hubert	2			
43	Kennedy, William	11	118	Roberts, W	2			
44	Macari, Lou	11	119	Wedge, Frank	2			
45	McNaught, James	11	120	Williams, Harry (1920s)	2			
46	Downie, Alex	10	121	Aitken, John	1			
47	McKay, Bill	10	122	Ambler, Alfred	1			
48	Robertson, Alex	10	123	Bain, James	1			
49	Bain, David	9	124	Barber, Jack	1			
50	Roberts, Charlie	9	125	Beadsworth, Arthur	1			
51	Rowley, Jack	9	126	Brown, Jimmy (1935–39)	1			
52	Smith, Tom	9	127	Carman, James	1			
53	Cartwright, Walter	8	128	Chalmers, Stewart	1			
54	McPherson, Frank	8	129	Chester, Reg	1			
55	Smith, Jack	8	130	Coppell, Steve	1			
56	Duckworth, Dick	7	131	Davidson, Will	1			
57	Erentz, Fred	7	132	Ferguson, John	1			
58	McIlroy, Sammy	7	133	Fitchett, John	1			
59	Morrison, Tommy	7	134	Foley, G	1			
60	Parkinson, Robert	7	135	Forsyth, Alex	1			
61	Stewart, William	7	136	Gardner, Dick	1			
62	Williams, Harry (1900s)	7	137	Griffiths, Jack	1			
63	Ball, Jack	6	138	Higson, James	1			
64	Dow, John	6	139	Hilditch, Clarence	1			
65	Draycott, Billy	6	140	Holt, Edward	1			
66	Hopkinson, Samuel	6	141	Lang, Tommy	1			
67	Houston, Stewart	6	142	McCartney, John	1			
68	Morgan, Billy	6	143	McCartney, William	1			
69	Bell, Alex	5	144	Miller, James	1			
70	Jenkyns, Caesar	5	145	Owen, W	1			
71	Lee, Edwin	5	146	Radford, Charlie	1			
72	Millar, George	5	147	Richards, Billy	1			
73	Pape, Albert	5	148	Richards, Charlie	1			
74	Boyd, William	4	149	Robertson, Sandy	1			
75	Coupar, Jimmy	4	150	Robertson, William	1			

ALL FA CUP MATCHES

#	PLAYER	GOALS	#	PLAYER	GOALS	#	PLAYER	GOALS
1	Law, Denis	34	76	Morris, Johnny	3	151	Heinze, Gabriel	1
2	Rowley, Jack	26	77	Mutch, George	3	152	Houston, Stewart	1
3	Best, George	21	78	Robins, Mark	3	153	Ince, Paul	1
4	Pearson, Stan	21	79	Saha, Louis	3	154	Johnsen, Ronnie	1
5	Charlton, Bobby	19	80	Sharpe, Lee	3	155	Kennedy, William	1
6	Hughes, Mark	17	81	Yorke, Dwight	3	156	Kinsey, Albert	1
7	Herd, David	15	82	Anderson, George	2	157	Larsson, Henrik	1
8	McClair, Brian	14	83	Byrne, Roger	2	158	Mackie, Charlie	1
9	van Nistelrooy, Ruud	14	84	Cantwell, Noel	2	159	Manley, Tom	1
10	Scholes, Paul	12	85	Connelly, John	2	160	Martin, Lee (1990s)	1
11	Mitten, Charlie	11	86	Downie, Alex	2	161	McLenahan, Hugh	1
12	Cantona, Eric	10	87	Giles, Johnny	2	162	Miller, Tom	1
13	Donaldson, Bob	10	88	Gowling, Alan	2	163	Moore, Graham	1
14	Giggs, Ryan	10	89	Greenhoff, Brian	2	164	Moran, Kevin	1
15	Robson, Bryan	10	90	Hanlon, Jimmy	2	165	Morgan, Billy	1
16	Spence, Joe	10	91	Hopkinson, Samuel	2	166	Morrison, Tommy	1
17	Turnbull, Sandy	10	92	Jackson, Bill	2	167	Moses, Remi	1
18	Whiteside, Norman	10	93	Jordan, Joe	2	168	Muhren, Arnold	1
19	Cassidy, Joe	9	94	Keane, Roy	2	169	Neville, Philip	1
20	Cole, Andrew	9	95	Lewis, Eddie	2	170	Nicholl, Jimmy	1
21	Greenhoff, Jimmy	9	96	McGrath, Paul	2	171	Nicholson, Jimmy	1
22	Halse, Harold	9	97	McQueen, Gordon	2	172	O'Shea, John	1
23	Ronaldo, Cristiano	9	98	Olsen, Jesper	2	173	Parker, Paul	1
24	Wall, George	9	99	Pallister, Gary	2	174	Pearson, Mark	1
25	Dawson, Alex	8	100	Partridge, Teddy	2	175	Peden, Jack	1
26	Kidd, Brian	8	101	Rossi, Giuseppe	2	176	Peters, James	1
27	Macari, Lou	8	102	Rothwell, Charles	2	177	Phelan, Mike	1
28	Rooney, Wayne	8	103	Smith, Dick	2	178	Redwood, Hubert	1
29	Solskjaer, Ole Gunnar	8	104	Strachan, Gordon	2	179	Rennox, Charlie	1
30	West, Enoch	8	105	Thomas, Mickey	2	180	Richards, Charlie	1
31	Irwin, Denis	7	106	Wallace, Danny	2	181	Roberts, Charlie	1
32	McPherson, Frank	7	107	Wrigglesworth, Billy	2	182	Sadler, David	1
33	Pegg, Dick	7	108	Allan, Jack	1	183	Sapsford, George	1
34	Picken, Jack	7	109	Anderson, John	1	184	Sartori, Carlo	1
35	Stapleton, Frank	7	110	Anderson, Viv	1	185	Scanlon, Albert	1
36	Beckham, David	6	111	Aston, John (junior)	1	186	Setters, Maurice	1
37	Bryant, William	6	112	Aston, John (senior)	1	187	Silvestre, Mikael	1
38	Burke, Ronnie	6	113	Bainbridge, Bill	1	188	Smith, Jack	1
39	Farman, Alf	6	114	Ball, Jack	1	189	Sneddon, J	1
40	Hill, Gordon	6	115	Banks, Jack	1	190	Stafford, Harry	1
41	McIlroy, Sammy	6	116	Bannister, Jimmy	1	191	Sweeney, Eric	1
42	Peddie, Jack	6	117	Barber, Jack	1	192	Taylor, Chris	1
43	Turnbull, Jimmy	6	118	Beadsworth, Arthur	1	193	Taylor, Ernie	1
44	Arkesden, Tommy	5	119	Bennion, Ray	1	194	Thomas, Harry	1
45	Daly, Gerry	5	120	Birch, Brian	1	195	Toms, Billy	1
46	Hanson, Jimmy	5	121	Birtles, Gary	1	196	Warner, Jack	1
47	Pearson, Stuart	5	122	Blackmore, Clayton	1	197	Webb, Neil	1
48	Schofield, Alf	5	123	Blanchflower, Jackie	1	198	Wilkins, Ray	1
49	Sheringham, Teddy	5	124	Boyd, Henry	1	199	Williams, Harry (1900s)	1
50	Taylor, Tommy	5	125	Bradley, Warren	1	200	Woodcock, Wilf	1
51	Viollet, Dennis	5	126	Buckle, Ted	1			
52	Bamford, Tommy	4	127	Butt, Nicky	1		own goals	12
53	Berry, Johnny	4	128	Carey, Johnny	1			
54	Coppell, Steve	4	129	Carrick, Michael	1			
55	Crerand, Pat	4	130	Chisnall, Phil	1			
56	Gillespie, Matthew	4	131	Collinson, Jimmy	1			
57	Kanchelskis, Andrei	4	132	Craig, T	1			
58	Morgan, Willie	4	133	Doughty, Roger	1			
59	Quixall, Albert	4	134	Downie, John	1			
60	Reid, Tom	4	135	Duxbury, Mike	1			
61	Richardson, Kieran	4	136	Edwards, Duncan	1			
62	Sagar, Charles	4	137	Evans, George	1			
63	Smith, Tom	4	138	Fisher, James	1			
64	Webster, Colin	4	139	Fitzpatrick, John	1			
65	Whelan, William	4	140	Forlan, Diego	1			
66	Williams, Fred	4	141	Forsyth, Alex	1			
67	Baird, Harry	3	142	Fortune, Quinton	1			
68	Beddow, John	3	143	Gallimore, Stanley	1			
69	Brennan, Shay	3	144	Gill, Tony	1			
70	Bruce, Steve	3	145	Gillespie, Keith	1			
71	Delaney, Jimmy	3	146	Goldthorpe, Ernie	1			
72	Doughty, Jack	3	147	Goodwin, Fred	1			
73	Edge, Alf	3	148	Graham, Deiniol	1			
74	Griffiths, Billy	3	149	Grassam, Billy	1			
75	Johnston, Billy	3	150	Grimes, Ashley	1			

ALL LEAGUE CUP MATCHES

#	PLAYER	GOALS	#	PLAYER	GOALS	#	PLAYER	GOALS
1	McClair, Brian	19	31	Wallace, Danny	3	61	Graham, Arthur	1
2	Hughes, Mark	16	32	Barnes, Peter	2	62	Greenhoff, Jimmy	1
3	Macari, Lou	10	33	Bellion, David	2	63	Herd, David	1
4	Best, George	9	34	Greenhoff, Brian	2	64	Lee, Kieran	1
5	Coppell, Steve	9	35	Houston, Stewart	2	65	May, David	1
6	Sharpe, Lee	9	36	Ince, Paul	2	66	McCreery, David	1
7	Whiteside, Norman	9	37	Jordan, Joe	2	67	Muhren, Arnold	1
8	Scholes, Paul	8	38	McGrath, Paul	2	68	Nevland, Erik	1
9	Charlton, Bobby	7	39	Miller, Liam	2	69	Nicholl, Jimmy	1
10	Giggs, Ryan	7	40	Moran, Kevin	2	70	Olsen, Jesper	1
11	Kidd, Brian	7	41	Quixall, Albert	2	71	O'Shea, John	1
12	Saha, Louis	7	42	Robins, Mark	2	72	Park, Ji-Sung	1
13	Solskjaer, Ole Gunnar	7	43	Ronaldo, Cristiano	2	73	Pearson, Mark	1
14	Bruce, Steve	6	44	Rooney, Wayne	2	74	Poborsky, Karel	1
15	McIlroy, Sammy	6	45	Thomas, Mickey	2	75	Rossi, Giuseppe	1
16	Stapleton, Frank	6	46	van Nistelrooy, Ruud	2	76	Sadler, David	1
17	Pearson, Stuart	5	47	Yorke, Dwight	2	77	Sheringham, Teddy	1
18	Robson, Bryan	5	48	Albiston, Arthur	1	78	Smith, Alan	1
19	Daly, Gerry	4	49	Anderson, Viv	1	79	Storey-Moore, Ian	1
20	Davenport, Peter	4	50	Beckham, David	1	80	Strachan, Gordon	1
21	Hill, Gordon	4	51	Cantona, Eric	1	81	Viollet, Dennis	1
22	McQueen, Gordon	4	52	Cooke, Terry	1	82	Webb, Neil	1
23	Moses, Remi	4	53	Dawson, Alex	1	83	Wilkins, Ray	1
24	Blackmore, Clayton	3	54	Djemba-Djemba, Eric	1		own goals	5
25	Brazil, Alan	3	55	Dublin, Dion	1			
26	Forlan, Diego	3	56	Ebanks-Blake, Sylvan	1			
27	Kanchelskis, Andrei	3	57	Edwards, Paul	1			
28	Law, Denis	3	58	Fitzpatrick, John	1			
29	Morgan, Willie	3	59	Giles, Johnny	1			
30	Richardson, Kieran	3	60	Gowling, Alan	1			

ALL EUROPEAN MATCHES

#	PLAYER	GOALS	#	PLAYER	GOALS	#	PLAYER	GOALS
1	van Nistelrooy, Ruud	38	31	Berry, Johnny	3	61	Chisnall, Phil	1
2	Law, Denis	28	32	Blanc, Laurent	3	62	Colman, Eddie	1
3	Giggs, Ryan	25	33	Coppell, Steve	3	63	Crerand, Pat	1
4	Scholes, Paul	23	34	Forlan, Diego	3	64	Davies, Alan	1
5	Charlton, Bobby	22	35	Kidd, Brian	3	65	Davies, Simon	1
6	Solskjaer, Ole Gunnar	20	36	Muhren, Arnold	3	66	Djemba-Djemba, Eric	1
7	Cole, Andrew	19	37	Sadler, David	3	67	Evra, Patrice	1
8	Beckham, David	15	38	Sharpe, Lee	3	68	Ferdinand, Rio	1
9	Herd, David	14	39	Smith, Alan	3	69	Graham, Arthur	1
10	Keane, Roy	14	40	Bellion, David	2	70	Kanchelskis, Andrei	1
11	Viollet, Dennis	13	41	Blackmore, Clayton	2	71	Larsson, Henrik	1
12	Ronaldo, Cristiano	12	42	Butt, Nicky	2	72	Macari, Lou	1
13	Rooney, Wayne	12	43	Carrick, Michael	2	73	May, David	1
14	Best, George	11	44	Fortune, Quinton	2	74	Morgan, Willie	1
15	Connelly, John	11	45	Foulkes, Bill	2	75	Nicholl, Jimmy	1
16	Taylor, Tommy	11	46	Heinze, Gabriel	2	76	O'Shea, John	1
17	Yorke, Dwight	11	47	Hill, Gordon	2	77	Pallister, Gary	1
18	Hughes, Mark	9	48	McIlroy, Sammy	2	78	Pearson, Stuart	1
19	Sheringham, Teddy	9	49	Neville, Gary	2	79	Robins, Mark	1
20	Robson, Bryan	8	50	Neville, Phil	2	80	Sartori, Carlo	1
21	Bruce, Steve	6	51	Pique, Gerard	2	81	Schmeichel, Peter	1
22	Cantona, Eric	5	52	Richardson, Kieran	2	82	Setters, Maurice	1
23	McClair, Brian	5	53	Silvestre, Mikael	2	83	Taylor, Ernie	1
24	Stapleton, Frank	5	54	Stiles, Nobby	2	84	Vidic, Nemanja	1
25	Whelan, William	5	55	Strachan, Gordon	2	85	Webb, Neil	1
26	Irwin, Denis	4	56	Aston, John (Jnr)	1	86	Webster, Colin	1
27	Pegg, David	4	57	Berg, Henning	1	87	Whiteside, Norman	1
28	Saha, Louis	4	58	Brazil, Alan	1	88	Wilkins, Ray	1
29	Tevez, Carlos	4	59	Brown, Wes	1		own goals	12
30	Veron, Juan-Sebastian	4	60	Burns, Francis	1			

ALL EUROPEAN CUP / CHAMPIONS LEAGUE MATCHES

#	PLAYER	GOALS	#	PLAYER	GOALS	#	PLAYER	GOALS
1	van Nistelrooy, Ruud	38	26	Berry, Johnny	3	51	Colman, Eddie	1
2	Giggs, Ryan	25	27	Blanc, Laurent	3	52	Crerand, Pat	1
3	Scholes, Paul	22	28	Forlan, Diego	3	53	Davies, Simon	1
4	Solskjaer, Ole Gunnar	20	29	Kidd, Brian	3	54	Djemba-Djemba, Eric	1
5	Cole, Andrew	19	30	Sadler, David	3	55	Evra, Patrice	1
6	Beckham, David	15	31	Smith, Alan	3	56	Ferdinand, Rio	1
7	Keane, Roy	14	32	Bellion, David	2	57	Kanchelskis, Andrei	1
8	Law, Denis	14	33	Bruce, Steve	2	58	Larsson, Henrik	1
9	Viollet, Dennis	13	34	Butt, Nicky	2	59	May, David	1
10	Ronaldo, Cristiano	12	35	Carrick, Michael	2	60	Morgan, Willie	1
11	Rooney, Wayne	12	36	Fortune, Quinton	2	61	O'Shea, John	1
12	Taylor, Tommy	11	37	Foulkes, Bill	2	62	Robson, Bryan	1
13	Yorke, Dwight	11	38	Heinze, Gabriel	2	63	Sartori, Carlo	1
14	Charlton, Bobby	10	39	Hughes, Mark	2	64	Taylor, Ernie	1
15	Best, George	9	40	Neville, Gary	2	65	Vidic, Nemanja	1
16	Sheringham, Teddy	9	41	Neville, Phil	2	66	Webster, Colin	1
17	Connelly, John	6	42	Pique, Gerard	2		own goals	9
18	Cantona, Eric	5	43	Richardson, Kieran	2			
19	Herd, David	5	44	Sharpe, Lee	2			
20	Whelan, William	5	45	Silvestre, Mikael	2			
21	Irwin, Denis	4	46	Stiles, Nobby	2			
22	Pegg, David	4	47	Aston, John (Jnr)	1			
23	Saha, Louis	4	48	Berg, Henning	1			
24	Tevez, Carlos	4	49	Brown, Wes	1			
25	Veron, Juan-Sebastian	4	50	Burns, Francis	1			

ALL EUROPEAN CUP-WINNERS' CUP MATCHES

#	PLAYER	GOALS	#	PLAYER	GOALS	#	PLAYER	GOALS
1	Law, Denis	6	11	Chisnall, Phil	1	21	Webb, Neil	1
2	Hughes, Mark	5	12	Davies, Alan	1	22	Whiteside, Norman	1
3	McClair, Brian	5	13	Graham, Arthur	1	23	Wilkins, Ray	1
4	Bruce, Steve	4	14	Hill, Gordon	1		own goals	2
5	Charlton, Bobby	4	15	Nicholl, Jimmy	1			
6	Robson, Bryan	4	16	Pallister, Gary	1			
7	Stapleton, Frank	4	17	Pearson, Stuart	1			
8	Coppell, Steve	3	18	Robins, Mark	1			
9	Herd, David	3	19	Setters, Maurice	1			
10	Blackmore, Clayton	2	20	Sharpe, Lee	1			

ALL UEFA CUP / INTER-CITIES' FAIRS CUP MATCHES

#	PLAYER	GOALS	#	PLAYER	GOALS	#	PLAYER	GOALS
1	Charlton, Bobby	8	7	Best, George	2	13	Macari, Lou	1
2	Law, Denis	8	8	Hughes, Mark	2	14	Schmeichel, Peter	1
3	Herd, David	6	9	McIlroy, Sammy	2	15	Scholes, Paul	1
4	Connelly, John	5	10	Strachan, Gordon	2	16	Stapleton, Frank	1
5	Muhren, Arnold	3	11	Brazil, Alan	1		own goal	1
6	Robson, Bryan	3	12	Hill, Gordon	1			

ALL OTHER COMPETITIVE MATCHES

#	PLAYER	GOALS	#	PLAYER	GOALS	#	PLAYER	GOALS
1	Halse, Harold	6	16	Berry, Johnny	1	31	McClair, Brian	1
2	Farman, Alf	4	17	Best, George	1	32	Meredith, Billy	1
3	Rowley, Jack	3	18	Blackmore, Clayton	1	33	Morgan, Willie	1
4	Taylor, Tommy	3	19	Burke, Ronnie	1	34	Silvestre, Mikael	1
5	Turnbull, Jimmy	3	20	Byrne, Roger	1	35	Smith, Alan	1
6	Boyd, Henry	2	21	Cassidy, Joe	1	36	Turnbull, Sandy	1
7	Butt, Nicky	2	22	Coupar, Jimmy	1	37	van Nistelrooy, Ruud	1
8	Cantona, Eric	2	23	Downie, John	1	38	Viollet, Dennis	1
9	Charlton, Bobby	2	24	Giggs, Ryan	1		own goal	1
10	Fortune, Quinton	2	25	Herd, David	1			
11	Keane, Roy	2	26	Hughes, Mark	1			
12	Robson, Bryan	2	27	Ince, Paul	1			
13	Wall, George	2	28	Jenkyns, Caesar	1			
14	Yorke, Dwight	2	29	Johnsen, Ronny	1			
15	Beckham, David	1	30	Law, Denis	1			

MANCHESTER UNITED
The Complete Record

Chapter 2.4
Substitutes and Their Goals

ALL COMPETITIVE MATCHES

	PREM		FLD 1		FLD 2		FAC		LC		EC/CL		ECWC		UEFA		OTHER		TOTAL	
	A	G	A	G	A	G	A	G	A	G	A	G	A	G	A	G	A	G	A	G
1 Solskjaer, Ole Gunnar	84	16	-	-	-	-	15	3	3	1	45	8	-	-	-	-	3	-	150	28
2 Scholes, Paul	67	4	-	-	-	-	12	1	5	-	11	2	-	-	1	1	-	-	96	8
3 Giggs, Ryan	59	2	7	1	-	-	7	2	5	1	11	3	-	-	-	-	1	-	90	9
4 Neville, Phil	53	-	-	-	-	-	6	-	1	-	22	-	-	-	-	-	3	-	85	-
5 Butt, Nicky	60	-	-	-	-	-	6	-	1	-	13	-	-	-	-	-	-	-	80	-
6 McClair, Brian	56	1	3	3	-	-	7	1	1	-	6	-	-	-	-	-	-	-	73	5
7 O'Shea, John	53	3	-	-	-	-	5	-	1	-	13	-	-	-	-	-	1	-	73	3
8 Forlan, Diego	40	4	-	-	-	-	2	-	2	-	15	1	-	-	-	-	2	-	61	5
9 McCreery, David	-	-	37	3	2	-	6	-	4	-	-	-	-	-	3	-	1	-	53	3
10 Sheringham, Teddy	31	4	-	-	-	-	5	3	-	-	11	1	-	-	-	-	5	-	52	8
11 Sharpe, Lee	16	-	17	-	-	-	7	-	8	-	-	-	2	-	-	-	-	-	50	-
12 Saha, Louis	34	4	-	-	-	-	4	-	-	-	10	-	-	-	-	-	-	-	48	4
13 Fletcher, Darren	28	-	-	-	-	-	7	-	-	-	9	-	-	-	-	-	2	-	46	-
14 Cole, Andrew	34	6	-	-	-	-	2	-	-	-	7	1	-	-	-	-	1	-	44	7
15 Blackmore, Clayton	2	-	34	3	-	-	6	-	2	-	-	-	-	-	-	-	-	-	44	3
16 Robins, Mark	-	-	29	4	-	-	4	1	7	2	-	-	2	-	-	-	1	-	43	7
17 Ronaldo, Cristiano	37	6	-	-	-	-	3	-	-	-	3	-	-	-	-	-	-	-	43	6
18 Beckham, David	28	6	-	-	-	-	2	-	2	-	4	2	-	-	-	-	2	-	38	8
19 Fortune, Quinton	23	1	-	-	-	-	1	-	-	-	12	-	-	-	-	-	2	-	38	1
20 Richardson, Kieran	21	-	-	-	-	-	2	1	2	1	11	2	-	-	-	-	1	-	37	4
21 Silvestre, Mikael	24	1	-	-	-	-	2	-	1	-	8	-	-	-	-	-	-	-	35	1
22 Beardsmore, Russell	-	-	26	1	-	-	4	-	1	-	-	-	3	-	-	-	-	-	34	1
23 Brown, Wes	23	-	-	-	-	-	2	-	2	-	7	-	-	-	-	-	-	-	34	-
24 Duxbury, Mike	-	-	25	-	-	-	5	1	2	-	-	-	-	-	1	-	-	-	33	1
25 Cruyff, Jordi	19	5	-	-	-	-	1	-	-	-	7	-	-	-	-	-	5	-	32	5
26 Yorke, Dwight	16	3	-	-	-	-	5	-	-	-	8	1	-	-	-	-	3	-	32	4
27 Smith, Alan	18	1	-	-	-	-	6	-	2	-	6	-	-	-	-	-	-	-	32	1
28 Grimes, Ashley	-	-	28	3	-	-	-	-	-	-	-	-	2	-	-	-	-	-	30	3
29 Park, Ji-Sung	21	-	-	-	-	-	2	-	-	-	7	-	-	-	-	-	-	-	30	-
30 Kanchelskis, Andrei	21	-	6	-	-	-	1	-	1	-	-	-	-	-	-	-	-	-	29	-
31 McIlroy, Sammy	-	-	21	2	1	-	3	-	3	1	-	-	-	-	-	-	-	-	28	3
32 Macari, Lou	-	-	16	1	2	-	3	-	5	-	-	-	-	-	1	-	-	-	27	1
33 Neville, Gary	15	-	-	-	-	-	3	-	1	-	6	-	-	-	1	-	1	-	27	-
34 Olsen, Jesper	-	-	20	-	-	-	3	-	3	-	-	-	-	-	1	-	-	-	27	-
35 Bellion, David	19	2	-	-	-	-	1	-	-	-	5	1	-	-	-	-	-	-	25	3
36 Martin, Lee (1990s)	-	-	17	-	-	-	1	-	2	-	1	-	4	-	-	-	-	-	25	-
37 Robson, Bryan	14	-	5	1	-	-	2	-	1	1	-	-	-	-	1	-	1	-	24	2
38 Davenport, Peter	-	-	19	-	-	-	2	-	2	-	-	-	-	-	-	-	-	-	23	-
39 Keane, Roy	17	2	-	-	-	-	2	-	2	-	1	-	-	-	-	-	-	-	22	2
40 Berg, Henning	17	1	-	-	-	-	-	-	-	-	4	-	-	-	-	-	1	-	22	1
41 Aston, John (Jnr)	-	-	16	1	-	-	2	1	3	-	-	-	-	-	-	-	-	-	21	2
42 Chadwick, Luke	14	2	-	-	-	-	2	-	-	-	5	-	-	-	-	-	-	-	21	2
43 Stapleton, Frank	-	-	19	2	-	-	-	-	1	-	-	-	-	-	1	-	-	-	21	2
44 Donaghy, Mal	-	-	13	-	-	-	-	-	5	-	-	-	3	-	-	-	-	-	21	-
45 Poborsky, Karel	14	3	-	-	-	-	-	-	-	-	5	-	-	-	-	-	1	-	20	3
46 May, David	17	-	-	-	-	-	-	-	-	-	2	-	-	-	-	-	1	-	20	-
47 van Nistelrooy, Ruud	13	4	-	-	-	-	3	2	1	-	2	1	-	-	-	-	-	-	19	7
48 Johnsen, Ronny	14	-	-	-	-	-	2	-	-	-	3	-	-	-	-	-	-	-	19	-
49 McGrath, Chris	-	-	16	-	-	-	-	-	2	-	-	-	-	-	1	-	-	-	19	-
50 O'Brien, Liam	-	-	15	-	-	-	2	-	2	-	-	-	-	-	-	-	-	-	19	-
51 Phelan, Mike	7	-	7	-	-	-	-	-	2	-	3	-	-	-	-	-	-	-	19	-
52 Rooney, Wayne	11	-	-	-	-	-	4	3	2	-	1	-	-	-	-	-	-	-	18	3
53 Whiteside, Norman	-	-	13	2	-	-	-	-	3	-	-	-	1	1	1	-	-	-	18	3
54 Wallace, Danny	2	-	9	-	-	-	2	1	3	-	-	-	2	-	-	-	-	-	18	1
55 Albiston, Arthur	-	-	15	-	-	-	-	-	2	-	-	-	-	-	1	-	-	-	18	-
56 Irwin, Denis	10	-	2	-	-	-	1	-	3	-	2	-	-	-	-	-	-	-	18	-
57 Wallwork, Ronnie	15	-	-	-	-	-	1	-	1	-	1	-	-	-	-	-	-	-	18	-
58 Young, Tony	-	-	6	-	8	-	-	-	4	-	-	-	-	-	-	-	-	-	18	-
59 Brazil, Alan	-	-	13	1	-	-	1	-	3	-	-	-	-	-	-	-	-	-	17	1
60 Nani	10	1	-	-	-	-	-	-	-	-	4	-	-	-	-	-	1	-	15	1
61 Sartori, Carlo	-	-	13	1	-	-	-	-	2	-	-	-	-	-	-	-	-	-	15	1
62 Carrick, Michael	11	1	-	-	-	-	1	-	1	-	1	-	-	-	-	-	-	-	14	1
63 Greening, Jonathan	10	-	-	-	-	-	1	-	-	-	2	-	-	-	-	-	1	-	14	-
64 Hughes, Mark	1	-	8	-	-	-	1	-	1	-	-	-	3	-	-	-	-	-	14	-
65 Evra, Patrice	6	-	-	-	-	-	2	-	2	-	3	1	-	-	-	-	-	-	13	1
66 Anderson	8	-	-	-	-	-	2	-	-	-	3	-	-	-	-	-	-	-	13	-
67 Burns, Francis	-	-	10	-	-	-	1	-	1	-	1	-	-	-	-	-	-	-	13	-
68 Nicholl, Jimmy	-	-	8	-	1	-	4	-	-	-	-	-	-	-	-	-	-	-	13	-
69 Djemba-Djemba, Eric	7	-	-	-	-	-	1	-	-	-	3	-	-	-	-	-	1	-	12	1
70 Gibson, Terry	-	-	9	-	-	-	1	-	2	-	-	-	-	-	-	-	-	-	12	-
71 McGarvey, Scott	-	-	12	-	-	-	-	-	-	-	-	-	-	-	-	-	-	-	12	-
72 van der Gouw, Raimond	11	-	-	-	-	-	-	-	1	-	-	-	-	-	-	-	-	-	12	-
73 Dublin, Dion	8	1	-	-	-	-	1	-	-	-	1	-	-	-	-	-	-	-	11	1
74 Hargreaves, Owen	7	-	-	-	-	-	-	-	-	-	3	-	-	-	-	-	-	-	11	-
75 Miller, Liam	6	-	-	-	-	-	2	-	-	-	3	-	-	-	-	-	-	-	11	-

continued../

ALL COMPETITIVE MATCHES (continued)

	PREM		FLD 1		FLD 2		FAC		LC		EC/CL		ECWC		UEFA		OTHER		TOTAL	
	A	G	A	G	A	G	A	G	A	G	A	G	A	G	A	G	A	G	A	G
76 Moses, Remi	–	–	7	–	–	–	–	–	2	–	–	–	1	–	–	–	1	–	11	–
77 Eagles, Chris	4	1	–	–	–	–	–	–	4	–	1	–	–	–	–	–	1	–	10	1
78 Curtis, John	9	–	–	–	–	–	–	–	–	–	–	–	–	–	–	–	1	–	10	–
79 Davies, Ron	–	–	–	–	8	–	2	–	–	–	–	–	–	–	–	–	–	–	10	–
80 Davies, Simon	7	–	–	–	–	–	–	–	2	–	–	–	1	–	–	–	–	–	10	–
81 Gowling, Alan	–	–	7	–	–	–	2	–	1	–	–	–	–	–	–	–	–	–	10	–
82 Ritchie, Andy	–	–	7	–	–	–	1	–	2	–	–	–	–	–	–	–	–	–	10	–
83 Tevez, Carlos	3	–	–	–	–	–	–	–	–	–	6	2	–	–	–	–	–	–	9	2
84 Parker, Paul	3	–	2	–	–	–	1	1	–	–	1	–	–	–	2	–	–	–	9	1
85 Blomqvist, Jesper	5	–	–	–	–	–	2	–	1	–	1	–	–	–	–	–	–	–	9	–
86 Clegg, Michael	5	–	–	–	–	–	1	–	1	–	2	–	–	–	–	–	–	–	9	–
87 Kidd, Brian	–	–	8	–	–	–	1	–	–	–	–	–	–	–	–	–	–	–	9	–
88 Pique, Gerard	6	–	–	–	–	–	–	–	2	–	1	–	–	–	–	–	–	–	9	–
89 Rossi, Guiseppe	4	1	–	–	–	–	–	–	2	–	2	–	–	–	–	–	–	–	8	1
90 Bardsley, Phil	5	–	–	–	–	–	1	–	1	–	1	–	–	–	–	–	–	–	8	–
91 Ferguson, Darren	2	–	5	–	–	–	–	–	1	–	–	–	–	–	–	–	–	–	8	–
92 Heinze, Gabriel	7	–	–	–	–	–	–	–	–	–	1	–	–	–	–	–	–	–	8	–
93 Sloan, Tom	–	–	7	–	–	–	–	–	1	–	–	–	–	–	–	–	–	–	8	–
94 Thornley, Ben	8	–	–	–	–	–	–	–	–	–	–	–	–	–	–	–	–	–	8	–
95 Gillespie, Keith	6	1	–	–	–	–	1	–	–	–	–	–	–	–	–	–	–	–	7	1
96 Sadler, David	–	–	6	1	–	–	1	–	–	–	–	–	–	–	–	–	–	–	7	1
97 Gill, Tony	–	–	5	–	–	–	2	–	–	–	–	–	–	–	–	–	–	–	7	–
98 Martin, Mick	–	–	6	–	1	–	–	–	–	–	–	–	–	–	–	–	–	–	7	–
99 McGrath, Paul	–	–	4	–	–	–	3	–	–	–	–	–	–	–	–	–	–	–	7	–
100 Stewart, Michael	2	–	–	–	–	–	1	–	2	–	2	–	–	–	–	–	–	–	7	–
101 Veron, Juan–Sebastian	6	–	–	–	–	–	–	–	1	–	–	–	–	–	–	–	–	–	7	–
102 Anderson, Trevor	–	–	6	–	–	–	–	–	–	–	–	–	–	–	–	–	–	–	6	–
103 Cooke, Terry	3	–	–	–	–	–	–	–	2	–	–	–	–	–	1	–	–	–	6	–
104 Fitzpatrick, John	–	–	6	–	–	–	–	–	–	–	–	–	–	–	–	–	–	–	6	–
105 Gibson, Colin	–	–	5	–	–	–	1	–	–	–	–	–	–	–	–	–	–	–	6	–
106 Kleberson, Jose	4	–	–	–	–	–	–	–	–	–	2	–	–	–	–	–	–	–	6	–
107 Law, Denis	–	–	4	–	–	–	2	–	–	–	–	–	–	–	–	–	–	–	6	–
108 Maiorana, Jules	–	–	5	–	–	–	–	–	1	–	–	–	–	–	–	–	–	–	6	–
109 Strachan, Gordon	–	–	5	–	–	–	–	–	1	–	–	–	–	–	–	–	–	–	6	–
110 Wilson, David	–	–	4	–	–	–	2	–	–	–	–	–	–	–	–	–	–	–	6	–
111 Anderson, Viv	–	–	4	–	–	–	–	–	1	–	–	–	–	–	–	–	–	–	5	–
112 Daly, Gerry	–	–	3	–	1	–	1	–	–	–	–	–	–	–	–	–	–	–	5	–
113 Fletcher, Peter	–	–	5	–	–	–	–	–	–	–	–	–	–	–	–	–	–	–	5	–
114 Graham, Arthur	–	–	4	–	–	–	–	–	–	–	–	–	1	–	–	–	–	–	5	–
115 Ince, Paul	–	–	3	–	–	–	1	–	1	–	–	–	–	–	–	–	–	–	5	–
116 Moran, Kevin	–	–	3	–	–	–	–	–	1	–	–	–	–	–	1	–	–	–	5	–
117 Muhren, Arnold	–	–	5	–	–	–	–	–	–	–	–	–	–	–	–	–	–	–	5	–
118 Paterson, Steve	–	–	3	–	–	–	–	–	–	–	–	–	–	–	2	–	–	–	5	–
119 Webb, Neil	1	–	4	–	–	–	–	–	–	–	–	–	–	–	–	–	–	–	5	–
120 Nevland, Erik	1	–	–	–	–	–	1	–	2	1	–	–	–	–	–	–	–	–	4	1
121 Blanc, Laurent	4	–	–	–	–	–	–	–	–	–	–	–	–	–	–	–	–	–	4	–
122 Buchan, George	–	–	3	–	–	–	–	–	1	–	–	–	–	–	–	–	–	–	4	–
123 Carroll, Roy	3	–	–	–	–	–	1	–	–	–	–	–	–	–	–	–	–	–	4	–
124 Ferdinand, Rio	1	–	–	–	–	–	1	–	1	–	1	–	–	–	–	–	–	–	4	–
125 Garton, Billy	–	–	2	–	–	–	–	–	1	–	–	–	–	–	1	–	–	–	4	–
126 Gidman, John	–	–	1	–	–	–	–	–	–	–	–	–	1	–	1	–	1	–	4	–
127 Givens, Don	–	–	4	–	–	–	–	–	–	–	–	–	–	–	–	–	–	–	4	–
128 Greenhoff, Jimmy	–	–	3	–	–	–	1	–	–	–	–	–	–	–	–	–	–	–	4	–
129 Kuszczak, Tomasz	1	–	–	–	–	–	1	–	–	–	2	–	–	–	–	–	–	–	4	–
130 Milne, Ralph	–	–	4	–	–	–	–	–	–	–	–	–	–	–	–	–	–	–	4	–
131 Pallister, Gary	–	–	3	–	–	–	–	–	–	–	–	–	1	–	–	–	–	–	4	–
132 Pugh, Danny	1	–	–	–	–	–	1	–	–	–	2	–	–	–	–	–	–	–	4	–
133 Simpson, Danny	2	–	–	–	–	–	1	–	1	–	–	–	–	–	–	–	–	–	4	–
134 Spector, Jonathan	1	–	–	–	–	–	1	–	1	–	–	–	–	–	1	–	–	–	4	–
135 Vidic, Nemanja	2	–	–	–	–	–	2	–	–	–	–	–	–	–	–	–	–	–	4	–
136 Wilson, Mark	2	–	–	–	–	–	–	–	–	–	2	–	–	–	–	–	–	–	4	–
137 Graham, Deiniol	–	–	1	–	–	–	1	1	1	–	–	–	–	–	–	–	–	–	3	1
138 Larsson, Henrik	2	1	–	–	–	–	1	–	–	–	–	–	–	–	–	–	–	–	3	1
139 Morgan, Willie	–	–	–	–	2	–	–	–	1	1	–	–	–	–	–	–	–	–	3	1
140 Ryan, Jimmy	–	–	3	1	–	–	–	–	–	–	–	–	–	–	–	–	–	–	3	1
141 Bruce, Steve	–	–	–	–	–	–	–	–	2	–	1	–	–	–	–	–	–	–	3	–
142 Casper, Chris	2	–	–	–	–	–	–	–	–	–	1	–	–	–	–	–	–	–	3	–
143 Coppell, Steve	–	–	1	–	1	–	–	–	–	–	–	–	–	–	1	–	–	–	3	–
144 Foggon, Alan	–	–	3	–	–	–	–	–	–	–	–	–	–	–	–	–	–	–	3	–
145 Forsyth, Alex	–	–	2	–	–	–	–	–	–	–	–	–	1	–	–	–	–	–	3	–
146 Foulkes, Bill	–	–	3	–	–	–	–	–	–	–	–	–	–	–	–	–	–	–	3	–
147 Greenhoff, Brian	–	–	1	–	2	–	–	–	–	–	–	–	–	–	–	–	–	–	3	–
148 Healy, David	1	–	–	–	–	–	–	–	2	–	–	–	–	–	–	–	–	–	3	–
149 Higginbotham, Danny	2	–	–	–	–	–	–	–	–	–	1	–	–	–	–	–	–	–	3	–
150 Nardiello, Daniel	–	–	–	–	–	–	–	–	2	–	1	–	–	–	–	–	–	–	3	–

continued../

ALL COMPETITIVE MATCHES (continued)

	PREM		FLD 1		FLD 2		FAC		LC		EC/CL		ECWC		UEFA		OTHER		TOTAL	
	A	G	A	G	A	G	A	G	A	G	A	G	A	G	A	G	A	G	A	G
151 Wilkins, Ray	–	–	2	–	–	–	–	–	1	–	–	–	–	–	–	–	–	–	3	–
152 Charlton, Bobby	–	–	2	1	–	–	–	–	–	–	–	–	–	–	–	–	–	–	2	1
153 Cunningham, Laurie	–	–	2	1	–	–	–	–	–	–	–	–	–	–	–	–	–	–	2	1
154 Davies, Alan	–	–	1	–	–	–	–	–	–	–	–	–	1	1	–	–	–	–	2	1
155 Lee, Kieran	–	–	–	–	–	–	–	–	2	1	–	–	–	–	–	–	–	–	2	1
156 Anderson, Willie	–	–	2	–	–	–	–	–	–	–	–	–	–	–	–	–	–	–	2	–
157 Bielby, Paul	–	–	2	–	–	–	–	–	–	–	–	–	–	–	–	–	–	–	2	–
158 Brazil, Derek	–	–	2	–	–	–	–	–	–	–	–	–	–	–	–	–	–	–	2	–
159 Campbell, Fraizer	1	–	–	–	–	–	–	–	1	–	–	–	–	–	–	–	–	–	2	–
160 Edwards, Paul	–	–	2	–	–	–	–	–	–	–	–	–	–	–	–	–	–	–	2	–
161 Graham, George	–	–	1	–	1	–	–	–	–	–	–	–	–	–	–	–	–	–	2	–
162 Grimshaw, Tony	–	–	1	–	–	–	–	–	1	–	–	–	–	–	–	–	–	–	2	–
163 Hogg, Graeme	–	–	1	–	–	–	–	–	1	–	–	–	–	–	–	–	–	–	2	–
164 Houston, Stewart	–	–	1	–	–	–	–	–	–	–	–	–	1	–	–	–	–	–	2	–
165 Jones, Richard	–	–	–	–	–	–	2	–	–	–	–	–	–	–	–	–	–	–	2	–
166 Kopel, Frank	–	–	2	–	–	–	–	–	–	–	–	–	–	–	–	–	–	–	2	–
167 O'Kane, John	1	–	–	–	–	–	–	–	1	–	–	–	–	–	–	–	–	–	2	–
168 Pilkington, Kevin	2	–	–	–	–	–	–	–	–	–	–	–	–	–	–	–	–	–	2	–
169 Rachubka, Paul	–	–	–	–	–	–	–	–	1	–	–	–	–	–	–	–	1	–	2	–
170 Ricardo, Felipe	1	–	–	–	–	–	–	–	–	–	1	–	–	–	–	–	–	–	2	–
171 Shawcross, Ryan	–	–	–	–	–	–	–	–	2	–	–	–	–	–	–	–	–	–	2	–
172 Sivebaek, Johnny	–	–	2	–	–	–	–	–	–	–	–	–	–	–	–	–	–	–	2	–
173 Stam, Jaap	–	–	–	–	–	–	1	–	–	–	–	–	–	–	–	–	1	–	2	–
174 Tomlinson, Graeme	–	–	–	–	–	–	–	–	2	–	–	–	–	–	–	–	–	–	2	–
175 Webber, Danny	–	–	–	–	–	–	–	–	1	–	1	–	–	–	–	–	–	–	2	–
176 Wood, Nicky	–	–	1	–	–	–	–	–	1	–	–	–	–	–	–	–	–	–	2	–
177 Wrattan, Paul	–	–	2	–	–	–	–	–	–	–	–	–	–	–	–	–	–	–	2	–
178 Pearson, Stuart	–	–	–	–	1	1	–	–	–	–	–	–	–	–	–	–	–	–	1	1
179 Appleton, Michael	–	–	–	–	–	–	–	–	1	–	–	–	–	–	–	–	–	–	1	–
180 Barnes, Michael	–	–	–	–	–	–	–	–	1	–	–	–	–	–	–	–	–	–	1	–
181 Barnes, Peter	–	–	1	–	–	–	–	–	–	–	–	–	–	–	–	–	–	–	1	–
182 Birtles, Gary	–	–	1	–	–	–	–	–	–	–	–	–	–	–	–	–	–	–	1	–
183 Brennan, Shay	–	–	1	–	–	–	–	–	–	–	–	–	–	–	–	–	–	–	1	–
184 Cantona, Eric	1	–	–	–	–	–	–	–	–	–	–	–	–	–	–	–	–	–	1	–
185 Clark, Jonathan	–	–	1	–	–	–	–	–	–	–	–	–	–	–	–	–	–	–	1	–
186 Connelly, John	–	–	1	–	–	–	–	–	–	–	–	–	–	–	–	–	–	–	1	–
187 Coyne, Peter	–	–	1	–	–	–	–	–	–	–	–	–	–	–	–	–	–	–	1	–
188 Crooks, Garth	–	–	1	–	–	–	–	–	–	–	–	–	–	–	–	–	–	–	1	–
189 Culkin, Nick	1	–	–	–	–	–	–	–	–	–	–	–	–	–	–	–	–	–	1	–
190 Davies, Wyn	–	–	1	–	–	–	–	–	–	–	–	–	–	–	–	–	–	–	1	–
191 Dempsey, Mark	–	–	–	–	–	–	–	–	–	–	–	–	1	–	–	–	–	–	1	–
192 Djordjic, Bojan	1	–	–	–	–	–	–	–	–	–	–	–	–	–	–	–	–	–	1	–
193 Dong, Fangzhuo	–	–	–	–	–	–	–	–	–	–	1	–	–	–	–	–	–	–	1	–
194 Dunne, Tony	–	–	–	–	–	–	1	–	–	–	–	–	–	–	–	–	–	–	1	–
195 Ebanks–Blake, Sylvan	–	–	–	–	–	–	–	–	1	–	–	–	–	–	–	–	–	–	1	–
196 Evans, Jonny	–	–	–	–	–	–	–	–	–	–	1	–	–	–	–	–	–	–	1	–
197 Gibson, Darron	–	–	–	–	–	–	–	–	1	–	–	–	–	–	–	–	–	–	1	–
198 Herd, David	–	–	1	–	–	–	–	–	–	–	–	–	–	–	–	–	–	–	1	–
199 Hill, Gordon	–	–	1	–	–	–	–	–	–	–	–	–	–	–	–	–	–	–	1	–
200 Howard, Tim	1	–	–	–	–	–	–	–	–	–	–	–	–	–	–	–	–	–	1	–
201 Jackson, Tommy	–	–	1	–	–	–	–	–	–	–	–	–	–	–	–	–	–	–	1	–
202 James, Steve	–	–	–	–	–	–	–	–	1	–	–	–	–	–	–	–	–	–	1	–
203 Johnson, Eddie	–	–	–	–	–	–	–	–	1	–	–	–	–	–	–	–	–	–	1	–
204 Jones, David (2004)	–	–	–	–	–	–	–	–	1	–	–	–	–	–	–	–	–	–	1	–
205 Jordan, Joe	–	–	–	–	–	–	1	–	–	–	–	–	–	–	–	–	–	–	1	–
206 Jovanovic, Nikki	–	–	1	–	–	–	–	–	–	–	–	–	–	–	–	–	–	–	1	–
207 Kelly, Jimmy	–	–	1	–	–	–	–	–	–	–	–	–	–	–	–	–	–	–	1	–
208 McCalliog, Jim	–	–	–	–	–	–	–	–	1	–	–	–	–	–	–	–	–	–	1	–
209 Mulryne, Philip	–	–	–	–	–	–	1	–	–	–	–	–	–	–	–	–	–	–	1	–
210 Notman, Alex	–	–	–	–	–	–	–	–	1	–	–	–	–	–	–	–	–	–	1	–
211 Rimmer, Jimmy	–	–	–	–	–	–	–	–	–	–	1	–	–	–	–	–	–	–	1	–
212 Roche, Lee	1	–	–	–	–	–	–	–	–	–	–	–	–	–	–	–	–	–	1	–
213 Sealey, Les	–	–	–	–	–	–	1	–	–	–	–	–	–	–	–	–	–	–	1	–
214 Timm, Mads	–	–	–	–	–	–	–	–	–	–	1	–	–	–	–	–	–	–	1	–
215 Twiss, Michael	–	–	–	–	–	–	1	–	–	–	–	–	–	–	–	–	–	–	1	–
216 Walsh, Gary	1	–	–	–	–	–	–	–	–	–	–	–	–	–	–	–	–	–	1	–
217 Wellens, Richard	–	–	–	–	–	–	–	–	1	–	–	–	–	–	–	–	–	–	1	–
218 Whelan, Anthony	–	–	1	–	–	–	–	–	–	–	–	–	–	–	–	–	–	–	1	–

ALL LEAGUE MATCHES

#	PLAYER	A	G
1	Solskjaer, Ole Gunnar	84	16
2	Scholes, Paul	67	4
3	Giggs, Ryan	66	3
4	Butt, Nicky	60	–
5	McClair, Brian	59	4
6	O'Shea, John	53	3
7	Neville, Phil	53	–
8	Forlan, Diego	40	4
9	McCreery, David	39	3
10	Ronaldo, Cristiano	37	6
11	Blackmore, Clayton	36	3
12	Cole, Andrew	34	6
13	Saha, Louis	34	4
14	Sharpe, Lee	33	–
15	Sheringham, Teddy	31	4
16	Robins, Mark	29	4
17	Beckham, David	28	6
18	Grimes, Ashley	28	3
19	Fletcher, Darren	28	–
20	Kanchelskis, Andrei	27	–
21	Beardsmore, Russell	26	1
22	Duxbury, Mike	25	–
23	Silvestre, Mikael	24	1
24	Fortune, Quinton	23	1
25	Brown, Wes	23	–
26	McIlroy, Sammy	22	2
27	Park, Ji-Sung	21	–
28	Richardson, Kieran	21	–
29	Olsen, Jesper	20	–
30	Cruyff, Jordi	19	5
31	Bellion, David	19	2
32	Stapleton, Frank	19	2
33	Robson, Bryan	19	1
34	Davenport, Peter	19	–
35	Macari, Lou	18	1
36	Smith, Alan	18	1
37	Keane, Roy	17	2
38	Berg, Henning	17	1
39	Martin, Lee (1990s)	17	–
40	May, David	17	–
41	Yorke, Dwight	16	3
42	Aston, John (Jnr)	16	1
43	McGrath, Chris	16	–
44	Albiston, Arthur	15	–
45	Neville, Gary	15	–
46	O'Brien, Liam	15	–
47	Wallwork, Ronnie	15	–
48	Poborsky, Karel	14	3
49	Chadwick, Luke	14	2
50	Johnsen, Ronny	14	–
51	Phelan, Mike	14	–
52	Young, Tony	14	–
53	van Nistelrooy, Ruud	13	4
54	Whiteside, Norman	13	2
55	Brazil, Alan	13	1
56	Sartori, Carlo	13	1
57	Donaghy, Mal	13	–
58	Irwin, Denis	12	–
59	McGarvey, Scott	12	–
60	Carrick, Michael	11	1
61	Rooney, Wayne	11	–
62	van der Gouw, Raimond	11	–
63	Wallace, Danny	11	–
64	Nani	10	1
65	Burns, Francis	10	–
66	Greening, Jonathan	10	–
67	Curtis, John	9	–
68	Gibson, Terry	9	–
69	Hughes, Mark	9	–
70	Nicholl, Jimmy	9	–
71	Dublin, Dion	8	1
72	Anderson	8	–
73	Davies, Ron	8	–
74	Kidd, Brian	8	–
75	Thornley, Ben	8	–

#	PLAYER	A	G
76	Davies, Simon	7	–
77	Djemba-Djemba, Eric	7	–
78	Ferguson, Darren	7	–
79	Gowling, Alan	7	–
80	Hargreaves, Owen	7	–
81	Heinze, Gabriel	7	–
82	Martin, Mick	7	–
83	Moses, Remi	7	–
84	Ritchie, Andy	7	–
85	Sloan, Tom	7	–
86	Gillespie, Keith	6	1
87	Sadler, David	6	1
88	Anderson, Trevor	6	–
89	Evra, Patrice	6	–
90	Fitzpatrick, John	6	–
91	Miller, Liam	6	–
92	Pique, Gerard	6	–
93	Veron, Juan-Sebastian	6	–
94	Bardsley, Phil	5	–
95	Blomqvist, Jesper	5	–
96	Clegg, Michael	5	–
97	Fletcher, Peter	5	–
98	Gibson, Colin	5	–
99	Gill, Tony	5	–
100	Maiorana, Jules	5	–
101	Muhren, Arnold	5	–
102	Parker, Paul	5	–
103	Strachan, Gordon	5	–
104	Webb, Neil	5	–
105	Eagles, Chris	4	1
106	Rossi, Guiseppe	4	1
107	Anderson, Viv	4	–
108	Blanc, Laurent	4	–
109	Daly, Gerry	4	–
110	Givens, Don	4	–
111	Graham, Arthur	4	–
112	Kleberson, Jose	4	–
113	Law, Denis	4	–
114	McGrath, Paul	4	–
115	Milne, Ralph	4	–
116	Wilson, David	4	–
117	Ryan, Jimmy	3	1
118	Buchan, George	3	–
119	Carroll, Roy	3	–
120	Cooke, Terry	3	–
121	Foggon, Alan	3	–
122	Foulkes, Bill	3	–
123	Greenhoff, Brian	3	–
124	Greenhoff, Jimmy	3	–
125	Ince, Paul	3	–
126	Moran, Kevin	3	–
127	Pallister, Gary	3	–
128	Paterson, Steve	3	–
129	Tevez, Carlos	3	–
130	Charlton, Bobby	2	1
131	Cunningham, Laurie	2	1
132	Larsson, Henrik	2	1
133	Anderson, Willie	2	–
134	Bielby, Paul	2	–
135	Brazil, Derek	2	–
136	Casper, Chris	2	–
137	Coppell, Steve	2	–
138	Edwards, Paul	2	–
139	Forsyth, Alex	2	–
140	Garton, Billy	2	–
141	Graham, George	2	–
142	Higginbotham, Danny	2	–
143	Kopel, Frank	2	–
144	Morgan, Willie	2	–
145	Pilkington, Kevin	2	–
146	Simpson, Danny	2	–
147	Sivebaek, Johnny	2	–
148	Stewart, Michael	2	–
149	Vidic, Nemanja	2	–
150	Wilkins, Ray	2	–

#	PLAYER	A	G
151	Wilson, Mark	2	–
152	Wrattan, Paul	2	–
153	Pearson, Stuart	1	1
154	Barnes, Peter	1	–
155	Birtles, Gary	1	–
156	Brennan, Shay	1	–
157	Campbell, Fraizer	1	–
158	Cantona, Eric	1	–
159	Clark, Jonathan	1	–
160	Connelly, John	1	–
161	Coyne, Peter	1	–
162	Crooks, Garth	1	–
163	Culkin, Nick	1	–
164	Davies, Alan	1	–
165	Davies, Wyn	1	–
166	Djordjic, Bojan	1	–
167	Ferdinand, Rio	1	–
168	Gidman, John	1	–
169	Graham, Deiniol	1	–
170	Grimshaw, Tony	1	–
171	Healy, David	1	–
172	Herd, David	1	–
173	Hill, Gordon	1	–
174	Hogg, Graeme	1	–
175	Houston, Stewart	1	–
176	Howard, Tim	1	–
177	Jackson, Tommy	1	–
178	Jovanovic, Nikki	1	–
179	Kelly, Jimmy	1	–
180	Kuszczak, Tomasz	1	–
181	Nevland, Erik	1	–
182	O'Kane, John	1	–
183	Pugh, Danny	1	–
184	Ricardo, Felipe	1	–
185	Roche, Lee	1	–
186	Spector, Jonathan	1	–
187	Walsh, Gary	1	–
188	Whelan, Anthony	1	–
189	Wood, Nicky	1	–

ALL PREMIERSHIP MATCHES

#	PLAYER	A	G	#	PLAYER	A	G	#	PLAYER	A	G
1	Solskjaer, Ole Gunnar	84	16	36	Carrick, Michael	11	1	71	Higginbotham, Danny	2	–
2	Scholes, Paul	67	4	37	Rooney, Wayne	11	–	72	Pilkington, Kevin	2	–
3	Butt, Nicky	60	–	38	van der Gouw, Raimond	11	–	73	Simpson, Danny	2	–
4	Giggs, Ryan	59	2	39	Nani	10	1	74	Stewart, Michael	2	–
5	McClair, Brian	56	1	40	Greening, Jonathan	10	–	75	Vidic, Nemanja	2	–
6	O'Shea, John	53	3	41	Irwin, Denis	10	–	76	Wallace, Danny	2	–
7	Neville, Phil	53	–	42	Curtis, John	9	–	77	Wilson, Mark	2	–
8	Forlan, Diego	40	4	43	Dublin, Dion	8	1	78	Campbell, Fraizer	1	–
9	Ronaldo, Cristiano	37	6	44	Anderson	8	–	79	Cantona, Eric	1	–
10	Cole, Andrew	34	6	45	Thornley, Ben	8	–	80	Culkin, Nick	1	–
11	Saha, Louis	34	4	46	Davies, Simon	7	–	81	Djordjic, Bojan	1	–
12	Sheringham, Teddy	31	4	47	Djemba–Djemba, Eric	7	–	82	Ferdinand, Rio	1	–
13	Beckham, David	28	6	48	Hargreaves, Owen	7	–	83	Healy, David	1	–
14	Fletcher, Darren	28	–	49	Heinze, Gabriel	7	–	84	Howard, Tim	1	–
15	Silvestre, Mikael	24	1	50	Phelan, Mike	7	–	85	Hughes, Mark	1	–
16	Fortune, Quinton	23	1	51	Gillespie, Keith	6	1	86	Kuszczak, Tomasz	1	–
17	Brown, Wes	23	–	52	Evra, Patrice	6	–	87	Nevland, Erik	1	–
18	Kanchelskis, Andrei	21	–	53	Miller, Liam	6	–	88	O'Kane, John	1	–
19	Park, Ji-Sung	21	–	54	Pique, Gerard	6	–	89	Pugh, Danny	1	–
20	Richardson, Kieran	21	–	55	Veron, Juan–Sebastian	6	–	90	Ricardo, Felipe	1	–
21	Cruyff, Jordi	19	5	56	Bardsley, Phil	5	–	91	Roche, Lee	1	–
22	Bellion, David	19	2	57	Blomqvist, Jesper	5	–	92	Spector, Jonathan	1	–
23	Smith, Alan	18	1	58	Clegg, Michael	5	–	93	Walsh, Gary	1	–
24	Keane, Roy	17	2	59	Eagles, Chris	4	1	94	Webb, Neil	1	–
25	Berg, Henning	17	1	60	Rossi, Guiseppe	4	1				
26	May, David	17	–	61	Blanc, Laurent	4	–				
27	Yorke, Dwight	16	3	62	Kleberson, Jose	4	–				
28	Sharpe, Lee	16	–	63	Carroll, Roy	3	–				
29	Neville, Gary	15	–	64	Cooke, Terry	3	–				
30	Wallwork, Ronnie	15	–	65	Parker, Paul	3	–				
31	Poborsky, Karel	14	3	66	Tevez, Carlos	3	–				
32	Chadwick, Luke	14	2	67	Larsson, Henrik	2	1				
33	Johnsen, Ronny	14	–	68	Blackmore, Clayton	2	–				
34	Robson, Bryan	14	–	69	Casper, Chris	2	–				
35	van Nistelrooy, Ruud	13	4	70	Ferguson, Darren	2	–				

ALL LEAGUE DIVISION 1 MATCHES

#	PLAYER	A	G	#	PLAYER	A	G	#	PLAYER	A	G
1	McCreery, David	37	3	36	Anderson, Trevor	6	–	71	Bielby, Paul	2	–
2	Blackmore, Clayton	34	3	37	Fitzpatrick, John	6	–	72	Brazil, Derek	2	–
3	Robins, Mark	29	4	38	Kanchelskis, Andrei	6	–	73	Edwards, Paul	2	–
4	Grimes, Ashley	28	3	39	Martin, Mick	6	–	74	Forsyth, Alex	2	–
5	Beardsmore, Russell	26	1	40	Young, Tony	6	–	75	Garton, Billy	2	–
6	Duxbury, Mike	25	–	41	Robson, Bryan	5	1	76	Irwin, Denis	2	–
7	McIlroy, Sammy	21	2	42	Ferguson, Darren	5	–	77	Kopel, Frank	2	–
8	Olsen, Jesper	20	–	43	Fletcher, Peter	5	–	78	Parker, Paul	2	–
9	Stapleton, Frank	19	2	44	Gibson, Colin	5	–	79	Sivebaek, Johnny	2	–
10	Davenport, Peter	19	–	45	Gill, Tony	5	–	80	Wilkins, Ray	2	–
11	Martin, Lee (1990s)	17	–	46	Maiorana, Jules	5	–	81	Wrattan, Paul	2	–
12	Sharpe, Lee	17	–	47	Muhren, Arnold	5	–	82	Barnes, Peter	1	–
13	Aston, John (junior)	16	1	48	Strachan, Gordon	5	–	83	Birtles, Gary	1	–
14	Macari, Lou	16	1	49	Anderson, Viv	4	–	84	Brennan, Shay	1	–
15	McGrath, Chris	16	–	50	Givens, Don	4	–	85	Clark, Jonathan	1	–
16	Albiston, Arthur	15	–	51	Graham, Arthur	4	–	86	Connelly, John	1	–
17	O'Brien, Liam	15	–	52	Law, Denis	4	–	87	Coppell, Steve	1	–
18	Whiteside, Norman	13	2	53	McGrath, Paul	4	–	88	Coyne, Peter	1	–
19	Brazil, Alan	13	1	54	Milne, Ralph	4	–	89	Crooks, Garth	1	–
20	Sartori, Carlo	13	1	55	Webb, Neil	4	–	90	Davies, Alan	1	–
21	Donaghy, Mal	13	–	56	Wilson, David	4	–	91	Davies, Wyn	1	–
22	McGarvey, Scott	12	–	57	McClair, Brian	3	3	92	Gidman, John	1	–
23	Burns, Francis	10	–	58	Ryan, Jimmy	3	1	93	Graham, Deiniol	1	–
24	Gibson, Terry	9	–	59	Buchan, George	3	–	94	Graham, George	1	–
25	Wallace, Danny	9	–	60	Daly, Gerry	3	–	95	Greenhoff, Brian	1	–
26	Hughes, Mark	8	–	61	Foggon, Alan	3	–	96	Grimshaw, Tony	1	–
27	Kidd, Brian	8	–	62	Foulkes, Bill	3	–	97	Herd, David	1	–
28	Nicholl, Jimmy	8	–	63	Greenhoff, Jimmy	3	–	98	Hill, Gordon	1	–
29	Giggs, Ryan	7	1	64	Ince, Paul	3	–	99	Hogg, Graeme	1	–
30	Gowling, Alan	7	–	65	Moran, Kevin	3	–	100	Houston, Stewart	1	–
31	Moses, Remi	7	–	66	Pallister, Gary	3	–	101	Jackson, Tommy	1	–
32	Phelan, Mike	7	–	67	Paterson, Steve	3	–	102	Jovanovic, Nikki	1	–
33	Ritchie, Andy	7	–	68	Charlton, Bobby	2	1	103	Kelly, Jimmy	1	–
34	Sloan, Tom	7	–	69	Cunningham, Laurie	2	1	104	Whelan, Anthony	1	–
35	Sadler, David	6	1	70	Anderson, Willie	2	–	105	Wood, Nicky	1	–

ALL LEAGUE DIVISION 2 MATCHES

#	PLAYER	A	G	#	PLAYER	A	G	#	PLAYER	A	G
1	Davies, Ron	8	–	6	Morgan, Willie	2	–	11	Martin, Mick	1	–
2	Young, Tony	8	–	7	Pearson, Stuart	1	1	12	McIlroy, Sammy	1	–
3	Greenhoff, Brian	2	–	8	Coppell, Steve	1	–	13	Nicholl, Jimmy	1	–
4	Macari, Lou	2	–	9	Daly, Gerry	1	–				
5	McCreery, David	2	–	10	Graham, George	1	–				

ALL FA CUP MATCHES

#	PLAYER	A	G	#	PLAYER	A	G	#	PLAYER	A	G
1	Solskjaer, Ole Gunnar	15	3	36	Cole, Andrew	2	–	71	Greenhoff, Jimmy	1	–
2	Scholes, Paul	12	1	37	Davenport, Peter	2	–	72	Greening, Jonathan	1	–
3	Giggs, Ryan	7	2	38	Davies, Ron	2	–	73	Hargreaves, Owen	1	–
4	McClair, Brian	7	1	39	Evra, Patrice	2	–	74	Hughes, Mark	1	–
5	Fletcher, Darren	7	–	40	Forlan, Diego	2	–	75	Ince, Paul	1	–
6	Sharpe, Lee	7	–	41	Gill, Tony	2	–	76	Irwin, Denis	1	–
7	Blackmore, Clayton	6	–	42	Gowling, Alan	2	–	77	Jordan, Joe	1	–
8	Butt, Nicky	6	–	43	Johnsen, Ronny	2	–	78	Kanchelskis, Andrei	1	–
9	McCreery, David	6	–	44	Keane, Roy	2	–	79	Kidd, Brian	1	–
10	Neville, Phil	6	–	45	Law, Denis	2	–	80	Kuszczak, Tomasz	1	–
11	Smith, Alan	6	–	46	Miller, Liam	2	–	81	Larsson, Henrik	1	–
12	Sheringham, Teddy	5	3	47	O'Brien, Liam	2	–	82	Martin, Lee (1990s)	1	–
13	Duxbury, Mike	5	1	48	Park, Ji-Sung	2	–	83	Mulryne, Philip	1	–
14	O'Shea, John	5	–	49	Robson, Bryan	2	–	84	Nevland, Erik	1	–
15	Yorke, Dwight	5	–	50	Silvestre, Mikael	2	–	85	Pugh, Danny	1	–
16	Rooney, Wayne	4	3	51	Wilson, David	2	–	86	Ritchie, Andy	1	–
17	Robins, Mark	4	1	52	Graham, Deiniol	1	1	87	Sadler, David	1	–
18	Beardsmore, Russell	4	–	53	Parker, Paul	1	1	88	Sealey, Les	1	–
19	Nicholl, Jimmy	4	–	54	Bardsley, Phil	1	–	89	Simpson, Danny	1	–
20	Saha, Louis	4	–	55	Bellion, David	1	–	90	Stam, Jaap	1	–
21	van Nistelrooy, Ruud	3	2	56	Brazil, Alan	1	–	91	Stewart, Michael	1	–
22	Macari, Lou	3	–	57	Burns, Francis	1	–	92	Twiss, Michael	1	–
23	McGrath, Paul	3	–	58	Carrick, Michael	1	–	93	Wallwork, Ronnie	1	–
24	McIlroy, Sammy	3	–	59	Carroll, Roy	1	–				
25	Neville, Gary	3	–	60	Clegg, Michael	1	–				
26	Olsen, Jesper	3	–	61	Cruyff, Jordi	1	–				
27	Ronaldo, Cristiano	3	–	62	Daly, Gerry	1	–				
28	Aston, John (Jnr)	2	1	63	Djemba–Djemba, Eric	1	–				
29	Richardson, Kieran	2	1	64	Dublin, Dion	1	–				
30	Wallace, Danny	2	1	65	Dunne, Tony	1	–				
31	Anderson	2	–	66	Ferdinand, Rio	1	–				
32	Beckham, David	2	–	67	Fortune, Quinton	1	–				
33	Blomqvist, Jesper	2	–	68	Gibson, Colin	1	–				
34	Brown, Wes	2	–	69	Gibson, Terry	1	–				
35	Chadwick, Luke	2	–	70	Gillespie, Keith	1	–				

ALL LEAGUE CUP MATCHES

#	PLAYER	A	G
1	Sharpe, Lee	8	–
2	Robins, Mark	7	2
3	Giggs, Ryan	5	1
4	Donaghy, Mal	5	–
5	Macari, Lou	5	–
6	Scholes, Paul	5	–
7	Eagles, Chris	4	–
8	McCreery, David	4	–
9	Young, Tony	4	–
10	McIlroy, Sammy	3	1
11	Solskjaer, Ole Gunnar	3	1
12	Aston, John (Jnr)	3	–
13	Brazil, Alan	3	–
14	Irwin, Denis	3	–
15	Olsen, Jesper	3	–
16	Wallace, Danny	3	–
17	Whiteside, Norman	3	–
18	Lee, Kieran	2	1
19	Nevland, Erik	2	1
20	Richardson, Kieran	2	1
21	Albiston, Arthur	2	–
22	Beckham, David	2	–
23	Blackmore, Clayton	2	–
24	Brown, Wes	2	–
25	Bruce, Steve	2	–
26	Cooke, Terry	2	–
27	Davenport, Peter	2	–
28	Davies, Simon	2	–
29	Duxbury, Mike	2	–
30	Evra, Patrice	2	–
31	Forlan, Diego	2	–
32	Gibson, Terry	2	–
33	Healy, David	2	–
34	Jones, Richard	2	–
35	Keane, Roy	2	–
36	Martin, Lee (1990s)	2	–
37	McGrath, Chris	2	–
38	Moses, Remi	2	–
39	Nardiello, Daniel	2	–
40	O'Brien, Liam	2	–
41	Phelan, Mike	2	–
42	Pique, Gerard	2	–
43	Ritchie, Andy	2	–
44	Rooney, Wayne	2	–
45	Rossi, Guiseppe	2	–
46	Sartori, Carlo	2	–
47	Shawcross, Ryan	2	–
48	Smith, Alan	2	–
49	Stewart, Michael	2	–
50	Tomlinson, Graeme	2	–
51	Vidic, Nemanja	2	–
52	Morgan, Willie	1	1
53	Robson, Bryan	1	1
54	Anderson, Viv	1	–
55	Appleton, Michael	1	–
56	Bardsley, Phil	1	–
57	Barnes, Michael	1	–
58	Beardsmore, Russell	1	–
59	Blomqvist, Jesper	1	–
60	Buchan, George	1	–
61	Burns, Francis	1	–
62	Butt, Nicky	1	–
63	Campbell, Fraizer	1	–
64	Carrick, Michael	1	–
65	Clegg, Michael	1	–
66	Dublin, Dion	1	–
67	Ebanks-Blake, Sylvan	1	–
68	Ferdinand, Rio	1	–
69	Ferguson, Darren	1	–
70	Garton, Billy	1	–
71	Gibson, Darron	1	–
72	Gowling, Alan	1	–
73	Graham, Deiniol	1	–
74	Grimshaw, Tony	1	–
75	Hogg, Graeme	1	–
76	Hughes, Mark	1	–
77	Ince, Paul	1	–
78	James, Steve	1	–
79	Johnson, Eddie	1	–
80	Jones, David (2004)	1	–
81	Kanchelskis, Andrei	1	–
82	Maiorana, Jules	1	–
83	McCalliog, Jim	1	–
84	McClair, Brian	1	–
85	Moran, Kevin	1	–
86	Neville, Gary	1	–
87	Neville, Phil	1	–
88	Notman, Alex	1	–
89	O'Kane, John	1	–
90	O'Shea, John	1	–
91	Rachubka, Paul	1	–
92	Silvestre, Mikael	1	–
93	Sloan, Tom	1	–
94	Spector, Jonathan	1	–
95	Stapleton, Frank	1	–
96	Strachan, Gordon	1	–
97	van der Gouw, Raimond	1	–
98	van Nistelrooy, Ruud	1	–
99	Veron, Juan-Sebastian	1	–
100	Wallwork, Ronnie	1	–
101	Webber, Danny	1	–
102	Wellens, Richard	1	–
103	Wilkins, Ray	1	–
104	Wood, Nicky	1	–

ALL EUROPEAN MATCHES

#	PLAYER	A	G
1	Solskjaer, Ole Gunnar	45	8
2	Neville, Phil	22	–
3	Forlan, Diego	15	1
4	Butt, Nicky	13	–
5	O'Shea, John	13	–
6	Scholes, Paul	12	3
7	Fortune, Quinton	12	–
8	Giggs, Ryan	11	3
9	Richardson, Kieran	11	2
10	Sheringham, Teddy	11	1
11	Saha, Louis	10	–
12	Fletcher, Darren	9	–
13	Yorke, Dwight	8	1
14	Silvestre, Mikael	8	–
15	Cole, Andrew	7	1
16	Brown, Wes	7	–
17	Cruyff, Jordi	7	–
18	Neville, Gary	7	–
19	Park, Ji-Sung	7	–
20	Tevez, Carlos	6	2
21	McClair, Brian	6	–
22	Smith, Alan	6	–
23	Bellion, David	5	1
24	Chadwick, Luke	5	–
25	Martin, Lee (1990s)	5	–
26	Poborsky, Karel	5	–
27	Beckham, David	4	2
28	Berg, Henning	4	–
29	Nani	4	–
30	Djemba-Djemba, Eric	3	1
31	Evra, Patrice	3	1
32	Anderson	3	–
33	Beardsmore, Russell	3	–
34	Donaghy, Mal	3	–
35	Hargreaves, Owen	3	–
36	Hughes, Mark	3	–
37	Johnsen, Ronny	3	–
38	McCreery, David	3	–
39	Miller, Liam	3	–
40	Parker, Paul	3	–
41	Phelan, Mike	3	–
42	Ronaldo, Cristiano	3	–
43	van Nistelrooy, Ruud	2	1
44	Whiteside, Norman	2	1
45	Clegg, Michael	2	–
46	Gidman, John	2	–
47	Greening, Jonathan	2	–
48	Grimes, Ashley	2	–
49	Irwin, Denis	2	–
50	Kleberson, Jose	2	–
51	Kuszczak, Tomasz	2	–
52	May, David	2	–
53	Paterson, Steve	2	–
54	Pugh, Danny	2	–
55	Robins, Mark	2	–
56	Rossi, Guiseppe	2	–
57	Sharpe, Lee	2	–
58	Stewart, Michael	2	–
59	Wallace, Danny	2	–
60	Wilson, Mark	2	–
61	Davies, Alan	1	1
62	Albiston, Arthur	1	–
63	Bardsley, Phil	1	–
64	Blomqvist, Jesper	1	–
65	Bruce, Steve	1	–
66	Burns, Francis	1	–
67	Carrick, Michael	1	–
68	Casper, Chris	1	–
69	Cooke, Terry	1	–
70	Coppell, Steve	1	–
71	Davies, Simon	1	–
72	Dempsey, Mark	1	–
73	Dong, Fangzhuo	1	–
74	Dublin, Dion	1	–
75	Duxbury, Mike	1	–
76	Eagles, Chris	1	–
77	Evans, Jonny	1	–
78	Ferdinand, Rio	1	–
79	Forsyth, Alex	1	–
80	Garton, Billy	1	–
81	Graham, Arthur	1	–
82	Heinze, Gabriel	1	–
83	Higginbotham, Danny	1	–
84	Houston, Stewart	1	–
85	Keane, Roy	1	–
86	Macari, Lou	1	–
87	McGrath, Chris	1	–
88	Moran, Kevin	1	–
89	Moses, Remi	1	–
90	Nardiello, Daniel	1	–
91	Olsen, Jesper	1	–
92	Pallister, Gary	1	–
93	Pique, Gerard	1	–
94	Ricardo, Felipe	1	–
95	Rimmer, Jimmy	1	–
96	Robson, Bryan	1	–
97	Rooney, Wayne	1	–
98	Simpson, Danny	1	–
99	Spector, Jonathan	1	–
100	Stapleton, Frank	1	–
101	Timm, Mads	1	–
102	Wallwork, Ronnie	1	–
103	Webber, Danny	1	–

ALL EUROPEAN CUP / CHAMPIONS LEAGUE MATCHES

#	PLAYER	A	G
1	Solskjaer, Ole Gunnar	45	8
2	Neville, Phil	22	–
3	Forlan, Diego	15	1
4	Butt, Nicky	13	–
5	O'Shea, John	13	–
6	Fortune, Quinton	12	–
7	Giggs, Ryan	11	3
8	Richardson, Kieran	11	2
9	Scholes, Paul	11	2
10	Sheringham, Teddy	11	1
11	Saha, Louis	10	–
12	Fletcher, Darren	9	–
13	Yorke, Dwight	8	1
14	Silvestre, Mikael	8	–
15	Cole, Andrew	7	1
16	Brown, Wes	7	–
17	Cruyff, Jordi	7	–
18	Park, Ji-Sung	7	–
19	Tevez, Carlos	6	2
20	McClair, Brian	6	–
21	Neville, Gary	6	–
22	Smith, Alan	6	–
23	Bellion, David	5	1
24	Chadwick, Luke	5	–
25	Poborsky, Karel	5	–
26	Beckham, David	4	2
27	Berg, Henning	4	–
28	Nani	4	–
29	Djemba–Djemba, Eric	3	1
30	Evra, Patrice	3	1
31	Anderson	3	–
32	Hargreaves, Owen	3	–
33	Johnsen, Ronny	3	–
34	Miller, Liam	3	–
35	Phelan, Mike	3	–
36	Ronaldo, Cristiano	3	–
37	van Nistelrooy, Ruud	2	1
38	Clegg, Michael	2	–
39	Greening, Jonathan	2	–
40	Irwin, Denis	2	–
41	Kleberson, Jose	2	–
42	Kuszczak, Tomasz	2	–
43	May, David	2	–
44	Pugh, Danny	2	–
45	Rossi, Guiseppe	2	–
46	Stewart, Michael	2	–
47	Wilson, Mark	2	–
48	Bardsley, Phil	1	–
49	Blomqvist, Jesper	1	–
50	Bruce, Steve	1	–
51	Burns, Francis	1	–
52	Carrick, Michael	1	–
53	Casper, Chris	1	–
54	Dong, Fangzhuo	1	–
55	Dublin, Dion	1	–
56	Eagles, Chris	1	–
57	Evans, Jonny	1	–
58	Ferdinand, Rio	1	–
59	Heinze, Gabriel	1	–
60	Higginbotham, Danny	1	–
61	Keane, Roy	1	–
62	Martin, Lee (1990s)	1	–
63	Nardiello, Daniel	1	–
64	Parker, Paul	1	–
65	Pique, Gerard	1	–
66	Ricardo, Felipe	1	–
67	Rimmer, Jimmy	1	–
68	Rooney, Wayne	1	–
69	Simpson, Danny	1	–
70	Spector, Jonathan	1	–
71	Timm, Mads	1	–
72	Wallwork, Ronnie	1	–
73	Webber, Danny	1	–

ALL EUROPEAN CUP-WINNERS' CUP MATCHES

#	PLAYER	A	G
1	Martin, Lee (1990s)	4	–
2	Beardsmore, Russell	3	–
3	Donaghy, Mal	3	–
4	Hughes, Mark	3	–
5	Grimes, Ashley	2	–
6	Robins, Mark	2	–
7	Sharpe, Lee	2	–
8	Wallace, Danny	2	–
9	Davies, Alan	1	1
10	Whiteside, Norman	1	1
11	Dempsey, Mark	1	–
12	Forsyth, Alex	1	–
13	Gidman, John	1	–
14	Graham, Arthur	1	–
15	Houston, Stewart	1	–
16	McGrath, Chris	1	–
17	Moses, Remi	1	–
18	Pallister, Gary	1	–

ALL UEFA CUP / INTER-CITIES' FAIRS CUP MATCHES

#	PLAYER	A	G	#	PLAYER	A	G	#	PLAYER	A	G
1	McCreery, David	3	–	7	Coppell, Steve	1	–	13	Moran, Kevin	1	–
2	Parker, Paul	2	–	8	Davies, Simon	1	–	14	Neville, Gary	1	–
3	Paterson, Steve	2	–	9	Duxbury, Mike	1	–	15	Olsen, Jesper	1	–
4	Scholes, Paul	1	1	10	Garton, Billy	1	–	16	Robson, Bryan	1	–
5	Albiston, Arthur	1	–	11	Gidman, John	1	–	17	Stapleton, Frank	1	–
6	Cooke, Terry	1	–	12	Macari, Lou	1	–	18	Whiteside, Norman	1	–

ALL OTHER COMPETITIVE MATCHES

#	PLAYER	A	G	#	PLAYER	A	G	#	PLAYER	A	G
1	Cruyff, Jordi	5	–	11	Cole, Andrew	1	–	21	Nani	1	–
2	Sheringham, Teddy	5	–	12	Curtis, John	1	–	22	Neville, Gary	1	–
3	Neville, Phil	3	–	13	Djemba-Djemba, Eric	1	–	23	O'Shea, John	1	–
4	Solskjaer, Ole Gunnar	3	–	14	Eagles, Chris	1	–	24	Poborsky, Karel	1	–
5	Yorke, Dwight	3	–	15	Gidman, John	1	–	25	Rachubka, Paul	1	–
6	Beckham, David	2	–	16	Giggs, Ryan	1	–	26	Richardson, Kieran	1	–
7	Fletcher, Darren	2	–	17	Greening, Jonathan	1	–	27	Robins, Mark	1	–
8	Forlan, Diego	2	–	18	May, David	1	–	28	Robson, Bryan	1	–
9	Fortune, Quinton	2	–	19	McCreery, David	1	–	29	Spector, Jonathan	1	–
10	Berg, Henning	1	–	20	Moses, Remi	1	–	30	Stam, Jaap	1	–

MANCHESTER UNITED
The Complete Record

Chapter 3.1
Day by Day, Month by Month

UNITED in JANUARY

OVERALL PLAYING RECORD

	P	W	D	L	F	A		P	W	D	L	F	A		P	W	D	L	F	A
1st	51	32	9	10	92	50	11th	20	11	5	4	38	23	22nd	19	13	3	3	34	14
2nd	22	8	6	8	35	30	12th	21	8	7	6	39	22	23rd	14	5	3	6	24	29
3rd	18	10	5	3	29	21	13th	15	7	4	4	28	15	24th	16	8	3	5	28	15
4th	15	7	5	3	33	24	14th	17	11	2	4	34	19	25th	14	6	5	3	17	9
5th	16	9	4	3	32	17	15th	17	10	3	4	26	17	26th	17	9	3	5	23	13
6th	14	6	3	5	27	17	16th	18	8	5	5	35	29	27th	14	9	3	2	25	13
7th	21	9	6	6	31	32	17th	13	2	3	8	11	18	28th	15	8	5	2	27	13
8th	15	5	7	3	23	17	18th	18	9	3	6	39	32	29th	14	10	2	2	25	7
9th	17	10	1	6	32	26	19th	17	9	3	5	30	18	30th	17	8	3	6	27	27
10th	15	10	1	4	27	21	20th	13	6	4	3	26	18	31st	19	8	4	7	26	21
							21st	17	5	2	10	23	36							

OVERALL 549 276 122 151 946 673

JANUARY 1

#	SEASON	DATE	COMPETITION / ROUND	MATCH RESULT	VENUE	ATT
1	1894/95	01/01/95	Football League Division 2	Newton Heath 3 Port Vale 0	Bank Street	5000
2	1895/96	01/01/96	Football League Division 2	Newton Heath 3 Grimsby Town 2	Bank Street	8000
3	1896/97	01/01/97	Football League Division 2	Newcastle United 2 Newton Heath 0	St James' Park	17000
4	1897/98	01/01/98	Football League Division 2	Newton Heath 4 Burton Swifts 0	Bank Street	6000
5	1900/01	01/01/01	Football League Division 2	Middlesbrough 1 Newton Heath 2	Linthorpe Road	12000
6	1901/02	01/01/02	Football League Division 2	Newton Heath 0 Preston North End 2	Bank Street	10000
7	1906/07	01/01/07	Football League Division 1	Manchester United 1 Aston Villa 0	Bank Street	40000
8	1907/08	01/01/08	Football League Division 1	Bury 0 Manchester United 1	Gigg Lane	29500
9	1908/09	01/01/09	Football League Division 1	Manchester United 4 Notts County 3	Bank Street	15000
10	1909/10	01/01/10	Football League Division 1	Bradford City 0 Manchester United 2	Valley Parade	25000
11	1911/12	01/01/12	Football League Division 1	Manchester United 2 Arsenal 0	Old Trafford	20000
12	1912/13	01/01/13	Football League Division 1	Manchester United 2 Bradford City 0	Old Trafford	30000
13	1913/14	01/01/14	Football League Division 1	Manchester United 1 West Bromwich Albion 0	Old Trafford	35000
14	1914/15	01/01/15	Football League Division 1	Manchester United 1 Bradford Park Avenue 2	Old Trafford	8000
15	1919/20	01/01/20	Football League Division 1	Liverpool 0 Manchester United 0	Anfield	30000
16	1920/21	01/01/21	Football League Division 1	Newcastle United 6 Manchester United 3	St James' Park	40000
17	1922/23	01/01/23	Football League Division 2	Manchester United 1 Barnsley 0	Old Trafford	29000
18	1924/25	01/01/25	Football League Division 2	Manchester United 1 Chelsea 0	Old Trafford	30500
19	1926/27	01/01/27	Football League Division 1	Manchester United 5 Sheffield United 0	Old Trafford	33593
20	1928/29	01/01/29	Football League Division 1	Manchester United 3 Aston Villa 2	Old Trafford	25935
21	1930/31	01/01/31	Football League Division 1	Manchester United 0 Leeds United 0	Old Trafford	9875
22	1934/35	01/01/35	Football League Division 2	Manchester United 4 Southampton 0	Old Trafford	15174
23	1935/36	01/01/36	Football League Division 2	Barnsley 0 Manchester United 3	Oakwell	20957
24	1936/37	01/01/37	Football League Division 1	Manchester United 2 Sunderland 1	Old Trafford	46257
25	1937/38	01/01/38	Football League Division 2	Newcastle United 2 Manchester United 2	St James' Park	40088
26	1947/48	01/01/48	Football League Division 1	Manchester United 5 Burnley 0	Maine Road	59838
27	1948/49	01/01/49	Football League Division 1	Manchester United 2 Arsenal 0	Maine Road	58688
28	1952/53	01/01/53	Football League Division 1	Manchester United 1 Derby County 0	Old Trafford	34813
29	1954/55	01/01/55	Football League Division 1	Manchester United 4 Blackpool 1	Old Trafford	51918
30	1956/57	01/01/57	Football League Division 1	Manchester United 3 Chelsea 0	Old Trafford	42116
31	1965/66	01/01/66	Football League Division 1	Liverpool 2 Manchester United 1	Anfield	53790
32	1971/72	01/01/72	Football League Division 1	West Ham United 3 Manchester United 0	Upton Park	41892
33	1973/74	01/01/74	Football League Division 1	Queens Park Rangers 3 Manchester United 0	Loftus Road	32339
34	1976/77	01/01/77	Football League Division 1	Manchester United 2 Aston Villa 0	Old Trafford	55446
35	1982/83	01/01/83	Football League Division 1	Manchester United 3 Aston Villa 1	Old Trafford	41545
36	1984/85	01/01/85	Football League Division 1	Manchester United 1 Sheffield Wednesday 2	Old Trafford	47625
37	1985/86	01/01/86	Football League Division 1	Manchester United 1 Birmingham City 0	Old Trafford	43095
38	1986/87	01/01/87	Football League Division 1	Manchester United 4 Newcastle United 1	Old Trafford	43334
39	1987/88	01/01/88	Football League Division 1	Manchester United 0 Charlton Athletic 0	Old Trafford	37257
40	1988/89	01/01/89	Football League Division 1	Manchester United 3 Liverpool 1	Old Trafford	44745
41	1989/90	01/01/90	Football League Division 1	Manchester United 0 Queens Park Rangers 0	Old Trafford	34824
42	1990/91	01/01/91	Football League Division 1	Tottenham Hotspur 1 Manchester United 2	White Hart Lane	29399
43	1991/92	01/01/92	Football League Division 1	Manchester United 1 Queens Park Rangers 4	Old Trafford	38554
44	1993/94	01/01/94	FA Premiership	Manchester United 0 Leeds United 0	Old Trafford	44724
45	1995/96	01/01/96	FA Premiership	Tottenham Hotspur 4 Manchester United 1	White Hart Lane	32852
46	1996/97	01/01/97	FA Premiership	Manchester United 0 Aston Villa 0	Old Trafford	55133
47	2000/01	01/01/01	FA Premiership	Manchester United 3 West Ham United 1	Old Trafford	67603
48	2002/03	01/01/03	FA Premiership	Manchester United 2 Sunderland 1	Old Trafford	67609
49	2004/05	01/01/05	FA Premiership	Middlesbrough 0 Manchester United 2	Riverside Stadium	34199
50	2006/07	01/01/07	FA Premiership	Newcastle United 2 Manchester United 2	St James' Park	52302
51	2007/08	01/01/08	FA Premiership	Manchester United 1 Birmingham City 0	Old Trafford	75459

JANUARY 2

#	SEASON	DATE	COMPETITION / ROUND	MATCH RESULT	VENUE	ATT
1	1896/97	02/01/97	FA Cup 4th Qualifying Round	Newton Heath 3 Nelson 0	Bank Street	5000
2	1898/99	02/01/99	Football League Division 2	Newton Heath 2 Burton Swifts 2	Bank Street	6000
3	1903/04	02/01/04	Football League Division 2	Bristol City 1 Manchester United 1	Ashton Gate	8000
4	1904/05	02/01/05	Football League Division 2	Manchester United 7 Bradford City 0	Bank Street	10000
5	1908/09	02/01/09	Football League Division 1	Manchester United 0 Preston North End 2	Bank Street	18000
6	1910/11	02/01/11	Football League Division 1	Manchester United 1 Bradford City 0	Old Trafford	40000
7	1914/15	02/01/15	Football League Division 1	Manchester City 1 Manchester United 1	Hyde Road	30000
8	1921/22	02/01/22	Football League Division 1	Sheffield United 3 Manchester United 0	Bramall Lane	18000
9	1923/24	02/01/24	Football League Division 2	Manchester United 1 Coventry City 2	Old Trafford	7000
10	1925/26	02/01/26	Football League Division 1	Manchester United 2 West Ham United 1	Old Trafford	29612
11	1931/32	02/01/32	Football League Division 2	Manchester United 0 Bradford Park Avenue 2	Old Trafford	6056
12	1932/33	02/01/33	Football League Division 2	Manchester United 4 Plymouth Argyle 0	Old Trafford	30257
13	1936/37	02/01/37	Football League Division 1	Manchester United 2 Derby County 2	Old Trafford	31883
14	1953/54	02/01/54	Football League Division 1	Newcastle United 1 Manchester United 2	St James' Park	55780
15	1959/60	02/01/60	Football League Division 1	Newcastle United 7 Manchester United 3	St James' Park	57200
16	1970/71	02/01/71	FA Cup 3rd Round	Manchester United 0 Middlesbrough 0	Old Trafford	47824
17	1977/78	02/01/78	Football League Division 1	Manchester United 1 Birmingham City 2	Old Trafford	53501
18	1981/82	02/01/82	FA Cup 3rd Round	Watford 1 Manchester United 0	Vicarage Road	26104
19	1983/84	02/01/84	Football League Division 1	Liverpool 1 Manchester United 1	Anfield	44622
20	1987/88	02/01/88	Football League Division 1	Watford 0 Manchester United 1	Vicarage Road	18038
21	1988/89	02/01/89	Football League Division 1	Middlesbrough 1 Manchester United 0	Ayresome Park	24411
22	2001/02	02/01/02	FA Premiership	Manchester United 3 Newcastle United 1	Old Trafford	67646

JANUARY 3

#	SEASON	DATE	COMPETITION / ROUND	MATCH RESULT	VENUE	ATT
1	1902/03	03/01/03	Football League Division 2	Manchester United 3 Gainsborough Trinity 1	Bank Street	8000
2	1904/05	03/01/05	Football League Division 2	Bolton Wanderers 2 Manchester United 4	Burnden Park	35000
3	1913/14	03/01/14	Football League Division 1	Bolton Wanderers 6 Manchester United 1	Burnden Park	35000
4	1919/20	03/01/20	Football League Division 1	Manchester United 0 Chelsea 2	Old Trafford	25000
5	1924/25	03/01/25	Football League Division 2	Manchester United 2 Stoke City 0	Old Trafford	24500
6	1930/31	03/01/31	Football League Division 1	Manchester United 1 Chelsea 0	Old Trafford	8966
7	1947/48	03/01/48	Football League Division 1	Charlton Athletic 1 Manchester United 2	The Valley	40484
8	1952/53	03/01/53	Football League Division 1	Manchester United 1 Manchester City 1	Old Trafford	47883
9	1958/59	03/01/59	Football League Division 1	Manchester United 3 Blackpool 1	Old Trafford	61961
10	1969/70	03/01/70	FA Cup 3rd Round	Ipswich Town 0 Manchester United 1	Portman Road	29552
11	1975/76	03/01/76	FA Cup 3rd Round	Manchester United 2 Oxford United 1	Old Trafford	41082
12	1976/77	03/01/77	Football League Division 1	Ipswich Town 2 Manchester United 1	Portman Road	30105
13	1980/81	03/01/81	FA Cup 3rd Round	Manchester United 2 Brighton 2	Old Trafford	42199
14	1982/83	03/01/83	Football League Division 1	Manchester United 0 West Bromwich Albion 0	Old Trafford	39123
15	1986/87	03/01/87	Football League Division 1	Southampton 1 Manchester United 1	The Dell	20409
16	1994/95	03/01/95	FA Premiership	Manchester United 2 Coventry City 0	Old Trafford	43130
17	1998/99	03/01/99	FA Cup 3rd Round	Manchester United 3 Middlesbrough 1	Old Trafford	52232
18	2005/06	03/01/06	FA Premiership	Arsenal 0 Manchester United 0	Highbury	38313

JANUARY 4

#	SEASON	DATE	COMPETITION / ROUND	MATCH RESULT	VENUE	ATT
1	1895/96	04/01/96	Football League Division 2	Leicester City 3 Newton Heath 0	Filbert Street	7000
2	1901/02	04/01/02	Football League Division 2	Gainsborough Trinity 1 Newton Heath 1	The Northolme	2000
3	1912/13	04/01/13	Football League Division 1	Manchester United 1 West Bromwich Albion 1	Old Trafford	25000
4	1929/30	04/01/30	Football League Division 1	Blackburn Rovers 5 Manchester United 4	Ewood Park	23923
5	1935/36	04/01/36	Football League Division 2	Bradford City 1 Manchester United 0	Valley Parade	11286
6	1946/47	04/01/47	Football League Division 1	Manchester United 4 Charlton Athletic 1	Maine Road	43406
7	1957/58	04/01/58	FA Cup 3rd Round	Workington 1 Manchester United 3	Borough Park	21000
8	1963/64	04/01/64	FA Cup 3rd Round	Southampton 2 Manchester United 3	The Dell	29164
9	1968/69	04/01/69	FA Cup 3rd Round	Exeter City 1 Manchester United 3	St James' Park	18500
10	1974/75	04/01/75	FA Cup 3rd Round	Manchester United 0 Walsall 0	Old Trafford	43353
11	1993/94	04/01/94	FA Premiership	Liverpool 3 Manchester United 3	Anfield	42795
12	1997/98	04/01/98	FA Cup 3rd Round	Chelsea 3 Manchester United 5	Stamford Bridge	34792
13	2002/03	04/01/03	FA Cup 3rd Round	Manchester United 4 Portsmouth 1	Old Trafford	67222
14	2003/04	04/01/04	FA Cup 3rd Round	Aston Villa 1 Manchester United 2	Villa Park	40371
15	2004/05	04/01/05	FA Premiership	Manchester United 0 Tottenham Hotspur 0	Old Trafford	67962

JANUARY 5

#	SEASON	DATE	COMPETITION / ROUND	MATCH RESULT	VENUE	ATT
1	1894/95	05/01/95	Football League Division 2	Newton Heath 4 Manchester City 1	Bank Street	12000
2	1900/01	05/01/01	FA Cup Supplementary Round	Newton Heath 3 Portsmouth 0	Bank Street	5000
3	1906/07	05/01/07	Football League Division 1	Notts County 3 Manchester United 0	Trent Bridge	10000
4	1923/24	05/01/24	Football League Division 2	Manchester United 3 Bradford City 0	Old Trafford	18000
5	1928/29	05/01/29	Football League Division 1	Manchester United 1 Manchester City 2	Old Trafford	42555
6	1934/35	05/01/35	Football League Division 2	Manchester United 3 Sheffield United 3	Old Trafford	28300
7	1945/46	05/01/46	FA Cup 3rd Round 1st Leg	Accrington Stanley 2 Manchester United 2	Peel Park	9968
8	1951/52	05/01/52	FA Cup 3rd Round	Stoke City 0 Manchester United 0	Victoria Ground	36389
9	1956/57	05/01/57	FA Cup 3rd Round	Hartlepool United 3 Manchester United 4	Victoria Ground	17264
10	1970/71	05/01/71	FA Cup 3rd Round Replay	Middlesbrough 2 Manchester United 1	Ayresome Park	41000
11	1973/74	05/01/74	FA Cup 3rd Round	Manchester United 1 Plymouth Argyle 0	Old Trafford	31810
12	1979/80	05/01/80	FA Cup 3rd Round	Tottenham Hotspur 1 Manchester United 1	White Hart Lane	45207
13	1984/85	05/01/85	FA Cup 3rd Round	Manchester United 3 Bournemouth 0	Old Trafford	32080
14	1992/93	05/01/93	FA Cup 3rd Round	Manchester United 2 Bury 0	Old Trafford	30668
15	1996/97	05/01/97	FA Cup 3rd Round	Manchester United 2 Tottenham Hotspur 0	Old Trafford	52445
16	2007/08	05/01/08	FA Cup 3rd Round	Aston Villa 0 Manchester United 2	Villa Park	33630

JANUARY 6

#	SEASON	DATE	COMPETITION / ROUND	MATCH RESULT	VENUE	ATT
1	1893/94	06/01/94	Football League Division 1	Everton 2 Newton Heath 0	Goodison Park	8000
2	1899/00	06/01/00	Football League Division 2	Newton Heath 1 Bolton Wanderers 2	Bank Street	5000
3	1905/06	06/01/06	Football League Division 2	Manchester United 5 Grimsby Town 0	Bank Street	10000
4	1911/12	06/01/12	Football League Division 1	Everton 4 Manchester United 0	Goodison Park	12000
5	1922/23	06/01/23	Football League Division 2	Manchester United 3 Hull City 2	Old Trafford	15000
6	1933/34	06/01/34	Football League Division 2	Lincoln City 5 Manchester United 1	Sincil Bank	6075
7	1950/51	06/01/51	FA Cup 3rd Round	Manchester United 4 Oldham Athletic 1	Old Trafford	37161
8	1961/62	06/01/62	FA Cup 3rd Round	Manchester United 2 Bolton Wanderers 1	Old Trafford	42202
9	1967/68	06/01/68	Football League Division 1	Manchester United 3 West Ham United 1	Old Trafford	54498
10	1972/73	06/01/73	Football League Division 1	Arsenal 3 Manchester United 1	Highbury	51194
11	1981/82	06/01/82	Football League Division 1	Manchester United 1 Everton 1	Old Trafford	40451
12	1995/96	06/01/96	FA Cup 3rd Round	Manchester United 2 Sunderland 2	Old Trafford	41563
13	1999/00	06/01/00	Club World Championship	Manchester United 1 Rayos del Necaxa 1	Maracana Stadium	50000
14	2001/02	06/01/02	FA Cup 3rd Round	Aston Villa 2 Manchester United 3	Villa Park	38444

JANUARY 7

#	SEASON	DATE	COMPETITION / ROUND	MATCH RESULT	VENUE	ATT
1	1892/93	07/01/93	Football League Division 1	Stoke City 7 Newton Heath 1	Victoria Ground	1000
2	1904/05	07/01/05	Football League Division 2	Bristol City 1 Manchester United 1	Ashton Gate	12000
3	1910/11	07/01/11	Football League Division 1	Manchester United 4 Nottingham Forest 2	Old Trafford	10000
4	1921/22	07/01/22	FA Cup 1st Round	Manchester United 1 Cardiff City 4	Old Trafford	25726
5	1927/28	07/01/28	Football League Division 1	Manchester United 1 Birmingham City 1	Old Trafford	16853
6	1932/33	07/01/33	Football League Division 2	Manchester United 1 Southampton 2	Old Trafford	21364
7	1938/39	07/01/39	FA Cup 3rd Round	West Bromwich Albion 0 Manchester United 0	The Hawthorns	23900
8	1949/50	07/01/50	FA Cup 3rd Round	Manchester United 4 Weymouth Town 0	Old Trafford	38284
9	1955/56	07/01/56	FA Cup 3rd Round	Bristol Rovers 4 Manchester United 0	Eastville	35872
10	1960/61	07/01/61	FA Cup 3rd Round	Manchester United 3 Middlesbrough 0	Old Trafford	49184
11	1974/75	07/01/75	FA Cup 3rd Round Replay	Walsall 3 Manchester United 2	Fellows Park	18105
12	1977/78	07/01/78	FA Cup 3rd Round	Carlisle United 1 Manchester United 1	Brunton Park	21710
13	1980/81	07/01/81	FA Cup 3rd Round Replay	Brighton 0 Manchester United 2	Goldstone Ground	26915
14	1983/84	07/01/84	FA Cup 3rd Round	Bournemouth 2 Manchester United 0	Dean Court	14782
15	1988/89	07/01/89	FA Cup 3rd Round	Manchester United 0 Queens Park Rangers 0	Old Trafford	36222
16	1989/90	07/01/90	FA Cup 3rd Round	Nottingham Forest 0 Manchester United 1	City Ground	23072
17	1990/91	07/01/91	FA Cup 3rd Round	Manchester United 2 Queens Park Rangers 1	Old Trafford	35065
18	2000/01	07/01/01	FA Cup 3rd Round	Fulham 1 Manchester United 2	Craven Cottage	19178
19	2002/03	07/01/03	League Cup Semi-Final 1st Leg	Manchester United 1 Blackburn Rovers 1	Old Trafford	62740
20	2003/04	07/01/04	FA Premiership	Bolton Wanderers 1 Manchester United 2	Reebok Stadium	27668
21	2006/07	07/01/07	FA Cup 3rd Round	Manchester United 2 Aston Villa 1	Old Trafford	74924

JANUARY 8

#	SEASON	DATE	COMPETITION / ROUND	MATCH RESULT	VENUE	ATT
1	1897/98	08/01/98	Football League Division 2	Arsenal 5 Newton Heath 1	Manor Field	8000
2	1909/10	08/01/10	Football League Division 1	Bury 1 Manchester United 1	Gigg Lane	10000
3	1920/21	08/01/21	FA Cup 1st Round	Liverpool 1 Manchester United 1	Anfield	40000
4	1926/27	08/01/27	FA Cup 3rd Round	Reading 1 Manchester United 1	Elm Park	28918
5	1937/38	08/01/38	FA Cup 3rd Round	Manchester United 3 Yeovil Town 0	Old Trafford	49004
6	1948/49	08/01/49	FA Cup 3rd Round	Manchester United 6 Bournemouth 0	Maine Road	55012
7	1954/55	08/01/55	FA Cup 3rd Round	Reading 1 Manchester United 1	Elm Park	26000
8	1965/66	08/01/66	Football League Division 1	Manchester United 1 Sunderland 1	Old Trafford	39162
9	1971/72	08/01/72	Football League Division 1	Manchester United 1 Wolverhampton Wanderers 3	Old Trafford	46781
10	1976/77	08/01/77	FA Cup 3rd Round	Manchester United 1 Walsall 0	Old Trafford	48870
11	1982/83	08/01/83	FA Cup 3rd Round	Manchester United 2 West Ham United 0	Old Trafford	44143
12	1991/92	08/01/92	League Cup 5th Round	Leeds United 1 Manchester United 3	Elland Road	28886
13	1999/00	08/01/00	Club World Championship	Manchester United 1 Vasco da Gama 3	Maracana Stadium	73000
14	2004/05	08/01/05	FA Cup 3rd Round	Manchester United 0 Exeter City 0	Old Trafford	67551
15	2005/06	08/01/06	FA Cup 3rd Round	Burton Albion 0 Manchester United 0	Pirelli Stadium	6191

JANUARY 9

#	SEASON	DATE	COMPETITION / ROUND	MATCH RESULT	VENUE	ATT
1	1896/97	09/01/97	Football League Division 2	Newton Heath 1 Burton Swifts 1	Bank Street	3000
2	1903/04	09/01/04	Football League Division 2	Manchester United 2 Port Vale 0	Bank Street	10000
3	1908/09	09/01/09	Football League Division 1	Middlesbrough 5 Manchester United 0	Ayresome Park	15000
4	1914/15	09/01/15	FA Cup 1st Round	Sheffield Wednesday 1 Manchester United 0	Hillsborough	23248
5	1925/26	09/01/26	FA Cup 3rd Round	Port Vale 2 Manchester United 3	Old Recreation Ground	14841
6	1931/32	09/01/32	FA Cup 3rd Round	Plymouth Argyle 4 Manchester United 1	Home Park	28000
7	1936/37	09/01/37	Football League Division 1	Manchester City 1 Manchester United 0	Maine Road	64862
8	1945/46	09/01/46	FA Cup 3rd Round 2nd Leg	Manchester United 5 Accrington Stanley 1	Maine Road	15339
9	1953/54	09/01/54	FA Cup 3rd Round	Burnley 5 Manchester United 3	Turf Moor	54000
10	1959/60	09/01/60	FA Cup 3rd Round	Derby County 2 Manchester United 4	Baseball Ground	33297
11	1964/65	09/01/65	FA Cup 3rd Round	Manchester United 2 Chester City 1	Old Trafford	40000
12	1970/71	09/01/71	Football League Division 1	Chelsea 1 Manchester United 2	Stamford Bridge	53482
13	1979/80	09/01/80	FA Cup 3rd Round Replay	Manchester United 0 Tottenham Hotspur 1	Old Trafford	53762
14	1985/86	09/01/86	FA Cup 3rd Round	Manchester United 2 Rochdale 0	Old Trafford	40223
15	1992/93	09/01/93	FA Premiership	Manchester United 4 Tottenham Hotspur 1	Old Trafford	35648
16	1993/94	09/01/94	FA Cup 3rd Round	Sheffield United 0 Manchester United 1	Bramall Lane	22019
17	1994/95	09/01/95	FA Cup 3rd Round	Sheffield United 0 Manchester United 2	Bramall Lane	22322

JANUARY 10

#	SEASON	DATE	COMPETITION / ROUND	MATCH RESULT	VENUE	ATT
1	1902/03	10/01/03	Football League Division 2	Burton United 3 Manchester United 1	Peel Croft	3000
2	1913/14	10/01/14	FA Cup 1st Round	Swindon Town 1 Manchester United 0	County Ground	18187
3	1919/20	10/01/20	FA Cup 1st Round	Port Vale 0 Manchester United 1	Old Recreation Ground	14549
4	1924/25	10/01/25	FA Cup 1st Round	Sheffield Wednesday 2 Manchester United 0	Hillsborough	35079
5	1930/31	10/01/31	FA Cup 3rd Round	Stoke City 3 Manchester United 3	Victoria Ground	23415
6	1947/48	10/01/48	FA Cup 3rd Round	Aston Villa 4 Manchester United 6	Villa Park	58683
7	1952/53	10/01/53	FA Cup 3rd Round	Millwall 0 Manchester United 1	The Den	35652
8	1958/59	10/01/59	FA Cup 3rd Round	Norwich City 3 Manchester United 0	Carrow Road	38000
9	1969/70	10/01/70	Football League Division 1	Manchester United 2 Arsenal 1	Old Trafford	41055
10	1975/76	10/01/76	Football League Division 1	Manchester United 2 Queens Park Rangers 1	Old Trafford	58302
11	1980/81	10/01/81	Football League Division 1	Manchester United 2 Brighton 1	Old Trafford	42208
12	1986/87	10/01/87	FA Cup 3rd Round	Manchester United 1 Manchester City 0	Old Trafford	54294
13	1987/88	10/01/88	FA Cup 3rd Round	Ipswich Town 1 Manchester United 2	Portman Road	23012
14	1997/98	10/01/98	FA Premiership	Manchester United 2 Tottenham Hotspur 0	Old Trafford	55281
15	1998/99	10/01/99	FA Premiership	Manchester United 4 West Ham United 1	Old Trafford	55180

JANUARY 11

#	SEASON	DATE	COMPETITION / ROUND	MATCH RESULT	VENUE	ATT
1	1895/96	11/01/96	Football League Division 2	Newton Heath 3 Rotherham United 0	Bank Street	3000
2	1903/04	11/01/04	FA Cup Intermediate Round 3rd Replay	Manchester United 3 Birmingham City 1	Hyde Road	9372
3	1907/08	11/01/08	FA Cup 1st Round	Manchester United 3 Blackpool 1	Bank Street	11747
4	1912/13	11/01/13	FA Cup 1st Round	Manchester United 1 Coventry City 1	Old Trafford	11500
5	1929/30	11/01/30	FA Cup 3rd Round	Manchester United 0 Swindon Town 2	Old Trafford	33226
6	1935/36	11/01/36	FA Cup 3rd Round	Reading 1 Manchester United 3	Elm Park	25844
7	1938/39	11/01/39	FA Cup 3rd Round Replay	Manchester United 1 West Bromwich Albion 5	Old Trafford	17641
8	1946/47	11/01/47	FA Cup 3rd Round	Bradford Park Avenue 0 Manchester United 3	Park Avenue	26990
9	1957/58	11/01/58	Football League Division 1	Leeds United 1 Manchester United 1	Elland Road	39401
10	1963/64	11/01/64	Football League Division 1	Manchester United 1 Birmingham City 2	Old Trafford	44695
11	1968/69	11/01/69	Football League Division 1	Leeds United 2 Manchester United 1	Elland Road	48145
12	1974/75	11/01/75	Football League Division 2	Manchester United 2 Sheffield Wednesday 0	Old Trafford	45662
13	1977/78	11/01/78	FA Cup 3rd Round Replay	Manchester United 4 Carlisle United 2	Old Trafford	54156
14	1985/86	11/01/86	Football League Division 1	Oxford United 1 Manchester United 3	Manor Ground	13280
15	1988/89	11/01/89	FA Cup 3rd Round Replay	Queens Park Rangers 2 Manchester United 2	Loftus Road	22236
16	1991/92	11/01/92	Football League Division 1	Manchester United 1 Everton 0	Old Trafford	46619
17	1999/00	11/01/00	Club World Championship	Manchester United 2 South Melbourne 0	Maracana Stadium	25000
18	2002/03	11/01/03	FA Premiership	West Bromwich Albion 1 Manchester United 3	The Hawthorns	27129
19	2003/04	11/01/04	FA Premiership	Manchester United 0 Newcastle United 0	Old Trafford	67622
20	2005/06	11/01/06	League Cup Semi-Final 1st Leg	Blackburn Rovers 1 Manchester United 1	Ewood Park	24348

JANUARY 12

#	SEASON	DATE	COMPETITION / ROUND	MATCH RESULT	VENUE	ATT
1	1894/95	12/01/95	Football League Division 2	Rotherham United 2 Newton Heath 1	Millmoor	2000
2	1897/98	12/01/98	Football League Division 2	Newton Heath 0 Burnley 0	Bank Street	7000
3	1900/01	12/01/01	Football League Division 2	Newton Heath 0 Burnley 0	Bank Street	10000
4	1906/07	12/01/07	FA Cup 1st Round	Portsmouth 2 Manchester United 2	Fratton Park	24329
5	1920/21	12/01/21	FA Cup 1st Round Replay	Manchester United 1 Liverpool 2	Old Trafford	30000
6	1923/24	12/01/24	FA Cup 1st Round	Manchester United 1 Plymouth Argyle 0	Old Trafford	35700
7	1926/27	12/01/27	FA Cup 3rd Round Replay	Manchester United 2 Reading 2	Old Trafford	29122
8	1928/29	12/01/29	FA Cup 3rd Round	Port Vale 0 Manchester United 3	Old Recreation Ground	17519
9	1934/35	12/01/35	FA Cup 3rd Round	Bristol Rovers 1 Manchester United 3	Eastville	20400
10	1951/52	12/01/52	FA Cup 3rd Round	Manchester United 0 Hull City 2	Old Trafford	43517
11	1954/55	12/01/55	FA Cup 3rd Round Replay	Manchester United 4 Reading 1	Old Trafford	24578
12	1956/57	12/01/57	Football League Division 1	Manchester United 6 Newcastle United 1	Old Trafford	44911
13	1965/66	12/01/66	Football League Division 1	Leeds United 1 Manchester United 1	Elland Road	49672
14	1973/74	12/01/74	Football League Division 1	West Ham United 2 Manchester United 1	Upton Park	34147
15	1979/80	12/01/80	Football League Division 1	Middlesbrough 1 Manchester United 1	Ayresome Park	30587
16	1984/85	12/01/85	Football League Division 1	Manchester United 0 Coventry City 1	Old Trafford	35992
17	1990/91	12/01/91	Football League Division 1	Manchester United 3 Sunderland 0	Old Trafford	45934
18	1993/94	12/01/94	League Cup 5th Round	Manchester United 2 Portsmouth 2	Old Trafford	43794
19	1996/97	12/01/97	FA Premiership	Tottenham Hotspur 1 Manchester United 2	White Hart Lane	33026
20	2004/05	12/01/05	League Cup Semi-Final 1st Leg	Chelsea 0 Manchester United 0	Stamford Bridge	41492
21	2007/08	12/01/08	FA Premiership	Manchester United 6 Newcastle United 0	Old Trafford	75965

JANUARY 13

#	SEASON	DATE	COMPETITION / ROUND	MATCH RESULT	VENUE	ATT
1	1893/94	13/01/94	Football League Division 1	Newton Heath 1 Sheffield Wednesday 2	Bank Street	9000
2	1899/00	13/01/00	Football League Division 2	Loughborough Town 0 Newton Heath 2	The Athletic Ground	1000
3	1905/06	13/01/06	FA Cup 1st Round	Manchester United 7 Staple Hill 2	Bank Street	7560
4	1911/12	13/01/12	FA Cup 1st Round	Manchester United 3 Huddersfield Town 1	Old Trafford	19579
5	1922/23	13/01/23	FA Cup 1st Round	Bradford City 1 Manchester United 1	Valley Parade	27000
6	1933/34	13/01/34	FA Cup 3rd Round	Manchester United 1 Portsmouth 1	Old Trafford	23283
7	1950/51	13/01/51	Football League Division 1	Manchester United 2 Tottenham Hotspur 1	Old Trafford	43283
8	1961/62	13/01/62	Football League Division 1	Manchester United 0 Blackpool 1	Old Trafford	26999
9	1972/73	13/01/73	FA Cup 3rd Round	Wolverhampton Wanderers 1 Manchester United 0	Molineux	40005
10	1983/84	13/01/84	Football League Division 1	Queens Park Rangers 1 Manchester United 1	Loftus Road	16308
11	1989/90	13/01/90	Football League Division 1	Manchester United 1 Derby County 2	Old Trafford	38985
12	1995/96	13/01/96	FA Premiership	Manchester United 0 Aston Villa 0	Old Trafford	42667
13	2000/01	13/01/01	FA Premiership	Bradford City 0 Manchester United 3	Valley Parade	20551
14	2001/02	13/01/02	FA Premiership	Southampton 1 Manchester United 3	St Mary's Stadium	31858
15	2006/07	13/01/07	FA Premiership	Manchester United 3 Aston Villa 1	Old Trafford	76073

JANUARY 14

#	SEASON	DATE	COMPETITION / ROUND	MATCH RESULT	VENUE	ATT
1	1892/93	14/01/93	Football League Division 1	Newton Heath 1 Nottingham Forest 3	North Road	8000
2	1898/99	14/01/99	Football League Division 2	Newton Heath 3 Glossop 0	Bank Street	12000
3	1904/05	14/01/05	FA Cup Intermediate Round	Manchester United 2 Fulham 2	Bank Street	17000
4	1910/11	14/01/11	FA Cup 1st Round	Blackpool 1 Manchester United 2	Bloomfield Road	12000
5	1921/22	14/01/22	Football League Division 1	Manchester United 0 Newcastle United 1	Old Trafford	20000
6	1927/28	14/01/28	FA Cup 3rd Round	Manchester United 7 Brentford 1	Old Trafford	18538
7	1930/31	14/01/31	FA Cup 3rd Round Replay	Manchester United 0 Stoke City 0	Old Trafford	22013
8	1932/33	14/01/33	FA Cup 3rd Round	Manchester United 1 Middlesbrough 4	Old Trafford	36991
9	1938/39	14/01/39	Football League Division 1	Manchester United 3 Grimsby Town 1	Old Trafford	25654
10	1949/50	14/01/50	Football League Division 1	Manchester United 1 Chelsea 0	Old Trafford	46954
11	1955/56	14/01/56	Football League Division 1	Manchester United 3 Sheffield United 1	Old Trafford	30162
12	1957/58	14/01/58	European Cup Quarter-Final 1st Leg	Manchester United 3 Red Star Belgrade 1	Old Trafford	60000
13	1960/61	14/01/61	Football League Division 1	Manchester United 2 Tottenham Hotspur 0	Old Trafford	65295
14	1966/67	14/01/67	Football League Division 1	Manchester United 1 Tottenham Hotspur 0	Old Trafford	57366
15	1977/78	14/01/78	Football League Division 1	Ipswich Town 1 Manchester United 2	Portman Road	23321
16	1988/89	14/01/89	Football League Division 1	Manchester United 3 Millwall 0	Old Trafford	40931
17	2005/06	14/01/06	FA Premiership	Manchester City 3 Manchester United 1	Eastlands Stadium	47192

JANUARY 15

#	SEASON	DATE	COMPETITION / ROUND	MATCH RESULT	VENUE	ATT
1	1897/98	15/01/98	Football League Division 2	Newton Heath 4 Blackpool 0	Bank Street	4000
2	1905/06	15/01/06	Football League Division 2	Manchester United 0 Leeds United 3	Bank Street	6000
3	1909/10	15/01/10	FA Cup 1st Round	Burnley 2 Manchester United 0	Turf Moor	16628
4	1920/21	15/01/21	Football League Division 1	Manchester United 1 West Bromwich Albion 4	Old Trafford	30000
5	1926/27	15/01/27	Football League Division 1	Manchester United 0 Liverpool 1	Old Trafford	30304
6	1937/38	15/01/38	Football League Division 2	Manchester United 4 Luton Town 2	Old Trafford	16845
7	1961/62	15/01/62	Football League Division 1	Manchester United 2 Aston Villa 0	Old Trafford	20807
8	1965/66	15/01/66	Football League Division 1	Fulham 0 Manchester United 1	Craven Cottage	33018
9	1971/72	15/01/72	FA Cup 3rd Round	Southampton 1 Manchester United 1	The Dell	30190
10	1974/75	15/01/75	League Cup Semi-Final 1st Leg	Manchester United 2 Norwich City 2	Old Trafford	58010
11	1976/77	15/01/77	Football League Division 1	Manchester United 2 Coventry City 0	Old Trafford	46567
12	1978/79	15/01/79	FA Cup 3rd Round	Manchester United 3 Chelsea 0	Old Trafford	38743
13	1982/83	15/01/83	Football League Division 1	Birmingham City 1 Manchester United 2	St Andrews	19333
14	1991/92	15/01/92	FA Cup 3rd Round	Leeds United 0 Manchester United 1	Elland Road	31819
15	1993/94	15/01/94	FA Premiership	Tottenham Hotspur 0 Manchester United 1	White Hart Lane	31343
16	1994/95	15/01/95	FA Premiership	Newcastle United 1 Manchester United 1	St James' Park	34471
17	2004/05	15/01/05	FA Premiership	Liverpool 0 Manchester United 1	Anfield	44183

JANUARY 16

#	SEASON	DATE	COMPETITION / ROUND	MATCH RESULT	VENUE	ATT
1	1896/97	16/01/97	FA Cup 5th Qualifying Round	Newton Heath 2 Blackpool 2	Bank Street	1500
2	1903/04	16/01/04	Football League Division 2	Manchester United 3 Glossop 1	Bank Street	10000
3	1906/07	16/01/07	FA Cup 1st Round Replay	Manchester United 1 Portsmouth 2	Bank Street	8000
4	1908/09	16/01/09	FA Cup 1st Round	Manchester United 1 Brighton 0	Bank Street	8300
5	1912/13	16/01/13	FA Cup 1st Round Replay	Coventry City 1 Manchester United 2	Highfield Road	20042
6	1914/15	16/01/15	Football League Division 1	Manchester United 4 Bolton Wanderers 1	Old Trafford	8000
7	1925/26	16/01/26	Football League Division 1	Arsenal 3 Manchester United 2	Highbury	25252
8	1931/32	16/01/32	Football League Division 2	Swansea City 3 Manchester United 1	Vetch Field	5888
9	1936/37	16/01/37	FA Cup 3rd Round	Manchester United 1 Reading 0	Old Trafford	36668
10	1953/54	16/01/54	Football League Division 1	Manchester United 1 Manchester City 1	Old Trafford	46379
11	1956/57	16/01/57	European Cup Quarter-Final 1st Leg	Athletic Bilbao 5 Manchester United 3	Estadio San Mames	60000
12	1959/60	16/01/60	Football League Division 1	Manchester United 3 Birmingham City 1	Old Trafford	47361
13	1964/65	16/01/65	Football League Division 1	Nottingham Forest 2 Manchester United 2	City Ground	43009
14	1970/71	16/01/71	Football League Division 1	Manchester United 1 Burnley 1	Old Trafford	40135
15	1987/88	16/01/88	Football League Division 1	Manchester United 0 Southampton 2	Old Trafford	35716
16	1990/91	16/01/91	League Cup 5th Round	Southampton 1 Manchester United 1	The Dell	21011
17	1995/96	16/01/96	FA Cup 3rd Round Replay	Sunderland 1 Manchester United 2	Roker Park	21378
18	1998/99	16/01/99	FA Premiership	Leicester City 2 Manchester United 6	Filbert Street	22091

JANUARY 17

#	SEASON	DATE	COMPETITION / ROUND	MATCH RESULT	VENUE	ATT
1	1902/03	17/01/03	Football League Division 2	Manchester United 1 Bristol City 2	Bank Street	12000
2	1913/14	17/01/14	Football League Division 1	Manchester United 0 Chelsea 1	Old Trafford	20000
3	1919/20	17/01/20	Football League Division 1	Chelsea 1 Manchester United 0	Stamford Bridge	40000
4	1922/23	17/01/23	FA Cup 1st Round Replay	Manchester United 2 Bradford City 0	Old Trafford	27791
5	1924/25	17/01/25	Football League Division 2	Coventry City 1 Manchester United 0	Highfield Road	9000
6	1926/27	17/01/27	FA Cup 3rd Round 2nd Replay	Manchester United 1 Reading 2	Villa Park	16500
7	1930/31	17/01/31	Football League Division 1	Newcastle United 4 Manchester United 3	St James' Park	24835
8	1933/34	17/01/34	FA Cup 3rd Round Replay	Portsmouth 4 Manchester United 1	Fratton Park	18748
9	1947/48	17/01/48	Football League Division 1	Manchester United 1 Arsenal 1	Maine Road	81962
10	1952/53	17/01/53	Football League Division 1	Manchester United 1 Portsmouth 0	Old Trafford	32341
11	1969/70	17/01/70	Football League Division 1	West Ham United 0 Manchester United 0	Upton Park	41643
12	1975/76	17/01/76	Football League Division 1	Tottenham Hotspur 1 Manchester United 1	White Hart Lane	49189
13	2003/04	17/01/04	FA Premiership	Wolverhampton Wanderers 1 Manchester United 0	Molineux	29396

JANUARY 18

#	SEASON	DATE	COMPETITION / ROUND	MATCH RESULT	VENUE	ATT
1	1889/90	18/01/90	FA Cup 1st Round	Preston North End 6 Newton Heath 1	Deepdale	7900
2	1901/02	18/01/02	Football League Division 2	Bristol City 4 Newton Heath 0	Ashton Gate	6000
3	1904/05	18/01/05	FA Cup Intermediate Round Replay	Fulham 0 Manchester United 0	Craven Cottage	15000
4	1907/08	18/01/08	Football League Division 1	Sheffield United 2 Manchester United 0	Bramall Lane	17000
5	1912/13	18/01/13	Football League Division 1	Everton 4 Manchester United 1	Goodison Park	20000
6	1929/30	18/01/30	Football League Division 1	Manchester United 0 Middlesbrough 3	Old Trafford	21028
7	1935/36	18/01/36	Football League Division 2	Manchester United 3 Newcastle United 1	Old Trafford	22968
8	1946/47	18/01/47	Football League Division 1	Middlesbrough 2 Manchester United 4	Ayresome Park	37435
9	1957/58	18/01/58	Football League Division 1	Manchester United 7 Bolton Wanderers 2	Old Trafford	41141
10	1963/64	18/01/64	Football League Division 1	West Bromwich Albion 1 Manchester United 4	The Hawthorns	25624
11	1968/69	18/01/69	Football League Division 1	Manchester United 4 Sunderland 1	Old Trafford	45670
12	1974/75	18/01/75	Football League Division 2	Sunderland 0 Manchester United 0	Roker Park	45976
13	1985/86	18/01/86	Football League Division 1	Manchester United 2 Nottingham Forest 3	Old Trafford	46717
14	1991/92	18/01/92	Football League Division 1	Notts County 1 Manchester United 1	Meadow Lane	21055
15	1992/93	18/01/93	FA Premiership	Queens Park Rangers 1 Manchester United 3	Loftus Road	21117
16	1996/97	18/01/97	FA Premiership	Coventry City 0 Manchester United 2	Highfield Road	23085
17	2002/03	18/01/03	FA Premiership	Manchester United 2 Chelsea 1	Old Trafford	67606
18	2005/06	18/01/06	FA Cup 3rd Round Replay	Manchester United 5 Burton Albion 0	Old Trafford	53564

JANUARY 19

#	SEASON	DATE	COMPETITION / ROUND	MATCH RESULT	VENUE	ATT
1	1900/01	19/01/01	Football League Division 2	Port Vale 2 Newton Heath 0	Cobridge Stadium	1000
2	1906/07	19/01/07	Football League Division 1	Manchester United 2 Sheffield United 0	Bank Street	15000
3	1923/24	19/01/24	Football League Division 2	Fulham 3 Manchester United 1	Craven Cottage	15500
4	1928/29	19/01/29	Football League Division 1	Manchester United 1 Leeds United 2	Old Trafford	21995
5	1930/31	19/01/31	FA Cup 3rd Round 2nd Replay	Manchester United 4 Stoke City 2	Anfield	11788
6	1934/35	19/01/35	Football League Division 2	Barnsley 0 Manchester United 2	Oakwell	10177
7	1951/52	19/01/52	Football League Division 1	Manchester United 1 Manchester City 1	Old Trafford	54245
8	1956/57	19/01/57	Football League Division 1	Sheffield Wednesday 2 Manchester United 1	Hillsborough	51068
9	1971/72	19/01/72	FA Cup 3rd Round Replay	Manchester United 4 Southampton 1	Old Trafford	50960
10	1973/74	19/01/74	Football League Division 1	Manchester United 1 Arsenal 1	Old Trafford	38589
11	1976/77	19/01/77	Football League Division 1	Manchester United 2 Bristol City 1	Old Trafford	43051
12	1982/83	19/01/83	League Cup 5th Round	Manchester United 4 Nottingham Forest 0	Old Trafford	44413
13	1990/91	19/01/91	Football League Division 1	Queens Park Rangers 1 Manchester United 1	Loftus Road	18544
14	1997/98	19/01/98	FA Premiership	Southampton 1 Manchester United 0	The Dell	15241
15	2001/02	19/01/02	FA Premiership	Manchester United 2 Blackburn Rovers 1	Old Trafford	67552
16	2004/05	19/01/05	FA Cup 3rd Round Replay	Exeter City 0 Manchester United 2	St James' Park	9033
17	2007/08	19/01/08	FA Premiership	Reading 0 Manchester United 2	Madejski Stadium	24135

JANUARY 20

#	SEASON	DATE	COMPETITION / ROUND	MATCH RESULT	VENUE	ATT
1	1896/97	20/01/97	FA Cup 5th Qualifying Round Replay	Blackpool 1 Newton Heath 2	Raikes Hall Gardens	5000
2	1899/00	20/01/00	Football League Division 2	Newton Heath 4 Burton Swifts 0	Bank Street	4000
3	1905/06	20/01/06	Football League Division 2	Manchester United 5 Glossop 0	Bank Street	7000
4	1911/12	20/01/12	Football League Division 1	Manchester United 1 West Bromwich Albion 2	Old Trafford	8000
5	1922/23	20/01/23	Football League Division 2	Manchester United 0 Leeds United 0	Old Trafford	25000
6	1933/34	20/01/34	Football League Division 2	Bolton Wanderers 3 Manchester United 1	Burnden Park	11887
7	1950/51	20/01/51	Football League Division 1	Charlton Athletic 1 Manchester United 2	The Valley	31978
8	1961/62	20/01/62	Football League Division 1	Tottenham Hotspur 2 Manchester United 2	White Hart Lane	55225
9	1964/65	20/01/65	ICFC 3rd Round 1st Leg	Manchester United 1 Everton 1	Old Trafford	50000
10	1967/68	20/01/68	Football League Division 1	Manchester United 4 Sheffield Wednesday 2	Old Trafford	55254
11	1972/73	20/01/73	Football League Division 1	Manchester United 2 West Ham United 2	Old Trafford	50878
12	1987/88	20/01/88	League Cup 5th Round	Oxford United 2 Manchester United 0	Manor Ground	12658
13	2000/01	20/01/01	FA Premiership	Manchester United 2 Aston Villa 0	Old Trafford	67533

JANUARY 21

#	SEASON	DATE	COMPETITION / ROUND	MATCH RESULT	VENUE	ATT
1	1892/93	21/01/93	FA Cup 1st Round	Blackburn Rovers 4 Newton Heath 0	Ewood Park	7000
2	1898/99	21/01/99	Football League Division 2	Walsall 2 Newton Heath 0	Fellows Park	3000
3	1904/05	21/01/05	Football League Division 2	Manchester United 4 Glossop 1	Bank Street	20000
4	1910/11	21/01/11	Football League Division 1	Manchester City 1 Manchester United 1	Hyde Road	40000
5	1921/22	21/01/22	Football League Division 1	Sunderland 2 Manchester United 1	Roker Park	10000
6	1927/28	21/01/28	Football League Division 1	Newcastle United 4 Manchester United 1	St James' Park	25912
7	1932/33	21/01/33	Football League Division 2	Manchester United 2 Tottenham Hotspur 1	Old Trafford	20661
8	1938/39	21/01/39	Football League Division 1	Manchester United 0 Stoke City 1	Old Trafford	37384
9	1949/50	21/01/50	Football League Division 1	Stoke City 3 Manchester United 1	Victoria Ground	38877
10	1955/56	21/01/56	Football League Division 1	Preston North End 3 Manchester United 1	Deepdale	28047
11	1960/61	21/01/61	Football League Division 1	Leicester City 6 Manchester United 0	Filbert Street	31308
12	1966/67	21/01/67	Football League Division 1	Manchester City 1 Manchester United 1	Maine Road	62983
13	1977/78	21/01/78	Football League Division 1	Manchester United 4 Derby County 0	Old Trafford	57115
14	1983/84	21/01/84	Football League Division 1	Manchester United 3 Southampton 2	Old Trafford	40371
15	1988/89	21/01/89	Football League Division 1	West Ham United 1 Manchester United 3	Upton Park	29822
16	1989/90	21/01/90	Football League Division 1	Norwich City 2 Manchester United 0	Carrow Road	17370
17	2006/07	21/01/07	FA Premiership	Arsenal 2 Manchester United 1	Emirates Stadium	60128

JANUARY 22

#	SEASON	DATE	COMPETITION / ROUND	MATCH RESULT	VENUE	ATT
1	1909/10	22/01/10	Football League Division 1	Manchester United 5 Tottenham Hotspur 0	Bank Street	7000
2	1920/21	22/01/21	Football League Division 1	West Bromwich Albion 0 Manchester United 2	The Hawthorns	30000
3	1926/27	22/01/27	Football League Division 1	Leeds United 2 Manchester United 3	Elland Road	16816
4	1937/38	22/01/38	FA Cup 4th Round	Barnsley 2 Manchester United 2	Oakwell	35549
5	1948/49	22/01/49	Football League Division 1	Manchester United 0 Manchester City 0	Maine Road	66485
6	1954/55	22/01/55	Football League Division 1	Manchester United 1 Bolton Wanderers 1	Old Trafford	39873
7	1965/66	22/01/66	FA Cup 3rd Round	Derby County 2 Manchester United 5	Baseball Ground	33827
8	1971/72	22/01/72	Football League Division 1	Manchester United 0 Chelsea 1	Old Trafford	55927
9	1974/75	22/01/75	League Cup Semi-Final 2nd Leg	Norwich City 1 Manchester United 0	Carrow Road	31621
10	1976/77	22/01/77	Football League Division 1	Birmingham City 2 Manchester United 3	St Andrews	35316
11	1982/83	22/01/83	Football League Division 1	Manchester United 2 Nottingham Forest 0	Old Trafford	38615
12	1991/92	22/01/92	Football League Division 1	Manchester United 1 Aston Villa 0	Old Trafford	45022
13	1993/94	22/01/94	FA Premiership	Manchester United 1 Everton 0	Old Trafford	44750
14	1994/95	22/01/95	FA Premiership	Manchester United 1 Blackburn Rovers 0	Old Trafford	43742
15	1995/96	22/01/96	FA Premiership	West Ham United 0 Manchester United 1	Upton Park	24197
16	2001/02	22/01/02	FA Premiership	Manchester United 0 Liverpool 1	Old Trafford	67599
17	2002/03	22/01/03	League Cup Semi-Final 2nd Leg	Blackburn Rovers 1 Manchester United 3	Ewood Park	29048
18	2004/05	22/01/05	FA Premiership	Manchester United 3 Aston Villa 1	Old Trafford	67859
19	2005/06	22/01/06	FA Premiership	Manchester United 1 Liverpool 0	Old Trafford	67874

JANUARY 23

#	SEASON	DATE	COMPETITION / ROUND	MATCH RESULT	VENUE	ATT
1	1903/04	23/01/04	Football League Division 2	Bradford City 3 Manchester United 3	Valley Parade	12000
2	1904/05	23/01/05	FA Cup Intermediate Round 2nd Replay	Manchester United 0 Fulham 1	Villa Park	6000
3	1908/09	23/01/09	Football League Division 1	Manchester United 3 Manchester City 1	Bank Street	40000
4	1914/15	23/01/15	Football League Division 1	Blackburn Rovers 3 Manchester United 3	Ewood Park	7000
5	1925/26	23/01/26	Football League Division 1	Manchester United 1 Manchester City 6	Old Trafford	48657
6	1931/32	23/01/32	Football League Division 2	Tottenham Hotspur 4 Manchester United 1	White Hart Lane	19139
7	1936/37	23/01/37	Football League Division 1	Sheffield Wednesday 1 Manchester United 0	Hillsborough	8658
8	1953/54	23/01/54	Football League Division 1	Manchester United 1 Bolton Wanderers 5	Old Trafford	46663
9	1959/60	23/01/60	Football League Division 1	Tottenham Hotspur 2 Manchester United 1	White Hart Lane	62602
10	1964/65	23/01/65	Football League Division 1	Manchester United 1 Stoke City 1	Old Trafford	50392
11	1981/82	23/01/82	Football League Division 1	Stoke City 0 Manchester United 3	Victoria Ground	19793
12	1988/89	23/01/89	FA Cup 3rd Round 2nd Replay	Manchester United 3 Queens Park Rangers 0	Old Trafford	46257
13	1990/91	23/01/91	League Cup 5th Round Replay	Manchester United 3 Southampton 2	Old Trafford	41903
14	1992/93	23/01/93	FA Cup 4th Round	Manchester United 1 Brighton 0	Old Trafford	33600

JANUARY 24

#	SEASON	DATE	COMPETITION / ROUND	MATCH RESULT	VENUE	ATT
1	1902/03	24/01/03	Football League Division 2	Glossop 1 Manchester United 3	North Road	5000
2	1913/14	24/01/14	Football League Division 1	Oldham Athletic 2 Manchester United 2	Boundary Park	10000
3	1919/20	24/01/20	Football League Division 1	West Bromwich Albion 2 Manchester United 1	The Hawthorns	20000
4	1924/25	24/01/25	Football League Division 2	Manchester United 0 Oldham Athletic 1	Old Trafford	20000
5	1930/31	24/01/31	FA Cup 4th Round	Grimsby Town 1 Manchester United 0	Blundell Park	15000
6	1947/48	24/01/48	FA Cup 4th Round	Manchester United 3 Liverpool 0	Goodison Park	74000
7	1952/53	24/01/53	Football League Division 1	Bolton Wanderers 2 Manchester United 1	Burnden Park	43638
8	1969/70	24/01/70	FA Cup 4th Round	Manchester United 3 Manchester City 0	Old Trafford	63417
9	1972/73	24/01/73	Football League Division 1	Manchester United 0 Everton 0	Old Trafford	58970
10	1975/76	24/01/76	FA Cup 4th Round	Manchester United 3 Peterborough United 1	Old Trafford	56352
11	1980/81	24/01/81	FA Cup 4th Round	Nottingham Forest 1 Manchester United 0	City Ground	34110
12	1986/87	24/01/87	Football League Division 1	Manchester United 2 Arsenal 0	Old Trafford	51367
13	1987/88	24/01/88	Football League Division 1	Arsenal 1 Manchester United 2	Highbury	29392
14	1997/98	24/01/98	FA Cup 4th Round	Manchester United 5 Walsall 1	Old Trafford	54669
15	1998/99	24/01/99	FA Cup 4th Round	Manchester United 2 Liverpool 1	Old Trafford	54591
16	1999/00	24/01/00	FA Premiership	Manchester United 1 Arsenal 1	Old Trafford	58293

JANUARY 25

#	SEASON	DATE	COMPETITION / ROUND	MATCH RESULT	VENUE	ATT
1	1901/02	25/01/02	Football League Division 2	Newton Heath 0 Blackpool 1	Bank Street	2500
2	1907/08	25/01/08	Football League Division 1	Manchester United 1 Chelsea 0	Bank Street	20000
3	1912/13	25/01/13	Football League Division 1	Manchester United 2 Sheffield Wednesday 0	Old Trafford	45000
4	1929/30	25/01/30	Football League Division 1	Liverpool 1 Manchester United 0	Anfield	28592
5	1935/36	25/01/36	FA Cup 4th Round	Stoke City 0 Manchester United 0	Victoria Ground	32286
6	1946/47	25/01/47	FA Cup 4th Round	Manchester United 0 Nottingham Forest 2	Maine Road	34059
7	1957/58	25/01/58	FA Cup 4th Round	Manchester United 2 Ipswich Town 0	Old Trafford	53550
8	1963/64	25/01/64	FA Cup 4th Round	Manchester United 4 Bristol Rovers 1	Old Trafford	55772
9	1968/69	25/01/69	FA Cup 4th Round	Manchester United 1 Watford 1	Old Trafford	63498
10	1985/86	25/01/86	FA Cup 4th Round	Sunderland 0 Manchester United 0	Roker Park	35484
11	1994/95	25/01/95	FA Premiership	Crystal Palace 1 Manchester United 1	Selhurst Park	18224
12	1996/97	25/01/97	FA Cup 4th Round	Manchester United 1 Wimbledon 1	Old Trafford	53342
13	2003/04	25/01/04	FA Cup 4th Round	Northampton Town 0 Manchester United 3	Sixfields Stadium	7356
14	2005/06	25/01/06	League Cup Semi-Final 2nd Leg	Manchester United 2 Blackburn Rovers 1	Old Trafford	61636

JANUARY 26

#	SEASON	DATE	COMPETITION / ROUND	MATCH RESULT	VENUE	ATT
1	1892/93	26/01/93	Football League Division 1	Notts County 4 Newton Heath 0	Trent Bridge	1000
2	1906/07	26/01/07	Football League Division 1	Bolton Wanderers 0 Manchester United 1	Burnden Park	25000
3	1923/24	26/01/24	Football League Division 2	Manchester United 0 Fulham 0	Old Trafford	25000
4	1928/29	26/01/29	FA Cup 4th Round	Manchester United 0 Bury 1	Old Trafford	40558
5	1934/35	26/01/35	FA Cup 4th Round	Nottingham Forest 0 Manchester United 0	City Ground	32862
6	1937/38	26/01/38	FA Cup 4th Round Replay	Manchester United 1 Barnsley 0	Old Trafford	33601
7	1945/46	26/01/46	FA Cup 4th Round 1st Leg	Manchester United 1 Preston North End 0	Maine Road	36237
8	1951/52	26/01/52	Football League Division 1	Manchester United 2 Tottenham Hotspur 0	Old Trafford	40845
9	1956/57	26/01/57	FA Cup 4th Round	Wrexham 0 Manchester United 5	Racecourse Ground	34445
10	1969/70	26/01/70	Football League Division 1	Manchester United 2 Leeds United 2	Old Trafford	59879
11	1973/74	26/01/74	FA Cup 4th Round	Manchester United 0 Ipswich Town 1	Old Trafford	37177
12	1984/85	26/01/85	FA Cup 4th Round	Manchester United 2 Coventry City 1	Old Trafford	38039
13	1990/91	26/01/91	FA Cup 4th Round	Manchester United 1 Bolton Wanderers 0	Old Trafford	43293
14	1993/94	26/01/94	League Cup 5th Round Replay	Portsmouth 0 Manchester United 1	Fratton Park	24950
15	2001/02	26/01/02	FA Cup 4th Round	Middlesbrough 2 Manchester United 0	Riverside Stadium	17624
16	2002/03	26/01/03	FA Cup 4th Round	Manchester United 6 West Ham United 0	Old Trafford	67181
17	2004/05	26/01/05	League Cup Semi-Final 2nd Leg	Manchester United 1 Chelsea 2	Old Trafford	67000

JANUARY 27

#	SEASON	DATE	COMPETITION / ROUND	MATCH RESULT	VENUE	ATT
1	1893/94	27/01/94	FA Cup 1st Round	Newton Heath 4 Middlesbrough 0	Bank Street	5000
2	1905/06	27/01/06	Football League Division 2	Stockport County 0 Manchester United 1	Edgeley Park	15000
3	1911/12	27/01/12	Football League Division 1	Sunderland 5 Manchester United 0	Roker Park	12000
4	1922/23	27/01/23	Football League Division 2	Leeds United 0 Manchester United 1	Elland Road	24500
5	1933/34	27/01/34	Football League Division 2	Manchester United 1 Brentford 3	Old Trafford	16891
6	1950/51	27/01/51	FA Cup 4th Round	Manchester United 4 Leeds United 0	Old Trafford	55434
7	1967/68	27/01/68	FA Cup 3rd Round	Manchester United 2 Tottenham Hotspur 2	Old Trafford	63500
8	1972/73	27/01/73	Football League Division 1	Coventry City 1 Manchester United 1	Highfield Road	42767
9	1981/82	27/01/82	Football League Division 1	Manchester United 1 West Ham United 0	Old Trafford	41291
10	1991/92	27/01/92	FA Cup 4th Round	Southampton 0 Manchester United 0	The Dell	19506
11	1992/93	27/01/93	FA Premiership	Manchester United 2 Nottingham Forest 0	Old Trafford	36085
12	1995/96	27/01/96	FA Cup 4th Round	Reading 0 Manchester United 3	Elm Park	14780
13	2006/07	27/01/07	FA Cup 4th Round	Manchester United 2 Portsmouth 1	Old Trafford	71137
14	2007/08	27/01/08	FA Cup 4th Round	Manchester United 3 Tottenham Hotspur 1	Old Trafford	75369

JANUARY 28

#	SEASON	DATE	COMPETITION / ROUND	MATCH RESULT	VENUE	ATT
1	1898/99	28/01/99	FA Cup 1st Round	Tottenham Hotspur 1 Newton Heath 1	Asplins Farm	15000
2	1910/11	28/01/11	Football League Division 1	Manchester United 2 Everton 2	Old Trafford	45000
3	1921/22	28/01/22	Football League Division 1	Manchester United 3 Sunderland 1	Old Trafford	18000
4	1927/28	28/01/28	FA Cup 4th Round	Bury 1 Manchester United 1	Gigg Lane	25000
5	1930/31	28/01/31	Football League Division 1	Manchester United 4 Sheffield Wednesday 1	Old Trafford	6077
6	1938/39	28/01/39	Football League Division 1	Chelsea 0 Manchester United 1	Stamford Bridge	31265
7	1949/50	28/01/50	FA Cup 4th Round	Watford 0 Manchester United 1	Vicarage Road	32800
8	1960/61	28/01/61	FA Cup 4th Round	Sheffield Wednesday 1 Manchester United 1	Hillsborough	58000
9	1966/67	28/01/67	FA Cup 3rd Round	Manchester United 2 Stoke City 0	Old Trafford	63500
10	1977/78	28/01/78	FA Cup 4th Round	Manchester United 1 West Bromwich Albion 1	Old Trafford	57056
11	1980/81	28/01/81	Football League Division 1	Sunderland 2 Manchester United 0	Roker Park	31910
12	1988/89	28/01/89	FA Cup 4th Round	Manchester United 4 Oxford United 0	Old Trafford	47745
13	1989/90	28/01/90	FA Cup 4th Round	Hereford United 0 Manchester United 1	Edgar Street	13777
14	1994/95	28/01/95	FA Cup 4th Round	Manchester United 5 Wrexham 2	Old Trafford	43222
15	2000/01	28/01/01	FA Cup 4th Round	Manchester United 0 West Ham United 1	Old Trafford	67029

JANUARY 29

#	SEASON	DATE	COMPETITION / ROUND	MATCH RESULT	VENUE	ATT
1	1897/98	29/01/98	FA Cup 1st Round	Newton Heath 1 Walsall 0	Bank Street	6000
2	1935/36	29/01/36	FA Cup 4th Round Replay	Manchester United 0 Stoke City 2	Old Trafford	34440
3	1937/38	29/01/38	Football League Division 2	Manchester United 3 Stockport County 1	Old Trafford	31852
4	1948/49	29/01/49	FA Cup 4th Round	Manchester United 1 Bradford Park Avenue 1	Maine Road	82771
5	1965/66	29/01/66	Football League Division 1	Sheffield Wednesday 0 Manchester United 0	Hillsborough	39281
6	1971/72	29/01/72	Football League Division 1	West Bromwich Albion 2 Manchester United 1	The Hawthorns	47012
7	1976/77	29/01/77	FA Cup 4th Round	Manchester United 1 Queens Park Rangers 0	Old Trafford	57422
8	1982/83	29/01/83	FA Cup 4th Round	Luton Town 0 Manchester United 2	Kenilworth Road	20516
9	1985/86	29/01/86	FA Cup 4th Round Replay	Manchester United 3 Sunderland 0	Old Trafford	43402
10	1996/97	29/01/97	FA Premiership	Manchester United 2 Wimbledon 1	Old Trafford	55314
11	1999/00	29/01/00	FA Premiership	Manchester United 1 Middlesbrough 0	Old Trafford	61267
12	2001/02	29/01/02	FA Premiership	Bolton Wanderers 0 Manchester United 4	Reebok Stadium	27350
13	2004/05	29/01/05	FA Cup 4th Round	Manchester United 3 Middlesbrough 0	Old Trafford	67251
14	2005/06	29/01/06	FA Cup 4th Round	Wolverhampton Wanderers 0 Manchester United 3	Molineux	28333

JANUARY 30

#	SEASON	DATE	COMPETITION / ROUND	MATCH RESULT	VENUE	ATT
1	1896/97	30/01/97	FA Cup 1st Round	Newton Heath 5 Kettering 1	Bank Street	1500
2	1903/04	30/01/04	Football League Division 2	Manchester United 1 Arsenal 0	Bank Street	40000
3	1908/09	30/01/09	Football League Division 1	Liverpool 3 Manchester United 1	Anfield	30000
4	1914/15	30/01/15	Football League Division 1	Manchester United 1 Notts County 2	Old Trafford	7000
5	1925/26	30/01/26	FA Cup 4th Round	Tottenham Hotspur 2 Manchester United 2	White Hart Lane	40000
6	1931/32	30/01/32	Football League Division 2	Manchester United 3 Nottingham Forest 2	Old Trafford	11152
7	1934/35	30/01/35	FA Cup 4th Round Replay	Manchester United 0 Nottingham Forest 3	Old Trafford	33851
8	1936/37	30/01/37	FA Cup 4th Round	Arsenal 5 Manchester United 0	Highbury	45637
9	1945/46	30/01/46	FA Cup 4th Round 2nd Leg	Preston North End 1 Manchester United 1	Deepdale	21000
10	1959/60	30/01/60	FA Cup 4th Round	Liverpool 1 Manchester United 3	Anfield	56736
11	1964/65	30/01/65	FA Cup 4th Round	Stoke City 0 Manchester United 0	Victoria Ground	53009
12	1970/71	30/01/71	Football League Division 1	Huddersfield Town 1 Manchester United 2	Leeds Road	41464
13	1981/82	30/01/82	Football League Division 1	Swansea City 2 Manchester United 0	Vetch Field	24115
14	1987/88	30/01/88	FA Cup 4th Round	Manchester United 2 Chelsea 0	Old Trafford	50716
15	1992/93	30/01/93	FA Premiership	Ipswich Town 2 Manchester United 1	Portman Road	22068
16	1993/94	30/01/94	FA Cup 4th Round	Norwich City 0 Manchester United 2	Carrow Road	21060
17	2007/08	30/01/08	FA Premiership	Manchester United 2 Portsmouth 0	Old Trafford	75415

JANUARY 31

#	SEASON	DATE	COMPETITION / ROUND	MATCH RESULT	VENUE	ATT
1	1902/03	31/01/03	Football League Division 2	Chesterfield 2 Manchester United 0	Saltergate	6000
2	1919/20	31/01/20	FA Cup 2nd Round	Manchester United 1 Aston Villa 2	Old Trafford	48600
3	1930/31	31/01/31	Football League Division 1	Grimsby Town 2 Manchester United 1	Blundell Park	9305
4	1932/33	31/01/33	Football League Division 2	Grimsby Town 1 Manchester United 1	Blundell Park	4020
5	1947/48	31/01/48	Football League Division 1	Sheffield United 2 Manchester United 1	Bramall Lane	45189
6	1952/53	31/01/53	FA Cup 4th Round	Manchester United 1 Walthamstow Avenue 1	Old Trafford	34748
7	1958/59	31/01/59	Football League Division 1	Manchester United 4 Newcastle United 4	Old Trafford	49008
8	1961/62	31/01/62	FA Cup 4th Round	Manchester United 1 Arsenal 0	Old Trafford	54082
9	1967/68	31/01/68	FA Cup 3rd Round Replay	Tottenham Hotspur 1 Manchester United 0	White Hart Lane	57200
10	1969/70	31/01/70	Football League Division 1	Manchester United 1 Derby County 0	Old Trafford	59315
11	1975/76	31/01/76	Football League Division 1	Manchester United 3 Birmingham City 1	Old Trafford	50724
12	1978/79	31/01/79	FA Cup 4th Round	Fulham 1 Manchester United 1	Craven Cottage	25229
13	1980/81	31/01/81	Football League Division 1	Manchester United 2 Birmingham City 0	Old Trafford	39081
14	1986/87	31/01/87	FA Cup 4th Round	Manchester United 0 Coventry City 1	Old Trafford	49082
15	1997/98	31/01/98	FA Premiership	Manchester United 0 Leicester City 1	Old Trafford	55156
16	1998/99	31/01/99	FA Premiership	Charlton Athletic 0 Manchester United 1	The Valley	20043
17	2000/01	31/01/01	FA Premiership	Sunderland 0 Manchester United 1	Stadium of Light	48260
18	2003/04	31/01/04	FA Premiership	Manchester United 3 Southampton 2	Old Trafford	67758
19	2006/07	31/01/07	FA Premiership	Manchester United 4 Watford 0	Old Trafford	76032

UNITED in FEBRUARY

OVERALL PLAYING RECORD

	P	W	D	L	F	A		P	W	D	L	F	A		P	W	D	L	F	A
1st	20	11	1	8	43	40	11th	18	8	5	5	36	34	21st	17	6	4	7	23	24
2nd	15	6	2	7	27	29	12th	13	5	3	5	23	19	22nd	16	9	5	2	25	12
3rd	20	14	3	3	36	19	13th	15	10	3	2	24	18	23rd	18	7	6	5	28	18
4th	15	8	4	3	23	14	14th	14	6	3	5	18	15	24th	15	8	2	5	29	19
5th	19	9	8	2	40	24	15th	14	8	4	2	28	13	25th	23	9	5	9	41	28
6th	18	12	3	3	40	14	16th	12	6	4	2	21	11	26th	21	10	7	4	45	29
7th	16	8	4	4	37	23	17th	15	5	7	3	20	19	27th	16	10	2	4	31	15
8th	11	2	6	3	16	15	18th	20	12	5	3	38	20	28th	16	6	6	4	28	19
9th	15	5	5	5	20	20	19th	17	8	1	8	29	29	29th	7	4	2	1	14	7
10th	20	14	2	4	37	17	20th	23	11	7	5	34	23							

OVERALL 479 237 119 123 854 587

FEBRUARY 1

#	SEASON	DATE	COMPETITION / ROUND	MATCH RESULT	VENUE	ATT
1	1895/96	01/02/96	FA Cup 1st Round	Newton Heath 2 Kettering 1	Bank Street	6000
2	1898/99	01/02/99	FA Cup 1st Round Replay	Newton Heath 3 Tottenham Hotspur 5	Bank Street	6000
3	1901/02	01/02/02	Football League Division 2	Stockport County 1 Newton Heath 0	Green Lane	2000
4	1907/08	01/02/08	FA Cup 2nd Round	Manchester United 1 Chelsea 0	Bank Street	25184
5	1912/13	01/02/13	FA Cup 2nd Round	Plymouth Argyle 0 Manchester United 2	Home Park	21700
6	1927/28	01/02/28	FA Cup 4th Round Replay	Manchester United 1 Bury 0	Old Trafford	48001
7	1929/30	01/02/30	Football League Division 1	Manchester United 4 West Ham United 2	Old Trafford	15424
8	1935/36	01/02/36	Football League Division 2	Manchester United 4 Southampton 0	Old Trafford	23205
9	1946/47	01/02/47	Football League Division 1	Arsenal 6 Manchester United 2	Highbury	29415
10	1957/58	01/02/58	Football League Division 1	Arsenal 4 Manchester United 5	Highbury	63578
11	1960/61	01/02/61	FA Cup 4th Round Replay	Manchester United 2 Sheffield Wednesday 7	Old Trafford	65243
12	1963/64	01/02/64	Football League Division 1	Manchester United 3 Arsenal 1	Old Trafford	48340
13	1968/69	01/02/69	Football League Division 1	Ipswich Town 1 Manchester United 0	Portman Road	30837
14	1974/75	01/02/75	Football League Division 2	Manchester United 0 Bristol City 1	Old Trafford	47118
15	1977/78	01/02/78	FA Cup 4th Round Replay	West Bromwich Albion 3 Manchester United 2	The Hawthorns	37086
16	1991/92	01/02/92	Football League Division 1	Arsenal 1 Manchester United 1	Highbury	41703
17	1996/97	01/02/97	FA Premiership	Manchester United 2 Southampton 1	Old Trafford	55269
18	2002/03	01/02/03	FA Premiership	Southampton 0 Manchester United 2	St Mary's Stadium	32085
19	2004/05	01/02/05	FA Premiership	Arsenal 2 Manchester United 4	Highbury	38164
20	2005/06	01/02/06	FA Premiership	Blackburn Rovers 4 Manchester United 3	Ewood Park	25484

FEBRUARY 2

#	SEASON	DATE	COMPETITION / ROUND	MATCH RESULT	VENUE	ATT
1	1894/95	02/02/95	FA Cup 1st Round	Newton Heath 2 Stoke City 3	Bank Street	7000
2	1906/07	02/02/07	Football League Division 1	Newcastle United 5 Manchester United 0	St James' Park	30000
3	1923/24	02/02/24	FA Cup 2nd Round	Manchester United 0 Huddersfield Town 3	Old Trafford	66673
4	1928/29	02/02/29	Football League Division 1	Manchester United 2 West Ham United 3	Old Trafford	12020
5	1934/35	02/02/35	Football League Division 2	Norwich City 3 Manchester United 2	The Nest	14260
6	1937/38	02/02/38	Football League Division 2	Barnsley 2 Manchester United 2	Oakwell	7859
7	1956/57	02/02/57	Football League Division 1	Manchester City 2 Manchester United 4	Maine Road	63872
8	1965/66	02/02/66	European Cup Quarter-Final 1st Leg	Manchester United 3 Benfica 2	Old Trafford	64035
9	1973/74	02/02/74	Football League Division 1	Coventry City 1 Manchester United 0	Highfield Road	25313
10	1979/80	02/02/80	Football League Division 1	Derby County 1 Manchester United 3	Baseball Ground	27783
11	1984/85	02/02/85	Football League Division 1	Manchester United 2 West Bromwich Albion 0	Old Trafford	36681
12	1985/86	02/02/86	Football League Division 1	West Ham United 2 Manchester United 1	Upton Park	22642
13	1999/00	02/02/00	FA Premiership	Sheffield Wednesday 0 Manchester United 1	Hillsborough	39640
14	2001/02	02/02/02	FA Premiership	Manchester United 4 Sunderland 1	Old Trafford	67587
15	2007/08	02/02/08	FA Premiership	Tottenham Hotspur 1 Manchester United 1	White Hart Lane	36075

FEBRUARY 3

#	SEASON	DATE	COMPETITION / ROUND	MATCH RESULT	VENUE	ATT
1	1893/94	03/02/94	Football League Division 1	Aston Villa 5 Newton Heath 1	Perry Barr	5000
2	1895/96	03/02/96	Football League Division 2	Newton Heath 2 Leicester City 0	Bank Street	1000
3	1899/00	03/02/00	Football League Division 2	Newton Heath 1 Sheffield Wednesday 0	Bank Street	10000
4	1905/06	03/02/06	FA Cup 2nd Round	Manchester United 3 Norwich City 0	Bank Street	10000
5	1911/12	03/02/12	FA Cup 2nd Round	Coventry City 1 Manchester United 5	Highfield Road	17130
6	1922/23	03/02/23	FA Cup 2nd Round	Tottenham Hotspur 4 Manchester United 0	White Hart Lane	38333
7	1925/26	03/02/26	FA Cup 4th Round Replay	Manchester United 2 Tottenham Hotspur 0	Old Trafford	45000
8	1933/34	03/02/34	Football League Division 2	Burnley 1 Manchester United 4	Turf Moor	9906
9	1936/37	03/02/37	Football League Division 1	Manchester United 1 Preston North End 1	Old Trafford	13225
10	1950/51	03/02/51	Football League Division 1	Manchester United 1 Middlesbrough 0	Old Trafford	44633
11	1961/62	03/02/62	Football League Division 1	Manchester United 3 Cardiff City 0	Old Trafford	29200
12	1964/65	03/02/65	FA Cup 4th Round Replay	Manchester United 1 Stoke City 0	Old Trafford	50814
13	1967/68	03/02/68	Football League Division 1	Tottenham Hotspur 1 Manchester United 2	White Hart Lane	57790
14	1968/69	03/02/69	FA Cup 4th Round Replay	Watford 0 Manchester United 2	Vicarage Road	34000
15	1978/79	03/02/79	Football League Division 1	Manchester United 0 Arsenal 2	Old Trafford	45460
16	1989/90	03/02/90	Football League Division 1	Manchester United 1 Manchester City 1	Old Trafford	40274
17	1990/91	03/02/91	Football League Division 1	Manchester United 1 Liverpool 1	Old Trafford	43690
18	1995/96	03/02/96	FA Premiership	Wimbledon 2 Manchester United 4	Selhurst Park	25380
19	1998/99	03/02/99	FA Premiership	Manchester United 1 Derby County 0	Old Trafford	55174
20	2000/01	03/02/01	FA Premiership	Manchester United 1 Everton 0	Old Trafford	67528

FEBRUARY 4

#	SEASON	DATE	COMPETITION / ROUND	MATCH RESULT	VENUE	ATT
1	1898/99	04/02/99	Football League Division 2	Port Vale 1 Newton Heath 0	Cobridge Stadium	6000
2	1910/11	04/02/11	FA Cup 2nd Round	Manchester United 2 Aston Villa 1	Old Trafford	65101
3	1927/28	04/02/28	Football League Division 1	Tottenham Hotspur 4 Manchester United 1	White Hart Lane	23545
4	1932/33	04/02/33	Football League Division 1	Manchester United 2 Oldham Athletic 0	Old Trafford	15275
5	1938/39	04/02/39	Football League Division 1	Manchester United 1 Preston North End 1	Old Trafford	41061
6	1949/50	04/02/50	Football League Division 1	Manchester United 3 Burnley 2	Old Trafford	46702
7	1955/56	04/02/56	Football League Division 1	Manchester United 2 Burnley 0	Old Trafford	27342
8	1960/61	04/02/61	Football League Division 1	Manchester United 1 Aston Villa 1	Old Trafford	33525
9	1966/67	04/02/67	Football League Division 1	Burnley 1 Manchester United 1	Turf Moor	40165
10	1983/84	04/02/84	Football League Division 1	Manchester United 0 Norwich City 0	Old Trafford	36851
11	1994/95	04/02/95	FA Premiership	Manchester United 1 Aston Villa 0	Old Trafford	43795
12	1996/97	04/02/97	FA Cup 4th Round Replay	Wimbledon 1 Manchester United 0	Selhurst Park	25601
13	2002/03	04/02/03	FA Premiership	Birmingham City 0 Manchester United 1	St Andrews	29475
14	2005/06	04/02/06	FA Premiership	Manchester United 4 Fulham 2	Old Trafford	67884
15	2006/07	04/02/07	FA Premiership	Tottenham Hotspur 0 Manchester United 4	White Hart Lane	36146

FEBRUARY 5

#	SEASON	DATE	COMPETITION / ROUND	MATCH RESULT	VENUE	ATT
1	1909/10	05/02/10	Football League Division 1	Preston North End 1 Manchester United 0	Deepdale	4000
2	1920/21	05/02/21	Football League Division 1	Manchester United 1 Liverpool 1	Old Trafford	30000
3	1926/27	05/02/27	Football League Division 1	Burnley 1 Manchester United 0	Turf Moor	22010
4	1935/36	05/02/36	Football League Division 2	Tottenham Hotspur 0 Manchester United 0	White Hart Lane	20085
5	1937/38	05/02/38	Football League Division 2	Southampton 3 Manchester United 3	The Dell	20354
6	1946/47	05/02/47	Football League Division 1	Manchester United 1 Stoke City 1	Maine Road	8456
7	1948/49	05/02/49	FA Cup 4th Round Replay	Bradford Park Avenue 1 Manchester United 1	Park Avenue	30000
8	1952/53	05/02/53	FA Cup 4th Round Replay	Walthamstow Avenue 2 Manchester United 5	Highbury	49119
9	1954/55	05/02/55	Football League Division 1	Huddersfield Town 1 Manchester United 3	Leeds Road	31408
10	1957/58	05/02/58	European Cup Quarter-Final 2nd Leg	Red Star Belgrade 3 Manchester United 3	Stadion JNA	55000
11	1965/66	05/02/66	Football League Division 1	Manchester United 6 Northampton Town 2	Old Trafford	34986
12	1971/72	05/02/72	FA Cup 4th Round	Preston North End 0 Manchester United 2	Deepdale	27025
13	1976/77	05/02/77	Football League Division 1	Manchester United 3 Derby County 1	Old Trafford	54044
14	1982/83	05/02/83	Football League Division 1	Ipswich Town 1 Manchester United 1	Portman Road	23804
15	1988/89	05/02/89	Football League Division 1	Manchester United 1 Tottenham Hotspur 0	Old Trafford	41423
16	1991/92	05/02/92	FA Cup 4th Round Replay	Manchester United 2 Southampton 2	Old Trafford	33414
17	1993/94	05/02/94	FA Premiership	Queens Park Rangers 2 Manchester United 3	Loftus Road	21267
18	1999/00	05/02/00	FA Premiership	Manchester United 3 Coventry City 2	Old Trafford	61380
19	2004/05	05/02/05	FA Premiership	Manchester United 2 Birmingham City 0	Old Trafford	67838

FEBRUARY 6

#	SEASON	DATE	COMPETITION / ROUND	MATCH RESULT	VENUE	ATT
1	1896/97	06/02/97	Football League Division 2	Newton Heath 6 Loughborough Town 0	Bank Street	5000
2	1903/04	06/02/04	FA Cup 1st Round	Notts County 3 Manchester United 3	Trent Bridge	12000
3	1908/09	06/02/09	FA Cup 2nd Round	Manchester United 1 Everton 0	Bank Street	35217
4	1914/15	06/02/15	Football League Division 1	Sunderland 1 Manchester United 0	Roker Park	5000
5	1923/24	06/02/24	Football League Division 2	Blackpool 1 Manchester United 0	Bloomfield Road	6000
6	1925/26	06/02/26	Football League Division 1	Burnley 0 Manchester United 1	Turf Moor	17141
7	1931/32	06/02/32	Football League Division 2	Chesterfield 1 Manchester United 3	Saltergate	9457
8	1934/35	06/02/35	Football League Division 2	Manchester United 2 Port Vale 1	Old Trafford	7372
9	1936/37	06/02/37	Football League Division 1	Arsenal 1 Manchester United 1	Highbury	37236
10	1953/54	06/02/54	Football League Division 1	Preston North End 1 Manchester United 3	Deepdale	30064
11	1956/57	06/02/57	European Cup Quarter-Final 2nd Leg	Manchester United 3 Athletic Bilbao 0	Maine Road	70000
12	1959/60	06/02/60	Football League Division 1	Manchester United 0 Manchester City 0	Old Trafford	59450
13	1964/65	06/02/65	Football League Division 1	Tottenham Hotspur 1 Manchester United 0	White Hart Lane	58639
14	1970/71	06/02/71	Football League Division 1	Manchester United 2 Tottenham Hotspur 1	Old Trafford	48965
15	1981/82	06/02/82	Football League Division 1	Manchester United 4 Aston Villa 1	Old Trafford	43184
16	1987/88	06/02/88	Football League Division 1	Manchester United 1 Coventry City 0	Old Trafford	37144
17	1992/93	06/02/93	FA Premiership	Manchester United 2 Sheffield United 1	Old Trafford	36156
18	1998/99	06/02/99	FA Premiership	Nottingham Forest 1 Manchester United 8	City Ground	30025

FEBRUARY 7

#	SEASON	DATE	COMPETITION / ROUND	MATCH RESULT	VENUE	ATT
1	1902/03	07/02/03	FA Cup 1st Round	Manchester United 2 Liverpool 1	Bank Street	15000
2	1913/14	07/02/14	Football League Division 1	Tottenham Hotspur 2 Manchester United 1	White Hart Lane	22000
3	1919/20	07/02/20	Football League Division 1	Sunderland 3 Manchester United 0	Roker Park	25000
4	1924/25	07/02/25	Football League Division 2	Manchester United 4 Leyton Orient 2	Old Trafford	18250
5	1930/31	07/02/31	Football League Division 1	Manchester United 1 Manchester City 3	Old Trafford	39876
6	1947/48	07/02/48	FA Cup 5th Round	Manchester United 2 Charlton Athletic 0	Leeds Road	33312
7	1948/49	07/02/49	FA Cup 4th Round 2nd Replay	Manchester United 5 Bradford Park Avenue 0	Maine Road	70434
8	1952/53	07/02/53	Football League Division 1	Manchester United 3 Aston Villa 1	Old Trafford	34339
9	1958/59	07/02/59	Football League Division 1	Tottenham Hotspur 1 Manchester United 3	White Hart Lane	48401
10	1969/70	07/02/70	FA Cup 5th Round	Northampton Town 2 Manchester United 8	County Ground	21771
11	1975/76	07/02/76	Football League Division 1	Coventry City 1 Manchester United 1	Highfield Road	33922
12	1980/81	07/02/81	Football League Division 1	Leicester City 1 Manchester United 0	Filbert Street	26085
13	1983/84	07/02/84	Football League Division 1	Birmingham City 2 Manchester United 2	St Andrews	19957
14	1986/87	07/02/87	Football League Division 1	Charlton Athletic 0 Manchester United 0	Selhurst Park	15482
15	1997/98	07/02/98	FA Premiership	Manchester United 1 Bolton Wanderers 1	Old Trafford	55156
16	2003/04	07/02/04	FA Premiership	Everton 3 Manchester United 4	Goodison Park	40190

FEBRUARY 8

#	SEASON	DATE	COMPETITION / ROUND	MATCH RESULT	VENUE	ATT
1	1895/96	08/02/96	Football League Division 2	Burton Swifts 4 Newton Heath 1	Peel Croft	2000
2	1907/08	08/02/08	Football League Division 1	Manchester United 1 Newcastle United 1	Bank Street	50000
3	1912/13	08/02/13	Football League Division 1	Blackburn Rovers 0 Manchester United 0	Ewood Park	38000
4	1929/30	08/02/30	Football League Division 1	Manchester City 0 Manchester United 1	Maine Road	64472
5	1935/36	08/02/36	Football League Division 1	Manchester United 7 Port Vale 2	Old Trafford	22265
6	1963/64	08/02/64	Football League Division 1	Leicester City 3 Manchester United 2	Filbert Street	35538
7	1968/69	08/02/69	FA Cup 5th Round	Birmingham City 2 Manchester United 2	St Andrews	52500
8	1974/75	08/02/75	Football League Division 2	Oxford United 1 Manchester United 0	Manor Ground	15959
9	1977/78	08/02/78	Football League Division 1	Manchester United 2 Bristol City 1	Old Trafford	43457
10	1991/92	08/02/92	Football League Division 1	Manchester United 1 Sheffield Wednesday 1	Old Trafford	47074
11	1992/93	08/02/93	FA Premiership	Leeds United 0 Manchester United 0	Elland Road	34166

FEBRUARY 9

#	SEASON	DATE	COMPETITION / ROUND	MATCH RESULT	VENUE	ATT
1	1900/01	09/02/01	FA Cup 1st Round	Newton Heath 0 Burnley 0	Bank Street	8000
2	1906/07	09/02/07	Football League Division 1	Manchester United 4 Stoke City 1	Bank Street	15000
3	1920/21	09/02/21	Football League Division 1	Liverpool 2 Manchester United 0	Anfield	35000
4	1923/24	09/02/24	Football League Division 2	Manchester United 0 Blackpool 0	Old Trafford	13000
5	1926/27	09/02/27	Football League Division 1	Manchester United 3 Newcastle United 1	Old Trafford	25402
6	1928/29	09/02/29	Football League Division 1	Newcastle United 5 Manchester United 0	St James' Park	34134
7	1934/35	09/02/35	Football League Division 2	Swansea City 1 Manchester United 0	Vetch Field	8876
8	1951/52	09/02/52	Football League Division 1	Preston North End 1 Manchester United 2	Deepdale	38792
9	1956/57	09/02/57	Football League Division 1	Manchester United 6 Arsenal 2	Old Trafford	60384
10	1964/65	09/02/65	ICFC 3rd Round 2nd Leg	Everton 1 Manchester United 2	Goodison Park	54397
11	1973/74	09/02/74	Football League Division 1	Manchester United 0 Leeds United 2	Old Trafford	60025
12	1979/80	09/02/80	Football League Division 1	Manchester United 0 Wolverhampton Wanderers 1	Old Trafford	51568
13	1984/85	09/02/85	Football League Division 1	Newcastle United 1 Manchester United 1	St James' Park	32555
14	1985/86	09/02/86	Football League Division 1	Liverpool 1 Manchester United 1	Anfield	35064
15	2002/03	09/02/03	FA Premiership	Manchester United 1 Manchester City 1	Old Trafford	67646

FEBRUARY 10

#	SEASON	DATE	COMPETITION / ROUND	MATCH RESULT	VENUE	ATT
1	1893/94	10/02/94	FA Cup 2nd Round	Newton Heath 0　Blackburn Rovers 0	Bank Street	18000
2	1899/00	10/02/00	Football League Division 2	Lincoln City 1　Newton Heath 0	Sincil Bank	2000
3	1903/04	10/02/04	FA Cup 1st Round Replay	Manchester United 2　Notts County 1	Bank Street	18000
4	1905/06	10/02/06	Football League Division 2	Bradford City 1　Manchester United 5	Valley Parade	8000
5	1911/12	10/02/12	Football League Division 1	Sheffield Wednesday 3　Manchester United 0	Hillsborough	25000
6	1922/23	10/02/23	Football League Division 2	Notts County 1　Manchester United 6	Meadow Lane	10000
7	1933/34	10/02/34	Football League Division 2	Manchester United 2　Oldham Athletic 3	Old Trafford	24480
8	1950/51	10/02/51	FA Cup 5th Round	Manchester United 1　Arsenal 0	Old Trafford	55058
9	1961/62	10/02/62	Football League Division 1	Manchester City 0　Manchester United 2	Maine Road	49959
10	1969/70	10/02/70	Football League Division 1	Ipswich Town 0　Manchester United 1	Portman Road	29755
11	1972/73	10/02/73	Football League Division 1	Manchester United 2　Wolverhampton Wanderers 1	Old Trafford	52089
12	1978/79	10/02/79	Football League Division 1	Manchester City 0　Manchester United 3	Maine Road	46151
13	1987/88	10/02/88	Football League Division 1	Derby County 1　Manchester United 2	Baseball Ground	20016
14	1989/90	10/02/90	Football League Division 1	Millwall 1　Manchester United 2	The Den	15491
15	1990/91	10/02/91	League Cup Semi-Final 1st Leg	Manchester United 2　Leeds United 1	Old Trafford	34050
16	1995/96	10/02/96	FA Premiership	Manchester United 1　Blackburn Rovers 0	Old Trafford	42681
17	2000/01	10/02/01	FA Premiership	Chelsea 1　Manchester United 1	Stamford Bridge	34690
18	2001/02	10/02/02	FA Premiership	Charlton Athletic 0　Manchester United 2	The Valley	26475
19	2006/07	10/02/07	FA Premiership	Manchester United 2　Charlton Athletic 0	Old Trafford	75883
20	2007/08	10/02/08	FA Premiership	Manchester United 1　Manchester City 2	Old Trafford	75970

FEBRUARY 11

#	SEASON	DATE	COMPETITION / ROUND	MATCH RESULT	VENUE	ATT
1	1892/93	11/02/93	Football League Division 1	Derby County 5　Newton Heath 1	Racecourse Ground	5000
2	1901/02	11/02/02	Football League Division 2	Newton Heath 2　Burnley 0	Bank Street	1000
3	1904/05	11/02/05	Football League Division 2	Lincoln City 3　Manchester United 0	Sincil Bank	2000
4	1910/11	11/02/11	Football League Division 1	Manchester United 3　Bristol City 1	Old Trafford	14000
5	1919/20	11/02/20	Football League Division 1	Manchester United 1　Oldham Athletic 1	Old Trafford	15000
6	1921/22	11/02/22	Football League Division 1	Manchester United 1　Huddersfield Town 1	Old Trafford	30000
7	1927/28	11/02/28	Football League Division 1	Manchester United 5　Leicester City 2	Old Trafford	16640
8	1932/33	11/02/33	Football League Division 2	Preston North End 3　Manchester United 3	Deepdale	15662
9	1938/39	11/02/39	Football League Division 1	Charlton Athletic 7　Manchester United 1	The Valley	23721
10	1949/50	11/02/50	FA Cup 5th Round	Manchester United 3　Portsmouth 3	Old Trafford	53688
11	1955/56	11/02/56	Football League Division 1	Luton Town 2　Manchester United 1	Kenilworth Road	16354
12	1960/61	11/02/61	Football League Division 1	Wolverhampton Wanderers 2　Manchester United 1	Molineux	38526
13	1966/67	11/02/67	Football League Division 1	Manchester United 1　Nottingham Forest 0	Old Trafford	62727
14	1977/78	11/02/78	Football League Division 1	Chelsea 2　Manchester United 2	Stamford Bridge	32849
15	1988/89	11/02/89	Football League Division 1	Sheffield Wednesday 0　Manchester United 2	Hillsborough	34820
16	1994/95	11/02/95	FA Premiership	Manchester City 0　Manchester United 3	Maine Road	26368
17	2003/04	11/02/04	FA Premiership	Manchester United 2　Middlesbrough 3	Old Trafford	67346
18	2005/06	11/02/06	FA Premiership	Portsmouth 1　Manchester United 3	Fratton Park	20206

FEBRUARY 12

#	SEASON	DATE	COMPETITION / ROUND	MATCH RESULT	VENUE	ATT
1	1897/98	12/02/98	FA Cup 2nd Round	Newton Heath 0　Liverpool 0	Bank Street	12000
2	1909/10	12/02/10	Football League Division 1	Newcastle United 3　Manchester United 4	St James' Park	20000
3	1920/21	12/02/21	Football League Division 1	Manchester United 1　Everton 2	Old Trafford	30000
4	1926/27	12/02/27	Football League Division 1	Manchester United 1　Cardiff City 1	Old Trafford	26213
5	1937/38	12/02/38	FA Cup 5th Round	Brentford 2　Manchester United 0	Griffin Park	24147
6	1948/49	12/02/49	FA Cup 5th Round	Manchester United 8　Yeovil Town 0	Maine Road	81565
7	1954/55	12/02/55	Football League Division 1	Manchester United 0　Manchester City 5	Old Trafford	47914
8	1965/66	12/02/66	FA Cup 4th Round	Manchester United 0　Rotherham United 0	Old Trafford	54263
9	1971/72	12/02/72	Football League Division 1	Manchester United 0　Newcastle United 2	Old Trafford	44983
10	1976/77	12/02/77	Football League Division 1	Tottenham Hotspur 1　Manchester United 3	White Hart Lane	46946
11	1978/79	12/02/79	FA Cup 4th Round Replay	Manchester United 1　Fulham 0	Old Trafford	41200
12	1983/84	12/02/84	Football League Division 1	Luton Town 0　Manchester United 5	Kenilworth Road	11265
13	1999/00	12/02/00	FA Premiership	Newcastle United 3　Manchester United 0	St James' Park	36470

FEBRUARY 13

#	SEASON	DATE	COMPETITION / ROUND	MATCH RESULT	VENUE	ATT
1	1896/97	13/02/97	FA Cup 2nd Round	Southampton 1　Newton Heath 1	County Cricket Ground	8000
2	1900/01	13/02/01	FA Cup 1st Round Replay	Burnley 7　Newton Heath 1	Turf Moor	4000
3	1903/04	13/02/04	Football League Division 2	Manchester United 2　Lincoln City 0	Bank Street	8000
4	1908/09	13/02/09	Football League Division 1	Sheffield United 0　Manchester United 0	Bramall Lane	12000
5	1914/15	13/02/15	Football League Division 1	Manchester United 2　Sheffield Wednesday 0	Old Trafford	7000
6	1925/26	13/02/26	Football League Division 1	Manchester United 2　Leeds United 1	Old Trafford	29584
7	1928/29	13/02/29	Football League Division 1	Liverpool 2　Manchester United 3	Anfield	8852
8	1936/37	13/02/37	Football League Division 1	Manchester United 1　Brentford 3	Old Trafford	31942
9	1953/54	13/02/54	Football League Division 1	Manchester United 2　Tottenham Hotspur 0	Old Trafford	35485
10	1959/60	13/02/60	Football League Division 1	Manchester United 1　Preston North End 1	Old Trafford	44014
11	1964/65	13/02/65	Football League Division 1	Manchester United 3　Burnley 2	Old Trafford	38865
12	1981/82	13/02/82	Football League Division 1	Wolverhampton Wanderers 0　Manchester United 1	Molineux	22481
13	1987/88	13/02/88	Football League Division 1	Chelsea 1　Manchester United 2	Stamford Bridge	25014
14	1993/94	13/02/94	League Cup Semi-Final 1st Leg	Manchester United 1　Sheffield Wednesday 0	Old Trafford	43294
15	2004/05	13/02/05	FA Premiership	Manchester City 0　Manchester United 2	Eastlands Stadium	47111

FEBRUARY 14

#	SEASON	DATE	COMPETITION / ROUND	MATCH RESULT	VENUE	ATT
1	1902/03	14/02/03	Football League Division 2	Blackpool 2 Manchester United 0	Bloomfield Road	3000
2	1913/14	14/02/14	Football League Division 1	Manchester United 0 Burnley 1	Old Trafford	35000
3	1919/20	14/02/20	Football League Division 1	Manchester United 2 Sunderland 0	Old Trafford	35000
4	1924/25	14/02/25	Football League Division 2	Crystal Palace 2 Manchester United 1	Selhurst Park	11250
5	1930/31	14/02/31	Football League Division 1	Manchester United 1 West Ham United 0	Old Trafford	9745
6	1947/48	14/02/48	Football League Division 1	Manchester United 1 Preston North End 1	Maine Road	61765
7	1952/53	14/02/53	FA Cup 5th Round	Everton 2 Manchester United 1	Goodison Park	77920
8	1969/70	14/02/70	Football League Division 1	Manchester United 1 Crystal Palace 1	Old Trafford	54711
9	1975/76	14/02/76	FA Cup 5th Round	Leicester City 1 Manchester United 2	Filbert Street	34000
10	1986/87	14/02/87	Football League Division 1	Manchester United 3 Watford 1	Old Trafford	35763
11	1992/93	14/02/93	FA Cup 5th Round	Sheffield United 2 Manchester United 1	Bramall Lane	27150
12	1998/99	14/02/99	FA Cup 5th Round	Manchester United 1 Fulham 0	Old Trafford	54798
13	2000/01	14/02/01	Champions League Phase 2 Match 3	Valencia 0 Manchester United 0	Mestalla	49541
14	2003/04	14/02/04	FA Cup 5th Round	Manchester United 4 Manchester City 2	Old Trafford	67228

FEBRUARY 15

#	SEASON	DATE	COMPETITION / ROUND	MATCH RESULT	VENUE	ATT
1	1895/96	15/02/96	FA Cup 2nd Round	Newton Heath 1 Derby County 1	Bank Street	20000
2	1901/02	15/02/02	Football League Division 2	Newton Heath 1 Glossop 0	Bank Street	5000
3	1907/08	15/02/08	Football League Division 1	Manchester United 1 Blackburn Rovers 2	Bank Street	15000
4	1912/13	15/02/13	Football League Division 1	Manchester United 4 Derby County 0	Old Trafford	30000
5	1929/30	15/02/30	Football League Division 1	Grimsby Town 2 Manchester United 2	Blundell Park	9337
6	1949/50	15/02/50	FA Cup 5th Round Replay	Portsmouth 1 Manchester United 3	Fratton Park	49962
7	1963/64	15/02/64	FA Cup 5th Round	Barnsley 0 Manchester United 4	Oakwell	38076
8	1965/66	15/02/66	FA Cup 4th Round Replay	Rotherham United 0 Manchester United 1	Millmoor	23500
9	1968/69	15/02/69	Football League Division 1	Wolverhampton Wanderers 2 Manchester United 2	Molineux	44023
10	1974/75	15/02/75	Football League Division 2	Manchester United 2 Hull City 0	Old Trafford	44712
11	1982/83	15/02/83	League Cup Semi-Final 1st Leg	Arsenal 2 Manchester United 4	Highbury	43136
12	1984/85	15/02/85	FA Cup 5th Round	Blackburn Rovers 0 Manchester United 2	Ewood Park	22692
13	1997/98	15/02/98	FA Cup 5th Round	Manchester United 1 Barnsley 1	Old Trafford	54700
14	2002/03	15/02/03	FA Cup 5th Round	Manchester United 0 Arsenal 2	Old Trafford	67209

FEBRUARY 16

#	SEASON	DATE	COMPETITION / ROUND	MATCH RESULT	VENUE	ATT
1	1897/98	16/02/98	FA Cup 2nd Round Replay	Liverpool 2 Newton Heath 1	Anfield	6000
2	1900/01	16/02/01	Football League Division 2	Newton Heath 0 Gainsborough Trinity 0	Bank Street	7000
3	1906/07	16/02/07	Football League Division 1	Blackburn Rovers 2 Manchester United 4	Ewood Park	5000
4	1923/24	16/02/24	Football League Division 2	Derby County 3 Manchester United 0	Baseball Ground	12000
5	1928/29	16/02/29	Football League Division 1	Manchester United 1 Burnley 0	Old Trafford	12516
6	1951/52	16/02/52	Football League Division 1	Derby County 0 Manchester United 3	Baseball Ground	27693
7	1956/57	16/02/57	FA Cup 5th Round	Manchester United 1 Everton 0	Old Trafford	61803
8	1958/59	16/02/59	Football League Division 1	Manchester United 4 Manchester City 1	Old Trafford	59846
9	1973/74	16/02/74	Football League Division 1	Derby County 2 Manchester United 2	Baseball Ground	29987
10	1976/77	16/02/77	Football League Division 1	Manchester United 0 Liverpool 0	Old Trafford	57487
11	1979/80	16/02/80	Football League Division 1	Stoke City 1 Manchester United 1	Victoria Ground	28389
12	2007/08	16/02/08	FA Cup 5th Round	Manchester United 4 Arsenal 0	Old Trafford	75550

FEBRUARY 17

#	SEASON	DATE	COMPETITION / ROUND	MATCH RESULT	VENUE	ATT
1	1893/94	17/02/94	FA Cup 2nd Round Replay	Blackburn Rovers 5 Newton Heath 1	Ewood Park	5000
2	1896/97	17/02/97	FA Cup 2nd Round Replay	Newton Heath 3 Southampton 1	Bank Street	7000
3	1899/00	17/02/00	Football League Division 2	Newton Heath 3 Birmingham City 2	Bank Street	10000
4	1905/06	17/02/06	Football League Division 2	Manchester United 0 West Bromwich Albion 0	Bank Street	30000
5	1911/12	17/02/12	Football League Division 1	Manchester United 0 Bury 0	Old Trafford	6000
6	1922/23	17/02/23	Football League Division 2	Manchester United 0 Derby County 0	Old Trafford	27500
7	1931/32	17/02/32	Football League Division 2	Manchester United 5 Burnley 1	Old Trafford	11036
8	1937/38	17/02/38	Football League Division 2	Sheffield United 1 Manchester United 2	Bramall Lane	17754
9	1950/51	17/02/51	Football League Division 1	Manchester United 2 Wolverhampton Wanderers 1	Old Trafford	42022
10	1961/62	17/02/62	FA Cup 5th Round	Manchester United 0 Sheffield Wednesday 0	Old Trafford	59553
11	1967/68	17/02/68	Football League Division 1	Burnley 2 Manchester United 1	Turf Moor	31965
12	1972/73	17/02/73	Football League Division 1	Ipswich Town 4 Manchester United 1	Portman Road	31918
13	1980/81	17/02/81	Football League Division 1	Manchester United 0 Tottenham Hotspur 0	Old Trafford	40642
14	1998/99	17/02/99	FA Premiership	Manchester United 1 Arsenal 1	Old Trafford	55171
15	2006/07	17/02/07	FA Cup 5th Round	Manchester United 1 Reading 1	Old Trafford	70608

FEBRUARY 18

#	SEASON	DATE	COMPETITION / ROUND	MATCH RESULT	VENUE	ATT
1	1898/99	18/02/99	Football League Division 2	Loughborough Town 0 Newton Heath 1	The Athletic Ground	1500
2	1904/05	18/02/05	Football League Division 2	Manchester United 4 Leicester City 1	Bank Street	7000
3	1910/11	18/02/11	Football League Division 1	Newcastle United 0 Manchester United 1	St James' Park	45000
4	1921/22	18/02/22	Football League Division 1	Birmingham City 0 Manchester United 1	St Andrews	20000
5	1927/28	18/02/28	FA Cup 5th Round	Manchester United 1 Birmingham City 0	Old Trafford	52568
6	1938/39	18/02/39	Football League Division 1	Blackpool 3 Manchester United 5	Bloomfield Road	15253
7	1949/50	18/02/50	Football League Division 1	Sunderland 2 Manchester United 2	Roker Park	63251
8	1952/53	18/02/53	Football League Division 1	Sunderland 2 Manchester United 2	Roker Park	24263
9	1955/56	18/02/56	Football League Division 1	Wolverhampton Wanderers 0 Manchester United 2	Molineux	40014
10	1956/57	18/02/57	Football League Division 1	Charlton Athletic 1 Manchester United 5	The Valley	16308
11	1960/61	18/02/61	Football League Division 1	Manchester United 3 Bolton Wanderers 1	Old Trafford	37558
12	1966/67	18/02/67	FA Cup 4th Round	Manchester United 1 Norwich City 2	Old Trafford	63409
13	1975/76	18/02/76	Football League Division 1	Manchester United 0 Liverpool 0	Old Trafford	59709
14	1983/84	18/02/84	Football League Division 1	Wolverhampton Wanderers 1 Manchester United 1	Molineux	20676
15	1988/89	18/02/89	FA Cup 5th Round	Bournemouth 1 Manchester United 1	Dean Court	12708
16	1989/90	18/02/90	FA Cup 5th Round	Newcastle United 2 Manchester United 3	St James' Park	31748
17	1990/91	18/02/91	FA Cup 5th Round	Norwich City 2 Manchester United 1	Carrow Road	23058
18	1995/96	18/02/96	FA Cup 5th Round	Manchester United 2 Manchester City 1	Old Trafford	42692
19	1997/98	18/02/98	FA Premiership	Aston Villa 0 Manchester United 2	Villa Park	39372
20	2005/06	18/02/06	FA Cup 5th Round	Liverpool 1 Manchester United 0	Anfield	44039

FEBRUARY 19

#	SEASON	DATE	COMPETITION / ROUND	MATCH RESULT	VENUE	ATT
1	1895/96	19/02/96	FA Cup 2nd Round Replay	Derby County 5 Newton Heath 1	Baseball Ground	6000
2	1900/01	19/02/01	Football League Division 2	New Brighton Tower 2 Newton Heath 0	Tower Athletic Ground	2000
3	1909/10	19/02/10	Football League Division 1	Manchester United 3 Liverpool 4	Old Trafford	45000
4	1926/27	19/02/27	Football League Division 1	Aston Villa 2 Manchester United 0	Villa Park	32467
5	1937/38	19/02/38	Football League Division 2	Manchester United 0 Tottenham Hotspur 1	Old Trafford	34631
6	1948/49	19/02/49	Football League Division 1	Aston Villa 2 Manchester United 1	Villa Park	68354
7	1954/55	19/02/55	FA Cup 4th Round	Manchester City 2 Manchester United 0	Maine Road	75000
8	1957/58	19/02/58	FA Cup 5th Round	Manchester United 3 Sheffield Wednesday 0	Old Trafford	59848
9	1963/64	19/02/64	Football League Division 1	Manchester United 5 Bolton Wanderers 0	Old Trafford	33926
10	1965/66	19/02/66	Football League Division 1	Stoke City 2 Manchester United 2	Victoria Ground	36667
11	1971/72	19/02/72	Football League Division 1	Leeds United 5 Manchester United 1	Elland Road	45399
12	1976/77	19/02/77	Football League Division 1	Manchester United 3 Newcastle United 1	Old Trafford	51828
13	1982/83	19/02/83	FA Cup 5th Round	Derby County 0 Manchester United 1	Baseball Ground	33022
14	1994/95	19/02/95	FA Cup 5th Round	Manchester United 3 Leeds United 1	Old Trafford	42744
15	1996/97	19/02/97	FA Premiership	Arsenal 1 Manchester United 2	Highbury	38172
16	2002/03	19/02/03	Champions League Phase 2 Match 3	Manchester United 2 Juventus 1	Old Trafford	66703
17	2004/05	19/02/05	FA Cup 5th Round	Everton 0 Manchester United 2	Goodison Park	38664

FEBRUARY 20

#	SEASON	DATE	COMPETITION / ROUND	MATCH RESULT	VENUE	ATT
1	1896/97	20/02/97	Football League Division 2	Newton Heath 2 Leicester City 1	Bank Street	8000
2	1903/04	20/02/04	FA Cup 2nd Round	Sheffield Wednesday 6 Manchester United 0	Hillsborough	22051
3	1908/09	20/02/09	FA Cup 3rd Round	Manchester United 6 Blackburn Rovers 1	Bank Street	38500
4	1914/15	20/02/15	Football League Division 1	West Bromwich Albion 0 Manchester United 0	The Hawthorns	10000
5	1920/21	20/02/21	Football League Division 1	Manchester United 3 Sunderland 0	Old Trafford	40000
6	1925/26	20/02/26	FA Cup 5th Round	Sunderland 3 Manchester United 3	Roker Park	50500
7	1931/32	20/02/32	Football League Division 2	Preston North End 0 Manchester United 0	Deepdale	13353
8	1936/37	20/02/37	Football League Division 1	Manchester United 0 Portsmouth 1	Old Trafford	19416
9	1953/54	20/02/54	Football League Division 1	Burnley 2 Manchester United 0	Turf Moor	29576
10	1959/60	20/02/60	FA Cup 5th Round	Manchester United 0 Sheffield Wednesday 1	Old Trafford	66350
11	1964/65	20/02/65	FA Cup 5th Round	Manchester United 2 Burnley 1	Old Trafford	54000
12	1970/71	20/02/71	Football League Division 1	Manchester United 5 Southampton 1	Old Trafford	36060
13	1978/79	20/02/79	FA Cup 5th Round	Colchester United 0 Manchester United 1	Layer Road	13171
14	1981/82	20/02/82	Football League Division 1	Manchester United 0 Arsenal 0	Old Trafford	43833
15	1987/88	20/02/88	FA Cup 5th Round	Arsenal 2 Manchester United 1	Highbury	54161
16	1992/93	20/02/93	FA Premiership	Manchester United 2 Southampton 1	Old Trafford	36257
17	1993/94	20/02/94	FA Cup 5th Round	Wimbledon 0 Manchester United 3	Selhurst Park	27511
18	1998/99	20/02/99	FA Premiership	Coventry City 0 Manchester United 1	Highfield Road	22596
19	1999/00	20/02/00	FA Premiership	Leeds United 0 Manchester United 1	Elland Road	40160
20	2000/01	20/02/01	Champions League Phase 2 Match 4	Manchester United 1 Valencia 1	Old Trafford	66715
21	2001/02	20/02/02	Champions League Phase 2 Match 3	Nantes Atlantique 1 Manchester United 1	Stade Beaujoire	38285
22	2006/07	20/02/07	Champions Lge 2nd Round 1st Leg	Lille Metropole 0 Manchester United 1	Stade Felix Bollaert	41000
23	2007/08	20/02/08	Champions Lge 2nd Round 1st Leg	Olympique Lyonnais 1 Manchester United 1	Stade de Gerland	39230

FEBRUARY 21

#	SEASON	DATE	COMPETITION / ROUND	MATCH RESULT	VENUE	ATT
1	1902/03	21/02/03	FA Cup 2nd Round	Everton 3 Manchester United 1	Goodison Park	15000
2	1913/14	21/02/14	Football League Division 1	Middlesbrough 3 Manchester United 1	Ayresome Park	12000
3	1919/20	21/02/20	Football League Division 1	Arsenal 0 Manchester United 3	Highbury	25000
4	1922/23	21/02/23	Football League Division 2	Manchester United 1 Notts County 1	Old Trafford	12100
5	1930/31	21/02/31	Football League Division 1	Arsenal 4 Manchester United 1	Highbury	41510
6	1933/34	21/02/34	Football League Division 2	Preston North End 3 Manchester United 2	Deepdale	9173
7	1947/48	21/02/48	Football League Division 1	Stoke City 0 Manchester United 2	Victoria Ground	36794
8	1952/53	21/02/53	Football League Division 1	Manchester United 0 Wolverhampton Wanderers 3	Old Trafford	38269
9	1958/59	21/02/59	Football League Division 1	Manchester United 1 Wolverhampton Wanderers 1	Old Trafford	62794
10	1961/62	21/02/62	FA Cup 5th Round Replay	Sheffield Wednesday 0 Manchester United 2	Hillsborough	62969
11	1969/70	21/02/70	FA Cup 6th Round	Middlesbrough 1 Manchester United 1	Ayresome Park	40000
12	1975/76	21/02/76	Football League Division 1	Aston Villa 2 Manchester United 1	Villa Park	50094
13	1980/81	21/02/81	Football League Division 1	Manchester City 1 Manchester United 0	Maine Road	50114
14	1986/87	21/02/87	Football League Division 1	Chelsea 1 Manchester United 1	Stamford Bridge	26516
15	1995/96	21/02/96	FA Premiership	Manchester United 2 Everton 0	Old Trafford	42459
16	1997/98	21/02/98	FA Premiership	Manchester United 2 Derby County 0	Old Trafford	55170
17	2003/04	21/02/04	FA Premiership	Manchester United 1 Leeds United 1	Old Trafford	67744

FEBRUARY 22

#	SEASON	DATE	COMPETITION / ROUND	MATCH RESULT	VENUE	ATT
1	1901/02	22/02/02	Football League Division 2	Doncaster Rovers 4 Newton Heath 0	Town Moor Avenue	3000
2	1907/08	22/02/08	FA Cup 3rd Round	Aston Villa 0 Manchester United 2	Villa Park	12777
3	1912/13	22/02/13	FA Cup 3rd Round	Oldham Athletic 0 Manchester United 0	Boundary Park	26932
4	1929/30	22/02/30	Football League Division 1	Manchester United 3 Portsmouth 0	Old Trafford	17317
5	1932/33	22/02/33	Football League Division 2	Manchester United 2 Burnley 1	Old Trafford	18533
6	1935/36	22/02/36	Football League Division 2	Sheffield United 1 Manchester United 1	Bramall Lane	25852
7	1946/47	22/02/47	Football League Division 1	Manchester United 3 Blackpool 0	Maine Road	29993
8	1957/58	22/02/58	Football League Division 1	Manchester United 1 Nottingham Forest 1	Old Trafford	66124
9	1963/64	22/02/64	Football League Division 1	Blackburn Rovers 1 Manchester United 3	Ewood Park	36726
10	1974/75	22/02/75	Football League Division 2	Aston Villa 2 Manchester United 0	Villa Park	39156
11	1985/86	22/02/86	Football League Division 1	Manchester United 3 West Bromwich Albion 0	Old Trafford	45193
12	1988/89	22/02/89	FA Cup 5th Round Replay	Manchester United 1 Bournemouth 0	Old Trafford	52422
13	1991/92	22/02/92	Football League Division 1	Manchester United 2 Crystal Palace 0	Old Trafford	46347
14	1994/95	22/02/95	FA Premiership	Norwich City 0 Manchester United 2	Carrow Road	21824
15	1996/97	22/02/97	FA Premiership	Chelsea 1 Manchester United 1	Stamford Bridge	28336
16	2002/03	22/02/03	FA Premiership	Bolton Wanderers 1 Manchester United 1	Reebok Stadium	27409

FEBRUARY 23

#	SEASON	DATE	COMPETITION / ROUND	MATCH RESULT	VENUE	ATT
1	1906/07	23/02/07	Football League Division 1	Manchester United 3 Preston North End 0	Bank Street	16000
2	1923/24	23/02/24	Football League Division 2	Manchester United 0 Derby County 0	Old Trafford	25000
3	1924/25	23/02/25	Football League Division 2	Sheffield Wednesday 1 Manchester United 1	Hillsborough	3000
4	1928/29	23/02/29	Football League Division 1	Cardiff City 2 Manchester United 2	Ninian Park	13070
5	1934/35	23/02/35	Football League Division 2	Oldham Athletic 3 Manchester United 1	Boundary Park	14432
6	1937/38	23/02/38	Football League Division 2	Manchester United 4 West Ham United 0	Old Trafford	14572
7	1954/55	23/02/55	Football League Division 1	Manchester United 2 Wolverhampton Wanderers 4	Old Trafford	15679
8	1956/57	23/02/57	Football League Division 1	Manchester United 0 Blackpool 2	Old Trafford	42602
9	1962/63	23/02/63	Football League Division 1	Manchester United 1 Blackpool 1	Old Trafford	43121
10	1970/71	23/02/71	Football League Division 1	Everton 1 Manchester United 0	Goodison Park	52544
11	1973/74	23/02/74	Football League Division 1	Manchester United 0 Wolverhampton Wanderers 0	Old Trafford	39260
12	1979/80	23/02/80	Football League Division 1	Manchester United 1 Bristol City 0	Old Trafford	43329
13	1982/83	23/02/83	League Cup Semi-Final 2nd Leg	Manchester United 2 Arsenal 1	Old Trafford	56635
14	1984/85	23/02/85	Football League Division 1	Arsenal 0 Manchester United 1	Highbury	48612
15	1987/88	23/02/88	Football League Division 1	Tottenham Hotspur 1 Manchester United 1	White Hart Lane	25731
16	2001/02	23/02/02	FA Premiership	Manchester United 1 Aston Villa 0	Old Trafford	67592
17	2004/05	23/02/05	Champions Lge 2nd Round 1st Leg	Manchester United 0 AC Milan 1	Old Trafford	67162
18	2007/08	23/02/08	FA Premiership	Newcastle United 1 Manchester United 5	St James' Park	52291

FEBRUARY 24

#	SEASON	DATE	COMPETITION / ROUND	MATCH RESULT	VENUE	ATT
1	1899/00	24/02/00	Football League Division 2	New Brighton Tower 1 Newton Heath 4	Tower Athletic Ground	8000
2	1905/06	24/02/06	FA Cup 3rd Round	Manchester United 5 Aston Villa 1	Bank Street	35500
3	1911/12	24/02/12	FA Cup 3rd Round	Reading 1 Manchester United 1	Elm Park	24069
4	1925/26	24/02/26	FA Cup 5th Round Replay	Manchester United 2 Sunderland 2	Old Trafford	58661
5	1933/34	24/02/34	Football League Division 2	Manchester United 0 Bradford Park Avenue 4	Old Trafford	13389
6	1950/51	24/02/51	FA Cup 6th Round	Birmingham City 1 Manchester United 0	St Andrews	50000
7	1959/60	24/02/60	Football League Division 1	Leicester City 3 Manchester United 1	Filbert Street	33191
8	1961/62	24/02/62	Football League Division 1	Manchester United 4 West Bromwich Albion 1	Old Trafford	32456
9	1964/65	24/02/65	Football League Division 1	Sunderland 1 Manchester United 0	Roker Park	51336
10	1967/68	24/02/68	Football League Division 1	Arsenal 0 Manchester United 2	Highbury	46417
11	1968/69	24/02/69	FA Cup 5th Round Replay	Manchester United 6 Birmingham City 2	Old Trafford	61932
12	1978/79	24/02/79	Football League Division 1	Manchester United 1 Aston Villa 1	Old Trafford	44437
13	1989/90	24/02/90	Football League Division 1	Chelsea 1 Manchester United 0	Stamford Bridge	29979
14	1990/91	24/02/91	League Cup Semi-Final 2nd Leg	Leeds United 0 Manchester United 1	Elland Road	32014
15	2006/07	24/02/07	FA Premiership	Fulham 1 Manchester United 2	Craven Cottage	24459

FEBRUARY 25

#	SEASON	DATE	COMPETITION / ROUND	MATCH RESULT	VENUE	ATT
1	1898/99	25/02/99	Football League Division 2	Newton Heath 2 Birmingham City 0	Bank Street	12000
2	1900/01	25/02/01	Football League Division 2	Walsall 1 Newton Heath 1	West Bromwich Road	2000
3	1904/05	25/02/05	Football League Division 2	Barnsley 0 Manchester United 0	Oakwell	5000
4	1910/11	25/02/11	FA Cup 3rd Round	West Ham United 2 Manchester United 1	Upton Park	26000
5	1919/20	25/02/20	Football League Division 1	Manchester United 1 West Bromwich Albion 2	Old Trafford	20000
6	1921/22	25/02/22	Football League Division 1	Manchester United 1 Birmingham City 1	Old Trafford	35000
7	1927/28	25/02/28	Football League Division 1	Cardiff City 2 Manchester United 0	Ninian Park	15579
8	1938/39	25/02/39	Football League Division 1	Manchester United 1 Derby County 1	Old Trafford	37166
9	1949/50	25/02/50	Football League Division 1	Charlton Athletic 1 Manchester United 2	The Valley	44920
10	1955/56	25/02/56	Football League Division 1	Manchester United 1 Aston Villa 0	Old Trafford	36277
11	1960/61	25/02/61	Football League Division 1	Nottingham Forest 3 Manchester United 2	City Ground	26850
12	1966/67	25/02/67	Football League Division 1	Manchester United 4 Blackpool 0	Old Trafford	47158
13	1969/70	25/02/70	FA Cup 6th Round Replay	Manchester United 2 Middlesbrough 1	Old Trafford	63418
14	1975/76	25/02/76	Football League Division 1	Manchester United 1 Derby County 1	Old Trafford	59632
15	1977/78	25/02/78	Football League Division 1	Liverpool 3 Manchester United 1	Anfield	49095
16	1983/84	25/02/84	Football League Division 1	Manchester United 2 Sunderland 1	Old Trafford	40615
17	1988/89	25/02/89	Football League Division 1	Norwich City 2 Manchester United 1	Carrow Road	23155
18	1994/95	25/02/95	FA Premiership	Everton 1 Manchester United 0	Goodison Park	40011
19	1995/96	25/02/96	FA Premiership	Bolton Wanderers 0 Manchester United 6	Burnden Park	21381
20	1997/98	25/02/98	FA Cup 5th Round Replay	Barnsley 3 Manchester United 2	Oakwell	18655
21	2000/01	25/02/01	FA Premiership	Manchester United 6 Arsenal 1	Old Trafford	67535
22	2002/03	25/02/03	Champions League Phase 2 Match 4	Juventus 0 Manchester United 3	Stadio Delle Alpi	59111
23	2003/04	25/02/04	Champions Lge 2nd Round 1st Leg	Porto 2 Manchester United 1	Estadio da Dragao	49977

FEBRUARY 26

#	SEASON	DATE	COMPETITION / ROUND	MATCH RESULT	VENUE	ATT
1	1897/98	26/02/98	Football League Division 2	Newton Heath 5 Arsenal 1	Bank Street	6000
2	1909/10	26/02/10	Football League Division 1	Aston Villa 7 Manchester United 1	Villa Park	20000
3	1912/13	26/02/13	FA Cup 3rd Round Replay	Manchester United 1 Oldham Athletic 2	Old Trafford	31180
4	1926/27	26/02/27	Football League Division 1	Manchester United 0 Bolton Wanderers 0	Old Trafford	29618
5	1937/38	26/02/38	Football League Division 2	Manchester United 2 Blackburn Rovers 1	Old Trafford	30892
6	1948/49	26/02/49	FA Cup 6th Round	Hull City 0 Manchester United 1	Boothferry Park	55000
7	1950/51	26/02/51	Football League Division 1	Sheffield Wednesday 0 Manchester United 4	Hillsborough	25693
8	1954/55	26/02/55	Football League Division 1	Cardiff City 3 Manchester United 0	Ninian Park	16329
9	1963/64	26/02/64	European CWC Quarter-Final 1st Leg	Manchester United 4 Sporting Lisbon 1	Old Trafford	60000
10	1965/66	26/02/66	Football League Division 1	Manchester United 4 Burnley 2	Old Trafford	49892
11	1968/69	26/02/69	European Cup Quarter-Final 1st Leg	Manchester United 3 Rapid Vienna 0	Old Trafford	61932
12	1971/72	26/02/72	FA Cup 5th Round	Manchester United 0 Middlesbrough 0	Old Trafford	53850
13	1976/77	26/02/77	FA Cup 5th Round	Southampton 2 Manchester United 2	The Dell	29137
14	1982/83	26/02/83	Football League Division 1	Manchester United 1 Liverpool 1	Old Trafford	57397
15	1990/91	26/02/91	Football League Division 1	Sheffield United 2 Manchester United 1	Bramall Lane	27570
16	1991/92	26/02/92	Football League Division 1	Manchester United 1 Chelsea 1	Old Trafford	44872
17	1993/94	26/02/94	FA Premiership	West Ham United 2 Manchester United 2	Upton Park	28832
18	1999/00	26/02/00	FA Premiership	Wimbledon 2 Manchester United 2	Selhurst Park	26129
19	2001/02	26/02/02	Champions League Phase 2 Match 4	Manchester United 5 Nantes Atlantique 1	Old Trafford	66492
20	2004/05	26/02/05	FA Premiership	Manchester United 2 Portsmouth 1	Old Trafford	67989
21	2005/06	26/02/06	League Cup Final	Manchester United 4 Wigan Athletic 0	Millennium Stadium	66866

FEBRUARY 27

#	SEASON	DATE	COMPETITION / ROUND	MATCH RESULT	VENUE	ATT
1	1896/97	27/02/97	FA Cup 3rd Round	Derby County 2 Newton Heath 0	Baseball Ground	12000
2	1908/09	27/02/09	Football League Division 1	Nottingham Forest 2 Manchester United 0	City Ground	7000
3	1914/15	27/02/15	Football League Division 1	Manchester United 1 Everton 2	Old Trafford	10000
4	1921/22	27/02/22	Football League Division 1	Huddersfield Town 1 Manchester United 1	Leeds Road	30000
5	1925/26	27/02/26	Football League Division 1	Tottenham Hotspur 0 Manchester United 1	White Hart Lane	25466
6	1931/32	27/02/32	Football League Division 2	Manchester United 3 Barnsley 0	Old Trafford	18223
7	1936/37	27/02/37	Football League Division 1	Chelsea 4 Manchester United 2	Stamford Bridge	16382
8	1953/54	27/02/54	Football League Division 1	Sunderland 0 Manchester United 2	Roker Park	58440
9	1959/60	27/02/60	Football League Division 1	Blackpool 0 Manchester United 6	Bloomfield Road	23996
10	1964/65	27/02/65	Football League Division 1	Manchester United 3 Wolverhampton Wanderers 0	Old Trafford	37018
11	1970/71	27/02/71	Football League Division 1	Manchester United 1 Newcastle United 0	Old Trafford	41902
12	1979/80	27/02/80	Football League Division 1	Manchester United 2 Bolton Wanderers 0	Old Trafford	47546
13	1981/82	27/02/82	Football League Division 1	Manchester United 1 Manchester City 1	Old Trafford	57830
14	1992/93	27/02/93	FA Premiership	Manchester United 3 Middlesbrough 0	Old Trafford	36251
15	1998/99	27/02/99	FA Premiership	Manchester United 2 Southampton 1	Old Trafford	55316
16	2006/07	27/02/07	FA Cup 5th Round Replay	Reading 2 Manchester United 3	Madejski Stadium	23821

FEBRUARY 28

#	SEASON	DATE	COMPETITION / ROUND	MATCH RESULT	VENUE	ATT
1	1902/03	28/02/03	Football League Division 2	Doncaster Rovers 2 Manchester United 2	Town Moor Avenue	4000
2	1913/14	28/02/14	Football League Division 1	Manchester United 2 Newcastle United 2	Old Trafford	30000
3	1919/20	28/02/20	Football League Division 1	Manchester United 0 Arsenal 1	Old Trafford	20000
4	1924/25	28/02/25	Football League Division 2	Manchester United 3 Wolverhampton Wanderers 0	Old Trafford	21250
5	1947/48	28/02/48	FA Cup 6th Round	Manchester United 4 Preston North End 2	Maine Road	74213
6	1952/53	28/02/53	Football League Division 1	Stoke City 3 Manchester United 1	Victoria Ground	30219
7	1958/59	28/02/59	Football League Division 1	Arsenal 3 Manchester United 2	Highbury	67162
8	1961/62	28/02/62	Football League Division 1	Wolverhampton Wanderers 2 Manchester United 2	Molineux	27565
9	1967/68	28/02/68	European Cup Quarter-Final 1st Leg	Manchester United 2 Gornik Zabrze 0	Old Trafford	63456
10	1969/70	28/02/70	Football League Division 1	Stoke City 2 Manchester United 2	Victoria Ground	38917
11	1975/76	28/02/76	Football League Division 1	Manchester United 4 West Ham United 0	Old Trafford	57220
12	1978/79	28/02/79	Football League Division 1	Manchester United 2 Queens Park Rangers 0	Old Trafford	36085
13	1980/81	28/02/81	Football League Division 1	Manchester United 0 Leeds United 1	Old Trafford	45733
14	1986/87	28/02/87	Football League Division 1	Manchester United 0 Everton 0	Old Trafford	47421
15	1997/98	28/02/98	FA Premiership	Chelsea 0 Manchester United 1	Stamford Bridge	35411
16	2003/04	28/02/04	FA Premiership	Fulham 1 Manchester United 1	Loftus Road	18306

FEBRUARY 29

#	SEASON	DATE	COMPETITION / ROUND	MATCH RESULT	VENUE	ATT
1	1895/96	29/02/96	Football League Division 2	Newton Heath 1 Burton Wanderers 2	Bank Street	1000
2	1907/08	29/02/08	Football League Division 1	Manchester United 1 Birmingham City 0	Bank Street	12000
3	1911/12	29/02/12	FA Cup 3rd Round Replay	Manchester United 3 Reading 0	Old Trafford	29511
4	1935/36	29/02/36	Football League Division 2	Manchester United 3 Blackpool 1	Old Trafford	18423
5	1963/64	29/02/64	FA Cup 6th Round	Manchester United 3 Sunderland 3	Old Trafford	63700
6	1971/72	29/02/72	FA Cup 5th Round Replay	Middlesbrough 0 Manchester United 3	Ayresome Park	39683
7	1991/92	29/02/92	Football League Division 1	Coventry City 0 Manchester United 0	Highfield Road	23967

UNITED in MARCH

OVERALL PLAYING RECORD

	P	W	D	L	F	A		P	W	D	L	F	A		P	W	D	L	F	A
1st	15	5	4	6	21	21	11th	16	9	6	1	26	12	22nd	19	11	5	3	36	17
2nd	17	6	6	5	23	20	12th	21	13	5	3	37	18	23rd	20	11	5	4	35	15
3rd	18	11	4	3	37	20	13th	18	9	6	3	25	17	24th	13	5	5	3	15	11
4th	18	6	6	6	28	25	14th	21	8	5	8	31	34	25th	21	8	3	10	28	34
5th	20	12	3	5	33	22	15th	22	7	9	6	31	28	26th	19	10	3	6	41	28
6th	16	12	2	2	28	15	16th	15	5	6	4	21	19	27th	20	4	7	9	28	33
7th	20	9	4	7	26	24	17th	19	8	5	6	33	25	28th	21	7	6	8	25	27
8th	15	6	1	8	19	21	18th	22	4	5	13	21	38	29th	19	11	5	3	36	20
9th	15	6	4	5	25	18	19th	24	13	7	4	45	21	30th	22	15	1	6	51	36
10th	18	4	8	6	27	30	20th	19	8	4	7	28	27	31st	28	15	3	10	48	33
							21st	18	8	5	5	29	19							

OVERALL 589 266 148 175 937 728

MARCH 1

#	SEASON	DATE	COMPETITION / ROUND	MATCH RESULT	VENUE	ATT
1	1901/02	01/03/02	Football League Division 2	Newton Heath 0 Lincoln City 0	Bank Street	6000
2	1912/13	01/03/13	Football League Division 1	Manchester United 2 Middlesbrough 3	Old Trafford	15000
3	1923/24	01/03/24	Football League Division 2	Nelson 0 Manchester United 2	Seed Hill	2750
4	1929/30	01/03/30	Football League Division 1	Bolton Wanderers 4 Manchester United 1	Burnden Park	17714
5	1946/47	01/03/47	Football League Division 1	Sunderland 1 Manchester United 1	Roker Park	25038
6	1951/52	01/03/52	Football League Division 1	Manchester United 1 Aston Villa 1	Old Trafford	38910
7	1957/58	01/03/58	FA Cup 6th Round	West Bromwich Albion 2 Manchester United 2	The Hawthorns	58250
8	1968/69	01/03/69	FA Cup 6th Round	Manchester United 0 Everton 1	Old Trafford	63464
9	1974/75	01/03/75	Football League Division 2	Manchester United 4 Cardiff City 0	Old Trafford	43601
10	1977/78	01/03/78	Football League Division 1	Manchester United 0 Leeds United 1	Old Trafford	49101
11	1979/80	01/03/80	Football League Division 1	Ipswich Town 6 Manchester United 0	Portman Road	30229
12	1985/86	01/03/86	Football League Division 1	Southampton 1 Manchester United 0	The Dell	19012
13	1996/97	01/03/97	FA Premiership	Manchester United 3 Coventry City 1	Old Trafford	55230
14	1999/00	01/03/00	Champions League Phase 2 Match 3	Manchester United 2 Girondins Bordeaux 0	Old Trafford	59786
15	2007/08	01/03/08	FA Premiership	Fulham 0 Manchester United 3	Craven Cottage	25314

MARCH 2

#	SEASON	DATE	COMPETITION / ROUND	MATCH RESULT	VENUE	ATT
1	1894/95	02/03/95	Football League Division 2	Newton Heath 1 Burton Wanderers 1	Bank Street	6000
2	1896/97	02/03/97	Football League Division 2	Newton Heath 3 Darwen 1	Bank Street	3000
3	1900/01	02/03/01	Football League Division 2	Newton Heath 1 Burton Swifts 1	Bank Street	5000
4	1906/07	02/03/07	Football League Division 1	Birmingham City 1 Manchester United 1	St Andrews	20000
5	1911/12	02/03/12	Football League Division 1	Manchester United 2 Notts County 0	Old Trafford	10000
6	1928/29	02/03/29	Football League Division 1	Birmingham City 1 Manchester United 1	St Andrews	16738
7	1934/35	02/03/35	Football League Division 2	Manchester United 0 Newcastle United 1	Old Trafford	20728
8	1956/57	02/03/57	FA Cup 6th Round	Bournemouth 1 Manchester United 2	Dean Court	28799
9	1958/59	02/03/59	Football League Division 1	Blackburn Rovers 1 Manchester United 3	Ewood Park	40401
10	1962/63	02/03/63	Football League Division 1	Blackburn Rovers 2 Manchester United 2	Ewood Park	27924
11	1967/68	02/03/68	Football League Division 1	Manchester United 1 Chelsea 3	Old Trafford	62978
12	1973/74	02/03/74	Football League Division 1	Sheffield United 0 Manchester United 1	Bramall Lane	29203
13	1982/83	02/03/83	Football League Division 1	Stoke City 1 Manchester United 0	Victoria Ground	21266
14	1984/85	02/03/85	Football League Division 1	Manchester United 1 Everton 1	Old Trafford	51150
15	1990/91	02/03/91	Football League Division 1	Manchester United 0 Everton 2	Old Trafford	45656
16	1993/94	02/03/94	League Cup Semi-Final 2nd Leg	Sheffield Wednesday 1 Manchester United 4	Hillsborough	34878
17	2002/03	02/03/03	League Cup Final	Manchester United 0 Liverpool 2	Millennium Stadium	74500

MARCH 3

#	SEASON	DATE	COMPETITION / ROUND	MATCH RESULT	VENUE	ATT
1	1893/94	03/03/94	Football League Division 1	Newton Heath 2 Sunderland 4	Bank Street	10000
2	1899/00	03/03/00	Football League Division 2	Newton Heath 1 Grimsby Town 0	Bank Street	4000
3	1905/06	03/03/06	Football League Division 2	Manchester United 5 Hull City 0	Bank Street	16000
4	1922/23	03/03/23	Football League Division 2	Manchester United 1 Southampton 2	Old Trafford	30000
5	1927/28	03/03/28	FA Cup 6th Round	Blackburn Rovers 2 Manchester United 0	Ewood Park	42312
6	1933/34	03/03/34	Football League Division 2	Manchester United 2 Bury 1	Old Trafford	11176
7	1950/51	03/03/51	Football League Division 1	Manchester United 3 Arsenal 1	Old Trafford	46202
8	1955/56	03/03/56	Football League Division 1	Chelsea 2 Manchester United 4	Stamford Bridge	32050
9	1961/62	03/03/62	Football League Division 1	Birmingham City 1 Manchester United 1	St Andrews	25817
10	1966/67	03/03/67	Football League Division 1	Arsenal 1 Manchester United 1	Highbury	63363
11	1972/73	03/03/73	Football League Division 1	Manchester United 2 West Bromwich Albion 1	Old Trafford	46735
12	1978/79	03/03/79	Football League Division 1	Bristol City 1 Manchester United 2	Ashton Gate	24583
13	1983/84	03/03/84	Football League Division 1	Aston Villa 0 Manchester United 3	Villa Park	32874
14	1989/90	03/03/90	Football League Division 1	Manchester United 4 Luton Town 1	Old Trafford	35327
15	1998/99	03/03/99	Champions Lge Quarter-Final 1st Leg	Manchester United 2 Internazionale 0	Old Trafford	54430
16	2000/01	03/03/01	FA Premiership	Leeds United 1 Manchester United 1	Elland Road	40055
17	2001/02	03/03/02	FA Premiership	Derby County 2 Manchester United 2	Pride Park	33041
18	2006/07	03/03/07	FA Premiership	Liverpool 0 Manchester United 1	Anfield	44403

MARCH 4

#	SEASON	DATE	COMPETITION / ROUND	MATCH RESULT	VENUE	ATT
1	1892/93	04/03/93	Football League Division 1	Newton Heath 0 Sunderland 5	North Road	15000
2	1898/99	04/03/99	Football League Division 2	Grimsby Town 3 Newton Heath 0	Abbey Park	4000
3	1904/05	04/03/05	Football League Division 2	Manchester United 2 West Bromwich Albion 0	Bank Street	8000
4	1910/11	04/03/11	Football League Division 1	Middlesbrough 2 Manchester United 2	Ayresome Park	8000
5	1932/33	04/03/33	Football League Division 2	Millwall 2 Manchester United 0	The Den	22587
6	1938/39	04/03/39	Football League Division 1	Sunderland 5 Manchester United 1	Roker Park	11078
7	1949/50	04/03/50	FA Cup 6th Round	Chelsea 2 Manchester United 0	Stamford Bridge	70362
8	1960/61	04/03/61	Football League Division 1	Manchester City 1 Manchester United 3	Maine Road	50479
9	1962/63	04/03/63	FA Cup 3rd Round	Manchester United 5 Huddersfield Town 0	Old Trafford	47703
10	1963/64	04/03/64	FA Cup 6th Round Replay	Sunderland 2 Manchester United 2	Roker Park	68000
11	1971/72	04/03/72	Football League Division 1	Tottenham Hotspur 2 Manchester United 0	White Hart Lane	54814
12	1977/78	04/03/78	Football League Division 1	Manchester United 0 Middlesbrough 0	Old Trafford	46322
13	1991/92	04/03/92	League Cup Semi-Final 1st Leg	Middlesbrough 0 Manchester United 0	Ayresome Park	25572
14	1994/95	04/03/95	FA Premiership	Manchester United 9 Ipswich Town 0	Old Trafford	43804
15	1995/96	04/03/96	FA Premiership	Newcastle United 0 Manchester United 1	St James' Park	36584
16	1997/98	04/03/98	Champions Lge Quarter-Final 1st Leg	Monaco 0 Manchester United 0	Stade Louis II	15000
17	1999/00	04/03/00	FA Premiership	Manchester United 1 Liverpool 1	Old Trafford	61592
18	2007/08	04/03/08	Champions Lge 2nd Round 2nd Leg	Manchester United 1 Olympique Lyonnais 0	Old Trafford	75520

MARCH 5

#	SEASON	DATE	COMPETITION / ROUND	MATCH RESULT	VENUE	ATT
1	1909/10	05/03/10	Football League Division 1	Manchester United 1 Sheffield United 0	Old Trafford	40000
2	1913/14	05/03/14	Football League Division 1	Preston North End 4 Manchester United 2	Deepdale	12000
3	1920/21	05/03/21	Football League Division 1	Sunderland 2 Manchester United 3	Roker Park	25000
4	1926/27	05/03/27	Football League Division 1	Manchester United 1 Bury 2	Old Trafford	14709
5	1931/32	05/03/32	Football League Division 2	Notts County 1 Manchester United 2	Meadow Lane	10817
6	1937/38	05/03/38	Football League Division 2	Sheffield Wednesday 1 Manchester United 3	Hillsborough	37156
7	1948/49	05/03/49	Football League Division 1	Charlton Athletic 2 Manchester United 3	The Valley	55291
8	1954/55	05/03/55	Football League Division 1	Manchester United 1 Burnley 0	Old Trafford	31729
9	1957/58	05/03/58	FA Cup 6th Round Replay	Manchester United 1 West Bromwich Albion 0	Old Trafford	60000
10	1959/60	05/03/60	Football League Division 1	Manchester United 0 Wolverhampton Wanderers 2	Old Trafford	60560
11	1965/66	05/03/66	FA Cup 5th Round	Wolverhampton Wanderers 2 Manchester United 4	Molineux	53500
12	1968/69	05/03/69	European Cup Quarter-Final 2nd Leg	Rapid Vienna 0 Manchester United 0	Wiener Stadion	52000
13	1976/77	05/03/77	Football League Division 1	Manchester United 3 Manchester City 1	Old Trafford	58595
14	1982/83	05/03/83	Football League Division 1	Manchester City 1 Manchester United 2	Maine Road	45400
15	1985/86	05/03/86	FA Cup 5th Round	West Ham United 1 Manchester United 1	Upton Park	26441
16	1987/88	05/03/88	Football League Division 1	Norwich City 1 Manchester United 0	Carrow Road	19129
17	1993/94	05/03/94	FA Premiership	Manchester United 0 Chelsea 1	Old Trafford	44745
18	1996/97	05/03/97	Champions Lge Quarter-Final 1st Leg	Manchester United 4 Porto 0	Old Trafford	53425
19	2002/03	05/03/03	FA Premiership	Manchester United 2 Leeds United 1	Old Trafford	67135
20	2004/05	05/03/05	FA Premiership	Crystal Palace 0 Manchester United 5	Selhurst Park	26021

MARCH 6

#	SEASON	DATE	COMPETITION / ROUND	MATCH RESULT	VENUE	ATT
1	1892/93	06/03/93	Football League Division 1	Aston Villa 2 Newton Heath 0	Perry Barr	4000
2	1919/20	06/03/20	Football League Division 1	Manchester United 1 Everton 0	Old Trafford	25000
3	1925/26	06/03/26	FA Cup 6th Round	Fulham 1 Manchester United 2	Craven Cottage	28699
4	1936/37	06/03/37	Football League Division 1	Manchester United 2 Stoke City 1	Old Trafford	24660
5	1947/48	06/03/48	Football League Division 1	Manchester United 3 Sunderland 1	Maine Road	55160
6	1953/54	06/03/54	Football League Division 1	Manchester United 1 Wolverhampton Wanderers 0	Old Trafford	38939
7	1956/57	06/03/57	Football League Division 1	Everton 1 Manchester United 2	Goodison Park	34029
8	1970/71	06/03/71	Football League Division 1	West Bromwich Albion 4 Manchester United 3	The Hawthorns	41112
9	1975/76	06/03/76	FA Cup 6th Round	Manchester United 1 Wolverhampton Wanderers 1	Old Trafford	59433
10	1981/82	06/03/82	Football League Division 1	Birmingham City 0 Manchester United 1	St Andrews	19637
11	1984/85	06/03/85	UEFA Cup Quarter-Final 1st Leg	Manchester United 1 Videoton 0	Old Trafford	35432
12	1990/91	06/03/91	European CWC 3rd Round 1st Leg	Manchester United 1 Montpellier Herault 1	Old Trafford	41942
13	1992/93	06/03/93	FA Premiership	Liverpool 1 Manchester United 2	Anfield	44374
14	2001/02	06/03/02	FA Premiership	Manchester United 4 Tottenham Hotspur 0	Old Trafford	67599
15	2003/04	06/03/04	FA Cup 6th Round	Manchester United 2 Fulham 1	Old Trafford	67614
16	2005/06	06/03/06	FA Premiership	Wigan Athletic 1 Manchester United 2	JJB Stadium	23574

MARCH 7

#	SEASON	DATE	COMPETITION / ROUND	MATCH RESULT	VENUE	ATT
1	1895/96	07/03/96	Football League Division 2	Rotherham United 2 Newton Heath 3	Millmoor	1500
2	1897/98	07/03/98	Football League Division 2	Burnley 6 Newton Heath 3	Turf Moor	3000
3	1902/03	07/03/03	Football League Division 2	Manchester United 1 Lincoln City 2	Bank Street	4000
4	1907/08	07/03/08	FA Cup 4th Round	Fulham 2 Manchester United 1	Craven Cottage	41000
5	1924/25	07/03/25	Football League Division 2	Fulham 1 Manchester United 0	Craven Cottage	16000
6	1927/28	07/03/28	Football League Division 1	Manchester United 0 Huddersfield Town 0	Old Trafford	35413
7	1930/31	07/03/31	Football League Division 1	Birmingham City 0 Manchester United 0	St Andrews	17678
8	1935/36	07/03/36	Football League Division 2	West Ham United 1 Manchester United 2	Upton Park	29684
9	1952/53	07/03/53	Football League Division 1	Manchester United 5 Preston North End 2	Old Trafford	52590
10	1958/59	07/03/59	Football League Division 1	Manchester United 2 Everton 1	Old Trafford	51254
11	1963/64	07/03/64	Football League Division 1	West Ham United 0 Manchester United 2	Upton Park	27027
12	1980/81	07/03/81	Football League Division 1	Southampton 1 Manchester United 0	The Dell	22698
13	1983/84	07/03/84	European CWC 3rd Round 1st Leg	Barcelona 2 Manchester United 0	Estadio Camp Nou	70000
14	1986/87	07/03/87	Football League Division 1	Manchester United 2 Manchester City 0	Old Trafford	48619
15	1994/95	07/03/95	FA Premiership	Wimbledon 0 Manchester United 1	Selhurst Park	18224
16	1997/98	07/03/98	FA Premiership	Sheffield Wednesday 2 Manchester United 0	Hillsborough	39427
17	1998/99	07/03/99	FA Cup 6th Round	Manchester United 0 Chelsea 0	Old Trafford	54587
18	1999/00	07/03/00	Champions League Phase 2 Match 4	Girondins Bordeaux 1 Manchester United 2	Stade Lescure	30130
19	2000/01	07/03/01	Champions League Phase 2 Match 5	Panathinaikos 1 Manchester United 1	Olympic Stadium	27231
20	2006/07	07/03/07	Champions Lge 2nd Round 2nd Leg	Manchester United 1 Lille Metropole 0	Old Trafford	75182

MARCH 8

#	SEASON	DATE	COMPETITION / ROUND	MATCH RESULT	VENUE	ATT
1	1901/02	08/03/02	Football League Division 2	West Bromwich Albion 4 Newton Heath 0	The Hawthorns	10000
2	1912/13	08/03/13	Football League Division 1	Notts County 1 Manchester United 2	Meadow Lane	10000
3	1923/24	08/03/24	Football League Division 2	Manchester United 0 Nelson 1	Old Trafford	8500
4	1929/30	08/03/30	Football League Division 1	Manchester United 2 Aston Villa 3	Old Trafford	25407
5	1946/47	08/03/47	Football League Division 1	Manchester United 2 Aston Villa 1	Maine Road	36965
6	1949/50	08/03/50	Football League Division 1	Manchester United 7 Aston Villa 0	Old Trafford	22149
7	1951/52	08/03/52	Football League Division 1	Sunderland 1 Manchester United 2	Roker Park	48078
8	1957/58	08/03/58	Football League Division 1	Manchester United 0 West Bromwich Albion 4	Old Trafford	63278
9	1968/69	08/03/69	Football League Division 1	Manchester United 0 Manchester City 1	Old Trafford	63264
10	1971/72	08/03/72	Football League Division 1	Manchester United 0 Everton 0	Old Trafford	38415
11	1974/75	08/03/75	Football League Division 2	Bolton Wanderers 0 Manchester United 1	Burnden Park	38152
12	1976/77	08/03/77	FA Cup 5th Round Replay	Manchester United 2 Southampton 1	Old Trafford	58103
13	1996/97	08/03/97	FA Premiership	Sunderland 2 Manchester United 1	Roker Park	22225
14	2004/05	08/03/05	Champions Lge 2nd Round 2nd Leg	AC Milan 1 Manchester United 0	Stadio San Siro	78957
15	2007/08	08/03/08	FA Cup 6th Round	Manchester United 0 Portsmouth 1	Old Trafford	75463

MARCH 9

#	SEASON	DATE	COMPETITION / ROUND	MATCH RESULT	VENUE	ATT
1	1902/03	09/03/03	Football League Division 2	Manchester United 3 Arsenal 0	Bank Street	5000
2	1903/04	09/03/04	Football League Division 2	Blackpool 2 Manchester United 1	Bloomfield Road	3000
3	1911/12	09/03/12	FA Cup 4th Round	Manchester United 1 Blackburn Rovers 1	Old Trafford	59300
4	1920/21	09/03/21	Football League Division 1	Everton 2 Manchester United 0	Goodison Park	38000
5	1928/29	09/03/29	Football League Division 1	Manchester United 1 Huddersfield Town 0	Old Trafford	28183
6	1934/35	09/03/35	Football League Division 2	West Ham United 0 Manchester United 0	Upton Park	19718
7	1956/57	09/03/57	Football League Division 1	Manchester United 1 Aston Villa 1	Old Trafford	55484
8	1962/63	09/03/63	Football League Division 1	Manchester United 0 Tottenham Hotspur 2	Old Trafford	53416
9	1963/64	09/03/64	FA Cup 6th Round 2nd Replay	Manchester United 5 Sunderland 1	Leeds Road	54952
10	1965/66	09/03/66	European Cup Quarter-Final 2nd Leg	Benfica 1 Manchester United 5	Estadio da Luz	75000
11	1975/76	09/03/76	FA Cup 6th Round Replay	Wolverhampton Wanderers 2 Manchester United 3	Molineux	44373
12	1984/85	09/03/85	FA Cup 6th Round	Manchester United 4 West Ham United 2	Old Trafford	46769
13	1985/86	09/03/86	FA Cup 5th Round Replay	Manchester United 0 West Ham United 2	Old Trafford	30441
14	1992/93	09/03/93	FA Premiership	Oldham Athletic 1 Manchester United 0	Boundary Park	17106
15	2003/04	09/03/04	Champions Lge 2nd Round 2nd Leg	Manchester United 1 Porto 1	Old Trafford	67029

MARCH 10

#	SEASON	DATE	COMPETITION / ROUND	MATCH RESULT	VENUE	ATT
1	1893/94	10/03/94	Football League Division 1	Newton Heath 0 Sheffield United 2	Bank Street	5000
2	1899/00	10/03/00	Football League Division 2	Arsenal 2 Newton Heath 1	Manor Field	3000
3	1905/06	10/03/06	FA Cup 4th Round	Manchester United 2 Arsenal 3	Bank Street	26500
4	1908/09	10/03/09	FA Cup 4th Round	Burnley 2 Manchester United 3	Turf Moor	16850
5	1925/26	10/03/26	Football League Division 1	Manchester United 3 Liverpool 3	Old Trafford	9214
6	1927/28	10/03/28	Football League Division 1	Manchester United 1 West Ham United 1	Old Trafford	21577
7	1933/34	10/03/34	Football League Division 2	Hull City 4 Manchester United 1	Anlaby Road	5771
8	1950/51	10/03/51	Football League Division 1	Portsmouth 0 Manchester United 0	Fratton Park	33148
9	1955/56	10/03/56	Football League Division 1	Manchester United 1 Cardiff City 1	Old Trafford	44693
10	1961/62	10/03/62	FA Cup 6th Round	Preston North End 0 Manchester United 0	Deepdale	37521
11	1964/65	10/03/65	FA Cup 6th Round	Wolverhampton Wanderers 3 Manchester United 5	Molineux	53581
12	1968/69	10/03/69	Football League Division 1	Everton 0 Manchester United 0	Goodison Park	57514
13	1972/73	10/03/73	Football League Division 1	Birmingham City 3 Manchester United 1	St Andrews	51278
14	1978/79	10/03/79	FA Cup 6th Round	Tottenham Hotspur 1 Manchester United 1	White Hart Lane	51800
15	1983/84	10/03/84	Football League Division 1	Manchester United 2 Leicester City 0	Old Trafford	39473
16	1990/91	10/03/91	Football League Division 1	Chelsea 3 Manchester United 2	Stamford Bridge	22818
17	1998/99	10/03/99	FA Cup 6th Round Replay	Chelsea 0 Manchester United 2	Stamford Bridge	33075
18	2006/07	10/03/07	FA Cup 6th Round	Middlesbrough 2 Manchester United 2	Riverside Stadium	33308

MARCH 11

#	SEASON	DATE	COMPETITION / ROUND	MATCH RESULT	VENUE	ATT
1	1904/05	11/03/05	Football League Division 2	Burnley 2 Manchester United 0	Turf Moor	7000
2	1910/11	11/03/11	Football League Division 1	Manchester United 5 Preston North End 0	Old Trafford	25000
3	1921/22	11/03/22	Football League Division 1	Manchester United 1 Arsenal 0	Old Trafford	30000
4	1932/33	11/03/33	Football League Division 2	Manchester United 1 Port Vale 1	Old Trafford	24690
5	1938/39	11/03/39	Football League Division 1	Manchester United 1 Aston Villa 1	Old Trafford	28292
6	1949/50	11/03/50	Football League Division 1	Middlesbrough 2 Manchester United 3	Ayresome Park	46702
7	1960/61	11/03/61	Football League Division 1	Newcastle United 1 Manchester United 1	St James' Park	28870
8	1962/63	11/03/63	FA Cup 4th Round	Manchester United 1 Aston Villa 0	Old Trafford	52265
9	1966/67	11/03/67	Football League Division 1	Newcastle United 0 Manchester United 0	St James' Park	37430
10	1971/72	11/03/72	Football League Division 1	Manchester United 2 Huddersfield Town 0	Old Trafford	53581
11	1977/78	11/03/78	Football League Division 1	Newcastle United 2 Manchester United 2	St James' Park	25825
12	1989/90	11/03/90	FA Cup 6th Round	Sheffield United 0 Manchester United 1	Bramall Lane	34344
13	1991/92	11/03/92	League Cup Semi-Final 2nd Leg	Manchester United 2 Middlesbrough 1	Old Trafford	45875
14	1995/96	11/03/96	FA Cup 6th Round	Manchester United 2 Southampton 0	Old Trafford	45446
15	1997/98	11/03/98	FA Premiership	West Ham United 1 Manchester United 1	Upton Park	25892
16	1999/00	11/03/00	FA Premiership	Manchester United 3 Derby County 1	Old Trafford	61619

MARCH 12

#	SEASON	DATE	COMPETITION / ROUND	MATCH RESULT	VENUE	ATT
1	1893/94	12/03/94	Football League Division 1	Newton Heath 5 Blackburn Rovers 1	Bank Street	5000
2	1903/04	12/03/04	Football League Division 2	Manchester United 3 Burnley 1	Bank Street	14000
3	1909/10	12/03/10	Football League Division 1	Arsenal 0 Manchester United 0	Manor Field	4000
4	1920/21	12/03/21	Football League Division 1	Manchester United 1 Bradford City 1	Old Trafford	30000
5	1926/27	12/03/27	Football League Division 1	Birmingham City 4 Manchester United 0	St Andrews	14392
6	1929/30	12/03/30	Football League Division 1	Arsenal 4 Manchester United 2	Highbury	18082
7	1931/32	12/03/32	Football League Division 2	Manchester United 2 Plymouth Argyle 1	Old Trafford	24827
8	1937/38	12/03/38	Football League Division 2	Manchester United 1 Fulham 0	Old Trafford	30636
9	1948/49	12/03/49	Football League Division 1	Manchester United 3 Stoke City 0	Maine Road	55949
10	1965/66	12/03/66	Football League Division 1	Chelsea 2 Manchester United 0	Stamford Bridge	60269
11	1976/77	12/03/77	Football League Division 1	Manchester United 1 Leeds United 0	Old Trafford	60612
12	1979/80	12/03/80	Football League Division 1	Manchester United 0 Everton 0	Old Trafford	45515
13	1982/83	12/03/83	FA Cup 6th Round	Manchester United 1 Everton 0	Old Trafford	58198
14	1984/85	12/03/85	Football League Division 1	Tottenham Hotspur 1 Manchester United 2	White Hart Lane	42908
15	1987/88	12/03/88	Football League Division 1	Manchester United 4 Sheffield Wednesday 1	Old Trafford	33318
16	1988/89	12/03/89	Football League Division 1	Aston Villa 0 Manchester United 1	Villa Park	28332
17	1993/94	12/03/94	FA Cup 6th Round	Manchester United 3 Charlton Athletic 1	Old Trafford	44347
18	1994/95	12/03/95	FA Cup 6th Round	Manchester United 2 Queens Park Rangers 0	Old Trafford	42830
19	2002/03	12/03/03	Champions League Phase 2 Match 5	Manchester United 1 Basel 1	Old Trafford	66870
20	2004/05	12/03/05	FA Cup 6th Round	Southampton 0 Manchester United 4	St Mary's Stadium	30971
21	2005/06	12/03/06	FA Premiership	Manchester United 2 Newcastle United 0	Old Trafford	67858

MARCH 13

#	SEASON	DATE	COMPETITION / ROUND	MATCH RESULT	VENUE	ATT
1	1896/97	13/03/97	Football League Division 2	Darwen 0 Newton Heath 2	Barley Bank	2000
2	1900/01	13/03/01	Football League Division 2	Newton Heath 1 Barnsley 0	Bank Street	6000
3	1908/09	13/03/09	Football League Division 1	Chelsea 1 Manchester United 1	Stamford Bridge	30000
4	1914/15	13/03/15	Football League Division 1	Manchester United 1 Bradford City 0	Old Trafford	14000
5	1919/20	13/03/20	Football League Division 1	Everton 0 Manchester United 0	Goodison Park	30000
6	1925/26	13/03/26	Football League Division 1	Huddersfield Town 5 Manchester United 0	Leeds Road	27842
7	1936/37	13/03/37	Football League Division 1	Charlton Athletic 3 Manchester United 0	The Valley	25943
8	1947/48	13/03/48	FA Cup Semi-Final	Manchester United 3 Derby County 1	Hillsborough	60000
9	1953/54	13/03/54	Football League Division 1	Aston Villa 2 Manchester United 2	Villa Park	26023
10	1964/65	13/03/65	Football League Division 1	Manchester United 4 Chelsea 0	Old Trafford	56261
11	1967/68	13/03/68	European Cup Quarter-Final 2nd Leg	Gornik Zabrze 1 Manchester United 0	Stadion Slaski	105000
12	1970/71	13/03/71	Football League Division 1	Manchester United 2 Nottingham Forest 0	Old Trafford	40473
13	1973/74	13/03/74	Football League Division 1	Manchester City 0 Manchester United 0	Maine Road	51331
14	1975/76	13/03/76	Football League Division 1	Manchester United 3 Leeds United 2	Old Trafford	59429
15	1990/91	13/03/91	Football League Division 1	Southampton 1 Manchester United 1	The Dell	15701
16	1998/99	13/03/99	FA Premiership	Newcastle United 1 Manchester United 2	St James' Park	36776
17	2000/01	13/03/01	Champions League Phase 2 Match 6	Manchester United 3 Sturm Graz 0	Old Trafford	66404
18	2001/02	13/03/02	Champions League Phase 2 Match 5	Manchester United 0 Bayern Munich 0	Old Trafford	66818

MARCH 14

#	SEASON	DATE	COMPETITION / ROUND	MATCH RESULT	VENUE	ATT
1	1895/96	14/03/96	Football League Division 2	Grimsby Town 4 Newton Heath 2	Abbey Park	2000
2	1907/08	14/03/08	Football League Division 1	Manchester United 3 Sunderland 0	Bank Street	15000
3	1911/12	14/03/12	FA Cup 4th Round Replay	Blackburn Rovers 4 Manchester United 2	Ewood Park	39296
4	1913/14	14/03/14	Football League Division 1	Manchester United 0 Aston Villa 6	Old Trafford	30000
5	1922/23	14/03/23	Football League Division 2	Derby County 1 Manchester United 1	Baseball Ground	12000
6	1924/25	14/03/25	Football League Division 2	Manchester United 2 Portsmouth 0	Old Trafford	22000
7	1927/28	14/03/28	Football League Division 1	Manchester United 1 Everton 0	Old Trafford	25667
8	1935/36	14/03/36	Football League Division 2	Manchester United 3 Swansea City 0	Old Trafford	27580
9	1952/53	14/03/53	Football League Division 1	Burnley 2 Manchester United 1	Turf Moor	45682
10	1958/59	14/03/59	Football League Division 1	West Bromwich Albion 1 Manchester United 3	The Hawthorns	35463
11	1961/62	14/03/62	FA Cup 6th Round Replay	Manchester United 2 Preston North End 1	Old Trafford	63468
12	1963/64	14/03/64	FA Cup Semi-Final	Manchester United 1 West Ham United 3	Hillsborough	65000
13	1969/70	14/03/70	FA Cup Semi-Final	Leeds United 0 Manchester United 0	Hillsborough	55000
14	1978/79	14/03/79	FA Cup 6th Round Replay	Manchester United 2 Tottenham Hotspur 0	Old Trafford	55584
15	1980/81	14/03/81	Football League Division 1	Aston Villa 3 Manchester United 3	Villa Park	42182
16	1986/87	14/03/87	Football League Division 1	Luton Town 2 Manchester United 1	Kenilworth Road	12509
17	1989/90	14/03/90	Football League Division 1	Manchester United 0 Everton 0	Old Trafford	37398
18	1991/92	14/03/92	Football League Division 1	Sheffield United 1 Manchester United 2	Bramall Lane	30183
19	1992/93	14/03/93	FA Premiership	Manchester United 1 Aston Villa 1	Old Trafford	36163
20	1997/98	14/03/98	FA Premiership	Manchester United 0 Arsenal 1	Old Trafford	55174
21	2003/04	14/03/04	FA Premiership	Manchester City 4 Manchester United 1	Eastlands Stadium	47284

MARCH 15

#	SEASON	DATE	COMPETITION / ROUND	MATCH RESULT	VENUE	ATT
1	1901/02	15/03/02	Football League Division 2	Newton Heath 0 Arsenal 1	Bank Street	4000
2	1908/09	15/03/09	Football League Division 1	Manchester United 2 Sunderland 2	Bank Street	10000
3	1910/11	15/03/11	Football League Division 1	Manchester United 3 Tottenham Hotspur 2	Old Trafford	10000
4	1912/13	15/03/13	Football League Division 1	Manchester United 1 Sunderland 3	Old Trafford	15000
5	1923/24	15/03/24	Football League Division 2	Manchester United 1 Hull City 1	Old Trafford	13000
6	1929/30	15/03/30	Football League Division 1	Derby County 1 Manchester United 1	Baseball Ground	9102
7	1946/47	15/03/47	Football League Division 1	Derby County 4 Manchester United 3	Baseball Ground	19579
8	1949/50	15/03/50	Football League Division 1	Manchester United 0 Liverpool 0	Old Trafford	43456
9	1951/52	15/03/52	Football League Division 1	Manchester United 2 Wolverhampton Wanderers 0	Old Trafford	45109
10	1957/58	15/03/58	Football League Division 1	Burnley 3 Manchester United 0	Turf Moor	37247
11	1964/65	15/03/65	Football League Division 1	Manchester United 4 Fulham 1	Old Trafford	45402
12	1968/69	15/03/69	Football League Division 1	Chelsea 3 Manchester United 2	Stamford Bridge	60436
13	1974/75	15/03/75	Football League Division 2	Manchester United 1 Norwich City 1	Old Trafford	56202
14	1977/78	15/03/78	Football League Division 1	Manchester United 2 Manchester City 2	Old Trafford	58398
15	1979/80	15/03/80	Football League Division 1	Brighton 0 Manchester United 0	Goldstone Ground	29621
16	1984/85	15/03/85	Football League Division 1	West Ham United 2 Manchester United 2	Upton Park	16674
17	1985/86	15/03/86	Football League Division 1	Queens Park Rangers 1 Manchester United 0	Loftus Road	23407
18	1994/95	15/03/95	FA Premiership	Manchester United 0 Tottenham Hotspur 0	Old Trafford	43802
19	1996/97	15/03/97	FA Premiership	Manchester United 2 Sheffield Wednesday 0	Old Trafford	55267
20	1999/00	15/03/00	Champions League Phase 2 Match 5	Manchester United 3 Fiorentina 1	Old Trafford	59926
21	2002/03	15/03/03	FA Premiership	Aston Villa 0 Manchester United 1	Villa Park	42602
22	2007/08	15/03/08	FA Premiership	Derby County 0 Manchester United 1	Pride Park	33072

MARCH 16

#	SEASON	DATE	COMPETITION / ROUND	MATCH RESULT	VENUE	ATT
1	1900/01	16/03/01	Football League Division 2	Newton Heath 1 Arsenal 0	Bank Street	5000
2	1906/07	16/03/07	Football League Division 1	Arsenal 4 Manchester United 0	Manor Field	6000
3	1911/12	16/03/12	Football League Division 1	Preston North End 0 Manchester United 0	Deepdale	7000
4	1928/29	16/03/29	Football League Division 1	Bolton Wanderers 1 Manchester United 1	Burnden Park	17354
5	1930/31	16/03/31	Football League Division 1	Manchester United 0 Portsmouth 1	Old Trafford	4808
6	1934/35	16/03/35	Football League Division 2	Manchester United 3 Blackpool 2	Old Trafford	25704
7	1956/57	16/03/57	Football League Division 1	Wolverhampton Wanderers 1 Manchester United 1	Molineux	53228
8	1962/63	16/03/63	FA Cup 5th Round	Manchester United 2 Chelsea 1	Old Trafford	48298
9	1967/68	16/03/68	Football League Division 1	Coventry City 2 Manchester United 0	Highfield Road	47110
10	1973/74	16/03/74	Football League Division 1	Birmingham City 1 Manchester United 0	St Andrews	37768
11	1975/76	16/03/76	Football League Division 1	Norwich City 1 Manchester United 1	Carrow Road	27787
12	1990/91	16/03/91	Football League Division 1	Nottingham Forest 1 Manchester United 1	City Ground	23859
13	1993/94	16/03/94	FA Premiership	Manchester United 5 Sheffield Wednesday 0	Old Trafford	43669
14	1995/96	16/03/96	FA Premiership	Queens Park Rangers 1 Manchester United 1	Loftus Road	18817
15	2001/02	16/03/02	FA Premiership	West Ham United 3 Manchester United 5	Upton Park	35281

MARCH 17

#	SEASON	DATE	COMPETITION / ROUND	MATCH RESULT	VENUE	ATT
1	1893/94	17/03/94	Football League Division 1	Newton Heath 2 Derby County 6	Bank Street	7000
2	1899/00	17/03/00	Football League Division 2	Newton Heath 3 Barnsley 0	Bank Street	6000
3	1901/02	17/03/02	Football League Division 2	Chesterfield 3 Newton Heath 0	Saltergate	2000
4	1905/06	17/03/06	Football League Division 2	Manchester United 4 Chesterfield 1	Bank Street	16000
5	1922/23	17/03/23	Football League Division 2	Bradford City 1 Manchester United 1	Valley Parade	10000
6	1925/26	17/03/26	Football League Division 1	Bolton Wanderers 3 Manchester United 1	Burnden Park	10794
7	1927/28	17/03/28	Football League Division 1	Portsmouth 1 Manchester United 0	Fratton Park	25400
8	1933/34	17/03/34	Football League Division 2	Manchester United 1 Fulham 0	Old Trafford	17565
9	1947/48	17/03/48	Football League Division 1	Grimsby Town 1 Manchester United 1	Blundell Park	12284
10	1950/51	17/03/51	Football League Division 1	Manchester United 3 Everton 0	Old Trafford	29317
11	1955/56	17/03/56	Football League Division 1	Arsenal 1 Manchester United 1	Highbury	50758
12	1961/62	17/03/62	Football League Division 1	Bolton Wanderers 1 Manchester United 0	Burnden Park	34366
13	1969/70	17/03/70	Football League Division 1	Manchester United 3 Burnley 3	Old Trafford	38377
14	1972/73	17/03/73	Football League Division 1	Manchester United 2 Newcastle United 1	Old Trafford	48426
15	1981/82	17/03/82	Football League Division 1	Manchester United 0 Coventry City 1	Old Trafford	34499
16	1983/84	17/03/84	Football League Division 1	Manchester United 4 Arsenal 0	Old Trafford	48942
17	1998/99	17/03/99	Champions Lge Quarter-Final 2nd Leg	Internazionale 1 Manchester United 1	Stadio San Siro	79528
18	2000/01	17/03/01	FA Premiership	Manchester United 2 Leicester City 0	Old Trafford	67516
19	2006/07	17/03/07	FA Premiership	Manchester United 4 Bolton Wanderers 1	Old Trafford	76058

MARCH 18

#	SEASON	DATE	COMPETITION / ROUND	MATCH RESULT	VENUE	ATT
1	1895/96	18/03/96	Football League Division 2	Burton Wanderers 5 Newton Heath 1	Derby Turn	2000
2	1898/99	18/03/99	Football League Division 2	Newton Heath 1 New Brighton Tower 2	Bank Street	20000
3	1904/05	18/03/05	Football League Division 2	Manchester United 2 Grimsby Town 1	Bank Street	12000
4	1910/11	18/03/11	Football League Division 1	Notts County 1 Manchester United 0	Meadow Lane	12000
5	1921/22	18/03/22	Football League Division 1	Manchester United 0 Blackburn Rovers 1	Old Trafford	30000
6	1932/33	18/03/33	Football League Division 2	Notts County 1 Manchester United 0	Meadow Lane	13018
7	1938/39	18/03/39	Football League Division 1	Wolverhampton Wanderers 3 Manchester United 0	Molineux	31498
8	1949/50	18/03/50	Football League Division 1	Manchester United 1 Blackpool 2	Old Trafford	53688
9	1960/61	18/03/61	Football League Division 1	Manchester United 1 Arsenal 1	Old Trafford	29732
10	1962/63	18/03/63	Football League Division 1	West Ham United 3 Manchester United 1	Upton Park	28950
11	1963/64	18/03/64	European CWC Quarter-Final 2nd Leg	Sporting Lisbon 5 Manchester United 0	de Jose Alvalade	40000
12	1966/67	18/03/67	Football League Division 1	Manchester United 5 Leicester City 2	Old Trafford	50281
13	1971/72	18/03/72	FA Cup 6th Round	Manchester United 1 Stoke City 1	Old Trafford	54226
14	1977/78	18/03/78	Football League Division 1	Manchester United 1 West Bromwich Albion 1	Old Trafford	46329
15	1980/81	18/03/81	Football League Division 1	Manchester United 1 Nottingham Forest 1	Old Trafford	38205
16	1988/89	18/03/89	FA Cup 6th Round	Manchester United 0 Nottingham Forest 1	Old Trafford	55040
17	1989/90	18/03/90	Football League Division 1	Manchester United 1 Liverpool 2	Old Trafford	46629
18	1991/92	18/03/92	Football League Division 1	Nottingham Forest 1 Manchester United 0	City Ground	28062
19	1997/98	18/03/98	Champions Lge Quarter-Final 2nd Leg	Manchester United 1 Monaco 1	Old Trafford	53683
20	1999/00	18/03/00	FA Premiership	Leicester City 0 Manchester United 2	Filbert Street	22170
21	2002/03	18/03/03	Champions League Phase 2 Match 6	Deportivo La Coruna 2 Manchester United 0	Estadio de Riazor	25000
22	2005/06	18/03/06	FA Premiership	West Bromwich Albion 1 Manchester United 2	The Hawthorns	27623

MARCH 19

#	SEASON	DATE	COMPETITION / ROUND	MATCH RESULT	VENUE	ATT
1	1897/98	19/03/98	Football League Division 2	Darwen 2 Newton Heath 3	Barley Bank	2000
2	1903/04	19/03/04	Football League Division 2	Preston North End 1 Manchester United 1	Deepdale	7000
3	1909/10	19/03/10	Football League Division 1	Manchester United 5 Bolton Wanderers 0	Old Trafford	20000
4	1920/21	19/03/21	Football League Division 1	Bradford City 1 Manchester United 1	Valley Parade	25000
5	1926/27	19/03/27	Football League Division 1	Manchester United 0 West Ham United 3	Old Trafford	18347
6	1931/32	19/03/32	Football League Division 2	Leeds United 1 Manchester United 4	Elland Road	13644
7	1937/38	19/03/38	Football League Division 2	Plymouth Argyle 1 Manchester United 1	Home Park	20311
8	1948/49	19/03/49	Football League Division 1	Birmingham City 1 Manchester United 0	St Andrews	46819
9	1954/55	19/03/55	Football League Division 1	Manchester United 1 Everton 2	Old Trafford	32295
10	1959/60	19/03/60	Football League Division 1	Manchester United 3 Nottingham Forest 1	Old Trafford	35269
11	1965/66	19/03/66	Football League Division 1	Manchester United 2 Arsenal 1	Old Trafford	47246
12	1968/69	19/03/69	Football League Division 1	Manchester United 8 Queens Park Rangers 1	Old Trafford	36638
13	1976/77	19/03/77	FA Cup 6th Round	Manchester United 2 Aston Villa 1	Old Trafford	57089
14	1982/83	19/03/83	Football League Division 1	Manchester United 1 Brighton 1	Old Trafford	36264
15	1985/86	19/03/86	Football League Division 1	Manchester United 2 Luton Town 0	Old Trafford	33668
16	1987/88	19/03/88	Football League Division 1	Nottingham Forest 0 Manchester United 0	City Ground	27598
17	1990/91	19/03/91	European CWC 3rd Round 2nd Leg	Montpellier Herault 0 Manchester United 2	Stade de la Masson	18000
18	1993/94	19/03/94	FA Premiership	Swindon Town 2 Manchester United 2	County Ground	18102
19	1994/95	19/03/95	FA Premiership	Liverpool 2 Manchester United 0	Anfield	38906
20	1996/97	19/03/97	Champions Lge Quarter-Final 2nd Leg	Porto 0 Manchester United 0	Estadio das Antas	40000
21	2001/02	19/03/02	Champions League Phase 2 Match 6	Boavista 0 Manchester United 3	Estadio do Bessa	13223
22	2004/05	19/03/05	FA Premiership	Manchester United 1 Fulham 0	Old Trafford	67959
23	2006/07	19/03/07	FA Cup 6th Round Replay	Manchester United 1 Middlesbrough 0	Old Trafford	71325
24	2007/08	19/03/08	FA Premiership	Manchester United 2 Bolton Wanderers 0	Old Trafford	75476

MARCH 20

#	SEASON	DATE	COMPETITION / ROUND	MATCH RESULT	VENUE	ATT
1	1896/97	20/03/97	Football League Division 2	Burton Wanderers 1 Newton Heath 2	Derby Turn	3000
2	1900/01	20/03/01	Football League Division 2	Newton Heath 2 Leicester City 3	Bank Street	2000
3	1908/09	20/03/09	Football League Division 1	Manchester United 0 Blackburn Rovers 3	Bank Street	11000
4	1914/15	20/03/15	Football League Division 1	Burnley 3 Manchester United 0	Turf Moor	12000
5	1919/20	20/03/20	Football League Division 1	Manchester United 0 Bradford City 0	Old Trafford	25000
6	1925/26	20/03/26	Football League Division 1	Manchester United 0 Everton 0	Old Trafford	30058
7	1936/37	20/03/37	Football League Division 1	Manchester United 1 Grimsby Town 1	Old Trafford	26636
8	1947/48	20/03/48	Football League Division 1	Manchester United 3 Wolverhampton Wanderers 2	Maine Road	50667
9	1953/54	20/03/54	Football League Division 1	Manchester United 3 Huddersfield Town 1	Old Trafford	40181
10	1961/62	20/03/62	Football League Division 1	Nottingham Forest 1 Manchester United 0	City Ground	27833
11	1964/65	20/03/65	Football League Division 1	Sheffield Wednesday 1 Manchester United 0	Hillsborough	33549
12	1970/71	20/03/71	Football League Division 1	Stoke City 1 Manchester United 2	Victoria Ground	40005
13	1975/76	20/03/76	Football League Division 1	Newcastle United 3 Manchester United 4	St James' Park	45048
14	1978/79	20/03/79	Football League Division 1	Coventry City 4 Manchester United 3	Highfield Road	25382
15	1981/82	20/03/82	Football League Division 1	Notts County 1 Manchester United 3	Meadow Lane	17048
16	1984/85	20/03/85	UEFA Cup Quarter-Final 2nd Leg	Videoton 1 Manchester United 0	Sostoi Stadion	25000
17	1992/93	20/03/93	FA Premiership	Manchester City 1 Manchester United 1	Maine Road	37136
18	1995/96	20/03/96	FA Premiership	Manchester United 1 Arsenal 0	Old Trafford	50028
19	2003/04	20/03/04	FA Premiership	Manchester United 3 Tottenham Hotspur 0	Old Trafford	67644

MARCH 21

#	SEASON	DATE	COMPETITION / ROUND	MATCH RESULT	VENUE	ATT
1	1897/98	21/03/98	Football League Division 2	Luton Town 2 Newton Heath 2	Dunstable Road	2000
2	1902/03	21/03/03	Football League Division 2	Manchester United 5 Leicester City 1	Bank Street	8000
3	1907/08	21/03/08	Football League Division 1	Arsenal 1 Manchester United 0	Manor Field	20000
4	1912/13	21/03/13	Football League Division 1	Manchester United 2 Arsenal 0	Old Trafford	20000
5	1922/23	21/03/23	Football League Division 2	Manchester United 1 Bradford City 1	Old Trafford	15000
6	1924/25	21/03/25	Football League Division 2	Hull City 0 Manchester United 1	Anlaby Road	6250
7	1930/31	21/03/31	Football League Division 1	Blackpool 5 Manchester United 1	Bloomfield Road	13162
8	1935/36	21/03/36	Football League Division 2	Leicester City 1 Manchester United 1	Filbert Street	18200
9	1958/59	21/03/59	Football League Division 1	Manchester United 4 Leeds United 0	Old Trafford	45473
10	1963/64	21/03/64	Football League Division 1	Tottenham Hotspur 2 Manchester United 3	White Hart Lane	56392
11	1969/70	21/03/70	Football League Division 1	Chelsea 2 Manchester United 1	Stamford Bridge	61479
12	1980/81	21/03/81	Football League Division 1	Manchester United 2 Ipswich Town 1	Old Trafford	46685
13	1983/84	21/03/84	European CWC 3rd Round 2nd Leg	Manchester United 3 Barcelona 0	Old Trafford	58547
14	1986/87	21/03/87	Football League Division 1	Sheffield Wednesday 1 Manchester United 0	Hillsborough	29888
15	1989/90	21/03/90	Football League Division 1	Sheffield Wednesday 1 Manchester United 0	Hillsborough	33260
16	1991/92	21/03/92	Football League Division 1	Manchester United 0 Wimbledon 0	Old Trafford	45428
17	1998/99	21/03/99	FA Premiership	Manchester United 3 Everton 1	Old Trafford	55182
18	1999/00	21/03/00	Champions League Phase 2 Match 6	Valencia 0 Manchester United 0	Mestalla	40419

MARCH 22

#	SEASON	DATE	COMPETITION / ROUND	MATCH RESULT	VENUE	ATT
1	1896/97	22/03/97	Football League Division 2	Newton Heath 1 Arsenal 1	Bank Street	3000
2	1901/02	22/03/02	Football League Division 2	Barnsley 3 Newton Heath 2	Oakwell	2500
3	1912/13	22/03/13	Football League Division 1	Manchester United 4 Aston Villa 0	Old Trafford	30000
4	1923/24	22/03/24	Football League Division 2	Hull City 1 Manchester United 1	Anlaby Road	6250
5	1946/47	22/03/47	Football League Division 1	Manchester United 3 Everton 0	Maine Road	43441
6	1947/48	22/03/48	Football League Division 1	Aston Villa 0 Manchester United 1	Villa Park	52368
7	1951/52	22/03/52	Football League Division 1	Huddersfield Town 3 Manchester United 2	Leeds Road	30316
8	1957/58	22/03/58	FA Cup Semi-Final	Manchester United 2 Fulham 2	Villa Park	69745
9	1964/65	22/03/65	Football League Division 1	Manchester United 2 Blackpool 0	Old Trafford	42318
10	1968/69	22/03/69	Football League Division 1	Manchester United 1 Sheffield Wednesday 0	Old Trafford	45527
11	1971/72	22/03/72	FA Cup 6th Round Replay	Stoke City 2 Manchester United 1	Victoria Ground	49192
12	1974/75	22/03/75	Football League Division 2	Nottingham Forest 0 Manchester United 1	City Ground	21893
13	1979/80	22/03/80	Football League Division 1	Manchester United 1 Manchester City 0	Old Trafford	56387
14	1982/83	22/03/83	Football League Division 1	Manchester United 2 West Ham United 1	Old Trafford	30227
15	1985/86	22/03/86	Football League Division 1	Manchester United 2 Manchester City 2	Old Trafford	51274
16	1993/94	22/03/94	FA Premiership	Arsenal 2 Manchester United 2	Highbury	36203
17	1994/95	22/03/95	FA Premiership	Manchester United 3 Arsenal 0	Old Trafford	43623
18	1996/97	22/03/97	FA Premiership	Everton 0 Manchester United 2	Goodison Park	40079
19	2002/03	22/03/03	FA Premiership	Manchester United 3 Fulham 0	Old Trafford	67706

MARCH 23

#	SEASON	DATE	COMPETITION / ROUND	MATCH RESULT	VENUE	ATT
1	1893/94	23/03/94	Football League Division 1	Newton Heath 6 Stoke City 2	Bank Street	8000
2	1894/95	23/03/95	Football League Division 2	Newton Heath 2 Grimsby Town 0	Bank Street	9000
3	1895/96	23/03/96	Football League Division 2	Port Vale 3 Newton Heath 0	Cobridge Stadium	3000
4	1900/01	23/03/01	Football League Division 2	Blackpool 1 Newton Heath 2	Bloomfield Road	2000
5	1902/03	23/03/03	Football League Division 2	Manchester United 0 Stockport County 0	Bank Street	2000
6	1911/12	23/03/12	Football League Division 1	Manchester United 1 Liverpool 1	Old Trafford	10000
7	1928/29	23/03/29	Football League Division 1	Manchester United 2 Sheffield Wednesday 1	Old Trafford	27095
8	1934/35	23/03/35	Football League Division 2	Bury 0 Manchester United 1	Gigg Lane	7229
9	1950/51	23/03/51	Football League Division 1	Manchester United 2 Derby County 0	Old Trafford	42009
10	1956/57	23/03/57	FA Cup Semi-Final	Manchester United 2 Birmingham City 0	Hillsborough	65107
11	1962/63	23/03/63	Football League Division 1	Manchester United 1 Ipswich Town 1	Old Trafford	32792
12	1963/64	23/03/64	Football League Division 1	Manchester United 1 Chelsea 1	Old Trafford	42931
13	1967/68	23/03/68	Football League Division 1	Manchester United 3 Nottingham Forest 0	Old Trafford	61978
14	1969/70	23/03/70	FA Cup Semi-Final Replay	Leeds United 0 Manchester United 0	Villa Park	62500
15	1973/74	23/03/74	Football League Division 1	Manchester United 0 Tottenham Hotspur 1	Old Trafford	36278
16	1976/77	23/03/77	Football League Division 1	Manchester United 2 West Bromwich Albion 2	Old Trafford	51053
17	1984/85	23/03/85	Football League Division 1	Manchester United 4 Aston Villa 0	Old Trafford	40941
18	1990/91	23/03/91	Football League Division 1	Manchester United 4 Luton Town 1	Old Trafford	41752
19	2001/02	23/03/02	FA Premiership	Manchester United 0 Middlesbrough 1	Old Trafford	67683
20	2007/08	23/03/08	FA Premiership	Manchester United 3 Liverpool 0	Old Trafford	76000

MARCH 24

#	SEASON	DATE	COMPETITION / ROUND	MATCH RESULT	VENUE	ATT
1	1893/94	24/03/94	Football League Division 1	Newton Heath 2 Bolton Wanderers 2	Bank Street	10000
2	1899/00	24/03/00	Football League Division 2	Leicester City 2 Newton Heath 0	Filbert Street	8000
3	1905/06	24/03/06	Football League Division 2	Port Vale 1 Manchester United 0	Cobridge Stadium	3000
4	1933/34	24/03/34	Football League Division 2	Southampton 1 Manchester United 0	The Dell	4840
5	1950/51	24/03/51	Football League Division 1	Burnley 1 Manchester United 2	Turf Moor	36656
6	1955/56	24/03/56	Football League Division 1	Manchester United 1 Bolton Wanderers 0	Old Trafford	46114
7	1961/62	24/03/62	Football League Division 1	Manchester United 1 Sheffield Wednesday 1	Old Trafford	31322
8	1968/69	24/03/69	Football League Division 1	Manchester United 1 Stoke City 1	Old Trafford	39931
9	1972/73	24/03/73	Football League Division 1	Tottenham Hotspur 1 Manchester United 1	White Hart Lane	49751
10	1978/79	24/03/79	Football League Division 1	Manchester United 4 Leeds United 1	Old Trafford	51191
11	1989/90	24/03/90	Football League Division 1	Southampton 0 Manchester United 2	The Dell	20510
12	1992/93	24/03/93	FA Premiership	Manchester United 0 Arsenal 0	Old Trafford	37301
13	1995/96	24/03/96	FA Premiership	Manchester United 1 Tottenham Hotspur 0	Old Trafford	50157

MARCH 25

#	SEASON	DATE	COMPETITION / ROUND	MATCH RESULT	VENUE	ATT
1	1898/99	25/03/99	Football League Division 2	Lincoln City 2 Newton Heath 0	Sincil Bank	3000
2	1904/05	25/03/05	Football League Division 2	Blackpool 0 Manchester United 1	Bloomfield Road	6000
3	1906/07	25/03/07	Football League Division 1	Manchester United 0 Sunderland 0	Bank Street	12000
4	1907/08	25/03/08	Football League Division 1	Liverpool 7 Manchester United 4	Anfield	10000
5	1909/10	25/03/10	Football League Division 1	Manchester United 2 Bristol City 1	Old Trafford	50000
6	1910/11	25/03/11	Football League Division 1	Manchester United 0 Oldham Athletic 0	Old Trafford	35000
7	1912/13	25/03/13	Football League Division 1	Bradford City 1 Manchester United 0	Valley Parade	25000
8	1920/21	25/03/21	Football League Division 1	Burnley 1 Manchester United 0	Turf Moor	20000
9	1921/22	25/03/22	Football League Division 1	Blackburn Rovers 3 Manchester United 0	Ewood Park	15000
10	1930/31	25/03/31	Football League Division 1	Manchester United 0 Leicester City 0	Old Trafford	3679
11	1931/32	25/03/32	Football League Division 2	Manchester United 0 Charlton Athletic 2	Old Trafford	37012
12	1932/33	25/03/33	Football League Division 2	Manchester United 1 Bury 3	Old Trafford	27687
13	1949/50	25/03/50	Football League Division 1	Huddersfield Town 3 Manchester United 1	Leeds Road	34348
14	1952/53	25/03/53	Football League Division 1	Manchester United 3 Tottenham Hotspur 2	Old Trafford	18384
15	1956/57	25/03/57	Football League Division 1	Manchester United 0 Bolton Wanderers 2	Old Trafford	60862
16	1960/61	25/03/61	Football League Division 1	Sheffield Wednesday 5 Manchester United 1	Hillsborough	35901
17	1966/67	25/03/67	Football League Division 1	Liverpool 0 Manchester United 0	Anfield	53813
18	1971/72	25/03/72	Football League Division 1	Manchester United 4 Crystal Palace 0	Old Trafford	41550
19	1977/78	25/03/78	Football League Division 1	Leicester City 2 Manchester United 3	Filbert Street	20299
20	1988/89	25/03/89	Football League Division 1	Manchester United 2 Luton Town 0	Old Trafford	36335
21	1999/00	25/03/00	FA Premiership	Bradford City 0 Manchester United 4	Valley Parade	18276

MARCH 26

#	SEASON	DATE	COMPETITION / ROUND	MATCH RESULT	VENUE	ATT
1	1893/94	26/03/94	Football League Division 1	Blackburn Rovers 4 Newton Heath 0	Ewood Park	5000
2	1903/04	26/03/04	Football League Division 2	Manchester United 2 Grimsby Town 0	Bank Street	12000
3	1909/10	26/03/10	Football League Division 1	Chelsea 1 Manchester United 1	Stamford Bridge	25000
4	1920/21	26/03/21	Football League Division 1	Huddersfield Town 5 Manchester United 2	Leeds Road	17000
5	1926/27	26/03/27	Football League Division 1	Sheffield Wednesday 2 Manchester United 0	Hillsborough	11997
6	1931/32	26/03/32	Football League Division 2	Manchester United 5 Oldham Athletic 1	Old Trafford	17886
7	1936/37	26/03/37	Football League Division 1	Manchester United 2 Everton 0	Old Trafford	30071
8	1937/38	26/03/38	Football League Division 2	Manchester United 4 Chesterfield 1	Old Trafford	27311
9	1947/48	26/03/48	Football League Division 1	Manchester United 0 Bolton Wanderers 2	Maine Road	71623
10	1948/49	26/03/49	FA Cup Semi-Final	Manchester United 1 Wolverhampton Wanderers 1	Hillsborough	62250
11	1950/51	26/03/51	Football League Division 1	Derby County 2 Manchester United 4	Baseball Ground	25860
12	1954/55	26/03/55	Football League Division 1	Preston North End 0 Manchester United 2	Deepdale	13327
13	1957/58	26/03/58	FA Cup Semi-Final Replay	Manchester United 5 Fulham 3	Highbury	38000
14	1959/60	26/03/60	Football League Division 1	Fulham 0 Manchester United 5	Craven Cottage	38250
15	1965/66	26/03/66	FA Cup 6th Round	Preston North End 1 Manchester United 1	Deepdale	37876
16	1969/70	26/03/70	FA Cup Semi-Final 2nd Replay	Leeds United 1 Manchester United 0	Burnden Park	56000
17	1982/83	26/03/83	League Cup Final	Manchester United 1 Liverpool 2	Wembley	100000
18	1987/88	26/03/88	Football League Division 1	Manchester United 3 West Ham United 1	Old Trafford	37269
19	2005/06	26/03/06	FA Premiership	Manchester United 3 Birmingham City 0	Old Trafford	69070

MARCH 27

#	SEASON	DATE	COMPETITION / ROUND	MATCH RESULT	VENUE	ATT
1	1896/97	27/03/97	Football League Division 2	Newton Heath 1 Notts County 1	Bank Street	10000
2	1908/09	27/03/09	FA Cup Semi-Final	Manchester United 1 Newcastle United 0	Bramall Lane	40118
3	1914/15	27/03/15	Football League Division 1	Manchester United 1 Tottenham Hotspur 1	Old Trafford	15000
4	1919/20	27/03/20	Football League Division 1	Bradford City 2 Manchester United 1	Valley Parade	18000
5	1925/26	27/03/26	FA Cup Semi-Final	Manchester United 0 Manchester City 3	Bramall Lane	46450
6	1934/35	27/03/35	Football League Division 2	Manchester United 3 Burnley 4	Old Trafford	10247
7	1936/37	27/03/37	Football League Division 1	Liverpool 2 Manchester United 0	Anfield	25319
8	1947/48	27/03/48	Football League Division 1	Huddersfield Town 0 Manchester United 2	Leeds Road	38266
9	1953/54	27/03/54	Football League Division 1	Arsenal 3 Manchester United 1	Highbury	42753
10	1958/59	27/03/59	Football League Division 1	Manchester United 6 Portsmouth 1	Old Trafford	52004
11	1963/64	27/03/64	Football League Division 1	Fulham 2 Manchester United 2	Craven Cottage	41769
12	1964/65	27/03/65	FA Cup Semi-Final	Manchester United 0 Leeds United 0	Hillsborough	65000
13	1966/67	27/03/67	Football League Division 1	Fulham 2 Manchester United 2	Craven Cottage	47290
14	1967/68	27/03/68	Football League Division 1	Manchester United 1 Manchester City 3	Old Trafford	63004
15	1975/76	27/03/76	Football League Division 1	Manchester United 3 Middlesbrough 0	Old Trafford	58527
16	1977/78	27/03/78	Football League Division 1	Manchester United 1 Everton 2	Old Trafford	55277
17	1978/79	27/03/79	Football League Division 1	Middlesbrough 2 Manchester United 2	Ayresome Park	20138
18	1981/82	27/03/82	Football League Division 1	Manchester United 0 Sunderland 0	Old Trafford	40776
19	1988/89	27/03/89	Football League Division 1	Nottingham Forest 2 Manchester United 0	City Ground	30092
20	1993/94	27/03/94	League Cup Final	Manchester United 1 Aston Villa 3	Wembley	77231

MARCH 28

#	SEASON	DATE	COMPETITION / ROUND	MATCH RESULT	VENUE	ATT
1	1901/02	28/03/02	Football League Division 2	Burnley 1 Newton Heath 0	Turf Moor	3000
2	1903/04	28/03/04	Football League Division 2	Stockport County 0 Manchester United 3	Edgeley Park	2500
3	1907/08	28/03/08	Football League Division 1	Manchester United 4 Sheffield Wednesday 1	Bank Street	30000
4	1909/10	28/03/10	Football League Division 1	Bristol City 2 Manchester United 1	Ashton Gate	18000
5	1920/21	28/03/21	Football League Division 1	Manchester United 0 Burnley 1	Old Trafford	28000
6	1924/25	28/03/25	Football League Division 2	Manchester United 0 Blackpool 0	Old Trafford	26250
7	1927/28	28/03/28	Football League Division 1	Derby County 5 Manchester United 0	Baseball Ground	8323
8	1930/31	28/03/31	Football League Division 1	Manchester United 1 Sheffield United 2	Old Trafford	5420
9	1931/32	28/03/32	Football League Division 2	Charlton Athletic 1 Manchester United 0	The Valley	16256
10	1935/36	28/03/36	Football League Division 2	Manchester United 2 Norwich City 1	Old Trafford	31596
11	1952/53	28/03/53	Football League Division 1	Sheffield Wednesday 0 Manchester United 0	Hillsborough	36509
12	1958/59	28/03/59	Football League Division 1	Burnley 4 Manchester United 2	Turf Moor	44577
13	1963/64	28/03/64	Football League Division 1	Manchester United 2 Wolverhampton Wanderers 2	Old Trafford	44470
14	1966/67	28/03/67	Football League Division 1	Manchester United 2 Fulham 1	Old Trafford	51673
15	1969/70	28/03/70	Football League Division 1	Manchester United 1 Manchester City 2	Old Trafford	59777
16	1974/75	28/03/75	Football League Division 2	Bristol Rovers 1 Manchester United 1	Eastville	19337
17	1980/81	28/03/81	Football League Division 1	Everton 0 Manchester United 1	Goodison Park	25856
18	1986/87	28/03/87	Football League Division 1	Manchester United 2 Nottingham Forest 0	Old Trafford	39182
19	1991/92	28/03/92	Football League Division 1	Queens Park Rangers 0 Manchester United 0	Loftus Road	22603
20	1997/98	28/03/98	FA Premiership	Manchester United 2 Wimbledon 0	Old Trafford	55306
21	2003/04	28/03/04	FA Premiership	Arsenal 1 Manchester United 1	Highbury	38184

MARCH 29

#	SEASON	DATE	COMPETITION / ROUND	MATCH RESULT	VENUE	ATT
1	1897/98	29/03/98	Football League Division 2	Newton Heath 5 Loughborough Town 1	Bank Street	2000
2	1901/02	29/03/02	Football League Division 2	Newton Heath 2 Leicester City 0	Bank Street	2000
3	1905/06	29/03/06	Football League Division 2	Leicester City 2 Manchester United 5	Filbert Street	5000
4	1912/13	29/03/13	Football League Division 1	Liverpool 0 Manchester United 2	Anfield	12000
5	1923/24	29/03/24	Football League Division 2	Manchester United 2 Stoke City 2	Old Trafford	13000
6	1928/29	29/03/29	Football League Division 1	Bury 1 Manchester United 3	Gigg Lane	27167
7	1929/30	29/03/30	Football League Division 1	Burnley 4 Manchester United 0	Turf Moor	11659
8	1936/37	29/03/37	Football League Division 1	Everton 4 Manchester United 3	Goodison Park	28395
9	1938/39	29/03/39	Football League Division 1	Manchester United 0 Everton 2	Old Trafford	18438
10	1946/47	29/03/47	Football League Division 1	Huddersfield Town 2 Manchester United 2	Leeds Road	18509
11	1947/48	29/03/48	Football League Division 1	Bolton Wanderers 0 Manchester United 1	Burnden Park	44225
12	1957/58	29/03/58	Football League Division 1	Sheffield Wednesday 1 Manchester United 0	Hillsborough	35608
13	1968/69	29/03/69	Football League Division 1	West Ham United 0 Manchester United 0	Upton Park	41546
14	1974/75	29/03/75	Football League Division 2	Manchester United 2 York City 1	Old Trafford	46802
15	1977/78	29/03/78	Football League Division 1	Manchester United 1 Aston Villa 1	Old Trafford	41625
16	1979/80	29/03/80	Football League Division 1	Crystal Palace 0 Manchester United 2	Selhurst Park	33056
17	1985/86	29/03/86	Football League Division 1	Birmingham City 1 Manchester United 1	St Andrews	22551
18	2005/06	29/03/06	FA Premiership	Manchester United 1 West Ham United 0	Old Trafford	69522
19	2007/08	29/03/08	FA Premiership	Manchester United 4 Aston Villa 0	Old Trafford	75932

MARCH 30

#	SEASON	DATE	COMPETITION / ROUND	MATCH RESULT	VENUE	ATT
1	1894/95	30/03/95	Football League Division 2	Arsenal 3 Newton Heath 2	Manor Field	6000
2	1900/01	30/03/01	Football League Division 2	Newton Heath 3 Stockport County 1	Bank Street	4000
3	1902/03	30/03/03	Football League Division 2	Manchester United 0 Preston North End 1	Bank Street	3000
4	1906/07	30/03/07	Football League Division 1	Bury 1 Manchester United 2	Gigg Lane	25000
5	1911/12	30/03/12	Football League Division 1	Aston Villa 6 Manchester United 0	Villa Park	15000
6	1922/23	30/03/23	Football League Division 2	Manchester United 3 South Shields 0	Old Trafford	26000
7	1928/29	30/03/29	Football League Division 1	Derby County 6 Manchester United 1	Baseball Ground	14619
8	1933/34	30/03/34	Football League Division 2	Manchester United 0 West Ham United 1	Old Trafford	29114
9	1934/35	30/03/35	Football League Division 2	Manchester United 3 Hull City 0	Old Trafford	15358
10	1955/56	30/03/56	Football League Division 1	Manchester United 5 Newcastle United 2	Old Trafford	58994
11	1956/57	30/03/57	Football League Division 1	Leeds United 1 Manchester United 2	Elland Road	47216
12	1958/59	30/03/59	Football League Division 1	Portsmouth 1 Manchester United 3	Fratton Park	29359
13	1959/60	30/03/60	Football League Division 1	Sheffield Wednesday 4 Manchester United 2	Hillsborough	26821
14	1962/63	30/03/63	FA Cup 6th Round	Coventry City 1 Manchester United 3	Highfield Road	44000
15	1963/64	30/03/64	Football League Division 1	Manchester United 3 Fulham 0	Old Trafford	42279
16	1965/66	30/03/66	FA Cup 6th Round Replay	Manchester United 3 Preston North End 1	Old Trafford	60433
17	1967/68	30/03/68	Football League Division 1	Stoke City 2 Manchester United 4	Victoria Ground	30141
18	1969/70	30/03/70	Football League Division 1	Manchester United 1 Coventry City 1	Old Trafford	38647
19	1973/74	30/03/74	Football League Division 1	Chelsea 1 Manchester United 3	Stamford Bridge	29602
20	1990/91	30/03/91	Football League Division 1	Norwich City 0 Manchester United 3	Carrow Road	18282
21	1993/94	30/03/94	FA Premiership	Manchester United 1 Liverpool 0	Old Trafford	44751
22	2001/02	30/03/02	FA Premiership	Leeds United 3 Manchester United 4	Elland Road	40058

MARCH 31

#	SEASON	DATE	COMPETITION / ROUND	MATCH RESULT	VENUE	ATT
1	1892/93	31/03/93	Football League Division 1	Newton Heath 1 Stoke City 0	North Road	10000
2	1893/94	31/03/94	Football League Division 1	Stoke City 3 Newton Heath 1	Victoria Ground	4000
3	1899/00	31/03/00	Football League Division 2	Newton Heath 5 Luton Town 0	Bank Street	6000
4	1905/06	31/03/06	Football League Division 2	Manchester United 5 Barnsley 1	Bank Street	15000
5	1908/09	31/03/09	Football League Division 1	Manchester United 0 Aston Villa 2	Bank Street	10000
6	1912/13	31/03/13	Football League Division 1	Tottenham Hotspur 1 Manchester United 1	White Hart Lane	12000
7	1922/23	31/03/23	Football League Division 2	Blackpool 1 Manchester United 0	Bloomfield Road	21000
8	1927/28	31/03/28	Football League Division 1	Aston Villa 3 Manchester United 1	Villa Park	24691
9	1933/34	31/03/34	Football League Division 2	Manchester United 2 Blackpool 0	Old Trafford	20038
10	1950/51	31/03/51	Football League Division 1	Manchester United 4 Chelsea 1	Old Trafford	25779
11	1955/56	31/03/56	Football League Division 1	Huddersfield Town 0 Manchester United 2	Leeds Road	37780
12	1957/58	31/03/58	Football League Division 1	Aston Villa 3 Manchester United 2	Villa Park	16631
13	1960/61	31/03/61	Football League Division 1	Blackpool 2 Manchester United 0	Bloomfield Road	30835
14	1961/62	31/03/62	FA Cup Semi-Final	Manchester United 1 Tottenham Hotspur 3	Hillsborough	65000
15	1964/65	31/03/65	FA Cup Semi-Final Replay	Manchester United 0 Leeds United 1	City Ground	46300
16	1968/69	31/03/69	Football League Division 1	Nottingham Forest 0 Manchester United 1	City Ground	41892
17	1969/70	31/03/70	Football League Division 1	Nottingham Forest 1 Manchester United 2	City Ground	39228
18	1972/73	31/03/73	Football League Division 1	Southampton 0 Manchester United 2	The Dell	23161
19	1974/75	31/03/75	Football League Division 2	Manchester United 3 Oldham Athletic 2	Old Trafford	56618
20	1978/79	31/03/79	FA Cup Semi-Final	Manchester United 2 Liverpool 2	Maine Road	52524
21	1983/84	31/03/84	Football League Division 1	West Bromwich Albion 2 Manchester United 0	The Hawthorns	28104
22	1984/85	31/03/85	Football League Division 1	Liverpool 0 Manchester United 1	Anfield	34886
23	1985/86	31/03/86	Football League Division 1	Manchester United 0 Everton 0	Old Trafford	51189
24	1989/90	31/03/90	Football League Division 1	Manchester United 3 Coventry City 0	Old Trafford	39172
25	1991/92	31/03/92	Football League Division 1	Norwich City 1 Manchester United 3	Carrow Road	17489
26	1995/96	31/03/96	FA Cup Semi-Final	Manchester United 2 Chelsea 1	Villa Park	38421
27	2000/01	31/03/01	FA Premiership	Liverpool 2 Manchester United 0	Anfield	44806
28	2006/07	31/03/07	FA Premiership	Manchester United 4 Blackburn Rovers 1	Old Trafford	76098

UNITED in APRIL

OVERALL PLAYING RECORD

	P	W	D	L	F	A		P	W	D	L	F	A		P	W	D	L	F	A
1st	21	13	4	4	45	22	11th	20	6	6	8	21	21	21st	28	10	8	10	40	34
2nd	27	15	5	7	40	18	12th	24	16	3	5	53	19	22nd	23	8	8	7	34	28
3rd	24	10	7	7	40	23	13th	27	12	5	10	38	35	23rd	24	11	5	8	35	31
4th	24	9	7	8	36	41	14th	23	12	5	6	47	30	24th	21	12	4	5	35	28
5th	21	11	2	8	32	29	15th	23	11	5	7	46	29	25th	20	9	7	4	25	22
6th	25	13	6	6	50	29	16th	24	12	7	5	40	25	26th	17	8	3	6	27	18
7th	23	10	6	7	32	26	17th	27	17	5	5	47	24	27th	19	11	3	5	34	27
8th	21	9	7	5	37	24	18th	24	10	8	6	36	30	28th	17	8	4	5	31	14
9th	25	10	6	9	34	31	19th	25	10	7	8	41	34	29th	19	9	4	6	36	23
10th	30	12	9	9	56	54	20th	18	9	3	6	32	20	30th	16	7	5	4	26	15

OVERALL   680   320   164   196   1126   804

APRIL 1

#	SEASON	DATE	COMPETITION / ROUND	MATCH RESULT	VENUE	ATT
1	1892/93	01/04/93	Football League Division 1	Newton Heath 2 Preston North End 1	North Road	9000
2	1896/97	01/04/97	Football League Division 2	Lincoln City 1 Newton Heath 3	Sincil Bank	1000
3	1898/99	01/04/99	Football League Division 2	Newton Heath 2 Arsenal 2	Bank Street	5000
4	1903/04	01/04/04	Football League Division 2	Chesterfield 0 Manchester United 2	Saltergate	5000
5	1904/05	01/04/05	Football League Division 2	Manchester United 6 Doncaster Rovers 0	Bank Street	6000
6	1906/07	01/04/07	Football League Division 1	Liverpool 0 Manchester United 1	Anfield	20000
7	1910/11	01/04/11	Football League Division 1	Manchester United 2 Liverpool 0	Old Trafford	20000
8	1921/22	01/04/22	Football League Division 1	Manchester United 0 Bolton Wanderers 1	Old Trafford	28000
9	1928/29	01/04/29	Football League Division 1	Manchester United 1 Bury 0	Old Trafford	29742
10	1932/33	01/04/33	Football League Division 2	Fulham 3 Manchester United 1	Craven Cottage	21477
11	1935/36	01/04/36	Football League Division 2	Fulham 2 Manchester United 2	Craven Cottage	11137
12	1938/39	01/04/39	Football League Division 1	Huddersfield Town 1 Manchester United 1	Leeds Road	14007
13	1949/50	01/04/50	Football League Division 1	Manchester United 1 Everton 1	Old Trafford	35381
14	1960/61	01/04/61	Football League Division 1	Manchester United 3 Fulham 1	Old Trafford	24654
15	1962/63	01/04/63	Football League Division 1	Manchester United 0 Fulham 2	Old Trafford	28124
16	1966/67	01/04/67	Football League Division 1	Manchester United 3 West Ham United 0	Old Trafford	61308
17	1971/72	01/04/72	Football League Division 1	Coventry City 2 Manchester United 3	Highfield Road	37901
18	1977/78	01/04/78	Football League Division 1	Arsenal 3 Manchester United 1	Highbury	40829
19	1999/00	01/04/00	FA Premiership	Manchester United 7 West Ham United 1	Old Trafford	61611
20	2005/06	01/04/06	FA Premiership	Bolton Wanderers 1 Manchester United 2	Reebok Stadium	27718
21	2007/08	01/04/08	Champions Lge Quarter-Final 1st Leg	Roma 0 Manchester United 2	Olympic Stadium	60931

APRIL 2

#	SEASON	DATE	COMPETITION / ROUND	MATCH RESULT	VENUE	ATT
1	1897/98	02/04/98	Football League Division 2	Grimsby Town 1 Newton Heath 3	Abbey Park	2000
2	1903/04	02/04/04	Football League Division 2	Leicester City 0 Manchester United 1	Filbert Street	4000
3	1909/10	02/04/10	Football League Division 1	Manchester United 2 Blackburn Rovers 0	Old Trafford	20000
4	1914/15	02/04/15	Football League Division 1	Manchester United 2 Liverpool 0	Old Trafford	18000
5	1919/20	02/04/20	Football League Division 1	Manchester United 0 Bradford Park Avenue 1	Old Trafford	30000
6	1920/21	02/04/21	Football League Division 1	Manchester United 2 Huddersfield Town 0	Old Trafford	30000
7	1922/23	02/04/23	Football League Division 2	South Shields 0 Manchester United 3	Talbot Road	6500
8	1925/26	02/04/26	Football League Division 1	Notts County 0 Manchester United 3	Meadow Lane	18453
9	1926/27	02/04/27	Football League Division 1	Manchester United 1 Leicester City 0	Old Trafford	17119
10	1931/32	02/04/32	Football League Division 2	Bury 0 Manchester United 0	Gigg Lane	12592
11	1933/34	02/04/34	Football League Division 2	West Ham United 2 Manchester United 1	Upton Park	20085
12	1937/38	02/04/38	Football League Division 2	Aston Villa 3 Manchester United 0	Villa Park	54654
13	1948/49	02/04/49	FA Cup Semi-Final Replay	Manchester United 0 Wolverhampton Wanderers 1	Goodison Park	73000
14	1954/55	02/04/55	Football League Division 1	Manchester United 5 Sheffield United 0	Old Trafford	21158
15	1955/56	02/04/56	Football League Division 1	Newcastle United 0 Manchester United 0	St James' Park	37395
16	1959/60	02/04/60	Football League Division 1	Manchester United 2 Bolton Wanderers 0	Old Trafford	45298
17	1968/69	02/04/69	Football League Division 1	Manchester United 2 West Bromwich Albion 1	Old Trafford	38846
18	1976/77	02/04/77	Football League Division 1	Norwich City 2 Manchester United 1	Carrow Road	24161
19	1979/80	02/04/80	Football League Division 1	Nottingham Forest 2 Manchester United 0	City Ground	31417
20	1982/83	02/04/83	Football League Division 1	Manchester United 3 Coventry City 0	Old Trafford	36814
21	1987/88	02/04/88	Football League Division 1	Manchester United 4 Derby County 1	Old Trafford	40146
22	1988/89	02/04/89	Football League Division 1	Manchester United 1 Arsenal 1	Old Trafford	37977
23	1990/91	02/04/91	Football League Division 1	Manchester United 2 Wimbledon 1	Old Trafford	36660
24	1993/94	02/04/94	FA Premiership	Blackburn Rovers 2 Manchester United 0	Ewood Park	20886
25	1994/95	02/04/95	FA Premiership	Manchester United 0 Leeds United 0	Old Trafford	43712
26	2001/02	02/04/02	Champions Lge Quarter-Final 1st Leg	Deportivo La Coruna 0 Manchester United 2	Estadio de Riazor	32351
27	2004/05	02/04/05	FA Premiership	Manchester United 0 Blackburn Rovers 0	Old Trafford	67939

APRIL 3

#	SEASON	DATE	COMPETITION / ROUND	MATCH RESULT	VENUE	ATT
1	1894/95	03/04/95	Football League Division 2	Newton Heath 9 Walsall 0	Bank Street	6000
2	1895/96	03/04/96	Football League Division 2	Newton Heath 4 Darwen 0	Bank Street	1000
3	1896/97	03/04/97	Football League Division 2	Arsenal 0 Newton Heath 2	Manor Field	6000
4	1898/99	03/04/99	Football League Division 2	Blackpool 0 Newton Heath 1	Raikes Hall Gardens	3000
5	1908/09	03/04/09	Football League Division 1	Sheffield Wednesday 2 Manchester United 0	Hillsborough	15000
6	1914/15	03/04/15	Football League Division 1	Newcastle United 2 Manchester United 0	St James' Park	12000
7	1919/20	03/04/20	Football League Division 1	Manchester United 1 Bolton Wanderers 1	Old Trafford	39000
8	1925/26	03/04/26	Football League Division 1	Manchester United 0 Bury 1	Old Trafford	41085
9	1930/31	03/04/31	Football League Division 1	Liverpool 1 Manchester United 1	Anfield	27782
10	1936/37	03/04/37	Football League Division 1	Manchester United 0 Leeds United 0	Old Trafford	34429
11	1947/48	03/04/48	Football League Division 1	Manchester United 1 Derby County 0	Maine Road	49609
12	1952/53	03/04/53	Football League Division 1	Charlton Athletic 2 Manchester United 2	The Valley	41814
13	1953/54	03/04/54	Football League Division 1	Manchester United 2 Cardiff City 3	Old Trafford	22832
14	1960/61	03/04/61	Football League Division 1	Manchester United 2 Blackpool 0	Old Trafford	39169
15	1964/65	03/04/65	Football League Division 1	Blackburn Rovers 0 Manchester United 5	Ewood Park	29363
16	1970/71	03/04/71	Football League Division 1	West Ham United 2 Manchester United 1	Upton Park	38507
17	1971/72	03/04/72	Football League Division 1	Manchester United 0 Liverpool 3	Old Trafford	53826
18	1973/74	03/04/74	Football League Division 1	Manchester United 3 Burnley 3	Old Trafford	33336
19	1975/76	03/04/76	FA Cup Semi-Final	Manchester United 2 Derby County 0	Hillsborough	55000
20	1981/82	03/04/82	Football League Division 1	Leeds United 0 Manchester United 0	Elland Road	30953
21	1984/85	03/04/85	Football League Division 1	Manchester United 2 Leicester City 1	Old Trafford	35950
22	1998/99	03/04/99	FA Premiership	Wimbledon 1 Manchester United 1	Selhurst Park	26121
23	2000/01	03/04/01	Champions Lge Quarter-Final 1st Leg	Manchester United 0 Bayern Munich 1	Old Trafford	66584
24	2003/04	03/04/04	FA Cup Semi-Final	Manchester United 1 Arsenal 0	Villa Park	39939

APRIL 4

#	SEASON	DATE	COMPETITION / ROUND	MATCH RESULT	VENUE	ATT
1	1892/93	04/04/93	Football League Division 1	Sunderland 6 Newton Heath 0	Newcastle Road	3500
2	1895/96	04/04/96	Football League Division 2	Newton Heath 2 Loughborough Town 0	Bank Street	4000
3	1898/99	04/04/99	Football League Division 2	Barnsley 0 Newton Heath 2	Oakwell	4000
4	1902/03	04/04/03	Football League Division 2	Manchester United 4 Burnley 0	Bank Street	5000
5	1907/08	04/04/08	Football League Division 1	Bristol City 1 Manchester United 1	Ashton Gate	12000
6	1913/14	04/04/14	Football League Division 1	Derby County 4 Manchester United 2	Baseball Ground	7000
7	1924/25	04/04/25	Football League Division 2	Derby County 1 Manchester United 0	Baseball Ground	24000
8	1930/31	04/04/31	Football League Division 1	Sunderland 1 Manchester United 2	Roker Park	13590
9	1935/36	04/04/36	Football League Division 2	Doncaster Rovers 0 Manchester United 0	Belle Vue Stadium	13474
10	1952/53	04/04/53	Football League Division 1	Manchester United 1 Cardiff City 4	Old Trafford	37163
11	1957/58	04/04/58	Football League Division 1	Manchester United 2 Sunderland 2	Old Trafford	47421
12	1958/59	04/04/59	Football League Division 1	Manchester United 3 Bolton Wanderers 0	Old Trafford	61528
13	1961/62	04/04/62	Football League Division 1	Leicester City 4 Manchester United 3	Filbert Street	15318
14	1963/64	04/04/64	Football League Division 1	Liverpool 3 Manchester United 0	Anfield	52559
15	1969/70	04/04/70	Football League Division 1	Newcastle United 5 Manchester United 1	St James' Park	43094
16	1971/72	04/04/72	Football League Division 1	Sheffield United 1 Manchester United 1	Bramall Lane	45045
17	1978/79	04/04/79	FA Cup Semi-Final Replay	Manchester United 1 Liverpool 0	Goodison Park	53069
18	1980/81	04/04/81	Football League Division 1	Manchester United 1 Crystal Palace 0	Old Trafford	37954
19	1982/83	04/04/83	Football League Division 1	Sunderland 0 Manchester United 0	Roker Park	31486
20	1986/87	04/04/87	Football League Division 1	Manchester United 3 Oxford United 2	Old Trafford	32443
21	1987/88	04/04/88	Football League Division 1	Liverpool 3 Manchester United 3	Anfield	43497
22	1993/94	04/04/94	FA Premiership	Manchester United 3 Oldham Athletic 2	Old Trafford	44686
23	1999/00	04/04/00	Champions Lge Quarter-Final 1st Leg	Real Madrid 0 Manchester United 0	Bernabeu Stadium	64119
24	2006/07	04/04/07	Champions Lge Quarter-Final 1st Leg	Roma 2 Manchester United 1	Olympic Stadium	77000

APRIL 5

#	SEASON	DATE	COMPETITION / ROUND	MATCH RESULT	VENUE	ATT
1	1900/01	05/04/01	Football League Division 2	Lincoln City 2 Newton Heath 0	Sincil Bank	5000
2	1903/04	05/04/04	Football League Division 2	Barnsley 0 Manchester United 2	Oakwell	5000
3	1911/12	05/04/12	Football League Division 1	Arsenal 0 Manchester United 1	Manor Field	14000
4	1912/13	05/04/13	Football League Division 1	Manchester United 2 Bolton Wanderers 1	Old Trafford	30000
5	1914/15	05/04/15	Football League Division 1	Bradford Park Avenue 5 Manchester United 0	Park Avenue	15000
6	1921/22	05/04/22	Football League Division 1	Arsenal 3 Manchester United 1	Highbury	25000
7	1923/24	05/04/24	Football League Division 2	Stoke City 3 Manchester United 0	Victoria Ground	11000
8	1925/26	05/04/26	Football League Division 1	Manchester United 0 Notts County 1	Old Trafford	19606
9	1929/30	05/04/30	Football League Division 1	Manchester United 2 Sunderland 1	Old Trafford	13230
10	1932/33	05/04/33	Football League Division 2	Bradford Park Avenue 1 Manchester United 1	Park Avenue	6314
11	1946/47	05/04/47	Football League Division 1	Manchester United 3 Wolverhampton Wanderers 1	Maine Road	66967
12	1951/52	05/04/52	Football League Division 1	Portsmouth 1 Manchester United 0	Fratton Park	25522
13	1957/58	05/04/58	Football League Division 1	Manchester United 0 Preston North End 0	Old Trafford	47816
14	1968/69	05/04/69	Football League Division 1	Manchester United 3 Nottingham Forest 1	Old Trafford	51952
15	1974/75	05/04/75	Football League Division 2	Southampton 0 Manchester United 1	The Dell	21866
16	1976/77	05/04/77	Football League Division 1	Everton 1 Manchester United 0	Goodison Park	38216
17	1979/80	05/04/80	Football League Division 1	Manchester United 2 Liverpool 1	Old Trafford	57342
18	1985/86	05/04/86	Football League Division 1	Coventry City 1 Manchester United 3	Highfield Road	17160
19	1992/93	05/04/93	FA Premiership	Norwich City 1 Manchester United 3	Carrow Road	20582
20	1996/97	05/04/97	FA Premiership	Manchester United 2 Derby County 3	Old Trafford	55243
21	2002/03	05/04/03	FA Premiership	Manchester United 4 Liverpool 0	Old Trafford	67639

APRIL 6

#	SEASON	DATE	COMPETITION / ROUND	MATCH RESULT	VENUE	ATT
1	1894/95	06/04/95	Football League Division 2	Newton Heath 5 Newcastle United 1	Bank Street	5000
2	1895/96	06/04/96	Football League Division 2	Newton Heath 2 Port Vale 1	Bank Street	5000
3	1900/01	06/04/01	Football League Division 2	Birmingham City 1 Newton Heath 0	Muntz Street	6000
4	1906/07	06/04/07	Football League Division 1	Manchester United 1 Manchester City 1	Bank Street	40000
5	1909/10	06/04/10	Football League Division 1	Manchester United 3 Everton 2	Old Trafford	5500
6	1911/12	06/04/12	Football League Division 1	Manchester United 0 Newcastle United 2	Old Trafford	14000
7	1914/15	06/04/15	Football League Division 1	Oldham Athletic 1 Manchester United 0	Boundary Park	2000
8	1919/20	06/04/20	Football League Division 1	Bradford Park Avenue 1 Manchester United 4	Park Avenue	14000
9	1927/28	06/04/28	Football League Division 1	Bolton Wanderers 3 Manchester United 2	Burnden Park	23795
10	1928/29	06/04/29	Football League Division 1	Manchester United 3 Sunderland 0	Old Trafford	27772
11	1930/31	06/04/31	Football League Division 1	Manchester United 4 Liverpool 1	Old Trafford	8058
12	1934/35	06/04/35	Football League Division 2	Nottingham Forest 2 Manchester United 2	City Ground	8618
13	1948/49	06/04/49	Football League Division 1	Huddersfield Town 2 Manchester United 1	Leeds Road	17256
14	1952/53	06/04/53	Football League Division 1	Manchester United 3 Charlton Athletic 1	Old Trafford	30105
15	1956/57	06/04/57	Football League Division 1	Manchester United 0 Tottenham Hotspur 0	Old Trafford	60349
16	1963/64	06/04/64	Football League Division 1	Manchester United 1 Aston Villa 0	Old Trafford	25848
17	1965/66	06/04/66	Football League Division 1	Aston Villa 1 Manchester United 1	Villa Park	28211
18	1967/68	06/04/68	Football League Division 1	Manchester United 1 Liverpool 2	Old Trafford	63059
19	1973/74	06/04/74	Football League Division 1	Norwich City 0 Manchester United 2	Carrow Road	28223
20	1984/85	06/04/85	Football League Division 1	Manchester United 5 Stoke City 0	Old Trafford	42940
21	1990/91	06/04/91	Football League Division 1	Aston Villa 1 Manchester United 1	Villa Park	33307
22	1995/96	06/04/96	FA Premiership	Manchester City 2 Manchester United 3	Maine Road	29668
23	1997/98	06/04/98	FA Premiership	Blackburn Rovers 1 Manchester United 3	Ewood Park	30547
24	2001/02	06/04/02	FA Premiership	Leicester City 0 Manchester United 1	Filbert Street	21447
25	2007/08	06/04/08	FA Premiership	Middlesbrough 2 Manchester United 2	Riverside Stadium	33952

APRIL 7

#	SEASON	DATE	COMPETITION / ROUND	MATCH RESULT	VENUE	ATT
1	1893/94	07/04/94	Football League Division 1	Nottingham Forest 2 Newton Heath 0	Town Ground	4000
2	1899/00	07/04/00	Football League Division 2	Port Vale 1 Newton Heath 0	Cobridge Stadium	3000
3	1901/02	07/04/02	Football League Division 2	Newton Heath 1 Middlesbrough 2	Bank Street	2000
4	1905/06	07/04/06	Football League Division 2	Leyton Orient 0 Manchester United 1	Millfields Road	8000
5	1922/23	07/04/23	Football League Division 2	Manchester United 2 Blackpool 1	Old Trafford	20000
6	1927/28	07/04/28	Football League Division 1	Manchester United 4 Burnley 3	Old Trafford	28311
7	1933/34	07/04/34	Football League Division 2	Bradford City 1 Manchester United 1	Valley Parade	9258
8	1938/39	07/04/39	Football League Division 1	Manchester United 0 Leeds United 0	Old Trafford	35564
9	1946/47	07/04/47	Football League Division 1	Manchester United 3 Leeds United 1	Maine Road	41772
10	1947/48	07/04/48	Football League Division 1	Manchester United 1 Manchester City 1	Maine Road	71690
11	1949/50	07/04/50	Football League Division 1	Manchester United 0 Birmingham City 2	Old Trafford	47170
12	1950/51	07/04/51	Football League Division 1	Stoke City 2 Manchester United 0	Victoria Ground	25690
13	1955/56	07/04/56	Football League Division 1	Manchester United 2 Blackpool 1	Old Trafford	62277
14	1957/58	07/04/58	Football League Division 1	Sunderland 1 Manchester United 2	Roker Park	51302
15	1961/62	07/04/62	Football League Division 1	Manchester United 5 Ipswich Town 0	Old Trafford	24976
16	1972/73	07/04/73	Football League Division 1	Manchester United 1 Norwich City 0	Old Trafford	48593
17	1978/79	07/04/79	Football League Division 1	Norwich City 2 Manchester United 2	Carrow Road	19382
18	1979/80	07/04/80	Football League Division 1	Bolton Wanderers 1 Manchester United 3	Burnden Park	31902
19	1981/82	07/04/82	Football League Division 1	Manchester United 0 Liverpool 1	Old Trafford	48371
20	1983/84	07/04/84	Football League Division 1	Manchester United 1 Birmingham City 0	Old Trafford	39896
21	1991/92	07/04/92	Football League Division 1	Manchester United 1 Manchester City 1	Old Trafford	46781
22	1998/99	07/04/99	Champions League Semi-Final 1st Leg	Manchester United 1 Juventus 1	Old Trafford	54487
23	2006/07	07/04/07	FA Premiership	Portsmouth 2 Manchester United 1	Fratton Park	20223

APRIL 8

#	SEASON	DATE	COMPETITION / ROUND	MATCH RESULT	VENUE	ATT
1	1892/93	08/04/93	Football League Division 1	Newton Heath 3 Accrington Stanley 3	North Road	3000
2	1897/98	08/04/98	Football League Division 2	Newton Heath 1 Gainsborough Trinity 0	Bank Street	5000
3	1898/99	08/04/99	Football League Division 2	Luton Town 0 Newton Heath 1	Dunstable Road	1000
4	1904/05	08/04/05	Football League Division 2	Gainsborough Trinity 0 Manchester United 0	The Northolme	6000
5	1907/08	08/04/08	Football League Division 1	Everton 1 Manchester United 3	Goodison Park	17000
6	1910/11	08/04/11	Football League Division 1	Bury 0 Manchester United 3	Gigg Lane	20000
7	1921/22	08/04/22	Football League Division 1	Bolton Wanderers 1 Manchester United 0	Burnden Park	28000
8	1932/33	08/04/33	Football League Division 2	Manchester United 2 Chesterfield 1	Old Trafford	16031
9	1938/39	08/04/39	Football League Division 1	Manchester United 1 Portsmouth 0	Old Trafford	25457
10	1946/47	08/04/47	Football League Division 1	Leeds United 0 Manchester United 2	Elland Road	15528
11	1949/50	08/04/50	Football League Division 1	Wolverhampton Wanderers 1 Manchester United 1	Molineux	54296
12	1954/55	08/04/55	Football League Division 1	Sunderland 4 Manchester United 3	Roker Park	43882
13	1960/61	08/04/61	Football League Division 1	West Bromwich Albion 1 Manchester United 1	The Hawthorns	27750
14	1968/69	08/04/69	Football League Division 1	Coventry City 2 Manchester United 1	Highfield Road	45402
15	1969/70	08/04/70	Football League Division 1	Manchester United 7 West Bromwich Albion 0	Old Trafford	26582
16	1971/72	08/04/72	Football League Division 1	Leicester City 2 Manchester United 0	Filbert Street	35970
17	1977/78	08/04/78	Football League Division 1	Manchester United 3 Queens Park Rangers 1	Old Trafford	42677
18	1988/89	08/04/89	Football League Division 1	Millwall 0 Manchester United 0	The Den	17523
19	1989/90	08/04/90	FA Cup Semi-Final	Manchester United 3 Oldham Athletic 3	Maine Road	44026
20	1995/96	08/04/96	FA Premiership	Manchester United 1 Coventry City 0	Old Trafford	50332
21	2002/03	08/04/03	Champions Lge Quarter-Final 1st Leg	Real Madrid 3 Manchester United 1	Bernabeu Stadium	75000

APRIL 9

#	SEASON	DATE	COMPETITION / ROUND	MATCH RESULT	VENUE	ATT
1	1897/98	09/04/98	Football League Division 2	Newton Heath 3 Birmingham City 1	Bank Street	4000
2	1900/01	09/04/01	Football League Division 2	Barnsley 6 Newton Heath 2	Oakwell	3000
3	1903/04	09/04/04	Football League Division 2	Manchester United 3 Blackpool 1	Bank Street	10000
4	1908/09	09/04/09	Football League Division 1	Manchester United 0 Bristol City 1	Bank Street	18000
5	1909/10	09/04/10	Football League Division 1	Nottingham Forest 2 Manchester United 0	City Ground	7000
6	1911/12	09/04/12	Football League Division 1	Tottenham Hotspur 1 Manchester United 1	White Hart Lane	20000
7	1920/21	09/04/21	Football League Division 1	Middlesbrough 2 Manchester United 4	Ayresome Park	15000
8	1926/27	09/04/27	Football League Division 1	Everton 0 Manchester United 0	Goodison Park	22564
9	1927/28	09/04/28	Football League Division 1	Manchester United 2 Bolton Wanderers 1	Old Trafford	28590
10	1931/32	09/04/32	Football League Division 2	Manchester United 2 Port Vale 1	Old Trafford	10916
11	1937/38	09/04/38	Football League Division 2	Manchester United 0 Norwich City 0	Old Trafford	25879
12	1948/49	09/04/49	Football League Division 1	Manchester United 1 Chelsea 1	Maine Road	27304
13	1954/55	09/04/55	Football League Division 1	Leicester City 1 Manchester United 0	Filbert Street	34362
14	1959/60	09/04/60	Football League Division 1	Luton Town 2 Manchester United 3	Kenilworth Road	21242
15	1962/63	09/04/63	Football League Division 1	Aston Villa 1 Manchester United 2	Villa Park	26867
16	1965/66	09/04/66	Football League Division 1	Manchester United 1 Leicester City 2	Old Trafford	42593
17	1976/77	09/04/77	Football League Division 1	Manchester United 3 Stoke City 0	Old Trafford	53102
18	1982/83	09/04/83	Football League Division 1	Manchester United 1 Southampton 1	Old Trafford	37120
19	1984/85	09/04/85	Football League Division 1	Sheffield Wednesday 1 Manchester United 0	Hillsborough	39380
20	1985/86	09/04/86	Football League Division 1	Manchester United 1 Chelsea 2	Old Trafford	45355
21	1994/95	09/04/95	FA Cup Semi-Final	Manchester United 2 Crystal Palace 2	Villa Park	38256
22	1996/97	09/04/97	Champions League Semi-Final 1st Leg	Borussia Dortmund 1 Manchester United 0	Westfalenstadion	48500
23	2004/05	09/04/05	FA Premiership	Norwich City 2 Manchester United 0	Carrow Road	25522
24	2005/06	09/04/06	FA Premiership	Manchester United 2 Arsenal 0	Old Trafford	70908
25	2007/08	09/04/08	Champions Lge Quarter-Final 2nd Leg	Manchester United 1 Roma 0	Old Trafford	74423

APRIL 10

#	SEASON	DATE	COMPETITION / ROUND	MATCH RESULT	VENUE	ATT
1	1896/97	10/04/97	Football League Division 2	Loughborough Town 2 Newton Heath 0	The Athletic Ground	3000
2	1902/03	10/04/03	Football League Division 2	Manchester City 0 Manchester United 2	Hyde Road	30000
3	1906/07	10/04/07	Football League Division 1	Manchester United 5 Sheffield Wednesday 0	Bank Street	10000
4	1908/09	10/04/09	Football League Division 1	Manchester United 2 Everton 0	Bank Street	8000
5	1913/14	10/04/14	Football League Division 1	Sunderland 2 Manchester United 0	Roker Park	20000
6	1914/15	10/04/15	Football League Division 1	Manchester United 2 Middlesbrough 2	Old Trafford	15000
7	1919/20	10/04/20	Football League Division 1	Bolton Wanderers 3 Manchester United 5	Burnden Park	25000
8	1924/25	10/04/25	Football League Division 2	Manchester United 2 Stockport County 0	Old Trafford	43500
9	1925/26	10/04/26	Football League Division 1	Blackburn Rovers 7 Manchester United 0	Ewood Park	15870
10	1935/36	10/04/36	Football League Division 2	Burnley 2 Manchester United 2	Turf Moor	27245
11	1936/37	10/04/37	Football League Division 1	Birmingham City 2 Manchester United 2	St Andrews	19130
12	1938/39	10/04/39	Football League Division 1	Leeds United 3 Manchester United 1	Elland Road	13771
13	1947/48	10/04/48	Football League Division 1	Everton 2 Manchester United 0	Goodison Park	44198
14	1949/50	10/04/50	Football League Division 1	Birmingham City 0 Manchester United 0	St Andrews	35863
15	1953/54	10/04/54	Football League Division 1	Blackpool 2 Manchester United 0	Bloomfield Road	25996
16	1961/62	10/04/62	Football League Division 1	Blackburn Rovers 3 Manchester United 0	Ewood Park	14623
17	1966/67	10/04/67	Football League Division 1	Sheffield Wednesday 2 Manchester United 2	Hillsborough	51101
18	1969/70	10/04/70	FA Cup 3rd Place Play-Off	Manchester United 2 Watford 0	Highbury	15105
19	1970/71	10/04/71	Football League Division 1	Manchester United 1 Derby County 2	Old Trafford	45691
20	1975/76	10/04/76	Football League Division 1	Ipswich Town 3 Manchester United 0	Portman Road	34886
21	1981/82	10/04/82	Football League Division 1	Everton 3 Manchester United 3	Goodison Park	29306
22	1990/91	10/04/91	European CWC Semi-Final 1st Leg	Legia Warsaw 1 Manchester United 3	Wojska Polskiego	20000
23	1992/93	10/04/93	FA Premiership	Manchester United 2 Sheffield Wednesday 1	Old Trafford	40102
24	1993/94	10/04/94	FA Cup Semi-Final	Manchester United 1 Oldham Athletic 1	Wembley	56399
25	1997/98	10/04/98	FA Premiership	Manchester United 1 Liverpool 1	Old Trafford	55171
26	1999/00	10/04/00	FA Premiership	Middlesbrough 3 Manchester United 4	Riverside Stadium	34775
27	2000/01	10/04/01	FA Premiership	Manchester United 2 Charlton Athletic 1	Old Trafford	67505
28	2001/02	10/04/02	Champions Lge Quarter-Final 2nd Leg	Manchester United 3 Deportivo La Coruna 2	Old Trafford	65875
29	2003/04	10/04/04	FA Premiership	Birmingham City 1 Manchester United 2	St Andrews	29548
30	2006/07	10/04/07	Champions Lge Quarter-Final 2nd Leg	Manchester United 7 Roma 1	Old Trafford	74476

APRIL 11

#	SEASON	DATE	COMPETITION / ROUND	MATCH RESULT	VENUE	ATT
1	1895/96	11/04/96	Football League Division 2	Lincoln City 2 Newton Heath 0	Sincil Bank	2000
2	1902/03	11/04/03	Football League Division 2	Preston North End 3 Manchester United 1	Deepdale	7000
3	1907/08	11/04/08	Football League Division 1	Manchester United 0 Notts County 1	Bank Street	20000
4	1913/14	11/04/14	Football League Division 1	Manchester United 0 Manchester City 1	Old Trafford	36000
5	1922/23	11/04/23	Football League Division 2	Southampton 0 Manchester United 0	The Dell	5500
6	1924/25	11/04/25	Football League Division 2	Manchester United 1 South Shields 0	Old Trafford	24000
7	1930/31	11/04/31	Football League Division 1	Manchester United 0 Blackburn Rovers 1	Old Trafford	6414
8	1935/36	11/04/36	Football League Division 2	Manchester United 4 Bradford Park Avenue 0	Old Trafford	33517
9	1951/52	11/04/52	Football League Division 1	Burnley 1 Manchester United 1	Turf Moor	38907
10	1952/53	11/04/53	Football League Division 1	Newcastle United 1 Manchester United 2	St James' Park	38970
11	1954/55	11/04/55	Football League Division 1	Manchester United 2 Sunderland 2	Old Trafford	36013
12	1956/57	11/04/57	European Cup Semi-Final 1st Leg	Real Madrid 3 Manchester United 1	Bernabeu Stadium	135000
13	1958/59	11/04/59	Football League Division 1	Luton Town 0 Manchester United 0	Kenilworth Road	27025
14	1972/73	11/04/73	Football League Division 1	Manchester United 2 Crystal Palace 0	Old Trafford	46891
15	1976/77	11/04/77	Football League Division 1	Sunderland 2 Manchester United 1	Roker Park	38785
16	1978/79	11/04/79	Football League Division 1	Manchester United 1 Bolton Wanderers 2	Old Trafford	49617
17	1980/81	11/04/81	Football League Division 1	Coventry City 0 Manchester United 2	Highfield Road	20201
18	1983/84	11/04/84	European CWC Semi-Final 1st Leg	Manchester United 1 Juventus 1	Old Trafford	58171
19	1989/90	11/04/90	FA Cup Semi-Final Replay	Manchester United 2 Oldham Athletic 1	Maine Road	35005
20	1998/99	11/04/99	FA Cup Semi-Final	Manchester United 0 Arsenal 0	Villa Park	39217

APRIL 12

#	SEASON	DATE	COMPETITION / ROUND	MATCH RESULT	VENUE	ATT
1	1894/95	12/04/95	Football League Division 2	Newton Heath 2 Bury 2	Bank Street	15000
2	1898/99	12/04/99	Football League Division 2	Newton Heath 5 Luton Town 0	Bank Street	3000
3	1903/04	12/04/04	Football League Division 2	Grimsby Town 3 Manchester United 1	Blundell Park	8000
4	1908/09	12/04/09	Football League Division 1	Bristol City 0 Manchester United 0	Ashton Gate	18000
5	1912/13	12/04/13	Football League Division 1	Sheffield United 2 Manchester United 1	Bramall Lane	12000
6	1923/24	12/04/24	Football League Division 2	Manchester United 5 Crystal Palace 1	Old Trafford	8000
7	1946/47	12/04/47	Football League Division 1	Brentford 0 Manchester United 0	Griffin Park	21714
8	1951/52	12/04/52	Football League Division 1	Manchester United 4 Liverpool 0	Old Trafford	42970
9	1957/58	12/04/58	Football League Division 1	Tottenham Hotspur 1 Manchester United 0	White Hart Lane	59836
10	1960/61	12/04/61	Football League Division 1	Manchester United 6 Burnley 0	Old Trafford	25019
11	1964/65	12/04/65	Football League Division 1	Manchester United 0 Leicester City 0	Old Trafford	34114
12	1967/68	12/04/68	Football League Division 1	Fulham 0 Manchester United 4	Craven Cottage	40152
13	1968/69	12/04/69	Football League Division 1	Newcastle United 2 Manchester United 0	St James' Park	46379
14	1970/71	12/04/71	Football League Division 1	Manchester United 1 Wolverhampton Wanderers 0	Old Trafford	41886
15	1971/72	12/04/72	Football League Division 1	Manchester United 1 Manchester City 3	Old Trafford	56362
16	1974/75	12/04/75	Football League Division 2	Manchester United 1 Fulham 0	Old Trafford	52971
17	1979/80	12/04/80	Football League Division 1	Manchester United 4 Tottenham Hotspur 1	Old Trafford	53151
18	1981/82	12/04/82	Football League Division 1	Manchester United 1 West Bromwich Albion 0	Old Trafford	38717
19	1987/88	12/04/88	Football League Division 1	Manchester United 3 Luton Town 0	Old Trafford	28830
20	1991/92	12/04/92	League Cup Final	Manchester United 1 Nottingham Forest 0	Wembley	76810
21	1992/93	12/04/93	FA Premiership	Coventry City 0 Manchester United 1	Highfield Road	24249
22	1994/95	12/04/95	FA Cup Semi-Final Replay	Manchester United 2 Crystal Palace 0	Villa Park	17987
23	1996/97	12/04/97	FA Premiership	Blackburn Rovers 2 Manchester United 3	Ewood Park	30476
24	2002/03	12/04/03	FA Premiership	Newcastle United 2 Manchester United 6	St James' Park	52164

APRIL 13

#	SEASON	DATE	COMPETITION / ROUND	MATCH RESULT	VENUE	ATT
1	1894/95	13/04/95	Football League Division 2	Newcastle United 3 Newton Heath 0	St James' Park	4000
2	1899/00	13/04/00	Football League Division 2	Newton Heath 3 Leicester City 2	Bank Street	10000
3	1900/01	13/04/01	Football League Division 2	Newton Heath 1 Grimsby Town 0	Bank Street	3000
4	1902/03	13/04/03	Football League Division 2	Manchester United 4 Doncaster Rovers 0	Bank Street	6000
5	1905/06	13/04/06	Football League Division 2	Chelsea 1 Manchester United 1	Stamford Bridge	60000
6	1906/07	13/04/07	Football League Division 1	Middlesbrough 2 Manchester United 0	Ayresome Park	15000
7	1908/09	13/04/09	Football League Division 1	Notts County 0 Manchester United 1	Trent Bridge	7000
8	1911/12	13/04/12	Football League Division 1	Sheffield United 6 Manchester United 1	Bramall Lane	7000
9	1913/14	13/04/14	Football League Division 1	West Bromwich Albion 2 Manchester United 1	The Hawthorns	20000
10	1924/25	13/04/25	Football League Division 2	Chelsea 0 Manchester United 0	Stamford Bridge	16500
11	1928/29	13/04/29	Football League Division 1	Blackburn Rovers 0 Manchester United 3	Ewood Park	8193
12	1934/35	13/04/35	Football League Division 2	Manchester United 0 Brentford 0	Old Trafford	32969
13	1935/36	13/04/36	Football League Division 2	Manchester United 4 Burnley 0	Old Trafford	39855
14	1956/57	13/04/57	Football League Division 1	Luton Town 0 Manchester United 2	Kenilworth Road	21227
15	1962/63	13/04/63	Football League Division 1	Liverpool 1 Manchester United 0	Anfield	51529
16	1963/64	13/04/64	Football League Division 1	Manchester United 2 Sheffield United 1	Old Trafford	27587
17	1965/66	13/04/66	European Cup Semi-Final 1st Leg	Partizan Belgrade 2 Manchester United 0	Stadion JNA	60000
18	1967/68	13/04/68	Football League Division 1	Southampton 2 Manchester United 2	The Dell	30079
19	1969/70	13/04/70	Football League Division 1	Tottenham Hotspur 2 Manchester United 1	White Hart Lane	41808
20	1970/71	13/04/71	Football League Division 1	Coventry City 2 Manchester United 1	Highfield Road	33818
21	1973/74	13/04/74	Football League Division 1	Manchester United 1 Newcastle United 0	Old Trafford	44751
22	1984/85	13/04/85	FA Cup Semi-Final	Manchester United 2 Liverpool 2	Goodison Park	51690
23	1985/86	13/04/86	Football League Division 1	Manchester United 0 Sheffield Wednesday 2	Old Trafford	32331
24	1993/94	13/04/94	FA Cup Semi-Final Replay	Manchester United 4 Oldham Athletic 1	Maine Road	32311
25	1995/96	13/04/96	FA Premiership	Southampton 3 Manchester United 1	The Dell	15262
26	2003/04	13/04/04	FA Premiership	Manchester United 1 Leicester City 0	Old Trafford	67749
27	2007/08	13/04/08	FA Premiership	Manchester United 2 Arsenal 1	Old Trafford	75985

APRIL 14

#	SEASON	DATE	COMPETITION / ROUND	MATCH RESULT	VENUE	ATT
1	1893/94	14/04/94	Football League Division 1	Newton Heath 1 Preston North End 3	Bank Street	4000
2	1899/00	14/04/00	Football League Division 2	Newton Heath 5 Walsall 0	Bank Street	4000
3	1905/06	14/04/06	Football League Division 2	Manchester United 1 Burnley 0	Bank Street	12000
4	1922/23	14/04/23	Football League Division 2	Leicester City 0 Manchester United 1	Filbert Street	25000
5	1925/26	14/04/26	Football League Division 1	Newcastle United 4 Manchester United 1	St James' Park	9829
6	1927/28	14/04/28	Football League Division 1	Bury 4 Manchester United 3	Gigg Lane	17440
7	1929/30	14/04/30	Football League Division 1	Manchester United 2 Sheffield Wednesday 2	Old Trafford	12806
8	1932/33	14/04/33	Football League Division 2	Nottingham Forest 3 Manchester United 2	City Ground	12963
9	1933/34	14/04/34	Football League Division 2	Manchester United 2 Port Vale 0	Old Trafford	14777
10	1950/51	14/04/51	Football League Division 1	Manchester United 3 West Bromwich Albion 0	Old Trafford	24764
11	1951/52	14/04/52	Football League Division 1	Manchester United 6 Burnley 1	Old Trafford	44508
12	1955/56	14/04/56	Football League Division 1	Sunderland 2 Manchester United 2	Roker Park	19865
13	1961/62	14/04/62	Football League Division 1	Burnley 1 Manchester United 3	Turf Moor	36240
14	1972/73	14/04/73	Football League Division 1	Stoke City 2 Manchester United 2	Victoria Ground	37051
15	1978/79	14/04/79	Football League Division 1	Liverpool 2 Manchester United 0	Anfield	46608
16	1980/81	14/04/81	Football League Division 1	Liverpool 0 Manchester United 1	Anfield	31276
17	1983/84	14/04/84	Football League Division 1	Notts County 1 Manchester United 0	Meadow Lane	13911
18	1986/87	14/04/87	Football League Division 1	West Ham United 0 Manchester United 0	Upton Park	23486
19	1989/90	14/04/90	Football League Division 1	Queens Park Rangers 1 Manchester United 2	Loftus Road	18997
20	1998/99	14/04/99	FA Cup Semi-Final Replay	Manchester United 2 Arsenal 1	Villa Park	30023
21	2000/01	14/04/01	FA Premiership	Manchester United 4 Coventry City 2	Old Trafford	67637
22	2005/06	14/04/06	FA Premiership	Manchester United 0 Sunderland 0	Old Trafford	72519
23	2006/07	14/04/07	FA Cup Semi-Final	Manchester United 4 Watford 1	Villa Park	37425

APRIL 15

#	SEASON	DATE	COMPETITION / ROUND	MATCH RESULT	VENUE	ATT
1	1894/95	15/04/95	Football League Division 2	Bury 2 Newton Heath 1	Gigg Lane	10000
2	1898/99	15/04/99	Football League Division 2	Newton Heath 2 Leicester City 2	Bank Street	6000
3	1904/05	15/04/05	Football League Division 2	Manchester United 5 Burton United 0	Bank Street	16000
4	1910/11	15/04/11	Football League Division 1	Manchester United 1 Sheffield United 1	Old Trafford	22000
5	1913/14	15/04/14	Football League Division 1	Liverpool 1 Manchester United 2	Anfield	28000
6	1921/22	15/04/22	Football League Division 1	Manchester United 0 Oldham Athletic 3	Old Trafford	30000
7	1926/27	15/04/27	Football League Division 1	Manchester United 2 Derby County 2	Old Trafford	31110
8	1932/33	15/04/33	Football League Division 2	Bradford City 1 Manchester United 2	Valley Parade	11195
9	1937/38	15/04/38	Football League Division 2	Burnley 1 Manchester United 0	Turf Moor	28459
10	1938/39	15/04/39	Football League Division 1	Arsenal 2 Manchester United 1	Highbury	25741
11	1948/49	15/04/49	Football League Division 1	Bolton Wanderers 0 Manchester United 1	Burnden Park	44999
12	1949/50	15/04/50	Football League Division 1	Manchester United 0 Portsmouth 2	Old Trafford	44908
13	1959/60	15/04/60	Football League Division 1	West Ham United 2 Manchester United 1	Upton Park	34969
14	1960/61	15/04/61	Football League Division 1	Manchester United 4 Birmingham City 1	Old Trafford	28376
15	1962/63	15/04/63	Football League Division 1	Manchester United 2 Leicester City 2	Old Trafford	50005
16	1967/68	15/04/68	Football League Division 1	Manchester United 3 Fulham 0	Old Trafford	60465
17	1969/70	15/04/70	Football League Division 1	Manchester United 2 Sheffield Wednesday 2	Old Trafford	36649
18	1971/72	15/04/72	Football League Division 1	Manchester United 3 Southampton 2	Old Trafford	38437
19	1973/74	15/04/74	Football League Division 1	Manchester United 3 Everton 0	Old Trafford	48424
20	1977/78	15/04/78	Football League Division 1	Norwich City 1 Manchester United 3	Carrow Road	19778
21	1988/89	15/04/89	Football League Division 1	Manchester United 0 Derby County 2	Old Trafford	34145
22	1994/95	15/04/95	FA Premiership	Leicester City 0 Manchester United 4	Filbert Street	21281
23	1999/00	15/04/00	FA Premiership	Manchester United 4 Sunderland 0	Old Trafford	61612

APRIL 16

#	SEASON	DATE	COMPETITION / ROUND	MATCH RESULT	VENUE	ATT
1	1897/98	16/04/98	Football League Division 2	Loughborough Town 0 Newton Heath 0	The Athletic Ground	1000
2	1903/04	16/04/04	Football League Division 2	Gainsborough Trinity 0 Manchester United 1	The Northolme	4000
3	1905/06	16/04/06	Football League Division 2	Manchester United 2 Gainsborough Trinity 0	Bank Street	20000
4	1909/10	16/04/10	Football League Division 1	Manchester United 2 Sunderland 0	Old Trafford	12000
5	1920/21	16/04/21	Football League Division 1	Manchester United 0 Middlesbrough 1	Old Trafford	25000
6	1926/27	16/04/27	Football League Division 1	Manchester United 2 Blackburn Rovers 0	Old Trafford	24845
7	1931/32	16/04/32	Football League Division 2	Millwall 1 Manchester United 1	The Den	9087
8	1937/38	16/04/38	Football League Division 2	Swansea City 2 Manchester United 2	Vetch Field	13811
9	1948/49	16/04/49	Football League Division 1	Burnley 0 Manchester United 2	Turf Moor	37722
10	1953/54	16/04/54	Football League Division 1	Manchester United 2 Charlton Athletic 0	Old Trafford	31876
11	1954/55	16/04/55	Football League Division 1	Manchester United 3 West Bromwich Albion 0	Old Trafford	24765
12	1957/58	16/04/58	Football League Division 1	Portsmouth 3 Manchester United 3	Fratton Park	39975
13	1959/60	16/04/60	Football League Division 1	Manchester United 1 Blackburn Rovers 0	Old Trafford	45945
14	1961/62	16/04/62	Football League Division 1	Manchester United 2 Arsenal 3	Old Trafford	24258
15	1962/63	16/04/63	Football League Division 1	Leicester City 4 Manchester United 3	Filbert Street	37002
16	1965/66	16/04/66	Football League Division 1	Sheffield United 3 Manchester United 1	Bramall Lane	22330
17	1976/77	16/04/77	Football League Division 1	Manchester United 1 Leicester City 1	Old Trafford	49161
18	1978/79	16/04/79	Football League Division 1	Manchester United 0 Coventry City 0	Old Trafford	46035
19	1982/83	16/04/83	FA Cup Semi-Final	Manchester United 2 Arsenal 1	Villa Park	46535
20	1985/86	16/04/86	Football League Division 1	Newcastle United 2 Manchester United 4	St James' Park	31840
21	1990/91	16/04/91	Football League Division 1	Manchester United 3 Derby County 1	Old Trafford	32776
22	1991/92	16/04/92	Football League Division 1	Manchester United 1 Southampton 0	Old Trafford	43972
23	1993/94	16/04/94	FA Premiership	Wimbledon 1 Manchester United 0	Selhurst Park	28553
24	2002/03	16/04/03	FA Premiership	Arsenal 2 Manchester United 2	Highbury	38164

APRIL 17

#	SEASON	DATE	COMPETITION / ROUND	MATCH RESULT	VENUE	ATT
1	1899/00	17/04/00	Football League Division 2	Walsall 0 Newton Heath 0	Fellows Park	3000
2	1907/08	17/04/08	Football League Division 1	Nottingham Forest 2 Manchester United 0	City Ground	22000
3	1908/09	17/04/09	Football League Division 1	Leicester City 3 Manchester United 2	Filbert Street	8000
4	1910/11	17/04/11	Football League Division 1	Sheffield Wednesday 0 Manchester United 0	Hillsborough	25000
5	1911/12	17/04/12	Football League Division 1	Middlesbrough 3 Manchester United 0	Ayresome Park	5000
6	1914/15	17/04/15	Football League Division 1	Sheffield United 3 Manchester United 1	Bramall Lane	14000
7	1919/20	17/04/20	Football League Division 1	Manchester United 1 Blackburn Rovers 1	Old Trafford	40000
8	1921/22	17/04/22	Football League Division 1	Manchester United 3 Sheffield United 2	Old Trafford	28000
9	1932/33	17/04/33	Football League Division 2	Manchester United 2 Nottingham Forest 1	Old Trafford	16849
10	1936/37	17/04/37	Football League Division 1	Manchester United 2 Middlesbrough 1	Old Trafford	17656
11	1947/48	17/04/48	Football League Division 1	Manchester United 5 Chelsea 0	Maine Road	43225
12	1953/54	17/04/54	Football League Division 1	Manchester United 2 Portsmouth 0	Old Trafford	29663
13	1964/65	17/04/65	Football League Division 1	Leeds United 0 Manchester United 1	Elland Road	52368
14	1970/71	17/04/71	Football League Division 1	Crystal Palace 3 Manchester United 5	Selhurst Park	39145
15	1975/76	17/04/76	Football League Division 1	Manchester United 2 Everton 1	Old Trafford	61879
16	1981/82	17/04/82	Football League Division 1	Manchester United 2 Tottenham Hotspur 0	Old Trafford	50724
17	1983/84	17/04/84	Football League Division 1	Watford 0 Manchester United 0	Vicarage Road	20764
18	1984/85	17/04/85	FA Cup Semi-Final Replay	Manchester United 2 Liverpool 1	Maine Road	45775
19	1989/90	17/04/90	Football League Division 1	Manchester United 2 Aston Villa 0	Old Trafford	44080
20	1992/93	17/04/93	FA Premiership	Manchester United 3 Chelsea 0	Old Trafford	40139
21	1994/95	17/04/95	FA Premiership	Manchester United 0 Chelsea 0	Old Trafford	43728
22	1995/96	17/04/96	FA Premiership	Manchester United 1 Leeds United 0	Old Trafford	48382
23	1998/99	17/04/99	FA Premiership	Manchester United 3 Sheffield Wednesday 0	Old Trafford	55270
24	2003/04	17/04/04	FA Premiership	Portsmouth 1 Manchester United 0	Fratton Park	20140
25	2004/05	17/04/05	FA Cup Semi-Final	Manchester United 4 Newcastle United 1	Millennium Stadium	69280
26	2005/06	17/04/06	FA Premiership	Tottenham Hotspur 1 Manchester United 2	White Hart Lane	36141
27	2006/07	17/04/07	FA Premiership	Manchester United 2 Sheffield United 0	Old Trafford	75540

APRIL 18

#	SEASON	DATE	COMPETITION / ROUND	MATCH RESULT	VENUE	ATT
1	1902/03	18/04/03	Football League Division 2	Manchester United 2 Port Vale 1	Bank Street	8000
2	1907/08	18/04/08	Football League Division 1	Manchester City 0 Manchester United 0	Hyde Road	40000
3	1913/14	18/04/14	Football League Division 1	Bradford City 1 Manchester United 1	Valley Parade	10000
4	1923/24	18/04/24	Football League Division 2	Leyton Orient 1 Manchester United 0	Millfields Road	18000
5	1924/25	18/04/25	Football League Division 2	Bradford City 0 Manchester United 1	Valley Parade	13250
6	1926/27	18/04/27	Football League Division 1	Derby County 2 Manchester United 2	Baseball Ground	17306
7	1929/30	18/04/30	Football League Division 1	Manchester United 1 Huddersfield Town 0	Old Trafford	26496
8	1930/31	18/04/31	Football League Division 1	Derby County 6 Manchester United 1	Baseball Ground	6610
9	1935/36	18/04/36	Football League Division 2	Nottingham Forest 1 Manchester United 1	City Ground	12156
10	1937/38	18/04/38	Football League Division 2	Manchester United 4 Burnley 0	Old Trafford	35808
11	1948/49	18/04/49	Football League Division 1	Manchester United 3 Bolton Wanderers 0	Maine Road	47653
12	1952/53	18/04/53	Football League Division 1	Manchester United 2 West Bromwich Albion 2	Old Trafford	31380
13	1954/55	18/04/55	Football League Division 1	Newcastle United 2 Manchester United 0	St James' Park	35540
14	1958/59	18/04/59	Football League Division 1	Manchester United 1 Birmingham City 0	Old Trafford	43006
15	1959/60	18/04/60	Football League Division 1	Manchester United 5 West Ham United 3	Old Trafford	34676
16	1963/64	18/04/64	Football League Division 1	Stoke City 3 Manchester United 1	Victoria Ground	45670
17	1966/67	18/04/67	Football League Division 1	Manchester United 3 Southampton 0	Old Trafford	54291
18	1972/73	18/04/73	Football League Division 1	Leeds United 0 Manchester United 1	Elland Road	45450
19	1978/79	18/04/79	Football League Division 1	Nottingham Forest 1 Manchester United 1	City Ground	33074
20	1980/81	18/04/81	Football League Division 1	Manchester United 2 West Bromwich Albion 1	Old Trafford	44442
21	1986/87	18/04/87	Football League Division 1	Newcastle United 2 Manchester United 1	St James' Park	32706
22	1991/92	18/04/92	Football League Division 1	Luton Town 1 Manchester United 1	Kenilworth Road	13410
23	1997/98	18/04/98	FA Premiership	Manchester United 1 Newcastle United 1	Old Trafford	55194
24	2000/01	18/04/01	Champions Lge Quarter-Final 2nd Leg	Bayern Munich 2 Manchester United 1	Olympic Stadium	60000

APRIL 19

#	SEASON	DATE	COMPETITION / ROUND	MATCH RESULT	VENUE	ATT
1	1896/97	19/04/97	Football League Test Match	Burnley 2 Newton Heath 0	Turf Moor	10000
2	1901/02	19/04/02	Football League Division 2	Port Vale 1 Newton Heath 1	Cobridge Stadium	2000
3	1912/13	19/04/13	Football League Division 1	Manchester United 3 Newcastle United 0	Old Trafford	10000
4	1914/15	19/04/15	Football League Division 1	Chelsea 1 Manchester United 3	Stamford Bridge	13000
5	1923/24	19/04/24	Football League Division 2	Crystal Palace 1 Manchester United 1	Sydenham Hill	7000
6	1925/26	19/04/26	Football League Division 1	Birmingham City 2 Manchester United 1	St Andrews	8948
7	1929/30	19/04/30	Football League Division 1	Manchester United 3 Everton 3	Old Trafford	13320
8	1946/47	19/04/47	Football League Division 1	Manchester United 4 Blackburn Rovers 0	Maine Road	46196
9	1951/52	19/04/52	Football League Division 1	Blackpool 2 Manchester United 2	Bloomfield Road	29118
10	1953/54	19/04/54	Football League Division 1	Charlton Athletic 1 Manchester United 0	The Valley	19111
11	1956/57	19/04/57	Football League Division 1	Burnley 1 Manchester United 1	Turf Moor	41321
12	1957/58	19/04/58	Football League Division 1	Manchester United 0 Birmingham City 2	Old Trafford	38991
13	1964/65	19/04/65	Football League Division 1	Birmingham City 2 Manchester United 4	St Andrews	28907
14	1968/69	19/04/69	Football League Division 1	Manchester United 2 Burnley 0	Old Trafford	52626
15	1970/71	19/04/71	Football League Division 1	Manchester United 0 Liverpool 2	Old Trafford	44004
16	1974/75	19/04/75	Football League Division 2	Notts County 2 Manchester United 2	Meadow Lane	17320
17	1975/76	19/04/76	Football League Division 1	Burnley 0 Manchester United 1	Turf Moor	27418
18	1976/77	19/04/77	Football League Division 1	Queens Park Rangers 4 Manchester United 0	Loftus Road	28848
19	1979/80	19/04/80	Football League Division 1	Norwich City 0 Manchester United 2	Carrow Road	23274
20	1982/83	19/04/83	Football League Division 1	Everton 2 Manchester United 0	Goodison Park	21715
21	1985/86	19/04/86	Football League Division 1	Tottenham Hotspur 0 Manchester United 0	White Hart Lane	32357
22	1996/97	19/04/97	FA Premiership	Liverpool 1 Manchester United 3	Anfield	40892
23	1999/00	19/04/00	Champions Lge Quarter-Final 2nd Leg	Manchester United 2 Real Madrid 3	Old Trafford	59178
24	2002/03	19/04/03	FA Premiership	Manchester United 3 Blackburn Rovers 1	Old Trafford	67626
25	2007/08	19/04/08	FA Premiership	Blackburn Rovers 1 Manchester United 1	Ewood Park	30316

APRIL 20

#	SEASON	DATE	COMPETITION / ROUND	MATCH RESULT	VENUE	ATT
1	1894/95	20/04/95	Football League Division 2	Newton Heath 3 Notts County 3	Bank Street	12000
2	1902/03	20/04/03	Football League Division 2	Birmingham City 2 Manchester United 1	St Andrews	6000
3	1907/08	20/04/08	Football League Division 1	Manchester United 1 Aston Villa 2	Bank Street	10000
4	1911/12	20/04/12	Football League Division 1	Manchester United 3 Oldham Athletic 1	Old Trafford	15000
5	1928/29	20/04/29	Football League Division 1	Manchester United 4 Arsenal 1	Old Trafford	22858
6	1934/35	20/04/35	Football League Division 2	Fulham 3 Manchester United 1	Craven Cottage	11059
7	1952/53	20/04/53	Football League Division 1	Manchester United 3 Liverpool 1	Old Trafford	20869
8	1956/57	20/04/57	Football League Division 1	Manchester United 4 Sunderland 0	Old Trafford	58725
9	1962/63	20/04/63	Football League Division 1	Manchester United 1 Sheffield United 1	Old Trafford	31179
10	1965/66	20/04/66	European Cup Semi-Final 2nd Leg	Manchester United 1 Partizan Belgrade 0	Old Trafford	62500
11	1967/68	20/04/68	Football League Division 1	Manchester United 1 Sheffield United 0	Old Trafford	55033
12	1973/74	20/04/74	Football League Division 1	Southampton 1 Manchester United 1	The Dell	30789
13	1981/82	20/04/82	Football League Division 1	Ipswich Town 2 Manchester United 1	Portman Road	25744
14	1986/87	20/04/87	Football League Division 1	Manchester United 1 Liverpool 0	Old Trafford	54103
15	1991/92	20/04/92	Football League Division 1	Manchester United 1 Nottingham Forest 2	Old Trafford	47576
16	2001/02	20/04/02	FA Premiership	Chelsea 0 Manchester United 3	Stamford Bridge	41725
17	2003/04	20/04/04	FA Premiership	Manchester United 2 Charlton Athletic 0	Old Trafford	67477
18	2004/05	20/04/05	FA Premiership	Everton 1 Manchester United 0	Goodison Park	37160

APRIL 21

#	SEASON	DATE	COMPETITION / ROUND	MATCH RESULT	VENUE	ATT
1	1896/97	21/04/97	Football League Test Match	Newton Heath 2 Burnley 0	Bank Street	7000
2	1899/00	21/04/00	Football League Division 2	Middlesbrough 2 Newton Heath 0	Linthorpe Road	8000
3	1901/02	21/04/02	Football League Division 2	Newton Heath 3 Burton United 1	Bank Street	500
4	1904/05	21/04/05	Football League Division 2	Chesterfield 2 Manchester United 0	Saltergate	10000
5	1905/06	21/04/06	Football League Division 2	Leeds United 1 Manchester United 3	Elland Road	15000
6	1922/23	21/04/23	Football League Division 2	Manchester United 0 Leicester City 2	Old Trafford	30000
7	1923/24	21/04/24	Football League Division 2	Manchester United 2 Leyton Orient 2	Old Trafford	11000
8	1925/26	21/04/26	Football League Division 1	Manchester United 5 Sunderland 1	Old Trafford	10918
9	1927/28	21/04/28	Football League Division 1	Manchester United 2 Sheffield United 3	Old Trafford	27137
10	1933/34	21/04/34	Football League Division 2	Notts County 0 Manchester United 0	Meadow Lane	9645
11	1936/37	21/04/37	Football League Division 1	Sunderland 1 Manchester United 1	Roker Park	12876
12	1948/49	21/04/49	Football League Division 1	Manchester United 1 Sunderland 2	Maine Road	30640
13	1950/51	21/04/51	Football League Division 1	Newcastle United 0 Manchester United 2	St James' Park	45209
14	1951/52	21/04/52	Football League Division 1	Manchester United 3 Chelsea 0	Old Trafford	37436
15	1955/56	21/04/56	Football League Division 1	Manchester United 1 Portsmouth 0	Old Trafford	38417
16	1957/58	21/04/58	Football League Division 1	Manchester United 0 Wolverhampton Wanderers 4	Old Trafford	33267
17	1961/62	21/04/62	Football League Division 1	Manchester United 1 Everton 0	Old Trafford	31926
18	1972/73	21/04/73	Football League Division 1	Manchester United 0 Manchester City 0	Old Trafford	61676
19	1975/76	21/04/76	Football League Division 1	Manchester United 0 Stoke City 1	Old Trafford	53879
20	1978/79	21/04/79	Football League Division 1	Tottenham Hotspur 1 Manchester United 1	White Hart Lane	36665
21	1983/84	21/04/84	Football League Division 1	Manchester United 4 Coventry City 1	Old Trafford	38524
22	1984/85	21/04/85	Football League Division 1	Luton Town 2 Manchester United 1	Kenilworth Road	10320
23	1989/90	21/04/90	Football League Division 1	Tottenham Hotspur 2 Manchester United 1	White Hart Lane	33317
24	1990/91	21/04/91	League Cup Final	Manchester United 0 Sheffield Wednesday 1	Wembley	77612
25	1992/93	21/04/93	FA Premiership	Crystal Palace 0 Manchester United 2	Selhurst Park	30115
26	1998/99	21/04/99	Champions Lge Semi-Final 2nd Leg	Juventus 2 Manchester United 3	Stadio Delle Alpi	64500
27	2000/01	21/04/01	FA Premiership	Manchester United 1 Manchester City 1	Old Trafford	67535
28	2006/07	21/04/07	FA Premiership	Manchester United 1 Middlesbrough 1	Old Trafford	75967

APRIL 22

#	SEASON	DATE	COMPETITION / ROUND	MATCH RESULT	VENUE	ATT
1	1892/93	22/04/93	Football League Test Match	Newton Heath 1 Birmingham City 1	Victoria Ground	4000
2	1898/99	22/04/99	Football League Division 2	Darwen 1 Newton Heath 1	Barley Bank	1000
3	1904/05	22/04/05	Football League Division 2	Liverpool 4 Manchester United 0	Anfield	28000
4	1906/07	22/04/07	Football League Division 1	Manchester United 3 Everton 0	Bank Street	10000
5	1907/08	22/04/08	Football League Division 1	Bolton Wanderers 2 Manchester United 2	Burnden Park	18000
6	1910/11	22/04/11	Football League Division 1	Aston Villa 4 Manchester United 2	Villa Park	50000
7	1913/14	22/04/14	Football League Division 1	Manchester United 2 Sheffield United 1	Old Trafford	4500
8	1921/22	22/04/22	Football League Division 1	Oldham Athletic 1 Manchester United 0	Boundary Park	30000
9	1924/25	22/04/25	Football League Division 2	Manchester United 1 Southampton 1	Old Trafford	26500
10	1929/30	22/04/30	Football League Division 1	Huddersfield Town 2 Manchester United 2	Leeds Road	20716
11	1932/33	22/04/33	Football League Division 2	Manchester United 1 West Ham United 2	Old Trafford	14958
12	1934/35	22/04/35	Football League Division 2	Southampton 1 Manchester United 0	The Dell	12458
13	1938/39	22/04/39	Football League Division 1	Manchester United 3 Brentford 0	Old Trafford	15353
14	1949/50	22/04/50	Football League Division 1	Newcastle United 2 Manchester United 1	St James' Park	52203
15	1956/57	22/04/57	Football League Division 1	Manchester United 2 Burnley 0	Old Trafford	41321
16	1960/61	22/04/61	Football League Division 1	Preston North End 2 Manchester United 4	Deepdale	21252
17	1962/63	22/04/63	Football League Division 1	Manchester United 2 Wolverhampton Wanderers 1	Old Trafford	36147
18	1966/67	22/04/67	Football League Division 1	Sunderland 0 Manchester United 0	Roker Park	43570
19	1971/72	22/04/72	Football League Division 1	Nottingham Forest 1 Manchester United 0	City Ground	35063
20	1977/78	22/04/78	Football League Division 1	Manchester United 3 West Ham United 0	Old Trafford	54089
21	1988/89	22/04/89	Football League Division 1	Charlton Athletic 1 Manchester United 0	Selhurst Park	12055
22	1991/92	22/04/92	Football League Division 1	West Ham United 1 Manchester United 0	Upton Park	24197
23	1999/00	22/04/00	FA Premiership	Southampton 1 Manchester United 3	The Dell	15245

APRIL 23

#	SEASON	DATE	COMPETITION / ROUND	MATCH RESULT	VENUE	ATT
1	1897/98	23/04/98	Football League Division 2	Newton Heath 3 Darwen 2	Bank Street	4000
2	1901/02	23/04/02	Football League Division 2	Newton Heath 2 Chesterfield 0	Bank Street	2000
3	1903/04	23/04/04	Football League Division 2	Manchester United 2 Burton United 0	Bank Street	8000
4	1909/10	23/04/10	Football League Division 1	Everton 3 Manchester United 3	Goodison Park	10000
5	1920/21	23/04/21	Football League Division 1	Blackburn Rovers 2 Manchester United 0	Ewood Park	18000
6	1926/27	23/04/27	Football League Division 1	Huddersfield Town 0 Manchester United 0	Leeds Road	13870
7	1931/32	23/04/32	Football League Division 2	Manchester United 1 Bradford City 0	Old Trafford	17765
8	1937/38	23/04/38	Football League Division 2	Manchester United 3 Bradford Park Avenue 1	Old Trafford	28919
9	1948/49	23/04/49	Football League Division 1	Manchester United 2 Preston North End 2	Maine Road	43214
10	1954/55	23/04/55	Football League Division 1	Arsenal 2 Manchester United 3	Highbury	42754
11	1957/58	23/04/58	Football League Division 1	Manchester United 1 Newcastle United 1	Old Trafford	28393
12	1959/60	23/04/60	Football League Division 1	Arsenal 5 Manchester United 2	Highbury	41057
13	1961/62	23/04/62	Football League Division 1	Manchester United 0 Sheffield United 1	Old Trafford	30073
14	1965/66	23/04/66	FA Cup Semi-Final	Manchester United 0 Everton 1	Burnden Park	60000
15	1968/69	23/04/69	European Cup Semi-Final 1st Leg	AC Milan 2 Manchester United 0	Stadio San Siro	80000
16	1972/73	23/04/73	Football League Division 1	Manchester United 1 Sheffield United 2	Old Trafford	57280
17	1973/74	23/04/74	Football League Division 1	Everton 1 Manchester United 0	Goodison Park	46093
18	1976/77	23/04/77	FA Cup Semi-Final	Manchester United 2 Leeds United 1	Hillsborough	55000
19	1979/80	23/04/80	Football League Division 1	Manchester United 2 Aston Villa 1	Old Trafford	45201
20	1982/83	23/04/83	Football League Division 1	Manchester United 2 Watford 0	Old Trafford	43048
21	1993/94	23/04/94	FA Premiership	Manchester United 2 Manchester City 0	Old Trafford	44333
22	1996/97	23/04/97	Champions Lge Semi-Final 2nd Leg	Manchester United 0 Borussia Dortmund 1	Old Trafford	53606
23	2002/03	23/04/03	Champions Lge Quarter-Final 2nd Leg	Manchester United 4 Real Madrid 3	Old Trafford	66708
24	2007/08	23/04/08	Champions Lge Semi-Final 1st Leg	Barcelona 0 Manchester United 0	Estadio Camp Nou	95949

APRIL 24

#	SEASON	DATE	COMPETITION / ROUND	MATCH RESULT	VENUE	ATT
1	1896/97	24/04/97	Football League Test Match	Newton Heath 1 Sunderland 1	Bank Street	18000
2	1904/05	24/04/05	Football League Division 2	Manchester United 3 Blackpool 1	Bank Street	4000
3	1908/09	24/04/09	FA Cup Final	Manchester United 1 Bristol City 0	Crystal Palace	71401
4	1919/20	24/04/20	Football League Division 1	Blackburn Rovers 5 Manchester United 0	Ewood Park	30000
5	1925/26	24/04/26	Football League Division 1	Sheffield United 2 Manchester United 0	Bramall Lane	15571
6	1936/37	24/04/37	Football League Division 1	West Bromwich Albion 1 Manchester United 0	The Hawthorns	16234
7	1947/48	24/04/48	FA Cup Final	Manchester United 4 Blackpool 2	Wembley	99000
8	1953/54	24/04/54	Football League Division 1	Sheffield United 1 Manchester United 3	Bramall Lane	29189
9	1961/62	24/04/62	Football League Division 1	Sheffield United 2 Manchester United 3	Bramall Lane	25324
10	1964/65	24/04/65	Football League Division 1	Manchester United 3 Liverpool 0	Old Trafford	55772
11	1967/68	24/04/68	European Cup Semi-Final 1st Leg	Manchester United 1 Real Madrid 0	Old Trafford	63500
12	1970/71	24/04/71	Football League Division 1	Manchester United 3 Ipswich Town 2	Old Trafford	33566
13	1975/76	24/04/76	Football League Division 1	Leicester City 2 Manchester United 1	Filbert Street	31053
14	1981/82	24/04/82	Football League Division 1	Brighton 0 Manchester United 1	Goldstone Ground	20750
15	1984/85	24/04/85	Football League Division 1	Manchester United 0 Southampton 0	Old Trafford	31291
16	1990/91	24/04/91	European CWC Semi-Final 2nd Leg	Manchester United 1 Legia Warsaw 1	Old Trafford	44269
17	1999/00	24/04/00	FA Premiership	Manchester United 3 Chelsea 1	Old Trafford	61593
18	2001/02	24/04/02	Champions League Semi-Final 1st Leg	Manchester United 2 Bayer Leverkusen 2	Old Trafford	66534
19	2003/04	24/04/04	FA Premiership	Manchester United 0 Liverpool 1	Old Trafford	67647
20	2004/05	24/04/05	FA Premiership	Manchester United 2 Newcastle United 1	Old Trafford	67845
21	2006/07	24/04/07	Champions League Semi-Final 1st Leg	Manchester United 3 AC Milan 2	Old Trafford	73820

APRIL 25

#	SEASON	DATE	COMPETITION / ROUND	MATCH RESULT	VENUE	ATT
1	1902/03	25/04/03	Football League Division 2	Barnsley 0 Manchester United 0	Oakwell	2000
2	1903/04	25/04/04	Football League Division 2	Bolton Wanderers 0 Manchester United 0	Burnden Park	10000
3	1905/06	25/04/06	Football League Division 2	Lincoln City 2 Manchester United 3	Sincil Bank	1500
4	1907/08	25/04/08	Football League Division 1	Manchester United 2 Preston North End 1	Bank Street	8000
5	1913/14	25/04/14	Football League Division 1	Manchester United 0 Blackburn Rovers 0	Old Trafford	20000
6	1924/25	25/04/25	Football League Division 2	Manchester United 4 Port Vale 0	Old Trafford	33500
7	1927/28	25/04/28	Football League Division 1	Manchester United 2 Sunderland 1	Old Trafford	9545
8	1935/36	25/04/36	Football League Division 2	Manchester United 2 Bury 1	Old Trafford	35027
9	1952/53	25/04/53	Football League Division 1	Middlesbrough 5 Manchester United 0	Ayresome Park	34344
10	1956/57	25/04/57	European Cup Semi-Final 2nd Leg	Manchester United 2 Real Madrid 2	Old Trafford	65000
11	1958/59	25/04/59	Football League Division 1	Leicester City 2 Manchester United 1	Filbert Street	38466
12	1963/64	25/04/64	Football League Division 1	Manchester United 3 Nottingham Forest 1	Old Trafford	31671
13	1965/66	25/04/66	Football League Division 1	Everton 0 Manchester United 0	Goodison Park	50843
14	1971/72	25/04/72	Football League Division 1	Arsenal 3 Manchester United 0	Highbury	49125
15	1977/78	25/04/78	Football League Division 1	Bristol City 0 Manchester United 1	Ashton Gate	26035
16	1978/79	25/04/79	Football League Division 1	Manchester United 1 Norwich City 0	Old Trafford	33678
17	1980/81	25/04/81	Football League Division 1	Manchester United 1 Norwich City 0	Old Trafford	40165
18	1983/84	25/04/84	European CWC Semi-Final 2nd Leg	Juventus 2 Manchester United 1	Stadio Comunale	64655
19	1986/87	25/04/87	Football League Division 1	Queens Park Rangers 1 Manchester United 1	Loftus Road	17414
20	1998/99	25/04/99	FA Premiership	Leeds United 1 Manchester United 1	Elland Road	40255

APRIL 26

#	SEASON	DATE	COMPETITION / ROUND	MATCH RESULT	VENUE	ATT
1	1896/97	26/04/97	Football League Test Match	Sunderland 2 Newton Heath 0	Newcastle Road	6000
2	1912/13	26/04/13	Football League Division 1	Oldham Athletic 0 Manchester United 0	Boundary Park	3000
3	1914/15	26/04/15	Football League Division 1	Manchester United 1 Aston Villa 0	Old Trafford	8000
4	1919/20	26/04/20	Football League Division 1	Manchester United 0 Notts County 0	Old Trafford	30000
5	1923/24	26/04/24	Football League Division 2	Manchester United 2 Sheffield Wednesday 0	Old Trafford	7500
6	1929/30	26/04/30	Football League Division 1	Leeds United 3 Manchester United 1	Elland Road	10596
7	1946/47	26/04/47	Football League Division 1	Portsmouth 0 Manchester United 1	Fratton Park	30623
8	1951/52	26/04/52	Football League Division 1	Manchester United 6 Arsenal 1	Old Trafford	53651
9	1954/55	26/04/55	Football League Division 1	Charlton Athletic 1 Manchester United 1	The Valley	18149
10	1957/58	26/04/58	Football League Division 1	Chelsea 2 Manchester United 1	Stamford Bridge	45011
11	1964/65	26/04/65	Football League Division 1	Manchester United 3 Arsenal 1	Old Trafford	51625
12	1974/75	26/04/75	Football League Division 2	Manchester United 4 Blackpool 0	Old Trafford	58769
13	1976/77	26/04/77	Football League Division 1	Middlesbrough 3 Manchester United 0	Ayresome Park	21744
14	1979/80	26/04/80	Football League Division 1	Manchester United 2 Coventry City 1	Old Trafford	52154
15	1985/86	26/04/86	Football League Division 1	Manchester United 4 Leicester City 0	Old Trafford	38840
16	1991/92	26/04/92	Football League Division 1	Liverpool 2 Manchester United 0	Anfield	38669
17	2007/08	26/04/08	FA Premiership	Chelsea 2 Manchester United 1	Stamford Bridge	41828

APRIL 27

#	SEASON	DATE	COMPETITION / ROUND	MATCH RESULT	VENUE	ATT
1	1892/93	27/04/93	Football League Test Match	Newton Heath 5 Birmingham City 2	Bramall Lane	6000
2	1894/95	27/04/95	Football League Test Match	Newton Heath 0 Stoke City 3	Cobridge Stadium	10000
3	1900/01	27/04/01	Football League Division 2	Newton Heath 1 Chesterfield 0	Bank Street	1000
4	1907/08	27/04/08	FA Charity Shield	Manchester United 1 Queens Park Rangers 1	Stamford Bridge	6000
5	1908/09	27/04/09	Football League Division 1	Manchester United 1 Arsenal 4	Bank Street	10000
6	1911/12	27/04/12	Football League Division 1	Bolton Wanderers 1 Manchester United 1	Burnden Park	20000
7	1928/29	27/04/29	Football League Division 1	Everton 2 Manchester United 4	Goodison Park	19442
8	1934/35	27/04/35	Football League Division 2	Manchester United 2 Bradford Park Avenue 0	Old Trafford	8606
9	1948/49	27/04/49	Football League Division 1	Everton 2 Manchester United 0	Goodison Park	39106
10	1956/57	27/04/57	Football League Division 1	Cardiff City 2 Manchester United 3	Ninian Park	17708
11	1962/63	27/04/63	FA Cup Semi-Final	Manchester United 1 Southampton 0	Villa Park	65000
12	1965/66	27/04/66	Football League Division 1	Manchester United 2 Blackpool 1	Old Trafford	26953
13	1967/68	27/04/68	Football League Division 1	West Bromwich Albion 6 Manchester United 3	The Hawthorns	43412
14	1973/74	27/04/74	Football League Division 1	Manchester United 0 Manchester City 1	Old Trafford	56996
15	1984/85	27/04/85	Football League Division 1	Manchester United 2 Sunderland 2	Old Trafford	38979
16	1993/94	27/04/94	FA Premiership	Leeds United 0 Manchester United 2	Elland Road	41125
17	1997/98	27/04/98	FA Premiership	Crystal Palace 0 Manchester United 3	Selhurst Park	26180
18	2001/02	27/04/02	FA Premiership	Ipswich Town 0 Manchester United 1	Portman Road	28433
19	2002/03	27/04/03	FA Premiership	Tottenham Hotspur 0 Manchester United 2	White Hart Lane	36073

APRIL 28

#	SEASON	DATE	COMPETITION / ROUND	MATCH RESULT	VENUE	ATT
1	1893/94	28/04/94	Football League Test Match	Newton Heath 0 Liverpool 2	Ewood Park	3000
2	1899/00	28/04/00	Football League Division 2	Newton Heath 2 Chesterfield 1	Bank Street	6000
3	1905/06	28/04/06	Football League Division 2	Manchester United 6 Burton United 0	Bank Street	16000
4	1922/23	28/04/23	Football League Division 2	Barnsley 2 Manchester United 2	Oakwell	8000
5	1925/26	28/04/26	Football League Division 1	Manchester United 1 Cardiff City 0	Old Trafford	9116
6	1927/28	28/04/28	Football League Division 1	Arsenal 0 Manchester United 1	Highbury	22452
7	1933/34	28/04/34	Football League Division 2	Manchester United 1 Swansea City 1	Old Trafford	16678
8	1947/48	28/04/48	Football League Division 1	Blackpool 1 Manchester United 0	Bloomfield Road	32236
9	1950/51	28/04/51	Football League Division 1	Manchester United 6 Huddersfield Town 0	Old Trafford	25560
10	1961/62	28/04/62	Football League Division 1	Fulham 2 Manchester United 0	Craven Cottage	40113
11	1964/65	28/04/65	Football League Division 1	Aston Villa 2 Manchester United 1	Villa Park	36081
12	1972/73	28/04/73	Football League Division 1	Chelsea 1 Manchester United 0	Stamford Bridge	44184
13	1978/79	28/04/79	Football League Division 1	Manchester United 0 Derby County 0	Old Trafford	42546
14	1983/84	28/04/84	Football League Division 1	Manchester United 0 West Ham United 0	Old Trafford	44124
15	1995/96	28/04/96	FA Premiership	Manchester United 5 Nottingham Forest 0	Old Trafford	53926
16	2000/01	28/04/01	FA Premiership	Middlesbrough 0 Manchester United 2	Riverside Stadium	34417
17	2006/07	28/04/07	FA Premiership	Everton 2 Manchester United 4	Goodison Park	39682

APRIL 29

#	SEASON	DATE	COMPETITION / ROUND	MATCH RESULT	VENUE	ATT
1	1907/08	29/04/08	FA Charity Shield	Manchester United 4 Queens Park Rangers 0	Stamford Bridge	6000
2	1908/09	29/04/09	Football League Division 1	Bradford City 1 Manchester United 0	Valley Parade	30000
3	1910/11	29/04/11	Football League Division 1	Manchester United 5 Sunderland 1	Old Trafford	10000
4	1911/12	29/04/12	Football League Division 1	Manchester United 3 Blackburn Rovers 1	Old Trafford	20000
5	1921/22	29/04/22	Football League Division 1	Manchester United 1 Cardiff City 1	Old Trafford	18000
6	1932/33	29/04/33	Football League Division 2	Lincoln City 3 Manchester United 2	Sincil Bank	8507
7	1935/36	29/04/36	Football League Division 2	Bury 2 Manchester United 3	Gigg Lane	31562
8	1938/39	29/04/39	Football League Division 1	Bolton Wanderers 0 Manchester United 0	Burnden Park	10314
9	1949/50	29/04/50	Football League Division 1	Manchester United 3 Fulham 0	Old Trafford	11968
10	1956/57	29/04/57	Football League Division 1	Manchester United 1 West Bromwich Albion 1	Old Trafford	20357
11	1960/61	29/04/61	Football League Division 1	Manchester United 3 Cardiff City 3	Old Trafford	30320
12	1966/67	29/04/67	Football League Division 1	Manchester United 3 Aston Villa 1	Old Trafford	55782
13	1971/72	29/04/72	Football League Division 1	Manchester United 3 Stoke City 0	Old Trafford	34959
14	1973/74	29/04/74	Football League Division 1	Stoke City 1 Manchester United 0	Victoria Ground	27392
15	1977/78	29/04/78	Football League Division 1	Wolverhampton Wanderers 2 Manchester United 1	Molineux	24774
16	1988/89	29/04/89	Football League Division 1	Manchester United 0 Coventry City 1	Old Trafford	29799
17	1999/00	29/04/00	FA Premiership	Watford 2 Manchester United 3	Vicarage Road	20250
18	2005/06	29/04/06	FA Premiership	Chelsea 3 Manchester United 0	Stamford Bridge	42219
19	2007/08	29/04/08	Champions Lge Semi-Final 2nd Leg	Manchester United 1 Barcelona 0	Old Trafford	75061

APRIL 30

#	SEASON	DATE	COMPETITION / ROUND	MATCH RESULT	VENUE	ATT
1	1903/04	30/04/04	Football League Division 2	Manchester United 5 Leicester City 2	Bank Street	7000
2	1909/10	30/04/10	Football League Division 1	Manchester United 4 Middlesbrough 1	Old Trafford	10000
3	1920/21	30/04/21	Football League Division 1	Manchester United 0 Blackburn Rovers 1	Old Trafford	20000
4	1926/27	30/04/27	Football League Division 1	Manchester United 0 Sunderland 0	Old Trafford	17300
5	1931/32	30/04/32	Football League Division 2	Bristol City 2 Manchester United 1	Ashton Gate	5874
6	1937/38	30/04/38	Football League Division 2	West Ham United 1 Manchester United 0	Upton Park	14816
7	1948/49	30/04/49	Football League Division 1	Newcastle United 0 Manchester United 1	St James' Park	38266
8	1954/55	30/04/55	Football League Division 1	Manchester United 2 Chelsea 1	Old Trafford	34933
9	1959/60	30/04/60	Football League Division 1	Manchester United 5 Everton 0	Old Trafford	43823
10	1965/66	30/04/66	Football League Division 1	West Ham United 3 Manchester United 2	Upton Park	36416
11	1976/77	30/04/77	Football League Division 1	Manchester United 1 Queens Park Rangers 0	Old Trafford	50788
12	1978/79	30/04/79	Football League Division 1	Southampton 1 Manchester United 1	The Dell	21616
13	1982/83	30/04/83	Football League Division 1	Norwich City 1 Manchester United 1	Carrow Road	22233
14	1987/88	30/04/88	Football League Division 1	Manchester United 2 Queens Park Rangers 1	Old Trafford	35733
15	1989/90	30/04/90	Football League Division 1	Manchester United 0 Wimbledon 0	Old Trafford	29281
16	2001/02	30/04/02	Champions Lge Semi-Final 2nd Leg	Bayer Leverkusen 1 Manchester United 1	Bayarena	22500

UNITED in MAY

OVERALL PLAYING RECORD

	P	W	D	L	F	A		P	W	D	L	F	A		P	W	D	L	F	A
1st	13	8	2	3	23	13	11th	10	5	2	3	14	12	22nd	2	2	0	0	5	0
2nd	12	4	4	4	13	18	12th	6	2	3	1	14	7	23rd	0	0	0	0	0	0
3rd	11	3	2	6	15	19	13th	5	1	1	3	4	8	24th	0	0	0	0	0	0
4th	13	9	2	2	25	11	14th	6	3	1	2	11	10	25th	1	1	0	0	3	1
5th	13	7	4	2	25	13	15th	7	5	2	0	13	6	26th	3	3	0	0	12	3
6th	10	4	2	4	20	15	16th	4	1	1	2	5	8	27th	0	0	0	0	0	0
7th	14	9	4	1	32	14	17th	3	3	0	0	7	2	28th	0	0	0	0	0	0
8th	7	1	4	2	6	7	18th	2	2	0	0	4	1	29th	1	1	0	0	4	1
9th	7	6	1	0	17	4	19th	4	0	2	2	2	5	30th	0	0	0	0	0	0
10th	6	2	1	3	8	9	20th	3	0	1	2	3	5	31st	1	1	0	0	3	2
							21st	4	1	3	0	5	4							

OVERALL 168 84 42 42 293 198

MAY 1

#	SEASON	DATE	COMPETITION / ROUND	MATCH RESULT	VENUE	ATT
1	1919/20	01/05/20	Football League Division 1	Notts County 0 Manchester United 2	Meadow Lane	20000
2	1925/26	01/05/26	Football League Division 1	Manchester United 3 West Bromwich Albion 2	Old Trafford	9974
3	1947/48	01/05/48	Football League Division 1	Manchester United 4 Blackburn Rovers 1	Maine Road	44439
4	1962/63	01/05/63	Football League Division 1	Manchester United 1 Sheffield Wednesday 3	Old Trafford	31878
5	1970/71	01/05/71	Football League Division 1	Blackpool 1 Manchester United 1	Bloomfield Road	29857
6	1975/76	01/05/76	FA Cup Final	Manchester United 0 Southampton 1	Wembley	100000
7	1981/82	01/05/82	Football League Division 1	Manchester United 1 Southampton 0	Old Trafford	40038
8	1993/94	01/05/94	FA Premiership	Ipswich Town 1 Manchester United 2	Portman Road	22559
9	1994/95	01/05/95	FA Premiership	Coventry City 2 Manchester United 3	Highfield Road	21885
10	1998/99	01/05/99	FA Premiership	Manchester United 2 Aston Villa 1	Old Trafford	55189
11	2003/04	01/05/04	FA Premiership	Blackburn Rovers 1 Manchester United 0	Ewood Park	29616
12	2004/05	01/05/05	FA Premiership	Charlton Athletic 0 Manchester United 4	The Valley	26789
13	2005/06	01/05/06	FA Premiership	Manchester United 0 Middlesbrough 0	Old Trafford	69531

MAY 2

#	SEASON	DATE	COMPETITION / ROUND	MATCH RESULT	VENUE	ATT
1	1920/21	02/05/21	Football League Division 1	Derby County 1 Manchester United 1	Baseball Ground	8000
2	1924/25	02/05/25	Football League Division 2	Barnsley 0 Manchester United 0	Oakwell	11250
3	1930/31	02/05/31	Football League Division 1	Manchester United 4 Middlesbrough 4	Old Trafford	3969
4	1935/36	02/05/36	Football League Division 2	Hull City 1 Manchester United 1	Anlaby Road	4540
5	1948/49	02/05/49	Football League Division 1	Manchester United 1 Middlesbrough 0	Maine Road	20158
6	1982/83	02/05/83	Football League Division 1	Arsenal 3 Manchester United 0	Highbury	23602
7	1986/87	02/05/87	Football League Division 1	Manchester United 0 Wimbledon 1	Old Trafford	31686
8	1987/88	02/05/88	Football League Division 1	Oxford United 0 Manchester United 2	Manor Ground	8966
9	1988/89	02/05/89	Football League Division 1	Manchester United 1 Wimbledon 0	Old Trafford	23368
10	1989/90	02/05/90	Football League Division 1	Nottingham Forest 4 Manchester United 0	City Ground	21186
11	1991/92	02/05/92	Football League Division 1	Manchester United 3 Tottenham Hotspur 1	Old Trafford	44595
12	2006/07	02/05/07	Champions Lge Semi-Final 2nd Leg	AC Milan 3 Manchester United 0	Stadio San Siro	78500

MAY 3

#	SEASON	DATE	COMPETITION / ROUND	MATCH RESULT	VENUE	ATT
1	1923/24	03/05/24	Football League Division 2	Sheffield Wednesday 2 Manchester United 0	Hillsborough	7250
2	1929/30	03/05/30	Football League Division 1	Manchester United 1 Sheffield United 5	Old Trafford	15268
3	1946/47	03/05/47	Football League Division 1	Liverpool 1 Manchester United 0	Anfield	48800
4	1957/58	03/05/58	FA Cup Final	Manchester United 0 Bolton Wanderers 2	Wembley	100000
5	1976/77	03/05/77	Football League Division 1	Liverpool 1 Manchester United 0	Anfield	53046
6	1979/80	03/05/80	Football League Division 1	Leeds United 2 Manchester United 0	Elland Road	39625
7	1985/86	03/05/86	Football League Division 1	Watford 1 Manchester United 0	Vicarage Road	18414
8	1992/93	03/05/93	FA Premiership	Manchester United 3 Blackburn Rovers 1	Old Trafford	40447
9	1996/97	03/05/97	FA Premiership	Leicester City 2 Manchester United 2	Filbert Street	21068
10	2002/03	03/05/03	FA Premiership	Manchester United 4 Charlton Athletic 1	Old Trafford	67721
11	2007/08	03/05/08	FA Premiership	Manchester United 4 West Ham United 1	Old Trafford	76013

MAY 4

#	SEASON	DATE	COMPETITION / ROUND	MATCH RESULT	VENUE	ATT
1	1928/29	04/05/29	Football League Division 1	Manchester United 0 Portsmouth 0	Old Trafford	17728
2	1934/35	04/05/35	Football League Division 2	Plymouth Argyle 0 Manchester United 2	Home Park	10767
3	1948/49	04/05/49	Football League Division 1	Manchester United 3 Sheffield United 2	Maine Road	20880
4	1956/57	04/05/57	FA Cup Final	Manchester United 1 Aston Villa 2	Wembley	100000
5	1962/63	04/05/63	Football League Division 1	Burnley 0 Manchester United 1	Turf Moor	30266
6	1965/66	04/05/66	Football League Division 1	West Bromwich Albion 3 Manchester United 3	The Hawthorns	22609
7	1967/68	04/05/68	Football League Division 1	Manchester United 6 Newcastle United 0	Old Trafford	59976
8	1975/76	04/05/76	Football League Division 1	Manchester United 2 Manchester City 0	Old Trafford	59517
9	1984/85	04/05/85	Football League Division 1	Norwich City 0 Manchester United 1	Carrow Road	15502
10	1986/87	04/05/87	Football League Division 1	Tottenham Hotspur 4 Manchester United 0	White Hart Lane	36692
11	1990/91	04/05/91	Football League Division 1	Manchester United 1 Manchester City 0	Old Trafford	45286
12	1993/94	04/05/94	FA Premiership	Manchester United 2 Southampton 0	Old Trafford	44705
13	1997/98	04/05/98	FA Premiership	Manchester United 3 Leeds United 0	Old Trafford	55167

			MAY 5			
#	SEASON	DATE	COMPETITION / ROUND	MATCH RESULT	VENUE	ATT
1	1927/28	05/05/28	Football League Division 1	Manchester United 6 Liverpool 1	Old Trafford	30625
2	1933/34	05/05/34	Football League Division 2	Millwall 0 Manchester United 2	The Den	24003
3	1950/51	05/05/51	Football League Division 1	Blackpool 1 Manchester United 1	Bloomfield Road	22864
4	1970/71	05/05/71	Football League Division 1	Manchester City 3 Manchester United 4	Maine Road	43626
5	1978/79	05/05/79	Football League Division 1	West Bromwich Albion 1 Manchester United 0	The Hawthorns	27960
6	1981/82	05/05/82	Football League Division 1	Nottingham Forest 0 Manchester United 1	City Ground	18449
7	1983/84	05/05/84	Football League Division 1	Everton 1 Manchester United 1	Goodison Park	28802
8	1989/90	05/05/90	Football League Division 1	Manchester United 1 Charlton Athletic 0	Old Trafford	35389
9	1995/96	05/05/96	FA Premiership	Middlesbrough 0 Manchester United 3	Riverside Stadium	29921
10	1996/97	05/05/97	FA Premiership	Manchester United 3 Middlesbrough 3	Old Trafford	54489
11	1998/99	05/05/99	FA Premiership	Liverpool 2 Manchester United 2	Anfield	44702
12	2000/01	05/05/01	FA Premiership	Manchester United 0 Derby County 1	Old Trafford	67526
13	2006/07	05/05/07	FA Premiership	Manchester City 0 Manchester United 1	Eastlands Stadium	47244

			MAY 6			
#	SEASON	DATE	COMPETITION / ROUND	MATCH RESULT	VENUE	ATT
1	1921/22	06/05/22	Football League Division 1	Cardiff City 3 Manchester United 1	Ninian Park	16000
2	1932/33	06/05/33	Football League Division 2	Manchester United 1 Swansea City 1	Old Trafford	65988
3	1938/39	06/05/39	Football League Division 1	Manchester United 2 Liverpool 0	Old Trafford	12073
4	1962/63	06/05/63	Football League Division 1	Manchester United 2 Arsenal 3	Old Trafford	35999
5	1966/67	06/05/67	Football League Division 1	West Ham United 1 Manchester United 6	Upton Park	38424
6	1984/85	06/05/85	Football League Division 1	Manchester United 2 Nottingham Forest 0	Old Trafford	41775
7	1986/87	06/05/87	Football League Division 1	Coventry City 1 Manchester United 1	Highfield Road	23407
8	1988/89	06/05/89	Football League Division 1	Southampton 2 Manchester United 1	The Dell	17021
9	1990/91	06/05/91	Football League Division 1	Arsenal 3 Manchester United 1	Highbury	40229
10	1999/00	06/05/00	FA Premiership	Manchester United 3 Tottenham Hotspur 1	Old Trafford	61629

			MAY 7			
#	SEASON	DATE	COMPETITION / ROUND	MATCH RESULT	VENUE	ATT
1	1920/21	07/05/21	Football League Division 1	Manchester United 3 Derby County 0	Old Trafford	10000
2	1926/27	07/05/27	Football League Division 1	West Bromwich Albion 2 Manchester United 2	The Hawthorns	6668
3	1931/32	07/05/32	Football League Division 2	Southampton 1 Manchester United 1	The Dell	6128
4	1937/38	07/05/38	Football League Division 2	Manchester United 2 Bury 0	Old Trafford	53604
5	1948/49	07/05/49	Football League Division 1	Manchester United 3 Portsmouth 2	Maine Road	49808
6	1965/66	07/05/66	Football League Division 1	Blackburn Rovers 1 Manchester United 4	Ewood Park	14513
7	1976/77	07/05/77	Football League Division 1	Bristol City 1 Manchester United 1	Ashton Gate	28864
8	1978/79	07/05/79	Football League Division 1	Manchester United 3 Wolverhampton Wanderers 2	Old Trafford	39402
9	1982/83	07/05/83	Football League Division 1	Manchester United 2 Swansea City 1	Old Trafford	35724
10	1983/84	07/05/84	Football League Division 1	Manchester United 1 Ipswich Town 2	Old Trafford	44257
11	1987/88	07/05/88	Football League Division 1	Manchester United 4 Portsmouth 1	Old Trafford	35105
12	1994/95	07/05/95	FA Premiership	Manchester United 1 Sheffield Wednesday 0	Old Trafford	43868
13	2004/05	07/05/05	FA Premiership	Manchester United 1 West Bromwich Albion 1	Old Trafford	67827
14	2005/06	07/05/06	FA Premiership	Manchester United 4 Charlton Athletic 0	Old Trafford	73006

			MAY 8			
#	SEASON	DATE	COMPETITION / ROUND	MATCH RESULT	VENUE	ATT
1	1957/58	08/05/58	European Cup Semi-Final 1st Leg	Manchester United 2 AC Milan 1	Old Trafford	44880
2	1981/82	08/05/82	Football League Division 1	West Ham United 1 Manchester United 1	Upton Park	26337
3	1988/89	08/05/89	Football League Division 1	Queens Park Rangers 3 Manchester United 2	Loftus Road	10017
4	1993/94	08/05/94	FA Premiership	Manchester United 0 Coventry City 0	Old Trafford	44717
5	1996/97	08/05/97	FA Premiership	Manchester United 0 Newcastle United 0	Old Trafford	55236
6	2001/02	08/05/02	FA Premiership	Manchester United 0 Arsenal 1	Old Trafford	67580
7	2003/04	08/05/04	FA Premiership	Manchester United 1 Chelsea 1	Old Trafford	67609

			MAY 9			
#	SEASON	DATE	COMPETITION / ROUND	MATCH RESULT	VENUE	ATT
1	1965/66	09/05/66	Football League Division 1	Manchester United 6 Aston Villa 1	Old Trafford	23039
2	1982/83	09/05/83	Football League Division 1	Manchester United 3 Luton Town 0	Old Trafford	34213
3	1986/87	09/05/87	Football League Division 1	Manchester United 3 Aston Villa 1	Old Trafford	35179
4	1987/88	09/05/88	Football League Division 1	Manchester United 2 Wimbledon 1	Old Trafford	28040
5	1992/93	09/05/93	FA Premiership	Wimbledon 1 Manchester United 2	Selhurst Park	30115
6	1998/99	09/05/99	FA Premiership	Middlesbrough 0 Manchester United 1	Riverside Stadium	34665
7	2006/07	09/05/07	FA Premiership	Chelsea 0 Manchester United 0	Stamford Bridge	41794

			MAY 10			
#	SEASON	DATE	COMPETITION / ROUND	MATCH RESULT	VENUE	ATT
1	1946/47	10/05/47	Football League Division 1	Preston North End 1 Manchester United 1	Deepdale	23278
2	1962/63	10/05/63	Football League Division 1	Birmingham City 2 Manchester United 1	St Andrews	21814
3	1988/89	10/05/89	Football League Division 1	Manchester United 1 Everton 2	Old Trafford	26722
4	1994/95	10/05/95	FA Premiership	Manchester United 2 Southampton 1	Old Trafford	43479
5	1997/98	10/05/98	FA Premiership	Barnsley 0 Manchester United 2	Oakwell	18694
6	2004/05	10/05/05	FA Premiership	Manchester United 1 Chelsea 3	Old Trafford	67832

MAY 11

#	SEASON	DATE	COMPETITION / ROUND	MATCH RESULT	VENUE	ATT
1	1967/68	11/05/68	Football League Division 1	Manchester United 1 Sunderland 2	Old Trafford	62963
2	1976/77	11/05/77	Football League Division 1	Stoke City 3 Manchester United 3	Victoria Ground	24204
3	1982/83	11/05/83	Football League Division 1	Tottenham Hotspur 2 Manchester United 0	White Hart Lane	32803
4	1984/85	11/05/85	Football League Division 1	Queens Park Rangers 1 Manchester United 3	Loftus Road	20483
5	1990/91	11/05/91	Football League Division 1	Crystal Palace 3 Manchester United 0	Selhurst Park	25301
6	1995/96	11/05/96	FA Cup Final	Manchester United 1 Liverpool 0	Wembley	79007
7	1996/97	11/05/97	FA Premiership	Manchester United 2 West Ham United 0	Old Trafford	55249
8	2001/02	11/05/02	FA Premiership	Manchester United 0 Charlton Athletic 0	Old Trafford	67571
9	2002/03	11/05/03	FA Premiership	Everton 1 Manchester United 2	Goodison Park	40168
10	2007/08	11/05/08	FA Premiership	Wigan Athletic 0 Manchester United 2	JJB Stadium	25133

MAY 12

#	SEASON	DATE	COMPETITION / ROUND	MATCH RESULT	VENUE	ATT
1	1964/65	12/05/65	ICFC Quarter-Final 1st Leg	Strasbourg 0 Manchester United 5	Stade de la Meinau	30000
2	1978/79	12/05/79	FA Cup Final	Manchester United 2 Arsenal 3	Wembley	100000
3	1981/82	12/05/82	Football League Division 1	West Bromwich Albion 0 Manchester United 3	The Hawthorns	19707
4	1983/84	12/05/84	Football League Division 1	Tottenham Hotspur 1 Manchester United 1	White Hart Lane	39790
5	1989/90	12/05/90	FA Cup Final	Manchester United 3 Crystal Palace 3	Wembley	80000
6	1998/99	12/05/99	FA Premiership	Blackburn Rovers 0 Manchester United 0	Ewood Park	30436

MAY 13

#	SEASON	DATE	COMPETITION / ROUND	MATCH RESULT	VENUE	ATT
1	1966/67	13/05/67	Football League Division 1	Manchester United 0 Stoke City 0	Old Trafford	61071
2	1984/85	13/05/85	Football League Division 1	Watford 5 Manchester United 1	Vicarage Road	20500
3	1988/89	13/05/89	Football League Division 1	Manchester United 2 Newcastle United 0	Old Trafford	30379
4	2000/01	13/05/01	FA Premiership	Southampton 2 Manchester United 1	The Dell	15526
5	2006/07	13/05/07	FA Premiership	Manchester United 0 West Ham United 1	Old Trafford	75927

MAY 14

#	SEASON	DATE	COMPETITION / ROUND	MATCH RESULT	VENUE	ATT
1	1957/58	14/05/58	European Cup Semi-Final 2nd Leg	AC Milan 4 Manchester United 0	Stadio San Siro	80000
2	1976/77	14/05/77	Football League Division 1	Manchester United 3 Arsenal 2	Old Trafford	53232
3	1982/83	14/05/83	Football League Division 1	Notts County 3 Manchester United 2	Meadow Lane	14395
4	1993/94	14/05/94	FA Cup Final	Manchester United 4 Chelsea 0	Wembley	79634
5	1994/95	14/05/95	FA Premiership	West Ham United 1 Manchester United 1	Upton Park	24783
6	1999/00	14/05/00	FA Premiership	Aston Villa 0 Manchester United 1	Villa Park	39217

MAY 15

#	SEASON	DATE	COMPETITION / ROUND	MATCH RESULT	VENUE	ATT
1	1962/63	15/05/63	Football League Division 1	Manchester City 1 Manchester United 1	Maine Road	52424
2	1967/68	15/05/68	European Cup Semi-Final 2nd Leg	Real Madrid 3 Manchester United 3	Bernabeu Stadium	125000
3	1968/69	15/05/69	European Cup Semi-Final 2nd Leg	Manchester United 1 AC Milan 0	Old Trafford	63103
4	1981/82	15/05/82	Football League Division 1	Manchester United 2 Stoke City 0	Old Trafford	43072
5	1990/91	15/05/91	European CWC Final	Manchester United 2 Barcelona 1	Feyenoord Stadion	50000
6	2003/04	15/05/04	FA Premiership	Aston Villa 0 Manchester United 2	Villa Park	42573
7	2004/05	15/05/05	FA Premiership	Southampton 1 Manchester United 2	St Mary's Stadium	32066

MAY 16

#	SEASON	DATE	COMPETITION / ROUND	MATCH RESULT	VENUE	ATT
1	1976/77	16/05/77	Football League Division 1	West Ham United 4 Manchester United 2	Upton Park	29904
2	1978/79	16/05/79	Football League Division 1	Manchester United 1 Chelsea 1	Old Trafford	38109
3	1983/84	16/05/84	Football League Division 1	Nottingham Forest 2 Manchester United 0	City Ground	23651
4	1998/99	16/05/99	FA Premiership	Manchester United 2 Tottenham Hotspur 1	Old Trafford	55189

MAY 17

#	SEASON	DATE	COMPETITION / ROUND	MATCH RESULT	VENUE	ATT
1	1946/47	17/05/47	Football League Division 1	Manchester United 3 Portsmouth 0	Maine Road	37614
2	1968/69	17/05/69	Football League Division 1	Manchester United 3 Leicester City 2	Old Trafford	45860
3	1989/90	17/05/90	FA Cup Final Replay	Manchester United 1 Crystal Palace 0	Wembley	80000

MAY 18

#	SEASON	DATE	COMPETITION / ROUND	MATCH RESULT	VENUE	ATT
1	1962/63	18/05/63	Football League Division 1	Manchester United 3 Leyton Orient 1	Old Trafford	32759
2	1984/85	18/05/85	FA Cup Final	Manchester United 1 Everton 0	Wembley	100000

MAY 19

#	SEASON	DATE	COMPETITION / ROUND	MATCH RESULT	VENUE	ATT
1	1964/65	19/05/65	ICFC Quarter-Final 2nd Leg	Manchester United 0 Strasbourg 0	Old Trafford	34188
2	1965/66	19/05/66	Football League Division 1	Manchester United 1 Leeds United 1	Old Trafford	35008
3	2000/01	19/05/01	FA Premiership	Tottenham Hotspur 3 Manchester United 1	White Hart Lane	36072
4	2006/07	19/05/07	FA Cup Final	Manchester United 0 Chelsea 1	Wembley	89826

MAY 20

#	SEASON	DATE	COMPETITION / ROUND	MATCH RESULT	VENUE	ATT
1	1962/63	20/05/63	Football League Division 1	Nottingham Forest 3 Manchester United 2	City Ground	16130
2	1990/91	20/05/91	Football League Division 1	Manchester United 1 Tottenham Hotspur 1	Old Trafford	46791
3	1994/95	20/05/95	FA Cup Final	Manchester United 0 Everton 1	Wembley	79592

MAY 21

#	SEASON	DATE	COMPETITION / ROUND	MATCH RESULT	VENUE	ATT
1	1976/77	21/05/77	FA Cup Final	Manchester United 2 Liverpool 1	Wembley	100000
2	1982/83	21/05/83	FA Cup Final	Manchester United 2 Brighton 2	Wembley	100000
3	2004/05	21/05/05	FA Cup Final	Manchester United 0 Arsenal 0	Millennium Stadium	71876
4	2007/08	21/05/08	Champions League Final	Manchester United 1 Chelsea 1	Luzhniki Stadium	67310

MAY 22

#	SEASON	DATE	COMPETITION / ROUND	MATCH RESULT	VENUE	ATT
1	1998/99	22/05/99	FA Cup Final	Manchester United 2 Newcastle United 0	Wembley	79101
2	2003/04	22/05/04	FA Cup Final	Manchester United 3 Millwall 0	Millennium Stadium	71350

MAY 25

#	SEASON	DATE	COMPETITION / ROUND	MATCH RESULT	VENUE	ATT
1	1962/63	25/05/63	FA Cup Final	Manchester United 3 Leicester City 1	Wembley	100000

MAY 26

#	SEASON	DATE	COMPETITION / ROUND	MATCH RESULT	VENUE	ATT
1	1946/47	26/05/47	Football League Division 1	Manchester United 6 Sheffield United 2	Maine Road	34059
2	1982/83	26/05/83	FA Cup Final Replay	Manchester United 4 Brighton 0	Wembley	92000
3	1998/99	26/05/99	Champions League Final	Manchester United 2 Bayern Munich 1	Estadio Camp Nou	90000

MAY 29

#	SEASON	DATE	COMPETITION / ROUND	MATCH RESULT	VENUE	ATT
1	1967/68	29/05/68	European Cup Final	Manchester United 4 Benfica 1	Wembley	100000

MAY 31

#	SEASON	DATE	COMPETITION / ROUND	MATCH RESULT	VENUE	ATT
1	1964/65	31/05/65	ICFC Semi-Final 1st Leg	Manchester United 3 Ferencvaros 2	Old Trafford	39902

UNITED in JUNE

OVERALL PLAYING RECORD

	P	W	D	L	F	A
6th	1	0	0	1	0	1
16th	1	0	0	1	1	2
OVERALL	2	0	0	2	1	3

JUNE 6

#	SEASON	DATE	COMPETITION / ROUND	MATCH RESULT	VENUE	ATT
1	1964/65	06/06/65	ICFC Semi-Final 2nd Leg	Ferencvaros 1 Manchester United 0	Nep Stadion	50000

JUNE 16

#	SEASON	DATE	COMPETITION / ROUND	MATCH RESULT	VENUE	ATT
1	1964/65	16/06/65	ICFC Semi-Final Replay	Ferencvaros 2 Manchester United 1	Nep Stadion	60000

UNITED in AUGUST

OVERALL PLAYING RECORD

	P	W	D	L	F	A		P	W	D	L	F	A		P	W	D	L	F	A
1st	1	0	0	1	1	2	11th	3	3	0	0	10	1	22nd	15	4	8	3	25	25
2nd	0	0	0	0	0	0	12th	5	1	2	2	7	7	23rd	22	14	6	2	46	22
3rd	1	0	1	0	1	1	13th	5	2	1	2	3	4	24th	15	8	3	4	28	22
4th	0	0	0	0	0	0	14th	6	2	2	2	9	8	25th	15	9	4	2	27	16
5th	1	0	1	0	1	1	15th	8	1	3	4	8	11	26th	17	6	5	6	21	22
6th	0	0	0	0	0	0	16th	4	3	0	1	10	4	27th	23	10	6	7	29	21
7th	1	0	1	0	1	1	17th	7	5	1	1	12	4	28th	21	12	6	3	36	17
8th	2	0	1	1	2	4	18th	7	2	5	0	15	11	29th	19	8	4	7	30	25
9th	3	1	1	1	5	5	19th	16	5	4	7	15	21	30th	23	8	5	10	34	30
10th	4	2	1	1	5	4	20th	13	11	1	1	32	12	31st	20	11	4	5	42	25
							21st	9	4	3	2	12	11							

OVERALL   286   132   79   75   467   337

AUGUST 1

#	SEASON	DATE	COMPETITION / ROUND	MATCH RESULT	VENUE	ATT
1	1999/00	01/08/99	FA Charity Shield	Manchester United 1 Arsenal 2	Wembley	70185

AUGUST 3

#	SEASON	DATE	COMPETITION / ROUND	MATCH RESULT	VENUE	ATT
1	1997/98	03/08/97	FA Charity Shield	Manchester United 1 Chelsea 1	Wembley	73636

AUGUST 5

#	SEASON	DATE	COMPETITION / ROUND	MATCH RESULT	VENUE	ATT
1	2007/08	05/08/07	FA Charity Shield	Manchester United 1 Chelsea 1	Wembley	80731

AUGUST 7

#	SEASON	DATE	COMPETITION / ROUND	MATCH RESULT	VENUE	ATT
1	1993/94	07/08/93	FA Charity Shield	Manchester United 1 Arsenal 1	Wembley	66519

AUGUST 8

#	SEASON	DATE	COMPETITION / ROUND	MATCH RESULT	VENUE	ATT
1	1999/00	08/08/99	FA Premiership	Everton 1 Manchester United 1	Goodison Park	39141
2	2004/05	08/08/04	FA Charity Shield	Manchester United 1 Arsenal 3	Millennium Stadium	63317

AUGUST 9

#	SEASON	DATE	COMPETITION / ROUND	MATCH RESULT	VENUE	ATT
1	1969/70	09/08/69	Football League Division 1	Crystal Palace 2 Manchester United 2	Selhurst Park	48610
2	1998/99	09/08/98	FA Charity Shield	Manchester United 0 Arsenal 3	Wembley	67342
3	2005/06	09/08/05	Champions League Qual. Round 1st Leg	Manchester United 3 Debreceni 0	Old Trafford	51701

AUGUST 10

#	SEASON	DATE	COMPETITION / ROUND	MATCH RESULT	VENUE	ATT
1	1968/69	10/08/68	Football League Division 1	Manchester United 2 Everton 1	Old Trafford	61311
2	1985/86	10/08/85	FA Charity Shield	Manchester United 0 Everton 2	Wembley	82000
3	1997/98	10/08/97	FA Premiership	Tottenham Hotspur 0 Manchester United 2	White Hart Lane	26359
4	2003/04	10/08/03	FA Charity Shield	Manchester United 1 Arsenal 1	Millennium Stadium	59293

AUGUST 11

#	SEASON	DATE	COMPETITION / ROUND	MATCH RESULT	VENUE	ATT
1	1996/97	11/08/96	FA Charity Shield	Manchester United 4 Newcastle United 0	Wembley	73214
2	1999/00	11/08/99	FA Premiership	Manchester United 4 Sheffield Wednesday 0	Old Trafford	54941
3	2004/05	11/08/04	Champions League Qual. Round 1st Leg	Dinamo Bucharest 1 Manchester United 2	National Stadium	58000

AUGUST 12

#	SEASON	DATE	COMPETITION / ROUND	MATCH RESULT	VENUE	ATT
1	1967/68	12/08/67	FA Charity Shield	Manchester United 3 Tottenham Hotspur 3	Old Trafford	54106
2	1972/73	12/08/72	Football League Division 1	Manchester United 1 Ipswich Town 2	Old Trafford	51459
3	1998/99	12/08/98	Champions League Qual. Round 1st Leg	Manchester United 2 LKS Lodz 0	Old Trafford	50906
4	2001/02	12/08/01	FA Charity Shield	Manchester United 1 Liverpool 2	Millennium Stadium	70227
5	2007/08	12/08/07	FA Premiership	Manchester United 0 Reading 0	Old Trafford	75655

AUGUST 13

#	SEASON	DATE	COMPETITION / ROUND	MATCH RESULT	VENUE	ATT
1	1969/70	13/08/69	Football League Division 1	Manchester United 0 Everton 2	Old Trafford	57752
2	1977/78	13/08/77	FA Charity Shield	Manchester United 0 Liverpool 0	Wembley	82000
3	1997/98	13/08/97	FA Premiership	Manchester United 1 Southampton 0	Old Trafford	55008
4	2000/01	13/08/00	FA Charity Shield	Manchester United 0 Chelsea 2	Wembley	65148
5	2005/06	13/08/05	FA Premiership	Everton 0 Manchester United 2	Goodison Park	38610

AUGUST 14

#	SEASON	DATE	COMPETITION / ROUND	MATCH RESULT	VENUE	ATT
1	1965/66	14/08/65	FA Charity Shield	Manchester United 2 Liverpool 2	Old Trafford	48502
2	1968/69	14/08/68	Football League Division 1	West Bromwich Albion 3 Manchester United 1	The Hawthorns	38299
3	1971/72	14/08/71	Football League Division 1	Derby County 2 Manchester United 2	Baseball Ground	35886
4	1994/95	14/08/94	FA Charity Shield	Manchester United 2 Blackburn Rovers 0	Wembley	60402
5	1999/00	14/08/99	FA Premiership	Manchester United 2 Leeds United 0	Old Trafford	55187
6	2002/03	14/08/02	Champions League Qual. Round 1st Leg	Zalaegerszeg 1 Manchester United 0	Ferenc Puskas Stadium	40000

AUGUST 15

#	SEASON	DATE	COMPETITION / ROUND	MATCH RESULT	VENUE	ATT
1	1970/71	15/08/70	Football League Division 1	Manchester United 0 Leeds United 1	Old Trafford	59365
2	1972/73	15/08/72	Football League Division 1	Liverpool 2 Manchester United 0	Anfield	54789
3	1987/88	15/08/87	Football League Division 1	Southampton 2 Manchester United 2	The Dell	21214
4	1992/93	15/08/92	FA Premiership	Sheffield United 2 Manchester United 1	Bramall Lane	28070
5	1993/94	15/08/93	FA Premiership	Norwich City 0 Manchester United 2	Carrow Road	19705
6	1998/99	15/08/98	FA Premiership	Manchester United 2 Leicester City 2	Old Trafford	55052
7	2004/05	15/08/04	FA Premiership	Chelsea 1 Manchester United 0	Stamford Bridge	41813
8	2007/08	15/08/07	FA Premiership	Portsmouth 1 Manchester United 1	Fratton Park	20510

AUGUST 16

#	SEASON	DATE	COMPETITION / ROUND	MATCH RESULT	VENUE	ATT
1	1969/70	16/08/69	Football League Division 1	Manchester United 1 Southampton 4	Old Trafford	46328
2	1975/76	16/08/75	Football League Division 1	Wolverhampton Wanderers 0 Manchester United 2	Molineux	32348
3	1980/81	16/08/80	Football League Division 1	Manchester United 2 Middlesbrough 0	Old Trafford	54394
4	2003/04	16/08/03	FA Premiership	Manchester United 4 Bolton Wanderers 0	Old Trafford	67647

AUGUST 17

#	SEASON	DATE	COMPETITION / ROUND	MATCH RESULT	VENUE	ATT
1	1963/64	17/08/63	FA Charity Shield	Everton 4 Manchester United 0	Goodison Park	54840
2	1968/69	17/08/68	Football League Division 1	Manchester City 0 Manchester United 0	Maine Road	63052
3	1974/75	17/08/74	Football League Division 2	Leyton Orient 0 Manchester United 2	Brisbane Road	17772
4	1985/86	17/08/85	Football League Division 1	Manchester United 4 Aston Villa 0	Old Trafford	49743
5	1991/92	17/08/91	Football League Division 1	Manchester United 2 Notts County 0	Old Trafford	46278
6	1996/97	17/08/96	FA Premiership	Wimbledon 0 Manchester United 3	Selhurst Park	25786
7	2002/03	17/08/02	FA Premiership	Manchester United 1 West Bromwich Albion 0	Old Trafford	67645

AUGUST 18

#	SEASON	DATE	COMPETITION / ROUND	MATCH RESULT	VENUE	ATT
1	1951/52	18/08/51	Football League Division 1	West Bromwich Albion 3 Manchester United 3	The Hawthorns	27486
2	1956/57	18/08/56	Football League Division 1	Manchester United 2 Birmingham City 2	Old Trafford	32752
3	1962/63	18/08/62	Football League Division 1	Manchester United 2 West Bromwich Albion 2	Old Trafford	51685
4	1971/72	18/08/71	Football League Division 1	Chelsea 2 Manchester United 3	Stamford Bridge	54763
5	1979/80	18/08/79	Football League Division 1	Southampton 1 Manchester United 1	The Dell	21768
6	1990/91	18/08/90	FA Charity Shield	Manchester United 1 Liverpool 1	Wembley	66558
7	1993/94	18/08/93	FA Premiership	Manchester United 3 Sheffield United 0	Old Trafford	41949

AUGUST 19

#	SEASON	DATE	COMPETITION / ROUND	MATCH RESULT	VENUE	ATT
1	1950/51	19/08/50	Football League Division 1	Manchester United 1 Fulham 0	Old Trafford	44042
2	1953/54	19/08/53	Football League Division 1	Manchester United 1 Chelsea 1	Old Trafford	28936
3	1961/62	19/08/61	Football League Division 1	West Ham United 1 Manchester United 1	Upton Park	32628
4	1967/68	19/08/67	Football League Division 1	Everton 3 Manchester United 1	Goodison Park	61452
5	1969/70	19/08/69	Football League Division 1	Everton 3 Manchester United 0	Goodison Park	53185
6	1970/71	19/08/70	Football League Division 1	Manchester United 0 Chelsea 0	Old Trafford	50979
7	1972/73	19/08/72	Football League Division 1	Everton 2 Manchester United 0	Goodison Park	52348
8	1975/76	19/08/75	Football League Division 1	Birmingham City 0 Manchester United 2	St Andrews	33177
9	1978/79	19/08/78	Football League Division 1	Manchester United 1 Birmingham City 0	Old Trafford	56139
10	1980/81	19/08/80	Football League Division 1	Wolverhampton Wanderers 1 Manchester United 0	Molineux	31955
11	1987/88	19/08/87	Football League Division 1	Manchester United 0 Arsenal 0	Old Trafford	43893
12	1989/90	19/08/89	Football League Division 1	Manchester United 4 Arsenal 1	Old Trafford	47245
13	1992/93	19/08/92	FA Premiership	Manchester United 0 Everton 3	Old Trafford	31901
14	1995/96	19/08/95	FA Premiership	Aston Villa 3 Manchester United 1	Villa Park	34655
15	2001/02	19/08/01	FA Premiership	Manchester United 3 Fulham 2	Old Trafford	67534
16	2007/08	19/08/07	FA Premiership	Manchester City 1 Manchester United 0	Eastlands Stadium	44955

AUGUST 20

#	SEASON	DATE	COMPETITION / ROUND	MATCH RESULT	VENUE	ATT
1	1949/50	20/08/49	Football League Division 1	Derby County 0 Manchester United 1	Baseball Ground	35687
2	1955/56	20/08/55	Football League Division 1	Birmingham City 2 Manchester United 2	St Andrews	37994
3	1956/57	20/08/56	Football League Division 1	Preston North End 1 Manchester United 3	Deepdale	32569
4	1960/61	20/08/60	Football League Division 1	Manchester United 1 Blackburn Rovers 3	Old Trafford	47778
5	1966/67	20/08/66	Football League Division 1	Manchester United 5 West Bromwich Albion 3	Old Trafford	41343
6	1971/72	20/08/71	Football League Division 1	Manchester United 3 Arsenal 1	Anfield	27649
7	1977/78	20/08/77	Football League Division 1	Birmingham City 1 Manchester United 4	St Andrews	28005
8	1983/84	20/08/83	FA Charity Shield	Manchester United 2 Liverpool 0	Wembley	92000
9	1985/86	20/08/85	Football League Division 1	Ipswich Town 0 Manchester United 1	Portman Road	18777
10	1994/95	20/08/94	FA Premiership	Manchester United 2 Queens Park Rangers 0	Old Trafford	43214
11	2000/01	20/08/00	FA Premiership	Manchester United 2 Newcastle United 0	Old Trafford	67477
12	2005/06	20/08/05	FA Premiership	Manchester United 1 Aston Villa 0	Old Trafford	67934
13	2006/07	20/08/06	FA Premiership	Manchester United 5 Fulham 1	Old Trafford	75115

AUGUST 21

#	SEASON	DATE	COMPETITION / ROUND	MATCH RESULT	VENUE	ATT
1	1948/49	21/08/48	Football League Division 1	Manchester United 1 Derby County 2	Maine Road	52620
2	1954/55	21/08/54	Football League Division 1	Manchester United 1 Portsmouth 3	Old Trafford	38203
3	1965/66	21/08/65	Football League Division 1	Manchester United 1 Sheffield Wednesday 0	Old Trafford	37524
4	1968/69	21/08/68	Football League Division 1	Manchester United 1 Coventry City 0	Old Trafford	51201
5	1976/77	21/08/76	Football League Division 1	Manchester United 2 Birmingham City 2	Old Trafford	58898
6	1991/92	21/08/91	Football League Division 1	Aston Villa 0 Manchester United 1	Villa Park	39995
7	1993/94	21/08/93	FA Premiership	Manchester United 1 Newcastle United 1	Old Trafford	41829
8	1996/97	21/08/96	FA Premiership	Manchester United 2 Everton 2	Old Trafford	54943
9	2004/05	21/08/04	FA Premiership	Manchester United 2 Norwich City 1	Old Trafford	67812

AUGUST 22

#	SEASON	DATE	COMPETITION / ROUND	MATCH RESULT	VENUE	ATT
1	1951/52	22/08/51	Football League Division 1	Manchester United 4 Middlesbrough 2	Old Trafford	37339
2	1953/54	22/08/53	Football League Division 1	Liverpool 4 Manchester United 4	Anfield	48422
3	1959/60	22/08/59	Football League Division 1	West Bromwich Albion 3 Manchester United 2	The Hawthorns	40076
4	1962/63	22/08/62	Football League Division 1	Everton 3 Manchester United 1	Goodison Park	69501
5	1964/65	22/08/64	Football League Division 1	Manchester United 2 West Bromwich Albion 2	Old Trafford	52007
6	1970/71	22/08/70	Football League Division 1	Arsenal 4 Manchester United 0	Highbury	54117
7	1979/80	22/08/79	Football League Division 1	Manchester United 2 West Bromwich Albion 0	Old Trafford	53377
8	1987/88	22/08/87	Football League Division 1	Manchester United 1 Watford 0	Old Trafford	38769
9	1989/90	22/08/89	Football League Division 1	Crystal Palace 1 Manchester United 1	Selhurst Park	22423
10	1992/93	22/08/92	FA Premiership	Manchester United 1 Ipswich Town 1	Old Trafford	31704
11	1994/95	22/08/94	FA Premiership	Nottingham Forest 1 Manchester United 1	City Ground	22072
12	1998/99	22/08/98	FA Premiership	West Ham United 0 Manchester United 0	Upton Park	26039
13	1999/00	22/08/99	FA Premiership	Arsenal 1 Manchester United 2	Highbury	38147
14	2000/01	22/08/00	FA Premiership	Ipswich Town 1 Manchester United 1	Portman Road	22007
15	2001/02	22/08/01	FA Premiership	Blackburn Rovers 2 Manchester United 2	Ewood Park	29836

AUGUST 23

#	SEASON	DATE	COMPETITION / ROUND	MATCH RESULT	VENUE	ATT
1	1947/48	23/08/47	Football League Division 1	Middlesbrough 2 Manchester United 2	Ayresome Park	39554
2	1948/49	23/08/48	Football League Division 1	Blackpool 0 Manchester United 3	Bloomfield Road	36880
3	1950/51	23/08/50	Football League Division 1	Liverpool 2 Manchester United 1	Anfield	30211
4	1952/53	23/08/52	Football League Division 1	Manchester United 2 Chelsea 0	Old Trafford	43629
5	1954/55	23/08/54	Football League Division 1	Sheffield Wednesday 2 Manchester United 4	Hillsborough	38118
6	1958/59	23/08/58	Football League Division 1	Manchester United 5 Chelsea 2	Old Trafford	52382
7	1961/62	23/08/61	Football League Division 1	Manchester United 3 Chelsea 2	Old Trafford	45847
8	1966/67	23/08/66	Football League Division 1	Everton 1 Manchester United 2	Goodison Park	60657
9	1967/68	23/08/67	Football League Division 1	Manchester United 1 Leeds United 0	Old Trafford	53016
10	1969/70	23/08/69	Football League Division 1	Wolverhampton Wanderers 0 Manchester United 0	Molineux	50783
11	1971/72	23/08/71	Football League Division 1	Manchester United 3 West Bromwich Albion 1	Victoria Ground	23146
12	1972/73	23/08/72	Football League Division 1	Manchester United 1 Leicester City 1	Old Trafford	40067
13	1975/76	23/08/75	Football League Division 1	Manchester United 5 Sheffield United 1	Old Trafford	55949
14	1978/79	23/08/78	Football League Division 1	Leeds United 2 Manchester United 3	Elland Road	36845
15	1980/81	23/08/80	Football League Division 1	Birmingham City 0 Manchester United 0	St Andrews	28661
16	1986/87	23/08/86	Football League Division 1	Arsenal 1 Manchester United 0	Highbury	41382
17	1993/94	23/08/93	FA Premiership	Aston Villa 1 Manchester United 2	Villa Park	39624
18	1995/96	23/08/95	FA Premiership	Manchester United 2 West Ham United 1	Old Trafford	31966
19	1997/98	23/08/97	FA Premiership	Leicester City 0 Manchester United 0	Filbert Street	21221
20	2002/03	23/08/02	FA Premiership	Chelsea 2 Manchester United 2	Stamford Bridge	41541
21	2003/04	23/08/03	FA Premiership	Newcastle United 1 Manchester United 2	St James' Park	52165
22	2006/07	23/08/06	FA Premiership	Charlton Athletic 0 Manchester United 3	The Valley	25422

AUGUST 24

#	SEASON	DATE	COMPETITION / ROUND	MATCH RESULT	VENUE	ATT
1	1949/50	24/08/49	Football League Division 1	Manchester United 3 Bolton Wanderers 0	Old Trafford	41748
2	1955/56	24/08/55	Football League Division 1	Manchester United 2 Tottenham Hotspur 2	Old Trafford	25406
3	1957/58	24/08/57	Football League Division 1	Leicester City 0 Manchester United 3	Filbert Street	40214
4	1960/61	24/08/60	Football League Division 1	Everton 4 Manchester United 0	Goodison Park	51602
5	1963/64	24/08/63	Football League Division 1	Sheffield Wednesday 3 Manchester United 3	Hillsborough	32177
6	1964/65	24/08/64	Football League Division 1	West Ham United 3 Manchester United 1	Upton Park	37070
7	1965/66	24/08/65	Football League Division 1	Nottingham Forest 4 Manchester United 2	City Ground	33744
8	1968/69	24/08/68	Football League Division 1	Manchester United 0 Chelsea 4	Old Trafford	55114
9	1974/75	24/08/74	Football League Division 2	Manchester United 4 Millwall 0	Old Trafford	44756
10	1976/77	24/08/76	Football League Division 1	Coventry City 0 Manchester United 2	Highfield Road	26775
11	1977/78	24/08/77	Football League Division 1	Manchester United 2 Coventry City 1	Old Trafford	55726
12	1985/86	24/08/85	Football League Division 1	Arsenal 1 Manchester United 2	Highbury	37145
13	1991/92	24/08/91	Football League Division 1	Everton 0 Manchester United 0	Goodison Park	36085
14	1992/93	24/08/92	FA Premiership	Southampton 0 Manchester United 1	The Dell	15623
15	2005/06	24/08/05	Champions League Qual. Round 2nd Leg	Debreceni 0 Manchester United 3	Ferenc Puskas Stadium	27000

AUGUST 25

#	SEASON	DATE	COMPETITION / ROUND	MATCH RESULT	VENUE	ATT
1	1923/24	25/08/23	Football League Division 2	Bristol City 1 Manchester United 2	Ashton Gate	20500
2	1928/29	25/08/28	Football League Division 1	Manchester United 1 Leicester City 1	Old Trafford	20129
3	1934/35	25/08/34	Football League Division 2	Manchester United 2 Bradford City 0	Old Trafford	27573
4	1951/52	25/08/51	Football League Division 1	Manchester United 2 Newcastle United 1	Old Trafford	51850
5	1956/57	25/08/56	Football League Division 1	West Bromwich Albion 2 Manchester United 3	The Hawthorns	26387
6	1962/63	25/08/62	Football League Division 1	Arsenal 1 Manchester United 3	Highbury	62308
7	1970/71	25/08/70	Football League Division 1	Burnley 0 Manchester United 2	Turf Moor	29385
8	1973/74	25/08/73	Football League Division 1	Arsenal 3 Manchester United 0	Highbury	51501
9	1979/80	25/08/79	Football League Division 1	Arsenal 0 Manchester United 0	Highbury	44380
10	1984/85	25/08/84	Football League Division 1	Manchester United 1 Watford 1	Old Trafford	53668
11	1986/87	25/08/86	Football League Division 1	Manchester United 2 West Ham United 3	Old Trafford	43306
12	1990/91	25/08/90	Football League Division 1	Manchester United 2 Coventry City 0	Old Trafford	46715
13	1996/97	25/08/96	FA Premiership	Manchester United 2 Blackburn Rovers 2	Old Trafford	54178
14	1999/00	25/08/99	FA Premiership	Coventry City 1 Manchester United 2	Highfield Road	22024
15	2004/05	25/08/04	Champions League Qual. Round 2nd Leg	Manchester United 3 Dinamo Bucharest 0	Old Trafford	61041

AUGUST 26

#	SEASON	DATE	COMPETITION / ROUND	MATCH RESULT	VENUE	ATT
1	1922/23	26/08/22	Football League Division 2	Manchester United 2 Crystal Palace 1	Old Trafford	30000
2	1933/34	26/08/33	Football League Division 2	Plymouth Argyle 4 Manchester United 0	Home Park	25700
3	1950/51	26/08/50	Football League Division 1	Bolton Wanderers 1 Manchester United 0	Burnden Park	40431
4	1953/54	26/08/53	Football League Division 1	Manchester United 1 West Bromwich Albion 3	Old Trafford	31806
5	1959/60	26/08/59	Football League Division 1	Manchester United 0 Chelsea 1	Old Trafford	57674
6	1961/62	26/08/61	Football League Division 1	Manchester United 6 Blackburn Rovers 1	Old Trafford	45302
7	1967/68	26/08/67	Football League Division 1	Manchester United 1 Leicester City 1	Old Trafford	51256
8	1972/73	26/08/72	Football League Division 1	Manchester United 0 Arsenal 0	Old Trafford	48108
9	1978/79	26/08/78	Football League Division 1	Ipswich Town 3 Manchester United 0	Portman Road	21802
10	1985/86	26/08/85	Football League Division 1	Manchester United 2 West Ham United 0	Old Trafford	50773
11	1989/90	26/08/89	Football League Division 1	Derby County 2 Manchester United 0	Baseball Ground	22175
12	1995/96	26/08/95	FA Premiership	Manchester United 3 Wimbledon 1	Old Trafford	32226
13	1998/99	26/08/98	Champions League Qual. Round 2nd Leg	LKS Lodz 0 Manchester United 0	LKS Stadion	8700
14	2000/01	26/08/00	FA Premiership	West Ham United 2 Manchester United 2	Upton Park	25998
15	2001/02	26/08/01	FA Premiership	Aston Villa 1 Manchester United 1	Villa Park	42632
16	2006/07	26/08/06	FA Premiership	Watford 1 Manchester United 2	Vicarage Road	19453
17	2007/08	26/08/07	FA Premiership	Manchester United 1 Tottenham Hotspur 0	Old Trafford	75696

AUGUST 27

#	SEASON	DATE	COMPETITION / ROUND	MATCH RESULT	VENUE	ATT
1	1921/22	27/08/21	Football League Division 1	Everton 5 Manchester United 0	Goodison Park	30000
2	1923/24	27/08/23	Football League Division 2	Manchester United 1 Southampton 0	Old Trafford	21750
3	1927/28	27/08/27	Football League Division 1	Manchester United 3 Middlesbrough 0	Old Trafford	44957
4	1928/29	27/08/28	Football League Division 1	Aston Villa 0 Manchester United 0	Villa Park	30356
5	1932/33	27/08/32	Football League Division 2	Manchester United 0 Stoke City 2	Old Trafford	24996
6	1938/39	27/08/38	Football League Division 1	Middlesbrough 3 Manchester United 1	Ayresome Park	25539
7	1947/48	27/08/47	Football League Division 1	Manchester United 2 Liverpool 0	Maine Road	52385
8	1949/50	27/08/49	Football League Division 1	Manchester United 1 West Bromwich Albion 1	Old Trafford	44655
9	1952/53	27/08/52	Football League Division 1	Arsenal 2 Manchester United 1	Highbury	58831
10	1955/56	27/08/55	Football League Division 1	Manchester United 3 West Bromwich Albion 1	Old Trafford	31996
11	1958/59	27/08/58	Football League Division 1	Nottingham Forest 0 Manchester United 3	City Ground	44971
12	1966/67	27/08/66	Football League Division 1	Leeds United 3 Manchester United 1	Elland Road	45092
13	1969/70	27/08/69	Football League Division 1	Manchester United 0 Newcastle United 0	Old Trafford	52774
14	1975/76	27/08/75	Football League Division 1	Manchester United 1 Coventry City 1	Old Trafford	52169
15	1977/78	27/08/77	Football League Division 1	Manchester United 0 Ipswich Town 0	Old Trafford	57904
16	1980/81	27/08/80	League Cup 2nd Round 1st Leg	Manchester United 0 Coventry City 1	Old Trafford	31656
17	1983/84	27/08/83	Football League Division 1	Manchester United 3 Queens Park Rangers 1	Old Trafford	48742
18	1988/89	27/08/88	Football League Division 1	Manchester United 0 Queens Park Rangers 0	Old Trafford	46377
19	1994/95	27/08/94	FA Premiership	Tottenham Hotspur 0 Manchester United 1	White Hart Lane	24502
20	1997/98	27/08/97	FA Premiership	Everton 0 Manchester United 2	Goodison Park	40079
21	1999/00	27/08/99	European Super Cup	Manchester United 0 Lazio 1	Stade Louis II	14461
22	2002/03	27/08/02	Champions League Qual. Round 2nd Leg	Manchester United 5 Zalaegerszeg 0	Old Trafford	66814
23	2003/04	27/08/03	FA Premiership	Manchester United 1 Wolverhampton Wanderers 0	Old Trafford	67648

AUGUST 28

#	SEASON	DATE	COMPETITION / ROUND	MATCH RESULT	VENUE	ATT
1	1920/21	28/08/20	Football League Division 1	Manchester United 2 Bolton Wanderers 3	Old Trafford	50000
2	1922/23	28/08/22	Football League Division 2	Sheffield Wednesday 1 Manchester United 0	Hillsborough	12500
3	1926/27	28/08/26	Football League Division 1	Liverpool 4 Manchester United 2	Anfield	34795
4	1937/38	28/08/37	Football League Division 2	Manchester United 3 Newcastle United 0	Old Trafford	29446
5	1948/49	28/08/48	Football League Division 1	Arsenal 0 Manchester United 1	Highbury	64150
6	1954/55	28/08/54	Football League Division 1	Blackpool 2 Manchester United 4	Bloomfield Road	31855
7	1957/58	28/08/57	Football League Division 1	Manchester United 3 Everton 0	Old Trafford	59103
8	1963/64	28/08/63	Football League Division 1	Manchester United 2 Ipswich Town 0	Old Trafford	39921
9	1965/66	28/08/65	Football League Division 1	Northampton Town 1 Manchester United 1	County Ground	21140
10	1968/69	28/08/68	Football League Division 1	Manchester United 3 Tottenham Hotspur 1	Old Trafford	62689
11	1971/72	28/08/71	Football League Division 1	Wolverhampton Wanderers 1 Manchester United 1	Molineux	46471
12	1974/75	28/08/74	Football League Division 2	Manchester United 0 Portsmouth 1	Old Trafford	42547
13	1976/77	28/08/76	Football League Division 1	Derby County 0 Manchester United 0	Baseball Ground	30054
14	1982/83	28/08/82	Football League Division 1	Manchester United 3 Birmingham City 0	Old Trafford	48673
15	1984/85	28/08/84	Football League Division 1	Southampton 0 Manchester United 0	The Dell	22183
16	1990/91	28/08/90	Football League Division 1	Leeds United 0 Manchester United 0	Elland Road	29174
17	1991/92	28/08/91	Football League Division 1	Manchester United 1 Oldham Athletic 0	Old Trafford	42078
18	1993/94	28/08/93	FA Premiership	Southampton 1 Manchester United 3	The Dell	16189
19	1995/96	28/08/95	FA Premiership	Blackburn Rovers 1 Manchester United 2	Ewood Park	29843
20	2004/05	28/08/04	FA Premiership	Blackburn Rovers 1 Manchester United 1	Ewood Park	26155
21	2005/06	28/08/05	FA Premiership	Newcastle United 0 Manchester United 2	St James' Park	52327

AUGUST 29

#	SEASON	DATE	COMPETITION / ROUND	MATCH RESULT	VENUE	ATT
1	1921/22	29/08/21	Football League Division 1	Manchester United 2 West Bromwich Albion 3	Old Trafford	20000
2	1925/26	29/08/25	Football League Division 1	West Ham United 1 Manchester United 0	Upton Park	25630
3	1927/28	29/08/27	Football League Division 1	Sheffield Wednesday 0 Manchester United 1	Hillsborough	17944
4	1931/32	29/08/31	Football League Division 2	Bradford Park Avenue 3 Manchester United 1	Park Avenue	16239
5	1932/33	29/08/32	Football League Division 2	Charlton Athletic 0 Manchester United 1	The Valley	12946
6	1936/37	29/08/36	Football League Division 1	Manchester United 1 Wolverhampton Wanderers 1	Old Trafford	42731
7	1951/52	29/08/51	Football League Division 1	Middlesbrough 1 Manchester United 4	Ayresome Park	44212
8	1953/54	29/08/53	Football League Division 1	Manchester United 1 Newcastle United 1	Old Trafford	27837
9	1956/57	29/08/56	Football League Division 1	Manchester United 3 Preston North End 2	Old Trafford	32515
10	1959/60	29/08/59	Football League Division 1	Manchester United 3 Newcastle United 2	Old Trafford	53257
11	1962/63	29/08/62	Football League Division 1	Manchester United 0 Everton 1	Old Trafford	63437
12	1964/65	29/08/64	Football League Division 1	Leicester City 2 Manchester United 2	Filbert Street	32373
13	1970/71	29/08/70	Football League Division 1	Manchester United 1 West Ham United 1	Old Trafford	50643
14	1973/74	29/08/73	Football League Division 1	Manchester United 1 Stoke City 0	Old Trafford	43614
15	1979/80	29/08/79	League Cup 2nd Round 1st Leg	Tottenham Hotspur 2 Manchester United 1	White Hart Lane	29163
16	1981/82	29/08/81	Football League Division 1	Coventry City 2 Manchester United 1	Highfield Road	19329
17	1983/84	29/08/83	Football League Division 1	Manchester United 1 Nottingham Forest 1	Old Trafford	43005
18	1987/88	29/08/87	Football League Division 1	Charlton Athletic 1 Manchester United 3	Selhurst Park	14046
19	1992/93	29/08/92	FA Premiership	Nottingham Forest 0 Manchester United 2	City Ground	19694

AUGUST 30

#	SEASON	DATE	COMPETITION / ROUND	MATCH RESULT	VENUE	ATT
1	1919/20	30/08/19	Football League Division 1	Derby County 1 Manchester United 1	Baseball Ground	12000
2	1920/21	30/08/20	Football League Division 1	Arsenal 2 Manchester United 0	Highbury	40000
3	1924/25	30/08/24	Football League Division 2	Manchester United 1 Leicester City 0	Old Trafford	21250
4	1926/27	30/08/26	Football League Division 1	Sheffield United 2 Manchester United 2	Bramall Lane	14844
5	1930/31	30/08/30	Football League Division 1	Manchester United 3 Aston Villa 4	Old Trafford	18004
6	1933/34	30/08/33	Football League Division 2	Manchester United 0 Nottingham Forest 1	Old Trafford	16934
7	1937/38	30/08/37	Football League Division 2	Coventry City 1 Manchester United 0	Highfield Road	30575
8	1947/48	30/08/47	Football League Division 1	Manchester United 6 Charlton Athletic 2	Maine Road	52659
9	1950/51	30/08/50	Football League Division 1	Manchester United 1 Liverpool 0	Old Trafford	34835
10	1952/53	30/08/52	Football League Division 1	Manchester City 2 Manchester United 1	Maine Road	56140
11	1958/59	30/08/58	Football League Division 1	Blackpool 2 Manchester United 1	Bloomfield Road	26719
12	1961/62	30/08/61	Football League Division 1	Chelsea 2 Manchester United 0	Stamford Bridge	42248
13	1969/70	30/08/69	Football League Division 1	Manchester United 3 Sunderland 1	Old Trafford	50570
14	1972/73	30/08/72	Football League Division 1	Manchester United 0 Chelsea 0	Old Trafford	44482
15	1975/76	30/08/75	Football League Division 1	Stoke City 0 Manchester United 1	Victoria Ground	33092
16	1977/78	30/08/77	League Cup 2nd Round	Arsenal 3 Manchester United 2	Highbury	36171
17	1978/79	30/08/78	League Cup 2nd Round	Stockport County 2 Manchester United 3	Old Trafford	41761
18	1980/81	30/08/80	Football League Division 1	Manchester United 1 Sunderland 1	Old Trafford	51498
19	1986/87	30/08/86	Football League Division 1	Manchester United 0 Charlton Athletic 1	Old Trafford	37544
20	1989/90	30/08/89	Football League Division 1	Manchester United 0 Norwich City 2	Old Trafford	41610
21	1997/98	30/08/97	FA Premiership	Manchester United 3 Coventry City 0	Old Trafford	55074
22	1999/00	30/08/99	FA Premiership	Manchester United 5 Newcastle United 1	Old Trafford	55190
23	2004/05	30/08/04	FA Premiership	Manchester United 0 Everton 0	Old Trafford	67803

AUGUST 31

#	SEASON	DATE	COMPETITION / ROUND	MATCH RESULT	VENUE	ATT
1	1929/30	31/08/29	Football League Division 1	Newcastle United 4 Manchester United 1	St James' Park	43489
2	1935/36	31/08/35	Football League Division 2	Plymouth Argyle 3 Manchester United 1	Home Park	22366
3	1938/39	31/08/38	Football League Division 1	Manchester United 2 Bolton Wanderers 2	Old Trafford	37950
4	1946/47	31/08/46	Football League Division 1	Manchester United 2 Grimsby Town 1	Maine Road	41025
5	1949/50	31/08/49	Football League Division 1	Bolton Wanderers 1 Manchester United 2	Burnden Park	36277
6	1955/56	31/08/55	Football League Division 1	Tottenham Hotspur 1 Manchester United 2	White Hart Lane	27453
7	1957/58	31/08/57	Football League Division 1	Manchester United 4 Manchester City 1	Old Trafford	63347
8	1960/61	31/08/60	Football League Division 1	Manchester United 4 Everton 0	Old Trafford	51818
9	1963/64	31/08/63	Football League Division 1	Manchester United 5 Everton 1	Old Trafford	62965
10	1966/67	31/08/66	Football League Division 1	Manchester United 3 Everton 0	Old Trafford	61114
11	1968/69	31/08/68	Football League Division 1	Sheffield Wednesday 5 Manchester United 4	Hillsborough	50490
12	1971/72	31/08/71	Football League Division 1	Everton 1 Manchester United 0	Goodison Park	52151
13	1974/75	31/08/74	Football League Division 2	Cardiff City 0 Manchester United 1	Ninian Park	22344
14	1981/82	31/08/81	Football League Division 1	Manchester United 0 Nottingham Forest 0	Old Trafford	51496
15	1985/86	31/08/85	Football League Division 1	Nottingham Forest 1 Manchester United 3	City Ground	26274
16	1987/88	31/08/87	Football League Division 1	Manchester United 3 Chelsea 1	Old Trafford	46616
17	1991/92	31/08/91	Football League Division 1	Manchester United 1 Leeds United 1	Old Trafford	43778
18	1994/95	31/08/94	FA Premiership	Manchester United 3 Wimbledon 0	Old Trafford	43440
19	2002/03	31/08/02	FA Premiership	Sunderland 1 Manchester United 1	Stadium of Light	47586
20	2003/04	31/08/03	FA Premiership	Southampton 1 Manchester United 0	St Mary's Stadium	32066

UNITED in SEPTEMBER

OVERALL PLAYING RECORD

	P	W	D	L	F	A		P	W	D	L	F	A		P	W	D	L	F	A
1st	24	14	4	6	42	21	11th	21	10	5	6	45	27	21st	19	12	3	4	40	18
2nd	24	12	6	6	48	35	12th	22	10	7	5	38	28	22nd	19	9	3	7	38	27
3rd	26	12	7	7	44	37	13th	18	12	2	4	40	20	23rd	20	9	9	2	39	24
4th	20	12	5	3	42	19	14th	23	10	6	7	37	35	24th	24	13	4	7	41	30
5th	21	7	6	8	36	31	15th	23	11	5	7	43	30	25th	22	11	4	7	50	30
6th	18	7	7	4	30	26	16th	26	15	6	5	51	28	26th	22	11	5	6	51	31
7th	28	14	9	5	53	25	17th	21	9	5	7	32	29	27th	16	5	7	4	27	20
8th	25	13	5	7	53	28	18th	21	10	8	3	35	20	28th	17	10	2	5	37	23
9th	23	13	4	6	44	28	19th	20	10	3	7	24	25	29th	20	11	4	5	34	17
10th	19	6	5	8	24	36	20th	17	7	6	4	28	23	30th	14	6	3	5	14	14

OVERALL 633 311 155 167 1160 785

SEPTEMBER 1

#	SEASON	DATE	COMPETITION / ROUND	MATCH RESULT	VENUE	ATT
1	1896/97	01/09/96	Football League Division 2	Newton Heath 2 Gainsborough Trinity 0	Bank Street	4000
2	1900/01	01/09/00	Football League Division 2	Glossop 1 Newton Heath 0	North Road	8000
3	1906/07	01/09/06	Football League Division 1	Bristol City 1 Manchester United 2	Ashton Gate	5000
4	1909/10	01/09/09	Football League Division 1	Manchester United 1 Bradford City 0	Bank Street	12000
5	1910/11	01/09/10	Football League Division 1	Arsenal 1 Manchester United 2	Manor Field	15000
6	1919/20	01/09/19	Football League Division 1	Manchester United 0 Sheffield Wednesday 0	Old Trafford	13000
7	1923/24	01/09/23	Football League Division 2	Manchester United 2 Bristol City 1	Old Trafford	21000
8	1924/25	01/09/24	Football League Division 2	Stockport County 2 Manchester United 1	Edgeley Park	12500
9	1928/29	01/09/28	Football League Division 1	Manchester City 2 Manchester United 2	Maine Road	61007
10	1934/35	01/09/34	Football League Division 2	Sheffield United 3 Manchester United 2	Bramall Lane	18468
11	1948/49	01/09/48	Football League Division 1	Manchester United 3 Blackpool 4	Maine Road	51187
12	1951/52	01/09/51	Football League Division 1	Bolton Wanderers 1 Manchester United 0	Burnden Park	52239
13	1954/55	01/09/54	Football League Division 1	Manchester United 2 Sheffield Wednesday 0	Old Trafford	31371
14	1956/57	01/09/56	Football League Division 1	Manchester United 3 Portsmouth 0	Old Trafford	40369
15	1962/63	01/09/62	Football League Division 1	Manchester United 2 Birmingham City 0	Old Trafford	39847
16	1965/66	01/09/65	Football League Division 1	Manchester United 0 Nottingham Forest 0	Old Trafford	38777
17	1973/74	01/09/73	Football League Division 1	Manchester United 2 Queens Park Rangers 1	Old Trafford	44156
18	1976/77	01/09/76	League Cup 2nd Round	Manchester United 5 Tranmere Rovers 0	Old Trafford	37586
19	1979/80	01/09/79	Football League Division 1	Manchester United 2 Middlesbrough 1	Old Trafford	51015
20	1982/83	01/09/82	Football League Division 1	Nottingham Forest 0 Manchester United 3	City Ground	23956
21	1984/85	01/09/84	Football League Division 1	Ipswich Town 1 Manchester United 1	Portman Road	20876
22	1990/91	01/09/90	Football League Division 1	Sunderland 2 Manchester United 1	Roker Park	26105
23	1993/94	01/09/93	FA Premiership	Manchester United 3 West Ham United 0	Old Trafford	44613
24	2007/08	01/09/07	FA Premiership	Manchester United 1 Sunderland 0	Old Trafford	75648

SEPTEMBER 2

#	SEASON	DATE	COMPETITION / ROUND	MATCH RESULT	VENUE	ATT
1	1893/94	02/09/93	Football League Division 1	Newton Heath 3 Burnley 2	North Road	10000
2	1899/00	02/09/99	Football League Division 2	Newton Heath 2 Gainsborough Trinity 2	Bank Street	8000
3	1905/06	02/09/05	Football League Division 1	Manchester United 5 Bristol City 1	Bank Street	25000
4	1907/08	02/09/07	Football League Division 1	Aston Villa 1 Manchester United 4	Villa Park	20000
5	1911/12	02/09/11	Football League Division 1	Manchester City 0 Manchester United 0	Hyde Road	35000
6	1912/13	02/09/12	Football League Division 1	Arsenal 0 Manchester United 0	Manor Field	11000
7	1914/15	02/09/14	Football League Division 1	Manchester United 1 Oldham Athletic 3	Old Trafford	13000
8	1922/23	02/09/22	Football League Division 2	Crystal Palace 2 Manchester United 3	Sydenham Hill	8500
9	1925/26	02/09/25	Football League Division 1	Manchester United 3 Aston Villa 0	Old Trafford	41717
10	1929/30	02/09/29	Football League Division 1	Leicester City 4 Manchester United 1	Filbert Street	20490
11	1931/32	02/09/31	Football League Division 2	Manchester United 2 Southampton 3	Old Trafford	3507
12	1933/34	02/09/33	Football League Division 2	Manchester United 1 Lincoln City 1	Old Trafford	16987
13	1936/37	02/09/36	Football League Division 1	Huddersfield Town 3 Manchester United 1	Leeds Road	12612
14	1950/51	02/09/50	Football League Division 1	Manchester United 1 Blackpool 0	Old Trafford	53260
15	1953/54	02/09/53	Football League Division 1	West Bromwich Albion 2 Manchester United 0	The Hawthorns	28892
16	1959/60	02/09/59	Football League Division 1	Chelsea 3 Manchester United 6	Stamford Bridge	66579
17	1961/62	02/09/61	Football League Division 1	Blackpool 2 Manchester United 3	Bloomfield Road	28156
18	1964/65	02/09/64	Football League Division 1	Manchester United 3 West Ham United 1	Old Trafford	45123
19	1967/68	02/09/67	Football League Division 1	West Ham United 1 Manchester United 3	Upton Park	36562
20	1970/71	02/09/70	Football League Division 1	Manchester United 2 Everton 0	Old Trafford	51346
21	1972/73	02/09/72	Football League Division 1	West Ham United 2 Manchester United 2	Upton Park	31939
22	1978/79	02/09/78	Football League Division 1	Manchester United 1 Everton 1	Old Trafford	53982
23	1980/81	02/09/80	League Cup 2nd Round 2nd Leg	Coventry City 1 Manchester United 0	Highfield Road	18946
24	1992/93	02/09/92	FA Premiership	Manchester United 1 Crystal Palace 0	Old Trafford	29736

SEPTEMBER 3

#	SEASON	DATE	COMPETITION / ROUND	MATCH RESULT	VENUE	ATT
1	1892/93	03/09/92	Football League Division 1	Blackburn Rovers 4 Newton Heath 3	Ewood Park	8000
2	1898/99	03/09/98	Football League Division 2	Gainsborough Trinity 0 Newton Heath 2	The Northolme	2000
3	1904/05	03/09/04	Football League Division 2	Port Vale 2 Manchester United 2	Cobridge Stadium	4000
4	1906/07	03/09/06	Football League Division 1	Derby County 2 Manchester United 2	Baseball Ground	5000
5	1910/11	03/09/10	Football League Division 1	Manchester United 3 Blackburn Rovers 2	Old Trafford	40000
6	1921/22	03/09/21	Football League Division 1	Manchester United 2 Everton 1	Old Trafford	25000
7	1923/24	03/09/23	Football League Division 2	Southampton 0 Manchester United 0	The Dell	11500
8	1927/28	03/09/27	Football League Division 1	Birmingham City 0 Manchester United 0	St Andrews	25863
9	1930/31	03/09/30	Football League Division 1	Middlesbrough 3 Manchester United 1	Ayresome Park	15712
10	1932/33	03/09/32	Football League Division 2	Southampton 4 Manchester United 2	The Dell	7978
11	1934/35	03/09/34	Football League Division 2	Bolton Wanderers 3 Manchester United 1	Burnden Park	16238
12	1938/39	03/09/38	Football League Division 1	Manchester United 4 Birmingham City 1	Old Trafford	22228
13	1947/48	03/09/47	Football League Division 1	Liverpool 2 Manchester United 2	Anfield	48081
14	1949/50	03/09/49	Football League Division 1	Manchester United 2 Manchester City 1	Old Trafford	47760
15	1952/53	03/09/52	Football League Division 1	Manchester United 0 Arsenal 0	Old Trafford	39193
16	1955/56	03/09/55	Football League Division 1	Manchester City 1 Manchester United 0	Maine Road	59162
17	1958/59	03/09/58	Football League Division 1	Manchester United 1 Nottingham Forest 1	Old Trafford	51880
18	1960/61	03/09/60	Football League Division 1	Tottenham Hotspur 4 Manchester United 1	White Hart Lane	55445
19	1963/64	03/09/63	Football League Division 1	Ipswich Town 2 Manchester United 7	Portman Road	28113
20	1966/67	03/09/66	Football League Division 1	Manchester United 3 Newcastle United 2	Old Trafford	44448
21	1969/70	03/09/69	League Cup 2nd Round	Manchester United 1 Middlesbrough 0	Old Trafford	38938
22	1977/78	03/09/77	Football League Division 1	Derby County 0 Manchester United 1	Baseball Ground	21279
23	1983/84	03/09/83	Football League Division 1	Stoke City 0 Manchester United 1	Victoria Ground	23704
24	1988/89	03/09/88	Football League Division 1	Liverpool 1 Manchester United 0	Anfield	42026
25	1991/92	03/09/91	Football League Division 1	Wimbledon 1 Manchester United 2	Selhurst Park	13824
26	2002/03	03/09/02	FA Premiership	Manchester United 1 Middlesbrough 0	Old Trafford	67464

SEPTEMBER 4

#	SEASON	DATE	COMPETITION / ROUND	MATCH RESULT	VENUE	ATT
1	1897/98	04/09/97	Football League Division 2	Newton Heath 5 Lincoln City 0	Bank Street	5000
2	1905/06	04/09/05	Football League Division 2	Manchester United 2 Blackpool 1	Bank Street	7000
3	1909/10	04/09/09	Football League Division 1	Manchester United 2 Bury 0	Bank Street	12000
4	1920/21	04/09/20	Football League Division 1	Bolton Wanderers 1 Manchester United 1	Burnden Park	35000
5	1922/23	04/09/22	Football League Division 2	Manchester United 1 Sheffield Wednesday 0	Old Trafford	22000
6	1926/27	04/09/26	Football League Division 1	Manchester United 2 Leeds United 2	Old Trafford	26338
7	1935/36	04/09/35	Football League Division 2	Manchester United 3 Charlton Athletic 0	Old Trafford	21211
8	1937/38	04/09/37	Football League Division 2	Luton Town 1 Manchester United 0	Kenilworth Road	20610
9	1946/47	04/09/46	Football League Division 1	Chelsea 0 Manchester United 3	Stamford Bridge	27750
10	1948/49	04/09/48	Football League Division 1	Manchester United 4 Huddersfield Town 1	Maine Road	57714
11	1950/51	04/09/50	Football League Division 1	Aston Villa 1 Manchester United 3	Villa Park	42724
12	1954/55	04/09/54	Football League Division 1	Manchester United 3 Charlton Athletic 1	Old Trafford	38105
13	1957/58	04/09/57	Football League Division 1	Everton 3 Manchester United 3	Goodison Park	72077
14	1965/66	04/09/65	Football League Division 1	Manchester United 1 Stoke City 1	Old Trafford	37603
15	1971/72	04/09/71	Football League Division 1	Manchester United 1 Ipswich Town 0	Old Trafford	45656
16	1976/77	04/09/76	Football League Division 1	Manchester United 2 Tottenham Hotspur 3	Old Trafford	60723
17	1982/83	04/09/82	Football League Division 1	West Bromwich Albion 3 Manchester United 1	The Hawthorns	24928
18	1985/86	04/09/85	Football League Division 1	Manchester United 3 Newcastle United 0	Old Trafford	51102
19	1990/91	04/09/90	Football League Division 1	Luton Town 0 Manchester United 1	Kenilworth Road	12576
20	1996/97	04/09/96	FA Premiership	Derby County 1 Manchester United 1	Baseball Ground	18026

SEPTEMBER 5

#	SEASON	DATE	COMPETITION / ROUND	MATCH RESULT	VENUE	ATT
1	1896/97	05/09/96	Football League Division 2	Burton Swifts 3 Newton Heath 5	Peel Croft	3000
2	1903/04	05/09/03	Football League Division 2	Manchester United 2 Bristol City 2	Bank Street	40000
3	1908/09	05/09/08	Football League Division 1	Preston North End 0 Manchester United 3	Deepdale	18000
4	1914/15	05/09/14	Football League Division 1	Manchester United 0 Manchester City 0	Old Trafford	20000
5	1925/26	05/09/25	Football League Division 1	Manchester United 0 Arsenal 1	Old Trafford	32288
6	1931/32	05/09/31	Football League Division 2	Manchester United 2 Swansea City 1	Old Trafford	6763
7	1936/37	05/09/36	Football League Division 1	Derby County 5 Manchester United 4	Baseball Ground	21194
8	1951/52	05/09/51	Football League Division 1	Manchester United 3 Charlton Athletic 2	Old Trafford	26773
9	1953/54	05/09/53	Football League Division 1	Manchester City 2 Manchester United 0	Maine Road	53097
10	1956/57	05/09/56	Football League Division 1	Chelsea 1 Manchester United 2	Stamford Bridge	29082
11	1959/60	05/09/59	Football League Division 1	Birmingham City 1 Manchester United 1	St Andrews	38220
12	1960/61	05/09/60	Football League Division 1	West Ham United 2 Manchester United 1	Upton Park	30506
13	1962/63	05/09/62	Football League Division 1	Bolton Wanderers 3 Manchester United 0	Burnden Park	44859
14	1964/65	05/09/64	Football League Division 1	Fulham 2 Manchester United 1	Craven Cottage	36291
15	1970/71	05/09/70	Football League Division 1	Liverpool 1 Manchester United 1	Anfield	52542
16	1973/74	05/09/73	Football League Division 1	Leicester City 1 Manchester United 0	Filbert Street	29152
17	1979/80	05/09/79	League Cup 2nd Round 2nd Leg	Manchester United 3 Tottenham Hotspur 1	Old Trafford	48292
18	1981/82	05/09/81	Football League Division 1	Manchester United 1 Ipswich Town 2	Old Trafford	45555
19	1984/85	05/09/84	Football League Division 1	Manchester United 1 Chelsea 1	Old Trafford	48398
20	1987/88	05/09/87	Football League Division 1	Coventry City 0 Manchester United 0	Highfield Road	27125
21	2000/01	05/09/00	FA Premiership	Manchester United 6 Bradford City 0	Old Trafford	67447

SEPTEMBER 6

#	SEASON	DATE	COMPETITION / ROUND	MATCH RESULT	VENUE	ATT
1	1902/03	06/09/02	Football League Division 2	Gainsborough Trinity 0 Manchester United 1	The Northolme	4000
2	1909/10	06/09/09	Football League Division 1	Manchester United 2 Notts County 1	Bank Street	6000
3	1913/14	06/09/13	Football League Division 1	Sheffield Wednesday 1 Manchester United 3	Hillsborough	32000
4	1919/20	06/09/19	Football League Division 1	Manchester United 0 Derby County 2	Old Trafford	15000
5	1920/21	06/09/20	Football League Division 1	Manchester United 1 Arsenal 1	Old Trafford	45000
6	1924/25	06/09/24	Football League Division 2	Stoke City 0 Manchester United 0	Victoria Ground	15250
7	1930/31	06/09/30	Football League Division 1	Chelsea 6 Manchester United 2	Stamford Bridge	68648
8	1947/48	06/09/47	Football League Division 1	Arsenal 2 Manchester United 1	Highbury	64905
9	1952/53	06/09/52	Football League Division 1	Portsmouth 2 Manchester United 0	Fratton Park	37278
10	1958/59	06/09/58	Football League Division 1	Manchester United 6 Blackburn Rovers 1	Old Trafford	65187
11	1967/68	06/09/67	Football League Division 1	Sunderland 1 Manchester United 1	Roker Park	51527
12	1969/70	06/09/69	Football League Division 1	Leeds United 2 Manchester United 2	Elland Road	44271
13	1972/73	06/09/72	League Cup 2nd Round	Oxford United 2 Manchester United 2	Manor Ground	16560
14	1975/76	06/09/75	Football League Division 1	Manchester United 3 Tottenham Hotspur 2	Old Trafford	51641
15	1980/81	06/09/80	Football League Division 1	Tottenham Hotspur 0 Manchester United 0	White Hart Lane	40995
16	1983/84	06/09/83	Football League Division 1	Arsenal 2 Manchester United 3	Highbury	42703
17	1986/87	06/09/86	Football League Division 1	Leicester City 1 Manchester United 1	Filbert Street	16785
18	1992/93	06/09/92	FA Premiership	Manchester United 2 Leeds United 0	Old Trafford	31296

SEPTEMBER 7

#	SEASON	DATE	COMPETITION / ROUND	MATCH RESULT	VENUE	ATT
1	1895/96	07/09/95	Football League Division 2	Newton Heath 5 Crewe Alexandra 0	Bank Street	6000
2	1896/97	07/09/96	Football League Division 2	Newton Heath 2 Walsall 0	Bank Street	7000
3	1901/02	07/09/01	Football League Division 2	Newton Heath 3 Gainsborough Trinity 0	Bank Street	3000
4	1903/04	07/09/03	Football League Division 2	Burnley 2 Manchester United 0	Turf Moor	5000
5	1907/08	07/09/07	Football League Division 1	Manchester United 4 Liverpool 0	Bank Street	24000
6	1908/09	07/09/08	Football League Division 1	Manchester United 2 Bury 1	Bank Street	16000
7	1912/13	07/09/12	Football League Division 1	Manchester United 0 Manchester City 1	Old Trafford	40000
8	1921/22	07/09/21	Football League Division 1	West Bromwich Albion 0 Manchester United 0	The Hawthorns	15000
9	1925/26	07/09/25	Football League Division 1	Aston Villa 2 Manchester United 2	Villa Park	27701
10	1927/28	07/09/27	Football League Division 1	Manchester United 1 Sheffield Wednesday 1	Old Trafford	18759
11	1929/30	07/09/29	Football League Division 1	Manchester United 1 Blackburn Rovers 0	Old Trafford	22362
12	1931/32	07/09/31	Football League Division 2	Stoke City 3 Manchester United 0	Victoria Ground	10518
13	1932/33	07/09/32	Football League Division 2	Manchester United 1 Charlton Athletic 1	Old Trafford	9480
14	1933/34	07/09/33	Football League Division 2	Nottingham Forest 1 Manchester United 1	City Ground	10650
15	1935/36	07/09/35	Football League Division 2	Manchester United 3 Bradford City 1	Old Trafford	30754
16	1938/39	07/09/38	Football League Division 1	Liverpool 1 Manchester United 0	Anfield	25070
17	1946/47	07/09/46	Football League Division 1	Charlton Athletic 1 Manchester United 3	The Valley	44088
18	1949/50	07/09/49	Football League Division 1	Liverpool 1 Manchester United 1	Anfield	51587
19	1955/56	07/09/55	Football League Division 1	Manchester United 2 Everton 1	Old Trafford	27843
20	1957/58	07/09/57	Football League Division 1	Manchester United 5 Leeds United 0	Old Trafford	50842
21	1963/64	07/09/63	Football League Division 1	Birmingham City 1 Manchester United 1	St Andrews	36874
22	1966/67	07/09/66	Football League Division 1	Stoke City 3 Manchester United 0	Victoria Ground	44337
23	1968/69	07/09/68	Football League Division 1	Manchester United 1 West Ham United 1	Old Trafford	63274
24	1971/72	07/09/71	League Cup 2nd Round	Ipswich Town 1 Manchester United 3	Portman Road	28143
25	1974/75	07/09/74	Football League Division 2	Manchester United 2 Nottingham Forest 2	Old Trafford	40671
26	1985/86	07/09/85	Football League Division 1	Manchester United 3 Oxford United 0	Old Trafford	51820
27	1991/92	07/09/91	Football League Division 1	Manchester United 3 Norwich City 0	Old Trafford	44946
28	1996/97	07/09/96	FA Premiership	Leeds United 0 Manchester United 4	Elland Road	39694

SEPTEMBER 8

#	SEASON	DATE	COMPETITION / ROUND	MATCH RESULT	VENUE	ATT
1	1894/95	08/09/94	Football League Division 2	Burton Wanderers 1 Newton Heath 0	Derby Turn	3000
2	1900/01	08/09/00	Football League Division 2	Newton Heath 4 Middlesbrough 0	Bank Street	5500
3	1906/07	08/09/06	Football League Division 1	Manchester United 0 Notts County 0	Bank Street	30000
4	1913/14	08/09/13	Football League Division 1	Manchester United 3 Sunderland 1	Old Trafford	25000
5	1919/20	08/09/19	Football League Division 1	Sheffield Wednesday 1 Manchester United 3	Hillsborough	10000
6	1923/24	08/09/23	Football League Division 2	Bury 2 Manchester United 0	Gigg Lane	19000
7	1924/25	08/09/24	Football League Division 2	Manchester United 1 Barnsley 0	Old Trafford	9500
8	1928/29	08/09/28	Football League Division 1	Leeds United 3 Manchester United 2	Elland Road	28723
9	1934/35	08/09/34	Football League Division 2	Manchester United 4 Barnsley 1	Old Trafford	22315
10	1937/38	08/09/37	Football League Division 2	Manchester United 2 Coventry City 2	Old Trafford	17455
11	1947/48	08/09/47	Football League Division 1	Burnley 0 Manchester United 0	Turf Moor	37517
12	1948/49	08/09/48	Football League Division 1	Wolverhampton Wanderers 3 Manchester United 2	Molineux	42617
13	1951/52	08/09/51	Football League Division 1	Manchester United 4 Stoke City 0	Old Trafford	48660
14	1954/55	08/09/54	Football League Division 1	Tottenham Hotspur 2 Manchester United 2	White Hart Lane	35162
15	1956/57	08/09/56	Football League Division 1	Newcastle United 1 Manchester United 1	St James' Park	50130
16	1958/59	08/09/58	Football League Division 1	West Ham United 3 Manchester United 2	Upton Park	35672
17	1962/63	08/09/62	Football League Division 1	Leyton Orient 1 Manchester United 0	Brisbane Road	24901
18	1964/65	08/09/64	Football League Division 1	Everton 3 Manchester United 3	Goodison Park	63024
19	1965/66	08/09/65	Football League Division 1	Newcastle United 1 Manchester United 2	St James' Park	57380
20	1973/74	08/09/73	Football League Division 1	Ipswich Town 2 Manchester United 1	Portman Road	22023
21	1979/80	08/09/79	Football League Division 1	Aston Villa 0 Manchester United 3	Villa Park	34859
22	1982/83	08/09/82	Football League Division 1	Manchester United 2 Everton 1	Old Trafford	43186
23	1984/85	08/09/84	Football League Division 1	Manchester United 5 Newcastle United 0	Old Trafford	54915
24	1990/91	08/09/90	Football League Division 1	Manchester United 3 Queens Park Rangers 1	Old Trafford	43427
25	2001/02	08/09/01	FA Premiership	Manchester United 4 Everton 1	Old Trafford	67534

SEPTEMBER 9

#	SEASON	DATE	COMPETITION / ROUND	MATCH RESULT	VENUE	ATT
1	1893/94	09/09/93	Football League Division 1	West Bromwich Albion 3 Newton Heath 1	Stoney Lane	4500
2	1899/00	09/09/99	Football League Division 2	Bolton Wanderers 2 Newton Heath 1	Burnden Park	5000
3	1905/06	09/09/05	Football League Division 2	Grimsby Town 0 Manchester United 1	Blundell Park	6000
4	1907/08	09/09/07	Football League Division 1	Manchester United 2 Middlesbrough 1	Bank Street	20000
5	1911/12	09/09/11	Football League Division 1	Manchester United 2 Everton 1	Old Trafford	20000
6	1922/23	09/09/22	Football League Division 2	Wolverhampton Wanderers 0 Manchester United 1	Molineux	18000
7	1933/34	09/09/33	Football League Division 2	Manchester United 1 Bolton Wanderers 5	Old Trafford	21779
8	1935/36	09/09/35	Football League Division 2	Charlton Athletic 0 Manchester United 0	The Valley	13178
9	1936/37	09/09/36	Football League Division 1	Manchester United 3 Huddersfield Town 1	Old Trafford	26839
10	1950/51	09/09/50	Football League Division 1	Tottenham Hotspur 1 Manchester United 0	White Hart Lane	60621
11	1953/54	09/09/53	Football League Division 1	Manchester United 2 Middlesbrough 2	Old Trafford	18161
12	1957/58	09/09/57	Football League Division 1	Blackpool 1 Manchester United 4	Bloomfield Road	34181
13	1959/60	09/09/59	Football League Division 1	Manchester United 6 Leeds United 0	Old Trafford	48407
14	1961/62	09/09/61	Football League Division 1	Manchester United 1 Tottenham Hotspur 0	Old Trafford	57135
15	1967/68	09/09/67	Football League Division 1	Manchester United 2 Burnley 2	Old Trafford	55809
16	1970/71	09/09/70	League Cup 2nd Round	Aldershot 1 Manchester United 3	Recreation Ground	18509
17	1972/73	09/09/72	Football League Division 1	Manchester United 0 Coventry City 1	Old Trafford	37073
18	1978/79	09/09/78	Football League Division 1	Queens Park Rangers 1 Manchester United 1	Loftus Road	23477
19	1989/90	09/09/89	Football League Division 1	Everton 3 Manchester United 2	Goodison Park	37916
20	1995/96	09/09/95	FA Premiership	Everton 2 Manchester United 3	Goodison Park	39496
21	1998/99	09/09/98	FA Premiership	Manchester United 4 Charlton Athletic 1	Old Trafford	55147
22	2000/01	09/09/00	FA Premiership	Manchester United 3 Sunderland 0	Old Trafford	67503
23	2006/07	09/09/06	FA Premiership	Manchester United 1 Tottenham Hotspur 0	Old Trafford	75453

SEPTEMBER 10

#	SEASON	DATE	COMPETITION / ROUND	MATCH RESULT	VENUE	ATT
1	1892/93	10/09/92	Football League Division 1	Newton Heath 1 Burnley 1	North Road	10000
2	1898/99	10/09/98	Football League Division 2	Newton Heath 3 Manchester City 0	Bank Street	20000
3	1904/05	10/09/04	Football League Division 2	Manchester United 4 Bristol City 1	Bank Street	20000
4	1910/11	10/09/10	Football League Division 1	Nottingham Forest 2 Manchester United 1	City Ground	20000
5	1921/22	10/09/21	Football League Division 1	Chelsea 0 Manchester United 0	Stamford Bridge	35000
6	1927/28	10/09/27	Football League Division 1	Manchester United 1 Newcastle United 7	Old Trafford	50217
7	1930/31	10/09/30	Football League Division 1	Manchester United 0 Huddersfield Town 6	Old Trafford	11836
8	1932/33	10/09/32	Football League Division 2	Tottenham Hotspur 6 Manchester United 1	White Hart Lane	23333
9	1938/39	10/09/38	Football League Division 1	Grimsby Town 1 Manchester United 0	Blundell Park	14077
10	1949/50	10/09/49	Football League Division 1	Chelsea 1 Manchester United 1	Stamford Bridge	61357
11	1952/53	10/09/52	Football League Division 1	Derby County 2 Manchester United 3	Baseball Ground	20226
12	1955/56	10/09/55	Football League Division 1	Sheffield United 1 Manchester United 0	Bramall Lane	28241
13	1960/61	10/09/60	Football League Division 1	Manchester United 1 Leicester City 1	Old Trafford	35493
14	1966/67	10/09/66	Football League Division 1	Tottenham Hotspur 2 Manchester United 1	White Hart Lane	56295
15	1975/76	10/09/75	League Cup 2nd Round	Manchester United 2 Brentford 1	Old Trafford	25286
16	1977/78	10/09/77	Football League Division 1	Manchester City 3 Manchester United 1	Maine Road	50856
17	1983/84	10/09/83	Football League Division 1	Manchester United 2 Luton Town 0	Old Trafford	41013
18	1988/89	10/09/88	Football League Division 1	Manchester United 1 Middlesbrough 0	Old Trafford	40422
19	2005/06	10/09/05	FA Premiership	Manchester United 1 Manchester City 1	Old Trafford	67839

SEPTEMBER 11

#	SEASON	DATE	COMPETITION / ROUND	MATCH RESULT	VENUE	ATT
1	1897/98	11/09/97	Football League Division 2	Burton Swifts 0 Newton Heath 4	Peel Croft	2000
2	1909/10	11/09/09	Football League Division 1	Tottenham Hotspur 2 Manchester United 2	White Hart Lane	40000
3	1920/21	11/09/20	Football League Division 1	Manchester United 3 Chelsea 1	Old Trafford	40000
4	1926/27	11/09/26	Football League Division 1	Newcastle United 4 Manchester United 2	St James' Park	28050
5	1929/30	11/09/29	Football League Division 1	Manchester United 2 Leicester City 1	Old Trafford	16445
6	1937/38	11/09/37	Football League Division 2	Manchester United 4 Barnsley 1	Old Trafford	22934
7	1946/47	11/09/46	Football League Division 1	Manchester United 5 Liverpool 0	Maine Road	41657
8	1948/49	11/09/48	Football League Division 1	Manchester City 0 Manchester United 0	Maine Road	64502
9	1954/55	11/09/54	Football League Division 1	Bolton Wanderers 1 Manchester United 1	Burnden Park	44661
10	1963/64	11/09/63	Football League Division 1	Manchester United 4 Blackpool 0	Old Trafford	47400
11	1965/66	11/09/65	Football League Division 1	Burnley 3 Manchester United 0	Turf Moor	30235
12	1971/72	11/09/71	Football League Division 1	Crystal Palace 1 Manchester United 3	Selhurst Park	44020
13	1974/75	11/09/74	League Cup 2nd Round	Manchester United 5 Charlton Athletic 1	Old Trafford	21616
14	1976/77	11/09/76	Football League Division 1	Newcastle United 2 Manchester United 2	St James' Park	39037
15	1982/83	11/09/82	Football League Division 1	Manchester United 3 Ipswich Town 1	Old Trafford	43140
16	1993/94	11/09/93	FA Premiership	Chelsea 1 Manchester United 0	Stamford Bridge	37064
17	1994/95	11/09/94	FA Premiership	Leeds United 2 Manchester United 1	Elland Road	39396
18	1996/97	11/09/96	Champions League Phase 1 Match 1	Juventus 1 Manchester United 0	Stadio Delle Alpi	54000
19	1999/00	11/09/99	FA Premiership	Liverpool 2 Manchester United 3	Anfield	44929
20	2002/03	11/09/02	FA Premiership	Manchester United 0 Bolton Wanderers 1	Old Trafford	67623
21	2004/05	11/09/04	FA Premiership	Bolton Wanderers 2 Manchester United 2	Reebok Stadium	27766

SEPTEMBER 12

#	SEASON	DATE	COMPETITION / ROUND	MATCH RESULT	VENUE	ATT
1	1896/97	12/09/96	Football League Division 2	Newton Heath 3 Lincoln City 1	Bank Street	7000
2	1903/04	12/09/03	Football League Division 2	Port Vale 1 Manchester United 0	Cobridge Stadium	3000
3	1908/09	12/09/08	Football League Division 1	Manchester United 6 Middlesbrough 3	Bank Street	25000
4	1914/15	12/09/14	Football League Division 1	Bolton Wanderers 3 Manchester United 0	Burnden Park	10000
5	1925/26	12/09/25	Football League Division 1	Manchester City 1 Manchester United 1	Maine Road	62994
6	1931/32	12/09/31	Football League Division 2	Manchester United 1 Tottenham Hotspur 1	Old Trafford	9557
7	1934/35	12/09/34	Football League Division 2	Manchester United 0 Bolton Wanderers 3	Old Trafford	24760
8	1936/37	12/09/36	Football League Division 1	Manchester United 3 Manchester City 2	Old Trafford	68796
9	1951/52	12/09/51	Football League Division 1	Charlton Athletic 2 Manchester United 2	The Valley	28806
10	1953/54	12/09/53	Football League Division 1	Bolton Wanderers 0 Manchester United 0	Burnden Park	43544
11	1956/57	12/09/56	European Cup Prel. Round 1st Leg	Anderlecht 0 Manchester United 2	Park Astrid	35000
12	1959/60	12/09/59	Football League Division 1	Manchester United 1 Tottenham Hotspur 5	Old Trafford	55402
13	1962/63	12/09/62	Football League Division 1	Manchester United 3 Bolton Wanderers 0	Old Trafford	37721
14	1964/65	12/09/64	Football League Division 1	Manchester United 3 Nottingham Forest 0	Old Trafford	45012
15	1970/71	12/09/70	Football League Division 1	Manchester United 2 Coventry City 0	Old Trafford	48939
16	1972/73	12/09/72	League Cup 2nd Round Replay	Manchester United 3 Oxford United 1	Old Trafford	21486
17	1973/74	12/09/73	Football League Division 1	Manchester United 1 Leicester City 2	Old Trafford	40793
18	1981/82	12/09/81	Football League Division 1	Aston Villa 1 Manchester United 1	Villa Park	37661
19	1987/88	12/09/87	Football League Division 1	Manchester United 2 Newcastle United 2	Old Trafford	45619
20	1992/93	12/09/92	FA Premiership	Everton 0 Manchester United 2	Goodison Park	30002
21	1995/96	12/09/95	UEFA Cup 1st Round 1st Leg	Rotor Volgograd 0 Manchester United 0	Central Stadion	33000
22	1998/99	12/09/98	FA Premiership	Manchester United 2 Coventry City 0	Old Trafford	55198

SEPTEMBER 13

#	SEASON	DATE	COMPETITION / ROUND	MATCH RESULT	VENUE	ATT
1	1902/03	13/09/02	Football League Division 2	Manchester United 1 Burton United 0	Bank Street	15000
2	1913/14	13/09/13	Football League Division 1	Manchester United 0 Bolton Wanderers 1	Old Trafford	45000
3	1919/20	13/09/19	Football League Division 1	Preston North End 2 Manchester United 3	Deepdale	15000
4	1924/25	13/09/24	Football League Division 2	Manchester United 5 Coventry City 1	Old Trafford	12000
5	1930/31	13/09/30	Football League Division 1	Manchester United 4 Newcastle United 7	Old Trafford	10907
6	1937/38	13/09/37	Football League Division 2	Bury 1 Manchester United 2	Gigg Lane	9954
7	1947/48	13/09/47	Football League Division 1	Manchester United 0 Sheffield United 1	Maine Road	49808
8	1950/51	13/09/50	Football League Division 1	Manchester United 0 Aston Villa 0	Old Trafford	33021
9	1952/53	13/09/52	Football League Division 1	Manchester United 1 Bolton Wanderers 0	Old Trafford	40531
10	1958/59	13/09/58	Football League Division 1	Newcastle United 1 Manchester United 1	St James' Park	60670
11	1969/70	13/09/69	Football League Division 1	Manchester United 1 Liverpool 0	Old Trafford	56509
12	1975/76	13/09/75	Football League Division 1	Queens Park Rangers 1 Manchester United 0	Loftus Road	29237
13	1980/81	13/09/80	Football League Division 1	Manchester United 5 Leicester City 0	Old Trafford	43229
14	1986/87	13/09/86	Football League Division 1	Manchester United 5 Southampton 1	Old Trafford	40135
15	1997/98	13/09/97	FA Premiership	Manchester United 2 West Ham United 1	Old Trafford	55068
16	2000/01	13/09/00	Champions League Phase 1 Match 1	Manchester United 5 Anderlecht 1	Old Trafford	62749
17	2003/04	13/09/03	FA Premiership	Charlton Athletic 0 Manchester United 2	The Valley	26078
18	2006/07	13/09/06	Champions League Phase 1 Match 1	Manchester United 3 Glasgow Celtic 2	Old Trafford	74031

SEPTEMBER 14

#	SEASON	DATE	COMPETITION / ROUND	MATCH RESULT	VENUE	ATT
1	1895/96	14/09/95	Football League Division 2	Loughborough Town 3 Newton Heath 3	The Athletic Ground	3000
2	1901/02	14/09/01	Football League Division 2	Middlesbrough 5 Newton Heath 0	Linthorpe Road	12000
3	1907/08	14/09/07	Football League Division 1	Middlesbrough 2 Manchester United 1	Ayresome Park	18000
4	1912/13	14/09/12	Football League Division 1	West Bromwich Albion 1 Manchester United 2	The Hawthorns	25000
5	1929/30	14/09/29	Football League Division 2	Middlesbrough 2 Manchester United 1	Ayresome Park	26428
6	1935/36	14/09/35	Football League Division 2	Newcastle United 0 Manchester United 2	St James' Park	28520
7	1946/47	14/09/46	Football League Division 1	Manchester United 1 Middlesbrough 0	Maine Road	65112
8	1955/56	14/09/55	Football League Division 1	Everton 4 Manchester United 2	Goodison Park	34897
9	1957/58	14/09/57	Football League Division 1	Bolton Wanderers 4 Manchester United 0	Burnden Park	48003
10	1960/61	14/09/60	Football League Division 1	Manchester United 6 West Ham United 1	Old Trafford	33695
11	1963/64	14/09/63	Football League Division 1	Manchester United 1 West Bromwich Albion 0	Old Trafford	50453
12	1966/67	14/09/66	League Cup 2nd Round	Blackpool 5 Manchester United 1	Bloomfield Road	15570
13	1968/69	14/09/68	Football League Division 1	Burnley 1 Manchester United 0	Turf Moor	32935
14	1974/75	14/09/74	Football League Division 2	West Bromwich Albion 1 Manchester United 1	The Hawthorns	23721
15	1977/78	14/09/77	European CWC 1st Round 1st Leg	St Etienne 1 Manchester United 1	Geoffrey Guichard	33678
16	1983/84	14/09/83	European CWC 1st Round 1st Leg	Manchester United 1 Dukla Prague 1	Old Trafford	39745
17	1985/86	14/09/85	Football League Division 1	Manchester City 0 Manchester United 3	Maine Road	48773
18	1991/92	14/09/91	Football League Division 1	Southampton 0 Manchester United 1	The Dell	19264
19	1994/95	14/09/94	Champions League Phase 1 Match 1	Manchester United 4 Gothenburg 2	Old Trafford	33625
20	1996/97	14/09/96	FA Premiership	Manchester United 4 Nottingham Forest 1	Old Trafford	54984
21	1999/00	14/09/99	Champions League Phase 1 Match 1	Manchester United 0 Croatia Zagreb 0	Old Trafford	53250
22	2002/03	14/09/02	FA Premiership	Leeds United 1 Manchester United 0	Elland Road	39622
23	2005/06	14/09/05	Champions League Phase 1 Match 1	Villarreal 0 Manchester United 0	El Madrigal Stadium	22000

SEPTEMBER 15

#	SEASON	DATE	COMPETITION / ROUND	MATCH RESULT	VENUE	ATT
1	1894/95	15/09/94	Football League Division 2	Newton Heath 6 Crewe Alexandra 1	Bank Street	6000
2	1900/01	15/09/00	Football League Division 2	Burnley 1 Newton Heath 0	Turf Moor	4000
3	1906/07	15/09/06	Football League Division 1	Sheffield United 0 Manchester United 2	Bramall Lane	12000
4	1923/24	15/09/23	Football League Division 1	Manchester United 0 Bury 1	Old Trafford	43000
5	1926/27	15/09/26	Football League Division 1	Manchester United 2 Arsenal 2	Old Trafford	15259
6	1928/29	15/09/28	Football League Division 1	Manchester United 2 Liverpool 2	Old Trafford	24077
7	1930/31	15/09/30	Football League Division 1	Huddersfield Town 3 Manchester United 0	Leeds Road	14028
8	1934/35	15/09/34	Football League Division 2	Port Vale 3 Manchester United 2	Old Recreation Ground	9307
9	1948/49	15/09/48	Football League Division 1	Manchester United 2 Wolverhampton Wanderers 0	Maine Road	33871
10	1951/52	15/09/51	Football League Division 1	Manchester City 1 Manchester United 2	Maine Road	52571
11	1954/55	15/09/54	Football League Division 1	Manchester United 2 Tottenham Hotspur 1	Old Trafford	29212
12	1956/57	15/09/56	Football League Division 1	Manchester United 4 Sheffield Wednesday 1	Old Trafford	48078
13	1962/63	15/09/62	Football League Division 1	Manchester United 2 Manchester City 3	Old Trafford	49193
14	1965/66	15/09/65	Football League Division 1	Manchester United 1 Newcastle United 1	Old Trafford	30401
15	1973/74	15/09/73	Football League Division 1	Manchester United 3 West Ham United 1	Old Trafford	44757
16	1976/77	15/09/76	UEFA Cup 1st Round 1st Leg	Ajax 1 Manchester United 0	Olympisch Stadion	30000
17	1979/80	15/09/79	Football League Division 1	Manchester United 1 Derby County 0	Old Trafford	54308
18	1982/83	15/09/82	UEFA Cup 1st Round 1st Leg	Manchester United 0 Valencia 0	Old Trafford	46588
19	1984/85	15/09/84	Football League Division 1	Coventry City 0 Manchester United 3	Highfield Road	18312
20	1993/94	15/09/93	European Cup 1st Round 1st Leg	Honved 2 Manchester United 3	Jozsef Bozsik Stadium	9000
21	2001/02	15/09/01	FA Premiership	Newcastle United 4 Manchester United 3	St James' Park	52056
22	2004/05	15/09/04	Champions League Phase 1 Match 1	Olympique Lyonnais 2 Manchester United 2	Stade de Gerland	40000
23	2007/08	15/09/07	FA Premiership	Everton 0 Manchester United 1	Goodison Park	39364

SEPTEMBER 16

#	SEASON	DATE	COMPETITION / ROUND	MATCH RESULT	VENUE	ATT
1	1893/94	16/09/93	Football League Division 1	Sheffield Wednesday 0 Newton Heath 1	Olive Grove	7000
2	1899/00	16/09/99	Football League Division 2	Newton Heath 4 Loughborough Town 0	Bank Street	6000
3	1905/06	16/09/05	Football League Division 2	Glossop 1 Manchester United 2	North Road	7000
4	1911/12	16/09/11	Football League Division 1	West Bromwich Albion 1 Manchester United 0	The Hawthorns	35000
5	1922/23	16/09/22	Football League Division 2	Manchester United 1 Wolverhampton Wanderers 0	Old Trafford	28000
6	1925/26	16/09/25	Football League Division 1	Manchester United 3 Leicester City 2	Old Trafford	21275
7	1931/32	16/09/31	Football League Division 2	Manchester United 1 Stoke City 1	Old Trafford	5025
8	1933/34	16/09/33	Football League Division 2	Brentford 3 Manchester United 4	Griffin Park	17180
9	1950/51	16/09/50	Football League Division 1	Manchester United 3 Charlton Athletic 0	Old Trafford	36619
10	1953/54	16/09/53	Football League Division 1	Middlesbrough 1 Manchester United 4	Ayresome Park	23607
11	1959/60	16/09/59	Football League Division 1	Leeds United 2 Manchester United 2	Elland Road	34048
12	1961/62	16/09/61	Football League Division 1	Cardiff City 1 Manchester United 2	Ninian Park	29251
13	1963/64	16/09/63	Football League Division 1	Blackpool 1 Manchester United 0	Bloomfield Road	29806
14	1964/65	16/09/64	Football League Division 1	Manchester United 2 Everton 1	Old Trafford	49968
15	1967/68	16/09/67	Football League Division 1	Sheffield Wednesday 1 Manchester United 1	Hillsborough	47274
16	1972/73	16/09/72	Football League Division 1	Wolverhampton Wanderers 2 Manchester United 0	Molineux	34049
17	1974/75	16/09/74	Football League Division 2	Millwall 0 Manchester United 1	The Den	16988
18	1978/79	16/09/78	Football League Division 1	Manchester United 1 Nottingham Forest 1	Old Trafford	53039
19	1986/87	16/09/86	Football League Division 1	Watford 1 Manchester United 0	Vicarage Road	21650
20	1989/90	16/09/89	Football League Division 1	Manchester United 5 Millwall 1	Old Trafford	42746
21	1990/91	16/09/90	Football League Division 1	Liverpool 4 Manchester United 0	Anfield	35726
22	1992/93	16/09/92	UEFA Cup 1st Round 1st Leg	Manchester United 0 Torpedo Moscow 0	Old Trafford	19998
23	1995/96	16/09/95	FA Premiership	Manchester United 3 Bolton Wanderers 0	Old Trafford	32812
24	1998/99	16/09/98	Champions League Phase 1 Match 1	Manchester United 3 Barcelona 3	Old Trafford	53601
25	2000/01	16/09/00	FA Premiership	Everton 1 Manchester United 3	Goodison Park	38541
26	2003/04	16/09/03	Champions League Phase 1 Match 1	Manchester United 5 Panathinaikos 0	Old Trafford	66520

SEPTEMBER 17

#	SEASON	DATE	COMPETITION / ROUND	MATCH RESULT	VENUE	ATT
1	1892/93	17/09/92	Football League Division 1	Burnley 4 Newton Heath 1	Turf Moor	7000
2	1898/99	17/09/98	Football League Division 2	Glossop 1 Newton Heath 2	North Road	6000
3	1904/05	17/09/04	Football League Division 2	Manchester United 1 Bolton Wanderers 2	Bank Street	25000
4	1910/11	17/09/10	Football League Division 1	Manchester United 2 Manchester City 1	Old Trafford	60000
5	1921/22	17/09/21	Football League Division 1	Manchester United 0 Chelsea 0	Old Trafford	28000
6	1927/28	17/09/27	Football League Division 1	Huddersfield Town 4 Manchester United 2	Leeds Road	17307
7	1932/33	17/09/32	Football League Division 2	Manchester United 1 Grimsby Town 1	Old Trafford	17662
8	1938/39	17/09/38	Football League Division 1	Stoke City 1 Manchester United 1	Victoria Ground	21526
9	1949/50	17/09/49	Football League Division 1	Manchester United 2 Stoke City 2	Old Trafford	43522
10	1955/56	17/09/55	Football League Division 1	Manchester United 3 Preston North End 2	Old Trafford	33078
11	1958/59	17/09/58	Football League Division 1	Manchester United 4 West Ham United 1	Old Trafford	53276
12	1960/61	17/09/60	Football League Division 1	Aston Villa 3 Manchester United 1	Villa Park	43593
13	1966/67	17/09/66	Football League Division 1	Manchester United 1 Manchester City 0	Old Trafford	62085
14	1969/70	17/09/69	Football League Division 1	Sheffield Wednesday 1 Manchester United 3	Hillsborough	39298
15	1977/78	17/09/77	Football League Division 1	Manchester United 0 Chelsea 1	Old Trafford	54951
16	1980/81	17/09/80	UEFA Cup 1st Round 1st Leg	Manchester United 1 Widzew Lodz 1	Old Trafford	38037
17	1983/84	17/09/83	Football League Division 1	Southampton 3 Manchester United 0	The Dell	20674
18	1988/89	17/09/88	Football League Division 1	Luton Town 0 Manchester United 2	Kenilworth Road	11010
19	1994/95	17/09/94	FA Premiership	Manchester United 2 Liverpool 0	Old Trafford	43740
20	1997/98	17/09/97	Champions League Phase 1 Match 1	Kosice 0 Manchester United 3	TJ Lokomotive	9950
21	2006/07	17/09/06	FA Premiership	Manchester United 0 Arsenal 1	Old Trafford	75595

SEPTEMBER 18

#	SEASON	DATE	COMPETITION / ROUND	MATCH RESULT	VENUE	ATT
1	1897/98	18/09/97	Football League Division 2	Newton Heath 1 Luton Town 2	Bank Street	8000
2	1909/10	18/09/09	Football League Division 1	Manchester United 1 Preston North End 1	Bank Street	13000
3	1920/21	18/09/20	Football League Division 1	Chelsea 1 Manchester United 2	Stamford Bridge	35000
4	1926/27	18/09/26	Football League Division 1	Manchester United 2 Burnley 1	Old Trafford	32593
5	1935/36	18/09/35	Football League Division 2	Manchester United 2 Hull City 0	Old Trafford	15739
6	1937/38	18/09/37	Football League Division 2	Stockport County 1 Manchester United 0	Edgeley Park	24386
7	1946/47	18/09/46	Football League Division 1	Manchester United 1 Chelsea 1	Maine Road	30275
8	1948/49	18/09/48	Football League Division 1	Sheffield United 2 Manchester United 2	Bramall Lane	36880
9	1954/55	18/09/54	Football League Division 1	Manchester United 1 Huddersfield Town 1	Old Trafford	45648
10	1957/58	18/09/57	Football League Division 1	Manchester United 1 Blackpool 2	Old Trafford	40763
11	1961/62	18/09/61	Football League Division 1	Aston Villa 1 Manchester United 1	Villa Park	38837
12	1965/66	18/09/65	Football League Division 1	Manchester United 4 Chelsea 1	Old Trafford	37917
13	1968/69	18/09/68	European Cup 1st Round 1st Leg	Waterford 1 Manchester United 3	Lansdowne Road	48000
14	1971/72	18/09/71	Football League Division 1	Manchester United 4 West Ham United 2	Old Trafford	55339
15	1976/77	18/09/76	Football League Division 1	Manchester United 2 Middlesbrough 0	Old Trafford	56712
16	1982/83	18/09/82	Football League Division 1	Southampton 0 Manchester United 1	The Dell	21700
17	1991/92	18/09/91	European CWC 1st Round 1st Leg	Athinaikos 0 Manchester United 0	Apostolos Nikolaidis	5400
18	1999/00	18/09/99	FA Premiership	Manchester United 1 Wimbledon 1	Old Trafford	55189
19	2001/02	18/09/01	Champions League Phase 1 Match 1	Manchester United 1 Lille Metropole 0	Old Trafford	64827
20	2002/03	18/09/02	Champions League Phase 1 Match 1	Manchester United 5 Maccabi Haifa 2	Old Trafford	63439
21	2005/06	18/09/05	FA Premiership	Liverpool 0 Manchester United 0	Anfield	44917

SEPTEMBER 19

#	SEASON	DATE	COMPETITION / ROUND	MATCH RESULT	VENUE	ATT
1	1896/97	19/09/96	Football League Division 2	Grimsby Town 2 Newton Heath 0	Abbey Park	3000
2	1903/04	19/09/03	Football League Division 2	Glossop 0 Manchester United 5	North Road	3000
3	1908/09	19/09/08	Football League Division 1	Manchester City 1 Manchester United 2	Hyde Road	40000
4	1914/15	19/09/14	Football League Division 1	Manchester United 2 Blackburn Rovers 0	Old Trafford	15000
5	1925/26	19/09/25	Football League Division 1	Liverpool 5 Manchester United 0	Anfield	18824
6	1927/28	19/09/27	Football League Division 1	Blackburn Rovers 3 Manchester United 0	Ewood Park	18243
7	1931/32	19/09/31	Football League Division 2	Nottingham Forest 2 Manchester United 1	City Ground	10166
8	1936/37	19/09/36	Football League Division 1	Manchester United 1 Sheffield Wednesday 1	Old Trafford	40933
9	1953/54	19/09/53	Football League Division 1	Manchester United 1 Preston North End 0	Old Trafford	41171
10	1959/60	19/09/59	Football League Division 1	Manchester City 3 Manchester United 0	Maine Road	58300
11	1964/65	19/09/64	Football League Division 1	Stoke City 1 Manchester United 2	Victoria Ground	40031
12	1970/71	19/09/70	Football League Division 1	Ipswich Town 4 Manchester United 0	Portman Road	27776
13	1981/82	19/09/81	Football League Division 1	Manchester United 1 Swansea City 0	Old Trafford	47309
14	1984/85	19/09/84	UEFA Cup 1st Round 1st Leg	Manchester United 3 Raba Vasas 0	Old Trafford	33119
15	1987/88	19/09/87	Football League Division 1	Everton 2 Manchester United 1	Goodison Park	38439
16	1990/91	19/09/90	European CWC 1st Round 1st Leg	Manchester United 2 Pecsi Munkas 0	Old Trafford	28411
17	1992/93	19/09/92	FA Premiership	Tottenham Hotspur 1 Manchester United 1	White Hart Lane	33296
18	1993/94	19/09/93	FA Premiership	Manchester United 1 Arsenal 0	Old Trafford	44009
19	2000/01	19/09/00	Champions League Phase 1 Match 2	Dynamo Kiev 0 Manchester United 0	Republican Stadium	65000
20	2007/08	19/09/07	Champions League Phase 1 Match 1	Sporting Lisbon 0 Manchester United 1	de Jose Alvalade	39514

SEPTEMBER 20

#	SEASON	DATE	COMPETITION / ROUND	MATCH RESULT	VENUE	ATT
1	1902/03	20/09/02	Football League Division 2	Bristol City 3 Manchester United 1	Ashton Gate	6000
2	1913/14	20/09/13	Football League Division 1	Chelsea 0 Manchester United 2	Stamford Bridge	40000
3	1919/20	20/09/19	Football League Division 1	Manchester United 5 Preston North End 1	Old Trafford	18000
4	1924/25	20/09/24	Football League Division 2	Oldham Athletic 0 Manchester United 3	Boundary Park	14500
5	1930/31	20/09/30	Football League Division 1	Sheffield Wednesday 3 Manchester United 0	Hillsborough	18705
6	1947/48	20/09/47	Football League Division 1	Manchester City 0 Manchester United 0	Maine Road	71364
7	1952/53	20/09/52	Football League Division 1	Aston Villa 3 Manchester United 3	Villa Park	43490
8	1958/59	20/09/58	Football League Division 1	Manchester United 2 Tottenham Hotspur 2	Old Trafford	62277
9	1967/68	20/09/67	European Cup 1st Round 1st Leg	Manchester United 4 Hibernians Malta 0	Old Trafford	43912
10	1969/70	20/09/69	Football League Division 1	Arsenal 2 Manchester United 2	Highbury	59498
11	1975/76	20/09/75	Football League Division 1	Manchester United 1 Ipswich Town 0	Old Trafford	50513
12	1980/81	20/09/80	Football League Division 1	Leeds United 0 Manchester United 0	Elland Road	32539
13	1989/90	20/09/89	League Cup 2nd Round 1st Leg	Portsmouth 2 Manchester United 3	Fratton Park	18072
14	1995/96	20/09/95	League Cup 2nd Round 1st Leg	Manchester United 0 York City 3	Old Trafford	29049
15	1997/98	20/09/97	FA Premiership	Bolton Wanderers 0 Manchester United 0	Reebok Stadium	25000
16	1998/99	20/09/98	FA Premiership	Arsenal 3 Manchester United 0	Highbury	38142
17	2004/05	20/09/04	FA Premiership	Manchester United 2 Liverpool 1	Old Trafford	67857

SEPTEMBER 21

#	SEASON	DATE	COMPETITION / ROUND	MATCH RESULT	VENUE	ATT
1	1895/96	21/09/95	Football League Division 2	Newton Heath 5 Burton Swifts 0	Bank Street	9000
2	1896/97	21/09/96	Football League Division 2	Walsall 2 Newton Heath 3	Fellows Park	7000
3	1901/02	21/09/01	Football League Division 2	Newton Heath 1 Bristol City 0	Bank Street	5000
4	1907/08	21/09/07	Football League Division 1	Manchester United 2 Sheffield United 1	Bank Street	25000
5	1912/13	21/09/12	Football League Division 1	Manchester United 2 Everton 0	Old Trafford	40000
6	1929/30	21/09/29	Football League Division 1	Manchester United 1 Liverpool 2	Old Trafford	20788
7	1935/36	21/09/35	Football League Division 2	Manchester United 0 Tottenham Hotspur 0	Old Trafford	34718
8	1946/47	21/09/46	Football League Division 1	Stoke City 3 Manchester United 2	Victoria Ground	41699
9	1957/58	21/09/57	Football League Division 1	Manchester United 4 Arsenal 2	Old Trafford	47142
10	1963/64	21/09/63	Football League Division 1	Arsenal 2 Manchester United 1	Highbury	56776
11	1968/69	21/09/68	Football League Division 1	Manchester United 3 Newcastle United 1	Old Trafford	47262
12	1974/75	21/09/74	Football League Division 2	Manchester United 2 Bristol Rovers 0	Old Trafford	42948
13	1985/86	21/09/85	Football League Division 1	West Bromwich Albion 1 Manchester United 5	The Hawthorns	25068
14	1986/87	21/09/86	Football League Division 1	Everton 3 Manchester United 1	Goodison Park	25843
15	1991/92	21/09/91	Football League Division 1	Manchester United 5 Luton Town 0	Old Trafford	46491
16	1994/95	21/09/94	League Cup 2nd Round 1st Leg	Port Vale 1 Manchester United 2	Vale Park	18605
17	1996/97	21/09/96	FA Premiership	Aston Villa 0 Manchester United 0	Villa Park	39339
18	2002/03	21/09/02	FA Premiership	Manchester United 1 Tottenham Hotspur 0	Old Trafford	67611
19	2003/04	21/09/03	FA Premiership	Manchester United 0 Arsenal 0	Old Trafford	67639

SEPTEMBER 22

#	SEASON	DATE	COMPETITION / ROUND	MATCH RESULT	VENUE	ATT
1	1894/95	22/09/94	Football League Division 2	Leicester City 2 Newton Heath 3	Filbert Street	6000
2	1900/01	22/09/00	Football League Division 2	Newton Heath 4 Port Vale 0	Bank Street	6000
3	1906/07	22/09/06	Football League Division 1	Manchester United 1 Bolton Wanderers 2	Bank Street	45000
4	1923/24	22/09/23	Football League Division 2	South Shields 1 Manchester United 0	Talbot Road	9750
5	1928/29	22/09/28	Football League Division 1	West Ham United 3 Manchester United 1	Upton Park	20788
6	1934/35	22/09/34	Football League Division 2	Manchester United 5 Norwich City 0	Old Trafford	13052
7	1951/52	22/09/51	Football League Division 1	Tottenham Hotspur 2 Manchester United 0	White Hart Lane	70882
8	1956/57	22/09/56	Football League Division 1	Manchester United 2 Manchester City 0	Old Trafford	53525
9	1962/63	22/09/62	Football League Division 1	Manchester United 2 Burnley 5	Old Trafford	45954
10	1965/66	22/09/65	European Cup Prel. Round 1st Leg	HJK Helsinki 2 Manchester United 3	Olympiastadion	25000
11	1973/74	22/09/73	Football League Division 1	Leeds United 0 Manchester United 0	Elland Road	47058
12	1976/77	22/09/76	League Cup 3rd Round	Manchester United 2 Sunderland 2	Old Trafford	46170
13	1979/80	22/09/79	Football League Division 1	Wolverhampton Wanderers 3 Manchester United 1	Molineux	35503
14	1981/82	22/09/81	Football League Division 1	Middlesbrough 0 Manchester United 2	Ayresome Park	19895
15	1984/85	22/09/84	Football League Division 1	Manchester United 1 Liverpool 1	Old Trafford	56638
16	1990/91	22/09/90	Football League Division 1	Manchester United 3 Southampton 2	Old Trafford	41288
17	1993/94	22/09/93	League Cup 2nd Round 1st Leg	Stoke City 2 Manchester United 1	Victoria Ground	23327
18	1999/00	22/09/99	Champions League Phase 1 Match 2	Sturm Graz 0 Manchester United 3	Schwarzenegger Stadium	16480
19	2001/02	22/09/01	FA Premiership	Manchester United 4 Ipswich Town 0	Old Trafford	67551

SEPTEMBER 23

#	SEASON	DATE	COMPETITION / ROUND	MATCH RESULT	VENUE	ATT
1	1893/94	23/09/93	Football League Division 1	Newton Heath 1 Nottingham Forest 1	Bank Street	10000
2	1899/00	23/09/99	Football League Division 2	Burton Swifts 0 Newton Heath 0	Peel Croft	2000
3	1905/06	23/09/05	Football League Division 2	Manchester United 3 Stockport County 1	Bank Street	15000
4	1911/12	23/09/11	Football League Division 1	Manchester United 2 Sunderland 2	Old Trafford	20000
5	1922/23	23/09/22	Football League Division 2	Coventry City 2 Manchester United 0	Highfield Road	19000
6	1933/34	23/09/33	Football League Division 2	Manchester United 5 Burnley 2	Old Trafford	18411
7	1950/51	23/09/50	Football League Division 1	Middlesbrough 1 Manchester United 2	Ayresome Park	48051
8	1961/62	23/09/61	Football League Division 1	Manchester United 3 Manchester City 2	Old Trafford	56345
9	1964/65	23/09/64	ICFC 1st Round 1st Leg	Djurgardens 1 Manchester United 1	Roasunda Stadion	6537
10	1967/68	23/09/67	Football League Division 1	Manchester United 3 Tottenham Hotspur 1	Old Trafford	58779
11	1969/70	23/09/69	League Cup 3rd Round	Manchester United 2 Wrexham 0	Old Trafford	48347
12	1972/73	23/09/72	Football League Division 1	Manchester United 3 Derby County 0	Old Trafford	48255
13	1978/79	23/09/78	Football League Division 1	Arsenal 1 Manchester United 1	Highbury	45393
14	1987/88	23/09/87	League Cup 2nd Round 1st Leg	Manchester United 5 Hull City 0	Old Trafford	25041
15	1989/90	23/09/89	Football League Division 1	Manchester City 5 Manchester United 1	Maine Road	43246
16	1992/93	23/09/92	League Cup 2nd Round 1st Leg	Brighton 1 Manchester United 1	Goldstone Ground	16649
17	1995/96	23/09/95	FA Premiership	Sheffield Wednesday 0 Manchester United 0	Hillsborough	34101
18	2000/01	23/09/00	FA Premiership	Manchester United 3 Chelsea 3	Old Trafford	67568
19	2006/07	23/09/06	FA Premiership	Reading 1 Manchester United 1	Madejski Stadium	24098
20	2007/08	23/09/07	FA Premiership	Manchester United 2 Chelsea 0	Old Trafford	75663

SEPTEMBER 24

#	SEASON	DATE	COMPETITION / ROUND	MATCH RESULT	VENUE	ATT
1	1892/93	24/09/92	Football League Division 1	Everton 6 Newton Heath 0	Goodison Park	10000
2	1898/99	24/09/98	Football League Division 2	Newton Heath 1 Walsall 0	Bank Street	8000
3	1904/05	24/09/04	Football League Division 2	Glossop 1 Manchester United 2	North Road	6000
4	1910/11	24/09/10	Football League Division 1	Everton 0 Manchester United 1	Goodison Park	25000
5	1921/22	24/09/21	Football League Division 1	Preston North End 3 Manchester United 2	Deepdale	25000
6	1927/28	24/09/27	Football League Division 1	Manchester United 3 Tottenham Hotspur 0	Old Trafford	13952
7	1932/33	24/09/32	Football League Division 2	Oldham Athletic 1 Manchester United 1	Boundary Park	14403
8	1938/39	24/09/38	Football League Division 1	Manchester United 5 Chelsea 1	Old Trafford	34557
9	1949/50	24/09/49	Football League Division 1	Burnley 1 Manchester United 0	Turf Moor	41072
10	1952/53	24/09/52	FA Charity Shield	Manchester United 4 Newcastle United 2	Old Trafford	11381
11	1955/56	24/09/55	Football League Division 1	Burnley 0 Manchester United 0	Turf Moor	26873
12	1960/61	24/09/60	Football League Division 1	Manchester United 1 Wolverhampton Wanderers 3	Old Trafford	44458
13	1966/67	24/09/66	Football League Division 1	Manchester United 4 Burnley 1	Old Trafford	52697
14	1975/76	24/09/75	Football League Division 1	Derby County 2 Manchester United 1	Baseball Ground	33187
15	1977/78	24/09/77	Football League Division 1	Leeds United 1 Manchester United 1	Elland Road	33517
16	1983/84	24/09/83	Football League Division 1	Manchester United 1 Liverpool 0	Old Trafford	56121
17	1985/86	24/09/85	League Cup 2nd Round 1st Leg	Crystal Palace 0 Manchester United 1	Selhurst Park	21507
18	1986/87	24/09/86	League Cup 2nd Round 1st Leg	Manchester United 2 Port Vale 0	Old Trafford	18906
19	1988/89	24/09/88	Football League Division 1	Manchester United 2 West Ham United 0	Old Trafford	39941
20	1994/95	24/09/94	FA Premiership	Ipswich Town 3 Manchester United 2	Portman Road	22559
21	1997/98	24/09/97	FA Premiership	Manchester United 2 Chelsea 2	Old Trafford	55163
22	1998/99	24/09/98	FA Premiership	Manchester United 2 Liverpool 0	Old Trafford	55181
23	2002/03	24/09/02	Champions League Phase 1 Match 2	Bayer Leverkusen 1 Manchester United 2	Bayarena	22500
24	2005/06	24/09/05	FA Premiership	Manchester United 1 Blackburn Rovers 2	Old Trafford	67765

SEPTEMBER 25

#	SEASON	DATE	COMPETITION / ROUND	MATCH RESULT	VENUE	ATT
1	1897/98	25/09/97	Football League Division 2	Blackpool 0 Newton Heath 1	Raikes Hall Gardens	2000
2	1909/10	25/09/09	Football League Division 1	Notts County 3 Manchester United 2	Trent Bridge	11000
3	1911/12	25/09/11	FA Charity Shield	Manchester United 8 Swindon Town 4	Stamford Bridge	10000
4	1920/21	25/09/20	Football League Division 1	Manchester United 0 Tottenham Hotspur 1	Old Trafford	50000
5	1926/27	25/09/26	Football League Division 1	Cardiff City 0 Manchester United 2	Ninian Park	17267
6	1937/38	25/09/37	Football League Division 2	Manchester United 1 Southampton 2	Old Trafford	22729
7	1948/49	25/09/48	Football League Division 1	Manchester United 3 Aston Villa 1	Maine Road	53820
8	1954/55	25/09/54	Football League Division 1	Manchester City 3 Manchester United 2	Maine Road	54105
9	1957/58	25/09/57	European Cup Prel. Round 1st Leg	Shamrock Rovers 0 Manchester United 6	Dalymount Park	45000
10	1963/64	25/09/63	European CWC 1st Round 1st Leg	Willem II 1 Manchester United 1	Feyenoord Stadion	20000
11	1965/66	25/09/65	Football League Division 1	Arsenal 4 Manchester United 2	Highbury	56757
12	1968/69	25/09/68	Inter-Continental Cup Final 1st Leg	Estudiantes de la Plata 1 Manchester United 0	Boca Juniors Stadium	55000
13	1971/72	25/09/71	Football League Division 1	Liverpool 2 Manchester United 2	Anfield	55634
14	1974/75	25/09/74	Football League Division 2	Manchester United 3 Bolton Wanderers 0	Old Trafford	47084
15	1976/77	25/09/76	Football League Division 1	Manchester City 1 Manchester United 3	Maine Road	48861
16	1982/83	25/09/82	Football League Division 1	Manchester United 0 Arsenal 0	Old Trafford	43198
17	1991/92	25/09/91	League Cup 2nd Round 1st Leg	Manchester United 3 Cambridge United 0	Old Trafford	30934
18	1993/94	25/09/93	FA Premiership	Manchester United 4 Swindon Town 2	Old Trafford	44583
19	1996/97	25/09/96	Champions League Phase 1 Match 2	Manchester United 2 Rapid Vienna 0	Old Trafford	51831
20	1999/00	25/09/99	FA Premiership	Manchester United 3 Southampton 3	Old Trafford	55249
21	2001/02	25/09/01	Champions League Phase 1 Match 2	Deportivo La Coruna 2 Manchester United 1	Estadio de Riazor	33108
22	2004/05	25/09/04	FA Premiership	Tottenham Hotspur 0 Manchester United 1	White Hart Lane	36103

SEPTEMBER 26

#	SEASON	DATE	COMPETITION / ROUND	MATCH RESULT	VENUE	ATT
1	1896/97	26/09/96	Football League Division 2	Newton Heath 4 Newcastle United 0	Bank Street	7000
2	1903/04	26/09/03	Football League Division 2	Manchester United 3 Bradford City 1	Bank Street	30000
3	1908/09	26/09/08	Football League Division 1	Manchester United 3 Liverpool 2	Bank Street	25000
4	1914/15	26/09/14	Football League Division 1	Notts County 4 Manchester United 2	Meadow Lane	12000
5	1925/26	26/09/25	Football League Division 1	Manchester United 6 Burnley 1	Old Trafford	17259
6	1931/32	26/09/31	Football League Division 2	Manchester United 3 Chesterfield 1	Old Trafford	10834
7	1936/37	26/09/36	Football League Division 1	Preston North End 3 Manchester United 1	Deepdale	24149
8	1953/54	26/09/53	Football League Division 1	Tottenham Hotspur 1 Manchester United 1	White Hart Lane	52837
9	1956/57	26/09/56	European Cup Prel. Round 2nd Leg	Manchester United 10 Anderlecht 0	Maine Road	40000
10	1959/60	26/09/59	Football League Division 1	Preston North End 4 Manchester United 0	Deepdale	35016
11	1964/65	26/09/64	Football League Division 1	Manchester United 4 Tottenham Hotspur 1	Old Trafford	53058
12	1970/71	26/09/70	Football League Division 1	Manchester United 1 Blackpool 1	Old Trafford	46647
13	1979/80	26/09/79	League Cup 3rd Round	Norwich City 4 Manchester United 1	Carrow Road	18312
14	1981/82	26/09/81	Football League Division 1	Arsenal 0 Manchester United 0	Highbury	39795
15	1984/85	26/09/84	League Cup 2nd Round 1st Leg	Manchester United 4 Burnley 0	Old Trafford	28383
16	1987/88	26/09/87	Football League Division 1	Manchester United 1 Tottenham Hotspur 0	Old Trafford	48087
17	1990/91	26/09/90	League Cup 2nd Round 1st Leg	Halifax Town 1 Manchester United 3	The Shay	6841
18	1992/93	26/09/92	FA Premiership	Manchester United 0 Queens Park Rangers 0	Old Trafford	33287
19	1995/96	26/09/95	UEFA Cup 1st Round 2nd Leg	Manchester United 2 Rotor Volgograd 2	Old Trafford	29724
20	2000/01	26/09/00	Champions League Phase 1 Match 3	PSV Eindhoven 3 Manchester United 1	Philipstadion	30500
21	2006/07	26/09/06	Champions League Phase 1 Match 2	Benfica 0 Manchester United 1	Estadio da Luz	61000
22	2007/08	26/09/07	League Cup 3rd Round	Manchester United 0 Coventry City 2	Old Trafford	74055

SEPTEMBER 27

#	SEASON	DATE	COMPETITION / ROUND	MATCH RESULT	VENUE	ATT
1	1902/03	27/09/02	Football League Division 2	Manchester United 1 Glossop 1	Bank Street	12000
2	1913/14	27/09/13	Football League Division 1	Manchester United 4 Oldham Athletic 1	Old Trafford	55000
3	1919/20	27/09/19	Football League Division 1	Middlesbrough 1 Manchester United 1	Ayresome Park	20000
4	1924/25	27/09/24	Football League Division 2	Manchester United 2 Sheffield Wednesday 0	Old Trafford	29500
5	1930/31	27/09/30	Football League Division 1	Manchester United 0 Grimsby Town 2	Old Trafford	14695
6	1947/48	27/09/47	Football League Division 1	Preston North End 2 Manchester United 1	Deepdale	34372
7	1952/53	27/09/52	Football League Division 1	Manchester United 0 Sunderland 1	Old Trafford	28967
8	1958/59	27/09/58	Football League Division 1	Manchester City 1 Manchester United 1	Maine Road	62912
9	1967/68	27/09/67	European Cup 1st Round 2nd Leg	Hibernians Malta 0 Manchester United 0	Empire Stadium	25000
10	1969/70	27/09/69	Football League Division 1	Manchester United 5 West Ham United 2	Old Trafford	58579
11	1975/76	27/09/75	Football League Division 1	Manchester City 2 Manchester United 2	Maine Road	46931
12	1980/81	27/09/80	Football League Division 1	Manchester United 2 Manchester City 2	Old Trafford	55918
13	1983/84	27/09/83	European CWC 1st Round 2nd Leg	Dukla Prague 2 Manchester United 2	Stadion Juliska	28850
14	1997/98	27/09/97	FA Premiership	Leeds United 1 Manchester United 0	Elland Road	39952
15	2003/04	27/09/03	FA Premiership	Leicester City 1 Manchester United 4	Walkers Stadium	32044
16	2005/06	27/09/05	Champions League Phase 1 Match 2	Manchester United 2 Benfica 1	Old Trafford	66112

SEPTEMBER 28

#	SEASON	DATE	COMPETITION / ROUND	MATCH RESULT	VENUE	ATT
1	1895/96	28/09/95	Football League Division 2	Crewe Alexandra 0 Newton Heath 2	Gresty Road	2000
2	1901/02	28/09/01	Football League Division 2	Blackpool 2 Newton Heath 4	Bloomfield Road	3000
3	1907/08	28/09/07	Football League Division 1	Chelsea 1 Manchester United 4	Stamford Bridge	40000
4	1912/13	28/09/12	Football League Division 1	Sheffield Wednesday 3 Manchester United 3	Hillsborough	30000
5	1929/30	28/09/29	Football League Division 1	West Ham United 2 Manchester United 1	Upton Park	20695
6	1935/36	28/09/35	Football League Division 2	Southampton 2 Manchester United 1	The Dell	17678
7	1946/47	28/09/46	Football League Division 1	Manchester United 5 Arsenal 2	Maine Road	62718
8	1957/58	28/09/57	Football League Division 1	Wolverhampton Wanderers 3 Manchester United 1	Molineux	48825
9	1963/64	28/09/63	Football League Division 1	Manchester United 3 Leicester City 1	Old Trafford	41374
10	1974/75	28/09/74	Football League Division 2	Norwich City 2 Manchester United 0	Carrow Road	24586
11	1985/86	28/09/85	Football League Division 1	Manchester United 1 Southampton 0	Old Trafford	52449
12	1986/87	28/09/86	Football League Division 1	Manchester United 0 Chelsea 1	Old Trafford	33340
13	1988/89	28/09/88	League Cup 2nd Round 1st Leg	Rotherham United 0 Manchester United 1	Millmoor	12588
14	1991/92	28/09/91	Football League Division 1	Tottenham Hotspur 1 Manchester United 2	White Hart Lane	35087
15	1994/95	28/09/94	Champions League Phase 1 Match 2	Galatasaray 0 Manchester United 0	Ali Sami Yen	28605
16	2002/03	28/09/02	FA Premiership	Charlton Athletic 1 Manchester United 3	The Valley	26630
17	2004/05	28/09/04	Champions League Phase 1 Match 2	Manchester United 6 Fenerbahce 2	Old Trafford	67128

SEPTEMBER 29

#	SEASON	DATE	COMPETITION / ROUND	MATCH RESULT	VENUE	ATT
1	1900/01	29/09/00	Football League Division 2	Leicester City 1 Newton Heath 0	Filbert Street	6000
2	1906/07	29/09/06	Football League Division 1	Manchester United 1 Derby County 1	Bank Street	25000
3	1923/24	29/09/23	Football League Division 1	Manchester United 1 South Shields 1	Old Trafford	22250
4	1928/29	29/09/28	Football League Division 1	Manchester United 5 Newcastle United 0	Old Trafford	25243
5	1934/35	29/09/34	Football League Division 1	Manchester United 3 Swansea City 1	Old Trafford	14865
6	1951/52	29/09/51	Football League Division 1	Manchester United 1 Preston North End 2	Old Trafford	53454
7	1956/57	29/09/56	Football League Division 1	Arsenal 1 Manchester United 2	Highbury	62479
8	1962/63	29/09/62	Football League Division 1	Sheffield Wednesday 1 Manchester United 0	Hillsborough	40520
9	1973/74	29/09/73	Football League Division 1	Manchester United 0 Liverpool 0	Old Trafford	53862
10	1976/77	29/09/76	UEFA Cup 1st Round 2nd Leg	Manchester United 2 Ajax 0	Old Trafford	58918
11	1979/80	29/09/79	Football League Division 1	Manchester United 4 Stoke City 0	Old Trafford	52596
12	1982/83	29/09/82	UEFA Cup 1st Round 2nd Leg	Valencia 2 Manchester United 1	Luis Casanova	35000
13	1984/85	29/09/84	Football League Division 1	West Bromwich Albion 1 Manchester United 2	The Hawthorns	26292
14	1990/91	29/09/90	Football League Division 1	Manchester United 0 Nottingham Forest 1	Old Trafford	46766
15	1992/93	29/09/92	UEFA Cup 1st Round 2nd Leg	Torpedo Moscow 0 Manchester United 0	Torpedo Stadion	11357
16	1993/94	29/09/93	European Cup 1st Round 2nd Leg	Manchester United 2 Honved 1	Old Trafford	35781
17	1996/97	29/09/96	FA Premiership	Manchester United 2 Tottenham Hotspur 0	Old Trafford	54943
18	1999/00	29/09/99	Champions League Phase 1 Match 3	Manchester United 2 Olympique Marseille 1	Old Trafford	53993
19	2001/02	29/09/01	FA Premiership	Tottenham Hotspur 3 Manchester United 5	White Hart Lane	36038
20	2007/08	29/09/07	FA Premiership	Birmingham City 0 Manchester United 1	St Andrews	26526

SEPTEMBER 30

#	SEASON	DATE	COMPETITION / ROUND	MATCH RESULT	VENUE	ATT
1	1893/94	30/09/93	Football League Division 1	Darwen 1 Newton Heath 0	Barley Bank	4000
2	1899/00	30/09/99	Football League Division 2	Sheffield Wednesday 2 Newton Heath 1	Hillsborough	8000
3	1905/06	30/09/05	Football League Division 2	Blackpool 0 Manchester United 1	Bloomfield Road	7000
4	1911/12	30/09/11	Football League Division 1	Blackburn Rovers 2 Manchester United 2	Ewood Park	30000
5	1922/23	30/09/22	Football League Division 2	Manchester United 2 Coventry City 1	Old Trafford	25000
6	1933/34	30/09/33	Football League Division 2	Oldham Athletic 2 Manchester United 0	Boundary Park	22736
7	1950/51	30/09/50	Football League Division 1	Wolverhampton Wanderers 0 Manchester United 0	Molineux	45898
8	1961/62	30/09/61	Football League Division 1	Manchester United 0 Wolverhampton Wanderers 2	Old Trafford	39457
9	1964/65	30/09/64	Football League Division 1	Chelsea 0 Manchester United 2	Stamford Bridge	60759
10	1967/68	30/09/67	Football League Division 1	Manchester City 1 Manchester United 2	Maine Road	62942
11	1972/73	30/09/72	Football League Division 1	Sheffield United 1 Manchester United 0	Bramall Lane	37347
12	1978/79	30/09/78	Football League Division 1	Manchester United 1 Manchester City 0	Old Trafford	55301
13	1981/82	30/09/81	Football League Division 1	Manchester United 1 Leeds United 0	Old Trafford	47019
14	1998/99	30/09/98	Champions League Phase 1 Match 2	Bayern Munich 2 Manchester United 2	Olympic Stadium	53000

UNITED in OCTOBER

OVERALL PLAYING RECORD

	P	W	D	L	F	A		P	W	D	L	F	A		P	W	D	L	F	A
1st	23	8	9	6	36	33	11th	13	5	3	5	20	23	22nd	20	13	3	4	48	24
2nd	16	9	3	4	31	20	12th	13	7	2	4	24	20	23rd	19	11	4	4	33	22
3rd	24	9	9	6	38	29	13th	14	7	4	3	29	18	24th	22	12	7	3	44	26
4th	17	7	5	5	24	26	14th	17	7	3	7	19	20	25th	19	7	4	8	30	26
5th	14	7	6	1	26	12	15th	18	11	5	2	49	23	26th	22	10	2	10	43	36
6th	20	12	4	4	42	24	16th	16	7	6	3	27	23	27th	20	10	7	3	48	30
7th	18	11	3	4	28	17	17th	17	5	6	6	29	27	28th	22	13	2	7	41	28
8th	18	8	3	7	31	33	18th	17	9	5	3	29	14	29th	18	8	4	6	25	20
9th	15	9	3	3	27	16	19th	21	7	7	7	30	31	30th	19	7	3	9	30	26
10th	16	10	2	4	26	18	20th	18	10	2	6	24	24	31st	16	5	6	5	23	24
							21st	16	7	2	7	32	30							

OVERALL   558 268 134 156 986 743

OCTOBER 1

#	SEASON	DATE	COMPETITION / ROUND	MATCH RESULT	VENUE	ATT
1	1892/93	01/10/92	Football League Division 1	West Bromwich Albion 0 Newton Heath 0	Stoney Lane	4000
2	1898/99	01/10/98	Football League Division 2	Burton Swifts 5 Newton Heath 1	Peel Croft	2000
3	1910/11	01/10/10	Football League Division 1	Manchester United 3 Sheffield Wednesday 2	Old Trafford	20000
4	1921/22	01/10/21	Football League Division 1	Manchester United 1 Preston North End 1	Old Trafford	30000
5	1927/28	01/10/27	Football League Division 1	Leicester City 1 Manchester United 0	Filbert Street	22385
6	1932/33	01/10/32	Football League Division 2	Manchester United 0 Preston North End 0	Old Trafford	20800
7	1938/39	01/10/38	Football League Division 1	Preston North End 1 Manchester United 1	Deepdale	25964
8	1949/50	01/10/49	Football League Division 1	Manchester United 3 Sunderland 3	Old Trafford	49260
9	1955/56	01/10/55	Football League Division 1	Manchester United 3 Luton Town 1	Old Trafford	34409
10	1960/61	01/10/60	Football League Division 1	Bolton Wanderers 1 Manchester United 1	Burnden Park	39197
11	1966/67	01/10/66	Football League Division 1	Nottingham Forest 4 Manchester United 1	City Ground	41854
12	1977/78	01/10/77	Football League Division 1	Manchester United 2 Liverpool 0	Old Trafford	55089
13	1980/81	01/10/80	UEFA Cup 1st Round 2nd Leg	Widzew Lodz 0 Manchester United 0	Stadio TKS	40000
14	1983/84	01/10/83	Football League Division 1	Norwich City 3 Manchester United 3	Carrow Road	19290
15	1988/89	01/10/88	Football League Division 1	Tottenham Hotspur 2 Manchester United 2	White Hart Lane	29318
16	1994/95	01/10/94	FA Premiership	Manchester United 2 Everton 0	Old Trafford	43803
17	1995/96	01/10/95	FA Premiership	Manchester United 2 Liverpool 2	Old Trafford	34934
18	1997/98	01/10/97	Champions League Phase 1 Match 2	Manchester United 3 Juventus 2	Old Trafford	53428
19	2000/01	01/10/00	FA Premiership	Arsenal 1 Manchester United 0	Highbury	38146
20	2002/03	01/10/02	Champions League Phase 1 Match 3	Manchester United 4 Olympiakos Piraeus 0	Old Trafford	66902
21	2003/04	01/10/03	Champions League Phase 1 Match 2	Stuttgart 2 Manchester United 1	Gottlieb-Daimler Stadium	53000
22	2005/06	01/10/05	FA Premiership	Fulham 2 Manchester United 3	Craven Cottage	21862
23	2006/07	01/10/06	FA Premiership	Manchester United 2 Newcastle United 0	Old Trafford	75664

OCTOBER 2

#	SEASON	DATE	COMPETITION / ROUND	MATCH RESULT	VENUE	ATT
1	1897/98	02/10/97	Football League Division 2	Newton Heath 2 Leicester City 0	Bank Street	6000
2	1909/10	02/10/09	Football League Division 1	Manchester United 1 Newcastle United 1	Bank Street	30000
3	1920/21	02/10/20	Football League Division 1	Tottenham Hotspur 4 Manchester United 1	White Hart Lane	45000
4	1926/27	02/10/26	Football League Division 1	Manchester United 2 Aston Villa 1	Old Trafford	31234
5	1937/38	02/10/37	Football League Division 2	Manchester United 0 Sheffield United 1	Old Trafford	20105
6	1948/49	02/10/48	Football League Division 1	Sunderland 2 Manchester United 1	Roker Park	54419
7	1954/55	02/10/54	Football League Division 1	Wolverhampton Wanderers 4 Manchester United 2	Molineux	39617
8	1957/58	02/10/57	European Cup Prel. Round 2nd Leg	Manchester United 3 Shamrock Rovers 2	Old Trafford	33754
9	1963/64	02/10/63	Football League Division 1	Chelsea 1 Manchester United 1	Stamford Bridge	45351
10	1968/69	02/10/68	European Cup 1st Round 2nd Leg	Manchester United 7 Waterford 1	Old Trafford	41750
11	1971/72	02/10/71	Football League Division 1	Manchester United 2 Sheffield United 0	Old Trafford	51735
12	1976/77	02/10/76	Football League Division 1	Leeds United 0 Manchester United 2	Elland Road	44512
13	1982/83	02/10/82	Football League Division 1	Luton Town 1 Manchester United 1	Kenilworth Road	17009
14	1991/92	02/10/91	European CWC 1st Round 2nd Leg	Manchester United 2 Athinaikos 0	Old Trafford	35023
15	1993/94	02/10/93	FA Premiership	Sheffield Wednesday 2 Manchester United 3	Hillsborough	34548
16	2007/08	02/10/07	Champions League Phase 1 Match 2	Manchester United 1 Roma 0	Old Trafford	73652

OCTOBER 3

#	SEASON	DATE	COMPETITION / ROUND	MATCH RESULT	VENUE	ATT
1	1891/92	03/10/91	FA Cup 1st Qualifying Round	Newton Heath 5 Manchester City 1	North Road	11000
2	1896/97	03/10/96	Football League Division 2	Manchester City 0 Newton Heath 0	Hyde Road	20000
3	1903/04	03/10/03	Football League Division 2	Arsenal 4 Manchester United 0	Manor Field	20000
4	1908/09	03/10/08	Football League Division 1	Bury 2 Manchester United 2	Gigg Lane	25000
5	1914/15	03/10/14	Football League Division 1	Manchester United 3 Sunderland 0	Old Trafford	16000
6	1925/26	03/10/25	Football League Division 1	Leeds United 2 Manchester United 0	Elland Road	26265
7	1931/32	03/10/31	Football League Division 2	Burnley 2 Manchester United 0	Turf Moor	9719
8	1936/37	03/10/36	Football League Division 1	Manchester United 2 Arsenal 0	Old Trafford	55884
9	1953/54	03/10/53	Football League Division 1	Manchester United 1 Burnley 2	Old Trafford	37696
10	1959/60	03/10/59	Football League Division 1	Manchester United 4 Leicester City 1	Old Trafford	41637
11	1964/65	03/10/64	Football League Division 1	Burnley 0 Manchester United 0	Turf Moor	30761
12	1970/71	03/10/70	Football League Division 1	Wolverhampton Wanderers 3 Manchester United 2	Molineux	38629
13	1972/73	03/10/72	League Cup 3rd Round	Bristol Rovers 1 Manchester United 1	Eastville	33957
14	1981/82	03/10/81	Football League Division 1	Manchester United 5 Wolverhampton Wanderers 0	Old Trafford	46837
15	1983/84	03/10/83	League Cup 2nd Round 1st Leg	Port Vale 0 Manchester United 1	Vale Park	19885
16	1984/85	03/10/84	UEFA Cup 1st Round 2nd Leg	Raba Vasas 2 Manchester United 2	Raba ETO Stadium	26000
17	1987/88	03/10/87	Football League Division 1	Luton Town 1 Manchester United 1	Kenilworth Road	9137
18	1989/90	03/10/89	League Cup 2nd Round 2nd Leg	Manchester United 0 Portsmouth 0	Old Trafford	26698
19	1990/91	03/10/90	European CWC 1st Round 2nd Leg	Pecsi Munkas 0 Manchester United 1	PMSC Stadion	17000
20	1992/93	03/10/92	FA Premiership	Middlesbrough 1 Manchester United 1	Ayresome Park	24172
21	1995/96	03/10/95	League Cup 2nd Round 2nd Leg	York City 1 Manchester United 3	Bootham Crescent	9386
22	1998/99	03/10/98	FA Premiership	Southampton 0 Manchester United 3	The Dell	15251
23	1999/00	03/10/99	FA Premiership	Chelsea 5 Manchester United 0	Stamford Bridge	34909
24	2004/05	03/10/04	FA Premiership	Manchester United 1 Middlesbrough 1	Old Trafford	67988

OCTOBER 4

#	SEASON	DATE	COMPETITION / ROUND	MATCH RESULT	VENUE	ATT
1	1890/91	04/10/90	FA Cup 1st Qualifying Round	Newton Heath 2 Higher Walton 0	North Road	3000
2	1902/03	04/10/02	Football League Division 2	Manchester United 2 Chesterfield 1	Bank Street	12000
3	1913/14	04/10/13	Football League Division 1	Manchester United 3 Tottenham Hotspur 1	Old Trafford	25000
4	1919/20	04/10/19	Football League Division 1	Manchester United 1 Middlesbrough 1	Old Trafford	28000
5	1924/25	04/10/24	Football League Division 2	Leyton Orient 0 Manchester United 1	Millfields Road	15000
6	1930/31	04/10/30	Football League Division 1	Manchester City 4 Manchester United 1	Maine Road	41757
7	1947/48	04/10/47	Football League Division 1	Manchester United 1 Stoke City 1	Maine Road	45745
8	1952/53	04/10/52	Football League Division 1	Wolverhampton Wanderers 6 Manchester United 2	Molineux	40132
9	1958/59	04/10/58	Football League Division 1	Wolverhampton Wanderers 4 Manchester United 0	Molineux	36840
10	1969/70	04/10/69	Football League Division 1	Derby County 2 Manchester United 0	Baseball Ground	40724
11	1975/76	04/10/75	Football League Division 1	Manchester United 0 Leicester City 0	Old Trafford	47878
12	1976/77	04/10/76	League Cup 3rd Round Replay	Sunderland 2 Manchester United 2	Roker Park	46170
13	1978/79	04/10/78	League Cup 3rd Round	Manchester United 1 Watford 2	Old Trafford	40534
14	1980/81	04/10/80	Football League Division 1	Nottingham Forest 1 Manchester United 2	City Ground	29801
15	1986/87	04/10/86	Football League Division 1	Nottingham Forest 1 Manchester United 1	City Ground	34828
16	1997/98	04/10/97	FA Premiership	Manchester United 2 Crystal Palace 0	Old Trafford	55143
17	2003/04	04/10/03	FA Premiership	Manchester United 3 Birmingham City 0	Old Trafford	67633

OCTOBER 5

#	SEASON	DATE	COMPETITION / ROUND	MATCH RESULT	VENUE	ATT
1	1895/96	05/10/95	Football League Division 2	Newton Heath 1 Manchester City 1	Bank Street	12000
2	1901/02	05/10/01	Football League Division 2	Newton Heath 3 Stockport County 3	Bank Street	5000
3	1907/08	05/10/07	Football League Division 1	Manchester United 4 Nottingham Forest 0	Bank Street	20000
4	1912/13	05/10/12	Football League Division 1	Manchester United 1 Blackburn Rovers 1	Old Trafford	45000
5	1929/30	05/10/29	Football League Division 1	Manchester United 1 Manchester City 3	Old Trafford	57201
6	1935/36	05/10/35	Football League Division 2	Port Vale 0 Manchester United 3	Old Recreation Ground	9703
7	1946/47	05/10/46	Football League Division 1	Manchester United 1 Preston North End 1	Maine Road	55395
8	1957/58	05/10/57	Football League Division 1	Manchester United 4 Aston Villa 1	Old Trafford	43102
9	1963/64	05/10/63	Football League Division 1	Bolton Wanderers 0 Manchester United 1	Burnden Park	35872
10	1968/69	05/10/68	Football League Division 1	Manchester United 0 Arsenal 0	Old Trafford	61843
11	1974/75	05/10/74	Football League Division 2	Fulham 1 Manchester United 2	Craven Cottage	26513
12	1977/78	05/10/77	European CWC 1st Round 2nd Leg	Manchester United 2 St Etienne 0	Home Park	31634
13	1985/86	05/10/85	Football League Division 1	Luton Town 1 Manchester United 1	Kenilworth Road	17454
14	1994/95	05/10/94	League Cup 2nd Round 2nd Leg	Manchester United 2 Port Vale 0	Old Trafford	31615

OCTOBER 6

#	SEASON	DATE	COMPETITION / ROUND	MATCH RESULT	VENUE	ATT
1	1894/95	06/10/94	Football League Division 2	Darwen 1 Newton Heath 1	Barley Bank	6000
2	1900/01	06/10/00	Football League Division 2	Newton Heath 1 New Brighton Tower 0	Bank Street	5000
3	1906/07	06/10/06	Football League Division 1	Stoke City 1 Manchester United 2	Victoria Ground	7000
4	1923/24	06/10/23	Football League Division 2	Oldham Athletic 3 Manchester United 2	Boundary Park	12250
5	1928/29	06/10/28	Football League Division 1	Burnley 3 Manchester United 4	Turf Moor	17493
6	1934/35	06/10/34	Football League Division 2	Burnley 1 Manchester United 2	Turf Moor	16757
7	1948/49	06/10/48	FA Charity Shield	Arsenal 4 Manchester United 3	Highbury	31000
8	1951/52	06/10/51	Football League Division 1	Manchester United 2 Derby County 1	Old Trafford	39767
9	1956/57	06/10/56	Football League Division 1	Manchester United 4 Charlton Athletic 2	Old Trafford	41439
10	1962/63	06/10/62	Football League Division 1	Blackpool 2 Manchester United 2	Bloomfield Road	33242
11	1965/66	06/10/65	European Cup Prel. Round 2nd Leg	Manchester United 6 HJK Helsinki 0	Old Trafford	30388
12	1971/72	06/10/71	League Cup 3rd Round	Manchester United 1 Burnley 1	Old Trafford	44600
13	1973/74	06/10/73	Football League Division 1	Wolverhampton Wanderers 2 Manchester United 1	Molineux	32962
14	1976/77	06/10/76	League Cup 3rd Round 2nd Replay	Manchester United 1 Sunderland 0	Old Trafford	47689
15	1979/80	06/10/79	Football League Division 1	Manchester United 2 Brighton 0	Old Trafford	52641
16	1982/83	06/10/82	League Cup 2nd Round 1st Leg	Manchester United 2 Bournemouth 0	Old Trafford	22091
17	1984/85	06/10/84	Football League Division 1	Aston Villa 3 Manchester United 0	Villa Park	37131
18	1991/92	06/10/91	Football League Division 1	Manchester United 0 Liverpool 0	Old Trafford	44997
19	1993/94	06/10/93	League Cup 2nd Round 2nd Leg	Manchester United 2 Stoke City 0	Old Trafford	41387
20	2007/08	06/10/07	FA Premiership	Manchester United 4 Wigan Athletic 0	Old Trafford	75300

OCTOBER 7

#	SEASON	DATE	COMPETITION / ROUND	MATCH RESULT	VENUE	ATT
1	1893/94	07/10/93	Football League Division 1	Derby County 2 Newton Heath 0	Racecourse Ground	7000
2	1899/00	07/10/99	Football League Division 2	Newton Heath 1 Lincoln City 0	Bank Street	5000
3	1905/06	07/10/05	Football League Division 2	Manchester United 0 Bradford City 0	Bank Street	17000
4	1911/12	07/10/11	Football League Division 1	Manchester United 3 Sheffield Wednesday 1	Old Trafford	30000
5	1922/23	07/10/22	Football League Division 2	Manchester United 1 Port Vale 2	Old Trafford	25000
6	1929/30	07/10/29	Football League Division 1	Sheffield United 3 Manchester United 1	Bramall Lane	7987
7	1933/34	07/10/33	Football League Division 2	Manchester United 1 Preston North End 0	Old Trafford	22303
8	1950/51	07/10/50	Football League Division 1	Manchester United 3 Sheffield Wednesday 1	Old Trafford	40651
9	1961/62	07/10/61	Football League Division 1	West Bromwich Albion 1 Manchester United 1	The Hawthorns	25645
10	1967/68	07/10/67	Football League Division 1	Manchester United 1 Arsenal 0	Old Trafford	60197
11	1970/71	07/10/70	League Cup 3rd Round	Manchester United 1 Portsmouth 0	Old Trafford	32068
12	1972/73	07/10/72	Football League Division 1	West Bromwich Albion 2 Manchester United 2	The Hawthorns	32909
13	1978/79	07/10/78	Football League Division 1	Manchester United 3 Middlesbrough 2	Old Trafford	45402
14	1981/82	07/10/81	League Cup 2nd Round 1st Leg	Tottenham Hotspur 1 Manchester United 0	White Hart Lane	39333
15	1986/87	07/10/86	League Cup 2nd Round 2nd Leg	Port Vale 2 Manchester United 5	Vale Park	10486
16	1987/88	07/10/87	League Cup 2nd Round 2nd Leg	Hull City 0 Manchester United 1	Boothferry Park	13586
17	1992/93	07/10/92	League Cup 2nd Round 2nd Leg	Manchester United 1 Brighton 0	Old Trafford	25405
18	2002/03	07/10/02	FA Premiership	Manchester United 3 Everton 0	Old Trafford	67629

OCTOBER 8

#	SEASON	DATE	COMPETITION / ROUND	MATCH RESULT	VENUE	ATT
1	1892/93	08/10/92	Football League Division 1	Newton Heath 2 West Bromwich Albion 4	North Road	9000
2	1898/99	08/10/98	Football League Division 2	Newton Heath 2 Port Vale 1	Bank Street	10000
3	1904/05	08/10/04	Football League Division 2	Bradford City 1 Manchester United 1	Valley Parade	12000
4	1910/11	08/10/10	Football League Division 1	Bristol City 0 Manchester United 1	Ashton Gate	20000
5	1921/22	08/10/21	Football League Division 1	Tottenham Hotspur 2 Manchester United 2	White Hart Lane	35000
6	1927/28	08/10/27	Football League Division 1	Everton 5 Manchester United 2	Goodison Park	40080
7	1932/33	08/10/32	Football League Division 2	Burnley 2 Manchester United 3	Turf Moor	5314
8	1938/39	08/10/38	Football League Division 1	Manchester United 0 Charlton Athletic 2	Old Trafford	35730
9	1949/50	08/10/49	Football League Division 1	Manchester United 3 Charlton Athletic 2	Old Trafford	43809
10	1955/56	08/10/55	Football League Division 1	Manchester United 4 Wolverhampton Wanderers 3	Old Trafford	48638
11	1958/59	08/10/58	Football League Division 1	Manchester United 0 Preston North End 2	Old Trafford	46163
12	1966/67	08/10/66	Football League Division 1	Blackpool 1 Manchester United 2	Bloomfield Road	33555
13	1969/70	08/10/69	Football League Division 1	Southampton 0 Manchester United 3	The Dell	31044
14	1973/74	08/10/73	League Cup 2nd Round	Manchester United 0 Middlesbrough 1	Old Trafford	23906
15	1975/76	08/10/75	League Cup 3rd Round	Aston Villa 1 Manchester United 2	Villa Park	41447
16	1977/78	08/10/77	Football League Division 1	Middlesbrough 2 Manchester United 1	Ayresome Park	26882
17	1980/81	08/10/80	Football League Division 1	Manchester United 3 Aston Villa 3	Old Trafford	38831
18	1994/95	08/10/94	FA Premiership	Sheffield Wednesday 1 Manchester United 0	Hillsborough	33441

OCTOBER 9

#	SEASON	DATE	COMPETITION / ROUND	MATCH RESULT	VENUE	ATT
1	1897/98	09/10/97	Football League Division 2	Newcastle United 2 Newton Heath 0	St James' Park	12000
2	1909/10	09/10/09	Football League Division 1	Liverpool 3 Manchester United 2	Anfield	30000
3	1920/21	09/10/20	Football League Division 1	Manchester United 4 Oldham Athletic 1	Old Trafford	50000
4	1926/27	09/10/26	Football League Division 1	Bolton Wanderers 4 Manchester United 0	Burnden Park	17869
5	1937/38	09/10/37	Football League Division 2	Tottenham Hotspur 0 Manchester United 1	White Hart Lane	31189
6	1948/49	09/10/48	Football League Division 1	Manchester United 1 Charlton Athletic 1	Maine Road	46964
7	1954/55	09/10/54	Football League Division 1	Manchester United 5 Cardiff City 2	Old Trafford	39378
8	1965/66	09/10/65	Football League Division 1	Manchester United 2 Liverpool 0	Old Trafford	58161
9	1968/69	09/10/68	European Cup 1st Round	Tottenham Hotspur 2 Manchester United 2	White Hart Lane	56205
10	1971/72	09/10/71	Football League Division 1	Huddersfield Town 0 Manchester United 3	Leeds Road	33458
11	1974/75	09/10/74	League Cup 3rd Round	Manchester United 1 Manchester City 0	Old Trafford	55169
12	1982/83	09/10/82	Football League Division 1	Manchester United 1 Stoke City 0	Old Trafford	43132
13	1984/85	09/10/84	League Cup 2nd Round 2nd Leg	Burnley 0 Manchester United 3	Turf Moor	12690
14	1985/86	09/10/85	League Cup 2nd Round 2nd Leg	Manchester United 1 Crystal Palace 0	Old Trafford	26118
15	1991/92	09/10/91	League Cup 2nd Round 2nd Leg	Cambridge United 1 Manchester United 1	Abbey Stadium	9248

OCTOBER 10

#	SEASON	DATE	COMPETITION / ROUND	MATCH RESULT	VENUE	ATT
1	1896/97	10/10/96	Football League Division 2	Newton Heath 1 Birmingham City 1	Bank Street	7000
2	1903/04	10/10/03	Football League Division 2	Manchester United 4 Barnsley 0	Bank Street	20000
3	1908/09	10/10/08	Football League Division 1	Manchester United 2 Sheffield United 1	Bank Street	14000
4	1914/15	10/10/14	Football League Division 1	Sheffield Wednesday 1 Manchester United 0	Hillsborough	19000
5	1925/26	10/10/25	Football League Division 1	Manchester United 2 Newcastle United 1	Old Trafford	39651
6	1931/32	10/10/31	Football League Division 2	Manchester United 3 Preston North End 2	Old Trafford	8496
7	1936/37	10/10/36	Football League Division 1	Brentford 4 Manchester United 0	Griffin Park	28019
8	1953/54	10/10/53	Football League Division 1	Manchester United 1 Sunderland 0	Old Trafford	34617
9	1959/60	10/10/59	Football League Division 1	Manchester United 4 Arsenal 2	Old Trafford	51626
10	1964/65	10/10/64	Football League Division 1	Manchester United 1 Sunderland 0	Old Trafford	48577
11	1970/71	10/10/70	Football League Division 1	Manchester United 0 Crystal Palace 1	Old Trafford	42979
12	1979/80	10/10/79	Football League Division 1	West Bromwich Albion 2 Manchester United 0	The Hawthorns	27713
13	1981/82	10/10/81	Football League Division 1	Manchester City 0 Manchester United 0	Maine Road	52037
14	1987/88	10/10/87	Football League Division 1	Sheffield Wednesday 2 Manchester United 4	Hillsborough	32779
15	1990/91	10/10/90	League Cup 2nd Round 2nd Leg	Manchester United 2 Halifax Town 1	Old Trafford	22295
16	2001/02	10/10/01	Champions League Phase 1 Match 3	Olympiakos Piraeus 0 Manchester United 2	Olympic Stadium	73537

OCTOBER 11

#	SEASON	DATE	COMPETITION / ROUND	MATCH RESULT	VENUE	ATT
1	1902/03	11/10/02	Football League Division 2	Stockport County 2 Manchester United 1	Edgeley Park	6000
2	1913/14	11/10/13	Football League Division 1	Burnley 1 Manchester United 2	Turf Moor	30000
3	1919/20	11/10/19	Football League Division 1	Manchester City 3 Manchester United 3	Hyde Road	30000
4	1924/25	11/10/24	Football League Division 2	Manchester United 1 Crystal Palace 0	Old Trafford	27750
5	1930/31	11/10/30	Football League Division 1	West Ham United 5 Manchester United 1	Upton Park	20003
6	1947/48	11/10/47	Football League Division 1	Manchester United 3 Grimsby Town 4	Maine Road	40035
7	1952/53	11/10/52	Football League Division 1	Manchester United 0 Stoke City 2	Old Trafford	28968
8	1958/59	11/10/58	Football League Division 1	Manchester United 1 Arsenal 1	Old Trafford	56148
9	1969/70	11/10/69	Football League Division 1	Manchester United 2 Ipswich Town 1	Old Trafford	52281
10	1972/73	11/10/72	League Cup 3rd Round Replay	Manchester United 1 Bristol Rovers 2	Old Trafford	29349
11	1975/76	11/10/75	Football League Division 1	Leeds United 1 Manchester United 2	Elland Road	40264
12	1980/81	11/10/80	Football League Division 1	Manchester United 0 Arsenal 0	Old Trafford	49036
13	1986/87	11/10/86	Football League Division 1	Manchester United 3 Sheffield Wednesday 1	Old Trafford	45890

OCTOBER 12

#	SEASON	DATE	COMPETITION / ROUND	MATCH RESULT	VENUE	ATT
1	1895/96	12/10/95	Football League Division 2	Liverpool 7 Newton Heath 1	Anfield	7000
2	1901/02	12/10/01	Football League Division 2	Burton United 0 Newton Heath 0	Peel Croft	3000
3	1907/08	12/10/07	Football League Division 1	Newcastle United 1 Manchester United 6	St James' Park	25000
4	1912/13	12/10/12	Football League Division 1	Derby County 2 Manchester United 1	Baseball Ground	15000
5	1929/30	12/10/29	Football League Division 1	Manchester United 2 Grimsby Town 5	Old Trafford	21494
6	1935/36	12/10/35	Football League Division 2	Manchester United 1 Fulham 0	Old Trafford	22723
7	1946/47	12/10/46	Football League Division 1	Sheffield United 2 Manchester United 2	Bramall Lane	35543
8	1957/58	12/10/57	Football League Division 1	Nottingham Forest 1 Manchester United 2	City Ground	47654
9	1968/69	12/10/68	Football League Division 1	Liverpool 2 Manchester United 0	Anfield	53392
10	1974/75	12/10/74	Football League Division 2	Manchester United 1 Notts County 0	Old Trafford	46565
11	1985/86	12/10/85	Football League Division 1	Manchester United 2 Queens Park Rangers 0	Old Trafford	48845
12	1988/89	12/10/88	League Cup 2nd Round 2nd Leg	Manchester United 5 Rotherham United 0	Old Trafford	20597
13	1996/97	12/10/96	FA Premiership	Manchester United 1 Liverpool 0	Old Trafford	55128

OCTOBER 13

#	SEASON	DATE	COMPETITION / ROUND	MATCH RESULT	VENUE	ATT
1	1894/95	13/10/94	Football League Division 2	Newton Heath 3 Arsenal 3	Bank Street	4000
2	1900/01	13/10/00	Football League Division 2	Gainsborough Trinity 0 Newton Heath 1	The Northolme	2000
3	1906/07	13/10/06	Football League Division 1	Manchester United 1 Blackburn Rovers 1	Bank Street	20000
4	1923/24	13/10/23	Football League Division 2	Manchester United 2 Oldham Athletic 0	Old Trafford	26000
5	1928/29	13/10/28	Football League Division 1	Manchester United 1 Cardiff City 1	Old Trafford	26010
6	1934/35	13/10/34	Football League Division 2	Manchester United 4 Oldham Athletic 0	Old Trafford	29143
7	1951/52	13/10/51	Football League Division 1	Aston Villa 2 Manchester United 5	Villa Park	47795
8	1956/57	13/10/56	Football League Division 1	Sunderland 1 Manchester United 3	Roker Park	49487
9	1962/63	13/10/62	Football League Division 1	Manchester United 0 Blackburn Rovers 3	Old Trafford	42252
10	1973/74	13/10/73	Football League Division 1	Manchester United 0 Derby County 1	Old Trafford	43724
11	1979/80	13/10/79	Football League Division 1	Bristol City 1 Manchester United 1	Ashton Gate	28305
12	1984/85	13/10/84	Football League Division 1	Manchester United 5 West Ham United 1	Old Trafford	47559
13	1999/00	13/10/99	League Cup 3rd Round	Aston Villa 3 Manchester United 0	Villa Park	33815
14	2001/02	13/10/01	FA Premiership	Sunderland 1 Manchester United 3	Stadium of Light	48305

OCTOBER 14

#	SEASON	DATE	COMPETITION / ROUND	MATCH RESULT	VENUE	ATT
1	1893/94	14/10/93	Football League Division 1	Newton Heath 4 West Bromwich Albion 1	Bank Street	8000
2	1899/00	14/10/99	Football League Division 2	Birmingham City 1 Newton Heath 0	Muntz Street	10000
3	1905/06	14/10/05	Football League Division 2	West Bromwich Albion 1 Manchester United 0	The Hawthorns	15000
4	1911/12	14/10/11	Football League Division 1	Bury 0 Manchester United 1	Gigg Lane	18000
5	1922/23	14/10/22	Football League Division 2	Port Vale 1 Manchester United 0	Old Recreation Ground	16000
6	1933/34	14/10/33	Football League Division 2	Bradford Park Avenue 6 Manchester United 1	Park Avenue	11033
7	1950/51	14/10/50	Football League Division 1	Arsenal 3 Manchester United 0	Highbury	66150
8	1961/62	14/10/61	Football League Division 1	Manchester United 0 Birmingham City 2	Old Trafford	30674
9	1967/68	14/10/67	Football League Division 1	Sheffield United 0 Manchester United 3	Bramall Lane	29170
10	1969/70	14/10/69	League Cup 4th Round	Burnley 0 Manchester United 0	Turf Moor	27959
11	1972/73	14/10/72	Football League Division 1	Manchester United 1 Birmingham City 0	Old Trafford	52104
12	1978/79	14/10/78	Football League Division 1	Aston Villa 2 Manchester United 2	Villa Park	36204
13	1989/90	14/10/89	Football League Division 1	Manchester United 0 Sheffield Wednesday 0	Old Trafford	41492
14	1995/96	14/10/95	FA Premiership	Manchester United 1 Manchester City 0	Old Trafford	35707
15	1997/98	14/10/97	League Cup 3rd Round	Ipswich Town 2 Manchester United 0	Portman Road	22173
16	2000/01	14/10/00	FA Premiership	Leicester City 0 Manchester United 3	Filbert Street	22132
17	2006/07	14/10/06	FA Premiership	Wigan Athletic 1 Manchester United 3	JJB Stadium	20631

OCTOBER 15

#	SEASON	DATE	COMPETITION / ROUND	MATCH RESULT	VENUE	ATT
1	1892/93	15/10/92	Football League Division 1	Newton Heath 10 Wolverhampton Wanderers 1	North Road	4000
2	1898/99	15/10/98	Football League Division 2	Birmingham City 4 Newton Heath 1	Muntz Street	5000
3	1904/05	15/10/04	Football League Division 2	Manchester United 2 Lincoln City 0	Bank Street	15000
4	1910/11	15/10/10	Football League Division 1	Manchester United 2 Newcastle United 0	Old Trafford	50000
5	1921/22	15/10/21	Football League Division 1	Manchester United 2 Tottenham Hotspur 1	Old Trafford	30000
6	1927/28	15/10/27	Football League Division 1	Manchester United 2 Cardiff City 2	Old Trafford	31090
7	1932/33	15/10/32	Football League Division 2	Manchester United 2 Bradford Park Avenue 1	Old Trafford	18918
8	1938/39	15/10/38	Football League Division 1	Manchester United 0 Blackpool 0	Old Trafford	39723
9	1949/50	15/10/49	Football League Division 1	Aston Villa 0 Manchester United 4	Villa Park	47483
10	1955/56	15/10/55	Football League Division 1	Aston Villa 4 Manchester United 4	Villa Park	29478
11	1960/61	15/10/60	Football League Division 1	Burnley 5 Manchester United 3	Turf Moor	32011
12	1963/64	15/10/63	European CWC 1st Round 2nd Leg	Manchester United 6 Willem II 1	Old Trafford	46272
13	1966/67	15/10/66	Football League Division 1	Manchester United 1 Chelsea 1	Old Trafford	56789
14	1974/75	15/10/74	Football League Division 2	Portsmouth 0 Manchester United 0	Fratton Park	25608
15	1977/78	15/10/77	Football League Division 1	Manchester United 3 Newcastle United 2	Old Trafford	55056
16	1983/84	15/10/83	Football League Division 1	Manchester United 3 West Bromwich Albion 0	Old Trafford	42221
17	1994/95	15/10/94	FA Premiership	Manchester United 1 West Ham United 0	Old Trafford	43795
18	2005/06	15/10/05	FA Premiership	Sunderland 1 Manchester United 3	Stadium of Light	39085

OCTOBER 16

#	SEASON	DATE	COMPETITION / ROUND	MATCH RESULT	VENUE	ATT
1	1897/98	16/10/97	Football League Division 2	Newton Heath 1 Manchester City 1	Bank Street	20000
2	1909/10	16/10/09	Football League Division 1	Manchester United 2 Aston Villa 0	Bank Street	20000
3	1920/21	16/10/20	Football League Division 1	Oldham Athletic 2 Manchester United 2	Boundary Park	20000
4	1926/27	16/10/26	Football League Division 1	Bury 0 Manchester United 3	Gigg Lane	22728
5	1937/38	16/10/37	Football League Division 2	Blackburn Rovers 1 Manchester United 1	Ewood Park	19580
6	1948/49	16/10/48	Football League Division 1	Stoke City 2 Manchester United 1	Victoria Ground	45830
7	1954/55	16/10/54	Football League Division 1	Chelsea 5 Manchester United 6	Stamford Bridge	55966
8	1965/66	16/10/65	Football League Division 1	Tottenham Hotspur 5 Manchester United 1	White Hart Lane	58051
9	1968/69	16/10/68	Inter-Continental Cup Final 2nd Leg	Manchester United 1 Estudiantes de la Plata 1	Old Trafford	63500
10	1971/72	16/10/71	Football League Division 1	Manchester United 1 Derby County 0	Old Trafford	53247
11	1976/77	16/10/76	Football League Division 1	West Bromwich Albion 4 Manchester United 0	The Hawthorns	36615
12	1982/83	16/10/82	Football League Division 1	Liverpool 0 Manchester United 0	Anfield	40853
13	1993/94	16/10/93	FA Premiership	Manchester United 2 Tottenham Hotspur 1	Old Trafford	44655
14	1996/97	16/10/96	Champions League Phase 1 Match 3	Fenerbahce 0 Manchester United 2	Fenerbahce	26200
15	1999/00	16/10/99	FA Premiership	Manchester United 4 Watford 1	Old Trafford	55188
16	2004/05	16/10/04	FA Premiership	Birmingham City 0 Manchester United 0	St Andrews	29221

OCTOBER 17

#	SEASON	DATE	COMPETITION / ROUND	MATCH RESULT	VENUE	ATT
1	1896/97	17/10/96	Football League Division 2	Blackpool 4 Newton Heath 2	Raikes Hall Gardens	5000
2	1903/04	17/10/03	Football League Division 2	Lincoln City 0 Manchester United 0	Sincil Bank	5000
3	1908/09	17/10/08	Football League Division 1	Aston Villa 3 Manchester United 1	Villa Park	40000
4	1914/15	17/10/14	Football League Division 1	Manchester United 0 West Bromwich Albion 0	Old Trafford	18000
5	1925/26	17/10/25	Football League Division 1	Manchester United 0 Tottenham Hotspur 0	Old Trafford	26496
6	1931/32	17/10/31	Football League Division 2	Barnsley 0 Manchester United 0	Oakwell	4052
7	1936/37	17/10/36	Football League Division 1	Portsmouth 2 Manchester United 1	Fratton Park	19845
8	1953/54	17/10/53	Football League Division 1	Wolverhampton Wanderers 3 Manchester United 1	Molineux	40084
9	1956/57	17/10/56	European Cup 1st Round 1st Leg	Manchester United 3 Borussia Dortmund 2	Maine Road	75598
10	1959/60	17/10/59	Football League Division 1	Wolverhampton Wanderers 3 Manchester United 2	Molineux	45451
11	1964/65	17/10/64	Football League Division 1	Wolverhampton Wanderers 2 Manchester United 4	Molineux	26763
12	1970/71	17/10/70	Football League Division 1	Leeds United 2 Manchester United 2	Elland Road	50190
13	1981/82	17/10/81	Football League Division 1	Manchester United 1 Birmingham City 1	Old Trafford	48800
14	1987/88	17/10/87	Football League Division 1	Manchester United 2 Norwich City 1	Old Trafford	39821
15	1998/99	17/10/98	FA Premiership	Manchester United 5 Wimbledon 1	Old Trafford	55265
16	2001/02	17/10/01	Champions League Phase 1 Match 4	Manchester United 2 Deportivo La Coruna 3	Old Trafford	65585
17	2006/07	17/10/06	Champions League Phase 1 Match 3	Manchester United 3 Copenhagen 0	Old Trafford	72020

OCTOBER 18

#	SEASON	DATE	COMPETITION / ROUND	MATCH RESULT	VENUE	ATT
1	1913/14	18/10/13	Football League Division 1	Manchester United 3 Preston North End 0	Old Trafford	30000
2	1919/20	18/10/19	Football League Division 1	Manchester United 1 Manchester City 0	Old Trafford	40000
3	1924/25	18/10/24	Football League Division 2	Southampton 0 Manchester United 2	The Dell	10000
4	1930/31	18/10/30	Football League Division 1	Manchester United 1 Arsenal 2	Old Trafford	23406
5	1947/48	18/10/47	Football League Division 1	Sunderland 1 Manchester United 0	Roker Park	37148
6	1952/53	18/10/52	Football League Division 1	Preston North End 0 Manchester United 5	Deepdale	33502
7	1958/59	18/10/58	Football League Division 1	Everton 3 Manchester United 2	Goodison Park	64079
8	1969/70	18/10/69	Football League Division 1	Manchester United 1 Nottingham Forest 1	Old Trafford	53702
9	1971/72	18/10/71	League Cup 3rd Round Replay	Burnley 0 Manchester United 1	Turf Moor	27511
10	1975/76	18/10/75	Football League Division 1	Manchester United 3 Arsenal 1	Old Trafford	53885
11	1980/81	18/10/80	Football League Division 1	Ipswich Town 1 Manchester United 1	Portman Road	28572
12	1986/87	18/10/86	Football League Division 1	Manchester United 1 Luton Town 0	Old Trafford	39927
13	1992/93	18/10/92	FA Premiership	Manchester United 2 Liverpool 2	Old Trafford	33243
14	1997/98	18/10/97	FA Premiership	Derby County 2 Manchester United 2	Pride Park	30014
15	2000/01	18/10/00	Champions League Phase 1 Match 4	Manchester United 3 PSV Eindhoven 1	Old Trafford	66313
16	2003/04	18/10/03	FA Premiership	Leeds United 0 Manchester United 1	Elland Road	40153
17	2005/06	18/10/05	Champions League Phase 1 Match 3	Manchester United 0 Lille Metropole 0	Old Trafford	60626

OCTOBER 19

#	SEASON	DATE	COMPETITION / ROUND	MATCH RESULT	VENUE	ATT
1	1892/93	19/10/92	Football League Division 1	Newton Heath 3 Everton 4	North Road	4000
2	1895/96	19/10/95	Football League Division 2	Newton Heath 2 Newcastle United 1	Bank Street	8000
3	1901/02	19/10/01	Football League Division 2	Glossop 0 Newton Heath 0	North Road	7000
4	1907/08	19/10/07	Football League Division 1	Blackburn Rovers 1 Manchester United 5	Ewood Park	30000
5	1912/13	19/10/12	Football League Division 1	Manchester United 2 Tottenham Hotspur 0	Old Trafford	12000
6	1929/30	19/10/29	Football League Division 1	Portsmouth 3 Manchester United 0	Fratton Park	18070
7	1935/36	19/10/35	Football League Division 2	Manchester United 3 Sheffield United 1	Old Trafford	18636
8	1946/47	19/10/46	Football League Division 1	Blackpool 3 Manchester United 1	Bloomfield Road	26307
9	1957/58	19/10/57	Football League Division 1	Manchester United 0 Portsmouth 3	Old Trafford	38253
10	1960/61	19/10/60	League Cup 1st Round	Exeter City 1 Manchester United 1	St James' Park	14494
11	1963/64	19/10/63	Football League Division 1	Nottingham Forest 1 Manchester United 2	City Ground	41426
12	1968/69	19/10/68	Football League Division 1	Manchester United 1 Southampton 2	Old Trafford	46526
13	1974/75	19/10/74	Football League Division 2	Blackpool 0 Manchester United 3	Bloomfield Road	25370
14	1977/78	19/10/77	European CWC 2nd Round 1st Leg	Porto 4 Manchester United 0	Estadio das Antas	70000
15	1983/84	19/10/83	European CWC 2nd Round 1st Leg	Spartak Varna 1 Manchester United 2	Stad Yuri Gargarin	40000
16	1985/86	19/10/85	Football League Division 1	Manchester United 1 Liverpool 1	Old Trafford	54492
17	1991/92	19/10/91	Football League Division 1	Manchester United 1 Arsenal 1	Old Trafford	46594
18	1994/95	19/10/94	Champions League Phase 1 Match 3	Manchester United 2 Barcelona 2	Old Trafford	40064
19	1999/00	19/10/99	Champions League Phase 1 Match 4	Olympique Marseille 1 Manchester United 0	Stade Velodrome	56732
20	2002/03	19/10/02	FA Premiership	Fulham 1 Manchester United 1	Loftus Road	18103
21	2004/05	19/10/04	Champions League Phase 1 Match 3	Sparta Prague 0 Manchester United 0	Toyota Arena	20654

OCTOBER 20

#	SEASON	DATE	COMPETITION / ROUND	MATCH RESULT	VENUE	ATT
1	1894/95	20/10/94	Football League Division 2	Burton Swifts 1 Newton Heath 2	Peel Croft	5000
2	1900/01	20/10/00	Football League Division 2	Newton Heath 1 Walsall 1	Bank Street	8000
3	1906/07	20/10/06	Football League Division 1	Sunderland 4 Manchester United 1	Roker Park	18000
4	1923/24	20/10/23	Football League Division 2	Manchester United 3 Stockport County 0	Old Trafford	31500
5	1928/29	20/10/28	Football League Division 1	Manchester United 1 Birmingham City 0	Old Trafford	17522
6	1934/35	20/10/34	Football League Division 2	Newcastle United 0 Manchester United 1	St James' Park	24752
7	1951/52	20/10/51	Football League Division 1	Manchester United 0 Sunderland 1	Old Trafford	40915
8	1956/57	20/10/56	Football League Division 1	Manchester United 2 Everton 5	Old Trafford	43151
9	1969/70	20/10/69	League Cup 4th Round Replay	Manchester United 1 Burnley 0	Old Trafford	50275
10	1973/74	20/10/73	Football League Division 1	Manchester United 1 Birmingham City 0	Old Trafford	48937
11	1976/77	20/10/76	UEFA Cup 2nd Round 1st Leg	Manchester United 1 Juventus 0	Old Trafford	59000
12	1979/80	20/10/79	Football League Division 1	Manchester United 1 Ipswich Town 0	Old Trafford	50826
13	1984/85	20/10/84	Football League Division 1	Manchester United 1 Tottenham Hotspur 0	Old Trafford	54516
14	1990/91	20/10/90	Football League Division 1	Manchester United 0 Arsenal 1	Old Trafford	47232
15	1993/94	20/10/93	European Cup 2nd Round 1st Leg	Manchester United 3 Galatasaray 3	Old Trafford	39346
16	1996/97	20/10/96	FA Premiership	Newcastle United 5 Manchester United 0	St James' Park	35579
17	2001/02	20/10/01	FA Premiership	Manchester United 1 Bolton Wanderers 2	Old Trafford	67559
18	2007/08	20/10/07	FA Premiership	Aston Villa 1 Manchester United 4	Villa Park	42640

OCTOBER 21

#	SEASON	DATE	COMPETITION / ROUND	MATCH RESULT	VENUE	ATT
1	1893/94	21/10/93	Football League Division 1	Burnley 4 Newton Heath 1	Turf Moor	7000
2	1896/97	21/10/96	Football League Division 2	Gainsborough Trinity 2 Newton Heath 0	The Northolme	4000
3	1899/00	21/10/99	Football League Division 2	Newton Heath 2 New Brighton Tower 1	Bank Street	5000
4	1905/06	21/10/05	Football League Division 2	Manchester United 3 Leicester City 2	Bank Street	12000
5	1911/12	21/10/11	Football League Division 1	Manchester United 3 Middlesbrough 4	Old Trafford	20000
6	1922/23	21/10/22	Football League Division 2	Manchester United 1 Fulham 0	Old Trafford	18000
7	1933/34	21/10/33	Football League Division 2	Bury 2 Manchester United 1	Gigg Lane	15008
8	1950/51	21/10/50	Football League Division 1	Manchester United 0 Portsmouth 0	Old Trafford	41842
9	1961/62	21/10/61	Football League Division 1	Arsenal 5 Manchester United 1	Highbury	54245
10	1972/73	21/10/72	Football League Division 1	Newcastle United 2 Manchester United 1	St James' Park	38170
11	1978/79	21/10/78	Football League Division 1	Manchester United 1 Bristol City 3	Old Trafford	47211
12	1981/82	21/10/81	Football League Division 1	Manchester United 1 Middlesbrough 0	Old Trafford	38342
13	1989/90	21/10/89	Football League Division 1	Coventry City 1 Manchester United 4	Highfield Road	19625
14	1995/96	21/10/95	FA Premiership	Chelsea 1 Manchester United 4	Stamford Bridge	31019
15	1998/99	21/10/98	Champions League Phase 1 Match 3	Brondby 2 Manchester United 6	Parken Stadion	40530
16	2000/01	21/10/00	FA Premiership	Manchester United 3 Leeds United 0	Old Trafford	67523

OCTOBER 22

#	SEASON	DATE	COMPETITION / ROUND	MATCH RESULT	VENUE	ATT
1	1892/93	22/10/92	Football League Division 1	Sheffield Wednesday 1 Newton Heath 0	Olive Grove	6000
2	1898/99	22/10/98	Football League Division 2	Newton Heath 6 Loughborough Town 1	Bank Street	2000
3	1904/05	22/10/04	Football League Division 2	Leicester City 0 Manchester United 3	Filbert Street	7000
4	1910/11	22/10/10	Football League Division 1	Tottenham Hotspur 2 Manchester United 2	White Hart Lane	30000
5	1921/22	22/10/21	Football League Division 1	Manchester City 4 Manchester United 1	Hyde Road	24000
6	1927/28	22/10/27	Football League Division 1	Manchester United 5 Derby County 0	Old Trafford	18304
7	1932/33	22/10/32	Football League Division 2	Manchester United 7 Millwall 1	Old Trafford	15860
8	1938/39	22/10/38	Football League Division 1	Derby County 5 Manchester United 1	Baseball Ground	26612
9	1949/50	22/10/49	Football League Division 1	Manchester United 3 Wolverhampton Wanderers 0	Old Trafford	51427
10	1955/56	22/10/55	Football League Division 1	Manchester United 3 Huddersfield Town 0	Old Trafford	34150
11	1957/58	22/10/57	FA Charity Shield	Manchester United 4 Aston Villa 0	Old Trafford	27293
12	1960/61	22/10/60	Football League Division 1	Manchester United 3 Newcastle United 2	Old Trafford	37516
13	1977/78	22/10/77	Football League Division 1	West Bromwich Albion 4 Manchester United 0	The Hawthorns	27526
14	1980/81	22/10/80	Football League Division 1	Stoke City 1 Manchester United 2	Victoria Ground	24534
15	1983/84	22/10/83	Football League Division 1	Sunderland 0 Manchester United 1	Roker Park	26826
16	1988/89	22/10/88	Football League Division 1	Wimbledon 1 Manchester United 1	Plough Lane	12143
17	1997/98	22/10/97	Champions League Phase 1 Match 3	Manchester United 2 Feyenoord 1	Old Trafford	53188
18	2003/04	22/10/03	Champions League Phase 1 Match 3	Glasgow Rangers 0 Manchester United 1	Ibrox Stadium	48730
19	2005/06	22/10/05	FA Premiership	Manchester United 1 Tottenham Hotspur 1	Old Trafford	67856
20	2006/07	22/10/06	FA Premiership	Manchester United 2 Liverpool 0	Old Trafford	75828

OCTOBER 23

#	SEASON	DATE	COMPETITION / ROUND	MATCH RESULT	VENUE	ATT
1	1897/98	23/10/97	Football League Division 2	Birmingham City 2 Newton Heath 1	Muntz Street	6000
2	1909/10	23/10/09	Football League Division 1	Sheffield United 0 Manchester United 1	Bramall Lane	30000
3	1920/21	23/10/20	Football League Division 1	Manchester United 1 Preston North End 0	Old Trafford	42000
4	1926/27	23/10/26	Football League Division 1	Manchester United 0 Birmingham City 1	Old Trafford	32010
5	1937/38	23/10/37	Football League Division 2	Manchester United 1 Sheffield Wednesday 0	Old Trafford	16379
6	1948/49	23/10/48	Football League Division 1	Manchester United 1 Burnley 1	Maine Road	47093
7	1954/55	23/10/54	Football League Division 1	Manchester United 2 Newcastle United 2	Old Trafford	29217
8	1965/66	23/10/65	Football League Division 1	Manchester United 4 Fulham 1	Old Trafford	32716
9	1971/72	23/10/71	Football League Division 1	Newcastle United 0 Manchester United 1	St James' Park	52411
10	1976/77	23/10/76	Football League Division 1	Manchester United 2 Norwich City 2	Old Trafford	54356
11	1982/83	23/10/82	Football League Division 1	Manchester United 2 Manchester City 2	Old Trafford	57334
12	1990/91	23/10/90	European CWC 2nd Round 1st Leg	Manchester United 3 Wrexham 0	Old Trafford	29405
13	1991/92	23/10/91	European CWC 2nd Round 1st Leg	Athletico Madrid 3 Manchester United 0	Vincente Calderon	40000
14	1993/94	23/10/93	FA Premiership	Everton 0 Manchester United 1	Goodison Park	35430
15	1996/97	23/10/96	League Cup 3rd Round	Manchester United 2 Swindon Town 1	Old Trafford	49305
16	1999/00	23/10/99	FA Premiership	Tottenham Hotspur 3 Manchester United 1	White Hart Lane	36072
17	2001/02	23/10/01	Champions League Phase 1 Match 5	Manchester United 3 Olympiakos Piraeus 0	Old Trafford	66769
18	2002/03	23/10/02	Champions League Phase 1 Match 4	Olympiakos Piraeus 2 Manchester United 3	Rizoupoli	13200
19	2007/08	23/10/07	Champions League Phase 1 Match 3	Dynamo Kiev 2 Manchester United 4	Olympic Stadium	43000

OCTOBER 24

#	SEASON	DATE	COMPETITION / ROUND	MATCH RESULT	VENUE	ATT
1	1896/97	24/10/96	Football League Division 2	Newton Heath 3 Burton Wanderers 0	Bank Street	4000
2	1903/04	24/10/03	Football League Division 2	Manchester United 3 Stockport County 1	Bank Street	15000
3	1908/09	24/10/08	Football League Division 1	Manchester United 2 Nottingham Forest 2	Bank Street	20000
4	1914/15	24/10/14	Football League Division 1	Everton 4 Manchester United 2	Goodison Park	15000
5	1925/26	24/10/25	Football League Division 1	Cardiff City 0 Manchester United 2	Ninian Park	15846
6	1931/32	24/10/31	Football League Division 2	Manchester United 3 Notts County 3	Old Trafford	6694
7	1936/37	24/10/36	Football League Division 1	Manchester United 0 Chelsea 0	Old Trafford	29859
8	1953/54	24/10/53	Football League Division 1	Manchester United 1 Aston Villa 0	Old Trafford	30266
9	1956/57	24/10/56	FA Charity Shield	Manchester City 0 Manchester United 1	Maine Road	30495
10	1959/60	24/10/59	Football League Division 1	Manchester United 3 Sheffield Wednesday 1	Old Trafford	39259
11	1960/61	24/10/60	Football League Division 1	Manchester United 2 Nottingham Forest 1	Old Trafford	23628
12	1962/63	24/10/62	Football League Division 1	Tottenham Hotspur 6 Manchester United 2	White Hart Lane	51314
13	1964/65	24/10/64	Football League Division 1	Manchester United 7 Aston Villa 0	Old Trafford	35807
14	1970/71	24/10/70	Football League Division 1	Manchester United 2 West Bromwich Albion 1	Old Trafford	43278
15	1981/82	24/10/81	Football League Division 1	Liverpool 1 Manchester United 2	Anfield	41438
16	1984/85	24/10/84	UEFA Cup 2nd Round 1st Leg	PSV Eindhoven 0 Manchester United 0	Philipstadion	27500
17	1987/88	24/10/87	Football League Division 1	West Ham United 1 Manchester United 1	Upton Park	19863
18	1992/93	24/10/92	FA Premiership	Blackburn Rovers 0 Manchester United 0	Ewood Park	20305
19	1994/95	24/10/94	FA Premiership	Blackburn Rovers 2 Manchester United 4	Ewood Park	30260
20	1998/99	24/10/98	FA Premiership	Derby County 1 Manchester United 1	Pride Park	30867
21	2000/01	24/10/00	Champions League Phase 1 Match 5	Anderlecht 2 Manchester United 1	Vanden Stock	22506
22	2004/05	24/10/04	FA Premiership	Manchester United 2 Arsenal 0	Old Trafford	67862

OCTOBER 25

#	SEASON	DATE	COMPETITION / ROUND	MATCH RESULT	VENUE	ATT
1	1890/91	25/10/90	FA Cup 2nd Qualifying Round	Bootle Reserves 1 Newton Heath 0	Bootle Park	500
2	1902/03	25/10/02	Football League Division 2	Arsenal 0 Manchester United 1	Manor Field	12000
3	1905/06	25/10/05	Football League Division 2	Gainsborough Trinity 2 Manchester United 2	The Northolme	4000
4	1913/14	25/10/13	Football League Division 1	Newcastle United 0 Manchester United 1	St James' Park	35000
5	1919/20	25/10/19	Football League Division 1	Sheffield United 2 Manchester United 2	Bramall Lane	18000
6	1924/25	25/10/24	Football League Division 2	Wolverhampton Wanderers 0 Manchester United 0	Molineux	17500
7	1930/31	25/10/30	Football League Division 1	Portsmouth 4 Manchester United 1	Fratton Park	19262
8	1947/48	25/10/47	Football League Division 1	Manchester United 2 Aston Villa 0	Maine Road	47078
9	1952/53	25/10/52	Football League Division 1	Manchester United 1 Burnley 3	Old Trafford	36913
10	1958/59	25/10/58	Football League Division 1	Manchester United 1 West Bromwich Albion 2	Old Trafford	51721
11	1967/68	25/10/67	Football League Division 1	Manchester United 4 Coventry City 0	Old Trafford	54253
12	1969/70	25/10/69	Football League Division 1	West Bromwich Albion 2 Manchester United 1	The Hawthorns	45120
13	1975/76	25/10/75	Football League Division 1	West Ham United 2 Manchester United 1	Upton Park	38528
14	1980/81	25/10/80	Football League Division 1	Manchester United 2 Everton 0	Old Trafford	54260
15	1986/87	25/10/86	Football League Division 1	Manchester City 1 Manchester United 1	Maine Road	32440
16	1989/90	25/10/89	League Cup 3rd Round	Manchester United 0 Tottenham Hotspur 3	Old Trafford	45759
17	1997/98	25/10/97	FA Premiership	Manchester United 7 Barnsley 0	Old Trafford	55142
18	2003/04	25/10/03	FA Premiership	Manchester United 1 Fulham 3	Old Trafford	67727
19	2006/07	25/10/06	League Cup 3rd Round	Crewe Alexandra 1 Manchester United 2	Gresty Road	10046

OCTOBER 26

#	SEASON	DATE	COMPETITION / ROUND	MATCH RESULT	VENUE	ATT
1	1895/96	26/10/95	Football League Division 2	Newcastle United 2 Newton Heath 1	St James' Park	8000
2	1901/02	26/10/01	Football League Division 2	Newton Heath 6 Doncaster Rovers 0	Bank Street	7000
3	1907/08	26/10/07	Football League Division 1	Manchester United 2 Bolton Wanderers 1	Bank Street	35000
4	1912/13	26/10/12	Football League Division 1	Middlesbrough 3 Manchester United 2	Ayresome Park	10000
5	1929/30	26/10/29	Football League Division 1	Manchester United 1 Arsenal 0	Old Trafford	12662
6	1935/36	26/10/35	Football League Division 2	Bradford Park Avenue 1 Manchester United 0	Park Avenue	12216
7	1946/47	26/10/46	Football League Division 1	Manchester United 0 Sunderland 3	Maine Road	48385
8	1957/58	26/10/57	Football League Division 1	West Bromwich Albion 4 Manchester United 3	The Hawthorns	52160
9	1960/61	26/10/60	League Cup 1st Round Replay	Manchester United 4 Exeter City 1	Old Trafford	15662
10	1963/64	26/10/63	Football League Division 1	Manchester United 0 West Ham United 1	Old Trafford	45120
11	1968/69	26/10/68	Football League Division 1	Queens Park Rangers 2 Manchester United 3	Loftus Road	31138
12	1974/75	26/10/74	Football League Division 2	Manchester United 1 Southampton 0	Old Trafford	48724
13	1982/83	26/10/82	League Cup 2nd Round 2nd Leg	Bournemouth 2 Manchester United 2	Dean Court	13226
14	1983/84	26/10/83	League Cup 2nd Round 2nd Leg	Manchester United 2 Port Vale 0	Old Trafford	23589
15	1985/86	26/10/85	Football League Division 1	Chelsea 1 Manchester United 2	Stamford Bridge	42485
16	1988/89	26/10/88	Football League Division 1	Manchester United 1 Norwich City 2	Old Trafford	36998
17	1991/92	26/10/91	Football League Division 1	Sheffield Wednesday 3 Manchester United 2	Hillsborough	38260
18	1994/95	26/10/94	League Cup 3rd Round	Newcastle United 2 Manchester United 0	St James' Park	34178
19	1996/97	26/10/96	FA Premiership	Southampton 6 Manchester United 3	The Dell	15253
20	2002/03	26/10/02	FA Premiership	Manchester United 1 Aston Villa 1	Old Trafford	67619
21	2004/05	26/10/04	League Cup 3rd Round	Crewe Alexandra 0 Manchester United 3	Gresty Road	10103
22	2005/06	26/10/05	League Cup 3rd Round	Manchester United 4 Barnet 1	Old Trafford	43673

OCTOBER 27

#	SEASON	DATE	COMPETITION / ROUND	MATCH RESULT	VENUE	ATT
1	1894/95	27/10/94	Football League Division 2	Newton Heath 2 Leicester City 2	Bank Street	3000
2	1900/01	27/10/00	Football League Division 2	Burton Swifts 3 Newton Heath 1	Peel Croft	2000
3	1906/07	27/10/06	Football League Division 1	Manchester United 2 Birmingham City 1	Bank Street	14000
4	1923/24	27/10/23	Football League Division 2	Stockport County 3 Manchester United 2	Edgeley Park	16500
5	1928/29	27/10/28	Football League Division 1	Huddersfield Town 1 Manchester United 2	Leeds Road	13648
6	1934/35	27/10/34	Football League Division 2	Manchester United 3 West Ham United 1	Old Trafford	31950
7	1951/52	27/10/51	Football League Division 1	Wolverhampton Wanderers 0 Manchester United 2	Molineux	46167
8	1956/57	27/10/56	Football League Division 1	Blackpool 2 Manchester United 2	Bloomfield Road	32632
9	1962/63	27/10/62	Football League Division 1	Manchester United 3 West Ham United 1	Old Trafford	29204
10	1964/65	27/10/64	ICFC 1st Round 2nd Leg	Manchester United 6 Djurgardens 1	Old Trafford	38437
11	1971/72	27/10/71	League Cup 4th Round	Manchester United 1 Stoke City 1	Old Trafford	47062
12	1973/74	27/10/73	Football League Division 1	Burnley 0 Manchester United 0	Turf Moor	31976
13	1976/77	27/10/76	League Cup 4th Round	Manchester United 7 Newcastle United 2	Old Trafford	52002
14	1979/80	27/10/79	Football League Division 1	Everton 0 Manchester United 0	Goodison Park	37708
15	1984/85	27/10/84	Football League Division 1	Everton 5 Manchester United 0	Goodison Park	40742
16	1990/91	27/10/90	Football League Division 1	Manchester City 3 Manchester United 3	Maine Road	36427
17	1993/94	27/10/93	League Cup 3rd Round	Manchester United 5 Leicester City 1	Old Trafford	41344
18	1999/00	27/10/99	Champions League Phase 1 Match 5	Croatia Zagreb 1 Manchester United 2	Maksimir Stadium	27500
19	2001/02	27/10/01	FA Premiership	Manchester United 1 Leeds United 1	Old Trafford	67555
20	2007/08	27/10/07	FA Premiership	Manchester United 4 Middlesbrough 1	Old Trafford	75720

OCTOBER 28

#	SEASON	DATE	COMPETITION / ROUND	MATCH RESULT	VENUE	ATT
1	1893/94	28/10/93	Football League Division 1	Wolverhampton Wanderers 2 Newton Heath 0	Molineux	4000
2	1899/00	28/10/99	FA Cup 3rd Qualifying Round	South Shore 3 Newton Heath 1	Bloomfield Road	3000
3	1905/06	28/10/05	Football League Division 2	Hull City 0 Manchester United 1	Anlaby Road	14000
4	1911/12	28/10/11	Football League Division 1	Notts County 0 Manchester United 1	Meadow Lane	15000
5	1922/23	28/10/22	Football League Division 2	Fulham 0 Manchester United 0	Craven Cottage	20000
6	1933/34	28/10/33	Football League Division 2	Manchester United 4 Hull City 1	Old Trafford	16269
7	1950/51	28/10/50	Football League Division 1	Everton 1 Manchester United 4	Goodison Park	51142
8	1961/62	28/10/61	Football League Division 1	Manchester United 0 Bolton Wanderers 3	Old Trafford	31442
9	1963/64	28/10/63	Football League Division 1	Manchester United 2 Blackburn Rovers 2	Old Trafford	41169
10	1967/68	28/10/67	Football League Division 1	Nottingham Forest 3 Manchester United 1	City Ground	49946
11	1970/71	28/10/70	League Cup 4th Round	Manchester United 2 Chelsea 1	Old Trafford	47565
12	1972/73	28/10/72	Football League Division 1	Manchester United 1 Tottenham Hotspur 4	Old Trafford	52497
13	1978/79	28/10/78	Football League Division 1	Wolverhampton Wanderers 2 Manchester United 4	Molineux	23141
14	1981/82	28/10/81	League Cup 2nd Round 2nd Leg	Manchester United 0 Tottenham Hotspur 1	Old Trafford	55890
15	1987/88	28/10/87	League Cup 3rd Round	Manchester United 2 Crystal Palace 1	Old Trafford	27283
16	1989/90	28/10/89	Football League Division 1	Manchester United 2 Southampton 1	Old Trafford	37122
17	1992/93	28/10/92	League Cup 3rd Round	Aston Villa 1 Manchester United 0	Villa Park	35964
18	1995/96	28/10/95	FA Premiership	Manchester United 2 Middlesbrough 0	Old Trafford	36580
19	1998/99	28/10/98	League Cup 3rd Round	Manchester United 2 Bury 0	Old Trafford	52495
20	2000/01	28/10/00	FA Premiership	Manchester United 5 Southampton 0	Old Trafford	67581
21	2003/04	28/10/03	League Cup 3rd Round	Leeds United 2 Manchester United 3	Elland Road	37546
22	2006/07	28/10/06	FA Premiership	Bolton Wanderers 0 Manchester United 4	Reebok Stadium	27229

OCTOBER 29

#	SEASON	DATE	COMPETITION / ROUND	MATCH RESULT	VENUE	ATT
1	1892/93	29/10/92	Football League Division 1	Nottingham Forest 1 Newton Heath 1	Town Ground	6000
2	1904/05	29/10/04	Football League Division 2	Manchester United 4 Barnsley 0	Bank Street	15000
3	1910/11	29/10/10	Football League Division 1	Manchester United 1 Middlesbrough 2	Old Trafford	35000
4	1921/22	29/10/21	Football League Division 1	Manchester United 3 Manchester City 1	Old Trafford	56000
5	1927/28	29/10/27	Football League Division 1	West Ham United 1 Manchester United 2	Upton Park	21972
6	1932/33	29/10/32	Football League Division 2	Port Vale 3 Manchester United 3	Old Recreation Ground	7138
7	1938/39	29/10/38	Football League Division 1	Manchester United 0 Sunderland 1	Old Trafford	33565
8	1949/50	29/10/49	Football League Division 1	Portsmouth 0 Manchester United 0	Fratton Park	41098
9	1955/56	29/10/55	Football League Division 1	Cardiff City 0 Manchester United 1	Ninian Park	27795
10	1960/61	29/10/60	Football League Division 1	Arsenal 2 Manchester United 1	Highbury	45715
11	1966/67	29/10/66	Football League Division 1	Manchester United 1 Arsenal 0	Old Trafford	45387
12	1977/78	29/10/77	Football League Division 1	Aston Villa 2 Manchester United 1	Villa Park	39144
13	1983/84	29/10/83	Football League Division 1	Manchester United 3 Wolverhampton Wanderers 0	Old Trafford	41880
14	1985/86	29/10/85	League Cup 3rd Round	Manchester United 1 West Ham United 0	Old Trafford	32056
15	1986/87	29/10/86	League Cup 3rd Round	Manchester United 0 Southampton 1	Old Trafford	23639
16	1994/95	29/10/94	FA Premiership	Manchester United 2 Newcastle United 0	Old Trafford	43795
17	2002/03	29/10/02	Champions League Phase 1 Match 5	Maccabi Haifa 3 Manchester United 0	Neo GSP Stadium	22000
18	2005/06	29/10/05	FA Premiership	Middlesbrough 4 Manchester United 1	Riverside Stadium	30579

OCTOBER 30

#	SEASON	DATE	COMPETITION / ROUND	MATCH RESULT	VENUE	ATT
1	1886/87	30/10/86	FA Cup 1st Round	Fleetwood Rangers 2 Newton Heath 2	Fleetwood Park	2000
2	1897/98	30/10/97	Football League Division 2	Newton Heath 6 Walsall 0	Bank Street	6000
3	1909/10	30/10/09	Football League Division 1	Manchester United 1 Arsenal 0	Bank Street	20000
4	1920/21	30/10/20	Football League Division 1	Preston North End 0 Manchester United 0	Deepdale	25000
5	1926/27	30/10/26	Football League Division 1	West Ham United 4 Manchester United 0	Upton Park	19733
6	1937/38	30/10/37	Football League Division 2	Fulham 1 Manchester United 0	Craven Cottage	17350
7	1948/49	30/10/48	Football League Division 1	Preston North End 1 Manchester United 6	Deepdale	37372
8	1954/55	30/10/54	Football League Division 1	Everton 4 Manchester United 2	Goodison Park	63021
9	1965/66	30/10/65	Football League Division 1	Blackpool 1 Manchester United 2	Bloomfield Road	24703
10	1971/72	30/10/71	Football League Division 1	Manchester United 0 Leeds United 1	Old Trafford	53960
11	1976/77	30/10/76	Football League Division 1	Manchester United 0 Ipswich Town 1	Old Trafford	57416
12	1982/83	30/10/82	Football League Division 1	West Ham United 3 Manchester United 1	Upton Park	31684
13	1984/85	30/10/84	League Cup 3rd Round	Manchester United 1 Everton 2	Old Trafford	50918
14	1988/89	30/10/88	Football League Division 1	Everton 1 Manchester United 1	Goodison Park	27005
15	1991/92	30/10/91	League Cup 3rd Round	Manchester United 3 Portsmouth 1	Old Trafford	29543
16	1993/94	30/10/93	FA Premiership	Manchester United 2 Queens Park Rangers 1	Old Trafford	44663
17	1996/97	30/10/96	Champions League Phase 1 Match 4	Manchester United 0 Fenerbahce 1	Old Trafford	53297
18	1999/00	30/10/99	FA Premiership	Manchester United 3 Aston Villa 0	Old Trafford	55211
19	2004/05	30/10/04	FA Premiership	Portsmouth 2 Manchester United 0	Fratton Park	20190

OCTOBER 31

#	SEASON	DATE	COMPETITION / ROUND	MATCH RESULT	VENUE	ATT
1	1908/09	31/10/08	Football League Division 1	Sunderland 6 Manchester United 1	Roker Park	30000
2	1914/15	31/10/14	Football League Division 1	Manchester United 2 Chelsea 2	Old Trafford	15000
3	1925/26	31/10/25	Football League Division 1	Manchester United 1 Huddersfield Town 1	Old Trafford	37213
4	1931/32	31/10/31	Football League Division 2	Plymouth Argyle 3 Manchester United 1	Home Park	22555
5	1936/37	31/10/36	Football League Division 1	Stoke City 3 Manchester United 0	Victoria Ground	22464
6	1953/54	31/10/53	Football League Division 1	Huddersfield Town 0 Manchester United 0	Leeds Road	34175
7	1959/60	31/10/59	Football League Division 1	Blackburn Rovers 1 Manchester United 1	Ewood Park	39621
8	1964/65	31/10/64	Football League Division 1	Liverpool 0 Manchester United 2	Anfield	52402
9	1970/71	31/10/70	Football League Division 1	Newcastle United 1 Manchester United 0	St James' Park	45140
10	1981/82	31/10/81	Football League Division 1	Manchester United 2 Notts County 1	Old Trafford	45928
11	1987/88	31/10/87	Football League Division 1	Manchester United 2 Nottingham Forest 2	Old Trafford	44669
12	1990/91	31/10/90	League Cup 3rd Round	Manchester United 3 Liverpool 1	Old Trafford	42033
13	1992/93	31/10/92	FA Premiership	Manchester United 0 Wimbledon 1	Old Trafford	32622
14	1998/99	31/10/98	FA Premiership	Everton 1 Manchester United 4	Goodison Park	40079
15	2000/01	31/10/00	League Cup 3rd Round	Watford 0 Manchester United 3	Vicarage Road	18871
16	2001/02	31/10/01	Champions League Phase 1 Match 6	Lille Metropole 1 Manchester United 1	Stade Felix Bollaert	38402

UNITED in NOVEMBER

OVERALL PLAYING RECORD

	P	W	D	L	F	A		P	W	D	L	F	A		P	W	D	L	F	A
1st	15	11	2	2	39	9	11th	16	9	4	3	23	14	21st	18	7	1	10	28	28
2nd	22	12	2	8	38	27	12th	19	3	8	8	15	29	22nd	16	8	5	3	32	20
3rd	15	7	6	2	30	21	13th	14	10	2	2	33	13	23rd	19	11	3	5	36	28
4th	19	8	4	7	28	22	14th	12	9	1	2	32	18	24th	14	3	6	5	22	22
5th	18	10	4	4	38	23	15th	15	3	6	6	13	19	25th	16	8	3	5	25	21
6th	15	7	5	3	22	16	16th	14	4	5	5	20	30	26th	17	5	8	4	24	23
7th	19	8	6	5	34	25	17th	15	6	3	6	25	24	27th	20	10	3	7	34	30
8th	17	4	6	7	22	27	18th	15	9	2	4	30	23	28th	15	8	3	4	27	17
9th	15	5	2	8	26	27	19th	19	16	1	2	44	16	29th	14	7	5	2	29	15
10th	17	7	4	6	29	24	20th	17	10	4	3	33	18	30th	21	12	3	6	44	27

OVERALL   498 237 117 144 875 656

NOVEMBER 1

#	SEASON	DATE	COMPETITION / ROUND	MATCH RESULT	VENUE	ATT
1	1902/03	01/11/02	FA Cup 3rd Qualifying Round	Manchester United 7 Accrington Stanley 0	Bank Street	6000
2	1913/14	01/11/13	Football League Division 1	Manchester United 3 Liverpool 0	Old Trafford	30000
3	1919/20	01/11/19	Football League Division 1	Manchester United 3 Sheffield United 0	Old Trafford	24500
4	1924/25	01/11/24	Football League Division 2	Manchester United 2 Fulham 0	Old Trafford	24000
5	1930/31	01/11/30	Football League Division 1	Manchester United 2 Birmingham City 0	Old Trafford	11479
6	1947/48	01/11/47	Football League Division 1	Wolverhampton Wanderers 2 Manchester United 6	Molineux	44309
7	1952/53	01/11/52	Football League Division 1	Tottenham Hotspur 1 Manchester United 2	White Hart Lane	44300
8	1958/59	01/11/58	Football League Division 1	Leeds United 1 Manchester United 2	Elland Road	48574
9	1969/70	01/11/69	Football League Division 1	Manchester United 1 Stoke City 1	Old Trafford	53406
10	1975/76	01/11/75	Football League Division 1	Manchester United 1 Norwich City 0	Old Trafford	50587
11	1980/81	01/11/80	Football League Division 1	Crystal Palace 1 Manchester United 0	Selhurst Park	31449
12	1986/87	01/11/86	Football League Division 1	Manchester United 1 Coventry City 1	Old Trafford	36946
13	1997/98	01/11/97	FA Premiership	Manchester United 6 Sheffield Wednesday 1	Old Trafford	55259
14	2003/04	01/11/03	FA Premiership	Manchester United 3 Portsmouth 0	Old Trafford	67639
15	2006/07	01/11/06	Champions League Phase 1 Match 4	Copenhagen 1 Manchester United 0	Parken Stadion	40000

NOVEMBER 2

#	SEASON	DATE	COMPETITION / ROUND	MATCH RESULT	VENUE	ATT
1	1895/96	02/11/95	Football League Division 2	Newton Heath 5 Liverpool 2	Bank Street	10000
2	1907/08	02/11/07	Football League Division 1	Birmingham City 3 Manchester United 4	St Andrews	20000
3	1912/13	02/11/12	Football League Division 1	Manchester United 2 Notts County 1	Old Trafford	12000
4	1929/30	02/11/29	Football League Division 1	Aston Villa 1 Manchester United 0	Villa Park	24292
5	1935/36	02/11/35	Football League Division 2	Manchester United 0 Leicester City 1	Old Trafford	39074
6	1946/47	02/11/46	Football League Division 1	Aston Villa 0 Manchester United 0	Villa Park	53668
7	1957/58	02/11/57	Football League Division 1	Manchester United 1 Burnley 0	Old Trafford	49449
8	1960/61	02/11/60	League Cup 2nd Round	Bradford City 2 Manchester United 1	Valley Parade	4670
9	1963/64	02/11/63	Football League Division 1	Wolverhampton Wanderers 2 Manchester United 0	Molineux	34159
10	1968/69	02/11/68	Football League Division 1	Manchester United 0 Leeds United 0	Old Trafford	53839
11	1974/75	02/11/74	Football League Division 2	Manchester United 4 Oxford United 0	Old Trafford	41909
12	1977/78	02/11/77	European CWC 2nd Round 2nd Leg	Manchester United 5 Porto 2	Old Trafford	51831
13	1983/84	02/11/83	European CWC 2nd Round 2nd Leg	Manchester United 2 Spartak Varna 0	Old Trafford	39079
14	1984/85	02/11/84	Football League Division 1	Manchester United 4 Arsenal 2	Old Trafford	32279
15	1985/86	02/11/85	Football League Division 1	Manchester United 2 Coventry City 0	Old Trafford	46748
16	1988/89	02/11/88	League Cup 3rd Round	Wimbledon 2 Manchester United 1	Plough Lane	10864
17	1991/92	02/11/91	Football League Division 1	Manchester United 2 Sheffield United 0	Old Trafford	42942
18	1994/95	02/11/94	Champions League Phase 1 Match 4	Barcelona 4 Manchester United 0	Estadio Camp Nou	114273
19	1996/97	02/11/96	FA Premiership	Manchester United 1 Chelsea 2	Old Trafford	55198
20	1999/00	02/11/99	Champions League Phase 1 Match 6	Manchester United 2 Sturm Graz 1	Old Trafford	53745
21	2002/03	02/11/02	FA Premiership	Manchester United 2 Southampton 1	Old Trafford	67691
22	2005/06	02/11/05	Champions League Phase 1 Match 4	Lille Metropole 1 Manchester United 0	Stade de France	65000

NOVEMBER 3

#	SEASON	DATE	COMPETITION / ROUND	MATCH RESULT	VENUE	ATT
1	1894/95	03/11/94	Football League Division 2	Manchester City 2 Newton Heath 5	Hyde Road	14000
2	1906/07	03/11/06	Football League Division 1	Everton 3 Manchester United 0	Goodison Park	20000
3	1923/24	03/11/23	Football League Division 2	Leicester City 2 Manchester United 2	Filbert Street	17000
4	1928/29	03/11/28	Football League Division 1	Manchester United 1 Bolton Wanderers 1	Old Trafford	31185
5	1934/35	03/11/34	Football League Division 2	Blackpool 1 Manchester United 2	Bloomfield Road	15663
6	1951/52	03/11/51	Football League Division 1	Manchester United 1 Huddersfield Town 1	Old Trafford	25616
7	1956/57	03/11/56	Football League Division 1	Manchester United 3 Wolverhampton Wanderers 0	Old Trafford	59835
8	1962/63	03/11/62	Football League Division 1	Ipswich Town 5 Manchester United 5	Portman Road	18483
9	1973/74	03/11/73	Football League Division 1	Manchester United 2 Chelsea 2	Old Trafford	48036
10	1976/77	03/11/76	UEFA Cup 2nd Round 2nd Leg	Juventus 3 Manchester United 0	Stadio Comunale	66632
11	1979/80	03/11/79	Football League Division 1	Manchester United 1 Southampton 0	Old Trafford	50215
12	1990/91	03/11/90	Football League Division 1	Manchester United 2 Crystal Palace 0	Old Trafford	45724
13	1993/94	03/11/93	European Cup 2nd Round 2nd Leg	Galatasaray 0 Manchester United 0	Ali Sami Yen	40000
14	2004/05	03/11/04	Champions League Phase 1 Match 4	Manchester United 4 Sparta Prague 1	Old Trafford	66706
15	2007/08	03/11/07	FA Premiership	Arsenal 2 Manchester United 2	Emirates Stadium	60161

NOVEMBER 4

#	SEASON	DATE	COMPETITION / ROUND	MATCH RESULT	VENUE	ATT
1	1893/94	04/11/93	Football League Division 1	Newton Heath 0 Darwen 1	Bank Street	8000
2	1899/00	04/11/99	Football League Division 2	Newton Heath 2 Arsenal 0	Bank Street	5000
3	1905/06	04/11/05	Football League Division 2	Manchester United 2 Lincoln City 1	Bank Street	15000
4	1911/12	04/11/11	Football League Division 1	Manchester United 1 Tottenham Hotspur 2	Old Trafford	20000
5	1922/23	04/11/22	Football League Division 2	Manchester United 0 Leyton Orient 0	Old Trafford	16500
6	1933/34	04/11/33	Football League Division 2	Fulham 0 Manchester United 2	Craven Cottage	17049
7	1950/51	04/11/50	Football League Division 1	Manchester United 1 Burnley 1	Old Trafford	39454
8	1961/62	04/11/61	Football League Division 1	Sheffield Wednesday 3 Manchester United 1	Hillsborough	35998
9	1967/68	04/11/67	Football League Division 1	Manchester United 1 Stoke City 0	Old Trafford	51041
10	1972/73	04/11/72	Football League Division 1	Leicester City 2 Manchester United 2	Filbert Street	32575
11	1978/79	04/11/78	Football League Division 1	Manchester United 1 Southampton 1	Old Trafford	46259
12	1986/87	04/11/86	League Cup 3rd Round Replay	Southampton 4 Manchester United 1	The Dell	17915
13	1989/90	04/11/89	Football League Division 1	Charlton Athletic 2 Manchester United 0	Selhurst Park	16065
14	1995/96	04/11/95	FA Premiership	Arsenal 1 Manchester United 0	Highbury	38317
15	1997/98	04/11/97	Champions League Phase 1 Match 4	Manchester United 5 Brondby 0	Old Trafford	53250
16	2000/01	04/11/00	FA Premiership	Coventry City 1 Manchester United 2	Highfield Road	21079
17	2001/02	04/11/01	FA Premiership	Liverpool 3 Manchester United 1	Anfield	44361
18	2003/04	04/11/03	Champions League Phase 1 Match 4	Manchester United 3 Glasgow Rangers 0	Old Trafford	66707
19	2006/07	04/11/06	FA Premiership	Manchester United 3 Portsmouth 0	Old Trafford	76004

NOVEMBER 5

#	SEASON	DATE	COMPETITION / ROUND	MATCH RESULT	VENUE	ATT
1	1892/93	05/11/92	Football League Division 1	Newton Heath 4 Blackburn Rovers 4	North Road	12000
2	1898/99	05/11/98	Football League Division 2	Newton Heath 3 Grimsby Town 2	Bank Street	5000
3	1904/05	05/11/04	Football League Division 2	West Bromwich Albion 0 Manchester United 2	The Hawthorns	5000
4	1910/11	05/11/10	Football League Division 1	Preston North End 0 Manchester United 2	Deepdale	13000
5	1921/22	05/11/21	Football League Division 1	Manchester United 3 Middlesbrough 5	Old Trafford	30000
6	1927/28	05/11/27	Football League Division 1	Manchester United 2 Portsmouth 0	Old Trafford	13119
7	1932/33	05/11/32	Football League Division 2	Manchester United 2 Notts County 0	Old Trafford	24178
8	1938/39	05/11/38	Football League Division 1	Aston Villa 0 Manchester United 2	Villa Park	38357
9	1949/50	05/11/49	Football League Division 1	Manchester United 6 Huddersfield Town 0	Old Trafford	40295
10	1955/56	05/11/55	Football League Division 1	Manchester United 1 Arsenal 1	Old Trafford	41586
11	1960/61	05/11/60	Football League Division 1	Manchester United 0 Sheffield Wednesday 0	Old Trafford	36855
12	1966/67	05/11/66	Football League Division 1	Chelsea 1 Manchester United 3	Stamford Bridge	55958
13	1977/78	05/11/77	Football League Division 1	Manchester United 1 Arsenal 2	Old Trafford	53055
14	1983/84	05/11/83	Football League Division 1	Manchester United 1 Aston Villa 2	Old Trafford	45077
15	1988/89	05/11/88	Football League Division 1	Manchester United 1 Aston Villa 1	Old Trafford	44804
16	1997/98	05/11/97	Champions League Phase 1 Match 4	Feyenoord 1 Manchester United 3	Feyenoord Stadion	51000
17	2001/02	05/11/01	League Cup 3rd Round	Arsenal 4 Manchester United 0	Highbury	30693
18	2002/03	05/11/02	League Cup 3rd Round	Manchester United 2 Leicester City 0	Old Trafford	47848

NOVEMBER 6

#	SEASON	DATE	COMPETITION / ROUND	MATCH RESULT	VENUE	ATT
1	1897/98	06/11/97	Football League Division 2	Lincoln City 1 Newton Heath 0	Sincil Bank	2000
2	1909/10	06/11/09	Football League Division 1	Bolton Wanderers 2 Manchester United 3	Burnden Park	20000
3	1920/21	06/11/20	Football League Division 1	Manchester United 2 Sheffield United 1	Old Trafford	30000
4	1926/27	06/11/26	Football League Division 1	Manchester United 0 Sheffield Wednesday 0	Old Trafford	16166
5	1937/38	06/11/37	Football League Division 2	Manchester United 0 Plymouth Argyle 0	Old Trafford	18359
6	1948/49	06/11/48	Football League Division 1	Manchester United 2 Everton 0	Maine Road	42789
7	1954/55	06/11/54	Football League Division 1	Manchester United 2 Preston North End 1	Old Trafford	30063
8	1965/66	06/11/65	Football League Division 1	Manchester United 2 Blackburn Rovers 2	Old Trafford	38823
9	1971/72	06/11/71	Football League Division 1	Manchester City 3 Manchester United 3	Maine Road	63326
10	1976/77	06/11/76	Football League Division 1	Aston Villa 3 Manchester United 2	Villa Park	44789
11	1982/83	06/11/82	Football League Division 1	Brighton 1 Manchester United 0	Goldstone Ground	18379
12	1991/92	06/11/91	European CWC 2nd Round 2nd Leg	Manchester United 1 Athletico Madrid 1	Old Trafford	39654
13	1994/95	06/11/94	FA Premiership	Aston Villa 1 Manchester United 2	Villa Park	32136
14	1999/00	06/11/99	FA Premiership	Manchester United 2 Leicester City 0	Old Trafford	55191
15	2005/06	06/11/05	FA Premiership	Manchester United 1 Chelsea 0	Old Trafford	67864

NOVEMBER 7

#	SEASON	DATE	COMPETITION / ROUND	MATCH RESULT	VENUE	ATT
1	1896/97	07/11/96	Football League Division 2	Newton Heath 4 Grimsby Town 2	Bank Street	5000
2	1903/04	07/11/03	Football League Division 2	Manchester United 0 Bolton Wanderers 0	Bank Street	30000
3	1908/09	07/11/08	Football League Division 1	Manchester United 0 Chelsea 1	Bank Street	15000
4	1914/15	07/11/14	Football League Division 1	Bradford City 4 Manchester United 2	Valley Parade	12000
5	1925/26	07/11/25	Football League Division 1	Everton 1 Manchester United 3	Goodison Park	12387
6	1931/32	07/11/31	Football League Division 2	Manchester United 2 Leeds United 5	Old Trafford	9512
7	1936/37	07/11/36	Football League Division 1	Manchester United 0 Charlton Athletic 0	Old Trafford	26084
8	1953/54	07/11/53	Football League Division 1	Manchester United 2 Arsenal 2	Old Trafford	28141
9	1959/60	07/11/59	Football League Division 1	Manchester United 3 Fulham 3	Old Trafford	44063
10	1964/65	07/11/64	Football League Division 1	Manchester United 1 Sheffield Wednesday 0	Old Trafford	50178
11	1970/71	07/11/70	Football League Division 1	Manchester United 2 Stoke City 2	Old Trafford	47451
12	1981/82	07/11/81	Football League Division 1	Sunderland 1 Manchester United 5	Roker Park	27070
13	1984/85	07/11/84	UEFA Cup 2nd Round 2nd Leg	Manchester United 1 PSV Eindhoven 0	Old Trafford	39281
14	1990/91	07/11/90	European CWC 2nd Round 2nd Leg	Wrexham 0 Manchester United 2	Racecourse Ground	13327
15	1992/93	07/11/92	FA Premiership	Aston Villa 1 Manchester United 0	Villa Park	39063
16	1993/94	07/11/93	FA Premiership	Manchester City 2 Manchester United 3	Maine Road	35155
17	2004/05	07/11/04	FA Premiership	Manchester United 0 Manchester City 0	Old Trafford	67863
18	2006/07	07/11/06	League Cup 4th Round	Southend United 1 Manchester United 0	Roots Hall	11532
19	2007/08	07/11/07	Champions League Phase 1 Match 4	Manchester United 4 Dynamo Kiev 0	Old Trafford	75017

NOVEMBER 8

#	SEASON	DATE	COMPETITION / ROUND	MATCH RESULT	VENUE	ATT
1	1902/03	08/11/02	Football League Division 2	Lincoln City 1 Manchester United 3	Sincil Bank	3000
2	1913/14	08/11/13	Football League Division 1	Aston Villa 3 Manchester United 1	Villa Park	20000
3	1919/20	08/11/19	Football League Division 1	Burnley 2 Manchester United 1	Turf Moor	15000
4	1924/25	08/11/24	Football League Division 2	Portsmouth 1 Manchester United 1	Fratton Park	19500
5	1930/31	08/11/30	Football League Division 1	Leicester City 5 Manchester United 4	Filbert Street	17466
6	1947/48	08/11/47	Football League Division 1	Manchester United 4 Huddersfield Town 4	Maine Road	59772
7	1952/53	08/11/52	Football League Division 1	Manchester United 1 Sheffield Wednesday 1	Old Trafford	48571
8	1958/59	08/11/58	Football League Division 1	Manchester United 1 Burnley 3	Old Trafford	48509
9	1967/68	08/11/67	Football League Division 1	Leeds United 1 Manchester United 0	Elland Road	43999
10	1969/70	08/11/69	Football League Division 1	Coventry City 1 Manchester United 2	Highfield Road	43446
11	1971/72	08/11/71	League Cup 4th Round Replay	Stoke City 0 Manchester United 0	Victoria Ground	40805
12	1975/76	08/11/75	Football League Division 1	Liverpool 3 Manchester United 1	Anfield	49136
13	1980/81	08/11/80	Football League Division 1	Manchester United 0 Coventry City 0	Old Trafford	42794
14	1983/84	08/11/83	League Cup 3rd Round	Colchester United 0 Manchester United 2	Layer Road	13031
15	1986/87	08/11/86	Football League Division 1	Oxford United 2 Manchester United 0	Manor Ground	13545
16	1998/99	08/11/98	FA Premiership	Manchester United 0 Newcastle United 0	Old Trafford	55174
17	2000/01	08/11/00	Champions League Phase 1 Match 6	Manchester United 1 Dynamo Kiev 0	Old Trafford	66776

NOVEMBER 9

#	SEASON	DATE	COMPETITION / ROUND	MATCH RESULT	VENUE	ATT
1	1895/96	09/11/95	Football League Division 2	Arsenal 2 Newton Heath 1	Manor Field	9000
2	1901/02	09/11/01	Football League Division 2	Newton Heath 1 West Bromwich Albion 2	Bank Street	13000
3	1907/08	09/11/07	Football League Division 1	Manchester United 4 Everton 3	Bank Street	30000
4	1912/13	09/11/12	Football League Division 1	Sunderland 3 Manchester United 1	Roker Park	20000
5	1929/30	09/11/29	Football League Division 1	Manchester United 3 Derby County 2	Old Trafford	15174
6	1935/36	09/11/35	Football League Division 2	Swansea City 2 Manchester United 1	Vetch Field	9731
7	1946/47	09/11/46	Football League Division 1	Manchester United 4 Derby County 1	Maine Road	57340
8	1957/58	09/11/57	Football League Division 1	Preston North End 1 Manchester United 1	Deepdale	39063
9	1963/64	09/11/63	Football League Division 1	Manchester United 4 Tottenham Hotspur 1	Old Trafford	57413
10	1968/69	09/11/68	Football League Division 1	Sunderland 1 Manchester United 1	Roker Park	33151
11	1974/75	09/11/74	Football League Division 2	Bristol City 1 Manchester United 0	Ashton Gate	28104
12	1985/86	09/11/85	Football League Division 1	Sheffield Wednesday 1 Manchester United 0	Hillsborough	48105
13	1997/98	09/11/97	FA Premiership	Arsenal 3 Manchester United 2	Highbury	38205
14	2002/03	09/11/02	FA Premiership	Manchester City 3 Manchester United 1	Maine Road	34649
15	2003/04	09/11/03	FA Premiership	Liverpool 1 Manchester United 2	Anfield	44159

NOVEMBER 10

#	SEASON	DATE	COMPETITION / ROUND	MATCH RESULT	VENUE	ATT
1	1894/95	10/11/94	Football League Division 2	Newton Heath 3 Rotherham United 2	Bank Street	4000
2	1900/01	10/11/00	Football League Division 2	Arsenal 2 Newton Heath 1	Manor Field	8000
3	1906/07	10/11/06	Football League Division 1	Manchester United 1 Arsenal 0	Bank Street	20000
4	1923/24	10/11/23	Football League Division 2	Manchester United 3 Leicester City 0	Old Trafford	20000
5	1928/29	10/11/28	Football League Division 1	Sheffield Wednesday 2 Manchester United 1	Hillsborough	18113
6	1934/35	10/11/34	Football League Division 2	Manchester United 1 Bury 0	Old Trafford	41415
7	1951/52	10/11/51	Football League Division 1	Chelsea 4 Manchester United 2	Stamford Bridge	48960
8	1956/57	10/11/56	Football League Division 1	Bolton Wanderers 2 Manchester United 0	Burnden Park	39922
9	1962/63	10/11/62	Football League Division 1	Manchester United 3 Liverpool 3	Old Trafford	43810
10	1973/74	10/11/73	Football League Division 1	Tottenham Hotspur 2 Manchester United 1	White Hart Lane	42756
11	1976/77	10/11/76	Football League Division 1	Manchester United 3 Sunderland 3	Old Trafford	42685
12	1979/80	10/11/79	Football League Division 1	Manchester City 2 Manchester United 0	Maine Road	50067
13	1982/83	10/11/82	League Cup 3rd Round	Bradford City 0 Manchester United 0	Valley Parade	15568
14	1984/85	10/11/84	Football League Division 1	Leicester City 2 Manchester United 3	Filbert Street	23840
15	1990/91	10/11/90	Football League Division 1	Derby County 0 Manchester United 0	Baseball Ground	21115
16	1994/95	10/11/94	FA Premiership	Manchester United 5 Manchester City 0	Old Trafford	43738
17	2004/05	10/11/04	League Cup 4th Round	Manchester United 2 Crystal Palace 0	Old Trafford	48891

NOVEMBER 11

#	SEASON	DATE	COMPETITION / ROUND	MATCH RESULT	VENUE	ATT
1	1893/94	11/11/93	Football League Division 1	Newton Heath 1 Wolverhampton Wanderers 0	Bank Street	5000
2	1899/00	11/11/99	Football League Division 2	Barnsley 0 Newton Heath 0	Oakwell	3000
3	1905/06	11/11/05	Football League Division 2	Chesterfield 1 Manchester United 0	Saltergate	3000
4	1911/12	11/11/11	Football League Division 1	Manchester United 0 Preston North End 0	Old Trafford	10000
5	1922/23	11/11/22	Football League Division 2	Leyton Orient 1 Manchester United 1	Millfields Road	11000
6	1933/34	11/11/33	Football League Division 2	Manchester United 1 Southampton 0	Old Trafford	18149
7	1950/51	11/11/50	Football League Division 1	Chelsea 1 Manchester United 0	Stamford Bridge	51882
8	1961/62	11/11/61	Football League Division 1	Manchester United 2 Leicester City 2	Old Trafford	21567
9	1964/65	11/11/64	ICFC 2nd Round 1st Leg	Borussia Dortmund 1 Manchester United 6	Rote Erde Stadion	25000
10	1967/68	11/11/67	Football League Division 1	Liverpool 1 Manchester United 2	Anfield	54515
11	1972/73	11/11/72	Football League Division 1	Manchester United 2 Liverpool 0	Old Trafford	53944
12	1978/79	11/11/78	Football League Division 1	Birmingham City 5 Manchester United 1	St Andrews	23550
13	1998/99	11/11/98	League Cup 4th Round	Manchester United 2 Nottingham Forest 1	Old Trafford	37337
14	2000/01	11/11/00	FA Premiership	Manchester United 2 Middlesbrough 1	Old Trafford	67576
15	2006/07	11/11/06	FA Premiership	Blackburn Rovers 0 Manchester United 1	Ewood Park	26162
16	2007/08	11/11/07	FA Premiership	Manchester United 2 Blackburn Rovers 0	Old Trafford	75710

NOVEMBER 12

#	SEASON	DATE	COMPETITION / ROUND	MATCH RESULT	VENUE	ATT
1	1892/93	12/11/92	Football League Division 1	Newton Heath 1 Notts County 3	North Road	8000
2	1898/99	12/11/98	Football League Division 2	Newton Heath 0 Barnsley 0	Bank Street	5000
3	1904/05	12/11/04	Football League Division 2	Manchester United 1 Burnley 0	Bank Street	15000
4	1910/11	12/11/10	Football League Division 1	Manchester United 0 Notts County 0	Old Trafford	13000
5	1921/22	12/11/21	Football League Division 1	Middlesbrough 2 Manchester United 0	Ayresome Park	18000
6	1927/28	12/11/27	Football League Division 1	Sunderland 4 Manchester United 1	Roker Park	13319
7	1932/33	12/11/32	Football League Division 2	Bury 2 Manchester United 2	Gigg Lane	21663
8	1938/39	12/11/38	Football League Division 1	Manchester United 1 Wolverhampton Wanderers 3	Old Trafford	32821
9	1949/50	12/11/49	Football League Division 1	Everton 0 Manchester United 0	Goodison Park	46672
10	1955/56	12/11/55	Football League Division 1	Bolton Wanderers 3 Manchester United 1	Burnden Park	38109
11	1960/61	12/11/60	Football League Division 1	Birmingham City 3 Manchester United 1	St Andrews	31549
12	1966/67	12/11/66	Football League Division 1	Manchester United 2 Sheffield Wednesday 0	Old Trafford	46942
13	1969/70	12/11/69	League Cup 5th Round	Derby County 0 Manchester United 0	Baseball Ground	38895
14	1975/76	12/11/75	League Cup 4th Round	Manchester United 2 Manchester United 0	Maine Road	50182
15	1977/78	12/11/77	Football League Division 1	Nottingham Forest 2 Manchester United 1	City Ground	30183
16	1980/81	12/11/80	Football League Division 1	Manchester United 0 Wolverhampton Wanderers 0	Old Trafford	37959
17	1983/84	12/11/83	Football League Division 1	Leicester City 1 Manchester United 1	Filbert Street	24409
18	1988/89	12/11/88	Football League Division 1	Derby County 2 Manchester United 2	Baseball Ground	24080
19	1989/90	12/11/89	Football League Division 1	Manchester United 1 Nottingham Forest 0	Old Trafford	34182

NOVEMBER 13

#	SEASON	DATE	COMPETITION / ROUND	MATCH RESULT	VENUE	ATT
1	1897/98	13/11/97	Football League Division 2	Newton Heath 0 Newcastle United 1	Bank Street	7000
2	1902/03	13/11/02	FA Cup 4th Qualifying Round	Manchester United 3 Oswaldtwistle Rovers 2	Bank Street	5000
3	1909/10	13/11/09	Football League Division 1	Manchester United 2 Chelsea 0	Bank Street	10000
4	1920/21	13/11/20	Football League Division 1	Sheffield United 0 Manchester United 0	Bramall Lane	18000
5	1926/27	13/11/26	Football League Division 1	Leicester City 2 Manchester United 3	Filbert Street	18521
6	1937/38	13/11/37	Football League Division 2	Chesterfield 1 Manchester United 7	Saltergate	17407
7	1948/49	13/11/48	Football League Division 1	Chelsea 1 Manchester United 1	Stamford Bridge	62542
8	1954/55	13/11/54	Football League Division 1	Sheffield United 4 Manchester United 0	Bramall Lane	26257
9	1965/66	13/11/65	Football League Division 1	Leicester City 0 Manchester United 5	Filbert Street	34551
10	1968/69	13/11/68	European Cup 2nd Round 1st Leg	Manchester United 3 Anderlecht 0	Old Trafford	51000
11	1971/72	13/11/71	Football League Division 1	Manchester United 3 Tottenham Hotspur 1	Old Trafford	54058
12	1974/75	13/11/74	League Cup 4th Round	Manchester United 3 Burnley 0	Old Trafford	46275
13	1982/83	13/11/82	Football League Division 1	Manchester United 1 Tottenham Hotspur 0	Old Trafford	47869
14	2002/03	13/11/02	Champions League Phase 1 Match 6	Manchester United 2 Bayer Leverkusen 0	Old Trafford	66185

NOVEMBER 14

#	SEASON	DATE	COMPETITION / ROUND	MATCH RESULT	VENUE	ATT
1	1891/92	14/11/91	FA Cup 3rd Qualifying Round	South Shore 0 Newton Heath 2	Bloomfield Road	2000
2	1908/09	14/11/08	Football League Division 1	Blackburn Rovers 1 Manchester United 3	Ewood Park	25000
3	1914/15	14/11/14	Football League Division 1	Manchester United 0 Burnley 2	Old Trafford	12000
4	1925/26	14/11/25	Football League Division 1	Manchester United 3 Birmingham City 1	Old Trafford	23559
5	1931/32	14/11/31	Football League Division 2	Oldham Athletic 1 Manchester United 5	Boundary Park	10922
6	1936/37	14/11/36	Football League Division 1	Grimsby Town 6 Manchester United 2	Blundell Park	9844
7	1953/54	14/11/53	Football League Division 1	Cardiff City 1 Manchester United 6	Ninian Park	26844
8	1959/60	14/11/59	Football League Division 1	Bolton Wanderers 1 Manchester United 1	Burnden Park	37892
9	1964/65	14/11/64	Football League Division 1	Blackpool 1 Manchester United 2	Bloomfield Road	31129
10	1970/71	14/11/70	Football League Division 1	Nottingham Forest 1 Manchester United 2	City Ground	36364
11	1998/99	14/11/98	FA Premiership	Manchester United 3 Blackburn Rovers 2	Old Trafford	55198
12	2004/05	14/11/04	FA Premiership	Newcastle United 1 Manchester United 3	St James' Park	52320

NOVEMBER 15

#	SEASON	DATE	COMPETITION / ROUND	MATCH RESULT	VENUE	ATT
1	1902/03	15/11/02	Football League Division 2	Manchester United 0 Birmingham City 1	Bank Street	25000
2	1913/14	15/11/13	Football League Division 1	Manchester United 0 Middlesbrough 1	Old Trafford	15000
3	1919/20	15/11/19	Football League Division 1	Manchester United 0 Burnley 1	Old Trafford	25000
4	1924/25	15/11/24	Football League Division 2	Manchester United 2 Hull City 0	Old Trafford	29750
5	1930/31	15/11/30	Football League Division 1	Manchester United 0 Blackpool 0	Old Trafford	14765
6	1947/48	15/11/47	Football League Division 1	Derby County 1 Manchester United 1	Baseball Ground	32990
7	1952/53	15/11/52	Football League Division 1	Cardiff City 1 Manchester United 2	Ninian Park	40096
8	1958/59	15/11/58	Football League Division 1	Bolton Wanderers 6 Manchester United 3	Burnden Park	33358
9	1967/68	15/11/67	European Cup 2nd Round 1st Leg	Sarajevo 0 Manchester United 0	Stadion Kosevo	45000
10	1969/70	15/11/69	Football League Division 1	Manchester City 4 Manchester United 0	Maine Road	63013
11	1971/72	15/11/71	League Cup 4th Round 2nd Replay	Stoke City 2 Manchester United 1	Victoria Ground	42249
12	1975/76	15/11/75	Football League Division 1	Manchester United 2 Aston Villa 0	Old Trafford	51682
13	1980/81	15/11/80	Football League Division 1	Middlesbrough 1 Manchester United 1	Ayresome Park	20606
14	1986/87	15/11/86	Football League Division 1	Norwich City 0 Manchester United 0	Carrow Road	22684
15	1987/88	15/11/87	Football League Division 1	Manchester United 1 Liverpool 1	Old Trafford	47106

NOVEMBER 16

#	SEASON	DATE	COMPETITION / ROUND	MATCH RESULT	VENUE	ATT
1	1895/96	16/11/95	Football League Division 2	Newton Heath 5 Lincoln City 5	Bank Street	8000
2	1901/02	16/11/01	Football League Division 2	Arsenal 2 Newton Heath 0	Manor Field	3000
3	1907/08	16/11/07	Football League Division 1	Sunderland 1 Manchester United 2	Roker Park	30000
4	1912/13	16/11/12	Football League Division 1	Aston Villa 4 Manchester United 2	Villa Park	20000
5	1929/30	16/11/29	Football League Division 1	Sheffield Wednesday 7 Manchester United 2	Hillsborough	14264
6	1935/36	16/11/35	Football League Division 2	Manchester United 2 West Ham United 3	Old Trafford	24440
7	1946/47	16/11/46	Football League Division 1	Everton 2 Manchester United 2	Goodison Park	45832
8	1957/58	16/11/57	Football League Division 1	Manchester United 2 Sheffield Wednesday 1	Old Trafford	40366
9	1963/64	16/11/63	Football League Division 1	Aston Villa 4 Manchester United 0	Villa Park	36276
10	1968/69	16/11/68	Football League Division 1	Manchester United 0 Ipswich Town 0	Old Trafford	45796
11	1974/75	16/11/74	Football League Division 2	Manchester United 2 Aston Villa 1	Old Trafford	55615
12	1985/86	16/11/85	Football League Division 1	Manchester United 2 Tottenham Hotspur 0	Old Trafford	54575
13	1991/92	16/11/91	Football League Division 1	Manchester City 0 Manchester United 0	Maine Road	38180
14	1996/97	16/11/96	FA Premiership	Manchester United 1 Arsenal 0	Old Trafford	55210

NOVEMBER 17

#	SEASON	DATE	COMPETITION / ROUND	MATCH RESULT	VENUE	ATT
1	1894/95	17/11/94	Football League Division 2	Grimsby Town 2 Newton Heath 1	Abbey Park	3000
2	1906/07	17/11/06	Football League Division 1	Sheffield Wednesday 5 Manchester United 2	Hillsborough	7000
3	1923/24	17/11/23	Football League Division 2	Coventry City 1 Manchester United 1	Highfield Road	13580
4	1928/29	17/11/28	Football League Division 1	Manchester United 0 Derby County 1	Old Trafford	26122
5	1934/35	17/11/34	Football League Division 2	Hull City 3 Manchester United 2	Anlaby Road	6494
6	1951/52	17/11/51	Football League Division 1	Manchester United 1 Portsmouth 3	Old Trafford	35914
7	1956/57	17/11/56	Football League Division 1	Manchester United 3 Leeds United 2	Old Trafford	51131
8	1962/63	17/11/62	Football League Division 1	Wolverhampton Wanderers 2 Manchester United 3	Molineux	27305
9	1965/66	17/11/65	European Cup 1st Round 1st Leg	ASK Vorwaerts 0 Manchester United 2	Walter Ulbricht	40000
10	1973/74	17/11/73	Football League Division 1	Newcastle United 3 Manchester United 2	St James' Park	41768
11	1979/80	17/11/79	Football League Division 1	Manchester United 1 Crystal Palace 1	Old Trafford	52800
12	1984/85	17/11/84	Football League Division 1	Manchester United 2 Luton Town 0	Old Trafford	41630
13	1990/91	17/11/90	Football League Division 1	Manchester United 2 Sheffield United 0	Old Trafford	45903
14	2001/02	17/11/01	FA Premiership	Manchester United 2 Leicester City 0	Old Trafford	67651
15	2002/03	17/11/02	FA Premiership	West Ham United 1 Manchester United 1	Upton Park	35049

NOVEMBER 18

#	SEASON	DATE	COMPETITION / ROUND	MATCH RESULT	VENUE	ATT
1	1905/06	18/11/05	Football League Division 2	Manchester United 3 Port Vale 0	Bank Street	8000
2	1911/12	18/11/11	Football League Division 1	Liverpool 3 Manchester United 2	Anfield	15000
3	1922/23	18/11/22	Football League Division 2	Bury 2 Manchester United 2	Gigg Lane	21000
4	1933/34	18/11/33	Football League Division 2	Blackpool 3 Manchester United 1	Bloomfield Road	14384
5	1950/51	18/11/50	Football League Division 1	Manchester United 0 Stoke City 0	Old Trafford	30031
6	1961/62	18/11/61	Football League Division 1	Ipswich Town 4 Manchester United 1	Portman Road	25755
7	1967/68	18/11/67	Football League Division 1	Manchester United 3 Southampton 2	Old Trafford	48732
8	1970/71	18/11/70	League Cup 5th Round	Manchester United 4 Crystal Palace 2	Old Trafford	48961
9	1972/73	18/11/72	Football League Division 1	Manchester City 3 Manchester United 0	Maine Road	52050
10	1978/79	18/11/78	Football League Division 1	Manchester United 2 Ipswich Town 0	Old Trafford	42109
11	1987/88	18/11/87	League Cup 4th Round	Bury 1 Manchester United 2	Old Trafford	33519
12	1989/90	18/11/89	Football League Division 1	Luton Town 1 Manchester United 3	Kenilworth Road	11141
13	1995/96	18/11/95	FA Premiership	Manchester United 4 Southampton 1	Old Trafford	39301
14	2000/01	18/11/00	FA Premiership	Manchester City 0 Manchester United 1	Maine Road	34429
15	2006/07	18/11/06	FA Premiership	Sheffield United 1 Manchester United 2	Bramall Lane	32584

NOVEMBER 19

#	SEASON	DATE	COMPETITION / ROUND	MATCH RESULT	VENUE	ATT
1	1892/93	19/11/92	Football League Division 1	Newton Heath 2 Aston Villa 0	North Road	7000
2	1898/99	19/11/98	Football League Division 2	New Brighton Tower 0 Newton Heath 3	Tower Athletic Ground	5000
3	1904/05	19/11/04	Football League Division 2	Grimsby Town 0 Manchester United 1	Blundell Park	4000
4	1910/11	19/11/10	Football League Division 1	Oldham Athletic 1 Manchester United 3	Boundary Park	25000
5	1921/22	19/11/21	Football League Division 1	Aston Villa 3 Manchester United 1	Villa Park	30000
6	1927/28	19/11/27	Football League Division 1	Manchester United 5 Aston Villa 1	Old Trafford	25991
7	1932/33	19/11/32	Football League Division 2	Manchester United 4 Fulham 3	Old Trafford	28803
8	1938/39	19/11/38	Football League Division 1	Everton 3 Manchester United 0	Goodison Park	31809
9	1949/50	19/11/49	Football League Division 1	Manchester United 2 Middlesbrough 0	Old Trafford	42626
10	1955/56	19/11/55	Football League Division 1	Manchester United 3 Chelsea 0	Old Trafford	22192
11	1960/61	19/11/60	Football League Division 1	Manchester United 3 West Bromwich Albion 0	Old Trafford	32756
12	1966/67	19/11/66	Football League Division 1	Southampton 1 Manchester United 2	The Dell	29458
13	1969/70	19/11/69	League Cup 5th Round Replay	Manchester United 1 Derby County 0	Old Trafford	57393
14	1977/78	19/11/77	Football League Division 1	Manchester United 1 Norwich City 0	Old Trafford	48729
15	1983/84	19/11/83	Football League Division 1	Manchester United 4 Watford 1	Old Trafford	43111
16	1988/89	19/11/88	Football League Division 1	Manchester United 1 Southampton 2	Old Trafford	37277
17	1991/92	19/11/91	European Super Cup	Manchester United 1 Red Star Belgrade 0	Old Trafford	22110
18	1994/95	19/11/94	FA Premiership	Manchester United 3 Crystal Palace 0	Old Trafford	43788
19	2005/06	19/11/05	FA Premiership	Charlton Athletic 1 Manchester United 3	The Valley	26730

NOVEMBER 20

#	SEASON	DATE	COMPETITION / ROUND	MATCH RESULT	VENUE	ATT
1	1897/98	20/11/97	Football League Division 2	Leicester City 1 Newton Heath 1	Filbert Street	6000
2	1909/10	20/11/09	Football League Division 1	Blackburn Rovers 3 Manchester United 2	Ewood Park	40000
3	1920/21	20/11/20	Football League Division 1	Manchester United 1 Manchester City 1	Old Trafford	63000
4	1926/27	20/11/26	Football League Division 1	Manchester United 2 Everton 0	Old Trafford	24361
5	1937/38	20/11/37	Football League Division 2	Manchester United 3 Aston Villa 1	Old Trafford	33193
6	1948/49	20/11/48	Football League Division 1	Manchester United 3 Birmingham City 0	Maine Road	45482
7	1954/55	20/11/54	Football League Division 1	Manchester United 2 Arsenal 1	Old Trafford	33373
8	1957/58	20/11/57	European Cup 1st Round 1st Leg	Manchester United 3 Dukla Prague 0	Old Trafford	60000
9	1965/66	20/11/65	Football League Division 1	Manchester United 3 Sheffield United 1	Old Trafford	37922
10	1971/72	20/11/71	Football League Division 1	Manchester United 3 Leicester City 2	Old Trafford	48757
11	1976/77	20/11/76	Football League Division 1	Leicester City 1 Manchester United 1	Filbert Street	26421
12	1982/83	20/11/82	Football League Division 1	Aston Villa 2 Manchester United 1	Villa Park	35487
13	1993/94	20/11/93	FA Premiership	Manchester United 3 Wimbledon 1	Old Trafford	44748
14	1996/97	20/11/96	Champions League Phase 1 Match 5	Manchester United 0 Juventus 1	Old Trafford	53529
15	1999/00	20/11/99	FA Premiership	Derby County 1 Manchester United 2	Pride Park	33370
16	2001/02	20/11/01	Champions League Phase 2 Match 1	Bayern Munich 1 Manchester United 1	Olympic Stadium	59000
17	2004/05	20/11/04	FA Premiership	Manchester United 2 Charlton Athletic 0	Old Trafford	67704

NOVEMBER 21

#	SEASON	DATE	COMPETITION / ROUND	MATCH RESULT	VENUE	ATT
1	1903/04	21/11/03	Football League Division 2	Manchester United 0 Preston North End 2	Bank Street	15000
2	1908/09	21/11/08	Football League Division 1	Manchester United 2 Bradford City 0	Bank Street	15000
3	1914/15	21/11/14	Football League Division 1	Tottenham Hotspur 2 Manchester United 0	White Hart Lane	12000
4	1925/26	21/11/25	Football League Division 1	Bury 1 Manchester United 3	Gigg Lane	16591
5	1931/32	21/11/31	Football League Division 2	Manchester United 1 Bury 2	Old Trafford	11745
6	1936/37	21/11/36	Football League Division 1	Manchester United 2 Liverpool 5	Old Trafford	26419
7	1953/54	21/11/53	Football League Division 1	Manchester United 4 Blackpool 1	Old Trafford	49853
8	1956/57	21/11/56	European Cup 1st Round 2nd Leg	Borussia Dortmund 0 Manchester United 0	Rote Erde Stadion	44570
9	1959/60	21/11/59	Football League Division 1	Manchester United 4 Luton Town 1	Old Trafford	40572
10	1964/65	21/11/64	Football League Division 1	Manchester United 3 Blackburn Rovers 0	Old Trafford	49633
11	1970/71	21/11/70	Football League Division 1	Southampton 1 Manchester United 0	The Dell	30202
12	1978/79	21/11/78	Football League Division 1	Everton 3 Manchester United 0	Goodison Park	42126
13	1981/82	21/11/81	Football League Division 1	Tottenham Hotspur 3 Manchester United 1	White Hart Lane	35534
14	1987/88	21/11/87	Football League Division 1	Wimbledon 2 Manchester United 1	Plough Lane	11532
15	1992/93	21/11/92	FA Premiership	Manchester United 3 Oldham Athletic 0	Old Trafford	33497
16	1998/99	21/11/98	FA Premiership	Sheffield Wednesday 3 Manchester United 1	Hillsborough	39475
17	2000/01	21/11/00	Champions League Phase 2 Match 1	Manchester United 3 Panathinaikos 1	Old Trafford	65024
18	2006/07	21/11/06	Champions League Phase 1 Match 5	Glasgow Celtic 1 Manchester United 0	Celtic Park	60632

NOVEMBER 22

#	SEASON	DATE	COMPETITION / ROUND	MATCH RESULT	VENUE	ATT
1	1902/03	22/11/02	Football League Division 2	Leicester City 1 Manchester United 1	Filbert Street	5000
2	1913/14	22/11/13	Football League Division 1	Sheffield United 2 Manchester United 0	Bramall Lane	30000
3	1919/20	22/11/19	Football League Division 1	Oldham Athletic 0 Manchester United 3	Boundary Park	15000
4	1924/25	22/11/24	Football League Division 2	Blackpool 1 Manchester United 1	Bloomfield Road	9500
5	1930/31	22/11/30	Football League Division 1	Sheffield United 3 Manchester United 1	Bramall Lane	12698
6	1947/48	22/11/47	Football League Division 1	Manchester United 2 Everton 2	Maine Road	35509
7	1952/53	22/11/52	Football League Division 1	Manchester United 2 Newcastle United 2	Old Trafford	33528
8	1958/59	22/11/58	Football League Division 1	Manchester United 2 Luton Town 1	Old Trafford	42428
9	1969/70	22/11/69	Football League Division 1	Manchester United 3 Tottenham Hotspur 1	Old Trafford	50003
10	1975/76	22/11/75	Football League Division 1	Arsenal 3 Manchester United 1	Highbury	40102
11	1980/81	22/11/80	Football League Division 1	Brighton 1 Manchester United 4	Goldstone Ground	23923
12	1986/87	22/11/86	Football League Division 1	Manchester United 1 Queens Park Rangers 0	Old Trafford	42235
13	1995/96	22/11/95	FA Premiership	Coventry City 0 Manchester United 4	Highfield Road	23400
14	1997/98	22/11/97	FA Premiership	Wimbledon 2 Manchester United 5	Selhurst Park	26309
15	2003/04	22/11/03	FA Premiership	Manchester United 2 Blackburn Rovers 1	Old Trafford	67748
16	2005/06	22/11/05	Champions League Phase 1 Match 5	Manchester United 0 Villarreal 0	Old Trafford	67471

NOVEMBER 23

#	SEASON	DATE	COMPETITION / ROUND	MATCH RESULT	VENUE	ATT
1	1895/96	23/11/95	Football League Division 2	Notts County 0 Newton Heath 2	Trent Bridge	3000
2	1901/02	23/11/01	Football League Division 2	Newton Heath 1 Barnsley 0	Bank Street	4000
3	1907/08	23/11/07	Football League Division 1	Manchester United 4 Arsenal 2	Bank Street	10000
4	1912/13	23/11/12	Football League Division 1	Manchester United 3 Liverpool 1	Old Trafford	8000
5	1929/30	23/11/29	Football League Division 1	Manchester United 1 Burnley 0	Old Trafford	9060
6	1935/36	23/11/35	Football League Division 2	Norwich City 3 Manchester United 5	Carrow Road	17266
7	1946/47	23/11/46	Football League Division 1	Manchester United 5 Huddersfield Town 2	Maine Road	39216
8	1957/58	23/11/57	Football League Division 1	Newcastle United 1 Manchester United 2	St James' Park	53890
9	1963/64	23/11/63	Football League Division 1	Manchester United 0 Liverpool 1	Old Trafford	54654
10	1968/69	23/11/68	Football League Division 1	Stoke City 0 Manchester United 0	Victoria Ground	30562
11	1974/75	23/11/74	Football League Division 2	Hull City 2 Manchester United 0	Boothferry Park	23287
12	1985/86	23/11/85	Football League Division 1	Leicester City 3 Manchester United 0	Filbert Street	22008
13	1988/89	23/11/88	Football League Division 1	Manchester United 1 Sheffield Wednesday 1	Old Trafford	30849
14	1991/92	23/11/91	Football League Division 1	Manchester United 2 West Ham United 1	Old Trafford	47185
15	1994/95	23/11/94	Champions League Phase 1 Match 5	Gothenburg 3 Manchester United 1	NYA Ullevi Stadium	36350
16	1996/97	23/11/96	FA Premiership	Middlesbrough 2 Manchester United 2	Riverside Stadium	30063
17	1999/00	23/11/99	Champions League Phase 2 Match 1	Fiorentina 2 Manchester United 0	Artemio Franchi	36002
18	2002/03	23/11/02	FA Premiership	Manchester United 5 Newcastle United 3	Old Trafford	67625
19	2004/05	23/11/04	Champions League Phase 1 Match 5	Manchester United 2 Olympique Lyonnais 1	Old Trafford	66398

NOVEMBER 24

#	SEASON	DATE	COMPETITION / ROUND	MATCH RESULT	VENUE	ATT
1	1894/95	24/11/94	Football League Division 2	Newton Heath 1 Darwen 1	Bank Street	5000
2	1900/01	24/11/00	Football League Division 2	Stockport County 0 Newton Heath 0	Green Lane	5000
3	1906/07	24/11/06	Football League Division 1	Manchester United 2 Bury 4	Bank Street	30000
4	1928/29	24/11/28	Football League Division 1	Sunderland 5 Manchester United 1	Roker Park	15932
5	1934/35	24/11/34	Football League Division 2	Manchester United 3 Nottingham Forest 2	Old Trafford	27192
6	1951/52	24/11/51	Football League Division 1	Liverpool 0 Manchester United 0	Anfield	42378
7	1956/57	24/11/56	Football League Division 1	Tottenham Hotspur 2 Manchester United 2	White Hart Lane	57724
8	1962/63	24/11/62	Football League Division 1	Manchester United 2 Aston Villa 2	Old Trafford	36852
9	1973/74	24/11/73	Football League Division 1	Manchester United 0 Norwich City 0	Old Trafford	36338
10	1979/80	24/11/79	Football League Division 1	Manchester United 5 Norwich City 0	Old Trafford	46540
11	1982/83	24/11/82	League Cup 3rd Round Replay	Manchester United 4 Bradford City 1	Old Trafford	24507
12	1984/85	24/11/84	Football League Division 1	Sunderland 3 Manchester United 2	Roker Park	25405
13	1993/94	24/11/93	FA Premiership	Manchester United 0 Ipswich Town 0	Old Trafford	43300
14	2007/08	24/11/07	FA Premiership	Bolton Wanderers 1 Manchester United 0	Reebok Stadium	25028

NOVEMBER 25

#	SEASON	DATE	COMPETITION / ROUND	MATCH RESULT	VENUE	ATT
1	1893/94	25/11/93	Football League Division 1	Sheffield United 3 Newton Heath 1	Bramall Lane	2000
2	1899/00	25/11/99	Football League Division 2	Luton Town 0 Newton Heath 1	Dunstable Road	3000
3	1905/06	25/11/05	Football League Division 2	Barnsley 0 Manchester United 3	Oakwell	3000
4	1911/12	25/11/11	Football League Division 1	Manchester United 3 Aston Villa 1	Old Trafford	20000
5	1922/23	25/11/22	Football League Division 2	Manchester United 0 Bury 1	Old Trafford	28000
6	1933/34	25/11/33	Football League Division 2	Manchester United 2 Bradford City 1	Old Trafford	20902
7	1950/51	25/11/50	Football League Division 1	West Bromwich Albion 0 Manchester United 1	The Hawthorns	28146
8	1961/62	25/11/61	Football League Division 1	Manchester United 1 Burnley 4	Old Trafford	41029
9	1967/68	25/11/67	Football League Division 1	Chelsea 1 Manchester United 1	Stamford Bridge	54712
10	1972/73	25/11/72	Football League Division 1	Manchester United 2 Southampton 1	Old Trafford	36073
11	1978/79	25/11/78	Football League Division 1	Chelsea 0 Manchester United 1	Stamford Bridge	28162
12	1989/90	25/11/89	Football League Division 1	Manchester United 0 Chelsea 0	Old Trafford	46975
13	1990/91	25/11/90	Football League Division 1	Manchester United 2 Chelsea 3	Old Trafford	37836
14	1998/99	25/11/98	Champions League Phase 1 Match 5	Barcelona 3 Manchester United 3	Estadio Camp Nou	67648
15	2000/01	25/11/00	FA Premiership	Derby County 0 Manchester United 3	Pride Park	32910
16	2001/02	25/11/01	FA Premiership	Arsenal 3 Manchester United 1	Highbury	38174

NOVEMBER 26

#	SEASON	DATE	COMPETITION / ROUND	MATCH RESULT	VENUE	ATT
1	1892/93	26/11/92	Football League Division 1	Accrington Stanley 2 Newton Heath 2	Thornleyholme Road	3000
2	1898/99	26/11/98	Football League Division 2	Newton Heath 1 Lincoln City 0	Bank Street	4000
3	1910/11	26/11/10	Football League Division 1	Liverpool 3 Manchester United 2	Anfield	8000
4	1921/22	26/11/21	Football League Division 1	Manchester United 1 Aston Villa 0	Old Trafford	33000
5	1927/28	26/11/27	Football League Division 1	Burnley 4 Manchester United 0	Turf Moor	18509
6	1932/33	26/11/32	Football League Division 2	Chesterfield 1 Manchester United 1	Saltergate	10277
7	1938/39	26/11/38	Football League Division 1	Manchester United 1 Huddersfield Town 1	Old Trafford	23164
8	1949/50	26/11/49	Football League Division 1	Blackpool 3 Manchester United 3	Bloomfield Road	27742
9	1955/56	26/11/55	Football League Division 1	Blackpool 0 Manchester United 0	Bloomfield Road	26240
10	1960/61	26/11/60	Football League Division 1	Cardiff City 3 Manchester United 0	Ninian Park	21122
11	1966/67	26/11/66	Football League Division 1	Manchester United 5 Sunderland 0	Old Trafford	44687
12	1977/78	26/11/77	Football League Division 1	Queens Park Rangers 2 Manchester United 2	Loftus Road	25367
13	1985/86	26/11/85	League Cup 4th Round	Liverpool 2 Manchester United 1	Anfield	41291
14	1994/95	26/11/94	FA Premiership	Arsenal 0 Manchester United 0	Highbury	38301
15	2002/03	26/11/02	Champions League Phase 2 Match 1	Basel 1 Manchester United 3	St Jakob Stadium	29501
16	2003/04	26/11/03	Champions League Phase 1 Match 5	Panathinaikos 0 Manchester United 1	Apostolos Nikolaidis	6890
17	2006/07	26/11/06	FA Premiership	Manchester United 1 Chelsea 1	Old Trafford	75948

NOVEMBER 27

#	SEASON	DATE	COMPETITION / ROUND	MATCH RESULT	VENUE	ATT
1	1897/98	27/11/97	Football League Division 2	Newton Heath 2 Grimsby Town 1	Bank Street	5000
2	1909/10	27/11/09	Football League Division 1	Manchester United 2 Nottingham Forest 6	Bank Street	12000
3	1920/21	27/11/20	Football League Division 1	Manchester City 3 Manchester United 0	Hyde Road	35000
4	1926/27	27/11/26	Football League Division 1	Blackburn Rovers 2 Manchester United 1	Ewood Park	17280
5	1937/38	27/11/37	Football League Division 2	Norwich City 2 Manchester United 3	Carrow Road	17397
6	1948/49	27/11/48	Football League Division 1	Middlesbrough 1 Manchester United 4	Ayresome Park	31331
7	1954/55	27/11/54	Football League Division 1	West Bromwich Albion 2 Manchester United 0	The Hawthorns	33931
8	1968/69	27/11/68	European Cup 2nd Round 2nd Leg	Anderlecht 3 Manchester United 1	Park Astrid	40000
9	1971/72	27/11/71	Football League Division 1	Southampton 2 Manchester United 5	The Dell	30323
10	1976/77	27/11/76	Football League Division 1	Manchester United 0 West Ham United 2	Old Trafford	55366
11	1982/83	27/11/82	Football League Division 1	Manchester United 3 Norwich City 0	Old Trafford	34579
12	1983/84	27/11/83	Football League Division 1	West Ham United 1 Manchester United 1	Upton Park	23355
13	1988/89	27/11/88	Football League Division 1	Newcastle United 0 Manchester United 0	St James' Park	20350
14	1993/94	27/11/93	FA Premiership	Coventry City 0 Manchester United 1	Highfield Road	17020
15	1995/96	27/11/95	FA Premiership	Nottingham Forest 1 Manchester United 1	City Ground	29263
16	1996/97	27/11/96	League Cup 4th Round	Leicester City 2 Manchester United 0	Filbert Street	20428
17	1997/98	27/11/97	Champions League Phase 1 Match 5	Manchester United 3 Kosice 0	Old Trafford	53535
18	2004/05	27/11/04	FA Premiership	West Bromwich Albion 0 Manchester United 3	The Hawthorns	27709
19	2005/06	27/11/05	FA Premiership	West Ham United 1 Manchester United 2	Upton Park	34755
20	2007/08	27/11/07	Champions League Phase 1 Match 5	Manchester United 2 Sporting Lisbon 1	Old Trafford	75162

NOVEMBER 28

#	SEASON	DATE	COMPETITION / ROUND	MATCH RESULT	VENUE	ATT
1	1896/97	28/11/96	Football League Division 2	Birmingham City 1 Newton Heath 0	Muntz Street	4000
2	1908/09	28/11/08	Football League Division 1	Manchester United 3 Sheffield Wednesday 1	Bank Street	20000
3	1914/15	28/11/14	Football League Division 1	Manchester United 1 Newcastle United 0	Old Trafford	5000
4	1925/26	28/11/25	Football League Division 1	Manchester United 2 Blackburn Rovers 0	Old Trafford	33660
5	1931/32	28/11/31	Football League Division 2	Port Vale 1 Manchester United 2	Old Recreation Ground	6955
6	1936/37	28/11/36	Football League Division 1	Leeds United 2 Manchester United 1	Elland Road	17610
7	1953/54	28/11/53	Football League Division 1	Portsmouth 1 Manchester United 1	Fratton Park	29233
8	1959/60	28/11/59	Football League Division 1	Everton 2 Manchester United 1	Goodison Park	46095
9	1964/65	28/11/64	Football League Division 1	Arsenal 2 Manchester United 3	Highbury	59627
10	1970/71	28/11/70	Football League Division 1	Manchester United 1 Huddersfield Town 1	Old Trafford	45306
11	1981/82	28/11/81	Football League Division 1	Manchester United 2 Brighton 0	Old Trafford	41911
12	1984/85	28/11/84	UEFA Cup 3rd Round 1st Leg	Manchester United 2 Dundee United 2	Old Trafford	48278
13	1990/91	28/11/90	League Cup 4th Round	Arsenal 2 Manchester United 6	Highbury	40844
14	1992/93	28/11/92	FA Premiership	Arsenal 0 Manchester United 1	Highbury	29739
15	2000/01	28/11/00	League Cup 4th Round	Sunderland 2 Manchester United 1	Stadium of Light	47543

NOVEMBER 29

#	SEASON	DATE	COMPETITION / ROUND	MATCH RESULT	VENUE	ATT
1	1902/03	29/11/02	FA Cup 5th Qualifying Round	Manchester United 4 Southport Central 1	Bank Street	6000
2	1913/14	29/11/13	Football League Division 1	Manchester United 3 Derby County 3	Old Trafford	20000
3	1924/25	29/11/24	Football League Division 2	Manchester United 1 Derby County 1	Old Trafford	59500
4	1930/31	29/11/30	Football League Division 1	Manchester United 1 Sunderland 1	Old Trafford	10971
5	1947/48	29/11/47	Football League Division 1	Chelsea 0 Manchester United 4	Stamford Bridge	43617
6	1952/53	29/11/52	Football League Division 1	West Bromwich Albion 3 Manchester United 1	The Hawthorns	23499
7	1958/59	29/11/58	Football League Division 1	Birmingham City 0 Manchester United 4	St Andrews	28658
8	1967/68	29/11/67	European Cup 2nd Round 2nd Leg	Manchester United 2 Sarajevo 1	Old Trafford	62801
9	1969/70	29/11/69	Football League Division 1	Burnley 1 Manchester United 1	Turf Moor	23770
10	1975/76	29/11/75	Football League Division 1	Manchester United 1 Newcastle United 0	Old Trafford	52624
11	1980/81	29/11/80	Football League Division 1	Manchester United 1 Southampton 1	Old Trafford	46840
12	1986/87	29/11/86	Football League Division 1	Wimbledon 1 Manchester United 0	Plough Lane	12112
13	1998/99	29/11/98	FA Premiership	Manchester United 3 Leeds United 2	Old Trafford	55172
14	2006/07	29/11/06	FA Premiership	Manchester United 3 Everton 0	Old Trafford	75723

NOVEMBER 30

#	SEASON	DATE	COMPETITION / ROUND	MATCH RESULT	VENUE	ATT
1	1895/96	30/11/95	Football League Division 2	Newton Heath 5 Arsenal 1	Bank Street	6000
2	1901/02	30/11/01	Football League Division 2	Leicester City 3 Newton Heath 2	Filbert Street	4000
3	1907/08	30/11/07	Football League Division 1	Sheffield Wednesday 2 Manchester United 0	Hillsborough	40000
4	1912/13	30/11/12	Football League Division 1	Bolton Wanderers 2 Manchester United 1	Burnden Park	25000
5	1929/30	30/11/29	Football League Division 1	Sunderland 2 Manchester United 4	Roker Park	11508
6	1935/36	30/11/35	Football League Division 2	Manchester United 0 Doncaster Rovers 0	Old Trafford	23569
7	1946/47	30/11/46	Football League Division 1	Wolverhampton Wanderers 3 Manchester United 2	Molineux	46704
8	1957/58	30/11/57	Football League Division 1	Manchester United 3 Tottenham Hotspur 4	Old Trafford	43077
9	1963/64	30/11/63	Football League Division 1	Sheffield United 2 Manchester United 1	Bramall Lane	30615
10	1966/67	30/11/66	Football League Division 1	Leicester City 1 Manchester United 2	Filbert Street	39014
11	1968/69	30/11/68	Football League Division 1	Manchester United 2 Wolverhampton Wanderers 0	Old Trafford	50165
12	1974/75	30/11/74	Football League Division 2	Manchester United 3 Sunderland 2	Old Trafford	60585
13	1983/84	30/11/83	League Cup 4th Round	Oxford United 1 Manchester United 1	Manor Ground	13739
14	1985/86	30/11/85	Football League Division 1	Manchester United 1 Watford 1	Old Trafford	42181
15	1991/92	30/11/91	Football League Division 1	Crystal Palace 1 Manchester United 3	Selhurst Park	29017
16	1993/94	30/11/93	League Cup 4th Round	Everton 0 Manchester United 2	Goodison Park	34052
17	1996/97	30/11/96	FA Premiership	Manchester United 3 Leicester City 1	Old Trafford	55196
18	1997/98	30/11/97	FA Premiership	Manchester United 4 Blackburn Rovers 0	Old Trafford	55175
19	1999/00	30/11/99	Inter-Continental Cup Final	Manchester United 1 Palmeiras 0	Olympic Stadium, Tokyo	53372
20	2003/04	30/11/03	FA Premiership	Chelsea 1 Manchester United 0	Stamford Bridge	41932
21	2005/06	30/11/05	League Cup 4th Round	Manchester United 3 West Bromwich Albion 1	Old Trafford	48924

UNITED in DECEMBER

OVERALL PLAYING RECORD

	P	W	D	L	F	A		P	W	D	L	F	A		P	W	D	L	F	A
1st	18	10	2	6	24	23	11th	12	5	5	2	23	22	22nd	14	7	1	6	30	19
2nd	15	10	1	4	32	20	12th	17	7	4	6	42	29	23rd	15	5	5	5	20	16
3rd	23	10	2	11	27	28	13th	14	7	6	1	32	19	24th	13	7	2	4	31	20
4th	16	9	5	2	32	13	14th	14	8	3	3	28	9	25th	33	14	10	9	50	42
5th	14	4	4	6	25	22	15th	17	10	3	4	32	20	26th	86	45	15	26	169	126
6th	17	10	3	4	32	22	16th	17	6	6	5	24	25	27th	30	11	7	12	43	51
7th	19	9	5	5	46	31	17th	22	11	1	10	37	32	28th	27	14	7	6	52	27
8th	18	9	4	5	37	23	18th	13	8	4	1	28	11	29th	16	7	5	4	24	15
9th	16	7	5	4	29	22	19th	15	5	3	7	28	31	30th	12	5	4	3	20	21
10th	18	7	3	8	29	27	20th	12	8	1	3	20	17	31st	16	9	4	3	40	20
							21st	14	8	2	4	21	14							

OVERALL   603 292 132 179 1107 817

DECEMBER 1

#	SEASON	DATE	COMPETITION / ROUND	MATCH RESULT	VENUE	ATT
1	1894/95	01/12/94	Football League Division 2	Crewe Alexandra 0 Newton Heath 2	Gresty Road	600
2	1900/01	01/12/00	Football League Division 2	Newton Heath 0 Birmingham City 1	Bank Street	5000
3	1906/07	01/12/06	Football League Division 1	Manchester City 3 Manchester United 0	Hyde Road	40000
4	1923/24	01/12/23	Football League Division 2	Leeds United 0 Manchester United 0	Elland Road	20000
5	1928/29	01/12/28	Football League Division 1	Manchester United 1 Blackburn Rovers 4	Old Trafford	19589
6	1934/35	01/12/34	Football League Division 2	Brentford 3 Manchester United 1	Griffin Park	21744
7	1951/52	01/12/51	Football League Division 1	Manchester United 3 Blackpool 1	Old Trafford	34154
8	1956/57	01/12/56	Football League Division 1	Manchester United 3 Luton Town 1	Old Trafford	34736
9	1962/63	01/12/62	Football League Division 1	Sheffield United 1 Manchester United 1	Bramall Lane	25173
10	1965/66	01/12/65	European Cup 1st Round 2nd Leg	Manchester United 3 ASK Vorwaerts 1	Old Trafford	30082
11	1976/77	01/12/76	League Cup 5th Round	Manchester United 0 Everton 3	Old Trafford	57738
12	1979/80	01/12/79	Football League Division 1	Tottenham Hotspur 1 Manchester United 2	White Hart Lane	51389
13	1982/83	01/12/82	League Cup 4th Round	Manchester United 2 Southampton 0	Old Trafford	28378
14	1984/85	01/12/84	Football League Division 1	Manchester United 2 Norwich City 0	Old Trafford	36635
15	1990/91	01/12/90	Football League Division 1	Everton 0 Manchester United 1	Goodison Park	32400
16	2001/02	01/12/01	FA Premiership	Manchester United 0 Chelsea 3	Old Trafford	67544
17	2002/03	01/12/02	FA Premiership	Liverpool 1 Manchester United 2	Anfield	44250
18	2004/05	01/12/04	League Cup 5th Round	Manchester United 1 Arsenal 0	Old Trafford	67103

DECEMBER 2

#	SEASON	DATE	COMPETITION / ROUND	MATCH RESULT	VENUE	ATT
1	1893/94	02/12/93	Football League Division 1	Newton Heath 0 Everton 3	Bank Street	6000
2	1899/00	02/12/99	Football League Division 2	Newton Heath 3 Port Vale 0	Bank Street	5000
3	1905/06	02/12/05	Football League Division 2	Manchester United 4 Leyton Orient 0	Bank Street	12000
4	1911/12	02/12/11	Football League Division 1	Newcastle United 2 Manchester United 3	St James' Park	40000
5	1922/23	02/12/22	Football League Division 2	Manchester United 3 Rotherham United 0	Old Trafford	13500
6	1933/34	02/12/33	Football League Division 2	Port Vale 2 Manchester United 3	Old Recreation Ground	10316
7	1950/51	02/12/50	Football League Division 1	Manchester United 1 Newcastle United 2	Old Trafford	34502
8	1961/62	02/12/61	Football League Division 1	Everton 5 Manchester United 1	Goodison Park	48099
9	1964/65	02/12/64	ICFC 2nd Round 2nd Leg	Manchester United 4 Borussia Dortmund 0	Old Trafford	31896
10	1967/68	02/12/67	Football League Division 1	Manchester United 2 West Bromwich Albion 1	Old Trafford	52568
11	1972/73	02/12/72	Football League Division 1	Norwich City 0 Manchester United 2	Carrow Road	35910
12	1995/96	02/12/95	FA Premiership	Manchester United 1 Chelsea 1	Old Trafford	42019
13	1998/99	02/12/98	League Cup 5th Round	Tottenham Hotspur 3 Manchester United 1	White Hart Lane	35702
14	2000/01	02/12/00	FA Premiership	Manchester United 2 Tottenham Hotspur 0	Old Trafford	67583
15	2006/07	02/12/06	FA Premiership	Middlesbrough 1 Manchester United 2	Riverside Stadium	31238

DECEMBER 3

#	SEASON	DATE	COMPETITION / ROUND	MATCH RESULT	VENUE	ATT
1	1892/93	03/12/92	Football League Division 1	Bolton Wanderers 4 Newton Heath 1	Pikes Lane	3000
2	1898/99	03/12/98	Football League Division 2	Arsenal 5 Newton Heath 1	Manor Field	7000
3	1904/05	03/12/04	Football League Division 2	Doncaster Rovers 0 Manchester United 1	Town Moor Avenue	10000
4	1910/11	03/12/10	Football League Division 1	Manchester United 3 Bury 2	Old Trafford	7000
5	1921/22	03/12/21	Football League Division 1	Bradford City 2 Manchester United 1	Valley Parade	15000
6	1927/28	03/12/27	Football League Division 1	Manchester United 0 Bury 1	Old Trafford	23581
7	1932/33	03/12/32	Football League Division 2	Manchester United 0 Bradford City 1	Old Trafford	28513
8	1938/39	03/12/38	Football League Division 1	Portsmouth 0 Manchester United 0	Fratton Park	18692
9	1949/50	03/12/49	Football League Division 1	Manchester United 1 Newcastle United 1	Old Trafford	30343
10	1955/56	03/12/55	Football League Division 1	Manchester United 2 Sunderland 1	Old Trafford	39901
11	1960/61	03/12/60	Football League Division 1	Manchester United 1 Preston North End 0	Old Trafford	24904
12	1963/64	03/12/63	European CWC 2nd Round 1st Leg	Tottenham Hotspur 2 Manchester United 0	White Hart Lane	57447
13	1966/67	03/12/66	Football League Division 1	Aston Villa 2 Manchester United 1	Villa Park	39937
14	1969/70	03/12/69	League Cup Semi-Final 1st Leg	Manchester City 2 Manchester United 1	Maine Road	55799
15	1977/78	03/12/77	Football League Division 1	Manchester United 3 Wolverhampton Wanderers 1	Old Trafford	48874
16	1983/84	03/12/83	Football League Division 1	Manchester United 0 Everton 1	Old Trafford	43664
17	1988/89	03/12/88	Football League Division 1	Manchester United 3 Charlton Athletic 0	Old Trafford	31173
18	1989/90	03/12/89	Football League Division 1	Arsenal 1 Manchester United 0	Highbury	34484
19	1994/95	03/12/94	FA Premiership	Manchester United 1 Norwich City 0	Old Trafford	43789
20	2002/03	03/12/02	League Cup 4th Round	Burnley 0 Manchester United 2	Turf Moor	22034
21	2003/04	03/12/03	League Cup 4th Round	West Bromwich Albion 2 Manchester United 0	The Hawthorns	25282
22	2005/06	03/12/05	FA Premiership	Manchester United 3 Portsmouth 0	Old Trafford	67684
23	2007/08	03/12/07	FA Premiership	Manchester United 2 Fulham 0	Old Trafford	75055

DECEMBER 4

#	SEASON	DATE	COMPETITION / ROUND	MATCH RESULT	VENUE	ATT
1	1909/10	04/12/09	Football League Division 1	Sunderland 3 Manchester United 0	Roker Park	12000
2	1920/21	04/12/20	Football League Division 1	Manchester United 5 Bradford Park Avenue 1	Old Trafford	25000
3	1926/27	04/12/26	Football League Division 1	Manchester United 0 Huddersfield Town 0	Old Trafford	33135
4	1937/38	04/12/37	Football League Division 2	Manchester United 5 Swansea City 1	Old Trafford	17782
5	1948/49	04/12/48	Football League Division 1	Manchester United 1 Newcastle United 1	Maine Road	70787
6	1954/55	04/12/54	Football League Division 1	Manchester United 3 Leicester City 1	Old Trafford	19369
7	1957/58	04/12/57	European Cup 1st Round 2nd Leg	Dukla Prague 1 Manchester United 0	Stadium Strahov	35000
8	1965/66	04/12/65	Football League Division 1	Manchester United 0 West Ham United 0	Old Trafford	32924
9	1971/72	04/12/71	Football League Division 1	Manchester United 3 Nottingham Forest 2	Old Trafford	45411
10	1974/75	04/12/74	League Cup 5th Round	Middlesbrough 0 Manchester United 0	Ayresome Park	36005
11	1982/83	04/12/82	Football League Division 1	Watford 0 Manchester United 1	Vicarage Road	25669
12	1991/92	04/12/91	League Cup 4th Round	Manchester United 2 Oldham Athletic 0	Old Trafford	38550
13	1993/94	04/12/93	FA Premiership	Manchester United 2 Norwich City 2	Old Trafford	44694
14	1996/97	04/12/96	Champions League Phase 1 Match 6	Rapid Vienna 0 Manchester United 2	Ernst Happel Stadion	45000
15	1999/00	04/12/99	FA Premiership	Manchester United 5 Everton 1	Old Trafford	55193
16	2004/05	04/12/04	FA Premiership	Manchester United 3 Southampton 0	Old Trafford	67921

DECEMBER 5

#	SEASON	DATE	COMPETITION / ROUND	MATCH RESULT	VENUE	ATT
1	1891/92	05/12/91	FA Cup 4th Qualifying Round	Newton Heath 3 Blackpool 4	North Road	4000
2	1908/09	05/12/08	Football League Division 1	Everton 3 Manchester United 2	Goodison Park	35000
3	1914/15	05/12/14	Football League Division 1	Middlesbrough 1 Manchester United 1	Ayresome Park	7000
4	1925/26	05/12/25	Football League Division 1	Sunderland 2 Manchester United 1	Roker Park	25507
5	1931/32	05/12/31	Football League Division 2	Manchester United 2 Millwall 0	Old Trafford	6396
6	1936/37	05/12/36	Football League Division 1	Manchester United 1 Birmingham City 2	Old Trafford	16544
7	1953/54	05/12/53	Football League Division 1	Manchester United 2 Sheffield United 2	Old Trafford	31693
8	1959/60	05/12/59	Football League Division 1	Manchester United 3 Blackpool 1	Old Trafford	45558
9	1964/65	05/12/64	Football League Division 1	Manchester United 0 Leeds United 1	Old Trafford	53374
10	1970/71	05/12/70	Football League Division 1	Tottenham Hotspur 2 Manchester United 2	White Hart Lane	55693
11	1981/82	05/12/81	Football League Division 1	Southampton 3 Manchester United 2	The Dell	24404
12	1987/88	05/12/87	Football League Division 1	Queens Park Rangers 0 Manchester United 2	Loftus Road	20632
13	1998/99	05/12/98	FA Premiership	Aston Villa 1 Manchester United 1	Villa Park	39241
14	2001/02	05/12/01	Champions League Phase 2 Match 2	Manchester United 3 Boavista 0	Old Trafford	66274

DECEMBER 6

#	SEASON	DATE	COMPETITION / ROUND	MATCH RESULT	VENUE	ATT
1	1893/94	06/12/93	Football League Division 1	Sunderland 4 Newton Heath 1	Newcastle Road	5000
2	1902/03	06/12/02	Football League Division 2	Burnley 0 Manchester United 2	Turf Moor	4000
3	1913/14	06/12/13	Football League Division 1	Manchester City 0 Manchester United 2	Hyde Road	40000
4	1919/20	06/12/19	Football League Division 1	Aston Villa 2 Manchester United 0	Villa Park	40000
5	1924/25	06/12/24	Football League Division 2	South Shields 1 Manchester United 2	Talbot Road	6500
6	1930/31	06/12/30	Football League Division 1	Blackburn Rovers 4 Manchester United 1	Ewood Park	10802
7	1947/48	06/12/47	Football League Division 1	Manchester United 1 Blackpool 1	Maine Road	63683
8	1952/53	06/12/52	Football League Division 1	Manchester United 3 Middlesbrough 2	Old Trafford	27617
9	1958/59	06/12/58	Football League Division 1	Manchester United 4 Leicester City 1	Old Trafford	38482
10	1969/70	06/12/69	Football League Division 1	Manchester United 0 Chelsea 2	Old Trafford	49344
11	1975/76	06/12/75	Football League Division 1	Middlesbrough 0 Manchester United 0	Ayresome Park	32454
12	1980/81	06/12/80	Football League Division 1	Norwich City 2 Manchester United 2	Carrow Road	18780
13	1992/93	06/12/92	FA Premiership	Manchester United 2 Manchester City 1	Old Trafford	35408
14	1997/98	06/12/97	FA Premiership	Liverpool 1 Manchester United 3	Anfield	41027
15	2000/01	06/12/00	Champions League Phase 2 Match 2	Sturm Graz 0 Manchester United 2	Schwarzenegger Stadium	16500
16	2003/04	06/12/03	FA Premiership	Manchester United 4 Aston Villa 0	Old Trafford	67621
17	2006/07	06/12/06	Champions League Phase 1 Match 6	Manchester United 3 Benfica 1	Old Trafford	74955

DECEMBER 7

#	SEASON	DATE	COMPETITION / ROUND	MATCH RESULT	VENUE	ATT
1	1895/96	07/12/95	Football League Division 2	Manchester City 2 Newton Heath 1	Hyde Road	18000
2	1901/02	07/12/01	Football League Division 2	Preston North End 5 Newton Heath 1	Deepdale	2000
3	1907/08	07/12/07	Football League Division 1	Manchester United 2 Bristol City 1	Bank Street	20000
4	1912/13	07/12/12	Football League Division 1	Manchester United 4 Sheffield United 0	Old Trafford	12000
5	1929/30	07/12/29	Football League Division 1	Manchester United 1 Bolton Wanderers 1	Old Trafford	5656
6	1935/36	07/12/35	Football League Division 2	Blackpool 4 Manchester United 1	Bloomfield Road	13218
7	1946/47	07/12/46	Football League Division 1	Manchester United 4 Brentford 1	Maine Road	31962
8	1957/58	07/12/57	Football League Division 1	Birmingham City 3 Manchester United 3	St Andrews	35791
9	1963/64	07/12/63	Football League Division 1	Manchester United 5 Stoke City 2	Old Trafford	52232
10	1968/69	07/12/68	Football League Division 1	Leicester City 2 Manchester United 1	Filbert Street	36303
11	1974/75	07/12/74	Football League Division 2	Sheffield Wednesday 4 Manchester United 4	Hillsborough	35230
12	1983/84	07/12/83	League Cup 4th Round Replay	Manchester United 1 Oxford United 1	Old Trafford	27459
13	1985/86	07/12/85	Football League Division 1	Manchester United 1 Ipswich Town 0	Old Trafford	37981
14	1986/87	07/12/86	Football League Division 1	Manchester United 3 Tottenham Hotspur 3	Old Trafford	35957
15	1991/92	07/12/91	Football League Division 1	Manchester United 4 Coventry City 0	Old Trafford	42549
16	1993/94	07/12/93	FA Premiership	Sheffield United 0 Manchester United 3	Bramall Lane	26746
17	1994/95	07/12/94	Champions League Phase 1 Match 6	Manchester United 4 Galatasaray 0	Old Trafford	39220
18	2002/03	07/12/02	FA Premiership	Manchester United 2 Arsenal 0	Old Trafford	67650
19	2005/06	07/12/05	Champions League Phase 1 Match 6	Benfica 2 Manchester United 1	Estadio da Luz	61000

DECEMBER 8

#	SEASON	DATE	COMPETITION / ROUND	MATCH RESULT	VENUE	ATT
1	1894/95	08/12/94	Football League Division 2	Newton Heath 5 Burton Swifts 1	Bank Street	4000
2	1900/01	08/12/00	Football League Division 2	Grimsby Town 2 Newton Heath 0	Blundell Park	4000
3	1906/07	08/12/06	Football League Division 1	Manchester United 3 Middlesbrough 1	Bank Street	12000
4	1923/24	08/12/23	Football League Division 2	Manchester United 3 Leeds United 1	Old Trafford	22250
5	1928/29	08/12/28	Football League Division 1	Arsenal 3 Manchester United 1	Highbury	18923
6	1934/35	08/12/34	Football League Division 2	Manchester United 1 Fulham 0	Old Trafford	25706
7	1951/52	08/12/51	Football League Division 1	Arsenal 1 Manchester United 3	Highbury	55451
8	1956/57	08/12/56	Football League Division 1	Aston Villa 1 Manchester United 3	Villa Park	42530
9	1962/63	08/12/62	Football League Division 1	Manchester United 5 Nottingham Forest 1	Old Trafford	27496
10	1973/74	08/12/73	Football League Division 1	Manchester United 0 Southampton 0	Old Trafford	31648
11	1979/80	08/12/79	Football League Division 1	Manchester United 1 Leeds United 1	Old Trafford	58348
12	1984/85	08/12/84	Football League Division 1	Nottingham Forest 3 Manchester United 2	City Ground	25902
13	1990/91	08/12/90	Football League Division 1	Manchester United 1 Leeds United 1	Old Trafford	40927
14	1996/97	08/12/96	FA Premiership	West Ham United 2 Manchester United 2	Upton Park	25045
15	1999/00	08/12/99	Champions League Phase 2 Match 2	Manchester United 3 Valencia 0	Old Trafford	54606
16	2001/02	08/12/01	FA Premiership	Manchester United 0 West Ham United 1	Old Trafford	67582
17	2004/05	08/12/04	Champions League Phase 1 Match 6	Fenerbahce 3 Manchester United 0	Sukru Saracoglu	35000
18	2007/08	08/12/07	FA Premiership	Manchester United 4 Derby County 1	Old Trafford	75725

DECEMBER 9

#	SEASON	DATE	COMPETITION / ROUND	MATCH RESULT	VENUE	ATT
1	1893/94	09/12/93	Football League Division 1	Bolton Wanderers 2 Newton Heath 0	Pikes Lane	5000
2	1905/06	09/12/05	Football League Division 2	Burnley 1 Manchester United 3	Turf Moor	8000
3	1911/12	09/12/11	Football League Division 1	Manchester United 1 Sheffield United 0	Old Trafford	12000
4	1922/23	09/12/22	Football League Division 2	Rotherham United 1 Manchester United 1	Millmoor	7500
5	1933/34	09/12/33	Football League Division 2	Manchester United 1 Notts County 2	Old Trafford	15564
6	1950/51	09/12/50	Football League Division 1	Huddersfield Town 2 Manchester United 3	Leeds Road	26713
7	1961/62	09/12/61	Football League Division 1	Manchester United 3 Fulham 0	Old Trafford	22193
8	1967/68	09/12/67	Football League Division 1	Newcastle United 2 Manchester United 2	St James' Park	48639
9	1972/73	09/12/72	Football League Division 1	Manchester United 0 Stoke City 2	Old Trafford	41347
10	1978/79	09/12/78	Football League Division 1	Derby County 1 Manchester United 3	Baseball Ground	23180
11	1989/90	09/12/89	Football League Division 1	Manchester United 1 Crystal Palace 2	Old Trafford	33514
12	1995/96	09/12/95	FA Premiership	Manchester United 2 Sheffield Wednesday 2	Old Trafford	41849
13	1998/99	09/12/98	Champions League Phase 1 Match 6	Manchester United 1 Bayern Munich 1	Old Trafford	54434
14	2000/01	09/12/00	FA Premiership	Charlton Athletic 3 Manchester United 3	The Valley	20043
15	2003/04	09/12/03	Champions League Phase 1 Match 6	Manchester United 2 Stuttgart 0	Old Trafford	67141
16	2006/07	09/12/06	FA Premiership	Manchester United 3 Manchester City 1	Old Trafford	75858

DECEMBER 10

#	SEASON	DATE	COMPETITION / ROUND	MATCH RESULT	VENUE	ATT
1	1892/93	10/12/92	Football League Division 1	Newton Heath 1 Bolton Wanderers 0	North Road	4000
2	1898/99	10/12/98	Football League Division 2	Newton Heath 3 Blackpool 1	Bank Street	5000
3	1904/05	10/12/04	Football League Division 2	Manchester United 3 Gainsborough Trinity 1	Bank Street	12000
4	1910/11	10/12/10	Football League Division 1	Sheffield United 2 Manchester United 0	Bramall Lane	8000
5	1921/22	10/12/21	Football League Division 1	Manchester United 1 Bradford City 1	Old Trafford	9000
6	1927/28	10/12/27	Football League Division 1	Sheffield United 2 Manchester United 1	Bramall Lane	11984
7	1932/33	10/12/32	Football League Division 2	West Ham United 3 Manchester United 1	Upton Park	13435
8	1938/39	10/12/38	Football League Division 1	Manchester United 1 Arsenal 0	Old Trafford	42008
9	1949/50	10/12/49	Football League Division 1	Fulham 1 Manchester United 0	Craven Cottage	35362
10	1955/56	10/12/55	Football League Division 1	Portsmouth 3 Manchester United 2	Fratton Park	24594
11	1960/61	10/12/60	Football League Division 1	Fulham 4 Manchester United 4	Craven Cottage	23625
12	1963/64	10/12/63	European CWC 2nd Round 2nd Leg	Manchester United 4 Tottenham Hotspur 1	Old Trafford	50000
13	1966/67	10/12/66	Football League Division 1	Manchester United 2 Liverpool 2	Old Trafford	61768
14	1977/78	10/12/77	Football League Division 1	West Ham United 2 Manchester United 1	Upton Park	20242
15	1983/84	10/12/83	Football League Division 1	Ipswich Town 0 Manchester United 2	Portman Road	19779
16	1988/89	10/12/88	Football League Division 1	Coventry City 1 Manchester United 0	Highfield Road	19936
17	1994/95	10/12/94	FA Premiership	Queens Park Rangers 2 Manchester United 3	Loftus Road	18948
18	1997/98	10/12/97	Champions League Phase 1 Match 6	Juventus 1 Manchester United 0	Stadio Delle Alpi	47786

DECEMBER 11

#	SEASON	DATE	COMPETITION / ROUND	MATCH RESULT	VENUE	ATT
1	1897/98	11/12/97	Football League Division 2	Walsall 1 Newton Heath 1	Fellows Park	2000
2	1920/21	11/12/20	Football League Division 1	Bradford Park Avenue 2 Manchester United 4	Park Avenue	10000
3	1926/27	11/12/26	Football League Division 1	Sunderland 6 Manchester United 0	Roker Park	15385
4	1937/38	11/12/37	Football League Division 2	Bradford Park Avenue 4 Manchester United 0	Park Avenue	12004
5	1948/49	11/12/48	Football League Division 1	Portsmouth 2 Manchester United 2	Fratton Park	29966
6	1954/55	11/12/54	Football League Division 1	Burnley 2 Manchester United 4	Turf Moor	24977
7	1965/66	11/12/65	Football League Division 1	Sunderland 2 Manchester United 3	Roker Park	37417
8	1971/72	11/12/71	Football League Division 1	Stoke City 1 Manchester United 1	Victoria Ground	33857
9	1982/83	11/12/82	Football League Division 1	Manchester United 4 Notts County 0	Old Trafford	33618
10	1993/94	11/12/93	FA Premiership	Newcastle United 1 Manchester United 1	St James' Park	36388
11	2002/03	11/12/02	Champions League Phase 2 Match 2	Manchester United 2 Deportivo La Coruna 0	Old Trafford	67014
12	2005/06	11/12/05	FA Premiership	Manchester United 1 Everton 1	Old Trafford	67831

DECEMBER 12

#	SEASON	DATE	COMPETITION / ROUND	MATCH RESULT	VENUE	ATT
1	1896/97	12/12/96	FA Cup 3rd Qualifying Round	Newton Heath 7 West Manchester 0	Bank Street	6000
2	1903/04	12/12/03	FA Cup Intermediate Round	Manchester United 1 Birmingham City 1	Bank Street	10000
3	1908/09	12/12/08	Football League Division 1	Manchester United 4 Leicester City 2	Bank Street	10000
4	1914/15	12/12/14	Football League Division 1	Manchester United 1 Sheffield United 2	Old Trafford	8000
5	1925/26	12/12/25	Football League Division 1	Manchester United 1 Sheffield United 2	Old Trafford	31132
6	1931/32	12/12/31	Football League Division 2	Bradford City 4 Manchester United 3	Valley Parade	13215
7	1936/37	12/12/36	Football League Division 1	Middlesbrough 3 Manchester United 2	Ayresome Park	11970
8	1953/54	12/12/53	Football League Division 1	Chelsea 3 Manchester United 1	Stamford Bridge	37153
9	1959/60	12/12/59	Football League Division 1	Nottingham Forest 1 Manchester United 5	City Ground	31666
10	1964/65	12/12/64	Football League Division 1	West Bromwich Albion 1 Manchester United 1	The Hawthorns	28126
11	1970/71	12/12/70	Football League Division 1	Manchester United 1 Manchester City 4	Old Trafford	52636
12	1984/85	12/12/84	UEFA Cup 3rd Round 2nd Leg	Dundee United 2 Manchester United 3	Tannadice Park	21821
13	1987/88	12/12/87	Football League Division 1	Manchester United 3 Oxford United 1	Old Trafford	34709
14	1992/93	12/12/92	FA Premiership	Manchester United 1 Norwich City 0	Old Trafford	34500
15	1998/99	12/12/98	FA Premiership	Tottenham Hotspur 2 Manchester United 2	White Hart Lane	36079
16	2001/02	12/12/01	FA Premiership	Manchester United 5 Derby County 0	Old Trafford	67577
17	2007/08	12/12/07	Champions League Phase 1 Match 6	Roma 1 Manchester United 1	Olympic Stadium	29490

DECEMBER 13

#	SEASON	DATE	COMPETITION / ROUND	MATCH RESULT	VENUE	ATT
1	1902/03	13/12/02	FA Cup Intermediate Round	Manchester United 1 Burton United 1	Bank Street	6000
2	1913/14	13/12/13	Football League Division 1	Manchester United 1 Bradford City 1	Old Trafford	18000
3	1919/20	13/12/19	Football League Division 1	Manchester United 1 Aston Villa 2	Old Trafford	30000
4	1924/25	13/12/24	Football League Division 2	Manchester United 3 Bradford City 0	Old Trafford	18250
5	1930/31	13/12/30	Football League Division 1	Manchester United 2 Derby County 1	Old Trafford	9701
6	1947/48	13/12/47	Football League Division 1	Blackburn Rovers 1 Manchester United 1	Ewood Park	22784
7	1952/53	13/12/52	Football League Division 1	Liverpool 1 Manchester United 2	Anfield	34450
8	1958/59	13/12/58	Football League Division 1	Preston North End 3 Manchester United 4	Deepdale	26290
9	1969/70	13/12/69	Football League Division 1	Liverpool 1 Manchester United 4	Anfield	47682
10	1975/76	13/12/75	Football League Division 1	Sheffield United 1 Manchester United 4	Bramall Lane	31741
11	1980/81	13/12/80	Football League Division 1	Manchester United 2 Stoke City 2	Old Trafford	39568
12	1986/87	13/12/86	Football League Division 1	Aston Villa 3 Manchester United 3	Villa Park	29205
13	2003/04	13/12/03	FA Premiership	Manchester United 3 Manchester City 1	Old Trafford	67643
14	2004/05	13/12/04	FA Premiership	Fulham 1 Manchester United 1	Craven Cottage	21940

DECEMBER 14

#	SEASON	DATE	COMPETITION / ROUND	MATCH RESULT	VENUE	ATT
1	1895/96	14/12/95	Football League Division 2	Newton Heath 3 Notts County 0	Bank Street	3000
2	1901/02	14/12/01	FA Cup Intermediate Round	Newton Heath 1 Lincoln City 2	Bank Street	4000
3	1907/08	14/12/07	Football League Division 1	Notts County 1 Manchester United 1	Trent Bridge	11000
4	1912/13	14/12/12	Football League Division 1	Newcastle United 1 Manchester United 3	St James' Park	20000
5	1929/30	14/12/29	Football League Division 1	Everton 0 Manchester United 0	Goodison Park	18182
6	1935/36	14/12/35	Football League Division 2	Manchester United 5 Nottingham Forest 0	Old Trafford	15284
7	1946/47	14/12/46	Football League Division 1	Blackburn Rovers 2 Manchester United 1	Ewood Park	21455
8	1957/58	14/12/57	Football League Division 1	Manchester United 0 Chelsea 1	Old Trafford	36853
9	1963/64	14/12/63	Football League Division 1	Manchester United 3 Sheffield Wednesday 1	Old Trafford	35139
10	1968/69	14/12/68	Football League Division 1	Manchester United 1 Liverpool 0	Old Trafford	55354
11	1974/75	14/12/74	Football League Division 2	Manchester United 0 Leyton Orient 0	Old Trafford	41200
12	1985/86	14/12/85	Football League Division 1	Aston Villa 1 Manchester United 3	Villa Park	27626
13	2002/03	14/12/02	FA Premiership	Manchester United 3 West Ham United 0	Old Trafford	67555
14	2005/06	14/12/05	FA Premiership	Manchester United 4 Wigan Athletic 0	Old Trafford	67793

DECEMBER 15

#	SEASON	DATE	COMPETITION / ROUND	MATCH RESULT	VENUE	ATT
1	1894/95	15/12/94	Football League Division 2	Notts County 1 Newton Heath 1	Trent Bridge	3000
2	1900/01	15/12/00	Football League Division 2	Newton Heath 4 Lincoln City 1	Bank Street	4000
3	1906/07	15/12/06	Football League Division 1	Preston North End 2 Manchester United 0	Deepdale	9000
4	1923/24	15/12/23	Football League Division 2	Port Vale 0 Manchester United 1	Old Recreation Ground	7500
5	1928/29	15/12/28	Football League Division 1	Manchester United 1 Everton 1	Old Trafford	17080
6	1934/35	15/12/34	Football League Division 2	Bradford Park Avenue 1 Manchester United 2	Park Avenue	8405
7	1951/52	15/12/51	Football League Division 1	Manchester United 5 West Bromwich Albion 1	Old Trafford	27584
8	1956/57	15/12/56	Football League Division 1	Birmingham City 3 Manchester United 1	St Andrews	36146
9	1962/63	15/12/62	Football League Division 1	West Bromwich Albion 3 Manchester United 0	The Hawthorns	18113
10	1965/66	15/12/65	Football League Division 1	Manchester United 3 Everton 0	Old Trafford	32624
11	1973/74	15/12/73	Football League Division 1	Manchester United 2 Coventry City 3	Old Trafford	28589
12	1979/80	15/12/79	Football League Division 1	Coventry City 1 Manchester United 2	Highfield Road	25541
13	1984/85	15/12/84	Football League Division 1	Manchester United 3 Queens Park Rangers 0	Old Trafford	36134
14	1990/91	15/12/90	Football League Division 1	Coventry City 2 Manchester United 2	Highfield Road	17106
15	1991/92	15/12/91	Football League Division 1	Chelsea 1 Manchester United 3	Stamford Bridge	23120
16	1997/98	15/12/97	FA Premiership	Manchester United 1 Aston Villa 0	Old Trafford	55151
17	2001/02	15/12/01	FA Premiership	Middlesbrough 0 Manchester United 1	Riverside Stadium	34358

DECEMBER 16

#	SEASON	DATE	COMPETITION / ROUND	MATCH RESULT	VENUE	ATT
1	1893/94	16/12/93	Football League Division 1	Newton Heath 1 Aston Villa 3	Bank Street	8000
2	1899/00	16/12/99	Football League Division 2	Newton Heath 2 Middlesbrough 1	Bank Street	4000
3	1903/04	16/12/03	FA Cup Intermediate Round Replay	Birmingham City 1 Manchester United 1	Muntz Street	5000
4	1911/12	16/12/11	Football League Division 1	Oldham Athletic 2 Manchester United 2	Boundary Park	20000
5	1922/23	16/12/22	Football League Division 2	Manchester United 1 Stockport County 0	Old Trafford	24000
6	1933/34	16/12/33	Football League Division 2	Swansea City 2 Manchester United 1	Vetch Field	6591
7	1950/51	16/12/50	Football League Division 1	Fulham 2 Manchester United 2	Craven Cottage	19649
8	1961/62	16/12/61	Football League Division 1	Manchester United 1 West Ham United 2	Old Trafford	29472
9	1964/65	16/12/64	Football League Division 1	Manchester United 1 Birmingham City 1	Old Trafford	25721
10	1967/68	16/12/67	Football League Division 1	Manchester United 3 Everton 1	Old Trafford	60736
11	1970/71	16/12/70	League Cup Semi-Final 1st Leg	Manchester United 1 Aston Villa 1	Old Trafford	48889
12	1972/73	16/12/72	Football League Division 1	Crystal Palace 5 Manchester United 0	Selhurst Park	39484
13	1978/79	16/12/78	Football League Division 1	Manchester United 2 Tottenham Hotspur 0	Old Trafford	52026
14	1983/84	16/12/83	Football League Division 1	Manchester United 4 Tottenham Hotspur 2	Old Trafford	33616
15	1989/90	16/12/89	Football League Division 1	Manchester United 0 Tottenham Hotspur 1	Old Trafford	36230
16	1998/99	16/12/98	FA Premiership	Manchester United 1 Chelsea 1	Old Trafford	55159
17	2007/08	16/12/07	FA Premiership	Liverpool 0 Manchester United 1	Anfield	44459

DECEMBER 17

#	SEASON	DATE	COMPETITION / ROUND	MATCH RESULT	VENUE	ATT
1	1892/93	17/12/92	Football League Division 1	Wolverhampton Wanderers 2 Newton Heath 0	Molineux	5000
2	1898/99	17/12/98	Football League Division 2	Leicester City 1 Newton Heath 0	Filbert Street	8000
3	1902/03	17/12/02	FA Cup Intermediate Round Replay	Burton United 1 Manchester United 3	Bank Street	7000
4	1904/05	17/12/04	Football League Division 2	Burton United 2 Manchester United 3	Peel Croft	3000
5	1910/11	17/12/10	Football League Division 1	Manchester United 2 Aston Villa 0	Old Trafford	20000
6	1921/22	17/12/21	Football League Division 1	Liverpool 2 Manchester United 1	Anfield	40000
7	1927/28	17/12/27	Football League Division 1	Manchester United 4 Arsenal 1	Old Trafford	18120
8	1932/33	17/12/32	Football League Division 2	Manchester United 4 Lincoln City 1	Old Trafford	18021
9	1938/39	17/12/38	Football League Division 1	Brentford 2 Manchester United 5	Griffin Park	14919
10	1949/50	17/12/49	Football League Division 1	Manchester United 0 Derby County 1	Old Trafford	33753
11	1955/56	17/12/55	Football League Division 1	Manchester United 2 Birmingham City 1	Old Trafford	27704
12	1960/61	17/12/60	Football League Division 1	Blackburn Rovers 1 Manchester United 2	Ewood Park	17285
13	1966/67	17/12/66	Football League Division 1	West Bromwich Albion 3 Manchester United 4	The Hawthorns	32080
14	1969/70	17/12/69	League Cup Semi-Final 2nd Leg	Manchester United 2 Manchester City 2	Old Trafford	63418
15	1977/78	17/12/77	Football League Division 1	Manchester United 0 Nottingham Forest 4	Old Trafford	54374
16	1988/89	17/12/88	Football League Division 1	Arsenal 2 Manchester United 1	Highbury	37422
17	1994/95	17/12/94	FA Premiership	Manchester United 1 Nottingham Forest 2	Old Trafford	43744
18	1995/96	17/12/95	FA Premiership	Liverpool 2 Manchester United 0	Anfield	40546
19	2000/01	17/12/00	FA Premiership	Manchester United 0 Liverpool 1	Old Trafford	67533
20	2002/03	17/12/02	League Cup 5th Round	Manchester United 1 Chelsea 0	Old Trafford	57985
21	2005/06	17/12/05	FA Premiership	Aston Villa 0 Manchester United 2	Villa Park	37128
22	2006/07	17/12/06	FA Premiership	West Ham United 1 Manchester United 0	Upton Park	34966

DECEMBER 18

#	SEASON	DATE	COMPETITION / ROUND	MATCH RESULT	VENUE	ATT
1	1909/10	18/12/09	Football League Division 1	Middlesbrough 1 Manchester United 2	Ayresome Park	10000
2	1920/21	18/12/20	Football League Division 1	Manchester United 2 Newcastle United 0	Old Trafford	40000
3	1926/27	18/12/26	Football League Division 1	Manchester United 2 West Bromwich Albion 0	Old Trafford	18585
4	1948/49	18/12/48	Football League Division 1	Derby County 1 Manchester United 3	Baseball Ground	31498
5	1954/55	18/12/54	Football League Division 1	Portsmouth 0 Manchester United 0	Fratton Park	26019
6	1965/66	18/12/65	Football League Division 1	Manchester United 5 Tottenham Hotspur 1	Old Trafford	39270
7	1971/72	18/12/71	Football League Division 1	Ipswich Town 0 Manchester United 0	Portman Road	29229
8	1974/75	18/12/74	League Cup 5th Round Replay	Manchester United 3 Middlesbrough 0	Old Trafford	49501
9	1976/77	18/12/76	Football League Division 1	Arsenal 3 Manchester United 1	Highbury	39572
10	1982/83	18/12/82	Football League Division 1	Swansea City 0 Manchester United 0	Vetch Field	15748
11	1996/97	18/12/96	FA Premiership	Sheffield Wednesday 1 Manchester United 1	Hillsborough	37671
12	1999/00	18/12/99	FA Premiership	West Ham United 2 Manchester United 4	Upton Park	26037
13	2004/05	18/12/04	FA Premiership	Manchester United 5 Crystal Palace 2	Old Trafford	67814

DECEMBER 19

#	SEASON	DATE	COMPETITION / ROUND	MATCH RESULT	VENUE	ATT
1	1896/97	19/12/96	Football League Division 2	Notts County 3 Newton Heath 0	Trent Bridge	5000
2	1903/04	19/12/03	Football League Division 2	Manchester United 4 Gainsborough Trinity 2	Bank Street	6000
3	1908/09	19/12/08	Football League Division 1	Arsenal 0 Manchester United 1	Manor Field	10000
4	1914/15	19/12/14	Football League Division 1	Aston Villa 3 Manchester United 3	Villa Park	10000
5	1925/26	19/12/25	Football League Division 1	West Bromwich Albion 5 Manchester United 1	The Hawthorns	17651
6	1931/32	19/12/31	Football League Division 2	Manchester United 0 Bristol City 1	Old Trafford	4697
7	1936/37	19/12/36	Football League Division 1	Manchester United 2 West Bromwich Albion 2	Old Trafford	21051
8	1953/54	19/12/53	Football League Division 1	Manchester United 5 Liverpool 1	Old Trafford	26074
9	1959/60	19/12/59	Football League Division 1	Manchester United 2 West Bromwich Albion 3	Old Trafford	33677
10	1970/71	19/12/70	Football League Division 1	Manchester United 1 Arsenal 3	Old Trafford	33182
11	1983/84	19/12/83	League Cup 4th Round 2nd Replay	Oxford United 2 Manchester United 1	Manor Ground	13912
12	1987/88	19/12/87	Football League Division 1	Portsmouth 1 Manchester United 2	Fratton Park	22207
13	1992/93	19/12/92	FA Premiership	Chelsea 1 Manchester United 1	Stamford Bridge	34464
14	1993/94	19/12/93	FA Premiership	Manchester United 3 Aston Villa 1	Old Trafford	44499
15	1998/99	19/12/98	FA Premiership	Manchester United 2 Middlesbrough 3	Old Trafford	55152

DECEMBER 20

#	SEASON	DATE	COMPETITION / ROUND	MATCH RESULT	VENUE	ATT
1	1902/03	20/12/02	Football League Division 2	Port Vale 1 Manchester United 1	Cobridge Stadium	1000
2	1913/14	20/12/13	Football League Division 1	Blackburn Rovers 0 Manchester United 1	Ewood Park	35000
3	1919/20	20/12/19	Football League Division 1	Manchester United 2 Newcastle United 1	Old Trafford	20000
4	1924/25	20/12/24	Football League Division 2	Port Vale 2 Manchester United 1	Old Recreation Ground	11000
5	1930/31	20/12/30	Football League Division 1	Leeds United 5 Manchester United 0	Elland Road	11282
6	1947/48	20/12/47	Football League Division 1	Manchester United 2 Middlesbrough 1	Maine Road	46666
7	1952/53	20/12/52	Football League Division 1	Chelsea 2 Manchester United 3	Stamford Bridge	23261
8	1958/59	20/12/58	Football League Division 1	Chelsea 2 Manchester United 3	Stamford Bridge	48550
9	1975/76	20/12/75	Football League Division 1	Manchester United 1 Wolverhampton Wanderers 0	Old Trafford	44269
10	1980/81	20/12/80	Football League Division 1	Arsenal 2 Manchester United 1	Highbury	33730
11	1986/87	20/12/86	Football League Division 1	Manchester United 2 Leicester City 0	Old Trafford	34150
12	2005/06	20/12/05	League Cup 5th Round	Birmingham City 1 Manchester United 3	St Andrews	20454

DECEMBER 21

#	SEASON	DATE	COMPETITION / ROUND	MATCH RESULT	VENUE	ATT
1	1895/96	21/12/95	Football League Division 2	Darwen 3 Newton Heath 0	Barley Bank	3000
2	1901/02	21/12/01	Football League Division 2	Newton Heath 1 Port Vale 0	Bank Street	3000
3	1903/04	21/12/03	FA Cup Intermediate Round 2nd Replay	Manchester United 1 Birmingham City 1	Bramall Lane	3000
4	1907/08	21/12/07	Football League Division 1	Manchester United 3 Manchester City 1	Bank Street	35000
5	1912/13	21/12/12	Football League Division 1	Manchester United 0 Oldham Athletic 1	Old Trafford	30000
6	1929/30	21/12/29	Football League Division 1	Manchester United 3 Leeds United 1	Old Trafford	15054
7	1957/58	21/12/57	Football League Division 1	Manchester United 4 Leicester City 0	Old Trafford	41631
8	1963/64	21/12/63	Football League Division 1	Everton 4 Manchester United 0	Goodison Park	48027
9	1968/69	21/12/68	Football League Division 1	Southampton 2 Manchester United 0	The Dell	26194
10	1974/75	21/12/74	Football League Division 2	York City 0 Manchester United 1	Bootham Crescent	15567
11	1985/86	21/12/85	Football League Division 1	Manchester United 0 Arsenal 1	Old Trafford	44386
12	1996/97	21/12/96	FA Premiership	Manchester United 5 Sunderland 0	Old Trafford	55081
13	1997/98	21/12/97	FA Premiership	Newcastle United 0 Manchester United 1	St James' Park	36767
14	2003/04	21/12/03	FA Premiership	Tottenham Hotspur 1 Manchester United 2	White Hart Lane	35910

DECEMBER 22

#	SEASON	DATE	COMPETITION / ROUND	MATCH RESULT	VENUE	ATT
1	1894/95	22/12/94	Football League Division 2	Newton Heath 3 Lincoln City 0	Bank Street	2000
2	1900/01	22/12/00	Football League Division 2	Chesterfield 2 Newton Heath 1	Saltergate	4000
3	1906/07	22/12/06	Football League Division 1	Manchester United 1 Newcastle United 3	Bank Street	18000
4	1923/24	22/12/23	Football League Division 2	Manchester United 5 Port Vale 0	Old Trafford	11750
5	1928/29	22/12/28	Football League Division 1	Portsmouth 3 Manchester United 1	Fratton Park	12836
6	1934/35	22/12/34	Football League Division 2	Manchester United 3 Plymouth Argyle 1	Old Trafford	24896
7	1951/52	22/12/51	Football League Division 1	Newcastle United 2 Manchester United 2	St James' Park	45414
8	1973/74	22/12/73	Football League Division 1	Liverpool 2 Manchester United 0	Anfield	40420
9	1978/79	22/12/78	Football League Division 1	Bolton Wanderers 3 Manchester United 0	Burnden Park	32390
10	1979/80	22/12/79	Football League Division 1	Manchester United 3 Nottingham Forest 0	Old Trafford	54607
11	1984/85	22/12/84	Football League Division 1	Manchester United 3 Ipswich Town 0	Old Trafford	35168
12	1990/91	22/12/90	Football League Division 1	Wimbledon 2 Manchester United 3	Plough Lane	9644
13	2001/02	22/12/01	FA Premiership	Manchester United 6 Southampton 1	Old Trafford	67638
14	2002/03	22/12/02	FA Premiership	Blackburn Rovers 1 Manchester United 0	Ewood Park	30475

DECEMBER 23

#	SEASON	DATE	COMPETITION / ROUND	MATCH RESULT	VENUE	ATT
1	1893/94	23/12/93	Football League Division 1	Preston North End 2 Newton Heath 0	Deepdale	5000
2	1899/00	23/12/99	Football League Division 2	Chesterfield 2 Newton Heath 1	Saltergate	2000
3	1905/06	23/12/05	Football League Division 2	Burton United 0 Manchester United 2	Peel Croft	5000
4	1911/12	23/12/11	Football League Division 1	Manchester United 2 Bolton Wanderers 0	Old Trafford	20000
5	1922/23	23/12/22	Football League Division 2	Stockport County 1 Manchester United 0	Edgeley Park	15500
6	1933/34	23/12/33	Football League Division 2	Manchester United 1 Millwall 1	Old Trafford	12043
7	1950/51	23/12/50	Football League Division 1	Manchester United 2 Bolton Wanderers 3	Old Trafford	35382
8	1967/68	23/12/67	Football League Division 1	Leicester City 2 Manchester United 2	Filbert Street	40104
9	1970/71	23/12/70	League Cup Semi-Final 2nd Leg	Aston Villa 2 Manchester United 1	Villa Park	58667
10	1972/73	23/12/72	Football League Division 1	Manchester United 1 Leeds United 1	Old Trafford	46382
11	1975/76	23/12/75	Football League Division 1	Everton 1 Manchester United 1	Goodison Park	41732
12	1989/90	23/12/89	Football League Division 1	Liverpool 0 Manchester United 0	Anfield	37426
13	2000/01	23/12/00	FA Premiership	Manchester United 2 Ipswich Town 0	Old Trafford	67597
14	2006/07	23/12/06	FA Premiership	Aston Villa 0 Manchester United 3	Villa Park	42551
15	2007/08	23/12/07	FA Premiership	Manchester United 2 Everton 1	Old Trafford	75749

DECEMBER 24

#	SEASON	DATE	COMPETITION / ROUND	MATCH RESULT	VENUE	ATT
1	1892/93	24/12/92	Football League Division 1	Newton Heath 1 Sheffield Wednesday 5	North Road	4000
2	1894/95	24/12/94	Football League Division 2	Port Vale 2 Newton Heath 5	Cobridge Stadium	1000
3	1898/99	24/12/98	Football League Division 2	Newton Heath 9 Darwen 0	Bank Street	2000
4	1904/05	24/12/04	Football League Division 2	Manchester United 3 Liverpool 1	Bank Street	40000
5	1910/11	24/12/10	Football League Division 1	Sunderland 1 Manchester United 2	Roker Park	30000
6	1921/22	24/12/21	Football League Division 1	Manchester United 0 Liverpool 0	Old Trafford	30000
7	1927/28	24/12/27	Football League Division 1	Liverpool 2 Manchester United 0	Anfield	14971
8	1932/33	24/12/32	Football League Division 2	Swansea City 2 Manchester United 1	Vetch Field	10727
9	1938/39	24/12/38	Football League Division 1	Manchester United 1 Middlesbrough 1	Old Trafford	33235
10	1949/50	24/12/49	Football League Division 1	West Bromwich Albion 1 Manchester United 2	The Hawthorns	46973
11	1955/56	24/12/55	Football League Division 1	West Bromwich Albion 1 Manchester United 4	The Hawthorns	25168
12	1960/61	24/12/60	Football League Division 1	Chelsea 1 Manchester United 2	Stamford Bridge	37601
13	1995/96	24/12/95	FA Premiership	Leeds United 3 Manchester United 1	Elland Road	39801

DECEMBER 25

#	SEASON	DATE	COMPETITION / ROUND	MATCH RESULT	VENUE	ATT
1	1896/97	25/12/96	Football League Division 2	Newton Heath 2 Manchester City 1	Bank Street	18000
2	1897/98	25/12/97	Football League Division 2	Manchester City 0 Newton Heath 1	Hyde Road	16000
3	1902/03	25/12/02	Football League Division 2	Manchester United 1 Manchester City 1	Bank Street	40000
4	1903/04	25/12/03	Football League Division 2	Manchester United 3 Chesterfield 1	Bank Street	15000
5	1905/06	25/12/05	Football League Division 2	Manchester United 0 Chelsea 0	Bank Street	35000
6	1906/07	25/12/06	Football League Division 1	Manchester United 0 Liverpool 0	Bank Street	20000
7	1907/08	25/12/07	Football League Division 1	Manchester United 2 Bury 1	Bank Street	45000
8	1908/09	25/12/08	Football League Division 1	Newcastle United 2 Manchester United 1	St James' Park	35000
9	1909/10	25/12/09	Football League Division 1	Manchester United 0 Sheffield Wednesday 3	Bank Street	25000
10	1911/12	25/12/11	Football League Division 1	Manchester United 0 Bradford City 1	Old Trafford	50000
11	1912/13	25/12/12	Football League Division 1	Chelsea 1 Manchester United 4	Stamford Bridge	33000
12	1913/14	25/12/13	Football League Division 1	Manchester United 0 Everton 1	Old Trafford	25000
13	1920/21	25/12/20	Football League Division 1	Aston Villa 3 Manchester United 4	Villa Park	38000
14	1922/23	25/12/22	Football League Division 2	Manchester United 1 West Ham United 2	Old Trafford	17500
15	1923/24	25/12/23	Football League Division 2	Manchester United 1 Barnsley 2	Old Trafford	34000
16	1924/25	25/12/24	Football League Division 2	Middlesbrough 1 Manchester United 1	Ayresome Park	18500
17	1925/26	25/12/25	Football League Division 1	Manchester United 2 Bolton Wanderers 1	Old Trafford	38503
18	1926/27	25/12/26	Football League Division 1	Tottenham Hotspur 1 Manchester United 1	White Hart Lane	37287
19	1928/29	25/12/28	Football League Division 1	Manchester United 1 Sheffield United 1	Old Trafford	22202
20	1929/30	25/12/29	Football League Division 1	Manchester United 0 Birmingham City 0	Old Trafford	18626
21	1930/31	25/12/30	Football League Division 1	Bolton Wanderers 3 Manchester United 1	Burnden Park	22662
22	1931/32	25/12/31	Football League Division 2	Manchester United 3 Wolverhampton Wanderers 2	Old Trafford	33123
23	1933/34	25/12/33	Football League Division 2	Manchester United 1 Grimsby Town 3	Old Trafford	29443
24	1934/35	25/12/34	Football League Division 2	Manchester United 2 Notts County 1	Old Trafford	32965
25	1936/37	25/12/36	Football League Division 1	Manchester United 1 Bolton Wanderers 0	Old Trafford	47658
26	1946/47	25/12/46	Football League Division 1	Bolton Wanderers 2 Manchester United 2	Burnden Park	28505
27	1947/48	25/12/47	Football League Division 1	Manchester United 3 Portsmouth 2	Maine Road	42776
28	1948/49	25/12/48	Football League Division 1	Manchester United 0 Liverpool 0	Maine Road	47788
29	1950/51	25/12/50	Football League Division 1	Sunderland 2 Manchester United 1	Roker Park	41215
30	1951/52	25/12/51	Football League Division 1	Manchester United 3 Fulham 2	Old Trafford	33802
31	1952/53	25/12/52	Football League Division 1	Blackpool 0 Manchester United 0	Bloomfield Road	27778
32	1953/54	25/12/53	Football League Division 1	Manchester United 5 Sheffield Wednesday 2	Old Trafford	27123
33	1957/58	25/12/57	Football League Division 1	Manchester United 3 Luton Town 1	Old Trafford	39444

DECEMBER 26

#	SEASON	DATE	COMPETITION / ROUND	MATCH RESULT	VENUE	ATT
1	1892/93	26/12/92	Football League Division 1	Preston North End 2 Newton Heath 1	Deepdale	4000
2	1894/95	26/12/94	Football League Division 2	Walsall 1 Newton Heath 2	West Bromwich Road	1000
3	1896/97	26/12/96	Football League Division 2	Newton Heath 2 Blackpool 0	Bank Street	9000
4	1898/99	26/12/98	Football League Division 2	Manchester City 4 Newton Heath 0	Hyde Road	25000
5	1899/00	26/12/99	Football League Division 2	Grimsby Town 0 Newton Heath 7	Blundell Park	2000
6	1900/01	26/12/00	Football League Division 2	Newton Heath 4 Blackpool 0	Bank Street	10000
7	1901/02	26/12/01	Football League Division 2	Lincoln City 2 Newton Heath 0	Sincil Bank	4000
8	1902/03	26/12/02	Football League Division 2	Manchester United 2 Blackpool 2	Bank Street	10000
9	1903/04	26/12/03	Football League Division 2	Burton United 2 Manchester United 2	Peel Croft	4000
10	1904/05	26/12/04	Football League Division 2	Manchester United 3 Chesterfield 0	Bank Street	20000
11	1906/07	26/12/06	Football League Division 1	Aston Villa 2 Manchester United 0	Perry Barr	20000
12	1908/09	26/12/08	Football League Division 1	Manchester United 1 Newcastle United 0	Bank Street	40000
13	1910/11	26/12/10	Football League Division 1	Manchester United 5 Arsenal 0	Old Trafford	40000
14	1911/12	26/12/11	Football League Division 1	Bradford City 0 Manchester United 1	Valley Parade	40000
15	1912/13	26/12/12	Football League Division 1	Manchester United 4 Chelsea 2	Old Trafford	20000
16	1913/14	26/12/13	Football League Division 1	Everton 5 Manchester United 0	Goodison Park	40000
17	1914/15	26/12/14	Football League Division 1	Liverpool 1 Manchester United 1	Anfield	25000
18	1919/20	26/12/19	Football League Division 1	Manchester United 0 Liverpool 0	Old Trafford	45000
19	1921/22	26/12/21	Football League Division 1	Manchester United 0 Burnley 1	Old Trafford	15000
20	1922/23	26/12/22	Football League Division 2	West Ham United 0 Manchester United 2	Upton Park	25000
21	1923/24	26/12/23	Football League Division 2	Barnsley 1 Manchester United 0	Oakwell	12000
22	1924/25	26/12/24	Football League Division 2	Manchester United 2 Middlesbrough 0	Old Trafford	44000
23	1927/28	26/12/27	Football League Division 1	Manchester United 1 Blackburn Rovers 1	Old Trafford	31131
24	1928/29	26/12/28	Football League Division 1	Sheffield United 6 Manchester United 1	Bramall Lane	34696
25	1929/30	26/12/29	Football League Division 1	Birmingham City 0 Manchester United 1	St Andrews	35682
26	1930/31	26/12/30	Football League Division 1	Manchester United 1 Bolton Wanderers 1	Old Trafford	12741
27	1931/32	26/12/31	Football League Division 2	Wolverhampton Wanderers 7 Manchester United 0	Molineux	37207
28	1932/33	26/12/32	Football League Division 2	Plymouth Argyle 2 Manchester United 3	Home Park	33776
29	1933/34	26/12/33	Football League Division 2	Grimsby Town 7 Manchester United 3	Blundell Park	15801
30	1934/35	26/12/34	Football League Division 2	Notts County 1 Manchester United 0	Meadow Lane	24599
31	1935/36	26/12/35	Football League Division 2	Manchester United 1 Barnsley 1	Old Trafford	20993
32	1936/37	26/12/36	Football League Division 1	Wolverhampton Wanderers 3 Manchester United 1	Molineux	41525
33	1938/39	26/12/38	Football League Division 1	Manchester United 3 Leicester City 0	Old Trafford	26332
34	1946/47	26/12/46	Football League Division 1	Manchester United 1 Bolton Wanderers 0	Maine Road	57186
35	1948/49	26/12/48	Football League Division 1	Liverpool 0 Manchester United 2	Anfield	53325
36	1949/50	26/12/49	Football League Division 1	Manchester United 2 Arsenal 0	Old Trafford	53928
37	1950/51	26/12/50	Football League Division 1	Manchester United 3 Sunderland 5	Old Trafford	35176
38	1951/52	26/12/51	Football League Division 1	Fulham 3 Manchester United 3	Craven Cottage	32671
39	1952/53	26/12/52	Football League Division 1	Manchester United 2 Blackpool 1	Old Trafford	48077
40	1953/54	26/12/53	Football League Division 1	Sheffield Wednesday 0 Manchester United 1	Hillsborough	44196
41	1955/56	26/12/55	Football League Division 1	Manchester United 5 Charlton Athletic 1	Old Trafford	44611
42	1956/57	26/12/56	Football League Division 1	Manchester United 3 Cardiff City 1	Old Trafford	28607
43	1957/58	26/12/57	Football League Division 1	Luton Town 2 Manchester United 0	Kenilworth Road	26458
44	1958/59	26/12/58	Football League Division 1	Manchester United 2 Aston Villa 1	Old Trafford	63098
45	1959/60	26/12/59	Football League Division 1	Manchester United 1 Burnley 2	Old Trafford	62376
46	1960/61	26/12/60	Football League Division 1	Manchester United 6 Chelsea 0	Old Trafford	50164
47	1961/62	26/12/61	Football League Division 1	Manchester United 6 Nottingham Forest 3	Old Trafford	30822
48	1962/63	26/12/62	Football League Division 1	Fulham 0 Manchester United 1	Craven Cottage	23928
49	1963/64	26/12/63	Football League Division 1	Burnley 6 Manchester United 1	Turf Moor	35764
50	1964/65	26/12/64	Football League Division 1	Sheffield United 0 Manchester United 1	Bramall Lane	37295

continued../

DECEMBER 26 (continued)

#	SEASON	DATE	COMPETITION / ROUND	MATCH RESULT	VENUE	ATT
51	1966/67	26/12/66	Football League Division 1	Sheffield United 2 Manchester United 1	Bramall Lane	42752
52	1967/68	26/12/67	Football League Division 1	Manchester United 4 Wolverhampton Wanderers 0	Old Trafford	63450
53	1968/69	26/12/68	Football League Division 1	Arsenal 3 Manchester United 0	Highbury	62300
54	1969/70	26/12/69	Football League Division 1	Manchester United 0 Wolverhampton Wanderers 0	Old Trafford	50806
55	1970/71	26/12/70	Football League Division 1	Derby County 4 Manchester United 4	Baseball Ground	34068
56	1972/73	26/12/72	Football League Division 1	Derby County 3 Manchester United 1	Baseball Ground	35098
57	1973/74	26/12/73	Football League Division 1	Manchester United 1 Sheffield United 2	Old Trafford	38653
58	1974/75	26/12/74	Football League Division 2	Manchester United 2 West Bromwich Albion 1	Old Trafford	51104
59	1977/78	26/12/77	Football League Division 1	Everton 2 Manchester United 6	Goodison Park	48335
60	1978/79	26/12/78	Football League Division 1	Manchester United 0 Liverpool 3	Old Trafford	54910
61	1979/80	26/12/79	Football League Division 1	Liverpool 2 Manchester United 0	Anfield	51073
62	1980/81	26/12/80	Football League Division 1	Manchester United 0 Liverpool 0	Old Trafford	57049
63	1983/84	26/12/83	Football League Division 1	Coventry City 1 Manchester United 1	Highfield Road	21553
64	1984/85	26/12/84	Football League Division 1	Stoke City 2 Manchester United 1	Victoria Ground	20985
65	1985/86	26/12/85	Football League Division 1	Everton 3 Manchester United 1	Goodison Park	42551
66	1986/87	26/12/86	Football League Division 1	Liverpool 0 Manchester United 1	Anfield	40663
67	1987/88	26/12/87	Football League Division 1	Newcastle United 1 Manchester United 0	St James' Park	26461
68	1988/89	26/12/88	Football League Division 1	Manchester United 2 Nottingham Forest 0	Old Trafford	39582
69	1989/90	26/12/89	Football League Division 1	Aston Villa 3 Manchester United 0	Villa Park	41247
70	1990/91	26/12/90	Football League Division 1	Manchester United 3 Norwich City 0	Old Trafford	39801
71	1991/92	26/12/91	Football League Division 1	Oldham Athletic 3 Manchester United 6	Boundary Park	18947
72	1992/93	26/12/92	FA Premiership	Sheffield Wednesday 3 Manchester United 3	Hillsborough	37708
73	1993/94	26/12/93	FA Premiership	Manchester United 1 Blackburn Rovers 1	Old Trafford	44511
74	1994/95	26/12/94	FA Premiership	Chelsea 2 Manchester United 3	Stamford Bridge	31161
75	1996/97	26/12/96	FA Premiership	Nottingham Forest 0 Manchester United 4	City Ground	29032
76	1997/98	26/12/97	FA Premiership	Manchester United 2 Everton 0	Old Trafford	55167
77	1998/99	26/12/98	FA Premiership	Manchester United 3 Nottingham Forest 0	Old Trafford	55216
78	1999/00	26/12/99	FA Premiership	Manchester United 4 Bradford City 0	Old Trafford	55188
79	2000/01	26/12/00	FA Premiership	Aston Villa 0 Manchester United 1	Villa Park	40889
80	2001/02	26/12/01	FA Premiership	Everton 0 Manchester United 2	Goodison Park	39948
81	2002/03	26/12/02	FA Premiership	Middlesbrough 3 Manchester United 1	Riverside Stadium	34673
82	2003/04	26/12/03	FA Premiership	Manchester United 3 Everton 2	Old Trafford	67642
83	2004/05	26/12/04	FA Premiership	Manchester United 2 Bolton Wanderers 0	Old Trafford	67867
84	2005/06	26/12/05	FA Premiership	Manchester United 3 West Bromwich Albion 0	Old Trafford	67972
85	2006/07	26/12/06	FA Premiership	Manchester United 3 Wigan Athletic 1	Old Trafford	76018
86	2007/08	26/12/07	FA Premiership	Sunderland 0 Manchester United 4	Stadium of Light	47360

DECEMBER 27

#	SEASON	DATE	COMPETITION / ROUND	MATCH RESULT	VENUE	ATT
1	1897/98	27/12/97	Football League Division 2	Gainsborough Trinity 2 Newton Heath 1	The Northolme	3000
2	1902/03	27/12/02	Football League Division 2	Manchester United 2 Barnsley 1	Bank Street	9000
3	1909/10	27/12/09	Football League Division 1	Sheffield Wednesday 4 Manchester United 1	Hillsborough	37000
4	1910/11	27/12/10	Football League Division 1	Bradford City 1 Manchester United 0	Valley Parade	35000
5	1913/14	27/12/13	Football League Division 1	Manchester United 2 Sheffield Wednesday 1	Old Trafford	10000
6	1919/20	27/12/19	Football League Division 1	Newcastle United 2 Manchester United 1	St James' Park	45000
7	1920/21	27/12/20	Football League Division 1	Manchester United 1 Aston Villa 3	Old Trafford	70504
8	1921/22	27/12/21	Football League Division 1	Burnley 4 Manchester United 2	Turf Moor	10000
9	1924/25	27/12/24	Football League Division 2	Leicester City 3 Manchester United 0	Filbert Street	18250
10	1926/27	27/12/26	Football League Division 1	Manchester United 2 Tottenham Hotspur 1	Old Trafford	50665
11	1930/31	27/12/30	Football League Division 1	Aston Villa 7 Manchester United 0	Villa Park	32505
12	1937/38	27/12/37	Football League Division 2	Manchester United 4 Nottingham Forest 3	Old Trafford	30778
13	1938/39	27/12/38	Football League Division 1	Leicester City 1 Manchester United 1	Filbert Street	21434
14	1947/48	27/12/47	Football League Division 1	Portsmouth 1 Manchester United 3	Fratton Park	27674
15	1949/50	27/12/49	Football League Division 1	Arsenal 0 Manchester United 0	Highbury	65133
16	1954/55	27/12/54	Football League Division 1	Manchester United 0 Aston Villa 1	Old Trafford	49136
17	1955/56	27/12/55	Football League Division 1	Charlton Athletic 3 Manchester United 0	The Valley	42040
18	1958/59	27/12/58	Football League Division 1	Aston Villa 0 Manchester United 2	Villa Park	56450
19	1965/66	27/12/65	Football League Division 1	Manchester United 1 West Bromwich Albion 1	Old Trafford	54102
20	1966/67	27/12/66	Football League Division 1	Manchester United 2 Sheffield United 0	Old Trafford	59392
21	1969/70	27/12/69	Football League Division 1	Sunderland 1 Manchester United 1	Roker Park	36504
22	1971/72	27/12/71	Football League Division 1	Manchester United 2 Coventry City 2	Old Trafford	52117
23	1975/76	27/12/75	Football League Division 1	Manchester United 2 Burnley 1	Old Trafford	59726
24	1976/77	27/12/76	Football League Division 1	Manchester United 4 Everton 0	Old Trafford	56786
25	1977/78	27/12/77	Football League Division 1	Manchester United 3 Leicester City 1	Old Trafford	57396
26	1980/81	27/12/80	Football League Division 1	West Bromwich Albion 3 Manchester United 1	The Hawthorns	30326
27	1982/83	27/12/82	Football League Division 1	Manchester United 0 Sunderland 0	Old Trafford	47783
28	1983/84	27/12/83	Football League Division 1	Manchester United 3 Notts County 3	Old Trafford	41544
29	1986/87	27/12/86	Football League Division 1	Manchester United 0 Norwich City 1	Old Trafford	44610
30	1995/96	27/12/95	FA Premiership	Manchester United 2 Newcastle United 0	Old Trafford	42024

DECEMBER 28

#	SEASON	DATE	COMPETITION / ROUND	MATCH RESULT	VENUE	ATT
1	1896/97	28/12/96	Football League Division 2	Leicester City 1 Newton Heath 0	Filbert Street	8000
2	1907/08	28/12/07	Football League Division 1	Preston North End 0 Manchester United 0	Deepdale	12000
3	1912/13	28/12/12	Football League Division 1	Manchester City 0 Manchester United 2	Hyde Road	38000
4	1925/26	28/12/25	Football League Division 1	Leicester City 1 Manchester United 3	Filbert Street	28367
5	1926/27	28/12/26	Football League Division 1	Arsenal 1 Manchester United 0	Highbury	30111
6	1929/30	28/12/29	Football League Division 1	Manchester United 5 Newcastle United 0	Old Trafford	14862
7	1935/36	28/12/35	Football League Division 2	Manchester United 3 Plymouth Argyle 2	Old Trafford	20894
8	1936/37	28/12/36	Football League Division 1	Bolton Wanderers 0 Manchester United 4	Burnden Park	11801
9	1937/38	28/12/37	Football League Division 2	Nottingham Forest 2 Manchester United 3	City Ground	19283
10	1946/47	28/12/46	Football League Division 1	Grimsby Town 0 Manchester United 0	Blundell Park	17183
11	1954/55	28/12/54	Football League Division 1	Aston Villa 2 Manchester United 1	Villa Park	48718
12	1957/58	28/12/57	Football League Division 1	Manchester City 2 Manchester United 2	Maine Road	70483
13	1959/60	28/12/59	Football League Division 1	Burnley 1 Manchester United 4	Turf Moor	47253
14	1963/64	28/12/63	Football League Division 1	Manchester United 5 Burnley 1	Old Trafford	47834
15	1964/65	28/12/64	Football League Division 1	Manchester United 1 Sheffield United 1	Old Trafford	42219
16	1974/75	28/12/74	Football League Division 2	Oldham Athletic 0 Manchester United 0	Boundary Park	26384
17	1982/83	28/12/82	Football League Division 1	Coventry City 3 Manchester United 0	Highfield Road	18945
18	1987/88	28/12/87	Football League Division 1	Manchester United 2 Everton 1	Old Trafford	47024
19	1992/93	28/12/92	FA Premiership	Manchester United 5 Coventry City 0	Old Trafford	36025
20	1994/95	28/12/94	FA Premiership	Manchester United 1 Leicester City 1	Old Trafford	43789
21	1996/97	28/12/96	FA Premiership	Manchester United 1 Leeds United 0	Old Trafford	55256
22	1997/98	28/12/97	FA Premiership	Coventry City 3 Manchester United 2	Highfield Road	23054
23	1999/00	28/12/99	FA Premiership	Sunderland 2 Manchester United 2	Stadium of Light	42026
24	2002/03	28/12/02	FA Premiership	Manchester United 2 Birmingham City 0	Old Trafford	67640
25	2003/04	28/12/03	FA Premiership	Middlesbrough 0 Manchester United 1	Riverside Stadium	34738
26	2004/05	28/12/04	FA Premiership	Aston Villa 0 Manchester United 1	Villa Park	42593
27	2005/06	28/12/05	FA Premiership	Birmingham City 2 Manchester United 2	St Andrews	28459

DECEMBER 29

#	SEASON	DATE	COMPETITION / ROUND	MATCH RESULT	VENUE	ATT
1	1894/95	29/12/94	Football League Division 2	Lincoln City 3 Newton Heath 0	John O'Gaunts	3000
2	1900/01	29/12/00	Football League Division 2	Newton Heath 3 Glossop 0	Bank Street	8000
3	1906/07	29/12/06	Football League Division 1	Manchester United 0 Bristol City 0	Bank Street	10000
4	1923/24	29/12/23	Football League Division 2	Bradford City 0 Manchester United 0	Valley Parade	11500
5	1928/29	29/12/28	Football League Division 1	Leicester City 2 Manchester United 1	Filbert Street	21535
6	1934/35	29/12/34	Football League Division 2	Bradford City 2 Manchester United 0	Valley Parade	11908
7	1951/52	29/12/51	Football League Division 1	Manchester United 1 Bolton Wanderers 0	Old Trafford	53205
8	1956/57	29/12/56	Football League Division 1	Portsmouth 1 Manchester United 3	Fratton Park	32147
9	1973/74	29/12/73	Football League Division 1	Manchester United 2 Ipswich Town 0	Old Trafford	36365
10	1979/80	29/12/79	Football League Division 1	Manchester United 3 Arsenal 0	Old Trafford	54295
11	1984/85	29/12/84	Football League Division 1	Chelsea 1 Manchester United 3	Stamford Bridge	42197
12	1990/91	29/12/90	Football League Division 1	Manchester United 1 Aston Villa 1	Old Trafford	47485
13	1991/92	29/12/91	Football League Division 1	Leeds United 1 Manchester United 1	Elland Road	32638
14	1993/94	29/12/93	FA Premiership	Oldham Athletic 2 Manchester United 5	Boundary Park	16708
15	1998/99	29/12/98	FA Premiership	Chelsea 0 Manchester United 0	Stamford Bridge	34741
16	2007/08	29/12/07	FA Premiership	West Ham United 2 Manchester United 1	Upton Park	34966

DECEMBER 30

#	SEASON	DATE	COMPETITION / ROUND	MATCH RESULT	VENUE	ATT
1	1899/00	30/12/99	Football League Division 2	Gainsborough Trinity 0 Newton Heath 1	The Northolme	2000
2	1905/06	30/12/05	Football League Division 2	Bristol City 1 Manchester United 1	Ashton Gate	18000
3	1911/12	30/12/11	Football League Division 1	Manchester United 0 Manchester City 0	Old Trafford	50000
4	1922/23	30/12/22	Football League Division 2	Hull City 2 Manchester United 1	Anlaby Road	6750
5	1933/34	30/12/33	Football League Division 2	Manchester United 0 Plymouth Argyle 3	Old Trafford	12206
6	1967/68	30/12/67	Football League Division 1	Wolverhampton Wanderers 2 Manchester United 3	Molineux	53940
7	1978/79	30/12/78	Football League Division 1	Manchester United 3 West Bromwich Albion 5	Old Trafford	45091
8	1989/90	30/12/89	Football League Division 1	Wimbledon 2 Manchester United 2	Plough Lane	9622
9	1995/96	30/12/95	FA Premiership	Manchester United 2 Queens Park Rangers 1	Old Trafford	41890
10	2000/01	30/12/00	FA Premiership	Newcastle United 1 Manchester United 1	St James' Park	52134
11	2001/02	30/12/01	FA Premiership	Fulham 2 Manchester United 3	Craven Cottage	21159
12	2006/07	30/12/06	FA Premiership	Manchester United 3 Reading 2	Old Trafford	75910

DECEMBER 31

#	SEASON	DATE	COMPETITION / ROUND	MATCH RESULT	VENUE	ATT
1	1892/93	31/12/92	Football League Division 1	Newton Heath 7 Derby County 1	North Road	3000
2	1898/99	31/12/98	Football League Division 2	Newton Heath 6 Gainsborough Trinity 1	Bank Street	2000
3	1904/05	31/12/04	Football League Division 2	Manchester United 6 Port Vale 1	Bank Street	8000
4	1910/11	31/12/10	Football League Division 1	Blackburn Rovers 1 Manchester United 0	Ewood Park	20000
5	1921/22	31/12/21	Football League Division 1	Newcastle United 3 Manchester United 0	St James' Park	20000
6	1927/28	31/12/27	Football League Division 1	Middlesbrough 1 Manchester United 2	Ayresome Park	19652
7	1932/33	31/12/32	Football League Division 2	Stoke City 0 Manchester United 0	Victoria Ground	14115
8	1938/39	31/12/38	Football League Division 1	Birmingham City 3 Manchester United 3	St Andrews	20787
9	1949/50	31/12/49	Football League Division 1	Manchester City 1 Manchester United 2	Maine Road	63704
10	1955/56	31/12/55	Football League Division 1	Manchester United 2 Manchester City 1	Old Trafford	60956
11	1960/61	31/12/60	Football League Division 1	Manchester United 5 Manchester City 1	Old Trafford	61213
12	1966/67	31/12/66	Football League Division 1	Manchester United 0 Leeds United 0	Old Trafford	53486
13	1977/78	31/12/77	Football League Division 1	Coventry City 3 Manchester United 0	Highfield Road	24706
14	1983/84	31/12/83	Football League Division 1	Manchester United 1 Stoke City 0	Old Trafford	40164
15	1994/95	31/12/94	FA Premiership	Southampton 2 Manchester United 2	The Dell	15204
16	2005/06	31/12/05	FA Premiership	Manchester United 4 Bolton Wanderers 1	Old Trafford	67858

MANCHESTER UNITED
The Complete Record

Chapter 3.2
Hat-Tricks and Better

6 GOALS IN A GAME

	PLAYER	DATE	COMPETITION / ROUND	MATCH RESULT	VENUE	ATT
1	Best, George	07/02/1970	FA Cup 5th Round	Northampton Town 2 Manchester United 8	County Ground	21771
2	Halse, Harold	25/09/1911	FA Charity Shield	Manchester United 8 Swindon Town 4	Stamford Bridge	10000

5 GOALS IN A GAME

	PLAYER	DATE	COMPETITION / ROUND	MATCH RESULT	VENUE	ATT
1	Cole, Andrew	04/03/1995	FA Premiership	Manchester United 9 Ipswich Town 0	Old Trafford	43804
2	Rowley, Jack	12/02/1949	FA Cup 5th Round	Manchester United 8 Yeovil Town 0	Maine Road	81565

4 GOALS IN A GAME

	PLAYER	DATE	COMPETITION / ROUND	MATCH RESULT	VENUE	ATT
1	Bamford, Tommy	13/11/1937	Football League Division 2	Chesterfield 1 Manchester United 7	Saltergate	17407
2	Cole, Andrew	30/08/1999	FA Premiership	Manchester United 5 Newcastle United 1	Old Trafford	55190
3	Dewar, Neil	23/09/1933	Football League Division 2	Manchester United 5 Burnley 2	Old Trafford	18411
4	Goldthorpe, Ernie	10/02/1923	Football League Division 2	Notts County 1 Manchester United 6	Meadow Lane	10000
5	Gowling, Alan	20/02/1971	Football League Division 1	Manchester United 5 Southampton 1	Old Trafford	36060
6	Hanson, Jimmy	14/01/1928	FA Cup 3rd Round	Manchester United 7 Brentford 1	Old Trafford	18538
7	Herd, David	26/11/1966	Football League Division 1	Manchester United 5 Sunderland 0	Old Trafford	44687
8	Law, Denis	03/11/1962	Football League Division 1	Ipswich Town 3 Manchester United 5	Portman Road	18483
9	Law, Denis	07/12/1963	Football League Division 1	Manchester United 5 Stoke City 2	Old Trafford	52232
10	Law, Denis	24/10/1964	Football League Division 1	Manchester United 7 Aston Villa 0	Old Trafford	35807
11	Law, Denis	02/10/1968	EC 1st Round 2nd Leg	Manchester United 7 Waterford 1	Old Trafford	41750
12	Manley, Tom	08/02/1936	Football League Division 2	Manchester United 7 Port Vale 2	Old Trafford	22265
13	Mitten, Charlie	08/03/1950	Football League Division 1	Manchester United 7 Aston Villa 0	Old Trafford	22149
14	Picken, Jack	30/04/1910	Football League Division 1	Manchester United 4 Middlesbrough 1	Old Trafford	10000
15	Rowley, Jack	04/12/1937	Football League Division 2	Manchester United 5 Swansea City 1	Old Trafford	17782
16	Rowley, Jack	30/08/1947	Football League Division 1	Manchester United 6 Charlton Athletic 2	Maine Road	52659
17	Rowley, Jack	08/11/1947	Football League Division 1	Manchester City 4 Huddersfield Town 4	Maine Road	59772
18	Smith, R	03/11/1894	Football League Division 2	Manchester City 2 Newton Heath 5	Hyde Road	14000
19	Solskjaer, Ole Gunnar	06/02/1999	FA Premiership	Nottingham Forest 1 Manchester United 8	City Ground	30025
20	Solskjaer, Ole Gunnar	04/12/1999	FA Premiership	Manchester United 5 Everton 1	Old Trafford	55193
21	Spence, Joe	12/04/1924	Football League Division 2	Manchester United 5 Crystal Palace 1	Old Trafford	8000
22	Spence, Joe	01/02/1930	Football League Division 1	Manchester United 4 West Ham United 2	Old Trafford	15424
23	Taylor, Tommy	09/10/1954	Football League Division 1	Manchester United 5 Cardiff City 2	Old Trafford	39378
24	Turnbull, Jimmy	12/09/1908	Football League Division 1	Manchester United 6 Middlesbrough 3	Bank Street	25000
25	Turnbull, Sandy	23/11/1907	Football League Division 1	Manchester United 4 Arsenal 2	Bank Street	10000
26	van Nistelrooy, Ruud	03/11/2004	CL Phase 1 Match 4	Manchester United 4 Sparta Prague 1	Old Trafford	66706
27	Viollet, Dennis	26/09/1956	EC Prelim. Round 2nd Leg	Manchester United 10 Anderlecht 0	Maine Road	40000

3 GOALS IN A GAME

	PLAYER	DATE	COMPETITION / ROUND	MATCH RESULT	VENUE	ATT
1	Allan, Jack	31/12/1904	Football League Division 2	Manchester United 6 Port Vale 1	Bank Street	8000
2	Anderson, George	18/10/1913	Football League Division 1	Manchester United 3 Preston North End 0	Old Trafford	30000
3	Bain, David	22/12/1923	Football League Division 2	Manchester United 5 Port Vale 0	Old Trafford	11750
4	Bamford, Tommy	05/09/1936	Football League Division 1	Derby County 5 Manchester United 4	Baseball Ground	21194
5	Bamford, Tommy	11/09/1937	Football League Division 2	Manchester United 4 Barnsley 1	Old Trafford	22934
6	Beddow, John	06/01/1906	Football League Division 2	Manchester United 5 Grimsby Town 0	Bank Street	10000
7	Beddow, John	13/01/1906	FA Cup 1st Round	Manchester United 7 Staple Hill 2	Bank Street	7560
8	Best, George	04/05/1968	Football League Division 1	Manchester United 6 Newcastle United 0	Old Trafford	59976
9	Best, George	18/09/1971	Football League Division 1	Manchester United 4 West Ham United 2	Old Trafford	55339
10	Best, George	27/11/1971	Football League Division 1	Southampton 2 Manchester United 5	The Dell	30323
11	Boyd, Henry	04/09/1897	Football League Division 2	Newton Heath 5 Lincoln City 0	Bank Street	5000
12	Boyd, Henry	11/09/1897	Football League Division 2	Burton Swifts 0 Newton Heath 4	Peel Croft	2000
13	Boyd, Henry	29/03/1898	Football League Division 2	Newton Heath 5 Loughborough Town 1	Bank Street	2000
14	Boyd, William	30/03/1935	Football League Division 2	Manchester United 3 Hull City 0	Old Trafford	15358
15	Bryant, William	24/12/1898	Football League Division 2	Newton Heath 9 Darwen 0	Bank Street	2000
16	Bryant, William	01/02/1899	FA Cup 1st Round Replay	Newton Heath 3 Tottenham Hotspur 5	Bank Street	6000
17	Bullock, Jimmy	08/11/1930	Football League Division 1	Leicester City 5 Manchester United 4	Filbert Street	17466
18	Cassidy, Joe	01/01/1896	Football League Division 2	Newton Heath 3 Grimsby Town 0	Bank Street	8000
19	Cassidy, Joe	26/09/1896	Football League Division 2	Newton Heath 4 Newcastle United 0	Bank Street	7000
20	Cassidy, Joe	24/10/1896	Football League Division 2	Newton Heath 3 Burton Wanderers 0	Bank Street	4000
21	Cassidy, Joe	30/01/1897	FA Cup 1st Round	Newton Heath 5 Kettering 1	Bank Street	1500
22	Cassidy, Joe	24/12/1898	Football League Division 2	Newton Heath 9 Darwen 0	Bank Street	2000
23	Cassidy, Joe	31/03/1900	Football League Division 2	Newton Heath 5 Luton Town 0	Bank Street	6000
24	Charlton, Bobby	18/02/1957	Football League Division 1	Charlton Athletic 1 Manchester United 5	The Valley	16308
25	Charlton, Bobby	18/01/1958	Football League Division 1	Manchester United 7 Bolton Wanderers 2	Old Trafford	41141
26	Charlton, Bobby	23/08/1958	Football League Division 1	Manchester United 5 Chelsea 2	Old Trafford	52382
27	Charlton, Bobby	27/02/1960	Football League Division 1	Blackpool 0 Manchester United 6	Bloomfield Road	23996
28	Charlton, Bobby	11/11/1964	ICFC 2nd Round 1st Leg	Borussia Dortmund 1 Manchester United 6	Rote Erde Stadion	25000
29	Charlton, Bobby	03/04/1965	Football League Division 1	Blackburn Rovers 0 Manchester United 5	Ewood Park	29363
30	Charlton, Bobby	05/02/1966	Football League Division 1	Manchester United 6 Northampton Town 2	Old Trafford	34986

3 GOALS IN A GAME (continued)

	PLAYER	DATE	COMPETITION / ROUND	MATCH RESULT	VENUE	ATT
31	Cole, Andrew	25/10/1997	FA Premiership	Manchester United 7 Barnsley 0	Old Trafford	55142
32	Cole, Andrew	05/11/1997	CL Phase 1 Match 4	Feyenoord 1 Manchester United 3	Feyenoord Stadion	51000
33	Cole, Andrew	13/09/2000	CL Phase 1 Match 1	Manchester United 5 Anderlecht 1	Old Trafford	62749
34	Connelly, John	06/10/1965	EC Prelim. Round 2nd Leg	Manchester United 6 HJK Helsinki 0	Old Trafford	30388
35	Coupar, Jimmy	26/10/1901	Football League Division 2	Newton Heath 6 Doncaster Rovers 0	Bank Street	7000
36	Daly, Gerry	24/08/1974	Football League Division 2	Manchester United 4 Millwall 0	Old Trafford	44756
37	Dawson, Alex	26/03/1958	FA Cup Semi-Final Replay	Manchester United 5 Fulham 3	Highbury	38000
38	Dawson, Alex	30/04/1960	Football League Division 1	Manchester United 5 Everton 0	Old Trafford	43823
39	Dawson, Alex	26/12/1960	Football League Division 1	Manchester United 6 Chelsea 0	Old Trafford	50164
40	Dawson, Alex	31/12/1960	Football League Division 1	Manchester United 5 Manchester City 1	Old Trafford	61213
41	Donaldson, Bob	15/10/1892	Football League Division 1	Newton Heath 10 Wolverhampton W. 1	North Road	4000
42	Donaldson, Bob	31/12/1892	Football League Division 1	Newton Heath 7 Derby County 1	North Road	3000
43	Donaldson, Bob	12/03/1894	Football League Division 1	Newton Heath 5 Blackburn Rovers 1	Bank Street	5000
44	Duckworth, Dick	01/04/1905	Football League Division 2	Manchester United 6 Doncaster Rovers 0	Bank Street	6000
45	Farman, Alf	31/12/1892	Football League Division 1	Newton Heath 7 Derby County 1	North Road	3000
46	Farman, Alf	27/04/1893	Football League Test Match	Newton Heath 5 Birmingham City 2	Bramall Lane	6000
47	Farman, Alf	02/09/1893	Football League Division 1	Newton Heath 3 Burnley 2	North Road	10000
48	Gillespie, Matthew	20/01/1900	Football League Division 2	Newton Heath 4 Burton Swifts 0	Bank Street	4000
49	Greenhoff, Jimmy	19/02/1977	Football League Division 1	Manchester United 3 Newcastle United 1	Old Trafford	51828
50	Hanlon, Jimmy	18/02/1939	Football League Division 1	Blackpool 3 Manchester United 5	Bloomfield Road	15253
51	Henderson, William	20/09/1924	Football League Division 2	Oldham Athletic 0 Manchester United 3	Boundary Park	14500
52	Herd, David	14/12/1963	Football League Division 1	Manchester United 3 Sheffield Wednesday 1	Old Trafford	35139
53	Herd, David	23/10/1965	Football League Division 1	Manchester United 4 Fulham 1	Old Trafford	32716
54	Herd, David	01/12/1965	EC 1st Round 2nd Leg	Manchester United 3 ASK Vorwaerts 1	Old Trafford	30082
55	Herd, David	26/02/1966	Football League Division 1	Manchester United 4 Burnley 2	Old Trafford	49892
56	Herd, David	17/12/1966	Football League Division 1	West Bromwich Albion 3 Manchester United 4	The Hawthorns	32080
57	Hill, Gordon	27/10/1976	League Cup 4th Round	Manchester United 7 Newcastle United 2	Old Trafford	52002
58	Hughes, Mark	26/09/1984	League Cup 2nd Round 1st Leg	Manchester United 4 Burnley 0	Old Trafford	28383
59	Hughes, Mark	23/03/1985	Football League Division 1	Manchester United 4 Aston Villa 0	Old Trafford	40941
60	Hughes, Mark	16/09/1989	Football League Division 1	Manchester United 5 Millwall 1	Old Trafford	42746
61	Hughes, Mark	23/01/1991	League Cup 5th Round Replay	Manchester United 3 Southampton 2	Old Trafford	41903
62	Jenkyns, Caesar	01/04/1897	Football League Division 2	Lincoln City 1 Newton Heath 3	Sincil Bank	1000
63	Kanchelskis, Andrei	10/11/1994	FA Premiership	Manchester United 5 Manchester City 0	Old Trafford	43738
64	Kennedy, William	03/04/1896	Football League Division 2	Newton Heath 4 Darwen 0	Bank Street	2000
65	Law, Denis	04/03/1963	FA Cup 3rd Round	Manchester United 5 Huddersfield Town 0	Old Trafford	47703
66	Law, Denis	16/04/1963	Football League Division 1	Leicester City 4 Manchester United 3	Filbert Street	37002
67	Law, Denis	03/09/1963	Football League Division 1	Ipswich Town 2 Manchester United 7	Portman Road	28113
68	Law, Denis	15/10/1963	ECWC 1st Round 2nd Leg	Manchester United 6 Willem II 1	Old Trafford	46272
69	Law, Denis	09/11/1963	Football League Division 1	Manchester United 4 Tottenham Hotspur 1	Old Trafford	57413
70	Law, Denis	25/01/1964	FA Cup 4th Round	Manchester United 4 Bristol Rovers 1	Old Trafford	55772
71	Law, Denis	26/02/1964	ECWC Quarter-Final 1st Leg	Manchester United 4 Sporting Lisbon 1	Old Trafford	60000
72	Law, Denis	09/03/1964	FA Cup 6th Round 2nd Replay	Manchester United 5 Sunderland 1	Leeds Road	54952
73	Law, Denis	27/10/1964	ICFC 1st Round 2nd Leg	Manchester United 6 Djurgardens 1	Old Trafford	38437
74	Law, Denis	18/09/1965	Football League Division 1	Manchester United 4 Chelsea 1	Old Trafford	37917
75	Law, Denis	18/09/1968	EC 1st Round 1st Leg	Waterford 1 Manchester United 3	Lansdowne Road	48000
76	Law, Denis	18/01/1969	Football League Division 1	Manchester United 4 Sunderland 1	Old Trafford	45670
77	Law, Denis	24/02/1969	FA Cup 5th Round Replay	Manchester United 6 Birmingham City 2	Old Trafford	61932
78	Law, Denis	17/04/1971	Football League Division 1	Crystal Palace 3 Manchester United 5	Selhurst Park	39145
79	Lawton, Nobby	26/12/1961	Football League Division 1	Manchester United 6 Nottingham Forest 3	Old Trafford	30822
80	Macari, Lou	20/08/1977	Football League Division 1	Birmingham City 1 Manchester United 4	St Andrews	28005
81	McClair, Brian	02/04/1988	Football League Division 1	Manchester United 4 Derby County 1	Old Trafford	40146
82	McClair, Brian	12/10/1988	Lge Cup 2nd Round 2nd Leg	Manchester United 5 Rotherham United 0	Old Trafford	20597
83	McIlroy, Sammy	03/10/1981	Football League Division 1	Manchester United 5 Wolverhampton W. 0	Old Trafford	46837
84	McPherson, Frank	28/12/1925	Football League Division 1	Leicester City 1 Manchester United 3	Filbert Street	28367
85	Morgan, Willie	19/03/1969	Football League Division 1	Manchester United 8 Queens Park Rangers 1	Old Trafford	36638
86	Morris, Johnny	29/11/1947	Football League Division 1	Chelsea 0 Manchester United 4	Stamford Bridge	43617
87	Mutch, George	08/09/1934	Football League Division 2	Manchester United 4 Barnsley 1	Old Trafford	22315
88	Olsen, Jesper	22/02/1986	Football League Division 1	Manchester United 3 West Bromwich Albion 0	Old Trafford	45193
89	Pearson, Stan	11/09/1946	Football League Division 1	Manchester United 5 Liverpool 0	Maine Road	41657
90	Pearson, Stan	13/03/1948	FA Cup Semi-Final	Manchester United 3 Derby County 1	Hillsborough	60000
91	Pearson, Stan	01/05/1948	Football League Division 1	Manchester United 4 Blackburn Rovers 1	Maine Road	44439
92	Pearson, Stan	27/01/1951	FA Cup 4th Round	Manchester United 4 Leeds United 0	Old Trafford	55434
93	Pearson, Stan	31/03/1951	Football League Division 1	Manchester United 4 Chelsea 1	Old Trafford	25779
94	Pearson, Stan	10/09/1952	Football League Division 1	Derby County 2 Manchester United 3	Baseball Ground	20226
95	Pearson, Stuart	02/11/1974	Football League Division 2	Manchester United 4 Oxford United 0	Old Trafford	41909
96	Peddie, Jack	17/12/1904	Football League Division 2	Burton United 2 Manchester United 3	Peel Croft	3000
97	Peddie, Jack	18/02/1905	Football League Division 2	Manchester United 4 Leicester City 1	Bank Street	7000
98	Peddie, Jack	29/03/1906	Football League Division 2	Leicester City 2 Manchester United 5	Filbert Street	5000
99	Pegg, Dick	29/11/1902	FA Cup 5th Qualifying Round	Manchester United 5 Southport Central 1	Bank Street	6000
100	Pegg, Dick	26/09/1903	Football League Division 2	Manchester United 3 Bradford City 1	Bank Street	30000
101	Peters, James	02/11/1895	Football League Division 2	Newton Heath 5 Liverpool 2	Bank Street	10000
102	Picken, Jack	24/02/1906	FA Cup 3rd Round	Manchester United 5 Aston Villa 1	Bank Street	35500
103	Picken, Jack	17/03/1906	Football League Division 2	Manchester United 4 Chesterfield 1	Bank Street	16000
104	Quixall, Albert	12/04/1961	Football League Division 1	Manchester United 6 Burnley 0	Old Trafford	25019
105	Quixall, Albert	07/04/1962	Football League Division 1	Manchester United 5 Ipswich Town 0	Old Trafford	24976
106	Rawlings, Bill	07/04/1928	Football League Division 1	Manchester United 4 Burnley 3	Old Trafford	28311
107	Rawlings, Bill	14/09/1929	Football League Division 1	Middlesbrough 2 Manchester United 3	Ayresome Park	26428
108	Reid, Tom	13/09/1930	Football League Division 1	Manchester United 4 Newcastle United 7	Old Trafford	10907
109	Reid, Tom	10/01/1931	FA Cup 3rd Round	Stoke City 3 Manchester United 3	Victoria Ground	23415
110	Reid, Tom	30/01/1932	Football League Division 2	Manchester United 3 Nottingham Forest 2	Old Trafford	11152

continued../

3 GOALS IN A GAME (continued)

	PLAYER	DATE	COMPETITION / ROUND	MATCH RESULT	VENUE	ATT
111	Reid, Tom	26/03/1932	Football League Division 2	Manchester United 5 Oldham Athletic 1	Old Trafford	17886
112	Reid, Tom	22/10/1932	Football League Division 2	Manchester United 7 Millwall 1	Old Trafford	15860
113	Reid, Tom	17/12/1932	Football League Division 2	Manchester United 4 Lincoln City 1	Old Trafford	18021
114	Rennox, Charlie	26/09/1925	Football League Division 1	Manchester United 6 Burnley 1	Old Trafford	17259
115	Ritchie, Andy	24/03/1979	Football League Division 1	Manchester United 4 Leeds United 1	Old Trafford	51191
116	Ritchie, Andy	12/04/1980	Football League Division 1	Manchester United 4 Tottenham Hotspur 1	Old Trafford	53151
117	Ronaldo, Cristiano	12/01/2008	FA Premiership	Manchester United 6 Newcastle United 0	Old Trafford	75965
118	Rooney, Wayne	28/09/2004	CL Phase 1 Match 2	Manchester United 6 Fenerbahce 2	Old Trafford	67128
119	Rooney, Wayne	28/10/2006	FA Premiership	Bolton Wanderers 0 Manchester United 4	Reebok Stadium	27229
120	Rowley, Harry	23/11/1935	Football League Division 2	Norwich City 3 Manchester United 5	Carrow Road	17266
121	Rowley, Jack	07/12/1946	Football League Division 1	Manchester United 4 Brentford 1	Maine Road	31962
122	Rowley, Jack	26/05/1947	Football League Division 1	Manchester United 6 Sheffield United 2	Maine Road	34059
123	Rowley, Jack	01/01/1948	Football League Division 1	Manchester United 5 Burnley 0	Maine Road	59838
124	Rowley, Jack	27/11/1948	Football League Division 1	Middlesbrough 1 Manchester United 4	Ayresome Park	31331
125	Rowley, Jack	18/08/1951	Football League Division 1	West Bromwich Albion 3 Manchester United 3	The Hawthorns	27486
126	Rowley, Jack	22/08/1951	Football League Division 1	Manchester United 4 Middlesbrough 2	Old Trafford	37339
127	Rowley, Jack	08/09/1951	Football League Division 1	Manchester United 4 Stoke City 0	Old Trafford	48660
128	Rowley, Jack	26/04/1952	Football League Division 1	Manchester United 6 Arsenal 1	Old Trafford	53651
129	Sagar, Charles	02/09/1905	Football League Division 2	Manchester United 5 Bristol City 1	Bank Street	25000
130	Sagar, Charles	31/03/1906	Football League Division 2	Manchester United 5 Barnsley 1	Bank Street	15000
131	Scanlon, Albert	17/09/1958	Football League Division 1	Manchester United 4 West Ham United 1	Old Trafford	53276
132	Scholes, Paul	01/04/2000	FA Premiership	Manchester United 7 West Ham United 1	Old Trafford	61611
133	Scholes, Paul	12/04/2003	FA Premiership	Newcastle United 2 Manchester United 6	St James' Park	52164
134	Sharpe, Lee	28/11/1990	League Cup 4th Round	Arsenal 2 Manchester United 6	Highbury	40844
135	Sheringham, Teddy	28/10/2000	FA Premiership	Manchester United 5 Southampton 0	Old Trafford	67581
136	Solskjaer, Ole Gunnar	29/01/2002	FA Premiership	Bolton Wanderers 0 Manchester United 4	Reebok Stadium	27350
137	Spence, Joe	29/10/1921	Football League Division 1	Manchester United 3 Manchester City 1	Old Trafford	56000
138	Spence, Joe	22/10/1927	Football League Division 1	Manchester United 5 Derby County 0	Old Trafford	18304
139	Spence, Joe	05/05/1928	Football League Division 1	Manchester United 6 Liverpool 1	Old Trafford	30625
140	Stapleton, Frank	19/11/1983	Football League Division 1	Manchester United 4 Watford 1	Old Trafford	43111
141	Stewart, William	15/10/1892	Football League Division 1	Newton Heath 10 Wolverhampton W. 1	North Road	4000
142	Taylor, Chris	21/04/1926	Football League Division 1	Manchester United 5 Sunderland 1	Old Trafford	10918
143	Taylor, Chris	01/05/1926	Football League Division 1	Manchester United 3 West Bromwich Albion 2	Old Trafford	9974
144	Taylor, Tommy	21/11/1953	Football League Division 1	Manchester United 4 Blackpool 1	Old Trafford	49853
145	Taylor, Tommy	25/12/1953	Football League Division 1	Manchester United 5 Sheffield Wednesday 2	Old Trafford	27123
146	Taylor, Tommy	26/09/1956	EC Preliminary Round 2nd Leg	Manchester United 10 Anderlecht 0	Maine Road	40000
147	Taylor, Tommy	22/10/1957	FA Charity Shield	Manchester United 4 Aston Villa 0	Old Trafford	27293
148	Turnbull, Jimmy	29/04/1908	FA Charity Shield Replay	Manchester United 4 Queens Park Rangers 0	Stamford Bridge	6000
149	Turnbull, Jimmy	20/02/1909	FA Cup 3rd Round	Manchester United 6 Blackburn Rovers 1	Bank Street	38500
150	Turnbull, Sandy	07/09/1907	Football League Division 1	Manchester United 4 Liverpool 0	Bank Street	24000
151	Turnbull, Sandy	19/10/1907	Football League Division 1	Blackburn Rovers 1 Manchester United 5	Ewood Park	30000
152	Turnbull, Sandy	20/02/1909	FA Cup 3rd Round	Manchester United 6 Blackburn Rovers 1	Bank Street	38500
153	van Nistelrooy, Ruud	22/12/2001	FA Premiership	Manchester United 6 Southampton 1	Old Trafford	67638
154	van Nistelrooy, Ruud	23/11/2002	FA Premiership	Manchester United 5 Newcastle United 3	Old Trafford	67625
155	van Nistelrooy, Ruud	22/03/2003	FA Premiership	Manchester United 3 Fulham 0	Old Trafford	67706
156	van Nistelrooy, Ruud	03/05/2003	FA Premiership	Manchester United 4 Charlton Athletic 1	Old Trafford	67721
157	van Nistelrooy, Ruud	27/09/2003	FA Premiership	Leicester City 1 Manchester United 4	Walkers Stadium	32044
158	Viollet, Dennis	16/10/1954	Football League Division 1	Chelsea 5 Manchester United 6	Stamford Bridge	55966
159	Viollet, Dennis	24/12/1955	Football League Division 1	West Bromwich Albion 1 Manchester United 4	The Hawthorns	25168
160	Viollet, Dennis	29/08/1956	Football League Division 1	Manchester United 3 Preston North End 2	Old Trafford	32515
161	Viollet, Dennis	04/01/1958	FA Cup 3rd Round	Workington 1 Manchester United 3	Borough Park	21000
162	Viollet, Dennis	21/03/1959	Football League Division 1	Manchester United 4 Leeds United 0	Old Trafford	45473
163	Viollet, Dennis	12/12/1959	Football League Division 1	Nottingham Forest 1 Manchester United 5	City Ground	31666
164	Viollet, Dennis	15/10/1960	Football League Division 1	Burnley 5 Manchester United 3	Turf Moor	32011
165	Viollet, Dennis	12/04/1961	Football League Division 1	Manchester United 6 Burnley 0	Old Trafford	25019
166	Wall, George	10/04/1907	Football League Division 1	Manchester United 5 Sheffield Wednesday 0	Bank Street	10000
167	Wall, George	12/12/1908	Football League Division 1	Manchester United 4 Leicester City 2	Bank Street	10000
168	Webster, Colin	11/12/1954	Football League Division 1	Burnley 2 Manchester United 4	Turf Moor	24977
169	West, Enoch	14/12/1912	Football League Division 1	Newcastle United 1 Manchester United 3	St James' Park	20000
170	Whelan, William	19/04/1957	Football League Division 1	Burnley 1 Manchester United 3	Turf Moor	41321
171	Whelan, William	24/08/1957	Football League Division 1	Leicester City 0 Manchester United 3	Filbert Street	40214
172	Whiteside, Norman	09/03/1985	FA Cup 6th Round	Manchester United 4 West Ham United 2	Old Trafford	46769
173	Williams, Fred	01/11/1902	FA Cup 3rd Qualifying Round	Manchester United 7 Accrington Stanley 0	Bank Street	6000
174	Yorke, Dwight	16/01/1999	FA Premiership	Leicester City 2 Manchester United 6	Filbert Street	22091
175	Yorke, Dwight	11/03/2000	FA Premiership	Manchester United 3 Derby County 1	Old Trafford	61619
176	Yorke, Dwight	25/02/2001	FA Premiership	Manchester United 6 Arsenal 1	Old Trafford	67535

CHRONOLOGICAL LISTING

DATE		PLAYER	COMPETITION / ROUND	MATCH RESULT	VENUE	ATT
1892/93						
15/10/1892	3	Donaldson, Bob	Football League Division 1	Newton Heath 10 Wolverhampton Wanderers 1	North Road	4000
15/10/1892	3	Stewart, William	Football League Division 1	Newton Heath 10 Wolverhampton Wanderers 1	North Road	4000
31/12/1892	3	Donaldson, Bob	Football League Division 1	Newton Heath 7 Derby County 1	North Road	3000
31/12/1892	3	Farman, Alf	Football League Division 1	Newton Heath 7 Derby County 1	North Road	3000
27/04/1893	3	Farman, Alf	Football League Test Match	Newton Heath 5 Birmingham City 2	Bramall Lane	6000
1893/94						
02/09/1893	3	Farman, Alf	Football League Division 1	Newton Heath 3 Burnley 2	North Road	10000
12/03/1894	3	Donaldson, Bob	Football League Division 1	Newton Heath 5 Blackburn Rovers 1	Bank Street	5000
1894/95						
03/11/1894	4	Smith, R	Football League Division 2	Manchester City 2 Newton Heath 5	Hyde Road	14000
1895/96						
02/11/1895	3	Peters, James	Football League Division 2	Newton Heath 5 Liverpool 2	Bank Street	10000
01/01/1896	3	Cassidy, Joe	Football League Division 2	Newton Heath 3 Grimsby Town 2	Bank Street	8000
03/04/1896	3	Kennedy, William	Football League Division 2	Newton Heath 4 Darwen 0	Bank Street	2000
1896/97						
26/09/1896	3	Cassidy, Joe	Football League Division 2	Newton Heath 4 Newcastle United 0	Bank Street	7000
24/10/1896	3	Cassidy, Joe	Football League Division 2	Newton Heath 3 Burton Wanderers 0	Bank Street	4000
30/01/1897	3	Cassidy, Joe	FA Cup 1st Round	Newton Heath 5 Kettering 1	Bank Street	1500
01/04/1897	3	Jenkyns, Caesar	Football League Division 2	Lincoln City 1 Newton Heath 3	Sincil Bank	1000
1897/98						
04/09/1897	3	Boyd, Henry	Football League Division 2	Newton Heath 5 Lincoln City 0	Bank Street	5000
11/09/1897	3	Boyd, Henry	Football League Division 2	Burton Swifts 0 Newton Heath 4	Peel Croft	2000
29/03/1898	3	Boyd, Henry	Football League Division 2	Newton Heath 5 Loughborough Town 1	Bank Street	2000
1898/99						
24/12/1898	3	Bryant, William	Football League Division 2	Newton Heath 9 Darwen 0	Bank Street	2000
24/12/1898	3	Cassidy, Joe	Football League Division 2	Newton Heath 9 Darwen 0	Bank Street	2000
01/02/1899	3	Bryant, William	FA Cup 1st Round Replay	Newton Heath 3 Tottenham Hotspur 5	Bank Street	6000
1899/1900						
20/01/1900	3	Gillespie, Matthew	Football League Division 2	Newton Heath 4 Burton Swifts 0	Bank Street	4000
31/03/1900	3	Cassidy, Joe	Football League Division 2	Newton Heath 5 Luton Town 0	Bank Street	6000
1901/02						
26/10/1901	3	Coupar, Jimmy	Football League Division 2	Newton Heath 6 Doncaster Rovers 0	Bank Street	7000
1902/03						
01/11/1902	3	Williams, Fred	FA Cup 3rd Qualifying Round	Manchester United 7 Accrington Stanley 0	Bank Street	6000
29/11/1902	3	Pegg, Dick	FA Cup 5th Qualifying Round	Manchester United 4 Southport Central 1	Bank Street	6000
1903/04						
26/09/1903	3	Pegg, Dick	Football League Division 2	Manchester United 3 Bradford City 1	Bank Street	30000
1904/05						
17/12/1904	3	Peddie, Jack	Football League Division 2	Burton United 2 Manchester United 3	Peel Croft	3000
31/12/1904	3	Allan, Jack	Football League Division 2	Manchester United 6 Port Vale 1	Bank Street	8000
18/02/1905	3	Peddie, Jack	Football League Division 2	Manchester United 4 Leicester City 1	Bank Street	7000
01/04/1905	3	Duckworth, Dick	Football League Division 2	Manchester United 6 Doncaster Rovers 0	Bank Street	6000
1905/06						
02/09/1905	3	Sagar, Charles	Football League Division 2	Manchester United 5 Bristol City 1	Bank Street	25000
06/01/1906	3	Beddow, John	Football League Division 2	Manchester United 5 Grimsby Town 0	Bank Street	10000
13/01/1906	3	Beddow, John	FA Cup 1st Round	Manchester United 7 Staple Hill 2	Bank Street	7560
24/02/1906	3	Picken, Jack	FA Cup 3rd Round	Manchester United 5 Aston Villa 1	Bank Street	35500
17/03/1906	3	Picken, Jack	Football League Division 2	Manchester United 4 Chesterfield 1	Bank Street	16000
29/03/1906	3	Peddie, Jack	Football League Division 2	Leicester City 2 Manchester United 5	Filbert Street	5000
31/03/1906	3	Sagar, Charles	Football League Division 2	Manchester United 5 Barnsley 1	Bank Street	15000
1906/07						
10/04/1907	3	Wall, George	Football League Division 1	Manchester United 5 Sheffield Wednesday 0	Bank Street	10000
1907/08						
07/09/1907	3	Turnbull, Sandy	Football League Division 1	Manchester United 4 Liverpool 0	Bank Street	24000
19/10/1907	3	Turnbull, Sandy	Football League Division 1	Blackburn Rovers 1 Manchester United 5	Ewood Park	30000
23/11/1907	4	Turnbull, Sandy	Football League Division 1	Manchester United 4 Arsenal 2	Bank Street	10000
29/04/1908	3	Turnbull, Jimmy	FA Charity Shield Replay	Manchester United 4 Queens Park Rangers 0	Stamford Bridge	6000
1908/09						
12/09/1908	4	Turnbull, Jimmy	Football League Division 1	Manchester United 6 Middlesbrough 3	Bank Street	25000
12/12/1908	3	Wall, George	Football League Division 1	Manchester United 4 Leicester City 2	Bank Street	10000
20/02/1909	3	Turnbull, Jimmy	FA Cup 3rd Round	Manchester United 6 Blackburn Rovers 1	Bank Street	38500
20/02/1909	3	Turnbull, Sandy	FA Cup 3rd Round	Manchester United 6 Blackburn Rovers 1	Bank Street	38500
1909/10						
30/04/1910	4	Picken, Jack	Football League Division 1	Manchester United 4 Middlesbrough 1	Old Trafford	10000
1911/12						
25/09/1911	6	Halse, Harold	FA Charity Shield	Manchester United 8 Swindon Town 4	Stamford Bridge	10000
1912/13						
14/12/1912	3	West, Enoch	Football League Division 1	Newcastle United 1 Manchester United 3	St James' Park	20000
1913/14						
18/10/1913	3	Anderson, George	Football League Division 1	Manchester United 3 Preston North End 0	Old Trafford	30000

CHRONOLOGICAL LISTING

DATE		PLAYER	COMPETITION / ROUND	MATCH RESULT	VENUE	ATT
1921/22						
29/10/1921	3	Spence, Joe	Football League Division 1	Manchester United 3 Manchester City 1	Old Trafford	56000
1922/23						
10/02/1923	4	Goldthorpe, Ernie	Football League Division 2	Notts County 1 Manchester United 6	Meadow Lane	10000
1923/24						
22/12/1923	3	Bain, David	Football League Division 2	Manchester United 5 Port Vale 0	Old Trafford	11750
12/04/1924	4	Spence, Joe	Football League Division 2	Manchester United 5 Crystal Palace 1	Old Trafford	8000
1924/25						
20/09/1924	3	Henderson, William	Football League Division 2	Oldham Athletic 0 Manchester United 3	Boundary Park	14500
1925/26						
26/09/1925	3	Rennox, Charlie	Football League Division 1	Manchester United 6 Burnley 1	Old Trafford	17259
28/12/1925	3	McPherson, Frank	Football League Division 1	Leicester City 1 Manchester United 3	Filbert Street	28367
21/04/1926	3	Taylor, Chris	Football League Division 1	Manchester United 5 Sunderland 1	Old Trafford	10918
01/05/1926	3	Taylor, Chris	Football League Division 1	Manchester United 3 West Bromwich Albion 2	Old Trafford	9974
1927/28						
22/10/1927	3	Spence, Joe	Football League Division 1	Manchester United 5 Derby County 0	Old Trafford	18304
14/01/1928	4	Hanson, Jimmy	FA Cup 3rd Round	Manchester United 7 Brentford 1	Old Trafford	18538
07/04/1928	3	Rawlings, Bill	Football League Division 1	Manchester United 4 Burnley 3	Old Trafford	28311
05/05/1928	3	Spence, Joe	Football League Division 1	Manchester United 6 Liverpool 1	Old Trafford	30625
1929/30						
14/09/1929	3	Rawlings, Bill	Football League Division 1	Middlesbrough 2 Manchester United 3	Ayresome Park	26428
01/02/1930	4	Spence, Joe	Football League Division 1	Manchester United 4 West Ham United 2	Old Trafford	15424
1930/31						
13/09/1930	3	Reid, Tom	Football League Division 1	Manchester United 4 Newcastle United 7	Old Trafford	10907
08/11/1930	3	Bullock, Jimmy	Football League Division 1	Leicester City 5 Manchester United 4	Filbert Street	17466
10/01/1931	3	Reid, Tom	FA Cup 3rd Round	Stoke City 3 Manchester United 3	Victoria Ground	23415
1931/32						
30/01/1932	3	Reid, Tom	Football League Division 2	Manchester United 3 Nottingham Forest 2	Old Trafford	11152
26/03/1932	3	Reid, Tom	Football League Division 2	Manchester United 5 Oldham Athletic 1	Old Trafford	17886
1932/33						
22/10/1932	3	Reid, Tom	Football League Division 2	Manchester United 7 Millwall 1	Old Trafford	15860
17/12/1932	3	Reid, Tom	Football League Division 2	Manchester United 4 Lincoln City 1	Old Trafford	18021
1933/34						
23/09/1933	4	Dewar, Neil	Football League Division 2	Manchester United 5 Burnley 2	Old Trafford	18411
1934/35						
08/09/1934	3	Mutch, George	Football League Division 2	Manchester United 4 Barnsley 1	Old Trafford	22315
30/03/1935	3	Boyd, William	Football League Division 2	Manchester United 3 Hull City 0	Old Trafford	15358
1935/36						
23/11/1935	3	Rowley, Harry	Football League Division 2	Norwich City 3 Manchester United 5	Carrow Road	17266
08/02/1936	4	Manley, Tom	Football League Division 2	Manchester United 7 Port Vale 2	Old Trafford	22265
1936/37						
05/09/1936	3	Bamford, Tommy	Football League Division 1	Derby County 5 Manchester United 4	Baseball Ground	21194
1937/38						
11/09/1937	3	Bamford, Tommy	Football League Division 2	Manchester United 4 Barnsley 1	Old Trafford	22934
13/11/1937	4	Bamford, Tommy	Football League Division 2	Chesterfield 1 Manchester United 7	Saltergate	17407
04/12/1937	4	Rowley, Jack	Football League Division 2	Manchester United 5 Swansea City 1	Old Trafford	17782
1938/39						
18/02/1939	3	Hanlon, Jimmy	Football League Division 1	Blackpool 3 Manchester United 5	Bloomfield Road	15253
1946/47						
11/09/1946	3	Pearson, Stan	Football League Division 1	Manchester United 5 Liverpool 0	Maine Road	41657
07/12/1946	3	Rowley, Jack	Football League Division 1	Manchester United 4 Brentford 1	Maine Road	31962
26/05/1947	3	Rowley, Jack	Football League Division 1	Manchester United 6 Sheffield United 2	Maine Road	34059
1947/48						
30/08/1947	4	Rowley, Jack	Football League Division 1	Manchester United 6 Charlton Athletic 2	Maine Road	52659
08/11/1947	4	Rowley, Jack	Football League Division 1	Manchester United 4 Huddersfield Town 4	Maine Road	59772
29/11/1947	3	Morris, Johnny	Football League Division 1	Chelsea 0 Manchester United 4	Stamford Bridge	43617
01/01/1948	3	Rowley, Jack	Football League Division 1	Manchester United 5 Burnley 0	Maine Road	59838
13/03/1948	3	Pearson, Stan	FA Cup Semi-Final	Manchester United 3 Derby County 1	Hillsborough	60000
01/05/1948	3	Pearson, Stan	Football League Division 1	Manchester United 4 Blackburn Rovers 1	Maine Road	44439
1948/49						
27/11/1948	3	Rowley, Jack	Football League Division 1	Middlesbrough 1 Manchester United 4	Ayresome Park	31331
12/02/1949	5	Rowley, Jack	FA Cup 5th Round	Manchester United 8 Yeovil Town 0	Maine Road	81565
1949/50						
08/03/1950	4	Mitten, Charlie	Football League Division 1	Manchester United 7 Aston Villa 0	Old Trafford	22149
1950/51						
27/01/1951	3	Pearson, Stan	FA Cup 4th Round	Manchester United 4 Leeds United 0	Old Trafford	55434
31/03/1951	3	Pearson, Stan	Football League Division 1	Manchester United 4 Chelsea 1	Old Trafford	25779

CHRONOLOGICAL LISTING

DATE		PLAYER	COMPETITION / ROUND	MATCH RESULT	VENUE	ATT
1951/52						
18/08/1951	3	Rowley, Jack	Football League Division 1	West Bromwich Albion 3 Manchester United 3	The Hawthorns	27486
22/08/1951	3	Rowley, Jack	Football League Division 1	Manchester United 4 Middlesbrough 2	Old Trafford	37339
08/09/1951	3	Rowley, Jack	Football League Division 1	Manchester United 4 Stoke City 0	Old Trafford	48660
26/04/1952	3	Rowley, Jack	Football League Division 1	Manchester United 6 Arsenal 1	Old Trafford	53651
1952/53						
10/09/1952	3	Pearson, Stan	Football League Division 1	Derby County 2 Manchester United 3	Baseball Ground	20226
1953/54						
21/11/1953	3	Taylor, Tommy	Football League Division 1	Manchester United 4 Blackpool 1	Old Trafford	49853
25/12/1953	3	Taylor, Tommy	Football League Division 1	Manchester United 5 Sheffield Wednesday 2	Old Trafford	27123
1954/55						
09/10/1954	4	Taylor, Tommy	Football League Division 1	Manchester United 5 Cardiff City 2	Old Trafford	39378
16/10/1954	3	Viollet, Dennis	Football League Division 1	Chelsea 5 Manchester United 6	Stamford Bridge	55966
11/12/1954	3	Webster, Colin	Football League Division 1	Burnley 2 Manchester United 4	Turf Moor	24977
1955/56						
24/12/1955	3	Viollet, Dennis	Football League Division 1	West Bromwich Albion 1 Manchester United 4	The Hawthorns	25168
1956/57						
29/08/1956	3	Viollet, Dennis	Football League Division 1	Manchester United 3 Preston North End 2	Old Trafford	32515
26/09/1956	3	Taylor, Tommy	EC Preliminary Round 2nd Leg	Manchester United 10 Anderlecht 0	Maine Road	40000
26/09/1956	4	Viollet, Dennis	EC Preliminary Round 2nd Leg	Manchester United 10 Anderlecht 0	Maine Road	40000
18/02/1957	3	Charlton, Bobby	Football League Division 1	Charlton Athletic 1 Manchester United 5	The Valley	16308
19/01/1957	3	Whelan, William	Football League Division 1	Burnley 1 Manchester United 3	Turf Moor	41321
1957/58						
24/08/1957	3	Whelan, William	Football League Division 1	Leicester City 0 Manchester United 3	Filbert Street	40214
22/10/1957	3	Taylor, Tommy	FA Charity Shield	Manchester United 4 Aston Villa 0	Old Trafford	27293
04/01/1958	3	Viollet, Dennis	FA Cup 3rd Round	Workington 1 Manchester United 3	Borough Park	21000
18/01/1958	3	Charlton, Bobby	Football League Division 1	Manchester United 7 Bolton Wanderers 2	Old Trafford	41141
26/03/1958	3	Dawson, Alex	FA Cup Semi-Final Replay	Manchester United 5 Fulham 3	Highbury	38000
1958/59						
23/08/1958	3	Charlton, Bobby	Football League Division 1	Manchester United 5 Chelsea 2	Old Trafford	52382
17/09/1958	3	Scanlon, Albert	Football League Division 1	Manchester United 4 West Ham United 1	Old Trafford	53276
21/03/1959	3	Viollet, Dennis	Football League Division 1	Manchester United 6 Leeds United 0	Old Trafford	45473
1959/60						
12/12/1959	3	Viollet, Dennis	Football League Division 1	Nottingham Forest 1 Manchester United 5	City Ground	31666
27/02/1960	3	Charlton, Bobby	Football League Division 1	Blackpool 0 Manchester United 6	Bloomfield Road	23996
30/04/1960	3	Dawson, Alex	Football League Division 1	Manchester United 5 Everton 0	Old Trafford	43823
1960/61						
15/10/1960	3	Viollet, Dennis	Football League Division 1	Burnley 5 Manchester United 3	Turf Moor	32011
26/12/1960	3	Dawson, Alex	Football League Division 1	Manchester United 6 Chelsea 0	Old Trafford	50164
31/12/1960	3	Dawson, Alex	Football League Division 1	Manchester United 5 Manchester City 1	Old Trafford	61213
12/04/1961	3	Quixall, Albert	Football League Division 1	Manchester United 6 Burnley 0	Old Trafford	25019
12/04/1961	3	Viollet, Dennis	Football League Division 1	Manchester United 6 Burnley 0	Old Trafford	25019
1961/62						
26/12/1961	3	Lawton, Nobby	Football League Division 1	Manchester United 6 Nottingham Forest 3	Old Trafford	30822
07/04/1962	3	Quixall, Albert	Football League Division 1	Manchester United 5 Ipswich Town 0	Old Trafford	24976
1962/63						
03/11/1962	4	Law, Denis	Football League Division 1	Ipswich Town 3 Manchester United 5	Portman Road	18483
04/03/1963	3	Law, Denis	FA Cup 3rd Round	Manchester United 5 Huddersfield Town 0	Old Trafford	47703
16/04/1963	3	Law, Denis	Football League Division 1	Leicester City 4 Manchester United 3	Filbert Street	37002
1963/64						
03/09/1963	3	Law, Denis	Football League Division 1	Ipswich Town 2 Manchester United 7	Portman Road	28113
15/10/1963	3	Law, Denis	ECWC 1st Round 2nd Leg	Manchester United 6 Willem II 1	Old Trafford	46272
09/11/1963	3	Law, Denis	Football League Division 1	Manchester United 4 Tottenham Hotspur 1	Old Trafford	57413
07/12/1963	4	Law, Denis	Football League Division 1	Manchester United 5 Stoke City 2	Old Trafford	52232
14/12/1963	3	Herd, David	Football League Division 1	Manchester United 3 Sheffield Wednesday 1	Old Trafford	35139
25/01/1964	3	Law, Denis	FA Cup 4th Round	Manchester United 4 Bristol Rovers 1	Old Trafford	55772
26/02/1964	3	Law, Denis	ECWC Quarter-Final 1st Leg	Manchester United 4 Sporting Lisbon 1	Old Trafford	60000
09/03/1964	3	Law, Denis	FA Cup 6th Round 2nd Replay	Manchester United 5 Sunderland 1	Leeds Road	54952
1964/65						
24/10/1964	4	Law, Denis	Football League Division 1	Manchester United 7 Aston Villa 0	Old Trafford	35807
27/10/1964	3	Law, Denis	ICFC 1st Round 2nd Leg	Manchester United 6 Djurgardens 1	Old Trafford	38437
11/11/1964	3	Charlton, Bobby	ICFC 2nd Round 1st Leg	Borussia Dortmund 1 Manchester United 6	Rote Erde Stadion	25000
03/04/1965	3	Charlton, Bobby	Football League Division 1	Blackburn Rovers 0 Manchester United 5	Ewood Park	29363
1965/66						
18/09/1965	3	Law, Denis	Football League Division 1	Manchester United 4 Chelsea 1	Old Trafford	37917
06/10/1965	3	Connelly, John	EC Preliminary Round 2nd Leg	Manchester United 6 HJK Helsinki 0	Old Trafford	30388
23/10/1965	3	Herd, David	Football League Division 1	Manchester United 4 Fulham 1	Old Trafford	32716
01/12/1965	3	Herd, David	EC 1st Round 2nd Leg	Manchester United 3 ASK Vorwaerts 1	Old Trafford	30082
05/02/1966	3	Charlton, Bobby	Football League Division 1	Manchester United 6 Northampton Town 2	Old Trafford	34986
26/02/1966	3	Herd, David	Football League Division 1	Manchester United 4 Burnley 2	Old Trafford	49892
1966/67						
26/11/1966	4	Herd, David	Football League Division 1	Manchester United 5 Sunderland 0	Old Trafford	44687
17/12/1966	3	Herd, David	Football League Division 1	West Bromwich Albion 3 Manchester United 4	The Hawthorns	32080

CHRONOLOGICAL LISTING

DATE		PLAYER	COMPETITION / ROUND	MATCH RESULT	VENUE	ATT
1967/68						
04/05/1968	3	Best, George	Football League Division 1	Manchester United 6　Newcastle United 0	Old Trafford	59976
1968/69						
18/09/1968	3	Law, Denis	EC 1st Round 1st Leg	Waterford 1　Manchester United 3	Lansdowne Road	48000
02/10/1968	4	Law, Denis	EC 1st Round 2nd Leg	Manchester United 7　Waterford 1	Old Trafford	41750
18/01/1969	3	Law, Denis	Football League Division 1	Manchester United 4　Sunderland 1	Old Trafford	45670
24/02/1969	3	Law, Denis	FA Cup 5th Round Replay	Manchester United 6　Birmingham City 2	Old Trafford	61932
19/03/1969	3	Morgan, Willie	Football League Division 1	Manchester United 8　Queens Park Rangers 1	Old Trafford	36638
1969/70						
07/02/1970	6	Best, George	FA Cup 5th Round	Northampton Town 2　Manchester United 8	County Ground	21771
1970/71						
20/02/1971	4	Gowling, Alan	Football League Division 1	Manchester United 5　Southampton 1	Old Trafford	36060
17/04/1971	3	Law, Denis	Football League Division 1	Crystal Palace 3　Manchester United 5	Selhurst Park	39145
1971/72						
18/09/1971	3	Best, George	Football League Division 1	Manchester United 4　West Ham United 2	Old Trafford	55339
27/11/1971	3	Best, George	Football League Division 1	Southampton 2　Manchester United 5	The Dell	30323
1974/75						
24/08/1974	3	Daly, Gerry	Football League Division 2	Manchester United 4　Millwall 0	Old Trafford	44756
02/11/1974	3	Pearson, Stuart	Football League Division 2	Manchester United 4　Oxford United 0	Old Trafford	41909
1976/77						
27/10/1976	3	Hill, Gordon	League Cup 4th Round	Manchester United 7　Newcastle United 2	Old Trafford	52002
19/02/1977	3	Greenhoff, Jimmy	Football League Division 1	Manchester United 3　Newcastle United 1	Old Trafford	51828
1977/78						
20/08/1977	3	Macari, Lou	Football League Division 1	Birmingham City 1　Manchester United 4	St Andrews	28005
1978/79						
24/03/1979	3	Ritchie, Andy	Football League Division 1	Manchester United 4　Leeds United 1	Old Trafford	51191
1979/80						
12/04/1980	3	Ritchie, Andy	Football League Division 1	Manchester United 4　Tottenham Hotspur 1	Old Trafford	53151
1981/82						
03/10/1981	3	McIlroy, Sammy	Football League Division 1	Manchester United 5　Wolverhampton W. 0	Old Trafford	46837
1983/84						
19/11/1983	3	Stapleton, Frank	Football League Division 1	Manchester United 4　Watford 1	Old Trafford	43111
1984/85						
26/09/1984	3	Hughes, Mark	League Cup 2nd Round 1st Leg	Manchester United 4　Burnley 0	Old Trafford	28383
09/03/1985	3	Whiteside, Norman	FA Cup 6th Round	Manchester United 4　West Ham United 2	Old Trafford	46769
23/03/1985	3	Hughes, Mark	Football League Division 1	Manchester United 4　Aston Villa 0	Old Trafford	40941
1985/86						
22/02/1986	3	Olsen, Jesper	Football League Division 1	Manchester United 3　West Bromwich Albion 0	Old Trafford	45193
1987/88						
02/04/1988	3	McClair, Brian	Football League Division 1	Manchester United 4　Derby County 1	Old Trafford	40146
1988/89						
12/10/1988	3	McClair, Brian	League Cup 2nd Round 2nd Leg	Manchester United 5　Rotherham United 0	Old Trafford	20597
1989/90						
16/09/1989	3	Hughes, Mark	Football League Division 1	Manchester United 5　Millwall 1	Old Trafford	42746
1990/91						
28/11/1990	3	Sharpe, Lee	League Cup 4th Round	Arsenal 2　Manchester United 6	Highbury	40844
23/01/1991	3	Hughes, Mark	League Cup 5th Round Replay	Manchester United 3　Southampton 2	Old Trafford	41903
1994/95						
10/11/1994	3	Kanchelskis, Andrei	FA Premiership	Manchester United 5　Manchester City 0	Old Trafford	43738
04/03/1995	5	Cole, Andrew	FA Premiership	Manchester United 9　Ipswich Town 0	Old Trafford	43804
1997/98						
25/10/1997	3	Cole, Andrew	FA Premiership	Manchester United 7　Barnsley 0	Old Trafford	55142
05/11/1997	3	Cole, Andrew	CL Phase 1 Match 4	Feyenoord 1　Manchester United 3	Feyenoord Stadion	51000
1998/99						
16/01/1999	3	Yorke, Dwight	FA Premiership	Leicester City 2　Manchester United 6	Filbert Street	22091
06/02/1999	4	Solskjaer, Ole Gunnar	FA Premiership	Nottingham Forest 1　Manchester United 8	City Ground	30025
1999/2000						
30/08/1999	4	Cole, Andrew	FA Premiership	Manchester United 5　Newcastle United 1	Old Trafford	55190
04/12/1999	4	Solskjaer, Ole Gunnar	FA Premiership	Manchester United 5　Everton 1	Old Trafford	55193
11/03/2000	3	Yorke, Dwight	FA Premiership	Manchester United 3　Derby County 1	Old Trafford	61619
01/04/2000	3	Scholes, Paul	FA Premiership	Manchester United 7　West Ham United 1	Old Trafford	61611
2000/01						
13/09/2000	3	Cole, Andrew	CL Phase 1 Match 1	Manchester United 5　Anderlecht 1	Old Trafford	62749
28/10/2000	3	Sheringham, Teddy	FA Premiership	Manchester United 5　Southampton 0	Old Trafford	67581
25/02/2001	3	Yorke, Dwight	FA Premiership	Manchester United 6　Arsenal 1	Old Trafford	67535
2001/02						
22/12/2001	3	van Nistelrooy, Ruud	FA Premiership	Manchester United 6　Southampton 1	Old Trafford	67638
29/01/2002	3	Solskjaer, Ole Gunnar	FA Premiership	Bolton Wanderers 0　Manchester United 4	Reebok Stadium	27350

CHRONOLOGICAL LISTING

DATE		PLAYER	COMPETITION / ROUND	MATCH RESULT	VENUE	ATT
2002/03						
23/11/2002	3	van Nistelrooy, Ruud	FA Premiership	Manchester United 5 Newcastle United 3	Old Trafford	67625
22/03/2003	3	van Nistelrooy, Ruud	FA Premiership	Manchester United 3 Fulham 0	Old Trafford	67706
12/04/2003	3	Scholes, Paul	FA Premiership	Newcastle United 2 Manchester United 6	St James' Park	52164
03/05/2003	3	van Nistelrooy, Ruud	FA Premiership	Manchester United 4 Charlton Athletic 1	Old Trafford	67721
2003/04						
27/09/2003	3	van Nistelrooy, Ruud	FA Premiership	Leicester City 1 Manchester United 4	Walkers Stadium	32044
2004/05						
28/09/2004	3	Rooney, Wayne	Champions Lge Phase 1 Match 2	Manchester United 6 Fenerbahce 2	Old Trafford	67128
03/11/2004	4	van Nistelrooy, Ruud	Champions Lge Phase 1 Match 4	Manchester United 4 Sparta Prague 1	Old Trafford	66706
2006/07						
28/10/2006	3	Rooney, Wayne	FA Premiership	Bolton Wanderers 0 Manchester United 4	Reebok Stadium	27229
2007/08						
12/01/2008	3	Ronaldo, Cristiano	FA Premiership	Manchester United 6 Newcastle United 0	Old Trafford	75965

HAT-TRICKS ON DEBUT

ONCE A CENTURY

Only two Manchester United players have scored hat-tricks on their competitive debuts. When Wayne Rooney netted three times on his debut against Fenerbahce on 28th September 2004 he repeated the achievement of Charles Sagar some 99 years earlier.

DATE		PLAYER	COMPETITION / ROUND	MATCH RESULT	VENUE	ATT
1905/06						
02/09/1905	3	Sagar, Charles	Football League Division 2	Manchester United 5 Bristol City 1	Bank Street	25000
2004/05						
28/09/2004	3	Rooney, Wayne	Champions League Phase 1 Match 2	Manchester United 6 Fenerbahce 2	Old Trafford	67128

SAME MATCH HAT-TRICKS

HIT FOR SIX

There have been six occasions when different Manchester United players have scored hat-tricks (or better) in the same match, although it is now over 40 years since this has occurred.

DATE		PLAYER	COMPETITION / ROUND	MATCH RESULT	VENUE	ATT
1892/93						
15/10/1892	3	Donaldson, Bob	Football League Division 1	Newton Heath 10 Wolverhampton Wanderers 1	North Road	4000
15/10/1892	3	Stewart, William				
31/12/1892	3	Donaldson, Bob	Football League Division 1	Newton Heath 7 Derby County 1	North Road	3000
31/12/1892	3	Farman, Alf				
1898/99						
24/12/1898	3	Bryant, William	Football League Division 2	Newton Heath 9 Darwen 0	Bank Street	2000
24/12/1898	3	Cassidy, Joe				
1908/09						
20/02/1909	3	Turnbull, Jimmy	FA Cup 3rd Round	Manchester United 6 Blackburn Rovers 1	Bank Street	38500
20/02/1909	3	Turnbull, Sandy				
1956/57						
26/09/1956	4	Taylor, Tommy	EC Preliminary Round 2nd Leg	Manchester United 10 Anderlecht 0	Maine Road	40000
26/09/1956	3	Viollet, Dennis				
1960/61						
12/04/1961	3	Quixall, Albert	Football League Division 1	Manchester United 6 Burnley 0	Old Trafford	25019
12/04/1961	3	Viollet, Dennis				

MANCHESTER UNITED
The Complete Record

Chapter 3.3
Won, Drawn, Lost

ALL COMPETITIVE MATCHES

	P	W	D	L	F	A
HOME	2483	1528	548	407	5089	2311
AWAY	2462	849	639	974	3500	3905
NEUTRAL	100	46	25	29	163	115
TOTAL	5045	2423	1212	1410	8752	6331

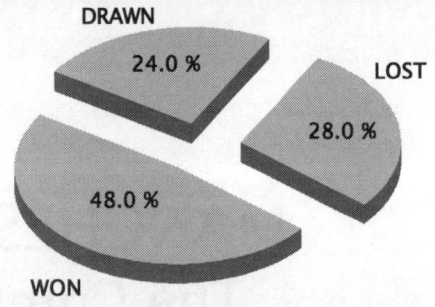

ALL LEAGUE MATCHES

	P	W	D	L	F	A
HOME	2088	1260	470	358	4219	1979
AWAY	2088	702	539	847	2957	3400
TOTAL	4176	1962	1009	1205	7176	5379

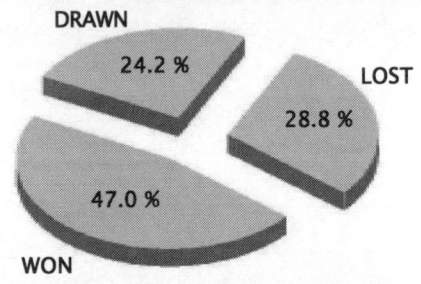

ALL PREMIERSHIP MATCHES

	P	W	D	L	F	A
HOME	310	224	60	26	669	195
AWAY	310	170	77	63	551	343
TOTAL	620	394	137	89	1220	538

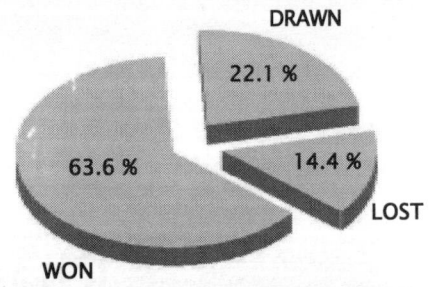

ALL LEAGUE DIVISION 1 MATCHES

	P	W	D	L	F	A
HOME	1370	758	339	273	2614	1440
AWAY	1370	404	365	601	1909	2435
TOTAL	2740	1162	704	874	4523	3875

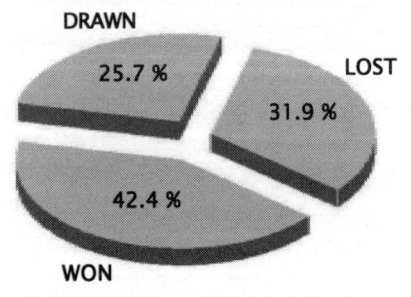

10

ALL LEAGUE DIVISION 2 MATCHES

	P	W	D	L	F	A
HOME	408	278	71	59	936	344
AWAY	408	128	97	183	497	622
TOTAL	816	406	168	242	1433	966

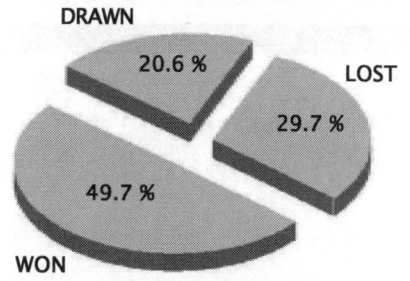

ALL FA CUP MATCHES

	P	W	D	L	F	A
HOME	186	119	36	31	390	168
AWAY	166	73	44	49	273	238
NEUTRAL	63	33	15	15	107	66
TOTAL	415	225	95	95	770	472

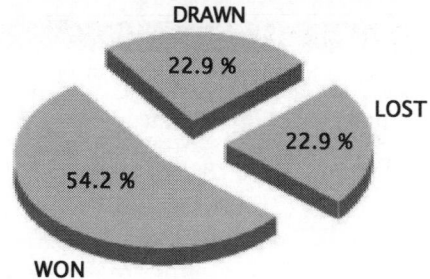

ALL LEAGUE CUP MATCHES

	P	W	D	L	F	A
HOME	75	54	11	11	154	63
AWAY	76	31	17	28	108	102
NEUTRAL	6	2	0	4	7	8
TOTAL	158	87	28	43	269	173

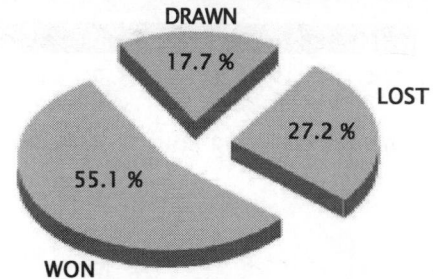

ALL EUROPEAN MATCHES

	P	W	D	L	F	A
HOME	125	91	27	7	308	92
AWAY	126	42	39	45	158	152
NEUTRAL	4	3	1	0	9	4
TOTAL	255	136	67	52	475	248

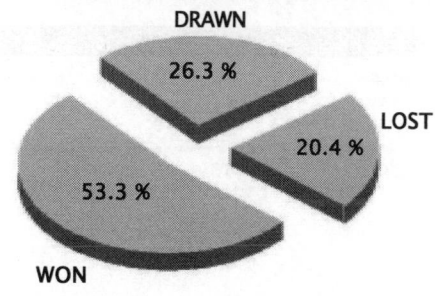

ALL EUROPEAN CUP / CHAMPIONS LEAGUE MATCHES

	P	W	D	L	F	A
HOME	95	73	15	7	243	73
AWAY	95	33	29	33	122	111
NEUTRAL	3	2	1	0	7	3
TOTAL	193	108	45	40	372	187

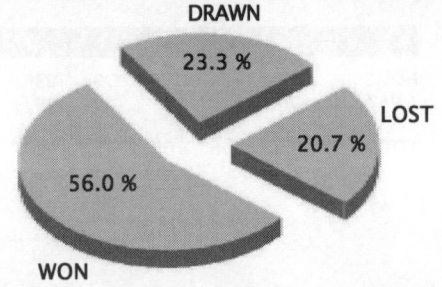

ALL EUROPEAN CUP-WINNERS' CUP MATCHES

	P	W	D	L	F	A
HOME	15	10	5	0	38	10
AWAY	15	5	4	6	15	24
NEUTRAL	1	1	0	0	2	1
TOTAL	31	16	9	6	55	35

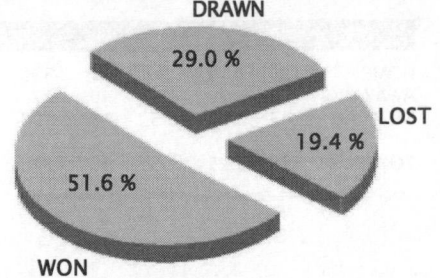

ALL UEFA CUP / INTER-CITIES' FAIRS CUP MATCHES

	P	W	D	L	F	A
HOME	15	9	6	0	32	9
AWAY	16	3	7	6	16	17
TOTAL	31	12	13	6	48	26

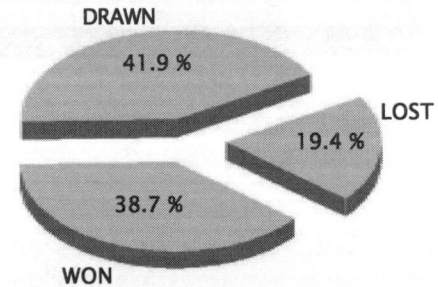

ALL OTHER COMPETITIVE MATCHES

	P	W	D	L	F	A
HOME	8	4	4	0	18	9
AWAY	6	1	0	5	4	13
NEUTRAL	27	8	9	10	40	37
TOTAL	41	13	13	15	62	59

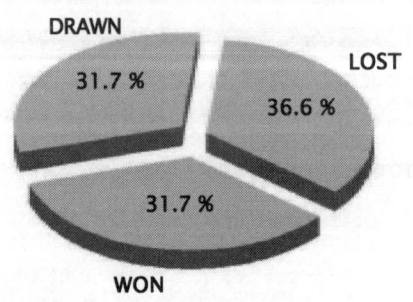

MANCHESTER UNITED
The Complete Record

Chapter 3.4
How Many Times

ALL COMPETITIVE MATCHES

#	OPPONENTS	GAMES	#	OPPONENTS	GAMES	#	OPPONENTS	GAMES
1	Arsenal	203	76	Bayern Munich	7	151	Olympique Marseille	2
2	Everton	175	77	Benfica	7	152	Partizan Belgrade	2
3	Liverpool	175	78	Bristol Rovers	7	153	Pecsi Munkas	2
4	Aston Villa	169	79	Wigan Athletic	7	154	Raba Vasas	2
5	Tottenham Hotspur	165	80	Anderlecht	6	155	Rotor Volgograd	2
6	Chelsea	151	81	Borussia Dortmund	6	156	Sarajevo	2
7	Manchester City	150	82	Burton Wanderers	6	157	Shamrock Rovers	2
8	Newcastle United	148	83	Crewe Alexandra	6	158	South Shore	2
9	Sunderland	125	84	Deportivo La Coruna	6	159	Sparta Prague	2
10	Sheffield Wednesday	124	85	Lille Metropole	6	160	Spartak Varna	2
11	Middlesbrough	120	86	New Brighton Tower	6	161	St Etienne	2
12	Burnley	118	87	Porto	6	162	Strasbourg	2
13	Leicester City	117	88	Roma	6	163	Stuttgart	2
14	West Ham United	115	89	South Shields	6	164	Torpedo Moscow	2
15	West Bromwich Albion	114	90	Swindon Town	6	165	Videoton	2
16	Bolton Wanderers	113	91	Valencia	6	166	Villarreal	2
17	Southampton	108	92	Accrington Stanley	5	167	Walthamstow Avenue	2
18	Leeds United	107	93	Exeter City	5	168	Waterford	2
19	Nottingham Forest	105	94	Wrexham	5	169	Widzew Lodz	2
20	Blackburn Rovers	103	95	Bayer Leverkusen	4	170	Willem II	2
21	Birmingham City	102	96	Dukla Prague	4	171	Yeovil Town	2
22	Derby County	100	97	Dynamo Kiev	4	172	Zalaegerszeg	2
23	Sheffield United	92	98	Fenerbahce	4	173	Aldershot	1
24	Wolverhampton Wanderers	90	99	Galatasaray	4	174	Barnet	1
25	Blackpool	87	100	Northampton Town	4	175	Bootle Reserves	1
26	Stoke City	87	101	Olympiakos Piraeus	4	176	Chester City	1
27	Coventry City	83	102	Olympique Lyonnais	4	177	Fleetwood Rangers	1
28	Preston North End	75	103	Panathinaikos	4	178	Hartlepool United	1
29	Portsmouth	70	104	PSV Eindhoven	4	179	Hereford United	1
30	Fulham	68	105	Rapid Vienna	4	180	Higher Walton	1
31	Charlton Athletic	59	106	Sporting Lisbon	4	181	Lazio	1
32	Norwich City	58	107	Sturm Graz	4	182	Oswaldtwistle Rovers	1
33	Ipswich Town	56	108	York City	4	183	Palmeiras	1
34	Bradford City	51	109	Ferencvaros	3	184	Peterborough United	1
35	Notts County	50	110	Nelson	3	185	Rayos del Necaxa	1
36	Queens Park Rangers	46	111	Red Star Belgrade	3	186	Rochdale	1
37	Huddersfield Town	45	112	Ajax	2	187	South Melbourne	1
38	Port Vale	45	113	ASK Vorwaerts	2	188	Southend United	1
39	Bury	44	114	Athinaikos	2	189	Southport Central	1
40	Oldham Athletic	44	115	Athletic Bilbao	2	190	Staple Hill	1
41	Crystal Palace	41	116	Athletico Madrid	2	191	Tranmere Rovers	1
42	Luton Town	39	117	Basel	2	192	Vasco da Gama	1
43	Barnsley	37	118	Boavista	2	193	West Manchester	1
44	Grimsby Town	37	119	Brondby	2	194	Weymouth Town	1
45	Bristol City	35	120	Burton Albion	2	195	Workington	1
46	Wimbledon	32	121	Cambridge United	2			
47	Lincoln City	29	122	Carlisle United	2			
48	Cardiff City	27	123	Colchester United	2			
49	Watford	24	124	Copenhagen	2			
50	Bradford Park Avenue	22	125	Croatia Zagreb	2			
51	Chesterfield	20	126	Debreceni	2			
52	Gainsborough Trinity	20	127	Dinamo Bucharest	2			
53	Hull City	20	128	Djurgardens	2			
54	Stockport County	19	129	Dundee United	2			
55	Walsall	17	130	Estudiantes de la Plata	2			
56	Brighton	16	131	Feyenoord	2			
57	Oxford United	16	132	Fiorentina	2			
58	Plymouth Argyle	16	133	Girondins Bordeaux	2			
59	Reading	16	134	Glasgow Celtic	2			
60	Swansea City	16	135	Glasgow Rangers	2			
61	Burton Swifts	14	136	Gornik Zabrze	2			
62	Glossop	14	137	Gothenburg	2			
63	Millwall	14	138	Halifax Town	2			
64	Brentford	13	139	Hibernians Malta	2			
65	Burton United	12	140	HJK Helsinki	2			
66	Darwen	12	141	Honved	2			
67	Juventus	12	142	Internazionale	2			
68	Leyton Orient	12	143	Kettering	2			
69	Loughborough Town	10	144	Kosice	2			
70	Rotherham United	10	145	Legia Warsaw	2			
71	Barcelona	9	146	LKS Lodz	2			
72	AC Milan	8	147	Maccabi Haifa	2			
73	Bournemouth	8	148	Monaco	2			
74	Doncaster Rovers	8	149	Montpellier Herault	2			
75	Real Madrid	8	150	Nantes Atlantique	2			

ALL LEAGUE MATCHES

#	OPPONENTS	GAMES	#	OPPONENTS	GAMES	#	OPPONENTS	GAMES
1	Arsenal	178	28	Preston North End	66	55	Watford	16
2	Everton	158	29	Charlton Athletic	56	56	Burton Swifts	14
3	Aston Villa	150	30	Fulham	56	57	Glossop	14
4	Liverpool	150	31	Portsmouth	54	58	Darwen	12
5	Tottenham Hotspur	142	32	Ipswich Town	50	59	Leyton Orient	12
6	Newcastle United	140	33	Norwich City	50	60	Millwall	12
7	Manchester City	138	34	Notts County	48	61	Plymouth Argyle	12
8	Chelsea	132	35	Bradford City	46	62	Walsall	12
9	Leicester City	112	36	Huddersfield Town	42	63	Brentford	10
10	Sheffield Wednesday	112	37	Bury	38	64	Burton United	10
11	Bolton Wanderers	110	38	Luton Town	38	65	Loughborough Town	10
12	Sunderland	110	39	Queens Park Rangers	38	66	Brighton	8
13	West Bromwich Albion	106	40	Grimsby Town	36	67	Doncaster Rovers	8
14	West Ham United	106	41	Oldham Athletic	36	68	Oxford United	8
15	Burnley	102	42	Port Vale	36	69	Burton Wanderers	6
16	Middlesbrough	100	43	Bristol City	34	70	New Brighton Tower	6
17	Nottingham Forest	96	44	Barnsley	32	71	Rotherham United	6
18	Leeds United	94	45	Crystal Palace	32	72	South Shields	6
19	Birmingham City	90	46	Lincoln City	28	73	Wigan Athletic	6
20	Blackburn Rovers	90	47	Wimbledon	28	74	Crewe Alexandra	4
21	Derby County	90	48	Cardiff City	26	75	Reading	4
22	Southampton	90	49	Chesterfield	20	76	Accrington Stanley	2
23	Sheffield United	88	50	Gainsborough Trinity	20	77	Bristol Rovers	2
24	Wolverhampton Wanderers	82	51	Bradford Park Avenue	18	78	Nelson	2
25	Blackpool	80	52	Stockport County	18	79	Northampton Town	2
26	Coventry City	74	53	Hull City	16	80	Swindon Town	2
27	Stoke City	70	54	Swansea City	16	81	York City	2

ALL PREMIERSHIP MATCHES

#	OPPONENTS	GAMES	#	OPPONENTS	GAMES	#	OPPONENTS	GAMES
1	Arsenal	32	14	Bolton Wanderers	18	27	Crystal Palace	8
2	Aston Villa	32	15	Coventry City	18	28	Norwich City	8
3	Chelsea	32	16	Charlton Athletic	16	29	Queens Park Rangers	8
4	Everton	32	17	Leicester City	16	30	Sheffield United	6
5	Liverpool	32	18	Sheffield Wednesday	16	31	West Bromwich Albion	6
6	Tottenham Hotspur	32	19	Wimbledon	16	32	Wigan Athletic	6
7	Newcastle United	30	20	Derby County	14	33	Bradford City	4
8	Blackburn Rovers	28	21	Fulham	14	34	Oldham Athletic	4
9	Middlesbrough	26	22	Sunderland	14	35	Reading	4
10	Southampton	26	23	Birmingham City	10	36	Watford	4
11	West Ham United	26	24	Ipswich Town	10	37	Barnsley	2
12	Leeds United	24	25	Nottingham Forest	10	38	Swindon Town	2
13	Manchester City	22	26	Portsmouth	10	39	Wolverhampton Wanderers	2

ALL LEAGUE DIVISION 1 MATCHES

#	OPPONENTS	GAMES	#	OPPONENTS	GAMES	#	OPPONENTS	GAMES
1	Arsenal	126	21	Leicester City	64	41	Bristol City	18
2	Everton	126	22	Leeds United	62	42	Crystal Palace	18
3	Aston Villa	114	23	Stoke City	62	43	Oldham Athletic	18
4	Liverpool	114	24	Blackburn Rovers	60	44	Grimsby Town	12
5	Manchester City	104	25	Preston North End	54	45	Watford	12
6	Tottenham Hotspur	102	26	Blackpool	48	46	Wimbledon	12
7	Chelsea	96	27	Coventry City	48	47	Brighton	8
8	Newcastle United	96	28	Southampton	44	48	Bradford Park Avenue	6
9	Sunderland	94	29	Huddersfield Town	42	49	Brentford	6
10	West Bromwich Albion	92	30	Ipswich Town	40	50	Oxford United	6
11	Sheffield Wednesday	84	31	Portsmouth	40	51	Millwall	4
12	Bolton Wanderers	80	32	Charlton Athletic	34	52	Swansea City	4
13	Burnley	76	33	Norwich City	34	53	Accrington Stanley	2
14	Sheffield United	76	34	Luton Town	30	54	Darwen	2
15	Wolverhampton Wanderers	74	35	Notts County	30	55	Leyton Orient	2
16	Nottingham Forest	72	36	Queens Park Rangers	30	56	Northampton Town	2
17	Derby County	70	37	Cardiff City	24			
18	Birmingham City	68	38	Fulham	24			
19	West Ham United	68	39	Bradford City	20			
20	Middlesbrough	66	40	Bury	20			

ALL LEAGUE DIVISION 2 MATCHES

#	OPPONENTS	GAMES	#	OPPONENTS	GAMES	#	OPPONENTS	GAMES
1	Port Vale	36	26	Bradford Park Avenue	12	51	Derby County	6
2	Blackpool	32	27	Manchester City	12	52	New Brighton Tower	6
3	Leicester City	32	28	Plymouth Argyle	12	53	Rotherham United	6
4	Barnsley	30	29	Preston North End	12	54	Sheffield United	6
5	Lincoln City	28	30	Sheffield Wednesday	12	55	South Shields	6
6	Burnley	26	31	Swansea City	12	56	Wolverhampton Wanderers	6
7	Grimsby Town	24	32	Walsall	12	57	Aston Villa	4
8	Bradford City	22	33	West Ham United	12	58	Brentford	4
9	Arsenal	20	34	Burton United	10	59	Chelsea	4
10	Chesterfield	20	35	Darwen	10	60	Crewe Alexandra	4
11	Gainsborough Trinity	20	36	Leyton Orient	10	61	Liverpool	4
12	Southampton	20	37	Loughborough Town	10	62	Portsmouth	4
13	Bury	18	38	Coventry City	8	63	Blackburn Rovers	2
14	Fulham	18	39	Doncaster Rovers	8	64	Bristol Rovers	2
15	Notts County	18	40	Leeds United	8	65	Cardiff City	2
16	Stockport County	18	41	Luton Town	8	66	Nelson	2
17	Bristol City	16	42	Middlesbrough	8	67	Oxford United	2
18	Hull City	16	43	Millwall	8	68	Sunderland	2
19	Burton Swifts	14	44	Norwich City	8	69	York City	2
20	Glossop	14	45	Stoke City	8			
21	Newcastle United	14	46	Tottenham Hotspur	8			
22	Nottingham Forest	14	47	West Bromwich Albion	8			
23	Oldham Athletic	14	48	Burton Wanderers	6			
24	Birmingham City	12	49	Charlton Athletic	6			
25	Bolton Wanderers	12	50	Crystal Palace	6			

ALL FA CUP MATCHES

#	OPPONENTS	GAMES	#	OPPONENTS	GAMES	#	OPPONENTS	GAMES
1	Liverpool	15	31	Watford	6	61	Notts County	2
2	Middlesbrough	14	32	West Bromwich Albion	6	62	Oxford United	2
3	Tottenham Hotspur	14	33	Barnsley	5	63	Rotherham United	2
4	Arsenal	13	34	Norwich City	5	64	South Shore	2
5	Southampton	13	35	Walsall	5	65	Swindon Town	2
6	Aston Villa	12	36	Bradford Park Avenue	4	66	Walthamstow Avenue	2
7	Fulham	12	37	Bury	4	67	Wrexham	2
8	Reading	12	38	Crystal Palace	4	68	Yeovil Town	2
9	Chelsea	11	39	Ipswich Town	4	69	Bootle Reserves	1
10	Stoke City	11	40	Newcastle United	4	70	Bristol City	1
11	Everton	10	41	Plymouth Argyle	4	71	Cardiff City	1
12	Portsmouth	10	42	Sheffield United	4	72	Chester City	1
13	Birmingham City	9	43	Accrington Stanley	3	73	Colchester United	1
14	Leeds United	9	44	Bolton Wanderers	3	74	Fleetwood Rangers	1
15	Preston North End	9	45	Bristol Rovers	3	75	Grimsby Town	1
16	Sheffield Wednesday	9	46	Exeter City	3	76	Hartlepool United	1
17	Sunderland	9	47	Huddersfield Town	3	77	Hereford United	1
18	Blackburn Rovers	8	48	Port Vale	3	78	Higher Walton	1
19	Derby County	8	49	Wimbledon	3	79	Lincoln City	1
20	West Ham United	8	50	Bradford City	2	80	Luton Town	1
21	Wolves	8	51	Brentford	2	81	Nelson	1
22	Manchester City	7	52	Burton Albion	2	82	Oswaldtwistle Rovers	1
23	Oldham Athletic	7	53	Burton United	2	83	Peterborough United	1
24	Blackpool	6	54	Carlisle United	2	84	Rochdale	1
25	Bournemouth	6	55	Charlton Athletic	2	85	Southport Central	1
26	Brighton	6	56	Hull City	2	86	Staple Hill	1
27	Burnley	6	57	Kettering	2	87	West Manchester	1
28	Coventry City	6	58	Leicester City	2	88	Weymouth Town	1
29	Nottingham Forest	6	59	Millwall	2	89	Workington	1
30	Queens Park Rangers	6	60	Northampton Town	2			

ALL LEAGUE CUP MATCHES

#	OPPONENTS	GAMES	#	OPPONENTS	GAMES	#	OPPONENTS	GAMES
1	Burnley	8	21	Leicester City	3	41	Aldershot	1
2	Arsenal	6	22	Norwich City	3	42	Barnet	1
3	Aston Villa	6	23	Nottingham Forest	3	43	Birmingham City	1
4	Middlesbrough	6	24	Sheffield Wednesday	3	44	Blackpool	1
5	Oxford United	6	25	Bournemouth	2	45	Brentford	1
6	Port Vale	6	26	Brighton	2	46	Charlton Athletic	1
7	Portsmouth	6	27	Bristol Rovers	2	47	Colchester United	1
8	Tottenham Hotspur	6	28	Bury	2	48	Oldham Athletic	1
9	Crystal Palace	5	29	Cambridge United	2	49	Southend United	1
10	Southampton	5	30	Crewe Alexandra	2	50	Stockport County	1
11	Stoke City	5	31	Derby County	2	51	Swindon Town	1
12	Blackburn Rovers	4	32	Exeter City	2	52	Tranmere Rovers	1
13	Chelsea	4	33	Halifax Town	2	53	West Ham United	1
14	Leeds United	4	34	Hull City	2	54	Wigan Athletic	1
15	Liverpool	4	35	Ipswich Town	2	55	Wimbledon	1
16	Manchester City	4	36	Newcastle United	2	56	Wrexham	1
17	Sunderland	4	37	Rotherham United	2			
18	Bradford City	3	38	Watford	2			
19	Coventry City	3	39	West Bromwich Albion	2			
20	Everton	3	40	York City	2			

ALL EUROPEAN MATCHES

#	OPPONENTS	GAMES	#	OPPONENTS	GAMES	#	OPPONENTS	GAMES
1	Juventus	12	31	Athletico Madrid	2	61	Partizan Belgrade	2
2	Barcelona	9	32	Basel	2	62	Pecsi Munkas	2
3	AC Milan	8	33	Boavista	2	63	Raba Vasas	2
4	Real Madrid	8	34	Brondby	2	64	Red Star Belgrade	2
5	Bayern Munich	7	35	Copenhagen	2	65	Rotor Volgograd	2
6	Benfica	7	36	Croatia Zagreb	2	66	Sarajevo	2
7	Anderlecht	6	37	Debreceni	2	67	Shamrock Rovers	2
8	Borussia Dortmund	6	38	Dinamo Bucharest	2	68	Spartak Varna	2
9	Deportivo La Coruna	6	39	Djurgardens	2	69	Sparta Prague	2
10	Lille Metropole	6	40	Dundee United	2	70	St Etienne	2
11	Porto	6	41	Everton	2	71	Strasbourg	2
12	Roma	6	42	Feyenoord	2	72	Stuttgart	2
13	Valencia	6	43	Fiorentina	2	73	Torpedo Moscow	2
14	Bayer Leverkusen	4	44	Girondins Bordeaux	2	74	Tottenham Hotspur	2
15	Dukla Prague	4	45	Glasgow Celtic	2	75	Videoton	2
16	Dynamo Kiev	4	46	Glasgow Rangers	2	76	Villarreal	2
17	Fenerbahce	4	47	Gornik Zabrze	2	77	Waterford	2
18	Galatasaray	4	48	Gothenburg	2	78	Widzew Lodz	2
19	Olympiakos Piraeus	4	49	Hibernians Malta	2	79	Willem II	2
20	Olympique Lyonnais	4	50	HJK Helsinki	2	80	Wrexham	2
21	Panathinaikos	4	51	Honved	2	81	Zalaegerszeg	2
22	PSV Eindhoven	4	52	Internazionale	2	82	Chelsea	1
23	Rapid Vienna	4	53	Kosice	2			
24	Sturm Graz	4	54	Legia Warsaw	2			
25	Sporting Lisbon	4	55	LKS Lodz	2			
26	Ferencvaros	3	56	Maccabi Haifa	2			
27	Ajax	2	57	Monaco	2			
28	ASK Vorwaerts	2	58	Montpellier Herault	2			
29	Athinaikos	2	59	Nantes Atlantique	2			
30	Athletic Bilbao	2	60	Olympique Marseille	2			

ALL EUROPEAN CUP / CHAMPIONS LEAGUE MATCHES

#	OPPONENTS	GAMES	#	OPPONENTS	GAMES	#	OPPONENTS	GAMES
1	AC Milan	8	21	Sturm Graz	4	41	HJK Helsinki	2
2	Juventus	8	22	Valencia	4	42	Honved	2
3	Real Madrid	8	23	ASK Vorwaerts	2	43	Internazionale	2
4	Bayern Munich	7	24	Athletic Bilbao	2	44	Kosice	2
5	Benfica	7	25	Basel	2	45	LKS Lodz	2
6	Anderlecht	6	26	Boavista	2	46	Maccabi Haifa	2
7	Barcelona	6	27	Brondby	2	47	Monaco	2
8	Deportivo La Coruna	6	28	Copenhagen	2	48	Nantes Atlantique	2
9	Lille Metropole	6	29	Croatia Zagreb	2	49	Olympique Marseille	2
10	Roma	6	30	Debreceni	2	50	Partizan Belgrade	2
11	Bayer Leverkusen	4	31	Dinamo Bucharest	2	51	PSV Eindhoven	2
12	Borussia Dortmund	4	32	Dukla Prague	2	52	Red Star Belgrade	2
13	Dynamo Kiev	4	33	Feyenoord	2	53	Sarajevo	2
14	Fenerbahce	4	34	Fiorentina	2	54	Shamrock Rovers	2
15	Galatasaray	4	35	Girondins Bordeaux	2	55	Sparta Prague	2
16	Olympiakos Piraeus	4	36	Glasgow Celtic	2	56	Sporting Lisbon	2
17	Olympique Lyonnais	4	37	Glasgow Rangers	2	57	Stuttgart	2
18	Panathinaikos	4	38	Gornik Zabrze	2	58	Villarreal	2
19	Porto	4	39	Gothenburg	2	59	Waterford	2
20	Rapid Vienna	4	40	Hibernians Malta	2	60	Zalaegerszeg	2
						61	Chelsea	1

ALL EUROPEAN CUP-WINNERS' CUP MATCHES

#	OPPONENTS	GAMES	#	OPPONENTS	GAMES	#	OPPONENTS	GAMES
1	Barcelona	3	6	Legia Warsaw	2	11	Sporting Lisbon	2
2	Athinaikos	2	7	Montpellier Herault	2	12	St Etienne	2
3	Athletico Madrid	2	8	Pecsi Munkas	2	13	Tottenham Hotspur	2
4	Dukla Prague	2	9	Porto	2	14	Willem II	2
5	Juventus	2	10	Spartak Varna	2	15	Wrexham	2

ALL UEFA CUP / INTER-CITIES' FAIRS CUP MATCHES

#	OPPONENTS	GAMES	#	OPPONENTS	GAMES	#	OPPONENTS	GAMES
1	Ferencvaros	3	6	Everton	2	11	Strasbourg	2
2	Ajax	2	7	Juventus	2	12	Torpedo Moscow	2
3	Borussia Dortmund	2	8	PSV Eindhoven	2	13	Valencia	2
4	Djurgardens	2	9	Raba Vasas	2	14	Videoton	2
5	Dundee United	2	10	Rotor Volgograd	2	15	Widzew Lodz	2

ALL OTHER COMPETITIVE MATCHES

CHARITY SHIELD

#	OPPONENTS	GAMES
1	Arsenal	6
2	Liverpool	5
3	Chelsea	3
4	Everton	2
5	Newcastle United	2
6	Queens Park Rangers	2
7	Aston Villa	1
8	Blackburn Rovers	1
9	Manchester City	1
10	Swindon Town	1
11	Tottenham Hotspur	1

TEST MATCHES

#	OPPONENTS	GAMES
1	Burnley	2
2	Birmingham City	2
3	Sunderland	2
4	Liverpool	1
5	Stoke City	1

EUROPEAN SUPER CUP

#	OPPONENTS	GAMES
1	Lazio	1
2	Red Star Belgrade	1

INTER-CONTINENTAL CUP

#	OPPONENTS	GAMES
1	Estudiantes de la Plata	2
2	Palmeiras	1

CLUB WORLD CHAMPIONSHIP

#	OPPONENTS	GAMES
1	Rayos del Necaxa	1
2	South Melbourne	1
3	Vasco da Gama	1

MANCHESTER UNITED
The Complete Record

Chapter 3.5
The Managers

COMPARE THE MANAGERS

	MANAGER	PLAYED	WON	DRAWN	LOST	FOR	AGAINST	PERCENTAGE		
								WON	DRAWN	LOST
1	Sir Alex FERGUSON	1210	702	287	221	2182	1096	58.02	23.72	18.26
2	Ernest MANGNALL	373	202	76	95	700	476	54.16	20.38	25.47
3	Sir Matt BUSBY	1141	576	266	299	2324	1566	50.48	23.31	26.21
4	Ron ATKINSON	292	146	79	67	461	266	50.00	27.05	22.95
5	Tommy DOCHERTY	228	107	56	65	333	252	46.93	24.56	28.51
6	John BENTLEY	82	36	16	30	127	110	43.90	19.51	36.59
7	James WEST	113	46	20	47	158	147	40.71	17.70	41.59
8	Dave SEXTON	201	81	64	56	290	240	40.30	31.84	27.86
9	Walter CRICKMER	119	47	32	40	203	188	39.50	26.89	33.61
10	Scott DUNCAN	235	92	53	90	371	362	39.15	22.55	38.30
11	John CHAPMAN	221	86	58	77	287	274	38.91	26.24	34.84
12	Frank O'FARRELL	81	30	24	27	115	111	37.04	29.63	33.33
13	Wilf McGUINNESS	87	32	32	23	127	111	36.78	36.78	26.44
14	Herbert BAMLETT	183	57	42	84	280	374	31.15	22.95	45.90
15	Clarence HILDITCH	33	10	10	13	38	47	30.30	30.30	39.39
16	John ROBSON	139	41	42	56	183	207	29.50	30.22	40.29
17	Jimmy MURPHY	22	5	7	10	27	42	22.73	31.82	45.45

UNITED under JAMES WEST (1900 - 1903)

ALL COMPETITIVE MATCHES							LEAGUE DIVISION TWO							FA CUP						
VENUE	P	W	D	L	F	A	VENUE	P	W	D	L	F	A	VENUE	P	W	D	L	F	A
HOME	59	35	11	13	111	43	HOME	51	30	9	12	90	36	HOME	8	5	2	1	21	7
AWAY	54	11	9	34	48	104	AWAY	51	10	9	32	43	93	AWAY	3	1	0	2	5	11
TOTAL	113	46	20	47	159	147	TOTAL	102	40	18	44	133	129	TOTAL	11	6	2	3	26	18

UNITED under ERNEST MANGNALL (1903 - 1912)

ALL COMPETITIVE MATCHES							ALL LEAGUE MATCHES							LEAGUE DIVISION ONE						
VENUE	P	W	D	L	F	A	VENUE	P	W	D	L	F	A	VENUE	P	W	D	L	F	A
HOME	184	129	29	26	431	178	HOME	167	117	26	24	387	161	HOME	114	72	21	21	230	124
AWAY	181	68	45	68	250	290	AWAY	167	64	40	63	227	263	AWAY	114	37	26	51	148	209
NEUTRAL	8	5	2	1	19	8														
TOTAL	373	202	76	95	700	476	TOTAL	334	181	66	87	614	424	TOTAL	228	109	47	72	378	333

LEAGUE DIVISION TWO							FA CUP							CHARITY SHIELD						
VENUE	P	W	D	L	F	A	VENUE	P	W	D	L	F	A	VENUE	P	W	D	L	F	A
HOME	53	45	5	3	157	37	HOME	17	12	3	2	44	17	HOME	0	0	0	0	0	0
AWAY	53	27	14	12	79	54	AWAY	14	4	5	5	23	27	AWAY	0	0	0	0	0	0
							NEUTRAL	5	3	1	1	6	3	NEUTRAL	3	2	1	0	13	5
TOTAL	106	72	19	15	236	91	TOTAL	36	19	9	8	73	47	NEUTRAL	3	2	1	0	13	5

UNITED under JOHN BENTLEY (1912 - 1914)

ALL COMPETITIVE MATCHES							LEAGUE DIVISION ONE							FA CUP						
VENUE	P	W	D	L	F	A	VENUE	P	W	D	L	F	A	VENUE	P	W	D	L	F	A
HOME	40	21	8	11	70	40	HOME	38	21	7	10	68	37	HOME	2	0	1	1	2	3
AWAY	42	15	8	19	57	70	AWAY	38	13	7	18	53	68	AWAY	4	2	1	1	4	2
TOTAL	82	36	16	30	127	110	TOTAL	76	34	14	28	121	105	TOTAL	6	2	2	2	6	5

UNITED under JOHN ROBSON (1914 - 1921)

ALL COMPETITIVE MATCHES							LEAGUE DIVISION ONE							FA CUP						
VENUE	P	W	D	L	F	A	VENUE	P	W	D	L	F	A	VENUE	P	W	D	L	F	A
HOME	69	26	20	23	93	73	HOME	67	26	20	21	91	69	HOME	2	0	0	2	2	4
AWAY	70	15	22	33	90	134	AWAY	67	14	21	32	88	132	AWAY	3	1	1	1	2	2
TOTAL	139	41	42	56	183	207	TOTAL	134	40	41	53	179	201	TOTAL	5	1	1	3	4	6

UNITED under JOHN CHAPMAN (1921 - 1926)

ALL COMPETITIVE MATCHES							ALL LEAGUE MATCHES							FA CUP						
VENUE	P	W	D	L	F	A	VENUE	P	W	D	L	F	A	VENUE	P	W	D	L	F	A
HOME	109	59	27	23	173	97	HOME	103	55	27	21	165	89	HOME	6	4	0	2	8	8
AWAY	111	27	31	53	114	174	AWAY	104	25	28	51	103	159	AWAY	7	2	3	2	11	15
NEUTRAL	1	0	0	1	0	3								NEUTRAL	1	0	0	1	0	3
TOTAL	221	86	58	77	287	274	TOTAL	207	80	55	72	268	248	TOTAL	14	6	3	5	19	26

LEAGUE DIVISION ONE							LEAGUE DIVISION TWO						
VENUE	P	W	D	L	F	A	VENUE	P	W	D	L	F	A
HOME	40	18	11	11	63	51	HOME	63	37	16	10	102	38
AWAY	41	9	5	27	45	94	AWAY	63	16	23	24	58	65
TOTAL	81	27	16	38	108	145	TOTAL	126	53	39	34	160	103

UNITED under CLARENCE HILDITCH (1926 - 1927)

ALL COMPETITIVE MATCHES							LEAGUE DIVISION ONE							FA CUP						
VENUE	P	W	D	L	F	A	VENUE	P	W	D	L	F	A	VENUE	P	W	D	L	F	A
HOME	17	7	6	4	23	15	HOME	16	7	5	4	21	13	HOME	1	0	1	0	2	2
AWAY	15	3	4	8	14	30	AWAY	14	3	3	8	13	29	AWAY	1	0	1	0	1	1
NEUTRAL	1	0	0	1	1	2								NEUTRAL	1	0	0	1	1	2
TOTAL	33	10	10	13	38	47	TOTAL	30	10	8	12	34	42	TOTAL	3	0	2	1	4	5

UNITED under HERBERT BAMLETT (1927 - 1931)

ALL COMPETITIVE MATCHES							LEAGUE DIVISION ONE							FA CUP						
VENUE	P	W	D	L	F	A	VENUE	P	W	D	L	F	A	VENUE	P	W	D	L	F	A
HOME	91	40	26	25	161	125	HOME	85	37	25	23	152	121	HOME	6	3	1	2	9	4
AWAY	91	16	16	59	115	247	AWAY	86	15	14	57	108	240	AWAY	5	1	2	2	7	7
NEUTRAL	1	1	0	0	4	2								NEUTRAL	1	1	0	0	4	2
TOTAL	183	57	42	84	280	374	TOTAL	171	52	39	80	260	361	TOTAL	12	5	3	4	20	13

UNITED under WALTER CRICKMER (1931 - 1932 / 1937 - 1945)

ALL COMPETITIVE MATCHES							ALL LEAGUE MATCHES							FA CUP						
VENUE	P	W	D	L	F	A	VENUE	P	W	D	L	F	A	VENUE	P	W	D	L	F	A
HOME	59	33	13	13	118	68	HOME	56	31	13	12	113	63	HOME	3	2	0	1	5	5
AWAY	60	14	19	27	85	120	AWAY	56	14	17	25	82	112	AWAY	4	0	2	2	3	8
TOTAL	119	47	32	40	203	188	TOTAL	112	45	30	37	195	175	TOTAL	7	2	2	3	8	13

LEAGUE DIVISION ONE							LEAGUE DIVISION TWO						
VENUE	P	W	D	L	F	A	VENUE	P	W	D	L	F	A
HOME	21	7	9	5	30	20	HOME	35	24	4	7	83	43
AWAY	21	4	7	10	27	45	AWAY	35	10	10	15	55	67
TOTAL	42	11	16	15	57	65	TOTAL	70	34	14	22	138	110

UNITED under SCOTT DUNCAN (1932 - 1937)

ALL COMPETITIVE MATCHES							ALL LEAGUE MATCHES							FA CUP						
VENUE	P	W	D	L	F	A	VENUE	P	W	D	L	F	A	VENUE	P	W	D	L	F	A
HOME	117	64	25	28	217	136	HOME	112	63	24	25	214	126	HOME	5	1	1	3	3	10
AWAY	118	28	28	62	154	226	AWAY	112	26	26	60	147	215	AWAY	6	2	2	2	7	11
TOTAL	235	92	53	90	371	362	TOTAL	224	89	50	85	361	341	TOTAL	11	3	3	5	10	21

LEAGUE DIVISION ONE							LEAGUE DIVISION TWO						
VENUE	P	W	D	L	F	A	VENUE	P	W	D	L	F	A
HOME	21	8	9	4	29	26	HOME	91	55	15	21	185	100
AWAY	21	2	3	16	26	52	AWAY	91	24	23	44	121	163
TOTAL	42	10	12	20	55	78	TOTAL	182	79	38	65	306	263

UNITED under SIR MATT BUSBY (1946 - 1969 / 1970 - 1971)

ALL COMPETITIVE MATCHES

VENUE	P	W	D	L	F	A
HOME	561	363	113	85	1324	598
AWAY	565	206	151	208	965	950
NEUTRAL	15	7	2	6	26	18
TOTAL	1141	576	266	299	2315	1566

LEAGUE DIVISION ONE

VENUE	P	W	D	L	F	A
HOME	485	306	99	80	1116	531
AWAY	487	174	132	181	826	830
TOTAL	972	480	231	261	1942	1361

ALL CUP MATCHES

VENUE	P	W	D	L	F	A
HOME	71	55	11	5	194	59
AWAY	74	31	19	24	135	111
NEUTRAL	15	7	2	6	26	18
TOTAL	160	93	32	35	355	188

FA CUP

VENUE	P	W	D	L	F	A
HOME	43	29	9	5	104	39
AWAY	43	23	9	11	89	62
NEUTRAL	14	6	2	6	22	17
TOTAL	100	58	20	22	215	118

LEAGUE CUP

VENUE	P	W	D	L	F	A
HOME	1	1	0	0	4	1
AWAY	3	0	1	2	3	8
TOTAL	4	1	1	2	7	9

EUROPEAN CUP

VENUE	P	W	D	L	F	A
HOME	19	18	1	0	53	12
AWAY	19	6	6	7	32	27
NEUTRAL	1	1	0	0	4	1
TOTAL	39	25	7	7	89	40

EUROPEAN CUP-WINNERS' CUP

VENUE	P	W	D	L	F	A
HOME	3	3	0	0	14	3
AWAY	3	0	1	2	1	8
TOTAL	6	3	1	2	15	11

INTER-CITIES' FAIRS CUP

VENUE	P	W	D	L	F	A
HOME	5	4	1	0	19	4
AWAY	6	2	2	2	10	6
TOTAL	11	6	3	2	29	10

OTHER MATCHES

VENUE	P	W	D	L	F	A
HOME	5	2	3	0	14	8
AWAY	4	1	0	3	4	9
TOTAL	9	3	3	3	18	17

CHARITY SHIELD

VENUE	P	W	D	L	F	A
HOME	4	2	2	0	13	7
AWAY	3	1	0	2	4	8
TOTAL	7	3	2	2	17	15

INTER-CONTINENTAL CUP

VENUE	P	W	D	L	F	A
HOME	1	0	1	0	1	1
AWAY	1	0	0	1	0	1
TOTAL	2	0	1	1	1	2

UNITED under JIMMY MURPHY (1958)

ALL COMPETITIVE MATCHES

VENUE	P	W	D	L	F	A
HOME	10	3	4	3	10	15
AWAY	9	1	2	6	10	20
NEUTRAL	3	1	1	1	7	7
TOTAL	22	5	7	10	27	42

LEAGUE DIVISION ONE

VENUE	P	W	D	L	F	A
HOME	7	0	4	3	4	14
AWAY	7	1	1	5	8	14
TOTAL	14	1	5	8	12	28

ALL CUP MATCHES

VENUE	P	W	D	L	F	A
HOME	3	3	0	0	6	1
AWAY	2	0	1	1	2	6
NEUTRAL	3	1	1	1	7	7
TOTAL	8	4	2	2	15	14

FA CUP

VENUE	P	W	D	L	F	A
HOME	2	2	0	0	4	0
AWAY	1	0	1	0	2	2
NEUTRAL	3	1	1	1	7	7
TOTAL	6	3	2	1	13	9

EUROPEAN CUP

VENUE	P	W	D	L	F	A
HOME	1	1	0	0	2	1
AWAY	1	0	0	1	0	4
TOTAL	2	1	0	1	2	5

UNITED under WILF McGUINNESS (1970 - 1971)

ALL COMPETITIVE MATCHES

VENUE	P	W	D	L	F	A
HOME	44	20	16	8	70	49
AWAY	39	11	14	14	55	61
NEUTRAL	4	1	2	1	2	1
TOTAL	87	32	32	23	127	111

LEAGUE DIVISION ONE

VENUE	P	W	D	L	F	A
HOME	33	11	14	8	50	42
AWAY	31	8	11	12	40	53
TOTAL	64	19	25	20	90	95

ALL CUP MATCHES

VENUE	P	W	D	L	F	A
HOME	11	9	2	0	20	7
AWAY	8	3	3	2	15	8
NEUTRAL	4	1	2	1	2	1
TOTAL	23	13	7	3	37	16

FA CUP

VENUE	P	W	D	L	F	A
HOME	2	2	0	0	5	1
AWAY	3	2	1	0	10	3
NEUTRAL	4	1	2	1	2	1
TOTAL	9	5	3	1	17	5

LEAGUE CUP

VENUE	P	W	D	L	F	A
HOME	9	7	2	0	15	6
AWAY	5	1	2	2	5	5
TOTAL	14	8	4	2	20	11

UNITED under FRANK O'FARRELL (1971 - 1972)

ALL COMPETITIVE MATCHES

VENUE	P	W	D	L	F	A
HOME	39	19	9	11	61	44
AWAY	42	11	15	16	54	67
TOTAL	81	30	24	27	115	111

LEAGUE DIVISION ONE

VENUE	P	W	D	L	F	A
HOME	32	17	5	10	50	37
AWAY	32	7	11	14	39	58
TOTAL	64	24	16	24	89	95

ALL CUP MATCHES

VENUE	P	W	D	L	F	A
HOME	7	2	4	1	11	7
AWAY	10	4	4	2	15	9
TOTAL	17	6	8	3	26	16

FA CUP

VENUE	P	W	D	L	F	A
HOME	3	1	2	0	5	5
AWAY	4	2	1	1	7	3
TOTAL	7	3	3	1	12	5

LEAGUE CUP

VENUE	P	W	D	L	F	A
HOME	4	1	2	1	6	5
AWAY	6	2	3	1	8	6
TOTAL	10	3	5	2	14	11

UNITED under TOMMY DOCHERTY (1972 - 1977)

ALL COMPETITIVE MATCHES

VENUE	P	W	D	L	F	A
HOME	118	74	28	16	209	95
AWAY	106	30	28	48	118	154
NEUTRAL	4	3	0	1	6	3
TOTAL	228	107	56	65	333	252

ALL LEAGUE MATCHES

VENUE	P	W	D	L	F	A
HOME	94	57	24	13	162	75
AWAY	94	27	25	42	105	133
TOTAL	188	84	49	55	267	208

ALL CUP MATCHES

VENUE	P	W	D	L	F	A
HOME	24	17	4	3	47	20
AWAY	12	3	3	6	13	21
NEUTRAL	4	3	0	1	6	3
TOTAL	40	23	7	10	66	44

LEAGUE DIVISION ONE

VENUE	P	W	D	L	F	A
HOME	73	40	21	12	117	63
AWAY	73	18	19	36	84	115
TOTAL	146	58	40	48	201	178

LEAGUE DIVISION TWO

VENUE	P	W	D	L	F	A
HOME	21	17	3	1	45	12
AWAY	21	9	6	6	21	18
TOTAL	42	26	9	7	66	30

FA CUP

VENUE	P	W	D	L	F	A
HOME	10	7	2	1	13	6
AWAY	5	2	1	2	9	9
NEUTRAL	4	3	0	1	6	3
TOTAL	19	12	3	4	28	18

LEAGUE CUP

VENUE	P	W	D	L	F	A
HOME	12	8	2	2	31	14
AWAY	5	1	2	2	4	8
TOTAL	17	9	4	4	35	22

UEFA CUP

VENUE	P	W	D	L	F	A
HOME	2	2	0	0	3	0
AWAY	2	0	0	2	0	4
TOTAL	4	2	0	2	3	4

UNITED under DAVE SEXTON (1977 - 1981)

ALL COMPETITIVE MATCHES

VENUE	P	W	D	L	F	A
HOME	97	51	30	16	159	83
AWAY	100	29	32	39	126	152
NEUTRAL	4	1	2	1	5	5
TOTAL	201	81	64	56	290	240

LEAGUE DIVISION ONE

VENUE	P	W	D	L	F	A
HOME	84	44	27	13	134	70
AWAY	84	26	26	32	109	127
TOTAL	168	70	53	45	243	197

ALL CUP MATCHES

VENUE	P	W	D	L	F	A
HOME	13	7	3	3	25	13
AWAY	16	3	6	7	17	25
NEUTRAL	3	1	1	1	5	5
TOTAL	32	11	10	11	47	43

FA CUP

VENUE	P	W	D	L	F	A
HOME	7	4	2	1	13	6
AWAY	8	2	4	2	9	8
NEUTRAL	3	1	1	1	5	5
TOTAL	18	7	7	4	27	19

LEAGUE CUP

VENUE	P	W	D	L	F	A
HOME	3	1	0	2	4	4
AWAY	5	1	0	4	7	12
TOTAL	8	2	0	6	11	16

EUROPEAN CUP-WINNERS' CUP

VENUE	P	W	D	L	F	A
HOME	2	2	0	0	7	2
AWAY	2	0	1	1	1	5
TOTAL	4	2	1	1	8	7

UEFA CUP

VENUE	P	W	D	L	F	A
HOME	1	0	1	0	1	1
AWAY	1	0	1	0	0	0
TOTAL	2	0	2	0	1	1

CHARITY SHIELD

VENUE	P	W	D	L	F	A
HOME	0	0	0	0	0	0
AWAY	0	0	0	0	0	0
NEUTRAL	1	0	1	0	0	0
TOTAL	1	0	1	0	0	0

UNITED under RON ATKINSON (1981 - 1986)

ALL COMPETITIVE MATCHES

VENUE	P	W	D	L	F	A
HOME	143	90	34	19	260	85
AWAY	140	51	43	46	185	171
NEUTRAL	9	5	2	2	16	10
TOTAL	292	146	79	67	461	266

LEAGUE DIVISION ONE

VENUE	P	W	D	L	F	A
HOME	112	68	28	16	203	70
AWAY	111	40	35	36	146	137
TOTAL	223	108	63	52	349	207

ALL CUP MATCHES

VENUE	P	W	D	L	F	A
HOME	31	22	6	3	57	15
AWAY	29	11	8	10	39	34
NEUTRAL	7	4	2	1	14	8
TOTAL	67	37	16	14	110	57

FA CUP

VENUE	P	W	D	L	F	A
HOME	8	7	0	1	17	5
AWAY	7	3	2	2	6	4
NEUTRAL	6	4	2	0	13	6
TOTAL	21	14	4	3	36	15

LEAGUE CUP

VENUE	P	W	D	L	F	A
HOME	14	10	2	2	26	6
AWAY	13	6	3	4	22	16
NEUTRAL	1	0	0	1	1	2
TOTAL	28	16	5	7	49	24

EUROPEAN CUP-WINNERS' CUP

VENUE	P	W	D	L	F	A
HOME	4	2	2	0	7	2
AWAY	4	1	1	2	5	7
TOTAL	8	3	3	2	12	9

UEFA CUP

VENUE	P	W	D	L	F	A
HOME	5	3	2	0	7	2
AWAY	5	1	2	2	6	7
TOTAL	10	4	4	2	13	9

CHARITY SHIELD

VENUE	P	W	D	L	F	A
HOME	0	0	0	0	0	0
AWAY	0	0	0	0	0	0
NEUTRAL	2	1	0	1	2	2
TOTAL	2	1	0	1	2	2

UNITED under SIR ALEX FERGUSON (1986 -)

ALL COMPETITIVE MATCHES

VENUE	P	W	D	L	F	A
HOME	583	404	119	60	1207	400
AWAY	581	277	155	149	904	648
NEUTRAL	46	21	13	12	71	48
TOTAL	1210	702	287	221	2182	1096

ALL LEAGUE MATCHES

VENUE	P	W	D	L	F	A
HOME	422	289	89	44	857	279
AWAY	423	202	118	103	682	486
TOTAL	845	491	207	147	1539	765

ALL CUP MATCHES

VENUE	P	W	D	L	F	A
HOME	160	114	30	16	349	121
AWAY	158	75	37	46	222	162
NEUTRAL	29	17	7	5	52	26
TOTAL	329	194	70	65	594	299

PREMIERSHIP

VENUE	P	W	D	L	F	A
HOME	310	224	60	26	669	195
AWAY	310	170	77	63	551	343
TOTAL	610	394	137	89	1220	538

LEAGUE DIVISION ONE

VENUE	P	W	D	L	F	A
HOME	112	65	29	18	188	84
AWAY	113	32	41	40	131	143
TOTAL	225	97	70	58	319	227

FA CUP

VENUE	P	W	D	L	F	A
HOME	44	31	8	5	90	29
AWAY	36	24	5	7	65	31
NEUTRAL	21	13	6	2	41	17
TOTAL	101	68	19	14	196	77

LEAGUE CUP

VENUE	P	W	D	L	F	A
HOME	33	26	3	4	68	27
AWAY	39	20	6	13	59	47
NEUTRAL	5	2	0	3	6	6
TOTAL	77	48	9	20	133	80

EUROPEAN CUP / CHAMPIONS LEAGUE

VENUE	P	W	D	L	F	A
HOME	75	54	14	7	179	60
AWAY	75	27	23	25	90	80
NEUTRAL	2	1	1	0	3	2
TOTAL	152	82	38	32	272	142

EUROPEAN CUP-WINNERS' CUP

VENUE	P	W	D	L	F	A
HOME	6	3	3	0	10	3
AWAY	6	4	1	1	8	4
NEUTRAL	1	1	0	0	2	1
TOTAL	13	8	4	1	20	8

UEFA CUP

VENUE	P	W	D	L	F	A
HOME	2	0	2	0	2	2
AWAY	2	0	2	0	0	0
TOTAL	4	0	4	0	2	2

ALL OTHER MATCHES

VENUE	P	W	D	L	F	A
HOME	1	1	0	0	1	0
AWAY	0	0	0	0	0	0
NEUTRAL	17	4	6	7	19	22
TOTAL	18	5	6	7	20	22

CHARITY SHIELD

VENUE	P	W	D	L	F	A
HOME	0	0	0	0	0	0
AWAY	0	0	0	0	0	0
NEUTRAL	12	2	5	5	14	17
TOTAL	12	2	5	5	14	17

INTER-CONTINENTAL CUP

VENUE	P	W	D	L	F	A
HOME	0	0	0	0	0	0
AWAY	0	0	0	0	0	0
NEUTRAL	1	1	0	0	1	0
TOTAL	1	1	0	0	1	0

CLUB WORLD CHAMPIONSHIP

VENUE	P	W	D	L	F	A
HOME	0	0	0	0	0	0
AWAY	0	0	0	0	0	0
NEUTRAL	3	1	1	1	4	4
TOTAL	3	1	1	1	4	4

EUROPEAN SUPER CUP

VENUE	P	W	D	L	F	A
HOME	1	1	0	0	1	0
AWAY	0	0	0	0	0	0
NEUTRAL	1	0	0	1	0	1
TOTAL	2	1	0	1	1	1

MANCHESTER UNITED
The Complete Record

Chapter 3.6
Reds on Tour

UNITED v TEAMS FROM ARGENTINA

INTER-CONTINENTAL CUP

VENUE	P	W	D	L	F	A
HOME	1	0	1	0	1	1
AWAY	1	0	0	1	0	1
TOTAL	2	0	1	1	1	2

#	SEASON	DATE	COMPETITION / ROUND	MATCH RESULT	VENUE	ATT
1	1968/69	25/09/68	Inter-Continental Cup Final 1st Leg	Estudiantes de la Plata 1 Manchester United 0	Boca Juniors Stadium	55000
2	1968/69	16/10/68	Inter-Continental Cup Final 2nd Leg	Manchester United 1 Estudiantes de la Plata 1	Old Trafford	63500

UNITED v TEAMS FROM AUSTRALIA

CLUB WORLD CHAMPIONSHIP

VENUE	P	W	D	L	F	A
HOME	0	0	0	0	0	0
AWAY	0	0	0	0	0	0
NEUTRAL	1	1	0	0	2	0
TOTAL	1	1	0	0	2	0

#	SEASON	DATE	COMPETITION / ROUND	MATCH RESULT	VENUE	ATT
1	1999/00	11/01/00	Club World Championship	Manchester United 2 South Melbourne 0	Maracana Stadium	25000

UNITED v TEAMS FROM AUSTRIA

EUROPEAN CUP / CHAMPIONS LEAGUE

VENUE	P	W	D	L	F	A
HOME	4	4	0	0	10	1
AWAY	4	3	1	0	7	0
TOTAL	8	7	1	0	17	1

#	SEASON	DATE	COMPETITION / ROUND	MATCH RESULT	VENUE	ATT
1	1968/69	26/02/69	European Cup Quarter-Final 1st Leg	Manchester United 3 Rapid Vienna 0	Old Trafford	61932
2	1968/69	05/03/69	European Cup Quarter-Final 2nd Leg	Rapid Vienna 0 Manchester United 0	Wiener Stadion	52000
3	1996/97	25/09/96	Champions League Phase 1 Match 2	Manchester United 2 Rapid Vienna 0	Old Trafford	51831
4	1996/97	04/12/96	Champions League Phase 1 Match 6	Rapid Vienna 0 Manchester United 2	Ernst Happel Stadion	45000
5	1999/00	22/09/99	Champions League Phase 1 Match 2	Sturm Graz 0 Manchester United 3	Schwarzenegger Stadium	16480
6	1999/00	02/11/99	Champions League Phase 1 Match 6	Manchester United 2 Sturm Graz 1	Old Trafford	53745
7	2000/01	06/12/00	Champions League Phase 2 Match 2	Sturm Graz 0 Manchester United 2	Schwarzenegger Stadium	16500
8	2000/01	13/03/01	Champions League Phase 2 Match 6	Manchester United 3 Sturm Graz 0	Old Trafford	66404

UNITED v TEAMS FROM BELGIUM

EUROPEAN CUP / CHAMPIONS LEAGUE

VENUE	P	W	D	L	F	A
HOME	3	3	0	0	18	1
AWAY	3	1	0	2	4	5
TOTAL	6	4	0	2	22	6

#	SEASON	DATE	COMPETITION / ROUND	MATCH RESULT	VENUE	ATT
1	1956/57	12/09/56	European Cup Preliminary Round 1st Leg	Anderlecht 0 Manchester United 2	Park Astrid	35000
2	1956/57	26/09/56	European Cup Preliminary Round 2nd Leg	Manchester United 10 Anderlecht 0	Maine Road	40000
3	1968/69	13/11/68	European Cup 2nd Round 1st Leg	Manchester United 3 Anderlecht 0	Old Trafford	51000
4	1968/69	27/11/68	European Cup 2nd Round 2nd Leg	Anderlecht 3 Manchester United 1	Park Astrid	40000
5	2000/01	13/09/00	Champions League Phase 1 Match 1	Manchester United 5 Anderlecht 1	Old Trafford	62749
6	2000/01	24/10/00	Champions League Phase 1 Match 5	Anderlecht 2 Manchester United 1	Vanden Stock	22506

UNITED v TEAMS FROM BOSNIA-HERZEGOVINA

EUROPEAN CUP

VENUE	P	W	D	L	F	A
HOME	1	1	0	0	2	1
AWAY	1	0	1	0	0	0
TOTAL	2	1	1	0	2	1

#	SEASON	DATE	COMPETITION / ROUND	MATCH RESULT	VENUE	ATT
1	1967/68	15/11/67	European Cup 2nd Round 1st Leg	Sarajevo 0 Manchester United 0	Stadion Kosevo	45000
2	1967/68	29/11/67	European Cup 2nd Round 2nd Leg	Manchester United 2 Sarajevo 1	Old Trafford	62801

UNITED v TEAMS FROM BRAZIL

ALL COMPETITIVE MATCHES							INTER-CONTINENTAL CUP							CLUB WORLD CHAMPIONSHIP						
VENUE	P	W	D	L	F	A	VENUE	P	W	D	L	F	A	VENUE	P	W	D	L	F	A
HOME	0	0	0	0	0	0	HOME	0	0	0	0	0	0	HOME	0	0	0	0	0	0
AWAY	0	0	0	0	0	0	AWAY	0	0	0	0	0	0	AWAY	0	0	0	0	0	0
NEUTRAL	2	1	0	1	2	3	NEUTRAL	1	1	0	0	1	0	NEUTRAL	1	0	0	1	1	3
TOTAL	2	1	0	1	2	3	TOTAL	1	1	0	0	1	0	TOTAL	1	0	0	1	1	3

#	SEASON	DATE	COMPETITION / ROUND	MATCH RESULT	VENUE	ATT
1	1999/00	30/11/99	Inter-Continental Cup Final	Manchester United 1 Palmeiras 0	Olympic Stadium, Tokyo	53372
2	1999/00	08/01/00	Club World Championship	Manchester United 1 Vasco da Gama 3	Maracana Stadium	73000

UNITED v TEAMS FROM BULGARIA

EUROPEAN CUP-WINNERS' CUP

VENUE	P	W	D	L	F	A
HOME	1	1	0	0	2	0
AWAY	1	1	0	0	2	1
TOTAL	2	2	0	0	4	1

#	SEASON	DATE	COMPETITION / ROUND	MATCH RESULT	VENUE	ATT
1	1983/84	19/10/83	ECWC 2nd Round 1st Leg	Spartak Varna 1 Manchester United 2	Stad Yuri Gargarin	40000
2	1983/84	02/11/83	ECWC 2nd Round 2nd Leg	Manchester United 2 Spartak Varna 0	Old Trafford	39079

UNITED v TEAMS FROM CROATIA

CHAMPIONS LEAGUE

VENUE	P	W	D	L	F	A
HOME	1	0	1	0	0	0
AWAY	1	1	0	0	2	1
TOTAL	2	1	1	0	2	1

#	SEASON	DATE	COMPETITION / ROUND	MATCH RESULT	VENUE	ATT
1	1999/00	14/09/99	Champions League Phase 1 Match 1	Manchester United 0 Croatia Zagreb 0	Old Trafford	53250
2	1999/00	27/10/99	Champions League Phase 1 Match 5	Croatia Zagreb 1 Manchester United 2	Maksimir Stadium	27500

UNITED v TEAMS FROM CZECH REPUBLIC

ALL COMPETITIVE MATCHES							EUROPEAN CUP / CHAMPIONS LEAGUE							EUROPEAN CUP-WINNERS' CUP						
VENUE	P	W	D	L	F	A	VENUE	P	W	D	L	F	A	VENUE	P	W	D	L	F	A
HOME	3	2	1	0	8	2	HOME	2	2	0	0	7	1	HOME	1	0	1	0	1	1
AWAY	3	0	2	1	2	3	AWAY	2	0	1	1	0	1	AWAY	1	0	1	0	2	2
TOTAL	6	2	3	1	10	5	TOTAL	4	2	1	1	7	2	TOTAL	2	0	2	0	3	3

#	SEASON	DATE	COMPETITION / ROUND	MATCH RESULT	VENUE	ATT
1	1957/58	20/11/57	European Cup 1st Round 1st Leg	Manchester United 3 Dukla Prague 0	Old Trafford	60000
2	1957/58	04/12/57	European Cup 1st Round 2nd Leg	Dukla Prague 1 Manchester United 0	Stadium Strahov	35000
3	1983/84	14/09/83	ECWC 1st Round 1st Leg	Manchester United 1 Dukla Prague 1	Old Trafford	39745
4	1983/84	27/09/83	ECWC 1st Round 2nd Leg	Dukla Prague 2 Manchester United 2	Stadion Juliska	28850
				(United won the tie on away goals rule)		
5	2004/05	19/10/04	Champions League Phase 1 Match 3	Sparta Prague 0 Manchester United 0	Toyota Stadium	20654
6	2004/05	03/11/04	Champions League Phase 1 Match 4	Manchester United 4 Sparta Prague 1	Old Trafford	66706

UNITED v TEAMS FROM DENMARK

CHAMPIONS LEAGUE

VENUE	P	W	D	L	F	A
HOME	2	2	0	0	8	0
AWAY	2	1	0	1	6	3
TOTAL	4	3	0	1	14	3

#	SEASON	DATE	COMPETITION / ROUND	MATCH RESULT	VENUE	ATT
1	1998/99	21/10/98	Champions League Phase 1 Match 3	Brondby 2 Manchester United 6	Parken Stadion	40530
2	1998/99	04/11/98	Champions League Phase 1 Match 4	Manchester United 5 Brondby 0	Old Trafford	53250
3	2006/07	17/10/06	Champions League Phase 1 Match 3	Manchester United 3 Copenhagen 0	Old Trafford	72020
4	2006/07	01/11/06	Champions League Phase 1 Match 4	Copenhagen 1 Manchester United 0	Parken Stadion	40000

UNITED v TEAMS FROM ENGLAND

ALL COMPETITIVE MATCHES

VENUE	P	W	D	L	F	A
HOME	2	1	1	0	5	2
AWAY	2	1	0	1	2	3
NEUTRAL	1	0	1	0	1	1
TOTAL	5	2	2	1	8	6

CHAMPIONS LEAGUE							EUROPEAN CUP-WINNERS' CUP							INTER-CITIES' FAIRS CUP						
VENUE	P	W	D	L	F	A	VENUE	P	W	D	L	F	A	VENUE	P	W	D	L	F	A
HOME	0	0	0	0	0	0	HOME	9	4	3	2	13	8	HOME	1	1	0	0	4	0
AWAY	0	0	0	0	0	0	AWAY	9	2	4	3	10	10	AWAY	1	1	0	0	6	1
NEUTRAL	1	0	1	0	1	1	NEUTRAL	1	1	0	0	2	1							
TOTAL	1	0	1	0	1	1	TOTAL	19	7	7	5	25	19	TOTAL	2	2	0	0	10	1

#	SEASON	DATE	COMPETITION / ROUND	MATCH RESULT	VENUE	ATT
1	1963/64	03/12/63	ECWC 2nd Round 1st Leg	Tottenham Hotspur 2 Manchester United 0	White Hart Lane	57447
2	1963/64	10/12/63	ECWC 2nd Round 2nd Leg	Manchester United 4 Tottenham Hotspur 1	Old Trafford	50000
3	1964/65	20/01/65	ICFC 3rd Round 1st Leg	Manchester United 1 Everton 1	Old Trafford	50000
4	1964/65	09/02/65	ICFC 3rd Round 2nd Leg	Everton 1 Manchester United 2	Goodison Park	54397
5	2007/08	21/05/08	Champions League Final	Manchester United 1 Chelsea 1 (United won the tie 6–5 on penalty kicks)	Luzhniki Stadium	67310

UNITED v TEAMS FROM FINLAND

EUROPEAN CUP

VENUE	P	W	D	L	F	A
HOME	1	1	0	0	6	0
AWAY	1	1	0	0	3	2
TOTAL	2	2	0	0	9	2

#	SEASON	DATE	COMPETITION / ROUND	MATCH RESULT	VENUE	ATT
1	1965/66	22/09/65	European Cup Preliminary Round 1st Leg	HJK Helsinki 2 Manchester United 3	Olympiastadion	25000
2	1965/66	06/10/65	European Cup Preliminary Round 2nd Leg	Manchester United 6 HJK Helsinki 0	Old Trafford	30388

UNITED v TEAMS FROM FRANCE

ALL COMPETITIVE MATCHES

VENUE	P	W	D	L	F	A
HOME	11	8	3	0	17	4
AWAY	11	4	5	2	16	9
TOTAL	22	12	8	2	33	13

CHAMPIONS LEAGUE							EUROPEAN CUP-WINNERS' CUP							INTER-CITIES' FAIRS CUP						
VENUE	P	W	D	L	F	A	VENUE	P	W	D	L	F	A	VENUE	P	W	D	L	F	A
HOME	8	7	1	0	14	3	HOME	2	1	1	0	3	1	HOME	1	0	1	0	0	0
AWAY	8	2	4	2	8	8	AWAY	2	1	1	0	3	1	AWAY	1	1	0	0	5	0
TOTAL	16	9	5	2	22	11	TOTAL	4	2	2	0	6	2	TOTAL	2	1	1	0	5	0

UNITED v TEAMS FROM FRANCE (continued)

#	SEASON	DATE	COMPETITION / ROUND	MATCH RESULT	VENUE	ATT
1	1964/65	12/05/65	ICFC Quarter-Final 1st Leg	Strasbourg 0 Manchester United 5	Stade de la Meinau	30000
2	1964/65	19/05/65	ICFC Quarter-Final 2nd Leg	Manchester United 0 Strasbourg 0	Old Trafford	34188
3	1977/78	14/09/77	ECWC 1st Round 1st Leg	St Etienne 1 Manchester United 1	Geoffrey Guichard	33678
4	1977/78	05/10/77	ECWC 1st Round 2nd Leg	Manchester United 2 St Etienne 0	Home Park	31634
5	1990/91	06/03/91	ECWC 3rd Round 1st Leg	Manchester United 1 Montpellier Herault 1	Old Trafford	41942
6	1990/91	19/03/91	ECWC 3rd Round 2nd Leg	Montpellier Herault 0 Manchester United 2	Stade de la Masson	18000
7	1999/00	29/09/99	Champions League Phase 1 Match 3	Manchester United 2 Olympique Marseille 1	Old Trafford	53993
8	1999/00	19/10/99	Champions League Phase 1 Match 4	Olympique Marseille 1 Manchester United 0	Stade Velodrome	56732
9	1999/00	01/03/00	Champions League Phase 2 Match 3	Manchester United 2 Girondins Bordeaux 0	Old Trafford	59786
10	1999/00	07/03/00	Champions League Phase 2 Match 4	Girondins Bordeaux 1 Manchester United 2	Stade Lescure	30130
11	2001/02	18/09/01	Champions League Phase 1 Match 1	Manchester United 1 Lille Metropole 0	Old Trafford	64827
12	2001/02	31/10/01	Champions League Phase 1 Match 6	Lille Metropole 1 Manchester United 1	Stade Felix Bollaert	38402
13	2001/02	20/02/02	Champions League Phase 2 Match 3	Nantes Atlantique 1 Manchester United 1	Stade Beaujoire	38285
14	2001/02	26/02/02	Champions League Phase 2 Match 4	Manchester United 5 Nantes Atlantique 1	Old Trafford	66492
15	2004/05	15/09/04	Champions League Phase 1 Match 1	Olympique Lyonnais 2 Manchester United 2	Stade de Gerland	40000
16	2004/05	23/11/04	Champions League Phase 1 Match 5	Manchester United 2 Olympique Lyonnais 1	Old Trafford	66398
17	2005/06	18/10/05	Champions League Phase 1 Match 3	Manchester United 0 Lille Metropole 0	Old Trafford	60626
18	2005/06	02/11/05	Champions League Phase 1 Match 4	Lille Metropole 1 Manchester United 0	Stade de France	65000
19	2006/07	20/02/07	Champions League 2nd Round 1st Leg	Lille Metropole 0 Manchester United 1	Stade Felix Bollaert	41000
20	2006/07	07/03/07	Champions League 2nd Round 2nd Leg	Manchester United 1 Lille Metropole 0	Old Trafford	75182
21	2007/08	20/02/08	Champions League 2nd Round 1st Leg	Olympique Lyonnais 1 Manchester United 1	Stade de Gerland	39230
22	2007/08	04/03/08	Champions League 2nd Round 2nd Leg	Manchester United 1 Olympique Lyonnais 0	Old Trafford	75520

UNITED v TEAMS FROM GERMANY

ALL COMPETITIVE MATCHES							EUROPEAN CUP / CHAMPIONS LEAGUE							INTER-CITIES' FAIRS CUP						
VENUE	P	W	D	L	F	A	VENUE	P	W	D	L	F	A	VENUE	P	W	D	L	F	A
HOME	10	5	3	2	17	8	HOME	9	4	3	2	13	8	HOME	1	1	0	0	4	0
AWAY	10	3	4	3	16	11	AWAY	9	2	4	3	10	10	AWAY	1	1	0	0	6	1
NEUTRAL	1	1	0	0	2	1	NEUTRAL	1	1	0	0	2	1							
TOTAL	21	9	7	5	35	20	TOTAL	19	7	7	5	25	19	TOTAL	2	2	0	0	10	1

#	SEASON	DATE	COMPETITION / ROUND	MATCH RESULT	VENUE	ATT
1	1956/57	17/10/56	European Cup 1st Round 1st Leg	Manchester United 3 Borussia Dortmund 2	Maine Road	75598
2	1956/57	21/11/56	European Cup 1st Round 2nd Leg	Borussia Dortmund 0 Manchester United 0	Rote Erde Stadion	44570
3	1964/65	11/11/64	ICFC 2nd Round 1st Leg	Borussia Dortmund 1 Manchester United 6	Rote Erde Stadion	25000
4	1964/65	02/12/64	ICFC 2nd Round 2nd Leg	Manchester United 4 Borussia Dortmund 0	Old Trafford	31896
5	1965/66	17/11/65	European Cup 1st Round 1st Leg	ASK Vorwaerts 0 Manchester United 2	Walter Ulbricht Stadium	40000
6	1965/66	01/12/65	European Cup 1st Round 2nd Leg	Manchester United 3 ASK Vorwaerts 1	Old Trafford	30082
7	1996/97	09/04/97	Champions League Semi-Final 1st Leg	Borussia Dortmund 1 Manchester United 0	Westfalenstadion	48500
8	1996/97	23/04/97	Champions League Semi-Final 2nd Leg	Manchester United 0 Borussia Dortmund 1	Old Trafford	53606
9	1998/99	30/09/98	Champions League Phase 1 Match 2	Bayern Munich 2 Manchester United 2	Olympic Stadium	53000
10	1998/99	09/12/98	Champions League Phase 1 Match 6	Manchester United 1 Bayern Munich 1	Old Trafford	54434
11	1998/99	26/05/99	Champions League Final	Manchester United 2 Bayern Munich 1	Estadio Camp Nou	90000
12	2000/01	03/04/01	Champions League Qtr-Final 1st Leg	Manchester United 0 Bayern Munich 1	Old Trafford	66584
13	2000/01	18/04/01	Champions League Qtr-Final 2nd Leg	Bayern Munich 2 Manchester United 1	Olympic Stadium	60000
14	2001/02	20/11/01	Champions League Phase 2 Match 1	Bayern Munich 1 Manchester United 1	Olympic Stadium	59000
15	2001/02	13/03/02	Champions League Phase 2 Match 5	Manchester United 0 Bayern Munich 0	Old Trafford	66818
16	2001/02	24/04/02	Champions League Semi-Final 1st Leg	Manchester United 2 Bayer Leverkusen 2	Old Trafford	66534
17	2001/02	30/04/02	Champions League Semi-Final 2nd Leg	Bayer Leverkusen 1 Manchester United 1 (United lost the tie on away goals rule)	Bayarena	22500
18	2002/03	24/09/02	Champions League Phase 1 Match 2	Bayer Leverkusen 1 Manchester United 2	Bayarena	22500
19	2002/03	13/11/02	Champions League Phase 1 Match 6	Manchester United 2 Bayer Leverkusen 0	Old Trafford	66185
20	2003/04	01/10/03	Champions League Phase 1 Match 2	Stuttgart 2 Manchester United 1	Gottlieb-Daimler Stadium	53000
21	2003/04	09/12/03	Champions League Phase 1 Match 6	Manchester United 2 Stuttgart 0	Old Trafford	67141

UNITED v TEAMS FROM GREECE

ALL COMPETITIVE MATCHES							CHAMPIONS LEAGUE							EUROPEAN CUP-WINNERS' CUP					
VENUE	P	W	D	L	F	A	VENUE	P	W	D	L	F	A	VENUE	P	W	D	L	F	A
HOME	5	5	0	0	17	1	HOME	4	4	0	0	15	1	HOME	1	1	0	0	2	0
AWAY	5	3	2	0	7	3	AWAY	4	3	1	0	7	3	AWAY	1	0	1	0	0	0
TOTAL	10	8	2	0	24	4	TOTAL	8	7	1	0	22	4	TOTAL	2	1	1	0	2	0

#	SEASON	DATE	COMPETITION / ROUND	MATCH RESULT	VENUE	ATT
1	1991/92	18/09/91	ECWC 1st Round 1st Leg	Athinaikos 0 Manchester United 0	Apostolos Nikolaidis	5400
2	1991/92	02/10/91	ECWC 1st Round 2nd Leg	Manchester United 2 Athinaikos 0	Old Trafford	35023
3	2000/01	21/11/00	Champions League Phase 2 Match 1	Manchester United 3 Panathinaikos 1	Old Trafford	65024
4	2000/01	07/03/01	Champions League Phase 2 Match 5	Panathinaikos 1 Manchester United 1	Olympic Stadium	27231
5	2001/02	10/10/01	Champions League Phase 1 Match 3	Olympiakos Piraeus 0 Manchester United 2	Olympic Stadium	73537
6	2001/02	23/10/01	Champions League Phase 1 Match 5	Manchester United 3 Olympiakos Piraeus 0	Old Trafford	66769
7	2002/03	01/10/02	Champions League Phase 1 Match 3	Manchester United 4 Olympiakos Piraeus 0	Old Trafford	66902
8	2002/03	23/10/02	Champions League Phase 1 Match 4	Olympiakos Piraeus 2 Manchester United 3	Rizoupoli	15000
9	2003/04	16/09/03	Champions League Phase 1 Match 1	Manchester United 5 Panathinaikos 0	Old Trafford	66520
10	2003/04	26/11/03	Champions League Phase 1 Match 5	Panathinaikos 0 Manchester United 1	Apostolos Nikolaidis	6890

UNITED v TEAMS FROM HUNGARY

ALL COMPETITIVE MATCHES						
VENUE	P	W	D	L	F	A
HOME	7	7	0	0	19	3
AWAY	8	3	1	4	10	9
TOTAL	15	10	1	4	29	12

EUROPEAN CUP / CHAMPIONS LEAGUE							EUROPEAN CUP-WINNERS' CUP							INTER-CITIES' FAIRS CUP / UEFA CUP					
VENUE	P	W	D	L	F	A	VENUE	P	W	D	L	F	A	VENUE	P	W	D	L	F	A
HOME	3	3	0	0	10	1	HOME	1	1	0	0	2	0	HOME	3	3	0	0	7	2
AWAY	3	2	0	1	6	3	AWAY	1	1	0	0	1	0	AWAY	4	0	1	3	3	6
TOTAL	6	5	0	1	16	4	TOTAL	2	2	0	0	3	0	TOTAL	7	3	1	3	10	8

#	SEASON	DATE	COMPETITION / ROUND	MATCH RESULT	VENUE	ATT
1	1964/65	31/05/65	ICFC Semi-Final 1st Leg	Manchester United 3 Ferencvaros 2	Old Trafford	39902
2	1964/65	06/06/65	ICFC Semi-Final 2nd Leg	Ferencvaros 1 Manchester United 0	Nep Stadion	50000
3	1964/65	16/06/65	ICFC Semi-Final Play-Off	Ferencvaros 2 Manchester United 1	Nep Stadion	60000
4	1984/85	19/09/84	UEFA Cup 1st Round 1st Leg	Manchester United 3 Raba Vasas 0	Old Trafford	33119
5	1984/85	03/10/84	UEFA Cup 1st Round 2nd Leg	Raba Vasas 2 Manchester United 2	Raba ETO Stadium	26000
6	1984/85	06/03/85	UEFA Cup Quarter-Final 1st Leg	Manchester United 1 Videoton 0	Old Trafford	35432
7	1984/85	20/03/85	UEFA Cup Quarter-Final 2nd Leg	Videoton 1 Manchester United 0	Sostoi Stadion	25000
				(United lost the tie 4-5 on penalty kicks)		
8	1990/91	19/09/90	ECWC 1st Round 1st Leg	Manchester United 2 Pecsi Munkas 0	Old Trafford	28411
9	1990/91	03/10/90	ECWC 1st Round 2nd Leg	Pecsi Munkas 0 Manchester United 1	PMSC Stadion	17000
10	1993/94	15/09/93	European Cup 1st Round 1st Leg	Honved 2 Manchester United 3	Jozsef Bozsik	9000
11	1993/94	29/09/93	European Cup 1st Round 2nd Leg	Manchester United 2 Honved 1	Old Trafford	35781
12	2002/03	14/08/02	Champions Lge Qualifying Round 1st Leg	Zalaegerszeg 1 Manchester United 0	Ferenc Puskas Stadion	40000
13	2002/03	27/08/02	Champions Lge Qualifying Round 2nd Leg	Manchester United 5 Zalaegerszeg 0	Old Trafford	66814
14	2005/06	09/08/05	Champions Lge Qualifying Round 1st Leg	Manchester United 3 Debreceni 0	Old Trafford	51701
15	2005/06	24/08/05	Champions Lge Qualifying Round 2nd Leg	Debreceni 0 Manchester United 3	Ferenc Puskas Stadion	27000

UNITED v TEAMS FROM IRELAND

EUROPEAN CUP						
VENUE	P	W	D	L	F	A
HOME	2	2	0	0	10	3
AWAY	2	2	0	0	9	1
TOTAL	4	4	0	0	19	4

#	SEASON	DATE	COMPETITION / ROUND	MATCH RESULT	VENUE	ATT
1	1957/58	25/09/57	European Cup Preliminary Round 1st Leg	Shamrock Rovers 0 Manchester United 6	Dalymount Park	33754
2	1957/58	02/10/57	European Cup Preliminary Round 2nd Leg	Manchester United 3 Shamrock Rovers 2	Old Trafford	45000
3	1968/69	18/09/68	European Cup 1st Round 1st Leg	Waterford 1 Manchester United 3	Lansdowne Road	48000
4	1968/69	02/10/68	European Cup 1st Round 2nd Leg	Manchester United 7 Waterford 1	Old Trafford	41750

UNITED v TEAMS FROM ISRAEL

CHAMPIONS LEAGUE

VENUE	P	W	D	L	F	A
HOME	1	1	0	0	5	2
AWAY	1	0	0	1	0	3
TOTAL	2	1	0	1	5	5

#	SEASON	DATE	COMPETITION / ROUND	MATCH RESULT	VENUE	ATT
1	2002/03	18/09/02	Champions League Phase 1 Match 1	Manchester United 5 Maccabi Haifa 2	Old Trafford	63439
2	2002/03	29/10/02	Champions League Phase 1 Match 5	Maccabi Haifa 3 Manchester United 0	GSP Stadion Cyprus	22000

UNITED v TEAMS FROM ITALY

ALL COMPETITIVE MATCHES							EUROPEAN SUPER CUP						
VENUE	P	W	D	L	F	A	VENUE	P	W	D	L	F	A
HOME	15	11	2	2	28	12	HOME	0	0	0	0	0	0
AWAY	15	3	2	10	12	25	AWAY	0	0	0	0	0	0
NEUTRAL	1	0	0	1	0	1	NEUTRAL	1	0	0	1	0	1
TOTAL	31	14	4	13	40	38	TOTAL	1	0	0	1	0	1

EUROPEAN CUP / CHAMPIONS LEAGUE							EUROPEAN CUP-WINNERS' CUP							UEFA CUP						
VENUE	P	W	D	L	F	A	VENUE	P	W	D	L	F	A	VENUE	P	W	D	L	F	A
HOME	13	10	1	2	26	11	HOME	1	0	1	0	1	1	HOME	1	1	0	0	1	0
AWAY	13	3	2	8	11	20	AWAY	1	0	0	1	1	2	AWAY	1	0	0	1	0	3
TOTAL	26	13	3	10	37	31	TOTAL	2	0	1	1	2	3	TOTAL	2	1	0	1	1	3

#	SEASON	DATE	COMPETITION / ROUND	MATCH RESULT	VENUE	ATT
1	1957/58	08/05/58	European Cup Semi-Final 1st Leg	Manchester United 2 AC Milan 1	Old Trafford	44880
2	1957/58	14/05/58	European Cup Semi-Final 2nd Leg	AC Milan 4 Manchester United 0	Stadio San Siro	80000
3	1968/69	23/04/69	European Cup Semi-Final 1st Leg	AC Milan 2 Manchester United 0	Stadio San Siro	80000
4	1968/69	15/05/69	European Cup Semi-Final 2nd Leg	Manchester United 1 AC Milan 0	Old Trafford	63103
5	1976/77	20/10/76	UEFA Cup 2nd Round 1st Leg	Manchester United 1 Juventus 0	Old Trafford	59000
6	1976/77	03/11/76	UEFA Cup 2nd Round 2nd Leg	Juventus 3 Manchester United 0	Stadio Comunale	66632
7	1983/84	11/04/84	ECWC Semi-Final 1st Leg	Manchester United 1 Juventus 1	Old Trafford	58171
8	1983/84	25/04/84	ECWC Semi-Final 2nd Leg	Juventus 2 Manchester United 1	Stadio Comunale	64655
9	1996/97	11/09/96	Champions League Phase 1 Match 1	Juventus 1 Manchester United 0	Stadio Delle Alpi	54000
10	1996/97	20/11/96	Champions League Phase 1 Match 5	Manchester United 0 Juventus 1	Old Trafford	53529
11	1997/98	01/10/97	Champions League Phase 1 Match 2	Manchester United 3 Juventus 2	Old Trafford	53428
12	1997/98	10/12/97	Champions League Phase 1 Match 6	Juventus 1 Manchester United 0	Stadio Delle Alpi	47786
13	1998/99	03/03/99	Champions League Quarter-Final 1st Leg	Manchester United 2 Internazionale 0	Old Trafford	54430
14	1998/99	17/03/99	Champions League Quarter-Final 2nd Leg	Internazionale 1 Manchester United 1	Stadio San Siro	79528
15	1998/99	07/04/99	Champions League Semi-Final 1st Leg	Manchester United 1 Juventus 1	Old Trafford	54487
16	1998/99	21/04/99	Champions League Semi-Final 2nd Leg	Juventus 2 Manchester United 3	Stadio Delle Alpi	64500
17	1999/00	27/08/99	European Super Cup	Manchester United 0 Lazio 1	Stade Louis II	14461
18	1999/00	23/11/99	Champions League Phase 2 Match 1	Fiorentina 2 Manchester United 0	Artemio Franchi	36002
19	1999/00	15/03/00	Champions League Phase 2 Match 5	Manchester United 3 Fiorentina 1	Old Trafford	59926
20	2002/03	19/02/03	Champions League Phase 2 Match 3	Manchester United 2 Juventus 1	Old Trafford	66703
21	2002/03	25/02/03	Champions League Phase 2 Match 4	Juventus 0 Manchester United 3	Stadio Delle Alpi	59111
22	2004/05	23/02/05	Champions League 2nd Round 1st Leg	Manchester United 0 AC Milan 1	Old Trafford	67162
23	2004/05	08/03/05	Champions League 2nd Round 2nd Leg	AC Milan 1 Manchester United 0	Stadio San Siro	78957
24	2006/07	04/04/07	Champions League Quarter-Final 1st Leg	Roma 2 Manchester United 1	Olympic Stadium	77000
25	2006/07	10/04/07	Champions League Quarter-Final 2nd Leg	Manchester United 7 Roma 1	Old Trafford	74476
26	2006/07	24/04/07	Champions League Semi-Final 1st Leg	Manchester United 3 AC Milan 2	Old Trafford	73820
27	2006/07	02/05/07	Champions League Semi-Final 2nd Leg	AC Milan 3 Manchester United 0	Stadio San Siro	78500
28	2007/08	02/10/07	Champions League Phase 1 Match 2	Manchester United 1 Roma 0	Old Trafford	73652
29	2007/08	12/12/07	Champions League Phase 1 Match 6	Roma 1 Manchester United 1	Olympic Stadium	29490
30	2007/08	01/04/08	Champions League Quarter-Final 1st Leg	Roma 0 Manchester United 2	Olympic Stadium	60931
31	2007/08	09/04/08	Champions League Quarter-Final 2nd Leg	Manchester United 1 Roma 0	Old Trafford	74423

UNITED v TEAMS FROM MALTA

EUROPEAN CUP

VENUE	P	W	D	L	F	A
HOME	1	1	0	0	4	0
AWAY	1	0	1	0	0	0
TOTAL	2	1	1	0	4	0

#	SEASON	DATE	COMPETITION / ROUND	MATCH RESULT	VENUE	ATT
1	1967/68	20/09/67	European Cup 1st Round 1st Leg	Manchester United 4 Hibernians Malta 0	Old Trafford	43912
2	1967/68	27/09/67	European Cup 1st Round 2nd Leg	Hibernians Malta 0 Manchester United 0	Empire Stadium	25000

UNITED v TEAMS FROM MEXICO

CLUB WORLD CHAMPIONSHIP

VENUE	P	W	D	L	F	A
HOME	0	0	0	0	0	0
AWAY	0	0	0	0	0	0
NEUTRAL	1	0	1	0	1	1
TOTAL	1	0	1	0	1	1

#	SEASON	DATE	COMPETITION / ROUND	MATCH RESULT	VENUE	ATT
1	1999/00	06/01/00	Club World Championship	Manchester United 1 Rayos del Necaxa 1	Maracana Stadium	50000

UNITED v TEAMS FROM MONACO

EUROPEAN CUP / CHAMPIONS LEAGUE

VENUE	P	W	D	L	F	A
HOME	1	0	1	0	1	1
AWAY	1	0	1	0	0	0
TOTAL	2	0	2	0	1	1

#	SEASON	DATE	COMPETITION / ROUND	MATCH RESULT	VENUE	ATT
1	1997/98	04/03/98	Champions League Quarter–Final 1st Leg	Monaco 0 Manchester United 0	Stade Louis II	15000
2	1997/98	18/03/98	Champions League Quarter–Final 2nd Leg	Manchester United 1 Monaco 1 (United lost the tie on away goals rule)	Old Trafford	53683

UNITED v TEAMS FROM NETHERLANDS

ALL COMPETITIVE MATCHES

VENUE	P	W	D	L	F	A
HOME	5	5	0	0	14	3
AWAY	5	1	2	2	5	6
TOTAL	10	6	2	2	19	9

CHAMPIONS LEAGUE

VENUE	P	W	D	L	F	A
HOME	2	2	0	0	5	2
AWAY	2	1	0	1	4	4
TOTAL	4	3	0	1	9	6

EUROPEAN CUP-WINNERS' CUP

VENUE	P	W	D	L	F	A
HOME	1	1	0	0	6	1
AWAY	1	0	1	0	1	1
TOTAL	2	1	1	0	7	2

UEFA CUP

VENUE	P	W	D	L	F	A
HOME	2	2	0	0	3	0
AWAY	2	0	1	1	0	1
TOTAL	4	2	1	1	3	1

#	SEASON	DATE	COMPETITION / ROUND	MATCH RESULT	VENUE	ATT
1	1963/64	25/09/63	ECWC 1st Round 1st Leg	Willem II 1 Manchester United 1	Feyenoord Stadion	20000
2	1963/64	15/10/63	ECWC 1st Round 2nd Leg	Manchester United 6 Willem II 1	Old Trafford	46272
3	1976/77	15/09/76	UEFA Cup 1st Round 1st Leg	Ajax 1 Manchester United 0	Olympisch Stadion	30000
4	1976/77	29/09/76	UEFA Cup 1st Round 2nd Leg	Manchester United 2 Ajax 0	Old Trafford	58918
5	1984/85	24/10/84	UEFA Cup 2nd Round 1st Leg	PSV Eindhoven 0 Manchester United 0	Philipstadion	27500
6	1984/85	07/11/84	UEFA Cup 2nd Round 2nd Leg	Manchester United 1 PSV Eindhoven 0	Old Trafford	39281
7	1997/98	22/10/97	Champions League Phase 1 Match 3	Manchester United 2 Feyenoord 1	Old Trafford	53188
8	1997/98	05/11/97	Champions League Phase 1 Match 4	Feyenoord 1 Manchester United 3	Feyenoord Stadion	51000
9	2000/01	26/09/00	Champions League Phase 1 Match 3	PSV Eindhoven 3 Manchester United 1	Philipstadion	30500
10	2000/01	18/10/00	Champions League Phase 1 Match 4	Manchester United 3 PSV Eindhoven 1	Old Trafford	66313

UNITED v TEAMS FROM POLAND

ALL COMPETITIVE MATCHES

VENUE	P	W	D	L	F	A
HOME	4	2	2	0	6	2
AWAY	4	1	2	1	3	2
TOTAL	8	3	4	1	9	4

EUROPEAN CUP / CHAMPIONS LEAGUE							EUROPEAN CUP-WINNERS' CUP							UEFA CUP						
VENUE	P	W	D	L	F	A	VENUE	P	W	D	L	F	A	VENUE	P	W	D	L	F	A
HOME	2	2	0	0	4	0	HOME	1	0	1	0	1	1	HOME	1	0	1	0	1	1
AWAY	2	0	1	1	0	1	AWAY	1	1	0	0	3	1	AWAY	1	0	1	0	0	0
TOTAL	4	2	1	1	4	1	TOTAL	2	1	1	0	4	2	TOTAL	2	0	2	0	1	1

#	SEASON	DATE	COMPETITION / ROUND	MATCH RESULT	VENUE	ATT
1	1967/68	28/02/68	European Cup Quarter-Final 1st Leg	Manchester United 2 Gornik Zabrze 0	Old Trafford	63456
2	1967/68	13/03/68	European Cup Quarter-Final 2nd Leg	Gornik Zabrze 1 Manchester United 0	Stadion Slaski	105000
3	1980/81	17/09/80	UEFA Cup 1st Round 1st Leg	Manchester United 1 Widzew Lodz 1	Old Trafford	38037
4	1980/81	01/10/80	UEFA Cup 1st Round 2nd Leg	Widzew Lodz 0 Manchester United 0 (United lost the tie on away goals rule)	Stadio TKS	40000
5	1990/91	10/04/91	ECWC Semi-Final 1st Leg	Legia Warsaw 1 Manchester United 3	Wojska Polskiego	20000
6	1990/91	24/04/91	ECWC Semi-Final 2nd Leg	Manchester United 1 Legia Warsaw 1	Old Trafford	44269
7	1998/99	12/08/98	Champions League Preliminary Round 1st Leg	Manchester United 2 LKS Lodz 0	Old Trafford	50906
8	1998/99	26/08/98	Champions League Preliminary Round 2nd Leg	LKS Lodz 0 Manchester United 0	LKS Stadion	8700

UNITED v TEAMS FROM PORTUGAL

ALL COMPETITIVE MATCHES							EUROPEAN CUP / CHAMPIONS LEAGUE							EUROPEAN CUP-WINNERS' CUP						
VENUE	P	W	D	L	F	A	VENUE	P	W	D	L	F	A	VENUE	P	W	D	L	F	A
HOME	9	8	1	0	27	9	HOME	7	6	1	0	18	6	HOME	2	2	0	0	9	3
AWAY	9	4	1	4	12	14	AWAY	7	4	1	2	12	5	AWAY	2	0	0	2	0	9
NEUTRAL	1	1	0	0	4	1	NEUTRAL	1	1	0	0	4	1							
TOTAL	19	13	2	4	43	24	TOTAL	15	11	2	2	34	12	TOTAL	4	2	0	2	9	12

#	SEASON	DATE	COMPETITION / ROUND	MATCH RESULT	VENUE	ATT
1	1963/64	26/02/64	ECWC Quarter-Final 1st Leg	Manchester United 4 Sporting Lisbon 1	Old Trafford	60000
2	1963/64	18/03/64	ECWC Quarter-Final 2nd Leg	Sporting Lisbon 5 Manchester United 0	de Jose Alvalade	40000
3	1965/66	02/02/66	European Cup Quarter-Final 1st Leg	Manchester United 3 Benfica 2	Old Trafford	64035
4	1965/66	09/03/66	European Cup Quarter-Final 2nd Leg	Benfica 1 Manchester United 5	Estadio da Luz	75000
5	1967/68	29/05/68	European Cup Final	Manchester United 4 Benfica 1	Wembley	100000
6	1977/78	19/10/77	ECWC 2nd Round 1st Leg	Porto 4 Manchester United 0	Estadio das Antas	70000
7	1977/78	02/11/77	ECWC 2nd Round 2nd Leg	Manchester United 5 Porto 2	Old Trafford	51831
8	1996/97	05/03/97	Champions League Quarter-Final 1st Leg	Manchester United 4 Porto 0	Old Trafford	53425
9	1996/97	19/03/97	Champions League Quarter-Final 2nd Leg	Porto 0 Manchester United 0	Estadio das Antas	40000
10	2001/02	05/12/01	Champions League Phase 2 Match 2	Manchester United 3 Boavista 0	Old Trafford	66274
11	2001/02	19/03/02	Champions League Phase 2 Match 6	Boavista 0 Manchester United 3	Estadio do Bessa	13223
12	2003/04	25/02/04	Champions League 2nd Round 1st Leg	Porto 2 Manchester United 1	Estadio da Dragao	49977
13	2003/04	09/03/04	Champions League 2nd Round 2nd Leg	Manchester United 1 Porto 1	Old Trafford	67029
14	2005/06	27/09/05	Champions League Phase 1 Match 2	Manchester United 2 Benfica 1	Old Trafford	66112
15	2005/06	07/12/05	Champions League Phase 1 Match 6	Benfica 2 Manchester United 1	Estadio da Luz	61000
16	2006/07	26/09/06	Champions League Phase 1 Match 2	Benfica 0 Manchester United 1	Estadio da Luz	61000
17	2006/07	06/12/06	Champions League Phase 1 Match 6	Manchester United 3 Benfica 1	Old Trafford	74955
18	2007/08	19/09/07	Champions League Phase 1 Match 1	Sporting Lisbon 0 Manchester United 1	de Jose Alvalade	39514
19	2007/08	27/11/07	Champions League Phase 1 Match 5	Manchester United 2 Sporting Lisbon 1	Old Trafford	75162

UNITED v TEAMS FROM ROMANIA

CHAMPIONS LEAGUE

VENUE	P	W	D	L	F	A
HOME	1	1	0	0	3	0
AWAY	1	1	0	0	2	1
TOTAL	2	2	0	0	5	1

#	SEASON	DATE	COMPETITION / ROUND	MATCH RESULT	VENUE	ATT
1	2004/05	11/08/04	Champions Lge Qualifying Round 1st Leg	Dinamo Bucharest 1 Manchester United 2	National Stadium	58000
2	2004/05	25/08/04	Champions Lge Qualifying Round 2nd Leg	Manchester United 3 Dinamo Bucharest 0	Old Trafford	61041

UNITED v TEAMS FROM RUSSIA

UEFA CUP

VENUE	P	W	D	L	F	A
HOME	2	0	2	0	2	2
AWAY	2	0	2	0	0	0
TOTAL	4	0	4	0	2	2

#	SEASON	DATE	COMPETITION / ROUND	MATCH RESULT	VENUE	ATT
1	1992/93	16/09/92	UEFA Cup 1st Round 1st Leg	Manchester United 0 Torpedo Moscow 0	Old Trafford	19998
2	1992/93	29/09/92	UEFA Cup 1st Round 2nd Leg	Torpedo Moscow 0 Manchester United 0	Torpedo Stadion	11357
				(United lost the tie 3–4 on penalty kicks)		
3	1995/96	12/09/95	UEFA Cup 2nd Round 1st Leg	Rotor Volgograd 0 Manchester United 0	Central Stadion	33000
4	1995/96	26/09/95	UEFA Cup 2nd Round 2nd Leg	Manchester United 2 Rotor Volgograd 2	Old Trafford	29724
				(United lost the tie on away goals rule)		

UNITED v TEAMS FROM SCOTLAND

ALL COMPETITIVE MATCHES							CHAMPIONS LEAGUE							UEFA CUP						
VENUE	P	W	D	L	F	A	VENUE	P	W	D	L	F	A	VENUE	P	W	D	L	F	A
HOME	3	2	1	0	8	4	HOME	2	2	0	0	6	2	HOME	1	0	1	0	2	2
AWAY	3	2	0	1	4	3	AWAY	2	1	0	1	1	1	AWAY	1	1	0	0	3	2
TOTAL	6	4	1	1	12	7	TOTAL	4	3	0	1	7	3	TOTAL	2	1	1	0	5	4

#	SEASON	DATE	COMPETITION / ROUND	MATCH RESULT	VENUE	ATT
1	1984/85	28/11/84	UEFA Cup 3rd Round 1st Leg	Manchester United 2 Dundee United 2	Old Trafford	48278
2	1984/85	12/12/84	UEFA Cup 3rd Round 2nd Leg	Dundee United 2 Manchester United 3	Tannadice Park	21821
3	2003/04	22/10/03	Champions League Phase 1 Match 3	Glasgow Rangers 0 Manchester United 1	Ibrox Stadium	48730
4	2003/04	04/11/03	Champions League Phase 1 Match 4	Manchester United 3 Glasgow Rangers 0	Old Trafford	66707
5	2006/07	13/09/06	Champions League Phase 1 Match 1	Manchester United 3 Glasgow Celtic 2	Old Trafford	74031
6	2006/07	21/11/06	Champions League Phase 1 Match 5	Glasgow Celtic 1 Manchester United 0	Celtic Park	60632

UNITED v TEAMS FROM SERBIA

ALL COMPETITIVE MATCHES							EUROPEAN CUP							EUROPEAN SUPER CUP						
VENUE	P	W	D	L	F	A	VENUE	P	W	D	L	F	A	VENUE	P	W	D	L	F	A
HOME	3	3	0	0	4	1	HOME	2	2	0	0	3	1	HOME	1	1	0	0	1	0
AWAY	2	0	1	1	3	5	AWAY	2	0	1	1	3	5	AWAY	0	0	0	0	0	0
TOTAL	5	3	1	1	7	6	TOTAL	4	2	1	1	6	6	TOTAL	1	1	0	0	1	0

#	SEASON	DATE	COMPETITION / ROUND	MATCH RESULT	VENUE	ATT
1	1957/58	14/01/58	European Cup Quarter-Final 1st Leg	Manchester United 2 Red Star Belgrade 1	Old Trafford	60000
2	1957/58	05/02/58	European Cup Quarter-Final 2nd Leg	Red Star Belgrade 3 Manchester United 3	Stadion JNA	55000
3	1965/66	13/04/66	European Cup Semi-Final 1st Leg	Partizan Belgrade 2 Manchester United 0	Stadion JNA	60000
4	1965/66	20/04/66	European Cup Semi-Final 2nd Leg	Manchester United 1 Partizan Belgrade 0	Old Trafford	62500
5	1991/92	19/11/91	European Super Cup	Manchester United 1 Red Star Belgrade 0	Old Trafford	22110

UNITED v TEAMS FROM SLOVAKIA

CHAMPIONS LEAGUE

VENUE	P	W	D	L	F	A
HOME	1	1	0	0	3	0
AWAY	1	1	0	0	3	0
TOTAL	2	2	0	0	6	0

#	SEASON	DATE	COMPETITION / ROUND	MATCH RESULT	VENUE	ATT
1	1997/98	17/09/97	Champions League Phase 1 Match 1	Kosice 0 Manchester United 3	TJ Lokomotive Stadium	9950
2	1997/98	27/11/97	Champions League Phase 1 Match 5	Manchester United 3 Kosice 0	Old Trafford	53535

UNITED v TEAMS FROM SPAIN

ALL COMPETITIVE MATCHES

VENUE	P	W	D	L	F	A
HOME	17	8	7	2	33	20
AWAY	17	1	7	9	15	32
NEUTRAL	1	1	0	0	2	1
TOTAL	35	10	14	11	50	53

EUROPEAN CUP / CHAMPIONS LEAGUE

VENUE	P	W	D	L	F	A
HOME	14	7	5	2	29	19
AWAY	14	1	7	6	14	25
TOTAL	28	8	12	8	43	44

EUROPEAN CUP-WINNERS' CUP

VENUE	P	W	D	L	F	A
HOME	2	1	1	0	4	1
AWAY	2	0	0	2	0	5
NEUTRAL	1	1	0	0	2	1
TOTAL	5	2	1	2	6	7

UEFA CUP

VENUE	P	W	D	L	F	A
HOME	1	0	1	0	0	0
AWAY	1	0	0	1	1	2
TOTAL	2	0	1	1	1	2

#	SEASON	DATE	COMPETITION / ROUND	MATCH RESULT	VENUE	ATT
1	1956/57	16/01/57	European Cup Quarter-Final 1st Leg	Athletic Bilbao 5 Manchester United 3	Estadio San Mames	60000
2	1956/57	06/02/57	European Cup Quarter-Final 2nd Leg	Manchester United 3 Athletic Bilbao 0	Maine Road	70000
3	1956/57	11/04/57	European Cup Semi-Final 1st Leg	Real Madrid 3 Manchester United 1	Bernabeu Stadium	135000
4	1956/57	25/04/57	European Cup Semi-Final 2nd Leg	Manchester United 2 Real Madrid 2	Old Trafford	65000
5	1967/68	24/04/68	European Cup Semi-Final 1st Leg	Manchester United 1 Real Madrid 0	Old Trafford	63500
6	1967/68	15/05/68	European Cup Semi-Final 2nd Leg	Real Madrid 3 Manchester United 3	Bernabeu Stadium	125000
7	1982/83	15/09/82	UEFA Cup 1st Round 1st Leg	Manchester United 0 Valencia 0	Old Trafford	46588
8	1982/83	29/09/82	UEFA Cup 1st Round 2nd Leg	Valencia 2 Manchester United 1	Luis Casanova	35000
9	1983/84	07/03/84	ECWC 3rd Round 1st Leg	Barcelona 2 Manchester United 0	Estadio Camp Nou	70000
10	1983/84	21/03/84	ECWC 3rd Round 2nd Leg	Manchester United 3 Barcelona 0	Old Trafford	58547
11	1990/91	15/05/91	ECWC Final	Manchester United 2 Barcelona 1	Feyenoord Stadion	50000
12	1991/92	23/10/91	ECWC 2nd Round 1st Leg	Athletico Madrid 3 Manchester United 0	Vincente Calderon	40000
13	1991/92	06/11/91	ECWC 2nd Round 2nd Leg	Manchester United 1 Athletico Madrid 1	Old Trafford	39654
14	1994/95	19/10/94	Champions League Phase 1 Match 3	Manchester United 2 Barcelona 2	Old Trafford	40064
15	1994/95	02/11/94	Champions League Phase 1 Match 4	Barcelona 4 Manchester United 0	Estadio Camp Nou	114273
16	1998/99	16/09/98	Champions League Phase 1 Match 1	Manchester United 3 Barcelona 3	Old Trafford	53601
17	1998/99	25/11/98	Champions League Phase 1 Match 5	Barcelona 3 Manchester United 3	Estadio Camp Nou	67648
18	1999/00	08/12/99	Champions League Phase 2 Match 2	Manchester United 3 Valencia 0	Old Trafford	54606
19	1999/00	21/03/00	Champions League Phase 2 Match 6	Valencia 0 Manchester United 0	Mestalla	40419
20	1999/00	04/04/00	Champions League Qtr-Final 1st Leg	Real Madrid 0 Manchester United 0	Bernabeu Stadium	64119
21	1999/00	19/04/00	Champions League Qtr-Final 2nd Leg	Manchester United 2 Real Madrid 3	Old Trafford	59178
22	2000/01	14/02/01	Champions League Phase 2 Match 3	Valencia 0 Manchester United 0	Mestalla	49541
23	2000/01	20/02/01	Champions League Phase 2 Match 4	Manchester United 1 Valencia 1	Old Trafford	66715
24	2001/02	25/09/01	Champions League Phase 1 Match 2	Deportivo La Coruna 2 Manchester United 1	Estadio de Riazor	33108
25	2001/02	17/10/01	Champions League Phase 1 Match 4	Manchester United 2 Deportivo La Coruna 3	Old Trafford	65585
26	2001/02	02/04/02	Champions League Qtr-Final 1st Leg	Deportivo La Coruna 0 Manchester United 2	Estadio de Riazor	32351
27	2001/02	10/04/02	Champions League Qtr-Final 2nd Leg	Manchester United 3 Deportivo La Coruna 2	Old Trafford	65875
28	2002/03	11/12/02	Champions League Phase 2 Match 2	Manchester United 2 Deportivo La Coruna 0	Old Trafford	67014
29	2002/03	18/03/03	Champions League Phase 2 Match 6	Deportivo La Coruna 2 Manchester United 0	Estadio de Riazor	25000
30	2002/03	08/04/03	Champions League Qtr-Final 1st Leg	Real Madrid 3 Manchester United 1	Bernabeu Stadium	75000
31	2002/03	23/04/03	Champions League Qtr-Final 2nd Leg	Manchester United 4 Real Madrid 3	Old Trafford	66708
32	2005/06	14/09/05	Champions League Phase 1 Match 1	Villarreal 0 Manchester United 0	El Madrigal Stadium	22000
33	2005/06	22/11/05	Champions League Phase 1 Match 5	Manchester United 0 Villarreal 0	Old Trafford	67471
34	2007/08	23/04/08	Champions League Semi-Final 1st Leg	Barcelona 0 Manchester United 0	Estadio Camp Nou	95949
35	2007/08	29/04/08	Champions League Semi-Final 2nd Leg	Manchester United 1 Barcelona 0	Old Trafford	75061

UNITED v TEAMS FROM SWEDEN

ALL COMPETITIVE MATCHES

VENUE	P	W	D	L	F	A
HOME	2	2	0	0	10	3
AWAY	2	0	1	1	2	4
TOTAL	4	2	1	1	12	7

CHAMPIONS LEAGUE

VENUE	P	W	D	L	F	A
HOME	1	1	0	0	4	2
AWAY	1	0	0	1	1	3
TOTAL	2	1	0	1	5	5

INTER-CITIES' FAIRS CUP

VENUE	P	W	D	L	F	A
HOME	1	1	0	0	6	1
AWAY	1	0	1	0	1	1
TOTAL	2	1	1	0	7	2

#	SEASON	DATE	COMPETITION / ROUND	MATCH RESULT	VENUE	ATT
1	1964/65	23/09/64	ICFC 1st Round 1st Leg	Djurgardens 1 Manchester United 1	Roasunda Stadion	6537
2	1964/65	27/10/64	ICFC 1st Round 2nd Leg	Manchester United 6 Djurgardens 1	Old Trafford	38437
3	1994/95	14/09/94	Champions League Phase 1 Match 1	Manchester United 4 Gothenburg 2	Old Trafford	33625
4	1994/95	23/11/94	Champions League Phase 1 Match 5	Gothenburg 3 Manchester United 1	NYA Ullevi Stadium	36350

UNITED v TEAMS FROM SWITZERLAND

CHAMPIONS LEAGUE

VENUE	P	W	D	L	F	A
HOME	1	0	1	0	1	1
AWAY	1	1	0	0	3	1
TOTAL	2	1	1	0	4	2

#	SEASON	DATE	COMPETITION / ROUND	MATCH RESULT	VENUE	ATT
1	2002/03	26/11/02	Champions League Phase 2 Match 1	Basel 1 Manchester United 3	St Jakob Stadium	29501
2	2002/03	12/03/03	Champions League Phase 2 Match 5	Manchester United 1 Basel 1	Old Trafford	66870

UNITED v TEAMS FROM TURKEY

EUROPEAN CUP / CHAMPIONS LEAGUE

VENUE	P	W	D	L	F	A
HOME	4	2	1	1	13	6
AWAY	4	1	2	1	2	3
TOTAL	8	3	3	2	15	9

#	SEASON	DATE	COMPETITION / ROUND	MATCH RESULT	VENUE	ATT
1	1993/94	20/10/93	European Cup 2nd Round 1st Leg	Manchester United 3 Galatasaray 3	Old Trafford	39346
2	1993/94	03/11/93	European Cup 2nd Round 2nd Leg	Galatasaray 0 Manchester United 0 (United lost the tie on away goals rule)	Ali Sami Yen	40000
3	1994/95	28/09/94	Champions League Phase 1 Match 2	Galatasaray 0 Manchester United 0	Ali Sami Yen	28605
4	1994/95	07/12/94	Champions League Phase 1 Match 6	Manchester United 4 Galatasaray 0	Old Trafford	39220
5	1996/97	16/10/96	Champions League Phase 1 Match 3	Fenerbahce 0 Manchester United 2	Fenerbahce Stadium	26200
6	1996/97	30/10/96	Champions League Phase 1 Match 4	Manchester United 0 Fenerbahce 1	Old Trafford	53297
7	2004/05	28/09/04	Champions League Phase 1 Match 2	Manchester United 6 Fenerbahce 2	Old Trafford	67128
8	2004/05	08/12/04	Champions League Phase 1 Match 6	Fenerbahce 3 Manchester United 0	Sukru Saracoglu	35000

UNITED v TEAMS FROM UKRAINE

CHAMPIONS LEAGUE

VENUE	P	W	D	L	F	A
HOME	2	2	0	0	5	0
AWAY	2	1	1	0	4	2
TOTAL	4	3	1	0	9	2

#	SEASON	DATE	COMPETITION / ROUND	MATCH RESULT	VENUE	ATT
1	2000/01	19/09/00	Champions League Phase 1 Match 2	Dynamo Kiev 0 Manchester United 0	Republican Stadium	65000
2	2000/01	08/11/00	Champions League Phase 1 Match 6	Manchester United 1 Dynamo Kiev 0	Old Trafford	66776
3	2007/08	23/10/07	Champions League Phase 1 Match 3	Dynamo Kiev 2 Manchester United 4	Olympic Stadium	43000
4	2007/08	07/11/07	Champions League Phase 1 Match 4	Manchester United 4 Dynamo Kiev 0	Old Trafford	75017

UNITED v TEAMS FROM WALES

EUROPEAN CUP-WINNERS' CUP

VENUE	P	W	D	L	F	A
HOME	1	1	0	0	3	0
AWAY	1	1	0	0	2	0
TOTAL	2	2	0	0	5	0

#	SEASON	DATE	COMPETITION / ROUND	MATCH RESULT	VENUE	ATT
1	1990/91	23/10/90	ECWC 2nd Round 1st Leg	Manchester United 3 Wrexham 0	Old Trafford	29405
2	1990/91	07/11/90	ECWC 2nd Round 2nd Leg	Wrexham 0 Manchester United 2	Racecourse Ground	13327

MANCHESTER UNITED
The Complete Record

Chapter 4
The Football Alliance
The War Leagues
Club Honours

SEASON 1889/90

Match # 1 Saturday 21/09/89 Football Alliance at North Road Attendance 3000
Result: **Newton Heath 4 Sunderland 1**
Teamsheet: Hay, Mitchell, Powell, Doughty R, Davies (Joe), Owen J, Tait, Stewart, Doughty J, Wilson, Gotheridge
Scorer(s): Doughty J, Stewart, Tait, Wilson

Match # 2 Monday 23/09/89 Football Alliance at Bootle Park Attendance 3000
Result: **Bootle 4 Newton Heath 1**
Teamsheet: Hay, Mitchell, Owen J, Doughty R, Davies (Joe), Burke, Tait, Stewart, Doughty J, Wilson, Gotheridge
Scorer(s): Tait

Match # 3 Saturday 28/09/89 Football Alliance at Gresty Road Attendance 2000
Result: **Crewe Alexandra 2 Newton Heath 2**
Teamsheet: Pedley, Mitchell, Powell, Doughty R, Davies (Joe), Owen J, Tait, Stewart, Doughty J, Wilson, Gotheridge
Scorer(s): Stewart, own goal

Match # 4 Saturday 19/10/89 Football Alliance at West Bromwich Road Attendance 600
Result: **Walsall 4 Newton Heath 0**
Teamsheet: Hay, Mitchell, Powell, Doughty R, Davies (Joe), Owen J, Tait, Stewart, Doughty J, Wilson, Gotheridge

Match # 5 Saturday 26/10/89 Football Alliance at St Georges Attendance 500
Result: **Birmingham St Georges 5 Newton Heath 1**
Teamsheet: Hay, Mitchell, Felton, Doughty R, Davies (Joe), Owen J, Tait, Stewart, Doughty J, Owen G, Gotheridge
Scorer(s): Doughty J

Match # 6 Saturday 09/11/89 Football Alliance at North Road Attendance 2500
Result: **Newton Heath 3 Long Eaton Rangers 0**
Teamsheet: Hay, Mitchell, Powell, Doughty R, Davies (Joe), Owen J, Farman, Stewart, Doughty J, Owen G, Wilson
Scorer(s): Doughty J 2, Farman

Match # 7 Saturday 30/11/89 Football Alliance at Olive Grove Attendance 5000
Result: **Sheffield Wednesday 3 Newton Heath 1**
Teamsheet: Hay, Mitchell, Powell, Doughty R, Davies (Joe), Owen J, Farman, Stewart, Doughty J, Felton, Wilson
Scorer(s): Doughty J

Match # 8 Saturday 07/12/89 Football Alliance at North Road Attendance 4000
Result: **Newton Heath 3 Bootle 0**
Teamsheet: Hay, Mitchell, Powell, Doughty R, Davies (Joe), Owen J, Farman, Stewart, Doughty J, Owen G, Wilson
Scorer(s): Doughty J, Farman, Stewart

Match # 9 Saturday 28/12/89 Football Alliance at Barley Bank Attendance 5000
Result: **Darwen 4 Newton Heath 1**
Teamsheet: Hay, Felton, Powell, Doughty R, Davies (Joe), Owen J, Farman, Craig, Doughty J, Owen G, Wilson
Scorer(s): Owen G

Match # 10 Saturday 25/01/90 Football Alliance at Newcastle Road Attendance 4000
Result: **Sunderland 2 Newton Heath 0**
Teamsheet: Hay, Felton, Harrison, Doughty R, Davies (Joe), Burke, Farman, Craig, Doughty J, Owen G, Wilson

Match # 11 Saturday 08/02/90 Football Alliance at Abbey Park Attendance 2400
Result: **Grimsby Town 7 Newton Heath 0**
Teamsheet: Harrison, Mitchell, Powell, Felton, Davies (Joe), Burke, Farman, Craig, Doughty J, Owen G, Wilson

Match # 12 Saturday 15/02/90 Football Alliance at Town Ground Attendance 800
Result: **Nottingham Forest 1 Newton Heath 3**
Teamsheet: Hay, Mitchell, Powell, Doughty R, Davies (Joe), Owen J, Farman, Stewart, Doughty J, Owen G, Wilson
Scorer(s): Stewart 2, Wilson

Match # 13 Saturday 01/03/90 Football Alliance at North Road Attendance 2000
Result: **Newton Heath 1 Crewe Alexandra 2**
Teamsheet: Harrison, Mitchell, Powell, Doughty R, Davies (Joe), Owen J, Farman, Stewart, Doughty J, Owen G, Wilson
Scorer(s): Owen G

Match # 14 Saturday 15/03/90 Football Alliance at Muntz Street Attendance 2000
Result: **Birmingham City 1 Newton Heath 1**
Teamsheet: Hay, Mitchell, Powell, Craig, Harrison, Owen J, Farman, Stewart, Doughty J, Owen G, Wilson
Scorer(s): Wilson

Match # 15 Saturday 22/03/90 Football Alliance at Long Eaton Attendance 2000
Result: **Long Eaton Rangers 1 Newton Heath 3**
Teamsheet: Hay, Mitchell, Powell, Doughty R, Davies (Joe), Owen J, Farman, Stewart, Doughty J, Craig, Wilson
Scorer(s): Wilson 2, Farman

Match # 16 Saturday 29/03/90 Football Alliance at North Road Attendance 5000
Result: **Newton Heath 2 Darwen 1**
Teamsheet: Hay, Mitchell, Powell, Doughty R, Davies (Joe), Owen J, Farman, Stewart, Doughty J, Craig, Wilson
Scorer(s): Davies (Joe), Stewart

Match # 17 Saturday 05/04/90 Football Alliance at North Road Attendance 4000
Result: **Newton Heath 0 Nottingham Forest 1**
Teamsheet: Hay, Mitchell, Powell, Doughty R, Davies (Joe), Owen J, Farman, Stewart, Doughty J, Tait, Wilson

Match # 18 Monday 07/04/90 Football Alliance at North Road Attendance 4000
Result: **Newton Heath 9 Birmingham City 1**
Teamsheet: Hay, Harrison, Powell, Doughty R, Davies (Joe), Owen J, Farman, Stewart, Doughty J, Craig, Wilson
Scorer(s): Stewart 3, Doughty J 2, Doughty R, Craig, Farman, Wilson

SEASON 1889/90 (continued)

Match # 19	Monday 14/04/90	Football Alliance	at North Road	Attendance 3000
Result:	**Newton Heath 0 Grimsby Town 1**			
Teamsheet:	Harrison, Mitchell, Powell, Doughty R, Davies (Joe), Craig, Farman, Stewart, Doughty J, Owen G, Wilson			

Match # 20	Saturday 19/04/90	Football Alliance	at North Road	Attendance 2500
Result:	**Newton Heath 2 Birmingham St Georges 1**			
Teamsheet:	Harrison, Mitchell, Burke, Doughty R, Davies (Joe), Craig, Farman, Stewart, Doughty J, Owen G, Tait			
Scorer(s):	Craig, Doughty J			

Match # 21	Monday 21/04/90	Football Alliance	at North Road	Attendance 1000
Result:	**Newton Heath 2 Walsall 1**			
Teamsheet:	Harrison, Mitchell, Powell, Doughty R, Davies (Joe), Owen J, Farman, Stewart, Doughty J, Craig, Wilson			
Scorer(s):	Davies (Joe), Stewart			

Match # 22	Saturday 26/04/90	Football Alliance	at North Road	Attendance 4000
Result:	**Newton Heath 1 Sheffield Wednesday 2**			
Teamsheet:	Harrison, Mitchell, Burke, Doughty R, Davies (Joe), Owen J, Farman, Stewart, Doughty J, Owen G, Craig			
Scorer(s):	Craig			

SEASON 1889/90 SUMMARY

APPEARANCES & GOALS

PLAYER	APPS	GOALS
Doughty J	22	9
Davies, Joe	21	2
Doughty R	20	1
Stewart	19	10
Wilson	19	6
Mitchell	19	0
Owen J	18	0
Farman	17	4
Powell	17	0
Hay	15	0
Owen G	12	2
Craig	11	3
Harrison	9	0
Tait	7	2
Felton	5	0
Burke	5	0
Gotheridge	5	0
Pedley	1	0
own goal		1

FINAL TABLE - FOOTBALL ALLIANCE

		P	W	D	L	F	A	W	D	L	F	A	PTS	GD
				HOME					AWAY					
1	Sheffield Wednesday	22	10	0	1	48	19	5	2	4	22	20	32	31
2	Bootle	22	11	0	0	49	8	2	2	7	17	31	28	27
3	Sunderland	22	9	0	2	43	13	3	2	6	24	31	26	23
4	Grimsby Town	22	9	0	2	42	17	3	2	6	16	30	26	11
5	Crewe Alexandra	22	6	2	3	42	27	5	0	6	26	32	24	9
6	Birmingham St Georges	22	7	2	2	36	22	3	1	7	31	30	23	15
7	Darwen	22	8	1	2	46	28	2	1	8	25	47	22	-4
8	NEWTON HEATH	22	7	0	4	27	11	2	2	7	13	34	20	-5
9	Walsall	22	6	3	2	27	19	2	0	9	17	40	19	-15
10	Birmingham City	22	5	3	3	33	18	1	2	8	11	48	17	-22
11	Nottingham Forest	22	3	4	4	19	20	3	1	7	12	42	17	-31
12	Long Eaton Rangers	22	3	1	7	18	29	1	1	9	17	45	10	-39

SEASON 1890/91

Match # 23   Saturday 06/09/90   Football Alliance   at North Road   Attendance 6000
Result: **Newton Heath 4 Darwen 2**
Teamsheet: Slater, Mitchell, McMillan, Doughty R, Ramsay, Owen J, Farman, Doughty J, Evans, Milarvie, Sharpe
Scorer(s): Doughty J, Evans, Farman, Owen J

Match # 24   Saturday 13/09/90   Football Alliance   at Abbey Park   Attendance 3000
Result: **Grimsby Town 3 Newton Heath 1**
Teamsheet: Slater, Mitchell, McMillan, Doughty R, Ramsay, Owen J, Farman, Stewart, Evans, Milarvie, Sharpe
Scorer(s): Stewart

Match # 25   Saturday 20/09/90   Football Alliance   at North Road   Attendance 5000
Result: **Newton Heath 1 Nottingham Forest 1**
Teamsheet: Slater, Powell, Stewart, Doughty R, Ramsay, Owen J, Farman, Doughty J, Evans, Milarvie, Sharpe
Scorer(s): Doughty J

Match # 26   Saturday 27/09/90   Football Alliance   at Victoria Ground   Attendance 2000
Result: **Stoke City 2 Newton Heath 1**
Teamsheet: Slater, Mitchell, Powell, Doughty R, Ramsay, Stewart, Farman, Doughty J, Evans, Milarvie, Sharpe
Scorer(s): Milarvie

Match # 27   Saturday 11/10/90   Football Alliance   at Bootle Park   Attendance 4000
Result: **Bootle 5 Newton Heath 0**
Teamsheet: Slater, Sadler, Powell, Doughty R, Ramsay, Owen J, Farman, Stewart, Evans, Milarvie, Sharpe

Match # 28   Saturday 18/10/90   Football Alliance   at North Road   Attendance 3000
Result: **Newton Heath 3 Grimsby Town 1**
Teamsheet: Slater, Mitchell, Powell, Doughty R, Ramsay, Owen J, Farman, Stewart, Evans, Milarvie, Sharpe
Scorer(s): Evans, Ramsay, Sharpe

Match # 29   Saturday 01/11/90   Football Alliance   at North Road   Attendance 4000
Result: **Newton Heath 6 Crewe Alexandra 3**
Teamsheet: Slater, Mitchell, Clements, Doughty R, Ramsay, Craig, Farman, Stewart, Evans, Milarvie, Sharpe
Scorer(s): Stewart 2, Craig, Evans, Farman, Ramsay

Match # 30   Saturday 08/11/90   Football Alliance   at West Bromwich Road   Attendance 3000
Result: **Walsall 2 Newton Heath 1**
Teamsheet: Slater, Mitchell, Clements, Doughty R, Ramsay, Sharpe, Farman, Stewart, Evans, Milarvie, Craig
Scorer(s): Sharpe

Match # 31   Saturday 22/11/90   Football Alliance   at Town Ground   Attendance 2000
Result: **Nottingham Forest 8 Newton Heath 2**
Teamsheet: Slater, Mitchell, Clements, Doughty R, Ramsay, Owen J, Farman, Stewart, Evans, Milarvie, Sharpe
Scorer(s): Farman, Ramsay

Match # 32   Saturday 29/11/90   Football Alliance   at North Road   Attendance 2000
Result: **Newton Heath 1 Sunderland 5**
Teamsheet: Slater, Mitchell, Clements, Doughty R, Ramsay, Owen J, Farman, Stewart, Evans, Milarvie, Sharpe
Scorer(s): Ramsay

Match # 33   Saturday 13/12/90   Football Alliance   at North Road   Attendance 1000
Result: **Newton Heath 3 Birmingham City 1**
Teamsheet: Slater, Mitchell, Clements, Doughty R, Ramsay, Craig, Farman, Stewart, Evans, Milarvie, Sharpe
Scorer(s): Milarvie, Sharpe, own goal

Match # 34   Saturday 27/12/90   Football Alliance   at North Road   Attendance 5000
Result: **Newton Heath 2 Bootle 1**
Teamsheet: Slater, Mitchell, Clements, Doughty R, Ramsay, Owen J, Farman, Stewart, Craig, Milarvie, Sharpe
Scorer(s): Milarvie, Stewart

Match # 35   Monday 05/01/91   Football Alliance   at North Road   Attendance 3000
Result: **Newton Heath 0 Stoke City 1**
Teamsheet: Slater, Mitchell, Clements, Doughty R, Ramsay, Owen J, Farman, Stewart, Stewart, Milarvie, Sharpe

Match # 36   Saturday 10/01/91   Football Alliance   at St Georges   Attendance 1000
Result: **Birmingham St Georges 6 Newton Heath 1**
Teamsheet: Slater, Felton, Clements, Doughty R, Ramsay, Owen J, Farman, Stewart, Craig, Milarvie, Phasey
Scorer(s): Farman

Match # 37   Saturday 17/01/91   Football Alliance   at North Road   Attendance 1500
Result: **Newton Heath 3 Walsall 3**
Teamsheet: Slater, Mitchell, Clements, Doughty R, Ramsay, Owen J, Farman, Stewart, Craig, Milarvie, Sharpe
Scorer(s): Milarvie, Owen J, Ramsay

Match # 38   Saturday 24/01/91   Football Alliance   at Olive Grove   Attendance 3000
Result: **Sheffield Wednesday 1 Newton Heath 2**
Teamsheet: Slater, Mitchell, Clements, Doughty R, Ramsay, Owen J, Farman, Stewart, Craig, Milarvie, Sharpe
Scorer(s): Sharpe, Stewart

Match # 39   Saturday 14/02/91   Football Alliance   at Gresty Road   Attendance 3000
Result: **Crewe Alexandra 0 Newton Heath 1**
Teamsheet: Slater, Mitchell, Clements, Evans, Ramsay, Owen J, Farman, Stewart, Craig, Milarvie, Sharpe
Scorer(s): Farman

Match # 40   Saturday 21/02/91   Football Alliance   at North Road   Attendance 4000
Result: **Newton Heath 1 Sheffield Wednesday 1**
Teamsheet: Slater, Mitchell, Clements, Doughty R, Ramsay, Owen J, Farman, Stewart, Craig, Milarvie, Sharpe
Scorer(s): Craig

SEASON 1890/91 (continued)

Match # 41	Saturday 07/03/91	Football Alliance	at Muntz Street	Attendance 2000
Result:	**Birmingham City 2 Newton Heath 1**			
Teamsheet:	Slater, Mitchell, Clements, Doughty R, Ramsay, Owen J, Farman, Stewart, Craig, Milarvie, Sharpe			
Scorer(s):	Sharpe			

Match # 42	Saturday 14/03/91	Football Alliance	at North Road	Attendance 2000
Result:	**Newton Heath 1 Birmingham St Georges 3**			
Teamsheet:	Slater, Mitchell, Clements, Doughty R, Ramsay, Owen J, Farman, Stewart, Craig, Milarvie, Sharpe			
Scorer(s):	Sharpe			

Match # 43	Saturday 28/03/91	Football Alliance	at Barley Bank	Attendance 2000
Result:	**Darwen 2 Newton Heath 1**			
Teamsheet:	Slater, Craig, Denman, Doughty R, Ramsay, Owen J, Farman, Stewart, Craig, Milarvie, Doughty J			
Scorer(s):	Ramsay			

Match # 44	Saturday 11/04/91	Football Alliance	at Newcastle Road	Attendance 3500
Result:	**Sunderland 2 Newton Heath 1**			
Teamsheet:	Slater, Denman, Clements, Doughty R, Ramsay, Owen J, Farman, Stewart, Craig, Milarvie, Sharpe			
Scorer(s):	Ramsay			

SEASON 1890/91 SUMMARY

APPEARANCES & GOALS

PLAYER	APPS	GOALS
Ramsay	22	7
Farman	22	5
Milarvie	22	4
Slater	22	0
Stewart	21	5
Doughty R	21	0
Sharpe	20	6
Owen J	18	2
Mitchell	17	0
Craig, T	15	2
Clements	15	0
Evans	12	3
Doughty J	4	2
Powell	4	0
Denman	2	0
McMillan	2	0
Felton	1	0
Phasey	1	0
Sadler	1	0
own goal		1

FINAL TABLE – FOOTBALL ALLIANCE

		P	W	D	L	F	A	W	D	L	F	A	PTS	GD
					HOME					AWAY				
1	Stoke City	22	9	2	0	33	15	4	5	2	24	24	33	18
2	Sunderland	22	9	2	0	47	6	3	4	4	22	22	30	41
3	Grimsby Town	22	9	2	0	31	9	2	3	6	12	18	27	16
4	Birmingham St Georges	22	9	0	2	41	22	3	2	6	23	40	26	2
5	Nottingham Forest	22	6	4	1	39	15	3	3	5	27	24	25	27
6	Darwen	22	7	3	1	45	20	3	0	8	19	39	23	5
7	Walsall	22	6	1	4	22	22	3	2	6	12	39	21	-27
8	Crewe Alexandra	22	5	1	5	28	29	3	3	5	31	38	20	-8
9	NEWTON HEATH	22	5	3	3	25	22	2	0	9	12	33	17	-18
10	Birmingham City	22	6	0	5	34	23	1	2	8	24	43	16	-8
11	Bootle	22	3	6	2	28	18	0	1	10	12	43	13	-21
12	Sheffield Wednesday	22	4	3	4	30	26	0	2	9	9	40	13	-27

SEASON 1891/92

Match # 45 Saturday 12/09/91   Football Alliance   at Peel Croft   Attendance 2000
Result: **Burton Swifts 3 Newton Heath 2**
Teamsheet: Slater, McFarlane, Clements, Doughty R, Stewart, Sharpe, Farman, Edge, Donaldson, Sneddon, Henrys
Scorer(s):   Donaldson, Farman

Match # 46 Saturday 19/09/91   Football Alliance   at North Road   Attendance 5000
Result: **Newton Heath 4 Bootle 0**
Teamsheet: Slater, McFarlane, Clements, Doughty R, Stewart, Owen J, Farman, Edge, Donaldson, Sneddon, Henrys
Scorer(s):   Edge 3, Farman

Match # 47 Saturday 26/09/91   Football Alliance   at St Georges   Attendance 300
Result: **Birmingham St Georges 1 Newton Heath 3**
Teamsheet: Slater, McFarlane, Clements, Doughty R, Stewart, Owen J, Farman, Edge, Donaldson, Sneddon, Henrys
Scorer(s):   Donaldson 2, Stewart

Match # 48 Saturday 10/10/91   Football Alliance   at North Road   Attendance 4000
Result: **Newton Heath 3 Manchester City 1**
Teamsheet: Slater, McFarlane, Clements, Sharpe, Stewart, Owen J, Farman, Edge, Donaldson, Sneddon, Henrys
Scorer(s):   Farman 2, Donaldson

Match # 49 Saturday 17/10/91   Football Alliance   at Abbey Park   Attendance 3000
Result: **Grimsby Town 2 Newton Heath 2**
Teamsheet: Slater, McFarlane, Clements, Sharpe, Stewart, Owen J, Farman, Edge, Donaldson, Sneddon, Henrys
Scorer(s):   Donaldson 2

Match # 50 Saturday 31/10/91   Football Alliance   at North Road   Attendance 4000
Result: **Newton Heath 3 Burton Swifts 1**
Teamsheet: Slater, McFarlane, Clements, Doughty R, Stewart, Owen J, Farman, Edge, Donaldson, Sneddon, Henrys
Scorer(s):   Doughty R, Edge, Farman

Match # 51 Saturday 07/11/91   Football Alliance   at Gresty Road   Attendance 3000
Result: **Crewe Alexandra 0 Newton Heath 2**
Teamsheet: Slater, McFarlane, Clements, Doughty R, Stewart, Denman, Farman, Edge, Donaldson, Sneddon, Henrys
Scorer(s):   Donaldson, own goal

Match # 52 Saturday 21/11/91   Football Alliance   at North Road   Attendance 6000
Result: **Newton Heath 10 Lincoln City 1**
Teamsheet: Slater, McFarlane, Clements, Doughty R, Stewart, Hood, Farman, Edge, Donaldson, Sneddon, Henrys
Scorer(s):   Donaldson 3, Hood 2, Stewart 2, Farman, Sneddon, own goal

Match # 53 Saturday 28/11/91   Football Alliance   at West Bromwich Road   Attendance 2500
Result: **Walsall 1 Newton Heath 4**
Teamsheet: Slater, McFarlane, Clements, Hood, Stewart, Owen J, Farman, Edge, Donaldson, Sneddon, Henrys
Scorer(s):   Donaldson 3, Farman

Match # 54 Saturday 12/12/91   Football Alliance   at Olive Grove   Attendance 4000
Result: **Sheffield Wednesday 2 Newton Heath 4**
Teamsheet: Slater, McFarlane, Clements, Owen J, Stewart, Hood, Farman, Edge, Donaldson, Sneddon, Henrys
Scorer(s):   Farman 2, Owen J, Sneddon

Match # 55 Saturday 19/12/91   Football Alliance   at Hyde Road   Attendance 13000
Result: **Manchester City 2 Newton Heath 2**
Teamsheet: Slater, Denman, Clements, Owen J, Stewart, Hood, Farman, Edge, Donaldson, Sneddon, Henrys
Scorer(s):   Farman 2

Match # 56 Saturday 26/12/91   Football Alliance   at North Road   Attendance 7000
Result: **Newton Heath 3 Birmingham City 3**
Teamsheet: Slater, Denman, Clements, Owen J, Stewart, Hood, Farman, Edge, Donaldson, Sneddon, Henrys
Scorer(s):   Edge 2, Farman

Match # 57 Friday 01/01/92   Football Alliance   at North Road   Attendance 12000
Result: **Newton Heath 1 Nottingham Forest 1**
Teamsheet: Slater, Henrys, Clements, Doughty R, Stewart, Owen J, Farman, Edge, Donaldson, Sneddon, Hood
Scorer(s):   Edge

Match # 58 Saturday 09/01/92   Football Alliance   at Bootle Park   Attendance 2000
Result: **Bootle 1 Newton Heath 1**
Teamsheet: Slater, Denman, Clements, Doughty R, Stewart, Owen J, Farman, Edge, Donaldson, Sneddon, Hood
Scorer(s):   Hood

Match # 59 Saturday 30/01/92   Football Alliance   at North Road   Attendance 3000
Result: **Newton Heath 5 Crewe Alexandra 3**
Teamsheet: Slater, McFarlane, Clements, Doughty R, Stewart, Owen J, Hood, Edge, Donaldson, Sneddon, Henrys
Scorer(s):   Donaldson 3, Doughty R, Sneddon

Match # 60 Saturday 20/02/92   Football Alliance   at North Road   Attendance 6000
Result: **Newton Heath 1 Sheffield Wednesday 1**
Teamsheet: Slater, McFarlane, Clements, Hood, Stewart, Owen J, Farman, Edge, Donaldson, Sneddon, Henrys
Scorer(s):   Hood

Match # 61 Saturday 27/02/92   Football Alliance   at Muntz Street   Attendance 3000
Result: **Birmingham City 3 Newton Heath 2**
Teamsheet: Slater, McFarlane, Clements, Doughty R, Stewart, Hood, Farman, Edge, Donaldson, Sneddon, Henrys
Scorer(s):   Farman, Sneddon

Match # 62 Saturday 05/03/92   Football Alliance   at North Road   Attendance 3500
Result: **Newton Heath 5 Walsall 0**
Teamsheet: Slater, McFarlane, Clements, Doughty R, Stewart, Hood, Farman, Edge, Donaldson, Sneddon, Henrys
Scorer(s):   Farman 2, Sneddon 2, McFarlane

SEASON 1891/92 (continued)

Match # 63	Saturday 19/03/92 Football Alliance	at Town Ground	Attendance 9000
Result:	**Nottingham Forest 3 Newton Heath 0**		
Teamsheet:	Slater, McFarlane, Clements, Doughty R, Stewart, Hood, Farman, Edge, Donaldson, Sneddon, Henrys		

Match # 64	Saturday 26/03/92 Football Alliance	at North Road	Attendance 6000
Result:	**Newton Heath 3 Grimsby Town 3**		
Teamsheet:	Davies (John), McFarlane, Clements, Doughty R, Stewart, Owen J, Farman, Hood, Donaldson, Sneddon, Mathieson		
Scorer(s):	Donaldson 2, Farman		

Match # 65	Saturday 02/04/92 Football Alliance	at John O'Gaunts	Attendance 2000
Result:	**Lincoln City 1 Newton Heath 6**		
Teamsheet:	Davies (John), McFarlane, Sneddon, Doughty R, Stewart, Owen J, Farman, Hood, Donaldson, Sneddon, Mathieson		
Scorer(s):	Mathieson, Sneddon, Unknown 4		

Match # 66	Saturday 09/04/92 Football Alliance	at North Road	Attendance 4000
Result:	**Newton Heath 3 Birmingham St Georges 0**		
Teamsheet:	Davies (John), McFarlane, Clements, Doughty R, Stewart, Owen J, Farman, Hood, Donaldson, Henrys, Mathieson		
Scorer(s):	Donaldson 2, Hood		

SEASON 1891/92 SUMMARY

APPEARANCES & GOALS

PLAYER	APPS	GOALS
Donaldson	22	20
Sneddon	22	7
Stewart	22	3
Farman	21	16
Clements	21	0
Edge	19	7
Slater	19	0
Henrys	19	0
McFarlane	18	1
Owen J	16	1
Hood	15	5
Doughty R	15	2
Denman	4	0
Mathieson	3	1
Sharpe	3	0
Davies, John	3	0
unknown		4
own goals		2

FINAL TABLE – FOOTBALL ALLIANCE

		P	W	D	L	F	A	W	D	L	F	A	PTS	GD
					HOME					AWAY				
1	Nottingham Forest	22	8	3	0	38	6	6	2	3	21	16	33	37
2	NEWTON HEATH	22	7	4	0	41	14	5	3	3	28	19	31	36
3	Birmingham City	22	8	2	1	32	11	4	3	4	21	25	29	17
4	Sheffield Wednesday	22	10	0	1	45	16	2	4	5	20	19	28	30
5	Burton Swifts	22	8	1	2	38	23	4	1	6	16	29	26	2
6	Grimsby Town	22	6	3	2	27	9	0	3	8	13	30	18	1
7	Crewe Alexandra	22	6	2	3	28	16	1	2	8	16	33	18	-5
8	Manchester City	22	5	3	3	28	21	1	3	7	11	30	18	-12
9	Bootle	22	7	1	3	27	19	1	1	9	15	45	18	-22
10	Lincoln City	22	4	4	3	23	20	2	1	8	14	45	17	-28
11	Walsall	22	6	1	4	28	18	0	2	9	5	41	15	-26
12	Birmingham St Georges	22	4	2	5	22	19	1	1	9	12	45	13	-30

1915/16

LANCASHIRE PRINCIPAL TOURNAMENT

Date	Opponent	H/A	Score
04/09/15	Oldham Athletic	A	2-3
11/09/15	Everton	H	2-4
18/09/15	Bolton Wanderers	A	5-3
25/09/15	Manchester City	H	1-1
02/10/15	Stoke City	A	0-0
09/10/15	Burnley	H	3-7
16/10/15	Preston North End	A	0-0
23/10/15	Stockport County	H	3-0
30/10/15	Liverpool	A	2-0
06/11/15	Bury	H	1-1
13/11/15	Rochdale	H	2-0
20/11/15	Blackpool	A	1-5
27/11/15	Southport Central	H	0-0
04/12/15	Oldham Athletic	H	2-0
11/12/15	Everton	A	0-2
18/12/15	Bolton Wanderers	H	1-0
25/12/15	Manchester City	A	1-2
01/01/16	Stoke City	H	1-2
08/01/16	Burnley	A	4-7
15/01/16	Preston North End	H	4-0
22/01/16	Stockport County	A	1-3
29/01/16	Liverpool	H	1-1
05/02/16	Bury	A	1-2
12/02/16	Rochdale	A	2-2
19/02/16	Blackpool	H	1-1
26/02/16	Southport Central	A	0-5

LANCASHIRE SUBSIDIARY TOURNAMENT

Date	Opponent	H/A	Score
04/03/16	Everton	H	0-2
11/03/16	Oldham Athletic	A	0-1
18/03/16	Liverpool	H	0-0
25/03/16	Manchester City	A	0-2
01/04/16	Stockport County	A	3-5
08/04/16	Everton	A	1-3
15/04/16	Oldham Athletic	H	3-0
21/04/16	Stockport County	H	3-2
22/04/16	Liverpool	A	1-7
29/04/16	Manchester City	A	1-2

1916/17

LANCASHIRE PRINCIPAL TOURNAMENT

Date	Opponent	H/A	Score
02/09/16	Port Vale	H	2-2
09/09/16	Oldham Athletic	A	2-0
16/09/16	Preston North End	H	2-1
23/09/16	Burnley	A	1-7
30/09/16	Blackpool	A	2-2
07/10/16	Liverpool	H	0-0
14/10/16	Stockport County	A	0-1
21/10/16	Bury	H	3-1
28/10/16	Stoke City	A	0-3
04/11/16	Southport Central	H	1-0
11/11/16	Blackburn Rovers	A	2-1
18/11/16	Manchester City	H	2-1
25/11/16	Everton	A	2-3
02/12/16	Rochdale	H	1-1
09/12/16	Bolton Wanderers	A	1-5
23/12/16	Oldham Athletic	H	3-2
30/12/16	Preston North End	A	2-3
06/01/17	Burnley	H	3-1
13/01/17	Blackpool	H	3-2
20/01/17	Liverpool	A	3-3
27/01/17	Stockport County	H	0-1
03/02/17	Bury	A	1-1
10/02/17	Stoke City	H	4-2
17/02/17	Southport Central	A	1-0
24/02/17	Blackburn Rovers	H	1-0
03/03/17	Manchester City	A	0-1
10/03/17	Everton	H	0-2
17/03/17	Rochdale	A	0-2
24/03/17	Bolton Wanderers	H	6-3
06/04/17	Port Vale	A	0-3

LANCASHIRE SUBSIDIARY TOURNAMENT

Date	Opponent	H/A	Score
31/03/17	Stoke City	A	1-2
07/04/17	Manchester City	H	5-1
09/04/17	Port Vale	H	5-1
14/04/17	Stoke City	H	1-0
21/04/17	Manchester City	A	1-0
28/04/17	Port Vale	A	2-5

1917/18

LANCASHIRE PRINCIPAL TOURNAMENT

Date	Opponent	H/A	Score
01/09/17	Blackburn Rovers	A	5-0
08/09/17	Blackburn Rovers	H	6-1
15/09/17	Rochdale	A	0-3
22/09/17	Rochdale	H	1-1
29/09/17	Manchester City	A	1-3
06/10/17	Manchester City	H	1-1
13/10/17	Everton	A	0-3
20/10/17	Everton	H	0-0
27/10/17	Port Vale	H	3-3
03/11/17	Port Vale	A	2-2
10/11/17	Bolton Wanderers	H	1-3
17/11/17	Bolton Wanderers	A	2-4
24/11/17	Preston North End	A	2-1
01/12/17	Preston North End	A	0-0
08/12/17	Blackpool	H	1-0
15/12/17	Blackpool	A	3-2
22/12/17	Burnley	H	5-0
29/12/17	Burnley	H	1-0
05/01/18	Southport Central	A	0-3
12/01/18	Southport Central	H	0-0
19/01/18	Liverpool	A	1-5
26/01/18	Liverpool	H	0-2
02/02/18	Stoke City	A	1-5
09/02/18	Stoke City	H	2-1
16/02/18	Bury	H	0-0
23/02/18	Bury	A	2-1
02/03/18	Oldham Athletic	H	2-1
09/03/18	Oldham Athletic	A	0-2
16/03/18	Stockport County	H	2-0
23/03/18	Stockport County	A	1-2

LANCASHIRE SUBSIDIARY TOURNAMENT

Date	Opponent	H/A	Score
29/03/18	Manchester City	A	0-3
30/03/18	Stoke City	H	2-1
01/04/18	Manchester City	H	2-0
06/04/18	Stoke City	A	0-0
13/04/18	Port Vale	H	2-0
20/04/18	Port Vale	A	0-2

1918/19

LANCASHIRE PRINCIPAL TOURNAMENT

Date	Opponent	H/A	Score
07/09/18	Oldham Athletic	H	1-4
14/09/18	Oldham Athletic	A	2-0
21/09/18	Blackburn Rovers	H	1-0
28/09/18	Blackburn Rovers	A	1-1
05/10/18	Manchester City	H	0-2
12/10/18	Manchester City	A	0-0
19/10/18	Everton	H	1-1
26/10/18	Everton	A	2-6
02/11/18	Rochdale	H	3-1
09/11/18	Rochdale	A	0-1
16/11/18	Preston North End	A	2-4
23/11/18	Preston North End	H	1-2
30/11/18	Bolton Wanderers	A	1-3
07/12/18	Bolton Wanderers	H	1-0
14/12/18	Port Vale	A	1-3
21/12/18	Port Vale	H	5-1
28/12/18	Blackpool	A	2-2
11/01/19	Stockport County	A	1-2
18/01/19	Stockport County	H	0-2
25/01/19	Liverpool	A	1-1
01/02/19	Liverpool	H	0-1
08/02/19	Southport Vulcan	A	1-2
15/02/19	Southport Vulcan	H	1-3
22/02/19	Burnley	A	2-4
01/03/19	Burnley	H	4-0
08/03/19	Stoke City	A	2-1
15/03/19	Stoke City	H	3-1
22/03/19	Bury	A	2-0
29/03/19	Bury	H	5-1
30/04/19	Blackpool	H	5-1

LANCASHIRE SUBSIDIARY TOURNAMENT

Date	Opponent	H/A	Score
05/04/19	Port Vale	A	3-1
12/04/19	Port Vale	H	2-1
18/04/19	Manchester City	A	0-3
19/04/19	Stoke City	H	0-1
21/04/19	Manchester City	H	2-4
26/04/19	Stoke City	A	2-4

1939/40

WESTERN DIVISION

Date	Opponent	H/A	Score
21/10/39	Manchester City	H	0-4
28/10/39	Chester City	A	4-0
11/11/39	Crewe Alexandra	H	5-1
18/11/39	Liverpool	A	0-1
25/11/39	Port Vale	H	8-1
02/12/39	Tranmere Rovers	A	4-2
09/12/39	Stockport County	A	7-4
23/12/39	Wrexham	H	5-1
06/01/40	Everton	A	2-3
20/01/40	Stoke City	H	4-3
10/02/40	Manchester City	A	0-1
24/02/40	Chester City	H	5-1
09/03/40	Crewe Alexandra	A	4-1
16/03/40	Liverpool	H	1-0
23/03/40	Port Vale	A	3-1
30/03/40	Tranmere Rovers	H	6-1
06/04/40	Stockport County	H	6-1
06/05/40	New Brighton	H	6-0
13/05/40	Wrexham	A	2-3
18/05/40	New Brighton	A	0-6
25/05/40	Stoke City	A	2-3
01/06/40	Everton	H	0-3

WAR LEAGUE CUP

Date	Opponent	H/A	Score
20/04/40	Manchester City	H	0-1
27/04/40	Manchester City	A	2-0
04/05/40	Blackburn Rovers	A	2-1
11/05/40	Blackburn Rovers	H	1-3

1940/41

NORTH REGIONAL LEAGUE

31/08/40	Rochdale	A	3-1
07/09/40	Bury	H	0-0
14/09/40	Oldham Athletic	A	1-2
21/09/40	Oldham Athletic	H	2-3
28/09/40	Manchester City	A	1-4
05/10/40	Manchester City	H	0-2
12/10/40	Burnley	A	1-0
19/10/40	Preston North End	H	4-1
26/10/40	Preston North End	A	1-3
02/11/40	Burnley	H	4-1
09/11/40	Everton	A	2-5
16/11/40	Everton	H	0-0
23/11/40	Liverpool	A	2-2
30/11/40	Liverpool	H	2-0
07/12/40	Blackburn Rovers	A	5-5
14/12/40	Rochdale	H	3-4
21/12/40	Bury	A	1-4
25/12/40	Stockport County	A	3-1
28/12/40	Blackburn Rovers	H	9-0
04/01/41	Blackburn Rovers	A	2-0
11/01/41	Blackburn Rovers	H	0-0
18/01/41	Bolton Wanderers	A	2-3
25/01/41	Bolton Wanderers	H	4-1
01/03/41	Chesterfield	A	1-1
08/03/41	Bury	H	7-3
22/03/41	Oldham Athletic	A	1-0
29/03/41	Blackpool	A	0-2
05/04/41	Blackpool	H	2-3
12/04/41	Everton	A	2-1
14/04/41	Manchester City	A	7-1
19/04/41	Chester City	A	6-4
26/04/41	Liverpool	A	1-2
03/05/41	Liverpool	H	1-1
10/05/41	Bury	A	1-5
17/05/41	Burnley	H	1-0

WAR LEAGUE CUP

15/02/41	Everton	H	2-2
22/02/41	Everton	A	1-2

1941/42

NORTH REGIONAL LEAGUE (1ST PHASE)

30/08/41	New Brighton	H	13-1
06/09/41	New Brighton	A	3-3
13/09/41	Stockport County	A	5-1
20/09/41	Stockport County	H	7-1
27/09/41	Everton	H	2-3
04/10/41	Everton	A	3-1
11/10/41	Chester City	A	7-0
18/10/41	Chester City	H	8-1
25/10/41	Stoke City	A	1-1
01/11/41	Stoke City	H	3-0
08/11/41	Tranmere Rovers	H	6-1
15/11/41	Tranmere Rovers	A	1-1
22/11/41	Liverpool	A	1-1
29/11/41	Liverpool	H	2-2
06/12/41	Wrexham	H	10-3
13/12/41	Wrexham	A	4-3
20/12/41	Manchester City	A	1-2
25/12/41	Manchester City	H	2-2

NORTH REGIONAL LEAGUE (2ND PHASE)

27/12/41	Bolton Wanderers	H	3-1
03/01/42	Bolton Wanderers	A	2-2
10/01/42	Oldham Athletic	H	1-1
17/01/42	Oldham Athletic	A	3-1
31/01/42	Southport	A	3-1
14/02/42	Sheffield United	A	2-0
21/02/42	Preston North End	H	0-2
28/02/42	Preston North End	A	3-1
21/03/42	Sheffield United	H	2-2
28/03/42	Southport	H	4-2
04/04/42	Blackburn Rovers	A	2-1
06/04/42	Blackburn Rovers	H	3-1
11/04/42	Wolves	H	5-4
18/04/42	Wolves	A	0-2
25/04/42	Oldham Athletic	H	5-1
02/05/42	Oldham Athletic	A	2-1
09/05/42	Blackburn Rovers	A	1-1
16/05/42	Blackburn Rovers	H	0-1
23/05/42	Manchester City	A	3-1

1942/43

NORTH REGIONAL LEAGUE (1ST PHASE)

29/08/42	Everton	A	2-2
05/09/42	Everton	H	2-1
12/09/42	Chester City	H	0-0
19/09/42	Chester City	A	2-2
26/09/42	Blackburn Rovers	A	2-4
03/10/42	Blackburn Rovers	H	5-2
10/10/42	Liverpool	H	3-4
17/10/42	Liverpool	A	1-2
24/10/42	Stockport County	A	4-1
31/10/42	Stockport County	H	3-1
07/11/42	Manchester City	H	2-1
14/11/42	Manchester City	A	5-0
21/11/42	Tranmere Rovers	A	5-0
28/11/42	Tranmere Rovers	H	5-1
05/12/42	Wrexham	H	6-1
12/12/42	Wrexham	A	5-2
19/12/42	Bolton Wanderers	A	2-0
25/12/42	Bolton Wanderers	H	4-0

NORTH REGIONAL LEAGUE (2ND PHASE)

26/12/42	Chester City	H	3-0
02/01/43	Chester City	A	1-4
09/01/43	Blackpool	A	1-1
16/01/43	Blackpool	H	5-3
23/01/43	Everton	H	1-4
30/01/43	Everton	A	5-0
06/02/43	Manchester City	A	0-0
13/02/43	Manchester City	H	1-1
20/02/43	Crewe Alexandra	A	7-0
27/02/43	Crewe Alexandra	A	3-2
06/03/43	Manchester City	H	0-1
13/03/43	Manchester City	A	0-2
20/03/43	Bury	H	4-1
27/03/43	Bury	A	5-3
03/04/43	Crewe Alexandra	H	4-1
10/04/43	Crewe Alexandra	A	6-0
17/04/43	Oldham Athletic	H	3-0
24/04/43	Oldham Athletic	A	1-3
01/05/43	Sheffield United	H	2-0
08/05/43	Liverpool	A	3-1
15/05/43	Liverpool	H	3-3

1943/44

NORTH REGIONAL LEAGUE (1ST PHASE)

28/08/43	Stockport County	H	6-0
04/09/43	Stockport County	A	3-3
11/09/43	Everton	H	4-1
18/09/43	Everton	A	1-6
25/09/43	Blackburn Rovers	H	2-1
02/10/43	Blackburn Rovers	A	1-2
09/10/43	Chester City	H	3-1
16/10/43	Chester City	A	4-5
23/10/43	Liverpool	A	4-3
30/10/43	Liverpool	H	1-0
06/11/43	Manchester City	A	2-2
13/11/43	Manchester City	H	3-0
20/11/43	Tranmere Rovers	H	6-3
27/11/43	Tranmere Rovers	A	1-0
04/12/43	Wrexham	A	4-1
11/12/43	Wrexham	H	5-0
18/12/43	Bolton Wanderers	H	3-1
25/12/43	Bolton Wanderers	A	3-1

NORTH REGIONAL LEAGUE (2ND PHASE)

27/12/43	Halifax Town	H	6-2
01/01/44	Halifax Town	A	1-1
08/01/44	Stockport County	A	3-2
15/01/44	Stockport County	H	4-2
22/01/44	Manchester City	H	1-3
29/01/44	Manchester City	A	3-2
05/02/44	Bury	A	3-0
12/02/44	Bury	H	3-3
19/02/44	Oldham Athletic	H	3-2
26/02/44	Oldham Athletic	A	1-1
04/03/44	Wrexham	A	4-1
11/03/44	Wrexham	H	2-2
18/03/44	Birmingham	A	1-3
25/03/44	Birmingham	H	1-1
01/04/44	Bolton Wanderers	A	0-3
08/04/44	Bolton Wanderers	H	3-2
10/04/44	Manchester City	A	1-4
15/04/44	Burnley	H	9-0
22/04/44	Burnley	A	3-3
29/04/44	Oldham Athletic	H	0-0
06/05/44	Oldham Athletic	A	3-1

1944/45

NORTH REGIONAL LEAGUE (1ST PHASE)

26/08/44	Everton	A	2-1
02/09/44	Everton	H	1-3
09/09/44	Stockport County	H	3-4
16/09/44	Stockport County	A	4-4
23/09/44	Bury	H	2-2
30/09/44	Bury	A	2-4
07/10/44	Chester City	A	0-2
14/10/44	Chester City	H	1-0
21/10/44	Tranmere Rovers	H	6-1
28/10/44	Tranmere Rovers	A	4-2
04/11/44	Liverpool	A	2-3
11/11/44	Liverpool	H	2-5
18/11/44	Manchester City	H	3-2
25/11/44	Manchester City	A	0-4
02/12/44	Crewe Alexandra	A	4-1
09/12/44	Crewe Alexandra	H	2-0
16/12/44	Wrexham	H	1-0
23/12/44	Wrexham	A	1-2

NORTH REGIONAL LEAGUE (2ND PHASE)

26/12/44	Sheffield United	A	4-3
30/12/44	Oldham Athletic	A	4-3
06/01/45	Huddersfield Town	H	1-0
13/01/45	Huddersfield Town	A	2-2
03/02/45	Manchester City	H	1-3
01/02/45	Manchester City	A	0-2
17/02/45	Bury	H	2-0
24/02/45	Bury	A	1-3
03/03/45	Oldham Athletic	H	3-2
10/03/45	Halifax Town	A	0-1
17/03/45	Halifax Town	H	2-0
24/03/45	Burnley	A	3-2
31/03/45	Burnley	H	4-0
02/04/45	Blackpool	A	1-4
07/04/45	Stoke City	H	6-1
14/04/45	Stoke City	A	4-1
21/04/45	Doncaster Rovers	A	2-1
28/04/45	Doncaster Rovers	H	3-1
05/05/45	Chesterfield	H	1-1
12/05/45	Chesterfield	A	1-0
19/05/45	Bolton Wanderers	A	0-1
26/05/45	Bolton Wanderers	H	2-0

1945/46

NORTH REGIONAL LEAGUE

25/08/45	Huddersfield Town	A	2-3
01/09/45	Huddersfield Town	H	2-3
08/09/45	Chesterfield	H	0-2
12/09/45	Middlesbrough	A	1-2
15/09/45	Chesterfield	A	1-1
20/09/45	Stoke City	A	2-1
22/09/45	Barnsley	A	2-2
29/09/45	Barnsley	H	1-1
06/10/45	Everton	H	0-0
13/10/45	Everton	A	0-3
20/10/45	Bolton Wanderers	H	1-1
27/10/45	Bolton Wanderers	A	2-1
03/11/45	Preston North End	H	6-1
10/12/45	Preston North End	A	2-2
17/11/45	Leeds United	A	3-3
24/11/45	Leeds United	H	6-1
01/12/45	Burnley	H	3-3
08/12/45	Burnley	A	2-2
15/12/45	Sunderland	H	2-1
22/12/45	Sunderland	A	2-4
25/12/45	Sheffield United	A	0-1
26/12/45	Sheffield United	H	2-3
29/12/45	Middlesbrough	H	4-1
12/01/46	Grimsby Town	H	5-0
19/01/46	Grimsby Town	A	0-1
02/02/46	Blackpool	H	4-2
09/02/46	Liverpool	H	2-1
16/02/46	Liverpool	A	5-0
23/02/46	Bury	A	1-1
02/03/46	Bury	H	1-1
09/03/46	Blackburn Rovers	H	6-2
16/03/46	Blackburn Rovers	A	3-1
23/03/46	Bradford	A	1-2
27/03/46	Blackpool	A	5-1
30/03/46	Bradford	H	4-0
06/04/46	Manchester City	H	1-4
13/04/46	Manchester City	A	3-1
19/04/46	Newcastle United	A	1-0
20/04/46	Sheffield Wednesday	H	4-0
22/04/46	Newcastle United	H	4-1
27/04/46	Sheffield Wednesday	A	0-1
04/05/46	Stoke City	H	2-1

Club Honours

European Champions Clubs' Cup

1968, 1999, 2008

European Cup-Winners' Cup

1991

FA Premiership

1993, 1994, 1996, 1997, 1999, 2000, 2001, 2003, 2007, 2008

Football League Division One

1908, 1911, 1952, 1956, 1957, 1965, 1967

Football League Division Two

1936, 1975

FA Challenge Cup

1909, 1948, 1963, 1977, 1983, 1985, 1990, 1994, 1996, 1999, 2004

Football League Cup

1992, 2006

Inter-Continental Cup

1999

European Super Cup

1991

FA Charity Shield

1908, 1911, 1952, 1956, 1957, 1983, 1993, 1994, 1996, 1997, 2003, 2007

Joint Holders

1965, 1967, 1977, 1990